1990
Britannica
Book of the Year

Encyclopædia Britannica, Inc.
Chicago
Auckland/Geneva/London/Madrid/Manila/Paris
Rome/Seoul/Sydney/Tokyo/Toronto

CONTENTS

CALENDAR 1990

JANUARY
1 New Year's Day
4 25th anniversary of the death of T.S. Eliot, U.S.-British author
7 Coptic Orthodox Christmas
15 U.S. federal holiday honouring Martin Luther King, Jr.
15 Bicentenary of the arrival of the British ship *Bounty* at Pitcairn Island. The ship was burned eight days later to conceal the whereabouts of the crew that mutinied against Capt. William Bligh
24 25th anniversary of the death of Winston Churchill, British leader during World War II
26 Australia Day
27 Chinese New Year's Day

FEBRUARY
6 Waitangi Day; 150th anniversary of the treaty that gave Britain sovereignty over New Zealand
11 Foundation Day; commemoration of the founding of Japan in 660 BC
14 Valentine's Day in U.S.
19 30th birthday of Prince Andrew, first child born to a reigning British monarch since 1857
19 U.S. observance of the birthday of George Washington
21 25th anniversary of the death of Malcolm X, prominent U.S. black militant leader
27 Mardi Gras, a day of often riotous celebrations on the eve of Ash Wednesday, the beginning of Lent

MARCH
7 25th anniversary of the historic first Selma to Montgomery (Ala.) voting rights march
15 15th anniversary of the death of Aristotle Onassis, Greek tycoon
17 St. Patrick's Day
18 25th anniversary of the death of Farouk I, king of Egypt until his ouster by Gamal Abdel Nasser
21 Holi, a fun-filled Hindu festival associated with the splashing of coloured water on passersby
24 10th anniversary of the murder of Roman Catholic Archbishop Oscar Romero in El Salvador
27 Projected first day of Ramadan, a month of fasting for Muslims

APRIL
2 150th anniversary of the birth of Émile Zola, French novelist
10 Jewish festival of Passover
13 Good Friday
15 Easter in the Western and Eastern Christian churches
17 Bicentenary of the death of Benjamin Franklin, U.S. scientist, printer, and diplomat; he helped frame the U.S. Declaration of Independence and Constitution
21 Birthday of Queen Elizabeth II
25 'Id al-Fitr, end of the Islamic month-long fast of Ramadan
27 25th anniversary of the death of Edward R. Murrow, U.S. radio and television broadcaster

MAY
1 May Day; International Labour Day
4 10th anniversary of the death of Josip Broz Tito, longtime leader of Yugoslavia
7 150th anniversary of the birth of Peter Tchaikovsky, Russian composer of classical ballet scores
13 Mother's Day in U.S.
21 Victoria Day in Canada
27 150th anniversary of the death of Niccolo Paganini, popular Italian violin virtuoso and composer
28 U.S. observance of Memorial Day
30 30th anniversary of the death of Boris Pasternak, Russian Nobel laureate in literature, whose works include *Doctor Zhivago*

JUNE
2 150th anniversary of the birth of Thomas Hardy, English novelist
12 Philippine Independence Day
13 25th anniversary of the death of Martin Buber, esteemed German-Jewish religious scholar
15 775th anniversary of the day King John of England placed his royal seal on the Magna Carta
17 Father's Day in U.S.
21 20th anniversary of the death of Sukarno, first president of independent Indonesia
25 40th anniversary of North Korea's invasion of South Korea; an estimated five million people died in the war that followed

JULY
1 Canada Day, formerly called Dominion Day, which commemorates the unification of the provinces of Canada in 1867
3 Centenary of Idaho's statehood. One week later Wyoming became the Union's 44th state
4 U.S. Independence Day
17 Bicentenary of the death of Adam Smith, Scottish economist and author of *The Wealth of Nations*
27 10th anniversary of the death of Mohammad Reza Pahlavi, autocratic ruler of Iran until January 1979
29 Centenary of the death of Vincent van Gogh, Dutch Expressionist painter

AUGUST
2 Islamic New Year's Day, provided the Moon is actually sighted
6 Annual Hiroshima peace festival
11 Centenary of the death of John H. Newman, leader of the Oxford Movement in the Church of England and later a Roman Catholic cardinal
11 25th anniversary of the outbreak of racial riots in the Watts section of Los Angeles
20 50th anniversary of the murder of Leon Trotsky near Mexico City
24 Tercentenary of the founding of Calcutta, India
27 25th anniversary of the death of Le Corbusier, renowned architect and city planner

SEPTEMBER
3 Labour Day in U.S. and Canada
11 40th anniversary of the death of Jan Smuts, South African scholar, military officer, and politician
17 10th anniversary of the death of Anastasio Somoza, last of the Somoza family to rule Nicaragua. In 1979 he went into exile in Paraguay, where he was slain
20 Rosh Hashana, Jewish New Year
27 150th anniversary of the birth of Thomas Nast, U.S. cartoonist
28 20th anniversary of the death of Gamal Abdel Nasser, Egyptian army officer and politician
29 Yom Kippur, or Day of Atonement; holiest day of the Jewish year

OCTOBER
2 Chusok, Korean Moon festival, a joyous three-day family celebration
8 Thanksgiving Day in Canada
11 Centenary of the founding in Washington, D.C., of the Daughters of the American Revolution
12 Columbus Day
14 Centenary of the birth of Dwight Eisenhower, 34th president of the U.S. and army general
22 25th anniversary of the death of Paul Tillich, German-U.S. theologian and philosopher
22 15th anniversary of the death of Arnold Toynbee, English historian
24 United Nations Day
31 Halloween

NOVEMBER
7 Anniversary of the Bolshevik Revolution in Russia (1917)
8 30th anniversary of the election of John F. Kennedy as 35th U.S. president. He was slain in 1963
8 Centenary of the death of César Franck, Belgian-French composer and organist
9 50th anniversary of the death of Neville Chamberlain, British prime minister who strove to prevent World War II by appeasing Hitler
11 Veterans Day in U.S.; Remembrance Day in Canada
14 150th anniversary of the birth of Claude Monet, French Impressionist
22 Thanksgiving Day in U.S.

DECEMBER
2 First Sunday of Advent
8 10th anniversary of the murder of John Lennon, British musician and member of the Beatles
12 First day of Hanukkah, the Jewish Festival of Lights
16 25th anniversary of the death of W. Somerset Maugham, English author
21 50th anniversary of the death of F. Scott Fitzgerald, author of *The Great Gatsby*
25 Christmas Day
26 Centenary of the death of Heinrich Schliemann, German archaeologist who excavated ancient Troy
26 Boxing Day in Britain and in many of its former colonies

The New Face of Eastern Europe

A Photo Essay

Winston Churchill, Franklin Roosevelt, and Joseph Stalin met in Yalta in February 1945 to draw up a blueprint for postwar Europe. That plan effectively sealed the fate of Eastern Europe for more than 40 years. Three months later Berlin fell to Soviet troops, but jubilation soon gave way to new dangers. Soviet tanks would roll into battle to suppress rebellions in Eastern Europe. The Berlin Wall would come to signify the cold war fiercely waged by the U.S. and the U.S.S.R. for some four decades. Then, almost overnight, winds of change turned into a tornado. In a year of drama unmatched in modern history, government after government collapsed in Eastern Europe. No longer able to stifle cries for freedom, East Germany allowed hundreds of thousands of its citizens to swarm through openings in the Berlin Wall to see for themselves how life was lived in the West. But the shape of things to come was not yet clear. The Soviet Union was in turmoil and the fate of Soviet leader Mikhail Gorbachev in doubt. One thing only was sure: 1989 was but the first chapter in a story still unfolding. The pictures on the following pages capture brief moments of history that reshaped the world in 1989.

(ABOVE) THE GRANGER COLLECTION; (ABOVE RIGHT) NOVOSTI/SOVFOTO; (BELOW) JACQUES WITT—SIPA

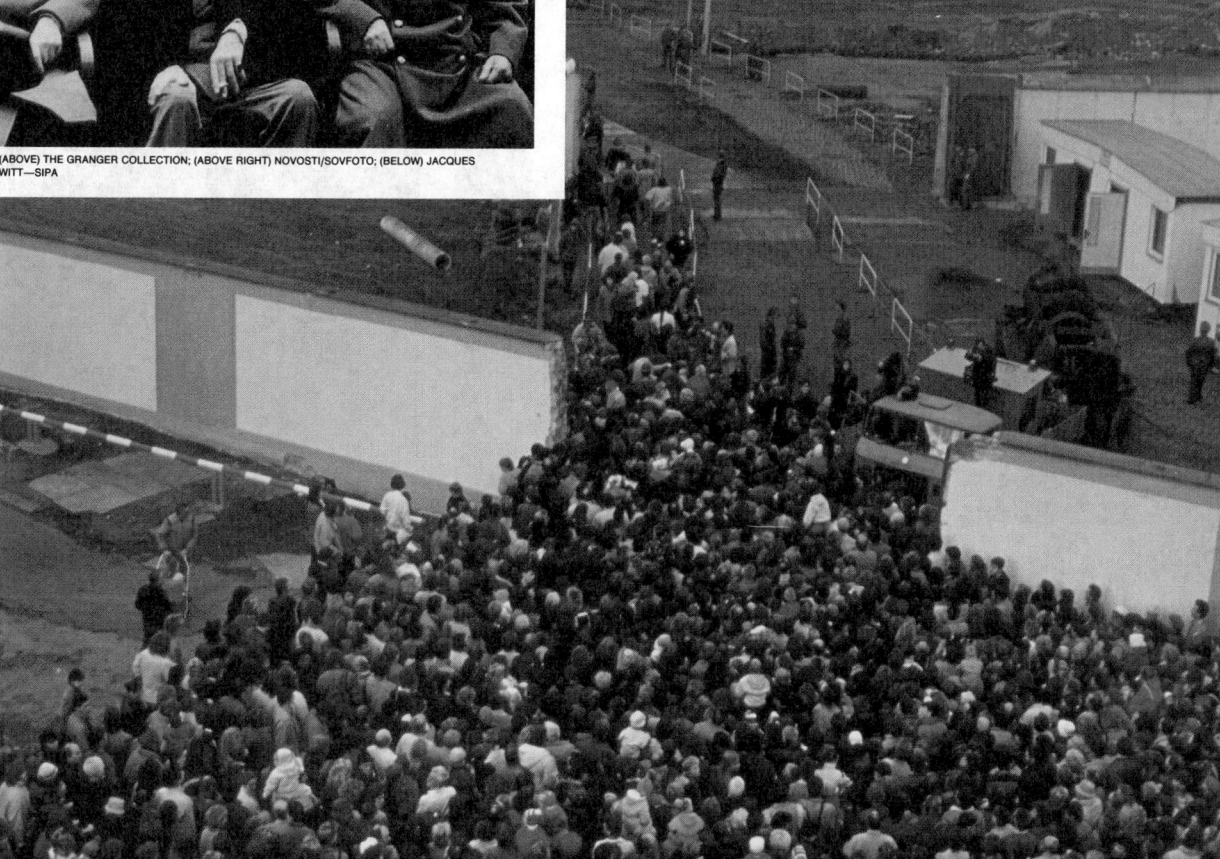

East Germany

For decades East Germany was a model hard-line Communist state. Deep inside its borders lay Berlin, the old capital of Germany, now divided into four zones of occupation. In 1948, in an effort to drive the Western powers out of Berlin, the Soviet Union blocked road and rail access to the city. U.S. Pres. Harry Truman responded with the Berlin airlift. During the next 11 months, well over two million tons of food, medicine, fuel, machinery, and other vital supplies were flown into the beleagured city. Then, in 1961, desperate to stop the flight of East Germans to the West, the government created the Berlin Wall. Two days after the first barbed wire barricades went up, an East German guard leaped to freedom. Escape routes, including second floor windows in nearby buildings, were sealed one by one. Chris Geoffroy was one of many would-be escapees who never made it.

By the spring of 1989 East Germans by the thousands
were fleeing to the West through other Eastern European
countries. In mid-October, after massive demonstrations
in Leipzig and elsewhere, Erich Honecker was ousted
after having ruled the country for 18 years. The country
had reached a point of no return. On November 7 and
8 the demoralized prime minister, his Cabinet, and most
of the Politburo resigned. On November 10, with official
approval, hundreds of thousands of East Germans swarmed
through openings in the Berlin Wall. With hammers,
chisels, picks, and make-do tools, Germans on both sides
of the graffiti-scarred wall began to pry away souvenirs.

(TOP) AP/WIDE WORLD; (CENTRE) GUSTAVO GILABERT—JB PICTURES; (RIGHT) EASTLIGHT/SABA

Hungary

Hungary was the first Eastern European nation to revolt openly against Soviet domination. In July 1953 Imre Nagy came to power. He was a committed Marxist but was even more devoted to his native land. The reforms he introduced to improve Hungarian life so distressed Moscow that Nagy was dismissed in 1955 and expelled from the party. In October 1956 a peaceful antigovernment demonstration turned violent when troops were ordered to fire into the crowd. When army troops joined

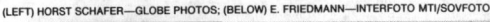

the protesters, a revolution was under way. Emboldened citizens mocked Stalin by severing the head of a huge bronze statue. Nagy was restored to power while Moscow temporized. The die was cast on November 1 when Hungary announced its withdrawal from the Warsaw Pact. Three days later Soviet troops seized control of Budapest, and the revolt was over. Nagy was captured and, in 1958, hanged. By June 16, 1989, the country had again changed so dramatically that Nagy's remains were removed from a potter's field and reburied with honours during an emotional ceremony attended by as many as 300,000 Hungarians. In late November, for the first time in 42 years, Hungarians voted in a free national election.

Czechoslovakia

The winds of political change also swept rapidly across Czechoslovakia. On November 24, just hours after some 350,000 Czechoslovak citizens gathered in Prague for the eighth consecutive day to demand democracy, Milos Jakes, head of the Communist Party, and other top leaders resigned. The crowd, brutally clubbed by police just a few days earlier, responded to the news by dancing in the streets. Alexander Dubcek, whose tenure as premier and program of liberalization (Prague Spring) had been abruptly terminated when Soviet-led Warsaw Pact troops invaded Czechoslovakia in 1968, was elected president of Parliament on Dec. 28, 1989. The legislature then elected the dissident playwright Vaclav Havel president.

Poland

Lech Walesa, an electrician in the Lenin Shipyard in Gdansk, planted the seeds of profound change in Poland when he organized a historic strike that led to the formation of the Solidarity trade union in September 1980. Less than 15 months later Solidarity was suspended, and then dissolved, by a government otherwise unable to meet the challenges the union posed. Nevertheless, the federation refused to die. Finally, desperate to secure the cooperation of the nation's work force, a reluctant government restored Solidarity's legal status in April 1989. In June Solidarity candidates scored a stunning victory in parliamentary elections. In August the unthinkable became reality: a prominent member of Solidarity became premier. It was the first instance of a non-Communist being chosen head of a Communist nation in Eastern Europe.

Bulgaria

Fully aware of what was happening in other Eastern European countries, Todor Zhivkov, Bulgaria's longtime leader, agreed to resign on November 10. Crowds vented their pent-up rage by angrily defacing Stalin's portrait. A new leader called for free elections in 1990.

Romania

No ruler in Eastern Europe was more fanatic than Romanian Pres. Nicolae Ceausescu, who, during more than 20 years in power, had communicated a like fanaticism to his armed followers. As Communist governments began to collapse around him, Ceausescu vowed never to relinquish power. On December 22, however, menacing crowds defiantly burned his picture as Ceausescu fled for his life. He was captured, tried in secret, and executed on Christmas Day. Meanwhile, the bodies of thousands of his latest victims were being exhumed from mass graves near Timisoara.

UPI/BETTMANN NEWSPHOTOS

(ABOVE) BLANCHE—GAMMA/LIAISON; (LEFT) PETER TURNLEY—BLACK STAR

Soviet Union

In one way or another, Soviet leader Mikhail Gorbachev was largely responsible for the political transformation that occurred in Eastern Europe in 1989. Unlike his predecessors, he sought to foster change and even viewed *perestroika* (restructuring) as the Soviet Union's last best hope for the future. However, *perestroika* and *glasnost* (openness) were also fraught with danger. Republics within the Soviet Union began demonstrating for greater freedom, some even straining for total independence. Others were wracked by violent ethnic conflict that even riot-control troops found difficult to quell. Meanwhile, hard-line conservatives watched from the sidelines to see if Gorbachev could foster change while keeping it within manageable limits. If not, his political enemies were ready to pounce.

TASS/SOVFOTO

The Future Has Started

BY THE RIGHT HONOURABLE BRIAN MULRONEY, PRIME MINISTER OF CANADA

The pace of change in international politics is straining mankind's capabilities of assimilation and assessment. In Western Europe, the outlines of a new supranationalism have become visible. In Central Europe, the echoes of history are heard again after 40 years of silence. And in Eastern Europe, Communism is in full-scale retreat under the implacable pressure of the truth and of rising expectations. In East-West relations, Yalta is yielding to Malta as the symbol of a new era. In Asia, countries that could scarcely feed themselves a generation ago have become dragons of economic competition. Almost everywhere, the computer and the microprocessor have revolutionized the ways we live and even the ways we think. And almost everywhere pluralistic democratic values—including economic liberty—dominate. When history turns this fast, statesmanship consists not so much in the control of events as in a sane response to them.

Meantime, the atrocities in Beijing (Peking) and Timisoara, the spectre of famine over the Horn of Africa, and the millions of children who die avoidable deaths each year remind us that not everything has changed.

It is clear that we are living in an age of expanding prosperity and economic opportunity, an age when swords might, at last, be beaten into plowshares. But it is also a time when new dangers will oblige us to broaden our definition of national security. Not long ago, national security was thought of almost exclusively in the traditional terms of diplomacy and belligerency, of deterrence and war. In latter years we have had to add economic competitiveness to our concept of security. Now we can perceive the outlines of more ominous threats of environmental degradation and social alienation, threats that are at once intrinsic and extrinsic to our societies.

Some of the features of the year 2000 are already clear. We know now that total world population will increase by one billion people, most of them in the poorer countries of the South. We know that this will mean accelerated industrial production, worldwide, and we know that will mean increased energy consumption. The world of the year 2000 is likely to be one of unprecedented economic prosperity, but with widening disparities between the richest countries and the poorest. Assuming progress can be made on the thorny question of debt, middle-income countries could grow briskly. Competition will be carried out on a global scale. A growing number of countries will acquire the capacity to produce sophisticated goods and services and to sell them abroad. Investment abroad will, perhaps, surpass exporting as the preferred means of conducting business internationally. It is certain to be an era of rapid technological change. The knowledge industry will predominate as information technology, materials science, and biotechnology evolve rapidly. Flexibility and adaptability will be the key. New production strategies, aimed at specific markets, will become increasingly important.

In this highly competitive environment, the quality of human resources will be a vital factor. Education systems will be decisive, and there will be a premium on scientific and engineering education. Since industry will increasingly need to develop an international orientation, language training will be important, as will experience abroad. Retraining will be a standard feature of working life. No country will be able to enjoy an across-the-board technological leadership, and vast amounts of capital will be needed to sustain technological progress. Health technology, for example, will be much advanced, making health care still more expensive and straining our capacity to provide the best available care to all who need it. The environment will have become a truly global issue, and progress will depend on all countries embracing a new environmental ethic based on the concept of sustainable development.

The Economic Revolution and Free Trade. In the space of 30 years—one generation—an international economic revolution has taken place. In 1960 world exports totaled $120 billion; in 1987 the figure was $2.3 trillion. Then the United States accounted for half of the developed world's gross national product; now it accounts for about 35%. Then, thanks to the Marshall Plan, Europe was on the road to recovery; now it is on the road to becoming one of the world's most powerful economic units. Then Japan was regarded as a low-cost producer of low-quality goods; now it is respected as a world leader in technologically advanced manufacturing.

A parallel revolution has taken place in finance. Thanks in part to the integration of computers, telecommunications, and satellites, a worldwide market has been created, with trillions of dollars pulsating through the global village. From London to New York and Tokyo to Toronto, the world has become one enormous, integrated banking machine. At the same time, this global financial economy has lost its link to the "real" economy of goods and services. The flow of investment capital can determine the exchange rates of national currencies with scant regard for such fundamentals as purchasing power parity. No longer does the flow of merchandise trade between countries determine the comparative values of national currencies, nor does the international flow of capital exist to facilitate the exchange of goods between nations. Now the profit or loss from the exchange of currencies itself can dwarf the rewards to be gained from the production and sale of a product.

This economic revolution has presented nations with a stark choice: competitiveness or protectionism—the vanguard of prosperity or the rear guard of decline. In the 1988 general election, Canadians made their choice, and they chose the optimistic vision. At issue was the free-trade agreement between Canada and the United States. The government stressed that a new economic relationship with the U.S. was needed. In 1960 trade between the U.S. and Canada totaled about $7 billion a year. It now amounts to an astonishing $200 billion, the largest volume of trade between two nations in the history of the world. U.S. trade with Canada is larger than U.S. trade with the U.K., France, West Germany, and Italy combined, and the U.S. exports more to one Canadian province, Ontario, than it does to Japan. Canada is a nation of only 26 million people, heavily dependent on trade and living next

A currency trader signals a deal at Tokyo's Dollar Trading Centre. The revolution in computers and communications networks has opened up a global market where financial deals are negotiated internationally by computer.

E. MIYAZAWA—BLACK STAR

door to the largest and richest market on Earth. Almost 75% of our exports, worth $108 billion, go to the U.S.

The growth in the size and breadth of the economic relationship between Canada and the U.S. outpaced the evolution of the international trading system. The General Agreement on Tariffs and Trade (GATT) rules were no longer sufficient for the scope and nature of the trade involved. Nor were the GATT rules likely to be updated as fully or as quickly as required. These factors, coupled with growing protectionist pressures in the U.S. that threatened to block our access to the market on which so many Canadian jobs depend, persuaded us that we needed a formal, bilateral agreement with the U.S. to complement our commitments to each other under the GATT.

Under the free-trade agreement, all tariffs on U.S. imports will be removed over the next 10 years. There will be no more U.S. quotas on Canadian uranium exports, no more U.S. import tax on Canadian oil exports, no more U.S. customs user fees on any Canadian exports. Most fundamentally, the agreement will replace the politics of trade with the rule of law, a feature that is of particular value to the smaller of the two partners. From now on, any U.S. trade legislation affecting Canada will have to be consistent with the agreement. From now on, all actions by the U.S. within the scope of the agreement—whether by the executive branch, the Congress, or independent regulatory bodies—will be subject to notification beforehand, to consultation, and, if necessary, to dispute-settlement procedures. From now on, final decisions on disputes regarding access to that vital market will be taken not just by Americans, as has been the case all too often in the past, but by Americans and Canadians together. This agreement builds on 50 years of bilateral and multilateral negotiations with the U.S. It takes a hodgepodge of existing agreements and ad hoc arrangements and translates them into a coherent and binding framework of rules tailored to the trade and investment realities of the 21st century.

In the U.S., our free-trade initiative was welcome. The Americans would benefit from more assured access to their largest market. Also, they wanted an instrument with which to counter rising protectionist pressure at home and abroad. By example, the free-trade agreement with Canada showed protectionists that selling into an expanding trading relationship was a better way to reduce

trade imbalances than impeding imports. The free-trade agreement is fully consistent with the GATT. In fact, many of the principles enunciated in the free-trade agreement are taken directly from the GATT. It raises no new barriers against any other nation. It extends trade policy frontiers, especially in services—including financial services—agriculture, investment, business travel, intellectual property, and dispute resolution.

Furthermore, the free-trade agreement was integral to our making Canada more competitive so we could develop markets abroad and meet competition from offshore. It is to make Canada more competitive that we have adopted a new element of our foreign trade policy called "Going Global," a program of trade and investment and science and technology initiatives, designed to position Canada strategically in its major markets—the U.S., Asia-Pacific, and Europe.

The New Protectionism. In 1983 our trade across the Pacific eclipsed our trade with Europe, and in 1989 our trade with Japan alone will be broadly equal to our trade with the four largest Western European countries combined. Four of our 10 largest markets are in Asia, and we expect that Canada's exports to this region will grow by another 50% by the year 2000. Despite the political, geographic, and cultural impediments to integration of the Asian countries, there is no doubt that a sense of community of interest is emerging there. This, combined with developments in Europe and North America, is generating fear in some quarters—both business and government—that regional blocs are inevitable and that the eclipse of the global trading system is only a question of time. The worry is that these blocs would favour freer trade among their component states but would raise barriers against third countries, thus promoting predatory, beggar-thy-neighbour policies with respect to trade and investment. Even the most cursory rereading of pre-World War II history makes clear that such an outcome would be very dangerous. Policies built on the mercantilist premise that the road to prosperity is a one-way street called export drive are not sustainable. No one would benefit if trade liberalization came to be regarded as a mug's game.

Mercantilist trade blocs are not inevitable, but if they are to be avoided we must guard against a drift into isolation and confrontation. The Uruguay round of GATT

negotiations is, in this sense, much more than just another round of trade liberalization talks. It is probably accurate to say that what is at issue in the Uruguay round is the future of economic multilateralism. But if the Uruguay round is a success, it will not be the definitive response to protectionism, nor will it blunt entirely any threat of the eventual emergence of trading blocs and the dangers they represent. That threat will still be present in the form of a new kind of mercantilism with nationalistic characteristics. It is apparent in a growing tendency in some quarters to seize and expand market share in technologically strategic industries, using a combination of national technology, trade, and competition policies.

Protectionism, until recently, has tended to be defensive, protecting declining industries with tariffs and with quotas, subsidies, and other nontariff barriers. The new threat to trade liberalization is offensive-minded. Taken together with the growing friction between the U.S., Japan, and Europe over conventional trade issues, this new, offensive strategy to dominate markets raises questions about the long-term viability of the free-trade ethic in international affairs. There are countervailing forces inherent in the process of globalization under way around the world, and the outcome is far from inevitable, but unchecked, high-tech mercantilism could well induce a drift into unilateralism, narrow reciprocity, more managed trade, and interbloc rivalry. Like agricultural subsidies, high-tech mercantilism could become a policy instrument available only to those major trading nations and trading companies with very deep pockets. In those circumstances, everyone else would lose, particularly the countries most dependent on foreign trade.

Canada has an enormous political and economic stake in keeping the system open. We already export 34% of what we produce, compared with 14% for Japan and 10% for the U.S. The challenge for all countries is to invest imagination and talent and wisdom in multilateral diplomacy rather than risk seeing the tendency to regional integration degenerate into neomercantilist, exclusionary blocs.

Beyond Economics. Leadership consists of recognizing world trends and acting to meet the challenges and to capitalize on the opportunities a new age presents. Interdependence makes this new age one of nearly boundless opportunities for those nations that are competitive, and of nearly limitless vulnerability for those that are not. We do not, however, see economic excellence, in the sense of competitiveness and a strong economy, as some Darwinian end in itself. We see it as a means to an end— an end that liberates our creative spirit, secures our social contract, expands our economic opportunities, protects our natural environment, and enhances our role in world affairs.

These goals are shared, in varying degrees, by many nations, but only the competitive nations will be able to realize them. Competitiveness depends on cooperation between government and industry, between business and universities, and between employers and employees. However, it is unmistakably clear in Canada, as in other successful economies, that private-sector individuals and corporations, not governments, are creating the new wealth that makes progress possible. I strongly believe that the role of government is to articulate the national vision and to create an economic climate in which the private sector can succeed. The role of the private sector is to create the wealth that makes progress possible and to lead the way in making us competitive.

In the period since 1950, Canada's gross domestic product (GDP), in constant dollars, has increased fivefold. This has been a time of unprecedented prosperity, fueled by direct foreign investment in resource development, tremendous productivity improvement in our agricultural sector, and the growth of sophisticated automotive, aerospace, and other industries competing in a global economy. As our people have moved from farms to the city, we have become one of the most urbanized societies in the world. With a population that today totals only 26 million, we have built an economy that ranks eighth in the world. As a trading nation, we rank seventh in absolute terms. Canadians enjoy a standard of living second only to that of the U.S. But we are mindful of the fact that in the new global economy, we must compete successfully or stagnate.

Over the last four years, we began to change the direction of our country to prepare it for the world ahead. We restored investor confidence, through our emphasis on fiscal responsibility; encouraged private initiative, by reforming our tax system; dismantled barriers to investment that had been hampering economic growth and deterring risk-taking by industry. We launched a process

WIDE WORLD PHOTOS/CANAPRESS PHOTO

Canadian Ambassador Allan Gotlieb, U.S. Trade Representative Clayton Yeutter, and former U.S. treasury secretary James Baker express their approval as Pres. Ronald Reagan signs legislation implementing the U.S.-Canadian free-trade agreement in September 1988.

15

of deregulation and privatization. We undertook initiatives that will ensure our growth in the 1990s and into the 21st century—free trade with the U.S.; multilateral negotiations in the GATT; new support for science and technology; and new regional agencies to promote entrepreneurship and small and medium-sized business.

We have made social programs more responsive to the needs of Canadians in the 1980s and 1990s and more attuned to the times ahead. We are, for example, reforming the unemployment insurance system. Canadians need a better system, one that trains them for the jobs of the future, not one that compensates them for the loss of the dead-end jobs of the past. A fundamental objective of our economic agenda is to ensure that we can continue to afford the generous health and social programs that bring us both peace of mind and pride in our citizenship.

But fostering economic prosperity without strengthening national unity is like building on quicksand, and no economic indicator will ever express the value of social solidarity, tolerance, and generosity. In Canada the legacy of the constitutional debates of the 1980s included an imperfect constitution, modified without the consent of Quebec, home of the majority of our francophone population. This, to me, was as dangerous to the future of our country as was economic stagnation.

The Living Constitution. I have always thought of the Canadian constitution as the expression of our collective will, as Canadians, to live in harmony, share our security and prosperity, and leave a better country to the next generation. It should, therefore, be an instrument for fashioning our future. It is a living document, and like all living things it must evolve and grow. The essence of our country, the "soul" of Canada, the principles that have been central to our existence since confederation—these do not change. Times change, however, and conditions change, and the purpose of constitutional reform is to ensure that unchanging principles can be applied to changing needs and circumstances.

In 1867 the fathers of confederation recognized our linguistic duality and the distinctiveness of Quebec. They acted to build a strong Canadian economy. They recognized, even then, special needs and circumstances in the Maritime provinces. They were determined not only to defend our physical territory but to establish Canada's sovereignty, independence, and national identity. Over the years, successive generations of Canadians have built, and built well, on the unique and precious concepts— of equality, of partnership, of respect for diversity, of sharing—that are the foundations of our nationhood.

Sometimes they have done so through constitutional reform. More often they have done so through federal or provincial policies and legislation—the Official Languages Acts of New Brunswick and of the federal Parliament; the equalization formula to assist less wealthy provinces; multiculturalism. These concepts, together with Aboriginal rights, have been enhanced by constitutional action: responsibilities with regard to English and French in the Manitoba Act of 1870; the expansion of Canada, bringing in British Columbia in 1871, Saskatchewan and Alberta in 1905, and, in the east, Prince Edward Island in 1873 and Newfoundland in 1949. Patriation, breaking the constitutional tie to Britain, and amendments to the constitution came in 1982. Successive generations have responded to the physical and geographic challenges posed by Canada— building the railways, the St. Lawrence Seaway, the ports and airports and highways, the communications systems, the infrastructure that Canada needed. Over the years, Canadians have developed the means of expressing our

The author enjoys a laugh with Soviet Pres. Mikhail Gorbachev during a visit to the Soviet Union. Gorbachev's sweeping reforms had already sparked profound change across the face of the Soviet Union and Eastern Europe.
CANAPRESS PHOTO

culture and identity—in broadcasting, publishing, the arts.

We Canadians know that we are the most fortunate of nations in many ways. The innumerable conflicts that persist around the world teach us that our structure— a bilingual, multicultural, federal, diversified, and united country—is the right one for Canada. And we know that each new generation must live up to the challenge of making that concept flourish. The coexistence of English- and French-speaking Canadians without either group assimilating the other is fundamental to our identity; it is also a noble and uplifting goal that teaches us the value of tolerance and generosity.

While this makes us unique, it also presents a constant challenge. In November 1976 Quebecers elected a pro-independence government, but when a referendum on sovereignty-association—the greatest threat to Canadian unity—was held in 1980, a majority of Quebecers voted for the promise of a renewed federalism. When the prime minister and the provincial premiers agreed on patriation and amendment of the constitution on Nov. 5, 1981, however, Quebec was left out. This clearly could not be left for the next generation to try to sort out. The premiers of the 10 provinces shared my sense of urgency and, together, we concluded the Meech Lake accord, which reunited the Canadian constitutional family. Three provinces— New Brunswick, Manitoba, and Newfoundland—wish to see changes in the accord, but I remain confident that the larger vision of Canada will prevail. The Meech Lake agreement is central to the kind of country Canada will be in the year 2000 and how we will meet the competition.

Canada and the World. We are not a superpower, but in an age when international influence is increasingly a function of economic strength, we rank as a major player on the international scene. We enjoy the unique privilege, and advantage, of membership in the Commonwealth, La Francophonie, the Organization of American States, and the Group of Seven major industrialized democracies. We are taking an active part in the multilateral trade negotiations. Other nations look to Canada to play a constructive role on regional political and economic issues and to contribute to peacekeeping operations. Canada is proud of its tradition of nearly four decades of peacekeeping, a task we have always willingly assumed. Canada has

participated in virtually every UN peacekeeping force, and this contribution, costly and difficult though it has often been, has assisted in bringing stability to explosive regions of the world. Today a significant portion of our armed forces are either involved in peacekeeping or training for further duty in the service of peace. The award of the 1988 Nobel Peace Prize to the UN peacekeeping forces was a splendid tribute both to the UN secretary-general and to those courageous men and women who patrol the world's danger spots under the UN flag.

Nowhere are more profound changes occurring than in the Soviet Union and Eastern Europe. The iron curtain is coming down and the Berlin Wall is open. In Poland, Hungary, and Czechoslovakia, free elections are producing new governments and new institutions for a new age. East Germany, Bulgaria, and Romania are embarked on the same path. This has happened at a pace that has confounded almost all the pundits and encouraged men and women of good will everywhere. These are circumstances in which there need be no losers; with such reform, both sides can win.

This process has been triggered by the Soviet leadership's domestic political reform program and forthright assurances—in keeping with its undertakings at the Conference for Security and Cooperation in Europe—that all nations are entitled to choose, without interference, their own way of development. A sterile period of East-West confrontation is ending, and a time of immensely more fruitful relations is starting, an era that holds the promise of genuine democracy in Eastern Europe, more liberalized trade and investment opportunities across that vast region, more predictable relations with the Soviet Union, and reduced emphasis on defense.

Eventually, as governments enjoying the freely given support of their people continue to emerge in Eastern Europe, European stability will be put on a durable basis. Nevertheless, the transition period will have to be managed carefully. In fact, the people of Eastern Europe and the leadership of the Soviet Union are handling the changing situation very prudently. In these swiftly changing circumstances, NATO retains its importance. NATO is a political as well as a military organization and is an indispensable part of the Western diplomatic infrastructure. It is the locus for discussion of the Western response to political change in the East and for coordinating positions in the crucial conventional arms reduction talks in Vienna and the superpower negotiations on strategic weapons in Geneva.

Elsewhere, we see less promise. The vicious cycle of repression and violence is unbroken in South Africa. We all know the cause: the massive and institutionalized violation of human rights called apartheid. International pressure on South Africa is increasing and, as the South African government itself has admitted, is having an impact. The entire world finds apartheid repugnant; the whole world must now join forces to bring it to an end. Canada has taken strong measures of its own to help rid the world of this unique evil. Trade with South Africa has been cut by 50% since we imposed sanctions. Agricultural trade has been stopped completely. Export credits have been cut off. And all high-level contacts have been proscribed.

Crisis in the South. The agenda of the new age will include topics that have entered the national consciousness only recently. Population growth, environmental deterioration, drug abuse, and social alienation—these issues will require foresight and leadership in unprecedented measure. None is as dramatic as war. None can galvanize public opinion the way war can. Ultimately, however, each presents grave threats to global security, and all demand we act cooperatively.

The demographics in the years ahead are chilling. In the next decade, when the world will add a billion people to its current population of five billion, 80% of the world's population will live in the poor countries of the South. These populations will make almost impossible demands on their governments for infrastructure, education, and shelter. They will place potentially unsustainable pressures on the environment for food, fuel, and resources. Deforestation, desertification, and destabilization are the quite-predictable results, with serious consequences for all of us. "Trouble spots" used to develop through the territorial ambitions of neighbours or the desire for hegemony. Now they are more likely to arise because of political instability

People crowd the streets of Cairo, which is one of the world's most densely populated cities. Within the next decade, the world's population is expected to increase by one billion people, most of whom will live in countries unable to support them.

North Canol Road, the source of the
South Macmillan River in the foothills of
the Selwyn Mountains (Yukon Territory),
remains unspoiled by litter or pollution.
Most Canadians feel that the environment
is a fundamental concern and cannot be
sacrificed in the name of progress.
GEORGE HUNTER—TSW-CLICK/CHICAGO LTD.

induced by hunger, income disparities, and the repression of economic aspirations. This turmoil will only add to the more than 80 million people already seeking to emigrate from their homelands.

These projections say as much about the present as about the future, and they are alterable if action is taken in time. Development assistance, of course, is one of the answers. Canada has always seen development assistance as a way to help newer nations raise their living standards toward the levels enjoyed by the leading industrialized nations. In fact, even with the constraints imposed by a difficult fiscal situation, Canada's per capita contribution as a percentage of GDP remains among the highest of the leading industrial countries.

Many less developed countries see an increasing share of their national incomes devoted to servicing debt owed to foreigners, whether governments or commercial banks. The debt was incurred in good faith on both sides, in the hope of stimulating a development boom that would enable the borrower nations to lay the economic foundations for a more prosperous future. The discipline of good faith between debtor and creditor must not be lightly abandoned if assistance of a similar kind is to be forthcoming in the future. However, the crushing burden of debt, sapping the will of the people to continue the effort to create self-sustaining development, must not be allowed to destabilize economic prospects and derail democratic practices. This is why Canada introduced a policy of forgiving official development assistance debt incurred by Commonwealth and francophone nations in Africa. In forgiving this debt, which would never have been repaid in any case, Canada was being both fair and realistic. It would be wise for all industrialized nations to regard the debt of these poorest countries in the same light. Acceptance of this approach by all of the leading industrial countries would eliminate 15% of all external debt owed by the poorest African nations.

At the same time, the industrialized countries owe it to themselves and to their partners to put their own fiscal houses in order. Excessive debt is not only a problem faced by less developed countries; it is also a problem in North America. In our first mandate, we succeeded in reducing Canada's deficit from 8.6% of GDP in 1984 to 4.7% in 1989. Even so, our debt today exceeds $320

billion. Investments in development assistance to the less developed nations and in our own future—science and technology, education, pensions, day care—cannot be afforded if we go on borrowing more and more just to pay interest on the national debt. This year alone, interest on our national debt will be more than we spend on health care, family allowances, old age security, and social assistance together. The deficit and the debt threaten the economic future of all Canadians. That is why we brought in a tough budget and comprehensive income tax reform and are moving ahead to replace our antiquated manufacturers' sales tax with a multistage goods and services tax, a value-added tax that will come into effect on Jan. 1, 1991.

By the end of our current fiscal planning period, 1993–94, our deficit, computed on a basis comparable to that used in the U.S. or the U.K., will be about $3 billion, or very close to zero. On a national accounts basis, we will be in surplus. Our government will then have freed up resources to attack our priorities.

Since 1984 our government has pursued a coherent agenda designed to get the government out of doing things it does not do well and to allow private initiative to get on with the business of creating durable growth and productive jobs. By almost every measure of economic performance, the returns have been substantial. Since 1984 our record of growth among the Group of Seven countries has been a close second to Japan. In the World Economic Forum's tabulation, our ranking in international competitiveness rose from 11th in 1983 to 4th in 1989.

Environmental Concerns. We are determined, however, that progress will not come at the cost of our natural environment. We Canadians care deeply about our environment. Our national soul breathes its life from our lakes and forests and plains and trees. They are part of us. The environment is a powerfully unifying force; it is fundamental to our identity. Preserving the environment for future generations is not merely a question of social responsibility; it is an act of national self-preservation.

It can also be, between neighbours, a test of friendship. Across the thousands of miles of our common border and along our common coasts on the rims of three oceans, Canadians and Americans meet and reach out to each other in uncounted ways, every day. On the whole,

the bilateral environmental record between Canada and the U.S. has been impressive—from the truly visionary Boundary Waters Treaty of 1909 to the renewal of the Great Lakes Water Quality Agreement, the Niagara River Toxics Management Plan, the Porcupine Caribou Herd Agreement, and the North American Waterfowl Management Plan of the past few years. But there remains one anomaly in this otherwise solid record of joint environmental stewardship. I am referring, of course, to acid rain. The one thing acid rain does not do is discriminate. Acid rain falls, corrosively and without respect to the values they represent, on the Washington Monument, the White House, the Capitol, and the Lincoln Memorial. In Canada our Parliament buildings are being similarly damaged. These facts symbolize the enormity of the damage our nations have been inflicting on their respective heritages.

In eastern Canada at least 14,000 lakes are now acid dead. Another 300,000 are damaged or vulnerable. In Nova Scotia many streams no longer support the salmon for which they were once famous, and throughout eastern Canada our magnificent forests—including, tragically, maple forests—are being seriously affected.

Acid rain offers a tough lesson in interdependence. Half of the acid rain that falls in Canada—and in some areas much more than half—originates in the U.S. Up to a quarter of the acid rain that falls in the northeastern U.S. originates in Canada. When the Progressive Conservative Party came to power in 1984, we were acutely conscious—and embarrassed—that Canada was asking the U.S. for action on acid rain when Canadian performance was also lacking. We set out to clean up our own backyard. We reached binding agreements with our seven easternmost provinces to cut sulfur dioxide emissions to 50% of 1980 allowable levels by 1994. We are well advanced in our program. Sulfur dioxide emissions in eastern Canada are down 40% already, and the amount of sulfur dioxide moving from Canada to the U.S. has been reduced by a third; Canadian firms and utilities have embarked on programs to install new processes and technologies that, when completed, will cost $500 million per year to operate.

I am encouraged by the progressive stance Pres. George Bush has taken on acid rain. The world needs the U.S. in the vanguard of environmental leadership because progress on the complex of global issues we face can be made only if the U.S. plays its full part. The environment is the common heritage of mankind; it is our destiny. We need to recognize that economic growth and environmental sensitivity are both indispensable. In Canada and abroad, we will work for the principle of sustainable development, the new international ethic for environmentally sound economic development. We believe we are making progress on our environmental agenda. We have passed a new Canadian Environmental Protection Act that is among the toughest in the world. We have adopted strict standards for handling polychlorinated biphenyls (PCBs). New emissions standards for buses and heavy-duty trucks, as strict as any in the world, came into effect in December 1988. We are cleaning up the Great Lakes and the St. Lawrence River. Under our "Environment Choice" program, we are giving our seal of approval to "environmentally friendly" products so Canadians can identify products that are not harmful to the environment. We plan new legislation on water quality and new regulations on toxic chemicals.

One of the most urgent problems facing our planet is ozone depletion. Chlorofluorocarbons (CFCs), used in everyday products like refrigerants and fire extinguishers,

are entering the upper atmosphere and depleting the ozone layer, the Earth's shield against ultraviolet radiation from the Sun. The results are very serious; not least among them, the incidence of skin cancer is increasing. The "holes" in the ozone layer that have appeared over both poles pose dangers that are still only partly understood. In Montreal in 1987, the first truly global treaty prescribing reductions in the use of CFCs was concluded. Canada, the U.S., and the European Communities and others have since pledged to stop using CFCs by the end of the next decade at the latest.

The Greenhouse Effect. Encouraging as this precedent is, a still more complex problem lies ahead—the warming of the Earth. Each year the world's 400 million automobiles discharge 550 million tons of carbon into the atmosphere. Each year forests the size of our province of Nova Scotia—forests that process carbon dioxide—disappear. What not long ago was merely a subject of scientific curiosity—the greenhouse effect—has burst onto our front pages. Coping with the threat of global warming will require more than high-minded urgings from the industrial countries to do as we say, not as we have done. It will take the cooperation of East and West and of North and South to combat this undesirable climate change.

We need, for example, to assign full value to natural resources and to the environment, to free ourselves of the misconception that natural resources achieve an economic value only when they are consumed—a dubious theoretical proposition at best and a self-evident error in the real world. By this reasoning, the Brazilian rain forest, perhaps nature's greatest cornucopia, would be of maximum value when it disappeared. That is why we, in Canada, are reexamining our system of national accounts. It is why the Group of Seven countries, at our suggestion, have requested the Organization for Economic Cooperation and Development to do more research on a system of environmental indicators so that factors previously ignored—including environmental factors—will be integrated into assessments of national wealth.

The industrialized countries have a special responsibility for leadership on energy use and environmental reform. They account for the lion's share of current world production of carbon dioxide. Global climate change is potentially the most dangerous and certainly the most complex challenge that governments face. Global problems require global solutions. That is why, at the landmark Toronto Conference on Climate Change in 1988, I called for an international convention to protect the atmosphere, akin to the convention that protects the seas. I would like to see that convention ready for signature at the UN Conference on the Environment in 1992. That is also why the countries participating in the environmental summit at The Hague in March 1989 endorsed the need for innovative institutions with the authority to combat global warming.

Governments must carry their share of the load, but industry and the public also have indispensable contributions to make. For industry, both energy producers and users, the challenges are every bit as difficult as they are for government, and the outcome is every bit as vital. The battle for sustainable development will be won only if industry is in the front lines. Significant gains can come from conservation; but technological development is critical. The main consumers of fossil fuels today are technologies—steam and the internal combustion engine—that have their origins in the 19th century. If we get our market signals right, private companies will prove to be among our most effective environmentalists; only

they have the capacity to bring environmentally sound products to market, cleaner new fuels and processes and the next generation of engines.

Challenges for Tomorrow. The epidemic of drug abuse is another, ominous threat to national and international security. When illegal drugs are involved, life is cheapened, crime rates soar, and young lives are ruined. Multinational drug syndicates even threaten the integrity of small countries. It is a problem that no nation can solve on its own, though some countries are suffering more than others. A new form of international diplomacy has been born—drug diplomacy. Unsanctioned production, illegal shipping, official corruption, money laundering are its targets, but so far self-interested supply continues to satisfy self-destructive demand. Only a concerted international approach can deal with a menace of such dimensions.

We must also foster international cooperation in the fight against new, widespread health problems such as AIDS. Undetected a decade ago, this illness has spared no region, exempted no country, and absolved no race. It is unimpressed by the state of health of those it infects. It is indifferent to their stations in life and contemptuous of their hopes and dreams. It has sown fear like few diseases before it. The disease affects all our lives. In a very real sense, we are all living with AIDS.

AIDS is teaching us all, rich nations and poor, a searing new lesson in interdependence. Worldwide, as many as 450,000 people may have contracted AIDS; as many as five million people, perhaps more, may be infected. In the cities of certain less developed countries, at least 10% of the population is testing positive for the HIV antibody, indicating exposure to the AIDS virus. Given the statistical relationship of the infection to the illness itself, the number of AIDS cases is certain to increase in the near future. This stark reality must spur us all to action. Our response must be built on cooperation of all sectors of society. This is not a problem that can be left to governments alone. Our tools are education and research—education to prevent further spread of the disease, to foster understanding and compassion for the afflicted, and to safeguard their rights; research to reveal the characteristics of the virus and how it can be defeated. All of these are, of course, interrelated.

Even the way we think about health is evolving. Health care will never again be thought of as a straightforward attack on disease. It now involves the marshaling of multidisciplinary expertise and individual genius to address a wide range of complex and often interrelated issues.

Embryo transplants, in vitro fertilization, genetic screening of fetuses—could we have known, even a decade ago, that the explosion in medical knowledge and scientific research would push to the forefront the ethical dilemmas we face in the field of reproductive technologies? Medical science has left open the fundamental questions and implications raised by these technologies. The health and well-being of women, the status and rights of people using or contributing to reproductive services, the social and legal arrangements for the children brought into the world through extraordinary medical means—these are moral issues that concern us all. This is why we have created a royal commission on the new reproductive technologies. This commission will be charged with the sobering responsibility of reviewing these technologies and their implications for Canadian society.

Reproductive technologies comprise only one aspect of the changing nature of health care. Basic prevention of disease is another, one in which all nations have an interest. In many nations the provision of water, free of

AIDS is a serious problem that cannot be ignored. The threat of the disease is already a global concern.
D. HUDSON—SYGMA

bacterial infection, is a major objective. The prevention and cure of simple diarrhea in children could save three million lives a year around the world. Once clean water is available, the general level of health in a society soars. Especially in developed nations, the maintenance of a safe water supply, free from toxic pollutants so water that looks safe is safe, has become a national priority.

Health care in the future will reach beyond the traditional medical model of curing and into improving the way we live as individuals and nations. In November 1986, at the first International Conference of Health Promotion, Canada introduced its own blueprint to guide the evolution of health care. It signaled a shift in our conception of health, away from mortality statistics and toward a greater concern for housing, education, and the quality of life. It goes beyond elaborate medical treatment systems to embrace the concepts of health promotion and disease prevention. It helps to transform individuals from passive patients into active participants and decision makers in their own care. Above all, it makes individuals, their communities, and their governments partners with health professionals.

The partnership takes many forms. In Canada, where it is estimated that tobacco constitutes the largest cause of preventable death, the partnership has led to passage of the Tobacco Products Control Act, legislation passed by my government last May that will prohibit the advertising of any tobacco products offered for sale in Canada. It creates new requirements for the labeling of tobacco products to inform users more clearly about the health risks they are incurring. Legislative action of this type is modern health policy. It is not easy. Many diverse interests bring their legitimate concerns to the debate. But in the end the nation's standard of health depends on citizens and their governments determining together the health care system they wish to create.

We are entering an age that calls for global values, values that recognize mankind's shared destiny, values based on social justice, tolerance, compassion, and liberty, values that are underwritten by broad economic prosperity and based on a profound sense of international responsibility. International collaboration is the most important condition of our success.

The key lies in recognizing that now, more than ever, our well-being and our security are indivisible from the well-being and security of all of mankind.

The Alma-Ata Declaration:
Health for All by the Year 2000?

BY KENNETH S. WARREN

To paraphrase a saying of Major Greenwood of the London School of Hygiene and Tropical Medicine 40 years ago, statistics is medicine with the tears wiped off. On a personal note, after 25 years as a tropical medicine specialist working in Brazil, the West Indies, Kenya, Egypt, Thailand, the Philippines, and China, both in hospitals and in the field, I was awakened to the reality of how easy it is to find ways to wipe such tears away. I was driving on a back road in the Rift Valley of Kenya when I passed a large, apparently unruly crowd of Masai who were attempting to wave me down. My first impulse was to put my foot on the accelerator, but in my rear-view mirror I noticed what appeared to be several limp children in their arms. I turned back, and five men and women carrying four unconscious children jumped into the car while others tried to force their way in as well. As we drove frantically to the nearest aid station, about eight kilometres (five miles) away, the adults moaned and cried while taking mouthfuls of cow's blood and milk from their gourds and blowing it on the children and all over the interior of the car. I don't think I've ever felt such a concentrated message of despair and fear as those people evinced.

Receiving that message, I suddenly realized how hardened I had become to the deaths of infants and children in the less developed world, and how I had assumed that the high death rates similarly inured parents to loss. In this case, happily, when we reached the aid station, the personnel were able to ascertain that the children had eaten poisonous berries and would probably recover.

The good outcome of that experience was pure chance and amazing luck for those involved. It would not have been surprising had the children been stricken with any of a myriad of more malevolent diseases such as African sleeping sickness, cholera, and measles. Each day, tens of thousands of children die in the world's less developed countries for lack of adequate health care.

More than 10 years ago, in 1978, a gathering of people aiming to change the state of such people's health took place in Alma-Ata, a city in central U.S.S.R. near the border with China and close to fabled Tashkent and Samarkand. The World Health Organization (WHO) and the United Nations Children's Fund (UNICEF) sponsored the meeting, which involved delegations from 134 countries and 67 UN organizations. It culminated in the adoption of the Declaration of Alma-Ata, which enshrined health as "a fundamental human right." The word *declaration* was used advisedly, suggesting that Alma-Ata would rank with those other great Declarations, of Independence and the Rights of Man. Its essential concern was with equity, the assurance that everyone have at least the minimal requisites for a healthy life.

Dr. Kenneth S. Warren is director for science at the Maxwell Communications Corp. in New York City. His books include Tropical and Geographical Medicine.

The Declaration: Crusade and Controversy. The International Conference on Primary Health Care met for six days in Alma-Ata, beginning Sept. 6, 1978. At the opening ceremony, Halfdan Mahler, the director general of WHO, speaking in the direct and uncompromising tone inherited from his Protestant clergyman father, challenged the delegates with eight questions:

1. Are you ready to address yourselves seriously to the existing gap between the health "haves" and the health "have nots" and to adopt concrete measures to reduce it?
2. Are you ready to ensure the proper planning and implementation of primary health care in coordinated efforts with other relevant sectors, in order to promote health as an indispensable contribution to the improvement of the quality of life of every individual,

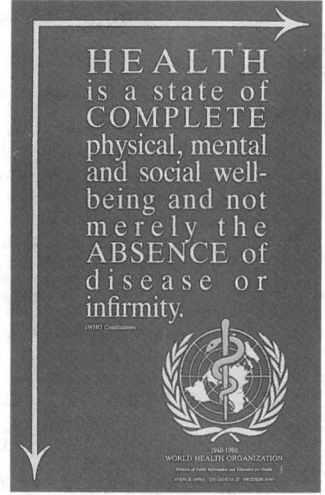

The World Health Organization's definition of health as a state of positive well-being, shown here on a poster, was incorporated into the Alma-Ata Declaration."

WORLD HEALTH ORGANIZATION

HEALTH is a state of COMPLETE physical, mental and social well-being and not merely the ABSENCE of disease or infirmity.

family and community as part of overall socioeconomic development?
3. Are you ready to make preferential allocations of health resources to the social periphery as an absolute priority?
4. Are you ready to mobilize and enlighten individuals, families and communities in order to ensure their full identification with primary health care, their participation in its planning and management, and their contribution to its application?
5. Are you ready to introduce the reforms required to ensure the availability of relevant manpower and technology, sufficient to cover the whole country with primary health care within the next two decades at a cost you can afford?
6. Are you ready to introduce, if necessary, radical changes in the existing health delivery system so that it properly supports primary health care as the overriding health priority?
7. Are you ready to fight the political and technical battles required to overcome any social and economic obstacles and professional resistance to the universal introduction of primary health care?
8. Are you ready to make unequivocal political com-

The Declaration of Alma-Ata

1. The conference strongly reaffirms that health, which is a state of complete physical, mental and social well-being, and not merely the absence of disease or infirmity, is a fundamental human right and that the attainment of the highest possible level of health is a most important world-wide social goal whose realisation requires the action of many other social and economic sectors in addition to the health sector.

2. The existing gross inequality in the health status of the people, particularly between developed and developing countries as well as within countries, is politically, socially and economically unacceptable and is, therefore, of common concern to all countries.

3. Economic and social development, based on a New International Economic Order, is of basic importance to the fullest attainment of health for all and to the reduction of the gap between the health status of the developing and developed countries. The promotion and protection of the health of the people is essential to sustained economic and social development and contributes to a better quality of life and to world peace.

4. The people have the right and duty to participate individually and collectively in the planning and implementation of their health care.

5. Governments have a responsibility for the health of their people which can be fulfilled only by the provision of adequate health and social measures. A main social target of governments, international organizations and the whole world community in the coming decades should be the attainment by all peoples of the world by the year 2000 of a level of health that will permit them to lead a socially and economically productive life. Primary health care is the key to attaining this target as part of development in the spirit of social justice.

6. Primary health care is essential health care based on practical, scientifically sound and socially acceptable methods and technology made universally accessible to individuals and families in the community through their full participation and at a cost that the community and country can afford to maintain at every stage of their development in the spirit of self-reliance and self-determination. It forms an integral part both of the country's health system, of which it is the central function and main focus, and of the overall social and economic development of the community. It is the first level of contact of individuals, the family and community with the national health system, bringing health care as close as possible to where people live and work, and constitutes the first element of a continuing health care process.

7. Primary health care:
1. reflects and evolves from the economic conditions and socio-cultural and political characteristics of the country and its communities, and is based on the application of the relevant results of social, biomedical and health services research and public health experience;
2. addresses the main health problems in the community, providing promotive, preventive, curative, and rehabilitative services accordingly;
3. includes at least: education concerning prevailing health problems and the methods of preventing and controlling them; promotion of food supply and proper nutrition; an adequate supply of safe water and basic sanitation; maternal and child health care, including family planning; immunization against the major infectious diseases; preven-

tion and control of locally endemic diseases; appropriate treatment of common diseases and injuries; and provision of essential drugs;
4. involves, in addition to the health sector, all related sectors and aspects of national and community development, in particular agriculture, animal husbandry, food, industry, education, housing, public works, communications and other sectors; and demands the coordinated efforts of all those sectors;
5. requires and promotes maximum community and individual self-reliance and participation in the planning, organization, operation and control of primary health care, making fullest use of local, national and other available resources, and to this end develops through appropriate education the ability of communities to participate;
6. should be sustained by integrated, functional and mutually-supportive referral systems, leading to the progressive improvement of comprehensive health care for all, and giving priority to those most in need;
7. relies, at local and referral levels, on health workers, including physicians, nurses, midwives, auxiliaries and community workers as applicable, as well as traditional practitioners as needed, suitably trained socially and technically to work as a health team and to respond to the expressed health needs of the community.

8. All governments should formulate national policies, strategies and plans of action to launch and sustain primary health care as part of a comprehensive national health system and in coordination with other sectors. To this end, it will be necessary to exercise political will, to mobilise the country's resources and to use available external resources rationally.

9. All countries should cooperate in a spirit of partnership and service to ensure primary health care for all people since the attainment of health by people in any one country directly concerns and benefits every other country. In this context the joint WHO/UNICEF report on primary health care constitutes a solid basis for the further development and operation of primary health care throughout the world.

10. An acceptable level of health for all the people of the world by the year 2000 can be attained through a fuller and better use of the world's resources, a considerable part of which is now spent on armaments and military conflicts. A genuine policy of independence, peace, détente and disarmament could and should release additional resources that could well be devoted to peaceful aims and in particular to the acceleration of social and economic development of which primary health care, as an essential part, should be allotted its proper share.

* * *

The International Conference on Primary Health Care calls for urgent and effective national and international action to develop and implement primary health care throughout the world and particularly in developing countries in a spirit of technical cooperation and in keeping with a New International Economic Order. It urges governments, WHO and UNICEF, and other international organizations, as well as multilateral and bilateral agencies, non-governmental organizations, funding agencies, all health workers and the whole world community to support national and international commitment to primary health care and to channel increased technical and financial support to it, particularly in developing countries. The Conference calls on all the aforementioned to collaborate in introducing, developing and maintaining primary health care in accordance with the spirit and content of this Declaration.

mitments to adopt primary health care and to mobilize international solidarity to attain the objective of health for all by the year 2000?

At the final plenary session, the Declaration of Alma-Ata was carried by acclamation. (*See* Sidebar.) In the words of Maggie Black in her book *The Children and the Nations: The Story of Unicef,* "In its own terms, the Alma-Ata conference was a triumph. It represented a watershed: the moment when primary health care ceased being the provenance of a few brave medical pioneers in dusty villages and a group of international protagonists on their behalf, and instead became an approach to which most of the governments of the world had given their endorsement, and many ministries of health committed themselves to carrying out."

From the beginning the Declaration of Alma-Ata has been controversial, particularly as regards its definition of health, its strategy to achieve it, and its timetable. It reaffirmed the definition of health set forth in the WHO constitution 30 years earlier: "a state of complete physical, mental and social well-being and not merely the absence of disease or infirmity." Its strategy was primary health care, which "reflects and evolves from the economic conditions and socio-cultural and political characteristics of the country and its communities, and is based on the application of the relevant results of social, biomedical and health services research and public health experience." Its timetable was the attainment "by all peoples of the world by the year 2000 of a level of health that will permit them to lead a socially and economically productive life."

Szeming Sze of China recently described how WHO's famous definition of health was created. He stated: "A lot of people did not think that we should define health. . . . I think there were three of us—Dr. Brock Chisholm from Canada (who became the first director general of WHO), Dr. Gregorio Berman from Argentina and myself. . . . Chisholm, being a psychiatrist, wanted to mention mental health, and I thought we should put in something that emphasized the importance of the preventive side of health. That's how we came up with the wording in the Constitution that defines health as not merely the absence of illness."

A state of complete physical, mental, and social well-being is an unattainable ideal. As physical well-being has increased in Europe and North America, mental illness has become more prominent. As social well-being has improved, both within and among countries, the disparity between wealth and poverty has become more pronounced. Primary health care, seemingly the key element in the battle, is difficult even to define. It is generally described as the first level of contact of individuals, the family, and the community with the National Health System, but in 1986 Susan Rifkind and Gil Walt of the London School of Hygiene and Tropical Medicine found it "still difficult to define, but reflecting the existing social, political and economic conditions of individuals and communities at a given time and place." But even if the final goal were achievable, the schedule is clearly too optimistic. It is now evident that health for all, as defined by WHO or even in far less demanding terms, will not be achieved by the year 2000, although many advances will have been made. The halfway point between Alma-Ata and its target year is a good time to examine the background of the Declaration, the efforts to implement it, the accomplishments and failures, and the outlook for the future.

Our World: How Healthy? The UNICEF publication *The State of the World's Children* for 1986 tells the story of Maria Auxilia Paja, from a rural area of South America where there was no organized health care. Two of her children had just died, one from a respiratory infection and the other from measles. As she described it, "For the baby boy, I tried to get help. But, as I was carrying him for help, he just died in my arms. My daughter was older. I had got used to playing with her, being with her. It's difficult . . . it's sad to remember those times with my children. She was alright when she went to bed. By midnight she was sick. She died just as day broke. I am not alone. It's happened to a lot of women."

At a meeting on nuclear war in Budapest in 1985, James Grant, the executive director of UNICEF, compared the 180,000 people killed by the first atomic bomb dropped on a city with the 60,000 children who, he said, die every day in the less developed countries of the world. Thus, he went on, "every three days constitutes a silent Hiroshima."

According to *The State of the World's Children* for 1984, 75% of the world's population, 97% of annual infant deaths (under one year of age), 98% of annual child deaths (from ages one to five), and 85% of annual births are found in the less developed world. (*See* Fig. 1.) Data for four less developed countries, Nepal, Pakistan, Indonesia, and Ghana, show the major causes of death among children to be diarrhea and malnutrition, measles, lower respiratory infections, tetanus, and malaria. (*See* Fig. 2.)

The plight of children is intimately related to that of their parents. The death of a mother does not bode well for surviving young children. In one incident that people in developed nations might find appalling, my chief technician and good friend for over a decade was born on the Zaire-Angola border to the youngest wife of a tribal chief. Unfortunately, his 14-year-old mother died in childbirth and, as was the custom, the living baby was placed out in the jungle to be disposed of by natural means. Fortunately for this child, the next day his amazed uncle found him still alive and took him to an American missionary family to be raised.

Because of the close tie between the fate of a mother and that of her child, it is important to realize that the commonest cause of death among women of reproductive age in the less developed world is complications of pregnancy! These complications are principally hemorrhage, infection, and obstructed labour. Ninety-nine percent of all maternal deaths in childbirth occur in the less developed world, one-third of them in Africa. A study conducted at the University Hospital in Zaria, Nigeria, found that for every maternal death, 15 women suffer permanent damage due to stroke, fistulas, and other complications of pregnancy. Over the child-bearing period of women in Africa, those who become pregnant suffer one chance in 21 of dying of pregnancy-related causes. For Asia, the figure is 1 in 54; for South America, 1 in 73; the Caribbean, 1 in 140; North America, 1 in 6,366; and northern Europe, 1 in 9,850.

It has been known for some time that the less developed world is going through what has been called the health transition. Its people are still suffering from the traditional diseases of the tropics and those related to wholesale poverty. At the same time, as socioeconomic development continues and life expectancy increases, they are also afflicted with the diseases of the developed world. Thus, in 1986 diseases of the circulatory system, a principal cause of death in the United States, was second only to respiratory diseases as a cause of death in the less developed world. These were followed by diarrhea, measles, injuries, and cancer (the latter attributable in part to high rates of

(TOP) SOURCE: *UNITED NATIONS WORLD DEMOGRAPHIC ESTIMATES* (JULY 1983);
(BOTTOM) SOURCE: ROBERT N. GROSSE, "INTERRELATION BETWEEN HEALTH AND POPULATION:
OBSERVATIONS DERIVED FROM FIELD EXPERIENCES," *SOCIAL SCIENCE AND MEDICINE* (JUNE 1980), VOL. 14C, NO. 2, P. 103

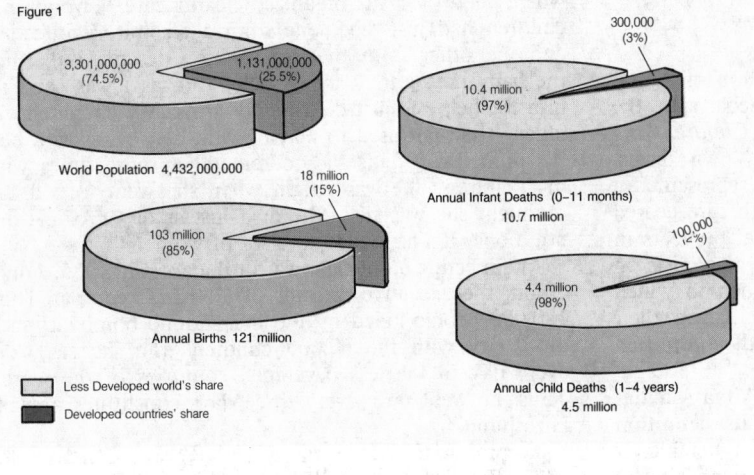

Figure 1

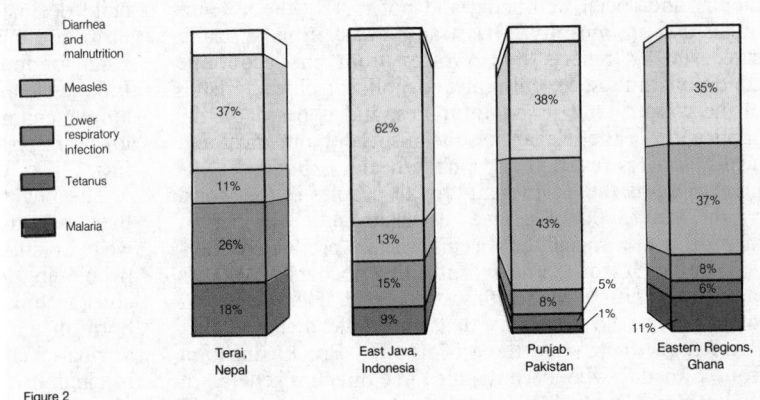

Figure 2

hepatitis B infection, leading to cancer of the liver, and to the increasing prevalence of cigarette smoking, resulting in cancer of the lungs).

Demographic indexes based on mortality figures, such as life expectancy at birth and infant and child mortality rates, are used almost exclusively to indicate health status because they are available, simple, and impersonal. Data concerning specific diseases have only recently come into vogue as they invoke children dying of cholera, pneumonia, and lockjaw. Morbidity or illness is rarely discussed because, thus far, it has been impossible to provide quantitative data. Suffice it to say that vast numbers of infants and young children in the less developed world are weakened by virtually continual upper respiratory infections and multiple bouts of severe diarrhea. Schoolchildren are weakened by the anemia and malnutrition induced by intestinal worms; mutilated by the "oriental sores" of leishmaniasis; blinded by onchocerciasis (river blindness), trachoma, measles, and vitamin A deficiency; and maimed by polio and dracunculiasis—"the fiery serpent."

The concern of the Alma-Ata Declaration was not only for the less developed world, with its overwhelming problems of poverty and inequity, but for vulnerable groups in the developed world as well. For example, life expectancy in the U.S. in 1987 was eighth in the world, after Japan, Sweden, Switzerland, Norway, The Netherlands, Canada, and Spain. The average was brought down largely by infant, child, and maternal mortality in inner-city ghettos and among migrant workers and other disfranchised groups. A recent editorial in the *New York Times* asked, "Is New York City a healthy place for children?" The answer was "not very . . . especially if the children are poor." In 1987 life expectancy in the U.S.S.R., which in the late 1950s surpassed that in the U.S., was ranked 38th, below Jamaica and Sri Lanka and on a par with Malaysia, South Korea, Guyana, Venezuela, and China. Health conditions in the Soviet Union worsened steadily after the mid-1960s. Major factors were increases in infant mortality, alcoholism, and farm and industrial accidents.

The Road to Alma-Ata. Historically, the tropical regions, where most of today's less developed countries are located, have always been associated with particularly high mortality rates among travelers and traders from the North. One of the earliest books on the subject was published in 1598 and was entitled *The Cure of the Disease in Remote Regions Preventing the Mortality in Forraine Attempts of the English Nation.* Toward the end of the 19th century, West Africa became known as "the white man's grave." High mortality rates existed also in the Caribbean, Latin America, and the Far East, mainly the result of such diseases as malaria, yellow fever, and cholera.

Concern over this situation led to the founding of the field of tropical medicine almost 100 years ago. From its beginning, the field divided into two camps. One was led by Sir Patrick Manson, who discovered the mosquito transmission of filariasis—the cause of elephantiasis—in Amoy, China, in the 1870s; the other by Sir Ronald Ross, who received the Nobel Prize for his work in Begumpett,

24

India, in the 1880s and 1890s showing that mosquitos spread malaria. Manson claimed, "I now firmly believe in the possibility of tropical colonization by the white races. Heat and moisture are not in themselves the direct causes of any important tropical disease. The direct causes of 99% of these diseases are germs. To kill them is simply a matter of knowledge." Ross's view was that the main determinants of health "were general living conditions, diet and sanitation." This was the beginning of a polarization of approaches to health in the less developed world that continues to the present day. The principal controversy for the last two decades has been between the so-called vertical approaches—direct, targeted programs using specific technologies such as drugs, vaccines, and insecticides—and horizontal approaches, which simultaneously utilize all means—medical, ecological, sociological, and political—to improve health.

One of the first large-scale vertical attempts to deal with rampant ill health in the tropical regions was the Rockefeller Foundation's campaign of 1913 to eradicate the hookworms that suck the blood and debilitate hundreds of millions of people. This campaign began in the southern United States and was then carried on in 52 countries, 6 continents, and 29 islands. The campaign failed because of the enormous reproductive potential of the worms, each capable of producing 20,000 eggs per day; the lack of highly effective nontoxic drugs; and the inadequacy of sanitary facilities. Today approximately one billion people are still infected with hookworm.

A second vertical Rockefeller campaign in the early 1920s was led by Gen. William Gorgas, the man who had made the building of the Panama Canal possible by controlling the mosquito carriers of yellow fever and malaria. He was convinced that yellow fever could be eradicated from the world by eliminating the *Aedes aegypti* mosquito from the cities of the Caribbean, South America, and Africa. He almost succeeded, but his efforts were confounded when it was discovered that jungle yellow fever, transmitted between monkeys and treetop mosquitoes, sporadically reseeds the urban environment. It is worth noting, however, that in the 1930s the Rockefeller Foundation was responsible for the development of a highly effective vaccine against yellow fever.

A publication commemorating WHO's 40th anniversary in 1988 noted that its initial programs were dominated by mass campaigns against tuberculosis, yaws, and malaria. The massive antimalaria effort begun in 1955 was prompted by the development during World War II of the insecticide DDT and of powerful new antimalarial drugs. Fifteen years later, because the malaria parasite and the mosquito carrier had developed resistance, respectively, to drugs and insecticides, WHO decided "to throw in the towel." Malaria had been eradicated from large areas of the world, including the U.S., Europe, and many islands, and 727 million people had been freed from risk (53% of the population of the originally malarious areas). Nevertheless, the failure to fulfill the promise to eliminate malaria from the world led to a major backlash, not only against the strategy of disease eradication but against the vertical approach in general.

As might be expected, horizontal approaches became more prominent as the backlash developed. In the period from 1965 to the early 1980s, many saw socioeconomic development as a panacea for all the less developed world's ills. Two great international statesmen, Lester Pearson of Canada and Willy Brandt of West Germany, chaired major commissions on international development issues, resulting in the publication of *Partners in Development*

in 1969 and *North-South: A Program for Survival* in 1980. It is remarkable that these two lengthy reports barely mentioned health as an issue, either as fostering development or as benefiting from it.

Support for a horizontal approach is not due solely to the perceived failures of vertical measures. In an influential book published in 1976, *The Modern Rise of Population,* Thomas McKeown of the department of social medicine at the University of Birmingham, England, observed that the population increase in Europe in the 19th and early 20th centuries was the result of a remarkable decline in infectious diseases, *due largely to socioeconomic progress and not to specific medical interventions.* "There need be no disappointment," he said, "with the conclusion that medical measures of immunization and treatment were relatively ineffective; they were also unnecessary." His graphs on such diseases as tuberculosis show a remarkable and continuing decline long before chemotherapy and vaccination were introduced. McKeown believed that water supplies and sanitation, decent housing, and, particularly, the availability of food were responsible for the dramatic improvement in health in the developed world. Extrapolating his theory to the less developed world of today, he suggested socioeconomic development as essentially the only viable strategy, despite the wide variety of immunizations, drugs, and other therapies now available. Recently McKeown chaired a report issued by WHO on *Health Research Strategy* to achieve health for all by the year 2000. Not surprisingly, it focused largely on disease origins rather than on intervention in disease mechanisms and stressed research on health systems rather than biomedical research.

Another important factor in the years preceding Alma-Alta was the growing awareness of the immense cost of hospital-based, so-called tertiary health care. Particularly severe in the United States, the problem gradually spread to the less developed world. Major hospitals in the capital cities of less developed countries, such as Kenyatta Hospital in Nairobi, Kenya, were taking up as much as 70% of the total health budget for the entire country. At the same time, primary health care, in both urban and rural areas, was grossly underfunded and in many places did not exist at all.

These factors—the failure of major vertical, global campaigns to eradicate or control disease, the emphasis on socioeconomic development in the less developed world to the exclusion of more immediate measures, and a tertiary health care system that was distorting the pattern of health care delivery in most countries—constituted the ground in which the seeds of Alma-Ata took root.

Strategies for Success. World health had been governed by three organizations—the Pan-American Sanitary Bureau in Washington, D.C., the International Office of Public Health in Paris, and the Health Organization of the League of Nations in Geneva—in the 30 years prior to the inauguration of WHO in June 1948. UNICEF, WHO's partner in Alma-Ata, was inaugurated as the United Nations International Children's Emergency Fund in December 1946 to deal with the aftermath of World War II. In 1953 the UN confirmed UNICEF's existence indefinitely, shifting its focus from the acute conditions of war to the chronic states of poverty and underdevelopment. In fact, the greater part of UNICEF's work was in the field of health. While the two organizations had different constituencies—that of WHO being the world's ministries of health, and that of UNICEF being far broader—they developed a good working relationship through the WHO/UNICEF Joint Committee on Health Policy.

A woman and child forage through a garbage dump in Guatemala City looking for food and things to sell. The plight of the world's poor, the most likely to suffer from malnutrition and life-threatening illnesses, illustrates the need for effective strategies for the creation of programs through which an acceptable level of health can be attained by all.
CHRIS WARREN

Just prior to the 1973 accession of Halfdan Mahler as director general of WHO, a working group completed a report on "basic health services" which concluded that there was "a failure to meet the expectations of the populations; an inability of the health services to deliver a level of national coverage adequate to meet the stated demands and the changing needs of different societies; a wide gap (which is not closing) in health status between countries, and between different groups within countries; rapidly rising costs without a visible and meaningful improvement in service; and a feeling of helplessness on the part of the consumer." The report recommended that WHO "should be participatory rather than advisory and should be directed towards a visible and objectively defined improvement in health services." UNICEF's response to the WHO report was that it was "yet another disheartening review of the slow rate at which health care was reaching people." Thus, from its beginnings, UNICEF was in full support of the initiative in primary health care that led to Alma-Ata.

The next step was the production of a joint WHO/UNICEF report on a range of successful or promising health systems in nine selected countries: Bangladesh, China, Cuba, India, Niger, Nigeria, Tanzania, Venezuela, and Yugoslavia. In 1975 *Alternative Approaches to Meeting Basic Health Needs in Developing Countries* was published. It concluded that "a virtual revolution" was needed to bring about "changes in the distribution of power, in the pattern of political decision-making, in the attitude and commitment of the health professionals and administrators in ministries of health and universities, and in people's awareness of what they are entitled to." The report emphasized the importance of primary health workers modeled after the so-called barefoot doctors of China.

The concept of these village workers, who were chosen from and by their communities to be trained in a short, intensive course, was essentially developed by John Grant (father of UNICEF's James Grant) and his Chinese colleagues in the 1920s and '30s. More than a million barefoot doctors were trained locally in commune hospitals for three months. While continuing their farm work, they learned environmental sanitation, health education, preventive medicine, first aid, and primary medical care, using both traditional Chinese and Western medicine.

These workers captured the imagination of the world community to such an extent that, according to a retired UNICEF official, the U.S.S.R. was moved to demonstrate its own forms of primary health care. After the World Health Assembly of 1975 endorsed the concept of primary health care, the U.S.S.R., at the Assembly in 1976, suggested a major international conference to initiate a global primary health care program. This suggestion came to fruition two and a half years later in the Alma-Ata conference.

WHO's principal tactics for implementing the Alma-Ata Declaration included an ongoing series of meetings in Geneva and many other parts of the world; a continuing series of glossy publications on issues such as formulating strategies; a global health strategy based on regional and national strategies; indicators for progress, management, evaluation, and plans of action for implementation; and the annual World Health Assemblies. In March 1988, a decade after Alma-Ata, a WHO meeting of 22 senior health experts was held in Riga, capital of the Latvian S.S.R. They reaffirmed their commitment to the principle of health for all and recommended strategies for accelerating progress toward that goal. By this time health for all through primary health care within a decidedly horizontal framework had become a crusade, not only for WHO but for some health care professionals in UNICEF, nongovernmental organizations, and academic institutions. Other approaches to improving health in the less developed world were often treated as heresies.

Questions about both the approach to and the viability of health for all were raised almost at the beginning of the crusade. Robert McNamara, in his annual president's report to the World Bank in 1978, said: "Even if the projected—and optimistic—growth rate in the developing world is achieved, some 600 million individuals at the end of the century will remain trapped in absolute poverty. Absolute poverty is a condition of life so characterized by malnutrition, illiteracy, disease, high infant mortality and low life expectancy as to be below any reasonable definition of human decency."

McNamara's statement was quoted at the beginning of a 1979 article in the *New England Journal of Medicine* entitled "Selective Primary Health Care: An Interim Strategy for Disease Control in Developing Countries," which I wrote in collaboration with Julia A. Walsh, then a

visiting research fellow at the Rockefeller Foundation and now an assistant professor of medicine at Harvard Medical School. The article went beyond the traditional composite indicators such as infant mortality or life expectancy at birth to look at specific causes of death. The major infectious diseases of the less developed world were placed in the order of their importance based on the number of people afflicted, the number of deaths produced, and the disabilities caused, ranging from weakness and inability to work and learn to crippling and disfigurement. This exercise had never been done in this way before, and it revealed that the two most important health problems in the less developed world were the diarrheal diseases and respiratory infections of infants and young children, each of which was responsible for billions of episodes and for 5 million to 10 million deaths each year. Other major diseases included malaria, measles, schistosomiasis, whooping cough, tuberculosis, tetanus, and diphtheria.

On the basis of these figures and the crucial element of feasibility of control (*i.e.,* the availability of adequate, low-cost means of preventing or treating these problems), the article concluded that application of four very low-cost (vertical) measures could save the lives of millions of children each year. Recommended were immunization against tuberculosis, polio, measles, diphtheria, whooping cough, and tetanus; use in diarrhea of highly effective salt-sugar-water mixtures (oral rehydration therapy); treatment of life-threatening malaria; and breast feeding of infants, which provides the child with protective antibodies present in mother's milk. The paper did not discourage application of the (horizontal) so-called comprehensive primary health care package of Alma-Ata but stated that until it could be made available to all, "services aimed at the few most important diseases may be the most effective means of improving the health of the greatest number of people."

The paper elicited a spate of critical letters. These were followed by two critical papers in the journal *Social Science and Medicine,* one entitled "Selective Primary Health Care: Old Wine in New Bottles" and the other subtitled "Is Efficient Sufficient?" Mack Lipkin of New York University School of Medicine, in a discussion of this controversy, concluded that "planners interested in the health of populations, I would think, would welcome this debate. It can do nothing but make choices more rational and thereby serve the interests of the people."

The debate has continued: in 1988 *Social Science and Medicine* published an entire issue on "Selective or Comprehensive Primary Health Care." In retrospect, Walsh and I realized that we had unwittingly entered directly into the great debate on vertical versus horizontal health interventions.

UNICEF and the Children's Revolution. The major reason for the continuing controversy was UNICEF's declaration early in 1983 of a "children's revolution." It noted the positive developments in basic education, primary health care, cleaner water, and safer sanitation in the less developed world, but it stated that "at the same time, new scientific and technological breakthroughs have also been made against some of the most widespread and intractable problems of health and nutrition. Put together, these social and scientific advances now offer vital new opportunities [oral rehydration therapy, universal child immunization, the promotion of breast feeding, and the use of growth charts] for improving the nutrition and health of the world's children. For all four actions, the cost of the supplies and technology would be no more than a few dollars a child. Yet they could mean that literally hundreds of millions of young lives would be

healthier. And within a decade, they could be saving the lives of 20,000 children each day."

These ideas elicited a negative response from many who were wholly committed to the Alma-Ata approach. For example, a noted Indian physician, D. Banerji, wrote that "there is an ominous similarity between the spread of a highly malignant cancerous tumour and the promotion of the technocentric approach by Western countries." The controversy centred around three basic issues: a negative versus a positive attitude toward science and technology; a belief in horizontal as opposed to vertical approaches; and whether the people or the "experts" make the decisions. Many were still disillusioned with the technically based vertical programs that had been organized by experts to eradicate specific diseases, malaria in particular. Even what may well be the greatest scientific triumph in the history of medicine, the eradication of smallpox certified by WHO in 1978, failed to mitigate the dispute.

The controversy led to a separation of the WHO and UNICEF strategies in the early 1980s. WHO had begun to distance itself from UNICEF in 1979 when it convened a donors' meeting to provide funds for the health for all campaign but did not invite its partner. At about the same time, Grant became UNICEF executive director; like Mahler, an individual of immense idealism and energy, he was, however, strongly committed to implementation rather than exhortation.

A major next step came with UNICEF's decision to focus its initial efforts in the children's revolution on immunization. On May 4, 1983, Jonas Salk, the developer of the first polio vaccine, and McNamara met with Grant at UNICEF headquarters to discuss the sorry state of immunization of the world's children. It was Salk's contention that WHO's Expanded Program on Immunization, an offshoot of the smallpox eradication campaign, was moving too slowly. Salk and McNamara had been working on development of an independent agency to spearhead the immunization effort, but after hearing of UNICEF's children's revolution they came to try to convince Grant to take over the leadership. Grant had just agreed to go along with them, using immunization as a "Trojan horse" under whose cover primary health care could be fostered, when an aide rushed in with a telex of Mahler's speech to the World Health Assembly that morning. In it Mahler castigated agencies that focus on vertical campaigns. In spite of this, it was agreed that everything should be done to persuade WHO to join UNICEF and the World Bank in a massive effort to achieve universal childhood immunization by 1990.

To that end, a meeting was organized at the Rockefeller Foundation's Bellagio conference centre in Italy on March 13–15, 1984. It included the heads of WHO, UNICEF, the UN Development Program (UNDP), the World Bank, and the Rockefeller Foundation, as well as the directors of many of the major agencies dispensing bilateral (country to country) aid, such as the U.S. Agency for International Development (USAID), and numerous technical experts. Mahler had agreed to take part in the endeavour, justifying his participation with the fact that the Expanded Program on Immunization was WHO's one vertical program. This focus was underlined when M. Peter McPherson, the USAID administrator, insisted on equal time for oral rehydration, which his agency was emphasizing, and Mahler canceled the meeting until McPherson agreed to limit discussion of that issue to his own presentation.

At the close of the Bellagio meeting, an ad hoc Task Force for Child Survival was formed to develop both country programs and research aspects of accelerated

Clean-water programs and health and nutrition classes (right) are examples of the so-called horizontal approach to health care, which simultaneously employs medical, ecological, sociological, and political means to improve health.

PHOTOGRAPHS, T. KELLY—WORLD HEALTH ORGANIZATION

immunization activities. William Foege, director of the U.S. Centers for Disease Control, agreed to be a joint consultant to WHO and UNICEF to direct this effort. He was responsible to a group consisting of the five convening agencies: WHO, UNICEF, the World Bank, UNDP, and the Rockefeller Foundation. The task force has met every three months in the five years since its inception, bringing together key figures from the five organizations and other relevant groups to plan strategies and coordinate efforts. Immediately following the Bellagio meeting, several countries took the initiative to immunize all of their children. Pres. Belisario Betancur of Colombia led a massive national effort, mobilizing all segments of society—from priests in the confessional to Boy Scouts and the Army—to immunize the children of his country. Two years later Bellagio II was held in Cartagena, Colombia, with 90 world leaders and public health experts in attendance. Not only was remarkable progress reported in several countries, but the world's two most populous nations, China and India, wholeheartedly joined the effort.

The third Bellagio conference was held on March 10–12, 1988, in Talloires, France, to ensure continued commitment to the goal of universal childhood immunization by 1990. The principal foci of the meeting were sustainability of immunization, the addition of new and better vaccines, and the introduction of other major cost-effective health initiatives. When the Expanded Program on Immunization began in 1974, only 5% of the children in the less developed world were immunized; when the Task Force for Child Survival began in 1984, 20% were immunized; in May 1987 WHO affirmed that immunization had exceeded 50%; and it is expected that in 1990 or shortly thereafter the long-term Expanded Program goal of 80% will have been achieved.

In the Western Hemisphere polio immunization has progressed to the point where it is now expected that the wild polio viruses (in contrast to the vaccine strains) will be eradicated by 1990. At Talloires there was a consensus that the global eradication of polio would be "a fitting gift from the 20th to the 21st century," and at the World Health Assembly in May 1989 that goal was ratified. With the development of molecular biology and genetic engineering, the capacity to produce new and better vaccines has been greatly accelerated. By sometime in the 1990s we can expect vaccines against such major killers

of children as the diarrheas, acute respiratory infections, and malaria.

Oral rehydration campaigns have also progressed. To complement the efforts of USAID and other bilateral agencies, WHO has established its own highly effective diarrhea-control program and recently added respiratory disease control. Global distribution of packets containing oral rehydration salts reached 300 million in 1986, and they were used by 23% of those who needed them. The goal of 50% was set for 1989. A major global campaign is under way under the rubric of Safe Motherhood, aimed at protecting mothers and also ensuring the safety of their children. Since experience has shown that people are willing to limit family size if they are confident their children will live to adulthood, it should act as a major factor in slowing the growth of world population.

A remarkable moment occurred at Talloires in which the strategies of WHO and UNICEF were reconciled. Toward the end of the meeting, Mahler moved to a blackboard and drew a horizontal line along the bottom. He then drew five vertical lines representing immunization, diarrheal diseases, acute respiratory infections, family planning, and AIDS. He said, in effect, that vertical programs could be inserted as low-cost, effective, and equitable measures into the overall plan for primary health care. Development, he said, consists of "knowledge and motivation"; the immunization campaign was delivering both; and the result was not a weakening of the primary health care movement, as had once been feared, but an improvement of it. This remarkable and generous reconciliation between the horizontal and vertical camps augurs well for the possibility that where reasonable expectations of physical health are concerned, a significant degree of success may be claimed by the year 2000.

Good Health at Low Cost. While the great multilateral international agencies were engaged in their geometric controversies—Gerald Keusch of Tufts University School of Medicine, Boston, suggested that we compromise by using the term *diagonal*—it seemed that some of the poorest countries in the world were quietly achieving remarkable health statistics on their own.

"Good Health at Low Cost" was the title of a meeting convened by the Rockefeller Foundation to bring together demographers, economists, and epidemiologists to verify this phenomenon. The four case studies were China,

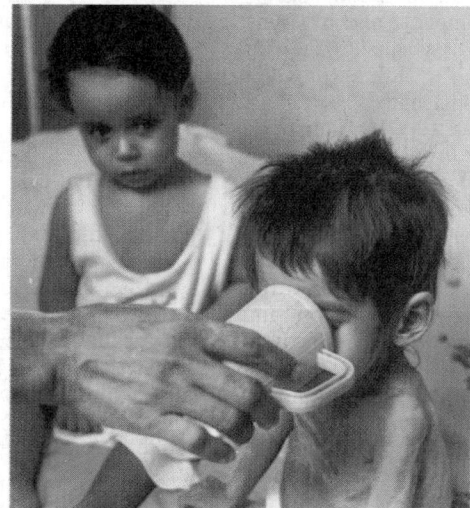
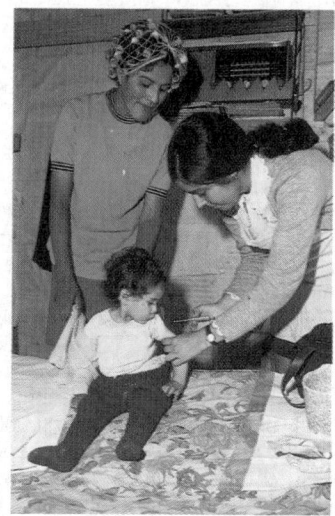

Sri Lanka, and Kerala state of India, with annual gross national product (GNP) per capita of $300 and life expectancies of 65, and Costa Rica, with corresponding figures of $1,300 and 75. It was not expected that the means by which they had achieved their results would be clear, but during the intensive analyses presented at the meeting, it became apparent that four similar factors were observed in each of these countries, and that these appeared to be largely responsible for their great success.

A summary of "Good Health at Low Cost" concluded, "When this meeting was being planned the approach fostering affluence was widely supported. Thus, for the last decade at least there has been a model for health in the developing world which can be called 'the northern paradigm.'" The evolution of good health in the developed world, often called the North, has been related to the process of development; i.e., the growth of a literate population living in spacious housing, provided with piped water and sanitary facilities, and supplied with the fruits of industry and agriculture via good roads and communication facilities. Furthermore, the medical system developed in the North had little to offer prior to the late 1930s and early '40s. On the basis of these premises, the governments of the less developed world, aided and abetted by multilateral, bilateral, and nongovernmental aid agencies, have been attempting to institute the northern model of health. The cost of this approach is staggering.

Meanwhile, the summary continued, it appears that certain countries of the South have quietly evolved a different model, which may be called the "southern paradigm," that has resulted in a remarkable reduction in infant and child mortality rates and increase in life expectancies. The key elements of this approach, as described by representatives from the four areas studied, appear to be only four: (1) political and social will; (2) education for all with emphasis on primary and secondary schooling; (3) equitable distribution throughout the urban and rural populations of public health measures and primary health care; and (4) assurance of adequate caloric intake for all.

Political will can come primarily from the top, as in the case of China, or from the bottom, as in Kerala, Sri Lanka, and Costa Rica. In the latter cases, in particular, the development of an educated and literate population was essential. Education thus appears to play a catalytic role and, in relation to the equitable distribution of health, appears to be highly synergistic, with the whole being

far greater than the sum of the parts. With respect to health systems, there has been a remarkable expansion of the power of modern medicine, beginning in the 1930s. Adequate calories for all can be assured by food subsidies and other devices such as food stamps. The cost must be kept within reasonable limits, and agricultural production must be fostered.

During the meeting, demographer/anthropologist Jack Caldwell of Australian National University became so involved he burst out, "One just can't wait for affluence." After the meeting he was inspired to do a major study comparing superior health achievers with poor health achievers. In it he provides a ranking of life expectancy relative to income. Among the superior health achievers, Kerala, Sri Lanka, and China rank highest. Among the poor health achievers, the oil providers—Oman, Saudi Arabia (with a per capita GNP of $16,000 and a life expectancy of 56), Iran, Libya, Algeria, and Iraq—rank lowest. "These findings are out of step with today's dominant economic and political ideologies in the development field. They show that low mortality is indeed within the reach of all countries."

Progress Report—Reasons for Hope? To understand what has transpired in the decade since the Declaration of Alma-Ata was proclaimed, one must consider three aspects of the problem: politics, economics, and implementation.

First of all, it must be understood that the Declaration and all the meetings and publications that have followed it are essentially political statements. Item 8 states that "all governments should formulate national policies, strategies and plans of actions . . . [for which] it will be necessary to exercise political will, to mobilise the country's resources and to use available external resources rationally." A major problem has been that by its constitution, WHO can deal only with ministries of health, which are generally thought to be among the least powerful of governmental ministries. UNICEF, by contrast, has been able to achieve direct access to heads of state and major regional organizations.

A recent editorial in The Lancet on the relevance of economics for medical students stated: "The gut response in many doctors would be to adopt the high moral stance that economics is irrelevant to medicine: it is ethical practice that the best be done for each patient and this view is incompatible with cost cutting. However, . . . economics is not merely about economy. Rather, its starting point is that the resources of human society are finite and scarce and that choices must necessarily be

made. . . . Economics, by valuing all costs and benefits on the single, universal metric of money, and by using techniques such as cost-benefit analysis, makes difficult choices rational and systematic, . . . Ethics provides justification for the desired goal or benefit."

The economic issue had been raised by McNamara in 1978 when he stated that "some 600 million individuals at the end of the century will remain trapped in absolute poverty." The 1979 *New England Journal of Medicine* article on selective primary health care called attention to a World Bank estimate that the cost of furnishing basic health services to all the poor in less developed countries by the year 2000 would be between $5.4 billion and $9.3 billion (at 1975 prices). This amount, which includes only initial capital investment and training costs, would provide one community health worker or auxiliary nurse-midwife for every 1,500 to 2,000 people and one health facility for every 8,000 to 12,000 people or every 10 sq km (3.9 sq mi), whichever is greater. The cost of providing community water supplies and sanitation to all those in need would add another $135 billion to $260 billion.

Soon after the Alma-Ata Declaration, the world went into recession. During that period many less developed countries accumulated enormous debts and had to cut back on their health services. In an economic evaluation of health for all, Mahesh Patel, an economist at the University of Manchester, demonstrated that in 1982 the weighted average for expenditures on health in the least developed countries was 0.4% of GNP and for middle-income less developed countries, 1.5%. Patel showed that expenditures of approximately 5% of GNP per annum would be needed to achieve the goal of health for all.

"Conceptual simplicity is essential to implementation," in the words of J.O. Field, agricultural sociologist at the School of Nutrition, Tufts University. "All too often in the social sector, intellectual aspiration and operational feasibility are inversely related. . . . Programs that call for extensive coordination are especially vulnerable as are programs that rely heavily on popular support and participation for their success. [The] longer the duration of implementation, the slimmer the possibility that the original policy will prevail." All these problems were present in the Alma-Ata strategy. Virtually every aspect of health and all the social, economic, and political factors that impinge on health were to be part of the program. There was no clear-cut prioritization, and no specific strategies were designed for countries at different socioeconomic levels.

In Mahler's last speech to the World Health Assembly in May 1988, he stated, "Another recently discovered principle is that it is possible to set targets for health, and to attain them," but his examples were the vertical smallpox and immunization campaigns. In his inaugural speech, Hiroshi Nakajima, the new director general of WHO, said the time had come to concentrate on practical implementation of the concept of health for all and the primary health care approach, which are now widely accepted.

The inevitable conclusion is that health for all by the year 2000 as defined by WHO will not be attained, although many poor countries in the less developed world have achieved good standards of health through their own efforts and through decades of gradual improvement in their socioeconomic status. What will be gained is a continuing decline in infant and child mortality through control of infectious diseases and malnutrition. Among the most important spin-offs of this development are a decrease in the rate of population growth and a probable overall decline in world population early in the 3rd millennium. In Latin America and Asia there has been a drastic decline in infant and child mortality and with it a decline in the population growth rate. Africa is the exception in that it has both the highest infant and child death rates and the highest birthrates and population growth.

In his Shattuck lecture, delivered to the Massachusetts Medical Society in 1981, John Evans, then director of the population, health, and nutrition department of the World Bank, described three stages in the evolution of health systems. The first is dominated by infectious diseases linked to poverty, malnutrition, and poor personal hygiene; the second by chronic diseases, particularly cardiac and cerebrovascular diseases, cancer, diabetes, arthritis, and mental disorders; and the third by environmental hazards. The industrialized countries evolved through the three stages over the course of more than a century, but the less developed countries face the challenge of coping with all three simultaneously.

With respect to the developed world of the North, it is worth reiterating that Black's study of health problems in the United Kingdom in the 1970s revealed mental illness as the major overall cause of encounters with the health system. Finally, concerning social well-being, in many of the wealthiest countries of the world there are immense pockets of poverty and ill health. This includes not only Saudi Arabia but also the two greatest powers in the world, the United States and the Soviet Union.

At the moment, in the wealthier countries, the most improvement in life expectancy in the near future can be achieved with diseases of life-style. This means behavioral change, including stopping smoking, eliminating alcohol abuse, changing diet, and increasing exercise. Prevention of injuries and improvement of environmental pollution will also increase longevity. Between 90 and 100 years of age, however, life expectancy drops precipitously, and for the foreseeable future there is nothing we can do about this, but we can work to improve the quality of life among the growing numbers of elderly. We can also try to escape the "paradox of health" described so graphically by Arthur Barsky of the Psychiatry Service at the Massachusetts General Hospital: "Although the collective health of the nation has improved dramatically in the past 30 years, surveys reveal declining satisfaction with personal health during the same period." This is what Aaron Wildavsky, while dean of the Graduate School of Public Policy at the University of California at Berkeley, called "doing better and feeling worse."

All this may sound pessimistic, but it relates largely to expectations and whether one sees the glass as half empty or half full. The world has made truly remarkable progress in the areas of health and life expectancy. Despite the vast increase in global population, science and technology have given us a better life. There is hope that as infant and child mortality decline in the less developed world, the population problem will also wane. There is hope as well that we may be entering an era of peace and disarmament (as hoped for in item 10 of the Declaration of Alma-Ata), thereby freeing resources for economic development and the improved health that will result. The world is slowly coming to a realization that the complex environment of the beautiful blue planet Earth as seen from the Moon must be preserved. Through education and the proper application of science and technology, we can achieve a realistic level of health and economic and social development so that the vast majority of people can enjoy the Earth's diverse and nourishing fruits.

Dyson, Freeman John

The distinguished physicist and educator Freeman John Dyson is best known for his speculative work on the possibility of extraterrestrial civilizations. The son of the musician and composer Sir George Dyson, he was born Dec. 15, 1923, in Crowthorne, Berkshire, England, and was educated at Winchester College and the University of Cambridge. As a boy he was an avid reader of such science fiction writers as Jules Verne and H.G. Wells. As a teenager he developed a passion for mathematics, but his mathematics studies at Cambridge were interrupted in 1943 when he was directed to the operational research section of RAF Bomber Command.

COURTESY OF JOHN FREEMAN DYSON

Back at Cambridge, he received a B.A. in 1945 and stayed on as a research fellow of Trinity College. In 1947 he won a Commonwealth Fund fellowship to study physics in the United States, and he spent the next two years at Cornell University, Ithaca, N.Y., and Princeton, where he studied under J. Robert Oppenheimer, then director of the Institute for Advanced Study. He returned to England in 1949 to become a research fellow at the University of Birmingham, but he was appointed professor of physics at Cornell in 1951 and two years later accepted the professorship of physics at the Institute for Advanced Study. He became an American citizen in 1957.

During a leave of absence in the late 1950s, he joined the Orion Project research team, which was attempting to build a manned spacecraft and send it to Mars. A working model was successfully tested, but for a variety of technological and environmental reasons, the government rejected it. A long-time advocate of exploration and colonization by earthlings of the solar system and beyond, Dyson has studied ways of searching for evidence of intelligent life, though he has admitted that too little is known as yet about the universe for scientists to conclude whether the existence of extraterrestrial intelligence is probable. Dyson is the author of several books, including *Disturbing the Universe* (1979), *Weapons and Hope* (1984), *Origins of Life* (1985), and *Infinite in All Directions* (1988).

Franklin, John Hope

Historian and educator John Hope Franklin devoted much of his life to the history of the South and of black Americans. He was born Jan. 2, 1915, in Rentiesville, Okla., the son of a prominent lawyer in Tulsa and one of the first blacks to practice law in Oklahoma. After being graduated magna cum laude from Fisk University in Nashville, Tenn., in 1935 with a major in history, Franklin went on to Harvard for graduate studies, gaining an M.A. in 1936 and a Ph.D. in 1941.

He began his teaching career at Fisk University in the 1936–37 academic year. From 1939 to 1943 he taught history at St. Augustine's College, Raleigh, N.C. While there he researched original sources on the status and economic position of free Negroes in North Carolina be-

fore the Civil War and published his findings in *The Free Negro in North Carolina, 1790–1860* (1943).

Franklin held appointments as professor of history at North Carolina College, Durham (1943–47), Howard University, Washington, D.C. (1947–56), and Brooklyn (N.Y.) College (1956–64), where he was also chairman of the

AMPIX PHOTOGRAPHY

history department. During a leave of absence in 1962–63 he served as Pitt professor of American history and institutions at the University of Cambridge. In 1964 he was appointed professor of American history at the University of Chicago, where he remained until 1982, serving as chairman of the history department from 1967 to 1970 and John Matthews Manly distinguished service professor from 1969 until he left the institution. In 1982 he moved to Duke University, Durham, N.C., as James B. Duke professor of history and three years later he became professor of legal history at Duke University Law School.

Franklin traveled and lectured extensively at home and abroad and was the recipient of many academic awards, fellowships, and honorary degrees. Among his books are *From Slavery to Freedom: A History of Negro Americans* (1947; 6th ed., with Alfred A. Moss, Jr., 1988); *The Militant South, 1800–1861* (1956); *Reconstruction: After the Civil War* (1961); *A Southern Odyssey: Travellers in the Antebellum North* (1976); *Racial Equality in America* (1976); *George Washington Williams: A Biography* (1985); and *Race and History, Selected Essays, 1938–1988* (1990).

PAULA M. LERNER—
WOODFIN CAMP & ASSOCIATES

Gould, Stephen Jay

Paleontologist and teacher of biology, geology, and the history of science at Harvard University, Stephen Jay Gould is also an author known for his gift of explaining scientific phenomena in terms comprehensible and even entertaining to lay readers. His column "This View of Life" in *Natural History* magazine won a National Magazine Award for essays and criticism in 1980, and his books have brought him the National Book Award in science in 1981 (for *The Panda's Thumb*, 1980) and the general nonfiction award of the National Book Critics Circle in 1982 (for *The Mismeasure of Man*, 1981). He was among the first group of MacArthur Foundation fellows in 1981.

Gould was born Sept. 10, 1941, in New York City and was brought up in Queens, where his father was a court stenographer. Taken to the American Museum of Natural History to see his first dinosaur when he was five, Stephen announced that he would become a paleontologist. He earned an A.B. degree from Antioch College, Yellow Springs, Ohio, in 1963 and a Ph.D. in paleontology at Columbia University, New York City, in 1967. He wrote his doctoral dissertation on fossil land snails in Bermuda. He joined the geology faculty at Harvard University in 1967, becoming professor of geology in 1973 and Alexander Agassiz professor of zoology in 1982.

Gould received a number of honorary degrees and fellowships and many distinguished awards, beginning in 1975 with the Schuchert Award of the Paleontological Society, given annually for excellence in research to a paleontologist under 40. In 1985 he was the subject of a profile on the television science program "Nova," which received a Westinghouse Science Film Award. His first book, *Ontogeny and Phylogeny* (1977), although addressed to an academic audience, showed him to be capable of capturing a nonscholarly audience and making complicated subjects understandable to the lay reader. Jeremy Bernstein, writing in *The New Yorker* of April 12, 1982, described his column "This View of Life" as "full of fun, totally without pretentiousness, and absolutely clear." Gould's other books include *Ever Since Darwin* (1977); *Hen's Teeth and Horse's Toes* (1983); *The Flamingo's Smile* (1985); *An Urchin in the Storm* (1987); *Time's Arrow, Time's Cycle* (1987); and *Wonderful Life* (1989).

Tunkin, Grigory I.

From humble origins in a peasant family, Grigory I. Tunkin rose to become an adviser to Soviet leaders Nikita Khrushchev and Mikhail Gorbachev. An advocate of peaceful coexistence of the Soviet and Western systems, he was influential during the middle and late 1950s and early 1960s, when his theory evolved into the concept of East-West détente, and again in the current period, when it has been the source of ideas, based in the concept of *perestroika* (restructuring), for East-West cooperation.

Tunkin was born Oct. 13, 1906, in the Arctic seaport of Archangel. He began his studies at the University of Moscow in 1923 at the age of 17 and took his doctorate there in 1938 (the Soviet doctorate is usually taken in professional midstream). After 26 years in government service, he accepted the chair of international law at the University of Moscow in 1964, an appointment that lasted until his retirement in 1988.

Tunkin joined the Soviet Foreign Ministry in 1938. During World War II he served in Canada, where he became fluent in both English and French. After the war he moved to the Treaty Division of the Foreign Ministry. His work, which involved both treaty drafting and negotiation, brought him close to Khrushchev. He initiated the theory of peaceful coexistence and exerted considerable influence in the period before Khrushchev's downfall in 1964. He played a role in the negotiations leading to several significant treaties, including the Antarctic Treaty of 1959, the Nuclear Test-Ban Treaty of 1963, the Outer Space Treaty of 1967, and the Treaty on the Non-proliferation of Nuclear Weapons of 1968. He was also a Soviet delegate to the UN General Assembly for many years.

Tunkin's theories have again gained influence in the era of *perestroika*. Essentially a theorist in international law and relations, he has written a number of major works, notably *Foundations of Modern International Law* (1956); *Problems of the Theory of International Law* (1962); *Ideological Struggle and International Law* (1967); *Theory of International Law* (1970); and *International Law in the International System* (1975).

Chronology of 1989

JANUARY

4 **U.S. downs Libyan fighters.** Two U.S. F-14 fighter planes shot down two Libyan MiG-23s over international waters about 110 km (70 mi) north of the Libyan port of Tobruk. The U.S. Navy claimed its pilots had tried to avoid a confrontation by changing their altitude, speed, and direction several times. The Navy pilots reportedly fired Sparrow and Sidewinder air-to-air missiles only after the Libyans continued to pursue them with "clear hostile intent." Libya called for an emergency meeting of the UN Security Council after accusing the U.S. of carrying out "a premeditated attack" on unarmed planes while they were on routine patrol. On January 6 the chief U.S. delegate to the UN displayed photos made from a videotape to support his contention that at least one of the Libyan planes was armed with missiles.

6 **Teledyne indicted for fraud.** Los Angeles-based Teledyne Industries was indicted by a federal grand jury in Washington, D.C., along with a navy officer and five other individuals. All were involved in the procurement of military weapons. The charges against them included conspiracy, bribery, racketeering, and theft of government property. Other indictments were expected to follow as a result of the two-year-old investigation. Shortly before the public announcement, the Hazeltine Corp. of Greenlawn, N.Y., pleaded guilty in a district court in Virginia to similar charges and agreed to pay a $1 million fine and $900,000 in other costs. Its parent company was the Emerson Electric Co. of St. Louis, Mo.

7 **Emperor of Japan dies.** Hirohito, the 124th emperor of Japan, died in Tokyo after a long illness. He was 87 years old. Known to his countrymen as the Showa ("Bright Peace") emperor, Hirohito occupied the Chrysanthemum Throne in 1926 and ruled 62 years, longer than any other emperor in recorded Japanese history. He was succeeded by 55-year-old Crown Prince Akihito, his eldest son, who would be known as the Heisei ("Achieving Peace") emperor. On February 24, after Shinto rituals and civil ceremonies were held, the Showa emperor was buried. Representatives of 163 foreign nations, including U.S. Pres. George Bush, attended the funeral. Also in attendance were numerous other presidents, kings, prime ministers, and governors general.

11 **Hungary sanctions opposition.** The Hungarian Parliament approved new legislation that would grant private citizens the right to form opposition political parties and to hold public demonstrations without government interference. Those rights, however, would not take effect until they were confirmed by Parliament. Justice Minister Kalman Kulcsar promised that Parliament would take up the matter before August 1. On January 28 Imre Pozsgay, a member of the Politburo, announced that a historical commission, after studying Hungary's postwar history, had determined that the landmark 1956 revolt had in fact been a popular uprising, not a foreign-supported counterrevolution, as the Communist Party had officially contended for the past 30 years.

Montenegro leaders resign. The entire state presidency and the leaders of the Communist Party in Montenegro, the smallest of Yugoslavia's six constituent republics, tendered their resignations after tens of thousands of workers and students demonstrated for two days in Titograd. The protesters denounced the leaders' abuse of power and demanded an end to economic hardship. A similar protest had led to the resignation of the country's prime minister, Branko Mikulic, less than two weeks earlier. On January 19 he was replaced by Ante Markovic, a member of the Croatian State Presidency.

12 **Moscow to govern troubled region.** In an effort to end ethnic violence in Nagorno-Karabakh, the Presidium of the Supreme Soviet of the U.S.S.R. decided to place the region temporarily under Moscow's direct rule. During that time it would continue to be an autonomous region incorporated in the Azerbaijan Soviet Socialist Republic. Despite the virtual imposition of martial law, the earthquake of December 1988, and numerous efforts to defuse demands by ethnic Armenians that their region of Azerbaijan be incorporated into the neighbouring Armenian S.S.R., the turmoil continued. Religious differences also divided the two groups. The Azerbaijanis were mostly Muslims, while the Armenians were predominantly Christian.

13 **North to face lesser charges.** Federal District Judge Gerhard A. Gesell dismissed two main charges against retired Marine Lieut. Col. Oliver North. The court had no other option, Gesell said, because the Reagan administration refused to release classified documents that the defense insisted were essential to its case. The previous day, U.S. Attorney General Dick Thornburgh had submitted a written statement to the court, at its insistence, saying he would block the use of certain classified documents on the grounds that to do otherwise would jeopardize national security. Although North would no longer have to defend himself against the charges of theft and of conspiring to defraud the government, he would still be tried on 12 other charges, all related to the Iran-*contra* affair.

16 **Miami killing sets off riots.** Three days of race-related riots began in the predominantly black Overtown section of Miami, Fla., after a Hispanic policeman shot and killed an unarmed black man fleeing the police on a motorcycle. The incident occurred at a time when the black community was complaining about alleged police brutality and voicing resentment over the loss of jobs that they claimed was due to the large influx of Hispanics into Miami. The rioting also spread to areas outside the 125 or so blocks cordoned off in Overtown by police. Although Mayor Xavier Suarez toured the area to plead for calm, the arson, looting, and random shooting continued. Six persons were reportedly shot and at least 300 arrested. A passenger on the motorcycle died of injuries the day after the vehicle crashed. On January 23 the police officer was arrested and charged with two counts of manslaughter.

18 **Estonians reinforce language.** The Estonian legislature approved a new law making Estonian the official language of the republic. The 204–50 vote underscored the growing resentment against perceived efforts by Moscow to impose the Russian language and cultural uniformity on minority groups within the Soviet Union. Supplementary legislation, if passed, would compel Soviet officials to respond in Estonian to any question asked in that language. The following week Lithuania, another Baltic republic, passed similar but more rigorous laws.

19 **Murders rile Colombian judges.** The 22,000 members of Colombia's judicial system began a two-day strike to protest the ambush murders the previous day of 12 members of a judicial commission. Three of the 15 intended victims survived the gunfire. After a meeting of the National Security Council, Gen. Miguel Maza Márquez told reporters that it was beyond doubt that the perpetrators were members of a right-wing paramilitary organization. They presumably acted because the commission had gathered incriminating evidence on previous massacres. About 140 paramil-

A Tokyo jewelry store displays Emperor Hirohito's portrait on a bed of pearls after his death on January 7. Hirohito, who was succeeded by his eldest son, had reigned for 62 years.
YAMAGUSHI—SYGMA

itary groups, financed by various vested interests, were believed to be operating in Colombia. One of their main missions was to neutralize guerrillas and those suspected of supporting them.

20 **George Bush assumes presidency.** George Bush was inaugurated as the 41st president of the United States during an outdoor ceremony at the Capitol. The oath of office was administered by Chief Justice William Rehnquist. Moments earlier Justice Sandra Day O'Connor had administered the vice presidential oath to former senator Dan Quayle of Indiana. During the course of his inaugural address, Bush pledged to do his part to end years of conflict between the executive and legislative branches of government, to launch new efforts to solve social problems, and to attack the federal budget deficit. The following day Bush personally greeted visitors who took the opportunity to tour the White House during an open house.

Israel closes Palestinian schools. Israel ordered the indefinite closing of all Palestinian schools in the occupied territories of the West Bank and Gaza Strip. Some 300,000 students were affected. The government contended that students were partly responsible for the increase in violence that over the previous month had resulted in the deaths of 30 Palestinians at the hands of Israeli soldiers.

23 **Court ruling affects minorities.** The United States Supreme Court declared unconstitutional a Richmond, Va., law requiring that 30% of public works funds be awarded to minority-owned construction companies. The 6–3 vote, which upheld an earlier ruling by the U.S. Court of Appeals for the 4th Circuit in Richmond, in effect ruled that the old statute denied white contractors their constitutional right of equal protection under the law. Justice Sandra Day O'Connor, writing for the majority, declared that such set-aside

programs could be justified only if they served compelling state interest or acted to redress "identified discrimination" by the government or private parties. Laws similar to those in Richmond had been passed by 36 states and by nearly 200 local legislative bodies.

Civilians seize army barracks. In an early-morning raid, some 50 Argentine men and women attacked La Tablada base, the headquarters of the 3rd Mechanized Infantry Regiment, on the outskirts of Buenos Aires. At least 36 persons were killed before 14 commandos surrendered to vastly superior forces after a day-long battle. The political views of the raiders and their motivation were unclear. Some believed the attackers were leftist guerrillas in search of arms. There was also speculation that they might be siding with disgruntled military officers who had staged three insurrections in less than two years to halt the prosecution of fellow officers accused of committing crimes during the government's counterinsurgency campaign of the 1970s.

24 **Recruit scandal rocks Japan.** Ken Harada, head of Japan's Economic Planning Agency, became the third person in six weeks to resign from Prime Minister Noboru Takeshita's Cabinet. All had been implicated in unsavoury financial dealings with Recruit Co., a data and real estate conglomerate. With the full extent of the scandal still unknown, it appeared certain that evidence would emerge showing that numerous other high-level officials had also made huge profits by receiving preflotation shares in the Recruit Co.

25 **El Salvador rejects rebel offer.** José Napoleón Duarte, president of El Salvador, rejected a list of conditions set down by Marxist-led guerrillas to secure their participation in the presidential election scheduled for March 19. The rebels, organized under the umbrella organization Farabundo Martí

National Liberation Front, had tried to disrupt the last five elections. This time, however, they offered to participate, and abide by the results, provided the government accepted 12 conditions. These included a postponement of the election until September, government guarantees of protection for leftist candidates, and a five-day cease-fire at the time of the election. Duarte's negative response was supported by members of other political parties who agreed that the rebel offer was little more than a propaganda ploy. A postponement of the election would also conflict with the constitution, which stipulated that an election had to be held at least 60 days before the beginning of June.

Honduran supporter of *contras* **slain.** Gustavo Álvarez Martínez, a fervent supporter of the Nicaraguan *contras* and chief of the Honduran armed forces from 1982 to 1984, was assassinated by six gunmen near his home in Tegucigalpa, the capital. In 1981, while serving as head of the national police, Álvarez reportedly informed William Casey, then head of the CIA, that the U.S.-supported *contras* could operate against Nicaragua's Sandinista government from bases inside Honduras.

31 **Probe of Chun Doo Hwan ends.** Government prosecutors in South Korea announced that they had completed their investigation of corruption and human rights abuses that occurred during the presidency of Chun Doo Hwan. Among the 47 persons arrested in connection with the probe were seven relatives of the former president. Also charged with crimes were the former mayor of Seoul, the former ministers of construction and transportation, and the former head of the nation's intelligence agency.

BRAD MARKEL—GAMMA/LIAISON

U.S. Pres. George Bush and his wife, Barbara, wave to crowds on Pennsylvania Avenue after Bush's inauguration.

FEBRUARY

3 **Alfredo Stroessner overthrown.** Alfredo Stroessner, Paraguay's dictatorial president for nearly 35 years, was overthrown in a military coup led by Gen. Andrés Rodríguez. Rodríguez, who reportedly organized the coup after being ordered to resign as Stroessner's second in command, immediately assumed the presidency and announced his new Cabinet. During heavy fighting between the rebels and those loyal to the president, as many as 300 people were killed. On February 5 Stroessner was forced to leave the country and was flown to Brazil. Rodríguez then announced that elections, for both the presidency and Congress, would be held within three months.

7 **U.S. Congress loses pay raise.** Members of the U.S. House of Representatives voted 380–48 against giving themselves and certain other federal employees a 51% pay increase. Shortly thereafter, the Senate voted 94–6 to reject the same proposal. Because having to vote publicly for a pay raise was always a great embarrassment to members of Congress, they had earlier devised a plan to get an automatic pay raise without having to vote. The public uproar was so intense that Congress killed the plan and called for a public vote. The increase was then decisively defeated in both houses of Congress.

9 **Jamaicans elect Manley.** The ruling Jamaica Labour Party of Prime Minister Edward Seaga was soundly defeated in parliamentary elections by the People's National Party led by former prime minister Michael Manley. Unlike the election in 1980, when more than 700 persons were killed, there was relatively little violence. During his previous term in office, Manley had closely allied himself with Cuban Pres. Fidel Castro and generally opposed U.S. policies in the area. During the recent campaign he pledged to follow a moderate course in the future and strive for better relations with the U.S. Manley also assured the voters he would seek financial assistance for Jamaica from the World Bank and the International Monetary Fund.

10 **Czechoslovak dissidents under attack.** The Czechoslovak government dismissed the editor of the Communist Party's weekly cultural newspaper in an apparent effort to stifle growing dissent within the party's ranks. On February 21 Vaclav Havel, a dissident author, was sentenced to nine months in prison after being declared guilty of inciting illegal protests. The court cited his participation in an abortive rally on January 16, which had been called to commemorate the 20th anniversary of the death of a student who had burned himself to death to protest the 1968 Soviet-led invasion of Czechoslovakia by Warsaw Pact nations. On February 22 another court sentenced seven others accused of illegal activities. Their punishment ranged from one year in prison to suspended sentences and fines.

14 **Latin leaders reach accord.** The presidents of Costa Rica, El Salvador, Guatemala, Honduras, and Nicaragua reached agreement on a plan to relocate Nicaraguan *contras* after closing their bases in Honduras; in exchange, Nicaragua promised to hold free elections in February 1990. Political opponents of the Sandinista government would have four months to organize political parties, then six months to campaign for national and local offices. During this period they would have guaranteed access to all the news media. Adolfo Calero, a prominent *contra* leader, questioned the workability of the agreement because it relied so heavily on promises made by Nicaraguan Pres. Daniel Ortega. Nicaragua also pledged to release most of the 3,300 *contras* and former national guardsmen presently held in prison; some would be freed immediately, others after the *contras* and their families had left Honduras.

Rushdie novel enrages Muslims. Ayatollah Ruhollah Khomeini, supreme religious leader in Iran, announced that Indian-born author Salman Rushdie had been "sentenced to death" for publishing *The Satanic Verses*. Khomeini called on all Muslims to seek out and execute Rushdie, a London resident, and those responsible for the publication of the book, which many Muslims considered insulting to the Prophet Muhammad and highly offensive to Muslims. Certain major bookstores temporarily removed the book from public display, fearful that employees or customers might be injured by bombs. Numerous others, however, vigorously defended Rushdie's right to express his views, no matter how unsavory they might be to certain segments of society. Several ardent advocates of free speech pointed out the ironic fact that very few of those who denounced the book had ever read it because copies were not available in their countries.

Bhopal lawsuit settled. The Supreme Court of India ordered Union Carbide Corp. to pay $470 million in damages to victims of the toxic gas leak that occurred at its pesticide plant in Bhopal on Dec. 3, 1984. Some 3,500 persons were killed and 200,000 others were affected. The court did not assign blame for the disaster, and it ordered the dismissal of all criminal and civil lawsuits filed in India against the company and then chairman Warren Anderson. The Indian government, which was given responsibility for distributing the money, had sought $3.3 billion in damages. Union Carbide never accepted responsibility for the tragedy, saying it had been perpetrated by a disgruntled Indian employee.

15 **Sri Lankans elect Parliament.** The United National Party of Sri Lankan Pres. Ranasinghe Premadasa won 125 seats in elections to the nation's 225-seat Parliament. The Sri Lanka Freedom Party, under the leadership of Sirimavo Bandaranaike, a former prime minister, won 67 seats and the Tamils 23. The remaining ten seats went to members of minor parties. During the campaign and election, some 1,000 people were believed killed as Sinhalese extremists and Tamil separatists tried to disrupt the election.

20 **Afghan prime minister resigns.** Mohammad Hassan Sharq, prime minister of Afghanistan, resigned after less than nine months in office. He was replaced the following day by his predecessor, Sultan Ali Keshtmand, who would have the title chairman of the executive committee of the Council of Ministers. Sharq's resignation was believed by outsiders to be linked to Pres. Mohammad Najibullah's apparent inability to bring together various factions within the government. The need for unity took on added importance because the last Soviet troops, which had supported Najibullah, left the country on February 15. On February 23, during a meeting in Pakistan, leaders of seven disparate Afghan guerrilla groups, anticipating the collapse of the government, elected a moderate as acting president and a Muslim fundamentalist as acting prime minister. The rebels then called for international recognition of their interim government-in-exile.

21 **Mandela bodyguards charged.** Two of Winnie Mandela's bodyguards were charged with abducting a 14-year-old boy on Dec. 28–29, 1988, then murdering him in Mandela's house. The two men, who were also

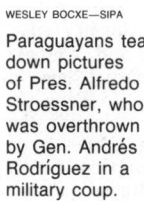

WESLEY BOCXE—SIPA
Paraguayans tear down pictures of Pres. Alfredo Stroessner, who was overthrown by Gen. Andrés Rodríguez in a military coup.

Muslim fundamentalists demonstrate against Salman Rushdie, author of *The Satanic Verses*. On February 14, Ayatollah Ruhollah Khomeini of Iran called for the death of Rushdie and others who were associated with the book, which Khomeini considered an offense against the Muslim faith.

M. ATTAR—SYGMA

26 **China prevents dissident from attending Bush banquet.** Fang Lizhi (Fang Li-chih), an astrophysicist and well-known Chinese dissident, was intercepted by police while on his way to a banquet given by President Bush at the Great Wall Sheraton Hotel in Beijing (Peking). Two other lesser-known critics of the government, however, were allowed to mingle with the 500 guests. During a meeting earlier in the day, Chinese Premier Zhao Ziyang (Chao Tzu-yang) had told Bush that support for people "who are dissatisfied with the Chinese government will not contribute to China's political stability and reform, nor will it help China's friendship with the United States." Even though Bush had not raised the question of human rights during the conversation, as most had expected him to do, Zhao introduced the topic. The government had already indicated its concern over such matters three days earlier when it denounced a local petition drive to grant amnesty to political prisoners.

Israel returns Taba to Egypt. After years of wrangling, Israel agreed to return the last piece of Sinai territory it had captured from Egypt during the 1967 Arab-Israeli war. Israel had long contended that regional border maps were incorrect and that the tiny beach resort of Taba rightly belonged to Israel all along. Nevertheless, Israel's inner Cabinet voted 9–1 to abandon Israel's claim to Taba and vacate the area by March 15. Despite Taba's relative insignificance, the protracted dispute had soured relations between the two countries.

28 **Venezuelans fight higher prices.** Venezuelan Pres. Carlos Andrés Pérez suspended certain constitutional rights and imposed a nationwide curfew the day after rioting erupted throughout the country. The rioting, which claimed some 300 lives, was in response to the government's new economic austerity program. The cost of transportation, consumer goods, and various services had risen dramatically once the government began to phase out price controls. Pérez had launched his economic program to demonstrate to the World Bank and the International Monetary Fund that Venezuela's efforts to reduce its $33 billion foreign debt and stabilize its economy merited continued financial support from the international institutions.

charged with kidnapping and beating three other young boys at the same time, had been arrested by South African police on February 19. Both were members of what was called the Mandela United Football Club. Nelson Mandela, an antiapartheid activist who had already served 26 years of a life sentence for conspiring to overthrow the government of South Africa, had reportedly urged his wife to disassociate herself from the club. Oliver Tambo, the head of the antiapartheid African National Congress, and Archbishop Desmond Tutu had also tried to dissuade Mandela from continuing her association with the club. On February 16 leaders of the antiapartheid movement distanced themselves from Mandela because she had such close ties with those charged with murder and brutality.

23 **Indonesia and China reconcile.** Indonesian President Suharto and Chinese Foreign Minister Qian Qichen (Ch'ien Ch'i-ch'en) agreed during a meeting in Tokyo to begin normalizing relations between their two countries. An Indonesian spokesman said the gradual process of restoring full diplomatic relations would be based on five principles:

noninterference in each other's affairs, nonaggression, mutual respect, beneficial relations, and peaceful coexistence. Indonesia had severed diplomatic ties in 1967 over alleged Chinese support of a failed Communist coup in 1965 that claimed more than 300,000 lives in Indonesia and eventually led to the removal of President Sukarno.

24 **Algerians approve constitution.** The Algerian government announced that more than 70% of those who voted the previous day had approved a proposed new constitution that would pave the way for the country's first multiparty system since Algeria gained independence from France in 1962. Other constitutional guarantees included free speech and a restricted right to strike. The move toward political liberalization had gained momentum after violent riots traumatized the country in October 1988. Government buildings and state-owned shops were destroyed before the Army was able to restore order. Unofficial reports put the death toll at more than 500. After pledging to support various reforms, Pres. Chadli Bendjedid was reelected to a third five-year term in December 1988.

MARCH

2 **Ozone shield to be protected.** The 12 nations constituting the European Communities agreed to eliminate, by the end of the century, the production and use of chemicals that harm the ozone layer protecting the Earth from harmful ultraviolet radiation. There would be an immediate effort to cut the production of such chemicals by 85%. On March 7 in London, during an international conference on the environment, 20 nations signed the Montreal Protocol, an agreement signed previously by some 30 nations, which resolved to cut in half the

production of ozone-destroying chemicals by the year 2000. The ultimate goal would be a permanent worldwide ban on such substances.

7 **Lhasa put under martial law.** After three days of violent clashes between Tibetans and Chinese police, China imposed martial law in Lhasa, the capital of Tibet. Li Peng (Li P'eng) signed a declaration blaming the unrest on separatists seeking independence from Chinese rule and announced that all gatherings, including meetings, parades,

and strikes, were illegal. According to official reports, at least a dozen persons were killed during the unrest; unofficial tallies were much higher. The level of violence posed the most serious challenge to Chinese rule since 1959, when the Dalai Lama fled to India after the Tibetans staged an unsuccessful uprising to secure independence.

Iran severs relations with U.K. Iran severed diplomatic relations with Great Britain because the latter had not met a one-week deadline to denounce Salman

Rushdie, the Indian-born author of *The Satanic Verses*. On February 14 Rushdie had been placed under sentence of death by Iran's Ayatollah Ruhollah Khomeini, who accused the London resident of deliberately insulting Islam in his novel.

12 **Latvians defend native tongue.** An estimated 200,000 Latvians staged the largest anti-Russian demonstration in the Soviet republic's history. It occurred in the capital city of Riga. The crowd, which encountered no police opposition, marched in support of the People's Front, which sought to establish Latvian as the dominant language of the republic. Although some demonstrators called for independence from the Soviet Union, the group was committed to working with the Communist Party to achieve reform. Two days later Estonia was the site of a very different demonstration, this one by non-Estonian ethnic Russians who claimed to be victims of discrimination. They also decried Estonia's "creeping counterrevolution." In Lithuania, the third Baltic republic, local leaders withdrew the candidacy of two persons running for congress, fearful that the movement for greater Lithuanian autonomy would be suppressed by hard-liners if two leading Communists were defeated.

13 **Vietnam refugees face curbs.** The six members (Brunei, Indonesia, Malaysia, the Philippines, Singapore, Thailand) of the Association of Southeast Asian Nations (ASEAN) announced that Vietnamese boat people would no longer be granted automatic refugee status when they arrived at an ASEAN port. As in Hong Kong, they would be screened to determine whether they had fled Vietnam merely to improve their lives economically. If this proved to be the case, they would not qualify for resettlement. During an international conference on refugees, scheduled for June in Geneva, the ASEAN plan would be studied, along with ways to deal with refugees in other parts of the world.

U.S. bans Chilean fruit. Following the discovery of two Chilean grapes bearing traces of nonlethal doses of cyanide, the U.S. Food and Drug Administration (FDA) advised consumers not to eat grapes or other fruit from Chile until further notice. U.S. officials had been on the lookout for contaminated fruit because on March 2 there had been a warning in Chile that poisoned fruit would be exported. Although stores holding perishable Chilean fruit faced serious financial losses, the U.S. government said it had no choice but to warn the public of the danger, small as it appeared to be. On March 15 Chile halted its fruit exports and promised to check all cargo before it was shipped overseas. On March 17 the FDA announced that most Chilean fruit would again be available in U.S. markets after it had been stringently inspected. The scare cost Chilean farmers millions of dollars.

15 **Opposition marches in Hungary.** An estimated 75,000 Hungarians protested and celebrated in commemoration of an unsuccessful 1848 uprising against Austrian rule. Demonstrations

included some 30,000 people in a march sanctioned by the authorities and tens of thousands more in unofficial protests. The holiday had not been officially declared since 1945. In recent years those opposed to the Communist regime had used the occasion to protest the near absolute political power of the government. The authorities had urged all parties to come together in one national celebration, but 31 opposition groups chose to celebrate on their own. The leader of the largest non-Communist organization declared in a public speech that the opposition sought "true, lasting national unity, but this cannot be built on a system of masters and servants." Another speaker remarked that not long ago the same people who now hold power had demonstrators beaten for demanding independence and democracy.

17 **Cheney named to defense post.** The U.S. Senate voted 92–0 to confirm the nomination of Dick Cheney, a Republican member of the House of Representatives, as secretary of defense. On March 9 the Senate had rejected (53–47) the nomination of John Tower, a longtime member of the Senate, after one of the bitterest debates in recent memory. During the hearings Tower had been intensely questioned about his private life and a possible conflict of interest because of his past association with military contractors. His rejection marked the first time in 30 years that a president's Cabinet nominee was not confirmed. Once Tower's fate was officially sealed, he read a statement saying it was time "for the bitterness, rancor, and anger to fade" and for government officials "to unite and be about the people's business." He added that he was departing Capitol Hill at peace with himself, knowing he had given a full measure of devotion to his country.

19 **Salvadorans elect Cristiani.** Amid widespread violence, Salvadorans elected Alfredo Cristiani, the candidate of the rightist Nationalist Republican Alliance (Arena), president of their troubled nation. Early returns indicated that Fidel Chávez Mena of the ruling Christian Democrats would finish a poor second in the field of seven. On June 1 Cristiani was scheduled to succeed José Napoleón Duarte, who had received U.S. support as a centrist holding ground between Arena on the right and guerrilla forces on the left. The rebels, who had called for a boycott of the polls, tried to disrupt the election through sabotage.

They succeeded in cutting off water and electricity from about 80% of the population and disrupted transportation.

French Socialists make gains. In the second and final round of municipal elections, the ruling Socialist Party of French Pres. François Mitterrand made significant gains at the expense of the far right, the conservatives, and the Communists. The Ecologist Party also did surprisingly well. Each of the major parties, however, retained control of many important cities where it had traditionally been strong. Jacques Chirac, a conservative who challenged Mitterrand for the presidency, was reelected mayor of Paris as expected. Former president Valéry Giscard d'Estaing acknowledged the Socialist gains but lamented the fact that France was still deeply divided by left and right ideologies and by divisions within each of these major groupings.

20 **Roh Tae Woo delays referendum.** South Korean Pres. Roh Tae Woo announced that he was indefinitely postponing a promised referendum on his first year in office to prevent a recurrence of past "confusion and violence" that had disrupted the nation. Before Roh's announcement, there was wide expectation that a referendum would be held in the near future and that Roh would win approval by a substantial margin. The announcement, therefore, came as a great surprise, even to Roh's political associates, but there was no significant negative reaction on the part of the general public.

24 **Exxon oil befouls Alaska.** A fully loaded Exxon oil tanker ruptured on charted reefs in Prince William Sound, Alaska, causing the worst tanker oil spill in U.S. history. By evening the *Exxon Valdez* had lost more than 200,000 bbl of crude oil in one of the world's finest marine habitats. Exxon's efforts to control the spill were ineffective, according to experts, in part because Exxon did not begin to put out cleanup booms for some ten hours. The president of Exxon Shipping Co. acknowledged on March 26 that the third mate was in command of the vessel when it ran aground on Bligh Reef, located three kilometres (two miles) away from shipping lanes. The third mate was in violation of federal regulations because he had no license to pilot a tanker through Prince William Sound. An investigating team reported that the captain of the ship was apparently intoxicated at the time of the accident.

GEOFFREY ORTH—SIPA

An oil-soaked bird sits on rocky coastland that was polluted after the *Exxon Valdez* ran aground and spilled more than 200,000 barrels of crude oil into Alaska's Prince William Sound.

Supporters campaign for Boris Yeltsin, the deposed party chief in Moscow and government critic, who defeated the party-backed candidate in the country's national elections.
LASKI—SIPA

25 **New coalition rules Sudan.** A political crisis ended in The Sudan with the formation of a new coalition government headed by Prime Minister Sadiq al-Mahdi of the Umma Party. The five-member Supreme Council then selected 17 persons for Cabinet posts. Four of the six remaining vacancies would be filled by southern Sudanese, who were at odds over who should represent them. The country was sharply divided between north and south. Southern rebels had long been waging war to prevent what they saw as efforts by the northern Muslims to dominate the south. Most Sudanese in that part of the country were either Christians or animists.

26 **Soviet people cast ballots.** In the freest national election since the 1917 October Revolution, Soviet citizens went to the polls to elect the Congress of People's Deputies. Although there was never any possibility that the Communist Party would lose control of the government, the stunning defeat of certain high-ranking officials caught almost everyone by surprise. Among those who failed to win were the first and second most powerful Communist officials in Moscow, the party leader in Leningrad, the two top officials in Kiev, both the president and the premier of Lithuania, the head of the KGB in Estonia, the commander of Soviet troops in East Germany, and the commander of the Northern Fleet. The most talked about candidate was Boris Yeltsin, the deposed party chief in Moscow and a critic of government policies, who won in a landslide.

28 **More arrests in Recruit scandal.** Japan's news media reported the arrest of Kunio Takaishi, a former deputy minister for education, for alleged involvement in the country's most sensational post-World War II political scandal. Takaishi became the 13th person arrested as a result of a broad investigation that had already forced three Cabinet officers to resign. All were suspected of receiving bribes of one sort or another from Recruit Co., usually in the form of stock at bargain prices before it was offered to the general public. On March 31 Prime Minister Noboru Takeshita admitted that Recruit had purchased the equivalent of $150,000 in tickets for a fund-raising party he had held two years earlier. Former prime minister Yasuhiro Nakasone was also reportedly under investigation.

30 **Palestinians choose Arafat.** Yasir Arafat, chairman of the Palestine Liberation Organization (PLO), was nominated by its executive committee to the post of president of the newly proclaimed Palestinian state. On April 2 the PLO's Central Council, meeting in Tunisia, formally elected Arafat president with a unanimous vote. Hard-line Palestinian groups continued to oppose Arafat and any compromise with Israel.

APRIL

2 **Gorbachev visits Fidel Castro.** Soviet leader Mikhail Gorbachev was warmly received in Havana by Fidel Castro, whose Communist government in Cuba had long been sustained by Soviet subsidies. Even though a treaty of friendship was signed by the two men on April 4, there were clear indications of basic disagreements. Castro declared that the new economic and political policies initiated by Gorbachev in the Soviet Union had no place in Cuba. Castro also refused to mitigate his bitter criticism of U.S. "imperialism." In a speech to the Cuban National Assembly, Gorbachev made no mention of future subsidies to Cuba, nor did he suggest that Cuba's sizable debt would be reduced or canceled.

Haiti claims coup foiled. The Haitian government announced that an attempt by army officers to overthrow Lieut. Gen. Prosper Avril, the nation's president, had been foiled by loyal troops. The rebels were intercepted while taking Avril to the airport to be deported. The insurrection was apparently linked to Avril's growing resolve to suppress drug traffic. The previous week, the government had announced the arrest of four top army officers who had been charged with drug trafficking.

5 **Shamir outlines peace plan.** During a visit to the U.S., Israeli Prime Minister Yitzhak Shamir suggested that Arab elections in the occupied territories could pave the way for a final settlement of the Arab-Israeli conflict. Shamir said that Arabs in the West Bank and Gaza Strip would be allowed to elect representatives who would, as a first step, negotiate limited self-rule for the Palestinians. The Palestinians, however, would first have to end their 16-month-old uprising. The U.S. appeared ready to support the proposal. On April 14 Palestinian leaders in the West Bank, initially cool to the idea, proposed international supervision of the elections and a partial withdrawal of Israelis. During a visit to Washington, D.C., cut short by price riots at home, King Hussein of Jordan expressed misgivings about the Israeli plan, but he said he fully supported President Bush's efforts to revive the peace process.

Vietnam to leave Kampuchea. Vietnam announced, without qualifications, that all its troops in Kampuchea would be brought home by the end of September. Vietnam's 1979 occupation of Kampuchea ended the brutal and catastrophic Khmer Rouge regime of Pol Pot. The makeup of the future government of Kampuchea was still to be negotiated. On one side was current Prime Minister Hun Sen; on the other, three disparate allies: Prince Norodom Sihanouk and his followers, the Khmer People's National Liberation Front, and Democratic Kampuchea (Khmer Rouge), whose military might was far greater than that of its allies.

6 **P.W. Botha to step down.** South African Pres. P.W. Botha, during a speech before Parliament, revealed he would relinquish the presidency after the general election later in the year. On February 3, F.W. de Klerk had been elected head of the ruling National Party, replacing the 73-year-old Botha, who had suffered a stroke on January 18. Following Botha's announcement, de Klerk appeared to be an odds-on favourite to win the presidency.

7 **Soviet Georgia in turmoil.** The Soviet government deployed troops and armoured personnel carriers along the streets of Tbilisi to stifle strikes and demonstrations in the capital city of the Georgian S.S.R. The people, who were demonstrating peacefully, were demanding greater political and economic

People in Soviet Georgia toss flowers at the site in Tbilisi where government troops had violently cracked down on those peacefully demonstrating for political and economic freedom.
LASKI—SIPA

independence from the central government in Moscow. On April 9 at least 19 persons were killed and many hundreds injured when troops moved against a crowd that had refused to disperse. The next day Foreign Minister Eduard Shevardnadze, the only native Georgian on the Politburo, flew to Tbilisi in an effort to restore calm. He later declared there was "no justification for the death of innocent people." On April 19 *Izvestiya*, the government newspaper, reported that an official investigation of the incident showed that numerous victims had been poisoned by chemical agents.

8   **Mexico arrests drug dealers.** Mexican authorities arrested 43-year-old Miguel Angel Félix Gallardo in Guadalajara. Mexico's attorney general announced that real estate, bank accounts, and businesses belonging to Félix Gallardo had also been seized. The suspect was considered Mexico's paramount trafficker in cocaine and had been accused by U.S. drug-enforcement agents of smuggling up to four tons of cocaine into the U.S. each month. The Mexican government crackdown also extended to Culiacán, Félix Gallardo's hometown, where scores of state and local police officers thought to be involved in the drug operation were rounded up.

13   **Congress votes *contra* aid.** The U.S. Congress approved $49.7 million in aid to Nicaraguan *contras* fighting the Sandinista government of Pres. Daniel Ortega. The vote in the House of Representatives was 309–110; that in the Senate, 89–9. The money, intended to support the *contras* until proposed elections were held in February 1990, was earmarked for food, clothing, medicine, shelter, and transportation. Unlike past debates on *contra* aid, there was broad congressional support for the legislation because it provided no direct military assistance to the *contras* but maintained

their organization during negotiations to end the hostilities.

Sri Lanka bomb kills dozens. Tamil separatists killed at least 38 people and wounded 56 others when they detonated a car bomb in a crowded bazaar in Trincomalee, Sri Lanka. Several of the victims were charred beyond recognition. The attack, which occurred at the beginning of a two-day holiday, was presumably intended to terrorize the Sinhalese into leaving an area the Tamil minority claimed as a homeland. Later in the day Sinhalese avenged the killings by murdering five Tamils in another part of the city.

16   **Amnesty for Uruguay's military.** Voters in Uruguay defeated a referendum that would have nullified the amnesty granted to members of the armed forces for alleged crimes committed

against the Tupamaro rebels during the years of military rule (1973–85). The Army had countered the bombings, political assassinations, bank robberies, and other acts of violence with a relentless campaign against real and suspected guerrillas. After their capture, some were reportedly killed and others tortured. Vice Pres. Enrique Tarigo declared that the vote put to rest "the last thorny question from the past."

17   **Solidarity regains legal status.** A court in Warsaw officially restored the legal status of Solidarity, the Polish federation of trade unions that had been declared illegal in October 1982 during martial law. When it was established in August 1980, Solidarity became the first independent trade union in Eastern Europe. The restoration of Solidarity was part of an April 5 agreement between labour leaders and government officials. The country was now looking forward to parliamentary elections, which would be the freest in Poland's postwar history.

18   **Beijing students hold rally.** Several thousand students marched through Beijing (Peking) in the early hours of the morning chanting demands for greater democratic freedom. The demonstration was also a declaration of admiration for Hu Yaobang (Hu Yao-pang), who had died on April 15. In January 1987, accused of being too tolerant of students lobbying for greater political freedom, he had been forced to resign as head of the Communist Party of China. On April 19 an estimated 10,000 people gathered in Tiananmen (T'ien-an-men) Square; some then tried to force their way into the compound where many of China's leaders lived and worked. Despite a ban on political protests, the same scenario was repeated the following day. On April 22 the crowd in Tiananmen swelled to more than 100,000, thousands of whom camped out overnight to prevent police from sealing off the square when it was empty. Two days later students began to boycott classes to reinforce their call for democratic changes. On April 27 at least 100,000 defied government troops

MITSUHIRO WADA—GAMMA/LIAISON

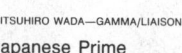
Japanese Prime Minister Noboru Takeshita announces his resignation amid the Recruit Co. scandal, in which many high-ranking government officials were charged with bribery and influence peddling.

by marching through the streets shouting slogans. The demonstration was called the largest antigovernment protest since the Communists came to power in 1949. On April 29, in an extraordinary attempt to calm the students, government officials appeared on national television to discuss the crisis with student representatives.

21 **Gandhi ousts chief minister.** Indian Prime Minister Rajiv Gandhi ordered the southern state of Karnataka placed under the direct rule of the central government; at the same time, the state's chief minister was dismissed and the legislature dissolved. The president signed a formal proclamation the same day. The opposition government in Karnataka had become a minority after 17 members of the ruling People's Party and one other legislator withdrew their support. Among the 25 Indian states, only 6 remained outside the control of the Congress Party.

23 **Egypt curbs fundamentalists.** Egyptian Interior Minister Zaki Badr, speaking at a Cairo police academy banquet, said that Muslim fundamentalists "are fueling religious strife in the country, and they must be met with force." Bahr was explaining and defending the government's arrest of about 1,500 Muslims in a renewed crackdown on members of clandestine fundamentalist groups known collectively as Jihad ("Holy War").

24 **Court backs apartheid foes.** After an 18-month trial, a South African judge ruled that the government had not proved its case against five black defendants charged with subversion and sedition. The men had set up the Alexandra Action Committee, which bypassed government offices in an attempt to upgrade the miserable living conditions of blacks living near the affluent white suburbs of Johannesburg. The judge concluded that such activity was not designed to replace Alexandra's town council or render the township ungovernable through protests.

25 **Kremlin purges "dead souls."** The leaders of the Soviet Union's Communist Party voted to remove 74 of the 301 members of the powerful Central Committee; all had full voting rights. In addition, 36 other high officials were also voted out of office; some were nonvoting members of the Central Committee, while others were members of the party's auditing commission. Generally, younger men were appointed to take their places. The overall size of the Central Committee was simultaneously reduced to 251. All those dismissed were called "dead souls,"

inactive officials considered impediments to Soviet leader Mikhail Gorbachev's program of reform. One official declared that the party was simply carrying out the wishes of those who voted "for renewal, for democracy, for *glasnost*, for economic reform" in the March election.

Noboru Takeshita to quit. Japanese Prime Minister Noboru Takeshita called a news conference in Tokyo to say he would resign in the near future because the Recruit scandal, which involved bribery and influence peddling, had tarnished his own reputation and that of the ruling Liberal-Democratic Party. The announcement was not unexpected; Takeshita had been under great pressure to step aside, especially after he testified on March 28 that the Recruit Co. had contributed $150,000 to his political war chest. On April 26 Ihei Aoki, Takeshita's close aide and chief fund-raiser, committed suicide.

Soviet tanks leave Hungary. With considerable fanfare, the Soviet Union began its promised cutback of military hardware deployed in Eastern Europe. With a corps of international reporters observing the operation near a provincial town some 145 km (90 mi) from Budapest, 31 heavy tanks began moving toward the Soviet Ukraine aboard flatbed railroad cars.

MAY

1 **Paraguay elects Andrés Rodríguez.** In an election described as the freest and most honest in Paraguay in more than 60 years, Gen. Andrés Rodríguez of the Colorado Party was elected president. He overwhelmed his seven opponents by winning a substantial majority of the ballots. In February Rodríguez had overthrown Pres. Alfredo Stroessner. The Colorado Party also gained control of the legislature by means of a law stipulating that two-thirds of the seats in each of the two houses of Congress

would go to the party that commanded a simple majority.

2 **Dutch government falls.** The seven-year-old coalition government of Dutch Prime Minister Ruud Lubbers collapsed when the People's Party for Freedom and Democracy, the junior partner in the coalition, refused to support the financing arrangements of a multibillion-dollar antipollution program. Even though Queen Beatrix was expected to accept the resignation of the Cabinet,

Lubbers' Christian Democrats would retain power as a caretaker government until early elections were held later in the year. Since World War II, no political party in The Netherlands had ever won an absolute majority in Parliament.

3 **Police killed on Pusan campus.** Six South Korean riot police lost their lives while attempting to rescue five officers held hostage by Dongeui University students in Pusan. The incident began on May 1 when police fired warning shots over the heads of students demonstrating outside a police station; several students were arrested. Outraged students took five plainclothes officers hostage on May 2. After fruitless nightlong negotiations, troops stormed the university library, where the students were holding the hostages. When, in response, students set a barricade soaked in paint thinner on fire, the riot police were engulfed in flames. The incident, described as one of the most violent student demonstrations in the nation's history, was but the latest in a series of events reflecting social upheaval. On March 30, for example, police had stormed the Hyundai shipyard in Ulsan to end a 109-day strike. On April 1 workers at Hyundai-affiliated companies were joined by student activists in protests. In an effort to end the turmoil, police arrested thousands of people who were staging sit-ins, leading strikes, or demonstrating.

4 **North convicted on three counts.** Oliver North, a retired lieutenant colonel in the U.S. Marine Corps and a former aide with the National Security Council, was convicted on 3

AFP PHOTO

Guillermo Ford, a vice presidential candidate of Panama's opposition party, is beaten by a pro-Noriega paramilitary force during a march called to protest widespread fraud in the country's national elections.

of 12 charges connected with the Iran-*contra* affair. North was found guilty of illegally accepting a $13,800 security system for his home, of altering and destroying government documents, and of obstructing Congress. On July 6 North was given a three-year suspended sentence, fined $150,000, and ordered to serve 1,200 hours of community service at an antidrug centre for youth in the nation's capital.

7 **Fraud vitiates Panama election.** Panamanian voters went to the polls in large numbers to elect a president. The voting was in effect a referendum on Gen. Manuel Noriega, the country's de facto ruler, whose surrogate candidate was Carlos Duque. The following day former U.S. president Jimmy Carter, a member of an international group of on-site observers, told reporters, "I hope there will be a worldwide outcry of condemnation against a dictator who stole this election from his own people." Exit polls reportedly showed the opposition winning by a 3–1 margin. Another member of the international delegation exclaimed, "I never thought the fraud would be this blatant. These people are absolutely shameless." On May 10 paramilitary forces used baseball bats and metal pipes to severely beat the opposition presidential and two vice presidential candidates. Soldiers standing nearby merely watched. That same day the government, in the face of mounting criticism, nullified the election.

9 **Coup foiled in Guatemala.** Troops loyal to Guatemalan Pres. Vinicio Cerezo Arévalo foiled an attempted coup by present and former members of the armed forces. No shots were fired. Some of the rebel officers had been cashiered out of the armed forces in May 1988 after an unsuccessful bid to overthrow Cerezo (who, in January 1986, had become head of the first civilian administration in 16 years). On May 15 a military tribunal charged the leaders of the insurgency with treason and rebellion.

14 **Menem victorious in Argentina.** Carlos Saúl Menem, candidate of the Peronists, was elected president of Argentina. His closest rival, Eduardo Angeloz of the ruling Radical Civic Union, conceded defeat late in the evening and congratulated Menem on his broad victory "in exemplary elections." Menem would be the first Peronist to lead the country since Isabel Perón was ousted as president in a 1976 military coup. Early returns indicated that Peronists would also probably win control of both houses of Congress.

Egypt to rejoin Arab world. An aide to Syrian Pres. Hafez al-Assad told reporters in Damascus that Egyptian Pres. Hosni Mubarak's attendance at the upcoming Arab conference in Casablanca, Morocco, would be a "natural and positive development." In effect, Egypt was being welcomed back to full participation in matters affecting the Arab world. Egypt's membership in the Arab League had been suspended after Pres. Anwar as-Sadat signed a peace treaty with Israel in 1979.

17 **Military coup fails in Ethiopia.** Ethiopian Pres. Mengistu Haile Mariam cut short a state visit to East Germany after senior military officers attempted to overthrow his Marxist government the previous day. After a brief period of heavy fighting, the rebellion was put down. The military was said to be extremely dissatisfied with the president's campaign against two separatist groups operating in the northern part of the country. According to official reports, at least eight generals involved in the coup were killed; several hundred other persons were arrested.

19 **Accord reached on Namibia.** Officials representing Angola, Cuba, and South Africa announced that they had resolved their differences and that the implementation of the United Nations plan for the independence of South West Africa/Namibia could continue. Cuba, which from bases inside neighbouring Angola had supported guerrillas of the South West Africa People's Organization, and South Africa, which effectively controlled the territory, were both committed to the withdrawal of their military personnel.

20 **Beijing put under martial law.** One day after China's Communist Party leader Zhao Ziyang (Chao Tzu-yang) visited Tiananmen (T'ien-an-men) Square to urge some 3,000 students to end the hunger strike they had begun on May 13, Premier Li Peng (Li P'eng) imposed martial law on the capital. Hundreds of thousands of people, most of whom flocked to the square in the centre of the city, had joined the call for greater freedom and democracy. Some called for the resignations of Li Peng and Deng Xiaoping (Teng Hsiao-p'ing), China's paramount leader. The students viewed both men as hard-liners unsympathetic to their demands. Zhao was considered a moderate, one willing to listen to student complaints and discuss "reasonable demands." When military units deployed in the Beijing (Peking) area tried to move into the centre of the city, they found their way blocked by barricades, vehicles of all sorts, and thousands upon thousands of students and their supporters. Many offered food and drink to the troops while pleading with them to turn back. There was no violence of any consequence on either side. Worldwide television coverage of the dramatic events was cut off, but it was then restored for those willing to share the Chinese government's satellite facilities. Early in the morning on May 30 the students moved a homemade 9-m (30-ft)-high statue of the "Goddess of Democracy" into Tiananmen Square and placed it facing the huge portrait of Chairman Mao Zedong (Mao Tse-tung).

22 **Baker urges Israel to change.** U.S. Secretary of State James Baker, in a speech before the American Israel Public Affairs Committee in Washington, D.C., declared: "For Israel, now is the time to lay aside, once and for all, the unrealistic vision of a greater Israel." He called on Israel to abandon its plan to annex the West Bank and Gaza Strip, to reopen Palestinian schools, to cease developing Jewish settlements in the occupied territories, and to rely on negotiations to establish a lasting peace in the Middle East. Baker also called on the Palestinians, who were deeply divided on the issue of negotiating with Israel, "to speak with one voice for peace." He urged the Palestinians to transform the "dialogue of violence" of the *intifada* ("uprising") that began in December 1987 "into a dialogue of politics and diplomacy."

25 **Gorbachev elected president.** Mikhail Gorbachev, head of the Soviet Union's Communist Party, was elected president of the U.S.S.R. by the newly constituted 2,250-member Congress of People's Deputies. His tenure would be limited to two five-year terms. The result of the secret balloting was 2,123–87. Before the voting Gorbachev was publicly and sharply questioned about his policies and was made, among other things, to defend his use of a plush official home in the Crimea. During the debates certain deputies contended that Gorbachev would rival Napoleon in power if he were both leader of the Communist Party and head of government. Among those in attendance was Boris Yeltsin, the former party leader in Moscow who had become a celebrity by challenging Gorbachev. Yeltsin failed to win a seat among the 542 members of the Supreme Soviet (the legislative body in the revamped government structure); the Congress responded to public indignation and voted on May 29 to allow Yeltsin to accept a seat offered to him by one of the victorious candidates.

U.S. chides trading partners. Carla Hills, the U.S. trade representative, announced that President Bush had concluded that Brazil, India, and Japan were guilty of unfair trading practices. As a consequence, the three countries would be required to relax their restrictions on U.S. imports within 12–18 months or face possible reprisals. These could include 100% tariffs on certain items exported to the U.S. Bush's decision appeased those members of Congress who were clamouring for such action, but it predictably angered the three nations that had been publicly rebuked.

Bhutto ousts powerful general. Pakistani Prime Minister Benazir Bhutto dismissed Lieut. Gen. Hamid Gul as head of the Inter-Service Intelligence directorate and named a retired general as his replacement. Gul, an appointee of the late president Mohammad Zia ul-Haq, had played a vital role in domestic and foreign affairs. His support of Afghan Muslim fundamentalists was at odds with Bhutto's support for a negotiated settlement to the civil war there. By removing Gul, Bhutto gained greater control over Pakistan's future.

29 **Japan ends Recruit probe.** Prosecutors investigating charges of bribery and influence peddling among Japan's leading politicians announced they had completed their probe of the Recruit scandal without uncovering significant evidence of criminal activity by the most prominent targets of the investigation, Prime Minister Noboru Takeshita and his predecessor, Yasuhiro Nakasone. The long investigation led to at least 16 indictments.

JUNE

2 **Uno chosen to replace Takeshita.** Sosuke Uno was elected prime minister of Japan by the House of Representatives, which was controlled by the ruling Liberal-Democratic Party (LDP). He replaced Noboru Takeshita, who was forced to resign after being implicated in the Recruit scandal. Powerful members of the LDP opposed Uno's appointment, in part because he had close ties to former prime minister Yasuhiro Nakasone, who felt compelled to resign from the LDP after his involvement in the Recruit affair became public knowledge.

3 **Ayatollah Khomeini dies in Iran.** Ayatollah Ruhollah Khomeini, who became Iran's supreme spiritual leader and unchallenged political authority after the 1979 overthrow of Shah Mohammad Reza Pahlavi, died. He had been in frail health for some time. An assembly of theologians quickly named Pres. Sayyed Ali Khamenei spiritual leader of the Islamic republic. On June 6 Khomeini was buried on the outskirts of Tehran. As many as three million people attended the Shi'ite Muslim ceremony. At one point Khomeini's body fell out of the coffin as hysterical mourners fought to touch his shroud.

4 **Troops crush Beijing protests.** Tens of thousands of Chinese troops made a determined drive into the centre of Beijing (Peking) to take back control of Tiananmen (T'ien-an-men) Square and nearby streets. As the troops moved relentlessly toward their objective, hundreds—possibly thousands—of students and workers were killed by automatic gunfire or by military vehicles. Many of those who watched the television coverage outside China used such words as *stunned, dismayed, horrified,* and *heartsick* to convey their feelings. U.S. print media, which overwhelmingly condemned the military assault for its perceived "brutality," most frequently described the bloodletting as a massacre or slaughter. France, the U.K., Italy, Japan, The Netherlands, Spain, the U.S., and West Germany were among the first nations to issue official statements deploring the government's order to shoot its own people simply because they were demanding an end to official corruption and pleading for democratic reforms. Chinese interviewed on the streets of Beijing said they were filled with anger and despair.

5 **Solidarity triumphs in election.** A spokesman for Poland's ruling Communist Party, in a televised announcement, declared that Solidarity had "achieved a decisive majority" in parliamentary elections. Solidarity's clear-cut victory in the popular vote did not translate directly into a corresponding number of seats in the legislature, but it was sure to shape the government in as yet unforeseeable ways. Solidarity candidates, moreover, were eligible for only 161 of the 460 seats in the lower house. Although Solidarity would virtually monopolize the Senate, that house's authority was limited to a veto over legislation. Lech Walesa, the head of Solidarity, said he would urge the labour federation's new legislators not to join a coalition government led by the Communist Party.

6 **New unrest in Soviet republics.** The Soviet government reported that at least 57 people had been killed in recent days during clashes in Uzbekistan. The Uzbek government blamed the violence on native Uzbeks who in a wild frenzy used wooden sticks and metal bars to kill 40 Meskhetians in Fergana on June 4. Hundreds of homes were also looted and set ablaze. The Meskhetians, a minuscule Turkish minority, had been relocated in 1944 on Joseph Stalin's orders. Their previous homes had been in southern Georgia, along the Turkish border. Although thousands of Soviet troops patrolled the area, they were unable to contain the marauding bands of Uzbeks. On June 9 there were reports that Uzbeks carrying automatic weapons, handguns, and knives had caused some 100 casualties in Kokand. On June 19 the Tass news agency reported that armed youths had gone on a rampage in Kazakhstan. Their anger seemed to be an expression of frustration over economic hardships and what they considered to be better conditions for migrant workers.

Foley elected House speaker. The Democratic majority in the U.S. House of Representatives—in a straight party-line vote—elected Thomas Foley speaker of the House. The post placed Foley, who represented a district in eastern Washington state, second in line to succeed to the presidency, after Vice Pres. Dan Quayle. Foley's predecessor, Jim Wright (Dem., Texas), in an address to members of the House on May 31, said he would resign as soon as a successor was chosen, although he continued to deny charges that he had violated House ethics rules regarding finances.

9 **China puts blame on Fang Lizhi.** During a Chinese television newscast, Fang Lizhi (Fang Li-chih), an eminent astrophysicist and well-known dissident, was identified as the main instigator of the Tiananmen (T'ien-an-men) protests and the violence that followed. Fang had already fled to the U.S. embassy with his wife on June 5 and had been granted political asylum. China, which later issued a warrant for his arrest, was incensed that the U.S. had involved itself in "China's internal affairs."

10 **Mammoth waste at HUD agency.** U.S. federal investigators revealed they had uncovered a nationwide financial scandal of mammoth proportions at the Department of Housing and Urban Development (HUD). Contractors working for HUD were said to have embezzled millions of dollars the government should have received from the sale of homes that had been foreclosed. A HUD agent in Maryland acknowledged she had taken

ERIC BOUVET—GAMMA/LIAISON

A sea of mourners crowd around the glass coffin bearing the body of Iran's spiritual leader, Ayatollah Ruhollah Khomeini.

CHIP HIRES—GAMMA/LIAISON

Chinese students fill Tiananmen (T'ien-an-men) Square in a pro-democracy demonstration before the violent crackdown by government forces.

as much as $5.5 million and given it to charity. The extent and duration of the scandal were blamed on mismanagement, near total lack of accountability by employees, and the wide discretion allowed staff members in the selection of projects. James Watt, secretary of the interior during the Reagan administration, bragged to a congressional panel investigating influence peddling at HUD that he had received more than $400,000 as a private consultant in federal low-income-housing projects. Although he had no background in housing and had never investigated the property he was promoting, his ready access to top government officials made it easy, he said, to get what he was after.

14 **Cuba arrests top general.** Cuba announced the arrest of Gen. Arnaldo Ochoa Sánchez, a popular hero of the revolution and one of the nation's most highly decorated military officers. After being tried before a military tribunal, Ochoa was found guilty of conspiring to ship tons of cocaine and marijuana into the U.S. On July 13 he and three other officers were executed by firing squad.

15 **Turmoil continues in China.** Despite Chinese government assurances that the country had returned to normal after the violence around Tiananmen Square, political ferment continued. On June 15 three pro-democracy youths were sentenced to death; then two days later eight more were added to the list. The first public executions took place on June 21. On June 20, dismissing China's official version of the Tiananmen incident—that there had been no gunfire and no deaths in the square on June 4—the White House suspended all high-level meetings between U.S. and Chinese officials. On June 24 Zhao Ziyang (Chao Tzu-yang) was ousted as head of the Communist Party and replaced by Jiang Zemin (Chiang Tse-min), the top party official in Shanghai. China meanwhile continued its manhunt for leaders of the pro-democracy demonstrations by urging citizens to notify police if they knew the whereabouts of the "counterrevolutionaries" whose pictures were being shown on television. Premier Li Peng (Li P'eng) had vowed they would be punished "without mercy." China was also endeavouring to revive tourism and

entice foreign businessmen back to the country.

16 **Hungary honours Imre Nagy.** Former Hungarian premier Imre Nagy, who had been hanged in 1958 for trying to establish a Communist government independent of the Soviet Union, was reburied with honours after a solemn funeral in Budapest. Nagy's remains had first to be identified from among many others disposed of in an unmarked mass grave. With the permission of the leaders of the political opposition but not as representatives of the Communist Party, the country's current prime minister, deputy prime minister, minister of state, and president of Parliament served as honorary pallbearers. An estimated 300,000 people attended the funeral. The eulogies to Nagy were uncompromising in their condemnation of Hungary's Communist Party and the Soviet Union.

18 **Papandreou party suffers defeat.** Greek Prime Minister Andreas Papandreou's Pan-Hellenic Socialist Movement (Pasok) lost its majority in Parliament after an opposition campaign that repeatedly called attention to the scandals that enmeshed the prime minister. The conservative New Democracy Party, led by Konstantinos Mitsotakis, won a plurality of the votes and 145 (+19) of the 300 seats in Parliament. Pasok captured 125 seats (−36), the Communist Alliance 28 (+15), and minor parties the 2 remaining seats. On July 1 Tzannis Tzannetakis, a member of the New Democracy Party, was sworn in as prime minister and head of a coalition government that included the Communist Alliance.

19 **Burma adopts new name.** Burma announced that it would henceforth be called the Union of Myanmar; the capital, Rangoon, would be known as Yangon. The change acknowledged the ethnic diversity of the nation by abandoning a name that referred exclusively to the country's most prominent ethnic group.

21 **Flag burning called free speech.** The U.S. Supreme Court, in a 5–4 decision, ruled in effect that the First Amendment to the Constitution, which guarantees free speech, invalidates

any laws that prohibit peaceful political activists from burning the U.S. flag as an act of protest. The court was directly addressing the case of Gregory Lee Johnson, who had been convicted of violating a Texas law in 1984 when he soaked a U.S. flag in kerosene and set it afire as a crowd chanted, "America, the red, white, and blue, we spit on you." Many Americans, angered by the court's decision, vowed to push for a constitutional amendment that would outlaw what they viewed as a desecration of the nation's most revered symbol.

22 **Cease-fire declared in Angola.** The Marxist-led government of Pres. José Eduardo dos Santos and the guerrilla forces of Jonas Savimbi, during a meeting in Zaire, agreed to observe a cease-fire in Angola beginning June 24. No one, however, expected the 14-year-old civil war to end without protracted and difficult negotiations. The U.S. said it would continue to provide military aid to the guerrillas until national reconciliation was an established fact.

28 **Sri Lankan foes accept cease-fire.** The Sri Lankan government and the Liberation Tigers of Tamil Eelam, the largest group of Tamil rebels, agreed to an immediate cease-fire. Both sides hoped to negotiate an end to their six-year-old conflict, in which some estimates put the number of deaths at over 10,000. The Tamils, who constituted a Hindu minority in predominantly Buddhist Sri Lanka, had long been demanding greater autonomy.

30 **Sudanese government ousted.** The Sudanese government of Prime Minister Sadiq al-Mahdi was overthrown in an early-morning military coup. There was no immediate report of casualties. The little-known leader of the coup announced that a Revolutionary Council would rule the country. Dissatisfaction with the government's failure to end the civil war between north and south and despair over the sorry state of the economy were seen as major causes of the revolt. According to international relief agencies, some 250,000 people had starved to death because the interdiction of food supplies to the south had been used as a weapon of war.

JULY

3 **Supreme Court rules on abortion.** In a 5–4 ruling the U.S. Supreme Court upheld three provisions of a 1986 Missouri law that placed state restrictions on abortion. Chief Justice William Rehnquist's majority opinion was shared by Justices Anthony Kennedy, Sandra Day O'Connor, Antonin Scalia, and Byron White. The anxiously awaited decision was widely viewed as a victory for "pro-life" advocates and a defeat for "pro-choice" groups. Although the court stopped short of overturning the landmark 1973 Roe v. Wade ruling, which established a woman's right to abortion, it upheld the right of individual states

to impose restrictions that for 16 years had been considered unconstitutional. The bitter battle over abortion was certain to continue, not only in state legislatures but also in the Supreme Court, which had agreed to consider three additional abortion cases when it convened for a new term in October.

10 **Soviet miners go on strike.** Coal miners in the Siberian city of Mezhdurechensk went on strike to reinforce their demands for better living conditions. Pravda, the Communist Party newspaper, reported on July 13 that work at all five mines had come to a halt.

Although the government agreed to certain concessions, the strike spread to other areas and involved some 100,000 miners. On July 17 the Soviet press reported that eight mines in the Ukraine had also closed. During a televised address on July 23, Soviet leader Mikhail Gorbachev told the miners he was inspired by their determination to take matters into their own hands to bring about changes that were necessary for the success of perestroika, his program for restructuring the nation's economy. Many strikers, heartened by Gorbachev's promise that their grievances would receive a positive response, began returning to work.

12 **Ireland gets its first coalition.** Charles Haughey, leader of Ireland's Fianna Fail, became prime minister for the fourth time after agreeing to accept the Progressive Democrats as partners in the nation's first coalition government. Desmond O'Malley, who had organized the Progressive Democrats after severing connections with Fianna Fail, joined Haughey in setting aside personal differences so the two could work together to solve Ireland's economic problems.

13 **France celebrates bicentennial.** French Pres. François Mitterrand presided over the opening of a week-long bicentennial celebration commemorating the French Revolution, which had begun on July 14, 1789, when an angry mob stormed the Bastille, a medieval fortress prison. The first major social event was the opening of a new opera house on the site once occupied by that prison. Numerous foreign dignitaries accepted Mitterrand's invitation to share in the celebration, including leaders of the seven principal industrialized democracies, who used the occasion to hold their 15th economic summit. The final communiqué called attention to three challenges. These included balancing and sustaining economic growth, controlling inflation, creating jobs, promoting social justice, and adjusting trade imbalances; alleviating the foreign debt and poverty of less developed nations; and safeguarding the environment.

18 **Kenya incinerates ivory tusks.** Kenyan Pres. Daniel arap Moi put the torch to a 12-ton pile of elephant tusks during a well-publicized gathering of environmentalists, government officials, and reporters in Nairobi National Park. The destruction of the ivory, valued at $3 million, was part of a government campaign to persuade the world community to ban international trade in ivory in order to halt the slaughter of Kenya's elephants. During the past decade, poachers, knowing there was a ready market for ivory, had killed about 75% of Kenya's elephants

19 **Jaruzelski wins presidency.** Gen. Wojciech Jaruzelski was elected president of Poland by the nation's newly elected Sejm (parliament). Although he ran unopposed, Jaruzelski received only 270 votes—the absolute minimum needed for victory. There were 233 votes against Jaruzelski, 34 abstentions, and 23 absentees. Even though the Communists had been soundly defeated by Solidarity candidates in the June parliamentary elections, they and their allies had been guaranteed 300 of the 560 seats. It was clear, therefore, that Jaruzelski had not received all the support he might have expected. On July 29 he resigned as leader of the party, as he had pledged to do if he won the presidency.

Khashoggi extradited to the U.S. Adnan Khashoggi, a wealthy Saudi arms broker, was extradited to the U.S., where he faced charges of implementing "illegal property deals" for former Philippine president Ferdinand Marcos. Before Khashoggi was flown from Switzerland to New York, Swiss authorities had assured him that he would be tried only for obstruction of justice and mail fraud, not for the more serious crimes of racketeering and conspiracy.

20 **Myanmar stifles opposition.** The military government of Myanmar, which had recently changed its name from Burma, placed Daw Aung San Suu Kyi under house arrest. She was one of the country's most prominent politicians and a leader of the National Unity Party (NUP). Her father, Aung San, a hero of the revolution that ended British rule in Burma, was assassinated in 1947. The NUP was a coalition of various groups that had demanded the legalization of more than one party. Their antigovernment demonstrations had led to thousands of deaths, mass arrests, the closing of universities, and the resignation of Ne Win, who had ruled the country with an iron fist for 26 years.

22 **Andreotti to lead Italy again.** Giulio Andreotti became Italy's prime minister for the sixth time since 1972. He succeeded Ciriaco De Mita, a fellow Christian Democrat, who had been in office a little more than a year before announcing his resignation in May. Andreotti's government would include the same four partners that formed the De Mita coalition: Socialists, Social Democrats, Republicans, and Liberals.

Israel reopens Arab schools. The Israeli government allowed some 200,000 Palestinian students to return to schools that six months earlier had been shut down in the occupied territories. The partial reopening permitted primary school students and high school seniors to resume their formal education. If the Israeli government was satisfied that the schools were not being used to support the ongoing Palestinian uprising, the entire high school student body would presumably be allowed to return to the classroom. The future of university students appeared more uncertain.

23 **Voters rebuff Japan's leaders.** Japan's ruling Liberal-Democratic Party (LDP) suffered its worst defeat at the polls in 34 years. When it became clear that the LDP had lost control of the upper house of the Diet (parliament), Prime Minister Sosuke Uno announced he would resign. He had been in office less than two months. Final tallies showed the LDP had won only 36 of the 69 LDP seats that were contested, giving it a new total of 109 seats (−33) in the House of Councilors; 127 constituted a majority. The Japan Socialist Party, having won 46 seats in the election, emerged with a new total of 66 (+24). Komeito ended up with 20 seats (−2), the Japan Communist Party 14 (−3), the Democratic Socialist Party 8 (−3), Rengo 12 (+11), and others 23 (+6). The LDP defeat was blamed on such things as the recent Recruit scandal, the unpopular consumption tax, the increase in agricultural imports, and the anger of female voters over Uno's liaison with a geisha.

25 **Kampuchea's future still in doubt.** Efforts to reach a general agreement on Kampuchea's future government ended in failure when representatives of the main factions could reach no compromise after a two-day meeting in France. On one side was Kampuchean Prime Minister Hun Sen, who had been installed by the Vietnamese; on the other, a coalition of three guerrilla organizations represented by Prince Norodom Sihanouk. The talks had been planned as a way to resolve basic differences before convening an international conference of 19 nations. One of the most difficult problems involved the Communist Khmer Rouge, which ruled the country from April 1975 to January 1979. During the brutal regime of Pol Pot, an estimated one million persons were killed. The Khmer Rouge could not be excluded from the discussions because they were by far the most powerful military force in the rebel coalition.

28 **Israelis kidnap Sheikh Obeid.** Operating from helicopters under cover of darkness, 12 Israeli commandos kidnapped Sheikh 'Abd-al Karim Obeid from his home in southern Lebanon. Two of his associates were also carried away. Israeli fighter planes provided a diversion by staging a mock air raid that drowned out the noise of the helicopters. Obeid was identified as a leader of the pro-Iranian Hezbollah (Party of God), which was believed to be holding 17 hostages in Lebanon, including three Israeli soldiers and nine Americans. Hezbollah had taken credit for numerous attacks against Israelis in a "security zone" Israel had established in southern Lebanon along the Israeli border. Obeid was "arrested" for instigating and sometimes planning the raids.

30 **Mozambique seeks end to war.** The ruling Mozambique Liberation Front (Frelimo) adjourned its party congress after drafting a new socialist agenda that generally lacked the government's accustomed Marxist-Lenin-

GROPP—SIPA

Protesters burn an effigy of the Supreme Court after the court's controversial ruling upholding state restrictions on abortion.

Saudi arms dealer Adnan Khashoggi is escorted to a police vehicle after his extradition to the U.S., where he was to face charges of implementing "illegal property deals."

VOGEL—GAMMA/LIAISON

ist rhetoric. In addition, Pres. Joaqim Chissanó's colleagues urged him to pursue peace negotiations with the insurgent Mozambique National Resistance (Renamo), which, with military support from South Africa, had disrupted public services and inflicted serious damage on the economy. During their "war for democracy," Renamo guerrillas had reportedly killed some 100,000 civilians. Their name also became a synonym for torture, rape, and kidnapping. Prospects for genuine peace in the foreseeable future were not considered bright, even though South Africa, Frelimo, and Renamo had all indicated a qualified willingness to end the conflict.

31 **U.S. colonel reported hanged.** The Organization for the Oppressed of the Earth, a group of Shi'ite Muslim extremists with close ties to the pro-Iranian Hezbollah, announced it had hanged Lieut. Col. William Higgins, a U.S. marine attached to the UN truce-monitoring force in Lebanon. Higgins had been abducted in February 1988. The group also released a low-quality videotape showing a gagged and bound man slowly twisting at the end of a rope. After careful study of the evidence, the CIA suggested that Higgins might have died at a much earlier date. A second Shi'ite Muslim group threatened to kill Joseph Cicippio unless the Israelis released Sheikh 'Abdal Karim Obeid. Cicippio, who had been attached to the American University of Beirut, Lebanon, was taken hostage in September 1986.

AUGUST

3 **Rafsanjani becomes president.** Hojatolislam Hashemi Rafsanjani, who had been speaker of Iran's Majlis (parliament), assumed the presidency during a ceremony in Tehran. The outcome of the July 28 presidential election had never been in doubt because Rafsanjani was the unequivocal choice of all of Iran's major political and religious parties. On August 29 the 270-member legislature approved all of Rafsanjani's 22 Cabinet nominees. It was a major political victory for the new president because he had pointedly omitted the name of Interior Minister Hojatolislam Ali Akbar Mohtashemi, a fiery opponent of rapprochement with the West. The new president also assumed the powers formerly invested in the prime minister; that office was abolished when voters approved a number of constitutional amendments.

6 **Paz Zamora takes oath of office.** Jaime Paz Zamora was formally installed as president of Bolivia, even though he had finished third in the presidential election held on May 7. In that election Gonzalo Sánchez de Lozada, of the ruling National Revolutionary Movement party (MNR), finished first in a field of ten with about 23% of the popular vote. Bolivian law, however, permitted Congress to select the president when no candidate won an absolute majority of the ballots cast. Congress selected Paz Zamora, but only after he and runner-up Hugo Bánzer Suárez had agreed to foster a national unity government. The MNR would thus relinquish the political power that the party had exercised since August 1985.

7 **Latin leaders oppose** *contras.* The presidents of five Central American countries (Costa Rica, El Salvador, Guatemala, Honduras, Nicaragua) reached unanimous agreement that by December 8 at the latest the Nicaraguan *contra* rebels operating from bases inside Honduras would be disbanded. The U.S. vigorously opposed the decision, claiming that the existence of organized and armed *contra* guerrillas would help ensure that Nicaragua would not back away from its commitment to hold free elections on Feb. 25, 1990. Among other things, the Latin accord also called for the establishment of an armed UN peacekeeping force that would guard the Honduran-Nicaraguan border against clandestine crossings and illicit arms shipments.

8 **Palmer to head New Zealand government.** New Zealand's ruling Labour Party chose Geoffrey Palmer as the nation's new prime minister. The previous day Prime Minister David Lange had announced he was retiring for health reasons. During his five-year tenure, Lange took a firm stand against allowing U.S. nuclear-powered or nuclear-armed warships to enter New Zealand ports. That decision effectively ended the ANZUS (Australia-New Zealand-U.S.) defense alliance.

U.S. resumes manned spaceflights. After an interval of three and a half years, the U.S. resumed its manned spaceflight program with the launching of the space shuttle *Columbia* from Cape Canaveral, Fla. Although the shuttle's mission was officially classified as secret, its principal goal was presumed to be the launching of a highly sophisticated spy satellite. U.S. manned spaceflights were halted in January 1986 after the shuttle *Challenger* exploded shortly after blast-off, killing all seven crew members.

9 **Kaifu becomes Japan's new leader.** Toshiki Kaifu, a member of the long-ruling Liberal-Democratic Party (LDP), formally became prime minister of Japan. He succeeded Sosuke Uno, who announced his resignation after the LDP lost control of the upper house of the Diet (parliament) in the July 23 elections. By law, the lower house prevailed when its choice of prime minister differed from that of the House of Councillors. It was, nonetheless, a historic moment in Japan when the upper house selected Takako Doi to be head of government. Doi, leader of the Japan Socialist Party, was the first woman to head a major political party and the first to be nominated for the prime ministership.

10 **Slaughter continues in Lebanon.** Cities, towns, and villages scattered across about a third of Lebanon were subjected to a severe barrage of some 20,000 rockets and artillery shells in the country's worst eruption of violence in many months. The firing began in the afternoon and lasted until dawn. Both Christian and Muslim strongholds were bombarded with reckless disregard for the civilian population. The fury resumed on August 12, upping the confirmed death toll to 47 and the number of wounded to more than 200. Gen. Michel Aoun, responding to an urgent UN Security Council plea, said he was prepared, as leader of the Christian forces, to accept a cease-fire. Muslim forces, however, appeared to be as determined as ever to oust Aoun, who in March had begun a campaign to drive 40,000 Syrian troops out of the country. That decision initiated a new round of violence in the 14-year-old civil war that had already claimed an estimated 100,000 lives.

12 **China cracks down on students.** The official *China Daily* reported that China's leaders had decided that most college graduates, especially those in the social sciences, should work for a year or two in villages and factories before continuing on to graduate school. The new program was generally viewed as an attempt to imbue the younger

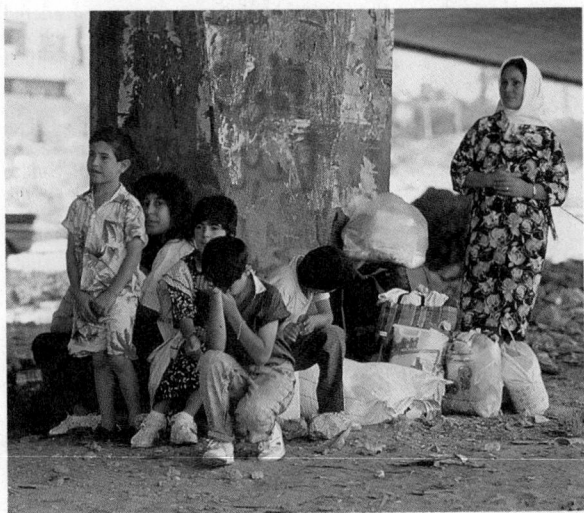

Refugees from West Beirut were forced to leave their homes after the city was hit by heavy shelling. About a third of Lebanon lay under siege when violence broke out between Christian and Muslim forces on August 10.
M. ATTAR—SYGMA

generation with Communist ideals and as retribution for the student-led pro-democracy demonstrations that were violently suppressed by the Army in early June. It was unclear how quickly the government planned to implement the program and how widely it would be applied. In addition, according to a report published in the *New York Times* on August 15, most freshmen planning to enter college in the fall would be required to serve in the military before beginning their four-year course of studies.

15 **De Klerk chosen acting president.** F.W. de Klerk, leader of South Africa's ruling National Party, took the oath of office as acting president. He was chosen by unanimous vote to succeed P.W. Botha, who had resigned the previous day. De Klerk told reporters, "We want to build a new South Africa in which all people will participate in decisions affecting their lives at all levels of government, but in such a way that no one group amongst the diversity which we have in South Africa will be in a position to dominate others." On August 28 de Klerk traveled to Zambia to meet Pres. Kenneth Kaunda, a severe critic of apartheid.

18 **Drug dealers murder Senator Galán.** Sen. Luis Carlos Galán, candidate of the Liberal Party in the campaign for the presidency of Colombia, was assassinated while addressing a political rally outside Bogotá. No one doubted that the gunmen were in the pay of Medellín drug dealers, who saw Galán as one of their most determined and fearless adversaries. Among other things, Galán had publicly endorsed the extradition of Colombian drug traffickers sought by the U.S.; they could then be tried by U.S. courts, whose officials were not intimidated by threats directed against them or their families. Outraged by the murder of Galán, Colombia quickly rounded up more than 10,000 persons believed to have ties to illegal drug operations.

21 **Egypt arrests Shi'ite Muslims.** Egypt announced it had arrested 41 persons believed to be mem-

bers of an underground Shi'ite Muslim group bent on overthrowing Pres. Hosni Mubarak and trained to attack U.S. and Israeli targets. An additional 16 persons were still being sought. Mubarak, like the vast majority of Egyptians, was a Sunni Muslim and had little sympathy for Shi'ite fundamentalists and their efforts to turn Egypt into an Islamic state. Mubarak was also the object of enmity because Egypt was the only Arab country formally at peace with Israel.

22 **Lithuania voids Soviet takeover.** A commission of the Lithuanian Supreme Soviet (parliament) officially declared that the 1940 occupation and annexation of Lithuania, Estonia, and Latvia by the Soviet Union was invalid. The next day hundreds of thousands of citizens in the three Baltic republics linked hands across their countries to dramatize their demand for independent statehood. The massive demonstrations were held on the 50th anniversary of the nonaggression pact signed by Joseph Stalin and Adolf Hitler; it included secret protocols that paved the way for Soviet annexation of the Baltic states and eastern Poland. The Baltic states were formally incorporated into the U.S.S.R. in August 1940.

24 **Poland gets Solidarity premier.** Tadeusz Mazowiecki, a prominent member of Solidarity, was confirmed by the Sejm (parliament) as Poland's new premier. He had been formally nominated on August 19 by Wojciech Jaruzelski, Poland's Communist president, who said a coalition government headed by Mazowiecki was the best hope for expeditiously overcoming the nation's severe economic problems, for implementing badly needed reforms, and for "satisfying the needs and aspirations" of the people. Doubts about the willingness of the United Workers' (Communist) Party to join such a coalition lingered until Soviet leader Mikhail Gorbachev had finished a lengthy phone conversation with the party's leader.

Voyager 2 ends historic flight. Voyager 2 completed its extraordinarily successful exploration of the solar system when it sped past Neptune at a distance of about 4,800 km (3,000 mi). From Neptune the Sun, which is some 4.5 billion km (2.8 billion mi) away, would appear to be a tiny but very brilliant spot of light. During its 12-year journey through space, Voyager 2 sent back remarkably clear pictures of Jupiter, Saturn, Uranus, and Neptune, as well as data about their environments. The information far exceeded the most fervent hopes of the scientific community. Having completed its planned mission, Voyager 2 headed out toward interstellar space. Pluto was now the only known planet that had not yet been visited by a spacecraft.

25 **Kim Dae Jung indicted in Seoul.** Kim Dae Jung and two other members of the opposition Party for Peace and Democracy were indicted in Seoul, but not jailed, for alleged complicity in a secret and illegal trip to North Korea by Suh Kyung Won, a fellow member of the National Assembly. The South Korean government contended that the three men knew about the trip in advance but failed to report it to the authorities. Kim flatly denied the charge, calling the indictment political persecution. Suh was confined in prison awaiting trial on espionage and other charges.

KUUS—SIPA

F.W. de Klerk was chosen to replace the outgoing president of South Africa, P.W. Botha, who had resigned the previous day.

SEPTEMBER

1 **Toshiki Kaifu visits U.S.** Japanese Prime Minister Toshiki Kaifu arrived at the White House for an informal meeting with President Bush. He also planned to visit Canada and Mexico before returning home. During their lengthy discussion of economic issues, Bush encouraged Kaifu to transform Japan into an "import superpower." Both men realized that an increase in U.S. imports would help alleviate tensions over Japan's $52 billion trade surplus with the U.S. On May 25 Carla Hills, the U.S. trade representative, had announced that Brazil, India, and Japan were, from a U.S. standpoint, guilty of unfair trade practices. As a consequence, these three nations would face possible reprisals if their restrictions on U.S. imports were not relaxed within a specified time limit.

2 **Anti-Sandinistas pick Chamorro.** Nicaragua's 14 anti-Sandinista political parties, known collectively as the National Opposition Union, chose Violeta Barrios de Chamorro as their presidential candidate in elections scheduled for Feb. 25, 1990. Chamorro was well known as the publisher of the country's main opposition newspaper, *La Prensa*, and as the widow of the former publisher, who had been a fearless critic of the government before he was assassinated, presumably at the behest of Pres. Anastasio Somoza. Because of her background, Chamorro had been named to the five-person junta that had ruled Nicaragua after Somoza was toppled in the successful 1979 Sandinista-led revolution. Nine months later, disillusioned with the Sandinistas, Chamorro resigned.

3 **Pretoria policies under attack.** As part of an ongoing campaign against apartheid, several thousand South African blacks invaded the whites-only section of Addington Beach in Durban, where they picnicked and waded for two hours without any violent confrontations before the police made 58 arrests. The previous day the police had used clubs and whips to break up a planned march on Parliament in Cape Town, the nation's legislative capital. On September 5 hundreds of thousands of blacks began a two-day boycott of jobs and schools to protest the exclusion of blacks from voting in parliamentary elections the following day. In those elections, the long-ruling National Party suffered a serious defeat at the hands of right-wing and liberal groups, but it managed to maintain control of the white chamber of the tricameral Parliament with a greatly reduced majority. On September 13 a large multiracial crowd of anti-apartheid protesters marched through the centre of Cape Town after receiving official authorization to do so. Two days later a similar march took place in Johannesburg.

4 **Nonbloc nations hold summit.** More than 100 members of the nonaligned movement convened their ninth summit in Belgrade, Yugos., the site of the first meeting in 1961. Following

months of negotiations, members of the movement formally approved a policy declaration, issued on September 7, that was far less critical of the U.S., Israel, and South Africa than had previously been the case. The shift toward more genuine neutrality was generally believed to be the principal reason why Iraq, Iran, and Cuba were not represented by their respective heads of government. Yugoslavia, which spearheaded the drive for adoption of a less belligerent stance, had reportedly pressed for a policy change because, among other things, the U.S. and U.S.S.R. were involved in negotiations that advanced the prospects for peace.

9 **Indian Army to leave Sri Lanka.** A Sri Lankan government official reported that during the meeting of nonaligned nations in Yugoslavia, India agreed to withdraw its estimated 42,000 troops from Sri Lanka before the end of the year. The soldiers had been welcomed in 1987 by the Sri Lankan government, which hoped the peacekeeping force could help implement an accord that granted Tamil separatists limited autonomy in their region of the country. The fighting continued, however, because the Liberation Tigers of Tamil Eelam, the most militant of the separatists, had fought off the Indian troops from the outset. Meanwhile, in other parts of the country, hundreds of people were being murdered by what most believed were rival pro- and antigovernment groups.

10 **East Germans fleeing to West.** The Hungarian government announced it had decided to permit thousands of East Germans, many of whom had refused to return home, to seek a new life in another "country of their choice." Tens of thousands of East Germans had already made their way to West Germany even though their travel documents were invalid for journeys outside Eastern Europe. Officials in both East and West Germany were clearly concerned that the migration from one Germany to the other might reach deluge proportions. By the end of the month, thousands of other East Germans who had invaded the grounds of the West German embassy in Prague were being allowed to travel to West Germany.

12 **Polish Cabinet wins approval.** The Polish Sejm (parliament) overwhelmingly approved the Cabinet selections of Prime Minister Tadeusz Mazowiecki, a leading member of Solidarity and the first non-Communist to head the Polish government since the 1940s. The voting (402–0 with 13 abstentions) underscored the willingness of all political factions to work together to extricate Poland from its desperate economic plight.

18 **Peace plan discussed in Cairo.** At the invitation of Egyptian Pres. Hosni Mubarak, Israeli Defense Minister Yitzhak Rabin arrived in Cairo to hold preliminary talks about an Egyptian peace proposal for the Middle East. Rabin

acknowledged the difficulty of speaking for a government that was deeply divided. Rabin himself and other Labour Party members of the Cabinet supported the Egyptian plan for elections in the Israeli-occupied West Bank and Gaza Strip, but the dominant Likud Party did not. Mubarak told reporters that Egypt's 10-point plan was "not the Ten Commandments" and could, therefore, be modified to the satisfaction of all concerned parties. His immediate aim, he said, was to break the stalemate and initiate a dialogue between Israel and the Palestinians. The makeup of the Palestinian delegation was a major problem that first had to be resolved.

20 **Gorbachev shakes up hierarchy.** Soviet Pres. Mikhail Gorbachev, exercising the authority he also possessed as head of the country's Communist Party, engineered the removal of five members of the party's hierarchy. Those named as replacements were expected to vigorously carry out Gorbachev's agenda and to reassert the supremacy of the party, especially in those regions clamouring for "unacceptable" change. Among those demoted were three voting members of the Politburo, the party's top policy-making body.

Papandreou to stand trial. Greece's 300-member Parliament voted 167–2 to have former prime minister Andreas Papandreou stand trial on charges of violating the constitutional rights of citizens by ordering illegal wiretaps during his eight years in power. If found guilty by a special court of senior judges, Papandreou could be given a 20-year prison sentence. Before the voting began, 124 Socialist deputies walked out in protest. In the June 18 elections, the Panhellenic Socialist Movement, headed by Papandreou, lost its majority in Parliament, and on July 2 Tzannis Tzannetakis became head of a new coalition government.

21 **Saudis execute Shi'ite terrorists.** Saudi Arabia publicly beheaded 16 Shi'ite Muslims in Mecca after convicting them of terrorist acts during the annual sacred pilgrimage to the holy city. The terrorists, identified as Kuwaitis of Saudi and Iranian origin, were found guilty of placing bombs near the Great Mosque. They also allegedly planned other acts of terrorism during the pilgrimage season. The leader of the pro-Iranian group reportedly confessed that he and his accomplices had been trained as terrorists by Iranian diplomats stationed in Kuwait.

22 **Cease-fire declared in Lebanon.** Lakhdar Ibrahimi, the assistant secretary-general of the Arab League, announced that Gen. Michel Aoun, military commander of the Lebanese Christian forces, had accepted the Arab League's cease-fire plan to end the 14-year-old civil war. Despite numerous failed cease-fires in the past, there were renewed but guarded hopes of a national reconciliation because both Muslim and

Christian forces had reached the point of near exhaustion after six months of relentless artillery bombardments. Almost immediately after the cease-fire was announced, people began returning to Beirut from the countryside and from mountain areas where thousands had fled out of fear for their lives.

25 **Bush urges cut in chemical arms.** In an address before the UN General Assembly, President Bush offered to destroy 80% of the U.S. arsenal of chemical weapons if the Soviet Union cut its stockpile to the new U.S. level. He further offered to do away with all chemical weapons after the signing of a worldwide treaty banning those weapons. Saying the time had come to rid the world of "this scourge," Bush also expressed the hope that negotiators in Geneva would move more quickly to reach agreement on the details of a global treaty banning chemical weapons. The following day Soviet Foreign Minister Eduard Shevardnadze, speaking before the same assembly, praised Bush and proposed an even more drastic cut in chemical arms by calling for a halt to the production of all chemical weapons, including binary weapons, which produce lethal poison when two chemicals inside a single missile are mixed. Because the U.S. was planning to produce such weapons, Bush had not included them in his proposal.

26 **Vietnam pulls out from Kampuchea.** Vietnam withdrew its last contingent of soldiers from Kampuchea (Cambodia), nearly 11 years after it invaded the country and overthrew the brutal Khmer Rouge regime of Pol Pot. Heng Samrin, the head of Kampuchea's Communist Party, used the occasion to urge his fellow countrymen to come together to prevent the Khmer Rouge from once again taking over the country. Observers agreed that the future of Kampuchea was very much in doubt. The current government under Prime Minister Hun Sen, who had been installed by the Vietnamese, was opposed by three rival but allied factions that claimed the right to head a new government. Among them was the Khmer Rouge, which could not be ignored or pushed aside because it was militarily the most powerful of the antigovernment groups.

27 **U.K. modifies Hong Kong policy.** In a speech delivered before the UN General Assembly, British Foreign Secretary John Major said his government planned to give an unspecified number of people who were considered "essential to Hong Kong's future stability and prosperity" the right to immigrate into Britain after the crown colony reverted

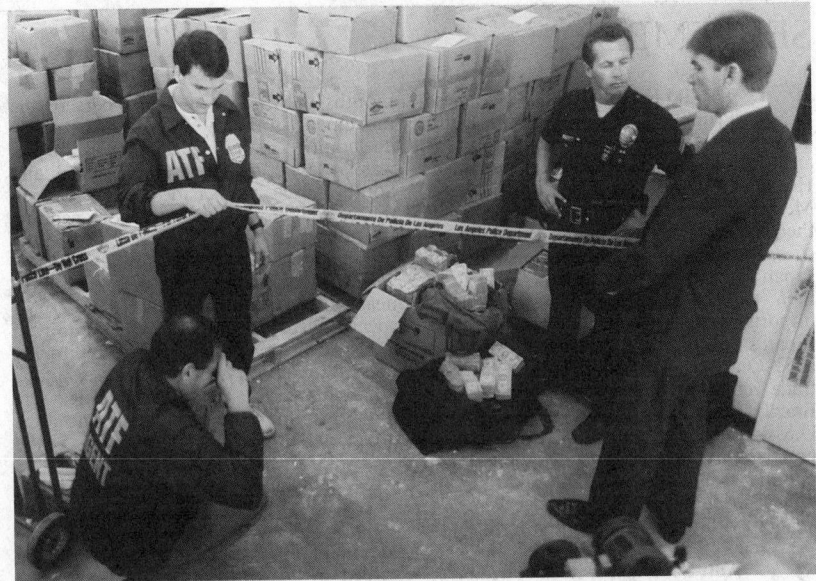

U.S. drug agents cordon off a cache of cocaine and cash discovered in a California warehouse. The discovery, estimated as worth over $2 billion, was the largest single drug seizure in history.
AP/WIDE WORLD

to China in 1997. The announcement was intended in part to encourage such people to remain in Hong Kong, secure in the knowledge that they had an "escape hatch" if the situation after 1997 became intolerable. Under current laws, Hong Kong citizens did not as a rule have the right to reside permanently in Britain.

28 **Ferdinand Marcos dies in Hawaii.** Ferdinand Marcos, who had ruled the Philippines for 20 years before he was forced into exile in 1986, died in Hawaii after a protracted illness. He had never been tried on U.S. criminal charges of looting the Philippines of vast sums of money during his years in office. Philippine Pres. Corazon Aquino denied a family request that Marcos be buried in Ilocos Norte, his native province. She said she was acting to protect "the safety of those who would take the death of Mr. Marcos in widely and passionately conflicting ways." Her right to make that decision was upheld by the Supreme Court on October 27.

29 **China confirms hard-line policy.** In a nationally televised address, Jiang Zemin (Chiang Tse-min), head of the Communist Party of China since June, said that the student-led pro-democracy movement had been stirred up by both internal and external hostile forces that were bent on overthrowing the Communist Party's leadership, subverting the socialist system, turning China into a

bourgeois republic, "and reducing it once again to a dependency of the Western capitalist powers." After noting that some people still favoured "bourgeois liberalization," he warned that such persons were in effect agents of Western civilization, "an extremely serious offense." He then assured his audience that the struggle against foreign and domestic adversaries would continue. The tone of the speech was not unexpected. On September 4, after a meeting of the Standing Committee of the National People's Congress, China's cultural minister, an advocate of artistic freedom, was replaced. At the same time, two other high officials and three Supreme Court judges were removed from their posts.

U.S. seizes huge cache of cocaine. U.S. drug agents discovered a cache of at least 20 tons of cocaine and more than $10 million in cash when they broke into an unguarded warehouse in California's San Fernando Valley. The wholesale value of the drugs, estimated to be in excess of $2 billion, represented the largest single drug seizure in history. Three men were arrested and another was being sought. The federal Drug Enforcement Administration (DEA) had been tipped off that large trucks were making suspiciously frequent stops at a warehouse located in an area that was largely residential. The DEA believed that the gangs handling the drugs were tied to ruthless traffickers in Medellín and Cali, Colombia.

OCTOBER

3 **Noriega survives bungled coup.** Several hundred soldiers under the command of Maj. Moisés Giroldi Vega attempted to overthrow Panamanian strongman Gen. Manuel Noriega. One contingent of dissident soldiers, assisted by

others who were already inside the military headquarters, attacked the compound shortly before 8 AM. The rebels also seized control of the national television and radio stations. The Bush administration acknowledged that it had been given

advance notice of the impending coup and fervently hoped that Noriega would be removed from power. Amid widely differing versions of what occurred during the fighting, it was impossible to determine immediately the actual chain of events

during the day and the nature and degree of U.S. involvement. In any case, Noriega was in complete control of the country by the end of the day. According to unconfirmed reports, Noriega himself shot and killed Giroldi, who had helped him put down an attempted coup 18 months earlier.

12 **Convicted Palme killer set free.** A Stockholm appeals court made up of four jurists and three lay assessors overturned the conviction of Christer Pettersson, a 42-year-old drifter and drug addict who had been sentenced to life imprisonment in July after being found guilty of murdering Swedish Prime Minister Olof Palme in 1986. No motive for the killing, which took place as Palme walked down a Stockholm street, was ever established. After unanimously agreeing that the evidence presented by the prosecution had been inadequate to justify a conviction, the court called for Pettersson's immediate release. The prosecution could still take the matter before the Supreme Court for a final ruling.

15 **South Africa releases dissidents.** The South African government released eight prominent political prisoners but not Nelson Mandela, the best known of all the black leaders committed to ending apartheid and minority white rule. There was wide speculation that Mandela would also be released in the near future if the government was satisfied with the behaviour of those already set free. On October 29 an estimated 70,000 supporters of the African National Congress (ANC) held a government-approved rally in a new soccer stadium near the black township of Soweto. During his speech 77-year-old Walter Sisulu, who had spent 26 years in prison, told the crowd that black leaders would not renounce their commitment to violence as a means of attaining their goals.

16 **Syse to head Norway's government.** Jan P. Syse took office as prime minister of Norway and head of a nonsocialist coalition made up of the Conservative Party, the Christian People's Party, and the Centre Party. The results of the September 11 balloting for seats in the Storting (parliament) gave the ruling Labour Party a total of 63 seats (−8) and the Conservatives 37 (−13). The success of the Progress Party, which increased its representation from 2 to 22 seats, contributed significantly to the cause of nonsocialists who had been highly critical of the government's austerity program, the socialized medical system, and an unemployment rate that was considered high by local standards. The future of Syse's government was viewed as precarious because its control of the Storting was weak and members of the coalition held quite different views on Norwegian participation in the European Communities.

17 **Quake ravages San Francisco area.** A violent earthquake measuring 7.1 on the Richter scale ravaged the San Francisco Bay area as tens of thousands of people were returning home from work. Among the 67 who died, most

were killed on Interstate 880 in Oakland when more than a mile of the upper deck of the freeway suddenly collapsed on the deck below. A 15-m (50-ft) section of the upper deck of the San Francisco-Oakland Bay Bridge also collapsed. In addition, a violent gas-fed fire destroyed a whole city block in the Marina district of San Francisco. Property damage was estimated to run into billions of dollars.

Gandhi calls for early election. After consultation with his Cabinet, Indian Prime Minister Rajiv Gandhi decided to call for a general election two months ahead of schedule. His five-year term would have expired in January 1990. The Election Commission then announced that parliamentary elections would be held in late November. Andhra Pradesh, Goa, and Sikkim would elect state assemblies at the same time. Although Gandhi's government had been under attack for alleged corruption and misuse of power, it was not certain that the opposition could unite effectively to defeat the ruling Congress Party.

18 **Honecker ousted in East Germany.** The East German Communist Party ousted Erich Honecker, a hard-liner who had been head of state and chairman of the Defense Council as well as leader of the country's Communist Party for 18 years. Egon Krenz, Honecker's 52-year-old protégé, assumed all of his mentor's responsibilities. Two days before Honecker was replaced, more than 100,000 East Germans took to the streets in Leipzig to demand reforms. On October 23 an estimated 300,000 demonstrated peacefully in East Berlin to demand such things as the legalization of opposition movements and independent labour unions and a clear separation of the powers invested in the government and in the Communist Party. Similar but smaller demonstrations also took place in other East German cities. On October 23 Parliament formally elected Krenz the nation's president. On October 30 some 300,000 once again marched in Leipzig calling for free elections, curbs on the secret police, and other reforms.

19 **Hungary sanctions opposition parties.** The Hungarian Parliament voted 323–4 with 15 abstentions to legalize opposition political parties, thus ending more than four decades of one-party Communist rule. There had been a brief multiparty government after the 1956 uprising that was crushed by Soviet troops. On October 18 Parliament had voted 333–5 with 8 abstentions to accept nearly 100 constitutional changes that gave the country a basic law devoid of Stalinist elements. The changes included the deletion of the word *People's* from the country's name, which would henceforth be known simply as the Republic of Hungary. New multiparty elections were expected to be held in 1990 after a new constitution was drawn up by Parliament.

24 **Bakker given 45-year sentence.** Jim Bakker, one of the best-known television evangelists in the U.S. and founder of the Christian PTL ministry, was sentenced by a federal judge in Charlotte, N.C., to serve 45 years in prison and pay a $500,000 fine. On October 5 Bakker had been convicted on all the 24 counts of fraud and conspiracy brought against him. During the six-week trial, the government had accused Bakker of bilking his followers out of $158 million by promising lifetime vacations he could not provide and by diverting some $3.7 million in donations to support an opulent life-style. Many of those who did not question the guilty verdict were nevertheless disturbed by the severity of the judge's sentence.

25 **Belgrade backs political pluralism.** Yugoslavia's official press agency reported that the Central Committee of the country's Communist Party had adopted a platform that supported the development of political pluralism and labour unions, individual rights, freedom of individuals, free and democratic elections, and an independent judiciary. The platform, however, did not explicitly endorse establishing opposition political parties. The platform was expected to be formally adopted during the Communist Party congress scheduled to convene in January 1990.

Qadhdhafi renounces terrorism. According to an interview published in *Al Mussawar*, a weekly magazine published in Cairo, Libyan leader Col. Mu'ammar al-Qadhdhafi acknowledged he had sponsored

PATRICK DURAND—SYGMA

Walter Sisulu, former secretary-general of the African National Congress, is greeted warmly after his release from prison. The South African government released eight political prisoners prominent in the antiapartheid movement, raising speculation that they would soon release antiapartheid leader Nelson Mandela.

terrorists until he discovered they were not motivated by a desire to promote the cause of all Arabs. Qadhdhafi also said he would welcome better relations with the U.S. The interview took place shortly after Qadhdhafi visited Egypt for the first time in 16 years to talk with Pres. Hosni Mubarak in the resort town of Marsa Matruh some 480 km (300 mi) from Cairo. Mubarak later agreed to continue the discussion in Tobruk, Libya. The meetings were not held in the national capitals because Libya and Syria were the only Arab countries still without formal diplomatic ties to Egypt. Egypt had been ostracized from the Arab world after Pres. Anwar as-Sadat concluded a peace treaty with Israel in 1979.

27 **Lubbers to head new coalition.** Queen Beatrix of The Netherlands asked Prime Minister Ruud Lubbers to form a new government after his Christian Democrats and the Labour Party announced they had reached agreement to cooperate in a coalition committed to a cleaner environment and greater welfare spending. The new government, which assumed power on November 7, was the first centre-left government in seven years. Lubbers had first tried, without success, to construct a parliamentary majority with the help of the Liberals, who had suffered a serious defeat at the polls in the September 6 elections.

28 **Nixon confers with China's leaders.** Richard Nixon arrived in Beijing (Peking) for personal talks with China's leaders. He was welcomed in China as the U.S. president who in 1972 reopened direct communication between the two countries after a 21-year estrangement. During a banquet given by Premier Li Peng (Li P'eng), Nixon spoke with unexpected frankness. Referring to the violent suppression of the Tiananmen (T'ien-an-men) Square pro-democracy demonstrations in early June, Nixon urged China not to retreat into a "backwater of oppression and stagnation." While acknowledging that the cultural, political, and ideological differences between China and the U.S. were "too great to permit a common understanding of this tragedy," he nonetheless urged both countries to strive for reconciliation and cooperation. On October 31 China's paramount leader Deng Xiaoping (Teng Hsiao-p'ing) told Nixon that it was up to the U.S. to take steps to improve relations with China.

A deep crevice runs through a driveway in Los Gatos, California. The city, on the outskirts of San Jose, was at the epicentre of the earthquake that struck the San Francisco Bay area.
JEFF REINKING—PICTURE GROUP

29 **Felipe González Márquez retains power.** Spanish Prime Minister Felipe González Márquez was assured of a third term in office when his Socialist Workers Party (SD) appeared to have won a precarious two-seat majority in the 350-member Chamber of Deputies. Although the Socialists could have remained in power with the support of minor parties, their popular support had been progressively eroding. In 1982 they had won 202 seats in the national legislature, compared with 184 in 1986 and 176 in the latest election. The most significant gains were made by the Communist-led United Left coalition, which appealed to poorer Spaniards, many of whom felt they were not sharing equitably in Spain's economic prosperity. On November 11, however, the election totals changed significantly when a provincial electoral committee ruled that one seat awarded to the SD rightly belonged to the United Left coalition. When other provincial committees also raised questions about previously declared totals, the validity of the entire election was called into doubt.

31 **Turkey elects new president.** The Turkish Parliament elected Prime Minister Turgut Ozal to the prestigious but largely ceremonial post of president. Although Ozal would not replace Pres. Kenan Evren until the latter's seven-year term expired in early

November, he was obliged to resign immediately as head of government. His decision to relinquish the reins of power was apparently prompted by recent heart bypass surgery. With all 155 opposition members of Parliament boycotting the election, Ozal was unable to secure the required two-thirds majority during balloting on October 20 and 24. The third ballot required only a simple majority. The new prime minister, who would be appointed by Ozal, was certain to be a member of the ruling Motherland Party.

U.S. approves new minimum wage. The U.S. Congress and the White House reached final agreement on legislation that would increase the minimum wage from $3.35 per hour to $3.80 per hour beginning April 1, 1990, the first such increase since 1981. One year later the minimum wage would rise to $4.25 per hour. The new bill also sanctioned a training wage of $3.35 per hour the first year and $3.61 per hour the second. The special training wage, however, would apply only to workers who were 16 through 19 years of age and holding their first jobs; no one, moreover, could be paid the training wage for more than six months. The U.S. Labor Department reported that some four million Americans currently worked for the minimum wage. Of that number, about 70% were identified as female employees and about 30% as teens.

NOVEMBER

7 **East German government falls.** Faced with the massive exodus of East Germans to the West and with clamorous demands for radical change, East German Premier Willi Stoph and his entire Council of Ministers agreed to step down as leaders of the Communist government. The following day most of the Politburo also resigned to give Egon Krenz, the new party leader, greater freedom to revamp the government. On November 9 East Germany removed virtually all

restrictions on travel to the West. The next day hundreds of thousands surged through an opening in the Berlin Wall to celebrate their new freedom, to shop, and to see for themselves how life in West Germany differed from their own. Most of those who traveled from East to West Berlin said they would return home.

8 **Jordanians elect new legislature.** For the first time since 1967, Jordanians went to the polls in

a national election to choose a new 80-seat legislature. Although women had been enfranchised in 1974, the event also marked the first time they were allowed to vote in a national election. Official vote tallies showed the fundamentalist Muslim Brotherhood had won 20 seats, other Islamic candidates 12 seats, and opposition leftist candidates and Arab nationalists 11. On November 10 King Hussein called upon all Jordanians to work together to move their country forward. At the same

time, he announced that a referendum would be held on a new charter, still in the formation stage, that would clarify the powers and responsibilities of the monarchy, the Cabinet, and the Parliament. He also promised, as one aspect of more liberal policies, "that the press law would be amended for the better." Although Islam remained the official religion of Jordan, Hussein said he intended to safeguard the "sacred rights" of all Jordanians, including those of secular Jordanians and of the Christian minority.

10 **Zhivkov out as Bulgaria's leader.** Todor Zhivkov, longtime president of Bulgaria and authoritarian head of the country's Communist Party, resigned both his posts following the dramatic ouster of Communist leaders in other Eastern European countries. There were indications that Zhivkov's resignation was not in fact voluntary. Petar Mladenov, Bulgaria's longtime foreign minister, was immediately named general secretary of the Communist Party. It was left to the National Assembly to chose a new president. On November 16 the party's Central Committee removed three of Zhivkov's most ardent supporters from the Politburo. The following day demonstrators renewed their demands for democracy and freedom, both of which Mladenov had promised. The crowds also reviled Zhivkov, defacing or destroying pictures of him to vent their anger.

11 **Namibia concludes five-day election.** South West Africa/Namibia concluded five days of voting to elect a constituent assembly that would draft a constitution for the future nation. The largest of the 10 competing political parties was the South West Africa People's Organization (SWAPO), which had waged guerrilla warfare for 23 years to end South Africa's control over the territory. On November 14 SWAPO was declared winner of the election. It failed, however, to win a two-thirds majority, which would have allowed it to disregard political adversaries who might disagree with certain provisions of a SWAPO-drafted constitution. Final tallies gave SWAPO 41 of the 72 assembly seats and the Democratic Turnhalle Alliance 21. The 10 remaining seats were allotted unequally to five other groups.

12 **U.S.S.R. to keep one-party system.** An article published in *Pravda*, the official newspaper of the Communist Party of the Soviet Union, stated: "There are no other public forces in this country apart from the party of Communists." The statement was apparently meant to end any speculation that the Soviet Union might soon follow the example of other Eastern European countries and adopt a multiparty political system. On November 16 Soviet Pres. Mikhail Gorbachev reconfirmed the Kremlin's position on two basic points when he said the country was not ready for private ownership of property or for competing political parties.

15 **Walesa addresses U.S. Congress.** Lech Walesa, founder of Solidarity, Poland's federation of labour

unions, addressed a joint meeting of the U.S. Congress. He besought the members to support Poland at a critical point in its history by approving a program of financial aid similar to the Marshall Plan, which helped rebuild Western Europe after World War II. Poland's economic situation was so desperate, Walesa warned, that without substantial aid there was little hope the political and economic transformation envisioned by Poland's new non-Communist government could become a reality.

20 **Romania's leader opposes change.** In a speech delivered to those attending a congress of Romania's Communist Party, Pres. Nicolae Ceausescu, who also headed the Communist Party, vowed that as long as he remained in power, Romania would never abandon socialism as other major countries of Eastern Europe had recently done. On November 24 tens of thousands of workers were herded into a square outside the Communist Party headquarters. Although the signs they carried expressed joy over Ceausescu's reelection as general secretary of the Communist Party, there was virtually no evidence of genuine enthusiasm. During the four-hour wait for Ceausescu's 10-minute speech, the police and military blocked all exits from the square.

22 **Gandhi's Congress (I) Party loses.** Hundreds of millions of Indian voters began casting votes for Parliament in an election that would determine the political future of Prime Minister Rajiv Gandhi. During the campaign Gandhi's political opponents had charged that his administration was guilty of corruption, incompetence, and arrogance. By November 27, after a five-day period of voting, incomplete returns indicated that Gandhi's Congress (I) Party had lost its majority in Parliament and with it an automatic right to govern the country. On November 29 Gandhi resigned, saying he accepted the verdict of the people, including those who had defected from his Congress (I) Party. On December 2 V.P. Singh took the oath of office as India's new prime minister. The leader of the Janata Dal Party, which formed the core of the National Front, expected to form a minority government that included both left-wing and conservative elements.

President of Lebanon murdered. René Moawad, who had been elected president of Lebanon on November 5 during a special session of members of Parliament, was assassinated when his motorcade was bombed in Beirut. At least 23 others were also killed. The 64-year-old Maronite Christian had advocated coexistence with Muslims and promised an equitable distribution of power between the two groups. Moawad had, accordingly, called upon all political factions to work together to reunify the country, which had been reduced to shambles during 14 years of civil war. Moawad had also urged acceptance of a role for Syria while Lebanon tried to get back on its feet. Meanwhile, Gen. Michel Aoun, the leader of the Christian forces, continued to maintain he had a right to the presidency. On November 24, in the Syrian-controlled town of Shtaura, Elias Hrawi was elected Moawad's successor.

23 **Coalition ends Greek stalemate.** After two inconclusive elections, Greece's leading politicians and technocrats agreed to end the political stalemate by forming an all-party coalition government. Cabinet posts were allotted on the basis of the popular vote received by the major parties on November 5. Xenophon Zolotas, the 85-year-old former governor of the Bank of Greece and a former minister of economic coordination, was chosen head of government. The New Democracy Party, a conservative group headed by Constantine Mitsotakis, was given 7 of the 21 Cabinet posts. The Socialists, who had run the government under former prime minister Andreas Papandreou, were given five posts. One post went to the Communists, the others to technocrats approved by the three major parties.

24 **Czechoslovakia's leaders quit.** Just hours after an estimated 350,000 Czechoslovak citizens gathered in central Prague for the eighth consecutive day to demand democracy, Milos Jakes, the general secretary of the Communist Party, and other top party leaders resigned. The Central Committee then chose 48-year-old Karel Urbanek, one of those who had resigned from the Politburo, as new party leader. The crowd responded to the resignations by singing and dancing in the streets. Just a few days earlier police had

Polish Solidarity leader Lech Walesa is applauded by members of the U.S. Congress, which he addressed on November 15. Walesa besought Congress for the financial support needed to rebuild Poland's ailing economy.

viciously clubbed numerous demonstrators in a futile effort to stifle protests. In an emotional emergence from obscurity, Alexander Dubcek addressed the crowd. In 1969 he had been ousted as party leader after a Soviet-led military invasion of Czechoslovakia by Warsaw Pact forces. The invasion had ended what had been called the "Prague Spring," Dubcek's program of liberalization that departed from hard-line Marxist orthodoxy. On November 28 the new party leaders, yielding to intense pressure, agreed to give up their monopoly of political power.

26 **Hungarians vote in free election.** For the first time in 42 years, Hungarians participated in a free national election to decide the date of the next presidential election. The government proposed Jan. 7, 1990, long before multiparty parliamentary elections were scheduled to be held in the spring. Those who urged a boycott of the referendum argued that the government was trying to steamroller the opposition to impose its will. Nonetheless, more than 50% of the eligible voters cast ballots, thereby validating the referendum. To the surprise of many, the government's timetable for a speedy presidential election was narrowly rejected by the voters.

National Party wins in Uruguay. Incomplete election returns indicated that Luis Alberto Lacalle, candidate of the National Party, had won a comfortable plurality of votes in an election for the presidency of Uruguay, which had a deep commitment to democracy. Sen. Jorge Batlle of the ruling Colorado Party, Lacalle's most potent challenger in the field of 12 candidates, conceded defeat late in the evening. The constitution prevented the incumbent, Pres. Julio María Sanguinetti Cairolo, from seeking reelection.

27 **Soviets denounce Lithuanian move toward independence.** A Lithuanian Communist official revealed that local party leaders had received a statement, signed by all members of the Soviet Politburo, vigorously condemning Lithuania's move toward greater freedom. Efforts to organize a local Communist Party independent of Moscow were called "illegal and undemocratic" because Lithuania was considered a constituent part of the Union of Soviet Socialist Republics. The Kremlin, however, was disposed to grant Lithuania, and its Baltic neighbours Latvia and Estonia, freedom to experiment with market economies.

DECEMBER

1 **Aquino survives sixth coup.** For the sixth time since Corazon Aquino assumed the presidency of the Philippines in February 1986, a clique of military officers attempted to overthrow her government. The latest assault was the most serious Aquino had yet faced. Rebel pilots used World War II-vintage aircraft to drop bombs on and near the presidential palace in Manila while others attacked a number of major military installations. They also seized control of two broadcast stations. When Aquino asked the U.S. for help, President Bush authorized F-4 jet fighters from Clark Air Base north of Manila to fly cover for loyal government troops. Even though the pilots fired no weapons, they effectively kept rebel aircraft on the ground and, according to many observers, probably turned the tide in Aquino's favour. The rebels, however, swept into Makati, the financial district of Manila, where they trapped some 2,000 foreigners in hotels. They also made virtual hostages of thousands of residents living or working in high-rise buildings. Vice Pres. Salvador Laurel, who had publicly split with Aquino in 1988 but remained in the post to which he had been independently elected, repeated his call for Aquino's resignation. On December 6, with the fighting still intense, the president imposed a nationwide state of emergency. That same day, during an arranged cease-fire, foreigners were allowed to leave their hotels unharmed. Many, but not all, of the heavily armed rebel soldiers in Manila finally surrendered after being assured they would be treated "fairly, justly, and humanely." They then returned to their barracks bearing loaded weapons. Rebel forces in Cebu laid down their arms on December 9. Gregorio Honasan, a cashiered army colonel who had led the previous failed coup in August 1987, was widely believed to have organized the revolt. He had been captured the following December but had arranged his escape a few months later and was still being sought by the government.

Gorbachev visits Pope John Paul II. Soviet Pres. Mikhail Gorbachev conferred with

Angry citizens and soldiers fight government supporters in the Romanian capital of Bucharest. During the overthrow of Romania's Communist government, Pres. Nicolae Ceausescu was arrested, tried, and executed.

I. NICHOLOS—SIPA

Pope John Paul II for about 75 minutes in the Vatican. It was the first time a leader of the Soviet Union and the head of the Roman Catholic Church had met. The two men, speaking Russian, spent the first five minutes behind closed doors. Gorbachev, who called the meeting "truly extraordinary," said the Soviet Union would soon enact a law guaranteeing freedom of conscience so people could "satisfy their spiritual needs." That same day Ukrainian officials announced that congregations of the Ukrainian Catholic Church could begin to register with authorities, thereby gaining legal recognition. Gorbachev and John Paul also discussed in positive terms the possibility of establishing diplomatic relations between their two states.

2 **Taiwan holds multiple elections.** About three-fourths of the 10 million eligible voters in Taiwan went to the polls to elect numerous local officials as well as members of the 276-seat national Legislative Yuan (parliament). As expected, the ruling Kuomintang (KMT, Nationalist Party) was victorious in a majority of the races. The KMT won 72 of the 101 contested seats in the national legislature, compared with 21 by the Democratic Progressive Party (DPP), the KMT's strongest political rival. The remaining eight seats went to independents. The results were historically important because the newly legalized DPP would have the required minimum of 20 seats needed to gain the right to introduce legislation in parliament.

Malaysian rebels end fighting. Leaders of the Communist Party of Malaya formally ended more than 40 years of antigovernment guerrilla warfare by agreeing "to terminate all armed activities and bring peace to the entire Thai-Malaysian border and Malaysia." The conflict had taken thousands of lives and at one time pitted some 70,000 British and Commonwealth troops against the insurgents. The Communists had begun their "war of liberation" in 1948 when the region, which was then called Malaya, was a British colony.

3 **East German leadership quits.** Egon Krenz, chief of East Germany's security police before he replaced Erich Honecker as Communist Party leader on October 18, resigned together with the party's entire Politburo and Central Committee. Large crowds greeted the news with unconcealed joy. They also demanded the total dissolution of the country's Communist Party and called for the reunification of East and

West Germany. On December 5 Honecker and other former top officials were placed under house arrest. Two days later, in an effort to defuse an explosive political situation, East Germany's Communist leaders and their counterparts among the opposition agreed on the need for free elections and a new constitution. On December 22, with the consent of both German governments, the Brandenburg Gate was opened. Standing just east of the Berlin Wall, it had become a potent symbol of the division between East and West Germany.

7 **New Czechoslovak premier takes office.** The political upheaval in Czechoslovakia continued with the resignation, under extreme pressure, of Premier Ladislav Adamec. Civic Forum, a powerful coalition of anti-Communist opposition forces, had demanded his removal. Adamec was immediately replaced by Marian Calfa, who had been appointed deputy premier just five days earlier. Calfa quickly announced that he would form a multiparty government with Communists in the minority. On December 9 Pres. Gustav Husak announced that he too would step down after a new government was formed. On December 10, after swearing in a new Cabinet that included seven ministers with no political affiliations, Husak kept his word. On December 28 Alexander Dubcek was unanimously elected chairman of Parliament. He had been ousted as party leader in 1968 after Warsaw Pact troops invaded Czechoslovakia. Another dramatic reversal of the old order took place on December 29 when Parliament elected Vaclav Havel president. Havel, a playwright, had spent years in prison for fearlessly criticizing the government's heavy-handed suppression of dissent.

9 **Bush sends top aides to China.** Brent Scowcroft, President Bush's national security adviser, and Lawrence Eagleburger, the U.S. deputy secretary of state, arrived in Beijing (Peking) for a two-day visit that had not been made public in advance. Scowcroft said his mission was "to bring new impetus and vigor" to U.S.-Chinese relations by exploiting areas of agreement, but to "isolate for another time" areas of disagreement. Members of Congress were among those who expressed outrage at Bush for "kowtowing" to China's leaders, who not only had honoured the soldiers who killed unarmed pro-democracy demonstrators at Tiananmen (T'ien-an-men) Square in Beijing but had then castigated the U.S. "for wanton interference in China's internal affairs" when the U.S. embassy in Beijing granted refuge to a Chinese dissident. China had also said that any improvement in relations between the two nations would have to be initiated by the United States. There was even greater indignation against Bush when it was revealed on December 18 that he had secretly sent Scowcroft on an even earlier mission to China in July, scarcely a month after the military crackdown.

10 **Kampuchea approves election.** Hun Sen, the Vietnamese-installed prime minister of Kampuchea,

U.S. troops occupy a street in Panama during the all-out effort to capture its de facto leader, Gen. Manuel Noriega.
RON HAVIV—SABA

announced that his government was prepared to disband its Council of Ministers before a United Nations-sponsored national election that would, it was hoped, end the 11-year-old civil war. Hun Sen had earlier rejected demands that he dissolve his government before elections were held. Hun Sen indicated he was also prepared to accept the active participation of the Khmer Rouge in the election, if United Nations officials ruled in their favour.

11 **Bulgaria backs free elections.** Petar Mladenov, who replaced Todor Zhivkov as general secretary of Bulgaria's Communist Party on November 10, told a plenary session of the party's Central Committee that he was in favour of having the National Assembly organize free elections by the end of May 1990, with actual voting the following month. He also called for a new constitution, to be drafted in 1990, that would no longer guarantee the Communist Party a leading role in national affairs. Several days earlier nine different opposition groups had joined forces as the Union of Democratic Forces in hopes of "accelerating the processes of democratization."

14 **Chileans choose new president.** Former senator Patricio Aylwin was elected president of Chile by winning a majority of the popular vote in a national election that featured three major candidates. Gen. Augusto Pinochet joined millions of others in choosing the man who would succeed him. The 73-year-old general had ruled Chile with an iron fist since 1973, but he had graciously accepted the results of a popular referendum that showed the people wished him to step aside. Aylwin, a 71-year-old Christian Democrat, headed a coalition that included Socialists and a motley group of smaller parties. Voters also elected a new Congress.

17 **Collor de Mello wins in Brazil.** In a runoff election between the two top vote getters in Brazil's incon-

clusive November 14 presidential election, 40-year-old conservative Fernando Collor de Mello emerged victorious. Incomplete returns indicated that Luís Inácio da Silva, a socialist, would be defeated by a few percentage points. Collor was the candidate of the National Reconstruction Party; da Silva represented the Workers' Party. Each had strong pockets of support in various parts of the country, but neither candidate carried his own hometown. The election had special significance because it was the first time in 29 years that Brazilians had been given an opportunity to elect a president.

20 **Bush sends troops into Panama.** Shortly after midnight U.S. troops began an all-out assault on preselected targets in Panama in an effort to capture Gen. Manuel Noriega, the de facto military ruler of the country. Noriega was being sought by U.S. authorities to face indictments on charges related to illegal trafficking in drugs. On November 13 an agency of the Organization of American States had issued a report declaring Noriega's government "devoid of constitutional legitimacy." The report accused Noriega of violating the most basic political rights of Panama's citizens by annulling the May presidential election, which, by all accounts, Noriega had decisively lost. When U.S. troops failed to locate Noriega, the U.S. government offered, without results, a $1 million reward for his capture. With Noriega on the run and effectively out of power, Guillermo Endara took the oath of office as president. Ricardo Arias Calderón and Guillermo Ford were sworn in as vice presidents. Meanwhile, attempts to control the streets of Panama City proved more difficult than anticipated as looters stripped stores clean of food, clothing, medicine, appliances, and other goods. Then on December 24, quite unexpectedly, news spread that Noriega had taken refuge at the Vatican nunciature in Panama City and had requested asylum. During the discussions that followed, the U.S. insisted that Noriega be turned over to the U.S. to face trial; the new government in Panama was in total agreement. Whatever the final outcome of the talks, the Vatican representatives appeared to insist that if Noriega did in fact leave the nunciature, he would do so voluntarily.

22 **Ceausescu overthrown in Romania.** Romanian Pres. Nicolae Ceausescu, the most brutal and fanatical Communist leader in Eastern Europe, fled Bucharest in fear as angry crowds fought to take over large areas of the capital. The battle with security forces loyal to Ceausescu was furious. That same day thousands of bodies were being uncovered in mass graves in the forest district of Timisoara, where troops had been ordered to kill anyone who opposed the Ceausescu regime. No one was sure which of many possible avenues of escape Ceausescu and his wife had taken, but on December 23 both were reported captured. During the secret trial that followed, Ceausescu was wildly defiant and refused to recognize the right of his accusers to try him. Nonetheless, he was convicted of genocide and gross abuse of power and was executed with his wife on December 25.

Major Revisions from the 1990 *Macropædia*

The purpose of this section is to introduce to continuing *Book of the Year* subscribers selected *Macropædia* articles or portions of them that have been completely revised or written anew. It is intended to update the *Macropædia* in ways that cannot be accomplished fully by reviewing the year's events or by revising statistics annually, because the *Macropædia* texts themselves—written from a longer perspective than any yearly revision—supply authoritative interpretation and analysis as well as narrative and description.

The four articles that have been chosen from the 1990 printing are all wholly new: ECONOMIC SYSTEMS (reprinted here in part); the section on *Strategy in the Nuclear Age* from The Theory and Conduct of WAR; the section on *Strategic Missiles* from The Technology of WAR; and the biography of MOZART.

Subscribers desiring a slipsheet to put in their encyclopædia to indicate that an article has been revised, and owners of older sets wishing information about the exact article being replaced by the reprints, should address their requests to Year Book Editorial, Encyclopædia Britannica, Inc., 310 South Michigan Avenue, Chicago, IL 60604. Be sure, please, to include an indication of the copyright year of your set.

Economic Systems

Economic systems refer to the ways in which humankind has arranged for its material provisioning. One would think that there would be a great variety of such systems, corresponding to the many cultural arrangements that have characterized human society. Surprisingly, that is not the case. Although a wide range of institutions and social customs have been associated with the economic activities of society, only a very small number of basic modes of provisioning can be discovered beneath this variety. Indeed, history has produced but three such kinds of economic systems—those based on the principle of tradition, those organized according to command, and the rather small number, historically speaking, in which the central organizing form is the market.

The very paucity of fundamental modes of economic organization calls attention to a central aspect of the problem of economic "systems"; namely, that the objective to which all economic arrangements must be addressed has itself remained unchanged throughout human history. This unvarying objective is the coordination of the individual activities associated with provisioning—activities that range from hunting and gathering in primitive societies to administrative or financial tasks in modern industrial systems. What may be called "the economic problem" is the orchestration of these activities into a coherent social whole—coherent in the sense of providing a social order with the goods or services it requires to assure its own continuance and to fulfill its perceived historic mission.

Social coordination can in turn be analyzed into two distinct tasks. The first of these is the production of the goods and services needed by the social order, a task that requires the mobilization of society's resources, including its most valuable and most resistive resource, human effort. Of nearly equal importance is the second task, the appropriate distribution of the product. This task must not only provide for the continuance of society's labour supply (even slaves must be fed) but must also accord with the prevailing values of different social orders, all of which favour some recipients of income over others—men over women, aristocrats over commoners, property owners over nonowners, or party members over nonmembers.

All modes of accomplishing the basic tasks of production and distribution rely on social rewards or penalties of one kind or another. Tradition-based societies depend largely on communal expressions of approval or disapproval. Command systems utilize the open or veiled power of physical coercion or punishment, or the bestowal of wealth or prerogatives. The third method—the market—also brings pressures and incentives to bear, but the stimuli of gain and loss are not usually within the control of any one person or group of persons. Instead, they emerge from the "workings" of the system itself, and, on closer inspection, those workings turn out to be nothing other than the efforts of individuals to gain pecuniary rewards by supplying the things that others are willing to pay for.

There is a paradoxical aspect to the manner in which the market resolves the economic problem. In contrast to the conformity that guides traditional society or the obedience to superiors that orchestrates command society, behaviour in a market society is mostly self-directed and seems, accordingly, an unlikely means for achieving social integration. Yet, as economists ever since Adam Smith have delighted in pointing out, the clash of self-directed wills becomes converted into just such a means within the setting of competition that is an indispensable legal and social precondition for a market system to operate. The unintended outcome of this competitive engagement of self-seeking individuals is the creation of the third, and by all odds the most remarkable, of the three modes of solving the economic problem.

This article is divided into the following sections:

THE EVOLUTION OF CAPITALISM

From mercantilism to commercial capitalism. It is usual to describe the earliest stages of capitalism as mercantilism, the word denoting the central importance of the merchant overseas traders who rose to prominence in 17th- and 18th-century England, Germany, and the Low Countries. In numerous pamphlets these merchants defended the principle that their trading activities buttressed the interest of the sovereign power, even when, to the consternation of the court, this required sending "treasure" (bullion) abroad. As the pamphleteers explained, treasure used in this way became itself a commodity in foreign trade, in which, as the great merchant Thomas Mun wrote about 1630, "we must ever observe this rule; to sell more to strangers than we consume of theirs in value."

For all its trading mentality, mercantilism was only partially a market-coordinated system. Smith complained bitterly about the government monopolies that granted exclusive trading rights to groups such as the East India or the Turkey companies, and modern commentators have emphasized the degree to which mercantilist economies relied on regulated, not free, prices and wages. The economic society that Smith described in *The Wealth of Nations* in 1776 is much closer to modern society, although it differs in many respects, as shall be seen. This 18th-century stage is called "commercial capitalism," although it should be noted that the word "capitalism" itself does not actually appear in the pages of Smith's great book.

Smith's society is nonetheless recognizable as capitalist precisely because of the prominence of those elements that had been absent in its mercantilist form. For example, with few exceptions, the production and distribution of all goods and services were entrusted to market forces rather than to the rules and regulations that had abounded a century earlier. The level of wages was likewise mainly determined by the interplay of the supply of, and the demand for, labour, not by the rulings of local magistrates. Profits were exposed to competition rather than protected by government monopoly.

Perhaps of greater importance in perceiving Smith's world as capitalist, as well as market-oriented, is its clear division of society into an economic and a political realm. The role of government had been gradually narrowed until Smith could describe its duties as consisting of only three functions: (1) the provision of national defense, (2) the protection of each member of society from the injustice or oppression of any other, and (3) the erection and maintenance of those public works and public institutions (including education) that would not repay the expense of any private enterpriser, although they might "do much more than repay it" to society as a whole. And if the realm of government had been greatly delimited, that of commerce had been greatly expanded. The accumulation of capital had become clearly recognized as the driving engine of the system. The expansion of "capitals"—Smith's term for firms—was the motive power by which the market system was launched on its historic course.

Thus in *The Wealth of Nations* it was possible for the first time to describe quite precisely the dynamics as well as the coordinative processes of capitalism. The latter were entrusted to the market mechanism—which is to say, to the universal drive for material betterment, curbed and contained by the necessary condition of competition.

Smith's great perception was that the combination of this drive and counterforce would direct productive activity toward those goods and services for which the public had the means and desire to pay, while forcing producers to satisfy those wants at prices that yielded no more than normal profits. Later economists would devote a great deal of attention to the question of whether competition in fact adequately constrains the workings of the acquisitive drive and whether a market system might not display cycles and crises unmentioned in *The Wealth of Nations*. These were questions unknown to Smith, because the institutions that would produce them, above all the development of large-scale industry, lay in the future. Given these historic realities, one can only admire Smith's perception of the market as a means of solving the economic problem.

Smith also saw that the competitive search for capital accumulation would impart a distinctive tendency to a society that harnessed its motive force. He pointed out that the most obvious way for a manufacturer to gain wealth was to expand his enterprise by hiring additional workers. As firms expanded their individual operations, manufacturers found that they could subdivide complex tasks into simpler ones and could then speed along these simpler tasks by providing their operatives with machinery. Thus the expansion of firms made possible an ever finer division of labour, and the finer division of labour, in turn, improved profits by lowering the costs of production, thereby encouraging the further enlargement of the firms. In this way the incentives of the market system gave rise to the augmentation of the wealth of the nation itself, endowing market society with its all-important historical momentum and at the same time making room for the upward striving of its members.

One final attribute of the emerging system must be noted. This is the tearing apart of the formerly seamless tapestry of social coordination. Under capitalism two realms of authority existed where there had formerly been only one—a realm of political governance for such purposes as war or law and order and a realm of economic governance over the processes of production and distribution. Each realm was largely shielded from the reach of the other. The capitalists who dominated the market system were not automatically entitled to governing power, and the members of government were not entrusted with decisions as to what goods should be produced or how social rewards should be distributed. This new dual structure brought with it two consequences of immense importance. The first was a limitation of political power that proved of very great importance in establishing democratic forms of government. The second, closer to the present theme, was the need for a new kind of analysis intended to clarify the workings of this new semi-independent realm within the larger social order. Thus did the appearance of capitalism give rise to the discipline now called economics.

From commercial to industrial capitalism. Commercial capitalism proved to be only transitional. The succeeding form would be distinguished by the pervasive mechanization and industrialization of its productive processes, a change that would not only vastly alter the social and physical landscape but would also set into motion new dynamic tendencies for the system.

The transformative agency was already present in Smith's day, observable in a few coal mines where steam-driven engines invented by Thomas Newcomen pumped water out of the pits. The diffusion and penetration of such machinery-driven processes of production during the first quarter of the next century has been traditionally called "the" Industrial Revolution, although historians today stress the long germination of the revolution and the many phases through which it passed. There is no doubt, however, that a remarkable confluence of advances in agriculture, cotton spinning and weaving, iron manufacture, machine tool design, and the harnessing of mechanical power began profoundly to alter the character of capitalism in the last years of the 18th century and the first decades of the 19th.

The alterations did not affect the driving motive of the system or its reliance on market forces as its coordinative principles. Their effect was rather on the social complexion

Emergence of mercantilism

Narrowed role of the state

Capitalism and productivity

Labour
under
capitalism

of the society that contained these new technologies and on the economic outcome of the processes of competition and capital accumulation. This aspect of industrialization was most immediately apparent in the advent of the factory as the archetypal locus of production. In Smith's time the individual enterprise was still small—the opening pages of *The Wealth of Nations* describe the effects of the division of labour in a 10-man pin factory—but by the early 19th century the increasing mechanization of labour, coupled with the application of water and steam power, had raised the size of the work force in an ordinary textile mill to several hundreds, by midcentury in the steel mills to several thousands, and by the end of the century in the railways to tens of thousands.

The increase in the scale of employment brought a marked change in the character of employment itself. In Smith's day the social distance between employer and labourer was still sufficiently small that the very word "manufacturer" implied an occupation (a mechanic) as well as a capitalist-like position. By the time of the "dark satanic mills" of the 1830s, a great gulf had opened between the manufacturers, who were now a propertied business class, and the men, women, and children who tended their machines for 10- and 12-hour stints. It was from the spectacle of mill labour, described in unsparing detail by the inspectors authorized by the first Factory Act of 1802, that Marx drew much of the indignation that animated his analysis of capitalism. More important, it was from this same factory setting, and from the urban squalor that industrialization also brought, that capitalism derived much of the social consciousness—sometimes revolutionary, sometimes reformist—that was to play so large a part in its subsequent political life.

The degradation of the physical and social landscape was the aspect of industrialization that first attracted attention, but it was its slower-acting impact on economic growth that was ultimately to be judged its most significant effect. A single statistic may dramatize this process. Between 1788 and 1839 the output of pig iron in Britain rose from 68,000 to 1,347,000 tons. For the significance of these numbers to be grasped, they must be translated into the huge multiplication of iron pumps, iron machine tools, iron pipes, iron rails, and iron beams that this increase in pig iron production made possible, and this multiplication of iron implements must in turn be translated into the strength and speed that they lent to production itself. This was the means by which the first industrial revolution promoted economic growth, not immediately but with gathering momentum. Thirty years later this effect would be repeated with even more spectacular results when the Bessemer converter ushered in the age of steel rails, ships, machines, girders, wires, pipes, and containers.

Industrial-
ization and
national
wealth

The most important consequence of the industrialization of capitalism was therefore its powerful effect on enhancing what Marx called "the forces of production"—the source of what is now called standard of living. The Swiss economic demographer Paul Bairoch has calculated that gross national product per capita in the developed countries rose from $180 in the 1750s (in dollars of 1960 purchasing power) to $780 in the 1930s and then to $3,000 in the 1980s, whereas the per capita income of the less developed countries remained unchanged at about $180–$190 from 1750 to 1930 and thereafter rose only to $410 in 1980. The single most important explanation for this difference is that the first group of countries became industrialized and the second did not.

A second major effect of the industrialization of the system was its increasing economic instability. Market systems are intrinsically susceptible to perturbations, because of mismatches and miscalculations in individual markets. Such disturbances bring relatively small effects in an economy of small enterprises, but they can have major repercussions as the scale of enterprises becomes larger. The difference can be likened to the contrast between a sand pile and a girdered structure: the sand pile absorbs blows without collapsing because of the adjustment of its many small particles, while a girdered structure can fail if a single beam buckles.

Not surprisingly, then, one side effect of industrialization

was the effort to minimize or prevent such shocks by linking firms together into cartels or trusts or simply into giant integrated enterprises. Although these efforts dampened the repercussions of individual miscalculations, they were insufficient to guard against the effects of speculative panics or commercial convulsions. By the end of the 19th century, economic depressions had become a worrisome and recurrent problem, and the Great Depression of the 1930s rocked the entire capitalist world.

From industrial to state capitalism. The problem of instability takes on further importance insofar as it is a principal cause of the next structural phase of the system. The new phase is often described as state capitalism because its outstanding feature is the enlargement in size and functions of the public realm. In 1929, for example, total U.S. government expenditures—federal, state, and local—came to less than 10 percent of the GNP; from the 1970s, they amounted to roughly one-third. This increase is observable in all major capitalist nations, many of which have reached considerably higher ratios of government disbursements to GNP than the United States.

At the same time, the function of government changed as decisively as its size. Already by the last quarter of the 19th century the emergence of great industrial trusts had provoked legislation in the United States (although not in Europe) to curb the monopolistic tendencies of industrialization. Apart from these antitrust laws and the regulation of a few industries of special public concern, however, the functions of the federal government were not significantly broadened from Smith's vision. Prior to the Great Depression, for example, the great bulk of federal outlays went for defense and international relations, for general administrative expense and interest on the debt, and for the post office.

Growth of
govern-
ment's role

The Great Depression radically altered this limited view of government in the United States, as it had earlier begun to widen it in Europe. The provision of old-age pensions, relief for the hungry and poor, and a dole for the unemployed were all policies inaugurated by the administration of President Franklin D. Roosevelt, following in the footsteps of similar enlargements of government functions in Britain, France, and Germany. From the 1970s forward, such new kinds of federal activities—under the designation of social security, health, education, and welfare expenditures—grew to be 20 to 50 percent larger than the traditional categories of federal spending.

Thus, one very important element in the advent of a new stage of capitalism was the emergence of the public sector as a guarantor of public economic well-being, a function that would never have entered Smith's imagination. A second and equally important departure was the government's assumption of responsibility for the general course of economic conditions themselves. This was a change of policy orientation that also emerged from the challenge of the Great Depression. Once regarded as a matter beyond remedy, the general level of national income came to be seen by the end of the 1930s as the responsibility of government, although the measures taken to improve conditions were on the whole timid, often wrongheaded (such as highly protectionist trade policies), and only modestly successful.

There is little doubt that capitalism in the 21st century will undergo still further structural alterations. Technological advances are rapidly reducing to near insignificance the once formidable barriers and opportunities of economic geography. Among the startling consequences of this technological leveling of the world have been the displacement of the economic centre of the globe from the Atlantic to the Pacific and the threat of large displacements of high-tech manufacture from Europe and North America to low-wage regions of Southwest Asia, Latin America, and possibly Africa. Another change has been the unprecedented growth of international finance to the point at which the total value of transactions in foreign exchange is estimated to be at least 20 times that of all foreign movements of goods and services.

Inter-
national-
ization of
finance

A third change again involves the international economy, this time through the creation of new institutions for the management of international economic trade. A number

of capitalist nations have met the challenges of the fast-growing international economy by joining the energies of the private sector (including organized labour) with the financial and negotiating powers of the state. This "corporatist" approach, most clearly evident in the organization of the Japanese economy, may become a common structural characteristic of capitalism in the 21st century, not only in managing foreign trade and production but also in dealing with domestic problems such as inflation.

These still-emergent trends seem likely to exert their pressures toward further growth of the governmental guiding role within capitalism. It is not necessary, however, to venture risky predictions as to the future. Rather, it seems more useful to conclude with two generalizations. The first emphasizes that capitalism in all its variations continues to be distinguished from other economic systems by the priority accorded to the drive for wealth and the centrality of the competitive mechanism that channels this drive toward those ends that the market rewards. The second generalization is that this driving force and constraining mechanism appear to be compatible with a wide variety of institutional settings, including substantial variations in the relationships between the private and public sectors. It is to this very adaptability that capitalism appears to owe its continued vitality.

CENTRALLY PLANNED SYSTEMS

No survey of comparative economic systems would be complete without an account of centrally planned systems, the modern descendants of the command economies of the imperial past. In sharpest possible contrast to those earlier tributary arrangements, however, modern command societies have virtually all been organized in the name of socialism—that is, with the function of command officially administered on behalf of the broad masses of the population.

Socialist central planning needs to be differentiated from the idea of socialism itself. The latter draws on moral precepts of concern for the needy that can be discovered in the Judeo-Christian tradition and derives its general social orientation from Gerrard Winstanley's Diggers movement during the English Civil Wars in the mid-17th century: "The Earth," Winstanley wrote, "was made by Almighty God to be a Common Treasury of livelihood to the whole of mankind . . . without respect of persons."

Socialism as a means of orchestrating a modern industrial system did not receive explicit attention until the Russian Revolution in 1917. In his brochure *The State and Revolution,* written before he came to power, Lenin envisaged the task of coordinating a socialist economy as little more than delivering production to central collecting points from which it would be distributed according to need—an operation requiring no more than "the extraordinarily simple operations of watching, recording, and issuing receipts, within the reach of anybody who can read and who knows the first four rules of arithmetic." After the revolution, it soon became apparent that the problem was a great deal more difficult than that. By the end of 1920 the system was at the verge of collapse.

Lenin's simplistic view

To forestall disaster, Lenin instituted the New Economic Policy (NEP), which amounted to a partial restoration of capitalism, especially in retail trade, small-scale production, and agriculture. Only the "commanding heights" of the economy remained in government hands. The NEP resuscitated the economy but opened a period of intense debate as to the use of market incentives versus moral suasion or more coercive techniques. The debate, which remained unresolved during Lenin's life, was brought to a conclusion at his death in 1924, when Joseph Stalin rose to power and rapidly forced the collectivization of the economy. By the 1930s a structure of centralized planning had been put into place that was to coordinate the Russian economy for the next half century.

Soviet planning. At the centre of the planning system was the Gosplan (*gos* means "committee"), the top economic planning agency of the Soviet state. Above the Gosplan were the political arms of the Soviet government, while below it were smaller planning agencies for the various Soviet republics. The Gosplan itself was staffed by economists and statisticians charged with drawing up what amounted to a blueprint for national economic activity, usually for a five- to seven-year period. This blueprint translated the major objectives determined by political decision (electrification targets, agricultural goals, transportation networks, and the like) into industry-specific requirements (outputs of generators, fertilizers, steel rails). These general requirements were then referred to ministries charged with the management of the industries in question, where the targets were further broken down into specific outputs (quantities, qualities, shapes, and sizes of steel plates, girders, rods, wires, and so forth) and where lower-level goals were fixed, such as budgets for firms, wage rates for different skill levels, or managerial bonuses.

Planning was not, therefore, entirely a one-way process. General objectives were indeed transmitted from the top down, but as each ministry and factory inspected its obligations, specific obstacles and difficulties were transmitted from the bottom up. The final plan was thus a compromise between the political objectives of the Central Committee of the Communist Party and the nuts-and-bolts considerations of the echelons charged with its execution. This coordinative mechanism worked quite well when the larger objectives of the system called for a kind of crash planning that resembled a war economy. The Soviet economy achieved unprecedentedly rapid progress in its industrialization drive before World War II and in repairing the devastation that followed the war. Moreover, in areas where the political stakes were high, such as space technology, the planning system was able to concentrate skills and resources regardless of cost, which enabled the Soviet Union on more than one occasion to outperform similar undertakings in the West. Yet, charged with the orchestration of a civilian economy in normal peacetime conditions, the system of centralized planning failed seriously.

Because of its failures, a far-reaching reorganization of the system was set into motion in 1985 by Mikhail Gorbachev, under the banner of *perestroika* ("restructuring"). The extent of the restructuring can be judged by these proposed changes in the coordinative system: (1) the scope and penetration of planning was to be greatly curtailed and directed mainly at general economic goals, such as rates of growth, consumption or investment targets, or regional development; (2) planning done for factory enterprises was to give way to planning by factories themselves, guided by considerations of profit and loss; (3) factory managers were no longer to be bound by instructions with respect to the sources of their inputs and the destination of their outputs, but were to be free to buy from and to sell to whomever they pleased; (4) managers were also to be free to hire and—more important—to fire workers, who formerly could not be easily discharged; and (5) many kinds of small private enterprises were to be encouraged, especially in farming and the retail trades.

Perestroika in Soviet planning

It is obvious that this program represents a dramatic retreat from the original idea of central planning. One cannot, however, say that it also represents a decisive turn from socialism to capitalism, for it is not clear to what extent the restructured planning system might embody other essential features of capitalism, such as private ownership of the means of production and the exclusion of political power from the normal operations of economic life.

Mixed economies. The efforts of the Soviet Union to find a more flexible amalgam of planning and market were anticipated by several decades of cautious experiment in the socialist countries of eastern Europe, especially Yugoslavia and Hungary, and by bold departures from central planning in China after 1979. All of these economies have long been in some degree of flux as their governments have sought configurations best suited to their institutional legacies, political ideologies, and general cultural traditions. Every indication, however, points toward the evolution of systems in which the market will play a much larger role than in the past, albeit with a continuing core of planning, and still under the banner of socialism.

Experiments in mixed economies

Something of this mixed system of coordination can also be seen in the less developed regions of the world. The

panorama of these economies is a kind of museum of economic systems, with tradition-dominated tribal societies, absolute monarchies, and semifeudal societies side by side with military socialisms and sophisticated, but very unevenly developed, capitalisms. To some extent this spectrum reflects the legacy of 19th-century imperialist capitalism, against whose cultural as well as economic hegemony all latecomers have had to struggle. Very little can be ventured as to the outcome of this astonishing variety of economic structures. Some few may follow the lead of the Pacific Rim success stories; too many are likely to remain destitute for a considerable time; the great majority will no doubt seek to use whatever institutions of market or planning appear to offer a chance to establish a viable place in the international arena. In this fateful drama, considerations of culture and politics are likely to play a more determinative role than any choice of economic instrumentalities.

APPRAISING ECONOMIC SYSTEMS

Problems of capitalism. Advocates and critics of capitalism agree that its distinctive contribution to history has been the encouragement of economic growth. Capitalist growth is not, however, regarded as an unalloyed benefit. The negative side derives from three dysfunctions that reflect its market origins.

The unreliability of growth. The first of these problems is already familiar from the above survey of the stages of capitalist development. It is the instability that has characterized and plagued the system since the advent of industrialization. Because capitalist growth is driven by profit expectations, it fluctuates with the adventitious opening of technological or social opportunities for capital accumulation. As opportunities appear, capital rushes in to take advantage of them, bringing as a consequence the familiar attributes of a boom. Sooner or later, however, the rush subsides, as the demand for the new products or services becomes saturated, bringing a halt to investment, a shakeout in the main industries caught up in the previous boom, and the advent of recession. Hence economic growth comes at the price of a succession of market gluts as booms meet their inevitable end.

This criticism did not receive its full exposition until the publication of Marx's *Das Kapital* in 1867. For Marx, the path of growth is not only unstable for the reasons just mentioned—Marx called such uncoordinated movements the "anarchy" of the market—but increasingly unstable. The reason for this is also familiar. It is the result of the industrialization process, which leads toward large-scale enterprises. As each saturation brings growth to a halt, a process of winnowing takes place in which the more successful firms are able to acquire the assets of the less successful. Thus the very dynamics of growth bring about an ever smaller number of ever larger firms. This leads to still more massive disruptions when the next boom ends, a process that terminates, according to Marx, only when the temper of the working class snaps and capitalism is replaced by socialism.

Marx's apocalyptic expectations have been largely replaced since the 1930s by the less violent but equally disquieting views of the English economist John Maynard Keynes, first set forth in his influential *The General Theory of Employment, Interest and Money* (1936). Keynes believed that the basic problem of capitalism is not so much its vulnerability to periodic saturations of investment as its likely failure to recover from them. He raised the possibility that a capitalist system could remain indefinitely in a condition of equilibrium despite high unemployment, a possibility not only entirely novel (even Marx believed that the system would recover its momentum after each crisis) but also one made plausible by the persisting unemployment of the 1930s. Keynes therefore raised the prospect that growth would end in stagnation, a condition for which the only remedy he saw was "a somewhat comprehensive socialization of investment."

The quality of growth. A second general criticism with respect to market-driven growth focuses on the negative externalities—the adverse side effects—generated by a system of production that is held accountable only to the test

of profitability. It is in the nature of a complex industrial society that the production processes of many commodities generate "bads" as well as "goods"—for example, smoke and toxic wastes or unhealthy working conditions, as well as useful outputs.

The catalog of such market-generated ills is very long. Smith himself warned that the division of labour, by routinizing work, would render workers "as stupid and ignorant as it is possible for a human creature to become," and Marx raised the spectre of alienation as the social price paid for the subordination of production to the imperatives of profit-making. A number of economists have warned that the introduction of technology designed to cut labour costs would create permanent unemployment. In modern times much attention has focused on the power of physical and chemical processes to surpass the carrying capacity of the environment—a concern made dramatically manifest by indications of various types of environmental damage arising from excessive discharges of industrial effluents and products. Because these social and ecological challenges spring from the extraordinary powers of technology, they can be viewed as side effects of socialist as well as of capitalist growth. But the argument can be made that market growth, by virtue of its overriding obedience to profit, is congenitally blind to such externalities.

Equity. A third criticism of capitalist growth concerns the fairness with which capitalism distributes its expanding wealth or with which it shares its recurrent hardships. This criticism takes on a specific and a general form.

The specific form focuses on disparities in income among layers of the population. In 1986 in the United States, for example, the lowest fifth of all families received only 4.6 percent of total income, whereas the topmost fifth received 43.7 percent. To an important degree this disparity results from the concentration of assets in the upper brackets. In addition, the disparity is the consequence of highly skewed patterns of corporate rewards that, for example, typically give chief executive officers of large companies 50 to 100 times more income than those of ordinary office or factory-floor employees.

At a more general level, the criticism may be broadened to an indictment of the market principle itself as the regulator of incomes. The advocate of market-determined distribution declares that in such a society, with certain exceptions, people tend to be paid what they are worth—that is, their incomes reflect the value of their contribution to production. Thus market-based rewards lead to the efficiency of the productive system, thereby maximizing the total income available for distribution. This argument is countered at two levels. Marxist critics contend that labour under capitalism is systematically paid less than its value by virtue of the superior bargaining power of employers, so that the claim of efficiency masks an underlying condition of exploitation. Other critics question the criterion of efficiency itself, one that counts every dollar of input and output but pays no heed to the moral or social or aesthetic qualities of either and that excludes workers from expressing their own preferences as to the most appropriate decisions for their firms.

The socialist alternative. The chief economic problem of socialism has been the efficient performance of the very task for which its planning apparatus exists, namely the effective coordination of the tasks of production and distribution. Conservative critics have even declared that a planned economy is impossible—that is, will inevitably become unmanageably chaotic—by virtue of the need for a planning agency to make the millions of dovetailing decisions necessary to bring into existence the gigantic catalog of goods and services of a modern society. Precisely such problems became manifest in the 1950s in the Soviet Union once the momentum of crash programs of industrialization or war recovery began to slacken. The problems appeared in such forms as severe shortages of housing, long queues that testified to inadequate distribution systems for even the most basic items, unattractive or even unacceptable consumer goods, the presence of *tolkachi* ("expediters") to arrange for the resolution of hopeless mismatches among planned inputs

Capitalism's boom-and-bust cycle

The externalities of economic activity

Failures of centralized planning

and outputs, and alarming statistics of waste, apathy, and absenteeism.

The proposed remedy for this, is the use of market arrangements within socialism, under which managers are free to conduct the affairs of their enterprises according to the dictates of supply and demand rather than those of a central authority. The difficulty with this solution lies in its political rather than its economic requirements. The acceptance of a market system entrusted with the coordination of the bulk of economic activity requires the tolerance of a sphere of private authority apart from that of public authority. A market mechanism may be compatible with a society of socialist principles, but it requires that the present forms of such a society be radically reorganized.

It seems likely, therefore, that socialism will encounter political problems to the extent that it comes to rely on market coordinative mechanisms, just as capitalism seems likely to encounter political problems as its own difficulties continue to push the system in the direction taken from the 1930s. To the extent that this is the case, economic systems may lose some of the decisive differences that have marked them in the past and come to suggest instead a continuum on which elements of both market and planning coexist in different proportions. Societies along such a continuum may continue to designate themselves as capitalist and socialist, but they are likely to reveal as many common aspects in the solutions to their economic problems as they may still display important differences.

(ROBERT L. HEILBRONER)

The Theory and Conduct of War

STRATEGY IN THE NUCLEAR AGE

Strategic thinking after World War II, at least with regard to conflict between the great powers, was dominated by two related developments. The first was nuclear weapons, which raised the prospect of war as the ultimate catastrophe. This led to a shift of focus in strategic thinking toward the deterrence of war rather than the waging and winning of war.

The second development was a decades-long continuity in the East–West conflict, with two alliances each dominated by a superpower—the North Atlantic Treaty Organization (NATO) by the United States and the Warsaw Pact by the Soviet Union. Although attempts to reproduce these alliances in continents other than Europe met with scant success, their stability within Europe meant that they were virtually taken for granted. Therefore, there was less postwar interest in the issues of alliance formation and disintegration, which had preoccupied earlier generations of strategists.

The atomic bomb and American strategic thought. The first successful test of the atomic bomb took place in New Mexico in July 1945, as the leaders of Britain, the Soviet Union, and the United States met at the Potsdam Conference to discuss the shape of the postwar world. This context coloured the early American appreciation of the potential foreign-policy role of the new weapons, with the result that nuclear strategy thereafter became bound up with the twists and turns of the Cold War between East and West.

However, the decision actually to use the bomb against Japan reflected the more immediate urge to end the war as soon as possible and certainly before it became necessary to mount an invasion of the mainland. The atomic bombing of Hiroshima and Nagasaki in August 1945 was a means of shocking Japan into surrender. The choice of civilian rather than purely military targets, and the consequent immense loss of life, reflected the brutalizing experience of the massive air raids that had become commonplace during the war. Afterward it was assumed that any future atomic bombing would also be against cities. As weapons of terror, they appeared to have brought 20th-century trends in warfare to their logical conclusion.

The first nuclear weapons were in the range of other munitions (the bomb that destroyed Hiroshima was equivalent to the load of some 200 B-29 bombers); also, at least initially, the weapons were scarce. The key development introduced by atomic bombs was less in the scale of their destructive power than in their efficiency. By the start of the 1950s, though, this situation had been transformed by two related developments. The first was the breaking of the U.S. monopoly by the Soviet Union, which conducted its first atomic bomb test in August 1949. Once two could play the nuclear game, the rules had to be changed. Anyone who thought of initiating nuclear war would henceforth need to consider the possibility of retaliation.

The second development followed from the first. In an effort to extend its effective nuclear superiority, the United States produced thermonuclear bombs, based on the principles of nuclear fusion rather than fission, upon which the atomic bombs were based. This made possible weapons with no obvious limits to their destructive potential. Opposition to this development by influential nuclear scientists, such as Robert Oppenheimer, was disregarded by President Harry S. Truman on the grounds that the Soviet Union would not suffer from any comparable moral inhibitions.

This move was not matched by a pronounced nuclear bias in U.S. strategy. The weapons were still scarce, and it seemed only a matter of time before whatever advantages accruing to the United States through its lead would be neutralized as the Soviet Union caught up. The Truman administration assumed that the introduction of thermonuclear weapons would extend the time available to the United States and its allies (including NATO) to build up conventional forces to match those of the Soviet Union and its satellites. A series of events, from the Berlin blockade of 1948 to the Korean War of 1950–53, had convinced the United States that the communists were prepared to use military means to pursue their political ambitions and that this could be countered only by a major program of Western rearmament.

Massive retaliation. The administration of President Dwight D. Eisenhower, which came to power in January 1953, saw things differently. It reflected on the frustrating experience of the inconclusive conventional war fought in Korea and wondered why the West had not made more of its nuclear superiority. Eisenhower was also extremely worried about the economic burden of conventional rearmament. Assigning a greater priority to nuclear weapons provided the opportunity to scale down expensive conventional forces. By this time the nuclear arsenal was becoming more plentiful and more powerful.

The strategy that emerged from these considerations became known as "massive retaliation," following a speech made by U.S. secretary of state John Foster Dulles in January 1954, when he declared that in the future a U.S. response to aggression would be "at places and with means of our own choosing." This doctrine was interpreted as threatening nuclear attack against targets in the Soviet Union and China in response to conventional aggression anywhere in the world.

Massive retaliation was widely criticized. In the United States the Democratic Party, whose policy under Truman was being reversed—and the army and navy, whose budgets were being cut at the expense of the air force's Strategic Air Command—charged that it placed undue reliance on nuclear threats, which would become less credible as Soviet nuclear strength grew. If a limited challenge developed anywhere around the Sino-Soviet periphery (the two communist giants were seen to constitute a virtual monolith), and the United States neglected its own con-

Weapons of terror

Endurance of conventional strategy

ventional forces, then a choice would have to be faced between "suicide or surrender."

First and second strikes. Massive retaliation was also criticized for failing to appreciate possible areas of Soviet superiority. This criticism grew after the Soviet Union demonstrated its technological prowess by successfully launching the first artificial Earth satellite (Sputnik 1) in October 1957, not long after it had also made the first tests of an intercontinental ballistic missile (ICBM), the SS-6. Concern grew that the Soviet Union was outpacing the United States in missile production, so leading to a "missile gap." (It might have been argued that after a certain level of destructive capability had been reached by both sides, an effective stalemate would be reached and extra weapons would make little difference, promising only, as British prime minister Winston Churchill put it, to make "the rubble bounce.")

However, by this time nuclear strategy was becoming much more sophisticated. With the RAND Corporation, a think tank based in Santa Monica, Calif., taking the lead, new analytical techniques were being developed. These were often drawn from engineering and economics, rather than the more traditional strategic disciplines of history and politics. In a celebrated RAND study of the mid-1950s, a team led by Albert Wohlstetter demonstrated that the air bases of the Strategic Air Command could be vulnerable to a surprise attack, after which retaliation would be impossible, thereby exposing the United States and its allies to Soviet blackmail.

A devastating surprise attack was considered possible because, with improved guidance systems, nuclear weapons were becoming more precise. Therefore, it was not inevitable that they would be used solely in "counter-value" strikes against easily targeted political and economic centres; instead it was just as likely that they would be used in "counterforce" strikes against military targets. A successful counterforce attack that rendered retaliation impossible—known as a "first strike"—would be strategically decisive. If, however, the attacked nation possessed sufficient forces to survive an attempted first strike with retaliatory weapons intact, then it would have what became known as a second-strike capability.

Other strategists, such as Thomas Schelling, warned that if both sides sought a first-strike capability, this could lead to an extremely unstable situation, especially during a period of high political tension when both were nervous as to the other's intentions. If it were feared that an enemy first strike was imminent, then there would be powerful pressures to attack first, and if the enemy recognized these pressures, then that would encourage him to get in his strike. Schelling described this as the "reciprocal fear of surprise attack."

On the other hand, if both sides were confident of their second-strike capabilities, then there would be considerable stability, as there would be no premium attached to unleashing nuclear hostilities. The benefits of a mutual second-strike capability led to the concept of arms control, by which potential adversaries would put less priority on simply lowering their force levels (as advocated by proponents of disarmament) and more on removing incentives to take the military initiative in the event of a severe crisis.

Mutual assured destruction. In the event, technological developments supported the second strike. Initially, long-range bombers had to be kept on continual alert to prevent them from being eliminated in a surprise attack. When ICBMs moved into full production in the early 1960s with such systems as the U.S. Titan and Minuteman I and the Soviet SS-7 and SS-8, they were placed in hardened underground silos, so that an unlikely direct hit would be required to destroy them. Even less vulnerable were submarine-launched ballistic missiles (SLBMs) such as the U.S. Polaris and the Soviet SS-N-5 and SS-N-6, which could take full advantage of the ocean expanses to hide from enemy attack.

Meanwhile, attempts to develop effective defenses against nuclear attack proved futile. The standards for antiaircraft defense in the nuclear age had to be much higher than for conventional air raids, since any penetration of the defensive screen would threaten the defender with catastrophe.

Progress was made using surface-to-air missiles (SAMs), such as the U.S. Nike series, in developing defenses against bombers, but the move to ICBMs, with their minimal warning time before impact, appeared to render the defensive task hopeless. Then, during the 1960s, advances in radars and long-range SAMs promised a breakthrough in antiballistic missile defense, but by the early 1970s these in turn were countered by improvements in offensive missiles—notably multiple independently targeted reentry vehicles (MIRVs), which could swamp any defenses. (The first MIRVed ICBMs were the U.S. Minuteman III and the Soviet SS-17.)

Measures of civil defense, which could offer little protection to the civilian populace against nuclear explosions and, at best, only some chance of avoiding exposure to nuclear fallout, also appeared hopeless in the face of the overwhelming destructive power being accumulated by both sides.

By the mid-1960s fears had eased of a technological arms race that might encourage either side to unleash a surprise attack. For the foreseeable future each side could eliminate the other as a modern industrial state. Robert McNamara, the U.S. secretary of defense for much of that decade, argued that so long as the two superpowers had confidence in their capacity for mutual assured destruction—an ability to impose "unacceptable damage" defined as 25 percent of population and 50 percent of industry—the relationship between the two would be stable.

The need to maintain strategic stability influenced the strategic arms limitation talks (SALT), which began in 1969 and became the centrepiece of President Richard M. Nixon's policy of détente with the Soviet Union. In 1972, with the ABM Treaty, the two sides agreed to ban nationwide antiballistic missile systems, thereby confirming the primacy of the offense. Attempts to consolidate the strategic standoff with a treaty limiting offensive weapons proved more difficult. (In 1972 only an interim freeze had been agreed.) The second round of talks was guided mainly by the concept of parity, by which a broad equality in destructive power would be confirmed. However, the difficulty in comparing the two nuclear arsenals, which differed in important respects, resulted in long and complex negotiations. A treaty called SALT II was agreed on in June 1979, but by this time détente was in decline, and it was dealt a final blow with the Soviet intervention in Afghanistan at the end of that year. In addition, the strategic underpinnings of arms control had been undermined by a growing dissatisfaction in the United States with the principles of mutual assured destruction.

Alternatives to assured destruction. Critics found the condition of mutual assured destruction—which had become known by its acronym MAD—alarming. If MAD failed to deter, then any war would soon lead to genocide. In addition, if the threat of retaliating with nuclear weapons was used to deter only nuclear attack, then the value of nuclear threats in deterring conventional aggression would be lost. In principle, this could undermine the commitments made to allies to use nuclear weapons on their behalf if they faced such aggression.

Particularly alarming was evidence that the nuclear strategy of the Soviet Union envisaged using nuclear weapons in a traditional military manner much as if they were conventional weapons—that is, at most to obtain a decisive military advantage in a conflict and at the very least to reduce the damage that an enemy might do to Soviet territory (if necessary, by launching preemptive strikes). During the negotiations that led to SALT II, critics also argued that the momentum behind the Soviet ICBM program, in combination with improved guidance systems that gave unprecedented accuracy to MIRVed missiles, had opened a "window of vulnerability" in the U.S. deterrent force. They expressed concern that the Soviet Union, by deploying the SS-17, SS-18, and SS-19 ICBMs, was building a force of such size and accuracy that just a portion of it could attack and destroy the U.S. Minuteman and Titan ICBM force without killing huge numbers of civilians. Although this would not be a true first strike, since U.S. bombers and submarines could retaliate, these latter delivery systems were not accurate enough to produce an

Counter-value and counter-force strikes

The futility of anti-nuclear defense

equivalent counterforce attack against Soviet missile silos. Instead, the United States would be forced to escalate the war by retaliating against cities. This repugnant act would be of no strategic value, however, because the rest of the untouched Soviet missile force would then be used to wipe out U.S. cities. The United States, therefore, would have placed itself in a position in which it would have to choose between surrender and slaughter.

The realism of this scenario may be doubted, given that no attack against U.S. ICBMs would be accurate enough to avoid massive civilian destruction; therefore, the Soviet Union could be certain that the United States would feel little repugnance at retaliating against Soviet cities. Nonetheless, it was used to criticize SALT II, a complicated treaty that offered few means of verification and did little to interfere with the Soviet ICBM program. It was also used to argue for the development of U.S. ICBMs comparable to the Soviet systems.

The first formal break with assured destruction came in 1974, when Secretary of Defense James Schlesinger announced that future U.S. nuclear targeting would be geared to selective strikes and not just the sort of massive attacks suggested by the philosophy of mutual assured destruction. Although President Jimmy Carter's secretary of defense, Harold Brown, was skeptical that either side would actually find such sophisticated nuclear strikes possible, he accepted the need to develop a range of targeting options to convince the Soviet Union that it could not gain the upper hand by such methods. This was the main theme of the "countervailing" strategy announced in 1980.

Ronald W. Reagan came to office the next year with a much more radical critique of MAD, and his presidency was devoted to attempts to escape from its constraints. Initially, this took the form of a search for offensive nuclear operations that would enable the United States to "prevail" in a protracted war with the Soviet Union, rather than just countervail. It involved upgrading the old civil-defense systems and deploying the MX, an experimental ICBM originally designed to survive a first strike through some form of mobile deployment. Neither of these ideas was politically popular. In the end, civil defense was rejected as impossible, and the MX (now named Peacekeeper) was deployed in Minuteman silos and in only a fraction of the originally proposed numbers.

In March 1983 Reagan announced the start of a second search for a means to escape from MAD. This time it was for a defensive system that could intercept ballistic missiles. Reagan spoke of his preference for protecting lives rather than avenging them, and of the possibility of rendering nuclear weapons "impotent and obsolete," but the vision could not be turned into reality. Although the Strategic Defense Initiative, or SDI (which critics dubbed Star Wars, after a science fiction movie), was given a high priority and billions of dollars for research, the idea of protecting society as a whole from nuclear attack soon appeared hopelessly impractical, given the diverse means of delivering nuclear weapons. The main question became whether SDI could protect key political and military assets from attack, but even here some of the more futuristic ideas—such as using space-based lasers to destroy ballistic missiles just as they were launched—proved technically demanding and expensive. Political support waned.

Meanwhile, Reagan had replaced talks on arms limitation with the Strategic Arms Reduction Talks (START). At first the Soviet Union argued that no progress on strategic arms control was possible so long as SDI was being pursued. Mikhail Gorbachev, who became the Soviet leader in 1985, offered his own vision of how to escape from assured destruction in a speech of January 1986, in which he set out a radical disarmament agenda leading toward a nuclear-free world by the end of the century. In October 1986, at a summit in Reykjavík, Ice., Reagan came close to embracing this vision, although no agreement was reached because he refused Gorbachev's demand to abandon SDI. Nevertheless, the concept of arms reduction had taken hold, and START proceeded with a new emphasis on deep cuts in nuclear arsenals.

The switch to arms reduction suggested that Reagan's critique of MAD had concluded with the view that, given

(margin note) Counter-vailing with limited strikes

(margin note) Arms reduction

the difficulties of designing and deploying both discriminating offensive options and effective ballistic missile defenses, it was better to do away with nuclear weapons altogether. This constituted a formidable challenge to the orthodox view that nuclear weapons exercised a stabilizing deterrence on international misbehaviour and were a reassurance to America's allies, who faced preponderant Soviet conventional forces. Reagan was prevailed upon to moderate his critique, but not before doubts had been created as to the strength of the U.S. commitment to guarantee the security of its allies with nuclear weapons.

On the other hand, the alacrity with which Gorbachev embraced complete nuclear disarmament reflected the greater freedom of maneuver available to any Soviet leader as well as the subordinate role of the Warsaw Pact allies. Whereas NATO's European members were anxious to lock the United States into their security arrangements for fear that they would be unable to stand alone, the Soviet Union had drawn its allies into a pact that met its own security requirements—that is, extending its form of government into eastern Europe and creating a buffer between it and the hostile capitalist forces of the West. Members of the Warsaw Pact might be beneficiaries of a Soviet nuclear guarantee, but there was no question of shared decision-making on nuclear matters. In fact, during the 1970s Soviet doctrine had appeared to have the goal of extracting the maximum regional benefit from its nuclear arsenal—vis-à-vis both western Europe and China—while maintaining Soviet territory as a sanctuary from nuclear devastation. Its priority in any nuclear conflict would have been to confine nuclear exchanges to central Europe, while showing a certain respect for U.S. territory as a sanctuary in the hope of reciprocal treatment by the United States. If escalation had appeared inevitable, however, or if the United States had appeared to be preparing a first strike, then Soviet doctrine would have called for a preemptive blow against the United States' long-range arsenal in an effort to reduce damage to the Soviet Union.

This approach was undermined by evidence that U.S. nuclear doctrine and deployment showed no respect for geographic sanctuary and by the Soviets' own recognition of the sheer difficulty of managing a nuclear exchange in such a way as to reduce the vulnerability of Soviet territory. Even before Gorbachev, there had been a discernible trend in military thinking toward emphasizing the opening conventional stage of a war and toward achieving victory within that stage. Gorbachev accelerated this trend. Because he was not prepared to allow overambitious nuclear doctrines to interfere with his objective of improving relations with the West, he was much more prepared than his predecessors to compromise in arms control negotiations. In addition, he was influenced by the April 1986 disaster at the Chernobyl nuclear power plant, which demonstrated that radioactive fallout had little respect for national boundaries.

(margin note) Orthodox Soviet doctrine

Flexible response. This gave a new twist to the long-standing debate within NATO over nuclear deterrence. The United States' allies had already learned to live with unavoidable doubts over the quality of the U.S. nuclear guarantee of European security. These began to surface in the 1950s, after the Eisenhower administration had embraced nuclear deterrence and the allies had agreed that it was natural to rely on the most advanced weapons available—especially those in which the United States then enjoyed a clear superiority. The alternative course—relying on conventional forces—would have caused severe economic strains, and there was deep pessimism as to the possibility of ever matching Soviet conventional strength.

The conventional buildup set in motion under the Truman administration had one important requirement: that the Federal Republic of Germany be rearmed. This set in motion a sharp debate in Europe that was coloured by memories of the recent war, but in 1955 a formula was found in which West Germany rearmed but was permitted no chemical or nuclear weapons and was part of NATO's military command. In return, the West German government sought a commitment by its new allies to the concept of forward defense, in which any aggression would be rebuffed at the border between East and West

Germany. (With its lack of depth and its concentration of population and industry close to the East, the Federal Republic had no wish for its allies to trade German soil for more time in responding to a Soviet attack.)

Once it was decided that NATO would not attempt to match Soviet conventional forces, then forward defense meant, in effect, that nuclear deterrence was linked to the inter-German border. European members of NATO had no qualms with this arrangement, because it saved them the expense of sustaining large-scale conventional forces, and they did not believe that the Soviet Union had any interest in invading western Europe that would be worth the slightest risk of nuclear war.

The threshold between conventional and nuclear war

In the early 1960s the administration of President John F. Kennedy, which confronted the Soviet Union over the Berlin Wall and the Cuban missile crisis, did not take such a relaxed view of Soviet intentions. Given what it saw as the Soviet capacity for retaliation, the United States thought it unlikely that any president would use nuclear weapons first, and it was hard to see how a credible deterrent could be fashioned out of an incredible nuclear threat. At the very least, the United States insisted, NATO should raise the nuclear threshold, that is, the point at which nuclear weapons would be necessary to stave off conventional defeat. This would be accomplished by extra conventional forces. New analyses suggested that it would be easier than hitherto assumed because previous assessments had exaggerated the strength of the Warsaw Pact. In addition, the Soviet leader, Nikita Khrushchev, who was convinced that nuclear weapons made it unnecessary to maintain vast armies, was imposing major reductions on his generals at that time.

European governments argued in response that conventional forces simply could not provide a sufficient deterrent. Since Soviet territory would not be vulnerable in a conventional war, the Kremlin might judge that the risks of conventional war were acceptable. And even if the Warsaw Pact were defeated, central Europe would still be devastated. Therefore, all war had to be deterred, not just nuclear war.

In 1967 a compromise was found in the doctrine of "flexible response." Under this compromise, the Europeans recognized the U.S. requirement for an extended conventional stage, so that the first shots across the Iron Curtain would not lead automatically to nuclear holocaust, and the United States accepted the need for a clear link between a land war in Europe and its own strategic nuclear arsenal.

Limited nuclear war. Flexible response did not prescribe a particular course of action; rather, it retained for NATO the possibility that it would be the first to use nuclear weapons and suggested that this initially would involve short-range, tactical weapons.

When tactical nuclear weapons such as the Honest John rocket were introduced into the NATO inventory during the 1950s, the U.S. Army had supposed that these could be considered quite separately from intercontinental strategic missiles. If anything, tactical nuclear weapons were closer to conventional weapons and were to be integrated with general-purpose forces. A number of strategic thinkers in the United States, including Henry Kissinger and Robert Osgood, hoped that, if the West could reinforce its military strength in this way, it would be possible to take on communists in limited nuclear wars without resort to incredible threats of massive retaliation.

However, once the widespread use of battlefield nuclear weapons by NATO was simulated in war games in the 1950s, it became apparent that they would result in such death and destruction that they could in no way be considered conventional. Also, as Warsaw Pact forces obtained comparable capabilities with such weapons as the SS-1 missile, any Western advantage seemed neutralized. Unless a retreating defender used nuclear weapons immediately, any later use could well be over his own territory and against a dispersed enemy. And, if tactical nuclear weapons were used to impose great costs on the enemy, there would be a risk that the conflict could soon escalate to strategic nuclear use. Limited nuclear war, therefore, appeared a contradiction in terms.

European governments were still loath to dispense with the weapons. Although they could not be considered ordinary weapons of war, their close integration with conventional forces meant that they were more likely than U.S. strategic nuclear forces to get entangled in a land war in Europe. The idea was to use the risk of escalating to total nuclear war with the United States as a powerful deterrent effect on the Soviet Union's actions in Europe. According to this strategy, deterrence did not require a certainty that nuclear weapons would be used, but only a risk. The consequences of miscalculation were so horrendous that a government would dare not gamble. However, the United States, whose own security was now being linked to peace in Europe, was still more concerned that miscalculation might nonetheless take place.

Linking U.S. to European security

Certainly, NATO's procedures for "going nuclear" were designed to reduce the risk of unauthorized use. But this created a tension between theory, which suggested that deterrence was served by the risk that a conflict might get out of control, and practice, which exhibited a determination not to lose control. The tension was reflected in discussions over how to replace the first generation of tactical nuclear weapons as they became obsolete in the 1970s. If the next generation were made smaller and more precise, then this would imply a readiness to use them to fight a nuclear war rather than simply deter. An apparent readiness to wage nuclear war was at the heart of a controversy over the "neutron bomb" (actually a thermonuclear missile warhead or artillery shell of enhanced radiation and reduced blast), which was criticized for blurring the boundary between conventional and nuclear weapons and thereby making it much easier to go nuclear.

Even greater controversy was generated by NATO's decision in 1979 to replace the Pershing IA, a medium-range ballistic missile, with two weapons that would constitute a more powerful intermediate nuclear force (INF): the Pershing II intermediate-range ballistic missile (IRBM) and the Tomahawk cruise missile. The origins of the program to modernize the INF lay in two western European concerns over the U.S. nuclear guarantee. The first concern resulted from the tendency of the United States in the Strategic Arms Limitation Talks to concentrate on achieving symmetry between the nuclear forces of the two superpowers, while paying little attention to the superiority, within the European theatre, of the Warsaw Pact in both nuclear and conventional weapons. Particularly worrisome was the Soviet SS-20, an IRBM that was first tested in 1974 and deployed in 1977. Although the SS-20 did not signal any shift in Soviet policy (U.S. military bases in Europe and the British, French, and Chinese nuclear forces had long been targeted), it was the first new missile designed for this purpose to have appeared in some time. In 1977 Chancellor Helmut Schmidt of West Germany argued that NATO should not tolerate Soviet superiority in such weapons. This suggested that the imbalance should be dealt with either through arms control or by an equivalent Western effort to upgrade its own INF.

The second concern placed far less stress on the SS-20 and more on the requirements, within NATO's strategy of flexible response, to be able to strike Soviet territory with systems based in western Europe in the event of full-scale war on the Continent. This requirement existed irrespective of the new Soviet missiles, and it was becoming problematic because of the age of NATO's medium bombers and the lack of any U.S. intermediate-range land-based missile in Europe. A modernized INF made more sense than systems designed for battlefield use, because they posed a direct threat to the Soviet homeland and thus challenged Soviet ideas of confining any nuclear exchanges to NATO and Warsaw Pact countries, with superpower territory accorded sanctuary status.

However, large-scale protests sprang up in Europe and North America after the decision to modernize. Voicing a concern that a new arms race was getting under way in Europe, they took on special urgency following the Soviet invasion of Afghanistan (two weeks after NATO's decision on the INF), with the decline of arms control, and with the election of Ronald Reagan, who had a hawkish reputation, to the U.S. presidency. The strength of the protests encouraged NATO to moderate its policy. The

rationale for modernizing the INF was switched from the requirements of flexible response to the more politically marketable aim of matching the deployment of the SS-20, and in November 1981, at the start of negotiations on this issue, Reagan offered to eliminate NATO's INF if all SS-20s were removed. This "zero option" was rejected by Leonid Brezhnev, and, despite warnings from the Soviet Union that deployment of a modernized INF would mean the end of negotiations, the first Tomahawk and Pershing II missiles were delivered in late 1983. Yury Andropov promptly broke off the INF talks, hoping to force a breach in the unanimity of the NATO allies, but, when the expected crisis failed to arise, Konstantin Chernenko agreed to resume negotiations. Soon afterward Gorbachev was in charge, and he decided that the zero option was in the Soviet interest: eliminating the INF would remove a direct threat to Soviet territory in return for removing a larger number of Soviet missiles that could strike only the allies of the United States. In December 1987, Gorbachev and Reagan signed the INF Treaty.

The INF Treaty: withdrawing nuclear deterrence

Although America's allies saw that the treaty had political benefits in improving East–West relations, some strategists worried that it sounded the death knell for nuclear deterrence. One response by NATO was to see whether it would be possible to build up other nuclear systems by way of compensation, but the difficulty here was that the improved political climate undermined public support for such moves. In West Germany the question of modernizing the short-range Lance missile was coloured by the direct and almost unique threat this weapon posed to German territory. There had always been the strongest official support for the traditional concept of nuclear deterrence in that country, but, with the political climate improving, West German politicians such as Chancellor Helmut Kohl came to argue that yet another nuclear modernization program would send the wrong signals to the East. They were also unhappy at the apparent readiness of the United States and Britain to retain Germany as a battlefield for short-range nuclear exchanges while securing the removal of intermediate- and long-range systems that threatened their own territories. The Soviet Union possessed large numbers of short-range missiles and had been modernizing them for a decade with such systems as the SS-21, but Gorbachev indicated a readiness to negotiate their complete elimination. British prime minister Margaret Thatcher and U.S. president George Bush insisted that this would be imprudent, and, following their lead, NATO agreed in 1989 to postpone modernizing the Lance in the hope that negotiations on conventional force reductions would reach a satisfactory conclusion and thus reduce the importance of nuclear weapons as a means of compensating for the Warsaw Pact's conventional superiority.

The Bush administration was more orthodox on nuclear matters than its predecessor, but Reagan's interest in a nuclear-free world—highlighted by SDI, the Reykjavík summit, and the INF Treaty—had already encouraged discussion among some Europeans of the possibility of a European defense community that would be less dependent upon the United States. In practice this would require the substitution of a French and British strategic nuclear guarantee for an American. Britain had always, officially at least, committed its strategic nuclear forces (which since the late 1960s had been SLBMs) to NATO. Britain's rationale for maintaining a national nuclear force involved a combination of the political influence that could be brought to bear on its allies, especially the United States, and a claim to be contributing to the overall deterrent posture. France, by contrast, had always had a much more nationalistic rationale, but after the 1970s, following the introduction of the Pluton short-range missile, which could only land on German territory, it was obliged to consider the role that its *force de frappe* might have in the defense of its allies. In any event, neither Britain nor France was eager to take over from the United States the broader deterrent role; nor were those who had previously sheltered under the U.S. umbrella interested in a European alternative.

Conventional strategy. The main consequence of the developing uncertainties surrounding nuclear deterrence

was an increased interest in conventional strategy. For the first two decades of the nuclear age, there had been little interest in this area; given the conviction that any war between the great powers would soon go nuclear, there seemed to be little point in preparing for nonnuclear engagements.

Meanwhile, France and Britain fought a number of colonial wars, with France's struggles in Indochina and Algeria particularly protracted and bitter. During the 1960s the United States became steadily involved in Vietnam, in which a weak pro-Western government in the South faced an insurgency backed by a communist government in the North. After 1965 there was a substantial commitment of all elements of U.S. military power, excluding nuclear weapons but including a bombing campaign against the North.

Partly as a result of these conflicts, interest began to revive in the likely character of a conventional war involving the major powers. In the West this was also a result of the adoption of flexible response, which demanded greater attention to conventional warfare. In the East as well, to some extent because of the shift in NATO doctrine, conventional warfare grew in importance. There was some irony in this. Flexible response reflected NATO's concern over Soviet conventional superiority, yet, under Khrushchev, Soviet forces had been cut back dramatically on the assumption that any future war would go nuclear from the start. After Khrushchev was ousted in 1964, the Soviet Union began a major buildup of conventional forces, and in 1967 military exercises were held that indicated the expectation of a substantial conventional stage at the start of a future war. Besides the need to remain strong in relation to NATO, by the early 1970s the Soviet buildup reflected concern over a possible threat from China, which had become extremely hostile and was rapidly improving relations with the West. Again, there was irony in this development. China and the Soviet Union had finally split in 1963 over Khrushchev's readiness to deal with the West, over his unwillingness to back the Chinese nuclear program, and also over a long-standing border dispute between the two countries. Later, the years of the Cultural Revolution (1966–76) convinced Brezhnev that the Chinese were dangerous and unstable; clashes on the border in 1969 led to hints from Moscow that it might take action against China's fledgling nuclear capability.

In the late 1970s this Warsaw Pact buildup, coupled with Soviet-supported operations in such Third World countries as Vietnam, Angola, and Ethiopia, stimulated NATO to improve its capacity to resist an offensive and mobilize quickly. This was based on the fear that, without sufficient warning to get mobilization under way, the strength of Soviet frontline and follow-on forces could overwhelm NATO's thin peacetime lines of defense. Growing doubts over the credibility and durability of nuclear deterrence also increased the importance of improving conventional forces.

Even with increased allocations to defense, NATO governments remained pessimistic about their ability to match Warsaw Pact forces. Although the total military power of NATO was much greater, geography favoured the Warsaw Pact, since reserves from the East could reach the front much more quickly than reserves from the United States, which would have to make a hazardous journey across the Atlantic Ocean. Against this pessimism it was noted that greater numbers were normally assumed to be required by the attacker (a ratio of three to one was often cited, although the critical factor was not the overall ratio but the strength of the offense at the point of attack). Technological advances were said further to favour the defense, in that extremely precise and comparatively simple guided weapons could be used to take on tanks and high-performance aircraft, the central actors in any offensive.

This optimism was questioned by other strategic analysts. They noted that the natural advantage accruing to the defense would do so only if the attacker had to force a way through well-prepared defensive positions, rather than simply outflanking them. The ability to impose attrition on the enemy would be reduced if the enemy was able to fight a war of maneuver, in which an immobile defense

Renewal of conventional strategy

might find itself caught off balance. Moreover, in a war of maneuver, the potential benefits of simple air-defense and antitank systems would soon be qualified by the need to make them mobile, which would put them in need of protection as well.

The proponents of maneuver warfare warned that this was the type favoured by the Warsaw Pact. The Soviet Union preferred the offensive because it would make it possible to defeat the enemy quickly, before the full weight of its power could be brought to bear. Soviet doctrine during the 1970s suggested that a key aspect of this offensive would be the neutralization of NATO's nuclear assets by overrunning key installations, with a possible shift to a regional nuclear offensive when the right moment arrived. By the early 1980s doubts over whether a war would last long enough for the right moment ever to arrive, and whether nuclear exchanges could be limited geographically, encouraged a greater stress by the Soviet military on obtaining a victory in the conventional stage.

Follow-on forces attack

The maneuver school eventually encouraged a shift in NATO thinking toward more mobile operations, as well as a greater willingness to contemplate attacks into Warsaw Pact territory in an effort to reduce the momentum of a Pact offensive. The strategy of follow-on forces attack (FOFA), for example, envisaged the holding of a Pact offensive on the ground while attacking the Pact's follow-on forces in the rear with air strikes. Such aggressive defense was criticized by peace movements as being too provocative. Instead, they proposed non-provocative strategies based on "defensive defense," which would lack any capability to go on the offensive. These ideas proved difficult to turn into practice, as any sort of mobile force could move forward, and few armies would tol-

erate being deprived of their capacity to counterattack.

Meanwhile, in the Soviet Union concern over the burden of high defense expenditures, combined with an awareness that the arms buildup of the 1970s had triggered a counterresponse from NATO, encouraged "new thinking" that actually picked up on the ideas of defensive defense. These ideas were received by Soviet military commanders with as little enthusiasm as they were received in the West. Nevertheless, they influenced cuts in Soviet forces, announced by Gorbachev in December 1988, that eliminated some military units of a clearly offensive nature without depriving the Warsaw Pact of its offensive options. However modest in themselves, the cuts raised the prospect of an end to the role of these forces in sustaining the Soviet Union's dominance over eastern Europe. When coupled with domestic political reforms in the Soviet Union, Poland, and Hungary, they also signaled the eventual demise of the postwar alliance system. The prospect of a declining Soviet hegemony, however, was clouded by growing disorder within eastern Europe (and even in the Soviet Union itself) and also by the considerable strength that Soviet military forces would retain in spite of the planned cuts. Moreover, there was no reason to presume that a security system in which the two superpowers played a less overbearing role would be free of conflict. This provided an argument for a continuing role for nuclear deterrence: to warn against the dangers of allowing any conflict to get out of hand, if not to deal with a specific military threat. Nevertheless, political changes within the Soviet bloc presented a historic opportunity to heal East–West divisions and, with that, to reduce the need for substantial armed forces of any kind.

(LAWRENCE D. FREEDMAN)

The Technology of War

STRATEGIC MISSILES

Strategic missiles represent a logical step in the attempt to attack enemy forces at a distance. As such, they can be seen as extensions of either artillery (in the case of ballistic missiles) or manned aircraft (in the case of cruise missiles). Ballistic missiles are rocket-propelled weapons that travel by momentum in a high, arcing trajectory after they have been launched into flight by a brief burst of power. Cruise missiles, on the other hand, are powered continuously by air-breathing jet engines and are sustained along a low, level flight path by aerodynamic lift.

Although experiments were undertaken before World War II on crude prototypes of the cruise and ballistic missile, the modern weapons are generally considered to have their true origins in the V-1 and V-2 missiles launched by Germany in 1944–45. Both of those Vergeltungswaffen, or "Vengeance Weapons," defined the problems of propulsion and guidance that have continued ever since to shape cruise and ballistic missile development.

Long-range missiles and nuclear warheads

Given the extremely long ranges required of strategic weapons, even the most modern guidance systems cannot deliver a missile's warhead to the target with consistent, pinpoint accuracy. For this reason, strategic missiles have almost exclusively carried nuclear warheads, which need not strike a target directly in order to destroy it. By contrast, missiles of shorter range (often called tactical- or battlefield-range) have been fitted with both nuclear and conventional warheads. For example, the SS-1 Scud, a ballistic missile with ranges of up to 185 miles (300 kilometres), was fielded with nuclear warheads by Soviet troops in eastern Europe from the 1950s through the 1980s; but in the "war of the cities" during the Iran–Iraq conflict of the 1980s, many SS-1s armed with conventional warheads were launched by both sides, killing thousands of civilians. Other "dual-capable" short-range ballistic missiles are the U.S. Lance, with a range of about 80 miles, and the Soviet SS-21 Scarab, with a range of 75

miles. (In this section, Soviet missile systems are referred to by their NATO designations, such as SS-21 Scarab.)

The exclusively nuclear capacity of strategic-range weapons has confined serious development of cruise and ballistic missile technology to the world's nuclear powers—particularly the United States and the Soviet Union. These two countries have taken different paths in exploiting missile technology. Soviet cruise missiles, for instance, have been designed mostly for tactical antiship use rather than for threatening strategic land targets (as has been the U.S. emphasis). Throughout the ballistic missile arms race, the United States has tended to streamline its weapons, seeking greater accuracy and lower explosive power, or yield. Meanwhile, the Soviet Union, perhaps to make up for its difficulties in solving guidance problems, has concentrated on larger missiles and higher yields. Most U.S. systems have carried warheads of less than one megaton, with the largest being the nine-megaton Titan II, in service from 1963 through 1987. The Soviet warheads have often exceeded five megatons, with the largest being a 20- to 25-megaton warhead deployed on the SS-7 Saddler from 1961 to 1980 and a 25-megaton warhead on the SS-9 Scarp, deployed from 1967 to 1982.

Most other countries pursuing missile technology have not developed strategic weapons to the extent of the United States and the Soviet Union. Nonetheless, several other nations have produced them; their emphasis, however, has been on ballistic rather than cruise missiles, because of the extremely sophisticated guidance systems required of cruise missiles. Also, as with any technology, there has occurred a transfer of ballistic missile technology to less-developed countries. Combined with the widespread capacity to produce chemical warheads, such weapons represent a potent addition to the arsenals of emerging powers of the Third World.

Ballistic missiles. Strategic ballistic missiles can be divided into two general categories according to their bas-

ing mode: those that are launched from land and those launched at sea (from submarines beneath the surface). They can also be divided according to their range into intermediate-range ballistic missiles (IRBMs) and intercontinental ballistic missiles (ICBMs). IRBMs have ranges of about 600 to 3,500 miles, while ICBMs have ranges exceeding 3,500 miles. Modern land-based strategic missiles are almost all of ICBM range, whereas all but the most modern submarine-launched ballistic missiles (SLBMs) have been of intermediate range.

Prelaunch survivability (that is, the ability to survive an enemy attack) has been a long-standing problem with land-based ICBMs. (SLBMs achieve survivability by being based on relatively undetectable submarines.) At first, they were considered safe from attack because neither U.S. nor Soviet missiles were sufficiently accurate to strike the other's launch sites; hence, early systems were launched from above ground. However, as missile accuracies improved, above-ground missiles became vulnerable, and in the 1960s both countries began to base their ICBMs below ground in concrete tubes called silos, some of which were hardened against nuclear blast. Later, even greater improvements in accuracy brought ICBM basing strategy back to above-ground systems. This time, prelaunch survivability was to be achieved by mobile ICBMs that would confound an attacker with multiple moving targets.

Most U.S. silos are designed for one-time "hot-launch" use, the rocket engines igniting within the silo and essentially destroying it as the missile departs. The Soviets pioneered the "cold-launch" method, in which the missile is expelled by gas and the rocket engine ignited after the missile clears the silo. This method, essentially the same system used with SLBMs, allows silos to be reused after minor repair.

In order to increase their range and throw weight, ballistic missiles are usually multistaged. By shedding weight as the flight progresses (that is, by burning the fuel and then discarding the pumps, flight controls, and associated

equipment of the previous stage), each successive stage has less mass to accelerate. This permits a missile to fly farther and carry a larger payload.

The flight path of a ballistic missile has three successive phases. In the first, called the boost phase, the rocket engine (or engines, if the missile contains two or three stages) provides the precise amount of propulsion required to place the missile on a specific ballistic trajectory. Then the engine quits, and the final stage of the missile (called the payload) coasts in the mid-course phase, usually beyond the Earth's atmosphere. The payload contains the warhead (or warheads), the guidance system, and such penetration aids as decoys, electronic jammers, and chaff to help elude enemy defenses. The weight of this payload constitutes the missile's throw weight, that is, the total weight that the missile is capable of placing on a ballistic trajectory toward a target. By mid-course, the warheads have detached from the remainder of the payload, and all elements are on a ballistic path. The terminal phase of flight occurs when gravity pulls the warheads (now referred to as the reentry vehicles, or RVs) back into the atmosphere and down to the target area.

Most ballistic missiles use inertial guidance to arrive at the vicinity of their targets. This technology, based on Newtonian physics, involves measuring disturbances to the missile in three axes. The device used to measure these disturbances is usually composed of three gyroscopically stabilized accelerometers mounted at right angles to one another. By calculating the acceleration imparted by external forces (including the rocket engine's thrust), and by comparing these forces to the launch position, the guidance system can determine the missile's position, velocity, and heading. Then the guidance computer, predicting the gravitational forces that will act on the reentry vehicle, can calculate the velocity and heading required to reach a predetermined point on the ground. Given these calculations, the guidance system can issue a command to the missile thrust system during boost phase to place the payload at

IRBMs and ICBMs

Boost, midcourse, and reentry phases

From L. Freedman, *Atlas of Global Strategy*, copyright © Equinox (Oxford) Ltd 1985

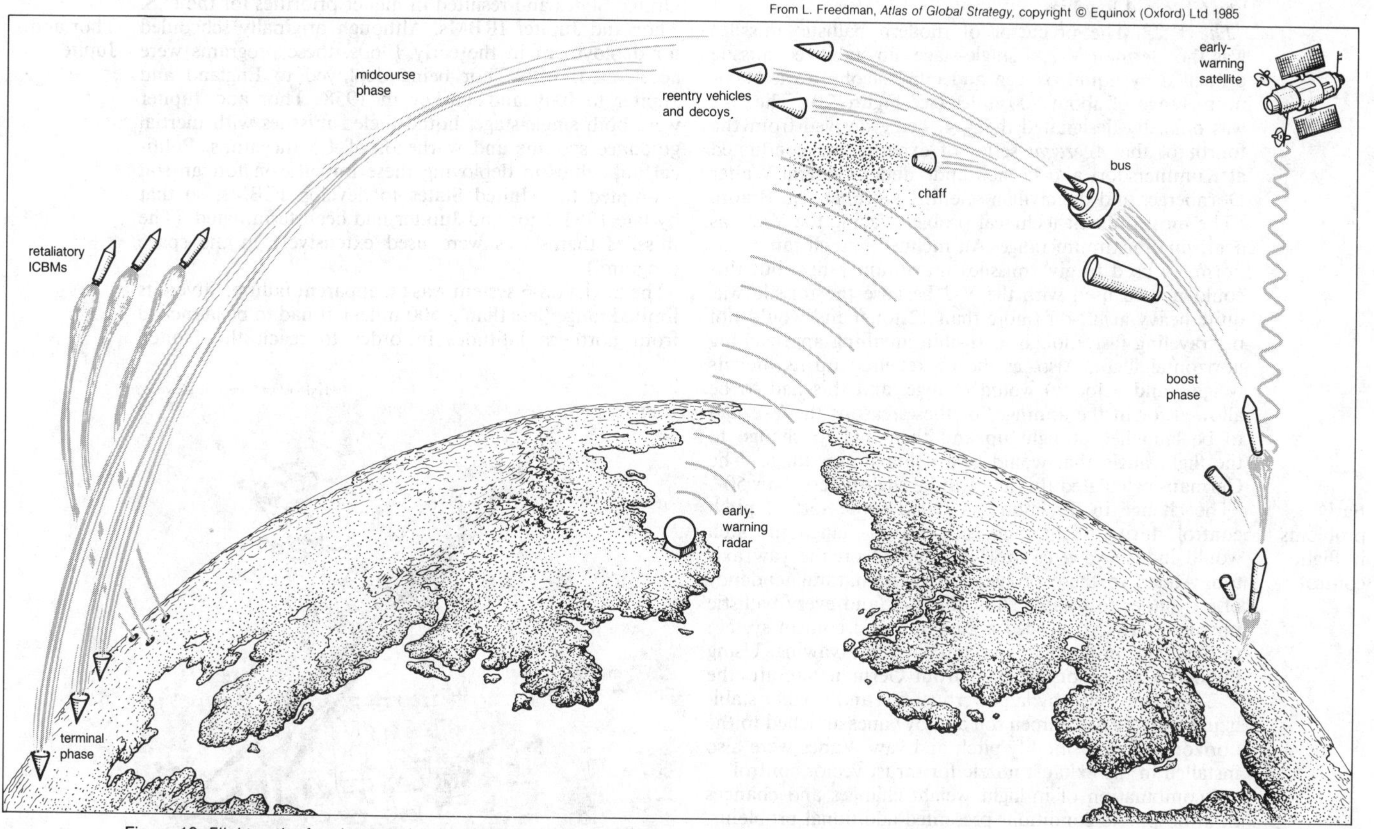

Figure 19: *Flight path of an intercontinental ballistic missile (ICBM).*
While being boosted into a ballistic trajectory beyond the Earth's atmosphere, the missile's final stage, called the bus, would dispense its nuclear warheads, or reentry vehicles. Decoys and a cloud of reflective chaff would confuse the enemy's radar-guided defenses, and the reentry vehicles would strike their targets within 30 minutes of launch. By that time, retaliatory ICBMs would probably be on their way.

a specific point in space, on a specific heading, and at a specific velocity—at which point thrust is shut off and a purely ballistic flight path begins.

Ballistic missile guidance is complicated by two factors. First, during the latter stages of the powered boost phase, the atmosphere is so thin that aerodynamic flight controls such as fins cannot work and the only corrections that can be made to the flight path must come from the rocket engines themselves. But, because the engines only provide a force vector roughly parallel to the missile's fuselage, they cannot be used to provide major course corrections; making major corrections would create large gravitational forces perpendicular to the fuselage that could destroy the missile. Nevertheless, small corrections can be made by slightly gimballing the main engines so that they swivel, by placing deflective surfaces called vanes within the rocket exhaust, or, in some instances, by fitting small rocket engines known as thrust-vector motors or thrusters. This technique of introducing small corrections into a missile's flight path by slightly altering the force vector of its engines is known as thrust-vector control.

Thrust-vector control

A second complication occurs during reentry to the atmosphere, when the unpowered RV is subject to relatively unpredictable forces such as wind. Guidance systems have had to be designed to accommodate these difficulties.

Errors in accuracy for ballistic missiles (and for cruise missiles as well) are generally expressed as launch-point errors, guidance/en-route errors, or aim-point errors. Both launch- and aim-point errors can be corrected by surveying the launch and target areas more accurately. Guidance/en-route errors, on the other hand, must be corrected by improving the missile's design—particularly its guidance. Guidance/en-route errors are usually measured by a missile's circular error of probability (CEP) and bias. CEP uses the mean point of impact of missile test firings, usually taken at maximum range, to calculate the radius of a circle that would take in 50 percent of the impact points. Bias measures the deviation of the mean impact point from the actual aim point. An accurate missile has both a low CEP and low bias.

The V-2. The precursor of modern ballistic missiles was the German V-2, a single-stage, fin-stabilized missile propelled by liquid oxygen and ethyl alcohol to a maximum range of about 200 miles (see Figure 20). The V-2 was officially designated the A-4, being derived from the fourth of the *Aggregat* series of experiments conducted at Kummersdorf and Peenemunde under General Walter Dornberger and the civilian scientist Wernher von Braun.

The most difficult technical problem facing the V-2 was achieving maximum range. An inclined launch ramp was normally used to give missiles maximum range, but this could not be used with the V-2 because the missile was quite heavy at lift-off (more than 12 tons) and would not be traveling fast enough to sustain anything approaching horizontal flight. Also, as the rocket used up its fuel its weight (and velocity) would change, and this had to be allowed for in the aiming. For these reasons the V-2 had to be launched straight up and then had to change to the flight angle that would give it maximum range. The Germans calculated this angle to be slightly less than 50°.

Early problems in flight control

The change in direction mandated some sort of pitch control during flight, and, because a change in pitch would induce yaw, control was needed on the yaw axis too. Added to these problems was the natural tendency of a cylinder to rotate. Thus, the V-2 (and every ballistic missile afterward) needed a guidance and control system to deal with in-flight rolling, pitching, and yawing. Using three-axis autopilots adapted from German aircraft, the V-2 was controlled by large vertical fins and smaller stabilizing surfaces to dampen roll and by vanes attached to the horizontal fins to modify pitch and yaw. Vanes were also installed in the exhaust nozzle for thrust vector control.

A combination of in-flight weight changes and changes in atmospheric conditions presented additional problems. Even over the fairly limited course of a V-2 trajectory (with a range of approximately 200 miles and an altitude of roughly 50 miles), changes in missile velocity and air density produced drastic shifts in the distance between the centre of gravity and the centre of aerodynamic pressure.

This meant the guidance system had to adjust its input to the control surfaces as the flight proceeded. As a result, V-2 accuracy never ceased to be a problem for the Germans.

Still, the missile caused a great deal of damage. The first V-2 used in combat was fired against Paris on Sept. 6, 1944. Two days later the first of more than 1,000 missiles was fired against London. By the end of the war 4,000 of these missiles had been launched from mobile bases against Allied targets. During February and March 1945, only weeks before the war in Europe ended, an average of 60 missiles was launched weekly. The V-2 killed an estimated five persons per launch (versus slightly more than two per launch for the V-1). Three major factors contributed to this difference. First, the V-2 warhead weighed more than 1,600 pounds (725 kilograms). Second, several V-2 attacks killed more than 100 people. Finally, there was no known defense against the V-2; it could not be intercepted and, traveling faster than sound, it arrived unexpectedly. The V-2 threat was eliminated only by bombing the launch sites and forcing the German army to retreat beyond missile range.

The V-2 obviously ushered in a new age of military technology. After the war there was intense competition between the United States and the Soviet Union to obtain these new missiles, as well as to obtain the German scientists who had developed them. The United States succeeded in capturing both Dornberger and von Braun as well as more than 60 V-2s; it was not revealed precisely what (or whom) the Soviets captured. However, given the relative immaturity of ballistic missile technology at that time, neither country achieved usable ballistic missiles for some time. During the late 1940s and early 1950s most of the nuclear competition between the two countries dealt with strategic bombers. Events in 1957 reshaped this contest.

The first ICBMs. In 1957 the Soviets launched a multistage ballistic missile (later given the NATO designation SS-6 Sapwood) as well as the first man-made satellite, Sputnik. This prompted the "missile gap" debate in the United States and resulted in higher priorities for the U.S. Thor and Jupiter IRBMs. Although originally scheduled for deployment in the early 1960s, these programs were accelerated, with Thor being deployed to England and Jupiter to Italy and Turkey in 1958. Thor and Jupiter were both single-stage, liquid-fueled missiles with inertial guidance systems and warheads of 1.5 megatons. Political difficulties in deploying these missiles on foreign soil prompted the United States to develop ICBMs, so that by late 1963 Thor and Jupiter had been terminated. (The missiles themselves were used extensively in the space program.)

Thor and Jupiter

The Soviet SS-6 system was an apparent failure. Given its limited range (less than 3,500 miles), it had to be launched from northern latitudes in order to reach the United

Bilderdienst im Suddeutschen Verlag

Figure 20: *German V-2 missile being erected for launch.* This "Vengeance Weapon" of World War II, which struck cities 200 miles away, was the precursor of modern ballistic missiles.

States. The severe weather conditions at these launch facilities (Novaya Zemlya and the Arctic mainland bases of Norilsk and Vorkuta) seriously degraded operational effectiveness; pumps for liquid propellants froze, metal fatigue was extreme, and lubrication of moving parts was nearly impossible. In 1960 a missile engine exploded during a test, killing Mitrofan Ivanovich Nedelin, chief of the Strategic Rocket Forces, and several hundred observers.

Possibly as a result of these technical failures (and possibly in response to the deployment of Thor and Jupiter), the Soviets attempted to base the SS-4 Sandal, an IRBM with a one-megaton warhead and a range of 900–1,000 miles, closer to the United States and in a warmer climate. This precipitated the Cuban missile crisis of 1962, after which the SS-4 was withdrawn to Central Asia. (It was unclear whether the United States' deactivation of Thor and Jupiter was a condition of this withdrawal.)

In the meantime, the United States was developing operational ICBMs to be based on U.S. territory. The first versions were the Atlas and the Titan I. The Atlas-D (the first version deployed) had a liquid-fueled engine that generated 360,000 pounds of thrust. The missile was radio-inertial guided, launched above ground, and had a range of 7,500 miles. The follow-on Atlas-E/F increased thrust to 390,000 pounds, used all-inertial guidance, and moved from an aboveground to horizontal canister launch in the E and, finally, to silo-stored vertical launch in the F. The Atlas E carried a two-megaton, and the Atlas F a four-megaton, warhead. The Titan I was a two-stage, liquid-fueled, radio-inertial guided, silo-launched ICBM carrying a four-megaton warhead and capable of traveling 6,300 miles. Both systems became operational in 1959.

From liquid to solid fuel. This first generation of missiles was typified by its liquid fuel, which required both a propellant and an oxidizer for ignition as well as a complex (and heavy) system of pumps. The early liquid fuels were quite dangerous, difficult to store, and time-consuming to load. For example, Atlas and Titan used so-called cryogenic (hypercold) fuels that had to be stored and handled at very low temperatures (−422° F [−252° C] for liquid hydrogen). These propellants had to be stored outside the rocket and pumped aboard just before launch, consuming more than an hour.

As each superpower produced, or was thought to produce, more ICBMs, military commanders became concerned about the relatively slow reaction times of their own ICBMs. The first step toward "rapid reaction" was the rapid loading of liquid fuels. Using improved pumps, the reaction time of the Titan I was reduced from over one hour to less than 20 minutes. Then, with a second generation of storable liquids that could be kept loaded in the missile, reaction time was reduced to approximately one minute. Examples of second-generation storable-liquid missiles were the Soviet SS-7 Saddler and SS-8 Sasin (the latter deployed in 1963) and the U.S. Titan II. The Titan II was the largest ballistic missile ever developed by the United States. This two-stage ICBM was more than 100 feet long and 10 feet in diameter. Weighing more than 325,000 pounds at launch, it delivered its single warhead (with a throw weight of about 8,000 pounds) to a range of 9,000 miles and with a CEP of about one mile.

Storable liquids

In about 1964 China began developing a series of liquid-fueled IRBMs given the NATO designation CSS, for Chinese surface-to-surface missile. (The Chinese named the series Dong Feng, meaning "East Wind.") The CSS-1 carried a 20-kiloton warhead to a range of 600 miles. The CSS-2, entering service in 1970, was fueled by storable liquids; it had a range of 1,500 miles and carried a one- to two-megaton warhead. With the two-stage CSS-3 (active from 1978) and the CSS-4 (active from 1980), the Chinese reached ICBM ranges of over 4,000 and 7,000 miles, respectively. The CSS-4 carried a warhead of four to five megatons.

Because storable liquids did not alleviate the dangers inherent in liquid fuels, and because the flight times of missiles flying between the United States and the Soviet Union shrank to less than 35 minutes from launch to impact, still faster reactions were sought with even safer fuels. This led to a third generation of missiles, powered by solid propellants. Solid propellants were, eventually, easier to make, safer to store, lighter in weight (because they did not require on-board pumps), and more reliable than their liquid predecessors. Here the oxidizer and propellant were mixed into a canister and kept loaded aboard the missile, so that reaction times were reduced to seconds. However, solid fuels were not without their complications. First, while it was possible with liquid fuels to adjust in flight the amount of thrust provided by the engine, rocket engines using solid fuel could not be throttled. Also, some early solid fuels had uneven ignition, producing surges or abrupt velocity changes that could disrupt or severely confound guidance systems.

The first solid-fueled U.S. system was the Minuteman I. This ICBM, conceived originally as a rail-mobile system, was deployed in silos in 1962, became operational the following year, and was phased out by 1973. The first Soviet solid-fueled ICBM was the SS-13 Savage, which became operational in 1969. This missile could carry a 750-kiloton warhead more than 5,000 miles. Because the Soviet Union deployed several other liquid-fueled ICBMs between 1962 and 1969, Western specialists speculated that the Soviets experienced engineering difficulties in producing solid propellants.

The French deployed the first of their solid-fueled S-2 missiles in 1971. These two-stage IRBMs carried a 150-kiloton warhead and had a range of 1,800 miles. The S-3, deployed in 1980, could carry a one-megaton warhead to a range of 2,100 miles.

The first SLBMs. Simultaneous with the early Soviet and U.S. efforts to produce land-based ICBMs, both countries were developing SLBMs. In 1955 the Soviets launched the first SLBM, the one- to two-megaton SS-N-4 Sark. This missile, deployed in 1958 aboard diesel-electric submarines and later aboard nuclear-powered vessels, had to be launched from the surface and had a range of only 350 miles. Partly in response to this deployment, the United States gave priority to its Polaris program, which became operational in 1960. Each Polaris A-1 carried a warhead of one megaton and had a range of 1,400 miles. The Polaris A-2, deployed in 1962, had a range of 1,700 miles and also carried a one-megaton warhead. The U.S. systems were solid-fueled, whereas the Soviets initially used storable liquids. The first Soviet solid-fueled SLBM was the SS-N-17 Snipe, deployed in 1978 with a range of 2,400 miles and a 500-kiloton warhead.

Polaris

Beginning in 1971, France deployed a series of solid-fueled SLBMs comprising the M-1, M-2 (1974), and M-20 (1977). The M-20, with a range of 1,800 miles, carried a one-megaton warhead. In the 1980s the Chinese fielded the two-stage, solid-fueled CSS-N-3 SLBM, which had a range of 1,700 miles and carried a two-megaton warhead.

Multiple warheads. By the early 1970s, several technologies were maturing that would produce a new wave of ICBMs. First, thermonuclear warheads, much lighter than the earlier atomic devices, had been incorporated into ICBMs by 1970. Second, the ability to launch larger throw weights, achieved especially by the Soviets, allowed designers to contemplate adding multiple warheads to each ballistic missile. Finally, improved and much lighter electronics translated into more accurate guidance.

The first steps toward incorporating these technologies came with multiple warheads, or multiple reentry vehicles (MRVs), and the Fractional Orbital Bombardment System (FOBS). The Soviets introduced both of these capabilities with the SS-9 Scarp, the first "heavy" missile, beginning in 1967. FOBS was based on a low-trajectory launch that would be fired in the opposite direction from the target and would achieve only partial earth orbit. With this method of delivery, it would be quite difficult to determine which target was being threatened. However, given the shallow reentry angles associated with a low trajectory and partial earth orbit, the accuracy of FOBS missiles was questionable. A missile carrying MRVs, on the other hand, would be launched toward the target in a high ballistic trajectory. Several warheads from the same missile would strike the same target, increasing the probability of killing that target, or individual warheads would strike separate targets within a very narrow ballistic "footprint."

(The footprint of a missile is that area which is feasible for targeting, given the characteristics of the reentry vehicle.) The SS-9, model 4, and the SS-11 Sego, model 3, both had three MRVs and ballistic footprints equal to the dimensions of a U.S. Minuteman complex. The only instance in which the United States incorporated MRVs was with the Polaris A-3, which, after deployment in 1964, carried three 200-kiloton warheads a distance of 2,800 miles. In 1967 the British adapted their own warheads to the A-3, and beginning in 1982 they upgraded the system to the A3TK, which contained penetration aids (chaff, decoys, and jammers) designed to foil ballistic missile defenses around Moscow.

MIRVs   Soon after adopting MRVs the United States took the next technological step, introducing multiple independently targetable reentry vehicles (MIRVs). Unlike MRVs, independently targeted RVs could be released to strike widely separated targets, essentially expanding the footprint established by a missile's original ballistic trajectory. This demanded the capacity to maneuver before releasing the warheads, and maneuvering was provided by a structure in the front end of the missile called the "bus," which contained the RVs. The bus was essentially a final, guided stage of the missile (usually the fourth), that now had to be considered part of the missile's payload. Since any bus capable of maneuvering would take up weight, MIRVed systems would have to carry warheads of lower yield. This in turn meant that the RVs would have to be released on their ballistic paths with great accuracy. As stated above, solid-fueled motors could be neither throttled nor shut down and restarted; for this reason, liquid-fueled buses were developed for making the necessary course corrections. The typical flight profile for a MIRVed ICBM then became approximately 300 seconds of solid-rocket boost and 200 seconds of bus maneuvering to place the warheads on independent ballistic trajectories.

The first MIRVed system was the U.S. Minuteman III. Deployed in 1970, this three-stage, solid-fueled ICBM carried three MIRVs of an estimated 170 to 335 kilotons. The warheads had a range of 8,000 miles with CEPs of 725–925 feet. Beginning in 1970 the United States also MIRVed its SLBM force with the Poseidon C-3, which could deliver up to 14 50-kiloton RVs to a range of 2,800 miles and with a CEP of about 1,450 feet. After 1979 this force was upgraded with the Trident C-4, or Trident I, which could deliver eight 100-kiloton MIRVs with the same accuracy as the Poseidon, but to a distance of 4,600 miles. Much longer range was made possible in the Trident by adding a third stage, by replacing aluminum with lighter graphite epoxies, and by adding an "aerospike" to the nose cone that, extending after launch, produced the streamlining effect of a pointed design while allowing the larger volume of a blunt design. Accuracy was maintained by updating the missile's inertial guidance during bus maneuvering with stellar navigation.

By 1978 the Soviet Union had fielded its first MIRVed SLBM, the SS-N-18 Stingray. This liquid-fueled missile could deliver three or five 500-kiloton warheads to a distance of 4,000 miles, with a CEP of about 3,000 feet. On land in the mid-1970s, the Soviets deployed three MIRVed, liquid-fueled ICBM systems, all with ranges exceeding 6,000 miles and with CEPs of 1,000 to 1,500 feet: the SS-17 Spanker, with four 750-kiloton warheads; the SS-18 Satan, with up to 10 500-kiloton warheads; and the SS-19 Stiletto, with six 550-kiloton warheads. Each of these Soviet systems had several versions that traded multiple warheads for higher yield. For instance, the SS-18, model 3, carried a single 20-megaton warhead. This giant missile, which replaced the SS-9 in the latter's silos, had about the same dimensions as the Titan II, but its throw weight of more than 16,000 pounds was twice that of the U.S. system.

Beginning in 1985, France upgraded its SLBM force with the M-4, a three-stage MIRVed missile capable of carrying six 150-kiloton warheads to ranges of 3,600 miles.

MX Peace-keeper   A second generation of MIRVed U.S. systems was represented by the Peacekeeper. Known as the MX during its 15-year development phase before entering service in 1986, this three-stage ICBM carried 10 300-kiloton war-

heads and had a range of 7,000 miles. Originally designed to be based on mobile railroad or wheeled launchers, the Peacekeeper was eventually housed in Minuteman silos. A second-generation MIRVed SLBM of the 1990s was the Trident D-5, or Trident II. Even though it was one-third again as long as its predecessor and had twice the throw weight, the D-5 could deliver 10 475-kiloton warheads to a range of 7,000 miles. Both the Trident D-5 and Peacekeeper represented a radical advance in accuracy, having CEPs of only 400 feet. The improved accuracy of the Peacekeeper was due to a refinement in the inertial guidance system, which housed the gyros and accelerometers in a floating-ball device, and to the use of an exterior celestial navigation system that updated the missile's position by reference to stars or satellites. The Trident D-5 also contained a star sensor and satellite navigator. This gave it several times the accuracy of the C-4 at more than twice the range.

Within the generally less-advanced guidance technology of the Soviet Union, an equally radical advance came with the solid-fueled SS-24 Scalpel and SS-25 Sickle ICBMs, deployed in 1987 and 1985, respectively. The SS-24 could carry eight or 10 MIRVed warheads of 100 kilotons, and the SS-25 was fitted with a single 550-kiloton RV. Both missiles had a CEP of 650 feet. In addition to their accuracy, these ICBMs represented a new generation in basing mode. The SS-24 was launched from railroad cars, while the SS-25 was carried on wheeled launchers that shuttled between concealed launch sites. As mobile-based systems, they were long-range descendants of the SS-20 Saber, an IRBM carried on mobile launchers that entered service in 1977, partly along the border with China and partly facing western Europe. That two-stage, solid-fueled missile could deliver three 150-kiloton warheads a distance of 3,000 miles with a CEP of 1,300 feet. It was phased out after the signing of the Intermediate-Range Nuclear Forces (INF) Treaty in 1987.

Ballistic missile defense. Although ballistic missiles followed a predictable flight path, defense against them was long thought to be technically impossible because their RVs were small and traveled at great speeds. Nevertheless, in the late 1960s the United States and Soviet Union pursued layered antiballistic missile (ABM) systems that combined a high-altitude interceptor missile (the U.S. Spartan and Soviet Galosh) with a terminal-phase interceptor (the U.S. Sprint and Soviet Gazelle). All systems were nuclear-armed. Such systems were subsequently limited by the Treaty on Anti-Ballistic Missile Systems of 1972, under a protocol in which each side was allowed one ABM location with 100 interceptor missiles each. The Soviet system, around Moscow, remained active and was upgraded in the 1980s, whereas the U.S. system was deactivated in 1976. Still, given the potential for renewed or surreptitious ballistic missile defenses, all countries incorporated penetration aids along with warheads in their missiles' payloads. MIRVs were also used to overcome missile defenses.

Maneuverable warheads. Even after updating a missile's guidance with stellar or satellite references, disturbances in final descent could throw a warhead off course. Also, given the advances in ballistic missile defenses that were achieved even after the ABM treaty was signed, RVs remained vulnerable. Two technologies offered possible means of overcoming these difficulties. Maneuvering warheads, or MaRVs, were first integrated into the U.S. Pershing II IRBMs deployed in Europe from 1984 until they were dismantled under the terms of the INF Treaty. The warhead of the Pershing II contained a radar area guidance (Radag) system that compared the terrain toward which it descended with information stored in a self-contained computer. The Radag system then issued commands to control fins that adjusted the glide of the warhead. Such terminal-phase corrections gave the Pershing II, with a range of 1,100 miles, a CEP of 150 feet. The improved accuracy allowed the missile to carry a low-yield 15-kiloton warhead.

Pershing II and Radag guidance

MaRVs would present ABM systems with a shifting, rather than ballistic, path, making interception quite difficult. Another technology, precision-guided warheads, or

PGRVs, would actively seek a target, then, using flight controls, actually "fly out" reentry errors. This could yield such accuracy that nuclear warheads could be replaced by conventional explosives.

Cruise missiles. The single most important difference between ballistic missiles and cruise missiles is that the latter operate within the atmosphere. This presents both advantages and disadvantages. One advantage of atmospheric flight is that traditional methods of flight control (*e.g.,* airfoil wings for aerodynamic lift, rudder and elevator flaps for directional and vertical control) are readily available from the technologies of manned aircraft. Also, while strategic early-warning systems can immediately detect the launch of ballistic missiles, low-flying cruise missiles presenting small radar and infrared cross sections offer a means of slipping past these air-defense screens.

The principal disadvantage of atmospheric flight centres around the fuel requirements of a missile that must be powered continuously for strategic distances. Some tactical-range antiship cruise missiles such as the U.S. Harpoon and the Soviet SS-N-19 Shipwreck have been powered by turbojet engines, and even some non-cruise missiles such as the Soviet SA-6 Gainful surface-to-air missile have used ramjets to reach supersonic speed, but at ranges of 1,000 miles or more these engines would require huge amounts of fuel. This in turn would require a larger missile, which would approach a manned jet aircraft in size and would thereby lose the unique ability to evade enemy defenses. This problem of maintaining balance between range, size, and fuel consumption was not solved until reliable, fuel-efficient turbofan engines were made small enough to propel a missile of radar-evading size.

The problem of guidance

As with ballistic missiles, guidance has been a long-standing problem in cruise missile development. Tactical cruise missiles generally use radio or inertial guidance to reach the general vicinity of their targets and then home onto the targets with various radar or infrared mechanisms. Radio guidance, however, is subject to line-of-sight range limitations, and inaccuracies tend to arise in inertial systems over the long flight times required of strategic cruise missiles. Radar and infrared homing devices, moreover, can be jammed or spoofed. Adequate long-range guidance for cruise missiles was not available until inertial systems were designed that could be updated periodically by self-contained electronic map-matching devices.

Beginning in the 1950s, the Soviet Union pioneered the development of tactical air- and sea-launched cruise missiles, and in 1984 a strategic cruise missile given the NATO designation AS-15 Kent became operational aboard Tu-95 bombers. But Soviet programs have been so cloaked in secrecy that the following account of the development of cruise missiles focuses by necessity on U.S. programs.

The V-1. The first practical cruise missile was the German V-1 of World War II, which was powered by a pulse jet that used a cycling flutter valve to regulate the air and fuel mixture. Since the pulse jet required airflow for ignition, it could not operate below 150 miles per hour. Therefore, a ground catapult boosted the V-1 to 200 miles per hour, at which time the pulse-jet engine was ignited. Once ignited, it could attain speeds of 400 miles per hour and ranges exceeding 150 miles. Course control was accomplished by a combined air-driven gyroscope and magnetic compass, and altitude was controlled by a simple barometric altimeter; as a consequence, the V-1 was subject to heading, or azimuth, errors resulting from gyro drift, and it had to be operated at fairly high altitudes (usually above 2,000 feet) to compensate for altitude errors caused by differences in atmospheric pressure along the route of flight.

The missile was armed in flight by a small propeller that, after a specified number of turns, activated the warhead at a safe distance from the launch. As the V-1 approached its target, the control vanes were inactivated and a rear-mounted spoiler, or drag device, deployed, pitching the missile nose-down toward the target. This usually interrupted the fuel supply, causing the engine to quit, and the weapon detonated upon impact.

Because of the rather crude method of calculating the impact point by the number of revolutions of a small propeller, the Germans could not use the V-1 as a precision weapon, nor could they determine the actual impact point in order to make course corrections for subsequent flights. In fact, the British publicized inaccurate information on impact points, causing the Germans to adjust their pre-flight calculations erroneously. As a result, V-1s often fell well short of their intended targets.

Following the war there was considerable interest in cruise missiles. Between 1945 and 1948, the United States began approximately 50 independent cruise missile projects, but lack of funding gradually reduced that number to three by 1948. These three—Snark, Navaho, and Matador—provided the necessary technical groundwork for the first truly successful strategic cruise missiles, which entered service in the 1980s.

Snark. The Snark was an air force program begun in 1945 to produce a subsonic (600-mile-per-hour) cruise missile capable of delivering a 2,000-pound atomic or conventional warhead to a range of 5,000 miles, with a CEP of less than 1.75 miles. Initially, the Snark used a turbojet engine and an inertial navigation system, with a complementary stellar navigation monitor to provide intercontinental range. By 1950, due to the yield requirements of atomic warheads, the design payload had changed to 5,000 pounds, accuracy requirements shrank the CEP to 1,500 feet, and range increased to more than 6,200 miles. These design changes forced the military to cancel the first Snark program in favour of a "Super Snark," or Snark II.

Control and propulsion problems with the Snark

The Snark II incorporated a new jet engine that was later used in the B-52 bomber and KC-135A aerial tanker operated by the Strategic Air Command. Although this engine design was to prove quite reliable in manned aircraft, other problems—in particular, those associated with flight dynamics—continued to plague the missile. The Snark lacked a horizontal tail surface, it used elevons instead of ailerons and elevators for attitude and directional control, and it had an extremely small vertical tail surface. These inadequate control surfaces, and the relatively slow (or sometimes nonexistent) ignition of the jet engine, contributed significantly to the missile's difficulties in flight tests—to a point where the coastal waters off the test site at Cape Canaveral, Fla., were often referred to as "Snark-infested waters." Flight control was not the least of the Snark's problems: unpredictable fuel consumption also resulted in embarrassing moments. One 1956 flight test appeared amazingly successful at the outset, but the engine failed to shut off and the missile was last seen "heading toward the Amazon." (The vehicle was found in 1982 by a Brazilian farmer.)

Considering the less than dramatic successes in the test program, the Snark, as well as other cruise missile programs, probably would have been destined for cancellation had it not been for two developments. First, antiaircraft defenses had improved to a point where bombers could no longer reach their targets with the usual high-altitude flight paths. Second, thermonuclear weapons were beginning to arrive in military inventories, and these lighter, higher-yield devices allowed designers to relax CEP constraints. As a result, an improved Snark was deployed in the late 1950s at two bases in Maine and Florida.

The new missile, however, continued to exhibit the unreliabilities and inaccuracies typical of earlier models. On a series of flight tests, the Snark's CEP was estimated to average 20 miles, with the most accurate flight striking 4.2 miles left and 1,600 feet short. This "successful" flight was the only one to reach the target area at all and was one of only two to go beyond 4,400 miles. Accumulated test data showed that the Snark had a 33-percent chance of successful launch and a 10-percent chance of achieving the required distance. As a consequence, the two Snark units were deactivated in 1961.

Navaho. The second postwar U.S. cruise missile effort was the Navaho, an intercontinental supersonic design. Unlike earlier efforts, which were extrapolated from V-1 engineering, the Navaho was based on the V-2; the basic V-2 structure was fitted with new control surfaces, and the rocket engine was replaced by a turbojet/ramjet combination. Known by a variety of names, the Navaho emerged into a missile more than 70 feet long, with canard fins

(*i.e.*, control surfaces set forward of the wing), a V tail, and a large delta wing. (These flight control designs would eventually make their way onto other supersonic aircraft, such as the experimental XB-70 Valkyrie bomber, several fighter planes, and the supersonic transport.)

With the exception of technologies associated with supersonic lift and control, few other aspects of the Navaho met designers' expectations. Most frustrating were difficulties with the ramjet engine, which was necessary for sustained supersonic flight. For a variety of reasons, including interrupted fuel flow, turbulence in the ramjet cavity, and clogging of the ramjet fire-ring, few of the engines ignited. This led engineers to label the project "Never Go, Navaho"—a name that stuck until the program was cancelled in 1958 after achieving only 1½ hours airborne. No missile was ever deployed.

Technologies explored in the Navaho program, besides those of flight dynamics, were used in other areas. Derivatives of the missile's titanium alloys, which were developed to accommodate surface temperatures at supersonic speed, came to be used on most high-performance aircraft. The rocket booster (which launched the missile until the ramjet ignited) eventually became the Redstone engine, which powered the Mercury manned spacecraft series, and the same basic design was used in the Thor and Atlas ballistic missiles. The guidance system, an inertial autonavigation design, was incorporated into a later cruise missile (Hound Dog) and was used by the nuclear submarine USS *Nautilus* for its under-the-ice passage of the North Pole in 1958.

Matador and other programs. The third postwar U.S. cruise missile effort was the Matador, a ground-launched, subsonic missile designed to carry a 3,000-pound warhead to a range of more than 600 miles. In its early development, Matador's radio-controlled guidance, which was limited essentially to the line of sight between the ground controller and the missile, covered less than the missile's potential range. However, in 1954 an automatic terrain recognition and guidance (Atran) system was added (and the missile system was subsequently designated Mace). Atran, which used radar map-matching for both en-route and terminal guidance, represented a major breakthrough in accuracy, a problem long associated with cruise missiles. The low availability of radar maps, especially of areas in the Soviet Union (the logical target area), limited operational use, however. Nonetheless, operational deployments began in 1954 to Europe and in 1959 to Korea. The missile was phased out in 1962,

Atran
guidance:
a major
break-
through

its most serious problems being associated with guidance.

While the U.S. Air Force was exploring the Snark, Navaho, and Matador programs, the navy was pursuing related technologies. The Regulus, which was closely akin to the Matador (having the same engine and roughly the same configuration), became operational in 1955 as a subsonic missile launched from both submarines and surface vessels, carrying a 3.8-megaton warhead. Decommissioned in 1959, the Regulus did not represent much of an improvement over the V-1.

A follow-on design, Regulus II, was pursued briefly, striving for supersonic speed. However, the navy's preference for the new large, angle-deck nuclear aircraft carriers and for ballistic missile submarines relegated sea-launched cruise missiles to relative obscurity. Another project, the Triton, was similarly bypassed due to design difficulties and lack of funding. The Triton was to have had a range of 12,000 miles and a payload of 1,500 pounds. Radar map-matching guidance was to have given it a CEP of 1,800 feet.

In the early 1960s the Air Force produced and deployed the Hound Dog cruise missile on B-52 bombers. This supersonic missile was powered by a turbojet engine to a range of 400–450 miles. It used the guidance system of the earlier Navaho. The missile was so large, however, that only two could be carried on the outside of the aircraft. This external carriage allowed B-52 crew members to use the Hound Dog engines for extra thrust on takeoff, but the extra drag associated with the carriage, as well as the additional weight (20,000 pounds), meant a net loss of range for the aircraft. By 1976 the Hound Dog had given way to the short-range attack missile, or SRAM, essentially an internally carried, air-launched ballistic missile.

ALCM, SLCM, and GLCM. By 1972, constraints placed on ballistic missiles by the SALT I treaty prompted U.S. nuclear strategists to think again about using cruise missiles. There was also concern over Soviet advances in antiship cruise missile technology, and in Vietnam remotely piloted vehicles had demonstrated considerable reliability in gathering intelligence information over previously inaccessible, highly defended areas. Improvements in electronics—in particular, microcircuits, solid-state memory, and computer processing—presented inexpensive, lightweight, and highly reliable methods of solving the persistent problems of guidance and control. Perhaps most important, terrain contour mapping, or Tercom, techniques, derived from the earlier Atran, offered excellent en route and terminal-area accuracy.

Tercom
guidance:
the prob-
lem solved

From L. Freedman, *Atlas of Global Strategy*, copyright © Equinox (Oxford) Ltd 1985

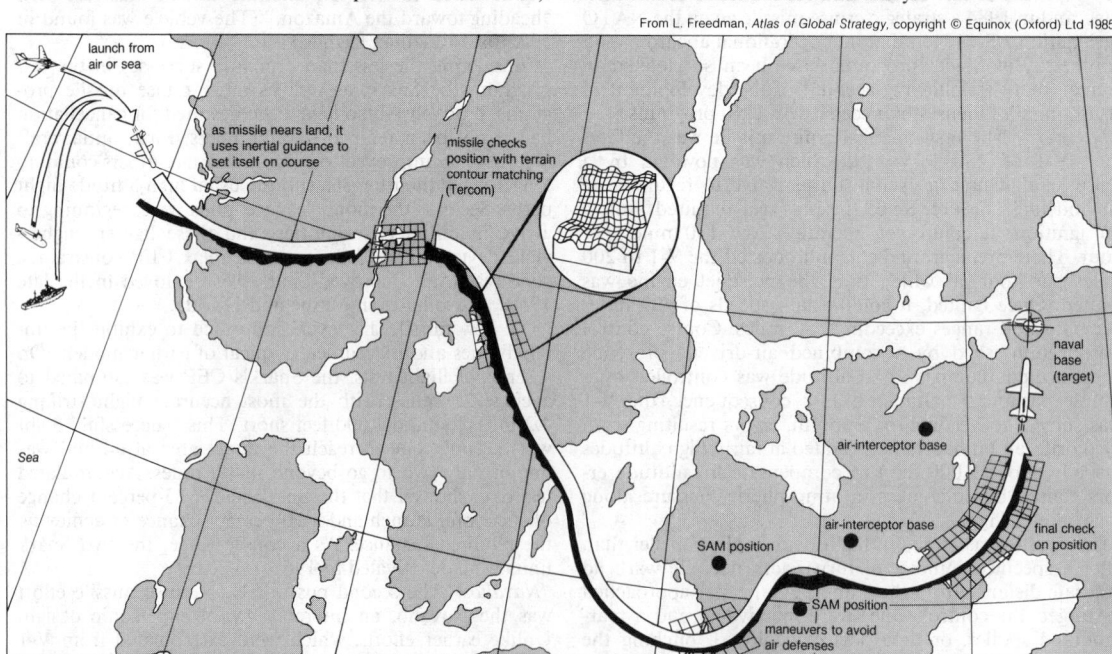

Figure 21: *Flight path of a cruise missile.*
Limited to subsonic speeds, the missile would rely on its small size and ground-hugging flight profile to evade detection. U.S. cruise missiles, guided by a digitalized map of the terrain along their routes, could strike their targets with a nuclear warhead after being launched from 1,500 miles away.

Tercom used a radar or photographic image from which a digitalized contour map was produced. At selected points in the flight known as Tercom checkpoints, the guidance system would match a radar image of the missile's current position with the programmed digital image, making corrections to the missile's flight path in order to place it on the correct course. Between Tercom checkpoints, the missile would be guided by an advanced inertial system; this would eliminate the need for constant radar emissions, which would make electronic detection extremely difficult. As the flight progressed, the size of the radar map would be reduced, improving accuracy. In practice, Tercom brought the CEP of modern cruise missiles down to less than 150 feet (see Figure 21).

Improvements in engine design also made cruise missiles more practical. In 1967 the Williams International Corporation produced a small turbofan engine (12 inches in diameter, 24 inches long) that weighed less than 70 pounds and produced more than 400 pounds of thrust. New fuel mixtures offered more than 30-percent increases in fuel energy, which translated directly into extended range.

By the end of the Vietnam War, both the U.S. Navy and Air Force had cruise missile projects under way. At 19 feet three inches, the navy's sea-launched cruise missile (SLCM; eventually designated the Tomahawk) was 30 inches shorter than the air force's air-launched cruise missile (ALCM), but system components were quite similar and often from the same manufacturer (both missiles used the Williams engine and the McDonnell Douglas Corporation's Tercom). The Boeing Company produced the ALCM, while the General Dynamics Corporation produced the SLCM as well as the ground-launched cruise missile, or GLCM. The SLCM and GLCM were essentially the same configuration, differing only in their basing mode. The GLCM was designed to be launched from wheeled transporter-erector-launchers, while the SLCM was expelled from submarine tubes to the ocean surface in steel canisters or launched directly from armoured box launchers aboard surface ships. Both the SLCM and GLCM were propelled from their launchers or canisters by a solid-rocket booster, which dropped off after the wings and tail fins flipped out and the jet engine ignited. The ALCM, being dropped from a bomb-bay dispenser or wing pylon of a flying B-52 or B-1 bomber, did not require rocket boosting.

As finally deployed, the U.S. cruise missiles were intermediate-range weapons that flew at an altitude of 100 feet to a range of 1,500 miles. The SLCM was produced in three versions: a tactical-range (275-mile) antiship missile, with a combination of inertial guidance and active radar homing and with a high-explosive warhead; and two intermediate-range land-attack versions, with combined inertial and Tercom guidance and with either a high-explosive or a 200-kiloton nuclear warhead. The ALCM carried the same nuclear warhead as the SLCM, while the GLCM carried a low-yield warhead of 10 to 50 kilotons.

The ALCM entered service in 1982 and the SLCM in 1984. The GLCM was first deployed to Europe in 1983, but all GLCMs were dismantled after the signing of the INF Treaty.

Although their small size and low flight paths made the ALCM and SLCM difficult to detect by radar (the ALCM presented a radar cross section only one one-thousandth that of the B-52 bomber), their subsonic speed of about 500 miles per hour made them vulnerable to air defenses once they were detected. For this reason, the U.S. Air Force began production of an advanced cruise missile, which would incorporate stealth technologies such as radar-absorbent materials and smooth, nonreflective surface shapes. The advanced cruise missile would have a range of over 1,800 miles.　　(STEPHEN OLIVER FOUGHT)

Mozart

Wolfgang Amadeus Mozart is widely recognized as one of the greatest composers in the history of Western music. With Haydn and Beethoven he brought to its height the achievement of the Viennese Classical school. Unlike any other composer in musical history, he wrote in all the musical genres of his day and excelled in every one. His taste, his command of form, and his range of expression entitle him to be considered the most universal of all composers.

Early life and works. Mozart was born in Salzburg, now in Austria, then in church lands, on Jan. 27, 1756. Although baptized Joannes Chrysostomus Wolfgangus Theophilus, he most commonly called himself Wolfgang Amadè or Wolfgang Gottlieb. His father, Leopold, came from a family of good standing, which included architects and bookbinders, and was the author of a famous violin-playing manual; his mother, Anna Maria Pertl, was born of a middle-class family active in local administration. Mozart and his sister Maria Anna ("Nannerl") were the only two of their seven children to survive.

The boy's early talent for music was remarkable. At three he was picking out chords on the harpsichord, at four playing short pieces, at five composing. There are anecdotes about his precise memory of pitch, about his scribbling a concerto at the age of five, and about his gentleness and sensitivity (he was afraid of the trumpet). Just before he was six, his father took him and Nannerl, also highly talented, to Munich to play at the Bavarian court, and a few months later they went to Vienna and were heard at the imperial court and in noble houses.

"The miracle which God let be born in Salzburg" was Leopold's description of his son, and he was keenly conscious of his duty to God, as he saw it, to draw the miracle to the notice of the world (and incidentally to

By courtesy of the Internationale Stiftung Mozarteum, Salzburg, Austria

Mozart, unfinished oil portrait by Joseph Lange, 1789. In the Internationale Stiftung Mozarteum, Salzburg, Austria.

profit from doing so). In mid-1763 he obtained a leave of absence from his position as deputy Kapellmeister at the prince-archbishop's court at Salzburg, and the family set out on a prolonged tour. They went to what were all the main musical centres of western Europe—Munich, Augsburg, Stuttgart, Mannheim, Mainz, Frankfurt, Brussels, and Paris (where they remained for the winter), then

First European tour

London (where they spent 15 months), returning through The Hague, Amsterdam, Paris, Lyon, and Switzerland, and arriving back in Salzburg in November 1766. In most of these cities Mozart, and often his sister, played and improvised, sometimes at court, sometimes in public or in a church. Leopold's surviving letters to friends in Salzburg tell of the universal admiration that his son's achievements aroused. In Paris they met several German composers, and Mozart's first music was published (sonatas for keyboard and violin, dedicated to a royal princess); in London they met, among others, Johann Christian Bach, Johann Sebastian Bach's youngest son and a leading figure in the city's musical life, and under his influence Mozart composed his first symphonies—three survive (K 16, K 19, and K 19a—K signifying the work's place in the catalog of Ludwig von Köchel). Two more followed during a stay in The Hague on the return journey (K 22 and K 45a).

After little more than nine months in Salzburg the Mozarts set out for Vienna in September 1767, where (apart from a 10-week break during a smallpox epidemic) they spent 15 months. Mozart wrote a one-act German singspiel, *Bastien und Bastienne,* which was given privately. Greater hopes were attached to his prospect of having an Italian opera buffa, *La finta semplice* ("The Feigned Simpleton"), done at the court theatre—hopes that were, however, frustrated, much to Leopold's indignation. But a substantial, festal mass setting (probably K 139/47a) was successfully given before the court at the dedication of the Orphanage Church. *La finta semplice* was given the following year, 1769, in the archbishop's palace in Salzburg. In October Mozart was appointed an honorary Konzertmeister at the Salzburg court.

La finta semplice

Still only 13, Mozart had by now acquired considerable fluency in the musical language of his time. The early Paris and London sonatas, the autographs of which include Leopold's helping hand, show a childlike pleasure in patterns of notes and textures. But the London and The Hague symphonies attest to his quick and inventive response to the music he had encountered, as, with their enrichment of texture and fuller development, do those he produced in Vienna (such as K 43 and, especially, K 48). And his first Italian opera shows a ready grasp of the buffo style.

The Italian tours. Mastery of the Italian operatic style was a prerequisite for a successful international composing career, and the Austrian political dominion over northern Italy ensured that doors would be open there to Mozart. This time Mozart's mother and sister remained at home, and the family correspondence provides a full account of events. The first tour, begun on Dec. 13, 1769, and lasting 15 months, took them to all the main musical centres, but as usual they paused at any town where a concert could be given or a nobleman might want to hear Mozart play. In Verona Mozart was put through stringent tests at the Accademia Filarmonica, and in Milan, after tests of his capacities in dramatic music, he was commissioned to write the first opera for the carnival season. After a stop in Bologna, where they met the esteemed theorist Giovanni Battista Martini, they proceeded to Florence and on to Rome for Holy Week. There Mozart heard the Sistine Choir in the famous *Miserere* of Gregorio Allegri (1582–1652), which was considered the choir's exclusive preserve but which Mozart copied out from memory. They spent six weeks in Naples; returning through Rome, Mozart had a papal audience and was made a knight of the order of the Golden Spur. The summer was passed near Bologna, where Mozart passed the tests for admission to the Accademia Filarmonica. In mid-October he reached Milan and began work on the new opera, *Mitridate, rè di Ponto* ("Mithradates, King of Pontus"). He had to rewrite several numbers to satisfy the singers, but, after a series of rehearsals (Leopold's letters provide fascinating insights as to theatre procedures), the premiere at the Regio Ducal Teatro on December 26 was a notable success. Mozart, in the traditional way, directed the first three of the 22 performances. After a brief excursion to Venice he and his father returned to Salzburg.

Rome

Plans had already been laid for further journeys to Italy: for a theatrical serenata commissioned for a royal wedding in Milan in October 1771 and for a further opera, again for Milan, at carnival time in 1772–73. Mozart was also commissioned to write an oratorio for Padua; he composed *La Betulia liberata* during 1771, but there is no record of a performance. The second Italian visit, between August and December 1771, saw the premiere of his *Ascanio in Alba,* which, Leopold gleefully reported, "completely overshadowed" the other new work for the occasion, an opera (*Ruggiero*) by Johann Adolph Hasse, the most respected opera seria composer of the time. But hopes that Leopold had entertained of his son's securing an appointment in Milan were disappointed. Back in Salzburg, Mozart had a prolific spell: he wrote eight symphonies, four divertimentos, several substantial sacred works, and an allegorical serenata, *Il sogno di Scipione.* Probably intended as a tribute to the Salzburg prince-archbishop, Count Schrattenbach, this work may not have been given until the spring of 1772, and then for his successor Hieronymus, Count Colloredo; Schrattenbach, a tolerant employer generous in allowing leave, died at the end of 1771.

The third and last Italian journey lasted from October 1772 until March 1773. *Lucio Silla* ("Lucius Sulla"), the new opera, was given on Dec. 26, 1772, and after a difficult premiere (it began three hours late and lasted six) it proved even more successful than *Mitridate,* with 26 performances. This is the earliest indication of the dramatic composer Mozart was to become. He followed *Lucio Silla* with a solo motet written for its leading singer, the castrato and composer Venanzio Rauzzini, *Exsultate, jubilate* (K 165), an appealing three-movement piece culminating in a brilliant "Alleluia." The instrumental music of the period around the Italian journeys includes several symphonies; a few of them are done in a light, Italianate style (*e.g.,* K 95 and K 97), but others, notably the seven from 1772, tread new ground in form, orchestration, and scale (such as K 130, K 132, and the chamber musical K 134). There are also six string quartets (K 155–160) and three divertimentos (K 136–138), in a lively, extroverted vein.

Third Italian journey

Early maturity. More symphonies and divertimentos, as well as a mass, followed during the summer of 1773. Then Leopold, doubtless seeking again a better situation for his son than the Salzburg court (now under a much less sympathetic archbishop) was likely to offer, took him to Vienna. No position materialized, but Mozart's contact with the newest Viennese music seems to have had a considerable effect on him. He produced a set of six string quartets in the capital, showing in them his knowledge of Haydn's recent Opus 20 in his fuller textures and more intellectual approach to the medium. Soon after his return he wrote a group of symphonies, including two that represent a new level of achievement, the "Little" G Minor (K 183) and the A Major (K 201). Also dating from this time was Mozart's first true piano concerto (in D, K 175; earlier keyboard concertos were arrangements of movements by other composers).

The year 1774 saw the composition of more symphonies, concertos for bassoon and for two violins (in a style recalling J.C. Bach), serenades, and several sacred works. Mozart was now a salaried court Konzertmeister, and the sacred music in particular was intended for local use. Archbishop Colloredo, a progressive churchman, discouraged lavish music and set a severe time limit on mass settings, which Mozart objected to but was obliged to observe. At the end of the year he was commissioned to write an opera buffa, *La finta giardiniera* ("The Feigned Gardener Girl"), for the Munich carnival season, where it was duly successful. It shows Mozart, in his first comic opera since his childhood, finding ways of using the orchestra more expressively and of giving real personality to the pasteboard figures of Italian opera buffa.

La finta giardiniera

A period of two and a half years (from March 1775) began in which Mozart worked steadily in his Salzburg post. The work was for him undemanding and by no means compatible with his abilities. During this period he wrote only one dramatic work (the serenata-like *Il rè pastore,* "The Shepherd King," for an archducal visit), but he was productive in sacred and lighter instrumental music. His most impressive piece for the church was the *Litaniae*

de venerabili altaris sacramento (K 243), which embraces a wide range of styles (fugues, choruses of considerable dramatic force, florid arias, and a plainchant setting). The instrumental works included divertimentos, concertos, and serenades, notably the *Haffner* (K 250), which in its use of instruments and its richness of working carried the serenade style into the symphonic without prejudicing its traditional warmth and high spirits. The five concertos for violin, all from this period (No. 1 may be slightly earlier), show a remarkable growth over a few months in confidence in handling the medium, with increasingly fanciful ideas and attractive and natural contexts for virtuoso display. The use of popular themes in the finales is typically south German. He also wrote a concerto for three pianos and three piano concertos, the last of them, K 271, showing a new level of maturity in technique and expressive range.

Mannheim and Paris.   It must have been abundantly clear by this time to Mozart as well as his father that a small, provincial court like that at Salzburg was no place for a genius of his order. In 1777 he petitioned the archbishop for his release and, with his mother to watch over him, set out to find new opportunities. The correspondence with his father over the 16 months he was away not only gives information as to what he was doing but also casts a sharp light on their changing relationship; Mozart, now 21, increasingly felt the need to free himself from paternal domination, while Leopold's anxieties about their future assumed almost pathological dimensions.

They went first to Munich, where the elector politely declined to offer Mozart a post. Next they visited Augsburg, staying with relatives; there Mozart struck up a lively friendship with his cousin Maria Anna Thekla (they later had a correspondence involving much playful, obscene humour). At the end of October they arrived at Mannheim, where the court of the Elector Palatine was musically one of the most famous and progressive in Europe. Mozart stayed there for more than four months, although he soon learned that again no position was to be had. He became friendly with the Mannheim musicians, undertook some teaching and playing, accepted and partly fulfilled a commission for flute music from a German surgeon, and fell in love with Aloysia Weber, a soprano, the second of four daughters of a music copyist. He also composed several piano sonatas, some with violin. He put to his father a scheme for traveling to Italy with the Webers, which, naive and irresponsible, met with an angry response: "Off with you to Paris! and that soon, find your place among great people—aut Caesar aut nihil." The plan had been that he would go on alone, but now Leopold felt that he was not to be trusted and made the ill-fated decision that his mother should go too. They reached Paris late in March 1778, and Mozart soon found work. His most important achievement was the symphony (K 297) composed for the Concert Spirituel, a brilliant D Major work in which he met the taste of the Parisian public (and musicians) for orchestral display without sacrifice of integrity; indeed he exploited the devices they admired (such as the opening coup d'archet—a forceful, unanimous musical gesture) to new formal ends.

Mother's death

By the time of its premiere, on June 18, his mother was seriously ill, and on July 3 she died. Mozart handled the situation with consideration, first writing to his father of her grave illness, then asking an abbé friend in Salzburg to break the news. He went to stay with Friedrich Melchior, Baron von Grimm, a German friend. Soon after, Grimm wrote pessimistically to Leopold about his son's prospects in Paris, and Leopold negotiated a better post for him in Salzburg, where he would be court organist rather than violinist as before, though still nominally Konzertmeister. Summoned home, Mozart reluctantly obeyed, tarrying en route in Mannheim and in Munich—where the Mannheim musicians had now mostly moved and where he was coolly received by Aloysia Weber. He reached Salzburg in mid-January 1780.

Salzburg and Munich.   Back in Salzburg, Mozart seems to have been eager to display his command of international styles: of the three symphonies he wrote in 1779–80, K 318 in G Major has a Parisian premier coup d'archet

and crescendos of the type favoured in Mannheim, and K 338 in C Major shows many features of the brilliant Parisian manner. His outstanding orchestral work of this period was, however, the sinfonia concertante for violin and viola K 364; the genre was popular in both cities, and there are many features of the Mannheim style in the orchestral writing, but the character of the work, its ingenious instrumental interplay, and its depth of feeling are unmistakably Mozartian. Also from this time came the cheerful two-piano concerto and the two-piano sonata, as well as a number of sacred works, including the best-known of his complete masses, the *Coronation Mass*.

But it was dramatic music that attracted Mozart above all. He had lately written incidental music to a play by Tobias Philipp von Gebler, and during 1779–80 he composed much of a singspiel, known as *Zaide,* although with no sure prospects of performance. So Mozart must have been delighted, in the summer of 1780, to receive a commission to compose a serious Italian opera for Munich. The subject was to be Idomeneus, king of Crete, and the librettist the local cleric Giambattista Varesco, who was to follow a French text of 1712. Mozart could start work in Salzburg as he already knew the capacities of several of the singers, but he went to Munich some 10 weeks before the date set for the premiere. Leopold remained at home until close to the time of the premiere and acted as a link between Mozart and Varesco; their correspondence is accordingly richly informative about the process of composition. Four matters dominate Mozart's letters home. First, he was anxious, as always, to assure his father of the enthusiasm with which the singers received his music. Second, he was concerned about cuts: the libretto was far too long, and Mozart had set it spaciously, so that much trimming—of the recitative, of the choral scenes, and even of two arias in the final acts—was needed. Third, he was always eager to make modifications that rendered the action more natural and plausible. And fourth, he was much occupied with accommodating the music and the action to the needs and the limitations of the singers.

In *Idomeneo, rè di Creta* Mozart depicted serious, heroic emotion with a richness unparalleled elsewhere in his operas. Though influenced by Christoph Gluck and by Niccolò Piccinni and others, it is not a "reform opera": it includes plain recitative and bravura singing, but always to a dramatic purpose, and, though the texture is more continuous than in Mozart's earlier operas, its plan, because of its French source, is essentially traditional. Given on Jan. 29, 1781, just after Mozart's 25th birthday, it met with due success. Mozart and his father were still in Munich when, on March 12, he was summoned to join the archbishop's retinue in Vienna, where the accession of Joseph II was being celebrated.

Idomeneo

Vienna: the early years.   Fresh from his triumphs in Munich, where he had mixed freely with noblemen, Mozart now found himself placed, at table in the lodgings for the archbishop's entourage, below the valets if above the cooks. Furthermore, the archbishop refused him permission to play at concerts (including one attended by the emperor at which Mozart could have earned half a year's salary in an evening). He was resentful and insulted. Matters came to a head at an interview with Archbishop Colloredo, who, according to Mozart, used unecclesiastical language; Mozart requested his discharge, which was eventually granted at a stormy meeting with the court steward on June 9, 1781.

Mozart, who now went to live with his old friends the Webers (Aloysia was married to a court actor and painter), set about earning a living in Vienna. Although eager for a court appointment, he for the moment was concerned to take on some pupils, to write music for publication, and to play in concerts (which in Vienna were more often in noblemen's houses than in public). He also embarked on an opera, *Die Entführung aus dem Serail* (*The Abduction from the Seraglio*). (Joseph II currently required that German opera, rather than the traditional Italian, be given at the court theatre.) In the summer of 1781, rumours began to circulate, as far as Salzburg, that Mozart was contemplating marriage with the third of the Weber daughters, Constanze; but he hotly denied them

Die Entführung aus dem Serail

in a letter to his father: "I have never thought less of getting married . . . besides, I am not in love with her." He moved lodgings to scotch the gossip. But by December he was asking for his father's blessing on a marriage with Constanze, with whom he was now in love and to whom, probably through the machinations of her mother and her guardian, he was in some degree committed. Because Constanze later destroyed Leopold's letters, for reasons that are easy to imagine, only one side of the correspondence exists; Leopold's reactions can, however, be readily inferred, and it would seem that this period marked a low point in the relationship between father and son.

Musically, Mozart's main preoccupation was with *Die Entführung* in the early part of 1782. The opera, after various delays, reached the Burgtheater stage on July 16. The story of the emperor's saying "very many notes, my dear Mozart" may not be literally true, but the tale is symptomatic: the work does have far more notes than any other then in the German repertory, with fuller textures, more elaboration, and longer arias. Mozart's letters to his father give insight into his approach to dramatic composition, explaining, for example, his use of accompanying figures and key relationships to embody meaning. He also had the original text substantially modified to strengthen its drama and allow better opportunities for music. Noteworthy features are the Turkish colouring, created by "exotic" turns of phrase and chromaticisms as well as janissary instruments; the extended Act 2 finale, along the lines of those in opera buffa but lacking the dramatic propulsion of the Italian type; the expressive and powerful arias for the heroine (coincidentally called Constanze); and what Mozart called concessions to Viennese taste in the comic music, such as the duet "Vivat Bacchus."

Die Entführung enjoyed immediate and continuing success; it was quickly taken up by traveling and provincial companies—as *La finta giardiniera* had been, to a lesser degree—and carried Mozart's reputation widely around the German-speaking countries. Later in the year he worked on a set of three piano concertos and began a set of six string quartets. He also started work on a mass setting, in C Minor, which he had vowed to write on his marriage but of which only the first two sections, "Kyrie" and "Gloria," were completed. Among the influences on this music, besides the Austrian ecclesiastical tradition, was that of the Baroque music (Bach, Handel, and others) that Mozart had become acquainted with, probably for the first time, at the house of his patron Baron Gottfried van Swieten, a music collector and antiquarian. The Baroque influence is noticeable especially in the spare textures and austere lines of certain of the solo numbers, though others are squarely in the decorative, south German late Rococo manner (this interest in "old-fashioned" counterpoint can also be seen in some of Mozart's piano music of the time and in his string arrangements of music from Bach's *The Well-Tempered Clavier*). Mozart and his wife visited Salzburg in the summer and autumn of 1783, when the completed movements were performed, with (as always intended) Constanze singing one of the solo soprano parts, at St. Peter's Abbey. On the way back to Vienna Mozart paused at Linz, where he hastily wrote the symphony known by that city's name for a concert he gave there.

The central Viennese period. Back in Vienna Mozart entered on what was to be the most fruitful and successful period of his life. He had once written to his father that Vienna was "the land of the piano," and his greatest triumphs there were as a pianist-composer. During one spell of little more than five weeks he appeared at 22 concerts, mainly at the Esterházy and Galitzin houses but including five concerts of his own. In February 1784 he began to keep a catalog of his own music, which suggests a new awareness of posterity and his place in it (in fact his entries are sometimes misdated). At concerts he would normally play the piano, both existing pieces and improvisations; his fantasias—such as the fine C Minor one (K 475) of 1785—and his numerous sets of variations probably give some indication of the kind of music his audiences heard. He would also conduct performances of his symphonies (using earlier Salzburg works as well as the two written since he had settled in Vienna, the *Haffner* of 1782, com-

posed for the Salzburg family, and the *Linz* [*Symphony No. 36 in C Major*]); but above all the piano concertos were the central products of his concert activity.

In 1782–83 Mozart wrote three piano concertos (K 413–415), which he published in 1785 with string and optional wind parts (so that they were suitable for domestic use) and described as "a happy medium between what is too easy and too difficult." Six more followed in 1784, three each in 1785 and 1786 and one each in 1788 and 1791. With the 1784 group he established a new level of piano concerto writing; these concertos are at once symphonic, melodically rich, and orchestrally ingenious, and they also blend the virtuoso element effectively into the musical and formal texture of the work. Much melodic material is assigned to the wind instruments, and a unique melodic style is developed that lends itself to patterns of dialogue and instrumental interplay. After the relatively homogeneous 1784 group (K 449, 450, 451, 453, 456, and 459), all of which begin with themes stated first by the orchestra and later taken up by the piano, Mozart moved on in the concertos of 1785 (K 466, 467, and 482) to make the piano solo a reinterpretation of the opening theme. These concertos are increasingly individual in character—one a stormy and romantic D Minor work, the next a closely argued concerto in C Major with a slow movement remarkable for its troubled beauty, and the third, in E-flat Major, notable for its military rhythms and wind colouring. The 1786 group begins with the refined but conservatively lyrical K 488, but then follow two concertos with a new level of symphonic unity and grandeur, that in C Minor (K 491), using the largest orchestra Mozart had yet called for in the concert hall, and the imperious concerto in C Major (K 503). The two final concertos (K 537 and 595) represent no new departures.

Mozart's other important contributions of this time come in the fields of chamber and piano music. The outpouring of 1784 included the fine piano sonata K 457 and the piano and violin sonata K 454 (written for a visiting violin virtuoso, it was produced in such haste that Mozart could not write out the piano part and played from blank paper at the premiere). He also wrote, in a style close to that of the concertos, a quintet for piano and wind instruments (K 452), which he considered his finest work to date; it was first heard at a concert in the house of his pupil Barbara Ployer, for whom two of the 1784 concertos had been written (K 449 and 453). The six string quartets on which he had embarked in 1782 were finished in the first days of 1785 and published later that year, dedicated to Haydn, now a friend of Mozart's. In 1785 Haydn said to Leopold Mozart, on a visit to his son in Vienna, "Your son is the greatest composer known to me in person or by name; he has taste, and what is more the greatest knowledge of composition."

From Figaro to Don Giovanni. In spite of his success as a pianist and composer, Mozart had serious financial worries, and they worsened as the famously fickle Viennese found other idols. One may calculate his likely income during his last five years, 1786–91, as being far larger than that of most musicians though much below that of the section of society with which he wanted to be associated; Leopold's early advice to be aloof ("like an Englishman") with his fellow musicians but friendly with the aristocracy had its price. His sense of being as good a man as any privileged nobleman led him and his wife into tastes that for his actual station in life, and his income, were extravagant. He saw a court appointment as a possible source of salvation but knew that the Italian musical influence at court, under the Kapellmeister Antonio Salieri, was powerful and exclusive—even if he and Salieri were never on less than friendly terms personally.

Success in the court opera house was all-important. Joseph II had now reverted to Italian opera, and since 1783 Mozart had been seeking suitable librettos (he had even started work on two but broke off when he came to realize their feebleness for his purpose). He had become acquainted with Lorenzo da Ponte, an Italian abbé-adventurer of Jewish descent who was a talented poet and librettist to the court theatre. At Mozart's suggestion he wrote a libretto), *Le nozze di Figaro*, based on Beau-

marchais's revolutionary comedy, *Le Mariage de Figaro*, but with most of the political sting removed. Nonetheless, the music of *Figaro* makes the social distinctions clear. *Figaro*, as well as the later opera *Don Giovanni*, treats the traditional figure of the licentious nobleman, but the earlier work does so on a more directly comic plane even though the undercurrents of social tension run stronger. Perhaps the central achievement of *Figaro* lies in its ensembles with their close link between music and dramatic meaning. The Act 3 Letter Duet, for instance, has a realistic representation of dictation with the reading back as a condensed recapitulation. The act finales, above all, show a broad, symphonic organization with each section worked out as a unit; for example, in the B-flat section of the Act 2 finale the tension of the count's examination of Figaro is paralleled in the tonal scheme, with its return to the tonic only when the final question is resolved: a telling conjunction of music and drama. These features, coupled with the elaborate commentary on character and action that is embodied in the orchestral writing, add depth to the situations and seriousness to their resolution and set the work apart from the generality of Italian opere buffe.

Figaro reached the stage on May 1, 1786, and was warmly received. There were nine performances in 1786 and a further 26 when it was revived in 1789–90—a success, but a modest one compared with certain operas of Martín y Soler and Giovanni Paisiello (to whose *Il barbiere di Siviglia* it was a sequel, and planned in direct competition). The opera did, however, enjoy outstanding popularity in Prague, and at the end of the year Mozart was invited to go to the Bohemian capital; he went in January 1787, giving a new symphony there and accepting a further operatic commission. He returned to Vienna in February 1787.

Mozart's concert activities in Vienna were now on a modest scale. No Viennese appearances at all are recorded for 1787. In April he heard that his father was gravely ill. Mozart wrote him a letter of consolation putting forward a view of death ("this best and truest friend of mankind") based on the teachings of Freemasonry, which he had embraced at the end of 1784. Leopold died in May 1787.

Mozart's music from this time includes the two string quintets K 515–516, arguably his supreme chamber works. Clearly this genre, with the opportunities it offered for richness of sonority and patterns of symmetry, had a particular appeal for him. The quintet in C Major (K 515) is the most expansive and most richly developed of all his chamber works, while the G Minor (K 516) has always been recognized for its depth of feeling, which in the circumstances it is tempting to regard as elegiac. From this period come a number of short but appealing lieder and three instrumental works of note: the *Musikalischer Spass* (*Musical Joke*), a good-humoured parody of bad music, in a vein Leopold would have liked (it was thought to have been provoked by his death until it was found that it was begun much earlier); *Eine kleine Nachtmusik*, the exquisite and much-loved serenade, probably intended for solo strings and written for a purpose that remains unknown; and a fine piano and violin sonata, K 526.

But Mozart's chief occupation during 1787 was the composition of *Don Giovanni*, commissioned for production in Prague; it was given on October 29 and warmly received. *Don Giovanni* was Mozart's second opera based on a libretto by da Ponte, who used as his model a libretto by Giovanni Bertati, set by Giuseppe Gazzaniga for Venice earlier in 1787. Da Ponte rewrote the libretto, inserting new episodes into the one-act original, which explains certain structural features. A difference in Mozart's approach to the work—a *dramma giocoso* in the tradition of Carlo Goldoni that, because of its more serious treatment of character, had a greater expressive potential than an opera buffa—is seen in the extended spans of the score, with set-piece numbers often running into one another. As in *Figaro*, the two act finales are again remarkable: the first for the three stage bands that play dances for different social segments, the second for the supper scene in which the commendatore's statue consigns Giovanni to damnation, with trombones to suggest the supernatural and with hieratic dotted rhythms, extreme chromaticism,

Don Giovanni

and wildly lurching harmony as Giovanni is overcome. But it remains a comic opera, as is made clear through the figure of Leporello, who from under a table offers the common man's wry or facetious observations; and at the end the surviving characters draw the moral in a cheerful sextet. The "demonic" character of the opera has caused it to exercise a special fascination for audiences, and it has given rise to a large critical, interpretative, and purely fanciful literature.

The last travels. On his return from Prague in mid-November 1787, Mozart was at last appointed to a court post, as *Kammermusicus*, in place of Gluck, who had died. It was largely a sinecure, the only requirement being that he should supply dance music for court balls, which he did, in abundance and with some distinction, over his remaining years. The salary of 800 gulden seems to have done little to relieve the Mozarts' chronic financial troubles. Their debts, however, were never large, and they were always able to continue employing servants and owning a carriage; their anxieties were more a matter of whether they could live as they wished than whether they would starve. In 1788 a series of letters begging loans from a fellow Freemason, Michael Puchberg, began; Puchberg usually obliged, and Mozart seems generally to have repaid him promptly. He was deeply depressed during the summer, writing of "black thoughts"; it has been suggested that he may have had a cyclothymic personality, linked with manic-depressive tendencies, which could explain not only his depression but also other aspects of his behaviour, including his spells of hectic creativity.

Financial difficulties

During the time of this depression Mozart was working on a series of three symphonies, in E-flat Major (K 543), G Minor (K 550), and C Major (the *Jupiter*, K 551), usually numbered 39, 40, and 41; these, with the work written for Prague (K 504), represent the summa of his orchestral output. It is not known why they were composed; possibly Mozart had a summer concert season in mind. The Prague work was a climax to his long series of brilliant D Major orchestral pieces, but the closely worked, even motivic form gives it a new power and unity. The E-flat Major work, scored with clarinets and more lyrical in temper, makes fewer departures, except in the intensity of its slow movement, where Mozart used a new palette of darker orchestral colours, and the epigrammatic wit of its finale. In the G Minor work the tone of passion and perhaps of pathos, in its constant falling figures, is still more pronounced. The *Jupiter* (the name dates from the early 19th century) summarized the series of C Major symphonies, with their atmosphere of military pomp and ceremony, but it went far beyond them in its assimilation of opera buffa style, profundity of expression (in its andante), and richness of working—especially in the finale, which incorporates fugal procedures and ends with a grand apotheosis in five-voice counterpoint.

Early in 1789 Mozart accepted an invitation to travel to Berlin with Prince Karl Lichnowsky; they paused in Prague, Dresden (where he played at court), and Leipzig (where he improvised on the Thomaskirche organ). He appeared at the Prussian court and probably was invited to compose piano sonatas for the princess and string quartets with a prominent cello part for King Friedrich Wilhelm II. He did in fact write three quartets, in parts of which he allowed the individual instruments (including the royal cello) special prominence, and there is one sonata (his last, K 576) that may have been intended for the Prussian princess. But it is unlikely that Mozart ever sent this music or was paid for it.

The summer saw the composition of the clarinet quintet, in which a true chamber style is warmly and gracefully reconciled with the solo writing. Thereafter Mozart concentrated on completing his next opera commission, the third of his da Ponte operas, *Così fan tutte*, which was given on Jan. 26, 1790; its run was interrupted after five performances when theatres closed because of the death of Joseph II, but a further five were given in the summer. This opera, the subtlest, most consistent, and most symmetrical of the three, was long reviled (from Beethoven onward) on account of its subject, female fickleness; but a more careful reading of it, especially in light of the

Così fan tutte

emotional texture of the music, which gains complexity as the plot progresses, makes it clear that it is no frivolous piece but a penetrating essay on human feelings and their mature recognition. The music of Act 1 is essentially conventional in expression, and conventional feeling is tellingly parodied in certain of the arias; but the arias of Act 2 are on a deeper and more personal level. Features of the music of *Così fan tutte*—serenity, restraint, poise, irony—may be noted as markers of Mozart's late style, which had developed since 1787 and may be linked with his personal development and the circumstances of his life, including his Masonic associations, his professional and financial situation, and his marriage.

The year 1790 was difficult and unproductive: besides *Così fan tutte*, Mozart completed two of the "Prussian" quartets, arranged works by Handel for performance at van Swieten's house (he had similarly arranged *Messiah* in 1789) and wrote the first of his two fantasy-like pieces, in a variety of prelude-and-fugue form, for a mechanical organ (this imposing work, in F Minor [K 594], is now generally played on a normal organ). In the autumn, anxious to be noticed in court circles, he went to Frankfurt for the imperial coronation of Leopold II, but as an individual rather than a court musician. His concert, which included two piano concertos and possibly one of the new symphonies, was ill timed, poorly attended, and a financial failure. Anxieties about money were a recurrent theme in his letters home.

The last year. But 1791 promised to be a better year. Music was flowing again: for a concert in March Mozart completed a piano concerto (K 595) begun some years before, reeled off numerous dances for the Redoutensaal, and wrote two new string quintets, the one in D (K 593) being a work of particular refinement and subtlety. In April he applied successfully for the role of unpaid assistant to the elderly Kapellmeister of St. Stephen's Cathedral, Leopold Hofmann (with the expectation of being duly appointed his successor, but Hofmann was to live until 1793).

An old friend of Mozart's, Emanuel Schikaneder, had in 1789 set up a company to perform singspiels in a suburban theatre, and in 1791 he engaged Mozart to compose *Die Zauberflöte* a score to his *Die Zauberflöte* (*The Magic Flute*); Mozart worked on it during the spring and early summer. Then he received another commission, anonymously delivered, for a requiem, to be composed under conditions of secrecy. In addition he was invited, probably in July, to write the opera to be given during Leopold II's coronation festivities in September. Constanze was away taking a cure at Baden during much of the summer and autumn; in July she gave birth to their sixth child, one of the two to survive (Carl Thomas, 1784–1858, and Franz Xaver Wolfgang, 1791–1844, a composer and pianist). Mozart's letters to her show that he worked first on *Die Zauberflöte,* although he must have written some of the Prague opera, *La clemenza di Tito* ("The Clemency of Titus"), before he left for the Bohemian capital near the end of August. Pressure of work, however, was such that he took with him to Prague, along with Constanze, his pupil Franz Xaver Süssmayr, who almost certainly composed the plain recitatives for the new opera. The work itself, to an old libretto by Pietro Metastasio, condensed and supplemented by the Dresden court poet Caterino Mazzolà, was long dismissed as a product of haste and a commission unwillingly undertaken; but in fact the spare scoring, the short arias, and the generally restrained style are better understood in terms of Mozart's reaction to the neoclassical thinking of the time and the known preferences of Leopold II. The opera was indifferently received by the court but quickly won over the Prague audiences and went on to become one of Mozart's most admired works over the ensuing decades.

Mozart was back in Vienna by the middle of September; his clarinet concerto was finished by September 29, and the next day *Die Zauberflöte* had its premiere. Again, early reactions were cautious, but soon the opera became the most loved of all of Mozart's works for the stage. Schikaneder took its plot from a collection of fairy tales by Christoph Martin Wieland but drew too on other literary sources and on current thinking about Freemasonry—all viewed in the context of Viennese popular theatre.

Musically it is distinguished from contemporary singspiels not merely by the quality of its music but also by the serious ideas that lie below what may seem to be merely childish pantomime or low comedy, welding together the stylistically diverse elements.

Mozart had been ill during the weeks in Prague, but to judge by his letters to Constanze in October he was in good spirits and, with some cause, more optimistic about the future. He wrote a Masonic cantata for his lodge and directed a performance of it on November 18. He was also working steadily on the commissioned requiem. Later in November he was ill and confined to bed; some apparent improvement on December 3 was not sustained, and on Dec. 5, 1791, he died. "Severe miliary fever" was the certified cause; later, "rheumatic inflammatory fever" was named. Other diagnoses, taking account of Mozart's medical history, have been put forward, including Schönlein–Henoch syndrome. There is no evidence to support the tale that he was poisoned by Salieri (a colleague and friend, hardly a real rival) or anyone else. He was buried in a multiple grave, standard at the time in Vienna for a person of his social and financial situation; a small group of friends attended the funeral.

Constanze Mozart was anxious to have the requiem completed, as a fee was due; it had been commissioned, in memory of his wife, by Count von Walsegg-Stuppach to pass off as his own. She handed it first to Joseph Eybler, who supplied some orchestration but was reluctant to do more, and then to Süssmayr, who produced a complete version, writing several movements himself though possibly basing them on Mozart's sketches or instructions. Although subject to criticism for its technical weaknesses, which editors have sought to remedy, this must remain the standard version by dint of its position as the only one with a source close to Mozart. The sombre grandeur of the work, with its restrained instrumental colouring and its noble choral writing, hints at what might have been had Mozart lived to take on the Kapellmeistership of St. Stephen's.

Mozart's place. At the time of his death Mozart was widely regarded not only as the greatest composer of the time but also as a bold and "difficult" one; *Don Giovanni* especially was seen as complex and dissonant, and his chamber music as calling for outstanding skill in its interpreters. His surviving manuscripts, which included many unpublished works, were mostly sold by Constanze to the firm of André in Offenbach, which issued editions during the 19th century. But Mozart's reputation was such that even before the end of the 18th century two firms had embarked on substantial collected editions of his music. Important biographies appeared in 1798 and 1828, the latter by Constanze's second husband; the first scholarly biography, by Otto Jahn, was issued on Mozart's centenary in 1856. The first edition of the Köchel catalog followed six years later, and the first complete edition of his music began in 1877.

The works most secure in the repertory during the 19th century were the three operas least susceptible to changes in public taste—*Le nozze di Figaro, Don Giovanni,* and *Die Zauberflöte*—and the orchestral works closest in spirit to the Romantic era—the minor-key piano concertos (Beethoven wrote a set of cadenzas for the one in D Minor) and the last three symphonies. It was only in the 20th century that Mozart's music began to be reexamined more broadly. Although up to the middle of the century Mozart was still widely regarded as having been surpassed in most respects by Beethoven, with the increased historical perspective of the later 20th century he came to be seen as an artist of a formidable, indeed perhaps unequaled, expressive range. The traditional image of the child prodigy turned refined drawing-room composer, who could miraculously conceive an entire work in his head before setting pen to paper (always a distortion of the truth), gave way to the image of the serious and painstaking creative artist with acute human insight, whose complex psychology demanded exploration by writers, historians, and scholars. But regardless of such shifting currents of interpretation, in public esteem and affection Mozart's place more than equals that of any other composer.   (STANLEY SADIE)

Completion of the requiem

First edition of the Köchel catalog

Bibliography: Recent Books

The following list encompasses some 174 recent books that have been judged significant contributions to learning and understanding in their respective fields. Each citation includes a few lines of commentary to indicate the general tenor of the work. The citations are organized by subject area, using the 10 parts of the *Propædia* as an outline.

Matter and Energy

A.C. Fabian (ed.), *Origins: The Darwin College Lectures* (1988), a book of stimulating essays on scientific understanding of the fundamentals of the world, both material and social.

J.L. Martin, *General Relativity: A Guide to Its Consequences for Gravity and Cosmology* (1988), a concise exposition of the theory underlying modern understanding of space and time.

Andrew Zangwill, *Physics at Surfaces* (1988), a broad survey of issues in the field of surface science.

John Briggs and F. David Peat, *Turbulent Mirror: An Illustrated Guide to Chaos Theory and the Science of Wholeness* (1989), an intriguingly organized and beautifully presented introduction to the duality of the physical concepts of chaos and order.

Tamas Viczek, *Fractal Growth Phenomena* (1989), an informative discussion of kinetic growth phenomena.

James M. Miller, *Chromatography: Concepts and Contrasts* (1988), a comprehensive introduction to the specifics of the chemical methods of separation and analysis.

A.B. Pippard, *Magnetoresistance in Metals* (1989), an examination of physical processes taking place in metals under the application of both an electric current and a magnetic field.

Harold Zirin, *Astrophysics of the Sun* (1988), a fascinating, if rather technical, exposition of everything modern science knows about this most important of stars.

Donat G. Wentzel, *The Restless Sun* (1989), a moderately technical discussion of solar phenomena.

Laurence A. Marschall, *The Supernova Story* (1988), an excellent literary treatment of stellar outbursts and their observation.

Martin Cohen, *In Darkness Born: The Story of Star Formation* (1988), a satisfying explanation of stellar evolution and astronomical observation of it, for informed lay readers.

The Earth

Kurt Lambeck, *Geophysical Geodesy: The Slow Deformations of the Earth* (1988), an authoritative introduction to the basic concepts defining the figure of the Earth and the gravitational field at the Earth's surface.

Lindsay McClelland *et al.* (eds.), *Global Volcanism 1975–1985* (1989), a detailed summary of volcanic activity.

Raymond Siever, *Sand* (1988), an excellently written and illustrated sedimentological survey.

Michael O'Donoghue, *Gemstones* (1988), a comprehensive description of geologic occurrences and properties of gem materials, branching into a survey of imitation stones.

Paul C. Hess, *Origins of Igneous Rocks* (1989), a detailed history of some of the main components of the Earth's crust.

Michael R. Rampino *et al.* (eds.), *Climate, History, Periodicity, and Predictability* (1987), a collection of outstanding though diverse writings with an extensive reference apparatus.

K.Ya. Kondratyev, *Climate Shocks: Natural and Anthropogenic*, trans. from Russian (1988), an important book on evidence of the consequences of mankind's activities on the climate.

Colin E. Thorn, *An Introduction to Theoretical Geomorphology* (1988), a discussion of a complex of disciplines describing the features of the Earth produced by geomorphic processes.

Donald L. Sparks, *Kinetics of Soil Chemical Processes* (1989), a substantial review of the chemical processes and factors affecting the formation of the Earth's soils.

Robert P. Sharp, *Living Ice: Understanding Glaciers and Glaciation* (1988), a beautifully illustrated and written literary treatment of the glacial environment of the world.

Jean M. Grove, *The Little Ice Age* (1988), a historical analysis of many glacial regions of the world.

Dean Edwin Abrahamson (ed.), *The Challenge of Global Warming* (1989), a survey of scientific thinking on the atmospheric "greenhouse effect."

Chris Park, *Acid Rain: Rhetoric and Reality* (1987), an examination of acid rain, with a focus on Europe.

James L. Regens and Robert W. Rycroft, *The Acid Rain Controversy* (1988), a survey of the same concerns in the U.S.

J.W. Cowie and M.D. Brasier (eds.), *The Precambrian-Cambrian Boundary* (1989), an authoritative summary of present knowledge and interpretation of the Earth's geologic record.

Life on Earth

Steven Vogel, *Life's Devices: The Physical World of Animals and Plants* (1988), an enticing introduction to natural sciences in general and biomechanics in particular.

Stephen Jay Gould, *Wonderful Life: The Burgess Shale and Nature of History* (1989), a very readable evolutionary treatment of the significance of fossil fauna for modern science.

Robert B. Gennis, *Biomembranes: Molecular Structure and Function* (1989), a detailed survey of the morphological elements of cell design and organization.

Andrew Scott, *Vital Principles: The Molecular Mechanisms of Life* (1988), a skillful but simple presentation of basic chemical, physical, and biological principles of life at the molecular level.

Jeremy Dale, *Molecular Genetics of Bacteria* (1989), a readable book on genetic engineering and applied genetics.

Niles Eldredge, *Macroevolutionary Dynamics: Species, Niches, and Adaptive Peaks* (1989), an important historical survey of the processes of evolution and the establishment of species.

J.W. Hart, *Light and Plant Growth* (1987), an attractive summary of the role of photosynthesis in plant physiology.

Rodney E. Langman, *The Immune System* (1989), an informative, readable survey of the biological defense system.

David H. Hubel, *Eye, Brain, and Vision* (1988), an examination of biological processing of visual information, written by a great pioneering authority in the field of neuroscience.

Richard E. Michod and Bruce R. Levin (eds.), *The Evolution of Sex: An Examination of Current Ideas* (1988), a study of advantages of sex as a way of genetic recombination.

Patrick Colgan, *Animal Motivation* (1989), a concise review of various approaches used to represent motivation in animals.

John L. Gittleman (ed.), *Carnivore Behavior, Ecology, and Evolution* (1989), a comprehensive and authoritative reference source on the flesh-eating animals.

A.A. Myers and P.S. Giller (eds.), *Analytical Biogeography: An Integrated Approach to the Study of Animal and Plant Distributions* (1988), a discussion of theoretical foundations of geography of biological populations and its applications.

Bernard Stonehouse, *Polar Ecology* (1989), a concise biogeographic summary of polar environments.

Henry F. Howe and Lynn C. Westley, *Ecological Relationships of Plants and Animals* (1988), a well-illustrated, readable examination of ecosystem dynamics.

John C. Kricher, *A Neotropical Companion: An Introduction to the Animals, Plants, and Ecosystems of the New World Tropics* (1989), a comprehensive study of a complex ecological system.

Human Life

Ian Tattersall, Eric Delson, and John Van Couvering (eds.), *Encyclopedia of Human Evolution and Prehistory* (1988), an informative compendium of diverse data on primate evolution.

C.G.N. Mascie-Taylor and G.W. Lasker (eds.), *Biological Aspects of Human Migration* (1988), an analysis of dynamics of the distribution of human populations.

Jillyn Smith, *Senses and Sensibilities* (1989), a study beginning with the anatomy and physiology of receptors and leading to an entertaining review of human interactions.

Andrea L. Bonnicksen, *In Vitro Fertilization: Building Policy from Laboratories to Legislatures* (1989), an informative description of the techniques of the controversial procedure and of the societal aspects of its development and influence.

Joan Jacobs Brumberg, *Fasting Girls: The Emergence of Anorexia Nervosa as a Modern Disease* (1988), a historical examination of the cultural and social nature of the disorder and its modern implications.

Blair Justice, *Who Gets Sick: Thinking and Health* (1987), a psychological exploration of the role of positive mental and social attitudes in the maintenance of health.

James H. Buchanan, *Patient Encounters: The Experience of Disease* (1989), an interpretive analysis of experiences of people battling catastrophic illnesses.

Jad Adams, *AIDS: The HIV Myth* (1989), a provocative exposition of alternative views on the etiology of AIDS.

Ronald Bayer, *Private Acts, Social Consequences: AIDS and the Politics of Public Health* (1989), an original and discerning treatment of the social effect of AIDS.

Lynn Payer, *Medicine & Culture: Varieties of Treatment in the United States, England, West Germany, and France* (1988), an involving analysis of historical, social, and cultural factors shaping medicine in industrialized societies.

Jerome Bruner and Helen Haste (eds.), *Making Sense: The Child's Construction of the World* (1987), an authoritative presentation of the role of social and cultural phenomena in the early cognitive development of humans.

William S. Robinson, *Brains and People: An Essay on Mentality and Its Causal Conditions* (1988), a well-structured, nonreligious consideration of nonphysical aspects of physical beings, such as sensations, intentionality, and morality.

Loraine K. Obler and Deborah Fein (eds.), *The Exceptional Brain: Neuropsychology of Talent and Special Abilities* (1988), a detailed survey of a new branch of psychology that attempts to provide definition of exceptional skills and abilities.

Linda Silka, *Intuitive Judgments of Change* (1989), a study of mass perception of social constancy and change.

Ruthellen Josselson, *Finding Herself: Pathways to Identity Development in Women* (1987), an account of an original longitudinal study resulting in a definition of the interpersonal character of identity in women.

Michael Ruse, *Homosexuality: A Philosophical Inquiry* (1988), a readable historical review of philosophical, legal, and moral issues of homosexuality.

Robert J. Sternberg and Michael L. Barnes (eds.), *The Psychology of Love* (1988), an original symposium of discussions of methodology and theory of a new branch of scientific study.

Barbara Lazear Ascher, *The Habit of Loving* (1989), a collection of literary essays, leading to the idea of love as an enduring, discerning, and insightful habit.

S.J. Rachman, *Fear and Courage,* 2nd ed. (1989), an appealing examination of theoretical issues combined with an account of behavioral observations.

Herbert Fingarette, *Heavy Drinking: The Myth of Alcoholism as a Disease* (1988), a provocative critique of the disease model of alcoholism.

Human Society

Ray Bull and Nichola Rumsey, *The Social Psychology of Facial Appearance* (1988), a balanced and comprehensive survey of the role of body image and personal attractiveness in social construction and interpersonal relationships.

Cynthia Eagle Russett, *Sexual Science: The Victorian Construction of Womanhood* (1989), an excellent social history focusing on the 19th-century understanding of the difference between men and women.

Fred Coalter (ed.), *Freedom and Constraint: The Paradoxes of Leisure* (1989), a collection of informative essays on the issues of free time in society.

Tovah Martin, *Once upon a Windowsill: A History of Indoor Plants* (1988), an original treatment of social factors that brought live plants into people's dwellings.

Georges Vigarello, *Concepts of Cleanliness: Changing Attitudes in France Since the Middle Ages* (1988; originally published in French, 1985), a dynamic exploration of the sources of many modern ideas on hygiene.

Elizabeth Wilson, *Adorned in Dreams: Fashion and Modernity* (1987), a penetrating study of fashion, placing it in a broad context of social and cultural history.

Geoffrey Hughes, *Words in Time: The Social History of English Vocabulary* (1988), a systematic, detailed discussion of social influences on the language.

Michael A. Hogg and Dominic Abrams, *Social Identifications: A Social Psychology of Intergroup Relations and Group Processes* (1988), an exploration of complicated attempts to reach a balance between an individual and a group.

Barbara Katz Rothman, *Recreating Motherhood: Ideology and Technology in a Patriarchal Society* (1989), a critical examination of modern values in reference to such issues as surrogate motherhood, birth control, infertility, and child care.

Kurt W. Back, *Family Planning and Population Control: The Challenges of a Successful Movement* (1989), an informative historical survey of the birth control movement.

Hyman Rodman, Betty Sarvis, and Joy Walker Bonar, *The Abortion Question* (1987), a balanced, informative analysis of a particularly controversial method of birth control.

Jacqueline Kasun, *The War Against Population: The Economics and Ideology of World Population Control* (1988), a persuasively presented alternative view on population control.

Shirley Radl, *Over Our Live Bodies: Preserving Choice in America* (1989), a polemic work defending the legality of abortion.

Robert Cherry, *Discrimination: Its Economic Impact on Blacks, Women, and Jews* (1989), a thorough review of issues of economic discrimination, including employment, family situation, and other aspects of the problem.

Martha Barron Barrett, *Invisible Lives: The Loving Alternative of Millions of Women* (1989), a study, based on interviews, of diverse social, religious, and cultural issues pertaining to lifestyles of lesbians.

Jerome D. Schein, *At Home Among Strangers* (1989), a comprehensive examination of the deaf, including a discussion of everyday problems.

Richard V. Ericson, Patricia M. Baranek, and Janet B.L. Chan, *Negotiating Control: A Study of News Sources* (1989), a thorough analysis of the process of creating news.

Grant McCracken, *Culture and Consumption: New Approaches to the Symbolic Character of Consumer Goods and Activities* (1988), a historico-economic study of the development of consumer society.

Edward Weisband (ed.), *Poverty Amidst Plenty: World Political Economy and Distributive Justice* (1989), a well-rounded collection of essays on problems of poverty in the world economy.

George Modelski and Sylvia Modelski (eds.), *Documenting Global Leadership* (1988), a massive though compact history of diplomacy and international politics, covering more than 500 years up to the mid-20th century.

Robert A. Dahl, *Democracy and Its Critics* (1989), a political scientist's analysis of the theory and practice of democratic organization of societies and political institutions.

Ellen L. Lutz, Hurst Hannum, and Kathryn J. Burke (eds.), *New Directions in Human Rights* (1989), a collection of studies on present-day human rights movements.

Richard L. Abel and Philip S.C. Lewis (eds.), *Lawyers in Society,* 3 vol. (1988–89), a comprehensive treatment of the influential profession, including a survey of the common law, the civil law, and the comparative theories defining the field all over the world.

Harry S. Broudy, *The Uses of Schooling* (1988), a penetrating examination of the significance of general education and common learning in life after school years.

Art

Ian Chilvers and Harold Osborne (eds.), *The Oxford Dictionary of Art* (1988), a well-written reference work covering Western painting, sculpture, graphic art, and design.

Kenneth Baker, *Minimalism: Art of Circumstance* (1988), an important analysis of an idiosyncratic contemporary art movement that has no similarities to traditional visual arts.

Calvin Tomkins, *Post- to Neo-: The Art World of the 1980s* (1988), a broad look at the world of modern art, its personalities, subjects, idols, custodians, and customers.

Linda Hutcheon, *A Poetics of Postmodernism: History, Theory, Fiction* (1988), a study of postmodernism, mostly in its literary incarnation, by a Canadian scholar.

Milan Kundera, *The Art of the Novel* (1988; originally published in French, 1986), a sophisticated and entertaining critical analysis of the European novel, by a master of the form.

Jean-Charles Seigneuret *et al.* (eds.), *Dictionary of Literary Themes and Motifs,* 2 vol. (1988), an encyclopaedic reference source covering themes, genres, and literary movements.

Jordan R. Young, *Acting Solo: The Art of One-Man Shows* (1989), a history of a specific genre of theatre that began in the 18th century.

Paul Monaco, *Ribbons in Time: Movies and Society Since 1945* (1988), a comparative sociological history of interpretive values reflected in the art of European film.

John Fiske, *Television Culture* (1987), an intelligent, readable analysis of the place of television in modern society.

Nicolas Slonimsky, *Lectionary of Music* (1989), a dictionary of musical terms, instruments, genres, works, and personalities, infused with humour.

Leo Treitler, *Music and the Historical Imagination* (1989), an erudite but readable analytic history of the Western musical tradition.

Deborah Jowitt, *Time and the Dancing Image* (1988), a social history of dance that places the art in the context of historical events and social influences.

Charles W. Moore, William J. Mitchell, and William Turnbull, Jr., *The Poetics of Gardens* (1988), a serious history of garden design and landscape architecture.

Mark Roskill, *The Interpretation of Pictures* (1989), an imaginative study of the interpretation of art in history.

Robert L. Herbert, *Impressionism: Art, Leisure, and Parisian Society* (1988), a beautifully illustrated treatment of the movement that epitomized the culture of the late 19th century.

Christopher Finch, *Twentieth-Century Watercolors* (1988), a richly illustrated inclusive survey of the genre as it contributed to the experimental developments of 20th-century painting.

Sarah Greenough *et al.*, *On the Art of Fixing a Shadow: One Hundred and Fifty Years of Photography* (1989), a retrospective history of photography in the form of an exhibition catalog.

Susanne K. Frantz, *Contemporary Glass: A World Survey from the Corning Museum of Glass* (1989), a well-illustrated work on a particular genre of decorative art.

John A. Walker, *Design History and the History of Design* (1989), a well-organized historiographic survey.

Technology

George Basalla, *The Evolution of Technology* (1988), an analysis of multifaceted factors that provide continuity of technological developments.

Leonard A. Doty, *Reliability for the Technologies,* 2nd ed. (1989), a clear though rather technical introduction to general problems of quality control and engineering reliability.

Peter Grootings, Bjørn Gustavsen, and Lajos Héthy (eds.), *New Forms of Work Organization in Europe* (1989), an intriguing if not quite conclusive survey of new tendencies in work organization.

Nelson E. Hay (ed.), *Guide to Natural Gas Cogeneration* (1988), a knowledgeable outline of a rapidly developing field of technology.

John B. Heywood, *Internal Combustion Engine Fundamentals* (1988), a massive historical review of the field of internal combustion, including the latest achievements in the direction of pollution control.

Don E. Bray and Roderick K. Stanley, *Nondestructive Evaluation: A Tool for Design, Manufacturing, and Service* (1989), a well-written presentation of both the theories and practices of nondestructive testing.

Randy Simon and Andrew Smith, *Superconductors: Conquering Technology's New Frontier* (1988), a moderately technical discussion of a promising field.

Don Paarlberg, *Toward a Well-Fed World* (1988), a history of the development of agriculture, based on biographies of important contributors to its advancement.

D.H. Cushing, *The Provident Sea* (1988), a well-illustrated historical treatment of a complex of scientific, technological, and industrial developments that resulted in the creation of modern productive fisheries.

Jean L. Marx (ed.), *A Revolution in Biotechnology* (1989), a comprehensive examination of all areas of biotechnology, from conventional production of pharmaceuticals to gene therapy.

Basil Greenhill, *The Evolution of the Wooden Ship* (1989), a nontechnical history of an ancient technological tradition.

Deborah Lynn Bleviss, *The New Oil Crisis and Fuel Economy Technologies: Preparing the Light Transportation Industry for the 1990s* (1988), a readable analysis of the influence of short supply of oil on technological advancement.

Scott A. Helmers, *Data Communications: A Beginner's Guide to Concepts and Technology* (1989), a nonmathematical introduction to the basic concepts of movement of information between computers.

John McAfee and Colin Haynes, *Computer Viruses, Worms, Data Diddlers, Killer Programs, and Other Threats to Your System* (1989), an overview of computer vulnerability and the insufficiency of data communications security.

Martin Van Creveld, *Technology and War: From 2000 B.C. to the Present* (1989), a thoughtful history of the role of technology in military art.

Robert E. Berlin and Catherine C. Stanton, *Radioactive Waste Management* (1989), a survey of a modern problem requiring both technological and managerial solutions.

Religion

Charles Wei-hsun Fu and Gerhard E. Spiegler (eds.), *Religious Issues and Interreligious Dialogues: An Analysis and Sourcebook of Developments Since 1945* (1989), a collection of excellent articles placing religious issues of our time in a broad sociophilosophical context.

John Hick, *An Interpretation of Religion: Human Responses to the Transcendent* (1989), a comprehensive look at world religions with an analysis of resemblances and pluralistic potential.

Walter Burkert, *Ancient Mystery Cults* (1987), an examination of religious rituals and organizations of ancient peoples.

Klaus K. Klostermaier, *A Survey of Hinduism* (1989), a detailed presentation of the Hindu religion.

W.H. McLeod, *The Sikhs: History, Religion, and Society* (1989), a concise survey of doctrine, culture, and history of the Sikhs.

Andrew Powell, *Living Buddhism* (1989), an accessible treatment of various schools of Buddhism.

Heinrich Dumoulin, *Zen Buddhism,* 2 vol. (1988–89), a historical exploration of the religious tradition spanning the cultures and beliefs of India, China, Japan, and Tibet.

H. Byron Earhart, *Gedatsu-Kai and Religion in Contemporary Japan: Returning to the Center* (1989), a provocative study of a Japanese tradition.

Michael A. Knibb, *The Qumran Community* (1987), a new translation of and research in the documents from the Dead Sea Scrolls.

Martin E. Marty and Frederick E. Greenspahn (eds.), *Pushing the Faith: Proselytism and Civility in a Pluralistic World* (1988), an interdisciplinary historical introduction to the concept of proselytism in Western religions.

Pedro Ramet (ed.), *Eastern Christianity and Politics in the Twentieth Century* (1988), a comprehensive survey of Eastern and Oriental Orthodox churches providing some rarely available data on religion in Communist countries.

David O'Brien, *Public Catholicism* (1989), a historical analysis of social involvement of the Roman Catholic Church, with a critique of unresolved problems of today.

Shireen T. Hunter (ed.), *The Politics of Islamic Revivalism: Diversity and Unity* (1988), a collection providing a broad coverage of Islamic movements in all major Muslim countries.

Leonard E. Barrett, Sr., *The Rastafarians: Sounds of Cultural Dissonance,* rev. and updated ed. (1988), a survey of an original religious movement characterized by militant messianic protest.

Omer C. Stewart, *Peyote Religion: A History* (1987), a study of a religion that originated as a tribal ritual and developed into the influential Native American Church.

Peter Bishop and Michael Darton (eds.), *The Encyclopedia of World Faiths* (1987), an excellent arrangement of informative essays on all major and many emerging religions, accompanied with impressive illustrations.

The History of Mankind

Barry J. Kemp, *Ancient Egypt: Anatomy of a Civilization* (1989), an insightful reexamination of what had been known of the ancient civilization, prompted by recent archaeological finds.

Hans J. Nissen, *The Early History of the Ancient Near East, 9000–2000 B.C.* (1988; originally published in German, 1983), a concise socioeconomic history of 70 centuries of the Middle East.

Xinru Liu, *Ancient India and Ancient China: Trade and Religious Exchanges, A.D. 1–600* (1988), a history of social, political, and religious issues that influenced trade of the period.

Andrew Wallace-Hadrill (ed.), *Patronage in Ancient Society* (1989), an accessible interdisciplinary collection introducing the subject on many levels of ideology and politics.

Lloyd A. Thompson, *Romans and Blacks* (1989), a historical study of Roman ethnocentricity and other specific attitudinal characteristics of the classical society.

John Julius Norwich, *Byzantium: The Early Centuries* (1989), an entertaining travelogue introducing five centuries of an illustrious culture.

Ann K.S. Lambton, *Continuity and Change in Medieval Persia: Aspects of Administrative, Economic, and Social History, 11th–14th Century* (1988), an important comprehensive presentation of the governmental, legal, economic, and cultural structures of medieval Iran.

Christopher I. Beckwith, *The Tibetan Empire in Central Asia: A History of the Struggle for Great Power Among Tibetans, Turks, Arabs, and Chinese During the Early Middle Ages* (1987), a thought-provoking history of the sudden emergence in the 7th century of a new power.

Serge Gruzinski, *Man-Gods in the Mexican Highlands: Indian Power and Colonial Society, 1520–1800* (1989; originally published in French, 1985), a readable history of a highly specific and local characteristic of Mexican society, taking its roots in the ancient Meso-American civilization.

Ira M. Lapidus, *A History of Islamic Societies* (1988), a monumental survey of 13 centuries of the history of Muslim communities all over the world.

Emmet Kennedy, *A Cultural History of the French Revolution* (1989), an excellent scholarly work, projecting the events of the period onto the following two centuries.

Sally Mitchell (ed.), *Victorian Britain: An Encyclopedia* (1988), a good introductory historical reference.

John Rickard, *Australia, a Cultural History* (1988), a combination of history and adventure that characterizes the identity of the nation in an engaging way.

Robert L. O'Connell, *Of Arms and Men: A History of War, Weapons, and Aggression* (1989), a provocative historico-philosophical look at the place of war in the life of humanity.

Michael Mandelbaum, *The Fate of Nations: The Search for National Security in the Nineteenth and Twentieth Centuries* (1988), a broad general account of world politics as characterized by international systems, not separate states.

Theodore H. Von Laue, *The World Revolution of Westernization: The Twentieth Century in Global Perspective* (1987), an analytic survey of wide-ranging effects of modernization and industrialization.

Héctor Pérez Brignoli, *A Brief History of Central America* (1989; originally published in Spanish, 1985), a balanced, nonpartisan, concise introduction to the region.

Rensselaer W. Lee III, *The White Labyrinth: Cocaine Trafficking and Political Power in the Andean Countries* (1989), a well-researched examination of a tragic contemporary phenomenon.

Stephen Uhalley, Jr., *A History of the Chinese Communist Party* (1988), an account of the growth and survival of an organization burdened with ruling the world's largest nation.

Harry Harding, *China's Second Revolution: Reform After Mao* (1987), a clear, substantial study of post-1976 events and the ensuing reforms, viewed without undue optimism.

Joseph J. Zasloff, *Postwar Indochina: Old Enemies and New Allies* (1988), an analysis of a complex political picture defined by relations among Vietnam, Kampuchea, Laos, the Soviet Union, China, and the U.S.

Anita Inder Singh, *The Origins of the Partition of India, 1936–1947* (1987), a detailed, persuasive history of the formation of Pakistan.

Catherine Coquery-Vidrovitch, *Africa: Endurance and Change South of the Sahara* (1988; originally published in French, 1985), a comprehensive history providing understanding of the current social, political, and economic situation in the region.

Joseph S. Nye, Graham T. Allison, and Albert Carnesale (eds.), *Fateful Visions: Avoiding Nuclear Catastrophe* (1988), a presentation of a futuristic, though not unrealistic, world.

The Branches of Knowledge

Sybil Wolfram, *Philosophical Logic: An Introduction* (1989), an original scholarly examination of those concepts of philosophical logic that extend into the philosophy of language.

Keith Devlin, *Mathematics: The New Golden Age* (1988), a survey of significant developments in mathematics from 1960 to 1985, meant for the open-minded lay reader.

Ivars Peterson, *The Mathematical Tourist: Snapshots of Modern Mathematics* (1988), a clear exposition of the fact that mathematical symbols and concepts represent ideas and that these can be expressed in the language of words as well.

Anthony O'Hear, *Introduction to the Philosophy of Science* (1989), a comprehensive, lucid survey of the concepts of the philosophy of science, analyzing science as intellectual activity that employs multiple approaches to problem resolution.

Milton A. Rothman, *A Physicist's Guide to Skepticism: Applying Laws of Physics to Faster-than-Light Travel, Psychic Phenomena, Telepathy, Time Travel, UFOs, and Other Pseudoscientific Claims* (1988), a polemical critique of extranormal phenomena, based on the atomic model of nature, which reinforces the author's attitude of "pragmatic skepticism."

Kevin Krisciunas, *Astronomical Centers of the World* (1988), a well-written and illustrated survey of the history, state of the art, and future of astronomy.

Stephen Boyden, *Western Civilization in Biological Perspective: Patterns in Biohistory* (1987), a well-documented exploration of human history through analysis of patterns of biological adaptation and efforts to achieve ecological stability.

Dean R. Gerstein (ed.), *The Behavioral and Social Sciences: Achievements and Opportunities* (1988), an anthology, authoritatively summarizing current research in various social and behavioral disciplines.

Joseph Finkelstein (ed.), *Windows on a New World: The Third Industrial Revolution* (1989), a collection of analytic essays, describing modern technological innovations as the third, information-based, industrial revolution, the first two having been based on mechanics and electronics, respectively.

David Anderson, *Artificial Intelligence and Intelligent Systems: The Implications* (1989), a provocative presentation of the idea that computers are capable of intelligent behaviour.

Richard B. Day, Ronald Beiner, and Joseph Masciulli (eds.), *Democratic Theory and Technological Society* (1988), an anthology of writings on modern thinking in the field of philosophy of technological society.

Bernard S. Katz and Ronald E. Robbins (eds.), *Modern Economic Classics—Evaluations Through Time* (1988), a collection of analytic critical reviews of influential writings.

Morris Weitz, *Theories of Concepts: A History of the Major Philosophical Tradition* (1988), an in-depth historical examination of philosophical theories of ideas, assessing the classics from a modern point of view.

People of 1989

BIOGRAPHIES

Altman, Sidney

In the early 1980s two researchers, working independently, made a discovery that reversed a three-quarter-century-old scientific dogma. The dogma was that enzymatic activity—the triggering and acceleration (catalysis) of vital chemical reactions within living cells—was the exclusive domain of protein molecules. The revolutionary find was that ribonucleic acid, or RNA—traditionally thought to be only a passive intracellular carrier of genetic information—also could function as an enzyme. The advance opened up new fields of research and biotechnology and caused scientists to rethink old theories of the way cells function and even of the way life on the Earth first began. For their discovery Sidney Altman of Yale University and Thomas R. Cech (*q.v.*) of the University of Colorado were awarded the 1989 Nobel Prize for Chemistry.

Altman was born May 7, 1939, in Montreal. He left Canada to attend the Massachusetts Institute of Technology, where he received a B.S. in physics in 1960. Seven years later he took a Ph.D. in biophysics from the University of Colorado, and he subsequently received research fellowships from Harvard University and the Medical Research Council Laboratory for Molecular Biology at the University of Cambridge. He joined the faculty of Yale University as an assistant professor in 1971 and was a professor of biology there from 1980. Altman also acted as dean at Yale College from 1985 until 1989. He became a U.S. citizen in 1984 while retaining his Canadian citizenship.

Altman's prizewinning work was done with a bacterial enzyme, ribonuclease P, that is composed of both RNA and protein components. He originally did not think that the RNA component served an active enzymatic function. His assumption was proved wrong, however, when in 1978 he and his colleagues found that ribonuclease P lost its enzymatic abilities when the RNA portion was removed. By 1983 the team had shown that, under certain conditions, the RNA portion alone could act as an enzyme in a chemical reaction. Since then scientists had identified about 100 catalytic RNA molecules, dubbed ribozymes, that are involved in important reactions.

The discovery of catalytic RNA inspired speculation that enzymatic RNA molecules may have been the key materials that made life on the Earth possible. The question of what kind of molecule first sparked life had long puzzled scientists because both catalysis and genetic-information storage are considered necessary preconditions for life, but no single biological molecule had been known that possessed both capabilities. The laureates' discovery of enzymatic RNA offered to solve the puzzle by supplying a molecule that can both carry genetic information and facilitate chemical reactions.

(CAROLYN D. NEWTON)

Aoun, Michel

"I will never surrender," declared Lebanon's defiant Gen. Michel Aoun in late November 1989, just before the newly elected president, Elias Hrawi, ordered the presidential palace Aoun had occupied surrounded by Syrian troops. The commander of Lebanon's Christian militia, Aoun saw his hopes and plans for saving

his country dwindle as the end of the year approached. In September 1988, when Parliament could not meet to elect a successor, Pres. Amin Gemayel had appointed Aoun to lead a transitional military government that consisted of six officers. Aoun was to serve as the Christian prime minister, and Selim al-Hoss was to be his Muslim counterpart. The arrangement fractured, so that Aoun, who previously had been the commander in chief of the Lebanese Army, controlled Christian East Beirut and al-Hoss led Muslim West Beirut. The transitional government was completely unsuccessful, and the country fell nearly into anarchy.

Staunchly nationalistic, Aoun believed his country's problems resulted from the intrusion of foreign invaders rather than from internal differences. In March Aoun declared a "war of liberation" against Syria. He believed that only after the Syrian military presence was eliminated from Lebanon could the country's other problems be solved. His Muslim counterparts were working closely with Syria, however, which led to an increasingly violent deadlock.

Meeting in Ta'if, Saudi Arabia, in October with the support of the Arab League, 62 Lebanese legislators created a new national charter for governing Lebanon. The arrangement called for Syria to redeploy its 40,000 troops into the Beqaa region over the next two years as a first stage toward possible eventual withdrawal from the country. The accord also redistributed political power between Muslims and Christians in the Parliament, neutralizing the Christian dominance mandated by Lebanon's 1943 constitution. Aoun rejected the accord, as did Walid Jumblatt, the Lebanese Druse leader, and representatives of the two main Shi'ite Muslim groups—the pro-Iranian Hezbollah and the pro-Syrian Amal militia.

In November Lebanon's Parliament elected René Moawad president. Aoun denounced the election and remained in the presidential palace in Baabda. Moawad's motorcade was blown up as he returned from an independence day ceremony. On the day of his funeral, Parliament elected Hrawi president. At year's end Aoun said he had postponed plans to hold an election of a rival government.

(FRANCINE SHONFELD SHERMAN)

Ayckbourn, Alan

The year 1989 was one of celebration for Alan Ayckbourn, Britain's most prolific and successful playwright. Son of the first violinist and deputy leader of the London Symphony Orchestra and stepson of his journalist mother's second husband, a bank manager, Ayckbourn on April 12 commemorated the 50th anniversary of his birth in Hampstead, London. The birthday cake, with its 50 candles, was shaped like the Stephen Joseph Theatre in the Round, the circular theatre in Scarborough, North Yorkshire, where all but four of his 39 plays (not counting revues and ad hoc entertainments) had their world premieres.

Ayckbourn, except for two years when he was at London's National Theatre, worked at Stephen Joseph's theatre not only as director and manager but, more importantly, as house dramatist. He joined Joseph as a small-part actor and assistant stage manager and got his

first playwriting assignment from him on being assured that there was "no mystique about playwriting. Only technique and talent were needed." He wrote his first play (*The Square Cat,* 1959), unpublished and since withdrawn, using the pen name Roland Allen. His latest play, *Body Language,* was due to open in Scarborough in February 1990, while *Man of the Moment,* his 35th, was scheduled to be transferred to London's West End in the same month.

From 1959 at least one new play by Ayckbourn was staged each year at Scarborough. Occasionally there might be as many as two or three, as happened in 1989; these three included *Invisible Friends,* which might be described as a "magic play" for children of all ages from seven years and upward. During the same 12 months, Ayckbourn's works were performed in more than 15 European countries, as well as in the U.S. and Japan.

Ayckbourn started writing playlets before he was 10, and in his middle teens this activity continued. At 15 he acted in school productions of Shakespeare that toured in Europe and the U.S. His plays were all set in southern England, usually in small towns and rural settings.

(OSSIA TRILLING)

Baker, James

At a formal ceremony at the White House on Jan. 27, 1989, James Addison Baker III was sworn in as the 61st U.S. secretary of state. Nominated in November 1988 by President-elect George Bush, Baker was confirmed by the Senate on Jan. 25, 1989. In years past the secretary of state's role was largely defined by matters of war and peace. Baker's immediate tasks, however, included the international drug war, the economic distress of less developed countries, the environment, and terrorism.

Baker, the son of a well-to-do attorney, was born on April 28, 1930, in Houston, Texas. His great-grandfather was a founder of Baker & Botts, one of Houston's first legal offices. His grandfather built Baker & Botts into one of the largest and most prestigious law firms in Houston. After graduating from Princeton University in 1952, Baker joined the U.S. Marine Corps, where he served as a lieutenant. Upon completion of his military service, he returned to Texas to study law at the University of Texas, earning his degree in 1957. Prevented from joining the family business by a company rule against nepotism, he went to work for Andrews, Kurth, Campbell & Jones, another major law firm in Houston. He became a partner and practiced law there until 1975.

Baker became actively involved in politics in 1970. In that year Bush, a longtime friend, announced his candidacy for the U.S. Senate and asked Baker to help manage his campaign. In 1975 Baker was appointed under secretary of commerce by Pres. Gerald Ford. Baker joined Ford's reelection campaign in 1976 as deputy chairman for delegate operations and in August of that year became national chairman of the Ford campaign. Despite Ford's loss in the election, Baker earned a reputation as a campaign tactician of uncommon ability.

In 1978 Baker ran for the office of state attorney general in Texas and lost to a conservative Democrat. From January 1979 to May 1980 he

was Bush's campaign chairman for the 1980 Republican presidential nomination. When Bush joined the Ronald Reagan ticket as the nominee for vice president, Baker served as a senior adviser. During the Reagan administration he served as chief of staff from January 1981 to January 1985 and as secretary of the treasury from February 1985 until August 1988, when he served, once again, as Bush's campaign chairman in his presidential election campaign.

(EDWARD PAUL MORAGNE)

Baker, Russell

In 1989 the Pulitzer Prize-winning journalist and author Russell Baker followed up his 1982 autobiography, *Growing Up*, with a sequel, *The Good Times*. The second volume picked up where the first ended—with his first job as a reporter for the *Baltimore* (Md.) *Sun*—and continued through 1963, ending with the assassination of U.S. Pres. John F. Kennedy and Baker's beginning his thrice-weekly newspaper column, "Observer," for the *New York Times*. His insightful, satirical commentary won him a wide readership and several journalism prizes, yet Baker's story of his own life struck many readers as melancholy and self-critical. The "good times," as he defined them, occurred at the start of his career, and thereafter he seemed to be trying to live up to unreachably high standards.

Russell Wayne Baker was born Aug. 14, 1925, in Loudoun county, Va. He was raised by his mother, having lost his father at the age of five. He interrupted his college education to serve with the U.S. Navy (1943–45), but after World War II he resumed his studies and received a bachelor's degree in English literature from Johns Hopkins University, Baltimore (1947).

Baker joined the *Baltimore Sun* as a police reporter—the paper's training ground—but by age 27 he had been promoted to London correspondent. (Characteristically, he attributed his rapid rise to luck and his skill as a typist.) He drew praise for his unusually well-drawn portraits of events in London, and upon his return to the U.S. after little more than a year, he was made White House correspondent for the *Sun*.

In 1954 the *New York Times* offered Baker a position with its Washington bureau, a job he had once declined. By now bored with the routine of covering the White House (which he saw as a matter of writing up prefabricated news items culled from official channels), and with some misgivings about biting the hand that had fed him, Baker accepted the *Times*'s offer. He reported on the State Department and Congress but later found himself once again at the White House. Throughout the 1950s his reputation as a lucid observer of political machinations and as a literate and humorous essayist had been growing. From 1962 Baker's syndicated column, "Observer," appeared on the editorial page of the *Times*.

Baker also wrote 12 books, including four collections of his columns, a children's book, and the two volumes of memoirs. In 1979 he won the Pulitzer Prize and the George Polk Award for commentary; in 1983 *Growing Up* won him another Pulitzer, this time for biography, and the Elmer Holmes Bobst Prize for nonfiction.

(LORRAINE MURRAY)

Barco Vargas, Virgilio

Colombia's drug mafia declared war on the government in 1989, and Pres. Virgilio Barco Vargas appealed to the international community for help. Barco's presidency had begun two years earlier on a somewhat different note, with a plan to attack absolute poverty, which he saw as the root cause of the violence pervading the country. In December 1986 details of the National Plan for the Eradication of Poverty had been announced. It called for the generation of stable and adequately remunerated employment and the meeting of basic needs in the violence-stricken areas. However, the worsening security situation called for more immediate action, which was not forthcoming.

From the beginning, Barco's administration was characterized by a sense of drift, arising

largely from the low profile that he adopted and the introduction of single-party government, bringing to an end almost three decades of power sharing between the Liberals and Conservatives. Barco's initial refusal to discuss the country's security issue outside Congress was in itself destabilizing. Politicians were unused to functioning in government and opposition parties, and, what was more, the Barco administration could not protect the lives of the legislators from the many death squads operating in the country. His increasing reliance on the military to deal with the security crisis was more incendiary than salutary. In April 1988 a report by Amnesty International explicitly referred to the military's involvement with the death squads.

No sooner had the government appeared to make headway against the leftist guerrillas than crimes related to drug trafficking flared up, with prominent people the victims of cold-blooded killings. Events forced Barco to resume the dialogue with the guerrillas begun by his predecessor and to concentrate his fire against the mafia. The Supreme Court twice ruled unconstitutional an extradition treaty with the U.S., but he signed it back into law and continued to strike at the heart of the drug trade by seizing cocaine shipments and destroying laboratories. He put forward a plan of action whose main points included curbing the demand for illegal drugs, controlling trade in chemicals used in the processing of drugs, reducing arms sales to drug traffickers and terrorists, and more effectively controlling money laundering.

Barco was born Sept. 17, 1921, in Cúcuta, Norte de Santander department. He was mayor of Bogotá in 1966–69.

(ALEXANDER JOHNS CAMPBELL)

Barenboim, Daniel

"There are two ways of dealing with an audience," explained Daniel Barenboim, conductor and pianist. "Either you go to it, or it comes to you. . . . Since there are 2,000 of them, it's easier for them to come to you." In his opinion, the most respectful way of treating an audience was to ignore it and to concentrate fully on the music, which should be performed as much to educate as to entertain. It was this nonpopulist approach and his insistence on paying high salaries for top performers and conductors, including himself, that contributed to his dismissal in January 1989 as artistic and music director of the French government's newly created Opéra de la Bastille.

That his problems in France were largely political was emphasized by the announcement, also in January, that Barenboim would replace the Chicago Symphony Orchestra's retiring and highly celebrated music director, Sir Georg Solti, a decision that had been made a year earlier. Barenboim afterward announced his resignation

ROBERT F. KUSEL

as music director of the Orchestre de Paris, where in 1975 he had also succeeded Solti.

In the early 1980s French Pres. François Mitterrand, a Socialist, proposed a modern, popular opera house, scheduled to open in July 1989. In 1987 it was the outgoing conservative government, however, that hired Barenboim as the opera's artistic director. After the Socialists took power again, Pierre Bergé, president of the Yves Saint-Laurent fashion house and a major contributor to Mitterrand's reelection campaign, became the opera's administrator. Bergé insisted that the $430 million opera house was wasting money and demanded a large cut in Barenboim's $1.1 million salary, the scheduling of more popular operas, veto power over Barenboim's artistic decisions, and an increase in performances. Barenboim objected, and Bergé fired him six months before the season's opening. Barenboim appealed to Mitterrand to choose between him and "the boss of a couture house." Mitterrand remained silent, but some of the world's most respected conductors and performers—including Solti, Herbert von Karajan, and Jessye Norman—threatened to cancel their commitments with the opera in protest.

Barenboim was born on Nov. 15, 1942, in Buenos Aires, Arg. He learned to play the piano from his parents, who were both accomplished pianists. Soon after his first concert appearance at the age of seven, he studied composition with Nadia Boulanger in Paris and conducting with Igor Markevich in Salzburg, Austria. Noted as a leading interpreter of music from the Classical and Romantic periods, he became one of the outstanding pianists of his generation.

(THOMAS J. RIGGS)

Barr, Roseanne

Fleshing out the role of harried housewife, Roseanne Barr became the biggest woman on television in 1989. The weekly series "Roseanne" starred the 80.2-kg (215-lb) comedian as a loudmouthed, softhearted wife and mother struggling to help her blue-collar family make ends meet. Punctuating and enlivening the series' slice-of-life episodes were Barr's

GLOBE PHOTOS

barbs, which the toothy, nasal-voiced actress directed—with offhand delight—at anyone who got in her way. Her engagingly sassy personality and the show's comically contentious family life (reminiscent of the classic shows "The Honeymooners" and "All in the Family") made "Roseanne" one of America's most highly watched television programs, often second only to "The Cosby Show." Writing her own lines and serving as a consultant on the show's scripts, Barr sought to convey a real, three-dimensional working mother. Her weight ironically aided the funny lady's cause. According to Barr, "Being fat means you take up more space, so you're seen—and probably heard—more easily."

Barr was first seen and heard in Salt Lake City, Utah, on Nov. 3, 1952, born to Jewish parents. To fit into that area's Mormon-dominated society, she was baptized and would spend Sundays in church after Saturdays in synagogue. The divided Barr proved a troubled, attention-seeking youth; at 16 she was struck by a car, an accident—or suicide attempt, according to some reports—that knocked her unconscious and later led to an eight-month stay in the psychiatric Utah State Hospital.

A few years later in Colorado she found herself in captivity of a more benevolent kind, keeping house for a husband and three children—an experience that would leave Barr with a mother lode of humour. Prodded by her younger sister, she worked as a stand-up comic for various Denver clubs during the early 1980s, but she did not develop a unique voice until 1986, when she was hired by the Comedy Store in Los Angeles. Her routines there—exploiting the Barr code to berate lazy husbands and wayward children—won Barr her own HBO cable-television special and several appearances on "The Tonight Show."

The next stop was network prime time. Her October 1988 debut in "Roseanne" made the chipmunk-cheeked comedian a household word. Her celebrity launched her book, *Roseanne: My Life as a Woman,* to the top of the best-seller lists and landed her a role in the movie *She-Devil.* A meaty woman whose husband leaves her for lean Meryl Streep, her character was—appropriately enough—a housewife with a vengeance.   (MICHAEL AMEDEO)

Bashir, Omar Hassan Ahmad al-
Lieut. Gen. Omar Hassan Ahmad al-Bashir, 45, became in 1989 the fourth military leader to overthrow a civilian government since Sudanese independence in 1956. In June he ousted Sadiq al-Mahdi's elected government and replaced it with a military regime, pledging not to restore a system of parliamentary democracy. A brigadier at the time of the coup, the heavily balding officer was hardly known outside army circles, where he had a reputation for toughness. He was the third-ranking officer in the paratroop division stationed in the isolated garrison of al-Muglad in south Kurdufan. He was believed to have served as a young soldier with the Egyptian Army in the defense of the Suez Canal. His brother, who was better known, was editor of a newspaper, *El-Sudani,* which supported the National Islamic Front, a Muslim fundamentalist movement. Although Bashir strongly denied that his military regime was linked to the Islamic Front, many of his ministerial and other appointees were known to be Muslim fundamentalists.

During his first months in power, Bashir showed little sign of having a clear political line. He identified himself closely with Egypt but also strengthened his ties with Libya. At one point he suggested the country might be partitioned between the Islamic north and the mainly non-Islamic south, but he later repudiated any such idea. He said he was unwilling to scrap the Shari'ah (Islamic law) but later suggested this was a matter for negotiation. (Imposition of the Shari'ah was one cause of the revolt in the south.) At first he ruled out any idea of continuing the war with the rebel Sudan People's Liberation Army, but subsequently he said that if his peace initiatives were rebuffed, the war would be resumed with all the resources of the country thrown into the effort. Under his leadership The Sudan continued to slide into deeper economic distress; famine stalked large areas; and the cease-fire in the fighting was ended in October.   (COLIN LEGUM)

Batman
In 1989, after 50 years of working the night shift, Batman finally got the American public to take him seriously. Caped, cowled, and a little crazy, a superhero without superpowers, he brought his obsession with crime fighting to the big screen in the $35 million *Batman,* which quickly became a "must-see" film. Though it

was cool and dark and its hero sombre and introspective, the film sold $250 million worth of tickets in the U.S. alone, making *Batman* one of the biggest hits in film history. As if to emphasize ironically Batman's half century, however, critics were 50-50 on the new film, the *New York Times* complaining that it "meanders mindlessly from one image to the next," *The New Yorker* countering that "its images sing," and *Time,* in a seeming compromise, calling it "half brilliant." Unaffected by the ambivalence, Americans not only filled up Bat screenings but also snatched up Bat products—an estimated $250 million worth of T-shirts, caps, buttons, and other items. According to social observers, Americans embraced Batman because he was a mortal who could do the near impossible: impose justice on an unjust world.

Batman was born in the May 1939 issue of *Detective Comics.* His mother/father was 18-year-old artist Bob Kane, who had sought to create a superhero who would rival the success of Superman. By day Kane's character functioned as bland millionaire Bruce Wayne, whose parents were murdered by thugs years before; by night he became the avenging Batman, who swung from shadow to shadow waiting for criminal prey. Lacking Superman's invulnerability, he needed the help of a junior partner, the tough and acrobatic Robin. Their exploits proved so popular with readers that Batman was given his own comic in 1940.

Changes in the comic took some of the edge off his character, and in the mid-1960s Batman even starred in a television series as a self-consciously campy superhero (played by Adam West). The biggest change came in 1984, however, when Robin left the Bat nest. His replacement, Jason Todd, was later killed, the result of a readers' poll that turned thumbs down on the new Robin.

A Batman grimmer and more rabid than the original took the streets in Frank Miller's *The Dark Knight Returns,* a 1986 comic book novel that would influence the makers of the 1989 movie. Seeing Batman as a rather disturbed guy, director Tim Burton antagonized fans by giving the role to the slightly built, wild-eyed Michael Keaton, who had played neurotic characters in a number of comedies. Unusually psychological for such a commercial production, Burton's film had Batman inadvertently creating his evil counterpart in the person of the green-haired, pasty-faced, smile-scarred Joker, played by Jack Nicholson as someone truly batty.

(MICHAEL AMEDEO)

Bennett, William
On Jan. 12, 1989, William Bennett was named director of the Office of National Drug Control Policy by U.S. President-elect George Bush. Bennett defined his mission: to oversee and coordinate all the government's drug efforts—as a Cabinet-level officer without a Cabinet department and without any control over the 58 government agencies already involved in the drug war.

A former U.S. secretary of education, one-time college football tackle, avowed philosopher, and lifelong rock and roll fan, Bennett was described as ambitious, impatient, abrasive, tough—a man looking for a challenge. He was given six months to prepare a report to Congress outlining his plans for a national drug strategy. Bennett was so successful in gaining the president's support that in Bush's first nationwide presidential address on September 5, Bennett's drug strategy was outlined. Key points included in the $7.9 billion antidrug package were specific goals for reducing drug use, financing antidrug efforts at the source (Colombia, Bolivia, and Peru), and placing more emphasis on individual accountability for drug use in schools and workplaces. Bennett allocated nearly 70% of the money for enforcement and earmarked the rest for prevention, education, and treatment. The one issue he refused to consider was legalizing drugs.

As secretary of education (1985–88), Bennett made headlines with his outspoken criticism of

the U.S. educational system. His forceful personality brought an unheard-of visibility to the Department of Education. Before he resigned on Sept. 20, 1988, he stated, "The one thing that I did not want said was that education reform fizzled out on my watch. We were true to the movement to reform schools in this country. Boy, were we true to it."

In 1976 Bennett cofounded the National Humanities Center in North Carolina, where he advanced his belief that the humanities "bring together the perennial questions of human life." The former Democrat joined the Republican Party in 1986.

William John Bennett was born in Brooklyn, N.Y., on July 31, 1943, graduated (1965) from Williams College in Williamstown, Mass., and "fell in with the world of ideas." He served as assistant to the president of Boston University (1972–76); executive director (1976–79) and president (1979–81) of the National Humanities Center, Research Triangle Park, N.C.; and associate professor at North Carolina State University (1979–81) and at the University of North Carolina (1979–81).

(VIRGINIA M. LAFLEUR)

Bishop, John Michael
The 1989 Nobel Prize for Physiology or Medicine went to two colleagues at the University of California Medical School in San Francisco for achievements in clarifying the origins of cancer. The researchers, J. Michael Bishop and Harold E. Varmus (*q.v.*), discovered that the viral genes that can cause cancer in humans and other animals do not originate within viruses, as had been previously suggested; instead, they begin as normal genes within healthy cells of the body where they serve to control cellular growth and division. The laureates' findings indicated that these benign genes can be picked up by certain viruses and then transformed into oncogenes; *i.e.,* genes capable of causing cancer. The discovery, published in 1976, dispelled a theory that distinct, potentially cancer-causing genes of viral origin exist in inactive form in all body cells. According to that theory, cancer results when the dormant viral genes are activated in some way—for example, by exposure to an environmental carcinogen.

Bishop, the son of a preacher, was born in York, Pa., Feb. 22, 1936. He attended Gettysburg (Pa.) College and graduated in 1957. Although he showed an interest in history, he entered Harvard University Medical School, where he discovered his passion and talent for biomedical science. There he took up the study of animal viruses and arranged with the dean of students to spend his fourth academic year doing research instead of attending classes. After graduating from Harvard with a medical degree in 1962 and spending two years in internship and residency at Massachusetts General Hospital, Boston, he became a researcher in virology at the National Institutes of Health, Bethesda, Md. In 1968 he joined the faculty of the University of California Medical Center in San Francisco, where he was a full professor from 1972. From 1981 he also served as director of the university's George F. Hooper Research Foundation. Bishop's research won him numerous honours, including the Biomedical Research Award from the American Association of Medical Colleges in 1981, the Albert Lasker Award for Basic Medical Research in 1982, and the American Cancer Society Medal of Honor in 1985.

In the mid-1970s Bishop and Varmus set out to test the theory that healthy body cells contain dormant viral oncogenes that, when triggered, cause cancer. They concentrated on the Rous sarcoma virus, known to cause tumours in chickens. Previous research had shown that the virus's cancer-causing ability is due to a particular gene within the virus. Bishop and Varmus found that, as would be expected, the gene was present in tumour cells. However, they also found a very similar gene in healthy cells. In 1976 they and two colleagues—Dominique Stehelin and Peter Vogt—published their findings, concluding that the virus had taken up the gene

responsible for the cancer from a normal cell. After the virus had infected the cell and begun its usual process of replication, it incorporated the gene into its own genetic material. Subsequent research done by Bishop, Varmus, and others showed that such genes can cause cancer in several ways. Bishop described these genes as "a keyboard on which various carcinogens can play." For instance, if a virus carrying such a gene inserts it into abnormal places in a cell's DNA where its action is no longer controlled, the gene can cause inappropriate or uncontrolled cellular growth characteristic of cancer. Even without viral involvement, these genes can be converted by certain chemical carcinogens into a form that allows uncontrolled growth.

Because the mechanism described by Bishop and Varmus seems common to all forms of cancer, their work proved invaluable to cancer research. By 1989 scientists had identified more than 40 genes having cancer-causing potential in animals. This work in turn was expected to lead to developments that would help doctors predict, diagnose, treat, and even prevent cancer in their patients. (CAROLYN D. NEWTON)

Border, Allan Robert

Allan Border was the epitome of the Australian cricketer—small, squat, broad-shouldered, and a fighter from the top of his baggy green Australian cap to the bottom of his boots. However, as the Australian coach Bobby Simpson said, that description did not do Border justice. He was the most prolific batsman in Australian test history, and in 1989 only the great Indian batsman Sunil Gavaskar had scored more than Border's 8,273 test runs. Perhaps even more remarkable was the fact that the little left-hander maintained a test average of 53 while, for a large part of his career, captaining a losing side. He captained his country a record 45 times and until 1989, when Australia beat England 4–0 to win back the Ashes trophy, had won only seven matches and one series.

Border was born on July 27, 1955, and became a professional cricketer in 1977. He played his first test in Melbourne in 1978–79 and was a permanent fixture in the Australian side from the day he scored 150 in both innings of the Lahore test against Pakistan in 1979–80. He was perhaps considered too quiet and unassuming to be a good captain, but when Kim Hughes resigned in the middle of the 1984–85 season, Border was thrust rather unwillingly into the limelight against a rampant West Indian side. His early years as captain were characterized by heroic rearguard innings in losing causes, which reached a head in 1986 when he threatened to resign if his players did not perform better. After that day he put his faith in youth and molded a fine young Australian side, which he led with great skill and obvious joy to victory over England in 1989, avenging the humiliating defeats of 1985 and 1986–87.

Brought up on grade cricket in his native Sydney, Border was not a stylish batsman. He had a short backlift, punching the ball away, particularly on his favourite cut and hook strokes. He had a phlegmatic temperament, though, and the ability when set to make big scores. He had the rare distinction for an Australian cricketer of being a very popular figure in England, partly because of his graceful acceptance of defeat in the 1985 Ashes series and partly because of his success playing with the English county Essex. Still only 34, he could, if he had the inclination, become the highest run-scorer ever in test cricket. (ANDREW LONGMORE)

Brown, Ron

On Feb. 10, 1989, Ron Brown was elected by acclamation to the chairmanship of the Democratic Party National Committee. As elections go, this one was historically significant mainly because Brown, a prominent Washington, D.C., lawyer and corporate lobbyist, became the first black to chair a major U.S. political party. "I wasn't running as a black candidate, and I wasn't running for a black position," he told the 400-plus committee members listening to

his acceptance speech. "I was seeking a position for which I was confident I was qualified and confident I could do a good job."

This self-confidence began manifesting itself at a very young age. Born on Aug. 1, 1941, in Washington, D.C., Ronald Harmon Brown was the only child of two Howard University graduates. Brown was reared in New York City and attended Hunter College Elementary School, where he was the only black student in his class. In 1958 he enrolled in Middlebury (Vt.) College, where he became the first black accepted into the Sigma Phi Epsilon fraternity. After graduating from Middlebury in 1962, he joined the U.S. Army, where he rose to the rank of captain. After leaving the Army in 1967, he worked as a welfare caseworker for the National Urban League by day and studied law at St. John's University, Jamaica, N.Y., by night. He received a law degree in 1970.

In 1971 Brown was elected district leader of the Democratic Party in Mount Vernon, N.Y. He moved to Washington, D.C., in 1973 and by 1978 held the position of vice president of the Urban League's Washington operations. The following year he became deputy manager of the presidential campaign of Sen. Edward Kennedy (Dem., Mass.). In 1980 Brown was named chief counsel to the Senate Judiciary Committee. In 1981 he joined Patton, Boggs & Blow as that law firm's first black partner.

For three months in 1988 Brown worked in the Rev. Jesse L. Jackson's presidential campaign, serving as its manager at the Democratic national convention. Five months after the convention Paul G. Kirk, Jr., announced that he would not seek a second four-year term as chairman of the Democratic National Committee. Brown decided to run, and in the final week of January 1989 he had gained enough significant endorsements to persuade his opponents to withdraw from the race. Because of his links with both Jackson and Kennedy, Brown spent considerable time before and after his election trying to dispel the seemingly indelible perception among Democratic Party leaders that he was "a clone of Jesse Jackson" and that his ascension would further fuel an image of liberalism that many in the party wanted to combat. (EDWARD PAUL MORAGNE)

Bush, Barbara

When Barbara Bush, wife of U.S. Pres. George Bush, was described, one of the most frequently heard phrases was "down to earth." She was unpretentious, especially about her appearance, and was always willing to poke fun at herself. She refused to dye her white hair or apologize for her matronly figure and acknowledged that her pearls were fakes. She also admitted that when she tells her children that she married the first man she ever kissed, "they just about throw up." Her honesty and irreverence endeared her to the public. One poll showed that the U.S. public preferred her over her predecessor, Nancy Reagan, by a 3–1 ratio, while another gave her a national approval rating higher than that of her husband.

She was born Barbara Pierce on June 8, 1925, in Rye, N.Y. She met Bush at a party in Greenwich, Conn., during Christmas vacation when she was a senior at Ashley Hall, a prep school in South Carolina. She dropped out of Smith College, Northampton, Mass., during her sophomore year to marry him. They had six children.

"The Silver Fox"—her children's nickname for her—became an activist first lady, maintaining a longtime involvement in a number of causes, chief among them the promotion of literacy. One reason for this interest was the dyslexia that one of her sons had to battle. More important was the impact that an improvement in literacy could have on a number of social problems. To aid this program, the Barbara Bush Foundation for Family Literacy was established in the spring of 1989 and supported reading programs throughout the U.S. Bush often personally encouraged her friends—and people she had just met—to become tutors,

CAROL T. POWERS—THE WHITE HOUSE

and she even appeared on the television show "Sesame Street."

Another of her concerns was the fight against leukemia. That, too, was motivated by personal experience: one of the Bushes' daughters died of the disease shortly before her fourth birthday. Bush later became honorary national chair of the Leukemia Society of America. She also became involved in a number of other medically oriented volunteer activities, aiding fund-raising efforts of a medical school and visiting patients in cancer wards and hospices, for example. As if that were not enough, she found time to help out in soup kitchens and shelters for the homeless. As first lady she was able to demonstrate prominently the effect that individuals could have if they would try to help where they saw a need. (BARBARA WHITNEY)

Bush, George Herbert Walker

On Jan. 20, 1989, George Bush was inaugurated as president of the United States, succeeding Ronald Reagan, a rival turned mentor. In his inaugural address, Bush said that his role was "to make kinder the face of the nation and gentler the face of the world." In his first 300 days in office, Bush made no major changes in Reagan's policies, but he adopted what seemed a more involved style. Bush met regularly with ranking officials, sought the advice of contacts around the world, and held frequent press conferences. Some federal offices went unfilled for weeks because of difficulties in recruiting and obtaining senatorial confirmation. However, the only major scandal in the executive branch involved appointees of Reagan—not of Bush—in the Department of Housing and Urban Development.

Some members of Bush's staff sharply criticized the opposition Democrats, who controlled both houses of Congress. Bush remained cordial with them, however, often negotiating written agreements—as that of March 25 on nonlethal aid to the *contras* (armed opponents of the Sandinista regime) in Nicaragua. Bush did use his veto against acts of Congress favourable to abortion and also to secure a minimum-wage law that reflected his own ideas. On October 16, under the deficit reduction law, he sequestered $16 billion from the federal budget and said that he preferred keeping it sequestered to signing a law calling for new taxes or for assignment of current expenditures to future budgets.

Bush applauded the efforts of Soviet Pres. Mikhail Gorbachev and leaders of other nations in the Warsaw Pact to reform their countries. In July Bush visited Poland and Hungary, and in December he held his first summit with Gorbachev in Malta. Elsewhere, Bush's foreign policy was more controversial. In February in Beijing (Peking), where he had been envoy (1974–75), he talked of freedom on Chinese television, then learned that a prominent dissident had been excluded from a banquet in his hon-

our. When the Chinese democracy movement was quelled in June, Bush imposed ineffective sanctions, and it was later revealed that he had sent secret delegations to Beijing in July and December. In October the U.S. Army watched a failed coup against Panama's de facto ruler, Gen. Manuel Noriega. At year's end, however, Bush sent in U.S. troops to oust Noriega, who was accused of corruption and drug trafficking.

Bush was generally well received by other heads of state. He met several in Tokyo on February 23–24 at Emperor Hirohito's funeral. Bush also attended the NATO summit in Brussels (May 29–30), met with the leaders of the other six major industrialized democracies in Paris (July 14–15), and conferred with Latin-American leaders at a regional conference in Costa Rica (October 27–28).

Born in Milton, Mass., on June 12, 1924, and raised in Greenwich, Conn., Bush graduated from Yale University in 1948 and worked in the Texas oil business. He entered politics in 1960 and was vice president of the U.S. under Reagan (1981–89).

(CHARLES JOHNSON TAGGART)

Carey, Peter

On Oct. 26, 1988, Great Britain's most prestigious literary award, the Booker Prize, was awarded to the Australian writer Peter Carey for his novel *Oscar and Lucinda*. The novel tells the story of Oscar Hopkins (who read Greats at Oriel) and Lucinda Leplastrier. They meet on a journey to Australia in the mid-19th century. Oscar is afraid of the sea, and when he decided to migrate to Australia on the *Leviathan*, he knew it would be a one-way journey. Oscar is drawn to Lucinda by their mutual gambling compulsion, the pair standing as the personification of the nation as a whole. Carey believed that Australia's history was "a history of orphans," and he used his novel (as he put it) like a "clever platform" to express the inevitable triumph of the antipodean environment over the individual, a phenomenon symbolized at the end of the novel by the destruction of a prefabricated glass church on its journey up a river.

Carey had been nominated for the Booker Prize once before, for *Illywacker* (1985). That novel, written in the first person, was the fictional biography of Herbert Badgery, a "terrible liar" who gave Carey the opportunity to expand on his themes of social disasters, tricksters, and morons.

Carey was born May 7, 1943, in Bacchus Marsh and was educated at Geelong Grammar School and Monash University. His intellectual awakening coincided with the efflorescence of explicit Australian cultural nationalism, and Carey was in contact with and influenced by such important figures as the cartoonist Bruce Petty, the film director Fred Schepsi, and the novelist Barry Oakley. Carey served a 10-year apprenticeship as an unpublished author working at various odd jobs before being discovered in 1974 following the publication of his collection of short stories *The Fat Man in History* (published in the U.K. in 1981 as *Exotic Pleasures*). His other works before his two Booker Prize nominations were *War Crimes* (1979; another short-story collection) and the novel *Bliss,* which was made into a highly successful film.

(A.R.G. GRIFFITHS)

Cech, Thomas Robert

The 1989 Nobel Prize for Chemistry was shared by Thomas R. Cech of the University of Colorado and Sidney Altman (*q.v.*) of Yale University. The researchers were recognized for their independent discoveries that ribonucleic acid, or RNA, traditionally considered to be only a passive messenger of genetic information, can also take on an enzymatic role in which it catalyzes, or facilitates, intracellular chemical reactions essential to life. Before these discoveries enzymatic activity had been attributed exclusively to proteins. According to the Royal Swedish Academy of Sciences, the laureates' work would "probably provide a new tool for gene technology, with potential to create

a new defense against viral infections." Scientists also speculated that such enzymatic RNA molecules, dubbed ribozymes, may have been the molecules from which sprang the first living organisms on the Earth.

Cech was born in Chicago on Dec. 8, 1947. He received a B.A. from Grinnell (Iowa) College in 1970 and a Ph.D. in chemistry from the University of California at Berkeley in 1975. In 1978, after a stint at the Massachusetts Institute of Technology as a National Cancer Institute fellow in molecular biology, he joined the faculty of the University of Colorado, where he became a full professor in 1983.

Cech was the first person to show that an RNA molecule could catalyze a chemical reaction. (Altman's earlier research had pointed strongly to such a conclusion, but his own demonstration of enzymatic activity by an RNA molecule was made in 1983, a year after Cech published his findings.) Cech began his prizewinning work in 1977 by trying to isolate the protein enzyme that was presumed to control a splicing reaction in which certain extraneous, or nonsense, segments are selectively removed from RNA molecules. While studying the reaction in a single-celled microorganism, he found that without external aid the RNA molecule cut away the nonsense segments from itself and rejoined the remainder into a new molecule. Still, the RNA molecule could not be considered a true enzyme because it could perform the operation only once and was itself changed in the process. True enzymes are defined as molecules that catalyze a reaction repeatedly while emerging from the reaction unchanged. One year later it was Altman who showed true enzymatic activity by an RNA molecule.

The laureates' work raised the possibility of using ribozymes to manipulate RNA molecules within cells. The discovery led to the development of a new kind of biotechnological tool called gene shears, which can cut RNA molecules at selected points. When the Nobel Prize was announced, Cech was involved in a patent dispute with Australian scientists over the commercial rights to this technology. Gene shears could one day be used to destroy RNA molecules that cause infections and to treat genetic disorders.

(CAROLYN D. NEWTON)

Cela, Camilo José

When the Swedish Academy chose Camilo José Cela as the winner of the 1989 Nobel Prize for Literature, they selected a "restless spirit" who personified a changing, modern Spain. In honouring Cela "for a rich and intensive prose, which with restrained compassion forms a challenging vision of man's vulnerability," the Academy bestowed the coveted prize on a longtime outspoken observer of the human condition.

Cela was born in 1916 in Iria Flavia in northwestern Spain. He studied medicine, philosophy, and law in Madrid; was badly wounded during the Civil War; and experimented with bullfighting, painting, and acting before becoming a serious writer. His first novel, *La familia de Pascual Duarte*, published in 1942, was widely acclaimed during the barren literary period that followed Gen. Francisco Franco's 1939 Civil War victory. Initially banned because of its candor, the novel became the second most popular in Spanish literature (after *Don Quixote*). Also significant to the Academy was Cela's publication of a literary magazine called *Papeles de Son Armadans*, which, during the Franco era, gave voice to young writers censored by the authorities. Cela became a member of the Academy of the Spanish Language in 1957; he won Spain's national literature prize in 1984 for his novel *Mazurca para dos muertos* ("Mazurka for Two Dead People"). Seven years earlier King Juan Carlos had appointed Cela to a Senate seat in the first post-Franco parliament.

This writer of 10 experimental novels, about 20 collections of stories, and numerous essays and travel accounts was the first to break literary sexual taboos that had developed in the puritanical writing styles of the Franco era. Cela

displayed an explicitness and a stark realism that electrified his readers. Two of his more unusual works were *Diccionario secreto* and *Enciclopedia del erotismo*, which reflect his fascination with the everyday language of Spaniards.

Critics argued that Cela had published nothing of importance after the 1950s and that most Spaniards recognized his name from gossip columns or as a television personality on a twice-weekly talk show. An opinionated figure who seemed to ignore most other opinions, Cela said upon winning, "Language is the instrument of the writer. Literature is the word and nothing else. The thinking of writers is in their books. In my case that's where people should look."

(BONNIE OBERMAN)

Chamorro, Violeta Barrios de

Was she truly a Chamorro or merely a Barrios? Was she a serious challenger for Nicaraguan president or just being used? On Sept. 2, 1989, Violeta Barrios de Chamorro, the owner of *La Prensa*, the daily opposition newspaper, became the official presidential candidate of the 14-party anti-Sandinista coalition, the National Opposition Union (UNO). She and UNO were closely identified with the U.S. and the *contras*. She belonged to no political party and had never run for political office, yet she carried the mantle of her late husband.

Doña Violeta, as she was respectfully called, was catapulted into politics on Jan. 10, 1978, when her husband, Pedro Joaquín Chamorro Cardenal, was assassinated by henchmen of dictator Anastasio Somoza. Chamorro was a prominent Conservative opposition figure and editor of the family-owned *La Prensa*. His murder galvanized moderate forces in Nicaragua against Somoza and thus helped lead to the triumph of the Sandinistas in 1979. It transformed Chamorro into a martyr for the revolution.

Doña Violeta served on the post-Somoza five-person revolutionary junta from June 1979. Citing ill health, she resigned in April 1980 and quickly turned *La Prensa* into a voice for those opposed to the government of Daniel Ortega. From then on, the paper was at the centre of controversy about the press, the *contras*, and efforts to overthrow the Nicaraguan government.

Violeta Barrios Torres was born in 1929 in Rivas, Nicaragua. She married Pedro Joaquín Chamorro in 1950 and spent the next 27 years raising a family. That family—sometimes compared to the Kennedys in the U.S.—and her right to the Chamorro name were now political issues. The government called her by her maiden name (Barrios). Her son Carlos was director of *Barricada*, the daily Sandinista newspaper; her brother-in-law Xavier was director of *El Nuevo Diario*, the country's third daily paper, which was generally pro-Sandinista; and her daughter Claudia was the former ambassador to Costa Rica. By contrast, daughter Cristina was editor of *La Prensa*, and her oldest son, Pedro Joaquín, its former editor and a former director of the *contra* Nicaraguan Resistance, lived in Miami.

If UNO should win the elections scheduled for February 1990, Doña Violeta said she would be most concerned with the nine Sandinista commandantes having to "look for new homes, because they are confiscated [from *contra* supporters]." In a country faced with inflation over 10,000%, the devastation of years of war and U.S. trade embargoes, and the destruction by Hurricane Joan in late 1988, this seemed the least worry awaiting the next Nicaraguan president.

(ELLEN FINKELSTEIN)

Cheney, Richard Bruce

On March 9, 1989, the U.S. Senate rejected Pres. George Bush's nomination of John Tower (*q.v.*) as secretary of defense amid allegations concerning his business interests and private conduct. The next day, Bush nominated Dick Cheney, a respected U.S. representative. Cheney took office on March 17 after having been confirmed by the Senate by a vote of 92–0. The process was speeded up because of the need to fill the job and also because of Cheney's acquaintance with senators, his administrative

experience, and his reputation for official and personal rectitude. It was noted, however, that his experience had not been military.

On April 25 Cheney proposed a departmental budget of $295.6 billion, about $10 billion less than had been proposed in January by Ronald Reagan as outgoing president. Cheney's budget called for reductions in personnel, elimination of some long-planned weapons systems, and the stretching out of work on others, such as the Strategic Defense Initiative. In July he announced plans to centralize the department's procurement system, as suggested in 1986, and draw up a code of ethics for those bidding on departmental contracts. On October 16 Bush sequestered $8.1 billion from the defense budget because of the deficit-reduction law, creating more hard choices for Cheney.

Richard Bruce Cheney was born in Lincoln, Neb., on Jan. 30, 1941, and lived in Casper, Wyo., from the age of 13. He received a B.A. in 1965 and an M.A. in 1966, both from the University of Wyoming, and studied for a Ph.D. in political science at the University of Wisconsin. In Washington, D.C., on a congressional fellowship in 1968, he caught the eye of Donald Rumsfeld, director of the Office of Economic Opportunity, and became Rumsfeld's special assistant in 1969. Cheney was on the White House staff in 1970–71 and served as an assistant director of the Cost of Living Council from 1971 to 1973, when Rumsfeld was director. When Rumsfeld became assistant to the president and chief of staff of the White House in 1974, Cheney was his deputy. From 1975 Cheney served first as assistant and then as chief of staff to Pres. Gerald Ford.

Cheney, a Republican, won the first of six consecutive terms as U.S. representative from Wyoming in 1978. He served on the Select Committee on Intelligence and became chairman of the Republican Conference in 1987 and minority whip in December 1988. In August of that year, he underwent coronary bypass surgery; his surgeon later advised no limits on his activities.   (CHARLES JOHNSON TAGGART)

Clements, the Rev. George
In the spring of 1989, the Rev. George Clements and the Rev. Michael Pfleger, both Roman Catholic priests, gained national attention when they waged their own small-scale war on the drug dealers that plagued the neighbourhoods around their churches in Chicago. The initial strategy was to put pressure on local stores to step selling drug paraphernalia. In June they made headlines after visiting the Good Deal One-Stop Distribution Co. This local wholesaler was openly selling drug paraphernalia and refused to let the two priests enter the building. Undaunted and determined, Clements shattered the glass door. Clements and Pfleger both were arrested and charged with criminal trespass and damage to property; the charges were dropped when the store clerk failed to appear at the trial. Shortly after the Good Deal incident, a law was passed in Illinois making it illegal for stores to sell drug paraphernalia. Clements and Pfleger worked to persuade the U.S. Congress to adopt a similar federal law.

A civil rights activist who marched at Selma, Ala., in 1965 with Martin Luther King, Jr., Clements was no novice at gaining the media's attention. In 1981 he made history and gained international exposure when he became the first Catholic priest to adopt a child. The late John Cardinal Cody, Clements' immediate superior at the time, forbade him to adopt a child and declared adoption by priests a violation of church law. However, Pope John Paul II learned of Clements' efforts, overruled Cody, and permitted Clements to adopt a 13-year-old boy. Soon afterward Clements founded One Church, One Child, an adoption program dedicated to finding black adoptive parents for black children. He himself later adopted three more sons. In December 1987 "The Father Clements Story," a two-hour television drama starring Academy Award winner Louis Gossett, Jr., in the title role, was shown on NBC.

Born in Chicago on Jan. 26, 1932, Clements had by the age of 12 decided to become a priest. After becoming the first black to graduate from Quigley Preparatory Seminary in Chicago, he studied philosophy and theology at St. Mary of the Lake Seminary in Mundelein, Ill., and received a B.A. degree and a M.A. degree in philosophy, a B.A. in sacred theology, and a licentiate of sacred theology. He was ordained a diocesan priest in May 1957. In July 1969 Clements became pastor of Holy Angels Church, where he gained renown for establishing a highly rated school in a poor inner-city neighbourhood. In 1977 he was honoured by the Association of Chicago Priests and presented with the Pope John XXIII Award as the Priest of the Year.
    (EDWARD PAUL MORAGNE)

Dalai Lama
The 1989 Nobel Peace Prize was awarded to the Dalai Lama, the exiled religious and political leader of Tibet, who had waged a nonviolent campaign for nearly 40 years to end Chinese domination of his native land. Following the violent June suppression of the pro-democracy movement in China and the imposition of martial law in Lhasa, Tibet's capital, the selection of the Dalai Lama seemed to signal support for such pro-democracy movements, although the Nobel Committee denied any political motivation.

Tenzin Gyatso, the son of peasants, was born June 6, 1935, in the Kokonor region of northeastern Tibet. At age five, having been chosen by the most venerated monks to be the 14th Dalai Lama, he was taken to Lhasa and enthroned in the Potala, a 1,000-room palace that overlooks the capital. In 1950 China invaded and occupied Tibet. When Chinese troops crushed an uprising in 1959 and murdered thousands, the Dalai Lama and 100,000 other refugees fled to India, where they were given political asylum. For 40 years the Tibetan leader continued to maintain a government-in-exile in the Himalayan town of Dharmsala, where his day began at two o'clock in the morning and consisted of several hours of meditating, two modest meals, gardening, and study. In 1987 he won the Albert Schweitzer Humanitarian Award. His books include several works on Buddhist theology and his autobiography, due to be published in 1990.

In 1988 the Dalai Lama offered the Chinese a compromise, recognizing their right to determine Tibet's foreign policy but allowing the small nation to be self-governing. Currently, Tibet was incorporated into China as the autonomous region of Xizang (Hsi-tsang). The Dalai Lama also agreed to a limited Chinese military presence on Tibetan soil until an area peace conference was convened. However, this search for a middle ground was blocked after the hard-liners gained control in Beijing (Peking).

All Tibetans fervently hoped the Nobel award would return their struggle to prominence. The Dalai Lama intended to give the $455,000 prize money to the Tibetan cause or to starving people elsewhere. His own life would not change. Upon learning of the award, he said, "I very much appreciate that kind of recognition about my beliefs. . . . I have always believed in love, compassion and a sense of universal respect. Every human being has that potential. My case is nothing special. I am a simple Buddhist monk—no more, no less." (BONNIE OBERMAN)

Daley, Richard M.
In 1989 the race for mayor of Chicago resulted in a Daley double. Richard M. Daley, son of the late Mayor Richard J. Daley, reached the finish line by beating black Acting Mayor Eugene Sawyer in the Democratic primary in February and black independent Alderman Timothy Evans in the general election in April. In a race shaped by race, Daley won by garnering the votes of more than 90% of the whites who cast ballots, including many of the affluent, independent-minded lakefront residents who had voted for Harold Washington, Chicago's first black mayor, in 1983 and 1987. Daley's election represented the first time since 1971 that a

ROBERT F. KUSEL

white had replaced a black as mayor of a major U.S. city. That fact alarmed some Chicago blacks, who feared that Daley would revive the "plantation politics" they felt had characterized his father's 21-year reign (1955–76). But the new mayor—whose tough, jowly face and mangled, tangled syntax were reminiscent of his father's—vowed to reach out to minorities, a promise he began to fulfill in May when he appointed blacks and Hispanics to head several of the city's largest departments. It was, at the very least, a sound political move by a man whose electoral platform—conservative on bureaucracy and law and order, more liberal on housing, education, and health care—had impressed national Democrats as the one the party needed to adopt in order to win key offices, especially the White House. Like Richard J., Richard M. proved to be a politician with a lot of horse sense.

Richard M., the first of four Daley sons out of the gate, was born April 24, 1942, in Bridgeport, a politically powerful, blue-collar ethnic community on Chicago's South Side. His father groomed him for public office, and the Daley political machine gave him a job in the city attorney's office after he passed the bar exam on the third attempt. Later, Daley won election to the Illinois Senate, filling a vacancy his father had arranged.

The death of his father in 1976 and the birth of a handicapped son in 1978 changed the young Daley forever. He became more independent and more compassionate, championing several social-welfare bills in the state Senate. In 1980 Daley was elected to the first of three terms as Cook County state's attorney, despite the opposition of several prominent Democrats, including Chicago Mayor Jane Byrne. Three years later he ran against Byrne for mayor, a move that split the white vote and ensured the historic election of Washington, who enjoyed monolithic support from the black community.

Washington's death from a heart attack in late 1987 cleared the path for another Daley run for mayor. Richard M. eventually won by a Daley-size margin: almost 15 points in the general election.   (MICHAEL AMEDEO)

Dehmelt, Hans Georg
Half of the 1989 Nobel Prize for Physics was shared by Hans G. Dehmelt of the University of Washington and West German scientist Wolfgang Paul (q.v.) of the University of Bonn for their development of methods for trapping individual electrically charged particles and atoms so that their properties could be studied with unprecedented precision. (The remainder of the prize went to Norman F. Ramsey [q.v.] of Harvard University.) Dehmelt was cited for the development in 1955 of the Penning trap, which uses a strong static magnetic field and a weak static electric field to capture electrons

and electrically charged atoms, or ions. The trap confines the electrons and ions in a small space for long periods of time in relative isolation from outside influences. In 1973, by means of his invention, Dehmelt became the first scientist to isolate a single electron for observation. In 1975 he devised a method for "cooling," or reducing the energy of, trapped electrons and ions in order to improve further the accuracy of measurements made on them. The cooling process made it possible for Dehmelt and other physicists to measure atomic frequencies and individual quantum jumps—the transitions between atomic energy levels—with a precision previously unattainable. Dehmelt and his colleagues used the Penning trap in another ground-breaking procedure when in the 1970s they measured an electron's magnetic moment to an accuracy of four parts in a trillion, the most precise measurement of that quantity at the time. Scientists subsequently used the measurement to test theoretical predictions of quantum electrodynamics.

Dehmelt was born Sept. 9, 1922, in Görlitz, now part of East Germany. He graduated from the Gymnasium Zum Grauen Kloster, Berlin, in 1940 and for the next six years served as a private in the German Army. Under an army program he studied physics at Breslau Technical University during World War II. In 1945 he was taken prisoner by American military forces near Bastogne, Belgium. After his release in 1946 he took up studies at the University of Göttingen, West Germany, where in 1950 he graduated summa cum laude with a doctoral degree in physics. For the next two years he worked as a research fellow at Göttingen.

Dehmelt traveled to the U.S. in 1952 for postdoctoral work at Duke University, Durham, N.C. In 1955 he joined the faculty of the University of Washington, where he was a full professor from 1961. He became a U.S. citizen in 1961. Dehmelt received numerous awards, including the Davisson-Germer Prize of the American Physical Society in 1970. In 1978 he was elected to the U.S. National Academy of Sciences.   (CAROLYN D. NEWTON)

de Klerk, F.W.

Frederik Willem de Klerk, 53, succeeded the ailing P.W. Botha as South Africa's president in September 1989, after an election in which the ruling National Party, which he had led in a campaign for the first time, emerged with a reduced majority in the all-white (and most powerful) chamber of the country's tricameral Parliament. Despite the electoral setback, de Klerk committed himself to speeding the reform program started by his predecessor and to initiating talks about a new postapartheid constitution with representative leaders of the country's four ethnic communities (white, Coloured, Indian, and black). Though faced with a strength-

ened right-wing opposition in Parliament in the form of the Conservative Party, the new president proceeded to release all important political prisoners except Nelson Mandela. In November he announced a major shift away from some of the remaining apartheid laws.

Born March 18, 1936, in Johannesburg, de Klerk was the son of a leading politician and brother of a prominent journalist, Willem ("Wimpie") de Klerk, who was one of the founders of the liberal opposition Democratic Party. Though politically far apart, the brothers maintained a close family relationship.

De Klerk passed his law degree with honours at Potchefstroom University in 1958. Soon afterward he began to establish a successful law firm in Vereeniging, becoming active in the civic and business affairs of that southern Transvaal industrial city. Although he was appointed professor of administrative law at Potchefstroom in 1972, he was elected to Parliament for the National Party in the same year and never took up the post. A careful, rather dull speaker, he was not a particularly distinguished parliamentary performer, but his legal talents and the respect in which he was held won him a number of key ministerial portfolios, including Mines, Social Welfare, National Education, Energy Affairs, and Internal Affairs. He was best known for his calm and moderate, if cautious, approach to sensitive political questions and for unfailing good nature and courtesy. Unlike his immediate predecessor, he had a quiet sense of humour and a total lack of arrogance. He owed his political success to the power base he built up in the Transvaal, where he was chairman of the provincial National Party, the NP's largest constituency in the country.   (COLIN LEGUM)

Dinkins, David

After 12 years of hearing Mayor Edward Koch ask New York City, "How am I doing?" the voting populace—apparently tiring of the city's problems—seemed to answer, "Not too well." On Sept. 12, 1989, David Dinkins defeated the 64-year-old incumbent in the Democratic Party mayoral primary. Then on November 7, Dinkins again seized victory when he defeated

his Republican opponent, former U.S. attorney Rudolph Giuliani, to become New York City's first black mayor.

Dinkins won the election with the support of a large number of blacks and Hispanics and with nearly one-third of the white vote. A far cry from the flamboyant, acerbic Koch, Dinkins had a soft-spoken, unassuming style that seemed to be just what New Yorkers were looking for to lead them into the 1990s. Accompanying Dinkins' sweet taste of victory was the bitter reality of the many problems that he would have to face. In addition to the $1 billion deficit that he would have to finance, there were the 50,000 homeless, the AIDS and

drug problems, and racial tensions. Prior to the election Dinkins was credited with staying neutral concerning a racially motivated killing in Brooklyn, and asking for calm. Racial harmony became a campaign issue, and Dinkins vowed to "bring New York City together."

David Dinkins was born July 10, 1927, in Trenton, N.J. A graduate of Howard University, Washington, D.C., he entered Brooklyn Law School in 1953. In 1965 he was elected to the New York state assembly. In 1973 Dinkins was named New York City's deputy mayor for planning, but he was forced to withdraw under the shadow of his having neglected to file income tax returns from 1969 to 1972. From 1975 to 1985 he served as city clerk and was then elected Manhattan borough president.

After the primary Dinkins told supporters, "You voted your hopes and not your fears." However, with Dinkins' easygoing style, many were doubtful that he would be able to successfully handle the labour unions and powerful pressure groups that supported him in the election. Felix Rohatyn, one of Dinkins' economic advisers, said, "He is so innately decent that he is really not used to having to disappoint people. And yet, in this job, he'll have to."

(ANTHONY L. GREEN)

Doi, Takako

With the startling defeat of Japan's ruling Liberal-Democratic Party (LDP) in the upper house elections on July 23, 1989, the premiership seemed open for Takako Doi. The LDP went into the election holding 69 of the 126 contested seats, but it won only 36. The Japan Socialist Party (JSP), led by Doi, had to defend 22 contested seats; it won 46. However, rattled

by a payoff scandal involving the notorious pachinko (pinball) trade and still in desperate search of viable new policies and persuasive counterproposals to the hated consumption tax, the JSP saw its popularity ratings dwindle from well over 30% in July to 21% in November. By year's end the JSP chairman had lost much of her earlier momentum, and the outcome in the decisive lower house elections slated for February 1990 was more uncertain.

Doi had waited a long time to influence Japanese politics. She was born the second daughter of a physician in Kobe on Nov. 30, 1928. She became a professor of constitutional law at her alma mater, Doshisha University in Kyoto, before being elected to the Diet (parliament) in 1969. After the JSP suffered its disastrous defeat in the 1986 general elections, she became the first woman ever to lead a political party in Japan.

Rocketed to the forefront of politics after three years in the relative anonymity of party vice-chairman, Doi was determined to rejuvenate the ailing JSP. From the outset she strove to bring the party more into the mainstream

on such divisive issues as defense and nuclear power. However, when the outline of a more pragmatic party platform appeared in September, many found it lacking in substance.

The party softened its traditional stance by accepting, within limits, a role for Japan's Self-Defense Forces, the U.S.-Japan security treaty, and the operation of existing nuclear power plants. Neither JSP left-wing ideologists nor the leaders of the other opposition parties, whose support Doi would need in a ruling coalition, were pleased.

Doi had much success wooing women voters, who appeared as a new power base in Japanese politics. Although she had done little to identify with feminist issues at the outset, she helped channel the dissatisfaction of women angered by money politics and the sex scandals plaguing the ruling party. Following her "madonna strategy," numerous freshman women candidates were successfully fielded in the summer campaign.

How well the JSP and the four centrist opposition parties could cooperate in the next general elections depended largely on the JSP leader.   (GERD LARSSON)

Englund, Robert

In 1989 actor Robert Englund remained America's dream man. He made hearts throb through Freddy Krueger, the tall, dark, and loathsome protagonist of the film *A Nightmare on Elm Street 5: The Dream Child.* His face a sneering, melting mass of pus, blood, and skin and his right hand an old leather claw with fingers as long and sharp as steak knives, the wise-cracking Freddy haunted, slashed, and murdered teenage characters—in their dreams. Freddy and his mayhem enabled *The Dream Child* and the four other *Nightmare* films to gross more than $320 million in ticket sales and videocassette rentals, with teenagers making up most of the customers. Young people's sympathy for the devil was reflected in the brisk trade in Freddy products—posters, bubble gum, plastic claws—and in the popularity of "Freddy's Nightmares," a late-night television program. Some critics also saw an artistic side to the films, citing their imaginative special effects and their reliance on psychological horror. A leading sleep researcher even claimed that few works captured the logic and anxiety of dreams as accurately as the *Nightmare* films. To those who argued that the unrelenting grimness of the films warped the young mind, Englund countered that they provided vicarious thrills that actually made viewers "feel more alive."

In 1984 Englund won the role by looking dead, by mesmerizing director Wes Craven through eyes encircled by black makeup. Inspired by actual news reports of three young men dying in their dreams, the first *Nightmare* established Englund's character as a child murderer incinerated by angry parents and later reborn in the dreams of their children—teenagers struggling with both their parents' guilt and their own fears and desires. According to Craven, the film showed young viewers that they must "stay awake" in the face of evil and other unpleasant truths. That metaphor was written, nay smeared, all over Englund's face through hideous makeup that regularly took from two to four hours to apply. Englund later submitted to the latex and glue in *A Nightmare On Elm Street 2: Freddy's Revenge* (1985), *3: Dream Warriors* (1987), and *4: The Dream Master* (1988).

Englund first awoke to the world on June 6, 1949, in Glendale, Calif., his parents' only child. Two decades later he dropped out of UCLA one year from graduation to study Shakespearean acting at the Michigan branch of the British Royal Academy. He eventually got parts in dozens of films and starred as Willy, the gentle lizard, in the television series "V." In 1989 his Freddy-filled résumé landed him the title role in a bloody *Phantom of the Opera.* Meanwhile, Englund/Freddy's biggest fans dreamed of what they hoped would be the unkindest cut of all: the coming *A Nightmare on Elm Street 6.*
                                        (MICHAEL AMEDEO)

Eyre, Richard

Richard Eyre, active in theatre, film, and television, made his mark as the director of the Royal National Theatre (RNT) after taking over from Sir Peter Hall on Sept. 1, 1988. In the RNT annual report the new chairman of the board, Lady Soames, wrote of the "remarkable partnership" set up by Eyre and the company's executive director, the lawyer David Aukin, which had brought its artistic reputation to an all-time high. By dividing responsibility for running the mammoth complex of the RNT between them, Eyre was able to concentrate on artistic matters, to the benefit of all.

Eyre was born March 28, 1943, in a small provincial town, Darnstaple, in Devonshire and, like Hall, finished his education at the University of Cambridge, where he spent much time acting in student drama. After graduation he became, at the age of 22, a full-time professional actor. He made his directing debut in Leicester's second civic theatre, the Phoenix, in 1965 and then acquired a wealth of experience in several regional theatres, notably at Edinburgh's Lyceum Theatre and Nottingham's Playhouse. While in Scotland he won three consecutive annual awards for best production on Scottish TV.

For one of Eyre's most successful productions, of his own adaptation of the Cole Porter film *High Society* at Leicester, later seen in London's West End, Hall gave him a leave of absence from the RNT. It became obvious that he was Hall's natural heir at the helm of the theatre where he had won two best director awards—for the musical *Guys and Dolls* and for Ben Jonson's *Bartholomew Fair.* When he took over from Hall, he was preparing his first 1989 production, that of *Hamlet,* which opened to acclaim in March.

Eyre's contributions to the new regime at the RNT were many. He promoted the work at its Studio, not least in encouraging new directors. He embarked on a coproduction policy with regional theatres, the first such being a highly praised new version of *The Misanthrope.* He dismantled Hall's scheme of dividing the RNT's ensemble into independent groups and carried on his policy of international exchange, welcoming four new troupes to London during the year, among them the Moscow Art Theatre with a new *Uncle Vanya.* He announced a wide-ranging world tour in 1990 of two forthcoming RNT productions: his own of *Richard III,* and another of *King Lear,* staged by Deborah Warner.   (OSSIA TRILLING)

Ezoe, Hiromasa

On June 18, 1988, the *Asahi Shimbun* reported that the deputy mayor of Kawasaki, a port city on Tokyo Bay, had accepted bribes in exchange for favourable consideration of a Recruit Co. building project. The story became international news as soon as other well-known public figures were suspected of bribe taking. Before long, 76 prominent Japanese, including Prime Minister Noboru Takeshita, were forced to resign.

The key figure in the scandal was Hiromasa Ezoe, the founder and chairman of Recruit Co., a gigantic job-placement, information, real estate, and communications conglomerate. Born in 1936 to a well-to-do family in Osaka, Ezoe graduated from Tokyo University before launching a magazine aimed at companies trying to recruit college graduates. His two-man office was on the rooftop of a prefabricated building in Tokyo. From business-information publishing he gradually branched out into real estate and other ventures. The Recruit Co. eventually comprised 32 companies with estimated 1988 revenues in excess of $3 billion.

During the prime ministership of Yasuhiro Nakasone, Ezoe became a member of two Education Ministry councils and joined a tax system research council. These posts, coupled with his influence as a wealthy businessman, provided easy access to government bureaucrats and business executives who were in a position to help or hinder Recruit's operations. Ezoe allegedly corrupted these people with the lure of Recruit stock that was sold under the table at bargain

prices. When the stock went public, Ezoe's influential friends were in a position to reap huge profits. Ezoe also reportedly provided luxurious meals, expense-paid outings, and generous cash gifts to friends for attending funerals, weddings, and other gatherings.

Ezoe resigned from Recruit on June 6, 1988, and was arrested the following February. After posting bail of 200 million yen in early June, he was released to await trial. He then managed to elude most reporters by staying overnight in one or another of his out-of-town villas or in hotels.

Before the Recruit trials got under way in November, thousands of witnesses had already been questioned and thousands of pieces of evidence gathered and sorted. It was taken for granted that definitive verdicts would not be rendered for at least 10 years.
                                     (KAY K. TATEISHI)

Foley, Thomas Stephen

On June 6, 1989, the Democratic majority in the U.S. House of Representatives met, facing a crisis in its leadership. James Wright (*q.v.*) had resigned as speaker and Tony Coelho as majority whip, both while under investigation for alleged ethical lapses. The caucus turned to Thomas Foley, the majority leader, who was well liked and had a spotless reputation, nominating him for speaker. Hours later, the House elected Foley to that office, 251 Democrats voting for him while 164 Republicans voted for Robert Michel; however, most Republicans seemed to welcome Foley's election. Although Foley said that maintaining decorum was his principal task, he remained a polite but firm party leader. He criticized Pres. George Bush's proposal for campaign reform and secured passage of a minimum-wage law differing from that favoured by Bush.

Thomas Stephen Foley was born in Spokane, Wash., on March 6, 1929. He attended Gonzaga University, Spokane, and the University of Washington, where he stayed after receiving a B.A. in 1951, taking courses in Far Eastern studies and, later, in law. In 1957 he received his law degree, was admitted to the bar, and formed the law firm of Higgins and Foley with a cousin in Spokane. He became assistant prosecuting attorney of Spokane county in 1958, assistant attorney general of Washington in 1960, and special counsel to the U.S. Senate's Committee on Interior and Insular Affairs in 1961. In 1964 a chance encounter with a major Democratic contributor in Spokane led him to resign as counsel and run for U.S. representative against Walt Horan, a senior incumbent Republican. Foley won an upset victory—and held a reception in Horan's honour. He continued to represent that Spokane area, where Republicans won most other elections. In 1974 he helped secure the passage of a rule allowing the Democratic caucus to remove committee chairmen. Urged to oppose W.R. Poage, the chairman of his own Committee on Agriculture, he instead nominated Poage, who lost. Poage gratefully nominated Foley, who served as chairman of the committee until 1981, when he became majority whip, responsible for obtaining the maximum possible Democratic support for the leaders' programs. He used polite persuasion effectively in a job in which predecessors had used bombast. In 1987 he became majority leader. His politeness contrasted well with Speaker Wright's often imperious style. Opposed to gun control, Foley favoured most of the federal social programs considered liberal and wanted abortion to remain legal.
                          (CHARLES JOHNSON TAGGART)

Glemp, Jozef Cardinal

Jozef Cardinal Glemp was named Archbishop of Gniezno and Warsaw in July 1981, just six months before martial law was imposed in Poland to crush the free trade union Solidarity. Overshadowed by his heroic predecessor, Stefan Cardinal Wyszynski (whose secretary he had been from 1967 to 1979, when he was made a bishop), he was outshone on the international stage by the first Polish pope. Born in Inowro-

CAMERA PRESS/GLOBE PHOTOS

claw Dec. 18, 1929, the son of a salt miner, Glemp spent World War II in forced labour on a German-run farm. He entered the seminary in 1950 and was ordained a priest in 1956.

In the early period of martial law, more ardent priests criticized his alleged collusion with the government. Shocked by the murder of Father Jerzy Popieluszko in 1984, he thought his main duty was "to defend the Church—both priests and laymen." The primate of Poland is responsible for all Poles wherever they are—for the wider Poland known as Polonia. Pope John Paul II cast him in another role as the agent of his *Ostpolitik.* If the pope could not go to Lithuania and Moscow, then Glemp could test the waters of *perestroika.* Early in 1989 he became the first cardinal to be interviewed by *Pravda.* Meanwhile, in Poland, the first semifree elections were held, the Communists were routed, and a Solidarity-led government took office in September.

However, much goodwill was dissipated in the summer of 1989 in the furor over the siting of a Carmelite convent at the Auschwitz concentration camp, where many of the victims of the Holocaust had died. Meeting in Geneva in February 1987, Jewish and Catholic authorities had agreed that a study and prayer centre would be built outside the camp area, and that the nuns would move into it within two years. That deadline passed, and on July 14 seven U.S. Jews tried to break into the convent and were roughly repelled by workmen. Glemp reacted defensively. He cautioned Jews against spreading anti-Polish sentiment in the "mass media that are easily at your disposal in many countries." For those familiar with prewar Poland, the suggestion of a conspiracy in the mass media raised sinister memories. It also seemed to some that the Catholic Church was incapable of keeping its word.

After pressure from the Vatican and promises of financial help, Glemp finally gave way in September. Writing to Sir Sigmund Sternberg, chairman of the Executive Committee of the International Council of Christians and Jews, Glemp said he was glad that "some of the shrill voices do not reflect the feelings of world Jewry and aggression is not part of Jewish philosophy." Even when conceding the case, Glemp sounded tactless.   (PETER HEBBLETHWAITE)

Goldsmith, Sir James

Sir James Goldsmith had few equals as a buyer, molder, and seller of companies. In 1989 he sought to crown his career by bidding £13 billion, mainly in junk bonds, for the ailing conglomerate British American Tobacco (BAT), which, despite its name, had long diversified into such areas as financial services, retailing, and paper and packaging.

Goldsmith was born on Feb. 26, 1933, in Paris to an English father and a French mother

and was educated at Eton (although he never finished). Goldsmith first generated headlines in 1953 when he eloped with Isabel Patino, a Bolivian heiress whom he married against her father's wishes. She died in childbirth, however, and Goldsmith faced his first of many court battles when he sought, and won, custody of his baby daughter.

From his early 20s, Goldsmith showed talent as an entrepreneur. His first major success came with Milical, a slimming (diet) aid that he produced in France and sold throughout Europe. He then mounted a series of takeovers, mainly of poorly managed British food companies. He created his own conglomerate, Cavenham Foods (named after his grandfather's estate), into which he slotted such enterprises as Carrs (a biscuit-maker), Procca (diet bread), Marmite (a savoury spread), and Liptons (a supermarket chain). He floated Cavenham on the stock exchange, but in the 1970s, wanting to regain undisputed personal control, he reorganized the company, selling some of its assets and repurchasing shares held by the public. He later operated the company through a family foundation based in Liechtenstein.

In the 1970s Goldsmith began to diversify out of food and, eventually, out of Europe. He bought the successful French newsmagazine *L'Express* and started an equivalent, *Now!,* in Great Britain. *Now!* was a flop and folded in 1981 after just 18 months' publication. In the early 1980s he made a series of audacious raids into the U.S., buying the forestry products group Diamond International Corp. in 1982 and bidding for the Goodyear Tire and Rubber Co. in 1986. Goodyear eventually persuaded Goldsmith to give up by making him an offer for his shares he could not refuse. If one decision above all gave him a springboard for the 1990s, however, it was to go liquid just before the 1987 stock market crash and preserve the monetary value of his assets when so many others saw theirs tumble.   (PETER KELLNER)

Haavelmo, Trygve

The 1989 Nobel Memorial Prize in Economic Science was awarded to Trygve Haavelmo, a relatively unknown 77-year-old Norwegian economics professor, who was a pioneer in what became the field of economic forecasting. His methods for testing economic theories, derived in the 1940s, dramatically changed the way economists used statistics to explain how various parts of the economy influence each other. Although economics is an inexact science, Haavelmo's theories allowed for more valid predictions.

Haavelmo was born on Dec. 13, 1911, in Skedsmo. After the outbreak of World War II he left Norway and delivered his doctoral dissertation, "The Probability Approach in Econometrics," at Harvard in 1941. Although he had two doctorates from the University of Oslo, his innovative thesis, cited by the Nobel committee for its influence, was first published in 1944 in *Econometrica,* an American periodical. Haavelmo worked at the University of Chicago during the 1940s (where he was also a visiting professor in the late 1950s) before returning to Norway in 1947. He retired from the University of Oslo faculty in 1979, becoming professor emeritus.

Because economics depends on data that may derive from uncertain observations, economists traditionally were able to draw only approximate conclusions. Haavelmo changed that by demonstrating that statistical probability theory could be integrated into economic formulations. All econometric models developed since the 1940s "rest on Haavelmo's work," said Robert M. Solow, the 1987 Nobel Economics winner. Assar Lindbeck, chairman of the prize committee, noted that it was Haavelmo's techniques that made possible the development of econometric models that predict how a change in one aspect of the economy will affect others. Indeed, contemporary predictions regarding the course of national economies and formulation of governmental economic policies depend on these

theories. Economists can predict the effect of the rise or fall of interest rates on personal consumption or how a particular tax reform might affect capital investments. They also know, for example, that when observing the level of imported goods in a particular nation's economy, they must consider not only exchange rates but interest and tax rates as well. One Nobel committee member called Haavelmo's contribution "the story of how economics was transformed from armchair instinct to empirical science."
    (BONNIE OBERMAN)

Harris, Barbara

When she became the first woman consecrated as suffragan (assistant) bishop in the Episcopal Church, the Rt. Rev. Barbara Clementine Harris broke a 2,000-year barrier for women in the Anglican Communion. At once a focus of unity and a symbol of divisions, the tough 58-year-old black activist was consecrated in February 1989 in a deeply moving three-hour ceremony attended by 55 Episcopal bishops and thousands

AP/WIDE WORLD

of guests and marked by joyous acclamation as well as strong protest.

Harris was born and raised in Philadelphia. Always a social activist, she marched in Selma, Ala., for civil rights; registered voters in Mississippi; and, in the late 1960s, joined the Church of the Advocate in Philadelphia, an urban cradle of black activism. To earn money throughout these years, Harris was a public relations executive—first at Joseph V. Baker Associates and then at the Sun Oil Co. She then became director of the Episcopal Publishing Co.

Her Church of the Advocate experiences in impoverished communities and in soup kitchens and as a prison chaplain led to her decision to enter the ministry. She was ordained a priest in 1980 and from the pulpit supported gay rights and criticized the Episcopal Church as "male-dominated" and "racist."

Fully aware of the controversy surrounding her ascension, Harris promised to soften her image as a political and religious radical and to concentrate on her sacramental and pastoral duties. While she had no intention of abandoning her causes, as the second in command of the 96,000-member Boston-based diocese she would not only help parishes develop programs and resources and solve problems but would also sit on diocesan commissions that handled pastoral care, social-justice issues, and the prison ministry.

While opponents throughout the church and as far away as England decried her appointment and mourned what they saw as the death of their church, this steadfast woman accustomed to the hot spot calmly declared: "I see myself as a Christian social activist following what I believe my Lord would have me do."

    (BONNIE OBERMAN)

Havel, Vaclav

On Jan. 16, 1989, Czechoslovakia's most prominent playwright and best known dissident, Vaclav Havel, was arrested in Prague for his participation in demonstrations commemorating the 20th anniversary of the suicide of a student who had immolated himself in protest against the 1968 Soviet-led invasion of Czechoslovakia. A little less than a year later, on December 29, he became the nation's first non-Communist president since 1948. No paradox better exemplifies the tumult and changes that were sweeping Eastern Europe at the year's end.

Havel was born in Prague on Oct. 5, 1936, into a prosperous family. His first essays were published when he was 19; his first plays were performed in the mid-1960s while he was resident playwright at the Theatre of the Balustrade. Although he became internationally recognized at that time, none of his plays was performed in Czechoslovakia after the 1968 invasion. His works were banned, and those already published were removed from libraries. Furthermore, having fought and spoken out against government abuses for more than 20 years, Havel was imprisoned repeatedly, spending a total of more than five years behind bars for his dissident activities. He served his first jail term in 1977 after the formation of Charter 77, a human rights organization that would prove influential in the 1989 overthrow of the Communist regime. During his most lengthy imprisonment, October 1979 to February 1983, he wrote steadily to his wife, detailing prison life as well as pondering universal truths. *Letters to Olga* was eventually published to wide acclaim and in 1989 was performed in New York City. His other works include the plays *The Memorandum* (1965), *The Conspirators* (1971), *Audience* (1975), and *Largo Desolato* (1985).

Upon accepting the mostly symbolic post of president, his election to which had been agreed upon by both the Communist leadership and the opposition Civic Forum, Havel insisted on free parliamentary elections. He announced that he would serve only until a new parliament was in place.

Throughout his years of tumultuous relations with the Czechoslovak government, Havel had repeatedly been urged to emigrate. He always refused, citing his reasons in a 1988 interview and echoing these sentiments upon his election as president. "I am Czech. This was not my choice, it was fate. . . . This is my language, this is my home. I live here like everyone else. I don't feel myself to be patriotic, because I don't feel that to be Czech is to be something more than French, or English, or European, or anybody else. . . . I try to do something for my country because I live here."

(BONNIE OBERMAN)

Helmsley, Leona

It was as much a public relations battle as a legal one as attorneys for the defense of self-styled hotel queen Leona Helmsley fought in 1989 to convince jurors of her innocence on charges of tax fraud and extortion. Helmsley and her husband, Harry, had been indicted in 1988 for allegedly defrauding the U.S. government of $1.2 million in the period 1983–85 by disguising personal luxuries as business expenses and claiming them as tax deductions. Although the 80-year-old Harry was declared mentally unfit to stand trial, proceedings continued against Leona. As a parade of government witnesses built up a picture of Leona as greedy, insecure, and despotic, her trial quickly turned into one of the year's media circuses.

Leona Mindy Rosenthal was born c. 1920 to a Brooklyn, N.Y., milliner and grew up in New York City. It was under the name Leona Roberts in the 1960s that she became a successful real estate broker. Two years after joining one of Harry Helmsley's companies as senior vice president in 1970, she married him. She took an active part in running the organization, which included in its management portfolio the Empire State Building and other large properties. In 1980 she was named president of

ADAM SCULL—RANGEFINDERS/GLOBE PHOTOS

Helmsley Hotels, Inc., and she gained public recognition from a series of print ads for the hotels that featured her prominently. In 1982 the International Hotel Industry voted her woman of the year. The Helmsleys' personal assets grew to some $1 billion, and the Helmsley organization was valued at $5 billion.

By the mid-1980s, however, Helmsley's reputed profligate spending and abusive treatment of employees had earned her many enemies, some of whom leaked documentation of tax evasion to the press. The ensuing federal investigation led to the couple's indictment. Throughout the nine-week trial the media played up, and the public followed avidly, the testimony of disgruntled business associates and former employees. The sensationalism of the trial led many to conclude that the press and the Internal Revenue Service intended to make an example of the case.

In August Helmsley was convicted on 33 counts of income tax evasion but was acquitted of extorting money and concessions from hotel suppliers. In December she was sentenced to four years in prison and ordered to pay $7.1 million in fines, $1.7 million in back taxes and penalties, and all court costs. At year's end the conviction was under appeal. Leona Helmsley once remarked that "only the little people pay taxes"; to many such "little people," her conviction seemed poetic justice.

(LORRAINE MURRAY)

Hnatyshyn, Ray

Once sworn in as Canada's 24th governor-general in January 1990, Ray Hnatyshyn would become the representative of the British sovereign in Canada. As such, he would assume duties that included opening and closing Parliament, signing Cabinet orders and proclamations, receiving credentials of foreign ambassadors, and investing citizens with the Order of Canada. He believed that the appointment was the greatest honour that could be bestowed on the average Canadian.

Born on March 16, 1934, in Saskatoon, Sask., Ramon John Hnatyshyn received bachelor of arts and bachelor of laws degrees from the University of Saskatchewan. After graduation, he practiced law in Saskatoon and lectured in law at the university (1966–74). He was elected a bencher of the Law Society of Saskatchewan in 1970 and became its president in 1973.

Son of a member of the Canadian Senate, Hnatyshyn entered federal politics in 1974 and was elected member of Parliament for the riding of Saskatoon West. His ability to bridge partisan differences by his personal charm and his sense of humour made him one of the most popular members of the House of Commons. When the Progressive Conservative Party came to power in 1979, Hnatyshyn was appointed

minister of state for technology and minister of energy, mines, and resources. He promised to make Canada energy self-sufficient by 1990, but the government lasted only a few months. When the Tories once again formed the government in 1984, Hnatyshyn was appointed government House leader. He introduced parliamentary reforms, including election of the speaker by secret ballot. In 1985 he was made president of the Privy Council of Canada.

In 1986 Hnatyshyn realized his lifelong ambition by becoming minister of justice and attorney general of Canada. He reformed the procedure for appointing judges and introduced legislation allowing judges to order criminals to compensate their victims and allowing police to seize the proceeds of crime before the perpetrator had been convicted. In the 1988 general election he fell victim to sentiment against the free-trade agreement with the U.S. and returned to the practice of law. Known as a person of great warmth, civility, and integrity, Hnatyshyn was expected to bring a popular touch to the office of governor-general. He believed his mandate was to foster both a sense of national purpose and a spirit of unity and understanding among Canadians.

(DIANE LOIS WAY)

Hoffman, Dustin

His head cocked to one side, the little man walked with precise, mincing steps, spoke in a fussy, dry whine, and kept citing mundane facts—"It's only ten minutes to 'Jeopardy'"—as if they were monumental truths. While he would not look anyone in the eye, would not allow himself to be touched, and could not participate in a normal conversation, the man could perform extraordinary feats of memory and mathematical calculation. This autistic savant named Raymond was not a true person, however; he was a true-to-life character played by Dustin Hoffman in the 1988 film *Rain Man*. Hoffman turned in a mono-saturated performance, giving his obsessively ritualistic and essentially unchanging character a lot of busy detail. Unimpressed, *The New Yorker* said *Rain Man* was "Dustin Hoffman humping one note on a piano for two hours and eleven minutes." Nevertheless, his autistic proved an artistic and commercial success, enabling the film to gross more than $170 million in the U.S. and in 1989 winning Hoffman an Oscar for best actor.

In being extensively researched and exhaustively performed, Raymond was similar to Hoffman's other roles, especially that of the unemployed actor who transforms himself into a flutter-voiced, southern-fried, strong-willed actress in the 1982 comedy *Tootsie*. The film earned Hoffman an Oscar nomination, and—because he had feuded with director Sydney Pollack during production—reinforced his reputation as a self-indulgent perfectionist. Three years earlier, under more peaceful conditions, Hoffman played a father determined to keep custody of his son in *Kramer vs. Kramer,* which won him his first Oscar.

That father was a son just 12 years earlier in Mike Nichols' *The Graduate,* which spoke to a generation rebelling against conventional values and established Hoffman as a counterculture hero. A 30-year-old Jew who convincingly played a 20-year-old WASP, Hoffman felt encouraged to take on such difficult roles as the limping, wheezing tramp Ratso in *Midnight Cowboy,* a 1969 film that already had critics calling him one of America's finest actors.

The star was born in Los Angeles on Aug. 8, 1937. Burdened by a little body and a big nose, an unhappy and insecure Hoffman looked for fulfillment in acting, eventually catching Nichols' eye with a 1967 performance in the Off-Broadway play *Eh?* Beginning with *Midnight Cowboy,* Hoffman's film career kept him from returning to the stage until 1983, when he played Willy Loman in Arthur Miller's *Death of a Salesman* on Broadway. Six years later he traded gridlock for Shylock, leaving home base Manhattan to perform in London's West End as the moneylender in Shakespeare's *The Merchant of Venice.*

(MICHAEL AMEDEO)

Icahn, Carl

Business observers throughout 1989 speculated about Carl Icahn's interest in taking over major U.S. corporations. Known to many as a corporate raider, Icahn was respected in the financial community for his remarkable business acumen that had led to success after financial success. Some of the companies he targeted were Texaco, Eastern Air Lines, and USX, formerly United States Steel Corp., which had also been a takeover target in 1986.

Icahn was born in Queens, New York, on Feb. 16, 1936. His mother was a teacher and his father a lawyer who also served as the cantor at their local synagogue. Icahn graduated from Princeton University with a degree in philosophy in 1957. While there he also learned to play chess, a game that he said had served him well as a model for planning ahead as well as anticipating his opponents' moves.

Icahn spent three unhappy years in medical school at New York University before dropping out to become an apprentice broker at the Dreyfus Corp. After three years there he became an options manager for Tessel, Patrick and Co. and then for Gruntal and Co. In 1968, with $400,000 borrowed from his uncle, he formed Icahn and Co. to trade stocks and bonds. He led the company into the options business and then into risk arbitrage and discount brokerage. Icahn made his first foray into corporate takeovers in 1978 when he began to buy quantities of stock in Tappan Co. He was elected to Tappan's board of directors, which accepted an offer from Sweden's AB Electrolux to buy the company. Icahn immediately sold his shares and walked away with a profit of almost $3 million.

In 1986 Icahn became chairman of Trans World Airlines after a takeover battle in which two labour unions threw their support to him. He turned the troubled company around, winning concessions from the unions and buying rival Ozark Air Lines in 1986. In 1989 Icahn bought large amounts of stock in Texaco, but he sold it all in June, leaving him with an estimated $1 billion in cash. That led to speculation as to what he would do with the money. Many thought it would be pumped into TWA, while others thought Icahn might just find another company to buy.

(FRANCINE SHONFELD SHERMAN)

Ito, Midori

Tiny Midori Ito, displaying dazzling finesse, amazing spins, soaring jumps, a variety of triple combinations, and innocent charm, electrified the crowded skating arena at the world figure skating championships at Paris in March 1989. She was the first female skater ever to complete a triple axel in international competition.

A freshman majoring in home economics at Nagoya Tokai Gakuen Junior College, Ito had spent more than half her life on the ice. She began skating when she was four years old and did not remember how many times she sustained injuries. To overcome frustrations and the temptation to give up, she simply intensified her determination. The result was eight All-Japan figure skating championships.

In 1986 Ito was asked to train with a group of Japanese skaters in the U.S., but she declined. She preferred to train under Machiko Yamada, her coach since primary school days, and to remain in the cozy atmosphere of her hometown rink in Nagoya.

Alex McGowan, coach of former U.S. champion Debi Thomas, described Ito as "the best female athletic jumper I've ever seen." Commenting on the phasing out of the school figures, Ito remarked, "Skaters like myself will have more opportunity to win in the future. I still believe school figures are good for a skater's basic technique." Nevertheless, she flashed a smile when she admitted, "I'm happy the school figures are going." Her next goal, she said, was to win the gold medal at the Winter Olympics in 1992.

With the retirement of Katarina Witt of East Germany, the 1984 and 1988 Olympic champion, and of Debi Thomas, Ito's chances of winning the gold increased dramatically. When questioned, she smiled and said she was ready for the challenge. "I like the audience, and when they get excited I get excited. That kind of atmosphere makes me skate well."

(KAY K. TATEISHI)

Jagger, Mick

"When I'm 33, I quit," proclaimed Mick Jagger in 1972, but in 1989 the 46-year-old front man of the Rolling Stones was more securely ensconced in his role as rock star than he had been for nearly a decade. During the year the Stones released an album, *Steel Wheels,* and mounted a North American tour that was expected to earn $65 million to $75 million.

The voice of the Rolling Stones, Michael Phillip Jagger, was born in Dartford, Kent, England, on July 26, 1943. Jagger's boyhood differed little from that of most middle-class English schoolboys of the 1950s except for his love for the music of such U.S. musicians as Muddy Waters, Bo Diddley, and Chuck Berry. After grammar school Jagger attended the London School of Economics, but he soon joined forces with guitarist Keith Richard (later Richards). Both avid fans of U.S. rhythm and blues, they found other like-minded musicians and formed the Rolling Stones. They made their debut in 1962 but were not at first appreciated. A promoter joked, "I honestly didn't know whether to laugh at them or send for an animal trainer." By the mid-1960s, however, the Stones were notorious as the bad boys of rock and roll—naughty counterparts to the clean-cut Beatles. Their image was largely realized through Jagger's "not nice" lyrics and his hyperactive cavorting on stage.

The partnership between Jagger, who wrote and sang most of the songs, and Richards, who wrote the music, resulted in numerous top-40 tunes. Many of the Stones' albums were considered classics, but as the band moved into the 1980s, some people thought it was just a bit silly for middle-aged rock stars to continue to pose as rebellious adolescents. Jagger himself admitted that he hoped "people don't laugh when we get out there."

Although the Stones toured in 1981, cracks in the Jagger-Richards affiliation began to appear. Their well-publicized bouts of name-calling and the release of Jagger's solo record albums, *She's the Boss* (1985) and *Primitive Cool* (1987), fueled rumours of the group's imminent breakup. In 1988, however, Richards made a solo album, and perhaps it restored the balance between the two driving forces of the Rolling Stones; their 35-year-old friendship seemed to be back on track. *Steel Wheels* was generally agreed to be more inspired than anything else the band had done in years; and the "world's greatest rock and roll band" managed to sell out performances of its 1989 tour in record time.

(ELIZABETH LASKEY)

Jiang Zemin

China's leadership underwent a major reshuffling in 1989 as a result of the student-led prodemocracy movement. At the fourth plenum of the 13th Central Committee of the Communist Party of China (CPC) in June, Jiang Zemin (Chiang Tse-min) was elected general secretary of the CPC replacing Zhao Ziyang (Chao Tzu-yang). Jiang's elevation to this top position followed the suppression of the democracy movement and the subsequent purge of the CPC leadership. Zhao was blamed, among other things, for "supporting the turmoil and splitting the party."

Jiang Zemin was born in Jiangsu (Kiangsu) province in 1926 and joined the CPC in 1946. After graduating from Jiaotong (Chiao-t'ung) University in Shanghai in 1947, he held various mid-level posts in a number of ministries, including the First Ministry of the Machine-Building Industry. He also spent a year at the Stalin Automobile Factory in Moscow in 1955 and became fluent in Russian and English.

In the early 1980s Jiang was appointed minister of the electronics industry. At about the same time, his political career gained impetus, notably with his election to the 12th Central Committee in 1982 and his elevation to the Political Bureau in 1987. He had already been named mayor of Shanghai in 1985 and secretary of its municipal party committee. As head of China's largest city, Jiang was a prominent supporter of China's economic modernization. Jiang endeared himself to Deng Xiaoping (Teng Hsiao-p'ing) by supporting law and order during the 1989 student-led demonstrations for democracy; he also fired Qin Benli (Ch'in Pen-li), the outspoken editor of the ultraliberal *World Economic Herald.*

Promoted to the position of general secretary over more senior political figures such as Li Peng (Li P'eng) and Qiao Shi (Ch'iao Shih), Jiang was reportedly a compromise choice who combined ideological toughness with a pragmatic commitment to continued economic reform. These were the twin themes he sounded in his speeches in the second half of 1989. At the fifth plenum of the Central Committee in November, in a significant attempt to boost Jiang's standing, Deng retired as chairman of the CPC's powerful Central Military Commission in favour of Jiang, whom he referred to as the "core" of the new party leadership.

(STEVEN I. LEVINE)

Kemp, Jack

When Jack Kemp was unanimously appointed U.S. secretary of housing and urban development (HUD) by the U.S. Senate on Feb. 2, 1989, he admitted hearing rumours "on the street" about the department's alleged mismanagement. Nevertheless, the seasoned Republican congressional veteran and former Buffalo Bills champion quarterback was astonished at the depth of corruption that surfaced in June. "I am outraged at what I have found. . . . I want to prove that my ideas can work. The risk is that I will fall flat on my face," Kemp exclaimed as hearings on Capitol Hill and Justice Department probes began to uncover charges of HUD misconduct.

When he was nominated HUD secretary by incoming Pres. George Bush on Dec. 19, 1988, Kemp vowed to wage a new war on poverty and pledged a steadfast commitment combined with "an audacious faith that together we can help recapture the American dream for our inner cities." His original initiatives included adding shelters for the homeless by using government property as temporary housing, promoting ownership for tenants living in public-housing projects, subsidizing low- and moderate-income housing, and permitting first-time home buyers to use tax-deferred savings accounts for down payments.

When Kemp began his Cabinet term, he targeted homelessness as his primary concern. He was faced with an additional challenge as the controversy surrounding former HUD secretary Samuel R. Pierce, Jr., continued. The subsequent investigation probing into HUD irregularities developed into a scandal that involved charges of political favouritism and influence peddling, mismanagement of mortgage-insurance programs, and fraud by prominent Republicans. In rapid response to the HUD disclosures, Kemp dismissed four senior officers in HUD's Washington, D.C., field office, suspended three corrupt housing programs, reviewed at least 50 other programs, and pledged sweeping reforms.

Jack French Kemp was born in Los Angeles on July 13, 1935, graduated (1957) from Occidental College in Los Angeles, and entered politics after playing professional football for 13 years. When he retired from the Buffalo Bills in 1969 after a series of injuries, the Bills organization permanently retired his number, 15. Kemp parlayed his success on the football field into a seat in the U.S. Congress as a representative from the Buffalo, N.Y., congressional district (1971–88). He was a contestant in the 1988 Republican presidential primary and candidly admitted that he "would like to step up the political ladder." (VIRGINIA M. LAFLEUR)

Kinnock, Neil Gordon

When Neil Kinnock was elected leader of the British Labour Party in October 1983, many thought the party would never see government again. By 1989 he had transformed its prospects, in part by jettisoning a number of policies, such as support for unilateral nuclear disarmament, that were loved by active party members but rejected by the electorate.

Kinnock was born in Tredegar, in the coal-mining area of South Wales, on March 28, 1942. He graduated from University College, Cardiff, in 1966 and, after four years as an adult education lecturer, entered Parliament in 1970. Kinnock declined ministerial service in the 1974–79 Labour government; he rejected what he saw as its right-wing policies. He acquired a reputation as one of Parliament's wittiest and most passionate speakers, although sometimes

his overly flowery language earned him the ep-ithet of "Welsh windbag."

After Labour's 1979 defeat, Kinnock joined the shadow cabinet and gradually broke with those elements of Labour's left wing that he thought destructive. When Michael Foot re-signed as Labour leader in 1983 after the party's worst election defeat since 1935, Kinnock was the candidate of the party's centre-left. He won easily but then began the harder task of win-ning over the electorate. In 1987 Labour gained 1.6 million extra votes in its first election un-der his leadership, but this fell far short of the target (five million) needed to unseat Margaret Thatcher's Conservatives. Personally, however, Kinnock emerged as an effective campaigner. Extracts from a speech used as part of a re-markable 10-minute campaign broadcast were subsequently copied by Joseph Biden as part of his campaign for the Democratic Party nomi-nation for the U.S. presidency in 1988.

In 1987, however, the process of transform-ing Labour's policies had barely begun. Kin-nock had abandoned Labour's opposition to the European Communities in 1983, but the party remained committed to the unilateral removal of nuclear weapons (including those of the U.S.) from the U.K. and to a large-scale program of public ownership of basic industries. By 1989 Kinnock had persuaded the party to abandon these policies and to bring greater internal democracy to the party's own operations. The new-look Labour Party won favour with the electorate in the June elections to the European Parliament and in a succession of opinion polls. By then the Conservatives were no longer con-fident that they could defeat Labour as easily in a future general election as they had done in 1983 and 1987. (PETER KELLNER)

Lee, Spike

If the most-watched film in 1989 was *Batman,* the most talked about—and argued over—was *Do the Right Thing.* And no wonder: it was

written, produced, and directed by Spike Lee, a black filmmaker known for having a lot to say—much of it controversial. Treating life on one multiracial, summer-baked block in Brook-lyn, N.Y., the film focused on the tension between two noisy black youths and the head-strong owner of the neighbourhood's only white business, a pizzeria. After the two sides come to blows and a white cop strangles one of the youths, a previously moderate character played by Lee heaves a trash can through the pizzeria's window, touching off a riot. The film had a dis-tinctive style, characterized by an imaginative, almost hyperactive use of the camera. However, it was the film's substance that caused the con-troversy, that left many people asking: Did Lee do the right thing? Some complimented him for dealing with race relations in an inspired and unflinching way, while others worried that his film would spark violence by blacks. Why did the short, slight, owl-eyed Lee want to kick up all that dust? "Because too many people have their head in the sand about racism," was his reply.

Not long after his birth in Atlanta, Ga., on March 20, 1957, Shelton Jackson Lee got the nickname "Spike" from his mother; he then spent the next 30-odd years living up to the piercing toughness it implied. In 1979–80, his first year in New York University's graduate film school, he created a film that attacked the racism of *Birth of a Nation* and that almost got him dismissed from school for using bad "film grammar." He proved his talent two years later, however, when he won an award from the Academy of Motion Picture Arts and Sciences for his thesis film, *Joe's Bed-Stuy Barbershop: We Cut Heads.*

Lee's professional debut as a director and actor came in 1986 with *She's Gotta Have It,* a cheaply but cleverly made comedy that de-lighted filmgoers with its story of a black woman blithely carrying on affairs with three men. The film's critical and financial success enabled Lee to obtain financing for the 1988 musical *School Daze,* which—like all his films—was scored by his father, Bill, a jazz musician. A story based on Lee's undergraduate experiences at More-house College, Atlanta, during the 1970s, *School Daze* received poor grades from reviewers who felt the musical genre was beyond Lee's tech-nical capabilities and from black leaders who resented the film's focus on the little-discussed conflict between light- and dark-skinned blacks. Against comments such as the latter, Lee ar-gued: "Something must be wrong if everybody agrees 100% on a film I do. I'm an instigator." (MICHAEL AMEDEO)

LeMond, Greg

Victory appeared hopeless for Greg LeMond on the morning of July 23, 1989. With one 27-km (15.2-mi) stage left in the 76th Tour de France bicycle race, he trailed Frenchman Lau-rent Fignon by 50 seconds. Gaining even one second per kilometre on him would be amazing.

LeMond already had reduced the amazing to the ordinary merely by competing seriously in one of the most demanding endurance events in sports. The 23-day race from Luxembourg to Paris covered 3,257 km (2,023 mi) in 21 stages, 6 of them through mountains. His body still carried more than 30 shotgun pellets from a hunting accident two years earlier that left him in critical condition.

His 55-km/h (34-mph) average speed on the sprint from Versailles was the fastest ever for one day in the Tour de France. His time of 26 min 57 sec was the day's fastest by 33 sec. It was enough to give LeMond his second Tour de France victory by eight seconds, the narrowest margin of victory in the history of the race.

Gregory James LeMond, born June 26, 1961, in Reno, Nev., began cycling when he was 14 and soon became a top amateur cyclist. In 1978 he was the first U.S. rider to win three medals in Olympic or world cycling competition, with gold, silver, and bronze medals in the junior world championship time trial. He won the Coors Classic stage race from San Francisco to Boulder, Colo., in 1981, his first year as a professional, and did not race in the U.S. again until he won that competition a second time in 1985.

Cycling's glamour event, the Tour de France, was also LeMond's best after the strong La Vie Claire team doubled his salary to $300,000 a year in 1984. Teams provide supplies and tac-tical support, setting paces and blocking oppo-nents, but the team got in LeMond's way after he finished third in his first Tour de France in 1984, the best finish ever by a non-European. On the 19th day of the Tour in 1985, he was pulling out of reach when his team manager ordered him to let teammate Bernard Hinault win a record-tying fifth time. Hinault, in turn, helped push Le Mond to his first victory in 1986.

The next spring LeMond was recovering from a broken hand at his home in Sacramento, Calif., when he went hunting for wild turkey on April 20, 1987, with his brother-in-law, Patrick Blades, and his uncle, Rod Barber. Blades mis-takenly shot him from 27.5 m (30 yd) with shot-gun pellets that collapsed his lung, broke two ribs, drained two pints of blood, and pierced his intestines, liver, diaphragm, kidney, and heart lining. His 1987 and 1988 seasons were wiped out by the accident and by an emergency ap-pendectomy four months later, an infected leg tendon, and a salary dispute that forced him to join the weak Belgian ADR team.

(KEVIN M. LAMB)

McBride, Patricia

In celebration of Patricia McBride's 30-year ca-reer with the New York City Ballet (NYCB), the company honoured her with a gala trib-ute on June 4, 1989. McBride, who had an-nounced her impending retirement, had had the longest, most consistently successful career of any woman in the history of the company. Forty-two of the more than 90 roles in her repertoire had been created for her, 22 of them by George Balanchine, NYCB's founding chore-ographer. The program of the gala featured a retrospective of roles identified with her ca-reer, with McBride herself dancing several of the 12 numbers presented. Many of her former partners and choreographers appeared onstage, and the final standing ovation found her being showered with bouquets, including 13,000 roses.

McBride was born on Aug. 23, 1942, in Tea-neck, N.J. She began taking ballet classes at the age of 7, and at 14 she won a scholarship to the School of American Ballet, NYCB's offi-cial school. She danced for a year with André Eglevsky's Petit Ballet Company and appeared Off-Broadway in *Come Play with Me* before be-coming, at 16, a member of NYCB's corps de ballet. In 1961 she became a principal dancer. She and Edward Villella were frequently cast as partners and, in addition to their NYCB

performances, often made guest appearances on television and at dance concerts and festivals. *Harlequinade, Tarantella,* the Tchaikovsky *Pas de deux,* and the "Rubies" section of *Jewels,* Balanchine ballets especially identified with them, spotlighted her strength of technique and stamina, as well as her sparkling personality.

She considered Jerome Robbins' *Dances at a Gathering* a turning point. It showed the intimacy of dancers dancing for each other and demonstrated her expansive lyricism. Other outstanding roles were those of Swanilda in *Coppélia,* the Pearly Queen in *Union Jack,* and the Sleepwalker in *La Sonnambula.* Her elegance was also showcased in *Who Cares?,* choreographed to a number of George Gershwin songs. Having begun her career at a time when ballet was dominated by European dancers, she was credited with changing the image of the ballerina in the U.S. to that of the "all-American girl."

In 1973 she married Jean-Pierre Bonnefoux, who at the time was a fellow NYCB dancer. Her plan after retirement was to move to Bloomington, Ind., where Bonnefoux was head of Indiana University's dance department.

(BARBARA WHITNEY)

Mackay of Clashfern, Lord
There were two senses in which Lord Mackay was an outsider in the Cabinet of U.K. Prime Minister Margaret Thatcher. First, he had no previous party political experience when Thatcher appointed him lord chancellor in 1987. Second, he came with little direct experience of English law to preside over the biggest reform of the English legal profession in the 20th century. Lord Mackay was a Scot and had devoted his career to the separate, and in some important respects very different, Scottish legal system.

James Mackay was born in Scourie, Sutherland, on July 2, 1927, and educated at Edinburgh's George Heriot's School, Edinburgh University, and Trinity College, Cambridge. He was called to the Scottish bar in 1955 and rose steadily through the country's ranks of barristers. When Thatcher became prime minister in 1979, she appointed Mackay as lord advocate—in effect, Scotland's senior law officer. It was a position that gave Mackay a seat in the House of Lords. He resigned as lord advocate and was then appointed a law lord in 1985.

In 1987 Thatcher suddenly needed a new lord chancellor when Lord Havers resigned because of ill health. Mackay's appointment came as a considerable surprise; he was the first member of the Scottish bar ever to hold the post. Mackay quickly showed that distance from English law did not make his heart grow fonder of it. He deplored many of the restrictive practices employed by barristers and solicitors and the overly rigid lines of demarcation between them. He instigated a series of reforms—for example, increasing the rights of solicitors to act as advocates in court and opening up the legal profession to greater competition.

Mackay was noted among his colleagues for his strong moral and religious feelings. These derived from his membership in Scotland's Free Presbyterian Church, a fiercely anti-Catholic sect. In November 1988, however, the Southern Presbytery suspended Mackay from communion and from his post as a church elder after he attended Roman Catholic requiem masses for two fellow judges. This suspension was held in abeyance until May 1989, when the Synod upheld the Presbytery's decision, stating that Mackay would be suspended until he repented his action and agreed not to repeat it. Mackay then resigned his membership in the church.

(PETER KELLNER)

McMurtry, Larry
In June 1989, as the newly elected president of PEN American Centre, an organization of novelists, poets, playwrights, essayists, and editors, Larry McMurtry packed his bags and set out across the U.S. to smooth the feathers of PEN members who felt they had been overlooked long enough by the New York headquarters.

McMurtry, a Texan, earned the distinction of being the first president of PEN since 1922 who did not hail from the state of New York (Booth Tarkington from Indiana was the last). For the rest of the country McMurtry would be remembered in 1989 for the television miniseries based on his Pulitzer Prize-winning novel, *Lonesome Dove* (1985).

Considered a regional writer, McMurtry succeeded with *Lonesome Dove* because of his familiarity with its place, time, and characters. As a boy growing up on his family's ranch in Archer county, Texas, he absorbed the stories his uncles and the cowboys told him about their experiences on cattle drives at the turn of the century. Careful to avoid romanticizing the Old West in his writing, McMurtry retained the actual gritty experiences and the reality of the life endured by cowboys on the trail, such as the death of a character when he rode into a nest of water moccasins. With Texas and Texas characters at the heart of his other novels, McMurtry incorporated a sense of reality into his writing. In *Horseman, Pass By* (1961; reprinted 1979) and *The Last Picture Show* (1966; reprinted 1979), he expressed the loneliness and problems of coming of age in a small town. He portrayed struggling and frustrated Texas characters in urban environments in *Terms of Endearment* (1975) and *Cadillac Jack* (1982).

McMurtry's relationship with Hollywood began with the film *Hud* (1963), an Academy Award-winning adaptation of *Horseman, Pass By.* He was coauthor, with Peter Bogdanovich, of the screenplay for *The Last Picture Show* (1971), which won the Academy Award for best screenplay based on material from another medium. *Terms of Endearment* (1983), based on McMurtry's novel, won the Academy Award for best picture.

Larry Jeff McMurtry, the son and grandson of ranchers, was born June 3, 1936, in Wichita Falls, Texas. He attended high school in Archer City, which he later used as the basis for his town, Thalia, in *The Last Picture Show.* He received degrees from North Texas State College (1958) and Rice University, Houston (1960). He maintained a full schedule, including running his rare book store and completing his latest works, *Anything for Billy* (1988) and *Some Can Whistle* (1989).

(SUSAN MARTS MYERS)

Major, John Roy
When Margaret Thatcher, the U.K.'s Conservative prime minister, asked John Major in July 1989 to become the country's new foreign secretary, Major was as startled as anyone. He had become known as one of the most effective of the younger Cabinet ministers, but nobody expected him to be catapulted from the number two post at the Treasury to one of the three great offices of state. Three months later came an even greater shock: he was switched to chancellor of the Exchequer following Nigel Lawson's sudden resignation.

Major's background was unusual for a Conservative. He was born on March 29, 1943, in Merton, South London, into a family that struggled to make ends meet. His father was a trapeze artist and not always in work. Major grew up in the multiracial inner-city London suburb of Brixton (which saw race riots in the early 1980s) and attended local state schools. Unlike others with that kind of upbringing, he decided that Conservatism and free enterprise offered the best hopes for struggling families, and he joined the party at the age of 16. His upbringing left another legacy: a passionate opposition to all forms of racism. Major worked as a banker while climbing the first rungs of the political ladder. He became a borough councillor in 1968, and in 1976 he was selected as Conservative candidate for the prosperous rural constituency of Huntingdon, 113 km (70 mi) north of London. He entered Parliament in 1979.

He soon impressed colleagues—and, in time, Thatcher—with his ability and dedication and with a toughness that belied his soft-spoken manner. He was an unexpected but inspired choice when he joined the Cabinet in 1987 as chief secretary to the Treasury, in charge of public spending. In two successive years he managed the remarkable feat of achieving negotiated deals with each minister within the government's overall spending plans—and emerging from the process more popular than when he started.

By early 1989 Major was being discussed by insiders as a possible successor to Thatcher after her retirement. His brief spell as foreign secretary did little to advance his cause. He seemed out of his depth at the Commonwealth heads of government conference in Kuala Lumpur, Malaysia, in October. His unexpected return to the Treasury, this time as chancellor, restored him to familiar territory. He now had a chance to demonstrate his talents—and, when necessary, his ability to act for himself rather than as Thatcher's poodle. More than anything, however, his political fortunes would henceforth be linked closely to those of the British economy.

(PETER KELLNER)

Marsalis, Wynton
It was astonishing to jazz lovers when trumpeter Wynton Marsalis, at 18, made his brilliant debut in 1980 with Art Blakey's Jazz Messengers, but equally astonishing had been his debut, at 14, with the New Orleans (La.) Philharmonic Orchestra playing Haydn's *Trumpet Concerto.*

Marsalis was born Oct. 18, 1961, in New Orleans. His first trumpet was given to him when he was six by renowned jazz trumpeter Al Hirt, leader of the band in which Marsalis' father was playing piano at the time. What really made Marsalis decide to take the jazz trumpet seriously, however, was a recording by jazz great Clifford Brown. Then, when he heard an album of Maurice André playing classical trumpet works, he resolved to master classical music as well. Marsalis excelled in both genres, and by the time he was 17, he was studying at the pres-

ROBERT F. KUSEL

tigious Berkshire Music Center at Tanglewood (near Lenox, Mass.). He received a scholarship from the Juilliard School of Music in New York City, but he left Juilliard when he began touring with the Jazz Messengers, finding that on-the-road experience with professional jazz players provided a more stimulating education.

By 1981 Marsalis was attracting attention in the jazz world with his exceptional technique and deft improvisation, but he was not neglecting the classical side. That year he signed a record contract in which he stipulated that he would record both kinds of music. The simultaneous release in 1983 of *Think of One* (jazz) and *Trumpet Concertos* (classical) was a success. Marsalis became the first musician ever to win (or even be nominated for) Grammy awards in both categories.

Later, Marsalis made the decision to devote himself exclusively to jazz. In a rather harsh bit

of self-criticism, he said, "I found there simply was not enough time for me to pay respects to both the unarguable greatness of European music or jazz. Every time I would mess up Haydn's concerto, I would have nightmares. . . . The time I spent bludgeoning Haydn could have been devoted to learning how to swing and reaching a functional appreciation for the blues."

Marsalis was well known for his strong opinions about the nature of jazz. He eschewed free-form and avant-garde approaches, and some found his definition of the music narrow and unimaginative. But to those who had feared that traditional jazz was dead, Marsalis' strict bebop- and swing-influenced playing was an answer to prayer, breathing a contemporary excitement into the traditional form.

(ELIZABETH LASKEY)

Mazowiecki, Tadeusz

Late in the summer of 1989, in a remarkable coup, Tadeusz Mazowiecki became the prime minister of Poland and formed the first non-Communist-dominated coalition government in the Soviet bloc since the early post-World War II years. Born in Plock on April 17, 1927, he graduated in law from the University of Warsaw. After a difficult start to his career as a journalist in the Stalinist '50s, he went on to set up the Warsaw chapter of the Catholic Intelligentsia Clubs (KIK) in 1957 and, a year later, the influential independent journal *Wiez*. Upon being elected to the Sejm (parliament) in 1961, he joined the Znak group of Catholic deputies, an island of open opposition unique in Communist legislative assemblies. His name became linked with every major demonstration of dissent, culminating with his condemnation of the excesses that ended the student demonstrations of March 1968. In general, however, he was a low-profile politician whose role in the creation and shaping of the key values and program of the Solidarity trade union movement was rarely perceived by the public. Chairman of the strike committee's advisory group in the Lenin Shipyard in Gdansk, he became the editor of the Solidarity weekly newspaper; with the imposition of martial law in December 1981, he was interned. Emerging a year later, he gradually became Lech Walesa's alter ego. An evocative image was that of the two men at the head of the apparently defeated workers leaving the Lenin Shipyard in May 1988. It was through Walesa's efforts that Mazowiecki obtained the premiership.

A popular choice, he was the first secular leader to outstrip the Catholic primate in public opinion polls. With food-price inflation running in the triple digits annually, he would need to draw on all of these reserves of goodwill, for he was not one to shirk difficult decisions. Official visits to Rome and Moscow signified his respect for the church as well as a desire to retain the confidence of his most powerful neighbour. It was his belief in dialogue with all, coupled to a vision of government as rooted in self-organized societal activity, that was the best guarantee of his ability to deal with a society where the springs of political, cultural, ethnic, and economic pluralism had broken through to the surface.

Not by nature a visionary, this widower and grandfather inspired confidence and trust through personal contact; his style was to allow his ministers to take responsibility for their offices. His influence was palpable as Poland struggled to stabilize its economy and maintain consensus coalition politics while at the same time recognizing its responsibility as a leading exemplar of the transformations being effected through much of the Eastern bloc.

(GEORGE KOLANKIEWICZ)

Menem, Carlos Saúl

With a violent streak, a populist style, and a fanatical interest in sport (including football [soccer], tennis, rally driving, and piloting his own aircraft), Carlos Saúl Menem modeled himself both physically and spiritually on the macho image of a local 19th-century Argentine chief-

PUCCIANO—CAMERA PRESS/GLOBE PHOTOS

tain, Juan Facundo Quiroga. He cultivated links with certain nationalistic members of the military who had participated in the Islas Malvinas/Falkland Islands war with the U.K. in 1982 as well as with such militaristic foreign leaders as Libya's Mu'ammar al-Qadhdhafi. These attributes appeared to consolidate grass-roots support among Argentina's Peronists sufficient to win him the presidential nomination on July 9, 1988, and the coveted presidency of Argentina in the elections held on May 14, 1989 (he took office early, on July 8).

Born on July 2, 1930, one of four sons of a Syrian immigrant family at Anillaco in Argentina's northeastern province of La Rioja, Menem graduated in law at Córdoba University in 1955. He began his career as a trade union lawyer in the city of La Rioja, defending predominantly poor and working-class clients. He joined the Peronist (Partido Justicialista) movement in 1956 and was imprisoned briefly for the first time in the same year after participating in a revolt that aimed to restore Juan Perón (who had been ousted from power) to the presidency. Menem won the post of president of the Peronist organization in his home province in 1963 and in 1973 was elected provincial governor, a post he held until 1976, when he was first imprisoned and then sent into internal exile by the military regime that took over from Perón's widow, Isabel.

Reentering active politics after 1981, Menem was returned to the governorship of La Rioja in 1983. During the six-year term of Pres. Raúl Alfonsín, Menem was able to extend his support base within the Peronists at a time when the party was being restructured toward more democratic practices, especially by such leaders as Antonio Cafiero, governor of the province of Buenos Aires. In sharp contrast to the new brand of Peronism, Menem remained loyal to the original version and retained his strong anti-establishment, anti-intellectual approach and distrust of rivals based in Buenos Aires.

(SUSAN CUNNINGHAM)

Mitchell, Kevin

Two years after Kevin Mitchell considered quitting baseball, he made National League pitchers wish he had. When he had 32 home runs in the San Francisco Giants' first 89 games, he was on pace to hit 56 home runs for the 1989 season. Nagging injuries slowed him after that, but no other major leaguer came within 10 of Mitchell's final total of 47.

The National League champions' cleanup hitter was an overwhelming choice for Most Valuable Player in the league. "Very few of Kevin's hits haven't caused some kind of damage," Giants pitcher Rich Gossage said. His home runs either tied a game or gave the Giants a lead 23 times. Only 16 were hit when the Giants were ahead. His 100th run batted in (RBI) on August

8 was the earliest that figure had been reached in the major leagues in 10 years.

Mitchell also led the major leagues with 125 RBIs, 345 total bases, 87 extra-base hits, and a .635 slugging percentage. Before 1989 his career highs for three major league seasons were only 19 home runs, 80 RBIs, 223 total bases, 51 extra-base hits, and a .442 slugging percentage. His .291 batting average in 1989 also was a career high. He batted .353 with two home runs and seven RBIs to help the Giants beat the Chicago Cubs four games to one in the National League championship series, and he had a home run and a .294 average in the Oakland A's four-game sweep of the Giants in the World Series.

Mitchell never had more than 15 home runs per season in the minor leagues, where he usually played third base in 1981–85. When he played six positions for the World Series champion New York Mets in 1986, it frustrated him to be considered a part-time utility man. The Mets traded him off-season to San Diego, where he was to play every day, but when he was traded again to the Giants half a season later, he was discouraged about being unwanted.

Josie Whitfield, Mitchell's grandmother, had to talk Mitchell out of quitting baseball. He attributed his 1989 improvement more to the contact lenses he bought at her suggestion than to his position switch from third base to left field.

Mitchell was born Jan. 13, 1962, in San Diego, Calif., where he played catcher and third base in high school and also starred at half-back and linebacker in football. He grew up in a rough neighbourhood and had three gunshot scars from his days with a street gang. He joined the Mets organization at 19. (KEVIN M. LAMB)

Montana, Joe

Where other people feel pressure, Joe Montana seizes opportunities. He sweats icicles when his San Francisco 49ers are behind in the fourth quarter. Montana quarterbacked the 49ers to victory on six of those occasions in 1989, starting with the Super Bowl on January 22 for the 1988 National Football League (NFL) championship. Driving from his own eight-yard line, Montana completed eight passes in less than three minutes for 92 yd, including the 10-yd touchdown that beat Cincinnati 20–16 with 34 seconds left, the latest winning touchdown in Super Bowl history. His 357 yd passing for the game set a Super Bowl record.

The climax turned out to be a catapult toward the best of Montana's 11 NFL seasons. The 49ers overcame fourth-quarter deficits in three of the first five games of 1989, including once when Montana threw for four touchdowns in the last 13 minutes 40 seconds. He was the NFL player of the month in September and November, and he won his first offensive player of the year award. His 112.4 passer rating broke a 29-year-old NFL record, and he also led the league with 9.12 yd per attempt, 6.7% of his passes for touchdowns, eight interceptions, and a completion percentage of .702, third best in NFL history. He was selected to his sixth Pro Bowl, and he was named man of the year by the *Sporting News*.

The 49ers, with a 14–2 won-lost record, won their seventh NFC West Division championship and eighth play-off berth in Montana's nine years as a regular starter. They already had won three Super Bowls, and Montana was most valuable player in the games for the 1981 and 1984 championships.

Joseph C. Montana grew up in New Eagle, Pa., where his hero was another Pittsburgh-area native, Joe Namath. Born June 11, 1956, he grew to a skinny 188 cm (6 ft 2 in) and 88 kg (195 lb) that made another 49er rookie mistake him for a punter at their first training camp. Despite appearances, he was an all-around athlete who pitched three perfect games and batted .500 in Little League baseball, high jumped 2.06 m (6 ft 9 in) at 15, and turned down a North Carolina State scholarship in basketball, in which he played every position.

He chose football for the opportunity to play

at Notre Dame, where he led the Fighting Irish to three fourth-quarter comebacks even before he became a full-time starter as a junior, the year Notre Dame won the 1977 national championship. Montana was a third-round draft choice in 1979 and the next year helped the 49ers set an NFL record by overcoming New Orleans' 35–7 halftime lead to win 38–35. It was the first of 20 times he overcame deficits in the fourth quarter.   (KEVIN M. LAMB)

Neil, Andrew Ferguson

No man rode the technological revolution in the media in Great Britain in the 1980s more enthusiastically than Andrew Neil, who started the decade as American correspondent for the magazine *The Economist* and ended it as both editor of *The Sunday Times* newspaper and chairman of the Sky Television satellite service—operations both owned by Rupert Murdoch's News Corp.

Neil was born in Paisley, Scotland, on May 21, 1949. After graduating from Glasgow University in 1971, he joined the Conservative Party's research department. In 1973 he joined *The Economist.* Three years as U.S. correspondent formed many of the attitudes he subsequently applied to the British media, where he sought to promulgate free-market economic ideas and liberal social values. One cause he espoused was the deregulation of television. He pursued it by opening a British branch of the U.S. antitrust consultancy National Economic Research Associates. This brought him into contact with Murdoch, who aspired to enter the British television market himself.

The two men immediately warmed to each other. In 1983 Murdoch appointed the 34-year-old Neil as editor of *The Sunday Times,* which Murdoch had bought (along with *The Times*) two years earlier. Neil's abrasive style provoked the departures of a number of senior journalists and, for a time, a declining circulation. In 1986 Murdoch's papers made an audacious overnight switch to a new high-technology printing and publishing centre in London's Docklands. Neil was Murdoch's most enthusiastic supporter of the move, which led to a bitter dispute with sacked printworkers. In time *The Sunday Times* settled down, regained readers, and added new sections and extra pages. By the end of the 1980s, it was twice as large and sold twice as many copies as its nearest rival in the "quality" Sunday market.

Neil's experience as chairman of Sky Television began less promisingly. The four-channel service opened in February 1989, but far fewer viewers than predicted bought receiving dishes. One result was that the venture lost $3 million a week through 1989, placing a strain on the finances of the Murdoch empire that it could not afford to suffer indefinitely.

(PETER KELLNER)

Nujoma, Sam

Sam Nujoma returned home to South West Africa/Namibia in September 1989 after 29 years in exile and led the South West Africa People's Organization (SWAPO) to victory in the UN-supervised November elections. Although his party won only 57% of the vote, this was twice as much as the next largest party and sufficient to make it reasonably certain that Nujoma would become independent Namibia's first president when South Africa finally relinquished its control over the territory in 1990.

Samuel Shafiihuma (literally "a time of trouble") Nujoma was born to a poor peasant family in the remote Ongandjera region of Ovamboland on May 12, 1929, and spent his early years tending the family's few cattle and goats. His primary education began at night school; his parents could not afford to send him on to secondary school, and at the age of 16 he became a railway dining car steward. After a fellow worker was sent home without compensation following a serious accident, Nujoma tried to form a union for railwaymen but was discharged. He subsequently worked as a clerk and a store assistant.

When SWAPO was formed on April 19, 1960, Nujoma was elected president, a position he still retained—a tribute to his political and organizational abilities. After several years of fruitlessly petitioning the UN to compel South Africa to comply with the conditions of its trusteeship over the former German colony, SWAPO embarked on an armed struggle in 1966. Although its guerrilla force, the People's National Liberation Army of Namibia (PLAN), failed to liberate any territory, it succeeded in focusing international attention on Namibia. In 1973 the UN General Assembly recognized SWAPO as the sole legitimate representative of the Namibian people, and in 1978 the Security Council adopted Resolution 435, which set out terms for the attainment of Namibian independence under UN supervision. After years of diplomatic jockeying, the resolution was finally accepted by South Africa in December 1988.

A short, burly figure with a bushy, white-flecked beard, Nujoma made an impressive appearance that was not matched by his hesitant speech and ponderous manner. But if his speech making was pedestrian, he showed a rare ability to command men and maintain control, sometimes by methods that drew criticism from human rights groups. A shrewd politician, he was remarkably free of bitterness and racial prejudice. Although often accused of being a Communist, he was in fact not an ideologue but was more drawn to the pragmatism of Scandinavian democratic socialism. He pledged himself to work for national reconciliation.

(COLIN LEGUM)

Oga, Norio

In the early 1950s, when Norio Oga was a young baritone student at the Tokyo National University of Fine Arts and Music, he thought constantly about ways to make a good tape recorder. His flair for electronics and mechanics landed him a job as consultant to the Sony Corp., which was then known as Tokyo Tsushin Kogyo. At that time, still determined to make singing his career, Oga spent four years studying voice at the Kunst Universitat in Berlin before being persuaded to formally join the electronics company in 1959.

Starting out as manager of the tape recorder division, he was soon also taking care of industrial design and product planning. Rapidly rising in the company, Oga was made president of the CBS/Sony Group, Inc., in 1970. During his tenure this joint venture grew into the largest record company in Japan. Oga then moved on to become chairman of the group in 1980. Two years later he was named president and chief operating officer of Sony. In July 1989 he moved to centre stage when he succeeded the firm's legendary cofounder, Akio Morita, as chief executive.

The son of a well-to-do lumber importer in Shizuoka prefecture, Oga was born on Jan. 29, 1930. Tall and portly, he enjoyed yachting and golfing. He chose to live in Tokyo with his wife, Midori, a professional piano player, who was once his classmate. Oga's reputation as a man possessed of tenacious confidence but not motivated by personal ambition endeared him to Morita, the company's chairman. Being rational and unsentimental, Oga was not always in tune with other Japanese managers, but he was admired for his sound business instincts and his ability to make quick judgments. While attending more to overall strategy than to fine details, he extended Sony's operations into new fields, particularly into entertainment software that complemented the company's mainstream consumer electronics.

Sony's $2 billion purchase of CBS Records in January 1988 was followed in October 1989 by the $3.4 billion takeover of Columbia Pictures, which sparked a heated debate in the media. Oga downplayed the criticism by maintaining that what counted most was whether five years hence "our American employees would be happy and American audiences would be praising us for making good movies."

(GERD LARSSON)

Palmer, Geoffrey

Geoffrey Winston Russell Palmer, 47, law professor and son of a newspaper editor, was his predecessor's nominee as prime minister of New Zealand. As deputy to David Lange, up to Lange's resignation and withdrawal to a non-Cabinet role, Palmer had provided a steady hand. It was needed, whether in fort-holding during Lange's forays to other countries or in providing solid backup for a leader whose forte was the bon mot and the footlights. It was Palmer who warned his colleagues against "speed wobbles" in Labour's frantic policies based on deregulation.

Different in background and style from Lange, he was no favourite among his party's "greenies" or among labour unions or dole-takers, but Labour MPs saw a different need. Geoff Palmer was born April 21, 1942, at Nelson, a resort city based on fruit growing, forestry, and

regional tourism, at the top of the thinly populated South Island. He was educated at Nelson College, then at Victoria University, Wellington. He completed a law degree, married his childhood sweetheart, and worked as a solicitor for a Wellington firm before gravitating back to university study and teaching. A term as a law professor at the Universities of Iowa and Virginia, combined with his family background in journalism, fanned an interest in liberalization of the laws of defamation. He became professor of English and New Zealand law at Victoria University in 1974.

He had declined an invitation to enter politics as a National Party candidate in Nelson in 1972. He was recruited for Labour by Bill Rowling, the party leader and a Nelson resident, in 1975 and became a member of Parliament at a by-election in 1979. Appointment as personal assistant to Rowling, a short-term prime minister, was the foot of the escalator. With Labour out of power and Rowling defeated for the leadership by Lange in 1983, Palmer narrowly was chosen deputy. He started on a five-year slog that established him, with Labour back in government, as a precise justice minister and monitor of the administration.

In U.S. eyes his formative years in America held the prospect of an end to the strained relationship arising out of Lange's ban on New Zealand port access for nuclear naval ships.

(JOHN A. KELLEHER)

Papandreou, Andreas Georgios

Neither indictment for alleged involvement in Greece's Bank of Crete scandal nor a widely publicized affair with a flight attendant half his age seemed to dampen Andreas Papandreou's spirits in 1989. The political party he formed in 1974, the Panhellenic Socialist Movement, or Pasok, made a strong-enough showing in the June and November elections to prevent the right-wing New Democracy Party from winning

a majority in Greece's Parliament. Despite the fact that Papandreou's eight-year term as prime minister was over, he still wielded considerable power.

Late in 1988 Papandreou's government struggled to overcome the effects of widespread allegations of fraud, bribery, and payoffs within Pasok. Bank of Crete executive George Koskotas fled to the United States but was jailed in Massachusetts pending extradition charges. He told a U.S. newsmagazine that payments of misappropriated funds and other irregularities in his business dealings involved high officials in the Greek government from 1986 to 1988. Papandreou staunchly denied the charges. Following new elections several months later, Parliament indicted the former prime minister, ordering Papandreou and four Pasok ministers to stand trial on charges including bribery and embezzlement.

At the same time that the corruption scandal was receiving worldwide attention, Papandreou's affair with Dimitra Liani was revealed. Papandreou announced his intention to divorce his wife of 38 years; the divorce became final on June 16, 1989, two days before the inconclusive national elections, and he and Liani were married July 13. Meanwhile, Papandreou was battling failing health. He underwent heart surgery in late 1988 in London and was hospitalized in June 1989 with heart, kidney, and lung problems. Nevertheless, the tenacious 70-year-old maintained a high profile in his efforts to guide Pasok to a continued role in Greece's Parliament. Under a November compromise among the main parties—Pasok, New Democracy, and Communist—a coalition would govern Greece until a third round of elections could be held in April 1990.

Papandreou was born on Feb. 5, 1919, in Chios, Greece. He studied law and was imprisoned briefly by the dictator Ionnis Metaxas. After being freed, he fled to the U.S. He received a Ph.D. from Harvard University in 1943 and taught economics at several U.S. and Canadian universities. When his father became prime minister of Greece in 1963, Papandreou returned to become involved in government and was jailed in 1967 for eight months after a military coup. In 1974 he formed Pasok, which won increasing shares of the vote in 1974 and 1977 before the sweeping victory in 1981 that was repeated in 1985. He served as prime minister of Greece until mid-1989. His tenure in office was characterized by anti-Americanism.

(FRANCINE SHONFELD SHERMAN)

Paul, Wolfgang
For his development of the Paul trap—an electromagnetic device that captures ions, or electrically charged atoms, and holds them so that their properties can be precisely measured—physicist Wolfgang Paul of the University of Bonn, West Germany, shared half of the 1989 Nobel Prize for Physics with Hans G. Dehmelt (q.v.) of the University of Washington. (The other half of the prize went to Norman F. Ramsey [q.v.] of Harvard University.) Paul's device used a radio-frequency current to maintain an alternating electric field that isolated and confined charged particles and atoms in a small space. The Paul trap was the first ion trap invented. Paul's fellow laureate Dehmelt built another kind of trap in 1955, for which he received his share of the prize. The traps of Paul and Dehmelt allowed physicists to study atomic properties and test physical theories with high degrees of precision, and they became key tools in modern spectroscopy.

Paul was born Aug. 10, 1913, in Lorenzkirch, now part of East Germany. He studied at the Munich and Berlin Institutes of Technology and received a doctorate from the Technical University in Berlin in 1939. In 1944 he became a lecturer at the University of Göttingen, now in West Germany, and taught there as a full professor from 1950. From 1952 he was also director of the Physics Institute and a member of the faculty of mathematical and natural sciences at the University of Bonn.

Paul's prizewinning work began in the 1950s when he conceived of a means whereby multipolar magnetic fields could be used to focus a beam of ions. He later invented a way of separating ions of different masses—the principle of which was widely used in modern spectrometers—and storing them in what came to be known as the Paul trap. According to the Nobel committee, the Paul trap "developed into a standard method for mass separation, now widely used."   (CAROLYN D. NEWTON)

Paz Zamora, Jaime
On his 101st day in office as president of Bolivia, Jaime Paz Zamora imposed a three-month state of siege in response to a widening teachers' strike; over 500 teachers and labour activists were arrested, and some strike leaders were sent into internal exile. They had protested that a promised counterinflationary bonus, equivalent to $100, had been denied the country's 80,000 teachers. Actions such as this confirmed that, once in office, Paz Zamora was committed to continuing the strict fiscal policies of his predecessor as well as rigidly upholding his end of the bargain by which he came into power. In an unusual alliance, former military dictator Hugo Banzer Suárez, of the right-wing Acción Democrática Nacionalista, and Paz Zamora, a self-proclaimed social democrat, joined forces to govern.

Paz Zamora was born April 15, 1939, in Cochabamba, Bolivia, and attended the Catholic University of Louvain, Belgium. After graduating Paz Zamora started his career by founding the Movimiento de la Izquierda Revolucionaria (MIR; Revolutionary Leftist Movement) in 1971, some three weeks after Banzer seized control of Bolivia. As leader of the MIR, Paz Zamora figured prominently in the movement as a proponent of "people's war" and anti-imperialism. In 1974 he was briefly jailed by the Banzer government for revolutionary activities, and he spent much of the rest of the decade in exile. On his return to Bolivia, he ran unsuccessfully for vice president in 1979 and then successfully the following year with Hernán Siles Zuazo of the left-leaning Unión Democrática y Popular as president (a military coup nullified the results). It was at this time that Paz Zamora was the sole survivor of a plane crash in an apparent assassination attempt by members of the military, leaving him with scars that remained visible. A split in the coalition took place after October 1982 elections that returned Siles and Paz Zamora to power; the MIR left the Cabinet, leaving Paz Zamora stranded in the vice presidency. He served until 1985.

The two years to 1982 were a period remembered in Bolivia as one of hyperinflation, strikes, and, finally, chaos. Nevertheless, they seemed to have provided the experience that allowed the unlikely coalition of Paz Zamora and Banzer to prosper. Locally, Paz Zamora had always been regarded as highly ambitious and tenacious. After he came to office, his pragmatism came to the fore. He discarded all pretense of radicalism, dismissing it as "sterile," and promptly signed an agreement with the International Monetary Fund.

On the international stage Paz Zamora attended the Rio Group's summit in Peru in October. There he backed the region's renewed fight against the international drug trade. He was at his most visible, however, in resisting the proposal to use U.S. ground troops against the drug dealers and appeared to have lost conditional U.S. aid to Bolivia as a consequence.

(MICHAEL WOOLLER)

Peacock, Andrew Sharp
On May 9, 1989, Andrew Peacock's parliamentary colleagues gave him a last chance to lead the conservative parties to victory in an Australian election. Calculating that the incumbent prime minister, R.J.L. Hawke, would have to call a general election within 12 months, the conservatives dumped their old leader, John Howard, and replaced him with Peacock, who, they hoped, would have a higher level of per-

CAMERA PRESS/GLOBE PHOTOS

sonal popularity than his predecessor. Speaking immediately after he became leader, Peacock said he wanted to see a fairer and more compassionate Australia. While Peacock supporters spoke of a phoenix rising from the ashes, Prime Minister Hawke called him a "recycled dunderhead." Peacock, however, was not deterred by his critics. He restored Howard to the opposition front bench and organized a successful dry-run election campaign, in which he coordinated the efforts of his major supporters.

Born Feb. 13, 1939, Peacock succeeded Sir Robert Menzies in the Melbourne establishment seat of Kooyong in 1966. From his earliest days it was expected that he would become prime minister. His most important early post, which launched his political career at centre stage, was as minister for the Army, 1969–72. During the Vietnam war Peacock performed so well as a minister that he was rewarded with the plum post of minister for foreign affairs (1975–80) in the Fraser government.

By 1989 Peacock was by far the most experienced minister in the conservative coalition, having held a wide variety of portfolios. He was successively minister advising the prime minister (1969–71), minister for external territories (1972), minister for the environment (two months in 1975), minister for industrial relations (1980–81), and minister for industry and commerce (1982–83). All that remained to crown his career was the prime ministership, but whether he had the capacity to lead the Liberal-National Party coalition to victory and defeat the Australian Labor Party was up to the judgment of the electorate.   (A.R.G. GRIFFITHS)

Pérez Rodríguez, Carlos Andrés
On Feb. 2, 1989, Carlos Andrés Pérez, a lifelong politician of the social democratic party, Acción Democrática (AD), took office as president of Venezuela for the second time, having won 54% of the vote in the December 1988 presidential elections. It was a historic occasion because no other Venezuelan president had ever been reelected under a constitution that forced former heads of state to wait for two consecutive five-year presidential terms to pass before seeking the office again.

Pérez was born Oct. 27, 1922, in the border state of Táchira and became involved in politics as a teenager. He was elected to the legislature as a member of AD in 1958, and as minister of the interior in the early 1960s he was responsible for the government's successful campaign to eradicate a leftist guerrilla movement. Pérez first held office as president in 1974–79, when oil prices rose steeply and oil-rich Venezuela was able to reap the benefits of a sudden increase in income to become the wealthiest country in Latin America. During his presidency the oil and iron ore industries were nationalized, and large industrial development

projects were undertaken. Financed with plentiful loans from commercial banks recycling Middle East petrodollars, the nation's economy grew rapidly. Venezuela's international standing also rose, and Pérez built a reputation as a spokesman for the Third World. However, he left office with a low popularity rating, and his government was widely accused of mismanagement, inefficiency, and corruption.

In the 10 years Pérez was out of office, interest rates increased markedly and oil prices were cut in half, creating serious financial problems for Venezuela. Pérez's elaborate inauguration ceremony, which 22 heads of state attended, belied the economic difficulties that he was inheriting. His first task was to put order into public finances and initiate a radical long-term restructuring program under the aegis of the International Monetary Fund and the World Bank. Tough economic measures were clearly going to induce a recession with a politically unpopular decline in real incomes, but the president and his ministers were unprepared for the violent response of the people. Increases in fuel and public transport prices provoked riots at the end of February. Hundreds of people were killed, and many more were injured. Pérez suspended constitutional rights and imposed a curfew. Nevertheless, his adroit handling of the situation soon allowed order to be restored without the economic program being derailed; concessions were granted to the poor and many workers received compensation. At the same time, the financial targets set with the IMF for midyear were met. (SARAH CAMERON)

Peterson, Oscar

Twelve-time winner of the Down Beat Award for best jazz pianist of the year, Oscar Peterson was noted for his ability to play with blazing speed and authority in all jazz piano styles. Early classical training developed Peterson's mechanically flawless technique. He attended the Montreal Conservatory of Music for one year before studying privately with Hungarian pianist Paul de Marky.

Born on Aug. 15, 1925, in Montreal, Oscar Emmanuel Peterson began his association with the piano at age seven. In 1939 he won a Canadian Broadcasting Corporation amateur contest. From 1944 to 1949, Peterson played with the Johnny Holmes Orchestra, then one of the most popular jazz bands in Canada. In 1949 impresario Norman Granz heard him play on a live broadcast in Montreal and immediately invited him to perform with Granz's touring concert unit, Jazz at the Philharmonic, in a Carnegie Hall concert. Peterson's performance drew a standing ovation, and his international career was launched.

Peterson toured throughout the world, first with Granz's group and then with his own trio, which he formed in 1952. He preferred to perform in Europe, saying that there jazz and jazz musicians were treated seriously. The Oscar Peterson Trio was nominated five times by the National Academy of Recording Arts and Sciences for recording the best album of the year.

In 1959 Peterson opened the Advanced School of Contemporary Music in Toronto. He was forced to close the school in 1963 because of the heavy demands of his concert tours, but he returned to teaching in the 1980s. In 1985 he founded the Oscar Peterson Scholarship for Jazz Studies at York University in Toronto, where he was named adjunct professor of music. In 1987 he received the Roy Thomson Hall Award for his outstanding contribution to the musical life of Toronto.

Peterson played in the mainstream of the 1940s tradition. Full-blown and joyous, his approach to the music celebrated jazz with energy, knowledge, intelligence, and inventiveness. Though known principally as a great interpreter of music, Peterson was also a composer. His *Canadiana Suite* (1963) memorialized several places in Canada. His *Royal Suite* (1981) was inspired by the wedding of the Prince of Wales. *Africa Suite*, completed in 1983, was written for ballet. In 1973 he was made an Officer of

the Order of Canada, and in 1989 the French government made him an Officer of the Order of Arts and Letters. (DIANE LOIS WAY)

Pons, Bobby Stanley

At a crowded press conference in Salt Lake City, Utah, on March 23, 1989, the chairman of the chemistry department at the University of Utah, B. Stanley Pons, and his mentor and frequent house guest, Martin Fleischmann of the University of Southampton, England, became unlikely celebrities. They announced that, at room temperature, nuclei of heavy hydrogen had been drawn to a negatively charged pole of a rare metal called palladium, absorbed by the palladium's unusual crystal, and induced to fuse, releasing four times as much energy as had used been to charge the pole. There had never before been a verifiable report of artificial nuclear fusion releasing more energy than was used.

Interest in a cheap energy source was widespread, but many scientists were alarmed about announcing the results at a press conference. Scientists usually released such information in special scientific journals, after peer reviews by other scientists who had worked in related areas. Pons and Fleischmann noted that their results were already being discussed inaccurately. They released no copies of their unpublished paper, claiming concern for patents, but copies of the paper soon circulated around the world. Scientists who tried to duplicate the experiment complained of a lack of detail. Results varied, and one team noted a flaw in a measuring device. On April 12 in Dallas, Texas, Pons was cheered at a meeting of the American Chemical Society, but physicists who were guests expressed doubt. A scientific journal published the paper after peer review in mid-April, but peer reviewers for another journal suggested changes in another article by Pons and Fleischmann, who withdrew the article. On May 2 seven physicists attending a meeting of the American Physical Society in Baltimore, Md., sharply criticized Pons and Fleischmann's interpretations of data. In July a committee of scientists appointed by the U.S. Department of Energy advised against further research of Pons and Fleischmann's claims.

Pons was born in Valdese, N.C., on Aug. 23, 1943. In 1965 he received a B.S. from Wake Forest University, Winston-Salem, N.C., and started work on a Ph.D. at the University of Michigan. For financial reasons he entered his family's textile business in 1967. He received a Ph.D from the University of Southampton in 1979, having worked there with Fleischmann. He joined the University of Utah faculty in 1983. (CHARLES JOHNSON TAGGART)

Powell, Colin Luther

On Aug. 10, 1989, U.S. Pres. George Bush nominated Colin Powell, who had been a four-star general in the Army for only four months, to be chairman of the Joint Chiefs of Staff. Powell, son of immigrants from Jamaica and the first black officer nominated to the highest military post in the U.S., would succeed Adm. William Crowe, who did not want another two-year term. Bush called Powell "the complete soldier," and Powell was said to prefer military command to other jobs. Even so, in jobs outside the military structure, he had shown skill in persuading others to work together.

Born in New York City on April 5, 1937, Colin Luther Powell graduated from the City College of New York in 1958. After graduation he was commissioned a second lieutenant in the Army. He served in Vietnam in 1962–63 and 1968–69 and was wounded on both tours. In 1971 he received an M.B.A. from George Washington University, Washington, D.C., and a year later, after an interview with Frank Carlucci, then deputy director of the Office of Management and Budget (OMB), Powell became a White House fellow and Carlucci's assistant. Powell commanded a battalion in South Korea in 1973–74 and worked in the Pentagon in 1974–75. In 1975 he became a colonel and

studied at the National War College. In 1979 he served briefly as executive assistant to the secretary of energy, became a major general, and was senior military assistant to the secretary of defense. He commanded the 4th Infantry Division at Ft. Collins, Colorado, in 1981–83.

In 1983 Caspar Weinberger, who had known Powell when both were in the OMB and who had become secretary of defense, made Powell his senior military assistant. Powell supervised the shipment of arms that was sold to Iran, but he would later testify that he had questioned the decision to sell them. He became a lieutenant general assigned to the V Corps in Europe in 1986. A year later Powell joined the staff of the National Security Council as deputy to Carlucci, then assistant to the president for national security affairs. Powell created a new structure for the staff. Late in 1987 U.S. Pres. Ronald Reagan appointed Powell to succeed Carlucci. Powell met regularly with the secretaries of state and defense and organized interdepartmental projects. Early in 1989 he took over the Army Forces Command. He became a four-star general in April. As chairman of the Joint Chiefs, he played a leading role in planning and executing the December invasion of Panama.

(CHARLES JOHNSON TAGGART)

Premadasa, Ranasinghe

Ranasinghe Premadasa was proud to have been poor. To alleviate any concerns of Sri Lankan voters, however, his party had him nominated for president by two high-caste members. While the island's civil unrest and faltering economy were major issues, Premadasa also campaigned as a man of the people. In December 1988

he defeated Sirimavo Bandaranaike, a former prime minister, to become the first leader of Sri Lanka from a low caste.

"I am happy to have been born among the poor and not in a castle with a silver spoon in my mouth," he once told the country's Parliament. He was born on June 23, 1924, in an impoverished neighbourhood of Colombo, Sri Lanka's capital. His family was in the dhobi (clothes washers) caste, one of the lowest in the country's traditional caste system. Indicative of Sri Lanka's high literacy rate, Premadasa, although poor and a Buddhist, attended a Roman Catholic college and later wrote numerous books, including novels and poetry.

The Temple of the Tooth, Sri Lanka's most sacred Buddhist shrine, was the site for Premadasa's oath of office on Jan. 2, 1989. Astrologers chose 10:40 AM as the most favourable moment for the ceremony, during which Premadasa spoke of his greatest challenge—to find an end to the conflict between the hard-liners of the minority Tamils in the north, who had been fighting for greater local autonomy and independence, and those of the majority Sin-

halese, who opposed any devolution of power to the Tamils. In his address he spoke in both Tamil and Sinhalese and appealed to the extreme factions that had boycotted the elections to lay down their arms. In the next six months, however, more than 1,700 people were killed in the continuing violence, and Premadasa was forced to reimpose the state of emergency that had been lifted when he took office.

As a youth Premadasa was involved in a social movement called Suchiritha (social consciousness among the low-caste people), and he later joined the trade union movement. In 1960, after serving in Colombo's Municipal Council, he gained a seat in the national Parliament as a member of the United National Party, and in 1978 he became the prime minister. Known as a good administrator and a charismatic speaker, he was popular among the poor for his promotion of low-income housing. Among his major political goals were eradicating poverty, restoring law and order, removing the Indian peace-keeping forces from Sri Lanka, and increasing foreign investment. (THOMAS J. RIGGS)

Ramsey, Norman Foster
For many observers the award to Norman F. Ramsey of half the 1989 Nobel Prize for Physics (shared with Hans G. Dehmelt and Wolfgang Paul [*qq.v.*]) was as much a recognition of his lifetime contribution to science as an acknowledgement of any particular achievement. Ramsey was cited for developing a technique, known as the separated oscillatory fields method, for inducing atoms to shift from one specific energy level to another. His work, carried out in the late 1940s, provided the basis for modern cesium atomic clocks, which set the international time standard and were used in many exacting applications, including digital telecommunications, satellite navigation, and measurements of continental drift. The Nobel committee also noted Ramsey's contribution to developing the hydrogen maser, a microwave-emitting relative of the laser, which likewise found applications in the precise measurement of time and frequency. Those specific citations, however, only touched on the highlights of a long, distinguished career.

Ramsey was born in Washington, D.C., Aug. 27, 1915, and attended Columbia University, New York City, where he received a Ph.D. in physics in 1940. Additional studies at the University of Cambridge culminated in a D.Sc. degree in 1954. He also received honorary degrees from Harvard University; Case Western Reserve University, Cleveland, Ohio; Middlebury (Vt.) College; the University of Oxford; and Rockefeller University, New York City. During the 1940s he held positions at the University of Illinois, the Massachusetts Institute of Technology Radiation Laboratory, and Columbia University. At Harvard he was an associate professor from 1947 to 1950, was a full professor from 1950, and in 1966 was named Higgins professor of physics.

In addition to teaching and research, Ramsey accepted numerous advisory and administrative posts, including consultant to the U.S. National Defense Research Committee (1940–45), expert consultant to the U.S. secretary of war (1942–45), science adviser to NATO (1958–59), and member of the general advisory committee of the U.S Atomic Energy Commission (1960–72). He also served as group leader and associate division head at the Los Alamos Scientific Laboratory (1943–45), head of the physics department at Brookhaven National Laboratory (1946–47), and chairman of the high-energy physics panel of the Science Advisory Board (1963). In 1989 he cochaired a federal committee to investigate the practical significance of cold nuclear fusion. Ramsey's many awards include the Presidential Order of Merit (1947) for his work in radar development during World War II, the E.O. Lawrence Award of the U.S. Atomic Energy Commission (1960), the Davisson-Germer Prize of the American Physical Society (1974), and the Columbia Award for excellence in science (1980). (CAROLYN D. NEWTON)

EXXON CORPORATION

Rawl, Lawrence G.
No sooner had the oil tanker *Exxon Valdez* run aground in Alaska's Prince William Sound than Exxon chairman and chief executive officer (CEO) Lawrence G. Rawl was catapulted into the nation's headlines. Widely criticized for not flying immediately to the spill site and for taking a week to make any type of public statement regarding the March 24, 1989, accident, Rawl finally announced that a lack of authorization from Alaskan and Coast Guard officials caused the delay in the cleanup of the largest oil spill in U.S. history. He carefully noted, however, that the oil-soaked beaches and rocks actually covered less than 10% of the Sound coastline. The following week Rawl advised a congressional panel that although the corporation's tracking of the *Valdez*'s captain, Joseph Hazelwood, a rehabilitated alcohol abuser, had been sufficient, Exxon was considering a revision of its policy that allowed former offenders to return to the command of a tanker.

In mid-April, in his first general news conference after the spill, Rawl again charged that official indecision rather than lack of company response caused the spill to spread uncontrollably. He charged that interdepartmental disagreements added to the delay, reminding observers that Exxon had its spraying equipment in place the day after the accident. (He also announced that 6,000 credit cards out of seven million had been returned to the company in protest.)

Rawl faced 1,700 Exxon shareholders for the first time at their annual meeting in Parsippany, N.J., in May. The meeting was hostile, but Rawl, ready to take the heat, had already rejected a call for his resignation the previous month in a hearing before the Senate Commerce Committee. He announced some rather vague corporate decisions pertaining to Exxon's honourable intentions regarding the environment and ultimately presided over a routine election of directors. When the cleanup was halted on September 15, it had a price tag of $1.2 billion, to be paid by a company whose 1988 earnings were $5.3 billion. In response to a lawsuit brought by Alaska, Exxon filed a countersuit in October.

Rawl was born in Lyndhurst, N.J., on May 4, 1928. He graduated from the University of Oklahoma in 1952, became a petroleum engineer at Exxon, and moved steadily up the corporate ladder of the nation's largest oil company. He became senior vice president in 1980 and was named chairman and CEO in 1986. He also served as a director at Exxon and at the American Petroleum Institute, Chemical Bank, Chemical Banking Corp., and Warner-Lambert Co. (BONNIE OBERMAN)

Rodríguez Pedotti, Andrés
Having brought to an end 34 years of dictatorship under Gen. Alfredo Stroessner with a coup early in the year, Gen. Andrés Rodríguez

Pedotti was democratically elected president of Paraguay on May 1, 1989. He justified his seizure of power on February 3 on the grounds that the dignity and honour of the armed forces had to be defended and that the country had to be set on the path to democracy. The real impetus for his rebellion, however, was alleged to have been Stroessner's plans to retire him from active service. Whatever the reason, the immediate consequence of Rodríguez' action was to settle once and for all the question of Stroessner's succession. This had already split the ruling Colorado Party into two factions—the "militants," staunch Stroessner supporters who favoured his son Gustavo for eventual succession, and the "traditionalists," members loyal to the Colorado ideals predating Stroessner who urged modest democratic reforms and wanted to distance themselves from the regime. Rodríguez sided with the "traditionalists," who later nominated him for the presidency.

Born in Borja on June 19, 1923, Rodríguez started his career in the Army in February 1942, when he joined the country's military college as a cadet. He graduated four years later as a cavalry junior officer. At the time that Stroessner seized power in 1954, Rodríguez was a captain. His rise in the Army began in August 1961, when Stroessner promoted him to colonel and put him in command of the 1st Cavalry Division, on the outskirts of the capital, Asunción; it was the biggest and best equipped of all the army divisions. In May 1967 Rodríguez became brigadier general and in May 1970 general, the second senior ranking officer after Stroessner.

During Stroessner's administration Rodríguez was a man of few words who preferred to keep a low profile. There were those who alleged that he used this time to amass a large fortune that made him one of the richest men in Latin America, with business interests that ranged from ranching to foreign exchange dealing. Busy polishing up his image and patching up relations with the church, which was a firm critic of his predecessor, Rodríguez undoubtedly had a negotiating ability that military men did not usually possess. He succeeded in gaining the maximum breadth of political support for the coup and in defusing the country's explosive problem of landless peasants.
(ALEXANDER JOHNS CAMPBELL)

Rose, Pete
The fall of Pete Rose from baseball's pantheon of immortals to its dungeon of immorals was a story out of Greek legend. Not only had he broken Ty Cobb's record for major league hits just four years earlier, Rose also had played 24 seasons with an overflowing enthusiasm that two generations of fathers told their sons to emulate. He was considered an idol who kept his uniform dirty and his nose clean.

By the end of 1989, however, Rose was under a lifetime suspension from the game that had been both career and passion. After six months of investigating Rose's alleged gambling, baseball commissioner A. Bartlett Giamatti (*see* OBITUARIES) suspended him August 23 for "a variety of acts which have stained the game." He was eligible to apply for reinstatement after one year, but none of the 14 people previously given lifetime suspensions from baseball had been reinstated.

Rose agreed to accept the suspension in return for a vague bill of particulars against him that did not specifically find him guilty of betting on baseball. Giamatti based his judgment on a 225-page report from special counsel John Dowd, who said he had nine witnesses and enough corroborating evidence to prove Rose had bet on baseball, and on his own team, from 1985 through 1987.

Rose said he was the victim of blackmailing attempts and called the principal witnesses, Ron Peters and Paul Janszen, unreliable because they were convicted felons. He denied the validity of betting sheets involving Reds games, which had his fingerprints and which a former FBI handwriting expert said were in his writing. Before agreeing to the suspension, his

lawyers challenged in court Giamatti's authority to judge him because they said he had taken a role that was more prosecutor than investigator. Rose damaged his case by contradicting himself several times in interviews, however, and he was further compromised by a grand jury investigation into his alleged tax evasion on several hundred thousand dollars in racetrack winnings. Though at first he denied having a gambling problem, by the end of the year he was being treated for it.

Peter Edward Rose was born April 14, 1941, in Cincinnati, Ohio, where he later starred as a player in 1963–78, returned as a player-manager Aug. 16, 1984, and led the Reds to four second-place finishes in 1985–88. The city renamed a street outside the Reds' stadium Pete Rose Way in 1985 when his 4,192nd hit that year broke Cobb's 57-year-old record. He was named man of the year in 1985 by *The Sporting News* and manager of the year by United Press International. He finished his playing career Aug. 17, 1986, with 4,256 hits and more than two dozen records. He led the National League in batting three times, and his 10 seasons with 200 hits set a major league record. His 1978 hitting streak of 44 consecutive games set a modern National League record. (KEVIN M. LAMB)

Rushdie, Salman

While many writers had walked a precarious tightrope between two cultures, rarely had the feat seemed as hazardous as it did in 1989 for the Indian-born British novelist Salman Rushdie. Having come from "too many places," he was able to look simultaneously at Western and Islamic societies from inside and outside. The resulting tensions did, indeed, "strike sparks." *The Satanic Verses* (published in late 1988 in England and released in 1989 in the U.S.) earned Rushdie the Whitbread Prize for fiction and the wrath of Muslims worldwide. He faced the "ultimate form of censorship"—a death sentence issued by Iran's Ayatollah Ruhollah Khomeini. Rushdie was forced into hiding.

Ahmed Salman Rushdie was born to a prosperous Muslim family in Bombay on June 19, 1947—just two months before India gained independence—and grew up speaking English and Urdu. In 1961 he was sent to Rugby, an elite school in England. While he struggled through school as an outsider, his family joined the Muslim exodus to Pakistan from predominantly Hindu India. He returned to King's College, Cambridge, to study history at the height of the India-Pakistan war, remained in London as a free-lance advertising copywriter, and began to write.

Rushdie's novels reflect his desire to acknowledge and integrate his divergent cultural heritages. Images have different resonances for different readers. For example, in *Midnight's Children* (1981) the nose of Saleem might recall

MARK GERSON

Cyrano de Bergerac and *Tristram Shandy* for Western readers, while Indian readers might recognize a comic version of the elephant-headed god of literature, Ganesh.

Rushdie's intimate knowledge of the history of the Indian subcontinent allowed him to explore the ways individual history interacts with national history. To Rushdie, history made sense only when seen in the form of individual lives, which must be seen in the context of history. *Midnight's Children*, which won the Booker Prize, is an allegory that examines modern Indian history through the lives of 1,001 children born within the first hour of independence. *Shame* (1983) mythologizes the partition of Pakistan and the resultant shame (a rich concept for Pakistanis). It was banned in Pakistan, primarily because of its portrayal of the regime of Pres. Mohammad Zia-ul-Haq.

Rushdie again used satire and allegory in *The Satanic Verses* to examine multiple cultures and an individual's relationship to his roots and history. The fictional scribe Salman changes the words of God as recited to him by the fictional prophet Mahound—a blasphemy punishable by death. In the novel Salman is spared; it remained to be seen whether the real-life author, condemned for his blasphemy against the faith, would be spared as well. (ELLEN FINKELSTEIN)

Ryan, Nolan

His right arm looked like many others. It had no bolts or springs. It was not five feet long. But it just did not seem to age. When Nolan Ryan struck out 301 American League batters for the Texas Rangers in 1989, it was the third year in a row in which he became the oldest pitcher ever to lead a major league in strikeouts.

At 42, more than 10 years after most power pitchers' arms would have broken down, Ryan's 16–10 won-lost record was the best percentage (.615) of his career. His strikeouts and .187 opponents' batting average were the best in either major league. It was the 10th time he had led a league in strikeouts, including seven of eight seasons in 1972–79. He extended his major league career record to an amazing 5,076 strikeouts, 940 more than second-ranked Steve Carlton.

Ryan had 41 records for one or both leagues, most of them for strikeouts. In 1989 he had his sixth season with 300 strikeouts, 13th with 200, and 23rd game with at least 15 strikeouts. His two one-hitters included a game that was two outs away from adding to his record of five no-hitters, and they boosted his record of one- and no-hit games to 16. Even for Ryan, though, power pitching had its downside; he led his league eight times in bases on balls and had the career record of 2,540.

Ryan's best season probably was 1973, one of his two 20-victory seasons, when he set single-season records with 383 strikeouts and 23 games with 10 strikeouts. He also pitched two no-hitters.

Ryan's fastball was timed at 162 km/h (100.90 mph) in the early 1970s, when he set records with 5.26 hits allowed per nine innings and three strikeouts on nine pitches in 1972. His 19 strikeouts in a nine-inning 1974 game was a record for 12 years. Even in 1989 he threw consistently at 151 km/h (94 mph) and as high as 158 (98), compared with the major league average of 140 (87).

Lynn Nolan Ryan, Jr., was born Jan. 31, 1947, in Refugio, Texas, and raised near Houston in Alvin, Texas. He played basketball at Alvin High School, but baseball was his sport from Little League through Babe Ruth League and high school, and he signed with the New York Mets at 18. After a brief appearance in 1966, he moved up to the major leagues to stay in 1968 and earned a save for the Mets in his only World Series game the next year. He pitched for the California Angels in 1972–79 and moved as a free agent to the Houston Astros in 1980 and to the Rangers in 1989. He planned to pitch in his 24th major league season in 1990, one short of the record. (KEVIN M. LAMB)

Sawyer, Diane

When Diane Sawyer, 10-year veteran CBS reporter and "60 Minutes" correspondent, left the network in the spring of 1989 for ABC and $1.6 million a year, she grabbed the first seat in what became a high-stakes game of media musical chairs in which the players were power personalities and the prize was prime time. When the music stopped, three of television's top female correspondents had switched networks for anchor spots on new prime-time news programs: Sawyer, NBC's Connie Chung, and CNN's Mary Alice Williams. Sawyer's ABC seat was next to Sam Donaldson on "Prime Time Live," a new one-hour weekly news program that featured a studio audience and town-meeting-like discussions.

Not since Barbara Walters left NBC's "Today Show" in 1976 for ABC and an unheard-of $1 million had there been so much talk about the high price of news personalities versus the value they brought to the news. "Is She Worth It?" *Time* magazine's August 7 cover asked, above Sawyer's knowing smile. ABC's executives thought so, betting the success of "Prime Time Live" on the chemistry between Donaldson, loud and caustic, and Sawyer, cool and classy; "a sonata for harp and jackhammer," Sawyer called it. However, it was not for the money that she made the switch, Sawyer said; CBS had virtually offered her a blank check to entice her to stay. Instead she wanted a chance to do live television and "to be in on a broadcast from the beginning." She passed off as "irrelevance" the attention she got for her glamorous job, for her 1988 marriage to film director Mike Nichols, and, most of all, for her beauty.

It was her looks, however, that first made her a celebrity. Sawyer, born in Glasgow, Ky., on Dec. 22, 1945, was, at 17, America's Junior Miss. After graduating from Wellesley (Mass.) College, the journalist who later delighted in "the breathtaking way we walk into people's lives and ask them anything we want and then leave," started out as a nearsighted weather reporter in Louisville, Ky. Sawyer's first break came when she got a job in the White House press office in 1970. For nearly eight years she worked devotedly for Richard Nixon, following him to California after his resignation as president to research his memoirs. A three-year reporting stint at CBS followed, and in 1981 Sawyer became co-anchor on the "CBS Morning News." In 1984 she became the first woman correspondent on "60 Minutes." Five years and 82 stories later, however, she was ready for something different. ABC Pres. Roone Arledge had been calling her for almost a year, and in February 1989 she finally said yes. (HOLLI RAE COSGROVE)

Shoemaker, Bill

Nearing his 58th birthday, the littlest big man in all of sports decided to retire after 41 seasons. Jockey Bill Shoemaker's farewell tour to horse racing began June 4, 1989, in Switzerland and was scheduled to end Feb. 4, 1990, at Santa Anita, his home track near Los Angeles. He was retiring after winning 22% of his more than 40,000 races and compiling a list of awards and achievements longer than his 150-cm, 44.5-kg (4-ft 11-in, 98-lb) body.

Shoemaker led the country in victories in 1950, 1953, 1954, 1958, and 1959 and in prize money every year from 1951 to 1964 except 1952 and 1955–57. His more than 8,800 victories included 11 in Triple Crown races, culminating with his fourth Kentucky Derby victory aboard Ferdinand in 1986. At 54 he was the oldest jockey by 12 years ever to win the Derby, rallying from last in a field of 16 to pay $37.40 on a $2 bet. He rode six winners in a day nine times, won the first Arlington Million aboard John Henry in 1981, and was the first jockey to earn more than $100 million.

On April 30 Shoemaker rode to his 1,000th stakes victory, his 254th worth at least $100,000. "I'm not as good as I was when I was 25, but I'm better than a lot of 25-year-olds," he said. He already had owners lined up for his next ca-

BOB V. NOBLE—GLOBE PHOTOS

reer as a trainer and, possibly, an exercise rider. "I love the life," he said. "I like everything about it, not just riding in the afternoon."

William Lee Shoemaker's doctor did not expect him to survive the night he was born, Aug. 19, 1931, to a family of tenant cotton farmers in Fabens, Texas, near El Paso. He was one month premature— 25.4 cm (10 in) long and weighing 822 g (29 oz). His grandmother wrapped him in a doll's blanket and kept him warm that night on the door of her kerosene oven.

Shoemaker was a good enough athlete to win the bantamweight boxing championship in the Los Angeles Golden Gloves tournament. He began rubbing down horses and cleaning their stalls at the Suzy Q Thoroughbred Ranch when he was in his mid-teens and eventually dropped out of high school to become an exercise rider in San Francisco. His first mount was March 19, 1949, at Golden Gate Park, and he won his first race there April 20, 1949, aboard Shafter V, a $3,000 claiming filly. His 485 victories in 1953 were a record that stood for 20 years. Quiet and even-tempered, he was nicknamed "Wee Willie" and "Silent Shoe" and became one of the first jockeys to win consistently by coaxing instead of whipping. He entered the Racing Hall of Fame in 1958 and passed Johnny Longden's record of 6,032 career victories on Sept. 7, 1970.   (KEVIN M. LAMB)

Starr, Patricia

In 1989 energetic Toronto fund-raiser Patti Starr became Canada's most notorious volunteer. Revelations concerning the gift of a refrigerator to a top Ontario government adviser quickly developed into a scandal that shook the foundations of Ontario Premier David Peterson's administration. He was forced to appoint a royal commission to investigate the relationship among Starr, Tridel Corp. (a multimillion-dollar real estate and development firm), and at least 25 Ontario politicians.

In 1984 Tridel made an agreement with Starr, a director of the Toronto Section of the National Council of Jewish Women. The council sponsored a housing project on land in Toronto owned by Tridel so Tridel could obtain municipal approval to develop the land. In return, Tridel paid consulting fees to a charitable foundation set up by the council. The foundation also collected sales tax rebates from construction of the project. This money was used by Starr to make political contributions (illegal for a charity). The president of Tridel was also the president of the Ontario Section of the Liberal Party of Canada, and many of the contributions went to Ontario Liberal Party politicians.

The Houlden Commission began hearings in September. There were approximately two months of testimony before the proceedings were suspended by court order. (A decision on

whether the inquiry would be allowed to proceed was expected in January 1990.) A former employee of the council testified that she had been fired when she insisted upon investigating Starr's political activities. These included constraining council members to make political contributions for which they were reimbursed by Starr's charitable foundation.

Patti Starr was introduced to the premier of Ontario by his brother Jim Peterson, a member of Parliament for Toronto. The Ontario government subsequently appointed her to the board of the Metro Toronto Housing Authority, where she promoted the interests of Tridel. She also became a member of the Ontario Liberal Party's central fund-raising committee.

Born about 1943, Patricia Starr grew up in Toronto. Her association with the National Council of Jewish Women began in 1963, and by 1981 she had risen to the presidency of the Toronto Section. In recognition of her contributions to the community, Starr received the Ontario Lieutenant-Governor's Award for Volunteerism, and the Ontario Ministry of Citizenship and Culture gave her a gold medal for good citizenship. In November 1989 the National Council of Jewish Women revoked her membership in the organization.

   (DIANE LOIS WAY)

Sununu, John Henry

U.S. President-elect George Bush announced in November 1988 that he would appoint John Sununu to be assistant to the president and chief of staff of the White House. Sununu, considered a strong governor of New Hampshire, was expected to become a promoter of the conservative agenda. Instead, he showed a remarkable ability to adjust to a secondary role, working on details for a president who seemed to have relatively little need for a chief of staff. Bush was accessible to ranking officials and planned his own calendar. Sununu claimed to express opinions on policy only when asked. A newcomer to Washington, Sununu was blamed by some Republicans for the Senate's rejection of John Tower (q.v.) as secretary of defense, but Sununu's reputation recovered. He had claimed to be a fast learner, and observers were soon agreeing with him.

John Henry Sununu, whose father was a U.S. citizen of Lebanese descent, was born in Havana on July 2, 1939, and was raised in New York City. In 1960 he founded Astro Dynamics, Inc., a consulting engineering firm, while an undergraduate at the Massachusetts Institute of Technology (MIT), from which he would receive a B.S. in 1961 and an M.S. in 1962. He reorganized his consulting business in 1965 as J.M.S. Engineering Co. In 1966 he received a Ph.D. from MIT—having used computers extensively on his dissertation—and became assistant professor of engineering at Tufts University, Medford, Mass. He continued to operate his consulting firm, even after becoming associate dean at Tufts and starting a second firm, Thermal Research, Inc., both in 1968. He became a resident of Salem, N.H., in 1969. In 1973 he ceased to be associate dean, became a Republican member of the New Hampshire House of Representatives, and was appointed to the Governor's Energy Council. He stayed on the council after leaving the House in 1974, becoming an associate professor at Tufts in 1975 and joining two other governor's boards in 1977.

Sununu left state government in 1978. In 1982 he ended his consulting, took leave from Tufts, and was elected to the first of three consecutive two-year terms as governor of New Hampshire. He used computers to control state spending and defended the controversial project of 16 electric utilities to build a nuclear generating plant at Seabrook, N.H. Gov. Michael Dukakis of Massachusetts opposed the project. Sununu did not seek reelection as governor in 1988 and was an outspoken supporter of Bush for president. He campaigned in many states and made barbed attacks on Dukakis, Bush's opponent.   (CHARLES JOHNSON TAGGART)

Syse, Jan Peder

Jan Peder Syse, who was chosen leader of Norway's Conservative (Høyre) Party in 1988, became the country's prime minister in October 1989 when a minority Conservative-led coalition replaced the minority Labour government that had ruled the country since 1986.

Syse was born Nov. 25, 1930, on the island of Nøtterøy. He took a law degree in 1957, and two years later he joined the Norwegian Wilhelmsen shipping group—one of Norway's largest—as head of its public relations department. He moved to the civil service in 1967 for a two-year stint at the Ministry of Trade. This was followed by two years as deputy minister of justice in a four-party, nonsocialist coalition. In 1971 he returned to Wilhelmsen as a lawyer and assistant director, a position from which he took leave (1983–85) to serve as industry minister.

A gifted public speaker, Syse started his political career early. In 1952 he was elected chairman of the Conservative Students' Association, and in the following year he became chairman of Norway's national association of students (Det Norske Studentersamfund). As chairman of Unge Høyres (1959–63), the Conservative Party's youth wing, he played an active part in the debate aimed at evolving a "modern" conservative ideology that would free Høyres from its traditional image as a party primarily for the wealthy and powerful. Central to this debate was the concept of "the property-owning democracy," about which Syse wrote a pamphlet in 1961. Over the next two decades he headed various party committees entrusted with formulating Conservative policy on key issues, ranging from industrial democracy to education and housing policy.

Syse was first elected to the Storting (parliament) in 1965, as a "deputy," or stand-in, member. In 1973 he became a full-time member. He headed the Storting's justice committee (1979-80) and its finance committee (1981–83). He became chairman of his party's group in the Storting in 1985.

In the international arena, Syse participated in delegations to the UN General Assembly (1973), a UN disarmament conference (1978), and the Nordic Council (1981–89; president 1988-89).

Syse lacked charisma and failed notably to win new voters for his party during the autumn 1989 election campaign. On the contrary, it lost thousands of votes to the far right Progress Party. Nevertheless, his cool, analytical attitude and his willingness to compromise might prove to be just the qualities needed to lead a minority coalition whose three partners disagreed with one another on many questions.

   (FAY GJESTER)

Tan, Amy

The overwhelming success that Amy Tan achieved with her first novel, *The Joy Luck Club* (1989), resulted in part from the vividness of her recollections of growing up as a Chinese American. *The Joy Luck Club* related the experiences of four Chinese mothers, their Chinese-American daughters, and the struggle of the two generations to communicate with one another. Although the novel dealt with the problems of bonding of Chinese-born parents with their Americanized children, Tan was reluctant to be considered a spokesperson for Asian Americans. She felt she was dealing with a personal conflict rather than with the raising of political consciousness.

The Joy Luck Club began as a series of short stories written for magazines. Working 90 hours a week as a well-established free-lance business writer, Tan decided in 1985 to turn her dream of writing fiction into a reality by attending a writer's workshop, reading certain books, and writing a short story within a year. The short story she created was "Endgame," about a young girl's success as a chess champion. "Endgame" eventually became a part of *The Joy Luck Club* in a section entitled "Rules of the Game." The strongest motivation for Tan to write a novel

occurred in 1986, when her mother, Daisy, was hospitalized with an apparent heart attack. Having once been chided by her mother, "You don't know little percent of me," Tan decided to get to know her mother, take her to China, and write a book. She was able to accomplish all her goals, including weaving parts of her mother's life into *The Joy Luck Club.*

In 1952 Amy Tan was born in Oakland, Calif., approximately two and a half years after her parents emigrated from China. Fiercely opposed to her Chinese background in her early years, she even went as far as sleeping with a clothespin on her nose hoping to narrow its Asian shape. After Tan's father and brother died within months of each other in the 1960s, her mother revealed that Tan had three half-sisters still in China. Tan felt sure that she was, in her own words, "the wicked daughter," so she became more rebellious and rejected her background with a renewed vigour. Finally, upon meeting two of her half-sisters on her trip to China with her mother in 1987, she admitted feeling a sense of belonging. She reflected this feeling in *The Joy Luck Club,* in which, after her mother's death, June Woo, one of Tan's main characters, is asked to take her mother's place in the mah-jongg group (the Joy Luck Club) and is told that she has two half-sisters who were left behind in China when her mother fled the Chinese Civil War. June Woo travels to China to meet her sisters and finds in her sisters a reflection of herself.

(SUSAN MARTS MYERS)

Thatcher, Margaret Hilda

On May 4, 1989, U.K. Conservative Prime Minister Margaret Thatcher celebrated her 10th anniversary in power. Born on Oct. 13, 1925, in Grantham, Lincolnshire, she was the first to achieve this record since Lord Liverpool 167 years earlier. Her anniversary, however, coincided with a spell of unpopularity for her third administration, which had commenced in June 1987. A succession of opinion polls found clear majorities of British voters opposed to her free-market philosophy. On June 15, in elections to the European Parliament, the Conservatives lost to Labour—the first defeat the party had suffered in a nationwide contest since Thatcher was elected leader of her party in February 1975.

Thatcher refused to respond to adversity by changing policies. In a stout defense of her record to the Conservative Party's annual conference in October, she told her followers that her policies would work and that the party would be rewarded in 1991 or 1992 with a fourth victory. Nevertheless, during 1989 she did seek to put a better face on government policy by reshuffling her Cabinet. This was intended as the last major reshuffle before the next election, but in October she was forced to find new people for all three of her most senior positions when Chancellor of the Exchequer Nigel Lawson suddenly resigned. Lawson's departure fractured Thatcher's already dented reputation. One opinion poll conducted immediately afterward showed that only 24% of British electors were satisfied with her as prime minister—the lowest figure since polling began more than 50 years earlier. In December, however, she easily survived the first real challenge to her party leadership.

It was one of Thatcher's more active years on the international stage. In March she was host to an international conference in London on the ozone layer, which called for an end to the use of chlorofluorocarbons. She also chose the environment as her theme when she addressed the UN General Assembly in November. In April Soviet Pres. Mikhail Gorbachev visited London and demonstrated the rapport he had built up with Thatcher since 1985. Elsewhere, Thatcher's diplomacy was less successful. At the NATO summit in May she was alone in wanting to press ahead with the modernization of NATO's short-range nuclear armoury. The event demonstrated that Thatcher would have a hard task in building the kind of close relationship with U.S. Pres. George Bush that she

had enjoyed with Ronald Reagan. At the June and December European Communities summits, Thatcher was isolated in her opposition to the notion of a "social charter" for the EC. At the meeting of Commonwealth heads of government in October, she was—as usual—in a minority of one opposing economic sanctions against South Africa.

(PETER KELLNER)

Tower, John

With the controversy over his choice of Dan Quayle for vice president not far behind him, U.S. Pres. George Bush, less than two months into office, again found himself having to defend one of his nominees. As one of his first major appointments after the 1988 election, Bush entered the name of John Tower as his nominee for secretary of defense.

There had been stories circulating around Washington for years concerning Tower's drinking and sexual misconduct. After reviewing the intensive FBI report compiled on Tower, the Senate Armed Services Committee voted 11–9 to reject his nomination, prompting committee chairman Sam Nunn to say, "His history of excessive drinking is such that he would not be selected to command a missile wing, a SAC [Strategic Air Command] bomber squadron, or a Trident missile submarine." The issue was then sent to the Senate with a recommendation not to confirm.

John Goodwin Tower was born in Houston, Texas, on Sept. 29, 1925. From 1961 to 1985 he represented Texas in the Senate and, ironically, served as chairman of the Armed Services Committee. For 30 years Tower was a close ally of Bush, even supporting him over Ronald Reagan in the 1980 presidential campaign. As chairman of the Iran-*contra* commission in 1987, Tower in his report in effect exempted Bush from blame. Consequently, as a result of the long-standing association, the president's support was unwavering. Bush refused to withdraw Tower's name from consideration.

Senate debate on Tower began on March 2, 1989. Although Nunn's committee could find no evidence that Tower had sexually harassed co-workers, Nunn did state that a number of examples had been found where Tower's judgment had been called into question. In addition to these charges, the committee also raised the question of $750,000 in consulting fees that Tower had received from defense contractors after he had served as negotiator in strategic nuclear arms talks with the Soviets.

Tower pledged to abstain from drinking alcohol during the term of his service if confirmed. In a last-ditch effort to save the nomination, Sen. Robert Dole (Rep., Kan.) even suggested that Tower be given a six-month probation period. Unimpressed, the Senate voted 53–47 on March 9 against confirmation. Tower was only the ninth Cabinet appointee in U.S. history to be rejected.

(ANTHONY L. GREEN)

Tyson, Mike

Without worthy opponents to test him, Mike Tyson turned to boxing against the clock. His first-round knockout of Carl ("The Truth") Williams on July 21, 1989, was his fifth fight in two years but only his 13th round of boxing during that span. It made Tyson's professional won-lost record 37–0 with 33 knockouts and nine successful defenses of his world heavyweight championship.

None of those five matches lasted beyond the fifth round. Williams went down in 93 seconds, two more than Tyson needed to knock out well-regarded Michael Spinks on June 27, 1988. Thus Tyson, before his 23rd birthday, was compared to boxing's all-time greats.

Tyson had become the youngest heavyweight champion in history Nov. 22, 1986, when he was 20 and his two-round knockout of Trevor Berbick won the World Boxing Council's crown. He was unanimously recognized as champion by all three sanctioning organizations after defeating Tony Tucker on Aug. 1, 1987.

Michael Gerard Tyson grew up in the Brownsville neighbourhood of Brooklyn, N.Y.,

where he was born June 30, 1966. He ran with street gangs and at 12 was sent to reform school in upstate New York. There, social worker Bobby Stewart noticed his boxing potential and directed him to the renowned trainer Cus D'Amato, who became his legal guardian. Tyson had a record of 24–3 as an amateur and turned professional on March 4, 1985, with a first-round knockout.

D'Amato taught Tyson a peekaboo boxing style, with hands held close to his cheeks, and a continuous bobbing motion in the ring that made his defense almost impenetrable. Tyson supplied the power of his fearsome offense. He lacked the classic heavyweight champion's appearance, looking short and squat at 181.6 cm

(5 ft 11½ in) and 98.9 kg (218 lb), but he boxed with surprising quickness and breathtaking aggressiveness.

Tyson's personal life began unraveling at the same time that his professional stature solidified, shortly after the deaths of D'Amato and manager Jimmy Jacobs. In 1988 he separated from wife Robin Givens after a brief marriage; sued manager Bill Cayton, Jacobs' associate, and aligned with promoter Don King despite Cayton's contract; fired trainer Kevin Rooney; broke his hand in a predawn street fight with boxer Mitch Green in New York City; and knocked himself out when he drove his car into a tree.

Still, his boxing remained flawless. Tyson earned $8 million on February 25 for his five-round technical knockout of Frank Bruno, whom he knocked down 12 seconds into the fight.

(KEVIN M. LAMB)

Varmus, Harold Elliot

Two researchers at the University of California Medical School in San Francisco, Harold E. Varmus and J. Michael Bishop (*q.v.*), shared the 1989 Nobel Prize for Physiology or Medicine. The scientists were recognized for their discovery that, under certain circumstances, normal genes in healthy cells of the body can cause cancer. These genes ordinarily control cellular growth and division, but if they are picked up by infecting viruses or affected by chemical carcinogens, they can be rendered capable of causing cancer. The laureates' research, carried out in the mid-1970s, disproved a theory that cancer is caused by viral genes, distinct from a cell's normal genetic material, that lie dormant in body cells until triggered into a cancer-causing state by carcinogens.

Varmus was born in Oceanside, N.Y., Dec. 18, 1939. He earned a B.A. in English from Amherst (Mass.) College in 1961 and studied 17th-century literature at Harvard University, where he graduated with an M.A. in 1962. He attended medical school at Columbia University, New York City, earning a medical degree in 1966, and then joined the National Cancer Institute, Bethesda, Md., where he took up

the study of bacteria. In 1970 he went to the University of California at San Francisco as a postdoctoral fellow. There he met Bishop and soon afterward embarked with him on the work that was to become their prizewinning research. Varmus remained on the faculty of the University of California, where he became a professor of biochemistry and biophysics in 1982. He also was made honorary professor of molecular virology by the American Cancer Society.

(CAROLYN D. NEWTON)

Wilson, Michael

The most credible member of Canada's Progressive Conservative (PC) government had his image severely tested in 1989. In April Finance Minister Michael Wilson's worst fear became reality: the confidential federal budget was leaked to the press before he was able to present it in the House of Commons. Although the opposition immediately called for his resignation on the principle of ministerial responsibility, Wilson refused to quit. He explained his failure to make full disclosure of the leak to the Commons by saying that the leak was the subject of a police investigation.

Perceived as reliable, responsible, and respectable by the public, Wilson had been chosen by Prime Minister Brian Mulroney in 1984 to lead the foray into tax reform. However, the personal income tax cut, implemented before the 1988 general elections, came too early to be associated with the new federal goods and services tax (GST) proposed in 1989. Negotiations with the provinces to integrate the GST with provincial sales taxes failed, and it was viewed by Canadians merely as a government tax grab. In response to the public outcry, the government lowered the initial tax rate from the proposed 9 to 7% while raising other rates and curtailing some tax credits.

Michael Holcombe Wilson was born in Toronto on Nov. 4, 1937, and graduated from the University of Toronto before embarking on a career as an investment dealer. Always certain of his ability to handle a top job, Wilson rose to become, by 1973, executive vice president of a major Toronto securities firm. In 1979 Wilson was elected to Parliament and was immediately appointed minister of state for international trade in Joe Clark's short-lived Tory government. During the next five years, Wilson served the PC as opposition critic for energy, finance, and regional economic expansion. One of Clark's most trusted advisers and firmest supporters, Wilson nonetheless was one of Clark's rivals in the 1983 contest for the leadership of the party.

When the Tories were swept back into power under Mulroney's leadership in 1984, Wilson was appointed minister of finance. He thus became head of the department where he had once worked as an analyst in the debt management and capital markets division (1964–66). His attempt to save money by deindexing the government old-age pension ended in a torrent of public opposition. More successful was his proposal to instate a lifetime income tax exemption on the first $100,000 in capital gains earned by an individual. Always more comfortable when dealing with the abstract, Wilson was noted for tackling his opponents with logic and statistics when he debated economic issues.

(DIANE LOIS WAY)

Wright, Jim

In June 1988 U.S. Rep. Newt Gingrich of Georgia filed a formal complaint against the speaker of the House of Representatives, Jim Wright. Thus, after having only recently ascended to the top seat in the House, Wright found himself the first U.S. speaker to be charged with rules violations and was faced with the prospect of being the first speaker to resign while his party held power in Congress.

After a 10-month inquiry conducted by the House Ethics Committee, headed by their outside counsel, Chicago lawyer Richard Phelan, a report was released accusing Wright of five counts of violating House rules on the accep-

tance of gifts and outside income. These charges detailed 69 specific instances of alleged wrongdoing that primarily dealt with Wright's sale of his book, *Reflections of a Public Man*, and his business relationship with Texas developer George Mallick.

With a vote of 10–2 the committee decided that several particular bulk sales of Wright's book appeared to be an attempt at circumventing the House limits on what could be earned in speaking fees. According to Phelan's report, Wright's royalty deal allowed him to keep 55% of the proceeds from its sale, and so he sold the book in lieu of speaking fees once he approached the House limits. The House had no limit on how much could be received in royalties.

In addition, the report indicated that between 1979 and 1988 Wright had received $145,000 in gifts from George Mallick. These gifts included reduced-rate housing, free use of an automobile, and a salary that was paid to Betty Wright for what appeared to be a no-show job—all of which should have been reported on Wright's financial disclosure forms.

After the formal announcement of the charges against Wright, the committee had to decide whether there was enough proof to find Wright guilty and, if there was, what the recommended punishment would be. Sensing the outcome of the situation, Wright announced in a tearful speech on May 31 that he would resign his seat in Congress as well as the speakership.

James C. Wright was born on Dec. 22, 1922, in Fort Worth, Texas. He rose to the rank of captain in the United States Air Force during World War II. He began his career in politics in 1946 when he won a seat to the Texas state legislature. In 1987 he succeeded Thomas ("Tip") O'Neill as speaker of the House.

(ANTHONY L. GREEN)

Wuer Kaixi

During the seven tumultuous weeks of the Chinese democracy movement in 1989, several student leaders gained worldwide recognition. The best known of these was perhaps Wuer Kaixi, a 21-year-old freshman at Beijing (Peking) Normal University. As head of the Capital Federation of Autonomous Student Unions, he helped coordinate the actions of Beijing-area colleges and universities. As a member of the Uighur national minority in Xinjiang (Sinkiang) province, he personally preferred to be called Uerkesh Daolet rather than Wuer Kaixi, a sinicized version of the same name.

Once the democracy movement got under way in mid-April, Wuer Kaixi quickly manifested a natural talent for leadership. His flair for dramatic oratory, his zest for confrontation, and his accessibility to the media linked him to Wang Dan, Chai Ling, and other student leaders. Wuer Kaixi helped draw up the list of political demands that the students presented

ROBERT F. KUSEL

to China's leaders. They insisted that the government recognize the patriotic character of the demonstrations and acknowledge their group as the authentic voice of the students. Wuer Kaixi also participated in the Tiananmen (T'ien-anmen) Square hunger strike that began on the eve of Soviet Pres. Mikhail Gorbachev's visit to China in mid-May.

One single event guaranteed Wuer Kaixi instant celebrity. It was his dramatic verbal confrontation with Premier Li Peng (Li P'eng) during a nationally televised meeting on May 18, in which he brashly berated the premier for arriving late. Wuer Kaixi and other student leaders insisted on being treated as equals and demanded substantive talks on various political issues that had been raised in the preceding weeks.

After the declaration of martial law in Beijing on May 19, Wuer Kaixi argued unsuccessfully for an end to the student occupation of Tiananmen Square. Following the military crackdown of June 3–4, he was among the 21 student leaders whose names appeared on the government's most-wanted list. He managed to elude capture and escaped to Hong Kong. In September Wuer Kaixi was elected vice president of the Federation for Democracy in China, a group of exiles and opposition figures, based in Paris, pressing for change in China. He then resumed his studies at Harvard University.

(STEVEN I. LEVINE)

Yeltsin, Boris

According to an opinion poll, Boris Yeltsin in 1989 was one of the most popular members of the U.S.S.R. Supreme Soviet. He was cochairman of the Interregional Group of Deputies, which advocated a more radical break with the past than did the government of Mikhail Gorbachev. A flamboyant, abrasive, fearlessly brave champion of the underdog, Yeltsin was the Soviet Union's scourge of the establishment. He was the target of many attacks, but at the year's end all had backfired. One of the most extraordinary occurrences was an article in the Soviet newspaper *Pravda* during his hugely successful visit to the U.S. in September 1989. *Pravda* reprinted material from an Italian newspaper describing Yeltsin as engaging in drinking bouts and other misdemeanours while on the visit. The public outcry in response to the article forced *Pravda* to retract it and apologize. This misjudgment contributed to the downfall of *Pravda*'s editor in chief shortly afterward.

Yeltsin was born in Sverdlovsk in the Urals on Feb. 1, 1931, and graduated from college as a construction engineer in 1955. He joined the Communist Party in 1961 and moved into full-time party work in 1968. In 1976 he became first secretary of the Sverdlovsk oblast party organization. His career really took off under Gorbachev. In 1985 he became a secretary in the then very powerful Central Committee Secretariat. He was then appointed party leader in Moscow, and there followed a tempestuous period until he was dismissed in ignominy in 1987. Yeltsin had all the qualities needed to clean up the corrupt Moscow organization except one—the tact a manager needs to carry the majority. Yeltsin engaged in furious rows with Egor Ligachev, secretary of the Central Committee Secretariat of the Communist Party, and in the end Gorbachev sacrificed Yeltsin in the interests of leadership stability. Popular support saved him from a minor posting away from Moscow, and he became a deputy minister for construction.

Yeltsin used his position as a member of the legislature to champion ordinary people and greater democracy. He accused Gorbachev of moving to the right and becoming a conservative in regard to *perestroika* (restructuring). He defended workers when they went on strike and used every opportunity to attack government bureaucracy. His critics claimed that his popularity was directly related to the disillusionment about *perestroika*. Once restructuring became widespread, they said, he would fade from the scene.

(MARTIN MCCAULEY)

OBITUARIES

Adamson, George, British conservationist (b. 1906, India—d. Aug. 20, 1989, Kora, Kenya), was a staunch protector of lions and their environment who became internationally known when the book *Born Free* (1960), written by his wife, Joy, recounted how the couple reared Elsa, an orphaned lion cub, to maturity and eventually returned her to her natural habitat. Adamson, who was born in India, arrived in Kenya in 1924; he worked as a gold prospector, goat trader, and by 1935 a professional safari hunter. Three years later he became an assistant game warden, and in 1939 he and Joy were married. He found a new occupation raising and releasing lions and, though he was once mauled by one, continued to delight in his self-appointed mission. In 1971 he separated from his wife; she was murdered in 1980 by a disgruntled employee. Adamson built a compound at Kora National Reserve, where he became a fierce protector of all animals, especially elephants and rhinoceros, which were being wiped out by heavy poaching. Adamson and two of his assistants were shot and killed, presumably by Somali poachers, when they attempted to foil a robbery by charging the bandits in Adamson's Land Rover.

'Aflaq, Michel, Syrian-born political theorist (b. 1910, Damascus, Ottoman Empire—d. June 23, 1989, Paris, France), was a leader in the pan-Arab nationalist movement during and after World War II and founder (with Salah ad-Din Bitar) of the Arab Socialist Ba'th Party, rival factions of which ruled Syria and Iraq. 'Aflaq, who promoted political and social unity throughout the Middle East, was also instrumental in forging what turned out to be an unsuccessful union of Syria and Egypt into the United Arab Republic (1958–61). 'Aflaq studied (1929–34) at the University of Paris and taught (1935–42) at a secondary school in Damascus until he resigned to devote his energies to the newly formed Ba'th Party. By 1958 'Aflaq and Bitar had built the party into a regional political force. The Ba'thists seized power in Syria in 1963, but intraparty disagreements led to a complete break between the radical and moderate factions of the party, and in 1966 'Aflaq and Bitar went into exile. 'Aflaq retained the support of the Iraqi branch of the party, and after the Ba'thists gained control of that country in 1968 he settled in Baghdad. Although 'Aflaq was later named pan-Arab secretary-general of the Iraqi Ba'th National Command, he remained a powerless figurehead.

Ahidjo, (Alhaji) Ahmadou, Cameroonian politician (b. Aug. 24, 1924, Garoua, Cameroon—d. Nov. 30, 1989, Dakar, Senegal), as (1960–82) the first elected president of independent Cameroon, established both an economically and a politically stable nation. After graduating from high school (1942) Ahidjo served as a radio operator (1942–46) before entering politics. He was elected (1947) to a regional representative assembly and reelected (1952) before rising to serve as its president (1956–57) and then as deputy prime minister (1957–58). Ahidjo formed (1958) his own party, the African *Union Camerounaise,* and became its president; he was credited with quelling anti-French rebellions; with offering amnesty to those who would surrender; and with attempting to unify northern French Cameroon with the southern British Cameroons. In 1960 Ahidjo was proclaimed president of the Republic of Cameroon. He was reelected four times, the last in April 1980. In 1966 he had founded and become president of the country's single party, the Union Nationale Camerounaise. Under his rule, Cameroon was self-sufficient in food and rich in oil. In November 1982, citing poor health, Ahidjo stepped down and named his prime minister, Paul Biya, to succeed him. Ahidjo later tried to regain

power, however, and Biya accused him (August 1983) of having instigated a plot against him; six months later a military tribunal condemned Ahidjo to death in absentia. He lived in exile in both Senegal and the south of France.

Ailey, Alvin, U.S. dancer, choreographer, and director (b. Jan. 5, 1931, Rogers, Texas—d. Dec. 1, 1989, New York, N.Y.), helped establish modern dance as a popular art form in the U.S., both as an exceptional dancer and as the creative founder in 1958 of the Alvin Ailey American Dance Theater, which served as a forum for his choreographic masterpieces including *Blues Suite* (1958), *Revelations* (1960), *Quintet* (1968), *Masekela Language* (1969), *Cry* (1971), and *The Lark Ascending* (1972). Ailey, who joined (1949) the Lester Horton company as part of the stage crew, made his dancing debut (1950) with that company. His vibrant and breathtaking style, coupled with his masterful technique, made him one of the greatest male dancers of his generation. In 1954 Ailey made his Broadway debut in *House of Flowers* and danced in the movie *Carmen Jones.* He stopped dancing in 1965 to develop himself as a choreographer. He used elements of classical ballet, jazz dance, Afro-Caribbean dance, and the modern dance idioms of Horton and Martha Graham in his works and also drew upon blues, spirituals, gospel music, and his own black heritage. Though his pieces formed the core of his company's repertory, he also presented signature pieces by Katherine Dunham, Pearl Primus, and Ted Shawn. Ailey's company also served as a showcase for such black choreographers as Talley Beatty, Donald McKayle, and George Faison. His troupe, which was exclusively black until it became multiracial in the mid-1960s, was among the most prominent and popular international modern dance groups and from the 1960s served as a cultural ambassador as it made extensive tours in Europe, Africa, Australia, and the Far East. Many of Ailey's 79 works also found expression in the repertory of such companies as the Joffrey Ballet, the American Ballet Theatre, the Paris Opéra Ballet, the London Festival Ballet (now English National Ballet), and the Royal Danish Ballet.

Allen, Sir George Oswald Browning ("GUBBY"), Australian-born British cricketer (b. July 31, 1902, Sydney, Australia—d. Nov. 29, 1989, London, England), as one of the last great amateur cricketers, played for England in 25 tests (captained 11), scoring 750 runs (average 24.19) and taking 81 wickets (average 29.37). Allen, a classic fast bowler, established a reputation for fair play when he refused to resort to short-pitched, leg-theory bowling on the infamous 1932–33 "bodyline" tour of Australia. When he returned to Australia as captain of England in 1936–37, he lost the Ashes but rebuilt the damaged relations with that country. In 1947–48 he led an ill-fated tour against the formidable West Indies team. Allen, a professional stockbroker, first played cricket for Eton and Cambridge. In a first-class career that lasted until 1954, he scored 9,232 runs (average 28.67), including 11 hundreds, and took 785 wickets (average 22.31). After his retirement as a player, he became an influential administrator. He was chairman of the test selectors (1955–61) and served the Marylebone Cricket Club (MCC) as president (1963–64), treasurer (1964–76), and Cricket Council representative (1968–82). Allen was made Commander of the Order of the British Empire in 1962 and was knighted in 1986.

Allison, Fran, U.S. television personality (b. 1908?, La Porte City, Iowa—d. June 13, 1989, Sherman Oaks, Calif.), delighted a generation of children as the human component of the unscripted live television program "Kukla, Fran and Ollie" (originally known as "Junior Jam-

boree" when it began local broadcasts in Chicago in 1947). The show featured the antics of the Kuklapolitans, a group of puppets created by Burr Tillstrom. Allison, who served as the endearing human foil to Kukla, a bubble-nosed worry wart, and Ollie, a carefree dragon sporting one tooth, used spontaneous dialogue to interact with them and with such other puppets as Fletcher Rabbit, Ophelia Oglepuss, Beulah Witch, Cecil Bill, Colonel Crackie, Mercedes, Dolores Dragon, and Olivia Dragon. "Kukla, Fran and Ollie" became extremely popular with both children and adults and aired nationally until 1957. Allison's professional singing and acting career began in 1937. She portrayed the gossipy spinster Aunt Fannie on the radio program "The Breakfast Club." During the 1960s Allison was the host of a show of films for children and after moving to Los Angeles was host of "Prime Time," a television program for senior citizens.

Alsop, Joseph Wright, U.S. journalist (b. Oct. 11, 1910, Avon, Conn.—d. Aug. 28, 1989, Washington, D.C.), was a longtime (1937–74) syndicated columnist who produced straightforward political reporting that was laced with strong opinions; at the time of his retirement his Washington political column, "Matter of Fact," was believed to be the longest-running nationally syndicated column of its kind, appearing in some 300 newspapers thrice weekly. After graduating magna cum laude from Harvard University in 1932, Alsop became a staff writer for the *New York Herald Tribune.* In 1937 he teamed up with Robert Kintner to write the column "The Capital Parade" for the North American Newspaper Alliance. Alsop abandoned the column in 1940 to join the U.S. Navy, and during World War II he served with the American Volunteer Group (Flying Tigers) on the staff of Gen. Claire L. Chennault. He was captured in Hong Kong by the Japanese in 1942 but later was released in a prisoner exchange. After the war he and his brother Stewart, self-styled New Deal liberals, collaborated (1946–58) on the column "Matter of Fact," which provided interpretations of foreign affairs as well as national news. Alsop's well-placed connections (Franklin D. Roosevelt and Theodore Roosevelt were distant cousins) were useful to his work, but he was not dependent on them. From 1958 to 1974 he was sole author of the column and adopted a more conservative stance, especially on foreign affairs. A staunch anti-Communist, he supported U.S. involvement in Vietnam. Alsop was the coauthor of such books as *The 168 Days* (1938), *Men Around the President* (1939), *American White Paper* (1940), and *The Reporter's Trade* (1958) and was the author of *FDR, 1882–1945: A Centenary Remembrance* (1982), among others.

Andrews, Harry, British actor (b. Nov. 10, 1911, Tonbridge, Kent, England—d. March 6, 1989, Salehurst, East Sussex, England), with his imposing air of authority and resonant voice, was a familiar face in a wide range of Shakespearean and other character roles on the British stage and screen. He was perhaps best known for his portrayal of tough, no-nonsense military men, notably in the motion picture *The Hill* (1965). Andrews made his stage debut in 1933 and two years later played Tybalt in the acclaimed West End production of *Romeo and Juliet* with John Gielgud and Laurence Olivier. After World War II Andrews appeared in numerous plays by Shakespeare at the Old Vic and the Shakespeare Memorial Theatre in Stratford-upon-Avon. He later expanded his repertoire to include Casanova in Tennessee Williams' *Camino Real* (1957), General Allenby in Terence Rattigan's *Ross* (1960), and Professor Serebryakov in Chekhov's *Uncle Vanya* (1982). Andrews made his first motion picture, *The Red Beret,* in 1952 and thereafter appeared in more than 50 films,

including *55 Days at Peking* (1955), *The Charge of the Light Brigade* (1968), *Entertaining Mr. Sloane* (1970), and *The Ruling Class* (1972). Andrews was made a Commander of the Order of the British Empire in 1966.

Arias Navarro, Carlos, Spanish politician (b. Dec. 11, 1908, Madrid, Spain—d. Nov. 27, 1989, Madrid), was the first civilian premier appointed in post-Civil War Spain and the last one to be appointed by dictator Gen. Francisco Franco. After Arias Navarro received his doctorate in law, he began serving in the Ministry of Justice in 1929. During the Spanish Civil War (1936–39), he became closely allied with Franco and Franco's authoritarian regime. Imprisoned by the Republicans, a group loyal to the republic, Arias Navarro was freed by Franco's forces and was made a military prosecutor. After the war Arias Navarro served as civil governor of the province of León (1944–49), governor of Navarre (1949), director general of security (1957–65), mayor of Madrid (1965–73), and minister of the interior (1973). His appointment as premier took place after the bombing death of Premier Luis Carrero Blanco in 1973. It was Arias Navarro who broke the news of Franco's death to the public in 1975. He resigned as premier under King Juan Carlos in 1976.

Ayer, Sir A(lfred) J(ules), British philosopher (b. Oct. 29, 1910, London, England—d. June 27, 1989, London), introduced the philosophical doctrines of Logical Positivism, or Logical Empiricism, to the English-speaking world through his controversial first book, *Language, Truth and Logic* (1936; revised 1946). Ayer, a philosophical follower of David Hume and Bertrand Russell, received his B.A. (1932) and M.A. (1936) from Christ Church College, Oxford. In 1932 he studied in Austria with the renowned Vienna Circle, the members of which applied the principle of verifiability to human knowledge and rejected as literally meaningless all statements that are not logical truths or cannot be confirmed through sense experience and observation. In applying this principle, Ayer dismissed theology and metaphysics as unverifiable and, therefore, meaningless. He also reduced ethics and aesthetics to individual expressions of feeling and advocated strict linguistic analysis as the only legitimate task of philosophy. Ayer served as a lecturer (1932–35) and researcher (1935–40) in philosophy at Oxford, Grote professor of philosophy at University College, London (1946–59), and Wykeham professor of logic at Oxford (1959–78). He was widely admired for his enthusiasm and for his ability to explain complex philosophical ideas with clarity and wit. He was also a familiar figure on British television, particularly on the popular program "Brains' Trust." His later books include *The Foundations of Empirical Knowledge* (1940), *The Problem of Knowledge* (1956), *The Origins of Pragmatism* (1968), *The Central Questions of Philosophy* (1973), two volumes of autobiography, and insightful studies of Hume, Russell, Voltaire, and Ludwig Wittgenstein. Ayer was elected a fellow of the British Academy in 1952 and was knighted in 1970.

Backus, Jim, U.S. actor (b. Feb. 25, 1913, Cleveland, Ohio—d. July 3, 1989, Santa Monica, Calif.), was best remembered for the booming, gravelly voice of the myopic Mr. Magoo, a crotchety, bald-headed cartoon character who bumbled through countless misadventures, and as the self-indulgent multimillionaire Thurston Howell III on the television series "Gilligan's Island," which ran from 1964 to 1967 and became a cult classic in syndication. Backus, a 1933 graduate of the American Academy of Dramatic Arts, New York City, specialized in character roles on radio and portrayed the long-suffering husband on the television program "I Married Joan" (1952–54). Besides his celebrated vocal portrayal of Mr. Magoo, Backus gained film laurels for his role as James Dean's ineffectual father in *Rebel Without a Cause* (1955).

Some of his other notable film credits include *Francis in the Navy* (1955) and *Man of a Thousand Faces* (1957). Backus wrote an autobiography, *Rocks on the Roof* (1958), and collaborated with his wife on *What Are You Doing After the Orgy?* (1962) and other humorous books. He also wrote radio and television scripts.

Ball, Lucille Désirée, U.S. comedienne (b. Aug. 6, 1911, Jamestown, N.Y.—d. April 26, 1989, Los Angeles, Calif.), became an American institution and one of the world's most beloved clowns, delighting millions of television viewers as the redheaded, scatterbrained, and scheming wife of Ricky Ricardo (Desi Arnaz) in "I Love Lucy" (1951–57), one of television's longest running situation comedies. The zany "Lucy" showcased her natural talents in such other successful series as "The Lucy Show" (1961–68) and "Here's Lucy" (1968–74). Ball worked as a waitress, soda jerk, and hat model before gaining attention as the Chesterfield Cigarette Girl in 1933 and securing a role as a chorus girl in the film *Roman Scandals*. She appeared in dozens of films, primarily in bit and supporting roles, before establishing herself as a first-rate comedienne, performing with Bob Hope and Red Skelton. After marrying Cuban-born band-

leader Desi Arnaz in 1940, she continued to appear on the silver screen, notably in *Dance, Girl, Dance* (1940), *The Dark Corner* (1946), *Sorrowful Jones* (1949), and *Fancy Pants* (1950), before persuading CBS television executives to broadcast "I Love Lucy." The milestone program was one of the first shows to be filmed rather than performed live at the time of broadcast; it was also the first to be filmed before a live audience. The smash hit series, featuring the adventures of the Ricardos and their best friends, Fred and Ethel Mertz (William Frawley and Vivian Vance, respectively), garnered more than 200 awards, including five Emmys. Ball's irrepressible humour, teamed with her perfect sense of timing and skillful pantomime routines, made her the undisputed queen of television. Ball and Arnaz established Desilu Productions, and the two amassed a fortune after securing rerun rights for the series. Ball also appeared with Arnaz in such films as *The Long, Long Trailer* (1954) and *Forever Darling* (1956) before they divorced in 1960. In 1961 Ball married nightclub comedian Gary Morton, who became vice-president of Desilu Productions when she purchased Arnaz's interest in the company in 1962. The indefatigable Ball starred in such motion pictures as *The Facts of Life* (1961), *Yours, Mine and Ours* (1968), and *Mame* (1974). She continued to perform on television, notably in 1985 as a spunky bag lady in the television movie "Stone Pillow." Her 1986 sitcom, "Life with Lucy," was not well received and was canceled shortly after its debut. Her death, a week

after undergoing heart surgery, was mourned throughout the world.

Baron, Salo Wittmayer, U.S. historian (b. May 26, 1895, Tarnow, Austria—d. Nov. 25, 1989, New York, N.Y.), was an eminent scholar who spent much of his life compiling the multivolume magnum opus *A Social and Religious History of the Jews,* which was published in 1937 in 3 volumes but was later revised and then expanded into 18 volumes. At the time of his death, Baron had been working on a 19th volume and had projected the addition of two more volumes to make the history complete through 1650. Baron, who was ordained a rabbi at the Jewish Theological Seminary in Vienna in 1920, earned three Ph.D. degrees from the University of Vienna—in philosophy (1917), political science (1922), and law (1923). He learned 20 languages and was able to lecture extemporaneously in five of them. On April 24, 1961, at the trial of Adolf Eichmann in Jerusalem, Baron expertly set the historic framework for the Israeli prosecution's case by testifying about anti-Semitism, European Jewry, and the atrocities committed by the Nazis. A prolific author, he wrote 13 works on Jewish history, many of them multivolume, and edited 4 other books. Baron served as professor at Columbia University, New York City, from 1930 until his retirement in 1963. In 1979 the university established the Salo Wittmayer Baron Chair of Jewish History, Culture and Society in his honour.

Barthelme, Donald, U.S. writer (b. April 7, 1931, Philadelphia, Pa.—d. July 23, 1989, Houston, Texas), was an innovative minimalist short-story writer and novelist who was credited with reviving the popularity of the short story during the 1960s with modernist "collages," which were marked by technical experimentation and a kind of melancholy gaiety. A onetime journalist, Barthelme also served as managing editor of *Location,* an art and literature review, and director (1961–62) of the Contemporary Arts Museum in Houston. Barthelme's first collection of short stories, *Come Back, Dr. Caligari,* was published in 1964; that was followed by his first novel, *Snow White* (1967), which initially had been published in the *New Yorker* magazine. Other collections of his stories include *City Life* (1970), *Sadness* (1972), *Sixty Stories* (1981), and *Overnight to Many Distant Cities* (1983). He wrote two additional novels, *The Dead Father* (1975) and *Paradise* (1986). Barthelme's children's book, *The Slightly Irregular Fire Engine or the Hithering Thithering Djinn* (1971), garnered the National Book Award in 1972. From 1974 to 1975 he was distinguished visiting professor of English at the City College of the City University of New York, and he remained a regular contributor to the *New Yorker*. Shortly before his death, Barthelme completed another novel, *The King,* which was scheduled to appear in 1990.

Baunsgaard, Hilmar Tormod Ingolf, Danish politician (b. Feb. 26, 1920, Slagelse, Den.—d. June 30, 1989), was a leading spokesman of the non–Socialist opposition during the 1960s and '70s and prime minister of the "bourgeois" Conservative-Liberal coalition that displaced the Socialist government from 1968 to 1971. Baunsgaard joined the youth organization of the Radical Liberal Party in 1936 and was on the executive committees of both the youth branch (1948–55; chairman 1948–51) and the party itself (1948–57; 1960–76). He entered the Folketing (parliament) in 1957 and served as minister of commerce (1961–64). As prime minister, Baunsgaard supported the abolition of the pornography laws and worked for Denmark's entry into the European Communities. During his tenure, however, the economy worsened, and the government was forced to increase taxes. After the Socialists regained power in the 1971 general election, Baunsgaard remained leader of the Radical Liberals. He retired from the Folketing in 1977 to return to the private sector as chairman of the daily newspaper *Politiken*.

Beadle, George Wells, U.S. geneticist (b. Oct. 22, 1903, Wahoo, Neb.—d. June 9, 1989, Pomona, Calif.), shared the 1958 Nobel Prize for Physiology or Medicine with Edward L. Tatum and Joshua Lederberg for "fundamental contributions in the field of biochemical and microbial genetics." Specifically, Beadle and Tatum were cited for their work on the genetic regulation of chemical processes, and Lederberg was cited for parallel work in bacterial genetics. After earning B.S. (1926) and M.S. (1927) degrees from the University of Nebraska, Beadle received a Ph.D. in genetics (1931) from Cornell University, Ithaca, N.Y., and in the same year undertook research on the fruit fly, *Drosophila melanogaster,* with Thomas Hunt Morgan at the California Institute of Technology (Caltech). There he concluded that genes influence heredity chemically. As a researcher at the Institut de Biologie in Paris, Beadle worked with Boris Ephrussi and devised a complex technique for determining the nature of these chemical effects in *Drosophila.* After serving (1936–37) as a professor at Harvard University, Beadle joined the faculty at Stanford University, where he conducted his Nobel Prize-winning research with Tatum. There they studied gene action in *Neurospora,* the red bread mold. By exposing the mold to X-rays, the two produced a variety of mutations and discovered that each gene determined the structure of a specific enzyme that, in turn, allowed a single chemical reaction to occur. Their findings revolutionized the production of penicillin and laid the foundations for the field of biochemical genetics. After serving as professor at Caltech from 1946 to 1961, Beadle became president of the University of Chicago in 1961, a post he held until 1968. Beadle was the author of such works as *An Introduction to Genetics* (with A.H. Sturtevant; 1939), *Genetics and Modern Biology* (1963), and *The Language of Life* (with Muriel M. Beadle; 1966).

Bechtel, Stephen Davison, U.S. construction engineer and business executive (b. Sept. 24, 1900, Aurora, Ind.—d. March 14, 1989, Oakland, Calif.), parlayed his family business into one of the world's largest construction companies as president (1935–60) of Bechtel Corp. (now Bechtel Group). During his tenure as president, Bechtel oversaw the construction of such megaprojects as the Hoover (Boulder) Dam on the Colorado River at the Arizona-Nevada border, the San Francisco-Oakland Bay Bridge in California, and the first commercial nuclear power plant. Bechtel dropped out of the University of California at Berkeley at the age of 19 to help in the family business. In 1935, two years after his father's death, he became president of the company and transformed it from a regional builder of railroads, highways, pipelines, and dams into an international giant; the firm diversified into the construction of nuclear power plants, petroleum refineries, and mines and became one of the leading construction companies in Saudi Arabia and other Middle Eastern countries. The imaginative Bechtel, who sometimes formulated designs on the backs of envelopes, also conceived of a plan to construct the Canadian Trans-Mountain Pipeline, a feat that some felt was impossible. Though Bechtel retired as president of the company in 1960, he remained as chairman until 1965 and then became a senior director. He continued to take an active role in the business and at the age of 84 helped negotiate a joint engineering venture with the government of China.

Beckett, Samuel Barclay, Irish-born novelist and playwright (b. April 13?, 1906, Foxrock, County Dublin, Ireland—d. Dec. 22, 1989, Paris, France), was the winner of the Nobel Prize for Literature (1969) and a dominating force in the genre that came to be called the Theatre of the Absurd. Although earlier playwrights had tested the limits of dramatic conventions, Beckett abandoned the conventions altogether in his breakthrough tragicomedy *En attendant Godot* (1952; *Waiting for Godot,* 1954). Beckett studied romance languages at Trinity Col-

JERRY BAUER

lege, Dublin (B.A., 1927), and taught in Paris and Dublin before eventually settling in France (1937), where he wrote a volume of poetry and his first novel, *Murphy* (1938). During World War II he worked as a labourer and joined the French Resistance (he later received the Croix de Guerre). During this period he also wrote the novel *Watt* (published 1953), the last of his works to be composed in English. Thereafter he wrote mainly in French and did his own English translations. Between 1946 and 1949 Beckett produced his most significant works, including *Godot* and a trilogy of novels, *Molloy* (1951; Eng. trans., 1955), *Malone meurt* (1951; *Malone Dies,* 1956), and *L'Innommable* (1953; *The Unnamable,* 1958). Beckett gained notoriety with the first productions of *Godot* in French (1953) and English (1955). Without a linear plot or definitive action and with a minimal use of sets, props, and costumes, Beckett created four characters in *Godot* that were at once universal types and distinct individuals. Vladimir and Estragon (usually presented as tramps, although the text does not specify this) resolutely wait for the eternally elusive Godot, while the master-slave pair, Pozzo and Lucky, move on- and offstage in equally futile activity. *Godot,* which combined slapstick comedy with the search for meaning in an apparently meaningless and absurd existence, influenced a generation of playwrights, including Eugène Ionesco, Jean Genet, Harold Pinter, Tom Stoppard, and David Mamet. Beckett's later plays (and stories) grew increasingly austere and abstract. These included *Fin de partie* (one act, 1957; *Endgame,* 1958), in which two of the characters are ensconced in ashbins; *Krapp's Last Tape* (one act, 1959), in which a man listens to the disembodied voice of his youth on a tape recorder; and *Happy Days* (1961), wherein a woman cheerfully details the mundane trivialities of her life as she is progressively buried up to her neck in dirt. In *Acte sans paroles* (1957; *Act Without Words,* 1958) Beckett abandoned the spoken word entirely.

Berkeley, Sir Lennox Randall Francis, British composer (b. May 12, 1903, Boars Hill, near Oxford, England—d. Dec. 26, 1989, London, England), crafted richly melodic works noted for their classical element. Berkeley graduated (1926) in modern languages from Merton College, Oxford, before studying (1927–32) with the renowned music teacher Nadia Boulanger in Paris. He became friends with, and was greatly influenced by, Maurice Ravel, Igor Stravinsky, François Poulenc, and Benjamin Britten, with whom he collaborated on an orchestral work, *Mont Juic* (1937). Berkeley composed four symphonies, one full-length opera, *Nelson* (1954), and concerti and sonatas for such diverse instruments as the piano, guitar, flute, and oboe. He achieved his greatest success, however, with

shorter pieces, such as *Serenade* (1939), *Divertimento* (1943), and the witty one-act opera *A Dinner Engagement* (1954). Berkeley's deeply religious vocal works included *Stabat Mater* (1947), written for Britten's English Opera Group, *Four Songs of St. Teresa of Avila* (1947), and the opera *Ruth* (1956). His later compositions, notably *Sonatina,* Opus 61 (1962), showed a marked atonal influence. Berkeley was made a Commander of the Order of the British Empire in 1957 and was knighted in 1974.

Berlin, Irving (ISRAEL ISIDORE BALINE), U.S. songwriter (b. May 11, 1888, Temum, Russia—d. Sept. 22, 1989, New York, N.Y.), saluted his adopted country with simply composed sentimental songs that echoed the fears, hopes, and fantasies of the average American. The all-time favourite "God Bless America" became an unofficial national anthem, and "White Christmas," his signature holiday greeting card, was regarded as a genuine carol. At the age of four, Berlin immigrated to the U.S. with his family. He began performing on the streets for nickels after the death of his father a few years later. Largely unschooled and unable to write musical notes, he was able to play the piano only in the key of F sharp. As a teenager he worked as a singing waiter in New York's Chinatown, and in 1911 he electrified audiences with his rendition of "Alexander's Ragtime Band," one of his first major hits. After the death of his first wife in 1912, only five months after their honeymoon, he wrote the tribute "When I Lost You," which sold two million copies. After establishing his own corporation in 1919, Berlin maintained strict control over all his copyrights. As an army draftee during World War I, he was commissioned to write the revue *Yip, Yip, Yaphank* (1918), which showcased the song "Oh, How I Hate to Get Up in the Morning," a tune revived for his World War II revue, *This Is the Army* (1943). With the advent of talkies, Berlin launched a career as a motion picture songwriter. He penned "Blue Skies" for *The Jazz Singer* (1927); "White Tie and Tails" and "Cheek to Cheek" for *Top Hat* (1935); and "White Christmas" for *Holiday Inn* (1942). Berlin's Broadway blockbusters included songbooks for *Annie Get Your Gun* (1950), *There's No Business like Show Business* (1954), *Call Me Madam* (1953), and *Mr. President* (1962), his last show. Of his more than 1,000 songs, many became classics, including "A Pretty Girl Is like a Melody," "Let's Have Another Cup of Coffee," "Easter Parade," "The Girl That I Marry," "Always," "Anything You Can Do I Can Do Better," "Remember," "I've Got My Love to Keep Me Warm," "How Deep Is the Ocean?," and "Say It Isn't So." Berlin won two Academy Awards for best song—for "Cheek to Cheek" and "White Christmas," which earned more than $1 million in royalties and became one of the most popular and frequently played songs ever written. He assigned the copyright to "God Bless America" to a fund that from 1940 supported the Boy and Girl Scouts of New York. After *Mr. President,* a critical failure, closed in 1962, Berlin retreated from the limelight. Though he endorsed the 1988 celebration of his 100th birthday for the benefit of Carnegie Hall and the American Society of Composers, Authors, and Publishers, he did not attend the festivities.

Bernhard, Thomas, Austrian writer (b. Feb. 9, 1931, Heerland, Neth.—d. Feb. 12, 1989, Gmunden, Austria), explored death, social injustice, and human misery in controversial literature that was deeply pessimistic about modern civilization in general and Austrian culture in particular. After surviving a life-threatening coma and repeated hospitalizations (1948–51) in tuberculosis sanatoriums, Bernhard studied music and drama in Salzburg and Vienna. He achieved little success with several collections of poetry in the late 1950s, but in 1963 he gained notoriety with his first novel, *Frost.* In such novels as *Verstörung* (1967; *Gargoyles,* 1970), *Das Kalkwerk* (1970; *The Lime Works,* 1973),

and *Korrektur* (1975; *Corrections,* 1979) he combined complex narrative structure with an increasingly misanthropic philosophy. In 1973 Bernhard withdrew his drama *Die Berühmten* ("The Famous") from the prestigious Salzburg Festival because of a controversy over staging. In 1984 his novel *Holzfällen* (*Woodcutters,* 1987) was seized by police for allegedly criticizing a public figure. Even before its premiere in November 1988, Bernhard's last play, *Heldenplatz* ("Heroes' Square"), a bleak indictment of anti-Semitism in contemporary Austria, provoked violent protests, a public call for censorship, and a personal rebuke by the Austrian president, Kurt Waldheim. Bernhard's memoirs were compiled in *Gathering Evidence* (1985).

Beuve-Méry, Hubert, French editor and publisher (b. Jan. 5, 1902, Paris, France—d. Aug. 6, 1989, Fontainebleau, France), founded the influential newspaper *Le Monde* and guided its rise to international importance. Beuve-Méry studied philosophy and law in Paris, and in 1928 he became director of the legal and economic section of the French Institute in Prague. He also served as foreign correspondent for several French publications, including the Parisian daily *Le Temps* from 1934. He quit the staff of *Le Temps,* however, when the newspaper failed to denounce the Nazi invasion of Czechoslovakia in 1938. *Le Temps* was refused government permission to publish again after the liberation, and Beuve-Méry, who had been working in the Resistance, got the chance to replace it. The first issue of *Le Monde* appeared on Dec. 18, 1944, with Beuve-Méry as editor, chief administrator, and editorial writer under the pseudonym Sirius. Beuve-Méry emphasized international news coverage, and under his leadership *Le Monde* grew in scope and influence. Despite official government support for the newspaper's inception, Beuve-Méry was frequently critical of Pres. Charles de Gaulle and of French foreign policy, particularly in Indochina and Algeria. Beuve-Méry retired from active editing in 1969, but he remained a consultant. He also wrote a number of books, including *Vers la plus grande Allemagne* (1939; "Toward a Greater Germany"), *Le Suicide de la IVᵉ République* (1958; "The Suicide of the Fourth Republic"), and *Onze Ans de règne: 1958–69* (1974; "An Eleven-Year Reign").

Blaik, Earl Henry ("RED"), U.S. football coach (b. Feb. 15, 1897, Dayton, Ohio—d. May 6, 1989, Colorado Springs, Colo.), was one of college football's most accomplished coaches, compiling an impressive 166–48–14 career record as head coach at Dartmouth College, N.H. (1934–40), and at the U.S. Military Academy at West Point, N.Y. (1941–58). A superb all-around athlete who lettered in baseball, basketball, and football while attending Miami University, Oxford, Ohio, Blaik entered West Point during World War I and became an all-America end while playing for Army in 1918 and 1919. After resigning his army commission in the cavalry in 1922, he briefly entered a real estate business before returning to his alma mater as an assistant coach in 1927. In 1934 he went to Dartmouth and propelled its teams to a 21-game winning streak and a seven-year 45-15-4 record. In 1940 his team ended Cornell's 18-game unbeaten streak. At Army he became the first civilian head football coach since 1911 and gained a reputation as a brilliant strategist who had a gift for anticipating opposing offensive and defensive plays; he led Army teams to national championships in 1944 and 1945 with daring and imaginative new plays. In 1951 his 45-man team was reduced to one player when the other members, including his son, were dismissed from the Academy for a violation of the honour code. Nonetheless, Blaik rebuilt the team and compiled a remarkable 121-33-10 record during his tenure at the Academy. He was the author of *You Have to Pay the Price* (1960) and *The Red Blaik Story* (1974). In 1986 he was awarded the Presidential Medal of Freedom.

Blaize, Herbert A., Grenadian politician (b. Feb. 26, 1918, Carriacou, Grenada, British West Indies—d. Dec. 19, 1989, near St. Georges, Grenada), served as head of government three times between 1960 and 1967 and, after 17 years out of office, became (Dec. 4, 1984) the country's first elected prime minister after the 1983 U.S.-led intervention in Grenada paved the way for general elections. In 1953 Blaize founded the Grenada National Party (GNP), and after taking a Law Society correspondence course he became a solicitor. Blaize entered the legislature in 1957 and three years later was appointed chief minister. In 1961 he was defeated by his rival, Eric Gairy, leader of the Grenada United Labour Party, but Blaize was returned to office in 1962 after Gairy was removed by the British government following accusations of corruption. During Blaize's five-year tenure, the country achieved internal self-government as an associated state. Gairy regained power in 1967, and in 1976 Blaize's GNP joined forces with the New Jewel Movement in an unsuccessful effort to unseat Gairy. Blaize kept a low profile during the years of revolutionary government until 1984, when he emerged to head a coalition of the GNP and other centre-right parties under the name New National Party. His party captured 14 of 15 seats in the legislature, and he was sworn in as prime minister. During his years in office (1984–89), Blaize, suffering from cancer and confined to a wheelchair, was sometimes criticized for being uncommunicative and authoritarian. During his last months he vehemently refused to step down, even though disavowed by his own party.

Blanc, Melvin Jerome, U.S. entertainer (b. May 30, 1908, San Francisco, Calif.—d. July 10, 1989, Los Angeles, Calif.), used his versatile voice to give life to such cartoon characters as stammering Porky Pig, pesky Woody Woodpecker, conniving Daffy Duck, foul-tempered Yosemite Sam, the devious canary Tweety Pie, Tweety's "puddy tat" nemesis Sylvester, the amorous French skunk Pépé le Pew, and the mischievous Bugs Bunny, famous for the catchphrase "What's up, doc?" Blanc, who had an abiding interest in music, was proficient on the bass, violin, and sousaphone. Shortly after marrying in 1933, however, he joined a daily radio program and created characters to provide a cast for the show. After moving to Los Angeles, Blanc joined Leon Schlesinger Productions, a cartoon workshop that later developed Warner Brothers' Looney Tunes and Merrie Melodies. Blanc's first Warner Brothers voice was that of a drunken bull in 1936. The next year, he became the voice of Porky Pig, and in 1940 Bugs Bunny (first named Happy Rabbit) made his debut. During more than 50 years in show business, Blanc provided voices for some 3,000 animated cartoons, and during the 1940s and '50s he breathed life into 90% of the Warner Brothers cartoon stable, including the flamboyant Mexican mouse Speedy Gonzales and the fleet-footed Road Runner. During the 1960s he was coproducer of "The Bugs Bunny Show," a Saturday morning television program featuring Looney Tunes characters, and he also provided the voices for Barney Rubble and Fred Flintstone's pet dinosaur, Dino, on "The Flintstones," the first animated situation comedy created for television. In 1988 he resurrected the voices of Bugs Bunny, Daffy Duck, Porky Pig, Tweety Pie, and Sylvester for the animation-live action film *Who Framed Roger Rabbit.* His autobiography, *That's Not All, Folks: My Life in the Golden Age of Cartoons and Radio,* was published that same year.

Blier, Bernard, French actor (b. Jan. 11, 1916, Buenos Aires, Arg.—d. March 29, 1989, Paris, France), was a popular character actor in some 150 motion pictures during a career that spanned more than 50 years. Blier, who was equally adept at comedy and drama, displayed his versatility in supporting parts ranging from credulous husbands and jilted lovers to cold-blooded gangsters and hard-boiled police inspec-tors. He made his film debut in *Trois, six, neuf* in 1937 and thereafter worked almost continuously, sometimes making five or more movies per year. His best-known films include *Hôtel du Nord* (1938), *La Symphonie fantastique* (1942), *Quai des orfèvres* (1947), *Dédée d'Anvers* (1948), *Manèges* (1949), *Les Misérables* (1957), *Germinal* (1963), *Lo straniero* (1967; *The Stranger*), *Le Grand Blond avec une chaussure noire* (1972; *The Tall Blond Man with One Black Shoe*), and *Buffet froid* (1979), which was directed by his son, Bertrand. Blier also made frequent stage appearances, notably in a series of Parisian "boulevard comedies." Only three weeks before his death, the French film industry honoured him with a special César award for outstanding lifetime achievement.

Bonnier, Albert, Jr., Swedish publisher (b. Aug. 18, 1907, Stockholm, Sweden—d. April 15, 1989, Stockholm), was the head of a vast family-owned business empire that included Sweden's largest book publisher, Åhlén & Åkerlunds, and two of the country's most widely read daily newspapers, the traditional *Dagens Nyheter* and the popular tabloid *Expressen.* Bonnier, whose great-grandfather founded the publishing house Albert Bonniers Förlag AB, studied publishing techniques throughout Europe and the U.S. In 1930 he joined Åhlén & Åkerlunds as chief of administration, later rising to managing director (1940–57) and chairman of the board (1957–89). In the 1950s Bonnier founded a new holding company, AB Bonnierföretagen, which he built into an international conglomerate with diversified interests in real estate, computers, and cinema, as well as publishing. Bonnier served as managing director (1959–81) and as chairman from 1981 until his retirement in early 1989.

Burns, Jethro (KENNETH C. BURNS), U.S. entertainer (b. March 10, 1920, Knoxville, Tenn.—d. Feb. 4, 1989, Evanston, Ill.), was Jethro of the Homer and Jethro country music comedy duo; the two delighted audiences with the cornball humour featured in their parodies of established tunes. The partnership was formed in 1932, and with Jethro playing the mandolin and Homer (Henry D. Haynes) strumming the guitar, they performed on radio station WNOX in Knoxville before becoming cast regulars in 1939 on the "Renfro Valley Barn Dance" radio program in Kentucky. The team broke up during World War II, but they reunited in 1945 and performed for a decade as regulars on the "National Barn Dance," broadcast from Chicago. The two later appeared on television, notably on such shows as "The Beverly Hillbillies," "The Tonight Show," and "The Johnny Cash Show." Burns also appeared on television's "Hee Haw," but the two were possibly best remembered for the zany commercials they made for Kellogg's cornflakes. Two of their most popular songs were "That Hound Dog in the Window" and "The Battle of Kookamonga," which earned them a Grammy award in 1959 for the best comedy performance. The two also produced a string of albums, including the all-time favourite *Homer and Jethro at the Country Club* (1960), a live comedy-music album, and *Playing It Straight,* which showcased their virtuoso talents as instrumentalists. After Haynes's sudden death from a heart attack in 1971, Burns began performing as a serious entertainer.

Busch, August Anheuser, Jr., U.S. corporate executive (b. March 28, 1899, St. Louis, Mo.—d. Sept. 29, 1989, St. Louis county), was a colourful beer baron who, as chairman (1946–75) of Anheuser-Busch Inc., built the moderately successful company into the world's largest brewery. He purchased the St. Louis Cardinals professional baseball team for $7.8 million in 1953 and, riding into Busch Stadium in a wagon drawn by Clydesdales, the horses indelibly identified with Budweiser beer wagons, became a familiar figure during league play-offs and World Series home games. Busch, the grandson of Adolphus A. Busch, who founded the company in 1876, started sweeping floors

and cleaning vats at the brewery in 1922, but by 1924 he was general superintendent of brewing operations. After his father died in 1934, Busch became head of the brewery department, and he was installed as president of Anheuser-Busch when his older brother unexpectedly died in 1946. "Gussie," as he was affectionately known, was also a major civic leader; he helped revive St. Louis during the 1950s and donated $5 million toward the construction of Busch Memorial Stadium. Busch, who used his considerable wealth to indulge his gusto for living, possessed a 114-ha (281-ac) estate that featured a cabin hand-built by Pres. Ulysses S. Grant, a 34-room French Renaissance château, and a private zoo. The beer-based company later branched out into foods and such entertainment enterprises as Busch Gardens in Tampa, Fla.

Bustamante y Rivero, José Luis, Peruvian lawyer, politician, and diplomat (b. Jan. 15, 1894, Arequipa, Peru—d. Jan. 11, 1989, Lima, Peru), was elected president of Peru in 1945 and served in office until he was ousted in a coup in 1948 led by his minister of the interior, Manuel Odría. Bustamante, educated at universities in Arequipa and Cuzco, was professor of civil law (1931–34) at the university in Arequipa. He was a politically independent lawyer, and during his tenure as president he extended Peruvian sovereignty to 200 mi out to sea, a law that was widely adopted by dozens of nations. After being ousted, Bustamante taught law and was dean of the law college in Lima. In 1961 he became a judge at the International Court of Justice in The Hague, Neth., and from 1967 to 1970 he served as its president. A skilled diplomat who had served as ambassador to Uruguay and Bolivia earlier in his career, Bustamante served as mediator in 1977 between El Salvador and Honduras, which were at war. The two countries signed a peace accord in 1980.

Cassavetes, John, U.S. motion-picture director and actor (b. Dec. 9, 1929, New York, N.Y.—d. Feb. 3, 1989, Los Angeles, Calif.), was an influential independent filmmaker who was regarded as a pioneer of U.S. cinema verité. His motion pictures relied on the improvisational abilities of actors, who were filmed at times with a hand-held camera. These unconventional techniques often produced a disturbing effect underscored by a gritty realism. Cassavetes majored in English at Colgate University before studying acting at the American Academy of Dramatic Arts in New York City. A method actor, he made his motion-picture debut as an extra in *14 Hours* (1951) and his first television appearance in a segment of "Omnibus" in 1953. From 1953 to 1956 he garnered more than 80 substantial television roles, appearing on "Studio One," "The Kraft Theater," "Playhouse 90," and "Alcoa Theater." In 1960 he made his directorial debut with the film *Shadows,* a semi-

HATAMI—CAMERA PRESS/GLOBE PHOTOS

improvised poignant production about a love affair between a white boy and a black girl. The film, which was shot on 16-mm stock at a cost of $40,000, captured the Critics Award at the Venice Film Festival. This success earned him two motion-picture studio commissions, *Too Late Blues* (1962) and *A Child Is Waiting* (1963), both of them commercial failures. He returned to independent filmmaking and appeared as an actor in a number of motion pictures, specializing in villainous roles. He gave memorable performances in *Rosemary's Baby* (1967) as the sinister husband helping the Devil impregnate his wife and in *The Dirty Dozen* (1967) as a psychopathic murderer, a role that earned him an Academy Award nomination for best supporting actor. As a director Cassavetes was masterful in dramatizing marital problems, notably in such films as *Faces* (1968), *Husbands* (1970), and *A Woman Under the Influence* (1974). The latter, which starred Cassavetes' wife, Gena Rowlands, was for him unique; it employed a finished script. Some of his other directorial efforts, including *The Killing of a Chinese Bookie* (1976), *Love Streams* (1984), and *Big Trouble* (1986), received mixed reviews from the critics.

Ceausescu, Nicolae, Romanian head of state (b. Jan. 26, 1918, Scornicesti, Rom.—d. Dec. 25, 1989, near Bucharest, Rom.), and **Elena,** Romanian government official (b. Jan. 7, 1919, Oltenia region, Rom.—d. Dec. 25, 1989, near Bucharest), ruled Romania with fists of iron for 24 years until they were overthrown in a bloody revolution, summarily tried, and executed by firing squad. Although he was a rigid Communist, Ceausescu initially drew praise from the West for his independent trade and foreign policies, especially his denunciation of the Warsaw Pact nations' 1968 invasion of Czechoslovakia. Within Romania, however, he reigned over an increasingly repressive regime that drove the country from relative economic well-being to near starvation. Ceausescu joined the Communist youth movement in the 1930s and was repeatedly imprisoned for subversive activities. While in prison he became a protégé of Gheorghe Gheorghiu-Dej, Romania's dictator from 1952. Ceausescu entered the Politburo in 1955, and after Gheorghiu-Dej died (1965) he stepped in unopposed as party general secretary and (from 1967) as president of the State Council. In 1974 he was elected to the newly created post of president of the republic. With the support of the Securitate (an elite security force that held allegiance only to the president), Ceausescu installed more than 30 of his relatives in positions of power, built a personal fortune that was estimated in the millions of dollars, and established a network of internal spies and informants that suppressed even minor opposition. In the 1980s, determined to pay off Romania's external debt of more than $10 billion, he exported most agricultural and manufactured goods, creating domestic shortages of food, fuel, energy, and other basic necessities. In 1939 he married Elena Petrescu, a devout Communist and, reportedly, a respected chemist (the extent of her scientific training later came under suspicion). She headed numerous scientific organizations, notably the Central Chemical Research Institute (from 1965) and the National Council for Science and Technology (from 1979). In 1980 she was raised to first deputy prime minister, with sweeping powers of her own. She instituted repressive policies that included razing entire villages for "development," banning birth control, and ordering physical examinations for all women of childbearing age to enforce a high birthrate. The Ceausescu regime collapsed after he ordered troops to fire on a crowd of protesters in Timisoara on December 17. The Ceausescus fled but were captured and were held by the armed forces, which had turned against them.

Chapman, Graham, British comedian and writer (b. Jan. 8, 1941, Leicester, England—d. Oct. 4, 1989, Maidstone, England), was a founding member of the Monty Python Flying Circus

troupe, which set a standard during the 1970s for its quirky, surreal, but engaging parodies and wacky humour on television and later in films. Chapman, who came from a working-class background, graduated from Emmanuel College, Cambridge (1962), and from St. Bartholomew's Hospital Medical School (1966). He practiced medicine briefly but turned to the entertainment industry, first as a writer for "The [David] Frost Report" and BBC shows starring comedian Marty Feldman and singer Petula Clark and then also as a performer in a 1967 series, "At Last the 1948 Show." On Oct. 5, 1969, in a time slot that had been reserved for a religious program, "Monty Python's Flying Circus" startled viewers with its send-ups of celebrity interviews and other standard television fare. Chapman, recognized by his tweed jackets and thoughtful puffs on a pipe, perfected absurd characters, notably the Colonel and Raymond Luxury-Yacht. Nevertheless, it was as King Arthur in *Monty Python and the Holy Grail* (1975) and as Brian in *Monty Python's Life of Brian* (1979), a parody of the life of Christ, that he is best remembered, both for his portrayals and for the script, which he wrote with fellow Python John Cleese. Chapman, who made no secret of his successful battle with alcoholism or his life as a homosexual, was reportedly preparing a sequel to *A Liar's Autobiography* (1980).

Chatwin, (Charles) Bruce, British travel writer and novelist (b. May 13, 1940, Sheffield, Yorkshire, England—d. Jan. 18, 1989, Nice, France), won international acclaim for a wide variety of books that were linked only by the author's passion for a nomadic life and a deep understanding of human frailties. In 1966 Chatwin abandoned a promising career as a director of Impressionist art at the auction firm Sotheby's in London to study archaeology at the University of Edinburgh. From 1973 he worked as a traveling correspondent for *The Sunday Times* (London), but he quit in 1976 to begin a pilgrimage through the Patagonia region of southern Argentina and Chile. The resulting book, *In Patagonia* (1977), won awards in Britain and the U.S. Chatwin focused on Africa in *The Viceroy of Ouidah* (1980; filmed as *Cobra Verde,* 1987), a fictionalized biography of a Brazilian slave trader in 19th-century Dahomey. In his first true novel, *On the Black Hill* (1982; filmed 1988), which won the 1982 Whitbread literary award, Chatwin turned away from exotic locales to explore the lives of twin brothers on an isolated 20th-century Welsh farm. *The Songlines* (1987), his most commercially successful work, was both a study of Australian Aboriginal creation myths and a philosophical reverie on the nature of nomads. Although he denied it, Chatwin apparently suffered from AIDS. During a brief period of remission he wrote his last novel, *Utz* (1988), which was nominated for the prestigious Booker Prize in 1988. *What Am I Doing Here?,* a collection of Chatwin's essays, was published posthumously.

Chen Boda (CH'EN PO-TA), Chinese revolutionary and propagandist (b. 1905, Huian, Fujian (Fu-chien) province, China—d. Sept. 20, 1989, Beijing (Peking), China), was Mao Zedong's (Mao Tse-tung's) personal secretary and speechwriter for over 30 years. After participating in the Northern Expedition (1926–27) that overthrew local warlords, Chen attended Sun Yatsen University in Moscow, and after his return to China in 1930, he taught under an alias. As Mao's political secretary, he was widely viewed as Mao's mouthpiece and was elected a full member of the Communist Party's Central Committee in 1946, serving as a major figure in the propaganda department. He was longtime editor of *Hongqi* (*Hung Ch'i*), the Central Committee's publication on ideology. With the publication of the essay "Mao Zedong's Theory of the Chinese Revolution Is the Combination of Marxism-Leninism with the Chinese Revolution" and the book *Mao Zedong on the Chinese Revolution* (1951), he established himself as the chief interpreter of Mao's thought. In 1965

Chen became a full member of the Politburo, and the following year he began orchestrating purges. Chen wielded considerable power during the Cultural Revolution as head of the Central Cultural Revolution Group, responsible for political purges but in the early 1970s fell from favour. In 1980 he was tried and convicted of authorizing the persecution of officials during that tumultuous period. He was sentenced to 18 years in prison in 1981 but was reportedly released later the same year. After his release from prison, Chen spent his final years studying history in Beijing.

Clarke, T(homas) E(rnest) B(ennett), British screenwriter (b. June 7, 1907, Watford, Hertfordshire, England—d. Feb. 11, 1989, London, England), wrote the scripts for some of the most popular and respected comedies in the post-World War II British film industry, including the Academy Award-winning screenplay for *The Lavender Hill Mob* (1951). Clarke worked as a free-lance journalist and novelist before joining Ealing Studios as a writer in 1943. He scripted several dramatic motion pictures, notably *The Blue Lamp* (1950), but it was the whimsical, idiosyncratic characters in such comedies as the Oscar-nominated *Passport to Pimlico* (1949), *Hue and Cry* (1950), *The Titfield Thunderbolt* (1953), and *Barnacle Bill* (1957) that brought him international acclaim. After Ealing closed in 1957, Clarke turned to Hollywood, where his work included screenplays for *A Tale of Two Cities* (1958) and *Sons and Lovers* (1960), which brought him his third Academy Award nomination. He gave up screenwriting in the mid-1960s to write novels and an autobiography, *This Is Where I Came In* (1974). Clarke was made an Officer of the Order of the British Empire in 1952.

Clubb, O(liver) Edmund, U.S. government official (b. Feb. 16, 1901, South Park, Minn.—d. May 9, 1989, New York, N.Y.), was a career officer in the Foreign Service and one of the U.S. State Department's valuable "China hands" before his reputation was irreparably tarnished as one of Wisconsin Sen. Joseph McCarthy's primary targets in his anti-Communist witch-hunts. Clubb, who spent 24 years in the Foreign Service, was stationed in China in 1946. As the last U.S. diplomat to remain after the Communist takeover in 1949, he was responsible, as consul general, for taking down the American flag in April 1950. After returning to the U.S., he was named chief of the China desk at the State Department but was suspended a year later as a security risk. Though Clubb was cleared of all charges, he was transferred to the division of historical research with no assignment. He resigned this post five days later and launched a new career as a writer, teacher, and lecturer. From 1966 to 1970 he served as a research associate at the East Asian Institute at Columbia University, New York City. Clubb detailed his experience in the 1974 book *The Witness and I* and published *China and Russia: The "Great Game"* in 1971.

Corbett, Harry, British puppeteer (b. 1918, Bradford, Yorkshire, England—d. Aug. 16, 1989, Blandford Forum, Dorset, England), created the puppet Sooty, which charmed millions of children for more than 35 years on television, on-stage, and in numerous books and toys. Corbett, an electrical engineer and amateur magician, bought the teddy bear glove puppet in 1948 to amuse his children. In 1952 his performance in a talent contest on closed-circuit television caught the attention of the BBC, and Corbett quit his job to appear in a limited-run television series. Sixteen years later it was front-page news when the BBC finally canceled the program and Corbett took the mischievous Sooty and his friends Sweep and Soo to the commercial channel, Thames Television. In 1975 Corbett suffered a severe heart attack and was forced to relinquish the program in favour of his son. Corbett was made an Officer of the Order of the British Empire in 1976.

Coulouris, George, British actor (b. Oct. 1, 1903, Manchester, England—d. April 25, 1989, London, England), despite a long and varied career, was best known for his portrayals of villainous characters such as Count Teck de Brancovis in both the stage (1941) and screen (1943) versions of Lillian Hellman's *Watch on the Rhine.* Coulouris studied at the Central School of Speech and Drama in London and drew critical acclaim for his performance as Yank in the 1928 Cambridge Festival Theatre production of Eugene O'Neill's *The Hairy Ape.* He made his London debut at the Old Vic in 1926 and his Broadway debut three years later. As an original member of Orson Welles's Mercury Theatre, Coulouris played Marc Antony in that company's renowned modern-dress staging (1937) of *Julius Caesar.* After appearing with Welles in the film *Citizen Kane* (1941), Coulouris moved easily between motion pictures and the theatre on both sides of the Atlantic. His notable films include *None but the Lonely Heart* (1944), *An Outcast of the Islands* (1951), *I Accuse* (1958), *Mahler* (1974), and *The Long Good Friday* (1980).

Cowley, Malcolm, U.S. literary critic and literary historian (b. Aug. 24, 1898, Belsano, Pa.—d. March 28, 1989, New Milford, Conn.), was an expatriate writer in Paris (1921–23) and as the author of the literary history *Exile's Return* (1934, rev. 1951), became the foremost chronicler of the so-called Lost Generation of authors, who established their literary reputations during and after World War I. The Lost Generation, so dubbed by Gertrude Stein, embraced such writers as Ernest Hemingway, F. Scott Fitzgerald, John Dos Passos, e.e. cummings, Archibald MacLeish, Hart Crane, Thornton Wilder, and Edmund Wilson, a generation of disillusioned American writers who matured in Paris during the 1920s.

Cowley attended Harvard University, but his education was interrupted during World War I when he served with the American Ambulance Service in France and then completed a year stint in a U.S. Army artillery officers' training school; he graduated cum laude from Harvard in 1920. After he returned to France, his critical thought was greatly influenced by the advanced studies he undertook at the University of Montpellier and by the social network he established with such writers as Hemingway, Ezra Pound, and the Parisian avant-garde. After returning to the U.S., he did free-lance writing and translating for the next five years before serving (1929–44) as literary editor of *The New Republic* with a reputation for championing the political left. With his editing of the anthology *Portable Faulkner* (1946), Cowley sparked renewed interest in the literary reputation of William Faulkner. He was also instrumental in advancing the career of John Cheever. Some of Cowley's other works include *The Literary Situation* (1954), *The Faulkner-Cowley File Letters and Memories, 1944–62* (1966), *Think Back on Us* (1967), *A Many-Windowed House* (1970), and *And I Worked at the Writer's Trade* (1978). From the 1940s until 1985, Cowley served as a literary adviser to Viking Press.

Cyrankiewicz, Jozef, Polish politician (b. April 23, 1911, Tarnow, Poland—d. Jan. 20, 1989, Warsaw, Poland), was prime minister (1947–52, 1954–70) and deputy prime minister (1952–54) of Poland throughout the upheavals that raised the country from near ruin after World War II to a central position in the Soviet-led Warsaw Pact. Cyrankiewicz, who attended Jagiellonian University in Krakow, became secretary of the Krakow branch of the Polish Socialist Party (PSP) in 1935. He was captured by German forces in 1939, but he escaped and joined the Polish underground. Recaptured in 1941, he spent the remainder of the war in the Nazi concentration camp at Auschwitz. Cyrankiewicz was named secretary-general of the pro-Soviet PSP Central Executive Committee in 1945. As prime minister he presided over the forcible merger (1948) of the PSP with the Soviet-backed Polish Workers' Party to form the Polish United Workers' Party. Although he was briefly demoted to deputy prime minister in July 1952, he was reinstated as chairman of the new Council of Ministers in March 1954. On Dec. 7, 1970, Cyrankiewicz and West German Chancellor Willy Brandt signed the treaty that formally established the West German-Polish border. Later that month Cyrankiewicz and controversial First Secretary Władysław Gomułka were forced out of office after food-price increases touched off riots in several Polish cities. Cyrankiewicz held the ceremonial post of chairman of the Council of State (president) until he retired in 1972.

Daché, Lilly, French-born milliner (b. *c.* 1904, Beigles, France—d. Dec. 31, 1989, Louvecienne, France), established a flourishing hat business in the U.S. with made-to-order creations, which she preferred to fashion on the heads of her clients. Daché, who left school at the age of 14 when her parents announced that they would no longer waste money on books for her, worked as an apprentice to her aunt, a milliner in Bordeaux. She also served as an apprentice to the famous milliner Caroline Reboux of Paris before moving to New York in 1924. Daché worked as a salesclerk at Macy's department store and then at a small milliner's shop until she saved enough money to buy out her employer. Some of her stunning innovations included the cloche hat, the turban, hats woven of kitchen twine, glass and Lucite-bedecked bonnets, and the swagger hat associated with Marlene Dietrich. In 1949 Daché expanded her operation to include dress designing, and later her signature appeared on lingerie, jewelry, and cosmetics. In 1968 Daché retired when her husband of some 37 years, Jean Despres, a cosmetics executive at Coty Inc., also retired.

Dalí, Salvador (FELIPE JACINTO), Spanish painter (b. May 11, 1904, Figueras, Catalonia, Spain—d. Jan. 23, 1989, Figueras), was perhaps the most recognized and influential Surrealist artist of the 20th century, yet he was as well known for his eccentric appearance and flamboyant behaviour as for the meticulous technique and powerful imagery of his art. Dalí studied in Madrid at the National School of Fine Arts, from which he was expelled in 1926. In 1928 he visited Paris, where he was introduced to the poet André Breton and the Surrealist movement. Dalí abandoned the classical and abstract art forms with which he had experimented and focused on the projection of the Freudian unconscious mind through a technique he called the "paranoiac-critical" method. He collaborated with the Spanish director Luis Buñuel on *Un Chien andalou* (1928; *An Andalusian Dog*) and *L'Âge d'or* (1930; *The*

Golden Age). Through these Surrealist films and such paintings as "The Persistence of Memory" (1931) and "Inventions of the Monsters" (1937), Dalí created images of melting watches, burning giraffes, and hallucinatory landscapes that came to represent Surrealism to the general public. Dalí, whose commercialism had already led Breton to dub him anagrammatically "Avida Dollars," moved to the U.S. in 1940. There he captured the public imagination with his highly waxed curled mustache, strangely erotic art, and self-promotional stunts, many of them intended to shock and outrage his audience. He also designed for the stage and cinema and created furniture, jewelry, and department store window displays. In 1948 Dalí returned to Catalonia and embraced right-wing politics and Roman Catholic mysticism, which dominated much of his later work. Eventually Dalí's bizarre activities and commercial exploitation overwhelmed the importance of his art, and his reputation suffered. It was later suggested that he had signed thousands of blank sheets of paper, which were used for forged lithographs. After the death in 1982 of his wife, Gala, his constant companion and artistic muse, Dalí became increasingly isolated. He was badly burned in a fire at his home in 1984; thereafter he lived under 24-hour nursing care in the tower of the Dalí Museum in Figueras. He was created Marqués de Dalí y de Pubol in 1982.

Davis, Bette (RUTH ELIZABETH DAVIS), U.S. actress (b. April 5, 1908, Lowell, Mass.—d. Oct. 6, 1989, Neuilly-sur-Seine, France), projected a majestic presence both on and off the silver screen and secured her position as a consummate actress with her intense characterizations—she masterfully portrayed suffering heroines in a string of melodramas; haughty, uncompromising females in films about independent women; and diabolical schemers in a series of horror films. Davis, an unconventional beauty who possessed large, expressive eyes, adopted a unique set of mannerisms. She used measured vocal inflections, batted her eyes, and

GLOBE PHOTOS

smoked cigarettes in a manner that was profoundly her own. Davis, who received little encouragement while pursuing an acting career, was fired by George Cukor during a summer stock engagement, was rejected as a student by Eva Le Gallienne, and was said to have "as much sex appeal as Slim Summerville" by then Universal Studio boss Carl Laemmle. The determined Davis, however, established herself as a superb dramatic actress, and after her motion picture debut in *Bad Sister* (1931) for Universal Studios, she signed a long-term contract with Warner Bros. Studios, where she demanded and eventually won the roles she coveted. She was nominated for Academy Awards 10 times and won for *Dangerous* (1935) and *Jezebel* (1938). During her longtime career, she appeared in

more than 80 films; dozens of them became classics, including *Of Human Bondage* (1934), *Dark Victory* (1939), *The Private Lives of Elizabeth and Essex* (1939), *The Letter* (1940), *The Little Foxes* (1941), *Now, Voyager* (1942), *Mr. Skeffington* (1944), *All About Eve* (1950), *The Star* (1952), and *Whatever Happened to Baby Jane?* (1962). The indomitable Davis continued to perform in such motion pictures as *Hush, Hush . . . Sweet Charlotte* (1964), *Burnt Offerings* (1976), and *The Whales of August* (1987) and garnered an Emmy award for her television performance in "Strangers—The Story of a Mother and Daughter" (1979). Her private life included four marriages, the last to actor Gary Merrill. Davis published two autobiographies, *The Lonely Life* (1962) and *This 'n That* (1987), the latter in response to her daughter B.D. Hyman's unflattering book, *My Mother's Keeper* (1985). Although ravaged by cancer, she delighted the audience at a tribute in her honour when she looked around and vehemently declared, "What a dump!" It was one of her most memorable lines.

Davis, Victor, Canadian swimmer (b. Feb. 10, 1964, Guelph, Ont.—d. Nov. 13, 1989, Montreal, Que.), was an aggressive competitor who, at the 1984 Summer Olympics in Los Angeles, captured a gold medal in the 200-m breaststroke and established a world record for that event that stood for five years. Davis also won a silver medal in the 100-m breaststroke at that Olympics. A controversial figure who, on national television, kicked over a chair in the presence of Queen Elizabeth II when the Canadian swimming team was disqualified from a men's medley relay, Davis was nonetheless respected by fellow competitors, who admired his dedication to the sport. A power during his heyday, Davis first made his mark at the 1982 world championships, in which he won a gold medal in the 200-m breaststroke and set a world record. He won a gold medal in the 100-m breaststroke in the 1986 world championships and a silver medal at the 1988 Olympics in Seoul, South Korea, as a member of the Canadian 4 × 100-m medley relay team. Davis, made an Officer of the Order of Canada in 1984, retired from competition in July 1989. He died two days after being hit by a car.

Davison, William ("WILD BILL"), U.S. musician (b. Jan. 5, 1906, Defiance, Ohio—d. Nov. 14, 1989, Santa Barbara, Calif.), electrified audiences with his hard-driven, brassy, and energetic playing style and was regarded as one of the world's finest jazz cornet players. During his 70-year-career Davison recorded some 800 songs and traveled extensively. After playing in Ohio, he moved to Chicago in the late 1920s and performed in legendary gangster-run clubs before becoming a regular at Eddie Condon's nightclub in New York City, where he performed from 1945 to 1957. Davison fronted his own band during his later years and toured Europe and Asia in the 1970s and '80s. His jazz band had been scheduled to appear in Britain and Switzerland in 1990.

Dennis, Nigel Forbes, British writer and critic (b. Jan. 16, 1912, Bletchingley, Surrey, England—d. July 19, 1989, Hertfordshire, England), used absurdist plots and witty repartee to satirize psychiatry, religion, and social behaviour, most notably in the novel *Cards of Identity* (1955) and the 1956 play based upon it. Dennis was reared in Southern Rhodesia (now Zimbabwe) and educated in Germany. He moved to Britain and in 1930 wrote his first novel, which was later lost. In 1934 Dennis traveled to New York City, where he helped translate the writings of the Austrian psychoanalyst Alfred Adler and worked as an editor and book reviewer for *The New Republic* (1937–38) and *Time* (1940–58). After his return to London in 1949, he also wrote reviews for the magazine *Encounter* (1960–63) and the *Sunday Telegraph* (1961–82) and served as joint editor of *Encounter* (1967–70). In *Boys and Girls Come Out to Play* (1949;

U.S. title *A Sea Change*), Dennis explored the Adlerian theme that each individual's personality adapts to suit the social context to which it is exposed, a theme he developed more fully in *Cards of Identity* and *A House in Order* (1966). He wrote two moderately successful plays, *The Making of Moo* (first performed in 1957), a satire on the psychological power of religious fervour, and *August for the People* (1961). Dennis' nonfiction included an incisive critical biography of Jonathan Swift (1964).

Deskey, Donald, U.S. industrial designer (b. Nov. 23, 1894, Blue Earth, Minn.—d. April 29, 1989, Vero Beach, Fla.), was instrumental in establishing industrial design as a profession with his innovative use of such experimental materials as plastic laminates and tubular steel. He was perhaps best known for his 1932 Art Deco designs and furnishings that adorn the interior of Radio City Music Hall. Deskey studied architecture at the University of California at Berkeley and attended the Mark Hopkins Art School in San Francisco and the Art Institute of Chicago. He had a brief career in advertising but in 1926 began designing window displays for Manhattan department stores. In these displays he used such ordinary industrial materials as corrugated iron and cork. During the late 1920s he created a special wallpaper using aluminum foil, and in 1940 he patented Weldtex, a textured plywood. In addition to his Radio City Music Hall designs, for which he used aluminum and bakelite, Deskey also designed the high-ceilinged apartment atop the Music Hall for the theatre's manager, Samuel L. ("Roxy") Rothafel. During a 20-year association with Procter and Gamble, he was responsible for the packaging on such products as Crest toothpaste, Aqua Velva after-shave lotion, Cheer and Oxydol laundry detergents, and Pampers disposable diapers. Deskey's consulting firm, founded in 1928, also produced projects for various world's fairs, including items for the New York exhibitions of 1939–40 and 1964–65 and the Seattle World's Fair of 1962. His first one-man show, which showcased his furniture designs from the 1920s and '30s, was at the Fifty/50 gallery in New York City in March 1989.

Diop, Birago Ismaël, Senegalese writer (b. Dec. 11, 1906, Dakar, French West Africa [now Senegal]—d. Nov. 25, 1989, Dakar), was a veterinarian and diplomat who shaped contemporary literature by writing in French the deceptively simple African folktales and legends that he said had been told to him by a *griot*, or storyteller, whom he named Amadou Koumba. Diop was also known for his poems, collected in *Leurres et lucurs* (1960; "Lures and Glimmerings"). Brought up in both Islamic and Wolof traditions, Diop won a scholarship when he was 15 to the Lycée Faidherbe in Saint-Louis, the capital of French West Africa, where he excelled in science and took a second degree in philosophy (1928). He served a year in the military before enrolling in the University of Toulouse, from which he graduated (1933) as a doctor of veterinary medicine. Soon after, in Paris, he met and collaborated with Léopold Sédar Senghor, who was to become the first president of Senegal in 1960. Encouraged by Jean-Paul Sartre and the poet Aimé Césaire, Senghor and Diop wrote poems that celebrated the traditional values of African life, and put them at the forefront of the literary movement known as *négritude*. Diop returned to Africa, where he served as a government veterinarian from 1934 to 1942; he was required to travel over vast expanses of what became Mali by whatever means he could find. He served in the Ivory Coast (now Côte d'Ivoire), Upper Volta (now Burkina Faso), and Mauritania in the 1940s and '50s. At Senghor's request, Diop served as ambassador to Tunisia (1961–65) before returning to Dakar to open a private veterinary practice. Beginning in 1947 he wrote down the stories that he had heard from the many storytellers he had encountered, especially in his own family, weaving graceful, subtle tales, and attributed

them to the composite Koumba. He published *Les Contes d'Amadou Koumba* (1947; *Tales of Amadou Koumba*, 1966), *Les Nouveaux Contes d'Amadou Koumba* (1959), and *Contes et lavanes* (1963; *Tales and Commentaries*), for which he won the 1964 Grand Prix Littéraire d'Afrique Noire. His autobiography, *La Plume raboutée* (*The Spliced Pen*), was published in 1978.

Diori, Hamani, Niger politician (b. June 6, 1916, Soudouré, Niger—d. April 23, 1989, Rabat, Morocco), was the first president (1960–74) of the Republic of Niger. Diori was educated in Dahomey (now Benin) and Senegal and worked as a teacher in Niger (1936–38, 1951–56) and at the Institute of Overseas Studies in Paris (1938–46). He was a founder member (1946) of the Rassemblement Démocratique Africaine and founder of its local branch, the Niger Progressive Party (PPN), and represented Niger in the French National Assembly (1946–51, 1956–58). During the transition period before Niger's independence, the French government banned (1959) all political parties except the PPN and chose Diori to serve as Niger's prime minister (1958–60) and president (1960). On Nov. 11, 1960, he was formally voted into office in the first postindependence elections. Despite pressure from France, he supported Nigeria during the secession (1967–70) of Biafra, and he gained worldwide respect for his attempts to negotiate a peaceful settlement to the conflict. Diori's administration, however, was rife with corruption, and he was unable to implement much-needed reforms or to alleviate the widespread famine brought on by the Sahelian drought of the early 1970s. He was deposed by the army chief of staff, Lieut. Col. Seyni Kountché, on April 15, 1974. Diori was released from prison in 1980, but he remained under house arrest until April 1987.

du Maurier, Dame Daphne, British writer (b. May 13, 1907, London, England—d. April 19, 1989, Par, Cornwall, England), wrote Gothic novels that combined psychological realism with suspense and became best-selling thrillers. The middle of three daughters of actor and manager Sir Gerald du Maurier, she grew up with the privileges of wealth—private tutors in Paris, glittering parties, and travel—but preferred to read and chose to follow in the path of her grandfather, novelist George du Maurier. Her early short stories were published when she was 21, and her first novel, *The Loving Spirit* (1931), revealed her rich imagination. Du Maurier's sophisticated storytelling was distinguished by the exploration of human emotions through complicated characters. Her fourth novel, *Jamaica Inn* (1936), captured the essence of Cornwall, with its rocky coast and turbulent seas. That place, her home since her early 20s, was the setting for the rest of her novels, including *Rebecca* (1938), her most famous. The latter, *Jamaica Inn,* and her story "The Birds" were made into motion pictures by Alfred Hitchcock. Among her 20 works are *My Cousin Rachel* (1951), which also was made into a movie; *The Scapegoat* (1957); *The Glassblowers* (1963), a historical novel; *Gerald: A Portrait,* a biography of her father; *Growing Pains* (1977), her autobiography; and *The Rebecca Notebook and Other Memories* (1981). She was created Dame Commander of the Order of the British Empire in 1969.

Eldridge, (David) Roy ("LITTLE JAZZ"), U.S. trumpeter (b. Jan. 30, 1911, Pittsburgh, Pa.—d. Feb. 26, 1989, Valley Stream, N.Y.), was a jazz virtuoso whose powerful and intense sound and staggering range served as the connecting link between the early innovations of Louis Armstrong and the modernist techniques introduced by Dizzy Gillespie. Eldridge, who expanded on Armstrong's innovations, was generally considered in a class by himself because he performed with a crackling intensity unequaled by his contemporaries; he earned the nickname Little Jazz in 1931 because he played incessantly. Eldridge

began playing the drums at the age of six and then took up the trumpet. He left home at the age of 16 to join a band called the Night Hawk Syncopaters and spent most of his time on the road before settling in New York City during the 1930s. He had stints in Teddy Hill's group and Fletcher Henderson's band before gaining celebrity as a featured soloist (both as a singer and trumpeter) with Gene Krupa's band from 1941 until it disbanded in 1943. Eldridge gained even greater renown when he joined Artie Shaw's band in 1944. He returned to Krupa's band in 1949 before touring with Benny Goodman in Europe. During his long career he developed a unique sound that was heard in such songs as "Wabash Stomp" and "Rockin' Chair" with Krupa, and the album *The Nifty Cat* combined the best of his early years with a new maturity. Eldridge, who toured with Jazz at the Philharmonic and other jazz concert groups, retired in 1980 after developing heart problems.

Evans, Maurice Herbert, British-born actor (b. June 3, 1901, Dorchester, England—d. March 12, 1989, Rottingdean, England), was a celebrated Shakespearean actor who gained fame on the English stage as Lieutenant Raleigh in *Journey's End* (1928) before going to the U.S. in 1935 to star as Romeo opposite Katharine Cornell's Juliet. Evans starred as Napoleon in *St. Helena* (1936), but it was not until 1937 when he mounted his interpretation of *Richard II* that he secured his reputation. The following year he brought a full-length *Hamlet* to the Broadway stage, and during the next decade he became one of the best-known Shakespearean actors in the U.S. His impressive list of credentials also includes roles as Falstaff in *Henry IV, Part I* (1939), Malvolio in *Twelfth Night* (1940), and the title role in *MacBeth* (1941). Evans became a U.S. citizen in 1941, and in 1942 he enlisted in the U.S. Army. He was commissioned a captain and was later promoted to major and put in charge of entertaining troops in the Central Pacific area. One of his productions was a shortened version of *Hamlet,* which was dubbed the "G.I. Hamlet"; after the war he successfully produced the play on Broadway. He appeared in *Man and Superman* (1947), *The Browning Version* (1949), *Harlequinade* (1949), and *The Devil's Disciple* (1950) before starring as Tony Wendice, a husband determined to kill his wife by devising the perfect murder in *Dial M for Murder*—his greatest commercial success—which ran from October 1952 until February 1954. Although Evans reprised many of his stage credits for television, he was perhaps best known in the U.S. as the warlock father on the television series "Bewitched." His film credits included *Kind Lady, Jack of Diamonds, Rosemary's Baby,* and *Planet of the Apes.* Evans also produced the Broadway hits *The Teahouse of the August Moon* (1953) and *No Time for Sergeants* (1955). At the end of the 1960s, he returned to England, where he lived quietly for the rest of his life.

Fain, Sammy (SAMUEL FEINBERG), U.S. composer (b. June 17, 1902, New York, N.Y.—d. Dec. 6, 1989, Los Angeles, Calif.), penned scores of enduring and heartfelt songs, including such all-time favourites as "Let a Smile Be Your Umbrella," "Wedding Bells Are Breaking Up That Old Gang of Mine," "I Can Dream, Can't I?," "April Love," "Strange Are the Ways of Love," "I'll Be Seeing You," and "Tender Is the Night." Fain, who was nominated 10 times for an Academy Award for best song, won twice, for "Secret Love" in 1953 and "Love Is a Many-Splendored Thing" in 1955. Fain began composing in 1925 and from 1927 to 1942 teamed up with lyricist Irving Kahal. Fain wrote music for the films *Alice in Wonderland, Peter Pan, Calamity Jane,* a 1953 version of *The Jazz Singer, Three Sailors and a Girl,* and *April Love;* his Broadway stage work included music for *Hellzapoppin, George White's Scandals,* and *Christine.* The self-taught composer, who played piano by ear, produced beautiful standard melodies that emerged as classics.

Francis Joseph II (MARIA ALOYS ALFRED KARL JOHANNES HEINRICH MICHAEL GEORG IGNATIUS BENEDIKTUS GERHARDUS MAJELLA VON UND ZU LIECHTENSTEIN), Liechtenstein monarch (b. Aug. 16, 1906, Frauenthal Castle, Austria—d. Nov. 13, 1989, Grabs, Switz.), was revered by his 28,000 subjects as the prince who built the impoverished but scenic 160-sq km (62-sq mi) country between Austria and Switzerland into Europe's richest nation. Franz Josef II, as he was called, studied forestry engineering at the Forestry and Agricultural University in Vienna. A nephew of Austrian Archduke Franz Ferdinand, whose assassination in 1914 triggered World War I, he was appointed to the throne of Liechtenstein in 1938 by his uncle, Francis I. Soon afterward, German troops marched into Austria. Francis Joseph II oversaw the formation of a national coalition government that kept Europe's fourth-smallest nation neutral during World War II; in 1945 Liechtenstein refused Soviet demands to extradite some 500 Soviets who had sought refuge there. Among family holdings were forests in Austria, real estate in Vienna, and an estimated 1,400 paintings by such old masters as Rembrandt, Rubens, and Van Dyck. The production of high-technology goods in conjunction with Switzerland built a strong industrial base. The family-owned Bank in Liechtenstein—with branches in London; Zürich, Switz.; New York; and Frankfurt, West Germany—made the principality a desirable tax haven for wealthy individuals and an estimated 30,000 to 80,000 foreign companies. The death of Francis Joseph II signaled the end of an era that had begun to change in 1984, when women earned voting rights and he installed his son, Prince Hans Adam, as regent.

Franco (L'OKANGA LA NDJU PENE LUAMBO MAKIADI), Zairian jazz musician and composer (b. June 6?, 1938, Sona-Bata, Belgian Congo (now Zaire)—d. Oct. 12, 1989, Brussels, Belgium), as a leader of the African pop music scene for over 30 years, blended the Latin-American rumba with jazz, gospel, and traditional African rhythms and melodies, creating the sound called soukous. He used the elements of Lingala (a tonal language), the likimbi hand piano, horn, and guitar as background for the social themes of his lyrics, which varied from politics to the struggle between men and women. As a youth Franco played guitar to attract customers to his mother's market store, made his recording debut, and cofounded OK Jazz (later TPOK Jazz). Franco wrote the successful songs "Independence Cha Cha" (1960), about Zairian independence from Belgium, "Mario" (1985), about the accusations wielded against a gigolo by his mistress, and "Beware of AIDS" (1987), about the battle against the disease. He recorded over 100 songs. Mobutu Sese Seko, president of Zaire, named Franco Grand Maître (Grand Master), and upon Franco's death Mobutu declared four days of national mourning.

Furillo, Carl, U.S. baseball player (b. March 8, 1922, Stony Creek Mills, Pa.—d. Jan. 21, 1989, Stony Creek Mills), was the intense right fielder for the star-studded Brooklyn Dodger professional baseball team during the late 1940s and early '50s, a team that boasted such superb players as Jackie Robinson, Roy Campanella, Gil Hodges, Carl Erskine, and Duke Snider. Furillo, who had a deadly throwing arm, was dubbed "the Reading Rifle." A tough competitor whose throws from right field often robbed batters of base hits, he spent his entire 15-year career (1946–60) with Dodger teams in Brooklyn and Los Angeles. This glory Dodger era, recounted in Roger Kahn's book *The Boys of Summer,* reached its zenith when the team captured the World Series in 1955. Furillo, who had a lifetime batting average of .299, slammed 192 home runs, batted in 1,058 runs, and compiled a more than .300 batting average in five seasons during his career; in 1953 he led the National League in batting with a .344 average. He was released from the Dodgers in 1960 after suffering a torn calf muscle. In a highly publicized lawsuit, the

bitter Furillo won back pay for what he felt was an unjustified dismissal after a baseball-related injury. He was the proprietor of a grocery store near Shea Stadium in New York City before returning to his hometown. In recent years Furillo had basked in his earlier triumphs as a regular staff member at the Dodgers' Fantasy Camp in Vero Beach, Fla.

Genda, Minoru, Japanese naval officer and politician (b. Aug. 16, 1904, Hiroshima, Japan—d. Aug. 15, 1989, Tokyo, Japan), was chosen by Adm. Yamamoto Isoroku to draft the air assault for the attack on Pearl Harbor, which crippled the American Pacific fleet and signaled the U.S. entry into World War II. He was credited with engineering attacks by low-flying torpedo bombers, which killed 2,450 Americans, sank or severely damaged 19 ships, and destroyed 177 planes. He became a fighter pilot after graduating from the Japanese Naval Academy in 1924 and was soon regarded as one of Japan's most brilliant naval officers. He was serving as a commander in the Navy when he was assigned to formulate the details of the surprise attack on Pearl Harbor. Genda ended the war as a captain. From 1959 to 1962 he served as chief of staff of the Air Self Defense Force, and from 1962 until his retirement in 1986, he served in the (upper) House of Councillors (Parliament). For many years he was also chairman of the National Defense Committee of the Liberal-Democratic Party.

Giamatti, A(ngelo) Bartlett, U.S. educator and sports executive (b. April 4, 1938, Boston, Mass.—d. Sept. 1, 1989, Oak Bluffs, Mass.), was a learned Renaissance scholar who taught literature at Yale University, served as president (1978–86) of Yale, and then abandoned an academic career to become president of baseball's National League; he would, however, probably best be remembered as the major league baseball commissioner who banned Cincinnati Reds player-manager Pete Rose from baseball. Giamatti earned his Ph.D. in comparative literature at Yale University in 1964 and taught at New York and Princeton universities before joining the faculty of his alma mater in 1966. In 1978, at the age of 40, Giamatti became Yale's youngest president; during his tenure he was dedicated to restoring the university to financial stability. As president he phased out 40 senior faculty positions, instituted a new billing system that required students to pay tuition earlier, launched intensive undergraduate writing programs, and persuaded the faculty to reinstate a foreign-language requirement. A lifelong Boston Red Sox fan, Giamatti, whose athletic skills were limited to keeping statistics and carrying sports equipment, fulfilled a lifelong dream when he entered big-league baseball as National League president. On April 1, 1989, Giamatti was named baseball commissioner; he became dedicated to upholding the integrity of the game. Just eight days before his death, Giamatti imposed on Pete Rose a lifelong suspension from baseball for betting on baseball games, including those involving his team. A prolific author, Giamatti wrote numerous articles and such books as *The Earthly Paradise and the Renaissance Epic* (1966) and *Play of Double Senses: Spenser's "Faerie Queene"* (1975).

Gibbons, Stella Dorothea, British novelist (b. Jan. 5, 1902, London, England—d. Dec. 19, 1989, London), captured the public's imagination and the 1933 Femina Vie Heureuse Prize with her first novel, *Cold Comfort Farm* (1932), a lively burlesque of both the pulp romance and the regional novels of D.H. Lawrence and Thomas Hardy. In the 1960s *Cold Comfort Farm* gained a new audience through popular adaptations for the musical stage and television. Although Gibbons never again equaled her early success, she produced more than 20 other novels, including *Ticky* (1943), *Here Be Dragons* (1956), and *The Woods in Winter* (1970). She also wrote several volumes of poetry and short stories.

Glushko, Valentin Petrovich, Soviet engineer (b. Sept. 2 [Aug. 20, old style], 1908, Odessa, Ukraine, Russia—d. Jan. 10, 1989, Moscow, U.S.S.R.), pioneered in the development of rocket propulsion systems and designed the innovative liquid-propellant engines that powered Soviet missiles and space rockets. After graduating (1929) from Leningrad State University, Glushko headed the Gas Dynamics Laboratory in Leningrad and began research on electrothermal, solid-fuel, and liquid-fuel rocket engines. He worked closely with the renowned rocket designer Sergey P. Korolyov from 1932 until Korolyov's death in 1966. Glushko and Korolyov achieved their greatest triumph in 1957 with the launching of the first intercontinental ballistic missile in August and of the first successful artificial satellite, Sputnik I, in October. Glushko received numerous official honours, including the Lenin Prize (1957) and election to the Academy of Sciences of the U.S.S.R. (1958). In 1974 he was named chief designer of the Soviet space program, where he oversaw development of the Mir space station.

Goldman, Eric Frederick, U.S. historian (b. June 17, 1915, Washington, D.C.—d. Feb. 19, 1989, Princeton, N.J.), was an eminent history professor (1942–85) at Princeton University, a special adviser (1963–66) to Pres. Lyndon B. Johnson, and a respected author whose best-known work, *Rendezvous with Destiny: A History of Modern American Reform* (1952), explored American liberalism. The book captured the Bancroft History Prize for "distinguished writing in American history" and became a standard text in high schools and colleges. Goldman, who earned a Ph.D. from Johns Hopkins University, Baltimore, Md., at 22 years of age, served as a lecturer (1938–41) at his alma mater and as a *Time* magazine staff writer before joining Princeton University as an assistant professor. Some of his other scholarly and authoritative writings include *The Crucial Decade, America 1945–55* (1956), which was updated in 1961 and published as a new edition under the title *The Crucial Decade—and After, America (1945–60)*, and *The Tragedy of Lyndon Johnson: A Historian's Personal Memoir* (1968), which illuminated the presidency of Johnson in light of Goldman's personal experience as a consultant to him. Though Goldman initially gave high praise to Johnson's "open administration," he later resigned his position when Johnson's distrust of academicians became apparent. Goldman became visible to the public as the moderator (1959–67) on the television discussion program "The Open Mind." Goldman, who had served as Rollins professor of history at Princeton since 1962, taught Modern America, the largest upper-class course in the university, until his retirement in 1985.

Gomez, Vernon ("LEFTY"), U.S. baseball player (b. Nov. 26, 1908, Rodeo, Calif.—d. Feb. 17, 1989, Larkspur, Calif.), as the jocular and colourful left-handed pitcher (1930–42) for the New York Yankees professional baseball team, compiled an outstanding career record of 189 wins and 102 losses and a near flawless performance in World Series appearances; he won six games without losing in seven starts. Gomez, of Irish and Spanish descent, was noted for his comedic quips and was dubbed "Goofy" by his contemporaries. When asked the secret of his success, Gomez replied, "Clean living and a fast outfield." His formula for winning helped propel powerful Yankee teams to five World Series championships (1932, 1936, 1937, 1938, and 1939). Gomez, who tabulated earned-run averages of 2.33 in both 1934 and 1937, was renowned for his superior performances while under pressure. In 1943 he spent his last year in professional baseball pitching for the Washington Senators. After his retirement he served as a recreational director, as a manager for the Yankee farm team in Binghamton, N.Y., and as a representative of the Wilson Sporting Goods Co. Gomez, who was inducted into the Baseball Hall of Fame in 1972, characteristically gave credit to his teammates. He applauded those who scored so many runs; outfielder Joe DiMaggio, who ran down so many of Gomez's mistakes; and Johnny Murphy, a superlative relief pitcher.

Gromyko, Andrey Andreyevich, Soviet diplomat (b. July 18 [July 5, old style], 1909, Starye Gromyki, Belorussia—d. July 2, 1989, Moscow, U.S.S.R.), directed Soviet affairs with the West for nearly 50 years, most notably as foreign minister, a position he held for 28 years (1957–85) under five Soviet leaders. Gromyko, who came from a peasant background, joined the Communist Party in 1931. He attended an agricultural school in Minsk, studying agriculture and economics. After completing postgraduate studies in 1936, he worked as a researcher at the Institute of Economics of the U.S.S.R. Academy of Sciences until Joseph Stalin sent him to the Soviet embassy in Washington in 1939. Gromyko was simultaneously (1943–46) the Soviet envoy to Cuba and ambassador to the U.S., where he made useful contacts with Western leaders and worked for the establishment of the UN. As the permanent representative (1946–48) to the UN Security Council, the taciturn Gromyko wielded the powerful Soviet veto 25 times, earning him the nickname "Mr. Nyet." Except for a brief stint (1952–53) as ambassador to Britain, he held the post of first deputy foreign minister from 1949 until 1957, when he was named foreign minister by Nikita Khrushchev. Although it was unclear exactly how great a role Gromyko played in formulating foreign policy, after Leonid Brezhnev became first secretary (1964) Gromyko's influence increased. He was instrumental in building a policy of détente under Brezhnev and his successors, Yury Andropov and Konstantin Chernenko. Gromyko was elevated to membership in the Politburo in 1973 and named first deputy chairman of the Council of Ministers in 1983. In March 1985 he put his considerable political weight behind Mikhail Gorbachev's candidacy for general secretary. Four months later Gromyko was replaced as foreign minister and promoted to the ceremonial post of president. He stepped down from the presidency and from the Politburo in September 1988. Gromyko's autobiography, *Memories,* was published in English shortly before his death.

Halliwell, Leslie, British writer and film historian (b. Feb. 23, 1929, Bolton, Lancashire, England—d. Jan. 21, 1989, Surrey, England), popularized film history with *Halliwell's Filmgoer's Companion* (1965; frequently revised), a concise encyclopaedia of the motion-picture industry, and *Halliwell's Film Guide* (1977; frequently revised), a collection of witty, incisive synopses and reviews of individual movies. Halliwell's influential, often idiosyncratic reviews demonstrated not only his extensive knowledge of motion-picture history but also his personal bias toward the films of the 1930s and '40s. After graduating from the University of Cambridge, Halliwell wrote for *Picturegoer* magazine and managed a small cinema in Cambridge. He joined Granada Television as a film researcher in 1959, but he soon advanced to program buyer. As film buyer for the Independent Television network (ITV; 1968–87) and for Channel 4 (1982–87), he introduced British television viewers to numerous older and seldom-seen motion pictures. Halliwell's other books include encyclopaedic guides to television programming, several works of fiction, and an autobiography, *Seats in All Parts* (1985).

Harding of Petherton, (Allan Francis) John Harding, BARON, British field marshal (b. Feb. 10, 1896, Somerset, England—d. Jan. 20, 1989, Nether Compton, Dorset, England), was a brilliant military strategist who rose from a part-time reservist in the Territorial Army to chief of the British Imperial General Staff (1952–55) and governor of Cyprus (1955–57). During World War II Harding commanded the 7th Armoured Division (the "Desert Rats") in its

acclaimed victory at the Battle of el-Alamein and crafted the plans for the Allied capture of Rome in 1944. After graduating (1912) from Ilminster Grammar School, Harding joined the Territorials. He was called to the regular army at the beginning of World War I and rose to the level of acting lieutenant colonel (a rank he lost after the war but officially regained in 1938) in command of a machine-gun battalion in the Middle East. At the outbreak of World War II, his regular posting was in India. He was transferred to the Middle East and in 1942 was chosen to head the Desert Rats. Harding was seriously wounded in January 1943, but he returned to the fighting in March 1944 as chief of staff under Gen. Sir Harold Alexander in the Italian campaign. After the war he succeeded Alexander as commander of the British forces in the Mediterranean. Harding, who was promoted to general in 1949 and field marshal in 1953, headed the British Far East Land Forces (1949–51) and the British Army of the Rhine (1951–52) before being named chief of the Imperial General Staff. He postponed his intended retirement in 1955 when he was appointed military governor and commander in chief in Cyprus. In 1956 he deported the Cypriot nationalist leader, Archbishop Makarios III. Harding was created a life peer soon after his retirement in 1958.

Harrington, Michael, U.S. socialist leader and writer (b. Feb. 24, 1928, St. Louis, Mo.—d. July 31, 1989, Larchmont, N.Y.), was in favour of adopting democratic socialism in the United States, served as a member of the national executive board of the Socialist Party from 1960 to 1968, and was named (1982) chairman and later cochairman of the Democratic Socialists of America. He gained national attention, however, as the author of *The Other America: Poverty in the United States* (1962), which sparked the War on Poverty, an initiative adopted by Pres. John F. Kennedy three days before his assassination in 1963 and later implemented by Pres. Lyndon B. Johnson. In his exhaustively researched book, Harrington contended that there existed an underclass of poor people who were unable to help themselves and were trapped in a "culture of poverty." His exposé led to the expansion of Social Security, Aid to Families with Dependent Children, and food stamps and the creation of programs for housing and medical care. After earning an M.A. from the University of Chicago in 1949, Harrington served as an associate editor of the *Catholic Worker,* a monthly magazine published in tabloid format; as organization secretary of the Workers Defense League; and as editor of *New American* magazine. In 1972 he was named professor of political science at Queens (N.Y.) College, and he became professor emeritus there in 1988, the same year he published an autobiography, *Long-Distance Runner.* Besides *The Other America,* for which he won the George Polk Award and the Sidney Hillman Award, Harrington's publications include *The Accidental Century* (1965), *Toward a Democratic Left: A Radical Program for a New Majority* (1968), *The Vast Majority: A Journey to the World's Poor* (1977), *The New American Poverty* (1984), and *Socialism: Past and Future* (1989), which appeared shortly before his death.

Hartung, Hans (HEINRICH ERNST), German-born French artist (b. Sept. 21, 1904, Leipzig, Germany—d. Dec. 8?, Antibes, France), pioneered European abstract "action" painting with calligraphic swirls that he typically applied—with a brush, his thumbs, a mop, or whatever else was handy—to large canvases of bright, pure colours. He once said his preference for lines rather than figures dated to his early childhood, when he preferred to draw lightning bolts rather than animals. Hartung studied (1924) philosophy and art history at the University of Leipzig and also studied (1926–32) with painters in Italy and France and in German art schools in Leipzig, Dresden, and Munich. His first one-man show (1931) was in Dresden and

his second (1932) in Oslo, Norway. Hartung moved (1933) to the Spanish island of Minorca in the Mediterranean but returned to Germany in 1935. His abhorrence of Nazism persuaded him to resettle in Paris, where he joined such other abstract artists as Wassily Kandinsky, Piet Mondrian, and Joan Miró. In 1939 Hartung joined the French Foreign Legion in North Africa, and in 1944 he sustained a battle injury that required the amputation of a leg. He returned to France, became a citizen in 1946, and continued to create abstract art. In 1960 he was awarded the Grand Prix for painting at the Venice Biennale. In 1976 he wrote his autobiography, *Autoportrait* ("Self-Portrait"). He was made Commander of the Legion of Honour in 1960.

Harvey, Douglas Norman, Canadian hockey player (b. Dec. 19, 1924, Montreal, Que.—d. Dec. 26, 1989, Montreal), was a superb defenseman who virtually dominated games by controlling the tempo (1947–61) for the Montreal Canadiens professional hockey team, which captured six Stanley Cups (1952–53, 1955–56, 1956–57, 1957–58, 1958–59, and 1959–60) while Harvey played for them. During his remarkable 19-year career, Harvey scored 88 goals, made 452 assists, and was named the recipient of the Norris Trophy as the National Hockey League's top defenseman seven times between 1955 and 1962. After Harvey was sold to the New York Rangers in 1961, he played for the team for two seasons and coached for one. In 1967 he played two games for the Detroit Red Wings, and the following year he was persuaded, at the age of 44, to join the St. Louis Blues. He retired in 1969 and was inducted into the Hockey Hall of Fame in 1973.

Haynsworth, Clement Furman, Jr., U.S. judge (b. Oct. 30, 1912, Greenville, S.C.—d. Nov. 23, 1989, Greenville), was quietly serving as a judge in the 4th Circuit Court of Appeals before becoming the centre of controversy in 1969 when Pres. Richard Nixon nominated him to the U.S. Supreme Court. After a bitter fight, Haynsworth's nomination was rejected 55–45 by the Senate. Haynsworth, a fifth-generation lawyer, graduated from Harvard University's School of Law in 1936 and served as a senior partner in the family firm until 1957, when Pres. Dwight D. Eisenhower appointed him to the federal bench. Following his nomination to the Supreme Court, Haynsworth, who had gained a reputation as a hard-working and competent judge, drew fire from labour and civil rights groups. He was also cited for having presided as a judge in several cases in which, arguably, his financial interests were linked to those of the litigants. After his nomination was defeated, Haynsworth returned to the 4th Circuit Court of Appeals; he retired as a senior judge in 1981.

Herrhausen, Alfred, West German banker (b. Jan. 30, 1930, Essen, Germany—d. Nov. 30, 1989, Bad Homburg, West Germany), was chairman of Deutsche Bank, West Germany's largest commercial bank, and was considered the most powerful force in moving that country's economy onto the international stage. Herrhausen launched (1952) his career in industry as an assistant manager with a company in his hometown. After receiving a Ph.D. (1955) from the University of Cologne, he joined the regional utility company in Dortmund, where he distinguished himself by planning its 1966 privatization; he was made financial director the following year. He joined Deutsche Bank as a deputy board member in 1970 and moved up the corporate ladder to become joint chairman (1985) and, in 1988, chairman. A visionary who sought to expand the influence of Deutsche Bank, Herrhausen led it into such ventures as management consultation and real estate; just a few days before his death, Deutsche Bank made a successful bid to acquire the U.K. merchant bank Morgan Grenfell. Herrhausen was considered a key adviser to West German

Chancellor Helmut Kohl, and he served on the boards of such companies as electric utilities, Daimler-Benz, Continental Gummi-werke, and the Xerox Corp. His opinions on easing Third World debt, supporting the economies of emerging Eastern European countries, and reunifying Germany increased his celebrity and reportedly made him a target of terrorists; he and his family lived under heavy security. The small terrorist group known as the Red Army Faction took credit for a remote-controlled bomb, wired to a bicycle parked along the street, that tore open Herrhausen's armoured Mercedes-Benz and killed him as he was being driven to work.

Hicks, Sir John Richard, British economist (b. April 8, 1904, Leamington Spa, Warwickshire, England—d. May 20, 1989, Blockley, Gloucestershire, England), with Kenneth J. Arrow was awarded the Nobel Memorial Prize in Economic Science in 1972 for "pioneering contributions to the general economic equilibrium theory." Hicks and Arrow demonstrated that economic equilibrium is achieved through the interaction of active forces that cancel each other out, rather than through passive cyclical trends. Hicks laid out many of his fundamental economic principles in *Value and Capital* (1939; rev. 1946) and in a 1937 paper on John Maynard Keynes's revolutionary theories, "Keynes and the 'Classics,'" which was often cited as the standard upon which later Keynesian economists based their own work. Hicks, an outspoken critic of monetarism, also had a significant effect on public policy decisions on trade, investments, and welfare. He attended the University of Oxford (B.A., 1927; M.A., 1931) and served on the faculties of the London School of Economics (1926–35) and the Universities of Cambridge (1935–38) and Manchester (1938–46). He returned to Oxford as an official fellow of Nuffield College in 1946. In 1952 Hicks was named a fellow at All Souls College and was elected to Oxford's Drummond Chair of Political Economy, from which he retired in 1965. His other influential books include *The Theory of Wages* (1932), *The Social Framework: An Introduction to Economics* (1942), *Capital and Growth* (1965), *The Crisis in Keynesian Economics* (1974), and *Collected Papers* (3 vol., 1981–83). Hicks was knighted in 1964.

Hillgruber, Andreas, West German historian (b. Jan. 18, 1925, Angerburg, East Prussia—d. May 8, 1989, Cologne, West Germany), provoked a furor with his book *Zweierlei Untergang: Die Zerschlagung des Deutschen Reiches und das Ende des europäischen Judentums* (1986; "Two Kinds of Destruction: The Shattering of the German Reich and the End of European Jewry"), in which he contended that the Holocaust was comparable to other atrocities in modern history. He also argued that the prolonged fighting by the Nazi troops on the Eastern Front at the end of World War II was justified because it allowed German civilians to escape to the West. Hillgruber insisted that he sought only to understand Adolf Hitler's regime within its historical context, but he was widely attacked as an apologist for the Nazis. Hillgruber obtained his Ph.D. (1953) from the University of Göttingen and taught modern and contemporary history at the universities of Marburg (1965–68), Freiburg (1968–72), and Cologne (1972–89). Despite the controversy over *Zweierlei Untergang,* he was highly respected for most of his detailed studies of World War II and the Third Reich, including *Hitlers Strategie, Politik und Kriegführung 1940–41* (1965) and *Der Zweite Weltkrieg 1939–1945* (1982).

Hirohito (MICHINOMIYA HIROHITO), Japanese emperor (b. April 29, 1901, Tokyo, Japan—d. Jan. 7, 1989, Tokyo), reigned from Dec. 25, 1926, to Jan. 7, 1989, as the 124th emperor of Japan during one of the country's most turbulent eras. He presided over Japan's period of expansion into Asia during the 1930s, the Sino-Japanese War, the bombing of Pearl Harbor in 1941, Japan's World War II surrender after

atomic bombs devastated Hiroshima and Nagasaki, and Japan's phenomenal postwar industrial growth, which made it an economic power in the free enterprise world.

Hirohito, born at the Aoyama Palace in Tokyo, was educated at the Peers' School and at the Crown Prince's Institute. He had an abiding interest in marine biology—he had a laboratory constructed on the palace grounds, published authoritative books on this subject, and was a leading expert on jellyfish. In 1921 when he visited Europe, Hirohito became the first Japanese crown prince to travel abroad. Shortly after his return, he was named prince regent when his father, Emperor Taisho, gave up the crown because of mental illness. After his father died on Dec. 25, 1926, Hirohito ascended the Chrysanthemum Throne; his reign was designated Showa, or "bright peace." As was the custom, Hirohito was revered as a god. His subjects never heard his voice until he broke the tradition of Imperial silence and on the radio announced Japan's World War II surrender (Aug. 15, 1945) and bid the Japanese to "endure the unendurable." Although Hirohito took full responsibility for Japan's role in the war, his actual involvement continued to be the subject of debate. Under the new constitution, drafted by U.S. occupation authorities, Japan became a constitutional monarchy. Hirohito renounced his claims to divinity and declared that sovereignty resided in the people. New traditions were established, and Hirohito permitted the publication of pictures and stories of his personal and family life. In 1959 his oldest son, Crown Prince Akihito, broke a 1,500-year tradition when he married Michiko Shoda, a commoner. When he made a 1971 tour of Europe, Hirohito again broke with custom by becoming the first reigning Japanese monarch to visit abroad. In 1975 he made a state visit to the U.S. On Sept. 18, 1988, Hirohito fell seriously ill, and on September 22 the Cabinet asked Crown Prince Akihito, heir to the throne, to assume the emperor's largely ceremonial duties. Two days later the Japanese press reported that Hirohito was suffering from cancer, thus breaking a national taboo against publicly mentioning the disease. Hirohito was the oldest and longest-reigning monarch in the world at the time of his death.

Hoffman, Abbie (ABBOTT HOFFMAN), U.S. political activist (b. Nov. 30, 1936, Worcester, Mass.—d. April 12, 1989, New Hope, Pa.), was a self-styled revolutionary who rose to prominence during the late 1960s with his theatrically staged Vietnam war protests, which he engineered as a founder (1968) of the Youth International Party (the Yippies). He gained his greatest notoriety and a reputation as a radical activist as one of the so-called Chicago Seven, who were charged, arrested, and tried for crossing state lines to incite a riot at the Democratic Party's national convention in Chicago in 1968. Hoffman, who attended Brandeis University and the University of California at Berkeley, was active in the civil rights movement before turning his energies to the peace movement and organizing the Yippies, who were dedicated to protesting the Vietnam war and the U.S. economic and political system. Hoffman became renowned for his successful media events. He gained worldwide attention when he dumped hundreds of dollars on the busy New York Stock Exchange trading floor, and millions of television viewers watched stockbrokers scramble for cash; he encircled the Pentagon in 1967 with 1,200 of his followers in an attempt to levitate the U.S. military headquarters. At his 1969 Chicago Seven trial, he attempted to make a mockery of Judge Julius Hoffman's court by suggesting that the judge was his illegitimate father and by coming to court dressed in a judicial robe. Hoffman was acquitted of conspiracy, but he and four of the other defendants were convicted of crossing state lines with intent to riot; the conviction was later overturned. From 1974 to 1980 Hoffman went underground to avoid charges of selling cocaine. He underwent plastic surgery, lived under the name Barry Freed, and worked as an environmental activist in New York. After resurfacing in 1980 he served a year in prison; he resumed his environmental efforts following his release. He was the author of such books as *Revolution for the Hell of It* (1968), *Steal This Book* (1971), and *The Best of Abbie Hoffman*, which was to be published posthumously.

Hook, Sidney, U.S. philosopher and educator (b. Dec. 20, 1902, New York, N.Y.—d. July 12, 1989, Stanford, Calif.), was a prominent exponent of the philosophy of pragmatism as advocated by John Dewey, his mentor. He was an expert on Marxism and became one of the earliest critics of the regime of terror and totalitarian rule promulgated in the U.S.S.R. by Joseph Stalin. Hook, who worked on his Ph.D. at Columbia University, New York City, under the tutelage of Dewey, taught at New York University (1927–72) until he joined the faculty of Stanford University as senior research fellow. A staunch anti-Communist, Hook denounced Sen. Joseph McCarthy's Communist witch-hunts during the early 1950s. Hook, opposed to all forms of totalitarianism, helped organize the Congress for Cultural Freedom in 1950, which was founded to dilute the concurrent formation of the Communist-sponsored Congress of Partisans for Peace. An influential professor who espoused liberal democracy as the most viable political structure for social and scientific advancements, he illuminated his views in more than 35 books, including *Towards the Understanding of Karl Marx: A Revolutionary Interpretation* (1933), *John Dewey: An Intellectual Portrait* (1939), *Education for Modern Man* (1946; rev. ed. 1963), *Revolution, Reform, and Social Justice* (1975), and an autobiography, *Out of Step: An Unquiet Life in the 20th Century* (1987). Hook was awarded the Presidential Medal of Freedom in 1985.

Horowitz, Vladimir, Russian-born pianist (b. Oct 1 [Sept. 18, old style], 1903, Berdichev, Russia—d. Nov. 5, 1989, New York, N.Y.), was regarded as one of the most spectacular keyboard virtuosos of the 20th century with his intense playing, exquisite interpretations of the music of Romantic composers, and brilliant, flawless technique; he was the highest-paid musician of his era and was renowned for his numerous retirements from the concert stage and his capricious yet legendary returns to stardom. Horowitz entered the Kiev conservatory at age 12 and studied piano and composing. Though he leaned more toward composing, he began giving piano recitals in exchange for food and clothing after his family lost most of their possessions in the Russian Revolution. Horowitz made his concert debut in 1922 in Kharkov and performed 15 times in that city before em-

barking on a series of 23 recitals in Leningrad, where he performed a total of more than 200 works by Liszt, Rachmaninoff, Chopin, Scriabin, Scarlatti, Moszkowski, and Prokofiev. Horowitz could deliver both powerful and delicate performances. In 1933 he married Arturo Toscanini's daughter, Wanda. In 1940 the couple settled in the United States, and in 1944 Horowitz became a U.S. citizen. He electrified audiences when he made his U.S. debut with the New York Philharmonic Orchestra, performing Tchaikovsky's *Piano Concerto No. 1*. Although Horowitz abandoned the concert stage four times (1936–38, 1953–65, 1968–74, and 1983–85), he continued to record; he made his final appearances as a performer in 1987. Known for his dynamic range and stupendous fortissimos, Horowitz was always firmly in control. He was highly temperamental and traveled with his own water-purification machine, insisted on his own cook, and frequently canceled engagements. He was awarded the U.S. Medal of Freedom in 1986.

Howard, Robin Jared Stanley, British dance company founder and administrator (b. May 17, 1924, London, England—d. June 11, London), used his considerable determination and personal finances to establish modern dance in England. Howard, a grandson of Prime Minister Stanley Baldwin and the eldest child of Sir Arthur and Lady Lorna Howard, was educated at Eton and served with the Scots Guard in World War II. In 1945 in The Netherlands he sustained injuries that resulted in the loss of both his legs; he returned to London and then to Trinity College, Cambridge, where he studied law. Though Howard passed the bar examination to become a lawyer, he instead entered the hotel business. In 1956 he formed the Hungarian Department of the United Nations Association in Britain to assist refugees and served (1956–63) as its director of international service. Howard became a full-time patron of modern dance in 1963, beginning with his sponsorship of performances by the Martha Graham Dance Company. He had first encountered the U.S. troupe in 1954, when he transferred his passion for ballet to the new form of dance that had been developed by the charismatic Graham. He persuaded her to return to Britain and appear at the 1963 Edinburgh Festival and in a London engagement. Following the company's successful tour, he established Graham-inspired classes and by 1967 had formed the London Contemporary Dance Group, since renamed London Contemporary Dance Theatre, and the Contemporary Dance Trust, of which he was director general (1966–88) and life president (1988–89). In 1969 Howard founded the Place dance school complex in London. He was created Commander of the Order of the British Empire in 1976.

Hu Yaobang (Hu Yao-pang), Chinese politician (b. 1915, Hunan province, China—d. April 15, 1989, Beijing (Peking), China), as the vibrant chairman of the Communist Party of China (1981–87), was instrumental along with his mentor, Deng Xiaoping (Teng Hsiao-p'ing), in introducing liberal policies that were designed to speed up economic growth in China. Hu, however, was forced to resign in January 1987 when students demanding greater political liberalization appeared to be getting out of control. Hu, a member of the Communist Party by 1933, was a veteran of the Long March (1934–35), serving as political commissar under Deng in the 2nd Field Army during the war against the Nationalists. In 1949 he and Deng led the Communist Army into Sichuan (Szechwan) province, where they remained until 1952. Hu later followed Deng to Beijing, where the latter joined the central government. Hu headed the Young Communist League until he was purged along with Deng at the beginning of the Cultural Revolution (1966–76). After being twice purged and twice rehabilitated, Hu became head of the Communist Party, replacing Hua Guofeng (Hua Kuo-feng), Mao Zedong's (Mao Tse-Tung's) handpicked successor. An effervescent leader who sometimes incensed party hard-liners by advocating Western-style democracy, Hu even suggested that chopsticks be abandoned in favour of knives and forks. When Hu stepped aside under intense pressure in 1987, he retained his seat on the Standing Committee of the Political Bureau but did not play an active role in policy-making. Hu's death sparked widespread demonstrations by students who eulogized him as a symbol of democracy and change.

Hull, Sir Richard Amyatt, British field marshal (b. May 7, 1907, Cosham, Hampshire, England—d. Sept. 17, 1989, Pinhole, Devon, England), achieved a distinguished military career that culminated in his appointment as chief of defense staff (1965), succeeding Lord Mountbatten. During World War II, Hull led the Blade Force in an unsuccessful attempt to capture Tunis before the Germans could do so. In 1944 after his promotion to major general, he was given the command of the 1st Armoured Division in Italy during the Coriano battles. Hull commanded (1954–56) the British troops in Egypt and was responsible for the withdrawal of British forces from the Suez Canal zone. In 1957 as deputy chief of the Imperial General Staff, Hull was credited with shaping the postwar Army. He served (1958–61) as commander in chief of the Far East Land Forces. As chief of the Imperial General Staff (1961–65), Hull deterred an Iraqi attack on Kuwait, ended the "confrontation" between Indonesia and Malaysia, and quelled the East African mutinies. He was educated at Charterhouse and Trinity College, Cambridge, and in 1928 he began his military career in the 17th/21st Lancers as a cavalryman. In 1980 Hull was created a Knight of the Garter.

Huynh Tan Phat, Vietnamese government official (b. 1913, near My Tho, Vietnam—d. Sept. 30, 1989, Ho Chi Minh City, Vietnam), was one of the leading theoreticians of the National Liberation Front (NLF), the guerrilla organization that opposed the U.S.-backed Saigon government until the collapse of South Vietnam in 1975. Phat earned a degree in architecture from Hanoi University and joined (1936) the underground movement that sought to liberate Vietnam from France. During World War II he opposed the Japanese occupation. After the war he joined the Vanguard Youth organization, became secretary-general of the liberal Democratic Party, and joined the Viet Minh, the Communist guerrilla organization formed by Ho Chi Minh to oppose the French. Though he was imprisoned twice during the Indochina War (1946–54), Phat served as director of the Viet Minh's information service. He returned to Saigon (1954) and established an office as an architect; he also remained active in the

Democratic Party. He went underground in 1959 when Vietnamese Pres. Ngo Dinh Diem began to crack down on opposition parties; the next year Phat became chairman of the Saigon-Cho Lon-Gia Dinh Special Zone Central Committee, which opposed the Diem government, and joined the newly formed NLF. He served (1964–66) as secretary general of the NLF's Central Committee, the most powerful position in the organization. From 1969 to 1976 Phat was president of the NLF's Provisional Revolutionary Government; from 1976 to 1982 he was a vice premier on the Council of Ministers. In 1982 he was named a vice president of the Council of State.

LEDRU—SYGMA

Ibárruri Gómez, (Isidora) Dolores, Spanish Communist leader (b. Dec. 9, 1895, Gallarta, Spain—d. Nov. 12, 1989, Madrid, Spain), gained a reputation as a passionate street and radio broadcast orator and, during the Spanish Civil War (1936–39), galvanized resistance to the fascism of Gen. Francisco Franco. One of her most notable broadcasts in 1936 ended with the rallying cry, "No pasarán!" ("They shall not pass"). Ibárruri, one of 11 children of a Basque iron-ore miner, was aware of the disparity between her life and that of wealthy mine owners. She left school at age 15, when lack of money thwarted her hopes of becoming a schoolteacher, and worked as a seamstress and as a housekeeper. She replaced her devotion to Roman Catholicism with the dogma of Marxism-Leninism. In 1918 Ibárruri began to write in a local newspaper for miners, using the name "La Pasionaria"; she joined the local Communist Party (1920) and served as a delegate (1921) to the national congress that founded the Spanish Communist Party (PCE). She became a member (1930) of PCE's Central Committee and was elected (1936) to the Cortes (parliament), where she became a strident critic of the military insurgents. On Radio Madrid (July 19, 1936), she said, "It is better to die on your feet than to live on your knees!" and she appealed to the women of Spain to stop the enemy as their forebears had resisted Napoleon, with knives and burning oil. When Franco's forces won the war (1939), Ibárruri fled Spain. She settled in Moscow, where she became an ardent supporter of most Soviet policies and played major roles in the Spanish Communist Party in exile, as secretary-general (1942–60) and from 1960 as president, a largely honorary post she held until her death. After Franco's death (1975) she returned (1977) to Spain and served (1977–79) as a delegate to the Cortes. In 1962 her autobiography, *El único camino* ("The Only Way"; Eng. trans., *They Shall Not Pass*, 1966) was published. Ibárruri was awarded the Order of Lenin in 1960.

Ignatieff, George, Canadian diplomat (b. Dec. 16, 1913, St. Petersburg, Russia—d. Aug. 10, 1989, Sherbrooke, Que.), as a staunch advocate of arms control, was dubbed "the peacemonger" and enjoyed a sterling diplomatic career under seven prime ministers of Canada. Ignatieff, the son of czarist aristocrats who fled to England after the 1917 Russian Revolution, settled in Canada in 1928. He earned a B.A. in 1935 from Trinity College, University of Toronto, and in the same year was named a Rhodes scholar. At the University of Oxford he earned an M.A. in 1938. Two years later Ignatieff joined Canada's Department of External Affairs and held a variety of posts before serving as a diplomatic adviser to the Canadian delegation to the UN Atomic Energy Commission. During his career Ignatieff was ambassador to Yugoslavia, Canada's permanent representative to the North Atlantic Treaty Organization, and ambassador to the UN; he also held senior posts in both London and Washington. From 1972 to 1979 he served as provost of Trinity College, and in 1980 he became chancellor of the University of Toronto, a post he held until 1986. His memoirs, *The Making of a Peacemonger*, appeared in 1985.

Ivens, Joris (GEORG HENRI ANTON), Dutch motion-picture director (b. Nov. 18, 1898, Nijmegen, Neth.—d. June 28, 1989, Paris, France), filmed more than 50 documentaries that explored both social and political concerns of the 20th-century left and the link between humans and their environment. Ivens, who studied at the Rotterdam (Neth.) School of Economics, served as a field artillery lieutenant in World War I and later studied photochemistry in Germany. He embraced socialist views as a student, as revealed in his autobiography, *The Camera and I* (1969). In 1926 Ivens returned to Amsterdam and joined the family business; he left after receiving acclaim for two early lyrical films, *De Brug* (1928; *The Bridge*) and *Regen* (1929; *Rain*). His success resulted in an invitation in 1930 to lecture in the Soviet Union, where he returned (1932) and made *Komsomol* (*Song of Heroes*), a celebration of the role of Communist youths in constructing a blast furnace. The following year he went to Belgium and filmed *Misère au Borinage* (1933), a powerful depiction of a miners' strike. In Spain (1937) with Ernest Hemingway he made *The Spanish Earth*, an anti-Franco report on the Spanish Civil War, and in China (1938) he produced *The Four Hundred Million*, a report on the Japanese attack on the Chinese. In 1940, at the invitation of the U.S. government, he made *The Power and the Land*, about the New Deal's rural electrification program, followed by *Our Russian Front* (1941). In 1944 he was named film commissioner for the Netherlands West Indies, but he resigned as a protest against Dutch colonialism. His pro-independence film, *Indonesia Calling* (1946), cost him his Dutch passport for 10 years and prompted his move to Eastern Europe, where he made most of his later documentaries. He returned to China to film *How Yukong Moves the Mountain* (1976), a look at ordinary life, and returned again to make *Une Histoire du Vent* (1988; *A Tale of the Wind*), his final film. Ivens received the 1955 World Peace Prize in Helsinki, Fin., numerous awards from film festivals, and in 1986 an award and a formal apology from the Dutch government.

James, C(yril) L(ionel) R(obert), Trinidadian-born cultural historian, cricket writer, and political activist (b. Jan. 4, 1901, Tunapuna, Trinidad—d. May 31, 1989, London, England), was an eloquent exponent of Marxist (notably Trotskyist) philosophy and a leading figure in the international Pan-African movement. James attended Queen's Royal College in Port of Spain, Trinidad, on a special scholarship and was certified as a teacher in 1918. In 1932 he moved to England, where he published *The Life of Captain Cipriani* (1932; revised as *The Case for West-Indian Self-Government*, 1933) with the personal and financial support of the West Indian cricketer and politician Learie (later Lord)

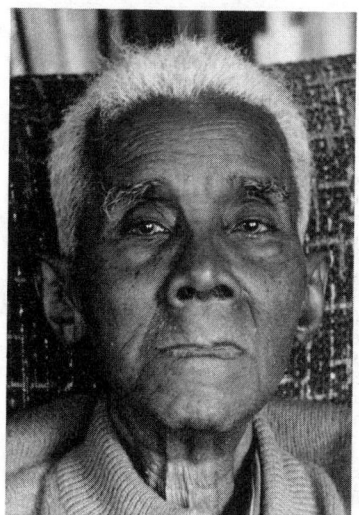

DAVID BROWN—CAMERA PRESS/GLOBE PHOTOS

Constantine. During the 1930s James served as cricket correspondent for the *Guardian* (Manchester) while becoming increasingly involved in Marxist politics and the African and West Indian independence movements. Shortly before leaving Britain for the U.S., he published *The Black Jacobins* (1938), a powerful Marxist study of the Haitian slave revolution of the 1790s that has been acclaimed as one of the outstanding works of history of the 20th century. James was expelled from the U.S. in 1953 (the ban was later lifted). Thereafter he moved between London and Trinidad, where he was secretary of the West Indies Federal Labour Party (1958–60). In 1963 he published *Beyond a Boundary,* a semiautobiographical study of cricket and its central importance to the British character and to the cultural and political development of the West Indies. James's other books include the novel *Minty Alley* (1936); *World Revolution* (1937); *Mariners, Renegades, and Castaways* (1953), an analysis of Herman Melville written while James was interned on Ellis Island; *Notes on Dialectics* (1971); *Nkrumah and the Ghana Revolution* (1977); and *Cricket* (1986), a collection of articles spanning the period 1935–85.

Jeffreys, Sir Harold, British scientist (b. April 22, 1891, Fatfield, Durham, England—d. March 18, 1989), made substantial contributions in the fields of geophysics, astronomy, and meteorology but was perhaps best known to the general public as a leading opponent of the theory of continental drift. Jeffreys studied at Armstrong College, Newcastle-upon-Tyne (B.S., 1910; D.Sc., 1917), and the University of Cambridge (B.A., 1913; M.A., 1917), where he was elected a fellow at St. John's College in 1914. After working in the Meteorological Office (1917–22), he served on the Cambridge faculty as a lecturer in mathematics (1923–32), a reader in geophysics (1932–46), and Plumian professor of astronomy and experimental philosophy (1946–58). Jeffreys' early research into seismology and the thermal history of the Earth led him to offer the first scientific hypothesis that the Earth's core is fluid, and in 1940 he coauthored the standard tables of travel times for earthquake waves. Jeffreys, who later applied his research to a study of the origin of the solar system, analyzed the long-term effects of tidal friction on planetary shape and devised models for the physical structure of Jupiter, Saturn, Uranus, and Neptune. He also did significant work on atmospheric circulation and on mathematical probabilities. His principal books include *The Earth: Its Origin, History and Physical Constitution* (1924; frequently revised), *Scientific Inference* (1931), *Earthquakes and Mountains* (1935), *Theory of Probability* (1939), and the six-volume *Collected Papers of Sir Harold Jeffreys* (1971–77). Jeffreys was knighted in 1953.

Johnson, Judy (WILLIAM JULIUS JOHNSON), U.S. baseball player (b. Oct. 26, 1899—d. June 14, 1989, Wilmington, Del.), was an outstanding third baseman and powerful line-drive hitter who batted over .300 during seven seasons with the Negro leagues. Johnson reached the peak of his career in 1929, when he batted .416; at the time, blacks were barred from playing in the major leagues. His extraordinary abilities were recognized in 1975 when he became the sixth black player to be elected to the Baseball Hall of Fame from the Negro leagues. After retiring as a player in 1937, ten years before the colour barrier was broken, Johnson worked for the Continental Can Co. before securing a major league job in 1954 as a baseball coach and scout for the Philadelphia Athletics. He later served as a scout for the Milwaukee Braves and for the Philadelphia Phillies.

Jorgensen, Christine, U.S. personality (b. May 30, 1926, New York, N.Y.—d. May 3, 1989, San Clemente, Calif.), captured international headlines in 1952 as the first person to undergo a successful sex-change operation. Jorgensen, born George Jorgensen, Jr., underwent surgery in Denmark after undergoing extensive psychotherapy and a series of hormone injections; on growing up, Jorgensen had become tormented by feelings of being a woman trapped in a man's body. Following the surgery she became an instant celebrity and lived comfortably on the proceeds from her lecture and nightclub circuit and from royalties from her 1967 book, *Christine Jorgensen: A Personal Biography.* Jorgensen, who never married, battled for two years against cancer, which was first detected in her bladder.

Kadar, Janos (JANOS CZERMANIK or CSERMANEK), Hungarian politician (b. May 26, 1912, Fiume, Hung. [now Rijeka, Yugos.]—d. July 6, 1989, Budapest, Hung.), rose to power during the Soviet suppression of the 1956 Hungarian uprising, but as premier (1956–58; 1961–65) and first secretary (1956–88) of the Communist Party, he presided over a prolonged period of political tolerance and economic prosperity. Kadar joined the then-outlawed Communist Party in 1931 and over the next four years was repeatedly arrested and jailed. During World War II he took the nom de guerre of Kadar for his work in the Hungarian resistance. He joined the Communist Party's Central Committee in 1942, and after the war he was elected (1945) to the Provisional National Assembly and held several government posts, including minister of internal affairs (1948–50). In 1951 Kadar was expelled from the party, imprisoned, and allegedly tortured. He was rehabilitated in 1954 and entered Prime Minster Imre Nagy's reformist Cabinet. Although Kadar appeared to support Nagy's liberal policies, on Nov. 4, 1956,

CAMERA PRESS/GLOBE PHOTOS

he denounced Hungary's withdrawal from the Warsaw Pact and, with Soviet support, took control of the government. Kadar instituted severe repressive measures under which Nagy was tried and executed (1958). By the early 1960s Kadar had begun to implement the "goulash Communism" that brought Hungary improved relations with the West, a measure of free enterprise, a rising standard of living, and relative freedom from Soviet intervention. The Hungarian economy stagnated in the 1980s, however, and in 1988 Kadar was shifted to the ceremonial post of party president. He was removed from that post and from the Central Committee shortly before his death.

Karajan, Herbert von, Austrian-born conductor (b. April 5, 1908, Salzburg, Austria—d. July 16, 1989, Anif, Austria), reigned supreme as principal conductor of the renowned Berlin Philharmonic Orchestra for 34 years (1955–89). Although he was celebrated as one of the premier conductors of the 20th century, Karajan's imperious manner, exacting perfectionism, and alleged Nazi sympathies frequently made him the centre of controversy. Karajan was a child prodigy and studied piano at the Salzburg Mozarteum and conducting at the Vienna Academy of Music and Drama. His professional debut in Ulm, Germany, led to his

CAMERA PRESS/GLOBE PHOTOS

appointment in 1929 as director of the Ulm municipal opera. He later conducted in Aachen, Germany (1935–41), and at the Berlin State Opera (1938–44). In 1946 Karajan, a former member (1933–42) of the Nazi Party, overcame a postwar prohibition and regained the podium at the Vienna Philharmonic and the London Philharmonia. He soon became principal conductor for the Vienna State Opera (director, 1956–64) and the Salzburg Festival (artistic director, 1956–60), as well as a leading guest conductor at La Scala in Milan, the New York Philharmonic, and L'Orchestre de Paris (director, 1969–70). He was named conductor for life of the Berlin Philharmonic in 1955, and in 1967 he founded the Salzburg Easter Festival. Karajan's U.S. debut (1955) provoked anti-Nazi protests, and the U.S. Justice Department admitted in 1989 that it was investigating his Nazi affiliations. Karajan was almost as well known for his demanding recording schedule as for his concert work, with more than 800 recordings, including some of the earliest long-playing discs and three recordings of the complete Beethoven symphonies. After a series of disputes in the 1980s that strained relations between the conductor and the members of the orchestra, Karajan resigned from the Berlin Philharmonic in April 1989 because of failing health. At the time of his death, however, he was conducting rehearsals at the Salzburg Festival.

Kaslik, Vaclav, Czechoslovak composer and conductor (b. Sept. 28, 1917, Policna, Czech.— d. June 4, 1989, Prague, Czech.), produced operas—his own and those of others—that featured live singers with often unorthodox sets and combinations of film, still projections, moving screens, and other theatrical techniques on European stages and on television. Kaslik studied at Charles University, Prague, the Prague Conservatory (1940), and the Conductors' Master School, Prague. He made his conducting debut (1940) in Prague and his operatic debut (1941) as producer and conductor of *Orfeo ed Euridice* in Brno. He served as assistant director (1941–43) of the National Theatre of Prague, and in 1945 he founded the opera ensemble (1945–48) of the Opera of May 5th (later renamed the Smetana Theatre) in Prague. He was (1952) conductor there before becoming (1961) chief opera director and later opera director of the National Theater. His collaborators were the designer Josef Svoboda and, on occasion, Alfred Radok. Kaslik's best-known opera was *Krakatit* (1960), which had an electronic score that combined orchestral, jazz, and popular music with a text exploring the positive and negative aspects of the use of atomic energy. His compositions embraced sound patterns he had heard in Moravian folk music when he was a child; his keen instincts for innovative touches were noted in a 1988 Kaslik-Svoboda production of *Don Giovanni* at the Prague Spring Festival.

Kateb, Yacine, Algerian writer (b. Aug. 6, 1929, Constantine, Alg.—d. Oct. 28, 1989, Grenoble, France), with his first novel, *Nedjma* (1956), broke from traditional storytelling and created a highly stylized, richly textured epic of intraclan conflict played against the violence and disunity of Algeria under French colonial rule. The work earned Kateb a place as one of North Africa's most respected literary figures. Kateb was educated in French colonial schools until May 8, 1945, when he was arrested in Setif with other young Algerians during the bloody suppression of an uprising. Though his formal education ended then, the event provided Kateb with material he would use as a writer. He published a volume of poems, *Soliloques* (1946), and worked as a reporter (1948–50) for *Alger Republicain* before traveling to Central Asia, Italy, and then West Germany. At the outbreak of the Algerian War in 1954, he joined the National Algerian Liberation Front (FNLA) and wrote from Europe about the conflict. Kateb's play about the French occupation, *Le Cadavre encerclé* (1955), was banned in France but staged in Brussels. He wrote another novel, *Le Polygone étoilé* (1966), but was better known for such plays as *L'Homme aux sandales de caoutchouc* (*The Man in the Rubber Sandals,* 1970) and *Mohammed prends ta valise* (*Mohammed, Get Your Suitcase,* 1971). Kateb returned to Algeria in the early 1970s and formed a popular theatre troupe that carried his messages to towns and villages.

Keogh, Eugene James, U.S. politician (b. Aug. 30, 1907, New York, N.Y.—d. May 26, 1989, New York), was a member of the U.S. House of Representatives from 1936 to 1966 and was the chief architect of the Keogh-Smathers bill. That bill, enacted in 1962, became the Self-Employed Individual Tax Retirement Act; it permitted professional and other self-employed persons to defer taxes on contributions to pension plans until the money was withdrawn at retirement. After earning a law degree from Fordham University, Bronx, N.Y., in 1930, Keogh practiced law before serving briefly in 1936 in the New York Assembly. As a Democratic congressman representing Brooklyn, he became a member of the influential Ways and Means Committee and was instrumental in drafting Medicare legislation. After leaving the House in 1966, Keogh returned to full-time legal practice.

Khaled, Sheikh Hassan, Lebanese religious leader (b. 1921, Beirut, Lebanon—d. May 16, 1989, Beirut), was the grand mufti (supreme Islamic legal authority) of Lebanon—the spiritual leader of the Sunni Muslim community—and a leading advocate of a peaceful solution to the crisis in Lebanon. Sheikh Khaled studied Shari'ah (Islamic law) at al-Makassed College and graduated (1949) from al-Azhar University, Cairo. He worked as a law clerk, lectured in logic at al-Makassed, and later served as a judge in the Shari'ah courts at Akkar and Mount Lebanon. After his election as mufti in 1966, Sheikh Khaled represented the religious and political interests of Lebanon's Sunni minority. Although he was considered a maverick at first, from the mid-1970s he sought to reunify the country and was an outspoken supporter of the Arab League's mediation efforts in the civil war. Sheikh Khaled's scholarly books include *Social Solidarity in Islam* and *Logic and Unicity.* He died when a car bomb was detonated as the motorcade in which he was riding passed by.

Khomeini, Ruhollah (Ruhollah Musawi), Iranian cleric (b. May 17, 1900?, Khomeyn, Iran— d. June 3, 1989, Tehran, Iran), as supreme spiritual leader of the Iranian Shi'ite Muslim community, spearheaded the 1979 overthrow of Mohammad Reza Shah Pahlavi and the subsequent establishment of the Islamic republic of Iran. Khomeini's unyielding demand for a return to Islamic religious purity and his steadfast rejection of westernization made him adored by his supporters and vilified by his opponents. In the early 1920s he settled in the Shi'ite holy city of Qom, where he completed his clerical studies, taught theology, wrote on Islamic philosophy and ethics, and took the name Khomeini. After the shah came to power in 1941, Khomeini gained prominence as a leading critic of the shah's modernization programs. In the 1950s Khomeini was acclaimed as an ayatollah, or major religious leader, and by the 1960s he had been elevated to grand ayatollah. In 1963 he was arrested for promoting rebellion, and after a year of internment and house arrest, he was exiled from Iran. He waged a vehement campaign against the shah from an-Najaf, Iraq, until he was expelled (1978) and then from Paris. Khomeini's writings and tape-recorded speeches calling for an Islamic revolution aroused fanatical support in Iran, especially among the poor. Massive civil unrest finally drove the ailing shah into exile, and on Feb. 1, 1979, Khomeini made his triumphant return to Iran. By the end of the year he had established a constitutional theocracy, largely controlled by Shi'ite clerics, with himself as final arbiter. All opposition to the regime was fiercely suppressed, and it was widely rumoured that tens of thousands of opponents were imprisoned or executed. Khomeini condemned both the U.S. and the U.S.S.R. as evil, but his avowed hatred of the U.S. showed its greatest impact when fundamentalist students seized the U.S. embassy in Tehran

JACQUES HAILLOT—CAMERA PRESS/GLOBE PHOTOS

on Nov. 4, 1979, and held the staff hostage for 444 days. After Iran was attacked by Iraqi forces in 1980, Khomeini devoted Iran's declining resources to fighting a prolonged war; he finally accepted a cease-fire in 1988, although subsequent peace talks made little progress. In February 1989, amid Western speculation that his health was failing, Khomeini regained the world stage when he denounced British novelist Salman Rushdie's book *The Satanic Verses* as blasphemous and exhorted devout Muslims to execute Rushdie and his publishers.

Kirkwood, James, U.S. librettist, actor, author, and playwright (b. Aug. 22, 1924, Los Angeles, Calif.—d. April 21, 1989, New York, N.Y.), together with Nicholas Dante wrote the book for the smash Broadway musical *A Chorus Line,* which premiered in 1975, was performed for a record 3,389th time in 1983, and continued to reign in 1989 as the longest-running musical in the history of Broadway. As the son of silent film stars Lila Lee and James Kirkwood, he followed his parents into show business, appearing on Broadway in *Junior Miss, Small Wonder,* and *Welcome Darlings* and in such films as *Mommie Dearest; Oh God, Book II;* and *The Supernaturals.* It was for *A Chorus Line,* however, that Kirkwood won acclaim; in 1976 he won both a Tony award and a Pulitzer Prize for the sensational story revealing the life stories of dancers auditioning for a Broadway musical. Kirkwood also wrote such plays as *Unhealthy to Be Unpleasant* (1966) and the comedy *Legends,* which toured the U.S. in 1986 and 1987. Among his books were *Hit Me with a Rainbow; Good Times-Bad Times; P.S. Your Cat Is Dead!,* which was adapted for the stage; and *There Must Be a Pony!,* which was adapted as a television movie in 1986 and starred Elizabeth Taylor. Kirkwood was also part of a comedy-satire team known as Jim Kirkwood and Lee Goodman; the two performed in nightclubs and on radio for several years.

Kirst, Hans Helmut, West German novelist (b. Dec. 5, 1914, Osterode, East Prussia—d. Feb. 23, 1989, Bremen, West Germany), wrote more than 40 popular novels, the most highly regarded of which conveyed—within a well-wrought political thriller or military satire—a sense of collective guilt over German complacency under Nazism. Although Kirst's novels were translated into more than two dozen languages, he was best known outside of West Germany for *Die Nacht der Generale* (1962; *The Night of the Generals,* 1963), which was made into a successful Hollywood motion picture in 1967. Kirst served (1933–45) in the German Army, rising to the rank of first lieutenant during World War II. After being disillusioned by his military experiences, he turned to fiction in 1950 with the anti-Nazi novel *Wir nannten ihn Galgenstrick* (*The Lieutenant Must Be Mad,* 1951). Kirst gained international acclaim with the witty satiric trilogy *Null-acht fünfzehn* (1954–55; *Zero Eight Fifteen,* 1955–57), the continuing story of an army private, Gunner Asch, and his personal battle with the absurdities of the German military system. Kirst's popularity faded somewhat in the 1970s.

Laing, R(onald) D(avid), British psychiatrist (b. Oct. 7, 1927, Glasgow, Scotland—d. Aug. 23, 1989, St. Tropez, France), polarized the mental health community with his first book, *The Divided Self* (1960), in which he theorized that schizophrenia might be a rational defensive reaction to unbearable pressures from family members and inappropriate psychiatric treatment. Laing rejected the prevailing theory that the symptoms characteristic of schizophrenia arose from genetic or biochemical causes and denounced the use of drugs, lobotomies, and electroshock therapy, then commonly prescribed for schizophrenics. After graduating (1951) in medicine from the University of Glasgow, Laing served (1951–53) as a British army psychiatrist. He taught (1953–56) at the University of Glasgow, trained in psychoanalysis, and conducted

research (1956–60) at the Tavistock Clinic in London. He then put his unorthodox theories into practice as an associate of the Tavistock Institute (1960–89), director of the Langham Clinic (1962–65), chairman of the Philadelphia Association (1964–82), and founding director of Kingsley Hall, an experimental community house in London. Laing's approach to madness as a form of individual free expression, combined with a series of well-publicized experiments in the therapeutic use of mescaline and LSD, earned him cult status in the antipsychiatry movement of the 1960s. He modified his theories somewhat in his later books, which included *Sanity, Madness and the Family* (1965), *The Politics of Experience* (1967), *The Politics of the Family* (1971), and the autobiographical *Wisdom, Madness and Folly: The Making of a Psychiatrist* (1985).

Laroche, Guy, French couturier (b. July 16, 1921, La Rochelle, France—d. Feb. 17, 1989, Paris, France), designed consistently elegant, flattering fashions that were widely admired for their superb cut and moderate prices. From 1949 Laroche trained under the Paris designer Jean Dessès and studied production and marketing techniques in the New York City garment district. In 1957 he showed his first solo collection in Paris, and four years later he opened a boutique for a new ready-to-wear line, which was an immediate sensation. In 1966 he launched a line of menswear and the first of many successful perfumes. Although Laroche stopped personally designing the ready-to-wear clothing in the 1970s to concentrate on haute couture, by the late 1980s his fashion empire included some 250 boutiques worldwide. In 1985 he received the coveted Golden Thimble, awarded by the international fashion press to the best Paris collection of the season; he received this award for the second time only three weeks before his death. In 1987 Laroche was made a Chevalier of the Legion of Honour.

Lattimore, Owen, U.S. scholar (b. July 29, 1900, Washington, D.C.—d. May 31, 1989, Providence, R.I.), as a renowned sinologist lived and traveled extensively throughout Manchuria, Mongolia, and the Chinese autonomous regions of Xinjiang (Sinkiang) and Inner Mongolia. He was fluent in the three main languages (Chinese, Russian, and Mongol) of those regions and penned a treasury of books on his experiences. Lattimore, who spent most of his childhood in China, received formal education in Europe beginning at the age of 12 but did not attend college. Instead he returned to China and briefly worked as a clerk in an import-export firm before embarking on a journey into Mongolia. He conducted research on the area at Harvard University from 1928 to 1929 and in Beijing (Peking) from 1930 to 1933. In 1938 he became a lecturer at Johns Hopkins University, Baltimore, Md. Returning to China, Lattimore served (1941–42) as Chinese Nationalist leader Chiang Kai-shek's personal American adviser. After returning (1943) to the U.S., he became deputy director of Pacific operations for the Office of War Information, and the following year he returned to Johns Hopkins. After the 1949 Communist takeover in China, Lattimore was accused in 1950 by Sen. Joseph McCarthy, then embarking on his anti-Communist crusade, of being "the top Soviet espionage agent in the United States." By 1958, after a lengthy investigation, Lattimore had been completely exonerated of all charges. At Johns Hopkins he was a lecturer until 1963 and also served as director (1939–53) of the university's Walter Hines Page School of International Relations. From 1963 until his retirement in 1975, Lattimore headed the department of Chinese studies at Leeds (England) University. His books include *The Desert Road to Turkestan* (1928), *Manchuria, Cradle of Conflict* (1932), *The Making of Modern China: A Short History* (with Eleanor Lattimore, 1944; rev. ed. 1947, *China: A Short History*), and *Ordeal by Slander* (1950), which recounted parts of the McCarthy episode.

Leach, Sir Edmund Ronald, British anthropologist (b. Nov. 7, 1910, Sidmouth, Devon, England—d. Jan. 6, 1989), was a leading figure in the development of cultural anthropology and an early champion of Claude Lévi-Strauss and structuralism (the analysis of cultures through the underlying structural relations of their elements). Leach graduated in engineering from the University of Cambridge in 1932. He was introduced to anthropology while working for a commercial firm in China, and on his return to England in 1937 he studied anthropology at the London School of Economics (LSE) under Bronisław Malinowski and Raymond Firth. At the outbreak of World War II, Leach was doing field research among the Kachin people in Burma, where he remained as a translator and intelligence worker in the British Burmese Army until 1945. In *Political Systems of Highland Burma* (1954), Leach incorporated his practical wartime experiences among the Kachin and his study of their history. Although this work was criticized for its lack of ethnographic data, it was highly influential, as were his later ethnographic studies on the peoples of Borneo and Ceylon (Sri Lanka) and his research on patterns of communication, notably the use of animal names in curses and insults. Leach taught social anthropology at LSE (1947–53) and Cambridge (1953–78). As provost of King's College, Cambridge (1966–79), he was instrumental in the admission of women students. His other important books include *Rethinking Anthropology* (1961), *Culture and Communication* (1976), and *Structuralist Interpretations of Biblical Myth* (1983). Leach was knighted in 1975.

Leone, Sergio, Italian motion-picture director (b. Jan. 3, 1929, Rome, Italy—d. April 30, 1989, Rome), injected new life into the Hollywood western as the creator of the "spaghetti westerns," low-budget, violence-packed cowboy films that were produced primarily in Italy. Leone, the son of Vincenzo Leone, a noted Roman director of silent motion pictures, launched his own career as an assistant to Vittorio De Sica when the classic *The Bicycle Thief* was made in 1948. During Hollywood's fascination in the 1950s with pseudoclassic, pseudobiblical "spear-and-sandal" epics, Leone worked in Rome with such American directors as William Wyler, Fred Zinnemann, and Mervyn LeRoy. In 1961 Leone made his debut as director with *The Colossus of Rhodes.* He made his fame and fortune, however, in 1964 with *A Fistful of Dollars,* a moody, violent film that both revived and parodied the American western genre. It was based on Akira Kurosawa's samurai film *Yojimbo* (1961). Leone used dramatic camera techniques, distinctive music, and often violent action to express the American male psyche. His mysterious, brooding gunman ready to exact frontier-style justice made Clint Eastwood, a little-known television performer, an international star in *Fistful* and its two sequels, *For a Few Dollars More* (1965) and *The Good, the Bad and the Ugly* (1966). Leone also directed *Once Upon a Time in the West* (1968), *Duck, You Sucker* (1972), and *Once Upon a Time in America* (1984). At the time of his death, he was planning a film, coproduced by the Soviet Union, about the German siege of Leningrad during World War II.

Liepa, Maris-Rudolf Eduardovich, Soviet ballet dancer (b. July 27, 1936, Riga, Latvia—d. March 25, 1989, Moscow, U.S.S.R.), as a principal dancer (1960–81) with the Bolshoi Ballet, charmed audiences with his elegant technique, good looks, and superb acting ability. Liepa studied in Riga and at the Bolshoi ballet school. He performed with the Riga Ballet (1955–56) and the Stanislavsky and Nemirovich-Danchenko Music Theatre (1956–60) before joining the Bolshoi. Liepa danced the romantic leading roles in such classical ballets as *Swan Lake, Sleeping Beauty, Don Quixote,* and *Giselle,* as well as in his own 1967 revival of *Le Spectre de la rose.* He was most admired, however, for his portrayal of the evil Crassus in a 1968 production

of Aram Khachaturian's *Spartacus,* and in 1970 he received the Lenin Prize for his stunning interpretation of the role. Later in his career Liepa acted in dramatic parts in motion pictures and on television. He also taught at the Moscow Choreographic School from 1963, wrote several books on dance, and directed the Bulgarian National Ballet. Liepa was made a People's Artist of the Latvian Republic in 1969 and a Merited Artist of the R.S.F.S.R. in 1976.

Lillie, Beatrice Gladys, Canadian-born actress (b. May 29, 1894, Toronto, Ont.—d. Jan. 20, 1989, Henley-on-Thames, England), was a natural comedienne who delighted stage and film audiences in North America and Britain for more than 50 years with her accomplished delivery of double entendres and barbed ripostes punctuated by flourishes of a long cigarette holder. Lillie's irrepressible humour, best suited to stage performances, was accentuated by her marvelous sense of timing as she arched an eyebrow, turned her longish face into a variety of shapes, twitched her nose, or turned a phrase in a such a way that audiences roared with laughter. Brooks Atkinson declared her the funniest woman in the world. Though she began her career as a serious singer in a trio with her mother and sister, her comic talents soon became apparent. She made her London stage debut in the 1914 revue *Not Likely* and made her Broadway bow in *Charlot's Revue of 1924.* In 1920 she married Sir Robert Peel and thus was formally addressed as Lady Peel, though she continued her career of skewering conventional behaviour. She became friends with such personalities as Winston Churchill, George Bernard Shaw, Charlie Chaplin, and Noël Coward. Onstage in the U.S. she shone in *This Year of Grace* (1928); *Third Little Show* (1931), in which she introduced the famous song "Mad Dogs and Englishmen"; and *At Home Abroad* (1935), in which her slightly tipsy character mangled an order for "two dozen double damask dinner napkins." During World War II Lillie spent much time entertaining the troops in the Mediterranean, Africa, the Middle East, and Germany. Her only son, Robert, an enlisted man in the Royal Navy, was killed in a Japanese air raid in 1942. After the war she returned to the U.S. and appeared onstage in *Seven Lively Arts* (1944) and *Inside U.S.A.* (1948) before showcasing her favourite routines in *An Evening with Beatrice Lillie* (1952), a performance that earned her a Tony award. Her last stage appearance was as Madame Arcati, the medium, in *High Spirits* (1964), a musical version of *Blithe Spirit.* Lillie's film credits include *Exit Smiling* (1926), *Around the World in 80 Days* (1956), and *Thoroughly Modern Millie* (1967). Her autobiography, *Every Other Inch a Lady,* was published in 1972.

Lorenz, Konrad Zacharias, Austrian zoologist (b. Nov. 7, 1903, Vienna, Austria—d. Feb. 27, 1989, Altenburg, Austria), along with Nikolaas Tinbergen and Karl von Frisch, was awarded the 1973 Nobel Prize for Physiology or Medicine for the advancement of the science of ethology, the study of animal behavioral patterns. Lorenz was particularly notable for his research into imprinting; he demonstrated that goslings and ducklings would learn to follow almost any conspicuous, moving object if it were presented with the appropriate stimuli during their first days after hatching and that the model established by imprinting would affect the birds' adult behaviour. Lorenz studied medicine at Columbia University, New York City (1922–23), before returning to Vienna to study medicine (M.D., 1928) and zoology (Ph.D., 1933). His first paper, on jackdaw behaviour, was published (1927) in a prestigious ornithology journal while he was still a student. Lorenz was a lecturer in comparative anatomy and animal psychology at the University of Vienna from 1937 until 1940, when he was chosen to head the new institute of comparative psychology at the University of Königsberg. He served as an army physician from 1941, but he was captured in 1944

HORST TAPPE

and interned by the Soviets. After his release in 1948, Lorenz directed Max Planck institutes for behavioral physiology in Altenberg, Austria (1949–51), Buldern, West Germany (1951–54), and Seewiesen, West Germany (1955–73). In 1973 he was named chairman of the department of animal sociology at the Austrian Academy of Sciences' Institute for Comparative Ethology in Altenberg. In perhaps his most controversial book, *Das sogenannte Böse* (1963; *On Aggression,* 1966), Lorenz extended his behavioral theories to explain human aggression as an innate drive. His other influential books include *Er redete mit dem Vieh, den Vögeln und den Fischen* (1949; *King Solomon's Ring,* 1952), *So kam der Mensch auf den Hund* (1950; *Man Meets Dog,* 1954), and *Das Jahr des Graugans* (1979; *The Year of the Greylag Goose,* 1980).

McAnally, Ray, Irish actor (b. March 30, 1926, Buncrana, County Donegal, Ireland—d. June 15, 1989, Ballinagore, County Wicklow, Ireland), was a fixture at Dublin's renowned Abbey Theatre, where he appeared in more than 150 plays between 1947 and 1963. He later reached a broader audience through his work with the Royal Shakespeare Company and in British motion pictures and television. A versatile character actor, McAnally was equally adept at portraying the cultured papal envoy in the film *The Mission* (1986), the tough Protestant work boss in the movie *Cal* (1984), the roguish Rick Pym in the 1987 television adaptation of John Le Carré's *A Perfect Spy,* and the charismatic Yorkshire steelworker elected prime minister in the miniseries *A Very British Coup* (1988). In 1987 McAnally achieved his own coup when he won the *Evening Standard*'s best actor award for his performances in both *The Mission* and the comedy *No Surrender.*

McCarthy, Mary Therese, U.S. novelist and critic (b. June 21, 1912, Seattle, Wash.—d. Oct. 25, 1989, New York, N.Y.), used her caustic wit to deliver sharp-tongued book reviews for the *Nation* and the *New Republic* and drew heavily on her own experiences to write novels that explored the social mores of intellectuals, marriage, sexual freedom, radicalism, the Vietnam war, and the role of women in contemporary urban America. Orphaned at the age of six, McCarthy was subjected to Dickensianlike cruelty while living with her great aunt in Minneapolis, Minn.; she recounted her ordeal in *Memories of a Catholic Girl* (1957), which came to be regarded as a landmark in autobiographical writing. When she was 11 years old, her maternal grandfather rescued her. McCarthy was educated at the Forest Ridge Convent in Seattle and at the fashionable Annie Wright Seminary in Tacoma, Wash.; she later chronicled these years in *How I Grew* (1988). After graduating from Vassar College, Poughkeepsie,

N.Y., in 1933, McCarthy served (1937–48) on the editorial board of the *Partisan Review.* She married four times, the second time to critic Edmund Wilson, who encouraged her to write fiction. McCarthy published such novels as *The Company She Keeps* (1942), *The Oasis* (1949), *The Groves of Academe* (1952), and *A Charmed Life* (1955) before gaining renown with the bestselling *The Group* (1963), a spicy story about eight Vassar graduates; the novel was made into

JERRY BAUER

a 1966 motion picture. Some of her later works included *Birds of America* (1971), *The Seventeenth Degree* (1974), *The Mask of State* (1974), and *Cannibals and Missionaries* (1979). As one of the lions of American literature, McCarthy was the recipient in 1984 of both the Edward MacDowell Medal and the National Medal for Literature. Her long-standing literary feud with Lillian Hellman was fueled by McCarthy's charges on national television that "everything she writes is a lie, including 'and' and 'the.'" Hellman, who filed a libel suit, died in 1984, before the case could come to trial.

McCloy, John Jay, U.S. lawyer and diplomat (b. March 31, 1895, Philadelphia, Pa.—d. March 11, 1989, Stamford, Conn.), was a trusted adviser to U.S. presidents from Franklin D. Roosevelt to Ronald Reagan and was a skilled administrator who was dubbed the "unofficial chairman of the Establishment" because of his longtime government service, which spanned some 60 years. In his most visible post as the U.S. high commissioner in postwar West Germany (1949–52), McCloy was instrumental in creating a civilian government following a fouryear military rule and in overseeing the contractual agreements that ended the U.S. occupation in 1955. A lawyer by profession, he established his reputation as a legal wizard when he proved that German secret agents were responsible for exploding (1916) a munitions factory in Hoboken, N.J., in order to prevent munitions from reaching the Allies during World War I; the case was settled in 1939. As assistant secretary of war (1941–45), McCloy helped to secure congressional approval of the Lend-Lease Act and oversaw the internment of Japanese-Americans following the bombing of Pearl Harbor. McCloy was also privy to the knowledge that the U.S. intended to drop an atomic bomb on Hiroshima to end World War II; he felt that the Japanese should have received an advance warning. McCloy later served as president of the World Bank (1947–49), chairman of the Chase Manhattan Bank (1953–60), chairman of the Ford Foundation (1958–65), and chief disarmament adviser to Pres. John F. Kennedy (1961). In 1979 he advised Pres. Jimmy Carter to admit the Shah of Iran into the U.S. for medical treatment, a move that sparked the Tehran hostage crisis. His one disappointment was the slow pace of arms control.

MacColl, Ewan (JAMES HENRY MILLER), British singer, composer, and playwright (b. Jan. 25, 1915, Auchterarder, Scotland—d. Oct. 22, 1989, London, England), helped to revive British folk music after World War II by incorporating in his performances some of the best folk and industrial workers' music of the U.S. MacColl's music and plays consistently honoured trade unionism and efforts to ban nuclear wars and end apartheid. Though MacColl joined the Communist Party at the age of 14, he abandoned the party during the 1960s. MacColl's father, William Miller, by trade an ironworker and agitator, was also a folksinger; so was his mother, Betsey, with whom MacColl later recorded traditional Gaelic music. MacColl began to write political songs as a youth; he quit school at 15 and worked in a wire mill until the firm went bankrupt. During the early 1930s he became active in theatre with a street group called the Red Megaphones. In 1934, with Joan Littlewood, he cofounded the Theatre Workshop, which performed MacColl's plays as well as classics. In 1953 he began to research and record traditional singers for the BBC's archives; he also ran small clubs in which he introduced British and American singers. Among them was Peggy Seeger, whom he later married; she was the sister of Pete Seeger and the daughter of folksingers who had documented Appalachian songs. With her, MacColl published a book, *Travellers' Songs from England and Scotland* (1978). Beginning in 1958 the two collaborated on compositions for BBC documentaries called "Radio Ballads." Though he shunned commercialism and was known for hard-edged, often bleak songs such as "Never Again!" and "Dirty Old Town," one of MacColl's compositions, written for his wife, became internationally popular after it was recorded (1972) by Roberta Flack—"The First Time Ever I Saw Your Face."

Magnuson, Warren Grant, U.S. politician (b. April 12, 1905, Moorhead, Minn.—d. May 20, 1989, Seattle, Wash.), as a six-term (1944–80) Democratic senator from Washington, wielded considerable power as chairman of the Appropriations Committee. He was a champion of legislation on health policy and safety standards and was instrumental in securing funds for water and public power projects. "Maggie," as he was known to his constituents and friends, earned a law degree from the University of Washington in 1929, served in the state legislature (1933–34), and was a special prosecuting attorney in Seattle for King county (1934–36). He served in the U.S. House of Representatives (1937–44) before his election to the Senate. During his term in office, Magnuson was also a ranking member on the powerful Commerce Committee. He lost his bid for reelection in 1980.

Malula, Joseph-Albert Cardinal, Zairian prelate of the Roman Catholic Church (b. Dec. 17, 1917, Léopoldville, Belgian Congo [now Kinshasa, Zaire]—d. June 14, 1989, Louvain, Belgium), sought a synthesis of Christian and African elements in the church, but he clashed with Pres. Mobutu Sese Seko when Mobutu, in a wide-reaching dewesternization program, demanded that all Zairian children be given local African names at the time of their baptism. Cardinal Malula rejected the use of nonChristian names, as well as the planned restrictions on religious education in Zaire, and in January 1972 the government confiscated the cardinal's official residence. Malula fled to exile in Rome, where he remained for five months, until Mobutu relented under pressure from the Vatican. Malula, who was ordained in 1946, was named archbishop of Kinshasa in 1964 and was elevated to cardinal in 1969. He frequently called for greater cultural pluralism in the church and antagonized many other Roman Catholic leaders by his incorporation of local tribal elements into the Zairian mass.

Mapplethorpe, Robert, U.S. photographer (b. Nov. 4, 1946, New York, N.Y.—d. March 9, 1989, Boston, Mass.), created intense black-and-

white images of classical beauty; he was especially noted for his austere photographs of flowers, his iconographic celebrity portraits, and his male nudes, some of them explicitly homoerotic. After studying at the Pratt Institute in New York City from 1963 to 1970, Mapplethorpe launched a career as an independent filmmaker and artist. He gained renown as a photographer with his masterfully sculptured nudes, which celebrated the power of the human form. He used sadomasochistic imagery, including chains, leather, and binding, to produce deeply disturbing photographs. Mapplethorpe, who credited sculpture as a leading influence, sometimes combined photographic images printed on linen and designed his own wooden frames. His photographs were widely exhibited, and at the time of his death, a retrospective of his works was on view at the Museum of Contemporary Art in Chicago. This show included haunting self-portraits that showed the ravages of AIDS on his once-handsome face. Collections of his photographs were included in such books as *Robert Mapplethorpe Photographs* (1978), *Lady: Lisa Lyon* (1983), and *Robert Mapplethorpe: Certain People* (1985).

Marcos, Ferdinand Edralin, Philippine lawyer and politician (b. Sept. 11, 1917, Sarrat, Phil.—d. Sept. 28, 1989, Honolulu, Hawaii), for 20 years was head of state of the Philippines. He had pledged to maintain democratic processes while fighting the Communist insurgency and to increase the economic growth rate but instead plunged the country into political and economic chaos while pillaging millions of dollars from government coffers; his autocratic regime was marred by government corruption, economic stagnation, inequities between the poor and rich, and the steady growth of a Communist guerrilla insurgency throughout the islands. Marcos, the son of a politician and landowner, earned a law degree from the University of the Philippines. After being tried for and found guilty in 1939 of the 1933 murder of one of his father's political opponents, he argued his appeal before the Supreme Court himself and was acquitted the following year. During World War II he served as an officer with the Philippine armed forces. Later, while campaigning for political office, he made exaggerated claims about his importance as a leader in the Filipino resistance movement against the Japanese; an examination of government archives revealed that he had played virtually no role in anti-Japanese activities between 1942 and 1945. In 1946–47 Marcos served as technical assistant to Manuel Roxas, the first president of the independent Philippines. In 1954, after an 11-day whirlwind romance, Marcos married Imelda Romanuldez, a former beauty queen. He was a member of the House of Representatives (1949–59) and of the Senate (1959–65) before waging a bitter presidential campaign as the Nationalist Party candidate opposing the Liberal president, Diosdado Macapagal. Marcos won the election and was inaugurated on Dec. 30, 1965. He was reelected in 1969, and though he made some progress in agriculture, industry, and education, his administration was plagued by student demonstrations and violent urban guerrilla activities. After imposing martial law on Sept. 21, 1972, Marcos jailed opposition politicians, notably Benigno Aquino, Jr., who was imprisoned for eight years; suspended the writ of habeas corpus; and promulgated a new constitution that increased his authority and established a parliamentary system with himself as prime minister and president. In 1983 Marcos' health began to fail, and he was widely implicated in the assassination of Aquino, who was shot dead moments after he stepped off a plane as he was returning to the Philippines from a self-imposed exile. When Marcos called elections in 1986, Aquino's widow, Corazon, became the presidential candidate of the opposition. Amid rumours of widespread voting fraud, Marcos was declared the winner, but after the middle class and portions of the Army rebelled against the tainted elections, Marcos was persuaded by the U.S. to seek exile in Hawaii. At the time of his death, Marcos, who had been declared too ill to stand trial, was, together with his wife, under indictment in the U.S. for stealing $103 million from the Philippines to buy art and real estate in Manhattan. His family fortune was estimated in the billions.

Martin, Billy (ALFRED MANUEL MARTIN), U.S. baseball player and manager (b. May 16, 1928, Berkeley, Calif.—d. Dec. 25, 1989, near Binghamton, N.Y.), during his 11 years as a player was a scrappy second baseman, notably for the New York Yankees professional baseball team, and was instrumental during the 1950s in helping the team capture five World Series championships with his smoking bat and excellent fielding; he was probably best remembered, however, as the inspirational yet tempestuous five-time manager (between 1975 and 1988) of the Yankees and as a colourful personality whose barroom brawls often made headlines. Martin, who entered the major leagues in 1950, played for the Yankees before being traded in 1957 to the Kansas City Athletics. He played for five other teams before retiring in 1961 with a .257 batting average and 333 runs batted in. He launched a managing career with a minor league team in Denver in 1956 before being named the Minnesota Twins' manager in 1969. He led them to a division title that year but joined the Detroit Tigers in 1971 and then (1973) the Texas Rangers before beginning his era with his beloved Yankees. His reigns as manager, dubbed Billy I, II, III, IV, and V, were punctuated by legendary confrontations with Yankee owner George Steinbrenner, who was attracted to Martin's dynamic managerial style but repulsed by his quick temper, which was savagely unleashed on losing teams. During his years as a manager, Martin's teams had 1,258 wins and 1,018 losses. After being fired as manager of the Yankees in 1988 after he was involved in a fight in the men's room at a topless bar in Texas, Martin was named a vice president of the Yankees. He was killed when his pickup truck, being driven by an intoxicated friend, veered off an icy road near Martin's home.

Matsushita, Konosuke, Japanese industrialist (b. Nov. 27, 1894, Wakayama prefecture, Japan—d. April 27, 1989, Osaka, Japan), built the small electric fixture plant that he founded in 1918 into the Matsushita Electric Industrial Co., the world's largest producer of consumer electric appliances. Matsushita, who began working at the age of nine, exhibited his aptitude for business early. He worked as an errand boy, and at the age of 16 left a job as an apprentice bicycle repairman to join the Osaka Electric Light Co. At the age of 23 he started his own company with about $50, three employees, and an electric light socket of his own design. Though the socket was a failure, he successfully marketed an electric attachment plug that sold for less than his competitors' products. In order to persuade shopkeepers to carry his battery-powered bicycle lamp that would shine three times longer than other models, he installed one in each store to prove his claim. In 1935 Matsushita reorganized the company, which was to become internationally famous for marketing such products as electric batteries, rice cookers, videocassette recorders, and computer chips under the Panasonic, Quasar, and National brand names. He was also widely admired for introducing a five-day workweek, for allowing unions to participate in management, and for guaranteeing his employees lifetime employment. His policy of *marugakae* ("total embrace") included providing houses, gymnasiums, hospitals, and schools for his workers. He even gave cash bonuses to employees who married fellow Matsushita workers. Though this philosophy appeared to be less popular with younger employees, who preferred increased wages, Matsushita employees showed their daily devotion by singing the company song, by reciting the company's seven "spiritual" values, and by using less than the allotted number of vacation days. In 1989 Matsushita's company had more than 150 factories worldwide making more than 14,000 products. The company's sales for 1988 were estimated at $42 billion.

Menen, Aubrey (SALVATOR AUBREY CLARENCE MENEN), British writer (b. April 22, 1912, London, England—d. Feb. 13, 1989, Trivandrum, Kerala, India), wrote witty, incisive essays and fiction, in which he explored cultural conflicts, the nature of nationalism, and the contrast between his own Irish-Indian ancestry and his traditional British upbringing. He was best known for his satiric novels, including *The Stumbling Stone* (1949), *The Backward Bride* (1950), *The Fig Tree* (1959), and *A Conspiracy of Women* (1965). After attending (1930–32) University College, London, Menen worked as a drama critic (1934) and stage director (1935–36). When World War II broke out, he was in India, where he organized pro-Allied radio broadcasts and edited film scripts for the Indian government. After the war he returned to London to work in advertising, but the success of his first novel, *The Prevalence of Witches* (1947), induced him to write full-time. Menen's nonfiction included travel books, popular essays about his experiences living in Italy, and two autobiographies, *Dead Man in the Silver Market* (1953) and *The Space Within the Heart* (1970).

Milanov, Zinka, Yugoslav-born opera singer (b. May 17, 1906, Zagreb, Yugos.—d. May 30, 1989, New York, N.Y.), reigned for some 30 years as the leading dramatic soprano at the Metropolitan Opera in New York City and was especially regarded for her exquisite pianissimo phrasing. Milanov, who studied at the Zagreb Academy of Music, made her operatic debut in 1927 as Leonora in *Il trovatore* at the State Opera in Ljubljana. From 1928 to 1935 she was a leading soprano at the Zagreb Opera, and in 1936 she sang at the German Theatre in Prague. In the next year, at the invitation of Arturo Toscanini, she brilliantly performed the soprano part in the Verdi *Requiem* at the Salzburg Festival and on the strength of this performance was engaged by the Metropolitan Opera. Milanov, accustomed to singing Italian roles in either German or her native Serbo-Croatian language, learned Italian and was unrivaled in her interpretations of 19th-century operas, notably those composed by Verdi, including *Aida, La forza del destino, Otello,* and *Il trovatore.* Though her acting was considered outdated by modern standards, the statuesque diva used her extraordinary voice to create powerful, sensitive, or dramatic interpretations as the music demanded. Milanov gave her last operatic performance on April 14, 1966, appearing in the role of Madeleine in *Andrea Chénier.*

Moawad, René Anis, Lebanese politician (b. 1925, Zgharta, Lebanon—d. Nov. 22, 1989, Beirut, Lebanon) and master conciliator, who was elected president of Lebanon on Nov. 5, 1989, in a special session of Parliament. He pledged to implement an Arab League-sponsored plan for peace between Muslims and Christians that included a Syrian role in the process, but he was killed just 17 days later by a car bomb that also took the lives of over 20 others. Moawad, a member of a powerful Maronite Christian family in the north of Lebanon, earned a law degree (1947) from Université Saint Joseph in Beirut and went into private practice. He became involved in politics and was a member of Parliament from 1957 to 1989. Between 1960 and 1982 he served in a number of posts, including chairman of the Administration of Justice Parliamentary Commission (1959–61), chairman of the Budget and Finance Commission (from 1960), minister of postal telephone and telegraph (1961–64), minister of public works (1969), and minister of education and fine arts (1980–82). In the latter role he cut through sectarian hatred and organized school examinations for Christian and Muslim children whose studies had been interrupted by the civil war that began in 1975. He was elected

president—a post Lebanon's 1943 charter specified had to be held by a Maronite—over the objections of Maronite Gen. Michel Aoun (*see* BIOGRAPHIES), who denounced Moawad as a Syrian puppet. The bombing took place as Moawad and other officials returned from a ceremony celebrating the 46th year of Lebanese independence from French rule.

Morris, Richard Brandon, U.S. historian (b. July 24, 1904, New York, N.Y.—d. March 3, 1989, New York), was a prolific writer who produced scholarly works that chronicled early American history. An expert on the Colonial period and the American Revolution, Morris was credited with uncovering evidence showing that during the U.S. War of Independence, France, a U.S. ally, had acted alone and secretly sought, through Swiss intermediaries, a compromise with the British to concede independence only to New England. Morris, who graduated from the City College of New York in 1924, earned an M.A. (1925) and Ph.D. (1930) from Columbia University, New York City. He taught (1927-49) at City College of New York before joining the faculty at Columbia, where he taught history (1949-73) and served as chairman of the history department (1959-61). He was the editor of the *Encyclopedia of American History* (1953; 7th rev. ed. under way at the time of his death) and of four volumes of the unpublished papers of the American statesman and first chief justice of the United States, John Jay; he coedited a 40-volume history, *The New American Nation Series.* Some of his influential writings include *Government and Labor in Early America* (1946), *The Peacemakers: The Great Powers and American Independence* (1965), *John Jay, the Nation and the Court* (1967), *Seven Who Shaped Our Destiny* (1973), and *The Forging of the Union (1781-1789)* (1987). When he retired from Columbia in 1973, Morris called for U.S. leaders to be more honest and less charismatic.

Mufti, Sa'id al-, Jordanian politician (b. 1898?, Amman, [now in Jordan]—d. March 25, 1989), was one of Jordan's most enduring and respected public figures and thrice served as prime minister (April–December 1950, May–December 1955, May–June 1956). He was also leader of the influential non-Arab Circassian community in Jordan. In 1924 Mufti entered local government service in Amman, where he vigorously opposed British rule. He joined the Cabinet as minister of communications in 1944 and held numerous other posts, notably that of interior minister (1944-45, 1948-50, 1951-53, 1957). As a member of the Circassian minority, Mufti was generally respected and trusted by the Palestinians living in Jordan, and after the formal annexation (1949-50) of the West Bank, he was named prime minister. Although he resigned a few months later, he became deputy prime minister. During the controversy (1955-56) over Jordan's possible membership in the Baghdad Pact mutual security organization, Mufti was recalled as prime minister by King Hussein in an effort to regain public support. In 1963 Mufti left the Cabinet to become speaker of the Senate, a position he held until 1974.

Naidoo, Stephen, South African prelate (b. Oct. 23, 1937, Durban, South Africa—d. July 1, 1989, London, England), as archbishop of Cape Town and therefore head of the Roman Catholic Church in South Africa, was a leader in the interdenominational struggle against apartheid. Naidoo, whose Indian parents had converted to Roman Catholicism, attended a Christian Brothers school near Durban and studied theology in Scotland and England. He was ordained in 1961, and in 1964 he received a Ph.D. in canon law from the Pontifical University of St. Thomas Aquinas in Rome. After his return (1968) to South Africa, Naidoo served as a monastery priest and taught in a seminary in Pretoria. He was named auxiliary bishop of Cape Town in 1974 and was elevated to archbishop in 1984. In February 1988 Naidoo was one of several South African clergymen who were briefly arrested for leading a protest march in Cape Town. Shortly afterward he joined with Anglican Archbishop Desmond Tutu and the Rev. Allan Boesak of the World Alliance of Reformed Churches to found the antiapartheid Committee for the Defense of Democracy, which was banned by the South African government within days.

Namora, Fernando Goncalves, Portuguese writer (b. April 15, 1919, Condeixa, Port.—d. Jan. 31, 1989, Lisbon, Port.), wrote vivid Neorealist poetry and fiction, much of it inspired by his years as a doctor in a remote mountainous area of Portugal. Namora studied medicine at the University of Coimbra and established a practice in the rural Beira Baixa region. His best-known work, *Retalhos da Vida de um Médico* (first series 1949, *Mountain Doctor,* 1956; second series 1963), was a collection of sketches about his attempts to overcome the mistrust of the superstitious farmers and miners he treated there. Namora, who grew to admire the stoic peasants, turned to antifascist Neorealist fiction to express his anger at the oppression and poverty he observed. In the early 1960s he worked at the Lisbon Cancer Institute, but he resigned in 1965 to write full time. After the revolution in 1974, Namora's work gained wider popularity, and *Retalhos de Vida de um Médico* was adapted for television and the cinema. Namora's other works include *Minas de São Francisco* (1946), *O Trigo e o Joio* (1954; *Fields of Fate,* 1970), and *Os Clandestinos* (1972). He received the Order of Henry the Navigator, Portugal's highest civilian award, in 1988.

Newton, Huey Percy, U.S. political activist (b. Feb. 17, 1942, New Orleans, La.—d. Aug. 22, 1989, Oakland, Calif.), was a cofounder of the Black Panther Party (originally called Black Panther Party for Self-Defense). He and Bobby Seale founded the party in 1966 in Oakland in response to police brutality and racism. Newton, as the party's "minister of defense," articulated the need for black self-reliance and self-defense. The party's "rhetoric of the gun" was perhaps best symbolized by the widely circulated poster of Newton wearing a black beret and leather jacket and holding a spear in one hand and a rifle in the other. At the height of its popularity during the late 1960s, the party had 2,000 members and chapters in several cities. Newton graduated from high school without learning how to read but then taught himself to read and enrolled in college, where he met Seale. In 1967 Newton was convicted of voluntary manslaughter in the death of a police officer. The call to "Free Huey" swept college campuses nationwide. His conviction was overturned 22 months later, and he was released from prison. In 1974 he was accused of another murder and fled to Cuba for three years before returning to face charges; two trials resulted in hung juries. In 1971 Newton had announced that the party would shift from its confrontational stance to adopt a nonviolent manifesto and dedicate itself to providing social services to the black community, including a breakfast program for children, a free health clinic, and a community school. The party was disbanded in 1982. In 1980 Newton earned a Ph.D. in social philosophy from the University of California at Santa Cruz; his dissertation, *War Against the Panthers,* was subtitled "A Study of Repression in America." He pleaded no contest in March 1989 to a charge of misappropriating public funds that had been intended for a Panther-founded Oakland school. Newton was found shot dead just blocks away from where the Panthers had been founded.

Nordmeyer, Sir Arnold Henry, New Zealand politician (b. 1901, Dunedin, N.Z.—d. Feb. 2, 1989, Wellington, N.Z.), was an influential figure in the New Zealand Labour Party for more than 30 years and served as party leader (1963-65) and finance minister (1957-60); however, he was responsible for the 1958 "Black Budget," which was blamed for the party's defeat in the 1960 general election. Nordmeyer graduated from the University of Otago and served as a Presbyterian minister from 1925 until he entered Parliament in 1935. He helped draft the Social Security Act of 1938, which formed the basis for the nation's modern welfare system, and then headed several ministries, including Health (1941-47) and Industries and Commerce (1947-49). Nordmeyer lost his reelection bid in 1949, but he returned to Parliament in 1951 and became finance minister in 1957. After the creation of the European Economic Community (1957), Nordmeyer responded to a perceived threat to New Zealand trade with an austerity budget that introduced heavy tax increases. In the resulting public uproar, support for Labour plunged, and the party lost control of the government. Nordmeyer, who was unable to rebuild public support, was ousted as leader of the opposition in 1965 and retired four years later. He was knighted in 1975.

Ochoa Sánchez, Arnaldo, Cuban general (b. 1932, Cuba—d. July 13, 1989, Havana, Cuba), commanded Cuban troops in Ethiopia, Angola, and Nicaragua and was a much-decorated military officer who served as vice-minister (1981-89) of the Revolutionary Armed Forces in Cuba before he was arrested, charged with drug smuggling and misuse of government funds, and executed by firing squad. Ochoa, who fought beside Fidel Castro in the mountains as part of Castro's 26 July Movement in the late 1950s, was chosen to join the officer corps of the new Revolutionary Army. He later helped support armed insurgents in South America and, as a trusted and respected friend of Castro, accompanied him on a tour of Africa shortly before Cuba's expansion of its military presence there. Popular with his troops and the general populace, Ochoa was passionately condemned at his trial by Fidel Castro's brother, Raúl, who perhaps feared that Ochoa would supplant him as his brother's successor. Ochoa, who was made a Hero of the Republic of Cuba in 1984, resignedly accepted the charges against him.

Olivier, Laurence Kerr (BARON OLIVIER OF BRIGHTON), British actor and director (b. May 22, 1907, Dorking, Surrey, England—d. July 11, 1989, Steyning, West Sussex, England), was the founding director (1962-73) of the British National Theatre and was hailed by many as the greatest actor of the 20th century. He dazzled audiences with brilliant acting, athleticism, and elaborate costumes, makeup, and vocal techniques. Olivier, who began acting as a child, attended the Central School of Speech Training and Dramatic Art and worked with the Birmingham Repertory Theatre Company (1926-28). His breakthrough came in Noël Coward's *Private Lives* (1930), and in *Romeo and Juliet* (1935), in which he alternated the roles of Romeo and Mercutio with John Gielgud, he

ALISTAIR MORRISON—GLOBE PHOTOS

began his distinguished classical career. Olivier gained international movie stardom and the first of 10 Academy Award nominations for his portrayal of Heathcliff in *Wuthering Heights* (1939). He followed this with popular romantic leads in *Rebecca* and *Pride and Prejudice* (both 1940). As codirector (1944–49) with Ralph Richardson of the rejuvenated Old Vic Theatre Company, Olivier specialized in Shakespearean roles, many of which he transferred to the screen, both as actor and as director. These included *Henry V* (1944), for which he received a special Oscar; *Hamlet* (1948), which won Oscars for best actor and best picture; *Richard III* (1955); and *Othello* (1965). Olivier also starred in several plays and films with his second wife, Vivien Leigh. In 1957 he broke away from classical roles and achieved new success with his portrayal of the seedy third-rate vaudevillian Archie Rice in John Osborne's *The Entertainer* (filmed 1960). In 1962 Olivier was named actor-manager of the new National Theatre, where he appeared in such varied plays as Shakespeare's *The Merchant of Venice,* August Strindberg's *Dance of Death,* and Anton Chekhov's *Three Sisters.* He retired from the stage in 1974 to focus on motion pictures and television. Although critics derided much of his later work, Olivier received Oscar nominations for *Sleuth* (1972), *Marathon Man* (1976), and *The Boys from Brazil* (1978). He also garnered five television Emmy awards, most notably for adaptations of Eugene O'Neill's *Long Day's Journey into Night* (1973), *Love Among the Ruins* (1975), and *Brideshead Revisited* (1982). In 1983 he starred in an acclaimed television staging of *King Lear.* Olivier was repeatedly stricken by debilitating illnesses in the 1970s and '80s, but he continued to act, making his last television appearance in *War Requiem* (1988). He published his memoirs in 1982, followed by *On Acting* (1986). Olivier was knighted in 1947, and in 1970 he was elevated to a life peerage, the first of his profession to be so honoured. As a final tribute from the nation, it was announced that Olivier would be the fifth actor in history to be buried in Westminster Abbey.

Onoe, Shoroku, II, Japanese Kabuki actor (b. March 28, 1913, Tokyo, Japan—d. June 25, 1989, Tokyo), was one of the foremost interpreters of the classical Kabuki plays and specialized in performing female roles (all Kabuki players are male). Born Yutaka Fujima, he was a pupil of the great Kikugoro Onoe VI; after starring in *Neiboku sendai hagi* ("The Disputed Succession") he adopted the dynastic name of his teacher. At the age of five Onoe made his debut as Ushiwakamaru in the famed Kabuki drama *Shusse Kagekiyo* at the Teikoku Theatre in Tokyo. Onoe later gave memorable performances in such Kabuki productions as *Yoshitsune Sembonzakura* ("The Thousand Cherry Trees"), *Tsuchigumo* ("Earth Spider"), and the comedy *Kanchincho* ("The Faithful Retainer"). Onoe was also at ease performing in works by Jean-Paul Sartre and Shakespeare. In 1972 Onoe was deemed an important intangible cultural property by the Japanese government, and in 1987 he was awarded the Order of Culture.

Panchen Lama (BSKAL-BZANG TSHE–BRTAN), Tibetan religious and political leader (b. Feb. 1938, Qinghai (Tsinghai) province, China—d. Jan. 28, 1989, Zhikatse, Tibet), was a venerated Buddhist spiritual leader in Tibet and, as a vice-chairman of China's National People's Congress (parliament), was instrumental in helping Beijing (Peking) deal with militant Tibetans protesting Chinese occupation of their homeland since 1949. As a boy he was recognized (1941) by Buddhist experts as the reincarnation of the first Panchen Lama, although he never underwent the usual exacting tests that determine rebirth. The Panchen Lama was revered by Tibetans as a "living Buddha." In 1952 he was enthroned as the head abbot of the influential Tashilhunpo monastery in Zhikatse. He remained in Tibet after the 1959 popular revolt against Chinese occupation, and he became

an even greater spiritual influence after the Dalai Lama fled into exile in India. Because the Panchen Lama refused to denounce the Dalai Lama, he fell out of favour with the Chinese authorities. The Panchen Lama was imprisoned and tortured during China's Cultural Revolution (1966–76); after his release he maintained an uneasy alliance with Chinese government officials. Though the Panchen Lama denounced the anti-Chinese activities of separatist Tibetan monks, he also criticized the violent way in which Chinese authorities handled riots in Tibet during 1988. A week before his death from a heart attack, the Panchen Lama presided at the dedication of the new Great Stupa at the Tashilhunpo monastery in Tibet, where the remains of five Panchen Lamas were reburied. Their remains had been dismembered and thrown away by Red Guards during the Cultural Revolution, but local people had recovered them. Government officials indicated that a shrine would be erected to entomb the Panchen Lama's remains.

Patané, Giuseppe, Italian conductor (b. Jan. 1, 1932, Naples, Italy—d. May 30, 1989, Munich, West Germany), was known for his expressive interpretations of operas, particularly those by Puccini and Verdi. The son of Franco Patané, an opera conductor, Patané studied piano and other instruments at the conservatory in Naples. When he was 19, he made his operatic debut at Naples' small Teatro Mercadante with Verdi's *La Traviata.* He repeated his performance before the San Carlo Opera in Naples later that year and joined the company as assistant conductor, a post that he held until 1956. Patané was sought after to conduct operas in Europe and became principal conductor (1961–62) of the Linz (Austria) opera and of the Deutsche Oper in West Berlin (1962–68). He made his American debut (1967) in San Francisco with Ponchielli's *La Gioconda* and first appeared before British audiences at the 1972 Edinburgh Festival with the Palermo Opera's performance of Verdi's *Attila.* Patané conducted the Vienna State Opera from 1977 to 1980. At the time of his death, he was conductor of the Bavarian Radio Orchestra and of Italian repertory works for the Bavarian State Opera, both in Munich, where he died after collapsing onstage while conducting Rossini's *Il Barbiere di Siviglia.* His final recordings, of *La Gioconda* and of Placido Domingo in Mascagni's *Iris,* were released posthumously.

Payne, John, U.S. actor (b. May 23, 1912, Roanoke, Va.—d. Dec. 6, 1989, Malibu, Calif.), as a boyishly handsome leading man during the 1940s, appeared opposite Alice Faye and Betty Grable in a succession of 20th Century-Fox musicals including *Tin Pan Alley* (1940), *Footlight Serenade* (1942), *Springtime in the Rockies* (1942), *Hello, Frisco, Hello* (1943), and *The Dolly Sisters* (1945) but was probably best remembered as the lawyer who defended Kris Kringle in the 1947 Christmas fantasy *Miracle on 34th Street.* After making his silver screen debut in *Dodsworth* (1936), Payne starred in musicals before moving on to westerns. He later starred in his own television series, "The Restless Gun." In 1973–74 Payne returned to the limelight, appearing opposite Faye in a revival of the stage musical *Good News.*

Pedersen, Charles John, U.S. chemist (b. Oct. 3, 1904, Pusan, Korea—d. Oct. 26, 1989, Salem, N.J.), conducted groundbreaking experiments as an industrial research chemist for E.I. du Pont de Nemours & Co. During the 1960s he synthesized a group of organic compounds that he named crown ethers, a loose flexible ring of carbon atoms punctuated at regular intervals by oxygen atoms. His discoveries were expanded independently by Donald James Cram and Jean-Marie Lehn, and the three shared the 1987 Nobel Prize for Chemistry for their work. Pedersen, the son of a Norwegian seaman who worked in Korea as a mechanical engineer, moved to the U.S. during the 1920s. After earning a B.A. in chemical engineering from the University of

Dayton, Ohio, he received an M.A. in organic chemistry from the Massachusetts Institute of Technology. Pedersen joined Du Pont in 1927 as a research chemist, and during his 42 years with the company, he wrote 25 technical papers and secured some 65 patents, primarily in petrochemicals. With his promotion in 1960 to the highest research post, that of research associate, Pedersen was given free rein to pursue his own line of investigations. It was then that he embarked on his Nobel Prize-winning research; his 1967 original paper, which detailed his findings, became a classic. His work led to the laboratory synthesis of molecules that could selectively react with other molecules in much the same way that enzymes and other natural biological molecules do. The discovery meant that scientists could design drugs that would be more effective against infections and tumours and that industrial substances could be synthesized in such a way that their release into the environment would be less damaging. Pedersen retired in 1969.

Pepper, Claude Denson, U.S. politician (b. Sept. 8, 1900, Dudleyville, Ala.—d. May 30, 1989, Washington, D.C.), gained a reputation as the undisputed champion of the elderly during his more than 60 years in public office serving as a liberal congressman (1962–89) and Democratic senator (1936–50) from Florida. Pepper, who earned a law degree from Harvard University, practiced law before his election in 1928 to the Florida legislature, where he sponsored a bill allowing senior citizens to fish without a license. As a senator, Pepper endorsed the New Deal policies of Pres. Franklin D. Roosevelt and ardently advocated the adoption of the legislation that created Social Security, a minimum wage, and medical assistance for the elderly and for handicapped children. The fiery-haired Pepper, who was called "Red Pepper" both for his red hair and for his liberal views, lost his Senate seat in 1950 as the era of McCarthyism began; he returned to private law practice. In 1962 he was elected to the House of Representatives. There he made his mark as the chairman of the House Select Committee on Aging, as chairman of the crucial Rules Committee, and as the principal architect of legislation, passed in 1986, that abolished mandatory retirement in the federal government, raised the retirement age from 65 to 70 in the private sector, and ensured continued health coverage for older workers. Pepper, the oldest member of Congress, was also instrumental in the passage of the Medicare Catastrophic Coverage Act of 1988. Pres. George Bush visited Pepper five days before his death to bestow on him the Medal of Freedom, the nation's highest civilian award.

Pritchard, Sir John Michael, British conductor (b. Feb. 5, 1921, London, England—d. Dec. 5, 1989, Daly City, Calif.), as perhaps Britain's most widely traveled conductor, was known for his unruffled interpretations of Mozart opera and for his expertise in mastering scores of contemporary works. He was chief conductor of the Cologne Opera (1978–89) and the BBC Symphony Orchestra (1979–89), as well as music director of the Belgian Opera Nationale (from 1981) and the San Francisco Opera (from 1986). Pritchard learned music from his father, a violinist in the London Symphony Orchestra; he attended Sir George Monoux Grammar School in London and then was sent to Italy to study viola, piano, and conducting. When his military service in World War II ended (1943) because of ill health, Pritchard became conductor of the Derby String Orchestra. In 1947 he joined the Glyndebourne Festival Opera, and he made his conducting debut (1949) with *Don Giovanni;* he later served (1969–78) as musical director at Glyndebourne, which he used as a base for his extensive travels. In 1952 he made his debut at Covent Garden, where he conducted the premieres of Benjamin Britten's *Gloriana* (1953) and Sir Michael Tippett's *Midsummer Marriage* (1955) and *King Priam* (1962). As musical director of the Royal Liverpool Philharmonic

(1957–63), he introduced to the United Kingdom the "Musica Viva" concept, in which a spoken introduction and musical examples precede the performance of a work. He was music director of the London Philharmonic (1962–66) and took that orchestra on tour in the Far East (1969) and China (1973). Pritchard was knighted in 1983.

Quayle, Sir (John) Anthony, British actor and director (b. Sept. 7, 1913, Ainsdale, England—d. Oct. 20, 1989, London, England), distinguished himself in classical roles on the stage, as a director who strengthened the foundations for what became the Royal Shakespeare Theatre, and as an actor in British and U.S. films and television. Quayle studied at the Royal Academy of Dramatic Art and made his stage debut (1931) at London's Q Theatre in a production of *Robin Hood.* He joined (1932) the Old Vic Company, appeared in such varied plays as *Anna Christie* (1934) and *Hamlet* (1935), and made his New York debut (1936) in *The Country Wife.* Quayle used the Old Vic as his base until 1939, when he enlisted in the Royal Army; he served in the artillery until 1945 and rose to the rank of major. His two books, *Eight Hours from England* (1945) and *On Such a Night* (1947), chronicled his military experiences. Quayle returned to the stage in *The Rivals* in 1945 and made his debut as a director with *Crime and Punishment* in 1946. He performed (1948–56) with the Shakespeare Memorial Theatre Company, Stratford-upon-Avon, and was instrumental in luring Laurence Olivier, Ralph Richardson, and John Gielgud to that repertory company. Quayle's stage credits include roles in *Long Day's Journey into Night* (1958), *Galileo* (1967), *Sleuth* (1970), *The Rivals* (1978), and *The Clandestine Marriage* (1984). He appeared in such films as *Saraband for Dead Lovers* (1948), *The Guns of Navarone* (1961), *Lawrence of Arabia* (1962), and *The Chosen* (1978). For television he appeared in such films as "QB VII" (1974) and "Dial M for Murder" (1981), produced "The Idiot" (1970), and directed "Caesar and Cleopatra" (1979). In 1984 Quayle founded a touring company, Compass, from which he retired in 1989. Quayle was made a Commander of the Order of the British Empire in 1952 and was knighted in 1985.

Radner, Gilda, U.S. comedienne (b. June 28, 1946, Detroit, Mich.—d. May 20, 1989, Los Angeles, Calif.), created a gallery of offbeat characters as one of the original cast members of "NBC's Saturday Night Live," a landmark comedy variety show first televised in 1975. Radner began her career performing with Toronto's Second City improvisational group. In 1974 she moved to New York City to work with John Belushi on the "National Lampoon Radio Hour," for which she wrote and performed. On "Saturday Night Live" Radner perfected such characters as the rambling loud-mouthed newscaster Rosanne Rosannadanna, the misinformation editorialist Emily Litella, the lisping Baba Wawa (a takeoff on Barbara Walters), and the nerdy teenager Lisa Loopner. In 1979 she took her act to Broadway and starred in the revue *Gilda Live,* which was filmed and released as a motion picture. Some of her other films include *First Family, The Woman in Red, Haunted Honeymoon, Hanky Panky,* and *It Came from Hollywood.* Some two years after her marriage in 1984 to actor and filmmaker Gene Wilder, Radner was diagnosed as having ovarian cancer. Her book, *It's Always Something,* appeared posthumously and was a poignant account of her battle with the disease.

Raposo, Joseph G., U.S. composer (b. Feb. 8, 1927, Fall River, Mass.—d. Feb. 5, 1989, Bronxville, N.Y.), together with Jim Henson and Jon Stone, created the revolutionary children's television program "Sesame Street" and, as its longtime musical director, composed some of the show's most popular songs. The program, designed to teach young children numbers, letters, and social concepts through the use of scenes as long as the average TV commercial, relied heavily on music, which was vital to the success of the program. Raposo garnered five Grammy awards during his career and created such delightful tunes as "Sing," "Bein' Green," "You Will Be My Music," "Winners," and "Somebody Come and Play." He was also coauthor of the play *You're a Good Man, Charlie Brown* and musical director of the public-television program "The Electric Company." He composed songs for Frank Sinatra and for the plays *Sing Muse, A Man's a Man,* and *Raggedy Ann.* At the time of his death, Raposo, who earned an Academy Award nomination for his music for the film *The Great Muppet Caper,* was creating music for "Sesame Street" to celebrate the show's 20th anniversary on public television.

Revie, Donald, British footballer and football manager (b. July 10, 1927, Middlesbrough, England—d. May 26, 1989, Edinburgh, Scotland), was an aggressive centre-forward who from 1945 to 1961 played professional football (soccer) with teams in Leicester, Hull, Manchester, Sunderland, and Leeds and was named Footballer of the Year in 1955; as player-manager and then manager (1961–74) of Leeds United, he led the pugnacious team to the Football Association (FA) Cup in 1972 and then served (1974–77) as manager of the England team. In 1978 he was suspended from the game for 10 years for securing a more lucrative job in Dubai when FA officials assumed he was in Finland scouting out England's competition, Italy, for the upcoming World Cup qualifying match. Revie, who successfully fought the ban in the High Court in 1978, was nonetheless characterized by the judge as, "greedy, selfish, and deceitful." As a coach Revie had a reputation for trying to win at all costs, and his teams during the 1960s were seen as ruthless. After coaching teams in the Middle East, he returned to England but never to British football. He later retired to Fife, Scotland, where he battled amyotrophic lateral sclerosis (Lou Gehrig's disease), a rare, incurable motor neuron disease.

Rive, Richard Moore, South African writer (b. March 1, 1931, Cape Town, South Africa—d. June 4?, 1989, Athlone, South Africa), was considered by many to be one of black South Africa's most important short-story writers and achieved international acclaim with his first novel, *Emergency* (1964). That book, which was banned by the South African government for a time, chronicled the racial strife that exploded into violence in Sharpeville, a black township in south central Transvaal in 1960. Rive grew up in the working-class area for Coloureds (people of mixed racial background) called District Six in Cape Town. It was in District Six that he learned about racism and degradation. Rising out of the ghetto through scholarship and athletics (he was a hurdling champion), he went on to obtain degrees from the University of Cape Town; Columbia University, New York City; and the University of Oxford. Although he traveled extensively, teaching and lecturing, he made his home near Cape Town, where he taught at South Peninsula High School and Hewat Training College. His imaginative works, written from a humanitarian perspective, reflected the social and political upheavals of the time and were praised for their technical power and realistic dialogue. His autobiographical novel, *Buckingham Palace, District Six* (1986), detailed the events surrounding the South African government's decision to rezone District Six exclusively for whites. The novel exposed the process of removing almost 40,000 nonwhite residents from the area. *Writing Black* (1981), an autobiography, described his years of traveling and studying in Africa and Europe. Two works, *Quartet: New Voices from South Africa* (1963) and *Advance, Retreat* (1983), are collections of his short stories. Shortly before a play based on *Buckingham Palace, District Six* was scheduled to open, Rive was found murdered in his home.

Robinson, Sugar Ray (WALKER SMITH), U.S. boxer (b. May 3, 1921, Detroit, Mich.—d. April 12, 1989, Culver City, Calif.), was a fighter whose dazzling footwork, devastating combination punches, lightning speed, and savvy timing made him, pound for pound, the greatest fighter in the world during his long boxing career (1940–65) and perhaps the best fighter ever; in 201 professional bouts he scored 109 knockouts. Robinson reigned as world welterweight champion from 1946 to 1951 and captured the world middleweight title five times between 1951 and 1960. As an amateur fighter he had scores of victories while fighting under his own name before he adopted the name of another fighter, Ray Robinson. He won Golden Gloves titles as a featherweight in 1939 and as a lightweight in 1940. As a professional boxer he captured 40 consecutive fights before losing to Jake LaMotta in 1943. Robinson became world welterweight champion on Dec. 20, 1946, after defeating Tommy Bell with a 15-round decision. Robinson gave up the welterweight crown when he knocked out LaMotta on Feb. 14, 1951, to capture the world middleweight championship. Although he was dethroned by Randy Turpin of England in July 1951, Robinson regained the crown when he knocked out Turpin in September of that year. In 1952 Robinson retired after being defeated by Joey Maxim for the world light heavyweight crown, but he returned to the ring in 1954 and regained the middleweight title from Carl ("Bobo") Olson in 1955. Robinson lost but then regained the crown from Gene Fullmer in 1957, yielded it to Carmen Basilio later in the year, and then recaptured it for the last time by defeating Basilio in a savage 1958 rematch. A legendary contract negotiator, Robinson spent millions maintaining a lifestyle that included an entourage of servants, a trademark flamingo-pink Cadillac, and such businesses as a dry cleaner, a barber shop, and a Harlem nightclub named Sugar Ray's. After his retirement he established a youth foundation in Los Angeles for inner-city children. The classic fighter, an inspiration to later champs including Muhammad Ali and Sugar Ray Leonard, was inducted into the Boxing Hall of Fame in 1967.

Rowicki, Witold, Russian-born conductor (b. Feb. 26, 1914, Taganrog, Russia—d. Oct. 1, 1989, Warsaw, Poland), helped to reestablish symphonic music in post-World War II Poland and became an internationally respected conductor and trainer of orchestras. He earned a degree (1938) in violin and composition from the Krakow Conservatory and, while studying in Vienna, he was introduced to the conducting of Richard Strauss and Anton Webern. Rowicki made his debut as a conductor in 1932. He also appeared as a violin soloist and chamber ensemble player and during World War II was said to have studied conducting with Rudolf Hindemith in Germany and to have played in the Krakow symphony during the Nazi occupation. In 1945 he was named head of music for Polish radio, based in Katowice, where he founded and directed (1945–50) the Polish Radio Symphony Orchestra. Rowicki served as conductor (1950–55) of the Warsaw Philharmonic and supervised the rebuilding of its concert hall; at its 1955 opening the orchestra was renamed the Polish National Philharmonic, which he served as artistic director and principal conductor until 1977. He was musical director (1965–70) of the Theatr Wielki, Warsaw's major opera and ballet theatre, and supervised the reconstruction of its building. Rowicki traveled widely with the National Philharmonic and was a frequent guest conductor of major orchestras on five continents; during the 1960s he recorded all of Dvorak's symphonies with the London Symphony Orchestra. His own compositions included a symphony (1957) and a concerto for orchestra (1976).

Rutherford, Charles, Canadian soldier (b. Jan. 9, 1892, Haldimand, Ont.—d. June 11, 1989, Ottawa, Ont.), was the last surviving World War I winner of the Victoria Cross, the highest British

honour for battlefield courage. Rutherford, who enlisted (1916) as a private in the Queen's Own Rifles of Canada, was twice wounded and garnered 12 other military medals for valour, including the Military Cross. He was awarded that medal for capturing the village of Arvillers on Aug. 8, 1918, and then holding it until French troops arrived to relieve him. Eighteen days later, in the action for which he won the Victoria Cross, Rutherford, who had been scouting alone, daringly and single-handedly captured 45 German soldiers guarding the town of Monchy-le-Preux, France, by convincing them that they were surrounded. After the war he bred pedigree cattle before returning to service during World War II in the Veterans' Guard, protecting the Duke of Windsor in the Bahamas and guarding prisoner-of-war camps in Canada.

Sakharov, Andrey Dmitriyevich, Soviet nuclear physicist and human rights activist (b. May 21, 1921, Moscow, U.S.S.R.—d. Dec. 14, 1989, Moscow), was the father of the Soviet hydrogen bomb and, as a tireless crusader for human rights, was awarded the 1975 Nobel Prize for Peace. Sakharov enjoyed rare Soviet prerogatives for having helped to create the hydrogen bomb, but then he raised such persistent, acute questions about its use and the flaws he found unconscionable in Soviet society that he was exiled (1980) until 1986, when Soviet leader Mikhail Gorbachev invited him to return to Moscow. Sakharov, an intellectual and brilliant student at Moscow State University, graduated in 1942 and worked in a military plant. After pursuing graduate studies (1945–48) in nuclear physics, he joined a top-secret nuclear weapons project. There, as he wrote in *Sakharov Speaks* (1974), he saw the bomb he created in the hands of "people who, though talented in their own way, were cynical." He tried but failed to persuade Nikita Khrushchev to cancel atmospheric tests in the late 1950s and championed the 1963 U.S.-U.S.S.R. treaty banning nuclear tests. In the 1960s he and other well-regarded Soviets protested a Kremlin plan to revive Stalinism; in 1968 the Soviet invasion of Czechoslovakia prompted Sakharov to circulate "Progress, Coexistence, and Intellectual Freedom," an essay highly critical of the increasing repression of Soviet dissidents. It was published in the *New York Times* and then broadcast back to the U.S.S.R. by the Voice of America. Sakharov refused to deny authorship and, though he lost top-level security clearance, he was allowed to remain a member of the prestigious Academy of Sciences and to keep his academy-assigned apartment and country house, car and driver, and a respectable job. In 1970 he and two other dissidents founded the Committee for Human Rights; in 1971 he married physician-dissident Yelena Bonner, gave up his official home, and was increasingly hounded for his outspoken-

SYGMA

ness. When Sakharov was awarded the Nobel Prize, he was not permitted to travel to Oslo, Norway, to receive it; Bonner did, and she delivered his speech, characteristically in support of intellectual freedom. Sakharov waged an increasingly lonely battle that peaked in December 1979, when he urged other nations to protest the Soviet invasion of Afghanistan by boycotting the 1980 Moscow Olympics. He was stopped by Soviet security officers, told he was stripped of state honours, and sent with Bonner to Gorky, an industrial city. Two hunger strikes and occasional letters smuggled by Bonner kept Sakharov in the world's eye until his 1986 return to Moscow. Though he supported Gorbachev's programs, he also warned against giving too much power to any one leader. In March 1989 Sakharov was elected a deputy to the Congress of People's Deputies. He became a leader of dissident deputies and on December 11 called for rallies and petitions to bring about an end to the Communist Party's monopoly of political power; the day he died Sakharov had exhorted fellow deputies to establish another political party. He was named a Hero of Socialist Labour three times and was awarded the Stalin Prize and the Order of Lenin.

Sauguet, Henri (HENRI-PIERRE POUPARD), French composer (b. May 18, 1901, Bordeaux, France—d. June 21, 1989, Paris, France), wrote hundreds of refined, melodic works for ballet, opera, orchestra, chamber groups, and voice, as well as for French films and television. Born Henri-Pierre Poupard, he began to study piano at the age of five, but his studies were interrupted during World War I, when he worked in local vineyards to support his family. At age 15 he began to play the organ in a local church. He moved to Montauban to study composition at age 18 and with a composer and poet in Bordeaux formed a musical group, "Les Trois," which was patterned after the group "Les Six," headed by composer Darius Milhaud, with whom he corresponded. Milhaud urged him to move to Paris to continue his studies. Adopting his mother's maiden name, Sauguet moved to Paris (1922) to study with Charles Koechlin and Erik Satie and was a founder of l'École d'Arcueil, an avant-garde chamber group. Sauguet received a commission and wrote his first major piece, a comic opera, *Le Plumet du colonel,* presented (1924) at the Champs-Élysées Theatre, followed by two ballets, *Les Roses* (1924) and *La Chatte* (1927), the latter directed by George Balanchine for Sergey Diaghilev at Monte Carlo. From 1928 to 1948 he also wrote music criticism for a number of journals. Of more than two dozen ballets, his best-regarded were *Les Mirages* (1943) and *Les Forains* (1945); *La Chartreuse de Parme* (1939), which had its premiere at the Paris Opera, was considered his best opera. Sauguet was elected (1975) to l'Académie des Beaux-Arts and was an officer of the Legion of Honour and a grand officer of the Order of Merit.

Schröder, Gerhard, West German politician (b. Sept. 11, 1910, Saarbrücken, Germany—d. Dec. 31, 1989, Kampen, Sylt Island, West Germany), was a cofounder of the centre-right Christian Democratic Union (CDU), a leader in the Bundestag (parliament) for some 30 years, and a key Cabinet minister in every West German government between 1953 and 1969. Schröder received a law degree (1933) and taught law in Bonn and Berlin until he entered the Army in 1939. In 1949 he was elected to the first Bundestag, representing the Protestant branch of the newly formed CDU. Schröder served three chancellors as minister of the interior (1953–61), foreign affairs (1961–66), and defense (1966–69). He ran for chancellor against Kurt Kiesinger in 1966, and in 1969 he lost a bid for the presidency by only six votes. In 1980 Schröder retired from the Bundestag, where he had been chairman of the Foreign Affairs Committee since 1969.

Sciascia, Leonardo, Italian writer (b. Jan. 8, 1921, Racalmuto, Sicily—d. Nov. 20, 1989,

Palermo, Italy), gained international recognition for his suspense-filled thrillers about political corruption and the Mafia. His first work, *Le parrocchie di Regalpetra* (1956; *Salt in the Wound,* 1969), written while he was an elementary school teacher in Racalmuto, was a collection of essays focusing on the church, the Fascist and Christian Democratic parties, the Mafia, and the suffering those groups caused the peasants. Sciascia used the format of a thriller as the basis for *Il giorno della civetta* (1961; *Mafia Vendetta,* 1963), about a policeman's attempt to solve a Mafia killing, and for *A ciascuno il suo* (1966; *A Man's Blessing,* 1968), about a man trying to solve the Mafia murder of his friend. Sciascia's political career began in the 1960s when he first joined the Communist Party. He later became a member of the Radical Party and was elected to the Italian legislature. In 1978 Sciascia publicly condemned the Red Brigade, an Italian terrorist group, for the death of Aldo Moro, the Christian Democratic leader; his controversial book *L'affaire Moro* (1978; "The Moro Affair") explored Moro's disappearance and death. In 1979 Sciascia was elected a deputy in the European Parliament. Besides essays, Sciascia also wrote *Il consiglio d'Egitte* (1963; *The Council of Egypt,* 1966), *Il contesto* (1971; *Equal Danger,* 1973), and *Chronacette* (1985; "Little Chronicles").

Scott, Sir Peter Markham, British naturalist (b. Sept. 14, 1909—d. Aug. 29, 1989, Bristol, England), was a leading spokesman for wildlife conservation and was both founder of the British Wildfowl Trust (later renamed the Wildfowl and Wetlands Trust) and a founder of the World Wildlife Fund (renamed the World Wide Fund for Nature). Scott, who was the only son of Antarctic explorer Robert Falcon Scott, attended the University of Cambridge and studied art at the Munich (Germany) State Academy and the Royal Academy in London. In the 1930s he gained renown as a painter of wildlife, particularly birds, and as an accomplished single-handed yachtsman, winning the Prince of Wales Cup three times and a bronze medal in the 1936 Olympic Games. After distinguished service in the Royal Navy during World War II, Scott founded (1946) the Slimbridge Refuge, a waterfowl sanctuary on the River Severn in Gloucestershire. He had tremendous success with conservation and breeding programs there, most notably in his efforts to save the Hawaiian goose, which had become nearly extinct by the 1950s. Scott guided the World Wildlife Fund for more than 25 years as chairman (1961–82), council chairman (1983–85), and honorary chairman (1985–89). As a member (1962–81) of the Species Survival Commission of the International Union for Conservation of Nature and Natural Resources, he created the Red Data Books, the IUCN's official lists of endangered species. He also led expeditions to such far-flung places as Antarctica and the Galápagos Islands, wrote 18 illustrated travel and wildlife books, and promoted conservation issues on the British television series "Look" and "Survival." Scott was knighted in 1973 and made a Companion of Honour in 1987.

Segrè, Emilio Gino, Italian-born U.S. physicist (b. Feb. 1, 1905, Tivoli, Italy—d. April 22, 1989, Lafayette, Calif.), made monumental contributions to the science of physics as codiscoverer—with Owen Chamberlain—of the antiproton, the negatively charged particle having the same mass as the proton; the two won the Nobel Prize for Physics in 1959 for their discovery. Segrè, the son of an Italian industrialist of Jewish descent, studied engineering at the University of Rome but later studied physics under Enrico Fermi and earned a Ph.D. in 1928. His association with Fermi, his mentor, spanned some three decades. Segrè was named assistant professor of physics at the University of Rome and conducted neutron experiments with Fermi, helping to lay the foundation for the development of atomic energy. In 1935 the two discovered slow neutrons, which have properties vital

to the operation of nuclear reactors. In 1936 Segrè became director of the physics laboratory at the University of Palermo, and the following year he discovered element 43, technetium, the first artificially produced element. While visiting in California in 1938, Segrè was fired from his university post in Italy by the Fascist government. He decided to remain in the U.S. and became a research associate at the University of California at Berkeley. There in 1940 he and his associates discovered element 85, astatine, and later with Glenn Seaborg, Segrè discovered plutonium-239, which was used in the atomic bomb dropped on Nagasaki, Japan. From 1943 to 1946 Segrè served as a group leader at the Los Alamos (N.M.) Scientific Laboratory before returning to Berkeley, where he remained a professor until 1972. He was appointed professor of nuclear physics at the University of Rome in 1974 but later returned to California. Segrè was the author of such scholarly works as *Nuclei and Particles* (1964), the biographical *Enrico Fermi, Physicist* (1970), *From X-rays to Quarks* (1980), and *From Falling Bodies to Radio Waves* (1984).

Sendic, Raúl, Uruguayan rebel leader (b.1935?, Uruguay—d. April 27, 1989, Paris, France), founded (1962) the leftist Tupamaro National Liberation Front, a guerrilla movement that waged a relentless battle (1967–72) against the police and the Army with a string of kidnappings, robberies, bombings, and murders. Sendic, the acknowledged leader of the movement, quit law school in the late 1950s to join the Socialist Party. When the party was defeated in two elections, he resigned to organize sugarcane workers' strikes and other rebellious activities, but he soon turned to more violent methods. The Tupamaros gained notoriety in the late 1960s with such exploits as Robin Hood–style distribution of stolen food to the poor and the bombing of an exclusive dance hall. In 1970 the Tupamaros kidnapped and killed Dan A. Mitrione, U.S. adviser to the Uruguayan police force; the events were the basis of *State of Siege,* a 1972 motion picture. In 1970 Sendic was captured, but in September 1971 he and over 100 other Tupamaro guerrillas escaped from Punta Carretas Prison by tunneling under the structure to a nearby house. Amid national instability the police and army security forces were then reorganized to form a combined antiguerrilla unit. In 1972 more than 2,000 Tupamaros, including Sendic, were arrested, and in 1973 Pres. Juan María Bordaberry Arocena dismissed Congress and increased the power of the military. The repressive regime, which ruled until 1985, reportedly dealt out harsh treatment to Tupamaro prisoners. Sendic, who spent some 13 years in prison before being released under a general amnesty in 1985, reorganized the Tupamaros as a legal political party.

Sewell, Truett Banks ("RIP"), U.S. baseball player (b. May 11, 1907, Decatur, Ala.—d. Sept. 3, 1989, Plant City, Fla.), as a right-handed pitcher for the Pittsburgh Pirates professional baseball team from 1938 to 1949, bedazzled fans with his "eephus ball," an arching blooper pitch that soared to a height of 8 m (25 ft) before coming straight down toward the plate. Sewell launched his major league career in 1932 with the Detroit Tigers. He returned to the minors until 1938, when he joined the Pirates. During his 13-year major league career, he compiled a record of 143 wins and 97 losses, and in 1943 he led the National League with 21 victories. After his retirement as a player, Sewell was instrumental in helping form baseball's pension fund. He was also an avid golfer, and even after both of his legs were amputated below the knees in 1972 because of circulation problems, he continued to play golf.

Shakhbut ibn Sultan an-Nahayan, Sheikh, former Arab potentate (b. 1905, Abu Dhabi—d. Feb. 11, 1989, al-'Ayn, Abu Dhabi, United Arab Emirates), ruled Abu Dhabi from 1928 until he was deposed in 1966. As ruler of the largest emirate within the British-controlled Trucial Coast, Sheikh Shakhbut maintained friendly relations with the U.K. and successfully resisted territorial incursions in a prolonged border dispute with Saudi Arabia. He was an early supporter of Western oil exploration and granted drilling rights that earned Abu Dhabi as much as $70 million per year in the mid-1960s. He was reluctant, however, to invest the emirate's oil earnings in schools and major development projects. On Aug. 6, 1966, a council of the Abu Dhabi royal family replaced him with his more progressive younger brother, Sheikh Zaid. After four years in exile Sheikh Shakhbut returned to Abu Dhabi to live quietly in the royal palace.

Shockley, William Bradford, U.S. physicist (b. Feb. 13, 1910, London, England—d. Aug. 12, 1989, Palo Alto, Calif.), had a brilliant career in physics that was later overshadowed by his controversial views on genetics and race. Shockley shared the 1956 Nobel Prize for Physics with John Bardeen and Walter H. Brattain for the development of the transistor, a tiny semiconductor that was used as a substitute for the bulkier, less efficient, and more expensive vacuum-tube amplifiers then used in radios and other electronics. He later became notorious for his philosophy of "retrogressive evolution," which held that intelligence was genetically transmitted. Shockley argued that blacks were genetically inferior to whites because they scored lower on IQ tests and that, because blacks were reproducing faster than whites, there was a retrogression in human evolution. Shockley graduated from the California Institute of Technology in 1932 and earned a Ph.D. from the Massachusetts Institute of Technology in 1936 before joining the staff of Bell Telephone Laboratories at Murray Hill, N.J. During World War II, he served as a director of research in the Antisubmarine Warfare Operations Research Group of the U.S. Navy. After the war, he returned to Bell Laboratories as director of the solid-state physics research program, and in 1947 he and his colleagues developed the transistor. In 1954–55 he was director of evaluation of weapons systems research for the U.S. Department of Defense. Shockley left Bell Labs in 1954 and launched his own semiconductor factory. A rebellion among his employees, who launched their own companies, sparked an electronics boom that created the area near Stanford University known as Silicon Valley. From 1963 to 1975 Shockley was a professor of electrical engineering at Stanford. During the 1970s he created a stir when, on more than one occasion, he contributed to a sperm bank that was offering to pass along the genes of "geniuses."

Simenon, Georges (JOSEPH CHRISTIAN), Belgian-French novelist (b. Feb. 13, 1903, Liège, Belgium—d. Sept. 4, 1989, Lausanne, Switz.), created the compassionate, streetwise French sleuth Inspector Jules Maigret and was perhaps the most widely published, best-known author of the 20th century. He was credited with more than 400 sparely written, characteristically short novels and two dozen other books, which were translated into at least 50 languages and read by an estimated 600 million people, and also with more than 1,000 articles and stories. Simenon left school at age 16 and worked at odd jobs before becoming a reporter for the *Gazette de Liège.* In 1922, after serving in the Belgian Army and after the death of his father, he moved to Paris. Working as secretary to a French marquis, Simenon had time to observe and, using 17 pseudonyms, to write pulp novels. He produced more than 200 between 1924 and 1933 and became very wealthy. The first novel published under his own name was *Pietr-le-Letton* (1931; *The Case of Peter the Lett*), in which he introduced the middle-aged, pipe-smoking police investigator Maigret, whose unassuming habits reportedly resembled those of Simenon's father and whose reliance upon intuition and curiosity about motivation set the standard for whodunits. After living in the U.S. (1945–55), he returned with his second

HORST TAPPE

wife to France and then went to Switzerland. He left their 26-room mansion after writing *Maigret et Monsieur Charles* (1972), with which he announced his retirement. In 1977 Simenon described his preoccupations with writing and with women, claiming to have intimately known 10,000 women. His understanding of compulsions, shared but never practiced by Maigret, was also explored by Simenon in two well-regarded novels, *La Neige était sale* (1948) and *L'Homme qui regardait passer les trains* (1938). His final book was *Mémoires intimes* (1981).

Siri, Giuseppe Cardinal, Italian prelate of the Roman Catholic Church (b. May 20, 1906, Genoa, Italy—d. May 2, 1989, Genoa), as archbishop of Genoa from 1946 to 1987, was twice the choice of more conservative cardinals for pope and was a rigid traditionalist who once wrote a pastoral letter denouncing women who wore trousers to church. Siri, the son of a dock-worker, earned a doctorate in theology from Pontifical Gregorian University, Rome. He was ordained a priest (1928) and became a professor of theology at the seminary of Genoa. In 1944 he was named auxiliary bishop of Genoa, where in 1945 he averted further German destruction of the port city by negotiating separately with retreating Nazi leaders and advancing leaders of the Italian resistance. He was named archbishop the following May and was elevated to cardinal (1953) by Pope Pius XII. Siri served as chairman of the Italian Episcopal Conference from 1955 to 1965. Though Siri was a leading candidate to succeed Pius XII, John XXIII was elected pope in 1958. Siri was openly critical of him and the Second Vatican Council (1962-65). In 1963 the conclave of cardinals chose Pope Paul VI; in 1978 it elected Pope John Paul II, reportedly to resolve a deadlock between Siri and a more liberal Italian cardinal, Giovanni Benelli. Supportive of John Paul II's emphasis on church tradition, Siri was reported to have remained deeply involved in Genoese sociopolitical life and scornful of liberal Catholics; he maintained that divorce was a multiple sin and that AIDS was a punishment from God.

Sopwith, Sir Thomas Octave Murdoch, British aircraft designer and industrialist (b. Jan. 18?, 1888, London, England—d. Jan. 27, 1989, King's Somborne, Hampshire, England), produced the airplanes that helped Britain win three wars over a period of more than 60 years. These planes included the Sopwith Camel, from which some 1,294 enemy aircraft were shot down in World War I; the Hawker Hurricane, which was used in the decisive Battle of Britain (1940) in World War II; and the Harrier, the vertical takeoff jet fighter used in the 1982 conflict in the Falkland Islands. Sopwith bought his first airplane in the autumn of 1910, taught himself to fly, and received his pilot's license

in November. By the end of December he had set British aerial duration and distance records, including one for a prizewinning flight to Belgium. In 1912 Sopwith established a flying school and formed the Sopwith Aviation Co., which supplied thousands of military aircraft—notably the Camel, Pup, and 1½ Strutter—during World War I. When Sopwith Aviation went bankrupt in 1920, he founded H.G. Hawker Engineering Co. Ltd. (from 1935, Hawker Siddeley Aircraft Ltd.), named for his partner and chief test pilot, Harry Hawker, who was killed in 1921. In the 1930s Sopwith anticipated the coming conflict and authorized the construction of hundreds of Hurricanes, with no guarantee of government orders. The Air Ministry did buy them, however, and in the Battle of Britain these fighters shot down more German planes than did the faster and better-known Spitfires. Sopwith retired in 1963 and thereafter held the title of founder and life president. However, he remained on the Hawker Siddeley board of directors until 1978. He also designed yachts and raced the *Endeavour* (1934) and *Endeavour II* (1937) in the America's Cup. He was knighted in 1953. In January 1988 the Royal Air Force honoured Sopwith's 100th birthday.

Stephenson, Sir William Samuel ("INTREPID"), Canadian-born British intelligence chief and industrialist (b. Jan. 11, 1896, Point Douglas, Man.—d. Jan. 31, 1989, Paget, Bermuda), was director of the U.S.-based British Security Coordination (BSC), the U.K.'s central intelligence-gathering office during World War II. Stephenson coordinated all British overseas espionage activities in the Western Hemisphere, recruited agents, established a secret base in Canada to train agents for missions behind enemy lines, and functioned as liaison between the BSC and the U.S. government until the Office of Strategic Services (OSS) assumed responsibility for U.S. intelligence in 1942. Stephenson served in World War I in the Royal Canadian Engineers (1914–15) and the British Royal Flying Corps (1915–18). His success as a fighter pilot and his escape from a German prison camp shortly before the armistice earned him the British Military Cross and Distinguished Flying Cross, as well as the French Legion of Honour and Croix de guerre avec palmes. In the 1920s he built an industrial empire, manufacturing such diverse products as steel, aircraft, and phonographs; he also patented the first process for the transmission of pictures over the wireless. Through his many business contacts, Stephenson gained valuable information in the 1930s about the buildup of German armaments and the development of the cipher machine Enigma. He conveyed this information to the British Secret Intelligence Service. When Winston Churchill became prime minister in 1940, he sent Stephenson to New York City to direct the BSC. After the war Stephenson, who personally financed many of the BSC's activities, returned to his business interests, mainly in Jamaica. He eventually retired to Bermuda. His exploits were later described in two popular biographies and a television miniseries. Stephenson was knighted in 1945 and received the U.S. Presidential Medal of Merit in 1946.

Stollmeyer, Jeffrey Baxter, Trinidadian cricketer (b. April 11, 1921, Port of Spain, Trinidad—d. Sept. 10, 1989, Melbourne, Fla.), as a stylish batsman for the West Indies team (1939–55), played in 32 tests (captain for 13 tests), scoring 2,159 runs with 4 centuries and an average score of 42.33. Stollmeyer was one of the last white captains for the West Indies team. He helped the team to a historic 3–1 victory over England (1950) and beat India (1952–53) when he scored 354 runs at 59. While Stollmeyer was president of the West Indies Board of Control in 1977, he opposed Australian Kerry Packer's formation of the World Series Cricket group and Packer's innovations, such as one-day cricket. Although Stollmeyer prevailed over Packer (World Series Cricket folded), Stollmeyer could not prevent the changes in the sport, including one-

day cricket and short-pitch fast bowling. He attended Queen's Royal College and managed his family's plantation. Stollmeyer was chairman of the Trinidad Publishing Company, and he served as a senator in the Trinidad and Tobago Parliament (1961–71).

Stone, I.F. (born ISIDOR FEINSTEIN), U.S. journalist (b. Dec. 24, 1907, Philadelphia, Pa.—d. June 18, 1989, Boston, Mass.), was a political muckraker who considered the pursuit of the truth his life's work and dispensed his liberal views in the influential four-page newsletter *I.F. Stone's Weekly* (1953–67; from 1967 to 1971 *I.F. Stone's Bi-Weekly).* That publication blended his unique wit with an erudite scholarship that appealed to such subscribers as Albert Einstein, Bertrand Russell, and Eleanor Roosevelt. As a child, Stone was a voracious reader though a mediocre student, and at age 14 he began his journalistic career when he and a classmate published a five-cent monthly newspaper. He attended the University of Pennsylvania while working at the *Philadelphia Inquirer* but left school in his junior year to be a full-time journalist. He was editorial writer at the *Philadelphia Record* in 1933 and concurrently served in the same position at the *New York Post* (1933–39). He was associate editor (1938–40) and Washington editor (1940–46) for the weekly *Nation,* and from 1942 to 1952 he undertook assignments for such newspapers as *PM,* the *New York Star,* the *New York Post,* and the *New York Daily Compass.* When the latter folded in 1952, Stone established *I.F. Stone's Weekly,* which was researched, written, and edited solely by Stone; his wife, Esther, handled business matters related to the weekly. He scrupulously canvassed public records and frequently developed major stories from details, contradictions, and inconsistencies he discovered while minutely examining the Congressional Record and other public documents. He supported civil rights and opposed Pres. Harry Truman's cold war policies, McCarthyism, and U.S. involvement in Vietnam. He routinely lambasted the government and took pride in the notion that he, "annoyed some of the people all of the time and all of the people at one time or another." When he discontinued publication of the biweekly in 1971, he became a contributing editor of the *New York Review of Books* and took up the study of classical Greek. The indefatigable gadfly published such books as *The Court Disposes* (1937), a treatise on the Supreme Court; *Business as Usual: The First Year of Defense* (1941), a condemnation of U.S. military waste and inefficiency; *Underground to Palestine* (1946), *The Hidden History of the Korean War* (1952), *The Killings at Kent State: How Murder Went Unpunished* (1971), and *The Trial of Socrates* (1988). Collections of his columns were compiled in *The Haunted Fifties* (1963), *In a Time of Torment* (1967), and *Polemics and Prophecies, 1967–70* (1971).

Stone, Irving, U.S. author (b. July 14, 1903, San Francisco, Calif.—d. Aug. 26, 1989, Los Angeles, Calif.), specialized in writing extensively researched biographical novels, including such popular successes as *Lust for Life* (1934), about Vincent Van Gogh; *The President's Lady* (1951), about Rachel Jackson; and *The Agony and the Ecstasy* (1961), based on the life of Michelangelo; all three were later made into motion pictures. Stone, who was born Irving Tennenbaum, later adopted the name of his stepfather. He earned an M.A. in economics in 1924 at the University of Southern California and was an instructor in economics (1924–26) at the University of California at Berkeley before embarking on a writing career. A prolific author whose first manuscripts were repeatedly turned down for publication, Stone enlisted the help of Jean Factor, a young editor, to help revise *Lust for Life,* which was published after 17 rejections and became an instant best-seller. The two later married, and his wife served as his lifelong editor. Stone also published such biographies as *Clarence Darrow for the Defense*

JERRY BAUER

(1941) and *Earl Warren* (1948). Some of his other fictionalized portraits featured Jack London in *Sailor on Horseback,* Abraham and Mary Lincoln in *Love Is Eternal,* Sigmund Freud in *The Passions of the Mind,* and Charles Darwin in *The Origin.*

Syme, Sir Ronald, British historian and classical scholar (b. March 11, 1903, Eltham, N.Z.—d. Sept. 4, 1989, Oxford, England), reinterpreted and clarified the history of ancient Rome in readable books that focused on the intrigues of the rulers and their lust for power and wealth. His first book, *The Roman Revolution* (1939), presented the fall of the ancient Roman republic in such a way that contemporary events in Europe—including Mussolini's march on Rome, Hitler's rise to power in Germany, and Stalin's purges—though not named, could not help but be recognized. Syme, educated in New Zealand at Victoria University College, Wellington, and at Auckland University College, went to Oriel College, Oxford (1925–27), where he graduated first in his class. He became a fellow of Trinity College and tutor in ancient history (1929) and traveled widely in central Europe. He served as British press attaché (1940–41) in Belgrade, Yugos., and then (1941–42) in Ankara, Turkey; he was (1942–45) professor of classical philology at the University of Istanbul. Syme returned to Trinity College (1945) and held Oxford's Camden chair of ancient history and was a fellow at Brasenose College (1949–70). His remarkable two-volume work, *Tacitus* (1958), breathed new life into one of Rome's key emperors. Syme served (1952–71) as secretary-general of the philosophical and humanities section of Unesco. He wrote *History in Ovid* (1978), *The Augustan Aristocracy* (1986), and *Some Arval Brethren* (1980); the last volumes in his *Roman Papers* (1979, 1984, 1988) were scheduled to appear posthumously. He was knighted in 1959 and was awarded the Order of Merit in 1976.

Talvela, Martti Olavi, Finnish opera singer (b. Feb. 4, 1935, Hiitola, Fin.—d. July 22, 1989, Juva, Fin.), thrilled audiences with his powerful bass voice and imposing physical stature in a wide range of operatic parts but was perhaps best known for his impassioned interpretation of the title role in Modest Mussorgsky's *Boris Godunov.* Talvela abandoned a career as a schoolteacher to study at the Lahti Academy of Music and made his professional debut in 1961 at the Swedish Royal Opera House in Stockholm. The next year, he was invited to appear at the prestigious Bayreuth Festival, and he was soon in demand throughout Europe and North America. As artistic director (1972–79) of the Savonlinna Festival, Talvela advanced the appreciation of opera in Finland by mounting productions of much of the standard repertory in Finnish and by commissioning new operas

from contemporary Finnish composers. Shortly before his death Talvela had been named director of the Finnish National Opera, beginning in 1992.

Taylor, E(dward) P(lunket), Canadian industrialist and sportsman (b. Jan. 29, 1901, Ottawa, Ont.—d. May 14, 1989, Lyford Cay, The Bahamas), amassed a fortune and became one of the country's wealthiest men as president of Canadian Breweries Ltd. (renamed Carling O'Keefe Ltd. in 1973). He used his wealth to build one of the most successful horse-breeding empires in the world, notably with his three-year-old colt Northern Dancer, the first Canadian horse to capture (1964) the Kentucky Derby. Taylor earned a degree in mechanical engineering from McGill University, Montreal, in 1922 but began working at one of his grandfather's brewing companies and in 1930, through a series of successful mergers and acquisitions, founded the Brewing Corp. of Canada, later Canadian Breweries Ltd. During World War II Taylor served as executive assistant to the minister of munitions and supply, vice-chairman of the British Supply Council in North America, and Canadian chairman of the joint war aid committee. By 1936 he had established Windfields Farm in Oshawa, Ont., for breeding thoroughbreds; his horse Northern Dancer by 1970 had become the world's leading sire, producing such champion thoroughbreds as Northfields, Laurie's Dancer, True North, and Nijinsky II. After World War II Taylor founded Argus Corp., an investment company with holdings in brewing, forestry, mining, and chemicals. When he retired as president of Argus in 1969, he sold Canadian Breweries and moved to The Bahamas, where he became interested in land development. When he resigned as chairman of Argus in 1972, the company had assets of some $177 million.

Terry, William Harold, U.S. baseball player (b. Oct. 30, 1898, Atlanta, Ga.—d. Jan. 9, 1989, Jacksonville, Fla.), was a feared hitter and first baseman (1923–36) for the New York Giants professional baseball team and as manager of the team (1932–41) won three National League pennants (1933, 1936, and 1937) and the 1933 World Series. Terry, who was in the minor leagues from 1914 to 1918, played semiprofessional baseball in Memphis, Tenn., until he signed with the Giants in 1922. Until 1927 he played only part-time. He became a premier fielder at first base and a powerful left-handed line-drive hitter. In 1930 Terry batted .401 and joined an elite group of only eight players to have topped .400 after 1900; he was the last player in the National League to do so. During his career Terry compiled an impressive record; he had a career batting average of .341 and had 2,193 hits, 154 home runs, and 1,078 runs batted in during his 14 years as a major league player. After serving as general manager of the Giants in 1942, Terry retired from baseball and amassed a fortune in oil and cotton speculation. He was inducted into the Baseball Hall of Fame in 1954.

Thomson, Virgil, U.S. composer, conductor, and music critic (b. Nov. 25, 1896, Kansas City, Mo.—d. Sept. 30, 1989, New York, N.Y.), composed pieces that blended homespun hymn tunes, waltzes, and marches into sophisticated structures, and exerted widespread influence as the opinionated music critic (1940–54) for the *New York Herald Tribune.* Thomson, who began playing the piano at the age of five, attended Harvard University before studying musical composition with Nadia Boulanger in Paris. There he was influenced by such 20th-century French composers as Erik Satie and the group known as Les Six. In 1926 Thomson began a collaboration with U.S. poet Gertrude Stein, and with Thomson writing the score and Stein the libretto, the two created the operas *Four Saints in Three Acts* (1934) and *The Mother of Us All* (1947), a tribute to Susan B. Anthony. Another opera, *Lord Byron* (1968), which took

seven years to complete, combined many of the styles in which Thomson composed. He also wrote instrumental music, choral works, chamber music, piano pieces, and film music, notably the scores for Pare Lorentz' pioneering documentaries *The Plow That Broke the Plains* (1936) and *The River* (1937), and for *Louisiana Story,* which won the 1948 Pulitzer Prize for music and was still the only film score ever to have been so honoured. His publications include *State of Music* (1939); *Virgil Thomson* (1966), an autobiography; *American Music Since 1910* (1971); *Selected Letters* (1988); and *Music with Words,* which was published posthumously.

Tovstonogov, Georgy Aleksandrovich, Soviet theatre director (b. Sept. 28 [Sept. 15, old style], 1915, Tbilisi, Georgia, Russian Empire—d. May 24, 1989, Leningrad, U.S.S.R.), as principal director of the Maksim Gorky Bolshoi Drama Theatre (the Gorky) in Leningrad from 1956, mounted innovative productions of Russian, English, and Soviet plays in which he combined realistic ensemble acting with unorthodox stagings. Tovstonogov graduated (1938) from the State Institute of Theatrical Arts in Moscow and served as director of the Tbilisi Griboyedov Russian Theatre (1938–46), the Moscow Central Children's Theatre (1946–49), and the Leningrad Lenin Komsomol Theatre (1950–56). In 1956 he moved to the Gorky, where his acclaimed productions included dramatizations of Dostoyevsky's *The Idiot* (1957; staged in London, 1966), Griboyedov's *Woe from Wit* (1962), Sholokhov's *Virgin Soil Upturned* (1964), Chekhov's *The Three Sisters* (1965), Gorky's *The Petty Bourgeoisie* (1967), Shakespeare's *Henry IV, Parts 1 and 2* (1969), and Gogol's *The Inspector General* (1972). He also taught (1960–89) at the Leningrad Institute of Theatre, Music, and Cinematography and wrote several books, notably *The Profession of the Stage Director* (1965; trans. 1972). Tovstonogov, who won two Orders of Lenin and a Lenin Prize, was named People's Artist of the U.S.S.R. in 1957.

Tuchman, Barbara, U.S. historian (b. Jan. 30, 1912, New York, N.Y.—d. Feb. 6, 1989, Greenwich, Conn.), was the Pulitzer Prize-winning author of *The Guns of August* (1962), a compelling narrative chronicling the events that precipitated World War I, and of *Stilwell and the American Experience in China, 1911–1945* (1971), an account of the general who led U.S. forces in the Far East against the Japanese during World War II. She was the daughter of Maurice Wertheim, an international banker, publisher, and philanthropist and the founder of the Theatre Guild. After receiving a bachelor of arts degree from Radcliffe College in 1933, she served as a research assistant (1933–35) for the Institute of Pacific Relations and worked as a writer and correspondent (1936–39)

JERRY BAUER

for *The Nation* magazine, covering the Spanish Civil War. After her 1940 marriage to physician Lester Reginald Tuchman, she devoted herself to raising three daughters; she began writing full time when the girls entered school. Tuchman, who never earned a Ph.D., felt that she was able to take a fresh approach to her work since her vision was untrained by the academic community; her scholarly historical works, written in a polished literary style, were immensely readable by the general public. She published *The Lost British Policy: Britain and Spain Since 1700* (1938), *Bible and Sword: England and Palestine from the Bronze Age to Balfour* (1956), and *The Zimmermann Telegram* (1958) before securing her reputation with *The Guns of August* (1962). Some of her other acclaimed works included *The Proud Tower: A Portrait of the World Before the War, 1890–1914* (1966); *A Distant Mirror: The Calamitous 14th Century* (1978), which cleverly re-created the tumultuous period in France marked by plague and war and was considered perhaps her most profound work; and *The March of Folly: From Troy to Vietnam* (1984), an examination of four case studies on political folly—the Trojan War, the battle between the Renaissance popes and the Protestants, the war between the British and the North American colonists, and U.S. involvement in Vietnam. Her last work, *The First Salute—A View of the American Revolution,* was published in 1988.

Twomey, Seamus, Northern Irish political activist (b. 1919, Belfast, Ireland—d. Sept. 12, 1989, Dublin, Ireland), a founder and twice chief of staff of the militant Provisional wing of the Irish Republican Army (IRA), was allegedly a mastermind of the 22 Belfast bombings that killed nine people on July 7, 1972, a day known as Bloody Friday. Twomey, whose father was reportedly tried for treason in Belfast, was born in the Roman Catholic district of Falls Road. He joined the Republican youth movement when he was 10 years old and was interned without trial as an IRA activist, reportedly on a prison ship off Belfast, at the outbreak of World War II. After the war he continued to work for Irish Republicanism. In 1969 he was a founding member of the Provisional ("green") IRA, which split from the Marxist Official ("red") IRA. In 1972 Twomey was one of several IRA leaders who traveled to London for talks that led to a brief cease-fire, whose end he was said to have spurred. He was arrested (1973) for armed robbery and sentenced to three years in Mountjoy Prison in Dublin; less than a month later, on Oct. 31, 1973, he and two fellow IRA prisoners made a dramatic escape in a helicopter airlift. He was arrested again in 1977 and released in 1982. Thereafter Twomey kept a low profile except for his appearances at several IRA fundraising events in North America.

Vanel, Charles-Marie, French actor (b. Aug. 21, 1892, Rennes, France—d. April 15, 1989, Cannes, France), enjoyed a remarkable 76-year career as a character actor in more than 200 films. Vanel grew up in a seafaring family in Saint-Malo; he wanted to attend naval college, but his poor eyesight prevented his admission. In 1904 his parents moved to Paris, and he discovered the theatre. When Vanel was 16 he made his debut in *Hamlet;* he appeared in his first film, *Jim Crow,* in 1912. For the next few years, except during a short period of military service in World War I, he concentrated on theatre work. His first major silent film role was as a brooding, beefy "heavy" in Robert Boudrioz' *L'Atre* (1922), the sort of role Vanel repeated many times. In 1929 he starred in and directed *Dans la nuit.* He received his greatest international recognition from two thrillers directed by Henri-Georges Clouzot: *The Wages of Fear* (1953), for which he won a citation at the Cannes Film Festival for his portrayal of an aging hoodlum, and *Les Diaboliques* (1954), in which he played a dispassionate, resolute detective. This role led to his part in Alfred Hitchcock's *To Catch a Thief* (1955). His last film was *The Seasons of Pleasure* (1988).

Vreeland, Diana, U.S. fashion editor (b. *c.* 1903, Paris, France—d. Aug. 22, 1989, New York, N.Y.), as fashion editor of *Harper's Bazaar* from 1937 to 1962 and editor in chief of *Vogue* from 1962 to 1971, was ordained the chic high priestess of fashion; she later mounted stunning fashion exhibitions at the Metropolitan Museum of Art in New York City, where visitors flocked in the millions to view her creations. Vreeland, who launched her legendary career in 1936 when she began writing the "Why Don't You . . ." column for *Harper's Bazaar,* possessed an eccentric charm. She never revealed her true age, remarking, "Whatever age you are, you're older than you ought to be." Vreeland was noted for her inimitable voice inflections, described as speaking in capital letters and italics. She introduced the Italian thong sandal, promoted see-through blouses, coined the term pizzazz, and declared the bikini "the most important thing since the atom bomb." With her jet-black slick of hair and understated yet chic clothes, Vreeland was an elegant and imposing presence; her colour predilection was for red, the hue of her polished fingernails, her office, and her Park Avenue living room. Her influence was so substantial that even though her experimental photographs taken with a wide-angle lens that distorted models—giving them big heads and small feet—were considered a failure, they were received with respect. Her memoirs, *D.V.,* appeared in 1984.

Warren, Robert Penn, U.S. novelist and poet (b. April 24, 1905, Guthrie, Ky.—d. Sept. 15, 1989, Stratton, Vt.), was a distinguished man of letters and a master stylist who made an extraordinary contribution to American literature with powerfully written novels and poems that explored the search for identity in a confused or corrupt South besieged by an erosion of its traditional rural values. He was the only U.S. writer to win Pulitzer Prizes for both fiction (once, in 1947) and poetry (twice, in 1958 and 1979), and in 1986 he was named the first official U.S. poet laureate. Warren, raised in a tobacco-farming region, culled memories of narratives, ballads, and folk legends he heard as a child as well as personal recollections to serve as inspiration for themes and subjects treated in his novels and poetry. As a student at Vanderbilt University, Nashville, Tenn., he joined a group of poets called the Fugitives, who together published an anthology of essays, *I'll Take My Stand* (1930), a testimony for the agrarian, Southern way of life. After graduating from Vanderbilt in 1925, he earned an M.A. (1927) from the University of California at Berkeley and studied at Yale before attending the University of Oxford as a Rhodes scholar. He was an inspirational and influential teacher (1930–57) at various universities, including Vanderbilt and the University of Minnesota. Warren, together with Cleanth Brooks, published *Understanding Poetry* (1938),

which was instrumental in ushering in the New Criticism, and the two also edited *The Southern Review,* perhaps the most influential American literary journal of its time. Warren published such novels as *Night Rider* (1939) and *At Heaven's Gate* (1943) before writing the Pulitzer Prize-winning *All the King's Men* (1946), said to have been loosely based on the career of Louisiana populist demagogue Huey Long; the film version earned an Academy Award for best picture in 1949. Though he published other novels, including *World Enough and Time* (1950), *Band of Angels* (1956), and *The Cave* (1959), Warren concentrated on writing poetry after the 1950s, notably such powerful narrative collections as *Promises, 1954–1956* (1957), *You, Emperors and Others* (1960), *Incarnations* (1968), *Audubon: A Vision* (1969), *Or Else, Poem* (1974), *Being Here* (1980), *Rumor Verified* (1981), *Chief Joseph of the Nez Perce* (1983), and *New and Selected Poems, 1923–1985* (1985).

Wedemeyer, Albert Coady, general (ret.), U.S. Army (b. July 9, 1897, Omaha, Neb.—d. Dec. 17, 1989, Ft. Belvoir, Virginia), was a brilliant military strategist who as a lieutenant colonel was the principal author of the 1941 Victory Program, a comprehensive war plan devised for the U.S. entry into World War II after the Japanese attack on Pearl Harbor. Wedemeyer, who drafted the "Germany first" strategy, formulated much of the Allied strategy in the Mediterranean and was instrumental in planning the successful Normandy invasion (June 6, 1944) in France by the Allies. After graduating from the U.S. Military Academy at West Point, N.Y., he studied Chinese while on assignment in Tientsin, China, during the early 1930s. He earned (1936) top honours at the Command and General Staff School at Ft. Leavenworth, Kansas, and was chosen to attend the *Kriegsakademie* (German War College) in Berlin. After returning to the U.S. in 1938, he penned a report on the German military mind and machine. After various assignments Wedemeyer joined the War Plans Division of the War Department General Staff in 1941 and quickly rose through the ranks. By 1942 he was a brigadier general and a protégé of Gen. George C. Marshall, chief of staff of the U.S. Army during World War II. In 1943 Wedemeyer was appointed deputy commander under Adm. Lord Mountbatten, the British head of the Southeast Asia Command. The following year Wedemeyer was appointed chief of staff to Gen. Chiang Kai-shek and commander of U.S. forces in China, a post he held until 1946. In 1947 Wedemeyer conducted a fact-finding mission to investigate the situation in China and Korea. His report, which warned of an imminent Communist triumph in China unless the U.S. gave greater support to the Nationalists, was deemed so sensitive that its publication was suppressed for two years. Three years after his 1951 retirement, Wedemeyer was promoted to the permanent rank of general. His autobiography, *Wedemeyer Reports!* (1958), principally chronicled the years 1941 to 1947, the most important period of his career.

Weiss, Paul Alfred, Austrian-born biologist (b. March 21, 1898, Vienna, Austria—d. Sept. 8, 1989, White Plains, N.Y.), made fundamental discoveries in the theory of cellular development, including breakthroughs in embryology, by demonstrating that an embryo's organization and growth are determined by the physical and chemical environment surrounding the newly multiplied cells. He also made significant inroads on the mechanics of nervous system development, nerve regeneration, and nerve repair. Weiss earned a Ph.D. at the University of Vienna in 1922 and, with the publication of his doctoral thesis, *Animal Behaviour as System Reaction,* introduced the landmark "systems" approach, which diverted from the mechanists' view that animal behaviour followed a rigid pattern of cause and effect. From 1922 to 1929 Weiss served as assistant director of the Biologi-

cal Research Institute of the Vienna Academy of Sciences, where he conducted pioneering studies of cell movement, tissue organization, and organ formation. In 1931 he immigrated to the U.S. to join the Yale University Laboratory, but in 1933 he moved to the University of Chicago, where he conducted experiments in embryology and in differentiation, the process by which tissues and organs develop from a single cell. His tenure there (1933–54) was interrupted during World War II when he was recruited by the U.S. government to improve methods of surgical nerve repair. He devised a technique for the sutureless splicing of severed nerves, a feat that earned him a merit citation from the U.S. War and Naval departments. From 1954 to 1964 Weiss was professor at the laboratory of developmental biology at the Rockefeller Institute, New York City, where he showed that, after being pulverized, individual cells from complex organs can reconstitute themselves. In 1962, together with A. Cecil Taylor, Weiss for the first time photographed nerve fibre under a powerful phase-contrast microscope and found that nerve fibre was a living, changing, adaptable tissue. In further experimentation he discovered that nerves could regenerate themselves. A prolific author of some 350 scientific articles, he also published 11 books, including *Principles of Development: A Text in Experimental Embryology* (1939) and *The Science of Life* (1973). In 1980 Weiss was awarded the National Medal of Science.

Weores, Sandor, Hungarian poet (b. June 22, 1913, Szombathely, Hung.—d. Jan. 22, 1989, Budapest, Hung.), wrote imaginative lyrical verse that encompassed a wide range of techniques and metric forms. Weores rejected the officially approved subject matter of Social Realism, choosing instead to explore such diverse areas as Eastern philosophy, Polynesian myths, and children's nursery rhymes. Weores, who published his first poem at the age of 15, attended the University of Pecs and worked as a librarian until 1951, at the same time producing several volumes of innovative and often surrealistic poetry. From 1949 to 1964 his poetry, except for widely admired translations of Chinese and Western European verse and a collection of children's rhymes, was suppressed by the government. *A hallgatas tornya* ("The Tower of Silence") was published during the brief period of relative freedom prior to the revolution of 1956. After the publication (1964) of *Tuzkut* ("The Well of Fire") in Paris, Weores' poetry again became acceptable in Hungary. His later works include *Psyche* (1972), a collection of letters and poems by a fictitious 19th-century woman, and several verse dramas. He also edited *Harom vereb hat szemmel* (1977), an influential anthology of Hungarian poetry. Weores received the Kossuth Prize, the nation's highest award, in 1970.

Wilde, Cornel, U.S. actor (b. Oct. 13, 1915, New York, N.Y.—d. Oct. 16, 1989, Los Angeles, Calif.), attained stardom with his sensitive portrayal of composer Frédéric Chopin in the motion picture *A Song to Remember* (1945), for which he received an Academy Award nomination. He later starred in and directed a series of action films, notably *The Naked Prey* (1966), *Beach Red* (1967), and *Shark's Treasure* (1975). Wilde, a prominent member of the

R. DOMINQUES—GLOBE PHOTOS

1936 Olympic fencing team, studied to become a physician before finding his niche as an actor. Some of his other film credits included *Leave Her to Heaven* (1945), *The Bandit of Sherwood Forest* (1946), *Centennial Summer* (1946), *Forever Amber* (1947), *Road House* (1948), *Shockproof* (1949), *The Greatest Show on Earth* (1952), and *The Fifth Musketeer* (1979). His last motion picture, *My Very Wilde Life,* was filmed in 1987.

Williams, Roy Lee, U.S. union leader (b. March 22, 1915, Ottumwa, Iowa—d. April 28, 1989, Leeton, Mo.), was president (1981–83) of the International Brotherhood of Teamsters before being convicted with four others of conspiring to bribe Howard Cannon, then a U.S. senator from Nevada, to use his influence to defeat a trucking industry deregulation bill. Williams, who was forced to step down as Teamster president, was sentenced to 10 years in prison but was released after serving 34 months. In 1935 Williams began his career by trucking livestock to Chicago. He later became active in the leadership of the Teamsters' Local 41 in Kansas City, Mo., and became influential in matters relating to the union's pension fund. As an executive Williams gained a reputation as a forceful bargainer with an expertise in trucking contracts. His rise to power was fueled by onetime Teamster boss James Hoffa, and in spite of an indictment that was pending on charges involving union misdeeds and reported links to organized crime, Williams was elected president of the Teamsters in 1981. During his imprisonment Williams testified as a government witness in criminal court cases; in 1987 he disclosed that he had been dominated by Nick Civella, who was identified at the trial as a Mafia boss in Kansas City. In return for his testimony, the ailing Williams was paroled in August 1988.

Wolman, Abel, U.S. sanitary engineer and educator (b. June 10, 1892, Baltimore, Md.—d. Feb. 22, 1989, Baltimore), together with Linn H. Enslow, developed in 1918 a formula for purifying drinking water with chlorine in specific amounts that would destroy pathogens yet be safe for human consumption. Wolman graduated from Johns Hopkins University, Baltimore, in 1913,

and in 1915 he became one of the first students to earn a B.S. degree from the university's newly established School of Engineering. Wolman worked for the U.S. Public Health Service and was chief engineer of the Maryland Department of Health before he joined the faculty of his alma mater in 1937 as chairman of the department of sanitary engineering. His expertise was widely sought, and Wolman advised more than 50 foreign governments on their water supplies. After World War II he conducted studies for the National Research Council to determine the public-health impact of radioactive wastes. His accomplishments were honoured in 1975 when he received the National Medal of Science and in 1976 when he shared the prestigious Tyler Ecology Award with two other scientists.

Yakovlev, Aleksandr Sergeyevich, Soviet aeronautical engineer (b. April 1 [March 19, old style], 1906, Moscow, Russia—d. Aug. 22, 1989, Moscow, U.S.S.R.), designed the Yak series of aircraft, the most important of which constituted more than half of the Soviet Union's World War II fighters. Yakovlev built his own glider in 1924 while working for aircraft designer Sergey V. Ilyushin as an engine mechanic. By the time Yakovlev entered the Zhukovsky Air Force Engineering Academy in 1927, he had designed and built the AIR-1, a light plane that later flew from Sevastopol to Moscow in world-record time. He completed his studies in 1931, and the next year he organized the Yak design bureau. As deputy aviation minister (1940–46), Yakovlev produced both piston- and jet-engine fighters, bombers, helicopters, and support aircraft. In 1957 he was named chief designer of the Soviet Ministry of the Aircraft Industry. Yakovlev built more than 70 types of aircraft, but in later years he concentrated mainly on the Yak-38 (Forger) jump jet and on commercial and sport planes.

Zaccagnini, Benigno, Italian politician (b. April 17, 1912, Faenza, Italy—d. Nov. 5, 1989, Ravenna, Italy), as national secretary of Italy's Christian Democratic Party from 1975 to 1980, helped to forge a short-lived "historic compromise" (1978) with the Italian Communist Party just before his colleague, Prime Minister Aldo Moro, was kidnapped and later murdered by Red Brigade terrorists. Zaccagnini was considered "Mr. Clean" for his ethical, conservative political record. While serving as a practicing physician, he became involved with the *Azione Cattolica* (Catholic Action) group during the Mussolini years. He served as a medical officer in the Balkans during World War II and then, in 1943, joined the Garibaldi Brigade near Ravenna, which resisted the German occupation of Italy. He was secretary (1943–45) of the National Liberation Committee of Ravenna and political secretary (1946) of the local Christian Democrats. In 1946 he also served as a member of the Constituent Assembly, which drafted Italy's postwar constitution. Zaccagnini was elected to the Chamber of Deputies (1948) and served until 1983. He stepped down as head of the Christian Democrats in 1980. In 1983 Zaccagnini was elected to the Senate; he was reelected in 1987.

Zavattini, Cesare, Italian screenwriter (b. Sept. 20, 1902, Luzzara, Italy—d. Oct. 13, 1989, Rome, Italy), played a central role in the founding of the post–World War II Neorealist movement in film. He wrote scripts that reflected his belief that "life is not what is invented in stories; life is another matter. To understand it involves a minute and patient search." In 1935 Zavattini wrote his first screenplay, the satirical comedy *Darò un milione* ("I'll Give a Million"). For nearly 30 years (1942–71) he collaborated with Italian director and actor Vittorio De Sica in creating such memorable films as *Sciuscià* (1946; *Shoeshine*) and *Ladri di biciclette* (1948; *The Bicycle Thief*), both of which won Academy Awards for best foreign film. Zavattini and De Sica achieved international acclaim for the film *Two Women* (1961). Zavattini con-

tinued to study ordinary people even in his last known script *La veritaaa* (1983; *The Truuuuth*), in which he made his acting debut. Some of his other major films were *Umberto D* (1952), *L'oro di Napoli* (1954; *The Gold of Naples*), and *Il giardino dei Finzi-Contini* (1971; *The Garden of the Finzi-Contini*). Zavattini's books included *Ipocrita* (1943), *Toto il buono* (1945), and a translation of some of his diaries, *Sequences from a Cinematic Life* (1970).

Zeman, Karel, Czechoslovak animator (b. Nov. 3, 1910, Ostromer, Moravia [now Czechoslovakia]—d. April 5, 1989, Gottwaldov, Czech.), pioneered the graphic special-effects film and was a leader of Czechoslovak puppetry and animated film. Zeman's short films tended toward political allegories; his most celebrated character, Mr. Prokouk, created in the late 1940s, was a much put-upon bureaucratic Everyman. Zeman was named National Artist in 1970 and received the Order of the Republic in 1980.

Zita of Bourbon-Parma, Italian-born empress of Austria and queen of Hungary (b. May 9, 1892, near Viareggio, Italy—d. March 14, 1989, Zizers, Switz.), was the consort of Charles I, the last ruler of the Habsburg Austro-Hungarian empire. Zita, the daughter of Princess Antonia of Portugal and the dispossessed duke Robert of Parma, was born Princess Zita Maria Grazia Adelgonda Michela Raffaella Gabriella Giuseppina Antonia Luisa Agnese of Bourbon-Parma. In 1911 she married Archduke Charles, who was crowned emperor of Austria and king of Hungary in 1916. Charles repeatedly sought to end World War I without losing the throne, and in 1917 Zita asked her brother Prince Sixtus to propose a separate peace for Austria-Hungary, but the secret talks failed. The emperor relinquished power on Nov. 11, 1918, but in 1921 he and the empress led two disastrous attempts to restore the Hungarian monarchy. After Charles's death (1922) in exile, Zita lived in Spain, Belgium, Canada, and the U.S.; she eventually settled in Switzerland. Although Zita continued to claim the Hungarian crown for her son Otto von Habsburg, through the intercession of King Juan Carlos of Spain she was finally allowed to return to Austria for a short visit in 1982. Her nationally televised funeral in Vienna was attended by thousands, notably Austrian president Kurt Waldheim, and included traditional imperial regalia borrowed from the Habsburg Museum at Schönbrunn Palace. A requiem mass was also said in Budapest.

Zymierski-Rola, Michal (MICHAL LYWINSKI), marshal of Poland (b. Sept. 4, 1890, Krakow, Poland—d. Oct. 15, 1989, Warsaw, Poland), served (1945–49) as marshal of the Polish Army before being relieved of his command in 1949 and imprisoned from 1952 to 1955, a period marked by Soviet leader Joseph Stalin's Sovietization of Poland. Zymierski was educated at the Jagiellonian University, Krakow, where he read law, Krakow Commercial Academy, and École Supérieure de Guerre in Paris. From 1914 to 1917 he served as an officer in Jozef Pilsudski's Polish Legion, fighting for Polish independence, which was won in 1918. During the following years Zymierski rose to the rank of colonel, and in 1920 he took part in the Polish-Soviet war. In 1924 he was promoted to the rank of brigadier general with responsibilities for the armament of the Army. Zymierski broke with Pilsudski in 1926 and was imprisoned until 1931. He then left for France but returned to Poland in 1938. During World War II Zymierski joined the People's Guard, later named the Polish People's Army, a military wing of the Polish Communist Party, and in 1944 he was nominated as its commander in chief. When the Polish Army, formed in the Soviet Union, returned to Poland, he was made its marshal. In 1952 during Stalinist purges, Zymierski was jailed for "right-nationalistic deviation." After his release from prison in 1955, he was rehabilitated and given a senior post in the National Bank, where he worked until his retirement in 1968.

Events of 1989

Agriculture and Food Supplies

A recovery from drought in North America in 1989 eased fears about global vulnerability to large-scale food shortages in the 1989–90 marketing year. However, world cereal stocks were again forecast to decline during 1989–90, leaving world food security once again, in 1990–91, unusually dependent upon 1990 harvests. Political developments in Eastern Europe led that region to emerge as a new major recipient of food aid, seen by some as competition with low-income, less developed countries. Favourable weather conditions helped defuse a major threat to African food security from the explosion of locust populations there. Food supplies were generally more ample in Africa, but Ethiopia once again was threatened by large-scale famine. World agricultural output (as defined by the Food and Agriculture Organization [FAO] production indexes; *see* TABLE 1) rose modestly in 1989, compared with the relatively flat performance of the four previous years. Output per capita also rose slightly after three years of decline.

In the contentious area of trade policy, the European Communities (EC) and the U.S. continued to be the most prominent protagonists. The Multilateral Trade Negotiations (MTN) dealing with agriculture were back on track but moving slowly after being derailed in December 1988 when the EC and the U.S. could not agree on their overall course. EC oilseed policies were censured in the General Agreement on Tariffs and Trade (GATT), as were the operations of the U.S. sugar-support program. The dispute between the U.S. and the EC over the use of growth hormones in cattle, which in 1988 had threatened to escalate into a major trade war, was contained in 1989, but an equally contentious issue involving the use of another hormone was emerging. The operations of the two remaining international agricultural commodity agreements with economic provisions, those dealing with coffee and cocoa, both broke down in 1989 under the pressure of excess supplies.

Food Security. The year 1988 ended amid fears that the drastic reduction in grain supplies in the fall, caused by the severe North American drought, would drive down global grain stocks by the end of the 1988–89 marketing year to a little more than 16% of total grain consumption. That would have approached the 15–16.5% recorded during the 1970s food crisis. In fact, grain production in 1988–89 turned out to be a little larger and consumption a little smaller than originally forecast. Although global grain

Table I. Selected Indexes of World Agricultural and Food Production
(1979–81 = 100)

Region or country	Total agricultural production						Total food production						Per capita food production					
	1984	1985	1986	1987	1988	1989¹	1984	1985	1986	1987	1988	1989¹	1984	1985	1986	1987	1988	1989¹
Developed countries	106	108	108	107	105	109	107	108	109	108	105	109	104	104	105	102	99	103
United States	102	107	100	99	94	103	102	108	102	100	94	104	98	102	96	93	87	95
Canada	108	113	123	116	101	110	109	113	123	118	101	110	104	107	117	109	94	101
Western Europe	109	107	107	108	106	106	109	107	107	107	106	108	108	105	105	105	103	103
Japan	107	106	106	101	97	100	108	108	108	103	99	103	105	104	104	99	95	97
Oceania	106	109	110	106	112	107	107	108	108	103	108	103	100	100	98	93	96	90
South Africa	89	95	97	102	106	115	88	94	97	103	106	116	81	85	85	88	89	95
Centrally planned economies	120	121	126	128	129	132	118	119	126	128	128	132	112	113	118	118	116	118
Eastern Europe	109	110	118	116	115	118	110	110	119	117	116	120	107	106	113	111	109	112
U.S.S.R.	109	110	117	116	116	119	110	110	119	118	117	121	106	106	112	110	109	111
China	134	132	135	142	143	146	129	129	135	140	140	144	122	122	126	128	127	129
Less developed countries	117	121	122	124	129	132	116	120	123	124	130	133	107	108	109	107	110	110
South and East Asia²	116	121	121	121	130	136	117	121	122	121	131	137	107	108	107	103	110	112
Bangladesh	107	113	113	111	112	115	108	112	113	112	113	116	98	97	96	93	91	91
India	121	124	123	121	135	142	121	124	124	122	137	144	111	112	109	105	115	119
Indonesia	124	127	137	138	143	148	126	128	139	140	145	151	117	116	124	122	125	128
Korea, South	108	109	108	105	109	110	109	111	109	107	111	112	102	103	100	97	99	99
Malaysia	122	134	131	142	150	160	130	148	152	159	167	180	119	132	132	133	139	146
Myanmar (Burma)	129	138	139	138	140	144	130	139	139	140	143	147	120	125	123	121	121	122
Pakistan	117	125	136	140	142	150	115	121	133	135	140	146	100	100	106	104	104	105
Philippines	99	101	106	106	110	112	99	100	106	106	110	112	89	88	90	88	89	89
Thailand	113	120	113	112	121	127	114	120	112	111	121	127	105	108	100	97	105	108
Vietnam	122	125	133	135	139	143	122	124	133	135	138	142	112	111	116	115	116	116
Western Asia	107	114	118	117	124	119	107	114	120	119	125	120	94	98	99	95	98	91
Iran	114	116	119	121	118	121	113	116	119	121	118	120	97	95	94	92	87	85
Turkey	105	109	114	113	120	112	105	109	115	114	120	112	96	95	99	97	100	91
Africa³	106	114	119	115	121	123	106	114	119	114	120	122	94	98	99	93	94	93
Egypt	110	116	120	127	127	130	115	120	126	135	138	139	103	105	107	112	111	110
Ethiopia	89	96	104	100	101	104	90	97	106	100	102	105	84	89	95	88	88	89
Morocco	107	121	149	121	155	152	106	120	147	120	155	151	96	105	127	100	125	119
Nigeria	109	124	133	115	131	133	110	124	134	115	131	133	96	105	109	91	100	98
Sudan, The	99	116	113	100	125	117	94	113	112	97	125	116	83	86	84	78	98	89
Latin America	108	113	111	115	118	120	109	114	113	116	120	122	100	102	99	100	101	100
Argentina	107	107	106	106	111	102	107	107	107	107	110	102	101	100	98	97	99	90
Brazil	112	125	114	129	132	134	113	124	118	126	136	137	104	111	104	110	114	113
Colombia	105	103	109	110	119	121	105	106	112	114	122	126	96	96	99	98	103	104
Mexico	108	112	111	112	111	123	110	114	112	113	112	124	100	101	97	96	93	101
Peru	113	109	107	119	124	122	115	111	111	122	127	125	104	98	95	102	104	99
Venezuela	103	104	117	110	112	109	103	103	116	107	110	108	92	89	98	89	88	84
World	111	114	115	116	117	121	111	114	116	116	117	121	104	105	104	102	102	103

¹Preliminary.   ²Excludes Japan.   ³Excludes South Africa.
Source: Food and Agriculture Organization of the United Nations, *FAO Quarterly Bulletin of Statistics*.

A farmer examines the parched soil in which he had planted his crop of winter wheat. A severe drought plagued the U.S. winter-wheat area, which, when combined with the previous year's drought conditions, contributed to a sharp decline in the world's grain supply.

JOHN FREEMAN

for less grain. However, considerable potential existed for those higher prices, if weather around the world in 1990 cooperated, to call forth further substantial increases in grain output in the 1990–91 marketing year. A rough indicator of this potential was that total area planted in grains in 1989–90 was about 36 million ha (89 million ac) less than the record 734 million ha (1,813,700,000 ac) planted in 1981–82. Although output per hectare for major grain categories was the highest ever, strong prices would likely lead to further growth in yields by inducing greater use of inputs such as fertilizers.

The threat of a spreading plague of locusts in Africa and parts of Asia at the beginning of 1989, said by the FAO to be the worst in 30 years, was contained by weather unusually unfavourable to those insects and aggressive countermeasures strongly supported by international donors. To avoid another explosive expansion of migratory swarms, substantial additional control measures would still be required in 1990 in remaining areas of concentration or where eggs had been laid.

The FAO warned that another, longer-term insect menace was threatening to emerge, through the establishment of the American screwworm fly (*Cochliomyia hominivorax*) in Libya. It had caused considerable damage to livestock in the Western Hemisphere and was expensive to control, partly because it could spread through infestation of wildlife. The insect, which also posed some danger to humans, had not been found outside Libya's borders by 1990, but the potential existed for its spread through other parts of Africa, the Middle East, and the southern part of Europe.

Food supplies were at relatively normal levels in most of Africa in 1989 thanks to an unusually good harvest overall in 1988 and generally good, although somewhat smaller, crops in 1989. However, Ethiopia, The Sudan, and Mozambique were major exceptions. The FAO warned in September that the Ethiopian drought in Eritrea and the northern and eastern parts of Tigrai threatened famine for some 1.5 million persons by mid-1990 in addition to a half million persons already experiencing severe food

stocks still fell an unprecedented 24% because consumption substantially exceeded production for the second straight year, the 1988–89 marketing year ended with stocks estimated (in December) at a more comfortable 18.7% of consumption.

Fortunately, grain production did recover in North America in 1989, and overall grain production outside the region was also expected to increase significantly. However, it seemed likely that grain utilization would resume its upward trend in 1989–90 so that it would again surpass production. Thus global grain stocks seemed likely to decline once more, perhaps to close to 17% of consumption. Wheat, by far the most important food grain in world trade, continued to be in the shortest supply among all the grains. World wheat stocks were forecast to fall very close to 21% of consumption during 1989–90, slightly above the lowest level in at least 30 years.

Therefore, the danger remained that poor harvests in the fall of 1990 could send grain prices soaring in 1990–91 and force drastic cuts in grain consumption, especially in the less developed countries. Grain importers in 1989 were already facing prices for wheat that averaged almost 50% higher than the unusually depressed prices in 1987. The FAO estimated that the 45 less developed countries in sub-Saharan Africa paid about $1 billion for their commercial imports in 1988–89, 40% more than a year earlier and

Table II. World Cereal Supply and Distribution
In 000,000 metric tons

	1986–87	1987–88	1988–89	1989–90[1]
Production				
Wheat	531	502	501	532
Coarse grains	835	792	729	807
Rice, milled	319	313	329	335
Total	1,685	1,606	1,558	1,674
Utilization				
Wheat	523	531	531	536
Coarse grains	810	812	797	821
Rice, milled	323	319	326	335
Total	1,655	1,662	1,654	1,692
Exports				
Wheat	91	105	98	97
Coarse grains	84	84	95	98
Rice, milled	13	12	15	13
Total	188	200	207	209
Ending stocks[2]				
Wheat	176	147	117	113
Coarse grains	234	213	145	131
Rice, milled	50	44	46	46
Total	460	404	309	291
Stocks as % of utilization				
Wheat	33.7%	27.6%	22.0%	21.2%
Coarse grains	28.9%	26.3%	18.2%	16.0%
Rice, milled	15.5%	13.8%	14.2%	13.7%
Total	27.8%	24.3%	18.7%	17.2%
Stocks held by U.S. in %				
Wheat	28.2%	23.4%	16.3%	10.7%
Coarse grains	65.2%	62.8%	45.5%	46.6%
Rice	3.4%	2.3%	1.9%	1.7%
Total	44.3%	41.9%	27.9%	25.5%

[1] Forecast.
[2] Series revised to include estimates of Chinese stocks, which especially affect rice estimates. Data not available for all countries, including parts of Eastern Europe and Asia.
Source: USDA, Foreign Agricultural Service, December 1989.

shortages. The agency in December repeated its warning that food supplies in those areas could be exhausted during the early months of 1990 unless prompt action was taken to ensure rapid distribution of increased international food assistance.

Commodity Developments. *Grains.* Fears that total grain stocks at the beginning of 1989–90 might approximate the dangerous levels experienced in the early 1970s were not realized because grain production the previous year was not as low, and grain consumption not as high, as had been suggested by many early forecasts. The two-year decline in world grain production, during which output fell 7.5%, seemed likely (in December) to be reversed in 1989–90, on the basis of Northern Hemisphere harvests through the fall of 1989 and those in the Southern Hemisphere at the year's end or in prospect in early 1990. The recovery was tempered by residual effects of the severe 1988 drought in the U.S. and Canada. Nevertheless, total grain utilization was expected to exceed output for the third year in a row, leading to a further decline in world grain stocks to the lowest levels, as a percentage of consumption, since 1977.

Total production of wheat and coarse grains in the EC in 1989–90 slightly exceeded the "maximum guaranteed quantity" of 160 million tons, which activates an automatic "price stabilizer" mechanism adopted in 1988 to restrict grain production and limit the EC's budgetary expenditures on grain subsidies. This mechanism was expected to trigger a further 3% reduction in 1990–91 intervention (support) prices for grains on top of the 3% reduction applied for the same reason in the 1989–90 season. Some analysts speculated that this would stimulate rather than inhibit production because farmers would increase output to maintain revenues on the expectation that export subsidies would compensate for reduced support prices. The

EC also adopted a voluntary set-aside program that paid farmers to idle land in a further effort to reduce surplus cereal production. The program got off to a slow start, with the EC estimating that about 1% of its arable land would be idled in 1990.

World wheat supplies remained the tightest among grains. Thanks to generally favourable harvests around the world, wheat production was catching up with consumption, which had remained nearly unchanged since 1987–88. Wheat stocks were still forecast to fall during 1989–90, however. World wheat prices, as reflected in the U.S. Gulf export price (f.o.b., 2HRW), which had fallen to an average of about $114 per metric ton in 1986 and 1987—the lowest since 1972—climbed to $146 in 1988 and averaged $168 per metric ton in November 1989.

The recovery in world coarse grain output, which had been hardest hit by the 1988 drought in North America, was stronger than for wheat, but utilization picked up again and still exceeded production for the third year in a row. As a result, stocks of coarse grains were expected to fall again during 1989–90 but to remain well above earlier lows expressed as a percentage of utilization. The price of coarse grains, as represented by corn (U.S. Gulf export, f.o.b., 2Yellow), jumped to nearly $130 per metric ton in mid-1988 before slipping to an average of $109 in November 1989.

World trade in coarse grains was expected to continue to expand in 1989–90, largely because of strong growth in Soviet imports. Soviet grain imports in the past had usually been reduced following a harvest as favourable as that in 1989, but the U.S.S.R. was expected to import considerably more feed grain than the 24.7 million tons in 1988–

Table III. World Production of Oilseeds and Products

In 000,000 metric tons

	1987–88	1988–89[1]	1989–90[2]
Production of oilseeds	208.3	202.7	214.3
Soybeans	103.3	107.9	107.7
U.S.	52.3	42.1	52.7
China	12.4	11.7	11.3
Argentina	9.7	6.6	10.5
Brazil	18.0	23.0	20.5
Cottonseed	31.2	32.2	31.2
U.S.	5.2	5.5	4.3
U.S.S.R.	4.5	5.0	4.8
China	7.2	7.1	7.0
Peanuts	20.3	23.3	22.5
U.S.	1.6	1.8	1.9
China	6.2	5.7	5.5
India	5.3	9.0	8.0
Sunflower seed	20.9	20.4	21.7
U.S.	1.2	0.8	0.8
U.S.S.R.	6.1	6.2	6.5
Argentina	2.8	2.9	4.0
Rapeseed	23.2	22.5	21.5
Canada	3.9	4.3	3.1
China	6.6	5.0	5.6
EC	6.0	5.2	5.0
India	3.2	4.2	3.5
Flaxseed	2.3	1.7	2.0
Copra	4.3	4.5	4.7
Palm kernel	2.7	2.9	3.1
Crushings of oilseeds	167.1	166.5	173.5
Soybeans	85.3	81.5	88.4
Ending stocks of oilseeds	23.8	22.1	23.4
Soybeans	19.7	18.1	20.4
World production[3]			
Total fats and oils	64.6	65.4	...
Edible vegetable oils	50.8	51.6	54.0
Soybean oil	15.3	14.7	15.8
Palm oil	8.4	9.3	10.0
Animal fats	11.7	11.7	...
Industrial and marine oils	2.0	2.1	2.2
High-protein meals[4]	109.6	107.8	113.4
Soybean meal	67.6	64.4	69.9

[1] Preliminary.
[2] Forecast.
[3] Processing potential from crops in year indicated.
[4] Converted, based on product's protein content, to weight equivalent to soybeans of 44% protein content.
Source: USDA, Foreign Agricultural Service, June and November 1989.

Table IV. Livestock Numbers and Meat Production in Major Producing Countries

In 000,000 head and 000,000 metric tons (carcass weight)

Region and country	1988	1989[1]	1988	1989[1]
	Cattle and buffalo		Beef and veal	
World total	1,029.2	1,035.0	45.30	45.19
Canada	11.0	11.1	0.97	0.96
United States	99.5	100.1	10.88	10.58
Mexico	35.0	31.9	1.75	2.14
Argentina	50.3	50.1	2.61	2.52
Brazil	98.3	100.3	2.50	2.40
Uruguay	10.1	9.1	0.32	0.35
Western Europe	85.3	84.6	8.22	8.06
EC	77.9	77.2	7.61	7.44
Eastern Europe	36.1	36.2	2.49	2.44
U.S.S.R.	119.6	120.2	8.47	8.55
Australia	24.3	25.3	1.53	1.45
India	269.2	273.5	0.55	0.67
China	98.0	101.4	0.94	1.02
	Hogs		Pork	
World total	756.0	742.5	62.16	62.34
Canada	10.8	10.7	1.19	1.15
United States	55.5	55.7	7.11	7.21
Mexico	9.0	8.3	0.96	0.94
Western Europe	110.8	110.5	13.65	13.43
EC	101.4	101.2	12.50	12.29
Eastern Europe	75.2	73.9	7.32	7.15
U.S.S.R.	78.1	78.5	6.48	6.60
Japan	11.9	11.9	1.58	1.57
China	342.2	332.0	20.17	20.53
	Poultry		Poultry meat[2]	
World total	...	...	30.23	31.21
United States	...	...	9.43	10.03
Brazil	...	...	2.00	2.13
EC	...	...	5.93	6.03
Eastern Europe	...	...	2.06	2.07
U.S.S.R.	...	...	3.18	3.22
Japan	...	...	1.47	1.48
	Sheep and goats		Sheep, goat meat	
World total	709.2	717.5	5.74	5.88
			All meat	
Total	...	...	143.43	144.61

[1] Preliminary livestock numbers at year's end. Consists of 51 countries for beef and veal, 38 for pork, 51 for poultry meat, 30 for sheep and goat meat, and roughly the same coverage for animal numbers. Includes nearly all European producers, the most significant in the Western Hemisphere, and scattered coverage elsewhere.
[2] Ready-to-eat equivalent.
Source: USDA, Foreign Agricultural Service, November and December 1989.

89 in order to fulfill popular desires for increased domestic production of meat and dairy products. The U.S.S.R. for the second consecutive year surpassed Japan as the world's largest importer of corn. In October the U.S. increased from 12 million to 16 million tons the combined limit for corn and wheat that the Soviets could purchase without consultation under the Long Term Agreement (LTA), which was to expire in December 1990. Negotiations for a new LTA were under way at the year's end.

World rice production continued to expand in 1989, aided by a recovery in Chinese production and continued high output in India. Those two countries together accounted for about 55% of both world production and consumption of rice. Low stocks, strong imports, and tight supplies in exporting countries by mid-1989 led to the highest prices for traded rice since 1981. Prices eased somewhat thereafter because of favourable crop prospects but remained well above levels of recent years. China in 1989 became a net importer of rice for the first time in its modern history.

Oilseeds. World output of oilseeds and their by-products was expected (in December) to register a strong increase in 1989–90, based largely on recovery in the U.S. soybean crop from the 1988 drought and on the expected recovery of the Argentine soybean crop to be harvested in early 1990. Unfavourable prices in Canada and the EC contributed to smaller rapeseed production, and cottonseed output also fell because of a less favourable market for cotton. Oilseed prices, as evidenced by soybeans, peaked at a little more than $350 per ton (c.i.f., Rotterdam, U.S. No. 2 yellow) in mid-1988; they slid downward thereafter, stabilizing at about $238 per ton in the late summer of 1989 before edging up to $246 in November.

Despite the 2.7% reduction in oilseed output in 1988–89, consumption of oilseed meals, as reflected in their crushings, fell only 0.4% because of the availability of adequate stocks. Stocks of oilseeds were expected to rebuild because of the larger 1989–90 crop. Global exports of oilseeds declined 20% in 1988–89 to 31.5 million tons, largely because fewer soybeans were available. Exports of oilseed meals (36.8 million tons) and vegetable oils (17.6 million tons) in 1988–89 changed little from a year earlier. Trade in oilseeds and their products was expected to expand only about 6–7% in 1989–90.

Although the recovery in production of oilseed meals in 1989–90 was outpacing that for vegetable oils, prices in international trade for both declined about one-third from their mid-1988 highs to their most recent lows in August 1989. Prices for oilseed meal, as reflected in those for soybean meal (c.i.f., Rotterdam), peaked at $317 per ton in mid-1988, fell gradually to about $255 in mid-1989, and stood at $226 in November 1989. World vegetable oil prices, as represented by soybean oil (f.o.b., Rotterdam), experienced their most recent high of $600 per ton in July 1988, fell off sharply thereafter, fluctuated around the average of $435 per ton in 1988–89, and stood at $433 in November 1989.

World consumption of rapeseed oil, which has the lowest saturated fat content of the vegetable oils, averaged 13.5% of total vegetable oil consumption in recent years, challenging sunflower seed (13.6%) and approaching palm oil (16.7%) but leaving soybean oil (28.4%) dominant. U.S. consumption of rapeseed oil increased dramatically after 1985, when the U.S. certified the safety of oil from new seed varieties. However, the amount consumed in the U.S. remained minuscule compared with other vegetable oils.

Meat and Livestock. World output of meat was expected (in November) to increase less than 1% in 1989, compared with a 3.3% rise in 1988, with poultry responsible for most of the increase. Annual growth in the production of beef and veal had already slowed to less than 1% in 1988, while that for pork was expected to be very small after expanding 5.2% in 1988. The world's cattle herd was estimated to have increased a little faster in 1989 than the 0.3% recorded in 1988, a figure that marked an end to declining cattle numbers since 1984. The decline in hog inventories in 1989 approximately matched the 1.9% increase a year earlier. Poultry production was estimated (in December) to have increased only slightly less rapidly in 1989 than the 3.4% rise in 1988. The expansion in output of lamb and mutton continued, supported by declining sheep numbers in New Zealand and despite greater retention of wool-producing sheep in Australia because of strong wool prices.

The steady decline since 1982 in the U.S. cattle herd was halted in 1988, and some herd rebuilding began in 1989. U.S. beef output, which had stabilized in 1987 and 1988, declined again in 1989. Among the other major beef exporters, cattle numbers continued similar but slowing long-term declines in the EC and Argentina, while herds were expanding in Australia and Brazil, suggesting an increase in the world total.

Australia regained from the EC its position as the world's leading beef exporter. The rapid expansion in the Australian cattle herd was tempered by competition for pasture from sheep, resulting from strong wool prices in recent years. U.S. meat exports grew more rapidly than those of the other leading exporters in the 1980s. As exporters free from foot-and-mouth disease, Australia, New Zealand, and the U.S. were reaping an increasing advantage in fast-growing Far Eastern import markets.

Table V. World Production and Stocks of Dairy Products[1]

Region and country	Production of cow milk 1987	1988	1989[2]
	In 000,000 metric tons		
North America	81.6	83.1	83.1
United States	64.7	66.0	65.9
South America	23.3	23.0	23.5
Brazil	13.3	13.2	13.2
Western Europe	127.3	124.3	123.7
EC	111.4	109.1	108.6
France	27.1	26.0	25.5
West Germany	24.4	24.0	24.3
Italy	10.3	10.7	10.7
Netherlands, The	11.7	11.4	11.7
United Kingdom	15.4	14.9	14.7
Other Western Europe	15.8	15.2	15.1
Eastern Europe	43.5	43.3	43.9
Poland	15.5	15.5	16.0
U.S.S.R.	103.4	106.4	106.8
China	3.3	3.7	3.6
India	21.2	22.0	23.0
Australia/New Zealand[3]	13.6	14.2	13.9
Japan/South Africa	9.7	10.1	10.2
Total	427.0	430.0	431.8

Product/Region	Production 1988	1989[2]	Year-end stocks 1988	1989[2]
	In 000 metric tons			
Butter	6,624	6,677	906	818
EC	1,683	1,680	545	428
U.S.	547	570	98	145
Cheese	10,482	10,613	1,426	1,377
EC	4,298	4,345	873	847
U.S.	2,527	2,570	181	155
Nonfat dry milk	3,240	3,304	481	496
EC	1,352	1,426	232	237
U.S.	444	390	24	18

[1]Based on 38 major producing countries. Those not shown individually include (North America) Canada and Mexico; (South America) Argentina, Brazil, Chile, Peru, and Venezuela; (EC) Belgium-Luxembourg, Denmark, Greece, Ireland, Portugal, and Spain; (Other Western Europe) Austria, Finland, Norway, Sweden, and Switzerland; and (Eastern Europe) Czechoslovakia, East Germany, Hungary, Romania, and Yugoslavia. Coverage of production and stocks of the other dairy products is not as comprehensive or uniform for the countries above not shown individually.
[2]Forecast.
[4]Year ended June 30 for Australia and May 31 for New Zealand.
Source: USDA, Foreign Agricultural Service, November 1989.

Dairy Products. The slow expansion of total output of cow milk by 38 major producing countries was thought (in November) to have continued in 1989, largely because of production gains in India, Poland, Argentina, and the U.S.S.R. Milk production declined for the third year in a row in the EC because of dry weather, even though new measures to reduce output were not adopted. Drought and high feed prices prevented an expansion of output in the U.S. Poland's increased output was the result of new incentives provided by the government that led to increased numbers of cows being retained for milk production. Cow numbers at the end of 1989 were estimated to be little changed from the beginning of the year, with significant declines in the U.S.S.R., Western Europe, and the U.S. and notable gains in Poland and India. Global consumption of fluid milk roughly kept pace with production.

Consumption of butter fell an estimated 3.5% in major producing countries, mainly because of declines in the EC, Eastern Europe, and the U.S. The EC's butter "mountain" continued to melt away and was estimated at the end of 1989 at only 40% of its size in 1986 as exports, though down sharply, remained high enough to offset decreased domestic consumption. Thus world butter stocks declined for a third year; this resulted in a steady increase in world trade prices for butter and butter oil, which by the fall of 1989 were double their level in the fall of 1987. In the U.S. output and stocks of butter reached their highest level in five years.

Growing demand for cheese led to widespread and more rapid increases in cheese consumption than production in the major producing countries. Cheese prices in world trade by the fall of 1989 were at their highest level in eight years. The decline in U.S. cheese stocks left virtually none available for overseas donation programs. U.S. import quotas for several cheese types remained unfilled, although the EC, a major source of U.S. imports, expanded its exports.

Total production of nonfat dry milk (NFDM) recovered in 1989 after two years of decline. Consumption was down sharply in the EC in 1989 because of reduced use for animal feed, while strong world trade prices drew NFDM away from consumption and into export channels in the U.S. Total stocks of NFDM increased for the first time in five years, but trade prices did not recede from the peaks reached during 1988.

Sugar. World production of sugar was not expected (in November) to increase significantly in 1989–90, with the result that sugar consumption was likely to exceed output for the fifth year in a row. Spot prices (Contract 11, f.o.b. Caribbean ports) of freely traded sugar averaged about 6.7 cents per pound in 1987 and 10.2 cents in 1988 and moved in the 14–15-cent range in the last half of 1989. Trade was expected to be slightly smaller than the 28.6 million tons of raw sugar shipped in 1988–89. World stocks of sugar as a percentage of consumption, which by the beginning of 1989–90 were already at their lowest point since the U.S. Department of Agriculture began making such estimates in 1974–75, were expected to fall even further by the year's end.

The drought-induced reduction in Brazil's 1989–90 sugar crop led to forecasts of the lowest sugar exports by that country since the mid-1970s, contributed to a rise in world sugar prices, and called into question Brazil's ability to fulfill its U.S. import-quota allocation. Brazil privatized all sugar exports in October 1989. However, the government set export quotas to guarantee that domestic sugar needs, including that for production of fuel alcohol, received first priority. In response to the high prices for imported petroleum in the early 1970s, Brazil promoted the substitu-tion of ethanol, produced from sugar, for gasoline. In 1989 about two-thirds of Brazil's 12.9 million automobile fleet used a mixture of gasoline and ethanol, and 4.2 million domestic vehicles were designed to use pure ethanol.

Coffee. The International Coffee Agreement (ICA) in effect collapsed in July when its governing council suspended export quotas for the remaining three months of the agreement, which was to expire at the end of September. The council took this action after it failed to resolve long-simmering issues over the form a new ICA was to take. Partly to gain time in which to find an end to the impasse, the council extended the ICA, but without economic provisions, for two more years. This maintained both a consultative mechanism and a system for computing official indicator prices but ended the verification of sales and stock holdings by members.

The sharp decline in export prices for coffee following the quota suspensions was of major significance not just to coffee drinkers but also to economies in many less developed countries heavily dependent upon coffee for earning badly needed foreign exchange. Several of the affected countries were also producers of cocoa, the price of which on the world market was at a 14-year low. Both crops could be grown in the same areas as coca, making them important in efforts to displace or prevent the production of cocaine in some countries. A prime example was Colombia, where one-half of the foreign exchange earnings from legitimate exports came from coffee.

The importing countries for the most part sought provisions in a new ICA that would guarantee the availability of the high-quality Arabica "milds," such as those produced in the high regions of Colombia and Central America, as opposed to the unwashed Arabica typical in Brazil and the Robustas common in much of Africa. In early periods of the ICA, when demand for high-quality Arabicas was relatively small, quota shares for individual countries had been largely based on their proportion of total production without regard to quality. Thus it had been possible for

Table VI. World Production of Centrifugal (Freed from Liquid) Sugar			
In 000,000 metric tons raw value			
Region and country	1987–88	1988–89	1989–90[1]
North America	10.4	9.9	10.1
United States	6.5	6.1	6.4
Mexico	3.8	3.7	3.5
Caribbean	8.8	9.5	9.5
Cuba	7.4	8.1	8.0
Central America	1.7	1.7	1.8
South America	13.4	13.6	12.3
Argentina	1.2	1.3	0.9
Brazil	8.5	8.6	7.5
Colombia	1.5	1.5	1.5
Europe	20.4	20.6	21.2
Western Europe	15.0	15.8	15.8
EC	14.2	14.8	14.7
France	4.0	4.4	4.1
West Germany	3.0	3.0	3.2
Eastern Europe	5.4	4.8	5.3
Poland	1.8	1.8	1.8
U.S.S.R.	9.6	8.9	9.0
Africa and Middle East	10.1	10.2	10.0
South Africa	2.2	2.5	2.4
Turkey	1.8	1.4	1.5
Asia	25.0	26.9	27.6
China	4.7	5.1	5.3
India	10.0	10.2	10.4
Indonesia	2.1	1.9	2.0
Pakistan	1.9	2.0	2.0
Philippines	1.4	1.6	1.8
Thailand	2.7	4.0	4.0
Oceania	4.0	4.2	4.3
Australia	3.5	3.7	3.8
Totals			
Production	103.4	105.5	105.7
Consumption	106.2	107.1	108.1
Exports	27.6	28.6	28.3
Ending stocks	20.4	19.2	18.2
As % of consumption	19.2%	17.9%	16.8%

[1]Preliminary.
Source: USDA, Foreign Agricultural Service, November 1989.

An entomologist from Cornell University goes over a field of cabbage with a spray containing a genetically-altered virus. If the virus proved effective in controlling agricultural pests, it might eventually replace the traditionally used chemicals.

MICHAEL J. OKONIEWSKI—GAMMA/LIAISON

excess supplies of lower-quality coffee to push down the composite indicator price just when prices were rising for higher-quality coffees in short supply. Until a compromise differentiating between Arabicas and Robustas was reached applicable only to the 1988–89 marketing year, the reductions in export quotas triggered by the indicator price were taken with little regard to what kind of coffee each country produced, so the resulting cutback in availability of higher-quality coffee could push its price even higher.

Divisions also existed among the exporting countries between those that had more rapidly expanding production and wanted larger market shares and those that wanted to maintain their existing share. Brazil, with the largest ICA share, was willing to accept an ICA that maintained its dominant position but also openly indicated that the new free market served its purpose of gaining a larger market share. Brazil, Indonesia, and Mexico were particularly aggressive in expanding sales immediately after the suspension of quotas.

Although world production of green coffee was expected (in December) to recover only partially in 1989–90 from sharply lower output a year earlier, excess supplies of exportable coffee continued to grow and depress prices. Falling prices had triggered reductions in export quotas in 1988, and the ICA composite indicator price (15-day moving average) had by January 1989 moved to an average of $1.29 per pound. However, prices fell thereafter, resulting in further quota reductions to the limit permitted for 1988–89. In June, just before the council met, the price fell below the ICA's lowest level at which intervention would be necessary, facing the council with the dilemma of agreeing on extraordinary cuts at a time when it was attempting to negotiate an extension of the ICA in which the operation of the quota system was a highly controversial issue. After suspension of the quotas the price plummeted to 62 cents per pound in November, the lowest since 1975.

Cocoa. The International Cocoa Agreement (ICCA) was in danger of foundering in 1989 as its resources, under the pressure of burgeoning supplies, proved inadequate to raise international prices of cocoa beans close to the ICCA's minimum. Cocoa bean production grew even faster in 1988–89 than previously estimated, resulting in a record large increase in stocks, and output was expected (in October) to continue expanding at about the same rate in 1989–90. Considerable short-term potential for further expansion existed, especially in Malaysia, Côte d'Ivoire, and Indonesia, where many cocoa trees had yet to reach their full bearing capacity. Cocoa consumption was believed to be nearly saturated in the developed countries, while low incomes and inadequate foreign exchange held down demand in many other areas. Cocoa bean production had exceeded cocoa grindings since 1984–85, leading to a large buildup in stocks and irresistible downward pressure on prices of cocoa beans.

Cocoa bean prices (New York futures, nearest three-month average) declined steadily from their most recent peak, an average of $1.06 per pound in 1984, to an average of 87 cents per pound in 1987 and 69 cents in 1988. Prices strengthened a little that winter after purchases filled the buffer stock to its maximum in June 1988. The ICCO (ICCA Council) met in January and September 1989 but could not agree on new measures. By September the price had fallen to 49 cents per pound. A special scheme to withhold specified quantities of cocoa from the market could not be implemented because many producers were in arrears on payment of the levy imposed on them to purchase the ICCA's buffer stock (over $120 million by October 1989), including the world's largest cocoa producers, Côte d'Ivoire and Brazil. Côte d'Ivoire, which had made no payments since joining the ICCA in 1986, was $70 million in arrears, and most producers had ceased paying the levy. ICCA members almost agreed on a package that would have reduced the lower price limit from 85 cents to 71 cents per pound and lowered the levy from $30 to $5 per ton, but accord was blocked by disagreement over how to treat the arrears. Malaysia in August repeated its refusal to join the ICCA. It expanded output from 100,000 tons in 1984–85 to a forecast 275,000 tons in 1989–90, and its growers wished to avoid any restrictions on output that membership in the ICCA might bring.

Cotton. World cotton stocks at the beginning of 1989–90 were at unusually low levels because of a strong drawdown in stocks outside the U.S. in 1988–89. It was estimated (in December) that world production of cotton would fall 4% in 1989–90 and would be less than cotton consumption for the second straight year. Increased planting restrictions and bad weather in some regions in the U.S. were responsible for most of the reduction. Among the other major exporters, production was estimated to be unchanged in China, where weak producer incentives had kept output below planned targets for several years; weather reduced production in the U.S.S.R.; and only Pakistan harvested a larger crop.

World use of cotton, estimated at 84.6 million bales in 1988–89, appeared to be expanding more rapidly in 1989–90 than the 0.7% recorded the previous year, largely because of population and income gains in major cotton-producing countries. In the U.S. cotton use was expected to reach a 30-year high, partly because the world of fashion once again had discovered denim. World stocks of cotton relative to use were projected to fall below 30% by the end of 1989–90, the lowest since World War II.

World export prices for cotton (Northern European "A" Index), after averaging 73.4 cents per pound in 1987–88,

slipped to an average of 66.3 cents in 1988–89 because of large 1988 harvests. They began to climb when it became apparent that the 1989 harvest would be much smaller and stabilized in the 82–83-cent range from mid-1989 to the end of the year. Rising prices restricted import growth in 1989–90, while low stocks were limiting exports by China, the U.S.S.R., and Pakistan. The result was that trade in cotton was expected to decline a little in 1989–90 after increasing almost 12% in 1988–89 and that world stocks of cotton would fall even further. China's once-large stocks continued to dwindle, contributing to reduced exports and a strong increase in imports in 1988–89.

International Trade Policy. *Trade Disputes.* The U.S. and the EC continued to be dissatisfied with each other's trade practices, but other countries also exchanged criticisms with them. The issues revolved around the types of government interventions and resulting conflicts that the ongoing MTN were attempting to eliminate or bring under control through mutual reforms in agricultural policies.

A GATT panel ruled in December that EC subsidies paid to its oilseed processors violated GATT provisions that required equal national treatment, while subsidies to producers impaired an earlier "zero duty" tariff concession given to the U.S. on soybeans. The U.S. argued that the subsidies had encouraged higher production of oilseeds in the EC because they had been sufficiently generous to permit processors to pass part of them along to producers in the form of higher prices. The EC accepted the report and

agreed to adopt legislation abolishing the subsidies before the end of 1990. Had the EC not accepted the report, the U.S. would have been obliged under U.S. law to retaliate. Some estimated that such a retaliation, sanctioned by GATT rules, could affect $5 billion in EC exports to the U.S.

European oilseed processors, on the other hand, asked the EC to investigate their claim that U.S. soybean meal exports to the EC constituted "dumping." They argued that U.S. domestic soybean oil prices were supported at artificially high levels by U.S. import tariffs that allowed U.S. soybean oil producers to sell the residual soybean meal in Europe at lower prices than they would otherwise. Brazilian vegetable oil producers wanted their government to take action against the U.S. in the GATT based on their claim that U.S. export subsidies under its Export Enhancement Program had depressed international prices of vegetable oils, creating unfair competition for Brazilian exporters. EC oilseed processors were overruled by the European Court of Justice on a complaint that Argentina's differential export taxes on soybeans (higher) and soybean oil (lower) constituted a form of export subsidy favouring soybean oil exports. The U.S. had raised a similar complaint against Argentina.

Multilateral Trade Negotiations. The inability of the EC and the U.S. to agree on the overall character of agricultural trade liberalization resulted in a breakdown of the MTN's midterm review at Montreal in December 1988, halfway between the beginning of the GATT negotiations and their scheduled conclusion in December 1990. The EC and the U.S. were more successful in narrowing their differences at the resumption of the review in Geneva in April 1989. The MTN participants there agreed that the long-term objective of the MTN was to achieve a "fair and market-oriented agricultural trading system" through the "substantial progressive reduction in agricultural support and protection resulting in correcting and preventing restrictions and distortions in world agricultural markets."

This language permitted the simultaneous negotiation of both long-term agricultural reforms and short-term measures for dealing with market imbalances. Previously, before negotiating short-term measures the U.S. had insisted on the adoption of a schedule for the total elimination of policies that distorted trade. The EC had proposed an immediate freeze on existing agricultural supports and other measures designed to stabilize markets in short-term disequilibrium and adamantly rejected the goal of total elimination of agricultural supports. The acceptance of "substantial progressive reduction" deferred to a later stage of the negotiations the question of just how far long-term agricultural reform was to go while permitting both sides

Table VII. World Green Coffee Production

In 000 60-kg bags

Region and country	1987–88	1988–89[1]	1989–90[2]
North America	17,204	16,930	17,475
Costa Rica	2,375	2,758	2,450
El Salvador	2,538	1,492	2,375
Guatemala	3,020	2,913	3,000
Honduras	1,553	1,635	1,740
Mexico	4,717	5,200	5,000
South America	55,473	41,070	44,170
Brazil	38,000	25,000	26,000
Colombia	13,300	10,700	13,000
Ecuador	1,663	2,150	2,000
Africa	19,069	19,689	20,010
Cameroon	1,251	2,253	1,415
Côte d'Ivoire	3,103	3,620	4,000
Ethiopia	3,100	2,900	3,000
Kenya	2,127	1,745	1,740
Uganda	2,600	3,000	3,200
Zaire	2,000	1,650	1,700
Asia and Oceania	11,096	13,924	12,145
India	2,050	3,590	2,250
Indonesia	5,965	6,400	6,450
Total production	102,842	91,613	93,800
Exportable[3]	80,141	68,904	69,645
Beginning stocks[4,5]	33,719	47,228	47,133
Exports[5]	66,620	69,292	77,708

[1]Preliminary.
[2]Forecast.
[3]Production minus domestic use.
[4]In exporting countries.
[5]Stocks and exports for 1987–88 and 1988–89 are August estimates.
Source: USDA, Foreign Agricultural Service, December 1989.

Table VIII. World Cocoa Bean Production

In 000 metric tons

Region and country	1987–88	1988–89	1989–90[1]
North and Central America	117	106	112
South America	555	493	510
Brazil	400	334	350
Ecuador	76	80	78
Africa	1,188	1,420	1,334
Cameroon	133	124	120
Côte d'Ivoire[2]	674	800	750
Ghana	187	305	275
Nigeria[3]	145	145	140
Asia and Oceania	326	344	404
Malaysia	227	230	275
Total	2,186	2,363	2,361

[1]Forecast.
[2]Includes some cocoa marketed from Ghana.
[3]Includes cocoa marketed through Benin.
Source: USDA, Foreign Agricultural Service, October 1989.

Table IX. World Cotton Production

In 000,000 480-lb bales

Region and country	1987–88	1988–89	1989–90
Western Hemisphere	23.1	23.5	20.0
United States	14.8	15.4	12.1
Mexico	1.0	1.4	0.8
Brazil	3.5	3.4	3.5
Europe	1.2	1.7	1.4
U.S.S.R.	11.3	12.7	12.0
Africa	6.1	6.2	5.9
Egypt	1.6	1.4	1.3
Sudan, The	0.6	0.7	0.6
Asia and Oceania[1]	39.2	40.1	41.2
China	19.5	19.1	19.0
India	7.4	8.3	9.0
Pakistan	6.8	6.6	7.1
Turkey	2.5	3.0	2.8
Australia	1.3	1.3	1.5
Total	81.0	84.3	80.6

[1]Includes Middle East.
Source: USDA, Foreign Agricultural Service, December 1989.

to maintain that their original goals were not precluded by the compromise.

In October 1989 the U.S. became the first country to submit a detailed concrete proposal for agricultural reform. Its early submission and comprehensive character tended to define the major issues in contention. The subsequent submissions by other countries, particularly that of the EC, could often be interpreted as responses to the U.S. paper. The EC's proposal was the last submitted, arriving a little before the deadline of the end of December.

The overall philosophy behind the U.S. proposal remained unchanged. Agricultural production and trade should be determined by each country's relative efficiency as measured and determined by the free operation of markets. As the U.S. saw it, government interventions that interfered substantially with free markets inevitably caused distortions in agricultural production, consumption, and trade that resulted in surpluses, massive government expenditures, inefficient allocation of resources, and trade conflicts. The solution was the comprehensive phased elimination of trade-distorting government interventions in agricultural markets, whether domestic or foreign.

The U.S. proposal for reducing import barriers called for "tariffication," the conversion of all nontariff trade barriers into tariffs that would be fixed by agreement at a specified level that could not be raised or offset by other measures without compensation. These "bound" tariffs would then be reduced to zero or to very low levels in 10 years. The U.S. also proposed to eliminate export subsidies within five years, except for bona fide food aid. In addition, all exemptions from GATT rules permitting restriction of imports provided under various "grandfather" agreements under GATT Article XI would be eliminated. Examples might be the U.S. "Section 22 waiver" that permitted otherwise forbidden restrictions when used to maintain domestic price-support programs; the variable import levies that constituted the EC's primary import restrictions; voluntary restraint agreements, such as those that limited meat exports to the U.S.; minimum import prices; and other import barriers not explicitly permitted by the GATT.

The U.S. also proposed to eliminate within five years all forms of export subsidies on a broad and comprehensive list of both raw and processed agricultural products. This shortening of the deadline by five years from an earlier U.S. proposal appeared to respond to the EC's focus on complaints about U.S. export subsidies under the Export Enhancement Program. Bona fide food-aid exports would be exempted, but guidelines might need to be adopted to ensure meeting the needs of aid recipients without distorting normal commercial sales.

The EC argued that the special characteristics of agriculture (low demand elasticities for agricultural products and production swings caused by weather) made it prone to chaotic and unacceptable destabilizing fluctuations. Thus government intervention to achieve stabilization objectives was both legitimate and necessary. Such interventions had, however, gotten out of hand, creating "structural imbalances" (surpluses) that resulted from steadily expanding output and saturated, slow-growing consumption in the industrialized countries. The solution, according to the EC, was not the end of government intervention in agricultural policy but better management of it. This required the mutual removal of excessive stimuli to production in a way that, quoting the Punta del Este Declaration initiating the MTN, reduced "the uncertainty, imbalances and instability in world agricultural markets." The proper aim was to reduce support progressively "to the extent necessary to reestablish balanced markets and a more market-oriented agricultural

trading system," not to set some final level of support.

All in all, neither party moved much closer to the other on major issues, although a more conciliatory tone appeared evident. Few expected either to give much away in the initial bargaining documents, and past negotiations suggested that a compromise, if it could be achieved, would most likely occur only near the December 1990 deadline.

Both some less developed countries and Japan called for certain exemptions based on considerations of food security. The positions of the less developed countries tended to focus on the need for government intervention to stimulate agricultural development, while Japan was most concerned about maintaining a high degree of agricultural self-sufficiency.

Food Aid. Food-aid availabilities in 1989–90 were estimated (in December) by the FAO to be the equivalent of 11 million tons of cereals, an unexpected increase over 1988–89, when shipments fell below the 10 million-ton target established at the 1974 World Food Conference. Action by donors to help aid new regimes in Eastern Europe trying to cope simultaneously with severe economic problems and rapid political transition was a major factor in the increase. For instance, the FAO reported that nearly two million tons of cereals had been allocated to Eastern Europe in 1989–90, including an additional 500,000 tons of wheat and 300,000 tons of other cereals for Poland from EC allocations. About the same level of food aid was expected to be available for shipment to low-income food-deficit countries as had been in 1988–89.

Pledges to the World Food Program's (WFP's) regular resources for the 1989–90 biennium by 71 donors through September 1989 totaled $935.7 million ($698 million of commodities and $237.7 million in cash), two-thirds of the $1.4 billion pledging target. For the 1987–88 biennium pledges by 85 donors amounted to $1,216,300,000 ($925.5 million in commodities and $290.8 million in cash), 87% of the $1.4 billion pledging target. The executive director of the WFP reported to the FAO Council in November that a marked reduction in the flow of multilateral food resources through the WFP would in 1990 hinder the effective operation of WFP development projects financed by those resources. Pledges in 1989 to the WFP's International Emergency Food Reserve by 21 donors through mid-November 1989 equaled 393,820 tons of cereals and 33,301 tons of noncereal commodities.

(RICHARD M. KENNEDY)

See also Gardening.
This article updates the *Macropædia* article The History of AGRICULTURE.

Table X. Shipments of Food Aid in Cereals

In 000 metric ton grain equivalent

Region and country	Average 1984–85, 1986–87	1987–88	1988–89[1]	1989–90[1]
Australia	393	355	348	330
Canada	1,133	1,062	1,170	850
EC	2,001	2,514	1,990	2,800
By members	960	1,094	1,108	...
By organization	1,041	1,420	882	...
Japan	425	547	440	400
Saudi Arabia	95	166	10	...
Sweden	77	115	132	80
United States	7,357	7,946	5,287	6,200
Others[2]	532	736	464	357
Total	12,013	13,441	9,841	11,017
Percentage to low-income food-deficit countries[3]	86%	79%	81%	73%

[1]Partly estimated.
[2]Includes Argentina, Austria, China, Finland, India, Norway, OPEC Special Fund, Switzerland, Turkey, and World Food Program, but not necessarily for all years.
[3]Per capita incomes under U.S. $940 in 1987.
Source: FAO, *Food Outlook*, December 1989.

FISHERIES

As the 1980s drew to a close, it was appropriate to note that 1989 reflected a continuation of trends that had emerged throughout the decade in the fishing industry. The period would be remembered as one of enormous changes in the world's fisheries, with further changes expected to come.

While it had long been accepted that the fishing industry worldwide is characterized by peaks and troughs corresponding to the abundance or scarcity of fish stocks, it was the extensive implementation, during the 1980s, of 200-mi exclusive economic zones (EEZs) by many coastal nations that was seen as the single most important cause of change. This move had the effect of regulating fishing activities in many grounds that had been freely fished. Thus some fishing nations, such as Japan, which relied to a large extent on catches obtained from foreign waters, suffered dire effects. Japan was generally acknowledged to be the world's largest and most discerning market for fish. In order to meet domestic consumer demand, Japanese fishing vessels had traditionally fished freely around the world, and the country had long ranked as the world's top catching nation. By 1989, however, it was pondering how much longer it could retain this position. The expulsion of Japanese fishing vessels from their traditional fishing grounds had had drastic social consequences. Many Japanese deep-sea fishermen had been forced to come ashore and either find work as coastal fishermen or leave the fishing industry entirely.

Conversely, the Soviet Union, which ranked as the world's second largest catching nation, had benefited, largely by successfully negotiating joint ventures in areas where it had political or commercial advantages. Evidence of its optimism for the future was confirmed by a major shipbuilding program that included the construction of 15 factory trawlers in Norway and another 15 in Spain; the last of three giant factory ships built in Finland was scheduled for delivery at the end of 1989. The Soviet Union signed almost 30 fishery cooperation agreements with China during the year, covering catching, processing, aquaculture, and fishing-boat construction and repairs. China received rights to fish in Soviet waters in return for access to Chinese shipbuilding and repair facilities and its expertise in aquaculture. China, the third-largest catching nation, also envisaged a positive future. It had negotiated several important joint ventures, including an agreement with Argentina to establish a joint venture company that would give it access to Argentine waters.

In the U.S. the program aimed at Americanizing the fishery included the implementation of an EEZ. Gradually, foreign fishing vessels had been replaced by U.S. vessels, ensuring that shipyards were kept busy, especially with new building and conversion work for the North Pacific fishery. By the year's end this fleet comprised 52 factory trawlers in service or under construction, mainly for surimi (processed minced fish) and fish fillet production. Nine of these vessels were fitted with equipment to utilize waste material from the factory as fish meal, a novel departure for U.S. vessels. The North Pacific fishery had grown so rapidly over the past few years that doubts were being expressed as to whether the industry was overcapitalized, whether fishing effort could be sustained at such high levels, and whether existing markets could absorb all the finished product that increased fishing effort would generate.

In Europe most fishing nations continued to struggle with the harsh realities of diminishing fish stocks and reduced catch quotas in their own fishing grounds. To make matters worse, stock assessments undertaken by scientists suggested that catch quotas and fishing effort should be reduced further to allow stocks to regenerate. The scientists' findings were perceived as an even greater threat to Europe's catching sector in coming years. Despite increased calls from the industry for decommissioning schemes or other incentives to encourage European fishermen to scrap old vessels and reduce fleet capacity, national and European Communities (EC) authorities appeared unwilling to provide financial compensation to fishermen who consented to leave the industry.

Against this background of increased regulation of the world's major fishing regions, there were still some fishing areas beyond the jurisdiction of 200-mi zones. However, the welfare of fish stocks in these areas caused international concern during the year. In particular, the southwest Pacific Ocean became a major focus of attention when several countries denounced the use there of gill, or drift, nets in the tuna fishery by Japanese, South Korean, and Taiwanese vessels. The technique, which became known as the "wall of death," was described as involving the indiscriminate use of nets stretching 50 km (30 mi) or more, which ensnared and killed most marine life in the area. Member countries of the Fisheries Agency of the South Pacific Forum formally denounced the practice at their summer conference. In December an agreement to phase out the use of large-scale drift nets by June 1992 was reached in the United Nations.

Shore-based processors, compelled to compete with the increasing trend toward on-board production of fish products, also had their share of difficulties. This trend showed

Table XI. World Fisheries, 1987[1]
In 000 metric tons

Country	Catch		Trade	
	Total	Inland	Imports	Exports
Japan	11,841.1	226.0	2,002.3	715.8
U.S.S.R.	11,159.6	988.4	491.3	771.3
China	9,346.2	3,937.9	246.0	238.6
United States	5,736.5	75.2	1,560.7	2,128.7
Chile	4,814.4	0.9	0.7	1,299.6
Peru	4,583.6	36.5	35.0	757.0
India	2,893.4	1,212.0	—	95.5
South Korea	2,876.4	57.0	301.1	536.7
Indonesia	2,609.7	641.8	64.3	120.3
Thailand	2,165.1	164.7	224.6	673.8
Philippines	1,988.7	562.8	105.4	71.1
Norway	1,929.3	0.4	91.5	711.7
North Korea	1,700.0	100.0	—	31.0
Denmark	1,695.7	23.8	397.6	696.3
Iceland	1,633.1	0.6	1.5	632.8
Canada	1,453.5	43.0	153.8	564.4
Mexico	1,419.2	173.4	6.1	127.6
Spain	1,393.4	28.7	590.0	237.6
United Kingdom	954.7	15.1	872.4	424.1
South Africa	902.1	0.8	101.6	125.8
Vietnam	871.4	251.0	—	28.5
France	843.7	39.9	679.1	232.2
Bangladesh	814.7	581.8	—	28.2
Brazil	793.1	215.0	113.1	47.0
Myanmar (Burma)	685.9	145.0	—	7.1
Ecuador	679.0	0.9	—	199.9
Poland	670.9	30.7	249.4	138.7
Turkey	625.7	44.8	3.6	32.7
Malaysia	607.5	9.0	256.3	174.0
Argentina	559.4	7.8	15.1	235.0
Italy	554.5	55.2	620.9	73.4
South West Africa/ Namibia	519.5	0.2	...	...
Morocco	491.0	1.3	0.8	180.6
The Netherlands	435.2	5.2	507.2	535.2
New Zealand	430.7	0.2	9.4	156.5
Pakistan	427.8	91.6	0.2	39.9
Portugal	395.2	2.4	179.7	65.5
Ghana	371.8	54.0	16.2	22.7
Faeroe Islands	355.4	—	4.2	141.6
Tanzania	313.5	265.8	0.1	0.7
Venezuela	303.5	27.4	0.1	20.5
Senegal	299.0	15.0	9.7	77.2
Romania	264.4	66.9	37.0	—
Egypt	250.0	201.7	132.2	0.7
Other	7,034.9	1,790.4	4,672.5	2,056.9
World	92,693.4	12,192.2	14,752.7	15,454.4

[1]Excludes whaling.
Source: United Nations Food and Agriculture Organization, *Yearbook of Fishery Statistics*, vols. 64 and 65.

A sea lion struggles fruitlessly against a drift net used by fishermen in the southwest Pacific to catch tuna. In response to increasing international pressure, countries that allowed such nets, which trapped and killed much marine life, were curtailing their use.
BOB SLOAN

no sign of being reversed, and many processors were forced to reassess their economic viability. Adding to their problems, processing plants in several European countries were faced with high water charges and a requirement to treat wastewater prior to discharge. Several research programs were being undertaken with the aim of reducing the cost of wastewater treatment, and two systems became commercially available during the year.

A subject of considerable debate concerned the implementation by January 1993 of the EC's single or integrated market. Several companies involved in the export of goods or services into the EC had already begun to establish a presence inside the Community in order to maintain access to this important market. Exporters of fish from North America and New Zealand began exploratory talks, while member countries of the European Free Trade Association, such as Norway and Iceland, which currently enjoyed significant export sales in the EC, conducted negotiations with EC officials with a view to securing access to EC markets.

In spite of the various problems that faced the fishing industry, there was agreement that fish stocks required protection to ensure their long-term survival in a world where consumer demand for fish was expected to exceed 100 million metric tons annually by the end of the century. What could not be agreed on was the most effective way of protecting both the fish and the industry, with the result that national and international disputes over catch quotas and territorial rights continued unabated.

(VIVIANNE AERS)

This article updates the *Macropædia* article Commercial FISH-ING AND MARINE PRODUCTS.

FOOD PROCESSING

Consumer demands on the food industry increased in 1989 as eating habits became more sensitive to the vagaries of fashion, political and health lobbyists exerted their influence, and—as a result of foreign travels—consumers demanded more exotic foods. The fastest growing sector of the European and U.S. food industries was frozen foods. In Europe two contradictory trends were noted: national and regional food differences became further blurred and, at the same time, food companies found specialized markets for regional and ethnic foods.

In all Western countries, particularly the U.S., the proportion of people over 40 continued to increase, resulting in consumer demands for fewer calories and less fat, salt, and sugar; more choice; and more natural and fresh products containing fewer additives. Paradoxically, a survey revealed that an astonishing 80% of consumers in Western Europe exhibited signs of nutritional disorder, particularly obesity, which was increasingly common in all prosperous countries. Contributing factors included life-style pressures, between-meal snacking, greater fast-food consumption, excessive smoking and drinking, and reduced intake of fruits and vegetables.

Epidemics of food poisoning continued to spread across the world, with many countries reporting large increases in illness; product tampering worsened. (*See* Special Report.)

Technology. The European Commission sponsored a research program to study food manufacturing in the areas of quality, safety, and nutrition. The program began in January 1989 and would end in mid-1993. The aim was to strengthen the European food industry in time for the removal of European Communities (EC) trade barriers in 1992 and to unite presently fragmented national research groups.

The use of additives in food products continued to increase overall, especially as flavours, flavour enhancers, acids for soft drinks, and high-intensity nonnutritive sweeteners. Tonnages of salt, yeast, colours, and preservatives declined.

In order to reduce the use of artificial additives, Rutgers, the State University of New Jersey, developed a process designed to extend the use of natural antioxidants in rosemary and sage, herbs that had long been used in meat preparation. The new process allowed their use in a much wider range of foods and was commercialized by a U.S. company.

Domestic use of microwave ovens in all developed countries increased. Forecasters predicted that by the end of 1990 penetration in the leading user countries would be U.S. 90%, Japan 69%, U.K. 58%, West Germany 22%, and France 22%. Manufacturers responded by launching more microwaveable products in special packaging.

A New Zealand company was the first in the world to use new susceptor technology to produce a package. An inner surface of film absorbs microwave energy and passes it on to the food in the form of radiant heat, which acts on the food in a way similar to heat in a conventional oven. This makes possible the microwave production of puff pastry, crusty bread, and browned bakery products.

A research program was started at the Leatherhead (England) Food Research Association to promote the use of refined and deodorized fish oils in food products. Some research findings had indicated that fish oils were beneficial in the prevention or amelioration of such major diseases of industrialized societies as heart disease and hypertension, but they had seldom been used in food products.

Experts gathered in Geneva expressed dismay at con-

Chilean grapes are removed from the shelves of a Chicago market in the midst of an international scare that broke out when two grapes in a shipment of fruit from Chile to the U.S. were found to have been injected with cyanide.

STEVE LEONARD—BLACK STAR

sumer rejection of food irradiation and said that this rejection, based on misunderstanding of what the process entailed, could hamper its use in those countries that would most benefit from it. The World Health Organization stated that irradiation could reduce vast food losses caused by spoilage and could help eliminate food-borne disease.

To ease its mounting economic crisis, Nigeria banned certain grain imports, including barley malt, thereby threatening to bankrupt the country's 36 breweries. A Danish company unveiled an enzyme system that promised to allow the use in brewing of such alternate indigenous grains as sorghum and corn (maize) instead of barley.

New Products and Ingredients. Product launches included a low-fat cottage cheese in Italy, the first in that market; a carbonated drink in Japan containing soluble dietary fibre; a high-fibre spaghetti in Australia; a rub-on powder in South Africa for browning meat, fish, and poultry in microwave ovens; and, in the U.S., fresh fruit and vegetable packs in controlled-atmosphere packaging (CAP) containers.

NutraSweet Co., manufacturer of the artificial sweetener Aspartame, estimated that in 1989 its product sweetened between a quarter and a third of all soft drinks. A competitor, Acesulfame-K manufactured by Hoechst of West Germany, was approved by the U.S. Food and Drug Administration in July 1988; food products containing the new sweetener stiffened competition in a market currently worth over $1 billion.

In spite of worldwide trends toward the reduced sale of alcoholic beverages, sales of beers with increased alcohol content soared in Japan. Termed "dry beers," they had 10% more alcohol, were being made by all leading Japanese brewers, and accounted for 40% of the beer market there. When dry beers were exported to the U.S., brewers there launched their own dry beer brands.

Packaging. Growing demand for convenience foods boosted the growth of CAP, microwaveable foods, and multilayer containers. CAP was forecast to become the fastest growing sector of food packaging during the next few years. It offered the retailer extended shelf life and the consumer a choice of fresh chilled products with no additives. The U.S., the U.K., and France showed the highest rate of CAP development.

Europe's food industry began to take seriously the recycling of food-packaging materials, namely glass, metal, and plastic. West Germany, which recycled 37% of its glass, had the highest total weight of glass recycled in Europe, while The Netherlands recycled the largest percentage, 62%; the U.K. and Ireland were Europe's poorest recycling performers.

Company Developments. Coca-Cola launched Europe's largest soft drink factory at Wakefield, England, and expected to spend $80 million to make it fully operational

(continued on page 141)

A Muffin a Day . . . ?

If years were defined by their most popular food item, then 1989 would have to be described as the year of oat bran. Unlike many previous food fads, however—croissants, quiche, and sushi, to name a few—this one had good health as its raison d'être.

It had long been known that consumption of insoluble dietary fibre—found in wheat products, for example—aids digestive health. In the 1980s, however, people had a more urgent concern—high blood cholesterol, a major risk factor for coronary heart disease. So when studies revealed that the fibre in oat bran—soluble fibre, which dissolves in water—lowers blood cholesterol, it was not long before oat bran was making headlines. The fact that such foods as broccoli, cauliflower, and beans are also excellent sources of soluble fibre seemed to be forgotten in the rush to jump on the oat "branwagon."

Numerous oat bran cereals appeared, as well as oat bran bagels, pretzels, pita bread, snack bars, cookies, animal crackers, and even potato chips. A favourite

staple of "oat cuisine" was the already fashionable muffin. Recipes abounded, mixes appeared on grocers' shelves, and bakeries and restaurants strove to maintain their supplies in the face of ever increasing demand.

There were a few notes of caution, however. Oat bran did not automatically make an item a health food; the amount of oat bran and the other ingredients had to be considered. Some muffins, for example, had a high fat content and were high in calories. The rest of the food in a person's diet was, of course, also important. Rich dairy products and fatty meats would negate the benefits of even large helpings of oat bran. It was not a magic pill or potion.

Even though innumerable fashionable foods had fallen from favour in the past, oat bran's popularity showed no signs of waning. Other fibres—psyllium, rice bran, corn bran—might be gaining in popularity, but oat bran remained the Cinderella food of the year.

(BARBARA WHITNEY)

Our Endangered Food Supply

BY CHRISTOPHER PARKES

About 100 years ago, when processed, packaged, and brand-named foodstuffs replaced commodities commonly sold loose from sacks, boxes, and barrels in Western markets, one of the greatest perceived benefits was that food supplies could be considered safe at last.

With a reputable manufacturer's trademark on the package, food of all kinds was freed from the unwelcome attentions of the tamperer and contaminator. Canning and other processes rendered food relatively secure from insect infestation and infection with microorganisms. Before then, unscrupulous wholesalers and grocers commonly watered down milk and contaminated flour with chalk and other cheap, makeweight ingredients. Bugs, microscopic and otherwise, multiplied unhindered.

After being kept at bay for most of this century, the spectre of unsafe food returned in new manifestations in the 1980s. Contamination once again became an issue of widespread public concern, but this time the issue was more subtle, insidious, and, in some forms, potentially more life-threatening than anything from the past. There were several elements that, taken together, confronted the public and the food industry with a considerable and complex dilemma.

Chemicals Cause Concern. The most problematic of these was the use of agricultural chemicals: pesticides, herbicides, and fungicides. Their residues linger in harvested crops and appear—either in their original form or modified during food-preparation processes—on the family table. At worst, residues were considered carcinogenic. At best, they were undesirable. In the U.S. alone, pesticide use more than doubled in the last 20 years.

In June 1989 Alar (daminozide), a spray applied to red apples, mainly for cosmetic purposes, was withdrawn from sale in the U.S. after the government acknowledged that the chemical had caused cancer in laboratory animals and might increase cancer risk in children. The alarm spread quickly to Britain and by September was beginning to be felt in continental Europe. By then another threat, the EBDC family of fungicides, which includes Maneb and Zineb and which produces by-products described by campaigners as "10 times more toxic than Alar," was becoming the issue of the moment in North America.

Food-Borne Illnesses. The incidence of food poisoning, originating mainly from such bacteria as *Salmonella, Listeria monocytogenes,* and *Campylobacter,* had increased exponentially in recent years and showed no sign of fading. While deaths were comparatively rare in industrialized countries, the very young, the very old, pregnant women, and people with impaired immune systems were at greater risk from these infections.

In early 1989 the U.S. and Britain were stricken more or less simultaneously with outbreaks of salmonella poisoning, specifically from eggs and chicken. By early spring U.K. egg consumption was 40% below normal, and sales were still down 12% six months later. Other scientific names gained popular currency as "listeria hysteria" struck Britain; the number of recorded cases of listeriosis in humans more than tripled between 1978 and 1988. The campylobacter "barbie bug," so called because of its links with undercooked barbecued chicken, also sprang to prominence. In June Britain recorded its first outbreak of botulism in more than 10 years. A batch of infected hazelnut puree, used to flavour yogurt, killed one of 26 afflicted persons. To compound matters, the United Kingdom basked in its hottest summer since 1976, making conditions ideal for bacteria to thrive.

Consumer Terrorism. Of less importance in terms of frequency but especially horrifying to the consumer was the "new terrorism." Fringe groups or individuals, for political or personal purposes, deliberately poisoned or otherwise contaminated food products from a particular company or country. Sometimes blackmailers sought gain from either manufacturers or retailers. However, while there was no easy way for consumers to detect chemical residues or bacteria in food, the new terrorists usually issued warnings. It was rare for their work to result in death or injury.

Among the dozens of reported cases of food tampering in 1989, two were widely publicized. The governments of the U.S., Japan, and Canada banned the importation of a billion dollars' worth of Chilean grapes after two single grapes were found laced with cyanide. In Britain one national supermarket chain promptly threw out $100,000 worth of Chilean grapes.

In Britain an extortionist contaminated baby food. The jars, spiked variously with pieces of razor blade or glass, pins, and caustic soda, caused a national furor and huge losses of sales. Within a month of the earliest report, the police had monitored more than 250 alleged instances of contaminated baby food. Two were the work of the blackmailer, and the others were either imagined or the work of "ordinary" people fraudulently seeking compensation from manufacturers.

The combined effect of these factors, compounded by the activities of consumer watchdog and political pressure groups, with each instance diligently, often colourfully, and sometimes inaccurately reported in the media, seriously shook the consumer's formerly unquestioning faith in the food industry.

Regulatory Efforts. Governments, regulatory authorities, and the industry itself appeared powerless to calm consumer fears. They seemed reluctant to impose statutory controls, maintaining that existing legislation was adequate to deal with criminal contamination and ensure the highest hygiene standards at all points in the food chain. As for agricultural chemicals, they deemed that the greatest body of international opinion, often underpinned by the World Health Organization, suggested that any residues carried nil or minimal risks to human health. Although some actions were taken to close legal loopholes, the message most heard was that enforcement officers should be more alert and that the buyer should beware.

However, some believed that the average buyer was ill-equipped to exercise proper judgment. The welter of publicity about previously unheard-of toxins and bacteria, accompanied by often conflicting opinions from reputable scientists, led to considerable confusion. Robert O. Aders, president of the U.S. Food Marketing Institute, attacked an activist group's campaign against fungicide residues. It was, he said, "based on a rehash of information

Christopher Parkes is editor of Business *magazine, London.*

and distortion that has been discredited by the scientific community and government. Food safety issues are too important for their resolution to be led by misguided zealots, charlatans, quacks and hucksters." John Gummer, Britain's agriculture minister, was more delicate. "Food faddists," he said, should be given no credibility. "We only confuse consumers if we bombard them with every possible and impossible fear."

Retailers Champion Consumers. In an attempt to cut through the confusion, food retailers in both the U.S. and Britain elected to present themselves as the consumers' champions. By operating as the interface between the food-production chain and the public, retailers stayed in close touch with consumer sentiment and were the first to feel the commercial effects when shoppers reduced purchases of "suspect" goods.

During September five U.S. and Canadian supermarket chains signed an agreement promising to eliminate all dangerous pesticides from fresh fruits and vegetables in hundreds of stores. In effect, they warned growers and suppliers that if they did not stop using a wide range of chemicals, they would lose the business of those chains.

Although worries over chemical residues were more subdued in Britain, retailers there posted reassuring notices on shelves displaying Alar-free apples, sought out and patronized "clean" egg and poultry producers, and imposed the most exacting hygiene controls on suppliers of all foodstuffs. At the time of the contaminated-baby-food scare, retailers ignored police advice and cleared shelves and warehouses of all suspect stock.

In an attempt to improve food hygiene, the British government declared during the year that it planned to legalize the use of gamma-ray irradiation as a means of preserving a wide range of foodstuffs. Aware of widespread public suspicion about anything connected with the nuclear industry, the country's leading stores declared they would not stock irradiated goods.

Retailers, especially large chains with considerable regional or national influence, were therefore emerging as the final arbiters in the current debates. Their marketing decisions were likely to have a considerable impact on all others in the food chain. Retailers had already demonstrated that they could force radical changes in production practice. Similarly, store owners in both the U.S. and Britain were pressuring farmers either to grow organic produce or to greatly reduce their use of chemicals.

Consumer Education. A fine balance would be needed between the perceived and the actual needs of consumers, however. Market research consistently indicated that people prefer fruit and vegetables that are unblemished and of consistent shape, size, and colour. Inconsistent with the laws of nature, such criteria were difficult, if not impossible, to achieve economically in chemical-free conditions.

Research also divined that people want fresher, only lightly processed foods without preservatives or other additives. Experience suggested that it was just such foods—ready-made microwave meals, for example—that were the source of at least a portion of the current food-poisoning epidemic because people did not understand how to store and prepare them safely and properly.

Suggestions that consumer education would resolve most of the problems could be valid in some instances, but it would take an educational campaign of some scale to bring the British and American public to appreciate that their new dietary requirements and their traditional perception that food is cheap were simply not compatible with the laws of economics.

(continued from page 139)

by 1991. Ganong Brothers, Canada's oldest chocolate company, opened a Can$12 million candy factory in New Brunswick. The U.K. brewers Courage opened a $4 million plant for producing low-alcohol lager at Reading, England. RHM Ingredient Supplies of the U.K. purchased for $18,250,000 Europe's largest food ingredients plant, which produced coatings, cereal ingredients, seasonings, and flavouring blends.

The U.S.S.R. bought a number of major installations from Western companies: four fruit- and juice-processing plants from Austria and Sweden, a fish-farming facility from Japan, 10 breakfast cereal plants and a bottling plant from France, which launched the U.S.S.R.'s entry into the plastic bottle field, and a cheese factory and three ice cream plants from the U.K.

Legislation. The EC proposed a Food and Flavours Directive that would replace the current list of prohibited flavours. It would change the way flavour companies did business, could eliminate 95% of the process flavours available in Europe, and would severely restrict the development of new flavours.

The increase in food poisoning throughout the world spurred authorities in many countries to improve hygiene and food-safety standards. In the U.S. the establishment of a single food-safety agency was recommended. In the U.K. a health minister resigned as a result of national concern about salmonellae in eggs. After a parliamentary report appeared severely criticizing the British Food Ministry's handling of the matter, the government set up a food-safety inquiry, unveiled a code of hygiene practice, and announced tough new laws regulating food handlers. Similar action was taken throughout the EC.

The U.K. government announced that food irradiation, already legal in Europe and many other countries, would be permitted in Britain. Opposition from consumer and food-industry groups continued, however, and major U.K. manufacturers of chilled foods said they had no intention of using the process.

Regulations banning the use of mineral oils in food processing were introduced in the U.K. They had been legally used to stop dried fruit from sticking, for coating citrus fruit and some cheese rinds, and in candy manufacture.

(ANTHONY WOOLLEN)

' *See also* Environment; Health and Disease; Industrial Review: *Beverages; Textiles; Tobacco.*
This article updates the *Macropædia* article FOOD PROCESSING.

Anthropology

Anthropology entered the 1990s as a much changed field of study. The discipline itself continued to be widely associated in the public mind with the hunt for remote exotic cultures or timeless pristine social laboratories. Few modern anthropologists, however, sought relics of a human past that might exist only in modern theory. Instead, most current anthropological studies reflected increasing awareness of the influences of history, politics, social context, and anthropologists themselves upon culture.

In New York City anthropologist Ansley Hamid worked in Harlem, gathering information on the effects of antidrug laws upon the crack trade. Hamid was one of a new breed of young urban anthropologists, known as "street ethnographers," who were studying the causes and consequences of crack addiction. Crack, a highly addictive cocaine derivative, had spread in epidemic waves through poor urban neighbourhoods across North America and was beginning

to appear in Europe. Hamid and his colleagues worked closely with criminologists, sociologists, psychologists, and other specialists to understand crack's disastrous impact on young people. Together they were providing policymakers with practical information that might help break crack's destructive cycle of crime, violence, and despair in America's poorest neighbourhoods.

Medical anthropologist Anna Kline was working to combat another problem associated with drug use and poverty. In the New Jersey cities of Newark, Jersey City, and Paterson, rates of AIDS infection among women and children were among the highest in North America. Intravenous drug use with contaminated needles was the primary mode of AIDS transmission in this population. Kline worked as a research scientist in New Jersey's Perinatal AIDS Prevention Project. This project, one of eight that was funded nationwide by the U.S. government's Centers for Disease Control, operated out of family-planning clinics, prenatal clinics, and community-based organizations. By working in communities where the need was greatest, Kline and other research scientists directly reached asymptomatic women who were infected with the AIDS virus and women at risk of AIDS infection in an effort to prevent the spread of the disease among this increasingly vulnerable population.

Anthropology museums responded to issues of concern to Native Americans and other tribal people during the late 1980s. The New York State Museum, for example, returned to the tribe wampum belts held in trust for the Iroquois League of six nations for more than 100 years. In Washington, D.C., the Smithsonian Institution agreed that where tribal origin had been established, human remains stored within its collections would be returned to tribes claiming them as ancestors. A U.S. bill signed into law on Nov. 25, 1989, established a National Museum of the American Indian incorporating the collections of the Smithsonian Institution and New York City's Museum of the American Indian, Heye Foundation. These actions reflected the museum community's growing awareness of the need to work with tribes and other ethnic communities as partners. (*See* ARCHAEOLOGY: *Western Hemisphere*.)

Anthropologist Waud Kracke assumed a particularly active role as an advocate for the Brazilian tribal people, whom he had studied as a field ethnographer since 1969. Abandoning the traditional role of participant-observer, Kracke and other anthropological advocates were assisting the estimated 200,000 Brazilian Amazon tribal people threatened by miners, loggers, and ranchers by helping them gain title to their land and avoid exploitation. These efforts often placed anthropological advocates in direct conflict with host government officials who administered Indian affairs or controlled access to tribal territories. Such confrontations sometimes placed tribal members and their advocates at risk, highlighting the dilemma faced by anthropologists who take a more active role in support of the people they study.

Political involvement was only one of the issues being actively addressed by the anthropological community. Hypotheses developed during the 1960s concerning models of hunter-gatherer life and upwardly revised estimates of pre-Columbian population were also undergoing particularly intensive scrutiny.

The 1968 publication of *Man the Hunter,* a symposium volume edited by anthropologists Richard B. Lee and Irven DeVore, challenged the prevailing views of hunting and gathering life as "nasty, brutish, and short" with an alternative vision of hunters and gatherers as "the original affluent society" composed of cooperative, peaceful, egalitarian nomadic foragers. Although many foraging cultures were discussed in the volume, the Kalahari Desert !Kung Bushmen as described by Lee came to be regarded as the model hunter-gatherer society.

As idealized models the !Kung came to represent not just themselves but the hunting and gathering way of life as it was lived by the ancestors of humans during the two million years preceding the invention of agriculture and settled society. Recent studies by Kristen Hawkes, Robert Foley, and other anthropologists, however, suggested that Lee's description of the sharing, nonviolent !Kung was romantic, idealistic, and too simplistic. They also showed that both modern *Homo sapiens* like the !Kung and the hunting and gathering lifeway they pursued did not emerge earlier than 200,000 years ago. These findings did not invalidate Lee's model as a framework for understanding modern desert foragers but did show that !Kung data should not be used as the definitive model describing human society during its earliest developmental stage.

Although specialists differed on their interpretations of !Kung culture, none denied their validity as a people. The same could not be said of another classic example of a simple, nomadic, nonviolent foraging society, the Tasaday (pronounced ta-SAH-dye) of the Philippines. The existence of the Tasaday was announced to the world in 1971 by the Philippine minority affairs minister, Manuel Elizalde, Jr. Initial reports identified them as a tiny, isolated, cave-dwelling, rain-forest, Stone Age tribe of about 25 people speaking a unique language who knew nothing of hunting, food production, violence, or the existence of other people beyond a shadowy group of jungle wife givers prior to the coming of a hunter from a nearby farming tribe named Dafal some years earlier.

Elizalde allowed several journalists, anthropologists, and celebrities to visit the Tasaday. None were permitted to stay for more than a few weeks, and all were closely supervised during their visits by Elizalde or his associates. In 1973 the Philippine government established an 18,700-ha (46,300-ac) reserve to protect the Tasaday and neighbouring tribes from land-hungry logging companies. One year later all contacts between the Tasaday and the outside world were broken off following the declaration of martial law.

The Tasaday were not revisited by outsiders until Swiss journalist Oswald Iten made his way to their cave in March 1986. Finding the caves empty and evidently uninhabited, he encountered Tasaday in a nearby village wearing Western clothing and playing Japanese radios. Believing them to be members of the neighbouring agricultural Tboli and Manubo-Blit tribes, Iten declared that the isolated Stone Age Tasaday were a hoax.

Iten's claim ignited a fire storm of controversy. Three scholarly symposia convened to examine the facts raised a number of questions requiring further investigation. Few anthropologists doubted that the Tasaday were a Philippine tribal people. Most, however, believed that original reports of the Tasaday as an isolated Stone Age people were a hoax, the purpose of which remained unclear.

Recent revised estimates of pre-Columbian population also stimulated spirited debate. Basing his estimates on ethnohistoric documents and epidemic disease mortality rates of from 50 to 90% among unexposed populations, Henry F. Dobyns in his influential 1966 article "Estimating Aboriginal American Populations" increased the estimate of the North American Indian population in 1492 by a factor of 20 to 18 million. Few scholars doubted the devastating effects of epidemic disease. Many, however, contested the high population estimates proposed by Dobyns and his supporters. Spurred by this upsurge in interest, scholars

on both sides of the issue were intensively reexamining historical records and reassessing the effectiveness of ethno-historic population reconstruction methods in determining what actually happened when the peoples of the Old World and the New met for the first time in 1492.

(ROBERT S. GRUMET)

See also Archaeology.

This article updates the *Macropædia* article SOCIAL SCIENCES: *Cultural Anthropology.*

Archaeology

Eastern Hemisphere. The year 1989 was marked by what should prove to be two spectacular finds—royal tombs at the ancient Hittite capital in Turkey and at the Assyrian capital of Nimrud in Iraq—but few details were available by year's end. Another spectacular find, a newly identified Mesopotamian city (Mashkan-Shapir), had its first excavation season. Of much more recent age, clearance for new commercial building in London exposed the remains of the Rose Theatre, where plays by Shakespeare and Marlowe were performed in their lifetimes.

For professional archaeologists and serious culture historians concerned over the loss of associated evidence when artifacts are acquired by illicit diggers and by theft, it was a bad year. The "antiquities market" flourished—for example, a geometrically simple Cyclades marble head (of unknown context) brought $2 million. An American dealer bought four illicitly acquired mosaics from a ruined Cypriot church for over $1 million but—sued by the Republic of Cyprus—was forced to return them. The enthusiasm for deep-sea diving for sunken treasure on old wrecks spread to Indochina. In Kampuchea there was concern over the quality of restoration work on Angkor Wat.

There were reports on new methods for testing possible faked artifacts, such as isotopic analysis of the marble of statues. The margin of error in radiocarbon age dating of ancient artifacts was sometimes found to be several times greater than claimed. There was increasing evidence (*New Scientist,* Feb. 11, 1989) suggesting that the great volcanic eruption of Santorini in the Aegean had worldwide climatic effects and that it happened about 1620 BC rather than 1500 BC. The eruption seems clearly to have been linked to the destruction of the great site of Knossos on Crete, making its date a key point for the archaeological history of the Aegean and the eastern Mediterranean. If this chronological change proved valid, it would have important consequences for ancient historical studies.

Pleistocene Prehistory. At a Paris conference there was—for the first time—general agreement concerning the presence of early hominids in Europe well before a million years ago. The use of fire over a million years ago was reported from Swartkrans Cave in South Africa. Studies of buried valleys in the Sahara, first located by space shuttle radar, yielded Acheulian artifacts from three separate non-desertic periods, up to 212,000 years ago. The region may well have been part of the scene of transition from the earlier *Homo erectus* to the *Homo sapiens* physical type. There was disagreement over a new suggestion that the Neanderthals did not actually bury their dead. A number of postglacial sites were tested in the high Alps in Italy and by a joint Portuguese-U.S. team in southern Portugal.

Middle East. In Egypt there was an unusual effort to recover evidence of the camps of the workers who constructed the Pyramids of Giza. A combined Yale–University of California at Berkeley group hoped to find evidence of the conditions of the labourers (not normally given attention)

as well as to learn more about how the Giza pyramids were actually built. An exceptionally early mummy was found near Giza. The director of the Coptic Museum in Cairo reported finding a wood- and leather-bound copy of the Book of Psalms, dating to *c.* AD 400. Perhaps because of the troubled political situation, there was not much word of activity in Israel, although a few foreign archaeologists had been at work. David Alon reported a group of 4th millennium BC "fiddle figurines" in the Negev. He claimed they were early evidence of monotheism, but Israeli colleagues disputed the interpretation. In Jordan a joint Yarmouk University–Free University of Berlin group made significant exposures on the early village site of Basta, south of Wadi Musa. Both the site and its finds were significant additions to information about the early range of village life before pottery vessels appeared. Radiocarbon dates ranged earlier than 6000 BC, and there was clear evidence of plant and animal domestication.

There was no archaeological news from strife-torn Lebanon or from Iran. The American School of Oriental Research began to publish a *Syrian Archaeology Bulletin* with useful notes on current activity. There were several salvage excavations on sites in the smaller river valleys in the trans-Euphrates region, where more flood pools would form when new dams were completed. A Yale expedition continued work at the large early city site at Tall Laylan. The information so far available on the so-called royal tomb at Nimrud concerned a *c.* 2,800-year-old burial chamber with the remains of two women and "hundreds of gold ornaments and pieces of jewelry." The clearances were made by the Iraq government's antiquity service. It was suggested that one of the women may have been the queen of Ashurnasirpal II. The site of Nimrud had been excavated, on and off, since the 1840s, mainly by the British. Another great Assyrian site, Nineveh, was again being excavated, this time by David Stronach of the University of California at Berkeley. Important salvage clearances were continuing in the upper Tigris Valley. In southern Iraq (classic southern Mesopotamia) the newly found city site of Mashkan-Shapir was being excavated by its discoverers, Elizabeth Stone (State University of New York at Stony Brook) and Paul Zimansky (Boston University). Occupation at least between 2050 and 1720 BC was already established, and the site's yield promised to be one of the most important of the post-World War II period.

In southeastern Turkey, new Turkish clearances continued at Cayonu and, by a German team, at Nevala Cori, both important early village sites. A surface survey for sites in the upper Tigris Valley floodplain continued. An ancient tin mine was located in the central Taurus Mountains. The second royal tomb find of the year took place at the ancient Hittite capital, Bogazkoy. The tomb appeared to be that of one of the kings named Suppiluliumas, but details as to which one and of the find in general were not yet available. Another German team completed the second of its new excavations at the site of Troy, and U.S. co-workers started an electromagnetometer surface survey to locate any underground features.

The Greco-Roman World. The local and long-established foreign research "schools" continued their usual activities in the regions where Greco-Roman developments took place, from nearer southwestern Asia westward to Britain. In Israel work continued on the Roman port of Caesarea Maritima and at the Roman city of Scythopolis. In Greece itself attention focused on surface surveys of (pre-Greek) sites of the Early Helladic II age, and much new evidence of early cultural development was recovered. In Italy a new, systematic approach to the recovery of traces of the actual

founding of the city of Rome and of developments in the early "Regal" period (*c.* 750 to 509 BC) was undertaken. Test soundings indicated, for example, that soil, rock, and clay fill was used (around 625 BC) to raise the level of the Tiber basin for the creation of the Forum.

The British journal *Current Archaeology* (August 1989) contained a note on the "ink-leaf tablets" (letters written on slivers of wood) being recovered in great numbers at early forts on Hadrian's Wall in northern England. Many were official reports and daily rosters, but some were personal letters. When the tablets were all read and interpreted, much would be learned of life among the Roman forces on the empire's frontier.

Africa and the Far East. In southeastern Nigeria several varieties of alloyed bronze were identified on metal artifacts over a thousand years old, incorporating elements not used as alloys that early in Europe. The single available note from China concerned the identification of a date for an eclipse of the Sun, in 1302 BC, made from a study of tests on "oracle bones" by a modern astronomer. In recent years there had been a marked rise in archaeological activity in the island regions of southeastern Asia and the western Pacific. The journal *Antiquity* (September 1989) contained a special group of papers on the subject. Occupation was now known to reach back 40,000 years, and the making of pottery began at least 3,500 years ago in the Bismarck Archipelago, north and east of New Guinea. The pottery was an element of the "Lapita complex," and the question of who the people who made it were, how they got there, and where they came from would increasingly become a new focus of archaeological attention.

(ROBERT J. BRAIDWOOD)

Western Hemisphere. The year in New World archaeology was marked by major discoveries concerning the origins and demise of Mayan culture, the beginnings of ceramic technology in South America, and new evidence that early man may have migrated to North America much earlier than had been previously believed. Within the U.S. the most noteworthy archaeological developments involved major changes in policy and legislation relative to museum collections and Native American rights rather than any specific field discoveries.

In a landmark move with long-term implications for the practice of North American archaeology and anthropology, Robert McCormick Adams of the Smithsonian Institution negotiated a new policy that would result in the return of thousands of human remains to modern Native American tribal groups. In response to years of intense lobbying by Native Americans disturbed by what they perceived as the desecration of ancestral remains, the Smithsonian agreed that, after a grace period of several years to permit the inventory of its massive collection, it would begin the return of processed remains to members of surviving tribal groups. The move overturned years of opposition from archaeologists and museum administrators concerned over maintaining continued access to human skeletal collections for scientific study. It also went far beyond the more restrictive position put forth by the American Anthropological Association, which would have limited the return of burials to confirmed family members. The Smithsonian decision paved the way for similar policy shifts by other museums and universities, including Stanford University, the University of Nebraska, the American Museum of Natural History in New York City, and the University of Minnesota. It helped to defuse tensions over civil versus scientific rights and led to the introduction of a series of bills in the U.S. Congress aimed at providing greater protection for both archaeological and human remains.

In a related development, the state of New York agreed to transfer the traditional tribal wampum belts of the Iroquois League, some representing important treaty agreements dating to the colonial period when the Iroquois controlled much of the upper Hudson Valley and western New York. Some of the 12 belts had been stored underground in a vault of the State Education Building in Albany since the 1880s. Included with the collection was the important Hiawatha Belt made of strands of woven purple and white whelk shells, which commemorated the formation of the Iroquois Confederacy in the 15th century. Following a similar return of wampum to Canadian Iroquois by the Museum of the American Indian in New York City the year before, the transfer marked a significant shift in museum policy to include the return not only of ancestral human remains but also of important religious and spiritual objects of significance to Native American peoples today.

Archaeologists from the University of Oklahoma announced the excavation of what might be the earliest evidence for the presence of man in North America. Don Wycoff of the University of Oklahoma reported the recovery from an as yet undisclosed site in Oklahoma of two stone tools and flakes from tool manufacture, found in association with bison bones in apparently undisturbed sediments of a buried and filled-in ancient stream channel. Radiocarbon tests of charcoal and snail shells found with the remains yielded age estimates of 30,000 to 40,000 years before the present. If confirmed through additional research at the site, the finds would rekindle the heated debate over the antiquity of early man in North America. The initial radiocarbon age determinations predate by tens of thousands of years the scientifically accepted age of 11,000 to 11,500 years before the present for the fluted points of the Clovis cultures, taken by most archaeologists as the earliest accepted artifactual evidence for the appearance of early man in the New World.

The year was also highlighted by the announcement of

Florence's Piazza della Signoria is torn up and closed off to visitors during an excavation by a team of Italian archaeologists. During the dig the archaeologists unearthed portions of a medieval city as well as artifacts dating as far back as the Bronze Age.

An antiquities inspector cleans a figure of lunet, a goddess of ancient Egypt, which was uncovered at the temple at Luxor. An investigation of the effect of seepage from the Nile River and from Luxor's sewage system led to the discovery of a cache of ancient figures that included King Amenhotep III, who built the courtyard where the statues were found as well as the main portion of the temple.

AP/WIDE WORLD

significant new findings and insights into the origins and demise of Mayan civilization. In a major announcement, Richard Hansen of the Institute of Archaeology at the University of California at Los Angeles presented the initial excavation results at what might be the earliest Mayan centre yet discovered. Guided by air photo coverage dating to the 1930s, and following an initial survey of the site by Ian Graham of the University of Pennsylvania in 1962, the archaeological team cut their way through the jungles of northern Guatemala to the site, where they recorded the presence of a large stone pyramid and other temples, as well as an elaborately carved limestone slab. The slab depicted two "kings" in royal costume facing one another, with one of them pointing upward toward a deity. Known as Nakbe, the centre was radiocarbon dated to between 400 and 600 BC, and pottery found during the excavation paralleled ceramic styles known to date to 600 BC elsewhere in Mexico.

Dating to the middle Pre-Classic period in Mesoamerican archaeology, the centre was several hundred years earlier than El Mirador some 16 km (10 mi) away, previously thought to be the earliest Maya centre. The presence of temples and ceremonial structures at this early date indicates that planned urban centres and centralized political systems had emerged at a period when archaeologists thought the early Mayan settlements were limited to small village communities with low stone platforms for houses. The antiquity and sophistication of architecture at Nakbe provided strong evidence that Mayan society emerged earlier than previously thought and more in parallel with cultural developments elsewhere in Mexico, such as those at the Olmec centres in Veracruz and Oaxaca.

Following six years of fieldwork in the Petén, archaeologists under the direction of Arthur A. Demarest of Vanderbilt University, Nashville, Tenn., came forward with new evidence relative to the collapse of Classic Mayan society. From one Late Classic site dating to after AD 900, the previously known centre of Dos Pilas, the Vanderbilt team found the remains of plain pottery and common house sites surrounded by defensive walls, apparently built in haste; these contrasted with the more elaborate urban architec-

tural facilities that characterized the earlier Classic Period phases at the same site. The team's data were fortified by the discovery of a second site, which remained unnamed to keep it safe from looters, belonging to the slightly earlier Classic Period and dating to c. AD 800. This second centre was built with extensive fortifications consisting of a defensive line of concentrically placed water-filled moats and backed by a massive stone wall on the inner perimeter. In a major reevaluation of traditional characterizations of Mayan society and the causes for its demise, Demarest used these two lines of evidence to argue that the end of the Mayans' social and economic power, and their political collapse, came about as a result of internal conflicts and internecine warfare rather than outside threats and attacks.

The jungles of Guatemala were the focus of archaeological concern because of the threat of intensive oil exploration in and around key archaeological sites in the heavily forested northern Petén. The confrontation over national patrimony versus economic development was particularly acute in this case. The exploration company, a subsidiary of Exxon, which had spent $21.4 million on initial tests, projected that the new wells would have made Guatemala completely self-sufficient in oil. Nevertheless, pressure from archaeologists and preservationists, who in some cases physically barred the drilling and survey crews from the ruins, brought a halt to the exploration. In August Exxon announced that it was abandoning plans for further drilling in this area of archaeological sensitivity.

Farther south, in the Andean region of South America, scientists reported some of the earliest traces of ceramic technology yet discovered in the New World. Using evidence of changing Pacific shorelines and sea level fluctuations, Jonathan Damp, formerly of the University of Calgary (Alta.), followed a hunch that if the coast is now more than a mile inland from former shoreline settlements with early pottery, even earlier sites might be discovered farther inland. Joint Equadorian and Chilean field teams excavated at the site of Alto Mayo, over 35 m (115 ft) above sea level and more than 4 km (2.5 mi) inland from the present shoreline. In the lowest levels of the excavation, they recovered several small burned clay objects

deeply buried below the levels containing Valdivia pottery, previously thought to represent the earliest evidence of ceramic technology along western South America. The ceramic pieces, which appeared to be both fired and molded, were radiocarbon dated to 6,000 years before the present. They appeared to represent the initial stages of New World ceramic development and added credence to the argument that this technology emerged locally in South America and not from Asia or Japan as a result of transpacific exchange.

(JOEL W. GROSSMAN)

See also Anthropology.

Architecture

In Britain architecture was frequently front-page news in 1989. This interest resulted from widespread publicity given since the mid-1980s to the various pronouncements of the Prince of Wales on architectural subjects. Architecture thus became a vibrant and important focus for debate, raising not only aesthetic but also social issues.

Prince Charles's encouragement of public debate on architecture began in 1984 when he spoke at the 150th anniversary celebration of the Royal Institute of British Architects at Hampton Court near London. He took that opportunity to attack specific projects then under discussion, including the proposed National Gallery extension in Trafalgar Square, which he likened in a famous simile to "a monstrous carbuncle on the face of a much loved and elegant friend." This speech provoked a dramatic public reaction, and eventually the proposals were scrapped. The prince also in that speech criticized the plan for the No. 1 Poultry site in the City of London, which at that time proposed an office tower block designed by Ludwig Mies van der Rohe.

Following the abandonment of the National Gallery proposals, the prince grew in confidence and enthusiasm for his subject and became more closely involved with current schemes. In September 1989 his book, *A Vision of Britain,* received a mixed reception from the public and the architectural profession. The prince set out therein ten principles that he believed should govern design. The lavishly illustrated book revealed that the prince's deep concern and sophisticated grasp of the subject was greater than some architects had realized. The book was launched in conjunction with an exhibition, also called "A Vision of Britain," at the Victoria and Albert Museum in South Kensington.

The ten principles set out by the prince included the requirements that buildings blend with their landscape and their size be in relation to their importance. Buildings should respond to human scale and be in tune with their neighbours, and a greater use of local materials was needed. The prince opined that modern buildings that lack decoration give "neither pleasure nor delight." Not all critics concurred with this view, but few would argue with the prince's view that the users of buildings should be more closely consulted by the designers.

A survey commissioned by the *Architects' Journal* showed that British architects did not uniformly agree with the prince. There was criticism of the prince's powerful influence on public opinion and local planning authorities. Some 41% of the architects surveyed believed that the prince was taking unfair advantage of his influence by expressing his views so publicly, though many others believed that he should continue to speak out about architecture, though not intervene in a manner that might influence planning.

There was wide disagreement with the prince's aesthetic views. The prince is well known to favour a classical revival, while most modern architects prefer the "Modern." Many disagreed that traditional or vernacular styles and materials were preferable to modern equivalents.

Commercial Buildings. Prince Charles's outspoken remarks about architecture coincided with a major development boom in London, particularly in the Docklands area to the east of the City of London. Many U.S. architectural firms were involved, and they may have been more accustomed than their British counterparts to developments on the scale being proposed and executed in the late 1980s. A number of buildings were for U.S. banking and multinational clients, and several of the major U.S. architectural firms set up London branches to serve them. The leading U.S. designer of office development in Britain was Skidmore, Owings & Merrill, whose best-known commission was the master plan of the Canary Wharf Development. Other U.S. designers involved in that project were Cesar Pelli, Kohn Pedersen Fox Associates, and I.M. Pei & Partners. The development would eventually comprise approximately 1.1 million sq m (12 million sq ft) of facilities. The design for the overall scheme featured three towers, shortened after objections by conservationists, and was criticized by some as being unexciting. Prince Charles, speaking in a television documentary that he wrote and narrated, said of the proposed Cesar Pelli Canary Wharf tower, "I personally would go mad if I had to work in a place like this."

Stylistic debate was not confined to Britain. In January 1989 the U.S. magazine *Progressive Architecture* reported that diversity was the only common thread in contemporary American architecture. Modernism had not died, nor had postmodernism turned out to be as transient as some of its early critics predicted. Diversity of opinion characterized debates on architectural form and, in particular, the degree to which architectural design should refer to historic form and detail or, by contrast, create new form and detail based on the technological and sociological concepts unique to the late 20th century. Only buildings of the highest quality (regardless of style and form) merited universal praise by architectural competition juries. Some architects still worked in opposing philosophies, displaying aspects of both modernism and postmodernism and somehow drawing together superficially unrelated strands of design and philosophy. Most critics and architects, however, did agree that sensitive response to the environment was essential, only rarely to be subordinated to originality. Only architectural genius might occasionally justify a building unfriendly to its context.

Rockefeller Plaza West by Kohn Pedersen Fox Associates was a notable New York City high-rise project, situated on Seventh Avenue near the existing Rockefeller Center. The 57-story skyscraper featured vertical limestone strips, stainless steel and glass, and a stepped-back main structure topped by a modernistic penthouse area. The bulk of the tower was broken by a glass 10-story-high section at its southeastern corner. The building was praised for conforming with the spirit of its environment while showing imagination in its use of the stepped-back section within an eroded corner. Inside, the building had column-free space and was technologically advanced while at the same time echoing skyscrapers of the 1920s.

A design competition in Columbus, Ohio, for the new Columbus Convention Center was won by Trott/Eisenman, which had earlier been successful in a project for the Ohio State University Visual Arts Center. The winning design consisted of a series of narrow, twisting volumes,

creating a streetscape along the major pedestrian access way. The forms were said by the architect to echo Ohio's prairie forms, referring to its ribbons of highway and rail yards. The building was expected to be completed by 1992, in time for the city's 500th-anniversary celebration of Columbus' voyage to the New World.

Another Ohio project was the proposed Progressive Insurance Co. building in Cleveland, a 50-story office tower. A collaboration between architect Frank O. Gehry and artists Claes Oldenberg and Coosje van Bruggen, it was to feature a whimsical giant folded newspaper on the roof.

A new regional banking headquarters for the North Carolina National Bank was designed by Harry Wolf with Odell Associates for downtown Tampa, Fla. The vast cylindrical shape contrasted with the nearby turrets of Tampa University and made a strong geometric statement. The headquarters comprised two distinct structures, a 31-story tower and a contrasting 7-story cubelike banking hall to the east. Both made lavish use of fine Texas shell limestone, and the tinted-glass windows were designed to minimize the effect of the Florida sun. The geometry of the whole was squarely within the Modern tradition of firms such as I.M. Pei and Skidmore, Owings & Merrill.

Another striking design was also commissioned by the North Carolina National Bank, this time for the centre of Charlotte. The NCNB Corporate Center was designed by architect Cesar Pelli and Associates of New Haven, Conn., with associated architects HKS of Dallas, Texas. A 60-story tower would dominate the centre, providing headquarters for the bank and also hotel and retail areas. The tower, the city's tallest building, was to feature a crown of silver rods at its apex.

Canary Wharf, a collaboration of Skidmore, Owings & Merrill and other U.S. architectural firms, was part of a development project of Docklands, an area east of the City of London, and would incorporate some 1.1 million square metres (12 million square feet) of space.

A 41,000-sq m (440,000-sq ft) headquarters for the People's Bank in Bridgeport, Conn., was dedicated in the spring. A major design by modernist architect Richard Meier, it was his first high-rise building and also the first time that he used a traditional material (in this case granite) so extensively. The central feature of the building was a 16-story white and gray tower with a concave facade. The limestone paving of an adjoining public garden echoed the geometric pattern of the banking hall.

Public and Cultural Buildings. The competition for the Walt Disney Concert Hall was won by Frank O. Gehry and Associates. This new concert hall for the Los Angeles Philharmonic, to be located near the existing Los Angeles Music Center, was to include an auditorium that would seat 2,500, a hall for chamber music, and a library and other support facilities. Gehry's dynamic grouping featured a central concert hall that was reminiscent of a grand conservatory, shaped like a flower with a radiating ceiling suggestive of petals. A dome topped a restaurant and bookstore, and a bridge linked the complex to the Music Center. Construction began in 1989, with completion planned for 1991.

A major new building for the Shepherd School of Music at Rice University, Houston, Texas, was to be designed by Ricardo Bofill and the Taller de Arquitectura in association with Kendall/Heaton/Associates of Houston. The design featured a strongly neoclassical and almost symmetrical structure with a long colonnade facing the campus. Distinctive landscaping would emphasize the formal nature of the buildings. In the selection of Bofill, Rice continued its recent tradition of commissioning major international architects.

The new Fine Arts Center at Arizona State University was designed by architect Antoine Predock of Albuquerque, N.M. Firmly in the Southwestern tradition, the complex included visual and performing arts spaces, with lavish use of open plazas. A museum, drama wing, playhouse, and dance studio were incorporated in the concrete and brick centre. The various elements were linked by passages, arcades, and courtyards.

In New York City Kevin Roche/John Dinkeloo, well known for their innovative and uncompromisingly modern designs for museums, extended the Jewish Museum by re-creating the French Renaissance style of the original 1908 structure, making it difficult to distinguish between new and old. Critics ranged from those who considered it appropriate to those who found it unimaginative. The architect saw his design as less a revival than a continuation, seeking to design as if the original architect himself were planning the extension. This approach certainly provided one solution to neighbourhood opposition to major additions not considered to be in harmony with the existing environment.

The difficulty of finding an acceptable solution to the need for an art museum to expand was well illustrated by the problems experienced by architect Michael Graves with his proposed addition to the Whitney Museum in New York City. He unveiled his third proposal in 1989, his first two—in 1985 and 1987—having received sharp criticism because they would have overwhelmed the original Marcel Breuer building. The new design, as abstract as the original building, apparently abandoned any attempt to harmonize with the surrounding street scene. The massing and geometry were similar to earlier designs, but the forms themselves had changed. The cylindrical feature of the earlier designs that linked the Breuer building to the new addition was gone, leaving the Breuer building as a distinct separate component. Graves had apparently abandoned his original

The architectural firm of Frank O. Gehry and Associates won the commission to design the Walt Disney Concert Hall, which would be used by the Los Angeles Philharmonic.
TOM BONNER

attempt to integrate the composition into one unit, and the new design emphasized the duality of separate parts.

In Washington, D.C., the new Canadian Chancery building on Pennsylvania Avenue by architect Arthur Erickson opened. It occupied a site away from other foreign embassies and within view of the Capitol and was the architect's first effort in postmodernism, a departure from his better-known modernist creations. A dignified and imaginative concept, it included a raised public courtyard surrounded by an interior cast-iron colonnade that echoed that of the nearby National Gallery. Planned landscaping would eventually soften the outlines of the rather horizontal facade.

More obviously postmodern, with strong references to early 20th-century Beaux Arts classicism, was the Harold Washington Library Center in Chicago designed by Hammond Beeby & Babka. The building was to house a ten-story central library for the city of Chicago, and its temple-like exterior form evoked other well-known Chicago structures, with a strong classical exterior organization featuring a bold projecting cornice. Inside, the flexibility required for a library was evident, yet the space was clearly organized and defined. Public spaces were confined to the base and top of the building, with services (stairs, elevators, and rest rooms) kept to the perimeter. One critic described it as a reinvention of classical architecture using contemporary techniques of building and materials. Other historically influenced projects under construction in Chicago included a small Gothic-style office block for the Chicago Bar Association and a classically inspired power station, both by architect Stanley Tigerman.

The much-heralded Pyramid by I.M. Pei, dominating the Cour Napoleon of the Louvre in Paris, finally opened in April and was widely judged a great success. As many as 50,000 visitors pressed through it on Sundays, descending to a varied underground world. The Pyramid created a front door for the Louvre and also an important visual anchor to the vast courtyard. In 1985, when the plans were first unveiled, reactions were not wholly favourable, but after the Pyramid opened, the public reaction was enthusiastic.

Preservation and modern design may have seemed unlikely partners, but in 1989 a number of pioneering modern buildings by the great masters of the 20th century were threatened. The well-known Price Tower in Bartlesville, Okla., by Frank Lloyd Wright stood vacant, used only for storage. The building itself never functioned particularly

well as a combined office and apartment building. The original owners of the tower eventually converted most of the apartments to office space, yet the building remained unworkable and, sadly, was considered unsafe.

The Villa Tugendhat in Brno, Czech., designed by Ludwig Mies van der Rohe and completed in 1930, was occupied for only eight years before the outbreak of World War II, during which it was seriously damaged. After many years of dereliction and disuse, work was begun in 1981 on the restoration of the building as a reception house for civic functions. Unfortunately, many of its unique details were lost.

In La Plata, Arg., a house designed by Le Corbusier, the Casa Dr. Currutchet, was restored after more than 20 years of abandonment and was opened to the public. The house, which was commissioned in 1948, was the architect's only executed residential project in the Western Hemisphere.

Awards. Late in 1988 U.S. Pres. Ronald Reagan announced another round of Presidential Awards for Design Excellence, to be given to federally sponsored or funded projects and awarded every four years. The president's definition of good design was "a process for increasing the efficiency and quality of our lives." The jury, representing a wide diversity of disciplines, commended 10 out of 500 projects that had been submitted, including one rural conservation scheme and Washington, D.C.'s Pennsylvania Avenue plan. The renovation of the Delaware River aqueduct was commended, as were two transportation-related projects.

The American Institute of Architects awarded its 1989 Gold Medal to San Francisco architect Joseph Esherick. He was commended for his contributions not only to design but also to education and practice. He was best known for his series of houses in northern California begun in 1939. The best known of these was the complex at the Sea Ranch, featuring shingles and shed roofs. His firm also designed the Architecture Building at the University of California at Berkeley (Wurster Hall) and the well-known Cannery retail project at Fisherman's Wharf in San Francisco.

The Royal Institute of British Architects awarded its Gold Medal to Renzo Piano. Piano, a native of Italy, gained international prominence in 1971 following his success, together with British architect Richard Rogers, in the competition for the design of the Georges Pompidou National Art and Cultural Centre in Paris. Piano, with the Building Workshop of Genoa, Italy, also won a design competition for the Kansai Airport in Osaka, Japan. Lo-

cated in Osaka Bay, the airport would eventually provide facilities for all Japan and would be completed in the mid-1990s at a projected cost of $800 million. The passenger building would be 1.6 km (one mile) long.

Canadian architect Raymond Affleck died in 1989 and received posthumously the Royal Architectural Institute of Canada's Gold Medal. He was best known for his design of Montreal's underground pedestrian network.

(SANDRA MILLIKIN)

See also Engineering Projects; Industrial Review: *Building and Construction.*

This article updates the *Macropædia* article The History of Western ARCHITECTURE.

Art Exhibitions and Art Sales

Despite seemingly prohibitive insurance costs, the "blockbuster" art exhibition had returned by 1989, in response to public interest and demand. Art galleries and museums were experiencing unprecedented popularity, and some important shows were so crowded that success made it almost impossible to enjoy the art. Fund drives concentrated on raising money for special exhibition galleries, and it was undoubtedly the traveling shows rather than the permanent collections that the public flocked to see. Museums and galleries appeared to compete with each other to attract or mount the most splendid exhibits.

More and more paintings and art objects were traveling farther and farther, protected by state-of-the-art packing, and the art and science of art transportation had become a major speciality among museum professionals. Manet's famous canvas "A Bar at the Folies-Bergère" was estimated to have clocked over 90,000 km (56,000 mi). Not all paintings traveled simply to illustrate points in art history. Some went for diplomatic reasons and others for commercial reasons, as fund-raising assets for the institution that owned them. Increased sophistication in packing and transport was accompanied, of course, by a major increase in costs. Lending institutions had imposed strict conditions to protect their holdings, and the cost of organizing major loan exhibitions had fallen on borrowing museums. Air fares and packing aside, human couriers were also usually required. Fortunately, travel-related accidents and damage had been rare.

In France a number of major exhibitions were mounted to mark the bicentennial of the start of the French Revolution, as part of the general celebrations held during the summer to commemorate that event. The largest was probably the vast exhibition organized by the Council of Europe, on view in the spring at the Grand Palais in Paris. The subject was difficult to portray in art, since the Revolution created almost no art, and the temptation was to present a panorama of culture in Europe in the 1790s. The exhibition incorporated 1,140 items, many quite large, and was not easy to view or appreciate. There were three main divisions: Europe before 1789; the main political and historical events; and the creative force of the Revolution. Portraits of reigning monarchs comprised one area of the prerevolutionary section. Another section was devoted to works from royal factories, including fine tapestry and porcelain. The catalog comprised three boxed volumes and weighed over 4.5 kg (10 lb)!

A smaller exhibition held at the Musée du Petit Palais between March and August was devoted to monuments erected in Paris in 1889 to celebrate the Revolution's centenary. Models and projects were shown, including the monument for the Place de la République. An exhibition devoted to costumes and French textiles was also shown in Paris before traveling to the Metropolitan Museum of Art in New York City in December. The Louvre museum showed a collection made during the Revolution by the geologist and priest Jean-Louis Soulavie (1752–1813). The 138 drawings, engravings, and caricatures depict all of the major events of the Revolution, from 1789 to the execution of Robespierre in 1794. Another exhibition at the Louvre was devoted to the paintings and drawings of Jacques-Louis David, probably the painter most closely connected with the Revolution in the public mind. It went on view in late October and was to remain until February 1990. Many provincial French museums also held exhibitions on the subject of the Revolution.

Such shows were not limited to France. A number were held in England, including "The Shadow of the Guillotine: Britain and the French Revolution," which was shown at the British Museum in the summer and included many caricatures by British artists. Commemorative medals, ceramics, and other artifacts were used to depict how British politics and culture were affected by the Revolution. There were also paintings and prints, and some of the best-known caricaturists of the period, including Thomas Rowlandson and James Gillray, were well represented. Most of the exhibits were drawn from the museum's own collections.

Bicentennial exhibitions were also mounted in the U.S., including a major show organized by the University of California at Los Angeles entitled "Politics and Polemics: French Caricature and the French Revolution 1789–99." This comprised about 200 prints, manuscripts, books, portraits, and the more familiar caricatures. Pamphlets documenting the English reform movement of the 1790s were included. An exhibition at the Pierpont Morgan Library in New York City, called "Words of Blood, Images of Fire," also successfully integrated many different media, combining manuscripts, drawings, engravings, books, and objects. One letter written by Marie Antoinette discussed the escape plans of the royal family, and another, by Charlotte Corday, was written to a lawyer shortly after she murdered Marat. The death warrant condemning Madame du Barry to the guillotine was another poignant reminder of the realities of the period. Other exhibitions in the U.S. focused on the centennial of the Eiffel Tower, erected as the centrepiece of the Paris Exposition of 1889. One traveling show, called "When the Eiffel Tower Was New: French Visions of Progress at the Centennial of the Revolution," was organized by the Mount Holyoke College Art Museum, South Hadley, Mass., where it was shown in the spring. The show later traveled to the Davison Art Center at Wesleyan University, Middletown, Conn., and in early 1990 was to be on view at the Massachusetts Institute of Technology Museum in Cambridge.

Impressionism and Postimpressionism remained immensely popular subjects for art exhibitions, and there were several notable shows in 1989. "The Annenberg Collection: Masterpieces of Impressionism and Post-Impressionism" was the title of a fine show of 50 works drawn from the collection of Mr. and Mrs. Walter H. Annenberg, on view from spring through late summer at the Philadelphia Museum of Art. Included (though of course not Impressionist or Postimpressionist) was a portrait of Walter Annenberg painted by Andrew Wyeth in 1978. There were also five works by van Gogh and a striking portrait by Cézanne. All the other major Impressionists and Postimpressionists were well represented by fine examples.

At the Grand Palais in Paris the show entitled "The Art

of Paul Gauguin" drew immense crowds in the spring. Previously seen at the National Gallery in Washington, D.C., and the Art Institute of Chicago, it was one of the most complete collections of the artist's works ever assembled. Loans from as far away as South America and the Soviet Union helped increase the range of works on show. Equal emphasis was given to Gauguin's abilities as sculptor, graphic artist, and ceramicist, as well as painter. The catalog included 280 items, but not all were on view at each venue in this joint French and American enterprise. Another significant Gauguin show was "Gauguin and the School of Pont-Aven," seen at the Royal Academy in London in the autumn and later in the year at the National Gallery of Scotland in Edinburgh. Pont-Aven was the village in Brittany where Gauguin lived for a short time in the mid-1880s before journeying to Tahiti. The exhibition concentrated on graphic art: woodcuts, lithographs, and engravings. The artists of the school were consciously primitive, reflecting the Breton landscape and culture. The hitherto little-considered Breton artist Armand Seguin, who refused Gauguin's invitation to accompany him to the South Seas, was perhaps the discovery of the show. His rugged works showed sophistication and power. Much admired by Gauguin, he died at the age of 34 from tuberculosis.

"Cézanne: The Bathers" was the title of a show at the Kunstmuseum Basel (Switz.) in the autumn. The first exhibition ever to have concentrated on this important aspect of the artist's work, it included 130 prints, drawings, oil sketches, watercolours, and paintings. The show was seen only at Basel. Cézanne first painted groups of bathers in about 1870, and he was to return to this theme frequently throughout his life. The bathers were always much admired by his colleagues, if not always appreciated by the public. Degas's own private collection, for example, included works on this subject by Cézanne, and they must have influenced his own paintings of women. An exhibition at the Tate Gallery Liverpool (England) was devoted entirely to representations of women by Degas. Although such subjects make up over two-thirds of Degas's work, this was the first show given over exclusively to them. Included were 10

of his rarely seen later pastels. In addition to bronzes, oils, and pastels from the Tate's own collection, there were items lent by the National Gallery and elsewhere. The subjects ranged from the better-known dancers and laundresses to society women.

The period just before Impressionism was represented by a major show devoted to the art of Gustave Courbet. Entitled "Courbet Reconsidered," it was organized by the Brooklyn (N.Y.) Museum and shown there and, later, at the Minneapolis (Minn.) Institute of Arts. It was the first major Courbet show to be organized in the U.S. in almost 30 years. Most of the artist's major works were lent, with the striking exceptions of the "Burial at Ornans" and "The Painter's Studio."

Increasing Western interest in Russian art was evident in 1989. This interest ranged from the innovative and experimental Russian art movements such as Constructivism and Suprematism, which had always enjoyed wide appreciation in the West, to a new and unprecedented interest in the works of Socialist Realist artists who had been completely out of fashion for many years. An exhibition mounted in the former Fiat car factory in Turin, Italy, entitled "Russian and Soviet Art 1870–1930," focused on a wide range of Russian painting. The venue was particularly appropriate since many of the great Russian painters studied in Italy. The exhibition comprised some 260 paintings, works on paper, and reliefs, mostly borrowed from Soviet collections.

An exhibition at the Stedelijk Museum in Amsterdam devoted to the Russian Suprematist Kasimir Malevich included over 200 works. Drawn from the major collections of the artist's work in Leningrad, Moscow, and at the Stedelijk Museum itself, they presented the entire range of his development, including his best-known Suprematist works. The exhibit "100 Years of Russian Art 1889–1989 from Private Collections in the USSR" was shown in London at the Barbican Art Gallery and in Oxford at the Museum of Modern Art in the summer. It featured a varied selection of Modernist and avant-garde works as well as prints, posters, and porcelain. The better-known Supre-

Claude Monet's "Camille Monet on a Garden Bench" was one of 50 paintings from the collection of Mr. and Mrs. Walter Annenberg shown at the Philadelphia Museum of Art as part of the exhibit "The Annenberg Collection: Masterpieces of Impressionism and Post-Impressionism."

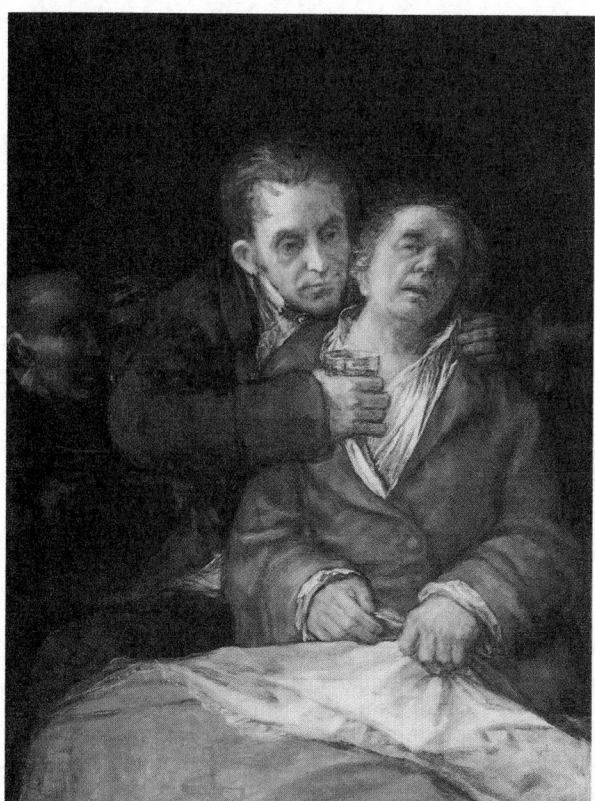

A doctor attends the ailing Goya in "Self Portrait with Dr. Arrieta."
"Goya and the Spirit of Enlightenment," an exhibit viewed in Spain and
the U.S., focused on Goya's role in the Spanish Enlightenment and
his place as social critic and emphasized his liberal beliefs.

matism and Constructivism were barely represented, but lesser-known periods and artists were featured. There was little from the period of Socialist Realism between the mid-1930s and about 1960, although a section was devoted to post-Socialist Realism paintings. In Finland the Turku Art Museum mounted a show entitled "Russian Avant-Garde" in the autumn. This extensive exhibition featured over 200 works of Russian art exhibited for the first time outside the Soviet Union. Russian art was also shown at Luzern, Switz., at the Kunstmuseum. A show in the summer was entitled "From the Revolution to Perestroika: Soviet Art from the Ludwig Collection."

Exhibitions devoted to photography and related aspects of that medium were numerous. "The Art of Photography 1839–1989," shown in the autumn at the Royal Academy in London, was described as a controversial look at the history of photography as an art medium and featured many original and pioneering prints. Experimental photography, focusing on the painter as photographer, was the subject of a show at the Getty Museum in Malibu, Calif., in the autumn. The Australian National Gallery held an exhibition in Canberra in the autumn devoted to portrait photography. The portraits by the famous Canadian photographer Yousuf Karsh were the subject of an exhibition at the National Gallery of Canada in Ottawa. (See PHOTOGRAPHY.)

The title of the exhibition "European Baroque Painting" was perhaps an overstatement, but the show included many rarely seen pictures of high quality. It was seen in Braunschweig, Cologne, and Munich, West Germany, and Utrecht, Neth. A comprehensive exhibition devoted to Sienese painting of the Renaissance was held at New York's Metropolitan Museum of Art. Entitled "Painting in

Renaissance Siena 1420–1500," it was the first such show to be devoted to this important Italian school. A major exhibition devoted to the drawings of Leonardo opened in January at the Hayward Gallery in London. The centrepiece of the exhibition, which comprised 119 drawings, was a collection of 88 drawings borrowed from the Royal Library at Windsor. The subjects ranged from anatomic and scientific drawings to allegorical and religious subjects. Also included was an 11-m (36-ft) model of a flying machine constructed from drawings by Leonardo. Computer graphics were used to explore perspective. The artist's inventiveness and powers of observation were clearly demonstrated.

The largest and finest of the exhibitions mounted to mark the 400th anniversary of the death of the Venetian artist Paolo Veronese, who died in 1588, was shown at the National Gallery in Washington in the winter of 1988–89. Entitled "The Art of Paolo Veronese 1528–1588," it featured 50 paintings and 55 drawings, many lent by European galleries. The richest display of modern Italian art from the early 20th century ever seen in England was on show at the Royal Academy. Entitled "Italian Art in the 20th Century," it featured painting and sculpture from 1900 to 1988. The contrast between movements such as Futurism, which were wholly modern, and artists working in the traditional manner of Italy's great cultural past was notable. An extensive area was devoted to Futurist works, including many early paintings by Giacomo Balla, Carlo Carrà, and Umberto Boccioni, the leaders of the movement. The Metaphysical movement, one of whose founders was Giorgio De Chirico, was also well represented. The selection of sculpture, though an important contribution by 20th-century Italian artists, was disappointingly limited.

"Andy Warhol: A Retrospective" was mounted in the summer at the Art Institute of Chicago. The enormous retrospective, organized by the Museum of Modern Art in New York City, featured a wide range of the artist's major works, including his depictions of Marilyn Monroe and his famous Campbell's soup cans. Prague's National Gallery showed paintings and sculptures from the Guggenheim collections in New York and Venice. The exhibition was on display in the winter of 1988–89. Two of Europe's greatest artists were celebrated in major exhibitions opening in the U.S. in the fall: "Velázquez" at the Metropolitan Museum of Art and "Franz Hals" at the National Gallery. Both shows were expected to travel to Europe in 1990.

Freedom of speech questions in relation to art exhibitions arose in the U.S. "Robert Mapplethorpe: The Perfect Moment," a retrospective of the photographer Robert Mapplethorpe (see OBITUARIES), which had been shown without incident in Philadelphia and Chicago, was canceled by the Corcoran Gallery of Art in Washington, D.C., in June. The gallery was attempting to avoid involvement in a controversy that had arisen in Congress over public funding (through the National Endowment for the Arts) of "objectionable" art, specifically, homoerotic images included in the Mapplethorpe show and a photograph by Andres Serrano of a crucifix in a jar of urine. Subsequently, however, a number of artists boycotted the Corcoran, and a major bequest was withdrawn. In September the gallery issued a statement of regret and apology for the cancellation, and the director resigned in December. In Congress, meanwhile, a measure introduced by Sen. Jesse Helms (Rep., N.C.) that would have prohibited federal financing of art broadly defined as offensive was rejected by Congress in favour of a milder restriction on art meeting the 1973 Supreme Court definition of obscenity. In Chicago the School of the Art Institute issued strict guidelines for student exhibitions. Twice within two years the school had been subjected to

protests and demonstrations because of student art, in one case a painting of the late Mayor Harold Washington in women's underclothes, in the other a work that included an American flag on the floor. Under the new guidelines, the school could remove student art that was "disruptive."

(SANDRA MILLIKIN)

ART SALES

A new phenomenon made the 1988–89 auction season one of the most spectacular in recent history. Collectors who had started buying during the Impressionist and modern boom of the 1980s, discouraged by the multimillion prices now demanded in that field, started to look for something cheaper, and their arrival had a dramatic impact on any collecting field they took a fancy to. Historically, collectors begin by buying cheaply and graduate to paying top prices only after their taste has become more sophisticated. This was the reverse process—big spenders searching for art that was expensive enough to deserve their attention.

Post-World War II American art was the first port of call for the disenchanted Impressionist collectors. Jasper Johns, the reclusive genius who provided a link between Abstract Expressionism and Pop Art, was raised to the status of "greatest living artist." Christie's sold his "White Flag" for a record $7,040,000 on Nov. 9, 1988, and the next day Sotheby's sold his "False Start" for $17,050,000. Throughout both sales, records fell like ninepins, Robert Rauschenberg at $6.3 million, Andy Warhol at $3,960,000, Mark Rothko at $2,750,000, Franz Kline at $2,310,000. . . .

The Impressionist sales, meanwhile, lost some of their sparkle. Degas's famous bronze of a ballerina wearing a real tutu, "Petite Danseuse de quatorze ans," just crept ahead of the $10,120,000 paid for another cast the previous summer to reach $10,175,000—setting a new price record for 20th-century sculpture by a whisker.

Picasso, on the other hand, emerged as one of the year's star turns. Synthetic Cubism is not his most highly regarded style, but "La Cage d'oiseaux" of 1923 set the first Picasso record of the year at $15.4 million. This was bested after only four days by the Blue Period "Maternité" at $24,750,-000. Two weeks later, as the action moved to London, a masterpiece of the even rarer Pink Period, "Acrobate et jeune arlequin," brought £20.9 million. In May 1989 a dashing self-portrait of 1901, inscribed "Yo Picasso," finished off the season's price spiral at $47,850,000.

Picasso apart, Impressionism and 20th-century art to 1940 or so were underpinned by investor buying, while the excitement and popular interest had switched to postwar art. Roughly 2,000 players crammed into Sotheby's May 1989 sale of contemporary art, and hands shooting up all over the room slowed the action to a crawl. (At the Impressionist sales, anonymous telephone bids accounted for 90% of purchases.) The landmark summer prices included $11,550,000 for Jackson Pollock's "Number 8," $6,270,-000 for Francis Bacon's "Triptych May–June," and $2.2 million for David Hockney's "A Grand Procession of Dignitaries in the Semi-Egyptian Style." The collectors eased out of the Impressionist market were joined by collectors eased out of the contemporary market as the season progressed. They seemed, in the main, to have stuck to the fine arts, dabbling in antique sculpture (a Cycladic marble head at $2,090,000 in December 1988), tribal art (a Benin bronze head at £1,320,000 in July), Renaissance bronzes (Susini's "Paris Carrying Off Helen" at F 21 million in Paris in April), Chinese bronzes (a buffalo of the 15th or 14th century BC at $2,970,000 in New York in December 1988).

They had a more serious impact on turn-of-the-century paintings, and any European or American artist whose style resembled that of the Impressionists was in high demand. The most interesting phenomenon, however, was the cautious invasion of the Old Master painting market by disenchanted modern art collectors. The sale of a Pontormo painting, identified by some as a portrait of Cosimo I de' Medici, for $35.2 million on May 31 to the Getty Museum was a turning point. It had been described as the most important Italian Renaissance painting in private hands, and there was disappointment in some quarters that the price did not top van Gogh's "Irises." But the punters recognized the price as proof that Old Masters were worth real money and began to buy seriously. On one hand, they stuck to museum pictures, sending a 15th-century Spanish altarpiece to F 21.5 million in Paris and Murillo's "Virgin of the Swaddling Clothes" to £1.7 million in London. At the same time, they began to buy paintings for their sheer decorative appeal. Most-favoured status was accorded to 18th-century Italian view painters—Canaletto and his school—and to 17th-century Dutch flower pictures or still lifes. A pedestrian Canaletto "View of the Piazza San Marco" made £968,000.

Chinese and Japanese collectors were responsible for a revolutionary change in prices for Chinese art. For decades moneyed connoisseurs of Chinese art had paid top prices for ceramics of antiquarian interest and archaic bronzes. Now the taste of Chinese expatriates began to impose a new pecking order on the market. A 14th-century handscroll entitled "The Imperial Autumn Hunting Party" set a new record for Chinese painting at Christie's in New York at $1,870,000 in June, three times presale expectations. Prices for contemporary painting were also rising sharply. Wu Guanzhong's (Wu Kuan-chung's) "View of the Ruins of Gaochang" set an auction record for the work of a living Chinese artist at HK$1,870,000 in Hong Kong in May. A Qing (Ch'ing) dynasty vase, painted with chrysanthemums for the Emperor Yongzheng (Yung-cheng), made ten times estimate at $1,650,000 in New York, and one of only two known examples of 13th-century guan ware made for the

AFP PHOTO

Sotheby representatives handle telephone auction bids for "Yo, Picasso," a self-portrait of the artist. The painting sold for $47.9 million, a record for a Picasso that stood until December, when "Pierrette's Wedding" brought $51.3 million.

emperor's use, a 20-cm (8-in) brush-washer in the form of a mallow flower, sold for HK$22 million in Hong Kong.

Book Sales. An unprecedented number of great book collections, elaborately cataloged, were sold at auction during the 1988–89 season. There were huge prices for rarities, and auction prices for ordinary books from the great collections ran far beyond those current in the trade. The year also saw the first purchase of a manuscript in the West by the Soviet government, the original manuscript of Turgenev's *Fathers and Sons.* It was consigned to Sotheby's for sale but withdrawn before the auction and sold, presumably around the £500,000 estimate. The West German government spent £1.1 million to acquire the manuscript of Franz Kafka's *The Trial* at Sotheby's in November 1988, a record price for a modern literary manuscript.

Christie's two-year, six-sale dispersal of the collection of Estelle Doheny ended on May 19, having realized a total of £21.6 million. The first sale of the season contained fine bindings that were hotly disputed between J. Paul Getty, Jr., and Henri Schiller, a French collector. A magnificent inlaid and painted binding by "the Queen's Binder B" enclosing a 1680 Oxford Bible made ten times estimate at $418,000. In February a copy of William Blake's "Songs of Innocence" with 27 hand-coloured plates made $330,-000 and, among American autographs, a letter by Caesar Rodney of Delaware dated July 4, 1776, made $440,000, the highest price on record for any letter. The last Doheny sale, in May, was devoted to the leader of the 19th-century Arts and Crafts Movement, William Morris, and his circle. It included a manuscript of Virgil's *Aeneid,* written and illuminated by Morris, at $1,320,000. Getty was believed to be the purchaser.

Christie's sold the collection of Japanese manuscripts formed by Donald and Mary Hyde in the 1960s and 1970s for £3.4 million, including the second-earliest extant manuscript of Sei Shonagon's *Pillow Book,* the most famous Japanese literary text, at $352,000. Fourteen illuminated pages, sold individually, from the Houghton *Shahnameh* or *Book of Kings*—the most important 16th-century Persian manuscript extant—made £976,800 at Christie's in London in October 1988.

Sotheby's kicked off 1989 by selling the investment collection they themselves had formed for the British Rail Pension Fund in the 1970s for £2.6 million. The British Rail collection of illuminated manuscripts was later sold privately to Getty for £3 million. In November Sotheby's sold the Chinese collection formed by Philip Robinson, the London book dealer, for £1.3 million, securing £209,000 for a map of the world printed in Beijing (Peking) in 1602 by the Jesuit Matteo Ricci, the highest price ever paid for a map. The 8th-century *Canons of the Church Councils* by Exiguus, the oldest Western manuscript in private hands, made £638,000. Sotheby's began the dispersal of 10,000 books and manuscripts from the collection of H. Bradley Martin by selling the four double elephant folio volumes of Audubon's *Birds of America* for $3,960,000.

(GERALDINE NORMAN)

This article updates the *Macropædia* articles The History of Western PAINTING; The History of Western SCULPTURE.

Astronomy

The year 1989 brought a welter of exciting astronomical discoveries that spanned the universe from the solar system's outermost giant gas planet, Neptune, to the most distant quasar discovered to date. While a new spacecraft was launched to study the microwave background radiation left over from the big bang and a decade-old Sun-watching satellite came tumbling down, the most exciting astronomical event of the year was the encounter of the U.S. Voyager 2 spacecraft with Neptune.

Solar System. Some 12 years and 11 billion km (7 billion mi) after launch, the planet-hopping Voyager 2 probe reached Neptune in August. It and its sibling craft, Voyager 1, had already made several other encounters with planets and their satellites, including flybys of Jupiter, Saturn, and Uranus, the three other gas giants of the solar system. Lying some 30 times farther from the Sun than does the Earth and receiving roughly a hundredth the solar radiation, Neptune had been expected to be a rather dull place. To many scientists' surprise it proved to be among the more remarkable visits on Voyager 2's long journey.

Like Jupiter, which has a Great Red Spot visible even from the Earth, Neptune was found to have a Great Dark Spot. The giant atmospheric storm lies at roughly the same latitude as Jupiter's Great Red Spot and measures about the same size in both its latitude and longitude, making it comparable in size to the Earth. This feature and other findings showed that Neptune's weather is much more dynamic than that of either Saturn or Uranus. Analysis of Voyager 2 images indicated that the jet stream winds blowing over the north side of the Great Dark Spot move at about 2,400 km/h (1,500 mph), the fastest winds discovered to date on any planet. Scientists found it difficult to explain how the heat left over from the formation of the planet is sufficient to drive such fast winds, since solar heating alone will not suffice.

Voyager 2's magnetometer found that Neptune has a magnetic field similar in strength to that of the Earth but tilted with respect to the planet's spin axis by about 55°. Even stranger, the magnetic field is offset from the centre of the planet by about four-tenths of Neptune's radius. Periodic variations in the radio emission associated with the rotation of the planet and its magnetic field revealed that Neptune turns on its axis once every 16.1 hours.

Whereas two Neptunian satellites, Triton and Nereid, had been known, six more were seen by Voyager 2, ranging in radius from 20 to 200 km (12 to 125 mi). The largest of the new discoveries is in fact larger than Nereid, the smaller of the previously known moons. Three moons appear to be irregular in shape and to have extremely dark surfaces. A large system of continuous rings around Neptune was also discovered, although some of the rings vary in density around their circumference. Equally exciting was the flyby of Neptune's largest moon, Triton. Prior to Voyager 2, even such basic facts as its size were unknown. By coming within about 40,000 km (24,800 mi) of its surface, Voyager found that the satellite is about 2,720 km (1,690 mi) in diameter and pink and blue in colour, with a very high reflectivity of nearly 70%. It was also found to be volcanically alive, having at least four volcanoes spewing plumes of nitrogen gas and ice.

Sun and Stars. The Sun advanced toward the peak of its 11-year sunspot cycle, expected to occur in 1990 or 1991. On the morning of March 6 a gigantic solar flare erupted from the centre of a group of sunspots seen on the east limb (edge) of the Sun. The largest flare observed in about five years, it released more energy in less than 10 minutes than humans had consumed throughout all of history. Within two days energetic particles swept by the Earth, producing auroral storms visible as far south as New York and Chicago. It was this rise in solar activity, causing an expansion of the Earth's upper atmosphere into space and thus an increased drag on satellites in low Earth orbit, that caused the early demise of the Solar Maximum Mission

spacecraft (Solar Max), which tumbled to the Earth late in the year. Launched in 1980 just after the last maximum in the sunspot cycle, Solar Max had made valuable contributions to an understanding of the active Sun.

Stars have a limited range of masses. If a star had more than about 100 times the mass of the Sun, it would literally blow itself apart from excessive radiation pressure. On the other hand, if an object had less than about a tenth of the Sun's mass, it would have insufficient mass to cause the hydrogen at its core to burn. The largest known planet, Jupiter, has a mass about a thousandth that of the Sun. In the range in between, from about a thousandth to a tenth of a solar mass, lies the realm of brown dwarfs, objects too small to be stars but too massive to be planets.

Do brown dwarfs exist? For decades astronomers sought to detect them either as the binary-star companions of otherwise easily observable stars or as single objects. In 1989 two different kinds of evidence were reported that argued for their existence. Using a newly developed near-infrared camera, William Forrest and collaborators from the University of Rochester, N.Y., reported that several objects in the Taurus star-forming region are cool and dim enough to fit the criteria for brown dwarfs. They suggested that the detected objects have masses about 5–15 times that of Jupiter. In a separate study David W. Latham of the Harvard-Smithsonian Center for Astrophysics, Cambridge, Mass., and collaborators reported spectroscopic evidence for a probable brown dwarf companion to the Sun-like star HD 114762. This star undergoes small periodic variations in its observed radial velocity, which the researchers attributed to an unseen orbiting companion having a mass about 11 times that of Jupiter. For many astronomers, however, uncertainties in the interpretation of both sets of observations still left the question of the existence of brown dwarfs tantalizingly open.

Somewhere near the centre of the Milky Way Galaxy lies an object that produces electrons and their antimatter counterparts, positrons, at a prodigious rate. Mutual annihilation of matter and antimatter particles gives rise to gamma rays, which are observed from the Earth as a spectral line with a characteristic energy of 511 kiloelectron volts (keV; thousands of electron volts). First observed in

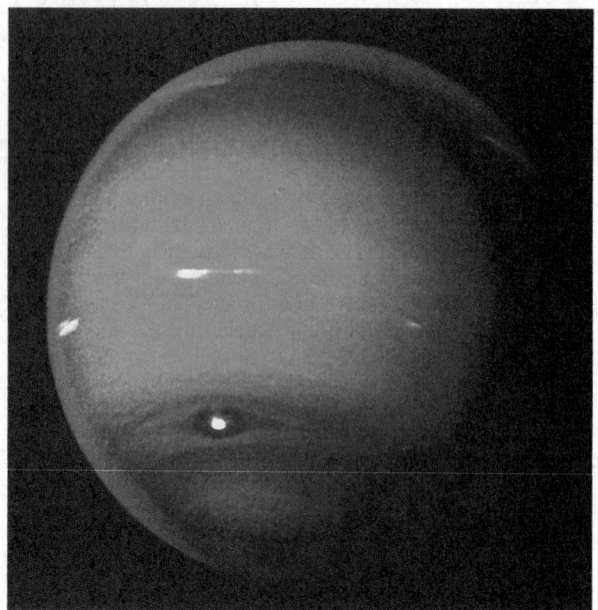

Methane gas in Neptune's atmosphere gives rise to the intense blue area in a false-colour image taken by the Voyager 2 spacecraft. In August pictures of the planet were transmitted to Earth by the probe, which had earlier visited Jupiter, Saturn, and Uranus.
JET PROPULSION LABORATORY

1970, the line has appeared and disappeared over the succeeding two decades. In 1989 astrophysicists from AT&T Bell Laboratories, Murray Hill, N.J., Sandia National Laboratories, Albuquerque, N.M., and NASA-Goddard Space Flight Center, Beltsville, Md., using a gamma-ray imaging spectrometer lofted by stratospheric balloon above much of the atmosphere, reported the reappearance of the source. If the source indeed lies at the distance of the centre of the Galaxy, it emits roughly 10,000 times the entire luminosity of the Sun in this one gamma-ray spectral line. Over the years many objects were proposed as the source of the radiation, including a young neutron star, a small black hole, and a black hole having a mass of some one million Suns. However, J.E. McClintock of the Harvard-Smithsonian Center and M. Leventhal of AT&T Bell Labs reported that an X-ray source in the direction of the galactic centre called GX1 + 4 increases and decreases in its X-ray output in coincidence with variations in the gamma-ray spectral line. If the association proved correct, it would leave a new puzzle as to how an X-ray source, which is believed to accrete matter from a binary companion, can so efficiently transform its energy into positrons.

In February 1987 the brightest supernova seen on Earth in more than three centuries, dubbed SN 1987A, appeared in the Large Magellanic Cloud, a nearby companion galaxy to the Milky Way. Despite its distance of more than 150,000 light-years from the Earth, the supernova, which marked the explosive death of a massive star, had been extensively studied since that time. Because pulsars—rapidly rotating magnetized neutron stars—had been found previously in old supernova remnants like the Crab Nebula, which exploded in AD 1054, astronomers eagerly sought evidence for a pulsar within the remnant of SN 1987A. Jerome A. Kristian of the Observatories of the Carnegie Institution of Washington and his collaborators, reporting on optical observations made January 18 at the Cerro Tololo Inter-American Observatory in Chile, announced detection of an optical pulsar lying within the SN 1987A remnant and rotating with a period of about 0.5 millisec-

Earth Perihelion and Aphelion, 1990

| Jan. 4 | Perihelion, 147,008,000 km (91,346,000 mi) from the Sun |
| July 4 | Aphelion, 151,994,000 km (94,444,000 mi) from the Sun |

Equinoxes and Solstices, 1990

March 20	Vernal equinox, 21:19[1]
June 21	Summer solstice, 15:33[1]
Sept. 23	Autumnal equinox, 06:55[1]
Dec. 22	Winter solstice, 03:07[1]

Eclipses, 1990

Jan. 26	Sun, annular (begins 17:13[1]), visible in the South Island of New Zealand, Antarctica, and southern and eastern South America.
Feb. 9	Moon, total (begins 16:19[1]), the beginning visible in New Zealand, Australia, the western Pacific Ocean, Alaska, all of Asia, the Arctic regions, Europe except the Iberian Peninsula, Africa except the northwestern extension and the southwestern coast, and the Indian Ocean; the end visible in western Australia, Asia, the Philippine Sea, the Arctic regions, Greenland, Europe, Africa, the eastern Atlantic Ocean, the Indian Ocean, and parts of Antarctica.
July 22	Sun, total (begins 00:40[1]), visible in the U.S.S.R., most of Scandinavia, the northern Pacific Ocean, northern Japan, the Arctic regions, northern Greenland, Alaska, and western Canada.
Aug. 6	Moon, partial (begins 11:29[1]), the beginning visible in Antarctica, the Pacific Ocean, California, southern Alaska, eastern Siberia and southeastern Asia, the eastern Indian Ocean, Australia, and New Zealand; the end visible in Antarctica, the western Pacific Ocean, all of Asia except the west, the southern half of the Middle East, the east coast of Africa, the Indian Ocean, Australia, and New Zealand.

[1]Universal time.
Source: *The Astronomical Almanac for the Year 1990* (1989).

onds (thousandths of a second). Unfortunately, whereas the reliability of the original detection was high, no subsequent observation confirmed the existence of the pulsar. Furthermore, theorists found themselves struggling to explain the existence of a star spinning some 2,000 times per second. At such a rate its surface would be moving at a third to a half the speed of light, and even its intense gravitational field could barely keep the star from flying apart.

SN 1987A produced another surprise in 1989 when M. Karovska and colleagues of the Harvard-Smithsonian Center reported what they believed to be the reappearance of the so-called mystery spot. This object lying near the supernova was first detected in March 1987 and then was not seen again for about two years. If the new detection was of the same object, it had been moving away from the supernova at about half the speed of light. The nature of the spot (or perhaps spots) was still unclear, though it might have resulted from an ejected fragment or from a jet from the reported half-millisecond pulsar.

Galaxies and Cosmology. Two fundamental observations in cosmology concern the distribution of matter and of radiation in the universe. One of them, the so-called microwave background radiation left over from the big bang event some 15 billion years ago, appears to be isotropic (uniform) regardless of the sweep of sky observed. In November the Cosmic Background Explorer (COBE) satellite was launched to improve the precision with which the spectrum and isotropy of this radiation is known. Equally important for cosmology is the study of the distribution of structures formed of observable matter, *i.e.,* galaxies, throughout the universe. To this end Margaret J. Geller and John P. Huchra of the Harvard-Smithsonian Center undertook a survey of galaxy distribution in a well-defined

JET PROPULSION LABORATORY

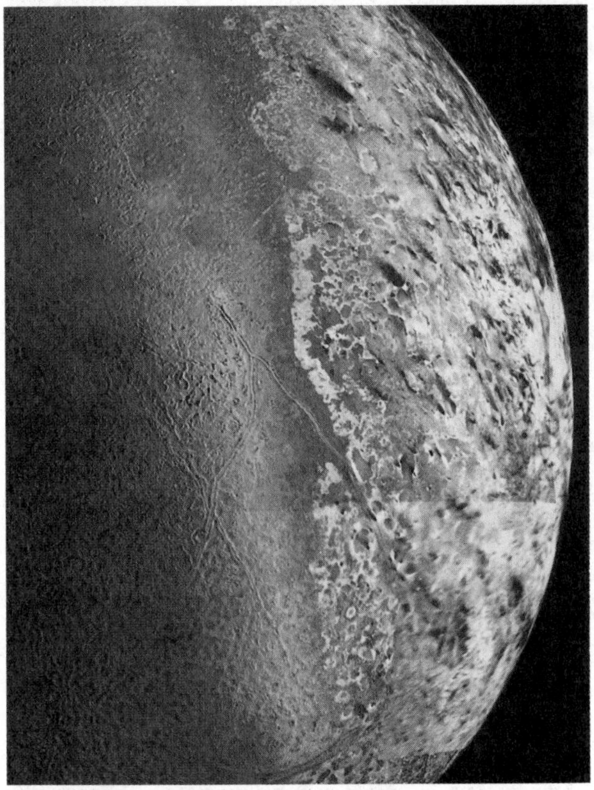

A Voyager 2 composite image of Triton, Neptune's largest moon, reveals volcanoes, frozen lakes, and giant fissures. Triton was also seen to have an atmosphere primarily of nitrogen and surface regions that presumably had been melted by volcanic heat and refrozen.

"slice" of space. The slice stretches some 135° across the sky and includes about 11,000 galaxies lying at distances between 200 million and 300 million light-years from the Earth. Although the volume studied represented only about a hundred-thousandth of the observable universe, it nevertheless contained many surprises. For instance, Geller and Huchra discovered the largest coherent structure in the universe found to date, an enormous sheet of galaxies nicknamed the Great Wall that extends across roughly 500 million light-years. It might even be larger since it reaches to the edge of the observed region. Given the isotropy of the microwave background radiation, which implies that the universe was very homogeneous early in its evolution, cosmologists were finding it challenging to explain how such large matter structures subsequently came about.

The year drew to a close with a report of the most distant object found to date, a quasar having a redshift of 4.73. The magnitude of the redshift implied such a distance for the quasar that the light from it now reaching the Earth was emitted when the universe was only about 7% of its present age. This observation further increased the difficulty of reconciling the extreme smoothness of the microwave radiation produced early in the evolution of the universe with the early appearance of lumpy structure in the form of galaxies and quasars that are seen today.

(KENNETH BRECHER)

See also Space Exploration.
This article updates the *Macropædia* articles The COSMOS; GALAXIES; The PHYSICAL SCIENCES: *Astronomy and Astrophysics;* The SOLAR SYSTEM; STARS AND STAR CLUSTERS.

Botanical Gardens and Zoos

Increasingly, in recent years, botanical gardens throughout the world have been presented with the almost impossible task of preserving plant species that no longer have a safe niche in the natural environment. Reflecting the need for global cooperation in meeting the challenge, international meetings and conferences have taken place more frequently than ever before. In August 1988 the South African National Botanic Gardens, Kirstenbosch, celebrated its 75th anniversary with a conference in Cape Town on research on threatened plants and the role of education and horticulture in conservation. A month later, at an international symposium in Nanjing (Nanking), China, 53 speakers addressed up to 300 delegates from 21 countries on similar issues. Sponsored by, among others, the International Union for Conservation of Nature (IUCN), the Worldwide Fund for Nature (WWF), and the International Association of Botanic Gardens (IABG), the meeting brought together representatives of different cultures. One result was an initiative to set up an Asian division of the IABG to address issues peculiar to the region.

In April 1989 the second International Botanic Gardens Conservation Congress was held on the Indian Ocean island of Réunion, organized by the IUCN Botanic Gardens Conservation Secretariat (BGCS) in collaboration with the Conseil Général de la Réunion and the Conservatoire et Jardins Botanique de Nancy, France. Its objective was to focus world attention on the needs of germ plasm conservation in botanical gardens, especially in the tropics, where the need is greatest. An extra session was devoted to examining practical linkages between botanical gardens in less developed and developed regions. The conference endorsed a final draft of the botanical gardens conservation strategy document prepared by BGCS. The document would be sent to all botanical gardens throughout the world, to

A pair of killer whales swim in a section of the five million-gallon pool at Sea World in San Diego, California. In August one killer whale was killed by another during a performance at Sea World, sparking debate about whether keeping the whales in close quarters makes them more aggressive.
AP/WIDE WORLD

governments and other international agencies, and to all organizations engaged in germ plasm conservation. It was intended to define the role of botanical gardens, show how they fit into a world network, and explain why they must receive support on an international level. The European and Mediterranean division of IABG held a meeting in Budapest during May. The theme was the developing role of botanical gardens, with particular emphasis on conservation.

The need for new botanical gardens in the tropics was well understood within the botanical garden community, and initiatives were being taken to develop new gardens in Guatemala, Nicaragua, and Ecuador. The last mentioned, although still in the early stages of development, was already linked with a new botanical garden at Wycliffe Hall, Durham, England. The botanical garden in São Paulo, Brazil, celebrated its 50th anniversary in 1988. In recent years it had functioned more as a park than as a research centre, but as a result of new policies the 18-ha (45-ac) site was to be redesigned by a team of landscape architects. Sections for specific plant collections, including rare and endangered species adapted to the region, were developed to support environmental education.

Plans were under way to create a new botanical garden at Aachen, West Germany. The intention was to interest amateurs by relating conservation themes to scientific and educational projects. The Adelaide Botanic Garden was celebrating Australia's bicentenary by opening a new Bicentennial Conservatory in November. It would be the largest conservatory in the Southern Hemisphere and would be used to display plants from Australasia, Malaysia, and the western Pacific. Approximately 750,000 persons visited the garden annually. At the Royal Botanic Gardens, Kew, England, the famous Palm House, built in 1848, was fully restored and replanted. As part of the restoration, the internal landscaping was greatly improved, and the basement boiler rooms were converted to house a new display of marine algae.   (REGINALD IAN BEYER)

Zoos. Four California condors (*Gymnogyps californianus*), hatched in incubators and subsequently hand-fed using puppet condor heads at the San Diego (Calif.) Wild Animal Park, raised the world population to 32 individuals. Two of the hatchlings were from separate single-egg clutches of the same parents that in 1988 produced Molloko, the first chick bred in captivity. The other two 1989

hatchlings came from two different pairs, while a third pair produced an egg that failed to hatch. DNA fingerprinting was used to help identify individuals and determine the relationships of all the wild-caught birds with unknown pedigrees. The information was used in pairing condors to reduce consanguinity and minimize potential loss of offspring. To help assess the feasibility of eventually reintroducing the California condor into the wild, captive-bred females of the closely related Andean condor (*Vultur gryphus*) were temporarily released into the California condor habitat in California. The progress of the project, especially the dramatic breeding successes of 1989, went a long way toward justifying the controversial decision to bring the last of the wild birds into captivity. It also boded well for the future of this species, which had hovered on the brink of extinction for many years.

Columbus (Ohio) Zoological Gardens announced pregnancies in three generations of its lowland gorilla (*Gorilla g. gorilla*) founder family. Colo, the world's first captive-born gorilla, was due to give birth to her fourth offspring at about the time of her 33rd birthday. Her 17-year-old daughter would deliver her sixth offspring, and her 10-year-old granddaughter's expected infant would represent the first fifth-generation member of the family and the fourth captive-bred generation.

Cincinnati (Ohio) Zoo and Botanical Garden continued its pioneering work on in vitro fertilization and interspecific embryo transfer with the successful birth of a male Indian desert cat (*Felis sylvestris ornata*) born to a domestic cat. Hopes were raised and then dashed at the National Zoological Park, Washington, D.C., with the birth on September 1 of a giant panda (*Ailuropoda melanoleuca*) and its death two days later. There was some consolation in the fact that the panda bred by artificial insemination in Japan in 1988 was progressing well.

Among the most important national and international meetings were the Captive Breeding Specialist Group (IUCN) meeting in San Antonio, Texas, in September, which was immediately followed by a meeting of the International Union of Directors of Zoological Gardens; an International Conference on Zoo Architecture in Paignton, England, in May; an international conference sponsored by the Soviet Ministry of Culture in August to celebrate the 125th anniversary of the Moscow Zoo and, three days later in Tallinn, Estonia, the 50th anniversary of the Tallinn

Zoo; and a meeting in Oman in February to discuss future plans for the continued reintroduction of captive-bred Arabian oryx (*Oryx leucoryx*) into Oman and Jordan and the need to broaden the genetic base of the herds already reintroduced and of the world's captive stock.

An incident that made headlines in August and caused much debate on the ethics of maintaining animals in captivity was the accidental killing of a killer whale (*Orcinus orca*) by another killer whale during a public performance at Sea World, San Diego.

New exhibits included Adventure Island at the Los Angeles Zoo; Sun Bear Forest at San Diego Zoo; Masai Mara exhibit at Zoo Atlanta, Ga.; the Living World at St. Louis (Mo.) Zoological Park; the Whale and Dolphin Pavilion at Indianapolis (Ind.) Zoo; a new ape house at Antwerp (Belgium) Zoo; and the Tropical Rain Forest Hall at Arnhem (Neth.) Zoo.

The zoo and conservation communities mourned the death of the naturalist Sir Peter Scott (*see* Obituaries) in August, just before his 80th birthday.　　　(P.J.S. OLNEY)

See also Environment; Gardening.

Chemistry

Electrochemistry. Fundamentally new approaches to nuclear fusion were reported during 1989 by chemists who conducted research in a field traditionally dominated by physicists. In one instance, British and U.S. chemists started an international scientific controversy in late March by claiming to have observed energy-producing nuclear fusion reactions in an electrochemical cell at ambient temperature and pressure. Other scientific groups, however, were unable to reproduce all of the results, raising doubts about the nature and existence of what had become known as cold fusion.

The unexpected fusion reactions between atoms of deuterium (D), a heavy isotope of hydrogen, were reported by Martin Fleischmann of the University of Southampton, England, and B. Stanley Pons (*see* Biographies) of the University of Utah. They used a modified version of a simple apparatus employed in the electrolysis of water, the dissociation of water into hydrogen and oxygen by an electric current. In a container of heavy water, or deuterium oxide (D_2O), the investigators dissolved lithium to form a lithium deuteroxide electrolyte solution, into which they inserted a platinum wire anode coiled around a palladium cathode. An electric current supplied to the electrodes caused decomposition of the electrolyte; deuterium was released at the palladium electrode, diffused into the metal, and packed into vacant sites in the metal's crystal lattice. Fleischmann and Pons reported that after several weeks of electrochemically charging the palladium, D-D fusion occurred and was detected in the form of expected byproducts—the isotope helium-3, neutrons, and substantial amounts of excess heat. (*See* Physics.)

Later in the year chemists at Brookhaven National Laboratory, Upton, N.Y., reported another new approach to D-D fusion. Robert Beuhler and his team used electric fields in a vacuum chamber to accelerate charged clusters of D_2O into a target of titanium deuteride, producing heat and compression at the point of impact that created a substantial rate of fusion reactions. It was not known whether the process could be applied on a larger scale in a practical fusion reactor.

Analytical Chemistry. Analysis of the abundance of rhenium and osmium can date geologic specimens with great accuracy and help in determining the origin of other noble metals—such as platinum, palladium, and gold—from their trace content of Re or Os. But Re and Os cannot be measured accurately with traditional analytical methods such as thermal ionization mass spectrometry. The metals are present in minute amounts (often lower than parts per billion), and a phenomenon called isobaric interference distorts the results of conventional analyses. Jack D. Fassett of the National Institute of Standards and Technology, Gaithersburg, Md., and Richard J. Walker of the U.S. Geological Survey, Reston, Va., developed a powerful new technique, resonance ionization mass spectrometry (RIMS), for measuring isotopic abundances of rhenium-187 and osmium-187. Traditional mass spectrometry, normally one of the analytic chemist's most sensitive techniques, cannot determine differences in abundance of the two isotopes because they have nearly identical masses. RIMS uses a tunable laser to prepare samples for mass spectrometry by selectively ionizing (removing electrons from) one isotope at a time, thus enabling the mass spectrograph to analyze each isotope separately. Scientists then can plot isotopic ratios of the two elements on a graph and arrive at highly accurate estimates of the age of rock samples.

Research groups from the Georgia Institute of Technology and the University of Georgia invented an interface that permitted integration of two important but previously incompatible methods of chemical analysis, infrared spectrometry and liquid chromatography. With no straightforward way of combining the two techniques, chemists in the past often turned to an alternative method of analysis, gas chromatography coupled with mass spectrometry (GC-MS). But GC-MS cannot be used to analyze many pharmaceuticals, food components, environmental pollutants, and other organic compounds. Indeed, fewer than 5% of the more than nine million compounds listed in the Chemical Abstracts Registry in the late 1980s could be measured with GC-MS. By contrast, more than 95% could be analyzed with the aid of the new interfacing device.

Physical Chemistry. Interest remained high in the characteristics and structure of zeolites. These crystalline compounds of aluminum, silicon, and oxygen have an open internal framework of microscopic pores that can be used to sort molecules and catalyze chemical reactions. W.M. Meier and G.O. Brunner of the Swiss Federal Institute of Technology, Zürich, discovered a relationship between the molecular structure of zeolites and pore size that promised to increase their applications substantially. Zeolites already had important applications as molecular sieves, in ion-exchange processes such as softening hard water, and in catalyzing chemical reactions that otherwise would occur slowly or not at all. But their versatility had been limited by a pore size too small to admit large hydrocarbon molecules. Meier and Brunner found that pore size can be enlarged by increasing the number of the smallest rings of tetrahedral atoms (T-atoms) in a zeolite's structure. The T-atoms consist of silicon and aluminum atoms arranged around oxygen atoms to make the basic pore structure of the zeolite. Zeolites with enlarged pores could be useful in the catalytic cracking of the large hydrocarbon molecules in heavy oils to yield gasoline, as a storage medium for natural gas, and in separating or catalyzing reactions involving large biomolecules, such as steroid and peptide hormones and sugars.

Organic Chemistry. Investigators at the General Electric Research and Development Center, Schenectady, N.Y., announced their development of a technique for polymerizing carbonates that could significantly expand commercial application of the products. Polycarbonates are extremely strong, impact-resistant plastics currently used as window-

panes and in electrical devices and industrial and sporting equipment. Polycarbonates previously could not be used in composites, products in which high-strength fibres of such materials as graphite or glass are embedded in a plastic matrix. Composites are extraordinarily light, strong plastics that have found growing applications in automotive, aerospace, and other industries. In the fabrication of a composite, the liquid plastic resin must flow readily enough to wet the reinforcing fibres thoroughly, filling up all voids to ensure a solid bond between resin and fibre once the resin hardens. Polycarbonates had proved too viscous to penetrate the fibre bundles easily in composite manufacture. The GE researchers solved the flow problem by using a cyclic (ring-containing) polycarbonate precursor that has the same chemical composition as the polymerized form but only $\frac{1}{50}$ of its molecular weight. When melted, the precursor flows almost as easily as light machine oil, filling tight spaces within the interstices of a fibre network. A special catalyst then is applied to open the cyclic structures and link them together in the long linear chains that account for the great strength of polycarbonates. The researchers believed that the technology could lead to a new generation of ultrastrong polycarbonate composites and also could be applied to aramids, polyarylates, and other resins.

[1.1.1]Propellanes are compounds formed by the arrangement of five atoms in a conformation resembling a propeller or paddle wheel with three flat triangular blades. Since the synthesis in 1982 of the first [1.1.1]propellane (1a), a carbon-based compound, there had been considerable interest in making structures in which carbon is replaced by atoms of those elements—silicon, germanium, tin, and lead—that are in the same group as carbon in the periodic table. The efforts succeeded in 1989 when the synthesis of a tin-based organometallic compound, a pentastannapropellane (1b), was reported by Lawrence R. Sita and Richard D. Bickerstaff of Carnegie Mellon University, Pittsburgh, Pa. The compound was seen as important in explaining chemical bonding in [1.1.1]propellanes. Sita also believed that it could be used to develop a class of compounds combining the electronic properties of metals with the versatile physical characteristics of polymers.

The mass extinctions at the end of the Cretaceous period 65 million years ago that killed the dinosaurs and perhaps 50–75% of other species on the Earth caught the attention of organic chemists during 1989. Meixun Zhao and Jeffrey L. Bada of the Scripps Institution of Oceanography, La Jolla, Calif., reported evidence in support of the theory that the extinctions were caused by the collision of a comet or asteroid with the Earth. They analyzed sediments from rock strata that marked the boundary between the Cretaceous and Tertiary periods; these layers previously had proved to be rich in iridium, an element rare in the Earth's crust but more common in extraterrestrial material. Zhao and Bada detected α-aminoisobutyric acid and racemic isovaline, two amino acids that are exceedingly rare on the Earth but are major amino acids in meteorites belonging to the carbonaceous chondrite group. Detection of racemic isovaline, which contains both left-handed and right-handed isomers of the compound, further argued for an extraterrestrial origin for the amino acids since only the right-handed form is synthesized by terrestrial organisms.

Demonstrating the power of contemporary organic synthesis, a Harvard University team headed by Yoshito Kishi synthesized palytoxin carboxylic acid (2), the largest single molecule ever made. The highly poisonous compound, first isolated in slightly different form from a Hawaiian coral, has more than 120 carbon atoms and possesses more than one sextillion (10^{21}) isomers, or variations of the same molecular structure, of which only one is the desired isomer. The extraordinarily complex synthesis was accomplished by making eight separate parts of the molecule and then assembling them. The synthesis should permit Kishi and his colleagues to modify portions of the palytoxin molecule systematically to understand its interactions with biological systems.

The total chemical synthesis of an all-carbon molecule, cyclo[18]carbon, was reported by François Diederich and colleagues of the University of California at Los Angeles. All-carbon molecules (C_n) were becoming the topic of an increasing number of experimental and theoretical studies in a variety of fields. They appear in the products of combustion and may be components of interstellar dust. The synthesis was expected to help elucidate the properties of all-carbon molecules by giving investigators the ability to synthesize them in a single size. The traditional technique,

1a: M = C (carbon)
     R = H (hydrogen)

1b: M = Sn (tin)
     R = 2,6-diethylphenyl

2   palytoxin carboxylic acid

laser vaporization of graphite, produces a mixture of cyclic and linear molecules having from 2 to more than 600 atoms. Diederich calculated that cyclo[18]carbon contains alternating single and triple bonds connected to form a monocyclic ring structure. (MICHAEL WOODS)

This article updates the *Macropædia* articles Physical and Chemical ANALYSIS AND MEASUREMENT; ATOMS: *Energy from atoms;* BIOCHEMICAL COMPONENTS OF ORGANISMS; CHEMICAL COMPOUNDS; CHEMICAL ELEMENTS; CHEMICAL REACTIONS; Principles, Methods, and Instruments of MEASUREMENT AND OBSERVATION; MOLECULES; The PHYSICAL SCIENCES: *Chemistry.*

Consumer Affairs

The international consumer movement continued to expand in 1989, encompassing several socialist countries of Eastern Europe where radical market-oriented reforms were being introduced. Since much of that region was plagued by severe product shortages and soaring prices, new consumer organizations began educating the public about their rights and how to exercise them, even when the demand for many goods far exceeded the supply.

At the initiative of the International Organization of Consumers Unions (IOCU), major consumer organizations from Western Europe and North America assembled in Warsaw in November for their first meetings with registered consumer groups from Bulgaria, Czechoslovakia, Hungary, Poland, Romania, the Soviet Union, and Yugoslavia. Information was exchanged on such subjects as consumer protection laws and their enforcement as well as on litigation, redress, product testing, and advertising and marketing codes. The meetings also explored future possibilities for the sharing of information and experience between organizations in the socialist countries and Western consumer groups.

For the seventh consecutive year World Consumer Rights Day was celebrated on March 15. A common theme, "The Right to Responsible Health Care," was taken up by consumer groups on every continent through campaigns and special activities that addressed a range of current concerns. Actions were undertaken to promote patients' rights and draw attention to the serious inequities that existed in the health care services of both developed and less developed countries.

Global consumer-health campaigns continued to concentrate on three issues: the promotion of sound infant feeding practices, the rational use of medicines, and efforts to halt tobacco promotion. In October the International Baby Food Action Network (IBFAN) held its International Forum on the Infant Feeding Crisis. The forum marked the 10th anniversary of IBFAN and brought together consumer leaders, health workers, and breast-feeding experts in discussions on hospital practices, the marketing of infant foods, and government measures to implement the 1981 World Health Organization (WHO)/United Nations Children's Fund (UNICEF) International Code of Marketing of Breastmilk Substitutes. Among its activities the Health Action International (HAI) network urged WHO to initiate a worldwide recall of the Dalkon Shield, an intrauterine contraceptive device known to cause serious injuries and sometimes death among users. IOCU's AGHAST Campaign (Action Groups to Halt Advertising and Sponsorship by Tobacco) was involved in the planning and production of a *Third World Tobacco Control Atlas* in preparation for the 1990 World Conference on Tobacco and Health.

Current threats to the environment reportedly had some impact on the public's buying preferences as well as influencing the priorities of many consumer organizations. Heightened environmental awareness spurred greater demand for "green" goods, ranging from phosphate-free washing powders and low-mercury batteries to ozone-safe aerosols. Quick to recognize the trend, manufacturers stepped up their marketing of environmentally friendly products, prompting some fear among consumer organizations that the unregulated proliferation of "green labels" could lead to false claims and other abuses. European consumer groups joined other lobbyists in calling for government regulations on product labeling, and the European Commission responded by announcing that it would draft new legislation for a European Communities (EC)-wide labeling system. Consumer groups throughout the world also disseminated information on harmful products while urging governments, intergovernmental bodies, UN agencies, and other authorities to take immediate steps to curb such threats as depletion of the ozone layer, rampant deforestation, air and water pollution, and the surreptitious dumping of hazardous wastes.

Food issues received increased attention in 1989 as outbreaks of food poisoning and a surge of reports about meat and produce tainted with pesticide residues, hormones, and carcinogenic chemicals generated worldwide concern. In the United Kingdom some four million consumers boycotted foods linked to salmonellosis, listeriosis, and botulism. Mounting consumer fears in the U.S. halted domestic sales of daminozide (Alar), a plant-growth regulator widely used on orchard crops, while some 70 consumer groups in South Korea launched a boycott that led to the government's banning of imported citrus fruit sprayed with that chemical. In Mauritius the Consumers' Health Action Network (CHAN) pressured authorities to ban imports of monosodium glutamate (MSG), a food flavouring known to cause serious side effects over time. (*See* AGRICULTURE AND FOOD SUPPLIES: *Special Report.*)

Food irradiation drew heavy criticism from consumer

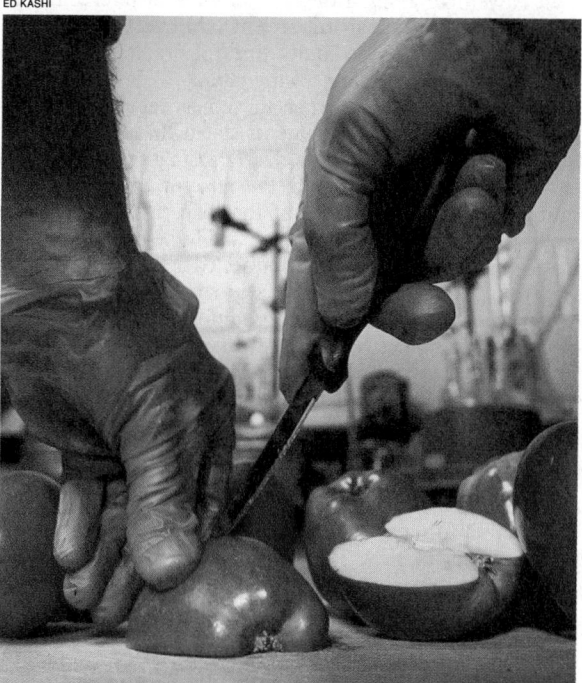

A technician wearing rubber gloves prepares apples for testing. After the Environmental Protection Agency determined that Alar, a chemical for promoting redness used on about 5% of all apples, was a carcinogen, many people refused to eat any apples at all.

groups. The controversial technology was used to preserve some 500,000 tons of food annually. Irradiation could also be used to mask previous contamination of food, however, and the possible hazardous effects of the process were not yet fully known. IOCU and consumer groups campaigned for a worldwide moratorium on the further use and development of food irradiation until all questions regarding nutrition, safety, labeling, and detection had been properly answered. In the state of New York a campaign by the Consumers Union of U.S., Inc., influenced a decision by state lawmakers to enact a moratorium on the sale of irradiated foods, while similar campaigns were also taken up by groups primarily in Europe and the Asia-Pacific region.

A task force of attorneys general from 10 states of the U.S. was formed in 1988 to protect consumers from the misleading health claims that were being used by food companies to gain a competitive advantage in the marketplace. According to Marketing Intelligence Services in Naples, N.Y., 40% of all food products introduced in the first half of 1989 used health messages to promote the product and boost sales. Food marketers contended that health claims make consumers more aware of proper dietary habits. Nutritionists and consumer activists, however, claimed that these messages were misleading and that there needed to be federal guidelines on the use of health claims in promoting products. In May 1989, as a result of the task force's efforts, Campbell Soup reached a settlement with nine states agreeing not to advertise that its soups were high in fibre and calcium. In September 1989 Sara Lee Corp. promised not to call a line of desserts "light" since they contained as many calories as regular desserts. The claim of Quaker Oats Co. concerning the healthful aspects of its products was the subject of a lawsuit initiated in Texas in late 1989. A Federal Trade Commission judge barred Kraft from claiming that its Kraft Singles cheese slices contained the same calcium as five ounces of milk. It was found that the individually wrapped ³⁄₄-oz slices contained about one-third less calcium than five ounces of milk.

In November 1989 stronger disclosure requirements for lenders and stricter loan rules went into effect for individuals applying for home-equity lines of credit. More than 3.5 million homeowners, owing about $75 billion, had home-equity credit lines when these new regulations went into effect. The new requirements stated that the payment terms had to be spelled out clearly, using an example of payments on a $10,000 loan; the fees for the loan application, points, maintenance of the loan, home appraisal, credit reports, and legal assistance had to be provided automatically when an individual requested a loan application. Experts claimed that the new regulations would protect homeowners by giving them more information before they pledged their homes as collateral. It would also help borrowers to better compare loans. The new rules prevented a lender from cutting off an individual's credit line, accelerating payments, or changing the terms of the loan once the credit line had been opened. Since the new regulations made it more difficult for lenders to change the rules once the loan was approved, borrowers would be given a shorter time period to repay the loan. Home-equity lines of credit in effect prior to Nov. 7, 1989, did not need to follow the new rules.

The nation's 180 Better Business Bureaus reported each year on consumer complaints. In July 1989 the Council of Better Business Bureaus announced a sharp decline in complaints about mail-order and telephone-order firms, from 68,500 in 1987 to 58,200 in 1988. The largest number of complaints in 1988 concerned retail outlets, with stores selling home furnishings topping the list. Non-automobile service firms were second, followed by home-improvement and remodeling companies and automobile, truck, and recreational vehicle dealers.

In 1989 Connecticut and Maryland passed legislation prohibiting the transmission of unsolicited advertising to owners of facsimile machines. As a result of the legislation, there was a $200 penalty for each message sent to one fax machine, making it very expensive for advertisers caught sending unsolicited messages. Lawmakers claimed that such "junk" faxes overstepped the bounds of privacy because they forced recipients to pay for messages that they might not want. Fax advertisers argued that the laws were violating their free-speech rights.

Automobile insurance rates ranked high on the legislative calendars of many states in 1989 as consumers complained to their representatives that these costs had risen twice as fast as inflation since 1980. An alliance of consumer groups, including Ralph Nader's Public Citizen Lobby, reported that reductions in waste and inefficiency by automobile insurance companies could save consumers $23 billion a year. In June the state legislature in Nevada, which had the fifth highest car insurance rates in the U.S., passed a measure to roll back rates to 15% below those of 1988.   (KEVIN G. COOK; EDWARD MARK MAZZE)

See also Economic Affairs: *World Economy;* Environment; Industrial Review: *Advertising.*

Crime, Law Enforcement, and Penology

Violent Crime. *Terrorism.* The level of international terrorist activity remained almost unchanged in 1989, following a record 856 incidents in 1988. According to U.S. State Department officials, the Middle East again had the highest incidence of terrorist attacks, followed by Asia, Western Europe, Latin America, and Africa.

The Middle East presented U.S. Pres. George Bush with his first hostage crisis in August. The crisis was precipitated by the abduction of a prominent pro-Iranian Muslim cleric, Sheikh 'Abd-al Karim Obeid, on July 28. Obeid, together with two associates, was seized by Israeli commandos in a night raid in southern Lebanon. Israeli authorities justified the action by describing Obeid as a central figure in Hezbollah, a pro-Iranian group thought to be responsible for the kidnapping of as many as 17 Western hostages believed to be held in Lebanon. Within three days of the Israeli raid, it was announced that one of these hostages, U.S. Marine Corps Lieut. Col. William Higgins, had been hanged in retaliation by a pro-Iranian group calling itself the Organization for the Oppressed of the Earth. The group, which released a grisly videotape to prove it had killed Higgins, also threatened the lives of other hostages. President Bush and his advisers sought to resolve the crisis by diplomatic rather than military means. Negotiations with Iran and its new president, Ali Akbar Hashemi Rafsanjani (*see* BIOGRAPHIES), were thought by many informed observers to provide the ultimate key to ending the dangerous standoff.

The potential for warmer relations between the U.S. and Iran, following the death of Ayatollah Ruhollah Khomeini (*see* OBITUARIES) in June, was chilled by speculation that Iran was linked to the bomb blast that destroyed Pan Am Flight 103 over Scotland in December 1988, killing 270 people. A worldwide investigative effort pointed suspicion at the Popular Front for the Liberation of Palestine—General Command (PFLP—GC), a radical Palestinian splinter

group led by Ahmed Jabril. The explosion was caused by Czechoslovak-made Semtex plastic explosives hidden in a portable radio-cassette player. Intelligence sources suggested that the PFLP—GC had been hired by the Iranian government to plant the explosives in retaliation for the destruction of an Iran Air jet by the USS *Vincennes* in the Persian Gulf in July 1988. This was also believed to be the motive behind an attempt on the life of Sharon Rogers, wife of the commander of the *Vincennes*.

A bomb like the one that destroyed Pan Am Flight 103 was believed responsible for a midair explosion on September 19 aboard a DC-10 jet belonging to the French airline UTA. The plane, en route from Brazzaville, Congo, to Paris, crashed in the Sahara shortly after taking off from N'Djamena, Chad. All 171 people on the aircraft perished. Several terrorist organizations claimed responsibility, including the Iranian-backed Islamic Jihad.

An international furor developed over the novel *The Satanic Verses* by Salman Rushdie (*see* BIOGRAPHIES). The novel was considered offensive by Muslims around the world, and Ayatollah Khomeini called for the author's execution, forcing Rushdie into hiding. (*See* PUBLISHING: *Sidebar.*) In late March a spiritual leader of Muslims in Belgium, Imam Abdullah al-Ahdal, who had criticized the order to kill Rushdie while condemning his book as "blasphemous," was assassinated in Brussels. Responsibility was claimed by a clandestine Beirut group called the Soldiers of Truth. In September, 16 Kuwaiti Shi'ites, arrested in July after a series of bomb explosions in Mecca, were decapitated by sabre in public in Saudi Arabia, in keeping with traditional Muslim practice. Less draconian punishment was imposed by a West German court in May, when Muhammad Ali Hamadei, one of the Lebanese hijackers of TWA Flight 847 in 1985, was sentenced to life imprisonment for air piracy and the murder of a U.S. Navy diver.

Alfred Herrhausen (*see* OBITUARIES), the head of West Germany's largest commercial bank, the Deutsche Bank A.G., was killed when a powerful bomb blew up his car on November 30. A note with the symbol of the Red Army Faction, an urban terrorist group active in West Germany in the 1970s, was found near the scene.

The bloody conflict between Protestants and Catholics in Northern Ireland spilled into England again on September 22, when an explosion at the Royal Marines School of Music in Kent left 10 military bandsmen dead and 22 injured. The Irish Republican Army (IRA) claimed responsibility. Meanwhile, the British government ordered a judicial inquiry into the case of the so-called Guildford Four, three men and one woman, all Irish, who had spent 15 years in jail for a 1974 pub bombing they did not commit. In October the English Court of Criminal Appeal set aside the convictions of the four after finding that the police had fabricated evidence.

Drug Trafficking. Violence associated with the burgeoning trade in illicit drugs from Latin-American countries to North America and Europe reached new levels of ferocity. Nowhere was this "narco terrorism" more pervasive than in Colombia, where on August 18 assassins gunned down a popular presidential candidate, Sen. Luis Carlos Galán, as he addressed a campaign rally. Galán had supported efforts to extradite suspected ringleaders of the major drug cartels to the U.S. to stand trial. His death prompted a government crackdown on the traffickers, who responded with a declaration of "total and absolute war," including a threat to kill 10 judges for every trafficker extradited to the U.S. Seeking U.S. aid, the Colombian justice minister, Mónica de Greiff, flew to Washington in late August. President Bush announced a $65 million emergency aid package for Colombia's drug war, but de Greiff, the eighth Colombian justice minister in three years, resigned in mid-September in the face of numerous death threats. A series of bombings of public targets, such as banks and schools, was blamed on the drug traffickers, as was the bomb that destroyed a Colombian airliner on November 27, killing 107 people. In the U.S. President Bush named William Bennett (*see* BIOGRAPHIES) as his "drug czar," and on September 5 he unveiled a comprehensive $7.9 billion antidrug plan to deal with what he called America's toughest domestic problem in decades.

Murder and Other Violence. In the U.S. both the major national crime-level indicators continued to rise in 1988, according to reports by the FBI and the Bureau of Justice Statistics (BJS). The FBI's Crime Index, based on reports from law-enforcement agencies across the country, showed a 3.1% increase in the overall rate of crime and a 5.5% increase in violent crimes. The BJS National Crime Survey, based on interviews nationwide with about 99,000 people, reported a 1.8% increase over 1987 in the number of respondents who said they had been the victims of crime. The BJS survey, which, unlike the FBI Crime Index, includes crimes not reported to the police, recorded a 9.3% increase in aggravated assault. In the U.S.S.R., prompted by the continuing spirit of *glasnost* (openness), Soviet authorities made the first disclosure of detailed crime statistics since 1933. Maj. Gen. Anatoly Smirnov of the Interior Ministry revealed in February that per capita crime in the U.S.S.R. had risen by almost 18% in 1988.

In the U.S. an upsurge in violent crimes committed by young people roused national concern. According to the FBI, between 1983 and 1987 arrests of those under 18 for murder rose more than 22%; for aggravated assault over 18%; and for rape more than 14%. Public anxiety was intensified in April by a widely publicized gang rape and near murder of a woman jogger in New York City's Central Park. The brutal attack by a group of youths, ranging in age from 14 to 17, was said to be a form of marauding

A group of children are tended at an elementary school in Stockton, California, after a gunman, wearing battle fatigues and carrying a semiautomatic rifle, opened fire. The gunman killed 5 and wounded 30 others before killing himself.

behaviour called "wilding." Americans were also shocked by two mass shootings. On January 17 Patrick Edward Purdy, a drifter with an extensive criminal background, walked onto the grounds of an elementary school in Stockton, Calif., wearing combat gear and began firing an AK-47 semiautomatic military assault rifle. Purdy killed 5 students and wounded 29 others and one teacher before taking his own life. On September 14 Joseph Wesbecker, also armed with an AK-47, opened fire in a printing plant in Louisville, Ky., where he had been an employee. Before shooting himself, Wesbecker killed 7 people and wounded 15. Both tragedies prompted calls for stricter gun controls, and following the Stockton massacre President Bush announced a ban on the importation of foreign-made assault weapons. However, possession of these weapons continued to be legal, and no steps were taken to prohibit the manufacture of equivalent U.S. guns. Canada, with strict gun-control laws and a far lower crime rate than the U.S., was shocked on December 6 when Marc Lépine, 25, entered the University of Montreal engineering school armed with a rifle and went on a rampage that left 14 women dead and 12 people wounded before killing himself. In a three-page suicide note he blamed all his troubles on "feminists."

In Africa on August 20 veteran international wildlife conservationist George Adamson (*see* OBITUARIES), 83, and two assistants were shot to death by bandits. Adamson was slain by the bandits near his remote Kenyan homestead, where he and his late wife, Joy, who was herself murdered in 1980, taught lions raised in captivity to live in the wild. The bandits were believed to be from a group of nomadic Somali tribesmen responsible for much of the animal poaching in Kenya. (*See* ENVIRONMENT.)

Nonviolent Crime. *Political Crime and Espionage.* The Recruit affair, Japan's worst political scandal in recent times, shook the stability of the nation's long-ruling Liberal-Democratic Party and led in April to the resignation of Prime Minister Noboru Takeshita. The scandal involved a complex scheme of insider trading, bribery, and influence peddling by the Recruit Co., a rapidly growing Japanese information services corporation. An ongoing investigation, headed by Tokyo Chief Prosecutor Yusuke Yoshinaga, resulted in a number of indictments during the year. (*See* WORLD AFFAIRS [East Asia]: *Japan.*)

In Greece in September former prime minister Andreas Papandreou and four members of his Cabinet were referred by Parliament for trial. Each faced charges of gross malfeasance, mainly in relation to the diversion of more than $200 million from the Bank of Crete. The scandal broke in March when George Koskotas, the Bank of Crete's owner and a confessed embezzler, claimed that Papandreou and his colleagues had received bribes and engaged in other illegal acts. Parliament also decided that Papandreou should be prosecuted for allegedly ordering the widespread tapping of phones during his term of office. (*See* WORLD AFFAIRS [Western Europe]: *Greece.*)

The death of former Philippines president Ferdinand Marcos (*see* OBITUARIES) appeared to make still more difficult the task of tracking down billions of dollars that Philippine officials claimed Marcos, his wife, and close associates had stolen. Fears were expressed that information about many of Marcos' secret accounts had died with him. One of Switzerland's most embarrassing scandals resulted in the resignation in December 1988 of Justice Minister Elisabeth Kopp. This followed allegations that she had used information gained in the course of her official duties to warn her husband that a company of which he was a director was being subjected to scrutiny for suspected money laundering by drug traffickers.

In May, after a 10-week jury trial in Washington, D.C., U.S. Marine Lieut. Col. Oliver North, a central figure in the long-running Iran-*contra* affair, was convicted on 3 of 12 counts relating to the case. He was fined $150,000, given a three-year suspended sentence, put on two years' probation, and ordered to perform 1,200 hours of community service. U.S. District Court Justice Gerhard A. Gesell imposed the relatively lenient penalties after saying he viewed North as not "a leader" in the affair "but really a low-ranking subordinate working to carry out initiatives of a few cynical superiors."

In March, after pleading guilty to charges of spying for six years for East German and Soviet authorities, U.S. Army Warrant Officer James Hall was sentenced to a 40-year prison term. Hall was believed to have crippled several multimillion-dollar electronic surveillance operations aimed at Eastern bloc countries.

White Collar Crime and Theft. Jim Bakker, a prominent U.S. television evangelist, was convicted in October by a Charlotte, N.C., jury on 24 counts of fraud and conspiracy; he was accused of bilking followers out of $158 million during his pastorship of the now-bankrupt PTL ministry. Bakker, whose ministry collapsed in 1987 in the wake of sexual and financial scandals, was sentenced to 45 years in prison and fined $500,000. He lodged an appeal against the sentence. In August the results were announced of a major FBI sting operation directed at commodities traders at the Chicago Board of Trade and the Chicago Mercantile Exchange. After FBI agents masquerading as brokers penetrated the trading pits, they uncovered wrongdoing that led to the indictment of 46 traders on charges ranging from defrauding customers to tax evasion and racketeering. Evidence was unearthed of widespread fraud in the Department of Housing and Urban Development, but Samuel Pierce, who had been HUD secretary throughout the Reagan years, refused to testify before a congressional committee on grounds that he might incriminate himself. Also refusing to testify was Charles Keating, whose

BLEIBTREU—SYGMA

Gen. Arnaldo T. Ochoa Sánchez, a decorated war hero, was one of four Cuban Army officers tried and executed for smuggling cocaine and marijuana to the U.S. Despite the trial and convictions, the U.S. remained skeptical of Cuba's crackdown on drug trafficking.

A drill instructor keeps a corps of young men in line at a correctional institution run much like a boot camp. Nine states had instituted programs whereby young first offenders convicted of drug or property crimes could serve their time at prisons that used military-like discipline to instill a "change of attitude."
BILLY GRIMES—TIME MAGAZINE

bankrupt Lincoln Savings and Loan Association, said to have been involved with questionable loans and fraudulent practices, was one of many such institutions that would cost taxpayers billions in bailout money. (*See* WORLD AFFAIRS [North America]: *United States.*)

Hong Kong authorities, seeking to rid the British colony of its reputation as a counterfeiting centre, continued a crackdown on illegally copied computer software and manuals. A software package priced at $800 in the U.S. was said to be available for a fraction of that cost at one of Hong Kong's pirating outlets. Some of these outlets were believed to be linked to Triad organized crime gangs, secret societies better known for their drug-trafficking, prostitution, and protection activities.

Illustrating the major increase in art theft, the New York-based International Foundation for Art Research listed about 1,300 works as stolen in 1979 and more than 30,000 a decade later. The theft problem was especially acute in Europe, where one criminal network was believed to have plundered more than $33 million of art from French manor houses during the mid-1980s. Many police forces, including those of France and Italy, were devoting more investigative resources to art theft, but recovery rates remained well below 50% in most cases.

Law Enforcement. Soviet authorities disclosed that current annual expenditure on the nation's 700,000-strong police force exceeded $5 billion. This excluded the cost of Interior Ministry troops, used during the year to break up violent demonstrations in southern Soviet republics. Interior Minister Vadim Bakatin suggested that the U.S.S.R. was considering joining Interpol, the international police organization based in Paris, "because organized crime in the U.S.S.R. is acquiring a transnational character."

An Italian parliamentary anti-Mafia commission was warned during the year by the governor of the Bank of Italy, Carlo Azeglio Ciampi, that political leaders needed to face up to the problem of billions of dollars in drug profits being recycled through national and international banking systems. This recycling, said Ciampi, would be further facilitated by the lifting of restrictions on the free movement of capital between eight European countries from July 1, 1990. Some financially powerful countries, including the U.S., Canada, the U.K., and Switzerland, were implementing or about to introduce legislation that would help law-enforcement officials trace the flow of illicit funds.

In what appeared to be a significant change of policy, a U.S. Justice Department ruling made public in October indicated that the U.S. had the right to arrest people in foreign countries who were wanted under U.S. law, without the consent of the country of asylum and whether or not they were U.S. citizens. The State Department confirmed that the FBI had been given this authority but said it would be exercised only at the discretion of the president.

In Sweden a successful conclusion seemed finally to have been reached to the lengthy hunt for the killer of Prime Minister Olof Palme, who was assassinated in a Stockholm street in February 1986. Christer Pettersson, a Swede with a long criminal record, was found guilty of the murder on July 27 by a Stockholm court and sentenced to life imprisonment. In October, however, an appeals court ordered Pettersson freed immediately, pending publication of its verdict on his case. One of the most intense police hunts in Australia's history began on January 10 following the assassination in Canberra of Federal Police Assistant Commissioner Colin Winchester. The brutal killing, the first of its type in Australia, remained unsolved at year's end.

In 1986 the Metro Toronto Police Force had not seen the highly addictive cocaine derivative known as crack, though they had been cautioned by their U.S. counterparts to prepare for the worst. In 1987 Toronto police made 177 crack arrests, in 1988, 726, and by 1989—duplicating developments in the U.S.—crack traffickers and users had transformed some public housing projects into virtual war zones. In the U.K. police chiefs expressed concern that this depressing scenario would be repeated shortly in Europe.

(DUNCAN CHAPPELL)

Prisons and Penology. Prison populations and the number of prison cells continued to increase in many countries. In the United States the total prison and jail population (including those awaiting trial) was estimated to be about one million. Many states were undertaking major prison construction programs, and in May President Bush announced that he would seek $1 billion for new federal prisons in addition to the $500 million already contained in the 1990 budget.

In England and Wales accommodations for an additional 3,000 prisoners were scheduled for construction, bringing the total prison-building program to 26,000 places and expanding the prison system by 60% between 1980 and 1996. As of 1989 Britain had a higher proportion of its population in prison than any other Western European country except Luxembourg. France also had an increasing prison

population but did, however, slightly reduce the scale of its prison-building plans. By contrast, in West Germany an increasing number of prisons stood empty, given the 20% reduction in the prison population since 1983. This unexpected downward trend was attributed to a shift among public prosecutors and judges in attitudes about the place of imprisonment. On the other hand, The Netherlands, long noted for its exceptionally low prison population, announced that prison capacity would be doubled by the early 1990s. This dramatic turnabout in Dutch penal policy reflected increased concerns about drug offenses and a hardening of political attitudes regarding crime.

In August Britain became the first European country to experiment with electronic tagging. Three magistrates' courts were equipped to use electronic surveillance as a bail condition, subject to the defendant's consent.

Prison Management and Prison Conditions. During the year attention was given to the growing interest by the private sector in the management of prisons, notably in Britain, the U.S., Australia, and France. To date, commercial involvement had been confined largely to prison construction. By the end of 1989 no decision had been made by the British government to widen that involvement to management, despite intense lobbying from the private sector. The government in France announced that, although there might be wider opportunities for commercial firms within the prison system, these would not include management of the facilities themselves.

Issues concerning prison conditions remained prominent in many countries. In France many prison officers were involved in strikes and other industrial action, in part reflecting concern that they had lost status in recent years. In Britain her majesty's chief inspector of prisons called for the installation of decent sanitation. In response, the home secretary agreed to speed up the renovation program. The pressure of numbers in several countries, notably the U.S., continued to result in deplorable conditions within many prisons. This situation was accentuated in many countries by the presence of growing numbers of prisoners with the AIDS virus, posing acute dilemmas about illegal drug usage and homosexual behaviour within the prison.

Punishment. Many countries continued to seek new ways of dealing with offenders in the community. Day fines (*i.e.,* units of daily disposable income) were introduced in Britain on an experimental basis in four parts of the country, and increased funding was provided for new accommodations for those who could not post bail as part of the strategy for reducing the number of people in prison awaiting trial. Not all such moves, however, could be described as being of liberal motivation. In the U.S. in Delaware a bill was introduced to revive public flogging for drug offenses. Another measure that some commentators regarded as regressive was the new power of prosecutors in England and Wales to appeal against "unduly lenient" sentences. On the other hand, it was argued that this step might encourage the development of sentencing guidelines. While the British judiciary had largely set its face against such guidelines, they were used at both the federal and state level in the U.S.

At the same time, there were pressures in the U.S. and elsewhere for more punitive sentencing arrangements. In May President Bush called for tougher penalties for federal crimes involving firearms and, indeed, for the revival of the death penalty with respect to certain killings. Bush also proposed, as part of a $1.2 billion federal anticrime package, a reduction in the frequency of plea bargaining to ensure that "federal charges always reflect . . . the seriousness of the defendant's conduct." In some countries, however,

there was some softening of the criminal law, especially in Communist countries seeking to loosen the shackles of the past. The Soviet Union amended the Law on Criminal Liability for Crimes against the State. The complete reworking of this provision, most frequently used to punish dissidents for "anti-Soviet agitation and propaganda," resulted in reduced maximum levels of imprisonment and fines. Similarly, in Poland the authorities pardoned persons punished for specified political offenses.

A wave of political executions continued in Iran, in addition to the execution of 300 "international drug traffickers." Iran featured prominently in a major survey of capital punishment published in April by Amnesty International. According to the report, *When the State Kills,* the death penalty was in force in 100 countries; during the previous three years 3,399 executions were known to have taken place (in addition to an unknown number in Iran and elsewhere).

In June the U.S. Supreme Court ruled in two 5–4 decisions that states were entitled to execute persons as young as 16 and those who are mentally retarded. The majority rejected the claim that this breached the Eighth Amendment (which prohibits the judicial use of "cruel and unusual punishment"). The court recommended that the mental age of a criminal be taken into consideration at the time of sentencing but found that it was not unconstitutional to execute the mentally retarded. This decision was condemned by the American Civil Liberties Union as a form of "legal barbarism." (ANDREW RUTHERFORD)

See also Law.

This article updates the *Macropædia* articles CRIME AND PUNISHMENT; POLICE.

Dance

North America. In many ways the 1980s were harsh years for American dance, and they ended with one marked by death, retirement, and jarring change. The New York City Ballet (NYCB) absorbed the most blows, beginning in late 1988 with the death of one of its principal patrons, Lawrence Wien. In 1989 Lincoln Kirstein retired from his positions as general director of NYCB and as president of the School of American Ballet (SAB). Alexandra Danilova, SAB's last living link to the prerevolutionary Mariinsky Theatre of Russia, retired from the faculty. Jerome Robbins announced his retirement from the position of co-ballet master in chief, effective Jan. 1, 1990. Suzanne Farrell, debatably George Balanchine's most important ballerina, retired prematurely from the stage at age 44, hostage to the restrictions imposed by an artificial hip. The day after her farewell in the last movement of *Vienna Waltzes* (one of her greatest performances of it), she was teaching NYCB company class. Earlier in the year Patricia McBride (*see* BIOGRAPHIES), another key Balanchine ballerina of Farrell's generation, also retired, going out with a gala evening that celebrated her roles. Finally, owing to a debilitating illness, NYCB's irreplaceable musical director and chief conductor, Robert Irving, quietly slipped from public view. The year's bright spot was the debut of SAB student Monique Meunier, now an NYCB apprentice and, experienced observers believed, the most brilliant danseuse to emerge from the school since Darci Kistler.

At American Ballet Theatre (ABT) there were two jolts. In June Mikhail Baryshnikov gave a year's notice that he would leave his position after 10 years as ABT's artistic director. Then, in the fall, he resigned overnight following a dispute with the board over the status of his assistant,

Finnish choreographer Reijo Kela's *081 05 2193V-237 . . .*, the full title of which encompassed all the dancers' social security numbers, was performed at the American Dance Festival at Duke University, Durham, North Carolina. Although modern dance had long been dominated by American choreographers, many dance festivals in 1989 drew from the field of international artists.

JAY ANDERSON

Charles France. No replacement had been named at the year's end. Baryshnikov also appeared onstage from time to time: in several galas with Martha Graham's company (the lead in her revised version of *American Document,* Oedipus in *Night Journey*) and on Broadway as Gregor Samsa, an actor-mime's role, in Steven Berkoff's *Metamorphosis,* for which Baryshnikov won a Tony nomination.

The death of popular modern dance choreographer Alvin Ailey (*see* OBITUARIES) just days before his company opened its New York season in December was another blow. Judith Jamison, who had danced with the Ailey troupe and was currently director of her own company, was named to succeed him as director of the Alvin Ailey American Dance Theater on December 20.

The year was also marked by increasing economic hardship for dancers. In New York City escalating rents drove more dance studios out of business, including that of Maggie Black, one of the city's most respected ballet teachers. It was also the last year for the adventuresome PepsiCo Summerfare, the 10-year-old international arts festival in Purchase, N.Y. Another bastion of experimentalism, the Brooklyn Academy of Music (BAM), began to withdraw its decade-long support of dancing in favour of opera and concert music. The only American dance presented at BAM in 1989 was the Bebe Miller company.

Among the year's new dances, the output of Merce Cunningham, at 70, was astonishing, both for its quantity and for its quality. His four new works, all masterpieces, excelled for their intricate detail and strength of purpose (*Cargo X, Field and Figures, Inventions,* and *August Pace*). Mark Morris took his company to Boston in his staging of Purcell's *Dido and Aeneas,* but his new dances remained in Belgium, his base of operations. Free-lance ballet choreographer Peter Anastos staged Edward Gorey's parable of *la danse, The Gilded Bat,* for Ballet West, with original Gorey designs. Christopher D'Amboise founded a chamber ballet company, Off Center Ballet, which began to present his work. Other dances that excited discussion during the year included Trisha Brown's lustrous *Astral Convertible,* Twyla Tharp's new works for ABT (*Bum's Rush, Quartet,*

Everlast), and Peter Martins' three ballets for NYCB, especially *Echo,* to a commissioned score by Michael Torke.

There were ambitious projects by tap dancers, notably by Brenda Bufalino for her American Tap Dance Orchestra. Gregory Hines showcased classic jazz tap through a TV special and his Hollywood movie, *Tap;* and the smash Broadway revue *Black and Blue* presented tap stars Bunny Briggs, Jimmy Slyde, and others. Still, one did not have a sense of tap as a vital art form but as a historical one. The same could be said of ballroom dancing, valiantly championed by the American Ballroom Theater, both on tour and in Tommy Tune's new Broadway show, *Grand Hotel.* On the other hand, it was a year notable for its revivals. Among them were the Tony-winning retrospective *Jerome Robbins' Broadway,* Bronislava Nijinska's *Le Train bleu* (Oakland Ballet), Charles Wiedman's *On My Mother's Side* (Douglas Nielsen), and Lucinda Childs's *Carnation.* Ann Hutchinson Guest staged a fascinating revision of Nijinsky's *L'Après-midi d'un faune*—based on her analysis of the choreographer's notations—for the Juilliard dancers and for Les Grands Ballets Canadiens.

Producers looked aggressively for imports from outside the U.S. and at previously unemphasized communities within it. Jacob's Pillow (Becket, Mass.) and the American Dance Festival (Durham, N.C.) imported richly diverse offerings from Europe, South America, and Asia. In June an ethnic dance festival was held in the San Francisco Bay area, and the Dance Critics Association, meeting there, devoted a day of its annual conference to ethnic dance issues. The young American Indian Dance Theatre enjoyed a sold-out tour within the U.S. Visiting Japanese dancers brought ballet, modern, Kabuki, and Noh. BAM imported several attractions from France (Maguy Marin) and West Germany's Ruhr Valley; the best of those was Susanne Linke, in a considered tribute to the late soloist Dore Hoyer.

The Leningrad Kirov Ballet enjoyed a successful tour of major U.S. cities, including New York—its first appearance there in 25 years. The program containing the Kirov's newly acquired Balanchine ballets—*Scotch Sym-*

Dancers performing at the Minskoff Theater bring back memories of all-black Broadway musicals in *Black and Blue,* a nostalgic revue featuring white tie and tails, sequined costumes, and tap dancing.
MARTHA SWOPE

phony, staged by Suzanne Farrell, and *Theme and Variations,* staged by Francia Russell—presented a window on the state of Soviet technique and, in reflection, on American. One Kirov dancer, Yury Zhukov, signed a nine-month contract with the San Francisco Ballet and did not need to defect to do so. Also touring the U.S. were the Red Army Chorus and Dancers, the Moscow Classical Ballet (with young virtuoso Vladimir Malakhov), the Donetsk Ballet, and a small group led by Bolshoi stars Ekaterina Maximova and Vladimir Vasiliev.

Awards included: Capezio (Edward Villella), the American Choreographers (Liz Lerman, Miriam Mahdaviani, Sara Pearson, Shapiro & Smith), and the Metropolitan Live/American Dance Festival Choreography Commission (Doug Elkins). The Scripps award went toward establishing an annual choreography fellowship in memory of Doris Humphrey, José Limón, and Charles Weidman. Alexandra Danilova captured the Kennedy Center Honors, a National Arts Institute medal, and New York City's Handel Medallion. Owing to the death of *Dance Magazine* editor William Como, there was no *Dance Magazine* award in 1989.

Other deaths included those of (in late 1988) Graham collaborator Isamu Noguchi and (in 1989) Harold Christensen, Lavinia Williams, Jeff Duncan, Angna Enters, Tim Wengerd, Ron Field, Michael Lland, Jim Clinton, and Parmenia Migel Ekstrom, ballet historian and founder and president of the Stravinsky-Diaghilev Foundation.

Canada. Tragedy struck Canadian ballet in 1989. Henny Jurriens, the new artistic director of the Royal Winnipeg Ballet (RWB), was killed with his wife, Judy, in an automobile accident before he had served a year in his position. André Lewis was appointed as interim artistic director, and RWB cofounder Arnold Spohr was called out of retirement to serve as artistic adviser. On top of this, David Peregrine, a leading RWB dancer, was killed in a plane crash, and RWB cofounder Betty Hey Farrally died of cancer.

The third Festival International de Nouvelle Danse took place in Montreal during November; it featured groups from Japan, Belgium, The Netherlands, France, and the U.S., as well as from throughout Canada. A symposium in Vancouver, B.C., was devoted to Leningrad's Kirov Ballet during the company's June appearances there. Nikita Dolgushin, one of the U.S.S.R.'s greatest Petipa stylists, taught and coached for the Goh Ballet in Vancouver.

At the National Ballet of Canada (NBC), Reid Anderson took over six months earlier than announced, and Glen Tetley, artistic associate, left his position six months earlier than expected. Tetley's newest ballet for the company, *Tagore,* about the Indian poet, was given its premiere in April.

Frank Augustyn, NBC principal dancer, was appointed artistic director of Ottawa's Theatre Ballet of Canada. Former Balanchine dancer Patricia Neary was named artistic director of Ballet British Columbia. Among awards were the First International New Choreographic Award to a Canadian artist (Andrea Smith) and the $8,000 Jean A. Chalmers Choreographic Award (David Allan).

(MINDY ALOFF)

Europe. Improved East-West relations had beneficial effects on dance. Leading Soviet artists were allowed increasing engagements in Britain and other Western countries; others from the West (and Australia) reciprocated in the U.S.S.R. Moscow's Bolshoi Ballet had an unprecedented six-week London season, followed by a week each in Birmingham, England, and in Dublin, and visits to the West were also made by the Byelorussian Ballet and the Tbilisi Ballet from the Soviet republic of Georgia.

The quality of Soviet dancing was generally more admired than its choreographic content. In London Yury Grigorovich, longtime artistic director of the Bolshoi Ballet, was attacked in most reviews for inferior choreographic revisions he had made to such established classics as *The Sleeping Beauty* and *Giselle.* Grigorovich vigorously defended himself in press interviews, a response that would have been unthinkable a few years earlier.

Soviet dance teaching was also made available. Irina Kolpakova, prima ballerina of the Kirov Ballet, spent time in London assisting former Kirov ballerina Natalia Makarova in staging a lavish new production of the 19th-century Marius Petipa classic *La Bayadère* for Britain's Royal Ballet. Soviet stars appeared in this in alternation with resident principals.

The Royal Ballet prepared to celebrate principal choreographer Sir Kenneth MacMillan's 60th birthday (December 11) with late fall and winter programs of his works. These supplemented his own new full-evening *The Prince of the Pagodas* to neglected original music by Benjamin Britten, first performed in 1957 to John Cranko choreography.

Modern dance continued to flourish in Britain. Robert Cohan presented a farewell program of four new works for London Contemporary Dance Theatre, which he had

directed from its formation in 1967, and was succeeded in the post in July by fellow U.S. dancer-choreographer Dan Wagoner. The change was shadowed by the death on June 11 of Robin Howard (*see* OBITUARIES), founder and chief executive of Contemporary Dance Trust, which established and managed the dance company and its associated school. Howard spent most of his own money in its support and was credited with having single-handedly "changed the face of dance in Britain."

A "Spring Loaded" season of modern dance in London and some regional centres by small companies and groups from Britain and abroad was added to the well-established fall season of "Dance Umbrella" events. The former put special focus on new dance and creative talent from The Netherlands (where the Netherlands Dance Theatre celebrated 30 years of activity in new dance work); Dance Umbrella focused on the fertile spread of new French dance.

The French emphasis took account of the Revolution bicentennial celebrations, in which dance played a major part in Paris and elsewhere. Besides regular Paris theatres, performances were given in the Grand Palais, the huge exhibition centre built in 1900 alongside the Champs-Élysées. These included a midsummer dance spectacular, *1789 . . . et nous,* devised by Maurice Béjart from his new base at Lausanne, Switz.

The Paris Opéra Ballet, directed by Rudolf Nureyev, followed the opera company's move to the new Bastille opera house, and the former Théâtre de l'Opéra officially became the Palais de la Danse. Nureyev "went missing" at the start

STEVE CARAS

Tatyana Terekhova soars during the Kirov Ballet's *Le Corsaire* at the Metropolitan Opera House in New York. The full-length *Le Corsaire*, a little-known work of virtuoso dancing, sparked the opening of the Kirov's eight-week, four-city tour of the U.S.

of the fall season, playing the king in a U.S. tour of *The King and I* while still under Paris contract. Pierre Bergé, the director of the Paris Opéra, objected to Nureyev's absence, and in November Nureyev resigned as director; however, he remained as "premier choreographer."

Regular training for modern dance in France was mainly located at the Centre National de Danse Contemporaine at Angers, but it was reliably estimated there were more than 200 performing groups nationwide in a "new wave" of nonclassical and experimental dance, drawing enthusiastic support from young audiences. In Denmark a Copenhagen festival of modern dance in its fourth year achieved "official" status as part of the Royal Theatre's longtime annual Ballet and Opera Festival.

The news was gloomier in Ireland, where both Dublin Contemporary Dance Theatre and Irish National Ballet were forced to disband by a February decision of the Irish Arts Council to withdraw all funding for dance on grounds of poor standards, poor public interest, and lack of educational infrastructure. After 15 years of activity, Irish National Ballet bowed out with *Oscar,* a full-evening production by their regular choreographer, Israeli-born Domy Reiter-Soffer, commemorating Oscar Wilde as one of the great Irish literary figures.

Another literary-based ballet received international acclaim: John Neumeier's *Peer Gynt,* after Ibsen, premiered by Hamburg (West Germany) State Ballet. It had Soviet collaboration in original music by Alfred Schnittke, rated in some reports "the best long ballet score for many years"; Schnittke created a disturbing precedent in asserting that his music could in future be played *only* in the context of Neumeier's ballet.

Italian ballerina Carla Fracci began her directorship of the San Carlo Ballet at Naples with a centennial tribute to Nijinsky. Fracci herself portrayed the famed Tamara Karsavina in a collage drawn from works Nijinsky danced, those he choreographed, and new choreography by Vasiliev (U.S.S.R.) and Wayne Eagling (U.K.). The Florence May Festival premiered Danish-born Flemming Flindt's *The Overcoat,* after Gogol, to a collage of Shostakovich music and featuring Nureyev as Gogol's protagonist.

In Budapest Antal Fodor became director of the Hungarian State Ballet and staged a unique triple bill of *The Miraculous Mandarin* to Bartók's celebrated music performed three times: with choreography by Gyula Harangozo (1945), by Laszlo Seregi (1970), and by Fodor himself. Hungary's Gyor Ballet visited London for the first time at Sadler's Wells.

U.S. dance companies maintained European touring. NYCB went to Paris, Glasgow, Scotland, and The Netherlands; Houston (Texas) Ballet to the Edinburgh Festival; Paul Taylor Dance Company to London for its first visit in 16 years; Alvin Ailey American Dance Theatre to France and Italy; Martha Graham Dance Company to Salzburg, Austria; and Merce Cunningham and Dancers to London and to Leicester, England, where a new international dance festival was inaugurated in March.

Deaths during the year included (besides Robin Howard): Maris Liepa, a former leading Soviet dancer (*see* OBITUARIES); British dancers Kerrison Cooke and Julian Hosking; Elsa Brunelleschi, leading British-based authority on Spanish dance; Jacques Garnier, director of the Paris experimental Groupe de Recherche Chorégraphique (GRCOP); and Simon Virsaladze, a Soviet ballet designer and Lenin Prize winner.   (NÖEL GOODWIN)

See also Music; Theatre.

This article updates the *Macropædia* article The History of Western DANCE.

Disasters

The loss of life and property from disasters in 1989 included the following:

Aviation

January 8, Near Kegworth, Leicestershire, England. A Boeing 737-400 crash-landed when the left engine caught fire and the crew mistakenly shut down the right engine; although experts initially suspected that alarm system wires were crossed when the plane was built, a subsequent investigation found no malfunction; 47 persons were killed in the crash, and 79 others survived, including the pilots.

January 31, Near Abilene, Texas. A KC-135A military refueling jet crashed in a ball of flames on takeoff at Dyess Air Force Base; of the 19 persons aboard, 17 lost their lives.

February 3, Rangoon, Burma. A Burma Airways turboprop Fokker Friendship 27 aircraft carrying 29 persons slammed into a tree during takeoff; 26 persons aboard the aircraft were killed.

February 8, Santa Maria, Portuguese Azores. A Boeing 707 jetliner slammed into a fog-enshrouded mountain and exploded in flames while making its approach to Santa Maria Airport; all 144 persons aboard lost their lives.

February 19, Southern California. A twin-engine chartered plane carrying 10 persons crashed into Pleasant Peak in Cleveland National Forest; there were no survivors.

February 23, Lake Constance, Austria. An Aerocommander AC-90 crashed into Lake Constance in dense fog; all 11 persons aboard were feared dead.

February 25, Near Tegucigalpa, Honduras. A DC-6 plane, carrying 10 persons returning from a mission to supply Nicaraguan rebels in Honduras, slammed into a hill; there were no survivors.

March 10, Near Lima, Peru. A twin-engine plane that appeared to be experiencing engine problems slammed into a building; all 10 persons aboard were killed.

March 10, Dryden, Ont. A twin-engine Fokker F-28 jet crashed in thick woods moments after taking off in heavy snow and with a buildup of ice on its wings; 45 persons miraculously survived the crash, but 24 others died; it was not known whether a fire aboard the aircraft erupted before or after the crash.

March 12, Near Tucson, Ariz. An Air Force CH-3E helicopter carrying 15 persons crashed on a night training mission; all aboard perished.

March 20, Near Pohang, South Korea. A CH-53D U.S. Marine Corps helicopter crashed while taking part in a major joint military exercise in South Korea; at least 21 marines were killed, and 13 others were injured.

March 21, Guarulhos, Brazil. A Transbrasil Boeing 707 jetliner crashed and exploded into pieces while preparing to make its landing; one of the plane's engines slammed into an apartment building, and burning wreckage slid down through a hillside shantytown killing at least 21 persons, including the 3 pilots, and severely burning some 200 others.

April 10, Near Leoncel, France. A Fokker 27 twin-engine turboprop plane carrying 22 persons slammed into Mt. Vercors; all aboard were presumed dead.

May 8, Oskarshamn, Sweden. A Beechcraft-99 twin-engine commuter airplane carrying 16 persons crashed and exploded while it attempted to land at the city's airport; all aboard were killed.

May 30, Off the coast of Okinawa Island, Japan. A CH-46 helicopter carrying 22 U.S. marines pitched over and slammed into the ocean upside down; 14 servicemen lost their lives.

June 7, Paramaribo, Suriname. A DC-8 jetliner crashed in dense fog in a jungle area near the airport; of the 182 persons aboard, only 13 survived the crash.

June 12, Hawaii. A twin-engine sight-seeing plane with 11 persons aboard disappeared between the islands of Maui and Hawaii; the wreckage from the craft was found the following day strewn across a rugged cliff in a remote valley of Hawaii; there were no survivors.

June 22, Near Tarma, Peru. A Peruvian Air Force transport plane carrying some 40 civilians crashed into a mountain and broke in two; all aboard were killed.

June 28, Near Hargeisa, Somalia. A Somali Airlines plane was apparently shot down by Somali rebels; all 30 persons aboard perished.

Late June, Near Kaohsiung, Taiwan. A Formosa Airlines plane crashed while taking off; 13 persons were killed.

Early July, Helmand province, Afghanistan. A government airliner crashed, and 35 persons lost their lives.

Mid-July, Vietnam. A Soviet military plane carrying a Soviet delegation and Vietnamese officials crashed; at least 20 persons were killed.

July 19, Sioux City, Iowa. A United Airlines DC-10 jumbo jet carrying 296 persons became disabled in the air en route from Denver, Colo., to Chicago when an engine's turbofan assembly ripped loose from its enclosure on the tail of the aircraft and severed all three of the plane's hydraulic lines, which control the aircraft; the veteran pilot flew the plane in right circles (the only way the plane would steer) until he could make an emergency landing at Sioux City, where the plane crashed just short of the runway and broke into pieces; miraculously, 186 persons survived the fiery crash, but one person later died in the hospital.

July 27, Tripoli, Libya. A Korean Air DC-10 carrying 199 persons crashed while attempting to land in heavy fog; 82 persons lost their lives, including 4 persons on the ground.

August 3, Samos, Greece. A Greek airliner crashed near a mountain while making its landing approach; all 34 persons aboard perished.

August 7, Near Dembidollo, Eth. A Twin Otter aircraft carrying an estimated 16 persons crashed on a remote rocky mountainside; all aboard were killed, including U.S. Rep. Mickey Leland (Dem., Texas).

August 8, South Island, New Zealand. A twin-engine sight-seeing plane crashed in rugged and remote terrain; at least 10 persons were aboard, and all were killed.

August 15, Shanghai. A Chinese airliner plunged into a river after an abortive takeoff; 34 persons were killed.

September 3, Havana. An Ilyushin 62-M Cubana Airlines jet carrying 126 persons crashed and burst into flames in a tiny village during a thunderstorm; the only survivor of the crash later died, and as many as 45 persons were killed on the ground in Cuba's worst aviation disaster to date.

September 3, Near São José do Xingu, Brazil. A Boeing 737 jetliner carrying 54 persons made a crash landing in the Amazon jungle after losing all its navigational equipment; 41 persons were rescued when a four-party group of survivors made their way through the thick jungle to get help at a nearby ranch.

September 8, Off the coast of Hirtshals, Den. A chartered twin-engine Convair 440 turboprop plane crashed in the Skagerrak, the eastern arm of the North Sea; all 55 persons aboard were lost.

Mid-September, Maharashtra state, India. An Indian plane with 11 persons aboard slammed into a dam; there were no survivors.

September 16, Irian Jaya province, Indon. A Twin Otter airplane carrying 22 persons disappeared over the jungle; all aboard were feared dead.

September 19, Niger. A DC-10 jetliner carrying 171 persons apparently exploded in midair over the Ténéré region of the Sahara; the craft, which originated its flight in Brazzaville, Congo, made a stopover in N'Djamena, Chad, and was en route to Paris when radio contact was lost; all those aboard persished; at least two terrorist groups claimed responsibility for the alleged bombing.

September 27, Near Tusayan, Ariz. A twin-engine Grand Canyon sight-seeing plane crashed while attempting to land at the airport; 10 of the 21 persons aboard were killed.

October 18, Near Nasosny, Azerbaijan S.S.R. An Ilyushin-76 Soviet military transport plane crashed into the Caspian Sea; all 57 persons aboard lost their lives.

October 20, Near Leninakan, Armenian S.S.R. A Soviet cargo plane carrying supplies to an earthquake-ravaged area crashed; all 17 persons aboard were killed.

October 21, Near Tegucigalpa, Honduras. A Boeing 727 jetliner slammed into a cloud-enshrouded mountain while attempting to land; 131 of the 146 persons aboard perished.

October 26, Petropavlovsk-Kamchatsky, U.S.S.R. A Soviet Antonov-26 military transport plane crashed into a mountain during bad weather; all 36 persons aboard were killed.

October 26, Near Chia Min, Taiwan. A China Airlines Boeing 737-200 slammed into a mountain minutes after takeoff; all 54 persons aboard died.

October 28, Molokai, Hawaii. An Aloha Island Air DH6 Twin Otter commuter plane carrying 20 persons, including members of a high school volleyball team, crashed into a wall of the Halawa Valley; there were no survivors.

November 21, Western Siberia, U.S.S.R. A twin-engine passenger plane crashed while attempting to land; 34 persons were killed.

November 27, Near Bogotá, Colombia. A passenger jet carrying 107 persons exploded in

A trail burned through an airport runway marks the path of the United Airlines DC-10 that crash-landed in Iowa after the plane's hydraulic lines were severed. Though the pilot was left with minimal steering ability and was unable to avoid a crash landing, 186 people survived.

The *Marchioness*, a British pleasure boat, sits on the bank of the Thames after being brought up from the river's bottom. The boat, which was being used for a party, was rammed from behind by a barge. It sank within minutes, killing 51 people.
AP/WIDE WORLD

midair and plunged to the ground shortly after takeoff; there were no survivors.

December 21, Near Guayaramerin, Bolivia. A Bolivian Air Force transport plane, being used to transport civilians, crashed in the jungle shortly after taking off with only three of its four engines working; of the 28 persons aboard, only 5 survived.

Fires and Explosions

January 1, Near Remer, Minn. A fast-spreading fire engulfed a two-story frame house; its 10 occupants, including 8 children, died in the blaze.

January 20, Henan (Honan) province, China. An explosion at a private firecracker company killed 26 persons and seriously injured 16 others when some 15 tons of explosives ignited and gutted the factory.

February 8, Mysore, India. A fire in a locked television studio erupted when firecrackers, which were set off during a wedding scene, ignited fabric, coconut fronds, and other props used in filming; at least 40 persons died, and 14 others were injured, 10 of them critically.

Mid-February, Toulon, France. An explosion caused a 200-year-old building to collapse, resulting in at least 15 deaths and injuries to 36 others.

March 3, Istanbul. A powerful explosion at a paint factory leveled the five-story structure and two adjacent buildings; the blast, apparently caused by a chemical reaction, killed at least 11 persons and injured 34 others.

March 3, Jamshedpur, India. A fire and subsequent stampede took place during a celebration in a tent; at least 28 persons were feared dead.

March 8, Belfort, France. A fast-burning fire devastated a five-story apartment building; 15 persons were killed, including 4 who jumped to their deaths.

April 19, Off the coast of Puerto Rico. An explosion and fire aboard the battleship *Iowa* occurred in one of the ship's three main turrets, which housed the world's largest naval guns; the fire was quickly contained, but 47 sailors stationed near the turret lost their lives.

June 4, Turin, Italy. A jail fire apparently started when a lighted paper was thrown onto a pile of rubber mattresses; eight women prisoners and two female wardens were overcome by asphyxiating fumes and died.

August 7, Mogilev-Podolsky, U.S.S.R. An explosion in a five-story apartment house occurred when a maintenance worker struck a match in the basement while investigating a gas leak; 18 persons were killed in the blast.

August 17, Near al-Hillah, Iraq. A giant explosion at an alleged Iraqi military installation destroyed at least a quarter of the complex and claimed the lives of up to 700 persons; Iraqi officials, however, claimed the explosion was at a petroleum depot and that only 19 persons were killed in the blast.

Mid-September, Northern Malaysia. A fire at a private religious school for girls killed 27 students.

October 23, Pasadena, Texas. A gigantic explosion at a petrochemical complex, presumably caused by a large leak of ethylene, was followed by a series of smaller explosions and a raging fire that burned out of control; 22 persons were feared dead.

December 3, Brussels. A gunpowder explosion in the basement of a shooting club occurred when a bullet apparently ricocheted and hit an ammunition store; 12 persons lost their lives in the blast.

December 24, Johnson City, Tenn. A fire at an 11-story retirement home claimed the lives of at least 16 residents; the cause of the blaze was unknown.

Marine

January 1, Off the coast of Guatemala. A ferry filled with New Year's revelers capsized and sank in Amatique Bay after it ran out of fuel and panicky passengers ran to one side of the vessel; 59 persons were reportedly drowned.

January 3, Off the coast of the Philippines. An overcrowded motor launch carrying more than 140 persons sank; at least 16 persons drowned off Romblon Island.

Mid-January, Punjab province, Pak. A riverboat carrying funeral mourners struck a length of iron bar laid across the river to fashion a temporary bridge, broke in two, and capsized; some 90 persons were feared drowned.

February 15, Skikda, Alg. A Dutch chemical tanker broke up and sank in shallow water during a gale; 27 of the 29 crew members were feared drowned.

February 22, Off the coast of Scotland. A freighter carrying a load of salt from Spain to Iceland sank during a fierce Atlantic storm; all 17 South Korean crewmen were feared drowned.

February 25–26, Atlantic Ocean. A fierce storm capsized or sank at least eight ships in the Atlantic Ocean; 8 persons drowned, 25 were missing and presumed dead, and 80 others were rescued.

Early March, Southern Bangladesh. A ferry capsized in crocodile-infested waters; at least 35 persons were killed, and 70 others were missing.

March 8, South China Sea. An overcrowded fishing boat carrying Vietnamese refugees collided with a Japanese tanker and capsized; at least 130 boat people were feared drowned, and 35 others were rescued.

Mid-March, Off the coast of Hainan Island, China. An overloaded sight-seeing boat carrying 182 persons capsized; 55 schoolchildren and 8 adults drowned.

March 19, Off the coast of Japan. A Liberian-registered tanker carrying a load of flammable chemicals drifted ablaze for five days before exploding and sinking; all 23 crewmen aboard were presumed drowned.

March 23, Off the coast of Virginia. A sport-fishing boat carrying 10 persons radioed the U.S. Coast Guard that it was taking on water; rescue ships battling rough seas found no trace of the boat or of survivors.

April 7, Norwegian Sea. A Soviet nuclear-powered submarine caught fire in the rear of the hull while submerged, briefly surfaced to allow crew members to escape, and then sank off the coast of Norway; 42 sailors died in the accident.

May 20, Off the coast of Bali, Indon. A ship loaded with mostly illegal workers bound for Malaysia capsized in rough seas; 30 were known dead, and at least 120 others were missing.

July 16, Near Manikganj, Bangladesh. A passenger ferry carrying some 70 persons capsized during a sudden rainstorm; at least 60 persons were feared drowned.

July 31, Off the coast of Morgan City, La. A barge serving as an oil rig capsized during high winds and turbulent waters fueled by Hurricane Chantal; 10 persons aboard the vessel were missing and presumed drowned.

August 20, Off the coast of London. A chartered pleasure boat carrying party revelers sank in the Thames within minutes after being rammed from behind by a barge; 51 persons lost their lives.

September 2, Off the coast of Java, Indon. A wooden passenger ferry sank in the Madura Straits; 37 persons drowned, and 90 others were missing and feared dead.

September 10, Near Galati, Rom. A Romanian cruiser carrying 179 persons collided with a Bulgarian tugboat that was pulling a convoy of loaded barges on the Danube River; only 18 persons were rescued from the cruiser.

September 26, Lake Victoria, Kenya. A boat carrying 40 fishermen and traders capsized; 33 persons were drowned.

October 28, Nigeria. An overloaded ferry split in half and capsized in the Cross River estuary; more than 200 persons were feared drowned.

December 7, Gulf of St. Lawrence. Two ships about 200 km (125 mi) apart sank shortly after issuing distress calls during a brutal storm; all 39 seamen aboard the ships were presumed dead.

Mining

January 20, Near Nazca, Peru. An explosion and fire, which produced deadly carbon monoxide gas, trapped some 200 gold miners in a mine; rescue attempts were hampered by the poisonous gas and fallen earth, and officials gave virtually no hope of finding survivors since equipment was not available to drive out the gas fumes.

March 9, Near Orkney, South Africa. A fire in a gold mine shaft claimed the lives of 10 miners, who were asphyxiated.

April 18, Luanping (Luan-p'ing) county, China. An explosion at a coal mine claimed the lives of at least 19 miners.

April 23, Northeastern Burundi. After heavy rain the walls of a gold mine collapsed on an unknown number of unauthorized prospectors; at least 100 persons were feared dead.

June 1, Mindanao Island, Phil. Heavy rains and faulty timbering triggered a landslide that caused cave-ins at 11 mine tunnels; 13 persons were killed, and hundreds of others were trapped.

Mid-June, Kasai province, Zaire. The collapse of shafts in a diamond mine led to the deaths of 36 persons.

Late June, Shanxi (Shansi) province, China. A gas explosion in a coal mine claimed the lives of 22 persons.

September 13, Near Wheatcroft, Ky. A methane gas explosion in a coal mine claimed the lives of 10 miners.

November 17, Aleksinac, Yugos. An explosion followed by a fire claimed the lives of 92 coal miners; the blast occurred while a conveyer was being welded.

Miscellaneous

March 4, Baroda, India. Illicit liquor, identified as methyl alcohol, killed at least 126 persons who drank the moonshine; some 200 others were hospitalized.

March 6, Northern India. A group of pilgrims stampeded into a temple and crushed at least 20 persons to death.

April 15, Sheffield, England. A severely overcrowded soccer stadium was strained beyond its capacity when fans surged forward in a standing area and those persons next to the security fence separating the field from spectators were literally crushed to death or trampled when they lost their footing; 95 persons died.

Late April, Ethiopia and The Sudan. A meningitis epidemic claimed the lives of as many as 20,000 persons in Ethiopia and spread to The Sudan, where at least 400 persons died of the disease.

Mid-May, Bolivia. A yellow fever epidemic in the country's central jungles killed at least 120 persons.

August 2, Kiev, Ukrainian S.S.R. A balcony rail on the main post office gave way and collapsed on a crowd of people during rush hour; at least 11 persons were killed.

August 13, Near Alice Springs, Australia. A hot-air balloon carrying 13 persons plummeted to the ground when its envelope was torn by another balloon passing overhead; there were no survivors.

September 14, Alexandria, Egypt. A crowded second-floor balcony of an old house gave way during a street wedding procession; at least 10 persons were killed.

Natural

Mid-January, Bangladesh. The coldest weather in 20 years claimed the lives of at least 70 persons who had lost their homes to floods or cyclones and were sleeping exposed to the icy elements.

Late January, Sumatra, Indon. A mountain landslide triggered by relentless rains killed at least 20 persons.

January 22, Tadzhik S.S.R. An earthquake measuring 5.3 on the Richter scale caused a gigantic mud slide to descend on the small village of Sharora; most of the 274 deaths reported were attributed to the mud slide, which virtually entombed the residents.

January 28–29, Réunion. Cyclone Firinga battered the island with winds of more than 200 km/h (125 mph), killing at least 10 persons, injuring 60 others, and leaving some 6,000 people homeless.

Early February, Samar Island, Phil. Monsoon rains inundated at least six towns and killed at least 121 persons.

Mid-February, Central Peru. Two rivers burst their banks, sending raging floodwaters through several villages; 57 persons were known dead.

February 25–26, Spain. Hurricane-force winds downed electricity lines and destroyed tons of citrus fruit; at least 12 deaths were attributed to the storm.

Late March, Yemen (Aden). Floods claimed the lives of at least 23 persons.

Late March, Eastern Somalia. The heaviest torrential rains in many years swept away roads, bridges, and homes and claimed the lives of at least 34 persons in the coastal towns of Skushuban, Bosasso, and Kandala.

April 12, Paraiba state, Brazil. Heavy rains killed at least 23 persons, many of them living in shantytowns.

April 19, Georgian S.S.R. A series of landslides, avalanches, and floods precipitated by rapidly melting snow killed more than 50 persons and destroyed or damaged more than 500 houses.

April 20, Sichuan (Szechwan) province, China. A brutal 30-minute hailstorm killed at least 157 persons and injured more than 6,000 others.

April 26, Central Bangladesh. A tornado devastated more than 20 villages, claimed the lives of as many as 1,000 persons, injured some

12,000 others, and left nearly 30,000 people homeless.

May 6, Southern U.S. A storm that spawned tornadoes and precipitated flooding roared through Texas, Virginia, North Carolina, Louisiana, South Carolina, and Oklahoma; storm-related deaths totaled 23, and more than 100 persons were injured.

May 18–20, Salvador, Brazil. Three days of mud slides killed at least 71 persons and left some 6,000 others homeless.

May 25–26, Central Vietnam. Typhoon Cecil devastated crops and some 36,000 homes, killed at least 140 persons, and left some 600 others missing.

May 27, Bangladesh and eastern India. A cyclone ripped across the two countries, destroying tens of thousands of mud and straw huts; some 200 persons were feared dead, including 150 fishermen missing in the Bay of Bengal.

Late May, Southern China. Typhoon Brenda killed 26 persons and injured some 48 others.

Early June, Sri Lanka. Heavy monsoon rains precipitated floods and landslides that killed more than 300 persons and trapped hundreds of others in debris; some 700 persons were injured, and 125,000 others were left homeless.

June 1–July, Sichuan province. Torrential rains unleashed widespread flooding that claimed the lives of more than 1,300 persons and affected some 10 million people.

June 7, Near Srinagar, India. A landslide buried a crowded bus on a mountain highway as it approached the village of Sheri; 41 persons were killed.

Mid-June, Ecuador. Heavy rains precipitated landslides and floods that claimed the lives of 35 persons and left some 30,000 others homeless.

Mid-June–July, Western China. A string of blizzards and bad weather stranded up to 8,000 gold prospectors, killing at least 67.

June 20, Shanxi province. A dam on a mountain burst and unleashed tons of water; 38 persons were killed.

July 16, Luzon, Phil. Typhoon Gordon pummeled the island and triggered landslides and floods; 33 persons lost their lives in the storm.

July 24, Thanh Hoa province, Vietnam. Typhoon Irving roared through the northern Vietnamese coast; at least 200 persons were killed, and nearly 500 others were injured.

Late July, South Korea. Typhoon Judy triggered landslides and severe flooding that claimed the lives of at least 17 persons.

Late July, Asia. Torrential monsoon rains inundated South Korea, where 81 persons perished in floods; southern India, where 750 persons died and 2,000 others were missing; Pakistan, where 17 persons were reported dead; Bangladesh, where some 200 persons were killed; and China, where monthlong flooding claimed some 1,500 lives.

Early August, Irian Jaya province, Indon. An earthquake killed at least 97 persons, including 60 persons who were buried in a landslide.

August 5, Northern India. A landslide buried

some 45 persons who had left passenger buses to remove boulders blocking the road.

September 4, Spain. A freak storm packing high winds and driving rain claimed at least 14 lives along the country's Mediterranean coastline.

September 11, Taiwan. Typhoon Sarah broke a Panamanian freighter in half and claimed the lives of at least 13 persons.

September 16, Zhejiang (Chekiang) province, China. Typhoon Vera, the worst storm to lash the province in 27 years, claimed the lives of 162 persons, left 354 others missing, and injured at least 692 persons.

September 17–21, Caribbean Sea and the U.S. East Coast. Hurricane Hugo, one of the fiercest storms of the decade, wreaked a path of destruction through the Caribbean islands from Guadeloupe to the Virgin Islands and Puerto Rico before lashing South and North Carolina; 71 deaths were attributed to the brutal storm, and damage to property was estimated in the billions of dollars.

Early October, The Philippines. Typhoon Angela swept away homes and claimed the lives of at least 50 persons.

October 2–13, Hainan (Hai-nan) province, China. Three typhoons blasted the southern province, resulting in the deaths of 63 persons and injuries to more than 700 others.

October 10, The Philippines. Typhoon Dan swept across the country and killed at least 43 persons; some 80,000 others were left homeless in 12 provinces.

October 17, San Francisco Bay area. An earthquake measuring 7.1 on the Richter scale shook the area for 15 seconds, claimed 67 lives, and inflicted billions of dollars in damage; the destruction included the collapse of more than a mile of Interstate 880 in Oakland, where 42 persons lost their lives when the upper deck crushed motorists driving on the lower deck, and the collapse of a span of the San Francisco–Oakland Bay Bridge and heavy damage to the Marina District, where three-story buildings were reduced to one level and a ruptured gas main sparked a raging fire.

October 18–19, Shanxi and Hebei (Ho-peh) provinces, China. At least five earthquakes shook the country and killed at least 29 persons; hardest hit was the village of Bucun in Shanxi, where all homes were destroyed.

October 19, The Philippines. Typhoon Elsie lashed the battered country and claimed 30 lives; some 332,000 people were left homeless by the latest storm.

October 29, Algeria. Two earthquakes, measuring 6 and 4.8 on the Richter scale, claimed the lives of some 30 persons.

November 4–5, Thailand. Typhoon Gay roared across the country, inflicting widespread damage and killing at least 365 persons, including 93 persons aboard a U.S. gas-drilling ship, which capsized in the Gulf of Thailand; 400 others were missing and feared dead, and nearly 30,000 dwellings were damaged or destroyed.

The upper deck of Oakland's two-tiered Interstate 880 collapsed onto the lower deck after a massive earthquake struck the San Francisco Bay area.

Rescue workers in the Soviet Union search the remains of two trains virtually destroyed in an explosion caused by a ruptured gas pipeline. The explosion was triggered when sparks from one of the trains ignited gas leaking from the pipeline.
SYGMA

November 9, Southern India. A cyclone swept across the coastal areas and claimed the lives of at least 50 persons.

November 15, Huntsville, Ala. A devastating tornado wreaked a path of destruction some 40 km (25 mi) long, leveling 119 homes and claiming the lives of 18 persons.

December 28, Newcastle, Australia. A rare earthquake, measuring 5.5 on the Richter scale, reduced buildings to rubble and claimed the lives of at least 11 persons; damages were estimated at $1 billion.

Late December, Northeastern Brazil. Heavy tropical rains caused extensive flooding, claiming the lives of 35 persons and leaving some 200,000 homeless.

Late December, India and Bangladesh. A bitter cold wave claimed the lives of at least 75 persons, many of them homeless, who died of exposure.

Railroad

January 15, Near Tongi, Bangladesh. An express train slammed head-on into a mail train carrying pilgrims to a religious festival; of the estimated 2,000 persons aboard both trains, 135 were killed and more than 1,000 others were injured in Bangladesh's worst rail disaster in history; railway officials speculated that the engineers may not have been familiar with a new signaling system recently installed.

January 17, Ahungalle, Sri Lanka. A school bus collided with a train at an unprotected crossing; at least 52 persons, most of them schoolchildren, were killed in the crash.

February 2, Near Chittagong, Bangladesh. Three coaches of an express train derailed, and some 20 persons lost their lives.

March 25, Blantyre, Malawi. A train crashed into a crowded bus; 12 persons were killed, and 43 others were seriously injured.

April 18, Near Jhansi, Uttar Pradesh, India. Twelve cars of a high-speed express train jumped the tracks and tumbled down an embankment; 67 persons were killed, and more than 130 others were injured.

April 29, Londiani, Kenya. A train carrying 800 passengers derailed and plunged over a cliff; at least 11 persons died, and some 114 others were injured.

Mid-May, Zambezia, Mozambique. Two trains collided on a poorly maintained rail line; at least 28 persons were known dead, and 48 others were injured.

May 15, Gujarat, India. A train slammed into a bus filled with some 80 persons returning from a wedding; 50 persons were feared dead.

June 3, Between Ufa and Chelyabinsk, U.S.S.R. A ruptured gas pipeline exploded and engulfed two passenger trains, traveling on the nearby Trans-Siberian Railroad, in flames; the blast, which was triggered when one of the trains threw off sparks from the rails, killed an estimated 462 persons and injured more than 700 others.

June 9, Kamenskaya-Pogorelovo, U.S.S.R. A train rammed into a bus after a railroad worker flagged the bus to proceed across the tracks;

31 persons were killed, and at least 14 others were injured.

June 26, Near Shanghai. A dynamite explosion aboard a passenger train claimed the lives of 28 persons; the blast occurred in the lavatory of the seventh passenger car.

August 4, Colón, Cuba. Two speeding passenger trains collided head-on; 25 persons were killed, and 100 others were injured.

August 9, Between Guasave and Guamuchil, Sinaloa state, Mexico. A train plunged into a rain-swollen river while crossing a bridge; at least 112 persons were killed, and some 500 others were injured.

Mid-September, Yugoslavia. A train collided with a school bus; 12 children were killed, and 20 others were injured.

November 1, Sakaldiha, India. Ten cars of an express train traveling from New Delhi to Calcutta derailed; at least 52 persons were killed, and more than 60 others were injured.

November 16, Calabria, Italy. Two trains collided, possibly because of a signal failure; at least 15 persons lost their lives in the crash.

December 12, Near Roman, Bulg. A passenger train traveling from Sofia to Varna derailed when it was rounding a curve at high speed; at least 15 persons were killed, and 100 others were injured.

Traffic

January 27, Dajabon province, Dominican Republic. A truck carrying Haitian sugarcane workers plunged off a cliff and crashed; at least 50 persons were killed, and 40 others were injured.

Late January, Near Barisal, Bangladesh. A bus carrying a bridal party fell into a river; some 45 passengers were feared drowned.

Late January, Abidjan, Côte d'Ivoire. A school bus fell into a culvert during a thunderstorm; 48 persons were feared dead, and 70 others were injured.

Early February, South Kalimantan, Indon. A truck carrying schoolchildren plunged into a ravine; 18 persons were killed, and 44 others were injured.

February 10, Bihar, India. A speeding truck overturned near the town of Gaya in eastern Bihar state; 22 persons were killed, and 15 others were injured.

Late February, Northern Taiwan. A tour bus crashed, and 12 persons lost their lives.

Mid-March, Northeastern Guinea. A truck loaded with several tons of oranges toppled into a ravine; 17 persons were smothered to death by the fruit.

Late March, Western Nepal. A bus that went out of control fell into a ravine; 14 persons were killed, and 60 others were injured.

June 11, Central Turkey. Two minibuses filled with wedding guests crashed when one hit the other, apparently from the rear, as they raced down the highway; 18 persons were killed.

Late June, Near Bareilly, India. A bus carrying a wedding party hit a high-voltage cable; 29 persons were electrocuted.

July 2, South Africa. A bus traveling to Transkei from the town of Harding in Natal skidded and plunged down an embankment; 56 persons were killed in the crash.

September 21, Alton, Texas. A bus carrying high school students plunged into a rain-filled gravel pit after being hit by a delivery truck; 19 students trapped in the submerged vehicle lost their lives.

October 8, Near Cap-Pele, N.B. A tractor-trailer truck skidded and dumped its load of logs onto a hayride; at least 11 persons lost their lives.

October 20, Near Grafton, New South Wales, Australia. A truck collided head-on with a bus carrying 46 persons; a total of 22 persons were killed in one of the worst traffic accidents in Australia's history.

November 23, Near Murewa, Zimbabwe. A bus plunged into the Chivake River after a tire blowout; at least 50 persons were killed.

December 10, Assam, India. A bus skidded off a road, and 19 persons were killed.

December 22, Near Kempsey, New South Wales. Two tour buses collided head-on while traveling on the Pacific Highway; at least 40 persons were killed in the crash.

AP/WIDE WORLD

An emergency team and curious onlookers examine the wreckage of two tour buses that collided on Australia's Pacific Highway near Kempsey, New South Wales. At least 40 people were killed, and many others were injured in the crash.

Earth Sciences

GEOLOGY AND GEOCHEMISTRY

The 28th International Geological Congress convened in Washington, D.C., in July 1989, five years after the previous congress in Moscow. Reviewing the status of the earth sciences, Umberto G. Cordani, president of the International Union of Geological Sciences, noted that geology was becoming more quantitative and increasingly global in perspective. The most important roles for the geosciences in the next decades would be to contribute to the worldwide effort to achieve sustainable development in the face of environmental damage, to assist in the discovery and management of resources, and to aid communities whose expansion was making them increasingly vulnerable to geologic hazards. Growing concern was expressed about possible changes to the global ecosystem as a result of human activities, which were now responsible for an annual flux of material equal to that moved in plate tectonics. In this light, Cordani emphasized the importance of bridging the knowledge gap between geologists and policymakers. The geologic record of past global changes provided the baseline against which the nature and significance of contemporary and future changes could be assessed, while elucidation of the dynamics of the solid Earth provided the framework for the mitigation of natural hazards. Frank Press, president of the U.S. National Academy of Sciences, informed the congress that he chaired an international group helping the United Nations plan an International Decade for Natural Disaster Reduction, which was to begin in 1990.

The external and internal engines that drive the geologic cycle brought two devastating natural disasters to North America within a month. Between September 17 and 21, Hurricane Hugo ripped across Puerto Rico, the Virgin Islands, the Caribbean, and North and South Carolina, killing more than 70 people (see *Meteorology,* below), and on October 17 an earthquake of magnitude 7.1 on the Richter scale (later named the Loma Prieta earthquake) with an epicentre near Santa Cruz, Calif., rocked the San Francisco Bay area, killing more than 60. For each of these paroxysms of nature, early estimates of the total financial loss exceed several billion dollars. The Loma Prieta quake added to the attention already being paid to earthquake engineering and urban geology after reports in 1989 confirmed that most of the damage and deaths incurred during the December 1988 shock in the Soviet republic of Armenia had resulted from poor construction. The mayor of Memphis, Tenn., aware of the neighbouring New Madrid Fault, which in 1811–12 generated the most powerful earthquakes known in North America, announced that he would push for a seismic building code for the city.

The part of the San Andreas Fault associated with the Loma Prieta earthquake had been identified as one with high potential for failure. The U.S. Geological Survey (USGS) in 1988 had reported a 30% chance that a magnitude-6.5 shock would occur in this section within 30 years. Failure along the San Andreas Fault is usually of the strike-slip variety, with the Pacific Plate moving to the north relative to the North American Plate. This movement usually produces a visible record in the form of a break (fault scarp) at the Earth's surface. Nevertheless, geologists who searched for such a surface rupture after the Loma Prieta shock saw no sign of the expected displacement, a finding that generated some debate. The focus of the earthquake, 18 km (11 mi) down, was nearly twice as deep as normal for the San Andreas. Preliminary analysis indicated that in addition to a lateral movement of 1.2–

1.8 m (4–6 ft), there was a vertical component of about 0.9 m (3 ft)—the first time a significant vertical movement had been recorded on any section of the San Andreas. It appeared that the fault zone in the vicinity of the earthquake might be more complex than previously realized. The USGS warned that the Loma Prieta quake was not the "big one" anticipated for the Bay Area sometime in the next few decades. Although it relieved stress stored in the Santa Cruz section of the fault south of San Francisco, it did not relieve the sections to the north, nearer the city, that had broken in the great earthquake of 1906.

A new study involving Landsat remote-sensing satellite imagery brought scientists one step closer to the goal of predicting hazardous volcanic eruptions. Pictures of an active volcano in Chile made from Earth orbit with a Landsat Thematic Mapper instrument recorded short-wavelength infrared radiation emanating from a localized "hot spot," whereas dormant volcanoes in Chile and Ethiopia did not show up in this way. The study, which was prompted by the extent to which Landsat images had revealed the 1986 Chernobyl nuclear reactor accident in the U.S.S.R., promised quantitative monitoring of the activity of individual volcanoes in a way that ground studies could not.

Space exploration efforts added to knowledge of active volcanoes on other bodies of the solar system. As the U.S. Voyager 2 spacecraft cruised past Neptune in August, it returned spectacular pictures of geyserlike eruptions that rose 8 km (5 mi) above the surface of Triton, Neptune's largest moon, and were then swept into streaks 145 km (90 mi) long across Triton's sky. The eruptions were from "ice volcanoes," which differ from the active volcanoes of Earth and of Jupiter's moon Io. The plumes may consist of pressurized nitrogen, which carries dark particles presumably of carbon-rich material as it escapes from the interior.

Volcanoes on Earth bring to the surface much information about internal geochemistry. Rare, explosive eruptions of kimberlite magma carry diamonds, made from carbon at high pressure, to the surface from depths far below the crust—175 km (110 mi) or more. Mineralogical and geochemical studies of diamonds and their inclusions, reported at a workshop at the International Geological Congress, provided much information about isotopes, trace elements, and gases in the Earth's mantle, information that would contribute to unraveling the history of the mantle, the lithosphere, and recycling of crust through the mantle.

Two discoveries confirmed that large masses of solid rock also can rise from great depths, bringing diamonds with them. A detailed study of graphite in the Beni Bousera peridotite massif of Morocco provided strong evidence that some of the octahedral and other crystalline forms found in the graphite are remnants of its former diamond crystal structure, confirming that the massif is a slice of the mantle that had been emplaced within the continental crust during collision tectonics and indicating that the mass had come from a depth of at least 150 km (90 mi), where diamonds are stable. Diamonds were also reported as inclusions in garnets of gneisses from a metamorphic complex in the Soviet republic of Kazakhstan—evidence that the continental rocks had been buried at least as deep as 120 km (75 mi).

That diamond was preserved in the Kazakhstan metamorphic complex but transformed to graphite in the Beni Bousera massif probably relates to the rates of uprise of the two rock masses. The metamorphic rocks must have been subducted and then risen rapidly under cool conditions unfavourable for diamonds encased in garnets to react. By contrast, the Beni Bousera rocks must have risen more slowly from a hot environment, the long period at high temperatures favouring the change to graphite.

New techniques involving a combination of geology, mineralogy, and geochemistry were yielding numbers for the rates of geologic processes associated with mountain building. Examination of garnets 3 cm (1.2 in) in diameter from 380 million-year-old schists in Vermont showed that they had rotated during growth, as indicated by spirals of inclusions. The garnets and their inclusions provided a sequential record of temperatures, chemical reactions, and deformation during metamorphism. Measurements of radial changes in strontium isotope ratios within single garnet crystals provided the time scale. Results included a heating rate of 5°–10° C (9°–18° F) per million years during garnet growth, an average growth rate of 1.4 mm (0.055 in) per million years, and a shear strain rate of 2.4×10^{-14} per second.

Rocks 3.96 billion years old from near Canada's Great Slave Lake replaced rocks from West Greenland, which are about 100 million years younger, as the world's oldest known rocks. Age was determined through measurements of uranium and lead contents of the mineral zircon in granitic rocks, using Australian National University's unique SHRIMP (sensitive high-mass-resolution ion microprobe) instrument. The discovery supported the idea that yet older rocks, an original crust, must have existed because granites are formed from preexisting rock. Furthermore, previous work had assigned a date of 4.3 billion years to individual zircon crystals taken from younger rocks, indicating that the crystals had been eroded from rocks of the same age as the zircons before incorporation into the younger rocks. (PETER JOHN WYLLIE)

GEOPHYSICS

Although 1989 was a year of moderate seismic activity, it was not devoid of tragedy due to earthquakes. The only great earthquake, that of magnitude 8 or greater on the Richter scale, happened on May 23 near remote Macquarie Island in the South Pacific. Its magnitude was 8.3, but it did no damage. By contrast, on January 22 a smaller shock of magnitude 5.3 left 274 dead and caused extensive damage in and around Gissar in the Soviet republic of Tadzhikistan. The densely populated Bay Area of California, which includes San Francisco and Oakland, was jolted October 17 by a quake having a magnitude of 7.1 and an epicentre along a section of the San Andreas Fault near Santa Cruz and about 80 km (50 mi) southeast of San Francisco. The shock collapsed a stretch of two-level interstate freeway in Oakland, killing 42 persons. Another 25 died from the quake, and thousands of structures were destroyed or heavily damaged by the shock or consequent fires. Total damage was estimated in the billions of dollars. (See *Geology and Geochemistry,* above.) On December 28 a magnitude-5.5 earthquake shook the industrial city of Newcastle, Australia, about 160 km (100 mi) north of Sydney—the first quake in the country's history to hit a heavily populated region. At least 10 people were killed, and more than 100 were injured; estimates of damage approached $1 billion.

Earthquakes frequently occur 400–700 km (250–435 mi) below the surface in regions of deep subduction. This fact had long puzzled geophysicists since, in theory, pressure at those depths should make any fault movement impossible. By subjecting small rock samples to temperatures as high as 15,000° C (27,000° F) and pressures thousands of times greater than the pressure at the Earth's surface, researchers at the University of California at Davis were able to produce defects called anticracks, which might provide an answer to the puzzle. These small lens-shaped cracks form when the mineral olivine is transformed under pressure to

denser spinel. After reaching a critical length they become unstable and form a fault, which results in a fracture. Such a process might explain the occurrence of earthquakes at depths where friction would otherwise inhibit them.

Volcanic activity continued at a low level among active volcanoes around the globe, creating few causes for alarm and no major eruptions. Investigators at Sandia National Laboratories, Albuquerque, N.M., challenged earlier ideas concerning the conditions and mechanisms that determine when a volcanic eruption will be a violent explosion or a quiet lava flow. Previous theory supposed the magma in the chamber below the volcano to be stratified, with a layer rich in water and other volatiles atop a layer of purer magma. In the earlier phases of an eruptive episode, which tend to be more violent than later ones, the vapour-rich magma rises first, and its trapped gases respond explosively to the decreased pressure. In the later phases the vapour-poor magma follows, producing a gradual discharge of lava. The new theory, based on a study of the 600-year-old Obsidian Dome volcano in California, proposed that the magma is not stratified. Instead, the character of the eruption is determined by the following mechanism and time sequence: As magma rises to the surface, it froths and forms pumice, the high porosity of which, under certain conditions, can allow gases in the magma to escape freely. In the earlier eruptive phases, the magma is likely to be forced through dense, gas-tight rock; it reaches the surface still highly charged with gas under pressure, and it explodes. The explosion creates a large cone-shaped crater, which collects pumice and other fall-back debris and funnels it

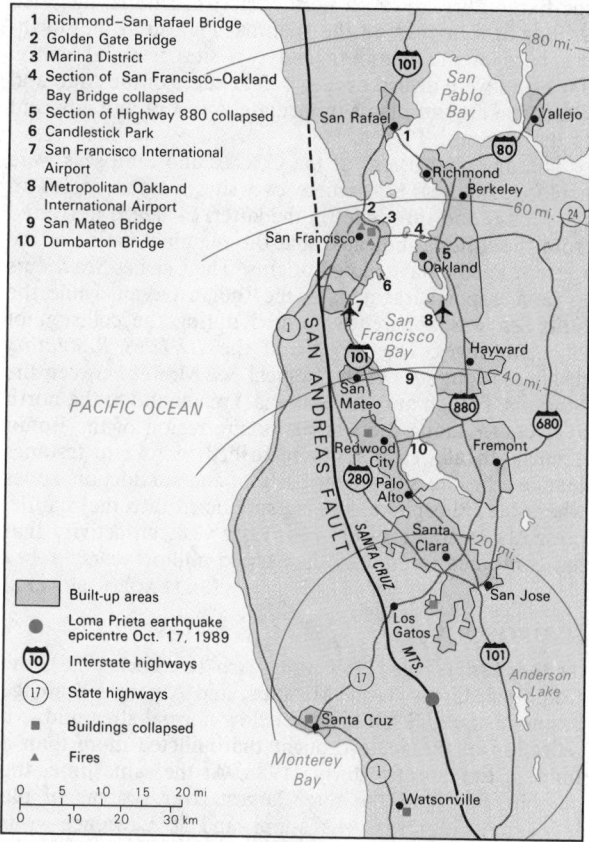

1 Richmond–San Rafael Bridge
2 Golden Gate Bridge
3 Marina District
4 Section of San Francisco–Oakland Bay Bridge collapsed
5 Section of Highway 880 collapsed
6 Candlestick Park
7 San Francisco International Airport
8 Metropolitan Oakland International Airport
9 San Mateo Bridge
10 Dumbarton Bridge

The epicentre of the massive earthquake that struck the San Francisco Bay area lies along a section of the San Andreas Fault near Santa Cruz. The quake, which struck the densely populated area during rush hour, caused a mile-long section of Interstate 880 to collapse, crushing many vehicles on its lower level, and ignited a raging fire that tore through San Francisco's Marina district.

into the vent through which subsequent magma must pass. The debris plug keeps the magma under pressure, but its porosity allows the gases to escape, thus turning later phases into nonexplosive lava flows.

Exploiting the Earth's heat as an energy source continued to grow and improve. In the U.S. average geothermal energy use during 1988 was 50 trillion joules per day, an increase of 58% over that reported in 1980. Argentina installed a 600-kw geothermal plant at Copahue, the first in South America, while Bolivia explored the geothermal resources of its Laguna Colorada area. Mexico completed its third plant, a 55-MW facility at Los Azufres, and was developing another at Cerro Prieto, which would raise the capacity of that field to 750 MW. In the Philippines work began on a $900 million program to drill 327 wells at 12 sites during the next 12 years, an effort expected to increase the country's geothermal energy output by 30%. England, France, West Germany, Japan, and the U.S. pursued research in extracting energy from hot dry rock. Heat transfer from these sources would be accomplished by means of fluid injection.

The international Ocean Drilling Program (ODP) completed and reported on Legs 121 through 125 in the Indian Ocean and far western Pacific. On Leg 121 the scientific drilling ship *JOIDES Resolution* drilled holes at four closely spaced sites on Broken Ridge, an east–west-aligned submarine plateau between Australia and the Ninetyeast Ridge, and at three sites along Ninetyeast Ridge, the volcanic trace of hot spots connected with the northward migration of the Indian Plate. Leg 122, which concentrated on the history of the rifting, breakup, and post-breakup of the Exmouth Plateau off northwestern Australia, included drilling at four sites on the Wombat Plateau at the northern edge of the Exmouth and two sites near its centre. Two sites were drilled on Leg 123 at edges of the Argo and Gascoyne abyssal plains immediately west of and adjacent to the Exmouth Plateau.

The marginal basins of the Celebes and Sulu seas were explored on Leg 124, where two sites were occupied in the former and three sites in the latter. Evidence recovered from the drilling indicated that the marginal basins of the western Pacific have varied origins. The Celebes Sea seems to be a trapped fragment of the Indian Ocean, while the Sulu Sea was apparently formed during the collision of adjacent ridges. Leg 125 found the *JOIDES Resolution* drilling at four sites at the Conical Sea Mount between the Mariana Trough and the Mariana Trench and to the north at five sites along the similar forearc region of the Bonin Trench. In all, 15 holes were drilled in forearc terranes that overlie the shallowest parts of the subduction zones where the lithosphere is being subducted into the mantle, presently at about 10 cm (4 in) per year, an activity that has continued for at least the past 45 million years.

(RUTLAGE J. BRAZEE)

HYDROLOGY

At the start of the 1989 water year (October 1988), the Columbia, Great Basin, Missouri, and Arkansas drainage basins of the U.S. all yielded below-normal streamflow, a reflection of the acute drought that afflicted more than a third of the country during 1988. At the same time, the combined flow of the three largest river systems of the U.S.—the Columbia, Mississippi, and St. Lawrence—was below normal. By late November, however, the drought had abated; the combined flow of the three river systems rose to normal levels and remained there through June 1989. In midsummer the combined flow was 18% above normal but declined to normal levels by late summer.

Much of the midwestern and eastern U.S., drought-stricken in 1988, experienced above-normal streamflow in the spring of 1989. On the other hand, streamflow for the 1989 water year was much below average over most of the western U.S. In Alaska streamflow ranged from much above average in the south-central region to much below average in the southeastern region of the state. Great Lakes water levels were at or slightly above median levels at the beginning of the summer season and continued at median levels through August.

Record-breaking rains produced floods in the vicinity of Anchorage, Alaska, in late August. August rains also resulted in extensive flooding in South Korea and in parts of Argentina. During the year the central and northern provinces of China experienced drought conditions severe enough to affect drinking-water supplies.

Many U.S. states recently established water information and education committees responsible for identifying water-resources education needs for children and adults. The American Water Resources Association charged an education committee with the task of developing an outreach program for secondary and primary schools. A Lake Superior Center, planned for construction on a waterfront site in Duluth, Minn., was intended to promote public understanding of the Great Lakes and freshwater issues. An American Groundwater Center, conceived as a private, nonprofit educational and museum facility, was to be completed in Wood River, Neb., in 1994.

Thirty-seven states enacted groundwater legislation during the period 1985–87. Whereas most states concentrated on specific groundwater concerns rather than statewide management strategies, Minnesota's 1989 legislature passed a groundwater protection act that emphasized the prevention of groundwater contamination. Suffolk County on Long Island, N.Y., began a $520 million program to purchase 12,960 ha (32,000 ac) of pine barrens overlying critical groundwater aquifers. The program was cited as the largest local government effort in the U.S. to protect groundwater resources.

The U.S. federal government planned to invest $225 million in scientific and technical activities focused directly on groundwater in 1990—a substantial increase over past years' funding levels. Hydrologic research priorities were changing in response to a general trend toward international-scale science. International research projects emphasizing regional and global hydrology were emerging. The U.S. announced a decade-long global change research program to be coordinated among several federal agencies. Planned funding for 1990 was $191.5 million. The highest research priority was to be climate and hydrologic systems.

The National Research Council's (NRC's) Committee on Opportunities in the Hydrologic Sciences, chaired by Peter Eagleson of the Massachusetts Institute of Technology, was engaged in identifying new research frontiers in the hydrologic sciences and developing a framework for improved hydrologic education. The NRC was of the opinion that fundamental advances in the hydrologic sciences were needed to generate solutions to complex water problems. The committee's report would be published in early 1990.

Wetlands, both natural and constructed, were being used to treat wastewater in many areas of the U.S. Wetland vegetation is capable of trapping and filtering pollutants found in sewage effluent and urban storm-water drainage.

The International Hydrological Program (IHP) began to put more emphasis on developing water-information systems. Because many less developed countries lacked the telecommunications infrastructure to participate, a truly international water resources data base would not be

achieved for several years. In addition, because inadequate funding would limit the scope of the initiative, the use of existing systems would be stressed. The IHP continued to develop hydrogeologic maps for less developed countries; one for Africa was in preparation in 1989.

The 1989 International Hydrology Prize, sponsored by the International Association of Hydrological Sciences, was awarded to J.E. Nash of University College, Galway, Ireland.

(BRUCE P. VAN HAVEREN)

METEOROLOGY

Hurricane Hugo, the most destructive and costly storm ever to strike the U.S., was among the more newsworthy meteorologic events of 1989. The vicious category-4 storm (on an intensity scale of 1 to 5) first struck Guadeloupe in the eastern Caribbean on September 17 with winds of 225 km/h (140 mph). It then hit the island of Montserrat and the next day plowed through St. Croix and Puerto Rico from San Juan eastward. When it hit Charleston, S.C., on September 21, Hugo was still carrying winds of 225 km/h, and storm tides as high as 6 m (20 ft) were recorded nearby. Hugo was the most intense hurricane to strike the U.S. since Camille, a category-5 storm, hit the Mississippi coast in 1969.

The death toll directly related to Hugo reached 71, while the cost of damage from the storm was estimated at $8.6 billion. Loss of life was minimized through concerted preparedness planning and actions by local, state, and federal emergency officials based on early and accurate warnings and wide dissemination of information by the media. It was estimated that more than a half million people from Savannah, Ga., to Cape Hatteras, N.C., heeded the warnings and evacuated their coastal and barrier island homes.

Ten tropical storms were recorded during the 1989 Atlantic hurricane season. Seven reached hurricane strength, and three of the hurricanes made landfall on the U.S. mainland. The first storm of the season, Allison, produced torrential rains in eastern Texas and the lower Mississippi Valley after making landfall June 26. Hurricane Chantal reached hurricane strength just before making landfall near Galveston, Texas, on August 1. The heavy rains and flooding caused by both Allison and Chantal took 11 lives each. On October 15 Jerry, the third tropical storm of the season to form in the Gulf of Mexico, became a hurricane nine hours before it, too, struck Galveston, killing three people.

Typhoons and tropical storms battered eastern and southeastern Asia. Seven storms brought excessive rains to Japan, which had its wettest September on record. Vietnam had two storms, in May and in October. Other regions that suffered damaging winds or flooding from tropical storms included Bangladesh, northeastern India, Thailand, Myanmar (Burma), the Philippines, and the Chinese island of Hainan.

The 1989 tornado season in the U.S. produced about 800 tornadoes that accounted for more than 40 deaths. In mid-November a devastating storm system in the eastern half of the U.S. generated unusually strong thunderstorms and killer tornadoes through seven states from the deep South through the Midwest and Northeast.

Unlike 1988, when a severe drought and midsummer heat wave dominated North America, 1989 was a year of highly variable precipitation patterns and less extreme temperatures. Whereas much of California had subnormal precipitation for the third consecutive year and the north central and southwestern U.S. was very dry, the south central, southern, and eastern U.S. experienced heavy precipitation and severe flooding. In the Northeast and Middle Atlantic regions, a dry, mild winter ended with unusually heavy snowstorms followed by an abnormally wet spring.

During the summer a prolonged heat wave prevailed across much of Europe and the Middle East, while infrequent showers kept the normally damp British Isles unexpectedly dry. Earlier, Europeans had had a very mild and dry winter followed by record warmth in March. An unusually mild winter prevailed in southeastern Siberia during the first half of 1989. Abnormally warm conditions also spread across North and South Korea, Japan, and northeastern China during most of the spring season. The 1989 Indian monsoon produced less rainfall than in 1988. Many locations in the western African Sahel measured near- to above-normal summer rainfall for the second consecutive season—the first time since the mid-1960s.

In the Southern Hemisphere a wide range of precipitation was also reported. Australia had unusually persistent heavy rains that soaked the central and eastern portions of the continent between March and July. In South America the first five months of the year were very dry in Uruguay, northern Argentina, and adjacent parts of Brazil and Paraguay.

Researchers monitoring atmospheric ozone concentra-

AP/WIDE WORLD

Pedestrians in the Philippine capital of Manila help a driver guide his car through a street flooded by heavy rain. A tropical storm caused massive flooding in the Philippines and set off a number of landslides that killed at least four people in the country's northern mountains.

Winds measuring up to 225 kilometres (140 miles) per hour smash into the Puerto Rican coast as Hurricane Hugo wends its way through the Caribbean. Hugo, which retained its powerful winds from Guadeloupe up through the Carolinas, was the most destructive and costly storm ever to hit the U.S.
GARY WILLIAMS—GAMMA/LIAISON

tions over Antarctica in 1989 reported that the seasonal ozone depletion, or hole, fell to levels approaching the record-breaking lows of 1987. The 1989 ozone hole reached its low point early in October before beginning to recover late in the month. Loss of stratospheric ozone, which shields life from damaging ultraviolet radiation from the Sun, was widely attributed to atmospheric chemical reactions caused by manufactured chlorofluorocarbons (CFCs) and related chlorine- and bromine-containing compounds. The same potentially ozone-destroying processes were observed in the Arctic stratosphere, although the loss there was not comparable to that of the Antarctic. (See *Oceanography,* below.)   (ELBERT W. FRIDAY, JR.)

This article updates the *Macropædia* article CLIMATE AND WEATHER.

OCEANOGRAPHY

Research in oceanography in 1989 was dominated by concern over the possibility that an increase in atmospheric carbon dioxide (CO_2) resulting from human activity might alter the balance between incoming solar radiation and outgoing infrared radiation that maintains the Earth's present temperature. In the late 1980s the concentration of CO_2 in the atmosphere indeed was about 25% higher than preindustrial levels and was predicted to double in the next few decades. Moreover, other human-released substances such as chlorofluorocarbons, whose potential effect on the radiation balance was even greater in proportion to their concentrations, were also building in the atmosphere. Computer models indicated that the total combined buildup could raise the Earth's surface temperature—the manifestation of the so-called greenhouse effect—by several degrees, with consequent major shifts in agricultural conditions and disastrous rises in sea level as polar ice melted. Because it can store and transport vast amounts of heat, CO_2, and other substances, the ocean was thought to play a crucial role in the response of the Earth's climate to these human interventions. That role was being studied in the World Climate Research Program (WCRP). One oceanic component of WCRP was the World Ocean Circulation Experiment (WOCE), whose planning had been under way for several years and whose fieldwork phase was scheduled to start in 1990.

WOCE aimed to achieve a first-ever global view of ocean circulation and to learn from that view how to monitor the ocean's effect on climate over decades. Part of WOCE

fieldwork was to be traditional: surface-to-bottom measurements of temperature and salinity made from ships circumnavigating or exploring major ocean basins. That effort alone, however, would not reveal the total amount of water, heat, or CO_2 and other substances being carried by the ocean from place to place. In WOCE such measurements, therefore, were to be combined with space-age observations. Satellites launched in the early 1990s would use techniques proved in earlier space missions to measure the travel time of radar pulses from satellite to sea surface, thus giving actual sea-level and surface-current data. Traditional and satellite measurements combined would then reveal how much water, heat, and substances the ocean transports at many depths.

Even this effort, however, could not reveal how the ocean dilutes its heat or CO_2. For such studies ocean currents had to be followed in greater detail. For years oceanographers had done studies at the surface by releasing thousands of drifters, floating instruments that moved with currents (but not with the wind or with waves) in the upper few metres of ocean. Each drifter carried a small radio transmitter by which satellites overhead could fix its position accurately several times a day. For WOCE a new kind of pop-up drifter was to be tested and deployed to track deep currents. While it was satellite-tracked like a surface drifter, the pop-up version could change its volume, allowing it to sink to a preprogrammed depth as great as several thousand metres. Once at depth it would drift with the deep current for many days, rise to the surface to report its position, and sink again. It could repeat this cycle 50–100 times. In WOCE several thousand pop-up drifters were to outline currents at various depths in unprecedented detail.

Other new ways of looking at the ocean would be tried out in WOCE. For example, because the speed of sound in water depends sensitively on water temperature and because sound crossing the ocean travels mainly in deep water, acoustic measurements might reveal changes in the heat content of the deep ocean. A deep-water warming of 0.005° C (0.009° F) in a year, a rate predicted in one theory of climate change, would decrease the time for sound to traverse the entire Pacific (which takes many hours) by about a fourth of a second—a decrease readily measured with current techniques. The fact that a small explosion at a depth of a few hundred metres near Heard Island in the southern Indian Ocean was easily detected in the ocean nearly halfway around the world at Bermuda suggested that

fluctuations in temperature of entire deep ocean basins could be monitored for years with fairly simple acoustic equipment. In WOCE enough independent observations of the deep ocean would be made to begin testing this idea.

Besides storing CO_2, the ocean helps set its concentration in the atmosphere. One way is by "pumping" carbon from near-surface waters to great oceanic depths through the process in which organic debris sinks out of the lighted waters. This pumping can be especially vigorous during the springtime bloom of phytoplankton, the rapid increase in microscopic free-floating upper-ocean algae as light penetrates into nutrient-rich subsurface waters. Seeing how the bloom develops and quantifying the action of the carbon pump was an important part of the Joint Global Ocean Flux Study (JGOFS), which began a five-nation program of field studies in the North Atlantic in the spring of 1989.

Photosynthesis in ocean phytoplankton, important in the carbon pump, could be affected by manufactured chlorofluorocarbons presently in the high atmosphere. These substances were widely believed to be the cause of the ozone depletion, or hole, first detected in the stratosphere over Antarctica in 1985 and reappearing particularly intensely in 1987 and 1989. Such an ozone hole could let enough additional solar ultraviolet radiation through to slow photosynthesis in the upper ocean. Since phytoplankton is at the base of a food chain that reaches up to fish, birds, and human beings, the consequences of such a change would be potentially far-reaching. As 1989 ended, researchers were divided over the extent to which photosynthesis in the ocean might change. They needed more definitive experiments in Antarctic waters under the ozone hole to reach a secure conclusion. (See *Meteorology,* above.)

(MYRL C. HENDERSHOTT)

See also Disasters; Energy; Environment; Life Sciences; Mining; Space Exploration.

This article updates the *Macropædia* articles ATMOSPHERE; The EARTH; EARTHQUAKES; The EARTH SCIENCES; GEOCHRONOLOGY; Principles, Methods, and Instruments of MEASUREMENT AND OBSERVATION; OCEANS; PLATE TECTONICS; RIVERS; SOLAR SYSTEM; VOLCANISM.

Economic Affairs

During 1989 the world economy was estimated to have produced a real growth of 3.1%. Although this was nearly one percentage point lower than the corresponding figure for the previous year, it was regarded as a satisfactory performance. Thus it represented the seventh successive year of the upturn in the world economy that began in 1983. It was still fast enough to bring about a further fall in unemployment and was well above the average annual rate of growth for the decade. In addition, given that late 1988 and early 1989 saw some signs of accelerating inflation, the slowdown in the overall level of activity was widely regarded as an essential development for reducing inflationary pressures and creating the conditions for sustainable growth in the 1990s.

As in 1988, industrially developed countries turned in the best performance, with a growth rate of 3.5%, down from the gain of 4.4% seen in the previous year. The slowdown was particularly pronounced in the U.S., where a relatively tight fiscal and monetary policy brought the growth rate from 4.5% in 1988 to an estimated 2.9%. Most other countries of the Organization for Economic Cooperation and Development (OECD) witnessed some slowdown, except West Germany, where gross domestic product (GDP) was thought to have risen by 4%, compared with an advance of 3.6% in the previous year. As in 1988,

the most dynamic economy in the developed world was that of Japan, which recorded a gross national product (GNP) gain of approximately 5%.

The less developed world also did reasonably well, although it, too, saw a weakening in activity and, as in previous years, it failed to match the advance of developed countries. On the basis of preliminary statistics, the less developed countries' growth rate was estimated at 3.2%, down one percentage point from the gain seen in 1988. Not unexpectedly, there were major discrepancies in performance from country to country. Although the relatively industrialized Asian economies saw a marked slowdown in growth from over 9 to 6.2%, they still managed to do nearly twice as well as the developed bloc as a whole. African countries, benefiting from structural improvements, foreign aid, and stable commodity prices, beat the general trend and accelerated their growth rate from 2.2 to 2.9%, but the debt-ridden less developed economies of the Western Hemisphere failed to produce any gain in the wake of their already poor growth of 0.7% in 1988. The Communist world, which experienced unprecedented political and social upheavals in 1989, remained firmly at the bottom of the league. Estimates by the International Monetary Fund (IMF) suggested a growth rate in the centrally planned economies of only 1.7%, compared with one of 2.2% in 1988.

The major reason for the slowdown in the expansion of the world economy was the widespread firming of monetary policies in the developed countries. This was mainly in response to stronger inflationary pressures but also because of the need to protect currencies against the unexpectedly strong U.S. dollar. Thus the upward trend of interest rates that started in 1988 continued throughout 1989. By late summer 1989, short-term interest rates were some 20% higher than in 1988 in the more important developed countries and, given a significant hike of European rates in the autumn, the consolidated figure for the final quarter was expected to show a further substantial increase. The absolute level of, and the rate of change in, national interest rates varied widely. In the United Kingdom, where pressure on the pound sterling and inflation were major problems, short-term rates rose from an average of 10.2% in 1988 to 13.8% in August 1989. In Japan, where inflation was less of a worry, the equivalent figures were 4.4 and 5.3%. Generally speaking, interest rate differentials among the principal countries tended to widen. The principal exception to this was West Germany, where the rapid rise in short-term rates that took place between 1988 and August 1989 had the effect of reducing the gap with most other countries.

Higher interest rates tended to restrain the two most important sources of domestic demand: consumer expenditure and capital investment. During 1989 the growth of private consumption was estimated to have slowed to 2.8% from the previous year's 3.7% in the major industrial countries, well below the average of the advance seen during the seven-year economic recovery. The slowdown in investment expenditures (from 7.9% to an estimated 5.6%) was more marked in relative terms, but this still left the absolute level of growth well above the average since 1982. The main reasons for this were the high capacity-utilization ratios, high levels of business confidence, and good corporate profitability. As a result of the rapid growth in demand since 1982, most major economies were utilizing new, record levels of existing productive capacity. This, together with widespread belief in the prospect for continued (albeit slower) growth, created a climate for buoyant investment activities, despite the steadily increasing cost

of borrowing. This development was widely seen as one of the most encouraging features in the world economy, since a high level of investment at a time of slower growth is a strong contributory factor to further, noninflationary growth in the medium-term future.

The slowdown in the level of economic activity in 1989 was consistent with a further fall in the level of unemployment. According to IMF estimates, the unemployment rate in the developed world fell from 7% in 1988 to 6.6%, compared with the peak of 8.6% reached in 1983. As usual, Japan boasted virtually full employment and faced an extremely tight labour market. The percentage of the labour force without a job in the U.S., which stood at 9.6% in 1982, was down to 5.3%. No European country was able to match these figures. The best performance in the European Communities (EC) was that of the U.K. at 6.7%, as against an EC average of 10%. In fact, with the exception of the U.K., the long-term progress of the EC in putting people back to work was fairly disappointing. Some countries such as France saw virtually no improvement; others such as Italy faced a steady worsening in the unemployment situation. Even West Germany had 7.7% of its labour force out of work, not significantly below the peak figure of 8.2% recorded in 1985.

Consumer prices were already rising in late 1988, a trend that continued well into 1989. Despite some signs of weakening inflationary pressures toward the end of 1989, consumer prices in the developed world were expected to rise by 4.5%, compared with increases of only 3.3, 3, and 2.4% in the three previous years. This was largely due to the pressure of demand, although the rise in oil prices and the weakening of the Japanese and European currencies against the dollar also played a part. The lowest inflation rates were achieved in West Germany (3%) and Japan (2.5%). At the other extreme were Italy and the U.K., with increases of 6.5 and 7.8%, respectively. Consumer price inflation in less developed countries accelerated from 70% in 1988 to an estimated 86%. However, this figure disguised massive variations in both the absolute rates and the year-to-year change in different parts of the less developed world. The rise in consumer prices fell from 14.6% in 1988 to some 13% in Asia, but it accelerated from 286 to 405% in the less developed countries of the Western Hemisphere, particularly Latin-American nations such as Bolivia, Peru, and Argentina.

The loss of buoyancy in the advanced economies appeared to have had quite a marked effect on the volume of world trade in 1989. IMF estimates suggested that, following an exceptionally rapid rise of 9% in 1988, trade volumes in 1989 rose by 6.9%. Most countries and areas shared in the slowdown, although less developed countries' exports suffered rather more than those of developed economies. However, unlike 1988, when the less developed bloc faced a deterioration in terms of trade, 1989 saw some improvement, largely because of higher oil prices. Higher oil prices also had a strong positive influence on the external payments balance of Middle Eastern oil producers, which was responsible for a modest reduction in the less developed world's overall current account deficit from $9.1 billion to $7.3 billion. In the developed world the problem of large external payments imbalance continued. The U.S.'s current account deficit totaled approximately $125 billion and was little changed from 1988, but as a percentage of GNP it fell modestly from 2.6 to 2.4%. At the same time, West Germany's surplus rose by some $4 billion to $53 billion, although this was more than offset by a small reduction of $8 billion to $72 billion in Japan's positive balance. All in all, the developed world's combined deficit rose to $78 billion from $54 billion. A significant part of this deterioration was attributable to the worsening external payments positions of the U.K., Canada, and Italy.

The foreign exchange markets were dominated by the unexpected strength of the dollar and the efforts of the international financial community to moderate its appreciation. Nevertheless, by late autumn the effective rate of the U.S. currency was some 6% higher than at the end of 1988. The dollar did particularly well against sterling, which, weakened by the growing U.K. external payments deficit and the public disagreement between Prime Minister Margaret Thatcher and the chancellor of the Exchequer, Nigel Lawson, gave up 14% of its value between January and November. The Japanese yen was also fairly vulnerable and lost about 11% of its dollar value by late November. The Deutsche Mark, which was relatively strong, depreciated by approximately 4% by September, but the weakening power of the Communist Party in East Germany in late autumn underpinned the West German currency and reversed the downward trend.

The reasons for the strength of the U.S. dollar were not clear, although narrowing interest rate differentials, relatively high interest rates, and confidence in the administration of Pres. George Bush were put forward as possible explanations. There were fears that this would undermine the export competitiveness of the U.S. and result in an increase in the already large U.S. external payments deficit. Nevertheless, as 1989 drew to a close, there were signs of some weakening in the dollar's underlying strength.

NATIONAL ECONOMIC POLICIES

Developed Market Economies. *United States.* During 1989 the U.S. economy made major gains toward its policymakers' goal of a "soft landing" (a gentle slowdown that would dampen inflation without triggering a recession). Real GNP, having risen by 4.4% in 1988 (up from 3.7% in 1987), was on track to slow down to a 2.9% growth rate during 1989. A gentle easing of monetary policy to allow interest rates to drop a little, coupled with strong growth in employment, abated fears of a recession.

Major components of demand charted a mixed course during the year. Consumer spending registered a 2% gain in the first two quarters, but it accelerated to 5.8% in the third quarter, stimulated by a cut in automobile prices to clear dealers' stocks. Real disposable income rose strongly during the year, up an annualized 5% in the first three quarters. This was largely attributable to lower tax payments and a lower inflation rate. As consumer spending recovered, the savings ratio deteriorated from 5.6% in the opening quarter to around 5% toward the close of the year. Even so, at this level it was still higher than the 3.4% that had been achieved in 1988.

Table I. Real Gross Domestic Products of Selected OECD Countries

% annual change

Country	1986	1987	1988	1989*
United States	2.7	3.7	4.4	2.9
Japan	2.5	4.5	5.7	4.9
West Germany	2.3	1.7	3.6	4.0
France	2.3	1.9	3.5	3.4
United Kingdom	3.2	4.5	4.2	3.0
Canada	3.1	4.5	5.0	2.6
Italy	2.6	3.0	3.9	3.2
Other developed countries	2.3	2.9	3.3	3.1
All developed countries	2.6	3.5	4.4	3.5
Seven major countries above	2.7	3.6	4.5	3.5
European countries	2.5	2.7	3.6	3.3
European Communities	2.6	2.7	3.7	3.4

*Estimated.
Source: International Monetary Fund, *World Economic Outlook*, October 1989.

U.S. Secretary of State James Baker (right) attends a meeting with Poland's Foreign Minister Krzstof Skubiszewski (second from left) and other Polish delegates before his meeting with the Group of 24 less developed nations.
AP/WIDE WORLD

The economic slowdown did not dent capital spending in the business sector, but the construction industry suffered from a fall in commercial and housing completions. A Commerce Department survey in July–August showed that industrialists expected to boost their capital expenditures on new plant and machinery by 7.7% in real terms. Although this was below the 8.9% gain in 1988, it was above the 1986 and 1987 levels, reflecting continuing confidence in the economic outlook.

The growth of industrial production continued in 1989, but at a much lower rate than in 1988. As the year-end approached, industrial production was up 3.5% over the year before, compared with a 5.7% gain in 1988. A large part of the slowdown could be attributed to the automobile sector. Capacity utilization reflecting industrial production eased back to 82% in October, compared with 84.7% in January 1989. While productivity in the business sector continued to rise throughout 1989, maintaining the uptrend in evidence from the second quarter of 1988, growth in employment remained strong. With nearly 2.5 million new jobs created during the first 10 months of the year, the level of unemployment settled around 5.2% at an annual rate, compared with 5.5% for the whole of 1988 and 6.2% in 1987. Because a large proportion of the new jobs were in the services sector and employed women and minority groups, this continued growth in employment did not give rise to undue pressures on wages. Hourly earnings gains averaged 4.5% in the third quarter, roughly in line with the rate of inflation. Partly because of soaring energy costs, consumer prices rose briskly in the first half of the year, reaching a seven-year peak of 5.4% in May but moderating to 4.2% in September. This raised expectations that the inflation rate for the year as a whole would remain below 5%.

The trade deficit continued to narrow after widening temporarily in the final quarter of 1988. However, the improvement in the external account was not as large as expected. The effect of the strong dollar, which had risen by over 6% from the beginning of the year, offset part of the improvement in competitiveness and slowed export growth.

In mid-September the dollar was 12% higher, on a trade-weighted basis, but it declined following the agreement in September by the Group of Seven industrialized nations to stem the dollar's value. A further drop occurred on October 13 when the stock market plunged unexpectedly. The monthly trade-gap figures remained volatile but ceased to shock the financial markets. Twice (in May and August) the monthly deficit went over $10 billion without causing any alarm. Despite the unmistakable downward trend, the decline in the deficit was not very fast. During the January–August period, exports rose by 15% and imports expanded by 9%, giving a cumulative trade gap of $73.1 billion, compared with $78.8 billion in the same period of 1988. At that rate of improvement, it would be 1993 before the U.S. achieved a trade surplus. Meanwhile, a deterioration in the invisibles account (services and transfers) produced a current account deficit of $30,990,000,000 for the second quarter, up from $30,390,000,000 recorded during the opening quarter.

The deficit had previously fallen to a three-year low of $28,680,000,000 in the fourth quarter of 1988. This led to expectations of a virtually unchanged current deficit during 1989 from the previous year's $126.5 million. There was little doubt that, given the fundamental strength of the U.S. economy, foreign funds would be available to fund the current account deficit, but many independent analysts worried that the rising stock of assets held by foreign investors would mean a larger outflow of dividends and other service payments. This would soon lead to a deficit in the invisibles account, which had already shown a substantial decrease in the surplus from $35 billion in 1980 to $15 billion in 1988.

Once again the objectives of containing inflation and reducing the external deficit by slowing the growth of

Table II. Percentage Changes in Consumer Prices in Selected OECD Countries

Country	1983	1984	1985	1986	1987	1988	1989*
United States	3.2	4.3	3.5	1.9	3.7	4.1	4.7
Japan	1.9	2.2	2.1	0.4	−0.2	0.5	2.6
West Germany	3.3	2.4	2.2	−0.2	0.2	1.2	2.9
France	9.6	7.4	5.8	2.7	3.1	2.7	3.4
United Kingdom	4.6	5.0	6.1	3.4	4.2	4.9	—
Italy	14.6	10.6	8.6	6.1	4.6	5.0	6.7
Canada	5.9	4.3	4.0	4.2	4.4	4.0	5.2
Austria	3.3	5.6	3.2	1.7	1.4	2.0	2.7
Belgium	7.7	6.3	4.9	1.3	1.6	1.2	3.2
Denmark	6.9	6.3	4.7	3.6	4.0	4.6	4.9
Finland	8.3	7.1	5.9	2.9	4.1	5.1	6.6
Greece	20.2	18.5	19.3	23.0	16.4	13.5	13.6
Iceland	86.5	30.9	31.9	22.2	18.3	25.7	17.6
Ireland	10.5	8.6	5.4	3.8	3.2	2.1	4.5
Luxembourg	8.7	4.6	4.1	0.3	−0.1	1.4	3.4
Netherlands, The	2.8	3.3	2.3	0.2	−0.5	0.7	1.1
Norway	8.4	6.2	5.7	7.2	8.7	6.7	4.6
Portugal	25.5	29.3	19.3	11.7	9.4	9.7	13.7
Spain	12.2	11.3	8.8	8.8	5.3	4.8	6.6
Sweden	8.9	8.0	7.4	4.3	4.2	5.8	6.3
Switzerland	3.0	3.0	3.4	0.7	1.5	1.8	3.0
Turkey	28.8	45.6	45.0	34.5	38.9	75.4	73.3
Australia	10.1	3.9	6.8	9.1	8.5	7.2	7.6
New Zealand	7.4	6.2	15.4	13.2	15.7	6.4	4.4
OECD Total	5.3	5.2	4.5	2.6	3.2	3.8	5.0

*Twelve-month rate of change in August 1989.
Sources: OECD, *Economic Outlook; Main Economic Indicators.*

(From left to right) European Communities Pres. Jacques Delors, Italian Prime Minister Ciriaco De Mita, German Chancellor Helmut Kohl, U.S. Pres. George Bush, French Pres. François Mitterrand, U.K. Prime Minister Margaret Thatcher, Canadian Prime Minister Brian Mulroney, and Japanese Prime Minister Sosuke Uno pose in front of the Louvre pyramid during the annual economic summit of the world's seven leading industrialized nations.
WITT—SIPA

domestic demand and encouraging higher private savings was furthered by the Federal Reserve Board (the Fed) through a tight monetary policy. Fiscal policy, on the other hand, remained lax, with insufficient cuts in expenditure or additional revenue generated to bring the budget deficit in line with the target stipulated by the Gramm-Rudman legislation.

Monetary policy remained tight throughout 1989, despite a cautious easing in the second half that allowed banks to drop the prime rate by half a percentage point in early May, late July, and early November. The success of this tight monetary policy could be seen when the Fed set monetary targets for 1989 slightly below the targets for 1988, which had been achieved, and then the money supply grew near the lower end of the target range for most of the year. On balance, the Fed was more worried about a recession than inflation, hence the modest easing of the monetary reins. Nevertheless, the target ranges for money supply for 1990 remained the same as in 1989. Many observers predicted a loosening in policy by the early part of 1990 at the latest.

The federal budget deficit in fiscal 1989 (ended September 30) was $152.1 billion, compared with $155.2 billion in fiscal 1988 and $149.7 billion in fiscal 1987. While this outcome was better than had originally been forecast, thanks to higher than expected tax revenues, it still exceeded the Gramm-Rudman target of $136 billion. The budget deficit for fiscal 1990 was expected to fall to $116 billion, according to the administration's Office of Management and Budget. Independent observers expected the outcome to be somewhere between the administration's figure and the $141 billion forecast by the Congressional Budget Office. In view of the gap between the government's projections and the Gramm-Rudman target, automatic spending cuts of $16 billion were triggered. The Gramm-Rudman legislation provided that the cuts could be restored if the deficit were cut to the required target.

United Kingdom. Although the rate of growth remained at an acceptable level, 1989 saw the emergence of a number of serious problems for the British economy. These included a sharp acceleration in inflation, a massive increase in the balance of payments deficit, a marked depreciation in the external value of the pound sterling, and a serious deterioration in business confidence. These—together with some overseas developments—forced the government to pursue a high-interest-rate policy (pushing rates to near-

record levels) in an attempt to choke off domestic demand, cut back the rise of imports, and defend the beleaguered sterling. As the year was drawing to a close, there was little evidence that the policy was anywhere near achieving its principal objectives, although there were some indications that high interest rates were slowly pushing the economy toward recession. The position was further complicated by an apparent difference of opinion between Prime Minister Thatcher and Chancellor of the Exchequer Lawson on the need to support sterling and early participation in the EC's exchange rate mechanism (ERM). To some extent, this undermined the credibility and effectiveness of the government's policy and aggravated uncertainty in foreign exchange markets. It resulted, at the end of October, in Lawson's dramatic resignation, which—despite Thatcher's assurances of no change in the high-interest-rate policy— threw financial markets into turmoil and caused a serious slide in both the sterling exchange rate and equity prices. Thus the year ended on a note of uncertainty. It was not clear whether the new chancellor, John Major (*see* BIOGRAPHIES), would persevere with his predecessor's

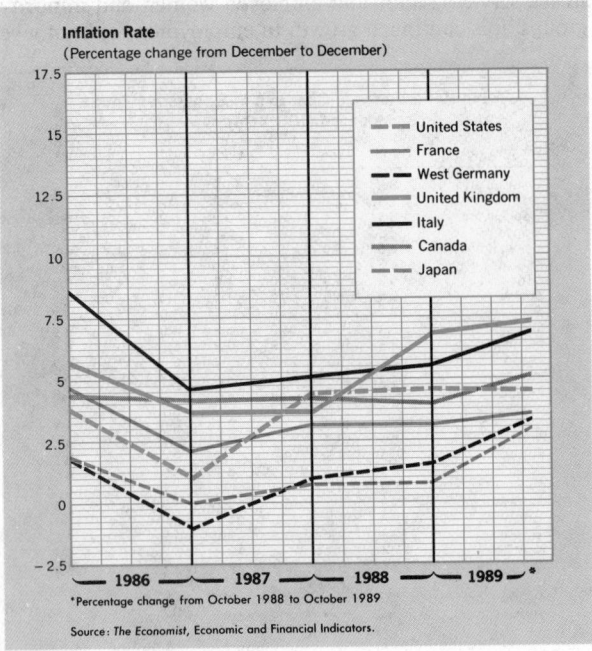

Inflation Rate
(Percentage change from December to December)

- - - - United States
——— France
– – – West Germany
——— United Kingdom
——— Italy
——— Canada
- - - - Japan

1986   1987   1988   1989 *
*Percentage change from October 1988 to October 1989

Source: *The Economist, Economic and Financial Indicators.*

policy of high interest rates even at the risk of pushing the economy into recession or whether he would seek to cut interest rates gradually and allow sterling to settle at a permanently lower level.

The principal source of problems in 1989 was, without doubt, the government's failure to moderate the unsustainably rapid growth of the economy during 1988. During this period GDP grew by 4.4% and, despite a steady hike in the base rate from 7.5 to 13%, growth in the first quarter of 1989 was still running at an unacceptably rapid rate of just under 3%. Furthermore, inflation was still gaining momentum, the trade gap continued to widen, and sterling came under considerable pressure. This caused Lawson to push the base rate up to 14% in May. Although GDP growth moderated to 2.2% by the second quarter, inflation and the external payments deficit were still moving in the wrong direction.

With consumer expenditure weakening rapidly as a result of the higher costs of housing and other credit, there was a general expectation that base rates would not have to rise further and that the rate of inflation could be reduced without a further squeeze on economic growth. However, sterling remained highly vulnerable, and when West German and other European interest rates rose by 1% in late September, the British government felt it necessary to follow suit and increase base rates to a near-record 15%. This was widely felt to be an overkill motivated not by domestic economic considerations but by the desire to peg the exchange rate, and it led, indirectly, to Lawson's resignation. Certainly by late 1989 many indicators pointed to a sharp slowdown in economic activity, with most estimates suggesting fourth-quarter GDP growth of only some 1%. GDP for the year was thought to have recorded an increase of just over 2%, just acceptable but only half the gain recorded in 1988.

Apart from steadying the nerves of holders of sterling, the main objective of high interest rates was to cut the growth of consumer expenditure. It was not surprising, therefore, that it was this component of domestic demand that saw the most marked turnaround. As a result of an acceleration in wage increases (aided by good corporate profitability), a fall in unemployment, an increase in consumer credit, and a decline in the savings ratio, the first quarter of 1989 saw a massive 8.3% increase in the volume of private consumption.

As the year progressed, the high cost of borrowing squeezed disposable incomes, especially those of the large number of homeowners who took out large mortgages during the property boom that ended in 1988. Retail sales, therefore, fell away sharply from the late spring onward, and consumer expenditure was thought to be growing at only about 2% in the closing quarter of 1989. For the year as a whole, growth was estimated at around 3%, compared with nearly 7% in 1988.

Unfortunately, the high cost of money and growing business uncertainty also had an adverse effect on investment. In 1988 fixed investment rose by 13%, ensuring both a good growth in productive capacity and an improvement in labour productivity. Indicators suggested that 1989 was unlikely to see an investment growth of more than 6%, with a marked slowdown in both residential and manufacturing investment only partially offset by higher spending in the oil and gas sectors. Inevitably, this had an adverse effect on the growth of productivity. In 1988 industry as a whole saw a gain of 2.6%, but in the first half of 1989 growth was down to 0.8%. The absolute level of industrial production also saw a significant change for the worse: following an increase of 3.5% in 1988, the first half of 1989 showed a gain of less than 0.5%, while both the July and September figures were below those recorded 12 months previously. In spite of this, unemployment continued to fall. In December 1988 the seasonally adjusted unemployment rate stood at 7.1%, having fallen from 9.1%. During the first nine months of 1989 the trend was steadily downward, with the result that by September the percentage of the available labour force without a job was only 5.9%. However, unfilled vacancies, which provided an early indication of the strength of the labour market, had been falling steadily since the latter half of 1988, suggesting that the slowdown in economic growth was about to make a mark on the trend of unemployment.

Despite slower economic growth, the trend of inflation was still upward. In 1988 retail prices rose by 4.9%, but the December-to-December figure registered a 6.8% gain. This was followed by a further steady rise for most of 1989, with the December figure heading for a gain of around 8% and an annual average increase of 7–7.5%. The principal reasons for this were the high level of interest rates, which increased mortgage costs, and the weakness of sterling, which had an adverse effect on the cost of imported products. This was only partially offset by manufacturers' and retailers' attempts to maintain sales growth in an increasingly sluggish market. One result (as well as a cause) of the accelerating rate of inflation was seen in the trend of wage settlements. Rising prices, together with falling unemployment, led to greater union militancy, with the result that employers faced tougher wage negotiations. The consequence was an acceleration in the rise of average earnings from 8.7% in 1988 to 9.3% in the first half of 1989. The second half saw several large wage disputes that were expected to be settled at or above the 10% mark, suggesting that there would be a further acceleration in the underlying trend.

On the external front, the two most notable features were the widening trade deficit and the weakness of the currency. Contrary to official forecasts, imports (fueled by strong private consumption) rose rapidly. For the January–August period the rise was over 15%, compared with one of only 12% for exports. The result was a trade deficit of £16.6 billion, as against £12.9 billion in the same period of 1988. At the same time, the surplus on invisible trade fell back from £4.3 billion to an estimated £3.2 billion. This resulted in a current account deficit of £13.9 billion, £5.4 billion more than in the corresponding eight months of the preceding year. All in all, 1989 was heading for a deficit of £20 billion, compared with £14.7 billion in 1988. Not unexpectedly, this and the disagreements between Lawson and Thatcher had an unsettling effect on foreign exchange markets. Sterling was under consistent pressure from the start of the year and, despite high interest rates and large-scale support operations by the Bank of England and other central banks, the currency lost ground on a wide front.

Table III. Unemployment Rates in Selected Developed Countries
% of total labour force

Country	1971–80	1986	1987	1988	1989*
Canada	6.9	9.5	8.8	7.8	7.8
United States	6.4	7.0	6.2	5.5	5.3
Japan	1.8	2.8	2.8	2.5	2.3
France	4.5	10.4	10.6	10.3	10.0
West Germany	2.7	7.9	7.9	7.7	7.1
Italy	6.7	11.1	12.0	12.0	12.0
United Kingdom	3.5	11.1	10.0	8.1	6.1
Other developed countries	3.9	10.5	10.3	9.9	9.5

*Estimated.
Source: International Monetary Fund, World Economic Outlook, October 1989.

Its rout was particularly pronounced against the Deutsche Mark, with a fall from DM 3.256 in January to DM 2.79 by late November. Against the dollar sterling fell 14% from $1.775 to $1.56, while the weighted average exchange rate showed a similar decline from 97.9 in January to 86.3 by late November. Furthermore, the support operations cost the Bank of England dearly in terms of foreign exchange reserves; by August these totaled £43.2 billion, as against £51.7 billion in January.

Japan. For the Japanese economy 1989 was a year of solid achievement. Overall economic growth, although somewhat slower than the exceptionally rapid progress recorded in the preceding year, was well above official expectations. Investment in manufacturing was maintained at a high level; consumption remained buoyant; and the large external payments surplus (the cause of so much disagreement between Japan and its trading partners) showed a small decline. There was a modest acceleration in the rate of inflation, although much of this could be attributed to the onetime effect of the small value-added tax (VAT) introduced in April. The fact that these achievements were secured against a background of considerable political uncertainty and upheaval was even more remarkable. Partly because of the unpopularity of the VAT, the ruling Liberal-Democratic Party (LDP) lost its long-standing majority in the (upper) House of Councillors. This resulted in the formation of a new LDP government that faced a significantly greater influence from the Japanese Socialist Party, but contrary to initial fears, this was not followed by any appreciable loss of business confidence.

During 1988 Japanese GNP rose by 5.8%, the highest rate of growth in some 10 years. The first quarter of 1989 opened on an extremely buoyant note, with the quarter-to-quarter annualized gain rising to 7.4%. This was followed by an annualized fall of 3.1% in April–June, giving rise to some fears that the official target of 4% growth for the year would be undershot by a significant margin. However, the second quarter's setback was largely a reaction to the imposition of the 3% VAT, which depressed private consumption, and in the third quarter the economy rebounded strongly to produce a real gain of 6.8%. The evidence available for the final three months of the year pointed to a good growth in most areas and suggested a GNP gain for 1989 of around 4.5%.

As in previous years, the mainstays of economic expansion were investment and private consumption, which collectively accounted for some 80% of GDP. Not unexpectedly, consumer expenditures were broadly in line with the fluctuations in the growth of the overall economy; a 3.9% year-to-year increase in the first quarter followed by a fall of 1.3% in the April–June period. In the second half of the year consumer spending recovered rapidly, with department store sales rising by around 9% in July–September, considerably faster than during the January–March period before the introduction of the VAT. In light of this and similar evidence, it was estimated that the full year saw a gain in consumer expenditure of around 4.5%, only half a percentage point below the increase recorded in 1988. This was principally the result of the continued rise in disposable income and strong underlying consumer confidence. Nominal wages during the first 10 months of the year rose by around 3.5%, but—with good summer bonus payments and a high level of overtime work—average earnings were estimated to have risen by around 6%, up from 4.5% in 1988. Thus there was a good increase in disposable income. At the same time, the tightness of the labour market and good employment prospects had a strong positive influence on consumer confidence.

The buoyancy of private demand had a beneficial effect on industrial output and investment. Industrial production during the first nine months of the year rose by some 6%, compared with a gain of 9.5% for the whole of 1988. There was evidence that the 1989 growth rate was constrained by lack of capacity—a fact that was reflected by a 4% rise in the capacity utilization ratio to its highest level in more than 10 years. This, together with continued business confidence in the future and good corporate profitability, exerted a positive influence on the level of investment in the industrial sector. Principal indicators such as machinery orders and investment surveys pointed to a strong performance in this sector of domestic demand. All in all, the year appeared to be heading for a gain in private plant and equipment investments of some 14%, compared with 16% in 1988. Housing investments, however, were relatively sluggish during the year. In the wake of extremely rapid growth in 1987 (22%) and 1988 (14%), residential construction fell to more normal levels, with an estimated growth of 6–7% in 1989.

The modest acceleration in the rate of inflation during 1989 arose from the new VAT and the relative weakness of the yen against the U.S. dollar, which had an adverse effect on the trend of import costs. As a result, the index of import prices, which declined 4.6% in 1988, recorded a steady increase throughout 1989, producing an average rise of 6.8% for the January–September period. Inevitably, this had a significant effect on the level of wholesale prices, which—after registering a 1% decrease in 1988—rose by 2.2% in the first nine months of 1989. In terms of consumer prices, the inflationary effect of these changes was reinforced by the VAT. Thus, following a quarter-to-quarter fall of 0.1% in the retail price index during January–March, the second quarter saw a hike of 2.2%. Although this was followed by an increase of only 0.2% in the subsequent three months, the net result for the year was a gain of 2.6%, compared with a rise of 1% in 1988. The extent of the increase was rather better than might have been expected under the circumstances. Despite buoyant consumer demand, manufacturers and retailers managed to absorb a significant part of both the increase in import costs and the new consumption tax.

There was also a small reduction in the country's external payments surplus, which had been a source of much friction with Washington and the principal EC countries. Partly because of the effect of the steady appreciation of the yen between 1985 and 1988, exports rose relatively slowly and registered a gain of only 6.6% in the first three quarters of the year, as against one of 15.6% in 1988. The rise in imports of 10.5% during January–September was considerably faster, with the result that the trade surplus was expected to total some $80 billion for 1989, compared with a total of $95 billion in 1988. The underlying trend of invisible transactions did not appear to change much, and the year was heading for a deficit of around $15 billion. The current account surplus was, therefore, expected to reach around $75 billion, still a very high figure but representing a considerable reduction from the positive balance of nearly $80 billion in 1988 and $87 billion in 1987.

Welcome as this development was in the context of the country's international economic relations, the second half of the year saw growing concern about an early reversal of this trend. This was largely due to the weakness of the yen throughout 1989, the effect of which was to make Japanese exports more competitive abroad and imports more expensive at home. In the closing quarter of 1988 the dollar was worth, on average, 125 yen. By the second quarter of 1989 the currency had depreciated to 138 yen, and by

November the rate was fluctuating at around 143 yen. This had less to do with the yen than with the unexpected, and largely unexplained, strength of the U.S. currency. Even the surprising plunge in Wall Street prices in early October failed to undermine the underlying strength of the dollar.

In terms of economic policy-making, the year was dominated by the attempt to reform the tax structure, with a view to bringing about a gradual reduction in the government deficit. The introduction of the 2% consumption tax was an integral part of this and played a major part in the ruling LDP's loss of its upper-house majority in the subsequent elections. This, in turn, brought forth a change of prime ministers and gave rise to the spectre of the party's losing its majority and right to govern in the elections for the (lower) House of Representatives due in 1990. It was, therefore, not surprising that no significant fiscal or monetary measures were taken, and it was perhaps fortunate that the economy was in a strong enough position not to require any major policy initiatives by government. The central bank, however, did increase the discount rate on two occasions. In May the rate went up by 0.25% to 3.25% as an anti-inflationary step, and in October there was a further increase to 3.75%, largely as a result of the hike in West German and other European interest rates.

West Germany. The West German economy performed strongly during 1989 and for the first time since 1979 grew at a higher rate than the OECD average. The real GNP, having risen by 4.6% during the first half of the year, was confidently expected to show a 4% volume growth as the year drew to a close. This represented a continuing improvement in the rate of growth that in 1988 had registered a 3.6% real gain, double the 1.7% increase recorded in 1987. Thus for the second year running, West Germany's buoyant economic performance baffled the pundits and the critics alike. Slower growth was originally expected for 1989, as tax increases held back consumer demand, but the government's forecast of 2.5% growth was revised upward to 3.5% and later to 4%.

The economic buoyancy was for the second consecutive year stimulated by an exceptionally mild winter, which led to a surge in construction during the opening quarter of 1989. A more lasting stimulus came from the growth in exports. Thanks to a decline in the Deutsche Mark that boosted exporters' competitiveness and also to strong economic growth and investment in European countries and the U.S., export demand rose by nearly 17% during the first nine months of the year. The trade surplus over the same period widened to DM 104.6 billion, compared with DM 90.9 billion in the corresponding period of 1988. The current account surplus, however, showed a larger gain.

The strong export demand delivered a boost to industrial production. During the first nine months of the year, it rose by 4.7%, compared with annual increases of 3.6 and 0.2% in 1988 and 1987, respectively. The increase in manufacturing led to a sharp rise in capital goods, which was accompanied by the highest capacity utilization levels since 1973 and record order books. Some of the capacity pressures were eased by a surge in new investment. An 8% increase in expenditure on machinery and equipment (7% in 1988 and 5.6% in 1987) was accompanied by a 10% gain in construction investment. The summer–autumn downturn in the growth rate of construction activity was expected to be reversed by the demand for housing from the influx of emigrants from East Germany and other Eastern European countries.

Consumer expenditure, which accounted for 56% of total GNP, held up better than expected despite an increase in consumer taxes in January. A combination of higher earnings, a reduction in savings from above trend levels, and anticipation of further tax cuts (effective January 1990) enabled retail sales to increase an estimated 3% during 1989—the same as in 1988.

The continuing strength of the economy had helped to bring unemployment down but not as much as expected. The mild winter and various training programs, together with early retirement schemes, removed 300,000 people from the unemployment register, but this was offset by nearly 500,000 Eastern European immigrants. Thus the rate of unemployment dipped gently to 7.1% from 7.7% in 1988.

The danger of an economic boom, of course, was overheating, as had happened in the U.K. The inflationary trends rose rapidly during 1989 and reached an annual rate of 3.3% in October—the highest rate in six years. At this level it was more than double the 1988 end rate of 1.6%. The upturn in the inflation rate in the opening quarter of 1989 was largely due to higher indirect taxes, which added 0.7% to the index. During the following months, higher import prices fed through before easing toward the end of the year. In the absence of an upward push from higher wages, the inflationary pressures appeared to be containable. Further relief came in November, when new weights used to calculate the inflation index showed a slightly slower increase.

Concern for the steepening inflation curve, monetary growth outside the target ranges, a weak currency, and potentially inflationary pressures from strong economic growth and capacity constraints spurred the Bundesbank to react repeatedly and raise key interest rates. The widely expected half-a-percentage-point rise in the discount and Lombard rates in mid-January was followed by a surprise decision by the Bundesbank to add another half a percentage point to both rates in April. A further touch on the monetary brakes followed in June, taking the discount rate to 5% and the Lombard rate to 7%, representing another half-a-percentage-point increase in both. This put

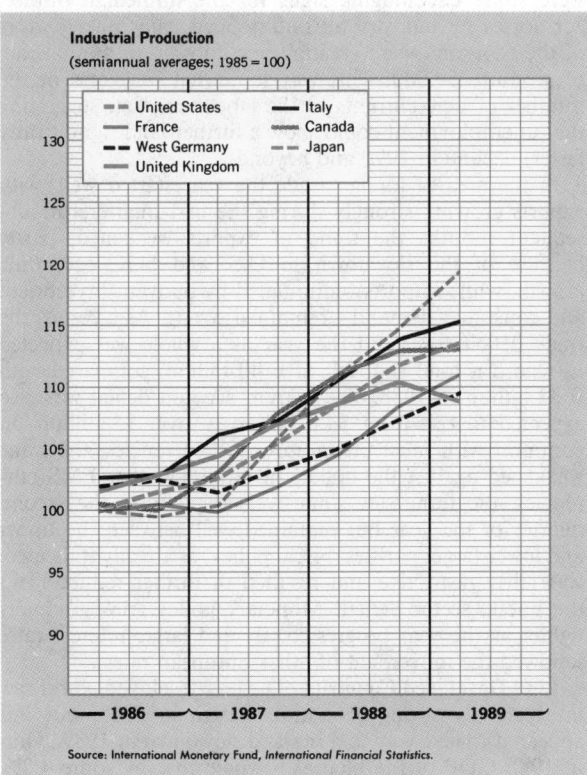

Industrial Production

(semiannual averages; 1985 = 100)

Legend: United States, France, West Germany, United Kingdom, Italy, Canada, Japan

1986   1987   1988   1989

Source: International Monetary Fund, *International Financial Statistics.*

interest rates at their highest level in almost seven years. To reinforce its anti-inflation goal against the backdrop of a robust economy, but with the danger of overheating ever present, the Bundesbank raised its discount and Lombard rates by a full 1% in October. This increase, which was followed widely in other European countries, appeared to have had the desired effect by strengthening the Deutsche Mark against the dollar and by dampening expectations of further price rises in 1990.

The progressively tighter monetary policy pursued by the Bundesbank was mirrored by the restrictive fiscal policy of the federal government. The aim was to consolidate the budget deficit before the next and final installment of the income tax cuts due in January 1990. In the event, the federal budget deficit declined further than planned, thanks to higher tax revenues and lower government expenditure. However, this did not exert an undue negative pressure on the economy.

France. Notwithstanding earlier fears of a slowdown in activity, the French economy turned in a generally satisfactory performance in 1989. Overall growth was maintained at a respectable level; investment stayed unexpectedly strong; the currency remained comfortably within the European Monetary System (EMS) parameters; and the size of the government deficit was cut back for the fourth successive year. There were, however, some less satisfactory features, including a rise in the trade and current account deficits, a modest acceleration in inflation, and a stubbornly high level of unemployment.

The year started off on a fairly buoyant note with the national accounts statistics pointing to first-quarter growth of 1.2%. This was followed by a gain of only 0.7% in the second quarter, but activity appeared to have gathered momentum in the second half of the year to produce overall annual growth of some 2.2%. Although this was a little slower than the 3.4% advance recorded in 1988, in the context of fears of a significant downturn and a modest slowdown in the growth of the world economy, it was a satisfactory performance. All sectors of demand recorded some growth, but the star performer was private investment. In the wake of an exceptionally fast increase of 7.2% in the previous year, 1989 was expected to see a significantly more modest performance. Business confidence remained unexpectedly strong, and the overall level of private investment was estimated to have recorded a gain of some 6.5%. In line with an official policy of reducing the deficit from F 115 billion in 1988 to F 100.5 billion in 1989, government expenditure rose a little less rapidly (around 2.1%, compared with 2.9% in the preceding year). The growth of consumer expenditure also witnessed a modest slowdown from 2.7% in 1988 to 2.3%. This was the result not of a lower rate of wage increases (the rise in average earnings was estimated to have been largely unchanged at 4.7%), but rather of a slight acceleration in inflation and the gradual fading of the effects of the tax reductions brought in during 1988.

Inflation showed an acceleration from 2.7% in 1988 to 3.5% in 1989. Virtually all of the acceleration was attributable to higher import costs, which arose from an increase in oil and commodity prices during the first half of the year and from depreciation in the external value of the franc in the second half. Domestic inflationary pressures remained largely unchanged, mainly because the continuing high level of plant and equipment investments brought forth additional productive capacity and because sustained moderation in the size of wage settlements, especially in the public sector, had a positive influence on the trend of labour costs. In addition, moderation in the wage-bargaining process was encouraged by the high level of unemployment.

The year opened with an unemployment rate of 10.1%, only marginally below the rate of 10.3% recorded 12 months earlier. Despite relatively buoyant economic growth, in the autumn of 1989 there were still some 2.3 million people out of work, accounting for 9.6% of the labour force. This was considerably higher than in most other European countries. By way of comparison, the OECD average stood at 5.9%. Nevertheless, as the year drew to a close, there were some encouraging signs for the immediate future. Job losses by industry all but stopped, and other sectors of the economy were creating new jobs at an annual rate of around 250,000. This was somewhat in excess of the number of new entrants to the labour market, suggesting that unemployment could show a further (and significantly faster) decline in 1990 and beyond.

In the area of foreign trade the year started well, with exports growing strongly during the first quarter. In subsequent months the trend of exports weakened, partly because of the slowdown in U.S. and U.K. economic growth, while imports—stimulated by buoyant investment and consumer demand—remained strong. As a result, the trade deficit rose, and the year as a whole was expected to record a total shortfall of F 40 billion, compared with F 33 billion in 1988. The current account deficit was also expected to rise from $4.3 billion to over $5 billion. In common with most other European currencies, the franc weakened against the dollar. In terms of other EMS currencies, the franc saw some weakening from the second quarter of the year but remained well between the upper and lower target parities. Fiscal policy, as already indicated, was fairly restrictive and resulted in further reduction in the public sector deficit. Monetary policy grew gradually tighter as the year progressed. By and large, interest rates followed the movement of other European rates.

Less Developed Countries. The less developed world saw unexpectedly strong economic growth in 1988, but this appeared to give way to a marked slowdown in 1989. Thus in 1988 GDP of the bloc as a whole rose by some 4.2%,

Table IV. Changes in Output in the Less Developed Countries

In %

| Area | Annual average 1971–80 | Change from preceding year | | | | |
		1985	1986	1987	1988	1989*
All less developed countries	5.5	3.9	4.2	3.6	4.2	3.2
Oil-exporting countries	6.6	1.6	0.4	−0.2	2.5	2.6
Non-oil less developed countries	5.1	5.0	5.9	5.4	4.9	3.3
Africa	3.8	4.0	2.3	1.0	2.2	2.8
Asia	5.3	6.9	6.7	7.9	9.2	6.1
Europe	5.3	2.1	4.3	2.7	1.2	1.9
Middle East	1.2	−0.2	0.6	−1.5	3.5	−3.5
Western Hemisphere	5.9	−3.5	4.0	3.0	0.7	—

*Estimated.
Source: International Monetary Fund, *World Economic Outlook*, October 1989.

Table V. Changes in Consumer Prices in the Less Developed Countries

In %

| Area | Annual average 1971–80 | Change from preceding year | | | | |
		1985	1986	1987	1988	1989*
All less developed countries	20.6	40.6	31.4	41.6	70.8	85.5
Oil-exporting countries	13.4	16.8	24.6	33.2	33.8	17.6
Non-oil less developed countries	24.0	53.6	34.6	45.4	88.6	119.1
Africa	14.1	13.2	14.5	15.0	19.7	16.8
Asia	10.5	7.8	9.1	9.8	14.6	13.0
Europe	13.2	27.2	26.8	35.5	62.5	92.2
Middle East	13.5	17.0	18.1	19.4	17.8	13.9
Western Hemisphere	39.8	145.3	87.8	130.9	286.4	404.6

*Estimated.
Source: International Monetary Fund, *World Economic Outlook*, October 1989.

A clock erected in New York City's Times Square keeps an up-to-the-second tally of the U.S. national debt, which was said to be increasing at a rate of about $8,000 per second.
AFP PHOTO

largely as a result of strong non-oil commodity prices and a rapid growth in world trade. By contrast, the evidence available in late 1989 suggested that GDP growth for the year would be around 3%, the lowest figure since 1982 and well below the average of 5.5% achieved in the 1971–80 period. The principal reasons for the relatively poor performance in 1989 were the rise in world interest rates and the relative weakness of commodity prices. Whereas the prices of non-oil commodities rose by around 20% in 1988, in 1989 they were broadly static. This had a serious effect on the ability of countries that exported food and metals or minerals to increase their foreign exchange earnings, although, because of a recovery in oil prices from the previous year's very low levels, oil producers were in a comparatively strong position. Foreign exchange positions were also adversely affected by the rising trend of interest rates, dictated by stronger inflationary pressures, in the developed world.

Despite attempts at restructuring, a substantial part of world debt was still subject to variable rates of interest, with the result that some countries (especially in Latin America) faced a marked increase in debt servicing problems. (*See* Special Report.) Another adverse external influence was the general slowdown in the growth of world trade from 9% in 1988 to an estimated 7% in 1989. Particularly serious was the sluggish growth in imports by the developed countries (down from 9.5 to 6.4%), which made it impossible for

the less developed world to maintain the relatively good export performance of 1988, when exports rose by 11%. Indications for 1989 suggested growth amounting to only around 6.5%.

Coupled with these external difficulties was a significant acceleration in the rate of inflation. Less developed countries traditionally had considerably higher inflation rates than their economically advanced counterparts. However, whereas in 1987 the inflation rate was 42% (nearly 13 times higher than in developed countries), in 1989 prices were thought to have risen by 86% (a multiple by nearly 20 of the comparable figure for the rest of the world). Although inflation varied widely (prices in the Western Hemisphere rose by 400%, while in Asia the rate was only 13%), the general result was to force governments to introduce tighter monetary policies as a means of combating inflation and of protecting external payments positions. In this respect, at least, the policies were broadly successful. The slowdown in the growth of exports was, to some extent, offset by a slowdown in the rise of imports from 10.2 to around 8.5%. The net effect of these and other changes was to ensure that there was no significant adverse movement in foreign payment deficits, and IMF estimates suggested that there might even have been a small improvement. At the end of 1989 it was estimated that the current account deficit for all less developed countries was around $7.3 billion, a reduction of some $1.5 billion from the shortfall recorded in the preceding year.

This was not the only positive feature of the outcome for 1989. It was also of some comfort that the overall slowdown in domestic growth was not shared by all groups within the less developed world. Thus the weaker GDP growth was entirely the result of the difficulties in Western Hemisphere countries and a slower rate of progress in Asian economies. Less developed countries in Latin America (including Argentina, Bolivia, Peru, Brazil, Chile, Mexico, Uruguay, and Venezuela) saw no increase in GDP, compared with a gain of 0.7% in 1988. By and large, this heavily indebted group was hard hit by the rise of interest rates and sluggish imports by developed countries, although a number of them derived some benefit from a strengthening in oil prices. They were also the most affected by accelerating inflation, which required policies to squeeze domestic demand, private consumption, and investment expenditures. Like other groups within the bloc, these Latin-American countries appeared to have been successful in preventing a further increase in their external payments deficit of some $11 billion.

The other major group where a weakening of economic growth was experienced consisted of Asia's more industrially developed economies. These economies were the most advanced within the less developed world, having seen by far the fastest growth rates. The slowdown in GDP growth from 9.2% in 1988 to 6.1% was, therefore, still a com-

Table VI. Balance of Payments on Current Account
In $000,000,000

Area	1984	1985	1986	1987	1988	1989*
		Change from preceding year				
All less developed countries	−27.5	−21.8	−41.3	4.1	−9.1	−7.3
Oil-exporting countries	−1.6	2.8	−31.4	−3.6	−19.1	−5.2
Non-oil less developed countries	−26.0	−24.6	−9.9	7.8	10.0	−2.1
Africa	−8.0	−1.2	−10.4	−5.1	−9.4	−8.3
Asia	−4.2	−14.0	3.8	21.5	12.3	4.3
Europe	−0.3	−0.2	−1.3	1.8	7.0	5.1
Middle East	−13.8	−3.6	−17.1	−3.6	−8.3	0.6
Western Hemisphere	−1.3	−2.9	−16.2	−10.4	−10.7	−9.0

*Estimated.
Source: International Monetary Fund, *World Economic Outlook*, October 1989.

paratively good performance and produced a good 4.6% growth in per capita income. This group, which included booming economies such as Taiwan, Singapore, Hong Kong, and South Korea, also managed to prevent inflation from accelerating over the previous year's level of around 14%. Because of the sluggish growth of imports by the developed world, Asian exports of industrial goods faced a fairly difficult climate, which led to a marked deterioration in their overall foreign payments position. Nevertheless, unlike most other groups in the less developed world, these countries ran a strong current account surplus, and the estimated reductions from $12.3 billion in 1988 to $4.3 billion remained consistent with a broadly satisfactory underlying position.

By contrast, Middle Eastern economies managed a significant improvement in their balance of payments position, turning a deficit of over $8 billion in 1988 to a modest surplus of around $1 billion in 1989. The main reason for this was the recovery in oil prices after the OPEC agreement on production quotas in November 1988, which, despite fairly volatile conditions for much of 1989, was estimated to have increased average prices by some 15–18%. Although foreign payment constraints on domestic growth were less serious than in 1988, monetary policies were not relaxed significantly, with the result that the inflation rate was thought to have fallen three to four percentage points below the 1988 increase of 18%, and GDP gain was maintained broadly unchanged at 3.5%.

Overall economic growth in Africa saw a modest acceleration from 2.2 to around 2.8%. Even the very poor and economically underdeveloped sub-Saharan African group was thought to have seen a modest increase. On the whole, much of the progress in 1989 was due to the implementation of structural reforms rather than external influences. Agricultural commodity prices were largely static, although one or two key products (coffee, cocoa) that were of major importance for many countries in the region worsened. Partly because of a cutback in the volume of imports and a relatively strong export performance in a weakening market, the external payments deficit remained largely unchanged at some $9 billion. This was a rather better

performance than expected, as was the estimated slowdown in the inflation rate from nearly 20 to around 17%.

The problem of external debt continued to dominate economic policy in many less developed countries during 1989. However, according to the World Bank and the IMF, 1988 showed some reduction in the overall level of world debt, and the available indications for 1989 pointed to a further modest drop. The main influences were a reduction in net external borrowings by several countries as well as various debt-reduction plans, including debt equity swaps and buybacks. Although this could be considered a modestly encouraging development, in 1989 the estimated total debt of just under $1.2 trillion still accounted for approximately 125% of the debtor countries' combined exports, significantly less than the peak figure of 171% reached in 1986 but still well in excess of the 95% seen in 1981. However, because of the various rescheduling schemes that were developed in the 1980s and despite the rise in world interest rates, the debt-servicing ratio expressed as a percentage of exports fell to an estimated 17% in 1989. This compared with 19.9% in 1988 and was the lowest figure seen since 1981.

Centrally Planned Economies. The wave of change that swept across Eastern Europe during 1989 was reflected in the working and functioning of the Council for Mutual Economic Assistance (CMEA, or Comecon). Its 45th session, which was due to be held in Budapest in June 1989, was at first postponed to November and then canceled. Instead, there were three separate meetings of Comecon Communist Party secretaries who headed economic departments in their respective countries.

The first meeting took place in March in Prague, the second in June in East Berlin, and the third in November, again in Prague. All the active member countries (Bulgaria, Hungary, Vietnam, East Germany, Cuba, Mongolia, Poland, Romania, Czechoslovakia, and the Soviet Union; Albania's membership had been inactive since 1961) sent

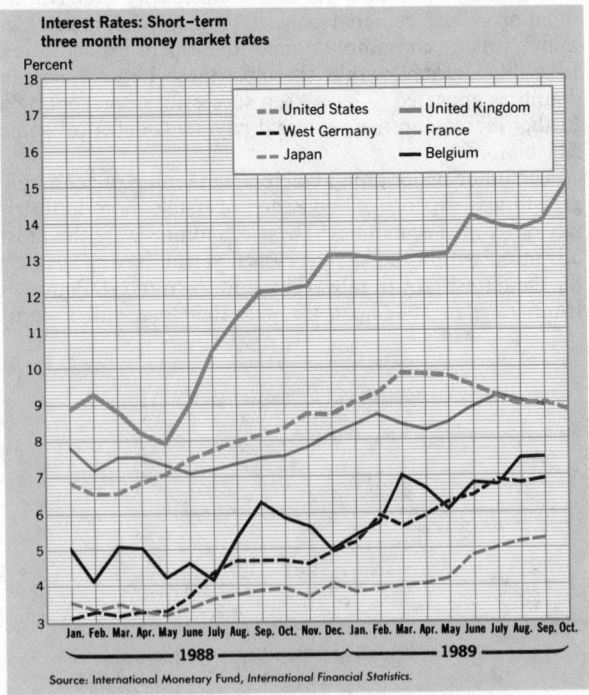

Source: International Monetary Fund, *International Financial Statistics.*

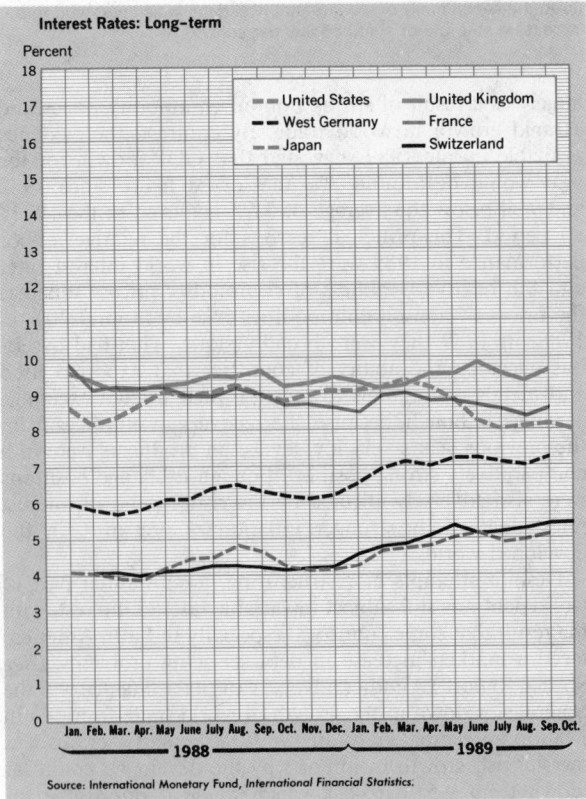

Source: International Monetary Fund, *International Financial Statistics.*

delegates to the November meeting, which was the most authoritative and meaningful of the three. Vyacheslav Sychev, the secretary of Comecon, was also present. It was questionable, however, whether the representatives of the Communist parties had any authority to make policy decisions given that in at least one country (Poland) there already was a coalition government dominated by non-Communists.

The Czechoslovak delegate, Ivan Knotek, stated that the Comecon market was not perfect. He believed it was desirable to build a single market gradually out of Comecon countries with economies that had properly functioning markets. He argued that in this way a Comecon single market would be capable of competing with economic organizations such as the EC.

The Hungarian delegate, Csaba Hamori, concluded that for the first time the Communist parties of the Comecon member countries recognized that there was a need to open up their economies to international competition. He added that Comecon could no longer survive in its present monolithic form and that future cooperation and development of Comecon would be determined by bilateral relations.

The Polish delegate, Zbigniew Michalek, criticized the workings of Comecon, saying that firm decisions had been taken but not acted upon. In spite of the recognized need for economic integration, customs barriers were being raised. Michalek believed there was an urgent need to radically reorganize Comecon's model of cooperation. He suggested that, in practical terms, the enterprises and not the states should be made accountable for failing to meet their obligations.

As the year progressed, it became clear that the Soviet Union's policy of *perestroika* (restructuring) was having a destabilizing effect on Comecon. Comecon's interstate trade agreements were essentially political arrangements that had little to do with market forces. The creation of freer markets in member countries would mean a complete change in the way Comecon operated. In the past its role had been made simple because of central planning. Although all active member countries eventually endorsed the need to create conditions for the free movement of goods and services and the decentralization of production, the Hungarian view was that the lack of free markets meant that there was no case for market unification.

The future of Comecon was extremely uncertain, especially as the changes in the economic systems of member countries were by no means uniform. In Poland, which implemented many of the changes first, the new government's program of economic reform envisaged the complete dismantling of the existing command economy. It was to be replaced by a market economy along the lines of those in Western Europe. The price system was being reformed, taxes simplified, and state monopolies and subsidies abolished, and the private and public sectors were to enjoy equal status in the future.

In October 1989 the Polish government adopted radical economic measures that attached great importance to economic relations with other Comecon members. At the same time, the program stressed that Poland was committed to a fundamental restructuring of the cooperation mechanisms within Comecon. In particular, Poland was in favour of the broad plan for commodity trade between member states being based on a different mechanism, with the existing centralized system replaced by one in which individual enterprises provided the input that would serve as the basis for decision making. The criteria for such decisions would be purely economic, and free currency settlements based on the prevailing international commodity prices would be encouraged. These changes were to be implemented more stringently in 1991. Until that time the five-year agreements signed within the Comecon framework were to continue in force.

At the end of November Poland's prime minister, Tadeusz Mazowiecki, the first non-Communist government leader in the Eastern bloc, visited Moscow. During economic negotiations the question of putting Polish-Soviet trade on a hard-currency basis for the first time (thus eliminating the transferable ruble) was discussed. Although the visit ended in a friendly atmosphere, no new agreement was signed.

In theory, *perestroika* was to devolve a great deal of responsibility to individual enterprises and drastically reduce the power of ministries and central planners. Because of bureaucratic resistance, however, the process of change in many countries was slow.

All the governments of the Comecon countries agreed that the Comecon system of bilateral trade agreements was crucial to the functioning of their economies and should not be abolished rapidly. It provided stable markets in the U.S.S.R. for Eastern European exports of industrial products and in return guaranteed steady supplies of Soviet fuels and raw materials. According to an informed Hungarian source, in 1989 the Soviet Union still provided over 60% of Hungary's oil and raw material needs. In the cases of some other member countries, the proportion was even higher.

The root of the difficulty facing Comecon lay in the failure of the centrally planned economies to function properly. All member countries of Comecon had been experiencing drastic slowdowns in economic growth, rising balance of payment deficits with the world's industrialized countries, and continuing deterioration in the environment, particularly in worsening levels of pollution. The technological gap between East and West had also widened, and the European member countries of Comecon were facing increased competition from the newly industrialized economies of Asia, most notably South Korea, Hong Kong, Taiwan, and Singapore.

Those Comecon countries that had already begun to change their economic systems were encountering prob-

Table VII. Output of Basic Industrial Products in Eastern Europe, 1988

In 000 metric tons unless otherwise stated

Country	Anthracite (hard coal)	Lignite (brown coal)	Natural gas (000,000 cu m)	Crude petroleum	Electric power (000,000 kw-hr)	Steel	Cement
Bulgaria	192	33,924	...	...	44,412	2,880	5,400
Czechoslovakia	25,908	99,924	29,880	144	81,360	15,384	10,368
East Germany	...	310,320	...	...	118,392	8,136	12,516
Hungary	2,256	18,624	231,072	1,944	29,160	3,384	3,876
Poland	193,008	73,488	179,220	...	144,336	16,872	16,980
Romania	...	...	...	...	...	...	...
U.S.S.R.	599,004	171,600	...	624,240	1,704,960	162,996	138,096

Source: UN, *Monthly Bulletin of Statistics.*

lems hitherto ignored or hidden, such as serious unemployment, falling levels of personal consumption, and galloping inflation.

A fundamental influence on the future of Comecon was the Soviet Union's Law on State Enterprise, which came into force in January 1988. According to this law, the powers of the ministries and central planners were to be drastically reduced, while individual enterprises were to be given more responsibilities and price reforms were to be instituted. The new prices would be raised to compensate for the abolition of state subsidies and to take into account the true costs of production. There was considerable bureaucratic resistance to the implementation of this law in the Soviet Union. The raising of prices to realistic levels would cause considerable hardship in many cases, at least in the short term, and to mitigate this the law was being implemented only slowly. Eventually, however, it was expected to be a major influence on trade relations among Comecon members.

There was no doubt that the dramatic changes taking place across Eastern Europe would influence the ongoing debate within the Comecon countries. On one side were those who until recently had supported, as the basis of cooperation, the long-term detailed coordination of national plans. On the other side were those who advocated more flexible arrangements, including more direct contacts between enterprises, the introduction of wholesale markets, and, what was probably most important, the establishment of convertible currencies. Up to the end of 1989 there was no clear-cut program for the restructuring of trade and economic cooperation within Comecon or for the creation of a unified Comecon market. Although Comecon was suffering the most severe crisis of its 40-year history, its continuing role, at least for the next several years, was not in question.

A crucial development that might influence the future of Comecon was the growing cooperation between some Comecon countries and the EC. Hungary and Poland were especially eager to have closer ties with the EC. In response to this growing interest, the European Commission in Brussels planned to establish permanent representations in Budapest and Warsaw in 1990. The EC planned to become more actively involved in helping Hungary and Poland—and any other country in Eastern Europe that undertook a program of democratization—to reform their economic systems. It was envisaged that links between Eastern and Western Europe would strengthen further during the course of 1990. West Germany even proposed the possibility of future unification with East Germany.

INTERNATIONAL TRADE AND PAYMENTS

In line with the modest slowdown in world economic growth, world trade also appeared to have lost some momentum in 1989. According to estimates by the IMF, 1989 probably recorded a volume gain of just under 7%. Although this fell short of the extraordinarily rapid increase of 9% seen in the previous year, it was still a very strong performance by historical standards. It was the third highest gain since 1981 and was well above the average annual growth rate of 5.7% achieved in the 10 years to 1980. More important, the 1989 figure appeared to reinforce the growing trend for international trade to become an increasingly important component of overall economic growth. In the 1970s world trade grew by one and a half percentage points for each percentage point of overall economic growth. In the first half of the 1980s the relationship between the two indexes varied wildly, but after 1987 the volume growth of world trade was approximately twice as fast as that of

the world economy. The reasons for this possibly structural change were not entirely clear, but it was thought that efforts to liberalize international trade, together with capacity shortages in many countries in the wake of one of the longest periods of economic boom, were a significant part of the explanation.

The overall figure marked some spectacular changes in a number of countries. Exports by the industrially advanced countries showed a relatively modest weakening from 8.9 to 7.4%, but the U.S., faced with an appreciating dollar, saw a sharp slowdown in its volume sales abroad to an estimated 12.5%, compared with 23.5% in the preceding year. By contrast, most other major advanced countries did better than in 1988, particularly Japan and West Germany, where exports benefited from increased competitiveness resulting from the stronger dollar. There was also a significant turnaround in the U.K., where a fall in exports in 1988 was turned into an increase in 1989, although the actual gain recorded (1.9%) was only a fraction of that seen by West Germany (11%) and Japan (6%). Imports by developed countries saw a relatively strong slowdown from around 9.5 to 6.5%.

Once again, the U.S. loomed large in the picture, cutting back its growth from 7 to about 4%, mainly as a result of some weakening in domestic economic activity. Japan, reacting to the adverse price effect of the stronger U.S. dollar, increased volume imports by only an estimated 6–7%, compared with nearly 17% in 1988. The U.K., similarly affected by the weakness of sterling and a slowdown in the growth of the economy, also saw a marked cutback in the rate of import growth from 13 to around 6%. In fact, the only major OECD country that went against the general trend was West Germany, which recorded a modest acceleration in import growth from 7 to 8% between 1988 and 1989.

In view of the foregoing it was not surprising that the less developed countries were faced with a marked slowdown in the growth of their volume exports in 1989. Official estimates suggested that 1989 showed an increase of around 6.5%, compared with 11% in 1988. Both oil producers and other less developed countries faced a loss of momentum, with oil producers experiencing a relatively sharp slowdown from 11.5 to 5% as a result of a rise in oil prices and consequent attempts to restrict consumption. Asian exports were also relatively weak. Manufactured

Table VIII. Soviet Trade with Eastern European Countries
In 000,000 rubles, current prices

Country	Exports			Imports		
	1986	1987	1988	1986	1987	1988
Bulgaria	6,787.8	6,276.3	6,093.7	6,191.3	6,551.7	6,873.1
Czechoslovakia	6,942.0	6,776.7	6,384.6	6,556.4	6,907.4	6,817.3
East Germany	7,884.2	7,635.9	7,193.2	7,128.1	7,093.2	7,024.4
Hungary	4,678.2	4,600.0	4,484.3	4,873.4	5,080.3	4,943.2
Poland	6,813.8	6,542.2	6,298.0	6,127.2	6,329.3	7,109.3
Romania	2,823.3	2,539.2	2,344.1	2,415.2	2,347.2	2,431.2

Source: U.S.S.R. Foreign Trade Statistics/Moscow.

Table IX. Soviet Crude Petroleum and Products Supplied to Eastern Europe
In 000 rubles

Country	1986	1987	1988
Bulgaria	2,256,362	1,910,394	1,559,539
Czechoslovakia	2,994,622	2,675,574	2,258,584
East Germany	3,126,569	2,860,031	2,439,076
Hungary	1,494,733	1,333,684	1,113,860
Poland	2,742,241	2,464,032	2,098,835
Romania	974,947	703,673	522,857

Source: U.S.S.R. Foreign Trade Statistics/Moscow.

Barber Conable, president of the World Bank, announces the bank's approval of a $1.5 billion loan to the government of Mexico. Under the terms set by the bank, Mexico would be able to use up to $375 million for debt-reduction arrangements.

AFP PHOTO

products accounted for a significant part of these, and the policy of restricting the growth of private consumption in the developed world had a pronounced effect on demand for consumer-related manufactures. Africa, however, which exported largely non-oil commodities, did relatively well and was thought to have maintained its 1988 growth rate of 3.5%.

In terms of import volumes, the less developed bloc saw some slowdown in growth (from 10.2 to 8.7%), but this was well below the comparable change in exports. Most parts of the less developed world saw a slowdown, except the Middle East, where the absence of any rise in imports in 1988 and higher prices for oil led to a volume gain of around 6%. In contrast, less developed economies in the Western Hemisphere, struggling with debt and foreign exchange problems, saw a decline in volume imports in the wake of a 4.5% rise in 1988.

Broadly speaking, the terms of trade moved in favour of the less developed world in 1989, but this was almost entirely the result of the recovery in oil prices in the wake of the massive decline of 1988. In foreign exchange terms, this was a major benefit for oil exporters. Although it had an adverse effect on less developed economies that were without significant oil resources, in overall terms they, too, registered a modest benefit because the stagnation of non-oil commodity prices was offset by a modest fall in world trade prices of manufactures. All in all, the IMF estimated a deterioration in the terms of trade for the developed world of around 1%. The corresponding measure for less developed economies pointed to a gain of 2%, with oil exporters benefiting by some 9% as against a gain of less than 1% for non-oil countries. In this respect the position was the mirror image of 1988, when non-oil exporters saw an improvement of 1.5% in their relative position compared with an 18% deterioration for oil producers.

There was considerable progress in the Uruguay round of trade-liberalization negotiations, and by the end of 1989 there were hopes that the discussions would be brought to a successful conclusion by late 1990. The year 1989 had started on a fairly pessimistic note, largely because of uncertainty about the commitment of the new U.S. administration to freer trade. This uncertainty reached its height in May, when Washington named Brazil, India, and Japan as unfair trading partners under the 1988 Trade Act in an attempt to promote bilateral negotiations. U.S. officials later indicated that, although they intended to fight for U.S. economic interests, they were prepared to work for an early conclusion of the Uruguay round. As a result, the 96 members of the General Agreement on Tariffs and Trade (GATT) agreed to a three-phase plan in June that was designed to bring the talks to a successful conclusion by the end of 1990. The plan provided for member countries to submit detailed proposals on the outstanding issues by early 1990. This was to be followed by a reconciliation of the inevitable differences and the drafting of the appropriate agreements by the end of 1990.

In line with the overall framework, the second half of 1989 saw much attention given to the major unresolved issues. These included trade in agricultural products, the protection of intellectual property rights, trade in textiles, and the nature and definition of antidumping safeguards. On the subject of agricultural trade, the U.S. proposal was for a conversion of import barriers into gradually reducing tariffs, an approach opposed by the EC but signifying some movement from previous positions. Washington continued to push for greater protection of intellectual property rights through patents and similar measures. This continued to be opposed by the more powerful less developed countries, but there were signs of a willingness to discuss the issues. Closely connected with the less developed countries' position was the liberalization of trade in textiles, where U.S. import restrictions were under heavy fire. On the question of antidumping regulations, the main issue was the EC practice, which was regarded as unfair by both the U.S. and Japan.

The year 1989 saw no fundamental change in world trade and payments balances. There was, however, an increase in the combined deficit of the developed countries from around $55 billion in 1988 to an estimated $77 billion in 1989. This was largely accounted for by a deterioration in the trade balances of Canada, Italy, and the U.K. Despite the higher interest rates designed to curb private consumption in the U.K., a relatively strong import growth resulted in a 20% rise in that country's deficit to $31 billion. There was also a marked rise in the deficits of the smaller developed economies from $12 billion to a total of $18 billion.

The huge U.S. adverse balance, which recorded a sizable reduction in 1988, remained broadly unchanged at $125 billion. This was offset by the persistent surplus earned by West Germany and Japan. In Japan this surplus declined from $80 billion to $72 billion, but West Germany saw an increase from $49 billion in 1988 to $54 billion. The existence of these large imbalances continued to cause concern, although there was widespread confidence that the international financial system was robust enough to manage any attendant instability. A note of confidence was also fostered by the ability of the less developed countries to control their deficits. Despite a slowdown in the growth of exports, their combined foreign payments shortfall was thought to have remained broadly unchanged at around $9 billion, and some estimates even suggested that there had been a modest decline.

On the foreign exchange front, the year was dominated by the onward march of the dollar, which—despite the persistence of the huge U.S. current account deficit—saw a strong appreciation against most other currencies. By late November 1989, the trade-weighted average value of the U.S. currency was some 6% higher than at the end of 1988, despite large-scale intervention by the bigger central banks in an attempt to prop up other currencies. The dollar performed particularly strongly against the British pound sterling (up by 14% between December 1988 and November 1989), which was also subject to pressure through rising inflation and other domestic economic developments. Against the Japanese yen the dollar saw a gain of 11% to

November 1989, largely because of interest rate differentials. The West German Deutsche Mark lost some 4% of its dollar value by September but regained all of this and more as a result of the optimism generated by the fall of the East German regime in October.

Much of the increase in the dollar was concentrated in the first eight months of the year. By late 1989 interest rate differentials had narrowed somewhat, and there was a growing realization that the loss of export competitiveness inherent in the strength of the dollar was likely to result in a serious rise in the already large U.S. balance of payments deficit. The result of these developments was to weaken support for the dollar; between August and November its effective rate lost 3.5%.

The problem of world debt remained a key feature of the international financial scene but was judged to be less of a problem than in previous years. On balance, debtor countries reduced their borrowings, which (together with various debt-reducing schemes) combined to cause a small reduction in total outstanding debt both in 1988 and in 1989. The major initiative was the plan launched by Nicholas Brady, the U.S. treasury secretary, in March. Brady recommended that commercial banks write off some existing debt and extend new loans in order to enable approved economic reforms to be implemented by debtor countries. While most commercial banks could see little difficulty with writing off some debts (this involved little more than facing reality), there was considerable reluctance to provide new credits. Nevertheless, after considerable effort a new package was put together for Mexico involving both public and commercial lenders. This provided for the acceptance of Mexican bonds against existing debt discounted by 35%, arrangements for reducing interest charges, and/or the granting of fresh loans. However, there seemed to be little enthusiasm for further schemes along these lines. The broad consensus was that while commercial lenders would be forced to write off more debt, a significant increase in new lending was unlikely.   (IEIS)

This article updates the *Macropædia* articles BANKS AND BANKING; ECONOMIC GROWTH AND PLANNING; GOVERNMENT FINANCE; INTERNATIONAL TRADE.

STOCK EXCHANGES

The world's major stock exchanges suffered a nasty jolt in October 1989, when New York's Dow Jones industrial average (DJIA) fell by 7% in two hours on Friday the 13th. A repeat of "Black Monday," Oct. 19, 1987, was feared. This time, however, a nervous calm returned quickly as the markets were reassured by the determination of the authorities to inject liquidity to avert another crash. Sentiment was also helped when it became clear that the immediate cause of the drop, the failure to raise $7.2 billion to finance a management buy-out of UAL Corp., did not mean the banks had closed the door on all buy-out bids. Rather, the UAL deal was correctly perceived as a particularly risky one, coming at a time when the New York market had been overbuoyed by highly leveraged buy-outs (LBOs) dependent on "junk" bonds (high-risk, high-yield debt).

With few exceptions, the October "minicrash" marked a turning point. Despite a subsequent hesitant recovery, many stock exchanges closed the year below their late summer-early autumn peaks but still 15–20% higher than their opening values at the beginning of the year (TABLE X).

Fixed-income securities, on the other hand, moved in the opposite direction to equities in response to higher interest rates worldwide. Commodity prices fell (in dollar terms), despite much higher oil prices and a sharp recovery in the price of gold during November.   (IEIS)

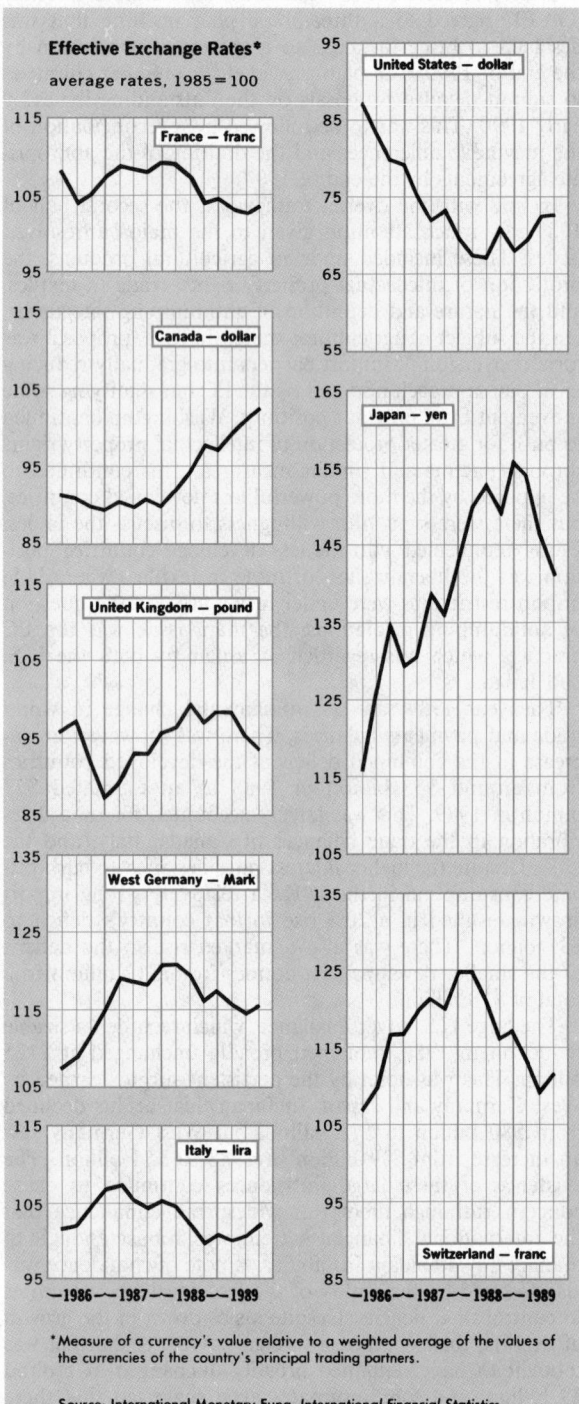

Effective Exchange Rates*

average rates, 1985 = 100

France — franc

Canada — dollar

United Kingdom — pound

West Germany — Mark

Italy — lira

United States — dollar

Japan — yen

Switzerland — franc

— 1986 — 1987 — 1988 — 1989

*Measure of a currency's value relative to a weighted average of the values of the currencies of the country's principal trading partners.

Source: International Monetary Fund, *International Financial Statistics.*

United States. The stock market rose strongly in 1989, despite persistent expectations of an early recession and the financial and psychological effects of the 190.58-point plunge on October 13. The DJIA made a full recovery from the shock of the 1987 crash. From a level of 2163.21 on the first trading day of 1989, the DJIA rose above 2700 in August for the first time in nearly two years, and it achieved a record high of 2754.56 on October 4. On the first trading day after the October minicrash, the market had its biggest one-day gain of the year, rising 88.12 points to close at 2657.38. By year's end the DJIA closed at 2753.20.

Program trading, usually identified with index arbitrage (trading based on price disparities between stocks, futures, and options), was blamed for much of the market's volatility, and a number of firms stopped it temporarily. After the October 13 plunge, program trading fell off.

The U.S. equity market was supported in 1989 by strong domestic and foreign demand. The dollar's bullish trend and the decline in interest rates were regarded as positive factors. The supply of stocks based on new stock sales, minus shares retired in mergers, LBOs, and stock buy-back programs, declined by about $100 billion. In 1988 the decline had been estimated at $122 billion. Weak corporate profits and fears of recession were bearish factors.

Institutional investors, pension funds, insurance companies, mutual funds, endowments, and other large investors, with almost $6 trillion under management, accounted for at least 60% of trades on the New York Stock Exchange (NYSE) and were responsible for much of the rise in volume. Turmoil in the junk-bond market showed no signs of easing. Prices on the more speculative bonds fell by more than 20%.

Economic growth slowed during 1989 as a result of the Fed's tight credit policy, which did not ease up until the end of the year. This helped control inflation, but it contributed to an erosion of corporate profits and to depressed bond prices. Corporate profits from current production declined quarter by quarter throughout the year. The prime rate was fixed at 10.5% throughout most of the year, although most other interest rates declined. GNP was estimated at an annual rate of $4,162,900,000,000, contrasted with $4,029,200,000,000 the previous year. Unemployment remained steady at 5.3%. Concerns about the vulnerability of the U.S. to a recession were based on the restrictive monetary policy, a flat to inverted yield curve, lower industrial commodity prices, a decrease in corporate net cash flow, increases in initial unemployment insurance claims, and declining sales of automobiles, houses, and other durable goods.

Wall Street's economics were changing rapidly in 1989 as employment in the securities industry continued to fall and the industry became more competitive, with increased emphasis on productivity and computerization. More than 5,000 workers were terminated during the year as securities firms struggled to improve the profitability of their retail brokerage business. While corporations issued a record $307.7 billion in domestic securities, an 11.9% increase over the $274.9 billion of 1988, most of the new issues were debt instruments. Equity issues dropped in 1989 to $30.8 billion, down 17% from 1988's $37.2 billion. Junk-bond prices plunged late in the year as issuers began to have problems.

The major securities firms increased their equity capital in order to compete effectively on a global level. The five largest securities firms ranked by equity capital were: Salomon Brothers, Inc. ($3,630,000,000), Merrill Lynch & Co. ($3,550,000,000), Shearson Lehman Hutton, Inc.

($2,010,000,000), Goldman, Sachs & Co. ($1,880,000,000), and Morgan Stanley & Co. ($1,860,000,000). The securities industry stopped fighting to preserve the 1933 Glass-Steagall Act's prohibition of the sale of corporate stocks and bonds to individuals by banks.

Merger and acquisition activity slowed down in 1989 because of the inability of buyers to complete a number of major financing deals. The general disfavour with which junk bonds were viewed made it difficult to raise the necessary capital. The biggest deal of the year was the completion of the acquisition of RJR Nabisco, Inc., by Kohlberg Kravis Roberts & Co., at a cost of $30.6 billion. During the year Time, Inc., and Warner Communications, Inc., agreed to combine, creating the world's biggest communications company.

Initial public offerings (IPOs) declined in 1989 both in number (245) and in value ($13,820,000,000). Merrill Lynch remained the nation's top underwriter of new stock and bond issues, with $45.4 billion (14.7%) of the $307.7 billion in debt and equity brought to market during the year. Goldman, Sachs ranked second with $41.9 billion, followed by First Boston Corp. in third place with $37.7 billion. Salomon Brothers, which had dominated the market through most of the 1980s, underwrote only $32 billion (10.4%) in 1989, while Morgan Stanley came in fifth with $28.8 billion.

Total share volume on the NYSE in 1989 was 41,-698,538,270, an increase of 3.1% over the 40,438,346,358 turnover of the previous year but well below the 1987 figure of 47,801,308,660. Total issues in 1989 were 2,279, compared with 2,263 in 1988. On the Big Board 1,565 issues advanced, 694 declined, and 20 remained unchanged for the year. The most active issues in terms of number of shares traded were AT&T, 462,065,100; IBM, 402,332,600; General Electric, 357,628,700; Exxon, 336,198,500; and Union Carbide, 316,854,100. Bond trading volume was $8,836,374,000, up 14.7% from the 1988 level of $7,702,-393,000. A seat on the NYSE sold for $420,000, the lowest price in four years. The record price of $1,150,000 had been set on Sept. 27, 1987. Seven seats were sold that year at prices of more than $1 million, but prices plunged after the crash.

The Big Board launched a major public information campaign aimed at the 47 million Americans who directly owned stocks or shares in stock mutual funds. A blue-ribbon panel was established to determine long-term public and private initiatives needed to control excess volatility of security prices. Member firms were asked to refrain from executing program trades for their own accounts and to request that their customers refrain from such trades whenever they would disrupt the market. The NYSE also began publishing weekly program trading statistics and initiated the Individual Investor Express Delivery System, which allowed individual orders to come into the market at any time and go to the head of the line, in front of program trades and other institutional orders. On October 16, when the Big Board handled a volume of more than 416 million shares, 96,000 individual orders took that fast lane. On October 26 the Big Board launched its own program trading plan. The new "baskets" of stocks allowed big investors to buy or sell all 500 stocks in the Standard & Poor's (S&P) Index in a single trade.

Volume on the American Stock Exchange (Amex) in 1989 was 3,125,030,000 shares, an increase of 24.2% over the 2,515,210,000 traded in 1988. The number of issues traded fell from 1,095 in 1988 to 1,059 in 1989. In all, 610 issues advanced, 425 declined, and 24 were unchanged.

(continued on page 193)

Consequences of Economic Austerity: Latin America and the Less Developed World

BY HOWARD HANDELMAN

During the past decade, Latin America endured the most intense economic suffering since the Great Depression of the 1930s. That deprivation has continued, largely unabated, during 1989. In Africa nations such as Côte d'Ivoire, Ghana, Nigeria, Zaire, and Zambia have also experienced sharp drops in their already-low standards of living. The picture for much of Asia during the 1980s has been brighter, with Indonesia, Hong Kong, Singapore, South Korea, and Taiwan enjoying robust economic growth. Elsewhere on that continent, however, countries such as the Philippines have also suffered a severe economic downturn.

Origins of the Debt Crisis. Ironically, the roots of the current crisis can be found in policies that contributed to considerable economic growth in the 1970s. At that time many Third World governments undertook state programs that severely strained their nations' economic resources, particularly in Latin America, where domestic rates of savings were much lower than in Asia. Throughout Africa and Latin America, governments frequently spent heavily on military purchases, economic-development projects, and consumer subsidies that reduced the prices of food, transportation, and energy. State bureaucracies also grew precipitously. Unable or unwilling to generate sufficient tax revenues to finance these programs, governments borrowed abroad from private commercial banks or from international lending agencies.

The low interest rates prevailing at that time and the large influx of petrodollars into the world banking system made borrowing relatively easy. Many Third World countries were also enjoying an export boom that convinced both their governments and lending institutions that they had sufficient resources to repay their loans. By the early 1980s the less developed world (outside of the Middle Eastern petroleum-exporting nations) had an external debt of over $700 billion. More than half of that amount was owed by the nations of Latin America. While the debts of sub-Saharan Africa were far smaller on an absolute basis, they frequently represented a higher proportion of the nations' gross national products (GNP). Some Asian nations also borrowed heavily. For the most part, however, Asian economies had sufficiently high export and savings levels to accommodate their borrowing.

Howard Handelman is professor and chairman of the department of political science, University of Wisconsin at Milwaukee. He is coeditor of Paying the Costs of Austerity in Latin America.

In much of Latin America, borrowing contributed to impressive economic growth during the 1970s. The region's GNP expanded at an average annual rate of 6%. To be sure, benefits tended to be distributed quite inequitably, as the urban middle and upper classes profited disproportionately. Some economic gains, however, did "trickle down" to the lower strata of society. Development projects, state enterprises, and expanded bureaucracies created employment, while government subsidies provided cheap food and transportation for the urban population.

Unfortunately, both the debtor nations and the lending institutions too frequently assumed that the favourable economic conditions that prevailed for most of the 1970s would continue into the future. By the end of the decade, however, a number of factors had adversely affected Third World debtors. Rising petroleum prices contributed to an economic recession in Europe and North America. Industrialized nations, in turn, sharply reduced imports of raw materials from the less developed world. Moreover, precisely when Third World countries were least able to finance their debts through exports, soaring interest rates greatly inflated the debt payments of countries that had borrowed from commercial banks at variable interest rates. Finally, less developed countries that imported petroleum faced increased import bills. Petroleum exporters, such as Mexico, Venezuela, and Nigeria, initially benefited from rising oil prices and continued to borrow heavily in anticipation of ever expanding export revenues. When petroleum prices fell sharply in the early 1980s, however, they, too, underwent a severe economic downturn. In 1982 Mexico announced that it was temporarily unable to pay the interest on its loans. Thereafter, commercial banks ceased offering Latin America credit, and the region entered into a decade-long debt crisis. Many African nations and selected Asian countries have experienced similar difficulties.

Since that time, Latin-American and African nations seeking further credit from the International Monetary Fund (IMF) or commercial banks have generally been required to undertake structural adjustment and stabilization policies. The purpose of such austerity programs is to reduce budget and balance of payments deficits so as to facilitate repayment of external debts. While adjustment and stabilization programs have sometimes achieved those goals, they constitute harsh economic medicine that brings great hardship upon much of the population.

The Human Costs of Economic Austerity Programs. Because orthodox austerity programs seek to reduce large government budget deficits, they usually involve sharp reductions in state subsidies for food, transportation, and other basic consumer needs. As a consequence, the prices of items such as bread, milk, rice, and cooking oil often rise substantially. The cost of living may be increased further by devaluation of the nation's currency. While designed to make the country's exports more competitive abroad, devaluation also increases the cost of imported machinery and raw materials needed for local manufacturing. Ironically, then, although the long-term objective of stabilization programs is to reduce inflation, they often create immediate price increases for basic consumer items needed by the poor.

Working-class standards of living are further eroded by government wage restraints that prevent incomes from keeping pace with the rising cost of living. While most Latin-American governments have introduced austerity packages since the early 1980s, few have brought prices under control. In 1989 Argentina, Brazil, Peru, and Nicaragua faced inflation rates of more than 1,000%.

There, and in many other Latin-American nations, workers' purchasing power has fallen some 20–50% since the start of the decade. Thus, a Mexican labourer who needed to work 45 minutes in 1982 in order to purchase a pound of chicken had to work 3.5 hours in 1989. As the real income of the lower class has deteriorated, nutritional levels have declined correspondingly. From 1977 to 1987 per capita beef consumption dropped by nearly 50% in Brazil. In Argentina, traditionally one of the less developed world's most affluent countries, many of the poor must now depend on soup kitchens, as runaway inflation, likely to reach 12,000% in 1989, led to hourly increases in food prices. Rampant inflation in several African nations has forced many of the urban poor to return to the countryside in order to engage in subsistence agriculture.

Because austerity produces an economic slowdown, urban unemployment also rises. From 1980 to 1984 joblessness increased by 50% in Chile and nearly doubled in Bolivia, Uruguay, and Venezuela. With few exceptions, unemployment rates have remained high since that time. In the absence of government welfare programs, many of the urban poor have moved into the "informal" sector of the urban economy, working as street vendors, day labourers, and the like. While such self-employment partially alleviates the deprivations of austerity, it is normally not financially rewarding. During the early 1980s an estimated 63% of Brazilian workers in the informal sector earned less than the equivalent of the legal minimum wage. Women and children are most likely to be employed in the informal economy. Consequently, school enrollments in countries such as Bolivia and Mexico have declined significantly in recent years.

Changes in internal and external migration patterns have also tended to mitigate the effects of austerity. In countries such as Colombia, Brazil, and Mexico, deteriorations in urban living conditions seem to have reduced the rate of rural-to-urban migration. At the same time, there has been a sharp increase in emigration (much of it illegal) from the Andean nations, Central America, and Mexico to the United States. In the short term, such emigration reduces economic strains at home and leads to the repatriation of funds from emigrant workers back to their families in Latin America. However, in countries such as Peru the long-run consequences may be very harmful, stripping the nation of some of its most talented young professionals and workers.

The Political Consequences of Austerity. Until this point, there have been surprisingly few negative political ramifications from the heavy economic costs of austerity. Most certainly the debt crisis has placed great strain on recently installed democracies in Latin America and the Philippines. Contrary to the expectations of many knowledgeable observers, however, those regimes have retained sufficient legitimacy and popular support to remain in power.

Orthodox austerity programs, however, have been associated with significant outbreaks of popular unrest in the past year. In February 1989 rising prices and the Venezuelan government's negotiations with the IMF on further austerity policies led to nationwide riots, in which some 250 people were killed and perhaps 2,000 wounded. Argentina also experienced major food riots during the past year. In Brazil deteriorating economic conditions led to the first nationwide strike in 30 years. Thus, unless a way can be found to alleviate the economic suffering brought on by austerity measures, further unrest and political instability may loom on the horizon.

(continued from page 191)

BAT Industries, a takeover target during the year, was the most active stock, with 173,681,600 shares traded. Bond trading on the Amex in 1989 was $708,836,000, up 17.4% from the $603,882,000 level of 1988.

Volume on the over-the-counter (OTC) market climbed by 7.9% to 33,303,859,005 shares, up from 31,070,000,000 in 1988. The National Association of Securities Dealers automated quotation (Nasdaq) composite index gained 15%. Of the 4,361 issues traded on the Nasdaq market, 1,737 advanced, 1,049 declined, and 1,575 were unchanged. High-technology companies were once again the most actively traded Nasdaq stocks, led by MCI Communication, with 485,377,200 shares changing hands, and Apple Computer, with 454,560,200 shares traded. In general, blue-chip stocks outperformed OTC stocks, especially in the second half of the year.

Assets of all mutual funds posted records in 1989 and probably exceeded $1 trillion, with money market funds accounting for about $366,010,000,000. Sales exceeded redemptions by increasing margins as the year wore on. In November 1989 mutual fund sales were $5,060,000,000, as contrasted with a $479 million outflow in November 1988, when redemptions exceeded sales.

The S&P 500 gained 31.64% for the year, assuming that dividends were invested. The composite index (TABLE XI) started the year at 285.41, progressed to a peak of 347.37 in October, and recovered from the minicrash to close the year at 353.40. The best performing industries were oil and gas drilling (up 79.4%), entertainment (65%), long distance telecommunications (63.7%), soft-drink beverages (62.9%), and hospital management (59%). The worst performers were machine tools (down 26.2%), computer systems (19.8%), electronic instrumentation (12.8%), miscellaneous transportation (10.8%), heavy duty trucks and parts (9.2%), and automobiles (8.2%). The index of 400 industrials started the year at 330.17 and peaked in September at 397.08, recording a gain of 20.2% before falling back in October. By year's end the S&P industrials index had reached 403.38 in a recovery from the October shock. Public utility stocks rose 25.3% from January through November, starting the year at 114.37 and closing at 156.34. Financial stocks also recorded significant gains. From a level of 25.51 in January, the index rose 27.3% by November to close the year at 31.30. The transportation index climbed 24.7% between the first of the year and October and reached a record high.

U.S. government long-term bond yields (TABLE XII) were at an average level of 9.07% in January and rose to 9.33% in March (their high for the year) before dropping to 8.95% in May and 8.15% in October. During the first four months of 1989, government bond yields were above 1988 levels, but they declined well below year-earlier levels by midyear. The 90-day treasury bill yield was 8% at year's end, down from 8.5% in 1988.

Triple A corporate bond yields were down 7.7% on a year-to-year basis in December 1989. From a level of 9.62% in January (TABLE XIII), the yield climbed to 9.8% in March and declined to 8.93% in July. After a modest recovery in August–September, the yield fell again until the end of the year. Junk-bond yields rose as a result of a combination of falling prices and substantial selling by institutions.

The options markets suffered from adverse publicity in 1989. In January Chicago's futures pits became the target of a major federal investigation that resulted in the indictment of 46 traders and brokers on charges of cheating customers, dodging taxes, and manipulating prices. In

May federal investigators visited the major commodity exchanges in New York City, seized records, and issued subpoenas as part of an inquiry into possible criminal and civil violations.

The Chicago Board of Trade took steps to tighten its regulatory procedures and reduce market volatility. It tightened the "circuit breakers" for its stock index futures contract on the major market index. (The "circuit breaker" was a halt on trading at lower prices for periods of half an hour to an hour or more to permit investors to reappraise market conditions.) The maximum amount of movement allowable each day was narrowed from 80 to 50 points. The major market index was based on 20 stocks and was intended to emulate the DJIA. The Commodity Futures Trading Commission approved new exchange rules governing a 20-point decline. After a 20-point decline, trading below that level had to be stopped for 30 minutes.

The Securities and Exchange Commission (SEC) was very active in the prosecution of insider-trading cases in 1989. The conviction of Drexel Burnham Lambert, Inc., one of the largest broker dealers in the U.S., on six felony counts carrying a $650 million fine established a major legal precedent. The indictment of Michael Milken, the "king of the junk-bond market," on charges of insider trading helped bring about that market's near collapse. The SEC was also investigating the stock loan business, in which firms lend stock to their institutional customers and to each other. Critics argued that such activities involved corruption and kickbacks. The SEC blocked the introduction of the "unbundled stock unit," a new product that attempted to divide a share of common stock into a bond, a share of preferred stock, and a warrant.

Canada. Prices on Canadian stock markets rose substantially in 1989 but lagged behind U.S. markets because of a rising Canadian dollar. The Canadian dollar strengthened to a 10-year high in 1989 as a result of the Bank of Canada's relatively tight monetary policy. Short-term interest rates were pushed above 12%, more than four percentage points above U.S. rates. The high rates caused the Canadian dollar to go from a low of 82.76 cents per U.S. dollar to a high of 86.24 cents on December 28. The stronger Canadian currency hurt profits and share prices of natural-resources companies, whose products were priced in U.S. dollars and who relied on exports.

Trading volume on the Canadian exchanges during the first nine months of 1989 were: Toronto 4,813,100,000 shares, representing 49.6% of the total traded; Vancouver 3,091,900,000 (31.9%); Montreal 1,240,300,000 (12.8%); and Alberta 557.4 million (5.7%). In value terms, the Toronto Stock Exchange led with $62,494,800,000 (76.5% of the total), and the Montreal exchange accounted for $15,582,000,000 (19.1%).

For the year as a whole, trading on the Toronto exchange rose by 37.6% with a total volume of 6,520,000,000 shares, up from 4,740,000,000 shares in 1988. The broadly based 300-stock composite index rose 17% to 3969.79, despite the severe decline on October 13. Gold mining led the industry groups, even though the price of gold gained just 3% to $401 per ounce during the year. Among the leading stocks in terms of year-to-year gains in 1989 were Laidlaw Transportation (up 52.5%), Placer Dome (34.1%), Royal Bank (32.5%), BCE, Inc. (22.5%), and Canadian Pacific (17%).

The Canadian securities exchanges witnessed above-average takeover activity, including the purchase of Texaco Canada, Inc., by Imperial Oil, Ltd., a subsidiary of Exxon Corp. Other major takeovers during the year included the purchase of Consolidated-Bathurst, Inc., by

Stone Container Corp., Institut Merieux S.A.'s acquisition of Connaught Biosciences, Inc., and the purchase of Falconbridge, Ltd. by Noranda, Inc., and Sweden's Trelleborg AB. Campeau Corp., formerly an aggressive investor in mergers and acquisitions, suffered severe losses because of debt problems associated with its previous purchases of Allied Stores Corp. and Federated Department Stores, Inc. Campeau's stock price fell from a high of $22.50 to a close of $3.65, and the company appeared to be moving toward bankruptcy.

(IRVING PFEFFER)

Table X. Selected Major World Stock Price Indexes*

Country	1989 range† High	Low	Year-end close	Percent change from 12/31/88
Australia	1782	1413	1649	+11
Austria	515	220	493	+125
Belgium	6805	5519	6476	+16
Canada	4038	3351	3970	+17
Denmark	363	275	363	+34
Finland	816	581	609	−17
France	562	418	554	+33
West Germany	741	536	741	+35
Hong Kong	3310	2094	2837	+6
Italy	735	577	687	+16
Japan	38,916	30,184	38,916	+29
Netherlands, The	211	167	203	+22
Norway	696	467	687	+47
Singapore	1488	1031	1481	+43
South Africa	2838	1961	2790	+44
Spain	329	269	297	+9
Sweden	4660	3334	4275	+23
Switzerland	829	613	761	+26
United Kingdom	2426	1783	2423	+35
United States	2791	2145	2753	+27

*Index numbers are rounded.
†Based on daily closing price.
Source: *The Financial Times.*

Table XI. U.S. Stock Market Prices

Month	Transportation (20 stocks) 1989	1988	Public utilities (40 stocks) 1989	1988	Industrials (400 stocks) 1989	1988	Composite (500 stocks) 1989	1988
January	114.37	106.13	114.37	106.13	330.17	288.36	285.41	250.48
February	116.88	110.67	116.88	110.67	339.70	296.46	294.01	258.13
March	116.65	107.24	116.65	107.24	337.74	308.04	292.71	265.74
April	119.91	104.12	119.91	104.12	348.47	305.78	302.25	262.61
May	127.74	103.11	127.74	103.11	360.88	297.39	313.93	256.12
June	133.50	109.86	133.50	109.86	370.36	312.78	323.73	270.68
July	137.22	108.49	137.22	108.49	379.45	310.87	331.92	269.05
August	140.47	107.89	140.47	107.89	396.63	303.12	346.61	263.73
September	140.98	109.67	140.98	109.67	397.08	307.40	347.33	267.97
October	142.71	113.00	142.71	113.00	396.34	319.05	347.37	277.40
November	...	111.70	143.37	111.70	388.11	311.84	340.22	271.02
December	...	113.02	...	113.02	...	319.07	...	281.28

Sources: U.S. Department of Commerce, *Survey of Current Business;* Board of Governors of the Federal Reserve System, *Federal Reserve Bulletin.* Prices are Standard & Poor's monthly averages of daily closing prices, with 1941–43 = 10.

Table XII. U.S. Government Long-Term Bond Yields

Month	Yield (%) 1989	1988	Month	Yield (%) 1989	1988
January	9.07	8.82	July	8.19	9.20
February	9.16	8.41	August	8.26	9.33
March	9.33	8.61	September	8.31	9.06
April	9.18	8.91	October	8.15	8.89
May	8.95	9.24	November	...	9.07
June	8.40	9.04	December	...	9.13

Source: U.S. Department of Commerce, *Survey of Current Business.* Yields are for U.S. Treasury bonds that are taxable and due or callable in ten years or more.

Table XIII. U.S. Corporate Bond Yields

Month	Yield (%) 1989	1988	Month	Yield (%) 1989	1988
January	9.62	9.88	July	8.93	9.96
February	9.64	9.40	August	8.96	10.11
March	9.80	9.39	September	9.01	9.82
April	9.79	9.67	October	8.92	9.51
May	9.57	9.90	November	...	9.45
June	9.10	9.86	December	...	9.57

Source: U.S. Department of Commerce, *Survey of Current Business.* Yields are based on Moody's Aaa domestic corporate bond index.

Western Europe. Stock markets in Europe closely tracked Wall Street with few exceptions. This meant a steady increase during the first 10 months and a sharp correction in mid-October, followed by a hesitant recovery. An overall gain of around 17% from the beginning of the year provided investors with another year of above-inflation returns. The best performers in Europe included the London and Paris stock exchanges with 24% and 25% gains, respectively. Madrid, with an 8% increase, was the only European bourse with a single-digit increase, and the Finnish market recorded an outright fall.

London, having seriously lagged behind the other European markets during 1988, sprang to life as the year drew to a close and increased by 16% during the first two months of 1989. The winter rally was sparked by several factors, particularly the resilience of the economy (in spite of higher interest rates) and the encouraging outlook for corporate profitability. A series of takeovers encouraged institutional investors to reevaluate the market and commit new funds.

The steep rise, exaggerated by a shortage of stock, continued unchecked until the March budget, which was marginally tighter than expected. The market then consolidated, with the *Financial Times*-Stock Exchange 100 (FT-SE 100) Index fluctuating in a narrow range between 2050 and 2150. A series of megatakeovers, including the £4.7 billion merger of SmithKline Beckman Corp. and the Beecham Group, Hanson Trust's £3.5 billion takeover of Consolidated Goldfields, and Isosceles' £2.1 billion bid for

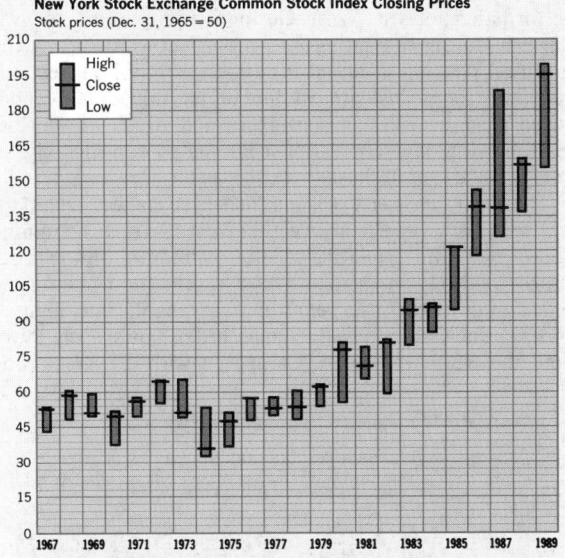

New York Stock Exchange Common Stock Index Closing Prices
Stock prices (Dec. 31, 1965 = 50)

Number of shares sold
In millions of shares

Sources: New York Stock Exchange; Barron's National Business and Financial Weekly; The Wall Street Journal.

Gateway Corp., underpinned the market and enabled it to shrug off the deteriorating economic fundamentals and rising interest rates. Another powerful rally developed during the long, hot summer as the London market, electrified by the audacious £13 billion bid for BAT Industries by Sir James Goldsmith (*see* BIOGRAPHIES), joined the Wall Street and the continental European rallies, which were also partly driven by takeovers.

At the end of August, the FT-SE 100 Index moved above the pre-October 1987 level and was within a whisker of the all-time high. The bubble burst in early October, however, when, a week before the ruling Conservative Party's annual conference, a full-blown sterling crisis forced a politically embarrassing 1% rise in interest rates. The 70-point net decline on Monday, October 16, mirroring Wall Street's plunge, and the subsequent recovery represented a minor blip in comparison with the 200-point retreat suffered after the October 5 interest rate rise. Although the economic outlook remained highly uncertain in late November–early December, the FT-SE 100 Index consolidated around the 2200 level. The market took the bombshell of the resignation of the chancellor of the Exchequer, Nigel Lawson, his subsequent replacement by John Major (*see* BIOGRAPHIES), and the good news of a better-than-expected trade deficit in its stride. The successful flotation of the water privatization bounced the London market to a higher level, and the FT-SE 100 ended the year above the 2400 level.

The Paris Bourse, having entered 1989 on a strong note, lost momentum, and by the end of February it had fallen below the opening level. It then rose steadily until the October 16 drop. Strong economic fundamentals (forecast 3.5% economic growth, strong consumer spending, investment growth, and a boost to exports) were supported by other favourable factors. Chief among these were exceptionally high earnings reported by some French companies in the first half of the year. LVMH's earnings were up 60%, while Matra's rose 88%, Pechiney's were up 69%, and earnings at CCF increased 38%.

By the summer the Paris Bourse had risen by nearly 20% and the CAC General Index reached the 500 level for the first time. It no longer looked cheap, considering the 40% gain registered the previous year, but it took heart from a fall in U.S. interest rates and demand from domestic and international investors, who were anticipating further potential from continuing restructuring before the emergence of the single European market in 1992. Major deals, such as Suez's F 27 billion acquisition of Victoire and Paribas' F 22.5 billion bid for Navigation Mixte, encouraged the investors and speculators to play the "spot the next bid target" game. They were not disappointed. In early October a new record high of 561.6 for the CAC Index was established, well above the precrash level of 370 regained at the end of 1988. Higher interest rates on October 5, in line with similar moves elsewhere in Europe, followed by the sharp decline on October 16, unnerved investors, who began to question the lack of strong underpinning from economic fundamentals. In the absence of further short-term growth potential, the Paris Bourse looked vulnerable, but it resisted the downward pressure to show a 28% gain and finish the year at 553.7.

West German stock markets underperformed their counterparts in France, despite stronger economic fundamentals. After a shaky start, which saw the FAZ Aktien Index fall below the opening level, the market recovered its poise as the government's GNP forecast of 2.5% was revised to 3.5%. At the same time, corporate profitability growth remained robust as export markets grew rapidly and capacity utilization approached the all-time high.

The flow of positive news enabled the West German markets to ride out the turbulence caused by the unexpected half-a-percentage-point rise in interest rates in April and again in June. Investors appeared to be convinced that the preemptive moves by the Bundesbank would contain the inflationary pressures, so a powerful summer rally developed, taking the FAZ Index to a peak of 670 in late August with a few minor corrections on the way up—a gain of 20% in just over three months. The prospects of a slowdown in the U.S., continuing high interest rates in the U.K., and a frothy Paris Bourse attracted overseas money to West German equities, pushing the FAZ Index to 692 in October. Consequently, when the minicrash occurred, the FAZ Index plunged by 13%, more than any other market, as investors took fright. They could no longer ignore bad news, such as the doubling of the inflation rate from 1.6% in 1988 to 3.2%, a money supply that was growing outside the target ranges, and the prospects of higher interest rates. The subsequent nervous recovery provided selling opportunities to many international investors, who were subsequently wrong footed by the bewildering speed of developments in East Germany that culminated in the opening of the Berlin Wall. Frankfurt's FAZ Index raced up by 6% in two days before pausing for breath. This brought the market within 40 points of the October peak, and the subsequent runup took the FAZ Index to a record 740.93 at year's end.

The smaller stock exchanges continued to benefit from the search by investors for undervalued situations and for potential beneficiaries from the approaching single market. The Vienna Bourse was the star performer, with a 92% increase seen in the Credit Aktien Index. This was a classic case of "discovery" by foreign investors pushing up a small, illiquid market to dizzying heights. By early October the Austrian market was 135% above January 1989 levels, and

not surprisingly it fell heavily in October. Further profit taking by investors during the subsequent recovery sent the Credit Aktien Index tumbling to around 400 from the autumn peak of 515, but it recovered to end the year at 493.07.

The Benelux countries were comparatively dull during 1989. Belgium, which was the scene of much takeover speculation activity in 1988, experienced an uneventful year tracking Wall Street. After a quiet first three months, reflecting restricted headroom, a late summer rally developed on the basis of the sound economic performance. By late September the Brussels Bourse Index had risen by 23% to 6805. It was swept up by the worldwide boom in stock exchanges. The October drop of 4.5%, while not out of line with other markets, generated so much volume that the bourse's computer system broke down. Despite some recovery, the Belgian market ended the year with a 16% gain at 6476.39, but it appeared to lack direction.

The Netherlands' performance was not dissimilar. Stronger economic growth (4% compared with 3% in 1988) was led by exports and business investments and the region's lowest rate of inflation (about 1%). This made The Netherlands an attractive destination for investors. The Amsterdam Stock Exchange rose steadily during the year, and the CBS General All Share Index reached an all-time high of 210.5 after the September general election. By early October it was 24% higher than at the beginning of the year. The General Index plunged on October 16, in line with the other stock exchanges, but at year's end it was 25% higher at 202.8.

The Swiss Bank General Index, mirroring the hesitant performance of the West German equity markets, was sluggish during the spring and moved upward during the summer, peaking at an all-time high of 829.1 in September. The Index lost almost 9% of its value on October 16 to close at 734.2, but it recovered much of the loss the following day. Thereafter it fluctuated considerably, to finish the year at 760.6.

The Scandinavian stock markets were mixed. Denmark was seen as a beneficiary of the West German economic boom and, with a relatively better economic outlook, declined modestly in October. As a result, the Copenhagen Index approached the year's end at an all-time high of 363.22. The Oslo Stock Exchange Index was slightly lower than the September peak, compared with an 8% decline

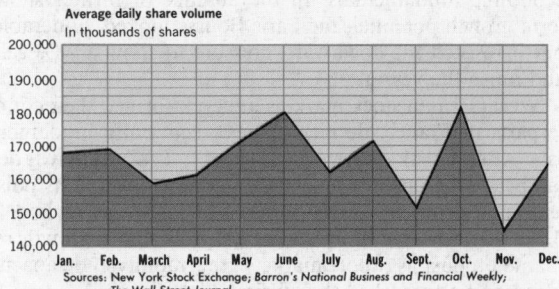

New York Stock Exchange Composite Index, 1989
Stock prices (Dec. 31, 1965 = 50)

Average daily share volume
In thousands of shares

Sources: New York Stock Exchange; Barron's National Business and Financial Weekly; The Wall Street Journal.

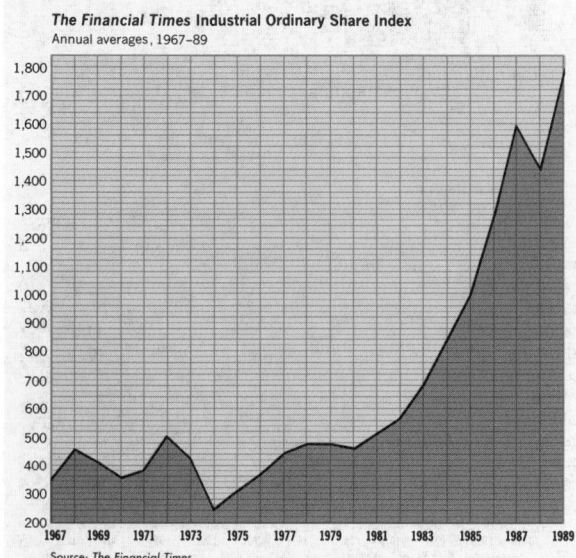

The Financial Times **Industrial Ordinary Share Index**
Annual averages, 1967–89

Source: The Financial Times.

from the August peak for the Jacobson & Ponsback Industrial Index in Sweden. Finland was the odd one out with an outright decline of 17% since the beginning of the year. The market got off to a promising start, and the Unitas General Index, which started the year at 727, peaked at 815.8 in late April. It declined gently after that but nose-dived in September as interest rates rose, the trade deficit worsened, inflation accelerated, and corporate earnings disappointed.

The other disappointing performer was Spain. A slowdown in economic growth, accelerating inflation, higher interest rates, and weak currency took the shine off the Madrid bolsa. After a sluggish start, the Madrid Stock Exchange Index gathered speed in the summer and peaked at 329 in early September, ahead of the general election, which returned Prime Minister Felipe González Márquez to office with a razor-thin majority. At its peak, the Madrid Index was up 23% above the January 1 level, but after the election-related sell-off and the October drop, the index ended the year only 8% higher than it had started.

The Italian stock market received more international investor interest during 1989 than previously, and the Banca Commerciale Italiana Index rose by 28% before peaking in September. Improving economy, moderate inflation, strong export demand, and higher corporate earnings were cited as the factors influencing the market. However, confidence dropped in the autumn and, following an 8% initial decline and the October shakeout, the Milan Stock Exchange ended the year nursing a 16.6% gain.

Other Countries. As the West's stock markets ended the year well below the autumn peaks, Tokyo once again charted a different course, and the Nikkei Average Price Index climbed to new highs. Encouraged by the strong economic fundamentals (GNP growth of 5%, strong export growth, and low inflation), buoyant corporate profitability, and the weakness of the yen against the dollar, the Tokyo stock market rose steadily during the spring. This enabled the Nikkei average to break through the 34,000 level.

Political sex scandals and worries over the defeat of the ruling Liberal-Democratic Party in the July election to the (upper) House of Councillors led to a sharp correction. The Nikkei average fell to 33,500, where it held. Political uncertainty eased with the appointment of Toshiki Kaifu as prime minister and, coupled with prospects of a nonrecession soft landing in the U.S., the Tokyo market resumed its jerky climb and almost touched 36,000. Wall Street's minicrash was barely felt in Tokyo—the market declined by around 1% to close at 34,468 before recovering swiftly. The fall of 650 points on October 16 was insignificant compared with a fall of around 400 points the previous week when interest rates were raised. Two days after the plunge the Nikkei average was above the 35,000 level. It continued upward and closed the year at a new high above 38,900.

Other Pacific Basin countries recorded strong gains during 1989. Rising commodity prices, especially for wool and gold, helped the Australian market to shrug off a 10-month downward drift and move to a new postcrash peak. Until the summer, Australian equity investments looked unattractive in view of the higher interest rates imposed by the government to cool an overheated economy. With other markets moving confidently ahead and Australia falling, the latter underperformed the world average by around 25% during the first four months of the year. Takeover activity in the early summer, coupled with a peak in interest rates, pushed Australia to join the Wall Street rally, taking the All Ordinary Index to 1781.8—a gain of 26% from the spring low. However, the market succumbed to profit taking and to further sell-off after the October minicrash. The

index declined by nearly 10% from the high and ended the year at around 1650, drifting as it was at the beginning but at a much higher trading level.

Hong Kong experienced the highest volatility among the established stock markets because of its sharp reaction to the massacre of student protesters in Beijing's (Peking's) Tiananmen (T'ien-an-men) Square on June 4. Until then the Hang Seng Index had been rising steadily and was 23% higher than the January level, reflecting sound economic fundamentals and good corporate profitability. It fell by over 30% after the Chinese Army crushed the student protests—more than two-thirds of the fall came in one day. Over the summer Hong Kong came to terms with the situation, and the markets recovered by over 20%. In the autumn the recovery ended with the Wall Street plunge, but investors were also worried about proposed legislation in China banning Hong Kong residents from antigovernment activities after 1997, when the British colony would revert to Chinese control. In the event, the October decline was not too severe, with a 6% correction that was more modest than in some regional markets. The Hang Seng Index finished the year up only about 5%. Indexes in Malaysia fell by 11.5% and in Singapore by 10% as foreign investors panicked and sold, but both recovered completely to post big gains by year's end.

Commodity Markets. Commodity prices weakened during 1989. The *Economist* commodity price index, which measured spot prices in U.S. dollars and sterling for 28 internationally traded foodstuffs, nonfood agricultural products, and metals, declined by around 14% in dollar terms from the beginning of the year. As the dollar gained strength during the year against the other currencies, the index, in sterling terms, remained unchanged.

The price of crude oil, which was not included in the *Economist* index, was volatile but upward in trend. Demand was stronger than expected, and producers in the OPEC countries exceeded their production quotas by a smaller margin than in the past. Crude oil prices rose from around $11 per barrel in January to around $16 in March. Lower output from the North Sea, due to a series of unexpected shutdowns, also played a role in the spring price rises. Following a short period of relative stability, crude oil prices declined in the summer, but the summer weakness did not last long, and the stable supply-demand relationship asserted itself. Oil prices were drifting upward toward the $19-per-barrel level as the year came to an end.

Two major sectors of the *Economist* index of dollar commodity prices declined by similar rates. The average 1989 level of the food index fell by 15%, while that of industrial raw materials declined by 14%. Within the industrial raw materials component, nonfood agricultural prices rose marginally (1.5%) but metals fell by 21%.

Gold ended a two-year period of decline by breaking through the $400 barrier in mid-November. During the spring there was no support for gold in view of rising interest rates, good economic growth, and inflation held under control. The revival in May did not last long, and the gold price traced its steps from $382 to $360 by September. The unexpected November rally was in part attributable to the events in Eastern Europe, which boosted the Deutsche Mark but depressed West German bonds. Gold-price watchers were more confident that the price would stay above the $400 level, in view of worsening global inflationary expectations and the potential demand from the Eastern European countries, where great uncertainty surrounded paper assets and higher demand was anticipated from fabricators.   (IEIS)

This article updates the *Macropædia* article MARKETS.

Education

Significant events on the education scene during 1989 included more international cooperation, greater autonomy for institutions in Eastern Europe, some altered investment patterns, efforts to increase enrollments, steps to improve the quality of education, concern for providing additional skilled education personnel, and a continuation of student political demonstrations.

Early in the year, under the auspices of the Unesco-affiliated International Bureau of Education, more than 500 educational and political leaders from 121 countries met in Geneva to identify methods of resolving difficulties in their systems of higher education. Many participants believed that postsecondary education in their countries lacked sufficient emphasis on practical vocational skills. They contended that unemployment among university graduates was due in part to the continued overenrollment of students in the humanities and underenrollment in technical fields. Delegates predicted that the future growth of higher education in most nations would take the form of alternatives to the traditional university pattern and would include such options as nondegree programs, "distance" education carried on by means of broadcast media and mail correspondence, evening and weekend classes, and work-study agreements between employers and universities. Two additional issues that were considered at the conference were the low level of funding for education in most nations of the Third World and the migration of well-educated citizens of less developed countries to the advanced industrialized nations.

There was increased cooperation across national borders in programs of instruction, research, and the exchange of students and scholars. In Western Europe plans toward unifying educational practices throughout the European Communities (EC) took a step forward when education ministers from the 12 member countries agreed on three issues related to the Community's goal of achieving a barrier-free economic market by 1992. First, technical education in all 12 countries would be divided into two cycles, one covering the last two years of high school and the other comprising specialized training for two or three years beyond high school. Second, every government would provide education for all students through age 16, thereby upgrading the current policy in Spain and Portugal, which required universal schooling through age 14. Third, in an effort to increase multilingual communication, a cooperative program called Lingua would provide financial assistance to teachers and to students aged 16 to 19 for short periods of language study in EC countries outside their own nation. The program was scheduled to begin in January 1990.

The World Bank continued major financing of educational efforts in less developed nations. Its investments moved further in the directions the Bank's commitments had taken in recent years, with less support going to diversified university vocational programs and more to basic primary education. The interest in raising the vocational content of general education that had marked the Bank's investments in the past had been abandoned. As the foundation for establishing educational programs, manpower forecasting had been replaced by labour-market analysis aimed at determining what students do after they leave school. Thus, emphasis was placed on measuring the effectiveness of educational programs in terms of student performance. As far as possible, attempts were being made to recover the cost of higher education.

Various efforts were launched to finance the rising expense of schooling. For the first time, the government of the Philippines enacted a program of financial aid to private secondary schools and colleges, primarily in the form of grants to students and faculty members. Pres. Corazon Aquino estimated that 70% of the 2.5 million students in the country's private institutions would benefit from the program. Subsidies for tuition, textbooks, scholarships, living expenses, and loans to students were included in the legislation, as well as funds for faculty development and the improvement of facilities. The Australian government, adopting a different approach toward coping with the cost of higher education, planned to consolidate many of the nation's 65 postsecondary institutions and to impose a "tuition tax" on students, thereby ending 15 years of free tertiary education.

Legislative measures to improve educational systems included the Indonesian government's new basic education law, replacing the original act of 1950. The 1989 act was far more comprehensive than the 1950 version, covering not only formal schooling but also nonformal education throughout life. It specifically outlawed discrimination in educational opportunity because of gender, ethnic status, religion, or socioeconomic condition. Mexico's new president, Carlos Salinas de Gortari, created a commission to organize a continuing national debate on educational improvement, focusing on the content, teaching methods, and structure of the education system. At the same time, Mexican educators were calling on the president to fulfill his campaign promise to increase spending on education from the current 2.7% of gross national product (GNP) to 8%.

U.S. Pres. George Bush, who had said during his campaign that he wanted to be an "education president," met with the nation's governors in September in an "education summit." Told in advance not to expect large increases in federal support, the governors discussed priorities and strategies for improving education in the U.S. Raising the level of education was widely seen as a way to regain the nation's competitive edge in the world economy. With hundreds of reporters on hand to observe the proceedings, the leaders agreed on the need for better preschool education for the poor, drug abuse prevention, dropout prevention, programs for minorities and the disadvantaged, and procedures for securing federal support. Nationwide performance goals were advocated, a break with the U.S. tradition that education is a local matter.

Shortly after his inauguration in January, President Bush outlined his education program. It included rewards for "merit schools" and outstanding teachers, programs for science and mathematics students, magnet schools to encourage better racial mixes, and flexible teacher certification to allow talented individuals to teach without having to undergo professional training. Bush resisted calls for large increases in federal support, choosing instead to fund programs that addressed specific education needs. The nation spent 6.8% of its GNP on education, an estimated $353 billion. Federal, state, and local spending exceeded the previous year's allocations by $23 billion. Business and industry invested some $40 billion in education in an effort to overcome workers' deficiencies and to improve their qualifications. The largest increase in education spending was for higher education, a 7.2% rise to $141 billion. The average cost to the full-time student was $14,923. Elementary and secondary expenditures rose 6.6%, to $212 billion. Per student expenditures reached a record $5,246, and teacher salaries averaged $31,200, up 5.5%. Principals generally earned twice as much.

Primary and Secondary. A number of countries launched major steps toward improving the quality of schooling. In Japan the Ministry of Education issued revised courses of study for all levels of education, from kindergarten through the upper secondary school. The updated curricula emphasized greater command of basic skills, the promotion of individualized instruction, the development of self-learning strategies and creativity, respect for national culture and tradition, and the fostering of international understanding. The Central Council for Education examined ways of reforming the education system, with the aim of enabling it to cope with the needs of a changing society. The state of Andhra Pradesh in India, with a population of over 60 million and a literacy rate of 30%, sought to improve primary-school instruction by instituting a massive child-centred teaching project. Over the next three years, the program would provide 4,107 new classrooms, in-service training in the new instructional methodology for 175,000 teachers, basic learning materials for 50,000 schools, and 250,000 teachers' handbooks.

In Singapore the Education Ministry announced a five-year plan that included converting all secondary schools to single-session rather than double-session institutions. In addition, four centralized vocational institutes would be built to teach a wide range of commercial and academic subjects to postsecondary students, replacing the present preuniversity classes in secondary schools. Although English would continue to be taught as the first language in schools, the ministry recommended teaching pupils their mother tongue (Chinese, Malay, or Tamil) as a second language in order to provide a strong cultural foundation and sense of Asian identity and values. Sri Lanka's new minister of education, W.L. Loku Bandara, instituted reforms that emphasized religion, national integration, and the revival of traditional cultural values. The reforms included requirements that prayers be said at morning assemblies and that teachers stay after school to make sure students prayed and meditated briefly before leaving the classroom. Newly appointed teachers were ordered to produce certificates attesting that they worshiped their parents daily and would abstain from alcohol and "other vices."

The British government, departing from its long tradition of local control over school curricula, began in late 1989 to implement a national curriculum for primary and secondary schools that had been authorized in the 1988 Education Reform Act. The national curriculum, comprising three core subjects (English, mathematics, science) and seven "foundation" subjects, was designed to take up 70% of students' study time, with the remaining 30% to be determined at the local level. To prepare the courses of study, working committees in the various subject-matter areas recommended curriculum contents to the National Curriculum Council. Reactions to the plans were then sought from representatives of industry, commerce, local governments, trade unions, and the teaching profession. In response to the report on teaching English in primary grades, the majority of these groups endorsed the plan to place more emphasis on information technology and on drama and less on formal grammar. A survey of the availability of microcomputers in schools cast doubt on the ability of schools to fulfill the computer-literacy requirement in the new curriculum, particularly at the primary level, where almost half of the schools had 50 to 100 pupils sharing a single microcomputer and one-fourth had 100 to 200 pupils per machine.

Both Denmark and New Zealand passed legislation granting local citizens more financial and pedagogical control over the operation of schools in their communities. In Denmark a local governing board for each of the nation's 1,800 *folkeskoler* (folk schools), attended by pupils aged 6 to 16, would include five to seven parents, with teaching staff and pupils represented by two members each. New Zealand's Prime Minister David Lange had decreed that schools would no longer be operated under educational authorities but instead would be governed by a board of trustees for each school, with parents making up the majority on each board. However, critics of Lange's proposal questioned whether parents would wish to face difficult decisions about teachers' qualifications, disciplinary issues, and teachers' pay.

In what was described as the most radical effort to restructure the schools ever undertaken in the U.S., Chicago

HOWARD SACHS—CONSOLIDATED PHOTOGRAPHERS OF WASHINGTON, D.C.

Pres. George Bush and his wife, Barbara, present a crystal apple to Mary V. Bicouvaris, a high school teacher of government-international relations, who was named the 1989 National Teacher of the Year. The award, which is sponsored by the Encyclopædia Britannica Companies, *Good Housekeeping* magazine, and the Council of Chief State School Officers, honours excellence in teaching.

A high school class watches a sample newscast of "Channel One," an independent news program designed by Whittle Communications for classroom use. Although the newscasts were well received, the network was criticized for showing its sponsors' commercials.

ERIC SANDER—GAMMA/LIAISON

began implementing a plan to place major operating powers in local school councils, composed of parents, teachers, and other citizens. The locally elected council would be responsible for budgets, school programs, selection of instructional materials, and the selection and retention of principals. Chicago was the nation's third largest school system. Joseph Fernandez, the new head of the largest, in New York City, began his job with a reputation for supporting decentralization, which he had effected in Miami, Fla. New York had decentralized its elementary and junior high schools, but several of the 32 districts had been troubled by charges of corruption, and as many as one-third had been under investigation.

Although the U.S. Department of Education reported a 10-year decline in dropout rates, Secretary of Education Lauro Cavazos still found them alarming, with 4.2 million young adults lacking high school diplomas. The rates for different groups varied greatly: whites 15%; blacks 22%; Hispanics 28%; and Native Americans and Alaskan natives, 35%. Asians had the lowest rate, 8%. Segregation of black and Hispanic students was increasing, according to the National School Boards Association. Blacks were commonly segregated in large Northern cities, while resegregation was occurring in the South. The black segregation rates ran as high as 83.8% in Illinois, 80.8% in New York, and 80.3% in Mississippi. For Hispanics, the proportion of segregated schooling was comparable in New York, New Jersey, and New Mexico. The U.S. courts maintained a low profile in education during the year. With half the sitting federal judges appointed by the Reagan administration, a generally conservative view prevailed in such matters as desegregation. The Supreme Court continued an earlier trend by upholding officials in a California school who had banned promotional publications for a student-led Bible-study group that met during noon hours.

Cross-national comparisons of the quality of education in terms of student test scores continued to be published by the International Association for the Evaluation of Educational Achievement (IEA). A report of the IEA's second mathematics study in 20 systems of education found achievement at the eighth-grade level to be highest in Japan, The Netherlands, Hungary, Flemish-speaking Belgium, and France. At the 12th-grade level the top mathematics scores were earned in Hong Kong, Japan, England, Finland, and Sweden. Results of a science-achievement study in 23 countries showed student scores were highest among 10-year-olds in Japan, South Korea, Finland, Sweden, and French-speaking Canada and among 14-year-olds in Hungary, Japan, The Netherlands, English-speaking Canada, and South Korea. The U.S. dropped from 7th place in 1970 to 15th.

The IEA report of its classroom-environment investigation in 17 nations indicated that teachers in all the countries continued to rely chiefly on whole-class instruction, with very little time dedicated to small-group instruction or group work. Classroom activities consisted mainly of lectures and seat work, with published textbooks assuming a central role in students' learning. Teachers tended to use homework assignments to identify pupils' learning deficiencies and to use more formal tests to assign marks. An IEA study of reading literacy, launched in 1989, involved testing the reading skills of 9-year-olds and 14-year-olds in 20 less developed nations and 20 advanced industrialized societies.

In releasing his department's annual "report card," Secretary Cavazos described education in the U.S. as stagnating. The sixth annual report card showed high school graduation rates and college entrance test scores declining in half of the states. Following a decade of gains, Scholastic Aptitude Test scores dropped slightly in 1988, according to the College Board. The SAT was the main college admissions examination used in 22 states. Lower scores were again reported for females and minorities compared with white males. The publisher attributed gender and ethnic differences to unequal opportunities. A slight drop was also noted in the ACT Assessment, the predominate test used in 28 states.

Guidelines for a new credentialing process for teachers in the U.S. were announced. The National Board for Professional Teaching Standards said it hoped to begin certification of teachers by 1993. Teachers seeking the voluntary certification would be required to have a B.A. degree, three years of experience, knowledge of professional skills, and knowledge of the age group and subject they would teach. Several measures of competence would be taken, including tests and observation of teaching.

Higher Education. The number of students studying abroad rose in 1989. Foreign students in Japan had increased by 3,000 annually over the past three years to reach a total of 25,000, most of them Asians in programs of advanced technology. Japanese students in the U.S. increased by 20% to 18,000. More foreign students also enrolled in institutions of higher learning in Australia, Britain, France, New Zealand, and West Germany, but the number in Canada fell by 10%, apparently because of less attractive educational provisions there for noncitizens.

In Eastern Europe there were significant moves toward more autonomy for institutions of higher education. The greatest changes took place in Hungary and Poland, while more modest advances were reported in the Soviet Union, Czechoslovakia, and East Germany. The faculties of Hungarian universities were accorded the right to appoint professors and administrators and to set curricula without first obtaining the approval of the Communist Party. More leeway was given to Hungarian institutions in their selection of students, and the practice of giving priority in admissions to children of peasants and workers was ended. As part of the Polish government's agreement to legalize the

A teacher in the Israeli-occupied West Bank conducts an illegal class outdoors after the schools in the region were shut down by the Israeli government. Israel, which felt that the schools had become centres of organizing for the Palestinian *intifada* (uprising), reopened a limited number of schools in response to pressure from its citizens, the United States, and other Western nations.
DAVID RUBINGER/TIME MAGAZINE

Solidarity trade union and create a more democratic political system, most of the restrictive aspects of the higher-education law of 1985 were suspended. For example, the minister of education could no longer veto the granting of advanced academic degrees, and university rectors could now authorize faculty travel to overseas conferences without obtaining government approval.

The Soviet Union's 1988 plan to democratize and upgrade the quality of higher education achieved mixed results in 1989. One positive outcome was that the faculties of 25% of the country's 895 higher-education institutions had now elected their own rectors. Furthermore, rectors gained control over how to spend funds in their institutions. Efforts to improve the quality of education included adopting more stringent entrance examinations, evaluating faculty members every five years, and ending the automatic promotion of students. However, some officials complained that too many school administrators and teachers were reluctant to display initiative after their experiences during the Brezhnev regime, when they were required to wait for orders from their superiors before they acted. To promote research, the Soviet Union and the U.S. agreed on a bilateral pact to increase formal cooperation between the two nations in the basic sciences, and the Soviet Union supported the idea of a European association of institutions to conduct research on higher education.

The British government, fearing a shortage of qualified graduates for the labour market, sought to increase university enrollments by providing additional money for higher education and by rewarding institutions for increasing class size. A 7% increase in the number of French secondary-school students successfully completing the 1989 school-leaving examination (*baccalauréat*) further strained the already crowded French university system. In 1987 three new universities had been opened to take the overflow of applicants to institutions in the environs of Paris, where one-quarter of the nation's more than one million higher-education students were enrolled. Two additional universities in the vicinity of the capital city were established in the fall of 1989.

West Germany's institutions of higher education, built to accommodate 850,000 students, enrolled 1.5 million in 1989, an overload that precipitated nationwide strikes and demonstrations by students and staff. In recent years, as enrollments increased, a declining portion of the nation's GNP had been allocated to higher education. At the same time, staff had been reduced, and equipment and books were in short supply. The government's response to the crisis was to pledge an additional DM 2.1 billion over the next seven years as a step toward relieving the chronic overcrowding. The Norwegian government, faced with an unemployment problem that accompanied the decline in oil prices, furnished additional funds to the country's four universities to receive students who could not find satisfactory places in the job market. The number of applicants rose as much as 60% in faculties of medicine, law, teacher training, and engineering.

In India the Indira Gandhi National Open University, modeled after the British Open University, enrolled 54,000 students in 1989, only four years after it had been established. The university had opened in 1985 with a single diploma course. By 1989 six more courses had been added, and the staff had been increased from 12 to 550. For instruction, students relied on printed materials and semimonthly visits to one of the 130 regional study centres, most of them located in existing educational institutions.

Around the world, students took to the streets to demonstrate against their governments. Protests resulted in violent clashes with the police in China, South Korea, El Salvador, Venezuela, Zaire, Zimbabwe, and South Africa. The most dramatic of these events occurred during May in China, where thousands of youths in Beijing (Peking) urged their government to permit more freedom of speech, control rising prices, and reduce corruption. The demonstrations ended when the Army shot or arrested scores of protesters. By midsummer the government had launched a new program of ideological indoctrination in the leading universities, with all members of the 1989 graduating class required to attend the indoctrination sessions in order to receive their diplomas. Students were compelled to engage

in self-criticism for having participated in the democracy movement. By late summer the government had imposed new limits on the number of students permitted to go abroad, particularly to North America. Chinese students already in the U.S. claimed they would face persecution if they returned. President Bush vetoed a bill that would have allowed them to overstay their visas, though he did provide such students administrative relief.

In South Korea students conducted periodic violent protests over a wide range of issues, including college tuition increases, reunification with North Korea, the presence of U.S. military forces in the country, farmers' rights, and the policies of their nation's president. Riots in Venezuela that forced the closing of many universities and resulted in 250 deaths were precipitated by the government's austerity program, which affected students' educational expenses. University students in Indonesia protested the ban on political activities on campuses, and they called on their government to stop the abuse of the environment, the eviction of small shop owners by developers, and the proliferation of massage parlors and brothels. Israeli students conducted demonstrations against a government plan to raise tuition fees by 25% and to double dormitory charges.

Protests in South Africa continued over such apartheid measures as the government ban on black student organizations in two of the country's five open universities. At the same time, the South African government announced that universities, upon making proper application, could open their dormitories to students of all races. On the eve of the September parliamentary elections, from which the nation's black majority was excluded, more than 600 university students and 150 faculty members were arrested for participating in antiapartheid demonstrations. Fewer blacks were going to college in the U.S. than in the mid-1970s, according to the American Council on Education. The council also reported that more than half of Hispanics and Native Americans in higher education were enrolled in two-year colleges, while the rate for the general population was 37%. At the same time, there was an upsurge of reports of racist incidents on the nation's campuses.

Concern over providing adequate instructional personnel for schools was apparent in many countries. In Australia the enrollment in higher education, totaling 500,000 students in 1989, was expected to increase by 20% over the next three years, when the shortage of faculty members would reach an estimated 8,400 to 12,000. The need for more school personnel throughout the world resulted not only from the growing school-age population but also from a shortage of youths entering teaching and an unwillingness of teachers to remain in the profession. The difficulty of retaining experienced educational personnel was partly the result of the inadequate level of pay for teaching. This issue was a significant cause for labour action among educators in a variety of countries. Professors demanding salary increases abandoned their classrooms in Greece, refused to administer final examinations in Britain, and assailed the government in France for according supplemental pay for extra services rather than increasing all instructors' pay. A further reason for a shortage of instructors was the continued "brain drain" of educators to other countries, most notably at the university level. In Britain a 32% drop in the number of philosophy positions in universities over the previous eight years resulted chiefly from the emigration of philosophy professors, particularly to the U.S.

(JOEL L. BURDIN; ROBERT MURRAY THOMAS)

See also Libraries; Motion Pictures.

This article updates the *Macropædia* articles History of EDU-CATION; TEACHING.

Energy

Events in energy during 1989 were dominated by the announcement in late March by two researchers at the University of Utah that they had discovered a way to accomplish nuclear fusion at room temperature. The implications of this astonishing claim were truly awesome, for it raised the possibility of virtually limitless cheap energy for all of humankind. "Cold fusion," as it was promptly dubbed by the media, is an impossibility according to existing theory, which calls for the temperature and pressure of the interior of the Sun for the establishment and maintenance of nuclear fusion. In this respect the claimed discovery was startlingly similar to the discovery of high-temperature superconductivity two years earlier, which also violated existing theory.

Confronted with this challenge, scientists throughout the world rushed to duplicate the results of the Utah experimenters and to understand the new phenomenon. However, unlike the experience with the superconductivity breakthrough, which was quickly proved to be a valid discovery, clear confirmation of cold fusion by other scientists was not forthcoming. As the year wore on, accumulated results of the various experiments continued to be frustratingly and tantalizingly ambiguous. On the one hand, the original claim could not be scientifically verified; on the other, there were hints suggesting that some previously unknown phenomenon had actually been discovered. As one scientific journal expressed it, "Confusion abounds." (*See* PHYSICS.)

Other developments in the field of unconventional energy were more mundane. Florida gave preliminary approval to a project in the Orlando area that would use "maglev" technology, in which a superstrong magnetic field levitates a train above the track and thus eliminates all rolling friction, permitting very high speeds. Trains would run a distance of 28 km (17.5 mi) in about seven minutes. In California's Imperial Valley the world's first manure-fired power plant began operation. The 15-MW plant burned some 1,000 tons of manure daily. In October Israel started up the first electric power plant fueled by the direct combustion of oil shale. Intended to reduce the country's almost total dependence on imported oil, the 15-MW facility was intended to demonstrate the feasibility of developing the 11 billion tons of Israeli oil-shale resources for this purpose.

Petroleum and Natural Gas. For the year as a whole, prices in world oil markets remained relatively stable. Through meetings with other oil-producing countries during January and February, several OPEC members were able to obtain the cooperation of seven of them (Angola, China, Egypt, Malaysia, Mexico, Oman, and the Soviet Union) in restricting production and thus maintaining price stability in the face of the chronic cheating by OPEC's own members on their production quotas. OPEC's effect on prices was overshadowed in March, however, by the disastrous oil spill in Prince William Sound, Alaska. (*See* ENVIRONMENT.) This led to the temporary inability of two of the major Alaskan producers to meet their commitments and raised fears that there could be a prolonged interference with a large portion of Alaskan supply. The market effect was dramatic—the sharpest increase in gasoline prices in history throughout the U.S.

This rise in U.S. prices spread to the world market when an explosion on a large producing platform in the British North Sea removed a significant fraction of British production. Together with other shutdowns for different reasons,

this reduced total British output by 31%. The market reaction was to push the price of crude oil to its highest level since the market collapse of 1986. It soon became apparent, however, that such a level could not be sustained in the face of the perennial cheating problem. Prices fell back to roughly the same level that prevailed at the beginning of the year. Price stability marked the second half of the year, although world demand continued to grow. At its September meeting OPEC took account of this increase by raising the total production ceiling of its members, but it was unable to assign new individual country quotas. The only effect of its action was a technical reduction in the total amount by which quotas were being exceeded. At the November meeting, however, the quota system was revised to reflect the ability of the large producers to meet increases in demand, thus tightening the Gulf states' grip on output and prices. The overall quota for the first six months of the year was raised from 20.5 million bbl a day to 22 million (still below actual production).

Other events concerning oil included imports exceeding domestic production in the U.S. during some months for the first time since 1977, the restoration of production at Iran's refinery at Abadan (once the world's largest) after its destruction during the Iran-Iraq war, and the discovery of another large oil field in the Prudhoe Bay area of Alaska's Beaufort Sea coast.

Two events involving natural gas occurred in the Soviet Union. In June it was reported that what might eventually prove to be the world's largest offshore gas field had been discovered in the Barents Sea about 400 km (250 mi) northeast of the Arctic port of Murmansk. According to initial estimates, the field's reserve could be five to six times larger than the United Kingdom's total reserves in the North Sea. Also in June a freak accident occurred near the town of Asha in the Ural Mountains, between the cities of Ufa and Chelyabinsk. By a ghastly coincidence two passenger trains on the Trans-Siberian Railroad were passing while a large liquid-natural-gas pipeline only one kilometre (0.6 mi) away from the rail line was leaking. A spark from a wheel on one of the trains was believed to have caused an explosion and fire. Negligence and mismanagement contributed to the tragedy; the pipeline operators had detected a loss of pressure three hours before the explosion but had responded by continuing to pump liquids into the pipeline

at a higher pressure. The total number of people killed, missing, or injured exceeded 1,000.

In the U.S. the major event concerning natural gas took place in July when Pres. George Bush signed a bill terminating federal controls on the price of natural gas at the wellhead. The date of Dec. 31, 1992, the effective end of all controls, would mark the end of 39 years of their existence, a subject of continuing controversy during the entire period.

Other events in the regulatory field also affected energy commodities and their use. After more than 30 years of struggling with an ever worsening air-pollution problem, authorities in southern California adopted a 20-year plan aimed at reducing smog-producing energy use in the Los Angeles area by 70%. Among the plan's provisions was the mandated conversion of most vehicles to alternative, less polluting fuels or to electricity. In a less drastic move toward the same end, Colorado enacted legislation offering a subsidy to vehicle owners for the conversion of their vehicles to alternative fuels. These actions had ominous implications for gasoline markets, prompting oil companies to introduce new, less polluting gasoline blends. Florida became the first state to establish limits on the strength of the magnetic field created by the flow of current in electric power transmission lines. According to one point of view, such fields have adverse health effects.

Labour Problems. Strikes were the events of note during 1989 in the coal industry. In April some 2,000 miners in Virginia and West Virginia went on strike against one U.S. coal company. By late June sympathy strikes by some 40,-000 other miners had spread to several other states, and in July almost all union mines east of the Mississippi River were shut down. Much of this action consisted of "wildcat" strikes (those not authorized by the national union) and, at the urging of union officials, most wildcat strikers soon returned to work. The original strike, however, persisted during the year. Although the period of wildcat strikes raised fears of serious adverse effects on the electric utility industry and U.S. export markets for coal, the general impact was minor. Only a few utilities experienced coal supply difficulties, and these were not serious.

By coincidence, at the same time the U.S. strike was spreading, coal miners in the Kuznetsk Coal Basin in Siberia also went on strike, a truly historic event for the

AP/WIDE WORLD

A cowboy in California's Imperial Valley grazes his cattle while a massive power plant operates in the distance. The plant, which was the first to be powered by burning manure, could generate the electricity needed for as many as 20,000 homes.

Soviet Union. The Soviet strike spread from its initial base to the Ukraine, the largest coal-mining region in the U.S.S.R. The government quickly moved to satisfy at least some of the miners' demands for better pay and working conditions, and a potential crisis for the Soviet economy was averted.

Electric Power. Three natural phenomena made the news in electric power during the year. In March an unusual burst of solar activity resulted in the worst magnetic storm in 100 years in the upper atmosphere over Quebec. In addition to producing spectacular occurrences of aurora borealis, or northern lights, the storm produced instabilities in the province's electric grid that knocked it completely out of service. Operations were not restored for nine hours. In September Hugo, a force-4 hurricane with winds of more than 180 km/h (100 mph), came ashore in South Carolina, destroying the state's power system. In Charleston, which took the brunt of the storm, distribution facilities were not replaced until more than a month later.

The third natural event was the strong earthquake in the San Francisco Bay area in October. Although electric utility (as well as gas) service was severely affected by the quake's violence, the utility system sustained surprisingly little damage except in a few localized areas. The region's oil pipelines and refineries were equally fortunate.

The beleaguered nuclear power industry in the U.S. continued to suffer setbacks. Residents of Sacramento, Calif., voted to shut down the city's 15-year-old Rancho Seco plant. This was the first such victory for nuclear opponents in 13 years and 14 other referenda. The high-temperature, gas-cooled reactor at Fort St. Vrain, Colo., the only one of its type ever built for power production in the U.S., was scheduled for voluntary shutdown in 1990 after 15 years of operation plagued by persistent problems. Nuclear proponents took some small comfort from the fact that the Seabrook reactor in New Hampshire, the subject of furious controversy over whether it should be allowed to operate after its completion, was permitted to begin a period of low-power testing. The status of another completed reactor, the Shoreham plant in New York, continued to remain in limbo.   (BRUCE C. NETSCHERT)

See also Engineering Projects; Industrial Review; Mining; Transportation.

This article updates the *Macropædia* articles ENERGY CONVERSION; Fossil FUELS.

Engineering Projects

Bridges. In the last year of the decade, high technology was the outstanding characteristic of bridge building. "European" cable stay and concrete segmental box techniques were dominant, though further advances in steels led to improvements in steel trusses. The development of ever larger cranes allowed the construction of steel or concrete girder viaducts, elevated roads, and approaches that would once have been bridges in their own right.

In Europe most major projects used those methods. The biggest was in Britain, where a new $146 million bridge over the Thames River for the London orbital M25 motorway (expressway) was under construction. This 450-m (1 m = 3.3 ft) main span bridge was to carry four road lanes to relieve two tunnels. The designer of the central steel cable stay with 80-m-high steel pylons was West Germany's Helmutt Homberg, designer of the world's longest single-plane cable-stayed bridge, the recently opened 450-m Chao Phya in Bangkok, Thailand.

For the Thames bridge two 30,000-ton caissons were floated into position to support 60-m-high concrete piers that sat beneath the pylons. Concrete foundations and six 53–68-m-long back spans using steel girders lifted in with a large floating crane were being designed and erected by Cementation Cleveland Bridge Consortium. This was part of the Trafalgar House group that was privately funding the project. As with the Channel Tunnel, costs were to be recovered from tolls.

A giant, just begun, was the French Pont de Normandie across the estuary of the Seine near Le Havre. Contractor Entrepose Quillery planned to build an 856-m main span, almost double the world-record 465 m.

High technology also brought problems. West Germany, which mainly developed cable stay for postwar rebuilding, had trouble with the Upper Argen viaduct in the Black Forest. This 258-m main steel span used only one A-shaped tower to support a 29-m-wide curving deck from one end. Cables passed under the deck about halfway to extend support, using underside cable struts. A short, simple steel span and a 391-m concrete box bridge completed the 730-m-long structure, which at the end of 1989 was at least two years past its construction deadline. In Spain complexity worried developers for the 1992 World's Fair, and one of

Japan's Yokohama Coastal Expressway extends over Yokohama Harbour via the newly opened Yokohama Bay Bridge. The bridge, with its span of 855 metres (2,800 feet), was the world's largest suspension bridge.
ASAHI SHIMBUN

the two elegant harp-shaped bridges planned for the site in Seville was abandoned.

Half a dozen river and estuarine crossings in North America included the 340-m main span SkyTrain lightweight mass transit bridge, in Vancouver, B.C.; the 339-m-long central span Talmadge Memorial highway bridge in Savannah, Ga., scheduled for completion in late 1990; and the BayTown bridge in the Houston harbour area in Texas. The latter, though not the longest, was one of the most dramatic. It featured double diamond-shaped main 135-m-high towers that had central crossover joints. Steel reinforcement for the huge X links had to be made in a 14.5-m-high crane lift frame to hold their 440 interlocking bars before concrete was "spooned" into the tight steel mesh. The bridge was designed to carry two parallel 26.6-m steel and concrete roadways.

BayTown design firm Figg & Muller originated in central Europe and was influential in using new methods, including precast segmental concrete bridges. These were controversial; U.S. contractors were more skilled at mass production beam-and-girder construction and initially had troubles. Construction time for the difficult San Antonio elevated highway in Texas was much longer than had been expected, but the six-lane elevated section, many kilometres in length, was elegant.

One of Europe's most prestigious projects, the Store Bælt waterway crossing in Denmark linking two of the country's main islands, incorporated two major bridges. The West bridge, subject to delay and controversy at the end of 1989 over letting of contracts against European regulations, was a 6.6-km (4.1-mi)-long concrete box structure to be constructed using a specially made crane ferrying into position elements weighing up to 6,000 tons. The East bridge was designed to use either 900–1,200-m cable-stay spans or up to 2,000-m suspension spans in order to cross 6.7 km (4.2 mi) of water. A decision as to which was expected early in 1990.

Finally, new advances in high-strength steel were revitalizing the much-used U.S. truss design. In Charleston, S.C., the 288-m main span Cooper River bridge by Howard Needles Tammen & Bergendorf used a 488-m-long steel truss to make an elegant flat parallel shape for the central 60-m-high river crossing. In Norway high-strength steel was used at Nord Sundet to create one of the longest lattice bridges in the world, with a 222.5-m main span.

(ADRIAN GREEMAN)

Buildings. Construction of tall buildings continued apace in several countries during 1989. In Kuwait the nation's tallest building, the Alahli Bank, was completed. Standing 112 m above ground and with two levels below ground, the building had a number of interesting technical features. For many years reinforced concrete had been the usual construction material in Kuwait. The Alahli Bank was the first building in the nation to use structural steelwork extensively. The main 26-story superstructure was supported on two slip-formed reinforced concrete cores, one at each end of the building, with a clear distance of 26 m between them. These cores, semicircular in plan, contained the elevators, staircases, and service ducts. Structural steel was used for the 26 × 16-m floors between the cores. In order to achieve an entirely column-free area at ground level, 10-m-deep trusses spanned the area between the cores at a distance between 17 and 27 m above ground; these supported the columns that carried the upper floors. This story was used to house environmental services equipment, as was another 4-m-deep story near roof level. Cork was used under parts of the base slab to control the load distribution and improve an otherwise undesirable settlement pattern.

The transfer of loads from one arrangement of columns to another that is spaced farther apart was a frequent problem in tall buildings, where large column-free areas were required at lower levels. Deep trusses as described above were one solution.

At the 222-m-high Pacific Place complex in Hong Kong, a 4.5-m-deep concrete slab was used as a transfer plate. Loads from perimeter concrete shear walls were transferred to fewer large columns below. Conventional reinforced concrete would have required a very large weight of steel, and a posttensioned prestressed concrete design was finally used.

Early in 1989 the Canary Wharf central tower in London started to rise above ground. This building was to be 237 m high and thus would have a significant effect on the city skyline. The structural frame of the building was in steelwork and, unlike the designs described above, the wind forces would be carried by the whole perimeter of the building acting as a perforated tube. This concept was developed by Fazlur Khan in the U.S. but had rarely been adopted in Europe.

The SkyDome in Toronto was completed during the year. The most interesting feature of this 55,000-seat stadium was its retractable roof, which covered 3.2 ha (1 ha

= 2.47 ac) and was designed to open or close in 20 minutes. The roof was in four sections formed in steel arched-lattice trusses supporting a thermally insulated steel deck. One of the sections of the roof was fixed above the 35 × 10-m electronic video scoreboard. The remaining three panels rotated and retracted over the fixed panel, leaving all the playing area and more than 90% of the seating area open to the sky. Because the roof panels were arched, they produced a horizontal as well as a vertical thrust at the supports, so they traveled on pairs of rails set at 45° to the horizontal.

Nearing completion in Barcelona, Spain, for the 1992 Olympic Games was the Palau Sant Jordi stadium. This was an indoor stadium for the gymnastics and volleyball events and had a 1.35-ha steel and glass roof with a maximum span of 128 m. The roof was in the form of an arched two-layer space grid, and the method of construction was of particular interest. A substantial central area was first fabricated at ground level complete with its decking, insulation, and environmental services equipment. This whole section was then lifted 45 m on 12 jacking towers situated around its edge to its final position. Once in place, the peripheral sections were fixed, after which the jacking towers were removed; this left the roof supported on 62 columns around the perimeter of the stadium.

A monumental lifting task was carried out in Yugoslavia during the year. This was the 4,000-metric ton, 39-m-diameter dome for St. Sava's cathedral in Belgrade. Construction of the cathedral was started in 1935, stopped in 1941, and did not resume again until 1985. The dome was constructed of precast concrete radial arch trusses clad with 60-mm (2.4-in) thick precast concrete slabs. This form of construction was chosen to minimize the weight to be lifted. The dome assembly with its ring beam was set into vertical grooves, one in each of the four main supporting columns. Two jacks in each groove were used in conjunction with thin concrete packing slabs to raise the dome gradually through 40 m. The piles of slabs in the grooves were restrained against buckling by steel bands and were subsequently filled with concrete.

(GEOFFREY M. PINFOLD)

Dams. The construction of eight new dams that would generate 2,635 MW of hydroelectric power was proposed for India. The nation's hydroelectric potential was about

Major World Dams Under Construction in 1989[1]

Name of dam	River	Country	Type[2]	Height (m)	Length of crest (m)	Volume content (000 cu m)	Gross reservoir capacity (000 cu m)
Altinkaya	Kizilirmak	Turkey	E,R	195	634	16,000	5,763,000
Arakhthos/Kalaritikos	Arakhthos	Greece	E	185	238	1,500	1,840,000
Ataturk	Euphrates	Turkey	E,R	184	1,820	84,500	48,700,000
Bakun	Rajang	Malaysia	R	210	900	29,400	43,800,000
Barakshetra	Sapta Kasi	Nepal	G	239	640	7,677	8,500,000
Boruca	Terraba	Costa Rica	E,R	267	700	43,000	14,960,000
Canales	Genil	Spain	E,R	158	340	7,248	70,000
Chapeton	Paraná	Argentina	E,G	35	224,000	296,200	60,600,000
Chisapani	Karnali	Nepal	E,R	210	850	35,000	15,000,000
Cipasang	Cimanuk	Indonesia	E,R	200	640	90,000	860,000
Corpus Posadas	Paraná	Argentina/Paraguay	E,R	65	8,474	18,200	13,000,000
Corumba	Corumba	Brazil	R	150	600	3,668	675,000
Dongfeng	Wujiang	China	A	166	250	622	1,025,000
Dongjiang	Laishui	China	A	157	438	943	8,120,000
Ertan	Yalongjiang	China	A	240	775	4,742	5,800
Garabi	Uruguay	Argentina/Brazil	E,G	60	3,960	19,884	5,810,000
Geheyan	Qingjiang	China	A	151	640	3,060	3,400,000
Guayllabamba	Guayllabamba	Ecuador	A	165	413	704	105,000
Hrusov-Dunakiliti-Gabcikovo	Dunaj	Czechoslovakia/Hungary	E,G	29	31,500	18,340	199,000
Ingapata	Paute	Ecuador	G	166	430	1,600	413,000
Kabalebo	Kabalebo	Suriname	E,R	45	1,650	3,790	19,000,000
Katse	Malibamatso	Lesotho	A	180	700	2,200	N/A
Katun	Katun	U.S.S.R.	E,R	185	760	32,700	5,800,000
Kayraktepe	Gaksu	Turkey	E,R	199	580	17,000	4,800,000
Kishau	Tons	India	E,R	253	360	18,850	2,400,000
Kouilou	Kouilou	Congo	A	137	345	390	35,000,000
Kumgang	North Itan	North Korea	E	215	1,120	N.A.	9,250,000
La Vueltosa	Caparo	Venezuela	E	118	1,200	15,000	5,300,000
Lijiaxia	Huang He	China	A	175	382	3,030	760,000
Maroun	Maroun	Iran	E,R	165	350	7,490	1,200,000
Menzelet	Ceyhan	Turkey	E,R	151	420	8,530	1,950,000
Naramata	Naramata	Japan	E,R	158	520	12,500	90,000
Nama Khuani	Rioni	U.S.S.R.	A	161	460	1,200	560,000
Pati	Paraná	Argentina	E,G	36	174,900	238,180	38,000,000
Piedra del Aquila	Limay	Argentina	E,G,R	163	820	2,520	11,300,000
Porto Primavera	Paraná	Brazil	E,R	38	11,300	37,644	20,000,000
Potrerillos	Mendoza	Argentina	E	146	550	17,120	860,000
Roncador	Uruguay	Brazil/Argentina	E,R	78	1,598	9,940	33,580,000
San Roque	Agno	Philippines	E	210	1,130	43,150	990,000
Sardar Sarovar	Narmada	India	G	163	1,202	6,869	9,500,000
Sera da Mesa	Tocantins	Brazil	E,R	144	1,544	11,498	54,400,000
Shuikou	Minjiang	China	G	101	940	3,560	23,400,000
Songwon	Chungmangang	North Korea	R	160	630	1,100	3,200,000
Tehri	Bhagirathi	India	E,R	261	570	27,032	3,540,000
Thein Dam Raqit	Ravi	India	E	160	565	14,213	3,280,000
Thissavros	Nestos	Greece	E	172	480	9,700	705,000
Tianshengqiao	Hongshui	China	E,R	185	1,250	19,300	9,550,000
Yacyreta-Apipe	Paraná	Paraguay/Argentina	E,G	43	69,600	81,000	21,000,000

Major World Dams Completed in 1988 and 1989[1]

Name of dam	River	Country	Type[2]	Height (m)	Length of crest (m)	Volume content (000 cu m)	Gross reservoir capacity (000 cu m)
Balbina	Uatuma	Brazil	E,R	33	2,930	6,724	17,533,000
Boguchany	Angara	U.S.S.R.	E,R	79	1,816	28,972	58,200,000
Casa de Piedra	Rio Colorado	Argentina	E	56	10,000	16,500	4,000,000
Gallilo Ciego	Jequetepeque	Peru	E,R	120	750	15,000	573,600
Guavio	Guavio	Colombia	E,R	243	390	17,755	1,020,000
Kilickaya	Kelkit	Turkey	E,R	140	405	6,700	1,400,000
Lhakwar	Yamuna	India	G	192	188	2,691	580,000
Michihuao	Limay	Argentina	E	70	6,700	29,840	5,860,000
Planicie Banderita	Neuquen	Argentina	E	35	350	1,194	43,000,000
Tokuyama	Ibi	Japan	E	161	420	15,000	660,000
Urra II	Sinu	Colombia	R	170	275	23,500	34,300,000

[1] Having a height exceeding 150 m (492 ft); or having a volume content exceeding 15 million cu m (19.6 million cu yd); or forming a reservoir exceeding 14,800 × 10⁶ cu m of capacity (12 million ac-ft).
[2] Type of dam: E = earth; R = rockfill; A = arch; G = gravity.

(T. W. MERMEL)

80,000 MW, only 16% of which had been developed. The Nathpa Jhakti Dam on the Sutlej River in the Himalayan state of Himachal Pradesh was to be 60 m high and develop 1,250 MW of power. Recent approval of this dam was given after assurances were made to 73 families that satisfactory resettlement would be provided. At Sardar Sarovar Dam, which was to be 163 m high, store 9.5 billion cu m of water for irrigation, and provide 1,250 MW of power, serious environmental problems were yet to be resolved. More than 70,000 people faced resettlement because of this project, and while power and irrigation were high on India's priority list, social unrest created bitter political conflicts that were not easy to resolve.

In China the Three Gorges project on the Chang Jiang (Yangtze River) was postponed for at least six years in favour of smaller dams on the main stream and its tributaries. Shortages of power required many Chinese industries to operate on a four-day-week schedule, and therefore it seemed that energy developments should be given high priority. China's exploitable hydroelectric potential was about 380,000 MW, less than 8% of which had been developed. More than 2,000 dam sites were identified for construction of large dams, with 200 suitable for development of dams that could generate 250 MW at each site. More than 10 such large dams were under construction.

Thailand was seeking approval of funds for two major dams, a 250-m-high dam at Kaeng Sua Ten for irrigation and another at Mae Wong. Peace talks in the area resurrected hopes for the Mekong River development and the Pa Mong and Nan Theun dams.

In Indonesia Java environmentalists and human rights organizations protested the construction of the Kedung Ombo Dam, where more than 1,800 families in the reservoir area were not properly compensated or resettled before the reservoir waters began flooding their lands.

In Malaysia the government shelved its plan to develop the 2,400-MW hydroelectric plant at the Bakun Dam. The project was opposed by environmental groups, but the large capital investment that was required might also have been a factor.

Zimbabwe decided to raise the height of two dams to add to their storage capacities. The Mayfair Dam, built in 1976, was to be raised five metres, which would increase the reservoir capacity from 97 million cu m to 176 million cu m (1 cu m = 35.3 cu ft). The Claw Dam, built in 1973, was to be raised 5½ m, and its reservoir capacity would be increased from 21 million cu m to 67 million cu m. Kariba Dam on the Zambezi River was to get a second power plant, which would add 300 MW. There were plans to install 800 MW on each side of the river to serve Zambia and Zimbabwe. The Kariba Dam impounded 180.6 billion cu m of water and was the world's largest man-made lake. The government also decided to make studies of the 190-m-high Batoka Gorge Dam on the Zambezi River, which was to be located downstream from Vielona Falls and upstream from Kariba Dam.

Lesotho's Orange River water-transfer project to South Africa was being delayed because of design changes for the 180-m-high Katse Dam and for the diversion tunnels. The purpose of the project was to transfer surplus waters to South Africa for use in that nation's expanding mining industry.

In Brunei water was being impounded behind the 22-m-high Benutan Dam, which was expected to increase the water supply to the capital city of Bandar Seri Begawan to 109,000 cu m daily. The dam had a storage capacity of 44 million cu m, which would assure the city a water supply during drought periods.

Kenya developed a plan to construct 5,000 small dams for storing water to benefit farmers in the arid areas of Baringo, Samburu, and Wajir. In Morocco the government adopted a program to free its agriculture from dependence on irregular rainfall by providing more storage reservoirs to catch more of the flood runoff. The program called for building one dam per year until the year 2000. As of the end of 1989 there were 20 dams under active construction. The largest of this group was to be the 87-m-high M'Jara Dam on the Oued Ouergha, a tributary of the Oued Sebou. The dam would impound 600 million cu m of water and develop 240 MW of hydroelectric power.

The Hungarian government decided to stop the construction of the hydroelectric project on the Danube River at Nagymaros. The decision affected relations with Czechoslovakia, which was building facilities at Gabcikovo designed to operate in connection with the canceled project, and with Austria, which had helped finance the Hungarian project. Czechoslovakia claimed it would demand about $3.5 billion in compensation from Hungary, while Austria asked for $1.3 billion.

Brazil decided to proceed with its Amazon River dams after assurances were given to environmentalists that the government would monitor and supervise the resettlement of displaced people from the rain forests to development areas. It also planned to establish new laws protecting the relocated people, make studies of soil and hydrology, and provide educational programs.

The Dominican Republic announced plans for two large dams. The Jiguey Dam on the Nizao River was to be a 110-m-high concrete gravity-arch type dam that would develop 100 MW. Farther downstream the Aquacate Dam, 48 m high, would feed an underground power plant with 50 MW installed. (T.W. MERMEL)

Roads. The trend toward privately financed toll highways gained momentum in both industrialized and less developed countries as a result of inadequate public funding for the construction and maintenance of roads. For example, a $2.2 billion toll road was planned to connect Kansas City, Mo., and Chicago. On the other side of the world, the 302-km (1 km = 0.62 mi) motorway from Hong Kong to Guangzhou (Canton), China, was being built by Hong Kong entrepreneur Gordon Wu as a private toll road at a cost of $1,020,000,000.

The U.S. Department of Transportation unveiled a master plan for transportation, including a reconstruction program for interstate highways, many of which were more than 30 years old. Chicago's 18-km Dan Ryan Expressway was reconstructed at a cost of $250 million. In Canada a six-lane freeway in metropolitan Toronto was part of a $570 million expansion program in the area.

The Inter-American Development Bank was financing the rehabilitation of portions of the Central American highway system in El Salvador, Honduras, and Costa Rica. The Mexican government was planning a 4,000-km network of toll roads. Construction of the first segment, a 262-km highway from Cuernavaca to Acapulco, began in September. A highway link was being built to connect La Paz, Bolivia, with the Brazilian city of Santos, with financing from the Inter-American Development Bank. In Paraguay the 98-km Tacuara–Santa Rosa highway linking Asunción with the north of the country was completed.

The Asian highway network, a 65,000-km system of roads designed to link 16 Asian countries, was significantly advanced when China joined it. The first Asian highway route in China was to be from Beijing (Peking) to Shenzhen (Shen-chen), 2,900 km distant. Eight expressways to be completed in 1990 were under construction in China.

A train engine enters the new 14.7-kilometre (9.1-mile) rail tunnel that stretches beneath Canada's Selkirk Mountains. It was the longest rail tunnel in the Western Hemisphere and would aid access to Canada's western ports and facilitate trade with Pacific Rim countries.

IAN LINDSAY/VANCOUVER SUN

What might be the world's most expensive highway, the $9 billion, 15-km Trans-Tokyo Bay Highway, was under construction and was expected to be opened to traffic in 1996. In South Korea a 24-km, $561 million expressway from Pangyo to Kuri was under construction; it was designed to reduce congestion in metropolitan Seoul.

Construction began on the $1 billion, 36-km Bangkok Expressway in Thailand. Indonesia was approaching completion of a road link between the capital city of Jakarta and the eastern provinces of Java. A $450 million loan from the World Bank was financing India's national highway project, aimed at linking the nation's villages and building India's first expressways. Two privately financed expressways were planned in New South Wales, Australia, at a cost of $170 million.

Britain announced an $18 billion program to build or reconstruct 43,000 km of highways. Emphasis was to be on the motorway program, including upgrading of London's M25 Ring Road and building access roads to the Channel Tunnel terminal.

Denmark was spending $470 million to build the 18-km road and rail crossing of the Store Bælt waterway between the islands of Sjælland and Fyn. Spain's 1989 road budget increased by 175% over the previous year. The last two sections of the Brussels-to-Luxembourg Motorway were completed, linking Belgium and The Netherlands with Switzerland, Italy, Spain, and southern France.

France built 340 km of expressways in 1989, including a 124-km segment of the Paris–Clermont Ferrand route. A 1,400-km privately funded expressway was to be built along the Adriatic coast of Yugoslavia.

(HUGH M. GILLESPIE)

Tunnels. The largest tunneling project in the world under construction, the triple-tube, 50-km-long Channel Tunnel being built between the south coast of England and northern France, was about half completed at the end of 1989. The tunnel was being built for the owner and operator, Eurotunnel, by a joint venture of five British and five French contractors called Transmanche-Link (TML). The underwater length was to be 38 km, making it the longest underwater crossing in the world, and the 22 km that were to be driven by three full-face tunnel-boring machines (TBMs) from a shaft on the British side would be the longest tunnels driven by TBMs in a single drive. Eurotunnel was financed by banks and private investors from all parts of the world, who would have to wait until June 1993 before they could expect to get any return on their money. More than half of the central 4.8-m-internal-diameter service tunnel had been excavated by September 1989, working from shafts on both sides of the Channel. Two separate 7.6-m-diameter rail tunnels, one to carry trains in each direction at speeds up to 160 km/h, were also being driven from each side. The total cost of the project, including financing, was likely to exceed £7 billion, with a possible additional £3.7 billion needed for a new high-speed railway, largely in tunnels, between the Kent coast and London.

The first phase of Denmark's road and rail crossing of the Store Bælt waterway between Fyn and Sjælland involved twin bored railway tunnels, each 7.7 m in internal diameter and 7,260 m in length. Four full-face TBMs were ordered from James Howden of Glasgow, Scotland, under a £44 million subcontract, the largest amount for TBMs in one order. The TBMs were of an exceptionally versatile design, enabling them to alternate quickly between open and closed modes, to crush boulders of substantial size, and to handle rocks up to 400 mm (16 in) across. As with the Channel Tunnel, the linings were to be precast concrete segment rings, except at cross passages, where the linings would be spheroidal graphite iron. The tunnels were due for completion in 1993.

Hong Kong was also the scene of major tunnel works, with the completion during 1989 of the Eastern Harbour Crossing (a HK$5 billion immersed tube tunnel carrying two two-lane roadways and twin subway rail tracks in separate tubes), good progress on the Tate's Cairn twin roadway road tunnel, and plans for yet another immersed-tube harbour crossing to take the Kowloon–Canton Railway (KCR) to a new terminal on Hong Kong Island. The need for a third harbour road crossing as part of a western corridor to China was identified and called for earlier than the year 2000.

Elsewhere, the U.S. proposed to build the world's largest scientific instrument, a 27-km-wide superconducting super collider in a circular tunnel 85 km in circumference at Waxahachie, Texas. In Boston tunneling began for 22 km of a large-diameter undersea rock tunnel.

The most notable technical developments of 1989 were the manufacture of more versatile hard- and soft-ground TBMs, especially TBMs with very large diameters; the greater use of the New Austrian Tunneling Method (NATM), with its application to a greater variety of jobs in a larger number of countries (its use even spread to Britain!); and various developments in tunnel linings and techniques, such as the application of the vacuum segment erector. The Channel Tunnel led to the design of machines using U.S. and Japanese technology that can work in waterlogged conditions in soft ground and convert as they go along to machines suitable for boring in mostly dry chalk.

(DAVID V. MARTIN)

This article updates the *Macropædia* articles BUILDING CONSTRUCTION; PUBLIC WORKS.

Environment

In the June 1989 elections to the European Parliament, the Greens made significant gains in several countries, most markedly in Britain. The United States suffered its worst oil pollution incident in March when the tanker *Exxon Valdez* ran aground off the coast of Alaska, spilling about 200,000 bbl of oil. Wildlife was severely affected, and the cleanup operation continued until September 15, when Exxon abandoned it for the winter. Climatic change caused by the greenhouse effect dominated environmental discussions at governmental and intergovernmental levels.

The Iranian supertanker *Kharg 5* on December 19 spilled some 72 million litres (19 million gal) of light crude oil into the Atlantic Ocean when an explosion tore a huge hole through its hull, igniting a fire and forcing the crew to abandon ship about 700 km (400 mi) north of the Canary Islands. Because the weather was mild, by the year's end the resulting 370-km (230-mi) oil slick had not reached the coast of Morocco, and about 40% of the spill had evaporated. Much of the oil sank to the ocean floor, where it might poison fish and oysters.

Environmentalists were appalled over the murder, in December 1988, of the Brazilian trade union leader Francisco Mendes Filho at his home in Xapuri. His campaign on behalf of impoverished rubber tappers led him to oppose deforestation and urge the preservation of the natural rain forest on which the rubber tappers depended. This won him wide support but brought him into conflict with landowners. In 1988 the UN presented him with the Global 500 Award.

INTERNATIONAL COOPERATION

In June 1989 the World Bank incorporated stringent environmental safeguards into a $20 million forestry loan to Sri Lanka. On Nov. 14, 1988, Robert Goodland, the bank's environment chief for Latin America, told participants at a Royal Geographical Society conference in London that the world had 10 years to prevent a breakdown in life-support systems resulting from the greenhouse effect and pollution. In August 1989, however, an internal study by the bank, said to represent a compromise between environmentalists and the energy department, acknowledged the potential impact of global warming but failed to recommend any change in funding policies. The bank's president, Barber Conable, noted that many less developed countries were wary of environmental constraints, which they regarded as a ruse by industrialized countries to restrict their development.

In March, 24 nations were represented at a conference on the environment, held under UN auspices in The Hague. It was suggested that the UN establish a new institution, to be called Globe, to protect the environment, with authority to enforce regulations, although several nations objected. There were also suggestions that offenders might be prosecuted in the International Court of Justice. The idea of a new international institution emerged again in late July when the environment ministers of France and West Germany announced plans to set up a joint environmental council at a forthcoming Franco-German summit. They hoped this would lead to a European Environment Agency, open to countries outside the European Communities (EC), that would have independent powers to provide scientific evaluation of environmental matters. Carlo Ripa di Meana, the EC environment commissioner, referred to the proposal during a visit to Britain, suggesting the agency might have an initial budget of £3.5 million a year.

At the summit of the seven leading industrial countries, held in Paris in July, environmental protection, especially the need to combat the greenhouse effect, was high on the agenda. The final communiqué called for "decisive action" to understand and protect the world's ecological balance and committed the governments to boost relevant scientific research.

World Resources 1988–89, published in December 1988 by the World Resources Institute, Washington, D.C., and the International Institute for Environment and Development, London, in collaboration with the UN Environment Program (UNEP), singled out damage to the ozone layer and tropical deforestation as the main environmental problems. Deforestation, it said, was proceeding at 11 million ha (27 million ac) a year. In June representatives of seven European countries, from both East and West, met in Prague for two days to work out a plan to protect the environment in Eastern Europe. It dealt especially with pollution of air and rivers.

MARK SHERMAN—BRUCE COLEMAN, INC.

The city of Los Angeles is covered by a dense layer of smog. In an effort to alleviate the city's pollution problem, officials in March 1989 adopted a 20-year plan specifying stiffer regulations on motor vehicles and on products damaging to the environment.

In the elections to the European Parliament, the Greens increased their seats from 20 to 23. They made a major advance in Britain, winning 15% of the national vote. This placed them third, behind Labour and the Conservatives, and they emerged for the first time as an important political force. However, because of the British electoral system, their 2.3 million votes won them no seats. In April the European Parliament voted in favour of bringing controls on vehicle emissions into line with those in the U.S. by 1993, two years earlier than previously proposed. The Council of Ministers approved the new controls in June. The European Commission announced on September 20 that it would take action against Britain in the European Court of Justice for failing to translate the 1985 Directive on Water Quality into national legislation and for the presence of excessive amounts of lead in water in Scotland and of nitrates in water in England. Action was also being taken against France and Belgium and might be taken against Luxembourg, Spain, West Germany, and Italy. In August discussions were held on plans to establish a Europe-wide code of labeling for consumer products to identify those least harmful to the environment.

NATIONAL DEVELOPMENTS

Australia. In Tasmanian state elections on May 13 and 14, the Greens won 18% of the vote and 5 seats, while the Liberals gained 17 seats (one short of an absolute majority) and Labor, 13. In June the Greens joined Labor to form a coalition government committed to a range of environmental improvements.

Brazil. Thousands of local people, led by the Kayapo tribe, protested at Altamira on February 21 against plans to build the Kararao Dam on the Xingu River as part of a hydroelectric project. The World Bank canceled a $500 million loan to Brazil for power-related projects, including the building of dams in connection with this scheme, and on March 28 it was reported that the Brazilian government had agreed to abandon the project and to accept a $400 million World Bank loan for projects related to energy conservation and the protection of tribal lands.

Britain. A team headed by David Pearce of University College, London, studied U.K. economic development and resource use in order to seek ways of measuring sustainable development. On August 16 Christopher Patten, the newly appointed secretary of state for the environment, commenting on the Pearce Report and accepting some of its recommendations, hinted at taxes on polluting substances. This idea was developed further in early September, when it was reported that officials at the Department of the Environment were working out details of a plan for taxing products on a scale that would increase in proportion to the harm they were believed to do.

Bulgaria. In October 1988 Nikolay Dyulgerov, head of the environment conservation committee of the Council of Ministers, announced a program—lasting until 2005—to clean up severely polluted areas including Sofia, Rousse on the Danube, and Varna on the Black Sea. Dyulgerov said 44% of Bulgarian air was polluted above maximum permitted levels. Meanwhile, an environmental protection organization called Ecoglasnost was established by Bulgarian dissidents.

China. China's first environmental lobby group was launched on Feb. 25, 1989, when more than 100 academics, writers, and scientists published a book—financed by themselves—criticizing plans to build the world's biggest dam. Sited in a seismically active area, the dam would form part of the Three Gorges hydroelectric project on the Chang Jiang (Yangtze River). The entire project would

cost $11 billion over 12 years and would involve the displacement of 1.1 million people. The river transports some 450 million tons of silt annually, and it was feared that the dam might silt up and eventually burst.

West Germany. In July East and West Germany announced a joint three-year program to transfer advanced antipollution technology from West to East and to build several new pollution-control facilities in the East. West Germany would contribute DM 300 million and East Germany, DM 120 million to provide advanced coal-burning technology, an incinerator to deal with wastes from a Dresden pharmaceutical plant, a water-purification plant for the Buna chemical works near Leipzig (the biggest single item in the program), and pilot cogeneration projects (for the simultaneous generation of electrical energy and heat), as well as the regular collection and exchange of standardized air-pollution data.

The Greens remained divided between "Fundis" and "Realos," with "Independents" forming a third force. In the West Berlin elections on January 29, the Greens won additional seats as part of the left-wing Alternative List, but soon afterward they were thrown into disarray when their best-known member, Otto Schily, advised the Social Democrats to make no concessions in negotiations to form a coalition. In March the federal Green Party conference at Duisburg elected a moderate executive, however, and on March 16 a coalition was formed. West Berlin thus became the first Land government in two years to have Green Party members. Community elections in Hesse in March also showed a surge in Green support.

Hungary. In April more than 500 people marched through Budapest to protest levels of atmospheric lead, which were said to exceed the internationally recommended limit by as much as 30 times. The government promised to do more to combat pollution.

Protesters in India rally against an irrigation and hydroelectric project in the Narmada River valley. In February protesters tried to halt work on one of the largest dams, the Sardar Sarovar Dam, whose reservoir would flood the land and homes of some 70,000 people.

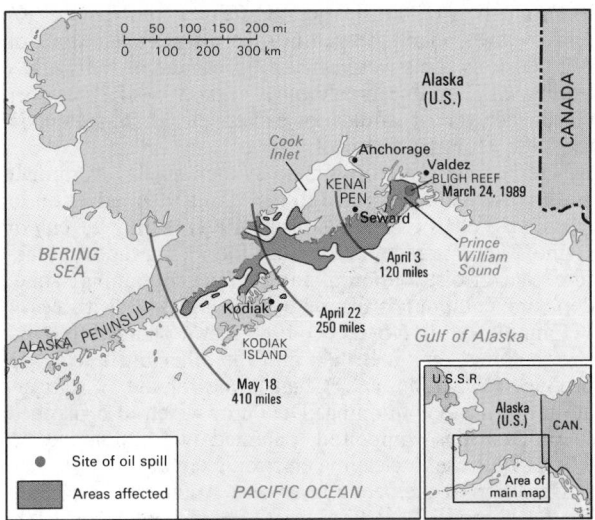

The extent of the spread of oil from the damaged *Exxon Valdez* was due to the lack of immediate efforts to contain the spill and to such natural conditions as strong winds and waves. The huge tanker spilled more than 200,000 barrels of oil into Prince William Sound after it ran aground on Bligh Reef. Over 700 kilometres (400 miles) of Alaskan coastline were polluted.

Controversy continued over the plan to build a dam at Nagymaros as part of the Austrian-financed joint Czechoslovak-Hungarian Gabcikovo-Nagymaros hydroelectric scheme. More than 5,000 people protested in Budapest on Oct. 30, 1988, and about 2,000 on May 26, 1989, when 160,000 people were said to have signed a petition calling for abandonment of the project. In December 1988 the Association of Young Democrats presented a petition with enough signatures to force Miklos Vida, deputy speaker of the Hungarian Parliament and a supporter of the Nagymaros scheme, to contest a by-election in his Budapest constituency. Two more constituencies took similar action in March. The Hungarian government reopened the debate on the issue and suspended work on the dam, but the project was being urged by the Czechoslovak government.

India. On February 22 about 200 people lay down in the road to halt work on the Sardar Sarovar Dam in Gujarat. They were taking part in a demonstration opposing the dam, which would fill a reservoir 214 km (133 mi) long, flooding the land and homes of 70,000 people.

The Netherlands. In what was said to be the first defeat of a government on an environmental issue, on May 3 the coalition government resigned over disagreements concerning the financing of its ambitious National Environment Plan. The caretaker government that took over announced, on May 25, a major program to reduce pollution by at least 70% by 2010, to be financed largely through higher taxes on fuel oils and gasoline (petrol) and on garbage and sewage disposal. The 1990 budget proposed in September by the new coalition government included £30 million for environmental improvement but made no provision for the National Environment Plan.

U.S. Results of the first nationwide survey of more than 320 toxic chemicals released into the air by industry, published in March and based on data collected by the Environmental Protection Agency (EPA), showed that those substances were being emitted in amounts that threatened public health. The most heavily polluted states were Rhode Island, New Jersey, Connecticut, Massachusetts, and Virginia; the cleanest were Nevada, New Mexico, and North and South Dakota.

On June 12 Pres. George Bush announced proposals to reduce air pollution and pollution from toxic chemicals. Coal-burning power stations would be required to cut emissions of sulfur dioxide by 10 million tons and those of nitrogen oxides by 2 million tons by 2000. Within six years there should be 500,000 cars that could run on such fuels as methanol, ethanol, and natural gas, and from 1996 one million such cars should be produced each year. Clean-muffler equipment would be required on gasoline-driven cars to reduce exhaust emissions by 40%. The proposals, embodied in a new Clean Air Act, were being considered by Congress.

In August the administration published *Our Changing Planet: The FY 1990 Research Plan,* a 196-page document produced by the Committee on Earth Sciences of the Federal Coordinating Council for Science, Engineering, and Technology, which outlined a program to distinguish between and predict the effects of natural and human-induced global changes, especially in climate. President Bush asked Congress for an increase in the 1990 budget from $139.9 million to $191.5 million for research into global change.

U.S.S.R. Moscow Radio reported in March that 170 million rubles were to be spent cleaning up Sumgait, an industrial district that, it was said, could be smelled from kilometres away. Two outbreaks of thallium poisoning were reported in April—one at Chernovtsy in the Ukraine, where several hundred children were affected; the other 6t Sillamae, Estonia, where 24 children became ill and 17 were sent to Moscow for treatment. The deputy public health minister, Aleksandr Baranov, blamed car exhausts.

MAJOR CONCERNS

Greenhouse Effect. As scientists continued to describe the possible consequences of global warming resulting from the greenhouse effect, climatic change emerged as a major political issue. In October 1988 participants at a UNEP conference at Split, Yugos., were warned that Venice, Alexandria in Egypt, and Split would be the first cities to be inundated if the Mediterranean were to rise, as predicted, by 13 to 55 cm (5 to 22 in) by 2025 and by up to 2 m (6.5 ft) by late in the 21st century. In November 1988 *The Impact of Climatic Variations on Agriculture,* a report by an international team of scientists, was published in Vienna. It predicted a northward shift of cereal-growing areas with increases in output in some areas but a return to dust-bowl conditions in the U.S. wheat belt. Mikhail Budyko, the Soviet climatologist who was one of the first to warn of the greenhouse effect, suggested at an international conference in the same month that the warming might bring generally increased rainfall and make tundra regions more productive.

In March 1989 scientists at the Meteorological Institute of the University of Bonn, West Germany, reported that the average temperature in the tropics had risen by nearly one degree Celsius since 1965, and the amount of water vapour over the equatorial Pacific had increased by 20 to 30%. In April Alan Strong of the U.S. National Oceanic and Atmospheric Administration (NOAA) reported a rise in sea-surface temperatures at a rate of about one degree Celsius every ten years between 1982 and 1988. In Britain the first results from the Biochemical Oceanic Flux Study, released in June, showed that large plankton blooms in the North Atlantic were absorbing substantial amounts of carbon dioxide, although scientists said this absorption might decrease as temperatures rose. Richard Peltier of the University of Toronto said in April that his calculations suggested the sea level might be rising about 2.4 mm (0.09

in) per year, twice as fast as previously estimated. Rising sea level around Australia was reportedly destroying large areas of low-lying tropical forest in parts of Queensland. In Britain there were warnings of increased coastal erosion, especially in eastern England. According to an EPA report published in October 1988, a one-metre (3.3-ft) rise in sea level would inundate one-quarter to three-quarters of all U.S. wetlands.

In September 1989 the director of the University of Cambridge's Scott Polar Research Institute produced data showing that the thickness of sea ice in an area north of Greenland had decreased from 6–7 m (20–23 ft) in 1976 to 4–5 m (13–16 ft) in 1987. Later the same month an assessment of the effects of building an airstrip at the British Antarctic base at Rothera revealed a rapid loss of ice due to a substantial rise in summer temperatures since 1982. Figures released in June by NOAA's Oak Ridge (Tenn.) National Laboratory showed global carbon dioxide emissions had increased by 10% since 1983, to a total of 5.6 billion tons of carbon a year. Measurements at the Mauna Loa Observatory in Hawaii, reported to a meeting of the National Academy of Sciences in March, showed a surge in atmospheric carbon dioxide between 1987 and 1988, probably due to bush fires caused by drought.

It was reported in October 1988 that UNEP's executive director, Mostafa Tolba, planned to produce a convention on climate change that would be ready for endorsement within three years. In May the British government was reported to be drafting such a convention for submission to the UN, but U.S. delegates to a May meeting in Geneva of the UN Intergovernmental Panel on Climate Change were instructed to drop their own proposal for an international convention and not to support that by Britain. At a meeting of environment ministers from 68 nations in The Netherlands in November, the U.S., Japan, and the Soviet Union blocked a Western European-backed timetable for limiting emissions of carbon dioxide.

Ozone Layer. Pressure continued for the complete phasing out of chlorofluorocarbon compounds (CFCs) and halons, which were implicated in the decrease in atmospheric ozone. On May 2, at a UNEP meeting in Helsinki, Fin., 80 nations agreed to a Finnish proposal to ban CFCs completely by 2000, on condition that the technologies needed to introduce substitutes were made available to Third World countries, and to phase out halons as soon as feasible. Support for a ban was not unanimous, however. In February it was reported that China planned to increase

its production of the refrigerants CFC11 and CFC12 10-fold by the end of the century, to an annual output of 132,000 tons. This would make China one of the world's leading CFC producers, although at 0.05 kg (1.76 oz) per person per year it would not exceed the limits set out in the 1987 Montreal Protocol.

A series of conventions signed by the French government and industry were expected to result in a 90% reduction in French use of CFCs and halons by 1991. In July the city of Irvine, Calif., passed an ordinance forbidding the manufacture, sale, or distribution of any product containing ozone-depleting compounds from July 1, 1990. The British firm ICI announced in November 1988 that it planned to build two factories, one in Britain and the other in the U.S., to produce HFC 134c, a CFC substitute for use in refrigeration and air conditioning. Du Pont, which also planned to produce this compound, patented two alternatives to CFC113 for use in cleaning electronic circuits.

Depletion of the ozone layer over Antarctica, measured by the Nimbus 7 satellite, was 15% in September 1988, compared with 50% a year earlier. Reporting these figures, the U.S. National Aeronautics and Space Administration attributed the decrease to unusual climatic conditions. By autumn of 1989, however, it appeared that the so-called ozone hole was increasing again. (*See* EARTH SCIENCES: *Meteorology.*) According to balloon studies at Kiruna, Sweden, reported in July, a depletion estimated at 3% of the total ozone column occurred over the Arctic during what had been the coldest January in at least 25 years.

Whaling. The Japanese whaling fleet sailed for Antarctic waters in January to hunt 300 minkes, but on arriving it was confronted by protesters from the *Gondwana,* a ship of the environmental organization Greenpeace, supported by a helicopter. The protest ended on February 2, after the *Gondwana* had been in collision with the factory ship *Nisshin Maru No. 3* and the crew of a Greenpeace inflatable had been thrown into the sea with grappling hooks and hosed with sea water. The fleet caught 241 whales. At the June meeting of the International Whaling Commission (IWC) in San Diego, Calif., Japan was refused permission to double its catch by exempting its traditional coastal whaling communities from the international moratorium and was denied an interim allocation of 320 minkes. The Japanese delegate said his country planned to take 400 minkes in the next season, and Norway planned to take 20. Iceland announced it would end scientific whaling for at least two years, and on August 1 Greenpeace ended its campaign for a boycott of Icelandic fish. (See *Wildlife Conservation,* below.)

Antarctica. In May French Prime Minister Michel Rocard said in a television interview that France would not ratify the Convention on the Regulation of Antarctic Mineral Resource Activities because it afforded too little protection. The convention, which had been signed in 1988, established guidelines for environmental protection during mineral exploration and exploitation in Antarctica, but environmentalists feared it would actually cause damage by permitting mineral exploitation to take place. Australia also refused ratification, citing the same reason as France. The convention required ratification by 16 of the 20 Antarctic consultative parties, including all seven countries with territorial claims, so the refusal of France and Australia, both claimant countries, would effectively veto it.

On January 28 the Argentine supply ship *Bahia Paraiso* ran aground on its way to the Esperanza base, spilling diesel fuel that washed ashore three kilometres (two miles) away. The 316 people on board were rescued before the

(continued on page 214)

Controlling Oil Spills

BY RICHARD GOLOB

Within 72 hours after the *Exxon Valdez* tanker ran aground on March 24, 1989, in Prince William Sound, Alaska, and spilled about 200,000 bbl of crude oil, cleanup crews had succeeded in recovering only 3,000 bbl of the spilled oil. This low recovery rate focused attention on the inability of current oil-spill technology to contain and recover massive spills in the open ocean. It also focused attention on the inadequacy of oil-spill equipment stockpiles and response teams to provide an effective response to massive open-ocean spills.

The problem with the technology for controlling oil spills is the problem with any technology: it has limitations. Whether the strategy is to contain, recover, or disperse the spilled oil, the technology involved operates effectively under a limited range of conditions. Once the winds, wave heights, and water currents reach certain levels, the spill-control technology becomes ineffective. Since a spill response in the open ocean is likely to encounter these conditions, the probability of mounting a successful open-ocean cleanup is unlikely.

At the same time, it is important to note that most oil spills do not take place in the open ocean. In fact, more than 95% of spills occur in inshore areas, such as ports and bays. In these sheltered areas the conditions tend to be less variable and less extreme and, as a result, the available technology has made possible the recovery of relatively large amounts of the oil.

In any spill an early response is the best response, simply because the available technology is most effective on freshly spilled oil. Once the spilled oil begins to move away from the spill site and form a slick, the task of containing it becomes increasingly difficult as winds and water currents carry the oil in changing directions.

At the same time that the oil forms a slick, it undergoes a weathering process whereby it loses certain components through several natural reactions, including evaporation, photochemical oxidation, and dissolution into the water. The weathering process causes the spilled oil to become more viscous, making it more difficult to recover mechanically or disperse chemically. In addition, turbulence may cause the oil and water to form a stable water-in-oil emulsion, or "mousse," which also presents problems for skimmers and dispersants.

Booms and Skimmers. In a spill response one of the first priorities is to deploy booms, or mechanical barriers, to contain and concentrate the oil near the spill source for recovery or to prevent it from reaching sensitive resources, such as marshes or oyster beds. Booms generally consist of a flotation device, a tension member, a skirt, and a freeboard section. The flotation device, such as a gas-filled chamber or a solid float, keeps the entire assembly afloat, while the tension member helps the device hold its shape in the presence of currents, waves, and winds. The skirt extends down into the water and helps prevent oil from escaping under the booms, while the freeboard

Richard Golob is president of World Information Systems and publisher of Golob's Oil Pollution Bulletin.

extends above the surface and helps keep the spilled oil from washing over the boom.

Booms are effective in containing spilled oil under relatively calm to moderate conditions. However, when the wave heights exceed 0.9–1.2 m (3–4 ft), or the water current speed at right angles to the boom increases above one knot, the boom loses its effectiveness in containing the oil. Under those conditions oil begins to seep under the boom and splash over the freeboard.

Once the spilled oil has been contained, skimmers provide a mechanical means for recovering it from the water surface. These devices make use of several different principles in order to remove the spilled oil without changing its chemical or physical characteristics. Some skimmers employ a power source to create a vacuum for sucking up the spilled oil, while others depend on material having a strong affinity for oil (oleophilic), formed into a belt, rope, or disk, to attract the spill, after which it can be scraped or squeezed off the material and collected in a storage area. Still others rely on the force of gravity to cause the floating oil to flow over a weir positioned at the oil-water interface and then down into a collection area, from which it is eventually removed. Each type of skimmer achieves the highest recovery rates on freshly spilled oil in thick concentrations and operates most effectively in relatively calm waters.

Dispersants and Other Chemical Treatments. The most controversial spill-control approach involves dispersants, chemicals that tend to break the slick up into small droplets, which then disperse into the upper layers of the water. The application of dispersants from either planes or boats provides a relatively rapid way to treat spilled oil over a large area. By dispersing the spilled oil into the water, the chemicals prevent the oil from contaminating birds and other surface organisms, including fish eggs, as severely as it otherwise might. In addition, by breaking up the slick into small droplets, the dispersants help to increase the rate of biodegradation of the oil.

At the same time, however, dispersants increase the oil concentrations in the upper layers of the water, thereby increasing the potential toxic effects of the oil on the marine organisms there. As a result, dispersants are not recommended for use in shallow waters with poor circulation or in protected bays and inlets.

In 1989 a U.S. National Research Council report concluded that the "use of dispersants as a first response option to oil spills should be considered along with mechanical cleanup." This conclusion represented a continuation of the trend to accept dispersants as an integral part of the spill-control arsenal, especially as the limitations of mechanical containment and recovery became apparent. Dispersants had been regarded cautiously in the U.S. since the *Torrey Canyon* tanker grounding and subsequent spill that occurred off southwestern England in March 1967, when dispersants with a high toxicity were used to treat the spilled oil and caused widespread damage to the marine life in the treated area. Subsequently, however, low-toxicity dispersants were developed, and application techniques improved.

For dispersants to be effective, they must be applied to freshly spilled oil. Otherwise, as the oil weathers, it will become increasingly viscous and less dispersible. In addition, dispersants function most successfully when there is moderate wave action to help mix the oil, water, and dispersants together.

In addition to dispersants, there are several other chemical treatments for combating spilled oil. Chemicals known as oil herders tend to keep the oil slick intact so

that it does not break up. Unfortunately, these chemicals are expensive per unit volume of oil treated.

Burning. Like the other options, burning has limitations. It is effective on relatively thick, freshly spilled oil. However, burning requires ignition, and since the ocean serves as a heat sink, it is difficult to provide a steady heat source to keep the oil's temperature above ignition. In addition, burning oil causes air pollution. The usefulness of burning has been demonstrated in cold environments, where the spilled oil is viscous because of the low temperatures and does not flow readily.

Cleanup on Shore. When spilled oil washes ashore, the cleanup options include doing nothing and, thereby, allowing the oil to degrade naturally. In many situations, however, where the oil has affected commercially valuable resources or environmentally sensitive areas, that approach is unacceptable. The techniques for actively recovering spilled oil from shoreline areas include using sorbents, high-pressure water, and bioremediation, in addition to simply using shovels and other manual methods.

Sorbents are oleophilic materials that recover oil either by adsorption or absorption. They work best on freshly spilled oil; as the oil increases in viscosity, the sorbents lose their effectiveness. The oleophilic material can consist of natural products such as peat or straw; mineral compounds such as ash, vermiculite, or perlite; or, most commonly, synthetic products such as polyethylene or polypropylene.

Steam and high-pressure water have been useful in removing oil from rocks, piers, and other structures. Once the oil is washed from the contaminated surface, it flows back into the water, where it is contained by booms and then recovered by skimmers.

Bioremediation has received increasing attention as a viable shoreline cleanup technique. In this approach, phosphorus and nitrogen nutrients are applied to the spilled oil along the beach to enhance the growth of naturally occurring oil-degrading bacteria. During the *Exxon Valdez* cleanup this technique was used on a limited basis and apparently resulted in visible changes to the treated shoreline areas.

PIRO. In the aftermath of the *Exxon Valdez* spill, the U.S. oil industry proposed the establishment of a Petroleum Industry Response Organization (PIRO), both to provide a response capability for massive open-ocean spills and to develop new spill-control technology. The industry announced the proposal in June 1989 and at that time estimated that the five-year program would cost $250 million. Since then, cost estimates have increased to almost double that amount. The plan would involve the establishment of five regional response centres nationwide, operated around the clock, and about 20 staging areas for equipment stockpiles. While PIRO would dramatically increase industry's response capabilities, part of the proposal involved the expenditure of $30 million to $35 million on research and development. PIRO would target research on technologies that would keep the spilled oil near the spill source, that would recover or treat it before it washed ashore, and that would ensure a rapid cleanup once it had contaminated the shoreline.

Although the oil industry has proposed a concerted effort to improve its response capabilities, it is not clear whether research and development will result in any cure-all technology. In the end, the best way to respond to oil spills is to prevent them. Prevention involves the possible use of double hulls and double bottoms on tankers, the implementation of traffic systems in major ports, and the imposition of severe penalties on spillers.

(continued from page 212)

ship sank on February 1. Peter E. Wilkniss, director of Polar Programs at the U.S. National Science Foundation, told the Senate Committee on Commerce, Science, and Transportation in September that the wreck was still slowly leaking diesel oil. The oil had affected krill and seabirds that were nearing the end of the breeding season at the time of the spill. The *Gondwana* arrived in early January at the French Dumont d'Urville base to protest against the building of an airstrip, and there were complaints about waste left behind at the Wilkes base, established in 1957 as a temporary U.S. station and handed over to Australia in 1964. Australian members of Greenpeace found 200 to 300 gasoline drums, many still full, old food sacks, and derelict buildings. They also claimed the U.S. replacement base, McMurdo, was discharging raw sewage and dumping spent batteries. In February the *Gondwana* crew collected and returned to the base seven 40-gal (151-litre) drums of untreated chemical waste from the sea outfall at McMurdo. (*See* WORLD AFFAIRS [Polar Regions]: *Antarctica.*)

Marine Pollution. On March 24 the U.S. suffered the worst oil pollution incident in its history when the tanker *Exxon Valdez* ran aground on Bligh Reef in Prince William Sound, Alaska, releasing some 200,000 bbl of its cargo of 964,000 bbl of oil. The ship was later refloated and towed away for repairs, but bad weather and delays in the arrival of suitable equipment hampered efforts to contain the spilled oil. By early April more than 3,600 sq km (1,400 sq mi) of water had been fouled. The slick did not break up until around April 14, when it had drifted into the Gulf of Alaska and was dispersed by heavy seas, but by that time about 1,770 km (1,100 mi) of coastline had been contaminated. Thousands of animals were killed, including some of Alaska's rarest species. By mid-September, when Exxon withdrew from the cleanup operation for the winter, the company had spent an estimated $1 billion on the operation, including about $90 million in settling claims. Both it and the Aleyska Pipeline Service Co. faced lawsuits. Exxon countersued the state of Alaska, claiming it had hindered the cleanup by opposing the use of oil-dispersing chemicals. The captain of the *Exxon Valdez,* Joseph Hazelwood, who according to some reports had been drinking and had left an inexperienced seaman at the wheel at the time of the accident, was indicted on criminal charges.

The U.S. suffered three more serious oil spills, two of which occurred on June 23. The Greek tanker *World Prodigy* struck Brenton Reef, near Newport, R.I., spilling about 10,000 bbl of light heating oil, which spread over about 130 sq km (50 sq mi), and a freighter and an oil barge collided in the Houston (Texas) Ship Canal, spilling about 5,950 bbl of crude oil from the barge and contaminating beaches in Galveston Bay. The third spill happened on the following day when the Uruguayan ship *Presidente Rivera* strayed from the marked channel and ran aground in the Delaware River, spilling about 19,000 bbl of heavy heating oil. Britain also suffered from oil spills. On Dec. 3, 1988, the Liberian-registered *El Omar* spilled more than 100 tons of light crude in Milford Haven estuary, Wales, contaminating more than 16 km (10 mi) of coastline. In August 1989 a fracture in a Shell pipeline released about 150 tons of crude oil into the River Mersey, contaminating 48 km (30 mi) of shoreline. (*See* Special Report.)

In November 1988 the Central Committee of the Soviet Communist Party announced a 20-year program to increase the flow of water into the Aral Sea. According to an article by Y.E. Ponarina, published in *Socialist Weekly* in June 1989, the health of two-thirds of the people in the Karakalpak Autonomous Region bordering the sea was

suffering because of pollution. The removal of water from the Amu Darya and Syrdarya rivers, which flow into the sea, had caused the area of the sea to shrink by at least one-third since 1960, concentrating pollutants in the remaining water.

On January 1 international controls came into force regulating the dumping at sea of rubbish from ships. It became illegal to dump articles made from plastics that do not degrade or any wastes within three miles of land. The dumping of other wastes was permitted more than 12 or 25 mi from land, depending on the nature and prior treatment of the waste.

Toxic Wastes. Some progress was made in regulating the international trade in toxic wastes when, on March 22, the Convention on the Transboundary Movements of Hazardous Waste was adopted at a conference in Basel, Switz. Although only 34 countries signed the convention, another 105 gave it general endorsement. The convention, prepared under the auspices of UNEP, establishes the right of countries to refuse to accept cargoes of hazardous wastes, sets out rules for the notification of planned shipments, and obliges the governments of originating countries to ensure that receiving countries have adequate storage and disposal facilities. In the case of illegal dumping, the agreement requires the exporting company or its government to find an alternative disposal site or to return the waste to its country of origin. Difficulties concerning substances that are considered toxic in some countries but not others remained unresolved.

In Europe, Commissioner Ripa di Meana said on September 13 that the European Commission had adopted a waste-management program under which dangerous waste would have to be disposed of at the nearest adequate centre. This would effectively ban competitive international bidding for waste disposal and would prevent the dumping of wastes in Third World or Eastern European countries. A report from the House of Commons Select Committee on European Legislation, published in August, indicated that the British government opposed the EC scheme on the grounds that it would inhibit the free movement of shipping and considered the International Maritime Organization a more appropriate body to deal with such matters. On August 15, however, the U.K. environment secretary, Christopher Patten, called on developed countries to process their own wastes and said he would urge EC environment ministers to support a halt to all shipments of toxic wastes among members of the Organization for Economic Cooperation and Development. At the same time, he warned that hasty action might lead to the dumping of wastes at sea.

Patten was reacting to the well-publicized arrival in early August of the Soviet freighter *Khudozhnik Saryan,* carrying the first of 15 consignments of wastes, including polychlorinated biphenyls (PCBs), from the St. Basile-le-Grand warehouse near Montreal, which was destroyed by fire in 1988. Greenpeace inflatables followed the ship as it approached Tilbury, and the port authority refused it entry. A second consignment, on board the *Nadezhda Obukhova,* was then refused entry to Liverpool. It was disclosed later that PCBs were routinely imported into Britain for incineration and that 100 containers of the compounds had already passed through Liverpool in 1989. When the first of the ships arrived back in Canada, at Baie Comeau, Que., several hundred protesters attempting to prevent the cargo from being unloaded were held back by riot police.

Deformities and deaths were alleged to have occurred among animals in the vicinity of Carrbrook, in Tameside, Greater Manchester, England, where high dioxin levels had been found. The source of the contamination was believed to be a chemical factory that had been destroyed in an explosion in 1981. High levels of tetrachlorinated dioxins were discovered in milk from 1,000 cows near a Rotterdam, Neth., waste incinerator in August. Greenpeace activists were arrested in March while protesting about a waste dump that was leaking chemicals, including the insecticide BHC, into the Gallego River in Spain. Water in Zaragoza and meat and vegetables from the surrounding area had been contaminated.

In January the U.S. Department of Energy released its estimate that $92 billion to $128 billion would be needed to clean up radioactive and chemical pollution from government-owned nuclear weapons and other plants. Sen. John Glenn (Dem., Ohio), chairman of the Senate Government Affairs Committee, said that when pollution from naval reactors was included, the true cost would be closer to $200 billion.

Chernobyl. On January 24 the Supreme Soviet of the U.S.S.R. voted an additional 243 million rubles for parts of Byelorussia affected by the 1986 nuclear reactor accident at Chernobyl. In August the government of the Byelorussian S.S.R. announced contingency plans for evacuating 103,-

DAVID WALBERG

A corncob and a newspaper that were recovered from a Phoenix, Arizona, landfill show little sign of decomposition, despite having been buried for more than 30 years. About 80% of U.S. garbage ended up in landfills, where little of it decomposed.

000 people from areas in Mogilev and Gomel provinces, where high caesium-137 levels had been discovered. In late February Vladimir Kolinko of Moscow News reported an increase in the number of animals born deformed at a collective farm in the Narodichi district, 50 km (31 mi) southwest of Chernobyl, outside the 30-km (18.5-mi) exclusion zone. In the five years before the accident, the farm had recorded three deformed piglets and no deformed calves, but 37 piglets and 27 calves were born seriously deformed in 1987, and in the first nine months of 1988, there were 41 deformed piglets and 35 calves. Medical workers had also noted an increase in chronic illness among humans and a doubling of new cancer cases, especially of the lip and thyroid gland. Tass reported that areas of woodland and countryside around the Chernobyl site were to be studied to evaluate the effects of radiation on wildlife. High radiation levels had been found in insects, fish, and small mammals, and some rodents showed genetic damage. Oak and acacia trees were reportedly producing unusually large leaves, while some pine needles were 10 times larger than normal.

Bhopal. On February 14 a final settlement was reached between the Indian government and Union Carbide Corp. over the 1984 industrial accident at Bhopal, India, that killed some 3,500 people. Criminal charges against company employees were dropped, and the company agreed to pay $470 million in full and final settlement of all claims.

(MICHAEL ALLABY)

WILDLIFE CONSERVATION

Poaching of rhinos and elephants continued to be of concern worldwide. The Zimbabwe Department of National Parks announced that it planned to dehorn a particularly vulnerable population of white rhinos, and in May Namibian officials started to cut off the horns of black rhinos in Damaraland. Poachers killed rhinos for the horn, which was used for dagger handles and as an aphrodisiac.

Over the past 10 years there had been massive declines in African elephant populations. Current numbers were estimated at 625,000, but the persistent demand for ivory and the high level of the illegal trade threatened the breeding potential of elephant family groups. The Ivory Trade Review Group set up by the International Union for Conservation of Nature and Natural Resources, in cooperation with the Convention on International Trade in Endangered Species of Wild Fauna and Flora (CITES), concluded that the level of take was far higher than could be sustained in the long term and that many elephant populations were heading for extinction. Kenya and Tanzania, in particular, were alarmed over the loss of tourist trade that could result from the decline of elephant herds—a popular tourist attraction—and the dangers posed by poaching activities. In a gesture aimed at dramatizing the situation, the Kenyan government, in July, publicly burned tusks, confiscated from poachers, with an estimated value of $3 million. In October CITES classified the African elephant as an endangered species, effectively banning international trade in elephant products. Five countries, however, said they would continue to trade outside the convention. They included Zimbabwe and Botswana, which had flourishing herds and relatively little poaching and which earned considerable revenue from ivory and other products obtained from culled animals.

There was much international concern over the destruction of rain forest, the irreplaceable habitat of innumerable animal species. In March a study prepared for the International Tropical Timber Organization showed that only 1% of the world's 800 million ha (1 ha = 2.47 ac) of productive tropical forest was being exploited without irreversible damage. The world had already lost half of the 1.5 billion ha of humid forest in existence at the beginning of the century, and 10 million–20 million ha of rain forest were being cleared or burned each year. On January 10 the Thai government banned all logging, just two months after flooding and mud slides, caused by deforestation, killed 430 people. Indonesia also banned exports of rough sawn timber from January, in part to slow the rate of deforestation. The Philippines, where more than 90% of virgin forests had been destroyed, announced a $1 million reforestation plan, and the Philippine House of Representatives approved a bill banning tree cutting in all but 9 of the country's 73 provinces. Papua New Guinea banned the export of logs of 10 tree species in June and planned to issue no more new log export permits after 1991.

Brazil was much in the news because of the destruction of Amazonian forests. A vast area—some reports estimated as much as 129,500 sq km (50,000 sq mi)—of virgin forest was reportedly lost in 1988; at the end of 1988 fires spread along a front of thousands of kilometres, shrouding northern South America in a pall of smoke that could be seen and smelled in Rio de Janeiro several thousand kilometres south.

Although new species of invertebrates and smaller animals are constantly being described, discoveries of new species of larger animals are rare. In February a new species of lemur—*Propithecus tattersalli* or the golden-crowned sifaka—was reported from northeastern Madagascar, where about 100 were estimated to live in a very restricted and fragmented habitat threatened by further deforestation. For the first time, the technique of DNA fingerprinting was applied to endangered species research. Geneticists were using the technique to investigate the relationships of the 28 Californian condors (*Gymnogyps californianus*), representing the total world population—all in captivity—so the best pairings for the future of the species could be made.

In June delegates at the annual meeting of the International Whaling Commission in California heard that the numbers of great whales in the Southern Hemisphere were far lower than had been calculated previously and that some—the blue whale with an estimated 200–1,100 individuals, the fin whale with an estimated 2,000, the sperm whale estimated at 10,000, and the humpback, believed

Conservationists in Namibia prepare to dehorn a drugged black rhinoceros. Although rhinos use their horns for defense and foraging, wildlife officials concluded that removing the valuable horns was the only means left to protect them from poachers.

to number some 4,000—were on the verge of extinction.

(JACQUI M. MORRIS)

See also Agriculture and Food Supplies; Botanical Gardens and Zoos; Energy; Life Sciences; Transportation.

This article updates the *Macropædia* article CONSERVATION OF NATURAL RESOURCES.

Fashion and Dress

The year 1989 was hardly a vintage year for high fashion, with no breakthrough for a new silhouette and no revolutionary line. The only message for the future was a new softness, with the hard edge of a mannish silhouette replaced by a new gentleness. Was it, perhaps, the start of a kinder, gentler world as envisioned by U.S. Pres. George Bush in his inaugural speech?

Attention turned to details, with focus on ornamentation, lavish embroidery, shimmering lamés and rich brocades for evening, and a great play of capes and stoles for day wear.

Despite the freshness of Neapolitan *cassata* colours, the warmth of deep purples and oranges inspired by the traveling Gauguin exhibition, and colourful designer collections and window displays, the street look in the springtime was black from head to toe. Never before was there such a discrepancy between theory and practice in the fashion world.

In the winter of 1988–89 the look was based on the tailored jumpsuit, all in one with ankle-clearing pants worn with a wide, low-waisted leather belt with metal buckle and a sprinkle of nails or knobs.

In the summer the jumpsuit softened into wide palazzo pants in a full-skirted effect. When separate, the top was a front or back crossover blouse, tied on one hip, in a sheer fabric such as crepe, chiffon, or a very fine jersey. For hot climates the top was strapless and gathered in bandeau style. The micromini or "tube skirt" pursued its urban career in Lycra mixture fabric for an ultraclinging effect, appearing in black for winter, with black tights in heavy maille, and debuting again in black for spring but with bare suntanned legs. Low, square-heeled bootees were worn for winter, and flat or low-heeled cyclist shoes, gillies, or ballerinas later on. T-shirts and knit pullovers were also featured in black. In the spring, tops turned to crisp white cotton or became romantic with white silk shirts or blouses with billowy sleeves.

A touch of drama was provided by large-brimmed hats in black felt with flat crowns, Spanish style. U.K. Prime Minister Margaret Thatcher wore one of these to the Paris summit meeting in July. Occasionally masses of flowers, also black, circled the crown, as on London's King's Road Fashion Walk.

Eccentricity and imagination broke loose for hats worn at the races. At Ascot in England and Chantilly in France, it was a case of the madder, the better. There were wide-brimmed Panamas, flowered cartwheel hats, winged horsehair ones, and the latest high-crowned, mannish, chimneypot shape in vividly coloured straw with a bunch of flowers centre front as a finishing touch.

The French Revolution bicentennial celebration inspired Paris fashion stylists to design in red, white, and blue. However, stripes—horizontal or vertical— were generally confined to window dressing and magazines. Few stripes ventured out on the streets except for those on belts, ribbons for the hair, and scarves.

A safe street look was provided by a long, tailored blazer worn over a mid-thigh, narrow, unmatched skirt or a pair

A model wears a silk floor-length evening gown in a soft floral print. The gentler, more feminine shapes in women's fashion were evidenced in casual wear as well as evening wear, showing a turn away from the sharply defined mannish silhouette.
AFP PHOTO

of shorts. An alternate jacket was cropped to just over the hipbone, double-breasted, with scoop neckline allowing a cluster of stones, beads, or pearls around the neck and braid trimming along the edges. A rash of gold buttons served as trimming down and across, and often up the sleeves from wrist to elbow. Another easy street look was suggested by the coatdress. Above the knee, slim, and wrapped like a bathrobe or buttoned up the front or to the side with gold buttons, it was made in crisp but, alas, not yet wrinkleproof linen.

Later in the summer the popular skirt was sarong shaped—crossed over and tied at the hip. It was a big look for the beach and, with a bare midriff, for evening. The Indian influence was visible in the length, from mid calf to ankle, and in the prints and colours: curry, saffron, navy, and burgundy in paisley patterns.

A trend for wildlife emerged in beige animal prints featuring endangered species, usually spotted leopards and striped tigers melded between jungle leaves. Spotted fake furs reappeared in the autumn for accessories— soft berets, bags, belts, and gloves.

In a move away from black, bright red—christened "Bastille red"—had its blaze of glory. However, an outsider appeared. An ecological thrust in politics and a love for nature were responsible for introducing a clear fresh green, a colour always avoided by the superstitious fashion world. In midsummer the tube skirt practically vanished overnight. The thigh-revealing skirt was replaced by black thermal pants clinging to mid calf. Then, as if a tidal wave had hit hemlines, skirts descended to just above the ankle, gained in fullness and softness, and were often divided.

A wave of boleros and vests appeared after the crossover blouse in such fluid and see-through fabrics as organza,

chiffon, and lace. There were also all sorts of breezy blouses worn with palazzo pants and without shoulder pads or bras by the under-30 age-group. The aim for vests and boleros was to emphasize the bust by using masses of jeweled embroidery, gold threads, beads, pearls, and black jet in pear drops. Boleros and vests were paired off with gauzy chiffon pants or easy, flowing above-ankle skirts. This was the main trend with the elegant evening audiences attending music festivals. For the daytime, summer vests were in white piqué, embroidered cotton, or lace.

The autumn version of vests appeared in speckled tweed, leather, suede, or velvet with a spattering of embroidery in Tyrolian style. With the profusion of costume jewelry available, there was no limit to the number of necklaces and chokers, bracelets, earrings, and rings for every finger. High-cuffed gold metal African-style bracelets vied with bracelets in clear or misty altuglass. Altuglass was also popular for sunglasses. Seashells in their original shape and substance turned up as cuff links or were combined into a cross, dangling on a chain of rock crystal. A twist of gold seashells became an earring. Wide silver or bronze rings with a centre colour stone could be traced to the Middle East.

Lycra, having done so well with the winter black, turned to white for an equal success in summer. Stretch dresses, bicycle shorts, and beachwear all owed their beautifying quality to Lycra's clinging nature. In the summer of 1989 a deep suntan was considered outdated. The formula was:

A strapless gown of sea green and midnight blue is modeled during a fashion show in the Louvre Museum's glass pyramid in Paris. As environmental protection became a global concern, natural greens, once avoided by the fashion world, were embraced.

just baked but never overbaked. On the beaches the golden girl selected two shades of mother-of-pearl for lipstick, one in the light copper range. Rose and again copper were combined on eyelids to brighten eyes set off by a terracotta base. Hair tended to be worn short, in a boyish cut with roots uplifted for extra volume. Long hair was carefully coiffed, braided or twisted and coiled into chignons held in place by coloured barrettes and combs. Swimsuits rallied to the one-piece suit with high cutouts on hips, low heart-shaped necklines, and, as a surprise effect, elbow-length sleeves. Some suits were trimmed with a narrow frill at the hem, ballet dancer style. Others were just the classic, plain "body" in luminous colours. There were also some dot prints and jeans effects in Lycra. The latest trend was a two-piece "retro" outfit with a high-waisted culotte and a classical bra that could be worn with a huge, floppy straw hat for sunbathing. Two-piece swimsuits combined distinct patterns, including two types of printed stripes or dots, and even appeared in conflicting colours.

Denim, true to type, was worn faded and ripped by the backpack crowd but, under the influence of black and white Japanese art, was seen printed with stripes, flowers, and checks.

Black and white had its say for autumn in checks of various sizes and speckled tweeds for suits, pants, separate jackets, and spencers.   (THELMA SWEETINBURGH)

Men's Fashions. Two factors—one predictable, the other unpredictable—were responsible for changes in men's fashions in 1989, the last year marking the era of the elegant '80s. Predictably, the adverse economic conditions in most countries of the world, especially those in Europe, resulted in less money being spent on clothes by men in all age groups. What had not been foreseen was the long, hot summer that resulted in men in most age groups wearing outfits more usually associated with leisure occasions than formal and business ones. Colourful T-shirts, mostly in cotton and in either floral or geometric patterns and sometimes emblazoned with a logo or advertising message, were worn unashamedly during all hours of the workday. Bermuda shorts, popular in the Americas, also became fashionable. When long pants were worn instead of shorts, they were either white or in soft pastel shades of primrose yellow, salmon pink, or sky blue.

Denim still held its ground as the preferred fabric for pants and jackets, but it met with a challenge from the crisp cottons, cool wool, linens, and some synthetic fibre blends.

Caps, usually in cotton or linen for the summer and wool tweeds for the autumn and winter months, were more fashionable than hats.

Both before and after the long, hot summer months, double-breasted styles overtook the single-breasted lounge suits. The double-breasted button six with a one-button fastening was followed by the emergence of suit jackets with long, rolling lapels. Patterns were more subdued, with blue and gray stripes predominating but in lighter shades. Attempts by men's clothing associations to persuade men to wear brown suits were not successful. White shirts once again emerged as an essential item in the wardrobe of the well-dressed man. More white shirts were sold and worn, to the exclusion of those in bold stripes on colourful grounds, which had been fashionable in previous years.

Vests, fashion garments in their own right, were featured in lightweight cottons and linens for summer and heavier meltons for winter.   (STANLEY H. COSTIN)

See also Industrial Review: *Furs.*

This article updates the *Macropædia* article DRESS AND ADORNMENT.

Gardening

Weather again played a prominent role on the garden scene in 1989. For a time it appeared that there would be a serious drought in the northeastern U.S., and water restrictions were planned. Instead, the East Coast experienced record-breaking rains, with the result that fungus diseases were rampant, and many beds of annual display flowers had to be replanted. At the same time, gardeners in the British Isles struggled to keep their gardens blooming in the face of severe drought. The summer was the second driest ever recorded in England and Wales.

Concern over the effect of gardening practices on the environment led to the formation of new consumer groups in the U.S., many initiated by mothers worried about the leaching of lawn and garden fertilizers into water sources. Other environmental problems were the casual use of pesticides by lawn services and homeowners and the stock of leftover pesticides and motor oils. Some localities instituted toxic-waste-disposal days, when homeowners were asked to bring their unwanted toxic materials to designated areas for safe, professional disposal.

A major step was taken toward conservation of the so-called minor or species bulbs. The major bulbs—tulips, hyacinths, and daffodils—are raised as crops in The Netherlands and exported worldwide, but many of the minor bulbs are dug from the wild in Mediterranean countries and sent to The Netherlands for marketing. Conservationists feared that this practice, together with grazing, was endangering the bulb populations. In response to these concerns, a group of conservation organizations and representatives of the Dutch bulb industry, meeting in The Netherlands, agreed on the introduction of protective marketing measures that, it was hoped, would save the wild bulb species from extinction.

THE COLLEGE OF ENVIRONMENTAL DESIGN,
DOCUMENTS COLLECTION, UNIVERSITY OF CALIFORNIA AT BERKELEY

"September Border Looking Down Through Laburnum Arch" is part of the photographic essay *Gertrude Jekyll: A Vision of Garden and Wood.* The book, which contains dozens of photos taken in Jekyll's gardens, is a celebration of the English garden at the turn of the century.

The popularity of perennials continued to soar, boosted by the advent of plastic containers that could be set out in rows at garden centres. Home gardeners appreciated these plants for their convenience and the almost "instant garden" they provided. Buyers were becoming more sophisticated in their selections, and a number of small mail-order nurseries had been established to supply the demand for specialties. Another trend was the incorporation into home gardens of native plants of the area. Roses continued to lead in popularity, however. A survey made for the All-America Rose Selections committee, a trade group, showed that one out of every four U.S. households, or about 23 million, had rosebushes in the garden and that the householders spent an average of $36 on new or replacement bushes each year. Hybrid teas were the favourites.

In the U.K., Wolseley Garden Park near Rugeley, Staffordshire, owned by Sir Charles and Lady Wolseley, was being developed into a major leisure and educational centre. Among other features, it would include a walled rose garden and a maze in the shape of the British Isles. Other gardens formed during the year included the Botanic Centre, developed on a 9-ha (23-ac) site near Middlesborough, and the National Gardening Centre at Capel Manor, Enfield, designed to provide a shop window for the horticultural industry. The most popular garden opened by the National Trust in 1989 was Stourhead Gardens in Wiltshire, which attracted over 214,000 visitors.

A National Waterlily Collection was established at Wycliffe Hall Botanical Gardens at Barnard Castle. Also at Wycliffe, the National Hyacinth Collection was planted and would come into bloom in the spring of 1990. A hundred historic gardens and parklands in Kent were now under the care of the Kent Gardens Trust, launched on October 17. Plantlife, a new conservation group supported by the Botanical Society for the British Isles, was founded in November.

Fleuroselect, the European seed-testing organization, awarded the first gold medal in its 19-year history to the *Coreopsis grandiflora* Early Sunrise. The perennial bedding plant grows to 46 cm (18 in) and produces an abundance of semidouble, golden-yellow blooms. Other Fleuroselect award winners included *Lobelia speciosa* Compliment Scarlet, *Dianthus* Telstar Crimson, and *Tagetes* Disco Orange, Disco Golden Yellow, and Orange Jacket. Glad Tidings, a rich crimson floribunda bush rose, was chosen Rose of the Year by the Rose Growers Association.

Innovations included a new aromatic form of the Mexican orange blossom called *Choisya* Aztec Pearl and Sensation, the first floribunda geranium. Ballerina trees, the first columnar fruit trees, were produced after 15 years of work at the Institute of Horticultural Research in East Malling. Four apple varieties had been developed, three eating apples and a crab apple. All four grow as a single column with no side branches and require virtually no pruning.

For the third successive year a new world record onion weight was established at the Kelsae Onion Festival in Harrogate. The winning onion weighed in at 4.4 kg (9 lb 11½ oz), surpassing the 1988 record by more than 0.24 kg (8½ oz). A new pumpkin record weight of 322 kg (710 lb) was set at the U.K. Giant Vegetable Championships on October 6, but three days later, at the World Pumpkin Weigh-Off in New York, a Canadian pushed the record to a massive 343 kg (755 lb).

(JOAN LEE FAUST; ADAM GERHOLD PASCO)

See also Agriculture and Food Supplies; Botanical Gardens and Zoos; Life Sciences.

This article updates the *Macropædia* article GARDENING AND HORTICULTURE.

Health and Disease

The year 1989 saw a number of significant developments in medicine, including improvements in diagnosis and treatment of disease, along with major advances in the understanding of disease processes at the molecular level. Among the year's notable developments were the identification of the gene responsible for cystic fibrosis, the most common genetic disorder in the Caucasian population; the finding that an experimental drug, levamisole, significantly increases the effectiveness of chemotherapy treatment for colon cancer; and the discovery that the drug zidovudine (Retrovir), also called AZT, the only drug approved in the U.S. for the treatment of AIDS (acquired immune deficiency syndrome), actually wards off the development of the disease in people who are infected but show no symptoms. Also during 1989, researchers at the U.S. National Institutes of Health (NIH) reported initial success in the first human experiment in gene transfer, in which a bacterial gene was used to monitor the progress of cancer therapy.

Controversy continued regarding the effects of both birth control pills and hormone replacement therapy on a woman's subsequent risk of breast cancer. In the U.S. the mandating of a new policy for the distribution of experimental drugs—not yet approved for marketing by the Food and Drug Administration (FDA)—to persons with AIDS and other life-threatening conditions was being closely watched for its effects on the process of clinical trial and approval.

AIDS. The *New England Journal of Medicine* reported in 1989 that an estimated 2.5 million people in the Western Hemisphere were infected with HIV-1 (human immunodeficiency virus, type 1), the virus that causes AIDS, and warned that if this organism continued to spread among the poor populations of Latin America and the Caribbean, a massive epidemic could occur in that region, paralleling the catastrophic spread of AIDS in Africa. In Brazil, the country with the most AIDS cases in Latin America, one report indicated that HIV infection was well established among homosexuals, bisexuals, and lower-class female prostitutes, bisexual men apparently acting as a "bridge" between the homosexual and heterosexual communities. The most draconian response to AIDS was being taken in Cuba, where the entire population was being screened for HIV and those found to be infected placed in virtual quarantine.

In the U.S. the most serious concern continued to focus on specific groups of high-risk individuals—in particular,

intravenous drug abusers and their sexual partners; persons previously infected with syphilis or other sexually transmitted diseases characterized by the presence of genital ulcers, which apparently facilitate the transmission of HIV; "crack" users, at increased risk because of the prevalent practice of sex-for-drugs barter and the consequent increased risk of both genital ulcer disease and AIDS; and infants born to HIV-infected mothers.

The growing concern about AIDS in newborns was not confined to the U.S. One French survey revealed that at least 27% of 117 infants born to infected mothers and followed up to 18 months were themselves infected. In Zaire HIV-positive women were found to be far more likely than uninfected women to give birth prematurely. Their babies had lower birth weights and a higher death rate during the first four weeks of life. Researchers at the U.S. Centers for Disease Control made an important advance in the diagnosis of AIDS in newborns, using the technique known as polymerase chain reaction, or PCR. This technique makes possible the amplification of minute amounts of DNA. Using PCR, researchers have been able to seek out tiny bits of viral DNA derived from HIV that have become incorporated into the cells of infected individuals. Thus they were able to detect direct evidence of HIV infection in newborns. It had not been possible to diagnose AIDS in newborns by means of antibody testing because of interference by maternal antibodies.

Of major importance in the control of the disease was the finding that the drug zidovudine could retard the development of AIDS in infected persons who had no symptoms, or only mild ones, but who showed a slight decline in immune function. Previously zidovudine, a prescription drug, had been approved by the FDA only for use in persons with AIDS or the group of symptoms known as ARC (AIDS-related complex). The new finding prompted federal health officials and many AIDS activist groups to urge all those who thought they might have been exposed to HIV to be tested for it and, if test results were positive, to begin to take zidovudine. It was not known, however, how long the drug remained effective in staving off development of the disease in infected individuals. Furthermore, there was evidence that over time HIV can become resistant to the drug.

Studies conducted by Philip Pizzo of the National Cancer Institute showed that AZT could prolong the lives of and reverse dementia in children with AIDS. In October 1989, on the basis of this finding, federal health officials—who had withheld approval of zidovudine treatment for children—finally approved the drug for administration to

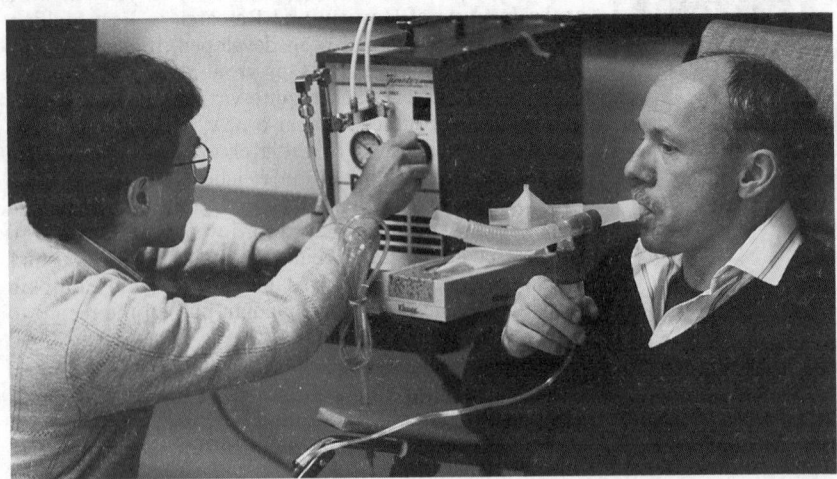

MARILYNN K. YEE/THE NEW YORK TIMES

A person with AIDS inhales an aerosol form of pentamidine, a drug used to treat and prevent pneumocystis pneumonia—the leading cause of death among AIDS patients. The drug was approved for marketing in June 1989 under the FDA's accelerated approval program but had been made available to seriously ill patients before that time.

A park official warns a group of hikers about Lyme disease, a debilitating disease transmitted via infected ticks. Lyme disease spread quickly throughout the United States and was found to affect animals as well as people.

JAMES D. WILSON/WOODFIN CAMP & ASSOCIATES

all children with AIDS; the drug's manufacturer, the Burroughs Wellcome Co., said it would distribute zidovudine free to children.

The concept of early intervention in AIDS was complicated by the discovery that HIV infection can occur long before antibodies against the virus become evident in the blood. Thus the standard blood test for AIDS, which detects antibodies, might not be as reliable as was first believed. Using PCR, researchers were able to find DNA from HIV in blood samples from healthy homosexual men months or, in some cases, years before their blood tested positive for antibodies to the virus. The phenomenon and extent of latent infection were not yet fully understood. Nonetheless, these findings raised the possibility that some people who had been tested for antibodies to HIV and found negative might want to be retested when PCR technology became more widely available. The finding of widespread latent infection could have profound implications for drug treatments that showed promise of delaying the onset of symptoms.

Two other drugs—ganciclovir (Cytovene), used to treat a viral eye disease that afflicts many AIDS patients, and the aerosol form of the antibiotic pentamidine (Nebupent), used to treat and prevent pneumocystis pneumonia, the most common serious opportunistic infection in AIDS patients—were approved for marketing in the U.S. in 1989 under the FDA's new accelerated approval program. A looming question was who would pay—not only for treatment of the increasing numbers of persons with AIDS, many of whom had insufficient or no insurance—but also for early intervention, which involved regular testing of those at risk, counseling of persons found to be HIV-positive, and monitoring of infected individuals for signs of disease. One calculation of the cost of early intervention for half of the estimated one million HIV-infected persons in the U.S. was $5 billion yearly. Burroughs Wellcome took one step toward making zidovudine more widely available, reducing its price by 20%, and the Lyphomed Corp., makers of the costly aerosolized pentamidine, began distributing it free to uninsured patients.

For other promising anti-AIDS drugs not yet on the market, a "parallel track" approach was initiated in 1989, enabling AIDS patients to receive the drugs while official studies of their safety and effectiveness were still in progress.

This new policy might have far-reaching consequences for drug testing and approval in general. For example, despite having been officially tested in only some 100 people, the drug dideoxyinosine, or DDI, which is similar in effect to zidovudine, was made available free to patients who could not tolerate or did not respond to zidovudine. Patients received DDI and other such drugs from private physicians or community-based research groups and had to be warned that they could suffer unanticipated toxic effects because full-scale clinical trials were not yet complete. Nonetheless, in the case of DDI, so many AIDS patients wanted to receive the drug that the FDA, in December 1989, had not been able to enroll a sufficient number of patients for a controlled clinical trial. In the clinical trial some patients—those in the "control" group—would not receive the drug being tested. Persons anxious to take DDI were therefore unwilling to enter the trial. This circumstance, some authorities feared, could undermine the entire formal drug-approval system.

In the meantime, underground networks for obtaining highly experimental drugs, mostly from abroad, remained active in the U.S. Controversy arose about one clandestine study in which several AIDS patients obtained the Chinese drug known as GLQ223, or "compound Q," which had been smuggled into the U.S. by an AIDS activist group, Project Inform. One patient who received the drug died a short time later, although apparently not as a direct effect of the drug. Tests of candidate vaccines also continued. Several appeared to be effective in halting infection with simian immune deficiency virus (SIV), an AIDS-like disease of monkeys, and the first vaccine approved for testing in humans was found, encouragingly, to boost immune responses against HIV in people already infected with the virus.

Genetics and Gene Therapy. The year's most spectacular breakthrough in the understanding of the molecular basis of disease was the identification of the gene that causes cystic fibrosis (CF). Two teams shared credit for the discovery, one led by Lap-Chee Tsui and John Riordan at Toronto's Hospital for Sick Children, the other by Francis Collins at the Howard Hughes Medical Institute of the University of Michigan. The protein encoded by the CF gene apparently regulates the movement of vital substances across cell membranes. An abnormality in the protein was believed

to be responsible for the development of the thick, sticky mucus that clogs the lungs and digestive systems of those with CF. The most immediate effect of the discovery was expected to be an improved method of prenatal diagnosis and carrier detection. Eventually it might be possible to treat the disorder by supplying the needed protein or even to correct the underlying defect in protein synthesis by means of gene therapy.

Advances in the area of gene therapy itself, which had attracted much interest in recent years, were proving more difficult to accomplish than researchers originally thought. In 1989, however, scientists at the NIH initiated the first human experiment in gene transfer, with encouraging results. The purpose of the experiment was not to treat a genetic defect but rather to monitor the progress of an experimental cancer therapy. The treatment consisted of delivering modified immune system cells, taken from patients' own tumours, back into their bodies, where, it was hoped, the modified cells would seek out and destroy the tumours. A bacterial gene whose presence could be detected easily was inserted into the immune system cells to serve as a marker, allowing the cells to be tracked. By year's end the NIH team had reported their first success; in at least one patient, the labeled gene reached the tumour, and the melanoma showed signs of regression. The modified cells remained in the patient's body up to 19 days.

Cancer. Breast cancer, the second most common cause of cancer deaths in women (lung cancer was first), commanded much attention during the year. There was renewed concern about the possibility that postmenopausal hormone replacement therapy (either estrogen alone or estrogen-progestin combinations) might cause breast cancer. A study conducted at University Hospital in Uppsala, Sweden, involving more than 20,000 women indicated that women using such hormones had 10% more breast cancers than expected; the figure rose to 70% for women who used the hormones for nine years or more. There was also a suggestion of a higher risk for women taking estrogen-progestin combinations for more than six years

CHARLES OSGOOD; © 1989 CHICAGO TRIBUNE COMPANY

A surgical team prepares to operate on Alyssa Smith, who was about to receive a section of her mother's liver. The operation was the first in the U.S. to use a section of a liver from a living donor, and, if successful, would revolutionize pediatric liver transplantation.

as compared with estrogen alone. These findings were understandably worrisome to the many women who took replacement hormones for protection against other ailments, such as osteoporosis and heart disease.

On the question of whether taking birth control pills increases a woman's risk of breast cancer, the already existing confusion was added to in 1989 as reports continued to come down on both sides of the issue. The results of a 10-year U.S. study, published in September in the *Journal of the National Cancer Institute,* indicated that women who did not begin using oral contraceptives until their mid-20s were at no increased risk of developing breast cancer in middle age. A British study published earlier in the year in *The Lancet* reported that women under 35 who had taken the pills for four years had a 43% increase in the risk of breast cancer; the risk rose to 74% after eight years. The author, Clair Chilvers of the Institute of Cancer Research in London, called upon physicians to fully inform women of the potential risks of oral contraceptives. Chilvers also advised women to seek birth control pills that had the lowest effective doses of hormones and to take them for the shortest possible time. Only one new study, conducted at University Hospital in Lund, Sweden, assessed the risk of breast cancer (premenopausal) in women who had started using oral contraceptives in their teenage or young adult years. It showed a greater than fivefold higher risk for such women. However, the birth control pills currently being used contained lower doses of hormones than the formulations taken by the women in the study, and there was as yet no information on the risk associated with the newer low-dose pills.

Disagreement continued over whether women with early-stage breast cancer that had not spread to adjacent lymph nodes ("node negative") should receive adjuvant (additional) therapy, either drug or hormonal, after surgery. The results of four studies, three U.S. and one European, published in February 1989 in the *New England Journal of Medicine,* indicated that adjuvant therapy was beneficial. Each of the studies demonstrated that more women who had received such therapy were alive without recurrence after four years than women who had not—although the ultimate survival rates of the two groups did not differ. An accompanying editorial, however, stated that even without additional treatment, which might entail severe side effects, 70% of node-negative women lived a long time without tumour recurrence; in addition, the editorial pointed out, some women died as a result of the adjuvant therapy itself. Therefore, it concluded, decisions on adjuvant therapy should be made on an individual basis. On the other hand, in another editorial in the same issue, Vincent T. DeVita, Jr., of the Memorial Sloan-Kettering Cancer Center in New York City, said that the four studies provided evidence that adjuvant therapy significantly decreases the risk of recurrence, and he recommended that such therapy be offered to all breast cancer patients except those with very small tumours.

Patients with another common type of cancer—colon cancer that has spread to adjacent lymph nodes—were shown definitely to benefit from adjuvant therapy. Two studies, one not yet completed, showed that the drugs fluorouracil, also called 5-FU (Adrucil), and levamisole, given after surgery, substantially reduced the death rate from this stage of the disease in treated patients as compared with those who received no treatment. Levamisole was not yet approved by the FDA for marketing in the U.S., but the National Cancer Institute (NCI), which sponsored the trials, said it would make the drug available to physicians treating colon cancer patients under a special arrangement similar

to the AIDS "parallel track" approach. Also, because NCI officials believed this therapy should now become the standard treatment for this stage of colon cancer, against which more promising therapies would be compared, they halted study arms of all clinical trials in which such patients had been randomly assigned to groups scheduled to receive no treatment or observation only. Those patients were told of the new findings and offered an opportunity to take the new drug regimen.

Cardiovascular Disease. The final report on aspirin from the U.S. Physicians' Health Study was published during the year. It demonstrated a 44% reduction in the risk of heart attack in physicians taking low-dose aspirin (325 mg every other day). The numbers of subjects who suffered strokes or died from cardiovascular disease, however, were too small for the effect of aspirin on these outcomes to be determined conclusively. Studies in Israel did establish that taking 100 mg of aspirin daily during the third trimester of pregnancy significantly reduced the incidence of pregnancy-induced hypertension in women at high risk for this complication.

Two investigations highlighted the significance of the menopause as a contributor to cardiovascular disease. Researchers at Erasmus University Medical School in Rotterdam, Neth., used radiography to study the amount of atherosclerosis in premenopausal and postmenopausal women. Even when adjusted for age, the results showed a 3.4 times greater risk of atherosclerosis in those who had natural menopause and a 5.5 times greater risk for those who had had both ovaries removed. The Dutch researchers concluded that the risk of atherosclerosis rises when estrogen production ceases, either naturally or after surgery. More detailed studies at the University of Pittsburgh, Pa., indicated that the menopause has unfavourable effects on fat metabolism, which might contribute to a heightened risk of heart disease, and that hormone replacement therapy might prevent some of those effects.

In a study designed to see whether certain drugs could not only suppress irregular heart rhythms (arrhythmias) that frequently occur after heart attack but also reduce the number of sudden deaths that ensue, researchers found to their surprise that patients treated with two of the three drugs being tested had a higher death rate from arrhythmias and other heart problems than patients in the control group, who received a placebo. The portions of the multicentre study using the two commercially available drugs, encainide (Enkaid) and flecainide (Tambocor), were halted. In another surprising turn of events, a study from the Albert Einstein College of Medicine, Bronx, N.Y., showed that in persons being treated with drugs to reduce mild or moderate hypertension, those who had either a large drop or a small drop in blood pressure had far more heart attacks than those who experienced only moderate drops in blood pressure. The reason was unknown; there was no evidence that the type of antihypertensive drug used mattered more than the decrease in blood pressure. Other studies had shown that treating hypertension, while it reduced the number of strokes, did not reduce the number of heart attacks. The Einstein researchers concluded that there was no "ideal" blood pressure, and therapy should be tailored to the individual.

Other Promising Developments. Among the many other newsworthy developments announced in 1989 were preliminary reports of the success of a new drug, known only by its code name FK-506, in preventing the rejection of transplanted organs. Some new hope was offered to persons newly diagnosed with Parkinson's disease; the drug deprenyl (Eldepryl), currently approved for use as an adjunct to levodopa (L-dopa) for those in advanced stages of the disease, was shown to delay the onset of symptoms when taken early in the course of the disease. Researchers at the Chiron Corp., Emeryville, Calif., announced that they had identified an elusive virus that causes the form of liver disease known as non-A, non-B hepatitis. A blood-screening test was almost immediately developed by Chiron to detect the so-called hepatitis C virus, and two research teams reported that treatment with alpha interferon was successful in controlling the devastating liver infection caused by the newly identified organism.

In the first operation of its kind in the U.S., doctors at the University of Chicago's Wyler Children's Hospital performed liver transplant surgery using a section of a liver from a living donor. The recipient was a 21-month-old girl; the donor was the girl's mother. It was predicted that the new procedure would revolutionize pediatric liver transplantation, increasing the availability of donor livers and thus making the surgery available to youngsters earlier, before they had become so ill that their chances of surviving the procedure were compromised by their desperate need for it.   (BERNARD DIXON; GAIL W. MCBRIDE)

MENTAL HEALTH

People born in the United States and Western Europe after World War II had benefited from economic prosperity by being physically healthier than their forebears, but the mental well-being of postwar generations became the focus of increasing concern as reports grew of high rates of depression, suicide, alcoholism, and substance abuse. In 1989 the *Journal of the American Medical Association* published a major "metaanalysis" (a study that draws conclusions from analysis of existing data) of this problem, carried out by Gerald Klerman of Cornell University Medical College, New York City, and Myrna Weissman of the New York State Psychiatric Institute.

Although previous studies indicated similar trends, some of this earlier research suffered from a lack of appropriate "control" populations for comparative purposes. By pooling data from earlier surveys in the U.S., Europe, and elsewhere and by using refined diagnostic criteria and new statistical techniques, Klerman and Weissman were able to compile the most complete picture yet published of recent and current trends in mental health. The results revealed several pronounced trends in the U.S., Canada, West Germany, Sweden, and New Zealand, but these were not evident in comparable studies conducted in South Korea and Puerto Rico or among Mexican-Americans living in the U.S. In addition to rising overall rates of major depression, there was a decline in the age at which depression began, with a marked increase in the number of victims in their late teenage years and early adulthood. The survey showed that women were two to three times more prone to depression than men but indicated that this differential was growing smaller as depression increased among young men. Klerman and Weissman called for continuing surveillance of rates of depression, suicide, and alcoholism using methods similar to those employed for monitoring physical health and economic and demographic trends.

Research conducted in recent years at several London hospitals shed new light on a biochemical characteristic of seriously depressed patients and provided a "marker" that can be used to distinguish between two different types of depression. Previous studies by this group of investigators had demonstrated an abnormality in the metabolism of tyramine in patients with endogenous depression (not traceable to any external cause) but not in those with the less severe reactive depression (which occurs in response

A therapist whose house was damaged by Hurricane Hugo leads a therapy session for a group of teachers who, in turn, were to help other victims of the disaster. After the hurricane many survivors were found to be suffering from posttraumatic stress disorder.

TOM SPAIN

to external influences). After taking tyramine by mouth, people diagnosed with endogenous depression excrete subnormal amounts of tyramine sulfate in their urine. A study of 30 patients with major depressive disorders showed that this abnormality correlates with a positive response to the antidepressant drugs known as tricyclics. It could, therefore, probably be used to predict which patients would be helped by such medication.

A study conducted at the U.S. National Institute of Mental Health (NIMH), Bethesda, Md., found that the tricyclic antidepressant clomipramine (Anafranil) was highly effective in the treatment of trichotillomania, a condition characterized by an irresistible impulse to pull out one's own hair. (Clomipramine, widely used in European countries as an antidepressant, became available in the U.S. in 1988 for experimental treatment of obsessive-compulsive disorders.) Trichottillomania usually begins in childhood but is most commonly seen in adolescent girls and young women. Its cause is unknown. As with other obsessive-compulsive disorders, psychotherapy and hypnosis sometimes provide relief, but relapses are common. The NIMH psychiatrists found clomipramine to be significantly more effective than desipramine (Norpramin; Pertofrane), another widely used tricyclic, in reducing the symptoms of trichotillomania. Writing in the same issue of the *New England Journal of Medicine* in which this finding was reported, psychiatrist Michael Jenike of Massachusetts General Hospital pointed out that obsessive-compulsive disorders were now believed to be much more common than was previously thought. As many as 2–3% of the U.S. population—more than four million people—might be affected.

Further evidence concerning the relationship between emotional stress and the recurrence of cancer was provided by a recent British study. Researchers at Guy's Hospital and Lewisham Hospital, London, studied 100 women who had undergone surgery for breast cancer. The cancer had recurred in half of the patients but not in the other half after an equivalent time following the operation. Amanda Ramirez and colleagues found that extremely stressful events and difficulties in everyday life were significantly

more frequent among those whose cancer recurred. The relative risk of tumour recurrence was 5.67 for those experiencing severely stressful life events, such as divorce or the death of a husband or child, and 4.75 for those facing severe difficulties (for example, the need to care for a severely handicapped child). The authors drew attention to U.K. census data indicating a link between stressful life events and deaths from cancer and suggested that psychological treatments could be devised to help cancer patients cope with the consequences of the disease and with subsequent stressful events. (BERNARD DIXON)

This article updates the *Macropædia* article MENTAL DISORDERS and Their Treatment.

DENTISTRY

In a study that was part of a cross-national survey on health behaviour in schoolchildren, conducted by the World Health Organization (WHO), the oral-hygiene habits of 30,000 children in 11 European countries received high marks. Age groups involved were 11-, 13-, and 15-yearolds. The percentages of children brushing at least once a day ranged from 98% in Sweden and 96% in Switzerland to 79% in Belgium and 68% in Spain. Girls were more frequent brushers in every country; toothbrushing frequency seemed to increase with age among girls but not among boys.

A U.S. government study released in 1989 found that only 7.6% of American schoolchildren had had dental sealants applied to their teeth. The National Institute of Dental Research (NIDR), Bethesda, Md., reported this surprising finding at the annual meeting of the American Dental Association in San Francisco. Preston A. Littleton, Jr., NIDR deputy director and deputy chief dental officer of the U.S. Public Health Service, said that U.S. dentists would like to see a much higher use of sealants. He noted that 25 years of research had proved sealants to be safe, effective, and very economical in preventing tooth decay. The promolars and molars to which the sealants are applied are the tooth surfaces least helped by fluorides and the ones most susceptible to cavities.

Dental researchers were attempting to make dentures, tooth crowns, and other ceramic dental appliances tougher by exposing them to the same "heat-tempering" process used to make car windshields shatter resistant. Researchers at the University of Florida College of Dentistry said that in laboratory tests the technique, called thermal tempering, had proved effective in increasing resistance to cracking, chipping, and fracturing of dental porcelain disks.They planned eventually to use the tempering process to produce crowns, bridges, and other porcelain dental appliances.

Researchers at the University of Pennsylvania found that braces can actually help prevent gum disease (periodontitis), a major cause of tooth loss. Because braces move poorly aligned teeth into different, corrected positions, bacteria that cause gum disease have difficulty settling into the gums. An added protective factor was that persons with braces also must be especially meticulous in their oralhygiene regimens.

In another development in the treatment of periodontal disease, researchers at Tel Aviv (Israel) University discovered a new antibiotic with "adhesive" qualities. The drug, a colourless compound that clings tightly to a variety of tissues, could be particularly useful in the treatment of diseased gum tissues. (LOU JOSEPH)

VETERINARY MEDICINE

Veterinary science was on the verge of a technological revolution comparable to the therapeutic revolution of the

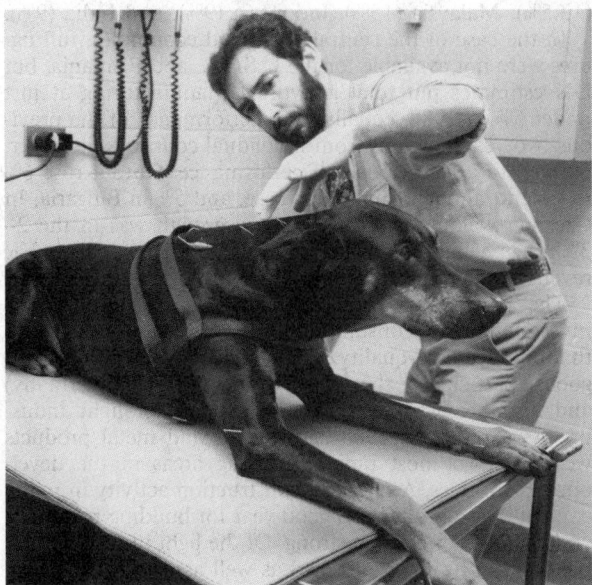

A Doberman pinscher patiently undergoes acupuncture treatment for wobbler syndrome, which results in spinal cord compression. The American Veterinary Medical Association officially recognized acupuncture as a valid treatment.

AP/WIDE WORLD

1960s. In August 1989 delegates at a joint meeting of the American Society of Animal Science and the American Dairy Science Association heard of the potential of a number of promising technological developments. Through the use of somatotropins (growth hormones), the milk yields of dairy cattle could be increased and the lean meat content of cattle and pig carcasses improved. Feed additives based on beta-adrenergic compounds could have a similar effect. Both growth hormones and feed additives increased by 10 to 20% the efficiency with which the animals utilized their feed. Gene transfer techniques, in which a gene containing desirable factors is introduced into an animal and can be passed on to its progeny, could be of immense importance in the breeding of livestock with enhanced resistance to disease. However, fears that such techniques might be subject to misuse led to calls for strict controls to regulate their application.

Princess Anne, who had the rare distinction of being an honorary associate member of the Royal College of Veterinary Surgeons, gave the opening address at the World Veterinary Poultry Association Congress at Brighton, England, in August. She noted in her remarks that poultry raising now provided the major source of meat protein in many parts of the world, and she emphasized the importance of the poultry veterinarians' role in helping to alleviate poverty and malnutrition in less developed countries. One problem in large-scale poultry production was infectious disease, which could rapidly destroy unprotected flocks. Vaccines were widely used to establish immunity; occasionally, however, infectious agents altered and became resistant to the vaccines in use. Such was the case with infectious bursal disease of poultry (Gumboró disease), outbreaks of which had been reported in the U.K., Europe, Israel, Turkey, and South Africa. Trials were under way to develop an effective vaccine against the disease.

The Battersea Dogs Home in London, a 128-year-old establishment that took in 22,000 strays a year, adopted an electronic method for identifying the dogs it found homes for. It involved a microchip, about the size of a rice grain, that was imprinted with a unique number and then inserted under the soft skin between the dogs' shoulders. The microchip remained in place permanently; the number could be read by a device similar to a supermarket bar code scanner. Apart from the obvious advantage of being able to trace lost pets, the device was expected to help in the tracking of animals that were spreading feces-transmitted diseases. Public health officials also hoped that widespread adoption of a satisfactory means of linking a dog with its owner would reduce attacks on humans by uncontrolled dogs.   (EDWARD BODEN)

See also Life Sciences; Populations and Population Movements; Social Security and Welfare Services.

This article updates the *Macropædia* articles DISEASE; MEDICINE.

Industrial Review

At the start of 1988 prospects for the world economy appeared anything but good. World stock markets had crashed the previous October, and the dollar was falling precipitously. The recovery in world activity, dating from late 1982, appeared to have run its course, and fears abounded that 1988 would be the year in which the long-awaited recession finally arrived. Yet 1988 proved to be a boom year. The growth of gross national product in the developed nations reached 4.5%, with manufacturing output 6% higher and world trade in manufactures rising an exceptionally rapid 8%. In the Western world as a whole, manufacturing advanced 6%, with the centrally planned economies slightly behind at 5%.

In retrospect it was the general relaxation of monetary policy immediately after the stock market crash rather than the crash itself that was the prime determinant of world activity in 1988. Lower interest rates, in combination with increasing pressure on capacity as the world upturn entered its sixth year, underpinned a worldwide boom in investment that had important repercussions on the composition of industrial output and also the direction of trade.

At the same time, the boom in activity—the most synchronized world upturn since the early 1970s—produced significant inflationary pressures. Commodity prices, oil and non-oil, rose sharply; labour markets tightened as unemployment fell to its lowest levels in many countries since the 1970s; and demand pressures pushed up wages

Table I. Annual Average Rates of Growth of Manufacturing Output, 1975–88
Percent

Area	1975–80	1980–85	1986	1987	1988
World[1]: Market economies	4.2	1.9	2.7	4.2	6.1
Industrial countries	3.9	1.6	1.7	3.3	6.1
Less industrialized countries	6.6	3.6	8.7	8.2	6.0
Centrally planned economies	5.5	3.7	4.9	4.5	4.9

[1] For definition *see* Table IV.
Source: UN, *Monthly Bulletin of Statistics.*

Table II. Manufacturing Production in the U.S.S.R. and Eastern Europe[1]
1980 = 100

Country	1984	1985	1986	1987	1988	%[3]
Bulgaria[2]	120	124	129	134	141	5
Czechoslovakia	111	116	119	122	124	2
East Germany[2]	117	122	127	131	135	3
Hungary	110	110	112	117	116	−1
Poland	94	97	102	105	111	6
U.S.S.R.[2]	115	120	126	130	...	...

[1] Romania not available.
[2] All industries.
[3] % change 1988–87.
Source: UN, *Monthly Bulletin of Statistics.*

and prices on a broad front. In response, the trend to tighter monetary policy, which had been interrupted by the stock market crash, was resumed. Led initially by the U.S. Federal Reserve System and followed to a greater or lesser extent by the European and Japanese authorities, interest rates were raised from the spring of 1988 onward. This had the dual effect of containing inflationary pressures and also ending the coordinated world upturn; the U.S. decelerated sharply, whereas for continental Europe the boom continued. In Europe 1989 was proving to be the peak of the cycle.

This was evident in the data for 1988, which showed European manufacturing (+5% over 1987) accelerating but still lagging behind the faster growing regions of North America (+6%) and Asia (+10%). Within Europe growth was remarkably uniform, in the 4–6% range in most countries. Only Norway and Sweden recorded significantly weaker growth, while only Ireland (13%) and the U.K. (7%) were appreciably stronger. What was also clear was that outside Asia the less developed countries were continuing to underperform the richer industrialized economies. Output growth in Central and South America was only 1.4%, and Australia and New Zealand also lagged behind. Within Asia the most rapid expansion again took place in Japan, where manufacturing output rose 10%, South Korea

(13.5%), Malaysia (15%), Indonesia (9%), and India (9%).

In the case of the centrally planned economies, full figures were not available for the U.S.S.R. and Romania, but UN estimates put total growth of manufacturing at just under 5% in 1988, equaling the performance of the previous two years. Figures from individual countries, however, pointed to a weaker overall performance. Output rose 6% in Poland, though from a low base, and 5% in Bulgaria. In Czechoslovakia and East Germany growth was in the 2–3% range, while in Hungary manufacturing contracted 1%, reversing the rapid gains of 1987.

The pattern of world demand—biased more toward investment than consumption—favoured those countries that produce high-quality, technologically advanced capital goods (particularly the U.S., Japan, and West Germany) and also heavy industry at the expense of light industry. As a result, in 1988 base metals and metal products were the two most rapidly growing areas in the developed economies. A boom in construction activity in many countries also produced a good year for building materials, and chemicals were also strong. Of the light industries only paper and printing performed as well as any of the heavy industries. For other light industries, notably textiles and clothing and footwear, 1988 proved to be a difficult year.

(GEOFFREY R. DICKS)

Table III. Pattern of Output, 1985–88

Percent change from previous year

	World[1]				Developed countries				Less developed countries				Centrally planned economies[2]			
	1985	1986	1987	1988	1985	1986	1987	1988	1985	1986	1987	1988	1985	1986	1987	1988
All manufacturing	4	3	4	6	3	2	3	6	6	9	8	6	5	5	5	5
Heavy industries	4	3	4	7	3	1	3	7	6	12	11	7	5	6	5	5
Base metals	1	−1	4	7	1	−4	3	9	3	8	10	3	2	4	3	3
Metal products	6	4	4	8	5	2	3	8	7	17	13	8	7	7	6	7
Building materials, etc.	1	3	3	5	−1	1	2	6	4	8	7	5	2	5	3	4
Chemicals	3	4	5	6	3	3	5	7	6	9	10	9	3	4	2	4
Light industries	2	3	4	4	1	3	3	4	5	6	5	4	3	4	4	4
Food, drink, tobacco	3	3	4	3	2	2	2	3	6	3	5	4	3	5	5	5
Textiles	2	3	3	1	1	2	2	0	5	7	5	0	3	2	2	3
Clothing, footwear	0	1	1	0	2	−1	−1	−2	1	8	7	4	3	1	2	3
Wood products	1	4	5	5	0	4	6	5	2	2	4	7	4	5	2	4
Paper, printing	3	5	6	7	1	5	5	7	15	7	9	10	3	6	3	4

[1] Excluding Albania, China, North Korea, and Vietnam.   [2] Excluding China.

Table IV. Index Numbers of Production, Employment, and Productivity in Manufacturing Industries

1980 = 100

Area	Relative importance[1]		Production		Employment		Productivity[2]	
	1980	1988	1987	1988	1987	1988	1987	1988
World[3]	1,000	1,000	118	125	...	...	...	...
Industrial countries	861	834	114	121	...	...	...	...
Less industrialized countries	139	166	140	149	...	...	...	...
North America[4]	282	289	120	128	...	...	...	...
Canada	22	23	121	128	...	...	...	...
United States	260	266	124	132	94	96	132	138
Latin America[5]	79	75	117	119	...	...	...	...
Argentina	12	...	92		...	...	...	...
Brazil	26	22	109	105	...	...	...	...
Mexico	18	16	109	112	...	...	...	...
Asia[6]	183	223	138	152	...	...	...	...
India	11	15	160	174	107	...	150	...
Japan	131	141	122	134	107	110	114	122
South Korea	6	13	244	277	...	...	...	...
Europe[7]	422	381	107	112	...	...	...	...
Austria	9	8	109	115	87	85	126	125
Belgium	13	12	108	114	...	...	...	...
Denmark	5	...	124	...	105	...	119	...
Finland	6	6	123	128	90	87	137	148

Area	Relative importance[1]		Production		Employment		Productivity[2]	
	1980	1988	1987	1988	1987	1988	1987	1988
France	75	63	100	105	84	...	119	...
West Germany	114	102	107	112	92	...	117	...
Greece	4	3	98	103	...	...	...	...
Ireland	2	3	150	169	81	80	185	212
Italy	54	47	103	108	84	...	123	...
Netherlands, The	14	13	111	116	...	...	...	...
Norway	5	4	110	109	91	...	120	...
Portugal	3	3	128	136	...	...	...	...
Spain	23	21	111	114	...	...	...	...
Sweden	13	12	119	119	91	...	131	...
Switzerland	13	12	107	115	...	...	...	...
United Kingdom	58	55	111	119	...	...	...	...
Yugoslavia	10	...	116		...	...	...	...
Rest of the world[8]	34	32	...	...	...	...	...	...
Oceania	15	13	104	107	...	...	...	...
South Africa	8	7	99	105	95	97	104	109
Centrally planned economies[9]	...	...	132	138	...	...	...	...

[1] The 1980 weights are those applied by the UN Statistical Office.
[2] This is 100 times the production index divided by the employment index, giving a rough indication of changes in output per person employed.
[3] Excluding Albania, Bulgaria, China, Czechoslovakia, East Germany, Hungary, Mongolia, North Korea, Poland, Romania, the U.S.S.R., and Vietnam.
[4] Canada and the United States.
[5] South and Central America (including Mexico) and the Caribbean islands.
[6] Asian Middle East and East and Southeast Asia; including Japan, Israel, and Turkey.
[7] Excluding Albania, Bulgaria, Czechoslovakia, East Germany, Hungary, Poland, Romania, and the U.S.S.R.
[8] Africa and Oceania.
[9] These are not included in the above world total and consist of the European countries listed in note 7 above.

ADVERTISING

An advertising code proposed in 1989 by a task force of retailers organized by the Council of Better Business Bureaus would set a U.S. benchmark for comparative advertising claims. The task force was composed of major retailers such as Sears, Roebuck and K-Mart. The code, which would be self-regulatory, was a response to charges leveled by state regulators and retailers concerning misleading claims about products made in competitors' advertisements. The code spelled out the substantiation an advertiser would need to support advertisements comparing prices in a variety of cases. Other claims addressed by the code included comparisons involving imperfect products and irregulars or seconds.

As in retailing, comparative advertising had become more widespread among manufacturers, with one company attacking the merits of another company's products. Starting in November 1989, a change in the Trademark Law Revision Act of 1988 made it easier for victims of attack advertising to sue. Under the Lanham Trademark Act of 1946, advertisers were prohibited from misrepresenting their own products. The new act prevented them from misrepresenting the qualities or characteristics of "another person's goods, services, or commercial activities."

Each year *Advertising Age* publishes a list of the top 100 U.S. advertisers of the previous year. In 1988 Philip Morris became the first company to spend more than $2 billion a year in advertising. It spent $2,060,000,000 in 1988, with 40% used to promote cigarette and beer products. Three companies, Proctor & Gamble, General Motors, and Sears, spent over $1 billion. The top 100 represented 27.3% of the estimated $118,050,000,000 total spent on all advertising in the U.S. in 1988. The top network television advertiser was General Motors, which increased its TV advertising budget by 62% to a total of over $400 million. Proctor & Gamble was the leading cable television advertiser, and Philip Morris was number one in magazine and outdoor advertising. The five leading newspaper advertisers were all retailers, headed by May Department Stores.

In October 1989 the governments making up the European Communities (EC) approved legislation that would create a single market in television broadcasting. The legislation, known as "Television Without Frontiers," would remove most of the barriers to intra-EC broadcasting by the end of 1992, when the new single European market would take effect. The act included a nonbinding recommendation that the majority of entertainment broadcasts be of European origin. In countries following this recommendation, U.S. syndicators of television programs would be precluded from selling a number of their programs to European broadcasting systems. Because of this and other changes resulting from the single market, major U.S. companies were reevaluating their approaches to advertising in Western Europe.

In recent years direct marketing had been used by an increasing number of advertisers to promote their products and services. According to the U.S. Office of Consumer Affairs, the most common consumer complaint was that information collected for one purpose, such as a credit application, was sold and used for direct marketing. In 1989 two bills were introduced in the U.S. Congress to curb automatic phone messages, outright fraud, and other telemarketing abuses. One would authorize the Federal Communications Commission to set up a national clearinghouse for consumers who wanted their names removed from selling lists. Since 1985, 950,-000 consumers had privately filed requests to have their names removed from mailing lists and more than 300,000 had notified telemarketers that they did not wish to be solicited by phone. An estimated seven million Americans a day received automatic telephone sales messages from an estimated 180,000 solicitors. Legislation to ban or at least restrict recorded messages was enacted or introduced in 27 state legislatures in 1989. More than 500 bills affecting direct marketers were pending at the state level.

There was a movement toward a "new puritanism" in television and television advertising in response to consumer complaints that network television was too lenient in its treatment of sex and violence. A

Michigan woman made national headlines when she called for advertisers to pull commercials from Fox Broadcasting Company's "Married . . . with Children" because of the way the program portrayed sex. A number of national advertisers, including Chrysler and Sears, removed their advertising support from NBC's "Nightingales" series after the American Nurses' Association started a letter-writing campaign to advertisers. Ralston Purina Co. and General Mills removed their advertising from NBC's "Saturday Night Live" because of questionable content in certain skits.

The four major television networks strengthened their broadcast standards operations, and advertisers and advertising agencies also initiated screening efforts to evaluate their television program sponsorships. Some advertisers also began to withdraw their support for programs coming under attack by special interest groups. In September 1989 a television special produced by the National Audubon Society, "Ancient Forests: Rage over Trees," was broadcast on Turner Broadcasting System without sponsors after eight advertisers withdrew their advertising because of pressure from the logging industry.

(EDWARD MARK MAZZE)

AEROSPACE

International air transport, the largest sector of aviation, in 1989 experienced huge orders for new aircraft and a growing shortage of airport capacity. Flights in Europe continued to be delayed by increasing congestion in the air, by the fragmented nature of national air-traffic control systems, and by the now-traditional strikes of French air-traffic controllers at peak holiday periods.

The upsurge in demand for new airliners continued. All three major international airframe builders—Boeing and McDonnell Douglas in the United States and Airbus Industrie in Europe—saw their order books grow as they tried to increase production rates. Both Boeing and McDonnell Douglas were criticized for delivery delays. Boeing's flagship, the new 747-400, entered service early in the year several months late, while the new MD-11 from McDonnell Douglas (a major revamp of the DC-10 trijet of the late 1960s and scheduled to fly early in 1990) was causing concern over predicted delays.

The industry was swamped by record-breaking orders. The call for 130 Boeing and Airbus transports placed by the International Lease Finance Corp. in May 1988 was eclipsed in 1989 by Guinness Peat Aviation's order for 308 airliners from all three builders, worth $16.8 billion. This order brought the Irish leasing company's fleet to 819 aircraft, valued at $30 billion. The leasing industry was coming into its own because predicted airline profits would buy outright only 10% of the 8,500 new aircraft that Boeing estimated would be needed over the next decade.

Individual airlines were making acquisition news, however; on just one day in February McDonnell Douglas announced orders and options from five airlines for aircraft worth $11 billion, a figure that included 50 MD-11 trijets for American Airlines.

Virtually all of these orders were placed to satisfy present and anticipated increases

THE NEW YORK TIMES

Tip O'Neill, former speaker of the U.S. House of Representatives, speaks from his suitcase in a commercial for Quality Inns. O'Neill appeared in a number of advertising campaigns, drawing criticism for what some saw as cashing in on his political career.

Technicians work on an assembly line of strategic B-2 Stealth bombers, which are covered with mats to protect their sensitive surface. Many breakthroughs achieved during the Stealth's manufacturing process resulted in advancements in machinery and computer technology.

NORTHROP CORPORATION

in demand rather than to replace older aircraft. The growth in air travel, along with long waits for new aircraft, obliged operators to keep old airliners rather than selling or retiring them, but mounting difficulties with them led to questions about how to guarantee their structural safety.

This problem came sharply into focus when in April 1988 an Aloha Airlines Boeing 737—one of the earliest 737s to be delivered—shed a large section of its fuselage roof; a flight attendant was killed when the resulting suction pulled her through the opening, and the plane's passengers were exposed to a 480-km/h (300-mph) wind. Further impetus to the investigations was given by the blowout of a large cargo door on a United Airlines 747 in February, from which nine people fell to their deaths in the Pacific. This plane also was one of the first of its type to enter service. The challenge facing the air transport industry, therefore, was how to limit the remaining number of flight hours permitted to elderly aircraft without unduly penalizing airlines by limiting their capacity.

The unducted fan experiments that had been conducted by U.S. firms during the past few years were shelved in 1989. Fuel costs—the rationale for these new devices—were not sufficiently high to justify the commercial launch of risky and expensive new technology at a time when airline profits were low. Also, the U.S. airframe industry had no spare resources for launching new ventures.

Nevertheless, the U.S. continued low-level studies of the HSCT, the High Speed Civil Transport, an environmentally acceptable aircraft that would travel as fast as five times the speed of sound and carry 250–300 passengers over ranges of 8,855 to 10,465 km (5,500 to 6,500 mi). No specific design was envisioned, only an investigation of the challenging technologies that developing the necessary special engines would require. Meanwhile, the 20th anniversary of the first flight of the supersonic Anglo-French Concorde was celebrated in January. Twelve of these aircraft

continued service between London, Paris, Washington, D.C., and New York City in 1989.

The surge in growth was also reflected in a healthy market for corporate and business planes. Companies such as Gulfstream, Canadair, and Learjet with their top-of-the-range corporate jets reported encouraging upturns in sales, but the operators faced pilot shortages (many going to better-paid jobs with the airlines, where there were also flight-crew shortages) and airport-access difficulties.

Soviet exhibitors provided the centre-stage attraction at the biennial Paris Air Show. Catapulted into the limelight by the policy of *glasnost* (openness), the comprehensive range of military and civil aircraft eclipsed the U.S.'s showing. The loss of a MiG-29 Fulcrum fighter during a flight display—its pilot was miraculously saved—did little to detract from the U.S.S.R.'s presentations. Dominating all others in size was the six-engined Antonov An-225 Mriya transport, by far the world's largest airplane, which had flown first at the end of 1988. Among many collaborative Western-Soviet arrangements subsequently announced, Sukhoi, a top U.S.S.R. fighter company, agreed to team with the U.S.'s Gulfstream Aerospace to study both a supersonic business jet for service entry in 1995 and a 50-seat commercial supersonic transport.

In August the U.S.S.R. staged a major Aviation Day air show at Tushino Airport near Moscow. Western observers were permitted to examine at close quarters aircraft not previously shown publicly, such as the Tupolev Tu-160 Blackjack bomber (externally a seeming copy of the U.S.'s B-1), Beriev's A-40 amphibian, the still-potent MiG-25R Foxbat D, and the Mil Mi-28 Havoc combat helicopter, similar to the U.S.'s McDonnell Douglas AH-64A Apache. The U.S.S.R.'s showing, at both Paris and Tushino, made it clear that the Soviets were aiming to capture world markets.

In the U.S. the year's military aviation

events were dominated by the first public disclosures of the Lockheed F-117A Stealth fighter in late 1988 and by the first flight of the Northrop B-2 Stealth bomber in July. The F-117A was an astonishing example of military secrecy in a democracy; the aircraft was designed, tested, and put into production and service (even apparently becoming operational in Europe) over a 10-year period without any formal acknowledgment of its existence or even a picture in the press.

In Europe a noteworthy event—perhaps a warning for the computer industry—was the crash of Sweden's first Gripen prototype fighter, possibly as a result of faulty software in the U.S.-developed flight-control system.   (MICHAEL WILSON)

AUTOMOBILES

Only two of the world's major automobile producers failed in 1988 to boost output over 1987: West Germany, down 0.2%, and Sweden, down 3.6%. The biggest gains were recorded by Canada, up 21% to 1,960,000 cars, trucks, and buses; Brazil, up 16% to 1,340,000; the U.K., up 11% to 1,530,000; South Korea, up 10.6% to 1,080,000; and Italy, up 10.4% to 2.1 million.

Europe, South America, China, and Australia. Western Europe recorded its highest ever car and commercial vehicle production in 1988, passing the 15 million level for the first time. Total automobile production increased from 13,364,811 units in 1987 to 13,846,032, and commercial vehicle output rose from 1,610,160 to 1,853,019. Total new vehicle sales in those nations (Belgium, France, West Germany, Italy, The Netherlands, Spain, and the United Kingdom) also reached a new high of 13,213,707 units, up from 12,521,404 in 1987. Those countries together accounted for 29% of total world automobile output, ahead of North America's 27% and Japan's 26%. Brazil and South Korea each produced about 2.2% of the world's motor vehicles in 1988, with the rest of the world, including Eastern Europe, Australia, and South Africa, producing the remaining 13%. Western Europe produced 32% of the world's passenger cars, ahead of Japan and North America, which accounted for just under 24% each.

In the first half of 1989 the Western European countries continued to experience growth in both car production and sales and seemed likely to register a fifth successive year of peak figures. New production peaks in the first half of 1989 were expected for France, Italy, West Germany, and Spain, and it was thought that the U.K. would reach its highest output since 1974. Most manufacturers also posted record or near-record profits in 1988 and could look forward to higher figures for 1989.

In the close-fought battle for European car market supremacy in 1988, Volkswagen Group of West Germany (including SEAT of Spain) finished just 8,000 units ahead of Italy's Fiat Group (including Alfa Romeo, Lancia, and Ferrari); each accounted for about 14.9% of total sales. France's Peugeot/Citroën was third with 12.9%, followed by Ford of Europe, 11.3%; General Motors (GM; Opel/Vauxhall), 10.4%; and Renault of France, 10.1%. The fastest volume growth was by Peugeot/Citroën.

European manufacturers were changing rapidly to meet ever growing challenges

from Japan. These included perceived superior Japanese productivity and, increasingly, product innovation; a rapidly growing Japanese manufacturing presence in Europe itself, particularly in Great Britain; the commitment of the EC to totally free trade by 1992; Japan's continuing success in winning sales from the Europeans in other parts of the world, particularly North America; and Japan's move into the former European-dominated territory of superluxury cars (Toyota Lexus and Nissan Infiniti) and sporting "supercars" (Honda N-SX and others anticipated in the early 1990s).

Major moves into the U.K. by the Japanese included Nissan, which began assembly there in 1986 and planned to move up from 200,000 cars a year to 400,000 by the late 1990s; Honda's 1989 acquisition of a 20% stake in the leading British carmaker, the Rover Group; and Honda's own plan to assemble 100,000 cars a year by 1994 following the start-up of a full-scale engine-manufacturing plant in England in mid-1989. The third major Japanese incursion into Europe was also destined for England; Toyota planned to assemble 100,000 cars a year there by 1995.

Mazda, 25% owned by the Ford Motor Co., was studying possible European assembly, as was Mitsubishi. In addition, major Japanese automotive components makers were following their vehicle manufacturing customers into Europe. By 1990 Japanese cars were expected to account for about 18% of the Western European market, compared with 11.3% in 1988. Additional pressure might come from exports to Europe of cars from Japanese plants in North America.

By no means did all product innovation emanate from Japan. This became evident with 1989 launches of cars such as the Mercedes Benz SL sports cars with optional five-speed automatic gearbox and many ingenious safety innovations; BMW's electronics-laden 850i coupe; the Citroën XM and Peugeot 605 luxury sedans; Opel's highly aerodynamic Calibra four-seat coupe; the Lotus (GM-owned) front-wheel-drive Elan sports car; a new four-litre Jaguar XJ6 and 5.3-litre XJ-S V12; and Rover Group's first major new four-wheel-drive car in 20 years, the VB Discovery. Late in the year Fiat acquired 49% of luxury carmaker Maserati.

In Eastern Europe production volumes changed little during the 1980s, totaling about 2.4 million cars and 1.1 million trucks each year. The Soviet Union planned to increase car output from 1.3 million in 1988 to 2 million in 1993. Poland's output fell back from the levels in the 1970s to about 350,000 cars in 1988, while East German, Yugoslav, and Czechoslovak production changed little.

Brazil continued to battle national inflation and other problems, including restriction on imports of high-technology components. Its three major makers were GM, Fiat, and Autolatina, the latter a slowly merging joint venture of the formerly independent Volkswagen and Ford organizations in Brazil and Argentina. Autolatina accounted for about 60% of a Brazilian car market that had been reduced from about one million units in 1980 to 600,000 in 1988. In Argentina's troubled economy automobile sales slumped to 164,000 in

1988, and production was down 15% from 1987 to 162,000, the same as in 1964.

Vehicle production in China expanded from 481,000 in 1987 to 647,000 in 1988. The great bulk of these were trucks, totaling 530,500. Japan and Western Europe were both playing key roles in the development of modern automobile production in China, but widespread shortages of raw materials and energy, recurrent austerity programs, and political uncertainty were expected to result in unsteady progress. Foreign companies involved in manufacture or negotiations included Volkswagen, GM, Toyota, Chrysler, Mercedes-Benz, and Citroën.

The Australian car and truck markets recovered markedly in 1988 compared with 1987 but remained depressed compared with the peak year of 1985. The government-inspired industry reorganization plan resulted in the merging of most of the interests of GM and Toyota in Australia and closer product links between Ford and Nissan. Mitsubishi alone remained totally independent. The firstfruits of these new links in product terms were the sharing by Ford and Nissan of certain four-wheel-drive (Patrol/Maverick), pickup (Falcon/Nissan "Ute"), and medium four-cylinder car (Pintara/Corsair) models in 1989. Similar model sharing took place in the new Toyota-Holden partnership of six-cylinder cars (Holden Commodore/Toyota Lexcen) and small and medium four-cylinder cars (Toyota Corolla/Holden Nova and Toyota Camry/Holden Apollo).

(JOHN R. WEINTHAL)

Japan. Having regained its position as Japan's top corporate earner in fiscal 1988, Toyota Motor Corp. in its 1989 accounting year that ended in June earned 625,-660,000,000 yen, up 2.5% from the previous year. The company's consolidated net profit rose 11.4% to 846,260,000,000 yen, and the consolidated sales rose 11.2% to

8,020,000,000,000 yen, topping 8 trillion yen for the first time, owing mainly to expanded domestic sales.

Production in Japan of both cars and commercial vehicles during January–July 1989 rose to 7,701,512 units, 3.6% above the corresponding period in 1988 and the largest volume ever for that period of the year. Of this total, cars accounted for 5,222,107 units, a 9.5% rise, and commercial vehicles stood at 2,479,405 units, a 7% decline.

Domestic sales of cars and commercial vehicles, excluding "minicars" of 550 cc displacement or less, during the January–August period totaled 3,574,305 units, up 10%. This more than made up for the leveling off of car exports during the same period and marked a new high, breaking the record sales achieved in the first eight months of 1988. Reflecting mainly sharply increased demand from service, wholesale, and retail industries, sales of trucks surged to 1,115,064 units, a significant 23.9% advance. Domestic sales of minicars of 550 cc displacement or less in the January–August period increased to 220,472 units, a surprising 118.5% jump, while those of minitrucks of 550 cc displacement or less decreased 12.9% to 906,524 units. Dealers and industry analysts ascribed the surges to lower prices resulting from the replacement of the high excise tax on motor vehicles by a 3% consumption tax in April and also to brisk sales campaigns by the carmakers.

Sales of imported cars increased 26% to 89,495 units in the first six months of 1989, far surpassing the previous record of 74,262 units in 1986. Accounting for this in large part were the lower loan rates applied to imported cars.

(MASATO MIYAHARA)

United States. Sluggish car sales early in the year in the U.S. were revived by massive industry incentive campaigns in

SAL DIMARCO JR./THE NEW YORK TIMES

Japan's new Mazda MX-5 Miata was praised by automotive experts as one of the five best cars in the world. Despite the decline in the U.S. car market, the auto was so popular that many buyers spent thousands of dollars above sticker price to purchase the relatively few Miatas that were available.

August and September to help the industry sell 15.1 million new cars and trucks in the 1989 model year, which ended September 30. Despite the boost from cash rebates and discount financing programs, the 1989 totals fell short of the 15.2 million vehicles sold in the previous model year.

As soon as the 1989 model year drew to a close, most automakers began offering a new round of rebates on the 1990 model cars and trucks. Analysts said that the incentives near the end of the 1989 model year brought buyers into the market who normally would have waited for the 1990s. As a result, fourth-quarter sales were down sharply.

For the 1989 model year domestic car sales totaled 7.4 million units, up from 7.3 million in 1988. Import sales declined to 2.9 million from 3.1 million in the previous model year, while light-duty truck sales remained even at 4.1 million units both years.

Among the domestic producers, GM sold 3.4 million cars in the model year, down from 3.5 million in the previous year; Ford sold 2.2 million, up from 2.1 million; Chrysler Corp. sold 968,116, down from 1,050,000; Honda sold 391,109, up from 360,035; Toyota sold 222,544, up from 60,076 in the previous year, when it was just beginning to build cars in the U.S.; Nissan sold 102,071, down from 110,517; Mazda sold 40,867, up from 23,040; and in its first year of U.S.-built car sales, Mitsubishi sold 21,630 units. In regard to specific makes, Ford outsold Chevrolet for the second year in a row. Ford sold more cars—1,490,000 to 1.4 million—and more trucks—1.5 million to 1.3 million.

The foreign producers who sold cars imported from Japan as well as those built in the U.S. generally experienced a decline in import sales and a gain in U.S.-made vehicle sales. This was intentional since the reason for setting up U.S. assembly plants in the first place was to counter rising prices caused by the increasing value of the Japanese yen against the U.S. dollar.

For the eighth consecutive year the Ford F-Series pickup truck was the industry's top-selling vehicle, with sales of 589,772 units. The top-selling car for the fourth straight year was the subcompact Ford Escort, with sales of 366,354 units. Rounding out the top 10 car-sales leaders were the Honda Accord, 362,435; Ford Taurus, 360,237; Chevrolet Beretta/Corsica, 352,-674; Chevrolet Cavalier, 306,518; Toyota Camry, 264,598; Ford Tempo, 241,608; Honda Civic, 238,967; Nissan Sentra, 224,-888; and Pontiac Grand Am, 217,169.

When the new model year began on October 1, the carmakers introduced a host of new vehicles for consumers to evaluate. GM brought out a trio of plastic-bodied minivans under the Chevrolet Lumina, Oldsmobile Silhouette, and Pontiac Trans Sport nameplates. Chevrolet introduced a Lumina two-door coupe and four-door sedan as well. Four-door sedans were brought out by Oldsmobile (Cutlass Supreme), Pontiac (Grand Prix), and Buick (Regal) in an attempt to counter the success of Ford's midsize, front-wheel-drive Taurus.

Buick also introduced a Reatta convertible, Oldsmobile a Supreme convertible, Chevrolet a Beretta convertible, and Chevrolet a 375-hp, 32-valve V-8 engine

A Chevrolet dealership advertises its low interest rates as an added incentive to car buyers. In an attempt to counteract sluggish car sales, the auto industry tried such incentives as low interest rates and cash rebates, but it was unable to match the previous year's sales numbers.
KEN KERBS

version of the Corvette officially called the ZR-1 but dubbed the King of the Hill by the media for its claimed 0–95-km/h (60-mph) time of roughly four seconds.

Ford brought out a new version of its luxury Town Car with rounded aerodynamic body lines, while Chrysler introduced new front-wheel-drive versions of old names, the Chrysler Fifth Avenue and Chrysler Imperial. A luxury version of Chrysler's minivan, called the Chrysler Town & Country, and a Dodge version of the Eagle Premier, called the Monaco, also bowed.

Among the imports, Toyota brought out a new luxury line called Lexus, a restyled sporty Celica, and a minivan; Nissan unveiled its own luxury car called Infiniti and a restyled Stanza; Honda introduced a larger version of its Accord; Mazda unveiled a two-seater roadster convertible called Miata; and Subaru for the first time moved up from strictly subcompacts with a new compact Legacy sedan. Mercedes redid its SL lineup with a new 300SL two-seater having a six-cylinder engine and a new 500SL with a V-8 engine. Mercedes also brought out two 300-series sedans with four-wheel drive and a pair of diesel-powered cars.

Chevrolet and Ford prepared to introduce the first four-door versions of their S-10 Blazer and Bronco II four-wheel-drive utility vehicles late in the model year. The Ford Bronco II was to be renamed Explorer.

The 1990 models that took the market by more than just a storm were the Miata and ZR-1, the V-8 version of the Corvette. Though the Miata's base price was only $13,800, tremendous demand for the roadster allowed dealers to ask from $20,000 to $40,000 for the vehicles and found consumers willing to pay those prices. The ZR-1 was priced at $58,995, the most expensive U.S.-made car for the model year. Some dealers were demanding $75,000.

For the 1990 model year there were a few other changes. The U.S. government required all automakers to equip their cars with passive restraints, either air bags

or safety belts that automatically fastened themselves around passengers. Chrysler was the only domestic automaker to offer air bags as standard equipment in all of its U.S.-built cars.

Air bags and a revised federal requirement dictating that each automaker obtain an average of 27.5 miles per gallon (mpg) from its fleet of cars, up from 26.5 mpg in the 1989 model year, helped contribute to higher prices for the 1990 cars. GM prices rose an average of 5.2%, or $525; Ford prices went up 4.9%, or $696; and Chrysler prices were up 5%, or $700. In order to encourage sales of small cars to help meet federal mileage laws, prices on many of these models were either reduced or frozen at 1989 levels.

In the annual Environmental Protection Agency rating of the fuel efficiency of new cars, the Chevrolet GEO Metro XFi powered by a one-litre, three-cylinder engine and five-speed manual transmission was the top-rated model, with mileages of 53 mpg in the city and 58 mpg on the highway. At the other end of the scale, the Lamborghini Countach, with its 5.2-litre, V-12 engine and five-speed manual transmission, was rated at 6 mpg in the city and 10 mpg on the highway.

In other developments, the federal government ruled in the long-standing controversy over sudden acceleration in Audi cars that the problem was caused by "pedal misapplication" of drivers, meaning that they applied their foot to the gas pedal instead of the brake. Chrysler Corp. reduced its holdings in Japanese partner Mitsubishi by selling off some of its stock. Chrysler cut its equity in Mitsubishi to 12.1 from 21.8% but obtained $309 million. GM announced plans to buy half of Saab-Scania's financially troubled auto-manufacturing unit.

U.S. Pres. George Bush surprised the industry by proposing that tougher Clean Air Act standards be imposed. The Bush proposal resulted in GM, Ford, and Chrysler getting together with the nation's 14 largest oil companies to study ways to develop fuel that burned more cleanly for cars in the future.   (JAMES L. MATEJA)

BEVERAGES

Beer. Anheuser-Busch of America remained the world's largest brewer. Its major brand, Budweiser, alone represented over 6% of the world's beer, almost three times more than its nearest rival, Kirin beer of Japan. Four American brewers were among the world's top ten beer producers, and the U.S. as a whole accounted for over 23% of world consumption. The U.S. also appeared close to regaining its title as the world's largest hop grower. U.S. exports of hops increased by 41% in 1988, with the largest increases in trade going to Brazil, Canada, and, ironically, West Germany, which overtook U.S. production in the mid-1980s. Competition from Chinese hops and a world surplus, however, led to a decline in average prices. Italy became the world's biggest importer of beer, overtaking Hungary. Per capita consumption of beer in Italy had more than doubled since 1970. The West Germans remained the biggest beer drinkers (141 litres per capita; 1 litre = 0.908 qt).

On March 1, 1989, beer became legal in Iceland following the final repeal of the General Prohibition Statute of 1915 by the Althing (parliament). To prepare for the lifting of the prohibition on beer, the state alcohol monopoly stockpiled over 1.5 million litres. Pubs and bars were reportedly booked by January. In Moscow, Allied-Lyons, the British food and brewing group, opened its first pub behind the iron curtain, the Hermitage Bar in the Savoy Hotel near Red Square.

Labatt, Canada's single largest brewer, took a majority holding in Birra Moretti, Italy's third largest. Australian brewers Elders continued to expand with a joint venture to brew Foster's under license by Pripps Bryggerier, which controlled 50% of the Swedish beer market. Österreichische Brau of Austria licensed its Steffl beer to be brewed in Hungary by Sopron Brewery, and Dutch brewer Heineken entered into a joint venture with the Mila Brewery of Shanghai.

(MICHAEL D. RIPLEY)

Spirits. Continued emphasis on healthier living styles, tougher restrictions on advertising, and a growing worldwide antidrink lobby combined to help ensure that 1989 was once again a year of lower-strength spirits and cocktails. Peach schnapps continued to enjoy phenomenal success in the U.S., while cream liqueurs also provided strong competition for traditional full-strength spirits. Typical of the new entries in the U.S. was a cognac and passion fruit mixture called Alize de France.

White spirits like vodka, gin, tequila, and white rum continued to increase in volume. It was a generally depressing picture for Scotch whisky, although the growth of profitable premium and single malt whisky to around 5% of sales provided a spark of comfort. A significant development for the Scotch Whisky Association was the agreement of the EC Council of Ministers to legislate that whisky should be at least 40% alcohol by volume. The council also recognized the geographic designation of Scotch.

In global terms, spirits consumption was declining dramatically. Sales of spirits in West Germany were down slightly at 90 million cases, while consumption continued to fall as the result of rising taxes. The spirits market in Belgium and Luxembourg declined to 3.5 million cases—nearly 1.5 million cases less than in 1982. In Canada a 5% drop in the spirits market was recorded between 1980 and 1989. Whiskey had suffered most, declining by 6% since 1980.

In the U.K. the main talking point was the relaxation of on-premise opening hours in line with other European countries. Early indications were that fears of increased drunk-driving or drunkenness convictions as a result were unfounded. The growth of beer and wine in China pushed spirits' share of the alcoholic beverage market down from 58% in 1980 to around 30% in 1989. A notable development was increased investment by leading brand producers in reduced-alcohol spirits.

(ANTONY C. WARNER)

Wine. Overproduction continued to plague the wine industry throughout the world in 1989 despite all the measures that had resulted in a decrease from previous years. The 1988 total was 274.2 million hectolitres (hl; 1 hl = 26.4 U.S. gallons), down from 319.6 million hl in 1987. Italy remained the leading producer in 1988, with 61,863,000 hl. France was second with 57,530,000 hl, followed by Spain with 21,565,000 hl and Argentina with 20,629,-000 hl. The case of the U.S.S.R. merited special attention; its maximum production of 34.4 million hl experienced a sharp decline as a result of the measures taken by the Soviet government to fight alcoholism, and in 1988 output totaled only 19,860,-000 hl. The U.S. showed a slow but constant increase.

An important reason for the worldwide surplus was that even though the three major wine-producing and wine-consuming countries—Italy, France, and Spain—decreased the cultivated areas, their productivity increased, thanks to restructuring and replanting, while their consumption did not. In the Americas, however, the situation was reversed, especially in the U.S., where consumption exceeded production by more than eight million hectolitres. In Argentina a balance between production and consumption was achieved.

Consumption worldwide rose slightly in 1988 to approximately 265.5 million hl, up from 264.8 million hl in 1987. For 1989 world wine production was expected to total approximately 255 million hl, of which 187.4 million hl were from Europe. Italy was once again expected to be the leading producer, with 70 million hl, followed by France with 57.5 million hl and Spain with 33.8 million.

After a mild winter, the hot and dry temperatures during the 1989 blooming season set the growing cycle forward as much as three weeks; harvests, consequently, were exceptionally early. There were good expectations in regard to quality; 1989 would most likely be a good year.

(MARIE-JOSE DESHAYES)

Table V. Estimated Consumption of Beer in Selected Countries

In litres[1] per capita

Country	1986	1987	1988
West Germany	146.4	144.2	143.0
East Germany	142.1	c. 143	143.0
Czechoslovakia	133.4	130.0	130.0
Denmark	125.78	118.05	119.86
Belgium	119.8	121.1	118.6
Austria	118.5	118.3	117.8
Luxembourg	119.3	116.5	115.8
New Zealand	120.8	121.7	115.2
Australia[2]	111.3	110.8	113.1
United Kingdom	108.1	110.5	111.2
Hungary	99.4	100.2	101
Ireland	104.5	93.5	96.7
United States	90.8	90.1	89.3
Netherlands, The	86.0	84.3	83.3
Canada[3]	81.9	83.0	...
Venezuela	60.7	72.4	75
Finland	65.4	68.1	74.1
Switzerland	69.4	69.3	68.8
Spain	62.0	66.8	68.7
Bulgaria	64.3	66.4	c. 66.5
Colombia	54.7	56.3	58.0
Sweden	50.0	51.5	54.8
Portugal	38.8	47.04	53.1
Norway	50.78	51.44	51.6
South Africa	41.8	46.4	50.9

[1] One litre = 1.0567 U.S. quart = 0.8799 imperial quart.
[2] Years ending June 30.
[3] Years ending March 31.

Table VI. Estimated Consumption of Spirits in Selected Countries

In litres[1] of pure alcohol per capita

Country	1986	1987	1988
East Germany	4.9	c. 5	5.2
Poland	4.7	4.7	4.6
Hungary	5.3	4.7	c. 4.5
Czechoslovakia	3.40	3.32	c. 3.3
Finland	3.17	3.22	3.13
Spain	c. 3	c. 3	c. 3
Bulgaria	3.41	2.83	c. 2.8
Luxembourg	c. 2.5	c. 2.5	c. 2.5
Canada[2]	2.53	2.50	...
Cyprus	2.3	2.4	2.5
France	2.34	2.40	2.47
Iceland	2.44	2.40	2.40
United States	2.45	2.41	2.4
Japan	2.4	2.3	2.4
West Germany	2.29	2.24	2.11
Netherlands, The	2.21	2.07	2.10
Romania	c. 2	c. 2	c. 2
Switzerland	2.08	2.04	1.99
Sweden	2.12	1.96	1.89
United Kingdom	1.71	1.73	1.81
Soviet Union	1.9	1.6	1.8
Ireland	1.7	c. 1.7	c. 1.7
Yugoslavia	2.2	1.8	1.6
Uruguay	1.5	1.6	1.6
Belgium	1.98	2.15	1.52

[1] One litre = 1.0567 U.S. quart = 0.8799 imperial quart.
[2] Years ending March 31.

Table VII. Estimated Consumption of Wine in Selected Countries

In litres[1] per capita

Country	1986	1987	1988
France	76.4	75.1	74
Italy	73.3	79.0	62.1
Luxembourg	55.4	58.5	58.3
Portugal	70.8	64.3	58
Argentina	59.2	57.9	55.8
Switzerland	48.6	49.5	49.9
Spain	47	54	47.4
Chile	35	35	35
Austria	32.8	32.1	32.9
Greece	23.7	31.8	32
Romania	c. 28	c. 28	c. 28
Uruguay	22.0	25.7	28
West Germany	23.3	25.8	25.9
Yugoslavia	27.5	26	25
Belgium	21.7	23.0	23.3
Bulgaria	22.1	22.5	c. 22.5
Hungary	23.2	21.5	22
Denmark	19.82	20.63	21.55
Australia[2]	20.6	20.6	19.1
New Zealand	16.2	15.3	14.8
Netherlands, The	14.90	14.60	14.79
Czechoslovakia	12.3	13.7	13.7
Cyprus	11.9	13.0	13.7
Sweden	11.96	11.83	12.12
East Germany	10.9	c. 10	12.1

[1] One litre = 1.0567 U.S. quart = 0.8799 imperial quart.
[2] Years ending June 30.

Source: Produktschap voor Gedistilleerde Dranken, *Hoeveel alcoholhoudende dranken worden er in de wereld gedronken?*

Soft Drinks. Per capita consumption of soft drinks in the U.S. in 1988 grew to 50.5 gal (1 U.S. gal = 3.8 litres). Industry volume increased 4.5% to 12,413,700,000 gal with a wholesale value of $27 billion. The number of households buying soft drinks reached 82.7 million, compared with 68.5 million 10 years earlier.

Gallonage of regular soft drinks rose 2.6%, while the diet market experienced an extraordinary 9.8% growth. Almost all new soft drinks were being introduced in both regular and diet versions. Much of the popularity of diet drinks was attributable to the current emphasis on fitness and health, but many consumers appeared to be buying them for the taste, thanks largely to the availability of the artificial sweetener aspartame. In 1989 saccharin and aspartame were still the only diet sweeteners approved for use in soft drinks in the U.S. Alitame and sucralose were being reviewed by the Food and Drug Administration, and the FDA was being petitioned to approve cyclamate for general use.

The juice-added category of soft drink, including both diet and regular, held a 4.5% share of the market in 1988. There was a change of emphasis in the promotion of juice-added drinks, from stressing their health benefits to presenting them as updated versions of such traditional drinks as orange soda and lemon-lime. Supermarkets were the leading distributors of soft drinks with 38% of the market. Other leading channels were: soda fountains 24.9%; vending machines 12.4%; and convenience stores 12.1%. Mergers and acquisitions in the industry continued.

More than 75% of all soft drinks were packaged in bottles or cans made from glass, plastic, aluminum, or steel; the balance was dispensed through fountain service. All soft drink containers being sold in the U.S. were recyclable. More than 55% of all 12-oz aluminum cans were being recycled annually. The glass-container recycling rate was 15%, and that for plastic soft drink bottles was 20%.

(DWIGHT C. REED)

BUILDING AND CONSTRUCTION

Based on U.S. Department of Commerce reports for the first nine months of the year, it appeared that construction spending in the U.S. in 1989 would be up because of higher prices, amounting to an estimated $415 billion. On a constant dollar basis (1982 = 100), however, the value of construction put in place in 1989 would probably be lower than the $352 billion reported for 1988. While the figures were preliminary, they were considered sufficiently accurate to assess general market conditions.

On the basis of dollar outlays for new construction put in place, residential and nonresidential building and private and public construction all showed gains in 1988 and the first half of 1989. However, it was expected that higher interest rates and the continuing effects of inflationary pressures would have a dampening effect in the last half of 1989 and in 1990. Housing starts continued to fall in 1989, following declines in 1987 and 1988. On a seasonally adjusted annual rate basis, all housing starts amounted to 1,260,000 units in September, the lowest level since October 1982. It was expected that starts for the year would total less than 1.4 million units, compared with 1,488,000 units in 1988. Builders were concerned about the large number of unsold homes and the possibility of higher interest rates.

The average price of a new house reached $162,300 in August. In the same month the Composite Construction Cost Index of the U.S. Department of Commerce reached 121.1 (1982 = 100). Average weekly and hourly earnings of construction workers had risen gradually from 1982 to 1989, and in June 1989 average hourly earnings were $13.27, compared with $11.63 in 1982.

The high rental rates for new apartments and the high average monthly payments for new homes excluded most low- and middle-income people from the market. The demolition of low-income unsubsidized housing, restrictive land use and building codes, and high rents for unsubsidized housing worked to make cheap housing unavailable to millions of poverty-level people. While there had been a substantial increase in dollar outlays for subsidized housing since 1980, a large majority of the poor continued to live in unsubsidized housing.

In Canada residential construction rose steeply in the last quarter of 1988 and continued at high levels in the first half of 1989, but there was a decline in the latter part of the year. There were clear signs of inflationary pressures, exerting an unfavourable effect on construction and housing investments. In Great Britain, where the government was concerned about the dangers of recession on the one hand and accelerating inflation on the other, the tightening of monetary policy in 1988 was having an effect on the housing market. Expected private investment in housing in 1989 was £11,334,000,000, down 5.8% from 1988. Expected public investment was £2,640,000,000, down 2.1%. The outlook for 1990 was less favourable.

The 1988 investment boom in West Germany moderated in 1989, but the expected lower rate of inflation and lower interest rates should stimulate housing and business investments. The outlook in France was similar. Italy's large public debt and high inflation rate were expected to have an unfavourable effect on building and construction. Japan's economic growth in 1989, the strongest in the past 10 years, was stimulated mainly by housing and business investment. While the annual increase in housing investment was not as great as in 1987, business investment continued to grow at greater rates. The Japanese housing industry was second only to that of the U.S.

(CARTER C. OSTERBIND)

CERAMICS

U.S. ceramic industry sales in 1988 were $35 billion, an increase over 1987 of almost 12%. The glass industry accounted for 59% of the sales. Glass containers, refractories, and dinnerware and fine china showed major increases in sales, and advanced ceramic sales were up on the basis of the strength of electronic ceramic sales in spite of a major decrease in sales of optical fibres. The continued strength of the U.S. economy, especially the building industry, and the decline in the value of the dollar were the major factors in the growth.

U.S. advanced ceramic sales increased to $4.5 billion in 1988. Sales of electronic substrates, electronic packages, and capacitors again dominated the market, if spark plugs and other low-voltage porcelains were excluded, making up 65% of the total and increasing 35%. However, optical fibre sales decreased more than 30%, and engineering ceramics dropped over 12%. The decrease in optical fibre sales was a result of the completion of many of the long-distance communications networks and the inability of increased sales for short-distance applications to compensate.

On a worldwide basis, the 1988 market for advanced ceramics was $12 billion. On a regional basis, Japan dominated the market with a share estimated at 57%, compared with 31% for the U.S. and 12% for Europe. Electronic ceramics accounted for 84% of the market, but this was expected to drop to 45–65% by the year 2000 as a result of projected increases in structural ceramic sales for engine applications.

The first ceramic-intensive automobile and truck engine, defined as containing six or more ceramic components with at least two in the hot zone, was expected to be introduced in Japan in 1995 and in the U.S. three or four years later. By 1989 several advanced ceramic components were being used, and many others were undergoing intensive engine tests. Ceramic gas turbine engines were expected to be introduced by 2015.

The worldwide market for high-temperature ceramic superconductors was expected to develop around 1995 and grow at 25% per year. The long-range market potential for these materials was projected to be $5 billion if they were used only in known applications, but it could reach $10 billion if new applications were developed. However, the market potential at the device and system level was expected to be many times higher. Although a similar situation existed for other advanced materials, the value added at the system level for high-temperature ceramic superconductors could be much greater than for the others. Therefore, the worldwide research-and-development effort was far greater than could be justified by the market for the materials alone.

Sales of refractories rose 18% in 1988 to $2 billion, primarily as a result of the strength of the steel industry. The backlog of orders at the end of 1988 was up 25% from a year earlier, indicating a strong start for 1989.

Whiteware sales in the U.S. totaled $3 billion in 1988. Sanitary ware sales were down, and tile sales were about level with 1987 in real dollars, while dinnerware and fine china combined were up almost 50%. The major factor in Lenox China's 60% increase in sales was direct sales through company-owned stores, and the Lenox China performance was a major factor in the strong performance of the dinnerware and fine china industry. At $4.6 billion, porcelain enamel sales in the U.S. in 1988 were nearly the same as in 1987.

(DALE E. NIESZ)

CHEMICALS

The extraordinarily strong year for the world chemical industry in 1988, during which U.S. production rose 8.5%, that of the U.K. and nine major European countries 6.6%, and that of Japan 8%, carried the industry into 1989 at a

pace that could not be sustained. However, 1988 provided momentum enough to shape 1989 into a fine year by all but the standards of 1988 and 1987. In 1989, overall, world chemical industry production was expected to increase about 4–5%, according to several of the industry's best regarded economists.

The U.S.S.R., which for years had made little data available on its chemical industry, revealed some information in 1989. During the last 20 to 25 years, an official said, its industry increased output by 3.8 to 6.3% per year. Its 1988 production of the raw material ethylene, for example, was put at 3,175,000 metric tons (U.S. production was 15,872,000 metric tons and West Germany's production was 2,775,000 metric tons in that year). In general, the spokesman said, demand far outstripped production.

Four factors in particular helped world chemical makers: a generally prosperous world economy, with stable currencies; stable prices for the petrochemical raw materials, oil and gas; a lean industry in terms of personnel at both management and labour levels, and almost no labour strife; and an improving political climate between East and West and in the Middle East following the cease-fire in the Gulf war between Iran and Iraq.

This combination of factors allowed chemical producers not only to record their fourth consecutive successful year in regard to both profits and production but also to view 1990 with measured optimism. Estimates were that world production would increase by at least 2% in 1990. World trade between nations set new records in 1988, according to estimates by *Chemical & Engineering News* magazine. At $249 billion, it was 14% above the 1987 mark. International traffic in chemicals remained high in 1989.

There were signs that the extremely high growth rates in both production and trade would slow down, however. By the spring of 1989, for example, prices of some major chemicals had been cut. Ethylene, the most important petrochemical build-

ing block material, declined almost 30% in price in 1989 from its peak level in late 1988. Benzene, essential for the production of styrene and polystyrene plastics but also important in detergent manufacture, varied wildly in cost in 1989. By the end of the year, the price was about $1.25 per pound (1 lb = 0.45 kg)—which industry experts considered low. Styrene expansions totaling four billion pounds a year were under way in 1989 in the U.S. and Canada alone; lower feedstock price would benefit them.

Also, it was becoming clear that three markets vital to U.S. chemical prosperity were slowing down: automobiles, housing (including appliances and furnishings), and farming. Output of the factories declined, while only farm production, thanks to a year of good weather, was up. The changes were not as marked in Europe and Japan, but production in both areas was down nonetheless.

These changes signaled to the chemical industry, which had a considerable supply of cash available for building and which had been cautiously readying for a new round of expansion, that it should think very carefully about a number of major projects. Worldwide, for example, plans that by 1993 could add about six billion pounds of ethylene per year to the world's supply were in one stage of execution or another. Although at least one $500 million ethylene plant was postponed in the U.S., and it appeared likely that several of the others, due to start producing in the early 1990s, would be delayed, out-and-out cancellations were rare.

Similarly, producers in the U.K. and Europe moved ahead cautiously with plans to enlarge their plants. Five major expansions (for more than 140 billion lb) were under way, as were a dozen lesser expansions.

At the same time that it weighed expansions, the chemical industry was finding the general public less enthusiastic about many of its products. Noteworthy was the disapproval directed toward chlorinated fluorocarbon compounds (CFCs). An increasing amount of evidence showed that

they may partially destroy the stratospheric ozone layer and thus allow potentially harmful (cancer-causing) solar radiation to reach the Earth.

Production of three main types of CFCs, which had gained essential roles in several industries—among them, refrigeration and air-conditioning, upholstery and insulating foams, and electronic parts degreasing—boomed in 1988, with increases of 13 to 18%. By 1989, however, CFC production was already slowing down, creating serious shortages, particularly in the air-conditioning and electronics industries, where substitute products were not available. The reason for the slowdown was industry's eagerness to get started on compliance with an international agreement known as the Montreal Protocol. Ratified by most of the world's industrial nations, the protocol called for CFC output to be halved (from 1987 levels) by 1999.

While in some arenas U.S. policies and attitudes in regard to chemicals appeared to lead the world (attitudes toward CFCs, water and air pollution, and pollution controls on automobiles, among them), Europe was leading in a matter of growing importance—the recycling of plastics. Unlike metals, which are comparatively easy to save, separate, and recycle, plastics are bulky, not readily distinguishable, and virtually unrefinable if mixed or melted together. Burning, to recover their hydrocarbon energy content, is quite feasible but not popular. Higher in public favour might be the making of low-cost materials from mixed plastics—lumberlike boards, for example—that would put plastics' toughness and water resistance into good secondary uses. Even in this case some sort of separation of materials is required, however, and European technology led the field for plants to separate the more costly and the more troublesome materials and to convert them into useful new products.

(J. ROBERT WARREN)

ELECTRICAL

Intervention by U.S. electrical giant General Electric Co. (GE) in February 1988 foiled an attempted asset-stripping takeover of the U.K.'s General Electric Co. (GEC) by a group led by the U.K. electronics company Plessey, which was itself under threat of a joint takeover by GEC and Siemens of West Germany. In a £1.5 billion collaboration, GE acquired 50% of GEC's consumer goods group; GEC's wholly owned Belgian subsidiary Vynckier was merged with GE's Compagnia Generale Elettromeccanica (Cogemec) of Italy to form a jointly owned low-voltage electrical transmission equipment company; GE took 10% of a new European gas turbine company formed by GEC (45%) and Alsthom of France (45%); and GE also acquired Picker International's U.K. medical equipment sales from GEC. These deals made GEC impregnable to the Plessey takeover attempt and, for GE, gave 4 of its 14 businesses an increased European participation.

A less important reason for the failure of the Plessey bid was the proposal that the French Compagnie Générale d'Électricité (CGE) merge its Alsthom subsidiary (power generation and transmission and rail transport) in a jointly owned company with the similar businesses of GEC. Fol-

The manager of a recycling company holds up food containers made of polystyrene plastics that would be recycled as plastic pellets to be used in packaging. Because of growing concern for the environment, many polystyrene companies were recycling their plastic containers.

lowing the GE intervention, this Anglo-French merger took place in March. Its importance exceeded that of the GE-GEC agreements in that the merged company, GEC Alsthom, had an annual turnover of £4 billion and a payroll of 85,000, making it the largest power engineering company in the EC. Earlier, the U.S. power- and process-plant construction giant Combustion Engineering pooled its boilermaking business with Alsthom. The new entity was owned jointly by Combustion Engineering and GEC Alsthom. In its last annual report, Alsthom recorded sales of F 28,104,-000,000 in 1988 and a net income of F 550.5 million, up 21% from 1987. In the year ended March 31, 1989, GEC recorded sales of £5,878,000,000, up 6% from the previous 12 months, giving net profits of £510.2 million, up 13.5%.

The Anglo-French merger was partly instigated by the requirement of the European Commission that nationalistic purchasing policies for public service contracts be halted. The market for power-generation products in the U.K. was the largest in Europe, and so this requirement, coming at the same time as the privatization of the U.K. electricity supply industry, worried GEC.

Although it was difficult to calculate the full effects of the recent U.S.-U.K.-French deals, it appeared that one result was to push Siemens, once supreme in Europe, into third place in electrical power engineering behind Asea Brown Boveri (ABB) and GEC Alsthom. Formed by the merger of Sweden's Asea and Switzerland's Brown Boveri companies in 1987, ABB was the world's largest electrical equipment manufacturer, with 170,000 employees in more than 800 companies in 140 countries. Sales in 1988, the first year of operation, were $17,832,000,000; operating earnings after depreciation were $854 million, yielding a net income of $386 million. A substantial increase in earnings was expected when the full effects of the restructuring that took place in 1988 were realized.

In Japan Toshiba's heavy electrical apparatus division recorded sales of 727 billion yen in the year ended March 31, 1989, a 17% decline from the previous year. Toshiba was the leading Japanese company in factory automation and was building Japan's first advanced boiling water nuclear power station.

In the U.S. GE recorded net earnings (after tax) of $3,386,000,000 in 1988, a 16% increase over 1987, on total revenues of $50,089,000,000. The combined sales of the two GE business sectors that compared directly with the electrical engineering activities of ABB, GEC Alsthom, and Siemens (industrial equipment and power systems) totaled $11,866,000,000 ($11,-657,000,000 in 1987), with an operating profit (before tax) of $1.3 billion ($500 million in 1987). In December GE announced plans to enter the Eastern European market by acquiring Tungsram, a Hungarian light-bulb maker and one of that country's largest firms.

Westinghouse Electric Corp. sales increased in 1988 to $11,718,900,000 ($10,-679,000,000 in 1987), with net income up 13% to $822.8 million. Looking ahead, Westinghouse determined that the most promising growth area was environmental services and recently acquired two com-

panies in this field, S&ME and Aptus. The environmental services market in the U.S. was growing at about 20% a year. In less than two years Westinghouse had become the leader in the garbage-burning generating plant business, turning waste into energy.

In Europe the largest growth market was said by the West German organizers of the 1989 Hanover Fair to be factory automation equipment. Estimates indicated that by 1990 worldwide demand would be DM 100 million, with a steady annual growth of 10% to the year 2000.

(T.C.J. COGLE)

FURNITURE

The year 1989 would go down as the one when the U.S. furniture industry went "international"—in identity, marketing strategies, and design influence. Most indicative of this change was the fact that High Point, N.C., established itself as the premier international furniture centre. On April 28 the Southern Furniture Market, a semiannual wholesale market begun in 1909, was renamed the International Home Furnishings Market to more accurately reflect its size and the geographic representation of exhibitors and visitors. At the nine-day October market 53,500 people from 50 countries (including the U.S.S.R.) attended, and there were approximately 1,600 exhibitors from 160 countries showing in 557,400 sq m (6 million sq ft) of display space. The central downtown complex, the International Home Furnishings Center, alone contained 232,250 sq m (2.5 million sq ft) of showroom space, more than either of the two next largest shows, in Milan, Italy, and Cologne, West Germany.

According to one source, this change was the result of behind-the-scenes political and economic activities begun in the late 1970s with the aim of expanding trade opportunities. One major roadblock had always been the fact that the furniture industry was made up largely of small "mom-and-pop" operations. However, the buyouts and consolidations that started in 1986 produced companies that could more realistically compete in the international arena. The industry's new strategy was also directly linked to the fact that during the past two years there had been little or no growth. According to the American Furniture Manufacturers Association, U.S. furniture shipments for 1988 rose by a higher-than-projected 2.9%, but shipments for 1989 were expected to increase no more than 1.1%, producing $16 billion. In spite of its new international awareness, the industry was still chided for being "export resistant" and not doing enough to penetrate overseas markets. While some inroads had begun to be made into Japan, the second largest market after the U.S., experts thought the industry should be focusing on the $4 trillion market that would be produced by the unified European market in 1992.

U.S. retail sales were expected to rise 1.5% in 1989 to $28.3 billion. Having started the year with large inventories, the retailers did better than the manufacturers.

Styles continued to be much the same as in the previous year—Victorian-influenced and very romantic. Here again the international theme emerged, with Russian designs and Scandinavian folk motifs

serving as important sources. The industry continued to rely on internationally famous name designers from the interior design and fashion industries to generate excitement. Joining the list were fashion designers Gucci and Fendi and the interior design firm McMillan, with a collection that included English, French, Dutch, American, Italian, and Chinese designs. A new name on this list of "concept designers" was Lynn Hollyn, whose fresh-looking collection of coordinated furnishings combined European and Swedish motifs.

In other developments, leather continued to enlarge its market share, with one company offering 700 colours. Technological advances—particularly computers and fax machines—were forcing a basically handicraft industry into the 21st century; introduced in October were computer programs that could lay out floor plans to scale and show exactly how a fabric would look on an upholstery frame. "Telecommuting"—the new term for those who work at home—was estimated to include 26.6 million persons in 1989, projected to rise to 32.9 million in 1992. This prompted many companies to begin developing furniture for home offices. (ABBY CHAPPLE)

FURS

Retail fur sales improved somewhat in 1989 in the important world markets, following two difficult years in which sales were adversely affected by unseasonably warm winters. Retailers took a generally cautious approach to the season, however, keeping inventories on the low side. Many had been hurt by the sharp declines in skin prices in the previous two years, which seriously depreciated the value of inventories. Although the volume of fur sales was about the same as in the previous year, the number of units sold was substantially higher, reflecting price declines of 20 to 30%.

There was a substantial increase in sales of fur and leather combinations and the shorn lambskins called shearlings. Retailers also sold more fur-trimmed cloth coats, fur-lined raincoats, and garments of other materials that reversed to furs. At the same time, there was less demand for such wild furs as raccoon, coyote, and muskrat, reflecting a shift in fashion toward flatter and shorter-haired furs.

Mink increased its domination over fur sales in 1989. In the U.S., mink accounted for between 70 and 75% of national sales, which were estimated to total about $1.8 billion. The world's mink ranchers, however, were overly optimistic when they put a record 42 million pelts on the international market. Mink breeding must be planned two years in advance, and planning for the 1989 crop reflected the record prices being paid for mink skins in early 1987, just before they began falling. Once in place, there was no way for ranchers to alter their plans, even when it became apparent that prices were likely to go lower yet.

Production plans put into effect in 1989 called for at least a 15% crop reduction in 1991. However, since this involved a reduction of the number of breeding animals held, there would be a temporary increase in pelts in 1990. Similar reductions had been put into place for ranched foxes, primarily in Finland, the largest producer.

U.S. wild fur crops would be down sharply in 1990 as a result of lower pelt prices.

Animal rights organizations continued to campaign against the use or exploitation of animals for human gain. Although targets included the meat, poultry, and dairy trades and woolen and silk mills, the most visible campaigns, sometimes marked by vandalism and violence, were directed against furriers and laboratories using animals for research. The fur industry, among others, launched a major education drive.

(SANDY PARKER)

GAMES AND TOYS

The international toy industry once again experienced upheaval in 1989 as manufacturers throughout the world came to terms with the complexities and differing fortunes of individual markets. In the U.S., for example, industry growth in 1988 was a moderate 3.9% in dollar terms ($8,646,-000,000, as compared with $8,227,000,000 in 1987), although volume sales actually decreased by 0.5%.

In Europe a storm of controversy was sparked when EC import quotas concerning Taiwan were enforced after France, and then West Germany, raised the matter in Brussels. The result was an extra 8% import duty on most toys and games from Taiwan from July 1, 1989. Previously, these imports had been duty free because Taiwan was considered to be a less developed nation.

Sales of games and toys in the U.K. grew by 7.5% in 1988, slightly ahead of inflation, to reach £935 million, while in Italy imports increased by a massive 24% from the previous year, with big gains from Asian manufacturers. In West Germany, too, imports rose by more than 14% although domestic production also increased by 3.9% to DM 1,783,000,000.

In Japan it was announced that the McDonald's Corp. would be opening joint venture stores with the $4 billion Toys

"Я" Us retail chain. McDonald's already had more than 700 stores in Japan, and its expertise in Japanese real estate was just what the world's largest toy retailer needed to break into a market that it had wanted to enter for some time. There were plans to open five Toys "Я" Us outlets in 1991, complete with McDonald's drive-through restaurants.

In Europe Mattel's flagship fashion doll, Barbie, was fighting a legal battle with her U.K.-designed rival, Sindy, now owned by U.S. multinational firm Hasbro. Mattel claimed that the resculpted, repackaged Sindy bore a striking resemblance to Barbie and applied for court injunctions to remove her from sale in France, Belgium, The Netherlands, and the U.K. The injunctions were upheld in Belgium and The Netherlands, and the case was under review in the other nations.

Japan strengthened its reputation for innovative toys when the entire international industry jumped on the "mini four-wheel-drive car" bandwagon. In 1987 Bandai had launched a series of small racing cars called HyperDrivers that traveled at high speeds. Race meetings held in Japan attracted more than 160,000 people, and Hasbro, Mattel, and Matchbox all introduced their versions of these cars during the year.

Fads had always been the lifeblood of the toy industry, and 1989 was notable for a revival of the yo-yo in the U.K. and the popularity in the United States of the Koosh Ball, a product that bore a striking resemblance to a pom-pom made of rubber. Among other popular toys of the year were Galoob's MicroMachines, small plastic cars, trucks, planes, and boats that often fit within one another; Galoob also developed car washes, gas stations, and other suitable facilities for the tiny vehicles. Fisher-Price's plastic foods and McDonald's portable restaurant and soda fountain were also best-sellers.

Board game sales continued at record high levels throughout the world, with Pictionary probably the biggest international hit. Trivial Pursuit continued to dominate the European market and even made it into a Soviet edition, as did the perennial best-seller Monopoly.

The year's changes of ownership included the purchase by Hasbro of Coleco, the company famous for its Cabbage Patch Kids. Games manufacturer Harbourdin in France was acquired by Spears in the U.K., and the leading French doll producer, Corolle, was bought by Mattel of the U.S.

Global conquest continued for the Nintendo Entertainment System, a Japanese home computer designed solely for playing video games. Sales soared in the U.S. as an estimated one in four households owned a system, and children were even treated to a Nintendo-licensed breakfast cereal and a TV series based on the best-known characters from Nintendo games. The company's sales reached 50 billion yen in the year ended August 1988.

(JONATHAN M. SALISBURY)

GEMSTONES

The year 1989 was marked by a continuation of the previous year's favourable trading conditions. The economy of the U.K., growing at a pace scarcely seen since World War II, continued to suck in imported goods, though late in the year the British government imposed high interest rates in an effort to keep the inflation rate down. This did not affect the jewelry trade as much as some others, however. The European trade also had a good year, with little sign of a downturn. The diamond stockpiles of De Beers continued to run down, and gemstones for investment, though traditionally a dangerous area for speculators, reappeared in advertisements. There were a number of sales of fine jewelry during the year; none matched the 1987 Duchess of Windsor sale in notoriety, though prices realized were as high as or higher than ever.

Many countries still concentrated on nine-carat gold jewelry, though many craftsmen felt this metal scarcely deserved the name of gold. Higher qualities were used by individual workers, and art-school exhibitions showed considerable initiative in the choice of metal, gemstones, and form. Coloured metals seemed to be making a comeback.

There was no sign of a diminution in the supply of fine gemstones, though the political scene in Sri Lanka was very grave. Fine rubies appeared in Thailand; some might have been treated Burmese material, though dealers expressed little concern over the possibility. Treatment had become the rule for many species. One recent development in this area was the use of nongemological facilities—medical equipment, for example—to treat suitable material. There were signs that amateurs trying to treat stones might be disregarding the possibility of latent radioactivity.

The gem trade laboratories were busy throughout the world, and many combined routine testing with the management of gem-testing courses. Though the enhancement of colour was hard to assess, laboratories were concerned with the increase in such materials as synthetic amethyst, new colours in cubic zirconia, and a

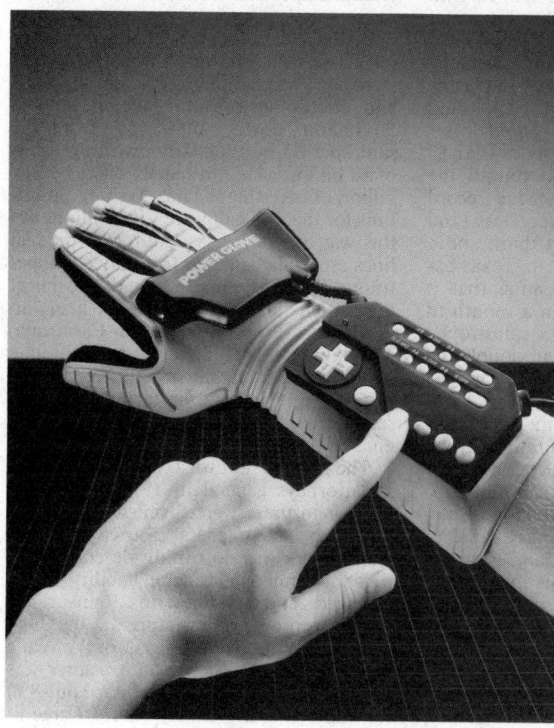

NINTENDO OF AMERICA INC.

Mattel's new Power Glove senses the Nintendo player's hand movements and imitates them in the game onscreen so that if, for example, the player's hand imitates grabbing a steering wheel and steering, the image on the screen holds the wheel and steers accordingly.

range of high-quality synthetic stones from Japan. These included alexandrite with a fine colour change and different colours of beryl. Synthetic gem-quality diamond, now reported from more than one manufacturer, had yet to come onto the market. Among natural stones, a very fine alexandrite was reported from the Hematita mine in Brazil.   (MICHAEL O'DONOGHUE)

GLASS

A feature of worldwide glass production in 1989 was the continued expansion in investment in producing facilities in China, the Far East generally, and South America. Correspondingly large production increases were recorded in those areas, while in the major industrial countries gains, where made at all, were much more modest.

Flat glass shipments in the U.S. followed the slowdown in the automobile and construction industries, which accounted for more than 80% of the U.S. flat glass market. Sales for the year were expected to be 3.7% lower than the 393,000,000 sq m (4,230,000,000 sq ft) recorded in 1988. Although there were some signs that the economy in Western Europe was also slowing down, new flat glass plants were being constructed in the U.K., West Germany, France, Spain, and Hungary, the last being a joint venture with a major U.S. manufacturer. The European flat glass market had grown an average of 2.5–3% each year over the past 10 years but 5.5–6% within the past five.

Glass container shipments in the United States were slightly lower in 1989 at a predicted 273.4 million gross units (as against 276.3 million in 1988). Sales of beer bottles, however, increased marginally, possibly because of the rising number of independent breweries. In Europe the glass container industry was subject to considerable restructuring, with major acquisitions by Saint-Gobain and BSN in Italy and Spain, respectively; the purchase of Redfearn (U.K.) by PLM of Sweden; and the sale of Guinness' 50% holding in United Glass to Owens-Illinois, which thus became sole owners of the company. The purchase of CWS's glass interests by Rockware made the latter one of the largest container companies in Western Europe. The market remained relatively buoyant, aided by the impact of environmental legislation, particularly in West Germany and The Netherlands, that tended to discourage the use of difficult-to-recycle plastics for beverage bottles.

The year was one of moderate growth for glass-reinforced plastics in the U.S., but several technical developments were reported. Owens-Corning Fiberglas introduced a roving (a slightly twisted roll or strand) especially designed for the expanding market for long-fibre composites and a fibreglass roving with a special glaze that could be processed at 415° C (780° F), compared with the limit of about 176° C (350° F) for standard fibres. In addition, PPG Industries announced the development of the first preform roving for structural reaction molding systems, the introduction of which could lead to commercially viable replacement of structural metal in cars and trucks. The European market for both reinforcement and insulation fibre showed some improvement during the year.

A roaring fire burns through a section of San Francisco's affluent Marina district after a massive earthquake struck the area. The earthquake, which caused extensive damage throughout the San Francisco area, resulted in a record $1 billion earthquake insurance loss.
MICHAEL WILLIAMSON/SACRAMENTO BEE—SYGMA

Sales of domestic glassware, particularly of crystal, declined in volume terms in many of the major glassmaking countries but showed strong increases in emerging countries, such as Turkey, South Korea, and Taiwan. The trend toward the replacement of pot furnaces by all-electric tank furnaces and the greater use of mechanized forming and processing methods were notable, even in the most traditional companies.   (PETER J. DOYLE)

INSURANCE

The global insurance business, which reported more than $1 trillion total sales for the first time during 1989, reeled from the effects of major catastrophic losses in the U.S. In March the biggest oil spill in U.S. history occurred when a tanker hit a reef off the Alaska coast; cleanup costs climbed past $1 billion. In September Hurricane Hugo became the most costly hurricane in U.S. history, with 500,000 claims and an estimated $4 billion of insured losses in Puerto Rico, the U.S. Virgin Islands, and the Carolinas. The next month the San Francisco area experienced a record $1 billion earthquake insurance loss (and uninsured losses many times that), and a Phillips petrochemical plant in Texas exploded, with estimates indicating that it could be the third loss within a month to exceed $1 billion. The year's catastrophe toll was expected to more than double the previous industrywide record of nearly $3 billion in 1985.

In the U.K. the underwriting profit cycle for general (nonlife) insurance turned downward by mid-1989, following a year when premiums rose almost 10% and profits totaled more than £2.4 billion. Rate-cutting was blamed as a primary cause of the reversal. Lloyd's of London results reported in 1989 (for 1986 on their three-year accounting base) were triple those of 1985, a record £650 million profit on premiums of £3.7 billion. Subsequent years were expected to be much less spectacular. In certain markets, motor (automobile) insurance results were satisfactory, but marine and aviation markets were not. U.K. life insurance companies reported premium income of almost £27 billion, an increase of 5%. Their invested funds rose from £190 billion to £216 billion. U.K. life insurers faced increased competition from banks and building societies in the provision of private pensions.

Elsewhere in Europe the insurance business hummed with excitement over the new open market for the EC, planned to be substantially completed in 1992. European insurers were positioning themselves to take advantage of the changes, with mergers—such as Groupe Victoire (France) with Colonia (West Germany)—becoming more common. Brokers and agency relationships were being reevaluated and restructured.

In the U.S. property-liability insurance results to midyear were discouraging and were not expected to improve before year's end. Pretax net operating income totaled $6 billion, down almost 15% from the same period in 1988. Underwriting losses of $8 billion were fortunately offset by $14 billion of investment gains. Written premiums for the first half were $103 billion, but this was less than a 3% gain. Commercial lines especially suffered from price competition. The midyear results did not reflect the anticipated increased losses likely to result from Proposition 103 in California. This law mandated 20% lower automobile insurance rates, a "fair rate of return" for insurers, and new rating factors based on safety record, annual mileage, and experience of drivers.

The federal antitrust lawsuits brought by attorneys general in 19 states against leading insurers were dismissed but were under appeal. A federal district judge declared there was no worldwide conspiracy to fix commercial general liability insurance rates and contract terms. Reinsurance rates for property insurance in the U.S. were starting to rise as a result of the year's catastrophes. One major auto insurer was the first to institute a discount (about 8%) for antilock brakes on all wheels. Large li-

ability insurance claims remained troublesome for insurers and policyholders, but medical malpractice rates were somewhat lower, and several court cases limited costly punitive damage awards in some states.

In the U.S. life insurance market, only universal life contracts showed increased sales (5%) for the first six months of 1989. Term life decreased 1% and whole life fell 8%. Single-premium products, including annuities, dropped 74% and variable products 59% compared with a year earlier; sharp decreases had been expected as a result of higher taxation of these policies under the Technical and Miscellaneous Revenue Act of 1988. Total face amount of life insurance in force was up by 1%. New products included accelerated death benefits for long-term care.

Health insurance costs continued to escalate. A Hewitt Associates study showed that employees were shouldering higher costs through more and larger deductibles, coinsurance provisions (80%), and paying part of the premiums (in three-fourths of the plans). AIDS-related life and health insurance claims rose more than 21% in 1988, costing insurers $590 million. Just before adjournment, Congress finally repealed the controversial Medicare Catastrophic Coverage Act, eliminating all its benefits and its much-disliked surtax on many of the elderly. Section 89 of the Internal Revenue Code was also repealed, postponing new antidiscrimination rules for employee benefit plans until further legislation was passed. Stricter pension-termination procedures and substantially increased premiums for employer payments to the Pension Benefit Guaranty Corporation were expected soon. (DAVID L. BICKELHAUPT)

IRON AND STEEL

World production increased by 6% in 1988 compared with the previous year to reach a new record level of 780,000 metric tons of crude steel. An additional increase was expected during 1989. This was the first time in 10 years that boom conditions had been experienced around the world in the steel industry. For most products delivery times lengthened and prices increased, but no serious shortages of supply occurred, which indicated that during this period of strong demand capacity was sufficient. There was an exception for coated sheets, where supply was unable to match demand because of the rapidly expanding market resulting from new applications in which they replaced other steel, as well as nonsteel, products. The result for the steel industry of working at efficient levels of capacity utilization, and with firm prices, was a large improvement in financial results. Toward the end of 1989 there were signs that demand had declined in certain regions but was being maintained at a high level in other parts of the world.

Trade in steel stabilized as producers tended to concentrate on maintaining supplies to customers in their own domestic markets. There was also a continuation of the trend toward more cross-border mergers and joint ventures, which could to some extent replace direct trade in steel products. The improved financial strength of the steel industry encouraged several governments to consider ways to liberalize the conditions for trade in steel.

Another key feature of 1988 and 1989 was the commissioning of new technology whereby the casting of very thin slabs was linked directly to a rolling mill in a continuous process, with considerable potential savings from energy and productive efficiencies. The success of such technology could encourage the further encroachment of smaller electric-arc production facilities into the traditional market areas of large integrated mills, notably in hot rolled wide flat products.

In the U.S. production increased 12% during 1988 and continued at similar high levels throughout the first half of 1989. There were, however, signs that demand had peaked and would decline toward the end of the year. During 1988 and 1989 two more Japanese steel companies entered into joint ventures with U.S. steel producers, bringing to a total of five the large Japanese firms that were linked to U.S. producers in schemes involving joint ventures or shared ownership. Often the expressed intention of such ventures was to develop products to supply Japanese automobile companies that had already established manufacturing facilities in the U.S. In December the Bush administration announced that agreements extending the arrangements that limited deliveries of steel to the U.S. market had been signed with 18 nations that provided some two-thirds of U.S. steel imports. The arrangements would last for two and a half years instead of the five-year term of the previous agreements, as had been urged by the steel industry. However, in a step the administration spokesman described as "historic," the 18 countries (the 12 members of the EC plus Japan, South Korea, Brazil, Mexico, Australia, and Trinidad and Tobago) had also agreed to end subsidies to their steelmakers. These agreements and

Table VIII. World Production of Crude Steel
In 000 metric tons

Country	1984	1985	1986	1987	1988	1989 Year to date	No. of months	Percent change 1989/88
World	710,320	719,000	713,120	735,920	779,990	—	—	—
U.S.S.R.	154,200	154,500	160,540	161,940	164,000[1]		2	
Japan	105,580	105,280	98,275	98,510	105,670	80,290	9	+2.1
U.S.	84,500	79,240	74,030	80,880	90,750	67,620	9	−0.8
China	43,360	46,700	51,900	56,020	59,000		2	
West Germany	39,390	40,500	37,140	36,250	41,010	31,230	9	+2.2
Italy	24,060	23,870	22,990	22,940	23,670	19,000	9	+9.2
France	19,000	18,820	17,900	17,690	19,000	14,790	9	+5.3
Brazil	18,390	20,450	21,230	22,230	24,620	18,750	9	+2.1
Poland	16,350	15,800	17,140	17,140	17,000[1]		2	
U.K.	15,120	15,720	14,720	17,430	19,010	14,350	9	+2.0
Czechoslovakia	14,830	14,960	15,110	15,420	15,400[1]		2	
Canada	14,700	14,650	14,080	14,740	15,180	11,870	9	+5.2
Romania	14,440	13,760	14,300	14,960	15,000[1]		2	
Spain	13,500	14,230	11,880	11,810	11,690	9,420	9	+7.2
South Korea	13,030	13,540	14,560	16,780	19,110	16,160	9	+12.3
Belgium	11,300	10,680	9,720	9,820	11,240	8,200	9	−1.3
India	10,550	11,940	12,200	13,100	14,200	10,680	9	+1.2
South Africa	7,730	8,510	8,900	8,730	8,750	6,980	9	+6.2
East Germany	7,573	7,840	7,970	8,240	8,250		2	
Mexico	7,480	7,260	7,170	7,570	7,790	5,980	9	+2.3
North Korea	6,500	6,500[1]	6,600	6,700	6,750		2	
Australia	6,300	6,410	6,670	6,100	6,300	4,970	9	+6.3
Netherlands, The	5,740	5,520	5,280	5,080	5,540	4,320	9	+4.8
Taiwan	5,010	5,090	5,550	5,790	8,310	6,490	9	+6.4
Austria	4,870	4,660	4,290	4,300	4,570	3,620	9	+6.1
Sweden	4,705	4,810	4,170	4,600	4,780	3,450	9	+0.7
Turkey	4,330	4,950	5,930	7,050	8,010	5,570	9	−6.1
Yugoslavia	4,290	4,470	4,520	4,370	4,470	3,480	9	+5.2
Luxembourg	3,990	3,945	3,710	3,300	3,660	2,830	9	+4.8
Hungary	3,750	3,620	3,730	3,620	3,500[1]		2	
Bulgaria	2,870	2,880	2,900	3,040	3,000[1]		2	
Venezuela	2,770	3,055	3,400	3,720	3,610	2,620	9	−6.1
Argentina	2,650	2,940	3,240	3,610	3,620	2,940	9	+13.4
Finland	2,640	2,520	2,590	2,670	2,790	2,150	9	+4.6
Iran	1,200	1,200	1,100	1,250	1,250		2	
Switzerland	980	990	1,080	870	825		2	
Norway	920	940	850	850	910	580	9	−12.3
Greece	900	990	1,010	910	970		2	

[1]Estimated.   [2]1989 figures not yet available.
Sources: International Iron and Steel Institute; United Nations.

Table IX. World Production of Pig Iron
In 000 metric tons

Country	1984	1985	1986	1987	1988
World	489,740	498,955	495,840	503,510	531,580
U.S.S.R.	110,800	109,980	113,840	113,900	114,000[1]
Japan	80,400	80,570	74,650	73,420	79,300
U.S.	47,090	45,760	39,870	43,920	50,460
China	40,000	43,540	49,940	50,200	51,000[1]
West Germany	30,200	31,530	28,590	28,120	31,890
Brazil	17,220	18,960	20,350	21,340	23,630
France	14,710	15,070	13,980	13,450	14,790
Italy	11,630	11,660	11,900	11,340	11,390
Canada	9,640	9,670	9,250	9,720	9,490
Czechoslovakia	9,560	9,560	9,600	9,790	9,800[1]
Romania	9,560	9,210	9,330	9,500	9,500[1]
Poland	9,540	9,440	10,100	10,020	10,000[1]
U.K.	9,490	10,380	9,690	12,020	12,970
India	9,460	9,840	10,510	10,920	11,710
Belgium	9,010	8,750	8,050	8,230	9,150
South Korea	8,760	8,830	9,000	11,060	12,590
North Korea	5,750	5,750	5,500	5,800	5,900
South Africa	5,530	5,040	5,770	6,320	6,110
Spain	5,340	5,480	4,803	4,820	4,640
Australia	5,330	5,600	5,850	5,580	5,720
Netherlands, The	4,930	4,820	4,630	4,570	5,000
Mexico	3,870	3,530	3,730	3,690	3,642
Austria	3,745	3,700	3,350	3,450	3,660
Taiwan	3,290	3,430	3,740	3,660	5,680[1]
Turkey	2,900	3,190	3,730	4,070	4,440
Yugoslavia	2,850	3,110	3,070	2,870	2,910
Luxembourg	2,770	2,750	2,650	2,310	2,520
East Germany	2,360	2,580	2,720	2,740	2,750[1]
Sweden	2,210	2,420	2,440	2,320	2,490
Hungary	2,100	2,100	2,080	2,110	2,050[1]
Finland	2,030	1,900	1,980	2,060	2,170
Bulgaria	1,580	1,710	1,600	1,660	1,650[1]
Argentina	920	1,310	1,640	1,750	1,610
Chile	590	580	590	610	780
Norway	550	610	570	370	370
Venezuela	330	440	490	470	500

[1]Estimated.
Sources: International Iron and Steel Institute; United Nations.

Steel pipes sit in a port in Seattle, Washington, after arriving from Japan. The restriction on steel imports was extended for another two and a half years—representing a compromise between the U.S. steel industry, which wanted the restrictions extended for another five years, and steel consumers, who wanted the restrictions dropped.

RICH FRISHMAN—PICTURE GROUP

the quota program would expire on March 31, 1992, but it was hoped that by then the provisions would have been incorporated into an "international consensus on steel" reached in the current (Uruguay) round of General Agreement on Tariffs and Trade (GATT) negotiations, with the aim of establishing a fair and open trading environment for steel.

In Japan production increased by 7% in 1988 and another 2% in 1989. Whereas imports into Japan had continued to increase and exports to decrease during 1988, trade levels stabilized in 1989. The financial results of Japanese steel producers continued to improve, and Nippon Steel, the world's largest steel company, was forecasting gross profits of approximately $1.3 billion in fiscal 1989.

In the EC similar strong market conditions prevailed, with production increasing by 8.5% in 1988 and with a further increase of 4% expected for 1989. The economic situation varied in the different member nations. Italy, for example, was notable for the strength of its growth in 1989, and this influenced the debate about an earlier decision to close the steel-making part of the Bagnoli works in return for authorization to pay subsidies. In West Germany a stronger financial position allowed firm proposals to be made for the state-owned company Peine Salzgitter to be privatized through a sale to Preussag, an engineering and trading concern. Continued restructuring and the prospects for the completion of the single internal market of the EC encouraged a number of cross-border purchases, joint ventures, or co-operation agreements. Usinor-Sacilor, the French state-owned producer and largest European steel company, was particularly active in this respect.

Among the newly industrialized countries, South Korea and Brazil again led production growth in 1988. The latter performed particularly strongly in export markets.   (IAN D. MATTHEWS)

MACHINERY AND MACHINE TOOLS

In 1988 the countries producing the greatest dollar value of metalworking machine tools (both cutting and forming, where cutting machines typically account for approximately four times the dollar value of forming machines) were Japan (total estimated value of production $8.6 billion), West Germany ($6.8 billion), the Soviet Union ($4.5 billion), Italy ($2.8 billion), and the United States ($2.4 billion). The above and subsequent figures for the Soviet Union are rough estimates based on fragmentary data.

The major countries exporting machine tools in 1988 were West Germany (where the total estimated value of machine tool exports was $4.1 billion), Japan ($3.4 billion), Switzerland ($1.6 billion), Italy ($1.3 billion), and East Germany ($1.3 billion). The major importers of machine tools in 1988 were the U.S. (with an estimated $2 billion), the Soviet Union ($1.8 billion), and West Germany ($1.1 billion). The major machine-tool consuming nations in 1988 were the Soviet Union (where machine tools with an estimated value of $6 billion were installed), Japan ($5.7 billion), the U.S. ($3.8 billion), West Germany ($3.8 billion), Italy ($2.2 billion), and the U.K. ($1.4 billion).

The use of numerically controlled (NC) machines, wherein the motion and actions of a machine are automatically controlled by numerical information processed by a specially designed and programmed computer-based device, had by 1989 become commonplace. Such NC machine tools could be programmed locally (at the machine) by means of a keyboard and an associated graphics display. Such displays could show an outline of the part and also the machine motions as they were programmed. Alternatively, machines could be remotely programmed on other computing equipment, with the resulting pro-

grams being transmitted electronically to the machine.

Indeed, by using various forms of local area networks, a number of reprogrammable machine tools and associated material-handling systems (such as robots and conveyors) were often electronically interconnected to provide what had come to be known as flexible manufacturing cells or systems (FMCs or FMSs). The controls of such cells or systems could in turn be interconnected to order-entry systems, inspection systems, part-and-tool routing systems, etc., to form what had become known as computer integrated manufacturing (CIM) systems. Such integrated systems were expected to gain even wider acceptance in the future as a means of achieving increases in manufacturing productivity.   (JOHN B. DEAM)

MICROELECTRONICS

Worldwide sales of semiconductors were projected to increase 9% in 1989 to $49 billion from $45 billion in 1988. This represented a steep drop from the 38% growth in 1988. The Semiconductor Industry Association (SIA) attributed about half of the 1988 increase to higher prices and changes in currency exchange rates. In 1989 neither factor was present. Price decreases resulted from alleviation of a memory-chip shortage and improvements in production techniques.

U.S. sales were expected to rise 9.7% to $14.7 billion from $13.4 billion in 1988. For Japan the SIA forecast a 6.8% growth to $19.3 billion in 1989, compared with $18.1 billion in 1988. European semiconductor sales were expected to gain 11.3% to reach $9 billion, compared with $8.1 billion in 1988. Both U.S. and Japanese companies increased their presence in Europe in expectation of Common Market rules that would require European-made microchips in products produced by EC members.

In 1989 Japanese firms adhered more closely to provisions of a three-year-old trade agreement prohibiting dumping (selling below market price) of chips in the U.S. and requiring the opening of markets in Japan to U.S. companies. Dumping stopped, and Toyota, the giant automaker, pledged to buy more semiconductors from the U.S. In June seven microelectronics companies announced the formation of U.S. Memories, a $1 billion joint venture to manufacture memory chips needed by commercial and military users in the U.S. The members were IBM, Digital Equipment Corp., Hewlett-Packard Co., Intel Corp., Advanced Micro Devices Inc., LSI Logic Corp., and National Semiconductor Corp.

In February Intel crossed a new microelectronics threshold by producing a 64-bit microprocessor containing one million transistors. The company followed up in April with a 32-bit logic chip holding 1.2 million transistors. The price of a silicon chip remains essentially the same no matter how many circuit elements are put onto it. Therefore, the more transistors per chip, the more functions a customer gets without a significant increase in cost. Also, increasing the number of transistors on a chip makes it operate faster because it takes less time for electric signals to go from element to element.

The new Intel chips were made with technology capable of printing circuit devices a scant one micrometre (0.00004 in) in thickness. The new frontier at microelectronics facilities was submicrometre technology and elements 0.8 micrometre in size. It was expected that Sematech, a U.S. government-industry partnership, would reduce this further to 0.5 micrometre and even 0.3 micrometre. (A human hair, for comparison, is between 0.5 and 0.75 micrometre thick.) IBM already had made a 0.4-micrometre device in its research division.

U.S. and Japanese companies began to produce a new product called a flash electrically erasable programmable read-only memory (flash E^{2}PROM). Other EPROMs were erased by ultraviolet light, a much slower process than the flash electrical erasure.   (WILLIAM J. CROMIE)

NUCLEAR INDUSTRY

Figures for 1988 released by the International Atomic Energy Agency (IAEA) during the year showed that 14 new reactors totaling 13,598 MW began producing electricity and that two units were shut down, bringing the number of commercial nuclear reactors in operation in 25 countries to 429. The total installed capacity at the beginning of the year was 310,812 MW. There were 105 units under construction, with a total rating of 84,871 MW. Nuclear units generated about 16% of the world's electricity production in 1988.

The World Association of Nuclear Operators (WANO) was inaugurated in a meeting in Moscow in May. The new organization provided a link between all the world's established and prospective nuclear plant operators. It was to act as a clearinghouse for information concerning operation and design in regard to safety, with centres in Paris, Moscow, Tokyo, and Atlanta, Ga., and a coordinating centre in London. The work of the new organization complemented the safety inspection and advisory service carried out by the operational safety review teams of the IAEA.

Modifications were undertaken on all Chernobyl-type reactors in the Soviet Union to overcome the design shortcomings that combined to cause the accident in 1986. Major restructuring in the organizations controlling nuclear power were announced during the year. A new Ministry for Nuclear Power Engineering and the Nuclear Power Industry was formed, replacing at least two previous ministries.

British government privatization plans for the state electrical utilities were dramatically changed with the sudden announcement in November that no nuclear stations, including the first British pressurized-water reactor (PWR) at Sizewell still in the early stages of construction, would be owned by the future private electricity companies. Originally, National Power, the larger of the two English generating companies to be sold by the government, and Scottish Nuclear Ltd., a jointly owned subsidiary of the two new private Scottish utilities, were to have acquired all the nuclear stations that had been operated by the Central Electricity Generating Board (CEGB) and its Scottish equivalent. It had originally been decided that National Power would inherit 70% of the existing nationalized industry to ensure that it was

of sufficient size to cope with the demands of owning nuclear plants.

As the new company began operation during the year as a division within the CEGB, it approached the government for subsidies to meet costs for irradiated fuel treatment and waste disposal. The government's first decision was that the Magnox reactors (Britain's original gas-cooled design) would remain under state ownership because they were so close to the end of their useful lives. However, with the later revelation that covering all nuclear costs would require still higher electricity prices, the final decision was made to keep all the nuclear plants in England and Scotland under government control. Two immediate repercussions were the resignation of Lord Marshall, the CEGB chairman and National Power chairman designate, and the CEGB's withdrawal of the proposal for a second British PWR station at Hinkley Point.

With more than 70% of all its electricity produced by nuclear stations, France decided to close down its four old Magnox units over the next four years. Électricité de France reported a loss in 1988 even though it exported a record 3.4 trillion watt-hours of electricity to the rest of Europe. The utility announced that it was making a significant increase in expenditures on maintenance and that prices to consumers would rise accordingly. The objective was to increase the useful life of the existing PWRs from 25 to 40 years.

The fast-breeder reactor Superphénix, at Creys-Malville, received a license to restart and run for eight months after almost two years of work to cure the liquid sodium leaks in the fuel storage drum. A long-standing plan to form a joint European fast-breeder development organization was finally signed by France, Britain, and West Germany.

Other countries might soon face the type of energy dilemma reported by the Swedish governing party, the Social Democrats. Swedish energy policy required that nuclear power be phased out from the mid-1990s, that rivers not used for hydroelectric production remain untouched, and that present levels of carbon dioxide emission not be allowed to increase. The report warned that there were "serious conflicts" in these policies.

The Nuclear Regulatory Commission approved the long-awaited simplified procedures for licensing nuclear plants in the U.S. The established procedure consisted of two stages, licenses had to be issued prior to construction and then prior to operation. This could now be combined into a single license, which, it was hoped, would allow project times as short as 6 years, compared with typical times of 12 years previously.

Delving into the ruined reactor vessel at Three Mile Island unit 2, 10 years after the accident in Pennsylvania, investigators finally succeeded in reaching the bottom of the vessel. A report from the U.S. Department of Energy's TMI2 Accident Evaluation Program indicated that about half the core (60 tons of fuel and cladding, etc.) melted, and about one-third of this material slumped onto the bottom of the reactor vessel. Prior to the accident such circumstances would have been expected to cause a failure of the vessel itself, but the water remaining in the vessel during the accident apparently provided enough cooling to avoid any danger of a vessel failure.

The U.S. Department of Energy awarded Westinghouse Electric and General Electric cost-sharing contracts of $50 million for the development and design of 600-MW advanced nuclear reactors. The basic objective for both the advanced pressurized water reactor and the boiling water

PHOTOGRAPHS, WADE SPEES/THE NEW YORK TIMES

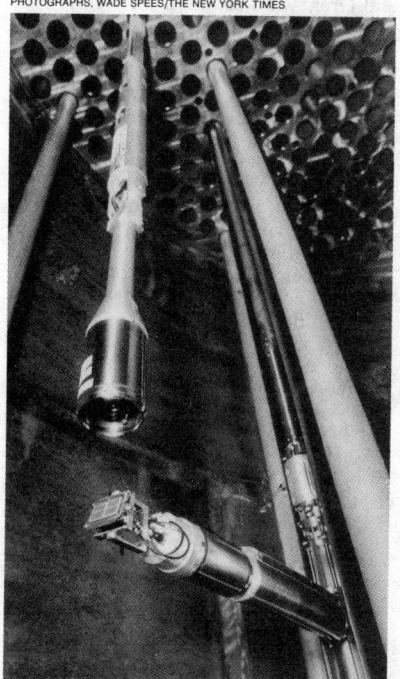

An engineer at the Savannah River nuclear weapons plant (right) guides a robotic arm (left) that can detect cracks in the walls of the plant's nuclear reactors. The robot is able to work in reactor areas that are too dangerous and too small for a person to examine directly.

reactor was to make the safety features of the design more "passive," meaning that fewer operational actions would be needed to ensure safety.

Other joint agreements announced by major nuclear engineering companies included one by Framatome (France) and Siemens/KWU (West Germany), which planned to cooperate on sales and service of PWR units outside of France and West Germany through a joint company, Nuclear Power International, to be based in Paris. Westinghouse and Asea Brown Boveri announced the formation of a joint nuclear services company, ABB Westinghouse Nuclear Services, which planned to offer services in Europe and other selected markets.

Lack of reactor sales by the Crown Corporation Atomic Energy of Canada (AECL) and the growing role in nuclear engineering of the provincial utility Ontario Hydro, which operated 20 of Canada's 22 Candu nuclear units, led to a review of AECL's funding by the federal government. Some of the profitable parts of the company were to be sold to private industry, and there was pressure for a greater proportion of AECL's funding to come from Ontario, the major user of the technology.

South Korea announced plans to have 14 nuclear power plants in operation by the year 2000. The plans called for five new nuclear units to be added to the existing program. The Indonesian National Atomic Energy Agency was to start evaluating sites for the country's first nuclear station following President Suharto's agreement to the project.

The Wackersdorf reprocessing plant under construction in West Germany was abandoned after prolonged political problems. Reprocessing of West Germany's irradiated fuel might be done in France or Britain, following a decision by the West German government to allow utilities to negotiate contracts with companies abroad.

(RICHARD A. KNOX)

PAINTS AND VARNISHES

After years of record growth, a distinct slowing down had become apparent by mid-1989, at least in the U.S. and the U.K. The growing maturity of the mainstream paint markets in the West was evident. Annual average growth rates of 1–2% in Europe and just over 2% in the U.S. contrasted markedly with the 5–6% expected from the paint markets of Southeast Asia. Powder and can coatings were seen as major opportunity areas, even in the West, but in the newly industrialized countries they were expected to increase at an annual rate in excess of 10%.

Corporate strategies responded accordingly, resulting in the industry's continuing internationalization on the one hand and growing specialization on the other. Takeovers continued, with European companies proving the most acquisitive. The U.S. market, by its sheer size, exerted a magnetic pull on European companies. Just as the purchase of Glidden in 1986 had brought Imperial Chemical Industries (ICI) world leadership, Akzo's 1989 acquisition of Reliance Universal (from the Tyler Corp. for $276 million) propelled the Dutch company from fifth to third place. Courtaulds of the U.K. also put down stronger U.S. roots by its acquisition, for

$260 million, of the Products Research and Chemical Corp. The purchase by Nippon Oil & Fats of the U.S. Paint Division from the Grow Group marked the entry of a major Japanese paint company into the U.S. market.

The Pacific area continued to prove attractive for joint ventures, that between ICI and Hong Kong-based Swire Pacific being a case in point. The new company was to produce automotive refinishes and can coatings, with China envisaged as the chief outlet. Joint ventures between Western companies and state-owned Eastern European enterprises were becoming more frequent. ICI's German subsidiary and the Soviet LNPO Pigment signed an agreement to establish a marketing and product-testing centre in Leningrad.

Toxicological and environmental concerns continued to impinge on the paint industry, though no major prohibitions were issued during the year. The EC was bringing about greater harmonization of regulations, standards, and practices. During the year, for instance, the limit value for lead in paint requiring a warning notice was reduced from 0.25 to 0.15%. Air pollution continued to occupy U.S. authorities. The Occupational Safety and Health Administration amended its Air Contaminants Standard by lowering 212 existing permissible exposure limits and setting 164 new ones.   (HELMA JOTISCHKY)

PHARMACEUTICALS

The generic drug makers in 1989 committed tactical blunders on a scale that undermined much of the advantage they had gained on major brand name manufacturers. Industry watchers suggested that the "FDA/Generic Drug Scandal" might have profound effects well into the 1990s in the way physicians and hospital pharmacists perceived generic drugs and the way these products were regulated by the Food and Drug Administration (FDA) and state pharmacy boards.

The scandal centred on the acceptance of illegal gratuities by three staffers in the FDA's Division of Generic Drugs, presumably in return for speeding up approvals of Abbreviated New Drug Applications (ANDAs). The House Oversight and Investigations Subcommittee, which investigated the scandal, was alerted by a whistle-blower (Mylan Laboratories, Inc., which complained about the slow progress of its ANDAs compared with those of its competitors) and the U.S. attorney's office in Baltimore, Md., which brought indictments against the three FDA employees and three drug company executives, all of whom were fined and sentenced. Other allegations emerged during the investigation. The FDA had per diem spending limits for personnel at industry conferences and seminars, but 20 or so FDA staffers were found to have accepted luxury-rate hotel and meal payments from the National Association of Pharmaceutical Manufacturers.

Even worse was the charge that the FDA had fallen for a variation of the "bait-and-switch" scam in the matter of samples submitted for bioequivalency testing. Instead of using their generic versions, companies utilized the very drug they were imitating. In the most glaring example, Bolar Pharmaceutical Co. and Vitarine Pharmaceuticals Inc. submitted samples of the hypertension

drug Dyazide (made by SmithKline Beckman) instead of their own versions.

The FDA and its parent, the Department of Health and Human Services, moved quickly to exert damage control. HHS sent its inspector general to investigate gratuities and hotel entertainment, while FDA Commissioner Frank Young set in motion a reorganization of the Division of Generic Drugs and asked for a review of ANDAs that led to revocation of FDA approval of a number of products and suspension of others. He also ordered a reinspection of manufacturing plants of a dozen leading generic manufacturers, later informing Rep. John Dingell (Dem., Mich.), the chairman of the subcommittee, that at least 10 infractions of Good Manufacturing Practices (GMPs) had been found.

Still to be assessed was how much confidence in generics remained among the medical establishment. In October only strong FDA assurances kept the American Academy of Family Physicians from recommending against prescribing generics for certain patients and certain illnesses. Ironically, at precisely the moment when they could have benefited from the scandal, brand name drug manufacturers encountered problems of their own. Because of GMP violations, Eli Lilly & Co. had to recall 18 lots of 10 drugs and to halt distribution from its Indianapolis, Ind., plant. Another giant, American Home Products Corp., found it necessary to suspend operations of its generic subsidiary, Quantum Pharmics Ltd.   (DONALD A. DAVIS)

PLASTICS

Increased demand for plastics was sustained for a fifth successive year, although some slowdown became evident, particularly in the U.S., toward the end of 1989. Overall, expansion was probably a little below the 7–8% or so of 1988, when consumption in the U.S. and Western Europe was estimated at 26 million tons each, and in Japan at 11 million tons. These three principal areas together accounted for two-thirds of a total world demand for plastics approaching 100 million tons.

The first half of 1989 was marked by sharp falls in the prices of all the large-tonnage commodity thermoplastics except polyvinyl chloride, which held up well. However, high-density polyethylene and polystyrene were less affected than low-density polyethylene, whose price plummeted in world markets. Some observers saw this fall as confirming expectations of a general downturn in activity, but this proved not to be the case. Rather, it was due to a feeling among customers that the material suppliers had pushed prices up too far and that stocks (then unusually high as a counter to the shortages of 1988) should be reduced. It became clear after the summer holidays that true demand remained strong. Prices began to recover, although not to the levels seen at the beginning of the year.

There were many announcements of new plants, especially in the Middle East, Latin America, Southeast Asia, and, more surprisingly, in Europe, on a scale not seen for a decade. Virtually every European petrochemicals producer expressed the intention of increasing output of ethylene and propylene monomer. These materials—the basis of all the large-tonnage

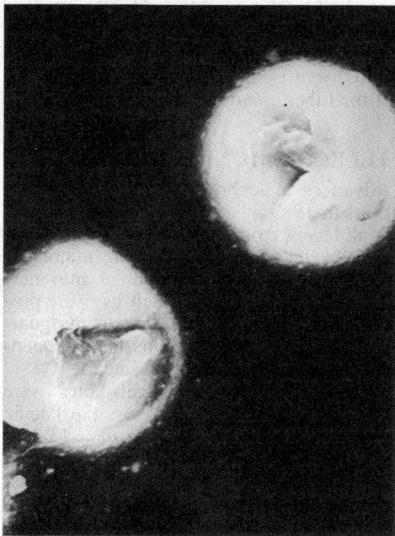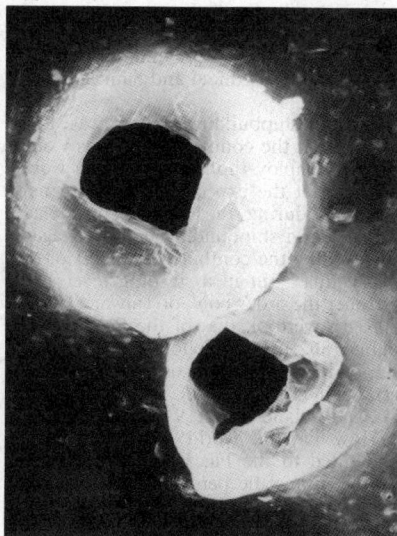

A closeup of degradable plastic reveals bits of cornstarch (left) that can be eaten by microbes, thus causing the plastic's disintegration to be speeded up (right). Manufacturers hoped this process would cut down on waste, but environmentalists felt it would do more harm than good.
PHOTOGRAPHS, UNIVERSITY OF MISSOURI, COLUMBIA

thermoplastics—were in short supply, and fears of overcapacity, like that blamed for the collapse of the industry in 1980, appeared to have been overcome.

Nevertheless, there were warning signs, particularly with polypropylene. Although this versatile material continued to enjoy above-average growth, the expanding surplus in Europe—set to get larger still—kept its price weak throughout the year. Firms either possessing or licensed to use the most modern production technology were seen as best placed to operate profitably. Himont, the world's largest polypropylene producer, announced its Catalloy process in which propylene is copolymerized with various other monomers, enabling material properties to be "tailored" and radically modified. Another important Himont development of 1989 was Valtec, a refinement of the Spheripol process in which stabilized pellets of polypropylene are produced directly from the reactor, cutting out the extrusion step.

The year brought confirmation that linear low-density polyethylene had not yet replaced conventional low-density polyethylene for packaging film in Europe to the extent that it had in the U.S. With ample availability, however, gradual market penetration would likely continue. The plants making low-density polyethylene by old high-pressure processes were aging and would eventually have to be replaced.

Growth in demand for high-performance plastics, including composite materials, continued to be steady at around 5% in 1989. Bayer of West Germany estimated that world consumption of engineering thermoplastics was as high as 4.9 million tons in 1988, a figure expected to grow to 5.8 million tons in 1992. The automotive industry was the largest customer, with the electrical and electronics sector a close second. (ROBIN C. PENFOLD)

PRINTING

Commercial changes marked the year in printing. Robert Maxwell, who only recently had expressed a desire to become the world's biggest printing tycoon, sold his holdings in Europe and North America and concentrated on publishing. Rupert Murdoch in New York increased printing history's largest press order to a value of some $550 million for news presses from MAN Roland. Komori Printing Machinery of Japan, frustrated a year earlier in its attempt to buy Harris Graphics' web press division, bought Chambon in France. Miller Printing Machinery was to be sold to MAN Roland, second largest pressmaker in the world after another West German firm, Heidelberg. The Graphic Systems Division of Rockwell International became number three, having bought Hantscho in the U.S., Crouzet-Loire in France, and Baker Perkins of Britain.

Du Pont and Fuji Photo Film of Japan jointly acquired Britain's Crosfield Electronics pre-press systems. Fuji also built new production facilities in the U.S. and The Netherlands. Anitec, now part of International Paper, acquired Ilford photographic from Ciba-Geigy in Switzerland. Earlier, Du Pont had bought Britain's Howson-Algraphy platemaking interests from Vickers. The British-based Cookson Group's Horsell offset plate company bought the West German Freundorfer company. Japan's printers, hitherto hesitant, began to look for acquisitions in North America and Europe.

Japanese technological advances were being pioneered to a considerable extent by the country's large printers. Dainippon Printing, the largest printing group in the world, and Toppan Printing had research and development facilities employing several hundred researchers each. Dainippon Screen of Japan introduced a new flatbed full-colour proof press. Automated guided vehicles were being introduced for paper reel handling. The pioneering work had been done in Japan.

Flexography became respectable for newspaper production. In West Germany Koenig & Bauer-Albert started up the Alfra CX anilox offset press for daily newspaper production, and MAN Roland made substantial installations for Flexoman presses in the U.S. (W. PINCUS JASPERT)

RUBBER

The consolidation of the rubber industry continued in 1989. France's Groupe Michelin ended a dispute as to who was the largest tire manufacturer in the world when it announced it would buy the Uniroyal Goodrich tire company for approximately $690 million; it also assumed Uniroyal Goodrich's outstanding debt, placing the overall value of the deal at $1.5 billion. Goodyear Tire of the U.S., the perennial leader, disputed claims that it had slipped to second place, insisting that sales figures showing Michelin in first were skewed by the exchange rate and that it was still tops in volume. However, Michelin's acquisition of Uniroyal Goodrich ended the debate. Michelin's sales in 1988 in the rubber industry amounted to $8.1 billion, Goodyear sales totaled $9.7 billion, and Bridgestone of Japan had sales of $8.1 billion. The acquisition also made Michelin the leader in tire capacity. Michelin's total capacity would be 630,000 units daily, while Goodyear's was 500,000. Michelin's purchase left only two U.S.-owned passenger tire manufacturers, as Japan's Yokohama bought Mohawk Rubber.

Bridgestone began construction of a $350 million radial truck-tire plant near Nashville, Tenn., which was expected to be fully operational in 1991. Firestone was spending $115 million for expansions and upgrades at its Wilson, N.C., plant that would increase manufacturing capacity by 30%. GTY Tire Co. broke ground for a new tire facility in Mt. Vernon, Ill. GTY, a joint venture between General Tire, the U.S. subsidiary of Continental West Germany, and Japan's Yokohama Rubber and Toyo Tire, would have an annual production capacity of 880,000 radial medium truck and bus tires when production began in 1991. General began expansion of its Charlotte, N.C., facility to increase the plant's capacity to nearly 30,000 radial tires daily from the current 25,000. The company was also spending $159 million at its Barrie, Ont., facility to double radial-tire production and convert the current bias-tire technology to radial passenger and light truck-tire technology. Continental formed a joint venture with Mabor S.A. of Porto, Port., to manufacture radial passenger tires in Portugal for the Western European market.

The truck-tire market, the last to go radial, had become extremely competitive. Radials accounted for about 70% of the 12 million-unit commercial truck-tire replacement market, and Goodyear estimated that radials would account for 85% of the market by 1993. A joint venture between Goodyear and Dunlop, South Pacific Tyres, started a $170 million investment program that would include construction of a steel radial truck-tire plant near Melbourne, Australia, the first new tire facility to be built in that country in 23 years. Goodyear sold its Uitenhage, South Africa, facilities to Consol Ltd., ending 42 years of business in South Africa.

In the nontire sector of the rubber industry, multinational companies were also trying to increase their presence in the North American market. Zeon Chemicals, a division of Japan's Nippon Zeon, purchased the elastomer division of B.F. Goodrich and began construction of a $20

million complex for synthetic rubber production in Pasadena, Texas. Nippon Zeon purchased the nitrile rubber division of BP Chemicals, located in Barry, Wales. BP sold its TPR thermoplastic rubber line to Monsanto of the U.S.

Another large U.S. synthetic rubber producer, Copolymer Rubber & Chemical, was bought by DSM of The Netherlands for $242.5 million plus other considerations. Other key acquisitions included purchase of U.S. rubber chemical producer Pennwalt for $1,050,000,000 by France's Elf Acquitaine; Cadillac Rubber & Plastics, a supplier of extruded and molded rubber products to the automotive market, for $57 million by Avon Rubber of Great Britain; and tire and rubber processing equipment maker Stewart Bolling by Kobe Steel of Japan.

Rubber industry suppliers began several capacity expansions in 1989. Exxon started expansion of its ethylene-propylene rubber capacity that would add 15,000 tons per year at its Notre-Dame-de-Gravenchon, France, facility. Polysar Ltd. of Canada completed a $25 million hydrogenated nitrile rubber facility in Orange, Texas, with a capacity of 1,600 metric tons annually. Firestone began a $22 million expansion at its Lake Charles, La., synthetic rubber facility to allow production of solution styrene butadiene rubber. Goodyear was spending $31.5 million at its Houston, Texas, facility.

Peter Bommarito, president of the United Rubber Workers from 1966 to 1981, died in September.

(DONALD SMITH)

SHIPBUILDING

The optimism engendered in shipping circles by the 2.6 million gross tonnage (gt) increase in the world order book in 1988 was justified by the mid-1989 figures issued by Lloyd's Register. They showed that the volume of tonnage in the world order book was 3,369,027 gt higher than for the same period in 1988. Tonnage under construction and orders not yet begun stood at a satisfying 27,336,535 gt. This was the eighth successive rise in quarterly order book figures since the nadir of March 1987.

The second-quarter figures for 1989 showed a confident Japan once again heading up the shipbuilding countries, having reversed the 1988 situation when South Korea took over the lead. Japan's order book increased by 1,789,436 gt to a total of 7,797,861 gt, or 28.53% of world tonnage. South Korea was second with 6,518,365 gt or 23.84%. Between them, the two shipbuilding giants accounted for 52.37% of the world's order book.

South Korea's performance was all the more remarkable because its shipbuilding industry faced severe financial problems during the year. Daewoo yard was said to have massive debts and, as part of a $1 billion rescue package, was forced to sell assets that included the Seoul Hilton Hotel. Both the Hyundai and Daewoo yards had to close for a period because of union troubles. Samsung yard was disrupted by strikes, and Korea Shipbuilding and Engineering Corp. was technically insolvent. By April Hyundai was back in full production. Daewoo workers returned to work in July after a bitter four-week strike. Later

in the year the South Korean government announced a financial rescue package for Daewoo and Korea Shipbuilding and Engineering Corp. Hyundai and Samsung were excluded.

Japan's shipbuilding union was forecasting that the country's shipyards would have to employ thousands of extra workers to meet the expected increase in new buildings during the 1990s. Third place in the world shipbuilding table was again achieved by the combined tonnages of the two Chinas, but in a startling reversal of fortunes the order book of Taiwan (1,019,-300 gt) overtook that of the People's Republic (862,176 gt). Following the Far East shipbuilders came Yugoslavia (1,442,626 gt), Spain (1,215,724 gt), Brazil (1,014,790 gt), and Poland (989,129 gt).

How far the world shipbuilding axis had tilted to the Far East could be seen by the minuscule percentage of the order book gained by formerly active European shipbuilding countries such as Belgium (0.36%), France (0.77%), Portugal (0.31%), Sweden (0.18%), and the U.K. (0.93%). In the U.K. the government sought to attack the problem by returning state-owned yards to private enterprise. A backer was found for the Harland and Wolff, Belfast, shipyard after Indian entrepreneur Ravi Tikkoo pulled out of talks with the Northern Ireland Office. Tikkoo had planned to build a $500 million cruise ship, the *Ultimate Dream*. The new deal, backed by Norwegian shipowner Fred Olsen, was a management-employee buyout of Harland and Wolff with Olsen making an investment of £12 million.

The percentages of principal ship types under construction or on order showed some slight changes from the same period in 1988: oil tankers 37.9% (down from 40.7%), bulk carriers 28.8% (up from 25.1%), and general cargo 17.8% (down from 18.1%). Of the general cargo component, containership tonnage continued to increase to 58.8% (2.9 million gt). This was a cause of some concern to the industry, since container shipping could face a perilous future if shipowners continued to

overbuild. Of the total world order book of 27.3 million gt, 72.9% was for registration in countries other than those where the ships were built. This included 5,966,239 gt for Liberia and 4,852,350 for Panama.

(EDWARD CROWLEY)

TELECOMMUNICATIONS

Advances in technology and new regulations in 1989 affected telecommunications at all levels, from global networks to shopping by telephone. There were major extensions of optical fibre cables into new areas, and standards for their use were promulgated. International agreements guaranteed to less developed nations frequencies for communication by satellite.

In 1989 undersea optical fibres were carrying telephone calls across the Pacific Ocean following completion of a 13,316-km (8,271-mi) cable between the U.S. and Japan during the year. Thirty companies paid $700 million to construct the Pacific link, which could carry about 40,000 calls simultaneously. Transpacific communications were increasing so rapidly that another fibre cable was planned for completion in 1992.

In Japan, Fujitsu Laboratories Ltd. began testing a broadband integrated services digital network (ISDN) to carry voice, data, text, and video signals over optical fibres. This system could transmit up to 150 megabits a second, the equivalent of 2,000 voice telephone circuits and much greater than the conventional 144 kilobit-per-second rate for narrowband ISDNs.

Fujitsu claimed that this network was the first to conform to standards recommended by the International Telegraph and Telephone Consultative Committee. These standards included what was known as SONET, a U.S. formula to standardize formats and rates for fibre communications. SONET required everyone to speak the same digital language at the same rates, in multiples of 1.5 megabits per second.

The use of optical fibres was extended to facsimile transmission in November 1988, when MCI Communications became the first U.S. long-distance company to offer a

JIM WILSON/THE NEW YORK TIMES

A hand-held device developed by Nynex Corp. can transmit the number of an incoming call as well as perform such other services as call tracing and automatic redial, which keeps dialing a busy line.

digital optical fibre network for domestic and international fax messages. To meet the soaring demand for sending printed information and pictures by telephone, MCI planned to construct the first digital fibre network solely for facsimile transmission. From 1987 to 1989 the number of facsimile machines in the U.S. doubled to more than 1.2 million. Falling prices for machines were expected to accelerate this demand.

Progress was also made during the year in the use of twisted-pair copper wire lines for high-speed services, including video images. Research laboratories in the U.S. and Japan transmitted moving video images with a quality approaching that of videocassette recorder pictures. Thus this technique might make possible the distribution of movies through telephone lines at a reasonable cost.

Paralleling the progress in connecting the businesses and homes of the developed world with fibres and wires were advances in linking the world via radio waves. The International Telecommunication Union (ITU) in 1988 allotted part of the geostationary orbit to every country. In this orbit the speed of an orbiting communications satellite matches that of Earth's rotation, effectively keeping the satellite stationary over one location. The ITU also allocated to each nation part of the ultrahigh and superhigh frequency bands. This guaranteed future access to space communications to countries that did not yet have the capability to launch satellites.

Satellites might soon be used for cellular transmissions, which would enable people in remote areas, continents apart, to talk with each other by means of pocket-sized radios. The growth of mobile radio phones had been phenomenal since the first commercial system went into operation in 1983. In the U.S. in 1989 more than one million customers used cellular phone services operating in hundreds of cities.

Such demand spurred a second generation of cellular phones based on digital technology. Digital signals (a series of on-off pulses) allowed more than one call to be carried per channel, overcoming a limitation of analog (sound or electrical wave) technology. Digital technology, therefore, could increase the volume of traffic carried within the frequencies allotted for cellular communications.

Additional regulatory action freed regional telephone companies to provide so-called gateways (connections) to services that offered information such as weather and shopping catalogs via voice or computer display. The gateway provided a single bill for all connect charges to the various sources. One such service, called Prodigy, provided news, weather, sports, games, financial data, and shopping information to IBM-compatible computers equipped with a modem.   (WILLIAM J. CROMIE)

TEXTILES

An earlier trend favouring natural fibres seemed to have stabilized in 1989, and world growth of synthetic fibre production resumed. The tendency for world textile manufacturing capacity to gravitate eastward was apparent not only in the countries of the Pacific Rim but also in Near Eastern countries such as Turkey, providing a major source of irritation to textile makers in

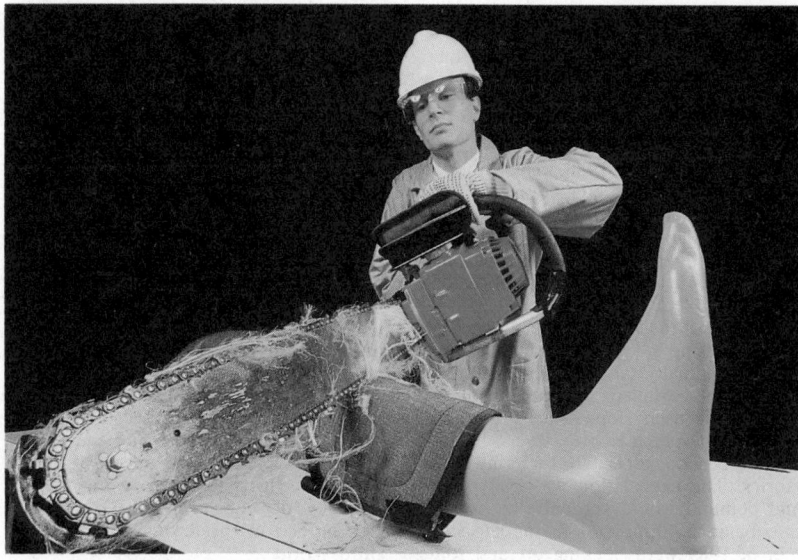

A technical specialist attempts to saw through a mannequin's leg covered with Du Pont's new Kevlar chaps. The Kevlar fibres disable the chainsaw, thus preventing it from cutting the leg.
DU PONT COMPANY

the EC. However, the attempts of certain Arab countries, such as Saudi Arabia, to establish a textile industry appeared to be more a matter of wishful thinking than a serious prospect.

The development of textile manufacturing in Africa had been virtually stagnant for some years. The countries north of the Sahara, including Egypt and The Sudan, had shown growth, but aside from Kenya those to the south had not advanced in line with developments elsewhere. A number of governments were attempting to generate economic environments in which producers of fibres, fabrics, and garments could expect to benefit from their efforts.

A German company collaborated with two other companies, one German and one Spanish, to convert what is known as "hard" waste (fabric clippings, thread waste, etc.) into acceptable commercial yarns. This recycling was a clear indication that the world textile industry was realizing at last that raw materials availability is finite.

China's political difficulties failed to stop the massive development of every aspect of the country's textile industry. Agreements were made whereby the Chinese could use the expertise of European textile-machinery makers, but with the understanding that they would not attempt to sell abroad.

(PETER LENNOX-KERR)

Wool. There was no sign of any deterioration in consumer demand for wool in 1989. Finer wool was still in favour as an apparel fibre and coarser wool for carpets and furnishings. The International Wool Secretariat was highly praised for its part in the market recovery of the previous three years. Fashion trends favoured worsted as opposed to knitwear.

The wool market situation, however, took a turn for the worse during the second half of the year. The Australian Wool Corporation's market indicator fell to 890 cents (Australian) per kilogram (1 kg = 2.2 lb) by the end of June, from an all-time peak of 1,266 cents in April 1988. The overall reserve price was left unchanged at 870 cents for the 1989–90 season, and

prices quickly fell to support level. By mid-October the AWC had stocks of over a million bales.

The collapse was due partly to increased Australian production, with growers hastening to put their wool onto the market when they saw no prospect of a price rise. Buyers also saw no reason to bear stock-holding costs when AWC stocks were so substantial. The absence of China from world markets in the latter half of the year was crucial. The June disturbances there exacerbated China's shortage of foreign exchange. However, industry leaders were confident that the downturn would be corrected in 1990, when offerings would be much lower and stock replenishment would be necessary.   (H.M.F. MALLETT)

Cotton. Because spinning of cotton-type yarns had been in a state of turmoil for a number of years, cotton growers found it difficult to decide on the best cotton to grow. As a simple "rule of thumb," the finer the cotton and the longer the fibre, the better the resulting product. However, with the increase in world capacity of rotor spinning, the call appeared to be for finer cottons, but of shorter length. This was because the tiny rotor cups used to form fibres into a yarn are of limited diameter, and the smaller the fibre is, the faster they can run.

India was making a considerable effort to expand production of extra-fine cottons by the 1990 season, as was Egypt, but it was the Soviet Union that dominated the trade, having massively increased output over the past few seasons. Much of this was irrigated cotton, and just how the changed political situation would influence this trend had yet to be seen. The very high environmental cost of growing cotton in the U.S.S.R. had to be taken into account.

Cotton production in 1990 was projected at 21.2 million bales (1 bale = 480 lb or c. 218 kg) in China, 15.4 million bales in the U.S., and 11.6 million bales in the U.S.S.R. Production of cotton yarn was dominated by China, followed by the U.S.S.R., India, and the U.S.

(PETER LENNOX-KERR)

Silk. In 1988 China was once again the largest producer of raw silk, at 34,400 metric tons, and Japan the largest consumer, at 21,420 tons. Up to December 1987 raw silk had been in plentiful and steady supply from China at reasonable prices, but thereafter shortages began to develop, reaching crisis level in July 1988. The situation was characterized by late shipments from China, a black market, consisting mostly of smuggled goods at high prices, in Hong Kong, and dwindling stocks in Japan and Europe. By the end of the year prices had almost doubled.

Because of the well-developed system of merchandising silk, few European manufacturers actually ran out, but production had to be curtailed. A number of peripheral silk users stopped using the fibre. However, despite high price levels, demand remained good, especially for printed silk fabrics. The expectation was that supply and demand would gradually be brought into balance. Shipments in the late summer of 1989 were catching up, and some very high prices for certain silk articles from Hong Kong (*e.g.,* spun silk yarn) were declining.

The higher price levels encouraged other countries to revive their interest in developing a silk industry. The Brazilians had been able to obtain higher prices for their production, but there were problems of poor supply for climatic reasons, and the long period of low Chinese prices had discouraged reinvestment. The industry in India continued to develop rapidly. Production now amounted to 9,000 tons, but the quality was still inferior. World production in 1987 was 64,278 tons.

(ANTHONY H. GADDUM)

Man-Made Fibres. A cellulose fibre made in Britain eliminated a number of production stages previously required for producing viscose rayon. The new fibre was both environmentally attractive and superior in certain physical properties. The concept relied on a substantial recovery (approximately 99%) of the costly solvent, and unless this could be assured, it was unlikely that the process would become well established. However, there was cause for optimism, given the burgeoning interest in "green" products.

Currently there were two groups of high-performance fibres, those that had emerged from efforts aimed at making high-tenacity versions of such synthetics as nylon, polyester, and, more recently, polypropylene and those based on complex and costly processes, such as the aramids and carbon-graphite fibres. Now an intermediate type of fibre was being made, and within two or three years it could fill the middle ground between the existing groups, which were widely separated by price. Italian-made polyethylene using British technology was an example of this type of development. One interesting development bridging the gap between natural and synthetic was the production of a multilayer yarn with a stretch-broken core of carbon fibres, around which have been wrapped a number of component layers of other fibres ending with an outer sheath of cotton. This provides unusual protective properties in such items as fire-fighting gear, but because of the outer sheath of cotton, the fabrics are very comfortable.

(PETER LENNOX-KERR)

TOBACCO

World use of cigarettes, by far the most popular form of tobacco consumption, rose again in 1989, to an estimated 5,250,000,000,000—a total that was predicted to reach 5.7 trillion by the end of the century. While developed countries were smoking a little less, the rest of the world, notably the less developed countries, where 53% of the world's cigarettes were sold, were smoking more.

In line with this trend, the world grew record quantities of tobacco in 1989. Of the 7,210,000 tons harvested, 60% was flue-cured, a key ingredient of mild, often American-blend cigarettes that were gaining favour everywhere at the expense of those made of dark tobacco. Increased environmental awareness and the vulnerability of tobacco to criticism explained redoubled efforts to improve the thermal efficiency of flue-curing and to replant trees burned in the drying process in the Third World.

Health concerns increasingly led smokers to choose lower-tar cigarettes, and manufacturers were deploying great ingenuity in reducing tar levels to meet this demand without sacrificing taste. One innovation was a cigarette, on sale in Italy, whose tar delivery could be varied up or down as the smoker twisted the filter. Some governments already decreed maximum tar levels, and the EC (which consumed 11% of the world's cigarettes) was under notice of severe tar-level limits as of 1993, to the alarm of EC growers who traditionally produced higher-tar tobaccos.

Although tobacco manufacture remained a state monopoly in more than half the world, the monopoly markets were opening, and the big transnational groups, mainly U.S. and British, were moving in with international brands. The cigarette export trade was booming as never before. However, these transnationals were having problems with corporate raiders. They had all used the strong cash flows the cigarette business produces to diversify out of tobacco. This policy (which monopolies in Japan and Spain were also adopting) exposed them to takeover bids by financiers

intent on dismembering the conglomerates. Thus the giant U.S. tobacco-and-food group R.J. Reynolds had been taken over, and the world's largest nonmonopoly business, the heavily diversified BAT Industries, came under attack and moved to shed some nontobacco activities.

(MICHAEL F. BARFORD)

TOURISM

The year 1989 marked a turning point for world tourism. Although demand for international travel remained buoyant, certain major tourist-receiving countries recorded zero growth or even slight declines. Government and industry circles agreed that this was symptomatic of a malaise affecting the business. Escalating prices, air traffic delays and strikes, poor quality, and environmentally insensitive accommodations were part of the problem. Low-margin, mass tourist flows that stretched infrastructure to the limit and alienated local host populations were another. For many traditional destinations the strategy for the 1990s was beginning to be clear: a restructuring of the industry involving closure of old, low-grade hotels and apartments in crowded coastal areas, a halt to new construction for the time being, development of new products such as special-interest tourism, and staggering of tourist flows to avoid overcrowding.

According to World Tourism Organization (WTO) figures, international arrivals worldwide in 1988 totaled 389 million, and receipts from international tourism were equal to $193,790,000,000. These figures represented increases over 1987 of 8.5% in the case of arrivals and 22.1% in the case of receipts. Despite the modest government support it enjoyed, tourism was the world's third most important traded item, after petroleum products and automobiles, and the world's leading traded service. Preliminary indications for 1989 suggested an easing of the growth rate in world tourism, essentially owing to stagnating growth in key European receiving countries. The trend was not identical in all regions, however, and international air transport—an important component of tourist travel—recorded a 9% increase in

JOSEPH MCNALLY—SYGMA

Two young visitors are fascinated by the creature from *Aliens* during Disney World's new Great Movie Ride. The trip through movie history was only part of Disney World's planned expansion that included a simulated trip through the human bloodstream.

revenue passenger-kilometres in the first half of the year.

In Europe, Spain expected zero growth in tourist arrivals in 1989, while in Italy there was a 2% decline. Yugoslavia, a major market for West German tourists, also experienced zero growth. In Israel arrivals for January–September 1989 rose 9% above the corresponding period in 1988. France, celebrating the bicentennial of the French Revolution, expected to take over from Italy as the second most important tourist destination in Europe, after Spain. France was host to the eighth General Assembly of the WTO. As *glasnost* swept Eastern Europe, Czechoslovakia reported a 47% increase in visitors, and Hungary, 26%. The weakness of the pound sterling against the U.S. dollar helped the U.K. mark up a 14% increase in tourists. Cyprus and Malta recorded growth rates of 23 and 14%, respectively.

The Asia/Pacific region continued to be a star performer. Arrivals in South Korea soared by 31% and in the Philippines by 27%. Though Japan was committed to a policy of exporting rather than receiving tourists, it still showed a 22% increase in visitors over 1988. Hong Kong and Singapore both welcomed 15% more tourists in 1989, a tribute to effective promotional strategies. In China tourism dipped after the suppression of the pro-democracy movement in June but recovered as overseas Chinese visited family and friends on October 1, the 40th anniversary of the establishment of the People's Republic. In Australia tourism declined by 15%.

According to revised figures released in 1989, the U.S. earned $29,202,000,000 from tourism in 1988 but spent $32,112,-000,000 abroad—over $7 billion more than the second biggest tourism spender, West Germany. Arrivals moved ahead strongly by almost 12% in 1989. The four countries sending the most visitors to the U.S. were Canada, Japan, the U.K., and Mexico, in that order. Among these countries, the U.K. showed the strongest growth at 24%. Canada could show only zero growth in tourist arrivals in 1989, apparently because of a fall in visitors from the U.S. Among Caribbean destinations, The Bahamas and Barbados reported gains of 5 to 6%, while Bermuda and Jamaica reported initial declines.

The tourism picture for Africa south of the Sahara was unclear, though South Africa reported a 13% increase in arrivals. North African countries showed increasing interest in their tourism prospects after completion of the EC internal market in 1992. The Tunisian prime minister, Hamed Karoui, announced a virtual relaunching of his country's tourism, with strong emphasis on cultural and desert tourism and the creation of new destinations.

The search for alternative forms of tourism with less negative impact on the environment intensified in 1989. In a keynote address delivered at the new North American tourism fair, ITIX '89, held in Chicago in April, the secretary-general of the WTO, Willibald P. Pahr, emphasized the need to pursue such a search with vigour. The need for environmental safeguards was also stressed by the first Interparliamentary Conference on Tourism, held in April in The Hague.

(PETER SHACKLEFORD)

WOOD PRODUCTS

The amount of public pressure for the preservation of the tropical rain forests intensified during 1989, and in Europe and North America demands for natural and leisure forests were stepped up. The tropical hardwood producers appeared to have reacted most strongly to pressure from the environmentalists. In July the Philippines banned sawn lumber exports, leaving a gap in supply, mainly in Europe, of 500,-000 cu m.

In October Indonesia levied a huge export tax on sawn timber, amounting to 40–50% of the contract price of the lumber. By far the largest hardwood producer in the Far East, Indonesia relied heavily on wood products exports, which were third only to oil and gas in the country's economy. The existence of measures to restrict rough sawn lumber exports reflected the country's need to foster its manufacturing industries more than any concession to environmentalists.

Europe would be most affected by these developments. According to the Economic Commission for Europe (ECE)/Food and Agriculture Organization (FAO) *Timber Bulletin for Europe* (1988), the EC had a net trade deficit in sawn broad-leaved timber of 4.6 million cu m, more than 3.6 million cu m of which was currently being satisfied by tropical hardwoods. The U.S. was gearing up to fill the gap. Its hardwood exports in 1988 topped $1 billion for the first time. This was some 37% higher than

in 1987 and included significant gains in European markets. According to FAO estimates, the U.S. produced approximately 13% of total world production of sawn hardwoods.

For wood products exporters around the world, the single European market scheduled for 1992 promised more than 320 million consumers operating under uniform standards. However, the codes of practice that were evolving had more exceptions than rules—a situation that was only to be expected since building requirements, for example, could not be the same in countries with climates as diverse as those of Italy and Britain.

Softwood consumption in Europe reached a record level in 1988. Imports topped 30 million cu m, though that figure was expected to decrease in 1989. However, of the top six wood users in Europe, few came close to meeting their softwood requirement.

The principal exporters to Europe seemed likely to retain their traditional shares: Sweden 6.6 million cu m; Finland 4.7 million cu m; U.S.S.R. 4 million cu m; Canada 3.1 million cu m; Czechoslovakia 1.1 million cu m; and the U.S. 1 million cu m.

The familiar production pattern in sheet materials persisted: world plywood and blockboard supply centres were outside Europe, but the EC countries were gathering force as suppliers of particleboard and fibreboard, including medium-density fibreboard. In October 1989 world production capacity of medium-density fibreboard was estimated at 7 million cu m, compared with 5.6 million cu m a year earlier. A further 1.3 million-cu m capacity was expected to come on stream in 1990–91, representing a 30% increase in capacity since 1988.

There was no doubt that environmentalist pressure to preserve the world's forests would grow in the years to come. However, the timber industry had not yet made a concerted effort to put forward its own messages, such as the environmental advantages of regular harvesting of trees and the ability of commercial and leisure forest uses to coexist.

World trade in logs, already declining sharply, was expected to diminish further, along with the supply of tropical hardwood lumber. Increasingly, investment in the less developed hardwood-exporting countries would be directed toward establishing manufacturing capability to produce finished components and furniture.

(JEAN CLARK CAMERON KLOOS)

See also Agriculture and Food Supplies; Consumer Affairs; Economic Affairs; Energy; Information Processing and Information Systems; Labour-Management Relations; Mining; Photography; Television and Radio; Transportation.

This article updates the *Macropædia* articles BEVERAGE PRODUCTION; ELECTRONICS; ENERGY CONVERSION; FORESTRY AND WOOD PRODUCTION; FURS, LEATHERS, AND HIDES; INDUSTRIAL GLASS AND CERAMICS; Chemical Process INDUSTRIES; Extraction and Processing INDUSTRIES; Manufacturing INDUSTRIES; Textile INDUSTRIES; INSURANCE; MARKETING AND MERCHANDISING; PRINTING, TYPOGRAPHY, AND PHOTOENGRAVING; TELECOMMUNICATIONS SYSTEMS; TOOLS.

Information Processing and Information Systems

After years of boom times, the U.S. computer industry suffered in 1989, and ailing companies laid off workers or were acquired by healthier foes. Because of intense competition in the market for computer workstations and because the increased strength of the U.S. dollar overseas reduced foreign buying, even the industry's largest firms had dour faces in 1989.

Computer users, though, seemed largely unworried by the industry downturn; one of their greatest concerns in 1989 was the spread of a type of destructive computer software called the virus. While many virus infections had been reported by the year's end, none approximated the destructive power of the virus that struck a nationwide defense and academic computer network in late 1988, affecting more than 6,000 computers and causing millions of dollars in damages.

For the companies of the U.S. computer industry, though, it was as if a financial virus were afoot in 1989. Among the hardest hit was Wang Laboratories Inc., a $3 billion maker of minicomputers that had helped launch the market for automated word processing in the 1970s. Wang reported a $424.3 million loss for fiscal 1989 and said that it did not expect to be profitable again until the third quarter of its 1990 fiscal year. Analysts blamed the company's high overhead; at 38% of revenue, Wang's overhead was 13% above the industry average. Also at fault were the low margins the company was earning on the sale of personal computers compatible with the IBM PC.

In response, the company began a round of layoffs that had, by the year's end, eliminated more than 3,000 jobs. Ultimately even company president Frederick Wang was replaced—by Richard Miller, a former General Electric executive familiar with running companies in crisis.

The financial hard times, however, were not confined to Wang. During the year, Data General Corp. eliminated 2,200 jobs, its largest of five consecutive annual work-force reductions, and Honeywell-Bull eliminated 1,600 jobs, 16% of its work force. Control Data Corp. pared roughly 10% of its total work force, in part by closing its six-year-old supercomputer subsidiary, and Prime Computer Inc. cut 2,500 jobs in the wake of its acquisition by a New York-based venture capital firm.

Even industry giants IBM and Digital Equipment Corp. reported downturns in net earnings in 1989. IBM's net income of $877 million for the year's third fiscal quarter represented a 30% decline from the level of a year earlier, and the company said that it expected net income for the entire year to be down as well. IBM was hurt when customers shifted to leasing computers. In addition, since half of its revenue comes from overseas, IBM also suffered from the increased strength of the dollar. At Digital Equipment net income for the first fiscal quarter declined 33% from the previous year, but analysts hoped that the company might turn in a better performance by the end of the fiscal year as the company's new line of computers began to bring in revenue.

The financial hard times in the industry reduced the stock prices of some computer companies, making them takeover targets. Cullinet Software, a 1,800-employee company that made a data-base program for mainframe computers, became the latest in a string of acquisitions by Computer Associates, a multiproduct software company with just over $1 billion in annual revenue. Also during the year, Prime Computer Inc. was purchased by a venture capital company for about $1.1 billion, a move that saved the company from a hostile takeover by another suitor and took the company private.

By far the biggest computer industry takeover of 1989, however, was the $476.4 million purchase by Hewlett-Packard Co. of Apollo Computer. While Hewlett-Packard's annual revenues of some $9.8 billion dwarfed Apollo's $653 million annual income, both companies had strengths in computer networking and in manufacturing workstations, powerful computers typically used by one worker at a time for applications such as computer-aided design. Workstation demand grew by more than 10% in 1989, and the takeover made Hewlett-Packard the nation's number-one workstation vendor; its estimated 30.5% market share just surpassed the 28% market share of Sun Microsystems, which had helped to launch the workstation industry.

Sun had other reasons to worry in 1989, as both Digital Equipment and Data General Corp. unveiled workstations that beat Sun's in price and performance and helped fuel a price war in an industry where prices had dropped 20% since 1987. Workstation performance is measured in MIPS, millions of instructions that can be processed per second. On that scale Digital's latest entry, the DECstation 3100, was clocked at 14 MIPS and cost $11,900. Data General's 1989 workstation market entry was priced even lower, offering 17 MIPS for $7,450. Sun's existing low-end line of Sparcstations, meanwhile, offered 12.5 MIPS at $12,995.

As if all of this were not bad enough, Sun, which in 1988 earned $1 billion, announced in 1989 that it would experience its first quarterly loss since it went public in 1986. One reason for this, according to Sun, was that it had sought only a 10% operating margin over four fiscal quarters in an attempt to increase its share of the market.

Besides the new workstations, perhaps the two best-remembered new products of 1989 were the portable version of Apple's Macintosh personal computer and the long-overdue arrival of the new version of Lotus Development's 1-2-3 spreadsheet, still the most-used program for financial analysis on IBM-compatible personal computers. While heavy (about 7 kg [16 lb] with battery and hard disk) and expensive ($6,449 with a hard disk), the new Macintosh had a brighter display than most other portable computers and more internal memory (one megabyte). It was hailed by Macintosh users even though it used a track ball instead of a mouse to move the screen's blinking cursor.

Lotus users, meanwhile, were pleased when the latest version of 1-2-3, Release 3.0, entered the marketplace. The new version cost $100 more than had been expected ($595) and could not be run on the early IBM PCs that used the 8088 and 8086 microprocessors. (Lotus released a special, less-powerful version for those computers.) The new 1-2-3 software was faster than its predecessor and allowed users to create spreadsheets of several dimensions.

On the hardware side, perennial foes IBM and Compaq Computer Corp. each vied to be the first to introduce a means by which IBM-compatible computer users could run a fast new microprocessor chip from Intel Corp., the I486. IBM's solution was to offer the chip on an upgrade board that could be plugged into its PS/2 Model 70 personal computer. Compaq, meanwhile, announced a new computer based upon the chip.

Intel itself introduced a new microprocessor in 1989 called the I860. Based on the reduced-instruction-set computer architecture, which simplified data processing for faster computing, the chip contained more than one million transistors.

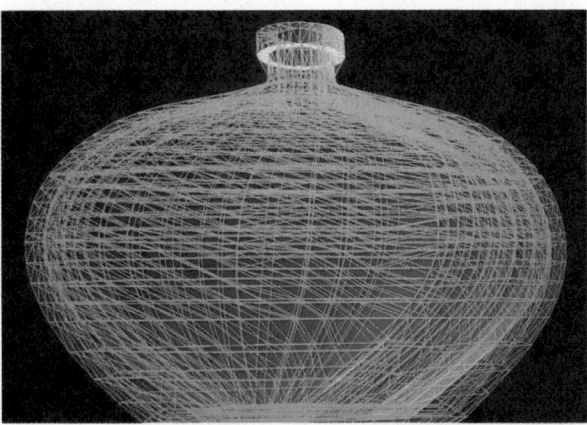

The 3-D image of a perfume bottle (top) generated by a computer can be used to guide a laser that will produce a working model (bottom) out of a polymer in a matter of hours. The technique, by 3-D Systems, Inc., significantly reduces the time spent in product design.

PHOTOGRAPHS, MAX AGUILERA-HELLWEG

Among computer users, though, the major developments of 1989 were the new breeds of computer viruses, software unleashed by malicious programmers. Viruses jump from infected computer programs to uninfected computers— or sometimes enter a computer through its network—and then hide for weeks to avoid detection. During October there was a spate of outbreaks of the newer viruses, which were given such names as Jerusalem Virus and Datacrime and which could wipe out the data on a personal computer's hard disk. Victimized were computers at the U.S. National Aeronautics and Space Administration (NASA), Mobil Oil Corp., and Prudential-Bache Securities. Data losses were minimal at each site, however, and, for the most part, computer users breathed a sigh of relief because, while highly publicized, viruses had so far been less of a threat than expected.

The virus threat was good news for the makers of computer security products, however. Sales of such products topped $588 million in 1988 and were expected to double by 1992, according to one market researcher.

Another piece of bright news also surfaced in 1989; computer memory chip prices, which had soared the year before, fell considerably. With the price of the popular one-megabit chips expected to drop 50% by the year's end, the cost of making computers was expected to decline as well, perhaps spurring users to buy more computers and raise the industry out of its dark times.   (EDWARD S. WARNER)

By the end of 1988 the Institute for New Generation Computer Technology (ICOT), the organization heading up the Fifth Generation Computer System project in Japan, had completed the design for a parallel inference machine (PIM) that interconnected 128 processors. ICOT planned to complete construction of the PIM by the end of 1989. NEC Corp., Fujitsu Ltd., and Mitsubishi Electric Corp. were among the private firms that announced the development of neural network computers, machines patterned after the neural networks in the human brain.

In the realm of interoperability, the Interoperability Technology Association for Information Processing (IN-TAP) in November 1988 succeeded in experimentally interconnecting four functional standard packaged devices, including one for file transfer access management. Japanese computer manufacturers successfully completed similar experiments in 1989. The information services industry in Japan was being transformed in line with changes in the Japanese industrial structure. This transformation was also deeply bound up with the changing roles of computer systems within corporate environments.

During 1988 the value of computers and related equipment produced in Japan totaled 5,054,000,000,000 yen, a 14.7% increase over the previous year.   (YUJI YAMADORI)

This article updates the *Macropædia* article INFORMATION PROCESSING AND INFORMATION SYSTEMS.

Labour-Management Relations

The economic environment more than any other factor had had the strongest influence on industrial relations in recent years. In the market economy countries in 1989, the economic forces at work were particularly manifested in heightened competition, necessitating continued efforts to maximize efficiency, notably through flexibility in labour utilization. Unemployment fell slightly, bringing the level across the Organization for Economic Cooperation and Development (OECD) countries back to the 1981 figure of about 7%. However, the reduction of unemployment and a shortage of labour in some areas, coupled with workers' expectations and anxieties about future rising prices, increased pressure for wage increases; this contributed to renewed inflationary pressures in several countries.

More notable than the developments in the Western world, though, were the signs of change in the Soviet Union and some of the Eastern European countries. The turnaround in the position of the trade union movement Solidarity in Poland signaled the extraordinary rise of non-Communist elements to positions of power in several Eastern bloc countries late in the year. The recognition of a limited right to strike in the Soviet Union and in Hungary was also of great importance.

United Kingdom. In Britain the government piloted a new Employment Bill through Parliament, its major provisions being concerned with easing restrictions on the employment of women and young workers and lessening employers' burdens in regard to dismissals and disciplinary procedures. A rash of strikes (railways, London Transport workers, BBC staff, and others) in the summer led the government to contemplate new steps to discourage such walkouts, notably those unofficial strikes that escaped the provisions of earlier legislation. The government was considering a measure to regulate strikes in essential public services, but a study of similar legislation in other countries led them to turn instead to a more general measure. The government's intentions were revealed at the Conservative Party's annual conference in October, when the employment secretary, Norman Fowler, announced that there

Workers at the Japanese-owned Nissan assembly plant in Smyrna, Tennessee, rejoice after the United Automobile Workers' (UAW) bid to represent them was turned down. Despite lengthy and costly campaigns by the union, the UAW was unable to organize any of the Japanese auto companies based in the U.S.
MARK HUMPHREY—AP/WIDE WORLD

would be a bill in the next parliamentary session obliging unions either to repudiate unofficial action organized by their unpaid officials or to take responsibility by arranging a strike ballot and allowing employers to dismiss individuals selectively from among those on strike. If the union subsequently organized action in support of those dismissed, it would lose its civil immunity from legal action.

In April the government announced the intended abolition of the National Dock Labour Scheme, which had been set up after World War II to end the use of casual labour on the docks. Special payments were envisioned for dockers who might lose their jobs as a result. Though the union concerned, the Transport and General Workers' Union, was strongly opposed to the abolition—and the announcement had been followed by wildcat strikes—it was determined not to run afoul of the law by calling a strike that would effectively be political. Instead, the union sought to turn the issue into a claim that the dock employers should enter into a national agreement on arrangements to replace the scheme. This the employers refused to do, and the union then proceeded with a strike ballot, which produced a three-to-one majority in favour; this was held to be legal by the Law Lords, who reversed an appeals court injunction against the strike. In the event, however, the strike crumbled within three weeks and was called off at the beginning of August. Meanwhile, the legislation had been passed and the scheme ended.

United States. The minimum wage legislation passed by Congress was vetoed by Pres. George Bush in June, and there was insufficient support to override the veto. On October 31, however, a compromise was reached between Democratic leaders and Bush that allowed an increase in the wage from the current $3.35 per hour to $3.80 an hour on April 1, 1990, and to $4.25 per hour on April 1, 1991.

On March 4, 8,500 mechanics and baggage handlers went on strike at Eastern Airlines (owned by Frank Lorenzo's Texas Air). Contrary to what the management appeared to expect, the pilots refused to cross picket lines. The company continued to operate, at a much reduced capacity, though it filed for bankruptcy under Chapter 11 of the bankruptcy code.

The Pittston Coal Group—the largest export-based coal operator in the U.S.—having seceded from the Bituminous Coal Operators' Association, declined to accept both the Operators' contract with the United Mine Workers (UMW) and a union proposal that it should enter into

a parallel agreement. After negotiations stalled, the union called a strike and about 1,700 members stopped work in the Appalachian coalfields on April 5. The issues involved were flexibility, job security, wages, and health and pension benefits. In October, U.S. Secretary of Labor Elizabeth Dole made an unexpected visit to the scene of the conflict and subsequently held a meeting in Washington, D.C., with Pittston chairman Paul Douglas and UMW president Richard Trumka, where it was agreed that a mediator should be appointed. Former secretary of labour William Usery was subsequently named to that post.

Australia. The Australian Industrial Relations Commission handed down an award, effective July 1, providing $A 20- to $A 30-a-week increases in wages. The big question in Australian industrial relations continued to be whether the accord originally established in 1983 and modified subsequently could continue to provide the degree of wage restraint the economy needed. The award of the commission on the national wage case was just about within the tolerable range, but a claim by the pilots of the domestic airlines for a 29.5% increase in pay (though later modified) pushed it beyond the limits. When the claim was refused, more than 1,600 members of flight crews resigned. Prime Minister Bob Hawke took a tough line, and the strike continued late into the year.

Continental Western Europe. *France.* On March 21 the central employers' organization in France signed a framework agreement with two of the union confederations concerning the reorganization of working time. The agreement, which set out guidelines rather than concrete rules, sought to balance the aspirations of workers and the pursuit of efficient working. Two long-running disputes in France attracted considerable attention during the year. A strike of Finance Ministry personnel, in support of a claim for better wages and conditions and more jobs, delayed the collection of various taxes. The Peugeot automobile company suffered its worst strike, lasting seven weeks in September and October. The strike was concerned with pay.

West Germany. In West Germany the emphasis in 1989 was on working hours. In March a 10-day strike in the printing industry centred on a union demand to limit weekend working. The controversy over opening hours of stores was not fully ended by a new law providing limited flexibility that came into force on October 1. The huge metalworkers' union, IG Metall, opened up its campaign for a 35-hour week and the abolition of weekend working.

Italy. Considerable strike activity, notably in the transport sector, took place in Italy during the year. Government tax measures had to be modified under union pressure. A general strike protesting health service charges that had been announced by the government involved about 16 million workers on May 10. The government withdrew its proposed decree. Employers' organizations and union confederations opened up a dialogue on a new industrial relations system.

Communist Countries. As mentioned above, there were significant changes in industrial relations in the Soviet Union and some of the Communist countries of Eastern Europe. Communist orthodoxy had long held that strikes had no place in a Communist society. The state was a workers' state, so why would workers strike against themselves? This did not prevent strikes from occurring, but they were usually put down fairly quickly and rarely made news. Trade unions, for their part, were regarded more as arms of the state than as representatives of working people. In 1989, however, these ideas underwent startling changes. In the Soviet Union, union delegates were elected to the new Congress of People's Deputies. New workers' unions and clubs sprang up in several parts of the country and held a first conference in Moscow in July. There were numbers of walkouts and wildcat strikes concerning pay and protesting such problems as breakdowns, unsafe working conditions, and shortages of supplies. A series of coal miners' strikes broke out, notably in Siberia and the Ukraine in July. More than 100,000 miners walked off the job. The text of a new law on strikes was adopted by the Supreme Soviet on October 9; it listed numbers of essential industries and services where strikes would not be allowed and provided for notice of strikes to be given and for conciliation to occur.

In a remarkable change of direction, the Polish government made it clear in January that it now regarded the banned trade union movement Solidarity as a potential partner. After lengthy discussions the union was relegalized, and after the parliamentary election in June a Solidarity newspaper editor became prime minister. In Hungary, where independent unions had also appeared, the official Central Council of Trade Unions decided to consider moving toward radical new structures. In April Parliament passed the country's first legislation concerning strikes. Employees were granted the right to strike for social and economic (but not political) reasons. Notice would have to be given, and strikes should start only after a seven-day conciliation period. Strikes in essential services were prohibited, and in the public sector they were limited.

International. On May 17 the Commission of the European Communities published the draft of a Charter of Fundamental Social Rights. The proposal dealt with a range of working conditions and social rights and also with freedom of association and collective bargaining, information, consultation, and participation. It was an issue at the heads of government meeting in Madrid in June, with Britain's Margaret Thatcher opposing it vigorously. A compromise was achieved, one that envisioned an eventual "solemn declaration" by governments and authorized the Commission to prepare a detailed program of action.

On February 13 the governing body of the International Labour Organization elected Michel Hansenne, a former Belgian employment minister and most recently minister for public services, as director general. He replaced Francis Blanchard, who retired. (R.O. CLARKE)

See also Economic Affairs: *World Economy;* Industrial Review.

This article updates the *Macropædia* article WORK AND EMPLOYMENT.

Law

Court Decisions. In 1989 the various judicial tribunals of the world decided a number of important cases, the most noteworthy of which, perhaps, were handed down by the U.S. Supreme Court and by various French and English courts. Significant cases mainly involved civil rights, including matters of free speech and rights of privacy respecting abortion and sterilization; banking and business law; and criminal law, particularly involving drugs.

Free Speech. By all odds the most newsworthy judicial decision in the United States during the year was *Texas* v. *Johnson.* After publicly burning an American flag, allegedly as a means of political protest, Gregory L. Johnson was convicted of desecrating the flag in violation of Texas law and sentenced to one year in prison. No one was physically injured at the demonstration in which the flag burning occurred. The U.S. Supreme Court held that the conviction was inconsistent with the First Amendment to the U.S. Constitution, which guarantees free speech. Under the circumstances of the flag burning, which coincided with the Republican national convention, it was clear to a majority of the court that the act constituted "expressive conduct," which, like the written or spoken word, is a form of speech. The court, however, rejected the contention that a limitless variety of conduct can be labeled "speech" simply because the person engaging in the conduct intends to express an idea. Rather, it said, conduct can be protected as "speech" only where it, under the circumstances, is used to convey a particularized message that is likely to be understood by the audience that views it. The court found that these criteria had been met.

The Johnson case generated a storm of criticism in the U.S., and Pres. George Bush proposed a constitutional amendment that would validate laws prohibiting flag burning. In his view, the Johnson case had clearly indicated that laws proscribing flag burning were unconstitutional and could not be rescued through artful drafting. Congress disagreed and enacted a criminal law prohibiting the burning of the American flag. This law was immediately put to the test by various protesters who burned flags. Ultimately, the Supreme Court would have to wrestle with these test cases.

Another freedom of speech case that engendered widespread interest in the U.S. involved the constitutionality of a federal criminal statute prohibiting obscene or indecent interstate telephone communications. The statute was aimed at suppressing the "dial-a-porn" industry, which offers sexually oriented prerecorded telephone messages to callers who pay for the service through charges to their phone bills. Sable Communications of California, Inc., which offered such services, conceded that Congress had the constitutional right to protect children from pornographic telephonic messages but complained that the statute, as implemented by Federal Communications Commission (FCC) regulations, was overbroad. Sable pointed out that the use of access codes, credit cards, and scrambling could dramatically reduce the number of calls from minors, and these technological features should have been used rather than a total ban. Congress had found that these uses of technology would not be completely effective in shielding children, and the FCC concluded that nothing less than a total ban on dial-a-porn messages could prevent children from gaining access to them.

The U.S. Supreme Court in *Sable Communications* v. *FCC* found the FCC's position less than completely persuasive. It held that the federal statute violated the First Amendment to the Constitution as to indecent commu-

nications but not as to obscene communications, which, it reaffirmed, are not constitutionally protected. Sexual expression that is indecent but not obscene is protected by the First Amendment but can be regulated in order to promote a compelling interest, such as the well-being of minors. Such a regulation, however, must be carefully tailored to achieve these compelling ends. Here, the court said, the legislation was not reasonably restricted to the evil with which it was said to deal.

In *Mme Kantor divorcee Colucci et autre* v. *S.A. Cogedi-Presse,* a French court held that it is legally impermissible for anyone, including the press, to print the features of a person on his or her deathbed unless consent is obtained from the family. The court said it made no difference that the person was famous, because one's image is legally protected, even beyond death. In another important French case, *Societe So.Ga.Ra.* v. *Societe So.Di.Car,* the Cour de Cassation, the highest court in France, broadly validated comparative advertising because it contributes to open choice and competition.

Abortion and Sterilization. Webster v. *Reproductive Health Services* gave the U.S. Supreme Court an opportunity to review its stance, announced most prominently in 1973 in *Roe* v. *Wade,* that a woman has a constitutional right to an abortion and that the power of the states to qualify that right is extremely limited. *Webster* involved a Missouri statute that included (1) a preamble stating that the life of each human being begins at conception; (2) some sections prohibiting the use of public funds to perform abortions or to encourage a woman to have an abortion, except where necessary to save the mother's life; and (3) a section prohibiting a physician from performing an abortion if he or she had reason to believe that the unborn child had an age of 20 or more gestational weeks. The lower federal courts held this statute unconstitutional as a violation of the due process clause of the 14th Amendment as construed in *Roe* v. *Wade.*

The Supreme Court reversed these decisions but refused to overturn *Roe* v. *Wade.* It held (1) that it was unnecessary to pass on the validity of the preamble, since it had no operational effect on the matter at hand; (2) that the sections prohibiting the use of public funds to perform or assist abortions were constitutional since they placed no governmental obstacles in the path of a woman who chose to terminate her pregnancy and left her in the same position she would have occupied had the state not elected to operate public hospitals at all; and (3) that "viability testing" is not inconsistent with prior Supreme Court precedents and, therefore, is constitutional. On this point, however, the members of the court forming the majority were sharply divided. Chief Justice William Rehnquist and Justices Byron White and Anthony Kennedy took the view that the trimester test of viability constituting the framework of *Roe* v. *Wade* should be abandoned in favour of viability testing. Justice Sandra Day O'Connor was content to say only that the Missouri viability-testing approach was constitutional and that there would be time enough to examine *Roe* v. *Wade* when the constitutional validity of an abortion statute actually turned on the validity of *Roe.* Justice Antonin Scalia would overturn *Roe.* A strong dissent was written by Justice Harry Blackmun, with whom Justices William Brennan and Thurgood Marshall joined.

In Great Britain the Court of Appeal held in *R.* v. *Tait* that a fetus is not a "person" distinct from its mother. The case involved a burglar who threatened a pregnant woman that he would kill her unborn child if she did not comply with his demands. The court held that this action did not constitute a threat to kill a "person" within the meaning of the Offences Against the Person Act of 1861. In *F.* v. *West Berkshire Health Authority,* the House of Lords, the highest court in Great Britain, held that it would not be improper to sterilize an adult mental patient who, because of her disability, was unable to give her consent to such an operation.

Banking and Business. In *Security Industry Association* v. *Clarke,* the U.S. Court of Appeals, 2nd circuit, perhaps the most highly respected commercial court in the U.S., held that a bank's sale of mortgage pass-through certificates was within the "business of banking" and did not violate the Glass-Steagall Act's prohibitions aimed at separating investment and commercial banking. As a result of this decision, the securities industry announced that it was considering giving up its long-standing effort to keep commercial banks out of the securities business. Along similar lines, India announced that banks possessing strong capital and assets would be permitted to issue commercial paper on money markets.

There had been considerable dispute as to the legal status of so-called letters of intent. These letters do not take the form of legal contracts but are designed to state the intention of the parties involved in negotiations and often are relied upon almost to the same extent as formal agreements. In *Kleinwort Benson Ltd.* v. *Malaysia Mining Corp.,* the English Court of Appeal held that a "letter of comfort" was not binding. The letter in question was written by a parent company to a potential lender; in it the parent stated that its policy was to ensure that its subsidiary repaid its loans. The purpose of the letter was to induce the lender to make a loan to the subsidiary. Nevertheless, the court held the letter could not be enforced as a contract. On almost identical facts, a French court reached an opposite result in *Soc. anon. Generale de Fonderie* v. *Soc. anon. Champex,* holding that a letter of intent, in spite of its unilateral character, may constitute a contractual commitment.

War on Drugs. As part of its effort to suppress illegal drugs, Congress in 1984 enacted the Comprehensive Forfeiture Act (CFA), which authorizes forfeiture of assets derived from specified criminal activities, including drug trafficking. The U.S. Supreme Court held this statute constitutional in *United States* v. *Monsanto.* The case involved an indictment against Peter Monsanto alleging that he had engaged in large-scale heroin distribution. It also alleged that three specific assets—a home, an apartment, and $35,000 in cash—had been accumulated as a result of this illegal narcotics activity. Monsanto wanted to use these assets to pay an attorney and otherwise defend himself against the charges, and he objected that freezing them would deprive him of a fair trial, guaranteed by the Constitution. The Supreme Court disagreed, holding in effect that the Sixth Amendment right to retain counsel of one's choice does not include the right to spend another person's money.

In *United States* v. *Sokolow,* the U.S. Supreme Court sustained the constitutionality of a "drug courier profile" as a justification for stopping and searching an individual without a warrant. Andrew Sokolow was stopped by drug-enforcement agents upon his arrival at Honolulu International Airport, and the agents found over 1,000 g of cocaine in his carry-on luggage. He claimed the agents had no reasonable suspicion to stop him, as required by the Fourth Amendment to the Constitution. They responded that he, and his actions, fit a "profile" of a drug courier that had been developed from empirical evidence. The court held that this provided reasonable suspicion.

The ability of drug-enforcement personnel to acquire

information from banks as to deposits made by suspects is critical to their investigative work. Thus, bank "secrecy laws" are of significant relevance respecting this effort. Luxembourg announced that it would continue to protect the confidential relationship that exists between banker and customer, but England and Brazil stated that they would relax this protection in proper circumstances.

(WILLIAM D. HAWKLAND)

International Law. The organs of international adjudication seemed in 1989 to acquire a status—and even popularity—they had rarely known before. This might have had some connection with the dramatic loosening and realignment of authoritarian regimes in Eurasia and the steady increase in attempts at interstate regional economic union.

Adjudication. The International Court of Justice (ICJ) emerged during the year as an almost workaday court, with four new cases brought, four others on its docket from previous years, and one major judgment delivered. Apart from three cases on maritime boundaries, the subject matter varied widely and illustrated a growing willingness of states to have recourse to the court. Proposals were introduced in the UN General Assembly by the U.S.S.R. and the nonaligned movement for fuller use of the ICJ, and the UN secretary-general announced the intention of the UN to create a "legal aid" trust fund, based on voluntary contributions, to assist states to settle their disputes through the ICJ.

The judgment of the court, delivered on July 20 in *United States* v. *Italy in re Elettronica Sicula SpA (ELSI),* like its older ruling in *Barcelona Traction,* concerned the rights of foreign shareholders in the disposal of a company and the piercing of the corporate veil. An Italian company producing electronic components in Palermo (Sicily), wholly owned by a U.S. corporation, became insolvent, ceased trading, dismissed its work force, and was thereupon requisitioned by the Italian authorities without payment of compensation to the owner. An action by the U.S. on behalf of the U.S. shareholder alleged breach of the U.S.-Italy Commercial Treaty of 1948. The ICJ, however, held in favour of Italy, ruling that because of the insolvency there was no breach of Article III (right of the American owners to control and manage the company), Article V (property rights), or Article VII (right to own and dispose of immovable property), and there was no disguised expropriation.

The new actions related to: (1) compensation for the shooting down by the USS *Vincennes* of an Iran Air civil airliner over the Persian Gulf in July 1988 (*Iran* v. *United States*); (2) rehabilitation of phosphate lands mined in Nauru under Australian administration in breach of the 1947 trusteeship agreement (*Nauru* v. *Australia*); (3) the refusal of Romania to permit access by the UN Economic and Social Council (Ecosoc) to a Romanian citizen, Dumitru Mazilu, who had been appointed special rapporteur of the Ecosoc Subcommission on the Prevention of Discrimination and Protection of Minorities (Ecosoc request for an advisory opinion); and (4) validity of the award in July 1989 by an arbitration tribunal on delimitation of the maritime boundary between Senegal and Guinea-Bissau (*Guinea-Bissau* v. *Senegal*). Pending cases included two more on maritime boundaries (*El Salvador* v. *Honduras* and *Denmark* v. *Norway*) and two arising from armed intervention in Nicaragua (*Nicaragua* v. *Honduras* and *Nicaragua* v. *United States*). Under a treaty signed in August among five Central American states, Nicaragua agreed to withdraw from both these latter cases.

Two new international courts were established. The fifth Islamic summit conference agreed to set up an International Islamic Court of Justice, to be situated in Kuwait,

once the agreement had been ratified by the individual states. The Court of First Instance of the European Communities had already been agreed upon the previous year in order to shoulder some of the burden of the European Court of Justice. The other European court (of Human Rights) faced the reverse as a Council of Europe committee of experts reported on the possibility of merging the court with the European Commission of Human Rights. The court itself delivered a particularly important judgment on extradition (*Soering* v. *United Kingdom*). A German national was arrested in England and threatened with extradition on a murder charge to the U.S. state of Virginia, where the death penalty was still allowable. The death penalty itself was not prohibited by the European Convention on Human Rights (even though neither West Germany nor the U.K. had such a provision) so the possibility of a death sentence in Virginia did not in itself invalidate the extradition. However, the court found that the lengthy appellate procedures in the U.S. did amount to inhuman and degrading treatment contrary to Article 3 of the convention, and extradition in such circumstances would be a breach of that article.

One innovation made during the year was the setting up of a panel under the U.S.-Canada free-trade agreement to resolve a long-standing dispute over a Canadian rule requiring U.S. fishermen to land their catches of Pacific coast salmon and herring in Canada before exporting them to the U.S. A dispute between the U.K. and Norway over their respective shares of the Statfjord oil field, which extends on both sides of their common continental shelf boundary in the North Sea, was referred to an independent expert for arbitration. The dispute between the U.S. and Iraq over the latter's missile attack on the USS *Stark* in the Persian Gulf in 1987 was concluded by Iraq's agreeing to pay $27,350,374 in compensation, which the U.S. would then distribute to the families of the 37 individuals killed in the attack.

Territory. Two border disputes continued to involve armed conflict: the Siachen Glacier in the Himalayas, where Indian and Pakistani troops had been fighting for some years; and the Western Sahara war between the Polisario Front and Morocco. It was thought the latter had ended with the UN cease-fire in 1988, but negotiations for a referendum of the inhabitants had not been pursued very seriously by Morocco, and in October fighting flared up again. Senegal and Mauritania referred to the UN Security Council the dispute over whether the border should continue to run down the middle of the Senegal River or along its right bank. The long-standing dispute between Chad and Libya over the Aozou Strip in northwestern Chad ended in a treaty to place the territory under the administration of an African observer group, withdraw the occupying Libyan troops, and negotiate a settlement within one year, failing which the matter would be referred to the ICJ.

The 1988 arbitration over the Taba beach strip on the Sinai shore of the Gulf of Aqaba, which went in favour of Egypt, had not been accepted wholeheartedly by Israel, and dispute continued over the precise placing of the border marker and the fate of the Israeli-built hotel and holiday camp situated in the part of the beach awarded to Egypt. Agreements were signed in February adopting a firm boundary and agreeing on compensation for the tourist establishments, thus constituting a final settlement of the affair. Minor adjustments to the land borders between France and Luxembourg were agreed to by treaty following construction of a road by a Luxembourg company that owned land on both sides of the border. The boundary between Sweden and Norway was readjusted following a

three-year review of the whole border by the two countries' boundary commissions.

The confederation between Senegal and The Gambia (Senegambia) was "frozen," and negotiations to dismantle it were initiated. On the other hand, the Caribbean Community (Caricom) agreed to establish a regional capital market as a step toward integrating the economies of the member states and creating a common market by 1993. In the eastern Caribbean proposals were published to merge the four Windward Islands of St. Vincent, St. Lucia, Dominica, and Grenada into a single state. Integration of the Andean states (Colombia, Ecuador, Peru, Venezuela, and Bolivia) was reaffirmed as a major goal by the summit of the Andean Pact at Cartagena, Colombia, in May.

In the Middle East the heads of state of Egypt, Iraq, Jordan, and Yemen (San'a'; North Yemen) agreed in February to form an Arab Cooperation Council (a permanent summit at two levels—the four heads of state and the four prime ministers) on the model of the already existing Gulf Cooperation Council. Shortly thereafter the heads of state of Algeria, Libya, Mauritania, Morocco, and Tunisia formed a more elaborate organization, the Arab Maghreb Union, with a supreme council (heads of state), a council of foreign ministers, a committee on integration, a consultative chamber, and a court, but no permanent secretariat.

The European Communities (EC) continued to attract other nations, and in August Austria applied to join. To discourage further applications, the EC encouraged the European Free Trade Association (EFTA) to develop as a valid partner, and negotiations began at a meeting on December 19 to draft an EC-EFTA treaty on a European Economic Space aimed at far-reaching integration of the two groups of states by 1993. There was also much discussion of how the Eastern European states might mesh with the Western European system. The first steps were taken by Hungary, which applied to join the Council of Europe, and by the Council of Europe, which granted special guest status to Hungary, Poland, Yugoslavia, and the Soviet Union.

Territorial sea limits were extended to 12 mi by Grenada (which at the same time defined its archipelagic waters, innocent passage, contiguous zone, continental shelf, and exclusive economic zone [EEZ]), Tanzania (with a 200-mi EEZ), the Falkland Islands, South Georgia, the South Sandwich Islands, St. Helena, and Turks and Caicos Islands. Interstate territorial sea boundaries were agreed to between France and the U.K. (Pas de Calais area), France and Italy (entry into force of the 1986 agreement on the Bouches de Bonifacio), and France and Dominica (between Dominica and the French islands of Guadeloupe and Martinique on either side of it). Fishery and continental shelf boundaries were agreed to between France and Canada (St. Pierre and Miquelon and Newfoundland), Sweden and Poland (the southern tip of the "white zone" off Gotland, which until 1988 had been in dispute between Sweden and the U.S.S.R.), and Denmark and East Germany (signed September 1988 and ratified during 1989).

Environment. Particularly noticeable during the year was increased treaty activity related to the protection of the environment. The Montreal Protocol on the safeguarding of the ozone layer entered into force on January 1. Later the same month the UN General Assembly passed a resolution on protection of the global climate. The states participating in the Vienna Convention and Montreal Protocol followed this in May with the Helsinki Declaration on the Protection of the Ozone Layer. The UN global convention on control of transborder movement of hazardous waste was adopted in March. A Hague Declaration on the Environment was adopted in March by 24 states, and in June the EC Council adopted a resolution on the greenhouse effect. A Latin-American and Caribbean meeting in March adopted a Declaration of Brasília on the Environment, which, however—like the Amazon Declaration by the heads of state of the eight Amazon countries two months later—emphasized the sovereign right of each country to manage its own affairs. The Organization for Economic Cooperation and Development adopted in February an environmental checklist for development assistance and, in July, a recommendation on the "polluter pays" principle to apply to accidental pollution.   (NEVILLE MARCH HUNNINGS)

See also Crime, Law Enforcement, and Penology; World Affairs: *United Nations.*

This article updates the *Macropædia* articles CONSTITUTIONAL LAW; INTERNATIONAL LAW.

Libraries

Book starvation continued to be a major problem in Africa in 1989. Most countries lacked adequate hard currency to buy books, journals, and reports from the main producers, most of whom were located in hard-currency countries. The situation was not helped by well-meaning but misguided attempts by charities to supply out-of-date or remaindered books to less developed countries. All too often these works were unsuitable in terms of the culture of the country where they were sent, used different spelling (*e.g.,* English versus American), or used a different system of measure (U.S. or imperial versus metric), raising the suspicion that the motive was partly to give tax relief to firms in the donor country. However, some supply agencies, such as the Ranfurly Trust, had begun to make a special effort to supply what was needed in the receiving country rather than what was not wanted in the country that did the supplying.

In Asian countries the main problem was piracy, with publishers from the developed countries being defrauded of millions of dollars through the illegal reprinting of books at reduced prices (and often in reduced condition). However, the fault lay partly with the publishers, who often asked unrealistic royalties for translation. Another growing practice that did not help libraries was the demand from some publishers in industrialized countries that their books be purchased only from their overseas branches or agents. This inevitably added markup that libraries and documentation centres in less developed countries could ill afford. As a result, educational institutions were looking for books from publishers who did not impose such conditions.

The financial problems currently besetting libraries arose from a number of conditions. First, libraries are essentially low-profile institutions; it is seldom that any but the greatest libraries make the news. Second, in almost all cases a library is a service to a service—a university library serves the university, a public library seeks to serve the community of which it is part, a documentation centre serves the specialists of its institution—and has little control over the policies of the parent body. Third, until very recently library education, especially in less developed countries, concentrated on paraprofessional training; like the libraries themselves, it did not respond speedily to the changes occurring in society. There were a few exceptions—for example, Nigeria, where professionals had played a leading role—but in general the statement held true for both industrialized and less developed nations.

As a result, in the current stringent financial climate, libraries and their staffs were in danger of becoming

marginal. Furthermore, preoccupation with technical library processes rather than service to readers and with unrealistic notions of worldwide information systems tended to alienate libraries from users. The World Bank pointed out the importance of literacy for the development process, but though the number of literates in the world was increasing, so was the proportion of illiterates in the world population. Librarians had not taken a broad enough view of their task, which should include playing a leading role in the eradication of illiteracy and in the encouragement of reading.

Libraries did make the headlines indirectly during the controversy over Salman Rushdie's novel *The Satanic Verses*. (*See* PUBLISHING: *Sidebar.*) While the book was admittedly offensive to Muslims, the general rule in Western democracies—and, on a more restricted scale, in Eastern Europe—has been that libraries are free to buy books and lend them to their patrons, provided their appearance is permitted by law. In some cases, books are lent under restricted conditions, but libraries are not forbidden to purchase them. Threats of violent action against libraries and bookshops that carried *Satanic Verses* added a new level of censorship, which librarians, on the whole, resisted.

(P. HAVARD-WILLIAMS)

In the U.S. several library systems implemented dial-in access to their electronic catalogs, allowing remote searches of the library's holdings from homes and offices. A user with a personal computer and modem could connect online to the catalogs of the Cuyahoga county (Ohio), Cleveland (Ohio), Santa Monica (Calif.), and Oklahoma county public libraries. The Ohio and Oklahoma systems reported that remote calls ran in the thousands each month. Lehigh

BALTHAZAR KORAB

The spacious design of the Michigan Library combines copious natural lighting and expansive holdings areas. The vast library is part of a newly built complex in Lansing, Michigan, that also includes a Historical Center.

University in Bethlehem, Pa., made its library catalog available to any personal computer user through Bell Atlantic's Gateway Service. Some library experts cautioned that mass on-line searching would create demands more suited to utilities than to the traditional resources of library staff.

Circulation at large public libraries continued to rise—some 2.5% in 1988, according to the University of Illinois' 1989 report. Voters approved several major bond issues to finance library expansion and renovation, including (figures rounded) $53 million in Los Angeles, $47 million in San Antonio, Texas, $27 million in Richland county, S.C., and $10 million in Tallahassee, Fla. A new central library for Eugene, Ore., was turned down, but the state allotted $17 million toward a $27 million library expansion at the University of Oregon in Eugene. Among new buildings were the spectacular 29,000-sq m (312,000-sq ft) Michigan Library and Historical Center in Lansing and the innovative Juneau, Alaska, downtown library atop an existing four-story parking garage. Hurricane Hugo devastated eight Charleston county, S.C., library buildings, and San Francisco's central library was closed in October as a result of earthquake damage. The National Endowment for the Humanities granted $15 million for preservation of collections.

Numerous tie-in events in children's services marked the observance of the Year of the Young Reader. The Dallas (Texas) Public Library opened a state-of-the-art Children's Center. September was proclaimed National Library Card Sign-Up Month by U.S. Pres. George Bush. Timothy S. Healy, a Jesuit priest and university administrator, succeeded Vartan Gregorian as president and chief executive officer of the New York Public Library, and Linda F. Crismond, formerly director of the Los Angeles County Public Library, became the first woman named executive director of the American Library Association (ALA). In the ALA American Association of School Librarians/Britannica Companies competition for best school media centre programs, the honourees were Norman (Okla.) public school district, Middletown (N.Y.) enlarged city school district, and Hickman High School, Columbia, Mo.

(ARTHUR PLOTNIK)

This article updates the *Macropædia* article LIBRARIES AND LIBRARY SCIENCE.

Life Sciences

ZOOLOGY

During 1989 scientific publications and conferences added to the burgeoning mass of communication in zoology. Among notable events in this regard was the first World Congress of Herpetology, held at the University of Kent, Canterbury, England. This first international-scale gathering of specialists in the study of reptiles and amphibians, which included scientists from more than 60 countries, allowed syntheses of previous work and saw the emergence of new findings in several subfields of zoology.

Conservation of animals and natural habitats remained a dominant theme during the year, reflecting worldwide concern about the elimination of species. Kristin H. Berry of the U.S. Department of the Interior's Bureau of Land Management reported that the desert tortoise (*Xerobates agassizii*) had suffered severe population declines throughout the western Mojave and Colorado deserts of California and attributed human influences as the primary cause in most cases. Among documented effects on desert tortoise numbers were poaching, vandalism, off-road vehicle use, and the loss, deterioration, and fragmentation of habitats.

Two new threats to the desert tortoise were recently identified. One was a 15-fold increase in numbers of the common raven (*Corvus corax*) in the Mojave Desert since the late 1960s. Ravens eat juvenile tortoises ranging from hatchlings to those about eight years of age. Predation was found to be so excessive among some populations that virtually no juvenile tortoises remained. The increase in ravens was blamed on local growth of human populations and consequent increases in year-round sources of food and water (road kills, garbage dumps, sewage ponds, and agricultural fields) for the birds and in perch sites (transmission towers, poles, and other structures). In many areas wild adult tortoises were also dying from an upper respiratory disease. The illness appeared to have been introduced to wild tortoises through unauthorized release of sick captives. Contagious and eliciting a high mortality rate, the disease was spreading through populations in California, Nevada, Utah, and Arizona.

In Argentina the tortoise *Chelonoidis chilensis* was also undergoing severe declines due to human activities. T. Waller, P.A. Micucci, and E. Richard of Fundación Vida Silvestre Argentina reported that although limited reserve areas existed to protect the tortoise and other native species, the presence of free-ranging cattle was detrimental to the tortoise. The investigators also reported major losses due to the capture of wild tortoises for commercial purposes. Although the practice was illegal, the specimens reached the international market under the guise of having come from breeding farms.

Wild-caught animals of species other than tortoises were being sold as captive-reared ones by poachers. To combat this common loophole in the illegal sale of African chimpanzees, the U.S. Fish and Wildlife Service made it illegal to import any chimpanzee from Africa regardless of its origin.

In India R.J. Rao of the National Chambal Sanctuary reported that a nationwide crocodilian conservation project begun in 1975 succeeded in increasing the numbers of gavials (*Gavialis gangeticus*), long-snouted relatives of alligators and crocodiles, by establishing protected habitats. The number of nesting gavials in the Chambal River region rose from 12 in 1978 to 50 in 1988. As a beneficial side effect, the environmental protection allowed recovery of several species of turtles and other animals that had been on the decline.

Research involving fish provided insight into mechanisms governing mating systems. Robert R. Warner of the University of California at Santa Barbara conducted experiments on a Caribbean coral reef fish, the bluehead wrasse (*Thalassoma bifasciatum*), demonstrating that the choice of mating sites was a culturally transmitted tradition rather than an individual assessment of site quality. The exact locations of spawning sites were determined in several coral reefs, and over a 12-year observation period the same sites were seen to be used by subsequent generations of fish. All bluehead wrasse were then removed from some reefs and replaced by ones from distant populations. The imported fish, which were naive to the sites previously used, chose new spawning sites randomly and continued to select these same sites in subsequent breeding bouts. Young females in a population apparently learn spawning site locations from experienced females. The study concluded that in locations where site quality does not vary appreciably, traditional behaviour is more efficient than careful assessment in selection.

During the year researchers added to evidence about the ways in which animals adjust to freezing temperatures. James A. Raymond of the Alaska Department of Fish and

A caterpillar of the moth species *Nemoria arizonaria* (right) looks like an oak tree's catkins upon which it feeds. Scientists found that the caterpillar resembled the catkins during their appearance in the spring, but when the catkins were gone, it resembled the oak's twigs.
ERICK GREENE, DEPARTMENT OF AVIAN SCIENCES, UNIVERSITY OF CALIFORNIA, DAVIS

Game and colleagues carried out studies to understand the workings of antifreeze agents produced in the blood of fish that live in polar waters between 0° and −2.5° C (32° and 27.5° F). They discovered that very different compounds from each of six species, representing three families, of Antarctic and North Atlantic fish affect the growth of ice in the same manner. The finding indicated that despite their differences, each antifreeze binds to similar faces on ice crystals. The antifreezes resist ice crystal growth and thus prevent the blood from freezing in subfreezing waters. Kenneth B. Storey of Carleton University, Ottawa, and colleagues found that baby painted turtles (*Chrysemys picta*) that overwinter in the nest and endure soil temperatures as low as −8° C (17.6° F) can survive the freezing of as much as 53% of their bodily fluids. Hatchling turtles exposed to subfreezing temperatures produced significantly higher levels of glucose, glycerol, and amino acids in the blood than did those kept at temperatures above freezing. The compounds presumably function in some manner as cold-protection products, but the mechanisms remained to be discovered.

The coldest body temperature known to be endured by a mammal was reported by Brian M. Barnes of the University of Alaska at Fairbanks for Arctic ground squirrels during hibernation. Squirrels were observed to withstand deep body temperatures as low as −2.9° C (26.8° F) and to remain below 0° C for several weeks without harm. Measured concentrations of substances in the blood of squirrels below 0° C were normal, and no antifreeze compounds could be detected. It was concluded that Arctic

ground squirrels somehow are able to maintain prolonged supercooling, a below-freezing condition in which water remains free of ice crystals. Supercooling in subfreezing hibernation may offer a metabolic savings, thus allowing the squirrel to conserve energy stores better during the long Arctic winters.

Zoological research in the vicinity of hydrothermal vents on the Atlantic Ocean seafloor at a depth of 3,600 m (11,800 ft) revealed that a shrimp formerly believed to be eyeless indeed has visual pigment. Cindy Lee Van Dover of Woods Hole (Mass.) Oceanographic Institution, Denis G. Pelli and Steven C. Chamberlain of Syracuse (N.Y.) University, and colleagues discovered that the species, which lacks the typical stalked eyes of other shrimp, has large organs on the back of its shell that appear to be photoreceptors. Rhodopsin, the pigment in the organs, would be sensitive to thermal radiation emanating from the hot water of the vents. One speculation was that the sensory structure evolved to allow the shrimp safe approach to the lethal 350° C (660° F) hot water plumes in order to feed on bacteria that live near the vent margins.

Long-term studies of freshwater turtles gave evidence of the responsiveness of natural populations to annual extremes in environmental variability. On the basis of individually marked turtles studied for two to four decades, Justin D. Congdon of the University of Georgia's Savannah River Ecology Laboratory reported that such critical features of life history as the fraction of nesting females and of surviving nestlings can vary dramatically from one year to another. In some years the number of adult females in populations of painted turtles (*Chrysemys picta*) that produce second clutches of eggs is only one-third that of other years. Likewise, nestling mortality ranges from almost 100% in some years to as low as 25% in others. Observations of turtles of known age, some more than 50 years old, documented not only the reproductive variability within individuals from year to year but also the extreme longevity of turtles in nature. One conclusion from the research was that short-term research projects do not adequately document the extent of environmental variability encountered by long-lived individuals during their individual history. (J. WHITFIELD GIBBONS)

Entomology. Studies of the apple maggot fly (*Rhagoletis pomonella*), a pest species of eastern North America, provided evidence that new species may be able to develop sympatrically—that is, within the same geographic region. Evolutionary biologists usually consider geographic separation, or allopatry, to be a requirement for speciation, since without isolation to prevent genetic mutations from mixing through the population, it is difficult for a new species to diverge genetically. Two teams of investigators discovered sympatric populations of *R. pomonella* that differ genetically, depending on whether they are found on hawthorn trees, their natural host, or on apple trees. Michigan fly populations sampled from the two tree species by Jeffrey L. Feder and Guy L. Bush of Michigan State University and Charles A. Chilcote of the University of Michigan had different genetic compositions. Bruce A. McPheron, D. Courtney Smith, and Stewart H. Berlocher of the University of Illinois, who reared populations of flies taken from apple and hawthorn trees in Illinois, likewise found genetic differences between the two. Working at the University of Utah, Smith determined that flies living on different tree species, which included apple, hawthorn, and dogwood, differ in their seasonal emergence patterns because of the differing fruiting patterns of their host plants. The seasonal patterns of the flies were found to be heritable, strongly suggesting that time rather than geography isolates the fly

populations and that such isolation allows sufficient genetic differentiation for sympatric speciation.

Observations and experiments involving the geometrid moth *Nemoria arizonaria* revealed that available food controls the morphology of the caterpillar. Those caterpillars that hatch in the spring feed on and assume the appearance of catkins, the golden, fuzzy male flowers of oaks. Those emerging in summer, when catkins are gone, eat oak leaves and look like twigs. Thus, during each season, individuals blend into the local environment and are camouflaged from predators. Erick Greene of Princeton University determined that in a laboratory environment diet alone determined the appearance of the caterpillars. Caterpillars fed a diet of catkins strongly resembled the flowers; those fed a diet of oak leaves resembled oak twigs. Furthermore, Greene suggested that plant chemicals known as tannins, found in the leaves but not the catkins, may be the determining factor, since caterpillars fed an artificial diet of tannins developed a twiglike appearance. Such dietary cues may be an important factor in the evolution of host specificity and may be more widespread as a cause of developmental differences within animal species than presently realized.

Although it is well known that honeybees communicate the location of food to the hive through a dance involving wing buzzing and abdominal waggling, until the past year no convincing evidence had been presented to show that bees can hear the accompanying sounds of the dance. By simulating the sounds generated by a dancing honeybee, William F. Towne of Princeton University and Wolfgang H. Kirchner of the Zoological Institute of the University of Würzburg, West Germany, demonstrated that bees actually perceive airborne sounds. The researchers repeatedly gave feeding honeybees a mild electric shock shortly after exposing them to the simulated sound of a dancing bee's wing vibrations (265 hertz, or cycles per second) or a dancer's abdominal waggling (14 hertz). They reasoned that if the bees could detect the sound being supplied, they should become conditioned to withdrawing from the food source when exposed to the sound alone. The research indicated that bees indeed do hear sound, both the low- and high-pitched frequencies, by sensing air-particle movement.

Other research involving bees could be helpful in battling a possible major threat to beekeepers. The parasitic varroa mite (*Varroa jacobsoni*), which feeds on both adult bees and developing drone larvae, can extensively damage a beehive, actually destroying the entire hive within a few years. Female mites have the ability to home in on open brood cells containing bee larvae, where they deposit their eggs. During development the mite larvae use the bee larvae as a food source. Yves Le Conte of the Laboratory of Invertebrate Comparative Neurobiology, Bures-sur-Yvette, France, and co-workers found that the female mite is guided to occupied brood cells by a chemical compound made by the bee larvae within, and they identified the substance as an ester, methyl palmitate. Commercially synthesized methyl palmitate used as a trap lure could offer an effective alternative to conventional pesticides, which had had only moderate success in controlling the destructive mite. (ANNE R. GIBBONS)

This article updates the *Macropædia* article INSECTS.

Ornithology. Growth continued in the comparatively new subdivision of ornithology concerned with birds in large towns and cities. The urban habitat had been expanding so extensively for so long that enough time passed for selective pressures to produce changed behaviour patterns in urban bird populations. Magpies in towns, for example, were known to build nests shaped differently from those

of their country congeners. The continued presence of cities also allowed urban colonization by species formerly found only in more natural habitats. Birds of prey were perhaps among the more surprising inner-city colonists. Kestrels were longtime residents in London and other large European urban agglomerations. Sparrow hawks appeared to be better established than formerly in brick-and-mortar surrounds in Bristol, England, and Århus, Den.; the same was observed for hobby falcons in West Berlin. In Canada the merlin, a bird that frequently nests on the ground on the open prairie, was seen occupying old nests of crows and other species in town parks in Regina and Moose Jaw, Sask., and Calgary and Edmonton, Alta. In Saskatoon, Sask., the city population of nesting merlins increased from a single pair in 1971 to 27 pairs in 1987.

The effects of aging on the reproductive behaviour of great and blue tits were studied. The onset of old age occurs in the larger species, the great tit, between four and five years of age. Old birds that lay later in the year (a little past optimal time) have less success at fledging young, and those offspring that do leave the nest die younger, a fact determined by the banding (ringing) of many nestlings. With the blue tit, the smaller species, only when the female reaches six does she have difficulty in laying early in the season. Otherwise blue tits "age" one year younger than great tits (as might be expected from their smaller size), having smaller broods from the age of three or four. Seven-year-old female blue tits raise fewer than half their clutch of eggs to fledging.

David and Barbara Snow, in an unusual, temperate-zone study of *Birds and Berries* (the title of their book), found undetected interactions between birds and plants and placed them in a wider ecological context. One such interaction is the defense of a food source; for example, the protection of individual holly trees and their berries by mistle thrushes (if necessary to the point of exhaustion) from other thrush species. The book makes important distinctions among fruit eaters, pulp eaters, and seedeaters. Some species' behaviour may straddle more than one category. The wood pigeon, for instance, may destroy some seeds in its crop but void others intact, thus involving itself in seed dispersal.

Long suspected of finding its carrion food by smell, the king vulture in Venezuela was presumed by Stewart B. Reid to fly too high for olfactory detection to be the case. Instead, its high flying probably allows it to observe lower flying turkey vultures (known definitely to nose out their food) and then to follow them down to their discoveries. The hoatzin, a neotropical leaf-eating bird, has earned the nickname stinkbird because it smells like fresh cow manure. Alejandro Grajal of the University of Florida and co-workers made the unexpected discovery that the bird's odour results from an active fermentation process taking place in its crop and esophagus, much like the process that occurs in the rumen of cattle. Symbiotic bacteria in the foregut break down fibrous plant material and release compounds that are important energy sources for the bird. Previously, foregut fermentation had been thought confined to ruminants, monkeys, marsupials, and other mammals.

Work in Norway by Svein Hofthorn and Randi Reinertzen showed how the willow tit, the smallest bird to winter north of the Arctic Circle, uses a spectrum of adaptations to help it through the cold and dark winter months. Of particular interest is nocturnal hypothermia, lowering the body temperature for the night by 10° C (18° F). Another energy-saving strategy is insulating the legs and beak, through which heat can easily be lost. The tit crouches to cover its legs with its belly feathers and tucks its beak into its scapular feathers. The latter posture also allows the bird to breathe warm rather than frosty air. By day in extreme cold the bird may hop on one leg to avoid losing heat through the other, which is tucked up inside the feathers of its underparts. One bird was observed to run on its wings across the snow rather than expose its legs. With only six hours of winter half-light in which to search for food, the bird takes the autumn precaution of hiding over 50,000 spruce and hemp nettle seeds, as well as hundreds of spiders and aphids. It uses tree cavities and specially excavated snow tunnels to help conserve heat. In blizzards or cold spells reaching as low as −40° C (−40° F), the tiny 10-g (0.35-oz) bird will stay self-buried for two whole days, sitting perfectly still to conserve the maximum amount of energy possible.   (JEFFERY BOSWALL)

This article updates the *Macropædia* article BIRDS.

MARINE BIOLOGY

In the oceans the fundamental biological process is photosynthetic fixation of carbon (primary production), the magnitude of which was still disputed by a factor of 10. This uncertainty continued to confound speculation as to whether ocean phytoplankton (photosynthetic members of plankton) could serve as a significant sink for the carbon dioxide that was building in the Earth's atmosphere and threatening to raise global surface temperatures via the greenhouse effect. An international Joint Global Ocean Flux Study (JGOFS) was initiated to study the problem; the unique collaborative program involved the meeting of five research vessels from the U.S., the U.K., West Germany, Canada, and The Netherlands in the North Atlantic study area, with a U.S. National Aeronautics and Space Administration (NASA) P3 research aircraft overhead. Initial results showed that surface water uptake of carbon dioxide is determined primarily by biological activity, indicating that feedback processes involving marine productivity need to be included in global climate models.

High-performance liquid chromatography analysis for plant and animal carotenoid pigments in copepods and cladocerans showed that carnivory represents an important mode of feeding for these crustaceans, additional to the herbivory usually attributed to small zooplankton (planktonic animal life). Remote sensing studies were advanced that made use of satellite images from the NOAA 6 Advanced Very High Resolution Radiometer and the Nimbus 7 Coastal Zone Color Scanner. Satellite-monitored changes in sea-surface temperatures and chlorophyll concentrations were correlated with the appearance and disappearance of plankton-feeding and predatory fish around Gulf of California seamounts.

Chilean researchers reported serious coastal disturbance by human harvesters collecting gastropod mollusks and the bull kelp *Durvillaea* even though islands and other inaccessible coastal refuges existed to facilitate repopulation of the harvested zones. Synchronous mass migration of an aggregation of juvenile queen conch (*Strombus gigas*) was reported for the first time. The migration was sustained for some months in the direction of ebb tidal currents off The Bahamas. Such migrations were presumed to occur mainly when conch densities are high, an uncommon occurrence in the heavily fished Caribbean region. Destruction of kelp beds off Nova Scotia by large populations of the sea urchin *Strongylocentrotus* was reinvestigated. Whereas the increased sea urchin population previously had been attributed to their reduced predation by overfished lobsters, new studies related urchin population increases to raised average sea temperatures during the period of urchin larval growth four to six years earlier. New Zealand studies ques-

tioned the paradigm that larval stages of coral reef fish are generally dispersed widely from their natal reefs by water currents. The behaviour of many such species of fish larvae was shown to be influenced by the proximity of coral reefs; the larvae did not behave simply as passive particles.

Adding to the few recorded on-site behavioral observations of large pelagic zooplankton, scuba divers in a British Columbia fjord observed predatory behaviour of the medusa (jellyfish) *Phacellophora camtschatica* upon another medusan species, *Aurelia aurita,* and found it to be size selective. In similar Yugoslav studies in the Adriatic, the medusa *Pelagia noctiluca* was observed to form subsurface aggregations and to exhibit characteristic foraging behaviour. Observations from a single-person untethered submersible at depths of as much as 1,000 m (3,300 ft) in the Monterey Canyon provided the first images of midwater bioluminescence made on-site. Most bioluminescence occurred after mechanical stimulation and was not spontaneous, a limitation that presumably reduces the risk of an animal's revealing its presence to predators.

(ERNEST NAYLOR)

This article updates the *Macropædia* articles CRUSTACEANS; FISHES; MOLLUSKS; etc.

BOTANY

Two ancient events of great importance in the evolution of plants were the migration of plants from water to land, which probably occurred between the Late Ordovician and Early Silurian epochs, more than 400 million years ago, and the unparalleled radiation of the angiosperms (flowering plants), which has taken place since the middle of the Cretaceous period, or within the last 100 million years. The most likely ancestors of the embryo-producing land plants were green algae, and it is possible that over the eons several attempts at life on land were made by members of this group. Because algae generally lack highly differentiated cells that contain the chemical lignin in their walls, it has been difficult to establish a clear lineage between early land plants and their algal ancestors. Organisms that lack lignin, a durable biological polymer (biopolymer) that serves as an important structural element in vascular plants, are not easily fossilized and thus are not always found as clear indicators of geologic time. In 1989 it was reported that ligninlike compounds and sporopollenin, another durable polymer found in the outer layer of pollen grains, exist in *Coleochaete,* a green alga thought to be on the evolutionary lineage that led to land plants, and that these biopolymers are similar to those found in *Anthoceros,* a genus of primitive land plants called horned liverworts. Thus it was suggested that *Coleochaete* or organisms similar to it might well be the early ancestors of land plants.

Although plants lack an immune system, it has long been obvious that defense mechanisms must exist to protect them from disease organisms (pathogens), particularly bacteria and fungi. Reports of physiological responses to wounding that are mediated by ethylene, a major plant hormone, appeared in the literature during the past several years, and the accumulated findings suggested that such enzymes as chitinase and glucanase, which attack and break down the biopolymers chitin and beta-glucan, respectively, accumulate in plant tissues that are wounded artificially or by pathogens. These enzymes and perhaps others were referred to generically as defense proteins, even though their exact function was not known. The appearance of chitinase and glucanase is of special interest since plants do not produce the polymers that these enzymes attack. Such compounds, however, are present in the external cell walls of fungi and bacteria.

Using specially labeled antibodies that were raised against these enzymes, researchers were able to identify the parts of the plant cell in which the enzymes were concentrated. Their findings resulted in a proposed model of a plant defense mechanism whereby a glucanase enzyme outside the cell releases signaling molecules (oligosaccharides) from the cell walls of the plants under attack. The signaling molecules move into the cell and either directly or indirectly turn on the synthesis of chitinase and glucanase, which are then shipped out of the cell's interior. Once in the cell wall, these enzymes attack and disrupt the cell walls of the invading pathogen. Thus the model explains one way that plants can fight off pathogen attack at the cellular level. Because the response is rather slow, it was suggested that the mechanism represents a last line of defense.

The revolution in molecular genetics technology recently led to the initiation of a heavily funded, much publicized, broad-based attack on human genetic defects by mapping and sequencing the entire human genome, or genetic endowment. A more modest project involving plants also was started, by the U.S. National Science Foundation. The attack on the plant genome would focus on *Arabidopsis thaliana,* a small, inconspicuous member of the mustard family. The reasons for choosing this particular plant were many and included the fact that it has a small genome with little repetitive DNA. Foreign DNA can be introduced to its genome by means of a well-developed technique, and the plant is so tiny that large numbers can be grown in such limited spaces as petri dishes. The organism was already being used for a variety of physiological studies, and genetic maps were available. The focused research project was to include storage centres for seeds, clones, and DNA and research centres devoted to physical mapping of the genome and to sequencing DNA fragments and ultimately the whole genome. The project should help bring botanical genetics more in line with the rest of the genetics community.

(PHILIP D. REID)

MOLECULAR BIOLOGY

Controlling Blood Pressure. Consider the circulatory system of the human body. The heart pumps blood into the large arteries, which branch repeatedly. At each branching the vessels grow smaller and more numerous until they become the microscopic arterioles, which branch further into a network of still smaller capillaries. It is in the capillary networks that the useful work is done—the exchange of oxygen for carbon dioxide and of nutrients for metabolic wastes. Then the blood is brought back into progressively larger vessels as capillaries fuse into venules, veins, and so back to the heart.

The viscous blood resists flow, particularly through the small vessels, and this resistance leads to a corresponding drop in pressure. Blood pressure is highest in the large arteries and lowest in the large veins. This pressure differential is what keeps the blood flowing, and it is the job of the heart to maintain it. The effort demanded of that living pump depends on the blood volume moved and the pressure against which it is working. The higher the arterial blood pressure is, the more the heart must labour and the greater the likelihood is that a vessel will balloon or burst catastrophically. Too low an arterial pressure, which means too low a pressure differential between arteries and veins, is also a recipe for disaster. Blood flow becomes insufficient for the tissues' needs, including those of the heart. It is clear that for health, blood pressure must be maintained within a narrow range.

If one assumes a constant rate of pumping by the heart, there are two ways that the body can manipulate blood

pressure. It must change either the volume of the blood itself or the volume of the system of vessels that contain it. The body exploits both options. Blood volume is adjusted by the kidneys, while the volume of the circulatory system is manipulated by muscle cells in the vessel walls, which can by contraction or relaxation either decrease or increase the bore of those vessels.

The kidneys excrete water and salts in a proportion designed to maintain a constant balance between water and solutes (dissolved substances) in the blood. If the concentration of solutes rises, water will pass from the body cells into the blood, and if the concentration falls, water will move in the opposite direction. Since the vital functions of cells, particularly nerve cells, are very sensitive to changes in solute concentrations, it is clear why the water-solute balance of the blood must be held constant. When the kidneys remove salts, in particular sodium (natrium) salts, from the blood, the net effect is a decrease in blood volume. A marvelously effective method of control would depend on the heart itself to signal the kidneys that blood volume needed lowering. In fact, the atria (upper chambers) of the heart do secrete a small peptide hormone that increases excretion of sodium salts by the kidneys. This recently discovered substance, called atrial natriuretic factor, is secreted into the blood in response to distension of the atria by increased blood pressure, and it tells the kidneys to lower blood volume and therefore blood pressure.

Regulating blood pressure by modifying the kidneys' salt excretion can be very effective, but it also is slow. Rapid adjustment in pressure often is needed to compensate for sudden changes, for example, in body position or in physical activity. Such adjustment can be achieved almost instantly by relaxing or contracting muscle cells in the vessel walls and thereby changing their internal diameter. One signal for these changes comes from the endothelial cells that line the interior of the blood vessels. These cells produce a substance that strongly relaxes the vessel walls. The discovery and identification of this substance, called endothelial-derived relaxing factor (EDRF), provided explanations for some long-standing puzzles and could open the door to rational and effective therapy for a very common, yet serious, disease—hypertension, or high blood pressure.

Early laboratory studies with dissected blood vessels showed that the muscle in the blood vessel wall contracted in response to contact with acetylcholine, a substance in the body that serves to transmit signals between nerves or from nerve to muscle. This observation, however, did not support other studies showing that intravenous injection of acetylcholine into the body caused blood pressure to fall rather than rise. Measurements of the effects of acetylcholine applied to arterial muscle had been made by means of strips of vessel wall attached to the lever of a recording device; contraction of the strip moved the lever and produced a recording. To help in cutting the strips, the blood vessel was first distended by insertion of a rod into its bore, a procedure that caused unrecognized damage to the endothelial lining. This technique was superseded by the use of electronic transducers to measure the diameter of the blood vessel. The new procedure involved slicing rings from the arterial segment. The rings were exposed to a test substance while any change in diameter was recorded.

The new technique yielded a result in direct contradiction to that obtained with arterial strips: acetylcholine relaxed the rings. The paradox was solved in 1980 by Robert F. Furchgott and Zbigniew A. Zawadski, both of Brown University, Providence, R.I. They realized that preparing the strips had damaged the endothelium, whereas slicing the rings had not. They showed that the rings would contract in response to acetylcholine, as the strips had done, when the endothelial cells were removed from the rings with a cotton swab. They proposed that acetylcholine prompted undamaged endothelial cells to secrete a substance—EDRF—that relaxed the underlying muscle.

The potential importance of EDRF was immediately recognized and came under intense scrutiny in many laboratories. All attempts to isolate and identify it were frustrated by its extreme instability. Indeed, even in neutral physiological salt solutions at body temperature, EDRF lost half of its activity in only six seconds. In 1986 Furchgott and Louis J. Ignarro, of the University of California at Los Angeles School of Medicine, independently proposed that EDRF might be the simple compound nitric oxide ($N = O$, or NO). There was good reason for this proposal in light of the long history of the use of nitro compounds to lower blood pressure. Amyl nitrite was first employed this way in 1867, and nitroglycerin came into similar use in 1879. Moreover, sodium nitroprusside, which contains $N = O$ bound to iron, is a modern blood-pressure-lowering agent. Identification of EDRF as nitric oxide was then established by Salvador Moncada of the Wellcome Research Laboratories, Beckenham, England, and his associates, who showed that NO could mimic all the biological and chemical properties of EDRF. They went on to find that NO is made in the endothelial cells from the amino acid L-arginine.

By producing NO the endothelial cells can regulate the bore of the blood vessels and thus blood pressure. Production of NO is responsive to a variety of factors including rate of blood flow, concentration of oxygen, and the presence of acetylcholine and certain other substances in the blood. NO is also important in maintaining fluidity of the blood by inhibiting aggregation of blood platelets and by preventing platelets from adhering to the endothelial lining. It thus exerts an anticlotting effect.

Nitric oxide might play a still wider role in living systems; cells other than endothelial cells recently were shown to make NO from L-arginine. It seemed likely that NO, because of its profound action and its chemical instability, is ideally suited to sending short-lived messages from cell to adjacent cell. The biological production and use of NO drove home once again the message that living things are incredibly complex and that human beings are only beginning to appreciate the level of their own complexity.

(IRWIN FRIDOVICH)

Genetic Engineering in the Garden. For millennia men and women have tilled the earth, reaping a harvest of grains, fruits, and vegetables that became mainstays of survival. As dependence on agricultural products has grown, so has the need to improve quality and yield. In theory and practice, crop characteristics and yield may be affected in either of two ways. The environment or cultivation methods may be changed, or the plants themselves may be changed. Much of the progress in agriculture to date centred on improving the way crops are grown, fertilized, and protected from disease, insects, and weeds. In addition, specific crop characteristics were altered over the centuries by such practices as selective breeding, which provided most of the produce enjoyed in the late 20th century. Manipulations like selective breeding, however, are slow and laborious. Moreover, they possess limits as to what characteristics may be altered and how they may change. Recent advances in plant molecular biology promised a new generation of crops having characteristics that might profoundly alter the pace and direction of agricultural progress.

The basis for much of the recent progress stemmed from the development of novel techniques for delivering new,

functioning DNA, or genetic material, into plants. In the 1970s methods first became available for adding foreign (*i.e.*, derived from other species) or altered DNA sequences to bacteria, animal cells, and some fungi. These techniques, collectively called genetic engineering, paved the way for important advances in the medical sciences. Whereas most DNA delivery methods for bacterial or animal cells depended on a chemical or electrical means of making the recipient cell permeable to the new DNA or used genetically engineered viruses as DNA carriers, or vectors, plant cells generally resisted these approaches. Only recently did genetic manipulation in plants begin to catch up with that in animals.

Most genetically engineered plants produced by 1989 owed their success to the plant disease agent *Agrobacterium tumefaciens*. In nature, susceptible plants that become infected by virulent strains of this bacterium develop large tumours known as crown galls. The utility of the bacterium as a means of gene transfer in plants was first proposed by Mary-Dell Chilton and colleagues at the University of Washington in 1977, when they showed that crown galls actually result from the transfer and integration of genes from the bacterium into the DNA of the plant cells. Subsequent studies led to identification of the Ti plasmid, a small circular piece of DNA found in *Agrobacterium* that is responsible for the gene transfer process.

In the late 1980s *Agrobacterium*-mediated gene transfer was accomplished with strains of the bacterium carrying "disarmed" Ti plasmids, from which the genes responsible for causing disease were removed and replaced with DNA destined for the recipient plant. Traits introduced this way into tomato and oilseed rape plants proved stable over at least five generations of the engineered species. The technique succeeded for a variety of species in the herbaceous dicot and woody dicot families ranging from petunias to soybeans to apple trees. Asparagus, a monocot, was also engineered via *Agrobacterium*. Unfortunately, many commercially important cereal monocots including rice, wheat, and corn were not.

Efforts to manipulate cereal plants genetically could benefit from the recent development of another, perhaps more novel method of gene transfer. In this system DNA to be introduced into plants is coated onto the surface of small metal particles, which are then literally shot into pieces of plant tissue (explants) with a "particle gun" at speeds as high as several hundred metres per second (1 m = 3.28 ft). At such speeds the metal particles can penetrate several layers of intact cells. The regeneration of whole cereal plants from tissue explants is then a routine task. During 1989 particle guns were involved in intensive efforts to engineer cereal plants.

The obvious purpose of developing efficient, stable methods of gene delivery into plants is to alter and improve various species. Initial research focused on strengthening resistance to herbicides, insect pests, and disease agents. Progress was rapid in these areas, and genetically engineered crops of soybean, cotton, rice, corn, oilseed rape, sugar beet, tomato, and alfalfa should enter the marketplace before the turn of the century.

A fundamental problem in weed control involved distinguishing weeds from crops. Although numerous herbicides selectively toxic to weeds were developed, very few showed absolute specificity. In short, crop plants were often damaged by the very compounds applied to protect them from competition by weeds. A genetic solution to this apparent paradox was to develop crops having improved herbicide tolerance. This approach was adopted by several large agrochemical companies, which in 1989 were developing and

field testing engineered crops better able to resist commercial herbicides.

Like weed control, modern methods of insect control relied heavily on specific chemical compounds. A genetic alternative would be to engineer plants resistant to insect attack. Such plants might produce substances in their tissues that are toxic to certain insect pests yet harmless to other insects, animals, and humans. One naturally occurring insecticide is a large protein molecule synthesized by the bacterium *Bacillus thuringiensis*. Most forms of this protein are toxic to moth and butterfly larvae (caterpillars), while some forms are also toxic to beetles and flies. Other insects, animals, and humans are not affected.

Introducing the bacterial gene for this protein into plants yielded strains of tomato, tobacco, and cotton plants that resisted caterpillar pests. In one field test, plants carrying the bacterial insecticide gene suffered no serious damage under conditions that resulted in total defoliation of nonengineered, or control, plants. Other natural insecticides were under study in an effort to apply the approach to a variety of crops and their respective pests.

A similar genetic approach benefited efforts to create disease-resistant crops. A large variety of commercially important plants naturally succumb to viral infections. In a 1986 article Patricia Powell Abel, then a graduate student at Washington University, St. Louis, Mo., and colleagues reported that plants could be made significantly resistant to infection by the tobacco mosaic virus if they carried a gene encoding the otherwise harmless coat protein of the virus. Although the mechanism of protection remained to be explained, by 1989 this approach, called transgenic viral-coat-protein–mediated cross-protection, had yielded engineered tomato, tobacco, and potato plants that resisted a broad variety of plant viruses including alfalfa mosaic virus, cucumber mosaic virus, potato virus X, and potato virus Y. Greenhouse and field tests showed that the engineered tomato plants suffered no yield loss following a viral inoculation that reduced the yield of control plants by 23–69%. These results were encouraging signs that genetic approaches could offer effective disease control in a variety of plant species.

Future prospects for genetic engineering in plants appeared both promising and complex during the year. As technical barriers toppled, new kinds of barriers arose to replace them. Such issues as regulatory approval, proprietary protection, and public perception of benefits and dangers presented both a safety net and a ball and chain to the development of engineered commercial crops. In the U.S. the procedure for Food and Drug Administration or Environmental Protection Agency approval of genetically engineered plants remained undefined, and uncertainties regarding patent rights concerning newly developed plants and the genes that they carry remained to be resolved.

On a grander scale, however, the progress made was clear, and the possibilities were awesome. Within the next few decades might come plants that thrive in harsher climates, provide improved nutrition and novel raw materials for industry, and require less chemical cultivation than those currently grown. Humankind would have created a new and powerful tool to help feed a hungry world.

(JUDITH L. FRIDOVICH-KEIL)

See also Earth Sciences; Environment.

This article updates the *Macropædia* articles AGRICULTURE; Animal BEHAVIOUR; BIOCHEMICAL COMPONENTS OF ORGANISMS; The BIOLOGICAL SCIENCES; BIOSPHERE; CIRCULATION AND CIRCULATORY SYSTEMS; CONSERVATION OF NATURAL RESOURCES; ECOSYSTEMS; The Principles of GENETICS AND HEREDITY; Biological GROWTH AND DEVELOPMENT; PROTOPHYTES; REPRODUCTION AND REPRODUCTIVE SYSTEMS.

Literature

The year 1989 was a bad one for the secular-minded, the "rationalists." A worldwide controversy surrounded *The Satanic Verses,* a novel by Salman Rushdie (*see* BIOGRAPHIES). Published in London in 1988, this book had been admired by critics in Britain and the United States, but in the Islamic world it was condemned as an insult to the Muslim faith. It was banned in Pakistan, Saudi Arabia, and (less predictably) India, not a Muslim state; the South African government followed India's example. In March Ayatollah Ruhollah Khomeini, the "supreme spiritual leader" of Iran, took the extraordinary step of issuing a *fatwah* against Rushdie, condemning him to death and offering money to anyone who killed him. The author, born in Bombay, lived in England, where he had been educated, and he was taken under the protection of the British police to live in seclusion at a secret address. (*See* PUBLISHING: *Sidebar.*)

The 1989 Nobel Prize for Literature was awarded to the Spanish novelist Camilo José Cela (*see* BIOGRAPHIES). Outside Spain, he was best known for his novels *The Hive* and *The Family of Pascual Duarte;* both had suffered from censorship under Gen. Francisco Franco's regime for their treatment of sex and violence. The latter novel was filmed in the 1970s, but it was not released in Britain because the production involved excessive cruelty to animals.

Despite his part-British ancestry, Cela's award was not welcomed in Britain, where it was objected that he had fought for Franco in the Spanish Civil War and had offered the dictatorship his services as an informer; the fact that he disconcerted and scandalized the regime offered no excuse. In Spain his much-publicized affair with a younger woman had been widely disparaged, and his most recent novel, *Cristo Versus Arizona,* was received with hostility by younger critics. Some Latin-American writers were appreciative. "He is probably the best writer in Spain," said Mario Vargas Llosa. Carlos Fuentes said: "He wrote two of the greatest novels in Spanish this century. And he did it from the heart of Franco. More power to him."

In France the Prix Goncourt was won by Jean Vautrin, with an epic novel about three generations of Cajun settlers in Louisiana, *Un Grand Pas vers le bon Dieu* ("A Big Step Toward God"). Criticism of the system of literary prizes focused on the allegation that Vautrin had deliberately moved to the publishing house of Grasset—one of the three French publishers who had regularly published the Goncourt winners. A new prize, the Prix Novembre, was instituted to challenge the Goncourt; the first winner was Guy Dupre, with his novel *Manoeuvres d'automne* ("Autumn Maneuvers").

Samuel Beckett (*see* OBITUARIES), playwright, author, and one of the giants of 20th-century literature, died December 22.

ENGLISH

United Kingdom. The furor aroused by *The Satanic Verses* evoked bewildering responses in the literary and political worlds. Muslims in Britain paraded and burned copies of the book, supporting the death sentence upon the author, and there were threats against bookshops and demands that the old, rarely used British law against blasphemy not be allowed to lapse but rather be extended to punish literary attacks against non-Christian religions. Rushdie was known to be hostile to Britain's Conservative Party government—whose literary adherents were quick to point out that he now required government protection, at considerable expense.

The novelist Fay Weldon published a pamphlet, *Sacred Cows,* denouncing Muslim customs and arguing that immigration to Britain should follow the "unicultural policy of the United States," with children attending schools where "one flag is saluted and one God worshiped." She did not consider the sensitivities of Hindus, for whom cows are sacred and many gods worshiped. Lisa Appignanesi and Sara Maitland published *The Rushdie File* (after many difficulties with nervous publishers and printers), attempting to set out the known facts about this international crisis—for literature, politics, race, and religion. Reviewing these two efforts, Christopher Hitchens wrote in the *London Review of Books* that the important point was that "Salman Rushdie was publicly condemned to death, and his murder made a holy obligation upon millions of true believers, by the theocratic and political head of a foreign state, because he had written a work of fiction which allegedly profaned" the teachings of the prophet Muhammad.

Hitchens insisted that "the Salman Rushdie case has no analogue and no precedent." Nevertheless, literary figures sought analogies. Tariq Ali, the well-known writer and radical politician (born in Lahore, Pak.), was cowriter of a play at London's Royal Court Theatre that presented the case as a variation on *The Arabian Nights.* The poet Tony Harrison wrote a verse drama, *The Blasphemers' Banquet,* comparing Rushdie, in his beleaguered situation, with Omar Khayyam, Byron, and Voltaire. This drama was presented on BBC Television despite an appeal from the Archbishop of Canterbury, who feared it would increase tension among Muslims.

Fear of religious fundamentalism provoked critical interest in books concerning the evangelical styles of Christianity promoted in the United States; many British readers feared that fervent and wealthy U.S. preachers would be able to wreak havoc on Britain's newly decontrolled commercial television. Much admired was Malise Ruthven's book *The Divine Supermarket: Travels in Search of the Soul of America.* Another useful account, by Douglas Kennedy (New York born, British based, and a traveler in the Deep South), was called *In God's Country: Travels in the Bible Belt, U.S.A.*

Fiction. It was reckoned to be a good year for British novelists, though there was a special acrimony about the prizes for literary fiction. Michael Frayn's witty novel *The Trick of It* had been expected to be on the lists of finalists (the shortlist) for the Booker Prize but failed to do so. It was the first novel Frayn had published in 16 years—and it was certainly literary enough. The story was told, in epistolary form, by an academic critic striving to evaluate the

Fay Weldon
JERRY BAUER

skill of a female novelist, a "major writer of our time"—trying to comprehend "the trick of it": he takes her to bed, but continues to misunderstand her. The detective stories of P.D. James were held by some readers to be worthy of acclaim as literary novels; her latest thriller, *Devices and Desires,* was found by some of her old admirers to be too literary, too much of a "straight novel."

Two old favourites, Iris Murdoch and Margaret Drabble, received less than their usual acclaim for their novels about civilized enclaves in a barbarous world. *A Natural Curiosity,* Drabble's 11th novel, continued the story of the three University of Cambridge graduates introduced in her previous novel, *The Radiant Way.* They were now professionally successful women in their 50s. One of them was pursuing an obsession with a convicted mass murderer who had killed one of her pupils; he seemed to be presented as a symptom of the nasty society surrounding the three cultivated women. Murdoch, with *The Message to the Planet* (her 24th novel, in her 70th year), concerned herself with a sage and his acolytes in a closed community. Some critics felt that it was too long, needing the attention of a publisher's editor.

Martin Amis failed to make the Booker shortlist with *London Fields* despite much publicity. The story concerned a young woman, doomed to be murdered by either an "upmarket" man or a "downmarket" man. Many reviewers applauded Amis' cruel description of the downmarket, or lower-class, assassin, but the female judges for the Booker Prize felt that the author had shown too little sympathy and respect for the female victim.

Similar acrimony beset the Whitbread Award for fiction. It was bestowed, at first, upon Alexander Stuart for his novel *The War Zone,* a story about incest, but the prize was withdrawn when a dissenting judge refused to accept the majority decision. The prize was given instead to Lindsay Clarke for *The Chymical Wedding.* Some readers (notably Martyn Goff, the administrator of the Booker Prize) blamed the administrators of the Whitbread Award for this debacle. However, the Whitbread Award for a first novel went, without trouble, to James Hamilton-Pater-

son for *Gerontius*—a novel concerning English melancholy, the composer Edward Elgar, and his travels in Latin America.

The Booker Prize went to Kazuo Ishiguro for *The Remains of the Day,* a novel about an elderly English butler coming to the conclusion that the aristocratic master whom he had loyally served, in prewar days, was a bad sort of nobleman, sympathetic to the Nazi enemy. Many readers admired the accomplishment of this peculiarly English novel, written by a man born in Japan, but some found it rather dull. Other contenders on the shortlist included Margaret Atwood, the Canadian feminist, with *Cat's Eye,* a sensitive memoir of youth in Toronto; and an almost autobiographical book by the cosmopolitan Sybille Bedford, *Jigsaw,* concerning an amusingly eccentric family. Other authors included Rose Tremain, with *Restoration,* a historical fantasy about the reign of Charles II; the Scottish writer James Kelman, with *A Disaffection,* the story of a Glasgow schoolteacher who fears he has betrayed his working-class origins; and the Irishman John Banville, with *The Book of Evidence,* the cheerless story of an upperclass Irish murderer.

Banville's book was compared (by Lawrence Lerner) with Albert Camus's *The Outsider* and (indirectly) with Mikhail Lermontov's *A Hero of Our Time.* "Yes, a hero of our time," wrote Lerner, "and a book of our time, well written: but not designed to make one love the time." Although unsuccessful with the Booker Prize, Tremain won the *Sunday Express* Prize, and Banville won the yet more remunerative Guinness Peat Aviation Award—another prize occasioning public disputes about the judging.

Stella Gibbons (*see* OBITUARIES), whose 1932 burlesque of the rural novel, *Cold Comfort Farm,* had never been out of print, died December 19 at 87.

Biography. The most noticed and controversial biography (in literary circles) was *Bitter Fame: A Life of Sylvia Plath* by Anne Stevenson. Plath, a U.S.-born poet, was married to Ted Hughes, the poet laureate of Britain, before her suicide in 1963. Other biographies had led readers to idealize Plath as a heroine. Stevenson, however, offered a less warmhearted account,

HORST TAPPE

Kazuo Ishiguro

assisted by friends of the married couple, particularly by Olwyn Hughes, the sister of Plath's husband. This biography tended to stimulate, rather than to lay to rest, speculations about Sylvia Plath's sufferings and psychological disturbance.

Earlier in the year came the first volume of *The Life of Graham Greene* by Norman Sherry. Encouraged by Greene, Sherry retraced (at some risk to himself) the novelist's youthful travels and presented a substantial account, instructive and amusing. Greene himself published (almost as appendixes to this biography) two books—one a collection of his provoking "letters to the editor" over the years, the other an account of the epigraphs to his books, discussing their sources. Greene also appeared in another sort of biography, *The Brideshead Generation: Evelyn Waugh and His Friends* by Humphrey Carpenter, linking such disparate contemporaries as John Betjeman, Henry Green, and Anthony Powell; this book was found to be entertaining but lacking in novelty. Another figure of (roughly speaking) "the Brideshead generation" received a whole new biography, *Osbert: A Portrait of Osbert Lancaster* by Richard Boston, who showed Lancaster to have many other accomplishments and achievements to his credit besides his celebrated cartoons and stage designs.

Coleridge: Early Visions, by Richard Holmes, won general approbation (and the Whitbread Award for Biography) with its eloquent appreciation of Samuel Taylor Coleridge. There was general admiration for the second volume of Michael Holroyd's large biography, *Bernard Shaw: 1898–1918, The Pursuit of Power;* as there was also for Alistair Horne's second volume, *Macmillan 1957–1986,* tracing the statesman's troubled career from the bitter aftermath of the Suez adventure. Another long, authorized biography, *Lawrence of Arabia* by Jeremy Wilson, appeared at last—a year too late for Lawrence's centenary; it was criticized by Humphrey Carpenter for its "unswerving blandness"—so that it seemed not so much a biography of this challenging man as "undigested history."

Poetry. The noticeable verse of the year was in *The Blasphemers' Banquet* by Tony Harrison—the televised verse-drama, mentioned above, written in support of the beleaguered Salman Rushdie. Secular critics (notably the *Sunday Telegraph*) deplored Harrison's rashness and reminded readers disapprovingly of the poet's earlier essay in televised poetry—his disturbing verse-drama called *V* (meaning "versus"); however, this tough-talking play, about football hooligans desecrating a graveyard, proved sufficiently popular to be staged at the Edinburgh Festival. The same Edinburgh honour was paid to Heathcote Williams, whose concern for endangered animals—whales and dolphins—had been first presented on television. In 1989 Williams turned his attention to saving the elephants; while giving his blessing to the good cause, Kingsley Amis was sharp about "much windy near-poetry" and observed that "if you like elephants, *Sacred Elephant* may not be the book for you." Amis was more satisfied by the quiet, undemonstrative verses of Roy Fuller, *Available for Dreams.*

Ted Hughes, the poet laureate, had often

Norman Sherry
WILLIAM E. SAURO—THE NEW YORK TIMES

been admired for his hard-eyed, unsentimental concern for the animal kingdom. His latest collection, *Wolfwatching,* won commendation for the poet's "toughness," seeming to "paralyze the high chatter that passes for criticism of the craft"; the critic was Derek Walcott, the West Indian poet who won the Queen's Award for Poetry in 1988. Walcott went on to praise some of Hughes's verses for being "predatory." Walcott wrote, "Our own eyes are harder than those of the beasts."

James Fenton had settled in the Philippines and (backing into the limelight) compelled his readers to apply for copies of his latest work, *Manila Envelope,* by writing to a private address there (28 Kayumanggi Street, Triangle Homes, Quezon City). "Nonsense and 'light verse' are yoked to the most harrowing material," wrote Neil Corcoran in the *London Review of Books.* There were menacing verses relating to Fenton's previous experiences in Vietnam and Kampuchea, and there was a "Ballad of the Imam and the Shah," presented as "an old Persian legend" about modern Iran; the concept reminded readers of the forces confronting Rushdie.

(D.A.N. JONES)

United States. *Fiction.* A remarkable richness characterized the publishing year in fiction in the United States, with little in the way of local scandal or tragedy to distract attention from the works themselves. Although U.S. writers did speak out against the threats by the Iranian leader Ayatollah Khomeini on the life of the Indian-born novelist Salman Rushdie, the national scene remained relatively calm.

Early in the year a number of established masters brought out new books, beginning with the latest novel by Joyce Carol Oates. *American Appetites,* her 19th work of fiction, presented, with Dreiserean force and fierce attentiveness to psychological detail, the death of a successful cookbook writer in the midst of a ferocious quarrel with her misunderstood husband. Many reviewers, this writer included, found the book to be an important turning away from the annoying gothicism of Oates's recent fiction

Saul Bellow
MARVIN LICHTNER—LEE GROSS, INC.

and a revelation as to the power of the maturing style of this enormously prolific novelist and critic. E.L. Doctorow, known nationwide for his excursion into America's early 20th century in his novel *Ragtime*, went to New York City's gangland days for *Billy Bathgate*, a novel about one boy's initiation into life by means of his rise in the mob. Saul Bellow, the dean of U.S. fiction writers, published two books in 1989, both of them novellas and both produced as paperback originals. The first of these slender volumes—neither of them much longer than 100 pages—was called *A Theft* and seemed the more successful. In telling the story of the crisis in the psychological life of a beautiful and capable New York executive, Bellow showed his genius in the creation of a full-scale and memorable female character. The second novella, *The Bellarosa Connection*, seemed more diffuse in its representation of an incident involving a Jewish refugee from Nazi-occupied Italy and the U.S. showman Billy Rose.

Fiction writer and naturalist Peter Matthiessen was represented by a range of interesting stories, from his apprentice work to current mastery, under the title *On the River Styx*. Far less interesting was the appearance of *The Shawl* by much-lauded story writer Cynthia Ozick, except insofar as it revealed the mannered emotiveness of two stories ("The Shawl" and "Rosa") that had won a lot of attention when these tales of the Holocaust and its aftermath first appeared in magazine form. Much more deserving of attention was a new novel by National Book Award winner Mary Lee Settle. *Charley Bland* tells of a lifelong passion for a West Virginia ne'er-do-well of great magnetism by a woman novelist who once lived in the region. Both a beautiful lyric re-creation of lost times and lost loves in this mountainous part of the South and a wisdom tale of great depth on the subjects of love, life, and vocation, this book showed a septuagenarian writer working at the top of her powers.

A younger generation of writers produced some noteworthy achievements during the year. Among these were *Some Can Whistle*, the latest work of fiction by Pulitzer Prize-winning novelist Larry McMurtry (*see* BIOGRAPHIES), and North Carolina writer Fred Chappell's little country masterpiece *Brighten the Corner Where You Are*. The title of Chappell's wonderfully comic yet deeply and seriously hu-

mane novel comes from an old church hymn. The power derives from the writer's passion for creating with great humour and telling detail one long day in the life of a rural North Carolina husband, father, and schoolteacher just after the end of World War II. John Irving's *A Prayer for Owen Meany* received mixed reviews, as did Thomas McGuane's elegantly composed but rather lacklustre novel about inheritance and vocation in the new West called *Keep the Change*. Key West, Fla., was the setting for *Mile Zero* by Thomas Sanchez, a daring attempt at producing a big novel in the old-fashioned romantic mode in which the larger American culture is portrayed in microcosm. "It is about water. It was about water in the beginning, it will be about water in the end. The ocean mothered us all. Water and darkness awaiting light. Night gives birth. An inkling of life over distant sea swells toward brilliance. Dawn emerges from Africa, strikes light between worlds, over misting mountains of Haiti, beyond the Great Bahama Bank, touching cane fields of Cuba, across the Tropic of Cancer to the sleeping island of Key West, farther to the Gold Coast of Florida, its great wall of condominiums demarcating mainland America." Sanchez' opening paragraphs boldly announce his broad and large intentions. The rest of the book, the intertwined stories of a burnt-out 1960s radical and a Cuban-American policeman in search of their happiness and the public tranquillity, more than amply enacts this drama of both social and psychological import.

Another success story is that of John Casey's *Spartina*. Casey, like Sanchez, had not published a novel in more than a decade but came back strong. The tale of his Rhode Island fishing boat captain Dick Pierce also has a lot to do with water and with men competing against the elements, both within and without. It won the 1989 National Book Award for fiction. Bob Shacochis, who won an American Book Award for *Easy in the Islands*, his first book of stories, returned with *The Next New World*, with some of these cannily told tales set, as in his earlier book, in the Caribbean and some in his native Virginia. Lynne Sharon Schwartz set her powerfully affecting short novel *Leaving Brooklyn* in her native borough; in that book a young girl with a congenital eye problem comes

JODI BUREN

Thomas McGuane

under the sexual thrall of an overmastering ophthalmologist. A superior novel of families and their sometimes destructive tendencies was *Mr. Field's Daughter* by Virginia novelist Richard Bausch. Twice a nominee for the prestigious PEN/Faulkner Prize for Fiction, Bausch used naturalistic techniques once again to create a novel of great sympathy and power with resonances that echo far beyond the realm of the naturalistic.

Chinese-American families took centre stage in *The Joy Luck Club*, the best-selling first novel by San Francisco writer Amy Tan (*see* BIOGRAPHIES). Cuban-Americans shared the spotlight in Oscar Hijuelos' much praised *The Mambo Kings Play Songs of Love*. In Allan Gurganus' enormously long first novel, some seven or eight years in the making, the antebellum South came again into focus, in the words of the loquacious narrator of *Oldest Living Confederate Widow Tells All*. As engaging as some reviewers found the book, others seemed to wish that the widow had told much less. Another accomplished novel was Robert Olen Butler's *The Deuce*, the story of a runaway named Võ Dinh Thanh or Tony, a sort of a Vietnamese-American Huck Finn who lights out for the squalor of New York City's Times Square district. It offered melodrama at the end but remained mostly successful. In *Long Distance Life* Marita Golden tells of her native Washington, D.C., over the course of three generations of a local black family. Pulitzer Prize winner M. Scott Momaday placed his new book, *The Ancient Child*, in the West, a region that comes to life in the beauty of fine descriptive passages; these help the reader accommodate to Momaday's deviations from conventional novelistic practice. The power of Craig Nova's prose in *Tornado Alley* showed off the tremendous abilities of this first-rate novelist, whose books had not always been as effectively dramatic as this new one.

Among younger writers novelist Terry McMillan brought out *Disappearing Acts*, her second book, a brusque but effective novel about a black female singer and composer and the construction worker she falls in love with, much to the chagrin of both. Jeanne Larsen, a poet and translator, showed her deft hand at historical fiction with an intelligent and entertaining novel set in 8th-century China called *Silk Road*. Darcey Steinke, a young Virginia writer, offered *Up Through the Water*, a lyrical novel set on Ocracoke Island off the coast of North Carolina. *The Rainbow Stories* by William Vollmann was a virtuoso performance that had all the earmarks of a cult classic in the making. *Still Life with Insects*, a slim first novel by Brian Kitely, demonstrated great economy and subtlety of craft.

Among best-selling writers with long track records, both Stephen King with *The Dark Half* and James Michener with *Caribbean* published novels that seemed destined to stay on the top-ten lists well into the new year. Also during the year much-praised short-story writer Donald Barthelme died (*see* OBITUARIES), and *The People*, a posthumous volume of unfinished work by the late Bernard Malamud, was published.

Nonfiction. The history of black America came under intense scrutiny during the

Amy Tan
ROBERT FOOTHORAP

year in a number of important books, beginning late in 1988 with Taylor Branch's *Parting the Waters: America in the King Years, 1954-1963;* it won a National Book Critics Circle Award in 1989 and was widely cited in news stories because of its striking portrait of Martin Luther King as private thinker as well as public leader. Less flattering to King was the warts-and-all portrayal in *And the Walls Came Tumbling Down* by his former colleague and friend the Rev. Ralph Abernathy. Historian Martin Bauml Duberman published *Paul Robeson,* a well-received biography of the black entertainer. Phyllis Rose did the same in *Jazz Cleopatra,* her treatment of Josephine Baker, the black American singer who lived many years in France.

A revisionist view of the French Revolution was presented in *Citizens* by Harvard University historian Simon Schama. Paul Fussell's controversial *Wartime* overturned the conventional wisdom about American ideas of World War II. In *The Control of Nature* the highly regarded nonfiction writer John McPhee presented ecological dramas set in Iceland, Hawaii, and southern California.

Some of the best fiction writers published nonfiction self-portraits: Whiting Award winner Tobias Wolff in the much lauded *This Boy's Life* and novelists Reynolds

ROBERT MAASS—PHOTOREPORTERS

Simon Schama

Price in *Clear Pictures,* John Updike in *Self-Consciousness,* and Nicholas Delbanco in *Running in Place,* the last an intelligent and elegantly composed travel book set in Provence that portrays the evolution of the art of a writer and family man. The expatriate writer and composer Paul Bowles was the subject in *An Invisible Spectator* by Christophe Sawyer-Laucanno, as was Nelson Algren in *Nelson Algren: A Life on the Wild Side* by Bettina Drew. Joseph Conrad biographer Frederick Karl turned his sights on U.S. literature in the massive *William Faulkner, American Writer.*

Poetry and Criticism. A number of accomplished poets published new volumes, among them Adrienne Rich (*Time's Power, Poems 1985-1988*), Robert Hass (*Human Wishes*), Stanley Plumly (*Boy on the Step*), and Pulitzer Prize winners Maxine Kumin (*Nurture*) and Rita Dove (*Grace Notes*). Two poets of enormous erudition and graceful technical expertise, Fred Chappell and David Slavitt, brought out, respectively, *First and Last Words* and *Equinox and Other Poems.* Brendan Galvin offered the book-length narrative poem *Wampanoag Traveller,* set in a fic-

NABOKOV—GAMMA/LIAISON

Bharati Mukherjee

tional 18th-century America. The highly regarded Stephen Dunn produced *Between Angels,* and the extraordinarily gifted Deborah Digges published *Late in the Millennium. A New Path to the Waterfall,* poems by the late short-story writer Raymond Carver, came out, with a moving introduction by his widow, poet Tess Gallagher.

Among books of criticism, *Moving Pictures* by Anne Hollander made a convincing argument for looking to 19th-century European painting for the origins of the composition of modern film images. In *Lipstick Traces* music critic Greil Marcus constructed a sweeping argument about the importance of seemingly marginal art in modern culture. Harvard psychiatrist and writer Robert Coles in *The Call of Stories* presented the therapeutic side of fiction. A posthumous volume of essays (*Along the Riverrun*) by Richard Ellmann was published. Poet and art critic John Ashbery brought out his essays on painting under the title *Reported Sightings,* as did novelist John Updike in *Just Looking.* Willard Spiegelman published *The Didac-*

tic Muse: Scenes of Instruction in Contemporary Poetry.

Awards and Prizes. The Pulitzer Prize for fiction for 1989 went to Anne Tyler's *Breathing Lessons.* Indian-born émigré Bharati Mukherjee won the National Book Critics Circle prize for fiction for her story collection *The Middleman and Other Stories,* and Donald Hall took the poetry award for *The One Day.* Thomas Friedman won the 1989 National Book Award for nonfiction for *From Beirut to Jerusalem.* Short-story writer and novelist James Salter won the PEN/Faulkner Award for fiction, the only U.S. fiction prize judged by U.S. fiction writers, for his collection titled *Dusk.*   (ALAN CHEUSE)

Canada. Fiction thrives on the actions of the rebel and outlaw, and there were plenty of bad apples in the 1989 crop of novels and short stories. Among the best of the bunch was the title character of Mordecai Richler's first novel in nine years, *Solomon Gursky Was Here,* a legendary figure who obsesses the young man searching for him. Then there was the "arrogant son of a bitch" who narrates Lesley Choyce's *The Second Season of Jonas MacPherson,* a man as full of wind as the ocean he claims is his mistress, veering from tender to bawdy, from clairvoyant to stupid, from fact to myth, in a single breath. David Helwig continued the mad parade with an excursion through *Old Wars,* a novel in which no characters are quite what they seem, whether they know it or not. The innocence of madness/the madness of innocence obsesses Minnie in Sandra Birdsell's *The Missing Child* until the forces of the outer world, and her own strength, enable her to work her way back into sanity. More extreme still is the introverted, introspective girl who stalks through Kristjana Gunnars' latest exploration of her Icelandic heritage, *The Prowler.*

However, there were also books in which more-or-less normal people lead more-or-less normal lives, as in Joan Barfoot's *Family News,* in which the disasters of the news hour are subtly echoed in more familiar catastrophes—at once less horrible and more painful than the world-class carnage the family reads and hears about. In *After the Fire,* Jane Rule presents five women as they struggle in their idiosyncratic, angry, and loving ways to come to terms with the difficulties of living, together and alone, amid the splendid solitudes of British Columbia's Gulf Islands. In *Homesick,* Guy Vanderhaeghe traces the bonds of family power, while in *A Good Baby,* Leon Rooke's latest issue, a number of young ideas are expressed in newborn prose. Rikki Ducornet, in her first novel, *The Fountains of Neptune,* floods the psyche with images of water and drowning in a story that wavers between fable and case history in its reconstruction of the depth dive into coma and the slow resurfacing that follows. In another first novel, *To All Appearances a Lady* by poet Marilyn Bowering, one man's quest for truth and identity leads him toward the liberating knowledge of death.

In her short-story collection *Before and After,* Katherine Govier goes beyond the moment of choice to the consequences, connecting her characters from one story to another in a manner befitting a novel. In Carol Shield's latest collection, *The Or-*

ange Fish, however, everyone feels unconnected, fish out of water.

Notable books of poetry published during the year included Erin Moure's *WSW (West South West),* an exploration of perspectives; Douglas Barbour's *Stories for a Saskatchewan Night,* in which the poet-cum-juggler nimbly entertains with his tricks of language and conceit; Marilyn Bowering's science-fiction-like fantasies in *Calling All the World: Laika and Folchakov; Dunino,* Stephen Scobie's humorous musings on his Scots heritage; Kristjana Gunnars' *Carnival of Longing,* in which poetry and prose are mated; a collection of Robert Kroetsch's longer works, *The Completed Field Notes: The Long Poems of Robert Kroetsch;* the robust satire of Nellie McClung's *I Never Met a Bad Cat;* the long-delayed official publication of George Bowring's first book of poems, *Sticks and Stones,* written in 1962; Tom Wayman's bittersweet and philosophical evocation of the woes and joys of working people, *In a Small House on the Outskirts of Heaven;* and Maggie Helwig's *Talking Prophet Blues,* three poetry sequences that celebrate three subtly sympathetic subjects—Simone Weil, Glenn Gould, and early Christian mystics.

Cathy Ford, in her *Saffron, Rose and Flame,* etches the life of Joan of Arc with painstaking clarity and breathtaking effect, while Francis Sparshott in *Sculling to Byzantium* brings the reader along with his crafty cargo of the funny, the formal, and the grotesque. Beth Jankola experiments with the choreography of sound in *She Dances into Light.* And George Woodcock, the editor of *The Dry Wells of India: An Anthology Against Thirst—Selected Poems from the Canadian Poetry Contest 1,* mingles poetry with reality in this presentation of the 6 winning poems, and 50 other outstanding entries, in a contest that raised money for an irrigation project.

(ELIZABETH WOODS)

FRENCH

The bicentennial of the French Revolution caused, as was to be expected, a flood of publications on the principal figures as well as the cultural, philosophical, and social upheavals of the period. Among works notable for their originality were those written or coauthored by the historian François Furet, such as the voluminous *Dictionnaire critique de la Révolution française.* In this book Furet and his collaborators restore the philosophical and cultural dimensions of 1789, aspects that 20th-century French historians had tended to ignore in favour of the purely political. *La Carmagnole des Muses,* produced under the direction of Jean-Claude Bonnet, shows how the Revolution, far from causing a decline in the arts (as had so often been asserted), passed on the new spirit of the Enlightenment and laid the groundwork for the cultural institutions of modern France.

Five years after his death on June 25, 1984, Michel Foucault continued to be the undisputed star of the French philosophical scene. A biography by Didier Eribon allows the reader to better understand Foucault as a man who became, in turn, a brilliant but psychologically brittle student, a lukewarm Communist, a flirting dandy, a temporary structuralist, and finally a man who, through his life and

Jean Cocteau
GISELE FREUND

works, tried to sabotage traps set by the powers that be. Eribon alludes to Foucault's homosexuality, a trait that he did not try to hide but refused to admit because admission would have amounted to an acknowledgement of those powers. A volume containing his *Résumes de cours,* which he composed every year, shows the work of Foucault the researcher. Finally, *Michel Foucault philosophe* synthesizes the papers and debates presented during an international seminar organized in Paris to study Foucault's works. Among the participants were Georges Canguilhem, Gilles Deleuze, Hubert Dreyfus, Manfred Frank, and Paul Veyne.

Several books fell somewhere between the essay and the autobiography. Michel Schneider, in his *La Tombée du jour,* depicted in erudite fashion the figure of Schumann but also touched on his experiences with grief. Arlette Farge (a disciple of Foucault) confessed in *Le Goût de l'archive* to an almost physical love for old papers and dusty old libraries. In *Le Remède dans le mal,* Jean Starobinski explored the development during the 17th and 18th centuries of a language that allowed society to disguise its behaviours and conventions. On the other hand, Starobinski published an impassioned short essay on Baudelaire: *La Mélancolie au miroir.*

Jean Cocteau would have been 100 years old in 1989. Two volumes of his *Journal* were published. The first, covering the years of the Occupation and Liberation (1942–45), shows a Cocteau who "does not understand politics at all." The second volume deals with the year 1954, when Cocteau achieved success with his play *La Machine infernale.* Some autobiographical texts entitled *La Vie est pleine de choses redoutables* by Jean Paulhan, the director of *La Nouvelle Revue Française,* were published, as well as his correspondence with the Italian poet Ungaretti. Also published were *Ecrits politiques* by the Surrealist writer René Crevel, who died tragically in 1935.

At 89 Nathalie Sarraute once again surprised critics and readers with *Tu ne t'aimes pas,* a funny and fierce portrait of those self-confident beings who love each other and experience self-doubts only with extreme difficulty. In *L'Acacia* Claude Simon takes up again some of his favourite topics—war, the South of France, the weather—but from a different angle and in a rich style that appears to be free of external constraints. Georges Perec contributed an unfinished novel, *53 Jours,* and two collections of short subjects, *L'Infra-ordinaire* and *Voeux.*

Pascal Quignard with his novel *Les Escaliers de Chambord* was the favourite in the competition for major literary prizes but came away empty-handed. The Prix Goncourt went to Jean Vautrin for *Un Grand Pas vers le bon Dieu.* (See *Introduction,* above.) Serge Doubrovsky received the Prix Médicis for *Le Livre brisé,* about a collector of miniatures obsessed with a childhood memory. The Renaudot went to Philippe Doumenc for *Les Comptoirs du Sud,* and the Fémina to Sylvie Germain for *Jours de colère.*

In *Lac,* his fourth novel, Jean Echenoz seemed a bit out of breath, repeating in a less convincing manner the turns of phrase and the tragicomic situations found in his previous books. In *Une Chambre dans les bois,* Patrick Drevet artfully demonstrated his talent for nuance and sketching. Christian Bobin chose writing as the theme for his subtle and successful *La Part manquante.*

In the world of poetry, *Elégie de la mort violente* by Claude Esteban was a deep and luminous collection. Franck Venaille published a beautiful essay on the Italian poet Umberto Saba, who lived and died in Trieste and whose singular genius was slowly being discovered by the French public.

A pseudonymous French translation of *The Satanic Verses* appeared in July, bearing the anagram that François Rabelais had used when he was being persecuted for his writings. While the publisher (Editions Christian Bourgois) took full responsibility, the book's back cover listed the support of 21 publishers and the French Ministry of Culture.

(FRANÇOIS POIRIÉ)

Canada. Eight years after *Le Matou,* with more than one million copies sold, Yves Beauchemin produced a similar, action-filled novel, *Juliette Pomerleau,* using the same narrative device: a series of plots and clustered subplots. Beauchemin's dominant motif is the quest. Juliette Pomerleau, the main character, undertakes to find her long-lost niece, Adèle Joannette, and the far-flung search is full of unexpected twists and turns. Beauchemin once said in an interview about *Le Matou* that the novelist is like a neighbour or a friend who grabs you by the collar and says: "Listen, something remarkable just happened to me, and I have to tell you about it." Without a doubt, *Juliette Pomerleau* tells an extraordinary story, though the fragile border between the "remarkable" and the "unlikely" is sometimes blurred. Nevertheless, it stood out in the literary year.

French-Canadian literature, particularly from Quebec, is often perceived as serious, if not tormented. Reading Guy Ménard's *Jamädhlavie* should put that notion to rest. Written in the style of the 18th century, *Jamädhlavie* relates the story of Axel, once abducted by bandits and sold to a Jamädhlave "fahqir." Axel, now an old man,

narrates the 10 years he spent in the city of Tzëvedzïhr and his visits to Këvk and Otwhõl. After several pages, one realizes that the novel is a transcription of the history and cultural particularities of Quebec, from the battle on the Plains of Abraham to the 1980 referendum on independence. This account of Quebec, unique in Québécois literature, is extremely amusing for insiders but could be rather disconcerting for those not well versed in Quebec history and culture.

In 1971 Juan Garcia received the *Études françaises* prize for a collection of poems, *Corps de gloire*. In 1989 l'Hexagone used the same title to group these and other poems from *Alchimie du corps* (1967), *Pacte avec ma poésie* (1982), and various journals, as well as several unpublished works. Juan Garcia, who was born in Morocco in 1945 and lived in Quebec from 1957 to 1967, was now established in Spain. This collection undoubtedly belonged both to Québécois and to universal literature.

(PIERRE HÉBERT)

GERMAN

West Germany, Austria, Switzerland. The spectre of the Third Reich continued to be a preoccupation. The paradoxes and hypocrisies in the relationship between Switzerland and its Nazi neighbour were treated in Otto F. Walter's *Zeit des Fasans,* a substantial novel centred on an industrialist family, told in a multiplicity of narrative styles, mingling historical research with mythological implications. Urs Widmer's *Der Kongress der Paläolepidopterologen* also demolishes the myth of Swiss neutrality during World War II. Gert Hofmann's *Vor der Regenzeit* is the account of a search for Germany's past, resolved by the narrator on a visit to South America, where his Nazi uncle had found refuge.

The Austrian dimension was provided by Alfred Kolleritsch, whose novel *Allemann,* set in a boys' boarding school during the Third Reich, presents sexuality as the true subversive counterforce to dictatorship. By contrast, Herbert Rosendorfer, in *Die Nacht der Amazonen,* suggests that, unlike most totalitarian states, that of the Nazis was anything but prudish. Gerhard Köpf's picaresque *Eulensehen* treats the transition from Third Reich to Federal Republic through the eyes of a provincial postman, whose experiences with the townsfolk do not suggest any genuine contrition.

The legacy of the past looms over Bernd Sülzer's thriller *Tage des Zorns,* a contemporary tale of secret deals between the Israeli secret service and the West German government. The division of Europe is at the heart of Herta Müller's *Reisende auf einem Bein.* Its protagonist, like its author, has left Romania for West Germany, where she finds a "cold land and cold hearts." Arnold Stadler's prizewinning *Ich war einmal* thematicizes the untrustworthiness of memory in its account of growing up in the "fairy-tale" world of Martin Heidegger's Messkirch. Hanns-Joseph Ortheil's *Agenten* describes the contemporary youth scene, ranging between drug addicts and yuppies. Michael Köhlmeier's *Die Musterschüler,* set in 1963, the year of the Kennedy assassination, portrays the dynamics affecting a class of boys at a boarding school.

Elfriede Jelinek's *Lust* was a best-seller, although presumably many of its purchasers got less than what the title seemed to promise. In this novel sex is sadomasochism, described unsensually with the woman invariably the subordinate, and the implications are not only gender-based power structures but economic ones as well. In Friedrich Dürrenmatt's satire *Durcheinandertal* not sex but religion is the key to contemporary society; its central figure proclaims the gospel of wealth as the passport to heaven.

Wilhelm Genazino uses the journey framework for his *Der Fleck, die Jacke, die Zimmer, der Schmerz,* but only to deny the public significance of literature altogether. Lukas Hammerstein takes a similar path in *Eine Art Gelassenheit,* a stream-of-consciousness narrative on the possibility or impossibility of making a public speech. Martin Grzimek's *Die Beschattung* is a vision of a totalitarian state in which imaginative literature has been replaced by pseudo-authentic biographies. Most radically, Gerhard Rühm's *Albertus Magnus Angelus* dispenses with narrative altogether; the relics of Albert the Great become an allegory of discontinuity and entropy.

Representative collections of poetry came from Michael Wildenhain (*Das Ticken der Steine*), Sarah Kirsch (*Schneewärme*), Michael Krüger (*Idyllen und Illusionen*), and H.C. Artmann (*gedichte von der wollust des dichtens in worte gefasst*).

East Germany. The extraordinary political events of the summer and autumn were foreshadowed by a perceptible slackening of censorship in the previous 12 months. The plays of Heiner Müller were made available in their entirety for the first time, and some of Volker Braun's most outspokenly critical works were reprinted. Most entertainingly, Hans-Eckardt Wenzel's *Reisebilder,* written in 1983 but only now published, satirizes the Democratic Republic's literary idiosyncrasies. Even a relatively conventional novel like Günter Görlich's *Drei Wohnungen* adumbrates the uncertainties confronting those who had hitherto taken the standard political line. Both Gerd Neumann's *Die Klandestinität der Kesselreiniger* and Wolfgang Hilbig's *Eine Übertragung* thematicize the conflict between literature and the "actually existing socialism"; although these books did

Christa Wolf

not appear in East Germany (but only in the West), this seemed likely to be rectified.

Two outstanding new works related to earlier political crises. Christa Wolf's bittersweet *Sommerstück* describes idyllic scenes from the summer of 1976; the story's impact for the reader stems from the awareness that many of those involved were now dead or had left the country. Christoph Hein's *Der Tangospieler* relates in kafkaesque manner the fate of a lecturer who, having been imprisoned for his chance involvement in a political cabaret in 1967, is equally arbitrarily rehabilitated in August 1968 at the time of the invasion of Czechoslovakia. Historical themes continued to be popular and were exemplified in Hans Pfeiffer's *Scharnhorst,* a novel about the Prussian general, and Werner Liersch's *Eine Tötung im Angesicht des Herrn Goethe,* which shows an aloof Goethe at Karlsbad in 1819 as decisive and reactionary political decisions are being taken around him.   (J.H. REID)

SCANDINAVIAN

Denmark. Helle Stangerup returned to the historical novel with *Spardame,* centred on Christian IV's redoubtable mother-in-law, Ellen Marsvin, and his morganatic wife, Kirsten Munk. More modern is the basis of Anders Bodelsen's *Mørklægning* (1988), set in occupied Denmark in 1944, about an apparently political murder. The Danish police are interned, and the detective obsessively seeking to solve the mystery is himself desperate to avoid capture. The 1960s are re-created by Bjarne Reuter in *Vi der valgte Mælkevejen,* while Marianne Larsen's first novel, *Gæt hvem der elsker diog,* uses the Denmark of the 1950s and '60s for its setting. In his short stories *Det svage køn,* Klaus Rifbjerg is in an iconoclastic mood, concentrating with energy and humour on the lower motions of the human body.

In *Apollons oprør,* Villy Sørensen retells the Greek myths, as he retold the Norse myths in the highly acclaimed *Ragnarok.* However, this book was more strictly philosophical, an extension of the ideas on society and human nature that Sørensen had published over the years. Islam colours Henrik Nordbrandt's *Nissen flytter med* (1988), reflections on his many homes, some of which were in Turkey. No Muslim himself, Nordbrandt knew Islam and understood its mind like few Danes.

Marianne Larsen's *Giv bare kærligheden skylden* is a collection of poems, written in concentrated language, on mankind and the world today. Like Villy Sørensen, both Jørgen Gustava Brandt and Vagn Steen celebrated their 60th birthdays in 1989, and both marked the occasion by publishing new poems, Vagn Steen with the retrospective *Træ: Du er min far* (1988) and Brandt with *Poppeldigte.* Pia Juul published her third volume of poems, *Forgjort,* while Poul Borum produced a new volume under the title *Nu ved jeg* (1988). More unusual was the comprehensive bilingual collection of Greenlandic poems edited and translated by Karen Nørregaard, *Inuit Nipaat. Grønlandske digte i 1980erne,* a selection of both established poets and their younger contemporaries.

Hans Lyngby Jepsen turned to autobiography in *Til Andrea,* while the former minister of finance, Thorkil Kristensen,

called his memoirs simply *Erindringer.* Halfdan Rasmussen was awarded the Danish Academy Prize in 1988, and Erik Knudsen received the 1989 Martin Andersen Nexø Prize.   (W. GLYN JONES)

Norway. A major event was the appearance of Frans Lasson's monumental two-volume *Olaf Bull. Brev fra en dikters liv,* containing letters from and to arguably the greatest Norwegian 20th-century poet. His private life was as beset by constant poverty, excessive use of alcohol, and marital upheavals as his fastidious poetry is a perfect world of beauty. Lasson's exemplary annotations turned this work into an outstanding biography.

Traditional storytelling of striking quality was provided by Johannes Heggland's novel *Guds husfolk,* centring on the repercussions of a financial scandal in a small western Norwegian farming community. Psychological aspects of a shipping dynasty on the brink of bankruptcy are dealt with in Øystein Lønn's *Tom Rebers siste retrett.* In her largely autobiographical novel *For alle vinder,* Gerd Brantenberg tells with humour how a teenage girl comes to terms with her lesbianism. Bergljot Hobæk Haff gives South African problems a new twist by letting Christ be reincarnated as a black in *Den guddommelige tragedie.* Highly unusual also was Terje Stigen's antiheroic novel *Krigen,* viewing the 1940 war in Norway in a humoristic vein. Tor Åge Bringsværd added a third volume, *Djevelens skinn og ben,* to his much praised 13th-century *Gobi* series. Ketil Bjørnstad's *Stormen* was a strong cocktail of complex sexual tensions.

Simon Flem Devold's documentary *Spikern. Historien om et medmenneske* is a moving account of the life of a homeless vagrant in Oslo, permanently scarred by the strain of serving in the underground movement during the German occupation. There were outstanding short-story contributions from Roy Jacobsen in the many-faceted collection *Det kan komme noen.* Social and political satire added spice to the poems in Jan Erik Vold's *Elg.* Stein Mehren in *Det andre lyset. Dikt 1989* saw human experience in the light of a cosmic time scale, whereas Harald Sverdrup in *Tranene danser* gave poetic expression to a more earthbound view of human activities. Centenary-inspired publications were Willy Dahl's critical biography *Arnulf Øverland* and a collection of articles on Øverland and his poetry, *Sverd og kjerte. Minneskrift ed Arnulf Øverlands 100-årsdag,* as well as the collected poems of Aslaug Vaa, *Dikt i samling.* Ebba Haslund continued her well-written memoirs in *Med vingehest i manesjen.*   (TORBJØRN STØVERUD)

Sweden. Family relationships were central to much of the year's literary work. In the third volume of his autobiography, Jan Myrdal portrayed a fat, awkward, independent-minded youngster determined not to be manipulated for the sake of the family image, thus continuing to throw an ironic light on the public adulation accorded during their lifetime to his distinguished parents. P.C. Jersild, with warmth—and a clinical exactitude doubtless derived from his medical background—described his early life and his parents' unhappy marriage in *Fem hjärtan i en tändsticksask.*

Journalist and author Marianne Fredriksson's suspenseful *Gåtan* confronted Swedish practical realism with repressed family guilt, incest, and the subconscious. In the slim *Skuggorna bakom oss,* Gunilla Linn Persson wrote with poetic suggestiveness of a young, horse-mad girl finally breaking free from her father fixation. Robert Kangas was clearly a man to watch; his powerful first novel, *Rötmånad,* spiced with grim humour, dealt with violent family clashes. A semidocumentary account of modern rural family life (with sickness, death, and also hopeful enterprise) was provided by Ann Marie and Bjarne Moelv in *Att bli kvar är också en resa.*

P.G. Evander wrote in *Medan dagen svalnar* of a patient, nonviolent attempt to persuade an armed youngster to abandon his protest against authority, while Björn Collarp in *Ingenmansland* provided a naturalistic account of tangled sexual relationships leading to violent death. Leading young novelist Stig Larsson's *Komedin I* was both praised and deplored for its stylistic brilliance and its amoral detachment. In *Gogols ansikte,* Kjell Johansson used the Russian author less for biographical purposes than as an exploration of what literature can teach about reality. Peter Nilsson's *Äventyret* was a mythological fantasy of considerable imaginative power. Lars Gyllensten published dialectical philosophico-religious and secular reflections culled from his notebooks in *Just så eller kanske det.*

Swedish poetry was enriched by Tomas Tranströmer's *För levande och döda,* Anna Rydstedt's delicate simplicity in *Genom nålsögat,* Majken Johansson's punning despair in *Djup ropar till rop,* and Kristina Lugn's feminist gallows humour in *Hundstunden.* The fourth and fifth volumes of *Den Svenska Litteraturen,* edited by L. Lönnroth and S. Delblanc, appeared during the year.   (KARIN PETHERICK)

ITALIAN

Amid heated polemics about the decay of the Italian language, Sebastiano Vassalli published *Il neoitaliano*—not a dictionary of new words and idioms adopted and adapted daily by Italians but an attempt to portray, through a grinning discussion of neologisms, a wider process of cultural massification and degradation. However, the impression from reading old and new writers alike was that such new vocabulary hardly impinged on literary language, which seemed to show little, if any, movement away from the lofty models of established 20th-century tradition. Narrative prose in particular continued to pursue a standard of expression that was clear, sharp, and unrhetorical.

The best-selling, most widely discussed, and, according to opinion polls, least read among the year's books was *Il pendolo di Foucault* by Umberto Eco, an exceedingly long thriller in which a fictional worldwide conspiracy, starting from the dissolution of the Templars in the 14th century, imitates reality so perfectly that it becomes real itself and turns against its three hapless perpetrators. Greek myths were the subject of *Le nozze di Cadmo e Armonia* by Roberto Calasso, who combined scholarship with narrative freshness and originality, revisiting the ancient myths with an underlying nostalgia for ways of being and knowing now irreparably lost. The myth of the Sirens inspired *Il canto delle Sirene* by

Umberto Eco
JERRY BAUER

Maria Corti; the book gives narrative form to a desire for knowledge that charms its author as much as the mysterious voices from the sea charm its protagonists.

Ancient history, this time Roman, provided the background for Roberto Pazzi's *Vangelo di Giuda.* There, the Emperor Tiberius, coming across a poem about a Jewish prophet, rewrites it with the aim of changing the course of history; but poetry prevails, and Christianity and the Roman Empire are shown to be indissolubly joined in the same destiny of mutual destruction. Less visionary was *L'ereditiera veneziana* by Fulvio Tomizza, another historical novel, concerning the unhappy life of a well-to-do 18th-century Venetian woman whose inherited illness leads to a premature death. An irresistible mix of dialect, national language, and English placed Luigi Meneghello's latest book, *Bau-sète,* in a category all its own: a witty recollection, poised between irony and nostalgia, of what it was like to be young, intelligent, and full of hope in provincial Veneto at the end of World War II.

Many novels were inspired, more or less directly, by current social and political preoccupations. *Il cavaliere e la morte* was another of Leonardo Sciascia's political thrillers; in the absence of real political terrorism, the powerful invent it so as to hold onto power. The faceless might of modern industrial organizations pervades *Le mosche del capitale* by Paolo Volponi, a grotesque apologue brimming with indignation over the hypocrisy and lies in which, as the narrator would have it, Italian industry, finance, and public life are hopelessly immersed. Much blander was the picture of the professional classes in *La grande sera* by Giuseppe Pontiggia, the story of the family, lovers, and friends of a man whose disappearance forces them to reassess their past and future lives. Gianni Celati in *Verso la foce* recorded his journey down the Po Valley; the dismal countryside he observes bears the signs of ecological decay, dereliction, and human loneliness, but his act of observing, apparently bereft of emotions, is no less disturbing.

Francesca Duranti confirmed her reputation as one of Italy's major writers with

Effetti personali, in which a woman seeks to find and interview a writer from Eastern Europe who in reality does not exist. Sex of a voyeuristic kind continued to preoccupy the octogenarian Alberto Moravia. In *Il viaggio a Roma* a young man travels from Paris to Rome to meet the father whom he has not seen since boyhood; the meeting raises the traumatic memory of his dead mother, caught again in the act of sexually betraying his father, her eyes obsessively staring at the boy. Ferdinando Camon in *Il canto delle balene* treated a similar theme but with a much lighter hand. Here social satire and a comic register replace Moravia's morbid view of the bourgeois condition: a husband is unfaithful to his wife, not so as to repay her in kind but because every time they make love she runs and tells her analyst about it.

Many works of fiction by young or new writers were distinguished for their quality of writing and originality of themes. Particularly noteworthy were *Grande raccordo* by Marco Lodoli and *Il nocchiero* by Paola Capriolo. Finally, the sensational *Volevo i pantaloni* by Lara Cardella, a Sicilian teenager, exposed the taboos, violence, and cruelty of contemporary Sicilian society. Ostracized by family, friends, and fellow Sicilians as a result of her writing, Cardella suddenly found herself thrown into the limelight and adopted by a national media thirsting for scandals. Her book was the first to dislodge Eco's *Pendolo* from the top of the best-seller list. (LINO PERTILE)

SPANISH

Spain. The award of the 1989 Nobel Prize for Literature to Camilo José Cela (*see* BIOGRAPHIES) inevitably upstaged the important recognition given to two writers whose contributions both embraced and transcended purely creative literary concerns. Late in 1988 the distinguished essayist María Zambrano became, at 84, the first woman to receive the Premio Cervantes, the highest award in Hispanic letters, for her elegant meditations on a wide range of literary, aesthetic, and philosophical themes, most of them written during a 45-year exile that began at the close of the Spanish Civil War in 1939. Ricardo Gullón, 81, earned the Príncipe de Asturias Prize in letters for his enormous output as a versatile critic of 19th- and 20th-century Spanish authors.

In new fiction, Antonio Muñoz Molina's *Beltenebros*, a well-wrought, introspective tale of double cross and revenge set in the Madrid of the 1960s, had been on the best-seller list for over 30 weeks when another fast-rising novelist, Soledad Puértolas, won the rich Planeta Prize with her fifth novel, *Queda la noche*, also in a spy-counterspy mode and also with a philosophical twist. The year's other best-seller was *La isla inaudita*, Eduardo Mendoza's story of a burned-out businessman's search for self-knowledge along the damp and decadent waterways of Venice. Retaining the setting of his *Herrumbrosas lanzas* cycle but departing from the symphonic complexity of those works, Juan Benet offered *En la penumbra*, an intimate, myth-laden reverie cast in delicately balanced dialogues.

Assumptions about the essence of the novel form and its linguistic constraints had not been safe since Julián Ríos released Book I of his audacious *Larva* cycle

in 1983 (Mondadori's expanded edition of Book II, *Poundemónium* [1986], appeared in 1989). In *Impresiones de Kitaj (La novela pintada)*, Ríos went a step further. Collaborating with the reclusive American painter R.B. Kitaj, Ríos created an ingenious, 600-page "fiction painting" in which the author, three characters liberated from *Larva*, and the artist all confront each other, the paintings, and themselves in multiple intersecting planes, teaching readers to "see between the lines and read between the images."

The works of Antonio Machado (1875–1939), a preeminent voice in modern Spanish poetry, had never been collected in a single source until a four-volume edition, meticulously annotated by the prominent Italian Hispanist Oreste Macrì, was published on the 50th anniversary of the poet's death. (ROGER L. UTT)

Latin America. Carlos Fuentes and Gabriel García Márquez were the most prominent and visible Latin-American writers during a year in which relatively few major novels were published. Other important figures were Octavio Paz, Manuel Mejía Vallejo, and Salvador Garmendia.

Fuentes' novel *Cristóbal Nonato* (1987) appeared in English as *Christopher Unborn* in the United States. At the same time, his novel *Old Gringo* (1985) was seen in a film version, first in the Hispanic world and later in the year in the United States. García Márquez' novel about Simón Bolívar, *El general en su laberinto* (late 1988), was a highly polemical best-seller throughout the Hispanic world. Poet and essayist Octavio Paz received the Alexis de Tocqueville Prize in France. The Colombian novelist Manuel Mejía Vallejo, author of over a dozen novels, crowned his distinguished career by receiving Latin America's most prestigious literary award, the Rómulo Gallegos Novel Prize. Venezuelan Salvador Garmendia published the novel *El capitán Kid*.

The two most accomplished novels to appear in Mexico were *Nos imputaron la muerte del perro* by Alejandro Hernández and *Puertas antiguas* by Federico Patán. Hernández creates the legendary and extraordinary characters associated with Juan Rulfo and his generation of Latin-American writers. Patán's *Puertas antiguas* is a brief, subtle, and exceptionally well-crafted novel of human relationships. Two talented women writers in Mexico, Carmen Boullosa and Laura Esquivel, published noteworthy novels. Boullosa's *Antes* is a postmodern work dealing with the adolescent protagonist's rite of passage. Esquivel's light and humorous *Como agua para chocolate* was a best-seller in Mexico. Luís Zapata's *La hermana secreta de Angélica María*, set in the 1960s, deals with a hermaphrodite. Other novels to appear were María Luisa Puga's *Antonia* and Ignacio Solares' *Madero, el otro*. The renowned poet José Emilio Pacheco published *Ciudad de la memoria*, poems of the 1986–89 period.

The most noteworthy novels in Colombia were Álvaro Mutis' *Un bel morir*, Rodrigo Parra Sandoval's *La amante de Shakespeare*, Marco Tulio Aguilera Garramuño's *El juego de las seducciones*, and Fernando Vallejo's *Años de indulgencia*. In *Un bel morir*, Mutis continues the spiritual trip of Maqroll, protagonist of his previous

Gabriel García Márquez
EVA RUBINSTEIN—LEE GROSS, INC.

novels. The subject of Parra Sandoval's *La amante de Shakespeare* is the role of women in Cali. Aguilera Garramuño explores the sexuality of adolescence in his fourth novel, *El juego de las seducciones*. In *Años de indulgencia*, Vallejo continues with the same irreverence as in his earlier fiction. Other Colombian fiction included Andrés Hoyos' *Por el sendero de los ángeles caídos*, Evelio Rosero Diago's *Cuento para matar un perro*, and Harold Kremer's *Rumor de mar*. The Guberek Foundation published several outstanding books, including Carlos José Restrepo López's *Para subir al cielo*, Joaquín Mattos Omar's *Páginas de un desconocido*, and Eduardo Mendoza Varela's *El mediterráneo es un mar joven*.

In Argentina, Enrique Medina published one of his best novels to date, *El secreto*. After having explored a variety of aspects of marginality and sexuality in his previous work, he portrays the experiences of a divorced woman in Argentina. Noé Jitrik wrote a brief and innovative work, *Limbo*. Other noteworthy Argentine novels were Liliana Heer's *La tercera mitad*, Juan Carlos Martini's *La construcción del héroe*, and Silvia Iparraguirre's *En el invierno de las ciudades*.

Several established writers from other regions of Latin America, in addition to some new figures, published novels. Venezuela's Denzil Romero published his fifth book, *Grand Tour*, and later *Tardía declaración de amor a Seraphine Louis*. The Chilean Diamela Eltit continued her feminist project with her third and most accessible novel, *El cuarto mundo*. Chile's Nelson Oxman published the stories *La leyenda escandinava*. The Nicaraguan Gioconda Belli published her first novel, *La mujer habitada*.

(RAYMOND LESLIE WILLIAMS)

PORTUGUESE

Portugal. With the publication of *Rosa*, Mário Cláudio, a former winner of the national prize for fiction, completed the narrative cycle he started in 1984. Three famous artists from northern Portugal are the chief characters of the trilogy. The prize-winning novel *Amadeo* tells the story of the brilliant modernist painter of that

name; *Guilhermina* is an admirable portrait of the internationally famous cellist Guilhermina Suggia; and *Rosa,* about an untutored peasant woman who learned the secret of sculpting in clay, is the fictionalized biography of Rosa Ramalho. In *Rosa,* a narrative made up of interviews with Rosa Ramalho and people who knew her, Mário Cláudio captures the creative moods of an intelligent woman, vigorously expressing the harshness of peasant life and its history as passed on by oral tradition.

The changes in psychological time brought about by Portugal's newly established democracy, which haunt *Rosa,* are poignantly present in *Missa in Albis* ("Mass in Albis") by Maria Velho da Costa. Skillfully structured in accordance with the parts of the mass, this novel spans the troubled decades that preceded and followed April 1974, when the dictatorship collapsed. The characters are set against a background of social hypocrisy, where the struggle for their own identity raises fears and obsessions. An atmosphere of disease and disintegration pervades this compelling narrative, full of challenging allusions and written in a poetic vein.

The pursuit of happiness in a changing world is the theme of *Gente Feliz com Lágrimas* ("Happy People in Tears"), the novel for which João de Melo was awarded the Great Prize for Fiction. The novel concerns the members of a family from the Azores who moved to Portugal and were dispersed over different continents. Written in a straightforward style, the novel conveys a certain optimism in the face of life's trials. (L.S. REBELO)

Brazil. In a year made turbulent by presidential campaigning, economic chaos, and vocal worldwide concern for the Amazon, literary criticism flourished. In addition to collected essays by Luíz Costa Lima, Silviano Santiago, and Augusto de Campos, works of note included: Moacir Werneck de Castro's biography of Mário de Andrade's "exile" in Rio de Janeiro; Normal Telles' critical overview of once renowned but now forgotten women writers; Elizabeth Rennó's evaluation of Ledo Ivo's poetry; Maria Lúcia Pinheiro Sampaio's psychoanalytical approach to Machado de Assis' *Dom Casmurro;* Benedito Nunes' new analysis of Clarice Lispector's works, *O Drama da Linguagem;* and Fernando Peixoto's evaluation of recent Brazilian theatre. Important critical works published abroad included Paul Dixon's *Retired Dreams,* which studies *Dom Casmurro* from the angle of literary and cultural anthropology; Robert DiAntonio's *Brazilian Fiction;* and David Brookshaw's *Paradise Betrayed: Brazilian Literature of the Indian.*

Rubem Fonseca's best-selling novel *Vastas Emocões e Pensamentos Imperfeitos* is a fast-paced adventure about a film director's madcap sojourn to Eastern Europe. Antônio Callado's semiautobiographical *Memórias de Aldenham House* symbolically deals with the contemporary Latin-American dilemma through a tale set in England in the early years of World War II. Lygia Fagundes Telles returned to the novel genre with *As Horas Nuas,* the story of an aging actress adjusting, with great difficulty, to her limitations.

Several interesting regional novels appeared: Milton Hatoun's *Relato de um Certo Oriente,* about an immigrant Lebanese family in Manaus; Apolo Herringer Lisboa's *Escândalo no Arraial das Formigas,* based on a true 1980s financial scandal in Minas Gerais; Luiz Vilela's *Graca,* set in a small town in Minas Gerais; and Raimundo Carrero's *Macã Agreste,* set in Pernambuco. Also of note were Jorge Amado's *O sumico da santa;* João Gilberto Noll's *Hotel Atlântico;* and Sônia Coutinho's *Atire em Sofia.* Notable collections of short fiction were Victor Giudice's *Salvador Janta no Lamas;* Moacyr Scliar's *As Orelhas de Van Gogh* (awarded the Cuban Casa de las Américas Prize in 1988); and Sérgio Sant'Anna's *A Senhorita Simpson.*

New poems were published by Olga Savary, *Berço Esplêndido;* Mário Quintana, *A Côr do Invisível;* and Zuleika Reis, *Espelhos em Fuga.* Fernando Paixão's debut as a poet was *Fogo dos Rios.* In *Rumor das Facas,* Pedro Paulo de Sena Madureira speaks of homosexual love. Denira Rozário's interviews with 20 contemporary poets appeared in print as *Palavra do Poeta.* Finally, the literary world mourned the deaths of Oswaldo Franca, Jr., and Paulo Leminiski. (IRWIN STERN)

RUSSIAN

Soviet Literature. Aleksandr Solzhenitsyn was once again available to Soviet readers. Selected chapters from *The Gulag Archipelago* were appearing in one of the leading literary monthlies. His short stories, Nobel lecture, several plays and essays, and occasional interviews also found their way into print. Shortly to appear were *Cancer Ward, The First Circle, The Red Wheel,* and seven volumes of selected works.

The writings of other civil rights campaigners—some forced to emigrate, others elbowed into obscurity, and many who gave their lives—were being offered to vast Soviet readerships. Among the best known were Anatoly Marchenko's fictionalized autobiography *Live like Anyone Else,* the works of Viktor Nekrasov and Yuli Daniel, Leonid Borodin's novellas, and Vadim Delonnais' verse and prose. Also new to the Soviet press were authors who had lived abroad after the Revolution, like Vladimir Nabokov, Ivan Shmelev, and Boris Zaitsev, and "Third Wave" émigrés who had fled during the last two decades to escape the stifling atmosphere and obstacles to publication.

Georgy Vladimov's novel *Faithful Ruslan,* a parable about the deadly influence of Stalinism on its loyal servants, was notable even in the context of 20th-century Russian literature. Vasily Aksyonov was triumphantly back in the Soviet press. Sasha Sokolov, with his novels *A Fools' School, Entre chien et loup,* and *Palisandria,* represented an esoteric trend in Russian artistic prose. Vladimir Voinovich's comic fantasy *The Life and Extraordinary Adventures of Private Ivan Chonkin* and his short novels *The Hat* and *By Mutual Exchange of Letters* attracted readers for their political satire and typically Russian self-irony. *Oktyabr,* a prominent national literary monthly, caused a sensation by carrying excerpts from Abram Tertz's (Andrey Sinavsky's) utterly unconventional *Walks with Pushkin.* Edward Limonov made his first appearance outside samizdat (underground publications) with the novel *We Had a Landmark Time,* about the late 1940s and early '50s.

Of great interest were the four-volume *Triumph and Tragedy,* a profile of Stalin as politician by Gen. Dmitry Volkogonov; *Twenty Letters to a Friend* by Svetlana Alliluyeva, Stalin's daughter; and Roy Medvedev's series of historical essays *They Surrounded Stalin* and his political biography of Khrushchev. Among newly begun editions were the *Encyclopaedia of Russian Authors: 1800–1917* and the long-awaited complete works of Anna Akhmatova, Mikhail Bulgakov, and Boris Pasternak.

The Soviet literary underground emerged into the daylight with a spate of homemade magazines. The major literary journals could be divided into two hostile camps: liberal-democratic (*Ogonyok, Znamya, Oktyabr, Yunost, Novy Mir,* and *Druzhba Narodov*) and neo-Slavophile conservative (*Nash Sovremennik, Molodaya Gvardia, Moskva,* and *Literaturnaya Rossia.* (SERGEI CHUPRININ)

Expatriate Russian Literature. Statistically, more works by émigré writers were published in the U.S.S.R. than abroad in 1989. Two highly significant Russian poets, Bakhyt Kenjeev and Aleksey Tzvetkov, and a previously denounced Byelorussian poet, Masey Sednew, appeared in the official Soviet press for the first time. The publications in the Soviet Union, however, consisted largely of reprints of works that had already appeared abroad.

Thanks to changes in official Soviet policy, a noticeable trend developed among émigrés of establishing closer ties to the mother country through visits and publications. While some writers were careful in dealing with the official Soviet press, many others eagerly sought out such opportunities. A new genre appeared in émigré periodicals—the "travelogue" recording observations from trips to the Soviet Union. Slavic conferences throughout the world were attended by an unprecedented number of Soviet intellectuals, and émigré newspapers and journals published papers by Soviet scholars.

The centenary of Anna Akhmatova's birth was celebrated jointly by Soviet and émigré scholars and writers at numerous conferences and commemorated by several publications. Among them were the selected poetry of Akhmatova, *Izbrannaia poezia,* edited by N.A. Struve; a collection of essays by both émigré and Soviet scholars, *Akhmatovskii Sbornik,* edited by S. Dediulin and G. Superfin; and a reprint of three works from the 1920s by B. Eikhenbaum, V. Vinogradov, and V. Zhirmunskii, *Tri knigi* ("Three Books").

Other noteworthy works of literary criticism included Vadim Kreyd's first full-length study of émigré poet Georgii Ivanov, *Peterburgskii period Georgiia Ivanova* ("The Petersburg Period of Georgii Ivanov"); Veronika Losskaia's collection of memoirs, *Marina Tsvetaeva v zhizni: Neizdannye vospominania sovremennikov* ("Marina Tsvetaeva in Life: Unpublished Recollections of Her Contemporaries"); and Efim Etkind's *Stikhi i liudi: Rasskazy o stikhotvoreniiakh* ("Poems and People: Stories About Poetry"). At the end of 1988 two important reference works appeared: *Zabytyi avangard* ("The Forgotten Avant-garde"), edited by K. Kuz'minskii, G. Janecek, and A. Ocheretianskii; and Temira Pachmuss' *Russian Literature in the Baltic Between the World Wars.*

Several new collections of poetry appeared during the year: Dimitry Bobyshev's *Zveri sviatogo Antoniia* ("St. Anthony's Animals"); Bakhyt Kenjeev's *Osen' v Amerike* ("Autumn in America"); Valentina Sinkevich's *Zdes' ia zhivu* ("Here I Live"); Jurii Kublianovskii's *Zat'mene* ("Eclipse"); and Aleksey Shel'vakh's *Chernovik otvagi* ("Notebook of Courage"), previously known only from samizdat. The collected works of the émigré poet and writer Igor Terentev, *Sobranie sochinenii*, were compiled by M. Marzaduri and I. Nikol'skaia. Irina Ratushinskaya published *Seryi—tsvet nadezhdy* ("Grey is the Colour of Hope"), a vivid record of life in a Moldavian labour camp.

(EDWARD J. CZERWINSKI; AGNIESZKA YURIEFF)

EASTERN EUROPEAN

The year 1989 would be remembered more in history than in literature. The upheavals in Poland, Hungary, Czechoslovakia, East Germany, and Bulgaria influenced every aspect of life in Eastern Europe. Even Romania broke from the ranks of totalitarian states, though Yugoslavia, with its continuing economic and political problems, was unable to extricate itself from its post-Tito syndrome.

Izabella Cywinska, Poland's newly appointed minister of culture, had long been known as "Iron Iza." As a director of the Nowy Theatre in Poznan, she was instrumental in developing such brilliant talents as the director Janusz Wisniewski and the superb actor Janusz Michalowski (her husband). In her acceptance speech, Cywinska pulled no punches: "I accept the position under the condition that weak artists will be removed from their posts and talented people will be given every opportunity to create."

Even before Cywinska's speech, a number of excellent works had appeared in both the official and independent press. The most anticipated was Maria Dabrowska's *Dzienniki* ("Diaries") in five volumes, covering the years 1914–65. According to Czeslaw Hernas, 39 phrases or sentences were excised by the official censor and then quickly published by the independent journal *Kultura niezalezna.* Marek Nowakowski's *Dwa Dni z aniolem* ("Two Days with an Angel") was published in Paris. Pawel Jasienica's *Polska anarchia* ("Polish Anarchy"), a collection of polemical essays, was published for the first time in Krakow, while Andrzej Szczepanski's *Poczatek* ("The Beginning") was published simultaneously in Poland and West Germany in 1988. Perhaps most exciting was Kazimierz Brandys' *Rondo* (translated by Jaroslaw Anders). The novelist-critic Phillip Lopate called the work "the summation of a lifetime's struggle for understanding."

Yugoslavia mourned the loss of one of its most talented novelist-dramatists, Danilo Kis, who for the last 10 years of his life lived in Paris. The greatest publishing sensation continued to be Milorad Pavic's *Dictionary of the Khazars: A Lexicon Novel in 100,000 Words.* One of Yugoslavia's greatest poets, Miodrag Pavlovic, published a collection, *Knjiga staroslovna* ("The Archaic Book"). Blaze Koneski, Macedonia's best poet, also published a critically acclaimed collection, *Seizmograf*

("Seismograph"). The final volume of Dobrica Cosic's trilogy, *Vreme zla* ("A Time of Evil"), received critical praise. The Battle of Kosovo was given a contemporary interpretation by Lujbomir Simovic in *Boj na Kosovu* ("Battle in Kosovo").

The best of Czech and Slovak literature continued to be published in Toronto by Sixty-Eight Publishers. Outstanding in 1989 was Milan Uhde's *Velice tiché Ave* ("A Very Silent Ave"). A few items appeared in Czechoslovakia's official press. Bohumil Hrabal's story of a waiter confronted by life's daily hazards, *Obsluhoval jsem anglického krále* ("I Served the English King"), was published in 190,000 copies, after having been printed in samizdat (underground publications; *petlice,* or "padlock," in Czech). His novel *Tanecni hodiny pro starsi a pokrocile* ("Dancing Classes for Older and Advanced") received critical acclaim, and a reprint of a selection of his stories, *Chcete videt zlatou Prahu?* ("Do You Want to See Golden Prague?"), appeared together with a 90-page critical study on the author—the first of its kind in Czechoslovakia. The trend toward liberalization could also be discerned in the publication of Jiri Suchy's *Pisnova tvorba Semaforu* ("The Semaphor's Songbook"), a memorial to the Semafor Theatre's golden days before and during the Soviet invasion. Two debuts received critical attention: Petr Bartunek's *Slavnostni odhaleni sochy* ("The Ceremonial Unveiling of a Statue") and Jan Kostrhun's *Svatba ve vypujcenych satech* ("A Wedding in Rented Clothes").

Bulgaria was also experiencing a metamorphosis. Although Stanislav Stratiev and Yordan Radichkov did not publish any new works, their plays continued to be popular. Ivailo Petrov's *Hajka za vyltsi* ("The Shooting Party for Wolves") finally was published in novel form, after having been censored in the midst of serialization in 1987.

(EDWARD J. CZERWINSKI; AGNIESZKA YURIEFF)

JEWISH

Hebrew. In 1989 significant works of fiction were published by Israel's veteran writers. These included Amos Oz's *Lada'at 'Isha,* Nissim Aloni's *ha'Ish Ba'al ha-Gavnon haKaful,* David Shahar's *Halom Leil Tammuz,* Aharon Appelfeld's *Katrina,* Shulamit Hareven's *Navi,* and the late Benjamin Tammuz' *haZikit Vehazamir.* Other works were penned by Yonat and Alexander Sened, Dan Tselka, Yehudit Haendel, David Schitz, Aharon Almog, Shulamit Lapid, and Gideon Telpaz.

Several new or young writers produced impressive works. Yitzhak Bar-Yosef wrote his first short-story collection, *Siparti et ze, Yehezkel,* and a first novel, *Hadar Milhama.* Aner Shalev penned a volume entitled *Opus 1,* and Miri Varon published her first collection, *Kala 'Afa.* New poetry collections included Leah Eilon's *Daniel Daniel,* Pinhas Sadeh's *Shirim 1985–88,* Gad Kenar's *Hayekha hakliniyim,* Dina Katan's *Milim Mafligot, Hibur Vehisur* by Hazi Leskali, and *Shirei Halon,* a first collection of poems by the novelist Shulamit Lapid.

Important critical studies published were Ziva Shamir's work on Nathan Alterman and Modernism, Yitzhak Bacon's *Agnon haTsa'ir,* Nurit Govrin's research on Eretz

Yisrael literature, Lilly Ratok's study of Aharon Appelfeld's fiction, and Hamutal Bar-Yosef's book on Zelda. Other volumes were penned by Ida Tsurit on Amir Gilboa, Hagit Halprin on Alexander Pen, and Dina Stern and Gavriel Moked with respective works on several S.Y. Agnon stories. Nurit Geertz and Ortsiyon Bartana published their respective critical perspectives on Israeli literature in the 1930s and in contemporary times.

A.B. Yehoshua penned a nonfiction volume on the "nonliterary reality" of the Israeli writer, and a collection of essays on Yehuda Amichai's work was published in the Hakibbutz Hameuchad series. Shmuel Werses, professor of Hebrew literature at the Hebrew University, was awarded the prestigious Israel Prize. Mourned in 1989 were the critic and teacher Dov Sadan, the poet Avraham Halfi, and the novelists Benjamin Tammuz and Dan Ben-Amotz.

(WARREN BARGAD)

Yiddish. Several welcome initiatives were apparent in 1989. *Steps to a Miracle,* a compelling volume of autobiographical sketches by the young Soviet writer Boris Sandler, was emblematic of the new voices that were emerging. *Vidervuks* ("New Growth"), an anthology of prose, poetry, and essays by 20 writers born after World War II, appeared in New York. *Yungvald* ("Young Growth"), a journal aimed at young student-readers, came out in Moscow.

Criticism occupied a major place, with analysis by Y. Kh. Biletski, *Lyricists in Yiddish Literature;* Yitskhak Korn's *Yiddish in Rumania;* Yoysef Ludin's second volume of essays, *Storm Warnings;* Dov Sadan's erudite and sometimes playful *Yiddish: Essence and Environment;* Moyshe Shapiro's provocative *Conversations About Yiddish;* and Chone Shmeruk's magisterial *Chapters from Yiddish Literary History.* Four other works merited special note: *Pearls of Yiddish Songs,* containing lyrics and music, by Yosl and Hannah Mlotek; *Sholem Aleykhem: His Life in Pictures,* assembled by Avrom Lis; Issakhar Ber Teller's medieval medical handbook, *The Wellspring of Living Waters,* edited by Arthur Teller; and number 125 of the Tel Aviv-based literary quarterly *Di goldene keyt,* observing 40 years of publication.

Significant works of poetry included M.M. Shaffir's *The Final Cluster;* a posthumous book of verse by Shloyme Shvarts, *Universes of Steel;* Hadasa Rubin's *On the Eve of Time;* and Rokhl Boymvol's *Occasional Poems.* Prose entries constituted an important segment of the year's output. Lili Berger's *In Flight from Time* demonstrated her great expressive power. Israel-based Yosl Birshteyn contributed *Your Little Streets, Jerusalem.* Nakhman Blits's *The Silent Princess* is made up of two novellas, and Yisroel Kaplan's *Footprints of Time* is divided into two amusing and touching tales. Leyzer Podriatshik's *Song and Prayer* was a striking collection of Soviet Yiddish writers. The two peaks of the year were Elye Shekhtman's *Rings on the Soul,* the conclusion of his sweeping epic of a Yiddish writer moving to the State of Israel, and a volume of stories, *The Prophecy of the Apple of Your Eye,* by Avrom Sutskever, the pivotal figure on the modern Yiddish literary scene.

(THOMAS E. BIRD)

CHINESE

During the first half of 1989 there was optimism that the recent upswing in literary accomplishment would continue in China. Although fewer literary magazines were being published, the quality, diversity, and boldness of their offerings fostered excitement. This optimism was shattered in early June as the nascent democracy movement was crushed in Tiananmen (T'ien-an-men) Square, and the year ended with the suspended publication of announced books and a noticeable drying up of contributions to literary magazines. Dozens of cultural figures fled to the West; of those who remained, some had been arrested and large numbers were under investigation.

The greatest harvest was reaped in fiction, most notably autobiographical novels of thought reform, political misadventures, and Cultural Revolution excesses. They included *Bathing* by Yang Jiang (Yang Chiang), *Walking Toward Chaos* by Cong Weixi (Ts'ung Wei-hsi), and the final volume of *Snow City* by Liang Xiaosheng (Liang Hsiao-sheng). A translation of Nien Cheng's *Life and Death in Shanghai* also appeared. The latest novels by Mo Yan (Mo Yen; *Thirteen Steps*) and Zhang Jie (Chang Chieh; *There Is Only One Sun*) appeared in magazines prior to June 4, but book publication was suspended. A fine collection of contemporary literature, *Chinese New Wave Fiction,* was published in Beijing (Peking) in April.

Avant-garde poets published prolifically in magazines, but few collections of worth found their way into bookstores. Volumes of essays, including one by the expatriate dissident Liu Binyan (Liu Pin-yen), whose Harvard speeches were being prepared in translation, were shelved.

Mainland Chinese literature was extremely popular in Taiwan, where novels by Mo Yan (*A Song of Garlic in Paradise* and *The Red Sorghum Clan*), Gu Hua (Ku Hua; *The Ivy-Covered Log Cabin* and *Scholars Park*), and Jia Pingwa (Chia P'ing-wa; *Turbulence,* the Mobil Corp. Pegasus Prize winner for 1989) were published, with royalties paid to the authors. Among indigenous writing in Taiwan, two

anthologies with the identical title of *The Hues of Love* appeared in response to reader interest in stories on the theme of romantic love, although some of the stories are decidedly nonromantic. Established authors like Chang Ta-ch'un, Chang Hsi-kuo, and Su Wei-chen published novels or story collections, but more exciting was the emergence of young writers like Ch'en Yeh, whose *Muddy River* broaches the heretofore forbidden subject of the brutal occupation of Taiwan by the Nationalists in 1948. The most significant literary event in Taiwan was the publication of the 12-volume *Compendium of Taiwan Literature: 1970–1989,* under the general editorship of the poet Yü Kuang-chung.

It was a banner year for English-language translations of Chinese literature in the U.S. and Great Britain. The focus began to shift from anthologies to volumes by individual authors. Noteworthy works included *Baotown,* the third book in translation by Wang Anyi (Wang An-yi); *The Piano Tuner* by her fellow Shanghai author Cheng Naishan (Ch'eng Nai-shan); a collection of stories by the avant-garde writer Duo Duo (To To), *Looking Out from Death; Bolshevik Salute* by Wang Meng, the recently deposed minister of culture; *Heavy Wings* by Zhang Jie (Chang Chieh); two excellent anthologies, *Spring Bamboo* and *Science Fiction from China: Eight Stories;* and the first serious gay novel in Chinese, *Crystal Boys* by the Taiwan novelist Pai Hsien-yung. At least two collections of poetry stemming from the Tiananmen incident were being prepared for publication in translation in the West. The immediate future of Chinese literature seemed brighter in the West than in China itself.   (HOWARD C. GOLDBLATT)

JAPANESE

There was much talk of the "Banana phenomenon" during the year. Banana Yoshimoto had written six books (collections of novelettes, short stories, and essays), whose total circulation already amounted to more than four million. One reason was the highly sympathetic response she roused among young women readers. Still in her 20s, she vividly expressed the mood,

Banana Yoshimoto

caprices, and fantasies of the young women of contemporary Japan, though her books could not be called feminist. *Shirakawa Yobune* ("Falling Sound Asleep"), the title story of her most recent book, concerned a young woman who could sleep well at any time of day. What could her "sleep" mean? Escape from actuality? Longing to secure "pure privacy"? Young Japanese seemed to be enjoying unprecedented prosperity and freedom, but they were actually insecure in their new status. Yoshimoto's tremendous success could be attributed to her subtle sense of this ambivalence.

Another literary phenomenon was the remarkable success of the biographical novel *Confucius* by Yasushi Inoue, an octogenarian writer. Confucius' works were standard texts for prewar high school students, but after the war the ancient Chinese sage was almost totally neglected. It would seem that Inoue's *Confucius* would appeal mainly to the older generation, but the responses of young readers also proved favourable. Perhaps they were looking for spiritual leadership. Indeed, Confucianism still seemed to be influential in the newly industrializing countries of Asia. Hideo Takubo's *Frozen Dream* was another impressive novel, both for its spiritual theme and for its technical virtuosity.

Two remarkable biographies appeared, both highly readable evocations of Japanese "eccentrics"—*Woman, Woman, and Woman* by Ei Muramatsu and *Story of Musoan* by Natsuhiko Yamamoto. The former is a life story of a popular novelist, by his own son, and the latter, a detailed exposé of a Japanese exile in prewar Paris, by his disciple. In literary criticism, Makoto Ooka's *Poetics of Blurring* is a sensitive analysis of the tragic career of the scholar-statesman Michizane Sugawara. Takaaki Yoshimoto's *Kenji Miyazazwa* and Shoichi Saeki's *The Essence of Shintoism* are both probing explorations of the religious basis of the Japanese imagination.

(SHOICHI SAEKI)

See also Art Exhibitions and Art Sales: *Art Sales;* Libraries; Publishing.

This article updates the *Macropædia* article The History of Western LITERATURE and articles on the literatures of the various languages.

Wang Anyi (left) and Cheng Naishan

Mathematics

Mathematicians' instinct is to find order, and thus predictable behaviour, in seemingly disordered situations. This is nowhere better evident than in the emerging theory of chaos, which in recent years has been used to model hundreds of irregular phenomena, from turbulence in fluids and the daily weather to disease epidemics and traffic jams. During 1989 chaos both grew in popularity and took on an element of controversy.

Chaos theory is a part of topological dynamics, which treats the behaviour of systems over time, and it has been motivated largely by developments in computers. Classically, mathematicians have used calculus to study dynamical systems. A collection of stars, for example, moves according to Newton's laws of motion, and one can determine a set of differential equations that, in principle, describes the motion of the system for all time. For large numbers of stars, however, great computational effort is needed to determine where each star will be after some time interval. Given initial positions and velocities of all the stars, Newton's laws predict (approximately) their new positions and velocities after some small interval. To predict these values farther in the future, one resorts to the tremendous "number-crunching" power of computers to repeat the process over and over again, substituting the new positions and velocities as initial values in the equations and recalculating.

A (discrete) dynamical system is the abstraction of this idea. Start with a function—a rule that takes numbers and assigns new numbers—and choose a particular number. Apply the function to get a new number, apply the function to this new number, and so on, always using the output as the next input—a process called iteration. The collection of numbers produced in this way is called the orbit of the starting number. For example, if the function is the rule "multiply by $\frac{1}{2}$," written $f(x) = x/2$, and if the initial number is 4, the orbit is the set of numbers 2, 1, $\frac{1}{2}$, $\frac{1}{4}$, ..., n, in which n gets closer and closer to zero. The same behaviour is true for any starting number except zero. The orbit of zero is zero itself (repeated infinitely often), and so zero is called a fixed point of the function. Another example is "multiply the product of x and $1 - x$ by 3," written $f(x) = 3x(1 - x)$. This time, when the initial value is any number between 0 and 1, the numbers in the orbit get closer and closer to $\frac{2}{3}$. The number $\frac{2}{3}$ itself remains fixed by the function.

The behaviour of the orbits in both examples is quite predictable—they are attracted to a fixed point. It is therefore surprising that a similar function, "multiply the product of x and $1 - x$ by 4," written $f(x) = 4x(1 - x)$, has an altogether different behaviour that makes it difficult to predict almost anything. With a starting number between 0 and 1, the numbers in the orbit appear to wander aimlessly over the interval. Moreover, if the orbits of two different but close starting values (say, 0.7 and 0.701) are compared, after just a few iterations the numbers are far apart; in other words, the orbits are sensitive to the starting points. The orbits appear to be random—chaotic, in the everyday sense of the word. In the midst of the randomness, however, there is hidden order and predictability. In fact, near any number between 0 and 1 there is another number with a completely predictable orbit; after a number of iterations, the orbit returns to the starting value and then repeats the process over again. (Such behaviour is called periodic.) These ingredients—the presence of orbits that wander over the interval and are sensitive to starting values, plus the presence of predictable orbits near any point—characterize what mathematicians mean by chaos.

The last two functions discussed suggest a whole family of simple dynamical systems for study; namely, "multiply the product of x and $1 - x$ by m," in which m is a number between 3 and 4. On one side, when $m = 3$, the orbits are predictable. On the other, when $m = 4$, they are chaotic. What happens in between? That is precisely what the theory of chaos tries to describe—how dynamical systems change from predictable to chaotic.

But is chaos theory a revolutionary new way of looking at dynamical systems and, by extension, of perceiving the physical world? During the year, mathematicians and scientists debated whether chaos is really new mathematics or merely old mathematics in new clothes and whether it is as incisive as its proponents claim in portraying the real universe as one of messy complexity rather than clockwork order. Considering the many research fronts on which chaos theory was being applied, some answers should not be long in coming. (JOHN EWING)

This article updates the *Macropædia* article GEOMETRY.

Military Affairs

Two major military actions took place at the end of 1989. On December 20 U.S. forces landed in Panama to replace military strongman Manuel Noriega with the democratic government of Guillermo Endara. Also in December the Romanian Army revolted against and overthrew Pres. Nicolae Ceaucescu after the latter's security police killed pro-democracy demonstrators in Timisoara.

The most significant defense event of 1989, however, was the December summit meeting off the coast of Malta between U.S. Pres. George Bush (*see* BIOGRAPHIES) and Soviet Pres. Mikhail Gorbachev, their first meeting since Bush's election. No major formal agreements were reached, although progress was made toward a START (Strategic Arms Reduction Talks) treaty (see *Arms Control and Disarmament,* below) and a full-scale summit was to be held early in 1991. This summit symbolized the change in the superpower relationship from one of high confrontation and low instability to one of low confrontation and high instability. This increased instability was especially evident in Eastern Europe, where the non-Soviet members of the Warsaw Pact were engaged in major political reforms that were changing the nature of the pact.

During the 40-year U.S.-Soviet cold war, the superpower relationship had been one of military and political confrontation. The Soviets had established and maintained their control over their Eastern European empire by their armies, which had crushed attempts at reform in East Germany (1953), Hungary (1956), and Czechoslovakia (1968). To contain the Soviets from further expansion, the U.S. and its Western European allies had formulated the North Atlantic Treaty Organization (NATO) and had built up their nuclear and conventional military forces to deter a potential attack by the U.S.S.R. The result was the world's largest confrontation of military forces on either side of an iron curtain stretching from the Baltic to the Balkans. Because this confrontation was at such a high level, however, it proved to be extremely stable. Despite the Soviets' large military advantages, successive Soviet leaders had decided that the possible gains for using their forces to threaten or to attack Western Europe were outweighed by the risks included, especially the risk of nuclear weapons being used. The result was that no war had been fought in Europe for more than 40 years.

Nevertheless, Gorbachev's reforms, though reducing the level of this East-West confrontation in Europe, were introducing new instabilities. In his Dec. 7, 1988, speech to the UN General Assembly, he had announced a major unilateral cutback in Soviet conventional forces totaling 500,000 personnel, and these cuts were indeed being made. Combining this with continued political reforms in Eastern Europe reduced the Soviet military threat to Western Europe and the Soviet ability to control their Eastern European empire and to prevent a breakup of the Warsaw Pact. The U.S.S.R. could not expect support for an attack on NATO from Poland's Solidarity government or from Hungary, Czechoslovakia, or Romania. Also, the decision by East Germany to allow free emigration to West Germany meant that a partial reunification of Germany was occurring that would make it impossible for the East German Army to attack the West German Army.

These changes were creating new sources of instability. In particular, they raised the question of how far Gorbachev could allow them to go before he lost the ability to control them. Even a limited Soviet use of force in Eastern Europe, though, would jeopardize his whole reform progress and could trigger a conflict with the Eastern Europe armies.

The need for the U.S. and Soviet leaders to keep these new instabilities within manageable bounds was a major issue for the December superpower summit. At the same time, it seemed that neither the U.S. nor the Soviets could exert the kind of influence they had exerted at the height of the cold war. This point was emphasized in an important speech in September by U.S. Deputy Secretary of State Lawrence Eagleburger. He said that the U.S. had won the cold war because the idea of democracy had triumphed over the idea of Marxism, but also that both superpowers had finished the cold war out of breath, with a much-reduced ability to influence events in a world of many major military and economic powers.

The Eagleburger doctrine of reduced superpower influence was certainly supported by the continuation of Third World conflicts and the proliferation of advanced military technology that made such conflicts more destructive. The two most dangerous weapons systems that were proliferating were short-to-medium-range ballistic missile systems (S/MRBM), with ranges up to about 1,000 km (620 mi), and chemical weapons, including nerve gas. Both weapons systems had been used extensively in the Iran-Iraq war, with Iraq's massive use of the latter violating the 1925 Geneva Protocol, which banned the first use of chemical weapons but did permit them to be employed for retaliatory purposes. The use of chemical weapons in the Iraq-Iran war violated the protocol's no-first-use rule and also represented the first wartime use of the much more deadly nerve gases that were developed after World War I.

Afghanistan Pres. Mohammad Najibullah's use of Soviet-supplied SS-1 Scud SRBM against the Muslim rebels further emphasized the proliferation and use of advanced weapons. However, the Soviets' continued support of Najibullah also emphasized the contradiction between Gorbachev's reforms and his support for old military policies.

The linked 1988 U.S.-Soviet and Pakistan-Afghanistan agreements committed the Soviets to withdrawing all of their military forces from Afghanistan by Feb. 15, 1989. The Afghanistan agreements included the concept of "positive symmetry," meaning that if the Soviets continued to supply their puppet government in Kabul with military equipment, the U.S. would continue to supply the rebels with sophisticated weapons, including the Stinger antiaircraft missiles that had proved highly effective. However, the Soviets claimed that this concept violated the agreement

and sharply increased their military aid to Najibullah, to about $300 million per year. The U.S.S.R. also provided military advisers and supported heavy bombing raids with Su-27 strike aircraft and Tu-26 Backfire strategic bombers, the first combat use of the latter.

The U.S. responded to these Soviet actions by increasing weapons supplies to the rebels and insisting that the Soviets observe the Afghanistan agreements, including the positive symmetry provision. President Bush remained committed to this policy. Afghanistan thus seemed set to provide the first major test of Gorbachev's new thinking in defense policy. To translate this new thinking into practice, the Soviets would have to observe the agreements, cut off aid, and risk the replacement of their puppet, President Najibullah, by a freely elected government. Alternatively, the Soviets could continue their support for Najibullah at the cost of straining the U.S.-Soviet relationship. At the year's end the U.S.S.R. continued to supply massive military aid to Najibullah.

UNITED STATES

The U.S. all-volunteer armed forces in 1989 totaled 2,124,-900 personnel (211,200 women). Both retention rates and personnel quality remained at record high levels. Defense spending for fiscal 1989, at $289.8 billion, represented some 6.4% of gross domestic product (GDP) and approximately 27% of the federal budget.

U.S. strategic nuclear forces (SNF) continued their modest modernization programs. The Strategic Air Command (SAC) had 97 new Rockwell B-1B strategic bombers, although these planes continued to suffer from defects limiting their effectiveness.

The elderly B-52 bomber force remained at 167 B-52Gs and 96 B-52Hs (first deployed in 1959 and 1962, respectively). Of the B-52Gs, 84 carried 12 AGM-86B air-launched cruise missiles (ALCM) each, while 61 were equipped with the Harpoon air-to-surface missile (ASM) and were intended for a nonnuclear antishipping role. SAC also had 62 FB-111A medium-range nuclear bombers. Development of the advanced technology (Stealth) bomber, the B-2, and the advanced cruise missile continued, with the B-2 making its first flight.

The land-based, fixed-silo intercontinental ballistic missile (ICBM) force remained vulnerable to a Soviet attack. It consisted of 1,000 silos, containing MX Peacekeeper, Minuteman II, and Minuteman III ICBM. The Peacekeeper, which was intended to modernize the ICBM force, was to have been deceptively based, but political pressures limited the deployment to 50 Peacekeepers in vulnerable Minuteman silos. All of these large missiles were operational, each weighing 88,000 kg (195,000 lb) and carrying 10 multiple independently targetable reentry vehicles (MIRV). The 500 Minuteman IIIs were modernized missiles, each carrying three MIRV. The 450 Minuteman II missiles were more than 20 years old. Development of the single-warhead Midgetman small ICBM, or SICBM, (about 11,350 kg [25,000 lb]) continued, but the high costs of this system made its deployment unlikely.

The ballistic missile nuclear submarine (SSBN) force totaled 35, carrying 608 submarine-launched ballistic missiles (SLBM). The nine new Ohio-class SSBN each carried 24 Trident I/C-4s, which were to be replaced by the Trident II/D-5 SLBM from 1989 onward. The first submersed firing test of a Trident II was unsuccessful, however, and so deployment of these missiles could be delayed. Older SSBN included 12 Franklin class (96 Trident I/C-4s and 96 Poseidon C-3s) and 14 Madison and Lafayette class (96 Trident I/C-4s and 128 Poseidon C-3s). The deploy-

ment of submarine-launched nuclear cruise missiles continued, with 10 nuclear cruise-missile submarines (SSGN) so equipped. Plans called for a total of about 750 BGM-109A Tomahawk sea-launched cruise missiles (SLCM). In addition, 2,300 conventionally armed Tomahawk SLCM were being deployed to give each vessel a mix of nuclear and conventionally armed missiles. Dispersing the nuclear SLCM would enhance their survivability.

The U.S. Navy at the end of 1989 totaled 229 principal surface combatants, 93 nuclear-powered attack submarines (SSN), and 583,900 personnel. These provided 14 carrier and 4 battleship groups, each carrier having an attack wing of some 86 aircraft plus escorting surface vessels and SSN. Of the 13 modern (post-1955) aircraft carriers, 5 were nuclear powered. Modern aircraft included 398 F-14A Tomcat interceptors, 340 A-6 Intruder/Prowler and 246 F/A-18A Hornet strike planes, and 86 E-2C electronic warfare/airborne early warning aircraft. All four World War II Iowa-class battleships were recommissioned with Tomahawk SLCM, but one, the *Iowa,* suffered an explosion that destroyed one of its three main gun turrets and killed 47 crew members. The 9 nuclear- and 32 conventionally powered guided-weapons (GW) cruisers included 14 new Ticonderoga-class ships equipped with the Aegis fleet air defense missile/radar system. Other major surface combatants included 37 GW and 31 gun/antisubmarine warfare (ASW) Spruance-class destroyers.

The Marine Corps, with 195,300 personnel, was organized in three divisions, each with its air wing. Modern aircraft included 186 F/A-18 Hornet interceptor/strike aircraft, 76 A-6 Intruder strike aircraft, and 141 AV-8A/C Harrier vertical/short takeoff and landing (V/STOL) interceptor/strike aircraft.

The 579,200-strong Air Force had approximately 3,577 combat aircraft plus 1,000 in storage. Among modern types were 642 F-15 Eagle interceptors, 1,083 F-16 Falcon fighter-bombers, and 34 E-3A Sentry airborne warning and control systems (AWACS). Older types included 677 F-4 Phantom fighter-bombers/reconnaissance, 219 F-111A/D/E/F medium bombers, and 538 A-10A Thunderbolt ground-support aircraft.

The Army, with 776,500 personnel, formed 14 heavy divisions (about 16,000 men each)—4 armoured, 7 mechanized, 1 infantry, 1 air assault; and 1 airborne division—plus 4 light infantry divisions (about 10,200 men each). The light infantry divisions were easier to transport and were intended as part of the Rapid Deployment Force for use outside NATO-Europe. Armour included 5,994 M-1/1A1 Abrams tanks and 4,883 M-2/3 Bradley mechanized infantry combat vehicles (MICV), plus some 8,887 M60A1/2 and M60A3 tanks and 18,080 M-113 armoured personnel carriers (APC).

The major overseas deployments of U.S. forces, including those afloat, were in Europe (326,400 personnel) and the Pacific/Far East (143,800) plus Latin America (19,300; not including 12,000 sent to Panama in late December).

U.S.S.R.

The Soviet military machine remained the world's most powerful, with about 4,250,000 personnel plus some 5.5 million in reserves and 570,000 paramilitary personnel. Western, including U.S., estimates of Soviet defense spending put it at 15–17% of gross national product (GNP), representing over $700 billion. This was a massive burden on the Soviet economy, one that had risen steadily.

Gorbachev's campaign for *perestroika* (restructuring) was badly handicapped by this high level of defense spending. It could not be reduced without weakening the Soviet's only

Table I. U.S./NATO–Soviet Strategic Nuclear Force Balance, June 1989

Weapons systems	Range[1] (km)	Payload[2] (000 kg)	Warheads, yield[3]	CEP[4]	Speed (Mach)	Number deployed
UNITED STATES Strategic Forces						
Intercontinental ballistic missiles (ICBM)						1,000
Minuteman II	11,300	0.7	1 × 1.2 mt	370	...	450
Minuteman III Mod 1	14,800	1.0	3 × 170 kt	220	...	200
Mod 2	12,900	1.1	3 × 335 kt	220	...	300
Peacekeeper (M-X)	11,000	3.2	10 × 300 or 400 kt	100	...	50
Submarine-launched ballistic missiles (SLBM; in 35 nuclear submarines)						608
Poseidon C-3	4,600	1.5	10 × 40 kt or 14 × 40 kt	450	...	224
Trident I/C-4	7,400	1.4	8 × 100 kt	450	...	384
Manned bombers and air-launched cruise missiles (ALCM)						
B-52G	4,600	29.5	20–24	...	0.95	167
B-52H	6,140	29.5	8–12 or 20–24	...	0.95	96
FB-111A	1,890	13.2	6	...	2.2	61
B-1B	4,580	61	30–38	...	1.25	99
AGM-86B ALCM	2,400	60	170–200 kt	...	0.66	1,650
Medium-range manned bombers						
U.S. F-111 E/F	1,750	13.1	3	...	2.5	140
BRITAIN (Strategic and Theatre Nuclear Forces)[5]						
Submarine-launched ballistic missiles (SLBM; in 4 nuclear submarines)						
Polaris A-3	4,600	0.7	3 × 200 kt	900	...	64
Strike aircraft						
Tornado	1,390	6.8			0.95	210
FRANCE (Strategic and Theatre Nuclear Forces)[5]						
Submarine-launched ballistic missiles (SLBM; in 6 nuclear submarines)						
MSBS M-20/TN-60	3,000	...	1 × 1 mt	...	...	64
MSBS M-4/TN-70	4,400+	...	6 × 150 kt	...	...	16
MSBS M-4/TN-71	6,000+	...	6 × 150 kt	...	...	—
Intermediate-range ballistic missiles (IRBM)						
SSBS S-3D/TN-61	3,500	...	1 × 1 mt	...	...	18
Strike aircraft/Air-to-surface missiles (ASM)						
Mirage IVP	930	9.3	1 × 60/1 × 150 kt ASMP ASM	...	2.2	18
Mirage IIIE	960	19	2 × 15 kt	...	1.8	15
Super Etendard	650	2.1	2 × 15/1 × 150 kt ASMP ASM	...	1.0	64
SOVIET UNION Strategic Forces						
Intercontinental ballistic missiles (ICBM)						c. 1,500+
SS-11 Mod 1	9,500	0.9	1 × 1 mt	1,400	...	} 400
Mod 2/3	11–13,000	1.1	3 × 100–300 kt	1,100	...	
SS-13 Mod 2	9,400	0.6	1 × 600 kt	1,800	...	60
SS-16	9–10,000	...	3 × 150 kt	...	...	c. 50[6]
SS-17 Mod 3	10,000	2.9	4 × 500 kt	...	...	138
SS-18 Mod 4/5	11,000	7.6	10 × 500 kt	250	...	308
SS-19 Mod 3	10,000	3.4	6 × 550 kt	300	...	350
SS-24	10,000	3.6	8–10 × 100 kt	200	...	30+
SS-25	10,500	0.7	1 × 550 kt	200	...	165+
Submarine-launched ballistic missiles (in 63 nuclear plus 12 diesel submarines)						c. 978[7]
SS-N-5 Sark	1,400	...	1 × 1 mt	2,800	...	18
SS-N-6 Mod 1,2	2,400	0.7	1 × 500 kt–1 mt	1,300	...	} 256
Mod 3	3,000	0.7	2 × 500 kt	1,300	...	
SS-N-8 Mod 1	7,800	0.7	1 × 500 kt–1 mt	1,500	...	} 286
Mod 2	9,100	...	1 × 800 kt	900	...	
SS-N-17	3,900	1.1	1 × 500 kt	1,400	...	12
SS-N-18 Mod 1	6,500	...	3 × 500 kt	1,400	...	} 224
Mod 2	8,000	...	1 × 500 kt–1 mt	900	...	
Mod 3	6,500	...	5 × 500 kt	900	...	
SS-N-20	8,300	...	6 × 100 kt	500	...	100
SS-N-23	8,300	...	10 × 100 kt	900	...	80
Manned bombers and air-launched cruise missiles (ALCM)						c. 420
Tu-95 Bear A/H	5,690	11.3	2–3 + 8 AS-15 ALCM	...	0.9	175
Tu-26 Backfire B	4,430	12	4	...	1.92	358
Tu-160 Blackjack	7,306	16.3	...	...	2.3	20+
AS-15 ALCM	1,600	...	250 kt	...	0.6	...
Medium-range manned bombers[8]						745
Tu-16 Badger	2,180	...	2	...	0.91	276
Tu-22 Blinder	1,500	10	2	...	1.4	160

[1] Range, for aircraft, is their radius of action in normal configuration, at optimum altitude, with a standard warhead, without in-flight refueling.
[2] Payload refers to a missile's throw weight or a bomber's weapons load.
[3] For MIRV and MRV the figure to the left of the multiplication sign gives the number of warheads and the figure to the right is the yield per warhead. For bombers, weapons per bomber are given.
[4] Circular Error Probable: the radius (in metres) of a circle within which at least half of the missile warheads aimed at a specific target will fall.
[5] British nuclear forces are under national control but may be assigned to NATO. French nuclear forces are controlled and targeted independently of NATO.
[6] Mobile SS-16 ICBM reported deployed, based on SS-20 V/IRBM.
[7] Includes 18 non-SALT/START counted SS-N-5 theatre missiles in 6 diesel submarines and 1 non-SALT/START counted SSBN.
[8] Total deployed worldwide. Of these, about half are allocated to Soviet Naval Aviation (some 135 Tu-16, 40 Tu-22, and 180 Tu-26). Two-thirds of the remaining strike bombers and ASM carriers are considered deployed against NATO. Tu-26 Backfire is now counted as strategic.
Sources: International Institute for Strategic Studies, *The Military Balance 1988–1989*; and *Aviation Week and Space Technology*. Figures for Soviet forces can only be estimates.

Table II. Approximate Strengths of Regular Armed Forces of the World

Country	Military personnel in 000s			Warships[1]			Jet aircraft[3]			
	Army	Navy	Air Force	Aircraft carriers/ cruisers	Submarines[2]	Destroyers/ frigates	Bombers and fighter-bombers	Fighters/ recon- nais- sance	Tanks[4]	Defense expenditure as % of 1987 GDP[5]
I. NATO										
Belgium	67.8	4.7	19.9	—		4 FFG	90 FB	36, 18 R	334	2.9
Canada[6]	23.5	17.1	24.2	—	3	11 FFH, 8 FF	128 FB, 33 MR	—	114	2.1
Denmark	17.0	7.7	6.9	—	3	3 FFG	93 FB	16	210	2.1
France[7]	292.5	65.5	94.1	2 CV, 1 CVV, 1 CG	10, 4 SSN, 6 SSBN	4 DDG, 36 FFG	18 B, 456 FB	129, 45 R, 33 MR	1,340	4.0
Germany, West	340.7	36.0	106.0	—	24	3 DDG, 4 DD, 6 FFG, 1 FF	587 FB	72 R, 19 MR	5,005	3.0
Greece	160.0	20.5	28.0	—	10	14 DD, 2 FFG, 5 FF	227 FB	70, 37 R	1,941	6.2
Italy	265.0	52.0	73.0	1 CVV, 3 CGH	10	4 DDG, 12 FFG, 10 FF	306 FB	30 R, 18 MR	1,720	2.4
Luxembourg	0.8	—	—	—	—	—	—	—	—	1.0
Netherlands, The	63.7	16.9	18.2	—	6	4 DDG, 11 FFG	207 FB	13 MR	913	3.1
Norway	19.0	5.3	9.1	—	12	5 FFG	89 FB	6 MR	117	3.3
Portugal	44.0	16.1	15.2	—	3	14 FF	93 FB	—	86	3.2
Spain	210.0	39.0[8]	36.0	1 CVV	8	4 DD, 8 FFG, 6 FF	98 FB	136, 24 R, 6 MR	838	2.4
Turkey	528.5	55.0	67.4	—	15	12 DD, 4 FFG, 6 FF	327 FB	30, 28 R	3,727	4.7
United Kingdom	155.5	64.6[8]	91.4	3 CVV	11, 16 SSN, 4 SSBN	13 DDG, 34 FFG	589 FB	193, 45 R, 39 MR	1,290	4.9
United States	766.5	779.2[8]	579.2	4 BBG, 5 CVN, 9 CV, 9 CGN, 32 CG, 6 LHA, 7 LPH, 13 LPD, 33 LSD/T	83 SSN, 35 SSBN, 10 SSGN,	37 DDG, 31 DD, 51 FFG, 51 FF	361 SB, 297 B, 3,450 FB	2,451, 270 R, 345 MR/ASW	15,992	6.4
II. WARSAW PACT										
Bulgaria	81.9	8.8	26.8	—	4	3 FF	45 FB	148, 35 R	2,200	4.7
Czechoslovakia	148.6	—	51.1	—	—	—	132 FB	245, 26 R	4,585	4.9
Germany, East	120.0	16.0	37.1	—	—	19 FF	60 FB	275	3,140	8.0
Hungary	68.0	—	23.0	—	—	—	—	101, 11 R	1,435	3.3
Poland	217.0	25.0	105.0	—	4	1 DDG, 1 FF	155 FB	360, 35 R	3,300	2.5
Romania	128.0	9.0	34.0	—	—	1 DDG, 4 FF	65 FB	230, 15 R	3,200	1.5
U.S.S.R.	3,074.0	437.0[8]	1,337.0[9]	4 CVV, 3 CVH, 3 CGN, 30 CG, 4 CA	117, 94 SSN, 63 SSBN, 6 SSB, 53 SSGN, 16 SSG	31 DDG, 21 DD, 33 FFG, 138 FF	533 SB, 612 B, 3,170 FB	4,405, 490 R, 180 MR	53,350	15–17 20–25
III. OTHER EUROPEAN										
Albania	31.5	2.0	7.2	—	2	—	45	50	190	4.0
Austria	38.0	—	4.5	—	—	—	16 FB	8	170	1.2
Finland	27.8	1.4	1.8	—	—	—	—	66	180	1.4
Ireland	11.2	1.0	0.8	—	—	—	—	—	—	1.5
Sweden[10]	44.5/725.0	12.0	8.0	—	11	—	110 FB	211, 48 R	785	3.0
Switzerland[10]	20.0/565.0	—	3.0/60.0	—	—	—	134 FB	134, 18 R	820	1.9
Yugoslavia	138.0	10.0	32.0	—	5	4 FFG	165 FB	146, 70 R	1,635	3.9
IV. MIDDLE EAST AND MEDITERRANEAN; SUB-SAHARAN AFRICA; LATIN AMERICA[11]										
Algeria	120.0	6.5	12.0	—	4	3 FF	84 FB	116, 7 R	900	1.9
Egypt	320.0	18.0	11.0	—	10	4 FFG	170 FB, 9 B	272, 20 R	2,425	8.0
Iran[12]	305.0	14.5	35.0	—	—	3 DDG, 5 FFG	40 FB	5 F, 8 R	500	3.0
Iraq[12]	955.0	5.0	40.0	—	—	5 FFG	20 B, 284 FB	243, 8 R	5,500	26.8
Israel[10]	104.0/598.0	9.0/10.0	28.0/37.0	—	3	—	552 FB	24 R	3,794	14.8
Jordan	74.0	0.25	11.0	—	—	—	59 FB	34	1,131	16.4
Kuwait	16.0	2.1	2.2	—	—	—	27 FB	40	275	7.2
Lebanon[13]	...	...	...				...	...		
Libya[14]	55.0	8.0	22.0	—	6	3 FFG	4 B, 189 FB	282, 13 R	1,980	6.3
Morocco	170.0	6.5	16.0	—	—	1 FFG	43 FB	21	224	5.0
Oman	20.0	2.5	3.0	—	—	—	40 FB	—	39	24.3
Qatar	6.0	0.7	0.3	—	—	—	6 FB	13	24	3.2
Saudi Arabia	38.0	7.2	16.5	—	—	8 FFG	83 FB	42, 10 R	550	22.7
Sudan, The	65.0	1.8	6.0	—	—	—	13 FB	18	175	6.9
Syria	300.0	4.0	100.0	—	3	2 FF	148 FB	311, 6 R	4,050	12.3
Tunisia	30.0	4.5	3.5	—	—	1 FF	12 FB	—	68	5.4
United Arab Emirates	40.0	1.5	1.5	—	—	—	26 FB	12	131	6.7
Yemen, North	35.0	0.5	1.0	—	—	—	43 FB	30	664	8.5
Yemen, South	24.0	1.0	2.5	—	—	—	77 FB	30	480	...
Angola[15]	91.5	1.5	7.0	—	—	—	98 FB	75	500	...
Ethiopia[16]	313.0	1.8	4.0	—	—	2 FF	138 FB	—	750	8.8

claim to superpower status, military power, but at the same time, it had to be reduced to supply the resources needed to make restructuring work and to provide the long-term economic base for that power. Thus the Soviet government faced a difficult series of choices. This was the background of Gorbachev's Dec. 7, 1988, speech to the UN, at which he announced a major unilateral cutback in Soviet conventional forces and a pullback of Soviet troops in Eastern Europe and along the Chinese border. By the end of 1989 these cuts seemed to be proceeding as scheduled. Observers pointed out, however, that the reductions would still leave Soviet conventional forces stronger than those of the West and that even those cuts might be resisted by the military.

The Strategic Nuclear Forces Command, a separate service with 287,000 troops, further increased its superiority over its U.S. counterpart in missile and warhead numbers and in warhead yields and accuracy. This gave the Soviets a first-strike capability that the U.S. would not have even after the year 2000. The figures shown in Table I underestimate the Soviet advantage because the U.S.S.R. also deployed 1,000–3,000 reload missiles for their ICBM and SLBM launchers. New systems being tested and deployed included two ICBM, the SS-24 and SS-25 (both mobile); one SLBM, the SS-N-23; and five long-range cruise missiles, all in the 3,000-km (1,860-mi) range. Continued increases in SS-24 and SS-25 deployments brought these up to a total of over 30 and over 165, respectively. The five Typhoon-class SSBN, each carrying 20 SS-N-20 MIRVed SLBM, were the world's largest, displacing 23,000 tons each.

The Strategic Aviation force included the first regiment of 20 new Blackjack A bombers, larger than the U.S. B-1B; 75 Bear-H, each carrying 8 ALCM; and 178 Tu-26M Backfire B/Cs. Additional medium-range bombers included 120 Tu-22 Blinder A/Bs and 140 obsolete Tu-16 Badgers. The

Country	Military personnel in 000s			Warships[1]			Jet aircraft[3]		Tanks[4]	Defense expenditure as % of 1987 GDP[5]
	Army	Navy	Air Force	Aircraft carriers/ cruisers	Submarines[2]	Destroyers/ frigates	Bombers and fighter-bombers	Fighters/ recon-naissance		
Kenya	19.0	1.1	3.5	—	—	—	11 FB	—	76	—
Madagascar	20.0	0.5	0.5	—	—	—	12 FB	—	—	1.8
Mozambique[17]	60.0	0.75	4.25	—	—	—	66 FB	—	150	...
Nigeria	80.0	5.0	9.5	—	—	2 FFG	63 FB	—	132	0.7
Somalia	61.3	1.2	2.5	—	—	—	20 FB	38	293	—
South Africa[10]	77.5	6.5	11.0	—	3	—	10 B, 111 FB	33, 7 R	250	4.1
Tanzania	45.0	0.7	1.0	—	—	—	—	24	30	—
Zaire	22.0	1.5	2.5	—	—	—	—	8	50	1.6
Zimbabwe	47.0	—	2.5	—	—	—	17 FB	48	43	7.9
Argentina	55.0	25.0[8]	15.0	1 CVS	4	6 DDG, 7 FFG	7 B, 111 FB	16 MR	360	1.5
Brazil	223.0	50.3[8]	50.7	1 CVS	7	9 DD, 7 FFG	30 FB	20	—	0.3
Chile	57.0	29.0[8]	15.0	—	4	6 DDG, 2 DD, 2 FFG	54 FB	15, 9 MR	171	4.5
Colombia	111.4	12.0[8]	7.0	—	2	4 FFG	22 FB	—	—	0.8
Cuba	145.0	13.5[8]	22.0	—	3	3 FF	60 FB	112	1,100	7.7
El Salvador	40.0	1.3	2.2	—	—	—	—	8	—	4.5
Mexico	105.5	28.0[8]	8.0	—	—	3 DD	—	11	—	0.3
Nicaragua	73.5	3.5	3.0	—	—	—	—	...	130	6.7
Peru	80.0	25.0[8]	15.0	2 CA	11	6 DD, 2 DDG, 4 FFG	21 B, 70 FB	28	350	1.4
Venezuela	34.0	10.0[8]	6.5	—	3	6 FFG	18 B, 76 FB	—	81	—
V. FAR EAST AND OCEANIA[11]										
Afghanistan[18]	50.0	—	5.0	—	—	—	145 FB	30	620	...
Australia	31.3	15.7	22.6	—	6	3 DDG, 9 FFG	22 B, 48 FB	20 MR	103	2.7
Bangladesh	90.0	7.0	6.0	—	—	3 FF	61 FB	12	50	1.2
China	2,300.0	260.0[8]	470.0	—	107, 1 SSG, 4 SSN, 1 SSBN	19 DDG, 26 FFG, 11 FF	600 B, 600 FB	4,600, 260 R, 10 MR	9,000	1.9
India	1,100.0	47.0	110.0	2 CVV	16, 1 SSGN	5 DDG, 3 FFG, 15 FF	440 FB	366, 18 R, 17 MR	3,150	3.8
Indonesia	215.0	43.0[8]	24.0	—	2	6 FFG, 6 FF	32 FB	14, 9 MR	—	1.9
Japan	156.0	44.0	46.0	—	14	6 DDG, 20 FFH, 37 FF	70 FB	250, 15 R, 73 MR	1,200	1.0
Korea, North	930.0	40.0	70.0	—	23	2 FF	80 B, 270 FB	180	3,200	9.3
Korea, South	550.0	60.0[8]	40.0	—	—	7 DDG, 4 DD, 17 FFG	252 FB	68, 10 R	1,560	5.7
Laos	52.5	0.7	2.0	—	—	—	30 FB	—	30	...
Malaysia	105.0	12.5	12.0	—	—	2 FFG, 2 FF	38 FB	18	—	4.6
Mongolia	21.0	—	0.5	—	—	—	—	30	650	10.9
Myanmar	182.0	9.0	9.0	—	—	—	—	—	26	3.3
New Zealand	5.7	2.5	4.2	—	—	4 FF	19 FB	6 MR	—	2.2
Pakistan	480.0	15.0	25.0	—	6	6 DD,1 DDH, 4 FFG, 6 FF	211 FB	210, 13 R, 4 MR	1,750	7.4
Philippines	68.0	28.0[8]	16.0	—	—	3 FF	—	18	—	2.1
Singapore	45.0	4.5	6.0	—	—	—	108 FB	42	—	5.6
Taiwan	270.0	65.5[8]	70.0	—	4	14 DDG, 12 DD, 10 FF	519 FB	3 R, 32 MR	309	6.3
Thailand	190.0	50.0[8]	43.0	—	—	5 FF, 1 FFG	23 FB	36, 6 R	104	3.7
Vietnam	1,100.0	37.0[8]	12.0	—	—	6 FF, 1 FFG	176 FB	206	1,950	...

Note: Data exclude paramilitary, security, and irregular forces. Naval data exclude vessels of less than 100 tons standard displacement. Figures are for June 1989. Because of substantive changes in national forces and reassessments of evidence, data may not be comparable with previous editions.

[1]Aircraft carrier (CV); aircraft carrier, nuclear (CVN); small (CVS); V/STOL and helicopter carrier (CVV); general purpose amphibious assault ship (LHA); amphibious transport dock (LPD); amphibious assault ship (helicopter) (LPH); dock/tank landing ship (LSD/T); battleship (BBG); heavy cruiser (CA); guided missile cruiser (CG); guided missile cruiser, nuclear (CGN); helicopter cruiser (CAH); destroyer (DD); guided missile destroyer (DDG); frigate (FF); guided missile frigate (FFG); N denotes nuclear powered.
[2]Nuclear-powered attack submarine (SSN); ballistic missile submarine (SSB); guided (cruise) missile submarine (SSG); coastal (C); N denotes nuclear powered.
[3]Bombers (B), fighter-bombers (FB), strategic bombers (SB), reconnaissance fighters (R); maritime reconnaissance (MR). Data include jet combat aircraft from all services including naval and air defense. MR also includes propeller drive ASW and ECM aircraft; data exclude light strike/counterinsurgency (COIN).
[4]Main battle tanks (MBT), medium and heavy, 31 tons and over.
[5]Figures are for gross domestic product (GDP).
[6]Of Canada's other military personnel, approximately 29,000 are not identified by service.
[7]French forces were withdrawn from NATO command structure in 1966, but France remains a member of NATO.
[8]Includes marines.
[9]Figure includes the Strategic Rocket Forces (287,000) and the Air Defense Force (502,000), both separate services.
[10]Second figure is fully mobilized strength.
[11]Sections IV and V list only those states with significant military forces.
[12]Losses in Iran-Iraq war made remaining force estimates uncertain.
[13]Lebanon's civil war and division mean that there are no longer any truly national forces, only militias.
[14]Some advanced Libyan aircraft are maintained and manned by Soviet/Warsaw Pact crews; figures reflect losses in 1987 conflict with Chad.
[15]Plus 50,000 Cubans and 500 East Germans serving with Angolan forces.
[16]Ethiopia also has 5,000 Soviet, Cuban plus other Soviet bloc troops; Army includes a 150,000-strong People's Militia.
[17]Plus Cuban, Warsaw Pact, and Chinese advisers and technicians.
[18]Figures approximate, given Soviet aid to Afghanistan government. Excludes Soviet advisers, and 40,000–120,000 *mujahideen* freedom fighters.

Sources: International Institute for Strategic Studies, 23 Tavistock Street, London, *The Military Balance 1989–1990, Strategic Survey 1988–89.*

450 Su-24 strike aircraft were transferred from Strategic Aviation to Theatre (TVD) Commands. Soviet strategic defensive forces were also large. The Air Defense Command (VPVO) formed a separate service with some 502,000 personnel, 2,225 interceptors, and 8,500 SAM launchers at 1,200 fixed sites. The latest SAM, the SA-X-12B, had a tactical antiballistic missile (ABM) capability. Soviet upgrading of the ABM system around Moscow, together with construction of other ABM radars, would enable the U.S.S.R. to field a nationwide ABM system.

The over two million-strong Army was organized into 53 tank, 153 motor rifle (mechanized), 18 artillery, 7 airborne, and 3 mobile divisions (10,500–12,500 men each) plus 490,000 railway and construction troops. Equipment—at much higher levels than for the U.S., its NATO allies, or China—included 53,350 tanks (modern types comprised 13,000 T-72/-80s and 9,700 T-64s, plus 30,300 older T-54/ -55/-62s); 28,500 armoured fighting vehicles (AFV); and 31,500 artillery pieces, including new self-propelled 203-mm, 180-mm, 152-mm, and 130-mm guns.

Soviet Army forces continued to be deployed roughly two-thirds against NATO-Europe and one-third against China. There were three major strategic theatre commands (GTVD), subdivided into five regional theatres of military operations (TVD), and a central strategic reserve military district with 16 divisions. Soviet forces stationed in Eastern Europe included 19 divisions in East Germany, 2 in Poland, 5 in Czechoslovakia, and 4 in Hungary.

WARSAW PACT

Poland maintained the largest military forces of the Eastern European nations, totaling 412,000 personnel and including a 217,000-strong army with 3,060 T-54/-55/-72 main battle tanks and a 105,000-strong air force with 565 com-

Gen. Colin L. Powell, who served as senior military assistant to Secretary of Defense Caspar Weinberger and then as national security adviser under Pres. Ronald Reagan, was chosen as chairman of the Joint Chiefs of Staff by Pres. George Bush.

CYNTHIA JOHNSON—TIME MAGAZINE

bat aircraft (325 MiG-21U interceptors). Czechoslovakia's 199,700-strong forces, the second largest, comprised an army of 148,600 with 4,585 T-54/-55/-72 tanks and an air force of 51,100 with 377 combat aircraft (245 MiG-21/-21U/-23 interceptors).

East Germany's armed forces totaled 173,100, including an army of 120,000 with 2,500 T-54/-55/-72 tanks (plus 640 T-34 in storage) and an air force of 37,100 with 335 combat aircraft, including 255 MiG-21/-23 interceptors. Hungary's armed forces, with 91,000 personnel, included an army of 68,000 with about 1,435 T-54/-55/-72 tanks and an air force of 23,000 with 101 MiG-21/-23 interceptors. All four countries allocated much lower proportions of their GDP to defense than did the U.S.S.R.

NATO

By late 1989 the fall of the Communist governments in five of the non-Soviet Warsaw Pact countries (Poland, Hungary, East Germany, Czechoslovakia, and Romania) and the removal of the Berlin Wall had changed the political and military balance between Eastern and Western Europe. The NATO alliance thus faced its greatest challenge since it was founded in 1949: how to assist the evolution of democratic governments in Eastern Europe and sharply reduce the military threat to Western Europe, while maintaining defenses adequate to deter the Soviets and to cope with any conflicts that emerged in the East.

For 40 years NATO had succeeded in its main aim—to deter the Soviets from using their superior conventional and nuclear forces to expand their empire beyond the iron curtain established by Joseph Stalin after the end of World War II. Stalin had used the Soviet Army to establish Communist puppet governments in Eastern Europe and to keep them obedient to Moscow, a policy continued by his successors. Gorbachev changed this policy, however, and refused to use Soviet troops to support those Communist governments against popular demands for democracy and the dismantling of the iron curtain. Provided that these changes continued, the result would be a transformation of the Warsaw Pact and of its relations with NATO.

The five major Eastern European members of the Pact would no longer function as Moscow's military satellites. Hungary was negotiating for the complete withdrawal of Soviet forces and neutral status; East Germany was rapidly moving toward effective unification with West Germany;

Poland was stressing its independence; and Czechoslovakia and Romania started to follow suit. All five were also relying on Western economic aid to rebuild their economies. Under these circumstances none of them would support a Soviet attack on NATO, and some of them could oppose it with their military forces. These forces were also being cut to save scarce resources.

At the NATO summit following the Malta meeting between Bush and Gorbachev, the alliance agreed on a two-track policy. It would give economic aid to the emerging Eastern European democracies and reduce the level of conventional forces through what was called the Conventional Forces in Europe (CFE). In principle, the initial CFE agreement was expected to eliminate Soviet (and Eastern European) advantages over NATO in conventional forces, estimated at 50% in major battle tanks alone. This agreement would also provide for an additional cut of about 15% in the remaining Warsaw Pact forces in Eastern Europe and in those of NATO. NATO also accepted Bush's goal of reaching this CFE agreement by the end of 1990, although this was a short time in which to negotiate such a complicated agreement.

Assuming the continuation of democratic reforms in Eastern Europe, most NATO members were also proposing additional reductions in their forces to follow the successful conclusion of the CFE agreement, with West Germany suggesting a 20% cut in military personnel. A CFE agreement would, if observed by the Soviets, provide NATO with greater security at lower costs. However, these additional cuts could reduce the alliance's defenses by too much and too quickly. As a voluntary alliance of democracies, NATO would find it very difficult to reverse any reductions it made, even if the Soviets reversed Gorbachev's policies of democratic reforms and cuts in military forces. In addition, the net effect of these NATO-Warsaw Pact force cuts would be to make NATO even more reliant on nuclear weapons to deter a Soviet attack, should such an offensive reemerge as a serious possibility.

UNITED KINGDOM

Defense expenditure for 1988–89 totaled $33,760,000,000 (4.7% of the 1987 GDP). The Army of 155,500 had 420

A Trident II missile spirals out of control after its test launch from a nuclear submarine, the USS *Tennessee*. Because the Trident II's first submersed test was unsuccessful, its deployment might be delayed.

AP/WIDE WORLD

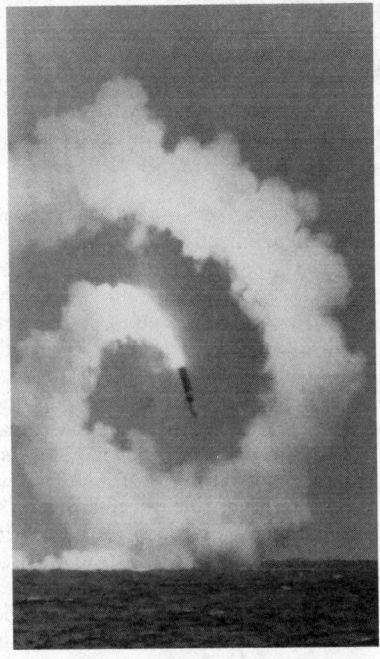

new Challenger and 870 Chieftain battle tanks plus 3,637 MICV/APC. The Royal Air Force (RAF), with 91,450 personnel, had about 600 combat aircraft. Some 221 of the new Tornado GR-1/-3 combat aircraft were being deployed in fighter, ground attack, and reconnaissance roles, replacing 90 Phantom fighters. Other modern aircraft included 51 Harrier GR-3/T-4 V/STOL, 87 Jaguar GR-1 ground-attack/reconnaissance planes, and 37 Nimrod MR-2 maritime reconnaissance aircraft.

The Royal Navy was the third largest naval force in the world, with 64,650 personnel, 27 attack submarines (16 nuclear), and 49 major surface combatants, including 2 small carriers with Sea Harriers, 13 GW destroyers, and 34 general-purpose frigates. Royal Marine personnel totaled some 7,700.

FRANCE

Defense spending in 1989 was estimated at $28,830,000,-000. Modernization of France's national nuclear forces continued, with five SSBN operational, one being refitted, and one under construction. The M-20 SLBM was being replaced with the M-4. Medium-range and tactical nuclear forces were also being increased.

Military personnel totaled 466,300 (292,500 in the Army). Equipment included 1,340 AMX-30 battle tanks (475 new AMX-30-B2), 960 AMX-10P/PC Milan MICV, and about 3,300 APC. These were organized in six armoured and two mechanized infantry divisions, plus a Rapid Action Force for overseas intervention consisting of one parachute, one air portable marine, one light armoured, one mountain, and one air-mobile division (averaging 7,000 to 8,000 personnel each). The Air Force of some 94,100 personnel had 598 combat aircraft, the newer models including 166 Mirage F-1C and 105 Mirage 2000 B/C-IV interceptors plus 50 Mirage 5F and some 122 Jaguar A ground-attack fighters. The 65,500-strong Navy's 43 major surface combatants included 2 light carriers, 4 GW destroyers, and 36 frigates; the Navy also had 14 attack submarines (4 nuclear).

WEST GERMANY

West Germany's defense budget amounted to $28,570,-000,000 in 1989. Standing armed forces totaled 494,300, more than half of them volunteers. The 340,700-strong Army included 12 divisions—6 armoured, 4 armoured infantry, 1 mountain, and 1 airborne. Armour included 2,000 new Leopard 2 and 2,130 Leopard 1 A1 battle tanks, plus about 2,130 MICV and 3,600 APC. Large numbers of artillery, antiaircraft guns and missiles, antitank guns, and guided weapons were also deployed.

The Air Force had 106,000 personnel with 507 combat aircraft. These included 198 new Tornados, 224 older F-4 Phantoms, and 165 Alpha Jet ground-attack fighters. The 36,000-strong Navy, designed for coastal warfare in the Baltic Sea, had 40 fast-attack craft equipped with guided missiles, 7 GW destroyers, 7 GW frigates, and 24 coastal submarines. The naval air arm consisted of 109 combat aircraft, including 95 Tornado attack/reconnaissance planes.

ARMS CONTROL AND DISARMAMENT

The most important arms control event of 1989 was Soviet Foreign Minister Eduard Shevardnadze's historic admission that the Krasnoyarsk radar installation in the U.S.S.R. was a violation of the 1972 ABM treaty. This was the first official admission by the Soviets that they had violated an arms control agreement; it resolved a long-standing U.S. debate in favour of those who had argued that the Krasnoyarsk radar was one of several Soviet violations. This

A U.S. Air Force Delta-2 rocket carrying a Navstar Global Positioning System satellite is launched at Cape Canaveral, Florida. The satellite was to be used to provide more precise measurements of the location, altitude, and velocity of military vehicles on land, at sea, and in the air.
AP/WIDE WORLD

argument had been made in successive reports on Soviet noncompliance with arms control agreements by U.S. Pres. Ronald Reagan and had been bitterly criticized by much of the arms control community as being incorrect. However, the Reagan administration's charge was now acknowledged as true by the Soviets.

This admission raised two important questions. First, would the U.S.S.R. reverse this violation by dismantling the Krasnoyarsk radar as promised? At the end of the year there was no evidence that it was being torn down. Second, how would the U.S. deal with other Soviet violations of arms control agreements and with violations of such agreements by other governments? The U.S. had charged the U.S.S.R. with a number of violations, including violation of the 1972 biological warfare convention, but had received no response. Nevertheless, it was now possible that the Soviets might admit these violations, including the alleged 1979 release of anthrax biological warfare agents from a Sverdlovsk facility. The U.S. thus needed to formulate a compliance policy that would respond to Soviet violations.

The U.S. also needed to respond to violations by other nations, the most flagrant being Iraq's massive use of chemical weapons, both in the Iran-Iraq war and against its Kurdish population, in violation of the 1925 Geneva Protocol. The 1989 Paris Conference, called to strengthen adherence to the protocol, had failed to do so. Iraq had not been penalized for its violation, and Libya had been left free to continue its construction of a plant at Rabta that would manufacture nerve gas.

The need for an effective U.S. compliance policy had

increased with the Bush administration's commitment to reaching arms control agreements that would involve deep cuts in nuclear and conventional forces and would eliminate chemical weapons. At the Malta summit it was decided that the U.S. and Soviets would reach an agreement in principle on a Strategic Arms Reduction Talks (START) treaty by the June 1990 summit. This treaty would cut their combined strategic nuclear warhead totals from about 12,000 to about 9,000. The proposed CFE Treaty would make large cuts in conventional forces in Europe (see *NATO,* above), and the proposed Chemical Weapons Convention would ban the manufacture and stockpiling of chemical weapons.

Because these agreements would make such deep reductions, they would also create much greater gains for governments that violated them. Thus there was a need for the U.S. and its allies to develop policies to enforce compliance with such agreements.

MIDDLE EAST

Syrian armed forces personnel totaled 404,000, with an army of 300,000 comprising five armoured and three mechanized divisions. Equipment included 950 new T-72 and 3,100 T-54/-55/-62 battle tanks and 3,800 BMP/BTR-series MICV/APC. The separate Air Defense Command had 60,000 personnel manning 95 batteries with Soviet SA-2/-3/-5/-6/-8 SAM. The 40,000-strong Air Force had some 499 combat aircraft, including 24 MiG-29 Fulcrum, 35 MiG-25 Foxbat E, 80 MiG-23 Flogger E, and 172 MiG-21 PF/MF interceptors and 60 MiG-23 Flogger F and 35 Su-20 fighter-bombers. Defense spending totaled $2,490,000,000 in 1989.

Israel remained the region's strongest military power, especially in the quality of its weapons. Its defense spending burden, which reached $6,370,000,000 for 1989, was difficult to support, even with massive U.S. aid. Defense had consumed 14.8% of GDP in 1987, compared with 21.2% in 1984. With a population of only 4,563,000, Israel raised standing armed forces of 141,000 that would increase to 645,000 on mobilization. The Army of 104,000 formed, on mobilization, 12 armoured divisions and 6 mechanized infantry and 4 artillery brigades. These forces had some 3,794 battle tanks and 5,900 MICV/APC. The 28,000-strong Air Force had 574 combat aircraft, including 53 U.S. F/TF-15 Eagles, 145 U.S. F-16A/D Falcons, 95 Israeli Kfir C1/C2/C7s, and 112 U.S. F-4E Phantom interceptor/fighter-bombers.

Egypt's armed forces totaled 448,000 personnel; defense spending was estimated at $6.8 billion in 1989–90. The nation's conversion from Soviet to Western equipment caused most Soviet equipment to be put in reserve. The Army of 320,000 had 785 U.S. M-60A3 battle tanks plus 1,640 Soviet T-54/-55/-62s in storage. Effective aircraft for the 30,000-strong Air Force comprised 33 F-4E Phantoms, 16 Mirage 5E2 and 76 Chinese J-6 fighter-bombers, plus 67 F-16A/C Falcon, 54 Mirage 5E, 16 Mirage 2000C, and 52 J-7 interceptors. Jordan's small but effective Army (74,000 personnel) had 870 effective battle tanks, and the Air Force (11,000) had 59 F-5E/F and 34 Mirage F-1CJ/EJ fighter-bombers.

Libya's forces remained numerically large, totaling 85,000 personnel with 1,800 battle tanks (1,200 in storage) and 515 combat aircraft. However, they had performed poorly in the war between Libya and Chad.

SOUTH, EAST, AND SOUTHEAST ASIA

The direct Soviet military occupation of Afghanistan was ended in 1989, but border incidents between Afghanistan and Pakistan remained a potential danger. With substantial U.S. military aid, Pakistan's armed forces had risen to 520,000 personnel, mainly an army of 480,000 with 1,750 battle tanks (mostly Chinese Type-59). The Air Force comprised 25,000 personnel and 451 combat aircraft, including 40 F-16 A/B Falcon and 58 Mirage 5 fighter-bombers. The defense budget in 1988–89 totaled $2,630,000,000.

India had become a major military power in the region, with armed forces that in 1989 totaled some 1,260,000 personnel. The 1.1 million-strong Army had some 3,150 battle tanks, including 650 new T-72s. The Air Force of 110,000 had 836 combat aircraft, including 72 MiG-27, 125 MiG-23, and 52 Mirage 2000 fighter-bombers. Defense spending in 1989–90 amounted to $9,120,000,000.

The Chinese Army's June 4, 1989, action against the Tiananmen (T'ien-an-men) Square demonstrators inflicted hundreds of casualties and increased the importance of the military. Reductions in forces and budgets were halted.

AP/WIDE WORLD

A group of Soviet SS-23 nuclear missiles at a military base in Kazakhstan wait to be destroyed. The graffiti-covered missiles were the last of the SS-23s to be destroyed under the terms of the U.S.-Soviet intermediate-range nuclear forces treaty.

The Soviet Union's new Blackjack A strategic bomber is flown publicly for the first time during a Moscow air show. According to the Pentagon the Blackjack was the world's largest and heaviest bomber.
AP/WIDE WORLD

China's total military personnel had been reduced to three million, but it appeared that they might again be increased. They had little modern equipment, while defense expenditure was sharply reduced from its 1978 level of 12% to 1.9% of GDP in 1987.

China's nuclear stockpile was small, with limited numbers of comparatively old, vulnerable delivery systems. These included about 8 ICBM (DF-4/-5), 60 DF-3 intermediate-range ballistic missiles (IRBM), and one Xia-class SSBN with 12 CSS-N-3 (J-1) SLBM (modified DF-3s). All 60 C55-1 (DF-2) MRBM were withdrawn. The Army had 2.3 million personnel but only 8,000 battle tanks (mostly T-59), while the 470,000-strong Air Force's 5,000 combat aircraft were modifications of old Soviet models, including 3,000 J-6/MiG-19 fighters.

Vietnam remained the largest active military power in Southeast Asia, with armed forces, mostly Army, totaling 1,249,000—the fourth largest army in the world. The Army had about 1,600 battle tanks, and the 12,000-strong Air Force had approximately 395 combat aircraft. Occupation forces in Kampuchea completed their withdrawal in 1989, and troops in Laos were reduced from 50,000 to 10,000–15,000.

North Korea's forces were so much larger than those of South Korea that the danger of a Northern invasion of the South remained. The balance was 1,040,000 personnel, 3,200 battle tanks, 1,600 APC, and 650 combat aircraft (mostly older types) for the North versus 650,000 personnel, 1,560 battle tanks, 1,550 APC, and 447 combat aircraft (mostly modern types) for the South.

Japan continued to exceed, marginally, its long-standing spending ceiling of no more than 1% of GNP on defense. Its 1989–90 defense expenditure was $30,090,000,000. Armed forces personnel totaled 247,000, including an army of 156,000 with 1,200 battle tanks. The Air Force had 46,000 personnel and 362 combat aircraft, including 70 Japanese-made F-1 fighter-bombers and 120 F-15J/DJ Eagle and 72 F-4EJ Phantom fighter-bombers. The 44,000-strong Navy had 6 GW destroyers, 57 frigates, and 14 submarines. Taiwan's armed forces, totaling 405,500 personnel, continued to provide a credible defense against China. The Army, with 270,000 personnel, had 309 battle tanks, and the 70,000-strong Air Force had 469 combat aircraft. Defense spending in 1989–90 was to total $7,640,000,000.

AFRICA SOUTH OF THE SAHARA

The war in Angola was reduced in intensity in 1989. Both the Soviet Union (and its ally Cuba) and South Africa wanted to avoid too deep an involvement in that conflict and in the guerrilla war for the control of neighbouring South West Africa/Namibia, and they finally supported the Crocker Plan to end these conflicts. U.S. Assistant Secretary of State Chester Crocker had negotiated a complex 1988 plan for the phased withdrawal of Cuban troops from Angola and of South African troops from Namibia, to be followed by UN-supervised elections in Namibia. At the end of 1989 the parties to the Crocker Plan appeared to have carried it out, although it was unclear what would become of the U.S.-backed rebel forces opposed to the Angolan government.

The Angolan government's armed forces, totaling 91,500 personnel with 500 battle tanks, had been reinforced by 48,000 Cuban military personnel and large quantities of Soviet military equipment. South Africa remained the region's dominant military power, with armed forces totaling 103,000 (rising to 528,000 on mobilization). Equipment included 250 battle tanks, 1,500 Ratel MICV, and 338 combat aircraft. Defense spending was estimated at $3,910,000,000 for 1989–90.

LATIN AMERICA

The two basic causes of instability in Central America remained the depressed economic and social conditions, which encouraged revolutionary movements. Central American armed forces, primarily internal-security infantry troops with little equipment, were poorly paid and often poorly led. They were also small relative to the size and population of their countries, as is apparent from Table II, and so the region was vulnerable to outside intervention. Costa Rica had no military forces and only a single Northern Border Security Battalion (7,700 personnel) of paramilitary forces. Honduras had total armed forces of 19,200 personnel, and Guatemala's personnel totaled 42,200. El Salvador's armed forces personnel totaled 56,000, mostly army, supported by U.S. economic and military aid in its fight against some 6,000 to 7,000 rebel guerrillas; the latter were aided by Cuban and Nicaraguan personnel and also by Soviet weapons and supplies.

In sharp contrast, Nicaragua's Pres. Daniel Ortega increased his total armed forces to 80,000 personnel, with 130 Soviet T-54/55 battle tanks and some 45 Mi-8/-17/24/-25 attack/assault helicopters. Nicaragua's anti-Sandinista guerrillas, the U.S.-backed *contras*, totaled 12,000 personnel. Their equipment included the U.S.-supplied Stinger SAM. Cuba remained the dominant Latin-American and Caribbean power, with armed forces of 180,500 personnel, including major overseas deployments in Angola (48,000), Nicaragua (4,000), and Ethiopia (2,800).

The U.S. intervention in Panama was triggered by the murder of a U.S. marine by the Noriega-controlled Panamanian Defense Force (PDF) and by other attacks that threatened the safety of U.S. personnel in the Canal Zone. Existing U.S. forces in Panama, which totaled approximately 12,000, were increased to some 24,000, and PDF resistance was quickly overcome. Noriega was forced to take refuge in the Vatican nunciature in Panama City.

(ROBIN RANGER)

See also Space Exploration.

This article updates the *Macropædia* article The Technology of WAR.

Mining

World mining output, as measured by UN production indexes (of value added in constant U.S. dollars), showed through the first two quarters of 1989 (*see* TABLE) that the metals sector, worldwide, was the only one that maintained any parity with manufacturing during the 1980–89 decade. Its strength, however, was more than offset by the decline in petroleum, which held the overall index below 100. Coal in the less developed countries (*see* TABLE notes) grew strongly, especially through the early part of 1989, reaching 167% of the 1980 level of output. The employment needs, development priorities, and structural importance of coal and petroleum in the economies of the centrally planned countries would assure their continued development in the 105 to 115 range that they maintained during the 1980s, despite world price levels, though it was by no means certain that central planning itself would survive into the 1990s. The overall low indexes of the developed countries, particularly the United States, probably reflected lessened demand in the late 1980s rather than the current health of the industry, which had survived the drastic restructuring of the early and mid-1980s to regain past confidence. *Business Week* magazine had proclaimed the mining industry "dead" in 1984 but during the year suggested that strenuous cost cutting and a modest rise in world prices had placed the industry in an enviable position, though still subject, it noted, to takeover pressures and also in need of scarce research and development capital to secure the continued gains in technology and productivity that analysts had noted as basic to future growth.

The total value of mineral output for the U.S. for 1988, the most recent year for which complete data were available, was estimated at $30,460,000,000, showing a gain of 15.6% over the previous year. About a quarter of this output came from only three states: California, $2,850,-000,000, Arizona, $2,829,000,000, and Nevada, $1,867,-000,000. About three-quarters of the gain was in the metals sector, which rose from $7,444,000,000 to $10,428,000,000 and represented a 40% increase in output; industrial minerals rose 6% to a value of $20,032,000,000. U.S. mining employment changed little during the year ended October 1989, up about 2.2% to 741,000; hours worked rose 2.7%. Utilization of capacity in the industry at the end of the third quarter, at 83.6%, was virtually identical to that of U.S. industry as a whole.

In September a second group of 25 individuals were named to the U.S. National Mining Hall of Fame, established in Leadville, Colo., in 1988. Among them were Alexander Agassiz (1835–1910), a marine zoologist, oceanographer, and mining engineer, who turned two unprofitable Lake Superior copper workings (Calumet and Hekla) into one of the world's foremost operations; James Dwight Dana (1813–95), another naturalist-geologist, whose *System of Mineralogy* (1837) and *Manual of Mineralogy* (1848) provide the classificational basis of modern mineralogy and were still published under his name; Charles Martin Hall (1863–1914), who developed the electrolytic process for refining aluminum; and William Morris Stewart (1825–1909), U.S. senator from Nevada, who laid much of the foundation for the General Mining Law of 1872, which had since governed the development of mining on U.S. public lands. (*See* below.)

Mining Journal's 22nd annual survey of the world's principal mines (those producing more than 150,000 metric tons of ore per year and representing about 90% of Western mining output for the 29 commodities surveyed) indicated a total of 1,186 such mines, 618 underground and 568 open pit. The 1989 total represented a 6% gain over the previous survey, mainly in small-volume gold mines. The survey involved closings as well as openings. Some, like the Rammelsberg copper, silver, and lead mine in West Germany, which closed in mid-1988 after 1,020 years as a producing operation, represented exhaustion of the natural resources; others, like the much newer Bougainville, Papua New Guinea, copper and gold mine at Panguna, closed since mid-May, represented concerns once thought irrelevant to mining operations, such as rights of indigenous peoples versus "national" interests in development and environmental pollution sanctioned by government but opposed by local economic interests.

Exploration. Several countries, including Vietnam and Mongolia, passed general mining or mineral resource laws

AFP PHOTO

Striking Ukrainian miners attend a meeting in Donetsk, Ukrainian S.S.R. The miners returned to work after Soviet leader Mikhail Gorbachev assured them that free local government elections would be held within each Soviet republic.

during 1989; others, like the U.S., examined the legal structure underlying the exploitation of public lands; still others, such as Indonesia, instituted tax incentives. The initial need was much the same everywhere: to stimulate prospecting and exploration. Depending on the scope of each national code, other issues might then be addressed: encouraging foreign investment while retaining essential control of strategic national resources; discouraging illegal mining and uncontrolled pollution; assuring balanced development of related industry and markets, domestic and foreign; and managing the transition to exhaustion of non-renewable resources.

The situation in South West Africa/Namibia as it approached independence exemplified some of those problems in the development of a national mining policy. Independence (perhaps by April 1990) would call into question much of the extensive South African-dominated mineral-development policy of recent decades. First National Development Corp. identified unexploited copper, tin/tungsten, rare earth, and industrial mineral deposits whose development might be not only feasible but also a principal means of financing further national development and utilizing a national labour force already long experienced in the mining of diamonds, uranium, lead, zinc, and copper. These accounted for about 85% of Namibia's export earnings in 1987. Strong incentives would exist for continued exploration to provide a continuing reserve base when current workings were exhausted.

Government and Labour Relations. In the U.S. two documents, one an annual statement of mining industry policy and the other a 117-year-old public law, highlighted problems common to the mining industry worldwide. The American Mining Congress, an industry association, adopted a "Declaration of Policy" in September that addressed a range of issues upon which, in its view, not only the industry but also U.S. security was seen to depend. These included markets and competition (supporting free trade and opposing uneconomic national subsidization programs), "multiple-use" exploitation of federally owned lands and waters, maintenance of the National Defense Stockpile (of strategic imported metals), protection of the environment, and "human resources," which included both safety and labour relations issues. Though the resolutions spoke optimistically and idealistically, it was nevertheless

the case that many of these issues represented subjects on which opposition to industry policies by labour, environmental groups, industries seeking the lowest-cost raw materials (whether subsidized or not), and others was substantial and of long standing.

Considerable consternation was aroused in the mining community by a March 10, 1989, report by the U.S. Congress's General Accounting Office (GAO) that recommended changes in the General Mining Law of 1872. This statute governed the exploitation of minerals on U.S. public lands, allowing individuals to obtain exclusive use of government land for mineral-development purposes. The mining industry found the report ill-founded and the GAO unwilling to document some of its more provocative claims (such as the extensive development of such "patented" land for nonmining purposes; *e.g.,* resorts). The report nonetheless generated substantial interest among several groups, including environmentalists, opponents of "multiple-use" public lands policies, and persons who believed too little revenue was accruing to the government under current law. The report recommended an end to the patenting process and held out the prospect of increased revenues from such land, though in the view of critics the GAO report had done little more than assert, with insufficient foundation, that patented land was being used extensively for purposes other than mineral development and that implementation of its recommendations would bring better exploration and development of the mineral resources of such lands. It probably could be agreed by both sides, however, that revenues could be improved, as patenting fees had not been raised since 1872.

Mining strikes often had national political significance, and in the heady atmosphere of *perestroika* (restructuring), the miners of Poland and the Soviet Union not only asserted their own views but in so doing gave voice to the concerns of others in the national labour force whose work did not have the potential to leave their country's homes, offices, and industries cold during the coming winter. The more than 100,000 strikers in three of the U.S.S.R.'s principal coal basins (the Kuzbass, Donbass, and Pechora Vorkuta) were actually cited in national media as supporting Soviet Pres. Mikhail Gorbachev, since their demands included reduction or elimination of local and national mining bureaucrats. Safety was also an issue; it was noted

Indexes of Production, Mining and Mineral Commodities
(1980 = 100)

	1984	1985	1986	1987	1988	1989 1st quarter	1989 2nd quarter
Mining (total)							
World[1]	88.0	86.9	89.7	90.8	93.8	94.9	...
Centrally planned economies[2]	106.4	108.1	111.8	113.6	116.0	117.5	115.6
Developed market economies[3]	102.9	105.2	102.3	103.6	105.2	107.4	101.4
Less developed market economies[4]	75.7	72.0	78.1	79.1	83.0	83.4	...
Coal							
World[1]	99.5	104.0	106.0	106.1	106.4	110.7	...
Centrally planned economies[2]	105.7	107.5	110.5	111.4	112.7	113.3	111.3
Developed market economies[3]	92.4	98.6	99.5	98.8	98.0	103.4	94.1
Less developed market economies[4]	123.7	132.0	138.3	140.1	145.0	167.7	...
Petroleum and natural gas							
World[1]	82.5	79.5	82.6	83.1	84.8	85.2	...
Centrally planned economies[2]	107.4	108.0	111.3	113.2	116.3	116.7	112.4
Developed market economies[3]	106.3	107.5	101.9	102.5	101.2	103.1	92.1
Less developed market economies[4]	72.2	67.5	73.8	74.2	77.2	77.0	...
Metals							
World[1]	104.3	108.5	109.1	112.9	124.0	126.0	...
Centrally planned economies[2]	97.8	99.5	102.0	103.6	107.4	109.1	107.2
Developed market economies[3]	106.6	110.1	110.6	116.1	128.1	133.0	135.2
Less developed market economies[4]	101.7	107.7	108.1	109.7	120.7	120.5	...
Manufacturing (total)	108.3	112.1	115.8	120.6	126.9	131.1	...

[1] Excluding Albania, China, North Korea, and Vietnam.
[2] Bulgaria, Czechoslovakia, East Germany, Hungary, Poland, Romania, and the U.S.S.R.
[3] North America, Europe (except centrally planned and Yugoslavia), Australia, Israel, Japan, New Zealand, and South Africa.
[4] Caribbean, Central and South America, Africa (except South Africa), Asian Middle East, East and Southeast Asia (except Israel and Japan), and Yugoslavia.
Source: UN, *Monthly Bulletin of Statistics* (November 1989).

that during the nine years of the Afghan war, in which some 15,000 Soviet soldiers had been killed, approximately 10,000 miners had also died.

Safety and Environment. During 1988, 100 deaths occurred in the U.S. mining industry, 52 in coal mining and 48 elsewhere. Not only was this a low total for the coal industry, traditionally one of the most dangerous workplaces, but the industry had also recently experienced a period of more than two years without a multiple-fatality accident. Similarly, the 1988 report of the South African Department of Mineral and Energy Affairs indicated continued improvement in what had long been considered a relatively dangerous arena, partly because of workplace safety practices but also because of the deep, difficult-to-mine geologic setting of the country's gold deposits. South Africa reported 674 fatalities, 510 of them in the gold mines. In terms of fatalities per 1,000 workers, the U.S. coal industry boasted a 0.3 rate, while the South African coal industry achieved a 0.5 rate. By comparison the South African gold mines had a rate nearly twice as high, 0.91. In terms of fatalities per million tons of coal mined, the South Korean industry in 1988 was among the most unsafe, with a rate of 6.5, compared with 2.3 for China, 1.6 for the U.S.S.R., 0.17 for the United Kingdom and South Africa, and 0.06 savethe U.S. Among the major disasters of 1989 were the deaths of 92 workers on November 17 at the Aleksinacki Rudnici mine in Yugoslavia, mostly by asphyxiation, and the deaths of as many as 100 clandestine gold prospectors at Masaka, Burundi, on April 23.

Among the most imaginative uses of reclaimed strip-mined land during the year was the donation of some 3,705 ha (9,154 ac) of reclaimed and reseeded land by the Ohio Power Co. to the International Center for the Preservation of Wild Animals, an organization founded by a consortium of zoos in Ohio and neighbouring states to create a wildlife preserve for African animals (black and white rhinoceros, cheetah, Grevy's zebra) and other endangered species. The ICPWA dedicated its first building, a 350-sq m (3,800-sq ft) visitors' centre and research facility, on December 2 at its rural home near Cumberland, in eastern Ohio. The first animals were due to arrive in 1990. Eighty hectares (200 ac) of exhibits, nature trails, a research clinic, animal hospital, and housing for researchers were planned or under construction.

Technology. Scale (size) continued to exercise a strong influence on planners of ore-handling equipment, at least above ground, where no limit on headroom usually existed. An order was placed during the year with the Marion (Ohio) Division of Dresser Industries for what was to be the world's largest two-crawler dragline, an excavating machine having a 17-cu m (22-cu yd) bucket and a 75-m (255-ft) boom. The dragline was being constructed for a coalfield in New South Wales, Australia.

Krupp Industries, Inc., of Bridgeville, Pa., accepted an order for 1990 delivery of the world's largest continuous surface miner, a machine capable of removing 3,500 tons per hour without blasting via an assembly of four bucket wheels that cut a channel 6.4 m (21 ft) wide and that could be tilted to follow the orientation of a seam. In South Africa the longest and heaviest train ever operated (660 ore cars; 70,543 tons) was assembled by South African Transport Services to carry iron ore 860 km (534 mi) from Sishen to Saldanha Bay, both in Cape Province.

(WILLIAM A. CLEVELAND)

See also Earth Sciences; Energy; Industrial Review: *Gemstones; Iron and Steel.*

This article updates the *Macropædia* article Extraction and Processing INDUSTRIES.

Motion Pictures

English-Speaking Cinema. *United States.* In a year without major landmarks, the biggest money earners were, predictably, Tim Burton's *Batman,* a dark-toned reincarnation of the 50-year-old comic-strip hero (*see* BIOGRAPHIES), and *Indiana Jones and the Last Crusade,* the third and best-scripted of the Indiana Jones series, directed by Steven Spielberg.

The bulk of Hollywood production, however, followed well-tried commercial formulas: horror film, high-school film, science fiction, police buddy thrillers (varied in a couple of examples—Rod Daniel's *K-9* and Roger Spottiswoode's *Turner and Hooch*—by giving the cop hero a dog as buddy). Sequels to commercial successes proliferated, generally confirming the law of diminishing returns, both artistic and economic. Among these were *The Fly II, Ghostbusters II, The Karate Kid III, A Nightmare on Elm Street 5, Halloween 5, Star Trek V: The Final Frontier, Back to the Future, Part II,* and *Friday the 13th Part VIII.* Only *Lethal Weapon 2,* directed by Richard Donner, improved on the original formula.

Notable work of the year included Steven Soderbergh's first film, *sex, lies and videotape,* a subtle and stylistically original examination of the sexual complications of a small-town quartet, which won the major prize of the Cannes Film Festival. Phil Alden Robinson's *Field of Dreams* used baseball as a metaphor for the importance of following where one's heart leads. Woody Allen made *Crimes and Misdemeanors,* a new treatment of moral choices and their results. James Ivory's adaptation of stories by Tama Janowitz, *Slaves of New York,* was a colourful evocation of Manhattan Bohemia. The Australian director Peter Weir filmed Tom Schulman's script *Dead Poets Society,* with Robin Williams playing a teacher who provocatively awakens students' creativity in a boys' prep school.

Exceptional thrillers were Ridley Scott's *Black Rain,* a self-conscious exercise in style, and Harold Becker's *Sea of Love.* Among the best comedies were Ron Howard's *Parenthood,* with Steve Martin exposed to the hazards of

Actor Michael Keaton played the caped crusader in one of the year's highest grossing films, *Batman.* In the dark-toned film, Keaton played a brooding Bruce Wayne with a personal vendetta against the Joker, played by superstar Jack Nicholson.

Andie MacDowell and James Spader play Ann and Graham, two
of the four central characters in *sex, lies, and videotape*. The
prizewinning film, which deals daringly with each character's sexual
problems, was a first effort by writer-director Steven Soderbergh.
MIRAMAX FILMS

bringing up children, and the Scots director Bill Forsyth's
Breaking In, from John Sayles's wry script about an aging
burglar (Burt Reynolds) teamed with a naive beginner.
Jim Jarmusch's uneven but often engaging *Mystery Train*
blended three stories set concurrently in a rundown, back-
street Memphis haunted by the ghost of Elvis Presley.

The Vietnam war returned to the screen, viewed from
new critical attitudes, in Brian DePalma's *Casualties of
War,* about a real-life atrocity committed in 1966 by
American GIs; in Patrick Duncan's first film, *84 Charlie
MoPic,* which used neodocumentary techniques to describe
the adventures and tensions of a single patrol; and in Eric
Weston's *The Iron Triangle,* which attempted to present
the view of both sides, through the story of a captured U.S.
officer and his 17-year-old Viet Cong guard.

Three black directors contributed interesting films. Spike
Lee (*see* BIOGRAPHIES) made *Do the Right Thing*, a dramatic allegory on racial intolerance set in the Bedford-
Stuyvesant area of Brooklyn, N.Y. Charles Lane made a
musical comedy on homelessness, *Sidewalk Stories*, inspired by silent film comedy; and Curtis Brown, like Lane
a debut director, made *The Game*, a strong story of corruption in a mayoral election campaign.

Several outstanding films were released late in the year.
They included Bruce Beresford's *Driving Miss Daisy,* an
effectively understated story about the 25-year relationship
between a Jewish widow in Atlanta and her black chauf-
feur; Edward Zwick's *Glory,* about the first regiment of
black soldiers to fight for the Union in the Civil War;
Blaze, Ron Shelton's recounting of the affair between
stripper Blaze Starr and Louisiana governor Earl Long;
Paul Mazursky's *Enemies, A Love Story,* concerning the
difficulties of Holocaust survivors living in New York City
in 1949; Danny DeVito's *The War of the Roses,* about a
very messy divorce; and Oliver Stone's *Born on the Fourth
of July,* with Tom Cruise playing against type as a bitter
Vietnam veteran. Animated features included Don Bluth's
All Dogs Go to Heaven, John Hancock's *Prancer,* and John
Musker's *The Little Mermaid.*

At the annual awards ceremony of the Academy of Motion Picture Arts and Sciences in Los Angeles in March,
Rain Man took Oscars for best picture, best actor (Dustin
Hoffman), best direction (Barry Levinson), and best original screenplay. Jodie Foster in *The Accused* won the award
for best actress. The awards for best supporting actor and

actress went to Kevin Kline (*A Fish Called Wanda*) and
Geena Davis (*The Accidental Tourist*). *Dangerous Liaisons*
took awards for best screenplay adaptation (Christopher
Hampton) and best costume design (James Acheson).
The best foreign-language film was *Pelle the Conqueror*
(Denmark).

Great Britain. As a result of uncertainty over government plans for television, TV investment in feature film
production—a major factor in the recent renascence of
British cinema—slackened, with a consequent falling off
in the extent and enterprise of production. In the mainstream commercial sector the most successful British film
of the year was, predictably, *Licence to Kill,* featuring
the new, younger James Bond, Timothy Dalton. Another
predestined commercial hit was Lewis Gilbert's *Shirley
Valentine,* adapted from Willy Russell's one-woman play
about a middle-aged provincial housewife's bid for eman-
cipation. Michael Caton-Jones's *Scandal,* painstakingly re-
creating a major political scandal of the 1960s, also enjoyed
commercial success. The most costly British-based production, Terry Gilliam's spectacular *The Adventures of Baron
Munchausen,* seemed unlikely to recoup even a fraction
of its $50 million investment even though it abounded in
extraordinary visual inventions that revealed the director's
early training in animated film.

Britain's most individualist directors, Peter Greenaway
and Derek Jarman, completed new features. Greenaway's
The Cook, The Thief, His Wife and Her Lover was a portrait of greed, violence, and vulgarity, superbly mounted
in the setting of a grand restaurant. Jarman's interpretation of *War Requiem*—Benjamin Britten's cantata on the
poems of Wilfred Owen—was a disappointingly literal and
uninspired work. The young Shakespearean actor Kenneth
Branagh risked comparison with Sir Laurence Olivier by
directing and playing the title role in *Henry V.*

From Scotland, Ian Sellar's *Venus Peter* was adapted
from a novel by Christopher Rush, set in the Orkney
Islands in the 1940s. From Ireland, Jim Sheridan's debut
film, *My Left Foot,* told the story of the Irish painter and
writer Christy Brown, whose talent transcended his handi-
caps of poverty and cerebral palsy.

Australia. Two women directors made striking feature
debuts. Jane Campion's *Sweetie* tellingly exposed the psychic disturbances lurking within an apparently ordinary
middle-class family. Ann Turner's *Celia* was the story of
the traumas and disillusions of a nine-year-old girl in the
1950s. In *Malpractice* Bill Bennett made a gripping drama
out of the aftermath of a childbirth bungled by the staff
of a hospital. Philip Noyce directed a virtuoso suspense
thriller set at sea, *Dead Calm.*

New Zealand. The best New Zealand motion picture of
the year was a first film by Martyn Sanderson, *Flying Fox
in a Freedom Tree.* It portrayed a young Samoan, caught
between Polynesian and European cultures.

Canada. Outstanding among English-language productions was Anne Wheeler's *Bye Bye Blues,* the odyssey, as
a band singer, of the wife of a missing soldier in World
War II. Bruce Pittman's independently produced *Where
the Spirit Lives* was an indictment of the days when the
federal government virtually kidnapped Indian children
from the reserves to give them "Christian" upbringing.

Speaking Parts, Atom Egoyan's third feature, used complex and original electronic imagery to tell the story of an
aspiring actor, hotel porter, and accidental gigolo. From
French Canada, Denys Arcand's *Jesus of Montreal* was an
ironic allegory about the leading actor in an experimental-
theatre group passion play who is made to carry his martyr
role into real life.

Western Europe. *France.* One of the few outstanding films of the year, Bertrand Tavernier's *La Vie et rien d'autre,* was the story of an army bureaucrat (Philippe Noiret) responsible for documenting the missing soldiers of World War I and also for finding a suitable candidate corpse for the tomb of the unknown soldier. Of other established directors, Alain Resnais made a mild comedy about the collisions with French culture of a U.S. cartoonist in Paris, *I Want to Go Home,* from a script by the U.S. cartoonist Jules Feiffer. Bertrand Blier's *Trop belle pour toi* was a stylish, witty sexual drama about a man who betrays his exquisite wife with a plain but warmhearted secretary. The expatriate Soviet Georgian director Otar Iosseliani created in *Et la lumière fut* (*Let There Be Light*) an allegory on human destruction of the world, set in a wholly invented primitive African society.

The most subversive commemoration of the bicentennial of the French Revolution was Henri Xhonneux's bawdy *Marquis.* Inspired and written by the satirist Roland Topor, it represented the Marquis de Sade and the most decadent representatives of the ancien régime by actors disguised as animals.

Italy. Coincidentally, two films celebrated the passing glories of the cinema and the days when the local movie house was a social focus for the whole community. Et-tore Scola's *Splendor* chronicled the vicissitudes of a small provincial theatre, with extracts from films that were the common cultural currency; Giuseppe Tornatore's *Nuovo Cinema Paradiso* was a sentimental saga of a Sicilian theatre. Scola also made *Che ora e?* (*What Time Is It?*), a slight but elegant anecdote, finely played by Marcello Mastroianni and Massimo Troissi, about a father's visit to his soldier son.

It was generally a good year for Italian cinema. Giuliano Montaldo adapted Ennio Flaiano's 1949 novel *Tempo di uccidere.* The gifted Pupi Avati dramatized the story of his own parents' farmhouse engagement party in *Storia di ragazzi e di ragazze.* Nanni Loy attempted a fresh look at the homeless and delinquent children of Naples in *Scugnizzi,* which centred on a musical show given by the inmates of a reformatory school. Mario Brenta's *Maicol* was an austere, unsentimental story centred on the lonely, loveless five-year-old son of an unmarried working mother. The Mexican enfant terrible Alejandro Jodorowsky made *Santa Sangre,* a lively and lurid horror film with an Oedipal theme.

West Germany. Filmmakers returned to history. The veteran Bernhard Wicki adapted Joseph Roth's saga about the adventures of a young former officer of World War I caught up in the beginnings of Nazism, *Das Spinnennetz.* Joseph Vilsmaier's *Herbstmilch* was a sensitive, neodocumentary adaptation of Anna Wimschneider's recollections of her teenage years on a Bavarian farm in the 1930s. Kai Wessel's *Marta Jellneck* was an effective drama about an old woman who avenges her half-brother's wartime murder.

On the lighter side, in *Rosalie Goes Shopping* Percy Adlon took the hefty star of *Bagdad Cafe,* Marianne Sägebrecht, back to the U.S. as a peacetime GI bride who masters the American credit system by becoming a computer hacker. Rudolph Thome's *Der Philosoph* was a strange sexual fairy tale about a shy young man who is adopted and sexually cosseted by a trio of beautiful young women.

Scandinavia. In Finland Aki Kaurismäki confirmed his place as the country's most prolific and inventive talent with *Leningrad Cowboys Go America,* the comic adventures of members of a painfully awful band who seek their fortune across the Atlantic. A notable new talent emerged in Ilkka Järvilaturi, whose *Homebound,* based on a real-life incident, was a grim picture of a young student trying to battle out of a brutal family life.

The most successful Swedish production of the year was a new episode in Lasse Aberg's series of successful comedies as actor-director, in the character of Stig-Helmer. In *SOS—Swedes at Sea,* Aberg teamed with a popular Norwegian comedian, Jon Skolmen. Katrin Ottarsdottir's *Atlantic Rhapsody,* the first film from Denmark's Faeroe Islands, was a witty collage of scenes of daily life in this self-governing and idiosyncratic community.

Eastern Europe. *U.S.S.R.* The effects of *glasnost* (openness) were very much in evidence as filmmakers dealt with themes previously impermissible: housing conditions, in Yury Mamin's fantastic comedy *Fountain;* the socially disadvantaged, in Sergey Bodrov's *Freedom Is Paradise;* the drug scene in Soviet Kazakhstan, in Rashid Nugmanov's *The Needle;* and realities of contemporary peasant life, in Viktor Arisov's visionary *It's Hard for the First Hundred Years.* Nijole Adomentajte's *Koma* was a searing dramatization of life in a "reeducation" camp for women in the early 1950s. Karen Shaknazarov's *Zero City,* an absurdist comedy about an engineer stranded in a bizarre town frozen in Stalinist times, was a powerful metaphor of the monolithic immobility of Soviet society.

The Chaplin Centenary

The worldwide celebration in 1989 of the centenary of the birth of Charles Chaplin demonstrated how potent the myth of his creation, the Little Tramp, remained more than half a century after its last major public release. The year happened also to be the 75th anniversary of the creation of the Tramp; the first members of the public to see him were the spectators at a soap-box car rally on Jan. 10, 1914, at Venice, Calif., where the Keystone Co. was filming a short improvised comedy.

Practically every country of the world paid tribute to the centenary, with exhibitions, screenings of the films, television programs, books, and articles. In Calcutta a street was named after Chaplin. In the Soviet Union audiences saw *The Great Dictator* for the first time (Stalin had viewed it but personally banned it from Soviet screens). In Chaplin's native London the birthday centenary was marked by a Royal gala, during which the Princess of Wales watched a screening of Chaplin's 1931 masterpiece, *City Lights,* with the original score performed live.   (DAVID ROBINSON)

AP/WIDE WORLD

Charlie Chaplin as the Little Tramp huddles against the cold in *The Gold Rush,* considered by many to be Chaplin's finest work. Many of Chaplin's films were given special screenings during film fests and celebrations that marked the 100th anniversary of his birth.

Documentary subjects included Marina Goldovskaya's *The Power of Solovki,* about the first Soviet gulag; Georgy Gavrilov's *Confession: A Chronicle of Alienation,* about drug abuse; Tofik Sharverdiev's *Stalin Is with Us,* which featured a group of people ardently wishing for the return of Stalinist discipline.

Poland. The one undoubted classic work of the year in world cinema was Krzysztof Kieslowski's great cycle of films on the Ten Commandments, *Dekalog.* These low-key dramas, all set in the vicinity of the same Warsaw high-rise apartment and each equally perfect in script, technique, and acting, definitively established Kieslowski as a cinema moralist on the level of Ingmar Bergman or Robert Bresson. The anecdotes demonstrated the inadequacy of the simple rules to deal with the ethical complexities of our times.

Hungary. Ildiko Enyedi's playful debut feature *My Twentieth Century,* a whimsical look at the start of the century through the eyes of twin girls taking different paths through society, was Hungary's major international success of the year. Other creditable productions were Peter Timar's perverse, stylish tale of sexuality and murder, *Before the Bat's Flight Is Done,* and Gyula Gazdag's gripping hostage melodrama, *Stand Off.* Peter Bacso's *Titania, Titania* broke new ground in Eastern European film with its ferocious ridicule of a Communist neighbour—the Romania of Pres. Nicolae Ceausescu.

Other films recalled the dark days of Stalinism. Ferenc Teglasy's *Never, Nowhere, to No One* told the story of a Budapest family in the early 1950s "relocated" as politically suspect. A remarkable documentary, *Recs, a Hungarian Gulag,* interviewed veteran officials and guards as well as former prisoners.

Czechoslovakia. In *The End of the Good Old Days,* Jiri Menzel made a disarming comedy, set just after World War I in a Bohemian castle, whose new rich owners ape the manners of their aristocratic predecessors. *Killing with Kindness,* the last film of the gifted Ewald Schorm, who died in January, told the story of a woman endeavouring to compensate for injuries she accidentally inflicted on her daughter in childhood.

Bulgaria. Bulgarian cinema flourished with *glasnost.* Many long-banned films were released, and the year's notable new productions included Ivan Nichev's *Ivan and Alexandra,* a story about small children forced to denounce their parents in the Stalinist 1950s, and Lyubomir Sharlandjiev's *The Prosecutor,* from a successful play about an official obliged to sign the warrant for the arrest of his friend during the Stalinist purges.

Middle East. *Israel.* In a gloomy year for Israeli films, Uri Barbash's *One of Us*—in which a commando officer investigating the death in custody of an Arab suspect is caught between loyalty to his peers and a sense of justice—was outstanding.

Latin America. *Argentina.* A Colombian-Venezuelan co-production, Sergio Dow's *El dia que me quieras* (*The Day You Love Me*), examined popular Latin myths through the legendary personalities of the great tango singer Carlos Gardel and the militant Marxist politician Pio Miranda.

Cuba. The most successful Cuban film of the year, Juan Carlos Tobio's *Plaff!,* was a farcical comedy about a mysterious egg pelter, incorporating irreverent criticism of contemporary Cuban society. *Juliana,* directed by Fernando Espinoz and Alejandro Legaspi, members of the Grupo Chaski cooperative, was a well-written and sensitive portrayal of a young slum girl on the run from home.

Asia. *India.* The giant of Indian cinema, Satyajit Ray, returned after a long period of illness to direct a low-key

local transmutation of Ibsen's *An Enemy of the People. Piravi* (*The Birth*), the first film by Shaji N. Karun, previously cinematographer to the Kerala director G. Aravindan, told of the agonies of the family of a young man abducted by the police during Indira Gandhi's state of emergency. Aravindan himself made *Masquerade,* an ingenious and visually compelling intertwining of traditional Kathakali play and murder mystery.

Japan. Coincidentally, two feature films dealt with the life of a 16th-century artist credited with perfecting the tea ceremony. Hiroshi Teshigahara's *Rikyu* was more subtle and authentic than Kei Kumai's decorative but pedestrian *Death of a Tea Master.* The second film of writer-director Kaizo Hayashi, *Circus Boys* (*The Boys' Own Book of the 20th Century*), revealed a major talent, able to mix comedy, tragedy, and poetic fantasy in a story of two brothers growing to maturity as circus performers. One of the most unconventional films of the year, Shusuke Kaneko's *Summer Vacation: 1999,* was a poetic fantasy of adolescent love and suicide among schoolboys—played by girls to stress their androgynous beauty.

China. Perhaps one of the last films from the period of liberalism, Huang Jianxin's (Huang Chien-hsin's) *Samsara* was an honest, anxious study of a young man trying to cope with the confusions of life in the changing China.

Hong Kong. In an inspired dramatic comedy, *Life Is Cheap,* the American-Chinese director Wayne Wang returned to Hong Kong to analyze the mood of the city on the verge of transfer to China. The box-office hit of the year was Clifton Ko's comedy *Chicken and Duck Talk,* with the comedian Michael Hui as the proprietor of a disastrously mismanaged restaurant.

TERRY O'NEILL—SYGMA

Kenneth Branagh stands bloodied and exhausted before his men in his film of Shakespeare's *Henry V.* With its gritty, realistic treatment of war, the film was a departure from the epic heroism of Laurence Olivier's classic 1944 version.

Taiwan. Taiwan had a year of notable successes—all taking as their theme the country's recent history. Hou Hsiao-hsien's fine *City of Sadness,* which won the Golden Lion of the Venice Festival, was a saga of one family in the years 1945 to 1949, between the end of Japanese occupation and separation from the Communist mainland. Wang T'ung's *Strawman* was a gentle, often comic picture of village life under Japanese occupation. Peter Wang's *First Date* set its story of a high-spirited young boy's self-discovery in the 1950s.

Philippines. In *Fight for Us* Lino Brocka, having used his cinema to fight the regime of Ferdinand Marcos, exposed the complicity of police and Army in the activities of right-wing guerrillas in the post-Marcos Philippines.

Africa. From Algeria, Muhammad Rachid Benhadj's *Rose of the Desert* forced the spectator to see in its protagonist—a man with no arms and a crippled leg—an attractive, intelligent young man leading a life of dignified independence in his desert village. From Burkina Faso, Idrissa Ouedraogo's *Yaaba* told a simple tale of the friendship of two children with an old woman outcast by the community and incidentally gave foreign spectators a vivid, intimate, human view of life in an African village.

Working in Botswana, Jamie Uys followed up his 1983 success with *The Gods Must Be Crazy 2,* another comedy about a bushman who becomes involved with the lunacies of white "civilization." (DAVID ROBINSON)

Nontheatrical Motion Pictures. Some of the top non-theatrical films in U.S. festivals in 1989 were not U.S. productions. Noteworthy were the two grand prize winners at the 1989 American Film Festival in New York City. Recipient of the prestigious Emily Award was *The Man Who Planted Trees,* produced by Frederic Back for the National Film Board of Canada. In an unusual animated film the "chief character moves as the embodiment of a legend," a successor to Johnny Appleseed. The other top American Festival film, receiving the Grierson Award, was *One Hundred Children Waiting for a Train.* Produced for Chilean television by Ignacio Aguero, the documentary portrays an energetic teacher who, through a film workshop, widens the horizon of children in a poor suburb of Santiago.

A U.S. film, *21st Century Forest,* was honoured at three European festivals, winning the Grand Prize at Kacskemet (Hung.) and taking bronze awards at the Santorem (Port.) Agriculture Film Festival and at Zaragoza (Spain). Produced by Peckham Productions, Tarrytown, N.Y., the film showed creative forest management that could result in superior forests in the next century. (THOMAS W. HOPE)

See also Photography; Television and Radio.

This article updates the *Macropædia* article MOTION PICTURES.

Museums

Deaccessioning, the process whereby museums sell works of art from their collections, reached a crescendo in 1989 amid controversy over its propriety. U.S. museums led the trend, with major sales generally designed to raise funds for additional purchases. Rising costs tempted institutions to sell to fund operating expenses, an activity much criticized as akin to selling the family silver. Sales to enable upgrading of collections were less controversial.

Two central factors behind the growth of sales in the U.S. were a dramatic drop in bequests to museums, stemming from 1986 changes in the tax laws that greatly lessened the personal tax deduction available to donors, and the continuing boom in the art market, which raised auction prices to new highs. A survey of 161 U.S. museums indicated that between 1986 and 1988 the value of donations had declined by an estimated $161 million, or 63%. Major deaccessioning was carried out by the Metropolitan Museum of Art in New York City and the Art Institute of Chicago, among others. Even the Getty Museum in Malibu, Calif., with an annual purchasing budget of around $50 million, found itself stretched for funds as a result of the high auction prices. The Getty sent 15 Impressionist and Postimpressionist pictures to London for sale in the autumn.

U.S. museums had always bought and sold, though rarely so publicly or on such a scale, but in England, where major museums are publicly financed, legal constraints had largely prevented deaccessioning to raise funds. Opponents

FRANK P. HERRERA

A self-portrait of the late artist Robert Mapplethorpe is projected onto the outside wall of the Corcoran Gallery of Art (Washington, D.C.) by a protester following the museum's cancellation of a scheduled Mapplethorpe exhibit. The show, which depicted such controversial themes as homosexuality and sadomasochism, had been canceled by the museum in response to congressional debate over the federal funding of art that was deemed "indecent."

Visitors to the Kennedy exhibit in what was formerly the Texas School Book Depository in Dallas peer at the corner window (centre)—the spot where Lee Harvey Oswald was standing when he shot Pres. John F. Kennedy. The exhibit was opened to the public for the first time since the assassination of the president in 1963.
GEORGE TAMES—THE NEW YORK TIMES

of legalization feared that it might mean further cuts in public funding and pressure on museums to "cash in" by selling their treasures. What one generation sells may be prized by the next, and disposition of works not to contemporary taste had led to major errors in the past.

In a move to help offset financial pressures, Walter H. Annenberg gave $15 million to the Metropolitan Museum of Art, specifically for acquisition, and similar awards of $5 million each to the National Gallery of Art in Washington, D.C., and the Philadelphia Museum of Art. Through a private bequest, the Metropolitan was able to extend its Friday and Saturday hours into the evening, while the Art Institute of Chicago received a $1 million gift to renovate its Asian art department. Other major grants included $2 million from the MacArthur Foundation for the educational program of Chicago's Museum of Contemporary Art and $5 million from the Ford Foundation to invigorate black and Hispanic museums in the U.S.

In London a major dispute between the director of the Victoria and Albert Museum and some senior curators (keepers) received wide publicity. In an attempt to save money, a new administrative structure was proposed that would separate curators' scholarly duties from the physical responsibility for objects. The curators objected that they would lose contact with the collections and that valuable objects might be mishandled and endangered, but after limited consultation, eight leading curators and scholars were made to resign. Many important figures in the art world protested, and debate continued over whether a museum should be a repository of elite scholarship or a challenge to a wider but less educated audience.

At the Louvre in Paris, a series of new rooms was opened on the second floor of the Cour Carrée as part of the major restoration of the court. Twelve new rooms were devoted to French painting of the 14th to 17th centuries. Such was the Louvre's popularity that delays of an hour or more to gain admission were not uncommon. In London's Docklands the much-publicized, privately funded Design Museum opened in July. Housed in a converted warehouse on the South Bank of the Thames, it was said to be the first museum in the world devoted entirely to industrial design. During the summer it was announced that a £10 million Museum of the British Empire and Commonwealth would be built at Temple Meads Station, Bristol. It would be

housed in the great train shed and would open in 1993.

In New York City the Whitney Museum of American Art unveiled the third version of its $37.5 million expansion plan. Two previous plans, in 1985 and 1987, had been set aside after preservationists protested that Michael Graves's designs would destroy the original 1966 facade. Preservationist pressure in that city had also led the Guggenheim Museum to alter the plans for its $18 million tower adjacent to the famous Frank Lloyd Wright structure.

The financially pressed Museum of the American Indian in New York City agreed to give part of its collection to the Smithsonian Institution, which would build a new 33,000-sq m (360,000-sq ft) National Museum of the American Indian on the Mall in Washington, D.C. Also in Manhattan, the Museum of American Folk Art, without gallery space for almost three years, opened the Eva and Morris Feld Gallery at Lincoln Square while plans continued for a museum structure on its nearby 53rd Street property. The Brooklyn (N.Y.) Museum received a $3.5 million gift to build a 460-seat auditorium, the first phase of the museum's master renovation plan.

A new $10 million research centre was established at the International Museum of Photography in Rochester, N.Y., while the adjoining 83-year-old George Eastman House underwent a $1.5 million restoration. In Kansas City, Mo., the Nelson-Atkins Museum of Art opened a 6.8-ha (17-ac) Henry Moore Sculpture Garden with 58 pieces from the Hall Family Foundation, including 12 monumental bronzes. The California Palace of the Legion of Honor and the M.H. de Young Memorial Museum in San Francisco were reorganized under a new director. The de Young would now display American art, while the Legion of Honor, formerly the only large U.S. museum entirely devoted to French art, would also show other European traditions.

The French art magazine *Connaissance des Arts* published a survey of its subscribers' museum-visiting habits. It concluded that social pressures and prestige were more important than interest in art in persuading people to visit museums and that the high rate of attendance reported among students dropped precipitously when education was completed.   (JOSHUA KIND; SANDRA MILLIKIN)

See also Art Exhibitions and Art Sales.
This article updates the *Macropædia* article MUSEUMS.

Music

Classical. The comings and goings of major conductors dominated the world of classical music in 1989. The resignation and death soon afterward of Herbert von Karajan (*see* OBITUARIES) was front-page news throughout the world, as was the dismissal of Daniel Barenboim (*see* BIOGRAPHIES) from Paris's Bastille Opera—even before its opening. The completion of the Bastille Opera was itself controversial, on levels political, financial, architectural, and musical. Such spectacles apart, the year offered the usual round of musical births and musicians' deaths. U.S. symphony orchestras had their familiar rounds of budget crises and contract deadlocks, even as period-instruments orchestras on both sides of the Atlantic prospered. The long-playing phonograph record nearly vanished into history, but the compact disc continued to energize the recording industry, and classical music videos—in both tape and disk form—made further inroads into the home-entertainment business.

Citing health reasons, Karajan resigned his position as conductor-for-life of the Berlin Philharmonic in April, but his relationship with the self-governing orchestra had been strained for some time. When he died three months later, the issue of his one-time Nazi Party membership again surfaced, but his more enduring legacy would surely be the orchestra he steel-wooled into a high gloss and the more than 800 recordings made over half a century. As his replacement, the Berlin orchestra chose an Italian, Claudio Abbado, music director of the Vienna State Opera. At the Salzburg Festival, of which Karajan had been the guiding spirit and resident conductor, Gérard Montier was named the new artistic director; it was announced that in the future there would be no Karajan-style permanent conductor.

Having been hired as the Bastille Opera's artistic and music director in 1987, Barenboim ran afoul of Pierre Bergé, director of the Yves Saint-Laurent fashion firm and newly appointed president of the Association of Paris Opera Theatres. Bergé objected to Barenboim's salary (in excess of $1 million a year) and programming and, in January, had him fired. Four months later a real dark horse, the South Korean pianist-conductor Myung Whun Chung, was named to the job.

The Bastille Opera opened on schedule, with a pair of July concerts commemorating the 200th anniversary of the French Revolution. The building, designed by Carlos Ott of Canada, was derided as an architectural monstrosity, but it promised the world's most sophisticated stage machinery in two very different performing spaces. Operatic productions were scheduled to begin early in 1990.

The year was marked by at least two dramatic returns to the stage. Thirty years after his historic first prize in the Tchaikovsky Competition and 11 years after retiring from public performances, pianist Van Cliburn made a comeback, appearing with the orchestras of Philadelphia and Dallas, Texas. And, after an apparently victorious two-year bout with leukemia, tenor José Carreras gave a triumphant Carnegie Hall recital. The most publicized new figure on the concert scene was probably the diminutive but fiery Soviet pianist Aleksey Sultanov, who won first prize in the Van Cliburn Competition; second and third prizes, respectively, went to José Carlos Cocarelli from Brazil and Benedetto Lupo from Italy.

Deaths in the musical world included composer-critic Virgil Thomson, conductors Giuseppe Patané and Witold Rowicki, soprano Zinka Milanov, mezzo Jan DeGaetani, bass Martti Talvela, pianists Vladimir Horowitz, John Ogdon, and Steven De Groote, violist Paul Doktor, hornist Alan Civil, and musicologist Karl Geiringer (*see* OBITUARIES). Also, it was a sad year for two popular U.S. music magazines; after nearly 40 years *High Fidelity* ceased publication in July, and two months later the nine-year-old *Ovation* did likewise.

Orchestras. Exactly two weeks after his firing from the Bastille Opera, Barenboim was named Sir Georg Solti's successor as music director of the Chicago Symphony Orchestra, effective in September 1991. In Los Angeles André Previn quit the city's Philharmonic in a huff, saying, "There is no room for a music director." (He was known to have feuded with its strong-willed executive director, Ernest Fleischmann.) The young Finnish conductor Esa-Pekka Salonen was named Previn's successor, starting in 1992.

The Baltimore (Md.) Symphony Orchestra, which had been prospering along with its newly refurbished city, began 1989 with what became a 21-week contract deadlock with musicians, and the Denver (Colo.) Symphony's fiscal woes led to early termination of its spring season. The Detroit (Mich.) Symphony was also in financial trouble, and even the revered Cleveland (Ohio) Orchestra returned from a triumphant European tour to post worrying deficits. On a happier note, and after nearly nine decades as a renter, the Dallas Symphony finally got a home of its own. Elegantly understated outside, opulent (both visually and

BEATRIZ SCHILLER

The fire god Loge emerges from a cloud of smoke in *Das Rheingold*, the first of four operas in Wagner's *Ring* cycle, performed at the Metropolitan Opera in New York City. The production combined traditional staging with monumental sets and effects.

acoustically) inside, the $81.5 million Morton H. Meyerson Symphony Center was designed by I.M. Pei.

What had come to seem a new golden age for U.S. composers writing for the orchestra continued with no dulling of its lustre. Among the year's premieres were new works by Stephen Paulus, Steven Stucky, Michael Torke, Joan Tower, and Ellen Taaffe Zwilich. The Chicago Symphony Orchestra's premiere of Jacob Druckman's *Brangle* got some unexpected publicity when supporters of the shadowy right-wing political figure Lyndon LaRouche marched outside with signs accusing the work of satanism (which Druckman, of course, denied). Literally on the subject of good versus evil (and based on Milton's *Paradise Lost*), Alexander Goehr's *Eve Dreams in Paradise* was premiered by England's City of Birmingham Symphony Orchestra. And the Cleveland Orchestra (with pianist Garrick Ohlsson and conductor Christoph von Dohnanyi) resurrected and recorded a rarity: Feruccio Busoni's monumental Piano Concerto.

Opera. Radically recast operas again captured their shares of headlines. An English National Opera *Masked Ball,* directed by the young American David Alden, was greeted with a mixture of boos and bravos and by front-page coverage in at least five international newspapers. Chicago's Lyric Opera mounted a wildly controversial Peter Sellars *Tannhäuser* that turned the medieval Minnesinger into a televangelist and Venusberg into a Las Vegas motel; Washington, D.C., was able to see the complete *Ring* in Götz Friedrich's bleakly modern Deutsche Oper production. And Sellars' sassy resetting (in New York City's Trump Tower) of the Mozart/Da Ponte trilogy (*The Marriage of Figaro, Don Giovanni,* and *Così fan tutte*) was one of the parting acts of PepsiCo Summerfare; based in Purchase, N.Y., the festival had been a lively one, and its passing was much mourned.

Of course, there were also more traditional productions of note. New York City's Metropolitan Opera performed its "mainstream" Otto Schenk *Ring* cycle, with such sturdy Wagnerians as Hildegard Behrens and James Morris onstage and James Levine in the pit. Levine also conducted a remarkable double bill of Bartok's *Bluebeard's Castle* and Schoenberg's *Erwartung,* with Jessye Norman very much centre stage. Across the Lincoln Center Plaza, the New York City Opera fell victim to yet another orchestra contract walkout; the fall season, which was to have included the first New York staging of Schoenberg's *Moses und Aaron,* was canceled. On a happier note, the Brooklyn (N.Y.) Academy of Music imported an elegant Lully *Atys,* done with period instruments and production values by Les Arts Florissants, a Paris-based company conducted by William Christie. Other novelties included the first U.S. production in 80 years of Catalani's *La Wally,* by the Sarasota (Fla.) Opera, and the first complete *Ring* in German ever mounted in Poland, with August Everding directing and Robert Satanowski conducting, in Warsaw's Grand Theatre. At Glyndebourne, England, Andrew Davis made his debut as the company's music director with Janacek's *Jenufa,* and Lotfi Mansouri took his leave of the Toronto-based Canadian Opera Company with a powerful *The Makropulos Case.*

There was no shortage of new operas. Robert Wilson directed the La Scala premiere of Giacomo Manzoni's *Doktor Faustus* (based on the Thomas Mann novel), while Hamburg (West Germany) Opera offered Alfred Schnittke's *Peer Gynt* (to a libretto by the company's ballet director, John Neumeir). At age 84 Sir Michael Tippett completed his fifth opera, *New Year,* which was premiered in a Houston (Texas) Grand Opera production conducted by John

Claudio Abbado, the music director of the Vienna State Opera, was chosen to succeed Herbert von Karajan as conductor of the Berlin Philharmonic. Karajan, who had fashioned the Berlin Philharmonic into a world-class orchestra, died in July 1989.
CLIVE BARDA/LONDON

DeMain, and Cleveland Opera introduced *Holy Blood and Crescent Moon* by Stewart Copeland (former drummer of the rock band The Police), with libretto by Susan Shirwen. Other premieres included Anthony Davis' *Under the Double Moon* (Opera Theatre of St. Louis, Mo.) and David Blake's *The Plumber's Gift* (English National Opera).

Authenticist Performances. What used to be called the early-music movement continued to be one of the liveliest musical forces of all. If a single name dominated this growing field, it was that of British conductor Roger Norrington. With the release of the final volume in his period-instruments recordings of all the Beethoven symphonies and the first four piano concerti (with fortepianist Melvyn Tan), Norrington consolidated his position as the most talked-about Beethoven conductor since Toscanini. Norrington took his London Classical Players and Schütz Choir on their first U.S. tour, presenting one of his two-day "Beethoven Experiences" at PepsiCo Summerfare and giving concerts at the Mostly Mozart, Great Woods, Tanglewood, and Ravinia festivals. With U.S. musicians he conducted a brilliant concert performance of Mozart's opera *Idomeneo* at the Boston Early Music Festival; he also was a guest conductor with several U.S. orchestras.

Also busy in the early-music movement was Britain's John Eliot Gardiner, who marked the 25th anniversary of his own Monteverdi Choir with a world tour; on the recording front, he taped the Monteverdi Vespers at San Marco in Venice and neared completion of his complete survey (with fortepianist Malcolm Bilson) of the Mozart piano concerti. Two more Englishmen were at work with U.S. period-instruments ensembles, Trevor Pinnock with the Classical Band, newly established in New York City, and Nicholas McGegan with San Francisco's Philharmonia Baroque Orchestra. It was evidence of the "mainstreaming" of the authenticist movement that an original-instruments *Figaro* turned up in no less a place than Glyndebourne, with Simon Rattle conducting the Orchestra of the Age of Enlightenment.

Recordings. As the decade came to a close, so did the just over four-decade history of the long-playing record; few new releases were being issued on LP, and sales of compact discs were challenging even the supremacy of cassette tapes. The huge new demand for CDs continued to make for considerable activity in the recording field, however, and there were some interesting shifts of allegiances among record companies. RCA records, now

owned by the German Bertelsman conglomerate, lured Gunther Hensler away from Polygram. CBS Masterworks was renamed Sony Classical, after its new Japanese owner, and former Deutsche Grammophon executive Gunther Breest was hired to run the label; one of Breest's first coups was issuing Carlos Kleiber's New Year's concert with the Vienna Philharmonic, and a new series of classical videos was announced.

Among the ongoing trends in the record business was the release of symphonic cycles by a number of the 20th century's more conservative composers. Chandos completed its survey of Arnold Bax symphonies and continued with those of Vaughan Williams and his teacher Charles Villiers Stanford; BIS carried on with the Estonian Eduard Tubin; in the U.S., Delos launched a Howard Hanson cycle and promised complete surveys of the symphonies of Walter Piston and David Diamond. Among the year's most highly praised recordings was the long-awaited Glyndebourne *Porgy and Bess* (with an all-American cast under Simon Rattle). A newly complete and "authentic" Jerome Kern/Oscar Hammerstein II *Show Boat,* with John McGlinn conducting the London Sinfonietta, was a prizewinner in both the International Record Critics Awards and *Gramophone* magazine's Record Awards.   (SCOTT CANTRELL)

Jazz. By the end of the 1980s, jazz existed in a circle of paradoxes. Though jazz clubs, concerts, and, especially, festivals continued to attract audiences of all ages, it was by no means a popular music in the same way as rock or country and western. Yet jazz's relatively low level of institutional support and its mode of presentation—it was most often heard in nightclubs, for example—also removed it from the status of a fine art. Though jazz is inherently an African-American art, the decline in size of the young black audience was significant. Moreover, by 1989 the early jazz musicians had long since vanished, few swing-era players remained active, the pioneers of bop had passed retirement age, and even the founders of free jazz were well into their middle years. Yet all of these jazz idioms, born of the conflicts of earlier 20th-century America, remained popular, though the majority of the musicians who were playing them grew up and were educated in the era of television and computers.

One of the year's major projects was the Jazz Masterwork Editions, announced by the Smithsonian Institution and Oberlin College's Conservatory of Music. The Editions were a massive program of transcribing classic jazz recordings and publishing them for use by schools and working bands; the scores were to be annotated to assist in the necessary interpretation. The first three volumes would present the music of the 1937–38 Count Basie band, the 1932–34 Fletcher Henderson band, and one of several projected collections of Duke Ellington's long works. The repertoires of other big swing bands were to follow, up to three editions a year during the 1990s. If jazz's masterworks were not re-created in live performance, said composer-educator Gunther Schuller, one of the Editions' executive board, "it will not be long before our jazz heritage, which now exists only on records, will disappear altogether."

The problem with concert revivals of classic jazz had always been in getting authentic expression and rhythmic feeling from players who were generations removed from the music's origins. For this reason the original recordings of a largely improvised music such as jazz, in which sound and expression are such crucial elements, were the essential documents of its heritage. The recording industry's rush to replace older recordings with digitally reprocessed recordings was endangering this heritage, however, for despite the digital process's promises of improved sound quality,

a fearful number of digitally reprocessed jazz reissues were far inferior to the original recordings. For example, 1989 saw reissues with Bix Beiderbecke's bell-like 1928 cornet tone turned shrill and scratchy, Billie Holiday in 1937–38 with her classic Freddie Green, Walter Page, and Jo Jones rhythm section inaudible, and Bessie Smith's rich voice reduced to tin. Indeed, the proliferation of this kind of careless, insensitive production raised the spectre of great jazz becoming as inaccessible to future generations as Mozart's piano improvisations.

The JVC Jazz Festival in New York City (formerly the Newport, then Kool Jazz Festival) celebrated its 35th year in 1989, while two Canadian festivals—Jazz City in Edmonton, Alta., and Montreal's International Jazz Festival—both celebrated their 10th years. The Montreal festival included a unique tribute to an artist by offering bassist Charlie Haden in seven nights of duet and trio concerts with a changing cast of costars that included trumpeter Don Cherry; guitarist Pat Metheny; pianists Geri Allen, Paul Bley, and, from Cuba, Gonzalo Rubalcava; and also a concert by Haden's Liberation Music Orchestra.

The gradual dissolving of the iron curtain found pianist Cecil Taylor and the ROVA Saxophone Quartet touring the Soviet Union. The former underground Soviet pianist Vyacheslav Ganelin, an important figure in 1980s jazz, began emphasizing his synthesizer playing and formed a new trio that recorded an album in Israel, his new home.

Elsewhere in international jazz, London's first 24-hour-a-day jazz radio station began broadcasting. An Australian trumpeter-trombonist, James Morrison, and a Czech-born pianist, Adam Makowicz, created an exceptional album, *Swiss Encounter,* for the East-West label. One of the decade's most ambitious recording projects was announced by West Berlin's FMP Records: the simultaneous release of 10 Cecil Taylor compact discs, including duets with five drummers (from East and West Germany, The Netherlands, South Africa, and the U.K.), a big band of European musicians, and a trio with cellist Tristan Honsinger and innovative saxophonist Evan Parker.

Charles Mingus' last major work, *Epitaph,* was at last given its first complete performance, 10 years after the composer's 1979 death, in New York City by an orchestra conducted by Schuller. Another major jazz composer, Benny Carter, brought his 1961 *Further Definitions* arrangements to a stimulating performance at the Chicago Jazz Festival. The fortunes of neglected composer-pianist Freddie Redd suddenly turned when Uptown Records released his *Lonely City* album and Mosaic reissued his complete 1959–61 Blue Note recordings in a boxed set.

One of jazz's great improvisers, Roy Eldridge (*see* OBITUARIES), whose daring trumpet flights were a major advance in both sensibility and technique during the swing era, died in 1989. The year's death toll also included saxophonist Arnett Cobb, guitarist Tiny Grimes, trumpeter Wild Bill Davison (*see* OBITUARIES), and trombonist-bandleader Will Bradley, from the swing era; bop pianist Phineas Newborn and late-bop trumpeter Woody Shaw; freely improvising bassist Donald Rafael Garrett; and Steve McCall, former drummer in the trio Air, whose unique sensitivity to dynamics made him a major figure in avant-garde jazz.

Among the year's books, biographies of Benny Goodman and Dexter Gordon and Miles Davis' autobiography were valued because of the importance of their subjects, while Martin Williams produced a valuable collection of essays, *Jazz in Its Time.* The year's major addition to the literature of jazz was *The Swing Era: The Development of Jazz, 1930–1945* by Schuller, the successor to his critical-historical landmark *Early Jazz.*   (JOHN LITWEILER)

Popular. The year 1989 was one in which many veterans of popular music returned with a vengeance, proving that success no longer depended just on youth or outrage but relied also on professionalism and staying power. Several of the major tours of the year were by bands that had first established their reputations in the 1960s and now, in middle age, were able to return to the big stadiums of the world, playing to audiences that included people who had not been born when the bands began performing.

British performers enjoying such a comeback included the former Beatle Paul McCartney, who released a well-received new album, *Flowers in the Dirt,* and then set out on a world tour, in which he revived many of his best-known songs from the Beatles era. The Rolling Stones also got together again for a tour, after releasing a new album, *Steel Wheels,* which was the best they had recorded during the 1980s. It showed that Keith Richards was still capable of gutsy and rousing guitar work, and the band, behind lead singer Mick Jagger (*see* BIOGRAPHIES), still had the energy and enthusiasm that had helped establish its reputation more than two decades earlier. It also provided a reminder that they had started out as often experimental blues musicians before becoming better known for their rebel stance. One track, "Continental Drift," featured wailing brass work from the traditional musicians of Joujouka, Morocco, a village that the band's former guitarist, the late Brian Jones, had visited in the 1960s.

Other veterans enjoying a comeback included The Who. Touring the U.S. and Britain with a new, augmented lineup, they gave special performances of their rock opera *Tommy,* in which they were joined by Billy Idol and Phil Collins. In October The Who were among those selected for induction into the Rock-and-Roll Hall of Fame. Van Morrison gained the biggest commercial success of his career with *Avalon Sunset.*

The same trend was repeated in the U.S., where Bob Dylan at long last recorded another classic album, *Oh Mercy,* which was hailed as his finest since *Blood on the Tracks* or even *Blonde on Blonde.* The songs ranged from slinky ballads to more up-tempo pieces and were concerned with global disintegration, religious themes, or soul-searching personal reflection, with a streak of good humour sneaking in through the gloom. It was remarkable for the quality of both the songwriting and the singing; Dylan performed with a powerful intimacy that had been lacking from much of his recent work.

If revivalism was one major trend during the year, then the other was the continued growth of the "world music" market. African music continued to expand its appeal, thanks to such artists as Salif Keita from Mali, whose *Ko-Yan* mixed traditional styles with a synthesized, highly contemporary backing and showed off his soulful, wailing, and mournful style. Youssou N'Dour, who had become the best-known African singer in the West following his tours on behalf of Amnesty International in the company of such superstars as Bruce Springsteen, showed the effects of such Western influence with his new album, *The Lion.* Perhaps the best African release of all came from South African artists recording in Paris. *Paris-Soweto* by the Soweto vocal team Mahlathini and the Mahotella Queens, was a rousing demonstration of their growling and soulful *mbaqanga* style.

Interest in African music was followed by interest in Latin-American styles, and in this area David Byrne, the singer and songwriter from Talking Heads, took the lead. During the year he compiled two anthologies of Brazilian music, which brought the work of such performers as Jorge Ben, Gilberto Gil, and Caetano Veloso to a new, non-

Superstar Mick Jagger of the Rolling Stones performs to a capacity crowd at Veterans Stadium in Philadelphia. The Rolling Stones and such other rock veterans as The Who and Paul McCartney returned to the stage with markedly successful revival tours.
PAUL NATKIN—PHOTO RESERVE INC.

Latin audience. He followed this by recording a solo album in which he was backed by a whole array of largely New York-based Latin musicians, whose brass, accordions, and percussion and light, lilting rhythmic backing were matched against the tuneful funk style of his writing. In many ways this was Byrne's answer to Paul Simon's African fusion album, *Graceland.*

In the more mainstream side of the Latin market, 1989 was another good year for Gloria Estefan and Miami Sound Machine, Miami-based performers who matched rousing, brassy dance songs inspired by Cuban styles with all-American soul ballads. Their album *Cuts Both Ways* and the single "Don't Wanna Lose You" were major hits on both sides of the Atlantic, and their previous album also returned to the best-seller list. Some of Estefan's songs were performed in Spanish and reflected the growing importance of the Spanish-speaking market in the U.S.

From black America, meanwhile, the most important development was the continued growth of the rhythmic "talk-over" style, rap. Popularized in the ghettoes of the East Coast cities as a form of do-it-yourself street protest music, the style spread into the black soul mainstream—thanks to such new stars as Salt-N-Pepa and L.L. Cool J—and also into the poor black areas of California, where a whole series of rappers emerged as major stars. Tone-Lōc matched his rap with a dash of guitar rock to create a style that would cross over into the white market, and his single "Wild Thing" reached second place on the U.S. charts, selling two million copies. Also from the West Coast, N.W.A. (Niggers with Attitude) provided a bleak report on those communities where poverty, drugs, and gang warfare were part of daily life. Their controversial album *Straight Outta Compton* showed that pop music could still shock, even in the year of revivals.

Two veterans of a still earlier era in popular music died during the year, the composers Irving Berlin, at the age of 101, and Sammy Fain (*see* OBITUARIES).

(ROBIN DENSELOW)

See also Dance; Motion Pictures; Television and Radio; Theatre.

This article updates the *Macropædia* article The History of Western MUSIC.

Philately and Numismatics

Stamps. Worldwide auction realizations confirmed a strong market for rarities during 1989, and there were indications that efforts to revive the hobby at more popular levels were taking effect. Exceptional realizations included: India 1854, 4 annas inverted head, £72,600 (Harmers, London); Spain 1852, 6 reales greenish-blue, used block of 12, Sw F 115,000 (Habsburg Feldman, Geneva); Cape of Good Hope 1861 "Woodblock," 1d vermilion used block of four including the 4d error, £104,500 (Sotheby, London); Bermuda 1937 "Revenue-Revenue" 12/6d postally used on cover to France, £10,000 (Temple Bar Auctions, Guernsey); Norway 1856, cover to Isle of Man franked with a pair of 3 skilling and six 4 skilling (two pairs and two singles) estimated at £750, sold at £20,900 (Christies/Robson Lowe, London). An 1860 Provisional Government of Tuscany 3 lire on an envelope addressed to the Marquis Bourbon del Monte went for a record 675 million lire.

The major international exhibition sponsored by the Fédération Internationale de Philatélie (FIP) was Philexfrance 89, held in Paris in July. The principal awards were: Grand Prix d'Honneur, Giuseppe Barcella for Papal States; Grand Prix International, Angelo Lima for Brazil; Grand Prix National (for French issues), Georges Dervin for French classic issues. At Sofia, Bulg., in May, the Federation of European Philatelic Associations was formed with Alan K. Huggins of the U.K. as chairman. The 53rd British Philatelic Federation Congress was held at Brighton, Sussex. Five collectors signed the Roll of Distinguished Philatelists: Enrique Martin de Bustamente, the first Spanish signatory since the Roll was founded in 1921; Prakaipet Indhusophon, the first Thai signatory and winner of the FIP Grand Prix d'Honneur at New Delhi in January; Roger Loeuillet (France), president of the French Chambre de Négociants et Experts en Philatélie; Christian C. Sundman (Finland), a leading specialist in Finnish stamps and postal stationery; and R. Martin Willcocks (U.K.), an authority on British postal history. The Congress Medal for 1989 was awarded to G. Franceska Rapkin, the fourth woman recipient in 31 years, and the Lichtenstein Medal of the Collectors Club of New York went to Susan M. McDonald, the first woman

CATHY MELLOAN

A new 25¢, peel-and-stick, self-adhesive stamp was introduced by the U.S. Postal Service in an attempt to do away with the older glue-coated stamps. The stamp, which carried an additional charge, was test-marketed in major cities throughout the U.S.

recipient. The Reginald M. Phillips Gold Medal, awarded every five years for outstanding work in the field of British stamp designing, went to Barry Robinson, head of design in the Royal Mail division of the Post Office.

The philatelic collections of the British Library were augmented by the transfer of 300 volumes of British postal history and stamps from 1660 to 1960. The collection had been bequeathed by the late H.G. Leslie Fletcher to the London Borough of Tottenham, whose council obtained the consent of the Charity Commissioners to transfer the collection into national safekeeping. The British police began investigations into claims of irregularities in the production and distribution of the stamps of Gibraltar and Tuvalu. The latter territory terminated its contract with Philatelic Distribution Corporation Ltd., a subsidiary of London & International Stamp Co. On August 22 the British Post Office issued its first undenominated stamps for restricted public use within Great Britain.

Henry Robert ("Bob") Holmes died in January aged 92. Holmes was a reforming president of the Royal Philatelic Society from 1961 to 1963. (KENNETH F. CHAPMAN)

Coins and Paper Money. Prices of exceedingly rare coins escalated during 1989 as Wall Street entered the numismatic marketplace. On July 7 in Chicago, a Louisiana company and a rare-coin limited partnership operated by Kidder, Peabody & Co. bought one of 15 known 1804 U.S. silver dollars for $990,000, the most ever paid for a single coin at public auction. The old record of $725,000 for a Brasher doubloon was set in 1979. In private transactions, a Minnesota money-management firm reportedly paid $1,350,000 for a U.S. pioneer gold coin that had sold for $325,000 in a 1980 auction, and two rare-coin companies announced that they had paid between $2 million and $4 million for nine U.S. coins known as the "King of Siam proof set," which included another of the 1804 dollars. The Wall Street firm of Salomon Brothers Inc. reported that rare coins went up 30.2% in value during the 12 months ended June 1, placing third in 13 categories of assets surveyed. Nevertheless, many old coins worn from use went down in value during 1989, in part because of a slumping silver and gold market throughout much of the year.

Canada's maple leaf was expected to rank as the world's most widely traded gold bullion coin for the second successive year, beating the U.S. American eagle, the Australian nugget, and the U.K.'s Britannia, among others. During 1988 Canada used 1.2 million troy ounces of gold to make maple leaf coins, about twice as much as the U.S. used to make eagles. Canada also completed its first full year of producing silver and platinum maple leafs; the silver coin was expected to rank second to the silver American eagle in worldwide sales for 1989 and the platinum coin, second to the Australian koala. In the U.S. some coin dealers called on the federal government to ban the importation of Chinese panda coins to protest the killing of student demonstrators in Beijing (Peking) in June.

U.S. lawmakers introduced bills in the 101st Congress that would require new designs on circulating coinage and a Christopher Columbus $1 coin to replace the $1 Federal Reserve note. A lobbyist predicted that a $1 coin would save taxpayers $120 million annually in the cost of printing money. In June Canada stopped issuing a $1 note, forcing its citizens to use a new coin that entered circulation in 1987. The U.S. Mint sold to collectors three types of 1989-dated coins commemorating the 200th anniversary of the U.S. Congress. Profits from sales were to be used to help pay for repairs to the Capitol. Several other countries also issued new commemorative coins, and Canada announced it would use a new portrait of Queen Elizabeth II on its

A rare 1804 U.S. silver dollar, featuring the bald eagle on one side and Lady Liberty on the other, was purchased by a rare-coin limited partnership and a company in Louisiana for a record $990,000.

coinage starting in 1990, the first such design change in 25 years.

Ongoing technical problems delayed until the early 1990s the introduction of U.S. paper money with additional anticounterfeiting devices, including microprinting and a security thread embedded in the paper, that were expected to make paper money more difficult to duplicate on colour copiers. In July the U.S. Secret Service confiscated $1 million worth of counterfeit "greenbacks" produced on colour copying machines, the largest such "take" to that time. U.S. collectors reported finding 1989-dated quarters that were missing their mint mark. Some dealers charged about $100 each for the error coins. The mint mark failed to form because part of the dies that made the coins became filled with grease. In late summer about 25,000 troy ounces of rare gold coins and bars were recovered from a ship that sank off South Carolina in 1857. Salvaging operations were to continue to mid-1990. (ROGER BOYE)

Photography

The year 1989 marked photography's 150th anniversary since the public introduction of the daguerreotype process in Paris on Aug. 19, 1839. The medium received virtually nonstop tributes around the world, ranging from postage stamps, exhibitions, and books to scholarly lectures and television documentaries. Coinciding with this lavish recognition, a number of photographic cultural institutions enlarged or enhanced their facilities, while the introduction of new cameras, some highly sophisticated and others utterly simple, gave users their widest choice ever.

Photo Equipment. A major new 35-mm single-lens-reflex (SLR) camera was the top-of-the-line Canon EOS-1, which combined sophisticated operating features and all-electronic controls within a modified version of the familiar ergonomically contoured EOS body. A multiblade focal-plane shutter provided speeds from 30 seconds to $1/_{8,000}$ second with flash synchronization up to $1/_{250}$ second. Exposure metering options included an evaluative system, which analyzed six segments of the picture area; centre-weighted averaging; 5.8% partial area; 2.3% spot; and through-the-lens (TTL) flash. In addition to standard EOS exposure modes—shutter- and aperture-priority autoexposure, shiftable program keyed to lens focal length, and metered manual—the EOS-1 added a mode that automatically selected an aperture and shutter-speed combination to provide a chosen depth of field. Programmable automatic three-frame exposure bracketing was yet another feature.

The camera's fast, sensitive autofocus system employed an image sensor that detected horizontal as well as vertical lines with lenses of $f/2.8$ and faster, and it focused from infinity to 46 cm (18 in) in 0.3 second with a 50-mm $f/1.8$ lens. Both single-shot and predictive continuous autofocus modes for tracking a moving subject were available. A unique feature was the Quick Control Dial, a knurled thumb wheel on the back of the camera. When activated, it allowed the user's right thumb to control autoexposure compensation or change manual apertures and shutter speeds, thus aiding one-handed camera operation.

Minolta filled out its line of autofocus SLR Maxxum cameras with the midrange 5000i ("i" for intelligent), which fit between its advanced 7000i and basic 3000i models and shared some features of each, including Minolta's Creative Expansion Cards, which programmed special operating features into the camera. With a top shutter speed of $1/_{2,000}$ second, lens-keyed programmed automatic and metered manual exposure control, and predictive autofocus system plus manual focus with a signal-light aid, the 5000i included a built-in TTL-metered zoom electronic flash that covered the field of view of 35-mm to 70-mm lenses.

As annual sales of point-and-shoot autofocus 35-mm cameras soared, the number of new models continued to proliferate. An innovative model was the Chinon 5001 Handyzoom, having a programmed electronic leaf shutter that offered speeds of $1/_4$ to $1/_{300}$ second, a Chinon 35–70-mm $f/3.7$–6.8 zoom lens, and a built-in zooming flash. The camera focused automatically by means of three infrared-emitting diodes arranged in a horizontal array. The diodes emitted beams in a left-to-right sequence across the picture area, thus measuring the distance of a subject even when it was not centred and providing information about its width. When activated, a unique microprocessor-based automatic picture composing system analyzed the subject situation and automatically drove the zoom motor to provide an appropriate image size.

Disposable cameras increased in popularity in both Japan and the U.S. Fuji added to its Fujicolor Quicksnap line with a telephoto model combining an 86-mm $f/11$ lens with a shutter speed of $1/_{150}$ second, and Kodak introduced two new throwaways. The Weekend 35, with a fixed-focus lens and a single shutter speed, was made waterproof and submersible to 3.7 m (12 ft) by a clear plastic outer casing. Kodak's Stretch 35 panoramic camera used a 25-mm $f/12$ lens to record a 78° horizontal view on a band across the middle of a standard 35-mm frame.

Kodak extended its premium Ektar line of colour print films with Ektar 125, which provided fine grain and sharpness nearly equal to that of Ektar 25 but at five times the latter's ISO speed rating, and introduced improved versions of Kodacolor Gold 400 and 1600. Fuji added five new colour print films to its lineup. ISO 100 Fujicolor Reala was an innovative film design in which a fourth, blue-green-sensitive emulsion layer was added to the traditional

Amateur photographer Ron Olshwanger won the Pulitzer Prize for spot news photography for his dramatic image of a fireman trying to revive a young child by mouth-to-mouth resuscitation, which appeared in the *St. Louis Post-Dispatch.*

ST. LOUIS POST-DISPATCH

blue-, green-, and red-sensitive layers. The results were a more natural colour rendition, neutral whites, and a less greenish cast with fluorescent lighting. Fujicolor Super HG 200 and 400 provided improved sharpness and finer grain, while Fujicolor Super HR-II 100 and 1600 offered longer shelf life and greater latent-image stability.

Electronic still video cameras designed for the amateur market were introduced, but with no hard-copy printers

available for home use, they remained more an advance guard than a true breakthrough. Exhibiting point-and-shoot simplicity, the palm-size Sony Mavica MCV-V1 included a 15-mm $f/2.8$ fixed-focus lens and shutter speeds of $1/60$ to $1/500$ second, and it recorded 50 pictures on a reusable video floppy disk. The pictures could be displayed on a TV set or monitor through a playback adapter.

Cultural Trends. Among tributes to photography's 150th anniversary were the balanced, comprehensive exhibition "On the Art of Fixing a Shadow: 150 Years of Photography," which opened at the National Gallery of Art, Washington, D.C., and the equally ambitious but more narrowly focused "The Art of Photography: 1839–1989" at the Museum of Fine Arts, Houston, Texas, which was curated chiefly by collector Daniel Wolf from the work of only 85 photographers. Martin W. Sandler's book *American Image—Photographing One Hundred Fifty Years in the Life of a Nation* gave a pictorial social history of America.

Photographic books included *In Our Time: The World as Seen by Magnum Photographers,* with text pieces by William Manchester, Fred Ritchin, and Jean Lacoutre, a coffee-table tribute to the Magnum Photos agency, founded in 1947. Trenchant images of business executives, workers, and consumers by a talented photographer who was killed in a plane crash in 1959 appeared in *America Worked: The 1950's Photographs of Dan Weiner,* with text by William A. Ewing. *Halsman at Work,* with text by the photographer's widow, Yvonne, is a delightful inside look at how Halsman created his often startling, surreal images.

The International Museum of Photography at George Eastman House, Rochester, N.Y., opened its impressive new building with greatly increased space to house exhibits, a library, study areas, and archives that included some 600,000 photographs, 7,000 films, and 11,000 pieces of equipment. In San Francisco, the Friends of Photography opened the Ansel Adams Center, a museum dedicated to creative photography and comprising five exhibition galleries, a bookstore and library, and a new headquarters for the 10,000-member Friends of Photography organization. In Great Britain the National Museum of Photography, Film, and Television opened its new Kodak Museum in Bradford to house the more than 50,000 artifacts and photographs donated by Kodak Ltd. from its former home at the Kodak facilities in Harrow.

©1989 CRISTINA GARCIA RODERO

The photograph of a religious procession was taken by Spanish photographer Cristina Garcia Rodero, who won the 10th annual W. Eugene Smith Grant in Humanistic Photography for her documentary depicting cultural life in rural Mediterranean Europe.

The death of Emperor Hirohito (see OBITUARIES) in January dominated the cultural aspects of photography in Japan in 1989. Numerous books and magazines, including issues of the *Asahi Graphic* and *Mainichi Graphic,* were devoted to his life and long reign, and many old historic photographs went on public display to commemorate the end of the Showa period. "The Works of Eleven Photographers, 1965–75," a retrospective exhibition, was the first tangible achievement of an effort, launched in 1988, to establish a museum in Japan specializing in photography.

In the U.S., photography precipitated a highly charged controversy involving artistic freedom and public policy. The Corcoran Gallery of Art, Washington, D.C., faced with the prospect of congressional displeasure, canceled a touring retrospective show, sponsored in part by the National Endowment of the Arts, of the work of the late Robert Mapplethorpe (see OBITUARIES). The exhibition included photographs depicting explicit homosexual and heterosexual erotic acts that were deemed offensive by some U.S. legislators, including Sen. Jesse Helms (Rep., N.C.), who proposed a bill to prohibit federal financing of art that violates broadly defined moral standards. The Corcoran later apologized for its cancellation of the show, and the Helms proposal was rejected by a congressional committee. Milder restrictions, however, were imposed on the National Endowment for the Arts, and the issues raised seemed far from settled.

At the 46th Pictures of the Year competition sponsored by the National Press Photographers Association and the University of Missouri School of Journalism, James Nachtwey of Magnum Photos won the Magazine Photographer of the Year award for a variety of essays; John Kaplan of the *Pittsburgh* (Pa.) *Press* received the Newspaper Photographer of the Year award for "Rodney's Crime," a picture essay that follows a young murder suspect through the Pennsylvania legal system; and Eugene Richards received the Canon Photo Essay Award for his *Life* magazine report on "Crack: The Downfall of a Neighborhood."

The 1989 Pulitzer Prize for spot news photography went to amateur photographer Ron Olshwanger for his wrenching image of a fireman trying to save a young girl's life with mouth-to-mouth resuscitation, published in the *St. Louis* (Mo.) *Post-Dispatch.* The feature photography Pulitzer went to Manny Crisostomo of the *Detroit* (Mich.) *Free Press* for his picture essay "A Class Act: The Life and Times of Southwestern High School." Spanish photographer Cristina Garcia Rodero won the 10th annual W. Eugene Smith Grant in Humanistic Photography for her ongoing documentation of vanishing aspects of cultural life in rural Mediterranean Europe.   (ARTHUR GOLDSMITH)

See also Motion Pictures.

This article updates the *Macropædia* article PHOTOGRAPHY.

Physics

Without doubt 1989 would be remembered as the year of cold fusion. The concept burst onto the international stage in late March as a possible answer to the energy problems of the world, but at the end of the year it sat under a considerable cloud. It had long been known that nuclear fusion can take place at temperatures of millions of degrees Celsius, but the announcement of fusion events occurring in great numbers at room temperature caught the whole scientific community by surprise.

When two nuclei from among the light elements (those with low atomic numbers) are brought sufficiently close, they can fuse into one heavier nucleus while releasing subatomic particles and substantial amounts of energy. Moving two nuclei together requires high energy because they are both positively charged; as they get nearer and nearer, their like charges repel one another more and more strongly. However, if they can be brought close enough, on the order of a ten-thousandth of a billionth of a centimetre (10^{-13} cm), it is possible for the nuclear force—the very short-range, attractive force that binds together the constituents of the nucleus—to overcome the electrostatic repulsion and pull the nuclei together. The energy needed for overcoming the repulsion can be supplied by heating matter to very high temperatures, producing a plasma in which the nuclei are free of the electrons that normally orbit them. When nuclei collide in a hot plasma, their extremely high kinetic energies can bring them close enough to fuse.

For decades, large-scale fusion experiments employing massive, expensive machines have been under way at several centres around the world in an effort to find a suitable means of containing a hot plasma of hydrogen isotopes long enough for fusion to occur. The ultimate goal, so far elusive, is to extract more energy from the fusion process than is invested in maintaining the hot plasma; in other words, to create a self-sustaining reaction whose excess energy then could be used to generate electric power.

When two light nuclei fuse, the product nucleus and emitted particles have a total mass that is slightly less than that of the reactants. This mass difference appears as released energy, which adds to the overall heating of the plasma. For example, the fusion of two nuclei of deuterium (D)—a heavy isotope of hydrogen made up of a proton (p) and a neutron (n) rather than the single proton nucleus of ordinary hydrogen—leads to at least two possible reactions:

$$(1)\ D + D \rightarrow {}^3He + n + 3.3\ MeV;$$
$$(2)\ D + D \rightarrow {}^3H + p + 4.0\ MeV.$$

In the reactions, ^3H is tritium, another heavy isotope of hydrogen made up of one proton and two neutrons, and ^3He is a light helium isotope comprising two protons and one neutron. Both reactions release substantial energy, which is expressed in millions of electron volts (MeV). This energy release is the reason that the Sun continues to burn; it is a giant self-sustaining fusion reactor converting hydrogen into helium. The liberated energy is also responsible for the tremendous destructiveness of the hydrogen bomb.

In light of this experience with fusion as being achievable only at very high temperatures, it is not difficult to understand the reactions of the scientific community when electrochemists B. Stanley Pons (see BIOGRAPHIES) of the University of Utah and Martin Fleischmann of the University of Southampton, England, announced their observation of cold fusion in a simple electrochemical cell at room temperature. In essence, what they reported was the generation of excess heat and fusion products from an electrolysis experiment in which an electrode of palladium metal absorbed a large amount of deuterium. They attributed these effects to deuterium-deuterium fusion.

The experimenters' apparatus consisted of a palladium cathode and a platinum anode immersed in an electrolytic bath of heavy water, or deuterium oxide (D_2O), with dissolved lithium. Palladium is known for its ability to absorb and store large amounts of hydrogen in spaces within its crystal lattice. When electric current was passed through the bath, the heavy water decomposed into its elements; oxygen was released at the platinum anode and deuterium at the palladium cathode. The liberated deuterium moved into the metal, which grew more and more saturated. Even-

tually, according to Pons and Fleischmann, the deuterium was squeezed ever closer together until the packing forced some deuterium nuclei near enough for fusion to occur.

Because of the nature of the fusion process, monitoring for fusion reactions can take two approaches: measuring the heat output (calorimetric) and watching for signs of the reaction products (nucleonic). Calorimetric measurements showed that after an incubation period of days or weeks, the electrolytic cell generated heat for an extended time. By late in the year, however, details of the incubation period and precise records of heat output had not been made available. Nucleonic monitoring was of three different kinds: determination of the amount of tritium that accumulated in the electrolyte from reaction (2), measurement of the neutron flux generated from reaction (1), and measurement of gamma rays from the interaction of emitted neutrons with water contained in a separate cell around the electrolytic bath. However, neither at the initial announcement nor during the ensuing weeks did complete, satisfactory details of these measurements or, in fact, of the experimental setup and procedure become disseminated.

The measurement data that the two electrochemists did release contained a major stumbling block to interpreting their results in terms of cold fusion. The heat generated in the electrolytic cell can be used to estimate a deuterium-deuterium reaction rate. Likewise, measurements of neutron and tritium products also can yield a reaction rate. Unfortunately, when the rates were calculated and compared, the one derived from calorimetric measurements was far higher, by a factor as high as a billion, than the other. Pons and Fleischmann later admitted to the possibility of error in their nucleonic data but stood by their claims of high heat generation.

The initial report of cold fusion, announced to the press in a blaze of publicity, caused excitement, surprise, and consternation in the scientific community. Within weeks laboratories around the world began attempts to reproduce the experiments, despite the lack of detailed published information. To criticism about the dearth of experimental detail was added criticism about the way the announcement was made. Normally scientific advances are presented first to other scientists, either at a conference where the researchers are available to answer questions or in a detailed article in the scientific literature. Before publication in a journal, the article is scrutinized by other experts (referees) in the field, who then recommend publication, amendment, or rejection. In the case of cold fusion the traditional practice of "scientists first" was sidestepped, perhaps because of the enormous economic and political implications of the results. Consequently, the work was not given the opportunity to benefit from valuable expert critique.

Soon after Pons and Fleischmann's announcement, a team from Brigham Young University, Provo, Utah, led by Steven Jones also reported signs of cold fusion. Jones's group had been independently pursuing cold fusion for some time in experiments similar to those of Pons and Fleischmann, and the two teams had discussed their approaches and data. Using a very sensitive detector, Jones's group reported finding neutrons, though at rates corresponding to a level of fusion too low even to be detectable by calorimetric means.

If any of the evidence for fusion neutrons reported from the two experiments is real, it may have some basis in a cold fusion process already familiar to physicists. By means of a phenomenon called tunneling, quantum mechanics allows for a definite, though very small, probability that two nuclei can fuse without having to overcome their mutual electrostatic repulsion. The major problem with tunneling-based fusion is that it occurs at a rate much too low to account for the heat measured by Pons and Fleischmann. Other, exotic fusion processes that yield heat but no neutrons or tritium were pondered, though there appeared to be no evidence for any other fusion process. Furthermore, although there were sporadic reports from other laboratories of unusual effects or partial confirmations in their own electrochemical experiments, no groups came forward during the year to support the University of Utah researchers in their claim for large amounts of fusion.

By the end of the year, room-temperature fusion in electrolytic cells remained unconfirmed, and many scientists were skeptical of Pons and Fleischmanns' results and interpretation. Nevertheless, the many as yet inadequately explained observations made by both Utah groups and others suggested the possibility that some unrecognized chemistry or physics was at work and promised researchers intriguing times in the months ahead.   (S.B. PALMER)

This article updates the *Macropædia* articles ATOMS: *Energy from atoms;* The PHYSICAL SCIENCES: *Physics.*

GEORGE FREY—TIME MAGAZINE

"Fusion in a jar" became a sobriquet used to refer to the cold fusion process claimed to have been observed by B. Stanley Pons and Martin Fleischmann in 1989. Their experimental apparatus was simple in construction, comprising a small glass container holding a platinum wire anode coiled around a palladium cathode. In operation the container was filled with a solution of lithium dissolved in heavy water, and an electric current was passed between the electrodes.

Populations and Population Movements

DEMOGRAPHY

World population stood at 5,234,000,000 as of July 1, 1989, according to Population Reference Bureau estimates, and was growing by about 93 million, or 1.78%, a year, up from 1.73% in 1988. These figures were higher than United Nations medium ("most probable") projections for 1989 prepared in the early 1980s, largely because of an unexpected rise in China's birthrate since 1985 and slower fertility decline and faster death rate decline than projected in India. The estimated mid-1989 populations of China (1,103,900,000) and India (835 million) together made up 37% of the world total. According to revised UN medium

projections released in 1988, world population would pass the six billion mark late in 1997, ten years after reaching five billion, and would be 6,251,000,000 in 2000 and 8,467,000,000 in 2025.

The United Nations Population Fund in its "State of World Population 1989" report pointed out that these projections were based on the optimistic assumption that fertility in the less developed countries of Africa, Asia (minus Japan), and Latin America would drop by a third in the next 30 to 40 years. That would require an increase in contraceptive use in these countries from the current average of 45% of women of childbearing age to 71% (the current average in more developed countries) by 2025. If this did not happen, world population in 2025 could be as high as the revised UN high projection of 9,423,000,000. In 1989 the less developed countries made up 77% of world population. The Population Reference Bureau estimated that annual natural increase (births minus deaths) averaged 2.1% a year in these countries and 0.6% in more developed countries. An estimated 41% of world population lived in urban areas about 1989.

U.S. Census Bureau estimates put the U.S. population (including armed forces overseas) at 248,777,000 on July 1, 1989, an increase of 2,448,000, or 1%, over a year earlier. Close to 1.8 million of this gain was due to natural increase and the remainder to net immigration (legal plus illegal immigration minus emigration). Blacks made up about 12.4% of the U.S. population in 1989, and Hispanics 8.2%. The urban proportion of the total was about 74%.

Birth Statistics. The National Center for Health Statistics provisionally estimated U.S. births in 1988 at 3,913,000, nearly 3% more than the 3,809,394 registered in 1987. This was the largest number reported since 1964, the last year of the "baby boom" that began in 1947. The estimated birthrate was 15.9 births per 1,000 population, 1% higher than the 1987 rate of 15.7, and the fertility rate was 67.3 births per 1,000 women aged 15–44, 2% above the 1987 figure of 66.1.

Numbers of births continued to increase in 1989. For the 12-month period ended in June, there were 85,000 more births than during the same period a year earlier. The birthrate for this period was 15.9, and the fertility rate, 67.5. Detailed data indicated that the increase in numbers of births resulted largely from sharp rises both in the number of women in their 30s, born during the peak baby boom years, and in the birthrates of these women, reflecting the ongoing trend of postponing childbearing to increasingly older ages.

The total fertility rate, which indicates the average lifetime births per woman if current fertility rates were to continue, was 1.87 for U.S. women as a whole in 1987, 1.77 for white women, and 2.29 for black women, up from the 1986 figures of 1.84, 1.74, and 2.23, respectively. The overall rate and the rate for white women were still below the "replacement" rate of 2.1 births per woman, but births continued to outstrip deaths because the number of women in the childbearing ages was inflated by those born during the baby boom. In 1987 there were 933,013 births to unmarried women in the U.S., 40% more than in 1980. New highs were again recorded for the proportion of all births occurring to unmarried women, 25%, and the birthrate per 1,000 unmarried women aged 15–44, 36. Although the nonmarital birthrate was still much higher for black women (85) than for white women (25), this racial difference was narrowing.

Worldwide estimates by the Population Reference Bureau of birthrates per 1,000 population about 1989 were 28 for the world as a whole, 15 for more developed countries,

and 31 for less developed countries, all unchanged from the previous year's estimates. China's official estimate of its birthrate for 1987 was revised from 21 to 23.3, compared with 18 in 1984 and 1985. This rise was attributed to the arrival in the childbearing ages of the generation born during China's baby boom of the 1960s, together with an easing of the government's one-child-per-couple policy. Birthrates among world regions about 1989 ranged from 45 in Africa, up one point from the previous annual estimate, to Europe's unchanged rate of 13.

The Population Reference Bureau estimated total fertility rates still at 3.6 births per woman for the world as a whole and 4.1 for less developed countries. The revision in China's officially estimated birthrate for 1987 suggested a rise in its total fertility rate from 2.4 to perhaps 2.6. India's estimated total fertility rate continued at 4.3. However, notable fertility declines were reported for some populous less developed countries. Kenya's total fertility rate, previously estimated to be nearly the world's highest at 8.1, was down to 6.7 according to preliminary results of a 1988 national survey. For South Korea a survey of the same year indicated a rate of 1.6, well below the replacement level. The average total fertility rate for more developed countries was again estimated at 1.9. However, the rates appeared to have stabilized or even risen from very low levels in some northwestern European countries, such as West Germany (up from 1.3 in 1985 to nearly 1.5) and Sweden (over 2 after a six-year rise). Italy's total fertility rate of 1.3 was recorded as currently the world's lowest.

Death Statistics. The provisional count of deaths in the U.S. in 1988 was 2,171,000. This was again a record annual high and reflected the increasing size of the population, especially at ages 65 and over, and the influenza outbreak of early 1988. The "crude" death rate edged up from 8.7 to 8.8 per 1,000 population, while the provisional age-adjusted death rate of 1988, 536 per 100,000 population, was the same as the record low rate of 1987. Human immunodeficiency virus infection (AIDS) was made a rankable cause of death and ranked 15th among the 15 leading causes of death in 1988. These causes, accounting for 87% of deaths during the year, were:

Causes of death	Estimated rate per 100,000 population
1. Diseases of the heart	312.2
2. Malignant neoplasms	198.6
3. Cerebrovascular diseases	61.1
4. Accidents and adverse effects	39.7
5. Chronic obstructive pulmonary diseases	33.3
6. Pneumonia and influenza	31.5
7. Diabetes mellitus	16.1
8. Suicide	12.3
9. Chronic liver disease and cirrhosis	10.6
10. Atherosclerosis	9.6
11. Homicide and legal intervention	9.0
12. Nephritis, nephrotic syndrome, and nephrosis	8.9
13. Septicemia	8.5
14. Conditions of the perinatal period	7.5
15. Human immunodeficiency virus infection (AIDS)	6.6

The death rate for the world as a whole was estimated at 10 per 1,000 population, as for the previous two years. The average for less developed countries, 10, continued to be scarcely higher than the average for more developed countries, 9, but combined with their birthrate of 31, it resulted in a high rate of natural increase of 2.1% a year. At that rate a population doubles in 33 years. India's rate of natural increase rose from 2 to 2.2% because of a drop in the death rate from 13 to 11 while the birthrate remained at 33. Natural increase was negative (fewer births than deaths) in Hungary and West Germany.

Infant Mortality. The provisional infant mortality rate for the U.S. in 1988 was again the lowest on record: 9.9 deaths under one year of age per 1,000 live births. Detailed

World's 25 Most Populous Urban Areas[1]

Rank	City and Country	City proper Population	Year	Metropolitan area Population	Year
1	Tokyo, Japan	8,323,699	1988 est.	27,824,000	1985 est.
2	Mexico City, Mexico	10,263,300	1988 est.	18,748,000	1986 est.
3	New York City, U.S.	7,346,352	1988 est.	18,120,200	1988 est.
4	Osaka, Japan	2,644,691	1988 est.	15,891,000	1985 est.
5	São Paulo, Brazil	7,032,547	1980 cen.	15,784,022	1986 est.
6	Los Angeles, U.S.	3,400,500	1989 est.	13,769,700	1988 est.
7	Shanghai, China	7,112,000	1988 est.	12,590,000	1989 est.
8	London, England	6,770,400	1987 est.	12,282,600	1987 est.
9	Buenos Aires, Arg.	2,924,000	1986 est.	10,750,000	1985 est.
10	Seoul, South Korea	[2]	[2]	10,513,000	1989 est.
11	Rio de Janeiro, Brazil	5,090,700	1980 cen.	10,489,360	1986 est.
12	Calcutta, India	3,305,006	1981 cen.	10,462,000	1985 est.
13	Paris, France	2,068,400	1987 est.	10,184,800	1987 est.
14	Bombay, India	8,243,405	1981 cen.	10,137,000	1985 est.
15	Beijing, China	5,468,540	1988 est.	9,926,150	1988 est.
16	Cairo, Egypt	6,052,836	1986 cen.	9,753,860	1986 cen.
17	Moscow, U.S.S.R.	8,769,000	1989 est.	8,967,000	1989 est.
18	Rhine-Ruhr, W.Ger.	[3]	[3]	8,730,000	1986 est.
19	Jakarta, Indonesia	[2]	[2]	8,498,709	1987 est.
20	Tianjin, China	4,314,271	1988 est.	8,324,515	1988 est.
21	Delhi, India	4,884,234	1981 cen.	8,200,000	1989 est.
22	Chicago, U.S.	2,994,100	1988 est.	8,180,900	1988 est.
23	Nagoya, Japan	2,147,667	1988 est.	8,139,000	1985 est.
24	Manila, Philippines	1,987,000	1986 est.	7,561,000	1988 est.
25	Karachi, Pakistan	4,776,000	1981 cen.	7,500,000	1987 est.

[1]Ranked by population of metropolitan area.
[2]Administrative unit within which a separate city proper is not distinguished.
[3]An industrial conurbation within which no single central city is defined.

data for 1986, however, showed that the rate for black infants in that year, 18, was more than twice the rate for white infants, 8.9, a larger gap than in 1960. The latest worldwide estimates reported by the Population Reference Bureau indicated two-point declines in average infant mortality rates to 75 for the world as a whole and 84 for less developed countries. The rate for more developed countries was unchanged at 15. The rates were lowest in Japan (4.9), Sweden (5.7), and Finland (5.8).

Life Expectancy. Life expectancy at birth for the total U.S. population in 1988 was the same as the record high of 1987, 74.9 years. Provisional data showed a rise of 0.1 year to 78.9 for white females, no change for white males (72.l) and black females (73.8), and a decline of 0.3 year to 65.1 for black males. The latest worldwide estimates of average life expectancy were unchanged at 63 years for the world as a whole, 73 for more developed countries, and 60 for less developed countries. The estimate for Africa, down one year to 51, was still the lowest among regions. Japan and Iceland reported the highest national life expectancy for men and women combined, 78 years.

Marriage and Divorce Statistics. Between 1987 and 1988, the number of marriages in the U.S. declined by 1% to 2,389,000, and the marriage rate per 1,000 population fell by 2% to 9.7, the lowest rate since 1967. The number of divorces in the U.S. in 1988, 1,183,000, was 26,000 more than in 1987, but the divorce rate was unchanged at 4.8 per 1,000 population. Although the divorce rate had been level since 1980, two University of Wisconsin demographers concluded from 1986 Census Bureau survey data that two-thirds of recent first marriages in the U.S. were likely to end in separation or divorce.

Censuses and Surveys. The U.S. Census Bureau agreed to consider adjusting decennial-census figures for possible undercount, following the census of April 1, 1990. The undercount of the 1980 census was estimated at only 1% overall but higher among minorities, especially in large cities. New York and other large cities contended in a suit that this had cost them their fair share of representation in Congress and state legislatures and of funds keyed to population numbers. In settlement of the suit, the bureau said the actual April 1990 counts would be reported within a year, as required by law, but subject to possible correction. By July 15, 1991, official adjusted figures would be released if these were deemed necessary by an independent panel of experts, based on results of a July 1990 national postenumeration survey.

Among 11 sub-Saharan African countries covered by the Demographic and Health Surveys program of 1985–90, Zimbabwe reported the highest proportion of married women of childbearing age using contraception, 43%, followed by Togo 34%, Botswana 33%, and Kenya 27%. Mali was lowest at 3%. Total fertility rates in the five years before the survey ranged from 5 births per woman in Botswana to 7.3 in Uganda.   (JEAN VAN DER TAK)

See also World Data.

INTERNATIONAL MIGRATION

Perhaps the biggest story of 1989 was the migration to the West of thousands of people from Eastern Europe, particularly East Germany. (*See* WORLD AFFAIRS [Eastern Europe and the U.S.S.R.]: *German Democratic Republic.*)

West Germany was expected to receive more than 100,-000 East Germans, plus 200,000 ethnic Germans from Poland and the Soviet Union. The liberalization of the political systems in Poland and Hungary provided an escape route for thousands of East Germans. This migration

AFP PHOTO

In Brownsville, Texas, an officer from the U.S. Immigration and Naturalization Service (INS) fingerprints one of many Central Americans who were attempting to immigrate to the U.S. Tens of thousands of refugees from Central America flocked to the U.S. for political asylum. In an attempt to discourage illegal border crossings in southern Texas, the INS began holding refugees in detention centres that were overcrowded and unsanitary.

was greeted by the political leaders and media in Western Europe and the United States as people fleeing to freedom. At the same time, refugees from the Third World were turned back in Western Europe and in the U.S. on the grounds that they were "economic refugees."

Britain sent back Kurdish refugees from Turkey and prevented many others from boarding planes in Turkey on the grounds that they were economic refugees. In June 1989 Britain required visas from all Turkish visitors, as it had done in 1988 for all Sri Lankans. As a result of British governmental resistance to granting political asylum, including new laws that fined shipping and airline companies that transported passengers with "inadequate" documents, the U.K. received only 4,000 applications for asylum, as opposed to 58,000 for West Germany and 28,000 for France.

In February 1989 scientists at Cellmark Diagnostics conducted genetic fingerprint tests on 1,500 immigrants who claimed parent-child ties with families already settled in Britain. They found that immigration officials were wrong to deny entry in approximately 90% of the cases. Despite this evidence, the Home Office refused to guarantee entry to applicants wrongly denied entry who had since gone over the age limit of 18 for joining their parents.

There was widespread concern that countries preparing for the 1992 single market in the European Communities (EC) would put up barriers against asylum seekers and immigrants from outside Europe. France, West Germany, and the Benelux countries, which were planning for the dismantling of border controls ahead of 1992, called for a "common deportation fund" and the tightening of border controls for aliens. Aliens would be able to cross the EC's external borders only at agreed points of entry and at fixed times and would be allowed entry only if they had proof of sufficient financial means and were not considered "as endangering public order or international relations of any of the contracting states."

The Chinese government's violent suppression of the pro-democracy movement led to increased emigration from Hong Kong and to demands from the colony that Britain provide guarantees to the people of Hong Kong that they would be allowed to enter Britain. In 1988 around 50,000 people left Hong Kong—24,588 went to Canada, 11,777 to the U.S., 7,846 to Australia, and 776 to Britain. It was estimated that some 500,000–600,000 people, or 10% of the population, would have left the colony by 1997 when Hong Kong reverted to China. In December the British government announced that it would grant up to 50,000 households full British citizenship.

The Hong Kong Chinese immigrants to Canada represented the largest group of immigrants in 1988. It was expected that the 1989 figures would be much higher. Nearly a quarter of immigrants from Hong Kong were business people who promised to create jobs or to invest large amounts in the economy. On Jan. 1, 1989, the Canadian government introduced tougher immigration laws that would allow officials to reject claimants at the airport and order them out of Canada within 72 hours. The immigration minister, Barbara McDougall, announced that there would be no amnesty for the 85,000 foreign nationals already in the country claiming political asylum.

In the United States the two major immigration issues were the fate of Central American refugees and the fate of Soviet Jews. Over 100,000 Central American refugees were expected to flee to the U.S. in 1989 from war and violence in their home countries. Since June 1988 more than 30,000 Nicaraguans had settled in the U.S.—many in Miami, Fla., where local services were severely overstretched. The

federal government refused to provide the sort of financial assistance that it had furnished when thousands of Cuban refugees arrived in Florida in the 1960s. The Immigration and Naturalization Service (INS) announced on Feb. 20, 1989, a plan to discourage refugees from entering the U.S. via Texas. Under the new procedures, which applied only to southern Texas, those who failed in their application for asylum, as well as all those taken into custody by border patrols, would be held in detention centres pending deportation. Reports by Helsinki Watch and Rio Grande Valley Watch concluded that the INS detention centres were "overcrowded, unsanitary and inhumane" and found that 80% of the refugees had no legal counsel. Helsinki Watch concluded that the INS policies violated the U.S. Refugee Act of 1980 and the UN Refugee Convention.

The number of Soviet Jews arriving in the U.S. increased dramatically as a result of Soviet relaxation of exit visa regulations. It was estimated that 48,000 Soviet Jews would immigrate to the U.S. in 1989, compared with approximately 19,000 in 1988 and 8,000 in 1987, and that the 1989 figure would double in 1990. Under new regulations, however, Soviet Jews who lacked relatives in the U.S. or other claims to residence would be ineligible for resettlement. In November the U.S. announced a sharp cut in the number of Poles and Hungarians admitted as refugees since they no longer had to fear persecution in their homelands.   (LOUIS KUSHNICK)

REFUGEES

Some 700,000 persons were added to the global refugee population in 1988 and, while over 400,000 had returned to their homelands since the beginning of 1987, the overall global figure at the end of 1988 stood at 13 million. The greatest refugee movements continued to be in Africa, where the most serious situation occurred when over 300,000 Somali refugees entered the Jijiga and Aware districts of Ethiopia. The number of Sudanese refugees in the four camps in southwestern Ethiopia rose from 260,000 to nearly 350,000, and some 30,000 Ethiopians fled into The Sudan itself in the latter half of 1988. In August 1988, 55,000 refugees from Burundi entered Rwanda. In southern Africa the displacement of persons continued, particularly of Mozambicans, of whom there were over 600,000 in Malawi alone by the end of 1988.

At the same time, repatriation occurred in impressive numbers. By the end of 1988 over 300,000 Ugandans had returned home from The Sudan since the start of the program. All but about 1,000 of the 55,000 refugees who fled from Burundi into Rwanda also returned home, and 1,000 Chadians, over 7,000 Ethiopians, 69,000 Mozambicans, and 3,300 Zimbabweans returned to their countries of origin. In South West Africa/Namibia the Dec. 22, 1988, agreement between Angola, Cuba, and South Africa paved the way for the organized return home of an estimated 58,000 Namibian refugees and exiles.

In Southeast Asia some 156,000 Indochinese asylum seekers were in camps in Hong Kong, Indonesia, Malaysia, the Philippines, Singapore, and Thailand. Thailand received 107,000 of these and an additional 300,000 displaced Khmer under the mandate of the UN Border Relief Operation (UNBRO) and the International Committee of the Red Cross (ICRC). With increasing arrivals of asylum seekers, particularly the Vietnamese boat people, which could not be offset by resettlement to third countries, important refugee developments took place. In June 1988 Hong Kong established, for the first time, mechanisms for examining refugee status claims. An international conference to consider a new multilateral approach to the prob-

lem of Indochinese asylum seekers, held in Geneva in June 1989, established a comprehensive plan of action. In 1988 Vietnam had declared its readiness to tackle the problem of the outflow of asylum seekers. Nevertheless, boat people continued to arrive in Hong Kong, which claimed it could no longer accommodate the influx. Voluntary repatriation failed to solve the problem, and on Dec. 12, 1989, 51 boat people were repatriated forcibly. The operation provoked an international outcry, but the British government said it expected involuntary repatriations to continue.

Afghan refugees, estimated at three million in Pakistan and over two million in Iran, continued to constitute the world's largest single refugee population. The mass repatriation that was expected to follow the announced withdrawal of foreign troops from Afghanistan did not occur, and toward the end of 1988 yet more Afghans had fled into Pakistan as a result of the intensified fighting in Afghanistan. Thus the care and maintenance programs for Afghan refugees continued. The UN High Commissioner for Refugees (UNHCR) also had to provide emergency relief to some 70,000 Iraqi Kurdish refugees who arrived in Iran in 1988. About 45,000 Iraqi Kurds returned to Iraq under the terms of an amnesty. Some 43,000 Sri Lankans had also returned home from India since July 1987.

Repatriation of 14,000 persons took place in Central America in 1988. This included some 2,500 Salvadorans and almost 8,000 Miskito and Sumo who repatriated from the Honduran Mosquito Coast. By the end of the year, 123,959 refugees remained in the Central American and Mexican region. A tripartite agreement was reached between France, Suriname, and UNHCR to prepare the way for the repatriation of up to 7,000 Surinamese refugees in the French overseas *département* of Guiana.

The UN High Commissioner for Refugees, Jean-Pierre Hocké of Switzerland, came under investigation for alleged misuse of travel funds and for his dictatorial treatment of the UNHCR staff. Hocké denied all wrongdoing, but on Oct. 26, 1989, he resigned the post. Gerald Hinteregger of Austria was named interim high commissioner.　(UNHCR)

This article updates the *Macropædia* article POPULATION.

Publishing

In a year dominated by upheavals in the Soviet Union and Eastern Europe, the crucial role of the media was graphically symbolized by the elevation of Solidarity newspaper editor Tadeusz Mazowiecki (*see* BIOGRAPHIES) as prime minister of Poland. In the Soviet Union a new press law ending formal censorship was being drafted, but it was unclear whether *glasnost* (openness) implied freedom of the press in the Western sense. During 1987 and 1988 it had appeared that there were no constraints, but in 1989 the newspapers discovered that certain areas were still sensitive, such as details of upheavals in Eastern Europe and criticism of Pres. Mikhail Gorbachev.

Pravda, the Soviet Communist Party daily, encountered serious trouble, with sales dropping 40% to 9.7 million, testimony to the crisis of faith in the party. In October editor Viktor Afanasyev was replaced by Ivan Frolov, a member of the Congress of People's Deputies. The shake-up followed publication of an attack on the radical Moscow politician Boris Yeltsin (*see* BIOGRAPHIES). *Argumenty i Fakty,* which had gone from sales of 3.5 million in 1987 to 20.5 million in 1989, and its editor, Vladislav Starkov, drew Gorbachev's displeasure during the year. The outspoken tabloid published an opinion poll suggesting that well-known liberals, such as Andrey Sakharov (*see* OBITUAR-

IES), were the most popular members of the new Soviet Parliament rather than the leader himself.

Six leading Western newspaper organizations launched an effort to help the newly independent Eastern European media, offering grants, for example, to ship a press from France's leading daily, *Le Monde,* to Poland's *Gazeta Wyborcia.* The Hungarian media, operating in the most westernized of Eastern European markets, became the target of Western attention. British publisher Robert Maxwell bought a 40% stake in the former government newspaper *Magyar Hirlap* and committed himself to launching a new weekly in 1990. Australian-born U.S. magnate Rupert Murdoch took a 50% share in the widely read weekly *Reform* and the daily *Mai Nap,* and West Germany's Axel Springer group set up a joint company with Hungarian partners.

Newspapers. Britain's national newspaper industry found itself under attack from politicians and the public over press standards, particularly those of the popular tabloids, the *Sun* and *News of the World.* On November 28 national newspaper editors, led by Andreas Whittam Smith of the *Independent,* responded with a code of conduct, designed to restore public confidence and avoid legal controls through self-regulation. The code offered a commitment to respect privacy; a fair opportunity for a right of reply; prompt, prominently placed corrections; curbs on payments for information; and elimination of irrelevant references to race, colour, or religion. Meanwhile, a wide-ranging review by an eminent lawyer, David Calcutt, was being undertaken to determine whether media law needed to be recast.

This domestic pressure coincided with worldwide concern about freedom of the press and broadcasting in Britain. Peter Galliner, director of the International Press Institute, described Britain as "the only black spot in Western Europe when it comes to Press freedom." The key development was the use of prepublication (prior restraint) injunctions by the government to prevent publication of controversial items. In April, for example, *The Observer* was forced to withdraw a special issue devoted to an unpublished government report on the takeover of Harrods department store by Middle Eastern interests.

September 17 saw the launch of the *Sunday Correspondent,* the first new quality Sunday broadsheet (full-size page) since 1961. It was designed to take readers away from *The Observer,* which had become steadily less influential under the proprietorship of Roland "Tiny" Rowland's Lonrho trading group, and from Murdoch's *Sunday Times.* It appeared to make a successful start and ended the year with sales somewhat above 300,000. However, *The Observer* was about to invest heavily in improvements, and a second new quality paper, the *Independent on Sunday,* was to be introduced in January. The owners of the *Daily* and *Sunday Telegraph* drove through a merger of staff on the two papers, along U.S. lines, in a bid to strengthen the reporting talents of the Sunday edition. All newspapers, however, entered 1990 facing an advertising recession, and the *Daily Mail* and *Daily Express* shut down their weekly magazine supplements.　(MAGGIE BROWN)

On the surface, the decline of competition in the U.S. newspaper industry appeared to continue in 1989. According to the 1989 *Editor & Publisher International Yearbook,* the total number of daily newspapers fell by four from the year before, to 1,642, and average daily circulation decreased from 62,826,273 to 62,694,816. Despite those losses, however, local competition was heating up in a number of major U.S. cities. Perhaps the year's most intriguing newcomer was the *St. Louis* (Mo.) *Sun,* which went up against one of the country's most distinguished

dailies, the *Post-Dispatch* (circulation 378,000), founded in 1878 by Joseph Pulitzer. The newborn *Sun* was started by the bearer of another distinguished newspaper name—Ralph Ingersoll II, whose father had founded *PM,* a New York City afternoon daily that lasted eight years in the 1940s. Unlike the full-size *Post-Dispatch,* Ingersoll's *Sun* was a breezy tabloid. If it survived, it would be the first successful big-city daily launched in the U.S. since *Newsday* on Long Island, N.Y., in 1940.

New York City, meanwhile, was experiencing its own newspaper war. While the broadsheet *New York Times* (circulation 1.1 million) had a comfortable lead in competition for the local advertising market, the city's three tabloids—the *Post* (circulation 535,000), the *Daily News* (1.2 million), and *Newsday* (698,000)—were slugging it out over the remainder. The competition heated up in 1988 when Peter Kalikow, a local real estate developer, bought the *Post* from Murdoch, who reportedly had lost $150 million in the 12 years he owned the paper. Under Kalikow, the *Post* toned down its Fleet Street-style sensationalism. Though a Sunday edition was dropped after seven months, Kalikow promised to give the remaining six-day-a-week paper whatever resources it needed.

In Dallas, Texas, the *Morning News* (circulation 370,-000) and its rival, the *Times Herald* (circulation 222,000), battled in court over the local rights to nationally syndicated features. The dispute, which reflected the growing importance of such features in building reader loyalty, began when the *Morning News* signed an agreement with Universal Press Syndicate giving the paper exclusive rights to 26 features that were currently running in the smaller *Times Herald.* A *Times Herald* motion to prevent the shift was denied by a Texas court, but the paper was expected to press a breach-of-contract suit.

In a less confrontational attempt to become competitive, two major dailies—the *Los Angeles Times* (circulation 1.1 million) and the *Boston Globe* (circulation 503,000)—introduced their first significant design changes in more than a decade, joining the growing number of U.S. dailies making heavier use of charts, photos, and colour printing.

In the realm of press freedom, the U.S. Supreme Court—which some commentators had described as growing increasingly conservative during the Reagan years—nonetheless issued several important rulings supportive of free speech. The court overturned a jury award against a small weekly, the *Florida Star,* for publishing the name of a rape victim. In another libel case, the justices upheld a local official's suit against the *Hamilton* (Ohio) *Journal-News* but pleased First Amendment supporters by reaffirming the "actual malice" standard. Established more than two decades earlier in *New York Times* v. *Sullivan,* the standard was intended to protect press criticism of public officials.

The Pulitzer gold medal for public service, the most prestigious of U.S. journalism prizes, was awarded to the *Anchorage* (Alaska) *Daily News* for its series on the high rates of alcoholism and suicide among Native American Alaskans. Donald L. Barlett and James B. Steel of the *Philadelphia Inquirer* received the national reporting award for their series on hidden tax breaks for the wealthy in the 1986 Tax Reform Act, and David Zucchino, another *Inquirer* reporter, received the feature writing prize for a nine-part series, "Being Black in South Africa." Other journalism Pulitzers were international reporting, jointly to Glenn Frankel, Jerusalem bureau chief of the *Washington Post,* and Bill Keller, Moscow bureau chief of the *New York Times;* general news reporting, the staff of the *Louisville* (Ky.) *Courier-Journal;* investigative reporting,

Bill Dedman of the *Atlanta* (Ga.) *Journal and Constitution;* explanatory journalism, David Hanners, William Snyder, and Karen Blessen of the *Dallas Morning News;* specialized reporting, Edward Humes of the *Orange County* (Calif.) *Register;* commentary, Clarence Page of the *Chicago Tribune;* criticism, Michael Skube of the *Raleigh* (N.C.) *News and Observer;* editorial writing, Lois Wille of the *Chicago Tribune;* spot news photography, Ron Olshwanger of St. Louis, an amateur, for his picture of a fireman giving mouth-to-mouth resuscitation to a child, later printed in the *St. Louis Post-Dispatch.* (DONALD MORRISON)

Magazines. The seemingly endless stream of new titles, mostly from West Germany, France, or Spain, that had revolutionized Britain's magazine market slowed to a trickle. The last big counterattack came from International Publishing Corp. (IPC), which successfully introduced a mass market women's weekly, *Me!,* in January. There had been a tough battle for readers and advertising revenue in a saturated market, and cover prices had also been rising. National Magazine Co., part of the U.S. Hearst organization, successfully tested a U.K. edition of the American title *House Beautiful* and planned to publish it monthly from February 1990. National Magazines decided to revamp *She,* one of its leading women's magazine titles, as a product aimed at mothers with babies and children. Condé Nast successfully introduced a British version of *GQ* (for Gentlemen's Quarterly) aimed at successful career men. It would go monthly in February.

The left-of-centre political weekly *New Statesman & Society,* a septuagenarian journal whose founders included the playwright George Bernard Shaw, was put up for sale following a financial crisis. As the year ended, it appeared that Australian businessman Robert Holmes à Court might be prepared to pay £2 million for it. (MAGGIE BROWN)

A failed takeover and a successful sale stole magazine headlines in the U.S. in 1989. After a wild attempt by Paramount to grab Time Inc., the latter defeated its foe when the Delaware Supreme Court ruled that a previous Time/Warner merger was legal. This left Time with a new partner and $10 billion in new revenues. (See *Books,* below.) At the other extreme, the *National Enquirer,* a favourite supermarket checkout title, was sold for over $400 million to New Macfadden Publications, the publishers of *True Story* and *Modern Romances.* Arguing that it would impose too great a burden on the publisher, a federal appeals court overturned a $9.4 million jury award that *Soldier of Fortune* magazine had been ordered to pay to relatives of a woman killed by a man hired through an ad in the magazine. The court said the case would set a dangerous precedent in that magazine publishers would have to screen all ambiguously worded advertisements.

One of the nation's most respected scientific journals admitted it had published a suspect paper. *Science,* in its July 14, 1989, issue, said a contributor had failed to acknowledge properly the source of his information on the physiology of pigments in vision. The incident was the latest of an apparently growing number of science frauds in periodicals. The problem involved all journal editors, and at an American Medical Association-sponsored conference on peer review in May, many questioned past editorial practices. A strong review system was advocated, but misunderstanding, fraud, and unrealistic expectations could not be eliminated entirely. Janet Malcom's two articles in *The New Yorker* (March 13, March 20) about the relationship between a murderer and an author who wrote about his crime stirred up a storm of criticism and questions about ethics in journalism. Malcom accused the author (Joe McGinniss) of deceiving the murderer and

then deserting him once he had enough information for his book, *Fatal Vision.*

Approximately 500 to 600 new commercial magazines were introduced to Americans in 1989, though the odds were that 8 out of 10 would fail. Among the most promising, *UpTime: The Disk Monthly* was a magazine about computers on a disk that could be read only on a computer. It claimed a circulation of over 50,000. Ziff-Davis published its *Computer Library* on a disk. The monthly, which carried the full text of articles from over 130 computer-oriented magazines, cost $720 a year. *Moxie,* a new life-style magazine, joined *Lear's* in appealing to women over 40, while for those just starting there was *Newlywed.* An old-fashioned approach to fiction and articles was offered by *Wigwag,* and *Memories* was one of several magazines catering to baby boom nostalgia. Among failures of the year, one headline asked: "Why didn't anyone want *Sylvia Porter's Personal Finance* magazine?" The six-year-old publication never recovered from the loss of interest that followed the October 1987 market crash.

An annual winner in the National Magazine Awards, *The New Yorker* came away with two prizes in 1989, one for reporting and the other for fiction. Among other 1989 prizewinners were two first timers, *Good Housekeeping,* for personal service, and *California,* for public interest. General excellence awards went to *Sports Illustrated, American Heritage,* and *Vanity Fair.* Does winning an award contribute to a magazine's prosperity? The *New York Times* put the question to publishing executives and found a wide range of opinion. An executive for *The Washingtonian* (which won a prize for reporting in 1988) said: "It absolutely makes a difference. The credibility of that award is significant in the business end." The publisher of the *National Journal* (award winner for reporting in 1981) countered: "To be recognized by our peers for doing terrific work was a big deal for us. It didn't particularly help with circulation, but it was a tremendous morale booster." The majority agreed that the awards did help, if not always with sales, at least with recognition for the staff.

(WILLIAM A. KATZ)

Books. The year was notable for the continuation of the flurry of mergers and takeovers, mainly involving U.K. companies, evident in previous years. In January News International finally won the battle to take over William Collins. In March Century Hutchinson bought Ebury, and in April Collins bought Thorsons. In June Century Hutchinson was itself taken over by Random House U.K. for £64 million, outbidding Groupe de la Cité, Simon & Schuster, and Little, Brown. In the same month, Stanley Thorsons bought Hutchinson Educational; Cassels acquired Ward Lock from Egremont (part of Gutenberghus); and Longman bought the Madrid educational publisher Editorial Alhambra. It was also announced that Collins/Harper & Row, the book empire of News International, would be sold to Media Partners International, itself jointly owned by News Corporation and Credit Suisse First Boston. In May it was rumoured that Collins was about to buy Gollancz. Meanwhile, Groupe de la Cité settled for the purchase of W. & R. Chambers for £2.4 million, while in August Pearson acquired the French medical publisher Tonus. Elsewhere in Europe the Italian group Mondadori took over Barcelona-based Ediciones Grijalbo in January, and in April Hatier of France took over Didascalia of Madrid.

The implications of the single European market were belatedly coming to the fore as 1992 approached. One key aspect was the issue of copyright. Under the Treaty of Rome, a British publisher could not use the U.K. Copyright Act to prevent the importation into the U.K. of books lawfully on the market in continental Europe and could not rely on contracts with other publishers to prevent their importing into the U.K. the books they had lawfully put into that market. Exclusive rights to the U.K. market were thus under threat from U.S. publishers gaining access to the U.K. via Europe. U.S. publishers argued that the additional transport costs involved ruled out this option, but exchange rate movements could nullify that objection. Eventually, rights might need to be assigned or licensed on an exclusive basis for the whole of the European Communities and held by either a U.K. or a U.S. agent. An asso-

". . . This merger of Time and Warner has gone too far!"

ciated development was the projected reform of Australian copyright laws. Currently, Australia had to wait until the U.K. edition of a title had been published and shipped. It was proposed that booksellers be free to buy from the U.S. unless supply from the U.K. could be guaranteed within 90 days of publication.

The debate about resale price maintenance (RPM) resurfaced. The French, who had abolished it only to change their minds with passage of the Lang Act, appeared to have confirmed that decision with the publication of the Arts Ministry's Cahart Report in 1988, which favoured RPM. However, in April 1989 the Finance Ministry published a study of the economic effects of the Lang Act, which concluded that it was against the interests of consumers. In Denmark the legal dispensation allowing RPM on books was partly revoked. RPM was henceforth to be permitted on new books only during the year of publication and the following full calendar year. In the U.K., in the face of attempts by the Pentos bookshop chain to have the Net Book Agreement referred to the Restrictive Practices Court, the director general of fair trading concluded that the matter should be set aside pending new restrictive practices legislation. Meanwhile, Australia's Price Surveillance Authority announced that it would hold an inquiry into the prices of both local and imported books.

It was generally agreed that the abolition of RPM would result in a reduction in the number of books published, but this was not necessarily a bad thing. In the U.K. a record 56,514 titles were published in 1988, including 43,188 that were new. The British Library decided that it could no longer keep a copy of every title published in the U.K. on its shelves. First to go were reprints, pamphlets, and romantic fiction. (PETER J. CURWEN)

The controversy surrounding Salman Rushdie's *The Satanic Verses* overshadowed all other events in publishing in 1989. (*See* Sidebar.) Presumably because of the headlines, it was Rushdie's most successful book to date, with one million copies sold worldwide, according to the publisher.

In January the U.S. Federal Trade Commission (FTC) charged six of the nation's largest publishers with illegal pricing policies that favoured chains over independent bookstores. At issue were the higher discounts and preferential credit terms offered to chains, which centrally order books in bulk. The gathering of evidence against the six houses—Harper & Row, William Morrow and its parent company, Hearst Books, Random House, Simon & Schuster, Putnam Berkley, and Macmillan—was expected to take at least a year.

On March 4, Time Inc. and Warner Communications announced intentions to merge, effective June 23, to create the world's largest communications conglomerate. Included in the new company would be several important book publishers—Little, Brown, Time-Life Books, Scott, Foresman educational publishers, and Warner Books, as well as the Book-of-the-Month Club. The projected annual revenues of the entire company, $10.7 billion, would dwarf the next largest conglomerate, Bertelsmann, with sales of $6.4 billion. The merger, however, did not progress smoothly. Paramount Communications offered $175 a share for Time Inc. on June 6, an offer rejected by Time. On June 23 the Paramount offer was sweetened to $200 a share but was also rejected. Time, meanwhile, offered to buy Warner for $14 billion, hoping to create a company too large for Paramount to acquire. The issue adjourned to the Delaware courts (all three companies were incorporated there), and on July 14 the court refused to block the Time Warner merger; by July's end the Paramount offer had been withdrawn. Time incurred debt of $15 billion in its takeover, and the cost of Paramount's unsuccessful takeover bid caused financial distress at Simon & Schuster, its publishing subsidiary.

Harcourt Brace Jovanovich (HBJ), the nation's largest educational publisher, continued to suffer the financial ill-effects of takeoveritis. Two years earlier HBJ had successfully resisted a takeover bid by Robert Maxwell and had recapitalized and taken on debt. To reduce its interest payments, HBJ sold its six theme parks and its land holdings to Anheuser Busch in October. In June it was announced that Grove Press, which Ann Getty had purchased in 1985, would merge with Weidenfeld & Nicolson, a publishing

The Rushdie Affair

A furor over the novel *The Satanic Verses* by Salman Rushdie (*see* BIOGRAPHIES) rocked the publishing world in 1989. The allegorical novel, published in the U.K. in late 1988, was acclaimed by critics and won the Whitbread Prize for fiction, but it was quickly proclaimed "blasphemous" by some Muslims. The book was banned in India, South Africa, and a number of Islamic countries. Anticipation of its release in the U.S. led to protests in early February in India and Pakistan that resulted in six deaths and numerous injuries. On February 14, Iran's Ayatollah Ruhollah Khomeini "sentenced to death" Rushdie and all those involved in the book's publication. The Indian-born British citizen and his family were placed in protective custody and went into hiding. The New York and London offices of the publisher, Viking Penguin, were disrupted by a series of bomb threats. Waldenbooks, Barnes & Noble, and B. Dalton—the largest booksellers in the U.S—ordered the book removed from their shelves to protect employees from terrorist attacks. (The book was restocked later but not displayed prominently.) Ironically, requests for the book soared.

Following an initial collective gasp, groups such as the PEN American Center, the Author's Guild, and the Association of American Publishers issued statements of support for Rushdie. Three members of the Swedish Academy of Letters (which awards the Nobel Prize for Literature) offered their letters of resignation because the Academy failed to condemn the death threat strongly enough. The U.S. and France denounced the threat, while the European Communities foreign ministers unanimously recalled their heads of missions in Iran for consultation. The U.K. withdrew its diplomatic staff from Tehran, and in March relations were cut off.

The intensity and vehemence of the anti-Rushdie sentiment—despite his apology for causing distress to Muslims—surprised many Westerners. Yet most Muslims—not just fundamentalists—deplored his satirical treatment of Islam and the Qur'an. There was an almost unanimous sense among them that Rushdie had dishonoured the faith, although not all believed that the correct punishment was death.

(ELLEN FINKELSTEIN)

(Left to right) Susan Sontag, Gay Talese, E.L. Doctorow, and Norman Mailer join other writers of the PEN American Center in support of author Salman Rushdie, whose novel *The Satanic Verses* spurred Iran's Ayatollah Ruhollah Khomeini to call for his death.

SARA KRULWICH—THE NEW YORK TIMES

company Getty had founded with George Weidenfeld, a British publisher, in 1986. Both were subsidiaries of the Getty-owned Wheatland Corp. The new firm, Grove Weidenfeld, rose from the ashes of a publishing company widely reported to have lost Getty at least $15 million.

On Halloween it was announced by Penguin USA that its subsidiary E.P. Dutton would cease its adult publishing operations and become an imprint of NAL, another Penguin USA subsidiary. More than 30 people, including Dutton's president, editor in chief, and executive editor, lost their jobs. Continuing losses at Dutton, whose children's publishing arm would be unaffected, were cited, but a £2.2 million loss suffered in the first half of the year by Pearson, Penguin USA's parent company, was rumoured to be the real reason. Costly problems encountered in combining the warehousing operations of NAL and Viking were also said to be partially at fault.

Best-sellers of 1988, as reported by *Publishers Weekly,* were, for fiction, Tom Clancy's *The Cardinal of the Kremlin* (1,277,000 copies) and Danielle Steel's *Zoya* (1,025,-000) and, for nonfiction, *The 8-Week Cholesterol Cure* by Robert Kowalski (961,000). Total book sales in 1988 reached $14,096,200,000, 9.1% over the previous year.

(WILLIAM W. GOLDSTEIN)

See also Literature.
This article updates the *Macropædia* article PUBLISHING.

Race Relations

The year 1989 was characterized by increasing levels of racial and ethnic conflicts throughout the world. In Africa, for example, at least 250 lives were lost in intercommunal massacres in Mauritania and Senegal; in the Balkans 300,000 members of Bulgaria's Turkish-speaking minority fled to Turkey; there were two weeks of anti-African riots in China; Western Europe witnessed the resurgence of extreme right-wing parties and an escalation of racial violence; and the United States was characterized both by political and legal measures against blacks and other racial minorities and by an increase in racial violence.

Asia. There were two weeks of anti-African riots and demonstrations in five Chinese cities, beginning on Dec. 24, 1988, in Nanjing (Nanking). African students denounced what they called "Chinese apartheid" and their treatment by the police. Many observers saw the events as reflecting both internal conflicts related to the growing insecurity of Chinese students and traditional Chinese chauvinist attitudes toward foreigners, particularly black foreigners.

The intercommunal conflict in Sri Lanka continued unabated and, indeed, escalated in 1989 as the Indian peacekeeping force marked its second year in the country. With 961 Indian soldiers and at least 5,000 civilians and Tamil rebels dead, the new president of Sri Lanka, Ranasinghe Premadasa, called for the withdrawal of Indian troops.

Tensions between the Fijian and Indian populations in Fiji continued high throughout the year. This was exacerbated by the imposition by the predominantly Christian Fijians of an almost total shutdown of life on Sundays and by increasing restrictions on the economic activities of ethnic Indians. There was an increasing level of outmigration among the Indian population.

Western Europe. Three extreme right-wing parties won 17 seats in the elections to the European Parliament on June 18. The French National Front (10 seats), the West German Republican Party (6 seats), and the Flemish-speaking Vlaams Blok of Belgium (1 seat) owed much of their support to their strong opposition to immigration of racial minorities. In West Germany right-wing parties also gained seats in local elections in West Berlin and Frankfurt. In the September general elections in Norway, the anti-immigrant Progress Party increased its parliamentary representation from 2 to 22 seats. It was suggested that the political framework within which these developments occurred was connected to the imminence of the single European market, due in 1992. Political leaders often stressed the specifically European racial character of Europe at the expense of its increasingly multiracial reality.

The level of racial violence in Britain increased during the year. Reports issued by committees in Sheffield, Leeds, and the Newham borough in London's East End identified high levels of racial harassment and violence against blacks and Asians. An interdepartmental government committee known as the Racial Attacks Group found that responses by police and the Crown Prosecution Service to racial attacks were often slow and depressingly ineffective. Although the committee found some examples of good practice, it concluded that overall "it is fair to say that there is still a very

low level of awareness about the problem generally and a great deal of confusion about who has responsibility for doing what."

Another series of studies released during the year found widespread racial discrimination in major sectors of British society. The National Association of Health Authorities found evidence of discrimination in both employment practices and service provision in the National Health Service. Figures released by the government revealed that not one person in the top three grades of the British civil service was from an ethnic minority group, and of the 18,644 people in the top seven grades only 207 were from ethnic minorities. Unemployment among ethnic minority workers was falling more rapidly than among white workers, but unemployment among the former was still more than one and a half times greater, and in certain minority areas youth unemployment reached 80%.

The controversy over Salman Rushdie's *The Satanic Verses* raged throughout 1989. There were reports throughout the country of increasing racial polarization, with *Muslim* being used as an epithet.

United States. A number of worrying statistics were published in the United States in 1989 that illustrated the problems of race relations. The National Center for Health Statistics found that for the first time in a century black life expectancy had declined for two years in a row. Another study found that although 8.8% of black households earned more than $50,000 a year, the gap between the income of black and white families had widened since the mid-1970s. Black median income was 57% that of whites, a decline of about four percentage points since the early 1970s. Incidents of racial harassment on several college campuses presented administrators with the problem of reconciling minority rights with free speech. More alarming was a rash of letter bombs late in the year apparently aimed at civil rights targets, rousing suspicions that the attacks were racially motivated. A U.S. appellate judge and a lawyer were killed.

The U.S. Supreme Court made a series of decisions in 1989 that were seen as significantly setting back, if not repealing, previous court decisions and legislative measures. In January the court overturned a 1980 decision allowing a quota on city construction contracts to be awarded to

minority-owned businesses in Richmond, Va. The ruling was seen as a devastating blow to affirmative-action plans. The court also overturned earlier decisions in workplace discrimination suits, shifting the burden of proof from employers to employees and allowing employees to challenge a voluntary affirmative-action settlement in which they had not joined. It was felt by some that this would have the effect of reopening many cases long believed closed.

In Virginia Democrat L. Douglas Wilder became the nation's first elected black governor. In an extremely close vote that led to an official recount, Wilder's pro-abortion stand was perhaps as decisive an issue among voters as his race.

Black candidates in major cities had varying degrees of success. Manhattan borough president David Dinkins (*see* BIOGRAPHIES) was elected New York City's first black mayor. Dinkins won some 30% of the white vote in the Democratic primary against incumbent Mayor Edward Koch and again in the general election against the Republican, former federal prosecutor Rudolph Giuliani. Dinkins' victory was seen as the result both of his overwhelming majority among black voters and of the desire among a significant proportion of New Yorkers for a less confrontational style of politics than that provided by Koch. This latter point was made especially relevant following the controversy surrounding the murder in August of Yusuf Hawkins, a 16-year-old black youth, in a white neighbourhood in Brooklyn. Black mayors were also elected in Seattle, Wash.; Cleveland, Ohio; and New Haven, Conn. Long-time Mayors Tom Bradley of Los Angeles and Coleman Young of Detroit were easily reelected.

The greatest defeat suffered by black political activists occurred in Chicago, where Richard M. Daley (*see* BIOGRAPHIES) defeated Acting Mayor Eugene Sawyer in the Democratic primary and Alderman Tim Evans, running as the candidate of the Harold Washington Party, in the general election. The vote was a reflection of a racially polarized community, with whites voting overwhelmingly for Daley and blacks voting overwhelmingly for Evans. Daley also won a high percentage of the Hispanic vote. It was the first defeat of a black mayor by a white candidate in a major city since 1971.

In Miami Cuban-born Mayor Xavier Suárez was re-

CARL J. BERGQUIST—THE NEW YORK TIMES

Two workers put the finishing touches on the Civil Rights Memorial, a sculpture of black granite and water by Maya Lin, who designed the Vietnam Memorial in Washington, D.C. The Civil Rights Memorial, a circular sculpture that stands in front of a curving wall in Montgomery, Alabama, features the names of 40 men, women, and children who were killed during the fight for civil rights.

elected, while Republican Ileana Ros-Lehtinen became the first Cuban-American to be elected to Congress. Ros-Lehtinen won largely because of a higher turnout in Hispanic neighbourhoods (58%) than in non-Hispanic white neighbourhoods (42%) and an even lower level in black neighbourhoods. It was calculated that of those who voted, 96% of blacks and 88% of non-Hispanic whites, including many Republicans, voted against the victor.

In January the Rev. Jesse Jackson declared that U.S. blacks should replace the label *black* with *African-American*. This provoked a hot debate among blacks as well as whites, and at year's end it remained unclear which term would prevail.

South Africa. South Africa's political system was in a state of flux in 1989. In January the newly formed Mass Democratic Movement organized hunger strikes by hundreds of black detainees that succeeded in forcing the Pretoria government to release many of them. There were massive strikes by blacks protesting the September elections to the white, Asian, and Coloured parliaments. More than three million workers stayed home on election day. The election outcome among the whites provided the ruling National Party with 48.6% of the white vote, the first time since 1953 that it had polled less than 50%.

In a move that was seen as being at least partly designed to weaken the demand for further sanctions at the Commonwealth heads of government meeting in October, the South African government released the "Rivonia 5," including African National Congress (ANC) leader Walter Sisulu, and three other black political prisoners. Nelson Mandela remained in detention, but in July he met with Pres. P.W. Botha. The South African Broadcasting Corporation, in a broadcast justifying the release of the eight political prisoners, said it had to be recognized that leaders of the ANC were regarded by sections of the population as "authentic black leaders." The move failed, however, and the Commonwealth meeting, despite the opposition of British Prime Minister Margaret Thatcher, announced its commitment to the maintenance of economic sanctions against South Africa. (*See* WORLD AFFAIRS [Africa South of the Sahara]: *South Africa.*)   (LOUIS KUSHNICK)

Religion

Soviet leader Mikhail Gorbachev's visit with Pope John Paul II, the church's role in the political changes sweeping Eastern Europe, and persecution of the churches in El Salvador were among the stories that made headlines in the world of religion in 1989.

The pope and Gorbachev concluded a historic December encounter with a decision to establish official and permanent relations, a first step toward full diplomatic ties after 72 years of estrangement. Gorbachev also pledged to increase religious freedom for all believers in the Soviet Union and invited John Paul to visit the U.S.S.R. In appealing for greater religious freedom in the Soviet Union, the pope indirectly referred to the hoped-for legalization of the Ukrainian or Uniate Catholic Church, which in 1946 was forcibly absorbed into the Russian Orthodox Church. Soviet authorities were said to be putting finishing touches on a new law on religious practices that would ease strictures on churches. Some reforms had already been put into practice without formal sanction. (See *The Orthodox Church,* below.)

Observers of Eastern bloc countries credited the churches with an important role in the newly chiseled openings in the Berlin Wall and the governmental and social reforms spreading rapidly through the countries of Eastern Europe in the waning weeks of 1989. Churches had for several years provided a free and open space to reform-minded groups. In East Germany, as a flood of emigrants departed for the West, church leaders urged their members to stay in the country and work for reform of the socialist society.

In El Salvador six Jesuit priests, their cook, and her daughter were brutally murdered in November, their deaths thought to be the work of right-wing death squads with ties to the military. Church workers engaged in humanitarian work amid the warfare between government troops and leftist guerrillas were accused of supporting the guerrillas. Some religious leaders received death threats, some church workers were abducted or detained, and more than 40 U.S. church workers were forced to flee the country. Church offices were ransacked. Roman Catholic, Lutheran, Episcopal, and Baptist churches were among those targeted. A number of U.S. church leaders called for an end to U.S. military aid to El Salvador and charged that those who had helped the poor were being singled out as enemies of the government.

British novelist Salman Rushdie (*see* BIOGRAPHIES), author of *The Satanic Verses* and a former Muslim, went into hiding after a "death sentence" was pronounced upon him by the Ayatollah Ruhollah Khomeini, Iran's spiritual leader, who himself died later in the year. (See *Islam,* below.) Some religionists in the West saw the attempted suppression of Rushdie's book as a press-freedom issue; others urged consideration for the sensitivities of Muslims, who deemed the book blasphemous and found it as offensive as a rabidly racist or anti-Semitic tract would be to the general public. (Meanwhile, religious statisticians noted that the U.S. Muslim population had grown to four million, surpassing the country's far more influential three million Episcopalians.)

Televangelist Jim Bakker, earlier defrocked by the Assemblies of God, was sentenced to 45 years in prison and fined heavily for defrauding his followers of $158 million. Evangelist Oral Roberts saw much of his religious empire in Tulsa, Okla., crumble as he was forced to close down his City of Faith hospital and medical school and sell his home in order to pay off debts and keep Oral Roberts University open. The National Religious Broadcasters rescinded TV evangelist Jimmy Swaggart's membership in the wake of a sexual scandal, declaring that a "minister's life should be above reproach." The broadcasting group also put in place a new ethics and financial integrity code for its member organizations. A TV evangelist whose prestige remained intact, Jerry Falwell, dissolved his Moral Majority organization and said he would devote more time to his duties as pastor of the Thomas Road Baptist Church in Lynchburg, Va. Falwell said the Moral Majority was no longer needed, having served its purpose of getting conservative evangelical Christians involved in electoral politics and helping to elect conservatives to public office, especially that of U.S. president.

Chinese Christian leaders were cautious in statements issued after the Tiananmen (T'ien-an-men) Square massacre in Beijing (Peking) in June, voicing only ambiguous support for youthful seekers of democracy. (*See* WORLD AFFAIRS [East Asia]: *China.*) It was not clear how the crackdown would eventually affect what had been a growing openness for churches in China.

In Poland an interreligious crisis was precipitated by the continued presence of a Roman Catholic convent at the site of the Auschwitz Nazi death camp, where Jews and other prisoners were gassed to death during World War II. The Polish primate, Jozef Cardinal Glemp, who first

refused to honour an agreement made by four cardinals with Jewish leaders to move the convent, finally agreed after pressure was exerted by the Vatican. Jewish leaders had long contended that the presence of the convent was inappropriate at the camp, which they believed should be left devoid of religious symbols as a reminder of the Holocaust. (See *Roman Catholic Church,* below.)

Barbara Clementine Harris (*see* BIOGRAPHIES) became the first woman bishop in the worldwide Anglican Communion. Harris was consecrated as suffragan (assistant) bishop of the Episcopal diocese of Massachusetts in a ceremony in Boston that included both joyous celebration and dire warnings by dissidents who saw her role as divisive. Episcopal traditionalists formed the Episcopal Synod of America, a nongeographic "church-within-a-church," at a meeting in Fort Worth, Texas. Later, traditionalist bishops achieved détente with the Episcopal House of Bishops. They agreed not to create a schism while, at the same time, church leaders agreed to consider dissidents as "loyal members of the family," despite their inability to accept the validity of a female bishop's ministries. (See *Anglican Communion,* below.)

Church struggles over the abortion issue heated up again as a U.S. Supreme Court ruling in a Missouri case, *Webster* v. *Reproductive Health Services,* cleared the way for more state regulation of abortion. (*See* LAW.) Activists on both sides of the issue, many of them motivated by religious convictions, mobilized for state-level campaigns. Within Protestantism, some mainline denominations moderated their strongly pro-choice stances and issued statements giving more weight to the sacredness of all life. The moves came under pressure from pro-life constituencies.

The Roman Catholic Church's relationship to its black U.S. constituency drew attention. George Stallings, a black priest, was suspended from the priesthood by Washington, D.C., Archbishop James Hickey for establishing an African-American Catholic congregation without authorization. Stallings argued that church officials were insensitive to the needs of black Catholics for liturgies in keeping with black cultural styles.

The image of U.S. mainline churches as "oldline" or even "sideline" became more pronounced as sociologists and journalists wrote about these churches' aging memberships, loss of influence, declining vitality, and financial problems. Agencies of the United Methodist Church, the Presbyterian Church (U.S.A.), and the Evangelical Lutheran Church in America (ELCA), among others, were forced by financial shortfalls to cut staff and programming. The spiraling cost of health insurance plans for church employees was one key element in budget crises.

The National Council of Churches, the major cooperative ecumenical organization for more than 30 mainline Protestant and Orthodox churches, spent the year in a state of crisis. The council prepared for a downscaling of its bureaucracy to address a growing deficit and a reorganization that would make it more responsive to member churches. The council's chief executive, Arie Brouwer, a Reformed Church in America cleric, was forced from office after the NCC governing board reached a stalemate on a motion for his dismissal. An authoritarian leadership style and a pattern of conflicts with other council leaders were blamed for the crisis that eventually led to his resignation.

The United Church of Christ voted to move its headquarters out of New York City to the less expensive environs of Cleveland, Ohio, becoming the third denomination to leave the East Coast for the "heartland" in recent years. (Earlier, the Presbyterian Church [U.S.A.] moved to Louisville, Ky., and the ELCA to Chicago.) Meanwhile,

(continued on page 309)

Televangelist Jim Bakker, who founded the multimillion-dollar PTL ministry, is led away after being sentenced to 45 years in prison and fined $500,000. Bakker had been charged with fraud and conspiracy for bilking money from his followers.

Satan and the American Spiritual Underground

BY MARTIN E. MARTY

A spiritual underworld, as old as human history and as widespread as the human race, was supposed to have disappeared with the rise of the modern world. That nether realm, made up of evil spirits and people who believed in them, of Satan or the devil and those who worked in his name, belonged, it was said, to the pre-modern world. That had been a time before rationality ruled and science cast its light into the dark corners of existence.

The spiritual underworld, however, did not go away just because modernity developed. Always a topic at the edges of the news, it has once again come to the centre. In recent seasons North America has seen a rise in incidents connected with Satan and evil spirits. One bizarre sign of interest occurred in the autumn of 1988, when television entrepreneur Geraldo Rivera broadcast a sensational program on the subject. Though the telecast received as many negative reviews as any program that year, it attracted the largest audience ever for a two-hour documentary. Pastors, police, and others, who before the broadcast had been queried on occasion about satanic cults, ritual killings, and evil spells, thereafter found themselves besieged. What was going on? How seriously should Americans take these evidences?

If the Rivera show was all sensation, a ritual killing in Matamoros in the Rio Grande Valley of Mexico in April 1989 confirmed the suspicion of many that satanism was on the rise. Mark Kilroy, a University of Texas student abducted off the street, was one of 13 victims of human sacrifice in ceremonies that employed black magic. The Matamoros incident at the Santa Elena Ranch was connected with drug-selling operations, but the commercial side of the venture was quickly obscured as authorities tried to come to terms with this evidence of activity in the spiritual underworld. The fact that Palo Mayombe, the belief system behind the killing, invoked African spirits and not the Satan who is, by definition, the "adversary" of the Christian God, was often lost on a public that translated all evidences into terms they best understood.

Assessing the Phenomenon. How seriously should one take the eruption? The Religion Newswriters Association (RNA) members, who cover religion for metropolitan newspapers, were curious or troubled enough to invite J. Gordon Melton to address the subject. The author of a two-volume *The Encyclopedia of American Religions,* Melton has kept computers busy tracing hundreds of religious groups, many of them of the underground sort. He brought perspective to the RNA members by noting that it is to some people's advantage to overaccent the survival and spread of satanism: "My sense is that the

real increase has been more in the attempts of promoting a fear of Satanism, not a rise in Satanism itself."

The notion that satanic worship might have a positive side was more popular 20 years ago than it has been recently. Anton Szandor LaVey, the author of *The Satanic Bible* (1969), founded the Church of Satan in 1966. Curious publics bought the book, but very few ever joined the church, which never amounted to much even in the years of mass rebellion and hippie experiment. The shock value soon wore off, and the devotees of extreme occult groups rejoined the mainstream culture, presumably finding new employment in the practical world of business and commerce.

The negative side of the phenomena somehow survives and, as Melton implied, there are people who have an interest in exaggerating its influence. Some Christians who had seen their belief in a literal Satan scorned by liberals found in the Rivera show and the Matamoros slaughter a confirmation of the existence of Satan, the devil. Some professionals who expose cults were happy to find a string of survivors of satanism on whom to concentrate in the late 1980s. Those who attacked heavy metal rock music and the violence it often portended could point to the destructiveness of its effects and show how often satanic imagery added to the lure of the entertainers. Police who had to deal with thousands of urban wall defacings, graffiti scribblings, acts of gang warfare, and menacing signs of teen rebellion, sometimes found in the figure of Satan an all-purpose explanation of what had gone wrong. And the likes of Geraldo Rivera located a huge public ripe for exploitation when signs of the devil showed up on the screen.

A Growth Industry. What was going on in all this? Those orthodox Christians who want the good and the bad judged by reference to Satan should not have a hard task. A Gallup Poll in 1978 determined that one out of three Americans believed that "the Devil is a personal being who directs evil forces and influences people to do wrong," while another one out of three thought of this devil as an impersonal force. Three years later the Gallup people again discovered that two-thirds of the public believed in the devil. Theologians who fear that accenting such a belief removes responsibility from people and locates evil outside of them, instead of in human will and desires, are outnumbered by those who say "the Devil made me do it."

Yet it is a far remove from the generalized belief that there is a devil to the practices of satanists, and the experts find themselves addressing that gap. Across the country, seminars, often sponsored by police, monitor and debate the issue. Typically, in the Fargo, N.D.–Moorhead, Minn., area, two agents of Christian Cops Against Illegal Drugs Ministries held a workshop at which they charged that Fargo-Moorhead was a nest for satanist cultists. The police chief and the theologians countered with charges of

Martin E. Marty is Fairfax M. Cone distinguished service professor of the history of modern Christianity at the University of Chicago and a senior editor of The Christian Century.

"hysteria" and "frenzy." John Helgeland of North Dakota State University recognized that "Satanism once again is a growth industry" but complained that "it gives the folks who are unsure of themselves a simple but deceptive way of explaining bad things that happen."

In San Francisco, Sandi Gallant helps alert police to satanism but minimizes the theological dimension. Most "satanic" crimes, in her interpretation, are acts by people who were "a few bubbles off center" on their own and who found in satanic ritual a high-powered way to act out their rebellion.

In Chicago detective Robert Simandl became an expert at studying this growth industry, which he called "the crime of the '90s," a message he carried to 200 seminars for law-enforcement officials. The New York State Sheriffs' Association finds satanism a "hot topic." John J. Joyce, who heads a project on the topic, says of the "growing fascination" that "we've gotten a lot of calls from sheriffs expressing an interest." He and his colleagues admit that many evidences are of the Halloween prank sort, but as Anthony Mosca, Westchester county's commissioner of public safety, stressed, "The scary part about this is it generally has a tendency to gain a momentum of its own."

The Underworld Persists. The presence of the satanic underground has led some anticultists to ask for legislation banning satanic ritual groups. But James Richardson, an expert at the University of Nevada at Reno, citing a case of a person who linked his suicide to heavy metal music, said, "Once you strike a blow against heavy metal, where do you stop?" Richardson pointed to the legal and definitional difficulties that are likely to make preventive legislation impossible. And Lee Coleman, a Berkeley, Calif., psychiatrist who has testified in some child molestation cases connected with satanism, alleged that this was a field crowded with hoaxsters. "It's the adult interviewers who are bringing these ideas to the children." Most child abuse occurs without benefit of rituals, satanic or other.

The sheriffs' associations, which estimate that 1.4 million teens and adults are somehow involved with satanic worship, might as well have given a figure a tenth that high or twice as large. No one knows with certainty. All depends on the definition and the eye of the beholder. What is clear is that two-thirds of the public do not need to be told to believe that there is a Satan. Millions will watch sensational television dealing with the subject. The heavy metal music industry will find profit in using satanic symbols. Rebellious teens will shock the adult world by painting pentagrams or the occult number 666 on the walls at the entrances to their hideaways. Police will remain puzzled and will keep holding seminars to make sense of things.

The experts who play down the statistics and who show how misused the belief in Satan can be perform a public service. Often reference to the devil does lead people away from discerning more banal causes of human evil or getting humans to take responsibility for their actions. Exaggerating satanism adds to its shock value, its mystique, and thus its lure. But the fact that the public has to deal with the subject at all is testimony to the fact that modernity did not purge the world of devils or belief in Satan. Underground religion does not belong only to ancient Greece and Rome or to the Europe of the Age of Witchcraft. It surfaces down the ranch road at Matamoros or in the suburbs of Westchester county, still puzzling those it threatens. And that, in an era of rebellion and lawlessness, means millions of people.

(continued from page 307)

the Christian Church (Disciples of Christ) broke ground for a new $15 million headquarters building in downtown Indianapolis, Ind. The nation's largest black denomination, the National Baptist Convention U.S.A. Inc., completed its first headquarters building—a $10 million edifice in Nashville, Tenn., construction of which had been urged by the group's powerful president, T.J. Jemison of Baton Rouge, La.

Several churches experienced tensions over the question of ordaining homosexuals to the ministry—an issue debated for more than a dozen years in some denominations. In The United Church of Canada, a pressure group claiming 3,000 members, including one-fourth of the church's clergy, mobilized to oppose the body's official stance of opening the ordained ministry to gays and lesbians. (See *The United Church of Canada,* below.) Two San Francisco congregations of the ELCA challenged the authority of church leaders by calling three homosexual seminary graduates as assistant pastors and proposing to ordain them without the local bishop's approval.

Two new revisions of the Bible were announced. The Revised English Bible—a revision of the 1970 New English Bible—was issued, with 50 cents from every copy sold to go to one of six charities. Publishers said the version, commissioned in 1973 by a multidenominational committee, would be the most accurate contemporary translation of the Bible to date. The NCC, holder of the copyright on the 1952 Revised Standard Version, announced that the New Revised Standard Version, the product of more than a decade's labours by a panel of Bible scholars, would be published in 1990. Changes in wording were made to eliminate archaic expressions, aid clarity for public reading, and get rid of "sexist" language not present in original texts. The gender of language referring to God was not altered.

Pope John Paul II drew criticism from 163 European Catholic theology professors who signed the "Cologne Declaration." The professors called the pontiff too authoritarian in limiting the rights of the laity, appointing ultraconservative bishops, and refusing to enter into dialogue with theologians. Vatican officials and 35 U.S. Catholic prelates met for a discussion of American church practices that the Vatican viewed as departures from church tradition and marked by secularizing influences. The U.S. bishops defended their practices on such matters as annulments, confessions, and the treatment of divorced church members.

U.S. churches involved themselves in several public issues. More than 240 religious leaders issued a statement supporting the United Mine Workers in their strike against the Pittston Coal Group in West Virginia and urging nonviolence in the conflict. Church-led ministries to persons with AIDS, their families and care givers were organized as the deadly disease continued its spread. Churches began to take a more active stance in fighting crack and other deadly drugs. The United Methodist Church, in an unprecedented move, released one of its bishops, Felton May of Harrisburg, Pa., from his regular duties for a year to lead an attack on drugs, with a Washington, D.C., neighbourhood serving as the site of a pilot project. Church-led campaigns to divest from South Africa continued. The churchwide assembly of the ELCA directed the church pension board to divest by September 1991 all funds from companies doing business in South Africa. The board rejected the directive, citing "fiduciary responsibility" under Minnesota law, which board leaders said required them to make profitability rather than social benefit the primary criterion for investment. (JEAN CAFFEY LYLES)

PROTESTANT CHURCHES

Anglican Communion. Debate over women in the office of bishop dominated discussions throughout the Anglican Communion for the second consecutive year, although tensions had eased before year's end. On Sept. 24, 1988, Barbara Harris (*see* BIOGRAPHIES) was elected as the suffragan (or assistant) bishop of the diocese of Massachusetts. She was consecrated in Boston as the first woman bishop in the Anglican Communion on Feb. 11, 1989. A week later, 44 Anglican bishops, including three from the U.S., issued a declaration warning that the ordination of women to the episcopacy threatened the future of Anglicanism.

Anglican unity, ecumenical relations, and evangelism were highlights at the meeting of Anglican primates held at Larnaca, Cyprus, April 26–May 3. The primates, who head the 27 autonomous provinces of the Anglican Communion, affirmed the Lambeth Conference's call to make the 1990s a "Decade of Evangelism." They also endorsed a report from the Eames Commission urging Anglicans to affirm the unity of the body of Christ despite their doctrinal differences over the role of women in the church. This commission, headed by Robert Eames, primate of the Church of Ireland, had been appointed by Robert Runcie, the Archbishop of Canterbury, with a mandate to discover how Anglicans could live in the "highest possible degree of communion" with differences over the question of women as bishops.

The synod of the Church of Ireland voted by large majorities to take steps to allow women to be ordained priests and bishops. If approved at the 1990 synod, women could be ordained in the Church of Ireland as early as 1991. Meanwhile, the Anglican Church of Australia defeated a similar proposal in August.

The Archbishop of Canterbury and Pope John Paul II met in Rome in the fall. They renewed their commitment to reunion but acknowledged that ordination of women was an insuperable obstacle. (See *Roman Catholic Church,* below.)

In the U.S. conservatives in the Episcopal Church met in Fort Worth, Texas, in June to establish the Episcopal Synod of America, which would be a "church within a church." Synod leaders—including six current and 20 retired bishops—emphasized that their goal was not schism but a determination "to maintain and propagate" the Christian faith according to "historic Anglicanism." The synod elected Clarence Pope, bishop of Fort Worth, as its first president. In September, however, bishops who helped form the synod reconciled with the church's House of Bishops and unanimously adopted a Statement of Unity. (See *Introduction,* above.)

The Episcopal Church mourned the death of John Walker, the first black bishop of Washington, D.C., on September 30.

(DAVID E. SUMNER)

Baptist Churches. Whether it was attributable to the decade-long fundamentalist-moderate political struggle or to other factors, the Southern Baptists showed losses in 21 of their state conventions in 1989. Despite their traditional commitment to evangelism, 7,244 Southern Baptist churches recorded no baptisms in 1988.

The denomination, however, showed a net gain of 111 new churches for a total of 37,-567. The fundamentalist faction elected its candidate, Jerry Vines, to a second term as president of the Southern Baptist Convention. The messengers (delegates) held their annual meeting in June in the unlikely city of Las Vegas, Nev., but only after several years of debate about the virtues of "witness" to the gambling culture of the city against the possibility that money spent there would support gambling interests. Meanwhile, a number of "moderate" organizations, such as the Southern Baptist Association, were being formed as a loyal opposition within the denomination.

The Baptist World Alliance, at its August meeting in Zagreb, Yugos., elected American Baptist (ABC/USA) Denton Lotz as general secretary for a five-year term. Sparked by an earlier visit by Lotz to Cuban Pres. Fidel Castro, permission was given to import 50,000 Bibles into Cuba and distribute them to evangelical churches there. The International Baptist Seminary in Ruschlikon, Switz., was to be taken over by the European Baptist Federation. The school had been heavily supported by Southern Baptists in the U.S., who withdrew support after the doctrinal purges being carried out among their own schools in the U.S. spread to the school in Switzerland.

Despite the chronic opposition of a number of member churches, the General Board of the ABC/USA resolved, by a vote of 166–5 with one abstention, to continue membership in both the National Council of Churches and the World Council of Churches. The General Board also voted to become an "official observer" in the National Association of Evangelicals. Among independent Baptists, 2,000 employees of Jerry Falwell's "Old-Time Gospel Hour" organization in Lynchburg, Va., were told that they had to join the evangelist's Thomas Road Baptist Church and begin tithing or face dismissal. The "Gospel Hour" reported a drop of more than $10 million in contributions during 1988, but an increase was predicted for 1989.

Thomas McDormand, former general secretary of the Baptist Federation of Canada, died at the age of 84.

(NORMAN R. DE PUY)

Christian Church (Disciples of Christ). By the end of February 1989, the Disciples had exceeded by nearly one-fourth their church-establishment goal for the decade. The Church Advance Now Program reported 121 new congregations established in the 1980s. In January the Disciples announced plans to build a $15 million–$18 million Disciples International Center in a section of downtown Indianapolis, Ind., currently undergoing redevelopment.

The Disciples' Commission on Theology issued a report reaffirming both the church's faith in Jesus Christ and its tolerance for different theological viewpoints. The Disciples and the United Church of Christ declared themselves in full communion, and neighbouring congregations of the two denominations were urged to share the Lord's Supper at least once or twice a year. The Disciples also affirmed the Consultation on Church Union's theological consensus. In August the Disciples became what was believed to be the first Protestant church ever to elect a Roman

Catholic priest as a full voting member of its governing body.

At its General Assembly, held in Indianapolis July 28–August 2, the Disciples reaffirmed the church's pro-choice position on the issue of abortion and decried the erosion of civil rights. K. David Cole of Kansas City, Mo., a black minister of a racially mixed congregation, was elected moderator for a two-year term.

(AUDREY BERTINA LEE)

Churches of Christ. The first legal shipment by churches of Christ of 50,000 Russian-language Bibles was distributed in Moscow in April 1989. Eastern European Mission planned to print and distribute 450,000 more Bibles by 1991. According to John Sudbury, president of the Houston (Texas)-based Bible printing and distribution ministry, EEM had sent 500,000 Bibles into the U.S.S.R. since 1982.

As part of a renewed emphasis on mission, 1,037 new congregations were established and 24,582 converts were baptized in India. A preacher-training seminar was held in Poland. The 25th annual Asian Mission Forum took place in Seoul, South Korea. The 13th annual National Youth meeting was held in Monclova, Mexico, with over 2,000 in attendance. A campaign in Nairobi, Kenya, resulted in 300 conversions.

A $13 million building for the College of Biblical Studies was dedicated at Abilene (Texas) Christian University. A significant development in the churches was the focus on different ministries for women as well as for men. Anticipating the new century, the monthly magazine *20th Century Christian* changed its name to *21st Century Christian.* (M. NORVEL YOUNG)

Church of Christ, Scientist. At their 94th annual meeting, held in Boston in June 1989, Christian Scientists from throughout the world rededicated themselves to Christian healing. As evidence that this rededication had already taken root, the church pointed to a significant increase in testimonies of healings submitted to church publications over the year. Members heard a discussion of the television airing of an award-winning documentary film on Mary Baker Eddy, the founder of Christian Science. They considered the public stirring over Christian healing and the opportunities it presented for helping the public understand why Christian Science families rely on prayer for their well-being.

During the year the church completed a worldwide shortwave radio network carrying programming from the denomination's newspaper, the *Christian Science Monitor,* and religious programs. The redesign of the *Monitor* and the successful launching in 1988 of a cable television news program, "World Monitor," and a monthly newsmagazine, *World Monitor,* were seen as significant accomplishments.

David Sleeper of Dallas, Texas, was named church president for 1989.

(NATHAN A. TALBOT)

Church of Jesus Christ of Latter-day Saints. Having become a worldwide church with more than seven million members in 100 countries, the Church of Jesus Christ of Latter-day Saints was experiencing the usual problems of size and of cultural pluralism. Ghana banished Mormon missionaries, while East Germany, for the first time since 1939, welcomed them. New

missions were also opened in Panama, Mauritius, and Réunion. The first meetinghouse in Poland was constructed, and the 100th stake (diocese) was organized in Mexico. There were bombings of Mormon chapels in Chile, Peru, and Bolivia, and two missionaries were killed.

George P. Lee, a member of the First Quorum of the Seventy since 1975 and the first Native American to serve as a general authority of the church, was excommunicated in September for "apostasy and other conduct unbecoming a member of the church." Lee, who claimed that the church was neglecting its Indian programs, was the first general authority to be excommunicated since 1943.

The Jerusalem Center for Near Eastern Studies of Brigham Young University, Provo, Utah, was dedicated in May 1989. New temples were completed and dedicated in Portland, Ore., and Las Vegas, Nev., the 42nd and 43rd temples built by the church. Significant assistance was rendered by church agencies in connection with natural disasters. The church marked the sesquicentennial of the Mormon settlement of Nauvoo, Ill., with numerous events, including a series of symposia and the production of films on the life of prophet-founder Joseph Smith.

(LEONARD J. ARRINGTON)

Jehovah's Witnesses. Over a thousand "Godly Devotion" conventions held by the Witnesses in 107 countries were highlights of 1989. Three were in Poland, a country undergoing profound changes. One of the three-day conventions was held in Katowice, not far from the Auschwitz concentration camp where hundreds of Witnesses were imprisoned during World War II and at least 153 perished. Thousands of delegates poured into Poland from 38 countries, including more than 12,000 from other Eastern European nations. Many had maintained their faith despite decades of opposition. The total attendance was 166,518.

The book *The Bible—God's Word or Man's?* was released at the conventions. A new 320-page book, *Questions Young People Ask—Answers That Work,* was designed to provide practical, Bible-based answers to young people's questions about morals and drugs and to help them get along with their parents and cope with depression, loneliness, and problems at school. In less than a year, nearly nine million copies of this book were produced in 14 languages.

(FREDERICK W. FRANZ)

Lutheran Communion. The eighth assembly of the Lutheran World Federation, to be held in February 1990 in Curitiba, Brazil, preoccupied the Lutheran Communion in 1989. It was the chief item on the agenda of the annual meeting in August of the LWF Executive Committee. The assembly theme was to be "I Have Heard the Cry of My People." The committee also endorsed a proposed restructuring of the LWF and a proposed new LWF constitution, to be presented to the assembly. If approved, one likely result would be a reduction of about 25% in the LWF Geneva staff of 125.

The latest LWF figures put the number of Lutherans worldwide at about 59 million, not counting another 10 million or so who maintained a Lutheran identity but belonged to regional churches in the two Germanys. In Namibia, where Lutherans formed the largest part of the Christian community, church leaders were prominent in efforts to monitor and assist the transition to independence from South Africa.

With the advent of *glasnost* (openness) and *perestroika* (restructuring) in the Soviet Union, Lutheranism in the Baltic republics of Latvia and Estonia (where it was the principal form of Christianity) came into prominence. A revived German Evangelical Lutheran Church in the U.S.S.R. joined the LWF. Lutheranism in East Germany was strongly involved in the ongoing debate on the role of the church in a Marxist-led society. Four-day *Kirchentage* (church congresses) in Leipzig (East Germany) and West Berlin drew tens of thousands of people.

In June, Pope John Paul II visited the five Nordic countries, all overwhelmingly Lutheran. Reaction varied, though in no case did the great crowds common on most papal journeys turn out. Nordic and Baltic Lutherans met with representatives of the (Anglican) Church of England to explore closer relationships.

The 5.3 million-member Evangelical Lutheran Church in America faced a shortfall of several million dollars in money passed on to the churchwide level, though overall giving at all ELCA levels increased more than the inflation rate. (See *Introduction,* above.) The 2.6 million-member Lutheran Church-Missouri Synod reelected Ralph Bohlmann for a fourth term as president, despite charges that he was insufficiently vigilant in opposing false doctrine and practice.

The 200,000-member Evangelical Lutheran Church in Canada and the Anglican Church in Canada declared a state of "interim sharing of the Eucharist" paralleling the relationship in the U.S. between the ELCA and the Episcopal Church.

(THOMAS HARTLEY DORRIS)

Methodist Churches. The United Methodist Church, the largest single body within the Methodist communion, holds quadrennial area general conferences. In the last months of 1988 and during 1989, several important general conferences were held, including those for Malaysia, Singapore, Central Europe, Central and Southern Europe, and West Germany. The quinquennial meeting of the North American Section of the World Methodist Council met under the theme "For Such a Time as This." Among other issues discussed were the challenges facing the Christian church in South Africa, Central America, and the Middle East.

Following a year in which it celebrated the 250th anniversary of the conversions of its founder, John Wesley, and his brother Charles, world Methodism took the anniversary of Wesley's decision, on April 2, 1739, to proclaim "in the highways the glad tidings of salvation" as an opportunity to renew its commitment to evangelism. Evangelism seminars were held in Fiji and Mexico, and the Pacific College for Evangelism opened in Sydney, Australia. H. Eddie Fox of Tennessee was appointed as the new director of world evangelism.

The joint commission between the World Methodist Council and the Roman Catholic Church met in Venice in February. The commission was encouraged to learn that the Nairobi Report of 1986, "Towards a Statement on the Church," had received close attention from the Congregation for the Doctrine of the Faith. The theme for the current five-year period was "Tradition," understood as "*koinonia* (communion, community) in time."

With effect from the beginning of 1989, the Methodist Church of South Africa decided—in line with an increasing number of Methodist churches around the world—to call its leaders bishops.

The World Methodist Council sent a goodwill mission to Fiji in March at the invitation of the Methodist Church of Fiji. Following relaxation of sabbatarian laws, some Methodists had set up roadblocks in an attempt to secure their enforcement. This led to a split in the church leadership. An agreement, drafted while the mission was in Fiji, called for reconciliation and for all to work together within the framework of the church's existing constitution.

The Executive Committee of the World Methodist Council met in Switzerland in September to complete plans for the World Conference, to be held in Singapore in 1991. Many committee members were concerned that the church in less developed countries should be more fully represented in the conference leadership.

(JOHN C.A. BARRETT)

Pentecostal Churches. Pentecostals and charismatics were involved in several major international conferences during 1989. In May 100 leaders gathered in Jerusalem to plan for a decade of world evangelization. Michael Harper, an Anglican, was chosen to head the group, known as the International Charismatic Consultation on World Evangelization.

Pentecostals in the U.S.S.R. were granted the right to form their own national union of churches in May. In July large numbers of Pentecostals attended the Lausanne II conference in Manila. The Lausanne statistical task force estimated that the number of Pentecostal/charismatic Christians reached 352 million in 1989, second only to the Roman Catholics. In September the 15th Pentecostal World Conference met in Singapore with some 3,800 registered delegates from over 40 nations. Thomas Zimmerman of the Assemblies of God, who had served as chairman of the Advisory Committee since 1961, retired and was replaced by Ray Hughes of the Church of God (Cleveland, Tenn).

In June the Pentecostal Church of God reelected James Gee as general superintendent in Joplin, Mo., while in August the Pentecostal Holiness Church, at its General Conference in Oklahoma City, Okla., elected B.E. Underwood as bishop and general superintendent. At their biennial General Council at Indianapolis, Ind., in August, the Assemblies of God celebrated their 75th year. Raymond Carleson was reelected to a second term as general superintendent.

(VINSON SYNAN)

Reformed, Presbyterian, and Congregational Churches. The World Alliance of Reformed Churches (WARC) held its 22nd General Council in Seoul, South Korea, Aug. 15–27, 1989. Much of the council's work involved church-state issues. Delegates adopted resolutions on the reunification of Korea, committing themselves to "reconciliation and reunification" and pledging their support to "Christians in

Korea [North and South] and elsewhere who struggled to achieve this important goal."

The council also reaffirmed the previous General Council's declaration on apartheid in 1982, which had resulted in the suspension of two member churches that refused to dismantle apartheid within their structures or in society. One withdrew; the other, the white Dutch Reformed Church, remained suspended. Sharpening the focus on apartheid, delegates stated that the apartheid government of South Africa was "illegitimate in light of the Bible and the Reformed tradition" and called upon Christians to "defy the authority of the illegitimate government in a way that is compatible with their Christian witness." The council pressed the church-state issue, endorsing civil disobedience specifically with respect to South Africa but broadening the mandate to include churches that give sanctuary to refugees illegally.

Other issues on which the council took positions included a continued witness on human rights violations in Romania; support for aboriginal land rights and democratic movements in New Caledonia; and a call for churches to press their governments to halt nuclear testing and the dumping of the nuclear wastes in parts of the Third World.

In the area of theology and ecumenical relations, the General Council called on the Department of Theology to undertake a contemporary theological study of the "just war" theory; to view and reflect on the various forms of Reformed worship at the close of the 20th century; and to follow up on the results of the dialogues with other Christian traditions that had taken up much of the department's work over the past seven years. Notably, the General Council applauded the results of the dialogues with the Disciples of Christ in which both Reformed and Disciples affirmed their common heritage and commitment to work toward unity.

For the first time in its 114-year history, the WARC reelected an incumbent to the presidency: Allan Aubrey Boesak, moderator of the Dutch Reformed Mission Church in South Africa was elected to a second seven-year term.

(JILL SCHAEFFER)

Religious Society of Friends. Quakers worldwide responded to the plight of the two Friends' high schools in Ramallah, in the West Bank, which like other schools in the West Bank and Gaza Strip had been closed by the Israeli government in reaction to the Palestinian *intifada* (uprising). Although an emergency appeal enabled them to offer scholarships and pay teachers' salaries during the year, it was by no means certain that the schools, serving both the Muslim and Christian communities, would survive.

The Quaker Council for European Affairs in Brussels celebrated its 10th anniversary in October. It had enabled Friends to make a contribution, together with other churches, in areas of European cooperation such as human rights, peace, immigrant workers, and relations with the less developed world.

British Friends faced the decision of whether to apply for membership in the new ecumenical bodies being set up to supersede the British Council of Churches.

Despite some hesitation, stemming mainly from the traditional refusal of Quakers to associate with anything resembling a "creed," the week-long Yearly Meeting of Friends, held in Aberdeen, Scotland, united in a decision to join the new bodies.

(DAVID FIRTH)

Salvation Army. The Salvation Army's current membership, totaling more than two million people, was larger than at any other time in its 124-year history. Geographically, Africa and South Korea were the areas of fastest growth. During the year the Army commenced work in El Salvador, the 91st country in which it now operated. ·

During 1988–89 the Army conducted a review of its principles and practices, under the title "Towards 2000—Vision and Task." This included a 10-day conference in Los Angeles, attended by leaders of the Army's work worldwide. Gen. Eva Burrows, the Army's international leader, told the conference the task was "to tackle the hard questions and seek solutions and new directions."

Among the latest developments in the Army's social service work was a pioneering approach to the home care of persons with AIDS in East Africa. The Army also continued to meet needs resulting from natural and man-made disasters, including Hurricane Hugo and the San Francisco earthquake.   (CHARLES KING)

Seventh-day Adventist Church. With accessions of almost half a million—the largest in its history—the Seventh-day Adventist Church increased its membership to 5,749,735 by Dec. 31, 1988. The church continued to grow fastest in Africa and Central and South America. An international task force developed plans for a global strategy to fulfill the church's mission. The church had established a presence in 184 countries.

The role of women in ministerial and other church leadership positions came to the fore. For several years women had served as ordained lay elders of congregations or as paid associate pastors. A 70-member commission of scholars and administrators recommended that women associate pastors be permitted to baptize and officiate at marriages but that they not be ordained to the gospel ministry. The matter was slated for consideration by the church's General Assembly in 1990.

Adventists in the Soviet Union dedicated a new seminary and church headquarters and were proceeding with steps toward their organization as the church's 11th division. In response to a request from the government of China, the church authorized negotiations for the management and operation of a new hospital in Hangzhou (Hangchow).

Robert H. Pierson, leader of the world church in 1966–78, died January 21.

(WILLIAM G. JOHNSSON)

Unitarian (Universalist) Churches. Over 3,200 Unitarian Universalists attended the 28th annual General Assembly of the Unitarian Universalist Association (UUA) on the campus of Yale University on June 22–27, 1989. Half of this number were delegates. Reelected unopposed to further four-year terms were William F. Schulz as president and Natalie W. Gulbrandsen as moderator. Launching its 50th anniversary, the UU Service Committee had programs

under way in Africa, India, the Caribbean, and Central America. U.S. seminaries contained 258 students for the UU ministry, 170 of whom were women. Females comprised 48% of all ministers settled in 1988.

The Australian and New Zealand Unitarian Association held its biennial conference in Auckland during Easter 1989. The theme was "Local Accents in a Universal Language." Resolutions were passed on the environment and pollution; the persecution of ethnic Hungarians, including Unitarians, in Romania; and support for the World Conference on Religion and Peace. In Japan the Dojin (Universalist) Christian Church, led by Michio Akashi, constructed a new church building and Dojin House.

The Canadian Unitarian Council met in Hamilton, Ont., in May, with 300 delegates addressing the theme "A Celebration of the Arts." A yearlong study was begun of the challenges raised by belonging to both a Canadian Council and the UUA, with a predominantly U.S. membership. At the General Assembly of the Unitarian and Free Christian Churches in Great Britain, held in Aberdeen, Scotland, just after Easter, a resolution was passed deploring the government's proposal for changing the National Health Service. Consultants advised that including the words "to promote civil and religious liberty" in a proposed revision of the Aims and Purposes of the General Assembly would jeopardize the charitable status of the denomination by being too "political."

(JOHN NICHOLLS BOOTH)

The United Church of Canada. "The United Church is alive, well and strong in spite of a year of turmoil and upset" was the message Moderator Sang Chul Lee gave members on the denomination's 64th anniversary, June 10, 1989. The "turmoil and upset" referred to an action of the 32nd General Council held in Victoria, B.C., in August 1988 stating (in part) "that all persons regardless of their sexual orientation, who profess faith in Jesus Christ and obedience to Him, are welcome to be or become full members" and that "all members . . . are eligible to be considered for ordered ministry." (*Considered* meant that all candidates would undergo a painstaking examination before being declared acceptable.)

Some ministers and members were still opposed to the ordination of homosexuals and lesbians, so the debate was certain to continue. Lee said, however, that he was "optimistic" about the final outcome. Some people had predicted that the issue would "split the church," but Douglas Flanders, director of the Department of Education and Information, stated in a news release that only 31 congregations had "suffered a significant loss" of members as a result of the controversy and only 36 of the 4,000 ministers had left the church.

A successful enterprise of the denomination was Vision-TV, a national multifaith satellite-to-cable network supported by the United Church and some 15 other faith groups, programmed regularly to audiences estimated by A.C. Nielsen as ranging from 50,000 to 120,000. The United Church produced a weekly program, "Spirit Connection," and monthly specials. In 1989 one of the latter was coproduced with the BBC. A forthcoming series would focus on issues and themes of the Seventh Assem-

bly of the World Council of Churches, to be held in 1991 in Canberra, Australia. Videotapes of programs were available to churches and groups. (NORMAN K. VALE)

United Church of Christ. Paul H. Sherry, executive director of the Community Renewal Society of Chicago, was elected the fifth president of the United Church of Christ at the church's 17th General Synod, held June 29–July 4 in Fort Worth, Texas. He succeeded Avery D. Post, who retired after serving three four-year terms.

The 17th Synod witnessed the passage of three foundational ecumenical votes: full communion with the Christian Church (Disciples of Christ), approval of the theological consensus of the nine-church Consultation on Church Union, and the affirmation of pulpit and altar fellowship with the Evangelical Lutheran Church of America and with the U.S. member churches of the World Alliance of Reformed Churches. In an action of considerable consequence, the Synod voted to establish the headquarters and the major offices of all national bodies of the church in Cleveland, Ohio. The move of headquarters from New York City was expected to be completed by 1991.

Other noteworthy actions of the Synod were the establishment of a mission partnership with the Middle East Council of Churches; the approval of Christian Education, Church Growth and Evangelism, and Integrity of Creation, Justice, and Peace as priorities of the church; the election of Charlotte P. Gosselink as moderator; the approval of pronouncements and proposals for action on genetic engineering, ministries to Pacific Islanders and Asian Americans, inclusive language and the Christian faith, and economic life and justice; and the approval of a major national fundraising campaign. In addition, the Synod took action on a broad range of issues, including AIDS, perils to the environment, solidarity with the Chinese people, sexual harassment in the church, reaffirmation of the UCC's support of freedom of reproductive choice, opposition to violence against gay and lesbian people, the resurgence of racism, and the boycott of Royal Dutch/ Shell Oil. (AVERY D. POST)

ROMAN CATHOLIC CHURCH

The year began with a flurry of theological protest. On the feast of the Epiphany, Jan. 6, 1989, a group of 163 German-speaking theologians objected to growing Vatican centralization that trampled on the rights of local churches, appointed unsuitable bishops, and turned the rejection of birth control into the chief norm of orthodoxy. French, Flemish, and Spanish theologians joined in, though in gentler tones, and by the time the Italians spoke up in May and the Brazilians in July, it was less a matter of disgruntled academics letting off steam and more an expression of Christian sadness at the way the pontificate was going. John Paul II brushed the theologians aside. Docile bishops continued to be appointed, especially in Brazil, where the Vatican asserted itself in August by closing down the seminaries in the Northeast associated with liberation theologian Dom Helder Cámara.

While U.S. theologians steered clear of these rows and let their bishops ably defend them, another conflict broke out when George A. Stallings, Jr., a black American priest of the Washington, D.C., diocese, broke with his archbishop, James Hickey, and set up his own African-American liturgical rite. Called the Imani (a Swahili word meaning "faith") Temple, it soon attracted several thousand worshipers. The 13 black Catholic bishops in the U.S. urged him to return, though some judged him right on the main issue but wrong in his strategy.

August saw another bitter controversy when Jozef Cardinal Glemp (*see* BIOGRAPHIES), the primate of Poland, said the departure of a Carmelite convent from the site of the Auschwitz death camp would be a "scandal." This was despite the decision of a joint commission of four cardinals and Jewish leaders in February 1987 that the sisters should withdraw out of respect for the victims of the *shoah*. Passions were envenomed when Glemp talked of "an anti-Polish conspiracy" in the mass media. On September 19, after a prolonged silence, John Paul finally intervened in the dispute, expressing support for relocation of the convent to a new interfaith prayer centre farther from the camp site and offering to help pay for its construction.

These events cast a shadow over what ought to have been a matter for rejoicing: Poland became the first country where the Communists, accepting electoral defeat in June, voluntarily loosened their grip on power. (*See* WORLD AFFAIRS [Eastern Europe and the U.S.S.R.]: *Poland.*) On the anniversary of the start of World War II in September, John Paul tried to recover ground with a letter to "all people of good will" in which he said, "The planned barbarism unleashed against the Jewish people will forever remain a shame of humanity." He also criticized the Yalta agreement of 1945 and did not hide his sympathy for the Baltic republics and the people of the Ukraine. This had a bearing on his meeting with Soviet leader Mikhail Gorbachev in December, for the role of nationalities in the U.S.S.R. had become one of the Soviet leader's main concerns. (See *Introduction,* above.)

John Paul wanted still more religious freedom for the Catholics of Lithuania and Latvia and the restoration to legality of

George A. Stallings, Jr., a priest of the Washington, D.C., diocese, defied the Catholic Church by initiating a new liturgical rite that he felt would better satisfy the needs of the black Catholic worshiper.

the Ukrainian Catholic Church (abolished by decree in 1946). On December 1 it was announced that the Ukrainian church was being granted legal status, although nothing was said concerning the fate of church buildings secularized or given to the Russian Orthodox Church. Elsewhere, great progress had been made toward religious freedom, especially in Lithuania, where the cathedral, formerly an art gallery, had been given back. Clearly, however, Gorbachev's concern was that these concessions should not stimulate separatist nationalism.

The visit of Robert Runcie, the Archbishop of Canterbury, at the beginning of October had fewer political consequences but was far from unproblematic. Runcie wanted to explain that he was in no way the "pope" of the Anglican Communion, that its 27 provinces were autonomous, and that there was little he could do about those Anglican churches that ordained women priests or even bishops. The pope replied, though politely, that there was little he could do with such a concept of "dispersed authority." The ordination of women, not being negotiable, was therefore a "fresh obstacle on the road to unity."

There were papal visits to Zambia, Malawi, and Madagascar in May, to Scandinavia in June, and to South Korea, Indonesia, and East Timor in October. The African visit was remarkable for the apparent reconciliation of church and state in "Marxist" but poverty-stricken Madagascar, for the way Archbishop Emmanuel Milingo, a faith healer exiled in Rome, was pointedly ignored in his own country of Zambia, and for the fact that no mention was made of the "African Synod" announced in January. The Scandinavian visit was notable for the indifference of the population, the rudeness of the Danish Lutheran bishops, and the welcome extended by the Lutheran Archbishop of Uppsala, the Swedish equivalent of the Archbishop of Canterbury. There was more tension than symbolism in the Far East. In South Korea Catholics made up 5% of the population, but they were growing. Indonesia, a mainly Muslim country, included East Timor, a former Portuguese colony that was three-quarters Catholic. It was still resisting Indonesian rule, making the visit probably the most dangerous the pope had undertaken.

The visits the pope does not make are as important as the ones he does make. On August 15 he wept publicly over what he called the "genocide" of the Maronite Christians in Lebanon, but his offer to go to Lebanon was not taken up. In October a projected stopover in Hong Kong was abandoned because, said the Vatican press office, the British government had no desire to be lectured about the Vietnamese refugees it was trying to send home.

(*See* WORLD AFFAIRS [Western Europe]: *Vatican City State.*)

(PETER HEBBLETHWAITE)

THE ORTHODOX CHURCH

The spectacular restoration and rebuilding of the church taking place in the Soviet Union, in connection with Mikhail Gorbachev's *perestroika,* was the single most important development in the Orthodox world. Reports indicated that more than 1,000 Orthodox communities had been established over the past year. Two new

A mosaic of the apostle Matthew is one of four 6th-century Byzantine mosaics that were stolen from a church in Cyprus. Found in the possession of an Indianapolis art dealer, the mosaics were ordered returned to the church.

MARY ANN CARTER

seminaries (in Belorussia and in Siberia) and several monasteries, including Optino in central Russia and Valaam on Lake Ladoga, were allowed to reopen. The church received frequent exposure in the media and, for the first time since the Revolution, began the publication of a newspaper (although the number of copies was a modest 50,000).

Technically, the highly restrictive "law on religious associations," published by Stalin in 1929, was still on the books, but it was no longer being applied literally. The publication of a new law by January 1989 was announced, but it had not taken place. It appeared that, once published, the law would recognize the church as a "legal person," entitled to own property, engage in some educational and social work, and receive protection of its rights in courts of law. The old law specifically excluded religious groups from all noncultic activities and deprived them of legal rights. Clearly, the situation allowed for great hopes, although critics maintained that the Orthodox episcopate, headed by the aged and sickly patriarch Pimen, was too accustomed to subservience and was not using all the newly available opportunities.

In Yugoslavia the Serbian Orthodox Church played an active role in reasserting the position of the Christian Serbian population in the province of Kosovo, which now had a Muslim Albanian majority. Serbian patriarch German presided at solemn celebrations of the 600th anniversary of the Battle of Kosovo against the Turks and on June 25 inaugurated the huge new Orthodox cathedral of St. Sava in Belgrade. In Romania, where the repressive regime of Nicolae Ceaucescu was overthrown in a bloody revolt at year's end, the church—still the most numerous Orthodox body in the Balkans—had suffered greatly. The policy of "consolidating" villages had endangered the traditional network of village churches.

In Greece the projects of the former Papandreou government to take over some church property and change structures of church authority were modified or dropped, mitigating the major causes of church-state confrontation. The government and the episcopate accepted two new texts, which according to some observers could eventually lead to separation of church and state.

In the U.S., Metropolitan Theodosius (Orthodox Church in America) and Metropolitan Philip (Antiochian Archdiocese) issued a joint encyclical calling for a more practical approach to the always burning issue of Orthodox administrative unity. Informally, both prelates expressed misgivings about the ineffectiveness of the "Standing Conference of Bishops," presided over by the Greek Archbishop Iakovos, of which they were also members.

(JOHN MEYENDORFF)

EASTERN NON-CHALCEDONIAN CHURCHES

Both centres of the Armenian church—the "supreme catholicossate of all Armenians" in Echmiadzin, U.S.S.R., and the catholicossate of Cilicia in Antelias, Lebanon—joined in providing material and spiritual relief to the victims of the December 1988 Armenian earthquake. This was significant because the two catholicoi had been at odds politically and administratively (Armenian communities in the U.S. gave allegiance to one or the other). Catholicos Karekin of Cilicia traveled three times to Echmiadzin, and a joint celebration took place in New York. In a communiqué (April 29, 1989), the two catholicoi called for "ecclesiastical, spiritual, educational, national and cultural" cooperation. A healing of the schism seemed to be in the making.

The Coptic pope, Shenuda III, was host to a meeting of the Joint Commission of dialogue between the Orthodox Church and the non-Chalcedonian churches on June 20–24. In September Shenuda visited the U.S., where immigration of Christian Copts from Egypt had increased in recent years.   (JOHN MEYENDORFF)

JUDAISM

A year of acute crisis in Judaism, 1989 witnessed one important occasion on which religious reconciliation, rather than division and strife, defined the focus. In São Paulo, Brazil, on June 11 the Jewish community and the Roman Catholic Church joined in conferring the Patriarch Abraham Award in recognition of lives spent strengthening ties of friendship between Catholics and Jews. The awards went to Johannes Cardinal Willebrands, president of the Vatican's Commission for Religious Relations with the Jews, and Gerhart M. Riegner, cochair of the Governing Board of the World Jewish Congress. Organized by Rabbi Henry I. Sobel, the coordinator of the national commission for Catholic-Jewish dialogue, under the auspices of the national conference of Brazilian bishops, the event brought as principal speaker Jehan as-Sadat, widow of Pres. Anwar as-Sadat of Egypt.

Two months later, in Brasília, Jacob Neusner addressed the Roman Catholic bishops of Brazil on the relationships between Judaism and Christianity in the 1st century and today. The address stressed that the two are completely different religions, each with its own system and message for its own world, but for that reason they can learn, also, to reach out to one another in respect.

This celebration of amity presented a marked contrast to the tensions within the various communities of Judaism. The Israeli elections of Nov. 1, 1988, had produced a strong delegation for the political parties identified with Orthodox Judaism. The Orthodox represented some 15% of Israeli society, but because of their strategic position between the leading parties, Likud and Labour, they had gained con-

MICHA BAR-AM/THE NEW YORK TIMES

Women leave Jerusalem's Western Wall, where police had fired tear gas at a group of Orthodox Jewish men who tried to disrupt the women's prayers. Claiming that the women were violating religious tradition by wearing prayer shawls and reading from the Torah, the Orthodox Jewish men had injured several of the women before the police were able to stop them.

siderable political preferment. In 1988–89 the Orthodox parties demanded a revision in Israel's Law of Return so that converts to Judaism by Reform and Conservative rabbis would not receive automatic Israeli citizenship upon their arrival in the State of Israel. The issue was pressed, in particular, by the Lubavitcher Hasidic movement, which is based in Brooklyn, N.Y., but exercises significant influence in Israeli life through its adherents in that country. Powerful U.S. Jewish opposition arose, however, and a coalition government was formed without a commitment to the change demanded by the Orthodox parties. (*See* WORLD AFFAIRS [Middle East and North Africa]: *Israel.*)

Another point of contention involved the perennial women's issue. While women had recently achieved equality within Conservative Judaism and were ordained as Conservative rabbis (Reform and Reconstructionist seminaries had been ordaining women for decades), the rights of women to liturgical equality remained a bitter issue. It was joined when a group of 50 women came to the Western (Wailing) Wall in Jerusalem, the holiest site of Judaism, on March 20 to conduct worship marking the Fast of Esther, which precedes the festival of Purim. The rabbinical authorities of the Wall had promised the women rights of free access, but Orthodox Jewish men disrupted their service by throwing chairs, rocks, and bottles over the partition that separated the women from men. The women had donned prayer shawls and had begun to read from the Torah. Women had been permitted to pray at the Wall, but conducting a service as a community, rather than worshiping as individuals, was regarded by the Orthodox as unacceptable. The State of Israel did not support the women, and they were warned that they would be arrested if they returned to the Wall and read the Torah again.

The future of Orthodox Judaic separatism in the State of Israel was called into question by Micha Odenheimer, writing in the *Jerusalem Post* on January 14. He pointed out that the internal structure of Orthodox society was changing because of economic pressures resulting from the very high birthrate. Housing, jobs, educating children—all involved the Orthodox with the secular world. The walls separating the different forms of Judaism were the subject of a powerful observation by Gary Rosenblatt in the *Baltimore Jewish Times* (Feb. 3, 1989). The problem, he observed, was that Orthodox Jews "find it difficult to believe that non-Orthodox Jews can have strong religious convictions," while non-Orthodox Jews see the Orthodox as "disengaged from the real world." Rosenblatt pointed to the central issue confronting Judaism in 1989: the shift in long-term tensions among different Judaisms from chronic to acute.

Pinchas H. Peli, Israeli Orthodox rabbi and professor of Jewish thought at Ben Gurion University of the Negev, and Salo Wittmayer Baron (*see* OBITUARIES), U.S. historian, died in 1989. (JACOB NEUSNER)

BUDDHISM

The liberalization of Indochina continued to benefit Buddhism during 1989, especially in Kampuchea. The government changed its constitution in April to make

The Dalai Lama (right) is escorted to the altar of a church in Mexico City during a trip to Mexico and Central America. For his persistent, peaceful efforts to free his native Tibet from Chinese rule, the Dalai Lama was awarded the 1989 Nobel Peace Prize.

JOHN HOPPER—AP/WIDE WORLD

Buddhism the country's state religion and abolished the prohibition on young men becoming monks. As Prime Minister Hun Sen began attending Buddhist festivals, Kampuchean monks began to reclaim their once-great political importance by participating in international peace talks and preaching Buddhist nonviolence among Khmer Rouge guerrillas. In July Cornell University, Ithaca, N.Y., publicized its plans to help rebuild the Cambodian National Library's collection of cultural and religious texts, decimated during the ascendancy of the Khmer Rouge.

Buddhism flourished in Singapore during 1989, due to the efforts of "missionary" Theravadan and Nichiren-sho-shu Buddhists. The Buddhist revival was fostered by Prime Minister Lee Kuan Yew in December 1988 when he praised Buddhist (and Hindu) ideals and denounced evangelical forms of Christianity and Islam.

The World Fellowship of Buddhists announced the computerization of the Tipitaka, the canon of the southern schools, in Thai and roman scripts, amounting to nearly 50 million characters. In May the Sri Lankan government ceremoniously announced the completion of the 30-year Buddha Jayanti translation of the canon into Sinhala; Pres. Ranasinghe Premadasa called it the most important event in the country's Buddhist history since the 1st century BC, when the canon was committed to writing. In February the Sri Lankan government announced its decision to create a Ministry of Buddha Sasana under the president's supervision, perhaps in an effort to control Buddhist monks, who were active throughout the year in antigovernment and anti-Indian demonstrations.

In March anti-Chinese rioting broke out in Tibet after Chinese soldiers opened fire on a small group of Buddhist monks and nuns protesting at Jokhang temple in Lhasa. The Chinese violently crushed the revolt. They were denounced by the Dalai Lama (*see* BIOGRAPHIES), who continued during 1989 to reject Beijing's settlement terms. The Dalai Lama received the 1989 Nobel Peace Prize. The pro-Beijing Panchen Lama (*see* OBITUARIES) died in January while in Tibet celebrating the erection of a stupa for the remains of five of his predecessors whose tombs were destroyed during the Cultural Revolution. The Thai supreme patriarch, Somdej Phra Ariyawongsa Katayana, died in March.

In November 1988 the World Fellowship of Buddhists held its 16th General Conference in Los Angeles.

(FRANK E. REYNOLDS;
JONATHAN S. WALTERS)

HINDUISM

In India there was an easing of tensions between Sikhs and Hindus. On March 3, 1989, Prime Minister Rajiv Gandhi announced that the remaining 188 of 366 Sikh militants originally imprisoned after the 1984 army attack on the Sikhs' holiest shrine, the Golden Temple in Amritsar, would be released. Gandhi also promised the removal of certain "emergency" restrictions on civil rights and a reduction in "antiterrorist" activity, which Indian human rights groups had protested as repressive.

By contrast, relations between India's Hindu and Muslim communities worsened. During the political campaigns for the December general elections, centuries-old animosities found a new focus in a dispute over a shrine in the state of Uttar Pradesh. In 1986 a local judge ruled that a temple-mosque at Ayodhya belonged to Hindus, and the building was opened to Hindu pilgrims. Militant Hindu groups, like the Vishwa Hindu Parishad, lauded the action, while Muslim organizations denounced it. The vacillation of the central government in the dispute occasioned stormy demonstrations and sporadic riots throughout the year. An already highly volatile situation was exacerbated by the stated intention of the Vishwa Hindu Parishad to tear down the mosque portion of the Ayodhya structure and erect a new temple. The organization used the great Kumbh Mela pilgrimage festival as the occasion for appealing to Hindu villagers to send bricks and stones for construction of the temple.

From mid-January to early March an estimated 30 million pilgrims visited the 10-sq km (4-sq mi) area at Allahabad marking the confluence of the Ganges, Yamuna, and mythical Sarasvati rivers, where once every three years the Kumbh Mela is held. At daybreak on February 6, the most auspicious of the mela days, some 15 million pilgrims bathed in the chilly waters, one of the four places on Earth where, according to Hindu tradition, divine nectar was spilled in a battle between the gods.

Vimla Mehra, director of a special police branch established to deal with crimes

against women, ordered police protection of women from sexual harassment during the annual spring celebration of Holi, which traditionally included sexual license. Mehra's action was in response to protests from increasingly influential women's rights groups. These groups also denounced the ancient practice of dedicating young women to sacred prostitution as devadasis or "slaves of god." Although prohibited by law, the practice persisted; in March, during the festival of Marg Purnima, over 3,000 minor girls were dedicated to the goddess Yellama as devadasis in a ceremony in the Belgaum district of Karnataka. It was feared many would eventually be sold into secular prostitution.

(H. PATRICK SULLIVAN)

ISLAM

The year 1989 began with a massive reaction throughout most of the Muslim world to the publication in late 1988 of *The Satanic Verses* by Salman Rushdie (*see* BIOGRAPHIES). The novel, read as blasphemous and scurrilous by almost all Muslim readers, was banned in most Muslim countries. Early in February Iran's Ayatollah Ruhollah Khomeini called on Muslims to kill Rushdie and the book's publishers, Viking Penguin. Demonstrations and riots broke out in many Muslim countries, although some of the violence masked old trouble spots. The violence tapered off during the summer. (*See* PUBLISHING: Sidebar.)

In China a book about sexual practices in which Islamic architecture was described in pejorative symbolic terms provoked demonstrations in several cities; some 2,500 Chinese students marched in Beijing early in May to protest, the first time Chinese Muslim students and sympathizers had organized a demonstration in the name of Islam. Muslims in the U.S.S.R. continued their activism, demonstrating in early February in Tashkent to press their religious demands, including the ouster of the chief mufti, whom they accused of impious behaviour. The government in The Sudan announced in March that it would not extend Islamic law to the Christian south, where civil war had been raging since 1973.

In the spring thousands of ethnic Turks fled to Turkey from Bulgaria, where they claimed the government was crushing their ethnic identity and religious expression. In Turkey, officially a secular state, concern continued over students' and others' interest in displaying Islamic symbols. In April the Israeli government, fearing disturbances, stopped most West Bank Palestinians from worshiping at the al-Aqsa Mosque on the Temple Mount in Jerusalem. A scandal occurred in Egypt when an investment fund, founded on Islamic principles of financial practice, was placed in receivership because of mismanagement. Mecca endured another terrorist attack in July, when two bombs exploded near the Ka'bah.

Islam continued to grow and to attract converts in many parts of the world. In the U.S. it was said to be the fastest growing religion; its converts were mainly American blacks, although the majority of Muslims in the U.S. were immigrants from the Middle East, Asia, and Africa. In Nigeria, Ibrahim Dasuki became the new sultan of Sokoto, spiritual head of 60 million Muslims in West Africa. The death of Ayatol-

lah Khomeini (*see* OBITUARIES) in June occasioned an outpouring of religious sentiment in Iran. Changes in the government following his death appeared to suggest a politically moderating policy, but no immediate changes in religious policies could be discerned. In Rome a mosque was under construction, the first to be built in that city. (REUBEN W. SMITH)

WORLD RELIGIOUS STATISTICS

The figures in the table below use definitions reflecting the UN Universal Declaration of Human Rights. A person's religion is what he says it is. Some 80% of the world's people professed religious faiths, and this percentage was growing slowly each year. The rapid growth of Muslims in North America and Europe, still almost entirely the result of emigration from Muslim lands, was especially noteworthy.

These figures do not represent merely nominal adherence. At least two-thirds of all religionists were active in their faiths. The figures for religious radio and television demonstrated this. The latest poll in Britain showed that 62% of the population watched Christian television programs regularly. Worldwide, 1.4 billion persons were listeners/viewers to Christian radio/TV. Similarly, Islam, Judaism, Baha'i, and many other religions broadcast to huge audiences daily. (DAVID B. BARRETT)

This article updates the *Macropædia* articles The Buddha and BUDDHISM; CHRISTIANITY; EASTERN ORTHODOXY; HINDUISM; Muhammad and the Religion of ISLAM; JUDAISM; PROTESTANTISM; The Study and Classification of RELIGIONS; ROMAN CATHOLICISM; and *Micropædia* entries on the various denominations.

Adherents of All Religions by Seven Continental Areas, Mid-1989

	Africa	Asia	Europe	Latin America	Northern America	Oceania	U.S.S.R.	World	%	Countries
Christians	293,547,000	236,700,000	410,310,000	410,240,000	234,600,000	21,700,000	104,800,000	1,711,897,000	32.9	251
Roman Catholics	110,264,000	111,028,000	260,450,000	381,800,000	95,200,000	7,660,000	5,300,000	971,702,000	18.7	242
Protestants	77,327,000	73,563,000	73,330,000	15,500,000	94,600,000	7,600,000	9,300,000	351,220,000	6.7	230
Orthodox	26,262,000	3,300,000	35,860,000	1,660,000	5,900,000	540,000	90,100,700	163,622,700	3.1	98
Anglicans	24,108,000	645,000	32,690,000	1,230,000	7,200,000	5,336,000	300	71,209,300	1.4	148
Other Christians	55,586,000	48,164,000	7,980,000	10,050,000	31,700,000	564,000	99,000	154,143,000	3.0	110
Muslims	263,132,000	608,500,000	12,360,000	1,200,000	5,220,000	99,500	34,100,000	924,611,500	17.8	172
Nonreligious	1,700,000	690,000,000	52,158,000	16,000,000	21,700,000	3,100,000	84,855,500	869,513,500	16.7	220
Hindus	1,450,000	685,000,000	594,000	750,000	1,100,000	310,000	1,100	689,205,100	13.2	88
Buddhists	14,000	310,000,000	222,000	495,000	400,000	17,000	290,000	311,438,000	6.0	86
Atheists	250,000	150,000,000	18,460,000	2,900,000	1,200,000	530,000	58,500,000	231,840,000	4.5	130
Chinese folk religionists	10,000	170,000,000	50,000	60,000	101,000	15,000	200	170,236,200	3.3	56
New-Religionists	15,000	125,000,000	35,000	460,000	1,300,000	9,000	500	126,819,500	2.4	25
Tribal religionists	66,240,000	23,500,000	200	950,000	50,000	70,000	0	90,810,200	1.7	98
Sikhs	23,000	17,350,000	217,000	7,000	230,000	8,000	100	17,735,100	0.3	20
Jews	300,000	4,310,000	1,447,000	1,010,000	7,100,000	90,000	3,100,000	17,357,000	0.3	125
Shamanists	900	10,500,000	400	200	500	200	200,000	10,702,200	0.2	10
Confucians	800	5,800,000	1,000	800	18,000	300	500	5,821,400	0.1	3
Baha'is	1,310,000	2,510,000	85,000	750,000	340,000	71,000	6,000	5,072,000	0.1	205
Jains	45,000	3,520,000	10,000	3,000	2,500	1,000	0	3,581,500	0.1	10
Shintoists	300	3,200,000	400	1,000	3,000	500	100	3,205,300	0.1	3
Other religionists	279,000	5,719,000	736,000	4,237,000	405,000	87,500	7,000	11,570,500	0.2	170
Total Population	**628,317,000**	**3,051,609,000**	**496,686,000**	**439,064,000**	**273,770,000**	**26,109,000**	**285,861,000**	**5,201,416,000**	**100.0**	**251**

NOTES:

Continents. These follow current UN demographic practice. UN practice in 1949 divided the world into five continents; then into 18 regions (1954); 8 major continental areas (called macro regions in 1987) and 24 regions (1963); and 7 major areas and 22 regions (1988). (See United Nations, *World Population Prospects 1988*, New York, 1989, with populations of all continents, regions, and countries covering the period 1950–2025.) The table above therefore combines its former columns "East Asia" and "South Asia" into one single continental area, "Asia."

Countries. The last column enumerates sovereign and nonsovereign countries in which each religion has a significant following.

Rows. The list of religions is arranged by descending order of magnitude of global adherents in 1989 (last two columns but one).

Adherents. As defined and enumerated for each of the world's countries in *World Christian Encyclopedia* (1982), projected to mid-1989, adjusted for recent data.

Christians. Followers of Jesus Christ affiliated to churches (church members, including children), plus persons professing in censuses or polls though not so affiliated.

Other Christians. Catholics (non-Roman), marginal Protestants, crypto-Christians, and adherents of African, Asian, black, and Latin-American indigenous churches.

Muslims. 83% Sunnite, 16% Shi'ites, 1% other schools. The definition excludes former ethnic Muslims in Communist lands who have now abandoned Islam.

Nonreligious. Persons professing no religion, nonbelievers, agnostics, freethinkers, dereligionized secularists indifferent to all religion.

Hindus. 79% Vaishnavites, 25% Shaivites, 2% neo-Hindus and reform Hindus.

Buddhists. 56% Mahayana, 38% Theravada, 6% Tantrayana.

Atheists. Persons professing atheism, skepticism, disbelief, or irreligion, including antireligious (opposed to all religion).

Chinese folk religionists. Followers of traditional Chinese religion (local deities, ancestor veneration, Confucian ethics, Taoism, universism, divination, some Buddhist elements).

New-Religionists. Followers of Asiatic 20th-century New Religions, New Religious movements, radical new crisis religions, and non-Christian syncretistic mass religions, all founded since 1800 and mostly since 1945.

Jews. 84% Ashkenazim, 10% Orientals, 4% Sephardim. The definition includes nonpracticing Jews, underground Jews, and crypto-Jews in Communist countries.

Confucians. Non-Chinese followers of Confucius and Confucianism, mostly Koreans in Korea.

Other religionists. Including 50 minor world religions and a large number of spiritist religions, New Age religions, quasi religions, pseudoreligions, parareligions, religious systems, mystic systems, religious and semireligious brotherhoods of numerous varieties.

Total Population. UN medium variant figures for mid-1989, as given in *World Population Prospects 1988*, pages 110–117.

(DAVID B. BARRETT)

Social Security and Welfare Services

Despite renewed economic growth that decreased the pressure on some social security programs in 1989, unemployment was a lingering problem for social policy in many countries, especially as regards certain specific groups and the long-term unemployed. The economic upturn had not spread to most less developed countries, where social protection often remained limited, so examples of countries that had instituted or expanded social security programs under difficult economic circumstances were especially encouraging.

National Developments in Social Security. In February Australia introduced a program for the long-term unemployed called Newstart, aimed at those who had been on unemployment benefit for more than one year. The purpose of the program, targeted at those between ages 21 and 54, was to provide special assistance for their reintegration into the labour market. A cash payment was provided when the person entered a job. If subsequently, through no fault of his own, the person lost the job (within 13 weeks), the waiting period for the receipt of unemployment benefits was waived. The program also allowed beneficiaries to continue to receive benefits while carrying out other activities, such as voluntary work.

In addition to the long-term unemployed, certain groups, such as young people and older workers, face special problems in entering or reentering the labour force. A new scheme for young people who were not working was introduced in New Zealand in January. Called the Youth Support scheme, the program combined three forms of assistance that had been administered separately: unemployment benefits, training allowances, and study allowances. An allowance was paid to young people aged 16 to 19 while they were unemployed, in training, or at school. The amount was linked to the rate of unemployment benefit for a single person and varied from 60% for youths aged 16 or 17 to 80% for those 18 years and over who were not living with their parents. Young people who were married or had dependent children received the full adult rate of benefit.

Another approach to the unemployment problem was exemplified by Finland, where, effective in July, a daily allowance was paid to unemployed persons who accepted part-time employment. The allowance, which was related to income, was also paid to partially unemployed workers for a period of not less than 150 days to a maximum of 18 months. This followed a series of measures taken in Finland over three years to improve benefits for the long-term unemployed, including liberalizing the means test for the basic unemployment benefit and increasing the amount that could be earned without loss of benefits.

In Venezuela a law was passed in September to implement an unemployment benefit program before the end of the year. The scheme, which would be funded by the government until regulations for employer and employee contributions were prepared, was based on a 1985 law that never took effect. However, because of the economic restructuring that Venezuela was currently undergoing, it was decided to institute an unemployment benefit program immediately.

In Africa, where social protection was still relatively limited, there were important legislative changes in a number of countries. In September Mozambique approved a law establishing a general social security scheme for employees. Benefits would initially include old-age, invalidity, and survivor pensions, cash sickness benefits, and death grants. A preexisting employment injury scheme, based on employer-provided compulsory insurance, would remain in force but would be under the control of the National Social Security Institute. Registration of insured persons began in September, and implementation of the new scheme was planned for January 1990, beginning with the province of Maputo and gradually expanding to the rest of the country. Similarly, in Angola a general law on social security, approved by the People's Assembly in July, provided for the creation of a national social security scheme that would include old-age, invalidity, and survivor pensions, employment injury benefits, cash sickness and maternity benefits, family allowances, and death and funeral grants. Implementation would be in stages.

Legislation passed in February in Ghana replaced the National Provident Fund, a kind of forced savings plan, with a social security pension program for all workers, both employees and self-employed, including most employees in the public sector. Benefits included an old-age pension, payable from age 60 at a rate of 50 to 80% of average earnings for the best three years based on the number of contributions paid. A reduced pension would be payable from age 55. Disability and survivors' pensions as well as death benefits would also be payable. The scheme would be financed by employer and employee contributions of 12.5 and 5% of monthly earnings, respectively. The new law also provided that benefits would be adjusted annually to reflect salary increases.

The scope of social protection in Honduras was substantially enlarged with a decree, effective in June, extending social security coverage to nearly the entire population and instituting new benefits and services. Certain previously excluded categories of workers, such as domestic workers, small-scale entrepreneurs and self-employed in the informal sector, and workers in cooperatives, would now be covered. The new benefits included family allowances and benefits in certain cases of unemployment, as well as expanded social services.

After overhauling the statutory health insurance in 1988, West Germany turned to social security pension reform in 1989. The reform was motivated by a concern to guarantee the future financial equilibrium of the pension scheme in view of the aging of the population. New legislation provided for gradually raising the minimum retirement age to 65 beginning in 2001. Currently old-age pensions could be drawn as early as age 60 under certain conditions. New provisions would be introduced for early retirement, as well as for a partial pension allowing persons to continue working part-time while drawing a reduced pension. Pension benefits for low-income persons would be increased but would require 35 years of contributions. The pension credit currently granted to persons leaving paid employment to care for a young child would be raised from one to three years of contributions. As for financing, the total contribution rate, which was divided between employers and employees, would increase gradually from 18.7 to 21.2% between 1993 and 2010. Additional state subsidies for the scheme were foreseen for the next two years.

In the U.K., as of October, it was possible to receive an old-age pension and continue working without any decrease in benefits. The Social Security Act of 1989, which received royal assent in July, eliminated the earnings limit that had reduced the old-age pensions of men under 70 and women under 65 if they had earnings of £75 per week or more. The aim was to remove disincentives to the participation of older workers in the labour force, particu-

larly in view of projected labour shortages in some fields.

A reform of the family pensions provided under the National Insurance Scheme in Sweden was passed by the Riksdag (parliament) in June. The reform was aimed at modifying the national basic (flat-rate) and supplementary (earnings-related) pensions paid to surviving relatives in response to the changes that had occurred as a result of increased participation of females in the labour force, new family structures, and social conditions in general. The existing widow's pension would be phased out gradually and a new system of pensions for surviving relatives established. This would include child pensions (for orphans up to age 18, or 20 if a full-time student), readjustment grants, and special survivor's pensions payable to both widows and widowers. The new benefits would come into effect on Jan. 1, 1990. Readjustment grants would be payable for a period of one year to a spouse or cohabitant who had lived with the insured person for at least five years. If the survivor was caring for a mutual child, benefits would be paid until the child reached age 12. Where there were no dependent children, a special survivor's pension would be payable if the survivor was unable to support her/himself from gainful employment. (LYNN VILLACORTA)

Major changes were made in two social policy areas in the U.S. in 1989—the minimum wage and medical care for the elderly—but legislation in two others—child care and the rights of disabled persons—did not win final congressional approval despite bipartisan support.

The new wage law would raise the minimum from $3.35 an hour (where it had been since 1981) to $3.80 an hour on April 1, 1990, and to $4.25 an hour a year later. The law also would allow employers to pay 16-to-19-year-old workers a subminimum wage—$3.35 an hour for the first year and 85% of the prevailing minimum after that—for up to three months. That subminimum provision would expire in 1993 unless Congress renewed it. In June Pres. George Bush vetoed a bill that would have raised the minimum wage to $4.55 an hour, but the measure was reintroduced, and the scaled-down compromise was reached in November. About four million U.S. workers received the minimum wage.

Two sweeping revisions were enacted in Medicare, the federal health insurance program for the elderly and disabled. Congress repealed the 1988 Medicare Catastrophic Coverage Act that was designed to shield 33 million Americans from astronomical hospital and doctors' bills. Senior citizens vigorously protested the income surtax that elderly persons making over $16,000 a year were required to pay to finance the extended benefits. In an effort to contain the soaring costs of Medicare and deal with disparities in fees, Congress overhauled the way Medicare pays doctors. The new system, which would be phased in gradually over several years, set a national fee schedule based on the relative value of medical services and procedures. Specialists like surgeons and radiologists would be paid less by the government than at present, while general practitioners would receive more. The revision also limited the amount doctors could bill their patients over and above the approved charge and provided for reducing the reimbursement schedule if billings in one year exceeded the target. The changes were not expected to affect Medicare's total costs.

Expectations were high at the beginning of the year that Congress would increase federal child-care assistance to low- and middle-income families. The Senate and House of Representatives passed separate child-care bills, but legislation was stalled in conference committee because of a jurisdictional dispute and philosophical differences. Democrats generally favoured providing subsidies to par-

ents plus grants to the states, while most Republicans, including President Bush, backed a less expensive increase in the earned-income tax credit, a negative income tax for the working poor. A second politically popular, but unresolved, piece of legislation was the Americans with Disabilities Act, which would give some 43 million physically and mentally disabled persons the civil rights protections that blacks and women were granted in the 1960s and '70s. The measure was passed by the Senate and had widespread support in the House and the Bush administration. It would prohibit discrimination based on disability in private-sector employment, public services (including transportation), and public accommodations, such as restaurants, stores, and office buildings. Both child care and rights of the disabled were expected to be priority items in Congress in 1990.

For the first time since 1981, both the House and Senate approved using Medicaid funds to finance abortions for poor women in cases of rape or incest, but President Bush vetoed the measure. Five child nutrition programs scheduled to expire in 1989, including the WIC feeding program for pregnant women, infants, and children, were reauthorized for five years at a projected cost of more than $13 billion.

Two proposed changes in the Social Security system had widespread support but did not win final passage. One would relax the Social Security "earnings test" that limited how much retirees aged 62 to 69 could earn each year and still draw full retirement benefits. The other would move the Social Security Administration from the Department of Health and Human Services and make it an independent agency. The Social Security Administration did get a new commissioner in 1989, Gwendolyn King. She was the first black to head the government's largest domestic program since it began in 1935. Social Security benefits and taxes would go up in 1990 as a result of a rise in the cost of living. The nation's 38.9 million Social Security recipients would receive a 4.7% boost—the largest in over seven years. It would increase the average monthly benefit for a retired worker from $541 to $566, and for an elderly couple from $923 to $966. Some 4.5 million recipients of Supplemental Security Income (SSI) also would receive a 4.7% increase in their benefits. The Social Security payroll tax in 1990 would be 7.65% each for employers and employees, up from 7.51% in 1989. The maximum wage subject to the tax would rise from $48,000 to $50,400, bringing the maximum tax to $3,855.60.

A Census Bureau study found that 18.3% of all Americans, or more than 40 million people, received welfare for at least one month during a 32-month period from 1983 to 1986 under one or more of five major federal or state programs. Half got benefits for two years or more. The welfare rate was higher for blacks, Hispanics, unmarried mothers, and children than for the general population. Another Census Bureau survey reported that 13.1% of Americans—or 31.9 million people—lived in poverty in 1988, including almost 12 million children aged 17 and under. The report said that the poorest fifth of American families received 4.6% of national family income in 1988, while the wealthiest fifth got 44%.

A study by the Social Security Administration found that social welfare spending by federal, state, and local governments had grown from $102 billion in 1950 to $770 billion in 1986, after adjusting for inflation. The federal government share was $472 billion. Social insurance, primarily Social Security and Medicare, accounted for just over half of the total. In 1950 spending on social programs represented 8.2% of the gross national product. By 1986 their cost had grown to 18.4% of a much larger GNP, but

that still represented a smaller share than many industrialized nations in Europe devoted to social welfare spending.

(DAVID M. MAZIE)

See also Education; Health and Disease; Industrial Review: Insurance.

This article updates the *Macropædia* article SOCIAL WELFARE.

Space Exploration

The return of the United States to planetary exploration highlighted 1989 in space, with the Magellan and Galileo spacecraft starting their journeys and Voyager 2 providing a spectacular finish to its interplanetary odyssey. Space shuttle missions continued without mishap, but the U.S. space station program was buffeted by budget and managerial woes that threatened its existence.

The year was also the 20th anniversary of the first manned landing on the Moon. In a celebratory speech U.S. Pres. George Bush advocated that the U.S. return to the Moon and establish a lunar outpost and then continue onward to Mars. No timetable was set, and a study was undertaken by the National Space Council.

Planetary Missions. Two hits, one error, and a home run marked 1989 as probes covered different parts of the solar system. The highlight was the Voyager 2 flyby of Neptune on August 25, 12 years after it was launched from Earth on a mission originally intended just to reconnoiter Jupiter and Saturn. Planetary scientists, however, took advantage of a rare alignment of the planets and aimed Voyager's Saturn encounter so that it would fly past Uranus (1986) and then Neptune.

Neptune presented a pale blue face with few features, the most notable being a Great Dark Spot (the size of Earth) and a few smaller dark spots, plus a few white clouds encircling the planet. The clouds move at 645 km/h (400 mph) in a direction opposite to that of the planet's rotation. On the inbound leg of the encounter, Voyager photographed what appeared to be partial rings around Neptune, prompting speculation as to what could cause such an unusual feature. As the spacecraft came closer, though, the "ring arcs" became longer, and a final set of images—backlit by the Sun—showed that the arcs are four complete rings that vary in density and structure.

The big surprise was Neptune's moon Triton, which Voyager passed after flying over Neptune at an incredibly close 4,900 km (3,044 mi). Triton turned out to be smaller (only 2,720 km [1,690 mi] wide) and brighter than expected. It has a thin nitrogen atmosphere and "volcanoes" of liquid nitrogen caused by pressure on liquid nitrogen more than 19 km (12 mi) deep. Triton's surface temperature is −205° C (−400° F), making it one of the coldest objects in the solar system. Voyager also discovered six smaller moons orbiting the planet, bringing the total to eight.

During the year the U.S. also restarted its stalled planetary exploration program. Magellan, a radar mapping spacecraft designed to peer through the clouds covering Venus and produce detailed maps of the planet's surface, was launched on May 4 by the space shuttle. Although radar mapping had been conducted earlier, the resolution from Magellan was expected to be much greater than that from previous spacecraft, and the mission was expected to yield important clues about the formation of Venus and whether plate tectonics (continental drift) is an active phenomenon on the planet. By October the spacecraft had reached the orbit of Venus, but the planet was not there. The best launch window was October, but because Galileo needed that window (*see* below), Magellan would have to make an orbit and a half around the Sun before being inserted in orbit around Venus in 1990.

Galileo was launched by the space shuttle on October 18 on a long path to Jupiter. This most complex planetary spacecraft was designed to drop a probe into the atmosphere of Jupiter before the main spacecraft went into orbit for almost two years of observations. Original launch plans required the use of high-energy rocket stages, launched from the shuttle, to send Galileo on its way, but various technical and safety problems canceled them. Engineers devised an innovative and complex means of launching Galileo with an existing medium-power rocket stage carried by the shuttle. Although lacking the energy to place Galileo on a trajectory to Jupiter, the stage could send it to Venus. Through a series of gravity assists at Venus (February 1990) and Earth (December 1990 and 1992), Galileo's trajectory could then be "cranked" outward until it was traveling to Jupiter (two asteroid flybys would also take place but would not affect the trajectory). Arrival was set for December 1995. Because this would take the spacecraft much closer to the Sun than was originally planned, and also would have it operating longer, solar shades and other modifications were necessary. About five months before arrival at Jupiter, Galileo would aim the probe at Jupiter and then change its own trajectory slightly. The probe was expected to provide some 20 minutes of data on winds, chemistry, and lightning until it was crushed by pressures equal to a depth of 180 m (600 ft) of water—while still in the uppermost levels of Jupiter's atmosphere.

The first legal challenge to a science launch took place when several antinuclear activists sued to delay Galileo on the grounds that NASA (the U.S. National Aeronautics and Space Administration) had not done the proper environmental studies or properly contained the plutonium that was to generate electricity by radioactive decay (similar units were used on the Voyager spacecraft) against a possible launch accident. The suit, filed on September 28, was dismissed two days before launch, and a threatened launch pad "sit-in" was not attempted.

AP/WIDE WORLD

The probe Magellan is launched from the space shuttle *Atlantis* at the onset of its mission to the planet Venus. The high resolution probe could view the planet through its cloud cover and was expected to send back detailed maps of the planet's surface.

The Soviets had less luck with their Phobos missions to Mars. Phobos 1 was lost in August 1988, a month after its launch. Phobos 2 arrived in Mars orbit on February 12, but on March 27, just hours short of its destination, the larger of Mars's two moons and its namesake, contact was lost. Despite the setbacks, the Soviets planned another mission to Phobos in 1996, plus missions to an asteroid in 1997 (with France), Venus in 1998, and Mercury in 2002. A manned mission to Mars by 2015, which the Soviets had touted in recent years, was judged too ambitious at the present time, a spokesman said.

Finally, NASA's fiscal 1990 budget began the funding for two planetary missions, the Comet Rendezvous/Asteroid Flyby (CRAF) and the Cassini/Huygens orbiter-and-probe to Saturn and its moon Titan. NASA also asked the science community to propose experiments for the Cassini orbiter. The European Space Agency (ESA) was to provide the Huygens probe that would enter the methane atmosphere of Saturn and possibly land on the surface.

Manned Flight. U.S. space shuttle missions continued in 1989 with NASA scheduling five flights during the year. The first, STS-29 (March 13–18), carried a Tracking and Data Relay Satellite (TDRS-D) and a test model of a heat pipe radiator for the planned space station. Commander Michael Coats, pilot John Blaha, and mission specialists James Bagian, James Buchli, and Robert Springer made up the crew. The second, STS-30 (May 4–8), launched Magellan. Commander David Walker, pilot Ronald Grabe, and mission specialists Norman Thagard, Mary Cleave, and Mark Lee made up its crew.

STS-28 (August 8–13) reportedly deployed a secret Strategic Response Satellite and carried a small research payload. In October Aviation Week & Space Technology magazine published photographs that, it claimed, showed the satellite to be tumbling out of control. The shuttle was crewed by commander Brewster Shaw, pilot Richard Richards, and mission specialists David Leestma, James Adamson, and Mark Brown.

The STS-34 mission (October 18–23) carried Galileo. It was crewed by commander Don Williams, pilot Michael McCulley, and mission specialists Shannon Lucid, Ellen Baker, and Franklin Chang-Diaz.

Two other shuttle missions were planned for late 1989. STS-33 (November 22–27) launched a classified defense satellite. The crew consisted of commander Frederick Gregory, pilot John Blaha, and mission specialists Story Musgrave, Kathryn Thornton, and Manley Carter. STS-32 was scheduled to launch in December a Syncom communications satellite for use by the military and then retrieve the Long Duration Exposure Facility (LDEF), which had been placed in orbit in 1984 and was in danger of reentering the atmosphere. However, problems with launching pad equipment forced a postponement of the mission until January 1990.

The long involvement of the U.S. Department of Defense with the shuttle ended in 1989, yet another result of the 1986 Challenger mishap. The Air Force Manned Spaceflight Control Squadron at Johnson Space Center in Texas was disbanded June 30. Most Department of Defense payloads were being shifted to expendable launchers.

The U.S. space station underwent an intense reassessment phase as NASA tried to find components that could be substituted or eliminated in order to meet drastic budget cuts expected from the U.S. Congress. NASA officials again threatened to cancel the program if adequate funding was not found.

Plans for a privately funded Commercially Developed Space Facility were all but killed by the National Research Council, which found "no compelling" need for the station despite an attempt in 1989 by U.S. Pres. Ronald Reagan to require that part of NASA's research be carried out aboard it. Another advanced project, the National Aerospace Plane (NASP), went through more severe gyrations including plans to transfer all work to NASA and attempts to eliminate its budget.

The Soviets did not launch their Buran shuttle in 1989, as that nation reassessed its space priorities. A second unmanned launch was planned for 1990; the first five manned missions were to be completed by 1995; and two more orbiters were under construction.

The Soviets were moderately active with their Mir space station. On April 27 cosmonauts Aleksandr Volkov, Sergey Krikalev, and Valery Polyakov returned from Mir after a stay that began Nov. 28, 1988, when Volkov and Krikalev were launched with French cosmonaut Jean-Loup Chretien aboard Soyuz TM-7 (Polykov was launched on an earlier mission). Chretien returned Dec. 21, 1988, with Vladimir Titov and Musa Manarov, who completed the first yearlong stay in space. Mir went unmanned for several months, leading to speculation that it had been abandoned. In truth, the Soviets were resolving technical and management problems. On September 6 the Soviets returned to the space station, with the Soyuz TM-8 spacecraft carrying cosmonauts Aleksandr Viktorenko and Aleksandr Serebrov. The two had to resort to a manual docking after experiencing a problem with the spacecraft's guidance system. On September 15 the Soviets launched Biocosmos 9. Although there were no humans on board, the spacecraft carried rhesus monkeys, rats, and other specimens on a two-week research mission.

Commercial Ventures. Business opportunities in space were given a lift, literally, with the first launches of space missions licensed by the U.S. Department of Transportation's Office of Space Transportation. On March 29 the Consort 1 rocket took off from the White Sands Missile Range in New Mexico. It carried a package of materials experiments that were conducted under weightless conditions for seven minutes and then fell back to Earth. While not technically daunting, this was the first mission to make its way through the regulatory process. Second was a Delta launch of a British communications satellite at Cape Canaveral, Fla., on August 27. One venture failed when, on October 5, an oxidizer valve on American Rocket's AMROC-1 stuck and the vehicle failed to achieve suborbital flight and burned on the launch pad.

The Soviets offered their powerful Energia booster rocket for commercial launches and suggested that it be used to orbit the U.S. space station. Florida established a "Spacecraft Florida" authority to reactivate old launch pads and attract new business to the state.

Other Projects. On March 24 a Delta vehicle launched the Delta Star satellite carrying laser radar, cameras, and infrared sensors for Strategic Defense Initiative tests. They were designed to observe various rocket launches and natural phenomena so that engineers would know what antimissile seekers would have to look for and through. The first Delta II rocket launched a Navstar navigational satellite on February 14. Additional Navstars followed on June 10 and October 20. The last two Titan 34D vehicles used by the U.S. Air Force were launched during the year, one on May 10 to orbit a spy satellite and the other to launch two defense communications satellites. The first Titan IV, a more powerful descendant capable of carrying shuttle-size payloads, was launched on June 14 with a missile early-warning satellite on board.

The last launch at Cape Canaveral of an expendable

Antinuclear activists protest the launch of the Galileo spacecraft from the Kennedy Space Center in Florida. Because the probe contained radioactive plutonium, activists filed a legal suit to delay the launch, questioning the effect an accident would have on the environment.
AP/WIDE WORLD

launch vehicle under NASA control took place on September 25, when an Atlas Centaur orbited FltSatCom, a U.S. Navy communications satellite. After that mission all expendable launches at Cape Canaveral were under U.S. Air Force or Department of Transportation auspices.

The ESA had its share of successes and failures during the year. The greatest disappointment was the Hipparcos satellite, launched August 8. Hipparcos carried a special twin telescope that was designed to measure precisely the relative positions of stars in two separate fields of view. Millions of such measurements over a period of years were expected to provide astronomers with a catalog of star positions 10 times more accurate than those currently possible. Unfortunately, the satellite's final stage failed to fire, and Hipparcos was left in a lopsided transfer orbit. Nevertheless, even this reduced mission was expected to improve star catalogs greatly.

ESA's other launches (all using Ariane vehicles) fared better. On March 6 the Meteosat 4 weather satellite was launched and soon started operations. Several communications satellites also went into orbit, including Scandinavia's Tele-X and West Germany's TV-Sat 2. Japan launched the EXOS-D X-ray astronomy satellite on February 22 and a weather satellite, GMS-4, on September 6.

The Hubble Space Telescope moved closer to orbit when it was transferred in a secret U.S. Air Force cargo carrier to Kennedy Space Center from Sunnyvale, Calif., just two weeks before the earthquake that struck the San Francisco Bay area in mid-October. When launched (in March 1990), the Hubble was expected to perform several times better than any terrestrial telescope and over a wider portion of the electromagnetic spectrum. NASA also announced plans to build four small Explorer satellites.

People. NASA received new leadership with the appointment of Richard Truly as administrator and J.R. Thompson as deputy administrator. Truly, a former astronaut (STS-2 and -8), had been serving as associate administrator for space flight since shortly after the *Challenger* accident. Thompson was director of the Marshall Space Flight Center, Huntsville, Ala., and had been manager of the shuttle main engine during its development phase.

Two other former astronauts were appointed to high positions, William Lenoir as associate administrator for space station and Robert Crippen as director of the National Space Transportation System. Meanwhile, the agency experienced a management crisis when several top managers resigned before a new ethics law took effect. The law banned retired government officials from working for companies that held contracts in areas they had previously supervised.

The Soviet Union lost one of its space pioneers, Valentin Glushko. He had led the designing of the U.S.S.R.'s major rocket systems; these included the R-7, which became the first intercontinental ballistic missile, and the A-series launchers that put Sputnik and all Soviet cosmonauts in orbit. The U.S. lost astronaut S. David Griggs on June 17 when the private plane that he was flying crashed in Arkansas while he was rehearsing stunts for an air show. Griggs had been training for a shuttle mission in November. The tragedy led NASA to tighten rules regarding activities by astronauts, especially when in training.

(DAVE DOOLING)

See also Astronomy; Earth Sciences; Industrial Review: *Aerospace; Telecommunications;* Military Affairs; Television and Radio.

This article updates the *Macropædia* article EXPLORATION: *Space Exploration.*

Sports and Games

AERIAL SPORTS

Veteran free-fall parachutist Sandra Williams of Orange City, Fla., and 78 other U.S. women jumpers made aerial history on Aug. 18, 1989, by achieving the largest-ever women's free-fall formation in a mass jump at Montgomery, N.Y. It was an accomplishment they made twice in one day. On their first attempt that afternoon, they put together a midair formation of 73 women in a successful jump, more than enough for the world's record. Because it went so well and conditions were so good that they felt confident of surpassing themselves, they went immediately aloft for another try, working five more women into their grouping.

The previous women's world record free-fall formation was set March 24, 1986, in Deland, Fla., by a group of 60 jumpers, including Williams. To qualify as an officially recognized formation, jumpers must be linked up hand to hand or hand to foot, and the grouping must be verified by photograph. There is no record category for male-only

free-fall jumps. The record for the largest formation of parachutists in history was set Aug. 8, 1988, at Quincy, Ill., by 144 jumpers, of whom 26 were women.

At the world relative work parachuting championships, held September 21–October 1 at Ampurabrava, Spain, the U.S. Army Golden Knights parachute team took first place in the 10-round, eight-way event with 138 points. The Soviet Union placed second with 133, and France was third with 125. In the four-way event the French were first with 152 points and the Soviets were second with 132. Both the U.S. and Chinese teams scored 131, but the U.S. was awarded third place after winning a tie-breaking jump-off 11 to 7.

The Fédération Aéronautique Internationale (FAI) certified a large number of world records set by Soviet parachutists at Fergana, U.S.S.R., in late 1988. These included Linger Abdurakhmanov's overall mark of 50 consecutive landings on a disk, Natalja Philinkova's daytime women's record of 41 landings on a disk, and Inessa Stepanova's nighttime women's record of 21 consecutive disk landings.

France took two of the three top honours at the 21st world gliding championships held May 11–26 at Weiner Neustadt, Austria. A total of 108 sailplanes were entered, representing 27 countries. Jean-Claude Lopitauz of France won the open-class challenge, accumulating 9,148 points in an ASW-22B. Ingo Renner of Australia was second with 9,123 in a Nimbus III. In the standard-class competition, Jacques Aboulin of France, flying a Discus, was first with 8,854 points, and Andrew Davis of Great Britain was second in a Discus with 8,819.

The 15-m class was won by Bruno Gantenbrink of West Germany, who gained 9,041 points in a Ventus-C. Justin Wills of Great Britain finished second with 8,761 in an LS-6.

West Germany's Hans Peter Elkmann, flying an ASW-22M from Boeghrost, West Germany, to Chanterelle, France, on May 15, set a world single-place motorglider straight distance record of 826.6 km (513.7 mi). The FAI confirmed the Nov. 29, 1988, world record claim of Beat Bunzli and Max Bachmann of Switzerland for multiplace motorglider speed over a 100-km (60-mi) course of 150.9 km/h (93.8 mph), flown in an ASH-25M from Bitterwasset, Namibia. The Oct. 27, 1988, out-and-return distance in a multiplace glider world record of 1,101.5 km (684.5 mi), claimed by New Zealand's Morris Walker and George Taylor flying a Twin Astri over a New Zealand course, also was confirmed.

Geoffrey Lyons of Great Britain, flying an Enterprise Wing from Dunlap Flight Park, Calif., set a world speed record of 30.4 km/h (18.9 mph) for flexible-wing hang gliders over a 25-km (15-mi) triangular course on Aug. 14, 1989. A straight-line distance world record for flex-wing hang gliders of 395.3 km (245.6 mi) was set by the U.S.'s Kewvin Christopherson in a UP Axis 15 out of Whiskey Peak, Wyo., on June 28. Helmut Denz of West Germany established a flex-wing hang glider world triangular distance mark of 127.8 km (79.4 mi) flying from Ruhpolding, West Germany, in a Zephyr CX on May 25.

First place at the world hot-air balloon championships, held November 20–25 at Saga, Japan, was won by Benedikt Haggeney of West Germany with a score of 16,381 points. Second place was taken by Al Nels of the U.S. with 14,563 points, and Bruce Comstock of the U.S. finished third with 14,146 points. The contest was judged mostly on the basis of the accuracy with which pilots reached predetermined goals.

The first human-powered helicopter flight in history was achieved December 12 at San Luis Obispo, Calif. Pilot Greg McNeil of the U.S. hovered his 44-kg (97-lb), 30-m (100-ft) Da Vinci III 20 cm (8 in) off the ground for 6.8 seconds.

A helicopter speed record was set by Vernon Albert and Dave Harvey of the U.S. on Aug. 4, 1989, flying a Sikorsky S76 312.1 km/h (193.9 mph) between Houston, Texas, and Lafayette, La. A helicopter altitude record of 5,937.5 m (19,480 ft) was set by Wayne Mulgrew of the U.S. in a Robinson R22 over Redding, Calif.   (MICHAEL D. KILIAN)

AUTOMOBILE RACING

Grand Prix Racing. The rules applying to International Formula One automobile racing were changed for 1989. A total ban was placed on 1½-litre turbocharged engines. This was expected to result in more competitive racing even if lap speeds were reduced. In fact, speeds were soon seen to be equal or faster, and the McLaren-Honda team was almost as dominant as previously, with fresh opposition from Ferrari.

The season opened at Rio de Janeiro. Honda had V10 engines and Ferrari V12s, while Renault provided V10s for Williams. Most of the others used V8s. The surprise winner was Nigel Mansell (U.K.) for Ferrari. The fastest lap, at 195.786 km/h (1 km = 0.62 mi), was by Riccardo Patrese of Italy in a Williams-Renault. The new Ferrari F1/89 thus posed a challenge to the previously dominant Japanese-engined McLarens. The old pattern returned, however, at San Marino, where Ayrton Senna (Brazil) and Alain Prost (France), both in McLaren-Hondas, finished first and second. Prost had the fastest lap, at 209.044 km/h.

On the street circuit at Monaco, Senna again led Prost home; and Prost again had the fastest lap, at 140.125 km/h. At Mexico Senna again won, with Patrese second. Mansell's Ferrari set the best lap, at 197.907 km/h, but did not finish the race. Prost gained the winner's circle in the United States race at Phoenix, Ariz., while Senna had the fastest lap (145.505 km/h).

The Canadian Grand Prix in Montreal was a Williams-Renault celebration, with Thierry Boutsen (Belgium) and Patrese finishing first and second. Great Britain's Jonathan Palmer had the quickest lap under difficult conditions in a Tyrrell-Cosworth, at 171.923 km/h. Prost was a popular winner of the French Grand Prix, strongly challenged by Mansell in a Ferrari. Then, before an enormous crowd, Mansell fought a terrific battle with Prost in the British Grand Prix at Silverstone, losing to the Frenchman by 19.369 seconds. Mansell lapped fastest at 238.931 km/h.

The McLaren-Hondas were back in form in the German Grand Prix at Hockenheim. Senna finished first and had the fastest lap at 231.094 km/h, while Prost placed

Formula One Grand Prix Race Results, 1989

Race	Driver	Car
Brazilian	N. Mansell	Ferrari
San Marino	A. Senna	McLaren-Honda
Monaco	A. Senna	McLaren-Honda
Mexican	A. Senna	McLaren-Honda
U.S.	A. Prost	McLaren-Honda
Canadian	T. Boutsen	Williams-Renault
French	A. Prost	McLaren-Honda
British	A. Prost	McLaren-Honda
German	A. Senna	McLaren-Honda
Hungarian	N. Mansell	Ferrari
Belgian	A. Senna	McLaren-Honda
Italian	A. Prost	McLaren-Honda
Portuguese	G. Berger	Ferrari
Spanish	A. Senna	McLaren-Honda
Japanese	A. Nannini	Benetton-Ford
Australian	T. Boutsen	Williams-Renault

WORLD DRIVERS' CHAMPIONSHIP: Prost 76 pt, Senna 60 pt, Patrese 40 pt.
CONSTRUCTORS' WORLD CHAMPIONSHIP: McLaren-Honda.

Ayrton Senna of Brazil (left) and Alain Prost of France (right) race around a curve during the San Marino Grand Prix in Imola, Italy. Senna and Prost, both driving McLaren-Honda cars, placed first and second, respectively.
DUOMO

second. In Hungary, however, Mansell's Ferrari took the checkered flag; Mansell lapped quickest, at 172.862 km/h. The pattern was back to normal at the Belgian Grand Prix, run over the fast and difficult Spa circuit. Senna led Prost home, this time by only 1.304 seconds. Prost had the fastest lap at 189.890 km/h.

In the Italian Grand Prix at Monza, Prost finished first with Gerhard Berger of Italy second for Ferrari. Prost had the fastest lap at 236.985 km/h, and his win put him in the lead for the world drivers' championship by 20 points over defending titleholder Senna. Drama then entered into championship prospects in the Portuguese race at Estoril. Mansell took the lead but then overshot his pit at the tire change and reversed into position. For this breaking of the rules he was shown the black flag for an immediate stop. He claimed later not to have seen the flag and continued racing, only to collide with Senna's car on lap 49. Both cars were eliminated from the 71-lap race, which Berger won from Prost. Berger had the fastest lap at 198.263 km/h. For his misdemeanours Mansell was heavily fined and excluded from the Spanish Grand Prix, which Senna won from Berger; Senna had the fastest lap at 177.022 km/h.

More drama occurred in the Japanese Grand Prix. Senna had to win to keep his championship challenge to Prost alive, and his determination resulted in another collision, which eliminated both McLaren-Hondas on lap 47 of the 53-lap race. Alessandro Nannini of Italy (Benetton-Ford) won, beating the Williams-Renault of Patrese. Prost, who lapped fastest at 203.779 km/h, was ultimately declared the world champion driver of 1989. The Australian Grand Prix, run in heavy rain, was the final event of the 1989 season. Prost gave up after one lap, and Senna and Mansell were among those who crashed, all without injury; only eight cars finished a race that was prudently stopped well before the intended distance. The winner was Boutsen in a Williams-Renault, and Nannini was second.

Rallies and Other Races. In 1988 British prestige ran high when Jaguar won at Le Mans, but in 1989 the famous French 24-hour race was a victory for the Sauber team of Mercedes-Benz, which finished in the first two places. Two Sauber Mercedes C9s finished ahead of a Porsche 962 in the Suzuka 480-km race, while a Porsche 962 won the Dijon (France) 480 km. At Brands Hatch, England, over 480 km, the Sauber Mercedes won from a Porsche and a Jaguar.

The Sauber Mercedes placed first and second ahead of a Porsche at the Nurburgring in West Germany, and they clinched the Championship for Sports Prototypes at Britain's Donington Park circuit by again winning the top two places. At the season's end Sauber Mercedes had 115 points and Jaguar 39.

The world's rally champion was Mike Biasion for Lancia, which also took the rally manufacturers' championship, topping Toyota and Mazda. Toyota driver David Llewellin took the British rally drivers' title.   (WILLIAM C. BODDY)

U.S. Racing. Emerson Fittipaldi dominated U.S. auto racing in 1989, winning five Championship Auto Racing Teams (CART) races. These included the 73rd Indianapolis 500, where he earned $1,001,604 out of a record $5.7 million purse. Fittipaldi won the classic on lap 199 of the 200 when he shouldered past Al Unser, Jr., on the inside as both were passing a slower car. Their wheels touched; Fittipaldi corrected a momentary slide of his Marlboro Chevrolet, while Unser's Lola Chevrolet spun into the wall. Fittipaldi led 158 laps, averaging 167.581 mph (1 mi = 1.61 km). Unser finished second. Of the 33 cars that started, 15 finished the race.

Fittipaldi and his Marlboro Chevrolet then won another $1 million, coming in first at Portland, Detroit, Cleveland, and Nazareth, Pa. This gained him the CART season title with 196 points to 186 for runner-up Rick Mears.

Chevrolet enjoyed equal success in the U.S. National Association for Stock Car Auto Racing (NASCAR) competition, winning the Winston Cup manufacturers' title. The comeback of Tennessean Darrell Waltrip (Chevrolet) was part of NASCAR's most competitive season in years. Waltrip won two NASCAR classics, the Daytona 500 in Florida and the Charlotte (N.C.) World 600. The real war for the title, however, was fought between three-time king Dale Earnhardt in a Chevrolet and Pontiac's Rusty Wallace. That battle continued to the final race of the season at Atlanta (Ga.) International Raceway. Earnhardt won the race, but Wallace's 15th-place finish gave him enough points for his first Winston Cup crown and the $1 million prize that went with it.

Former ARCA star Grant Adcox of Chattanooga, Tenn., became NASCAR's first race fatality in five Winston Cup years in the Atlanta Journal 500. It was a one-car accident.

In the International Motor Sports Association (IMSA) Camel GT road racing series for Grand Touring Prototypes, Nissan and its drivers were in firm command, with Jaguar the only successful opposition most of the year. The drivers' championship was a duel between Geoff Brabham and Chip Robinson, both of Nissan; the latter finished second after a disastrous finale at Del Mar, Calif. A Porsche won the 24 Hours of Daytona and at West Palm Beach, Fla., and a Jaguar won at Del Mar, Tampa, Fla., and at

(continued on page 325)

The Seamy Side of Sports

BY D.G. MYERS

The lifetime banishment from professional baseball of Pete Rose—perhaps the greatest hitter of all time—damaged more than the man and his sport. Rose's case was only the most widely noticed scandal to tar sports in the U.S. during 1989. Racketeering and fraud among players' agents, drug abuse, crime and low graduation rates among college athletes, and under-the-table payments to student athletes by their coaches—all these raised serious questions about what sports had become in the U.S.

Although sports are, in the words of the late baseball commissioner A. Bartlett Giamatti (*see* OBITUARIES), an "important, enduring American institution," the scandals suggested that perhaps they had become more than that. Perhaps they had become not specialized human endeavours with principles and standards of their own, but a region of human life exempt from any principles of conduct or standards of character whatsoever. The exposure of the seamy side of sports, by revealing the self-importance and cavalier lawlessness of sports figures, may have shown that sports in the U.S. are treated as more important than they really are.

The Rose Affair. When Pete Rose (*see* BIOGRAPHIES), manager of the Cincinnati Reds, was accused of placing bets on games involving his own team, it was the most serious charge to be made against someone in uniform since the 1919 Black Sox scandal. The accusations first surfaced during spring training. It was reported that a check from Rose to a man later convicted of bookmaking had turned up in a 1984 gambling raid. Soon unnamed sources were telling two different newspapers that Rose had given a bookie his 1974 World Series ring in payment of gambling debts. A onetime friend of Rose was said to be on the verge of testifying before a federal grand jury that Rose had wagered and consorted with drug traffickers. The U.S. Internal Revenue Service was reportedly investigating Rose for income-tax evasion.

Rose insisted that the charges were untrue, maintaining that he had never bet on major league baseball games. Even so, former Reds teammate Johnny Bench recommended that Rose quit baseball for the good of the game. Commissioner Giamatti, however, said publicly only that he had appointed a special counsel to investigate the allegations. In May Giamatti received a report detailing Rose's gambling activities. He also scheduled a hearing at which Rose would be given a chance to answer the charges and counter the evidence. Rose declined to attend a hearing. After obtaining a one-month postponement and then unsuccessfully challenging the commissioner's authority in court, he cut a deal with Giamatti—a "compromise," he called it—in August. Giamatti agreed to make no "formal findings or determinations" on the

gambling allegations. In return, Rose acknowledged that Giamatti had a "factual basis" for penalizing him. He was ousted as manager of the Reds and banned from baseball for life.

Rose's supporters—and they were not silent—pointed out that he had never been accused of betting *against* the Reds. No one had ever suggested that Rose had tried to fix or throw games, as members of the Chicago White Sox had done in the 1919 World Series. But this seemed an odd defense of a man who had often said that his life was baseball. The rules of major league baseball explicitly forbid the placing of bets on "any baseball game in connection with which the bettor has a duty to perform." Or were his defenders implying that Rose's intense desire to win—a desire that would presumably only be fueled by a side bet on the game—somehow exempted him from the rules?

The fact that Rose's apologists continued to praise him for his single-mindedness—even his refusal to admit that he had a gambling problem was said to reveal that he knew no other way to play the game—spoke volumes about the American attitude toward sports. The aggrandizement of the will to win apparently forgave all sins.

The Degradation of Collegiate Athletics. Not everyone who blackened the name of sports during 1989 was a sporting legend with fans who were ready to explain away his misdeeds. In April sports agents Norby Walters and Lloyd Bloom were found guilty of racketeering and fraud in connection with the signing of 43 college athletes. Walters and Bloom had been indicted in August 1988 after a 17-month investigation by the FBI. According to the indictment, athletes were offered between $2,500 and $5,000 in illegal payments to sign a contract before their collegiate eligibility was up. If a client tried to back out of his contract, Walters and Bloom allegedly threatened to have a mob enforcer break the athlete's legs.

Several well-known athletes testified against Walters and Bloom, including running back Paul Palmer of the Kansas City Chiefs and Philadelphia Eagles wide receiver Cris Carter, both of whom admitted to accepting money from the agents while still in college. The athletes' testimony gained wide notice, and afterward U.S. attorney Anton Valukas complained it had overshadowed the ugliest aspect of the entire affair—the infiltration of organized crime into the ranks of sports agents. But observers appeared to be more interested in a behind-the-scenes glimpse into the lives of college athletes than in what such uncritical attention had permitted collegiate athletics to become.

"The problem is that we're turning institutions of higher education into entertainment centers," said former University of North Carolina president William C. Friday. A study commissioned by the National Collegiate Athletic Association (NCAA) found that college athletes spent more of their time on sports (an average of 30 hours per week throughout the school year) than in studying for class (25 hours per week). As might be expected, their priorities influenced athletes' academic performance. At more than half of 93 major football schools surveyed by the U.S. General Accounting Office (GAO), fewer than 40% of the players graduated within five years. The graduation rate among basketball players was even worse, the GAO found, but when the NCAA attempted to raise academic standards for athletic scholarships, coaches protested that the new standards were unfair.

The presence of agents with mob contacts, the degradation of their educational mission—these were only some of the problems facing colleges with athletic programs. On some campuses ethical indiscretions and even crime

D.G. Myers, an assistant professor of English at Texas A & M University, has written articles for the New York Times Book Review, Sewanee Review, New Criterion, and other journals.

had become the problem. Gang rapes, cocaine arrests, and shootings; hush money and cash payments to recruits via air express; easy courses, grade changes, cheating on entrance exams; players making extra money by scalping tickets—the dark side of collegiate athletics, when turned to the light, was crawling with worms.

Steroids. The worst of it was drugs. In his book *Personal Fouls,* Peter Golenbock reported the rumour that North Carolina State's basketball team intentionally lost a tournament game for fear of what NCAA-administered drug tests would have discovered if they had won. Seattle Seahawks linebacker Brian Bosworth claimed that he witnessed players at Oklahoma ingesting cocaine on game days. The use of performance-enhancing steroids, Bosworth added, is commonplace among college athletes. Even Columbia University, loser of a record 44 consecutive football games, was forced to investigate possible steroid use among football players.

The use of steroids by some athletes had been an open secret for years. But the sports establishment did little to solve the problem—or even to address it—until Canadian sprinter Ben Johnson tested positive for traces of stanozolol, a steroid taken in pill form, after dashing 100 m in a world-record 9.79 seconds at the 1988 Summer Olympics. Stanozolol is believed to cause cancer of the liver, and trainers who had examined Johnson commented privately on the yellowness of his eyes, an indication of the strain that the drug was putting on his liver.

The International Amateur Athletic Federation (IAAF) passed a rule in September stripping world records from any athlete who admitted to using steroids. The new rule nullified Johnson's records in the 60- and 100-m dashes. Despite the IAAF action, however, many athletes said anonymously that they doubted that drug use would decline significantly. Some estimates pegged steroid use among players in the National Football League (NFL) at 40%, while reckonings of the number of athletes at the Olympics who had used performance-enhancing drugs were even higher—50% or more. Pete Rozelle, commissioner of the NFL, announced in March that the league would suspend players who tested positive for steroids. With five months' advance notice, steroid users were able to take precautions. When it came time to test players in August, only 13 active players returned positive results and were suspended.

The abuse of steroids was treated not as an ethical or even a medical dilemma but as an unfair competitive advantage. Baseball players who flashed unaccustomed home-run power, or abilities above the norm, were greeted with singsong chants of "Steroid! Steroid!" Few people, however, asked whether such a response, with its implied envy and approval, was not itself one cause of the abuse of steroids. Indeed, it might be asked if the response to steroids was not simply the latest example of collective denial among Americans about the true nature of sports in their country.

If a manager who bet on his own team was not generally recognized as a cheat and if it could not yet be widely admitted that college football and basketball players were not really college students, then what could be wrong with athletes whose physical development was not truly theirs? The widespread and unspoken belief seemed to be that these things do not really matter if someone is a fine athlete. Even the attitudes that were said to breed success in sports—giving 110%, playing hurt, winning ugly—were urged as the keys to success in other areas of life, where moderation and proportion and elegance might have been better.

(continued from page 323)

Portland, Ore.; but the Electromotive Nissans won 9 of the 15 events. The XJR-9 Jaguars finished the first seven races of the season in second place, and drivers Price Cobb, Bob Nielsen, and Jan Lammers were in the top three in 13 of the 15 events. Meanwhile, the unsupercharged Camel Light class was dominated by Buick-engined vehicles, with Scott Schubot beating Charles Morgan for the drivers' crown.

Sports Car Club of America Trans Am production car racing enjoyed a banner year, with Mustang and Camaro fighting for supremacy. Dorsey Schroeder and Mustang won season honours. In drag racing the season champions were Gary Ormsby in Top Fuel, Bruce Larson in Funny Car, and Bobby Glidden in Pro Stock.

(ROBERT J. FENDELL)

BADMINTON

China swept the 1988 World Cup, which was held in Bangkok, Thailand, on Aug. 31–Sept. 4, 1988. Yang Yang won the men's singles title and Han Aiping the women's championship. Tian Bingyi and Li Yongbo captured the men's doubles crown and Guan Weizhen and Lin Ying the women's doubles championship. Wang Pengren and Shi Fangjing completed the sweep with a victory in the mixed doubles. In the 1988 Grand Prix finals, held in Hong Kong in January 1989, China again dominated the competition by winning four of the five titles.

The prestigious All-England championships were held in March in Wembley, England. Yang defeated Morten Frost (Den.) in the men's singles while Li Lingwei (China) overcame Susi Susanti (Indon.) to win the women's singles. In the men's doubles, Lee Sang Bok and Park Joo Bong (South Korea) defeated Rudy Gunawan and Eddy Hartono (Indon.). The women's doubles title went to Chung Myung Hee and Chung So Young (South Korea). Park Joo Bong and Chung Myung Hee took home another trophy for South Korea with a victory in the mixed doubles.

Two competitions highlighted the biennial World Badminton Championships held in Jakarta, Indon., in May–June. In the World Team Championships, the big news was South Korea's victory over heavily favoured China in a semifinal match. Indonesia later won the first Sudirman Cup team title by defeating South Korea in five sets. The next day competition for the World Individual Championships got under way. Chinese players rebounded by winning four of the five titles. Their only defeat came in the mixed doubles, which was won by the South Korean team of Park Joo Bong and Chung Myung Hee.

(WARREN K. EMERSON)

BASEBALL

Major league baseball enjoyed another fruitful season during 1989, withstanding several traumatic events, including the death of commissioner A. Bartlett Giamatti (*see* OBITUARIES) and the lifetime suspension of former superstar Pete Rose (*see* BIOGRAPHIES). All but one franchise—the Atlanta Braves—reached the one million mark in paid spectators, while two teams, the St. Louis Cardinals and the Toronto Blue Jays, exceeded three million. The 12 National League teams attracted a total of 25,323,273, an increase of 824,005 over 1988. The 14 franchises of the American League recorded an aggregate of 29,851,391, an increase of 1,351,755.

World Series. The Oakland Athletics, vanquished favourites in the 1988 World Series against the Los Angeles Dodgers, swept the San Francisco Giants in the best-of-seven finale to claim their fourth World Series title since

Members of the Oakland A's look around San Francisco's Candlestick Park in confusion after a major earthquake struck the area on October 17. After the quake, which measured 7.1 on the Richter scale, baseball commissioner Fay Vincent postponed the San Francisco-Oakland World Series.
AP/WIDE WORLD

the franchise moved from Kansas City in 1968. The 1989 World Series was completed after being interrupted by an earthquake that caused great destruction in the San Francisco Bay area.

On October 14 at Oakland Coliseum, A's ace Dave Stewart stifled the Giants to win the first game 5–0, and it was much the same story one evening later when Mike Moore won for Oakland 5–1. The Giants staked their hopes for a revival in the first "Bay Area Series" on a return to Candlestick Park, where they had crafted the National League's best home field record during the regular season. But baseball became a decidedly secondary issue on Tuesday, October 17. At 5:04 PM, about 20 minutes before the third game was to begin, an earthquake measuring 7.1 on the Richter scale struck the region, causing Candlestick Park to sway while some 60,000 fans awaited pregame introductions of the players. Members of the A's and Giants spilled from their respective dugouts, in search of families and friends in the stands.

When it was announced that the game had been postponed because of the calamity, spectators evacuated the stadium in orderly fashion. Baseball commissioner Francis T. ("Fay") Vincent declared the following day that the World Series would be resumed on Tuesday, October 24, provided that studies of Candlestick Park proved it to be structurally sound. Also, Vincent said that the condition of surrounding communities and their citizens would influence the fate of "our modest little sporting event here."

On Sunday, October 22, after consulting with civic leaders, Vincent delayed game three until Friday, October 27. He dismissed options such as transferring the World Series to a neutral site, perhaps San Diego, or canceling the event altogether. He opined that the World Series might heal the Bay Area's spirits, but only after a proper period of time. Most observers hailed Vincent's compassion and sense of priorities.

The long delay begat the latest World Series conclusion in history, though the A's hardly seemed affected. On October 27, 62,038 spectators bowed heads in Candlestick Park for a moment of silence to honour those who perished during the quake. Then Oakland picked up where it had left off, routing the Giants 13–7 behind another capable performance by Stewart and five home runs, two by Dave Henderson. On October 28 in San Francisco, the A's roared to an 8–0 lead and clinched the title with a 9–6 triumph.

Though A's manager Tony LaRussa had agreed to allow his players to celebrate their well-earned accomplishment, the team was relatively subdued afterward. Oakland-born Stewart, voted the most valuable participant in the World Series, spoke for all when he said that "baseball doesn't matter as much when you see the devastation we've seen." Vincent revealed that major league baseball would contribute $1.4 million to earthquake victims. Members of the A's and Giants and the Players Association also pledged significant donations.

The World Series itself was among the most lopsided ever—the Giants never led and were outscored 32–14—and the Oakland team was pegged as a dynasty in the making. "They've got what it takes to keep winning for a few years," said San Francisco manager Roger Craig.

The A's had advanced to the World Series by defeating the Toronto Blue Jays four games to one in the American League championship play-off series, while the Giants claimed the National League pennant by eliminating the Chicago Cubs, also four games to one.

Regular Season. Though bedeviled by several injuries during the early weeks of the season, the talented A's captured the American League West by seven games with a

Final Major League Standings, 1989

AMERICAN LEAGUE East Division					NATIONAL LEAGUE East Division				
Club	W.	L.	Pct.	G.B.	Club	W.	L.	Pct.	G.B.
Toronto	89	73	.549	–	Chicago	93	69	.574	–
Baltimore	87	75	.537	2	New York	87	75	.537	6
Boston	83	79	.512	6	St. Louis	86	76	.531	7
Milwaukee	81	81	.500	8	Montreal	81	81	.500	12
New York	74	87	.460	14½	Pittsburgh	74	88	.457	19
Cleveland	73	89	.451	16	Philadelphia	67	95	.414	26
Detroit	59	103	.364	30					

West Division					West Division				
Club	W.	L.	Pct.	G.B.	Club	W.	L.	Pct.	G.B.
Oakland	99	63	.611	–	San Francisco	92	70	.568	–
Kansas City	92	70	.568	7	San Diego	89	73	.549	3
California	91	71	.562	8	Houston	86	76	.531	6
Texas	83	79	.512	16	Los Angeles	77	83	.481	14
Minnesota	80	82	.494	19	Cincinnati	75	87	.463	17
Seattle	73	89	.451	26	Atlanta	63	97	.394	28
Chicago	69	92	.429	29					

mark of 99 victories and 63 losses, the best in either league. Toronto rebounded from a ragged start to beat out the Baltimore Orioles in the American League East division.

The Giants survived pitching inconsistencies to win the National League West by three games over the San Diego Padres. In the National League East the surprising Cubs beat the heavily favoured New York Mets by six games.

Kirby Puckett of the Minnesota Twins won the American League batting title with an average of .339. San Diego's Tony Gwynn took the National League crown with .336. At age 42, Nolan Ryan (*see* BIOGRAPHIES) of the Texas Rangers continued his amazing career as he raised his record strikeout total to 5,076; this was 940 more than retired runner-up Steve Carlton.

Voted Most Valuable Player in the National League was San Francisco outfielder Kevin Mitchell (*see* BIOGRAPHIES), who led both leagues in home runs with 47 and in runs-batted-in with 125. Milwaukee outfielder Robin Yount, who batted .318 and hit 21 home runs, won the corresponding prize in the American League. Cy Young Awards for outstanding pitcher in each league were won by reliever Mark Davis of San Diego in the National League and Bret Saberhagen of Kansas City in the American. Rookies of the year were Chicago outfielder Jerome Walton in the National League and Baltimore relief pitcher Gregg Olson in the American. Don Zimmer of Chicago was National League manager of the year, and Frank Robinson of Baltimore won the award in the American League.

A. Bartlett Giamatti. Only five months after succeeding Peter Ueberroth as commissioner of baseball, Giamatti

Pete Rose, the manager of the Cincinnati Reds, addresses the press on charges brought against him for gambling. Although Rose denied all charges, an investigation revealed he had gambled on games, and he was banned for life from baseball.

succumbed to a massive heart attack at his summer home in Edgartown, Mass., on September 1. He was 51. A much-revered scholar, Giamatti had been the president of Yale University before accepting the post of National League president in 1986.

One of Giamatti's first moves as commissioner was to install Fay Vincent as his deputy commissioner. Shortly after Giamatti's death, Vincent was elected commissioner.

Pete Rose. On August 24, after several months of investigation, Giamatti banned Rose from baseball for life. The 48-year-old Rose, who was managing the Cincinnati Reds at the time of his suspension, was exiled for betting on games, though Rose denied the commissioner's judgment that he had wagered frequently on games involving the Reds.

Rose, the sport's all-time hit leader upon his retirement as an active player in 1986, became the first person banned from baseball since 1943 and the 15th in history. None of the previous 14 was ever reinstated, but Rose promised to seek reinstatement after one year. He signed a document that was "not an admission or a denial of guilt," but it did resolve that "the Commissioner has a factual basis to impose the (lifetime) penalty imposed."

Rose was summoned to the New York office of then-commissioner Ueberroth in late February, after which it was revealed that baseball was probing "serious allegations" involving Rose's gambling habits. During spring training and the first few months of the regular season, Rose reacted to daily scrutiny by saying he would be vindicated. However, John Dowd, baseball's special counsel, produced a 225-page report on Rose's off-field activities and associations. After a series of court battles, attorneys for Rose agreed to the settlement that left one of the game's all-time heroes on the permanently ineligible list and with only a seemingly remote chance of reentry.

(ROBERT WILLIAM VERDI)

Latin America. The Zulia Eagles, from Venezuela, won Latin America's most prestigious baseball tournament, the Caribbean Series, which was played during February in Mazatlán, Mexico. The Venezuelans collected five wins in the four-team round-robin meet, dropping only the final game—after the championship had been decided—to the second-place Mayagüez Indians from Puerto Rico, who finished with a record of four and two.

Considered the hosts of the tournament although their home is hundreds of kilometres away from Mazatlán, the Mexicali Eagles enjoyed the support of the Mexican crowd, but they managed to gain only a third-place finish with two wins and four losses. The 1988 Caribbean champions, the Escogido Lions from the Dominican Republic, had only a single victory.

The Zulia Eagles had previously won the Venezuelan national winter pennant after beating Aragua in the final play-off. In Puerto Rico the Mayagüez Indians defeated the San Juan Metros in the championship series.

In the Mexican Pacific League hopes were high that a true home team would act as host of the Caribbean Series after the Mazatlán Deer made it to the play-offs. They were eliminated, however, by the Navojoa Mayos, who were later beaten by the Mexicali Eagles. The Escogido Lions took the Dominican championship after defeating the Cibao Eagles and the Licey Tigres in consecutive play-off series.

During the summer the Owls of the Two Laredos (Nuevo Laredo, Mexico, and Laredo, Texas), the most successful team during the regular season, won the AAA Mexican League. They defeated the Yucatán Lions four games to two in the championship series.

Cuba continued to dominate amateur baseball. In August the Cuban national team was undefeated in its quest for the Intercontinental Cup, played in Puerto Rico. Japan placed second after losing the final game 8–2 to the Cubans. Puerto Rico finished third. Other participants included South Korea, Taiwan, Italy, the United States, and Mexico.   (SERGIO SARMIENTO)

Japan. Osaka's Kintetsu Buffaloes almost won their first-ever Japan Series title, but Tokyo's Yomiuri Giants rallied to defeat them four games to three. The Buffaloes, three-time Pacific League champions, won the first three games of the best-of-seven postseason championship contest 4–3, 6–3, and 3–0. Then Isao Kouda, starter of the fourth game for the Giants, turned the tide, pitching a 5–0 three-hitter. The Giants, 25-time Central League champions and 16-time Japan Series titleholders, then won the remaining games 6–1, 3–1, and 8–5 for their 17th championship in the Japan Series' 40-year history. The Giants' pitching corps, with a combined earned-run average of 2.95 (against the Buffaloes' 3.84) and the batting of Norihiro Komada (.522) and Warren Cromarty (.346), contributed to the Giants' rally. Komada was voted the most valuable player of the series.

The Giants clinched the Central League pennant rather easily, despite the fact that the 1988 champion Chunichi Dragons were preseason favourites. The Dragons were not able to contend because of injuries to two pitchers, Tatsuo Komatsu, who had been the best starter for the team, and Kuo Yuan-tzu, with 37 saves the best reliever in the league in 1988. For the Giants the emergence of young players was a major reason for their success. Among them, pitcher Masaki Saito, 24, won 20 games (7 losses), including 11 consecutive complete-game victories (Japan's professional baseball record).

In the Pacific League the Buffaloes clinched the pennant in their 129th game (of the 130-game season). Their final winning percentage was .568; the Orix Braves were .567 and the Seibu Lions, .566. Early in the season the Braves, with a strong batting corps that Japanese media dubbed the "Blue Thunder Machine," were once eight games ahead of the Buffaloes. The Buffaloes were led by outfielder and designated hitter Ralph Bryant, who hit 49 home runs and batted in 121 runs, and left-handed pitcher Hideyuki Awano, who won 19 games against 8 losses.

(TOSHIHIKO SUZUKI)

BASKETBALL

United States. *College.* The drama that brought opposing coaches Steve Fisher of Michigan and P.J. Carlesimo of Seton Hall face-to-face in the 1989 National Collegiate Athletic Association (NCAA) tournament contributed an astonishing chapter to the rich history of this event. Both men had traveled hard roads to their confrontation in one of the most exciting finishes to a tournament noteworthy for such things. In overtime Michigan and Fisher edged Seton Hall and Carlesimo 80–79, adding a basketball crown to the football laurels won by the Wolverines a few months earlier in the Rose Bowl.

The national championship hung in the balance until Michigan's Rumeal Robinson sank a pair of free throws with three seconds left in the five-minute extra period. Seton Hall had fought back from a 12-point deficit to tie the score at 71–71 in the final 25 seconds of the second half. The scrappy Pirates from East Orange, N.J., built a 79–76 lead in overtime but could not hang on in a game neither team deserved to lose.

Immediately afterward, Carlesimo displayed championship class by defending the official who had called a controversial blocking foul on Seton Hall's Gerald Greene. It sent Robinson to the free-throw line for his decisive one-and-one attempt. Robinson had cost Michigan a game at Wisconsin during the season by missing his first shot in the same situation, but he did not do so this time. With a Seattle Kingdome crowd of 39,187 holding its breath, Robinson calmly hit the first shot to tie the score and then did it again on the bonus try. Michigan's Glen Rice scored 31 points in the championship game to win most valuable player honours.

Rice also set an NCAA tournament scoring record by tallying 184 points in six games, in addition, the 2-m (6-ft 7-in) forward made an equally vital contribution on defense. He kept the Wolverines alive by forcing the Pirates' John Morton to miss two shots in the final minutes of overtime.

Despite the bitter defeat, reaching the NCAA finals vindicated Carlesimo, who had come close to being fired a year earlier. Seton Hall caught fire in the second half of the game even though Michigan's Mike Griffin and Sean Higgins were combining to limit Australian Olympic hero Andrew Gaze, the Pirates' best outside shooter, to a single basket. An upset was in the making until All-American Rice brought the Wolverines back to life.

In the semifinal round Seton Hall overcame an early deficit to oust Duke 95–78, and Michigan nipped its Big Ten rival Illinois 83–81 after losing twice to the Illini during the regular season. That put two unlikely teams into the finals for a showdown that started cautiously, then grew in intensity.

FOCUS ON SPORTS

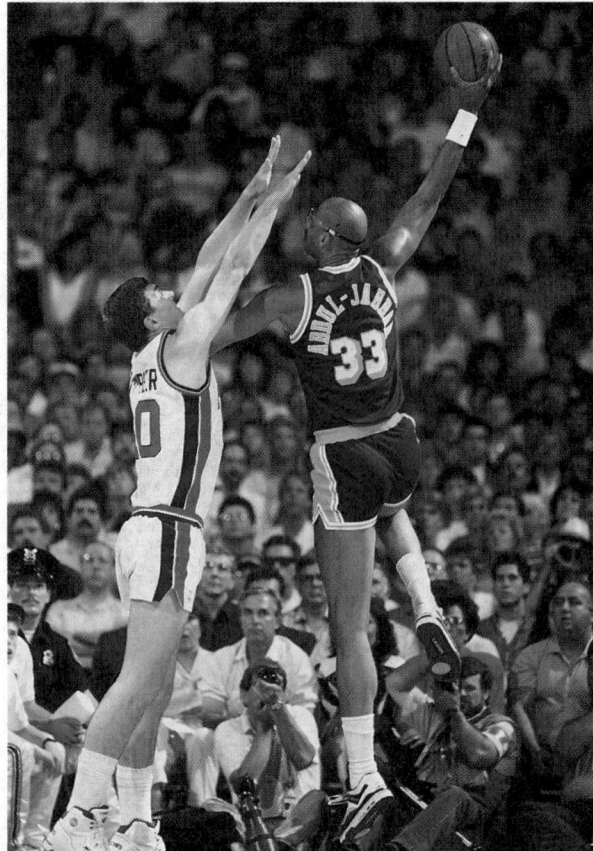

Bill Laimbeer of the Detroit Pistons tries to block a shot by Kareem Abdul-Jabbar of the Los Angeles Lakers (right) during the NBA championship. Abdul-Jabbar played the last game of his career at the series. Both the game and the championship went to the Pistons.

Still, the outcome was overshadowed by the success story of Steve Fisher. The soft-spoken Michigan assistant had stepped out of the shadows when Michigan coach Bill Frieder shocked the university by quitting on the eve of the tournament. Fisher had expected to leave Frieder's staff and become head coach at Western Michigan after the tournament. After seven years as an aide and recruiter at Michigan, he was ready to run his own program.

Nobody, least of all Fisher, dreamed that his chance would come at Michigan, especially in such storybook fashion. When Frieder announced he was moving to Arizona State just two days before the Wolverines' tourney opener, pandemonium reigned in Ann Arbor. In desperation, Michigan's athletic director, Glenn E. ("Bo") Schembechler, turned to Fisher, asking him to take over until the team was eliminated from the NCAA. Schembechler planned to launch a nationwide search for a new head coach.

That search was canceled by the Wolverines' incredible march to the national championship under Fisher. From total chaos on March 15 to the pinnacle in the Kingdome on April 3, the former assistant coach glued the shaken Wolverines' confidence back together and guided their victory march. Fisher was rewarded with a three-year contract as Michigan's head coach.

In the women's NCAA tournament, Tennessee pulled away from Auburn for a convincing 76–60 victory and the national championship. The Lady Volunteers found their once-comfortable lead trimmed to 50–47 midway through the second half, but Bridgette Gordon hit three consecutive shots from outside to pace a 13–2 Tennessee surge. That doomed Auburn (32–2) to a second straight defeat in the final game.

Gordon's 27 points led all scorers, but Tennessee (35–2) got plenty of help from centre Sheila Frost, who blocked five shots, made three steals, and added 12 rebounds, powering the winners to a 45–30 advantage on the boards. It was the second time in three years that coach Pat Summitt had taken Tennessee to the top.

Professional. After coming close a year earlier, the Detroit Pistons were not to be denied in 1989. They swept the Los Angeles Lakers out of their path in four straight games to capture the 1988–89 National Basketball Association (NBA) crown. It was the first world championship for the franchise that had started in Fort Wayne, Ind., in 1948.

Living up to their "bad boys" image, the Pistons ended a two-year Los Angeles grip on the NBA title. An injury to Lakers' playmaker Earvin ("Magic") Johnson in the second game virtually assured quick elimination in the best-of-seven series, but the defending champions put up a good fight.

The Pistons led the NBA with 63 regular-season victories and went 12–2 in the play-offs. Both of those play-off setbacks were to the Chicago Bulls and their magnificent Michael Jordan in the Eastern Conference finals. The Bulls actually led that tension-packed series 2–1, but Detroit guard Joe Dumars shackled Jordan in the pivotal fourth game, and Detroit did not lose again en route to its long-awaited championship.

Dumars was the main man once more in the finals, averaging 27.3 points per game in the 4–0 sweep over the Lakers. That, combined with inspired defensive play, made the 1.9-m (6-ft 3-in) guard an overwhelming choice as most valuable player of the championship round.

Nevertheless, veteran Kareem Abdul-Jabbar of the Lakers won the plaudits of fans across the nation with a gallant end to his 20-year professional career. With a 24-point outburst, Abdul-Jabbar did his best to pull the Lakers through in the third game, but to no avail. The 2.2-m (7-ft 2-in) centre managed only seven points in his last NBA appearance, and the Pistons prevailed 105–97 to wrap up the series. However, even the Detroit bench rose to join the Forum crowd's ovation when Abdul-Jabbar left the floor for the final time.

(ROBERT G. LOGAN)

World Basketball. The International Basketball Federation (FIBA) abolished all distinctions between professional and other players at its world congress in April 1989 in Munich, West Germany. Nevertheless, difficulties still arose with the movement of players between the NBA and Europe. Yugoslavs Drazen Petrovic and Dino Radja were signed by the Portland Trail Blazers and Boston Celtics, respectively, amid debate regarding their contracts in Europe. Real Madrid of Spain agreed to release Petrovic to Portland for $1,150,000. Petrovic had scored 22 points for Madrid against the Boston Celtics in the final of the McDonald's Basketball Open in Madrid in October 1988, which Boston had won 111–96, led by 29 points from Larry Bird.

Radja, the 21-year-old star of Jugoplastika of Split, Yugos., led his club to success in the European Champions' Cup. The young team, without any U.S. players, upset Maccabi Tel Aviv of Israel 75–69 in the final in the Olympic Hall in Munich on April 6. Radja then became the centre of a legal dispute when he signed with Boston. Judge Douglas Woodlock ruled in favour of Jugoplastika, and Radja was ordered to return to Yugoslavia; Boston appealed the decision.

Soviet stars Sarunas Marchulenis and Aleksandr Volkov joined the Golden State Warriors and Atlanta Hawks, respectively. By contrast, Danny Ferry, the number two overall pick in the NBA draft, gave up the Los Angeles Clippers to sign for Il Messaggero of Rome.

Yugoslavia dominated the European scene, acting as host and winning the European men's championship at Zagreb, Yugos., in June. Greece shocked the U.S.S.R. 81–80 in a semifinal, thanks to 45 points from Nik Gallis, but could do nothing to stop Yugoslavia from winning the final 98–77. Neither Rik Smits (The Netherlands) nor Detler Schrempf (West Germany) was able to gain release from his NBA team to play in the tournament.

Jugoplastika Split was joined by Partizan Belgrade (European Korac Cup for men) and J.A. Tuzla (women's champions) in winning European Cups for Yugoslavia. Petrovic ensured that Yugoslavia also featured prominently in the European Cup Winners' Cup final. He notched 62 points for Real Madrid as it overcame Snaidero Caserta of Italy 117–113 in overtime. Brazilian star Oscar Schmidt scored 44 for the losers. CSKA Moscow won the Ronchetti Women's Cup.

NBA Final Standings, 1988–89

EASTERN CONFERENCE			WESTERN CONFERENCE		
Team	Won	Lost	Team	Won	Lost
Atlantic Division			**Midwest Division**		
*New York	52	30	*Utah	51	31
*Philadelphia	46	30	*Houston	45	37
*Boston	42	40	*Denver	44	38
Washington	40	42	Dallas	38	44
New Jersey	26	56	San Antonio	21	61
Charlotte	20	62	Miami	15	67
Central Division			**Pacific Division**		
*Detroit	63	19	*L.A. Lakers	57	25
*Cleveland	57	25	*Phoenix	55	35
*Atlanta	52	30	*Seattle	47	35
*Milwaukee	49	33	*Golden State	43	39
*Chicago	47	35	*Portland	39	43
Indiana	28	54	Sacramento	27	55
			L.A. Clippers	21	61

*Gained play-off berth.

Rumeal Robinson of Michigan (left) tries to block a jump shot by Seton Hall's John Morton during the NCAA championship game. Michigan edged out Seton Hall by a score of 80–79 after Robinson sank a pair of free throws in overtime.

ROBERT BECK—ALLSPORT USA

Puerto Rico upset the U.S. 88–80 in the final to win the Americas Championship in Mexico City, while the women's crown went to Cuba, victors 87–84 over Brazil in São Paulo. The Asian women's title was won by South Korea, which gained a 73–72 victory over China in the final game in Hong Kong, but China captured both the junior men's and junior women's Asian titles.

In the McDonald's Basketball Open, held in Rome in October, the Denver Nuggets of the NBA won the title by defeating Jugoplastika Split 135–129 in the final. Radja scored 29 for Jugoplastika, as did Danny Schayes for Denver.   (MELVIN D. WELCH)

BILLIARD GAMES

Carom Billiards. The Billiard World Cup Association (BWA) conducted its second professional tour to determine a world three-cushion champion, sanctioning six events in Paris, West Berlin, Tokyo, Antwerp (Belgium), Valkenburg (Neth.), and Mallorca (Spain). Although the format of best three out of five 15-point games to win a match was disconcerting to many players and fans (who preferred the more traditional 60-point single-game matches), the combination of a $200,000 purse and the discontinuance of the Union Mondial de Billiard (UMB) world amateur championship resulted in a strong field. Torbjorn Blomdahl of Sweden, generally considered as heir apparent to the throne of the legendary Raymond Ceulemans of Belgium, proved himself most worthy by winning the BWA World Cup by a wide margin in the scoring. He won four of the six events and in the process set a new record scoring average (for 15-point game sets) of 1.947 per inning. In second place was frequent UMB runner-up Nobuaki

Kobayashi of Japan, with 19-time UMB world champion Ceulemans finishing third.

The 47th European three-cushion championships in Viersen, West Germany, was also a Blomdahl victory, but it was the veteran Lennart Blomdahl, father of the BWA champion, who took this prestigious title home to Sweden. He defeated Richard Bitalis of France in the final match. The younger Blomdahl was a close third.

A field of 20 battled for the South American three-cushion championship in Quito, Ecuador. A 50-point game format was employed, and José Arguello of Argentina narrowly edged out Mexico's José Paniagua, though Paniagua posted the high run of 15 and high average of 2.173 per inning.

Highly regarded newcomers won top honours in the All-Japan three-cushion championship. Yoshihiko Mano was first and Joji Kai second in the tourney held in Tokyo.

Major national federation championships in Europe included the 60th Dutch tournament at Rosmalen, where Rini van Bracht won his record-tying eighth national crown; the Danish national championship, won by Danny Korte with an average of 1.081, in Odense; the Austrian nationals in Vienna, where an average of 0.996 was enough to clinch the title for Franz Stenzel; and the hard-fought Belgian championships, won by Paul Stroobants with a 50–37 victory in the final game over Ceulemans (tournament-high run of 15).

The $30,000 international championships brought 36 of the world's finest players to Astoria (New York City) for the year's major U.S. three-cushion competition. Raymond Steylaerts, another of the many talented Belgian players, won the $7,000 first prize while averaging 1.058 billiards per inning. Hans Laursen of Denmark placed second.

Pocket Billiards. The steady (if somewhat slow) expansion of the U.S. professional pocket billiard tournament circuit was buoyed by several developments during the year. First, the Brunswick Corp. of Bristol, Wis., confirmed that it would sponsor several major nineball tournaments; such backing from within the industry was considered to be critical to pool's acceptance as a "big-time" sport that could attract television sponsors. Second, the Men's Professional Billiard Association (MPBA) appointed the able and well-respected Joe Kerr of Akron, Ohio, as its president. Third, several nonindustry advertisers began to use pool as a vehicle; positive returns from their cautious testing of the waters could result in important support for the sport.

The 1987–88 tour drew to a close with clear domination by Earl Strickland of Hillsboro, N.C., in the men's division and Loree Jon Jones of Hillsborough, N.J., in the women's. They were named 1988 Players of the Year by both *Pool and Billiard Magazine* and *Billiards Digest*.

Both Jones and Strickland played well in the 1988–89 tour, although the unofficial kickoff event, the $36,400 U.S. Nineball Open, was won by Mike LeBron of Philadelphia and Ewa Mataya of Grand Ledge, Mich. Strickland won several men's events, including the $23,000 Lexington All-Star crown.

It was Nick Varner of Owensboro, Ky., however, who chalked up not only 10 victories by the summer's end but also the richest and toughest events—the $38,600 Rakm-Up Classic, the $30,000 Glass City Open, the $47,000 Sands Regent Open, the $50,000 Brunswick World's Open, the $36,000 Governor's Cup, and the $48,200 Sands Regent Open. This run of victories ranked as the most dominant in tour history.

In women's competition, by contrast, no one player was able to dominate the action. Mary Kenniston of Las Vegas, Nev., won the McDermott Masters and the Brunswick

World's Open; Robin Bell of Costa Mesa, Calif., topped the fields of the GinaCue Open and the WPBA (Women's Professional Billiard Association) Cleveland Open; Bonnie Hoffman of St. Petersburg, Fla., snared the 1988 Cleveland Open and the Carolina's Cup; Lori Shampo of Charlotte, N.C., was best at the Cleveland Women's Pro Open; and Jones was champion of the BC Open and the WPBA Nationals, both held in New York state.

The Association of College Unions-International conducted its 39th intercollegiate championships at Georgia Tech. Gary Asbell (Florida State) and Cathy Petrowski (North Texas State) won the men's and women's divisions, respectively.

The Billiard Congress of America (BCA) inducted Mike Sigel of Baltimore, Md., into its Hall of Fame in ceremonies at the BCA Trade Expo in Nashville, Tenn. Luther ("Wimpy") Lassiter, legendary pocket billiard champion and member of the BCA Hall of Fame, died on Oct. 25, 1988, at the age of 69 in Elizabeth City, N.J.

(BRUCE H. VENZKE)

Snooker. Steve Davis of England reaffirmed his mastery at professional snooker in May 1989 by winning the world championship for the sixth time, defeating his fellow countryman John Parrott in the final by 18 frames to 3. In September Davis won the season's first ranking tournament by beating Stephen Hendry of Scotland 9–4 in the final. On winning the Grand Prix at Reading in October with a 10–0 victory over another Englishman, Dean Reynolds, in the final, Davis achieved his 50th tournament triumph in 11 years.

(SYDNEY E. FRISKIN)

BOWLING

World Tenpins. The major international bowling competition of 1989 took place at World Games III in Karlsruhe, West Germany, in late July. It consisted of mixed doubles and singles competitions. Ma Ying-chieh and Yüan Yueh-huang of Taiwan won the mixed doubles over Jorge Fernandez and Arianne Cerdena of the Philippines 4,708–4,646.

Ma became a double gold medalist when he defeated Darold Meisel of the U.S. for the men's singles title 424–380. In women's singles Canada's Jane Amlinger edged Cerdena 364–352.

The most important singles tournament of the year, the World Cup, was held in December 1988 at Guadalajara, Mexico. Muhammad Khalifah of the United Arab Emirates became the first bowler from the Gulf states to capture a major international title when he defeated Australia's Ian Bradford 246–197 in the final game. In the women's final Linda Kelly of Union, Ohio, beat Diana Tanlimco of the Philippines 199–170.

(YRJÖ SARAHETE)

U.S. Tenpins. Tom Jordan, a little-known left-hander from Paterson, N.J., came within one pin of achieving bowling's perfect three-game score when he totaled 899 in a doubles league in Union, N.J. Jordan, a welder by trade, bowled games of 300, 299, and 300 on March 7. It was a four-game league, and Jordan then added another 299. Jordan's score surpassed the American Bowling Congress (ABC) record 886 rolled by Allie Brandt of Lockport, N.Y., in 1939 and tied earlier in the 1988–89 season by Pat Landry in Lansing, Mich.

Virtually all of the ABC tournament records were shattered in the 86th annual event, which took place over 103 days in Wichita, Kan. A new type of synthetic surface was used for the lanes. The most notable feat was the total of 45 perfect games bowled; the most 300s in a previous ABC meet was four. Other records included: team series, Chilton Vending, Wichita, 3,481; doubles, Gus Yannaras

and Gary Daroszewski, Milwaukee, Wis., 1,499; all-events, George Hall, Mundelein, Ill., 2,227.

In the ABC Bud Light Masters Tournament, on the same lanes, another 17 perfect games were bowled. Mike Aulby of Indianapolis, Ind., already the winner of three championships on the Professional Bowlers Association (PBA) tour, won the championship by defeating Mike Edwards of Tulsa, Okla., in the title game. Pete Weber of Florissant, Mo., won the PBA national championship tournament at Toledo, Ohio, and Del Ballard, Jr., was winner of the Firestone Tournament of Champions at Fairlawn, Ohio.

A 21-year-old Australian, Carol Gianotti, won the Queens Tournament sponsored by the Women's International Bowling Congress (WIBC) in Bismarck, N.D. Gianotti defeated two-time Queens champion Aleta Sill of Dearborn, Mich., in the semifinal match and beat amateur Sandra Jo Shiery of Bronson, Mich., to gain the $10,000 prize.

In the 70th annual WIBC tournament, also held in Bismarck, the Open Division winners were: team, Robby's, Glendale, Calif., 3,000; singles, Lorraine Anderson, Northville, Mich., 683; doubles, Diana Goodman, Chino Hill, Calif., and Rene Fleming, Oklahoma City, Okla., 1,283; all-events, Nancy Fehr, Cincinnati, Ohio, 1,911.

In a rare occurrence a bowler competing in Division I (averages 151–170) outscored all Open Division entrants with 694 in singles and thus was declared the WIBC champion in that category. The surprise champion was Sandy Flint of Sioux Falls, S.D.

(JOHN J. ARCHIBALD)

BOXING

Mike Tyson (U.S.; *see* BIOGRAPHIES) retained the undisputed world heavyweight championship and his undefeated record and, though only 23, staked a claim for inclusion among all-time greats like Jack Dempsey, Joe Louis, Rocky Marciano, and Muhammad Ali. He began the year by hammering Frank Bruno (England) in five rounds and later dismissed Carl ("The Truth") Williams (U.S.) in only 93 seconds. This was his ninth defense of the title and his 37th victory, 17 of which ended in the first round. Tyson was scheduled for another defense against Donovan ("Razor") Ruddock (Canada) in November but canceled the event owing to slight illness while in training.

The cruiserweight division was thrown wide open by the decision of Evander Holyfield (U.S.) to join the heavyweights, with his target to face Tyson in a title clash. Before moving to the new weight class he was, like Tyson, recognized as champion by boxing's three controlling organizations, the World Boxing Council (WBC), the World Boxing Association (WBA), and the International Boxing Federation (IBF). After Holyfield relinquished his crown, the WBC championship was won by Carlos de León (P.R.), a former champion who had been defeated by Holyfield. De León beat Sammy Reeson (England) in nine rounds in London. The WBA recognized Taoufik Belbouli (France) when he defeated Michael Green (U.S.) at Casablanca, Morocco, giving France three world champions over a six-week period, but later the WBA declared this championship vacant as the Frenchman was put out of action by a knee operation. Robert Daniels (U.S.) was matched with Dwight Muhammad Qawi (U.S.) for the vacant title in France in December, with Daniels winning a split decision. Glenn McCrory (England) won the IBF version with a win on points against Patrick Lumumba (Kenya) and retained it by stopping Siza Makhathini (South Africa) in nine rounds.

Dennis Andries (Australia) gained the WBC light heavyweight title for the second time, stopping Tony Willis (U.S.)

in five rounds, but lost it again when he was defeated by Jeff Harding (Australia). Harding continued his reign by beating Tom Collins (England) in two rounds at Brisbane, Australia. Virgil Hill (U.S.) kept a tight hold on the WBA crown by defeating three U.S. challengers: Bobby Czyz, Joe Lasisi, and James Kinchen. Charles Williams (U.S.) remained IBF champion.

The legendary Sugar Ray Leonard (U.S.) only just held onto the WBC super middleweight crown when old rival Thomas Hearns (U.S.) held him to a draw. In December in their first bout in nine years, Leonard defeated Roberto Durán (Panama) in a unanimous 12-round decision.

Baek In Chul (South Korea) halted Fulgencio Obelmejias (Venezuela) in 11 rounds to become the WBA champion and later stopped Ron Esset (U.S.) also in 11 rounds. The IBF championship became vacant when Graciano Rocchigiani (West Germany) relinquished it to compete with the light heavyweights.

Durán outpointed Iran Barkley (U.S.) to win the WBC middleweight title at 37 and his fourth world title in 91 contests spread over 21 years. The WBA stripped Sumbu Kalambay (Italy) of its crown and recognized Mike McCallum (Jamaica) after he outpointed Herol Graham (England). Michael Nunn (U.S.) retained the IBF championship, knocking out Kalambay in one round and outpointing Iran Barkley.

René Jacquot (France) lifted the WBC junior middleweight crown from Don Curry (U.S.) but lost it to John Mugabi (Uganda) in one round. Julian Jackson (U.S.) retained the WBA crown by stopping Francisco De Jesus (Brazil) and Terry Norris (U.S.). Darrin Van Horn (U.S.) beat Robert Hines (U.S.) to win the IBF title but then lost it to Gianfranco Rosi (Italy). After capturing the WBC welterweight title from Lloyd Honeyghan (England), Marlon Starling (U.S.) beat Chung Yung Kil (South Korea) twice. Mark Breland (U.S.) won the WBA title that had been vacated by Tomas Molinares (Colombia) and then defeated Rafael Pineda (Colombia), Mauro Martelli (Switz.), and Fujio Ozaki (Japan). Simon Brown (U.S.) retained the IBF crown by beating Jorge Maysonet (P.R.) in Budapest, the first professional world championship to be staged in a Warsaw Pact country. Brown later successfully defended his title. Julio César Chávez (Mexico) became the first of his countrymen to win three world titles when he beat WBC junior welterweight champion Roger Mayweather (U.S.). Juan Coggi (Arg.) retained the WBA version with wins against Harold Brazier (U.S.) and Akinobou Hiranaka (Japan). Meldrick Taylor (U.S.) carried on as IBF champion, stopping John Meekins (U.S.) in seven rounds.

The WBC lightweight crown, which had been given up by Chávez when he moved to the heavier weight, was won by Pernell Whitaker (U.S.), who outpointed José Luis Ramírez (Mexico). Whitaker had become IBF champion in February. The WBA version was taken by Edwin Rosario (P.R.) when he stopped Anthony Jones (U.S.). Azumah Nelson (Ghana) and Brian Mitchell (South Africa) retained, respectively, the WBC and WBA junior lightweight championships. Nelson stopped Mario Martínez (Mexico) and Jim McDonell (England), each contest ending in the 12th round. Mitchell brought his successful defenses of the title to 10 after stopping Salvatore Bottiglieri (Italy) and Irving Mitchell (U.S.). After beating Rocky Lockridge (U.S.) and Tyrone Jackson (U.S.), Tony Lopez (U.S.) lost the IBF crown to Juan Molina (P.R.).

Jeff Fenech, the first Australian to hold three world titles (WBC bantamweight, junior featherweight, and featherweight), announced his retirement because of hand injuries after retaining the title by outpointing Marcos Villasana (Mexico) at Melbourne, Australia, in April. He later decided not to end his career, however, and announced that he would continue to fight in the same division. Antonio Esparragoza (Venezuela) remained supreme in the WBA, knocking out Mitsuru Sugiya (Japan), Jean-Marc Renard (Belg.), and Eduardo Montoya (Mexico). Jorge Paez (Mexico) was the IBF champion, stopping Calvin Grove (U.S.), Steve Cruz (U.S.), José López (Arg.), drawing with Louie Espinoza (U.S.), and defeating Lupe Gutierrez (U.S.).

Daniel Zaragoza (Mexico) and Fabrice Benichou (France) retained their WBC and IBF junior featherweight crowns, but Juan Estrada (Mexico) lost his WBA title to Jésus Salud (U.S.). Raul Pérez (Mexico) kept the WBC bantamweight title, but the WBA championship changed three times. Kaokor Galaxy (Thailand) regained the title from Moon Sung Kil (South Korea) but lost it in one round to Lusito Espinosa (Phil.). Orlando Canizales (U.S.) became the IBF champion.

Nana Konadu (Ghana) scored a major upset when he outpointed WBC super flyweight champion Gilberto Román (Mexico). Kaosai Galaxy (Thailand) retained the WBA version for the 11th time when stopping Alberto Castro (Colombia). Juan Polo Pérez (Colombia) captured the IBF title from Elly Pical (Indon.). Sot Chitalada (Thailand), a former champion, took the WBC flyweight crown from Kim Yong Kang (South Korea), while Jésus Rojas (Venezuela) surprisingly won the WBA version from Fidel Bassa (Colombia). The IBF title was taken from Duke McKenzie (England) by Dave McAuley (Northern Ireland). Two changes took place in the WBC junior flyweight

---

World, European, and Commonwealth Boxing Champions
as of Dec. 31, 1989

Division	WBC[1]	WBA[2]	IBF[3]	Europe	Commonwealth
Heavyweight	M. Tyson (U.S.)	M. Tyson (U.S.)	M. Tyson (U.S.)	vacant	D. Williams (England)
Cruiserweight	C. de León (P.R.)	R. Daniels (U.S.)	G. McCrory (England)	A. Wamba (France)	D. Angol (England)
Light heavyweight	J. Harding (Australia)	V. Hill (U.S.)	C. Williams (U.S.)	E. Nicoletta (France)	G. Waters (Australia)
Super middleweight	R. Leonard (U.S.)	Baek In Chul (South Korea)	vacant	vacant	R. Carr (Australia)
Middleweight	R. Durán (Panama)	M. McCallum (Jamaica)	M. Nunn (U.S.)	E. dell' Aquila (Italy)	T. Waters (Australia)
Junior middleweight	J. Mugabi (Uganda)	J. Jackson (U.S.)	G. Rosi (Italy)	G. Dele (France)	T. Waters (Australia)
Welterweight	M. Starling (U.S.)	M. Breland (U.S.)	S. Brown (U.S.)	N. La Rocca (Italy)	D. Boucher (Canada)
Junior welterweight	J.C. Chávez (Mexico)	J. Coggi (Argentina)	M. Taylor (U.S.)	E. Calamati (Italy)	T. Ekubia (England)
Lightweight	P. Whitaker (U.S.)	E. Rosario (Puerto Rico)	P. Whitaker (U.S.)	P. Díaz (Spain)	N. Daho (England)
Junior lightweight	A. Nelson (Ghana)	B. Mitchell (South Africa)	J. Molina (Puerto Rico)	D. Londas (France)	M. Reefer (England)
Featherweight	J. Fenech (Australia)	A. Esparragoza (Venezuela)	J. Paez (Mexico)	P. Hodkinson (England)	O. Commey (Ghana)
Junior featherweight	D. Zaragoza (Mexico)	J. Salud (U.S.)	F. Benichou (France)	V. Belcastro (Italy)	R. Minus (Bahamas)
Bantamweight	R. Pérez (Mexico)	L. Espinosa (Philippines)	O. Canizales (U.S.)	—	—
Super flyweight	N. Konadu (Ghana)	K. Galaxy (Thailand)	J.P. Pérez (Colombia)	E. Can (Turkey)	A. Kotey (Ghana)
Flyweight	S. Chitalada (Thailand)	J. Rojas (Venezuela)	D. McAuley (N. Ireland)	—	—
Junior flyweight	H. González (Mexico)	Yuh Myung Woo (South Korea)	M. Kittikasem (Thailand)	—	—
Straw weight	J.H. Choi (South Korea)	B. Kim (South Korea)	E. Chavez (Philippines)	—	—

[1]World Boxing Council.   [2]World Boxing Association.   [3]International Boxing Federation.

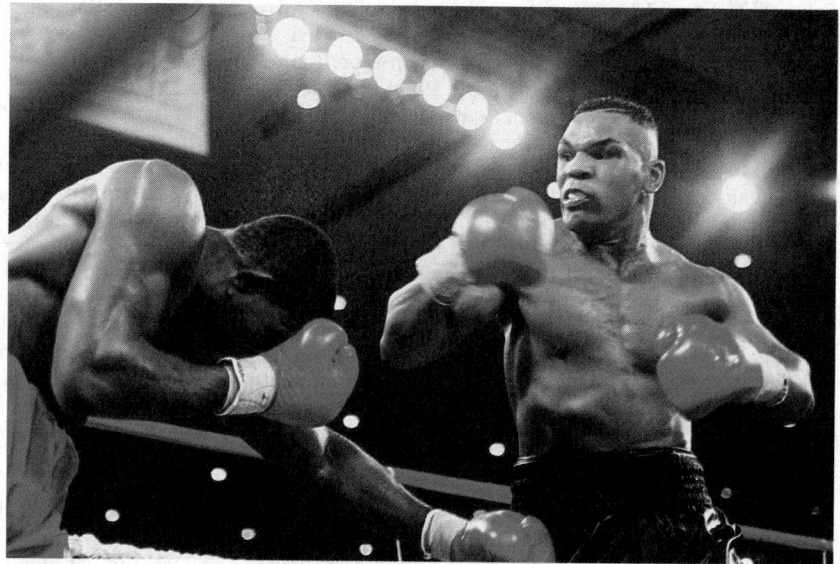

Heavyweight champ Mike Tyson (right) hammers challenger Frank Bruno of the U.K. during their bout in Las Vegas, Nevada. Tyson defeated Bruno in five rounds and later trounced Carl Williams of the U.S. to retain his title as heavyweight champion of the world.
AP/WIDE WORLD

competition. After Lee Yul Woo (South Korea) beat German Torres (Mexico), he lost on points to Humberto González (Mexico). Yuh Myung Woo (South Korea) remained unrivaled in the WBA, successfully defending his title 12 times. Muangchai Kittikasem (Thailand), a former kick boxer, gained the IBF championship from Tacy Macalos (Phil.).

After dominating the WBC straw weights, Napa Kiatwanchai (Thailand) lost the title to Jeum Hwan Choi (South Korea). Kim Bon Jung (South Korea) took over the vacant WBA crown, defeating Augustus García (Colombia). The IBF title changed twice. Nico Thomas (Indon.) took it from Samuth Sithnaruepol (Thailand) but was later knocked out in four rounds by Eric Chávez (Phil.).

Italy was not as dominant in the European championships as in previous years but still held four championships. England headed the Commonwealth with six championships, while Australia claimed four.

Boxing throughout the world was mainly manipulated by television's almost unbelievable fees, which made Mike Tyson, with $22 million, the biggest earner in any sport in 1989. International television demanded world title fights and was happy to screen WBC, WBA, and IBF championships. The importance of television money to promotions was the reason that the British Boxing Board of Control agreed during the year to affiliate with the IBF as well as with the WBC and WBA. A fourth international controlling body, the World Boxing Organization, launched in 1988 following a walkout by some members of the WBA, continued to strive for worldwide recognition.

If the WBO should be fully accepted, there could be 68 different world champions, far removed from a few decades earlier, when only 8 world champions were accepted. Finance might rule and control boxing, but many genuine lovers of the sport would like to see one world controlling body and a maximum of 17 champions.

A further change was anticipated as a result of the Soviet Union's decision to allow professional boxing for the first time. Following the world title fight in Hungary, a small professional tournament took place in Moscow, and later two established amateurs were given permission to become the first Soviet professionals to box abroad—in London. Andrey Oreshkin (heavyweight) had no difficulty in stopping Carl Gaffney, a little-known English novice, in 71 seconds, while Viktor Egorov, winner of a European

championship as a middleweight, defeated Mustapha Cole (U.S.) in five rounds. The Soviets sent a boxing team to Helsinki, Fin., in 1952 when they entered the Olympic Games for the first time. As of late 1989 there were about 300,000 amateur boxers in the U.S.S.R. and 10 who had turned professional. Many more were expected to be attracted by the big purses offered in the West.

(FRANK BUTLER)

CHESS

World chess champion Garry Kasparov of the U.S.S.R. was again the centre of attention in 1989, challenged by the increased playing strength both of the Polgar sisters from Hungary and of computer programs. Kasparov won the inaugural World Cup by a decisive margin in the sixth and final tournament of the 1988–89 cycle, though he was even in points with perennial Soviet rival Anatoly Karpov in the sixth contest, which ended at Skelleftea, Sweden, on September 2. Karpov had collapsed in the fifth contest at Rotterdam, Neth., in June, losing his last three games to compatriot Valery Salov, Ljubomir Ljubojevic (Yugos.), and John Nunn (U.K.). The top finishers in the World Cup were Kasparov 83, Karpov 81, Salov 68½, Jaan Ehlvest (U.S.S.R.) 68, Ljubojevic 66½, Nunn 65½, Nigel Short (U.K.) and Aleksandr Belyavsky (U.S.S.R.) 63½, and Jan Timman (Neth.) and Robert Hübner (West Germany) 57½.

Kasparov went on to achieve his heart's desire when his outstanding score of 12 points in 14 games at the Tilburg (Neth.) tournaments, September 14–October 2, ensured that he surpassed the previous highest world rating, the 2,785 achieved by Bobby Fischer of the U.S. in 1972. Some, however, believed that Fischer reached this pinnacle before a slight inflationary element was added to the rating system in the 1980s.

Meanwhile, the world championship semifinals in London resulted in narrow victories for the favourites: Karpov 4½–3½ against fellow Soviet Artur Yusupov and the same margin for Timman against Jonathan Speelman of the U.K. Karpov and Timman thus would meet in March 1990 to contest the right to meet Kasparov for the world championship later that year.

The right to organize this match of 24 games was given to Lyon, France, under controversial circumstances when the world ruling body, the Fédération Internationale des

Échecs (FIDE), under pressure from the claims of the GMA (Grand Masters Association, founded 1987), decided to resolve the site and conditions for the match more than a year before its scheduled date (October 1990) and without consulting the finalists. This break with rule and tradition produced an angry reaction from Kasparov, who reserved the right to make other dispositions through the GMA and thus threatened a schism in the chess world. Parallel world title matches seemed in prospect should the disagreements persist.

A new event, the World Blitz Championship, was held in Mazatlán, Mexico, in December 1988. Karpov, Viktor Gavrikov (U.S.S.R.), Rafael Vaganian (U.S.S.R.), and Maxim Dlugy (U.S.) tied for first, but the title was awarded to Karpov on the basis of his record during the tournament.

Kasparov made headlines throughout the world in mid-October when he visited the U.S. to play two exhibition games, Human versus Machine, with the powerful Deep Thought computer. Human won both games at the New York Academy of Art in New York City on October 22. Kasparov demonstrated the benefit of having studied earlier games in which the computer had bested such grand masters as Denmark's Bent Larsen.

Meanwhile, it was widely thought that three Hungarian sisters, Zsuzsa, Zsofia, and Judit Polgar, might provide as realistic a challenge to Kasparov as the computer in the 1990s. Zsuzsa, at age 20 the oldest of the trio, was the least realistic of the potential contenders for the world crown, as she was "merely" a strong grand master but not an outstanding player for that age. The younger sisters had many years in which to develop, and both gave notice of their potential in the first half of the year.

Judit, 12, already on top of the women's rating list in January 1989, owing to her score of 12½ points in 13 games at the late-1988 World Chess Olympiad, took part in January in the Hastings Challengers, the section below the elite top group. She scored 8/10, taking first place ahead of several male grand masters. This was an unprecedented performance, superior to that achieved at this age by earlier prodigies such as Fischer or Kasparov.

In February at an open tournament in Rome for 66 players, the 14-year-old Zsofia Polgar finished first with a score of 8½/9, beating several grand masters to achieve a tournament performance rated at 2,930. For the significance of this, one should remember the rating of around 2,790 for the mature Fischer and Kasparov, as mentioned above.

One noteworthy point was that among the defeated contestants in Rome were several Soviet grand masters, now able to play abroad more freely than in previous years. The news of the Hungarian girl's achievement was widely publicized in the West but not in the U.S.S.R. until the late summer, when it was realized that the Soviet participants at Rome had not formally reported the result. Apparently they wanted the result to remain unknown in order to protect their rating figures, upon which tournament invitations and appearance fees depend. The players who failed to report the scores were excluded from the Soviet internal rating list as part of the attempt to maintain discipline in chess matters.

A similar attempt to revert to stronger discipline was the so-called Havana Declaration of February 9, when senior chess officials of the chess federations of the Warsaw Pact countries and Cuba declared that chess players of the "socialist countries" should not be allowed to travel abroad for chess contests without the permission of their national chess federations. This was a defensive measure against the growing influence of the GMA, but it was honoured

mainly in the breach, as far more Soviet players traveled abroad at their own expense in 1989 than followed the traditional route of being nominated as part of an official chess delegation.

Youth continued to come to the fore in many countries. Michael Adams, 17, won the British championship in August, learning halfway through the 11-round contest that he had gained the grand master ranking from FIDE. He thus followed in the footsteps of Nigel Short, who won the Hastings Premier for the second consecutive year.

The world junior championships in Colombia in August was won by a little-known Bulgarian, Vasil Spasov. Another strong tournament was the Linares (Spain) all-play-all in late February–early March. Vasily Ivanchuk, 19, of the U.S.S.R. scored 7½/10, half a point ahead of Karpov, with other leading figures such as Ljubojevic, Short, Timman, and Yusupov farther down in the standings. The Soviet championship was won in October by Rafael Vaganyan.

The U.S. Chess Federation celebrated its 50th anniversary in December, but U.S. chess still was looking in vain for a successor to Fischer. The leading U.S. players specialized in winning big-money contests of the Swiss system type (many hundreds of entrants contributing to a large prize fund) rather than in honing their talent in smaller all-play-alls from which future world title contenders tend to emerge.   (BERNARD CAFFERTY)

CONTRACT BRIDGE

The World Bridge Federation took steps during the year to control the proliferation of highly artificial bidding systems. The Executive Committee of the WBF meeting in Perth, Australia, appointed a panel of experts to examine a new concept based on guidelines laid down by the federation. The panel was to be chaired by Chip Martel (U.S.), with Gabriel Chagas (Brazil), Tony Forrester (Great Britain), Edgar Kaplan (U.S.), Ron Klinger (Australia), and P.O.

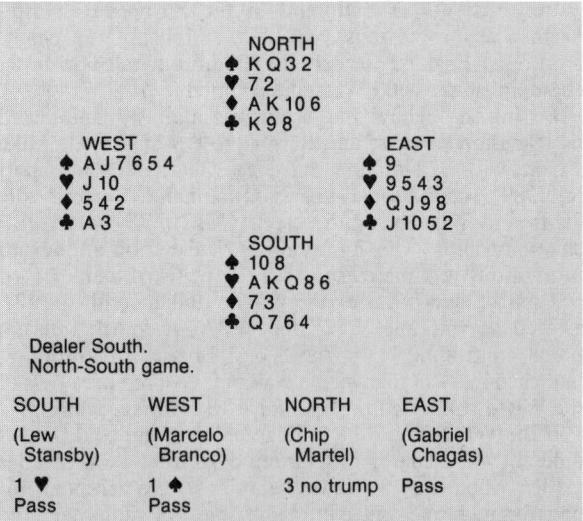

Dealer South.
North-South game.

SOUTH	WEST	NORTH	EAST
(Lew Stansby)	(Marcelo Branco)	(Chip Martel)	(Gabriel Chagas)
1 ♥	1 ♠	3 no trump	Pass
Pass	Pass		

East led the queen of diamonds, and Martel ducked. East switched to the three of hearts, and declarer took time out to evaluate the situation. West's play to the opening lead showed a probable three-card holding. East's heart lead precluded the possibility of a 3–3 division of the suit, and East's failure to lead a spade marked him with at most two cards in the suit.

Martel played a low heart from dummy, and West won and returned a heart. Martel won with the ace and cashed his king of diamonds, followed by four heart winners, leaving himself with ♠ K Q and ♣ K 9 8, while West was reduced to three spades and two clubs. A club to the king was followed by a club, ducked in dummy, and West had to concede two more tricks and the contract.

Sundelin (Sweden) as its other members. The panel was scheduled to report back to the WBF in May 1990, but its recommendations, if approved, would not be implemented before 1991.

In Perth the U.S. defended both world team championships—the Bermuda Bowl (Open teams) and the Venice Cup (women's teams). The U.S. retained the Venice Cup, defeating The Netherlands (European champions) by the narrowest of margins, 325½–318½, while in the play-off for the bronze medal, Canada defeated West Germany 153–151. The U.S., however, surrendered the Bermuda Bowl, which it had held for 10 years, when it was defeated by Brazil 442–388. It was the third world championship for Brazil, which had previously won Olympic pairs and team titles. Chip Martel of the U.S. shone on the diagrammed hand from the final.

Members of Brazil's championship team in the Bermuda Bowl were Gabriel Chagas and Marcelo Branco, Pedro Branco and Roberto Mello, and Ricardo Janz and Carlos Camacho. The first-place U.S. women's team in the Venice Cup included Kerrie Shuman and Karen McCallum, Lynn Deas and Beth Palmer, and Kitty Bethe and Margie Gwozdzinsky.

The World Bridge Federation during the year reached an ever greater number of players. The 1989 Epson Worldwide Bridge Contest simultaneous pairs was played in clubs in no fewer than 90 countries and would have attained a record entry of 100,000 players save for the insurrection in Beijing (Peking).

The world championships scheduled for Geneva in August 1990 were to involve players of all levels, thanks to a formula devised by president emeritus of the WBF Jaime Ortiz-Patiño. The three championship events, the Rosenblun Knock-out Teams and the open and ladies' pairs championships, would be unchanged, as would the mixed pairs. The major innovation of the tournament was to be a continuous pairs championship with two sessions a day for 14 days. There would be no limit to the number of pairs who could compete, subject to the approval of the national body. Initially they would play among themselves, but the pairs eliminated from the main events as these proceeded could join in the continuous pairs competition. Thus club players would have the opportunity to compete with those players of international and world class.

(HAROLD FRANKLIN)

CRICKET

There were two dominant forces in international cricket during the 1988–89 seasons. On the field, the West Indies comfortably beat Australia and India to prove beyond doubt its position as the best cricketing nation. Off the field, the politics of South Africa caused the cancellation of England's proposed tour of India and led to a controversial ban by the International Cricket Conference (from September the International Cricket Council). In January the ICC agreed that any cricketer who played or coached in South Africa would be automatically banned from international cricket for a minimum of five years. The South African response to that threat was predictable enough. By the end of July a team of 16 English players, led by the former England captain M.W. Gatting, had been recruited by the South African Cricket Union to tour South Africa in 1989–90 and 1990–91.

The announcement of that touring team coincided with the heavy defeat of England by Australia, its oldest cricketing enemy, and deprived England of eight current test players. England, led by D.I. Gower, lost the six-match series 5–0, equaling its heaviest defeat ever by Australia. The Australian batsmen S.R. Waugh, M.A. Taylor, and D.M. Jones scored two centuries each and averaged over 70; captain A.R. Border (see BIOGRAPHIES) averaged 73; and T.M. Alderman took 41 wickets. In contrast, only R.A. Smith, playing for England, did himself justice, scoring two centuries and averaging 61. England's leading bowler was N.A. Foster with 12 wickets.

Australia's margin of victory was as wide as it was unexpected. In Leeds for the first test, the two teams seemed to be well matched. For the first four days, on a wicket that behaved rather better than it had in previous years, the batsmen dominated the bowlers. Taylor (136) and Waugh (177 not out) scored their maiden test centuries in Australia's total of 601 for seven. A.J. Lamb hit 125 in reply. A draw looked likely, but on the final day bad batting by England and intelligent bowling by Alderman, who took 10 wickets in the match, brought Australia victory by 210 runs.

Australia, led by another unbeaten century by Waugh and backed up by 94 from D.C. Boon, dominated the second test at Lord's, winning by six wickets despite a welcome 106 by Gower. After a drawn third test, Smith

Test Series Results, September 1988–September 1989

Test	Host country	Ground	Scores	Result
1st	Pakistan	Karachi	Pakistan 469; Australia 165 and 116	Pakistan won by an innings and 188 runs
2nd	Pakistan	Faisalabad	Pakistan 316 and 378; Australia 321 and 67 for 3	Match drawn
3rd	Pakistan	Lahore	Australia 340 and 161 for 3 dec; Pakistan 233 and 153 for 8	Match drawn
1st	India	Bangalore	India 384 for 9 dec and 141 for 1 dec; New Zealand 189 and 164	India won by 172 runs
2nd	India	Bombay	New Zealand 236 and 279; India 234 and 145	New Zealand won by 136 runs
3rd	India	Hyderabad	New Zealand 254 and 124; India 358 and 22 for 0	India won by 10 wkt
1st	Australia	Brisbane	Australia 167 and 289; West Indies 394 and 63 for 1	West Indies won by 9 wkt
2nd	Australia	Perth	West Indies 449 and 349 for 9 dec; Australia 395 for 8 dec and 234	West Indies won by 169 runs
3rd	Australia	Melbourne	West Indies 280 and 361 for 9 dec; Australia 242 and 114	West Indies won by 285 runs
4th	Australia	Sydney	West Indies 224 and 256; Australia 401 and 82 for 3	Australia won by 7 wkt
5th	Australia	Adelaide	Australia 515 and 224 for 4 dec; West Indies 369 and 233 for 4	Match drawn
1st	New Zealand	Dunedin	Match abandoned without a ball bowled	
2nd	New Zealand	Wellington	New Zealand 447 and 186 for 8; Pakistan 438 for 7 dec	Match drawn
3rd	New Zealand	Auckland	Pakistan 616 for 5 dec; New Zealand 403 and 99 for 3	Match drawn
1st	West Indies	Guyana	West Indies 437; India 86 for 1	Match drawn—rain
2nd	West Indies	Barbados	India 321 and 251; West Indies 377 and 196 for 2	West Indies won by 8 wkt
3rd	West Indies	Trinidad	West Indies 314 and 266; India 150 and 213	West Indies won by 217 runs
4th	West Indies	Jamaica	India 289 and 152; West Indies 384 and 60 for 3	West Indies won by 7 wkt
1st	England	Leeds	Australia 601 for 7 dec and 230 for 3 dec; England 430 and 191	Australia won by 210 runs
2nd	England	Lord's	England 286 and 359; Australia 528 and 119 for 4	Australia won by 6 wkt
3rd	England	Birmingham	Australia 424 and 158 for 2; England 242	Match drawn
4th	England	Manchester	England 260 and 264; Australia 447 and 81 for 1	Australia won by 9 wkt
5th	England	Nottingham	Australia 602 for 6 dec; England 255 and 167	Australia won by an innings and 180 runs
6th	England	The Oval	Australia 468 and 219 for 4 dec; England 285 and 143 for 5	Match drawn

and R.C. Russell made centuries in either innings for England at Manchester, but Australia, batting solidly and with Lawson taking nine wickets in the match, won by nine wickets to take the series. England faced another massive defeat, by an innings and 180 runs in Nottingham, after the Australian openers Taylor (219) and G.R. Marsh (138) had put on a record partnership of 329 for the first wicket. The final test at the Oval was drawn.

Australia's victory capped a remarkable recovery for Border and his team, who had earlier in the season been outplayed by the West Indies at home. The West Indies, led by I.V.A. Richards and with a fearsome trio of fast bowlers that included M.D. Marshall, C.E.L. Ambrose, and C.A. Walsh (who took a hat trick in the first test), won the first three test matches by nine wickets, 169 runs, and 285 runs, respectively. Richards (146 in the second test at Perth), D.L. Haynes (100 at Perth and 143 in the fourth test at Sydney), R.B. Richardson (122 in the third test at Melbourne and 106 in the fifth test at Adelaide), and C.G. Greenidge (104 in the fifth test) scored centuries for the touring team. G.M. Wood (111 in the second test), Boon (149 in the third), and Jones (216 in the fifth) replied with centuries for Australia. The series also included remarkable pieces of bowling by the Australian fast bowler M.G. Hughes, who took 13 for 217 in the second test (including a hat trick), and by Border, an occasional left-arm spinner, whose match figures of 11 for 96 on a turning wicket at Sydney helped Australia to victory by seven wickets in the fourth test.

Prior to its series with the West Indies, Australia had visited Pakistan, where there was more controversy over the standard of umpiring. On a wicket made for spin in the first test, Australia succumbed to its heaviest defeat by Pakistan. Iqbal Qasim took 9 for 84 in the match, and Abdul Qadir took 5 for 88 after the Pakistan captain, Javed Miandad, had made 211. Both Border and the Australian manager, R.B. Simpson, criticized the umpires, and there was even a chance the Australian team would return home immediately. However, the Australians responded on the field instead, drawing the second test and coming to within two wickets of winning the last, when only stubborn resistance by the ninth wicket pair of Qasim and Tausif Ahmed prevented an Australian victory. Miandad scored 412 runs in the series at an average of 82. The tour further highlighted the need for a panel of top-class umpires to officiate in all test matches.

India played two series, beating New Zealand 2–1 in the first and losing 3–0 to the West Indies in the second. In the first test against New Zealand, R.J. Hadlee took his 374th wicket to become the highest wicket-taker in test history. Hadlee had 17 more wickets in the series, but they were matched by the combination of off-spinner Arshad Ayub and leg-spinner Najendra Hirwani, who took 41 wickets between them. New Zealand returned home to play a dull series against Pakistan, in which the first test was abandoned because of rain and the next two drawn. Apart from Hadlee's record, other milestones in the season were passed by Richards, who scored his 100th first-class hundred, Marshall, who became the ninth bowler to take 300 test wickets, and Kapil Dev of India, who joined I.T. Botham as the only men to score 4,000 runs and take 300 wickets in tests.

In one-day cricket, the West Indies won the triangular World Series Cup, beating Pakistan in the qualifying matches and Australia in the last of the three-match final. In domestic cricket in England, Essex was the unluckiest side of the season, losing the Benson and Hedges final to Nottinghamshire off the last ball and the Britannic Assur-

ance Championship by just six points to Worcestershire after being deducted 25 points for producing a wicket deemed unsuitable for first-class cricket by the authorities. Lancashire won the Refuge Assurance Sunday League, and Warwickshire surprised everyone by beating Middlesex in the NatWest Trophy. Western Australia retained the Sheffield Shield; Eastern Province won the South African Currie Cup; and in the West Indies, Jamaica retained the Red Stripe Cup.   (ANDREW LONGMORE)

CYCLING

United States rider Greg LeMond (*see* BIOGRAPHIES) astounded the cycling world in 1989 by becoming only the fifth competitor to win both the Tour de France and world professional road race championship in the same season. Still carrying lead pellets in his body from a shooting accident in April 1987 that almost ended his life, LeMond had struggled for over a year to recover his form, also undergoing an appendectomy and a leg operation.

His results at the start of 1989 were unimpressive, and LeMond finished well behind overall winner Laurent Fignon in the Tour of Italy, which ended on June 11. However, a little more than three weeks later LeMond, to general astonishment, was wearing the yellow jersey of

1989 Cycling Champions		
Event	Winner	Country
WORLD AMATEUR CHAMPIONS—TRACK		
Men		
Sprint	B. Huck	East Germany
Tandem sprint	F. Colas, F. Magne	France
Individual pursuit	V. Ekimov	U.S.S.R.
Team pursuit	S. Blochwitz, G. Fulst, T. Liese, C. Wolf	East Germany
1,000-m time trial	J. Glucklich	East Germany
50-km points	M. Satybaldiev	U.S.S.R.
50-km motor paced	R. Konigshofer	Austria
Women		
Sprint	E. Salumiae	U.S.S.R.
Individual pursuit	J. Longo	France
30-km points	J. Longo	France
WORLD PROFESSIONAL CHAMPIONS—TRACK		
Sprint	C. Golinelli	Italy
Individual pursuit	C. Sturgess	Great Britain
50-km points	U. Freuler	Switzerland
One-hour motor paced	G. Renosto	Italy
Keirin	C. Golinelli	Italy
WORLD AMATEUR CHAMPIONS—ROAD		
Men		
Individual road race	J. Halupczok	Poland
Team time trial	F. Boden, M. Kummer, M. Landsmann, J. Schur	East Germany
Women		
Individual road race	J. Longo	France
Team time trial	N. Kibardina, N. Melekhina, T. Poliakova, L. Zilporitee	U.S.S.R.
WORLD PROFESSIONAL CHAMPION—ROAD		
Individual road race	G. LeMond	U.S.
WORLD CHAMPIONS—CYCLO-CROSS		
Amateur	D. Glajza	Czechoslovakia
Professional	D. De Bie	Belgium
MAJOR PROFESSIONAL ROAD-RACE WINNERS		
Tour de France	G. LeMond	U.S.
Tour of Italy	L. Fignon	France
Tour of Spain	P. Delgado	Spain
Tour of Switzerland	B. Breu	Switzerland
Milan–San Remo	L. Fignon	France
Tour of Flanders	E. van Hooydonck	Belgium
Paris–Roubaix	J-M. Wampers	Belgium
Liège–Bastogne–Liège	S. Kelly	Ireland
Amstel Gold	E. van Lancker	Belgium
Wincanton Classic	F. Maassen	The Netherlands
G.P. of the Americas	J. Muller	Switzerland
Championship of Zurich	S. Bauer	Canada
San Sebastian G.P.	G. Zadrobilek	Austria
Paris–Nice	M. Indurain	Spain
Ghent–Wevelgem	G. Solleveld	The Netherlands
Flèche Wallonne	C. Criquielion	Belgium
Dunkirk 4-Day	C. Mottet	France
Paris–Brussels	J. Nijdam	The Netherlands
Tour of Britain	R. Millar	Great Britain
Milk Race[1]	B. Walton	Canada
Peace Race[2]	U. Ampler	East Germany

[1] Mixed professional and amateur.
[2] Amateur.

Jeannie Longo of France races to a new world cycling record in the women's 5,000-metre outdoor track event with a time of 6:14.13. Longo dominated women's cycling in 1989 by winning the women's Tour de France as well as world titles in the individual pursuit, 30-kilometre points, and road race.
AFP PHOTO

overall leader of the Tour de France, the sport's most prestigious event, after the fifth stage, a 73-km individual time trial from Dinard to Rennes. Fignon took over the lead after the tenth stage, and the advantage changed twice more between the two riders until LeMond, starting the day 50 seconds behind, won the closing 25-km time trial from Versailles to Paris and the 23-day race. His winning margin was only eight seconds, the narrowest in the race's 86-year history.

The world championship road races took place at Chambery, France, in August. After 6¾ hours of racing, LeMond beat Dimitry Konychev, the first professional medalist from the Soviet Union, in a sprint finish.

The inaugural World Cup professional road race series comprised one team and 11 individual events and was contested in Italy, France, Belgium, The Netherlands, the U.K., Canada, Spain, and Switzerland. It began with the Milan to San Remo race in mid-March and ended seven months later with the Tour of Lombardy. For the first time since computer lists were introduced in April 1984, Sean Kelly of Ireland was displaced—by Charly Mottet of France—as the world's top-ranked professional.

The world championship track program took place at the Parc de la Tête d'Or velodrome in Lyon, France. Urs Freuler of Switzerland claimed his eighth professional 50-km points title in nine years, while Colin Sturgess of England became the youngest professional pursuit champion at 20. Italy's Claudio Golinelli, stripped of his sprint silver medal in 1988 after a positive test for drugs, returned to become the first rider to win both the professional sprint and keirin in the same year.

Women's racing was dominated by Jeannie Longo of France. She won the women's Tour de France for the third time and went on to take three world titles in the individual pursuit, 30-km points, and road race.

(JOHN R. WILKINSON)

FIELD HOCKEY

Australia and West Germany were the sporting barons of field hockey in 1989. Australia gained the distinction of becoming the first nation to win the Champions Trophy four times by finishing ahead of The Netherlands, West Germany, Pakistan, Great Britain, and India in the round-robin event at West Berlin in June. In September West Germany defeated Australia 3–2 and then won a five-nation tournament at Hamburg, West Germany; Australia finished second, the Soviet Union third, Argentina fourth, and Spain fifth. In October Australia won the International Classic at Luton, England, ahead of The Netherlands, England, and Argentina. West Germany then defeated The Netherlands and England in a three-nation round-robin event played at Bonn, West Germany; Utrecht, Neth.; and Preston, England. The Netherlands placed second and England third.

Pakistan retained the Indira Gandhi Gold Cup at Lucknow, India, in January with a 2–1 victory over The Netherlands in the final. India finished third, followed by Kenya, Poland, Malaysia, the Soviet Union, and Spain. In Amsterdam in March, India's matches with The Netherlands and England each ended in a 2–2 tie. England and The Netherlands tied 3–3, but England then won 5–4 in a penalty stroke competition to gain the trophy.

At Madison, N.J., in July The Netherlands won the Intercontinental Cup with a 5–1 victory over Canada in the final. India was third and France fourth, followed by Ireland, Malaysia, Poland, New Zealand, Egypt, Chile, the U.S., and Zimbabwe. Indoors, England emerged as Home Countries champions, winning all three matches at Glasgow, Scotland. The host team placed second, followed by Ireland in third and Wales in fourth.

South Korea, a new force in women's hockey, carried off the Champions Trophy at Frankfurt, West Germany, in September. Australia was second, followed by West Germany, Great Britain, The Netherlands, and Canada. South Korea had previously won a four-nation tournament in Amsterdam, in which England was second, The Netherlands third, and West Germany fourth. The U.S. Women's Classic at Trenton, N.J., in June was won by Scotland, with West Germany second, the U.S. third, and the Soviet Union fourth. At the end of August in The Hague, Great Britain won an international tournament; The Netherlands was second, followed by the U.S. and Canada. Wales won the Home Countries title, with England second, Scotland third, and Ireland fourth; but indoors Scotland was first, England second, Ireland third, and Wales fourth.

(SYDNEY E. FRISKIN)

FOOTBALL

Association Football (Soccer). Although the qualifying tournament for the 1990 World Cup finals occupied attention at the national level, the ever present problem of hooliganism clouded the association football scene in 1989. The continuing ban on English clubs participating in the three major European club competitions worried the sport's authorities, who failed in their attempt to enlist the U.K. government's unreserved support for reinstatement of the English clubs. Elsewhere in Europe most countries were experiencing outbreaks of trouble. Several playing fields were temporarily closed in Greece after fan violence, and firebombs were even thrown onto a field in East Germany. There was damage to trains and a subway station in Hungary, rioting in Yugoslavia, street battles in Italy between gangs of rival factions, and street riots in Stockholm before a World Cup qualifying match between England and Sweden.

In April 95 people died at the Hillsborough Stadium in Sheffield, England, when a surge of spectators crushed or trampled them (*see* Sidebar). The verdict of the 1985 Heysel Stadium tragedy in Brussels, in which 39 spectators died during a riot, was announced shortly after the Hillsborough disaster. Fourteen Liverpool fans were found guilty of manslaughter. Ten others were released, as the case against them was not proved.

On the positive side, attendance at Football League matches in England rose for the third successive season to 18.4 million, the level achieved six years earlier. Steaua Bucharest, Romania's army club, enjoyed an unbeaten domestic season, dropping points only in 3 tied games out of 34 played, in which they scored 121 goals. In Bulgaria the former army club CSKA Sofia, re-formed as Sredets and then renamed CFKA Sredets, achieved its 25th League title, a postwar record.

European Champions' Cup. In Barcelona, Spain, on May 24, AC Milan of Italy defeated Steaua Bucharest of Romania 4–0, exhibiting the most effective playing since the Dutch team Ajax Amsterdam achieved three European Cup successes in the early 1970s. It was no coincidence that AC Milan owed much to three Dutch players, Frank Rijkaard, Marco van Basten, and Ruud Gullit, whose individual flair combined with traditional Italian discipline and tactical expertise to produce a memorable performance.

Gullit opened the scoring from close range after 17 minutes, following up when Angelo Colombo's drive was blocked by goalkeeper Silviu Lung. Nine minutes later the Steaua defense failed to clear a corner. Mauro Tassotti eluded Iosif Rotariu to cross the ball, and Gullit took two opponents with him to the near post, leaving van Basten unchallenged to head in. Gullit scored his second goal and Milan's third in the 38th minute of the contest from a centre by Roberto Donadoni on the left and, 18 seconds after the second half began, Rijkaard on the left set up van Basten, who completed the scoring inside Lung's left-hand post.

European Cup-Winners' Cup. Italian hopes of three European titles vanished in Bern, Switz., on May 10, when Sampdoria of Genoa lost 2–0 to Spain's Barcelona. The Spaniards opened the scoring after only four minutes. England's Gary Lineker, playing in the uncustomary wing role that coach Johan Cruyff had decided to give him, broke through on the right and crossed to the far post, where Julio Salinas headed in. The second goal was created and completed by Barcelona's two substitutes in the 79th minute of the game. Miguel Soler ran through on a counter attack, and López Rekarte, who had been on the field for only four minutes, timed his run perfectly before hitting a low shot past goalkeeper Gianluca Pagliuca's left hand.

UEFA Cup. Despite being stunned by falling behind by a goal on its own field, Italy's Napoli recovered to beat Stuttgart of West Germany by an aggregate score of 5–4. In the first leg in Naples on May 3, Maurizio Gaudino scored for Stuttgart following a free kick in which the ball eluded the grasp of Napoli goalkeeper Giuliano Giuliani. It was not until the team's captain, Diego Maradona, converted a penalty in the 68th minute that Napoli took command after Gunter Schafer was alleged to have handled Maradona's shot. Three minutes before the end of the game Maradona escaped his marker and crossed perfectly for Antonio Careca to stab the ball in for a 2–1 victory. On May 17 in Stuttgart it was Napoli's turn to score early through Brazilian Ricardo Alemão from a pass by his fellow countryman Careca. Jurgen Klinsmann tied the score after 27 minutes, only to have Ciro Ferrera restore Napoli's advantage 6 minutes before halftime from a Maradona centre. The Italians went ahead 5–2 on aggregate in the 62nd minute when Maradona again supplied the pass for Careca to score Napoli's third goal of the day. However, a goal by Fernando De Napoli eight minutes later and a fourth for Stuttgart by substitute Olaf Schmaler in the final seconds gave some respectability to the West Germans, who had been largely outplayed throughout the two games.

Hillsborough disaster

On April 15, 94 people were either crushed or trampled to death and nearly 200 were injured by a surge of spectators that pushed them against a fence at the Leppings Lane end of the Hillsborough playing field in Sheffield, England, at the start of the FA Cup semifinal between Liverpool and Nottingham Forest. Another victim died in the hospital two days later. It was Britain's worst sporting disaster. The match was abandoned after six minutes of play.

The late arrival of hundreds of Liverpool spectators had caused congestion outside the stadium, and police decided to open the exit gate to relieve pressure. Unfortunately, the centre pens of the terraces behind the goal were already overfull because no safe maximum capacities had been established. The failure to cut off fans' access to tunnels leading to the terraces was responsible for the tragedy.

The report of the interim inquiry conducted by Lord Justice Peter Taylor held that the main reason for the disaster was the failure of the police to exercise sufficient control, with the blame falling on the senior officers. The Sheffield Wednesday Football Club was also criticized for confused and inadequate signs and ticketing. The reaction of the police on duty inside the ground to the crush was said to have been sluggish, and there was poor liaison between officers stationed there and those outside the stadium. Lord Justice Taylor made 43 recommendations for ground safety rules to be implemented as a matter of priority.

(JACK ROLLIN)

Table I. Association Football National Champions

Nation	League winners	Cup winners
Albania	17 Nentori	Dinamo
Argentina	Independiente	
Austria	Tirol	Tirol
Belgium	Mechelen	Anderlecht
Bolivia	Bolívar	
Brazil	Bahia	
Bulgaria	CFKA Sredets	CFKA Sredets
Chile	Cobreloa	
Colombia	Millonarios	
Cyprus	Omonia	AEL
Czechoslovakia	Sparta Prague	Sparta Prague
Denmark	Brøndby	Brøndby
Ecuador	Emelec	
El Salvador	Luis Angel Firpo	
England	Arsenal	Liverpool
Finland	HJK Helsinki	Haka
France	Marseille	Marseille
Germany, East	Dynamo Dresden	Dynamo Berlin
Germany, West	Bayern Münich	Borussia Dortmund
Greece	AEK Athens	Panathinaikos
Guatemala	Municipal	
Honduras	Olimpia	
Hungary	Honved	Honved
Iceland	Fram	Valur
Ireland	Derry City	Derry City
Italy	Internazionale	Sampdoria
Luxembourg	Spora	Union
Malta	Sliema Wanderers	Hamrun Spartans
Mexico	América	
Netherlands, The	PSV Eindhoven	PSV Eindhoven
Northern Ireland	Linfield	Ballymena
Norway	Rosenborg	Rosenborg
Paraguay	Olimpia	
Peru	Sporting Cristal	
Poland	Ruch Chorzow	Legia Warsaw
Portugal	Benfica	Belenenses
Romania	Steaua Bucharest	Steaua Bucharest
Scotland	Rangers	Celtic
Spain	Real Madrid	Real Madrid
Sweden	Malmö	Norrköping
Switzerland	Lucerne	Grasshoppers
Turkey	Fenerbahce	Besiktas
U.S.S.R.	Dnepr	Dnepr
U.S.	San Diego	
Uruguay	Danubio	
Venezuela	Mineros	
Wales	—	Swansea City
Yugoslavia	Vojvodina	Partizan

In an early-round match for the 1990 UEFA Cup, unruly behaviour by an Amsterdam crowd forced the cancellation of a game between Ajax Amsterdam and Austria Vienna. Ajax was subsequently banned from European competition for at least two years.

North America. Baltimore was the regular-season champion of the Major Indoor Soccer League. In the championship series of the play-offs, San Diego defeated Baltimore four games to three. (JACK ROLLIN)

Latin America. After several years of knocking at the door, a Colombian team in 1989 finally won the Libertadores de América Cup, South America's team championship. The coveted trophy, however, was not gained by either of the traditional powerhouses of Colombian football, América of Cali or Millonarios of Bogotá, but rather by Nacional of Medellín, which defeated a Paraguayan team, Olimpia of Asunción. The two final games, in Asunción and in Medellín, ended in 2–2 ties. Nacional, however, edged Olimpia 5–4 in a penalty shoot-out.

The América Cup, South America's championship for national teams, was played in Brazil. The home team, however, had to face unfriendly crowds during the first round of play, which took place in the northern cities of Salvador and Recife, because the Brazilian technical director had decided to exclude from the team the most popular player from northern Brazil. In the final play-off, held in Rio de Janeiro, crowd support was present, and Brazil easily defeated the other three finalists—Argentina, Paraguay, and Uruguay, which finished second.

Brazil's participation in the tournament to select qualifiers to the 1990 World Cup was fraught with controversy. In the final decisive game, a firecracker exploded near the Chilean team's goalkeeper and apparently wounded him. The Chileans protested loudly and walked out of the stadium without the referee's permission. Although television tapes showed what seemed to be blood on the Chilean goalkeeper's face, the International Federation of Association Football (FIFA) ruled that he had not been hurt by the firecracker and disqualified Chile for having abandoned the field of play. The apparent blood, the FIFA claimed, was Mercurochrome. In December FIFA suspended the goalkeeper, Roberto Rojas, from football for life and banned Chile from competing for the 1994 World Cup.

Brazil thus qualified for the 1990 World Cup, to be played in Italy. Argentina was automatically in by virtue of being the defending champion. The other two South American qualifiers were Uruguay and Colombia.

In the North American, Central American, and Caribbean zone, Mexico, the traditional powerhouse, was disqualified from playing for having used illegal players in a previous juvenile championship. This, coupled with the fact that two places were available from that area, provided an opportunity for Costa Rica, which qualified for the World Cup for the first time in history. Also traveling to Italy would be the U.S. team. (SERGIO SARMIENTO)

Rugby. *Rugby Union.* The main event of 1988–89 in rugby union was the Lions' tour of Australia, which took place in June and July 1989. This was the first tour of Australia ever made by the Lions independently of a tour to New Zealand.

Captained by Finlay Calder, the Scotland flanker, the Lions played 12 matches, winning all except the first of three tests against the Wallabies. This test, played at Sydney, was won impressively by the Wallabies 30–12. In the second test, at Brisbane, the Lions' forwards played with greatly improved skill and commitment, and with a score of 19–12 in the Lions' favour, the series was tied. The decisive third test, at Sydney, could not have been closer, the Lions winning by a single point 19–18. They were again indebted to their forwards and also to their full back, Gavin Hastings of Scotland, who kicked five penalty goals in six attempts.

While the Lions were in Australia, the French toured New Zealand for a meeting between the two finalists from the inaugural World Cup of 1987. The New Zealanders retained their supremacy, winning the first of the two tests 25–17 in Christchurch and the second 34–20 in Auckland.

In August and September 1989 South Africa received its first officially authorized visit in six years when an international team played two tests against the Springboks on a tour to mark the centenary of the South African Rugby Board. The Springboks won the first test 20–19 in Cape Town and the second 22–16 in Johannesburg.

Also in August the rivalry between New Zealand and Australia continued with the staging of the Bledisloe Cup match in Auckland. The game was won by New Zealand 24–12, the team's 17th straight international victory.

The Five Nations Championship, played in the early months of 1989, was won by France but not without some difficulties. In France's first match, against Ireland in Dublin, the Irish at one time led 15–0 and then 21–7. It said much for the character of the French team, captained by Pierre Berbizier from scrum half, that they fought back and won 26–21. They defeated Wales 31–12 in Paris but were then beaten 11–0 by England at Twickenham. They made sure of the championship by defeating Scotland 19–13 in Paris on the same day that England was beaten 12–9 by Wales at Cardiff.

Rugby League. In the 50th test between the two countries, Great Britain defeated France 30–8 at Avignon,

thus achieving its seventh consecutive victory over the French. The British had earlier beaten France 26–10 at Wigan. Both matches were played early in 1989.

(DAVID FROST)

U.S. Football. *College.* The University of Miami won its third national championship of college football in seven years on voting that was hotly debated because no major team was undefeated. Miami, with an 11–1 won-lost record, won 33–25 over Alabama (10–2) in the Sugar Bowl at New Orleans, La., Jan. 1, 1990, while Notre Dame (12–1), ranked second by the Associated Press poll, was winning 21–6 over No. 4 Colorado (11–1) in the Orange Bowl at Miami, Fla. No. 3 Florida State (10–2) won the Fiesta Bowl at Phoenix, Ariz., 41–17 over Nebraska (10–2).

The top four spots in the various polls were close because Florida State defeated Miami, which defeated Notre Dame, which defeated Big Eight champion Colorado, which was undefeated and ranked No. 1 after the regular season. Notre Dame had the toughest college schedule and played nine bowl teams, all at least eight-game winners, while Miami played only five such teams. But Notre Dame's defeat was by Miami, 27–10. Florida State won its last 10 games but lost its first 2.

The other team that lost only one game was No. 5 Tennessee (11–1), which won the Cotton Bowl at Dallas, Texas, 31–27 over No. 13 Arkansas (10–2), the Southwest Conference champion. No. 9 Alabama won the Southeastern Conference through a tiebreaking formula over Tennessee and No. 6 Auburn (10–2), which had identical conference records. Tennessee also had the biggest improvement, up from 5–6 in 1988. Pacific 10 champion Southern California (9–2–1) beat Michigan (10–2) in the Rose Bowl 17–10 at Pasadena, Calif., and both teams were ranked seventh and eighth in different polls.

Miami's defense led Division I-A of the National Collegiate Athletic Association (NCAA) by allowing 216.5 yd and 9.3 points per game, and it finished second to Southern California's 61.5 yd rushing yield per game. Miami broke a record by allowing only two yards in punt returns. Kansas State was the pass defense leader, allowing 129.3 yd per game largely because it ranked last in rushing defense; Illinois was the pass defense runner-up at 140.5. Nebraska's top rushing offense gained 375.3 yd per game.

The most impressive team statistically was No. 14 Houston (9–2), which was on probation for recruiting violations and ineligible for postseason play. Houston set Division I-A yardage records with regular-season per-game averages of 511.3 yd passing and 624.9 yd total offense, and its average of 53.5 points per game was second to Army's 56 with Doc Blanchard and Glenn Davis in 1944. Using four wide receivers, one running back, and no tight end, Houston also set a record with 55 touchdown passes and led the country with 23 field goals, 75 touchdowns, and 32 pass interceptions. It set single-game records of 771 yd passing and 1,021 yd offense in a 95–21 victory over Southern Methodist, which had missed two seasons as punishment for recruiting violations.

Houston quarterback Andre Ware broke 13 NCAA records and won the Heisman Trophy as college player of the year in a close vote over Indiana halfback Anthony Thompson. Ware's season records included 4,661 yd total offense (less than the passing total because of quarterback sacks), 4,699 yd passing, and 4.18 touchdown passes per game (46 total). Thompson, who won the Maxwell Award, set career records with 65 touchdowns and 394 points, set a single-game record with 377 yd rushing, and led Division I-A with 1,793 yd rushing, 25 touchdowns, and 154 points.

Other new season records were Emmanuel Hazard's 142 catches and 22 touchdown catches for Houston, Chuck Weatherspoon's 9.63 yd per rushing attempt for Houston, Roman Anderson's 131 kicking points for Houston, and Ty Detmer's 11.07 yd per pass attempt and 8.92 yd per offensive play for Brigham Young. Detmer's 175.6 passer-efficiency rating points and Hazard's 1,689 yd receiving led the country, as did Mike Pringle's 2,690 all-purpose yards for California State-Fullerton. New Mexico's Terance Mathis set career records with 263 catches and 4,254 yd receiving, as did Duke's Clarkston Hines with 38 touchdown catches and Air Force's Dee Dowis with 3,612 yd rushing by a quarterback.

Virginia (10–3) won the Atlantic Coast Conference in a tiebreaker over Duke (8–4), as did Yale (8–2) in the Ivy League over Princeton (7–2–1). Other conference champions were Brigham Young (10–3) in the Western Atlantic, Idaho (9–3) in the Big Sky, Fresno State (11–1) in the Big West, Holy Cross (10–1) in the Colonial, and Ball State (7–3–2) in the Mid-American.

Other NCAA divisions decided their championships in play-off tournaments. Undefeated Georgia Southern won its third Division I-AA championship in five years and

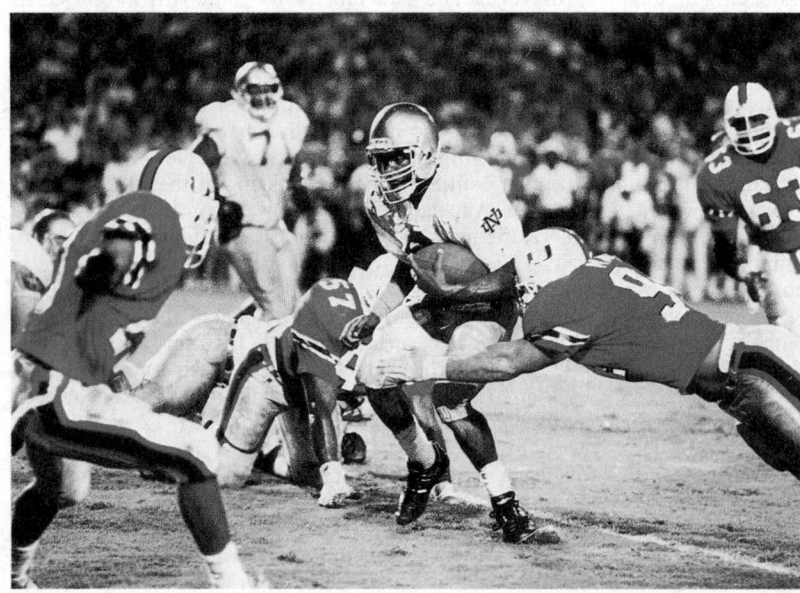

Notre Dame quarterback Tony Rice is brought down by the Miami defense during the game that broke Notre Dame's 23-game winning streak. Miami's victory gained it the college football national championship.

Joe Montana of the San Francisco 49ers (right) and John Elway of the Denver Broncos (far right) were two of the four quarterbacks headed for the NFL play-offs, which would determine the teams playing in the Super Bowl. The 49ers were champions of the NFC West Division, while the Broncos won the AFC West.

PHOTOGRAPHS, AP/WIDE WORLD

became the first school in the 20th century to win 15 games in a season when it won 37–34 against Stephen F. Austin of Texas (12–2–1). Mississippi College (11–3) won the Division II crown 3–0 over Jacksonville (Fla.) State. Dayton of Ohio (13–0–1) won the Division III title 17–7 over Union of New York (13–1).

Michigan State linebacker Percy Snow won the Butkus and Lombardi awards for the best linebacker and lineman, respectively. Brigham Young offensive guard Mohammed Elewonibi won the other lineman's award, the Outland Trophy. Texas A&I halfback Johnny Bailey won his third consecutive Harlon Hill Trophy for the outstanding player in Division II of the NCAA. Bailey became the all-time leading college rusher with 6,320 yd.

Bo Schembechler resigned after 21 years as Michigan's coach with 13 Big Ten championships and a 234–64–8 record in 27 college seasons, the most wins among active Division I-A coaches. The Big Ten announced that Penn State was to join its conference.

Professional. The San Francisco 49ers had the most successful season by a defending National Football League (NFL) champion since 1984 when they won 14 of 16 regular-season games and reached the National Conference (NFC) championship game against the Los Angeles Rams on Jan. 14, 1990. They had won their third Super Bowl in eight years by defeating the Cincinnati Bengals 20–16 at Miami on Jan. 22, 1989. Their winning drive of 92 yd ended with 34 seconds to play, making it the second Super Bowl decided in the last minute. Coach Bill Walsh retired after the victory and was replaced by George Seifert.

The 49ers' 1989 NFC West Division championship was their fourth in a row and gave them a chance to be the first repeating Super Bowl champions since Pittsburgh 10 years earlier. Buffalo in the American Conference (AFC) East was the only other repeating division champion.

Pittsburgh's five-year absence from the play-offs was the longest to end. Minnesota, winning the NFC Central for the first time since 1980, was the only division champion without a crown in the previous three years. The New York Giants won the NFC East, and division winners Cleveland of the AFC Central and Denver of the AFC West played their third AFC championship game in four years.

Green Bay's improvement from a 4–12 won-lost record in 1988 to 10–6 in 1989 was the league's biggest and made Lindy Infante the coach of the year. Chicago fell the farthest, from 12–4 to 6–10.

San Francisco quarterback Joe Montana (*see* BIOGRAPHIES), the NFL's most valuable player, broke a 29-year-old league record with his passing-efficiency rating of 112.4.

Montana also led the NFL in three of its four components of efficiency, with 9.12 yd per attempt and percentages of .702 for completions and .067 for touchdowns. His .021 interception percentage was second to Chris Miller's .019 for Atlanta, but Montana's eight interceptions were the NFL low. The 49ers led the NFL with 27.6 points and 391.8 yd per game. Jerry Rice led NFL receivers with 1,483 yd and 17 touchdowns, and 49er teammate John Taylor set an NFL record by catching two touchdown passes of at least 90 yd in one game. Placekicker Mike Cofer led the NFL with 136 points.

Minnesota led the NFL defensively by allowing 156.3 passing yards and 261.5 total yards per game. The Vikings' 71 quarterback sacks were one short of Chicago's five-year-old record. Chris Doleman led the league with 20.5, and Keith Millard, the defensive player of the year, set a league record for defensive tackles with 18.

Washington led the NFL with 271.8 yd passing per game and became the second NFL team with three receivers to gain at least 1,000 yd apiece. Green Bay's passing game produced league leaders Don Majkowski with 4,318 yd passing and Sterling Sharpe with 90 catches.

The Rams had three individual league leaders: Henry Ellard with 19.7 yd per catch, Jim Everett with 29 touchdown passes, and Greg Bell with 25 rushing touchdowns. Willie ("Flipper") Anderson's 336 yd on pass receptions set an NFL record on November 26.

Cincinnati, the AFC total offense leader, led the NFL with 381.3 yd rushing per game. Other AFC leaders were Buffalo in points and Miami in passing yards. New Orleans' best NFL rushing defense allowed 82.9 yd per game. Kansas City led the AFC in total and passing defense, while Denver's defense led the AFC in points and rushing yards allowed.

The rookies of the year were Kansas City linebacker Derrick Thomas on defense and Detroit tailback Barry Sanders on offense. Detroit's radical offense made it the first NFL team to play an entire season without a tight end.

Seattle wide receiver Steve Largent caught the 100th touchdown pass of his career, breaking Don Hutson's 44-year-old record. Largent finished his 14-year career after extending his records for catches to 819, for receiving yardage to 13,089, and for consecutive games with at least one catch to 177. He passed the runners-up by 69 catches, 934 yd, and 27 games.

Chicago placekicker Kevin Butler set a record with 24 consecutive field goals. Eddie Murray of Detroit tied the one-year accuracy rate for the second consecutive season with 20 field goals in 21 attempts (95.2%). Rich Karlis of

Table II. NFL Final Standings and Play-offs, 1989

AMERICAN CONFERENCE	W	L	T	NATIONAL CONFERENCE	W	L	T
Eastern Division				**Eastern Division**			
*Buffalo	9	7	0	*New York Giants	12	4	0
Indianapolis	8	8	0	*Philadelphia	11	5	0
Miami	8	8	0	Washington	10	6	0
New England	5	11	0	Phoenix	5	11	0
New York Jets	4	12	0	Dallas	1	15	0
Central Division				**Central Division**			
*Cleveland	9	6	1	*Minnesota	10	6	0
*Houston	9	7	0	Green Bay	10	6	0
*Pittsburgh	9	7	0	Detroit	7	9	0
Cincinnati	8	8	0	Chicago	6	10	0
				Tampa Bay	5	11	0
Western Division				**Western Division**			
*Denver	11	5	0	*San Francisco	14	2	0
Kansas City	8	7	1	*Los Angeles Rams	11	5	0
Los Angeles Raiders	8	8	0	New Orleans	9	7	0
Seattle	7	9	0	Atlanta	3	13	0
San Diego	6	10	0				

*Qualified for play-offs.

Play-offs

Wild-card round
Los Angeles Rams 21, Philadelphia 7
Pittsburgh 26, Houston 23

Minnesota tied another record with seven field goals in one game and led the league with 31 field goals.

Eric Dickerson of Indianapolis set a league rushing record with his seventh straight 1,000-yd season. Randall Cunningham of Philadelphia became the first modern quarterback to lead his team three straight years in rushing.

Commissioner Pete Rozelle resigned after 29 years in office and was replaced by former league attorney Paul Tagliabue. NFL owners also formed a subsidiary league to begin play in the spring of 1991 with teams in at least four European cities.

The NFL set an attendance record in its 70th season with an average of 60,833 per game, but it finished its third season without a collective bargaining agreement between players and management. The NFL Players Association withdrew itself as the players' bargaining agent and pursued its lawsuit seeking to abolish the draft of college players and restrictions on the movement of veteran players among teams. The NFL Management Council allowed the first free movement for players not designated among the top 37 on their teams. Plan B, as it was called, resulted in 229 players' changing teams.

Thirteen players received the NFL's first punishments for using anabolic steroids, 30-day suspensions for testing positive in scheduled tests. Washington defensive end Dexter Manley was the third player banned for life under the league's drug-abuse policy, which allowed application for reinstatement after one year.

Canadian Football. The Saskatchewan Roughriders won the 1989 Canadian Football League (CFL) championship by defeating the Hamilton Tiger-Cats 43–40 in the highest-scoring Grey Cup game, on November 26 at Toronto. David Ridgway's 35-yd field goal with two seconds left decided the game. Saskatchewan had finished third in the Western Division with a 9–9 record but reached the Grey Cup by upsetting 10–8 Calgary and 16–2 Edmonton, which had set a CFL record for victories. Hamilton won the Eastern Division with a 12–6 record.

Edmonton quarterback Tracy Ham, the league's most outstanding player, led the CFL with 30 touchdown passes, 8.4 yd per attempt, and an 85.2 efficiency rating. Teammate Reggie Taylor led with 1,503 yd rushing. Edmonton ranked first in seven of eight team categories for offensive and defensive points, total yards, rushing yards, and passing yards, with Saskatchewan first in passing offense. For

Hamilton, Tony Champion led CFL receivers with 1,656 yd, 95 catches, and 15 touchdowns, and Paul Osbaldiston led the kickers with 233 points and tied Ridgway with 54 field goals.

(KEVIN M. LAMB)

GOLF

While Jack Nicklaus could still be regarded as the most successful golfer of all time, he could no longer claim to have won the most money. In 1989 Tom Kite was for the second time in his career the leader of the U.S. Professional Golfers' Association (PGA) tour money list, his earnings of $1,395,278 increasing his career total to $5,600,691. Nicklaus in 1988 had been the first man to pass the $5 million mark. By the end of 1989 there were four: Kite, Tom Watson ($5,160,244), Nicklaus ($5,102,420), and Curtis Strange ($5,015,720).

Money, however, was only half the story. While Nicklaus had won 18 of the world's major championships as a professional, Watson 8, and Strange 2, Kite had still, at the age of 40, failed to win any. Fate had not smiled kindly on this slight, bespectacled, and most dependable of golfers. Victories in the Player's championship at Ponte Vedra, Fla., the Nestle Invitational at Bay Hill, Fla., and the Nabisco championship at Harbour Town, S.C., in which he beat Payne Stewart in the victory that decided first place on the 1989 money list, undoubtedly gave him satisfaction. However, there was one much greater disappointment. In the United States Open championship at Oak Hill Country Club near Rochester, N.Y., Kite led the field by three strokes with 15 holes to play in the final round. Never had he had a better chance to achieve his dearest ambition, but the drive he hit into the water and the seven he took to complete the fifth hole left him in disarray.

Instead it was the methodical Curtis Strange, who reeled off par after par for a round of 70 and a total of 278, two under par, who took the title for the second successive year. He won by one stroke from two other Americans, Mark McCumber and Chip Beck, and the Welshman Ian Woosnam. Not since Ben Hogan in 1950–51 had anyone triumphed in successive U.S. Open championships.

For the first time ever in tournament golf, four players scored holes in one in the U.S. Open. Within two hours of each other during the second round, Doug Weaver, Jerry Pate, Nick Price, and Mark Wiebe, each using a 7 iron, aced the same hole (the sixth) at the Oak Hill course.

European golf had enjoyed unprecedented success through the 1980s, and another notable landmark was achieved in 1989 when Britain's Nick Faldo followed his fellow countryman Sandy Lyle as the winner of the Masters at Augusta, Ga. Just as Lyle had won in thrilling style in 1988, hitting a fairway bunker shot close enough to the flag to sink the birdie putt that took the crown, so did Faldo's victory come in equally gripping circumstances. Trailing Ben Crenshaw by four strokes going into the last round, Faldo shot a brilliant 65 to force a play-off with Scott Hoch of the U.S., both players finishing with totals of 283, five under par. At the first extra hole, Hoch missed the shortest putt (0.6 m [2 ft]) on which a major championship had ever depended, and in gathering darkness Faldo exacted full punishment by sinking at the second extra hole a birdie putt of 7.6 m (25 ft). It was his second major championship, for in 1987 he had won the British Open at Muirfield, Scotland.

U.S. golfers, nevertheless, still had the better of the major championships, for in addition to Strange in the U.S. Open, Mark Calcavecchia won the British Open at Royal Troon, Scotland, and Payne Stewart the PGA at Kemper Lakes Golf Club near Chicago.

Betsy King is victorious after making a shot at the U.S. Women's Open championship. King had lost a comfortable lead in the third round but later recovered to win the Open with a 6-under-par score.
AFP PHOTO

Calcavecchia was a golfer of growing reputation, and his victory in another play-off concluded one of the best British Opens in some years, blessed at last with hot and sunny weather. For three days the pace was largely set by Wayne Grady of Australia, who led after both 36 and 54 holes. On the last day, however, it was another Australian, Greg Norman, who attracted all the attention when he scored birdies at each of the first six holes and, in due course, a final round of 64. It gave him a total of 275, 13 under par, which Calcavecchia, with a birdie on the 18th hole for a 69, and then Grady (71) equaled.

In the play-off over four holes, Norman resumed where he had left off with birdies on the first two holes, but the mistake he made at the third (the 17th of the golf course) allowed Calcavecchia to catch him. With Grady already out of the running, Norman tangled with too many bunkers on the last hole and conceded before Calcavecchia went through the formality of holing out with his second birdie of the day at the 18th.

Stewart's record in the major championships had for some time been consistent, but his first victory, in the PGA, was unexpected, for Mike Reid, also of the U.S., was in full control through the first 69 holes. He had begun with a 66, followed it with rounds of 67 and 70, and with three holes to play led by three strokes. Stewart's final round of 67 for a total of 276 did not, therefore, appear to be an insurmountable target until Reid suddenly collapsed by dropping one stroke at the 16th and two at the 17th, leaving him in a three-way tie for second place with Strange and Andy Bean.

The U.S. scored further successes in the Dunhill Cup at St. Andrews, Scotland, and in the Four Tours championship in Tokyo. In the Dunhill Calcavecchia, Kite, and Strange defeated, in turn, South Korea, Argentina, and England and then overcame Japan in the final. In Tokyo the U.S. was victorious over Europe in the final for the third successive year.

However, the U.S. did not win back the Ryder Cup at the Belfry, near Birmingham, England. The U.S. had lost in both 1985 and 1987, and the 14–14 tie in 1989 allowed Europe to retain the cup for another two years. It was, as expected, a thrilling contest, with Europe having the better of the first two days and leading by two points with the 12 singles matches still to be played. On the last afternoon the balance of power shifted four times, first Europe strengthening its grip and then the U.S. coming back so strongly that victory seemed inevitable, only to have Europe recover so well that the cup seemed theirs for the taking. At the last gasp, however, the U.S. won each of the last four singles, and the honours, very properly, were shared.

No fewer than 8 of the 12 singles were decided on the last hole and 5 of the 16 players hit either their drives or their approach shots—and sometimes both—into the water that was such a feature of the 18th. It proved particularly costly to Stewart and Calcavecchia, both of whom lost, and also to Severiano Ballesteros and Faldo, who were beaten as well.

The two outstanding players on each side were José-María Olazábal of Spain, who scored 4½ points out of a possible 5, and Chip Beck of the U.S., who scored 3½ points out of 4. The match marked the end of Tony Jacklin's reign as European captain. He had served through four terms since 1983 and, having won two, tied one, and lost one, departed with a record that would be difficult to surpass.

Much of Europe's success over the past 10 years had been due to their "big five"—Ballesteros, Faldo, Woosnam, Sandy Lyle, and Bernard Langer—all of whom by 1989 were in their early 30s. However, in 1989 Ronan Rafferty, aged 25, was the year's leading money winner with £400,311. As in the U.S., everything depended on the last tournament, the Volvo Masters at Sotogrande, Spain, and Rafferty, a Northern Irishman, won it in the most convincing manner to overtake Olazábal, who until then had led him by some £2,000.

Rafferty's play on the last 9 holes of 32, to beat Faldo by a stroke over a difficult course, was the culmination of a splendid season in which he had also won the Italian and Scandinavian opens, his first successes in Europe. Even so Faldo was generally regarded as the European golfer of the year. Not only did he become the second Briton to win the Masters but he also took the Volvo PGA championship, the Dunhill Masters, the French Open, and, with his best golf of the year, the Suntory world match-play championship at Wentworth, England. In the final he came back from three down with seven holes to play to beat Woosnam with an eagle three at the last hole.

The best team performance was by Britain's amateurs when they won the Walker Cup at the Peachtree Country Club near Atlanta, Ga. It was their first victory on U.S. soil since they first met the United States at the National Golf Links on Long Island in 1922. Needing only 1½ points from the singles for the victory, the British got them from three players who had been on the verge of defeat. Andrew Hare won the last two holes to finish even with Doug Martin; Eoghan O'Connell caught Phil Mickelson, having been one down and two to play; and Jim Milligan tied with Jay Sigel, having been two down with three to play.

A week later the Americans gained partial compensation when Chris Patton beat Danny Green by three and one to win the U.S. amateur championship at the Merion Golf Club near Philadelphia. None of the British contingent survived for long, including Stephen Dodd, who had won the British amateur championship at Royal Birkdale, Lancashire, beating Craig Cassells by five and three in the final. With teammates Duncan Evans, Philip Parkin, and Paul Mayo, Dodd was the third Welshman to take the title in the '80s.

After conceding the U.S. Women's Open to Laura Davies of Britain and Liselotte Neumann of Sweden in 1987 and 1988, Betsy King returned the cup home again

U.S. gymnast Brandy Johnson sails through her vault during the U.S. national gymnastics championships. Johnson placed first in four of the five competitions, which included the women's all-around championships.
FOCUS ON SPORTS

with a convincing victory at Indianwood Country Club near Detroit, Mich. King won by four strokes from Nancy Lopez, and she was also the Ladies Professional Golfers' Association (LPGA) tour's leading money winner.

Another American, Jane Geddes, won the British Women's Open at Ferndown, Dorset, England, beating Florence Deschamps of Belgium by two strokes. Third was Marie Laure de Lorenzi of France, who for the second consecutive year was the leading money winner on the Women's Professional Golfers' European tour.

The U.S. women's amateur champion was Vicki Goetz. She beat Brandie Burton by four and three in the final at Pinehurst, N.C. Helen Dobson, the British women's amateur champion, defeated Elaine Farquharson by six and five in the final at Hoylake, England. The 18-year-old Dobson also won the British stroke-play title, the English championship, and the English girls' championship.

(MICHAEL WILLIAMS)

GYMNASTICS

The Soviet Union continued to dominate international gymnastics competition, winning the world team and all-around individual competitions in Stuttgart, West Germany. For the fifth time in six years, the Soviet men won the team title, easily defeating East Germany 587.250 to 580.850 (out of a possible 600). The Soviet women nosed out Romania 396.793 to 394.931 (out of a possible 400).

A newcomer to world competition, Igor Korobchinski of the Soviet Union, won the men's all-around title by the narrow margin of 0.1 point over 1988 Olympic Games champion Vladimir Artyomov, also of the Soviet Union. The women's all-around winner was Svetlana Boginskaya of the Soviet Union, the recently crowned European champion. She also tied for first in the floor exercises with Daniela Silivas of Romania. Silivas also won on the balance beam and tied for first with China's Fan Di on the uneven parallel bars.

Olessia Dudnik of the Soviet Union received a perfect 10 to win the vault. She also placed second to Silivas on the balance beam. Brandy Johnson of the U.S. tied for second on the vault. It was the first medal won by the U.S. in the world championships in eight years.

The U.S. women finished fourth in the team competi-

tion, trailing the Soviets, Romania, and China. The Soviet women won four gold medals to three for Romania and also scored five perfect 10s.

The first four teams in the men's competition were the Soviet Union, East Germany, China, and Japan. Overall, the Soviets accounted for five gold medals, while China won two and East and West Germany earned one apiece.

In addition to his gold medals in the team and all-around individual competitions, Korobchinski finished first in the floor exercises. Artyomov won a gold medal in the team competition, tied for first on the parallel bars, placed second on the horizontal bar, finished third on the vault, and placed sixth in the all-around competition.

Other gold medalists in the men's finals were Andreas Aguilar of West Germany, rings; Valentin Mogilny of the Soviet Union, pommel horse; Li Chunyang of China, horizontal bar; Li Jing of China, tied for first on the parallel bars; and Joerg Behrend of East Germany, vault.

The world championships attracted many new faces to replace the veterans who completed their careers in the 1988 Olympic Games. The "risk, originality, and virtuosity" of the gymnasts' routines continued to improve. The judges responded with a record number of perfect 10s in scoring the routines. (CHARLES ROBERT PAUL, JR.)

HORSE RACING

Thoroughbred Racing and Steeplechasing. *United States and Canada.* Sunday Silence, which engaged in a season-long rivalry with Easy Goer, seemed certain to be named horse of the year when he won the Eclipse Award for three-year-old colt of the year. Sunday Silence and Easy Goer met four times, with the former scoring wins in the Kentucky Derby, Preakness, and Breeders' Cup Classic. Easy Goer won the Belmont, thwarting Sunday Silence in his bid to become a Triple Crown champion.

Easy Goer made a strong case for year-end honours by scoring five other major stakes victories during the year, including stunning triumphs over older horses in the Woodward and the Jockey Club Gold Cup. It was Sunday Silence's victory by a neck over Easy Goer in the Breeders' Cup Classic at Gulfstream Park in Florida that tipped the balance in his favour.

In the voting conducted among representatives of the

Daily Racing Form, the Thoroughbred Racing Association, and the National Turf Writers Association, eight of nine divisional champions were unanimous choices. In addition to Sunday Silence, they included Go For Wand (two-year-old filly), Open Mind (three-year-old filly), Blushing John (older male), Steinlen (male turf horse), Brown Bess (female turf horse), Safely Kept (sprinter), and Bayakoa (older female). The only split decision came in the two-year-old colt division with Rhythm taking the honours over Grand Canyon and Summer Squall. In the 10th division, a special committee selected among the three voting bodies unanimously voted Highland Bud the champion steeplechaser. The only champion to repeat was Open Mind, which had been voted the best two-year-old filly of 1988.

Ogden Phipps, who the previous season had won Eclipse Awards as outstanding owner and breeder, repeated in 1989 as champion owner. Outstanding breeder honours went to Mr. and Mrs. Franklin Groves of North Ridge Farm. Michael Luzzi received the Eclipse Award as the nation's outstanding apprentice jockey of 1989.

Sunday Silence set a single-season earnings record of $4,578,454, the first horse in thoroughbred racing history to top $4 million in yearly earnings. His total, which included a $1 million bonus for best performance in the Triple Crown races, topped Alysheba's 1988 mark of $3,808,600.

Bayakoa, the champion older female, won 9 of 11 starts, including seven Grade I stakes, for $1,406,403 in earnings. Her campaign was headlined by an impressive victory in the Breeders' Cup Distaff.

Open Mind, the champion three-year-old filly, won the first two legs of the New York Racing Association's Triple Tiara, the Acorn and the Mother Goose. She was upset by a nose by Nite of Fun in the third leg, the Coaching Club American Oaks, but was awarded the victory when the winner was disqualified.

Outstanding owner Ogden Phipps raced seven stakes winners in 1989, all homebreds. Phipps horses earned $5,439,154, the leading total for an owner. Easy Goer was Phipps's leading money winner with $3,837,150. Phipps also campaigned Dancing Spree, which proved his versatility by winning the 1¼-mi Suburban Handicap and the six-furlong Breeders' Cup Sprint.

Leading breeder Franklin Groves was the breeder of champion older male horse Blushing John. Groves's North Ridge Farm was also represented by 1989 Grade I stakes winners Ruhlmann, Sabona, and Trumpet's Blare.

Luzzi won 225 races in 1989. The 20-year-old native of Wilmington, Del., campaigned at tracks in Maryland. The nation's leading race-winning jockey for the third straight year was 19-year-old Kent Desormeaux, who set a record for the most victories by a jockey in a single season. He rode his 547th winner of the year on November 30 at Laurel in Maryland to break the old mark of 546 set by Chris McCarron in 1974.

José Santos led all riders in earnings for the fourth straight year. The defending Eclipse Award-winning rider accounted for purses of $13,838,389, short of the record $14,876,157 he earned in 1988.

D. Wayne Lukas led the nation's trainers in both victories and purse earnings. His stable accounted for $16,-103,998, short of his record $17,842,358 set in 1988 and breaking his streak of six consecutive record seasons.

With Approval was voted Sovereign Awards as Canada's horse of the year and three-year-old male of the year by virtue of becoming the first Canadian Triple Crown champion in 26 years. The three races constituting Canada's Triple Crown were the Queen's Plate Stakes, the Prince of Wales Stakes, and the Breeders' Stakes.

Kinghaven Farms, which was represented by homebreds in five of nine divisions honouring the champions of Canadian racing in 1988, had three homebreds honoured in 1989. They included With Approval, Steady Power (champion older male), and Passing Mood (brood mare).

The remaining Sovereign Award winners were Sky Classic (two-year-old male), Wavering Girl (two-year-old filly), Blushing Katy (three-year-old filly), Proper Evidence (older female), Charlie Barley (grass horse), Mr. Hot Shot (sprinter), Kinghaven Farms (owner and breeder), Roger Attfield (trainer), Don Seymour (jockey), and Maree Richards (apprentice jockey).   (JOHN G. BROKOPP)

Europe and Australia. Arab owners dominated flat racing in Europe in a way that had been predicted for several years. Controversy continued as to whether their oil-rich presence was good or bad for racing, both as a sport and as an industry. They brought a higher quality of racehorses and breeding stock to Europe, mainly from the United

Easy Goer surges to the finish to take the Belmont Stakes. Easy Goer's win prevented Sunday Silence (who had won the Kentucky Derby and the Preakness) from taking the Triple Crown.

States. However, any change in their involvement in horse racing, as a result of either events at home or a simple alteration in their racing policy, would have a significant impact on the sport in Europe and on the bloodstock industry on both sides of the Atlantic. For the moment, though, racing in Europe had not been home to so many star performers for decades, while the international bloodstock market stood at a higher level than expected, entirely thanks to Arab investment.

Sheikh Muhammad al-Maktoum from Dubai was the leading owner in Britain for the fifth consecutive year, with 90 winners of 130 races worth £1,296,933. All three figures were records, and he amassed an additional £800,-337 in place money. The sheikh was also leading owner in Ireland, where he won the first four classics with four different horses, all trained in Britain, and in France, where he was represented by two top-class milers, Golden Opinion and Polish Precedent. Golden Opinion won the Coronation Stakes at Royal Ascot and finished second by a head to Cadeaux Genereux in the July Cup. The British-trained Old Vic won the Prix du Jockey-Club (Derby) in France by seven lengths. He then won the Irish Derby by four lengths on July 2 to make his score five out of five for the year, but he did not race again.

Old Vic was expected to return in 1990, however, while Nashwan, the general choice as best horse in Europe in 1989, was retired to stud. Both colts had raced twice as two-year-olds but without encountering the leaders of their generation. Nashwan, which was bred and owned by Sheikh Hamdan al-Maktoum, won both his races at two and followed with four consecutive victories, all in Group I events, at three. However, he did not appear to be improving in midsummer and, when he returned after eight weeks of rest, he was beaten by Golden Pheasant and French Glory, two French-trained colts of average ability, at Longchamp on September 17. The idea of contesting the Prix de l'Arc de Triomphe (the Arc) was abandoned, as were alternate plans to bid for the Dubai Champion Stakes when Nashwan ran a high temperature a few days before that race.

Sheikh Hamdan was the second leading owner in Britain, while his elder brother Sheikh Maktoum finished fifth, and their nephew, Mana al-Maktoum, was sixth. Prince Khaled Abdulla from Saudi Arabia was third, and the Aga Khan, the only non-Arab in the top six, finished fourth. Mana al Maktoum owned just one horse, Zilzal, unbeaten in five races in Britain, in the last of which he halted the sequence of seven victories established by his French-trained rival for Europe's miling crown, Polish Precedent.

Carroll House, an Italian-owned but British-trained four-year-old, created a 19–1 surprise when he beat Behera by 1½ lengths in the Arc. Like the previous Arc winner, Tony Bin, Carroll House was later bought by Zenya Yoshida, to run in the Japan Cup in November; he finished second to last. Japanese owners acquired two other winners of Group I races, Assatis and Sheriff's Star.

Machiavellian, U.S.-bred and trained in France, was Europe's outstanding two-year-old. He was undefeated in three races and was prevented from extending his winning streak when he coughed shortly before the Grand Critérium. Coughing was a general problem in late summer and early autumn after a prolonged dry spell.

Pat Eddery, a rider for Prince Khaled, was champion jockey in Britain for the seventh time, his 171 winners being 8 more than his principal rival, Steve Cauthen. Michael Kinane, who rode Carroll House to win the Arc, finished well ahead of his rivals in Ireland, while Cash Asmussen was similarly dominant in France in spite of missing the

Major Thoroughbred Race Winners, 1989

Race	Won by	Jockey
United States		
Acorn	Open Mind	A. Cordero, Jr.
American Derby	Awe Inspiring	C. Perret
Arlington Classic	Clevor Trevor	D. Pettinger
Arlington Million	Steinlen	L. Pincay, Jr.
Belmont	Easy Goer	P. Day
Blue Grass	Western Playboy	R. Romero
Breeders' Cup Juvenile	Rhythm	C. Perret
Breeders' Cup Juvenile Fillies	Go For Wand	R. Romero
Breeders' Cup Sprint	Dancing Spree	A. Cordero, Jr.
Breeders' Cup Mile	Steinlen	J. Santos
Breeders' Cup Distaff	Bayakoa	L. Pincay, Jr.
Breeders' Cup Turf	Prized	E. Delahoussaye
Breeders' Cup Classic	Sunday Silence	C. McCarron
Brooklyn	Forever Silver	J. Vásquez
Champagne	Adjudicating	J. Vásquez
Charles H. Strub Stakes	Nasr El Arab	P. Valenzuela
Coaching Club American Oaks	Open Mind	A. Cordero, Jr.
Flamingo	Awe Inspiring	C. Perret
Florida Derby	Mercedes Won	E. Fires
Futurity	Senor Pete	J. Santos
Gulfstream Park Handicap	Slew City Slew	A. Cordero, Jr.
Haskell Invitational	King Glorious	C. McCarron
Hialeah Turf Cup	El Senor	H. McCauley
Hollywood Derby	Live The Dream	A. Solis
Hollywood Futurity	Grand Canyon	A. Cordero, Jr.
Hollywood Gold Cup	Blushing John	P. Day
Hollywood Invitational	Great Communicator	R. Sibille
Hollywood Turf Cup	Frankly Perfect	C. McCarron
International	Caltech	R.R. Douglas
Jockey Club Gold Cup	Easy Goer	P. Day
Kentucky Derby	Sunday Silence	P. Valenzuela
Kentucky Oaks	Open Mind	A. Cordero, Jr.
Man o' War	Yankee Affair	J. Santos
Meadowlands Cup	Mi Selecto	J. Santos
Metropolitan	Proper Reality	J. Bailey
Preakness	Sunday Silence	P. Valenzuela
Santa Anita Derby	Sunday Silence	P. Valenzuela
Santa Anita Handicap	Martial Law	M. Pedroza
Suburban	Dancing Spree	A. Cordero, Jr.
Super Derby Invitational	Sunday Silence	P. Valenzuela
Travers	Easy Goer	P. Day
Turf Classic	Yankee Affair	J. Santos
United Nations	Yankee Affair	P. Day
Whitney	Easy Goer	P. Day
Wood Memorial Invitational	Easy Goer	P. Day
Woodward	Easy Goer	P. Day
England		
One Thousand Guineas	Musical Bliss	W.R. Swinburn
Two Thousand Guineas	Nashwan	W. Carson
Derby	Nashwan	W. Carson
Oaks	Aliysa	W.R. Swinburn
St. Leger	Michelozzo	S. Cauthen
Coronation Cup	Sheriff's Star	R. Cochrane
Ascot Gold Cup	Sadeem	W. Carson
Eclipse Stakes	Nashwan	W. Carson
King George VI and Queen Elizabeth Diamond Stakes	Nashwan	W. Carson
Sussex Stakes	Zilzal	W.R. Swinburn
International Stakes	Tle de Chypre	A. Clark
Dubai Champion Stakes	Legal Case	R. Cochrane
France		
Poule d'Essai des Poulains	Kendor	M. Philipperon
Poule d'Essai des Pouliches	Pearl Bracelet	A. Gibert
Prix du Jockey-Club	Old Vic	S. Cauthen
Prix de Diane	Lady in Silver	A. Cruz
Prix Royal-Oak	Top Sunrise	F. Head
Prix Ganay	Saint Andrews	A. Badel
Prix Lupin	Galetto	E. Legrix
Grand Prix de Paris	Dancehall	C. Asmussen
Grand Prix de Saint-Cloud	Sheriff's Star	T. Ives
Prix Vermeille	Young Mother	A. Badel
Prix de l'Arc de Triomphe	Carroll House	M. Kinane
Grand Critérium	Jade Robbery	C. Asmussen
Ireland		
Irish Two Thousand Guineas	Shaadi	W.R. Swinburn
Irish One Thousand Guineas	Ensconse	R. Cochrane
Irish Derby	Old Vic	S. Cauthen
Irish Oaks	Alydaress	M. Kinane
Irish St. Leger	Petite Ile	R. Quinton
Phoenix Champion Stakes	Carroll House	M. Kinane
Italy		
Derby Italiano	Prorutori	M. Roberts
Gran Premio del Jockey-Club	Assatis	G. Baxter
West Germany		
Deutsches Derby	Mondrian	K. Woodburn
Grosser Preis von Baden	Mondrian	K. Woodburn
Grosser Preis der Berliner Bank	Mondrian	K. Woodburn
R & V Europa Preis	Ibn Bey	T. Quinn

final seven weeks of the season after injuring his neck in a fall. Lanfranco Dettori, whose father was Italian champion 13 times, equaled the post-World War II British record for an apprentice with 71 winners.

André Fabre, who supplied Asmussen with most of his best winners, was the leading trainer in France. Dermot Weld, Kinane's employer, was best in Ireland, and Michael Stoute, trainer of Zilzal, Aliysa, Shaadi, and Musical Bliss, ranked first in Britain. However, Henry Cecil, who trained Old Vic, would be at the top if earnings outside Britain were included.

Desert Orchid, an instantly recognizable near-white 10-year-old gelding, which had become the most popular horse in Britain, gained his 20th win in 33 steeplechase appearances when he caught Yahoo near the finish in the Cheltenham Gold Cup. He was not as dominant as Katko, the leading French jumper, a six-year-old that gained his 14th success in his last 15 outings when he won the Prix La Haye Jousselin at Auteuil on November 19. Katko took the wrong course on the occasion of his only defeat, on May 29; his rider was suspended for one month.

The 30–1 Tawrrific beat his 25–1 stable-companion, Super Impose, by 2¼ lengths in the Melbourne Cup, running the 3,200 m in a record 3 min 17.1 sec. Almaarad, an Irish-bred seven-year-old trained in Britain until late 1988, won both the Group I Caulfield Stakes and Australasia's richest nonhandicap event, the W.S. Cox Plate, in October but had to miss the Melbourne Cup because of injury. Poetic Prince, the leading performer of the 1988–89 season, beat the British-trained Top Class by three-fourths of a length in the Tancred International Stakes. Four months later, on July 22, Top Class finished third to Nashwan and Cacoethes in the King George VI and Queen Elizabeth Diamond Stakes. Carroll House was another four lengths back in fifth.

(ROBERT W. CARTER)

Harness Racing. At the Meadowlands in New Jersey in July, Dexter Nukes, with John Campbell driving for octogenarians Tom and Mildred Dexter, won the $852,-000 Meadowlands Pace. From post 7 behind the newly devised slanting mobile gate, he scored easily in 1 min 51.6 sec, a time bettered in the race only by Nihilator's 1 min 50.6 sec in 1985. The $907,000 Woodrow Wilson Pace, which highlighted the Meadowland's "Million Dollar Babies Night," was won by Sam Francisco Ben, driven by 33-year-old Ron Pierce.

At the Meadowlands early in August, Park Avenue Joe was awarded the $1,131,000 Hambletonian Trot after an epic tussle that climaxed with his dead heat in the race-off with Probe—the first in the long history of the race. In two heats earlier in the day, Park Avenue Joe finished first and second while Probe was first (in fastest time) and ninth. Probe's owners subsequently appealed; a judgment was expected before the running of the 1990 contest. On the previous night Lou Guida's Park Avenue Stable and driver Ron Waples had also been successful after three heats with Park Avenue Kathy in the $423,000 Hambletonian Oaks.

Camtastic joined the elite 1-min 50-sec group when he paced a time trial in 1 min 49.6 sec at Springfield, Ill., in August to share the world record for four-year-old pacers with Call For Rain. Dancing Master won the $248,484 final of the $621,210 Cane Pace Series at Yonkers (N.Y.) Raceway in September. A week prior to the Cane, Canada's Goalie Jeff, which in June had won the $1 million North America Cup in his homeland, clashed with Meadowlands Pace winner Dexter Nukes in the $632,500 Prix d'Ete series at Blue Bonnets in Montreal. Goalie Jeff coasted to an easy win in 1 min 52.2 sec in the $253,000 final, equaling the world record for three-year-old colt pacers on a half-mile

track. Goalie Jeff also won the Little Brown Jug before a crowd of 50,792 at Delaware in Ohio in September. Soon afterward, at Freestate Raceway in Maryland, Sandman Hanover, a $300,000 Guida purchase a month earlier and $30,000 supplementary entry, won the $315,748 Messenger Stakes, with Goalie Jeff his runner-up.

Three-year-old filly Peace Corps posted the second fastest trotting mile in history—1 min 52.8 sec—beating the colts in the $600,000 World Trotting Derby at Du Quoin, Ill., in September. Peace Corps then equaled the all-age world record for trotters on a half-mile track when she won the $61,722 Buckette in 1 min 56 sec. John Campbell, the driver of more world record champions than any other reinsman, declared OK Bye "the best two-year-old I have sat behind" after the colt's 1-min 54.6-sec world record win in the $230,151 Lou Babic Memorial at Freehold, N.J., in September.

In Europe at Vincennes, France, the Prix d'Amerique was won by Queila Gede and the Prix de France by Poroto. The great French trotter Ourasi in May won the Oslo Grand Prix at Bjerke in Norway at a 1-min 58-sec mile rate for 2,100 m. Sweden's $332,000 Elitlopp at Solvalla in Stockholm in May was won by Swedish-owned Napoletano. Mack Lobell, also now owned in Sweden, came back into his own, winning the $250,000 Campionato Europeo at Cesena in Italy in September. In the United Kingdom the National Pacing Derby, run for three-year-olds over 1½ mi at York Raceway in June, was won comfortably by Flag Forever in 3 min 14.2 sec.

At Gloucester Park, Western Australia, in December 1988, eight-year-old pacing star Village Kid recorded his fourth win in Perth's richest race, the $A 250,000 Benson & Hedges Cup Final. Westburn Grant blitzed the cream of New Zealand's talent in the Derby series at Addington, Christchurch.

(RONALD W. BISMAN)

ICE HOCKEY

North America. In the 1988–89 season, the 17th in their history, the Calgary Flames won their first National Hockey League (NHL) Stanley Cup championship. The season was marked by spectacular play by two centres—Wayne Gretzky of the Los Angeles Kings and Mario Lemieux of the Pittsburgh Penguins. In a league in which the average salary was $188,000, they were the highest-paid players, Gretzky earning $2 million and Lemieux $1.6 million.

Regular Season. From October 1988 to April 1989, each of the NHL's 21 teams played 80 games. The best records were achieved by Calgary (54 victories, 17 defeats, and 9 ties) and the Montreal Canadiens (53–18–9).

The division champions were Calgary with 117 points, Montreal with 115, the Washington Capitals with 92, and the Detroit Red Wings with 80. They led 16 teams into the play-offs.

Play-offs. Calgary reached the finals by eliminating the Vancouver Canucks (four games to three, with the deciding game settled in overtime), Los Angeles (4–0), and the Chicago Blackhawks (4–1). Montreal got there by defeating the Hartford Whalers (4–0), the Boston Bruins (4–1), and the Philadelphia Flyers (4–2).

Calgary relied on hard hitting and a ferocious power play. Montreal countered with a strong, smart defense and play-off experience. The Canadiens had won the last nine championship series in which they appeared.

In the play-off finals May 14–25, Montreal won two of the first three games. Then Calgary won three straight, 4–2, 3–2, and 4–2, to win the championship series, four games to two.

Al MacInnis of Calgary, with 31 points, became the first

Hockey star Wayne Gretzky is congratulated by hockey legend Gordie Howe (right) after breaking Howe's career point record with 1,851 points. Gretzky's wife and father look on. Gretzky scored the record point in a game against his former team, the Edmonton Oilers.

CANAPRESS PHOTO

defenseman to lead the play-offs in scoring. He won the Conn Smythe Trophy as the most valuable player in the play-offs.

Honours. Many hockey followers considered Gretzky the greatest player in history. In a monumental trade in August 1988, the Edmonton Oilers traded him to Los Angeles in a deal that involved five players, three draft choices, and $15 million. Los Angeles benefited immediately, moving from 18th to 4th place in the overall standings and selling out 24 games, compared with 5 the previous season. At the start of the 1989–90 season Gretzky, at 28, broke Gordie Howe's record of 1,850 points, made over 26 seasons.

Gretzky had won seven consecutive scoring titles until the 1987–88 season, when he missed 13 games because of a knee injury. He finished second in scoring that season to Lemieux, and in 1988–89 Lemieux beat him again, 199 points to 168. Centre Steve Yzerman of Detroit finished third with 155. Right wing Joe Mullen of Calgary scored 110 points, the most ever by a U.S.-born player.

Lemieux also led the league in goals (85), power-play goals (31), and shorthanded goals (13). He tied with Gretzky for first place in assists (114).

In a poll of players conducted by the NHL Players Association, Yzerman won the Lester Pearson Award as the league's outstanding player. In a poll of writers conducted by the league, Gretzky finished first in the voting for the Hart Trophy as the league's most valuable player. Gretzky won the award for a record ninth time.

Of the other official awards, Lemieux won the Art Ross Trophy as the scoring champion, Chris Chelios of Montreal the Norris Trophy for defensemen, Patrick Roy of Montreal the Vezina Trophy for goaltending, Guy Carbonneau of Montreal the Selke Trophy for defensive forwards, Mullen the Lady Byng Trophy for sportsmanship and gentlemanly play, defenseman Brian Leetch of the New York Rangers the Calder Trophy as rookie of the year, and Pat Burns of Montreal the Adams Trophy as coach of the year.

Violence. The NHL tried to reduce stick fouls by ejecting players who received major penalties for injuring an opponent with a hockey stick. The campaign resulted in less fighting and fewer infractions involving the use of sticks.

The league also increased punishment for players who instigated fights and injured opponents intentionally. Typically, it barred such players for 6 to 12 games. In the play-offs, after Ron Hextall, the Philadelphia Flyers' goalie, attacked Chelios without using a stick, the league suspended Hextall for the first 12 games of the 1989–90 season.

Soviets. In recent years the NHL rosters had included numerous players from Sweden and Finland as well as from Canada and the U.S. Late in the 1988–89 season and after the play-offs, Soviet officials allowed several of their players to join NHL teams. In return, the NHL clubs that held rights to those players compensated the Soviet hockey federation.

Right wings Sergey Priakin and Sergey Makarov signed with Calgary, defensemen Vyacheslav Fetisov and Sergey Starikov with the New Jersey Devils, and centre Igor Larionov with Vancouver. Aleksandr Mogilny, a 20-year-old forward, defected during the world championships in Stockholm in May and signed with the Buffalo Sabres. In September goaltender Sergey Mylnikov signed with the Quebec Nordiques and left wing Vladimir Krutov with the Vancouver Canucks. In addition, Helmut Balderis, a 37-year-old right wing who had been coaching in Japan, signed with the Minnesota North Stars.   (FRANK LITSKY)

European and International. A record entry of 29 nations contested the 53rd world ice hockey championships, divided for the second time into four groups. The U.S.S.R. won all of its 10 matches to recapture the title lost in 1987 to Sweden, which played host in Stockholm to the eight Group A contenders from April 15 to May 1, 1989. The attendance figures for the group's 40 matches totaled 387,427, an average of 9,686 per game. The major contests took place in the Swedish capital's impressive new Globe Arena, which was filled ten times to its capacity of 13,850.

The other seven teams were dominated by the Soviets in the preliminary round-robin. No opponent led them at any stage, and only the Canadians managed to outshoot them, 30–22, while losing 4–3. Sweden, Canada, and Czechoslovakia qualified to start afresh with the U.S.S.R. in the four-team medal round, their earlier matches not being carried forward. The preliminary games, however, did count in the final reckoning for Finland, the U.S., Poland, and West Germany in contesting the relegation round.

As usual, Canada and the U.S. could not use players concurrently needed for the Stanley Cup play-offs, but the Canadians nevertheless defeated both the Czechoslovaks and the Swedes to finish second, denied the title when beaten 5–3 by the Soviets in a worthy decider. Czechoslovakia placed third and the host nation fourth. A highlight of the relegation round was the crucial 2–0 victory by West Germany over Poland.

The tournament's four top scorers, each with 14 points, were Brian Bellows (Canada), Vladimir Ruzicka (Czechoslovakia), Kari Jalonen (Finland), and Kent Nilsson (Sweden). Some 160 journalists cast votes for an all-star lineup comprising the Czechoslovak goaltender, Dominik Hasek, defensemen Vyacheslav Fetisov (U.S.S.R.) and Anders Eldebrink (Sweden), and forwards Vyacheslav Bykov and Sergey Makarov, both Soviets, and Canada's Steve Yzerman.

The eight Group B countries competed in Norway at Lillehammer and Oslo from March 30 to April 9. The host nation gained promotion to Group A (replacing Poland) after defeating the second-place Italians 3–1. Denmark lost every contest and was demoted with Japan to Group C for 1990.

They were to be replaced by The Netherlands and Yugoslavia, first and second, respectively, in the Group C competition at Sydney, Australia, on March 18–27. The top two gained victories over all the other six participants, and so their confrontation was the centrepiece of the tour-

nament, won convincingly by the Dutch 8–3. Australia failed to win a point and, with South Korea, had to drop back into the bottom group.

Great Britain, returning to the championships for the first time in eight years, failed narrowly to gain promotion from Group D, contested at Geel and Heist, Belgium, on March 16–22. Romania topped the five-team section, earning a move up to Group C along with second-place Belgium.

The European Cup for club teams was won for the 19th time by the U.S.S.R. Army team, CSKA Moscow, after a six-match, four-team round-robin final on February 17–19 in Cologne, West Germany. The runner-up was VSZ Kosice from Czechoslovakia, with the local Cologne Sharks third and Farjetads of Karlstad, Sweden, fourth. League champions from 18 nations competed.

Table I. NHL Final Standings, 1989

	Won	Lost	Tied	Points
Prince of Wales Conference				
PATRICK DIVISION				
*Washington	41	29	10	92
*Pittsburgh	40	33	7	87
*New York Rangers	37	35	8	82
*Philadelphia	36	36	8	80
New Jersey Devils	27	41	12	66
New York Islanders	28	47	5	61
ADAMS DIVISION				
*Montreal	53	18	9	115
*Boston	37	29	14	88
*Buffalo	38	35	7	83
*Hartford	37	38	5	79
Quebec	27	46	7	61
Clarence Campbell Conference				
NORRIS DIVISION				
*Detroit	34	34	12	80
*St. Louis	32	35	12	78
*Minnesota	27	37	16	70
*Chicago	27	41	12	66
Toronto	28	46	6	62
SMYTHE DIVISION				
*Calgary ·	54	17	9	117
*Los Angeles	42	31	7	91
*Edmonton	38	34	8	84
*Vancouver	33	39	8	74
Winnipeg	26	42	12	64

*Gained play-off berth.

Table II. World Ice Hockey Championships, 1989

Country	Won	Lost	Tied	Goals	Goals against	Points
GROUP A Championship Section						
U.S.S.R.	3	0	0	11	4	6
Canada	2	1	0	12	11	4
Czechoslovakia	1	2	0	5	6	2
Sweden	0	3	0	5	12	0
GROUP A Relegation Section						
Finland	5	4	1	35	27	11
United States	4	5	1	37	40	9
West Germany	1	7	2	22	41	4
Poland	1	9	0	12	76	2
GROUP B						
Norway	5	1	1	28	18	11
Italy	5	1	1	37	16	11
France	4	1	2	29	18	10
Switzerland	5	2	0	40	21	10
East Germany	3	4	0	22	29	6
Austria	2	5	0	27	32	4
Japan	2	5	0	20	34	4
Denmark	0	7	0	9	44	0
GROUP C						
Netherlands, The	7	0	0	48	15	14
Yugoslavia	6	1	0	55	14	12
China	4	2	1	31	29	9
Hungary	3	3	1	32	30	7
Bulgaria	3	3	1	35	35	7
North Korea	2	5	0	26	40	4
South Korea	1	5	1	26	46	3
Australia	0	7	0	14	58	0
GROUP D						
Romania	3	0	1	77	10	7
Belgium	3	1	0	38	17	6
Great Britain	2	1	1	45	16	5
Spain	1	3	0	29	27	2
New Zealand	0	4	0	3	122	0

Women overcame an important hurdle by receiving official approval to compete from the International Ice Hockey Federation, which accepted registrations rather than see the formation of a separate women's organization. Canada, where the women's game made most headway, expressed interest in acting as host for an inaugural world championship for women in 1990.   (HOWARD BASS)

ICE SKATING

An aura of progress pervaded competitive ice skating in 1989, the next to last season with compulsory figures and the beginning of an era granting full Olympic status to indoor short-track speed racing. With no sign of abatement in the worldwide growth of new rinks, the sport's rising popularity as a public recreation was self-evident, and high television viewing figures reflected the strong appeal of skating's visual elegance.

Figure Skating. At the 79th world championships, in Paris on March 14–19, Kurt Browning of Canada captured the men's crown with a breathtaking array of hazardous triple leaps and a tremendous quadruple toe-loop jump. Only one quadruple had ever been landed before, also by Browning at the previous year's meet in Budapest. Drawn to skate before his main rivals, Browning, 22, from Edmonton, Alta., received scores of 5.9 for technical merit from seven of the nine judges. Christopher Bowman, the U.S. runner-up, strove hard but in vain to match the champion and was visibly tired at the end. Aleksandr Fadeev of the Soviet Union, the 1985 winner who had led before the final, fell from a triple and dropped to fourth, below Grzegorz Filipowski of Poland.

When little Midori Ito (see BIOGRAPHIES) became Japan's first queen of the ice, nobody could deny that this new women's champion was a worthy one. The power-packed 19-year-old from Nagoya beamed with delight when she sprang into the *Guinness Book of Records* with the first successful women's triple axel jump in an international contest. This awesome leap, more than half her height and involving 3½ midair rotations, was one of an unprecedented seven triples in a faultless performance, endorsed by five maximum scores of 6.0. Claudia Leistner, the West German silver medalist who had been favoured to win, landed four triples but fell from a fifth, an error that had no bearing on a clear-cut outcome because Ito, though only sixth in the compulsory figures, proved finally far too good overall. Jill Trenary of the U.S. could manage only two of the three triples she attempted, but her all-round ability was enough to take the bronze medal. Her tiny Californian compatriot Kristi Yamaguchi—making her international debut at 17—finished sixth in this event and fifth in the pairs, exciting much speculation about her prospects in the 1992 Olympic Games.

Ekaterina Gordeeva and Sergey Grinkov regained the pairs title, skating a complex and flawless long program in admirable unison, spurring eight of the nine judges to award 5.9 for the Soviet partnership's repertoire of daring triple throws and overhead lifts. Canadians Cindy Landry and Lyndon Johnston were surprise silver medalists, having skated together for only nine months. Soviets Elena Bechke and Denis Petrov gained third place, and when Yamaguchi finished fifth with Rudi Galindo, one wondered whether she would continue to compete in two events.

After four successive years as runners-up, the graceful Marina Klimova and Sergey Ponomarenko at last gained the ice dance title, finishing comfortably ahead of their Soviet compatriots Maya Usova and Aleksandr Zhulin. The controversially creative French brother and sister Paul and Isabelle Duchesnay were a popular third.

Midori Ito of Japan concentrates on a jump during her original program at the world figure skating championships in Paris. Midori entered the *Guinness Book of Records* as the first woman to complete a successful triple axel jump in an international competition.

VANDYSTADT—ALLSPORT USA

Speed Skating. Leo Visser of The Netherlands achieved the overall title in the men's world championships, in Oslo, Norway, on February 11–12. His compatriot Gerard Kemkers placed second without winning any of the four distances, followed by Geir Karlstad of Norway. Visser emphasized his versatility by winning both the 1,500 m and the 5,000 m. Karlstad took the 10,000 m, and Nikolay Gulyaev of the U.S.S.R. was first in the 500 m. Constanze Moser proved supreme in the women's world championships, at Lake Placid, N.Y., on February 4–5, finishing ahead of her fellow East German Gunda Kleeman. The bronze medal was won by Yvonne van Gennip of The Netherlands, the 1988 triple Olympic gold medalist.

In the separate world sprint championships, at Heerenveen, Neth., on February 25–26, Igor Zhelezovsky of the U.S.S.R. gained the men's crown, equaling the world record time of 1 min 12.58 sec for the 1,000 m. Jens-Uwe Mey of East Germany placed second, and another Soviet racer, Andrey Bakhvalov, finished third. Bonnie Blair took the women's title for the U.S., followed by Christa Rothenburger Luding of East Germany and Seiko Hashimoto of Japan.

The third World Cup series was dominated by East Germans, who won six of the eight distances. Winners of the men's events were Mey (500 and 1,000 m), Eric Flaim of the U.S. (1,500 m), and Kemkers (5,000). The successful women were Luding (500 m), Angela Hauck (1,000 m), Moser (1,500 m), and Heike Schalling (3,000).

(HOWARD BASS)

LAWN BOWLS

Scotland's Richard Corsie, at the age of 22, won the Embassy world indoor championship in Preston, England, in March 1989 to give credibility to the assertion that level-green bowling was no longer a game just for those of advanced years. Indoor bowls was being played extensively throughout the United Kingdom by all its leading lawn bowlers, and to win the title Corsie defeated fellow Scotsman Willie Wood, runner-up to David Bryant at the last four annual world outdoor championships. Bryant was also among the competitors, who included bowlers from the British Isles, Australia, New Zealand, Hong Kong, and Zimbabwe.

England and Australia, each of which had at least half a million players, continued to be the strongest of the bowling countries, and they dominated the year's two principal events, the Mazda Pacific Championships held in Suva, Fiji, and England's annual Woolwich International Masters. Eleven nations, including the U.S. and Canada, competed for the Pacific titles. Australia won all four of the men's events as Rob Farrella scored a double by taking the singles and then the pairs with Dennis Katurarich. Millie Khan (New Zealand) won the women's singles.

Bryant once again dominated the Woolwich International Masters, defeating Wood in the final at Worthing in June—a repeat of the last world championships in New Zealand in 1988. Ken Williams (Australia) ousted John Ottaway (England), who later in the year won the English singles title. Japie Deventer of Zambia outbowled Garin Beare of Zimbabwe to win the gold medal at the 1989 African States championships held in Zambia in May.

(DONALD J. NEWBY)

MOTORBOATING

What could easily be dubbed a year of firsts in U.S. boat racing, the 1989 season of the American Power Boat Association (APBA) was one to liven up the pages of the history books. The unexpected, the unusual, and the unforeseen were truly the buzzwords of the year.

Because of a driver change in the *Miss Budweiser* Unlimited hydroplane camp halfway through the 1989 season, for the first time in 14 years the U.S. champion driver did not drive the champion boat. With Jim Kropfeld driving the first half of the season and Tom D'Eath piloting the second, *Miss Budweiser* scored more than 11,000 total points to take the boat title, while the driver championship went to *Circus Circus* pilot Chip Hanauer. Although Hanauer won the driver title, he was not as successful in his quest for the coveted APBA Gold Cup. Trying for his eighth consecutive Gold Cup win, he suffered a loss of power in his rig in the race's final heat, and D'Eath scored a down-to-the-wire win in *Miss Budweiser*.

In the APBA's U.S. Formula One circuit, endurance and consistency were the key factors in 1989. While not necessarily having the upper hand on speed, North Carolina's Buck Thornton put his equipment to the durability test and won the series championship. He won only two of the season's six events but finished every race.

Competing in his first full year of APBA Offshore racing, Charles Marks clinched the Superboat national championship before he even entered the last race of the season, earning six first-place finishes and 2,656 total points. However, in the Offshore world championships gear problems kept him from the winner's circle, and Pete Markey won the title.

Prior to the last race of the 1989 APBA International Outboard Grand Prix (IOGP) circuit, only seven points

separated the top five drivers who were vying for the title in the series' Champ Boat class. When the final Champ race was completed, however, only one driver stood out from the rest in the points standings: Billy Seebold in his *Bud Light* tunnel hull. The SST-140 series title went to Mark Miller, who won four of the five series events. In the closely contested Mod VP class, Rusty Campbell won his third straight championship, this time by only a two-point margin.

(RENEE MAHN OLEJNIK)

POLO

Europe's premier international tournament, for the Coronation Cup and the Silver Jubilee Cup, took place in Windsor, England, in July and was attended by an estimated 27,000 people, an all-time record. For the Coronation Cup, England (A. Hine, J. Hipwood, A. Kent, and Lord C. Beresford) produced a workmanlike performance to win 7–5 against Australasia (J. Gould, C. Forsyth, S. Mackenzie, and J. Gilmore). In a much more exciting supporting contest for the Silver Jubilee Cup, North America (R. Gonzales, M. Azzarro, O. Rinehart, and D. Smicklas) turned in a scintillating team performance to defeat the Prince of Wales's team (H. Galindo, C. Gracida, E. Trotz, and the Prince of Wales) 7–6.

Some of the best polo seen in Great Britain in more than 50 years took place when Buenos Aires (P. Merlos, J. Badiola, E. Trotz, and E. Heguy) drew 6–6 with The Rest of the World (M. Azzarro, G. Donoso, O. Rinehart, and H. Hipwood).

In the much-publicized 14-goal world championships, held in West Berlin in August, the U.S. (J. Arellano, J. Wigdahl, C. Bostwick, and H. Schwartz) became world champions by defeating Hurlingham (representing Great Britain; A. Brodie, W. Lucas, J. Lucas, and J. Dixon). The most surprising result of this competition was the 9–6 defeat of Argentina by Hurlingham in the semifinals. In a women's international tournament held in England, a Rest of the World team defeated Great Britain 3½–3.

(COLIN J. CROSS)

RODEO

Discord was the byword in the Professional Rodeo Cowboys Association (PRCA) during 1989. A Texas group, known as PRCA-Texas, tried unsuccessfully to merge with the PRCA and thereby gain influence and promote changes in the structure and management of professional rodeo. The ill-fated plan was conceived by a group of dissatisfied PRCA members who felt that the organization did not concern itself enough with the welfare of the cowboys who participate in rodeo.

In 1985 the National Finals Rodeo was moved from Oklahoma City, Okla., to Las Vegas, Nev. The move was one of the reasons that the prize money increased from $901,000 to $1.8 million. The prize money for the 1989 NFR grew to $2.3 million, and an agreement signed in 1989 assured that the finals would continue to be held in Las Vegas until at least 1995.

The star of the 1989 National Finals was all-around champion Ty Murray of Odessa, Texas. He competed in two events at the finals, saddle bronc riding and bareback riding. His prize money there, added to his year-long winnings in those events plus bull riding, earned him $134,806. At 20 years of age Murray became the youngest man ever to win the all-around title. (The prestigious championship goes to the cowboy who wins the most money throughout the season in two or more events.) Other 1989 champions included Clint Johnson, Spearfish, S.D., $89,687 in saddle bronc riding (his fourth championship); Marvin Garrett,

Gillette, Wyo., $105,931 in bareback riding (second title); Richard ("Tuff") Hedeman, Bowie, Texas, $122,765 in bull riding (second title); Rabe Rabon, San Antonio, Fla., $89,301 in calf roping; John W. Jones, Jr., Morro Bay, Calif., $94,304 in steer wrestling (third championship); Jake Barnes, Bloomfield, N.M., and Clay O'Brien Cooper, Gilbert, Ariz., $90,455 each in team roping (fifth consecutive title); and Charmayne James Rodman, Galt, Calif., $96,651 in barrel racing (sixth consecutive world championship).

The 1989 single steer roping champion was Guy Allen of Lovington, N.M. He earned $44,386 during the year and won the championship at the National Finals Steer Roping in Guthrie, Okla.

At the International Professional Rodeo Association finals, held in January 1989 in Tulsa, Okla., Dan Dailey of Peaster, Texas, won his 11th all-around title and became the all-around champion for the IPRA for 1988. The Canadian Professional Rodeo Association all-around championship was won by Duane Daines of Innisfail, Alta. He won $22,242 and placed ninth in the PRCA standings with $51,204.

The 1989 National Intercollegiate Rodeo Association men's all-around champion was Murray. The women's all-around title was won by Cathy Dennis.

Tragedy marked the year in professional rodeo when 1987 PRCA bull-riding champion Lane Frost was killed by a bull at the Cheyenne (Wyo.) Frontier Days Rodeo. Frost had successfully ridden the bull to a second-place 85-point score but was gored and trampled before he could get away.

(DARRELL ARNOLD)

ROWING

East Germany regained its supremacy in world rowing in 1989 with seven titles in open competition. Romania and West Germany followed with three championships each, and the other nations in the top 10 in world ranking included Italy, The Netherlands, the United States, China, Austria, Norway, and Great Britain. East Germany dominated men's and women's open rowing, while West Germany and the U.S. did likewise in men's and women's lightweight classes.

In the world championships on Lake Bled, Yugos., 22 nations won medals in the 22 events. In the men's open events, East Germany's outstanding new coxless pair—Thomas Jung and Uwe Kellner—outclassed their opponents; Thomas Lange of East Germany repeated his 1988 Olympic Games triumph in single sculls; and in coxless fours the East Germans narrowly denied the fast-finishing U.S. the title by 0.98 sec.

The Netherlands was involved in the closest men's final, holding off Italy by 0.27 sec in quadruple sculls, but the Dutch rowers had to give way to Norway in double sculls by 1.28 sec. Romania was less hard pressed in winning the coxed fours, while the Italian brothers Carmine and Giuseppe Abbagnale added the coxed pairs to their four previous world titles and two Olympic championships. In eights West Germany defeated East Germany and Great Britain.

East Germany and Romania dominated the women's open events, taking all but two silver and three bronze of the available medals. East Germany defeated China by 2.64 sec in the new coxless fours event (which replaced coxed fours) and was also a clear winner over Romania in coxless pairs and double sculls and over the Soviet Union in quadruple sculls. Romania narrowly turned the tables in eights, however, defeating East Germany by 0.27 sec, and also won the single sculls.

The West Germans stole the limelight in men's lightweight events with two gold and two bronze medals. They defeated Italy in coxless fours and Switzerland in double sculls. Austria was pushed to the limit to capture the double sculls from Spain by 0.20 sec. The Netherlands won the single sculls.

The U.S. and China were the stars of the women's lightweight events. China fulfilled expectations by retaining the coxless fours, beating Great Britain by 3.18 sec. In sculls the U.S. was more than two seconds faster than Belgium in singles and New Zealand in doubles.

The world junior championships in Szeged, Hung., attracted 28 nations, of which a dozen won medals. East Germany and the Soviet Union took five of the men's titles, with the remainder going to Great Britain, West Germany, and Yugoslavia. East Germany dominated the women's events with four winners, leaving the two other titles to Australia and the Soviet Union.

In England the Henley Royal Regatta celebrated its 150th anniversary with a record entry of more than 400 crews, including 60 from the U.S. Only four trophies went overseas. Finalists broke records in ten events headed by the Hansa Dortmund eight from West Germany, who won the Grand Challenge Cup and later became world champions. Italy took the Queen Mother Cup (quadruple sculls), and the double sculls went to The Netherlands; in the Diamond Sculls, Vaclav Chalupa of Czechoslovakia became the first Henley winner from his country.

In the 135th University Boat Race, Oxford won against expectations by 2½ lengths to close the Cambridge lead in the series to 69–65 with one dead heat.   (KEITH OSBORNE)

SAILING

The Admirals Cup returned to Britain in 1989. The winning three-yacht team consisted of Alan Gray's Farr-designed 50-footer *Jamarella,* Mike Peacock's Castro-designed 45-footer *Juno IV,* and Graham Walker's Andrieu one-tonner *Indulgence VII.* On their way to victory the British encountered a tough fight from the Danish and U.S. teams, and the result might have been different had those two teams not suffered crippling breakages on leading yachts. The New Zealanders and West Germans did not quite live up to their reputations. A total of 14 teams competed for the cup, fewer than in previous years. There were a good number of new yachts spread among the teams.

The America's Cup's future continued to languish in U.S. courts; the New Zealanders took first blood in the courts, but on appeal the U.S. victory was upheld. New

Class	Winner	Class	Winner
Albacore	John Clark (Canada)	Laser	Glenn Bourke (Australia)
Contender	Steve Daniel (United Kingdom)	Laser 2	Chris Hancock (Canada)
Dragon	Poul Hoj-Jenson (Denmark)	OK	Per Haggstrom (Sweden)
Europe (women)	Chiara Calligaris (Italy)	Star	Alan Alder (Brazil)
Fireball	John Dransfield (Australia)	6 Metre	John Kostecki (United States)
Flying Dutchman	Albert Batzill (West Germany)	Tasar	Charlie McKee (United States)
505	Krister Bergstrom (Sweden)	¼ Ton	Pompeo Businello (Italy)
470 (men)	Tao Tsutsumi (Japan)	½ Ton	Alain Pointet (France)
470 (women)	Susan Meyer (West Germany)	1 Ton	Pasquale Landolfi (Italy)
Hornet	Chris Vine (United Kingdom)	50 Footers	Rich DeVos (Sweden)
INT 14	Neal McDonald (United Kingdom)	Maxi	Gianni Barasi (Italy)
J24	Larry Klein (United States)		

1989 World Class Boat Champions

Zealand announced that it would appeal that ruling to New York state's highest court; a decision was not expected until well into 1990. Meanwhile, within the new America's Cup rules, testing of new designs by some 20 potential challengers and defenders was under way. However, with no firm date or place established for the next series, little interest in building new yachts was shown.

The world match race championship was held in Christchurch Bay off the south coast of England on September 6–9. Chris Dickson, New Zealand's reigning world champion, retained his title but only after the mast of Peter Gilmour, winner of the first race, broke in two places. While leading in the second race in his Beneteau Europe class boat, Gilmour, of Australia, attempted a jibe, spinnaker set at the wing mark of the triangular course; however, the spinnaker filled before the running backstay was set to stabilize the mast, and the mast collapsed. With several masts coming down in this and earlier competitions, the mast design of this new class appeared to leave little margin for error.

The Whitbread Round the World race began on September 2 at Plymouth, England. In the first leg Peter Blake's *Steinlager II* from New Zealand appeared to be in a class of its own and, assuming it did not suffer any serious breakages, would finish back in England again in May 1990 with a huge lead. Pierre Fehlmann's Swiss entry *Merit* was a distant second, followed by the second New Zealand yacht, *Fisher and Paykel,* and Britain's *Rothmans.*

AP/WIDE WORLD

The yacht *Thursday's Child* heads toward San Francisco's Golden Gate Bridge. With a crew of three, *Thursday's Child* broke the 135-year-old New York–San Francisco sailing record of 89 days 8 hours by completing the trip in just 81 days.

The death on September 7 of Tom Blackaller of the U.S. at the age of 49 robbed the yachting world of one of its most colourful and talented racing skippers. His most recent success was sailing the U.S. Admirals Cup yacht *Great News* to victory in the Fastnet race. In earlier years he had won world titles in both the Star and 6 Metre classes and raced yachts in several America's Cup series.

(ADRIAN JARDINE)

SKIING

A continuing upsurge of recreational skiing in 1989 featured a marked increase of transatlantic package holidays in both directions, considerably widening the choice of terrain for many enthusiasts. Worldwide television coverage of world championships and World Cup events, both alpine and Nordic, enhanced awareness and support of top-flight competition.

Alpine Racing. Opened by former U.S. president Gerald Ford against a spectacular backdrop of the Colorado Rockies, the world alpine ski championships—the first in 39 years in which the U.S. acted as host—took place at Vail and Beaver Creek, Colo., from January 29 to February 12. Eight nations shared the medals in five men's and five women's events. A mouse that roared to defy the might of Switzerland was West Germany's Hansjoerg Tauscher, who surprisingly snatched the men's downhill crown. While the big names faltered and faded, Rudolf Nierlich of Austria asserted his claim to greatness by becoming Vail's only double gold medalist, in the giant slalom and slalom. Martin Hangl of Switzerland took the supergiant slalom, outpacing compatriot Pirmin Zurbriggen, who was hampered by a training injury. The alpine combination predictably went to Luxembourg's Marc Girardelli, who used his physical strength and unorthodox stance to telling effect.

Maria Walliser convincingly retained the women's downhill title, and her fellow Swiss Vreni Schneider became undisputed queen of the championships after a masterly and decisive giant slalom victory; she had already placed second in the slalom, behind Mateja Svet of Yugoslavia, and in the combination, in which Tamara McKinney thrilled appreciative crowds with a popular victory for the home country. Ulrike Maier won the supergiant slalom for Austria with only 0.03 sec to spare over her more experienced compatriot Sigrid Wolf.

Girardelli and Schneider were impressive overall winners in the 23rd Alpine World Cup series, which overcame an unusually mild winter with the help of snowmaking machines. Girardelli, the 1985 and 1986 victor, achieved the unique feat of race wins in all four disciplines and secured the prestige downhill crown as well as the overall title, beating defender Zurbriggen by 98 points. Alberto Tomba of Italy finished third. Dominating the women's events, Schneider became the first skier to win all seven slaloms in a season. Her 14 victories in the series, including six giant slaloms and one combined event, beat the previous record of 13 set by Sweden's Ingemar Stenmark in 1979. Eleven of Schneider's wins were consecutive, surpassing by one the previous best run, by Annemarie Moser-Proell of Austria in 1973. Schneider finished 115 points ahead of Walliser, with defending cup holder Michela Figini third in a Swiss sweep of the event. Stenmark skied the final race of his career in March after earlier extending his record number of race wins to 86, spanning 16 seasons. The concurrently decided Nations' Cup for men and women was won by Switzerland for a seventh consecutive year, with Austria runner-up and West Germany third.

Nordic Events. Home skiers gained the lion's share of medals, 15 out of 45, in the 37th Nordic world champi-

Lars-Boerje Eriksson of Sweden shoots past a gate in the men's Super G race of the World Cup in Aspen, Colorado. Eriksson, whose winning time of 1:17.98 brought him his first World Cup victory, became the first Swede to win a World Cup speed event.
AFP PHOTO

onships, on February 17–26 at Lahti, Fin., but the most successful individual was a Swede, Gunde Svan, who won three golds, in the 50-km and 15-km freestyle cross-country events and as a member of his country's 4 × 10-km relay team. The classical 15 km went to Finland's Harri Kirvesniemi and the 30 km to the Soviet racer Vladimir Smirnov.

In the women's 15-km classical event, Marjo Matikainen edged out her fellow Finn Marja-Liisa Kirvesniemi, who had won the 10 km on the opening day. Elena Valbe of the U.S.S.R. won both freestyle events, 10 km and 30 km. Matikainen, on the winning 4 × 5-km relay team, also collected a silver and two bronze medals to become the first skier to collect five medals at the same world Nordic championships.

Jens Weissflog of East Germany was declared winner of the 70-m ski jump with the best first-round mark; the second round was subsequently wiped out by a combination of fog and wind. Jari Puikkonen of Finland won the high-hill 90-m jump, denying runner-up Weissflog a double victory. Finland won the team jumping. The individual and team combination events went to Trond Einar Elden and his Norwegian team.

In the 10th Nordic World Cup series for cross-country racing, Svan retained the men's title, ahead of Norway's Vegard Ulvang and another Swede, Torgny Mogren. The women's prize was won by Valbe, followed by Alzbeta Hovrancikova of Czechoslovakia and Tamara Tikhonova of the U.S.S.R. The U.S.S.R. won the Nations' Cup, with Norway runner-up and Sweden third. Jan Boklöv of Sweden was victor in the jumping World Cup series, with Weissflog placing second.

Other Events. The world biathlon championships, in February at Freistitz, Austria, produced individual men's victories for Frank Luck of East Germany (10 km) and Erik Kvalfoss of Norway (20 km). The top women were Anne Elvebækk of Norway (7.5 km) and West Germany's Petra Schaaf (15 km).

The world championships in freestyle skiing, held in March at Oberjoch, West Germany, resulted in men's and women's overall victories for, respectively, Chris Simboli of Canada and Melanie Palenik of the U.S.

(HOWARD BASS)

SQUASH RACKETS

After several years in a supporting role, Martine Le Moignan, from Guernsey, captured for England the 1989 women's world individual squash rackets title from Susan Devoy of Rotorua, N.Z., who had been unbeaten in world-level competition since 1985. Seeded third in the tournament, held in The Netherlands in March, Le Moignan overcame Sarah FitzGerald in the semifinals before beating Devoy; earlier, Le Moignan had served notice of her improvement by winning the British national championship in December 1988. England also won the world team championship, defeating Australia in the final. However, Devoy gained revenge in the final of the British Open in April 1989 when she beat Le Moignan to secure her sixth consecutive British Open title. In August England completed a clean sweep of world titles by winning the world junior women's championship in New Zealand; Donna Vardy of England beat Lynora Hati of New Zealand to take the individual crown.

The main question in men's competition in the spring was whether Pakistan's Jahangir Khan could win his eighth British Open title and so equal the record held by Geoff Hunt from Australia. Since Hunt beat Jahangir in the 1981 final, the Pakistani had played seven different opponents and defeated them all. In 1989 that pattern was broken when his opponent of 1988, Rodney Martin from Sydney, Australia, again reached the final. In what turned out to be an exceedingly close match, Jahangir overcame an assertive opponent and the perceived (by Jahangir) shortcomings of the referee to eventually triumph over Martin. At the World Open in Kuala Lumpur, Malaysia, in October Jansher Khan of Pakistan defeated Australia's Chris Dittmar in the final; Dittmar had beaten Jahangir Khan in a semifinal. At the world team championships in Singapore, defending champion Pakistan lost its title to Australia 3–0 in the final.

On May 1 the rules of squash were amended by the International Squash Rackets Federation (ISRF). The main change was a fundamental one in that from that date players would not have a second serve if the first were a fault and so would lose the service to their opponent. Additionally, the time gap between most games was extended from a maximum of one minute to 90 seconds.

(ANDREW SHELLEY)

SWIMMING

After the 1988 Olympic Games, during which 17 world records were set, a letdown was expected in 1989, but no one anticipated that there would be so few new marks. Men and women swimmers could set only seven, and two of those were in the same event, the 200-m breaststroke; the first new mark in this event was tied before a new record was set. The expected decline in the number of new world records emphasized the general mediocrity of competition on the world scene. Most of the U.S. and European medalists retired or took a year's break from hard training.

The first world record of 1989 was set at the U.S. national championships at the University of Southern California. On August 3 Mike Barrowman of Rockville, Md., in the preliminaries, lowered by 0.44 sec—from 2 min 13.34 sec to 2 min 12.90 sec—the 200-m breaststroke record set by Victor Davis of Canada (*see* OBITUARIES) in the 1984 Olympic Games. On August 18, at the European championships in Bonn, West Germany, Nick Gillingham of the U.K. tied Barrowman's mark.

Two days later Barrowman took 0.01 sec off the record with a time of 2 min 12.89 sec in Tokyo during the Pan Pacific championships. His record, which was not recognized by the world governing body, was one of four set on the same day by U.S. swimmers. Janet Evans of Placentia, Calif., who won three gold medals at the 1988 Olympic Games, shaved nearly a second from her 1988 record in the 800-m freestyle, lowering the mark from 8 min 17.12 sec to 8 min 16.22 sec. Evans' record was the only one achieved by a woman in 1989. David Wharton of Warminster, Pa., lowered the 200-m individual medley world record to 2 min 0.11 sec, 0.06 sec under the 2 min 0.17 sec time set by Tomas Darnyi of Hungary in 1988. Finally, Thomas Jager of Collinsville, Ill., swam the 50-m freestyle in 22.12 sec to erase by 0.02 sec Matt Biondi's 1988 record of 22.14 sec.

Two world records were set at the European championships at Bonn. On August 15 Georgio Lamberti became the first male swimmer from Italy to set a world record, bettering the 200-m freestyle by 0.56 sec, from 1 min 47.25 sec to 1 min 46.69. The previous record was set by Duncan Armstrong of Australia in 1988. On the same day, Adrian Moorhouse of the U.K. lowered Steve Lundquist's 1988 100-m breaststroke record of 1 min 01.65 sec by 0.16 sec, to 1 min 01.49 sec.

The tournament was marked by the absence of Vladimir Salnikov, the Soviet holder of two world records, and by the failure of the traditionally dominant East German women to set a single world record. Though the East German women won 14 out of 16 events, France's Catherine Plewinski was the outstanding woman competitor, finishing first in the 50-m freestyle and the 100-m butterfly. The East German women won 14 gold, 6 silver, and 5 bronze medals. Anke Mohring of East Germany lowered the European record for the 400-m freestyle by 0.10 sec for a time of 4 min 5.84 sec.

In addition to his world record, Lamberti, the outstanding male swimmer, also set a European record of 49.24 sec, slicing 0.11 sec from the 100-m freestyle. He won his third gold by anchoring the Italian 4 × 200-m freestyle relay. Darnyi won three events, the 200-m and 400-m individual medleys and the 200-m butterfly, but with lacklustre

DAN HELMS—DUOMO

Mike Barrowman is ecstatic after hearing that he has just broken the world's record for the 200-m men's breaststroke. When his winning time of 2:12.90 was tied 15 days later, Barrowman responded two days after that with a time of 2:12.89.

World Swimming Records Set in 1989

Event	Name	Country	Time
	MEN		
50-m freestyle	Thomas Jager	U.S.	22.12 sec
200-m freestyle	Giorgio Lamberti	Italy	1 min 46.69 sec
100-m breaststroke	Adrian Moorhouse	U.K.	1 min 01.49 sec
200-m breaststroke	Mike Barrowman	U.S.	2 min 12.90 sec
200-m breaststroke	Nick Gillingham	U.K.	2 min 12.90 sec
200-m individual medley	David Wharton	U.S.	2 min 00.11 sec
	WOMEN		
800-m freestyle	Janet Evans	U.S.	8 min 16.22 sec

clockings. Italy led the medal count with four golds and two bronzes, Hungary won three golds and one bronze, while the Soviet Union took two golds, five silvers, and one bronze.

At the Pan Pacific championships the U.S. men won 13 gold, 11 silver, and 4 bronze medals in 14 individual and 3 relay events. Australia finished second with two golds, three silvers, and three bronzes. In women's competition the U.S. won 10 golds, 7 silvers, and 8 bronzes. China surprised many observers by garnering three golds, three silvers, and four bronzes, followed by Canada with two golds, three silvers, and one bronze.

The U.S. defeated the Soviet Union 201–136 in a dual meet at Atlanta, Ga., in August. It was the sixth victory for the Americans in the six dual competitions between the two nations. Janet Evans became the first woman in the dual meet series to win three individual events. The U.S. won 22 of the 30 events.

With the exception of Barrowman's record performance in the U.S. national championships at Los Angeles, mediocre swims were the rule in almost every event. Wharton broke his U.S. record in the 400-m individual medley with a time of 4 min 15.93 sec, 0.19 sec faster than his two-year-old record. Evans captured four titles, winning the 400-m and 800-m freestyles and the 200-m and 400-m individual medleys.

Diving. At the U.S. national outdoor diving championships at Raleigh, N.C., in August, Wendy Lucero of Aurora, Colo., and Kent Ferguson of Boca Raton, Fla., won the 3-m springboard events. Matt Scoggin of Great Falls, Va., and Wendy Wyland of Boca Raton successfully defended their 10-m platform championships.

Divers from China swept all four events at the Australian international meet in February at Brisbane. In the men's competition Wang Yijie won the 3-m springboard and Tu Junhui the 10-m platform. Lin Xiaoni won the women's 3-m springboard and Chen Xiaodan the 10-m platform. China won three of four events in the World Diving Cup at Indianapolis, Ind., in May. In the men's events Tan Liangde was the 3-m springboard champion, and Xiong Ni won the platform. Gao Min won the women's 3-m springboard and Wendy Williams of Bridgeton, Mo., the platform. At a triangular meet with China and the Soviet Union in Fort Lauderdale, Fla., in May, Kent Ferguson of the U.S. defeated Tan for the 3-m springboard crown, and Scoggin outpointed Vladimir Timoshinin of the Soviet Union for the platform title. China swept the women's events, Gao taking the springboard and Chen the platform.

The Soviets and East Germans dominated the women's events in the European championships. Marina Babkova of the U.S.S.R. won the 3-m springboard on her last dive, scoring 514.23 points to 510.72 for Brita Baldus of East Germany. Ute Wetzig of East Germany won the platform over Inga Afonina of the U.S.S.R. Albin Killat of West Germany outpointed Aleksandr Gladchenko of the U.S.S.R for the men's 3-m springboard title, and Georgiy

Chogovadze of the Soviet Union won his second straight European platform championship, coming from behind to overtake Jan Hempel of East Germany 639.69–578.43.

Synchronized Swimming. Swimmers from Walnut Creek, Calif., won two of three events in the U.S. national synchronized championships at Durham, N.C., on March 27–April 3. Kristen Babb won the solo event and then paired with Tracy Long to win the duet. Santa Clara won the trio event. Walnut Creek won the team title. Thirteen countries competed in the first junior world championships at Cali, Colombia, in July. Becky Dryoen of the U.S. won the solo and, with Jill Suddeth, the duet. The U.S. won the team title.

At the fourth Synchronized Swimming World Cup in Paris in September, Long led the U.S. to victories in all three events. In the solo event she outpointed Sylvie Frechette of Canada 192.64 to 192.40. Mikako Kotani of Japan was third at 191.76. Long and Michelle Svitenko won the duet over Japan's Kotani and Aki Takayama 191.03 to 190.03. The Canadian duo of Frechette and Nathalie Guzey placed third with 189.45. The U.S. won the team championship, narrowly defeating Canada 188.94 to 188.86. Japan was third with 186.70.

In the European championships Karine Schuler of France missed a clean sweep by less than two points. Khristina Falasinidi of the U.S.S.R. became the first Soviet gold medal winner in the sport, scoring 184.56 to Schuler's 182.87. In the duet Schuler and Marianne Aeschbacker outpointed the Soviet Union's Maria Cherniaeva and Elena Forschevskaia 182.502–179.970. In the team event France scored 180.365 to the U.S.S.R.'s 179.945.

(ALBERT SCHOENFIELD)

TABLE TENNIS

The biennial world championships got under way in Dortmund, West Germany, in April. The men's team from Sweden finished ahead of China and was awarded the Swaythling Cup. North Korea was third. China captured the women's team title and received the Marcel Corbillon Cup. South Korea was runner-up and Hong Kong third. In individual competitions, Jan-Ove Waldner (Sweden) won the men's singles championship and Qiao Hong (China) the women's. West Germany won the men's doubles, China the women's doubles, and South Korea the mixed doubles. During the tournament the International Table Tennis Federation ruled that the Swaythling Cup would no longer be decided by the best-of-nine singles matches. Instead, there would be one doubles and four singles matches involving three players on each team.

In September the 16 top-ranked men players in the world met for World Cup play in Nairobi, Kenya. In the final, Ma Wenge (China) defeated Andrzej Grubba (Poland) in five sets. Mikael Applegren (Sweden) earned third place with a victory over Jean-Michel Saive (Belgium). The Commonwealth tournament was dominated by Hong Kong and England. (ARTHUR KINGSLEY VINT)

1989 Table Tennis World Rankings

MEN	WOMEN
1. Jan-Ove Waldner (Sweden)	1. Qiao Hong (China)
2. Jorgen Persson (Sweden)	2. Chen Jing (China)
3. Andrzej Grubba (Poland)	3. Li Bun Hui (North Korea)
4. Jiang Jialiang (China)	4. Hyun Jung Hwa (South Korea)
5. Yoo Nam Kyu (South Korea)	5. Chen Zihe (China)
6. Mikael Appelgren (Sweden)	6. Li Huifen (China)
7. Erik Lindh (Sweden)	7. Daniela Guergueltcheva (Bulgaria)
8. Chen Yongcan (China)	8. Li Jun (China)
9. Yu Shentong (China)	9. Csilla Batorfi (Hungary)
10. Teng Yi (China)	10. Olga Nemes (West Germany)

TENNIS

A radical change in the administration of men's tennis took place in 1989. The Association of Tennis Professionals, founded in 1972, withdrew from the Men's Tennis Council (MTC), the tripartite body that controlled Grand Prix tournaments and that consisted of ATP, the International Tennis Federation (ITF), and representative tournament organizers. ATP organized its own series for 1990 and signed a five-year agreement with the International Management Group, a commercial concern. IMG, manager of many leading players, guaranteed a minimum $56,100,100 sponsorship for the first three years.

The authority of the ITF, for 76 years the world governing body, was diminished by the change. It retained control of the four Grand Slam tournaments—the championships of Australia, France, Wimbledon, and the U.S.—as well as the Davis Cup. Its membership grew to 157. South Africa, a founding member, was suspended. Brian Tobin (Australia) was appointed as the ITF's first executive vice president.

The possibility loomed of a difference in rules between tournaments. The women's game was not affected. The MTC dissolved itself at the end of the year.

Men's Competition. Mats Wilander of Sweden, the 1988 winner of the Australian, French, and U.S. championships, was designated "world champion" for 1989. During the year, however, he failed to match his previous performance, losing all three titles and reaching the quarterfinals only in the French and Wimbledon events.

The Australian title was won by Ivan Lendl (Czech.) for the first time. Lendl beat John McEnroe (U.S.) 7–6, 6–2, 7–6 in the quarterfinals, Thomas Muster (Austria) 6–2, 6–

REUTERS/BETTMANN NEWSPHOTOS

Tennis champ Chris Evert bids her fans farewell at the U.S. Open after playing the last match of her career. During her 19 years of professional play, "Chrissy" won 18 Grand Slam titles. She also set an unequaled match record of 1,304–145.

4, 5–7, 7–5 in the semifinals, and Miloslav Mecir (Czech.) 6–2, 6–2, 6–2 in the final. Stefan Edberg (Sweden), the 1985 and 1987 champion, defaulted to Muster in the quarterfinals. Wilander lost in the second round to Ramesh Krishnan (India).

Michael Chang (U.S.) was an unexpected winner of the French championship in Paris, where Andrey Chesnokov (U.S.S.R.) beat defending champion Wilander in the quarterfinals. Chang defeated Chesnokov 6–1, 5–7, 7–6, 7–5 in one semifinal, while in the other Edberg beat Boris Becker (West Germany) 6–3, 6–4, 5–7, 3–6, 6–2. Chang then defeated Edberg in the final 6–1, 3–6, 4–6, 6–4, 6–2. At 17 years 111 days he was the youngest champion of the French tournament.

Becker won the Wimbledon championship in London for the third time since 1985. Lendl did not fulfill his top seeding when Becker beat him 7–5, 6–7, 2–6, 6–4, 6–3 in the semifinals. McEnroe defeated Wilander 7–6, 3–6, 6–3, 6–4 in the quarterfinals but then lost in his semifinal to Edberg 7–5, 7–6, 7–6. In the final Becker beat Edberg 6–0, 7–6, 6–4 to reverse the result of 1988.

Becker went on to win the U.S. Open at Flushing Meadows in New York City for the first time. He survived a perilous second-round contest when he saved two match points in the fourth set in his defeat of Derrick Rostagno (U.S.) 1–6, 6–7, 6–3, 7–6, 6–3. Subsequently, he beat Yannick Noah (France) 6–3, 6–3, 6–2 in the quarterfinals; Aaron Krickstein (U.S.) 6–4, 6–3, 6–4 in the semifinals; and Lendl 7–6, 1–6, 6–3, 7–6 in the final. Lendl, the champion from 1985 through 1987, was in the final for the eighth successive year. In the quarterfinals he beat Tim Mayotte (U.S.) 6–4, 6–0, 6–1 and in the semifinals Andre Agassi (U.S.) 7–6, 6–1, 3–6, 6–1. Jimmy Connors (U.S.), champion in 1974, 1976, 1978, 1982, and 1983, reached the quarterfinals, where Agassi beat him 6–1, 4–6, 0–6, 6–3, 6–4. Pete Sampras (U.S.) defeated Wilander 5–7, 6–3, 1–6, 6–1, 6–4 in the second round.

In the men's doubles Rick Leach (U.S.) and Jim Pugh (U.S.) had the best record in the four top tournaments. They won the Australian title and placed second at Wimbledon. McEnroe won the U.S. title with Mark Woodforde (Australia), his first Grand Slam success since 1984. Patrick McEnroe, John's brother, won the French title with Jim Grabb (U.S.). John Fitzgerald (Australia) and Anders Jarryd (Sweden) were first-time Wimbledon champions.

A record 79 nations competed in the Davis Cup tournament. Belgium, Ghana, Chile, and Pakistan won their section finals to gain promotion from Group II to Group I in their zones. Switzerland, Hungary, Great Britain, The Netherlands, Peru, Argentina, New Zealand, and South Korea won sections to earn entry to the qualifying round for the World Group. In a change of format they competed against the first-round losers in the World Group for eight vacant places in the 1990 competition. The nations who thus qualified were Argentina, Switzerland, Australia, Israel, Italy, New Zealand, the U.S.S.R., and The Netherlands. Great Britain lost 3–2 to Argentina to be denied access to the top group for the third year.

West Germany, the defending champion, and Sweden dominated the 16 nations in the World Group. Austria beat Australia, not at full strength, 5–0 in the first round. In the quarterfinals Sweden defeated Austria 3–2, Yugoslavia triumphed over Spain 4–1, the U.S. beat France 5–0, and West Germany defeated Czechoslovakia 3–2. In the semifinals Sweden beat Yugoslavia 4–1, and West Germany defeated the U.S. 3–2 to qualify for the final.

West Germany won its second consecutive Davis Cup, defeating Sweden 3–2 at Stuttgart, West Germany, in De-

Michael Chang of the U.S. is exuberant after beating Sweden's Stefan Edberg in the final match of the French Open. The 17-year-old Chang was the first American to win the French championship since Tony Trabert in 1955.

VANDYSTADT—ALLSPORT

cember. Becker won both of his singles matches, 6–2, 6–2, 6–4 over Edberg and 6–2, 6–0, 6–2 over Wilander. He teamed with Eric Jelen to win the doubles in five sets over Anders Jarryd and Jan Gunnarsson.

Women's Competition. Steffi Graf of West Germany, the designated world champion of 1988, was again the dominant player and won three of the four major championships. Martina Navratilova (U.S.) failed to win back her former top status. Chris Evert (U.S.) competed at Wimbledon for the 18th successive year and in the U.S. Open for the 19th. After the latter tournament she indicated that 1989 would be her last year of competition.

Graf won the Australian championship for the second year. In the semifinal she beat Gabriela Sabatini (Arg.) 6–3, 6–0, and then in the final she defeated Helena Sukova (Czech.) 6–4, 6–4. She lost no set in any round.

Graf's failure to retain her French title was a major upset. She beat Monica Seles (Yugos.) 6–3, 3–6, 6–3 in the semifinals after her 15-year-old opponent beat Manuela Maleeva (Bulg.) 6–3, 7–5 in the quarterfinals. Graf's unexpected opponent in the final was Arantxa Sánchez Vicario (Spain), who had a quarterfinal win against Jana Novotna (Czech.) 6–2, 6–2 and a semifinal triumph over Mary Joe Fernandez (U.S.) 6–2, 6–2. In the final Sánchez Vicario beat Graf 7–6, 3–6, 7–5, the most surprising result of the season. At 17 years 175 days she joined the men's champion, Chang, in being the youngest winner of that tournament on record.

Graf reasserted her supremacy at Wimbledon, where she was champion for the second year in a row. She beat

Sánchez Vicario in the quarterfinals 7–5, 6–1 and Evert 6–2, 6–1 in the semifinals, reaching the final without the loss of a set. Navratilova was again her opponent and, with eight titles to her credit, was there for the 10th time. As in 1988, Graf won in three sets, 6–1, 6–7, 6–1.

Graf then won the U.S. Open, also for the second straight year. She was extended in the semifinals, where, despite a cramp, she beat Sabatini 3–6, 6–4, 6–2. Navratilova beat Maleeva 6–0 6–0 in the quarterfinals and Zina Garrison (U.S.) 7–6, 6–2 in the semifinals to reach the final for the seventh time. Graf then won the final 3–6, 7–5, 6–1 to gain the third of the four Grand Slam titles. A nostalgic match was the quarterfinal in which Garrison beat Evert 7–6, 6–2. In the previous round Evert, the champion from 1975 through 1978 and in 1980 and 1982, beat Seles 6–0, 6–2 for her 101st singles win in the tournament where she had played without a break from 1971.

In 19 years, since the age of 16, Evert achieved a consistently successful record. She won the Australian title twice, the French seven times, Wimbledon three, and the U.S. Open six times. In the Wightman Cup competition from 1971 to 1985, she won 26 of 26 singles matches, and in the Federation Cup she won 35 of 37 singles from 1977 to 1987. Her double-fisted backhand became orthodox as others followed her example. Her fine ball control, command of length, and cool temperament combined with impeccable sportsmanship to make her a universal favourite.

In doubles play Navratilova won two major titles, the Australian with Pam Shriver (U.S.) and the U.S. with Hana Mandlikova (Australia). Larisa Savchenko and Natalia Zvereva of the U.S.S.R. won the French title and finished second to Novotna and Sukova at Wimbledon.

The Federation Cup, held in Tokyo with 40 challengers, was won for the 13th time by the U.S. (Navratilova, Evert, Garrison, and Shriver) when they won five rounds without a loss. In the semifinals the U.S. beat the defending champion Czechoslovakia, and Spain defeated Australia. In the final the U.S. beat Spain (Sánchez Vicario, Conchita Martínez, each only 17 years old) 3–0.

In Williamsburg, Va., the U.S. (Lori McNeil, Fernandez, Jennifer Capriati, Betsy Nagelsen, Patty Fendick) beat Great Britain (Jo Durie, Sara Gomer, Clare Wood, Anne Hobbs) 9–7 to win the Wightman Cup for the 51st time in 61 contests. Capriati, at 13 years 168 days, was the youngest player ever to compete in the tournament; she won her singles match 6–0, 6–0. (LANCE TINGAY)

TRACK AND FIELD SPORTS

Despite keen competition throughout the year, the world's track and field athletes produced less excitement than in the previous two years. This was not surprising, however, 1987 being the year of the quadrennial world championships and 1988 that of the Olympic Games.

Men's International Competition. The World Cup competition in Barcelona, Spain, involved many of track and field's top athletes, but the unique structure of the meet limited the entry list. Nine teams participated, and each team was allowed only one contestant per event. The United States topped the men's results, outscoring a European team 133 to 127 with Great Britain (119) and East Germany (116½) in close pursuit. Africa (107), Americas (not including the U.S.; 97), Asia (68½), Spain (64½), and Oceania (64½) trailed.

Most of the outstanding performances during the year were recorded in invitational meets participating in the Grand Prix circuit. Certain meets are designated as Grand Prix contests and therefore are eligible to offer money to the high scorers. Points are earned by placing in the events

that are recognized by the Grand Prix (GP). Approximately half the regular events are designated GP events each year, with the other half so named the following year. The concluding meet of the circuit brings together the highest point scorers in each GP event. Leaders in each event earn cash prizes, and the athlete who scores the most points for the season earns an additional $25,000.

The overall winner in 1989 was Said Aouita of Morocco, who had won the circuit before and who added another world record in the process. The event was the 3,000-m run, a distance not contested in the Olympics. The old record, set by Henry Rono of Kenya in 1978, was considered by many as the toughest distance record to break. Aouita had come within striking distance at least four times earlier, and then on August 20 in Cologne, West Germany, he ran an all-out 7 min 29.45 sec to erase Rono's 7-min 32.1-sec mark. The veteran runner thus added a fourth world mark to go with his global bests at 1,500 m, 2,000 m, and 5,000 m. Another world record was produced at 3,000 m by another African runner. Peter Koech of Kenya covered the 3,000-m steeplechase in 8 min 5.35 sec at Stockholm on July 3. The previous record had, again, been set by Rono, whose time was just 0.05 sec slower.

Arturo Barrios, perhaps best known as a runner for his successes on the road, proved he could also win on the track. On August 18 in West Berlin he ran 25 times around a 400-m track in a time of 27 min 8.23 sec to lower the previous 10,000-m best of 27 min 13.81 sec by Fernando Mamede of Portugal. Barrios became the first Mexican to claim a world record in any track and field event other than the walks.

The sole world record by a U.S. athlete came by the narrowest of margins in the 110-m hurdles. The site was Zürich, Switz., where eight years earlier Renaldo Nehemiah of the U.S. set a hard-to-believe record of 12.93 sec before leaving track and field to try his talents as a professional football player. By 1989 he was back in track and doing well, but he was only a spectator as Roger Kingdom charged home in 12.92 sec. Kingdom had won Olympic gold medals in the hurdles in 1984 and 1988.

Only one field event saw record-breaking action. In the high jump Javier Sotomayor of Cuba early in the year set an indoor world record of 2.43 m (7 ft 11½ in) to match the outdoor mark he had set in 1988. The quest to be the first at eight feet thus continued until July 29, when

Sotomayor finally achieved that goal during a meet at San Juan, P.R.

Indoor competition produced world records in five events, the busiest of which was the pole vault. Soviet athletes continued to dominate the event. At the start of the year Sergey Bubka was the record holder and leader of the vaulters, as he had been for the past six years. However, he lost the honour of becoming the first to clear 6 m (19 ft 8¼) to teammate Rodion Gataullin, who improved his record to 6.02 m (19 ft 9 in). Bubka later reclaimed the record with a vault of 6.03 m (19 ft 9¼ in).

Only two world indoor running records were broken, both by non-U.S. athletes who either were attending or had graduated from U.S. colleges. Paul Ereng of Kenya and the University of Virginia sped through 800 m in 1 min 44.84 sec. Ireland's Marcus O'Sullivan, a graduate of Villanova University, scored with a world best in the 1,500 m, running this distance in 3 min 35.6 sec, en route to a nonrecord time of 3 min 51.66 sec in the mile. Sotomayor's 2.43-m high jump accounted for one of the field records, while the other fell to Randy Barnes of the U.S., who put the shot 22.66 m (74 ft 4¼ in).

As had been usual in post-Olympic years, the season was relatively modest in terms of high-quality performances. A number of stars of 1988 either stayed out of competition or trained less intensely. Such was the case of Carl Lewis, winner of four gold medals in the 1984 Olympics and two more in 1988. During the year he was not nearly as active. He ran only in relays for about half the season and obviously was not in top form in the individual events. He lost about as often as he won in the sprints. Even in the long jump, where he extended his unbeaten string to 62 meets, he was not at his best.

Women's International Competition. For women there was a significant decline in the quality of the performances in 1989. A major reason for this was the absence of both Florence Griffith Joyner and Jackie Joyner-Kersee. Between them they had collected five gold medals and one silver in the 1988 Olympics. Griffith Joyner retired, while sister-in-law Joyner-Kersee competed infrequently.

Other big stars were also missing, and for the first time in years there were no new women's world records in Olympic events. Best of the 1989 marks was the 4-min 15.61-sec mile by Paula Ivan of Romania. There is official approval of the mile, but it is not an Olympic event. Galina

Javier Sotomayor of Cuba clears the bar during the New York Games. At the Caribbean championships the following week, Sotomayor set a new world high-jump record of 2.44 metres (8 feet) and thus became the first man to break this long-standing barrier.

Chistyakova of the Soviet Union, holder of the long-jump record, triple jumped 14.52 m (47 ft 7¾ in) for a best-ever mark in a nonapproved event. The walkers were busy breaking the 5,000-m and 10,000-m records twice each. Kerry Saxby of Australia lowered both marks during the Southern Hemisphere's summer, but she lost them in June when Ileana Salvador of Italy walked the 5,000 m in 20 min 27.59 sec and the 10,000 m in 42 min 39.2 sec.

As with the men, the women of 1989 were not up to the 1988 standards. Competition was plentiful, however, and a frequent visitor to the victory stand was Ana Quirot of Cuba. Unable to attend the 1988 Olympics because of her nation's boycott, she had a 1989 season that combined quantity and quality, extending her string of consecutive wins to 33 races. Primarily an 800-m runner, Quirot won both the 400 m and 800 m in the World Cup, her time of 1 min 54.44 sec putting her third on the all-time 800-m listings. Teammate Silvia Costa achieved the fourth-best high jump ever with a leap of 2.03 m (6 ft 8¼ in).

Highlight of the indoor season was the world indoor championships in Budapest, where Elly van Hulst of The Netherlands lowered the 3,000-m mark to 8 min 33.82 séc. Outdoors the only international team meet was the World Cup. Leading the nine teams was East Germany with 124 points. The Soviet Union placed second with 106, followed by Americas (94), Europe (89), United States (84½), Asia (67½), Africa (58), Spain (48), and Oceania (40).

U.S. Competition. More than a dozen U.S. national records were set in 1989, including Barnes's world indoor title in the shot put and Kingdom's mark in the 110-m hurdles. Strangely, there were only two field-event records, the others coming from the track, with or without hurdles. Hollis Conway joined Barnes as an exception with his high jump of 2.37 m (7 ft 9¼ in). The six other indoor U.S. male records included Joe De Loach's 20.59 sec in the 200 m, Antonio McKay's 45.59 sec in the 400 m, 1 min 46.07 sec and 1 min 45.85 sec by Ocky Clark in the 800 m, and 7 min 39.94 sec by Steve Scott in the 3,000 m. Women's indoor marks were set by Dawn Sowell and Gwen Torrence (7.16 sec), Alice Brown (7.13 sec), and Gwen Torrence (7.10 sec, 7.07 sec) in the 60 m; Sowell, 22.87 sec in the 200 m; Diane Dixon, 51.77 sec in the 400 m; Kim McKenzie, 6.84 sec in the 50-m hurdles; Joyner-Kersee, 7.81 sec in the 60-m hurdles; and PattieSue Plumer, 14 min 59.99 sec for the 5,000 m.

Team competition generally reaches its peak in the National Collegiate Athletic Association tournament, and this was dramatically confirmed in the 1989 contest. For the first time in history both team titles, men's and women's, were won by the same school, Louisiana State University. LSU had no trouble in the women's division, which it won for the third time in a row. Heading the team was Sowell, who won three gold medals and earned two collegiate

Roger Kingdom of the U.S. takes his victory lap after setting a new world record in the 110-metre hurdles. Kingdom, a two-time Olympic champ, set the new record of 12.92 seconds during the Weltklasse track and field meet in Zürich, Switzerland.
AP/WIDE WORLD

records, running 10.78 sec in the 100 m, 22.04 sec in the 200, and running second in the 4 × 100-m relay. Sowell's 100-m time was the third fastest in history, trailing only Griffith Joyner and Evelyn Ashford. LSU won in a runaway, scoring 86 points to 47 for UCLA, 37 for Nebraska, 34 for Texas Southern, and 23 for Arizona. Men's competition was close, as LSU edged Texas A & M 53 to 51, with Florida getting 39, Oregon 36, and Texas 33. Hollis Conway, runner-up in the Olympic high jump, became holder of the national outdoor record when he cleared 2.38 m (7 ft 9¾ in).

At the other annual championships, TAC (the Athletics Congress), many of the best U.S. athletes did not attend. Among them were Lewis and DeLoach, both passing up the meet in their hometown (Houston, Texas). However, another Houston sprinter almost made their absence unimportant. He was Leroy Burrell, who came close to beating Lewis' U.S. record of 9.92 sec in the 100 m as he blazed home in 9.94 sec, making him the fourth fastest ever at that distance. Sandra Farmer-Patrick set a U.S. record of 53.75 sec in the 400-m hurdles on the same day that her husband won the same event in the men's division.

Off the Track. Much attention during the year was paid to the subject of drug abuse. Those found guilty suffered such penalties as suspensions and forfeiture of medals and records. The most prominent athlete involved was Ben Johnson. The Canadian sprinter won the 100 m in the 1988 Olympics in world-record time but was later found to have used banned substances. His victory was negated, as were his world records in the 100 m and indoor 60 m.

Table I. World 1989 Outdoor Records—Men

Event	Competitor and country	Performance
3,000-m steeplechase	Peter Koech (Kenya)	8 min 5.35 sec
3,000-m	Said Aouita (Morocco)	7 min 29.45 sec
10,000-m	Arturo Barrios (Mexico)	27 min 8.23 sec
110-m hurdles	Roger Kingdom (U.S.)	12.92 sec
High jump	Javier Sotomayor (Cuba)	2.44 m (8 ft)

Table II. World 1989 Outdoor Records—Women

Event	Competitor and country	Performance
One mile	Paula Ivan (Romania)	4 min 15.61 sec
5,000-m walk	Ileana Salvador (Italy)	20 min 27.59 sec
10,000-m walk	Ileana Salvador (Italy)	42 min 39.2 sec

Charges against Johnson were upheld in a special hearing in the Canadian courts.

Internationally, plans were made for the U.S. and the Soviet Union to check each other's drug-control procedures. Random testing was ordered for top athletes of each country.

Marathon Running and Cross Country. Kenya dominated the annual international men's cross country competition, winning the individual event and three of the four team races. John Ngugi of Kenya won the 12,000-m (7.43-mi) race for his fourth consecutive victory, and Kenya's men's team duplicated the four-in-a-row feat. The races, at Stavanger, Norway, also saw Annette Sergent of France winning her second title in the women's competition. Leading the men's junior race was Addis Abebe of Ethiopia, while Malin Overlof, a 16-year-old from Sweden, took home the women's junior trophy. Both junior team races were won by Kenya.

The U.S. men's cross country championships were won by Pat Porter for an unparalleled eighth time in a row, and Lynn Jennings won her third consecutive title. In college competition the winners were John Nuttall of Iowa State and Vicky Huber of Villanova. Iowa State won the men's team trophy, and Villanova took the women's.

Abebe Mekonnen of Ethiopia won the Boston marathon with a time of 2 hr 9 min 6 sec, and Ingrid Kristiansen of Norway was the women's champion in 2 hr 24 min 33 sec. In the New York City marathon the men's race was won by Juma Ikangaa of Tanzania in 2 hr 8 min 1 sec, lowering the course record by 12 seconds, while Kristiansen finished first for the women in 2 hr 25 min 30 sec. Douglas Wakiihuri of Kenya won the London marathon in 2 hr 9 min 3 sec, and Veronique Marot of England was the top runner for the women with a time of 2 hr 25 min 56 sec. Victors in the Chicago marathon were Paul Davies-Hale of the U.K. in 2 hr 11 min 25 sec for the men and Lisa Weidenbach of the U.S. in 2 hr 28 min 15 sec for the women. Ken Martin of the U.S. triumphed in the Pittsburgh (Pa.) marathon in 2 hr 15 min 28 sec, and Margaret Groos of the U.S. led the women home with a time of 2 hr 32 min 39 sec.   (BERT NELSON)

VOLLEYBALL

Cuba, which boycotted the 1988 Olympic Games, established itself in 1989 as the best team in both men's and women's volleyball. Cuba won both the men's and women's World Cup, held in Japan in November, and also won the men's and women's Norceca (North and Central America and the Caribbean) zone championships in July.

The Cuban men's national team was joined in its top world ranking by the Soviet Union, and strong showings were made by the men's national teams of Italy, The Netherlands, and Brazil. The U.S. men's team during the year underwent its greatest transition since it became established as a world volleyball powerhouse in 1984. The entire starting lineup of the 1988 Olympic champion team, including Karch Kiraly and Steve Timmons, left the team during the year. The U.S. did win its sixth consecutive USA Cup in June, defeating the Soviet Union (2nd), Brazil (3rd), and Korea (4th). The USA Cup marked the retirement of Kiraly and Timmons from amateur play.

The U.S. women's team also lost players in 1989 but was mostly affected by injuries to its remaining starters. Despite these difficulties, the U.S. defeated traditional favourites Cuba (2nd) and China (3rd) at the Canada Cup in March. The Soviet Union's national women's team (1988 Olympic gold medalist), China, and Japan remained strong during 1989.   (JENNIFER WALSH)

WEIGHT LIFTING

The 1989 world weight-lifting championships, held in Athens in September, became essentially a dual meet between the Soviet Union and Bulgaria. The Soviets won 5 of the 10 weight classes to 4 for Bulgaria. The other gold medal went to Naim Suleymanoglu of Turkey in the 60-kg (132-lb) class. Suleymanoglu was one of three 1988 Olympic Games champions to win gold medals. The others were Soviets Anatoly Khrapaty at 90 kg (198 lb) and super heavyweight Aleksandr Kurlovich.

Bulgaria and the Soviet Union each won 8 medals out of a possible 30. However, Bulgaria won the team title, outscoring the Soviets 411 to 407. The Soviets lost when Yury Zakharevich in the 110-kg (242-lb) class failed in the clean and jerk.

Winners of three medals were China and Romania, while East Germany and North Korea each won two and Cuba and Poland took one apiece. Great Britain's Andrew Davies finished second in the 110-kg class, the only lifter from a nonsocialist country to win a medal. Thirty-one countries competed. The best performance by a U.S. lifter was an eighth place for Richard Schutz in the 110-kg class.

The most impressive performance was a 415-kg (913-lb) total lift by Khrapaty. His effort equaled that of the 110-kg champion, Bulgaria's Petar Stefanov. For the first time since drug testing was introduced, there were no reported disqualifications for substance abuse.

(CHARLES ROBERT PAUL, JR.)

WRESTLING

At the 1989 world championships in Martigny, Switz., the Soviet Union once again emerged in first place. In freestyle competition September 1–3, the Soviet team placed 8 of their 10 wrestlers, gaining four first, two second, and two third places for a total of 79 points. Garnering 70 points for second place, the United States had six finalists, the most it had ever achieved, and claimed two first and four second places. Turkey finished third with 49 points. In what turned out to be the battle of Olympic champions, Ken Monday of the U.S. defeated Arsen Fadzaev of the Soviet Union in the 74-kg (163-lb) weight class. Both were Olympic champions in 1988, at which time Fadzaev had wrestled in the 68-kg (149.5-lb) weight class.

In Greco-Roman wrestling August 24–27, the Soviet Union continued its domination by placing 9 of 10 wrestlers in the top three places—five firsts, two seconds, and two thirds—for a total of 90 points. Hungary placed second with 53 points and Bulgaria third with 45.

At the National Collegiate Athletic Association tournament March 16–18 in Oklahoma City, Oklahoma State University dethroned the Sun Devils of Arizona State to claim first place, topping the collegiate ranks with a total of 91.25 points. Arizona State placed second with 70.5 points, and Iowa State was third with 63 points.

(MARVIN G. HESS)

World Wrestling Champions, 1989

Weight class	Freestyle	Greco-Roman
48 kg (105.5 lb)	J. Kim (S.Korea)	O. Kucherenko (U.S.S.R.)
52 kg (114.5 lb)	V. Iordanov (Bulg.)	A. Ignatenko (U.S.S.R.)
57 kg (125.5 lb)	S. Yeung (N.Korea)	E. Ivanov (Bulg.)
62 kg (136.5 lb)	J. Smith (U.S.)	K. Madzhidov (U.S.S.R.)
68 kg (149.5 lb)	B. Budaev (U.S.S.R.)	C. Passarelli (W.Germany)
74 kg (163 lb)	K. Monday (U.S.)	D. Turlykhanov (U.S.S.R.)
82 kg (180.5 lb)	E. Jabraylov (U.S.S.R.)	T. Komaromi (Hung.)
90 kg (198 lb)	M. Khadartsev (U.S.S.R.)	M. Bullmann (E.Germany)
100 kg (220 lb)	A. Atatov (U.S.S.R.)	G. Himmel (W.Germany)
130 kg (286 lb)	A. Soleimani (Iran)	A. Karelin (U.S.S.R.)

Sporting Record

ARCHERY

FITA Outdoor World Target Archery Championships

year	men's individual		men's team		women's individual		women's team	
	winner	points	winner	points	winner	points	winner	points
1981	K. Laasonen (Fin.)	2,541	United States	7,547	N. Butuzova (U.S.S.R.)	2,514	U.S.S.R.	7,455
1983	R. McKinney (U.S.)	2,617	United States	7,812	Kim Jin Ho (S.Kor.)	2,616	South Korea	7,704
1985	R. McKinney (U.S.)	2,601	South Korea	7,660	I. Soldatova (U.S.S.R.)	2,595	U.S.S.R.	7,721
1987	V. Esheyev (U.S.S.R.)	329	West Germany	891	Ma Xiangjun (China)	330	U.S.S.R.	884
1989	S. Zabrodsky (U.S.S.R.)	332	U.S.S.R.	985	Kim Soo Nyung (S.Kor.)	338	South Korea	995

ATHLETICS

World Cup Championship—men

	100 metre	200 metre	400 metre	800 metre	1,500 metre
1981	A. Wells (Europe)	M. Lattany (U.S.)	C. Wiley (U.S.)	S. Coe (Europe)	S. Ovett (Europe)
1985	B. Johnson (Americas)	R. Caetano da Silva (Americas)	M. Franks (U.S.)	S. Koskei (Africa)	O. Khalifa (Africa)
1989	L. Christie (Gr.Brit.)	R. Caetano da Silva (Americas)	R. Hernandez (Americas)	T. McKean (Gr.Brit.)	A. Bile (Africa)

	5,000 metre	10,000 metre	Steeplechase	110-m hurdles	400-m hurdles
1981	E. Coghlan (Europe)	W. Schildhauer (E.Ger.)	B. Maminski (Europe)	G. Foster (U.S.)	E. Moses (U.S.)
1985	D. Padilla (U.S.)	W. Bulti (Africa)	J. Kariuki (Africa)	T. Campbell (U.S.)	A. Phillips (U.S.)
1989	S. Aouita (Africa)	S. Antibo (Europe)	J. Kariuki (Africa)	R. Kingdom (U.S.)	D. Patrick (U.S.)

	4 × 100 relays	4 × 400 relays	Triple jump	High jump	Pole vault
1981	Europe	United States	J. de Oliveira (Americas)	T. Peacock (U.S.)	K. Volkov (U.S.S.R.)
1985	United States	United States	W. Banks (U.S.)	P. Sjoberg (Europe)	S. Bubka (U.S.S.R.)
1989	United States	Americas	M. Conley (U.S.)	P. Sjoberg (Europe)	P. Collet (Europe)

	Long jump	Shot put	Discus throw	Hammer throw	Javelin throw
1981	C. Lewis (U.S.)	U. Beyer (E.Ger.)	A. Lemme (E.Ger.)	Yu. Sedykh (U.S.S.R.)	D. Kula (U.S.S.R.)
1985	M. Conley (U.S.)	U. Timmerman (E.Ger.)	G. Kolnootchenko (U.S.S.R.)	Yu. Tamm (U.S.S.R.)	U. Hohn (E.Ger.)
1989	L. Myricks (U.S.)	U. Timmermann (E.Ger.)	J. Schult (E.Ger.)	H. Weis (Europe)	S. Backley (Gr.Brit.)

	Team	Marathon
1981	Europe	
1985	United States	1985 A. Salah (Djibouti)
1989	United States	1987 A. Salah (Djibouti)
		1989 K. Metaferia (Ethiopia)

World Cup Championship—women

	100 metre	200 metre	400 metre	800 metre	1,500 metre
1981	E. Ashford (U.S.)	E. Ashford (U.S.)	J. Kratochvílová (Europe)	L. Veselkova (U.S.S.R.)	T. Sorokina (U.S.S.R.)
1985	M. Göhr (E.Ger.)	M. Koch (E.Ger.)	M. Koch (E.Ger.)	C. Wachtel (E.Ger.)	H. Korner (E.Ger.)
1989	S. Echols (U.S.)	S. Moller (E.Ger.)	A. Quirot (Americas)	A. Quirot (Americas)	P. Ivan (Europe)

	3,000 metre	10,000 metre	100-m hurdles	400-m hurdles	4 × 100 relays
1981	A. Zauber (E.Ger.)	—	T. Anisimova (U.S.S.R.)	E. Neumann (E.Ger.)	East Germany
1985	U. Bruns (E.Ger.)	A. Cunha (Europe)	C. Oschkenat (E.Ger.)	S. Busch (E.Ger.)	East Germany
1989	Y. Murray (Europe)	K. Ullrich (E.Ger.)	C. Oschkenat (E.Ger.)	S. Farmer-Patrick (U.S.)	East Germany

	4 × 400 relays	High jump	Long jump	Shot put	Discus throw
1981	East Germany	U. Meyfarth (Europe)	S. Ulbricht (E.Ger.)	I. Slupianek (E.Ger.)	E. Jahl (E.Ger.)
1985	East Germany	S. Kostadinova (U.S.S.R.)	H. Daute Drechsler (E.Ger.)	N. Lisovskaya (U.S.S.R.)	M. Optiz (E.Ger.)
1989	Americas	S. Costa (Americas)	G. Chistyakova (U.S.S.R.)	Zhihong Huang (Asia)	I. Wyludda (E.Ger.)

	Javelin throw	Team	Marathon
1981	A. Todorova (Europe)	East Germany	
1985	O. Gavrilova (U.S.S.R.)	East Germany	1985 K. Dörre (E.Ger.)
1989	P. Felke (E.Ger.)	East Germany	1987 Z. Ivanova (U.S.S.R.)
			1985 S. Marchiano (U.S.)

S. Antibo (no. 3): 10,000-m World Cup championship—men (1989)

STEVEN E. SUTTON—DUOMO

For records of previous years, *see* the entry SPORTING RECORD in the Micropædia.

World Track-and-Field Championships—men

event	1983	1987
100 m	C. Lewis (U.S.)	B. Johnson (Can.)
200 m	C. Smith (U.S.)	C. Smith (U.S.)
400 m	B. Cameron (Jam.)	T. Schoenlebe (E.Ger.)
800 m	W. Wülbeck (W.Ger.)	B. Konchellah (Kenya)
1,500 m	S. Cram (U.K.)	A. Bile (Som.)
5,000 m	E. Coghlan (Ire.)	S. Aouita (Mor.)
10,000 m	A. Cova (Italy)	P. Kipkoech (Kenya)
steeplechase	P. Ilg (W.Ger.)	F. Panetta (Italy)
110-m hurdles	G. Foster (U.S.)	G. Foster (U.S.)
400-m hurdles	E. Moses (U.S.)	E. Moses (U.S.)
marathon	R. de Castella (Australia)	D. Wakihuru (Kenya)
20-km walk	E. Canto (Mex.)	M. Damilano (Italy)
50-km walk	R. Weigel (E.Ger.)	H. Gauder (E.Ger.)
4 × 100 m relay	United States (E. King, W. Gault, C. Smith, C. Lewis)	United States (L. McRae, L. McNeil, H. Glance, C. Lewis)
4 × 400 m relay	U.S.S.R. (S. Lovachev, A. Troschilo, N. Chernetsky, V. Markin)	United States (D. Everett, R. Haley, A. McKay, H. Reynolds)
high jump	G. Avdeyenko (U.S.S.R.)	P. Sjöberg (Swed.)
pole vault	S. Bubka (U.S.S.R.)	S. Bubka (U.S.S.R.)
long jump	C. Lewis (U.S.)	C. Lewis (U.S.)
triple jump	Z. Hoffman (Pol.)	C. Markov (Bulg.)
shot put	E. Sarul (Pol.)	W. Guenther (Switz.)
discus throw	I. Bugár (Czech.)	J. Schult (E.Ger.)
hammer throw	S. Litvinov (U.S.S.R.)	S. Litvinov (U.S.S.R.)
javelin throw	D. Michel (E.Ger.)	S. Raty (Fin.)
decathlon	D. Thompson (U.K.)	T. Voss (E.Ger.)

World Track-and-Field Championships—women

event	1983	1987
100 m	M. Göhr (E.Ger.)	S. Gladisch (E.Ger.)
200 m	M. Koch (E.Ger.)	S. Gladisch (E.Ger.)
400 m	J. Kratochvilová (Czech.)	O. Bryzgina (U.S.S.R.)
800 m	J. Kratochvilová (Czech.)	S. Wodars (E.Ger.)
1,500 m	M. Decker (U.S.)	T. Samolenko (U.S.S.R.)
3,000 m	M. Decker (U.S.)	T. Samolenko (U.S.S.R.)
10,000 m*		I. Kristiansen (Nor.)
100-m hurdles	B. Jahn (E.Ger.)	G. Zagorcheva (Bulg.)
400-m hurdles	Ye. Fesenko (U.S.S.R.)	S. Busch (E.Ger.)
marathon	G. Waitz (Nor.)	R. Mota (Port.)
10-km walk*		I. Strakhova (U.S.S.R.)
4 × 100 m relay	East Germany (S. Gladisch, M. Koch, M. Göhr, I. Auerswald)	United States (A. Brown, D. Williams, F. Griffith, P. Marshall)
4 × 400 m relay	East Germany (K. Walther, D. Rubsam, M. Koch, S. Busch)	East Germany (D. Neubauer, K. Emmelmann, P. Mueller, S. Busch)
high jump	T. Bykova (U.S.S.R.)	S. Kostadinova (Bulg.)
long jump	H. Daute (E.Ger.)	J. Joyner-Kersee (U.S.)
shot put	H. Fibingerová (Czech.)	N. Lisovskaya (U.S.S.R.)
discus throw	M. Opitz (E.Ger.)	M. Hellmann (E.Ger.)
javelin throw	T. Lillak (Fin.)	F. Whitbread (U.K.)
heptathlon	R. Neubert (E.Ger.)	J. Joyner-Kersee (U.S.)

*Event added in 1987.

Boston Marathon

year	men	h:min:s	women	h:min:s
1985	G. Smith (Eng.)	2:14:05	L. Larsen (U.S.)	2:34:06
1986	R. de Castella (Australia)	2:07:51	I. Kristiansen (Nor.)	2:24:55
1987	T. Seko (Japan)	2:11:50	R. Mota (Port.)	2:25:21
1988	I. Hussein (Kenya)	2:08:43	R. Mota (Port.)	2:24:30
1989	A. Mekonnen (Ethiopia)	2:09:06	I. Kristiansen (Nor.)	2:24:33

New York Marathon

year	men	h:min:s	women	h:min:s
1985	O. Pizzolato (U.S.)	2:11:34	G. Waitz (Nor.)	2:28:34
1986	G. Poli (Italy)	2:11:06	G. Waitz (Nor.)	2:28:06
1987	I. Hussein (Kenya)	2:11:01	P. Welch (U.K.)	2:30:17
1988	S. Jones (Wales)	2:08:20	G. Waitz (Nor.)	2:28:07
1989	J. Ikangaa (Tanzania)	2:08:01	I. Kristiansen (Nor.)	2:25:30

America's Marathon/Chicago

year	men	h:min:s	women	h:min:s
1985	S. Jones (U.K.)	2:07:13	J. Benoit Samuelson (U.S.)	2:21:21
1986	T. Seko (Japan)	2:08:27	I. Kristiansen (Nor.)	2:27:08
1987	not held			
1988	A. Cruz (Mexico)	2:08:57	L. Weidenbach (U.S.)	2:29:17
1989	P. Davies-Hale (U.K.)	2:11:25	L. Weidenbach (U.S.)	2:28:15

G. Zagorcheva: 100-m hurdles world track and field championships—women (1987)

TONY DUFFY—ALLSPORT

World Cross-Country Championship—men (12,000 m)

year	individual	team
1984	C. Lopes (Port.)	Ethiopia
1985	C. Lopes (Port.)	Ethiopia
1986	J. Ngugi (Kenya)	Kenya
1987	J. Ngugi (Kenya)	Kenya
1988	J. Ngugi (Kenya)	Kenya
1989	J. Ngugi (Kenya)	Kenya

World Cross-Country Championship—women (5,000 m)

year	individual	team
1984	M. Puica (Rom.)	United States
1985	Z. Budd (U.K.)	United States
1986	Z. Budd (U.K.)	England
1987	A. Sergent (Fr.)	United States
1988	I. Christiansen (Nor.)	U.S.S.R.
1989	A. Sergent (Fr.)	U.S.S.R.

J. Ikangaa: New York Marathon (1989)

PAUL J. SUTTON—DUOMO

AUTOMOBILE RACING

United States Auto Club Champions

year	driver
1984/85	D. Sullivan
1985/86	B. Rahal
1986/87	A. Unser
1987/88	R. Mears
1988/89	C. Gurney

Indianapolis 500

year	winner	avg. speed in mph
1985	D. Sullivan	152.982
1986	B. Rahal	170.722
1987	A. Unser	162.175
1988	R. Mears	144.809
1989	E. Fittipaldi	167.581

International Cup for Formula One Manufacturers

year	car	year	car
1984	McLaren/Porsche-TAG	1987	Williams/Honda
1985	McLaren/Ferrari	1988	McLaren/Honda
1986	Williams/Honda	1989	McLaren/Honda

World Championship of Drivers

year	winner	car
1985	A. Prost (Fr.)	McLaren/Porsche-TAG
1986	A. Prost (Fr.)	McLaren/Porsche-TAG
1987	N. Piquet (Braz.)	Williams/Honda
1988	A. Senna (Braz.)	McLaren/Honda
1989	A. Prost (Fr.)	McLaren/Honda

Le Mans 24-hour Grand Prix d'Endurance

year	car	drivers
1985	Porsche	K. Ludwig, J. Winter, P. Barilla
1986	Porsche	D. Bell, H. Stuck, A. Holbert
1987	Porsche	H. Stuck, D. Bell, A. Holbert
1988	Jaguar	J. Lammers, J. Dumfries, A. Wallace
1989	Mercedes-Benz	J. Mass, M. Reuter, S. Dickens

Monte-Carlo Rally

year	car	driver, codriver
1985	Peugeot 205 Turbo	Vatanen, Harryman
1986	Lancia Martini Delta	Toivonen, Cresto
1987	Lancia Delta HF	Biasion, Siviero
1988	Lancia Delta 4WD	Saby, Fauchille
1989	Lancia	Biasion, Siviero

National Association for Stock Car Auto Racing (NASCAR) Winston Cup Champions

year	winner	year	winner
1984	T. Labonte	1987	D. Earnhardt
1985	D. Waltrip	1988	B. Elliott
1986	D. Earnhardt	1989	R. Wallace

E. Fittipaldi: Indianapolis 500 (1989)
FOCUS ON SPORTS

Mercedes-Benz—J. Mass, M. Reuter, S. Dickens: Le Mans 24-hour Grand Prix (1989)
DUOMO

BADMINTON

World Badminton Championships

year	men's singles	women's singles	men's doubles	women's doubles
1980	R. Hartono (Indon.)	W. Verawaty (Indon.)	A. Chandra, C. Hadinata (Indon.)	N. Perry, J. Webster (U.K.)
1983	I. Sugiarto (Indon.)	Li Lingwei (China)	S. Fladberg, J. Helledie (Den.)	Lin Ying, Wu Dixi (China)
1985	Han Jian (China)	Han Aiping (China)	Park Joo Bong, Kim Moon Soo (S.Kor.)	Han Aiping, Li Lingwei (China)
1987	Yang Yang (China)	Han Aiping (China)	Li Yongbo, Tian Bingyi (China)	Lin Ying, Guan Weizhen (China)
1989	Yang Yang (China)	Li Lingwei (China)	Li Yongbo, Tian Bingyi (China)	Lin Ying, Guan Weizhen (China)

All-England Championships—singles

year	men	women
1985	Zhao Jianhua (China)	Han Aiping (China)
1986	M. Frost (Den.)	Kim Yun Ja (S.Kor.)
1987	M. Frost (Den.)	K. Larsen (Den.)
1988	I. Frederiksen (Den.)	Gu Jiaming (China)
1989	Yang Yang (China)	Li Lingwei (China)

Uber Cup (women)

year	winner	runner-up
1977–78	Japan	Indonesia
1980–81	Japan	Indonesia
1983–84	China	England
1985–86	China	Indonesia
1987–88	China	S.Korea

Thomas Cup (men)

year	winner	runner-up
1978–79	Indonesia	Denmark
1981–82	China	Indonesia
1983–84	Indonesia	China
1985–86	China	Indonesia
1987–88	China	Malaysia

BASEBALL

Oakland Athletics: World Series (1989)

FOCUS ON SPORTS

Baseball Hall of Fame

year elected	members
1985	Hoyt Wilhelm, Enos Slaughter, Lou Brock, Joseph Floyd (Arky) Vaughan
1986	Willie McCovey, Bobby Doerr, Ernie Lombardi
1987	Billy Williams, Jim (Catfish) Hunter, Ray Dandridge
1988	Willie Stargell
1989	Johnny Bench, Carl Yastrzemski

World Series*

year	winning team	losing team	results
1985	Kansas City Royals (AL)	St. Louis Cardinals (NL)	4–3
1986	New York Mets (NL)	Boston Red Sox (AL)	4–3
1987	Minnesota Twins (AL)	St. Louis Cardinals (NL)	4–3
1988	Los Angeles Dodgers (NL)	Oakland Athletics (AL)	4–1
1989	Oakland Athletics (AL)	San Francisco Giants (NL)	4–0

*AL—American League; NL—National League.

Japan Series*

year	winning team	losing team	results
1985	Hanshin Tigers (CL)	Seibu Lions (PL)	4–2
1986	Seibu Lions (PL)	Hiroshima Tōyō Carp (CL)	4–3
1987	Seibu Lions (PL)	Yomiuri Giants (CL)	4–2
1988	Seibu Lions (PL)	Chunichi Dragons (CL)	4–1
1989	Yomiuri Giants (CL)	Kintetsu Buffaloes (PL)	4–3

*CL—Central League; PL—Pacific League.

BASKETBALL

National Basketball Association (NBA) Championship

season	winner	runner-up	results
1984–85	Los Angeles Lakers	Boston Celtics	4–2
1985–86	Boston Celtics	Houston Rockets	4–2
1986–87	Los Angeles Lakers	Boston Celtics	4–2
1987–88	Los Angeles Lakers	Detroit Pistons	4–3
1988–89	Detroit Pistons	Los Angeles Lakers	4–0

World Amateur Basketball Championship—men

year	winner	runner-up
1980	Yugoslavia	Italy
1982	U.S.S.R.	United States
1984	United States	Spain
1986	United States	U.S.S.R.
1988	U.S.S.R.	Yugoslavia

World Amateur Basketball Championship—women

year	winner	runner-up
1980	U.S.S.R.	Bulgaria
1983	U.S.S.R.	United States
1984	United States	South Korea
1986	United States	U.S.S.R.
1988	United States	Yugoslavia

Division I National Collegiate Athletic Association (NCAA) Championship—men

year	winner	runner-up	score
1985	Villanova	Georgetown	66–64
1986	Louisville	Duke	72–69
1987	Indiana	Syracuse	74–73
1988	Kansas	Oklahoma	83–79
1989	Michigan	Seton Hall	80–79

Division I National Collegiate Athletic Association (NCAA) Championship—women

year	winner	runner-up	score
1985	Old Dominion	Georgia	70–65
1986	Texas	Southern California	97–81
1987	Tennessee	Louisiana Tech	67–44
1988	Louisiana Tech	Auburn	56–54
1989	Tennessee	Auburn	76–60

National Invitation Tournament (NIT) Championship

year	winner	runner-up	score
1985	UCLA	Indiana	65–62
1986	Ohio State	Wyoming	73–63
1987	Southern Mississippi	LaSalle	84–80
1988	Connecticut	Ohio State	72–67
1989	St. John's	St. Louis	73–65

Tennessee: NCAA championship—women (1989)

AUBURN UNIVERSITY

BILLIARDS

World Amateur Three-Cushion Championship

year	winner
1985	R. Ceulemans (Belg.)
1986	A. Rico (Spain)
1987	T. Blomdahl (Swed.)
1988	T. Blomdahl (Swed.)
1989	T. Blomdahl (Swed.)

World Professional (English) Billiards Champions

year	winner
1985	R. Edmonds
1986	R. Foldvari
1987	N. Dagley
1988	N. Dagley
1989	M. Russell

BOWLING

ABC Bowling Championships—Regular Division

year	singles	score	all-events	score
1986	J. Mackey	774	E. Marzka	2,116
1987	T. Taylor	749	R. Shafer	2,044
1988	S. Hutkowski	774	R. Steelsmith	2,053
1989	P. Tetreault	813	G. Hall	2,227

WIBC Bowling Championship—Open Division

year	singles	score	all-events	score
1985	P. Schwarzel	694	A. Rzepecki Sill	1,900
1986	D. Stewart	698	Romeo, Lewis (tie)	1,877
1987	R. Jonak	728	L. Barrette	1,972
1988	M. Meyer-Welty	690	L. Wagner	1,988
1989	L. Anderson	683	N. Fehr	1,911

FIQ World Bowling Championship—men

year	singles	pairs	triples	fives	eights
1975	M. Stoudt (U.S.)	United Kingdom		Finland	West Germany
1979*	G. Bugden (U.K.)	Australia	Malaysia	Australia	
1983	T. Cariello (U.S.)	Australia	Sweden	Finland	
1987	P. Rolland (Fr.)	Sweden	United States	Sweden	

*In 1979 eights were discontinued and triples were introduced.

Professional Bowlers Association (PBA) Firestone Tournament of Champions

year	champion	runner-up
1985	M. Williams	B. Handley
1986	M. Holman	M. Baker
1987	P. Weber	J. Murtishaw
1988	M. Williams	T. Westlake
1989	D. Ballard	W.R. Williams

FIQ World Bowling Championship—women

year	singles	pairs	triples	fours	fives
1975	A. Haefker (W.Ger.)	Sweden		Japan	Japan
1979*	L. de la Rosa (Phil.)	Philippines	United States		United States
1983	L. Sulkanen (Swed.)	Denmark	West Germany		Sweden
1987	E. Piccini (Mex.)	United States	United States		United States

*In 1979 fours were discontinued and triples were introduced.

BOWLS

World Lawn Bowls Championships

year	singles	pairs	triples	fours	team
1972	M. Evans (Wales)	Hong Kong	United States	England	Scotland
1976	D. Watson (S.Af.)	South Africa	South Africa	South Africa	South Africa
1980	D. Bryant (Eng.)	Australia	England	Hong Kong	—
1984	P. Bellis (N.Z.)	United States	Ireland	England	Scotland
1988	D. Bryant (Eng.)	New Zealand	New Zealand	Ireland	England

BOXING

World heavyweight champions—no weight limit

WBA	WBC
Greg Page (U.S.; 12/1/84)	Tim Witherspoon (U.S.; 3/9/84)
Tony Tubbs (U.S.; 4/29/85)	Pinklon Thomas (U.S.; 8/31/84)
Tim Witherspoon (U.S.; 1/17/86)	Trevor Berbick (Can.; 3/22/86)
James Smith (U.S.; 12/12/86)	Mike Tyson (U.S.; 11/22/86)
Mike Tyson (U.S.; 3/7/87)	

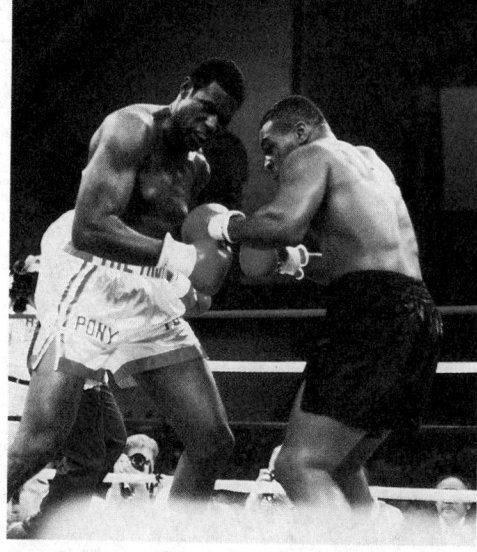

M. Tyson (right): WBA and WBC heavyweight champion (1989)

World cruiserweight champions—top weight 195 pounds

WBA	WBC
Dwight Muhammad Qawi (U.S.; 7/27/85)	Bernard Benton (U.S.; 9/21/85)
Evander Holyfield (U.S.; 7/12/86)	Carlos de León (P.R.; 3/22/86)
gave up title in 1988	Evander Holyfield (U.S.; 4/9/88)
Taoufik Belbouli (Fr.)	gave up title in 1988
declared vacant in 1989	Carlos de León (P.R.; 5/17/89)

World junior middleweight champions—top weight 154 pounds (also called super welterweight)

WBA	WBC
Roberto Durán (Pan.; 6/16/83)	Gianfranco Rosi (Italy; 10/2/87)
gave up title in 1984	Donald Curry (U.S.; 7/8/88)
Mike McCallum (Jam.; 10/19/84) vacant	René Jacquot (Fr.; 2/11/89)
Julian Jackson (Virgin Is. U.S.; 11/21/87)	John Mugabi (Uganda; 7/8/89)

World light heavyweight champions—top weight 175 pounds

WBA	WBC
Marvin Johnson (U.S.; 2/9/86)	Don Lalonde (Can.; 11/27/87)
Leslie Stewart (Trinidad and Tobago; 5/23/87)	Sugar Ray Leonard (U.S.; 11/7/88)
Virgil Hill (U.S.; 9/5/87)	gave up title in 1988
	Dennis Andries (U.K; 2/89)
	Jeff Harding (Australia; 6/24/89)

World welterweight champions—top weight 147 pounds

WBA	WBC
Mark Breland (U.S.; 2/6/87)	Donald Curry (U.S.; 12/6/85)
Marlon Starling (U.S.; 8/22/87)	Lloyd Honeyghan (U.K.; 9/27/86)
Tomas Molinares (Colom.; 7/29/88)	Jorge Vaca (Mex.; 10/28/87)
vacant	Lloyd Honeyghan (U.K.; 3/29/88)
Mark Breland (U.S.; 2/4/89)	Marlon Starling (U.S.; 2/4/89)

World middleweight champions—top weight 160 pounds

WBA	WBC
Marvin Hagler (U.S.; 9/27/80)	Sugar Ray Leonard (U.S.; 4/6/87)
stripped of title in 1987	retired
Sumbu Kalambay (Italy; 10/23/87)	Thomas Hearns (U.S.; 10/29/87)
stripped of title in 1989	Iran Barkley (U.S.; 6/6/88)
Mike McCallum (Jam.; 5/13/89)	Roberto Duran (Pan.; 2/24/89)

World junior welterweight champions—top weight 140 pounds (also called super lightweight)

WBA	WBC
Gene Hatcher (U.S.; 6/1/84)	Tsuyoshi Hamada (Japan; 7/24/86)
Ubaldo Sacco (Arg.; 7/21/85)	René Arrendondo (Mex.; 7/22/87)
Patrizio Oliva (Italy; 3/15/86)	Roger Mayweather (U.S.; 11/12/87)
Juan Martin Coggi (Arg.; 7/4/87)	Julio César Chávez (Mex.; 5/13/89)

World lightweight champions—top weight 135 pounds

WBA	WBC
Livingstone Bramble (Vir.Is.; 6/1/84)	José Luis Ramírez (Mex.; 7/19/87)
Edwin Rosario (P.R.; 9/26/86)	Julio Cesar Chávez (Mex.; 10/29/88)
Julio César Chávez (Mex.; 11/21/87)	gave up title in 1989
gave up title in 1989	Pernell Whitaker (U.S.; 8/20/89)
Edwin Rosario (P.R.; 7/9/89)	

World junior lightweight champions—top weight 130 pounds (also called super featherweight)

WBA	WBC
Rocky Lockridge (U.S.; 2/26/84)	Julio César Chavez (Mex.; 9/13/84)
Wilfredo Gómez (P.R.; 5/19/85)	gave up title
Alfredo Layne (Pan.; 5/24/86)	Azumah Nelson (Ghana; 2/29/88)
Brian Mitchell (S.Af.; 9/27/86)	

World featherweight champions—top weight 126 pounds

WBA	WBC
Cecilio Lastra (Spain; 12/17/77)	Juan LaPorte (P.R.; 9/15/82)
Eusebio Pedroza (Pan.; 4/15/78)	Wilfredo Gómez (P.R.; 3/31/84)
Barry McGuigan (N.Ire.; 6/8/85)	Azumah Nelson (Ghana; 12/8/84)
Steve Cruz (U.S.; 6/23/86)	gave up title in 1988
Antonio Esparragoza (Venez.; 3/6/87)	Jeff Fenech (Australia; 3/7/88)

World junior featherweight champions (also called super bantamweight)—top weight 122 pounds

WBA	WBC
Bernardo Pinango (Venez.; 3/5/88)	Samart Payakaroon (Thai.; 1/18/86)
Juan José Estrada (Mex.; 5/28/88)	Jeff Fenech (Australia; 5/8/87)
Jesus Salud (U.S.; 12/11/89)	gave up title in 1988
	Daniel Zaragoza (Mex.; 2/29/88)

World bantamweight champions—top weight 118 pounds

WBA	WBC
Wilfredo Vásquez (P.R.; 10/4/87)	Alberto Davila (U.S.; 9/1/83)
Khaokor Galaxy (Thai.; 5/9/88)	stripped of title in 1985
Moon Sung Kil (S.Kor.; 8/14/88)	Daniel Zaragoza (Mex.; 5/4/85)
Kaokor Galaxy (Thai.; 7/9/89)	Miguel Lora (Colom.; 8/9/85)
Luisita Espinosa (Phil.; 10/18/89)	Raul Pérez (Mex.; 10/29/88)

World junior bantamweight champions (also called super flyweight)—top weight 115 pounds

WBA	WBC
Gustavo Ballas (Arg.; 9/12/1981)	Gilberto Román (Mex.; 3/30/86)
Rafael Pedroza (Pan.; 12/5/81)	Santos Laciar (Arg.; 5/16/87)
Watanabe Jiro (Japan; 4/8/82)	Jesús Rojas (Colom.; 8/9/87)
stripped of title in 1984	Gilberto Román (Mex.; 4/8/88)
Kaosai Galaxy (Thai.; 11/21/84)	Nana Konadu (Ghana; 11/7/89)

J.C. Chávez (left): WBC junior welterweight champion (1989)
ALLSPORT USA

World flyweight champions—top weight 112 pounds

WBA	WBC
Santos Laciar (Arg.; 5/1/82)	Kobayashi Koji (Japan; 1/18/84)
gave up title in 1985	Gabriel Bernal (Mex.; 4/9/84)
Hilario Zapata (Pan.; 10/5/85)	Sot Chitalada (Thai.; 10/8/84)
Fidel Bassa (Colom.; 2/13/87)	Kim Young Kang (S.Kor.; 7/24/88)
Jesús Rojas (Venez.; 9/30/89)	Sot Chitalada (Thai.; 6/89)

World junior flyweight champions—top weight 108 pounds

WBA	WBC
Tokashiki Katsuo (Japan; 12/16/81)	Hilario Zapata (Pan.; 7/20/82)
Lupe Madera (Mex.; 7/10/83)	Chang Jung Koo (S.Kor.; 3/26/83)
Francisco Quiroz (Dom.Rep.; 5/19/84)	German Torres (Mex.)
Joey Olivo (U.S.; 3/29/85)	Lee Yul Woo (S.Kor.)
Yuh Myung Woo (S.Kor.; 12/8/85)	Humberto Gonzalez (Mex.; 6/89)

CHESS

World Chess Championships—men

year	winner	runner-up
1975	A. Karpov (U.S.S.R.)*	*
1978	A. Karpov (U.S.S.R.)	V. Korchnoy (U.S.S.R.)
1981	A. Karpov (U.S.S.R.)	V. Korchnoy (U.S.S.R.)
1984–85	G. Kasparov (U.S.S.R.)	A. Karpov (U.S.S.R.)
1986	G. Kasparov (U.S.S.R.)	A. Karpov (U.S.S.R.)
1987	G. Kasparov (U.S.S.R.)	A. Karpov (U.S.S.R.)

*By default. R. Fischer (U.S.) was stripped of the title for failure to comply with an FIDE ruling, and Karpov was declared the new world champion.

World Chess Championships—women

year	winner	runner-up
1978	M. Chiburdanidze (U.S.S.R.)	N. Gaprindashvili (U.S.S.R.)
1981	M. Chiburdanidze (U.S.S.R.)	N. Aleksandriya (U.S.S.R.)
1984	M. Chiburdanidze (U.S.S.R.)	I. Levitina (U.S.S.R.)
1986	M. Chiburdanidze (U.S.S.R.)	E. Akhmilovskaya (U.S.S.R.)
1988	M. Chiburdanidze (U.S.S.R.)	N. Ioseliani (U.S.S.R.)

International Team Chess Championships—men

year	winner	runner-up
1982	U.S.S.R.	Czechoslovakia
1984	U.S.S.R.	United Kingdom
1986	U.S.S.R.	United Kingdom
1988	U.S.S.R.	United Kingdom
1989	U.S.S.R.	Yugoslavia

International Team Chess Championships—women

year	winner	runner-up
1980	U.S.S.R.	Hungary
1982	U.S.S.R.	Romania
1984	U.S.S.R.	Bulgaria
1986	U.S.S.R.	Hungary
1988	Hungary	U.S.S.R.

CONTRACT BRIDGE

Bermuda Bowl

year	winner	runner-up
1985	United States	Austria
1987	United States	United Kingdom
1989	Brazil	United States

World Contract Bridge Pair Championship

year	open winner	women's winner	mixed winner
1978	Brazil	United States	United States
1982	United States	United States	Canada
1986	United States	United States	United States

World Team Olympiad

year	open winner	open runner-up	women's winner	women's runner-up
1984	Poland	France	United States	United Kingdom
1988	United States	Austria	Denmark	United Kingdom

CRICKET

All-time First-class Test Cricket Standings (as of August 31, 1989)

	England wins draws losses			Australia w d l			South Africa w d l			West Indies w d l			New Zealand w d l			India w d l			Pakistan w d l			Sri Lanka w d l		
England v.	—	—	—	88	79	101	46	38	18	21	35	39	30	32	4	29	34	11	13	29	5	2	1	0
Australia v.	101	79	88	—	—	—	29	13	11	28	17*	22	10	9	5	20	17*	8	11	11	9	2	0	0
South Africa v.	18	38	46	11	13	29	—	—	—	†			19	6	2	†			†			†		
West Indies v.	39	35	21	22	17*	28	†			—	—	—	8	12	4	26	30	6	9	10	6	†		
New Zealand v.	4	32	30	5	9	10	2	6	19	4	12	8	—	—	—	5	11	12	3	16	10	4	2	0
India v.	11	34	29	8	17*	20	†			6	30	26	12	11	5	—	—	—	4	29	7	3	3	1
Pakistan v.	5	29	13	9	11	11	†			6	10	9	10	16	3	7	29	4	—	—	—	5	3	1
Sri Lanka v.	0	1	2	0	0	2	†			†			0	2	4	1	3	3	1	3	5	—	—	—

*Including one tie.   †No matches.

CURLING

International Olympic Committee President's Cup

year	winner	runner-up
1985	Canada	Sweden
1986	Canada	Scotland
1987	Canada	West Germany
1988	Norway	Canada
1989	Canada	Switzerland

World Curling Championship—women

year	winner	runner-up
1985	Canada	Scotland
1986	Canada	West Germany
1987	Canada	West Germany
1988	West Germany	Canada
1989	Canada	Norway

CYCLING

Tour de France

year	winner	km
1985	B. Hinault (Fr.)	4,100
1986	G. LeMond (U.S.)	4,091
1987	S. Roche (Ire.)	4,100
1988	P. Delgado (Spain)	3,300
1989	G. LeMond (U.S.)	3,215

Cycling World Track Championships—women (amateur)

year	sprint	3-km pursuit
1985	I. Nicoloso (Fr.)	R. Twigg (U.S.)
1986	C. Rothenburger (E.Ger.)	J. Longo (Fr.)
1987	E. Salumyae (U.S.S.R.)	R. Twigg-Whitehead (U.S.)
1988	E. Salumyae (U.S.S.R.)	J. Longo (Fr.)
1989	E. Salumyae (U.S.S.R.)	J. Longo (Fr.)

Cycling World Road-Racing Championships

year	men (amateur)	men (professional)	women (amateur)
1985	L. Piasecki (Pol.)	J. Zoetemelk (Neth.)	J. Longo (Fr.)
1986	U. Ampler (E.Ger.)	M. Argentin (Italy)	J. Longo (Fr.)
1987	R. Vivien (Fr.)	S. Roche (Ireland)	J. Longo (Fr.)
1988	O. Ludwig (E.Ger.)	M. Fondriest (Italy)	M. Knol (Neth.)
1989	J. Halupczok (Pol.)	G. LeMond (U.S.)	J. Longo (Fr.)

G. LeMond: Tour de France (1989)
VANDYSTADT—ALLSPORT USA

Cycling World Track Championships—men

year	sprint (amateur)	sprint (professional)	pursuit (amateur)	pursuit (professional)	motor-paced (amateur)	motor-paced (professional)
1985	L. Hesslich (E.Ger.)	Nakano K. (Japan)	V. Ekimov (U.S.S.R.)	H.-H. Oersted (Den.)	R. Dotti (Italy)	B. Vicino (Italy)
1986	M. Hübner (E.Ger.)	Nakano K. (Japan)	V. Ekimov (U.S.S.R.)	T. Doyle (U.K.)	M. Gentili (Italy)	B. Vicino (Italy)
1987	L. Hesslich (E.Ger.)	Tawara N. (Japan)	G. Umaras (U.S.S.R.)	H.-H. Oersted (Den.)	M. Gentili (Italy)	M. Huerzeler (Switz.)
1988	L. Hesslich (E.Ger.)	S. Pate (Australia)	G. Umaras (U.S.S.R.)	L. Piasecki (Pol.)	V. Colamartino (Italy)	D. Clark (Australia)
1989	B. Huck (E.Ger.)	C. Golinelli (Italy)	V. Ekimov (U.S.S.R.)	C. Sturgess (U.K.)	R. Konigshofer (Austria)	G. Renosto (Italy)

FENCING

World Fencing Championships—men

year	individual			team		
	foil	épée	sabre	foil	épée	sabre
1985	M. Numa (Italy)	P. Boisse (Fr.)	G. Nebald (Hung.)	Italy	West Germany	U.S.S.R.
1986	A. Borella (Italy)	P. Riboud (Fr.)	S. Mindirgasov (U.S.S.R.)	Italy	West Germany	U.S.S.R.
1987	M. Gey (W.Ger.)	V. Fischer (W.Ger.)	J.-F. Lamour (Fr.)	West Germany	U.S.S.R.	U.S.S.R.
1988	S. Cerioni (Italy)	A. Schmitt (W.Ger.)	J.-F. Lamour (Fr.)	U.S.S.R.	France	Hungary
1989	A. Koch (W.Ger.)	M. Pereira (Spain)	G. Kirienko (U.S.S.R.)	U.S.S.R.	Italy	U.S.S.R.

World Fencing Championships—women

year	individual foil	team foil
1985	C. Hanisch (W.Ger.)	West Germany
1986	A. Fichtel (W.Ger.)	U.S.S.R.
1987	E. Tufan (Rom.)	Hungary
1988	A. Fichtel (W.Ger.)	West Germany
1989	O. Velitchko (U.S.S.R.)	West Germany

San Francisco 49ers: Super Bowl (1989)

FOCUS ON SPORTS

The European Cup of Champion Clubs

season	result			
1985–86	Steaua Bucharest*	0	Barcelona	0
1986–87	Porto (Port.)	2	Bayern Munich	1
1987–88	PSV Eindhoven (Neth.)*	0	Benfica (Port.)	0
1988–89	A.C. Milan	4	Steaua Bucharest	0

*Won on penalty kicks.

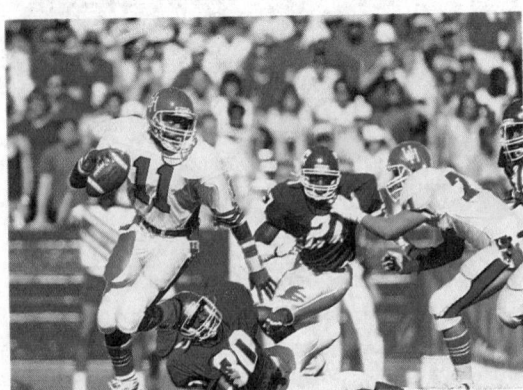

A. Ware: Heisman Memorial Trophy winner (1989)

D. STROHMEYER—ALLSPORT USA

FIELD HOCKEY

World Cup Field Hockey Championships—men

year	winner	runner-up
1982	Pakistan	West Germany
1986	Australia	England

World Cup Field Hockey Championships—women

year	winner	runner-up
1983	The Netherlands	Canada
1986	The Netherlands	West Germany

FOOTBALL

FIFA World Cup

year	result			
1982	Italy	3	West Germany	1
1986	Argentina	3	West Germany	2

European Cup-Winners' Cup

season	result			
1984–85	Everton (Eng.)	3	Rapid Vienna	1
1985–86	Dinamo Kiev	3	Atlético Madrid	0
1986–87	Ajax Amsterdam	1	Lokomotiv Leipzig	0
1987–88	KV Mechelen (Belg.)	1	Ajax Amsterdam	0
1988–89	Barcelona	2	Sampdoria (Italy)	0

Libertadores de América Cup

year	winner (country)	runner-up (country)	scores
1986	River Plate (Arg.)	América de Cali (Colom.)	2–1, 1–0
1987	Peñarol (Uruguay)	América de Cali (Colom.)	1–2, 2–1, 1–0
1988	Nacional (Uruguay)	Newell's Old Boys (Arg.)	0–1, 3–0
1989	Nacional of Medellín (Colom.)	Olimpia (Par.)	0–2, 2–0, 5–4*

*Winner determined in penalty shootout after tiebreaking game.

U.S. Football—professional

Super Bowl

	season	result			
XIX	1984–85	San Francisco 49ers (NFC)	38	Miami Dolphins (AFC)	16
XX	1985–86	Chicago Bears (NFC)	46	New England Patriots (AFC)	10
XXI	1986–87	New York Giants (NFC)	39	Denver Broncos (AFC)	20
XXII	1987–88	Washington Redskins (NFC)	42	Denver Broncos (AFC)	10
XXIII	1988–89	San Francisco 49ers (NFC)	20	Cincinnati Bengals (AFC)	16

U.S. Football—college

U.S. College Football National Champion

season	champion
1986	Penn State
1987	Miami (Fla.)
1988	Notre Dame
1989	Miami (Fla.)

Heisman Memorial Trophy winner

year	player	school
1985	Bo Jackson	Auburn
1986	Vinnie Testaverde	Miami (Fla.)
1987	Tim Brown	Notre Dame
1988	B. Sanders	Oklahoma State
1989	Andre Ware	Houston

Rose Bowl

season	result			
1985–86	UCLA	45	Iowa	28
1986–87	Arizona State	22	Michigan	15
1987–88	Michigan St.	20	Southern California	17
1988–89	Michigan	22	Southern California	14
1989–90	Southern California	17	Michigan	10

Orange Bowl

season	result			
1985–86	Oklahoma	25	Penn State	10
1986–87	Oklahoma	42	Arkansas	8
1987–88	Miami (Fla.)	20	Oklahoma	14
1988–89	Miami (Fla.)	23	Nebraska	3
1989–90	Notre Dame	21	Colorado	6

Sugar Bowl

season	result			
1985–86	Tennessee	35	Miami (Fla.)	7
1986–87	Nebraska	30	Louisiana State	15
1987–88	Auburn	16	Syracuse	16
1988–89	Florida St.	13	Auburn	7
1989–90	Miami (Fla.)	33	Alabama	25

Cotton Bowl

season	result			
1985–86	Texas A&M	36	Auburn	16
1986–87	Ohio State	28	Texas A&M	12
1987–88	Texas A&M	35	Notre Dame	10
1988–89	UCLA	17	Arkansas	3
1989–90	Tennessee	31	Arkansas	27

Canadian football—professional

Grey Cup

year	result			
1985	British Columbia Lions (WFC)	37	Hamilton Tiger-Cats (EFC)	24
1986	Hamilton Tiger-Cats (EFC)	39	Edmonton Eskimos (WFC)	15
1987	Edmonton Eskimos (WFC)	38	Toronto Argonauts (EFC)	36
1988	Winnipeg Blue Bombers (EFC)	22	British Columbia Lions (WFC)	21
1989	Saskatchewan Roughriders (WFC)	43	Hamilton Tiger-Cats (EFC)	40

Rugby Union football

Record of International Test matches 1871 to September 30, 1989

	England wins	draws	losses	Scotland wins	draws	losses	Ireland wins	draws	losses	Wales wins	draws	losses	British Isles wins	draws	losses
England v.	—	—	—	50	17	38	57	8	36	36	12	47	—	—	—
Scotland v.	38	17	50	—	—	—	50	4	45	39	2	52	—	—	—
Ireland v.	36	8	57	45	4	50	—	—	—	31	5	56	—	—	—
Wales v.	47	12	36	52	2	39	56	5	31	—	—	—	—	—	—
British Isles* v.													—	—	—
South Africa v.	6	1	2	5	0	3	8	1	1	6	1	0	20	6	14
New Zealand v.	12	0	3	11	2	0	8	1	0	11	0	3	24	3	5
Australia v.	10	0	6	5	0	7	6	0	6	5	0	8	3	0	14
France v.	24	7	33	29	3	28	32	5	25	23	3	36			

	South Africa wins	draws	losses	New Zealand wins	draws	losses	Australia wins	draws	losses	France wins	draws	losses
England v.	2	1	6	3	0	12	6	0	10	33	7	24
Scotland v.	3	0	5	0	2	11	7	0	5	28	3	29
Ireland v.	1	1	8	0	1	8	6	0	6	25	5	32
Wales v.	0	1	6	3	0	11	8	0	5	36	3	23
British Isles* v.	14	6	20	5	3	24	14	0	3			
South Africa v.	—	—	—	20	2	15	21	0	7	12	4	3
New Zealand v.	15	2	20	—	—	—	61	5	21	21	0	5
Australia v.	7	0	21	21	5	61	—	—	—	6	2	10
France v.	3	4	12	5	0	21	10	2	6	—	—	—

*The British Isles ("British Lions") is a combined team from the four "Home Unions" (England, Ireland, Scotland, and Wales).

Five Nations Championship

year	result
1985	Ireland†
1986	France, Scotland*
1987	France‡
1988	Wales†
1989	France

*Tied. †Triple Crown (all three matches, excluding France) and Grand Slam (all four matches) winner. ‡Grand Slam winner.

Rugby League football

Record of Test matches from January 25, 1908, to September 30, 1989

	Great Britain wins	draws	losses	Australia wins	draws	losses	New Zealand wins	draws	losses	France wins	draws	losses
Great Britain v.				50	4	46	48	3	25	32	3	13
Australia v.	48	4	50				38	0	22	24	3	12
New Zealand v.	25	3	45	22	0	38				15	3	11
France* v.	13	3	32	12	3	24	11	3	15			

*France began playing in this series of matches in 1954.

GOLF

British Open Golf Tournament—men

year	winner
1986	G. Norman (Australia)
1987	N. Faldo (U.K.)
1988	S. Ballesteros (Spain)
1989	M. Calcavecchia (U.S.)

United States Open Golf Championship—men

year	winner
1986	R. Floyd (U.S.)
1987	S. Simpson (U.S.)
1988	C. Strange (U.S.)
1989	C. Strange (U.S.)

Masters Tournament

year	winner
1985	B. Langer (W.Ger.)
1986	J. Nicklaus (U.S.)
1987	L. Mize (U.S.)
1988	S. Lyle (Scot.)
1989	N. Faldo (U.K.)

U.S. Professional Golfers' Association (PGA) championship

year	winner
1986	B. Tway (U.S.)
1987	L. Nelson (U.S.)
1988	J. Sluman (U.S.)
1989	P. Stewart (U.S.)

C. Strange (far left): U.S. Open golf championship—men (1989)

M. Calcavecchia (left): British Open golf tournament—men (1989)

PHOTOGRAPHS, FOCUS ON SPORTS

British Amateur Golf Championship—men

year	winner
1985	G. McGimpsey (Ire.)
1986	D. Curry (U.K.)
1987	P. Mayo (U.K.)
1988	C. Hardin (Swed.)
1989	S. Richardson (U.K.)

United States Amateur Golf Championship—men

year	winner
1985	S. Randolph (U.S.)
1986	B. Alexander (U.S.)
1987	B. Mayfair (U.S.)
1988	E. Meeks (U.S.)
1989	C. Patton (U.S.)

Ladies' British Open Golf Championship

year	winner
1985	B. King (U.S.)
1986	L. Davies (U.K.)
1987	A. Nicholas (U.K.)
1988	C. Dibnah (Australia)
1989	J. Geddes (U.S.)

British Ladies Amateur Golf Championship

year	winner
1985	L. Behan (Ire.)
1986	J. Thornhill (U.K.)
1987	J. Collingham (U.K.)
1988	J. Furby (U.S.)
1989	H. Dobson (U.K.)

United States Women's Open champions

year	winner
1985	K. Baker (U.S.)
1986	J. Geddes (U.S.)
1987	L. Davies (U.K.)
1988	L. Neumann (Swed.)
1989	B. King (U.S.)

United States Women's Amateur Golf Championship

year	winner
1985	Hattori M. (Japan)
1986	K. Cockerill (U.S.)
1987	K. Cockerill (U.S.)
1988	P. Sinn (U.S.)
1989	V. Goetze (U.S.)

Ladies' Professional Golf Association (LPGA) champions

year	winner
1985	N. Lopez (U.S.)
1986	P. Bradley (U.S.)
1987	J. Geddes (U.S.)
1988	S. Turner (U.S.)
1989	N. Lopez (U.S.)

Team events

Walker Cup—men (amateur)

year	result	tied	place
1981	United States 15, Britain and Ireland 9	0	Monterey, Calif., U.S.
1983	United States 13, Britain and Ireland 10	1	Hoylake, Cheshire, Eng.
1985	United States 13, Britain and Ireland 11	2	Pine Valley, N.J., U.S.
1987	United States 16, Britain and Ireland 7	1	Sunningdale, Berkshire, Eng.
1989	Britain and Ireland 9, United States 8	7	Atlanta, Ga., U.S.

World Cup—men (professional)

year	winner
1984	Spain (J. Cañizares and J. Rivero)
1985	Canada (D. Halldorson and D. Barr)
1986	not held
1987	Wales (I. Woosnam and D. Llewellyn)

Ryder Cup—men (professional)

year	result	tied	place
1981	United States 18, Great Britain 9	1	Walton Heath, Surrey, Eng.
1983	United States 13, Great Britain 12	3	Palm Beach Gardens, Fla., U.S.
1985	Europe 16, United States 11	1	Belfry, West Midlands, Eng.
1987	Europe 13, United States 11	4	Dublin, Ohio, U.S.
1989	Europe 14, United States 14	0	Belfry, West Midlands, Eng.

Curtis Cup—women (amateur)

year	result	tied	place
1980	United States 11, Britain and Ireland 3	4	Chepstow, Gwent, Wales
1982	United States 14, Britain and Ireland 3	1	Denver, Colo., U.S.
1984	United States 9, Britain and Ireland 8	1	Muirfield, East Lothian, Scot.
1986	Britain and Ireland 11, United States 3	4	Hutchinson, Kan., U.S.
1988	Britain and Ireland 11, United States 7	0	Sandwich, Kent, U.K.

GREYHOUND RACING

British Greyhound Derby

year	winning dog	time (s)	year	winning dog	time (s)
1982	Laurie's Panther	29.60	1986	Tico	28.69
1983	I'm Slippy	29.40	1987	Signal Spark	28.83
1984	Whisper Wishes	29.43	1988	Hit the Lid	
1985	Pagan Swallow	29.04*	1989	Lartigue Note	28.79

*In 1985 the distance was lowered from 500 m to 480 m.

GYMNASTICS

World Gymnastics Championships—men

year	all-around team	all-around individual	horizontal bar	parallel bars
1985	U.S.S.R.	Y. Korolyov (U.S.S.R.)	Tong Fei (China)	S. Kroll (E.Ger.)* V. Mogilny (U.S.S.R.)*
1987	U.S.S.R.	D. Bilozerchev (U.S.S.R.)	D. Bilozerchev (U.S.S.R.)	V. Artyomov (U.S.S.R.)
1988	U.S.S.R.	V. Artyomov (U.S.S.R.)	V. Artyomov (U.S.S.R.)* V. Lyukin (U.S.S.R.)*	V. Artyomov (U.S.S.R.)
1989	U.S.S.R.	I. Korobchinski (U.S.S.R.)	Li Chunyang (China)	V. Artyomov (U.S.S.R.)* Li Jing (China)*

year	pommel horse	rings	vault	floor exercise
1985	V. Mogilny (U.S.S.R.)	Li Ning (China)* Y. Korolyov (U.S.S.R.)*	Y. Korolyov (U.S.S.R.)	Tong Fei (China)
1987	D. Bilozerchev (U.S.S.R.)* Z. Borkai (Hung.)*	Y. Korolyov (U.S.S.R.)	S. Kroll (E.Ger.)* Lou Yun (China)*	Lou Yun (China)
1988	D. Bilozerchev (U.S.S.R.)* Z. Borkai (Hung.)* L. Gueraskov (Bulg.)*	H. Behrendt (E.Ger.)* D. Bilozerchev (U.S.S.R.)*	Lou Yun (China)	S. Kharkov (U.S.S.R.)
1989	V. Mogilny (U.S.S.R.)	A. Aguilar (W.Ger.)	J. Behrend (E.Ger.)	I. Korobchinski (U.S.S.R.)

*Tied.

I. Korobchinski: all-around individual world gymnastics championships

VANDYSTADT—ALLSPORT USA

S. Boginskaya: all-around individual world gymnastics championships—women (1989)

VANDYSTADT—ALLSPORT USA

World Gymnastics Championships—women

year	all-around team	all-around individual	balance beam
1985	U.S.S.R.	Y. Shushunova (U.S.S.R.)* O. Omelyanchik (U.S.S.R.)*	D. Silivas (Rom.)
1987	Romania	A. Dobre (Rom.)	A. Dobre (Rom.)
1988	U.S.S.R.	Y. Shushunova (U.S.S.R.)	D. Silivas (Rom.)
1989	U.S.S.R.	S. Boginskaya (U.S.S.R.)	D. Silivas (Rom.)

year	uneven parallel bars	vault	floor exercise	rhythmic
1985	G. Fahnrich (E.Ger.)	Y. Shushunova (U.S.S.R.)	O. Omelyanchik (U.S.S.R.)	
1987	D. Silivas (Rom.) E. Thuemmler (E.Ger.)	Y. Shushunova (U.S.S.R.)	Y. Shushunova (U.S.S.R.) D. Silivas (Rom.)	
1988	D. Silivas (Rom.)	S. Boginskaya (U.S.S.R.)	D. Silivas (Rom.)	M. Lobach (U.S.S.R.)
1989	Fan Di (China)* D. Silivas (Rom.)*	O. Dudnik (U.S.S.R.)	S. Boginskaya (U.S.S.R.)* D. Silivas (Rom.)*	B. Panova (Bulg.)

*Tied.

HORSE RACING

2,000 Guineas

year	horse	jockey	owner	trainer
1985	Shadeed	L. Piggott	M. al-Maktoum	M. Stoute
1986	Dancing Brave	G. Starkey	K. Abdullah	G. Harwood
1987	Don't Forget Me	W. Carson	J. Horgan	R. Hannon
1988	Doyoun	W. Swinburn	Aga Khan IV	M. Stoute
1989	Nashwan	W. Carson	H. al-Maktoum	D. Hern

The Derby

year	horse	jockey	owner	trainer
1985	Slip Anchor	S. Cauthen	Lord H. de Walden	H. Cecil
1986	Shahrastani	W.R. Swinburn	Aga Khan IV	M.R. Stoute
1987	Reference Point	S. Cauthen	L. Freedman	H. Cecil
1988	Kahyasi	R. Cochrane		
1989	Nashwan	W. Carson	H. al-Maktoum	D. Hern

Triple Crown champions—British

year	winner
1915	Pommern
1917	Gay Crusader
1918	Gainsborough
1935	Bahram
1970	Nijinsky

The St. Leger

year	horse	jockey	owner	trainer
1985	Oh So Sharp	S. Cauthen	Sheikh Mohammed	H. Cecil
1986	Moon Madness	P. Eddery	Duchess of Norfolk	J. Dunlop
1987	Reference Point	S. Cauthen	L. Freedman	H. Cecil
1988	Minster Son	W. Carson	Lady Beaverbrook	N. Graham
1989	Michelozzo	S. Cauthen	C. St. George	H. Cecil

The American Thoroughbred classics

The Kentucky Derby

year	horse	jockey	owner	trainer
1985	Spend a Buck	A. Cordero, Jr.	D. Diaz	C. Gambolati
1986	Ferdinand	W. Shoemaker	E. Keck	C. Whittingham
1987	Alysheba	C. McCarron	D. & P. Scharbauer	J. Van Berg
1988	Winning Colors	G. Stevens	E. Klein	D.W. Lukas
1989	Sunday Silence	P. Valenzuela	A. Hancock, others	C. Whittingham

The Preakness Stakes

year	horse	jockey	owner	trainer
1986	Snow Chief	A. Solis	C. Grinsted, B. Rochelle	M. Stute
1987	Alysheba	C. McCarron	D. & P. Scharbauer	J. Van Berg
1988	Risen Star	E. Delahoussaye	R. Lamarque, L. Roussel	L. Roussel
1989	Sunday Silence	P. Valenzuela	A. Hancock, others	C. Whittingham

The Belmont Stakes

year	horse	jockey	owner	trainer
1986	Danzig Connection	C. McCarren	H. de Kwiatkowski	W. Stephens
1987	Bet Twice	C. Perret	Cisley Stable	J. Croll
1988	Risen Star	E. Delahoussaye	R. Lamarque, L. Roussel	L. Roussel
1989	Easy Goer	P. Day	O. Phipps	S. McGaughey

Harness racing

The Hambletonian Trot

year	horse	driver
1985	Prakas	B. O'Donnell
1986	Nuclear Kosmos	U. Thoresen
1987	Mack Lobell	J. Campbell
1988	Armbro Goal	J. Campbell
1989	Park Avenue Joe	R. Waples

Australian Thoroughbred racing

Melbourne Cup

year	horse	jockey	owner	trainer
1985	What a Nuisance	P. Hyland	Mr. & Mrs. L.J. Williams	J.F. Meagher
1986	At Talaq	M. Clarke	Sheikh al-Maktoum	C. Hayes
1987	Kensei	L. Olsen	Six-man syndicate	L. Bridge
1988	Empire Rose	T. Allan	F.R. & T.J. Bodle	L. Laxon
1989	Tawrrific	R.S. Dye	B.F. Avery, others	D.L. Freedman

Triple Crown champions—U.S.

year	horse
1946	Assault
1948	Citation
1973	Secretariat
1977	Seattle Slew
1978	Affirmed

Sunday Silence: Kentucky Derby (1989)
FOCUS ON SPORTS

ICE HOCKEY

The Stanley Cup

season	winner	runner-up	games
1984–85	Edmonton Oilers	Philadelphia Flyers	4–1
1985–86	Montreal Canadiens	Calgary Flames	4–1
1986–87	Edmonton Oilers	Philadelphia Flyers	4–3
1987–88	Edmonton Oilers	Boston Bruins	4–0
1988–89	Calgary Flames	Montreal Canadiens	4–2

World Amateur Hockey Championships

year	winner
1985	Czechoslovakia
1986	U.S.S.R.
1987	Sweden
1988	U.S.S.R.
1989	U.S.S.R.

Calgary Flames: Stanley Cup (1989)
ALLSPORT USA

ICE SKATING

World figure skating champions—women	
year	winner
1985	K. Witt (E.Ger.)
1986	D. Thomas (U.S.)
1987	K. Witt (E.Ger.)
1988	K. Witt (E.Ger.)
1989	M. Ito (Japan)

World figure skating champions—pairs	
year	winners
1985	E. Valova, O. Vasilev (U.S.S.R.)
1986	E. Gordeeva, S. Grinkov (U.S.S.R.)
1987	E. Gordeeva, S. Grinkov (U.S.S.R.)
1988	E. Valova, O. Vasilyev (U.S.S.R.)
1989	E. Gordeeva, S. Grinkov (U.S.S.R.)

World figure skating champions—men	
year	winner
1985	A. Fadeyev (U.S.S.R.)
1986	B. Boitano (U.S.)
1987	B. Orser (Can.)
1988	B. Boitano (U.S.)
1989	K. Browning (Can.)

World ice dancing champions	
year	winners
1985	N. Bestemyanova, A. Bukin (U.S.S.R.)
1986	N. Bestemyanova, A. Bukin (U.S.S.R.)
1987	N. Bestemyanova, A. Bukin (U.S.S.R.)
1988	N. Bestemyanova, A. Bukin (U.S.S.R.)
1989	M. Klimova, S. Ponomarenko (U.S.S.R.)

E. Gordeeva, S. Grinkov: world figure skating champions—pairs (1989)

PAUL J. SUTTON—DUOMO

K. Browning: world figure skating champion—men (1989)

STEVEN E. SUTTON—DUOMO

World all-around speed skating champions—men	
year	winner
1985	H. Vergeer (Neth.)
1986	D. Jansen (U.S.)
1987	N. Gulyaev (U.S.S.R.)
1988	E. Flaim (U.S.)
1989	L. Visser (Neth.)

World all-around speed skating champions—women	
year	winner
1985	A. Schöne (E.Ger.)
1986	K. Kania (E.Ger.)
1987	K. Kania (E.Ger.)
1988	K. Kania (E.Ger.)
1989	C. Moser (E.Ger.)

World Speed Skating Sprint Championships		
year	men	women
1985	I. Zhelezovsky (U.S.S.R.)	C. Rothenburger (E.Ger.)
1986	I. Zhelezovsky (U.S.S.R.)	K. Kania (E.Ger.)
1987	A. Kuroiwa (Japan)	K. Kania (E.Ger.)
1988	D. Jansen (U.S.)	C. Rothenburger (E.Ger.)
1989	I. Zhelezovsky (U.S.S.R.)	B. Blair (U.S.)

JUDO

World Judo Championships				
year	open weights	60 kg	65 kg	71 kg
1981	Y. Yamashita (Japan)	Y. Moriwaki (Japan)	K. Kashiwazaki (Japan)	Park Chong Hak (S.Kor.)
1983	H. Saito (Japan)	K. Tletseri (U.S.S.R.)	N. Solodukhin (U.S.S.R.)	H. Nakanishi (Japan)
1985	Y. Masaki (Japan)	S. Hosokawa (Japan)	Y. Sololov (U.S.S.R.)	Keun Ahn Byung (S. Kor.)
1987	N. Ogawa (Japan)	Kim Jae Yup (S.Kor.)	Y. Yamamoto (Japan)	M. Swain (U.S.)
1989	N. Ogawa (Japan)	A. Totikasvili (U.S.S.R.)	D. Becanovic (Yugos.)	T. Koga (Japan)

year	78 kg	86 kg	95 kg	+ 95 kg
1981	N. Adams (U.K.)	B. Tchoullouyan (Fr.)	T. Khubuluri (U.S.S.R.)	Y. Yamashita (Japan)
1983	N. Hikage (Japan)	D. Ultsch (E.Ger.)	A. Preschel (E.Ger.)	Y. Yamashita (Japan)
1985	N. Hikage (Japan)	P. Seisenbacher (Austria)	H. Sugai (Japan)	Chul Cho Yong (S.Kor.)
1987	H. Okada (Japan)	F. Canu (Fr.)	H. Sugai (Japan)	G. Veritchev (U.S.S.R.)
1989	Kim Bying Ju (S.Kor.)	F. Canu (Fr.)	K. Kurtanidze (U.S.S.R.)	N. Ogawa (Japan)

T. Murray: men's world all-around rodeo championship (1989)

PROFESSIONAL RODEO COWBOYS ASSOCIATION

MOTORBOAT RACING

Gold Cup Championship

year	boat	driver
1986	Miller American	C. Hanauer
1987	Miller American	C. Hanauer
1988	Miller American	C. Hanauer
1989	Miss Budweiser	T. D'Eath

POLO

Coronation Cup

year	result			
1985	Mexico	8	England I	6
1986	Mexico	8	England	4
1987	United States	8	England	5
1988	England	8	North America	7
1989	England	7	Australasia	5

Copa de las Americas

year	winner
1936	Argentina
1950	Argentina
1966	Argentina
1969	Argentina
1980	Argentina

RODEO

Men's World All-Around Rodeo Championship

year	winner
1985	L. Feild
1986	L. Feild
1987	L. Feild
1988	D. Appleton
1989	T. Murray

ROWING

World Rowing Championship—men

year	single sculls	min:s	double sculls	min:s	coxed pairs	min:s
1985	P. Karppinen (Fin.)	6:48.08	U. Heppner, T. Lange (E.Ger.)	6:15.49	G. Abbagnale, C. Abbagnale (Italy)	6:53.40
1986	P.-M. Kolbe (W.Ger.)	6:54.09	A. Belgeri, I. Pescialli (Italy)	6:33.64	A. Holmes, S. Redgrave (U.K.)	6:51.66
1987	T. Lange (E.Ger.)	7:36.41	D. Yorddanov, V. Dadev (Bulg.)	7:03.33	G. Abbagnale, C. Abbagnale (Italy)	7:40.81
1988	T. Lange (E.Ger.)	6:49.86	R. Florijan, N. Rienks (Neth.)	6:21.13	G. Abbagnale, C. Abbagnale (Italy)	6:58.79
1989	T. Lange (E.Ger.)	6:58.14	R. Thorsen, L. Bjoenness (Nor.)	6:23.40	G. Abbagnale, C. Abbagnale (Italy)	6:54.81

year	coxless pairs	min:s	coxed fours	min:s	coxless fours	min:s	eights	min:s
1985	N. Pimenov, Yu. Pimenov (U.S.S.R.)	6:38.39	U.S.S.R.	6:07.23	West Germany	6:00.19	U.S.S.R.	5:33.71
1986	Yu. Pimenov, N. Pimenov (U.S.S.R.)	6:42.37	East Germany	6:03.81	United States	6:03.53	Australia	5:33.54
1987	S. Redgrave, A. Holmes (U.K.)	7:11.20	East Germany	6:41.74	East Germany	6:39.70	United States	5:58.83
1988	S. Redgrave, A. Holmes (U.K.)	6:36.84	East Germany	6:10.74	East Germany	6:03.11	West Germany	5:46.05
1989	T. Jung, U. Kellner (E.Ger.)	6:39.95	Romania	6:14.90	East Germany	6:06.94	West Germany	5:43.88

World Rowing Championships—women

year	single sculls	min:s	double sculls	min:s	quadruple sculls	min:s
1985	C. Linse (E.Ger.)	7:40.37	S. Schwabe, M. Schröter (E.Ger.)	6:58.80	East Germany	6:22.47
1986	J. Hampe (E.Ger.)	7:29.60	S. Schwabe, B. Schramm (E.Ger.)	6:57.71	East Germany	6:13.91
1987	M. Georgieva (Bulg.)	8:59.26	S. Madina, V. Ninova (Bulg.)	7:47.89	East Germany	6:58.42
1988	J. Behrendt (E.Ger.)	7:47.19	B. Peter, M. Schröter (E.Ger.)	7:00.48	East Germany	6:21.06
1989	E. Lipa (Rom.)	7:27.96	J. Sorgers, B. Schramm (E.Ger.)	7:01.71	East Germany	6:16.62

year	coxless pairs	min:s	coxed fours*	min:s	eights	min:s
1985	R. Arba, E. Florea (Rom.)	7:25.08	East Germany	6:50.08	U.S.S.R.	6:14.00
1986	R. Arba, O. Homeghi (Rom.)	7:12.20	Romania	6:43.86	U.S.S.R.	6:08.76
1987	R. Arba, O. Homeghi (Rom.)	8:00.73	Romania	7:30.12	Romania	6:55.61
1988	R. Arba, O. Homeghi (Rom.)	7:28.13	East Germany	6:56.00	East Germany	6:15.17
1989	K. Haaker, J. Zeidler (E.Ger.)	7:26.97	East Germany	6:45.81	Romania	6:07.92

*Coxless fours from 1989.

The Diamond Challenge Sculls

year	winner	min:s
1985	S. Redgrave (Marlow R.C.)	8:28
1986	B. Eltang (Den.)	*
1987	P.-M. Kolbe (Ruder-Club Hamburg)	7:52
1988	H. McGlashan (Melbourne Univ.)	
1989	V. Chalupa (Dukla Praha, Czech.)	7:23

*Not rowed out.

Grand Challenge Cup

year	winner	min:s
1985	Harvard University, U.S.	6:27
1986	Nautilus R.C.	6:18
1987	Soviet Army	6:11
1988	Great Britain Olympic team	
1989	Hansa Dortmund (W.Ger.)	5:58

SKIING

World Nordic (Cross-country) Skiing Championships—men

year	15-km classic	30-km classic	50-km freestyle	relay
1984	G. Svan (Swed.)	N. Zimyatov (U.S.S.R.)	T. Wassberg (Swed.)	Sweden
1985	K. Haerhoenen (Fin.)	G. Svan (Swed.)	G. Svan (Swed.)	Norway
1987	M. Albarello (Italy)	T. Wassberg (Swed.)	M. De Zoll (Italy)	Sweden
1988	M. Deviatiarov (U.S.S.R.)	A. Prokurorov (U.S.S.R.)	G. Svan (Swed.)	Sweden
1989	H. Kirvesniemi (Fin.)	V. Smirnov (U.S.S.R.)	G. Svan (Swed.)	Sweden

World Nordic (Cross-country) Skiing Championships—women

year	5-km classic	10-km classic	20-km freestyle	relay
1984	M.-L. Hämäläinen (Fin.)	M.-L. Hämäläinen (Fin.)	M.-L. Hämäläinen (Fin.)	Norway
1985	A. Boe (Nor.)	A. Boe (Nor.)	G. Nykelmo (Nor.)	U.S.S.R.
1987	M. Matikainen (Fin.)	A. Jahren (Nor.)	M.-H. Westin (Swed.)	U.S.S.R.
1988	M. Matikainen (Fin.)	V. Ventsene (U.S.S.R.)	T. Tikhonova (U.S.S.R.)	U.S.S.R.
1989	not held	M.-L. Kirvesniemi (Fin.)	not held	Finland

World Nordic Skiing Championships—ski jump

year	jump (70 m)	special jump (90 m)	combined
1984	J. Weissflog (E.Ger.)	M. Nykänen (Fin.)	T. Sandberg (Nor.)
1985	J. Weissflog (E.Ger.)	P. Bergerud (Nor.)	H. Weinbach (W.Ger.)
1987	J. Parma (Czech.)	A. Felder (Austria)	T. Loekken (Nor.)
1988	M. Nykänen (Fin.)	M. Nykänen (Fin.)	H. Kempf (Switz.)
1989	J. Weissflog (E.Ger.)	J. Puikkonen (Fin.)	T.E. Elden (Nor.)

G. Svan: world Nordic skiing championships—50-km freestyle (1989)
PASCAL RONDEAU—ALLSPORT

World Alpine Skiing Championships—slalom

year	men's slalom	men's giant slalom	women's slalom	women's giant slalom
1984	P. Mahre (U.S.)	M. Julen (Switz.)	P. Magoni (Italy)	D. Armstrong (U.S.)
1985	J. Nilsson (Swed.)	M. Wasmaier (W.Ger.)	P. Pelen (Fr.)	D. Roffe (U.S.)
1987	F. Woerndl (W.Ger.)	P. Zurbriggen (Switz.)	E. Hess (Switz.)	V. Schneider (Switz.)
1988	A. Tomba (Italy)	A. Tomba (Italy)	V. Schneider (Switz.)	V. Schneider (Switz.)
1989	R. Nierlich (Austria)	R. Nierlich (Austria)	M. Svet (Yugos.)	V. Schneider (Switz.)

World Alpine Skiing Championships—downhill

year	men	women
1984	B. Johnson (U.S.)	M. Figini (Switz.)
1985	P. Zurbriggen (Switz.)	M. Figini (Switz.)
1987	P. Müller (Switz.)	M. Walliser (Switz.)
1988	P. Zurbriggen (Switz.)	M. Kichl (W.Ger.)
1989	H. Tauscher (W.Ger.)	M. Walliser (Switz.)

World Alpine Skiing Championships—combined

year	men	women
1978	A. Wenzel (Liech.)	A. Moser-Proell (Austria)
1982	M. Vion (Fr.)	E. Hess (Switz.)
1987	M. Girardelli (Lux.)	E. Hess (Switz.)
1988	H. Strolz (Austria)	A. Wachter (Austria)
1989	M. Girardelli (Lux.)	T. McKinney (U.S.)

V. Schneider: world Alpine skiing championships—giant slalom (1989)
PAUL J. SUTTON—DUOMO

Alpine World Cup

year	men	women
1985	M. Girardelli (Lux.)	M. Figini (Switz.)
1986	M. Girardelli (Lux.)	M. Walliser (Switz.)
1987	P. Zurbriggen (Switz.)	M. Walliser (Switz.)
1988	P. Zurbriggen (Switz.)	M. Figini (Switz.)
1989	M. Girardelli (Lux.)	V. Schneider (Switz.)

Nordic World Cup

year	men	women
1985	G. Svan (Swed.)	A. Boe (Nor.)
1986	G. Svan (Swed.)	M. Matikainen (Fin.)
1987	T. Mogren (Swed.)	M. Matikainen (Fin.)
1988	G. Svan (Swed.)	M. Matikainen (Fin.)
1989	G. Svan (Swed.)	E. Valbe (U.S.S.R.)

SQUASH RACKETS

British Open Championships—men

year	winner
1984–85	Jah. Khan (Pak.)
1985–86	Jah. Khan (Pak.)
1986–87	Jah. Khan (Pak.)
1987–88	Jah. Khan (Pak.)
1988–89	Jah. Khan (Pak.)

British Open Championships—women

year	winner
1984–85	S. Devoy (N.Z.)
1985–86	S. Devoy (N.Z.)
1986–87	S. Devoy (N.Z.)
1987–88	S. Devoy (N.Z.)
1988–89	S. Devoy (N.Z.)

World Open Championships—men

year	winner
1985–86	Jah. Khan (Pak.)
1986–87	R. Norman (N.Z.)
1987–88	Jah. Khan (Pak.)
1988–89	Jah. Khan (Pak.)
1989–90	Jan. Khan (Pak.)

World Open Championships—women

year	winner
1981–82	R. Thorne (Australia)
1983–84	V. Cardwell (Australia)
1985–86	S. Devoy (N.Z.)
1987–88	S. Devoy (N.Z.)
1988–89	M. Le Moignan (U.K.)

SWIMMING

World Swimming Championships—men

	freestyle				backstroke	
year	100 m	200 m	400 m	1,500 m	100 m	200 m
1975	A. Coan (U.S.)	T. Shaw (U.S.)	T. Shaw (U.S.)	T. Shaw (U.S.)	R. Matthes (E.Ger.)	Z. Verraszto (Hung.)
1978	D. McCagg (U.S.)	B. Forrester (U.S.)	V. Salnikov (U.S.S.R.)	V. Salnikov (U.S.S.R.)	B. Jackson (U.S.)	J. Vassallo (U.S.)
1982	J. Woithe (E.Ger.)	M. Gross (W.Ger.)	V. Salnikov (U.S.S.R.)	V. Salnikov (U.S.S.R.)	D. Richter (E.Ger.)	R. Carey (U.S.)
1986	M. Biondi (U.S.)	M. Gross (W.Ger.)	R. Henkel (W.Ger.)	R. Henkel (W.Ger.)	I. Polyansky (U.S.S.R.)	I. Polyansky (U.S.S.R.)

	breaststroke		butterfly		individual medley	
	100 m	200 m	100 m	200 m	200 m	400 m
1975	D. Wilkie (U.K.)	D. Wilkie (U.K.)	G. Jagenburg (U.S.)	B. Forrester (U.S.)	A. Hargitay (Hung.)	A. Hargitay (Hung.)
1978	W. Kusch (W.Ger.)	N. Nevid (U.S.)	J. Bottom (U.S.)	M. Bruner (U.S.)	G. Smith (Can.)	J. Vassallo (U.S.)
1982	S. Lundquist (U.S.)	V. Davis (Can.)	M. Gribble (U.S.)	M. Gross (W.Ger.)	A. Sidorenko (U.S.S.R.)	R. Prado (Braz.)
1986	V. Davis (Can.)	J. Szabo (Hung.)	P. Morales (U.S.)	M. Gross (W.Ger.)	T. Darnyi (Hung.)	T. Darnyi (Hung.)

	team relays			diving	
	4 × 100-m freestyle	4 × 200-m freestyle	4 × 100-m medley	springboard	platform
1975	United States	West Germany	United States	P. Boggs (U.S.)	K. Dibiasi (Italy)
1978	United States	United States	United States	P. Boggs (U.S.)	G. Louganis (U.S.)
1982	United States	United States	United States	G. Louganis (U.S.)	G. Louganis (U.S.)
1986	United States	East Germany	United States	G. Louganis (U.S.)	G. Louganis (U.S.)

World Swimming Championships—women

	freestyle				backstroke	
year	100 m	200 m	400 m	800 m	100 m	200 m
1975	K. Ender (E.Ger.)	S. Babashoff (U.S.)	S. Babashoff (U.S.)	J. Turrall (Australia)	U. Richter (E.Ger.)	B. Treiber (E.Ger.)
1978	B. Krause (E.Ger.)	C. Woodhead (U.S.)	T. Wickham (Australia)	T. Wickham (Australia)	L. Jezek (U.S.)	L. Jezek (U.S.)
1982	B. Meineke (E.Ger.)	A. Verstappen (Neth.)	C. Schmidt (E.Ger.)	K. Linehan (U.S.)	K. Otto (E.Ger.)	C. Sirch (E.Ger.)
1986	K. Otto (E.Ger.)	H. Friedrich (E.Ger.)	H. Friedrich (E.Ger.)	A. Strauss (E.Ger.)	B. Mitchell (U.S.)	C. Sirch (E.Ger.)

	breaststroke		butterfly		individual medley	
	100 m	200 m	100 m	200 m	200 m	400 m
1975	H. Anke (E.Ger.)	H. Anke (E.Ger.)	K. Ender (E.Ger.)	R. Kother (E.Ger.)	K. Heddy (U.S.)	U. Tauber (E.Ger.)
1978	J. Bogdanova (U.S.S.R.)	L. Kachushite (U.S.S.R.)	J. Pennington (U.S.)	T. Caulkins (U.S.)	T. Caulkins (U.S.)	T. Caulkins (U.S.)
1982	U. Geweniger (E.Ger.)	S. Varganova (U.S.S.R.)	M.T. Meagher (U.S.)	I. Geissler (E.Ger.)	P. Schneider (E.Ger.)	P. Schneider (E.Ger.)
1986	S. Gerasch (E.Ger.)	S. Hörner (E.Ger.)	K. Gressler (E.Ger.)	M.T. Meagher (U.S.)	K. Otto (E.Ger.)	K. Nord (E.Ger.)

	team relays			diving	
	4 × 100-m freestyle	4 × 200-m freestyle	4 × 100-m medley	springboard	platform
1975	East Germany		East Germany	I. Kalinina (U.S.S.R.)	J. Ely (U.S.)
1978	United States		United States	I. Kalinina (U.S.S.R.)	I. Kalinina (U.S.S.R.)
1982	East Germany		East Germany	M. Neyer (U.S.)	W. Wyland (U.S.)
1986	East Germany	East Germany	East Germany	Gao Min (China)	Chen Lin (China)

K. Otto: world swimming championships—100-m freestyle and 200-m individual medley (1986)

PAUL J. SUTTON—DUOMO

TABLE TENNIS

World Table Tennis Championships—men

year	St. Bride's Vase (singles)	Iran Cup (doubles)	Swaythling Cup (team)
1983	Guo Yuehua (China)	D. Surbek, Z. Kalinic (Yugos.)	China
1985	Jiang Jialiang (China)	M. Appelgren, U. Carlsson (Swed.)	China
1987	Jiang Jialiang (China)	Chen Longcan, Wei Qingguang (China)	China
1989	J.-O. Waldner (Swed.)	J. Rosskopf, S. Fetzner (W.Ger.)	Sweden

World Table Tennis Championships—women

year	G. Geist Prize (singles)	W.J. Pope Trophy (doubles)	Corbillon Cup (team)
1983	Cao Yanhua (China)	Shen Jianping, Dai Lili (China)	China
1985	Cao Yanhua (China)	Dai Lili, Geng Lijuan (China)	China
1987	He Zhili (China)	Hyun Jung Hwa, Yang Young Ja (S.Kor.)	China
1989	Qiao Hong (China)	Qiao Hong, Deng Yaping (China)	China

World Table Tennis Championships—mixed

year	Heydusek Prize
1981	Xie Saike, Huang Junqun (China)
1983	Guo Yuehua, Ni Xialian (China)
1985	Cai Zhenhua, Cao Yanhua (China)
1987	Hui Jun, Geng Lijuan (China)
1989	Yoo Nam Kyu, Hyung Jung Hwa (S.Kor.)

Table Tennis World Cup

year	winner
1985	Chen Xinhua (China)
1986	Chen Longcan (China)
1987	Teng Yi (China)
1988	A. Grubba (Pol.)
1989	Ma Wenge (China)

TENNIS

B. Becker (far left):
U.S. Open tennis
championships—singles
(1989)

S. Graf (left): All-England
(Wimbledon) tennis
championships—singles
(1989)

(LEFT) PAUL J. SUTTON—DUOMO;
(RIGHT) BOB MARTIN—ALLSPORT

All-England (Wimbledon) Tennis Championships—singles

year	men	women
1985	B. Becker (W.Ger.)	M. Navratilova (U.S.)
1986	B. Becker (W.Ger.)	M. Navratilova (U.S.)
1987	P. Cash (Australia)	M. Navratilova (U.S.)
1988	S. Edberg (Swed.)	S. Graf (W.Ger.)
1989	B. Becker (W.Ger.)	S. Graf (W.Ger.)

French Open Tennis Championships—singles

year	men	women
1985	M. Wilander (Swed.)	C. Evert Lloyd (U.S.)
1986	I. Lendl (Czech.)	C. Evert Lloyd (U.S.)
1987	I. Lendl (Czech.)	S. Graf (W.Ger.)
1988	M. Wilander (Swed.)	S. Graf (W.Ger.)
1989	M. Chang (U.S.)	A. Sánchez Vicario (Spain)

All-England (Wimbledon) Tennis Championships—doubles

year	men	women
1985	H. Gunthardt/B. Taroczy	K. Jordan/E. Smylie
1986	J. Nystrom/M. Wilander	M. Navratilova/P. Shriver
1987	R. Seguso/K. Flach	C. Kohde-Kilsche/H. Sukova
1988	R. Seguso/K. Flach	S. Graf/G. Sabatini
1989	J. Fitzgerald/A. Jarryd	J. Novotna/H. Sukova

French Open Tennis Championships—doubles

year	men	women
1985	M. Edmondson/K. Warwick	M. Navratilova/P. Shriver
1986	J. Fitzgerald/T. Smid	M. Navratilova/A. Temesvari
1987	R. Seguso/A. Jarryd	M. Navratilova/P. Shriver
1988	E. Sánchez/A. Gomez	M. Navratilova/P. Shriver
1989	J. Grabb/P. McEnroe	L. Savchenko/N. Zvereva

United States Open Tennis Championships—singles

year	men	women
1985	I. Lendl (Czech.)	H. Mandlikova (Czech.)
1986	I. Lendl (Czech.)	M. Navratilova (U.S.)
1987	I. Lendl (Czech.)	M. Navratilova (U.S.)
1988	M. Wilander (Swed.)	S. Graf (W.Ger.)
1989	B. Becker (W.Ger.)	S. Graf (W.Ger.)

Australian Open Tennis Championships—singles

year	men	women
1985	M. Wilander (Swed.)	C. Evert Lloyd (U.S.)
1986	S. Edberg (Swed.)	M. Navratilova (U.S.)
1987	S. Edberg (Swed.)	H. Mandlikova (Czech.)
1988	M. Wilander (Swed.)	S. Graf (W.Ger.)
1989	I. Lendl (Czech.)	S. Graf (W.Ger.)

United States Open Tennis Championships—doubles

year	men	women
1985	K. Flach/R. Seguso	C. Kohde-Kilsche/H. Sukova
1986	A. Gómez/S. Zivojinovic	M. Navratilova/P. Shriver
1987	S. Edberg/A. Jarryd	M. Navratilova/P. Shriver
1988	S. Casal/E. Sánchez	G. Fernandez/R. White
1989	J. McEnroe/M. Woodforde	M. Navratilova/H. Mandlikova

Australian Open Tennis Championships—doubles

year	men	women
1985	M. Edmondson/S. Stewart	M. Navratilova/P. Shriver
1986	P. Annacone/C. van Rensburg	M. Navratilova/P. Shriver
1987	S. Edberg/A. Jarryd	M. Navratilova/P. Shriver
1988	R. Leach/J. Pugh	M. Navratilova/P. Shriver
1989	R. Leach/J. Pugh	M. Navratilova/P. Shriver

Davis Cup

year	winner
1985	Sweden
1986	Australia
1987	Sweden
1988	West Germany
1989	West Germany

Wightman Cup

year	winner
1985	United States
1986	United States
1987	United States
1988	United States
1989	United States

Federation Cup

year	winner	runner-up	results
1985	Czechoslovakia	United States	2–1
1986	United States	Czechoslovakia	3–0
1987	West Germany	United States	2–1
1988	Czechoslovakia	U.S.S.R.	2–1
1989	United States	Spain	3–0

VOLLEYBALL

World Volleyball Championships

year	men	women	year	men	women
1978	U.S.S.R.	Cuba	1984	United States	China
1980	U.S.S.R.	U.S.S.R.	1986	United States	China
1982	U.S.S.R.	China	1988	United States	U.S.S.R.

WRESTLING

World Wrestling Championships—Freestyle

year	48 kg	52 kg	57 kg	62 kg	68 kg
1984	R. Weaver (U.S.)	S. Trstena (Yugos.)	H. Tomiyama (Japan)	R. Lewis (U.S.)	You I.T. (S.Kor.)
1985	Kim Chol Hwan (N.Kor.)	V. Iordanov (Bulg.)	S. Beloglazov (U.S.S.R.)	V. Alekseev (U.S.S.R.)	A. Fadzaev (U.S.S.R.)
1986	Y. Li (N.Kor.)	K. Sik (N.Kor.)	S. Beloglazov (U.S.S.R.)	K. Isaev (U.S.S.R.)	A. Fadzaev (U.S.S.R.)
1987	Li Jae Sik (N.Kor.)	V. Iordanov (Bulg.)	S. Beloglazov (U.S.S.R.)	J. Smith (U.S.)	A. Fadzaev (U.S.S.R.)
1988	T. Kobayashi (Japan)	M. Sato (Japan)	S. Beloglazov (U.S.S.R.)	J. Smith (U.S.)	A. Fadzaev (U.S.S.R.)
1989	J. Kim (S.Kor.)	V. Jordanov (Bulg.)	S. Yeung (N.Kor.)	J. Smith (U.S.)	B. Bovdayev (U.S.S.R.)

year	74 kg	82 kg	90 kg	100 kg	130 kg
1984	D. Schultz (U.S.)	M. Schultz (U.S.)	E. Banach (U.S.)	L. Banach (U.S.)	B. Baumgartner (U.S.)
1985	R. Cascaret (Cuba)	M. Schultz (U.S.)	B. Scherr (U.S.)	L. Khabelov (U.S.S.R.)	D. Gobedzhishvili (U.S.S.R.)
1986	R. Cascaret (Cuba)	V. Modozyan (U.S.S.R.)	M. Khadartsev (U.S.S.R.)	A. Khadartsev (U.S.S.R.)	B. Baumgartner (U.S.)
1987	A. Varaev (U.S.S.R.)	M. Schultz (U.S.)	M. Khadartsev (U.S.S.R.)	L. Khabelov (U.S.S.R.)	A. Khadartsev (U.S.S.R.)
1988	K. Monday (U.S.)	Han Myang Woo (S. Kor.)	M. Khadartsev (U.S.S.R.)	V. Puscasu (Rom.)	D. Gobedzhishvili (U.S.S.R.)
1989	K. Monday (U.S.)	E. Jabraylov (U.S.S.R.)	M. Khadartsev (U.S.S.R.)	A. Atavov (U.S.S.R.)	A.R. Soleimani (Iran)

World Wrestling Championships—Greco-Roman style

year	48 kg	52 kg	57 kg	62 kg	68 kg
1984	V. Maenza (Italy)	A. Miyahara (Japan)	P. Passarelli (W.Ger.)	Kim W.K. (S.Kor.)	V. Lisjak (Yugos.)
1985	M. Allakhverdiev (U.S.S.R.)	J. Ronningen (Nor.)	S. Balov (Bulg.)	J. Vangelov (Bulg.)	S. Negrisan (Rom.)
1986	M. Allakhverdiev (U.S.S.R.)	S. Dudyaev (U.S.S.R.)	E. Ivanov (Bulg.)	K. Madzhidov (U.S.S.R.)	L. Dzhulfalakyan (U.S.S.R.)
1987	M. Allakhverdiev (U.S.S.R.)	P. Roque (Cuba)	P. Mourier (France)	J. Vanguelov (Bulg.)	A. Abaev (U.S.S.R.)
1988	V. Maenza (Italy)	J. Ronningen (Nor.)	A. Sike (Hung.)	K. Madzhidov (U.S.S.R.)	L. Dzhulfalakyan (U.S.S.R.)
1989	O. Koucherenko (U.S.S.R.)	A. Ignatenko (U.S.S.R.)	E. Iwanov (Bulg.)	K. Madjidov (U.S.S.R.)	C. Passarelli (W.Ger.)

year	74 kg	82 kg	90 kg	100 kg	130 kg
1984	J. Salomaki (Fin.)	I. Draica (Rom.)	S. Fraser (U.S.)	V. Andrei (Rom.)	J. Blatnick (U.S.)
1985	M. Mamiashvili (U.S.S.R.)	B. Daras (Pol.)	M. Houck (U.S.)	A. Dimitrov (Bulg.)	I. Rostotsky (U.S.S.R.)
1986	M. Mamiashvili (U.S.S.R.)	not awarded	A. Malina (Poland)	T. Gaspar (Hung.)	T. Johansson (Swed.)
1987	J. Salomaki (Fin.)	T. Komaromi (Hung.)	V. Popov (U.S.S.R.)	G. Guedekhaorui (U.S.S.R.)	I. Rostorotski (U.S.S.R.)
1988	Kim Young Nam (S.Kor.)	M. Mamiashvili (U.S.S.R.)	A. Komchev (Bulg.)	A. Wronski (Pol.)	A. Karelin (U.S.S.R.)
1989	D. Tourlykhanov (U.S.S.R.)	T. Komaromi (Hung.)	M. Bullmann (E.Ger.)	G. Himmel (W.Ger.)	A. Karelin (U.S.S.R.)

YACHTING

America's Cup

year	winning yacht	owner	skipper	losing yacht	owner
1974	*Courageous* (U.S.)	Courageous syndicate	T. Hood	*Southern Cross* (Australia)	A. Bond
1977	*Courageous* (U.S.)	Courageous syndicate	T. Turner	*Australia* (Australia)	A. Bond and syndicate
1980	*Freedom* (U.S.)	Maritime College at Fort Schuyler Foundation, Inc.	D. Conner	*Australia* (Australia)	A. Bond and syndicate
1983	*Australia II* (Australia)	A. Bond and syndicate	J. Bertrand	*Liberty* (U.S.)	Maritime College at Fort Schuyler Foundation, Inc.
1987	*Stars & Stripes* (U.S.)	Sail America syndicate	D. Conner	*Kookaburra III* (Australia)	K. Parry and syndicate
1988	*Stars & Stripes* (U.S.)	Sail America syndicate	D. Conner	*New Zealand* (New Zealand)	M. Fay

Stars & Stripes: America's Cup (1988)

BOB GRIESER—GAMMA/LIAISON

Bermuda Race

year	winning yacht	owner
1978	*Babe*	A. Gay
1980	*Holger Danske*	R. Wilson
1982	*Brigadoon III*	B. Morton
1984	*Pamir*	F. Curren, Jr.
1986	*Silver Star* and *Puritan*	D. Clarke D. Robinson

Transpacific Race

year	winning yacht	owner
1979	*Arriba*	D. Choate
1981	*Sweet Okole*	D. Treadway
1983	*Bravura*	I. Loube
1985	*Montgomery Street*	D. Denning
1987	*Merlin*	D. Campion

Fastnet Cup

year	winning yacht	owner
1983	*Condor*	B. Bell (U.K.)
1985	*Panda*	P. Whipp (U.K.)
1987	*Irish Independent Pelt*	S. Fein (Ire.)
1989	*Great News*	R. Short (U.S.)

Television and Radio

The dominance of radio and television as the major sources of the world's news and entertainment could be seen in the number of radio and television sets in use. According to the latest statistics provided by Unesco, 1,914,789,000 radio sets and 749,424,000 television receivers were providing access to news, information, and entertainment to people throughout the world. Unesco's 1988 *Statistical Year Book* revealed that more than 500 million of the radio sets and 195 million of the television receivers were in use in the U.S. The Soviet Union ranked second in both categories, with 185 million radio and 90 million television sets. China ranked third in the number of radio sets, with 150 million, and Japan was third in the number of television sets, with 71 million. In Europe the United Kingdom was served by the most radio receivers, 65 million, and television sets, 30 million.

Organization of Services. For eight years the radio and television industries in the U.S. had been regulated by a Federal Communications Commission (FCC) that saw as its mission the dismantling of much of the regulatory structure that had been built up over the past 50 years. The marketplace, the commission felt, provided a more efficient regulatory mechanism. Thus it was a matter of no little moment when the commission was given three new members during the summer, including a chairman.

Alfred C. Sikes, a lawyer and former broadcaster who had served in the Reagan administration as the Commerce Department's assistant secretary for communications and information, was U.S. Pres. George Bush's choice for chairman. He replaced Dennis Patrick, who, like his predecessor, Mark Fowler, had made deregulation the principal item on his agenda. The other new appointees were Sherrie Marshall, a Washington, D.C., attorney with strong ties to the White House, and Andrew Barrett, recruited from the membership of the Illinois Commerce Commission. They filled two long-vacant seats.

Together with holdover member James Quello (with the departure in September of Patricia Diaz Dennis, the fifth seat became vacant), they were viewed by members of the broadcasting and cable television industries as constituting, on balance, a basically conservative commission. "'Pragmatic'" rather than "ideological" was the thumbnail description of the Sikes commission.

Pragmatism, broadcasters soon learned, cut two ways, however. The U.S. Senate Commerce Committee, in the confirmation hearing it held on the three nominations, made it clear that Congress expected the FCC to crack down on indecency and obscenity in broadcasting. Such programming had long been a matter of concern to members of Congress, not to mention the religious groups that had been pressuring Congress and the commission on the issue for years. The three nominees acknowledged Congress's role in setting policy; the commission's, they said, was to carry it out.

Thus it did not come as a complete surprise that one of the FCC's first actions under Sikes was to send letters to three radio stations asserting that their "shock jocks"—disc jockeys with a penchant for ribald humour—might have violated the federal statute barring indecent programming. The stations were asked to help the commission determine if a violation had occurred. A few weeks later the commission dispensed with the letter-writing phase of its new enforcement policy with the issuance of a tentative decision (a notice of apparent liability) to fine WLLZ (FM) in Detroit, Mich., for airing a song two years earlier that a listener, and the commission staff, considered indecent.

Then, in October, the FCC staff reported that it had cleaned up a two-year backlog of indecency complaints. It had sent notices of apparent liability to four radio stations and letters of inquiry to four others. For a variety of reasons the staff had dismissed the remaining 87. Nor was that all. The commission issued a notice of inquiry aimed at producing a record to answer the question of whether a rule it had adopted in response to a congressional directive to ban indecent broadcasts on a round-the-clock basis was constitutional. The U.S. Court of Appeals in Washington had ordered the commission to hold such a proceeding.

Beyond the changes at the FCC, the major story involving broadcasting and cable was another chapter in the takeover game. This one, though, topped the earlier ones. There was, for instance, the merger of Time Inc. and Warner Communications into the largest media and entertainment company in the world, a vertically integrated leader in several fields. The new Time Warner included one of the top three Hollywood film studios, the largest producer of television programming in the world, and the largest magazine publisher, the largest pay television programmer, and the second-largest cable operator in the U.S.

The Time-Warner merger was only one of several examples of companies throughout the world seeking to become major players in the international entertainment marketplace. Sony Corp. in September reached an agreement to purchase the stock of Columbia Pictures for $3.4 billion.

HARRY BENSON

Veteran reporters Sam Donaldson and Diane Sawyer were the hosts of "Prime Time Live," ABC's new hour-long weekly news program. Each of the three major networks introduced an hour-long weekly newsmagazine.

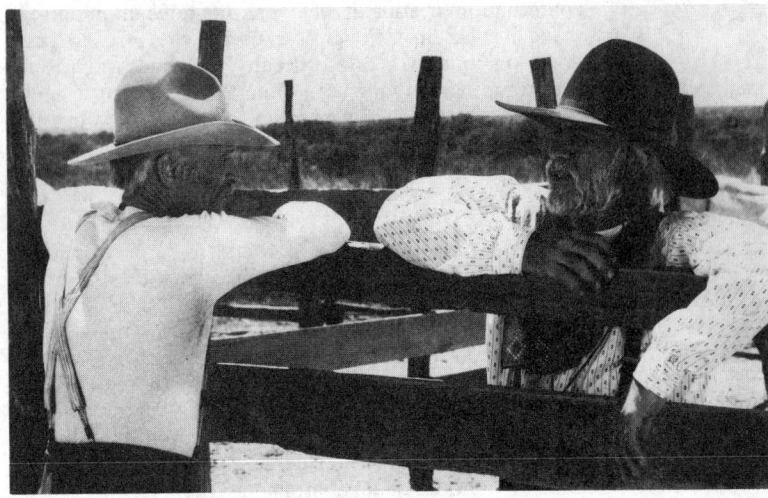

Robert Duvall (left) and Tommy Lee Jones play former Texas Rangers on a last great adventure in CBS's "Lonesome Dove," an epic miniseries based on the best-selling novel by Larry McMurtry.

TONY ESPARZA—CBS

The purchase, which was completed on October 31, put Sony in control of an enormous film library—about 3,000 films and some 2,600 television shows—that could be transferred to the 8-mm videotape cassette, video disc, and even the high-definition television (HDTV) technologies that Sony had developed.

The European Communities' (EC's) directive "Television Without Frontiers" was finally adopted in the face of deep divisions between member nations over proposals that would restrict the importation of U.S. programming. After objections from West Germany, Belgium, Denmark, The Netherlands, and Greece, the proposal to impose a 46.9% quota on non-EC programming was accepted as a "political objective" rather than as a firm restriction. U.S. producers, whose sales to Europe during the year were estimated at $900 million, protested vigorously against the quota even though the volume of U.S. imports across all channels never exceeded 20% and the new guidelines were unlikely to slow down the market.

The essence of the directive was to require member nations of the EC to ensure freedom of broadcast reception and not restrict retransmission in their territory of broadcasts from other member nations. The directive also restricted both the times allowed for advertising and the subject matter for advertisements. Particular controls were placed on advertising to children to ensure that their youth or their credulity would not be exploited in attempts to exhort them to purchase products. In addition, children should not be encouraged to persuade parents to buy the goods advertised.

The advance toward advertising-supported programming services continued unabated throughout Europe. A financial review of European television by the British magazine *Broadcast* revealed a growth in advertising, which, it was estimated, would more than double TV advertising revenue within 10 years. No Western European country appeared able to stem the tide of commercialized TV. The last bastion of public service purity, Scandinavia, had already given way with a commercial channel, TV2, well established in Denmark, a new commercial channel in Norway, and Sweden prepared to follow at the end of 1990.

Elsewhere in the EC, Spanish broadcasting was undergoing the most rapid increase, with three franchises awarded to challenge the state broadcaster RTVE's monopoly. New commercial channels were also scheduled to open in Portugal and Ireland. Austria decided to have a national referendum on deregulation of broadcasting, while in Italy, the least regulated broadcasting system in the EC, the state

broadcaster RAI made a remarkable recovery, winning audience ratings against its aggressive commercial competitor, Silvio Berlusconi's three Milan-based networks, Canale 5, Italia 1, and Rete 4.

In France the privatized national channel TF1 made a small profit, but the two private commercial stations, Metropole 6 and La 5, lost money. However, TF1 ran into problems with the broadcasting regulatory body, the Conseil Superieur de L'Audiovisuel (CSA), for failing to adhere to restrictions on imported programming. TF1 was informed that if it did not comply with regulations, it faced fines of up to $10,300 for every hour it fell below the quotas. TF1 complied, dropping some 670 hours of programming, mainly from the U.S.

In the U.K. the government's declared policy of seeking bids for regional independent television (ITV) franchises was tempered by a decision to place a quality requirement on contenders. The government also proposed a new national commercial channel, Channel 5, that would be bid for on the same basis as ITV regional licenses and would eventually reach 65–75% of the population. The BBC license fee remained linked to the retail price index.

In Eastern Europe advertising made inroads into the traditional state-owned systems. In the Soviet Union former newspaper editor Mikhail Nenashev was appointed to head Gosteleradio, the state Committee for TV and Radio, which made arrangements with Western advertising agencies to screen commercials. Hungary announced its first private channel, partially financed by the West German publisher Axel Springer. Commercial TV fared less well in Australia, where three major networks all faced financial difficulties due, in the main, to a heavy burden of debt.

Programming. The A.C. Nielsen Co., the leading TV audience-measurement service, reported in September that cable television was continuing to expand; it was reaching 56.4% of U.S. homes equipped with television, compared with 52.8% a year earlier. The popularity of videocassette recorders (VCRs), which record and play back television programs as well as playing prerecorded movies and other programming, also continued to grow. They could be found in 62% of the nation's 92.1 million TV households, compared with 56% a year earlier, according to the Electronic Industries Association. Also, independent television stations were seen as siphoning off audiences once regarded as virtually owned by the networks. (*See* Special Report.)

The news regarding the networks was not entirely bleak, however. During the summer, as they prepared for the

(continued on page 382)

The "Big Three" Become "Just Three More"

BY KENNETH R. CLARK

It is a perversity of human nature, most pronounced among Americans, that the only thing people enjoy more than raising up an idol is watching an idol fall. That is probably why one hears no wailing in the streets over the fate of ABC, CBS, and NBC in the decade of the '80s.

They are, of course, still very much in business, and in an advertising marketplace estimated by New York City advertising agencies at $10 billion for the 1989–90 television season, they are likely to stay in business for a long time. Most of that $10 billion in advertising dollars will even wind up in their coffers, but the wealth and power they wielded of old, when they were known, collectively, as the "Big Three," have gone the way of the Roman Empire.

Rise and Fall. The "Big Three" evolved in varying stages from the primordial soup of early television, the chief ingredients of which were test patterns, minute-long commercials, J. Fred Muggs, Milton Berle, and doctors endorsing cigarettes. The families of such sitcoms as "Father Knows Best" and "Leave It to Beaver" were blandly perfect, highly improbable, relentlessly cheerful, and, because they were the sole alternative, immensely popular.

In the earliest days, CBS and NBC split the fledgling television audience between them. ABC, dubbed in its infancy the "Almost Broadcasting Company," grew up a bit later. But by the 1970s the "Big Three" were in place, and if they were not a monopoly, they were at least a communications oligarchy commanding up to 95% of the nation's total television audience. What was left went, like crumbs from the king's table, to independent stations scratching like beggars at the gate.

Cable television, in its prototype stage, consisted of a few rural companies stringing wire to transmitters so the "Big Three" signal might be received in remote valleys and mountain communities with no other access. The videocassette recorder (VCR) belonged to science fiction. But cable came of age, science fiction became fact, and the end of the 1988–89 season found the three-network audience share at an all-time low of 68%.

The rest of the audience had gone to about 40 basic and 10 pay-cable services and to the once-struggling independents, which, according to the New York City advertising agency Bozell, Inc., gained some 27% of the networks' loss in 1988. The rise of the independents was fueled by aggressive marketing and by programming drawn from a booming syndication business that gave them everything from off-network reruns at a fraction of

Kenneth R. Clark is national media writer for the Chicago Tribune.

the original production cost to news programs and game shows independently produced.

With the increasing spread of VCRs into American living rooms, "home videos" added substantially to the network audience drain, which was evident all across the schedule, from daytime soap operas and game shows to prime time. According to Bozell, by the end of 1989 VCR owners could browse for rent or purchase among 40,000 movie titles, including 9,000 X-rated offerings.

According to the A.C. Nielsen Co., whose sample "families" determine what network shows make the "Top 10" each week, in 1989 VCRs were functioning in 62% of U.S. homes, and nearly 40 basic and 10 pay-cable programmers fed up to 50 channels (only three of which were ABC, CBS, NBC, and their affiliates) into 56.4% of U.S. homes equipped with television. Cable, once wholly dependent on network leavings for its schedule, used its new-found economic muscle in the 1980s to start producing its own fare. Nickelodeon aired 1,400 hours of its own programming in 1989.

To be sure, the audience base, first measured in 1950 when only 4.6 million television sets had been purchased, was considerably larger than it had been when ABC, CBS, and NBC divided it so exclusively. At the networks' zenith, in 1975, the number of sets had grown to 69.6 million, and Nielsen estimated that by Jan. 1, 1990, there were 92.1 million television homes serving 235,230,000 viewers in the 50 states. With rampant technology pushing such new horizons as high-definition sets, giant screens, broadcasts directly from satellite to dish antenna, and stereo sound, there would seem to be no limit to the growth.

Americans love television, watching, on average, seven hours and two minutes a day (as measured by Nielsen in the 1988–89 broadcast year), but the "Big Three" that initially gave it to them were just "Three More" now, and they have had to tailor their programming and promotion accordingly.

Rear Guard Action. The networks did not yield to either cable or the VCR without a fight. Many early cable companies, functioning then as "community antenna television" systems, found themselves in court when they attempted to boost network programming into signal-

Al Bundy (Ed O'Neill) lectures his wife, Peg (Katey Sagal), in an episode of "Married . . . with Children." The show, which was known for its coarse, adult humour, prompted a letter-writing campaign that persuaded several major sponsors to pull their commercial support.

poor rural areas. The networks did not mind adding those audiences to their base, but they did worry about copyrights and the prospect of someone else making a profit on their fare. "Copyright" also was the shibboleth raised in 1975 when Sony introduced the first VCR to the United States. This time, it was the networks' Hollywood surrogates, the big production companies that turn out network prime-time fare, who carried the ball—all the way to the U.S. Supreme Court, where they finally lost in 1984—in a bid to get the new technology either banned or heavily surcharged in the U.S. Home-taping of network programming, they claimed, was a "piracy" that would endanger their copyrights and cut into syndication profits. New technologies, however, almost always turn out to be unstoppable, and neither cable nor the VCR proved to be an exception.

As it turned out, home copying of television shows was less of a peril to the producers and the networks than the sale and rental of videocassettes. Audiences watching VCR movies are not watching the networks, so, in one of those practical compromises so common in the free marketplace, ABC, CBS, and NBC all developed cross-promotional deals with the makers of VCRs and tapes in which they beg viewers to tape their shows and view them later. Carrying the hucksterism one step further, NBC—the reigning ratings champion—joined Sears, Continental Airlines, and Buick in the fall of 1989 in an unprecedented cross-promotion to woo and win back the dwindling audience.

All the bells and whistles in the world, however, are not going to bring back all the strays. Unlike the networks, which depend on the varied tastes and sensibilities of the mass audience for their existence, cable "narrowcasts" straight to its chosen target—ESPN and Sportschannel to sports fans, Lifetime to women, CNN to news junkies, FNN to people worried about their money.

On the "Decency" Front. Because cable does not use the "public airwaves" to disseminate its fare, and because it sells its services only to viewers who want them, cable is not governed by the "decency" standards imposed—until the Reagan administration, at least—on the networks. HBO or Showtime can run, uncut and unexpurgated, the most explicitly sexy or mindlessly violent feature films, along with stand-up comics whose language would blister the paint on the walls of a National Football League locker room.

Let the networks try it—and under a deregulation-minded Federal Communications Commission they have wider license to do so—and the "pro-family" activists descend upon them with stones and cudgels. Yet, with large audience segments being lured away by cable's more "adult" offerings, they must try, as NBC did in 1988–89 with "Favorite Son" and as Fox, the fledgling "fourth network," was doing every week with its raunchy, sexist, much-protested, and heavily watched "Married . . . with Children."

In the long run, network television increasingly could be expected to press the boundaries established by feature films and cable, and most advertising agencies predicted that the audience drain would level off at a plateau giving the networks somewhere in the neighbourhood of 60% of the total audience. Since sponsor boycotts, the only weapon available to those who would "clean up television," seldom have any lasting effect, a return to the bland, good old days of "Father Knows Best" and "Leave It to Beaver" was highly unlikely. Like the television era of the "Big Three" supremacy, the age of innocence also was over.

(continued from page 380)

start of the fall season, the networks were reporting sales of almost $1 billion more than they had recorded at that time in 1988. Most of the increase was apparently due to higher prices generated by increased advertiser demand. Also, if estimates by financial analysts proved correct, the three networks could double the $600 million in profits they reported in 1988. In addition, the networks' optimism was heightened by the first week of the new season, when they managed to win back viewers who traditionally abandoned them in the summer months.

However, the new season was not greeted with uniform enthusiasm by the critics. The *New York Times*'s John J. O'Connor, for instance, said that as the more than 20 new weekly shows began developing their personality and character, "the overall programming landscape looks increasingly bleak." Not one, he said had the calibre of "Hill Street Blues" or "The Wonder Years" or even last year's "Roseanne." The networks did not need that kind of downbeat appraisal to begin preparing replacements. By the time the new season had passed the three-week mark, they were preparing series to take over the slots of struggling shows.

If for nothing else, the 1988–89 season might be remembered as the one that produced the biggest disappointment and the happiest surprise in regard to miniseries. ABC's massive production of Herman Wouk's "War and Remembrance"—19½ hours spread over 11 evenings in November 1988 and May 1989—was a sequel to the 1983 success "Winds of War" and was supposed to achieve high ratings. It was a disappointment, however, in both November and May, and was said to have cost the network between $30 million and $40 million. On the other hand, CBS's "Lonesome Dove," based on Larry McMurtry's best-selling novel set in the old West, demonstrated that westerns had not lost their appeal for viewers and that the miniseries was not dead as an art form on television. The four-part series in February won its time period on each of the four nights and propelled CBS to a strong second place in the ratings race for the February sweeps period; it proved to be CBS's third-highest-rated miniseries ever.

Broadcast news continued to prove its fascination and its worth in some of the major stories it covered in 1989. For almost a week in August the networks relayed pictures from Voyager 2 as it approached and flew by Neptune. Viewers were seeing the pictures and hearing of the discoveries from the space probe almost as soon as the National Aeronautics and Space Administration scientists monitoring the event completed their analyses.

Earlier in the summer U.S. radio and television journalists joined others from around the world in covering the upheaval in China. For months the journalists camped in Beijing (Peking), covering the protests of students and workers calling for democracy and an end to corruption in government. Late in the year the revolutionary events in Eastern Europe and two natural disasters—the San Francisco Bay area earthquake and Hurricane Hugo—received extensive coverage.

News was seized upon by the three major networks as providing a vehicle for one-hour prime-time programs. The most highly touted was ABC's "Prime Time Live," featuring two of the most celebrated news personalities in television, Sam Donaldson, known for the tenacity of his questioning of presidents, and Diane Sawyer, wooed away from CBS for the show. CBS's new offering, "Saturday Night with Connie Chung," employed something new for news programs, the use of prominent actors in dramatic re-creations of historic events. The third new program, "Yes-

terday, Today and Tomorrow" from NBC, was aired three times in the summer and was scheduled for three more times later in the year. It, too, made use of dramatic re-creations. This technique came under particular scrutiny as a result of the controversy generated by ABC's use of "simulations" in its report, on a newscast, of the U.S. government's suspicions that a high-ranking U.S. diplomat, Felix Bloch, had passed government secrets to the Soviet secret service.

Although CBS did poorly in the ratings contest in 1988, it won bragging rights in terms of the number of Emmys its shows garnered—27 in all, 2 more than NBC and 14 more than ABC. However, the 41st annual Emmy awards night, on September 17, was not an unrelieved joy for CBS. "Lonesome Dove" had been nominated for 18 Emmys but won only one in a major category (direction of a miniseries or special) and seven in all. By contrast, "War and Remembrance," a major commercial disappointment and not a hit with the critics, won the award for the outstanding miniseries. James Woods won an Emmy for the outstanding lead actor in a miniseries or special for his role in ABC's "My Name Is Bill W." Robert Duvall, who starred in "Lonesome Dove," had been seen as a virtually certain winner in that category. In the news department the Public Broadcasting Service (PBS) was dominant with 18 Emmys; CBS was second with 16, while ABC received 8 and NBC 5.

Sports continued to play a major role in the programming offered by radio and television, and the sports universe was expanding. According to a survey by *Broadcasting* magazine, ABC, CBS, NBC, and the cable sports network ESPN paid a combined total of $531 million for rights to televise National Football League games in the 1989–90 season. CBS, ABC, and ESPN paid another $45 million for the rights to carry college football. However, a number of college conferences sold their rights to cable television networks.

Broadcasters and cable operators also contributed to the treasuries of major league baseball teams. Those teams collected some $478 million in national and local radio and television (including regional broadcast and cable television) revenue, according to a *Broadcasting* survey. The total represented an increase of 18.6%, or $75 million, over the amount the teams collected in 1988. ABC-TV and NBC-TV announced that they were giving up their association with major league baseball for at least four years. CBS, with a reported offer of $1.1 billion, won the exclusive right to carry the World Series, the American and National League championship series, and 12 regular-season games during each of the four years from 1990 to 1993.

Basketball was also generating revenue for professional and college teams. A *Broadcasting* survey showed that national broadcast and cable television networks and local television and radio stations were producing close to $160 million for rights to National Basketball Association games during the 1988–89 season. The total was about $22 million more than the league earned from the sale of its broadcast rights in the previous year. After a 17-year relationship with CBS, NBA officials announced in November that the right to cover the league's games for the next four years belonged to NBC. The network agreed to pay the league $600 million, which would more than triple the NBA's annual broadcast revenue.

Basketball was also a revenue producer for U.S. colleges. CBS paid $55.3 million for the rights to some 20 National Collegiate Athletic Association tournament games and the national championship that concludes the tournament. In addition, the six top major conferences, each with about

A woman turns over letters to reveal the solution on "La Roue de la fortune," a French version of "Wheel of Fortune." A flood of U.S. game shows and soap operas on European television prompted the European Communities to recommend quotas on such shows.
Y. RIVOALLAN—KIPA

10 teams, were said to be selling their rights at a rate of about $1 million per team—some $60 million in all.

As for radio programming, a *Broadcasting* survey of the top 10 stations of the leading 50 metro service areas indicated that U.S. tastes in music had not changed very much during recent years. So-called adult contemporary and its variants—soft or "lite" adult contemporary—remained the most popular, as they had for the past several years. The gap between that music and the format that traditionally trailed it, top 40 or contemporary hit radio, was narrowing fast, however. Album-oriented rock was said to be the third-most-popular format and country music the fourth.

In Eastern Europe, as *glasnost* (openness) in its various forms thawed the political system, television emerged as one of the significant engines of change. In East Germany leading members of the government submitted themselves to a televised forum, answering questions from members of the public in an exercise in direct democracy, and the media attempted to report the appointment of Communist Party leader Egon Krenz as if it were a Western-style election.

In the Soviet Union the cameras covered striking miners, and news bulletins reported openly on the anti-Soviet demonstrations in the Baltic republics. A breakfast program, "120 Minutes," won widespread popularity, while at the other end of the schedule Vladimir Molchanov emerged as the TV personality with the largest public following for his "Before and After Midnight" discussion series, in which leading political figures were invited to discuss the major issues of the day.

The most dramatic manifestation of television in a closed political system during 1989 was in China, where the cameras were permitted to record the confrontation between student protesters on hunger strike and government leaders. However, the authorities used footage from Western TV coverage of the subsequent military action against student activists to identify and imprison dissidents, raising serious and as-yet-unresolved questions concerning the moral responsibility of the media.

In Western Europe the questions of morality that faced broadcasters were of a more conventional nature. The issue of "soft-porn" programs transmitted by satellite channels exercised broadcast authorities, while in the U.K. the government remained agitated over what it described as "trial by TV" in the coverage of Northern Ireland affairs. The stance of the broadcasters in this matter was partially

vindicated by the role of the Yorkshire ITV documentary series "First Tuesday" in alerting the public to the case of four young Irish people wrongfully imprisoned for 14 years for an Irish Republican Army bombing in the English town of Guildford. The program spent some five years of research and three investigative documentaries in successfully demonstrating the innocence of the "Guildford Four."

In the field of entertainment a global survey by the magazine *TV World* revealed that game shows and family drama continued to dominate audience ratings in virtually every country. Australia appeared to be ousting the U.S. as the leading producer of daytime dramas around the world. Not everyone relied on imported "soaps," however. One of the most successful domestic productions was Sweden's "Varuhuset" ("Department Store"), which created wide public interest and press debate by the manner in which it treated such sensitive subjects as alcoholism and AIDS. At its peak the serial attracted four million viewers, more than 50% of the potential Swedish audience.

Game shows were mostly local versions of U.S. formats. "Wheel of Fortune," known in German as "Gluecksrad" on the satellite channel Sat-1, received more than 8,000 requests a day from people wanting to compete. In France, as TF1's "La Roue de la fortune," it dominated the early evening schedule with a 26% audience rating.

At the International Television Festival Awards, the U.K.'s London Weekend ITV company won the Golden Rose of Montreux light entertainment award with the comedians "Hale and Pace"; RAI 2 from Italy won the Golden Nymph of Monte Carlo production award for a dramatic reconstruction of the origin of the Russian Revolution, "Lenin's Train"; the Prix Italia drama was the Soviet Union's "A Dog's Heart," a satire about the early days of the Revolution; and the documentary winner was Polish TV for "The Parade," lampooning the dictator worship of Kim Il Sung in North Korea.

A controversial drama from the independent producers Skreba Film for Britain's Channel 4, "A Very British Coup," about the overthrow of a future left-wing Labour government, won a number of important awards, including the Grand Prix at Banff, Alta. The disappointment of the year was an extravagant Anglo-French production of "A Tale of Two Cities" to mark the 200th anniversary of the French Revolution. It failed to capture either the imagination of the audience or the acclaim of the critics.

(MARTIN JACKSON; LAWRENCE B. TAISHOFF;
LEONARD ZEIDENBERG)

Amateur Radio. During the devastating Hurricane Hugo in September, ham radio operators on U.S. possessions in the Caribbean Sea proved to be the only link between the National Hurricane Center in Coral Cables, Fla., and Puerto Rico, the Virgin Islands, and other islands that had lost their electrical power and telephone service. Hams also provided emergency service in a number of lesser crises during the year, among them the 3,200-ha (8,000-ac) Summit fire in northeastern Oregon.

The FCC reported 464,800 licensed radio operators in the U.S. at the end of September 1988, about 28,000 more than in 1987. Estimates for the total number of hams worldwide were not available, but representatives of the American Radio Relay League put the number—exclusive of those in the U.S.S.R., for which no estimates were available—at about two million.

(LAWRENCE B. TAISHOFF; LEONARD ZEIDENBERG)

See also Industrial Review: *Advertising; Telecommunications; Motion Pictures; Music.*

This article updates the *Macropædia* article BROADCASTING.

Theatre

Great Britain and Ireland. Criticism mounted and angry voices continued to be raised by underfunded arts organizations, as well as by Peter Palumbo, the new chairman of the Arts Council of Great Britain, and by lobbyists from the National Campaign for the Arts, accusing Arts Minister Richard Luce and the Treasury of breaking their promise to raise grants in step with inflation. Although the government was finally shamed into admitting that it had been remiss, the level of the next year's grant was increased only 1.8%. The ensuing shortfall threatened bankruptcy or partial closing of some arts bodies, notably in the theatre. The relatively small rise in subsidies and in business sponsorship and the unexpected increase in box-office receipts from transfers of lucrative nonprofit productions to the private sector, by such bodies as the Royal National Theatre (RNT) and the Royal Shakespeare Company (RSC), served only as a mild palliative. An important victim of misguided governmental thrift was the "promising new playwright," whose diminishing numbers were directly attributable to the cuts in grants in the subsidized theatre. Britain's most successful playwright, Alan Ayckbourn (*see* BIOGRAPHIES), lamented this fact at the *Evening Standard* (ES) award ceremony, when he was handed his sixth award for best comedy, the science-fiction horror-comedy *Henceforward.* . . .

Of the awards given by the ES, *Plays and Players* (PP), *Time Out* (TO), and the Society of West End Theatre's Laurence Olivier (LO) jury, only the LO awards applied to productions from 1988 as well as 1989. Altogether, 34 awards for 1989 were won by the subsidized theatre. Of those, 12 went to the RSC and 7 to the RNT. The commercial theatre, including the privately owned Old Vic, which was subsidized by its owner, the Canadian entrepreneur Ed Mirvish, won 13 awards; 4 of those were LO awards for 1988 productions, including best designer to Richard Hudson for the season's six designs and best musical to Leonard Bernstein's *Candide,* a guest production originally seen at the Scottish Opera in Glasgow.

Other LO awards went to Willy Russell's *Shirley Valentine* (best comedy) and to its star, Pauline Collins (best actress in a new play). The ES and PP chose *Miss Saigon,* the exotic "operetta" by the French team of Claude-Michel Schönberg and Alain Boublil, as best musical and its director, Nicholas Hytner, as best director, while PP also picked its designer, John Napier, as best designer for his superb decor. Both ES and PP also cited Hytner as best director for his audacious production at the RNT of the controversial concentration-camp drama *Ghetto,* which earned its author, Joshua Sobol, the ES and one of the PP best play awards. In addition to the award for *Ghetto,* PP also cited Hytner as best director for the RSC production of *The Tempest.* Three players won awards in the private sector: Con O'Neill, the best actor in a musical LO award in Willy Russell's *Blood Brothers;* Felicity Kendal, the best actress ES award in *Much Ado About Nothing* and *Ivanov;* and Sarah Woodward, the Clarence Derwent Award (best supporting actress). The Irish actor Nial Buggy won the second Clarence Derwent Award (best supporting actor).

The RNT won the LO supporting role award for Eileen Atkins' two moving performances, in Harold Pinter's brief antitorture drama *Mountain Language* and in *Cymbeline.* In the same category one of the PP 1989 awards went to Michael Bryant for his crusty Polonius in Richard Eyre's (*see* BIOGRAPHIES) *Hamlet* at the RNT, and its best actress award went to the former RSC actress Fiona Shaw for her

(From left to right) Jonathan Pryce, Simon Bowman, and Lea Salonga rehearse a scene from *Miss Saigon,* a musical playing at London's Theatre Royal Drury Lane. Set in Saigon in the Vietnam war era, *Miss Saigon* is a modern adaptation of *Madame Butterfly.*

AP/WIDE WORLD

versatile interpretation in the twofold role of kindly Shen Te and her cruel fictitious brother Shui Ta in Deborah Warner's *The Good Person of Sichuan,* her first stint at the RNT since becoming an associate director there. The PP best actress in a revival award went to Shaw in RSC productions of *Electra* and *As You Like It.* TO chose the Royal Court Theatre for a citation for its general achievements and for director Max Stafford-Clark's production of Timberlake Wertenbaker's LO prizewinner of 1988, *Our Country's Good.* The ES and PP most promising playwright awards went to Stephen Jeffreys for the Hampstead Theatre production of his "yuppie" comedy *Valued Friends,* which also divided the TO best play award with *House of America* by Edward Thomas, staged by the Company Cwmni. Another PP promising playwright award went to Charlotte Keatley for *My Mother Said I Never Should,* a tearful family drama about four generations of Manchester women. *Poor Beast in the Rain,* an Irish comedy by Billy Roche, at the Bush Theatre, also shared that award.

Other awards to the RSC were three LOs from 1988 to Harriet Walters for three separate roles, to Brian Cox for his Titus Andronicus, and to Deborah Warner's austere and much-acclaimed—also in Europe—production of Shakespeare's horror-drama of that name. Trevor Nunn's studio production of *Othello* earned Ian McKellen the PP and ES acting awards in the role of Iago and Zoë Wanamaker the PP best supporting actress award for Emilia. Simon Russell-Beale was cited twice by PP for the supporting roles of Sir Fopling Flutter in George Etherege's *The Man of Mode* and of Henry McNeil in the world premiere of the RSC-commissioned satirical *Some Americans Abroad* by U.S. author Richard Nelson. This was one of the plays sharing the PP best play award. Another was Peter Flannery's drama of a modern Wandering Jew, *Singer,* with Antony Sher in the title role.

Sir Alec Guinness (LO) and Stephen Sondheim (ES) received special awards for services to theatre. The Benjamin Franklin medal of the Royal Society for the Arts was given to U.S. actor Sam Wanamaker for his promotion of the rebuilt Globe Theatre.

New and revived U.S. plays of note included works by David Mamet at the RNT and at Hampstead, August Wilson and John Steinbeck at the RNT, and David Henry Hwang, Donald Freed, Neil Simon, and Robert Harling in the West End (London commercial theatre). U.S. musicals that enjoyed long runs were *Anything Goes* and *A Little Night Music,* but *The Baker's Wife* closed early. British

musicals, new and revived, included *Metropolis, Aspects of Love* (another Andrew Lloyd Webber blockbuster), Ian Dury's *Apples,* Alan Jones's *Buddy* (the life of rock singer Buddy Holly), and the science-fiction extravaganza *Return to the Forbidden Planet.*

Other highlights at the RNT included *Juno and the Paycock;* David Storey's *The March on Russia,* featuring Bill Owen as a cynical ex-miner in Thatcherite Britain; and Peter Wood's stylish handling of *The Beaux' Stratagem.* Richard Eyre announced the production of *Racing Demon,* a new David Hare drama about religion and politics in modern Britain, for February 1990, followed by Sondheim's *Sunday in the Park with George* and Tony Harrison's latest new play. The RSC's repertoire of new plays included Frank McGuinness' *Mary and Lizzie,* a surreal skit on Marxism, seen through Irish eyes, and Stephen Poliakoff's *Playing with Trains,* a spiritual sequel to his *Breaking the Silence* of 1984. Several Stratford productions, notably *The Plantagenets, King John,* and *A Midsummer Night's Dream,* transferred to the Barbican, where Adrian Noble's production of Ibsen's *The Master Builder* was highly acclaimed. Jonathan Miller's bold new staging at the Old Vic included *King Lear,* with Eric Porter, and the hilarious British premiere of Corneille's *The Liar,* starring Alex Jennings.

Elsewhere new works or productions of special merit were Caryl Churchill's jazz-inspired *Icecream* (a TO citation) and Iain Heggie's *American Bagpipes* at the Royal Court, McGuinness' *Carthaginians* at Hampstead, and, in the West End, *The Black Prince* (Iris Murdoch), *Another Time* (Ronald Harwood's semiautobiographical view of South African apartheid, with Albert Finney brilliantly doubling as father and son), *Shadowlands* (William Nicholson), about Professor and Mrs. C.S. Lewis' life together, and *Jeffrey Barnard Is Unwell* (Keith Waterhouse), with Peter O'Toole irresistible as the drunken newspaper columnist of the title.

The death of Laurence Olivier (*see* OBITUARIES) was mourned throughout the land. The second Critics' Circle Drama Section award went to Sir Alec Guinness.

Despite the abolition of the Harvey Theatre Awards, the Dublin Festival survived, with fine productions at the Abbey Theatre, under interim manager Noel Pearson, of Tom Murphy's study of a suicide, *Too Late for Logic,* and Thomas Gilroy's updated version of Ibsen's *Ghosts.* At Dublin's newest theatre, the Tivoli, the Druid Theatre Company was seen in Ken Bourke's comic melodrama

Wild Harvest. Notable at the Belfast Festival were *Heart-break House,* staged by Nancy Meckler, the British Actors' Touring Company's *Antony and Cleopatra,* and the premiere of John McClelland's *Charlie Gorilla.*

France, Italy, Spain, Low Countries. As he embarked on his "Black Theatre" season in Paris, Peter Brook received the second European Community Theatre Prize. Other prizes in France were won by Ariane Mnouchkine (the Arletty), Brigitte Jaques (director's), René de Obaldia (Dramatists' League), Marion Bierry (the Gautier), Robert Hossein (the Dominique), and Catherine Samy (the "Plaisir du Théâtre"). The "Molières" went to Patrice Chéreau's two designers and Gérard Desarthes, star of *Hamlet;* Régis Stanton (director's); François Billetdoux (best new play); Hennequin and Véber (best comedy); *Cats* (best musical); and the players Maria Casarès, Christine Murillo, and Étienne Chicot, with a special prize to Eugène Ionesco.

Amid an increasing number of new French plays of merit, the numbers of foreign dramas and revivals on the Paris stage also increased. Outstanding were the Japanese suicide drama *The Hunting Gun,* by Yasushi Inoue; Rojas' *La Célestine,* with Jeanne Moreau, at the Comédie Française; *A Month in the Country,* with Isabelle Huppert; and André Engel's own version of *The Book of Job,* at the Chaillot.

Italian theatre was notable for Peter Stein's "fascist" *Titus Andronicus* in Rome; Giorgio Strehler's Piccolo productions of *As You Desire Me,* with his wife, Andrea Jonasson, and of *Arlecchino* (his sixth and last of the Goldoni comedy), with Jonasson and Ferruccio Soleri; Botho Strauss's *The Visitors,* produced in Turin with Vittorio Gassman; and *The Giants of the Mountain,* staged by Bolognini in Agrigento with Irene Pappas. Special in Madrid was Federico García Lorca's posthumous fragment *Play with No Title,* staged by Lluis Pasqual, and in Barcelona there was Fabià Puigserver's striking version of *The Marriage of Figaro.*

The 1989 Europalia Festival in Belgium was devoted to Japanese arts, in which the theatre was represented by the Grand Kabuki company, the Noh Theatre, Bunraku, the Buto dancers, and the Noda and Ninagawa companies. The two outstanding entries at the third Netherlands Theatre Festival, directed by Arthur Sonnen in Rotterdam, were from West and East Germany, respectively. *War,* by Rainald Goetz, was staged by the new Rotterdamse Schouwburg (Playhouse) company, while Volker Braun's *Nibelungen Paraphrase* was the Bonn City Theatre's production of a new play by an East Berlin dramatist.

Switzerland, East and West Germany, Austria. The bilingual, simultaneous coproduction, directed by Benno Besson, of the world premiere of Max Frisch's drama about Swiss military service, *Jonah and His Veteran,* was staged in Lausanne and Zürich, where Achim Benning became head of the Schauspielhaus. At his theatre, *Purification* by Czechoslovak Pres. Vaclav Havel (*see* BIOGRAPHIES), winner of the German Booksellers' Peace and Vienna's Karl Renner prizes, won high praise. The Hamburg "FVS" Prize went to Peter Shaffer, the Mühlheim to Tankred Dorst, and the Kortner to actors Rolf Boysen and Thomas Holzmann.

Premieres in West Berlin were Rolf Hochhuth's drama of surrogate motherhood, *Immaculate Conception,* and the late Thomas Bernhardt's (died 1988) antifascist *Elizabeth II,* both at the Schiller; and, at the Schaubühne, Virginia Woolf's *Orlando,* starring Jutta Lampe in a one-woman version adapted and staged by Robert Wilson. Premieres at the East Berlin Berliner Ensemble were Manfred Wasworth's prizewinning version of Nikolay R. Erdman's *The Suicide*

and the Schiller Foundation prizewinner, Georg Seidel's *Carmen Kittel.* Top events in Vienna were three much-debated novelties at the Burgtheater—Bernhardt's anti-Nazi *Heroes Square,* Peter Zadek's hard-hitting *The Merchant of Venice,* and Manfred Karge's *Dear Niembtsch*—and Hannelore Hoger's directing debut, *Spring Awakening,* at the Josefstadt.

Eastern Europe, Scandinavia, Israel. Nikolay Gubenko left the Taganka Theatre in Moscow to become cultural minister and was replaced by Yury Lyubimov, who revived Boris Mozhayev's banned *Fyodor Kuskin* (1969) as *Alive* and his own version of Pushkin's *The Plague-Time Feast.* After revivals of *Dead Souls* and Mikhail A. Bulgakov's *Molière,* the Moscow Art Theatre staged *The Crucible* and *Equus.*

A trenchant new Hungarian play was Andres Suto's *Dream Commando* at the Budapest Comedy Theatre. The last festival in Belgrade, planned by the late Mira Trailovic (died 1989), awarded two first prizes—to Hungary for the Jozsef Katona Theatre's *The Government Inspector,* and to West Germany for the Theater an der Ruhr's *Kaspar* by Peter Handke, staged by Roberto Ciulli, who won the *Politika* director's prize.

Ingmar Bergman's thrilling productions of Mishima's *The Marquise of Sade* and Ibsen's *A Doll's House* earned rave notices at the Royal Dramatic Theatre in Stockholm, where *The Phantom of the Opera* had its European premiere at Oscars. Stein Winge, new head of the Oslo National from 1990, celebrated the theatre's 90th birthday with his telling production of *King Lear,* starring Espen Skjønberg, and Kirsten Sørlie's of Eugene O'Neill's *Long Day's Journey into Night.* Paul Hammerich and Bent Fabricius' musical version of Nathansen's epoch-making drama of Danish anti-Semitism, renamed *Esther,* broke box-office records at Copenhagen's Royal Theatre under its new manager, Boel Jørgensen.

High points of the Israel Festival were visitors from Japan and South Korea, along with the Berliner Ensemble's *Galileo,* the Tbilisi Rustaveli in *The Caucasian Chalk Circle* and *Richard III,* and the Vienna Kreis in Tabori's *Masada.* Among many novelties in Israel, Mike Alfreds' version of *Ghosts,* starring Hanna Maron, stood out.

(OSSIA TRILLING)

United States and Canada. Broadway's theatrical year was seemingly miraculous as, yet again, the "Fabulous Invalid" staged its own recovery. During the first six months of 1989, the commercial theatre in New York City, symbol of the U.S. stage, was inactive as the number and quality of shows reached a record low. At Tony award time in June, there were not even enough shows to go around for nominations in the various categories. Indeed, a revival won the prize for best musical. That was *Jerome Robbins' Broadway,* a compilation of musical numbers from the director-choreographer's past hits, such as *West Side Story* and *Fiddler on the Roof.* Another contender for this award was *Black and Blue,* a tribute to black music, dancing, and performers of the 1930s. This highly picturesque, scriptless song-and-dance show evoked the musical spirits of Duke Ellington and Josephine Baker with a rare continentalism and chic.

Winning the Tony award for the year's best play was Wendy Wasserstein's *The Heidi Chronicles,* a comedy-drama that chronicles a young woman's development from collegiate ardour during the protest-filled 1970s to modern adulthood as a lecturer in fine arts. Using the fresh device of art lectures and projections for its dramatic format, *The Heidi Chronicles* reached its audience with a strong but not strident feminist theme, a humorous perspective, and

dynamic acting by Joan Allen and, subsequently, Christine Lahti in the title role.

Other plays in the meagre first half of 1989 included Ken Ludwig's *Lend Me a Tenor,* which was not only about opera but was performed with the zest and zaniness of Italian comic opera. There were also revivals of Hy Kraft's *Cafe Crown* (with Eli Wallach and Anne Jackson as a couple of stars of the old Yiddish Art Theatre) and Garson Kanin's political comedy *Born Yesterday* with Ed Asner and Madeline Kahn. Only *Lend Me a Tenor* succeeded to any degree, and by June the Broadway theatre was generally conceded to be at death's door.

Then, quite inexplicably, the patient underwent a startling, spontaneous recovery. Within three months Broadway was positively thriving. Some 21 productions opened between September and year's end, the most for that period since 1982. Leading the parade were a thrilling new musical, two star-led productions as the newly formed, transatlantic Peter Hall Company arrived brandishing Vanessa Redgrave and Dustin Hoffman, and a new play by the estimable Tom Stoppard.

The musical, *Grand Hotel,* based on the Vicki Baum novel and the subsequent Greta Garbo-John Barrymore movie, was not entirely a new show. In an earlier incarnation, with music by Robert Wright and George Forrest and a script by Luther Davis, it had been unsuccessfully produced in Los Angeles. Freshly directed and choreographed by Tommy Tune, however, with a script revised by Peter Stone and with many new songs by Maury Yeston, it became a thoroughly new work. Visually spectacular, *Grand Hotel* proved that in a musical theatre dominated by such all-sung shows as *Les Miserables* or *Phantom of the Opera,* it was still possible for Broadway's choreographers and directors to have something to stage.

The two Peter Hall productions (originating in London) were star vehicles rather than stimulating plays adventurously staged. Vanessa Redgrave was rather oddly cast in Tennessee Williams' *Orpheus Descending.* While arguably the greatest actress in current English-speaking theatre, even she had her limitations and one of them might have been the playing of Southern heroines in Tennessee Williams plays, especially second-rate ones. Hall's second presentation was of another lesser play, albeit one written by the master of masters. Shakespeare's *The Merchant of Venice* probably endured because of the notoriety of its anti-Semitism rather than for real artistic quality. That notoriety and the presence of Dustin Hoffman (*see* BIOGRAPHIES) as Shylock assured sold-out houses in New

In Alan Ayckbourn's futuristic *Henceforeward . . .,* Ian McKellen plays Jerome, a frustrated composer, and Serena Evans plays Zoe, one of the two women in his life. The play also features the robot counterparts of both women.
DONALD COOPER—PHOTOSTAGE

York City, as it had done during the spring in London. Successful as these two productions were on both sides of the Atlantic, they belied the notion of a company—an ensemble of actors devoted to teamwork. "The Peter Hall Company," instead, seemed to be a star-oriented enterprise geared to commercial theatre events, and as such its debut was a financial rather than an artistic success.

After *Grand Hotel* the new Tom Stoppard play, *Artist Descending a Staircase,* provided the second real boost for Broadway's miraculous recovery. A mere 90 minutes long (without an intermission), it was one of the rare plays to deal visually with painting and yet (after *The Heidi Chronicles*) the second one to do so in 1989. Stoppard's play is a possible murder mystery and a romantic enigma in fractured time; that is, it is typical of the author in its ingenuity, originality, and wit.

The third stimulating event in Broadway's 1989 revival was, in fact, a revival. The musical classic *Gypsy* was brought back with its brassy Jule Styne-Stephen Sondheim songs and the Arthur Laurents script about a monstrous stage mother who propels her two unwilling daughters to

MARTHA SWOPE

Henry Foustka (David Strathairn) is raised upside down in the midst of fiendish debauchery in *Temptation,* the Faustian play by the Czechoslovak playwright Vaclav Havel. *Temptation,* which was banned in Czechoslovakia, portrays the modern-day Faust as a misguided scientist who ultimately sells his soul to the state.

Joan Allen plays the title role in *The Heidi Chronicles,* winner of the Tony award for best play. Written by Wendy Wasserstein, *Heidi Chronicles* centres around feminist art scholar Heidi Holland, who comes of age during the social upheaval of the baby-boom era.

GERRY GOLDSTEIN—PLAYWRIGHTS HORIZONS

stardom. Demanding a cyclonic performance in the central role originated by Ethel Merman, the production got just that from Tyne Daly (of television's "Cagney and Lacey"). Daly proved more than equal to her role's dramatic and vocal challenges, making the revival of *Gypsy* the year's surprise hit.

The renewed activity on New York's Great White Way by no means drained energy from Off-Broadway, which itself had so recently revived. Exemplifying the variety of entertainments succeeding in the city's smaller playhouses were three diverse successes—Jerry Sterner's *Other People's Money,* an old-fashioned naturalistic drama dealing with the new subject of Wall Street takeovers; Jim Geoghan's *Only Kidding!* about a somewhat different kind of competition, a throat-cutting kind among television comedians;

and Charles Busch's *The Lady in Question,* a campy send-up, much of it with actors playing opposite sexes, of the Marlene Dietrich subcategory of wartime movie thriller.

Such diversity shamed the country's not-for-profit theatres, which were supposed to be doing the artistic alternate but instead had been programming close to the commercial vest because of federal cutbacks in arts subsidies. In New York the Lincoln Center Theater performed the musical *Anything Goes* for most of the year, perhaps at a profit but at an artistic loss and certainly offering nothing new to its subscribers. The Circle in the Square put on another revived musical, Stephen Sondheim's *Sweeney Todd,* for most of its season.

Elsewhere, the original purposes of institutional theatre—the production of less commercial but artistic plays—was remembered. For instance, the Hartford (Conn.) Stage Company produced Ibsen's *Peer Gynt,* and the Mark Taper Forum in Los Angeles staged Pedro Calderon de la Barca's *The Mayor of Zalamea.*

Oddly enough, Canada's usually conservative (even stodgy) Stratford Festival was downright perky in this fourth and final year of the reign of artistic director John Neville (David William was to take the helm in 1990). The twin jewels of the season were a *Henry V* reset in the trenches of World War I, with incidental music drawn from Gilbert and Sullivan, and a production of Cole Porter's *Kiss Me Kate.* (MARTIN GOTTFRIED)

See also Dance; Music.

This article updates the *Macropædia* article The History of Western THEATRE.

Transportation

Although some of the impetus toward outright privatization of transport systems had slackened in 1989, many countries continued to make plans to sell off sections of their utilities. Toll-financed projects and those involving private-sector collaboration remained a strong and growing trend, particularly in less developed countries. The great dilemma facing governments and cities was that demand for transport, particularly urban transport, was far outstripping the means of infrastructure supply. Achieving a correct balance between competing modes within an environmental framework was a more widely recognized problem.

The year was marked by a number of major disasters. The most notable was the collapse of over 1 km (1 km = 0.621 mi) of the Interstate 880 double-decked viaduct and damage to the Oakland Bay Bridge during the California earthquake in October. (JOHN H. EARP)

MARTHA SWOPE

The cast of *Metamorphosis* is mystified by Gregor Samsa, played by Mikhail Baryshnikov, who has turned into a giant insect. Baryshnikov's talent as a dancer illuminated Gregor's transformation.

AVIATION

Security was the major concern of the world airline industry during 1989 following the explosion, as 1988 ended, aboard a Pan American Boeing 747 over Lockerbie, Scotland, resulting in the deaths of all 259 on board and 11 people on the ground. While the hunt continued for the terrorists responsible for the tragedy, airlines and airport authorities stepped up searches of passengers and their baggage, at a heavy but unquantifiable cost in both money and delayed flights. Norman Jackson, senior technical director of the International Air Transport Association (IATA), noted at the association's annual meeting in Warsaw in October that there had been a shift from hijacking to sabotage, using difficult-to-detect devices and, in some cases, perpetrated by terrorists who were "prepared to die as martyrs for a cause." Jackson believed such politically inspired interference with air transport could be virtually ended if all governments adhered to the terms of the relevant security conventions.

Despite such worries, the number of people who flew during the year rose some 6% from the 1.1 billion recorded in 1988, and the International Civil Aviation Organization forecast in September that the 2 billion mark would be reached around the turn of the century. During the same period, air freight traffic, which stood at 54 billion metric ton-km in 1988, would rise to 124 billion. IATA forecast worldwide international scheduled passenger traffic growth for 1989–90 at 8%, with Asia and the Pacific remaining the fastest-growing region. Freight traffic would grow 6%, with northeastern Asia and southern South America showing the biggest gains.

As in the previous year, the smooth flow of air transport was disrupted by airport and airway congestion, although hastily introduced palliative measures, along with a decline in charter holiday flights, improved the situation slightly in Europe. Even so, delays due to congestion cost one airline, British Airways, some £15 million, mainly through extra fuel burned. Pressure grew for an integrated system of air traffic control centres throughout Europe, equipped with compatible software and hardware and linked by a common communications network. Such a system would function irrespective of state boundaries.

The various airworthiness authorities around the world became tougher on the subject of aging airliners following several incidents blamed on structural corrosion. No arbitrary limit on the life of airliners was to be introduced, but operators were instructed to carry out a series of deep checks on their older aircraft—checks that were expensive and stretched the industry's skilled engineering manpower. Skill shortages in both the maintenance and flight crew areas led many airlines to establish their own apprenticeship training plans. Another shortage that manifested itself during the year was that of new airliners, with most of the main aerospace manufacturers unable to promise delivery in less than four years. New and increasingly stringent noise regulations covering older aircraft were debated during 1989, and fears were expressed in the industry that enforced early retirement of such aircraft could exacerbate the delivery situation. IATA would like well-maintained airliners to have a life of 30 years, but this produced a reaction from the "green" lobby to the effect that populations living around airports were entitled to the benefits of the latest generation of quiet jet engines.

Heavy investment by the airlines in computer reservations systems (CRS) came to fruition in 1989 as both the Galileo and Amadeus European projects came on stream. All of the major European airlines were members of one

Angry union members protest the latest cost-cutting measures by Frank Lorenzo of Eastern Airlines. Lorenzo's campaign to trim the airline's huge deficit resulted in a war between labour and management that forced Eastern to file for bankruptcy.
STEVE STARR—PICTURE GROUP

of the two groupings, which enabled travel agents to offer their customers a wide range of travel options, from airline tickets to theatre bookings. Concern remained that individual airline members of CRS consortia would use the new systems to highlight their own services, to the detriment of their partners, and the European Civil Aviation Conference adopted a code of conduct for CRS, which came into effect on August 1.

Despite all of the pressures on it, the world air transport industry did well financially in 1989. Gunter Eser, director general of IATA, reporting that member airlines made a net profit of $6.2 billion in 1988, commented that the 1989–90 outlook was "very promising." In the area of safety, 20 jet transports were lost in 1988, and it appeared that the 1989 figure would be similar. There was, however, one worrisome trend—the human factor was considered to be the dominant cause in 80% of the accidents. IATA planned to hold a special conference on the subject within the next two years. (ARTHUR REED)

SHIPPING AND PORTS

The shipping industry in 1989 enjoyed a stability founded on three years of recovery and strong global economic growth. Dry cargo freight rates continued to rise slowly, and by the middle of the year the tanker market, particularly in the Middle East loading area, showed a marked degree of buoyancy. However, freight rates, especially in the tanker market, had some way to go before a new building contracted at 1989 prices could be justified. As a result, many owners were considering life-extension schemes for their tankers. Early in the year freight rates firmed up for the largest ships. Entry of the U.S.S.R. into the market to secure tonnage for grain cargoes placed upward pressure on rates. The oil market was also optimistic, with crude oil prices maintaining their levels despite continuing OPEC overproduction.

South Korea decided to spend $2.3 billion on the development of eight major ports up to the year 2000. The port of Oakland, Calif., started preparations for a new 15-ha (38-ac) container terminal, and in the U.K. the Port of Sheerness started a $9.3 million expansion plan that would treble its capacity. In Greece the first 70,000 sq m (750,000 sq ft) of the new Piraeus container terminal came into service, with two 45-ton gantry cranes and 400 m (1 m = 3.3 ft) of serviceable quay.

Passengers aboard the American-European Express toast each other in the train's elegant dining car. The luxuriously remodeled train offered sumptuous accommodations, gourmet dining, and first-rate entertainment for the traveler who could afford the very best.
RED MORGAN

Cruising continued to be a growth area. However, a leading U.S. Coast Guard official warned that cruise ships operating to U.S. ports could expect much tougher checks if their specifications predated the 1974 Safety of Life at Sea Convention. The U.K. Royal Institution of Naval Architects (RINA) voiced concern over the speed of research into long-term design considerations for roll-on/roll-off ships and the attention being paid to modifying existing vessels. RINA believed these ferries were still not safe enough.

The volume of laid-up tonnage fell again. In October 1989 there were 302 ships of 5,197,000 deadweight tons (dwt) in layup, compared with 445 ships of 8,647,000 dwt the previous October. At the height of the shipping depression in 1983, the figure was 1,726 ships totaling 52 million dwt. The total tonnage of the world fleet, at 410.5 million gross tons (gt), showed a significant 7.1 million-gt increase over the previous year. For 1989 the principal merchant fleets by flag registry were: Liberia 47.9 million gt, Panama 47.3 million gt, Japan 28 million gt, the U.S.S.R. 25.8 million gt, Greece 21.3 million gt, and the U.S. 20.5 million gt. The principal ship types in the world fleet were: oil tankers 123.7 million gt, bulk/ore carriers 109.5 million gt, general cargo ships 51.6 million gt, containerships 22.7 million gt, liquefied gas carriers 10 million gt, and pure chemical carriers 3.4 million gt.   (EDWARD CROWLEY)

FREIGHT AND PIPELINES

Despite the political disturbances in China, the continued growth of intraregional trade in the Far East maintained the region's lead in container freight activity. Hong Kong's seven container terminals handled over four million 20-ft equivalent units (TEU) in 1988, and it remained the world's busiest container port. Singapore showed the largest growth of traffic in the region. China's $1.3 billion port development plan was supported by a $100 million World Bank loan. Total throughput at world ports was estimated at 70 million TEU. Rotterdam, Neth., still Europe's largest port, was developing a $143 million automated container terminal. Total freight movement in the European Communities (EC) had grown to over one trillion ton-kilometres: 63% by road, 17% by rail, and 20% by inland waterway or pipeline. There were significant freight terminal developments in progress to take advantage of the Channel Tunnel, due to be completed in 1993.

In the U.S. railroads had set intermodal traffic records every year since deregulation in 1981. The growth of freight affected the inland terminals; the Virginia Port Authority developed a $10 million terminal at Front Royal, 350 km inland from its marine terminal.

Among new freight routes developed in 1989 were the 200-km roll-on/roll-off rail/ferry services between Uusikaupunki in Finland and Hargshamn in Sweden and 60 km of road across the Mato Grosso in Brazil to Bolivia, designed to eliminate the need to use Atlantic ports and reduce some freight routes to the U.S. West Coast by 4,000 km.

During 1988 pipeline construction rebounded sharply, with worldwide installations totaling 36,700 km. The forecast for 1989 was 31,800 km, 50% of which was in the U.S. Prospects for the international market for gas lines were good, but the outlook for liquid/crude lines was less optimistic. Most of the strategic crude oil network in the Middle East area had been completed, but new natural gas lines were being planned for Iran, Iraq, Kuwait, and Qatar.

ROADS AND TRAFFIC

Many new highway projects throughout the world were to be constructed as toll roads. The new west link of the Dublin Ring Road, the $146 million, 20-km Dulles Toll Road extension to the Leesburg, Va., area, and the 800-km, $1.5 billion, privately funded Malaysian peninsular spine road were good examples. Among the cities providing additional capacity, Boston planned a new 7.3-km Third Harbour Tunnel, and Charleston, S.C., was building a 2-km stretch of elevated highway with two major bridges on Interstate 526. With the end of hostilities in the Gulf war, work was restarted on Iraq's 1,300-km Expressway No. 1 from the Syrian border through Baghdad to Kuwait, the longest expressway (motorway) under construction anywhere in the world. In the United Arab Emirates, strict weight limits on trucks were to be introduced following severe deterioration of new highways from overloading.

A major link in the European road network would be provided by the 6.5-km Western (road/rail) and 6.7-km Eastern (road) Store Bælt crossings linking the Danish islands of Sjælland and Fyn. The project had been the centre of an EC dispute over bidding procedures. Denmark was also building a 460-m immersed tube tunnel to take the Germany–Sweden expressway under Guldborg Sound. In

Norway a 3.6-km, eight-lane cross-city tunnel using 400-m immersed tubes was being completed in Oslo. Austria had the largest European road-tunneling program, with 14 major projects under way. The 7.8-km Karawanken tunnel connecting Austria to Yugoslavia was due to open in 1991. In Australia work on the Sydney Harbour Tunnel 2.3-km dual carriageway link included a 960-m immersed-tube section using eight precast-reinforced sections. The tunnel, which was due to open in 1992, would ease congestion on the Sydney Harbour Bridge, the world's second busiest toll crossing, with over 65 million vehicle crossings in 1988.

INTERCITY RAIL

Over $21 billion was being invested in railways in 60 countries during 1989, with most of the expenditure going to track improvements and infrastructure. U.S. railways alone were investing $5 billion. Worldwide expenditure on locomotives doubled over 1988 levels, and spending on freight cars (wagons) rose 75%. In the U.S., Amtrak reached record levels in ridership and revenue, while the renaissance of railways in Europe continued into 1989, following a 5% increase in traffic in 1988 to 248 billion passenger-km. Freight traffic rose by 6% in the first quarter of 1989. These trends underpinned the development of a comprehensive European high-speed rail network that would use the Channel Tunnel as a key link to the U.K. A single rail authority to manage all European track was being planned.

The new French TGV-Atlantique 280-km network introduced 300-km/h services in September, reducing travel time between Paris and Le Mans from 100 to 55 minutes. Many other European countries continued to take steps toward their own high-speed lines.

The highly successful Japanese Shinkansen celebrated its 25th anniversary. The 2,000-km network, which carried over 200 million passengers in 1988, was to be extended to Yamagata by 1992.

Rail services were resumed between Casablanca, Morocco, and Algiers and between Yugoslavia and Albania. New services included a cross-Taipei tunnel and a special Brussels–Luxembourg–Strasbourg express for EC officials. In South America there were plans to set up a 3,500-km transcontinental corridor linking Buenos Aires, Arg., with La Paz, Bolivia. Norway was to introduce a freight line to the Soviet Union via Murmansk. The movement of refrigerated containers between Japan and northern Europe via the Trans-Siberian Railway was begun.

High capacity double-deck passenger coaches were introduced in a number of locations, including Long Island, N.Y., Austria, and Australia. Other technical innovations included the diesel-powered Class 610 Pendolino tilting sleeping car trains and 160-ton stainless steel iron-ore cars with four independent self-steering axles.

URBAN MASS TRANSIT

Urban railways continued to show remarkable growth during the year. Since 1985 approximately 1,120 km of new urban railway had been opened in 101 cities. Some 70 countries had more than 200 projects under construction in 1989, amounting to 1,675 km of railway metro (subway) system; an additional 2,200 km were being designed, and more than 7,000 km were in the feasibility study stage. The U.S. overtook the U.S.S.R. in terms of further development, with projects in 11 locations. The projects included a wide range of facilities, from conventional subways to light-rail systems and automated people movers. The fastest growing sector was light rail. At year's end more than 60 light-rail systems were operating in continental Western Europe.

New light-rail systems opened in 1989 in Guadalajara and Monterrey, Mexico, and numerous other projects were under construction. Only one new metro system (Taipei) was opened during the year, but several were extended. The Soviet Union offered to plan and build a 36-km system for Delhi, India. The Singapore system, opened in 1988, was now carrying 500,000 passengers per year.

One significant technical development was a dual-voltage system in Karlsruhe, West Germany. Specialist applications of automated guided transit were introduced or extended in Kobe, Japan, and Vancouver, B.C. Kuala Lumpur, Malaysia, approved $105 million for a 20-km monorail to replace an aerobus project, now declared an expensive failure. Trolley buses were ordered for a number of cities. The O-Bahn bus system in Adelaide, Australia, was doubled in size to 12 km, but no other significant systems had been developed, and guided buses were not seen as a threat to light rail. With new air-quality standards to come into effect in the U.S. in 1991, experiments using methanol-powered buses in Los Angeles, oil fuel/hydrogen in Moscow, and natural gas in Sweden were of considerable interest.

(JOHN H. EARP)

See also Energy; Engineering Projects; Environment; Industrial Review: *Aerospace; Automobiles.*

This article updates the *Macropædia* article TRANSPORTATION.

New York City's last graffiti-covered train is taken out of commission as part of the city's five-year program to rid its subways of graffiti. Once covered with slogans, names, and drawings, the trains of New York City's subways were all replaced, rebuilt, or scrubbed clean.

World Affairs

As 1989 began, a new Republican administration took over in Washington facing a Democratic Congress; James A. Baker served as Pres. George Bush's secretary of state. But events in the Soviet Union, China, and Eastern Europe overshadowed Western initiatives as well as Third World developments. The first (partly) freely elected Soviet parliament convened in Moscow during the summer. Mikhail Gorbachev strengthened his position in both party and state, removing several of his leading adversaries from positions of influence. Even earlier, in February, all Soviet troops had been withdrawn from Afghanistan. Contrary to widespread expectations, the Kabul government did not fall, as the resistance groups spent more time fighting each other than the common enemy. (Later in the year Vietnam was to withdraw its troops from embattled Kampuchea.)

But the setbacks suffered by the reform movement in the Soviet Union were even more striking than its achievements. It became increasingly clear that the new economic program worked badly and that public indifference and conservative resistance had seemingly combined forces to defeat the liberalization of society. Nationalist-separatist movements in Central Asia, the Caucasus, and the Baltic region, forcibly suppressed for decades, resurfaced and endangered the cohesion of the Soviet Union. The slogan of the reform party ("there is no other way") was not dropped, but pessimistic assessments of the chances of success increased steadily. Conviction was growing that it was not so much a question of revitalizing a sluggish economy as of confronting a grave cultural and moral crisis.

The June elections in Poland gave the trade union Solidarity, hitherto illegal, an overwhelming majority. Gen. Wojciech Jaruzelski was reelected president, but for the first time in post-World War II history, a Communist party was compelled to give up its monopoly of power and to share it with the opposition. In Hungary, where political democratization was making great strides, the Communist Party renounced Marxism and changed its name.

The events that took place during the fall and winter of 1989 made it a veritable annus mirabilis for Eastern Europe. As a result of mass demonstrations, the Communist governments of Czechoslovakia, East Germany, Romania, and Bulgaria fell or, at the very least, were compelled to carry out far-reaching purges in their ranks. In Romania the secret police offered armed resistance, and after a short but bloody confrontation, Pres. Nicolae Ceausescu and his wife were executed. Elsewhere, the (partial) transfer of power proceeded more or less peacefully. In Czechoslovakia a leading dissident, Vaclav Havel (see BIOGRAPHIES), became president, whereas in East Germany and Bulgaria a new generation of Communists kept the key positions for the time being. The economic problems facing Eastern Europe, however, were tremendous. The question of whether and how to help began to preoccupy the West.

China, too, was severely affected by the general ferment in the Communist world. After several years of an economic upsurge and (limited) liberalization, the movement for greater political freedom gathered momentum, culminating in mass demonstrations in Beijing (Peking) and other major Chinese cities. The showdown between the conservative government and the reformers in April–May wholly overshadowed Gorbachev's visit to China, the first Sino-Soviet summit in several decades. Martial law was eventually imposed, the pro-reform elements in the party

World Affairs: Contents

For your convenience this article groups the countries of the world by the geopolitical regions to which they belong. Certain related topics, such as United Nations, Dependent States, and various regional affairs articles (e.g., Latin-American Affairs), are also included. An alphabetical list of these topics appears below, indicating the page where each may be found. Articles on the various countries update the *Macropædia* articles of the same name (except where otherwise noted), as do the more extensive statistical treatments in the *World Data* section.

leadership (such as General Secretary Zhao Ziyang [Chao Tzu-yang]) purged. Many among the student demonstrators were killed, and a large number were arrested. China's international position and its economic situation were adversely affected, with economic growth hampered by inflation and the return to a centralized system.

The death of the Ayatollah Ruhollah Khomeini on June 3 did not bring about a basic reorientation in Iranian domestic and foreign policy. The tug-of-war among the contenders for power in Iran was likely to continue for a long time. A peace with Iraq seemed as yet a distant possibility, nor was there any progress in the negotiations (mainly indirect) between Israel and the Palestinians. The *intifada* continued, and in the Lebanese civil war some of the heaviest fighting took place in the spring between Christian units and the forces supported by Syria. An armistice in September between the warring factions and negotiations in Saudi Arabia—although inconclusive—provided a ray of hope in this long and bloody conflict. The violent suppression of the Kurds in Iraq and Iran continued to exact a high toll.

Disputes among the Western allies about NATO strategy were settled, at least temporarily, at the Brussels meeting in May. The members agreed to start negotiations on short-range nuclear missiles with the Soviet Union in mid-1990, but only if progress had been made in the Vienna talks on reduction of conventional forces in Europe. Further arms control proposals were agreed upon in the meetings in the U.S. in September between Secretary Baker and Soviet Foreign Minister Eduard Shevardnadze. While it was clear that the basic issues in the field of arms reduction would be subject to negotiations for years to come, the climate in which the various visits and talks took place was infinitely more relaxed and positive than during past negotiations.

In Western Europe preparations continued for 1992, which was to be another watershed in the economic unification of the European Communities. Despite some reservations on the part of certain governments (*e.g.*, the U.K.), there was little doubt that the majority would not be deflected from their previous decision. Leading officials in the U.S., the Eastern bloc, and the Third World were pondering the implications of this new stage in European cooperation for the rest of the world.

If the danger of a great war receded, civil wars and terrorist attacks continued unabated. Among civil wars, the struggle in Sri Lanka should be mentioned; the warring factions there temporarily made common cause, demanding withdrawal of the "peacekeeping" force of 45,000 Indian troops. Narco-terrorism intensified, above all in Colombia but also in several other Latin- and Central American countries. Strongman Manuel Noriega of Panama, who was generally thought to be providing assistance to the narcotics traffickers, survived yet another attempted coup in October, only to be ousted by a U.S. armed intervention in Panama in December. In general, the drug issue moved to a high place in the global agenda, even though concerted international action was still far from being widespread or effective.   (WALTER LAQUEUR)

This article updates the *Macropædia* article 20th-Century INTERNATIONAL RELATIONS.

UNITED NATIONS

On Feb. 27, 1989, in New Delhi, Indian Pres. Ramaswamy Venkataraman presented UN Secretary-General Javier Pérez de Cuéllar with the Jawaharlal Nehru Award for International Understanding ($100,000 and a plaque) for steering the UN through troubled times. The president called the UN mankind's hope of transcending "narrow

. . . considerations which have caused so much turmoil and pain around the world."

U.S. Pres. George Bush also praised the secretary-general and the UN, but praise did not translate into dollars. The U.S. ended the year without contributing to the UN Population Fund and owing the UN $430 million, more than any other member (South Africa owed $37.3 million, Iran $11.9 million, and the U.S.S.R. $2.6 million).

Peacekeeping continued as a major UN activity, with new UN forces and observer units dispatched to Central America and Namibia.

Central America. At the request of Nicaragua and the Organization of American States (OAS), the UN dispatched two groups to Nicaragua to ensure free and fair elections on Feb. 25, 1990. One, a civilian unit, was the first UN observer group to supervise an election in an independent country and the first to go to Latin America; it reported (December 12) that voter registration had concluded "very satisfactorily" but warned that political violence could still threaten the elections. The other, the Observer Mission in Central America (created November 7), was the first UN military mission in the Western Hemisphere. The 260 unarmed observers, equipped with helicopters and light aircraft, would monitor the Central American governments' commitment not to aid the 11,000 Nicaraguan *contra* forces based in Honduras.

Nicaraguan Pres. Daniel Ortega ended his cease-fire with the *contras* (November 1) because they were stepping up attacks on government forces. Further talks between the two sides were inconclusive, and on December 5, the deadline set for the *contras* to disband, Nicaragua reinstituted a case against Honduras before the International Court of Justice (ICJ).

On December 12, at San José, Costa Rica, the five Central American presidents called for the UN to extend its peacekeeping efforts to El Salvador. On December 29, by a vote of 75–20 (39 abstentions), the General Assembly, meeting in emergency session, "strongly" deplored the U.S. invasion of Panama (December 20).

Namibia and Angola. A 70-man UN "verification mission" began (January 10) to supervise the withdrawal of 50,000 Cuban troops from Angola. After long debate, the Security Council unanimously accepted (February 16) the secretary-general's design of a transition assistance group (4,650 troops costing $416 million) to help prepare South West Africa/Namibia for independence. African states feared that the reduced UN force (from a proposed 7,500 troops costing $700 million) would allow South Africa to block elections. However, China, the U.S., and the U.S.S.R. backed the smaller force, the first time they had jointly opposed a Third World request. The group was still the largest the UN had deployed since it sent 19,000 troops to the Congo (now Zaire) between 1960 and 1964.

The secretary-general assured the Africans that the Council would send additional troops if needed, and on May 11 the Security Council president announced that the secretary-general was doubling (from 500 to 1,000) the Namibian force's police unit. This followed an incursion into Namibia by South West Africa People's Organization (SWAPO) troops, and African complaints that South African-controlled local police were intimidating Namibians. After six weeks of conflict and intensive negotiations, implementation of the UN independence plan resumed.

On June 6 South African Pres. P.W. Botha ended apartheid (racial separation) in Namibia and granted amnesty to guerrillas returning from Angola. Subsequently, 41,000 refugees and political exiles came back, some assisted by a six-week-long UN airlift begun June 12. Among

them was SWAPO president Sam Nujoma (*see* BIOGRA-PHIES). Voting on November 7–11 for a constituent assembly to draft a Namibian constitution was supervised by UN officials, 1,695 UN-trained supervisors, and South African observers. Over 90% of the some 700,000 registered voters participated, and SWAPO received a majority of 57.3%. The UN declared the election peaceful, free, and fair.

Armaments. Debate at the 44th General Assembly (opened September 19) was remarkable for its optimism and lack of rancour. Bush, speaking to the delegates for the first time as U.S. president, urged them (September 25) "to rid the earth" of chemical weapons and offered to destroy 80% of the U.S. stockpile (an estimated 30,000 tons) if the U.S.S.R. cut its store (50,000 tons) to U.S. levels. He also promised to eliminate all U.S. chemical arms within a decade if nations agreed on a treaty outlawing chemical weapons that the 40-nation UN Disarmament Conference was drafting in Geneva. The next day, Soviet Foreign Minister Eduard A. Shevardnadze accepted Bush's proposal and urged both countries to stop producing all chemical weapons, including "binary" weapons, which produce lethal poison when two chemicals inside one missile are mixed together. The U.S. excluded them from its proposals, but when Bush met at Malta with Soviet Pres. Mikhail Gorbachev (December 2), he offered to stop producing them if the U.S.S.R. accepted other U.S. arms proposals.

Economic and Social Matters. *Environment.* The UN Environment Program announced (March 22) a successful end to 18 months of negotiations when experts from 117 countries, meeting in Basel, Switz., adopted an agreement restricting shipments of hazardous wastes across national frontiers. UNEP also sponsored meetings in Helsinki, Fin., where 80 states declared (May 2) that by the year 2000 they would stop producing chlorofluorocarbons that threaten the Earth's ozone layer. The existing Montreal Protocol (1987), also promoted by the UN, called for states to cut production in half by 1998. At the Economic and Social Council, the U.K. urged states (May 8) to draft an international convention to stop global warming. British Prime Minister Margaret Thatcher repeated this call to the Assembly (November 8), requesting a 1992 deadline. In the fall a UN-sponsored working group in Geneva and a majority of 68 countries meeting in The Netherlands supported quicker action to stabilize carbon dioxide emissions at 1988 levels by the year 2000 and to reduce them a further 20% by 2005. Britain, Japan, the U.S.S.R., and the U.S. opposed strict timetables, however, and the delegates agreed only to act "as soon as possible." At the General Assembly meetings, 159 member states committed themselves to drafting a treaty to stabilize the Earth's climate and convening a world conference in Brazil in 1992 to discuss ways of reducing the environmental impact of economic development.

Economics. The UN reported (January 5) that the world economy grew by 4% in 1988, faster than at any other time since 1984, but that one-fifth of the world's five billion people, especially in Africa and Latin America, still lived in poverty. Officials of the International Monetary Fund (IMF), the World Bank, and the UN Conference on Trade and Development (UNCTAD) called for debt relief and new loans to Third World countries whose living conditions were endangered by lagging investment and the weight of heavy external debt. (*See* ECONOMIC AFFAIRS: *Special Report.*) The World Bank reported that in 1988 less developed countries paid $142 billion to creditors but received only $92 billion in new aid. The IMF reported that 10% of its outstanding loans represented bad debts and that it was short of cash just when member states

wanted it to do more. However, Fund officials announced on September 25 that by year's end states were likely to increase IMF resources by as much as 67% ($80 billion) to cushion against economic shocks in the 1990s and to allow the Fund to expand its role in Eastern Europe. On December 29 the General Assembly unanimously approved a call for humanitarian aid for the new government in Romania.

Human Rights. The Assembly unanimously adopted a Convention on the Rights of the Child on November 20, the 30th anniversary of its declaration on the subject. The convention, drafted over 10 years by a 42-nation working group of the Commission on Human Rights, consolidated international law on children's rights and established standards to protect children from drug abuse and sexual exploitation, safeguard them in adoptions across frontiers, guarantee access to juvenile courts, and bar military service before age 15.

AIDS. Meeting under World Health Organization (WHO) auspices, experts on March 2 announced guidelines for testing vaccines against AIDS aimed at making vaccines available to poor countries without cost and allowing researchers to pay those who participate in tests but without inducing them to risk their health for money. WHO expected the number of AIDS cases to rise from the current 600,000 to 6 million–8 million by the year 2000.

Kampuchea. At a 19-nation conference in Paris, conferees accepted (August 1) the secretary-general's proposal to send a fact-finding team to Kampuchea (Cambodia) to examine "technical aspects" of monitoring a possible comprehensive settlement there. On September 26 Vietnam announced that it had withdrawn all its troops from Kampuchea, but Kampuchean opposition leaders challenged the claim. On November 16 the Assembly overwhelmingly (124–17, 12 abstentions) urged a comprehensive Kampuchean political settlement that would allow the UN to verify the Vietnamese withdrawal and supervise elections. Alluding to the brutal four-year rule of the Khmer Rouge in the 1970s, the Assembly warned against returning to the "universally condemned policies and practices of the recent past," although it left the way open for Khmer Rouge officials to join an interim government. On December 11 Kampuchea conditionally agreed to hold UN-supervised elections in 1991.

Middle East. *Arab-Israeli Relations.* On February 17 the U.S. vetoed a Security Council resolution, supported by the other 14 members, that deplored Israel's treatment of Palestinians in the Israeli-occupied territories. U.S. spokesmen said that they opposed "certain Israeli practices, for example, expulsion of Palestinian residents, collective punishment, [and] use of live fire in non-life threatening situations" but criticized the resolution for not sufficiently taking into account the context of the other side's "excesses." However, a similar resolution, condemning Israel's persistent violations of Palestinian rights, succeeded in the Assembly on October 6 (140–2 [U.S. and Israel], 6 abstentions).

Iranian Hostages. On July 28 Israeli commandos kidnapped Sheikh Abdul Karim Obeid, a Lebanese Shi'ite leader, and offered to exchange him and 300 other Shi'ite prisoners for three Israeli soldiers and 18 Western hostages held in Lebanon. Retaliating, a pro-Iranian extremist group announced that it had hanged U.S. Lieut. Col. William R. Higgins, kidnapped in February 1988 while serving with the UN International Force in Lebanon. On August 8, Marrack Goulding, UN under secretary-general for special political affairs, went to the Middle East to investigate. He asked Israel to free the Shi'ite cleric, but Israel refused to do so without a quid pro quo.

Lebanon. On August 15, acting on his own authority under Article 99 of the UN Charter, Pérez de Cuéllar asked the Security Council to try to halt the bloodshed in Lebanon. It was the first time since 1979 that a secretary-general had invoked his power to summon the Council. The next day the Council called for a "total and immediate cease-fire" in the 14-year-old civil war and asked all parties to open lines of communication and lift their sieges in Beirut. It also fully supported the efforts of an Arab League committee to mediate the dispute and repeated that support on September 20. The Arab plan led ultimately to agreement on political reforms, a charter for national reconciliation, and the election on November 5 of René Moawad (*see* OBITUARIES) as president. However, Moawad was assassinated November 22. The Lebanese Parliament then elected Elias Hrawi as president on November 24. Hrawi immediately challenged Gen. Michel Aoun (*see* BIOGRAPHIES), a Maronite Christian leader who had rejected the settlement, to surrender the presidential palace and give up his pretensions of being head of state. The general, who began a "war of liberation" in March to drive Syria from Lebanon, maintained that Parliament had exceeded its jurisdiction and put Lebanon under a "Syrian mandate."

Iran-Iraq War. Sixteen rounds of face-to-face negotiations and three meetings with the secretary-general had not managed to get Iran and Iraq to advance beyond a cease-fire. From October 30 to mid-November, UN mediator Jan Eliasson of Sweden shuttled between Baghdad and Tehran in an effort to persuade the parties to comply with the Security Council peace plan, calling for both armies to withdraw behind recognized frontiers, exchange prisoners, and sign a peace treaty.

Vincennes Case. On May 18 Iran asked the ICJ to award it compensation for the aircraft the USS *Vincennes* shot down in July 1988. The U.S. had said it would compensate the families of persons killed or injured but not the government of Iran, maintaining that it destroyed the plane in self-defense. The U.S. was planning to contest the action, the firstfruits of a Soviet-U.S. agreement to allow the ICJ a larger role in settling international disputes.

(RICHARD N. SWIFT)

This article updates the *Macropædia* article UNITED NATIONS.

COMMONWEALTH OF NATIONS

Pakistan, which withdrew its membership in 1972, returned to the Commonwealth as the 49th member following the resumption of civilian rule and the election of Benazir Bhutto as prime minister. Previously, India had led objections to Pakistan's return because it was governed by the military. Pakistan officially rejoined on October 1, and Bhutto joined 45 other leaders at the biennial heads of government meeting, held in Kuala Lumpur, Malaysia, on October 18–24. Of those present, 34 were heads of government, including two kings and a sultan (Swaziland, Lesotho, and Brunei, respectively). Only Dominica was absent (its prime minister being ill). The two smallest members, Tuvalu and Nauru, did not attend summits.

Under the chairmanship of Malaysian Prime Minister Mahathir bin Mohamad, the meeting was notable for a large number of initiatives. Most important were the Langkawi Declaration on the Environment (named after the island where the leaders spent their weekend retreat) and a statement on southern Africa called "The Way Ahead." Concerning the environment, the leaders agreed that it was neither desirable nor to be expected that the less developed countries should slow their economic growth. They would need considerable financial help if they were to avoid adding to the global pollution problems. This

British Prime Minister Margaret Thatcher and an aide prepare to depart from a session of the Commonwealth heads of government meeting. Thatcher was alone among the Commonwealth government heads in opposing sanctions against South Africa.
AFP PHOTO

meant increasing transfers of technology from the rich to the poor.

The statement on southern Africa dealt with the new situation that had arisen in South Africa following the coming to power of Pres. F.W. de Klerk. Differences remained between Britain and the rest of the Commonwealth on the application of sanctions. All nations except Britain wanted more proof of genuine change in the country and real moves to demolish apartheid before they would consider relaxing sanctions. In the meantime, they proposed further economic squeezes.

British Prime Minister Margaret Thatcher caused a storm because an hour or two after agreeing to the Commonwealth communiqué section on southern Africa (which included four British reservations), she issued her own statement, taking her further away from the spirit of the communiqué. Whereas she had originally agreed that such encouraging signs as there were had been very much the product of a combination of internal and external pressures, she later said that sanctions did not have the political effects claimed for them.

The leaders generated considerable optimism about the Commonwealth's future and set up a committee of 10 presidents and prime ministers to examine roles that the Commonwealth might be expected to play in the 1990s. The 10 countries represented, with Mahathir as chairman, were to be Australia, The Bahamas, Britain, Canada, India, Jamaica, Malaysia, Nigeria, Singapore, and Zambia. Another initiative in Kuala Lumpur was the decision to take the first diplomatic steps toward a resumption of the North-South economic dialogue that had lapsed after the Cancún (Mexico) summit in 1981.

On the opening day of the meeting in Malaysia, the leaders elected Chief Emeka Anyaoku of Nigeria as the third Commonwealth secretary-general. Chief Anyaoku held the post of deputy secretary-general (political) and had served in the Secretariat since 1966, except for a short break when he served as foreign minister of Nigeria. He was opposed by former Australian prime minister Malcolm Fraser. Chief Anyaoku's five-year term was to begin on June 1, 1990.

(DEREK INGRAM)

POLITICAL PARTIES

The following table is a general world guide to the political parties of the world. All countries that were independent on Dec. 31, 1989, are included; there are a number for which no analysis of political activities can be given, such as one-party states. Parties are included in most instances only if represented in parliaments (in the lower house in bicameral legislatures); the last column indicates the number of seats obtained in the last general election (figures in parentheses are those of the penultimate one) and excludes nonelective seats and seats still in dispute. The date of the most recent election follows the name of the country.

The code letters in the affiliation column show the relative political positions of the parties within each country; there is, therefore, no entry in this column for single-party nations. There are obvious difficulties involved in labeling parties within the political spectrum of a given country. The key chosen is as follows: F-fascist; ER-extreme right; R-right; CR-centre right; C-centre; CL-centre left; L-non-Marxist left; SD-social democratic; S-socialist; EL-extreme left; and K-Communist.

The percentages in the column "Voting strength" indicate proportions of the valid votes cast for the respective parties, or the number of registered voters who went to the polls in single-party states.   (K.M. SMOGORZEWSKI)

Political Parties

Country / Name of party	Affiliation	Voting strength (%)	Parliamentary representation
Afghanistan (April 1988)			
National Front of Afghanistan	—	—	184
Albania (February 1987)			
Albanian Labour (Communist)	—	100	250 (250)
Algeria (February 1987)			
National Liberation Front	—	87	295 (281)
Angola (August 1980)			
Movimento Popular de Libertaçao de Angola (MPLA)	—	—	203
Antigua and Barbuda (March 1989)			
Antigua Labour Party	C	63.8	15 (16)
United National Democratic Party	C	31.0	1 —
Barbuda People's Movement	—	...	1 —
Barbuda National Party	—	...	— (1)
Argentina (May 1989)			
Movimiento Justicialista Nacional (Peronist)	CR	47.3	127 (105)
Unión Cívica Radical	C	36.9	93 (117)
Others	—	15.8	34 (32)
Australia (July 1987)			
National	R	11.5	19 (21)
Liberal	C	34.3	43 (45)
Labor	L	45.8	86 (82)
Austria (November 1986)			
Freiheitliche Partei Österreichs	R	9.7	18 (12)
Österreichische Volkspartei	C	41.3	77 (81)
Sozialistische Partei Österreichs	SD	43.3	80 (90)
Vereinigte Grüne Österreich (Greens)	—	4.8	8 (0)
Bahamas, The (June 1987)			
Progressive Liberal Party	CR	53	31 (32)
Free National Movement	L	...	16 (8)
Others	—	...	2 (3)
Bahrain			
Emirate, no parties	—	—	—
Bangladesh (March 1988)			
Jatiya Party	—	...	251 (183)
Combined opposition	—	...	18 —
Awami League Party	—	(Boycotted)	(76)
Other parties	—	...	5 (39)
Independents	—	...	25 (32)
Barbados (May 1986)			
Democratic Labour Party	C	59.5	24 (7)
Barbados Labour Party	L	40.4	3 (17)
Belgium (December 1987)			
Vlaams Blok	ER	1.9	2 (1)
Volksunie	R	8.0	16 (16)
Front Démocratique des Francophones	R	1.2	3 (3)
Liberals { Flemish	CR	11.5	25 (22)
Liberals { French	CR	9.4	23 (24)
Social Christians { Flemish	C	19.5	43 (49)
Social Christians { French	C	8.0	19 (20)
Socialists { Flemish	SD	14.9	32 (32)
Socialists { French	SD	15.7	40 (35)
Others	—	7.1	9 (10)
Belize (September 1989)			
United Democratic Party	R	48.2	13 (21)
People's United Party	C	50.0	15 (7)
Benin (June 1989)			
People's Revolutionary Party	—	—	206 (196)
Bhutan			
A monarchy without parties	—	—	—
Bolivia (May 1989)			
Acción Democrática Nacionalista	R	...	36 (52)
Movimiento Nacionalista Revolucionario	C	...	38 (60)
Others	—	...	56 (41)
Botswana (October 1989)			
Botswana Democratic Party	C	...	31 (29)
Botswana People's Party	L	...	— (1)
Botswana National Front	EL	...	3 (4)

Country / Name of party	Affiliation	Voting strength (%)	Parliamentary representation
Brazil (November 1986)			
Partido do Movimento Democrático Brasileiro (coalition)	R & L	...	479 (200)
39 other parties	—	...	8 (277)
Brunei			
Legislative Council (nonelected)	—	—	—
Bulgaria (June 1986)			
Fatherland Front			
Bulgarian Communist Party	} —	99.9 { 276	400 (400)
Bulgarian Agrarian People's Union		99	
Independents		25	
Burkina Faso			
National Revolutionary Council since August 1983	—	—	—
Burma (October 1985)			
Burma Socialist Program Party	—	...	489 (475)
Burundi			
Military Committee for National Salvation took power September 1987	—	—	—
Cameroon (April 1988)			
Rassemblement Démocratique du Peuple Camerounais	—	90.1	180 (120)
Canada (November 1988)			
Progressive Conservative	CR	43	170 (211)
Liberal	C	32	82 (40)
New Democratic	L	20	43 (30)
Others	—	5	0 (1)
Cape Verde (December 1985)			
African Party for the Independence of Cape Verde and independents	—	94	83 (56)
Central African Republic (August 1987)			
Rassemblement Démocratique Centrafricain	—	...	52
Chad			
Military government since 1975	—	—	—
Chile (December 1989)			
National Renovation and allied parties	R	...	48
Christian Democrats and allied parties	CL	...	69
Others	L	...	2
Independents	—	...	1
China, People's Republic of (March–April 1988)			
Communist (Kungchantang) National People's Congress	—	...	2,978
Colombia (March 1986)			
Partido Conservador	R	...	82 (84)
Partido Liberal	C	49	100 (114)
Nuevo Liberalismo	C	...	7 —
Unión Patriótica	EL	...	10 —
Comoros (March 1987)			
Federal Assembly	—	65	42 (38)
Congo (September 1989)			
Parti Congolais du Travail	—	—	59 (153)
Others (preapproved by party)	—	...	74 —
Costa Rica (February 1986)			
Partido de Liberación Nacional	L	...	29 (33)
Partido Unidad Social Cristiana	CR	...	25 (18)
Others	—	...	3 (6)
Côte d'Ivoire (November 1985)			
Parti Démocratique	—	...	175 (100)
Cuba (December 1986)			
Partido Comunista Cubano	—	...	499 (499)
Cyprus			
Greek Zone (December 1985)			
Democratic Rally	CR	33.56	19 (12)
Democratic Party (DIKO)	C	27.65	16 (8)
Socialist Party (EDEK)	SD	11.07	6 (3)
Communist Party (AKEL)	K	27.43	15 (12)

Country / Name of party	Affiliation	Voting strength (%)	Parliamentary representation
Turkish Zone (June 1985)			
National Turkish Party	—	...	24
Communal Liberation Party	—	...	10
Turkish Republican Party	—	...	12
New Dawn Party (Renaissance)	—	...	4
Czechoslovakia (May 1986)			
National Front	—	99.4	200 (200)
Denmark (May 1988)			
Conservative	R	19.3	35 (38)
Liberal Democratic (Venstre)	CR	11.8	22 (19)
Christian People's	CR	2.0	4 (4)
Progress	C	9.0	16 (9)
Radical Liberal (Radikale Venstre)	C	5.6	10 (11)
Centre Democrats	C	4.7	9 (9)
Social Democrats	SD	29.8	55 (54)
Common Course	L	1.9	0 (4)
Socialist People's	EL	13.0	24 (27)
Left Socialists	EL	0.6	0 (0)
Faeroe Islands and Greenland	—	...	4 (4)
Djibouti (April 1987)			
Rassemblement Populaire pour le Progrès	—	87	65 (65)
Dominica (July 1985)			
Freedom Party	C	59.0	15 (17)
Labour Party	L	...	5 (2)
Independents	—	...	1 (2)
Dominican Republic (May 1986)			
Partido Reformista Social Cristiano	R	...	56
Partido Revolucionario Dominicano	L	...	48
Partido de la Liberación Dominicana	EL	...	16
Ecuador (January 1988)			
Frente de Reconstrucción Nacional			
Partido Social Cristiano	} R & CR	... 16 {	7 15
Partido Conservador			1 (1)
Partido Liberal Radical			1 (3)
Concentración de Fuerzas Populares			5 (4)
Frente Radical Alfarista			2 (3)
Others			0 (1)
Frente Progresista Democrática			
Izquierda Democrática	} L & EL	... 55 {	31 (17)
Democracia Popular			8 (8)
Partido Socialista Ecuatoriano			4 6
Movimiento Popular Democrático			2 (4)
Frente Amplio de Izquierda			2 (3)
Partido Roldosista Ecuatoriano			8 (5)
Others			0 (1)
Egypt (April 1987)			
New Wafd Party	R	7.8	35 (57)
National Democratic Party	CR	77.2	346 (391)
Socialist Labour Party and allies parties	L	13.4	60 (0)
Independents	—	1.6	7 (0)
El Salvador (March 1988)			
Alianza Republicana Nacionalista (Arena)	R	55	30 (13)
Partido Auténtico Institucional Salvadoreño	R	...	0 (1)
Partido de Conciliación Nacional	CR	...	7 (12)
Partido Acción Democrática	CR	...	0 (1)
Partido Cristiano Democrático	C	...	23 (33)
Equatorial Guinea (July 1988)			
National Assembly	—	...	41
Ethiopia (June 1987)			
Shengo (National Assembly)	—	85.4	835
Fiji			
Military government suspended constitution May 1987	—	—	—
Finland (March 1987)			
National Coalition Party (Conservative)	R	23.2	53 (44)
Swedish People's	R	5.3	13 (11)

Political Parties

Country / Name of party	Affiliation	Voting strength (%)	Parliamentary representation
Centre (including former Liberal)			
Party	C	17.6	40 (38)
Christian Union	C	2.6	5 (3)
Rural Party	C	6.3	9 (17)
Social Democratic	SD	24.3	56 (57)
People's Democratic League			
(Communist)	K	9.4	16 (17)
Green Party	—	4.0	4 (10)
Democratic Alternative	—	4.2	4 (10)
Others	—	6.1	0 (1)
France (June 1988)			
Front National	F	1.1	1 (35)
Rassemblement pour la République	R	23.1	127 (147)
Union pour la Démocratie Française	R	21.1	129 (130)
Diverse right		2.6	16 (14)
Parti Socialiste	SD	45.3	260 ⎫
Mouvement des Radicaux			⎬ (207)
de Gauche	SD	1.3	9 ⎭
Diverse left	—	2.1	7 (9)
Parti Communiste	K	3.4	27 (35)
Other	—	...	1 —
Gabon (February–March 1985)			
Parti Démocratique Gabonais	—	95.44	111 (84)
Gambia, The (March 1987)			
People's Progressive Party	C	59.2	31 (27)
National Convention Party	—	...	5 (4)
German Democratic Republic (June 1986)			
National Front	—	99.7	500 (500)
(Sozialistische Einheitspartei and others)			
Germany, Federal Republic of (January 1987)			
Christlich-Demokratische Union	R	34.5	174 (191)
Christlich-Soziale Union		9.8	49 (53)
Freie Demokratische Partei	C	9.1	46 (34)
Sozialdemokratische Partei			
Deutschlands	SD	37.0	186 (193)
The Green (Ecology) Party	—	8.3	42 (27)
Ghana			
Military dictatorship since Dec. 31, 1981	—	—	—
Greece (November 1989)			
New Democracy Party	CR	46.2	148 (145)
Panhellenic Socialist Movement			
(Pasok)	SD	40.7	128 (125)
Communist Alliance	K	11.0	21 (28)
Independents	—	1.3	3 (2)
Grenada (December 1984)			
New National Party	C	...	14
Grenada United Labour Party	R	...	1
Guatemala (November 1985)			
Movimiento de Liberación Nacional	ER	6.3	6
Partido Institucional Democrático	R	6.3	6
Central Auténtica Nacionalista	R	6.3	1
Partido Nacionalista Renovador	CR	3.2	1
Partido Democracia Cristiana	C	38.7	51
Unión del Centro Nacional	C	20.2	22
Partido Revolucionario/Partido de Democrático de			
Conciliación Nacional	C	13.8	11
Partido Socialista Democrático	SD	3.2	2
Guinea			
Military Committee for National Redress in power since April 1984	—	—	—
Guinea-Bissau (June 1989)			
African Party for the Independence of Guinea and Cape Verde	—	...	150
Guyana (December 1985)			
People's National Congress	S	77.0	42 (41)
People's Progressive Party	K	11.0	8 (10)
Others		0.5	3 (0)
Haiti			
Military government since February 1986	—	—	—
Honduras (November 1989)			
Partido Nacional	R	...	67 (63)
Partido Liberal	CR	...	60 (67)
Others		...	1 (4)
Hungary (June 1985)			
Patriotic People's Front	—	...	361
Independents	—	...	25
Iceland (April 1987)			
Independence Party	R	27.2	18 (23)
Citizen's Party	R	10.9	7
Progressive (Farmers') Party	C	18.9	13 (14)
Social Democratic Party	SD	15.2	10 (6)
People's Alliance	K	13.3	8 (10)
Women's Alliance		10.1	6 (3)
Others		...	1 (4)
India (November 1989)			
Bharatiya Janata	R	...	88
Congress (I)	C	...	192 (395)
Janata Dal	C	...	141
Communist parties	K	...	43 (28)
Other parties	—	...	43
Independents	—	...	16

Country / Name of party	Affiliation	Voting strength (%)	Parliamentary representation
Indonesia (April 1987)			
Golkar (Functional Groups)	—	73.0	299 (246)
United Development Party	—	16.0	61 (94)
Indonesian Democratic Party	—	11.0	40 (24)
(merger of five nationalist and Christian parties)			
Iran (April–May 1988)			
Consultative Assembly, no parties since 1987	—	...	270
Iraq (April 1989)			
Ba'th Party and others	—	...	250
Ireland (June 1989)			
Fianna Fáil (Sons of Destiny)	C	43.7	77 (81)
Fine Gael (United Ireland)	C	29.6	55 (51)
Progressive Democrats	C	5.0	6 (14)
Irish Labour Party	L	8.0	15 (12)
Workers' Party	K	5.6	7 (4)
Others	—	8.2	6 (4)
Israel (November 1988)			
Tehiya	ER	...	3 (5)
Shas	R	...	6 (4)
Likud	R	...	39 (41)
National Religious	CR	...	5 (4)
Agudat Israel	C	...	5 (2)
Labour Alignment ⎰ Labour	SD	...	38 ⎱ (44)
⎱ Mapam	SD	...	3 ⎰
Citizens' Rights	SD	...	5 (3)
Hadash	K	...	5 (4)
Other parties	—	...	11 (13)
Italy (June 1987)			
Movimento Sociale Italiano	F	5.9	35 (42)
Partito Liberale Italiano	CR	2.1	11 (16)
Democrazia Cristiana	C	34.3	234 (225)
Partito Repubblicano Italiano	C	3.7	21 (29)
Partito Social-Democratico Italiano	L	3.4	17 (23)
Partito Socialista Italiano	SD	14.3	94 (73)
Partito Radicale	EL	2.6	13 (11)
Partito Comunista Italiano	K	26.6	177 (198)
Democrazia Proletariana	K	1.7	8 (7)
Greens	—	2.5	13 —
Others	—	...	7 (6)
Jamaica (February 1989)			
Jamaica Labour Party	L	44.1	15 (60)
People's National Party	SD	55.8	45 —
Japan (July 1986)			
Liberal-Democratic Party	R	49.6	300 (250)
Komeito (Clean Government)	C	...	57 (58)
Democratic Socialist Party	SD	...	28 (38)
Japan Socialist Party	S	...	87 (112)
Japan Communist Party	K	...	27 (26)
Others	—	...	13 (27)
Jordan (November 1989)			
Islamic fundamentalists	R	...	32
Leftist democratic bloc	L	...	16
Others	—	...	32
Kampuchea (May 1981)			
Kampuchean United Front for National Salvation (Vietnamese-backed)	—	99.0	117
Kenya (March 1988)			
Kenya African National Union	—	48.0	188
Kiribati (March 1987)			
House of Assembly, no parties	—	84.0	39 (36)
Korea, North (November 1986)			
Korean Workers' (Communist) Party	—	...	...
Korea, South (April 1988)			
Democratic Justice Party	C	33.9	125
Party for Peace and Democracy	L	19.3	70
Reunification Democratic Party	L	23.8	59
New Democratic Republican Party	L	15.6	35
Others	—	7.4	10
Kuwait			
National Assembly abolished July 1986	—	—	—
Laos, People's Democratic Republic of (March 1989)			
Lao People's Revolutionary Party	—	47	79
Lebanon (April 1972)			
Maronites (Roman Catholics)	—	...	30
Sunni Muslims	—	...	20
Shi'ah Muslims	—	...	19
Greek Orthodox	—	...	11
Druzes (Muslim sect)	—	...	6
Melchites (Greek Catholics)	—	...	6
Armenian Orthodox	—	...	4
Other Christian	—	...	2
Armenian Catholics	—	...	1
Lesotho			
Military Council in power from January 1986	—	—	—
Liberia (October 1985)			
National Democratic Party	R	...	45
Opposition	L	...	19
Libya			
Military government since Sept. 1, 1969	—	—	—

Country / Name of party	Affiliation	Voting strength (%)	Parliamentary representation
Liechtenstein (March 1989)			
Vaterländische Union	CR	47.15	13 (8)
Fortschrittliche Bürgerpartei	C	42.13	12 (7)
Luxembourg (June 1989)			
Parti Chrétien Social	CR	...	22 (25)
Parti Libéral	C	...	11 (14)
Parti Ouvrier Socialiste	SD	...	18 (21)
Parti Communiste	K	...	1 (2)
Ecologists	—	...	4 (2)
Madagascar (May 1989)			
Advance Guard of the Malagasy Revolution (Arema)	C	...	120 (115)
Madagascar Independence Congress	L	...	2 ⎫
Madagascar Independence Congress—Renewal	L	...	3 ⎬ (9)
Movement for Proletarian Power	L	...	7 (3)
People's Party for National Unity	L	...	4 (7)
Madagascar National Independence Movement (Monima)	L	...	1 (2)
Malawi (May 1987)			
Malawi Congress Party	—	...	112 (101)
Malaysia (August 1986)			
National Front (Barisan Nasional) Coalition			
United Malays National Organization ⎫		83	
Malaysian Chinese Association		17	
Malaysian Indian Congress ⎬	57.4	6	148 (133)
Malaysian People's Movement		5	
Sabah and Sarawak parties ⎭		37	
Opposition Parties			
Democratic Action Party		15.6	24 ⎫
Pan-Malaysian Islamic Party		...	1 ⎬ 29 (21)
Independents		...	4 ⎭
Maldives (December 1984)			
Citizens' Assembly	—	...	40
Mali (June 1988)			
Union Démocratique du Peuple Malien	—	...	82
Malta (May 1987)			
Nationalist Party	R	50.9	35 (31)
Labour Party	SD	48.9	34 (34)
Mauritania			
Military government since April 25, 1981	—	—	—
Mauritius (August 1987)			
Mouvement Socialiste Mauricien ⎫		26	
Mauritius Labour Party		9	
Parti Mauricien Social Démocrate ⎬ C		4	(43)
Org. du Peuple Rodriguais ⎭		2	
Mouvement Militant Mauricien ⎫			
Mouvement Travailliste Démocrate ⎬ L		21	(19)
Front des Travailleurs Socialiste ⎭		...	
Mexico (July 1988)			
Partido Acción Nacional	CR	...	101
Partido Revolucionario Institucional	CR	...	261
National Democratic Front	L	...	138
Monaco (January 1988)			
Union Nationale et Démocratique	—	...	18 (18)
Mongolia (June 1986)			
Mongolian People's Revolutionary Party	—	99.9	370 (354)
Morocco (September 1984)			
Union Constitutionelle	CR	...	83 —
Rassemblement National des Indépendants	CR	...	61 (141)
Mouvement Populaire	CR	...	47 (44)
Istiqlal (Independence)	C	...	41 (49)
Union Socialiste des Forces Populaires	L	...	36 (16)
Others	—	...	38 (14)
Mozambique (November–December 1986)			
Frente da Libertação de Moçambique (Frelimo)	—	...	250 (210)
Nauru (January 1987)			
Independents	—	...	18 (18)
Nepal (May 1986)			
140-member Parliament, 122 elected and 28 appointed by the king; no parties	—	—	—
Netherlands, The (September 1989)			
Christen Democratisch Appèl	CR	35.3	54 (54)
Volkspartij voor Vrijheid en Democratie	C	14.6	22 (27)
Democraten 1966	C	7.9	12 (9)
Partij van de Arbeid	SD	31.9	49 (52)
Groen Links	—	4.1	6 (3)
Others	—	6.2	7 (5)
New Zealand (August 1987)			
National (Conservative) Party	CR	45.0	39 (37)
Democratic Party	C	6.0	0 (2)
Labour Party	L	47.0	58 (56)
Nicaragua (November 1984)			
Democratic Conservative Party	CR	14.0	14
Independent Liberal Party	C	9.6	9
Popular Social Christian Party	C	5.6	6
Sandinista National Liberation Front	L	66.8	61
Socialist Party of Nicaragua	EL	1.4	2
Communist Party of Nicaragua	K	1.5	2

Political Parties

Country / Name of party	Affiliation	Voting strength (%)	Parliamentary representation
Marxist-Leninist Popular Action Movement	K	1.0	2
Niger (December 1989)			
Mouvement National pour la Société en Developpement	—	—	99 93
Nigeria			
Military government since December 1983	—	—	—
Norway (September 1989)			
Progress Party	R	13.0	22 (2)
Høyre (Conservative)	R	22.2	37 (50)
Kristelig Folkeparti	CR	8.5	14 (16)
Senterpartiet (Agrarian)	C	6.5	11 (12)
Venstre (Liberal)	C	3.2	0 (0)
Arbeiderpartiet (Labour)	SD	34.3	63 (71)
Sosialistisk Venstreparti (Socialist Left)	S	10.1	17 (6)
Independent	—	0.3	1 (0)
Oman			
Independent sultanate, no parties	—	—	—
Pakistan (November 1988)			
Islamic Democratic Alliance	R	...	54
Jamit-i-Ulema-i-Islam	R	...	7
Pakistan People's Party	C	...	93
Mohajir Qaumi Movement	—	...	13
Other parties	—	...	11
Independents	—	...	27
Panama (May 1989)			
Results annulled May 10, 1989	—	—	—
Papua New Guinea (June–July 1987)			
Pangu Party	—	14.7	26 (51)
People's Democratic Movement	—	10.8	18 —
National Party	—	5.1	12 (13)
Melanesian Alliance	—	5.6	7 (8)
People's Action Party	—	3.2	6 (7)
People's Progress Party	—	6.1	5 (14)
Others	—	...	14 (12)
Independents	—	41.2	21 (4)
Paraguay (May 1989)			
Partido Colorado	R	72.8	48 (48)
Partido Liberal Radical Auténtico	C	20.1	19 } (24)
Other parties	—	...	5 }
Peru (April 1985)			
Convergencia Democrática	R	...	12
Acción Popular	CR	...	10
Alianza Popular Revolucionaria Americana	SD	...	107
Izquierda Unida	L	...	48
Izquierda Nacionalista	L	...	1
Independents	—	...	2
Philippines (May 1987)			
House of Representatives	—	...	200
Poland (June 1989)			
Polish United Workers' Party	K	...	173 (245)
Solidarity Citizens' Committee	—	...	161 —
Others	—	...	126 (215)
Portugal (July 1987)			
Social Democratic Centre Party	R	4.4	4 (22)
Democratic Renewal Party	CR	4.9	7 (45)
Social Democratic Party	C	50.2	148 (88)
Socialist Party	SD	22.2	60 (57)
United People's Alliance	K	12.1	31 (38)
Qatar			
Independent emirate, no parties	—	—	—
Romania (March 1985)			
Social Democracy and Unity Front	—	99.99	369 (369)
Rwanda (December 1988)			
National Revolutionary Development Movement	—	...	70
Saint Kitts and Nevis (March 1989)			
People's Action Movement	CR	...	6 (6)
Nevis Reformation Party	CR	...	2 (3)
Labour Party	L	...	2 (2)
Concerned Citizens' Movement	...	...	1 —
Saint Lucia (April 1987)			
United Workers' Party	C	52.7	9 (14)
St. Lucia Labour Party	S	38.1	8 (2)
Progressive Labour Party	EL	9.2	0 (1)
Saint Vincent and the Grenadines (May 1989)			
St. Vincent Labour Party	CR	30.4	0 (4)
New Democratic Party	C	66.2	15 (9)
United People's Movement	L	...	0 (0)
San Marino (May 1988)			
Partito Comunista	...	...	18 (15)
Partito Socialista	...	...	7 ...
Partito Socialista Unitario	...	...	8 (8)
Christian Democrats	...	...	27 (26)
Other parties	...	...	0 (2)
São Tomé and Príncipe (August–September 1985)			
Movimento Libertaçao	—	—	40
Saudi Arabia			
Royal government, no parties	—	—	—
Senegal (February 1988)			
Parti Socialiste	CR	71.3	103 (111)
Parti Démocratique Sénégalais	L	24.7	17 (8)
Other parties	—	4.0	0 (1)
Seychelles (December 1987)			
People's Progressive Front	—	...	23 (23)
Sierra Leone (May–June 1986)			
All People's Congress and independents	—	...	105 (85)
Singapore (September 1988)			
People's Action Party	CR	61.8	80 (77)
Workers' Party	L	...	0 (1)
Democratic Party	—	...	1 (1)
Solomon Islands (February 1989)			
Liberal Party	—	...	4 (1)
United Party	—	...	6 (13)
People's Alliance Party	—	...	14 (12)
Solomone Ano Sagufenua	—	...	0 (4)
Nationalistic Front for Progress	—	...	3 —
Labour Party	—	...	2 —
Independents	—	...	9 (7)
Somalia (December 1984)			
Somalian Revolutionary Socialist Party	—	99.86	171 (171)
South Africa (September 1989)			
Herstigte Nasionale Party	ER	...	0 (0)
Conservative Party	R	31.3	39 (22)
National Party	R	48.6	93 (123)
Democratic (including former Progressive Federal) Party	L	20.0	33 (21)
Spain (October 1989)			
Partido Popular (formerly Alianza Popular)	R	25.8	106 (105)
Centro Democrático y Social	C	7.9	14 (19)
Convergència (Catalan nationalists)	C	5.0	18 (18)
Partido Socialista Obrero Español	SD	39.6	176 (184)
Izquierda Unida (Communists)	K	9.0	17 (7)
Partido Nacionalista Vasco	—	1.2	5 (6)
Herri Batasuna (Basque radicals)	—	1.1	4 (5)
Others	—	...	10 (6)
Sri Lanka (February 1989)			
United National Party	R	51	125 (140)
Freedom Party	C	32	67 (8)
Tamil groups	—	...	23 (18)
Communists and others	—	...	10 (2)
Sudan, The (April 1986)			
National Islamic Front	R	...	51
National Umma Party	C	...	99
Democratic Unionist Party	L	...	63
South Sudan Political Alliance	—	...	9
39 other parties	—	...	42
Suriname (November 1987)			
National Democratic Party	—	...	2
Front for Democracy and Development (three-party coalition)	—	...	42
Others	—	...	7
Swaziland (November 1987)			
House of Assembly, no parties	—	...	40
Sweden (September 1988)			
Conservative	R	18.4	66 (76)
Centre	CR	11.4	42 (44)
Liberal	C	12.2	44 (51)
Social Democrats	SD	43.6	156 (159)
Communists	K	5.9	21 (19)
Greens	—	5.5	20 (0)
Switzerland (October 1987)			
Christian Democrats	R	...	42 (42)
National Campaign	R	...	3 (5)
Evangelical People's	R	...	3 (3)
Swiss People's	CR	...	25 (23)
Radical Democrats	C	...	51 (54)
League of Independents	C	...	8 (8)
Liberal Democrats	L	...	9 (8)
Social Democrats	SD	...	41 (47)
Progressive Organization (Socialists)	EL	...	4 (3)
Communist Party	K	...	1 (1)
Environmentalist Party	—	...	9 (3)
Others	—	...	4 (3)
Syria (February 1986)			
Ba'th Party	—	...	129
National Progressive Front	—	...	57
Communist Party	—	...	9
Taiwan (December 1989)			
Nationalist (Kuomintang)	—	...	72
Democratic Progressive Party	—	...	21
Others	—	...	8
Tanzania (October 1985)			
Chama Cha Mapinduzi	—	...	169 (111)
Thailand (July 1988)			
Prachakorn Thai	ER	8.7	31 (24)
Chart Thai	R	24.4	87 (63)
Democrat Party	C	13.4	48 (100)
Social Action Party	C	15.1	54 (51)
United Democratic Party	C	1.4	5 (38)
United Thai Party	—	9.8	35 (19)
Others	—	27.1	97 (52)
Togo (March 1985)			
Rassemblement du Peuple Togolais	—	96.0	77 (67)
Tonga (February 1987)			
Legislative Assembly	—	—	9
Trinidad and Tobago (December 1986)			
People's National Movement	C	32	3 (26)
National Alliance for Reconstruction (four parties)	—	66	33 —
Tunisia (April 1989)			
National Front (led by the Constitutional Democratic Assembly)	—	80.5	141 (138)
Turkey (November 1987)			
Right Path	CR	19.2	59 —
Motherland	CR	36.2	292 (212)
Social Democratic Populist	C	24.8	99 —
Democratic Left	L	8.5	0 —
Others	—	10.9	0 (188)
Tuvalu (October 1989)			
House of Assembly, no political parties	—	—	12 (12)
Uganda (February 1989)			
National Resistance Council	—	—	168 (98)
Union of Soviet Socialist Republics (March 1989)			
Communist Party of the Soviet Union and independents	—	...	1,500
United Arab Emirates			
Federal government of seven emirates	—	—	—
United Kingdom (June 1987)			
Conservative	R	42.3	375 (397)
Alliance			
Liberal	C	12.8	17 (17)
Social Democratic	SD	9.8	5 (6)
Labour	L	30.8	229 (209)
Communist	K	...	0 (0)
Scottish National Party	—	1.3	3 (2)
Plaid Cymru (Welsh Nationalists)	—	0.4	3 (2)
Ulster Unionists (three groups)	—	1.2	13 (15)
Social Democratic and Labour Party	—	...	3 (1)
Sinn Fein (Northern Ireland)	—	...	1 1
Other (speaker)	—	...	1 —
United States (November 1988)			
Republican	CR	...	173 (177)
Democratic	C	...	262 (258)
Uruguay (November 1989)			
Colorado Party (Conservative)	R	...	30 (40)
Unión Cívica	CR	...	(2)
National (Blanco) Party	C	...	39 (36)
Christian Democrats	CL	...	9 } (21)
Partido por el Gobierno del Pueblo			
Frente Amplio (Broad Front)	L	...	21 }
Vanuatu (November 1987)			
Union of Moderate Parties	CR	42.0	20 (12)
Vanuaaku Parti	C	47.0	26 (24)
Others	—	11.0	0 (3)
Venezuela (December 1988)			
COPEI (Social Christians)	CR	33.33	67 ...
Acción Democrática	L	48.26	97 (118)
Movimiento al Socialismo } Movimiento de Izquierda Revolucionaria }	SD	8.96	18 ...
Other parties	—	9.45	19 ...
Vietnam (April 1987)			
Vietnam Fatherland Front	—	...	496
Yemen, People's Democratic Republic of (October 1986)			
Yemen Socialist Party and independents	—	...	111
Yemen Arab Republic (July 1988)			
Consultative Council	—	...	128
Yugoslavia (May 1986)			
Communist-controlled Federal Chamber	K	...	220 (220)
Zaire (September 1987)			
Mouvement Populaire de la Révolution	—	...	210 (268)
Zambia (October 1988)			
United National Independence Party	—	67.0	125
Zimbabwe (June–July 1985)			
Zimbabwe African National Union	—	77.0	63 (57)
Zimbabwe African People's Union	—	20.0	15 (20)
United African National Council	—	...	0 (3)
Zimbabwe African National Union (Sithole)	—	...	1 (0)
white roll			
Conservative Alliance of Zimbabwe	—	...	15 (20)
Independent Zimbabwe	—	...	4 —
Independent	—	...	1 (0)

Africa South of the Sahara

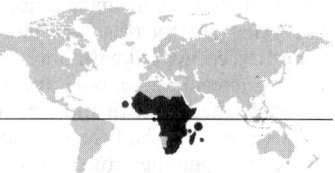

AFRICAN AFFAIRS

The continent's main concerns in 1989 were economic recovery and the effects of the destabilizing wars in the Horn of Africa and southern Africa. The relative absence of drought for the second successive season, along with the economic reform programs adopted by most governments, relieved the acute food-shortage problems of the earlier part of the decade and at least slowed down the economic deterioration of most countries. AIDS continued to be a major threat in a dozen countries, none of which had the resources to cope adequately with the disease. Successful coups occurred in The Sudan and Comoros. While conflicts in the Horn worsened, tensions in the south were eased by the successful implementation of the UN operation to bring independence to Namibia and by the beginning of the withdrawal of foreign troops from Angola.

Organization of African Unity. The 26th annual summit of African heads of state, held in Addis Ababa, Eth., was unusual for the absence of the major controversial issues that had been features of past summit meetings. Discussions focused on two main questions: the burden of foreign indebtedness, which was identified as a major obstacle to economic recovery, and the situation in southern Africa. Proposals to initiate an international conference on the debt problem were rejected by the governments of the less developed countries. While welcoming the agreements on Angola and Namibia, the OAU decided to monitor closely the transition process in the latter country. The OAU protested strongly against the UN Security Council's decision to reduce the size of the UN military contingent sent to help supervise the security arrangements in the period leading up to Namibian elections in November.

The OAU summit supported the idea of an international conference to settle the conflicts in the Middle East. It reiterated its strong support for the Palestinian cause, but apart from a pious resolution urging member nations not to break the OAU's diplomatic boycott of Israel, it proposed no action against the increasing number of countries that had done so. Kenya was the latest country to resume relations, increasing the total who had restored diplomatic links with Israel to 11.

Apart from political and international questions, the summit devoted much of its time to discussing the continent's social problems, especially those affecting the welfare of women, children, and refugees. The African Commission for Human and People's Rights, set up by the OAU in 1987, was provided with new headquarters in Banjul, The Gambia. The commission of 11 members was composed mainly of jurists chosen for their "integrity and morality." Thirty complaints were registered with the commission.

Southern Africa. The implementation of UN Security Council Resolution 435 began on April 1. After an initial flurry of concern due to the incursion of guerrillas of the South West Africa People's Organization (SWAPO) into Namibia, the transition process was accomplished despite continuous complaints about the role of the South African administration and intimidation by its police. In the elections, held November 11, SWAPO gained a majority of seats in the constituent assembly but not enough to give it complete control. In December the assembly agreed in principle on a Western-style constitution.

The withdrawal of 50,000 Cuban combat troops from Angola began in January, more than two months ahead of schedule and one month before South African troops began to leave the country. The phased withdrawal of Cubans continued without a hitch throughout the year. However, the civil war between the Angolan government and Jonas Savimbi's National Union for the Total Independence of Angola (UNITA) continued, though at a lower level of intensity than in recent years. At a summit meeting of 20 OAU member nations, masterminded by Pres. Mobutu Sese Seko of Zaire, the warring parties were brought together at Gbadolite, Zaire, in June. However, the agreement was immediately repudiated by Savimbi, who claimed that the announced terms were different from those on which he had agreed.

The signing of the Angolan and Namibian agreements and the détente with Mozambique improved the security problems on South Africa's borders, but that country's internal political crisis deepened. The newly established Mass Democratic Movement, which broadly supported the banned African National Congress (ANC), sharpened the campaign against apartheid in defiance of the state of emergency, in its fourth year in 1989. Pres. P.W. Botha's successor, F.W. de Klerk (*see* BIOGRAPHIES), promised he would resolutely work for reforms to eliminate white domination.

Horn of Africa. The conflicts in the three main nations in the Horn—The Sudan, Ethiopia, and Somalia—worsened considerably in 1989. Only Djibouti remained an enclave of tranquillity. In The Sudan a military coup, led by Brig. Gen. Umar Hasan Ahmed al-Bashir (*see* BIOGRAPHIES), overthrew the elected government of Sadiq al-Mahdi at the end of June. Although the new regime proposed negotiations with the challenging Sudan People's Liberation Army (SPLA), led by Col. John Garang, its initiative met with no success, principally because of conflicts over Islamic law, the Shari'ah. With the SPLA controlling much of the southern provinces, the military regime admitted that the war was unwinnable. In this painful deadlocked situation, the SPLA succeeded in winning support from a number of African governments.

In Ethiopia the Army continued to suffer heavy military defeats in Tigrai province, losing some 20,000 men in battles in September. Pres. Mengistu Haile Mariam's position also seemed to be seriously weakened by an abortive military coup in May led by many of his senior officers. More than 30 senior officers were killed and 400 officers, troops, and others arrested. Facing these setbacks, Mengistu agreed to open negotiations with the Eritrean People's Liberation Front (EPLF) and the Tigrai People's Liberation Front, renamed the Ethiopian People's Revolutionary Democratic Movement. Former U.S. president Jimmy Carter was accepted as a mediator by the Ethiopian government and the EPLF. Preliminary talks in Atlanta, Ga., in September produced some agreement on procedures for pursuing the negotiations.

In Somalia the Army behaved with great ruthlessness in seeking to meet the military challenge of the Somali National Movement. Thousands of people were killed or wounded in and around the northern capital of Hargeisa. The Army's methods were widely condemned by the Somali government's allies, including the U.S. and Britain.

Inter-African Affairs. The long-standing conflict between Chad and Libya appeared to be finally over with the restoration of diplomatic relations between the two countries and an agreement to refer the dispute over the contested Aozou Strip to the International Court at The Hague for juridical decision.

A bitter new conflict developed between Senegal and Mauritania in April over grazing rights on the border between the two countries. This resulted in attacks on Mauritanians in Dakar and on Senegalese in Mauritania. The two countries came close to the brink of war, but this was averted. An attempt at mediation by the OAU failed to resolve the difficulties, and the situation remained tense.

The desert war in the Western Sahara continued but with only occasional engagements. OAU attempts to mediate between Morocco and the Sahara Arab Democratic Republic (which claimed sovereignty over the Western Sahara) were unsuccessful. Senegal and The Gambia agreed in September to end their ailing seven-year old Senegambia confederation and to replace it with new cooperation agreements.

External Relations. The major issue affecting relations between Africa and the Western democracies remained the refusal by major donor countries and international banks to give greater relief to the foreign indebtedness of most sub-Saharan countries. Meanwhile, African nations continued to support the South-South Commission, headed by former Tanzanian president Julius Nyerere, which sought to promote increased trade and other economic relations between Third World countries.

Soviet leader Mikhail Gorbachev was widely praised for helping to ease superpower rivalries in Africa. There was, however, concern in some quarters about the U.S.S.R.'s firm stand against the value of the armed struggle by the ANC against apartheid, and over Moscow's apparent willingness to adopt a more conciliatory attitude toward South Africa. China, while maintaining its low-level economic aid program, continued to adopt a fairly low profile in the continent.

Relations between many African states and Israel showed further signs of improving. In addition to the 11 countries that maintained diplomatic ties with Israel, another 10 (including Nigeria) continued to expand their economic connections. However, Israeli policy concerning the West Bank and Gaza attracted considerable criticism from most OAU members.

Social and Economic Conditions. The mid-1989 review of the UN Economic Commission for Africa (ECA) was largely discouraging. The overall economic performance of the continent showed no significant improvement over 1988. The average growth in gross domestic products decelerated in the first half of the year to 2.2%, compared with 2.5% in the same period in 1988. The terms of trade continued to decline; although oil prices rose modestly, prices of non-oil primary commodities continued to fall. The external debt of sub-Saharan countries stood at $138 billion, as compared with only $14 billion in 1975. Because of the increases in population, the gross national product per capita declined for most countries in the region.

Africa in 1989 had the largest population growth rate in the world, ranging from 2.7% in North Africa and 2.9% in Central Africa to 3.1% in East Africa and 3.3% in West Africa. A World Bank report estimated that the population in sub-Saharan Africa would rise to 487 million by 1990 and to 695 million by 2000. If the North African population was included, this would put the continent's population in 2000 at 834 million.

Growing dissatisfaction with the operations of the World Bank and International Monetary Fund led the ECA and OAU to initiate the African Alternative Framework to Structural Adjustment Programs for Socio-Economic Recovery and Transformation. It stressed the need for African countries to reorient their economies toward both domestic consumers and other African nations for markets and sources of finance and technical assistance. Special emphasis was given to the importance of land reform.

Africa's illiteracy rate continued to rise despite greater expenditure and efforts to promote education. According to a Unesco finding, the rate was 54%.   (COLIN LEGUM)

See also *Dependent States,* below.

ANGOLA

A people's republic, Angola is located on the Atlantic coast in southwestern Africa. The small exclave of Cabinda is separated from Angola by a strip of Zaire. Area: 1,246,700 sq km (481,354 sq mi). Pop. (1989 est.): 9,739,000. Cap.: Luanda. Monetary unit: kwanza, with (Oct. 2, 1989) a free rate of 29.38 kwanzas to U.S. $1 (47.53 kwanzas = £1 sterling). President in 1989, José Eduardo dos Santos.

Under the terms of an agreement signed on Dec. 22, 1988, by the foreign ministers of Angola, South Africa, and Cuba, Cuban troops were to begin a withdrawal from Angola that would be complete by July 1991. Before returning to Cuba the troops would be withdrawn from southern Angola and redeployed farther north. The first contingent of Cubans left the country on Jan. 10, 1989, under the supervision of a UN verification mission. The agreement, however, made no reference to the internal struggle between the government and the National Union for the Total Independence of Angola (UNITA) guerrillas. Early in the same month, South Africa announced that it would cease to give sup-

AP/WIDE WORLD

Former U.S. president Jimmy Carter (right) stands by as Ashegre Yigletu (centre) of the Ethiopian government and Alamin Mohamed Saiyed of the insurgent Eritrean People's Liberation Front shake hands at a press conference held before negotiation meetings in Atlanta, Georgia.

Cuban soldiers wait at the Luanda International Airport to depart from Angola. Cuba began to withdraw its troops from Angola as part of an agreement signed by Angola, South Africa, and Cuba that called for the removal of all Ouban troops and the independence of Namibia.

AP/WIDE WORLD

port to UNITA immediately, but the U.S. refused to cut off supplies of military equipment to UNITA until the U.S.S.R. put an end to its assistance to the government.

The first initiative aimed at an internal settlement came from Pres. Félix Houphouët-Boigny of Côte d'Ivoire in February and appeared to have the approval of the UNITA leader, Jonas Savimbi, who said that he was prepared to hold talks with neighbouring African countries aimed at reopening the Benguela railway line, a prime target of his military operations. Angolan Pres. José Eduardo dos Santos, however, refused to take part in any negotiations involving Savimbi.

In an attempt to bring the civil war to an end, dos Santos himself was the host of a meeting on May 16 in Luanda that was attended by leaders of seven other African nations. This conference was followed by talks in Kinshasa, Zaire, on June 22–23 that were attended by 18 heads of African states, including dos Santos, as well as Savimbi. Dos Santos had hesitated to meet his opponent but agreed to do so under pressure from other African leaders. The outcome of the talks appeared hopeful when the two opposing leaders shook hands on an agreement that was said to include a cease-fire, the withdrawal of Savimbi from the political scene, and the integration of UNITA supporters into all aspects of Angola's governing political organization.

Almost at once each side accused the other of violating the cease-fire, the worst incident involving the shooting down of an Angolan airliner over UNITA-held territory on July 23 with the loss of 42 lives. Although UNITA denied responsibility, efforts to establish peace were undermined, and they received a further setback in August when Savimbi announced that UNITA had withdrawn from the agreement reached in Zaire. By mid-September fighting had escalated, but with a change of tone, Savimbi claimed that this was only to be expected in view of the hurried fashion in which the supposed agreement had been reached and that he still believed that talks could result in peace. He failed, however, to attend a meeting of African leaders in Kinshasa on September 18 at which it had been hoped he would formally sign the original agreement in Zaire. On December 3, after talks with Zairian Pres. Mobutu Sese Seko, he announced his willingness to sign a cease-fire immediately. The Angolan government offered counterproposals December 30.

Early in the year the full text of Law 13 of 1988 was published. Its aim was to encourage foreign investment, and although foreign investors were excluded from becoming involved in all public services, as well as in defense, security, and the central bank, foreign companies would not now be hindered in their operations in other parts of the economy. Net profits as well as the proceeds of any sale could also be transferred abroad, and compensation was promised in the event of expropriation. Also, in September Angola was admitted to membership in the International Monetary Fund. Assistance from every available source was needed to help revive the country's economy, which still depended heavily upon the proceeds of the sale of Cabinda's oil supplies. The extent of the problem was emphasized at a conference in September in Luanda at which an appeal was launched for international aid to meet the needs of nearly 1.5 million people who had suffered as a result of the civil war. (KENNETH INGHAM)

This article updates the *Macropædia* article SOUTHERN AFRICA: *Angola*.

BENIN

The people's republic of Benin is on the southern coast of West Africa, on the Gulf of Guinea. Area: 112,600 sq km (43,450 sq mi). Pop. (1989 est.): 4,592,000. Cap.: Porto-Novo (official); Cotonou (de facto). Monetary unit: CFA franc, with (Oct. 2, 1989) a par value of CFAF 50 to the French franc and a free rate of CFAF 317.90 to U.S. $1 (CFAF 514.37 = £1 sterling). President in 1989, Brig. Gen. Mathieu Kérékou.

During 1989 Benin again experienced severe economic difficulties, caused by a combination of adverse external conditions and past mismanagement and corruption. The collapse of the Banque Commerciale du Bénin, the country's only commercial bank, at the end of 1988 was followed in early January by a student strike over unpaid grants and by rioting in Porto-Novo. In June Pres. Mathieu Kérékou finally bowed to the pressure, signing an agreement with the International Monetary Fund for a 21.9 million Special Drawing Rights structural adjustment loan. The Fund's "seal of approval" opened the door to additional World Bank and bilateral aid, as well as external debt rescheduling, but was expected to cause a severe contraction of economic activity in the public sector.

On June 18 elections were held, on a single party list, to the National Revolutionary Assembly. Official results showed an 89% "yes" vote, on an 86% turnout, and on August 2 the new Assembly elected Kérékou to another five-year term as head of state. A declared critic of the government, Robert Dossou, was unexpectedly appointed minister of planning. On December 8 Kérékou announced that Marxism-Leninism would no longer be the state ideology. (NIM CASWELL)

This article updates the *Macropædia* article WESTERN AFRICA: *Benin*.

BOTSWANA

A landlocked republic of southern Africa, Botswana is a member of the Commonwealth. Area: 581,730 sq km (224,607 sq mi). Pop. (1989 est.): 1,250,000. Cap.: Gaborone. Monetary unit: pula, with (Oct. 2, 1989) a free rate of 2 pula to U.S. $1 (3.24 pula = £1 sterling). President in 1989, Quett Masire.

Record earnings from diamonds, nickel, and beef exports ($234.6 million in the first two months of 1989, more than 80% above 1988) gave the country an economic boost, and Botswana benefited throughout the year from generally high world mineral prices. International sanctions against South Africa increased Botswana's importance as a potential outlet for South Africa's exports. Thus Botswana's diamonds, marketed by De Beers, helped mask international sales of South Africa's own diamonds. At the same time, the development of Botswana's soda ash deposits, to be purchased mainly by South Africa, put that country in an unusual position of dependence on its small neighbour.

Nevertheless, the economy suffered from a basic imbalance. Mineral royalties and diamonds accounted for 57.4% of income and the Southern African Customs Union for another 16.2%; on the other hand, agriculture provided only 3.9% of gross domestic product and manufacturing only 6%. In theory, average per capita income amounted to $1,410, but 25% of the labour force was unemployed.

In elections on October 3, the ruling Botswana Democratic Party won overwhelmingly, gaining 31 of the 34 parliamentary seats. Botswana joined Malawi, Mozambique, Zambia, and Zimbabwe in forming a cartel to market ivory, in defiance of the movement to ban international trade in elephant products.   (GUY ARNOLD)

This article updates the *Macropædia* article SOUTHERN AFRICA: *Botswana*.

BURKINA FASO

Burkina Faso is a landlocked country of West Africa. Area: 274,200 sq km (105,869 sq mi). Pop. (1989 est.): 8,714,000. Cap.: Ouagadougou. Monetary unit: CFA franc, with (Oct. 2, 1989) a par value of CFAF 50 to the French franc and a free rate of CFAF 317.90 to U.S. $1 (CFAF 514.37 = £1 sterling). President (chairman) of the Popular Front and head of state and government in 1989, Capt. Blaise Compaoré.

On Sept. 19, 1989, it was announced that the second- and third-ranking members of Burkina Faso's Popular Front (PF) government, Commandant Jean-Baptiste Lingani and Capt. Henri Zongo, had been executed by firing squad for plotting to overthrow Pres. Blaise Compaoré. This left only Compaoré alive out of the four young officers who had seized power in 1983; the fourth, former president Thomas Sankara, was assassinated in October 1987. Two other officers were executed in the immediate wake of what the official media described as "a sordid plot by militant fascist elements." On December 26 the government announced that it had foiled a coup attempt by "foreign mercenaries."

Earlier in the year there had been signs that the government was gaining in confidence and was shaking off the quirky revolutionary style that had marked the Sankara regime. In April the Organization for Popular Democracy/Labour Movement was launched, apparently as the first step toward a one-party state. Other leftist groupings lost influence in the Cabinet reshuffle that followed on April 25, and they failed to attend the first session of the PF Coordinating Committee on June 16–17.   (NIM CASWELL)

This article updates the *Macropædia* article WESTERN AFRICA: *Burkina Faso*.

BURUNDI

Burundi is a landlocked republic of central Africa. Area: 27,834 sq km (10,747 sq mi). Pop. (1989 est.): 5,287,000. Cap.: Bujumbura. Monetary unit: Burundi franc, with (Oct. 2, 1989) a free rate of FBu 156.67 to U.S. $1 (FBu 253.50 = £1 sterling). President in 1989, Maj. Pierre Buyoya; prime minister, Adrien Sibomana.

During 1989 a fragile but growing sense of possible rapprochement between Tutsi and Hutu followed the Cabinet changes of October 1988, which for the first time gave the Hutus a majority of ministers. Pres. Pierre Buyoya, who had been in office since September 1987, showed considerable flexibility, and it was a tribute to his moderate policies that by mid-1989 almost all the 40,000 Hutu who had fled the country after the 1988 massacres had returned home. The president was encouraging the Hutu to join the Army, which had been virtually a Tutsi preserve. Educational opportunities, however, were still weighted heavily toward the Tutsi; only 20% of university places went to Hutu, who represented 85% of the population. In April the new (Hutu) prime minister, Adrien Sibomana, visited Brussels to inform the European Commission of developments, including measures to solve the national unity issue.

The president was working hard to secure his economic reforms. Inflation was only 3.9%, and an International Monetary Fund program was in place. However, Burundi remained heavily dependent on aid. Coffee was the staple of the economy, accounting for 75% of foreign exchange earnings, while agriculture as a whole accounted for between 50 and 60% of gross domestic product. The country's debts, at $551 million, were equivalent to 50% of GDP.

(GUY ARNOLD)

This article updates the *Macropædia* article CENTRAL AFRICA: *Burundi*.

CAMEROON

A republic of western central Africa, Cameroon lies on the Gulf of Guinea. Area: 465,458 sq km (179,714 sq mi). Pop. (1989 est.): 11,407,000. Cap.: Yaoundé. Monetary unit: CFA franc, with (Oct. 2, 1989) a par value of CFAF 50 to the French franc and a free rate of CFAF 317.90 to U.S. $1 (CFAF 514.37 = £1 sterling). President in 1989, Paul Biya.

The World Bank and the International Monetary Fund (IMF) were both involved in drafting Cameroon's 1989–90 budget as Pres. Paul Biya continued his economic policy of austerity. The budget provided for expenditures of CFAF 600 billion, which was unchanged from 1988–89. This represented a decline in real terms, as Cameroon's annual inflation rate was 4.5%. However, the government recouped the loss by reducing the provision for debt servicing, which was CFAF 97 billion, down from the previous year's CFAF 170 billion. This savings made it possible for Cameroon to increase funding for higher education, agriculture, and housing significantly.

International lending institutions were generally pleased with Cameroon's economic policies, though the IMF criticized the administration for not depositing export revenue within the Franc Zone, investing instead in banks in the United States. The Paris Club of Western creditor governments agreed to reschedule $550 million in public external debt in 1989, and the World Bank also demonstrated its general approval by granting Cameroon a $9 million loan.

(TIMOTHY D. CLEAVELAND)

This article updates the *Macropædia* article WESTERN AFRICA: *Cameroon*.

CAPE VERDE

The republic of Cape Verde occupies an island group in the Atlantic Ocean about 620 km (385 mi) off the west coast of Africa. Area: 4,033 sq km (1,557 sq mi). Pop. (1989 est.): 337,000. Cap.: Praia. Monetary unit: Cape Verde escudo, with (Oct. 2, 1989) a free rate of 82.21 escudos to U.S. $1 (133.02 escudos = £1 sterling). President in 1989, Aristides Pereira; prime minister, Pedro Pires.

During 1989 the government reconverted part of the armed forces, putting them "at service" for the battle of national development. As the armed forces minister explained: "Our good relations with all the world's countries make the threat of external aggression unlikely." Thus the Army was directed to provide assistance for development projects; a number of troops were also demobilized.

With both arable land and water in short supply, many people were leaving the rural areas and moving to the towns, where there was a growing shortage of housing. The government launched an urban housing program which depended on international aid, mainly from the European Communities. Cape Verde continued to experience a permanent, relatively massive trade deficit as well as generally low production. It remained dependent upon aid for most of its development as well as for balancing the budget.

(GUY ARNOLD)

This article updates the *Macropædia* article WESTERN AFRICA: *Cape Verde*.

CENTRAL AFRICAN REPUBLIC

The Central African Republic is a landlocked state in central Africa. Area: 622,436 sq km (240,324 sq mi). Pop. (1989 est.): 2,813,000. Cap.: Bangui. Monetary unit: CFA franc, with (Oct. 2, 1989) a par value of CFAF 50 to the French franc and a free rate of CFAF 317.90 to U.S. $1 (CFAF 514.37 = £1 sterling). President in 1989, Gen. André Kolingba.

Pres. André Kolingba visited Israel in July 1989. He had intended to make the visit in May but was forced to turn back when The Sudan denied his plane the use of its airspace. Kolingba immediately broke diplomatic relations with The Sudan. The purpose of the visit was to obtain assistance in dealing with domestic security problems, which were concentrated along the border with The Sudan. The conflict seemed to have been generated by a group called Zarguina, which was suspected of having ties to Gen. François Bozize. Bozize, who was involved in a 1982 coup attempt, was arrested in Benin on July 24 and extradited to the Central African Republic a month later.

The nation's economic problems continued. Weak prices offset increases in coffee and cotton production. The World Bank withheld the second installment of its structural adjustment loan, demanding that Kolingba trim the bureaucracy and make salary cuts. On May 10 some 50 Central African students in Côte d'Ivoire occupied their nation's embassy in Abidjan to demand payment of their government stipends.   (TIMOTHY D. CLEAVELAND)

This article updates the *Macropædia* article CENTRAL AFRICA: *Central African Republic*.

CHAD

Chad is a landlocked republic of central Africa. Area: 1,284,000 sq km (495,755 sq mi). Pop. (1989 est.): 5,538,000. Cap.: N'Djamena. Monetary unit: CFA franc, with (Oct. 2, 1989) a par value of CFAF 50 to the French franc and a free rate of CFAF 317.90 to U.S. $1 (CFAF 514.37 = £1 sterling). President in 1989, Hissen Habré.

Relations between Chad and its northern neighbour, Libya, continued to improve during 1989. The restoration of diplomatic relations between the two countries, announced on Oct. 3, 1988, led to an agreement on Aug. 31, 1989, in which the two nations allowed themselves one year to resolve the status of the disputed Aozou Strip; after that the matter would be referred to the International Court of Justice at The Hague. In the interim the 114,000-sq km (44,000-sq mi) territory was to be administered by an African observer force. Following the agreement France confirmed that it was reducing its forces in Chad from 1,700 in late 1988 to approximately 1,200 in recognition of the diminished threat to Chad's sovereignty.

Domestically, the progressive rallying of opposition movements to the ruling Union Nationale pour l'Indépendance et la Révolution came to a head in November 1988 when Acheikh ibn Oumar, the leader of the largest remaining opposition faction, returned to N'Djaména. He was appointed foreign minister in a Cabinet reshuffle on March 3. A new constitution to replace the defunct *loi fondamentale* of 1982 was drafted.

Pres. Hissen Habré nevertheless continued to face hostility from a range of sources. In April it was announced that loyal forces had foiled an attempted coup led by two of his closest military collaborators, Hassan Djamouss and Idriss Deby. Djamouss was killed, but Deby managed to flee to The Sudan with a small band of followers; from there he continued to harass the regime. Those arrested in the wake of the attempt included the minister of internal affairs, Mahamat Itno, and others of his Zaghawa ethnic group, confirming the breakup of the northern ethnic coalition that had brought Habré to power.   (NIM CASWELL)

This article updates the *Macropædia* article WESTERN AFRICA: *Chad*.

COMOROS

The republic of Comoros is an island state in the Indian Ocean off the east coast of Africa. Area: 1,862 sq km (719 sq mi), excluding the island of Mayotte, which continued to be a de facto dependency of France. Pop. (1989 est., excluding Mayotte): 448,000. Cap.: Moroni. Monetary unit: Comorian franc, with (Oct. 2, 1989) a par value of CF 50 to the French franc and a free rate of CF 317.90 to U.S. $1 (CF 514.37 = £1 sterling). Presidents in 1989, Ahmed Abdallah to November 26 and Said Mohammed Djohar (interim).

On Nov. 4, 1989, the public apparently approved an amendment to the constitution that allowed Pres. Ahmed Abdallah to serve a third six-year term. However, the referendum was followed by rioting. One reason for the discontent was the foreign military presence in Comoros. Since 1984 South Africa had contributed $5 million per year to the Presidential Guard in exchange for use of the islands as a base from which to supply the Mozambican rebels. The guard, whose officers were French and Belgian mercenaries, was led by Bob Denard, a Frenchman. In 1989 the South African government became dissatisfied with the mercenary force, and in April the quasi-official South African attaché was ordered out of Comoros, apparently at Denard's behest.

On the night of November 26–27 the president was assassinated. Initial reports indicated that the shooting took place during an abortive military coup, but other reports suggested Denard himself was behind the killing, a charge Denard denied. Said Mohammed Djohar, the head of the Supreme Court, was named interim president but remained under virtual house arrest while the Presidential Guard seized control of the islands. South Africa and France cut off aid to Comoros, and the French carried on a war of

nerves, with warships patrolling off Moroni. Finally, on December 15, after several days of negotiations, Denard surrendered to French military authorities and left with his followers for South Africa, although Pretoria made it clear that he would not be welcome to stay. He was wanted in France on charges relating to an attempted coup in Benin in 1977. Djohar reportedly asked French forces to remain in Comoros and help to restore order.

(TIMOTHY D. CLEAVELAND)

This article updates the *Macropædia* article INDIAN OCEAN ISLANDS: *Comoros.*

CONGO

A people's republic, Congo is in central Africa on the Atlantic Ocean. Area: 342,000 sq km (132,047 sq mi). Pop. (1989 est.): 2,245,000. Cap.: Brazzaville. Monetary unit: CFA franc, with (Oct. 2, 1989) a par value of CFAF 50 to the French franc and a free rate of CFAF 317.90 to U.S. $1 (CFAF 514.37 = £1 sterling). President in 1989, Col. Denis Sassou-Nguesso; prime ministers, Ange-Édouard Poungui and, from August 7, Alphonse Poaty-Souchlaty.

Denis Sassou-Nguesso was reelected in 1989 as head of the Parti Congolais du Travail, Congo's only political party, for a third five-year term. Because of depressed petroleum prices, the Congolese Parliament voted its fourth consecutive austerity budget. In 1985 petroleum revenues had amounted to CFAF 230 billion, while in 1988 they were only CFAF 35 billion. Total Congolese revenues were CFAF 125.4 billion in 1988, while expenditures were CFAF 310.8 billion. This economic situation began to create serious social problems. Congo's unemployment rate in 1989 was 23%, and it was likely to rise rapidly because roughly 70% of the population were under 35 years of age.

Relations between Zaire and Congo became strained when a reported 5,000 Zairians were expelled from Congo and sent back to Zaire's capital, Kinshasa, during a single week in April. Most of the deported Zairians were market traders living in Brazzaville, directly across the Congo River from Kinshasa. However, Sassou-Nguesso and Pres. Mobutu Sese Seko of Zaire met on April 27 and declared that the recent troubles were minor incidents that would not affect relations between the two countries.

(TIMOTHY D. CLEAVELAND)

This article updates the *Macropædia* article CENTRAL AFRICA: *Congo.*

CÔTE D'IVOIRE

A republic of West Africa, Côte d'Ivoire lies on the Gulf of Guinea. Area: 320,763 sq km (123,847 sq mi). Pop. (1989 est.): 12,135,000. Cap., Abidjan; capital designate, Yamoussoukro. Monetary unit: CFA franc, with (Oct. 2, 1989) a par value of CFAF 50 to the French franc and a free rate of CFAF 317.90 to U.S. $1 (CFAF 514.37 = £1 sterling). President in 1989, Félix Houphouët-Boigny.

Pres. Félix Houphouët-Boigny's health began to fail in 1989 as he turned 84. In April he visited Pope John Paul II and offered the Holy See a basilica that was under construction in Yamoussoukro, the capital designate and the president's place of birth. This project was criticized within Côte d'Ivoire, as it continued Houphouët-Boigny's policy of spending large sums to convert the small, agricultural town into a sophisticated city.

Falling prices for cocoa and coffee, the nation's two leading exports, led Houphouët-Boigny to comply with World Bank and International Monetary Fund recommendations in order to qualify for debt rescheduling. Consequently, the government halved the price paid to cocoa and coffee farmers for the 1989–90 crop.

Côte d'Ivoire's marketing problems were further complicated by diplomatic considerations. In 1989 Philbro, a U.S. company, purchased 280,000 tons of unprocessed cocoa from Côte d'Ivoire, thus breaking the unofficial monopoly of Sucden, a French concern. However, Houphouët-Boigny rejected a similar offer from Philbro for the 1989–90 and 1990–91 harvests, fearing that such a deal might endanger French financial aid.

(TIMOTHY D. CLEAVELAND)

This article updates the *Macropædia* article WESTERN AFRICA: *Côte d'Ivoire.*

DJIBOUTI

The republic of Djibouti is in the Horn of northeastern Africa on the Gulf of Aden. Area: 23,200 sq km (8,950 sq mi). Pop. (1989 est.): 512,000. Cap.: Djibouti. Monetary unit: Djibouti franc, with (Oct. 2, 1989) a pegged rate of DF 177.72 to U.S. $1 (DF 287.55= £1 sterling). President in 1989, Hassan Gouled Aptidon; prime minister, Barkat Gourad Hamadou.

Despite severe floods early in the year, 1989 brought Djibouti some cause for economic optimism. France agreed to maintain its military and economic aid at $160 million,

BARRY IVERSON—TIME MAGAZINE

The massive Basilica of Our Lady of Peace rises from the earth near Côte d'Ivoire's capital designate, Yamoussoukro. The basilica, offered to the pope as a gift from Pres. Félix Houphouët-Boigny, was widely criticized because of its hefty price tag.

roughly half of Djibouti's gross domestic product. A 113-km (70-mi) road linking the southern and northern regions of the country was completed with $33.5 million from Saudi Arabia. The World Bank and a multidonor group led by Italy contributed $8.9 million and $22 million, respectively, to a geothermal power project in the Lake Assal area. Japan donated $7 million to finance rice imports and construct new port facilities. Finally, ar-Rahbani, a private Saudi company, was financing the construction of Djibouti's first oil refinery.

Djibouti's ethnic communities experienced political instability during the year. In March there were clashes in the capital between the Gadaboursis and the Issas, and in April between the Gadaboursis and Issaqs. One reason for the conflict was that ethnic groups in Djibouti supported different sides in the civil war in neighbouring Somalia. However, some of the tension was generated within Djibouti itself. On April 19 Afars in the northern region of Tadjoura accused an Issa administrator of distributing flood-relief supplies improperly. Five prominent Afar politicians were arrested, and Afar youth subsequently sacked the state representative's office. On May 2 one of the arrested politicians, Abdulqader Daoud, died in prison.

(TIMOTHY D. CLEAVELAND)

This article updates the *Macropædia* article EASTERN AFRICA: *Djibouti.*

EQUATORIAL GUINEA

The republic of Equatorial Guinea consists of Río Muni, on the Atlantic coast of West Africa, and the offshore islands of Bioko and Annobon. Area: 28,051 sq km (10,831 sq mi). Pop. (1989 est.): 343,000. Cap.: Malabo. Monetary unit: CFA franc, with (Oct. 2, 1989) a par value of CFAF 50 to the French franc and a free rate of CFAF 317.90 to U.S. $1 (CFAF 514.37 = £1 sterling). President in 1989, Brig. Gen. Teodoro Obiang Nguema Mbasogo; prime minister, Capt. Cristino Seriche Bioko.

In January 1989 Pres. Teodoro Obiang Nguema Mbasogo pardoned Joe Luis Jones, the senior opposition figure sentenced to 17 years in prison for conspiring against the president in September 1988. The president's official visit to Madrid at the end of January was rewarded by the writing off of a third of Equatorial Guinea's 500 million peseta debt to Spain; the balance was to be paid off over 14 years, with 8 years' grace.

The presidential election on June 25 passed peacefully; the only candidate was the president himself, although voters were allowed to register a "no" to express dissatisfaction. In order to ensure a maximum turnout, the times of church services were altered, the sale of alcohol was banned, and traffic was kept off the streets. The president was reelected for another seven-year term by 99.96% of the votes cast. These first national elections since independence in 1968 were, supposedly, to familiarize the population with democratic procedures. Meanwhile, opponents of the regime were still in exile, although the president had invited them to return home. (GUY ARNOLD)

This article updates the *Macropædia* article WESTERN AFRICA: *Equatorial Guinea.*

ETHIOPIA

The people's republic of Ethiopia is in the Horn of northeastern Africa, on the Red Sea. Area: 1,223,500 sq km (472,400 sq mi). Pop. (1989 est.): 48,898,000. Cap.: Addis Ababa. Monetary unit: birr, with (Oct. 2, 1989) a par value of 2.07 birr to U.S. $1 (free rate of 3.35 birr = £1 sterling). President in 1989, Lieut. Col. Mengistu Haile Mariam; prime ministers, Fikre Selassie Wogderess and, from November 8, Hailu Yemenu.

An attempted coup d'état in mid-May was the most visible evidence in 1989 of widespread dissatisfaction with the government's military policies and its attempts to construct a Marxist state.

The revolt, embracing both the Army and the Air Force and a significant number in the high command, was crushed quickly and resulted in the death of at least 30 senior officers in Addis Ababa and Asmara and the arrest of a much larger group, including some civilians. The highest placed of these was Teffera Wonde, a deputy prime minister. Only one of the known plotters, Maj. Gen. Kumelachew Dejene, previously deputy commander in Eritrea, escaped from Ethiopia. The national legislature (Shengo) set up a special military tribunal to try those arrested.

Throughout the year there was continual rather than sporadic conflict, and army casualties were heavy. Using standard guerrilla tactics, the Eritrean and Tigrean dissident groups repeatedly cut off government forces, temporarily occupying parts of the main road system while avoiding fixed battles. During the year these activities extended southward into the Welo region and westward into the Gonder and Gojam regions. The Army was often fighting in conditions that limited the effectiveness of its heavy armour. The government call for "everything to the war front" contributed massively to the wrecking of the economy, but at year's end there was a larger area outside effective government control than ever before.

The Army's problems also stemmed from declining levels of external support and an obvious unwillingness in the Soviet Union to support the kinds of development policies that were being rapidly dismantled in the U.S.S.R. In September the last contingent of Cuban troops was withdrawn from Ethiopia.

In Ethiopia's continuing search for external support, diplomatic activity intensified. Diplomatic relations with Israel were resumed in November after a 16-year break. There was also increasing pressure on the government to engage in talks with the rebel groups. After visits by former U.S. president Jimmy Carter, this was given official sanction at a one-day extraordinary session of the Shengo on June 5 with a call for "unconditional talks." The formal agreement that these would take place in Atlanta, Ga., under the patronage of Carter was announced in mid-August.

Several factors limited the scope and possible outcome of these peace talks. Their "unconditional" nature was denied the following day by Ethiopian Pres. Mengistu Haile Mariam, who placed secession outside the discussion and underlined unwillingness to talk to the Tigrai Peoples Liberation Front (TPLF). A second factor was the parallel series of discussions between the government and "lowland Eritreans," initiated in Khartoum, The Sudan, in April and followed by discussions in Addis Ababa on a petition for autonomy presented by a group from the northern and western areas of Eritrea. The Shengo sanctioned continued negotiations as evidence of the government's willingness to talk. The Eritrean People's Liberation Front played no part in these activities and continued its support for the proposals made by Carter. The Atlanta talks focused on procedural and technical questions. There was sufficient agreement for a continuing series of meetings in African capitals, the first in Nairobi, Kenya. The central issue was the nature of the autonomy that could be provided to Eritrea.

Although there were claims that overall agricultural output increased from 1988, this was from a very low level and actually represented a decline in per capita production. In addition, an estimated 2% of the cultivated land was being

A U.S. Air Force helicopter lowers a serviceman to join a military team that had been sent to retrieve the bodies of U.S. Rep. Mickey Leland (Dem., Texas) and 15 others after their airplane crashed in western Ethiopia.
AFP PHOTO

lost annually because of soil erosion at the same time that the population was increasing 2.9% annually. To reverse these trends large investments were needed, but there was little likelihood that these could be provided. During a review of the agricultural sector in August, which included visits to the resettlement areas, the light plane carrying U.S. Rep. Mickey Leyland (Dem., Texas) crashed in bad weather on the western escarpment, killing him and the 15 others on board.

The economy also suffered from a fall in coffee prices. Though Ethiopia supplies only a fraction of world output, coffee is its most important export. The boost to the economy that had been expected from the "joint ventures" proclamation of 1983 had not taken place. The call in 1989 for domestic investors to participate more actively in economic development was inhibited by the statement that successful enterprises could be taken over by the state.

The unstable structures in the Rift Valley region produced significant tremours in the Arba Minch area of Gemu Gofa region. In August earth movements totally disrupted traffic on the crucial road link between the highlands and the port of Aseb.

In September there was the customary amnesty for prisoners; 907 were released, the majority of them common criminals. Included were 87 political prisoners, 3 of whom were members of the royal family.

This article updates the *Macropædia* article EASTERN AFRICA: *Ethiopia*.

GABON

Gabon is a republic of central Africa, on the Atlantic Ocean. Area: 267,667 sq km (103,347 sq mi). Pop.: in 1989 estimates ranged from 930,000 to 1,530,000 (UN est., 1,245,000). Cap.: Libreville. Monetary unit: CFA franc, with (Oct. 2, 1989) a par value of CFAF 50 to the French franc and a free rate of CFAF 317.90 to U.S. $1 (CFAF 514.37 = £1 sterling). President in 1989, Omar Bongo; prime minister, Léon Mébiame.

Early in 1989 Pres. Omar Bongo announced measures designed to streamline the state bureaucracy and liberalize the economy. This was an attempt to implement the suggestions of the World Bank and other international financial institutions. One of the reform measures would have allowed the payment of employees on a piecework basis. However, hundreds of workers protested against the measure in front of the presidential palace, and the proposal was withdrawn in July.

Oil production had decreased in recent years, and the subsequent loss of export revenue was the primary cause of Gabon's budgetary problems. In an effort to increase production, the Gabonese administration persuaded the International Finance Corporation to provide $160 million in loans to the new onshore drilling project at the Rabi-Kounga oil field. The administration hoped that this project would double oil exports by 1991. Other extractive industries remained healthy. The Ogooué mining company (Comilog), one of the top manganese producers in the world, reported profits in 1988 of CFAF 693 million, up from CFAF 555 million in 1987.

In June Gabon initiated a program to study and preserve the nation's native languages and literature. Until recently the study of Gabonese languages had been neglected in favour of French, partly in an effort to forge national unity. (TIMOTHY D. CLEAVELAND)

This article updates the *Macropædia* article CENTRAL AFRICA: *Gabon*.

GAMBIA, THE

A republic and member of the Commonwealth, The Gambia extends from the Atlantic Ocean along the lower Gambia River in West Africa; it is surrounded by Senegal. Area: 10,689 sq km (4,127 sq mi). Pop. (1989 est.): 835,000. Cap.: Banjul. Monetary unit: dalasi, with (Oct. 2, 1989) a free rate of 7.75 dalasis to U.S. $1 (12.54 dalasis = £1 sterling). President in 1989, Sir Dawda Jawara.

A Cabinet reshuffle in February 1989 followed the resignation of the minister of finance, Sheriff Sisay, for reasons of health. On the occasion of the 24th anniversary of national independence, Pres. Dawda Jawara pardoned 50 prisoners, opened a $7 million Saudi-financed mosque in Banjul, and opened a new 7.5 million dalasi plastics and knitwear factory.

Good relations with the U.S. were reemphasized during President Jawara's private visit to Washington, D.C., in May, when he met with U.S. Pres. George Bush. Yundum Airport in Banjul was selected by the U.S. National Aeronautics and Space Administration as its first choice for emergency landings for stricken space shuttles.

The Gambia enjoyed a substantial economic recovery (including considerable international aid inflows) during 1989. Following a loan from the World Bank, the nation liberalized the marketing of peanuts, opening it to all private traders. At the end of September, the Senegambia confederation was dissolved. In August Senegal, without consultation, withdrew the troops it had stationed in The

Gambia in 1981; then in September Senegal Pres. Abdou Diouf said that the seven-year confederation had failed and was not worth continuing.   (GUY ARNOLD)

This article updates the *Macropædia* article WESTERN AFRICA: *The Gambia*.

GHANA

A republic of West Africa and member of the Commonwealth, Ghana lies on the Gulf of Guinea. Area: 238,533 sq km (92,098 sq mi). Pop. (1989 est.): 14,566,000. Cap.: Accra. Monetary unit: cedi, with (Oct. 2, 1989) a free rate of 321.38 cedis to U.S. $1 (520 cedis = £1 sterling). Chairman of the Provisional National Defense Council in 1989, Jerry John Rawlings.

Ghana's economic recovery appeared to be on course in 1989. Agriculture now accounted for 50% of gross domestic product and employed 55% of the labour force, while cocoa, also recovering well, earned 54% of foreign exchange. Gold was the second major earner, accounting for 15%. Gold resources stood at 2.3 million fine troy ounces and would last for ten years at current rates of extraction. The Economic Recovery Program relied on expansion of cocoa exports and a continuing inflow of aid. The aim was to increase productivity to 300,000 metric tons of cocoa by 1991. In Paris at the end of February, the fifth Consultative Group for Ghana pledged $900 million in aid, well above the $800 million the World Bank had said was needed.

While the economy was being liberalized to attract investment capital, freedom of expression was under greater restraints. In June the president of the Ghana Bar Association, Peter Ala Adjetey, and the secretary, Nutifafa Kuenyehia, were arrested prior to a series of lectures to commemorate three high court judges kidnapped and killed in 1982. The government also banned a number of religious sects (in the national interest), including the Jehovah's Witnesses, the Mormons, and two indigenous Christian churches. Increasingly it appeared that only groups overtly loyal to the ruling Provisional National Defense Council were left alone.   (GUY ARNOLD)

This article updates the *Macropædia* article WESTERN AFRICA: *Ghana*.

A woman passes by one of the many currency exchanges that opened in Accra, Ghana, after the start of the Economic Recovery Program. The program's expansion of export trade and influx of foreign aid had so far proved successful.

GUINEA

The republic of Guinea is located in West Africa, on the Atlantic Ocean. Area: 245,857 sq km (94,926 sq mi). Pop. (1989 est.): 6,705,000. Cap.: Conakry. Monetary unit: Guinean franc, with (Sept. 30, 1989) a free rate of GF 615 to U.S. $1 (GF 999.50 = £1 sterling). President in 1989, Brig. Gen. Lansana Conté.

The year 1989 opened to renewed rumours of unrest in the armed forces. At a military parade on Oct. 2, 1988, the 30th anniversary of independence, a truck had sped out of control in front of the presidential tribune and had killed one spectator. The government strongly denied that this had been an assassination attempt, however, and pressed ahead with plans announced the previous day to return the country to civilian rule. Pres. Lansana Conté later indicated that within the framework of a two-party political system, to be put in place during a five-year period, a head of state would be elected to a five-year term by all eligible voters. On June 30, 1989, senior military officers switched positions during a Cabinet reshuffle; the only important civilian ministerial change was the movement of Edouard Benjamin from planning to finance.

The structural adjustment program received backing from the International Monetary Fund, the World Bank, and bilateral donors; in April the Paris Club of Western creditor nations agreed to debt rescheduling on favourable terms. Prospective new investments included a Soviet proposal for a second bauxite mine at Djandjan in the north, a French-backed hydroelectric station on the Konkouré River, and iron ore mining on the border with Liberia.

(NIM CASWELL)

This article updates the *Macropædia* article WESTERN AFRICA: *Guinea*.

GUINEA-BISSAU

A republic of West Africa, Guinea-Bissau lies on the Atlantic Ocean. Area: 36,125 sq km (13,948 sq mi). Pop. (1989 est.): 953,000. Cap.: Bissau. Monetary unit: Guinea-Bissau peso, with (Oct. 2, 1989) a free rate of 650 pesos to U.S. $1 (1,052 pesos = £1 sterling). President in 1989, João Bernardo Vieira.

Nine nations and ten international organizations guaranteed sufficient financing to enable Guinea-Bissau to achieve its growth target of 4% for 1989–90. According to Manuel Maria dos Santos, the minister for economic coordination, commerce, and tourism, the country needed $120 million, of which 40% would be used to support the balance of payments and the balance to meet general financial requirements. To accompany the moves toward economic liberalization that had been made since 1987, the government established a national commission to revise the constitution and a second commission to reform the electoral law.

National elections in June resulted in an overwhelming mandate for the ruling party. João Vieira was reelected president, and Col. Iafai Camara, minister of the armed forces, became first vice president. Guinea-Bissau submitted to the international community a five-year health plan that would concentrate on primary health care and ensure that the population had access to drinkable water. The discovery of oil in Senegal's territorial waters reopened an old border dispute between the two countries; Guinea-Bissau claimed that its border should be moved farther north.

(GUY ARNOLD)

This article updates the *Macropædia* article WESTERN AFRICA: *Guinea-Bissau*.

KENYA

A republic and member of the Commonwealth, Kenya is in eastern Africa, on the Indian Ocean. Area: 582,646 sq km (224,961 sq mi), including 11,230 sq km of inland water. Pop. (1989 est.): 23,883,000. Cap.: Nairobi. Monetary unit: Kenya shilling, with (Oct. 2, 1989) a free rate of 21.51 shillings to U.S. $1 (34.80 shillings = £1 sterling). President in 1989, Daniel arap Moi.

In 1989 former vice president and long-term government critic Oginga Odinga created a political stir. In December 1988 police had arrested his associate, Dave Owak. Early in 1989 Pres. Daniel arap Moi claimed that certain dissidents were trying to enlist Odinga's support, yet barely two weeks later Odinga surprised and puzzled observers by calling upon his countrymen to support the government. His intentions remained unclear until June, when Moi released all political prisoners detained without trial, including Raila Odinga, Odinga's son, and offered an amnesty to opponents living in exile.

After President Moi returned from a European trip in April, he delivered a speech at Nairobi airport condemning gambling; he stated categorically that in his absence from the country there was no acting president. His remarks were interpreted as being leveled against Vice Pres. Josephat Karanja, who had invested in a gambling house in Nairobi. Almost at once Karanja was accused of arrogance and of promoting the interests of his Kikuyu ethnic group. In Parliament he was charged with receiving funds from Uganda to destabilize the government. Following a vote of no confidence, Karanja resigned at the beginning of May and was suspended from membership in the Kenya African National Union (KANU) with the recommendation that he be expelled from the party.

Karanja's downfall, after only 12 months in office, provided further evidence of the power at the president's disposal and of the ease with which he could control Parliament. President Moi also called upon KANU to purge itself further and to drive all elements of disloyalty and subversion from the body politic. It was an opportunity to settle political scores that most did not hesitate to seize.

As part of a general Cabinet reshuffle aimed at strengthening the president's position still further, Karanja was succeeded as vice president by George Saitoti, formerly minister of finance, and as minister for home affairs by Davidson Ngubuini Kuguru. The appointment of Saitoti, a Masai, tipped the balance increasingly against the Kikuyu. In June, after President Moi criticized reports published in the country's leading newspaper, the *Daily Nation,* Parliament banned that paper from reporting its sessions and from having access to information about its activities. The president was equally hostile to external criticism, upbraiding Arab countries that had condemned his decision to restore diplomatic relations with Israel on Dec. 30, 1988, and rejecting outside interference in Kenya's affairs.

On May 15, 1989, the International Monetary Fund approved funding to enhance a structural facility worth $310.8 million. The measure supported the country's 1989–91 economic and financial program. The shortage of jobs was acute, particularly among school dropouts, and was a potential source of serious discord. The income from the tourist industry, the main foreign exchange earner, was also threatened. In April three vacationers were wounded when bandits opened fire on their minibus. This followed the 1988 death of a British photographer, Julie Ward, on a popular game reserve. Originally the authorities indicated that she had been killed by wild animals, but her father accused the police of a cover-up, and in October a Nairobi magistrate ruled that she had been murdered. More palatable was the news that in July Moi had burned more than $3 million worth of confiscated ivory as part of a campaign to stop the ivory trade and save elephants from extinction.

(KENNETH INGHAM)

This article updates the *Macropædia* article EASTERN AFRICA: *Kenya.*

LESOTHO

A monarchy of southern Africa and member of the Commonwealth, Lesotho forms a landlocked enclave within South Africa. Area: 30,355 sq km (11,720 sq mi). Pop. (1989 est.): 1,715,000. Cap.: Maseru. Monetary unit: loti (plural: maloti), at par with the South African rand, with (Oct. 2, 1989) a free rate of 2.69 maloti to U.S. $1 (4.35 maloti = £1 sterling). King, Moshoeshoe II; chairman of the Military Council in 1989, Maj. Gen. Justin Metsino Lekhanya.

A major scandal shook the country in June 1989 with revelations that Maj. Gen. Justin Metsino Lekhanya, the chairman of the ruling Military Council, had been re-

WILLETS CAMERAPIX—GAMMA/LIAISON

Pres. Daniel arap Moi of Kenya sets fire to a hill of confiscated elephant tusks of some 2,000 animals, worth more than $3 million. The president hoped that the action would emphasize the government's determination to stop poachers and to end the world's ivory trade, which could soon wipe out Kenya's elephant population.

sponsible for shooting a 20-year-old agricultural student, George Ramone, the previous December at Maseru's Agricultural College. The story was originally hushed up, but at a staff meeting of 16 senior government figures, the general admitted he had done the shooting. There was no explanation as to why he was on the campus in the middle of the night, although it was suggested that he and the student were seeking the favours of the same young woman. Lekhanya had become increasingly unpopular, particularly for his known close ties with South Africa. A number of accusations of corruption had also been leveled against him.

The budget, at R 593 million, emphasized restraining expenditure and improving revenue collection; R 425 million was earmarked for recurrent expenditure and the balance for development. Agricultural production rose 5% during the year, thanks largely to favourable weather. A European Communities project worth 7.7 million European Currency Units was launched to develop manpower for the natural resources sector.   (GUY ARNOLD)

This article updates the *Macropædia* article SOUTHERN AFRICA: *Lesotho*.

LIBERIA

The republic of Liberia is located in West Africa, on the Atlantic Ocean. Area: 99,067 sq km (38,250 sq mi). Pop. (1989 est.): 2,508,000. Cap.: Monrovia. Monetary unit: Liberian dollar, at par with the U.S. dollar, with a free rate (Oct. 2, 1989) of L$1.62 to £1 sterling. President in 1989, Gen. Samuel K. Doe.

Liberia experienced a troubled year in 1989, both politically and economically. The defense minister, Gray D. Allison, long considered the second most powerful man in the country, was sacked and then tried for involvement in ritual murder. Allison was accused of having conspired to murder a local policeman in order to obtain body parts, needed for a potion to be used against Pres. Samuel K. Doe. He was found guilty and sentenced to death by firing squad. Another attempt to bring down Doe's government was reportedly crushed by the Army in December, when

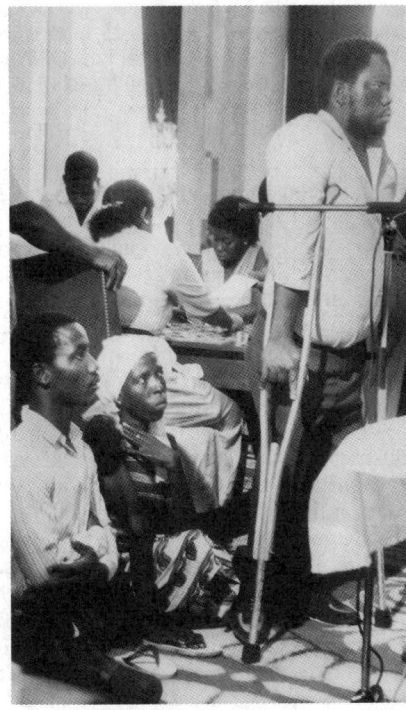

KENNETH B. NOBLE—THE NEW YORK TIMES

Disabled Liberians wait to add their pennies to the fund to pay back some of the country's $183 million debt to the United States.

hundreds of Liberians were said to have fled into Côte d'Ivoire.

In March the U.S. threatened to stop further aid to Liberia unless it repaid its $7 million backlog of debts by May. President Doe launched a nationwide drive to raise the money by voluntary donations, and the deadline was met. The success of this drive led Doe to launch another in September to collect money toward the $183 million total owed to the U.S. Meanwhile, four agreements were reached with the U.S. providing $9.5 million in aid for development.

At the end of July the Liberian-American-Swedish mining consortium, LAMCO, closed its iron-ore mining operations, with the loss of 15,000 jobs, and in September Japanese-owned Firestone decided to close two of its rubber plantations. Revenue declined through the year, and by September the government was holding talks with the International Monetary Fund.

On the ninth anniversary of the coup that brought Doe to power, the U.S.-based human rights group Africa Watch issued a bulletin detailing systematic human rights abuses taking place in Liberia. The Movement for Justice in Africa led demands for the release of William Gabriel Kpolleh, the leader of the Liberian Unification Party, and other political prisoners. The Press Union of Liberia condemned the government for closing down the Roman Catholic radio station.   (GUY ARNOLD)

This article updates the *Macropædia* article WESTERN AFRICA: *Liberia*.

MADAGASCAR

The republic of Madagascar occupies the island of the same name and minor adjacent islands in the Indian Ocean off the southeast coast of Africa. Area: 587,041 sq km (226,658 sq mi). Pop. (1989 est.): 11,602,000. Cap.: Antananarivo. Monetary unit: Malagasy franc, with (Oct. 2, 1989) a free rate of FMG 1,458 to U.S. $1 (FMG 2,359 = £1 sterling). President in 1989, Didier Ratsiraka; prime minister, Lieut. Col. Victor Ramahatra.

In March 1989 Didier Ratsiraka was elected to his third seven-year term as president of Madagascar. Though his margin of victory was much narrower than in previous elections, success was ensured by the fact that the opposition was split among three major candidates. Opposition leaders accused Ratsiraka of election fraud, and riots followed the announcement of his victory. In July the government said armed men had seized the state radio to announce a coup, but the attempt had been foiled.

Madagascar doubled coffee production in 1989 to 80,-000 tons, which represented 40% of total export earnings. Nevertheless, because of the combined effect of falling coffee prices and rising prices for rice, the trade deficit worsened. Though 80% of Madagascar's agricultural land was devoted to rice, the country could not fully supply its own needs. Madagascar in 1989 was the world's greatest per capita consumer of rice.

Despite foreign aid and the purchase of debt by charitable organizations, the nation's economy continued to decline. In 1989 the rate of inflation was about 30%, and an estimated 250,000 urban workers were unemployed. The government adopted a program of "structural adjustment," a policy of economic liberalization and privatization. President Ratsiraka found it necessary to institute the program in order to qualify for additional loans from international lending institutions and development associations.

(TIMOTHY D. CLEAVELAND)

This article updates the *Macropædia* article INDIAN OCEAN ISLANDS: *Madagascar*.

MALAWI

A republic and member of the Commonwealth, Malawi is a landlocked state in eastern Africa. Area: 118,484 sq km (45,747 sq mi). Pop. (1989 est.): 8,515,000. Cap.: Lilongwe. Monetary unit: Malawi kwacha, with (Oct. 2, 1989) a free rate of 2.74 kwacha to U.S. $1 (4.43 kwacha = £1 sterling). President in 1989, Hastings Kamuzu Banda.

In July 1989 Malawi celebrated 25 years of independence. President Banda's keynote speech stressed the peace and economic prosperity the country had enjoyed, but his optimism was challenged by a number of developments that adversely affected the country. The continuation of the resistance movement in Mozambique meant that Malawi's most convenient trade outlets remained closed, and the cost of transporting goods to and from South African ports amounted to almost half the country's export earnings. Industrial growth was hampered by the extremely low purchasing power of the people, while many landowners, unable to grow enough even to support their own households, were compelled to work on plantations for minuscule wages. A UNICEF report pointed out that one-third of the country's children died before the age of five, while the level of malnutrition among the survivors was high even by the standards of Malawi's neighbours.

In March British Prime Minister Margaret Thatcher visited the country and promised increased aid. The U.S. announced in November that it was canceling its share of Malawi's official debt. Pope John Paul II visited Malawi and praised the country for accepting 650,000 refugees from the war in Mozambique. It was praise that was received with muted enthusiasm in view of the heavy cost of maintaining the refugees.   (KENNETH INGHAM)

This article updates the *Macropædia* article SOUTHERN AFRICA: *Malawi*.

MALI

Mali is a landlocked republic of West Africa. Area: 1,240,192 sq km (478,841 sq mi). Pop. (1989 est.): 7,911,000. Cap.: Bamako. Monetary unit: CFA franc, with (Oct. 2, 1989) a par value of CFAF 50 to the French franc and a free rate of CFAF 317.90 to U.S. $1 (CFAF 514.37 = £1 sterling). President in 1989, Gen. Moussa Traoré.

Malian Pres. Moussa Traoré spent much of the first half of 1989 traveling in his capacity as chairman of the Organization of African Unity, pleading the case for debt alleviation and mediating the continent's various disputes. The expiration of his OAU term in July was preceded on June 8 by a sweeping Cabinet reshuffle in Mali in which seven ministers were ousted and top posts consolidated in the hands of his closest associates. Otherwise, the president appeared to be in a conciliatory mood, as shown by the appointment of former finance minister Soumana Sacko as auditor general in late 1988. Sacko's dismissal in 1987, after a brief but zealous campaign against corruption in high places, had dismayed both aid donors and many of the Malian middle class.

Reforms of trade and investment regulations, the domestic grain market, and the banking system pressed ahead with backing from France, among others. A World Bank–International Monetary Fund joint mission to Bamako was, nevertheless, reported to be dissatisfied with progress on the structural adjustment program. Excellent rains ensured a bumper 1988–89 harvest.   (NIM CASWELL)

This article updates the *Macropædia* article WESTERN AFRICA: *Mali*.

MAURITANIA

The republic of Mauritania is on the Atlantic coast of West Africa. Area: 1,030,700 sq km (398,000 sq mi). Pop. (1989 est.): 1,946,000. Cap.: Nouakchott. Monetary unit: ouguiya, with (Oct. 2, 1989) a free rate of 83.62 ouguiya to U.S. $1 (135.30 ouguiya = £1 sterling). President of the Military Committee for National Salvation and prime minister in 1989, Col. Maaouya Ould Sidi Ahmed Taya.

The year 1989 was dominated by the explosion into violence of previously simmering racial tensions between the politically dominant "white" (Bidan) Moors and the mainly Poular-speaking black population. The first concrete sign of trouble occurred in January, when a brief trade war broke out with Senegal over alleged violations of cross-border grazing quotas. Then, on April 9, two Senegalese peasants were killed, apparently by Mauritanian border guards, in a clash over grazing rights in a border area.

Subsequent looting of Mauritanian premises in several Senegalese towns sparked revenge attacks on blacks in Mauritania on April 24–25, news of which brought Senegalese gangs onto the streets of their cities during the following days, murdering and looting. Widespread atrocities on both sides resulted in the deaths of perhaps 300 people, while up to a quarter of a million more fled their homes for the other nation. Diplomatic relations were broken off at the end of August.

Domestic politics—which had been moving cautiously toward democratization—were polarized by these events, and in September the government announced postponement of municipal elections and educational reforms scheduled for 1990. Internationally, the effect was to reinforce Mauritania's increasing closeness to the Arab world.

(NIM CASWELL)

This article updates the *Macropædia* article WESTERN AFRICA: *Mauritania*.

MAURITIUS

The constitutional monarchy of Mauritius, a member of the Commonwealth, occupies an island in the Indian Ocean about 800 km (500 mi) east of Madagascar and includes the island dependencies of Rodrigues, Agalega, and Cargados Carajos Shoals. Area: 2,040 sq km (788 sq mi). Pop. (1989 est.): 1,061,000. Cap.: Port Louis. Monetary unit: Mauritian rupee, with (Oct. 2, 1989) a free rate of Mau Rs 15.53 to U.S. $1 (Mau Rs 25.13 = £1 sterling). Queen, Elizabeth II; governor-general in 1989, Sir Veerasamy Ringadoo; prime minister, Aneerood Jugnauth.

Still enjoying remarkable economic success, Mauritius continued in 1989 to pursue open-market policies that had only recently become popular in other parts of Africa. The government embarked on an ambitious $90 million environmental protection program with help from its main trading partners and international agencies. The program involved such developments as sewage-treatment facilities and improvements to the infrastructure in the areas mainly affected by the island's heavy tourist trade. It also included creation of an industrial zone designed specifically for industries that are environmentally hazardous.

Mauritius had demonstrated some years earlier how to make a free-trade zone work efficiently; this approach was ideally suited to a small country with a large population in comparison with total resources and a relatively highly educated population as well. By 1989 the Mauritius free-trade zones were contributing $500 million annually in export earnings while accounting for 100,000 jobs, 10% of the island's total. This compared with 600 jobs in 1971, when the free-trade zones were first developed. Perhaps

the greatest contribution of the free-trade zones was to lessen Mauritius' dependence upon sugar; by 1989 sugar accounted for slightly less than 40% of exports.

Since 1984 the nation's gross domestic product had been growing at an average annual rate of 7%. Clearly a favourite of the International Monetary Fund and the World Bank, Mauritius' economic program was so successful that the country was facing a different kind of problem: constraints on the labour supply and an overconcentration of the export business on garments and textiles.   (GUY ARNOLD)

This article updates the *Macropædia* article INDIAN OCEAN ISLANDS: *Mauritius.*

MOZAMBIQUE

The people's republic of Mozambique is located in eastern Africa, on the Indian Ocean. Area: 799,380 sq km (308,642 sq mi). Pop. (1989 est.): 15,293,000. Cap.: Maputo. Monetary unit: metical, with (Oct. 2, 1989) a free rate of 808 meticais to U.S. $1 (1,307 meticais = £1 sterling). President in 1989, Joaquim Chissanó; prime minister, Marío de Graça Machungo.

Although 1988 ended with an attack by saboteurs on Maputo's power supply and 1989 began with a guerrilla attack on a sugar complex 70 km (44 mi) north of Maputo that left 27 people dead and many more wounded, prospects for an end to the civil war seemed to improve as the year progressed. The improvement came none too soon. The war had taken a heavy toll. A report prepared jointly by UNICEF and the Mozambican authorities and published in March estimated that 600,000 people had been killed in the struggle and 494,000 children had died from causes directly attributable to malnutrition associated with the war. A radio report during the same month stated that 3,500 people had died of starvation in the northeastern Memba coastal district, mainly as a result of drought though guerrilla operations had exacerbated the situation. By contrast, although the guerrillas had been less active in Tete province, floods were causing serious difficulties there. An estimated 7.7 million people throughout the country were dependent on food aid, and more than 900,000 tons of food were urgently needed to meet their requirements. Hoping to extend the sources of aid to his country, Pres. Joaquim Chissanó visited West Africa and western Europe in March.

In an effort to save lives and to promote national harmony at home, Chissanó had extended for one year from Dec. 31, 1988, the amnesty offered to antigovernment guerrillas. He did not, however, reduce the military pressure on his opponents, and in the middle of the year government forces, cooperating with troops from Zimbabwe, launched a powerful offensive in Sofala province, where the headquarters of the Mozambican National Resistance (Renamo) was located. These military operations coincided with a congress of the ruling Frelimo Party at which the party announced a swing away from its left-wing ideology and said that it wished to have talks with the guerrillas, but on its own terms. Frelimo rejected any suggestion of sharing power with Renamo but said that individual rebel supporters might be appointed to official posts if they renounced their opposition to the government. The government had taken as the models for its new approach to its opponents the developments in neighbouring Zimbabwe and the attempts of the Angolan government to achieve a settlement with its own guerrilla fighters.

The leaders of Renamo seemed in a responsive mood, for in August Afonso Dhlakama, together with other officials of the movement, held talks in Nairobi, Kenya, with Mozambican church leaders in an attempt to plan a new peace initiative. At the same time, Pres. Robert Mugabe of Zimbabwe was also in Nairobi, having agreed to act alongside Pres. Daniel arap Moi of Kenya as mediator in any discussions that might take place between Renamo and the Mozambican government.

Chissanó's abandonment of Marxism-Leninism was the official acknowledgement of the changes that resulted from the demands made on Mozambique by the International Monetary Fund in return for assistance. Large sectors of the economy had to be freed from state control. The currency was severely devalued and in the middle of the year stood at barely 7% of its value at the beginning of 1987. Wage increases had failed to keep up with the rising cost of essentials such as domestic fuel and bus fares. At the same time, while the majority of the people found it difficult even to survive, as a result of the new financial arrangements, stores and markets in Maputo became well stocked with consumer goods that only the wealthy could afford. The capital itself took on the appearance of normality after years of decay.   (KENNETH INGHAM)

This article updates the *Macropædia* article SOUTHERN AFRICA: *Mozambique.*

NIGER

Niger is a landlocked republic of West Africa. Area: 1,186,408 sq km (458,075 sq mi). Pop. (1989 est.): 7,523,000. Cap.: Niamey. Monetary unit: CFA franc, with (Oct. 2, 1989) a par value of CFAF 50 to the French franc and a free rate of CFAF 317.90 to U.S. $1 (CFAF 514.37 = £1 sterling). President of the Supreme Military Council (Supreme Council of National Orientation from May 17) to Dec. 20, 1989, and president from that date, Gen. Ali Saibou; prime minister to December 20, Mamane Oumarou.

Consolidation and democratization were the watchwords for 1989 in Niger, where the president, Ali Saibou, continued to enjoy widespread popular support. The Cabinet reshuffle that included replacement of the former finance minister, Beïdari Mamadou, in November 1988 was followed by a more wide-ranging government reorganization on May 19.

This followed the ending on May 18 of the constituent congress of the National Movement of the Society of Development, henceforward to be Niger's sole political party. The Supreme Council of National Orientation succeeded the former Supreme Military Council as the country's top executive body, and Saibou's official title changed to president of the CSON. A new constitution was approved by 99.28% of voters in a referendum on September 24, and elections for president and a 93-seat National Assembly were held December 10. The civilian government, with Saibou as president, took office December 20. The CSON and the post of prime minister were abolished.

(NIM CASWELL)

This article updates the *Macropædia* article WESTERN AFRICA: *Niger.*

NIGERIA

A republic and member of the Commonwealth, Nigeria is located in West Africa, on the Gulf of Guinea. Area: 923,768 sq km (356,669 sq mi). Pop. (1989 est.): 115,973,000. Cap., Lagos; capital designate, Abuja. Monetary unit: naira, with (Oct. 2, 1989) a free rate of 7.33 naira to U.S. $1 (11.86 naira = £1 sterling). President and chairman of the Armed Forces Ruling Council in 1989, Maj. Gen. Ibrahim Babangida.

The year 1989 was an uneasy one for Nigeria, dominated by two issues—the state of the economy and moves toward a return to civilian rule in 1992. The country was presented

in January with an austerity budget, which attracted the approval of the world financial institutions; the International Monetary Fund (IMF) made available $650 million in standby credits and the World Bank $720 million in loans. The budget included a two-tier price for gasoline: 42 kobo (100 kobo = 1 naira) per litre for commercial users and 60 kobo for private users.

The austerity resulted from the continuing decline in crude-oil exports; projected earnings for 1989 were only $4.4 billion, the lowest in a decade. The economy remained far too dependent upon oil—all other exports accounting for only $890 million—and the future outlook suggested little change. The debt service requirement stood at 37% of export earnings. New projections during the year suggested that $3,445,000,000 would be required for servicing the debt in 1989, rising to $4,043,000,000 in 1992, when the country was scheduled to return to civilian rule. According to the IMF and the World Bank, these figures, moreover, were regarded as the most optimistic for Nigeria.

At the beginning of May, shortly before he went on a state visit to Britain, Maj. Gen. Ibrahim Babangida lifted the five-year ban on party political activity. The visit to Britain turned out to be highly successful; it put the seal on the loans promised at the time of the budget and ended a phase of poor Anglo-Nigerian relations that had begun in 1984 with the attempted kidnapping in London of the former Nigerian transport minister, Umaru Dikko.

Political parties, meanwhile, were readying themselves to contest the first hurdle before 1992, the local elections set for December 1989. It was increasingly difficult to determine who would compete since the old politicians were banned from running. Two groups—the Federalists and the Progressives—appeared to be emerging as front-runners; at the same time, a constant juggling of names occurred as the parties sought well-known leaders who were not banned from competing.

At the end of May Nigeria experienced some of the worst riots in years as anger against the austerity measures (the structural adjustment program, or SAP) exploded in a number of cities, causing many casualties and extensive destruction of property. The government retaliated with mass arrests and the closing down of six universities for a year. In addition, Babangida felt obliged to cancel his state visit to Paris scheduled for June.

In an effort to lessen the impact of the SAP following the riots, the government adopted a series of measures (almost a midyear minibudget) that included additional finances for the National Directorate of Employment to enable it to create an immediate 62,000 jobs. The most important measure was the order to works ministries to employ large additional numbers of staff and offer jobs to professionals, many of whom had been unemployed ever since their university graduation. However, Nigeria's economic problems remained daunting, and food prices rose steadily through the year.

In mid-October Babangida sprang a major surprise when he rejected the credentials of all 13 political parties that had emerged after the ban on political activities was lifted. Babangida announced that instead the Armed Forces Ruling Council would create two new parties that all unbanned politicians would be free to join. The reason given for the move was that the new politicians were behaving too much like the old ones. On December 7 it was announced that the local elections were being postponed to late 1990, although the scheduled return to civilian rule remained the same.   (GUY ARNOLD)

This article updates the Macropædia article WESTERN AFRICA: Nigeria.

RWANDA

The landlocked republic of Rwanda is situated in central Africa. Area: 26,338 sq km (10,169 sq mi). Pop. (1989 est.): 6,989,000. Cap.: Kigali. Monetary unit: Rwanda franc, with (Oct. 2, 1989) a free rate of RF 80.25 to U.S. $1 (RF 129.85 = £1 sterling). President in 1989, Maj. Gen. Juvénal Habyarimana.

Sluggish agricultural growth during 1988 probably produced a drop in the country's per capita gross domestic product. In addition, depressed world prices for coffee, Rwanda's principal export, had an adverse impact on the balance of payments and the budget, even though special measures were taken to control expenditure. The result, unsurprisingly, was to emphasize the degree to which Rwanda remained dependent upon international aid.

By 1989 West Germany had become one of Rwanda's main sources of aid, its assistance totaling more than DM 44 million per year. A program sponsored by the European Communities was aimed at rehabilitating the Kigali–Butare road, while the European Investment Bank made available 4 million European Currency Units (ECU) for small- and medium-sized enterprises in the industrial, agro-industrial, mining, and tourism sectors. A ECU 30 million program funded by foreign aid was designed to modernize the country's telecommunications network.

To mark the beginning of a new term of office, Pres. Juvénal Habyarimana commuted death sentences and reduced life jail sentences, although not for political prisoners, embezzlers of public funds, or those convicted of armed robbery.   (GUY ARNOLD)

This article updates the Macropædia article CENTRAL AFRICA: Rwanda.

SÃO TOMÉ AND PRÍNCIPE

The republic of São Tomé and Príncipe comprises two main islands and several smaller islets that straddle the Equator in the Gulf of Guinea, off the west coast of Africa. Area: 1,001 sq km (386 sq mi). Pop. (1989 est.): 118,000. Cap.: São Tomé. Monetary unit: dobra, with (Oct. 2, 1989) a free rate of 106.35 dobras to U.S. $1 (172.07 dobras = £1 sterling). President in 1989, Manuel Pinto da Costa; prime minister, Celestino Rocha da Costa.

In June 1989 the nation was afflicted by a cholera epidemic that caused 30 deaths; Minister of Health Armindo Vaz de Almeida called on the international community for help. Portugal sent two tons of medicine, and the French provided a medical team and additional supplies. The inability to cope with the epidemic emphasized the tiny size of the economy and infrastructure and the continuing dependence in most respects on assistance from outside. Economic development remained minuscule.

São Tomé continued to obtain regular assistance from Angola, including a military detachment, while East Germany bought most of the cocoa crop at above world prices. There was a need to diversify away from dependence on cocoa, but there was a problem as to what the new products should be. Only fishing and tourism offered any real possibilities for expansion.

In August the 43 persons implicated in the March 1988 coup attempt went on trial. Evidence against Alfonso dos Santos, the leader of the banned Revived Resistance Front of São Tomé and Príncipe, included a resignation letter for Pres. Manuel da Costa to sign and a proclamation making dos Santos new head of state.   (GUY ARNOLD)

This article updates the Macropædia article CENTRAL AFRICA: São Tomé and Príncipe.

SENEGAL

The republic of Senegal is located in West Africa, on the Atlantic Ocean; it surrounds the country of The Gambia. Area: 196,722 sq km (75,955 sq mi). Pop. (1989 est.): 7.4 million Cap.: Dakar. Monetary unit: CFA franc, with (Oct. 2, 1989) a par value of CFAF 50 to the French franc and a free rate of CFAF 317.90 to U.S. $1 (CFAF 514.37 = £1 sterling). President in 1989, Abdou Diouf.

Political unrest dating back to the February 1988 presidential and legislative elections gave Senegal's Parti Socialiste (PS) government, led by Pres. Abdou Diouf, a distinctly embattled look as 1989 opened, with "roundtable" talks with the opposition suspended, separatist agitation in the Casamance region, an impending strike by university teachers, and the resignation on Dec. 9, 1988, of the president of the National Assembly, Daouda Sow. An extraordinary congress of the PS on March 4–5 agreed to internal reforms designed to breathe life into the increasingly moribund party. Rioting marred the Independence Day celebrations on April 4.

A border incident in the Sénégal River valley on April 9 and the subsequent outbreak of ethnic violence between Mauritanians and Senegalese helped President Diouf regain the domestic initiative but raised new and urgent problems. (See *Mauritania,* above.) Commercial circuits were shattered as the Moors who had previously dominated retail trade fled north, while tens of thousands of Senegalese and expelled black Mauritanians crowded refugee camps on the southern side of the river valley, exacerbating tensions by their raids into Mauritanian territory. Diplomatic relations with Mauritania were broken in August. Guinea-Bissau took advantage of Dakar's other preoccupations to reject a ruling on July 31 by an international arbitration panel on the disputed maritime border between the two countries. At the end of September the confederation that had linked Senegal and The Gambia since 1982 was dissolved, amid mutual recriminations. Meanwhile, a poor farming season meant no easing of austerity. (NIM CASWELL)

This article updates the *Macropædia* article WESTERN AFRICA: *Senegal.*

Shopkeepers from Senegal's Mauritanian community wait with their goods in the Mauritanian embassy in Dakar. Many Mauritanians abandoned their homes and businesses in Senegal to escape the growing number of racial attacks.

SEYCHELLES

A republic and member of the Commonwealth, the Seychelles consists of about 100 islands in the Indian Ocean, 1,450 km (900 mi) from the east coast of Africa. Area: 453 sq km (175 sq mi). Pop. (1989 est.): 67,100. Cap.: Victoria. Monetary unit: Seychelles rupee, with (Oct. 2, 1989) a free rate of SR 5.75 to U.S. $1 (SR 9.30 = £1 sterling). President in 1989, France-Albert René.

Tourism remained the backbone of the economy in 1989. The government set a limit—and a target—of 4,000 tourists a day by 1994, although there were some who wanted to double that figure. The government also recognized a need to diversify the source of tourists, who came overwhelmingly from Europe, South Africa, and Japan.

The second major commercial activity was fishing, and in recent months there had been an increase in the tuna catch. The 60 foreign vessels that each paid an annual fee of $200,000 to operate in Seychelles' waters dominated the trade, however, and the government wanted to replace them with local boats. Efforts to improve agriculture and boost food security were a top priority. A major objective was the reclamation and development of agricultural land through drainage, irrigation, and the building of access roads, while food security was to be improved by the promotion of fruit, vegetable, milk, and meat production. Seychelles in 1989 was self-sufficient in poultry production and hoped to raise the current level of beef production—20% of needs—to 40%.

France-Albert René, running unopposed, was elected to a third term as president in June. (GUY ARNOLD)

This article updates the *Macropædia* article INDIAN OCEAN ISLANDS: *Seychelles.*

SIERRA LEONE

A republic of West Africa and member of the Commonwealth, Sierra Leone lies on the Atlantic Ocean. Area: 71,740 sq km (27,699 sq mi). Pop. (1989 est.): 3,957,000. Cap.: Freetown. Monetary unit: leone, with (Oct. 2, 1989) an official rate of 65.36 leones to U.S. $1 (105.75 leones = £1 sterling). President in 1989, Maj. Gen. Joseph Saidu Momoh.

In April 1989 Sierra Leone celebrated 28 years of independence in the midst of what appeared to be a long-term economic crisis. The country's refineries were operating at only 40% of capacity owing to a lack of available crude oil to process. The two main foreign exchange earners—gold and diamonds—were regularly smuggled out of the country, causing a major loss to the national treasury. A new mining policy required each diamond exporter to show a turnover of $500,000 a month in order to retain his license and also to give 60% of foreign exchange earned to the central bank. Though there were 22 exporters who met this condition, it was believed that 90% of the nation's diamonds were being smuggled into neighbouring countries or flown out through Freetown airport.

The 10th National Delegates Conference of the All Peoples' Congress at the beginning of the year produced a code of conduct for political leaders and public servants. In September 2,000 civil servants in Freetown went on strike for their back pay, one more symptom of a generally troubled economic year. After a long trial and appeal process, the former vice president, Francis Minah, and five others were hanged for treason for the attempted overthrow of the government in March 1987. (GUY ARNOLD)

This article updates the *Macropædia* article WESTERN AFRICA: *Sierra Leone.*

SOMALIA

A republic in the Horn of northeastern Africa, the Somali Democratic Republic, or Somalia, lies on the Gulf of Aden and the Indian Ocean. Area: 637,000 sq km (246,000 sq mi). Pop. (1989 est.): 7,339,000. Cap.: Mogadishu. Monetary unit: Somali shilling, with (Oct. 2, 1989) a free rate of 410 Somali shillings to U.S. $1 (663.38 Somali shillings = £1 sterling). President in 1989, Maj. Gen. Muhammad Siyad Barrah; prime minister, Lieut. Gen. Muhammad Ali Samatar.

In response to criticism of Somalia's human rights record and the withdrawal, and threats of withdrawal, of urgently needed aid, the government launched a diplomatic campaign at the beginning of 1989 to try to win foreign support for its efforts to restore peace in the north following the civil war in 1988. Pres. Muhammad Siyad Barrah visited Egypt, Kuwait, and Iraq, while Prime Minister Muhammad Ali Samatar traveled to Western Europe and the U.S. These moves were accompanied by the offer of amnesty to people imprisoned for their involvement in the war. The government also said that it intended to streamline and reform its military forces. In April Samatar suggested that there were to be changes in the economy that would reduce state control and encourage private investment.

These moves appeared to have little effect on the discontent expressed with varying degrees of violence in different parts of the country. The demotion of Maj. Gen. Adan Abdullahi Nuur had been unpopular among his fellow Ogadeni, who formed a large proportion of the rank and file of the Army. In March Ogadeni soldiers mutinied in Kismayo, winning support from their fellow clansmen in that region; although the rebellion was suppressed, fighting in southern Sudan continued for several months. Late in July government troops attacked members of the Ogadeni clan near Kismayo, and hundreds of refugees streamed over the border into Kenya. The government insisted that only bandits or poachers fleeing from security forces had been involved, but the Kenya government disputed the claim.

Somali government forces were also heavily engaged by troops of the Somali National Movement, which claimed that it controlled most of the rural areas of the country. So severe did the fighting become that in May staff of the UN and other aid agencies were forced to withdraw from the country, causing grave concern about the fate of 140,000 Ethiopian refugees who were heavily reliant upon charitable sources for their survival.

The assassination of the Roman Catholic bishop of Mogadishu on July 9 was the signal for further acts of violence by the Army and police. These followed a demonstration on July 14 by Muslims protesting the arrest of some of their leaders who had said that the promise to execute the assassin when apprehended was too severe. At least 450 were believed to have been killed and 1,000 wounded in the violence; many more were held in detention, and some of those were summarily executed. As a result, the popularity of President Barrah declined even in the capital, where order was maintained by troops commanded by the president's son and by secret police. Meanwhile, rebels claimed that the commander of the government forces in Hargeisa, Col. Ahmed Omar Gees, had defected along with ten other officers. Bowing to rebel pressure, the government announced on August 30 that it would hold the first multiparty elections since Barrah came to power in 1969.

(KENNETH INGHAM)

This article updates the *Macropædia* article EASTERN AFRICA: *Somalia*.

SOUTH AFRICA

The Republic

South Africa occupies the southern tip of Africa, with the Atlantic Ocean to the west and the Indian Ocean to the east. It partially surrounds the four republics of Bophuthatswana, Ciskei, Transkei, and Venda (whose independence from South Africa is not recognized by the international community). Area: 1,123,226 sq km (433,680 sq mi). Pop. (1989 est.): 30,244,000. (Area and population figures exclude the four republics.) Executive cap., Pretoria; judicial cap., Bloemfontein; legislative cap., Cape Town. Monetary unit: South African rand, with (Oct. 2, 1989) a financial rate of R 3.89 to U.S. $1 (R 6.30 = £1 sterling) and a commercial rate of R 2.69 to U.S. $1 (R 4.35 = £1 sterling). State presidents in 1989, Pieter Willem Botha until January 19 and from March 15 to August 14; acting presidents, J. Christian Heunis from January 19 to March 15 and Frederik W. de Klerk from August 15 to September 20; president from September 20, de Klerk.

The Republic. *Domestic Affairs.* During 1989 P.W. Botha, head of government since 1978, was replaced as state president by Frederik W. de Klerk, former minister of education and leader of the National Party (NP) in the Transvaal (*see* BIOGRAPHIES). Botha suffered a stroke in January. De Klerk was elected national leader of the NP on February 2. Returning to his desk in March, Botha stated his intention of continuing as state president. After increasingly open dissension between him and de Klerk, the Cabinet, and NP parliamentarians, however, Botha resigned on August 14.

The Botha government, which had over the previous decade introduced a number of reforms of apartheid, the official policy of racial separation, had by 1989 become increasingly paralyzed and reliant on military-police means of repression. In the early part of the year, commissions exposed corruption linked to NP members of Parliament, causing several resignations.

An election for the tricameral (whites, Coloureds—those of mixed race—and Indians) Parliament, one of the Botha reforms, was held on September 6. The NP retained its majority in the (white) House of Assembly but suffered its most serious loss of seats there since the 1950s, to the Conservative Party to its right and the Democratic Party to its left. The results (with one seat tied; previous figures

Blacks in South Africa hold up banners of the African National Congress (ANC) during a rally held after the release of Walter Sisulu, former ANC secretary-general. Such mass demonstrations had been legalized as part of Pres. F.W. de Klerk's reforms.

in parentheses) were NP 93 (123), CP 39 (22), DP 33 (21). Results for the (Coloured) House of Representatives and (Indian) House of Delegates were overshadowed by the overwhelmingly successful boycott of those elections called by the extraparliamentary movement.

The white results showed that the shift of voters toward the CP, apparent in 1988, had stalled. An important factor in this development were events in Boksburg and Carletonville, where CP municipal councils elected in 1988 reimposed some aspects of apartheid, resulting in black boycotts of white business in those areas. The message to whites was the difficulty of attempting to implement the CP policy of a return to racial partition in the face of an increasingly numerous and confident black majority.

The Democratic Party was launched in April as a merger of parties under the joint leadership of Dennis Worrall (Independent Party), Wynand Malan (National Democratic Party), and Zac de Beer (Progressive Federal Party). Both Worrall and Malan were former NP members.

The replacement of Botha by de Klerk, and the elections, took place under the shadow of a state of emergency (in existence from 1986) and severe legal restrictions, imposed in February 1988, on extraparliamentary political organizations and on the one million-strong Congress of South African Trade Unions (COSATU). Despite these measures, there was during 1989 a massive revival of organized defiance by the disenfranchised black majority.

This defiance became apparent early in the year in the continuation of a rent strike by thousands of households in Soweto and other black townships in Transvaal, the Boksburg and Carletonville boycotts, hunger strikes by political detainees, campaigns against the antiunion Labour Relations Amendment Act by organized workers, a revival of a boycott movement in African and Coloured schools, and the continued observation of Sharpeville Day (March 21), May Day, and June 16 (commemoration of the 1976 Soweto massacre) as public holidays, official or not.

The strong opposition among organized workers to the Labour Act was also apparent at the workers' summits in March and August and at the third COSATU congress, held in July. The workers' summits were unprecedented in that only workers had delegate status and that they brought together members of COSATU and members of the rival National Congress of Trade Unions, whose leaders adhered to ideas of "black consciousness" rather than the nonracialism of COSATU. As a result of these protests, a number of big companies, foreign and local, declared that they would not make use of controversial clauses in the Labour Act. In August defiance was given shape in an official antisegregation campaign launched by the Mass Democratic Movement (COSATU, United Democratic Front, and other organizations). It involved actions to desegregate hospitals, parks, and beaches—as well as spontaneous activity in workplaces to desegregate rest rooms, locker rooms, and other facilities.

In protest against the exclusion of the black majority from the September 6 election, the Mass Democratic Movement called a two-day general strike, in which three million participated on election day. There was an upsurge of mass protest against the elections in the African townships, particularly in the Western Cape; this resulted in action by the riot police that culminated in as many as 28 demonstrators being shot dead on election night. In an unprecedented step a Coloured police lieutenant, Gregory Rockman, publicly denounced the riot police and was supported by the most senior Coloured police officer.

Under de Klerk's leadership the NP campaigned in the election on the basis of a five-year plan for moving away from apartheid and for negotiation of a new constitution with representative leaders from all communities, including the African majority. The plan, however, rejected majority rule, endorsing instead the right of minorities to retain control over their "own affairs." After the elections de Klerk took steps to implement this program. Among them were the legalization of mass protest demonstrations for the first time since 1976. Starting on September 13 in Cape Town, there followed a series of marches and demonstrations by tens of thousands in major cities and small towns, which, taken as a whole, represented the biggest such events in the history of South Africa. The flag of the banned African National Congress (ANC) dominated these demonstrations.

On September 15 the government released from prison Walter Sisulu, former secretary-general of the ANC, and seven other political prisoners. All except one had been serving sentences since the early 1960s. This was seen as testing the ground for the release of the country's most famous political prisoner, Nelson Mandela.

On October 29 Sisulu and the other released prisoners spoke in Soweto at a rally of 70,000 under the banners of the ANC and the (banned) South African Communist Party. Government tolerance of the rally indicated the possibility that it was moving toward unbanning the ANC and lifting the state of emergency. These steps, together with the release of all political prisoners and the right of return for political exiles, were preconditions named by the Mass Democratic Movement and the ANC for entering negotiations with the government.

In November de Klerk ordered that all of the nation's beaches and four residential areas be opened to all races. He met with Mandela in December to discuss South Africa's future and on December 24 invited church leaders to join the government in similar talks. Several of these leaders maintained that talks could not take place until the ANC was legalized, Mandela and other political prisoners were freed, and troops were withdrawn from black townships.

Despite the easing of the climate of repression in the latter part of the year, detentions and trials of antiapartheid activists continued. Between October 1988 and August 1989, more than 860 people were charged in 248 political trials, according to the Human Rights Commission. Of these, 350 were convicted, 172 were acquitted, and 341 had charges against them withdrawn. The case of the "Upington 14," sentenced to death for participation in a demonstration in 1985 in which a black policeman was killed, received international attention. They, along with other political offenders, remained on death row. There were estimated to be 3,000 political prisoners. On the other hand, union leader Moses Mayekiso and four associates were acquitted of treason in April, and in December the nation's Appeals Court reversed the conviction of five Africans found guilty of terrorism in 1988.

In Natal the violent conflict between vigilante supporters of Chief Gatsha Buthelezi's Inkatha movement and supporters of the UDF and COSATU continued unabated, despite the attempts of the leaders of the two latter groups to reach a peace agreement. Talks between the two sides took place during the year. Following a peace-seeking letter from Nelson Mandela to Buthelezi in April, there were attempts to organize a meeting between Inkatha and the ANC leadership abroad. In September Chief Buthelezi broke off all talks with the ANC organizations.

Foreign Affairs. The limited sanctions against South Africa by Western powers remained in force. Attempts at the Commonwealth conference in October to intensify sanctions were frustrated by the opposition of British Prime Minister Margaret Thatcher and by the postelection

climate in South Africa. Despite attempts by antiapartheid organizations to block it, the South African government was able to announce that agreement had been reached with the major creditor banks to reschedule $8 billion of debt.

Considerable easing of the tension between South Africa and its southern African neighbours took place during the year. The agreement reached by South Africa at multinational talks in 1988 on resolving the linked questions of Namibian independence and war in Angola began to be implemented. A UN task force took up its position on April 1 to oversee elections for a constitutional assembly in November, leading to projected independence for Namibia in 1990. Cuban troops began to withdraw from Angola in January.

De Klerk visited Mozambique, Zambia, and Zaire during the year. His visit to Zambia provoked Botha's resignation. The major item of discussion in the visit to Zaire was the South African-supported National Union for the Total Independence of Angola (UNITA), whose leader, Jonas Savimbi, was reluctant to halt his war against the government. Attempts by African governments to establish the terms of a peace agreement between Savimbi and the government had broken down.

Economy. South Africa's economy slowed during 1989. The gross domestic product (GDP) had grown in 1988 by 3.2%, the highest figure in some years but still less than the 5% rate needed even to absorb new entrants to the labour market (let alone the estimated three million to six million unemployed). GDP was projected to grow by no more than 2% in 1989. The growth was stimulated in part by consumer credit, but nongold exports also received a stimulus from the continued growth in the world economy. A good year for agriculture also contributed. On the other hand, the price of gold (generally the nation's main export), which fell to a low of $360 per ounce during the year, had a detrimental effect on growth and on the balance of payments.

Fixed investment, which rose in 1988 (by 6.4%) for the first time since 1981, continued to grow. However, the underlying weakness of the economy was reflected in the fact that, while the index of manufacturing output rose for the first time above its 1981 peak, capacity in manufacturing industry was shrinking.

Government policy was directed toward cooling the economy because of balance of payments problems and rising inflation, though this was balanced against the government's need to avoid recession in an election year. A main method was to raise interest rates, with the bank rate reaching 18% by October. The budget was relatively neutral in its effects, except for a 1% rise in the general sales tax, but in May an austerity package was introduced, including restrictions on hire purchase (installment) credit and a loan levy on companies.

On the surface the current account of the balance of payments appeared healthy. Against a surplus of R 2.9 billion in 1988, the surplus was projected to be R 3.5 billion–R 4 billion in 1989. However, South Africa continued to be subjected to heavy capital outflow (approximately 4% of GDP a year since 1985) and a heavy debt-repayment burden. Despite the rescheduling agreement this involved repayment of some $1.8 billion in 1989, $3.5 billion in 1990–92, and more than $7 billion within 10 years—requiring a contraction of imports to allow continued surpluses in the current account. Growth was increasingly being sustained, in this context, at the expense of foreign reserves, which in August had fallen to a dangerous level, equivalent to only 1.3 months of imports.

Government spending in the 1988–89 fiscal year rose 18.4% (against a projected increase of 12.6%), but revenue rose 25% as against a projection of 16.3%. The deficit before borrowing was R 9.1 billion. The 1989–90 budget projected a deficit before borrowing of R 9.5 billion (4.1% of GDP). From an annualized rate of 12.5% in 1988, inflation was anticipated to rise to the 15–18% range by the end of 1989, partly as a result of an increase of 27% in broad money supply (M3) during 1988, which continued to increase at a somewhat slower rate during 1989.

The floating of the Iron and Steel Corp. on the nation's stock exchange in November represented a step in the government's privatization program. The governor of the Reserve Bank, Gerhard de Kock, resigned and died later in the year; he was replaced by Chris Stals.

Bophuthatswana

The republic of Bophuthatswana consists of seven discontinuous, landlocked geographic units, entirely surrounded by South Africa except for one unit that borders Botswana on the northwest. Area: 44,000 sq km (16,988 sq mi). Pop. (1989 est.): 1,914,000. Cap.: Mmabatho. Monetary unit: South African rand. President in 1989, Lucas Mangope.

Ciskei

Bordering the Indian Ocean in the south, Ciskei is surrounded on land by South Africa. Area: 7,760 sq km (2,996 sq mi). Pop. (1989 est.): 824,000. Cap.: Bisho. Monetary unit: South African rand. President in 1989, Lennox Sebe.

Transkei

Bordering the Indian Ocean and surrounded on land by South Africa, Transkei comprises three discontinuous geographic units, two of which are landlocked and one of which borders Lesotho. Area: 43,653 sq km (16,855 sq mi). Pop. (1989 est.): 3,224,000. Cap.: Umtata. Monetary unit: South African rand. Head of the Military Council in 1989, Maj. Gen. Bantu Holomisa.

Venda

The landlocked republic of Venda is located in extreme northeastern South Africa. Area: 7,176 sq km (2,771 sq mi). Pop. (1989 est.): 506,000. Cap.: Thohoyandou. Monetary unit: South African rand. President in 1989, Frank Ravele.

The four former homelands, regarded as "independent" of South Africa only by the South African government, continued to depend on revenue from the South African economy. This consisted mainly of wages paid to migrant workers and direct and indirect payments from the government of the republic.

Together with the six "nonindependent" homelands, Bophuthatswana, Ciskei, Transkei, and Venda were voted more than R 9 billion in the March budget, a 24% increase over 1988–89. It was estimated in 1986–87 that internally generated budget revenue comprised 24% of the total in Transkei, 23% in Bophuthatswana, 12% in Venda, and 10% in Ciskei.

Evidence of corruption continued to mount in these states. The de Wet Commission investigating Ciskei and the Harms Commission investigating Transkei discovered corruption, bribery, maladministration, and mismanagement of money, involving not only officials in these homelands but white South Africans as well. Former Transkei Chief Minister George Matanzima was jailed for bribery.

Bophuthatswana police engaged in mass arrests in Leeuwfontein in July after a protest movement against

the township's incorporation into Bophuthatswana led to an incident in which nine policemen were killed. Trials of those involved in the abortive 1988 coup against the Bophuthatswana government continued.

In a surprising development, rapprochement appeared to be developing between Transkei's ruler, Maj. Gen. Bantu Holomisa, and the ANC. Holomisa announced plans to lift the ban on COSATU and the ANC in Transkei and a possible referendum to determine whether the homeland wished to end its "independence." This followed the reburial in October of the pro-ANC Chief Sabata Dalindyebo (who had died in exile in 1986 and been buried by order of the Matanzimas in a commoners' grave) at a funeral attended by Holomisa and representatives of COSATU, the UDF, and the ANC. This loosening of the government was accompanied by a wave of strikes and demonstrations.

In Venda youth and student protest continued against ritual murders blamed on government officials.

(MARTIN LEGASSICK)

See also *Dependent States,* below.

SUDAN, THE

A republic of North Africa, The Sudan has a coastline on the Red Sea. Area: 2,503,890 sq km (966,757 sq mi). Pop. (1989 est.): 27,268,000. Cap.: Khartoum. Monetary unit: Sudanese pound, with (Oct. 2, 1989) a par value of LSd 4.50 to U.S. $1 (free rate of LSd 7.28 = £1 sterling). Chairman of the Supreme Council to June 30, 1989, Ahmad al-Mirghani; prime minister until June 30, Sadiq al-Mahdi; president of the National Salvation Revolution Command Council from June 30, Brig. Gen. Omar Hassan Ahmad al-Bashir.

On June 30, 1989, the government of Sadiq al-Mahdi was overthrown in a bloodless military coup. Army officers had been pressing al-Mahdi since December 1988 to implement the peace arrangements made privately by the Democratic Unionist Party with the Sudan People's Liberation Army, which for six years had been conducting a civil war in the south. Al-Mahdi, partly to retain the support of the fundamentalist National Islamic Front, which was violently opposed to peace negotiations, and partly because of his own religious convictions, had consistently resisted the Army's pressure, knowing that a precondition of any settlement with the rebels would be the abolition of Islamic law in the south. The successes of the SPLA, however, made al-Mahdi's position impossible.

Although the new military government, led by Brig. Gen. Omar al-Bashir (*see* BIOGRAPHIES), took immediate steps to punish anyone involved in corruption or dishonest dealing and declared a cease-fire to facilitate talks with the rebels, it failed to win either the hearts of the people or the confidence of external aid donors. Severe restrictions on prices led to shortages of essential goods, and while the cease-fire enabled foreign aid agencies to resume their relief operations in the south and thereby avoid a repetition of the famine of 1988, the reluctance of the SPLA commander, Col. John Garang, to open negotiations with the government dimmed the enthusiasm of the people for the new regime. The reason for Garang's misgivings was that the government had decided to leave the question of the retention or abolition of Islamic law to a national referendum. This, in a country with a population that was 70% Muslim, offered little consolation to the rebels. Western nations were also wary of recognizing a government that in the interests of efficiency had abolished political parties, banned newspapers, and renounced democratic rule for the foreseeable future. Hundreds of villagers in the south were reported killed by Arab militiamen in late December.

(KENNETH INGHAM)

SWAZILAND

Swaziland is a landlocked monarchy of southern Africa and a member of the Commonwealth. Area: 17,364 sq km (6,704 sq mi). Pop. (1989 est.): 746,000. Administrative cap., Mbabane; royal and legislative cap., Lobamba. Monetary unit: lilangeni (plural: emalangeni), at par with the South African rand, with (Oct. 2, 1989) a free rate of 2.69 emalangeni to U.S. $1 (4.35 emalangeni = £1 sterling). King, Mswati III; prime ministers in 1989, Sotsha Dlamini and, from July 12, Obed Dlamini.

Swaziland continued to keep a low profile in 1989, although the young king, Mswati III, made a growing impression of being on the side of the progressives rather than the traditionalists. The economy continued to perform well, with a low debt ratio and inflation under 10%. However, Swaziland was especially vulnerable to developments in South Africa since the lilangeni was tied to the rand. Tourist trade was increasing, although most visitors came from South Africa for short stays. Swaziland was attracting investments that formerly would have gone to South Africa, and South African companies were investing in Swaziland as a hedge against possible future sanctions. Because of unsettled conditions in Mozambique, most of Swaziland's freight was using the route through Richards Bay in South Africa rather than Maputo.

In July the prime minister, Sotsha Dlamini, was dismissed for failing to obey orders and was replaced by Obed Dlamini. Ambrose Zwane, the opposition leader, was arrested for possession of prohibited pamphlets. He insisted

Children in The Sudan wait behind rows of plates for food that arrived from the United Nations' "Operation Lifeline Sudan." A cease-fire between the new military government and rebels in the south made it possible for relief groups to distribute food and supplies among people suffering from shortages caused by the country's civil war.

that he had received them through the mail and appealed to African leaders to intervene on his behalf.

(GUY ARNOLD)

This article updates the *Macropædia* article SOUTHERN AFRICA: *Swaziland.*

TANZANIA

The republic of Tanzania, a member of the Commonwealth, consists of Tanganyika, on the east coast of Africa, and Zanzibar, just off the coast in the Indian Ocean, which includes Zanzibar Island, Pemba Island, and small islets. Area: 945,037 sq km (364,881 sq mi). Pop. (1989 est.): 23,729,000. Cap.: government in process of being transferred from Dar es Salaam to Dodoma. Monetary unit: Tanzania shilling, with (Oct. 2, 1989) a free rate of 144.25 shillings to U.S. $1 (233.40 shillings = £1 sterling). President in 1989, Ali Hassan Mwinyi; prime minister, Joseph Warioba.

The celebrations planned to mark the 25th anniversary of the Jan. 12, 1964, revolution in Zanzibar were watched with some concern by the mainland government, which was conscious of the growing support on the islands for constitutional reform that would strengthen Zanzibar's autonomy. The movement, promoted mainly by Muslims who feared that the Christian-dominated government of the mainland showed insufficient concern for the islands' well-being, was concentrated behind the person of Zanzibar's former chief minister, Seif Shariff Hamad. The celebrations took place peacefully, but the government saw fit to station 6,000 members of the Tanzanian People's Defence Force on Pemba.

Julius Nyerere, the former president and current chairman of Chama Cha Mapinduzi (CCM), the ruling party, was intent on welding the mainland and the islands firmly together. His task was made more difficult, however, by the weakness of Zanzibar's economy at a time of recession in the clove industry, which encouraged the people to believe that economic development was being impeded by restrictions imposed by the government. Speaking in Zanzibar in March, Nyerere said the CCM would deal ruthlessly with those who tried to reduce the nation to chaos. Though his remarks were couched in general terms, they were clearly a response to the campaign of criticism being waged against the ruling party and its leaders by Hamad. On May 10, after he had called for a referendum on union with the mainland, Hamad was arrested and charged with attending illegal meetings.

The power of Nyerere's personality was also felt on the mainland, where his continuing hostility toward the International Monetary Fund created problems for Pres. Ali Hassan Mwinyi. Nyerere was becoming increasingly isolated in his campaign, however. Though openly committed to its old socialist program, the CCM leaders were aware that they needed to accept—at least covertly—some move toward a mixed economy if they were not to lose the initiative in developing the country. In March Mwinyi took the final steps to rid his Cabinet of those who were reluctant to give him wholehearted support. Despite the party's unwillingness to agree to price controls and its belated acceptance of further devaluation, the president's attempts to reform the system were boosted by measures to promote business, mainly the relaxation of import controls and the arrival of foreign businessmen interested in investing in the country. This success was accompanied by some less appealing features, such as the prevalence of bribery, and progress was hampered by the lack of an official investment code.

The first meeting of the joint commission for cooperation with Zaire took place in September, when it was agreed to expand trading and cultural relations. Particular attention was paid to Zaire's use of the trade route to the Indian Ocean, across Lake Tanzania and along the Kigoma–Dar es Salaam railway, but the agreement also dealt with agriculture and security and with other communications issues.

(KENNETH INGHAM)

This article updates the *Macropædia* article EASTERN AFRICA: *Tanzania.*

TOGO

A republic of West Africa, Togo is situated on the Bight of Benin. Area: 56,785 sq km (21,925 sq mi). Pop. (1989 est.): 3,622,000. Cap.: Lomé. Monetary unit: CFA franc, with (Oct. 2, 1989) a par value of CFAF 50 to the French franc and a free rate of CFAF 317.90 to U.S. $1 (CFAF 514.37 = £1 sterling). President in 1989, Gen. Gnassingbe Eyadema.

A Cabinet reshuffle on Dec. 19, 1988, resulted in the departure of three senior ministers of the older generation and the entry into the government of Pres. Gnassingbe Eyadema's military second in command, Gen. Yao Amegi, with responsibility for the interior and security. The following day the trade and transport minister was also dismissed, for alleged financial improprieties. He was the first of a number of senior figures to fall from grace under a well-publicized campaign against corruption in high places. In June 1989 Lieut. Col. Seyi Memene, the commander of the armed forces, was arrested on allegations that he had embezzled funds intended for arms and equipment.

Rock-bottom world prices for Togo's principal export commodities, coffee and cocoa, continued to depress economic performance and forced the government to reduce producer prices for the 1989 season. Continuing economic reforms included the closing of the troubled Cimao cement works, jointly owned with Ghana and Côte d'Ivoire.

(NIM CASWELL)

This article updates the *Macropædia* article WESTERN AFRICA: *Togo.*

UGANDA

A landlocked republic and member of the Commonwealth, Uganda is located in eastern Africa. Area: 241,040 sq km (93,070 sq mi), including 44,000 sq km of inland water. Pop. (1989 est.): 16,452,000. Cap.: Kampala. Monetary unit: Uganda shilling, with (Oct. 2, 1989) a par value of 200 shillings to U.S. $1 (free rate of 323.60 shillings = £1 sterling). President in 1989, Yoweri Museveni; prime minister, Samson Kisekka.

In February 1989 Pres. Yoweri Museveni took two steps aimed at strengthening his authority. First, he appointed a commission to hold nationwide consultations and to draw up constitutional proposals. This meant, effectively, that the question of the future constitution of the country was postponed. Then he held the first parliamentary elections since 1980, thereby fulfilling the promise he had made when he first took office. The membership of the legislature, the National Resistance Council (NRC), was at the same time increased from 98 to 278.

Only the initial stages of the electoral process at village level were by direct election, the remaining steps in the voting being carried out by electoral colleges. Although several parties contested the elections, they had little opportunity to organize an effective campaign because political meetings were banned. Museveni himself derived the greatest benefit from the elections, as he had always intended and as the electoral system made reasonably certain. The personal popularity of the president in some parts of the country ensured the success of his supporters in those districts; in addition, 38 seats were set aside for the original members of

the NRC, who were close associates of Museveni from the days of the civil war. Ten seats were given to the National Revolutionary Army, and 20 members were nominated by the president himself.

In spite of his victory, Museveni produced no long-term strategy setting out how the country should be governed. Though he claimed to be opposed to sectarianism, he made all his ministerial appointments on a sectarian or ethnic basis. Real power, however, remained in the hands of his close supporters, many of whom held appointments as deputies to senior ministers, on whom they were able to keep a close watch. The success of these tactics as far as Museveni himself was concerned could be measured by the fact that in October the new NRC extended the term of office of the government by five years.

The president needed all the power he could muster to deal with the country's problems. There was a brief crisis when former president Idi Amin arrived in Zaire on January 3 with a false passport, intent, it would seem, on reentering Uganda clandestinely. The Zairian authorities refused Uganda's request for his extradition but finally sent him back to his reluctant hosts in Saudi Arabia. More disturbing was the influx into northern Uganda of thousands of refugees from The Sudan in February and March. Only the timely supply of aid by relief agencies averted the prospect of famine in the regions affected by the arrival of the refugees.

Shortly afterward, Amnesty International accused the government of human rights violations, claiming that although there had been some reforms, abuses similar to those perpetrated by the former regimes of Amin and Milton Obote persisted, including the torture of civilians by members of the security forces. The report also condemned the Army for its practice of burning crops, homes, and food stores in an attempt to crush rebel activities. The state-run newspaper, *New Vision,* admitted that there had been abuses by the Army but denied that human rights violations were increasing.

Relations with Kenya remained strained, mainly because of allegations of border infringements. Museveni claimed that an alleged incursion into Kenya by Ugandan troops was, in fact, the work of cattle rustlers, and he denied that the government was in any way involved in the bombing of the northwestern Kenyan village of Lokichoggio by three aircraft in March. Kenya was not impressed by his assertions and, after carrying out investigations, accused Uganda of participating in a plot with The Sudan and Libya to carry out the bombing.   (KENNETH INGHAM)

This article updates the *Macropædia* article EASTERN AFRICA: *Uganda.*

ZAIRE

The republic of Zaire is located in central Africa with a short coastline on the Atlantic Ocean. Area: 2,345,095 sq km (905,446 sq mi). Pop. (1989 est.): 33,336,000. Cap.: Kinshasa. Monetary unit: zaïre, with (Oct. 2, 1989) a free rate of 418.23 zaïres to U.S. $1 (676.70 zaïres = £1 sterling). President in 1989, Mobutu Sese Seko; first state commissioner (prime minister), Kengo Wa Dondo.

The tension that had developed in Zaire's relations with Belgium in the closing weeks of 1988 became more acute in 1989. The first strains occurred in November 1988 when Belgian journalists and members of Parliament criticized their government's proposal to reschedule Zaire's debt. The critics claimed that aid sent to Zaire had been misappropriated and that Pres. Mobutu Sese Seko's government was little more than a corrupt dictatorship. Mobutu responded by rejecting the rescheduling offer and by ordering all Zairian nationals in Belgium, about 15,000 in number, to return to their homeland. The foreign minister, Nguza Karl-I-Bond, said that Zaire intended to repay all its debts to Belgium and that the criticisms by the Belgian government were insulting. An attempt by Belgian Foreign Minister Léo Tindemans to effect a reconciliation was thwarted when a Belgian judge ordered the seizure of all of Mobutu's assets in Belgium to compensate a Belgian company for assets nationalized by the Zairian government in 1973. When Mobutu threatened to sever diplomatic ties, the order was lifted.

The two governments then engaged in a series of measures and countermeasures. Zaire's statement that it would halt all debt repayments to Brussels was matched by Belgium's decision to fund no new development projects in Zaire. Mobutu's order that passenger flights between Belgium and Zaire be halved, and later suspended entirely, was followed by a threat of legal action from Belgium. Late in January all Zairian-owned companies moved their operations out of Belgium.

When it appeared that Mobutu might substitute France for Belgium as its major European trading partner, Belgium suddenly appeared extremely anxious to heal the rift. After further discussions, Belgium agreed to cancel the whole of Zaire's public debt and a third of its commercial debts, with interest-free rescheduling of the rest over 25 years. In addition, interest already due on the debt would, when paid, be put into a fund to support development projects in Zaire. After these concessions were made, relations between the two countries gradually returned to normal.

Mobutu scored another victory in March when the UN Commission on Human Rights and Amnesty International removed Zaire from their lists of countries under surveillance for violating human rights. The economy, too, showed signs of improvement. In November 1988 Mobutu had reappointed as prime minister Kengo Wa Dondo, the man who had been dismissed as the scapegoat for the unpopular measures earlier called for by the International Monetary Fund (IMF). In June 1989 it was announced that Zaire had paid off all its debts to the IMF. This repayment opened the way to the signing of a new accord with the IMF; in addition, the World Bank gave Zaire access to funds frozen since June 1988, when the government suspended repayment of its debts as a protest against IMF demands. France and the U.S. also offered aid, and the prospect for further bilateral agreements increased. Shortly afterward, an announcement was made that Zaire had repaid all its debts to the African Development Bank, that the monthly inflation rate had dropped from 12 to 2% in the first half of the year, and that the discrepancy between the official and unofficial exchange rates had been severely cut. In July the Paris Club of Western creditor nations agreed to reschedule a further slice of Zaire's debt.

On the diplomatic front Mobutu played a significant role in discussions aimed at ending the civil war in Angola. Zaire's relations with Congo, often inclined to be brittle, threatened to break down in April when the Congolese authorities sent 5,000 Zairians back to Kinshasa. Hasty discussions between the two governments resulted in apparent amity, however.

Internal dissent surfaced in February when students took to the streets in Kinshasa to protest an 80% increase in the cost of public transportation. The problem arose when the price of oil was doubled in response to pressure from the IMF. Further student demonstrations followed in Lubumbashi after the discovery of a student's body near a military camp. The government denied claims that as many as 52

Pres. Mobutu Sese Seko of Zaire (left) and acting president of South Africa F.W. de Klerk (right) attend a reception during de Klerk's August visit to Zaire. De Klerk had gone to Zaire to discuss the faltering cease-fire in Angola.
AFP PHOTO

people had been killed in the demonstrations but admitted that one student had been shot dead and 14 others injured, in addition to two soldiers. Institutions of higher education were then closed on Mobutu's orders on February 15 and reopened March 15. Allegations that some of the protesters were not students resulted in the extension of the investigation into the disturbances to include other sections of the population. On March 11 opposition leader Etienne Tshisekedi wa Mulumba's wife, Marthe, was arrested. The opposition claimed that her arrest was meant to pressure Tshisekedi into confessing that he had instigated the disturbances. In May an officer who had authorized his troops to fire on the students in Lubumbashi was sentenced to five years' hard labour. Shortly afterward Tshisekedi himself was arrested.

Another problem arose when a Zairian newspaper reported that the illegal sale of drugs had become a serious problem in Kinshasa. Most of the drugs were of inferior quality or had been adulterated, and they appeared to emanate from a variety of sources including medical staff and employees in pharmaceutical depots.

In May Mobutu reclaimed the defense portfolio that he had conferred on Gen. Singa Boyenge Mosambay six months earlier. The general, however, continued as minister of territorial security.   (KENNETH INGHAM)

This article updates the *Macropædia* article CENTRAL AFRICA: *Zaire.*

ZAMBIA

A landlocked republic and member of the Commonwealth, Zambia is in eastern Africa. Area: 752,614 sq km (290,586 sq mi). Pop. (1989 est.): 8,148,000. Cap.: Lusaka. Monetary unit: kwacha, with (Oct. 2, 1989) a free rate of 16.07 kwacha to U.S. $1 (26 kwacha = £1 sterling). President in 1989, Kenneth Kaunda; secretary-general of the United National Independence Party, Alexander Grey Zulu; prime ministers, Kebby Musokotwane and, from March 15, Gen. Malimba Masheke.

With a foreign debt of $6 billion, inflation running at 100%, and average annual income per household down to $300 from $500 at independence, economic measures were the dominant issue in Zambia throughout 1989. At the beginning of the year, Pres. Kenneth Kaunda announced a five-year plan in an attempt to halt his country's decline and to revive International Monetary Fund (IMF) support. The target was 3% economic growth and a reduction in the rate of population growth, which had played an important role in depressing the economy.

At midyear stern measures were introduced to make the

plan effective. The currency was devalued by 37.5% and, at the same time, the Bank of Zambia raised base interest rates from 19 to 29%. As a result, it was possible to make a new agreement with the IMF and World Bank on September 19. In his address on the 25th anniversary of independence in October, the president was able to claim that there was a good prospect of economic recovery, as long as people did not misuse the new opportunities for private enterprise by indulging in smuggling and black marketeering.   (KENNETH INGHAM)

This article updates the *Macropædia* article SOUTHERN AFRICA: *Zambia.*

ZIMBABWE

A republic and member of the Commonwealth, Zimbabwe is a landlocked state in eastern Africa. Area: 390,759 sq km (150,-873 sq mi). Pop. (1989 est.): 9,122,000. Cap.: Harare. Monetary unit: Zimbabwe dollar, with (Oct. 2, 1989) a free rate of Z$2.21 to U.S. $1 (Z$3.57 = £1 sterling). President in 1989, Robert Mugabe.

Only with difficulty and by dint of firm leadership did Pres. Robert Mugabe ride out the wave of unpopularity that threatened his government in 1989. The accusations of corruption against government ministers made by Edgar Tekere, former secretary-general of the Zimbabwe African National Union (Patriotic Front) (ZANU [PF]), which had led to his expulsion from the party in October 1988, were taken up vigorously by the *Bulawayo Chronicle* newspaper. In December 1988 the defense minister, Enos Nkala, the main target of the attacks, threatened to send the Army to the newspaper offices to arrest both the editor, Geoff Nyarota, and the deputy editor, Davison Maruziva. In February 1989 Nyarota was removed from his position by his employers, the Mass Media Trust, and transferred to the post of public relations officer with the trust's subsidiary, Zimbabwe Newspapers.

The criticism continued, however. On February 28 Tekere accused the government of creating a personality cult around the president. He condemned its handling of the economy, referring particularly to the recent purchase of $92 million worth of air defense systems, aircraft, and missiles from China at a time when many people were hungry and there was widespread unemployment. Once again he drew attention to the work of the commission, under the chairmanship of Judge Wilson Sandura, that had been appointed by the president to investigate accusations of corruption against the government. It was time, Tekere claimed, to get rid of these dishonest leaders. Two days later

he reiterated his view that the time had come to appoint new leaders, and less than a week later his demand began to be vindicated. Frederick Shava, the minister of state for political affairs, announced his resignation from the government because he had lied to the Sandura commission about the illegal profits he had made from automobile deals. This was followed almost at once by the more significant confession to similar illegal activities and perjury of Nkala, who also resigned as minister of defense. Only hours before the publication of the commission's report in April, the president received an even greater blow when his close friend Maurice Nyagumbo, a leader in the long struggle for majority rule, also felt compelled to resign in light of the commission's findings. Nyagumbo committed suicide a week later. A few days after his resignation, three other senior ministers resigned.

It was at this point that Mugabe showed his leadership qualities to the full. While paying generous tribute to the contributions made to the country by all the disgraced ministers, he insisted that corruption had to be sought out, and he ordered the members of the commission to renew their investigations. Emboldened by these events, Tekere announced on April 30 the formation of a new party, the Zimbabwe Unity Movement, to contest the 1990 parliamentary elections, and he invited the white leaders of the Conservative Alliance of Zimbabwe to join him.

Economic issues added their quota to the list of the nation's problems. During a visit to Zimbabwe in March, British Prime Minister Margaret Thatcher again disagreed with the president over the desirability of economic sanctions against South Africa—a disagreement that found further expression at the meeting of Commonwealth heads of government in October—but she also promised to increase the £15 million offered to assist land resettlement in October 1988 by an additional £10 million. During an independence day address in April, Mugabe announced a new program aimed at encouraging foreign investment. This, he hoped, would help to overcome some of Zimbabwe's major economic problems, notably unemployment. Earlier policies, involving controls on prices and incomes and intended to narrow the gap between rich and poor, had, he said, helped to slow economic growth and had caused unemployment. In the future, salaries and wages would be negotiated by means of collective bargaining, though minimum wages would still be enforced in those areas where the government believed employees needed protection. An investment centre would also be set up to facilitate quick decision making, and there would be greater flexibility with regard to the remittance of dividends and the use of surplus funds.

In May the finance minister, Bernard Chidzero, added further details to the president's plan. To coincide with his visit to the U.K. to take part in a conference organized by the Confederation of British Industry to discuss investment in Zimbabwe, Chidzero released a new investment code. This relaxation of socialist principles was criticized by some members of ZANU (PF), but Chidzero was convinced that the country's desperate unemployment problem could not be tackled by any other means, and his view won instant approval in Britain.

Trouble broke out in another quarter when 300 junior government physicians went on strike in June over low wages and long working hours. Their action was also stimulated by fears that the government's health care program would break down under the strain imposed on the medical staff. Sixty-three physicians were arrested, but once again the personal intervention of the president brought about a settlement, and the doctors returned to work.

The government was equally successful in meeting a challenge from Tekere's party in a by-election in July, though for less creditable reasons. Although Tekere had been prevented from holding any rallies in Harare and the pro-government press had refused to advertise his movement while attacking it on every pretext, his candidate was still widely believed to present a serious threat to the ZANU (PF) nominee. In the election, however, the electorate demonstrated its lack of enthusiasm for any political party by virtually ignoring the poll. Only a little over 10,000 out of 64,000 registered voters cast their votes, and the ZANU (PF) candidate was victorious.

University students were less apathetic. Late in July, riot police broke up a meeting at the University of Zimbabwe that was being addressed by Tekere, and violence broke out between students and police. The differences between the students and the government were evident once again in October, when further violence erupted after the president and the secretary-general of the students' union had been arrested on October 4. The students shouted their condemnation of Mugabe and declared their support for the Zimbabwe Unity Movement. The university was closed, but it was reopened temporarily two weeks later to allow students who had given a guarantee of good behaviour to write their examinations.

In a further attempt to check the decline in support for ZANU (PF), the government published a draft bill, to take effect after the election in 1990, that would deny members of the House of Assembly the right to change parties while retaining their parliamentary seats. In December ZANU (PF) merged with its chief opponent, Joshua Nkomo's Zimbabwe African People's Union, and Mugabe expressed his desire for a one-party state.   (KENNETH INGHAM)

This article updates the *Macropædia* article SOUTHERN AFRICA: *Zimbabwe.*

Middle East and North Africa

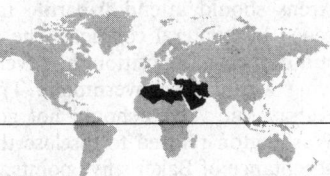

MIDDLE EASTERN AND NORTH AFRICAN AFFAIRS

With Secretary of State James Baker's five-point plan for Palestinian elections, the U.S. took centre stage in the quest for a Middle East peace settlement in 1989. The plan was initially hailed as a diplomatic breakthrough but appeared stalled on predictable opposition from Israel. Progress was also slow in the UN-sponsored peace talks between Iran and Iraq. In the Arab world, however, 1989 was a year of new regional alliances and reconciliations. The Arab Maghreb Union was formed in February, with 50 North African members of its assembly meeting in Rabat, Morocco, in October. The Arab Cooperation Council was founded in February in Baghdad, Iraq, by Egypt, Iraq, Jordan, and Yemen (San'a'; North Yemen). After a 10-year estrangement, Egypt was readmitted to the Arab League.

At the end of 1988 the Palestinian uprising, or *intifada,* in Israel's occupied territories had entered its second year with increasing evidence of the use of weapons and the rapid expansion of the Islamic Resistance Movement (Hamas). It was seen as a sign of disillusion with the moderate strategies outlined by the Palestine Liberation Organization (PLO) leader, Yasir Arafat, as was a growing pattern of revenge killings and assassinations.

The Arab World and Arab-Israeli Relations. In April Israeli Prime Minister Yitzhak Shamir presented a four-point proposal for "free elections" on the West Bank and the Gaza Strip. Pres. Hosni Mubarak of Egypt countered with a 10-point plan. In September Mubarak recommended that the 140,000 Palestinians living in East Jerusalem be allowed to vote in the elections, which would be monitored by international observers. Israeli troops would be withdrawn from polling areas prior to the elections. The proposal also involved the acceptance of Israeli plans for a period of limited autonomy in the occupied territories, with a proviso that it be followed by a comprehensive peace plan. Mubarak suggested a meeting in Cairo of Israeli officials and a Palestinian delegation that would include representatives who had been deported from the occupied territories. Shamir, however, said he was prepared to meet only with those from within the occupied territories and not with the PLO, either directly or indirectly.

In October Baker proposed his five-point framework after Israel's inner Cabinet rejected Mubarak's plan. Baker implicitly supported Mubarak's ideas on the composition of the Palestinian delegation. He also envisaged that the Palestinians should be allowed to discuss issues at the talks other than those relating directly to the elections in the territories, but Shamir rejected this. On December 31 Shamir dismissed from his Cabinet the science minister, Ezer Weizman, charging Weizman with meeting with leaders of the PLO; Weizman, a member of the Labour Party, denied the charge.

The Baker plan was designed to bring together Israeli, Egyptian, and U.S. foreign ministers in advance of direct Israeli-Palestinian talks in Cairo about elections in the occupied territories. Diplomats said the PLO had been put under pressure to accept an "invisible" role in the process and to concur with Egypt's acceptance of the Baker plan.

Tel Aviv at first responded positively. The Israeli Cabinet agreed by majority decision that Foreign Minister Moshe Arens should attend tripartite talks in Washington preceded by bilateral contacts. The announcement met with stiff domestic opposition, however, not least from the right wing within the government. Transport Minister Moshe Katsav said Arens should not go to the U.S. as long as Washington refused to disclose the exact terms of Cairo's acceptance of Baker's five points.

On December 11 Arens himself backed away from Israel's acceptance of the Washington meeting. He said he wanted assurances that the PLO would be excluded from the eventual direct talks. "If it is clear that Egypt simply represents the PLO, I would say that given the course we've embarked on now, we would not come," he said. U.S. Pres. George Bush insisted that he had no intention of pressuring Israel into negotiating with the PLO. Vice Pres. Dan Quayle called on the UN to scrap its 1975 resolution equating Zionism with racism. Quayle said Arab willingness to abandon this resolution would "send a powerful signal to Israel."

The Baker plan received backing from the three-strong ministerial team of the European Communities (EC) charged with dealing with the matter. France's foreign minister, Roland Dumas, said the 12-nation EC supported the Baker proposals but believed a full settlement could be reached only through an international conference.

The PLO central council, meeting in Baghdad in October, urged "firm confrontation against American policy, which is based on the rejection of the Palestinian people's right to self-determination." On October 4, Palestinian sources had released the names of 12 Palestinians, reportedly agreed upon with the PLO, who could be negotia-

tors with Israel. They included Hanna Siniora, Faisal al-Husseini, Ghassan Shakaa, Elias Freij, and Mustafa Natshe, all of whom were leading West Bank citizens. Among those who lived outside the occupied territories was newspaper editor Mohammed Milhem, the former mayor of Halhoul and a PLO executive committee member.

In the meantime, Arafat was strengthening his position. In April the PLO council elected him president of the self-proclaimed state of Palestine. Meeting from August 3 to 9 in Tunis at its first congress since 1980, more than 1,100 delegates of the al-Fatah movement (the PLO's largest faction) backed the PLO leader, electing him al-Fatah Central Committee chairman.

Elections to the Central Committee brought in nine new members, including Intissar al-Wazir (Umm Jihad), the widow of Khalil al-Wazir (Abu Jihad), the PLO military commander killed by Israeli commandos in April 1988. Hakam Balawi, PLO ambassador to Tunisia and the main contact with the U.S. since the diplomatic initiative was launched, also got promoted. The only member to lose his job was Rafiq an-Natshe, the PLO ambassador to Saudi Arabia, who was criticized for failing to raise enough money from the kingdom and for expressing doubts about Arafat's diplomatic moves.

In light of the claimed success of the *intifada* in the West Bank and Gaza Strip, delegates also voted for resolutions supporting the campaign for an independent Palestinian state. About 10% voted against the resolutions, but they pledged to abide by the majority decision. No explicit mention was made of controversial matters, such as Arafat's earlier statements recognizing Israel and his renunciation of terrorism.

Violence in the occupied territories continued to increase throughout the year. Eight Palestinians were killed in two days in the second week of September. Israeli Chief of Staff Dan Shomron ordered Israeli soldiers not to humiliate or mistreat Arab protesters or use excessive force. According to claims by human rights organizations, several of the more than 600 Palestinians who had been killed by December had been beaten to death by soldiers.

The Gaza Strip was sealed off on November 14 as Israel tried to avoid demonstrations on the first anniversary of the declaration of an independent Palestinian state by the Palestine National Council (sometimes referred to as a "parliament in exile"). The PLO claimed that 93 countries recognized Palestine. Other observers said the PLO's claim that the end of the occupation was approaching was farfetched. Palestinians continued to be killed as collaborators by fellow Arabs, a trend attributed to frustration over the lack of political progress.

The Arab League summit in Casablanca, Morocco, on May 23–26 saw the readmission of Egypt, whose membership had been suspended in 1979 after it signed a bilateral peace treaty with Israel. Syria's Pres. Hafez al-Assad and Mubarak were publicly reconciled, and relations continued to improve subsequently. A decision to reopen air links was made on December 12. Both Egypt and Syria were eager to contain Iraq's regional ambitions in the wake of the Gulf war cease-fire.

The summit was dominated, however, by the Lebanon crisis. Agreement was reached on a political process that led to the convening of a meeting of Lebanese deputies in Saudi Arabia. Egyptian officials made clear their deep disapproval of Iraq's role in backing the campaign of Gen. Michel Aoun (*see* BIOGRAPHIES) to eject Syrian forces from Lebanon. In Cairo's view, Iraq had been motivated entirely by spite in its anti-Syrian intervention in Lebanon and as such was doing harm to inter-Arab cooperation.

Hostages. A fresh Middle East hostage crisis erupted following Israel's abduction of a Lebanese cleric and the subsequent announcement of the hanging of Lieut. Col. William Higgins, a U.S. officer serving with the UN peacekeeping forces in southern Lebanon until his kidnapping in February 1988.

The abduction of Sheikh 'Abd-al Karim Obeid on July 28 from his home in Jibshit, just north of Israel's security zone, was the most spectacular Israeli military action since the raid on Entebbe airport in July 1976. It provoked the Organization of the Oppressed of the Earth, a faction of the Iranian-backed Hezbollah, to threaten Higgins' execution. Evidence was provided on July 31 of his death, followed by similar threats to kill two more captives, Joseph Cicippio of the United States and the Archbishop of Canterbury's envoy Terry Waite.

U.S. attempts to defuse the crisis involved calling on "all parties who hold hostages in the Middle East to release them forthwith." A task force, including an aircraft carrier and battleships, was dispatched in the direction of Lebanon in a show of strength. Prime Minister Shamir offered to trade 150 Shi'ite prisoners for all the Western captives and three Israeli prisoners. In any event, extremists failed to carry out their threats against Cicippio and Waite, but the apparent stalemate left another smoldering crisis in the Middle East.

Gulf War. Indirect negotiations between Iran and Iraq were planned for mid-December in New York City, UN Secretary-General Javier Pérez de Cuéllar said on November 28. The Security Council issued a statement on the same day that, with both countries' support, the UN peace plan, based on Resolution 598 (1987), would be implemented speedily. This resolution called for a cease-fire and withdrawal of troops from occupied territories as a first step. A cease-fire had gone into effect on Aug. 20, 1988, but Iraq refused to withdraw its troops from some 2,500 sq km (965 sq mi) of Iranian territory unless Iran agreed to surrender joint sovereignty over the Shatt al-Arab waterway. Iraq also wanted to exchange an estimated 100,000 prisoners of war first. In November 1989 Tehran offered a prisoner exchange, but this was rejected. Iran in December rejected an Iraqi demand that the border between the two countries be redrawn.

Regional Considerations. The Arab Cooperation Council (ACC) foundation meeting on February 16 in Baghdad was preceded by a meeting in Amman, Jordan, on February 12 of the four ACC member states' prime ministers. The ACC aimed to cement economic ties between the four member countries, which had a combined population of about 80 million, on lines similar to those of the EC and the Gulf Cooperation Council (GCC). The mid-June ACC summit held in Alexandria, Egypt, produced directives abolishing visa requirements and promoting the free movement of workers between member states. President Mubarak's political adviser Osama al-Baz emphasized that the ACC had no intention of cooperating in the military sphere. Helmi Nammar, an Egyptian economics professor, was appointed secretary-general. The ACC was viewed with some suspicion by Saudi Arabia, which feared, in particular, closer integration between North Yemen and Yemen (Aden; South Yemen); the two countries did indeed announce a draft constitution linking them late in the year. In a resolution released on September 26 at an ACC summit in San'a', however, the four governments expressed support for the Arab League peace plan for Lebanon, which was essentially a Saudi initiative. They also called for an exchange of prisoners and the clearing of the Shatt al-Arab waterway to resolve the deadlocked Gulf war peace process. The summit reiterated its support for the *intifada* and made no reference to Mubarak's moves on Palestinian elections.

In a parallel move, the Arab North African countries of Algeria, Morocco, Tunisia, Libya, and Mauritania announced in February the formation of the Arab Maghreb Union. On October 19 the 50-member Maghreb Assembly (a legislative body of the Union) met for the first time in Rabat. King Hassan of Morocco opened the meeting. The assembly's first president was Ahmed Osman, one of Morocco's most senior politicians. The meeting was an important step forward after fears that the unity initiative was running out of steam, with political tensions mounting over the renewed fighting in Western Sahara.

The GCC was engaged in intense dialogue with the EC over trade liberalization in 1989. The Europeans had ended all special duty-free access provisions included in its annual generalized system of preferences for GCC petrochemicals. The first joint industrial cooperation conference of the GCC and the EC was scheduled to be held in early 1990 in Granada, Spain.

The U.S. administration again targeted the Middle East for much of its foreign aid. On November 21 President Bush signed a bill that authorized $3 billion in aid to Israel and $2 billion to Egypt out of a total of $14.6 billion in foreign aid. Washington expressed concern over Tel Aviv's nuclear support for South Africa and equivocation over the Middle East peace processes, but this did not affect the decision to aid Israel.

King Hassan II of Morocco (left) and Pres. Hosni Mubarak of Egypt greet each other at the Arab summit held in Casablanca, Morocco. In May Egypt was welcomed back to the Arab League after having been barred from membership in 1979, when Egypt signed a bilateral peace treaty with Israel.

Within OPEC, the Arab countries were uneasily united behind the organization's production agreement for the first six months of 1990, which raised the OPEC output ceiling by 7.7% to just over 22 million bbl a day. The United Arab Emirates (U.A.E.) signed the deal, but the country's oil and minerals resources minister said the U.A.E. would not observe its new quota of approximately 1.1 million bbl a day.

A meeting of Islamic Conference Organization (ICO) foreign ministers in March condemned Salman Rushdie's novel *The Satanic Verses,* as well as condemning the author as an apostate. The ICO's political committee had stopped short of supporting the call for Rushdie to be killed, made originally in February by Ayatollah Ruhollah Khomeini of Iran. The ICO's 46 members included all Arab states.

North African Affairs. The Arab Maghreb Union's formation signaled improving regional relationships. President Mubarak of Egypt and Libya's leader, Col. Mu'ammar al-Qadhdhafi, met on October 16–17 at Marsa Matruh, Egypt, and Tobruk, Libya. The discussions focused on reconciliation. Libya sought to mend fences and to shed its image as the region's maverick state.

The control of the Western Sahara continued to be the thorn in the side of peace in the Maghreb. In October a battle at Guelta Zemmour resulted in the deaths of a Moroccan colonel and several hundred troops. King Hassan canceled a round of talks with the Popular Front for the Liberation of Saguia el Hamra and Río de Oro (Polisario Front). The Saharan guerrilla organization claimed King Hassan was blocking the peace process. Polisario representatives alleged that the king canceled talks on five occasions in 1989.

In the economic sphere, on November 17 European North-South Commissioner Abel Juan Matutes said there would be a complete overhaul of trade and aid agreements with the EC's southern Mediterranean trading partners. Measures might include direct financial support to soften the blow of austerity measures attached to International Monetary Fund economic stabilization programs. The plan called for more European investment to create jobs in North Africa, with an emphasis on establishing small and medium-sized companies, promoting human resources, and developing local financial institutions. Detailed arrangements still had to be worked out. The preferential trade pacts signed with 12 of the 14 Mediterranean countries were expected to remain in force.   (JOHN WHELAN)

ALGERIA

Algeria is a republic of North Africa on the Mediterranean Sea. Area: 2,381,741 sq km (919,595 sq mi). Pop. (1989 est.): 24,579,000. Cap.: Algiers. Monetary unit: Algerian dinar, with (Oct. 2, 1989) a free rate of 8.10 dinars to U.S. $1 (13.11 dinars = £1 sterling). President in 1989, Col. Chadli Bendjedid; prime ministers, Kasdi Merbah and, from September 9, Mouloud Hamrouche.

In the wake of the riots of October 1988, Algeria in 1989 was obsessed with the twin problems of economic and political reform. A new national constitution that dropped all mention of socialism, permitted political plurality, and granted the right to strike was approved in February by 74% of the 79% of the electorate that participated. Anxiety was expressed over the level of participation, which was far below the levels of the past, thereby indicating some disaffection. Nonetheless, the government pressed ahead with political reforms.

At the beginning of July, the National Assembly adopted a new political associations law that required political

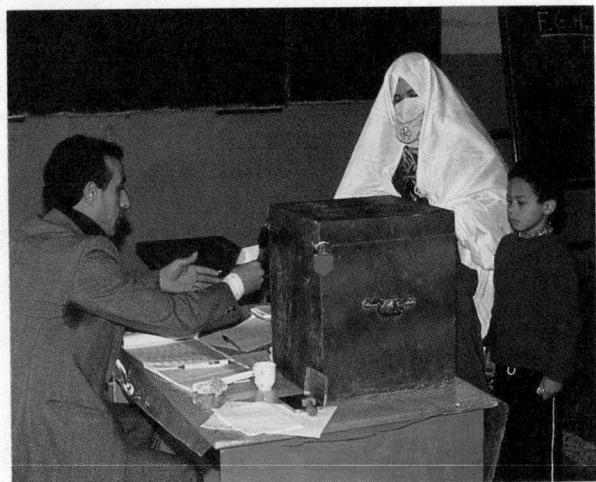

An Algerian woman casts her ballot on a proposed new constitution. Though voter turnout was lower than usual, more than 70% of those who did vote endorsed the constitution, which allowed free speech and a multiparty political system and granted the right to strike.
ZAOURAR—SIPA

movements to avoid platforms based on language or religion. At the end of the same month, a new electoral law was passed that required any political party to obtain a minimum of 10% of the vote in any constituency to qualify for representation. It also awarded all seats in a multiseat constituency to any party with more than 50% of the vote, otherwise awarding seating in proportion to each competing party's votes.

Both laws were seen by the Algerian League of Human Rights as supporting the dominance of the former single political party, the National Liberation Front (FLN), the political associations law discriminating against the Islamist movements and Berber groupings and the electoral law increasing the strength of the FLN in the National Assembly. These anxieties were enhanced by the new information law, passed by the Assembly on July 27. This ensured that the government would continue to control the press and television and radio, with the FLN taking over the major newspapers, although rights of reply and freedom of expression were guaranteed.

Nonetheless, there were major advances to report. In the wake of the political relations law, 20 new groups emerged. By the end of September, five new parties, in addition to the FLN, were registered. The political liberalization movement also encountered setbacks, however. Municipal elections, due in September, were postponed, and at the start of the same month, Algerian Pres. Chadli Bendjedid abruptly dismissed Prime Minister Kasdi Merbah, who had also been security chief under the former president, replacing him with a former presidential adviser, Mouloud Hamrouche. Merbah initially refused to leave office on constitutional grounds. Observers suggested that the real reason for the firing was that Bendjedid believed he had lost control of the government and the FLN and wished to reassert his role. At a three-day congress of the FLN that ended December 1, several figures prominent during the presidency of the late Houari Boumédienne were returned to the Central Committee.

On October 29 two earthquakes struck 12 minutes apart on the coast near Algiers. Measuring 6 and 4.8 on the Richter scale, they left some 30 dead and 250 injured and caused heavy property damage.   (GEORGE JOFFÉ)

This article updates the *Macropædia* article NORTH AFRICA: *Algeria.*

BAHRAIN

The monarchy (emirate) of Bahrain consists of a group of islands in the Persian Gulf between the Qatar Peninsula and Saudi Arabia. Area: 691 sq km (267 sq mi). Pop. (1989 est.): 489,000. Cap.: Manama. Monetary unit: Bahrain dinar, with (Oct. 2, 1989) a free rate of 0.38 dinar to U.S. $1 (0.61 dinar = £1 sterling). Emir in 1989, Isa ibn Sulman al-Khalifah; prime minister, Khalifah ibn Sulman al-Khalifah.

The aftermath of the war between Iran and Iraq left Bahrain in a position to consolidate its hold on the regional services industry, particularly in banking and tourism. Trading on the floor of the Bahrain stock exchange opened on June 17, 1989, with 29 local and joint venture companies quoted. No early decision was made to allow transshipment of freight from Mina Sulman, the island's main port, but on June 26 the Cabinet received recommendations for a new port industrial area and free zone.

Bahrain expected oil income in 1989 to total $650 million and then rise to $663 million in 1990, but annual government spending exceeded $1.4 billion. To boost tourism, which was already popular with Saudis, a 250-bed hotel was being built at Sanabis—the island's only beach resort. Bahrain's relaxed attitude to night life and hotel bars made the island a favoured weekend retreat, although the government sought to stress family tourism.

The aluminum industry was boosted by high metal prices, and a $130 million expansion plan was under way to increase the capacity of Aluminium Bahrain's smelter to 400,000 tons a year. Aluminum, refining, and tourism were the biggest employers outside government service.

To enhance the island's defenses it was announced in May that Bahrain had bought seven battlefield rocket systems from the United States for $93 million. The multiple-launch rocket system fires quick volleys of short-range conventional rockets. Bahrain wanted the system to forestall attacks by assault landing craft.   (JOHN WHELAN)

This article updates the *Macropædia* article ARABIA: *Bahrain*.

CYPRUS

An island republic and member of the Commonwealth, Cyprus is in the eastern Mediterranean Sea. Island area: 9,251 sq km (3,572 sq mi). Island pop. (1989 est.): 733,000. Area of the Turkish Republic of Northern Cyprus (TRNC), proclaimed unilaterally (1983) in the occupied northern third of the island (controlled by Turkish Cypriots since 1974): 3,355 sq km (1,295 sq mi); pop. (1989 est.): 169,000. Cap.: Nicosia. Monetary unit: Cyprus pound, with (Oct. 2, 1989) a free rate of £C 0.49 to U.S. $1 (£C 0.80 = £1 sterling). President in 1989, George Vassiliou. President of TRNC in 1989, Rauf Denktash.

When he was elected in 1988, Cypriot Pres. George Vassiliou had declared the problem of divided Cyprus to be a simple one, and he pledged to work with Turkish Cypriot leader Rauf Denktash to draft a skeleton settlement by mid-1989. When July 1989 brought the 15th anniversary of the Turkish invasion of Cyprus, however, the island was even further from a solution. One reason was the Greek Cypriot Women Walk Home movement, whose members made several attempts to storm Turkish military lines. The movement, which had begun about four years earlier as a campaign by exiled women to return to their occupied homes in northern Cyprus, had increasingly grabbed world headlines.

In November 1988 more than 2,000 young Greek Cypriots tore through barbed wire with their bare hands and fought with UN peacekeeping troops to mark the fifth anniversary of Denktash's unilateral declaration of a Turkish Cypriot republic in the north. In March more than 3,000 women, backed by feminist supporters from the U.S., Australia, and Europe, successfully broke through defense lines in several places. The two Cypriot leaders did meet in New York in June, and UN Secretary-General Javier Pérez de Cuéllar said he was confident that an early and lasting settlement in Cyprus was a real possibility. Both the Cypriot leaders described the talks as "productive," but few details emerged. Vassiliou was praised by the media for declining to react to Denktash's "provocative" offer to Ankara to resettle ethnic Turks fleeing Bulgaria in the abandoned Greek Cypriot city of Varosha.

Greek Cypriots were more disturbed by political instability in Greece following the collapse of the scandal-ridden Papandreou government. Nicosia feared that Athens would be too preoccupied to pursue its traditional policy of supporting Greek Cypriots in their dispute with Turkey. In Nicosia the UN peacekeeping force managed to persuade Greek and Turkish Cypriot troops to dismantle 24 sentry posts on a dangerous narrow sector of the Green Line boundary. One Turkish Cypriot and two Greek Cypriot soldiers were killed in shooting incidents during the year. On the invasion anniversary in July, the Women Walk Home movement was back in action on the Green Line. Turkish troops and police were condemned for brutality as they beat more than 100 women and dragged them into custody.

The Cypriot House of Representatives in June approved a resolution urging the government to apply for full membership in the European Communities. The economy remained healthy. There were worries over declining demand for Cypriot exports, but the 4% fall in domestic export value in 1988 was offset by a 30% growth in reexport trade. High demand for imports pushed the trade deficit to £C 482 million in 1988, compared with £C 366 million the previous year.   (THOMAS O'DWYER)

EGYPT

A republic of North Africa, Egypt has coastlines on the Mediterranean and Red seas. Area: 997,739 sq km (385,229 sq mi). Pop. (1989 est.): 51,748,000. Cap.: Cairo. Monetary unit: Egyptian pound (LE), with (Oct. 2, 1989) a free rate of LE 2.57 to U.S. $1 (LE 4.16 = £1 sterling). President in 1989, Hosni Mubarak; prime minister, Atef Sedki.

Egypt rejoined the Arab League in 1989, and Pres. Hosni Mubarak took the chair of the Organization of African Unity (OAU), pushing Egypt into the centre of the regional stage. The authorities continued to crack down on suspected members of extremist Islamic groups. Israel returned the Taba strip to Egypt but was lukewarm about Mubarak's 10-point plan for elections in the West Bank and Gaza Strip.

The Arab summit that opened on May 23 in Casablanca, Morocco, was attended by Mubarak; he was publicly reconciled with Syria's Pres. Hafez al-Assad and held talks with Libya's Col. Mu'ammar al-Qadhdhafi. In the following weeks the Egyptian-Libyan border was opened, air traffic between the two countries was resumed, and Libya agreed to pay compensation to the 10,000 Egyptian workers it had expelled in 1985. On October 16–17 Qadhdhafi met Mubarak for talks at the Libyan port of Tobruk amid signs that formal diplomatic ties would be resumed. In a separate move, Egypt on May 13 was formally readmitted to the Organization of Arab Petroleum Exporting Countries.

In February Egypt, Iraq, Yemen (San'a'; North Yemen), and Jordan agreed to form the Arab Cooperation Council, and a summit conference was held in Alexandria. The

three days of meetings set the final seal on agreements between the four countries about trade, defense, and security cooperation. Although Egypt and Iraq were dominant members of the ACC, Egyptian spokesmen made it clear that the council members had no intention of cooperating in the military sphere. In early September it was reported that Egypt's ambition to develop the long-range Condor II missile in cooperation with Iraq and Argentina had received a setback a few weeks earlier. On August 17 a huge explosion wrecked the secret military complex near al-Hillah, south of Baghdad, where the missile was being modified. The fire caused Egyptian casualties.

In late July Mubarak was unanimously elected chairman of the 49-nation OAU, reinforcing Egypt's rehabilitation from the political wilderness it entered after the bilateral peace with Israel in 1979. Mubarak offered to mediate between The Sudan's new military rulers and the southern rebels. Other disputes in which he might become involved included the Chad-Libya confrontation and the conflict between Morocco and the Polisario Front over Western Sahara. Mubarak also emerged as a spokesman for debtor nations. At the Paris bicentennial celebrations in July he joined the leaders of Venezuela, Mexico, and Indonesia in advocating a joint proposal to resolve Third World indebtedness.

The Taba strip on the Red Sea was returned to Egypt on March 13 following an international arbitration panel ruling that obliged Israel to withdraw. Egypt planned to develop the area, and the Hilton Hotel group began managing a hotel there. Mubarak and Israel's Defense Minister Yitzhak Rabin agreed on September 18 that Israel and the Palestinians should negotiate face to face, but they failed to resolve who should represent the Palestinian side. On October 6 Mubarak's plan was formally rejected by Israel's inner cabinet, leaving Labour and Likud ministers sharply divided. Mubarak had suggested a list of 12 Palestinians who could be involved in negotiations. Mubarak's 10-point plan for elections in the West Bank and Gaza Strip was negatively received by the Palestine Liberation Organization and its supporters.

Egypt's higher profile on the international scene, which included a visit to Washington April 1–4 for talks with

A fence separating the resort area of Taba from the rest of the Sinai territory of Egypt is cut down after an international arbitration panel ruled that Israel should return the area to Egypt.

Pres. George Bush, contrasted with some heavy-handed moves against domestic political opposition. Some Egyptians had hoped that the June 8 elections to the Shura, if fairly conducted, would enable this purely consultative body to develop into a second chamber. As it turned out, all but one of the Shura's 153 contested seats was won by the ruling National Democratic Party.

The authorities dealt severely with suspected members of extremist Islamic organizations. Sheikh Omar Ahmad Rahman, the blind spiritual leader of Islamic Jihad, one of the most militant groups, was rearrested in mid-August after a court had ordered his release. Eight years earlier the sheikh had been accused of inciting Jihad to assassinate Pres. Anwar as-Sadat but was acquitted. With popular sympathy for the more aggressive Islamic factions reduced, the authorities evidently had concluded that the time was ripe for confronting Islamic militancy in general and Jihad in particular. In late August the security police arrested 41 alleged members of a Shi'ite Muslim organization accused of planning to attack U.S., Israeli, Saudi, Iraqi, and Kuwaiti interests in Egypt. Clashes between police and militants in Asyut in December left 40 wounded. The security services were severely criticized by the U.K.-based human rights organization Amnesty International, which alleged that only about 5% of those arrested for security-related offenses in recent years had ever been brought to trial. On the other hand, on Jan. 1, 1989, the government received an important message of support from the leading Islamic scholar Sheikh Muhammad Mitwali ash-Shaarawi.

In line with its repression of Islamic critics, the regime also hit back at secular enemies. In late May a "Communist cell," linked to the illegal Egyptian Communist Party, was broken up, and six of its members were charged with possessing seditious material. In early August workers taking industrial action at the Helwan iron and steel plant were attacked by security police. One worker was killed, 15 were injured, and more than 600 were arrested in the worst case of industrial unrest since Mubarak came to power in 1981. Later in the month 52 prominent intellectuals, newsmen, and attorneys were arrested.

The new defense minister, Gen. Youssef Abu Taleb, made his first visit to Washington in early August. His appointment in April followed the sacking of Field Marshal Abdel-Halim Abu Ghazalah, who had been regarded as President Mubarak's heir apparent. Washington provided indirect debt relief to Cairo by using a moratorium interest fund for U.S. military debt payments rescheduled in 1987 to meet outstanding interest payments on the military debt until November 1989. Mubarak was expected to visit Moscow in early 1990, a sign of improving relations with the Kremlin. On October 9 Mubarak's political adviser and the Soviet ambassador in Cairo discussed preparations for the visit. Relations with Moscow were broken off in 1981 but were restored by Mubarak in 1984.

The International Monetary Fund (IMF) was negotiating with Egypt over a new standby-credit accord that would pave the way for a fresh rescheduling of debt with the Paris Club of Western creditor nations. This would cover $8 billion–$10 billion in debt service payments due between June 1988 and December 1990. Egypt would be eligible for up to $500 million a year in IMF standby credits. With arrears on repayments mounting, Cairo planned to take significant steps to meet IMF demands on reducing its budget deficit, moving toward unifying its multiple exchange rate system, and encouraging the private sector.

After years of relative inactivity, oil and gas exploration was at a new high. In the first six months of 1989, 35 new exploration agreements were awarded, making it a

record year. The activity had some urgency. If domestic consumption of energy continued to increase at the current annual rate of 10% a year and no new large finds were made, Egypt, already short of foreign exchange for essential imports such as wheat, would have to face importing oil by early in the next century. Revenues earned by the Suez Canal in fiscal 1988–89 rose to a record $1,340,000,000, up 12% from the previous year. A $2 million feasibility study on widening and deepening the canal to accommodate fully laden tankers of up to 270,000 dead weight tons (dwt) was commissioned by the Suez Canal Authority. Currently the canal could handle tankers of up to 150,000 dwt, but it was being deepened and widened to accommodate ships up to 200,000 dwt by the end of 1990.

Egypt and Saudi Arabia were planning to build a $500 million road to link Sinai with the Saudi coast via Tiran island, lying at the mouth of the Gulf of Aqaba. The road, to be paid for by tolls on traffic, was expected to boost Saudi investment in Egypt. King Fahd of Saudi Arabia visited Cairo in late March, giving Mubarak the opportunity to clarify the reasons behind the formation of the ACC. Included on Fahd's itinerary was the Deversoir area, east of the Suez Canal, where private Saudi investors were financing a tourist complex with an estimated worth of $900 million. Tourism continued to boom. In the first four months of 1989 the number of visitors to Egypt was 11% above the corresponding period of 1988. Income from tourism had grown from less than $1 billion a year in the mid-1980s to $2.2 billion in 1988, making it Egypt's largest hard currency earner after expatriate remittances. Egypt's resumed ties with the Arab world had helped this process.

(JOHN WHELAN)

IRAN

The Islamic republic of Iran is in southwestern Asia on the Caspian and Arabian seas and the Persian Gulf. Area: 1,648,196 sq km (636,372 sq mi). Pop. (1989 est., including up to 2 million Afghan and 500,000 Iraqi refugees): 54,333,000. Cap.: Tehran. Monetary unit: Iranian rial, with (Oct. 2, 1989) an official exchange rate of 72.25 rials to U.S. $1 (116.90 rials = £1 sterling). Rahbars (spiritual leaders) in 1989, Ayatollah Ruhollah Khomeini and, from June 4, Ayatollah Sayyed Ali Khamenei; presidents, Sayyed Ali Khamenei and, from August 3, Hojatolislam Hashemi Ali Akbar Rafsanjani; prime minister, until August 3, Mir Hossein Moussavi.

The Islamic republic of Iran celebrated its 10th anniversary in February. During the same month, outrage was generated in Iran and in much of the Muslim world by the novel Satanic Verses by Salman Rushdie (see BIOGRAPHIES), which had been published in late 1988. In the aftermath Iran's spiritual leader, Ayatollah Ruhollah Khomeini, denounced all "liberals." (See PUBLISHING; Sidebar.)

On June 3 Ayatollah Khomeini died (see OBITUARIES). Since the revolution in 1979 he had been universally acknowledged as the velayat-e faqih (guardian of true jurisprudence) and the marja al-taqlid (source of emulation) among Shi'ite Muslims. He was also the unchallenged leader of the Iranian revolution. He was buried in Tehran amid scenes of great mourning by crowds estimated at more than two million.

The succession to Khomeini was managed without an overt political struggle. Sayyed Ali Khamenei was appointed as rahbar, or spiritual leader of the Islamic republic. He gave up the presidency, for which elections were arranged for July together with a plebiscite on modification of the constitution. Hojatolislam Hashemi Ali Akbar Rafsanjani was elected president with 94.51% of the vote and took office on August 3. Amendments to the constitution

Iran's new president, Hojatolislam Hashemi Ali Akbar Rafsanjani (bottom), delivers his inaugural address before the Iranian Majlis (parliament) and its speaker, Hojatolislam Mehdi Karrubi (top).
FARNOOD—SIPA

were accepted, eliminating the post of prime minister and strengthening the position of president. The new Cabinet was notable for its omissions, with the extreme radicals such as Ali Akbar Mohtashemi, Mohammad Mohammedi Reyshari, former prime minister Mir Hossein Moussavi, and Ahmad Khomeini absent from the new appointees.

Only 68.5% of Iranians voted in the elections in July. Solidarity within the regime was attained, however, and the transition to a presidential system was achieved without disruption. The new president stated that economic affairs would be his principal concern. Most opposition groups had called for a boycott of the elections. Suppression of political opponents of the regime continued after the election, and in September the UN Committee on Human Rights criticized Iran. On July 13 Abdolrahman Qassemlu, an Iranian leader of the opposition Kurdish Democratic Party, and his deputy were assassinated in Vienna.

Peace talks with Iraq under the auspices of the UN made little progress during the year. In February a mixed military working party was set up to oversee the cease-fire, but negotiations for substantive peace talks were abortive. As prerequisites for talks, Iran insisted that all Iraqi troops withdraw from its soil, while the Iraqis demanded control of navigation on the Shatt al-Arab. UN attempts in April to get movement toward a settlement were unsuccessful. Frustrations on the Iranian side manifested themselves in September when President Rafsanjani threatened a renewal of fighting to drive Iraqi troops from Iran.

Iran remained internationally isolated despite a drive for normalization of diplomatic relations early in the year. The main obstacle to improving contacts abroad was the eruption in February of a vitriolic campaign against Rushdie, whose death was called for by Ayatollah Khomeini. The United Kingdom, which had reestablished diplomatic links only in the closing days of 1988, withdrew its staff and requested that official Iranian representatives leave London. Members of the European Communities withdrew their ambassadors for a month beginning February 20 and, following a call on May 5 by Rafsanjani for the killing by Palestinians of five U.S., British, or French nationals for every Palestinian killed by the Israelis, Iranian links with the West as a whole deteriorated markedly.

Iranian relations with the U.S.S.R. improved. Soviet Foreign Minister Eduard Shevardnadze visited Tehran on February 26–27 and again on July 31, while Rafsanjani traveled to the U.S.S.R. on June 20 to sign $6 billion worth of economic and technical cooperation agreements. These included a resumption of Iranian natural gas deliveries to the U.S.S.R. and joint oil explorations in the Caspian Sea area.   (KEITH S. MCLACHLAN)

IRAQ

A republic of southwestern Asia, Iraq has a short coastline on the Persian Gulf. Area: 435,052 sq km (167,975 sq mi). Pop. (1989 est.): 17,215,000. Cap.: Baghdad. Monetary unit: Iraqi dinar, with (Oct. 2, 1989) a par value of 0.31 dinar to U.S. $1 (free rate of 0.50 dinar = £1 sterling). President in 1989, Saddam Hussein at-Takriti.

Pres. Saddam Hussein survived a coup attempt planned for Army Day in January 1989 by disaffected officers. His grip on the country had weakened somewhat following the cease-fire in the Gulf war with Iran, and his personal standing had been damaged by allegations of marital infidelity. Nevertheless, Hussein remained determined to speed up a process of political reform, introducing more democracy into what had previously been virtually a one-party state. At the National Assembly elections on April 1, more than seven million Iraqis voted for 953 candidates contesting 59 constituencies. Candidates were members of the official Ba'th Party and the affiliated Progressive National Front or were independents. Candidates were obliged to attest their support for the 1968 revolution and the Gulf war.

On March 30 Izzat Ibrahim, Revolution Command Council vice-chairman, said that the new assembly would mark a transitional state in Iraq's political life. It was expected to endorse the new constitution that was being drawn up by a special committee. The permanent constitution—the 1970 version was only provisional—would allow political parties and freedom of the press. Ibrahim said that in the future the Cabinet would be responsible to the National Assembly, which would have the power to withdraw its confidence in the Cabinet or in individual ministers. This power was used for the first time in 1988 in dismissing the health minister.

In the elections two former Cabinet ministers, Hatem Abdel-Rasheed and Hisham Hassan Tawfig, were elected, as was Ba'th Party regional command member Sasdi Mahdi Saleh. The only current Cabinet minister to run for office, Hashim Aqrawi, was defeated. Elections for the Kurdish autonomous region's 50-man council were held on September 9.

In June Iraq confirmed that it was preparing a 30-km (19-mi)-wide buffer zone along the length of its 1,600-km (1,000-mi) border with Iran and Turkey. All towns and villages in the zone—except for two—were to be demolished. Kurdish opposition groups estimated that 300,000 Kurds had already been resettled.

As Iraq adjusted to peace, four army divisions were to be demobilized in October, according to an announcement on September 27. The decision was a sign of Iraq's confidence in its defense capability. One division had been demobilized earlier in the year, together with 200,000 conscripts.

Security remained a concern, however. A grenade attack on an expatriate club in Baghdad on September 20 injured 25 people. As many as 700 people were reported killed in a huge explosion at a defense industry complex on August 17 near the town of al-Hillah, 70 km (43 mi) from Baghdad. The Iraqis said the death toll was only 19. The London newspaper the *Independent* alleged that the

site was a project to develop a version of the Argentinian Condor II missile, with Egyptian assistance. In December it was reported that Iraq had launched a rocket large enough to put a satellite in orbit.

On May 5 Deputy Prime Minister and Defense Minister Adnan Khairallah was killed when his helicopter crashed in a sandstorm near Mosul. His replacement was 69-year-old Gen. Abdel-Jabbar Khalil ash-Shansal, former minister of state for defense. Khairallah, the president's brother-in-law, was the third senior army officer to die in a plane crash in 18 months.

The economy was stimulated by a successful rescheduling of French debt signed on September 14 in Baghdad, covering some $1.2 billion worth of debt repayments and arrears. The completion of a new crude-oil pipeline and the reopening of Gulf oil export terminals provided greater flexibility for oil exports. Iraq also obtained from OPEC a new oil export quota of 3,140,000 bbl a day.

Iraq made rapid progress in rebuilding areas devastated by war, starting with the southern city of Basra and then proceeding to the Fao Peninsula. Iraq anxiously courted Western aid for this task but also looked to the Soviet Union for a new economic agreement. President Hussein, however, criticized the Soviet Union's action in supplying weapons to Iran.   (JOHN WHELAN)

ISRAEL

A republic of southwestern Asia, Israel is situated on the Mediterranean Sea. Area: 20,700 sq km (7,992 sq mi), not including territory occupied in the June 1967 war. Pop. (1989 est.): 4,563,000. Cap.: Jerusalem (but *see* Israel table in *World Data* section). Monetary unit: new (Israeli) sheqel, with (Oct. 2, 1989) a free rate of 2 sheqalim to U.S. $1 (3.24 sheqalim = £1 sterling). President in 1989, Chaim Herzog; prime minister, Yitzhak Shamir.

In 1989 Israel once again faced the harsh realities to which it was becoming accustomed: the state of the country's economy, the Palestinian "uprising" (the *intifada*) in the occupied territories; and the process that was supposed to lead to peace. Everyone involved was producing "peace initiatives": the Palestine Liberation Organization (PLO), U.S. Secretary of State James Baker, Egyptian Pres. Hosni Mubarak, Israeli Prime Minister Yitzhak Shamir, and many others. Peace plans and peace hopes fueled the basically unrealistic public discussion. Private Israeli preoccupations were more down to earth—how to make national and personal economic ends meet and how to come to terms with the *intifada*.

The political life of Israel was dominated by these two considerations. The country was in a state of permanent political uncertainty about the ruling coalition—the so-called national unity government—and also about its principal components: the right-wing Likud, the Labour Alignment, and the grouping of four disparate and rival religious parties. All were in a permanent state of conflict with one another and within themselves. Yet despite continuous strife the national unity coalition did not break up, and the divided and warring parties composing it did not split. What held them together in the final analysis was the unspoken consensus that was at the root of Israeli thinking—that the PLO demands, whether expressed through the *intifada* or through its diplomatic offensive at the United Nations, in Washington, D.C., and in Cairo, were unacceptable if Israel wanted to survive as a Jewish state. It was, despite all the domestic conflicts and party differences, the one issue on which the great majority of Israelis remained united.

Palestinians are issued computerized identity cards by Israeli soldiers while a roomful of others endure a long wait. Palestinians living in the Israeli-occupied Gaza Strip were required to carry the ID cards in order to enter Israel, where many of them worked.

M. MILNER—SYGMA

Within this framework of national unity, Israel's 27 political and religious parties felt that they could exploit to the full the luxury of personal, political, and sectarian partisanship; and this they did, knowing all the time that the Shamir government could be rocked but would not capsize. For the secret of the Shamir government's survival was the same formula that had dictated national unity on so many previous difficult occasions—*Ein Breira,* no alternative.

Another factor in this equation that Israelis would have to discover during the year was the personality of their prime minister, Yitzhak Shamir. Unlike most of his predecessors, he was a retiring and very private person. In contrast to Menachem Begin, whom he had loyally served, he was pragmatic rather than dogmatic; his faith in Israel was national rather than religious; he was calculating rather than intuitive; and he commanded the commodity so few politicians seemed to understand—patience, apparently endless patience. Thus, despite appearances to the contrary, he was a formidable political practitioner. The emergence of Shamir as prime minister in the mold of Israel's legendary first prime minister, David Ben-Gurion, was one of the notable features of the year for Israeli politics. Shamir's patience and toughness—and his innate understanding of political infighting—began to pay off as the year wore on; his powerful and more charismatic rivals were to discover to their cost that Shamir was very much the man in charge.

Out of the plethora of Cabinet ministers and their deputies—more than 40 of the Knesset's (parliament's) 120 members—only two others stood out in the policy-making of the Shamir government. One was the deputy prime minister and finance minister, Shimon Peres, leader of the Labour Alignment and former prime minister. The other was his Labour colleague Defense Minister Yitzhak Rabin, who had virtually assumed personal responsibility for taking on the *intifada.* This trio of strongmen, despite their party and personal differences, provided the inner strength of the Shamir government and held it together through its recurring crises. Shamir did not interfere—and

did not allow other ministers to interfere—with the virtual autonomy of Peres and Rabin.

Thus, when Peres presented his budget to the Knesset on January 31, it had the independent quality that he had shown during his period in office as prime minister. The economy was in a bad state. Inflation was increasing, and growth was stagnant. Unemployment was rising to unacceptable proportions. The labour force had become distorted; barely half its civilian sector was employed in productive industry and agriculture. Peres proceeded to challenge the sacred cows of his own left and of the majority Likud right. His estimated budget expenditure of $26 billion was severely controlled. Once again, debt repayment and defense dominated Peres' spending plans. Between them they accounted for 60% of all budget expenditure: debt repayment consumed $10.5 billion and defense $5.3 billion. Only $3 billion was available for the endless demands on public spending and less than $2 billion for investment in the infrastructure and for credits to industry, the municipalities, and institutions.

In addition, the Treasury had to determine the costs incurred as a result of the *intifada.* The Bank of Israel had estimated that the "troubles" on the West Bank and in Gaza cost Israel $650 million in 1988 (and more in 1989) in lost exports and tourist income. Ironically, the number of Palestinians working in Israel during the first year of the *intifada* increased from 103,000 to 109,000—11% of those employed in Israel's private sector. It all added up to a difficult scenario for the finance minister.

By the end of the year, however, the economy was in better shape; inflation was declining, exports had improved, and there had been some improvement in the hard-hit agricultural sector—especially the cooperative and communal settlements. The Bank of Israel noted on November 9 that the recession had been halted and that—despite the *intifada*—the economy was beginning to recover. There was, however, a long, hard road ahead before Israel's economy would be adequately readjusted to the new challenges at home and in Europe.

The fundamental weakness of the *intifada* was demonstrated during the year. The damage it inflicted on Israel's national economy was considerable but not insurmountable. The same was true of physical casualties. Israeli loss of life totaled 20 Israelis killed in two years; by contrast, 2,600 had died in 18 days during the Yom Kippur War. The *intifada* was uncomfortable and unpleasant for Israel in terms of public relations, but Israelis—especially the families of troops serving in the occupied territories—were coming to terms with what they accepted as a necessary hardship but never as a threat.

There was a singular consensus that Israel would not and could not submit to the demands of the *intifada.* If necessary, Israel could face a long war of attrition on the West Bank with only a fraction of the cost and strain that the *intifada* imposed on the Palestinian Arabs. Since the start of the *intifada,* the latter had lost some 500 dead; at least 150 of these were killed in "executions" carried out by masked Arab youths attached to one of the many groups claiming to represent the Palestinians.

In December the Israeli Army issued an order that forbade Faisal Husseini, one of the best-known leaders of the Palestinians, to enter either the occupied West Bank or the Gaza Strip for the next six months. The Army charged Husseini with helping to foment protest and violence in the territories several times during recent months. Husseini said that he would abide by the order, even though he believed that it came as a result of pressure from the Israeli right.

With these symptoms of internal pressure and disintegration of the *intifada*, pressures for a political settlement increased. They came from many interested quarters, but especially from the conference of Arab heads of state that met in Casablanca, Morocco, in May. This summit adopted virtually the full set of demands voiced by the PLO and by the mainstream groups of the *intifada*. These included an Israeli withdrawal from all territories occupied by Israel in 1967, including Jerusalem, and also the designation of the PLO as the only organization that could name the Palestinian Arabs who would negotiate the calling of the international conference that would oversee the establishment of an independent Palestinian state and the return of all Palestinian refugees to their former homes.

Israel's municipal elections on February 28 gave control of most major cities and of virtually all development towns to Prime Minister Shamir's Likud Party. Likud retained control of Tel Aviv, Herzliyya, and Natanya and wrested control from Labour and the religious parties in Holon, Ramat Gan, Beersheba, Petah Tiqwa, and Tiberias. In Jerusalem Mayor Teddy Kollek, a member of the Labour Party, was returned with a large majority, but his supporters lost control of the city council. With his Likud Party in unchallenged control of the political heights, Shamir turned in a confident mood to addressing the pressures from the U.S. and from his own military intelligence community to counter the *intifada* with an Israeli political initiative.

The direct impetus to achieve this end came on March 21, three weeks after the municipal elections. The annual assessment of Israel's military intelligence community advised the prime minister that the Arab countries and the PLO had concluded that the only way to end the *intifada* was through a political settlement. Moreover, the Arab countries except for Saudi Arabia had refused to meet their commitments to fund the Palestinian Arab "uprising," and they had difficulties in funding their own defense budgets. The time was ripe, therefore, for an Israeli peace initiative.

Accordingly, Prime Minister Shamir submitted a four-point proposal to the U.S. at the beginning of April that envisioned the holding of "free elections" on the West Bank and in Gaza. The objective of the elections was to bring about the establishment of a Palestinian Arab delegation that would participate in negotiations on an interim settlement in which a self-governing Palestinian Arab administration would be established.

The proposal was rejected by the PLO, expanded by Egypt's President Mubarak into a 10-point document, and finally refined by U.S. Secretary of State Baker on October 12 into a five-point compromise. Israel accepted the Baker version on November 5 with six minor "reservations." Prime Minister Shamir met U.S. Pres. George Bush and Baker in Washington, D.C., on November 15 to discuss the proposal. At the meeting Shamir stated that Israel would not negotiate directly or indirectly with the PLO; Baker said that the U.S. could not support this position unreservedly without undermining the entire Middle East peace process. Shamir backed up his stand on December 31, when he dismissed Science Minister Ezer Weizman, a veteran Labour Party politician, for allegedly holding talks with PLO leaders. (JON KIMCHE)

JORDAN

A constitutional monarchy, Jordan is located in southwestern Asia and has a short coastline on the Gulf of Aqaba. Area: 88,947 sq km (34,343 sq mi). Pop. (1989 est.): 3,059,000. Cap.: Amman. Monetary unit: Jordan dinar, with (Oct. 2, 1989) a free rate of 0.67 dinar to U.S. $1 (1.08 dinars = £1 sterling). King, Hussein I; prime ministers in 1989, Zaid ar-Rifai to April 24, Sharif Zaid ibn Shaker from April 27 to December 4, and, from December 4, Mudar Badran.

Jordan's stability was undermined in April 1989 by a wave of unrest that spread through much of the East Bank heartland. It was the worst outbreak of violence since the civil war ended in 1971. The trouble, sparked by price increases, resulted in the dismissal by King Hussein of the administration of Zaid ar-Rifai and the appointment of a new prime minister, Sharif Zaid ibn Shaker.

King Hussein appointed a new Cabinet on April 27 to meet popular demands, including a drive against corruption and preparations for parliamentary elections, the first since 1967. He also called for greater press freedom, within limits. Ibn Shaker was well known for his role in quelling the 1970–71 rebellion by Palestinian guerrillas. His background as head of the Army from 1976 to 1988 signaled more emphasis on security than liberalization. The new Cabinet contained seven ministers of Palestinian origin, viewed as a reward for the fact that Palestinians played little part in the riots.

On July 5 the prime minister announced that parlia-

Jordanian men present their voting cards before voting in the country's general elections, which were held for the first time in 22 years.

mentary elections would take place on November 8 and that changes were expected to occur in the electoral law, including the expansion of the lower house to 80 seats from 72. The extra representation would be in the governorates of Amman, Zarqa, Irbid, and Balqa. The allocation of nine seats for Christians and three for Circassians or Shishanis would be maintained. Interior Minister Salem Masadeh said on July 6 that he was opposed to the continued allocation of separate seats because all Jordanians, whatever their religious or ethnic background, should be treated equally. He added that at present, however, there was no way of changing the system. The ban on political parties, allowed under the constitution but outlawed since 1964, also remained. Nevertheless, it was clear that all political factions would be represented, including Islamic fundamentalists. In the election, on November 8, Islamic fundamentalists won 32 seats, the leftist democratic bloc 16, and other parties 32. In December King Hussein appointed Madar Badran as prime minister.

The rioting, triggered by price increases of up to 50% on goods including fuel but not staple foods, began on April 18 in the southern town of Ma'an; it spread quickly to Karak, Tafilah, and Shobek. King Hussein was forced to cut short a foreign tour to deal with the crisis, in which eight people died. Violence was directed at government offices but did not appear to be targeted at the monarchy.

Prime Minister Zaid ibn Shaker, a distant cousin of King Hussein, began an immediate tour of the country to raise morale and to listen to grievances. There was general consensus among businessmen on the need to shake up all government departments and agencies to improve efficiency, bring in new ideas, and promote greater integrity. In May Kuwait promised $40 million in aid to Jordan and another $40 million from oil sales. Oman and Iraq offered $20 million each and Iraq a further $30 million by the end of 1989. The Bush administration pressed the U.S. Congress for $35 million in economic aid to Jordan and $48 million in military assistance for 1990.

On the international front, Jordan in February joined with Egypt, Iraq, and Yemen (San'a'; North Yemen) in forming an Arab Cooperation Council, seen in regional terms as a counterbalance to the Arab Maghreb Union and the Gulf Cooperation Council. (JOHN WHELAN)

KUWAIT

A constitutional monarchy (emirate), Kuwait is in the northeastern Arabian Peninsula, on the Persian Gulf. Area: 17,818 sq km (6,880 sq mi). Pop. (1989 est.): 2,048,000. Cap.: Kuwait City. Monetary unit: Kuwaiti dinar, with (Oct. 2, 1989) a free rate of 0.29 dinar to U.S. $1 (0.48 dinar = £1 sterling). Emir, Sheikh Jabir al-Ahmad al-Jabir as-Sabah; prime minister in 1989, Crown Prince Sheikh Saad al-Abdullah as-Salim as-Sabah.

Kuwait remained at the centre of regional tensions following the end of the war between Iran and Iraq. Iraq made no early moves to settle Kuwait's claim to sovereignty over Babiyan Island, although a water agreement was signed. This was seen as scant reward for Kuwaiti financial backing for Iraq during the eight-year war.

On May 9 an armed Kuwaiti Coast Guard patrol boat was seized by Iranian revolutionary guards. The Kuwaiti vessel had been in hot pursuit of illegal immigrants near the maritime border. The boat was subsequently released, but the incident followed an arrest in March by Iran of a Kuwaiti yacht with cadet members of the royal family aboard. Both incidents strained Kuwait's supposedly "normal" relations with Iran.

Kuwait played a wider role in Arab affairs by chairing an Arab League committee to settle the Lebanese civil war, but in May Kuwait abruptly resigned in apparent frustration over the lack of progress. Links with Egypt were strengthened by a visit from Pres. Hosni Mubarak in February and the first shipment, in March, of Egyptian-built Amoun surface-to-air missiles.

Internally, 30,000 people signed a petition in March calling for the restoration of the elected National Assembly. A total of 33 people, many being tried in absentia, were accused of subversion in Kuwait's biggest-ever show trial, which began on May 13.

On June 8 in Vienna Kuwaiti Oil Minister Sheikh Ali al-Khalifah al-Athbi as-Sabah said that his nation's share of combined OPEC production should be 9–12%. He complained that Kuwait had long suffered an inequitable position in the organization. At the November OPEC meeting Kuwait was assigned a quota of 1.5 million bbl a day for the first six months of 1990. (JOHN WHELAN)

This article updates the *Macropædia* article ARABIA: *Kuwait*.

LEBANON

A republic of southwestern Asia, Lebanon is situated on the Mediterranean Sea. Area: 10,230 sq km (3,950 sq mi). Pop. (1989 est.): 2,897,000 (including Palestinian refugees estimated to number about 300,000). Cap.: Beirut. Monetary unit: Lebanese pound, with (Oct. 2, 1989) a free rate of LL 459.15 to U.S. $1 (LL 742.90 = £1 sterling). Presidents in 1989, René Moawad from November 5 to November 22 and, from November 24, Elias Hrawi; prime ministers, Selim al-Hoss (civilian government) and Michel Aoun (provisional military government).

The year 1989 in Lebanon was characterized by renewed civil war, assassinations (including that of the newly elected president, René Moawad; *see* OBITUARIES), and continued deadlock over Western hostages. Army commander Michel Aoun (*see* BIOGRAPHIES) emerged as the key Christian leader, while Arab League mediation appeared to provide the best means to resolve the long-standing conflict.

Saudi Arabia made available the resort of Ta'if for a meeting of deputies from the National Assembly to consider the Arab peace initiative. They appeared to be on the brink of agreement in mid-October when Aoun intervened, claiming that the Christian deputies were in danger of making too many concessions to Syria.

The deputies were debating a charter drawn up by Arab League mediators that aimed to reconcile demands from the Christians for a Syrian withdrawal with Muslim calls for political reform. The Arab plan specified that a meeting of the National Assembly take place in Beirut to elect a new president once the charter was approved in Ta'if. The deputies reached agreement on political reform clauses in the charter but continued to argue about the clause on sovereignty. This provided for a Syrian redeployment in the Beqaa Valley within two years of the charter's approval but failed to specify when Syrian troops would withdraw altogether from Lebanon.

The deputies of the National Assembly met on November 5 and elected René Moawad, a moderate Christian, president of Lebanon. Seventeen days later he was killed by a car bomb in predominantly Muslim West Beirut. The deputies on November 24 elected Elias Hrawi, another Christian, president. Aoun threatened to hold elections for a legislature to rival the National Assembly.

Both Druse leader Walid Jumblatt and Shi'ite Muslim Amal leader Nabih Berri criticized the Ta'if charter for allegedly failing to address the need for radical reform. Both men wanted the size of the new National Assembly

increased from 108 to 128 seats. They believed that the practice of apportioning political posts according to religion should be abolished immediately and that the Army should be completely restructured.

The year's major round of fighting began on March 14; more than 40 people were killed when Aoun and the Christian Lebanese Forces militia pounded West Beirut. Three days later 15 people died in a huge car bomb explosion in the eastern sector of the city. Aoun then threw down the gauntlet to Syria and its allies, launching a "war of liberation" and declaring that he would be satisfied with nothing less than the total expulsion of the Syrians from Lebanon.

Aoun's action failed to stop the wave of killings. On May 16 Sunni Muslim leader Sheikh Hassan Khaled died in a car bomb blast with 21 others. Considered to be a moderate, he was leader of 700,000 Lebanese Sunni Muslims.

In response to the growing chaos and a mandate from the Arab summit in May, heads of state from Morocco, Algeria, and Saudi Arabia met in the Algerian port of Oran on June 27. The summit ended with proposals to invite members of the National Assembly to meet outside Lebanon to "prepare a charter of national harmony." As the talks proceeded, fighting in Beirut continued. (By the time an uneasy truce took effect in late September, more than 800 people had died and some 4,500 had been wounded; the truce was broken in December.)

The Arab mediation committee subsequently ran into difficulty over differences with Syria about the concept of Lebanese sovereignty. In Jidda on September 13 the committee reached a compromise, effectively withdrawing its criticism of Syria in return for Syrian pledges to cooperate in enforcing a cease-fire. Syria was refusing to withdraw its forces in the face of Aoun's onslaught unless asked to do so by a government of national unity.

On September 6 the U.S. evacuated its embassy in East Beirut in the face of increasing hostility from Aoun's supporters. Aoun had said on September 3 that the U.S. lacked the moral courage to support him. He claimed that the U.S. was part of a conspiracy with Israel and Syria to dismember Lebanon.

KENNETH WOOD—GAMMA/LIAISON

Lebanon's newly elected Pres. René Moawad (centre), flanked by his bodyguards, arrives in Beirut to negotiate the formation of a new government. Moawad, who advocated the peaceful coexistence of Lebanon's warring Muslim and Christian factions, was assassinated after 17 days in office.

The U.S. administration had been hauled into the Lebanon crisis after Israel's abduction of a Lebanese cleric, Sheikh 'Abd-al Karim Obeid, from his home on July 28. Three days later terrorists announced the revenge hanging of a U.S. hostage, Lieut. Col. William Higgins, a U.S. officer who had been serving with the UN in southern Lebanon. He had been held since 1988 by the Organization for the Oppressed of the Earth, a faction of the Iranian-backed Hezbollah.

The U.S. response was largely diplomatic, and on August 3 the Revolutionary Justice Organization announced the suspension of threats to execute another U.S. hostage, Joseph Cicippio. While the crisis was not over, it had been defused. Hopes were also raised—prematurely as it turned out—for a general release of Western hostages, including the Archbishop of Canterbury's envoy Terry Waite and British journalist John McCarthy.   (JOHN WHELAN)

LIBYA

A socialist country of North Africa, Libya lies on the Mediterranean Sea. Area: 1,757,000 sq km (678,400 sq mi). Pop. (1989 est.): 4,080,000. Cap.: Tripoli; capitals designate, Hun and Surt (Sidra). Monetary unit: Libyan dinar, with (Oct. 2, 1989) a free rate of 0.30 dinar to U.S. $1 (0.48 dinar = £1 sterling). De facto chief of state in 1989, Col. Mu'ammar al-Qadhdhafi; secretary of the General People's Congress (nominal chief of state), Mifta al-Usta Umar; secretary of the General People's Committee (premier), Umar Mustafa al-Muntasir.

In 1989 Libya celebrated the 20th anniversary of its First of September Revolution, which brought Mu'ammar al-Qadhdhafi to power. The anniversary occasioned a great deal of looking back and, on the part of the leadership, some celebration, although this was much less extravagant than in 1979. The reason for the muted style of the 20th celebration was the state of the economy. The 10th anniversary had marked the end of a decade of unimaginable expansion and development, with Libya beginning to enjoy the additional benefits of a second surge in oil prices. By 1984, however, revenues had fallen from the 1981 peak of $23 billion to an estimated $5 billion, with dramatic negative consequences for domestic consumption and for the ambitious programs of economic and social development.

During the year, Libya continued to cultivate and improve its relations with Algeria and Tunisia. This culminated in September in formal discussions about cooperation in the region. In late 1988 the flamboyant commitment of the Libyan leadership to a liberalization of economic and political systems at home was accompanied by the granting of free access to Tunisians, which resulted in a large influx of workers. Relations with Egypt also improved; the Egyptian border, closed since 1976, was opened, and Pres. Hosni Mubarak and Colonel Qadhdhafi crossed the land border to visit border towns in October.

World news was dominated in the first weeks of 1989 by an anti-Libyan scare. Awareness that Libya had been building a chemical plant at Rabta, south of Tripoli, with a capacity for manufacturing chemical weapons led to threats that there might be a U.S. air strike against the plant. Events took a serious turn when two Libyan MiGs were shot down on January 4 by U.S. F-14s off the coast of northeastern Libya. The U.S. found itself without allied support for the strike, and gradually the tension was defused, although the status of the Rabta plant was not clarified. The departure on January 13 of the U.S. 6th Fleet from its intimidating position close to Libyan waters signaled the end of the confrontation. In May it was announced that the chemical plant would be available for inspection by the time of the September celebrations, al-

though experts remained skeptical because the plant could easily be converted for the production of gas for military purposes.

Throughout the year Colonel Qadhdhafi was at pains to project a conciliatory profile, and even during the tension over the Rabta plant in January, he arranged to release the body of one of the U.S. airmen killed during the 1986 raid on Tripoli. He also welcomed evidence confirming his contention that the security agencies of the Western powers had sought in the past to destroy him. This came in September when an Italian inquiry revealed that the shooting down of an Italian domestic flight, IH870, from Bologna to Palermo on June 27, 1980, had occurred when an airplane carrying Qadhdhafi had been flying in the same corridor northward to Warsaw. The Libyan jet turned sharply eastward just south of Sicily, and soon afterward the Italian DC9 was hit by a missile, killing 81 passengers and crew. The evidence emerged as the result of a confession by an Italian military radar technician.

The national development program continued to concentrate resources on the Great Man-Made River Project. A major effort was made to open the 500-km (310-mi) section of the twin pipeline from Sarir to Ajdabiyah on September 1 as part of the 20th-anniversary celebrations, but this was not achieved. The project was reevaluated during the year with regard to how the water would be used. It became evident, as had long been predicted by many observers, that the expensive water conveyed by the pipeline should not be allocated to uneconomic ventures.

(J.A. ALLAN)

This article updates the *Macropædia* article NORTH AFRICA: *Libya*.

MOROCCO

A constitutional monarchy of North Africa, Morocco has coastlines on the Atlantic Ocean and the Mediterranean Sea. Area: 458,730 sq km (177,117 sq mi). Pop. (1989 est.): 24,530,000. (Area and population figures refer to Morocco as constituted prior to the purported division of Western Sahara between Morocco and Mauritania and the subsequent Moroccan occupation of the Mauritanian zone in 1979.) Cap.: Rabat. Monetary unit: dirham, with (Oct. 2, 1989) a selling rate of 8.46 dirhams to U.S. $1 (13.69 dirhams = £1 sterling). King, Hassan II; prime minister in 1989, Azzedine Laraki.

The issue of the Western Sahara continued to dominate Morocco's horizons during 1989. The year began with the visit to Marrakesh of a delegation from the Popular Front for the Liberation of Saguia el Hamra and Río de Oro (Polisario Front) in the wake of a statement by King Hassan that the doors of his palace would always be open to Moroccans. The Polisario Front declared a unilateral truce in the Western Sahara, which held effectively until the end of September, when Polisario units attacked an observation post. This was followed by two major attacks launched from Mauritanian territory.

In the wake of the attacks, King Hassan annulled plans for further talks with the Polisario Front, although these had been promised to the Algerian leader, Chadli Bendjedid, during a meeting of Maghrebi heads of state in September. Despite these events, the United Nations proceeded with preparations for a referendum in the Western Sahara.

In February the Maghrebi leaders, meeting in Marrakesh, decided to form the Arab Maghreb Union (Union Maghreb Arabe; UMA). Article 15 of the charter of the new organization, which was intended primarily to coordinate the Maghreb's response to the single European market in 1992, provided that an attack on any member state is the responsibility of all member states. By year's end this had already obliged Algeria to wind down its military support for the Western Saharan movement.

In other respects, Morocco's diplomatic situation improved. Diplomatic relations with Syria, broken off in 1986, were restored. Morocco finally ratified the 1972 border treaty with Algeria, and the two countries agreed on closer economic relations. Morocco was host to an extraordinary Arab League summit in May and joined Algeria and Saudi Arabia on the League's conciliation commission for the Lebanese conflict. British Prime Minister Margaret Thatcher visited Morocco in March.

The domestic scene remained calm, although unemployment rose over one million, according to opposition sources. The strike at the Jerada coal-mine complex, which had begun the previous November, ended in mid-February. Despite two amnesties, the Moroccan human rights organization, L'Organisation Marocaine des Droits de l'Homme, claimed that there were still 226 political prisoners.

As a result of an excellent cereal harvest of seven million tons, the government had sufficient leeway to continue its economic liberalization program. A privatization law, affecting 687 state companies, was approved by the Chamber of Deputies in May. The tax reforms were completed with a reform of personal taxation. Partly because of improved tax collection, the budget anticipated a 21% decline in the deficit. At the year's end Morocco asked for help in preventing an oil spill, caused by the explosion of an Iranian tanker, from reaching its shore.

(GEORGE JOFFÉ)

This article updates the *Macropædia* article NORTH AFRICA: *Morocco*.

OMAN

The sultanate of Oman occupies the southeastern part of the Arabian Peninsula, facing the Persian Gulf, the Gulf of Oman, and the Arabian Sea. A small part of the country lies to the north and is separated from the rest of Oman by the United Arab Emirates. Area: 300,000 sq km (120,000 sq mi). Pop.: in 1989 estimates ranged from 1.2 million to an official 2 million; no census has ever been taken (UN est., 1,422,000). Cap.: Muscat. Monetary unit: rial Omani, with (Oct. 2, 1989) a par value of 0.38 rial to U.S. $1 (free rate of 0.62 rial = £1 sterling). Sultan and prime minister in 1989, Qabus ibn Sa'id.

The 20th anniversary of Sultan Qabus ibn Sa'id's succession would be the major event of 1990. It should provide a much-needed boost for the sultanate, whose economy was sluggish and suffering from weak oil prices.

On May 3, 1989, the sultanate announced that it was suspending plans to buy eight Tornado bomber aircraft from the U.K. The official Oman News Agency said the move was for operational and management reasons. Oman would buy the cheaper Hawk aircraft from British Aerospace and surface-to-air Javelin missiles made by Short Brothers, also of the U.K.

The balance of payments was in deficit in 1988—by $363 million, compared with a 1987 surplus of $187 million. Oman remained a good credit risk, however. A $500 million loan to the government was signed on June 28. The Muscat Stock Exchange opened on May 20 listing 48 companies, but trading volumes were low. An indication of lack of interest in exporting to Oman was the failure to take advantage of a $5 million Canadian line of credit set up in 1988 by the Export Development Corporation of Canada. In an unrelated development, South Korea's Overseas Fisheries Company withdrew from a long-term deep-sea fishing concession because of a dispute over production sharing with the government. This move coincided with a decision to close the Korean trade centre in Muscat.

In July Petroleum Development Oman, the national oil company, announced its largest gas discovery in 22 years at the Saih Nihayda field in the central region. A test well produced 600,000 cu m (21 million cu ft).

(JOHN WHELAN)

This article updates the *Macropædia* article ARABIA: *Oman.*

QATAR

A monarchy (emirate) on the Arabian Peninsula, Qatar occupies a desert peninsula on the west coast of the Persian Gulf. Area: 11,337 sq km (4,377 sq mi). Pop. (1989 est.): 427,000. Cap.: Doha. Monetary unit: Qatar riyal, with (Oct. 2, 1989) a free rate of 3.64 riyals to U.S. $1 (5.89 riyals = £1 sterling). Emir and prime minister in 1989, Sheikh Khalifah ibn Hamad ath-Thani.

The first government reshuffle since 1978 on July 18, 1989, resulted in the retirement of seven senior ministers and the appointment of 11 newcomers. Many of the new ministers were under the age of 40 and had been promoted from the ranks of civil servants. The 15,000-strong ath-Thani clan continued to dominate the government, but the new team suggested the growing influence of the heir apparent, Sheikh Hamad ibn Khalifah ath-Thani, the ruler's son. His increasingly active participation in government appeared to be preparing him for his future role.

For the economy, which had to be weaned from dependence on depleting oil reserves, an important appointee was the new industry minister, Ahmad Muhammad Ali as-Subaie, a commoner, who was chairman of the Qatar Steel Company and head of the aluminum project steering committee. Qatar was considering investment in an aluminum smelter to complement existing plants in Bahrain and Dubai. The new foreign affairs minister was Abdullah ibn Khalifah al-Attiya, former adviser to the heir apparent, and the information portfolio was given to a royal, Sheikh Hamad ibn Suhaim at-Trani.

Qatar's industrial ambitions hinged on the North Field, a gas deposit containing 4% of the known world reserves. Development work was under way for a 1990 commissioning of facilities to produce 22.6 million cu m (800 million cu ft) of gas per day, enough to serve local industry and help conserve the oil supplies. Qatar General Petroleum Corporation was borrowing $400 million from international banks to promote the project.

(JOHN WHELAN)

This article updates the *Macropædia* article ARABIA: *Qatar.*

SAUDI ARABIA

The kingdom of Saudi Arabia occupies four-fifths of the Arabian Peninsula, with coastlines on the Red Sea and the Persian Gulf. Area: 2,240,000 sq km (865,000 sq mi). Pop. (1989 est.): 13,592,000. Cap.: Riyadh. Monetary unit: Saudi Arabian riyal, with (Oct. 2, 1989) a free rate of 3.75 riyals to U.S. $1 (6.07 riyals = £1 sterling). King and prime minister in 1989, Fahd.

The progress of Saudi efforts to bring about a political settlement in Lebanon put the kingdom into the centre of the regional stage in 1989. Violence once again marred the hajj pilgrimage season. On his deathbed Ayatollah Ruhollah Khomeini (*see* OBITUARIES) of Iran denounced Saudi Arabia's King Fahd as "a traitor to God," reducing Saudi pleasure over the end of the Khomeini era.

There were growing signs of Saudi impatience with Lebanese Christian leader Gen. Michel Aoun's rejection of the political agreement reached by Lebanese deputies meeting in the Saudi resort of Ta'if. The Ta'if meetings in the fall of 1989 went further toward bringing about a set-

tlement of the Lebanese civil war than any other forum in the past 10 years. King Fahd had reentered the picture on Lebanon after the Arab summit in Casablanca, Morocco, in May, which gave the Saudi monarch, Pres. Chadli Bendjedid of Algeria, and King Hassan II of Morocco the task of negotiating the formation of a government of national unity for Lebanon within six months.

Although the hajj season passed with only two bomb attacks in Mecca, on July 10 when one Pakistani pilgrim was killed and on July 16 when a second blast occurred without casualties, the atmosphere remained tense. On September 21, 16 Kuwaitis accused of being responsible for the bombings were beheaded in public. King Fahd later said that anyone disrupting the hajj or threatening the kingdom's security would receive similar punishment. In apparent retaliation, gunmen assassinated a Saudi diplomat, Muhammad Ali Marzouki, in Beirut, Lebanon, on November 1. The terrorist group Islamic Jihad claimed responsibility. The death of Ayatollah Khomeini on June 3 was followed by conciliatory gestures to Tehran by Riyadh, despite the broadcast of the deathbed statement by the Iranian spiritual leader. The Saudis refused, however, to lift the 45,000 limit on Iranian hajj pilgrims, claiming logistical problems in the holy cities. The Saudi leadership was eager to have better relations with Iran, but not at any price. Shi'ites mourning the death of Khomeini in the Eastern province were harshly treated by the Saudi police.

Syria's declaration of a week's official mourning for Khomeini's death was badly received by Riyadh, but King Fahd was undoubtedly pleased by Syrian Pres. Hafez al-Assad's acquiescence over the readmission of Egypt into the Arab League. Riyadh was less happy about the formation in February of the Arab Cooperation Council, a grouping of Yemen (San'a'; North Yemen), Egypt, Iraq, and Jordan. Saudi Arabia was troubled by a number of border incidents in 1989 with both North Yemen and Yemen (Aden; South Yemen) and might oppose the joint Yemeni plans to develop oil fields straddling the border between the two Yemens. North Yemen's Pres. Ali Abdullah Saleh indicated that if King Fahd accepted an invitation to visit San'a', the Yemenis hoped to sign a nonaggression pact similar to the one Saudi Arabia had concluded with Iraq in March. Saudi Arabia was directly concerned with rioting that took place in southern Jordan in April. One of the seeds of the riots was related to illicit border trade in grain. Traders from Ma'an in Jordan were crossing the border and selling subsidized Jordanian wheat and barley as Saudi products. A crackdown by Saudi officials sparked the trouble in Jordan.

On May 15 Saudi Justice Minister Ibrahim ibn Muhammad ibn Ibrahim ash-Shaikh resigned for health reasons and was replaced by Muhammad ibn Muhammad ibn Jubair. The retiring minister was one of two sons of Sheikh Muhammad ibn Ibrahim ash-Shaikh, grand mufti until his death in 1970. The fact that he was not replaced by another member of the same family confirmed that the family's liberalizing influence in the kingdom was on the wane. France reasserted itself as a major weapons supplier to Saudi Arabia with two deals, for missiles and frigates, having an overall value of some $2.8 billion. The Mistral portable missile was a replacement for the U.S. Stinger, supply of which had been blocked by Congress. The other deal, confirming France's dominant role in Saudi naval supplies, was for two, or possibly three, helicopter-carrying frigates.

Within OPEC, Saudi Arabia succeeded in weakening the organization's commitment to an $18-per-barrel reference price. At the June OPEC meeting, however, the kingdom

failed to achieve a pro-rata raising of the overall production ceiling to 20 million bbl per day. However, in November OPEC agreed to raise the overall ceiling to 22 million bbl per day for the first six months of 1990; the Saudi quota would be 5,380,000 bbl per day. The kingdom's moderation on oil pricing was expressed on October 19 by Petroleum Minister Hisham Nazer when he declared, "Too high a price merely sets the stage for too low a price." He added that OPEC and non-OPEC producers realized that the price of oil was "the price of moderation and stability."

Industry reports said Saudi Aramco, the national oil company, planned to spend around $15 billion on a drive to raise the kingdom's oil capacity to 10 million bbl per day in the mid-1990s. This compared with current production of 6.5 million bbl per day and export capacity of 14 million bbl per day. In early June Saudi Aramco announced the first discovery of an oil field since it took over the Saudi oil industry in November 1988. The al-Hawtah field, some 190 km (118 mi) from Riyadh, was the first discovery to be made outside the Eastern province and the Rub' al-Khali (Empty Quarter). It raised hopes that the central region would yield more world-scale finds. Saudi Aramco held its first board meeting on March 14 under Nazer's chairmanship. In a related development, King Fahd appointed five independent Saudi businessmen to the Supreme Oil Council, in apparent recognition of the kingdom's desire to allow the private sector to take over more responsibility for running the economy.

A major new project, estimated to cost $750 million–$800 million, was the private-sector aluminium smelter planned for Yanbu on the Red Sea. The Alujain Corp. signed a major alumina supply contract with Australia's Gove Aluminium, part of the CSR Group. Foreign companies would provide 40% of the equity, with the balance from local and Gulf Corporation Council investors. The scope of the public debate between government and business over privatization of some sectors of the economy widened at the end of May. The fourth Saudi Businessmen's Conference drew up a four-point plan covering privatization and three other areas: restructuring the private sector, Saudization of the work force, and promoting local investment.

In a widely reported public *majlis* (assembly) in April, King Fahd explained the rationale of the state's social security expenditure. It was, he said, intended to help the needy and the poor. The king stated the government's belief that one-quarter of social welfare and social security allocations went astray. It was not believed, however, that the kingdom was about to introduce any form of means testing, since the cost of running it would undoubtedly be more than the savings. At the end of April the king was also quoted as saying he did not believe in imprisoning debtors. The monarch said that a man unable to pay his debts when free was less likely to do so in prison. In situations where the debtor ended up in prison, King Fahd implied, the lender had erred, both in lending to someone who was incapable of repayment and in suing him before the court and putting him in jail, thereby depriving his family of their livelihood.   (JOHN WHELAN)

This article updates the *Macropædia* article ARABIA: *Saudi Arabia.*

SYRIA

A republic of southwestern Asia, Syria is on the Mediterranean Sea. Area: 185,180 sq km (71,498 sq mi). Pop. (1989 est.): 11,719,000. Cap.: Damascus. Monetary unit: Syrian pound, with (Oct. 2, 1989) an official rate of LS 11.225 to U.S. $1 (free rate of LS 18.16 = £1 sterling). President in 1989, Gen. Hafez al-Assad; prime minister, Mahmoud Zuabi.

Syria during 1989 was under pressure to accept the principle of a withdrawal of its forces from Lebanon, as part of a political settlement between rival factions. In mid-March Lebanese Christian military commander Michel Aoun (*see* BIOGRAPHIES), with the active support of Iraq, opened a military campaign to drive out Syrian forces, amounting to some 40,000 troops. Diplomatic pressure intensified at the Arab summit in Casablanca, Morocco, in May, when Pres. Hafez al-Assad was forced to make two key concessions—acquiescence in Egypt's return to the Arab League after a decade of exclusion and agreement to the establishment of a tripartite Arab committee charged with ending the Lebanese impasse. On April 3 the Shi'ite Muslim Amal and Hezbollah organizations concluded a united front with Syria against the Lebanese Christians. This coincided with a visit to Damascus by the Iranian foreign minister, Ali Akbar Velayati, for talks with President Assad and Foreign Minister Faruq ash-Shara. The Iranian government provided moral and financial support to extremist Shi'ite Muslim groups in Lebanon.

Despite its alliance with Muslim organizations and its forces' numerical advantage over the Christians in Lebanon, Syria's power base there was fragile. President Assad, who was anxious to improve his image in the West, failed to halt hostage taking by Hezbollah and some of the newer Palestinian splinter groups. However, during May and June Damascus managed to secure, through Amal, the release of two West Germans in return for an Arab jailed in Cyprus. Iraq's support for the Christians in Lebanon further polarized the divisions between these two Arab states. At the Casablanca summit Iraq's Pres. Saddam Hussein launched a bitter attack on Syria. In Geneva in April, Iraq sponsored the launch of a broad-based National Alliance for the Liberation of Syria. The move in February to create an Arab Cooperation Council composed of Iraq, Egypt, Yemen (San'a'; North Yemen), and Jordan further exposed Syria's isolation and impelled President Assad, who rarely

Yasir Arafat, the chairman of the Palestine Liberation Organization (PLO), raises the Palestinian flag at the new Palestinian embassy in Riyadh, Saudi Arabia, on Jan. 1, 1989; the Saudis had granted the PLO full diplomatic status the previous week.

traveled abroad, to visit Libya, Algeria, and Tunisia in late March. In December Syria and Egypt agreed to resume diplomatic relations.

There were sharp diplomatic exchanges with France when Foreign Minister ash-Shara visited Paris on March 21–22, and matters took a turn for the worse after France sent a hospital ship to a Christian Lebanese port. On April 12 Pres. François Mitterrand of France was obliged to make a public statement to the effect that French aid was humanitarian and was not targeted at any special group. Links with the United States remained frosty, particularly after the brief detention on March 3 of two U.S. military attachés, 60 km (37 mi) from Damascus. Relations with the Soviet Union were also in transition. Soviet Foreign Minister Eduard Shevardnadze began his Middle East tour in Damascus on February 17. Defense Minister Dimitry Yazov visited at the end of March, and indications were that a deal for Soviet SU-24 ground attack jets would go through. However, the Kremlin was eager to distance itself from the charge of supplying excessive weaponry to Syria. Partly as a result of Soviet pressure, President Assad moved to mend relations with Palestine Liberation Organization chairman Yasir Arafat. In June Syria released 164 Palestinians from the pro-Arafat al-Fatah movement; 500 Syrian and Lebanese political prisoners were also released, some of whom had been held since the Hamah uprising of 1982.

On June 23 Michel 'Aflaq (see OBITUARIES), founder of the Ba'th Party, died in exile in Paris. He had been sentenced to death in absentia in 1971.

Syria's economy suffered from poor harvests resulting from lack of rain. The Omar oil field proved a disappointment, yielding only some 30,000 bbl a day by midyear instead of the expected 100,000 bbl. However, over the past two years seven U.S. and European oil companies had signed production-sharing agreements with Syria. Effective from June 1 a 25% pay increase was awarded to public servants, including the Army and police, and pensions rose by 15%. This $500 million handout of public money was to be paid for by sharply increased customs duties and fuel prices.　　　　　　　　　　　　　　　　(JOHN WHELAN)

TUNISIA

A republic of North Africa, Tunisia lies on the Mediterranean Sea. Area: 154,530 sq km (59,664 sq mi). Pop. (1989 est.): 7,973,000. Cap.: Tunis. Monetary unit: Tunisian dinar, with (Oct. 2, 1989) a selling rate of 0.95 dinar to U.S. $1 (1.54 dinars = £1 sterling). President in 1989, Gen. Zine al-Abidine Ben Ali; prime ministers, Hedi Baccouche and, from September 27, Hamed Karoui.

Domestic issues dominated the Tunisian political scene during 1989. On April 2 presidential and legislative elections were held as the culmination of the process of political conciliation that had begun in 1988. The presidential election was a foregone conclusion since there was only one candidate, the incumbent, Zine al-Abidine Ben Ali, who was reelected with 99% of the vote. In the legislative election the Constitutional Democratic Rally, the successor to the Destourian Socialist Party, won all 141 seats.

In the wake of the election, the government of Prime Minister Hedi Baccouche was reshuffled. No major posts changed hands, and the reshuffle essentially removed some minor figures from the Bourguiba era while increasing the government's technocratic content. In midyear a general amnesty was announced, and over 5,400 political prisoners were released. The amnesty excluded those convicted of embezzlement or fraud; consequently, the former prime

minister, Mohammed Mzali, remained imprisoned. In September Pres. Ben Ali replaced Baccouche with Hamed Karoui after the former expressed growing opposition to Ben Ali's economic reforms.

The harvest in 1989, after initial promise, was once again a disaster, with yields reaching only 400,000 tons (20% of the average yield) as a result of locusts and drought. In August food subsidies on bread, flour, semolina, sugar, and cooking oil were cut by an average of 14%.

The government continued to implement economic reforms introduced in 1987. Private investment was expected to account for 64% of total investment and to create 46,-000 new jobs. Foreign investment continued to be strong, despite a 5% fall during 1988. The privatization program was slowed during the year in order to avoid popular unrest over further job losses.

The poor harvest was responsible for a significant rise in imports in 1988, when the trade deficit rose by 50%. Despite a strong export growth of 39% in the first eight months of 1989, a substantial deficit persisted. Oil output was expected to decline further as Tunisia approached becoming a net oil importer. Tunisia was able to control its level of foreign debt and to avoid further significant loans. Foreign debt, however, still stood at $5 billion, with debt service during 1989 placed at $1.2 billion.

In the international field bilateral relations with Libya improved, and Libyan leader Col. Mu'ammar al-Qadhdhafi visited Tunisia in February. Joint Libyan-Tunisian projects, including offshore oil developments and the trans-Tunisia pipeline from Algeria to Libya, moved ahead. Links with France, Spain, Saudi Arabia, and Syria were also strengthened.　　　　　　　　　　　(GEORGE JOFFÉ)

This article updates the *Macropædia* article NORTH AFRICA: *Tunisia*.

TURKEY

A republic of Asia Minor and southeastern Europe, Turkey has coastlines on the Aegean, Black, and Mediterranean seas. Area: 779,452 sq km (300,948 sq mi), including 23,764 sq km in Europe. Pop. (1989 est.): 55,541,000. Cap.: Ankara. Monetary unit: Turkish lira, with (Oct. 2, 1989) a free rate of 2,230 liras to U.S. $1 (3,609 liras = £1 sterling). Presidents in 1989, Gen. Kenan Evren and, from November 9, Turgut Ozal; prime ministers, Turgut Ozal and, from November 9, Yildirim Akbulut.

Turkish refugees wait with their belongings at a train station near the Turkish-Bulgarian border. Some 310,000 ethnic Turks fled from Bulgaria to Turkey to escape a forced assimilation plan that forbade them to speak Turkish and required them to take Slavic names.

The popularity of the ruling conservative Motherland Party (MP) slumped in 1989 in line with a sharp drop in economic growth. In the local government elections held on March 26, the MP finished third with 22% of the total poll. The Social Democratic Populist Party, led by Erdal Inonu, was first with 28%, winning six of the eight metropolitan areas (including the largest, Istanbul; the capital, Ankara; and the cities of Izmir and Adana). It was followed, with 26%, by the conservative Right Path Party, led by former prime minister Suleyman Demirel (who had been ousted by the military in 1980). The opposition thereupon demanded a dissolution of the National Assembly before the latter could elect a new president of the republic to succeed Kenan Evren, whose seven-year term expired on November 9. Arguing that the local poll did not affect the five-year mandate that he had won in the November 1987 parliamentary elections, Prime Minister Turgut Ozal himself ran for the presidency and was duly elected on October 31, by 263 votes of the MP members of the assembly, while the opposition boycotted the proceedings. In accordance with the constitution, Ozal then resigned the leadership of the MP. On November 9 he appointed Yildirim Akbulut as the new prime minister.

In the economy, stagnation was accompanied by inflation. The growth rate, which had been revised down to 3.4% for 1988, dropped further in 1989, largely as the result of a drought that necessitated large-scale wheat imports. Inflation continued at an annual rate above 70%. It was restrained by a decline in investments but was fed by large raises in public-service salaries, which had been preceded by the first important wave of labour agitation since the 1980 coup. However, the cutback in investments and a fall in internal demand allowed Turkey to end 1988 with a record surplus of $1.5 billion in its external current account and to remain solvent, while meeting its foreign debt repayment schedule, in 1989.

Relations with Syria continued to be strained by the facilities afforded in Syrian-controlled Lebanon to the terrorists of the secessionist Kurdish PKK (Kurdish Workers' Party). A summer campaign by Turkish security forces against PKK bands in the mountains of the southeast failed to stem terrorist activity.

Foreign affairs were dominated by the dispute with Bulgaria over its maltreatment of its Turkish minority (whose numbers were estimated at between one million and 1.5 million). Following the expulsion by Bulgaria of ethnic Turkish human rights activists, Turkey suspended visa requirements for Bulgarian citizens on May 30. By August 22, when Turkey reimposed visas, some 310,000 ethnic Turks had fled to Turkey. While several thousand more were then given Turkish entry visas, the inability of Turkish authorities to care adequately for the refugees caused a large number of them (estimated at 60,000 at the end of November) to return to Bulgaria. Turkey insisted that Bulgaria should negotiate a proper migration agreement while putting an end to its policy of forcible assimilation of the Turkish minority. Thanks to the mediation of the Organization of the Islamic Conference, Turkish Foreign Minister Mesut Yilmaz and Bulgarian Deputy Prime Minister Georgy Yordanov met in Kuwait on October 30 and started to discuss the problem. On December 29 a senior Bulgarian official announced that Bulgarian Turks would be allowed to adopt Muslim names, forbidden as part of the assimilation campaign.

Trade with the U.S. increased and cooperation continued, notably in the buildup of Turkey's defense industries. Turkey fitted in smoothly with East-West efforts to promote stability in Europe.　　　　(ANDREW MANGO)

UNITED ARAB EMIRATES

Consisting of Abu Dhabi, Ajman, Dubayy, al-Fujayrah, Ra's al-Khaymah, ash-Shariqah, and Umm al-Qaywayn, the United Arab Emirates is a federation of seven largely autonomous emirates located on the eastern Arabian Peninsula. Area: 77,700 sq km (30,000 sq mi). Pop. (1989 est.): 1,827,000. Provisional cap.: Abu Dhabi. Monetary unit: United Arab Emirates dirham, with (Oct. 2, 1989) a free rate of 3.67 dirhams to U.S. $1 (5.94 dirhams = £1 sterling). President in 1989, Sheikh Zaid ibn Sultan an-Nahayan; prime minister, Sheikh Rashid ibn Said al-Maktum.

The former ruler of Abu Dhabi, Sheikh Shakhbut ibn Sultan an-Nahayan (see OBITUARIES), died on Feb. 11, 1989, aged 83. This royal death—Shakhbut abdicated in 1966 after ruling the emirate for 38 years—marked a break with the past, emphasizing the U.A.E.'s transition into a new era. On October 12 Deputy Prime Minister Sheikh Hamdan ibn Muhammad an-Nahayan's death was announced by the presidential court. Sheikh Hamdan, a cousin of the U.A.E. president, was another influential figure in the years after the formation of the federation in December 1971.

With the Gulf war effectively over, the U.A.E. embarked on a new program of expansion in tourism and economic development. It was estimated that by early 1990 the Jebel Ali free zone outside Dubayy would have attracted some $1 billion in private investment. Emirates, the international airline of the U.A.E., opened services to Jidda in Saudi Arabia in March, Bandar Abbas in Iran in June, and Kuwait in July. The local Almulla group in Dubayy was building a new 350-room luxury hotel that would be open in 1992. As part of this open-market strategy, diplomatic relations with the Eastern bloc countries were being strengthened. Poland was recognized on September 4.

Pres. Sheikh Zaid ibn Sultan an-Nahayan visited the U.K. in July. A defense deal involving supply of $170 million worth of British Aerospace Hawks was under discussion between the U.A.E. and the U.K.　(JOHN WHELAN)

This article updates the Macropædia article ARABIA: United Arab Emirates.

YEMEN, PEOPLE'S DEMOCRATIC REPUBLIC OF

The People's Democratic Republic of Yemen (Yemen [Aden]; South Yemen) is located in the southern coastal region of the Arabian Peninsula, on the Gulf of Aden and the Arabian Sea. Area: 336,869 sq km (130,066 sq mi). Pop. (1989 est.): 2,406,000. Cap.: Aden. Monetary unit: Yemeni dinar, with (Oct. 2, 1989) a par value of 0.35 dinar to U.S. $1 (free rate of 0.56 dinar = £1 sterling). Chairman of the Presidium of the Supreme People's Council in 1989, Haidar Abu Bakr al-Attas; prime minister, Yasin Said Numan.

In March 1989 an amnesty was announced for some 35 persons convicted of treason following the 1986 coup, which left 4,000 dead. Former president Ali Nasir Muhammad Husani, in exile in the Yemen Arab Republic (Yemen [San'a']; North Yemen), welcomed the news and indicated that he had no further presidential ambitions.

On June 22 Yemen Socialist Party leader Ali Salem al-Beidh made the first telephone call on South Yemen's direct dial international link to Pres. Ali Abdullah Saleh of North Yemen; the two discussed Yemeni political unity. On December 1 the two countries announced agreement on a constitution for a unified state.

In September the ruling party introduced political reforms both to reconcile the former president's supporters to the regime and to end administrative and policy duplication between the party and the Marxist-oriented government. An agreement was reached on August 18 with North

Yemen to establish an oil-exploration consortium in the Ma'rib-al-Jawf neutral zone between the two countries. Reported clashes on the Saudi border in June caused disruption to oil exploration in the Sirr Hazar region. Although both countries were eager to minimize the importance of the incidents, the French oil company Elf Aquitaine was forced to break off seismic work. In October talks were held with the U.S. (JOHN WHELAN)

This article updates the *Macropædia* article ARABIA: *People's Democratic Republic of Yemen.*

YEMEN ARAB REPUBLIC

The Yemen Arab Republic (Yemen [San'a']; North Yemen) is situated in the southwestern coastal region of the Arabian Peninsula, on the Red Sea. Area: 195,000 sq km (75,300 sq mi). Pop. (1989 est.): 8,834,000. Cap.: San'a'. Monetary unit: Yemen rial, with (Oct. 2, 1989) a par value of 9.76 rials = U.S. $1 (15.79 rials = £1 sterling). President in 1989, Col. Ali Abdullah Saleh; prime minister, Abdel Aziz Abdel Ghani.

In 1989 the Arab Cooperation Council, a new group consisting of Egypt, Iraq, Jordan, and North Yemen, held its first summit in San'a' on September 25–26. The heads of state signed several economic and trade accords. The four states hoped that the measures would shape an alliance, announced in February, into a coherent common market. There were signs that the People's Democratic Republic of Yemen (Yemen [Aden]; South Yemen) was interested in joining the group. The presence of Palestine Liberation Organization chairman Yassir Arafat in San'a' during the summit indicated a new Arab alignment and highlighted Syria's political isolation. A draft constitution for a unified Yemen was made public on December 1. It was to be referred for ratification to the legislatures of North and South Yemen within six months.

Oil exports, which first started in the fall of 1987, were running at 200,000 bbl a day in 1989. In October Pres. Ali Abdullah Saleh announced the ratification of an oil production-sharing agreement with Canada's International Petroleum Corporation—the fifth such deal with foreign oil companies since the early 1980s. There were also indications that exploration would proceed in the border area with South Yemen following reported agreement on August 18 to award a concession. (See *Yemen, People's Democratic Republic of,* above.) (JOHN WHELAN)

This article updates the *Macropædia* article ARABIA: *Yemen Arab Republic.*

East Asia

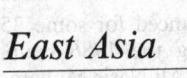

CHINA

The People's Republic of China is situated in eastern Asia, with coastlines on the Yellow Sea and the East and South China seas. Area: 9,572,900 sq km (3,696,100 sq mi), including Tibet and excluding Taiwan. (See *Taiwan,* below.) Pop. (1989 est., excluding Taiwan): 1,104,275,000. Cap.: Beijing (Peking). Monetary unit: renminbi yuan, with (Oct. 2, 1989) a free rate of 3.72 yuan to U.S. $1 (6.02 yuan = £1 sterling). General secretaries of the Communist Party of China in 1989, Zhao Ziyang (Chao Tzu-yang) and, from June 24, Jiang Zemin (Chiang Tse-min); presidents, Li Xiannian (Li Hsien-nien) and, from April 8, Yang Shangkun (Yang Shang-k'un); premiers, Zhao and, from April 9, Li Peng (Li P'eng).

In the spring of 1989, a crisis that had been brewing in China for more than two years erupted in a wide-scale popular movement for political change that shook the foundations of Communist rule. Unlike Communist rulers in Eastern Europe who made unprecedented concessions in the face of similar challenges, the senior leaders of the Communist Party of China (CPC), after weeks of indecisive high-level political infighting, ordered a military crackdown on the student-led democracy movement. The June 4 massacre of roughly a thousand unarmed students and their supporters in Beijing (Peking) not far from China's symbolic centre, Tiananmen (T'ien-an-men) Square, shocked the world as few recent events had done and ushered in a new period of political repression in China.

In the aftermath of what they chose to call a "counter-revolutionary rebellion," China's leaders continued to proclaim their adherence to the economic reform policies of the past decade. At the same time, however, they began to recentralize economic controls and to rein in the flourishing private sector of the economy. In the realm of foreign affairs, the normalization of relations with the Soviet Union was finally accomplished during Soviet leader Mikhail Gorbachev's visit to Beijing in May 1989, but this undoubted achievement was offset by a crisis in relations with the U.S. that was provoked by the Tiananmen massacre.

As a tidal wave of democratization rolled across the European part of the Communist world, the meaning of the Chinese model became dramatically altered. The earlier view of China as a positive example of enlightened transformation worthy of emulation did not survive the military crackdown. In the rapidly changing Communist world, as well as in the West, the "Chinese solution" became a new code name for political repression, and the actions of China's elderly, hard-line rulers a grim reminder of the totalitarian reflexes of Leninist-style political systems.

Domestic Affairs and the Economy. The early successes of the economic reform program initiated by senior leader Deng Xiaoping (Teng Hsiao-p'ing) in 1978 were significant and had long obscured from view the lack of any concomitant program of substantive political reforms in China. Beginning with the imprisonment of the Democracy Wall activists in 1979 and continuing through the suppression of the student movement of December 1986–January 1987, Deng and his associates had repeatedly demonstrated that they would brook no opposition to the CPC's political monopoly. They viewed any autonomous political activity as a dangerous challenge to their own and the party's authority.

During this same time, however, the pressures for political change were building up within the Communist Party itself as well as within Chinese society as a whole. These pressures were created by the very reform policies that Deng had initiated. As the CPC loosened its control over the economy, liberalized its policies toward intellectuals, and opened China to the outside world, Chinese society gradually liberated itself from the grip of Maoist-era repression and orthodoxy. Within the party, radical young reformers pushed for thoroughgoing price reforms and the further privatization of the economy.

In the political realm, however, the Deng regime proved unwilling to deal with the consequences of its own policies. It failed to create new political institutions for consultation and power sharing through which the political aspirations of significant sectors of Chinese society could be articulated and their demands accommodated. This failure led directly to the confrontation between the Communist regime and a significant portion of the Chinese people it claimed to

represent. Unable to find an institutional outlet for expressing their interests, Chinese students, soon joined by a wide spectrum of workers and other urban residents, took to the streets of Beijing and dozens of other Chinese cities in the largest popular political demonstrations that China had ever witnessed.

By 1988 the reform movement had reached a critical juncture. The economic reforms of the preceding decade had brought new prosperity to a considerable part of the Chinese countryside. A flourishing, consumer-oriented urban economy had replaced the Spartan poverty of the Mao Zedong (Mao Tse-tung) era, and a burgeoning foreign trade linked China's coastal cities to the outside world.

At the same time, serious problems had emerged for which the regime appeared to have no workable solutions. Among the most important of these was a rate of inflation that was probably twice the officially estimated figure of nearly 20%. The inflation hit particularly hard at those on fixed incomes—including intellectuals and salaried workers—who had no supplemental sources of income. Second, there was a rapidly rising crime rate, caused in part by the influx of rural people into the cities in search of work, which produced a vast population of homeless, marginal labourers. Third, corruption permeated the government bureaucracy. Leading party officials had long enjoyed numerous special privileges. In the newly permissive atmosphere that sanctioned personal enrichment, many officials brazenly abused their official positions to advance their own and their families' economic interests through private business deals, bribery, and the siphoning off of public funds.

The democracy movement of 1989 was the culmination of repeated efforts by party and nonparty intellectuals to achieve the democratization of Chinese socialism through peaceful means. Deng himself had often proclaimed the need for political reform, but he invoked the Four Cardinal Principles—adherence to the socialist road, the people's democratic dictatorship, leadership by the CPC, and Marxist-Leninist-Maoist thought—to define the boundaries of acceptable political action. In practice these criteria served to block political change. Party leaders viewed any unsanctioned political activity as a threat to their monopoly of power. By the mid-1980s the Chinese reform coalition had become fundamentally divided into radical and conservative wings. The former pushed for ad-

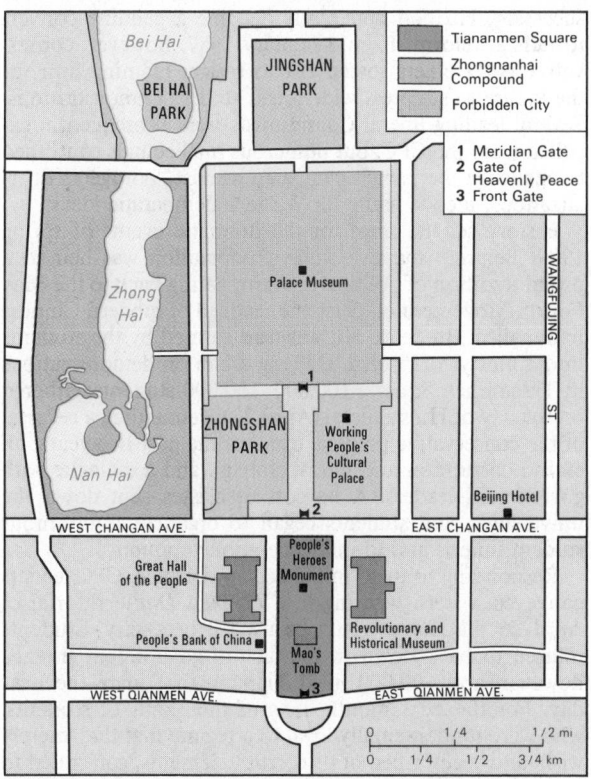

Tiananmen Square, the symbolic heart of China, was the scene of a protest that began in April when students defied a ban on demonstrations in the square. On May 20 martial law was instituted. Nonviolent popular resistance kept troops from the centre of the city for several weeks, but on June 3–4 they moved in, clearing the square and killing civilians in the surrounding area.

ditional economic changes, including price reforms, while the latter opposed further reforms by invoking the spectre of a loss of party authority and by claiming that socialism was endangered.

The death of former CPC general secretary Hu Yaobang (Hu Yao-pang; *see* OBITUARIES) on April 15, 1989, was the spark that ignited perhaps the most remarkable six weeks in modern Chinese history. An idiosyncratic figure who had nevertheless been chosen by Deng in 1980 as his

STUART FRANKLIN—MAGNUM

A lone man faces down a column of tanks en route to Tiananmen Square, where Chinese students were demonstrating for democracy. He pleaded with the soldiers in the lead tank before being pulled away by bystanders.

successor, Hu had apparently become a genuine convert to radical reform. In mid-January 1987, however, conservative party elders forced Hu to resign, blaming him for the failure to suppress widespread student demonstrations. Several leading liberal Communists were subsequently expelled from the CPC, but numerous intellectuals continued to challenge the party's campaign against "bourgeois liberalization," a code name for Western democratic ideas.

History set the stage for the dramatic events of spring 1989. Beijing's massive student population was heir to a proud tradition of political activism dating back to the May Fourth Movement of 1919, the seedbed of modern Chinese nationalism. In death Hu was transformed by the students into a martyr of reform. Defying a ban on demonstrations in Tiananmen Square, 100,000–150,000 students gathered on the day of Hu's funeral (April 22), demanding a reversal of the conservative political trend of the past two years, an end to corruption and bureaucratism, and a dialogue with government leaders. A boycott of classes shut down the universities, and students began to organize autonomous student unions and to influence public opinion.

Responding to these initial acts of defiance, CPC leaders conveyed a stern warning in a *People's Daily* editorial of April 26 that force would be used if necessary. Students refused to back down in the face of government threats, however, and 100,000 filled Tiananmen Square the next day. For the next month, tens of thousands of students, who were fundamentally loyal to a regime that they merely wished to see purified of its corrupt elements, continued to occupy the centre of Beijing.

Caught off balance by the massive outpouring of public support for the students, China's divided leadership temporized while the students perfected their organizations and escalated their demands. There quickly emerged a group of young student leaders, including such figures as Wuer Kaixi (Uerkesh Daolet; *see* BIOGRAPHIES), Wang Dan (Wang Tan), Chai Ling (Ch'ai Ling), and many others who demonstrated an impressive capacity for leadership and self-governance. Meanwhile, in the nation's capital, groups of workers, office personnel, journalists, and even policemen and public security cadres organized themselves to support what had become a truly popular movement. By that time, the news from Beijing had ignited similar protests and demonstrations in dozens of other Chinese cities. Shortly before Gorbachev arrived in Beijing on May 15, as many as three thousand students on a hunger strike occupied Tiananmen Square to dramatize their demands, which now included the ouster of Premier Li Peng (Li P'eng). The world media, which had gone to Beijing to cover the Sino-Soviet summit, were on hand to provide unparalleled coverage of the pro-democracy movement, which included reports of one million people demonstrating in Beijing on May 17; the reports were then beamed back into China by shortwave radio.

In the protracted inner-party debate over how to handle the crisis, CPC General Secretary Zhao Ziyang (Chao Tzu-yang), who favoured making concessions, was first isolated within, then removed from, the ruling Political Bureau Standing Committee. With Deng supporting a military solution to the crisis, Li announced on May 20 the imposition of martial law in parts of Beijing; army troops from outside the capital were also deployed on the outskirts of the city. Yet for two more weeks nonviolent popular resistance prevented the soldiers from advancing to the student encampment in Tiananmen Square. There the student occupation was slowly winding down, but in a last burst of defiant energy, a plaster statue of the Goddess of Democracy, which subsequently became a widely recognized symbol of the democratic movement, was erected in the north end of the square.

With Zhao now out of the way, CPC hard-liners moved to reassert their badly damaged authority and regain control of events. On the night of June 3–4, heavily armed troops of the 27th Army cleared Tiananmen Square of its remaining occupants and attacked and killed perhaps a thousand demonstrators in the nearby streets and alleys. Similar bloodshed occurred in Chengdu (Ch'eng-tu), the capital of Sichuan (Szechwan) province, and elsewhere as troops and security personnel violently suppressed the pro-democracy movement. On June 8 Deng congratulated the Army on suppressing what was officially termed a "counterrevolutionary rebellion" purportedly aimed at overthrowing the socialist system in China. The security forces arrested thousands of those who had led or participated in the democratic movement and publicly executed more than two dozen persons accused of violent counterrevolutionary crimes. In the universities, research institutes, and other institutions where the democratic movement had made significant inroads, an atmosphere of repression reigned. Campaigns to indoctrinate students and intellectuals with Marxist-Leninist ideology were undertaken as the regime reverted to the control mechanisms of the Maoist past.

At the fourth plenum of the Central Committee in late June, Zhao, who stood accused of responsibility for the "counterrevolutionary rebellion," was formally stripped of his power, and a wide-scale purge of his supporters ensued. In his place, Jiang Zemin (Chiang Tse-min; *see* BIOGRAPHIES), the former Shanghai Communist Party boss, was promoted to general secretary. A new Political Bureau Standing Committee was also selected, consisting of Jiang Zemin, Li Peng, Qiao Shi (Ch'iao Shih), Yao Yilin (Yao Yi-lin), Song Ping (Sung P'ing), and Li Ruihan (Li Jui-han). Behind these men stood such elderly first-generation revolutionaries as Deng, Pres. Yang Shangkun (Yang Shang-k'un), Chen Yun (Ch'en Yün), and Peng Zhen (P'eng Chen), who had ordered the military crackdown.

Deng's two previous attempts to ensure an orderly political succession had singularly failed. First Hu and then Zhao were found wanting. Then Deng attempted to confer his authority on Jiang, whom he designated as the "core" of the new party leadership. Most significantly, at the fifth plenum of the Central Committee in November, Deng retired from his last official position, the chairmanship of the CPC's powerful Military Commission, and was replaced by Jiang. By occupying both the top party and military positions, Jiang leapfrogged over his potential rival for power, Li Peng, whose unpopularity had become evident during the spring. Yet Jiang's political longevity was uncertain at best. Not only did he lack the personal prestige of the old revolutionaries and an independent power base, but he also faced the formidable task of restoring the shattered authority of the party and the Army and of reviving faith in an ideology that many Chinese no longer took seriously. Moreover, the collapse of the hard-line Communist regimes in Bulgaria, Czechoslovakia, East Germany, and Romania and the self-emancipation of Hungary and Poland were ill omens for China's leaders.

Quite a few leaders of the democratic movement escaped abroad, where they vowed to continue the struggle for political reform. Meeting in Paris on July 20, 1989, such prominent figures as the intellectuals Liu Binyan (Liu Pin-yen), Yan Jiaqi (Yen Chia-ch'i), and Su Shaozhi (Su Shao-chih), student leader Wuer Kaixi, and the industrialist Wan Runnan (Wan Jun-nan) established the Democratic Chinese Alliance with the long-term goal of establishing political pluralism and democratic socialism in China.

With the liberal reformers in eclipse, the conservative party leaders pursued policies of economic retrenchment and recentralization. Instead of moving toward a rationalized price system and additional market-oriented reforms, they instituted new administrative measures and initiated political campaigns to combat corruption, price gouging, and the proliferation of shoddy or dangerous goods. The economy slowed down considerably as investment in construction was slashed, and millions of unemployed workers were urged to return to the countryside. Inflation proved very difficult to control. The state moved to severely restrict rural and urban private enterprises, which not only had provided employment opportunities for large numbers of persons but had also created an autonomous social sphere outside the party's direct control. The new leadership favoured a rationalized form of the old, highly centralized state planning system that had long been one of the key defining characteristics of Soviet-style socialism.

The political turmoil in China and the uncertain future of the new leadership so disturbed international financial groups that they withheld offers of new loans and investments. China no longer seemed to be a modernizing, politically stable country. Tourism, a lucrative source of foreign exchange, plummeted in the second half of 1989, and the foreign trade deficit grew.

Foreign Affairs. The long-awaited Sino-Soviet summit meeting (May 15–18, 1989) turned out to be an embarrassment for China's leaders because the hundreds of thousands of demonstrators occupying the centre of Beijing necessitated changes in Gorbachev's schedule. Nevertheless, the visit served the important symbolic purpose of ending the long-standing Sino-Soviet conflict. Amid affirmations of mutual friendship and respect for the principles of sovereignty and nonintervention in each other's internal affairs, Deng and Gorbachev initiated a new era in the relations between their two countries. Chinese leaders looked toward the further expansion of Sino-Soviet trade and scientific and technological exchanges, but there was no reason to suppose that the U.S.S.R. could do more than supplement China's reliance on the non-Communist market economies for its further economic modernization.

The crisis in Beijing's relations with Washington was foreshadowed by Sino-American sparring over various human rights issues and the situation in Tibet. After June 4, China charged the U.S. with aiding and abetting the "counterrevolutionary rebellion" and condemned the U.S. for providing sanctuary in its Beijing embassy to two leading intellectual critics of the Communist regime, Fang Lizhi (Fang Li-chih) and his wife, Li Shuixian (Li Shuihsien). Chinese officials bitterly condemned the economic sanctions that the U.S. Congress passed in response to the Tiananmen massacre and responded by restricting the flow of Chinese students to the U.S. Most of the 40,000 Chinese studying in the U.S. had vigorously supported the democracy movement and were unwilling to return home. At the same time, Beijing repeatedly assured American investors and businessmen that China's open-door policy remained in effect. In December Pres. George Bush, at pains to prevent a complete Sino-U.S. rupture, vetoed a bill extending the visas of Chinese students (though he said he would take the same steps administratively), waived some economic sanctions, and sent a high-level delegation to Beijing. It was also revealed that a similar delegation had gone to Beijing in July. Some congressional leaders threatened legislation to counter these moves when Congress reconvened in January 1990. In retrospect, 1989 would undoubtedly be viewed as a watershed in modern Chinese history.

(STEVEN I. LEVINE)

JAPAN

A constitutional monarchy in the northwestern Pacific Ocean, Japan comprises an archipelago with four main islands (Hokkaido, Honshu, Kyushu, and Shikoku), the Ryukyus (including Okinawa), and minor adjacent islands. Area: 377,835 sq km (145,883 sq mi). Pop. (1989 est.): 123,120,000. Cap.: Tokyo. Monetary unit: yen, with (Oct. 2, 1989) a free rate of 139.52 yen to U.S. $1 (225.75 yen = £1 sterling). Emperors, Hirohito and, from Jan. 7, 1989, Akihito; prime ministers, Noboru Takeshita to June 2, Sosuke Uno to August 9, and Toshiki Kaifu.

The year 1989 was one of transition for Japan. The death of Emperor Hirohito (*see* OBITUARIES) after a 62-year reign (the longest in Japanese history) brought an end to the Showa era. The period (1926–88) had witnessed the growth of incipient democracy in the 1920s; the rise of militarism, imperialism, and aggression in the 1930s; a disastrous military defeat in the 1940s; and the recovery of Japan, which by the 1980s had become a major economic power. Some measure of the nation's status was revealed by the fact that about 160 representatives of countries and 26 delegates from international organizations attended the emperor's funeral, which was held in Tokyo on February 24.

At the same time, however, domestic politics were in disarray. Wracked by a scandal arising out of "money politics," the ruling Liberal-Democratic Party (LDP) suffered a loss in a general election for the first time in three decades. In less than three months no fewer than three LDP leaders occupied the post of prime minister.

Domestic Affairs. On January 7 Hirohito, the Showa emperor, died of duodenal cancer at the age of 87. Immediately, a succession ceremony was held for his son Akihito, whose reign was named Heisei ("Achieving Peace"). In his first audience with representatives of the nation on January 9, the new emperor promised to be "at one with the people." In a news conference held August 4 at the Imperial Palace, Emperor Akihito stressed his desire to abide

M. WADA—GAMMA/LIAISON

Takako Doi, leader of the Japan Socialist Party, gives the victory sign after opposition parties won a majority of seats in Japan's upper house. The Socialist Party gained significant ground in the wake of scandals that had plagued the ruling Liberal-Democratic Party.

by the constitution of Japan, which limits his role to being "a symbol of the state and of the unity of the people."

Meanwhile, the unity of the people was being sorely tested by a scandal affecting the LDP. In August 1988 opposition party spokesmen had first pressed for an investigation of private sales of unlisted stocks in a fast-growing real-estate firm, the Recruit Cosmos Co. By June 12, after a 260-day inquiry, the Justice Ministry made a final report to the Diet. By that time, former prime minister Yasuhiro Nakasone had been publicly questioned and his staff implicated, although he was not indicted. A sitting prime minister, Noboru Takeshita, had been forced to resign. Three Cabinet ministers had left their posts. At least 16 businessmen and politicians (including 2 Diet members) were indicted; 14 were arrested; and almost all of the leaders of the LDP were included in the list of "gray" figures tainted by the probe.

Finance Minister Kiichi Miyazawa (one of the "three new leaders" of the LDP, with Takeshita and Secretary-General Shintaro Abe) had resigned in December 1988. On December 27 Prime Minister Takeshita had reshuffled his Cabinet, pledging to make 1989 a "year of political reform," but three days later his new justice minister, Takashi Hasegawa, resigned after it was revealed that his funding organization had received Recruit money. On January 24 the director of the Economic Planning Agency (EPA), Ken Harada, also stepped down. The Recruit inquiry also entered the realm of private business. Late in 1988 the chairman of the publicly regulated Nippon Telegraph & Telephone Corp. (NTT), Hisashi Shinto, resigned when it was revealed that preflotation Recruit shares were purchased for him. On February 13 former Recruit chairman Hiromasa Ezoe (*see* BIOGRAPHIES), an aide, and two former NTT executives were arrested for involvement in bribery. On March 6 Shinto and his former secretary, Kozo Murata, were held on charges of accepting bribes from Recruit. Ezoe and Shinto were indicted on March 5 and 27, respectively.

When the 114th session of the Diet resumed on February 10, party strength was apportioned as follows: in the (lower) House of Representatives, LDP 297, Japan Socialist Party (JSP) 85, Clean Government Party (Komeito) 56, Democratic Socialist Party (DSP) 29, Japan Communist Party (JCP) 27, independents 6, vacancies 12 (total 512); in the (upper) House of Councillors, LDP 143, JSP 42, Komeito 23, DSP 12, JCP 17, minor parties and independents 14, vacancies 1 (total 252).

Despite its solid majorities, the LDP faced delay in the Diet as opposition parties demanded, on March 6, that former prime minister Nakasone be subpoenaed to testify on his connections with Recruit. On March 29 Kyodo News Service announced that public support for the Takeshita Cabinet had plummeted to 12.6%, the lowest rating in three decades of surveys. On April 7 leaders of the four major opposition parties called for the resignation of the prime minister, a dissolution of the lower house, and a snap general election. The trouble was, opposition leaders were also caught up in the scandal. On February 7 the DSP chairman, Saburo Tsukamoto, announced his resignation from the party. In May Komeito Dietman Katsuya Ikeda was indicted, and on May 17 the chairman of Komeito, Junya Yano, resigned because of Recruit ties.

On April 11 Takeshita admitted to the Diet that his support groups had received cash and stock worth about $1.2 million from Recruit. On April 25 the prime minister, bowing to the inevitable, announced that he would step down "in order to regain the trust of the people." He stated, however, that before resigning, he would proceed with a planned visit to Southeast Asia. Finally, on May 28, after offering testimony in the Diet, former prime minister Nakasone announced that he would leave the LDP and resign his position as head of an 86-member faction, but he would not relinquish his seat in the lower house.

On June 2 Foreign Minister Sosuke Uno was elected by the Diet to be Japan's 47th prime minister. He pledged a "fresh" start to reorganize the LDP into a "clean" party. Widely recognized as a caretaker leader, he lasted only 53 days before announcing his resignation. He was brought down not so much by the Recruit affair as by reports of a personal liaison with "Ms. A.," a part-time geisha, and by the Liberal-Democrats' electoral losses.

The majority party had campaigned for the regular triennial House of Councillors election at a disadvantage. Continuing distrust arising from the Recruit scandal, popular resentment over a new consumption tax, farmers' rebellion against liberalization of Japan's agricultural market, and women's denunciation of Uno's private life—all served to work against the LDP. Voters in the Tokyo Metropolitan Assembly election had sent an ominous signal to the majority party on July 3, when the LDP lost 20 of its 63

AFP PHOTO

Members of Japan's Liberal-Democratic Party applaud Toshiki Kaifu (standing) upon his election as prime minister. Kaifu, a former education minister, had been challenged by Socialist Party leader Takako Doi but was elected prime minister by vote of the Diet's lower house.

seats. On July 23, in the upper house election (for 126 or half the seats in the chamber), the LDP won only 36 seats (of 69 at risk). With 73 seats uncontested, the party held 109 seats (down from 142). Under their triumphant leader, Takako Doi (*see* Biographies), the JSP parlayed 22 seats at risk into 46 (total 66). For the first time, the strength of combined opposition parties was greater than that of the LDP. Ideological fractures, however, continued to split the opposition.

On August 8 the LDP selected a former education minister, Toshiki Kaifu, to fill out Uno's term as party president, due to end in October. The next day the lower house nominated him to be prime minister. The upper house, however, chose Doi, the first woman ever named by a chamber to be prime minister. By law, in such a deadlock, the will of the lower house prevails, and Kaifu was elected prime minister. At age 58 he became the second youngest occupant of that office in Japan's history.

Although the Cabinet offices were, as usual, proportionately distributed according to major LDP factions, Kaifu did break new ground. Responding to the power of women's votes in recent elections, he appointed two women: Mayumi Moriyama (to head the Environment Agency) and Sumiko Takahara (director of the EPA). When Chief Cabinet Secretary Tokuo Yamashita resigned on August 25 amid reports of extramarital affairs, Kaifu moved Moriyama up to the slot of Cabinet spokesperson, the first woman to hold this sensitive position. In October Kaifu was elected LDP president (and therefore prime minister) for a full two-year term. At about the same time, a new scandal was surfacing, involving contributions to both the LDP and opposition parties from the lucrative pachinko (pinball) industry.

The Economy. In late December 1988 the LDP had rammed through the Diet a controversial 3% consumption tax bill. The JSP and JCP had boycotted the session; the DSP and Komeito attended but voted against the bill. The levy went into effect on April 1 amid confusion over how the sweeping tax reform was to be implemented. Without doubt, the new tax contributed to LDP losses in by-elections (Fukuoka, Niigata, and Tokyo) and in the July general election for the upper house.

Although the Takeshita Cabinet in January approved a 60.4 trillion yen budget for the fiscal year beginning April 1, proceedings were stalled in the Diet because of the Recruit scandal. In late April the LDP unilaterally passed the budget through the lower house. Overall expenditures (in effect May 27) rose 6.6% over the fiscal 1988 level. Defense spending was increased by 5.9% and official development assistance (ODA) by 7.8%. The nominal gross national product (GNP) for fiscal 1988, according to the EPA, reached 371.3 trillion yen. The real GNP growth rate was 5.1% (surpassing the official projection of 4.9%). In January the Cabinet predicted that Japan would have 4% real growth in fiscal 1989 (ending March 31, 1990).

Foreign Affairs. Although their tenure tended to be uncertain at home, all three prime ministers were busy on the diplomatic front in 1989. On February 2 Prime Minister Takeshita became the first foreign leader to call on newly elected U.S. Pres. George Bush. While in the U.S., Takeshita also visited UN Secretary-General Javier Pérez de Cuéllar in New York City. Back in Tokyo, the prime minister met Bush again on February 24, on the occasion of Emperor Hirohito's funeral. In late April, before he left office, he made a nine-day tour of member states of the Association of Southeast Asian Nations (ASEAN).

As foreign minister, Uno had accompanied Takeshita on the trip to Washington. His next meeting with President Bush came on July 14, at the Paris summit meeting of seven leading industrial democracies. Uno won praise for his pledge to provide more than $40 billion in aid to less developed nations and to improve the world environment. One of Prime Minister Kaifu's first steps, possibly to bolster his stature at home, was to schedule a meeting with Bush in Washington on September 1. Economic issues, including Japan's $52 billion trade surplus, were discussed "at great length" during three hours of talks.

During the year, the U.S. and Japan settled one issue, but difficult negotiations left dissatisfaction on both sides. In November 1988 the two countries had signed a memorandum of intent concerning coproduction of an experimental fighter aircraft, the FSX (modeled on the F-16), for Japan's Self-Defense Forces. In mid-February it became apparent that final agreement was being delayed by interagency differences in Washington. The Departments of Defense and State favoured the deal because it would strengthen U.S.–Japanese military ties. Commerce and U.S. Trade Representative Carla Hills opposed it on the grounds that it would give Japan access to high technology that could be used to make the Japanese aviation industry more competitive. The Japanese openly threatened an alternative: building a fighter alone. On May 16, after vigorous debate, the Senate defeated a resolution that would have scrapped the FSX pact. Under the arrangement, U.S. military contractors were to receive 40% of actual production.

Tokyo did not do so well on another issue. On May 25, on the recommendation of Trade Representative Hills, President Bush named Japan an unfair trader, under provision 301 of the 1988 Trade Act. Washington targeted supercomputers, lumber products, and intellectual properties (patents, copyrights, and trademarks). The law provided that the cited practices had to stop in 12–18 months or the U.S. would take retaliatory measures. Tokyo refused to negotiate under the "unilateral" 301 threat and said it would appeal under the General Agreement on Tariffs and Trade.

In May, during a visit to Moscow by Foreign Minister Uno, Soviet leader Mikhail Gorbachev announced postponement of an expected late-1989 visit to Japan. Diplomatic relations—including signature of a peace treaty—continued to be hampered by what Japanese called the "Northern Territories" issue. The dispute involved certain islands northeast of Hokkaido in the Kurils, occupied by Soviet forces since 1945 but claimed by Japan.

On April 16 Chinese Premier Li Peng (Li P'eng) concluded a five-day visit to Tokyo by obtaining a pledge of continuing economic cooperation. Japan had been China's largest foreign-aid donor, contributing 68% of its bilateral aid to the mainland. A five-year government loan of about $6 billion was scheduled to begin in 1990. Mindful of Japan's transgressions in China during the Pacific War (World War II), Foreign Minister Hiroshi Mitsuzuka was moderate in his complaint about Beijing's (Peking's) forceful repression of pro-democracy demonstrations in June. Although some organizations called for stronger criticism, business circles were aware that in 1988 two-way trade with China had increased 23% over the previous year to reach a record $19,330,000,000.

Japan had normalized relations with the Republic of (South) Korea in 1965. Indeed, in 1988 Prime Minister Takeshita had attended the inauguration of Pres. Roh Tae Woo in Seoul. On the other hand, the Democratic People's Republic of (North) Korea was the only nation with which Japan had no diplomatic relations. Nonetheless, on April 4 the North Korean leader, Kim Il Sung, reacted positively to a statement by Prime Minister Takeshita. For the first

time, the latter clearly expressed "remorse and regret" for the "serious damage and pain" inflicted by Japan on the Korean peninsula between 1910 and 1945, when it was under Japanese control. Normal ties were delayed, however, because of a dispute involving the capture, in the early 1980s, of five Japanese fishermen by Pyongyang.

(ARDATH W. BURKS)

KOREA

A country of northeastern Asia, bordered by the Sea of Japan, the Korea Strait, and the Yellow Sea, Korea is divided into two parts roughly at the 38th parallel.

South Koreans began 1989 on a wave of "reunification fever" when veteran industrialist Chung Ju Yung, the 73-year-old founder of the giant Hyundai conglomerate, flew to Pyongyang, North Korea, on January 23 to discuss joint-venture business deals with his nation's once-reviled Communist neighbour. Chung's government-approved trip seemed to signal a dramatic easing of tensions with the North. Since July 1988 South Korean Pres. Roh Tae Woo had promoted his version of "Nordpolitik"—détente with Communist countries.

The euphoria triggered by Chung's pioneering trip was not destined to last, however. On February 8, just one week after his return, a meeting between North and South representatives at the truce village of Panmunjom foundered when South Korea refused to call off its annual "Team Spirit" joint military maneuvers with the United States. The meeting was to have paved the way for a first-ever prime ministers' summit. A meeting of parliamentary delegations set for February 10 was also canceled.

If Roh's overtures to North Korea had proved fruitless, his diplomatic initiatives to other Communist countries paid off handsomely. In February Hungary became the first Eastern bloc government to establish full diplomatic ties with South Korea, prompting North Korea to downgrade its relations with Hungary. Poland and Yugoslavia were expected to follow Hungary's example. The Soviet Union opened a trade office in Seoul in April, and South Korea reciprocated by opening an office in Moscow in July. That same month a contingent of South Korean businessmen traveled to China to attend that nation's international trade fair in Beijing (Peking).

Nonetheless, North-South relations were what counted, and progress on that front was dismayingly slow. There were signs, however, that behind-the-scenes overtures were continuing. U.S. diplomats reportedly met several times with North Korean officials in Beijing early in the year to discuss security issues. And South Korean opposition leader Kim Young Sam, while on a surprise visit to Moscow in June, met—with his government's approval—with Ho Dam, head of North Korea's reunification committee. Both China and the Soviet Union pressured North Korea to demonstrate moderation in its relations with the South.

In July North Korea invited the world to its own sports extravaganza to rival Seoul's 1988 Olympics. On July 1–8 more than 25,000 young people from about 160 countries attended the 13th World Youth and Student Festival in Pyongyang. The largest international gathering ever held in North Korea, it opened the rigidly totalitarian society to Western reporters, rock music, and even a human rights demonstration.

The annual South Korea-U.S. security meeting, held in Washington in July, focused for the first time in more than a decade on cutting back the U.S. military presence on the peninsula. South Korea was worried by growing

sentiment in the U.S. Congress that favoured pulling out all or part of the 43,000 U.S. soldiers in the South. Just before the talks the South Koreans leaked confidential U.S. intelligence data indicating that North Korea was building a nuclear reprocessing plant in Yongbyon, some 95 km (60 mi) northwest of Pyongyang, that could eventually produce weapons-grade plutonium. At the meeting U.S. Secretary of Defense Richard Cheney pledged that U.S. troops would remain in Korea as long as South Korea wanted them. For its part South Korea agreed to pick up more of the cost of maintaining the U.S. presence.

Republic of Korea (South Korea)

Area: 99,237 sq km (38,316 sq mi). Pop. (1989 est.): 42,380,-000. Cap.: Seoul. Monetary unit: won, with (Oct. 2, 1989) a free rate of 670 won to U.S. $1 (1,085 won = £1 sterling). President in 1989, Roh Tae Woo; prime minister, Kang Young Hoon.

Pres. Roh Tae Woo entered his second year of democratic rule plagued by militant students, political dissidents, and labour unrest. On January 22 an alliance of 20 dissident groups staged a 10,000-strong demonstration in downtown Seoul. Their key demands included the withdrawal of U.S. troops from South Korea and reunification of the peninsula. Roh surprised both the left and the right ends of the political spectrum when he announced in a nationwide broadcast on March 20 that he was indefinitely postponing a promised referendum on his rule. The news was welcomed by most South Koreans, including the major opposition parties. The referendum had promised to be divisive, with the left seeking to oust the ruling Democratic Justice Party and the right anticipating a mandate to crush dissent. The postponement angered hard-liners in the military, however. On March 28 Roh quickly moved to shore up his authority by ordering a military reshuffle. Many of the 49 generals reassigned had been appointed by Roh's predecessor and longtime friend, Chun Doo Hwan. Roh replaced them with his own men.

Roh also showed a firm hand against labour unrest. At

The Rev. Moon Ik Hwan is escorted from court after being sentenced to 10 years in prison for an unauthorized trip to North Korea. Moon, a leading dissident from South Korea, had met with North Korean leader Kim Il Sung to promote reunification.

first the government had tolerated the widespread strikes that accompanied democratization, but on March 30 some 10,000 riot police stormed Hyundai Heavy Industries shipyard in Ulsan, crushing a 3½-month-old strike there. The new get-tough policy included a crackdown on leftists. The government was enraged when the Rev. Moon Ik Hwan, a leading dissident, made a secret trip to North Korea and embraced that nation's leader, Kim Il Sung, in the cause of reunification. On his return to Seoul on April 13, the maverick clergyman was promptly arrested and charged with violating national security laws. Opposition assemblyman Suh Kyong Won was arrested on June 28 after he admitted that he secretly traveled to North Korea in August 1988 and met with Kim Il Sung. In December he was convicted of spying but received a relatively light 15-year sentence. Kim Dae Jung, head of the Party for Peace and Democracy, to which Suh belonged, had persuaded him to turn himself in. On August 25, however, Kim himself was indicted for failing to report Suh's trip earlier. On October 5 the Reverend Moon was sentenced to 10 years in prison.

Roh reorganized his government on July 19, dismissing six ministers and his intelligence chief, Park Seh Jik. Park, who as minister of sports had successfully organized the 1988 Olympic Games in Seoul, was blamed for not preventing the trips north by dissidents. Roh's most trusted aide, Park Chul On, the architect of the government's northern policy, was promoted to first minister for political affairs. Although Roh managed to forge a working relationship with the opposition-dominated National Assembly, legislators would not compromise on demands for a full investigation of the excesses of the Chun administration. In February prosecutors ended their probe of the Chun era, indicting 47 of the former president's relatives and aides for corruption. Following an agreement between Roh and the opposition, Chun, who had entered a Buddhist monastery late in 1988, testified on his rule before a December 31 session of the National Assembly that was repeatedly disrupted by yelling and scuffling.

Democratic People's Republic of Korea (North Korea)

Area: 122,370 sq km (47,250 sq mi). Pop. (1989 est.): 22,418,-000. Cap.: Pyongyang. Monetary unit: won, with (Oct. 2, 1989) a nominal exchange rate of 0.97 won to U.S. $1 (1.57 won = £1 sterling). General secretary of the Central Committee of the Workers' (Communist) Party of Korea and president in 1989, Marshal Kim Il Sung; chairman of the Council of Ministers (premier), Yong Hyong Muk.

Years of effort and some $4.5 billion went into staging the eight-day World Youth and Student Festival held in Pyongyang in July. New construction included several stadiums; new hotels, theatres, and cultural centres; and a bank of high-rise apartments. Though shops were well stocked to impress foreign guests, consumer goods were in short supply, and power shortages were chronic.

A third "Work Harder" campaign launched in April indicated that the government was having difficulty achieving its economic goals. In August the party called for workers to increase dramatically the output of light industrial products. South Korea and its Western allies had hoped that the economic and political liberalization sweeping Eastern Europe and the Soviet Union would spur North Korea into opening up to the world. Instead, the Workers' Party intensified its campaign to promote its Juche (self-reliance) philosophy. The news media failed to report the student unrest in China in May and June.

North Korea's 77-year-old leader, Kim Il Sung, maintained his firm grip on the Army and foreign policy,

including relations with the South, but day-to-day management of the government fell increasingly to his son and heir apparent, 47-year-old Kim Jong Il. The younger Kim was steadily moving his former Kim Il Sung University classmates into positions of power, but other factions also gathered influence, particularly sons of Kim Il Sung's old comrades and a cadre of young grass-roots party leaders. The Army remained a potent force. Although North Korea claimed that it had cut its troop strength by about 100,000, the U.S. estimated in January that the number of men under arms actually increased to about one million. In August Kim Il Sung admitted in a radio broadcast that military expenditures were hampering economic development.

(JOSEPH L. NAGY)

MONGOLIA

A landlocked people's republic of eastern Asia, Mongolia occupies the geographic area known as Outer Mongolia. Area: 1,566,500 sq km (604,800 sq mi). Pop. (1989 est.): 2,096,000. Cap.: Ulan Bator. Monetary unit: tugrik, with (Oct. 2, 1989) a free rate of 3.35 tugriks to U.S. $1 (5.43 tugriks = £1 sterling). First secretary of the Mongolian People's Revolutionary (Communist) Party and chairman of the Presidium of the People's Great Khural (chief of state) in 1989, Jambyn Batmönh; chairman of the Council of Ministers (premier), Dumaagiyn Sodnom.

A meeting of the party Central Committee in December 1988 gave an important boost to economic and sociopolitical reform when it adopted Politburo proposals to end bureaucracy and inertia; for the first time Yumjaagiyn Tsedenbal, the former leader deposed in 1984, was named as the cause of the country's "stagnation." The proposals sought to develop popular initiative through greater media openness and the democratization of some election practices. A more nationalist view of Genghis Khan and the Mongol Empire was permitted.

According to a census taken in January 1989, the annual rate of population increase was 2.8%, but the proportion of the population of working age was rising by 3.4% and unemployment, at 27,480, was expected to reach 60,000 or so by 1990. To increase employment, the authorities were planning two- and three-shift work in industry, a five-day workweek, and the development of cooperative enterprises.

The second stage of the partial Soviet troop withdrawal began in May, with 75% of the troops remaining after the first stage (completed in 1987) due to leave in 1989–90. Mongolia planned to halve its armed forces to two motor-rifle divisions and cut the defense budget by 11% in 1990. Tserenpilyn Gombosüren paid an official visit to Beijing (Peking)—the first by a Mongolian foreign minister in the 40 years since the establishment of diplomatic relations with China.

(ALAN J.K. SANDERS)

TAIWAN

Taiwan, which consists of the island of Taiwan and surrounding islands off the coast of China, is the seat of the Republic of China (Nationalist China). Area: 36,000 sq km (13,900 sq mi), including the island of Taiwan and its 85 outlying islands, 21 in the Taiwan group and 64 in the Pescadores group. Pop. (1989 est.): 20,024,000. (Area and population figures exclude the Quemoy and Matsu groups, which are administered as an occupied part of Fujian [Fukien] province.) Cap.: Taipei. Monetary unit: New Taiwan dollar, with (Oct. 2, 1989) an official rate of NT$25.53 to U.S. $1 (NT$41.30 = £1 sterling). President in 1989, Lee Teng-hui; presidents of the Executive Yuan (premiers), Yu Kuo-hwa and, from May 21, Lee Huan.

After more than two decades of rapid economic growth, Taiwan had graduated into the ranks of developed countries,

and its 20 million citizens, with an annual per capita income approaching $7,000, enjoyed a level of prosperity scarcely imaginable just one generation ago. At the same time, the accelerating pace of political change transformed a once stodgy authoritarian regime into an increasingly free and open democratic system in which the remnants of the old order were steadily losing their battle against the forces of change. Pres. Lee Teng-hui's skillful and flexible diplomacy expanded Taiwan's foreign contacts, diminishing the sense of international isolation that had prevailed since the late 1970s.

Following the death of Pres. Chiang Ching-kuo on Jan. 13, 1988, his constitutional successor, Lee Teng-hui, accelerated the process of political change and democratization that had been under way for a decade. The first chairman of the ruling Kuomintang (KMT) to have been born in Taiwan, Lee strengthened the position of young, liberal reformers on the powerful Central Standing Committee and encouraged the retirement of old-line party stalwarts. He also edged away from the old dream of retaking the mainland of China. The transition to a new leadership was completed with the resignation on May 21, 1989, of Premier Yu Kuo-hwa, a relatively unpopular elder statesman, and his replacement by KMT Secretary-General Lee Huan, a key figure in the revitalization of the party. Meanwhile, a new generation of mostly U.S.-trained technocrats strengthened their positions in the KMT and government hierarchies.

The Democratic Progressive Party (DPP), established in 1986 and representing the major opposition force, assumed an increasingly active role in the Legislative Yuan (parliament). However, it remained split between a moderate faction led by party chairman Huang Hsin-chieh—re-elected to that post in late 1989—and a more radical group led by Yao Chia-wen. Official results of the December 2 elections—the first islandwide competitive elections in Taiwan's history—gave the KMT 72 parliamentary seats, to 21 for the DPP and 8 for independents. The KMT won 21 county magistrate and mayoral positions, the DPP 6, and an independent 1.

Taiwan's heavily trade-dependent economy continued to grow at a healthy 6–7% pace in 1988–89. The perennially worrisome trade surplus soared in 1989 despite the appreciation of the Taiwan dollar, and foreign investments during the year achieved a record high, projected at $1.8 billion. Taiwan turned increasingly toward Europe to reduce its chronic dependency on U.S. and Japanese markets. Unemployment remained below 2%, and inflation lagged well behind rising wage levels. Government attempts to limit the money supply and dampen speculation failed to curb a runaway stock market fueled by the dreams of millions of small investors.

Pioneering a new, flexible diplomacy, Lee Teng-hui made the first presidential trip abroad since 1977 when he paid a state visit to Singapore in March 1989. Taiwan derived some small satisfaction when it received diplomatic recognition from The Bahamas, Liberia, and Belize, and China severed its ties with those nations in retaliation. In May Finance Minister Shirley Kuo became the first Taiwan Cabinet minister to visit China since 1949.

The June 1989 military crackdown in China, vividly reported on the spot by Taiwan journalists, produced a sense of outrage on the part of many Taiwanese citizens. Expectations about an eventual reconciliation between Taiwan and China were badly damaged by these events, and the gulf between a democratizing and prosperous Taiwan and a repressive, economically troubled China again widened noticeably.   (STEVEN I. LEVINE)

South Asia

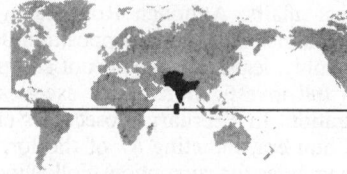

AFGHANISTAN

Afghanistan is a landlocked people's republic in central Asia. Area: 652,225 sq km (251,825 sq mi). Pop. (1989 est.): 14,-825,000 (excluding Afghan refugees estimated to number about 3.6 million in Pakistan and 2.1 million to 2.3 million in Iran). Cap.: Kabul. Monetary unit: afghani, with (Oct. 2, 1989) a par value of 50.60 afghanis to U.S. $1 (free rate of 81.87 afghanis = £1 sterling). General secretary of the People's Democratic (Communist) Party and president in 1989, Mohammad Najibullah; prime ministers, Mohammad Hassan Sharq and, from February 21, Sultan Ali Keshtmand.

ALFRED—SIPA

Women in Kabul hold up ration booklets, clamouring for their allotment of food. After the Soviet troops withdrew from Afghanistan, the Muslim rebels stepped up their battle for Kabul and set up blockades that cut off food shipments from Pakistan.

The last Soviet soldiers rode out of Afghanistan on Feb. 15, 1989, ending a nine-year intervention that left 15,000 Soviet troops dead and that failed to defeat Muslim rebels seeking the government's overthrow. The guerrillas had been fighting Afghanistan's government since the Communists seized power in a bloody 1978 coup. The Soviet forces, which intervened in December 1979, withdrew under a UN-mediated accord. Predictions by Western governments that Pres. Mohammad Najibullah's regime would fall as soon as the Soviets left proved wrong. The 43-year-old former secret police chief showed himself to be a shrewd political infighter and deftly appealed to nationalistic sentiments in his war-ravaged nation.

Three days after the Soviet pullout Najibullah declared a state of emergency, and on February 19 he replaced seven members of his Cabinet who did not belong to the governing People's Democratic (Communist) Party of Afghanistan with party members, a move aimed at consolidating the party's powers. Prime Minister Mohammad Hassan Sharq, another non-party member, resigned on February 20. Sultan Ali Keshtmand, a ranking member of the Politburo and a Communist hard-liner, was named de facto prime minister on February 21 after a 21-member Supreme Defense Council effectively assumed power.

The Muslim rebels, meanwhile, set up an interim government in Pakistan. On February 23, after three weeks of fractious debate, an assembly of 440 delegates elected an interim government with Sibghatullah Mojaddedi, considered a moderate, as president. Rasul Sayaf, a hard-line fundamentalist from the Ittehad-i-Islami rebel group, was elected prime minister. Afghan Shi'ite guerrillas, most of whom were in Iran, boycotted the assembly after the Pakistan-based rebels, the majority of whom were Sunnites, refused to give them the representation they sought. The Shi'ites constituted only 17% of the Afghan population but made up 40% of the refugees, who provided many of the guerrillas. The rebel government was officially recognized by Saudi Arabia on March 9, and Bahrain, Malaysia, and The Sudan also announced their recognition. The U.S. and Pakistan, the rebels' main backers, withheld recognition until a functioning administration was established, but the U.S. named a special presidential envoy to the Afghanistan resistance, with the rank of ambassador.

These developments had no military effect. The Kabul regime successfully pushed back rebel forces from several areas, including the strategic city of Jalalabad in July. Jalalabad, 70 km (42 mi) west of the Pakistani border, was the country's third largest city. Najibullah made repeated offers to start a policy of national reconciliation, but rebel leaders rejected them. On November 1 the UN General Assembly passed an unprecedented resolution calling on the Afghan government and the rebels to open negotiations to establish a coalition government. Afghanistan's relations with Pakistan deteriorated further. Pakistan did not turn away refugees during the year, but the strain on its economy was increasing since other countries cut their contributions after the Soviet withdrawal. International relief agencies and government officials estimated that about 100,000 Afghans had returned home, but the flow was difficult to gauge because of the country's porous borders.

A group of 15 former top officials and military officers formed what they called a third force to try to bridge the gap between Kabul and the guerrillas. Calling themselves the National Salvation Society, they issued a manifesto in October calling for an end to both Soviet and U.S. interference. Most of them served the deposed King Zahir Shah, and the government did not oppose the group because it might help lure the 74-year-old former monarch home

from exile in Italy. The king was still a popular figure in Afghanistan, and his return might lend Najibullah the legitimacy he sought at home and abroad. The king's return might also fracture the squabbling rebel alliance, since the leaders of the seven Pakistan-based rebel groups ranged from bitter antimonarchists to former palace advisers.

(DILIP GANGULY)

BANGLADESH

A republic and member of the Commonwealth, Bangladesh is in the northeastern part of the Indian subcontinent, on the Bay of Bengal. Area: 143,998 sq km (55,598 sq mi). Pop. (1989 est.): 110,290,000. Cap.: Dhaka. Monetary unit: taka, with (Oct. 2, 1989) a market auction rate of 31.52 taka to U.S. $1 (51 taka = £1 sterling). President in 1989, Lieut. Gen. Hossain Mohammad Ershad; prime ministers, Moudud Ahmed and, from August 12, Kazi Zafar Ahmed.

Bangladesh in 1989 reeled under drought, floods, and other natural disasters that killed more than 1,500 people and injured 15,000 others. There was huge crop loss, plunging the country, one of the world's poorest, into deeper economic crisis. Floods and resulting diseases killed at least 300 people by unofficial count. In 1988 floods had claimed over 2,000 lives and submerged three-fourths of the country. In April at least 1,000 people died in a cyclonic storm, and in May the government said spring crops worth $93 million had been lost owing to drought. A train accident in January killed 135 people near Dhaka.

The opposition, fragmented in about 15 political parties, made feeble attempts to force Pres. Hossain Mohammad Ershad to step down and announce new elections under a neutral caretaker government. The campaign drew the attention of the U.S. government. Rep. Stephen Solarz (Dem., N.Y.), chairman of the House of Representatives Subcommittee on Asian and Pacific Affairs, said more democracy in Bangladesh should become "a major American priority in South Asia." Solarz, who visited Bangladesh during the year, said he would recommend a legislative link between future U.S. aid to Bangladesh and progress toward free and fair elections.

Ershad, whose Jatiya Party held 251 of the 300 parliamentary seats, rejected all opposition demands. In July a constitutional amendment bill was passed limiting the presidency to 10 years. Ershad, who said he made the constitutional change for the good of democracy, could now seek reelection to another five-year term in 1991 but would be ineligible for a third term. Bangladesh had had nine presidents since it gained independence from Pakistan in 1971, all of whom had taken office through military intervention. Ershad had governed Bangladesh longer than any other leader. In July Ershad dismissed Justice Nurul Islam as vice president, allegedly for inefficiency, and replaced him with the prime minister, Moudud Ahmed. Kazi Zafar Ahmed took over the prime minister's post.

In its first attempt at grass-roots democracy, Bangladesh held district council elections in June in the Chittagong Hill Tracts, a remote region of primeval forests where a bush war had simmered and periodically flared for 14 years. More than 4,000 people had died in the 13,468-sq km (5,200-sq mi) area that stretches along the border with India and Burma. The indigenous inhabitants—Chakmas, Tripuras, and 11 other tribes—resented the in-migration of Bangladeshi from the plains. The tribespeople now made up 60% of the population, as against 90% some 40 years earlier. In 1989 at least 100 people died in bush war violence and police actions in the area.

The country's main opposition leader, Sheikh Hasina

Wajad, escaped what she said was an attempt on her life on August 11 in Dhaka. Hasina, daughter of Bangladesh's first prime minister (and later president), Sheikh Mujibur Rahman, who was assassinated in 1975, was in her house when a group of men fired 25 rounds into it and exploded a hand grenade. She was unhurt. Police arrested about 1,000 Marxist guerrillas during a drive in June. The Marxists had been blamed for 100 deaths during the previous year.

Bangladesh continued to depend heavily on foreign assistance. The 1989–90 annual development budget of $1.8 billion, unveiled in June, had a foreign assistance component of 87%. Defense got $15 million. Annual per capita income remained at $160.

Dhaka continued to maintain good relations with China, Pakistan, India, and the Islamic world. The Chinese vice-premier Ni Zhifu (Ni Chih-fu) visited Bangladesh in March and inaugurated a road bridge built with Chinese aid. Palestine Liberation Organization Chairman Yasir Arafat visited Dhaka in March. In February President Ershad made his first official visit to the U.K. (DILIP GANGULY)

BHUTAN

The monarchy of Bhutan is a landlocked state situated in the eastern Himalayas between China and India. Area: 47,000 sq km (18,150 sq mi). Pop. (1989 est.): 1,408,000. Cap.: Thimphu. Monetary unit: ngultrum, at par with the Indian rupee (which is also in use), with (Oct. 2, 1989) a free rate of 17 ngultrums to U.S. $1 (27.50 ngultrums = £1 sterling). Druk gyalpo (king) in 1989, Jigme Singye Wangchuk.

King Jigme Singye Wangchuck formally married his four wives at a public ceremony in 1989, nine years after the union was consecrated. After the ceremony the king's eldest son, nine-year-old Jigme Gesar Namgyal Wangchuk, was designated as heir to the throne of "the land of the thunder dragon," as the kingdom is also known. The 35-year-old king, the fourth ruler of the dynasty, had four sons and four daughters from his wives.

Bhutan continued to follow the policy of restricting foreign tourists. In 1989 only 2,500 visas were issued. The policy was established to protect the culture and heritage of the country from tourists who ravaged shrines and stole objects of worship.

Bhutan's relations with India remained friendly, but there were signs that the kingdom wanted to reduce its economic dependence on its large neighbour. The first two five-year development plans, as well as more than 90% of the third, were financed exclusively by India, but that nation's share in the 1987–92 plan was less than 70% of the total outlay.

During the year, the government expelled 9,000 foreign workers who did not have identification cards. Though India denied it, many of the workers were Indians.

(DILIP GANGULY)

This article updates the *Micropædia* article BHUTAN.

INDIA

A federal republic of southern Asia and member of the Commonwealth, India is situated on a peninsula extending into the Indian Ocean with the Arabian Sea to the west and the Bay of Bengal to the east. Area: 3,166,414 sq km (1,222,559 sq mi), including the Indian-administered portion of Jammu and Kashmir. Pop. (1989 est.): 835,812,000, including Indian-administered Jammu and Kashmir. Cap.: New Delhi. Monetary unit: Indian rupee, with (Oct. 2, 1989) a free rate of Rs 17 to U.S. $1 (Rs 27.50 = £1 sterling). President in 1989, Ramaswamy Venkataraman; prime ministers, Rajiv Gandhi and, from December 2, Vishwanath Pratap Singh.

Domestic Affairs. The major event of 1989 was the general election held in November, which brought the defeat of Rajiv Gandhi's government. The Congress (I) Party was able to secure only 192 seats in the Lok Sabha (House of the People; lower house) out of 525 for which polling took place on November 22, 24, and 26. (For tabulated results, see *Political Parties,* above.) No election was held in Assam because the voters' lists were not yet ready. Vishwanath Pratap Singh, leader of the Janata Dal, which won 141 seats, was sworn in on December 2 as prime minister, heading a minority National Front government with assurance of support from the Bharatiya Janata Party (88 seats) and the Left Front, including the two Communist parties (43 seats). Devi Lal was named deputy prime minister.

Elections were also held to the state assemblies of Andhra Pradesh, Karnataka, Uttar Pradesh, Sikkim, and Goa. The Congress (I) was triumphant in the first two states, and M. Chenna Reddy and Veerendra Patil became chief ministers. In Uttar Pradesh the Janata Party, as the largest single party, formed the government with Mulayam Singh Yadav as chief minister. The Sikkim Sangram Parishad swept the polls in Sikkim, and N.B. Bhandari formed the government. In Goa there was a tie between the Congress (I) and the Maharashtra Gomantakawadi Party, and the governor recommended president's rule.

Gandhi sprang a surprise by announcing the election six weeks ahead of the expiration of the old Lok Sabha's term. The opposition parties sought to avoid contests among themselves and to present a united front, despite the ideological incompatibilities between the leftists and the religious parties. This was the first election in which the voting age was 18. Earlier in the year the constitution had been amended to lower it from 21, thus enlarging the electorate by about 50 million.

Throughout the year the opposition groups had vociferously demanded the resignation of the government over the Bofors affair, involving purchase of 155-mm towed guns for the Army from the Bofors Co. of Sweden. They asserted that persons close to the government had received substantial kickbacks as part of the $1.3 billion agreement, signed in March 1986. V.P. Singh openly accused the prime minister of corruption and prevarication. The comptroller and auditor-general, in a report introduced in Parliament in May, after portions had appeared in newspapers, spoke of lapses in the evaluation of the guns and in fixing their price, which had resulted in financial losses. The government maintained that the guns had been adjudged the most efficient and suitable and that, to its knowledge, no commissions had been paid. One hundred and six opposition members of the Lok Sabha resigned over the issue. In October newspapers published documents identifying the agents and the payments to them. The defense minister asserted in Parliament that the government had hidden nothing and that investigators were to be sent to Sweden and Switzerland to find out about the payments. Bofors was one of the principal election issues. On December 26 V.P. Singh announced that India would make no more purchases from Bofors until the company revealed the names of Indians who had received kickbacks. During the campaign members of the ruling party accused Ajeya Singh, son of V.P. Singh, of stashing away large sums of money in a bank in St. Kitts, but this was denied by both son and father.

Elections to three state assemblies were held in January. The Dravida Munnetra Kazhagam secured a majority in Tamil Nadu, and M. Karunanidhi formed a government. In Nagaland the Congress (I) was successful, and S.C. Jamir was sworn in as chief minister. Mizoram also witnessed a

Congress (I) victory under Lalthanhawla. Karnataka was placed under president's rule after the Janata Dal government lost its majority. Two other states had new chief ministers, Motilal Vora succeeding Arjun Singh in Madhya Pradesh in January and Satyendra Narain Sinha taking over from Bhagwat Jha Azad in Bihar in March.

The Bodos, a tribal group in northeastern India, launched a yearlong plan of agitation, demanding that their region be declared a union territory. Yet another tribal group, inhabiting areas in Bihar, West Bengal, and Orissa, pressed for the formation of a separate Jharkhand state. Buddhist groups in Ladakh demanded separation from Jammu and Kashmir state and recognition as a union territory. In December the daughter of Home Affairs Minister Mohammed Sayeed was kidnapped by members of the (Muslim) Jammu and Kashmir Liberation Front; she was freed after five Muslim separatists were released from prison. Feelings between Hindus and Muslims were strained because of the decision of the Vishwa Hindu Parishad to build a temple of Lord Rama in Ayodhya at a spot where a mosque stands. (*See* RELIGION: *Hinduism*.) There were clashes between the two religious communities in several towns, notably Jaipur, Indore, Badaun, Srinagar, and Bhagalpur. The declaration of Urdu as an additional official language in Uttar Pradesh also sparked riots. Extremists continued their antigovernment activities in Punjab. In March the Union government announced a package of measures to promote reconciliation in the state. In January Kehar Singh and Satwant Singh, convicted of the assassination of Indira Gandhi, were hanged after the Supreme Court rejected their petitions.

Among important initiatives by the government during the year were the Jawahar Rozgar Yojana and bills to amend the constitution to give more powers to village councils (*panchayats*) and municipalities (*nagar palikas*). The aim of the Jawahar Rozgar Yojana, launched on November 14, the centenary of the birth of Jawaharlal Nehru, was to provide at least one job to every family below the poverty line in rural areas. Rs 21 billion was set apart for the project, which was to create 44 million jobs. Two parallel projects, the Nehru Rozgar Yojana and the Indira Mahila Yojana, were aimed at tackling unemployment in urban areas and promoting women's welfare, respectively. The Panchayati Raj Bill and the Nagar Palikas Bill were adopted by the Lok Sabha in August but failed in the Rajya Sabha (Council of States; upper house).

Several commemorative functions were held to mark the birth centenaries of Nehru and Abul Kalam Azad, two of the nation's founding fathers. A U.S. court in October re-

jected a defamation suit that former prime minister Morarji Desai had filed against a U.S. journalist, Seymour Hersch, who had called Desai a paid CIA agent. The Supreme Court in February decreed that Union Carbide Corp. of the U.S. should pay $470 million to the government of India, to be distributed as compensation to victims of toxic fumes that had escaped from that company's plant at Bhopal in December 1984. The award of the 1989 Nobel Prize for Peace to the Dalai Lama (*see* BIOGRAPHIES), resident in India, was welcomed by the people and government.

The Economy. The index of wholesale prices stood at 167.9 (1981–82 = 100) on October 7, compared with 154.7 the previous August. In October the government announced new incentives for agriculture. The budget of the Union government, presented on February 28, estimated revenue and expenditure for 1989–90 at Rs 526.3 billion and Rs 596,420,000,000 and capital receipts and expenditure at Rs 221,940,000,000 and Rs 225,190,000, resulting in an overall deficit of Rs 73,370,000,000. The allocation for defense was Rs 130 billion, a reduction of Rs 2 billion from the revised estimate for 1988–89. The Economic Survey for 1988–89 said that there had been 9% growth during the year, with agricultural production rising 17% and industrial output 7.5%. The inflation rate had come down to 5%. In June the Aid India Consortium assured assistance of $6.7 billion in 1989–90.

India's fourth nuclear power plant was inaugurated at Narora in October. Earlier, superthermal power stations began operating at Talcher and Singrauli. The World Bank offered assistance of $645 million for the Sutlej hydroelectric project in Himachal Pradesh and a loan of Rs 4,780,000,000 for irrigation projects.

Foreign Relations. Indo-Sri Lankan relations and the continuing hostility in Sri Lanka between Sinhalese and Tamils remained a cause for concern. After a visit by the Sri Lankan foreign minister to Delhi, India announced in August that it would carry out early and total withdrawal of the Indian peacekeeping troops from that country and urged Sri Lanka to take steps to ensure the safety of Tamils. The deinduction process began in October, but several battalions had, in fact, been recalled earlier.

Prime Minister Gandhi attended the summit of nonaligned nations in Belgrade, Yugos., in September, where he proposed the establishment of a Planet Protection Fund, with universal membership, for promoting conservation-compatible technologies. In Belgrade Gandhi had a special meeting with King Birendra of Nepal. A Nepalese move to alter the status of Indian nationals caused concern. In July Gandhi visited France for the bicentenary of the French

India's new prime minister, Vishwanath Pratap Singh (right), is congratulated by the outgoing prime minister, Rajiv Gandhi. Although neither Gandhi nor Singh was able to secure a majority in the national elections, Singh became prime minister as leader of Janata Dal.

Revolution, as well as the Soviet Union and Pakistan. The visit to Islamabad signaled a major effort to improve relations between India and Pakistan. Talks were held with Pakistani officials about the Siachen Glacier, where skirmishes over a disputed area had been taking place, and both sides reiterated their determination to resolve the problem peacefully. A three-year protocol was signed for expanding cultural relations, trade, and tourism.

Following Gandhi's visit to China in December 1988, a systematic attempt was made to improve relations with that country. The Chinese vice-premier Wu Xueqian (Wu Hsüeh-ch'ien) visited Delhi in October. Gandhi was unable to participate in the Commonwealth heads of government meeting in Kuala Lumpur, Malaysia, in October because of the elections. The president, Ramaswamy Venkataraman, attended the funeral of Emperor Hirohito in Tokyo in February and paid state visits to Tanzania, Zambia, Zimbabwe, and West Germany. Among important visitors to India during the year were Pres. François Mitterrand of France, the presidents of Nauru, Maldives, Mongolia, and Cyprus, Prime Minister Robert Hawke of Australia, Vietnamese Communist Party leader Nguyen Van Linh, Yasir Arafat of the Palestine Liberation Organization, and Javier Pérez de Cuéllar, the UN secretary-general.

(H.Y. SHARADA PRASAD)

MALDIVES

A republic and member of the Commonwealth in the Indian Ocean, Maldives consists of about 2,000 small islands southwest of the southern tip of India. Area: 298 sq km (115 sq mi). Pop. (1989 est.): 209,000. Cap.: Male. Monetary unit: rufiyaa, with (Oct. 2, 1989) a free rate of 9.01 rufiyaa to U.S. $1 (14.58 rufiyaa = £1 sterling). President in 1989, Maumoon Abdul Gayoom.

The economic policies of Maldives were endorsed during the year by the nation's principal donor countries. Although remaining one of the least developed countries in the world, Maldives nonetheless achieved an economic growth of 10% in its gross domestic product (GDP) during the 1980s. By the end of 1989 there was also a balance of payments surplus.

Pres. Maumoon Abdul Gayoom made education the top government priority, initiating a literacy drive, and also worked to encourage commercial enterprises. Half the work force were engaged in the fishing industry, which provided 25% of GDP. The other principal arm of the economy was tourism, which was stimulated by a new (1981) airport. Maldives maintained its nonaligned political stance; it had played a prominent role in backing the moves to make the Indian Ocean a peace zone and also turned down lucrative offers by big powers to provide facilities for military bases. Political stability returned to Maldives during 1989 after the traumatic events of 1988 when Sri Lankan mercenaries invaded the country and Indian forces had to come to its rescue. In August, 16 people were condemned to death for their part in the coup attempt. (GUY ARNOLD)

This article updates the Macropædia article INDIAN OCEAN ISLANDS: Maldives.

NEPAL

A constitutional monarchy, Nepal is a landlocked country in the Himalayas between India and the Tibetan Autonomous Region of China. Area: 147,181 sq km (56,827 sq mi). Pop. (1989 est.): 18,452,000. Cap.: Kathmandu. Monetary unit: Nepalese rupee, with (Oct. 2, 1989) a free rate of NRs 24 to U.S. $1 (NRs 38.83 = £1 sterling). King, Birendra Bir Bikram Shah Deva; prime minister in 1989, Marich Man Singh Shrestha.

A trade dispute with India in 1989 caused Nepal to seem like a state under siege. Gasoline was rationed; many restaurants were closed because of lack of provisions; and housewives stood in long lines at stores. Trouble between landlocked Nepal and politically and militarily powerful India peaked in a dispute over a trade and transit treaty. India, miffed at being perceived as the big bully, accused Nepal of discrimination against Indians who had been running businesses and working freely in Nepal under a transit treaty that allowed unrestricted travel by citizens of the two countries. Nepal, which sought to diversify its trade, wanted a trade treaty that would not be paired with the transit treaty; India disagreed. When the treaty expired in March, India closed 13 of the 15 crossing points on the 1,750-km (1,085-mi) frontier. India maintained that this did not constitute trade blockage, as Nepal charged. Government ministers continued to travel between the two capitals, but there was no sign of an agreement. In July Nepal abolished the free exchange of Nepalese and Indian currencies.

King Birendra ruled Nepal in 1989 with firmness, and the government suppressed pro-democracy campaigns. In September police arrested 624 activists of the outlawed Nepali Congress Party. Those arrested were observing "awareness week," but they were charged with carrying out propaganda critical of the government. (DILIP GANGULY)

PAKISTAN

A federal republic and, from October, a member of the Commonwealth, Pakistan is in the northwestern part of the Indian subcontinent, on the Arabian Sea. Area: 796,095 sq km (307,-374 sq mi), excluding the 83,716-sq km Pakistani-controlled section of Jammu and Kashmir. Pop. (1989 est., including some 3 million Afghan refugees and 3 million residents of Pakistani-controlled Jammu and Kashmir): 118,820,000. Cap.: Islamabad. Monetary unit: Pakistan rupee, with (Oct. 2, 1989) a free rate of PRs 21.32 to U.S. $1 (PRs 34.50 = £1 sterling). President in 1989, Ghulam Ishaq Khan; prime minister, Benazir Bhutto.

Benazir Bhutto, who assumed the prime ministership of Pakistan in December 1988, found that governing a restless nation of 117 million people burdened by poverty, ethnic unrest, drug problems, illiteracy, a civil war in neighbouring Afghanistan, and a history of tense relations with India posed a formidable challenge. Following the death of Gen. Mohammad Zia ul-Haq in a plane crash in August 1988, Bhutto, of the left-leaning Pakistan People's Party, became the first woman to lead a modern Muslim nation.

While her political power at the federal level remained intact in 1989, squabbling in all four provinces interfered with Bhutto's effort to implement a populist socioeconomic program focused on local projects to improve health, education, and public works. Buoyed by the prime minister's pro-labour election platform, a number of trade unions—including teachers, transport workers, office clerks, and airline pilots—went on strike several times in 1989. Bhutto narrowly survived a no confidence vote on November 1. In a subsequent Cabinet reshuffle, three opposition politicians who had supported her received ministerial appointments.

Death threats were made against Bhutto following the government's declaration of war on the heroin trade and the powerful drug barons who had grown rich from it. Western countries estimated that 80% of the heroin that arrived in the U.S. and Europe in 1989 came from, or through, Pakistan. Drug abuse in Pakistan soared from near zero in 1979 to an estimated one million addicts in 1989. The government unveiled a plan to employ an anti-drug army and a U.S.-funded elite commission to hunt

down narcotics dealers. The bulk of the problem, however, was Afghanistan, where an estimated 1,500 to 2,000 tons of poppies were harvested in 1989, compared with 120 tons in Pakistan. Poppies are the raw materials used in the production of heroin. Pakistan shares a 2,250-km (1,400-mi) frontier with Afghanistan, a border that is controlled by tribal chiefs. The government in 1989 identified 150 different heroin-smuggling routes from Afghanistan into Pakistan.

Dozens of people died in 1989 in ethnic violence in Sind province. Among the groups in conflict were militant secessionists, Muslim immigrants from India, and Pakistani migrants from poorer provinces.

The government claimed that the rate of inflation fell to 8% from 13% in 1988, but prices of all essential goods soared in 1989. Bhutto cut government spending by 14% and raised property and excise taxes.

On the international front Bhutto made several gains. She traveled to the U.S., Britain, Turkey, and Bangladesh, which had been part of Pakistan until 1971, when it gained independence in a nine-month liberation war.

Pakistan rejoined the 48-member Commonwealth in October after a 17-year absence. Pakistan had left the organization in 1972 in protest against its admission of Bangladesh. Britain continued to be Pakistan's largest single investor. In 1988 Pakistan sold goods worth £283 million to Britain, and Britain gave back £23 million in aid.

Pakistan's relations with the U.S. remained warm in 1989. The U.S. agreed to sell to Pakistan 60 F-16 jets, each costing about $25 million. The jets, to be delivered in late 1992, would help Pakistan maintain its ratio of one plane to every three of India's. Pakistan received $230 million in military aid and $215 million in economic aid in 1989, ranking it third, after Israel and Egypt, among recipients of U.S. foreign assistance during the year.

Pakistan's relations with India remained uneasy despite

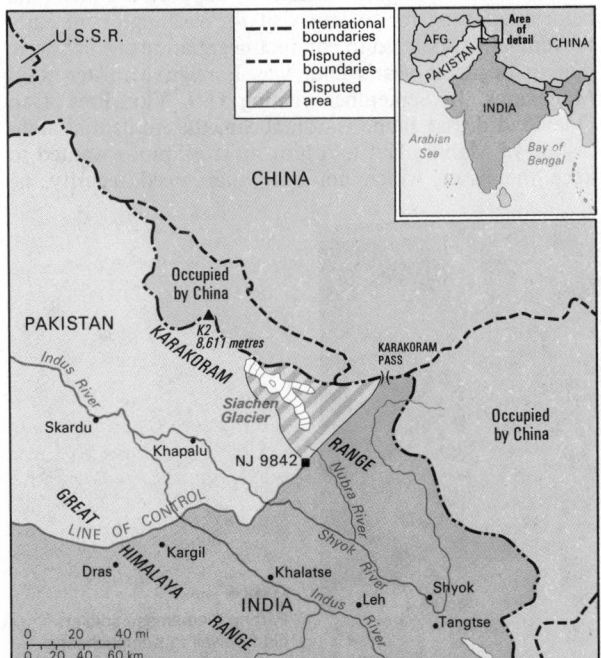

The "line of control," a cease-fire line agreed to by Pakistan and India in 1971, lies within the disputed territory of Jammu and Kashmir and extends eastward only to NJ 9842, a point defined by a 1949 cease-fire. Fighting continued in the areas east of those defined by the agreement, but both Pakistan and India were losing more lives to the harsh elements than to combat.

public pledges by the leaders of both nations to improve relations. Indian Prime Minister Rajiv Gandhi visited Pakistan in July. Relations became strained over the issue of control of the 6,000-m (20,000-ft)-high Siachen Glacier, which is part of the Karakoram mountain range at the northern edge of the Himalayas.   (DILIP GANGULY)

SRI LANKA

A republic and member of the Commonwealth, Sri Lanka occupies an island in the Indian Ocean off the southeast coast of peninsular India. Area: 65,610 sq km (25,332 sq mi). Pop. (1989 est.): 16,842,000. Legislative and judicial cap., Sri Jayawardenapura Kotte; administrative cap., Colombo. Monetary unit: Sri Lanka rupee, with (Oct. 2, 1989) a free rate of SL Rs 40.17 to U.S. $1 (SL Rs 65 = £1 sterling). Presidents in 1989, Junius Richard Jayawardene and, from January 2, Ranasinghe Premadasa; prime ministers, Premadasa and, from March 3, Dingiri Banda Wijetunge.

Sri Lanka, once famed as an idyllic tourist resort, continued to be plagued by ethnic violence in 1989. Amnesty International estimated that more than 1,000 people were being killed each month in violence blamed on radical Sinhalese, Tamil separatists, and police actions. The government's efforts to halt the bloodshed, including an offer to hold new elections, failed to silence the guns.

Prime Minister Ranasinghe Premadasa (see BIOGRAPHIES), of the United National Party, was sworn in as president on January 2 after winning the December 1988 presidential election by polling 50.4% of the vote. The five-and-a-half-year-old state of emergency was lifted on January 11, but mounting violence, including the murders of some 1,705 people, forced Premadasa to reimpose emergency regulations on June 20. Among the victims of militancy were Appapillai Amirthalingam, general secretary of the moderate Tamil United Liberation Front, who was assassinated on July 13, and Rohana Wijeweera, chairman of the (Sinhalese) People's Liberation Front, who died November 13 under mysterious circumstances after being arrested by government forces.

Sri Lanka's relations with neighbouring India soured in 1989 over the continued presence of Indian peacekeeping troops in Sri Lanka. Since 1987 Indian soldiers had occupied Sri Lanka's Tamil-dominated northeast in an effort to disarm Tamil guerrillas fighting for an independent homeland. They were initially deployed to supervise an India-sponsored accord under which the Sri Lankan government offered Tamils limited autonomy in exchange for an arms surrender. The most powerful of the Tamil groups, the Liberation Tigers of Tamil Eelam, rejected the agreement, however, and turned their guns on the Indians. India was reluctant to withdraw its troops from Sri Lanka because of the danger to the minority Tamil population. In September, however, India agreed to withdraw all its 42,000 troops by December 31, thus avoiding a showdown with Sri Lanka, which had threatened to take the issue to the United Nations.

The Tamils, who formed 18% of Sri Lanka's nearly 17 million people, alleged they were discriminated against by the Sinhalese, who made up 75% of the population and controlled the government and the military. At least 11,000 people, including 1,000 Indian soldiers, had been killed in the fighting since the Tamils launched their campaign in 1983. About 5,000 people had also been killed in fighting between the Sinhalese extremists and the government since Sinhalese radicals launched their campaign in July 1987, claiming the government had given too many concessions to the Tamil minority under the 1987 accord.

(DILIP GANGULY)

Southeast Asia

SOUTHEAST ASIAN AFFAIRS

The withdrawal of Vietnamese troops from Kampuchea, completed on Sept. 26, 1989, was the culmination of several years' intense diplomatic efforts, especially on the part of the Association of Southeast Asian Nations (ASEAN). It did not, however, bring an end to the long civil war. ASEAN members—Thailand, Indonesia, Malaysia, Singapore, the Philippines, and Brunei—had long supported a postwithdrawal interim power-sharing formula for Kampuchea that included the Hanoi-backed government of Prime Minister Hun Sen and all three of the resistance factions that had waged a ten-year struggle against the occupying Vietnamese: the China-backed Khmer Rouge, the followers of former head of state Prince Norodom Sihanouk, and the Khmer People's National Liberation Front (KPNLF) led by Son Sann. An international gathering in Jakarta, Indon., in February and a Hun Sen-Sihanouk meeting there in May raised hopes that a permanent peaceful settlement might be reached.

The search for an acceptable compromise was pursued at a conference held in Paris throughout August, chaired jointly by Indonesia and France and attended by 23 delegations from 19 countries and the UN; among those participating were foreign ministers of the U.S., the Soviet Union, China, Japan, the Indochina states, and the ASEAN countries. Progress was stymied by the refusal of Vietnam and the Hun Sen government to countenance participation of the Khmer Rouge in an interim government leading to elections and by the refusal of China to accept anything less than a "comprehensive settlement" that would include them. Thailand, unwilling to damage relations with China, declined to prohibit the passage of Chinese arms through its territory. ASEAN's position was that no formula that excluded the strong, well-disciplined Khmer Rouge stood any chance of ending the long civil war. There was widespread revulsion, especially in the U.S., to any kind of role for the ruthless fanatics who had

brought untold misery to Kampuchea during their four-year regime. The U.S. State Department, however, could see no workable solution without them.

The evacuation of Vietnam's troops had apparently been hastened by the unwillingness of the Soviet Union, under Mikhail Gorbachev's vigorously promoted policies of global détente, to continue underwriting the Vietnamese military presence with money and weapons. Despite skepticism about the unsupervised troop withdrawal, most analysts were satisfied that no significant hidden pockets of soldiers remained. However, far from bringing peace to the war-ravaged land, by November it appeared likely that the pullout would merely shift the conflict into a new phase as the Hun Sen government struggled to retain control. In late October the town of Pailin near the Thai border fell to the Khmer Rouge. The Sihanoukists and the KPNLF also claimed local victories near the border. By year's end no settlement was in sight, and the possibility of a Vietnamese return was not being discounted in the event of major Khmer Rouge victories.

Debate over the military presence of the U.S. in the Philippines generated much concern throughout the region. There was strong support in the Philippine Senate for not renewing lease agreements for the Subic Bay naval base and Clark Air Base, due to expire in September 1991. Other ASEAN countries were clearly alarmed at the prospect of a strategic power vacuum in the event of a U.S. withdrawal but were reluctant to endorse a new treaty publicly, for fear of being accused of interfering in the affairs of the Philippines and of compromising their positions on nonalignment. Fifteen of 23 Philippine senators voted for a resolution in September that called for evacuation of the two bases and four smaller facilities, with 38,000 U.S. personnel including dependents. The House of Representatives, however, endorsed a proposal, introduced by Speaker Ramon Mitra, to hold a nonbinding referendum to assess public opinion.

Pres. Corazon Aquino tentatively supported a plebiscite before departing for a state visit to Washington in early November. Appointed to conduct negotiations, which were due to begin at year's end, was Foreign Minister Raul Manglapus. In September visiting U.S. Vice Pres. Dan Quayle said that Jaime Cardinal Sin, the influential archbishop of Manila, had told him most Filipinos wanted to keep the bases, which not only guaranteed security, he

J. LANGEVIN—SYGMA

Parting Vietnamese soldiers bid farewell to Kampucheans as they leave the city of Battambang. After having occupied Kampuchea since the 1979 overthrow of the Khmer Rouge, the Vietnamese troops completed their withdrawal in September 1989.

said, but provided employment for 70,000 Filipinos. Annual spending was estimated at $400 million, in addition to $481 million in aid under the agreement negotiated in October 1988.

On August 4 the Singapore minister of state for foreign affairs, George Yeo, announced in Parliament that Singapore was prepared to provide base facilities for the U.S. Prime Minister Lee Kuan Yew later commented that the offer was intended to "make it easier for the Philippines to continue to host American bases without it being said they are lackeys of the imperialists." Reaction, however, was swift and negative in both Malaysia and Indonesia, in whose airspace any Singapore-based aircraft would have to operate. Both declared the proposal at odds with the ASEAN commitment to Zopfan (zone of peace, freedom, and neutrality). Thailand said it did not object in principle, but Vietnam and China expressed strong disapproval. It was revealed that a U.S. survey team had visited Singapore to assess facilities for stationing two squadrons of F-16 fighters. The government made it clear later that this was not to be considered a base.

All governments in the region were deeply concerned about possible wider repercussions of the June 4 crackdown on dissent in Beijing (Peking). Some worried that China's newly harsh and uncompromising attitudes would affect security. Beijing's position on Kampuchea did appear to become more intransigent, but otherwise the effects were chiefly economic. In this the ASEAN countries tended to benefit, since foreign investment deflected from China found a welcome in Southeast Asia, especially Thailand. Indonesian President Suharto intimated after June that he would go ahead with talks aimed at establishing diplomatic ties with China. Singapore was expected to follow suit, since Prime Minister Lee had suggested over the years that his country would recognize China after Indonesia did so. Lee visited Suharto in October.

In Brunei in early August, Sultan Hassanal Bolkiah, head of state and prime minister, was host to a gathering of ASEAN heads of government at ceremonies marking the coming of age of his 15-year-old son, Prince al-Muhtadee Billah. Although it was stressed that the meeting was not to be considered a formal summit, and no communiqué was issued, the leaders—President Suharto, President Aquino, Prime Minister Lee, Prime Minister Mahathir bin Mohamad of Malaysia, Prime Minister Chatichai Choonhavan of Thailand, and the Sultan of Brunei—discussed matters of regional concern, including Kampuchea and the U.S. bases.

A month earlier Brunei, for the first time, had been host to the annual ASEAN foreign ministers' conference. At the conclusion of their two-day meeting, the six ministers were joined by U.S. Secretary of State James Baker, the foreign ministers of Japan, Australia, New Zealand, and Canada, and a representative of the European Communities. The Australian foreign minister, Sen. Gareth Evans, strenuously promoted an Asia-Pacific Forum, a meeting of Pacific Rim countries in Canberra scheduled for November to address the establishment of a Pacific Community to pursue regional cooperation. Secretary Baker enthusiastically supported this "new mechanism," and there was strong support from Japan. The plan was not received with enthusiasm by ASEAN ministers, who nevertheless attended the 12-nation conference, which opened in Australia November 5.

Vietnamese "boat people" set sail in increasing numbers, straining the resources and exhausting the compassion of the "countries of first asylum," chiefly Hong Kong, Malaysia, Thailand, Indonesia, and the Philippines. In March a 29-nation, U.S.-sponsored conference on refugees in Kuala Lumpur, Malaysia, called for a screening process to separate genuinely persecuted persons from the great majority, who were merely seeking a better life abroad. Over the objections of the Vietnamese vice-foreign minister, Vu Khoan, support was expressed for forced repatriation of economic immigrants. In June a 50-nation gathering in Geneva pursued the idea but endorsed only voluntary repatriation. Both Malaysia and Thailand were turning refugee boats back to sea. By November there were 60,000 Vietnamese refugees in Hong Kong camps, and overcrowding had given rise to gang fights and riots. The issue of forced repatriation was also raised in October at the meeting of Commonwealth heads of government in Malaysia. In early December the Hong Kong authorities forcibly repatriated 51 Vietnamese but suspended the operation in the face of an international outcry.   (ROBERT WOODROW)

BRUNEI

The sultanate of Brunei is located on the northern coast of the island of Borneo, on the South China Sea. Area: 5,765 sq km (2,226 sq mi). Pop. (1989 est.): 251,000. Cap.: Bandar Seri Begawan. Monetary unit: Brunei dollar, with (Oct. 2, 1989) a free rate of Br$1.96 to U.S. $1 (Br$3.18 = £1 sterling). Sultan and prime minister in 1989, Sir Muda Hassanal Bolkiah Mu'izzadin Waddaulah.

A concerted effort was made during the year to overcome the widespread perception that the sultan of Brunei was "the richest man in the world." This assessment, which failed to differentiate personal assets from national reserves (about $25 billion), was seen as shallow and misleading. To clarify the government's view, Sultan Hassanal Bolkiah, who also served as prime minister, gave a television interview (his first) to former British minister of state Lord Chalfont. He observed that his 1,788-room palace incorporated government offices and provided a focus for national aspirations. Asked about democracy, the 29th hereditary ruler said that he would introduce elections and establish a legislature "when I see evidence of interest on the part of a responsible majority of the people."

In August coming-of-age rites for the sultan's 15-year-old eldest son were attended by President Suharto of Indonesia, Pres. Corazon Aquino of the Philippines, Prime Minister Mahathir bin Mohamad of Malaysia, Prime Minister Chatichai Choonhavan of Thailand, and Prime Minister Lee Kuan Yew of Singapore. They discussed regional interests but issued no communiqué.

The fifth national development plan, scheduled to end in 1990, was only marginally successful in lessening dependence on oil, which accounted for almost all the country's $2.5 billion in exports and about half the $1.6 billion in government revenues (the rest came from investments). A Ministry of Industry and Primary Resources was created to promote diversification.   (ROBERT WOODROW)

This article updates the Macropædia article EAST INDIES: Brunei.

INDONESIA

A republic of Southeast Asia, Indonesia consists of the major islands of Sumatra, Java, Kalimantan (Indonesian Borneo), Celebes, and Irian Jaya (West New Guinea) and approximately 3,000 smaller islands and islets. Area: 1,919,443 sq km (741,101 sq mi). Pop. (1989 est.): 177,046,000. (Area and population figures include East [former Portuguese] Timor.) Cap.: Jakarta. Monetary unit: rupiah, with (Oct. 2, 1989) a free rate of 1,788 rupiah to U.S. $1 (2,892 rupiah = £1 sterling). President in 1989, Suharto.

Indonesian police club demonstrators in the Indonesian province of East Timor, where, moments before, Pope John Paul II had called for an end to the country's human rights abuses.
AP/WIDE WORLD

For the first time since President Suharto came to power in 1966, Indonesians talked openly about changing their country's consensus-based method of selecting the head of state. In early 1988 Suharto had been named to his fifth five-year term by the 1,000-member People's Consultative Assembly, composed of members of Parliament and regional and sectoral delegates. No voting had taken place, since the Assembly's task was to arrive at a consensus as to who the sole candidate should be. Barely one year into his latest term, however, Suharto faced strong suggestions from politicians both in and out of government that the Assembly be allowed to vote on more than one presidential candidate. One retired general—the military was highly influential politically—even called for "pure and genuine" presidential polls.

The rising crescendo of demands eventually forced Suharto to speak out. At midyear, in a lengthy speech to the Cabinet that was made public, the president warned officials "not to make statements outside their field of competence. If people start talking about succession now, they're just wasting their time." Later in the year he went further. Talking to reporters while flying home from Moscow after a six-day visit to the Soviet Union, Suharto issued a warning to would-be usurpers. "I will clobber them," he said, "whoever they are." His words seemed to be in response to rumours circulating in Jakarta at the time that a group consisting mainly of retired generals planned to generate a political crisis and force Suharto and Vice President Sudharmono to step down.

The campaign for increased political openness extended beyond the succession question. Education authorities considered easing restrictions on political activity on university campuses even as students repeatedly took to the streets in largely peaceful protests over a variety of issues; one of the most significant of them was a 25% hike in electricity rates. Of greater concern to the administration was resistance to government expropriation of farmland for development. One of the most controversial cases involved the Kedung Ombo project in central Java, where a multipurpose dam displaced some 5,400 families. The dam was to provide water and electricity to 300 villages in an area where only about 17% of the local population had access to adequate

supplies of these commodities. However, about one-third of the families refused to give up their land, citing insufficient compensation.

Land expropriated for conservation was reportedly one cause of a village revolt in southern Sumatra that the Army put down, with more than 30 civilian casualties. The authorities blamed a Muslim sect for the trouble, saying that it had spread antigovernment sentiments among villagers in the area. Later, officials came under fire for the manner in which the incident was handled.

On the international front Indonesia and China began negotiations to resume diplomatic relations after a historic meeting between Suharto and Chinese Foreign Minister Qian Qichen (Ch'ien Ch'i-ch'en) in Tokyo during the funeral of Emperor Hirohito. Indonesia had suspended ties in 1967 because of suspicions that China had played a role in the bloody abortive coup of 1965.

In a year in which the fifth five-year national development plan (Repelita V) was launched, the government continued its efforts to liberalize the economy. Foreign investment rules were relaxed further. Companies were allowed to come in with only $250,000 in paid-up capital, down from the previous minimum of $1 million. The government also reduced the number of economic sectors closed to foreign investment from 273 to 75. The investments had to be labour-intensive, however. Repelita V also called for a greater role for the private sector, especially in the face of declining oil revenues for the government.

(ZOHER F. ABDOOLCARIM)

This article updates the *Macropædia* article EAST INDIES: *Indonesia.*

KAMPUCHEA (CAMBODIA)

A "state" of Southeast Asia, Kampuchea occupies the southwestern part of the Indochinese Peninsula, on the Gulf of Thailand. Area: 181,035 sq km (69,898 sq mi). Pop. (1989 est.): 8,055,000. Cap.: Phnom Penh. Monetary unit: riel, with (Oct. 2, 1989) a free market rate of 150 riels to U.S. $1 (242.70 riels = £1 sterling). Secretary-general of the People's Revolutionary (Communist) Party of Kampuchea and chairman of the Council of State (president) in 1989, Heng Samrin; chairman of the Council of Ministers (prime minister), Hun Sen.

During the first half of 1989 there were signs that the conflict in Kampuchea could be settled, but by September efforts to find a peaceful solution had failed, and the war intensified. The year began with an unprecedented visit by Hun Sen, Phnom Penh's prime minister, to Bangkok. He went at the invitation of Thai Prime Minister Chatichai Choonhavan, who had pledged, after coming to power in August 1988, to "turn Indochina's battlefields into a marketplace." They made progress on opening up bilateral trade, but the stalemate continued as Thailand remained, along with China, a chief supporter of the Kampuchean resistance.

A second informal meeting of the four Kampuchean factions, the six members of the Association of Southeast Asian Nations (ASEAN), Vietnam, and Laos took place in Indonesia in February but produced no progress on key issues. In May Hun Sen had a third meeting, also in Indonesia, with Prince Norodom Sihanouk, the leader of the tripartite resistance coalition. The two made progress on how to end the fighting and set up a future government. They were spurred by Hun Sen's announcement of liberal changes to his administration's constitution. The country's name was no longer the People's Republic of Kampuchea but the State of Cambodia; Buddhism had been reestablished as the national religion; private ownership of property was allowed; and a new flag had been adopted. In July the National Assembly declared the country permanently neutral and passed a foreign investment law.

In early April, Vietnam announced that it would finish the phased withdrawal of its troops from Kampuchea by the end of September. That seemed timed to affect the meeting between Soviet leader Mikhail Gorbachev and Chinese leader Deng Xiaoping (Teng Hsiao-p'ing) in Beijing (Peking) in May. The summit, however, brought little movement on Kampuchea. Meanwhile, fighting between the Khmer Rouge, militarily the strongest of the resistance factions, and the Phnom Penh government with its Vietnamese allies increased in May and June as each side fought for territory. Both sides were reported to have received new consignments of weapons. The U.S. Congress voted in July to increase aid to the two non-Communist resistance members and, for the first time, did not insist that the aid be used for nonlethal purposes.

France and Indonesia brokered an international conference on Kampuchea in Paris throughout August. The session set up working groups and sent a UN fact-finding mission to assess the possibilities for some kind of control mechanism for the period during and after the Vietnamese withdrawal. However, when the conference reconvened in late August, the talks foundered. The main obstacle was the role of the Khmer Rouge, with its unsavoury history of brutality. The Phnom Penh government and its allies insisted that the group be excluded from a future government, but the resistance and its supporters called for it to be part of a four-way interim government before elections.

Without a settlement, the UN had no brief to oversee the Vietnamese withdrawal in September. Although a number of official observers and several hundred journalists went to watch, there was no independent verification. China and the resistance insisted that many Vietnamese troops remained and, though Chatichai made 11th-hour efforts to bring about a cease-fire, the conflict continued. The more than 300,000 refugees along the Thai border had been expecting to return home but were disappointed. The Khmer Rouge stepped up fighting around Pailin, the ruby-mining centre in western Kampuchea. In December Prince Sihanouk's group announced that the two non-Communist factions had joined forces with the Khmer Rouge in attacking government strongholds. Meanwhile, international interest was being shown in an Australian proposal to make Kampuchea a UN trusteeship pending elections.

Kampuchea's economy rebounded as Thailand expanded trade. The expected boom after the Vietnamese withdrawal failed to materialize, however, as China, the West, and ASEAN maintained their official embargo. A drought at midyear cut the area under rice to only 45% of what the government had planned.   (JUDITH L. CLARKE)

This article updates the *Macropædia* article Mainland SOUTH-EAST ASIA: *Kampuchea.*

LAOS

A landlocked people's republic, Laos is in the northern part of the Indochinese Peninsula. Area: 236,800 sq km (91,400 sq mi). Pop. (1989 est.): 3,936,000. Cap.: Vientiane. Monetary unit: kip, with (Oct. 2, 1989) a free rate of 583 kip to U.S. $1 (943.29 kip = £1 sterling). President in 1989 (interim), Phoumi Vongvichit; chairman of the Council of Ministers (prime minister), Kaysone Phomvihan.

Laos continued to liberalize its economy in 1989. After a new foreign investment law was passed in July 1988, the government in a little over a year received 124 applications for investment projects and approved 60 of them. Joint ventures included those with Thai, Soviet, and Australian companies. Food production at home was boosted by a return to family-based farms from cooperatives and state-owned enterprises. The lack of a constitution made it difficult to protect investments, however, so a committee to draft a constitution was set up by the party Politburo in August.

Laos held its first parliamentary election on March 26. There were 121 candidates for the 79 seats in the Supreme People's Assembly, but many were officials of the government or the ruling Lao People's Revolutionary Party or their relatives. A 98.44% turnout of the 1.8 million eligible voters was claimed.

Laos during the year maintained its good relations with Vietnam. A high-level delegation, led by Vietnamese Communist Party leader Nguyen Van Linh and Premier Do Muoi, visited Laos in July. The Laotians also improved relations with Vietnam's enemy, China. The two countries inaugurated party-to-party relations in August, and Prime Minister Kaysone Phomvihan went to China for the first time in October.

Relations with Thailand continued to improve. In November 1988 Chatichai Choonhavan became the first Thai prime minister to visit Vientiane in nearly 10 years. The new closeness came largely at the instigation of the two countries' armies. Gen. Sisavat Keobounphan, Laotian military leader, visited Bangkok in August 1989, and Thai commander in chief Gen. Chaovalit Yongchaiyuth went to Vientiane in October and signed a pact on bilateral ties. The relationship had taken a turn for the worse in July when Vientiane radio accused Thailand of undermining Laos economically. It blamed Chatichai's policy of opening Indochina up to trade, but its real target was unscrupulous Thai traders, some with army connections, who had taken advantage of the new investment law. Thailand was incensed, and Laos announced that the broadcast was not official. In August and September Laos increased taxes on imports and exports and added extra requirements for Thai investors. Bilateral trade dropped by more than 25% in September. In October the Thais agreed to scrap the last 29 items on a list of "strategic" goods whose export to Laos was banned.

Laos continued to survive largely off foreign aid. A drought in the south brought extra help from Japan and the UN. Australia provided financing for a satellite station to be set up by February 1990.   (JUDITH L. CLARKE)

This article updates the *Macropædia* article Mainland SOUTH-EAST ASIA: *Laos.*

MALAYSIA

A federal constitutional monarchy of Southeast Asia and member of the Commonwealth, Malaysia consists of the former Federation of Malaya at the southern end of the Malay Peninsula (excluding Singapore) and Sabah and Sarawak on the northern part of the island of Borneo. Area: 330,442 sq km (127,584 sq mi). Pop. (1989 est.): 17,421,000. Cap.: Kuala Lumpur. Monetary unit: ringgit, with (Oct. 2, 1989) a free rate of 2.69 ringgit to U.S. $1 (4.35 ringgit = £1 sterling). Paramount rulers in 1989, with the title of *yang di-pertuan agong,* Tuanku Mahmood Iskandar ibni al-Marhum Sultan Ismail and, from April 26, Tuanku Azlan Muhibbudin Shah ibni al-Marhum Yusuff Ghafarullahu-Lahu Shah; prime minister, Datuk Seri Mahathir bin Mohamad.

Prime Minister Datuk Seri Mahathir bin Mohamad began 1989 in physical and political difficulty. In January he suffered a heart attack and underwent bypass surgery. Mahathir's hospitalization occurred at a time when the ruling Barisan Nasional (National Front) coalition, which was dominated by the premier's New United Malays National Organization, or UMNO Baru, was facing a stiff challenge from political forces marshaled by Razaleigh Hamzah, a former Cabinet minister.

Razaleigh's political vehicle was known as the "Spirit of '46," named after the year the original UMNO, declared illegal in 1988 on a technicality, was founded. In an unprecedented challenge to Barisan, the "46ers" joined forces with the fundamentalist Parti Islam and two smaller political parties to form an informal alliance, the Angkatan Perpaduan Ummah (Muslim Unity Front, or APU). The APU also worked closely with the main opposition party, the Chinese-backed Democratic Action Party.

As the year progressed, however, Barisan asserted itself over the APU, winning all but one of a series of parliamentary and state assembly by-elections. Moreover, the influential former deputy prime minister Musa Hitam was wooed back to the government camp. Musa had broken with Mahathir in 1986 and lent his support to Razaleigh. In a dramatic about-face, Musa joined UMNO Baru in early 1989 and was later named Malaysia's representative to the United Nations with ministerial rank. By the end of the year, Mahathir had recovered fully.

Sultan Azlan Shah of Perak state became Malaysia's ninth *yang di-pertuan agong*—the "one who is chief among the most prominent," or king. Under a unique system of constitutional monarchy, the country's nine hereditary state rulers took turns for the kingship every five years. Tuanku Jaafar Abdul Rahman of Negri Sembilan state was named deputy king.

Parliament passed an amendment to the Internal Security Act (ISA) limiting judges' powers to review procedural matters in national security cases. The ISA allowed for detention without trial when national security was at issue. In late 1987 the government had arrested more than 100 social activists, politicians, and educators under the act for allegedly fueling racial tensions. Many of those arrested contested their detentions in court. Three succeeded, but all had been released by April anyway. The government had long been at odds with the judiciary over various issues.

In October Malaysia acted as host to the biennial Commonwealth heads of government meeting. Mahathir had once considered pulling Malaysia out of the Commonwealth because he thought the institution irrelevant, but he said that he changed his mind after his government conducted a review of the organization and determined that there were useful aspects to it.

The government launched the National Economic Consultative Council, a 150-member body that was to deliberate on a successor to the controversial New Economic Policy (NEP). The NEP, devised in 1970 to correct economic imbalances among Malaysia's different ethnic groups, was scheduled to expire in 1990.

A guerrilla war that had dragged on for 41 years ended on December 2 when the Communist Party of Malaya agreed to abandon its insurgency. Under the agreement, Malaysia and Thailand guaranteed fair treatment for the approximately 1,200 guerrillas, who promised to relinquish their arms and return to civilian life.

The economy continued to improve. Bank Negara Malaysia, the central bank, reported that the economy grew by 8.1% in 1988, slightly higher than expected and up substantially from 1987's figure of about 5%.

(ZOHER F. ABDOOLCARIM)

This article updates the *Macropædia* article Mainland SOUTH-EAST ASIA: *Malaysia.*

MYANMAR (BURMA)

Myanmar (Burma until May 26, 1989) is a republic of Southeast Asia with coastlines on the Bay of Bengal and the Andaman Sea. Area: 676,577 sq km (261,228 sq mi). Pop. (1989 est.): 40,810,000. Cap.: Yangon (Rangoon). Monetary unit: kyat, with (Oct. 2, 1989) a free rate of 6.66 kyats to U.S. $1 (10.78 kyats = £1 sterling). Chairman of the State Law and Order Restoration Council in 1989, Gen. Saw Maung.

Burma's military rulers gave the country a new name in 1989—"The Union of Myanmar"—to make clear that the country was composed of various ethnic groups, not just the majority Burmans. Rangoon's name was changed to Yangon. For four decades about a dozen ethnic-based

SANDRO TUCCI/TIME MAGAZINE

Daw Aung San Suu Kyi, a leading member of Myanmar's opposition, was placed under house arrest as part of the government's crackdown on the country's pro-democracy movement.

Soldiers conceal themselves behind a tank during an attempted military coup against Philippine Pres. Corazon Aquino. The December coup attempt marked the sixth and the most serious attempt to overthrow the Aquino government.
SYGMA

guerrilla groups, controlling vast territory, had been fighting for greater autonomy.

The 1988 pro-democracy movement had been crushed in September of that year, when Gen. Saw Maung seized power and his troops cleared the streets by shooting thousands of demonstrators. A new wave of arrests, including several leading opposition figures, began in July 1989 following small-scale protests. The military government made a series of mostly superficial, tentative changes in the economy and the political system. Elections were promised for April or May 1990, and a total of 223 political parties registered in February under a government directive. A draft law set 18 as the voting age and reduced the minimum age for candidates from 24 to 21.

Burmese troops clashed with Thai troops several times in 1989 during campaigns against Karen rebels. The Karens had begun their revolt in 1949, a year after Burma achieved independence from Britain, on the grounds that the government had reneged on its promise of more autonomy for ethnic minorities. The Karen National Union was the largest of 12 ethnic groups joined in the National Democratic Front, which claimed a total of 35,000 troops and said it controlled half the country.   (DILIP GANGULY)

PHILIPPINES

Situated in the western Pacific Ocean off the southeast coast of Asia, the republic of the Philippines consists of an archipelago of about 7,100 islands. Area: 300,000 sq km (115,800 sq mi). Pop. (1989 est.): 59,906,000. Cap.: Manila. Monetary unit: Philippine peso, with (Oct. 2, 1989) a free rate of 21.76 pesos to U.S. $1 (35.20 pesos = £1 sterling). President in 1989, Corazon Aquino.

Pres. Corazon Aquino survived the sixth and most serious attempt to overthrow her government when an attempted military coup was put down in early December 1989. During the year the government made gains against the still-strong insurgency of the Communist Party of the Philippines and its guerrilla force, the New People's Army. Improved economic conditions reduced the Communists' appeal, and the armed forces were patrolling more actively and improving their village support programs.

Under pressure, guerrillas hunted in their own ranks for informers, killing many Communists just on suspicion and causing others to defect. In May defectors showed authorities the graves south of Manila of 48 victims of the guerrilla witch-hunt. Police arrested a Communist leader, Satur Ocampo, in Manila on July 27, four days after the reward for such captures was raised to $45,000. The Communists were accused of atrocities, including the murder of at least 39 worshipers at a provincial church on June 25. Human rights activists said that the Philippine Army also used terror against Communists.

Blaming the United States for helping Aquino's forces, the Communists targeted Americans in the Philippines. On April 6 an attempt to blow up a bus carrying 30 U.S. servicemen near Clark Air Base failed. On April 21 gunmen in Manila killed Col. James Rowe, the chief of the army division at the Joint U.S. Military Assistance Group, who had been a prisoner of war for five years in Vietnam. On September 26 two Americans working for the U.S. military were killed near Clark—just hours before U.S. Vice Pres. Dan Quayle arrived in Manila to discuss the use by the U.S. of military bases in the Philippines after the current agreement ended in 1991. Renewal of the U.S. leases was politically controversial.

Aquino's political opponents began preparing for the 1992 presidential election by reviving the Nationalist Party that had been led by former president Ferdinand Marcos (see OBITUARIES). Vice Pres. Salvador Laurel became the party's president, and former defense minister Juan Ponce Enrile was named secretary-general. Marcos died on September 28 at the age of 72 in Hawaii, where he had fled when a 1986 popular uprising brought Aquino to power. She refused to allow his body to be brought home for burial because of apprehension about demonstrations.

The abortive coup was launched on December 1, when rebel troops seized military bases and television stations, bombed the presidential palace, and turned parts of downtown Manila into battle zones. With air cover provided by U.S. F-4s from Clark, government forces were able to defeat the attempt, although pockets of resistance held out for several days. Rebel troops holding Manila's financial district did not surrender until December 7, and the air

base at Cebu, 560 km (350 mi) south of Manila, was in rebel hands until two days later. At least 98 people were killed and more than 500 wounded in the fighting. Aquino declared a state of emergency on December 6. In what was described as an effort to ameliorate conditions that led to the coup attempt, she reshuffled her Cabinet on December 31.

After years of economic problems and a rapidly rising population, the government sought to push gross national product (GNP) per capita back to its 1981 level by 1992 with a restructuring program intended to achieve 6.5% economic growth annually. The International Monetary Fund agreed on March 6 to help the program, and at a meeting on July 4–5 in Tokyo, 19 nations and 7 international financial institutions pledged $3.5 billion in aid to the Philippines over the next 12 months. Economic problems remained grave, however. The trade deficit for the first half of 1989 was more than double that of the first six months of 1988, and the inflation rate rose to 10.3% in July, the highest in three years.   (HENRY S. BRADSHER)

SINGAPORE

Singapore, a republic of Southeast Asia and member of the Commonwealth, occupies a group of islands, the largest of which is Singapore, at the southern extremity of the Malay Peninsula. Area: 622 sq km (240 sq mi). Pop. (1989 est.): 2,674,000. Monetary unit: Singapore dollar, with (Oct. 2, 1989) a free rate of S$1.96 to U.S. $1 (S$3.18 = £1 sterling). President in 1989, Wee Kim Wee; prime minister, Lee Kuan Yew.

Court cases provided the focus of much attention throughout the year. Tried in absentia, opposition politician Francis Seow, a former solicitor general and president of the Law Society, was convicted in December 1988 of income-tax evasion. A fine of $9,500 prevented him from taking the seat in Parliament that he had won three months earlier under a modified electoral system. Another ousted parliamentarian, J.B. Jeyaretnam, who had been disbarred in 1987, was reinstated by the Privy Council in London (Singapore's highest court of appeal). The judges declared Jeyaretnam not guilty of misdirecting party funds, the charge on which he had been convicted, disbarred, and removed from Parliament. In January a law was introduced to abolish Privy Council appeals against disbarment, and the government also declined to lift a ban on Jeyaretnam's participation in elections.

In August Prime Minister Lee Kuan Yew caused a furor by declaring Singapore open to the idea of accommodating limited United States military facilities. The prime minister's announcement was poorly received in Malaysia and Indonesia, especially after U.S. experts had visited Singapore in June to survey sites. In early October, upon returning from a visit to Indonesia, Lee said that while there would be no bases as such, U.S aircraft and naval vessels might use Singapore as a way station for servicing.

A diplomatic row erupted with Thailand in March over Singapore's treatment of illegal immigrant workers. Singapore warned that those convicted would be imprisoned and flogged, a practice called "barbaric" in Bangkok. An amnesty led to the repatriation into Thailand, assisted by the Thai government, of almost 10,000 workers. The resulting acute labour shortage in Singapore's construction industry forced a speedy revision of policy, and the majority of the workers returned with visas.

The nation's economy continued to prosper in 1989, with a first-half growth in gross domestic product of 8.4%. Tourism picked up after a five-year slump, raising hotel occupancy to 80%. Industry was, however, plagued by a worsening labour shortage.   (ROBERT WOODROW)

This article updates the *Macropædia* article Mainland SOUTH-EAST ASIA: *Singapore*.

THAILAND

Thailand is a constitutional monarchy in Southeast Asia, on the Andaman Sea and the Gulf of Thailand. Area: 513,115 sq km (119,115 sq mi). Pop. (1989 est.): 55,258,000. Cap.: Bangkok. Monetary unit: baht, with (Oct. 2, 1989) a free rate of 25.96 baht to U.S. $1 (42 baht = £1 sterling). King, Bhumibol Adulyadej; prime minister in 1989, Maj. Gen. Chatichai Choonhavan.

AP/WIDE WORLD

Border police in Thailand escort two of Kampuchea's government soldiers captured inside Thailand. In September Thai president Chatichai Choonhavan met with Kampuchean prime minister Hun Sen to discuss a cease-fire between the Kampuchean government and its resistance movement.

Thailand continued to prosper in 1989 under the business-minded administration of Chart Thai party leader Chatichai Choonhavan. New investment poured in, much of it from Japan, Taiwan, and Hong Kong, and 11% growth for 1989 was projected in October. The Cabinet held sessions in the south and northeast, announcing new development plans for those areas, including a deep-sea port at the southern town of Krabi. A record number of tourists had visited Thailand by October.

The prime minister's promotion of the country's business interests was reflected in his foreign policy. He had announced in 1988 that he would "turn Indochina's battlefields into a marketplace," a reversal of Thailand's previous hostility toward Indochina. In January Chatichai welcomed to Bangkok Hun Sen, prime minister of Kampuchea, even though Thailand did not recognize his administration and continued to support the resistance forces in Kampuchea. Hun Sen visited Thailand twice more, in May and in September. Chatichai unsuccessfully tried to arrange a cease-fire in Kampuchea in September.

Although the prime minister's foreign policy stance was popular in business circles, there was strong opposition from some other quarters. China, the main backer of the Kampuchean resistance movement, imparted its disapproval when Chatichai visited Beijing (Peking) in March. Foreign Minister Siddhi Savetsila remained opposed to Chatichai's rapprochement with Hun Sen despite his own ground-breaking visit to Vietnam in January.

The Army, which had long supported the Kampuchean resistance, also opposed Chatichai's views on Indochina. However, Chatichai made an ally of the commander in chief, Gen. Chaovalit Yongchaiyuth, and gave him a leading role in foreign policy, allowing him, among other things, to participate in the meetings with Hun Sen. Chatichai also gave Chaovalit an almost free hand in relations with Burma and Laos. The prime minister himself visited Laos in November 1988, signing an agreement to build an Australian-financed bridge linking the two countries across the Mekong River.

The Army was also critical of the increase in corruption that had occurred after Chatichai came to power. When Chaovalit spoke out against corruption in the government in August, he became involved in a clash with the prime minister's advisory team of young academics. Adviser Sukhumbhand Paribatra, an international relations expert, replied to Chaovalit's charges by implying that the military was also corrupt. The army protest that ensued led to Sukhumbhand's resignation.

Chatichai steered his coalition through the May–September parliamentary session, surviving a motion of no-confidence in four of his ministers in July. A conflict arose when two ministers, both members of the Democrat Party, suggested that certain Chart Thai Cabinet members had bribed the opposition to take their names off the no-confidence list, and there was talk of replacing the Democrats in the coalition. Parliament's elected lower house won a small victory on July 10 when it pushed through a constitutional amendment making its own speaker parliamentary president instead of the speaker of the appointed Senate.

Health and environmental issues loomed large in 1989. The seriousness of the spread of AIDS in Thailand became recognized. Although still low by world standards, the incidence was the highest in Asia by far. By October 31 health officials said there were eight full-blown cases, 73 AIDS-related complex cases, and 11,281 HIV-infected cases. After heavy rains in the south in late 1988 caused landslides in overlogged areas, killing more than 400 people, the prime minister in December ordered a regional logging ban, which was extended to the entire nation the following month. The ban became law in May, but illegal logging continued. (JUDITH L. CLARKE)

This article updates the *Macropædia* article Mainland SOUTHEAST ASIA: *Thailand.*

VIETNAM

The socialist republic of Vietnam occupies the eastern part of the Indochinese Peninsula in Southeast Asia and is bounded on the south and east by the South China Sea. Area: 331,688 sq km (128,065 sq mi). Pop. (1989 est.): 64,747,000. Cap.: Hanoi. Monetary unit: dong, with (Oct. 2, 1989) a par value of 4,500 dong to U.S. $1 (7,281 dong = £1 sterling). General secretary of the Communist Party in 1989, Nguyen Van Linh; chairman of the State Council (president), Vo Chi Cong; chairman of the Council of Ministers (premier), Do Muoi.

Vietnamese Foreign Minister Nguyen Co Thach attended the international conference on Kampuchea in Paris in July 1989. China, which backed the Khmer Rouge, insisted on including that group in a four-way interim Kampuchean government, a configuration that Vietnam rejected, and the conference ended without result. Vietnam went ahead with its final troop pullout in September, but Beijing (Peking) refused to accept the withdrawal as genuine because there was no independent UN verification. Diplomatic and defense experts, however, acknowledged that most Vietnamese troops had gone. Still, the U.S., which had demanded the withdrawal as a condition for lifting its trade and aid embargo, now stood with China and the Association of Southeast Asian Nations (ASEAN) in demanding a "comprehensive solution" for Kampuchea. Washington's embargo, shared to some extent by Western Europe, Japan, and ASEAN, remained in place.

Early in the year there was some improvement in Vietnam's relations with China. A Vietnamese vice-foreign minister visited Beijing twice. Tension along the common border deescalated, and trade boomed as Vietnamese bought consumer items long unavailable at home. China even implied that it would reduce arms to the Khmer Rouge when Vietnam took its troops out of Kampuchea. By August, however, there was a new coolness as the two disagreed over Kampuchea. They also quarreled over the Spratly Islands, which both claimed.

Toward the end of 1988, the economy was in a dire state, despite some successes of the *doi moi* (renovation) program of reform instituted at the sixth Communist Party congress in late 1986. Faced with severe rice shortages and inflation estimated at 1,000% a year, the government embarked on an austerity program recommended by the International Monetary Fund. It devalued the dong to its black market rate, cut subsidies to state enterprises and employees, instituted some changes in the complex tax structure, and began to streamline banking, including the provision of reasonable interest rates. The measures produced results. The dong held its value, so the black market for the currency declined. Inflation was estimated at 5% per month in September, and private business flourished. Vietnam was also profiting from its foreign investment code of December 1987. Between September 1988 and June 1989 officials claimed 64 foreign investment plans worth $640 million had been approved.

Rice production improved despite the usual typhoon destruction in the north. Vietnam was expected to produce 21 million tons of rice by the end of 1989. Rice exports in 1989 were forecast to total one million tons, about 13 times the figure for 1988. Good harvests were the main reason, but the relaxing of socialist laws, allowing rice farmers to lease their own land and openly sell produce surplus to

government quotas, made more rice available. However, severe dislocations continued. The sudden availability of goods from China led to thefts of private and state property to trade for items from across the border. The competition forced many state factories, which were producing inferior goods, out of business. About 18–20% of the work force was estimated to be unemployed, and their numbers were swollen by troops returning from Kampuchea. Corruption among government and party officials continued, and crime was still widespread. Students protested against their low stipends and living conditions in April and May, encouraged by the democracy protests in Beijing, but the government nipped the movement in the bud by raising allowances.

Despite the decidedly capitalist-style economic reforms, the leadership maintained its Marxist-Leninist principles. A group of highly regarded southern Communists pressed strongly for more liberal economic and political reforms. A Central Committee plenum in March endorsed the economic reforms but stressed that there would be no political changes. The Central Committee was summoned again in August, and Communist Party leader Nguyen Van Linh made it clear that the liberals were regarded as deviationists. The official media had already condemned the political reforms in Eastern Europe. In the same month, the Politburo admitted that parts of Communist Party founder Ho Chi Minh's will had not been followed. He had not been cremated, as he requested (his body lay in a mausoleum in Hanoi), and his call for a one-year moratorium on agricultural taxes had been disregarded. Also, he had died on Sept. 2, 1969, not September 3 as had been announced. The date had been changed so as not to spoil the mood of National Day on September 2.

Vietnam kept up good relations with Laos—Nguyen Van Linh and Premier Do Muoi visited Vientiane in July—and Kampuchea's president, Heng Samrin, led a delegation to Hanoi in September. Relations with the Soviet Union continued to be prickly. Moscow was believed to have pressured Hanoi to remove its troops from Kampuchea in compliance with a request from Beijing. Thai Foreign Minister Siddhi Savetsila visited Hanoi in January, and trade increased under the business-minded government of Prime Minister Chatichai Choonhavan. However, Chatichai's planned visit to Hanoi failed to come off as the Kampuchean situation worsened. Hanoi complained that Vietnamese resistance groups operated out of Thailand. In August Laotian troops killed or captured 68 Vietnamese apparently on their way from Thailand to Vietnam. Relations with the U.S. were smooth despite Washington's refusal to lift the embargo or open diplomatic ties. Hanoi handed over more remains of some of the 1,700 U.S. servicemen still listed as missing in action during the Vietnam war. The government also opened a dialogue with South Korea.

Vietnamese continued to flee in boats, landing mostly in Hong Kong but also in Thailand, Malaysia, Indonesia, and even Japan. A conference in Geneva decided that countries of first asylum would accept the Vietnamese but would screen them to determine whether they were genuine political refugees, sending back those who were not. Hanoi, however, said it would refuse to take back those who did not want to return. It accepted 51 Vietnamese who were forcibly repatriated from Hong Kong in December, but it sent a strong protest to the British ambassador and said it reserved the right to refuse such groups in the future.

(JUDITH L. CLARKE)

This article updates the *Macropædia* article Mainland SOUTH-EAST ASIA: *Vietnam.*

Western Europe

WESTERN EUROPEAN AFFAIRS

The European Communities (EC, comprising the European Economic Community [EEC], the European Coal and Steel Community [ECSC], and Euratom) confronted two powerful but potentially conflicting pressures during 1989: pressure to accelerate internal economic and political integration and pressure to open its doors to new member states. The year ended with a major debate under way about the extent to which enlargement of the Community beyond its present 12 member countries might threaten greater internal integration.

The Community's formal political agenda during the year was largely dominated by the issues surrounding the single European market, due to be completed by 1992, and a parallel plan to move to progressive economic and monetary union. The proposal to move to economic and monetary union (EMU)—including the possible introduction of a single European currency—proved controversial and aroused the special opposition of the British government. There was intermittent commercial friction between the EC and its major world trading partners, notably the U.S. and Japan. But while continued economic growth was a feature of 1989, the year ended with some fears that the long international economic recovery could be drawing to a close.

By general consensus, the EC benefited from a continuing sense of political dynamism during 1989, in marked contrast to the years of stagnation that ended only with the changes to the EC's constitution, known as the Single European Act, made in 1987. This sense of greater self-confidence was reflected at the biannual EC summit of heads of state and government held in Madrid on June 26 and 27. At that meeting, the EC leaders discussed the far-reaching proposals for economic and monetary union made by a committee of experts, chaired by the president of the EC's executive Commission, Jacques Delors. The committee's report, first published in April, suggested a three-stage move toward full union, including the eventual establishment of an EC central banking system, a single European currency, and greater supranational determination of common economic and monetary policies.

The general aims of EMU were endorsed by the great majority of the EC governments, with only the British government indicating opposition in principle, although some others, notably the West German Bundesbank, expressed doubts about a too rapid move to supranational union. Nevertheless, the year-end EC summit in Strasbourg set late 1990 as the date for an intergovernmental conference to open the way for monetary union. The British government's critical stance on EMU was matched by its unhappiness with other aspects of EC policy, and U.K. ministers frequently expressed their growing unease about the direction being taken by the Community. During the year British ministers found themselves involved in bitter arguments with both the Commission and other member states over a range of proposed EC policies, including a planned Social Charter of Workers' Rights, greater harmonization of indirect tax rates, and the scope of EC authority in educational policy. Only the U.K. withheld approval of the Social Charter at the Strasbourg summit.

European writers demonstrate outside the Palais de l'Europe, Strasbourg, France, where the European Parliament was discussing the influx of American television programs. Many Europeans believed that the preponderance of U.S. shows on European television stifled cultural diversity. AFP PHOTO

During the first half of the year, the presidency of the EC Council of Ministers passed to the Spanish government, which in June announced its enthusiastic support for the goal of greater European integration by preparing to peg the Spanish peseta within the fixed exchange rate regime of the European Monetary System. This left only sterling outside the EMS system. At the Madrid summit, British Prime Minister Margaret Thatcher indicated that the U.K. might agree to participate when the first stage of monetary union began in July 1990, provided other EC governments had abolished controls over the movement of capital. The EC governments agreed that the first stage of EMU should be restricted to greater intergovernmental cooperation on economic and monetary policy. However, Delors, in a speech before the College of Europe in the Belgian city of Brugge on September 17, proposed moving to the more ambitious second and third stages no later than Dec. 31, 1992, the deadline for the single market.

Progress to make a reality of the barrier- and frontier-free European market proved somewhat slow during the year, and the French government, which took over the EC presidency in July, made this its top priority for the second half of 1989. Only a little over half of the 270 pieces of European legislation needed to achieve the single market had been passed by the middle of the year. Moreover, serious disagreements among governments remained over key issues, such as whether to completely abolish national frontier controls over the movement of peoples from one EC country to another and what system of indirect controls should be implemented when the borders were opened. On the other hand, the prospects for agreement on the creation of a single financial market seemed brighter, and experts seemed confident that the process of creating the internal market was now irreversible.

The attractions of the single market for other countries were undeniable. A summit meeting of the prime ministers of the six governments of the European Free Trade Association (Austria, Finland, Iceland, Norway, Sweden, and Switzerland), held in Oslo, Norway, on March 14–15, was followed by negotiations on the creation of a single "economic space" involving all 18 EC and EFTA countries. However, it was uncertain whether negotiations between the two blocs would lead to agreed structures for administering the new market. This doubt led Austria to formally apply for full EC membership in July, and there was speculation during the Norwegian general election in

September that it too might pursue the option of EC membership. With a membership application from Turkey already on the table, the first response of the Commission was none too enthusiastic. There was general agreement that there could be no negotiations to enlarge the present Community before the completion of the single market.

In the early months of 1989, final agreements on commercial and economic cooperation were signed between the EC and both Hungary and Poland, marking a new state in the evolution of those countries toward a more market-based economic system. A limited protocol agreement was signed between the EC and Comecon, the Eastern bloc trading organization, and in December the EC signed a 10-year trade agreement with the Soviet Union. Following the meeting of leaders of the main Western industrialized nations in Paris during July, the Commission was charged with coordinating a major program of aid to Hungary and Poland.

In the closing months of the year, there was renewed speculation about the form political links between the Eastern European countries and the EC should take. The liberalization taking place in East Germany and the opening of the East-West German border revived apprehension in EC capitals that German reunification might be coming back onto the political agenda. Some EC leaders expressed worries that West German preoccupation with German unity might slow the pace of internal integration among the EC countries, but this was denied by the government in Bonn. The Strasbourg summit issued a declaration recognizing the German people's right to "regain unity through free self-determination" but including a number of conditions, among them recognition of the inviolability of the post-World War II borders.

A major event of the year was the third direct election to the European Parliament, held in June. It produced a significant swing to the left in the political composition of the 518-member assembly, with notable gains for the antinuclear left-wing Green parties and some of the EC socialist parties. However, neofascist groups also won additional votes in both France and West Germany. The newly elected Parliament lost no time in making clear its determination to play a bigger and more influential role in the Community's decision-making process. European parliamentarians served notice that they would take advantage of any amendment to the Treaty of Rome, the constitution of the EC, to press for an increased legislative

role. In October they warned that if national governments blocked or diluted the proposed Social Charter, they might delay ratification of other legislation needed to implement the single market. The Parliament also lent its weight to the growing pressure for tougher EC-wide protection of the environment. This strengthened the authority of the Commission in its campaign to enforce higher environmental standards. A number of member states were taken before the European Court of Justice in Luxembourg for failure to observe agreed EC standards of water purity.

There were continued difficulties in commercial relations with both the U.S. and Japan. A sharp disagreement between Brussels and Washington over an EC ban on imported meat containing artificial hormones, introduced in January, led to a series of trade sanctions and countersanctions that threatened to sour negotiations within the General Agreement on Tariffs and Trade for a freer global trading system. Although diplomatic action defused the hormone crisis, lingering doubts about protectionist tendencies in both the U.S. and the EC continued to overshadow relations across the Atlantic. These were revived during October following a decision by the Council of Ministers to discourage the use of non-European-made TV programs and films, a move criticized in Washington as a reversion to "Fortress Europe" policies. Similar charges were made by Japan, which pressed the EC to remove national import restrictions on Japanese cars as part of its single market program. For their part, the Europeans complained about the size of the Japanese trade surplus and the obstacles put in the way of European companies trying to enter the Japanese market.

Inevitably, the Council of Europe, a body linking 23 Western European governments, was overshadowed by the Community during 1989. However, the Council was addressed by Soviet leader Mikhail Gorbachev in July, when he made a renewed appeal for "a common European home" linking nations from the Urals to the Atlantic. This was followed by an agreement that Hungary, Poland, the Soviet Union, and Yugoslavia would be given observer status in the Council, which hitherto had excluded Eastern bloc countries.

The membership of the Western European Union, an organization linking the principal European members of NATO, remained at nine. Discussions continued about the need to strengthen the "European pillar" of NATO and the division of responsibility for European security policy between the WEU and the EC. However, developments in Eastern Europe and the continuing disarmament "offensive" of the Soviet government highlighted divisions within both bodies about future security strategy. The participation of socialist ministers in the Belgian and Dutch coalition governments strengthened those, headed by West Germany, arguing for more rapid progress in arms control and a greater denuclearization of NATO defense policy—a development opposed by the British and U.S. governments in particular.   (JOHN PALMER)

See also Economic Affairs; Military Affairs.

ANDORRA

A landlocked independent coprincipality of Europe, Andorra is in the Pyrenees Mountains between Spain and France. Area: 468 sq km (181 sq mi). Pop. (1989 est.): 50,000. Cap.: Andorra la Vella. Monetary units: French franc and Spanish peseta. Coprinces: the president of the French Republic and the bishop of Urgel, Spain, represented by their veguers (provosts) and batlles (prosecutors); chief executive in 1988, Josep Pintat-Solans. An elected Council General of 28 members elects the first syndic, in 1989 Francesc Cerqueda Pascuet.

The completion of the single market within the European Communities, scheduled for 1992, continued to be the main item of political concern in Andorra in 1989. Since a great amount of Andorra's income was obtained from trading in duty-free goods, the economy would be severely affected if developments within the EC brought this trade to an end.

The preoccupation of the Andorran government was to negotiate a special relationship with the Community. Andorra's trading status was being reviewed by the EC, and in April representatives of the Andorran government held negotiations with EC officials in Brussels over establishing a commercial agreement between the two sides. Advocates of devolution of some of the powers of the coprinces won a narrow majority in parliamentary elections held in December.   (ALUN JONES)

This article updates the Micropædia article ANDORRA.

AUSTRIA

The republic of Austria is a landlocked state of central Europe. Area: 83,857 sq km (32,377 sq mi). Pop. (1989 est.): 7,603,000. Cap.: Vienna. Monetary unit: Austrian Schilling, with (Oct. 2, 1989) a free rate of 13.18 Schillings to U.S. $1 (21.33 Schillings = £1 sterling). President in 1989, Kurt Waldheim; chancellor, Franz Vranitzky.

In July 1989 Austria requested admission into the European Communities (EC). Apart from the Greens, all Austrian parliamentary parties supported the petition. It was assumed that long, difficult negotiations would follow, after which a referendum would have to be held before Austria could formally join the EC. Concerns were voiced in Austria, the EC, and the Soviet Union regarding the possible conflict between Austria's status as a neutral nation and EC membership since the EC was also a military alliance. However, the decreased tensions between East and West and the growing integration of Europe could make such neutrality superfluous. Austria's entry into the EC could become a precedent for other neutral European countries. Relations with the EC were strained late in the year when Austria passed a night ban on noisy trucks, many of which carried perishables to EC markets.

The softening of the Communist systems in Eastern Europe afforded Austria more opportunity for cooperation. Many people, particularly in Hungary and Yugoslavia, looked to Austria's neutrality and strong social democratic system as a possible model upon which to base their own futures. The opening of the Austria-Hungary border by Hungary in 1989 led to a mass escape to Western Europe, especially by East Germans, through Hungary and Austria.

In 1988–89 Austria's economy experienced a 4% annual growth rate. The export and tourism sectors set records, and a low inflation rate of about 3% was recorded. Unemployment remained stable at or below 5%, but the country lacked some 10,000 skilled workers and apprentices.

Scandals continued to shake Austria in 1989. A parliamentary fact-finding committee was formed to uncover the possible misuse of public offices for private criminal activity in the "Lucona affair," an alleged 1977 insurance fraud that resulted in six deaths. In January Interior Minister Karl Blecha and Leopold Gratz, president of the Parliament, resigned amid allegations that they had interfered with previous investigations. Udo Proksch, a key suspect in the Lucona affair who had disappeared in early 1988, was arrested in transit at the Vienna airport in October.

The "Noricum affair" revolved around the delivery of weapons to Iran in 1985 and 1986 by the state-owned arms manufacturer Noricum, in violation of a law banning

Hungarian soldiers remove the barbed-wire fence separating Hungary from Austria. Hungary's removal of the fence and the opening of its common border with Austria sparked a mass exodus of people hoping to escape from Eastern Europe to the West.
ERIC BOUVET—GAMMA/LIAISON

the sale of weapons to nations at war. Eighteen Noricum managers went on trial in November, and a parliamentary committee was created to investigate the involvement of politicians. Chancellor Franz Vranitzky's call for an end to all arms exports led to discussions about Austrian arms production. The problem was that weapons could be produced only in large quantities that exceeded domestic requirements. The debate also revolved around the federal army itself, which some people argued should be changed to a militia or completely abolished.

Voter dissatisfaction was clearly expressed through election results. In the provincial elections in Lower Austria in October 1988 and in Kärnten, Salzburg, and Tirol in March 1989, the Socialist Party (SPÖ) and the People's Party (ÖVP) that formed the government coalitions lost high percentages of votes to the opposition parties. In Kärnten the leader of the right-wing Freedom Party (FPÖ), Jörg Haider, was elected provincial governor. The poor showing by the ÖVP reflected badly on the federal party chief, Alois Mock, who resigned in April as ÖVP leader and as vice-chancellor, although he remained foreign minister. Josef Riegler was elected at the ÖVP congress in May to replace Mock.

Zita of Bourbon, the last empress of Austria, was buried in Vienna with full royal regalia in a nationally televised funeral in March. Austria also lost two great men of culture in 1989: the important German-language playwright Thomas Bernhard and Herbert von Karajan, world-renowned conductor of the Berlin Philharmonic Orchestra. (*See* OBITUARIES.)   (ELFRIEDE DIRNBACHER)

BELGIUM

A constitutional monarchy, the Benelux country of Belgium is situated on the North Sea coast of northwestern Europe. Area: 30,518 sq km (11,783 sq mi). Pop. (1989 est.) 9,878,000. Cap. Brussels. Monetary unit: Belgian franc, with (Oct. 2, 1989) a commercial rate of BF 39.34 to U.S. $1 (BF 63.65 = £1 pound sterling) and a financial rate of BF 39.46 to U.S. $1 (BF 63.85 = £1 pound sterling). King, Baudouin I; prime minister in 1989, Wilfried Martens.

The second stage in the federalization of Belgium was ushered in by a vote in the Senate on Jan. 16, 1989; it provided for the transfer to the regions and communities of two major ministerial departments, Education and Public Works, as well as a number of specific powers. Also approved was an extension of the powers of the Court of Arbitration. Disagreements appeared with respect to the third and last stage of the reform of the state structures, which would modify the existing two-chamber system, provide for direct election of the members of the regional and community assemblies, grant the regions and communities the right to conclude international treaties, and transfer residual powers to the regions and communities. The French Socialist chairman, Guy Spitaels, as well as the Flemish Nationalists (Volksunie), wanted to transfer additional national ministries to the regions, although they did not agree on which ones. The Social Christians had doubts about the urgency and contents of the third stage.

As provided in the second stage, elections were organized for the new Brussels regional assembly on June 18. Of the 75 seats, 64 went to French-speaking parties and only 11 to the Flemish parties. The government coalition parties formed the new five-member executive in which the Flemish group was granted fixed representation. The steps toward federalization did not pacify relations between the language communities. In Voeren (Fourons) in Dutch-speaking Flanders, José Happart, who as mayor had caused a crisis by refusing to speak Dutch, was succeeded by a party friend. The new mayor's decision to set up polling stations for the European Parliament elections in a French school was countered by the minister of the interior, Louis Tobback, who dispatched civil defense trucks to serve as polling stations. A decision by local authorities in Overijse, on the outskirts of Brussels, to issue building permits only to Flemish-speaking citizens created further animosity.

Results of the European elections on June 18 were disappointing for most of the coalition parties. The leading vote getters were outgoing foreign minister Léo Tindemans (433,172 votes) and Happart (308,112). The extreme right, with a platform directed against Arab immigrants, made considerable headway in the elections for both the European Parliament and the Brussels regional assembly.

Relations with Zaire reached a low ebb when the Belgian government refused to forgive its former colony's debt. Following mediation by King Hassan of Morocco, an agreement was signed in Rabat in July whereby Belgium agreed to release Zaire from a major part of its debt, amounting to nearly BF 11 billion. For its part, Zaire canceled all the measures it had taken against Belgian interests. (*See* Africa South of the Sahara: *Zaire,* above.)

In order to reduce the 1990 budget deficit to BF 405

billion, or 6.5% of gross national product, excise duties on cigarettes and motor fuel were increased and previously granted tax deductions were partially rescinded. A vote by a Senate commission favouring legalized abortion under certain circumstances was vehemently opposed by all the Belgian bishops. The introduction of high-speed train service was delayed because the Flemish and French parties could not agree on the route. A study revealed that 75% of rivers and lakes in Flanders were badly or very badly polluted.

Early in the year the abduction of former prime minister Paul Vanden Boeynants, a wealthy businessman, created a sensation. He was released after 30 days following payment of a ransom. Later it appeared the abduction was organized by Patrick Haemers, a notorious criminal who was later arrested in Brazil.   (JAN R. ENGELS)

This article updates the *Macropædia* article The Low COUNTRIES: *Belgium.*

DENMARK

A constitutional monarchy of north central Europe, Denmark lies between the North and Baltic seas. Area: 43,093 sq km (16,638 sq mi), excluding the Faeroe Islands and Greenland. Pop. (1989 est.): 5,135,000. Cap.: Copenhagen. Monetary unit: Danish krone, with (Oct. 2, 1989) a free rate of 7.30 kroner to U.S. $1 (11.81 kroner = £1 sterling). Queen, Margrethe II; prime minister in 1989, Poul Schlüter.

There was no end to Denmark's economic woes in 1989, as the centre-right minority government of Poul Schlüter, the country's first Conservative prime minister of the century, negotiated with opposition parties to secure backing for an economic plan for "growth and progress" in the 1990s. Schlüter's plan called for major reforms of Denmark's tax and social security systems, along with moves toward tax harmonization with the rest of the European Communities (EC) before the introduction of the single European market in 1992. It envisaged 40 billion kroner a year in tax cuts. Danes pay the highest personal income taxes in the EC, and these, along with the 50% corporate tax rate, were the major targets of the government's planned reductions. Company taxes would drop to 35% and income taxes to between 45 and 52% from the present 52–68%, with purchase taxes slashed on gasoline (petrol) and a variety of consumer goods. The cuts, to be phased in over four years from 1991, would be financed by reductions in state and local authority spending, lower unemployment and health service benefits, and slashes in tax compensation.

The plan was immediately attacked by Svend Auken, the leader of the Social Democratic Party, the main opposition grouping. The Social Democrats issued their own plan, which called for tax cuts for the lower paid and a drive to slash unemployment. In early December, however, after months of negotiations, Schlüter put together a compromise satisfactory to all six nonsocialist parties, including the populist Progress Party, which had never supported a finance bill before. Among other changes, the compromise bill reduced company taxes to 40%. A controversial item was abolition of the three-year-old tax penalty on borrowing for purposes other than student loans or mortgages, which had sharply reduced consumer spending.

Overshadowing the negotiations on the plan were serious economic problems, notably unemployment at over 9% of the work force, a balance of payments deficit forecast to rise to 13.5 billion kroner in 1989, and a state budget shortfall in the region of 16 billion kroner. Denmark, which had the highest material standard of living in the EC, had foreign debts of 300 billion kroner, the equivalent

of $8,200 per Danish citizen. Although an Economy Ministry report published in the autumn saw Denmark's gross national product growing by 2% in 1989 (after two years of stagnation) and industrial exports by over 7%, most analysts were not optimistic about Denmark's chances for a quick economic revival. With eight wrangling political parties in the Folketing (parliament) and a tradition of minority coalition governments, consensus was the name of the game in Danish politics, making agreement on the tough economic measures difficult in the extreme. Some analysts prophesied intervention by the International Monetary Fund in the early 1990s as the only solution.

Denmark froze its military expenditure within NATO at an annual 13 billion kroner for the next three years. It became the first country to legalize civil marriages between homosexuals, and Pope John Paul II was given a cool reception during his five-day visit to what is a bastion of Lutheranism. Denmark's Protestant church still strongly resented the excommunication of Martin Luther by the Roman Catholic Church in the 16th century during the Protestant Reformation. In the summer elections to the European Parliament, Danes showed their traditional disinterest in European affairs with a dismal 46% voter turnout, the lowest in any Danish election in the century.
                    (CHRISTOPHER FOLLETT)

FINLAND

The republic of Finland is in northern Europe, on the Gulf of Bothnia and the Gulf of Finland. Area: 338,145 sq km (130,559 sq mi). Pop. (1989 est.): 4,960,000. Cap.: Helsinki. Monetary unit: Finnish markka, with (Oct. 2, 1989) a free rate of 4.27 markkaa to U.S. $1 (6.91 markkaa = £1 sterling). President in 1989, Mauno Koivisto; prime minister, Harri Holkeri.

Finland came close to full employment in 1989, although the government continued to complain because the 4% unemployment rate was accompanied by a rise in the inflation rate to an estimated 6.5%. Another troubling aspect of the economy was persistent heavy borrowing from abroad. The problem of the swelling deficit in the current account was compounded in September by news that the National Board of Customs had fumbled its statistics earlier in the year and the country was running a larger than expected deficit in visible trade.

The government's 1990 draft budget, with the traditional emphasis on social security and education, was the third balanced budget in a row. Nevertheless, it was quickly condemned by banking and industrial circles as too lax. The government, which consisted mainly of Social Democrats and Conservatives with a few representatives from the Swedish and Rural parties, showed greater stringency when, in September, it imposed a tax on the building of hotels, restaurants, services, and cultural and sports premises to counteract what it described as overheating in the construction sector.

Wartsila Marine, a major producer of passenger cruise liners and icebreakers, admitted in the summer that it was in severe financial difficulties despite a fat order book; it was bailed out by the government. Another company, Nokia, which had been spearheading Finland's high-technology drive, was embroiled during the year in a patent case with the U.S. corporation Motorola over sales in the U.S. of its mobile cellular telephones.

The big political story of the year had its origins early in the decade. In his memoirs, published in August, former prime minister Ahti Karjalainen accused Paavo Väyrynen, the current leader of the opposition Centre Party, of having conspired with the Soviets to affect Finnish internal

Demonstrators in Helsinki, Finland, march outside the presidential palace, where Soviet Pres. Mikhail Gorbachev was visiting, carrying signs that refer to the Finnish Karelia region. Finland lost the region to the Soviet Union during World War II.
AP/WIDE WORLD

affairs. According to Karjalainen, in 1981 Väyrynen, then minister for foreign affairs, consulted a senior Soviet official on ways the Soviet Union might help defeat Mauno Koivisto, a Social Democrat, in the 1982 presidential election. Koivisto was ultimately elected and went on to win a second six-year term in 1988.

Amid charges in the press that his action was close to treason, Väyrynen admitted to having had talks at the Soviet embassy with former ministerial counsellor Viktor Vladimirov, widely reported in the press to be a general in the Soviet security police, the KGB. However, he denied that he had done anything to harm the country. President Koivisto said publicly that he believed the charge. He noted, however, that such behaviour—which had prompted aspersions within the international community of "Finlandization," or undue readiness to accept Moscow's interference in Finnish affairs—was a thing of the past. The press did not unanimously agree with his assessment, but he received some backing from Soviet Pres. Mikhail Gorbachev, who during a visit in October said the U.S.S.R. had no right to interfere in the affairs of its neighbours.

Elsewhere on the political scene, the Finnish Communist Party, one of the world's oldest and formerly a fixed part of coalition governments, continued to decline. In the summer it decided to merge into a new Alliance of the Left, to be created in 1990.

Parliament remained split over policy on economic integration within the European Communities. The EC was Finland's most important trading partner, and the government insisted that an accommodation with it had to be found if Finland was not to suffer severely, although Finnish neutrality excluded the possibility of eventual full membership. The opposition persisted in emphasizing the need to maintain Finland's subsidized farming and protected markets. Finland, which belonged to the European Free Trade Association, planned to approach the EC through that organization.   (EDWARD M. SUMMERHILL)

FRANCE

A republic of western Europe, France includes the island of Corsica in the Mediterranean Sea and has coastlines on the English Channel, the Mediterranean, and the Atlantic Ocean. Area: 543,965 sq km (210,026 sq mi). Pop. (1989 est.): 56,107,-000. Cap.: Paris. Monetary unit: franc, with (Oct. 2, 1989) a free rate of F 6.36 to U.S. $1 (F 10.29 = £1 sterling). President in 1989, François Mitterrand; prime minister, Michel Rocard.

The year 1988 was full of political events, such as the reelection of Pres. François Mitterrand and the election of a new National Assembly. In 1989, however, the public showed little interest in the municipal elections, in the European Parliament elections, which showed a record number of abstentions, or in the partial renewing of the Senate. On the other hand, the French showed great enthusiasm over the celebration in all its aspects of the bicentennial of the French Revolution. (See Sidebar.)

Domestic Affairs. Mitterrand started out the year with a bang. During his speech to the nation delivered from Strasbourg, he referred to the bicentennial of the Revolution and the Declaration of Human Rights and requested that the government carry on a bolder policy to address the problem of the "excluded" and the "marginals," starting with the immigrants. This presidential initiative would take shape also through the contemplated reform of the penal code.

A few weeks later on television, Mitterrand, who had not made any general comments on the state of the nation since July 1988, reaffirmed his leftist loyalties and his faith in the "union of popular forces." Half of this two-hour broadcast was devoted to business and particularly to the serious political-financial scandal surrounding the takeover of Triangle Industries by Péchiney and the insider trading investigation involving Mitterrand's longtime friend Roger-Patrice Pelat, who died suddenly while under indictment.

In March a little over 30 million voters were asked to renew the municipal councils of 36,736 communes in France and its overseas territories. The second round of elections confirmed the apparent successes of the Socialist Party (PS) in the first round. The PS was victorious in 35 of 42 cities with populations of more than 20,000. The rightist Rassemblement pour la République (RPR) and Union pour la Démocratic Françoise (UDF), as well as the Communist Party (PC), lost more large cities than they gained. The Greens (environmentalists) and the extreme right-wing National Front retained their victories from the first round and made inroads in a large number of municipal councils.

On a more personal level, three leading political figures experienced exceptional triumphs by winning all the districts of the three great cities where they campaigned for mayor. Former prime minister Jacques Chirac (RPR) was elected mayor for the second time in Paris, while former trade minister Michel Noir (RFPR) in Lyon defeated

both the outgoing mayor, Francisque Collomb, and former prime minister Raymond Barre (UDF). Robert Vigouroux, incumbent mayor of Marseille and a dissident within the PS, was reelected over Jean-Claude Gaudin (UDF).

Conservative leaders Valéry Giscard d'Estaing and Chirac made an appeal for the unification of the rightist opposition without delay in order to face the elections to the European Parliament on June 18. In truth, the right had not come up with satisfactory responses to the challenges in its path since its defeat in the presidential elections of May 1988.

In the European elections the result of this joint appeal was the success of the roll of candidates presented by the opposition union of the UDF and the RPR, which outpolled the Socialists led by Laurent Fabius. However, the three main government parties—the UDF, the RPR, and the PS—won only a little more than half of the votes. The National Front of Jean-Marie Le Pen ranked third, confirming his presence on the political gameboard. The good showing of Antoine Waechter and the Greens rekindled the demand for a renovation of the French political system as a whole.

Moreover, with the exception of the 1988 referendum on the future of New Caledonia, the European elections on June 18, 1989, established a record of abstentions for a national turnout; more than one out of every two French citizens avoided the ballots. Only 18,690,692 (48.8%) of the 38,297,496 registered voters went to the polls. The UDF-RPR coalition took the lead, with 5,242,038 votes (28.87%) and 26 seats. The PS obtained 4,286,354 votes (23.61%) and 22 seats; the National Front got 2,129,668 votes (11.73%) and 10 seats; the Greens received 1,922,945 votes (10.59%) and 9 seats; the centrists won 1,529,346 votes (8.42%) and 7 seats; and the PC got 1,401,171 votes (7.71%) and 7 seats.

The renewal of 102 of the 321 Senate seats resulted in a loss of influence for the centre group, to the benefit of the RPR, which gained 11 seats. The following week Alain Poher was elected president of the Senate for the eighth consecutive time.

At the beginning of May, all of France was shocked to hear of the murder in New Caledonia of two independence leaders, Jean-Marie Tjibaou and Yeiwené Yeiwené, both native Caledonians who had signed the Matignon agreements of 1988. The Caledonian Union, the main element of the FLNKS (Kanak Socialist National Liberation Front), immediately confirmed that it intended to bring to a conclusion the process started in 1988, adding that the two murdered leaders "left a heritage of tolerance and wisdom which the movement owes to itself to continue with courage and strength." Prime Minister Michel Rocard, who attended the funeral services of the two leaders of the FLNKS, announced without delay his intention of keeping to the schedule set out in the Matignon agreements for New Caledonia's future. "Tolerance will not take a back seat to fanaticsm," he stated.

The new Assembly sessions to discuss the national budget did not manage to disguise the underlying social conflicts; the main payoffs were an increase in salaries and an improvement in the status of workers. At the beginning of the year, the Paris transport commission broke the ban on strikes, thereby plunging the capital into chaos. Protests by nurses, doctors, and schoolteachers were followed by strikes by prison guards, general discontent within the military and the police, and an impasse in the dialogue with Corsica. After a seven-week strike, work was finally resumed at the Peugeot factories in Mulhouse and Sochaux. At the end of October the union of financial agents, and particularly tax agents, still continued its five-month-long strike, which completely paralyzed many of the country's financial services.

Foreign Affairs. Foreign relations and defense were matters reserved for the head of state, and President Mitterrand devoted himself wholeheartedly to this task. Trips abroad followed in quick succession. The first was to Prague, Mitterrand's first visit to Central Europe since his reelection. This was followed by a French-African summit meeting in Casablanca, Morocco, where Morocco confirmed its reentry into the continental scene, and a conference in Paris on chemical warfare, at which Mitterrand acted as host, which came to a conclusion later at the UN.

Mitterrand paid the first visit by a French head of state to Bulgaria in January. Several months later in Boston, during a meeting between U.S. Pres. George Bush and

---

The Bicentennial of the French Revolution

It should come as no surprise that, in view of the lacklustre political scene, the French took up with such great enthusiasm the bicentennial celebrations that started the first of the year. The festivities included a reenactment in Versailles of the Jeu de Paume oath and the meeting of the Estates-General. In addition, some 500,000 people showed up at the Champ de Mars for the party organized by the city of Paris to celebrate the 100th anniversary of the Eiffel Tower.

On July 13 the 33 heads of state and government leaders invited to Paris by Pres. François Mitterrand went to the Trocadero for a midday ceremony to commemorate the Rights of Man. That night a grand ball was held to inaugurate the Opera Bastille. The next day came the main event at the Champs-Élysées to celebrate the 200th anniversary of the storming of the Bastille. Fireworks completed a lavish parade designed by the advertising genius Jean-Paul Goude and admired by a million people, not counting hundreds of thousands of TV viewers. The parade was kicked off with a magnificent military display along the Champs-Élysées to the Place de la Concorde, as proof of the modernization of the French Army. Later, under the floodlights and to the enthusiastic applause of the crowd, more than 6,000 multinational performers—ranging from a Florida A&M band to Italian lancers to Sri Lankans with their elephants—took part in the Festival of the Planet's Tribes, climaxed by the singing of the French national anthem, *La Marseillaise* by the American soprano Jessye Norman.

Numerous celebrations were held in the provinces, but during a week of festivities, Paris was aflame in a whirlwind of joie de vivre. The French sought not to remember certain bloody episodes of the Revolution (such as the Reign of Terror) but rather to renew the ideas of liberty, equality, and brotherhood. As for Mitterrand, he undoubtedly achieved a personal triumph in the foreign and the French eye by emphasizing the "history" and the "message" of France.

(JEAN KNECHT)

Celebratory fireworks marked the 100th anniversary of the Eiffel Tower and the 200th anniversary of the French Revolution. The week-long festivities drew many visitors and heads of state from around the world.
ERIC BRISSAUD—GAMMA/LIAISON

Mitterrand, the latter was able to observe a substantial change in the U.S. attitude toward Europe. The U.S. president wished for a "new partnership" between the United States and Europe. In December he met with Soviet Pres. Mikhail Gorbachev in Kiev and, later in the month, with Bush again on the Caribbean island of St. Martin.

During the course of the year, Mitterrand also visited India for three days and attended the funeral services in Tokyo of Emperor Hirohito. He was the host of the 53rd French-German summit with West German Chancellor Helmut Kohl. Later, in Paris, he welcomed Palestinian leader Yasir Arafat for the first time, a visit that caused great commotion within the French Jewish community. Mitterrand visited Poland to reassure the Polish people that France would furnish all aid needed for the nation's economic recovery.

As an accompaniment to the celebrations of the bicentennial of the French Revolution, Paris served as the site for the 15th summit meeting of the seven principal industrialized countries. The meetings, held in the controversial new Grand Arch de la Défense and in a new addition to the Louvre, took place in a harmonious atmosphere and concluded with the publication of an economic declaration and several political texts that showed considerable progress over the previous summit.

Two new topics were brought up for the first time: the war on drugs and the deterioration of the environment. However, the main decision reached by the seven—eight after the president of the European Commission, Jacques Delors, joined the group—concerned East-West relations. In effect, the summit entrusted the European Communities (EC) with the task of coordinating all Western aid to

Poland and Hungary and with following up on the Eastern European reforms. Gorbachev's five-page letter, addressed to Mitterrand as president of the summit and requesting closer economic cooperation between East and West, caused a certain stir by revealing the Soviet desire to be fully integrated into the international community.

On a Latin-American tour in the autumn, Mitterrand met with his counterpart in Caracas, Venezuela, Carlos Andrés Pérez, to renew the North-South dialogue and to advance negotiations on the reduction of outstanding debts by less developed countries. Mitterrand also signed a cooperation agreement in the war against drugs. During this trip, Mitterrand visited Guadaloupe, which had been hit by Hurricane Hugo, to offer France's goodwill toward the victims. He also visited Ecuador and, before returning to Paris, showed his support for President Bush's war on drugs by making an unscheduled stop in Colombia to reassure Pres. Virgilio Barco Vargas of France's and the EC's support in the fight against drug dealers.

At the end of October Mitterrand met with Spanish Prime Minister Felipe González Márquez in a summit without precedent in European history. Also in October, Mitterrand declared in a speech to the European Parliament that it was imperative to offer help to the Soviet Union and to Gorbachev and that the only possible response to the events that had shaken the Eastern European countries would be the construction of a political Europe. He particularly pleaded in favour of a European monetary union (EMU). In order to fulfill his promises, Mitterrand announced an aid package to Poland amounting to almost F 4 million over a three-year period.

The 54th French-West German summit took place on November 2–3 in Bonn. Kohl and Mitterrand met privately several times to discuss the Eastern European situation and to prepare for the EC summit, which convened on December 8 in Strasbourg. Mitterrand stirred up strong reactions at the summit by again stressing the need for an EMU and caution over possible German unification.

(JEAN KNECHT)

See also *Dependent States,* below.

GERMANY, FEDERAL REPUBLIC OF

The Federal Republic of Germany (West Germany) is in central Europe, on the North and Baltic seas. Area: 248,709 sq km (96,027 sq mi). Pop. (1989 est.; including West Berlin, which is an enclave within East Germany, and excluding some 600,000 immigrants and refugees arriving in 1989 from East Germany, the Soviet Union, Poland, and elsewhere in Eastern Europe): 61,131,000. Provisional cap.: Bonn. Monetary unit: Deutsche Mark, with (Oct. 2, 1989) a free rate of DM 1.87 to U.S. $1 (DM 3.03 = £1 sterling). President in 1989, Richard von Weizsacker; chancellor, Helmut Kohl.

The Federal Republic of Germany (FRG; West Germany) marked its 40th anniversary during 1989 and, with maturity, seemed to find new confidence to accept international responsibility in keeping with its position as a world economic superpower. East-West relations dominated the political scene throughout the year, and the government recognized a need for major financial aid to help emerging democracies in the Eastern bloc. The main interest, however, was in the turbulence caused by the movement for reform in the German Democratic Republic (GDR; East Germany), which made the German Question a live topic once again.

The mass movement of ethnic German refugees from the GDR and other parts of the Soviet empire created short-term problems and was a major reason behind the strong and unexpected support for the radical right-wing Repub-

licans in a series of elections. This shocked the established parties and forced a change in tactics by the government coalition led by the Christian Democratic Union (CDU). The Social Democratic Party (SPD), meanwhile, succeeded in forming a "red-green" coalition with the environmentally oriented Alternative List to rule in West Berlin. Economically the country continued to move ahead, maintaining its dominant position inside the European Communities (EC). However, bank interest rates were raised four times in response to signs of overheating and inflation.

Terrorism proved a serious problem. West German investigators were deeply involved in the inquiries into the midair bombing of a Pan Am flight over Lockerbie, Scotland, on Dec. 21, 1988, and a series of attacks on British targets for which the Irish Republican Army (IRA) claimed responsibility. On November 30 Alfred Herrhausen (*see* OBITUARIES), chief executive of the Deutsche Bank and one of the country's most powerful men, was killed in a bomb attack in Bad Homburg. The killing bore the marks of the Red Army Faction, a leftist urban guerrilla group that had been active in the late 1960s and early '70s. Most of its members were dead or in prison, but a small remnant was still at large.

Domestic Affairs. The year began badly for Chancellor Helmut Kohl with the disclosure in the press that West German companies had been involved in the construction of a plant in Libya capable of manufacturing poison gas. Although it later emerged that the government had been warned of this by the United States on a number of occasions in 1988, the revelation that U.S. intelligence had listened to telephone conversations between Libya and Imhausen-Chemie—the main company involved in constructing the plant—angered public opinion. A criminal investigation was begun against Imhausen; tougher penalties were introduced to punish companies exporting sensitive materials to "irresponsible" countries; and the government was strengthened in its resolve to take a more independent stand within NATO.

There was already strong grass-roots pressure for this course. Local citizens groups had been campaigning for reduction or abolition of low-level training flights by NATO air forces and for curbs on large-scale army maneuvers. In January the government had agreed to activate unpopular legislation to increase the length of military service from 15 to 18 months, and this added further resentment. Conveniently, the government found new figures in April that enabled it to postpone implementation of the longer service period until 1992. The main public concern, however, was with NATO plans to modernize short-range nuclear weapons, largely based in West Germany. Hans-Dietrich Genscher, the foreign minister, led opposition to the idea, arguing that it would send the wrong kind of signal to the Soviet Union at a time when that country needed encouragement in introducing *perestroika* (restructuring) and *glasnost* (openness).

Chancellor Kohl backed this position and, despite strong argument from British Prime Minister Margaret Thatcher at Anglo-German summit meetings in February and April, he maintained the view that a decision on modernization could be postponed until 1992—well after the next general election. That was ultimately agreed to by the NATO summit in May, which also accepted the West German case that there should be negotiations on short-range nuclear reductions "at the earliest possible point in time." In September the Allies promised to reduce the time and speed of training flights, and the British Army agreed to some reductions in the use made of its training ground on Lüneburg Heath.

The CDU suffered its first and most serious election setback of the year in West Berlin on January 29, when its populist mayor, Eberhard Diepgen, lost control, largely because of the emergence of the radical right-wing Republicans, who took 7.5% of the votes. The result meant that the SPD leader, Walter Momper, was able to form a coalition with the Alternative List. The CDU lost out again during local elections in Hesse on March 12, when the Republicans and the extreme right-wing National Democratic Party won council seats in inner-city areas, and the SPD was able to form a ruling coalition with the Greens in 10 of the 29 local authorities, including Frankfurt. Franz Schönhuber, the former Waffen SS sergeant who founded the Republicans, denied he was in any way a Nazi and predicted his party would soon hold the balance of power in the government.

Kohl responded with a major Cabinet reshuffle on April 13 and a new government program, spelled out on April 27. He dismissed Rupert Scholz, his hawkish defense minister, replacing him with Gerhard Stoltenberg, the experienced finance minister. The finance portfolio was given to Theo Waigel, leader of the Christian Social Union (CSU), the CDU's Bavarian sister party. The Republicans were strongest in Bavaria, where the right-wing vote had been held for the CSU only by the charismatic Franz Josef Strauss, who died in October 1988. The new government program introduced measures aimed at curbing the number of ethnic German settlers arriving—to satisfy the Republicans—and tax incentives for environmentally friendly cars—to placate the Greens.

The voters in the elections to the European Parliament on June 18 seemed unimpressed. The CDU/CSU took

A couple display their new West German passports after fleeing the East. The influx of East Germans influenced local elections, causing an unexpected shift to the right. The coalition government was forced to change its tactics in order to win back conservative voters.

38% of the votes, the SPD won 36.7%—but the Republicans took 7.3% in their first nationwide test, just behind the Greens with 8.3%. The Free Democratic Party (FDP), thanks to the personal popularity of Genscher, its best-known member, scored 5.5%. The results were mirrored in local elections held the same day in Saarland, where Republicans won some support at the expense of the SPD, and in Rhineland-Palatinate, Kohl's home area, where the CDU was overtaken by the SPD.

After due reflection, Kohl decided to dismiss Heiner Geissler, the CDU's general secretary for the past 12 years, who had been trying to broaden the party's base to the left and was therefore blamed for prompting desertions to the Republicans. The chancellor's choice of Volker Rühe as a "new generation" replacement was endorsed by the CDU's conference in Bremen on September 11–13. On October 1, however, CDU voters in North Rhine-Westphalia's local elections continued to desert the party, which dropped nearly 5% of the support it had there five years earlier. The Republicans again did well in the big cities. The same trend away from the CDU continued in the local elections in Baden-Württemberg on October 23, where the Republicans scored up to 14.2%. With a growing housing shortage seen as a looming electoral issue, the government agreed to a major building program in November, at a cost of DM 2 billion a year until 1993.

The economy moved serenely ahead, with real gross domestic product growing by 4% and unemployment leveling out at 1.8 million, while the number of available jobs rose steadily. Surveys showed that West German companies were leading the EC in preparations for the removal of internal frontiers in 1992, although the transport and insurance sectors continued to drag their feet. Daimler-Benz was allowed to purchase Messerschmitt-Bölkow-Blohm, thus becoming a major force in the European aerospace industry as well as an important arms producer.

British forces in West Germany were put on red alert in the summer as the 20th anniversary of troops going into Northern Ireland approached. It proved only too necessary as the IRA began to claim responsibility for a series of attacks on British military personnel and their families. The antiterrorist unit of the Federal Criminal Police Office (BKA) was also involved in the investigation into the Pan Am bombing, with inquiries centring on two members of the Popular Front for the Liberation of Palestine—General Command, who had been arrested in October 1988 at a bomb-making factory in Neuss. The BKA was not able to establish a link between the two and the actual bombing, however, and in November they were charged with attempted murder for blowing up two U.S. troop trains in 1987 and 1988. In May one of the Palestinian hijackers of a TWA flight over the Mediterranean in 1985 was given a life sentence.

Foreign Affairs. West Germany was host to both U.S. Pres. George Bush and Soviet Pres. Mikhail Gorbachev within the space of two weeks in the early summer. The U.S. president, fresh from the NATO summit, which had agreed with his disarmament proposals, chose Mainz to make an important speech on May 31. He called on Europe to be "whole and free," on the East German regime to tear down the Berlin Wall, and on the Soviets to end the cold war. To the delight of his hosts, Bush said the U.S. and West Germany were now "partners in leadership." Aware of U.S. concern that his country was being increasingly tempted to look east, Kohl promised that the FRG would remain loyal to the West and to NATO. Nevertheless, when Gorbachev arrived for a four-day visit on June 12, he was given a far more rapturous reception by

the public than had been accorded the U.S. president. He was mobbed by crowds in Bonn and Stuttgart and cheered by the steelworkers of the Ruhr. At the end of the visit he signed a joint declaration with Kohl to work to achieve military balance in Europe and "to build a better future together."

Genscher worked through the year to help Poland and Hungary find the economic help needed to provide the stability that would allow democracy to take firm root. This argument was accepted by the Western economic summit meeting in Paris on July 14–15, which agreed to coordinate aid through the EC. However, negotiations with Poland on a bilateral aid package proved difficult, particularly after Waigel affirmed that the true borders of Germany legally remained those of the Third Reich in 1937—including Silesia and Pomerania, which are part of postwar Poland—and that the ethnic German population there should be able to choose freely in which country they wanted to live. This argument, strongly supported by the right wings of the CDU and the CSU, embarrassed Kohl, who could not afford to denounce it publicly since it simply restated the Basic Law which forms the country's constitution. As the reform movement in East Germany gathered strength, however, the need for agreement with Poland became more and more urgent. The government recognized that if Polish reforms were allowed to fail because of lack of money, the chances of similar reforms succeeding in East Germany were minimal. In October agreement was reached on an aid package for Poland, totaling some DM 3 billion in credits, and the chancellor agreed to a joint declaration accepting the 1970 Warsaw Treaty, which said the existing border was "inviolable."

On November 9 Kohl left for Poland on a visit of reconciliation, but within 24 hours he was forced to return to take charge of the situation created by the East German government's decision to open its borders to the West. Throughout the autumn, as the crisis in the GDR developed, West German politicians had tried to maintain a low profile. However, in agreeing unconditionally to grant citizenship to any ethnic German refugee, Bonn did precipitate the crisis. At the beginning of August, the West German representation in East Berlin was forced to close its doors because 131 would-be refugees invaded it, demanding the right to leave. In Budapest, Warsaw, and, later, Prague, West Germany's embassies were besieged by refugees. On September 11 Hungary opened its border with Austria, and the refugees began to stream out. They arrived in Bavaria to a rapturous, highly organized welcome, the first of a huge army of 100,000 and more mostly young, illegal refugees, whose departure largely forced the East German regime to resign and the new one to make concession after concession.

This allowed Kohl to dictate terms. He told the Bundestag in a state of the nation speech on November 8 that he would provide the economic aid needed to finance reform, but only if genuine Western-style democracy were introduced in the GDR. For the first time he spoke openly and confidently of a reunification of the country: "We have less reason than ever to be resigned to the long-term division of Germany into two states." On November 28 he outlined a 10-point plan for the development of common political and economic institutions, leading to federation of the two Germanys and eventual unification. Meanwhile, the huge influx of refugees was causing problems. There was insufficient housing available for them, and fears grew that unemployment would rise. But the real prospect of a reunited Germany fired the popular imagination. When the GDR opened its borders with the West on the night

of November 9, thousands rushed to the Berlin Wall to celebrate, greeting their fellow citizens with champagne, laughter, and cheers.

On November 28 Kohl put forward a 10-point plan for helping East Germany, which, he told the Bundestag, aimed at eventual reunification. He promised that the final decision would lie with the East Germans but made clear his belief that unity was only a matter of time. At the European summit in Strasbourg on December 8–9, he showed his new self-confidence in international affairs by forcing the meeting to agree that an intergovernmental conference on European monetary and currency union would be held in a year's time, after the West German elections. On December 19 he traveled to Dresden for a "German-German" summit with East German Premier Hans Modrow, and the two leaders drew up a blueprint for cooperation in a treaty to be signed the following spring.   (IAN MURRAY)

This article updates the *Macropædia* article GERMANY: *Federal Republic of Germany.*

GREECE

The republic of Greece occupies the southern part of the Balkan Peninsula and several adjoining island groups in southeastern Europe, in and between the Ionian and Aegean seas. Area: 131,957 sq km (50,949 sq mi). Pop. (1989 est.): 10,096,000. Cap.: Athens. Monetary unit: drachma, with (Oct. 2, 1989) a free rate of 164.49 drachmas to U.S. $1 (266.15 drachmas = £1 sterling). President in 1989, Christos Sartzetakis; prime ministers, Andreas Papandreou, Tzannis Tzannetakis from July 2, Yiannis Grivas (caretaker) from October 11, and Xenophon Zolotas from November 23.

The Panhellenic Socialist Movement (Pasok) of Prime Minister Andreas Papandreou, which was swept into power in 1981 and won a second term in 1985, was defeated in the general elections held on June 18, 1989. However, its main adversary, the conservative New Democracy Party of Konstantinos Mitsotakis, while winning first place, was six seats short of an overall majority in a hung Parliament of 300 members.

For a country that had had no experience of coalition government in 36 years, new elections seemed the only way out. However, two parties, New Democracy and the Communist-controlled Left Alliance, had focused their campaigns on "catharsis," a pledge to punish those responsible for a series of scandals blamed on the socialist regime. Brushing aside not only ideological differences but also bitter memories of the 1946–49 civil war in which they had fought in opposite camps, the conservatives and Communists gave joint support to an interim coalition government under Tzannis Tzannetakis, a well-liked New Democracy backbencher. It was sworn in on July 2. The object was to give Parliament time to institute criminal proceedings against the responsible socialist ministers, forestalling their exoneration under a special statute of limitations. The investigation and indictment procedure lasted the full 14-week span of Parliament's life. Papandreou and four of his ex-ministers were ordered to stand trial before special tribunals on charges of corruption, fraud, and illegal telephone tapping.

Papandreou, who was still recovering from a serious heart operation and had survived a dangerous relapse after the June elections, dismissed the accusations against himself as a U.S.-instigated conspiracy. The 70-year-old politician sought to eliminate another source of embarrassment, his conspicuous love affair with Dimitra Liani, a former flight attendant half his age, by marrying her in church on July 13, shortly after obtaining a divorce from his American-born wife of 38 years.

The Tzannetakis Cabinet, its mission completed, resigned on October 7 and was succeeded by a caretaker government under Yiannis Grivas, the Supreme Court president, which organized new elections on November 5. An awkward voting system, a backlash within the Communist camp as a result of the pact with the conservatives, and Papandreou's personal charisma all contributed to deny New Democracy the minimum parliamentary majority of 151 by a mere 3 seats. (For tabulated results, see *Political Parties,* above.) Bogged down by a second hung Parliament and hoping to spare the country the ordeal of a third general election in less than six months, Greek political leaders agreed on November 21 to form an all-party government headed by Xenophon Zolotas, 85, a former governor of the central bank. The Cabinet, which did not include either Mitsotakis or Papandreou, was to serve until mid-April 1990, when Parliament would elect a new president.

In this tense political setting, terrorists struck again. Pavlos Bakoyiannis, a New Democracy deputy, party spokesman, and the leader's son-in-law, was killed by unknown gunmen on September 26. Responsibility was claimed by the November 17 terrorist group, whose members still evaded arrest after at least 14 political assassinations of prominent Americans and Greeks since 1975. The same group had claimed a car-bomb attack on May 8 against George Petsos, one of Papandreou's Cabinet ministers charged with taking bribes. Three attacks in January against senior magistrates, two of whom were killed, reinforced the view that terrorists were trying to intimidate judges investigating scandals blamed on Pasok officials and personal friends of Papandreou.

Internal political troubles so preoccupied the Greeks that all other major issues were left to fester. For the first time, the country's overall public debt exceeded its gross

DANILIDES—GAMMA/LIAISON

A campaigner carries an anti-Papandreou sign during a rally for the New Democracy Party. The corruption of the former Papandreou government spurred Greece's Communist and New Democracy parties to form a coalition government to prosecute former officials.

national product. Inflation was expected to soar to 16% by the year's end, and unemployment stood at 8.5%. The current account deficit at the end of September had trebled to $1.6 billion, while reserves declined from $5.2 billion to $3.9 billion. The all-party agreement that produced the Zolotas government included an economic accord, giving the new Cabinet a mandate to attack the country's failing economy.

Equally urgent was the need to resume negotiations on the future of U.S. military bases in Greece, which the Pasok government had broken off before the June elections. The previous five-year bases agreement had lapsed in December 1988, and the 17-month grace period for completing the dismantling of the four bases and 20 lesser facilities if no new agreement was reached was slipping away. U.S. Secretary of State James Baker paid a one-day visit to Athens on February 14 to impress on Papandreou the need to speed up the bases talks and also to warn him on another pending bilateral issue—the extradition of Muhammad Rashid, a Palestinian terrorist suspect held in Greece, who was wanted in the U.S. for a 1982 airliner bombing. The Papandreou government had left this question in abeyance, as did the Tzannetakis interim Cabinet and the caretaker Cabinet that succeeded it. Washington considered the Rashid affair a test case for Greek-U.S. relations.

Relations with Turkey also were frozen for the duration of the political upheaval. Friction continued, however, and Greek officials were concerned over Turkey's growing interest in the Turkish-speaking Muslim minority of 120,000 living in western Thrace. Attempts by minority politicians to take advantage of the elections to press for equal rights prompted hostile Greek reactions and encouraging comments from Turkey, adding another sore point to the long list of grievances between the two neighbours.

(MARIO MODIANO)

ICELAND

Iceland is an island republic in the North Atlantic Ocean, near the Arctic Circle. Area: 103,000 sq km (39,769 sq mi). Pop. (1989 est.): 252,000. Cap.: Reykjavík. Monetary unit: Icelandic króna, with (Oct. 2, 1989) a free rate of 60.96 krónur to U.S. $1 (98.63 krónur = £1 sterling). President in 1989, Vigdís Finnbogadóttir; prime minister, Steingrímur Hermannsson.

The Icelandic economy slipped into recession in the middle of 1988, and it failed to improve in 1989. The gross national product in real terms fell by 3.3% in 1989 after a 1.8% decline in 1988; the decline was expected to continue in 1990. The recession was attributed primarily to overfishing of stocks in the sea and to cutbacks in fishing due to stricter catch quotas. The strong 1986–87 expansion also led to greater overinvesting and overborrowing, which brought difficulties to many enterprises, chiefly fisheries and commerce. One of the main tasks of the government was to establish a fund for restructuring the debt of enterprises that were in difficulty and for injecting new equity capital.

For three years Iceland had pursued a scientific whaling program and had caught between 80 and 100 whales a year for research purposes. The whales were processed for their meat and sold to finance the research. This activity led to intense pressure from international environmental groups, which had some success in organizing boycotts against Icelandic products in foreign markets. On July 20, 1989, the last whale was caught under the three-year program, which was then disbanded. The boycott also ended.

Pope John Paul II visited Iceland for 23 hours on June

3–4, and during his short stay he celebrated two outdoor masses before large crowds. By stopping in Iceland on his 10-day tour of the Scandinavian countries, the pope did much to encourage the small Catholic community in Iceland, which had an overwhelmingly Lutheran population.

On March 1 the sale of alcoholic beer became legal after having been banned since 1915. The new-found beverage quickly became the favourite of Icelanders, pushing aside wine and liquor, sales of which dropped sharply. The euphoria quickly subsided in the following months as the novelty wore off, and drinking habits returned to normal levels.

The left-of-centre government of Steingrímur Hermannsson was backed by a very scant majority in the Althing, Iceland's parliament, and thus had difficulty mustering sufficient votes for its legislative program in the 1988–89 parliamentary session. Though Prime Minister Hermannsson had hoped to gain the support of the Citizen's Party, which had seven members in the Althing, the party's leader, Albert Gudmundsson, was intractably opposed to an agreement. A solution was found when Gudmundsson, an illustrious presence in Icelandic politics for many years, was appointed ambassador to France. Following his departure, the Citizen's Party split, and four of its seven members in the Althing opted to join the government. Two of the four were offered Cabinet posts, bringing the number of ministers to 11.

The economic recession made all wage agreements more difficult than before. The Union of University-Educated Public Employees went on a five-week strike in April, closing down many secondary schools and a number of government agencies. The strike ended with fairly small pay increases that had difficulty keeping pace with inflation.

The squeeze on profits in fisheries and commerce brought on by the recession led to a wave of bankruptcies and mergers of firms. The four largest insurance companies in the country merged into two. Three small commercial banks—the Industrial Bank, the Bank of Commerce, and the Union Bank—merged and took over the government-owned Fisheries Bank, which two years earlier had been reorganized as a corporation with the government owning a majority of the shares. When the National Bank, the country's largest commercial bank, took over another small commercial bank, the Cooperative Bank, the number of commercial banks was reduced from seven to three.

(BJÖRN MATTHÍASSON)

IRELAND

The republic of Ireland, separated from Great Britain by the North Channel, the Irish Sea, and St. George's Channel, shares its island with Northern Ireland to the northeast. Area: 70,285 sq km (27,137 sq mi). Pop. (1989 est.): 3,515,000. Cap.: Dublin. Monetary unit: Irish pound (phunt), with (Oct. 2, 1989) a free rate of Ir£0.70 to U.S. $1 (Ir£1.14 = £1 sterling). President in 1989, Patrick J. Hillery; prime minister, Charles Haughey.

In January 1989 Charles Haughey's minority Fianna Fail government launched the second phase of its economic recovery program with a cautious budget that set out to stimulate new jobs through Ir£126 million in tax concessions and through increased capital investment. Exchequer borrowing requirements would be reduced to 5.3% of gross national product (GNP), down from the 1988 target of 8.2%. A net gain of 13,000 jobs was forecast, with unemployment falling by 10,000 to 232,000 by the end of the year. It was considered a popular budget by most people and greatly enhanced Fianna Fail's standing in the coun-

try. An opinion poll showed it to have the support of 54% of the population—a high figure for a party in office.

The government was clearly performing well, and on all major economic issues it had the overwhelming support of the Dail (parliament). Nevertheless, two defeats on minor issues, against a background of opinion poll predictions that in an election at that time Haughey would return to power with a clear majority, were too great a temptation for a leader who had already failed on four occasions to achieve that goal. There was the added advantage that the general election could be combined with the European Parliament elections.

The basic issues in the general election, which was set for June 15, were unemployment and health cuts, but the real issue was whether the Irish electorate would give Haughey the mandate he sought. There was a high turnout—77%— on polling day, but the result proved inconclusive and no one party was able to form a government. (For tabulated results, see *Political Parties,* above. The two significant trends in the voting were the move to the left in most Dublin city constituencies and the election of the first-ever Green Party candidate. This movement to the left was also reflected in the elections to the European Parliament, which saw a Workers' Party candidate returned for the first time. John Cushnahan, the former leader of Northern Ireland's Alliance Party, won a seat in Munster.

Haughey having failed, for the fifth time, to secure an overall majority, strenuous efforts were made to ensure his reelection as prime minister of a minority government, but the Dail met twice without success. Days of uncertainty followed, with various coalitions being considered and rejected and the ever present threat of a second general election becoming more likely. Then, in a dramatic turn of events, intense discussions over several days were held with Desmond O'Malley of the Progressive Democrats; these concluded with the agreement that his party should be the junior partner in a Fianna Fail-led coalition. It was the fifth coalition since the foundation of the state but the first ever entered into by Fianna Fail. Since it was O'Malley's disagreement with Haughey that had caused the breakaway from Fianna Fail in 1986 and the subsequent formation of the Progressive Democrats, this was a particularly ironic situation.

The tough bargaining position taken by the Progressive Democrats meant that they ended up with two senior ministries and one junior ministry, thus winning a share in power disproportionate to their numerical strength in the Dail. Haughey, who had spoken strongly against the idea of coalition government during the election campaign, was placed in a difficult position, but he quickly recovered and hailed the event as a historic political departure. He was reelected prime minister on July 12.

Although many Fianna Fail deputies and party members throughout the country found the idea of coalition unpalatable, only one deputy resigned from the parliamentary party. It was generally felt that the coalition represented stability and that the government would be able to complete its planned four-year program for economic and social progress. Moreover, the result of the election ensured that Fianna Fail would find it difficult to return to its old populist position and that Fine Gael, which gained four seats, could recover the former socialist democratic ground that it had held until recession forced it to the right in 1986 and 1987.

Despite the government's optimistic forecasts, the unemployment rate of 17.9%, one of the highest in the European Communities, continued to cause concern. However, confidence in the economy continued to grow, with the

central bank forecasting a rise in GNP to 4.25%, ahead of the government's prediction of slightly more than 3% growth. Late in the year inflation rose slightly to 4.5%.

The Anglo-Irish agreement came under strain after allegations were made against the Ulster Defence Regiment, and the situation further deteriorated when the director of public prosecutions rejected the British application to have Patrick Ryan, a Roman Catholic priest, tried in Ireland for alleged arms offenses under the Criminal Law Jurisdiction Act, on the grounds that there was insufficient evidence. Earlier in the year Britain had sought the extradition of Ryan on explosives and conspiracy charges. Following his expulsion from Belgium, Ryan had sought refuge in Ireland, where he subsequently stood as a candidate in the European elections on an antiextradition platform. Although he was not elected, he polled surprisingly well, gaining 30,000 first-preference votes.

Two new universities were established in Limerick and Dublin during the year. They were already operating as National Institutes of Higher Education, and their upgrading to become the first new universities since 1908 was seen as a historic development.

In 1989 Ireland's environmental awareness was increased. The hot summer caused water levels in rivers to fall, and uncontrolled distribution of slurry caused a number of rivers to become polluted, resulting in serious fish kills. Following strong lobbying by local residents, the Merrell Dow chemical company withdrew its request for permission to locate a new plant in Cork.

In May the Church of Ireland General Synod voted overwhelmingly in favour of the ordination of women as priests and bishops. The official Roman Catholic observer at the synod said that this decision could represent an additional obstacle to unity between the Roman Catholic and Anglican churches.   (MAVIS ARNOLD)

See also *United Kingdom,* below.

ITALY

A republic of southern Europe, Italy occupies the Apennine Peninsula, Sicily, Sardinia, and a number of smaller islands in the Mediterranean Sea. Area: 301,277 sq km (116,324 sq mi). Pop. (1989 est.): 57,436,000. Cap.: Rome. Monetary unit: Italian lira, with (Oct. 2, 1989) a free rate of 1,372 lire to U.S. $1 (2,220 lire = £1 sterling). President in 1989, Francesco Cossiga; prime ministers, Ciriaco De Mita and, from July 23, Giulio Andreotti.

The political year in Italy in 1989 was marked by the continuing slow decline in the voting strength of the Communist Party, the emergence of the Green Party, and the return of Giulio Andreotti as prime minister for the sixth time.

The first two facts were probably related. Young Italians had often voted for the Communists, or for the somewhat maverick Radicals, either as a nonconformist gesture or as a protest against the always dominant Christian Democrats. Now they had another alternative in the Greens, and in 1989 that party won seats in virtually every municipal election where it was in the running—as well as in the June election to the European Parliament. In the span of three years it had become Italy's fourth largest party. The Green leaders were an attractive bunch, highly politicized, not concerned only with environment, and they had shown caution in joining coalitions their supporters would find unacceptable. That sense of propriety could never be attributed to the more orthodox parties. So far, the Greens had been like a breath of fresh air, and it was to be hoped that they would not let themselves be used as mere

Students fill the streets in Rome to demonstrate against drugs. Italy, with the highest incidence of drug addiction in Europe, had become a centre for heroin and cocaine trafficking between Latin America and the United States.

RUDI FREY/TIME MAGAZINE

deodorants in the stale air of Italy's political chambers.

The Communists, under their new leader, Achille Occhetto, lost ground except in their traditional strongholds. Elsewhere, they polled about one quarter of the votes, leaving them still the second largest party, after their perpetual rivals, the Christian Democrats, who held onto about one-third of the votes. It was useful to remember that more than 80% of the Italians actually go to the polling stations and vote, and in the European election the figure was 88% of those eligible. It was a trying year for Communist parties everywhere, particularly in Eastern Europe and in China, and the Italian Communist Party decided that it would change its name at a party congress due early in 1990. Occhetto formally created his own shadow cabinet, taking the British parliamentary custom as his model. However, the chances of the PCI shadow cabinet actually taking over government posts remained as remote as ever.

The Socialists, under would-be strongman Bettino Craxi, continued to make small gains in elections, but only in a few localities did they cross over the 15% line. Even so, Craxi exerted an influence in national coalitions beyond the strength of the Socialist vote. He knew that the Christian Democrats needed his 14% of the seats in Parliament, and he made them squirm with frequent threats to walk out of the coalition. Both the Catholic and the Socialist parties had a bumper crop of corruption charges laid against their men at various levels in 1989. The editor of Rome's *La Repubblica* newspaper, Eugenio Scalfari, wrote that the rise of the Socialists under Craxi had coincided with a decline of integrity in his party.

Ciriaco De Mita began the year wearing two hats, that of secretary-general (or chairman) of the Christian Democrat Party and that of sitting prime minister. It could be said that De Mita was a better party leader than he was a prime minister, and the second job was one he had never sought. At the party conference in February, De Mita was forced to resign as party boss, and that position was taken over once again by the easygoing Arnaldo Forlani. His party, abetted by Craxi, then proceeded to undermine the De Mita premiership as well, and De Mita resigned that post in May after 13 months in office. It was true that a relatively minor scandal had surfaced involving large sums of public funds, destined for victims of the 1980 earthquake in southern Italy, that had found their way to a small bank in De Mita's home province of Avellino, but his main fault was that his Avellino life-style did not go down well with the party or the country.

Andreotti, who entered his first government as an under secretary in 1947 and had presided over five previous Cabinets, relinquished his post as foreign minister in July to become, at age 70, the new prime minister. Andreotti had been around so long and had circumvented so many scandals that he had become a living national monument, even implicitly admired by the Communists. The public admired him for his sense of humour and his proven ability as a navigator. What they may not have realized was that the boat was going nowhere because the skipper had no chartered map.

All elections confirmed that the honoured old parties, the Liberal, Social Democrat, and Republican, though members of most governments during the 1980s, seemed to be heading for oblivion at the polls. The Liberal vote had fallen below 2%.

The state of Italian justice was never regarded as healthy, even by those operating in that sector. In February a court handed down a verdict of complete acquittal for two well-known neofascists accused of having organized and carried out the first terrorist crime in post-World War II Italy. It happened in December 1969 when a bomb carried into a Milan bank in a suitcase exploded, killing 16 people and injuring 87. The police immediately rounded up the usual left-wing suspects, who remained in prison without trial for more than four years, even though the press and part of the public recognized their innocence. Eventually, two neofascists were accused and finally brought to trial, only to be acquitted. "No one is guilty" was the headline in several papers responding to the court's verdict. In April a television program took up another mysterious instance of nonjustice in Italy, the case of a DC-9 airliner that fell into the sea in 1980, taking the lives of all 81 persons aboard, during a scheduled flight from Bologna to Palermo. The TV show obliged the government to admit that the plane had been downed by a missile. The affair appeared to involve an elaborate cover-up by the Italian military, but the nationality of the missile might well remain a mystery.

The good news in the field of justice was that as of Oct. 25, 1989, court procedures were radically changed to bring them somewhat into line with what might be called Anglo-American procedures or, as the Italians chose to put it, "bringing in Perry Mason." (The old television series of that name had been very popular.) What this reform meant was that the old inquisitorial formula, whereby the judge was generally expected to ratify the accusations of the public prosecutor, was no more. Cross-examination was allowed for the first time. The defendant entered the courtroom still innocent. The judge entered the courtroom ignorant of the case, rather than having spent months studying the prosecutor's charges against the accused. For the first time, a defense attorney could call out, "Your Honour, I object" without being himself ejected from the courtroom. There was a heady feeling in the Italian courts. Everyone seemed pleased.

Tourism, one of Italy's major industries, was troubled during the summer by banks of floating slime being washed ashore at the country's resorts along the Adriatic. The

slime was ugly but not toxic, consisting only of seaweed, or algae, that had become overnourished by chemical fertilizers used on farms and eventually carried out to sea by Italian rivers. It would take years before that situation could be totally remedied. European television repeatedly showed film footage of the floating dead and decomposing seaweed, and some resorts had 40% of their reservations canceled. A good wind usually carried the seaweed away from shore.

In another centre for tourism, Florence, a study made of 106 foreign tourists who were brought to a hospital after feeling faint or giddy seemed to confirm that there really was something called (now) the Stendhal filerome. The name came from the French writer's 1817 travel book in which he described himself as feeling faint after seeing so many beautiful things in a Florence church. The patients examined in Florence were first-time visitors of different ages who appeared to be suffering from visual and mental indigestion caused by a surfeit of beauty. And perhaps more wine than they were accustomed to.

Italy's larger banks had good reason to be concerned about the arrival in 1992 of foreign banks from other countries in the European Communities, where an effort was usually made to attract and serve the small client. They feared the loss of the small client and also the larger client seeking greater efficiency. Italian banks had had branches abroad for many years, and the country's biggest bank (and the only one owned by the State Treasury), the Banca Nazionale del Lavoro, was the centre of a scandal in the late summer. Its branch in Atlanta, Ga., was found by U.S. officials to have granted $3 billion in credit to Iraq. The bank headquarters in Rome claimed to know nothing about that operation, and the bank president was obliged to resign.

Italian voters in the June 19 European election were also given a referendum ballot, asking if they were in favour of greater political unity in the European Communities and of giving the European Parliament legislative powers. As stated above, 88% of those eligible to vote in the election did so and, of those, 88% voted "yes" in the referendum. This suggested to one observer that Italians, who at that date were again without a government of their own, were reaching beyond their national frontiers for something lacking at home.   (GEORGE ARMSTRONG)

LIECHTENSTEIN

A landlocked constitutional monarchy of central Europe, Liechtenstein is united with Switzerland by a customs and monetary union. Area: 160 sq km (62 sq mi). Pop. (1989 est.): 28,300. Cap.: Vaduz. Monetary unit: Swiss franc, with (Oct. 2, 1989) a free rate of Sw F 1.62 to U.S. $1 (Sw F 2.63 = £1 sterling). Sovereign princes, Francis Joseph II to November 13, 1989, and Hans Adam; head of government, Hans Brunhart.

Francis Joseph II (see OBITUARIES), sovereign prince of Liechtenstein and the longest reigning chief of state in Europe, died Nov. 13, 1989. His wife, Princess Gina, had died the preceding month. He was succeeded by his son, Prince Hans Adam, who had exercised executive power in the principality since 1984.

In a general election on March 3, 1989, the balance of seats between the two ruling coalition parties, the Fatherland Union (VU) and the Progressive Citizens Party (FBP), remained essentially unchanged, although the number of seats in the Landtag (parliament) had been increased from 15 to 25. The VU led by Hans Brunhart, head of government since 1978, won 13 seats with 47.15% of the vote, and the FBP led by Herbert Wille won 12 seats with

42.13%. The Free Voters' List again failed to win the 8% needed for representation.

Parliament had been dissolved on January 23, prematurely, after FBP members walked out following an acrimonious debate on the building of a new art gallery to house the collection of the ruling family. Funds for the gallery had been approved in a 1980 referendum, but opponents had demanded a new vote. The president of the high court, Erich Seeger, had refused to permit a second referendum to be held, while his political opponents claimed that this decision was illegal.   (ALUN JONES)

This article updates the Micropædia article LIECHTENSTEIN.

LUXEMBOURG

The Benelux country of Luxembourg is a landlocked constitutional monarchy in western Europe. Area: 2,586 sq km (999 sq mi). Pop. (1989 est.): 377,000. Cap.: Luxembourg. Monetary unit: Luxembourg franc, at par with the Belgian franc, with (Oct. 2, 1989) a free rate of Lux F 39.34 to U.S. $1 (Lux F 63.65 = £1 sterling). Grand duke, Jean; prime minister in 1989, Jacques Santer.

In 1989 Luxembourg's outward self-confidence—born of rapidly growing prosperity, an enviable degree of social harmony, and the special position it had occupied in the geographic (and political) centre of the European Communities (EC)—was beginning to look fragile. Pressure came from the European Commission's efforts to harmonize value-added tax (VAT) throughout the EC, and the question was being raised as to whether the EC's tiniest member would be allowed to retain what amounted to a paradise for financiers as the EC's barrier-free internal market took shape. However, the Grand Duchy had overcome the decline of its once-dominant steel industry and the diminishing attractions of its core wholesale banking activities, and observers expected it to fight the latest threat with equal determination. Some thought Luxembourg's best card was that the EC ultimately needed it as much as it needed the EC. If Luxembourg ceased to be a financial haven, its customers might leave the Community for another shelter, such as the Cayman Islands.

In elections held on June 17, the ruling coalition parties, the Christian Democrats and the Socialists, both lost seats but retained a comfortable majority. (For tabulated results, see Political Parties, above.)

On April 18 Luxembourg celebrated its 150th anniversary. Guests included British Prime Minister Margaret Thatcher, French Prime Minister Michel Rocard, and West German Chancellor Helmut Kohl.   (ALUN JONES)

This article updates the Macropædia article The Low Countries: Luxembourg.

MALTA

The republic of Malta, a member of the Commonwealth, comprises the islands of Malta, Gozo, and Comino in the Mediterranean Sea between Sicily and Tunisia. Area: 316 sq km (122 sq mi). Pop. (1989 est.): 349,000. Cap.: Valletta. Monetary unit: Maltese lira, with (Oct. 2, 1989) a free rate of 0.35 lira to U.S. $1 (0.56 lira = £1 sterling). Presidents in 1989, Paul Xuereb (acting) and, from April 4, Censu Tabone; prime minister, Eddie Fenech Adami.

On Sept. 21, 1989, Malta celebrated the 25th anniversary of its independence from Britain. Several foreign dignitaries attended the festivities held to mark the occasion. Censu Tabone, 76, was elected president of Malta on April 4. He had served as foreign minister since 1987.

Malta's commitment to improving international rela-

tions continued. Prime Minister Eddie Fenech Adami addressed the UN General Assembly in New York City on September 28, and in October he attended the Commonwealth heads of government meeting in Malaysia.

The year was marked by Malta's debut as an offshore business centre and by the liberalization of trade. An important aid agreement was signed between the government and Malta Drydocks, which was expected to break even for the first time in many years. Malta continued to upgrade its infrastructure with the introduction of an avant-garde telecommunications network and construction of a new power station, water desalination plants, and a modern international airport.

In early December Malta was host to the first summit meeting between U.S. Pres. George Bush and Soviet Pres. Mikhail Gorbachev. The meeting was delayed briefly by a gale that stranded Bush aboard a U.S. naval vessel.

(ALBERT GANADO)

MONACO

A sovereign principality on the northern Mediterranean coast, Monaco is bounded on land by the French département of Alpes-Maritimes. Area: 1.9 sq km (0.73 sq mi). Pop. (1989 est.): 29,100. Monetary unit: French franc, with (Oct. 2, 1989) a free rate of F 6.36 to U.S. $1 (F 10.29 = £1 sterling). Chief of state, Prince Rainier III; minister of state in 1989, Jean Ausseil.

The latest figures available as of 1989 revealed that the industrial sector provided approximately 40% of Monaco's business turnover, while 30% came from real estate and 25% from tourism. Banking and finance accounted for more than 38% of the turnover of the services sector. Monaco continued to be an important centre for the administration of "offshore" companies and for foreign deposits, though the country's subjection to French controls on foreign exchange had prevented it from becoming a major offshore banking centre. It was hoped that these controls would be relaxed following completion of the single European market in 1992.

Reports during the year suggested that Monaco was trying to alter its image from that of a shelter for wealthy tax exiles to a home for small industries, service businesses, and banking enterprises. The banking sector now comprised 30 different banks, including virtually all the big international names. The principality was also trying to put itself on the international sports calendar by holding major tennis and golf tournaments.

(ALUN JONES)

This article updates the *Micropædia* article MONACO.

NETHERLANDS, THE

A constitutional monarchy of northwestern Europe, The Netherlands, a Benelux country, is on the North Sea. Area: 41,863 sq km (16,163 sq mi). Pop. (1989 est.): 14,846,000. Cap., Amsterdam; seat of government, The Hague. Monetary unit: Netherlands guilder, with (Oct. 2, 1989) a free rate of 2.12 guilders to U.S. $1 (3.43 guilders = £1 sterling). Queen, Beatrix; prime minister in 1988, Ruud Lubbers.

On Jan. 27, 1989, the Dutch Parliament supported Justice Minister Frederik Korthals Altes in releasing two World War II German war criminals. On that day Franz Fischer and Ferdinand H. aus der Fünten, both sentenced to life imprisonment, were transported over the Dutch-German border. Arguments based on legal principles had prevailed in an emotional debate, in which former members of the Resistance and representatives of war victims had participated.

On May 2 Joris Voorhoeve, leader of the right-wing

People's Party for Freedom and Democracy (VVD) in Parliament, vetoed a national environmental plan. By this action the VVD, the junior partner in the coalition government, caused the fall of Prime Minister Ruud Lubbers' second Cabinet. On May 3 Lubbers offered the resignation of the Cabinet to Queen Beatrix. The reason for the veto was that 1 billion guilders of the total budget of almost 7 billion guilders was to be financed by the abolition of tax reductions for transportation costs. Although two VVD ministers, Ed Nijpels (Environment) and Neelie Smit-Kroes (Transport and Public Works), supported the environmental policy, the plan was not acceptable to the VVD in Parliament. Frustration over the arrogant behaviour of the senior coalition partner, the Christian Democratic Appeal (CDA), was also said to have played a major role in Voorhoeve's decision. The Cabinet fell a few months after the government had finished its most important project, the adoption in Parliament on February 2 of a radical tax reform. This tax reform, named after the chairman of the tax reform commission, C.J. Oort, was intended to reduce the complexity of the existing tax system and to be introduced by Jan. 1, 1990.

On June 18 elections for the European Parliament took place. They were expected to give a general indication of shifts in public opinion after the fall of the Lubbers Cabinet. The VVD and the leading opposition party, the Labour Party (PvdA), suffered significant losses, while the CDA stabilized its position. The Green Alliance, a new party formed by the fusion of the Progressive Party, the Communist Party, and the Socialist Pacifists, gained. The results were difficult to interpret, however, because of a very low voter turnout (47.2%).

On September 6 general elections were held. The turnout of 80.1% was much higher than in the elections of June 18 but more than 5% lower than in the 1986 general election. The CDA equaled its 1986 results and retained 54 seats, while the VVD lost 5 seats. Among the opposition parties, the social-democratic PvdA kept 49 seats (a painful loss of 3); the left-wing Democrats 1966 (D66) got 12 seats (a gain of 3); and the Greens won 6 seats (a gain of 3). (For

People outside the Dutch Parliament protest the release of two Nazi war criminals, Franz Fischer and Ferdinand H. aus der Fünten. The two had been serving life sentences for their involvement in the transportation and extermination of some 10,000 Jews.

tabulated results, see *Political Parties,* above.) The former coalition partners together held 76 of 150 seats in Parliament, but this majority was considered too small to restore a centre-right Cabinet. The CDA remained the biggest party in Parliament, however, so Lubbers announced that he would form a new centre-left government.

The CDA used all its power to exclude D66 from membership in the new Cabinet, and on October 13 it reached a coalition agreement with the PvdA. The new Cabinet was sworn in on November 7, with PvdA leader Wim Kok as vice-prime minister. Compared with Lubbers' two previous Cabinets, the main shifts in government policies were that there would be more emphasis on environmental policy, social justice, and the fight against unemployment, despite the maintenance of a very restricted budget policy.

(KLAAS J. HOEKSEMA)

See also *Dependent States,* below.

This article updates the *Macropædia* article THE LOW COUNTRIES: *The Netherlands.*

NORWAY

A constitutional monarchy of northern Europe, Norway occupies the western part of the Scandinavian Peninsula, with coastlines on the Skagerrak, the North Sea, the Norwegian Sea, and the Arctic Ocean. Area: 323,878 sq km (125,050 sq mi), excluding the Svalbard Archipelago and Jan Mayen Island. Pop. (1989 est.): 4,228,000. Cap.: Oslo. Monetary unit: Norwegian krone, with (Oct. 2, 1989) a free rate of 6.92 kroner to U.S. $1 (11.19 kroner = £1 sterling). King, Olav V; prime ministers in 1989, Gro Harlem Brundtland and, from October 16, Jan Peder Syse.

The minority Labour government headed by Gro Harlem Brundtland resigned on Oct. 13, 1989, after three and a half years in office, and King Olav V invited the leader of the Conservative Party, Jan Peder Syse (*see* BIOGRAPHIES), to form a new government. Brundtland's resignation came in the wake of parliamentary elections, on September 11, and after three of the four nonsocialist parties in the Storting (parliament) had agreed on a joint program. With Syse as prime minister, the government was to include members of the Storting's two small, middle-of-the-road parties, the Christian Democrats and the Centre (farmers') Party. Excluded because of its extremist views was the radical, rightist Progress Party.

The Syse coalition would, however, depend heavily on receiving at least passive support from Progress. Its three member parties controlled only 62 seats in the newly elected, 165-member Storting, one less than Labour and 18 fewer than the socialist bloc as a whole, which also included the Socialist Left Party. The 1989 elections marked a breakthrough for the Progress Party, led by the charismatic Carl I. Hagen, who campaigned on a platform calling for big cuts in taxes and public spending, plus tough controls on immigration. His party increased its representation in the Storting by 20 to 22 and its share of the popular vote from 3.7% in 1985 to 13%. Its advance was mainly at the expense of the Conservatives, whose share of the popular vote dropped from 30.4 to 22.2%. On the left, the Socialist Left Party saw its share of the vote rise by 4.6 percentage points to 10.1%, while Labour slipped to 34.3% from 40.8% four years earlier. In the middle, the Christian Democrat and Centre parties held their ground, the former with a 0.2 percentage point rise to 8.5%, the latter with a 0.1 percentage point decline to 6.5%. (For tabulated results, see *Political Parties,* above.)

Unemployment was a major issue in the election campaign. Mainly because of the government's austerity policies, it had been rising since the middle of 1988. By mid-August 1989 the number of registered jobless had hit a post-World War II record of almost 94,000—4.3% of the labour force. Another 40,000 were on public works projects. Voters on both the left and right felt that belt-tightening had been carried too far. Even the Labour Party said its 1990 budget would include modest tax cuts, designed to stimulate the economy without triggering inflation. For many who favoured such a stimulus, this was not enough; they turned from Labour and the other "establishment" party, the Conservatives, to the Progress Party or the Socialist Left.

The draft budget for 1990, introduced by the outgoing Labour government on October 12, was expansive, envisaging a deficit of 9.7 billion kroner. It provided for increases in both public and private consumption, with reductions in direct taxes that were not offset by the proposed increases in indirect taxes. Presenting the budget, Labour Finance Minister Gunnar Berge pointed to the successes achieved during three and a half years of austerity: a sharp drop in the inflation rate, a dramatic turnaround in the balance of payments (expected to show a surplus of 25 billion kroner in 1989), an increase in productivity, and a marked decline in interest rates. There was now room, he claimed, for "moderate" increases in private and public consumption, but holding down costs and keeping the payments balance in surplus had to continue to be two main goals of economic policy. In addition, efforts would have to be made to reduce Norway's dependence on offshore oil and gas. On November 3 the incoming coalition announced changes in the Labour budget, including, among other things, an increase in the proposed tax concessions, which Syse criticized as inadequate. The 7% rise in expenditure called for by Labour was reduced to 6%, though spending on the environment, foreign aid, and defense remained largely unchanged.

(FAY GJESTER)

See also *Dependent States,* below.

PORTUGAL

A republic of southwestern Europe, metropolitan Portugal is on the Atlantic coast of the Iberian Peninsula, which it shares with Spain. Area: 92,389 sq km (35,672 sq mi), including the Azores and Madeira island groups/archipelagoes in the Atlantic. Pop. (1989 est.): 10,372,000. Cap.: Lisbon. Monetary unit: Portuguese escudo, with (Oct. 2, 1989) a free rate of 158.96 escudos to U.S. $1 (257.20 escudos = £1 sterling). President in 1989, Mário Soares; prime minister, Aníbal Cavaço Silva.

The ruling Social Democratic Party (PSD) suffered a reverse in the June 1989 contest for the country's 24 seats in the European Parliament. It polled 32.5% of the vote and gained 9 seats, but with 750,000 fewer votes than in the 1987 European election. The Socialist Party (PSP), in coalition with the tiny Democratic Renovation Party, received 28.9% of the vote and gained two seats for a total of eight. The Communists won four seats (up by one), and the Christian Democrats lost a seat, reducing their total to three. The 51% turnout, the lowest since the return to overt democracy in 1975, was interpreted as a protest vote by many of the PSD's mostly middle-class supporters against the government's high-handed efforts to reform the country's professions, efforts that had alienated many civil servants, policemen, doctors, and the financial community.

Prime Minister Aníbal Cavaço Silva personally blamed the PSD's poor showing on the March tax and labour reforms and the higher interest rates imposed to cool growth in the economy. Also, higher-than-forecast inflation resulted in the erosion of real wages and the collapse of the National Wages and Prices Pact. There were strikes

throughout the year, especially in the public sector. For the first time, the Socialist-backed UGTP and the Communists' CGTP trade unions overcame their often bitter rivalry enough to cooperate in pressuring the government in such areas as job security and pension rights.

With the necessary two-thirds majority provided by the PSD and PSP, the Assembly passed a bill on June 1 allowing amendment of the constitution. Pres. Mário Soares signed the updated constitution into law on July 7. The redrafted document omitted all references to socialism and deleted those clauses referring to nationalizations as irreversible gains of the working class. As a result of the bill's passage, the government was able to begin its privatization program in earnest; 49% of the shares in Unicer, the public-sector brewery, the Banco Totta e Acroes, and Aliança Segurdora were offered to the public, and all three issues were oversubscribed. The government's policy was eventually to return all 68 firms nationalized since 1975 to the private sector, except for Cimpor, the cement company, where the authorities would retain a majority stake for strategic reasons. However, there was concern over how well the market would absorb more privatizations before the elections scheduled for 1991.

Foreign business interest in Portugal continued to grow, particularly on the part of firms wishing to benefit from the European Communities (EC) 1992 single market process. Spanish banks bid up prices to gain entrance to the previously restricted Portuguese market in the auction for Banco Totta shares. Ford announced an investment of $130 million, the biggest foreign investment in the country since Renault, to establish a high-tech electronics plant. The EC was very active in financing infrastructural and energy-related projects, including roads, rail, and airports. The European Investment Bank (EIB) was expected to raise its loans to Portugal from 560.9 million European Currency Units (ECUs) in 1988 to 700 million ECUs in 1989. The EIB budgeted 2.8 billion ECUs up to 1994, mainly for infrastructural work and to help construct a gas pipeline. The EIB had been able to raise funds in the local escudo market for the first time, on the basis of Portugal's high local savings rate and the current strict limits to growth in bank lending.

On September 21 the composition of the ECU was redefined for the first time since Sept. 17, 1984, to incorporate both Iberian currencies. The escudo was given a weight of 0.8 in the European unit, the same as the Greek drachma. Following Spain's surprise adherence to the European Monetary System (EMS) in June, Prime Minister Cavaço Silva stated that, starting July 1, 1990, Portugal would speed up its efforts to join the EMS by increasing coordination of monetary policy, with a view to bringing the escudo into the fixed exchange rate system thereafter. The prime minister's main reason for not joining sooner was high inflation, plus the feeling that it would not be in Portugal's best interests to join while the U.K., a major trading partner, remained outside.

On October 17 the government introduced a budget for 1990 aimed at raising economic growth to 4.4%, or slightly above the 1989 forecast. Higher priority was to be given to education and health, which would absorb nearly 39% of total spending. Inflation was expected to fall from 12–13% to 9.5–10.5% in 1990. Total spending in 1990 was to rise 15% to 2,554,000,000 escudos, and revenue was forecast at 1,796,000,000 escudos. The budget deficit, representing 7.5% of gross domestic product in both 1989 and 1990, was expected to rise from 439 billion escudos to over 601 billion escudos. (MICHAEL WOOLLER)

See also *Dependent States,* below.

SAN MARINO

The republic of San Marino is a landlocked enclave in northeastern Italy. Area: 61 sq km (24 sq mi). Pop. (1989 est.): 22,900. Cap.: San Marino. Monetary unit: Italian lira, with (Oct. 2, 1989) a free rate of 1,372 lire to U.S. $1 (2,220 lire = £1 sterling). The republic is governed by two *capitani reggenti,* or coregents, appointed every six months by a popularly elected Great and General Council. Executive power rests with the Congress of State, headed by the coregents and composed of three secretaries of state and seven ministers.

In 1988–89 San Marino greatly increased its participation in international affairs. The republic was admitted to the United Nations in the role of permanent observer, and as such it appointed a formal delegation to the UN High Commissioner for Refugees. In late 1988 the Council of Europe approved San Marino's membership application. In keeping with this upgrading from observer status to full membership, San Marino ratified the Council's 1950 European Convention for the Protection of Human Rights. In January 1989 the republic was a signatory to the historic Vienna Concluding Document, which was issued by the Conference on Security and Cooperation in Europe after more than two years of negotiations. San Marino also established diplomatic relations with Austria, Sweden, France, and Egypt.

The most significant event domestically was the reorganization of San Marino's judiciary. The government approved the institution of a new Administrative Tribunal to serve as the nation's final court of review. Unlike the Council of Twelve, which it replaced, the autonomous Tribunal would be outside political jurisdiction.

In local administrative elections in 1989, the parties of the governing coalition received almost the same percentages of votes as they had in the 1988 general election. The Christian Democrats received 47% of the vote, while their junior partners, the Communist Party, got 27%. (ALUN JONES)

This article updates the *Micropædia* article SAN MARINO.

SPAIN

A constitutional monarchy of southwestern Europe with coastlines on the Bay of Biscay, the Atlantic Ocean, and the Mediterranean Sea, Spain shares the Iberian Peninsula with Portugal; it includes the Balearic and Canary island groups, in the Mediterranean and the Atlantic, respectively, and enclaves in northern Morocco. Area: 504,783 sq km (194,898 sq mi). Pop. (1989 est.): 39,159,000. Cap.: Madrid. Monetary unit: Spanish peseta, with (Oct. 2, 1989) a free rate of 119 pesetas to U.S. $1 (192.55 pesetas = £1 sterling). King, Juan Carlos I; prime minister in 1989, Felipe González Márquez.

Prime Minister Felipe González Márquez and the leaders of the Comisiones Obreras (CCOO) and the Unión General de Trabajadores (UGT) trade unions held talks in January 1989 following the general strike of Dec. 14, 1988, Spain's first since 1934. Despite concessions by the government, negotiations broke down in early February. Apart from differences over social payments and the way the government was dividing the benefits of economic growth, the major cause of the breakdown in relations with the UGT, traditionally a major supporter of the ruling Partido Socialista Obrero Español (PSOE), was the party's attempt to set up a network of political representatives in factories, creating a parallel organization competing with the union at grassroots level.

The conflict with the unions dominated González' state of the nation address to the Cortes (parliament) on February 14, with the prime minister attacking the unions for

not caring what sacrifices would have to be made if the unions' demands were met. In the event, more money was made available with the cooperation of the Partido Popular. Some 197 billion pesetas were cut from the 1990 defense and public works budgets and used to finance bigger payments to the unemployed and wage increases for civil servants, but the government's largess amounted to only a little over half of the unions' demands. On February 16 the CCOO and the UGT had agreed to put in a joint wage claim for the first time in 10 years. On July 10 the secretaries-general of both unions formalized their pact by signing a joint declaration favouring medium-term policies opposed to those proposed by Gonzáles and the PSOE.

In a move aimed at contesting the centre ground of Spanish politics, the Alianza Popular changed its name in January to the Partido Popular (PP). By May the PP had convinced the Democrática Cristiana, Partido Liberal, and Centro Democrático y Social (CDS) members in the Cortes to join together under the leadership of PP's Manuel Fraga Iribarne. However, Fraga Iribarne refused to let his name be put forward as the PP candidate for prime minister, and his dithering over who that person should be left the party without a candidate when a snap general election was called on September 1. His eventual choice was José María Aznar, a competent but little-known leader of Castilla-León's regional government. In the June 15 election for the European Parliament, the PSOE received 39.5% of the votes and 27 seats. The PP won 15 seats.

Following the announcement of a cease-fire in the Basque region on January 8, talks between the secretary of state for security, Rafael Varón, and Eugenio ("Antxón") Etxebeste of the Euzkadi ta Azkatasuna (ETA) took place in Algeria. On March 18 approximately 10% of the Basque population staged a demonstration for peace on the streets of Bilbao, but the talks subsequently broke down. The government dispersed ETA prisoners among Spanish jails, provoking a spate of letter bombs sent to prison officials. In the fall six Basque separatists were sentenced to long prison terms for terrorist bombings. Three members of the ETA who had been elected to the Cortes in October were expelled from the opening session of the legislature on December 4 for failing to swear allegiance to the Spanish constitution in the correct manner.

Spain took over as head of the European Communities (EC) Council of Ministers for the first half of the year and gained a reputation as an efficient and determined chairman. What could be of longer-term importance to Spain was the country's surprise decision in mid-June to join the exchange-rate mechanism of the European Monetary System, with a 6% fluctuation margin. Subsequently, the peseta was one of the stronger members of the EMS.

Surging profits, a stock market boom propelled by a state policy of privatizing quasi-monopoly firms, and strong foreign capital inflows pushed economic growth ahead at an unsustainable 4.75% in 1989, compared with the even higher 5% registered the year before. Reflecting overheating in the economy and a rebound in food prices, inflation rose from 4% in mid-1988 to 6.8% in September 1989. Strong investment and domestic demand resulted in an import surge and a marked rise in the current account deficit. Central bank measures in February helped keep broad money supply growth within its 6.5–9.6% target range, but by July concern about deterioration on the trade and current accounts forced the government to take further action. Withholding tax on stock market dividends and treasury bonds was raised to 25%, and the commercial banks' obligatory deposits with the central bank were raised by a full percentage point.

Encouraged by the PSOE's fair showing in the EC election, Prime Minister González dissolved the Cortes on September 1 and called general elections for October 29, eight months early. The PSOE was hoping to benefit from the evident muddle among the opposition, and there was also a growing conviction that tougher measures would be required for controlling overheating in the economy. Officially the decision was attributed to the need to "renew PSOE support before preparations for the European single market and 1992 were put into effect." The PSOE was returned to power. The Socialist vote dropped by 800,000, and the party lost 8 of the 184 seats it had won in the previous election. The main beneficiary was the Izquierda Unida (IU), which picked up one million votes and gained 10 more Cortes seats for a total of 17. The PP under its new leader did better than expected, gaining one seat for a total of 106. (For tabulated results, see *Political Parties,* above.) In early December magistrates in the province of Mureia ruled that because of "incorrect procedures" a new election would have to be held. Until the results of the election for the province's nine seats were known, the PSOE would be unable to tell whether it would hold an absolute majority in the Cortes, where it controlled 176 seats until new polls could take place.   (MICHAEL WOOLLER)

SWEDEN

A constitutional monarchy of northern Europe, Sweden occupies the eastern side of the Scandinavian Peninsula, with coastlines on the North and Baltic seas and the Gulf of Bothnia. Area: 449,964 sq km (173,732 sq mi). Pop. (1989 est.): 8,498,000. Cap.: Stockholm. Monetary unit: Swedish krona, with (Oct. 2, 1989) a free rate of 6.43 kronor to U.S. $1 (10.41 kronor = £1 sterling). King, Carl XVI Gustaf; prime minister in 1989, Ingvar Carlsson.

The 1986 assassination of Prime Minister Olof Palme continued to cast a long shadow over life in Sweden in 1989. Carl Gustav Christer Pettersson, a 42-year-old drifter with a history of substance abuse, was convicted in July 1989

TONI SICA—GAMMA/LIAISON

Christer Pettersson, who had been imprisoned for the assassination of Sweden's Prime Minister Olof Palme, talks to the press after his release from prison. Pettersson's earlier conviction was overturned because of lack of evidence.

and sentenced to life imprisonment for the assassination. On October 12, however, a seven-member Swedish appeals court unanimously overturned the conviction because of insufficient evidence. The affair renewed questions concerning the validity of the Swedish judicial system, already accused by a number of the nation's most prominent lawyers of permitting both hearsay and circumstantial evidence to be admitted and thus favouring the state over the individual.

Pettersson was convicted primarily on the evidence given by Lisbet Palme, the widow of the assassinated prime minister. In a face-to-face court confrontation, she identified Pettersson as the killer. A police officer, who had arrived at the scene shortly after the murder, testified for the defense at the appeal proceedings, however, and claimed that Mrs. Palme had been hysterical and in no condition to identify the assassin. Pettersson announced via his lawyers that he fully intended to sue the state for what would almost certainly be record damages. He was held in custody for nearly a year and had received death threats from Palme's supporters.

The Palme assassination had also precipitated the "Ebbe Carlsson affair," which continued in the public eye in 1989. Carlsson, a prominent book publisher, had led a private investigation into the murder that included the smuggling of illegal electronic bugging devices into Sweden to spy on Kurdish extremists suspected of the murder. The disclosure of the investigation had led to the resignation of the justice minister in mid-1988, and Carlsson's theories were later discredited.

Though Finance Minister Kjell-Olof Feldt balanced the budget, more than 10,000 schoolchildren protested public spending cuts. Feldt was severely criticized for proposing a one-time tax on large company profits and a system of compulsory savings in which a percentage of a citizen's salary would be paid into a state bank account to be repaid later with interest. However, both industry and the population in general reacted more favourably to his plans to cut income taxes. Following talks between Prime Minister Ingvar Carlsson and opposition leaders, it was agreed that the corporate tax, at present 52%, should be cut to 40% and that marginal income tax rates should be reduced to a maximum of 50% by 1991. Other taxes would be increased to make up for the cuts.

The country's policy of strongly defended neutrality was dealt a severe blow in February when a prototype of the JAS 39 Gripen, a new generation of jet fighter, crashed while landing on its maiden flight. The pilot escaped unhurt, but the JAS program was delayed for a year, and extra costs of 1 billion kronor were incurred. The crash was a setback for the Saab-Scania aerospace and automobile company, which also experienced trouble with its car division, badly hit by falling sales in the U.S. In December General Motors Corp., announced that it would buy half of Saab-Scania's car-making operations. Volvo announced record profits of 7.1 billion kronor; however, most of this was attributed to increased truck sales.

Mats Lundberg, former marketing chief for the arms company Bofors, and Malmö director Karl-Erik Schmitz were found not guilty of smuggling explosives to Iran. Investigations into alleged bribes paid by Bofors to secure a large Indian order were abandoned by the Swedish police. However, three other former Bofors officials—Martin Ardbo, Hans Ekblom, and Lennart Palsson—were charged with illegal sale of ground-to-air missiles to Dubai and Bahrain.

Authors Lars Gyllensten, Werner Aspenström, and Kerstin Ekman, members of the Nobel Prize for Literature selection committee, submitted their resignations to Sweden's Academy of Letters because the Academy had failed to condemn Ayatollah Ruhollah Khomeini's "death sentence" against Indian-born British author Salman Rushdie. His novel *The Satanic Verses* had been deemed blasphemous by Muslim fundamentalists. Their resignations were refused under the Academy's rules of lifelong tenure.

(CHRIS MOSEY)

SWITZERLAND

A landlocked federal state in west central Europe, Switzerland consists of a confederation of 26 cantons (6 of which are demicantons). Area: 41,293 sq km (15,943 sq mi). Pop. (1989 est.): 6,689,000. Cap.: Bern. Monetary unit: Swiss franc, with (Oct. 2, 1989) a free rate of Sw F 1.62 to U.S. $1 (Sw F 2.63 = £1 sterling). President in 1989, Jean-Pascal Delamuraz.

Though hardly an inflationary ripple disturbed its placid surface of general prosperity, Switzerland confronted several worrying problems in 1989. They included drugs, the influx of asylum seekers from less developed countries, continuing environmental concerns, especially worsening air pollution from motor vehicles and heating systems, and an acute shortage of urban accommodations at reasonable prices. In early autumn Parliament hurriedly endorsed a ban on the instant resale of property, on which millions were being made.

Beyond these loomed the now urgent question of how best to react to the economic integration of the European Communities in 1992. The EC surrounded Switzerland on all sides and comprised its main trading partner. The extent to which this was exercising the government was indicated when the Cabinet commissioned a high-level expert group to assess the consequences of possible EC membership, particularly in relation to Switzerland's federal system, sovereignty, and traditional neutrality. "No insurmountable juridical barrier prevents Switzerland's joining the Common Market," the experts' report concluded. Parliamentary commissions were still discussing it behind closed doors at year's end.

Meanwhile, the public at large was deeply troubled by the plight of the country's drug addicts, an estimated 10,000–15,000 of them on heroin and many infected with the AIDS (acquired immune deficiency syndrome) virus. Switzerland had, proportionately, the second highest incidence of AIDS in any developed country, after the U.S. In an effort to curb the spread of the disease, Bern, Zürich, and Basel were making available free disposable syringes and needles—up to 4,000 a day at Zürich's Platzspitz Park. The concentration of addicts there, many homeless, led people to question how much this turning to drugs by the young in one of the world's most affluent societies could be blamed on growth of excessive materialism compensating for a compulsive work ethic. The anxiety over drugs also focused attention on investigations into sweeping allegations that proceeds from large-scale drug trafficking were being laundered in Switzerland.

This attention served to highlight the dramatic setback to feminist aspirations—women gained the vote less than two decades ago—in the sudden departure from office at the end of 1988 of the justice and police minister, Elisabeth Kopp, the first Swiss woman to attain Cabinet rank. Amid charges of violating official secrecy, she quit after admitting she had tipped off her husband, a Zürich business lawyer, that an enterprise with which he was connected was suspected of money laundering.

For would-be refugees, the attraction of a wealthy Switzerland with full employment combined with the real-

Drug addicts shoot up openly in a Swiss park. The widespread sharing of needles by Switzerland's many drug addicts prompted the government to distribute free disposable syringes as a means of slowing the spread of AIDS.
PATA—SIPA

ization that if only they could enter the country, they were probably assured of food and accommodation at public expense until an official decision was made on whether they were genuine political refugees entitled to asylum. More than 20,000 entered Switzerland in 1989—mostly Turkish Kurds, Sri Lankans, Yugoslavs, and Pakistanis— bringing the total awaiting a decision to over 40,000. The acceptance rate was below 4%. A xenophobic reaction was a series of highly suspect fires—one causing four deaths— at premises housing refugees. Public outrage resulted in November when police stood by as members of a notorious neo-Nazi extremist group smashed the kitchen, broke windows, and manhandled the director of the Steinhausen (Zug) transit centre.

It was reassuring, therefore, to solid citizens that a November 26 national referendum proposal to "abolish the Swiss Army" was, as expected, decisively rejected. The government was already working on well-publicized plans for a one-third reduction, as from 1995, in the 625,000-strong militia-type force. Meanwhile, the Army itself continued its programs for further acquisitions of sophisticated new weaponry—including new machines for the three bicycle regiments. It also maintained 10,000 packhorses and mules, still the surest transport on perilous Alpine paths.

(ALAN MCGREGOR)

UNITED KINGDOM

A constitutional monarchy in northwestern Europe and member of the Commonwealth, the United Kingdom comprises the island of Great Britain (England, Scotland, and Wales) and Northern Ireland, together with many small islands. Area: 244,110 sq km (94,251 sq mi), including 3,218 sq km of inland water but excluding the crown dependencies of the Channel Islands and Isle of Man. Pop. (1989 est.): 57,218,000. Cap.: London. Monetary unit: pound sterling, with (Oct. 2, 1989) a free rate of £0.62 to U.S. $1 (U.S. $1.62 = £1 sterling). Queen, Elizabeth II; prime minister in 1989, Margaret Thatcher.

Domestic Affairs. The 10th anniversary of the May 1979 election that propelled Prime Minister Margaret Thatcher (*see* BIOGRAPHIES) to power might have been an occasion to ease up on her program of free market reforms. Some of her fellow Conservatives wished that this were so as the party stumbled to defeat in elections to the European Parliament, but the pace of reform was maintained.

Two major new privatization bills passed into law. Parliament agreed to the sale of the water and electric-

ity industries, by far the biggest sell-offs of state-owned companies in the Thatcher era. The bills provided for 10 regional water companies to be sold separately and for Great Britain's electricity-generation industry to be divided into two. The government announced in November, however, that it would keep Britain's nuclear power stations (providing about 15% cent of the country's electricity) in public ownership. In the case of water, controversy was intensified by disclosures that the quality of drinking water in some parts of Britain fell below European Communities (EC) standards. The government argued that privatization, accompanied by firm regulation, provided the best guarantee of clean water (and efficient electricity supplies) in the future. Opinion polls showed that few voters shared the ministers' optimism.

The government also unveiled plans to open up the legal profession and the National Health Service. In July, following a bitter debate in which many barristers and judges urged the lord chancellor, Lord Mackay of Clashfern (*see* BIOGRAPHIES), to dilute his initial proposals, firm plans were unveiled that would remove some of the protected rights enjoyed by barristers and solicitors. Barristers would no longer have exclusive rights of audience in higher courts, while financial institutions like banks and building societies would be able to compete with solicitors in the provision of house conveyancing services.

Throughout the year the medical profession was locked in dispute with the health secretary, Kenneth Clarke, over his plans, unveiled in January, to reform the National Health Service. Clarke's proposals included encouragement to hospitals and general practitioners to estimate the cost of their services more accurately, to offer greater value for money, and to take greater care with their budgets. The British Medical Association (BMA) argued that these plans threatened doctors' duties to exercise their best clinical judgment according to the needs of each patient, and it launched a major publicity campaign against the reforms. One advertisement that aroused particular controversy consisted of the question "What do you call a man who does not listen to his doctor?" and the answer "Mr. Clarke." Clarke, who denounced the BMA campaign as "extremely unscrupulous," was confident that the Conservatives' 100-seat majority in the House of Commons would allow him to pass his reforms into law.

Like the plans to privatize water and electricity, the government's proposals for the health service encountered

widespread public disapproval. At the same time, rising interest rates were making life uncomfortable for many homeowners. (See *Economic Affairs,* below.) One result was the first defeat for the Conservatives in a national election since Thatcher became leader of her party in 1975. In the European Parliament elections on June 15, the Conservatives won 34.8% of the vote, while Labour won 40.3%. The Conservatives won 32 seats, to Labour's 45—exactly the reverse of the outcome of the previous contest in 1984. (The Scottish Nationalists held their single seat in Scotland; as usual, the main parties did not contest any of the three seats in Northern Ireland.)

Labour Party leader Neil Kinnock (*see* BIOGRAPHIES) regarded his party's win as an emphatic endorsement of Labour's policy review, which had begun after its 1987 general election defeat. The results were published during the European election campaign under the title "Meet the Challenge, Make the Change." The new policy document, endorsed at Labour's annual conference at Brighton in October, swept away a number of policies that Kinnock maintained had cost Labour votes. The most dramatic change concerned defense. In 1983 and 1987 Labour had promised to scrap Britain's nuclear weapons unilaterally and to eject U.S. nuclear weapons based on British soil. Following the policy review, Labour promised only that it would seek to negotiate an end to British ownership of nuclear weapons as part of the strategic arms limitation talks. Elsewhere in "Meet the Challenge, Make the Change," Labour abandoned its commitment to renationalize all the industries privatized by the Conservatives and committed itself to the operation of a market economy. In December Labour also decided that it would no longer support the closed shop (compulsory union membership).

The European Parliament elections were also notable for the sudden emergence of Britain's Green Party as an electoral force. Their 15% of the vote won them no seats. (Britain, alone among EC countries, continued to operate a "first-past-the-post" rather than a proportional system.) It was, however, the largest share of the vote that any Green party had won at any national election anywhere in the world. The result was made even more surprising by the fact that the party, founded in 1973, had won only 1.4% on average in those constituencies where it fielded candidates in the 1987 general election. Opinion polls and analysis suggested that concern over environmental issues

was augmented by middle-class disenchantment with the performance of the government—and the failure of the centre parties to present an effective alternative.

All parties responded to the Greens' advance by proclaiming their own environmental credentials. The government, which had mounted a successful international conference in March to discuss measures to protect the ozone layer, published a report by David Pearce of University College, London, in August. It argued that the best way to preserve the environment was to assign a monetary value to it. Taxes should then be applied to "dirty" goods and production processes to make sure they reflected their full environmental cost.

The greatest losers in the European Parliament elections were the Social and Liberal Democrats (SLD), formed only a year earlier as the result of a messy merger between the Liberals and the Social Democratic Party (SDP). The SLD won only 6.1% of the vote and no seats—the worst result by the main centre party at any British election since the 1950s. One continuing problem for the SLD was not settled until October—its name. The party's leader, Paddy Ashdown, and most former Social Democrats favoured "Democrat" as the party's short name, but most former Liberal MPs wanted "Liberal Democrat." Eventually the matter was settled by a ballot of individual members. Seventy percent opted for "Liberal Democrat."

In July Thatcher conducted her midterm Cabinet reshuffle, designed to bring younger blood into the Cabinet and to give some of its occupants more suitable roles. However, the desired impact was blunted by a semipublic row between Thatcher and her foreign secretary, Sir Geoffrey Howe. Howe wanted to keep his job; Thatcher wanted to move him, not least because she regarded him as too enthusiastic about the EC. Howe eventually agreed to move to leader of the House (in effect, becoming responsible for securing passage of the government's business through the House of Commons) but with the added title of "deputy prime minister." The deal nearly came unstuck when Thatcher's office briefed journalists the following day to the effect that the title was meaningless. Thatcher's main new appointments were: foreign secretary, John Major (*see* BIOGRAPHIES); environment secretary, Christopher Patten (previously overseas development minister, outside the Cabinet); defense secretary, Tom King (previously Northern Ireland secretary); chairman of the Conservative Party,

Kenneth Baker (previously education secretary). On October 26 Nigel Lawson's resignation as chancellor of the Exchequer (*see* below) provoked a further reshuffle. Major became the new chancellor; Douglas Hurd moved from the Home Office to become foreign secretary; and David Waddington (formerly chief whip) became home secretary.

Perhaps the unluckiest dismissal from the Cabinet in the July reshuffle was that of Paul Channon, the transport secretary. He had the misfortune to carry ministerial responsibility for a series of fatal accidents and was thought to have shown indecision in his response to them. The main accidents during his last eight months were: Dec. 12, 1988, Clapham, South London, 35 killed in triple train crash; December 21, Lockerbie, Scotland, 259 killed when terrorist bomb explodes on Pam Am jumbo jet; Jan. 8, 1989, Kegworth, East Midlands, 47 killed when British Midland 737 crashes on motorway (expressway) attempting emergency landing; March 4, Purley, Surrey, 5 killed in train crash; March 6, Glasgow, 2 killed in train crash. Another major accident occurred on April 15, when 95 football fans were crushed to death in Sheffield. A subsequent public inquiry found that the police had mishandled the situation by admitting extra fans, without tickets, to the grounds and then refusing to open gates from the terraces onto the pitch when pressure built up in the stands. (*See* SPORTS AND GAMES: *Football: Soccer:* Sidebar.)

Late in the year Sir Anthony Meyer became the first person to challenge Thatcher for the leadership of the Conservative Party since she was elected in 1975. In the vote, by Conservative members of Parliament in December, Thatcher won 314–33 with 24 spoiled ballots and 3 abstentions. Meyer had not expected to win but had hoped to demonstrate enough opposition to Thatcher to provoke her resignation before the next general election, scheduled for July 1992.

The year marked a series of new developments for British television. In February Rupert Murdoch's Sky satellite television service started transmitting four channels, including Britain's first 24-hour television news station. However, sales of satellite dishes in the early months were less than anticipated, and losses mounted at £2 million a week. (*See* BIOGRAPHIES: *Neil, Andrew.*) In June the government announced its latest plans for the reform of terrestrial television. The BBC's license-fee income would be preserved until the mid-1990s; independent television channels would be auctioned to the highest bidders in each region, subject to safeguards regarding quality and range of programming. November saw the introduction of television cameras to the House of Commons, amid fears in some quarters—and hopes in others—that television would lead to a change in MPs' behaviour. The first and most noticeable consequence was an increase in MPs' attendance.

On February 14 Iran's Ayatollah Ruhollah Khomeini issued a "death sentence" against Indian-born British author Salman Rushdie (*see* PUBLISHING: *Sidebar*).

Economic Affairs. Chancellor Lawson had raised interest rates in the second half of 1988 to tame an economy that threatened to unleash both high inflation and a balance of payments crisis, but the patient seemed slow to respond. By October 1989 the base interest rate had risen to 15% and, as the year closed, inflation remained uncomfortably near the peak of 8% a year it had reached in May. Provisional estimates put the balance of trade deficit for the year at £20 billion. Both the trade and inflation figures were substantially worse than Lawson had forecast at the time of his annual budget speech in March.

The opposition parties, and some Conservatives, criticized Lawson for his "one-club golf" policy of relying on interest rates to cool the economy. Critics suggested that higher taxes, direct credit controls, or both should be applied. Lawson's response was that taxes already exceeded government spending by around £15 billion a year, and credit controls, even if desirable, were no longer practical following the abolition of exchange controls in 1979 and deregulation of the financial markets in 1987. Lawson did, however, believe that his objectives could be more easily obtained if the U.K. joined the exchange rate mechanism of the European Monetary System (EMS). This would tie sterling to such currencies as the West German Deutsche Mark and the French franc and (so the supporters of British participation claimed) enable monetary discipline to be maintained at lower interest rates. However, Thatcher, guided by her economic adviser, Sir Alan Walters, remained adamantly opposed to this course.

When the issue of Britain's full membership in the EMS was discussed at the EC summit in Madrid in June, Thatcher and Lawson agreed on a compromise position: the U.K. would join the exchange rate mechanism when and if Britain's inflation rate fell to that of other EC countries and they, in turn, abolished exchange controls as the U.K. had done. The compromise did not prevent a dispute that led to Lawson's resignation. Lawson held that Walters' public and semipublic utterances were weakening his (Lawson's) position. Matters came to a head in October, following publication in the U.S. of an article by Walters in which he described the exchange rate mechanism as a "half-baked" scheme. On October 26 Lawson told Thatcher he could not remain chancellor if Walters stayed as Thatcher's adviser, and when Thatcher refused to sack Walters, he resigned. The news reached Walters in the U.S., whereupon he also resigned. At the EC summit in Strasbourg, France, in December, Thatcher maintained her opposition to the EMS.

One bright spot for the U.K. economy was unemployment, which continued to fall from its 1986 peak of 3.2 million; by the end of 1989 the published figure had halved to less than 1.7 million. A significant part of this reduction, however, resulted from changes in the definition of unemployment and the methods used to measure it. Independent estimates put the true reduction since 1986 at between 500,000 and one million.

Foreign Affairs. In June the shock waves from China's imposition of martial law reached London. In 1984 Thatcher had signed a declaration returning Hong Kong to China in 1997, following the expiration of a 99-year lease granted to the U.K. in 1898. The 1984 agreement stipulated that for 50 years after 1997, Hong Kong's "previous capitalist system and life-style shall remain unchanged." However, some of the colony's 3.3 million U.K. passport holders said they did not trust China's word and wanted the right to settle in the U.K. They received little comfort from the U.K. government, which, with the support of the Labour Party, said that only a small number with particular ties to the U.K. (such as crown employees) would be admitted.

The arrival of George Bush at the White House in Washington in January produced a slight but significant change in U.K.-U.S. relations. Thatcher did not strike up as close a relationship with Bush as she had with Ronald Reagan. When NATO held its summit at the end of May, Thatcher was isolated in her enthusiasm for the modernization of short-range nuclear weapons in Europe; Bush had moved some way toward the West German position of caution on this issue. Thatcher still claimed a close personal rapport with Pres. Mikhail Gorbachev of the Soviet Union, who visited London in April. At the Conservative Party confer-

British soccer fans watch in horror as other fans are crushed against a fence at the Hillsborough Stadium in Sheffield. Some 95 people were killed and many others injured when hordes of soccer fans rushed into the already overcrowded standing area.

THOMAS—GAMMA/LIAISON

ence in Blackpool in October, Thatcher claimed that her concept of political and economic freedom had inspired the reform movements in Eastern Europe.

At the Commonwealth heads of government conference in Malaysia in October, Britain continued to be in a minority of one in its attitude toward sanctions against South Africa. A compromise appeared to have been reached when Britain agreed with the other 48 governments to a communiqué that said sanctions should stay until there was "fundamental political change" in South Africa. Within hours, the British government issued a statement reaffirming that sanctions had little role to play in producing change.

Northern Ireland. Twenty years after the arrival of British troops, initially to defend Catholic communities in Northern Ireland, the Irish Republican Army (IRA) stepped up its terror campaign against the British Army, attacking a series of "soft" targets in mainland Britain and West Germany, as well as in Northern Ireland. A British corporal was killed by a car bomb in Hanover, West Germany, in July, and the wife of a soldier was shot dead outside her home in Dortmund in September. The worst attack occurred at Deal, in Kent, on September 22, when 10 musicians were killed at the Royal Marines School of Music. Ireland's Prime Minister Charles Haughey said the attack renewed his determination to end all such "barbaric acts of terrorism in our democracies."

Attempts by Northern Ireland's police force, the Royal Ulster Constabulary, to maintain the trust of the Catholic communities were dented by a series of disclosures in September that RUC officers were leaking information and photographs relating to people suspected, but not convicted, of republican activities. Some of this information had been leaked to Protestant terrorist groups, some sent anonymously to British newspapers.

In October the Appeal Court in London suddenly released four people who had been convicted in 1975 of planting bombs that had killed five people in Guildford, Surrey, in October 1974. The "Guildford Four" had been convicted on the strength of confessions that they said had been obtained under duress. In January 1989 Home Secretary Douglas Hurd ordered the Court of Appeal to reexamine their case in light of new evidence. A subsequent police inquiry found that the four were right, and that the Surrey police had withheld evidence from the initial trial.

(PETER KELLNER)

See also *Commonwealth of Nations,* above; *Dependent States,* below.

VATICAN CITY STATE

The independent sovereignty of Vatican City State is surrounded by but is not part of Rome. As a state with territorial limits, it is properly distinguished from the Holy See, which constitutes the worldwide administrative and legislative body for the Roman Catholic Church. Area: 44 ha (109 ac). Pop. (1989 est.): 750. As sovereign pontiff, John Paul II is the chief of state. Vatican City is administered by a pontifical commission of five cardinals headed by the secretary of state, in 1989 Camerlingue Sebastiano Cardinal Baggio.

On December 24 Panamanian strongman Manuel Noriega took refuge in the Vatican nunciature from U.S. troops that had invaded Panama City. During the following days the papal nuncio, Sebastian Laboa, played a central role in the negotiations between Noriega and the U.S. forces.

A number of important events in 1989 marked the evolving relations between the Holy See and Eastern Europe. Several bishops were nominated in Czechoslovakia; with the consent of the Soviet authorities, a bishop was nominated to head the diocese of Minsk, vacant for three years; and the dioceses in Lithuania were reorganized with the nomination of an archbishop of Vilnius, an archbishop of Kaunas, and one titular bishop to vacant dioceses. Diplomatic relations between Poland and the Vatican, severed since 1939, were reestablished. Finally, Mikhail Gorbachev met with the pope in December, during the Soviet leader's trip to Italy.

The Institute for Religious Works (the Vatican bank) was reorganized and given an administrative council, composed of five experts, which in turn was under the direction of a council of five cardinals. In a message marking the 50th anniversary of the start of World War II, Pope John Paul II condemned the "planned barbarity against the Jewish people, which remains forever a disgrace for humanity."

The pope journeyed to Madagascar, Réunion, Zambia, and Malawi in April; to Scandinavia in June; and to South Korea, Indonesia, and Mauritius in October. He made the pilgrimage to the shrine of Santiago de Compostela in Spain, where hundreds of thousands of young people had gathered. Visitors to the Vatican included U.S. Pres. George Bush, UN Secretary-General Javier Pérez de Cuéllar; Irish Pres. Patrick Hillery; Portuguese Pres. Mário Soares, and Nobel laureate Andrey Sakharov.   (MAX BERGERRE)

See also RELIGION: *Roman Catholic Church.*

This article updates the *Micropædia* article VATICAN CITY STATE.

Eastern Europe and the U.S.S.R

EASTERN EUROPEAN AFFAIRS

The year 1989 entirely transformed the face of Eastern European politics. At the start of the year only Hungary was taking very tentative steps toward multiparty, competitive politics; by December the political monopoly of the Communist Party was fast disappearing not only in Hungary but in Poland, East Germany, Czechoslovakia, Bulgaria, and Romania as well. This left only Albania maintaining its firm adherence to the neo-Stalinist system, while in Yugoslavia two very different conceptions of government—one nationalist and one democratic—were struggling for supremacy.

A number of broad reasons, applicable to all the countries involved, helped to explain why the Communist system was crumbling. The removal of an aging, longtime party leader proved to be significant in Hungary, East Germany, Bulgaria, Czechoslovakia, and Romania in that it eliminated an element of conservatism, a refusal to recognize that far-reaching change was needed. In Poland, though, Gen. Wojciech Jaruzelski underwent a conversion and accepted that the Communist Party could no longer rule on its own.

A second factor was the readiness of a section of the intellectuals in those countries to reject the Communist Party's monopoly and to launch criticism of Communist policies, strategies, and dogmas. When this criticism reached a certain quantity and quality, it became increasingly difficult for the ruling elite to ignore it, especially when it began to find expression in the public media. This breaching of surface unanimity, a key factor in maintaining the elite's self-confidence, was a broad signal that major changes could be imminent. This stage was reached in Hungary and Poland in 1988; in the other countries intellectual criticism became more trenchant as 1989 progressed.

A third factor was the involvement of the general population, leading to fear by the rulers that popular discontent would spill over into the streets. Once these leaders could see that a divided and disorganized population was capable of unified action, their morale crumbled rapidly. In many ways being at the top in a Communist system for many years is poor preparation for facing the challenge of mass demonstrations. The elite concluded that the only alternatives were to give way to popular demands or to use force. The hostile world reaction to the use of force in China earlier in the year was a severe disincentive to adopting this policy in Eastern Europe.

In Poland the strikes of 1988 and the fear that a growing section of the working population would listen neither to the government nor to the Solidarity trade union movement impelled the Jaruzelski government to broach negotiations with Solidarity at the beginning of 1989. Hungary never really went through this stage; the demonstrations that took place there were, in effect, aligned with the changes taking place in the political system. In East Germany, on the other hand, it was the sight of large numbers of East Germans leaving the country and then, subsequently, the mass demonstrations in various cities that finally broke the nerve of the leadership and prompted it to open the Berlin Wall on November 9. In both Czechoslovakia and Bulgaria mass rallies, and in the former a two-hour general

strike, brought it home to the rulers that the introduction of a multiparty system could no longer be avoided.

To these should be added a fourth factor—the fear of economic collapse and the recognition by the ruling Communist parties that their economic policies were in tatters. One after another, leaders were forced to conclude that their planned economies were not succeeding—that there were severe shortages of consumer goods and, in some cases, foodstuffs; that the threat of inflation and unemployment could not be averted; and that finally only a genuine competitive market economy could save the situation. This loss of faith in Communism by the ruling elites powerfully reinforced their sense of drift and thus made them vulnerable to the challenges, not least because they understood that the alternatives were collapse or repression.

A fifth factor was the international situation. At some stage the Soviet leadership decided that the Communist nations of Eastern Europe were no longer viable under Communist leadership and that their stability and economic future could be guaranteed only by a thoroughgoing transformation. From the Soviet standpoint this was a dangerous situation because collapse in any Eastern European country might drag the Soviet Union into intervention, a circumstance that the Soviet leadership wanted to avoid at any cost. Consequently, Soviet Pres. Mikhail Gorbachev repeatedly encouraged the pro-reform elements in Eastern Europe to remove the antireform elements and open up their systems to change. This was clearly what happened in East Germany; Gorbachev's apparently critical remarks about longtime East German leader Erich Honecker, made at the 40th anniversary of the founding of the nation, were instrumental in bringing about Honecker's removal. The seal on this process was set at the Warsaw Pact summit in December when the members officially recognized that the invasion of Czechoslovakia in 1968 had been an error.

In Romania, where the lid was held on most tightly, the eventual explosion was the most violent and the subsequent situation the most chaotic. Unlike his counterparts elsewhere in Eastern Europe, Nicolae Ceausescu, who had caustically rejected any hint of *perestroika,* was overthrown in a bloody revolution and executed.

The Soviet Union's calculation presumably was that the Eastern European states were unstable without reform, that the old leaderships would not reform, and that, even if Communist parties were largely eliminated, Soviet interests would be better served by stable though friendly governments in the area. In effect, the Soviet Union accepted that a status similar to the one it maintained with Finland was the best on which to base relationships with its Eastern European allies. It was, under the circumstances, impossible to know exactly how the Soviet Union defined its basic interests in the region, but the assumption was that membership in the Warsaw Pact was still not negotiable and, perhaps, that the Communist Party should retain some residual role in the affairs of the various countries.

The events of the year, therefore, contributed to a complete reevaluation and redefinition of Europe. In Soviet eyes, evidently, the loosening of the reins in Eastern Europe was a part of the process of moving back toward the European mainstream from which the 1917 revolution had excluded it. For the Eastern Europeans the process was reintegration into political, intellectual, and economic currents from which they were excluded after the Communist seizure of power. And for the Western Europeans the prospect of an undivided and integrated continent was enormously exciting and a source of concern at the same time.　　　　　　　　　　　　　(GEORGE SCHÖPFLIN)

See also Economic Affairs; Military Affairs.

ALBANIA

A socialist republic in the western Balkan Peninsula of southeastern Europe, Albania is situated on the Adriatic Sea. Area: 28,748 sq km (11,100 sq mi). Pop. (1989 est.): 3,197,000. Cap.: Tirane. Monetary unit: lek, with (Oct. 2, 1989) a free rate of 6.20 leks to U.S. $1 (10.03 leks = £1 sterling). First secretary of the Albanian (Communist) Party of Labour and chairman of the Presidium of the People's Assembly (president) in 1989, Ramiz Alia; chairman of the Council of Ministers (premier), Adil Carcani.

Although Ramiz Alia, the party leader, consolidated his position in 1989, there were no signals that Albania was embarking on a Soviet-style *perestroika* (restructuring). The absence of significant economic reforms suggested that conservative elements within the leadership still exercised considerable influence. Albania's perennial economic problems of low productivity, inefficiency, and outmoded technology were compounded by a long drought that affected agricultural production and seriously disrupted supplies of hydroelectricity.

The continued improvement of relations with West Germany culminated in the signing in March of a two-year agreement on technical and financial cooperation worth DM 20 million. In the wake of Foreign Minister Reis Malile's visit to France in March (the first such visit since World War II), talks were under way on the possibility of joint Albanian-French oil extraction in Albania. Other signs that Albania was gradually emerging from diplomatic isolation included the strengthening of relations with Greece, Bulgaria, and Turkey. Tirane also was host to the Balkan deputy foreign ministers' conference in January. Although Albania condemned the violence in the Yugoslav province of Kosovo in the spring as an act of "state terror" against the Albanian population, it was careful not to burn its bridges with Yugoslavia, which remained its main trading partner.   (PATRICK ARTISIEN)

BULGARIA

The socialist republic of Bulgaria is on the eastern Balkan Peninsula of southeastern Europe, along the Black Sea. Area: 110,994 sq km (42,855 sq mi). Pop. (1989 est.): 8,987,000. Cap.: Sofia. Monetary unit: lev, with (Oct. 2, 1989) a free rate of 0.82 lev to U.S. $1 (1.33 leva = £1 sterling). General secretaries of the Bulgarian Communist Party in 1989, Todor Zhivkov and, from November 10, Petar Mladenov; chairmen of the State Council (presidents), Zhivkov to November 10 and, from November 17, Mladenov; chairman of the Council of Ministers (premier), Georgy Atanasov.

Economic reform continued in January 1989 when Decree No. 56 announced that henceforth the basic economic unit in Bulgaria would be the "firm." Though not precisely defined, the firm would be allowed to issue dividend-bearing shares to its employees. Firms could be established by existing economic concerns, by local authorities, and by citizens.

Existing independent and dissident organizations grew stronger as the year went on, and new ones were founded. The main groups were the Independent Association for the Defense of Human Rights, established in January 1988, and the Discussion Group for the Support of Glasnost and Perestroika, set up the following November. Bulgaria's first independent trade union and a number of environmental organizations also appeared. The government reacted harshly, expelling some prominent dissenters and intimidating others. It was forced to make some accommodation, however, and in February the Politburo held an extraordinary meeting with leading intellectuals. At the meeting

A line of people surround Bulgaria's National Assembly demanding democratic reforms. The protesters called for more personal freedoms, a restructuring of the economy, and the resignation of the Communist Party's Central Committee.
AFP PHOTO

party leader Todor Zhivkov called for "socialist pluralism," which seemed to mean officially registered societies providing little more than token opposition.

In May ethnic Turks in Bulgaria and their supporters became more assertive in opposing Bulgaria's five-year-old assimilation policy. Hunger strikes spread in the Turkish areas of the northeast, and there were clashes with the police in which a number of Turks died. In a nationwide broadcast on May 29, Zhivkov associated himself with the policy of assimilation and, in response to criticisms from Ankara, called upon Turkey to open its borders to Bulgaria's Turks. The Bulgarian government had recently promised its subjects a liberalization of passport regulations, and Zhivkov's speech was a veiled bluff: if Bulgaria's Turks were as disaffected as Ankara alleged, they would leave Bulgaria. They were and they did. By the end of August, 300,000 of them had left, and the Turkish government had been forced to close its border with Bulgaria. The assimilation policy had brought Bulgaria unwelcome attention from the Organization of the Islamic Conference, the United Nations, the European Parliament, and other bodies.

The Turkish problem was thought to have been a precipitating factor behind Zhivkov's resignation on November 10. At 78, he had been in power for 35 years, the longest-serving leader in Eastern Europe. He was succeeded as both party head and president by his longtime foreign minister, Petar Mladenov, who was generally perceived as being more open to Soviet-style change. Mladenov lost no time in shaking up the government; after purges on November 17 and December 8, only three Zhivkov-era members remained on the Politburo. Zhivkov himself was expelled from the party on December 13. Meanwhile, starting with a small gathering of environmentalists in early November, rallies in Sofia had grown increasingly larger and more insistent on change. On December 7 nine leading opposition groups formed the Union of Democratic Forces. Against this background, the government approved constitutional changes that would end the party's monopoly of power, agreed to wide-ranging talks with the opposition,

and promised free elections in the spring. On December 29 it was announced that Turks would be permitted to use Muslim names.   (RICHARD J. CRAMPTON)

CZECHOSLOVAKIA

The federal republic of Czechoslovakia is a landlocked state of central Europe. Area: 127,900 sq km (49,382 sq mi). Pop. (1989 est.): 15,636,000. Cap.: Prague. Monetary unit: koruna, with (Oct. 2, 1989) a noncommercial rate of 9.75 koruny to U.S. $1 (15.78 koruny = £1 sterling). General secretaries of the Communist Party of Czechoslovakia in 1989, Milos Jakes, Karel Urbanek, from November 24, and, from December 20, Ladislav Adamec; presidents, Gustav Husak until December 10 and, from December 29, Vaclav Havel; federal premiers, Ladislav Adamec until December 7 and, from December 10, Marian Calfa.

The political transformation of Czechoslovakia in 1989 seemed to come suddenly from nowhere and to take place at lightning speed. Between November 17 and year's end, the country changed its rigid Communist system and acquired a government with a majority of non-Communist ministers.

Early in the year the Communist leadership appeared to be well entrenched. In December 1988 the arch-conservative Vasil Bilak was dropped from the party's Politburo, but this was no more than a part of a general rejuvenation process. The party leader, Milos Jakes, made it clear that there was no intention to adopt the policies of *perestroika* (restructuring) and *glasnost* (openness) urged on Eastern Europe by the Soviet Union.

The economy continued in its old, unreformed way and, as a result, problems were accumulating. The projected growth figure for the domestic economy was reduced by the planners from 3.5 to 2.2%, in itself an admission of failure. Even worse, the growth figure for the 1986–90 five-year plan was subject to a severe shortfall—it was likely to achieve no more than a 13–14% increase, rather than the planned 19%. In June Premier Ladislav Adamec warned Czechoslovaks that the situation was bleak, that no improvement could be expected, and that the reforms had barely begun to touch the surface of the problem. This last was reflected in increased shortages of consumer goods and consequent popular unrest.

However, the heart of the conflict was political rather than economic. In January Prague saw six days of demonstrations, largely by young people, in favour of democratization. The initial demonstration, to commemorate the 20th anniversary of the death of Jan Palach, a student who burned himself to death in 1969 in protest against the 1968 Soviet invasion of Czechoslovakia, had been organized by the political opposition. The continuation of the protests, however, was spontaneous and was, in effect, provoked by violent police reactions, which exacerbated matters by making no distinction between demonstrators and passers-by. Other protests took place later in the year, notably on August 21, the anniversary of the 1968 invasion.

More worrisome for the regime was the growing number of those willing to sign petitions from inside official institutions. Petitions calling for a dialogue between rulers and ruled were signed by more than 3,000 people in January and February. A second document, entitled "Just a Few Sentences," calling for democratization, attracted more than 31,000 signatures by mid-October.

There was a wave of protests both in Czechoslovakia and abroad over the arrest and imprisonment in February of the dramatist and political essayist Vaclav Havel (*see* BIOGRAPHIES) on charges of breach of the peace (he was given a nine-month sentence but was released in May). The

Alexander Dubcek addresses a crowd of people after the resignation of Communist leader Milos Jakes. Dubcek, Czechoslovakia's leader during its liberal Prague Spring, was elected chairman of the parliament on December 28.
ERIC BOUVET—GAMMA/LIAISON

Archbishop of Prague called for an end to religious and political repression. By the early summer the non-Communist opposition had substantially broken out of the political ghetto into which it had been pressed by the regime. Many people not previously active politically were ready to sign petitions protesting governmental policies, and there were a growing number of unofficial, unsanctioned organizations.

The government was also worried by the evidence of restiveness and apathy in the Communist Party and resignations from it. There was increasing criticism in the media, though in an oblique form, of the previous 20 years as a time of stagnation and indecision. Finally, one of the Communist Party's allies, the previously subservient Czechoslovak People's Party, began to show signs that it was no longer prepared to accept its subordinate role and demanded greater participation in the political process.

Despite these developments, the magnitude of the revolt against the regime was unexpected. A student demonstration on November 17 was dispersed by the police with needless brutality, and this galvanized large sections of the population into action. There was a massive demonstration in Prague two days later, and that night an unofficial loose opposition coalition, the Civic Forum, was formed.

The Civic Forum demanded the democratization of the government, the resignations of the Communist Party leaders, freedom of the media, and the end of the Communist Party's leading role. The Politburo's initial reaction was to ignore the demands, but throughout the following week the centre of Prague was filled by enormous, spontaneous demonstrations, and these were echoed by protests in some provincial centres. Jakes and the Prague party boss, Miroslav Stepan, resigned on November 24, and negotiations began between the new party leader, Karel Urbanek, and Adamec for a new government to reflect popular feeling. A call for a two-hour general strike on November 27 was well supported.

After a few days Adamec resigned as premier, and his place was taken by a Slovak, Marian Calfa, who then announced the country's first non-Communist government since 1948. The president, Gustav Husak, who was intimately associated with the repression of the previous 20 years, also resigned. On December 20 Urbanek was ousted after less than a month and replaced as party general secretary by Adamec. With the support of the Civic Forum, Alexander Dubcek, the reformer who led the government during the 1968 Prague Spring, was unanimously elected chairman of the parliament on December 28. The following day the parliament named Havel, the acknowledged opposition leader, interim president. The new government announced a series of reforms; the leading role of the party was abolished; more than 30 important party members were suspended or expelled; a multiparty system was to be established; and general elections were planned for 1990.

A principal factor underlying the transformation was the deteriorating economic situation, which the party was not prepared to tackle seriously, as this would have involved a major adjustment of political and economic power relations—to the disadvantage of the rulers. There was also the change of generations. The younger generation had no memory of the trauma of 1968 and its suppression or of the 1970s and was, therefore, less cautious in its demands for change. To some extent this new mood also affected a section of the country's intellectual establishment, notably the economists, whose criticisms grew more direct as they saw the leadership's inaction.

Finally, many people in Czechoslovakia began to feel that they were being left behind by events abroad. The Soviet Union had for some time been pressing the Czechoslovak leadership to reform; both Poland and Hungary contributed to the process of destabilization by supporting reform; and the sudden change in East Germany, a nation that the Prague leadership had viewed as a particularly close ally, was likewise disturbing.   (GEORGE SCHÖPFLIN)

GERMAN DEMOCRATIC REPUBLIC

A socialist republic, the German Democratic Republic (East Germany) is in central Europe on the Baltic Sea. Area: 108,333 sq km (41,827 sq mi). Pop. (1989 est.): 16,613,000. Cap.: Berlin (East). Monetary unit: Mark of Deutsche Demokratische Republik, with (Oct. 2, 1989) a free rate of M 1.87 to U.S. $1 (M 3.03 = £1 sterling). General secretaries of the Socialist Unity (Communist) Party in 1989, Erich Honecker, Egon Krenz from October 18 to December 3 and, from December 9, Gregor Gysi; chairmen of the Council of State (presidents), Honecker, Krenz from October 24, and, from December 6, Manfred Gerlach; chairmen of the Council of Ministers (premiers), Willi Stoph and, from November 13, Hans Modrow.

The German Democratic Republic (GDR; East Germany) experienced the most turbulent period in its 40-year history in 1989. It started out as the most hard-line member of the Warsaw Pact. By late October it was in turmoil, with a changed leadership struggling to contend with the problems created by a mass exodus of young people and to control huge, nationwide demonstrations demanding change. In November the border to the West was opened, and plans for free, democratic elections were announced.

For Erich Honecker, leader of the country since 1971, the year began calmly enough. He may have been a bit worried by figures showing that 40,000 people left the country in 1988, compared with just 12,000 the previous year. However, he continued to hold to his particularly firm brand of Communism and to be suspicious of reforms in the Soviet Union. The GDR was host to the Pact meeting on April 11–12, when NATO was challenged to start separate talks on eliminating all tactical nuclear weapons from Europe.

Meanwhile, dissident church groups were preparing for local elections on May 7. In a system where every candidate had to be approved by the Communist Party, the dissidents urged people to abstain as the best means of recording a protest. The official result, announced by Egon Krenz, the Politburo member in charge, was a 98.77% vote for party candidates—down from the 99.38% five years earlier. Krenz admitted to 142,301 "no" votes and the failure of over 300,000 of the 12.5 million electors to go to the polls. Church groups immediately claimed that up to 10% had voted "no" in some areas. In Leipzig, where there had been a small demonstration against the electoral system on polling day, there were a number of arrests. This initiated a series of public meetings that grew into the protest movement.

Another result of the election was that more and more young people began to believe that there was no hope of reform. The easy reception of West German television showing life in the West made their life-style seem drab by comparison, while news of reforms in Poland and Hungary proved unsettling. After a meeting in June with Mayor Walter Momper of West Berlin, Honecker agreed to allow multiple entry passes to West Germans visiting relatives in the East and to various plans for cross-border cooperation. The package failed to satisfy the growing mood for change, however, and the trickle of refugees trying to reach the West began to grow. Under strong international pressure, Honecker revoked orders to shoot escapers, but the borders stayed firmly closed to the West. The only possible escape was to the east, through West Germany's embassies or through its mission in East Berlin.

Honecker suffered a gall bladder attack in mid-July and subsequently underwent surgery in August. During his long convalescence, refugees began to pack the embassies. On August 8 the West German mission in East Berlin had to be closed because it was too full to take any more people. Others began to arrive at the embassies in Budapest, Warsaw, and Prague. On August 19 Hungary allowed border guards to unlock a gate and let 900 people into Austria, and on September 10 the Budapest government decided to open its border indefinitely. As conditions deteriorated in the Prague embassy complex, deals were struck to allow thousands of others to leave by special trains for the West—provided they traveled across the GDR to be stripped of their papers. This attempt at disgracing them backfired as dozens more refugees scrambled aboard the trains as they passed through. A second deal was struck on October 3, but this time the GDR closed its border with Czechoslovakia, effectively trapping the East Germans inside their country.

It was against this background that Communist leaders gathered in East Berlin for the GDR's 40th anniversary celebrations on October 7. Soviet Pres. Mikhail Gorbachev took the opportunity to warn Honecker that he must not take too long bringing in reforms. On the evening of the anniversary thousands of people demonstrated in the streets of East Berlin and were dispersed only after a violent battle with the police. From then on demonstrations erupted all over the country, with the main protests in Dresden and in Leipzig, where regular Monday evening meetings at the Nikolaikirche had been gaining support throughout the autumn. In marked contrast to the refugees, the demonstrators marched under the slogan: "We are staying." Krenz, as head of internal security, issued orders that the police stop using violence. On October 18 Honecker was forced to resign, and Krenz was chosen to take his place. The change in leadership did nothing to stop either the exodus or the

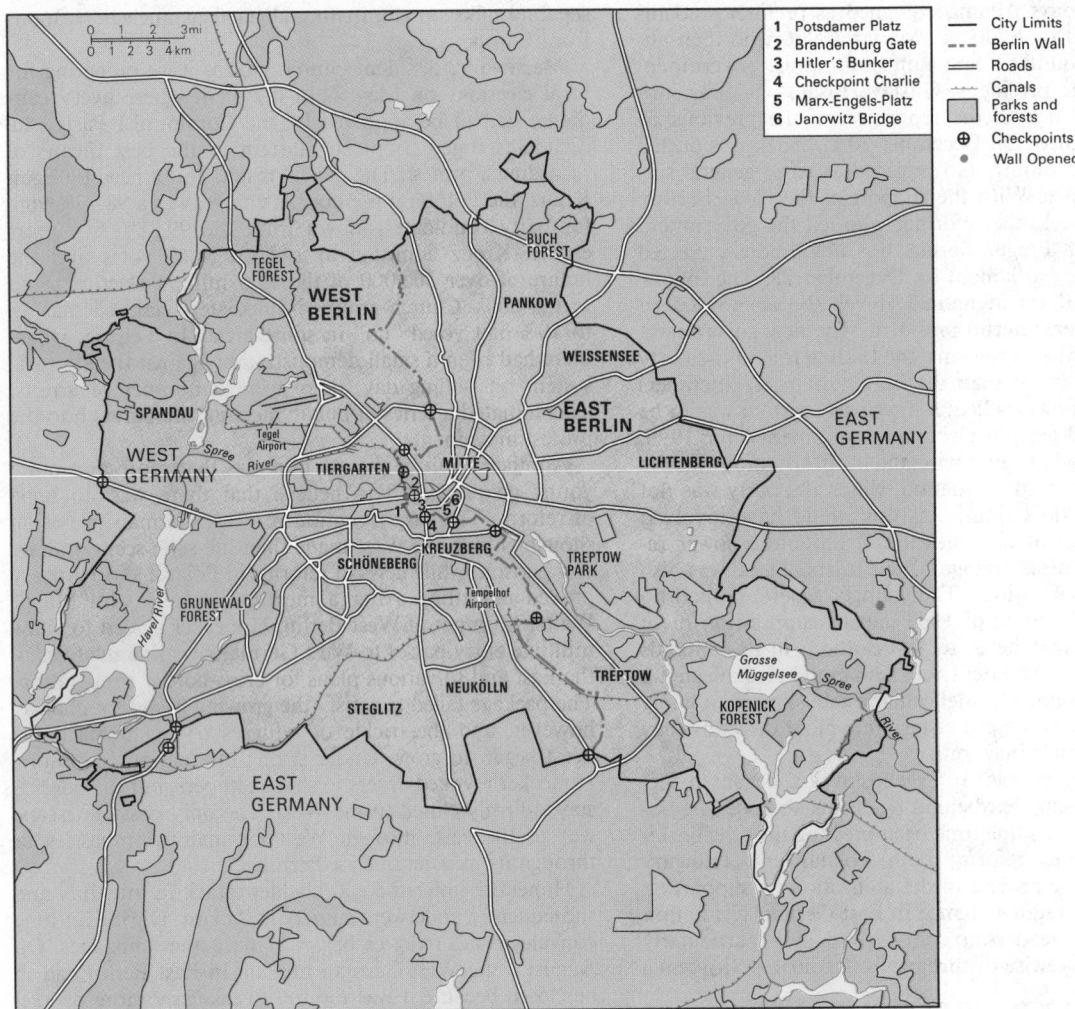

1 Potsdamer Platz	—— City Limits
2 Brandenburg Gate	--- Berlin Wall
3 Hitler's Bunker	═══ Roads
4 Checkpoint Charlie	⋯⋯ Canals
5 Marx-Engels-Platz	▢ Parks and forests
6 Janowitz Bridge	⊕ Checkpoints
	• Wall Opened

demonstrations, however. Krenz offered dialogue, granted an amnesty for all refugees and jailed demonstrators, and promised to make foreign travel easier.

Events moved with increasing speed. On November 4 the border with Czechoslovakia was reopened, and permission was given for refugees to travel on to the West. On November 6 a new travel law was proposed and promptly rejected by Parliament's legal committee as insufficiently liberal. On November 7 the entire government resigned, and on November 8 the Politburo resigned and was replaced by a smaller one of 11 members. On November 9 the decision was made to open the border to the West. Within 24 hours hundreds of thousands of people had swarmed across for a visit (though only 2,500 decided to stay on afterward), and throughout the weekend the Berlin Wall, the supreme emblem of the cold war, was the scene of what observers described as a gigantic party. On November 10 Krenz announced that he was working for free, democratic, and secret elections. On November 13 Parliament chose Hans Modrow, the Dresden party chief who was considered to be a proponent of liberalization, as the new premier. Communists held 17 posts in his 28-member Cabinet, with four allied parties sharing the remainder. Meanwhile, mass demonstrations continued to exert pressure for change. On the first weekend after the Berlin Wall was opened, three million people crossed to visit the West, while the number of refugees dropped to what became an average of 2,000 a day opting to settle in the West.

At the same time, allegations of corruption against former members of the Politburo, including Honecker, began to surface, building up to a crescendo that forced the entire new Politburo to resign on December 3. Krenz was replaced as head of state by Manfred Gerlach, leader of the tiny Liberal Democratic Party, but it was seen as a stopgap appointment until after the general elections, fixed for May 6, 1990. Control of the government was left in the hands of Modrow, who was not involved in any of the corruption allegations. On December 8 the ruling Socialist Unity (Communist) Party held a special all-night congress, at which Gregor Gysi, a prominent lawyer, was chosen as the new leader, and it was agreed to change the party name. A week later a second special congress added "Democratic" to the party's name, and delegates prepared to fight the election in which it had already been conceded that the Communists would lose their power monopoly. Other reform groups also began organizing into political parties, such as New Forum, Democracy Now, and Democratic Awakening, but all said East Germany should continue as a separate socialist alternative to West Germany. Demonstrations in Leipzig and other cities, however, began to show increasing support for the idea of reunification, as did the politically symbolic reopening of the Brandenburg Gate on December 22, and the issue was set to top the political agenda in the year ahead.   (IAN MURRAY)

This article updates the *Macropædia* article GERMANY: *German Democratic Republic.*

HUNGARY

A republic, Hungary is a landlocked state in central Europe. Area: 93,033 sq km (35,920 sq mi). Pop. (1989 est.): 10,-580,000. Cap.: Budapest. Monetary unit: forint, with (Oct. 2, 1989) a free rate of 59.89 forints to U.S. $1 (96.90 forints = £1 sterling). General secretary of the Hungarian Socialist Workers' (Communist) Party in 1989, Karoly Grosz to October 7 when title was abolished; ceremonial president of the Hungarian Socialist Workers' Party to May 8, Janos Kadar; collective presidency of the Hungarian Socialist Workers' Party from June 24, Rezso Nyers (president of the Hungarian Socialist Workers' Party), Grosz, Imre Pozsgay (minister of state), and Miklos Nemeth (chairman of the Council of Ministers), replaced by the president of the Hungarian Socialist Party (renamed Hungarian Socialist Workers' Party), Nyers from October 9; chairman of the Presidential Council (chief of state) to October 18, Bruno Ferenc Straub; interim president from October 18, Matyas Szuros; chairman of the Council of Ministers (prime minister), Nemeth.

A slow but apparently irreversible shift away from Communism and toward democracy dominated the year in Hungary. The change was significantly more gradual than in neighbouring Czechoslovakia and was not attended by large spontaneous demonstrations. On the contrary, it was as if Hungary's Communist rulers had simply concluded that loss of power was inevitable and that they might as well bow to it.

In effect, the last attempt by the party to repel the forces of pluralism came at the end of 1988, when party leader Karoly Grosz issued a warning about the threat of a "white terror," which he was obliged to withdraw in a few days after a very hostile public reaction. By December 1988 the first signs of a renascent multiparty system were discernible.

These signs multiplied in the first few months of 1989 as an increasing number of people concluded that the political climate really had altered and that the Communists would not use their monopoly of force to suppress opposition activities. By the spring a vast number of political parties had come into being, most of them of little consequence.

The parties that did count formed the Opposition Round Table in order to negotiate with Communist Party leadership and other opposition factions for an orderly transition from Communism to democracy, for which there was no precedent anywhere in the world. The main participants in the Round Table were the Hungarian Democratic Forum, the Alliance of Free Democrats, the Young Democrats, and the Social Democrats. The Round Table negotiations continued through the summer and were concluded in September. It was agreed that Hungary would become a democratic republic, with a sovereign, unicameral legislature elected by universal suffrage. There would be a relatively weak president and a constitutional court. In December Parliament voted to dissolve itself on March 16, 1990, and elections were scheduled for March 25.

The leading figure among the reformers was Imre Pozsgay, who had evidently decided by the spring that only the acceptance of genuine democracy, and the consequent redistribution of power, would prevent a collapse of the Communist Party. The party reformers played a major role in the transformation. In February Pozsgay publicly accepted that the revolution of 1956, on the suppression of which the old elite had based its legitimacy, had in fact been a popular uprising and not a counterrevolution. This opened the way to the rehabilitation and ceremonial reinterment of Imre Nagy, the leader of the 1956 revolution, which took place on June 16, the 31st anniversary of his execution. It was attended by enormous crowds, estimated

at as many as 300,000. Major demonstrations were also held to commemorate the country's national day, March 15, and the anniversary of the 1956 revolution, October 23.

A number of by-elections were held during the summer and, where results were declared, the seat was captured by the Hungarian Democratic Forum; this boded ill for the prospects of the Communists, whose popularity was waning continuously. It was clearly to avoid electoral elimination that the reformers pressed for the transformation of the Communist Party into a democratic socialist party.

At their extraordinary congress in early October, a messy compromise was struck. The party changed its name from the Hungarian Socialist Workers' Party to the Hungarian Socialist Party. However, because many of the conservative old guard stayed within the new party, public opinion concluded that the change was only skin deep. On the other hand, by formally dissolving the Communist Party as they did, reformers also brought about a situation where party discipline disappeared and the entire network of institutions controlled by the Communists was suddenly liberated.

The consequences were far-reaching and dramatic. Parliament passed a package of laws effectively destroying the party's power base; this was accomplished by dissolving the workers' militia (the party's private army), by ordering the Communists to give up their network of cells in factories and offices, and by insisting that the party make a full public accounting of all its properties. A change in the constitution also ended the Communist Party's leading role, the formal legal basis for its political monopoly.

The government, now likewise freed from Communist control, moved to introduce a number of measures but could take no tough action regarding the economy since it lacked the legitimacy that derived from popular election. In fact, the economic situation continued to deteriorate, and only irregular injections of short-term credits prevented Hungary from sliding into bankruptcy. However, the government declared its intention to have a market economy in operation by the beginning of 1990.

On the international front, tacit or active encouragement of reform by the Soviet Union evidently played a major role in ensuring that the reform process continued. Hints were even dropped that the U.S.S.R. could live with Hungarian neutrality at some time in the future. The acceleration of reforms in Poland also served to encourage the reformers.

In the spring the Hungarian government symbolically opened its frontier by removing stretches of the barbed wire that formed the iron curtain. This provided an opening for East Germans who wanted to move to West Germany, and several thousand of them took refuge in Hungary. The government, despite great pressure from East Germany, allowed the East Germans to cross to the West and thereby contributed to the subsequent changes in East Germany as well.   (GEORGE SCHÖPFLIN)

POLAND

A socialist republic of eastern Europe, Poland is on the Baltic Sea. Area: 312,683 sq km (120,727 sq mi). Pop. (1989 est.): 37,875,000. Cap.: Warsaw. Monetary unit: zloty, with (Oct. 2, 1989) an official rate of 1,395 zlotys to U.S. $1 (2,258 zlotys = £1 sterling). First secretaries of the Polish United Workers' (Communist) Party in 1989, Gen. Wojciech Jaruzelski and, from July 29, Mieczyslaw Rakowski; chairman of the Council of State to July 19 and president from that date, General Jaruzelski; chairmen of the Council of Ministers (premiers), Rakowski, Czeslaw Kiszczak from August 2, and, from August 24, Tadeusz Mazowiecki.

Tadeusz Mazowiecki of Poland's Solidarity party was elected Poland's first non-Communist prime minister since World War II.

CHIP HIRES—GAMMA/LIAISON

Few observers could have surmised that the roundtable talks between Poland's Communist government and the Solidarity opposition, which had been a condition for ending the strikes of August 1988, would have such far-reaching consequences. Held over a period of eight weeks, between Feb. 6 and April 5, 1989, the negotiations ranged across the full spectrum of problems accumulated after 45 years of Communist rule. Health, housing, education, agriculture, mining, the environment, local government, the malaise affecting Poland's disaffected youth, and the economic system itself came under critical scrutiny.

It was, however, the relegalization of Solidarity as a trade union and the agreement to hold partially free parliamentary elections that appeared to have opened the Pandora's box of radical reforms whose impact spilled over into other countries of the Soviet bloc. At the ballot box in June, Solidarity utilized to the full its symbolic power, gained from seven years in opposition, as well as capitalizing on the people's antipathy to the perpetrators of martial law, the Polish United Workers' (Communist) Party (PUWP). In their first opportunity to vote freely since 1947, the voters gave Solidarity all 35% (161) of the seats in the Sejm (parliament) accorded to the various opposition groupings and 99 of the 100 Senate places in the new bicameral National Assembly. The "coalition" made up of the ruling PUWP, the Peasant Front, the Democratic Front, and the tame Catholic parties received a humiliatingly low share of the votes, though it was guaranteed 65% of the seats. (For tabulated results, see *Political Parties,* above.) Nowhere was this defeat more obvious than in the ignominious rejection of 33 of the 35 elite candidates on the national list, who ran unopposed but failed to gain 50% voter approval.

Political events then moved at a pace that seemed to leave both sides bewildered. Gen. Wojciech Jaruzelski was ensconced in the newly created office of president, by the narrowest of margins and with the overt support of key Solidarity figures. Shortly thereafter he resigned as first secretary of the PUWP and was replaced by Mieczyslaw Rakowski, who had been prime minister. Subsequent attempts by Gen. Czeslaw Kiszczak, the minister of internal affairs and an initiator of the roundtable, to form a govern-

ment collapsed. The newly revivified Peasant and Democratic parties then dropped their senior coalition partner, the PUWP, and with an eye to the fully free elections scheduled for 1992, joined the political wing of Solidarity, the Citizens Parliamentary Club (OKP), in coalition. Solidarity leader Lech Walesa produced, seemingly from nowhere, his nominee, the Catholic intellectual editor Tadeusz Mazowiecki (*see* BIOGRAPHIES), and Poland's first non-Communist prime minister since World War II was in place. Inevitably the government that emerged bore all the hallmarks of political horse-trading. Twelve ministerial posts went to Solidarity and six to minor parties. Of necessity, the Defense and Internal Affairs ministries were two of the four granted the PUWP.

The second half of the year was given over to the burgeoning economic crisis. Food-price increases of 78% during August alone, brought about largely by the outgoing government's inept introduction of market pricing for agricultural produce, pointed Poland toward 900% hyperinflation by Christmas. A 240% rise in the cost of foodstuffs over the preceding year had led to strikes and demands for full wage indexation, and there was concern as to whether additional market-oriented reforms could be successfully introduced into such a pauperized society. In the climate of discontent, the official trade unions were eagerly taking on the populist mantle of Solidarity in order to embarrass the latter. Agricultural production, assisted by favourable weather, was higher than in the previous year (grain was up by 2.3 million tons, rapeseed by 29%). Milk sales rose by 1.6%, but meat delivered to processing plants was as much as a third lower than in 1988. European Communities (EC) and U.S. assistance in foodstuffs had some small impact on the provisioning crisis, but it was to rescheduling of the $37.3 billion and 6.4 transferable ruble foreign debt that Poland looked for help.

Despite Western exhortations, Poland's ability to help itself appeared limited. National income was 8.3% below the high of 1978, and the twin evils of decapitalization and underutilization emphasized the need for foreign aid. Declining annual industrial output by the state sector was only partly offset by the increase in private sector production, which rose 30% compared with 1988 and amounted to 8% of state sector production. Nearly 1.4 million persons were employed in the nonagricultural private sector, an increase of 18% for the year. Declining coal output, caused largely by the elimination of compulsory Saturday working for miners, coupled with a fall in liquid gas deliveries posed serious problems for the winter. It would be some time before measures aimed at energy conservation in highly wasteful industries could compensate for this shortfall. Though it occupied one of the lowest places in the European foreign trade league, Poland had a current account balance of trade surplus. However, the dollar surplus had shrunk considerably while the ruble surplus was nearly 50% above 1988.

In the realm of economic policy, short-term stabilization measures were aimed, first and foremost, at cutting back inflation. These were to be followed by the longer-term institutional transformation of the economic system, to begin Jan. 1, 1990. To this end, Poland sought Western understanding concerning its debt repayments since simultaneous action on all three fronts was impossible. Since wages were outstripping production, which was itself falling, the only short-term option was to cut incomes. Unemployment levels of 20% were a real possibility, and appropriate safety-net social measures were being taken, albeit by a government committed to rolling back the state. Longer-term institutional changes would involve the pri-

vatization of state enterprises. Government bonds issued on October 1, with a six-month redemption period and generating 86% interest per year, helped to stabilize the now legalized private dollar exchange at 8,000 zlotys. It was hoped that new forms of taxation (*e.g.,* progressive income tax and value-added tax instead of turnover tax) would instill in the population the sense that they support the state and thus make them interested in limiting state expenditure. However, times would be hard at least until the end of 1990. Not to be outdone, the defense sector cut its expenditure to 5.5% of the state budget, said to be the lowest level since World War II. Defense industries were producing civilian goods.

A major inheritance bequeathed to the new government was a catastrophic environmental and health situation. Polluted water supplies, massive sulfur dioxide emissions affecting 65% of Poland's forests, and poisoned soil all contributed to producing an environment where 35% of the population inhabiting 11% of the country lived in conditions of ecological breakdown. Not surprisingly, industrial diseases were on the increase, and psychological disorders had grown by nearly 30% per year.

Criminality and deviance in general had decreased, but crimes against property were on the rise. Since 1980 over 400,000 Polish citizens had extended their stay abroad by more than six months over their original stated intention.

(GEORGE KOLANKIEWICZ)

ROMANIA

A socialist republic on the Balkan Peninsula in southeastern Europe, Romania has a coastline on the Black Sea. Area: 237,500 sq km (91,699 sq mi). Pop. (1989 est.): 23,168,000. Cap.: Bucharest. Monetary unit: leu, with (Oct. 2, 1989) a noncommercial rate of 8.79 lei to U.S. $1 (14.22 lei = £1 sterling). General secretary of the Romanian Communist Party, president of the republic, and president of the State Council to Dec. 25, 1989, Nicolae Ceausescu; interim president of the National Salvation Front from December 26, Ion Iliescu; chairman of the Council of Ministers (prime minister) to December 25, Constantin Dascalescu; prime minister of the National Salvation Front from December 26, Petre Roman.

The efforts of Pres. Nicolae Ceausescu (*see* OBITUARIES) to hold back the tide of change sweeping Eastern Europe in 1989 ended in December in a bloody revolution. Throughout most of the year, Ceausescu had confirmed in word and deed that he would not bow to persistent international criticism and change his internal policies. Relations with the European Communities (EC), the U.S., and neighbouring Hungary were strained over alleged human rights violations arising from Ceausescu's vast "systematization" or rural resettlement program and from his attempts to silence domestic dissent. In April Ceausescu announced that Romania had completely paid off its external debt, which in 1982 had reached a peak of $10.2 billion. This feat, however, was achieved at the expense of a sharp drop in living standards. Ceausescu declared that there would be no reduction in the export of foodstuffs despite food shortages and the rationing of bread, flour, and sugar.

Ceausescu's plans to complete the urbanization or "systematization" of about half of Romania's 13,000 villages by the year 2000 continued to provoke international criticism. The coercive application of this policy involved the bulldozing of villagers' private houses and the destruction of their plots of land in order to force them into small blocks of apartments in new "agro-industrial" complexes. The program was harshly criticized in the West, and the EC broke off trade negotiations with Romania in April. Romania also sustained criticism from its Eastern bloc allies. In March the UN Human Rights Commission in Geneva voted to investigate alleged violations by Romania; the Soviet Union, Bulgaria, and East Germany abstained from voting, but Hungary joined the resolution's sponsors.

Romania's relations with Hungary, already tense because of the latter's charges that Ceausescu's regime was persecuting the two million-strong Hungarian minority in Transylvania, were further strained by the application of the systematization program. Most Hungarians believed that the program was designed to assimilate the Hungarian minority by destroying their cultural identity and heritage. The growing rift between the two countries was exacerbated by the publicity Hungary gave throughout the year to the plight of some 6,000 Romanian citizens, mostly Hungarians from Transylvania, who fled Romania because of chronic food shortages. They joined some 20,000 of their compatriots who since 1985 had sought refuge in Hungary.

Concern about the situation in Romania was expressed in March in an open letter to Ceausescu from six retired senior figures in the Romanian Communist Party, among them Gheorghe Apostol, a former party secretary, and Silviu Brucan, former ambassador to the U.S. and editor of the party daily *Scinteia.* The signatories called upon Ceausescu to relax his demands for increased exports, release more food for internal consumption, invest in new technology for outmoded industries, halt the vastly expensive program of prestige projects of doubtful economic value, and end systematization because it had seriously damaged the country's international image. President Ceausescu responded by first placing the signatories under house arrest and then relocating them to markedly inferior accommodations.

Against this background of increasing pressure upon her husband, both from within Communist Party circles and from leading intellectuals, Elena Ceausescu made increas-

A soldier in Romania tries to calm an angry mob in pursuit of two people believed to be loyal to Nicolae Ceausescu's government. Although the Communist government of Ceausescu had been overthrown by civilians and soldiers, fighting remained heavy between government loyalists and the rebel forces until pictures of the captured dictator were televised nationally.

ing efforts to advance her political credentials. Vice president in all but name (she was a member of the Politburo and first deputy prime minister), she was given greater prominence in the Romanian media throughout the year. The 14th party congress, held on November 20–25, confirmed the dominant position of the presidential couple.

The outside world's first intimation that there might be serious cracks in Ceausescu's defenses came in mid-December. The locus of the trouble was, again, Transylvania, where, on December 15, demonstrators in Timisoara tried to prevent the arrest of Laszlo Tokes, an activist Protestant clergyman. The demonstrations grew, and on the following day security forces opened fire on the crowds. Estimates of the number killed varied, but later hundreds and possibly thousands of corpses were found in mass graves. On December 20 Ceausescu, who had been on a state visit to Iran, declared a state of emergency in western Romania, but by the 21st the demonstrations had spread to Bucharest. State television showed the shock on the president's face when he was shouted down while addressing what he had presumed was a "tame" rally. On December 22 army units defected to the demonstrators, and the Ceausescus fled while a Council of the National Salvation Front announced that it had overthrown the government. Fierce fighting went on, however, as elements of the security forces continued to resist. The loyalists did not begin to surrender until after the Ceausescus had been captured, tried, and executed on Christmas Day, and their bodies shown on national television. An interim government was formed by the National Salvation Front with Ion Iliescu, a former Cabinet member and party secretary, as president and Petre Roman as prime minister. Foods missing from stores for years were put on sale, discovered among the caches of luxury goods enjoyed by the Ceausescus and their circle. Rebuilding the shattered economy, however, would not be an easy matter. Some of the old regime's repressive laws were repealed, and elections were scheduled for April. A new flag was adopted, with the state seal removed from the centre.

(DENNIS J. DELETANT)

UNION OF SOVIET SOCIALIST REPUBLICS

The Union of Soviet Socialist Republics is a federal state covering parts of eastern Europe and northern Asia. Area: 22,403,000 sq km (8,649,800 sq mi). Pop. (1989 est.): 287.8 million. Cap.: Moscow. Monetary unit: ruble, with (Oct. 2, 1989) a free rate of 0.63 ruble to U.S. $1 (1.02 rubles = £1 sterling). General secretary of the Communist Party of the Soviet Union and chairman of the Presidium of the Supreme Soviet (president) in 1989, Mikhail S. Gorbachev; chairman of the Council of Ministers (premier), Nikolay I. Ryzhkov.

In a remarkable year, the first Soviet parliament since 1918 convened in Moscow in 1989, Soviet Pres. Mikhail Gorbachev and U.S. Pres. George Bush held their first summit on warships off the coast of Malta, Soviet control over some non-Russian republics declined, and Eastern Europe began to abandon Communism. Throughout the year Gorbachev enhanced his position as general secretary of the Communist Party of the Soviet Union (CPSU). He won great acclaim abroad but failed to provide any tangible improvement in Soviet living standards. Hence his standing outside the country was greater than at home.

Domestic Affairs. In April Gorbachev achieved the astonishing feat of convincing 110 full and alternate members of the Central Committee (CC) of the CPSU to resign "voluntarily." The device of a collective letter of resignation kept within party rules, which stipulate that members can be dropped only at the five-yearly party congresses, except for the occasional expulsion for political or crimi-

nal misdeeds. Gorbachev was able to promote 24 alternate members to full membership in the CC, but new members can be added only at a party congress. As a result, 50 of the 301 CC seats were left vacant. Among those dropped was Andrey Gromyko (*see* OBITUARIES), Gorbachev's predecessor as Soviet president.

In September Gorbachev effected more changes in the Politburo than he had made on any other single occasion since he came to power in 1985. Three full members and two alternate members were dropped. The most prominent casualty was Vladimir Shcherbitsky, party leader in the Ukraine, who was regarded as a remnant of the Brezhnev era. Gen. Viktor Chebrikov, chairman of the CC's Legal Commission—which appeared to be dragging its feet over legislation on such sensitive matters as religious affairs and press freedom—also departed the scene. So did Viktor Nikonov, deputy chairman of the CC's Agricultural Commission, but his departure might have been a victory for Egor Ligachev, chairman of the Agricultural Commission and Gorbachev's most formidable conservative critic in the Politburo. Yury Maslyukov, chairman of the State Planning Commission (Gosplan), was advanced to full Politburo membership, as was Gen. Vladimir Kryuchkov, head of the KGB. Both were important to Gorbachev if *perestroika* (restructuring) was to succeed.

Gen. Dmitry Yazov remained an alternate member of the Politburo, confirming the loss of status of the military. Boris Pugo, chairman of the party Control Committee, charged with enforcing party discipline and combating corruption, became an alternate member. Pugo, a former head of the KGB in Latvia, provided the Baltic republics with a voice in the Politburo but also enhanced the standing of the new-look KGB. Evgeny Primakov, chairman of the U.S.S.R. Supreme Soviet, also became an alternate member, providing the increasingly influential Soviet parliament with a voice in party decision making. Four new CC secretaries were named: Egor Stroyev, party leader in the Orel region; Yury Manayenkov; Gumer Usmanov, party leader in the Tatar Autonomous Republic; and Andrey Girenko, from the Crimea. When questioned, all confessed they were not certain what their new duties would be. Their promotion might be connected with the convening of the next party congress in 1990 and the need to revise the party program and rules.

Elections to the U.S.S.R. Congress of People's Deputies took place in March and April. This new body consisted of 2,250 deputies: one-third elected directly by the population, another third elected along nationality lines, and the rest reserved for social and political organizations—100 for the CPSU, 100 for the trade unions, 75 for the Communist youth movement, the Komsomol, and so on. A criticism of this arrangement was that it was possible for some persons to have up to six votes. The election results shocked the party establishment and astounded the world at large. Many officially backed candidates holding senior party and government positions were defeated in favour of almost anyone who stood against them. The most prominent casualty was Yury Solovev, a Politburo alternate member and party leader in Leningrad oblast, who failed to obtain the necessary 50% of the votes even though he was unopposed. The most stunning result was in Moscow, where Boris Yeltsin (*see* BIOGRAPHIES) obtained 89% of the vote against the official candidate. In the Baltic republics candidates (including leading party officials) supported by the popular fronts swept the board.

The People's Congress was elected for five years, and one-fifth of its members were to be replaced annually. It was the highest body of state power in the Soviet Union. It

DISASTERS

- ● Earthquake
- ○ Chernobyl nuclear plant accident
- ✝ Nuclear submarine accident
- ▲ Soviet cruise ship accident
- ▬ Train accident

DONETS BASIN Coal basins

▨ Republics demanding greater autonomy

- ● Capital cities
- • Other cities

AREAS OF ETHNIC VIOLENCE
1 Nagorno-Karabakh Autonomous Oblast
2 Abkhaz Autonomous S.S.R.
3 Fergana
4 Mangishlak

ACCOMPLISHED
100,300 Soviet troops were withdrawn from Afghanistan by Feb. 15, 1989.

TROOP WITHDRAWAL

PROPOSED
A. Proposed armed force reduction in Czechoslovakia, East Germany, and Hungary would consist of 10,000 tanks, 8,500 artillery systems, and 800 combat aircraft.

B. About 75% of Soviet troops stationed in Mongolia were scheduled to be withdrawn.

The U.S.S.R.'s ailing economy forced the introduction of *perestroika* (restructuring) and prompted the end to its Afghan adventure, the planned withdrawal of other costly occupying forces, and action on such economic problems as those that caused strikes in its main coal basins.

elected a new Committee of Constitutional Review, which was to ensure that the changes to the constitution were implemented and supervise the coming into being of a law-governed state. Another of the Congress's important tasks was the selection of 542 of its members to sit in the U.S.S.R. Supreme Soviet, the U.S.S.R.'s first parliament since the Constituent Assembly was dispersed by force in 1918. The new U.S.S.R. Supreme Soviet replaced the old Supreme Soviet, which voted itself out of existence. The new Supreme Soviet was to meet annually for two sessions of three to four months each (the practice of meeting for 40-day sessions appeared to have been established). It consisted of two chambers, the Soviet of the Union and the Soviet of Nationalities, with one-fifth of the deputies being replaced annually by the People's Congress. The Soviet of the Union was responsible for social and economic questions, the process of government, the rights, freedoms, and duties of Soviet citizens, and foreign, security, and state security issues. The Soviet of Nationalities was to

concentrate on ensuring national equality and the rights of the various Soviet nationalities and on regulating relations among them.

The U.S.S.R. Supreme Soviet elected Gorbachev as its chairman, and thereby he became Soviet president. Anatoly Lukyanov became deputy chairman. The Supreme Soviet appoints the chairman of the Council of Ministers (premier) and confirms government ministers in office. Nikolay Ryzhkov, the premier, discovered to his embarrassment that parliament rejected several of his nominees. In all, about one in three ministers was new. One striking departure from past practice was the appointment of Nikolay Vorontsov, a non-Communist, as minister for the environment. The government was restructured, and the number of ministries reduced to 57—often by the merging of two ministries to form a new one. Many observers considered it doubtful that this reform would improve the efficiency of the administration.

The Supreme Soviet also appointed the Council of De-

Soviet dissident Andrey Sakharov addresses the Soviet Union's Congress of People's Deputies. As a prominent dissident and member of the People's Congress, Sakharov frequently spoke out against Soviet Pres. Mikhail Gorbachev's programs. He was elected a chairman of the Inter-Regional Group shortly before his death.

TASS/SOVFOTO

fense (headed by the president) and the top military personnel; the Committee of People's Control; and the members of the state arbitration service. Parliament's duties included interpreting Soviet law, supervising the planning process, ratifying international treaties, ordering military mobilization, declaring war, and ordering Soviet troops abroad. Legislation could be initiated by any deputy but in practice emanated from the various parliamentary committees and commissions. A simple majority of both houses was necessary to pass legislation.

Supreme Soviet deputies, unlike their predecessors, were full-time politicians. Indirect elections to the Supreme Soviet ensured that many radicals were not chosen. About 300 members of the People's Congress impatient with the pace of change set up the Inter-Regional Group and elected Yeltsin and Andrey Sakharov (see OBITUARIES), physicist and long-time dissident, as two of its chairmen. Yeltsin used his position to criticize Gorbachev for being conservative and continued his attacks on bureaucratic privilege. His popularity was underlined during a visit to the U.S. in September. When *Pravda* reprinted an article from an Italian newspaper that exaggerated Yeltsin's drinking bouts in the U.S., the resulting outcry forced *Pravda* to retract the article, and the misjudgment was a factor in the dismissal of Viktor Afanasyev, its editor in chief.

The Congress gradually developed into a forum for national debate, and it was no respecter of persons. Several of Gorbachev's proposals were defeated. The wave of labour unrest during the summer alarmed the Soviet leader and led to his advocating a ban on all strikes until the end of 1990. This was rejected, but eventually strikes were banned in energy and all essential services. Another issue that resulted in defeat for Gorbachev was his proposal that elections to republican Supreme Soviets or parliaments in the spring of 1990 should be indirect, following the pattern of the U.S.S.R. Supreme Soviet. Instead, republican elections would be direct, making it more difficult for the party to influence selection. In December, however, Gorbachev succeeded in blocking debate on whether the Communist Party should relinquish its monopoly on political power and won approval of his economic program to delay price reforms and other free-market innovations.

National conflict increased throughout the year. Generally, non-Russians became much more assertive. In Moldavia, Romanian was proclaimed the republic's language; in Uzbekistan, Uzbek. The conflict between Azerbaijan and Armenia over Nagorno-Karabakh defied solution,

even though Moscow had installed its own emissary in the disputed territory. Many deaths were reported, including some of the security forces. A long transport strike that isolated Armenia from its neighbour was broken only by putting soldiers on the trains. In December angry crowds in the Azerbaijani city of Dzhalilabad expelled the Communist Party leadership, police officers, and other officials after the police fired on protesters, killing one and wounding 150. In Georgia Abkhazians and Georgians clashed violently in July, leaving several dead. Abkhazians were protesting against Georgian plans to found a branch of Tbilisi University in their territory. In Uzbekistan bloody clashes between Uzbeks and Meskhetians throughout the summer left over 100 dead and over 1,000 injured. The intra-Muslim conflict appeared to have economic roots. Many of the Meskhetians were resettled in the central Volga region.

In the Baltic republics efforts continued to secure political and economic independence from Moscow. On the occasion of the 50th anniversary of the Hitler-Stalin pact of Aug. 23, 1939, a human chain extended across the three republics. The pact was denounced and declared null and void. Moscow eventually conceded that the pact was illegal but claimed that the decision of the three Baltic republics to join the U.S.S.R. was unrelated to it. In November the Communist Party of Lithuania defied the CPSU (of which it was a part) and in December voted to establish independent Communist parties. Lithuania also voted to legalize alternative political parties. Russians in non-Russian republics began to coordinate their efforts. They were particularly concerned about the dominance of the republican languages, since few of them spoke those languages fluently. They launched many strikes and had some success; for instance, in Estonia legislation disfranchising those who had moved to the republic recently was withdrawn. Nevertheless, the overall impression was that Russian minorities throughout the U.S.S.R. would find life more difficult in the future. The lack of economic progress exacerbated national tensions.

In Tbilisi, Georgia, on April 9 the violent assault by Soviet military units on unarmed Georgian demonstrators left 20 dead and many hundreds injured. The troops used poison gas and hand shovels. Georgian police tried to protect the demonstrators and were themselves attacked. Some onlookers claimed the soldiers appeared drugged. The troops, from the Transcaucasian Military District, had been invited in by the Georgian authorities. At the end of the year it was still unclear who had given the order to assault the demonstrators and why gas was used. The incident led to furious recriminations between the military and the Ministry of Internal Affairs (MVD) and between Georgians and the military and led to the decision not to use the military in a police role if at all possible. Troops were involved in Azerbaijan and Armenia but were little in evidence elsewhere. The minister of internal affairs, Vadim Bakatin, warned that the MVD did not have the resources to cope with the interethnic violence and rising crime rate.

Prison camp violence continued to increase alarmingly. From 15 cases of hostage taking by prisoners in 1988, the number jumped to 35 during the first five months of 1989. Eight camp officials had died, and 130 had been seriously injured. One reason given was that over the past three years about 40% of prisoners had been released in amnesties. Of those who remained, over 30% had been sentenced for crimes of violence.

The U.S.S.R.'s human rights record improved during the year. Amnesty International estimated that in 1989 there were 90 political prisoners, compared with 600 in

1986. There was a drop of 80% in the number of religious believers arrested in 1989.

The anniversary of the October Revolution on November 7 was marked in Moscow by a counterdemonstration, the first since 1927. All references to Marxism-Leninism were dropped by the official parade, but the unofficial happening came up with the snappiest slogans: "72 years on the road to nowhere"; "workers of the world—sorry!"; "We shall defend perestroika against its architect." In Moldavia the parade was disrupted and abandoned, and on November 10 the republic's Ministry of the Interior was attacked and set ablaze. Over 2,000 MVD troops were flown in, and calm was restored after the hard-line party leader, Semyon Grossu, was dismissed.

The Economy. During the first nine months of the year, it became clear that key industrial sectors, including oil and coal, would not achieve their plan targets. Food production rose by only 3.2% instead of the planned 11%, and consumer goods by 5.7% instead of 10%. Between January and September industrial output rose 2.2%, but the income of the population rose 12.2%, fueling inflation. The cooperative sector expanded, though the 100,000 co-ops, employing 3.6 million persons, accounted for only 1% of national production. There was considerable animosity toward co-ops in various parts of the country. A common accusation was that they stole from the state sector and sold the goods at exorbitant prices.

The CC plenum on agriculture, many times postponed, finally convened in March. Gorbachev's speech included some daunting facts: 22 million ha (55 million ac) of arable land and 3 million ha (7 million ac) of irrigated land written off; 20% of agricultural output lost through mismanagement (30 or 40% for some products). The plenum did not resolve the conflict over the leasing system. Gorbachev favoured family farming, but the majority did not. The harvest was estimated at 209 million metric tons, up from 1988. U.S.S.R. Gosagroprom, created by Gorbachev in 1985 to run agriculture, was dissolved.

Labour unrest became a major problem during the summer when about half of the country's miners went on strike. Miners in the Kuzbass, in western Siberia, spearheaded the protest against poor food and living conditions. Gorbachev appeared on television and appealed for a resumption of work. The authorities appeared to panic and conceded all the miners' political and economic demands, but the government was incapable of honouring its side of the bargain. Lost production in the Kuzbass alone amounted to about 3 billion rubles. Vorkuta miners, in the Arctic, went on strike for four weeks in October–November. Strikes continued despite the ban on work stoppages in energy and essential services.

In November Leonid Abalkin, deputy premier responsible for economic reform, spelled out a detailed timetable of new measures up to the year 2000. Unprofitable industries were to be closed (no mention was made of unemployment); farmers were to be encouraged to take over unprofitable collective and state farms; and a commercial banking sector was to operate in a market regulated by interest rates and credit controls. However, furious debate raged over these objectives, which many considered deviations from socialism.

Joint ventures between Soviet and foreign firms continued to proliferate. In August 1989 there were 835, compared with 86 in August 1988. Foreign companies had so far invested $1.2 billion. Most enterprises were small, with 56% of joint ventures having nominal capital below 1 million rubles. Few appeared to be making a profit, partly because of overhasty arrangements.

Natural and man-made disasters continued to haunt the Soviet Union. An earthquake in Tadzhikistan in January buried some villages, and there were some appalling railroad disasters. The worst was an explosion of a natural gas pipeline near Chelyabinsk in the Urals. The Trans-Siberian express happened to be there at the time, and an estimated 462 died and over 700 were injured.

Foreign Affairs. The highlight of the year was the first summit between Gorbachev and Bush, on warships off Malta on December 2 and 3. Although there was no formal agenda and no documents were signed, talks centred on *perestroika* in the U.S.S.R. and the momentous changes in Eastern Europe. A summit had not been planned by the U.S. side before the spring or early summer of 1990, but successful talks between Soviet Foreign Minister Eduard Shevardnadze and U.S. Secretary of State James Baker in Wyoming in September led to the meeting. This underlined the urgency felt by the Soviet side in contrast to the wait-and-see attitude of the Bush administration. The Soviets needed arms reduction agreements so they could cut back on defense expenditure. The Soviet defense budget was put at 77.3 billion rubles in 1990, and U.S. Secretary of Defense Richard Cheney stated in November that the U.S. had perceived a reduction in Soviet defense spending.

Gorbachev's standing abroad continued to rise as a result of his many foreign visits. The most remarkable was to West Germany in June, where he was given a rapturous welcome. He visited Britain in April and invited Queen Elizabeth II to visit the Soviet Union (a visit was planned for 1991). U.K. Prime Minister Margaret Thatcher stopped off in Moscow on her return from an official visit to Japan in September. In July Gorbachev addressed the Council of Europe in Strasbourg, France, and once again spoke of the "common European house." In Finland in October he stressed his support of closer links between Finland and Estonia. Not everything went right, however. His visit to China in May was almost a fiasco because of the activities of the pro-democracy demonstrators. (*See* East Asia: *China,* above.) In Cuba in April he was visibly irritated when Fidel Castro lectured him on Marxism-Leninism. He displayed little sympathy for Erich Honecker's brand of socialism in East Berlin in October.

The remarkable changes in Eastern Europe found the Soviets concerned with their own domestic troubles. Gorbachev seized every opportunity to voice his support for reform Communists and indirectly influenced change in East Germany and Czechoslovakia. On the reunification of Germany and Eastern Europe generally, he adopted a two-track policy. On the one hand, he stated that the various nations were at liberty to forge their own futures, but on the other he stressed that the postwar borders in Europe were to stay. He also made it clear that socialism would remain the dominant ideology.   (MARTIN MCCAULEY)

YUGOSLAVIA

A federal socialist republic, Yugoslavia is in southern Europe on the Adriatic Sea. Area: 255,804 sq km (98,766 sq mi). Pop. (1989 est.): 23,710,000. Cap.: Belgrade. Monetary unit: Yugoslav dinar, with (Oct. 2, 1989) a free rate of 37,050 dinars to U.S. $1 (59,947 dinars = £1 sterling). Presidents of the Presidium of the League of Communists in 1989, Stipe Suvar and, from May 17, Milan Pancevski; presidents of the Collective Presidency, Raif Dizdarevic and, from May 15, Janez Drnovsek; presidents of the Federal Executive Council (premiers), Branko Mikulic (acting) and, from March 16, Ante Markovic.

For Yugoslavia, 1989 was a year of political turbulence amid fears of political disintegration and economic collapse.

A dramatic deterioration occurred between Serbia, the country's biggest federal republic, and Croatia and Slovenia, the two western republics. Under its hard-line populist leader, Slobodan Milosevic, Serbia sought to consolidate its hold over its two autonomous provinces, Kosovo and Vojvodina. A drastic purge of anti-Milosevic party and government officials was carried out in January in Vojvodina under its new pro-Milosevic leadership, which had come to power there in October 1988.

In February in Kosovo ethnic Albanians, who made up about 90% of the province's population, staged strikes against the plan to give Serbia full direct control over Kosovo's police, courts, and territorial defense. The demonstrators demanded the resignation of three pro-Milosevic ethnic Albanian officials: Rahman Morina, the former police chief appointed party leader in the province after the sacking, under pressure from Belgrade, of Azem Vlasi; Ali Sukrija, a member of the Yugoslav Communist Party's Central Committee; and Husamedin Azemi, party boss in Pristina, the provincial capital. The strikes ended after the three ostensibly agreed to resign, but then all three withdrew their resignations. Widespread protests were crushed with violence in at least nine towns of the province after the acceptance by Kosovo's provincial assembly on March 23 of amendments, already adopted by the Serbian assembly, that gave Serbia increased control over the province. In the riots that followed, at least 24 people were killed. Vlasi was arrested on charges of "counterrevolutionary activity."

Fears of a possible Milosevic-inspired imposition of a centralist regime on the whole of Yugoslavia under the guise of a state of emergency led to the adoption by the Slovene assembly on September 27 of a series of constitutional amendments, including the right to self-determination up to and including secession and the sole right of the Slovene assembly to decide whether a state of emergency imposed in peacetime applied to Slovene territory. The adoption of these amendments provoked demonstrations in Serbia as well as in Montenegro, which since January 1989 had been under pro-Milosevic leadership. When Slovenia forbade the staging in Ljubljana, on December 1, of a demonstration by Serbian groups from Belgrade, Serbia declared a commercial boycott of Slovenia. Croatia, which had for some time stood on the sidelines, took Slovenia's side in this matter. At the December congress of the Croatian Communists in Zagreb, the republic's capital, free elections with a multiparty system were promised. Also in December the Serbian Communist leaders reversed their long-standing policy and declared that they would allow other parties to compete in free elections in 1990. Throughout the year, the Yugoslav Army leadership continued to criticize calls for political liberalization.

Political conflicts effectively blocked attempts by Premier Ante Markovic, a former businessman and an advocate of a free-market economy, to push through decisive changes, notably by introducing the three free markets abolished when the Communists took power in 1945: those of commodities, labour, and capital. The Law on Enterprises, which came into force in January 1989 (and was further amended after Markovic's assumption of power in March), granted public-sector enterprises freedom from political control as well as the right to establish joint ventures with foreign firms. Separate legislation allowed for majority holding by foreign investors. The question of who actually owned enterprises remained unresolved, however, owing to bitter opposition of party hard-liners to proposals that would allow privatization of public-sector enterprises. Meanwhile, Yugoslavia's annual inflation rate exceeded 2,000%. (K.F. CVIIC)

North America

CANADA

Canada is a federal parliamentary state and member of the Commonwealth covering North America north of conterminous United States and east of Alaska. Area: 9,970,610 sq km (3,849,675 sq mi). Pop (1989 est.): 26,189,000. Cap.: Ottawa. Monetary unit: Canadian dollar, with (Oct. 2, 1989) a free rate of Can$1.18 to U.S. $1 (Can$1.91 = £1 sterling). Queen, Elizabeth II; governor-general in 1989, Jeanne Sauvé; prime minister, Brian Mulroney.

Domestic Affairs. The Progressive Conservative government of Brian Mulroney, reelected in a general election on Nov. 21, 1988, pressed forward with major changes in Canada's taxation system in 1989. During the previous year its election victory had allowed it to approve a comprehensive free-trade agreement with the United States (effective Jan. 1, 1989). In addition, it had embarked upon a sweeping reform of Canada's tax structure, the first phase of which, a reduction in personal income taxes, also came into effect on January 1. The second phase, the introduction of a goods and services tax (GST), emerged as the most important item on the Mulroney government's agenda for 1989.

Parliament, which had been recalled after the election to pass the free-trade measure, adjourned before Christmas and was not brought back into session until April 3. Sittings lasted until June 29, followed by a summer recess and the resumption of the session on September 25. The government's legislative program was restricted by Canada's large and accumulating public deficit, the interest charges on which ate up slightly more than one-third of the federal government's revenues. Faced with this limitation, the Mulroney government was forced to defer some of its earlier promises.

Finance Minister Michael Wilson (*see* BIOGRAPHIES) had proposed in 1987 a national value-added sales tax, which would combine the federal government's tax on manufactured goods (12% at the time but raised to 13.5% in 1989) with retail sales taxes levied by the provinces. (These ranged from 12% in Newfoundland to no sales tax at all in Alberta.) Discussions with the provinces went on until April 24, when Wilson told Parliament that he had been unable to reach agreement with them on the form of a national tax. Under these circumstances, Wilson said, the federal government would move alone with "its sales tax reform." Alberta had flatly rejected involvement with a national tax, and Quebec had claimed that its authority to raise revenues was threatened by the proposed measure. (Under Canada's constitution the central government has unlimited taxing power while the provinces are restricted to direct taxation.)

Three days later, when the finance minister delivered his budget to Parliament, he outlined the main features of the proposed GST. It would tax all goods at every stage of production, from raw materials to final consumer products, as well as a host of services, many of which were not presently taxed by Ottawa. A number of services would be excluded from the new tax: health and dental care, education, life insurance, and mortgages. Basic groceries and prescription drugs would also be exempt. An initial rate of 9% was proposed for the GST, as well as a system of tax

credits to relieve low-income earners from the effect of the tax. The measure would take effect on Jan. 1, 1991.

A storm of controversy erupted over the GST. It was claimed that it would lead to a damaging rise in the cost of living, that it would impose an impossible burden on small businesses, and that its collection would become an administrative nightmare. A House of Commons committee began countrywide hearings during the summer to discover the public's view of the measure. In December the government relented and lowered the rate to 7%. Other taxes would be raised to make up the revenue shortfall.

The 1988 election gave the Progressive Conservative Party a solid majority of 170 seats in the 295-seat House of Commons. This block of seats shrank slightly during 1989. In January a judicial recount turned an Ontario seat over to the Liberals, while in March a by-election in Alberta resulted in a Conservative loss to a representative of the newly formed Reform Party. Taking as its motto "The West Wants In," the Reform Party claimed to speak for western disenchantment with the dominance of central Canada in Canadian politics. In May a Quebec Conservative member of Parliament convicted of fraud and breach of trust resigned from the legislature. These losses reduced the number of Conservative MPs to 167, while the Liberals rose to 83 seats and the New Democratic Party (NDP; socialist) remained at 43 seats. There were one Reform Party member and one vacancy in the House.

The leaders of the two major opposition parties resigned during 1989. John Turner, the Liberal leader, first elected to Parliament in 1962 and a minister under Lester Pearson and Pierre Trudeau, decided to leave politics following his second defeat by the Conservatives under Mulroney in 1988. Chosen leader in 1984, Turner had failed to give the Liberal Party the unity and sense of purpose it had enjoyed in earlier times. Edward Broadbent, leader of the NDP since 1974, also resigned his post. He had led the party through four elections; in most of them it had increased its standing in Parliament, although its share of the popular vote remained frozen at 18–20%.

Mulroney announced a substantial Cabinet shuffle on January 30, two months after the election. Six ministers had been defeated in November, and they were replaced by new faces. Another 19 Cabinet members exchanged portfolios. The Cabinet was reduced from 40 to 39 members. Significantly, the most powerful and effective ministers were kept at their posts: Joe Clark in external affairs, Michael Wilson in finance, John Crosbie in international trade, Barbara McDougall in employment and immigration, and Donald Mazankowski as deputy prime minister. Mazankowski was also given the portfolio of agriculture. The Cabinet lost a promising younger member in August when Bernard Valcourt, a representative of the French-speaking Acadian people in New Brunswick, resigned following a conviction on an impaired driving charge. Valcourt had been injured in a motorcycle accident.

The Meech Lake accord, concluded in 1987, dominated debate on the future of Canada's federal system in 1989. The accord proposed several changes in the constitution designed to reinforce Quebec's position as a "distinct society," an island of French-speakers in the sea of English-speaking North Americans. Quebec promised, if the Meech Lake changes were approved by the rest of the country, to assent to the revised federal constitution worked out by Prime Minister Pierre Trudeau and the other nine provinces in 1982. It was provided that if the accord was not ratified by the federal Parliament and the 10 provinces by June 1990, it would die. In 1989 the agreement had been approved by Parliament and eight provinces.

Throughout the year opposition to the accord mounted. A major factor was Quebec Premier Robert Bourassa's decision in December 1988 to prohibit the use of the English language on exterior commercial signs in Quebec. This action was seen in other parts of Canada as undercutting the rights of the English-speaking residents of the province, and it produced a widespread mood of disenchantment with Quebec across the country. The federal government was criticized for having made too many concessions to Quebec, a province that was intent on achieving its own objectives without reference to the interests of Canada as a whole.

Following Bourassa's language decision, Manitoba withdrew the Meech Lake accord from further discussion in its legislature, directing a legislative committee to hold public hearings on the document and bring in a report recommending suitable changes. The government of New Brunswick, which had changed from Progressive Conservative to Liberal after the accord was drawn up, took the same action. In May an election in Newfoundland brought a Liberal government to power, and the new premier, Clyde Wells, declared that he was unhappy with the accord. On the other hand, Bourassa, his hand strengthened by a Liberal election victory in Quebec in September, insisted that the accord had to be approved by the remaining provinces without change. To alter it would be to unravel it, he declared.

Four provinces and a federal territory held elections in 1989. The most important was in Quebec, where Bourassa led the Liberals to a solid victory on September 25, winning 92 seats in the 125-seat National Assembly. The separatist Parti Québécois, openly campaigning for independence under a new leader, Jacques Parizeau, won 29 seats and 40% of the popular vote. A party representing English-speaking Montrealers took four seats. To many Canadians the ap-

Canadian Prime Minister Brian Mulroney (left) strolls with U.S. Pres. George Bush during Bush's February visit to Canada. During the visit, Mulroney pressed for a bilateral treaty to reduce acid rain but was unable to get a commitment from Bush.

pearance of a rejuvenated separatist movement in Quebec was disturbing.

In Newfoundland on April 20 a 17-year Progressive Conservative government was toppled by the opposition Liberal Party. In the tiny province of Prince Edward Island, the Liberals under Joseph Ghiz were decisively reelected on May 29. In Alberta on March 20 the governing Progressive Conservatives under Premier Don Getty were reelected with slightly fewer seats in the 83-seat legislature than they had held before. The federal territory of Yukon, with 15,000 voters, reelected an NDP administration on February 20. The Yukon government was the only one in Canada controlled by the NDP. Among the 10 provinces, there were five Liberal administrations, four Progressive Conservative ones, and one legislature (British Columbia) controlled by the Social Credit Party.

Ramon Hnatyshyn (*see* BIOGRAPHIES), a Saskatchewan lawyer who had been minister of justice, government House leader, and minister of energy in the Brian Mulroney and Joe Clark governments, was named to succeed Jeanne Sauvé as governor-general. He would take office in January 1990.

The Economy. After several years of vigorous growth, the Canadian economy slowed in 1989. The most marked change was in foreign trade, where the surplus of merchandise exports was the lowest since 1978. An appreciating Canadian dollar, lower wheat sales, and reduced demand for some Canadian products in the United States were blamed for the relative decline in exports. Domestic demand remained strong, however, both in consumer spending and in business outlays for plant and equipment. The real gross domestic product (GDP) rose only 1.3% in the second quarter of 1989, giving a seasonally adjusted annual rate of Can$643.7 billion. Unemployment stood at 7.3% of the labour force in September, a rate virtually unchanged for half a year. The consumer price index rose to 5.2% in September, although it was estimated that 1% of the increase derived from higher sales and excise taxes. The Bank of Canada pursued a tight money policy to subdue inflation. At the beginning of October the bank's rate, used to determine commercial lending terms, hovered around 12.4%.

Finance Minister Wilson's budget, normally presented first to Parliament, was dramatically released to the country at a late-night news conference on April 26. The minister took this step to avoid possible insider profiteering on Canada's financial markets following a leak of a summary of the budget to an Ottawa television station earlier in the day. A police investigation of the leak led to the arrest of five men, one a television reporter, on charges of possession of stolen goods and theft. Wilson delivered his budget formally in the Commons the next day. Opposition critics, demanding that Wilson take responsibility for the breach of security by resigning, walked out of the chamber.

Wilson's budget message was straightforward: "Cut spending and increase taxes." The message was given urgency by the rapid growth in Canada's accumulated public debt, up from $200 billion to $320 billion in five years. Interest charges, the minister pointed out, would reach $39 billion in 1989–90, more than the government spent on health care, family allowances, old age security, and social assistance programs combined. For the fiscal year 1989–90 the government predicted revenues of $112.4 billion and expenditures of $142.9 billion, leaving a deficit of $30.5 billion. Wilson promised to cut $5 billion from the growth of the deficit in 1989–90. More than two-thirds of this reduction was to be obtained by raising taxes, the remainder from spending restrictions. Increases were announced

on sales and excise taxes and on corporate and personal income taxes. Unemployment insurance premiums were raised. Two universal social programs were cut back: family allowance benefits and old age pensions. This was to be achieved through a tax "claw-back" from individuals earning over $50,000 a year.

Reductions in spending were an important feature of the budget. The controversial plan to acquire nuclear-propelled submarines for use in the Arctic would not be carried out, and other purchases of tanks, long-range patrol aircraft, and tracked vehicles would be shelved or delayed. Fourteen military bases would be closed or scaled down. Other reductions were announced in the provision of official development assistance, in transfer payments to the provinces for health care and postsecondary education, and in the subsidies to Canada's passenger rail service and to the state broadcasting system, the Canadian Broadcasting Corporation (CBC). A Progressive Conservative election promise to provide $4 billion to the provinces to double day-care spaces was put off indefinitely, although the government offered $2.3 billion in tax benefits to families requiring child care over the next seven years.

Foreign Affairs. Declining cod stocks in the Northwest Atlantic brought Canada into two international disputes in 1989. The grave position of Canada's east coast fishing industry was highlighted in February when a panel of scientists recommended a 53% cut in the amount of northern cod allowed to be taken in 1989. The government declined to implement such a drastic reduction, asking instead that the quotas for 1989 be reduced to 235,000 metric tons from 266,000 tons in 1988. Offshore trawlers were required to absorb the cuts. Inshore fishermen, responsible for a smaller proportion of the total catch, were exempted from the quotas.

A long-standing dispute with France over the extent of that country's maritime jurisdiction around its tiny possession of Saint Pierre and Miquelon in the Gulf of St. Lawrence was carried on against the background of declining resources. On March 31 an agreement with France was announced under which the dispute would be sent to a five-member international tribunal for settlement. France accepted this mode of solution in return for greater access to cod in the disputed waters during the period of arbitration. The arrangement was bitterly denounced by the Newfoundland government, by the fishing companies, and by their employees, who claimed that it would result in serious overfishing.

The other fishing dispute was with the European Communities (EC) and especially with Spain and Portugal, whose trawlers were accused of grossly depleting stocks of northern cod on the Grand Banks. These waters lie beyond the 200-mi economic zone over which Canada exercises exclusive fisheries jurisdiction, but it was obvious that practices in international waters affected inshore fisheries. Voluntary quotas for the Banks had been laid down by the Northwest Atlantic Fisheries Organization (NAFO), but its fishing limits for the countries of the EC had been consistently ignored by Spain and Portugal. The Canadian government pressed its case at a four-day meeting of the EC in Brussels in September, but the Community refused to accept quotas proposed by NAFO. In December the EC announced its own limits, which Canada considered dangerously high. Expressing anger, the Canadian government planned to bypass the EC by appealing directly to its people to conserve the important Atlantic fish stocks.

Canada moved to establish cordial relationships with the new U.S. administration of Pres. George Bush. On February 10, a few weeks after his inauguration as president,

Bush paid a visit to Canada, his first to a foreign country since taking office. He and Prime Minister Mulroney discussed the need to reduce sulfur dioxide smokestack emissions, which cause acid rain, on both sides of the border. Mulroney pressed for a bilateral treaty on the subject, but Bush announced that he would take no action until legislation his administration was preparing was submitted to Congress. On May 4 Mulroney was in Washington to receive an environmental award and to open a new Canadian embassy on Pennsylvania Avenue. During a meeting with Bush, he returned to the subject of an acid rain treaty and confirmed Canada's desire to see a 50% reduction in transborder pollution from acid rain by 1994. President Bush remained noncommittal on the subject at the time. A third meeting between the two leaders took place at Bush's summer residence at Kennebunkport, Maine, on August 30 and 31.

At a meeting in Costa Rica on October 27, Prime Minister Mulroney announced that Canada would join the 32-nation Organization of American States (OAS). For many years Canada had resisted membership in the organization, fearing pressures from the U.S. or the Latin-American countries that would restrict its freedom of action. Now, following the implementation of· free trade with the U.S., there seemed a need for Canada to pay closer attention to the economic, social, and political problems in Latin America.   (D.M.L. FARR)

See also Feature Article: THE FUTURE HAS STARTED.

UNITED STATES

The United States of America is a federal republic composed of 50 states, 49 of which are in North America and one of which consists of the Hawaiian Islands. Area: 9,372,571 sq km (3,618,770 sq mi), including 205,856 sq km of inland water but excluding the 156,492 sq km of the Great Lakes that lie within U.S. boundaries. Pop. (1989 est.): 248,777,000. Cap.: Washington, D.C. Monetary unit: U.S. dollar, with (Oct. 2, 1989) a free rate of U.S. $1.62 to £1 sterling. Presidents in 1989, Ronald Reagan and, from January 20, George Bush.

George Bush (*see* BIOGRAPHIES) got off to a slow start in his first year as president. He was widely criticized for excessive caution in foreign affairs, especially his response to the tumultuous changes in the Soviet Union and Eastern Europe. He was faulted for his tendency to make bold proclamations—declaring war on drugs, for instance, or calling for sweeping educational reforms—and then failing to specify how such initiatives would be funded. He was even chided for his sluggish pace in filling many senior government jobs. According to some estimates, at year's end nearly one-quarter of his administration's top 300 sub-Cabinet posts were still vacant. In the last days of the year, however, Bush belied his image of timidity when he ordered U.S. troops into Panama to overthrow the government of Gen. Manuel Noriega, who was accused by the U.S. of corruption and dealing in drugs.

Bush did score a few symbolic successes earlier in his inaugural year. He was cheered by crowds in Poland and Hungary during a state visit in July. More significant was his first summit with Soviet Pres. Mikhail Gorbachev, a cordial shipboard meeting in the Mediterranean Sea off Malta. Though the session produced no concrete agreements, Bush and Gorbachev supported the quick completion of three arms control treaties. Those unfinished agreements would end production of chemical weapons, slash long-range nuclear missiles by as much as 50%, and reduce troops, tanks, artillery, and other conventional forces in Europe. Bush also offered to lift U.S. import restrictions on Soviet goods in return for a liberalization of Soviet emigration policy

Businessman Charles Keating, Jr., gave over $1 million in campaign contributions to five U.S. senators in hopes that they would use their influence to save Keating's failing savings and loan.
R. REID/THE PHOENIX GAZETTE

and to support the U.S.S.R.'s participation in the General Agreement on Tariffs and Trade (GATT), a framework for lowering barriers to global commerce. The two leaders agreed to meet again in June 1990.

On the domestic front, the Bush administration took a number of steps, ranging from a proposal for seriously reducing automobile emissions to a largely symbolic ban on the importation of assault rifles. Yet overall, the new president's domestic performance seemed marked by hesitation, lassitude, and concern over the short-term swings of public opinion.

In the view of many Americans, that was precisely the right course. After eight years of Ronald Reagan's ideological approach to government and his frequent confrontations with Congress, Bush's moderation came as a soothing respite. The first 100 days of a new presidency have traditionally been scrutinized for clues about future performance. While Reagan spent that period furiously overturning a generation of social programs on the domestic front and projecting a more strident anti-Communism abroad, Bush's first 100 days were relatively quiet. The new president's approval rating—the percentage of opinion-poll respondents who felt he was doing a good job—hit an unusually high 70% in the first months of his presidency.

Perhaps even more popular than Bush was his wife, Barbara (*see* BIOGRAPHIES), whose ample figure and down-to-earth style stood in contrast to the brittle, fashion-conscious persona of her predecessor, Nancy Reagan. For her part, Mrs. Reagan remained much in the public eye with the publication of a memoir, *My Turn,* in which she struck back at a number of her and her husband's critics. Chief among the book's targets was Donald Regan, the former White House chief of staff, whose own 1988 best-seller had revealed that the First Lady relied on a San Francisco astrologer to determine the timing of presidential activities.

Foreign Affairs. In the field of foreign policy, the Bush administration spent much of its first year reviewing U.S. positions on a number of major questions, such as arms control and the Middle East. As a result, while the U.S. reviewed, the Soviets took the initiative in bilateral dealings, and events tended to outrun U.S. policy. In Panama, for instance, the U.S. stood by idly as a coup attempt by junior military officers against the dictatorship of General Noriega ended in failure in October. The Bush administration had been talking openly about toppling Noriega, but because of miscommunication between the coup plotters and U.S. officials, as well as indecision and intelligence failures in Washington, the 12,700 U.S. troops stationed in Central America were unable to assist in the operation. As

a result, the U.S. missed an opportunity to oust Noriega. In apparent frustration over the incident, senior U.S. officials said that they were reconsidering a 1976 executive order that prohibited the CIA from participating in the assassination of foreign leaders. And when rebels tried to overthrow the U.S.-backed government of Philippines Pres. Corazon Aquino in early December, the Bush administration made sure it acted quickly to support Aquino. Bush even ordered U.S. fighter jets stationed in the Philippines to keep rebel planes out of the sky.

Before long, Bush was presented with another opportunity to oust Noriega. This time he did not hesitate. After the shooting death of a U.S. serviceman and several other violent incidents, Bush sent 14,000 additional U.S. troops to join those stationed in Panama in mounting a full-scale invasion of the country. Amid the heavy fighting that ensued, Noriega was driven into hiding, and the elected civilians he had prevented from taking office earlier in the year were installed in his place.

In the Middle East, where years of U.S. peace efforts had come to naught, the Bush administration had only slightly more success than its predecessors. As the Palestinian *intifada* (uprising) entered its second year in the Israeli-occupied West Bank and Gaza Strip, U.S. Secretary of State James Baker (*see* BIOGRAPHIES) proposed a plan for peace talks between Palestinians and Israelis. The Cabinet of Israeli Prime Minister Yitzhak Shamir accepted the plan but attached reservations that were unacceptable to the Palestinians. The Israelis insisted, for instance, that the Palestine Liberation Organization be excluded from such talks, realizing that no important Palestinian would talk to the Israelis without the blessing of the PLO. More than 40 Israelis and 600 Palestinians had been killed since the uprising began.

On arms control the Soviets continued to score public relations points at the expense of the U.S. At a September meeting with Secretary of State Baker in Wyoming's Grand Teton National Park, Soviet Foreign Minister Eduard Shevardnadze made an unexpected concession in the long-standing Soviet opposition to the U.S. antimissile Strategic Defense Initiative, popularly known as Star Wars. Shevardnadze dropped the demand that reductions in ballistic weapons be linked to limits on U.S. testing of the antimissile system. The foreign minister also proposed separate discussions on submarine-launched nuclear cruise

missiles (SLCMs), abandoning an earlier Soviet insistence that such talks be part of the overall strategic-arms discussions. When the U.S. offered to destroy 80% of its chemical weapons arsenal, the Soviets upped the ante by proposing that both superpowers eliminate 100% of their existing chemical arms and cease all future production—a notion the U.S. was not prepared to accept immediately. Bush retrieved some of the arms control momentum by proposing a significant reduction in the conventional U.S. forces in Europe, but he did so only after the Soviets had made a somewhat less drastic proposal of their own. At the Malta summit Bush came off somewhat better, presenting a detailed list of proposals, including a relaxation of the U.S. stand on chemical weapons.

Despite his attempts to keep up with Soviet diplomatic initiatives, Bush was generally caught off-balance by the year's dramatic, Soviet-encouraged developments in Eastern Europe. In the case of Poland, the president responded to a request by the newly installed non-Communist government for economic assistance by offering a relatively stingy $119 million. After widespread criticism he eventually raised the sum to a still modest $455.5 million, including $125 million in food aid. Congress later approved more than twice that amount.

Another source of controversy was Bush's slowness to declare publicly that the U.S. had a stake in ensuring the success of Gorbachev's reforms in the Soviet Union. Some foreign policy analysts expressed concern that the deteriorating Soviet economy would undermine Gorbachev's hold on power and that it was in the best interests of the U.S. to provide assistance to him. Yet many in the Bush administration asserted that there was not really much the U.S. could do to help Gorbachev, given the immense problems of the Soviet economy and the danger of provoking his conservative opponents by appearing to interfere in Soviet domestic affairs. As a practical matter, increased U.S. investment in the U.S.S.R. was hampered by, among other impediments, the inconvertibility of the Soviet ruble, the lack of local experience with modern business techniques, and the dearth of Soviet products that could compete in world markets. As for the broader criticism that the Bush administration was slow to respond to Soviet initiatives, the president's supporters countered that he had not made any major foreign policy mistakes and that inaction was sometimes preferable to hasty overreaction.

Samuel R. Pierce (centre), former secretary of housing and urban development (HUD), confers with his lawyers before attending a congressional subcommittee hearing. Pierce and other HUD employees during the Reagan administration were under investigation for their involvement in questionable practices and political favouritism shown by HUD in awarding its contracts.

Domestic Affairs. Bush was more assertive on a number of domestic issues, though not always successfully. He lost one of his first major battles with Congress when former U.S. senator John Tower (*see* BIOGRAPHIES), a Republican from Texas, was rejected by the Senate for the job of secretary of defense. Tower's congressional opponents had raised questions about his drinking habits and other alleged improprieties. The defense post went instead to Richard Cheney (*see* BIOGRAPHIES), a Republican U.S. representative from Wyoming.

The early months of the Bush presidency were enlivened by a scandal at the Department of Housing and Urban Development, though the alleged misdeeds took place during the previous administration. Press reports and testimony before Congress revealed a long list of questionable practices and flagrant favouritism that flourished under the eye of former HUD secretary Samuel Pierce during his eight-year stewardship of the agency. Late in the year Pierce appeared before a congressional panel investigating the scandal and refused to answer questions, citing the Fifth Amendment's protection against self-incrimination.

Though the federal government's losses in the HUD mess headed steadily toward $1 billion, they did not come close to those of another government-related scandal, this one involving savings and loans. Those institutions had traditionally concentrated on taking deposits from individual savers and lending the money out in the form of home mortgages. With financial deregulation in the 1980s, however, they had moved into more speculative investments. Many of those ventures went sour, jeopardizing the savings of vast numbers of Americans. With Bush's backing, Congress stepped in to bail out the industry with a package of guarantees that, by some estimates, would ultimately cost the government hundreds of billions of dollars.

The year was marked by a long list of scandals involving individual members of Congress. Most prominent among them was Democrat James Wright of Texas (*see* BIOGRAPHIES), the speaker of the House of Representatives, who was forced to resign over allegations of financial improprieties that included questionable royalties from a book he had written. The speaker's job thereupon went to Thomas Foley of Washington (*see* BIOGRAPHIES), who had been the majority leader. The man thought to be in line to succeed Foley as majority leader, Tony Coelho of California, also resigned. Coelho decided to quit after disclosures involving a $100,000 low-quality "junk" bond sold to him by the firm of Drexel Burnham Lambert, whose chief junk-bond executive, Michael Milken, was indicted in 1989 for insider trading. Meanwhile, the Republican who led the drive to oust Jim Wright from the speakership, Newt Gingrich of Georgia, was himself investigated by the House Ethics Committee for alleged financial misdeeds, including improper payments involving a book he had co-written. Gingrich remained in office.

Across the aisle five U.S. senators were under fire for taking a total of more than $1 million in campaign contributions from a businessman who was being sued for racketeering, fraud, and conspiracy. The five were Democrats Dennis DeConcini of Arizona, John Glenn of Ohio, Alan Cranston of California, and Donald Riegle of Michigan, as well as Republican John McCain of Arizona. They had met with federal banking authorities on behalf of Charles Keating, Jr., owner of a California savings and loan. The Department of Justice and several congressional committees were investigating the matter. In addition, two other Republicans were under investigation by the Senate Ethics Committee: Alfonse D'Amato of New York for his alleged role in the HUD scandal and David Durenberger of Minnesota for purportedly violating—by means of a book deal—the limits set on outside income.

Some commentators complained that Congress was more interested in self-righteous investigations of its members than in passing legislation. Indeed, the Center for Media and Public Affairs counted 1,086 news stories on congressional ethics scandals, involving 27 House members and 20 senators, during the first nine months of the year. At the same time, the legislative record of the 101st Congress was slim. In addition to approving the savings and loan bailout and aid to Poland and Hungary, Congress agreed to raise the minimum wage from $3.35 to $4.25 an hour, spend $8.8 billion to fight illegal drugs ($900 million more than President Bush had requested), and send a limited amount of nonmilitary aid to the *contra* rebels fighting the leftist government of Nicaragua. Each house also passed a large pay increase for its members. Problems left unresolved included clean air, child care, the disabled, and housing.

The long-running Iran-*contra* scandal reached a conclusion of sorts in 1989. A jury in Washington, D.C., found former Marine Corps lieutenant colonel Oliver North, a National Security Council aide during the Reagan years, guilty of aiding and abetting an obstruction of Congress, of destroying White House documents, and of receiving an illegal gratuity. He was sentenced to two years' probation, fined $150,000, and ordered to perform 1,200 hours of community service. North had been accused of masterminding a wide-ranging conspiracy to evade congressional limits on arms shipments to the *contras*. At his trial, he had insisted that his activities were authorized by superiors, including President Reagan. North's testimony indicated that George Bush, who was then vice president, may have known of his activities, but Bush continued to deny any knowledge of the conspiracy. The jury's verdict was a partial vindication for North, who was found innocent on several of the more serious charges against him.

Though Bush generally avoided comment on the Iran-*contra* scandal, there was one controversy he did not hesitate to join: the national debate over abortion. He praised a U.S. Supreme Court ruling in July that states could pass laws restricting abortions and vetoed a bill to permit Medicaid to pay for abortions for victims of rape and incest. He also vetoed the congressionally approved annual budget for the District of Columbia on grounds that the measure included Medicaid funds for abortion. Nonetheless, despite the Supreme Court decision and Bush's strong stand on the issue, the pro-choice movement seemed to be gaining supporters late in 1989 after a period of decline. Though Pennsylvania imposed restrictions on abortion, similar attempts in Illinois and Florida were rebuffed. In New Jersey and Virginia voters rejected antiabortion candidates for governor. Meanwhile, U.S. opinion remained sharply divided over the abortion question. In one typical survey, a *New York Times*/CBS poll of 1,297 adults taken late in the year, 41% of respondents said that abortion should be "generally available," while 42% favoured stricter limits than currently existed.

Bush had a difficult time with Congress in his first year. In addition to rejecting his first nominee to head the Department of Defense, the legislators declined to approve one of the president's most cherished legislative goals: a reduction in the tax rate on capital gains, profits from the sale of securities or tangible property. Under the Tax Reform Act of 1986, capital gains were taxed at the same rate as regular income. Bush insisted that a preferential rate for such gains would help encourage investment and that the resulting economic activity would produce more tax revenue than would be lost by cutting the gains rate.

His crusade foundered, however. Congress and the White House had trouble agreeing on a budget for the 1990 fiscal year. As a result, the Gramm-Rudman-Hollings law went into effect, imposing across-the-board cuts in all major federal spending categories. Action on the capital gains question was deferred until 1990. Bush, meanwhile, remained largely faithful to his oft-quoted campaign pledge of "no new taxes" but, as a result, was unable to make much of a dent in the 1990 federal budget deficit. That gap soared past the $200 billion mark, according to the Congressional Budget Office, though some bookkeeping tricks allowed the White House to assert that the figure was closer to the $110 billion target specified by the Gramm-Rudman-Hollings law. Mindful of the deficit—and of the dramatic improvement in U.S.-Soviet relations—Secretary of Defense Cheney proposed that defense spending be lowered by $180 billion, or about 5%, for the years 1992–94.

The Economy. Some analysts feared that the huge federal deficit would exert a negative effect on the U.S. economy, forcing the government to borrow more money and thus driving up interest rates, which would then choke off economic growth. By the year's end, however, those fears had not yet come to pass. The U.S. economy grew at a rate of nearly 3% in 1989, the seventh straight year of expansion. The inflation rate was up somewhat from the previous year's 4.1% but was still substantially below the double-digit rates of 1979–81.

There were, however, signs that a recession was approaching. Consumer spending, which traditionally accounted for two-thirds of all domestic economic activity, was slowing. Automobile sales were off, and corporate profits fell in the third quarter of 1989 by more than 20% from the previous year's level. More and more firms were strapped for cash after a frenetic era of takeovers, junk bonds, and leveraged buyouts. A shiver of anxiety about the economy swept through the financial community on October 13, when the Dow Jones industrial average plunged 190 points in a single trading session.

Nonetheless, some Americans believed that the economy could sidestep a truly ugly recession. Optimists expected that the Federal Reserve Board, which regulated the country's money supply, would ease its previously tight monetary policy and stimulate at least modest growth. If U.S. exports then picked up a little steam, that could be enough to keep the expansion going. Such expectations helped the stock market recover most of its October 13 loss.

Drugs. In opinion polls a large number of Americans indicated that their prime worry was not, as in previous years, the future of the economy or even that perennial spectre, the possibility of global nuclear war. Instead, many citizens believed that the country's biggest problem was the illegal drug trade. William Bennett (*see* BIOGRAPHIES), the Bush administration's chief antidrug official, proposed a $7.9 billion program, including $1 billion in new funds, to attack the problem. Bennett's plan included federal aid to state and local police agencies for law enforcement, as well as a controversial proposal for getting tough on casual users of illegal drugs. The administration, which was criticized for vagueness on how this proposal would be financed, also offered $65 million to aid Colombia in its war against the drug cartel and prepared to file charges against Noriega for his dealings in the drug trade in Panama.

Church Membership in the United States

Religious body	Total clergy	Inclusive membership	Religious body	Total clergy	Inclusive membership
Baptist bodies			Independent Fundamental Churches of America	1,366	120,446
American Baptist Association	1,760	250,000	Jehovah's Witnesses	None	804,639
American Baptist Churches in the U.S.A.	8,276	1,549,563	Jews	6,500	5,935,000
Baptist Bible Fellowship, International	4,500	1,405,900	Latter Day Saints (Mormons)		
Baptist General Conference	1,700	135,125	Church of Jesus Christ of Latter-day Saints	29,714	4,000,000
Baptist Missionary Association of America	2,630	227,897	Reorganized Church of Jesus Christ of L.D.S.	17,048	190,950
Conservative Baptist Association of America	...	204,496	Lutherans		
Free Will Baptists	2,895	204,382	Evangelical Lutheran Church in America	16,083	5,251,534
General Baptists (General Association of)	1,483	74,086	Lutheran Church—Missouri Synod	8,193	2,604,278
Liberty Baptist Fellowship	...	200,000	Wisconsin Evangelical Lutheran Synod	1,538	418,691
National Baptist Convention of America	28,574	2,668,799	Mennonites		
National Baptist Convention, U.S.A., Inc.	27,500	5,500,000	Mennonite Church	2,469	92,682
National Primitive Baptist Convention	636	250,000	Old Order Amish Church	3,049	68,040
Primitive Baptists	...	72,000	Methodists		
Progressive National Baptist Convention	863	521,692	African Methodist Episcopal Church	6,550	2,210,000
Regular Baptist Churches, General Association of	2,150	260,000	African Methodist Episcopal Zion Church	6,060	1,220,260
Southern Baptist Convention	63,625	14,812,844	Christian Methodist Episcopal Church	2,340	718,922
Buddhist Churches of America	115	100,000	Free Methodist Church of North America	1,802	73,647
Christian and Missionary Alliance	2,261	259,612	United Methodist Church	37,999	9,124,575
Christian Brethren	500	98,000	Wesleyan Church	3,783	185,861
Christian Congregation	1,460	107,902	North American Old Roman Catholic Church	150	62,611
Church of God (Anderson, Ind.)	3,315	198,842	Pentecostals		
Church of the Brethren	1,553	151,169	Assemblies of God	30,552	2,147,041
Church of the Nazarene	8,988	552,264	Church of God	2,737	75,890
Churches of Christ—Christian Churches			Church of God (Cleveland, Tenn.)	7,544	582,203
Christian Church (Disciples of Christ)	6,849	1,073,119	Church of God in Christ	10,426	3,709,661
Christian Churches and Churches of Christ	6,596	1,070,616	Church of God in Christ, International	1,600	200,000
Churches of Christ	...	1,626,000	Church of God of Prophecy	7,573	74,588
Community Churches, International Council of	350	250,000	Full Gospel Fellowship of Churches and Ministers, Intl.	850	65,000
Congregational Christian Churches, Natl. Assn. of	575	90,000	International Church of the Foursquare Gospel	5,076	198,715
Eastern Churches			Pentecostal Church of God	1,584	86,000
American Carpatho-Russian Orthodox Greek Catholic Ch.	66	100,000	Pentecostal Holiness Church, International	3,314	116,764
Antiochian Orthodox Christian Archdiocese of N. Am.	172	300,000	United Pentecostal Church, International	7,279	500,000
Apostolic Catholic Assyrian Ch. of the East, N. Am. Dioc.	109	120,000	Polish National Catholic Church of America	141	282,411
Armenian Church of America, Diocese of the	61	450,000	Presbyterians		
Bulgarian Eastern Orthodox Church	11	86,000	Cumberland Presbyterian Church	725	91,491
Coptic Orthodox Church	44	160,000	Evangelical Presbyterian Church	225	50,300
Greek Orthodox Archdiocese of N. and S. America	655	1,950,000	Presbyterian Church in America	1,722	190,960
Orthodox Church in America	531	1,000,000	Presbyterian Church (U.S.A.)	19,746	2,929,608
Romanian Orthodox Episcopate of America	67	60,000	Reformed bodies		
Russian Orthodox Church Outside of Russia	168	55,000	Christian Reformed Church in North America	1,075	222,408
Serbian Eastern Orth. Ch. in the U.S.A. and Canada	82	67,000	Reformed Church in America	1,698	333,798
Ukrainian Orthodox Church in the U.S.A.	131	87,745	United Church of Christ	10,145	1,644,787
Episcopal Church	14,694	2,455,422	Roman Catholic Church	52,948	54,918,949
Evangelical Covenant Church of America	1,260	87,750	Salvation Army	5,198	433,443
Evangelical Free Church of America	1,484	95,722	Seventh-day Adventist Church	4,537	687,200
Friends United Meeting	601	54,501	Unitarian Universalist Association	1,140	178,623

Table includes churches reporting a membership of 50,000 or more and represents the latest information available.
Source: National Council of the Churches of Christ in the U.S.A.

(CONSTANT H. JACQUET)

Meanwhile, a federal study indicated that the number of Americans using illicit drugs at least once a month was 14.5 million. Though down substantially from earlier years, this was still enormously high by any measure. Moreover, the number of weekly cocaine users had risen by one-third in the previous three years, to a total of 862,000 people. As increasingly potent forms of cocaine proliferated, drug-inspired violence rose to epidemic proportions. The number of murders in the first half of 1989 increased 5% over the same period a year earlier, according to the FBI. Murders soared 15% in cities with populations between 500,000 and one million, and drugs were blamed for most of the increase. Washington, D.C., the nation's capital, seemed destined to become its murder capital as well, registering more than one killing a day.

Racial Problems. Racial tensions continued to plague the U.S. In New York City a 16-year-old black youth was killed by a mob after he ventured into the all-white Bensonhurst section of Brooklyn. The incident, which touched off protest marches by blacks, came only a few months after a public outcry over the rape and beating of a white female jogger in New York's Central Park, a crime for which a group of young blacks were charged. Miami, Fla., braced for racial violence as a Hispanic policeman went on trial for shooting a black motorcyclist to death in the city's black Overtown ghetto. The policeman was found guilty, and violence was averted. In Philadelphia a young Hispanic was killed by a white mob. Across the country racial incidents increased on college campuses. *Do the Right Thing,* by actor-director Spike Lee (*see* BIOGRAPHIES), became one of the year's most controversial films because of its frank treatment of the subject of racial violence.

Commentators had various explanations for the seeming epidemic of bigotry. The alarming growth of the black underclass and fears of drug-related crime had created a widening gulf of mutual misunderstanding between the races. Blacks and whites in declining urban neighbourhoods were becoming increasingly frustrated with their economic plight and seemed more eager to blame racial discrimination for it. Young people, black and white alike, had grown up without an appreciation for the civil rights struggles of the 1950s and 1960s and were thus insensitive to the perils of racism. The federal government's commitment to civil rights and affirmative action had weakened during the Reagan years. Against that background a major study of race relations in the U.S. concluded that virtually no progress had been made since the urban upheavals of the

1960s. *A Common Destiny: Blacks and American Society,* produced by the National Research Council, reported that "the economic status of blacks relative to whites has, on average, stagnated or deteriorated" since the early 1970s. In addition, the study noted that there had been almost no improvement in racial integration of housing and that whites continued to be reluctant to come into direct contact with blacks at all levels of society.

Environment. Another concern that captured considerable attention in 1989 was the environment, the subject of countless inquiries in the press and the halls of government. Perhaps the biggest ecological outcry came when the oil tanker *Exxon Valdez* ran aground in Prince William Sound, Alaska. The resulting oil spill, the worst in the country's history, fouled beaches and killed wildlife along Alaska's coastline. (*See* ENVIRONMENT.) Less serious oil and chemical spills occurred in other parts of the country during the year, and local environmental disputes proliferated. In a departure from its usual practice of naming a "Man of the Year," *Time* magazine chose the endangered Earth as "Planet of the Year."

Natural disasters claimed more than 150 American lives in 1989, the highest toll from hurricanes, earthquakes, and tornadoes in 15 years. Two events were especially devastating. In September the southeastern states were battered by Hurricane Hugo, the most destructive storm in U.S. history. In South Carolina alone at least 17 people died, more than 36,000 homes were destroyed, and 224,000 people were thrown out of work at least temporarily. Total property damage in the 24-county region of South Carolina that bore the brunt of the storm was estimated at more than $5 billion.

Barely a month later an earthquake registering 7.1 on the 12-point Richter scale rocked northern California. Known officially as the Loma Prieta Quake, after a mountain perched almost atop the epicentre, the tremor caused heavy damage in nearby Santa Cruz and in the highly urbanized San Francisco Bay area some 95 km (60 mi) away. A total of 67 people died in the disaster, 3,000 were injured, and 14,000 were made homeless. Property damage was estimated at up to $10 billion. Devastating as it was, the Loma Prieta Quake was not the "big one" that millions of Californians living along the active San Andreas Fault had long been expecting. Instead, with characteristic California casualness, they referred to the 1989 quake as the "pretty big one."   (DONALD MORRISON)

See also *Dependent States,* below.

Developments in the States in 1989

No other issue carried such fearful political consequences for state officials in 1989 as abortion. Delivered back to the states by a conservative U.S. Supreme Court, abortion played a major role in the first round of state elections. In the only two gubernatorial races of the year, pro-choice candidates won. One of those candidates, in Virginia, made history as the country's first elected black governor.

U.S. Pres. George Bush told the nation that he wanted to be the "education president" but warned that "we have more will than wallet; but will is what we need." At the education summit that was all he could offer as governors searched for new ways to stop the decline in academic performance.

The federal budget deficit also left states to open their own fronts in the war on drugs. The prison population increased, as did the number of executions.

Many states took the lead in cleaning up the environment, enacting numerous anti-pollution laws. Continuing a trend that characterized much of the decade, states also took the initiative in a wide range of other matters.

Party Strengths. The two gubernatorial elections in 1989 resulted in a gain of one state for the Democrats. In New Jersey, Democrat James Florio, an eight-term congressman, succeeded outgoing Republican Thomas Kean. Florio defeated his opponent, Rep. Jim Courter, in a landslide election that was noteworthy only for its extreme nastiness.

In Virginia, Democrat Douglas Wilder became the first elected black governor in U.S. history. During the campaign he de-emphasized the issue of race, preferring instead to portray himself as a moderate and making his pro-abortion position the centrepiece of the election. The final vote was much closer than predicted by the polls—897,139 to 890,285, or 50.19 to 49.81%—leading pundits to speculate that racism was indeed a factor. His opponent, former Virginia attorney general J. Marshall Coleman, demanded a recount.

Since it was an odd-year election, only 180 legislative seats were up for grabs. In New Jersey, Democrats regained the General Assembly, giving them control of both houses. In Virginia the House of Delegates remained in Democratic hands, but Republicans picked up four seats. After November there were 29 Democratic and 21 Republican governors. Democrats controlled the governorship and both legislative chambers in 15 states, while Republicans did so in only 4 states. Democrats controlled both houses in 29 states, up one from the previous year, while Republicans stayed the same with 8, and 12 were split.

Government Structures, Powers. As the new legislative session began, well-entrenched house speakers in Connecticut and North Carolina were overthrown by unexpected bipartisan coalitions. The vote for house speaker is traditionally a partisan affair, but there was speculation that party loyalty and discipline were weakening in a new era of independent legislators. This trend worried some political scientists, who believed that the decline of strong party structure would lead to instability and the demise of loyalty. In Oklahoma the Democratic house speaker was ousted by a bi-partisan coalition nine days before the end of the session.

Ballot initiatives remained popular. Texas, where voters rejected a proposal to triple the $7,200 annual salary of state lawmakers, had 21 propositions. Texan voters did allow officeholders to drop a 113-year-old provision ordering them to swear publicly that they did not pay bribes to get into office. Voters in Oklahoma shortened the legislative session by approximately one month.

To the embarrassment of the national Republican Party, which had increasingly been reaching out to black voters, the former grand wizard of the Knights of the Ku Klux Klan, David Duke, running as a Republican, was elected to the Louisiana state legislature. He subsequently announced his intention to run for the U.S. Senate. Republican National Chairman Lee Atwater called Duke a "pretender, a charlatan and a political opportunist."

By one vote the state Senate in Arizona passed a bill restoring the observance of Martin Luther King, Jr.'s birthday. The holiday had been rescinded in 1987 by former governor Evan Mecham, an act that cost the state more than $200 million by alienating conventioneers and tourists. In restoring the holiday, Arizona legislators rescinded Columbus Day's status as a state holiday.

Government Relations. State governments continued to assume more responsibility for domestic affairs, the result of a lack of political will on the part of Congress and a new judicial mind-set in the Supreme Court. Congress spent much of the year preoccupied with internal scandals and the problem of giving itself a raise. In contrast, the court actively handed the states more authority over decisions on abortion, antitrust cases, drug testing, and criminal justice. In addition, there were unprecedented numbers of rulings favouring the states in areas such as constitutional rights and discrimination. The one major ruling against the states said that they could be forced to pay for cleaning up hazardous-waste sites.

Overshadowing all else was the spectre of abortion as this politically charged issue was thrown into the reluctant hands of state legislators. The constitutional rights granted in the landmark 1973 decision *Roe* v. *Wade* seemed for the first time in danger of being nibbled away, if not actually overthrown, when the Supreme Court decided in favour of a Missouri law restricting abortion. The decision unleashed a flood of activity as pro-life and pro-choice advocates prepared to do battle in state legislatures. Florida's governor immediately called a special session to enact a series of antiabortion measures, an effort that failed. Louisiana, one of 20 states still having on the books pre-1973 statutes making abortion a crime, called for tough enforcement of such laws. Pennsylvania passed the nation's most restrictive antiabortion bill. In a California election that received nationwide attention, a pro-choice candidate who had been barred by her Roman Catholic bishop from receiving communion was elected to the state Senate, tipping the legislative balance in favour of abortion.

Finances. Most state budgets were in fairly healthy condition in 1989. Fiscal conditions actually improved for many states as a result of a stable national economy. Nevertheless, it was an active year financially, with 42 states making important changes in tax policy. There were tax increases in 30 states, decreases in 11, and one revenue-neutral change. The result was a net tax increase of $3.5 billion, up from $600 million in 1988.

Excise taxes were the most popular vehicle by which states increased revenues. Twenty-three states raised motor fuel taxes, 13 raised cigarette taxes, and 7 increased taxes on alcoholic beverages. Increases in cigarette taxes ranged from 3.7 to 81.3%, with Connecticut having the highest tax at 40 cents a pack. Connecticut also had the highest sales tax in the nation, rising from 7.5 to 8%, and the highest corporate tax rate, which rose from 11.5 to 20%. California officials planned to place a constitutional amendment on the 1990 ballot that would allow them to tax beyond the spending limits of the 1978 law known as Proposition 13.

Spending was up 7.2% over 1988. Education spending, which accounted for

MICHAEL L. ABRAMSON

A wagon train wends its way through South Dakota as part of the state's centennial celebration. South Dakota, North Dakota, and Montana celebrated their 100th anniversaries of statehood with such special events as rodeos, wild West shows, and cattle drives.

nearly half of all state expenditures, increased 8% for elementary and secondary education and 7.7% for higher education. Prison expenditures grew by 14.2% and Medicaid by 10%.

The Northeast, where economic expansion had slowed, experienced financial difficulties, continuing a recent downward trend. Eight northeastern states enacted revenue measures accounting for almost 50% of the total revenue to be raised. The "Massachusetts Miracle" was history as that state grappled with proposed tax increases in order to balance its $13 billion budget, a requirement of state law. The estimated deficit was $1.2 billion, the worst in Massachusetts history. New York predicted a $500 million shortfall by the end of the fiscal year, and estimates of a $100 million to $200 million shortfall were predicted for the next fiscal year.

Two states facing unexpected financial crises were South Carolina and California. In South Carolina Hurricane Hugo caused at least 17 deaths and an estimated $5 billion in damages. A fiscal 1991 deficit of $100 million to $200 million was anticipated. In California a devastating earthquake in the San Francisco Bay area took 67 lives and caused nearly $10 billion in damages, making it the costliest natural disaster in U.S. history. California raised the state sales tax from 4.75 to 5% for one year to raise $800 million in emergency relief.

Ethics. One year to the day after Arizona Gov. Evan Mecham was removed from office, he announced his intention to run for the post again. The Republican governor was impeached after his conviction in the state Senate of obstruction of justice and misusing state funds. Mecham had managed to infuriate and embarrass many citizens of his state by first canceling a state holiday honouring Martin Luther King, Jr., and then later making unfavourable references to homosexuals. At the time of his impeachment, the governor was facing a recall election.

A three-year investigation by the FBI into political corruption in the California legislature led Assembly Speaker Willie Brown to announce creation of a select committee on ethics. The probe netted its first indictment when Sen. Joseph Montoya was charged with 12 counts of racketeering, extortion, and money laundering. The 50-year-old Democratic lawmaker pleaded innocent.

In Kentucky a gravedigger at the Louisville Crematories and Cemetery called the state attorney general's office to report that graves were being used for multiple burials. The remains of more than 45,000 people were discovered to have been placed in graves occupied by other bodies in a practice dating back to the 1920s. Some graves held the remains of more than five people. Cemetery officials were charged in a 60-count indictment, including abuse of corpses.

Education. For only the third time in history, a U.S. president called the nation's governors together for a working session on an issue of major national importance. With test results in standard academic subjects an international embarrassment, educators and politicians alike were eagerly searching for new approaches to education reform. At the education summit in Char-

lottesville, Va., however, officials faced a paradox: in its third annual report on school reforms, the National Governors' Association said, "While states and localities have primary responsibility for education . . . it is time to set national education goals that reflect the performance the nation needs from the education system as it approaches the 21st century."

The concept of parental choice gained ground. By 1990 parents in Minnesota would be able to send their children to any public school in the state, providing desegregation efforts were not thwarted. Nebraska, Arkansas, Iowa, Ohio, and 11 other states were moving to or had already adopted freedom of choice.

The Texas Supreme Court ruled unanimously that the state's method of public school financing was unconstitutional because of "glaring disparities" between the richest and poorest school districts. Nine other states faced lawsuits or court orders challenging inequities in school financing. The implications of the ruling extended far beyond Texas. The prospect of national performance standards and goals raised the question of equality of financing among states, not just within them.

Kentucky was ordered by the state Supreme Court to rebuild its entire educational system. In an unprecedented ruling the court held that not only school financing procedures but all aspects of the system failed to provide for an "efficient system of common schools."

Ohio passed legislation requiring schools to award differentiated diplomas. They were divided into four categories: a certificate of attendance, a diploma of basic competency, a diploma with distinction, and a diploma of commendation.

Health, Welfare. As Americans spent a staggering $1.5 billion a day on health care, state governments grappled with the problem of ensuring access to such care for the country's 37 million citizens who lacked medical insurance. Oregon passed legislation to guarantee basic health care for its 400,000 uninsured, sharing the financial burden with business. Minnesota introduced legislation to offer coverage for all state residents. Washington began a health insurance plan to be financed by taxpayers that would cover low-income families.

New Jersey became the first state to offer universal access to prenatal care. New York planned to test all newborns for syphilis. Almost every state addressed legislation dealing with some aspect of the AIDS crisis. Illinois repealed its requirement that individuals undergo AIDS tests before getting a marriage license.

A Tennessee court gave custody of seven frozen embryos to a divorced woman who planned to use them to become pregnant. The judge ruled that "human life begins at the moment of conception," rejecting arguments by the father that this was a property dispute. The case attracted wide attention and was seen as a victory for antiabortion forces. The Michigan legislature approved a bill requiring teenage girls to seek parental consent before obtaining an abortion. However, Democratic Gov. James Blanchard promised to veto it. Illinois eliminated the requirement that abortion clinics be equipped and staffed like hospital operating rooms but retained the authority to inspect clinics and enforce

rules considered necessary for protecting the health and safety of patients.

Voters in the heart of tobacco country, Greensboro, N.C., approved an antismoking initiative. The law designated smoke-free areas in large restaurants and banned smoking in elevators and some stores. New York adopted comprehensive legislation banning smoking in a wide variety of public areas and requiring the creation of smoke-free work areas by employers. Vending machine owners felt under attack in Minnesota, where bans on cigarette vending machines were spreading throughout the state.

Drugs. More legislation was submitted to state legislatures on the subject of drug abuse than on any other single issue. More than half the states passed laws to deal with the problem. President Bush's new drug offensive included an increase of $200 million in federal aid to state and local law-enforcement agencies. The administration targeted four areas—New York City; Miami, Fla.; Los Angeles; and the border with Mexico—to receive additional funds.

Illinois state police nabbed 16 school bus drivers in Operation S.K.I.D. (School Kids in Danger). The drivers were indicted for selling cocaine, marijuana, and heroin while driving their regular bus routes with children on board. A new Illinois law required school superintendents to run criminal background checks on school bus drivers. In the first initiative of its kind, voters in Kansas City, Mo., agreed to a quarter-cent increase in their sales tax to raise $98 million over the next seven years to combat drugs.

Texas banned possession of beepers by public school students when at school or at school functions "unless the student is in attendance in the capacity of an active member of a volunteer fire-fighting or emergency medical services organization." Illinois passed similar legislation. Beepers had been used by drug dealers.

Law, Justice. California became the first state to ban the sale, possession, or manufacture of semiautomatic weapons. In a dramatic gesture Attorney General John Van de Kamp stood before the California Assembly clutching an AK-47 assault rifle. "You are lucky that I am the attorney general and not a nut," he said. The bill had faced strong, well-financed opposition from the National Rifle Association, but a shooting incident that captured headlines nationwide made passage of the bill inevitable. A young drifter with an AK-47 opened fire on dozens of children at an elementary school. Five children were killed, and many others were wounded. The man then killed himself with a pistol.

Eighteen other states proposed gun-control legislation, the most common requiring background checks and a waiting period. Florida passed an innovative gun-control law providing stiff sentences for adults whose weapons were used by minors in fatal or very injurious shootings. Five children in Florida were shot in less than one month, two fatally, by other children who were playing with guns.

Connecticut found itself in a complicated mess when it was discovered that state police had been taping phone conversations between suspects and their lawyers. The revelation that most of the telephone lines at all 12 state police barracks were

equipped to record conversations resulted in the forced resignation of Connecticut's public safety commissioner, who was also commander of the state police. In addition to lawsuits by criminal defendants, a federal civil rights and racketeering suit was filed against the state on behalf of the Connecticut Criminal Lawyers Association.

The New York State Court of Claims awarded more than $1 million in damages to seven former inmates of Attica state prison who were present at the time of the infamous 1971 riot.

Prisons. As it had in recent years, the population of state prisons increased. At midyear, according to the Bureau of Justice Statistics, the number of prisoners in state facilities reached 618,847, an increase of 7.1%. The number of women incarcerated rose from 29,350 at the end of 1988 to 33,301 by July 1989, an increase of 13.5%. Since the beginning of the 1980s, the routine annual increase had caused a percentage rise of more than 100% nationwide in state prisons, with several states experiencing an increase of more than 200%.

California had the largest growth in its prison population, with 6,700 new prisoners, an increase of 8.8%. Eight states and the District of Columbia had double-digit increases, including Rhode Island with an increase of 20.3%, South Dakota with 19.9%, and Connecticut with 18.4%.

According to the Legal Defense Fund of the National Association for the Advancement of Colored People (NAACP), there were 17 executions in 1989, up from 11 in 1988. The number of prisoners on death row grew to 2,210 from 2,151 a year earlier.

Expenditures for prisons underwent a 14.2% growth over 1988. States faced with overcrowded prisons employed several approaches to meet the problem that did not require construction of new facilities. At least 16 states passed legislation dealing with prison release mechanisms. Ten states approved or expanded boot camp facilities. New York, whose correctional system was operating at 120% of capacity, opened its first SI (shock incarceration) camp for female offenders. Illinois planned to build three new prisons with a total of 1,725 beds at a cost of $97 million. The state also was to spend $6 million to lease space in Missouri for a year for up to 250 prisoners.

Gambling. New records were set in two state lotteries. In Illinois a $69.9 million jackpot had four winners. In Pennsylvania 14 winners shared a jackpot of $115.5 million.

In the hope of attracting tourists, two states legalized casino gambling, keeping it on a small scale and restricting it to fairly benign locations. In Iowa paddleboats on the Mississippi River were to have casinos run by nonprofit organizations starting in 1991. Bets were to be no higher than $5 a game, and no one would be permitted to lose more than $200 a trip. In Mississippi casino gambling was legalized for cruise ships in the Gulf of Mexico.

Oregon instituted the first state-sponsored betting for professional football games. Game cards were to be sold at 1,300 lottery outlets, and estimates were that the betting would produce revenues for the state of about $8 million.

Environment. Alaska became the scene of the largest oil spill in U.S. history when the tanker *Exxon Valdez* plowed into a reef in Prince William Sound. As officials bungled initial efforts at containment, thousands of barrels of oil escaped from the ship's ruptured hull. When a spring storm blew in three days later, the oil spread out of control. Over 200,000 bbl contaminated 1,700 km (1,100 mi) of shoreline. More than 33,000 birds died in the disaster and nearly 1,000 otters. The cleanup effort involved more than 10,000 people and 1,385 vessels and planes. Transportation Secretary Samuel Skinner estimated the cost to Exxon at $1.9 billion, and the company faced at least 145 lawsuits, including one brought by the state of Alaska.

Federal officials rated Grand Canyon National Park in Arizona as having the worst air pollution of all the national parks. The source was traced to the Navajo Generating Station, a coal-fired power plant in Arizona that did not have modern pollution-control equipment.

At least 30 states enacted legislation dealing with source reduction and recycling. The U.S. got its first diaper law in Nebraska, where by 1993 disposable diapers would have to be biodegradable. In Minnesota Minneapolis and St. Paul planned to ban all nonbiodegradable plastic food packaging that could not be recycled. Experts argued that biodegradability was not the ultimate answer, though; if all 18 billion diapers used annually were biodegradable, it would still cost $300 million for their disposal. West Virginia reformed its solid-waste system by establishing landfill controls and solid-waste authorities at the county level.

California and eight northeastern states announced new rules to restrict toxic emissions of motor vehicles. Antipollution devices lasting 161,000 km (100,000 mi) would also be required. The new rules would become applicable beginning with the 1993 models.

More than two dozen states introduced ozone-protection legislation. Vermont passed the toughest such law against chlorofluorocarbons (CFCs) by banning the substance in model 1993 car air-conditioning systems. Ford and General Motors said that they did not expect to meet Vermont's deadline, although they did plan to convert to nonpolluting systems by the mid-1990s. Hawaii became the first state to ban over-the-counter sales of refrigerants containing CFCs.

Alabama, which had the nation's largest toxic-waste landfill, banned shipments of hazardous waste from 22 states and the District of Columbia. South Carolina had already taken similar steps to ban shipments of waste.

Energy. California voters were the first to succeed in closing down a nuclear power plant. The 15-year-old Rancho Seco plant had a history of problems. Over the years the plant had more than 100 unplanned shutdowns, one of which lasted more than two years. Rancho Seco was also found to be discharging unacceptable levels of waste and was fined $100,000 by the Nuclear Regulatory Commission.

The Nevada legislature passed a joint resolution opposing a high-level radioactive-waste repository at Yucca Mountain. Voters in Maine ratified a contract to send their low-level nuclear waste to Beatty, Nev.

Equal Rights. The year would not be remembered as the most auspicious one for equal rights. In January the U.S. Supreme Court invalidated a Richmond, Va., minority business program that required setting aside 30% of the city's public works funds for minority-owned construction companies. The consequences of that decision could be fairly widespread, as 36 states had similar affirmative action programs that presumably were now threatened. In the first involving one of them, the Supreme Court in March overturned a Michigan statute that called for 7% of state contracts to be awarded to minority-owned businesses and 5% to businesses owned by women.

Massachusetts became the second state, after Wisconsin, to pass a comprehensive law barring discrimination against homosexuals. Eleven states and 80 municipalities had laws prohibiting discrimination in such areas as housing and employment.

New York state was found to discriminate against girls by granting scholarships solely on the basis of SAT scores. The court's decision was believed to be the first to find that standardized achievement tests were biased.

In legislation known as Potty Parity, New York would soon require new buildings to provide larger bathroom facilities for women than for men. A study of lines outside public rest rooms concluded that women spent nearly twice as long (79 sec) as men in such facilities. Other states considering the issue were Colorado, Florida, Michigan, and Oregon.

A report by New Jersey's Task Force on Minority Concerns found the state's judicial system biased against black and Hispanic defendants. The report made 33 recommendations, among them "sensitivity training." The panel found that rather than being manifested in overt prejudice, the problem was "oftentimes subtle or totally unrecognized."

Consumer Protection. More than a year after California voters passed a sweeping insurance reform measure known as Proposition 103, officials were still sorting it out. The initiative called for 20% cutbacks on most property and casualty insurance rates. In 1989 the California Supreme Court upheld the law in opposition to insurance industry lawsuits but included a proviso that rate rollbacks had to afford companies a "fair and reasonable" profit. As the year ended, a six-month freeze on automobile insurance rates was in effect, and public hearings were scheduled. Proposition 103 also created the first new elective post in California in the 20th century.

Credit card customers in New York would no longer have to provide their address or telephone number on credit-card sales receipts. The law was aimed at preventing merchants from compiling lists to be used for mail and telephone solicitation. Six states passed laws making it illegal for businesses to use fax machines for commercial solicitation without prior approval from the recipient.

Consumers in California would no longer have to worry about losing a whole day waiting for deliveries or repairmen. A new law required businesses to arrive at a customer's house within a specified four-hour period or be liable for monetary damages. (MELANIE A. COOPER)

Latin America and the Caribbean

LATIN-AMERICAN AFFAIRS

For most countries in the region, 1989 saw a worsening of economic problems. Apart from Chile, where the economy expanded by around 8%, low to sharply negative growth prevailed, with the worst results in Venezuela, Peru, Argentina, Nicaragua, and Panama; Panama's economy suffered even more after the U.S. invasion in December. Inflationary pressure was also evident, particularly in Argentina (where the monthly inflation rate peaked at almost 200% in July) and Brazil (with rates of around 40% per month in the latter part of the year). Mexico, however, succeeded in reducing its annual rate to well under half the 51.7% of 1988. The economic position was complicated in Argentina, Brazil, and Chile by presidential elections.

Limited progress was achieved with respect to foreign debt difficulties, although important new deals were struck by Mexico and Costa Rica under the so-called Brady initiative, launched by U.S. Treasury Secretary Nicholas Brady on March 10. Only a few weeks earlier, there had been bloody riots in Venezuela, prompted by austerity measures introduced by the new administration of Carlos Andrés Pérez (*see* BIOGRAPHIES) as part of an effort to stabilize the economy. Unlike its predecessor, the Baker plan, Brady placed the emphasis on future debt reduction by commercial banks, with supporting funds provided by the International Monetary Fund (IMF) and the World Bank (although banks were expected to come up with fresh finance for debtors where appropriate). (*See* ECONOMIC AFFAIRS: *Special Report*.)

The agreement on a new deal for Mexico covering $54 billion of bank debt over the period 1989–92 was reached on July 23, after months of difficult negotiations. Commitments by 60% of banks were received by mid-November, with some 50% of banks opting for the reduction of debt principal by swapping old debt for discounted bonds. Despite delays in completing the debt deal, the administration of Carlos Salinas de Gortari was able to secure the cooperation of business and labour unions for the extension of its anti-inflation strategy until March 1990. The growing challenge from the left—notably the new Party of the Democratic Revolution led by Cuauhtémoc Cárdenas—was also kept in check, but the ruling Institutional Revolutionary Party had to concede a provincial governorship in Baja California Norte to the right-wing National Action Party candidate after elections in July.

In Argentina and Brazil the approach of presidential elections contributed to a deterioration in economic management, and a formidable task awaited the incoming administrations. The Peronist candidate, Carlos Saúl Menem (*see* BIOGRAPHIES), won the presidency in Argentina with 47% of the vote and took office early, on July 8 rather than December 10, by agreement with outgoing Pres. Raúl Alfonsín. Menem embarked on a strategy of rapprochement with the U.K., which resulted in the normalization of trade between the two countries from August and progress on the restoration of diplomatic links, broken since the Falklands/Malvinas war in 1982. The new Argentine administration also moved swiftly to stabilize an economy that was seriously out of control. The country had reached an accord with the IMF in late September for a $1.4 billion

standby loan, followed in early November by exploratory meetings with the country's leading commercial bankers over plans for dealing with its more than $60 billion debt. Argentina had ceased interest payments to banks in 1988 and had accumulated arrears of well over $4.4 billion.

In Brazil, which had concluded a major debt-rescheduling package in late 1988, problems with international creditors began to surface by early 1989, both in the context of a sharp deterioration in economic performance and over the criteria for disbursement of World Bank loans for the energy sector. While these were temporarily overcome, Brazil's failure to meet IMF targets meant that its standby loans were suspended, and this held up other agreed loans from multilateral, official, and commercial bank sources. In its last months of office, the outgoing government of Pres. José Sarney proved unable to adjust the economy to creditors' satisfaction. An impasse over bank interest payments came in mid-September, and from then on the country remained in arrears. Resumption of payments might well have to wait until mid-March 1990, when the new administration would take office. There was also some easing of formerly tense relations with the U.S. over trade matters. In the second round of the presidential election on December 17, Fernando Collor de Mello of the National Reconstruction Party (PRN) emerged as the victor. The new president would face the unenviable task of dealing with an economy riven by hyperinflation, record domestic indebtedness, and flagging business confidence, while the 1990 political agenda would be dominated by the approach of congressional and gubernatorial elections.

The region's longest-ruling military dictator, Gen. Alfredo Stroessner of Paraguay, was ousted in a coup by Gen. Andrés Rodríguez (*see* BIOGRAPHIES) in February. Rodríguez subsequently secured a comfortable victory in presidential elections on May 1. In Chile, Gen. Augusto Pinochet Ugarte, defeated in the October 1988 plebiscite over extension of his term in office, was forced to make concessions to the opposition prior to presidential elections on December 14. The new president, Patricio Aylwin of the Christian Democratic Party, would take office in March 1990.

In Peru the faltering economic policies of Pres. Alan García's administration were further undermined by the activities of the Sendero Luminoso (Shining Path) guerrillas. Municipal elections in early November 1989 produced a strong swing to the right, whose presidential candidate, the writer Mario Vargas Llosa, was favoured to win the presidency in 1990. Uruguay's presidential elections in late November resulted in a victory for Luis Alberto Lacalle of the centrist National Party, but a Marxist coalition gained control of the Montevideo city government. Jamaica saw the return to power of Michael Manley in elections on February 9. In a switch from his earlier period in office, Manley was eager to foster cooperation with the U.S.

The Central American peace process encountered further obstacles to full realization of the peace accord reached in August 1987, as economic difficulties and guerrilla activity persisted in El Salvador, Guatemala, and Nicaragua. In El Salvador the election of a new right-wing president, Alfredo Cristiani, prompted a major offensive by leftist guerrillas in the capital of San Salvador during November. Guatemalan Pres. Vinicio Cerezo Arévalo survived a coup attempt in May. A cease-fire with the *contra* rebels was in effect for much of the year in Nicaragua, but it was ended by Pres. Daniel Ortega at the beginning of November. Elections scheduled for February 1990 were being vigorously contested by the 14-party National Opposition Union led by Violeta Barrios de Chamorro (*see* BIOGRAPHIES).

The five Central American presidents (from left to right), Vinicio Cerezo Arévalo of Guatemala, Oscar Arias Sánchez of Costa Rica, José Azcona Hoyo of Honduras, Alfredo Cristiani of El Salvador, and Daniel Ortega Saavedra of Nicaragua, sign an accord that outlines the disbandment of Nicaragua's *contra* rebels.

BLEIBTREU—SYGMA

Throughout Central America, the economic position was exacerbated by low international coffee prices, especially in the second half of the year after the collapse of the International Coffee Organization's quota agreement. Against this background, the Central American Common Market remained in the doldrums. Low coffee prices also contributed to a worsening of Colombia's export performance, although this was partly offset by higher oil and coal revenues. Soon after the assassination of Liberal presidential candidate Luis Carlos Galán, Pres. Virgilio Barco Vargas (*see* BIOGRAPHIES) escalated the government's offensive against drug traffickers. Barco obtained financial and military support from the U.S., although this did not prevent more political murders by members of the Medellín drug cartel and their hirelings. In Panama the results of general elections in May were annulled by de facto ruler Gen. Manuel Noriega, who installed his nominee as president. Noriega resisted efforts by representatives of the Organization of American States to set up a government of national reconstruction. His intransigence and antidemocratic stance over these and other matters (not least his alleged involvement in drug trafficking and money laundering) led to the invasion of Panama by U.S. troops in December (see *Panama,* below).

At a two-day summit in Ica, Peru, in October, leaders of the Group of Eight, which included Argentina, Brazil, Colombia, Mexico, Peru, Uruguay, Venezuela, and, until 1988, Panama, agreed to further reduce trade barriers by 1992 in an effort to build a regional common market. No major initiatives were forthcoming from the Latin American Integration Association (LAIA; Argentina, Bolivia, Brazil, Chile, Colombia, Ecuador, Mexico, Paraguay, Peru, Uruguay, Venezuela) or the Andean Pact (Bolivia, Colombia, Ecuador, Peru, Venezuela), but members appeared committed to the central objective of increasing intraregional trade. The most impressive example of the integration process remained the bilateral program of Argentina and Brazil. Initially in Brazil's favour, the bilateral trade balance rebounded to Argentina's advantage in 1989. During the first eight months of the year, Argentina had a surplus on its Brazil trade of $225 million, compared with annual surpluses in Brazil's favour of around $200 million in previous years.

In the Caribbean the 13-member Caricom grouping agreed at its annual summit, held in Grenada in July, to establish a regional capital market, eventually leading to a unified exchange rate, as part of intensified efforts to create a common market by 1993. Caricom was approached by Lieut. Gen. Prosper Avril of Haiti concerning the possibility of membership for his country, but this was initially refused pending evidence of political improvements. Worries concerning future prospects for Caricom exports to the European Communities (EC) after 1992 were heightened in late 1989 by the momentous political changes in Eastern Europe. Caribbean officials meeting in Barbados during November feared that the EC might refocus its trading activity, to the detriment of the Africa-Caribbean-Pacific group.   (SUSAN CUNNINGHAM)

ANTIGUA AND BARBUDA

A constitutional monarchy and member of the Commonwealth, Antigua and Barbuda comprises the islands of Antigua, Barbuda, and Redonda in the eastern Caribbean Sea. Area: 442 sq km (171 sq mi). Pop. (1989 est.): 78,400. Cap.: Saint John's. Monetary unit: Eastern Caribbean dollar, with (Oct. 2, 1989) a par value of EC$2.70 to U.S. $1 (free rate of EC$4.37 = £1 sterling). Queen, Elizabeth II; governor-general in 1989, Sir Wilfred E. Jacobs; prime minister, Vere Cornwall Bird.

In a general election held on March 9, 1989, the governing Antigua Labour Party (ALP) was returned to power, winning 15 of the 16 Antigua seats. The opposition United National Democratic Party (UNDP) won one seat, and the lone Barbuda seat went to the Barbuda People's Movement. The defeated UNDP candidates in seven constituencies filed election petitions on the grounds of irregularities in the conduct of the poll; when the first of the petitions was upheld in the High Court, new elections were called. The UNDP boycotted them, however, and the ALP was returned unopposed in all seven seats.

Real gross domestic product was expected to increase more slowly in 1989 than in 1988, when a growth rate of 6.5% was recorded. Finance Minister John St. Luce reported in his 1989 budget in March that the external debt had increased slightly to $250 million, with EC$54 million earmarked for debt servicing, compared with total recurrent expenditure of EC$264 million.

Although Antigua and Barbuda were not in the direct path of Hurricane Hugo, the September storm caused some $37 million in damage.   (ROD PRINCE)

This article updates the *Macropædia* article The WEST INDIES: *Antigua and Barbuda.*

ARGENTINA

The federal republic of Argentina occupies the eastern section of the Southern Cone of South America, along the Atlantic Ocean. Area: 2,780,092 sq km (1,073,399 sq mi). Pop. (1989 est.): 32,425,000. Cap.: Buenos Aires. Monetary unit: austral, with (Oct. 2, 1989) an official rate of 653 australes to U.S. $1 (1,056 australes = £1 sterling). Presidents in 1989, Raúl Alfonsín and, from July 8, Carlos Saúl Menem.

Domestic Affairs. The drama of political and economic events surrounding the May 14 presidential (and partial congressional) elections marked 1989 as one of the most turbulent years in Argentina's recent history. During the first four months of the year, the outgoing government led by Pres. Raúl Alfonsín of the Unión Cívica Radical (UCR) struggled through a series of crises. As the year began, Alfonsín managed to win support from major business leaders for an extension to midyear of the Primavera ("Spring") Plan, the price-restraint pact launched in August 1988. The plan had helped reduce inflation to well under 10% in the final quarter of 1988, and it was hoped that it would succeed in keeping inflation down and stabilizing the economy until after the elections, thus increasing the chances of the UCR presidential candidate, Eduardo Angeloz. None of this materialized, however, and the Peronists' (Partido Justicialista) candidate, Carlos Saúl Menem (*see* BIOGRAPHIES), won with 47% of the vote.

In late January Alfonsín had to deal with a damaging episode involving the invasion of the La Tablada barracks outside of Buenos Aires by a group of armed civilian guerrillas. The attack came less than two months after a military rebellion led by the nationalist-inspired Col. Mohamed Ali Seineldín, which sought, among other demands, amnesty for officers involved in human rights abuses, the appointment of a new army chief of staff, and better conditions. At La Tablada there was an efficient and bloody response by the military, but the incident put President Alfonsín under immense pressure. Shortly thereafter a five-year, $4 billion military investment program was put before Congress. This helped quell rumblings from the military until after the elections.

From February onward, efforts to keep the economy under control had little effect, and it became clear that the powerful Argentine Industrial Union (UIA) would withdraw support for holding down prices. The largely Peronist-controlled labour unions, however, were fairly restrained, part of a strategy aimed at demonstrating the movement's responsible approach. With inflation mounting and the exchange rate under pressure, Economy Minister Juan Sourrouille and his team resigned at the end of March.

He was replaced by Juan Carlos Pugliese, a veteran UCR politician, who launched a series of stopgap measures.

Within a few weeks of the election date, Angeloz appeared to be gaining ground, but Menem won a convincing victory, helped by strong support in the provinces, which command disproportionately large representation in the 600-member electoral college. In the Chamber of Deputies, where 127 of the 254 seats were contested, the Peronists increased their representation from 107 to 125 (they already controlled the Senate). After the UCR's defeat, the economic situation deteriorated further, and emergency measures enacted in late May by yet another economy minister, Jésus Rodríguez, provoked unrest and rioting in some areas. According to the constitution, the new president would take office on December 10, but such a long wait was untenable for Alfonsín without the cooperation of the Peronists. Alfonsín resigned at the end of June, and Menem was inaugurated on July 8. Since the new members of Congress would not take office until December, however, Menem was forced to enlist support from smaller parties, especially the Union of the Democratic Centre.

Having assembled his economic team with top-level support from Bunge y Born (BB), one of Argentina's leading corporations, and having made most of his Cabinet appointments known by mid-June, Menem lost no time in announcing a new economic stabilization plan. BB supplied the economy minister, Miguel Roig, and when Roig died less than a week after the plan was announced, he was replaced by another BB executive, Néstor Rapanelli. The strong business links helped secure support from industrial leaders for a fresh round of price restraint, to last 90 days, and similar undertakings on wages were obtained from the labour unions. A rapprochement with the U.K. was begun in July–August. Although the issue of sovereignty over the Falkland Islands/Islas Malvinas was left aside, foreign trade links were restored and a special meeting in Madrid in October reestablished diplomatic links at the consular level. The stabilization program, combined with positive developments with the U.K., helped Menem's cause in negotiating a fresh $1.4 billion standby loan with the International Monetary Fund (IMF). Despite some popular opposition, Menem signed a general pardon in October affecting most of the military involved in human rights abuses.

Although initially successful in stabilizing the economy and easing social tensions, Menem ran into increasing difficulties during the final quarter of 1989. Treasury chief Rodolfo Frigeri resigned in October, and the head of the central bank, Javier González Fraga, resigned in November. Modifications to the economic program were made in early December, but the situation continued to deteriorate,

Carlos Saúl Menem is congratulated by supporters after being elected president of Argentina. Menem, who evoked the style and memory of the late president Juan Perón, drew strong support from poor and working-class people and inspired hope for an improvement in Argentina's ailing economy.

and Rapanelli resigned in mid-December. He was replaced by Hernán González, a close adviser of Menem, who had been minister of social affairs.

The Economy. Following a year in which gross domestic product growth was negative (−3.1%) and annual inflation almost 388%, 1989 did not begin on a positive note. Consumer price rises were still below 10% per month but on an upward trend. Extension of the price restraint agreement with business in January and adjustments to the Primavera Plan announced in early February (including the introduction of a three-tier exchange rate system, more rapid depreciation of the austral, and withdrawal of central bank support for the free financial rate) failed to reverse the situation. Inflation began to accelerate in March, especially after the collapse of the Primavera Plan following the Alfonsín government's failure to agree on new targets for price and wage increases. The public sector deficit was rising sharply, and disbursement of loans under the World Bank's $1.2 billion structural adjustment program was suspended. International reserves, which had totaled about $3.5 billion at the end of 1988, were being rapidly depleted, even though the country's trade position was showing signs of improvement, and debt service payments to banks were not being met.

After the elections the economic crisis intensified, with inflation reaching 78.6% in May and 114.5% in June despite emergency measures in late May. The Menem administration's economic program included a 54% devaluation of the austral against the U.S. dollar and the imposition of a single fixed exchange rate, the introduction of new taxes and steep rises (200–900%) in public sector utility rates, and the reduction of tariffs to encourage both exports and imports. Legislation was issued declaring a state of emergency in the public sector, paving the way for public spending cuts and an expanded schedule of privatization. After rising to 196.6% in July, the inflation rate fell to 37.9% in August and under 10% per month in the September–November period. The World Bank agreed to restore some of the funds suspended earlier in the year, and commercial bank creditors held preliminary meetings with Argentina's finance team in October with a view to beginning negotiations on debt rescheduling.

However, the targets agreed with the IMF (growth of 5% after an expected negative rate of at least −5% in 1989; inflation not exceeding 15% per annum) were looking increasingly unrealistic by November. Problems were intensified by discontent among labour unions over the government's wage policy guidelines which limited raises to approximately 15% until early 1990, and in October the main union confederation split from the wage-restraint agreement. In November currency speculation gathered momentum, and there was a rash of strikes. A series of adjustments were announced December 10–12, including a 34.8% devaluation of the austral to 1,000 = $1, reintroduction of a two-tier exchange rate, hikes in domestic oil prices (59%) and public sector tariffs (averaging 40%), and immediate wage raises for public- and private-sector workers of $24–$30. Prices of most basic goods, which had been regulated by the government, were also freed, although business agreed to exercise restraint. This led to sharp increases in the prices of some goods in the second week of December.

On December 26 the austral lost 27% of its value against the dollar. Prices of consumer goods continued to rise rapidly, as much as 100% in a single day, and interest rates for the month of December reached 300%. A new economic policy was expected to be announced by the government early in 1990.   (SUSAN CUNNINGHAM)

BAHAMAS, THE

A constitutional monarchy and member of the Commonwealth, The Bahamas comprises an archipelago of about 700 islands in the North Atlantic Ocean just southeast of the United States. Area: 13,939 sq km (5,382 sq mi). Pop. (1989 est.): 249,000. Cap.: Nassau. Monetary unit: Bahamian dollar, with (Oct. 2, 1989) a par value of B$1 to U.S. $1 (free rate of B$1.62 = £1 sterling). Queen, Elizabeth II; governor-general in 1989, Sir Henry Taylor; prime minister, Sir Lynden O. Pindling.

Expectations of continued economic growth in 1989 were pinned principally on a satisfactory performance from the tourist industry, despite the loss of flights by Eastern Airlines from the United States. Figures for the first quarter showed a 5.3% increase in stopover arrivals, which had suffered a slight decline in 1988; cruise ship passenger arrivals rose by 7.9%. The state airline, Bahamasair, reported increased passenger loadings after Eastern's collapse and enlarged its fleet of aircraft to cope with the new traffic.

Following a pay increase to workers in the public sector in the last quarter of 1988, the government reported a budget deficit of B$22.2 million in the first quarter of 1989. Consequently, tax increases were expected. The balance of payments showed a smaller deficit on current account for the first quarter of 1989 than for the same quarter of 1988, despite a larger trade deficit. The external debt at the end of 1988 was B$91.4 million, compared with B$108.5 million a year earlier.

Allegations of failure by the government to cooperate fully with the U.S. authorities on measures to curb trafficking in drugs continued during the year, but a motion to "decertify" The Bahamas for U.S. aid was defeated in the U.S. Senate in May.   (ROD PRINCE)

This article updates the *Macropædia* article The WEST INDIES: *The Bahamas.*

BARBADOS

The constitutional monarchy of Barbados, a member of the Commonwealth, occupies the most easterly island in the southern Caribbean Sea. Area: 430 sq km (166 sq mi). Pop. (1989 est.): 255,000. Cap.: Bridgetown. Monetary unit: Barbados dollar, with (Oct. 2, 1989) a par value of BDS$2.01 to U.S. $1 (free rate of BDS$3.25 = £1 sterling). Queen, Elizabeth II; governor-general in 1989, Sir Hugh Springer; prime minister, Erskine Sandiford.

The two-party pattern of Barbadian politics was broken in February 1989 when the former finance minister, Richard Haynes, resigned from the governing Democratic Labour Party (DLP) to form the National Democratic Party. He was joined by three other DLP members of Parliament and was appointed opposition leader in the national legislature, displacing Henry Forde of the Barbados Labour Party. The launching of the new party followed disagreements between Haynes and Prime Minister Erskine Sandiford over taxation policy and other aspects of economic management.

Economic growth in 1989 was expected to be about 2.5%, as compared with 3.5% in 1988, with tourism and construction again providing the main impetus. Stopover arrivals increased 7% in the first five months of 1989 compared with the corresponding period of 1988, and a new record of nearly 500,000 was expected for the entire year. However, rowdy behaviour by some British tourists gave rise to criticism of the expansion program.

The government's efforts to reduce the fiscal deficit continued with the imposition of tax increases in the 1989–90 budget; the aim was to bring the overall deficit down

from 4.8% of gross domestic product to 4%. A record trade deficit of BDS$809.7 million was registered in 1988; for the first half of 1989 the deficit declined marginally from the corresponding 1988 half year, while net foreign reserves fell 18.5% to BDS$321.9 million.   (ROD PRINCE)

This article updates the *Macropædia* article The WEST INDIES: *Barbados*.

BELIZE

A constitutional monarchy and member of the Commonwealth, Belize is on the Caribbean coast of Central America. Area: 22,965 sq km (8,867 sq mi). Pop. (1989 est.): 185,000. Cap.: Belmopan. Monetary unit: Belize dollar, with (Oct. 2, 1989) a par value of BZ$2 to U.S. $1 (free rate of BZ$3.24 = £1 sterling). Queen, Elizabeth II; governor-general in 1989, Dame Minita Gordon; prime ministers, Manuel Esquivel and, from November 7, George Cadle Price.

In peaceful general elections held on Sept. 4, 1989, the People's United Party (PUP) defeated the ruling United Democratic Party (UDP) by winning 15 of 28 seats in the House of Representatives. The UDP was victorious (winning 6 out of 10 seats) in the city votes but lost in the districts and neighbouring towns, giving the total election victory to the PUP for another five years. George Cadle Price became the new prime minister.

At midyear, economic earnings increased. Sugar exports, Belize's largest agricultural earner, rose by 19.9%, bananas by 19.9%, citrus by 10.5%, and manufacturing by 40%. Tourism earnings also increased 34%.

The European Communities agreed to provide a grant of $3.2 million and a loan of $6.5 million for the construction of a 100-bed hospital in Belize City. The remaining $1 million needed for construction would be provided by the Belize government.

Meetings of the Belize-Guatemala joint commissions on border disputes were held in January, February, and June in efforts to draft a treaty. Areas that continued to provoke controversy were the corridor from Guatemala to international waters, the movement of people and goods to both countries, the location of joint economic development zones, and immigration.   (INES T. BAPTIST)

This article updates the *Macropædia* article CENTRAL AMERICA: *Belize*.

BOLIVIA

Bolivia is a landlocked republic in central South America. Area: 1,098,581 sq km (424,164 sq mi). Pop. (1989 est.): 7,193,000. Judicial cap., Sucre; administrative cap., La Paz. Monetary unit: boliviano, with (Oct. 2, 1989) an official rate of 2.85 bolivianos to U.S. $1 (4.61 bolivianos = £1 sterling). Presidents in 1989, Víctor Paz Estenssoro and, from August 6, Jaime Paz Zamora.

Following a peaceful campaign, voting for the nation's president, vice president, and both houses of Congress took place on May 7. All major parties contesting the election were united on the need for nonalignment as a foreign policy, for securing Bolivia an outlet to the sea, and on an economic policy based on the demands of the International Monetary Fund austerity program. In the election the winner was Gonzalo Sánchez de Lozada of the ruling Movimiento Nacionalista Revolucionario (MNR). Finishing second was Hugo Banzer Suárez of the Acción Democrática Nacionalista (ADN), and third was Jaime Paz Zamora of the Movimiento de la Izquierda Revolucionario (MIR). No candidate won a majority of the votes, and so under the constitution the choice of president was left to Congress. On August 2 Banzer announced that his ADN

A Bolivian woman casts her ballot in the country's national election. When no presidential candidate received a majority, the third-place party of Jaime Paz Zamora allied itself with the second-place party, enabling Paz Zamora's election by Congress.
AP/WIDE WORLD

party would form a government with the MIR and that he would withdraw in favour of Paz Zamora as president. His action gave the MIR a 97–50 majority in Congress.

On August 6 Paz Zamora took office as the country's third president since the return to democratic rule. Ossio Sanjines of the Christian Democrat Party, also in alliance with the ADN, became vice president. In the Cabinet the MIR held the Education and Labour portfolios, while Foreign Affairs, Defense, Finance, Transport, Mining, Agriculture, and Information were held by the ADN.

President Paz Zamora promised to maintain the free-market policies of his relative, former president Víctor Paz Estenssoro of the MNR; these had helped Bolivia escape from its extreme inflation and resume some economic growth. Paz Zamora also promised fiscal discipline, guarantees for dollar convertibility at a free exchange rate, and prices and interest rates determined by the market. The chief break with the past was the new president's emphasis on national production to provide the country's food and raw materials.

Paz Zamora promised continuing cooperation with the U.S. to help fight the cocaine trade. His incentive was a strong one. If progress was not made, U.S. government assistance to Bolivian drug administration personnel plus $100 million in aid per year would be at risk. European nations, including the U.K., channeled their contributions toward coca eradication through the UN Fund for Drug Abuse Control. The dilemma for Bolivia was that in just one of the country's three main producing areas, the Chaparé, 250,000 people depended on drug industry earnings for their livelihood. As of 1989 Bolivia supplied about a

quarter of the U.S. cocaine market and a somewhat larger proportion of Europe's, but only $200 million per year was reportedly repatriated by the drug trade.

Bolivia's tin production was expected to rise to 14,600 tons in 1989 from only 10,573 tons in 1988. Tin earnings in 1989 were expected to be the highest since the collapse in 1985 of the tin contract on the London Metal Exchange. The U.S. and Bolivian governments signed a $2 million accord under a U.S. trade and development program to survey and report on the mineral resources of the high plateau and western mountain ranges.

(MICHAEL WOOLLER)

BRAZIL

Brazil is a federal republic in eastern South America on the Atlantic Ocean. Area: 8,511,965 sq km (3,286,488 sq mi). Pop. (1989 est.): 147,404,000. Cap.: Brasília. Monetary unit: new cruzado, with (Oct. 2, 1989) a free rate of 3.79 new cruzados to U.S. $1 (6.13 new cruzados = £1 sterling). President in 1989, José Sarney.

Domestic Affairs. Events surrounding the first presidential election in 29 years dominated the political scene during 1989. The climate of uncertainty this engendered was not helped by difficulties arising from provisions contained in the country's new constitution, which had been finally approved on Oct. 5, 1988, and from the often unhelpful maneuverings of Congress. These factors contributed to an impasse over many aspects of economic policy as the outgoing government, led by Pres. José Sarney and Finance Minister Maílson da Nóbrega, became increasingly unable or unwilling to take effective action. A series of problems thus confronted the new administration headed by President-elect Fernando Collor de Mello. These included the control of inflation (which had risen to 54% in December) and the domestic debt (estimated at over $90 billion by the end of 1989), as well as difficulties over privatization (which Sarney had set in motion but suspended in October) and wages.

At the start of the year the favourite candidate for the presidency was Leonel Brízola of the Democratic Labour Party (PDT), although the populist former governor of Rio de Janeiro state attracted no more than a fifth of the votes in early polls. Support for his main rival, Workers' Party (PT) leader Luís Inácio da Silva ("Lula"), was at least several points behind, while that for Ulysses Guimarães, head of the largest single party, the Brazilian Democratic Movement Party (PMDB), lagged even farther. During March–April the polls revealed the ascendance of a new force in Brazilian politics—Fernando Collor de Mello, the youthful ex-governor of the northeastern state of Alagoas. Collor, whose political stance was essentially centrist but with a radical twist on certain issues such as the handling of the country's foreign debt, was backed by a new grouping, the National Reconstruction Party (PRN), which was formed in late March. Despite his relative inexperience and lack of a well-established party machine, Collor rose steadily in popularity and pulled well ahead of all other candidates, with support rising to about 32% in May and 40–45% by mid-June.

In the election, held on November 15, Collor finished first with 27% of the votes, and Lula narrowly defeated Brízola for second place. Because no candidate received a majority of the votes, a runoff between Collor and Lula was scheduled for December 17. Collor won the election with close to 43% of the vote, compared with approximately 38% for Lula, who did best in the large cities. The remaining ballots were disallowed or left blank.

The Economy. The stagnation of the economy that was evident in 1988, when real gross domestic product (GDP) declined by 0.3% (after modest growth of 2.9% in 1987), continued in 1989. Against a background of falling industrial output combined with mounting inflationary pressure, the authorities attempted to correct the position in mid-January by launching a new anti-inflation package—the Summer Plan (Plano Verão). This included large price increases (ranging from 15% for electricity, 20–30% for gasoline and fuel alcohol, 46% for milk, and 188% for telephone charges); a freeze on the prices of certain goods for a specified period; a 17% devaluation of the currency combined with the introduction of a new currency (the new cruzado) initially at a fixed exchange rate (roughly at parity with the U.S. dollar); and the elimination of indexing for inflation (raising wages to keep up with the increasing cost of living). Additional proposals were made to help streamline the public sector and reduce the operational deficit

Fernando Collor de Mello flashes the victory sign during his campaign for Brazil's presidency. Collor, whose campaign centred on Brazil's need for modernization and free-market growth, won the December election.

(around 4.5% of GDP at the end of 1988), including the dismissal of up to 90,000 civil servants.

The Summer Plan measures at first boosted the inflation rate, which had been almost 29% in December 1988 (with a year-end total figure of 933.6%). The rate for January 1989 was announced at over 70%. There was a sharp drop to 3.6% in February, but prices started to climb again, especially after April 18, when adjustments to the plan—including the return of indexation and regular small devaluations of the currency—were put into effect.

During the first five months of 1989, the abolition of wage indexation and the lack of a new wage policy contributed to mounting labour unrest. A two-day general strike was held in mid-March, and subsequently many unions continued to take individual action, prompting Sarney to announce restrictive measures. Although unrest was rather less marked in the second half of the year, widespread dissatisfaction continued over wages and working conditions as inflation, running in excess of 25% per month from June and pushed higher by record domestic interest rates and the burgeoning domestic debt, cut back real incomes.

The Sarney administration ran into fresh difficulties with international creditors during 1989. Having concluded refinancing deals in the second half of 1988 involving the International Monetary Fund, World Bank, and commercial creditors, Brazil was committed to achieving a series of economic targets for 1988 and 1989 in order to release loans and trade credits. Failure to meet 1988 targets in full resulted in some difficulties over loan disbursements early in the new year, but these were temporarily overcome. Problems intensified at midyear when it became clear that the government's economic policies were leading to an overrun on key indicators such as inflation and the public sector deficit (which was estimated to end the year at 6–7% of GDP rather than the 2% agreed on with the IMF), although Brazil had succeeded in raising the 1988 trade surplus to over $19 billion (from $11.2 billion in 1987). In these circumstances, creditors made it clear that disbursement of the final series of bank loans ($600 million) would be suspended, along with more than $2 billion of other loans pledged by the IMF, World Bank, and Japan, until a new accord was reached with the IMF. Later the banks indicated a willingness to keep available until January 1990 the $600 million of credits due in 1989.

(SUSAN CUNNINGHAM)

CHILE

The republic of Chile extends along the Pacific coast of the Southern Cone of South America. Area: 756,626 sq km (292,135 sq mi), not including Chile's Antarctic claim. Pop. (1989 est.): 12,961,000. Cap.: Santiago. Monetary unit: Chilean peso, with (Oct. 2, 1989) a free rate of 268.71 pesos to U.S. $1 (434.78 pesos = £1 sterling). President in 1989, Maj. Gen. Augusto Pinochet Ugarte.

The holding of presidential and congressional elections on December 14 marked a new stage in the country's transition to democracy. In October 1988 the people had rejected via a plebiscite the continuation of Maj. Gen. Augusto Pinochet Ugarte's military regime. As generally predicted by the preelection opinion polls, Patricio Aylwin Azócar, a 71-year-old Christian Democrat and leader of the 17-member opposition Coalition of Parties for Democracy, was elected president with 55.2% of the vote. The remainder was split between Hernán Büchi, the government's candidate and a former finance minister, who gained 29.4%,

Chile's Patricio Aylwin votes in the nation's constitutional reform referendum in July. Aylwin, a member of the opposition Christian Democratic Party and leader of a 17-party alliance, was the front-runner in the December presidential elections.
AFP PHOTO

and Juan Francisco Javier Errazuriz, a right-wing independent, who obtained 15.4%. Voting went smoothly with the exception of one incident, the assassination of a policeman at a polling station on the outskirts of Santiago. Both the government and the opposition condemned the killing.

Although Aylwin's coalition won 72 of the 120 seats in the Chamber of Deputies, it gained only 22 of the 48 seats in the Senate (including 9 seats for government-appointed senators and one for Pinochet himself). Given the strong presence in Congress of the Christian Democratic Party on the centre-left and the National Renovation Party on the right, the country's future political reforms would largely be negotiated between those two parties.

Important steps toward the country's transition to democracy had already been taken earlier in the year. Despite Pinochet's initial refusal, negotiations started in March between the government (including pro-government political parties) and the opposition on ways to render the presidential and congressional elections more democratic, facilitate future reform of the 1980 constitution, and reduce the continued influence of the armed forces on civilian life. Agreement between the parties having been reached in May, a referendum was held on July 30; it gave overwhelming support to the constitutional amendments: 85.7% of the vote in favour of them and only 8.2% against. The amendments, which fell short of the opposition demands, included revocation of the controversial Article Eight, which had banned Marxist parties. In addition, the first presidential term was reduced from eight to

four years; the presidential powers to exile opponents and dissolve Congress were removed; the number of elected senators was increased from 26 to 38, thus reducing the relative importance of the nonelected senators; and civilian and military representatives were given equal parity on the National Security Council, a body empowered to overrule executive and legislative decisions on matters involving national security. Also, it would become easier for future amendments to the constitution to be adopted; they could be approved by a two-thirds vote in each of the two legislative chambers.

During the year, the regime worked on the few final pieces of legislation that would prevent any future civilian government from undoing what it had achieved in 16 years of government. In April the military junta approved a law defining 60 electoral districts, each of which would be eligible to elect two deputies. They also confirmed the system requiring at least 66.7% of the vote in order to elect both deputies in a given district. As the results of the congressional elections showed, this rule virtually eliminated the possibility that the candidates of minority parties could be elected. Only two left-wingers and one independent were elected deputies; no members of the Communist Party were elected.

In December the law that made the central bank an autonomous institution went into effect. The bank thus became wholly responsible for financial and exchange rate policies. By assuming the right to appoint the first five directors of the bank, Pinochet ensured that the current guiding economic principles would remain unchanged for years after he left office. In December, however, Pinochet agreed, despite strong initial objections, to appoint to the board two technocrats recommended by the opposition, as well as a consensus candidate as the director.

With the nomination of 9 judges out of 10 to the Supreme Court, Pinochet also secured a strong conservative element in the judicial system. Some of the former judges were enticed to retire with substantial benefits. Despite the opposition's threat that it would not recognize the privatizations undertaken after the October 1988 plebiscite, the government accelerated the pace at which state-owned companies were transferred to the private sector. Some of the new total or partial privatizations included the national airline, a lithium mining company, and the state insurance institute.

Although the political system created by Pinochet might be eroded after he stepped down in March 1990, the economic model that he crafted seemed likely to survive much longer. Aylwin campaigned on a platform of political and social change, with pledges to assist those who had been excluded from the benefits of the regime's free-market economy. He appeased the business community with promises of continued support for the export sector, which had been the country's main engine of growth during most of the 1980s, and for the further integration of Chile into the world economy with the assistance of foreign investment.

After increasing 7.4% in 1988, the gross domestic product expanded by a further 8.5% in 1989 as a result of higher prices for the country's exports and the initiation of a number of large export-oriented investment projects. Reflecting this increased activity, imports also rose, leading to a deterioration in the current account surplus. Also, inflation rekindled to an annual rate of about 18% after slowing to 12.7% in 1988. Under a highly successful debt-conversion program, the country's total external debt was reduced to $16.7 billion in 1989 from $20.4 billion in 1988.   (ALEXANDER JOHNS CAMPBELL)

COLOMBIA

A republic in northwestern South America, Colombia has coastlines on the Caribbean Sea and the Pacific Ocean. Area: 1,141,748 sq km (440,831 sq mi). Pop. (1989 est.): 32,317,000. Cap.: Bogotá. Monetary unit: Colombian peso, with (Oct. 2, 1989) a free rate of 406.29 pesos to U.S. $1 (657.38 pesos = £1 sterling). President in 1989, Virgilio Barco Vargas.

National security continued to dominate events in 1989. Following the government's increased crackdown on the activities of local drug traffickers, the drug dealers viciously retaliated with a series of killings, touching the nation's nerve with the assassination on August 18 of Luis Carlos Galán, the ruling party's presidential hopeful in the 1990 election. A state of emergency was declared, and the order to seize those assets believed to have been purchased with drug money was backed by the reinstatement of a suspended extradition treaty with the U.S. The drug dealers quickly responded with further killings and bombings in Bogotá and the other two largest cities, Medellín and Cali, the seats of the country's two drug cartels. They also promised to take the lives of 10 judges for every drug trafficker extradited. Thousands of people were arrested, but most of the drug barons wanted in the U.S. eluded capture. One, José Gonzalo Rodríguez Gacha, was killed in a police shoot-out December 15.

The U.S. assisted the Colombian government with military hardware, trained personnel, and $65 million. It also provided a $2.5 million package for the judiciary, which was paralyzed by the government's inability to protect the judges. Following the murder of Carlos Ernesto Valencia, an appeals court judge who dared to uphold an arrest warrant for the leader of the Medellín cartel, the nation's 4,379 judges went on strike for a week. Violence continued throughout the year. The offices of a newspaper and three banks in Bogotá were bombed, and in the week of October 28–November 4, a magistrate, a congressman, a left-wing political leader, and six policemen were killed. The crash of a Colombian jet aircraft on November 27, in which 107 people died, was believed to have been the result of a bomb planted by drug traffickers. A truck bomb outside a police building in Bogotá on December 6 killed 35 people and wounded hundreds.

The National Liberation Army (ELN), a left-wing guerrilla organization, continued its attacks on the poorly defended economic targets in the oil- and gold-producing areas of Arauca and Magdalena. However, some progress was achieved with another guerrilla group, the April 19 Movement (M-19), and with some factions of the Colombian Revolutionary Armed Forces (FARC) and the Popular Liberation Army (EPL) following a peace offer by Colombian Pres. Virgilio Barco Vargas (*see* BIOGRAPHIES) in September 1988. A blow to the process was delivered early in the year by the withdrawal of the Patriotic Union (UP) from its mediatory role in the talks when its vice president, José Antequera, was killed on March 3; the assassination was widely believed to have been the work of the country's far-right death squads.

President Barco reshuffled his Cabinet in late July, replacing four ministers. The most significant new appointment was to the Ministry of Energy and Mines, where Margarita Mena, a seasoned technocrat, replaced Oscar Mejía, who had mishandled negotiations with the ELN. In September Justice Minister Mónica de Greiff resigned and moved to the U.S., fearing assassination by the drug dealers.

Economic growth slowed to an estimated 3.2% in 1989

Soldiers in Medellín, Colombia, check the belongings of pedestrians as part of the government security measures imposed in response to a series of drug-related bombings. When the government renewed its efforts to clamp down on the drug trade, Colombia's drug barons responded with a rash of threats and violence aimed at many businesses and government officials.

AFP PHOTO

from 3.7% in 1988. Consumer price increases of about 28% were high by historical standards. The need to increase expenditure in the violence-stricken areas put pressure on the fiscal deficit, and the guerrilla-induced losses on exports of oil, coal, and bananas led to a reduced trade surplus. Although the country finally succeeded in reaching an agreement with its international creditor banks for disbursement of a $1,650,000,000 voluntary loan in June, doubts remained about Colombia's ability to service its external debt in the future.

(ALEXANDER JOHNS CAMPBELL)

COSTA RICA

The Central American republic of Costa Rica has coastlines on the Caribbean Sea and the Pacific Ocean. Area: 51,100 sq km (19,730 sq mi). Pop. (1989 est.): 2,941,000. Cap.: San José. Monetary unit: Costa Rican colón, with (Oct. 2, 1989) a free rate of 82.45 colones to U.S. $1 (133.40 colones = £1 sterling). President in 1989, Oscar Arias Sánchez.

During 1989 both main political parties faced allegations that their 1986 campaigns had been financed by drug money. The claims were the result of a National Legislature Narcotics Investigation Commission inquiry into Costa Rica's role in cocaine transshipment between Colombia and the U.S. in the mid-1980s. Incumbent Pres. Oscar Arias Sánchez of the National Liberation Party (PLN) and his opponent, Rafael Angel Calderón Fournier of the Social Christian Unity Party (the party's candidate for the 1990 presidential election), denied the charges. The PLN candidate for 1990 was Carlos Manuel Castillo.

Arias' concentration on foreign affairs again brought criticism that he was not attending to domestic matters. In addition to attending the August summit of Central American presidents in Tela, Honduras, he met both sides in the Nicaraguan conflict and offered to mediate between the new Salvadoran government and that nation's guerrillas.

Despite record inflation of 25.3% in 1988, the government's adherence to the terms of the 1985 World Bank structural adjustment loan was seen as a success. Inflation was expected to be halved in 1989. (BEN BOX)

This article updates the *Macropædia* article CENTRAL AMERICA: *Costa Rica.*

CUBA

The socialist republic of Cuba comprises the island of Cuba and several thousand smaller islands and cays in the Caribbean Sea. Area: 110,861 sq km (42,804 sq mi). Pop. (1989 est.): 10,540,000. Cap.: Havana. Monetary unit: Cuban peso, with (Oct. 2, 1989) a free rate of 0.76 peso to U.S. $1 (1.23 pesos = £1 sterling). President of the Councils of State and Ministers in 1989, Fidel Castro Ruz.

Cuba enjoyed political stability and made limited economic progress in 1989. Elections in 169 municipal assemblies took place from April 30 to May 7, with 7.1 million people voting. A total of 14,246 delegates were elected, of whom 6,544 were reelected. A second round was required in 431 electoral districts, where no candidate obtained the necessary 50% of the vote in the first. Relations with Latin-American countries continued to improve, as witnessed by Pres. Fidel Castro Ruz's February visit to Caracas, Venezuela, for the inauguration of Pres. Carlos Andrés Pérez. Diplomatic relations were also established with the European Communities. In keeping with agreements signed on Dec. 22, 1988, for the independence of Namibia and the withdrawal of an estimated 50,000 Cuban troops from Angola by July 1, 1991, a total of 1,200 Cuban troops left Angola during 1989.

The Castro government was gravely embarrassed by a drug trafficking and embezzlement scandal that came to light in June. Gen. Arnaldo Ochoa Sánchez (*see* OBITUARIES), one of the top five army commanders, was arrested together with 13 other officers, including nine from the Interior Ministry. Ochoa, a 57-year-old former head of military missions in Ethiopia, Angola, and Nicaragua, was a member of the Central Committee of the Communist Party and had been a close confidante of Castro for more than ten years. Another officer, Col. Antonio de la Guardia Font, was head of the Interior Ministry department that coordinated undercover operations to circumvent the U.S. economic blockade. Ochoa, de la Guardia, and five other officers were accused of conspiring with Colombia's Medellín drug cartel to transport six tons of cocaine to the U.S. in exchange for $3.4 million. Their trial was held from June 30 to July 4, and more than 20 hours of the

"Welcome Comrade Mikhail Gorbachev" reads a sign made in preparation for the Soviet leader's visit to Cuba. Gorbachev was warmly welcomed upon his arrival in Havana, where he and Cuban Pres. Fidel Castro signed a 25-year treaty of friendship and cooperation.
LARRY REIDER—SIPA

proceedings were televised. Ochoa, de la Guardia, and two other officers were executed on July 13, and the others were given long prison sentences.

An anticorruption drive carried out in connection with the trial forced the interior minister, Gen. José Abrantes Fernández, to resign on June 29. He was placed under arrest in July with other officials of the Interior Ministry, including the heads of customs and immigration. A former transport minister, Diocles Torralba González, was sent to jail for 20 years. The head of the Interior Ministry finance department, Col. Rafael Alvares Cueto, committed suicide on August 6.

Soviet leader Mikhail Gorbachev visited Havana from April 2 to 5. No pressure was put on Cuba to pursue *perestroika* (restructuring) and *glasnost* (openness), but a 25-year treaty of friendship and cooperation was signed between the two countries. In a speech to the National Assembly on April 4, Gorbachev emphasized the need for greater efficiency and quality in Cuban economic performance and the need for an element of competition in bilateral trade. In December President Castro reaffirmed in a speech his determination to resist the reforms sweeping Eastern Europe. He also banned two Soviet publications advocating reforms: *Sputnik* and *Moscow News*.

Relations with the U.S. continued to be strained. President Castro stated in July that the administration of Pres. George Bush was more threatening and insolent than that of his predecessor, Pres. Ronald Reagan. Informal contacts to establish cooperation in combating drug smuggling had begun early in 1988 but ceased in July 1989.

Good weather following a four-year drought was the main factor in attaining economic growth of 2.3% in 1988, compared with a decline of 3.2% in 1987. The 1988–89 sugar crop was estimated at eight million tons, and non-sugar agriculture recovered. Industrial output grew by 2.7% and labour productivity by 0.5%. Total exports increased by 2.2% to $5,401,000,000, and the overall trade deficit was reduced from $2,210,000,000 in 1987 to $2,061,000,000 in 1988. Convertible currency exports grew by 7.6% to $1,049,000,000, of which oil reexports represented $296 million. Growth of 2% was expected in 1989, with a larger sugar crop and increased farm and nickel production.

Cuba's convertible foreign currency debt rose to $6,450,-000,000 in December 1988 from $6,055,000,000 in December 1987. Because servicing of medium- and long-term debt was suspended in July 1986, creditors were reluctant to proceed with rescheduling negotiations unless some arrears were paid off. Cuba's debt to the U.S.S.R. and other member countries of the Council of Mutual Economic Assistance (Comecon) was not known but was estimated at between $9 billion and $34 billion.

Because of insufficient funding for infrastructure development, progress was slower than expected on a program designed to increase tourism to 350,000 visitors by 1992. Nonetheless, a total of 225,018 tourists visited Cuba in 1988, compared with 195,143 in 1987; income rose by 20.7% to $131 million. Tourists from Western Europe comprised 52.2% of all visitors, followed by Latin America with 23.1% and Canada with 20.1%. During the year, hotel capacity was expanded to 3,145 rooms at Varadero, the main beach resort.　　　　　　　　　　(ROBIN CHAPMAN)

This article updates the *Macropædia* article The WEST INDIES: *Cuba*.

DOMINICA

An island republic within the Commonwealth, Dominica is in the eastern Caribbean Sea. Area: 750 sq km (290 sq mi). Pop. (1989 est.): 82,800. Cap.: Roseau. Monetary unit: Eastern Caribbean dollar, with (Oct. 2, 1989) a par value of EC$2.70 to U.S. $1 (free rate of EC$4.37 = £1 sterling). President in 1989, Clarence Augustus Seignoret; prime minister, Eugenia Charles.

A further improvement in government finances was reported in 1989, with a current account surplus of EC$22.6 million expected for the 1989–90 fiscal year. The annual budget included a new round of concessions on income and consumption taxes. Economic growth, which reached 5.6% in 1988, as compared with a forecast of 4%, was expected to continue in 1989, stimulated by a buoyant construction sector. However, as a result of heavy rainfall and widespread destruction by Hurricane Hugo in September, banana production was expected to decline sharply from the more than 70,000 tons in 1988. Banana export earnings in 1988 were EC$103.3 million, 70% of total exports.

The pace of economic development reduced the unemployment level by May 1989 to below 10%, compared with

18% in 1981; labour shortages were reported in agriculture and construction. The increase in consumer prices for 1988 was only 1.7%, compared with 5.3% in 1987.

Work continued on infrastructural projects, including road improvements and development of a hydroelectric plant. The tourist business, although small, experienced a 16% increase in stopover arrivals in 1988 and a modest increase in hotel capacity in 1989. (ROD PRINCE)

This article updates the *Macropædia* article The WEST INDIES: *Dominica.*

DOMINICAN REPUBLIC

The Dominican Republic covers the eastern two-thirds of the Caribbean island of Hispaniola, which it shares with Haiti. Area: 48,443 sq km (18,704 sq mi). Pop. (1989 est.): 7,012,000. Cap.: Santo Domingo. Monetary unit: Dominican peso, with (Oct. 2, 1989) a free rate of 6.41 pesos to U.S. $1 (10.37 pesos = £1 sterling). President in 1989, Joaquín Balaguer.

The Dominican Republic experienced political and economic difficulties in 1989. Pres. Joaquín Balaguer became increasingly unpopular for his failure to deal with accelerating inflation and a deepening public utilities crisis, with electricity and water shortages. In August he made several Cabinet changes designed to improve the image of his administration before the presidential and legislative elections scheduled for May 1990. Guillermo Carram was appointed finance minister and Manuel Estrada Molina interior minister, replacing Roberto Martínez Villanueva and Juan Peralta Pérez, respectively. Rising popular discontent culminated in a widely supported general strike on June 19 and 20 to back demands for a reduction in prices for basic foods, a doubling of the minimum wage for public employees, and lower taxes.

Gross domestic product was expected to grow by 1% in 1989, the same as in 1988. Consumer prices rose by 55% in the year ended in August, fueled by spending on public works that resulted in a public-sector deficit estimated at 8% of GDP. External payments difficulties continued, and in September payment was suspended on the $777 million accumulated commercial debt. A policy program had not been arranged with the International Monetary Fund by December 1989. (ROBIN CHAPMAN)

This article updates the *Macropædia* article The WEST INDIES: *Dominican Republic.*

ECUADOR

The republic of Ecuador is in western South America, on the Pacific Ocean. Area: 269,178 sq km (103,930 sq mi), including the Galápagos Islands. Pop. (1989 est.): 10,490,000. Cap.: Quito. Monetary unit: sucre, with (Oct. 2, 1989) a free market rate of 584.86 sucres to U.S. $1 (946.30 sucres = £1 sterling). President in 1989, Rodrigo Borja Cevallos.

In 1989 the government concentrated on consolidating the progress made in stabilizing the economy, the main aim being to lower inflation. A tight monetary policy and fiscal adjustments succeeded in reducing the underlying rate of inflation, although the cost-of-living index remained heavily weighted toward basic foodstuffs, the prices of which fluctuated widely during the year. A shortage of rice early in the year, caused by lack of credit to planters during the previous season and an inefficient and corrupt importing system, drove up inflation to an annual rate of nearly 100%. The ensuing scandal caused the resignation of the minister of agriculture and several other officials as Pres. Rodrigo Borja Cevallos promised to punish all those involved.

Despite political opposition, the government approached the International Monetary Fund and other foreign creditors for support for its economic policies. In September the IMF approved an 18-month 110 million Special Drawing Rights standby agreement, noting the progress made so far in reducing the budget deficit and reducing inflation to about 70%. A World Bank mission to Quito in October was expected to prepare a longer term strategy for structural adjustment and sustainable growth. Negotiations with commercial bank creditors took place intermittently during the year.

President Borja pledged solidarity with the government of Colombia in the war against drugs and deported an alleged racketeer to Colombia for trial and possible deportation to the U.S. It was widely feared that the drug barons were moving part of their operations to Ecuador, and it was noted that imports of chemicals were rising rapidly and that a plentiful supply of dollars was keeping the free exchange rate unusually stable. (SARAH CAMERON)

EL SALVADOR

The republic of El Salvador is situated on the Pacific coast of Central America. Area: 21,041 sq km (8,124 sq mi). Pop. (1989 est.): 5,138,000. Cap.: San Salvador. Monetary unit: Salvadoran colón, with (Oct. 2, 1989) a par value of 5 colones to U.S. $1 (free rate of 8.10 colones = £1 sterling). Presidents in 1989, José Napoleón Duarte and, from June 1, Alfredo Cristiani.

As the civil war in El Salvador entered its 10th year, presidential elections were held on March 19, 1989. Alfredo Cristiani of the right-wing Nationalist Republican Alliance (Arena) captured 54% of the vote. Fidel Chávez Mena (Christian Democratic Party) got 36%, while the National Conciliation Party came third and the Democratic Convergence, allied with leftist guerrilla forces, was fourth. Polling was held in an atmosphere of violence; at least 23 people died, including three journalists, two of them killed by the military. The rebels of the Farabundo Martí National Liberation Front (FMLN) mounted attacks in some 20 towns. With many municipalities not even holding polls, the abstention rate was about 50%.

The outcome reflected the failure of Pres. José Napoleón

El Salvador's outgoing president, José Napoleón Duarte (left), congratulates newly elected Pres. Alfredo Cristiani at his inauguration. With Cristiani's election, the far-right Arena solidified its grasp on power in the war-torn country.

Duarte's Christian Democratic government to bring peace, stabilize the economy, and end widespread corruption. It also underlined the inability of the United States to establish a popularly supported centre movement. After the elections the attorney general, Roberto García Alvarado, was murdered, and during an upsurge in violence after Cristiani's accession in June, José António Rodríguez Porth, the new minister of the presidency, was shot. Each killing was blamed by Arena on the FMLN, which had vowed to make the country ungovernable, but right-wing death squads were suspected of involvement in these and other atrocities.

Despite this high level of tension, a number of moves toward peace were initiated in 1989. Negotiations in February on an FMLN proposal to end the conflict foundered on the demand that the elections be postponed until September. President Duarte subsequently offered an extension until April, but this did not satisfy the FMLN. On taking office, Cristiani appointed an unsuccessful commission for dialogue, but he also proposed a restrictive new penal code that would crack down on all dissent and peaceful protests. He was one of five Central American presidents to sign an accord in Honduras in August calling for a political solution to the conflict. Despite antagonism from the extreme right of his own party and the military, in September Cristiani sent a delegation to Mexico City to discuss a new FMLN proposal that called for a cease-fire by November 15 and an end to hostilities by Jan. 31, 1990. Meetings between the two sides were held on October 16–18 in San José, Costa Rica, and more were scheduled to be held in Venezuela. Negotiations were broken off, however, after 10 people were killed in the bombing of a leftist labour federation office on October 31.

On November 11 the rebels launched the strongest offensive of the civil war. For the first time, extensive fighting took place in San Salvador, where it spread to affluent neighbourhoods. On November 16 six Jesuit priests, their cook, and her daughter were tortured and murdered in a predawn raid on their quarters at José Simeón Cañas University of Central America. It was asserted that a death squad was responsible, but the Army was also under suspicion. Although Cristiani denied any connection with the killings, international opinion turned against him. The U.S. continued to support Arena while demanding a full investigation. Meanwhile, the government intensified its crackdown on other religious groups. (*See* RELIGION: *Introduction.*) In December Cristiani soothed relations with neighbouring states at a regional summit, but the fighting continued.

Before the rebel offensive, tough austerity measures were instituted to revive the economy. These included lifting price controls, raising public service tariffs, freeing exchange rates, and raising interest rates. The conservative business community approved the return to private ownership of land appropriated under land reform and the end of state control of the coffee trade.   (BEN BOX)

This article updates the *Macropædia* article CENTRAL AMERICA: *El Salvador.*

GRENADA

A constitutional monarchy within the Commonwealth, Grenada (with its dependency, the Southern Grenadines) is in the eastern Caribbean Sea. Area: 345 sq km (133 sq mi). Pop. (1989 est.): 96,600. Cap.: Saint George's. Monetary unit: Eastern Caribbean dollar, with (Oct. 2, 1989) a par value of EC$2.70 to U.S. $1 (free rate of EC$4.37 = £1 sterling). Queen, Elizabeth II; governor-general in 1989, Sir Paul Scoon; prime ministers, Herbert A. Blaize to December 19 and, from December 20, Ben Jones.

Tensions within the governing New National Party (NNP) led to an open break in July 1989, when Prime Minister Herbert Blaize (*see* OBITUARIES) dismissed the minister of communications and works, Keith Mitchell, who had defeated Blaize for the party leadership at the NNP annual convention in January. A junior minister was also dismissed, and two Mitchell supporters resigned from the government, reducing the prime minister's parliamentary strength to only 6 of the 15 members. In August Blaize terminated Parliament two days before a scheduled sitting at which it was expected that motions of no confidence in the government would be debated. Blaize, who had been in ill health for some time, died on December 19. The following day the governor-general, Sir Paul Scoon, named Deputy Prime Minister Ben Jones to succeed him until elections were held in 1990.

In his annual budget, presented in April, Blaize made changes in the application of the value-added tax, admitting that difficulty in collecting the tax had led to revenue shortfalls. He forecast a surplus on current account for the first time in a decade, with real growth in the gross domestic product of about 5%, similar to the 1988 result.

(ROD PRINCE)

This article updates the *Macropædia* article The WEST INDIES: *Grenada.*

GUATEMALA

A republic of Central America, Guatemala has coastlines on the Caribbean Sea and the Pacific Ocean. Area: 108,889 sq km (42,042 sq mi). Pop. (1989 est.): 8,935,000. Cap.: Guatemala City. Monetary unit: quetzal, with (Oct. 2, 1989) a regulated market rate of 2.78 quetzales to U.S. $1 (4.50 quetzales = £1 sterling). President in 1989, Marco Vinicio Cerezo Arévalo.

In a coup attempt on May 9, 1989, almost a year to the day since the last, 17 military officers and 9 civilians were implicated in a plot reportedly to remove the ministers of defense and interior from office. A number of candidates had already registered for the November 1990 elections. The ruling Christian Democrat candidate, Alfonso Cabrera Hidalgo, received death threats amid an increase in violence; estimates of the number of killings ranged from 40 to about 200 per month. Many accused the government of lack of concern as right-wing extremists carried out a campaign of terror against unionists, journalists, church activists, and human rights workers.

Meanwhile, the Guatemalan National Revolutionary Unity guerrillas, active in half the country's provinces, extended operations, having survived the armed forces' offensive at the end of 1988. Pres. Vinicio Cerezo attended the Central American summit in Tela, Honduras, where the presidents focused on the situation in Nicaragua and thus did not press for the simultaneous solution of all the region's civil wars.

A strike by teachers began on May 30, at one stage drawing in 50,000 public-sector workers; it ended inconclusively on August 17. Strain on the economy was caused by the high level of current and capital expenditure, as well as capital flight, a rising foreign debt, and loan delays. The quetzal was devalued from 2.70 to 2.78 to the U.S. dollar in August, partly in response to the fall in the price of coffee. Oil exports were hit by Amoco's decision to withdraw from Guatemala following guerrilla harassment; Exxon halted its exploration program in the protected El Ceibal national park after intense opposition from environmentalists and archaeologists.   (BEN BOX)

This article updates the *Macropædia* article CENTRAL AMERICA: *Guatemala.*

A street in Port-au-Prince near Haiti's presidential palace is blocked by burning tires set afire by civilians showing support for an attempted coup. In April the government was shaken by two coup attempts that were triggered by Pres. Prosper Avril's efforts to dismiss four senior officers who were implicated in drug trafficking.

LYN WARBERG—GAMMA/LIAISON

GUYANA

A republic and member of the Commonwealth, Guyana is situated in northeastern South America, on the Atlantic Ocean. Area: 215,000 sq km (83,000 sq mi). Pop. (1989 est.): 754,000. Cap.: Georgetown. Monetary unit: Guyana dollar, with (Oct. 2, 1989) a par value of G$30 to U.S. $1 (free rate of G$48.54 = £1 sterling). President in 1989, Desmond Hoyte; prime minister, Hamilton Green.

Following lengthy and complex negotiations, the International Monetary Fund (IMF) approved a monitoring agreement at the end of April 1989 involving a bridging loan to Guyana from an international support group to enable arrears to the Fund and other bodies to be paid off. The agreement followed a 70% devaluation of the Guyana dollar, announced in the annual budget on March 31. The budget also raised interest rates, among other measures aimed at satisfying the IMF as to the viability of the government's Economic Recovery Program.

It was expected that $181 million would be made available toward the end of 1989 from an IMF Enhanced Structural Adjustment Facility, in addition to $80 million from a standby facility. However, a prolonged strike in the sugar and bauxite industries led to serious production losses. Following a visit by IMF officials in August, it appeared that revisions to Fund conditions for the two facilities would be required, including the possibility of a further devaluation.

Production was badly affected by persistent breakdowns of the electric power supply throughout the year. However, the government succeeded in obtaining the rescheduling of $755 million of the $1,270,000,000 of external debt.

(ROD PRINCE)

This article updates the *Macropædia* article THE GUIANAS: *Guyana.*

HAITI

The republic of Haiti occupies the western one-third of the Caribbean island of Hispaniola, which it shares with the Dominican Republic. Area: 27,400 sq km (10,579 sq mi). Pop. (1989 est.): 5,520,000. Cap.: Port-au-Prince. Monetary unit: gourde, with (Oct. 2, 1989) a par value of 5 gourdes to U.S. $1 (free rate of 8.09 gourdes = £1 sterling). President in 1989, Lieut. Gen. Prosper Avril.

The government of Pres. Prosper Avril was shaken by two coup attempts in April 1989, which exposed the worst conflicts within the military since 1957. On April 2 members of the Leopards Corps, the elite antisubversion squad, seized Avril and attempted to deport him to the Dominican Republic. He was rescued by members of the Presidential Guard. On April 5 elements of the elite Jean-Jacques Dessalines battalion, based in Port-au-Prince, and members of the Leopards staged a revolt, which was finally suppressed on April 10. The unrest was triggered by Avril's decision on March 30 to dismiss four senior officers who were implicated in drug trafficking and to establish an antidrug unit in the Army. The Leopards Corps and Dessalines battalion were disbanded, and the Army was reduced from 7,500 to about 6,000. Military unrest continued throughout the year.

On March 13 Avril partially restored the 1987 constitution, although he omitted 37 articles that would restrict the powers of the president and the Army. In late September he announced that elections for a civilian president would be held in October and November 1990.

The U.S. strongly backed the Avril government, partially resuming food aid—up to $10 million—and requesting that $41 million be made available in the 1989–90 fiscal year. The International Monetary Fund provided $21 million, and the World Bank offered $44 million. The Haitian economy experienced its seventh year of stagnation in 1989.

(ROBIN CHAPMAN)

This article updates the *Macropædia* article THE WEST INDIES: *Haiti.*

HONDURAS

A republic of Central America, Honduras has coastlines on the Caribbean Sea and the Pacific Ocean. Area: 112,088 sq km (43,277 sq mi). Pop. (1989 est.): 4,530,000. Cap.: Tegucigalpa. Monetary unit: lempira, with (Oct. 2, 1989) a par value of 2 lempiras to U.S. $1 (free rate of 3.24 lempiras = £1 sterling). President in 1989, José Azcona Hoyo.

In elections held on Nov. 26, 1989, Rafael Leonardo Callejas of the National Party (PN) defeated the candidate of the ruling Liberal Party (PL), Carlos Roberto Flores Facussé. Also running were Enrique Aguilar Paz of the Innovation and National Unity Party (PINU) and Efraín Díaz Arri-

Michael Manley, leader of the People's National Party, greets supporters on Jamaica's general election day. Manley, who was Jamaica's prime minister during most of the 1970s, was expected to continue the policies of the outgoing prime minister, Edward Seaga.
ALAN WEINER—GAMMA/LIAISON

villaga, a Christian Democrat. The main issue dividing the PL and the PN was the devaluation of the lempira, historically fixed at 2 to the U.S. dollar. The PN favoured devaluation and economic austerity, both rejected by the government. Callejas was scheduled to take office on Jan. 17, 1990.

The World Bank and the International Monetary Fund both demanded modification of the exchange rate, higher taxation, and a restructured public sector as conditions for aid. Talks collapsed in March, prompting the U.S., which had been expected to provide $70 million in balance of payments support, to refuse disbursement. One month earlier the coordinating committee of commercial bank creditors had disbanded, leaving the banks to resolve their debts individually with the government. Also in March, the central bank formally ceased paying principal and interest on the $3.5 billion foreign debt.

Further strain was put on the budget by a series of strikes in the public sector, most of which were ended with wage increases. Honduras could not expect continued, unconditional financial support from the U.S. Under the agreement signed in Tela in August by the five Central American presidents, the Nicaraguan *contras,* whose presence in Honduras assured the supply of U.S. funds, were to be disbanded. Pres. José Azcona Hoyo insisted that the rebels leave the country.

The presence of U.S. military personnel in Honduras also caused renewed resentment, including attacks by left-wing guerrillas. Violence in general increased, with victims among both left- and right-wing sympathizers.   (BEN BOX)

This article updates the *Macropædia* article CENTRAL AMERICA: *Honduras.*

JAMAICA

A constitutional monarchy within the Commonwealth, Jamaica occupies an island in the Caribbean Sea. Area: 10,991 sq km (4,244 sq mi). Pop. (1989 est.): 2,376,000. Cap.: Kingston. Monetary unit: Jamaica dollar, with (Oct. 2, 1989) a free rate of J$5.48 to U.S. $1 (J$8.87 = £1 sterling). Queen, Elizabeth II; governor-general in 1989, Sir Florizel Glasspole; prime ministers, Edward Seaga and, from February 10, Michael Manley.

The general election of Feb. 9, 1989, brought the People's National Party led by Michael Manley to power, with 45 seats to 15 for the Jamaica Labour Party of Edward Seaga, the outgoing prime minister. The new administration maintained a high degree of continuity with the policies of the outgoing government, emphasizing the role of the private sector in economic development. Relations with the United States remained cordial.

A new International Monetary Fund program was inaugurated in July, providing $66 million up to March 1990. The program in operation since August 1988 had been suspended in March owing to certain performance targets not being met in the wake of Hurricane Gilbert. Strong demand for foreign exchange in August and early September led to a fall in the value of the Jamaica dollar from J$5.50 to J$5.92 = U.S. $1 on September 12. New credit restrictions were imposed in September to reduce demand.

Real growth in the gross domestic product, which was only 0.5% in 1988, was expected to accelerate to about 4% in 1989. Bauxite and alumina production was expected to increase about 20%, and the tourist industry was also performing strongly.   (ROD PRINCE)

This article updates the *Macropædia* article The WEST INDIES: *Jamaica.*

MEXICO

A federal republic of North America, Mexico has coastlines on the Pacific Ocean, the Gulf of Mexico, and the Caribbean Sea. Area: 1,958,201 sq km (756,066 sq mi). Pop. (1989 est.): 84,275,000. Cap.: Mexico City. Monetary unit: Mexican peso, with (Oct. 2, 1989) a free rate of 2,598 pesos to U.S. $1 (4,204 pesos = £1 sterling) and a controlled rate of 2,550 pesos to U.S. $1 (4,126 pesos = £1 sterling). President in 1989, Carlos Salinas de Gortari.

Mexico's new president began 1989 with a dramatic assertion of his authority when he sent troops to arrest Joaquín Hernández Galicia ("La Quina"), leader of the oil workers' union and the most powerful union boss in the country. Other top officials and business associates of La Quina were also detained. La Quina had crossed swords earlier with

Carlos Salinas de Gortari when, as secretary of planning and budget, Salinas had attempted to bring the spending of the state oil company, Pemex, under budgetary control. Salinas soon proved that this arrest was not an isolated event. Others included a prominent stock broker, accused of selling expired government bonds and not reporting the transactions to the authorities; the former head of the country's political police, who was charged with masterminding the death of a journalist; and the alleged head of the Sinaloa and Jalisco drug rings. Other union leaders were removed, and many unions accepted reorganization of their industries with relatively little reward.

In May the Party of the Democratic Revolution (PRD) was formally established, and the defeated presidential contender, Cuauhtémoc Cárdenas, became its head. The party grew out of the Democratic Current, led by Cárdenas and other defectors from the ruling Institutional Revolutionary Party (PRI), which later became part of the loose coalition that contested the 1988 presidential elections under the name National Democratic Front. Its influence was felt primarily in pushing the PRI toward reform.

President Salinas took action to clean up election malpractices in June when, for the first time, a PRI mayor, in Hermosillo, was charged with vote rigging and fraud. The cleanup was designed as a warning to the party before the July gubernatorial and mayoral elections in six states, which were hotly disputed between the PRI, the centre-left PRD, and the centre-right National Action Party (PAN). Three states in particular were watched carefully: Michoacán, the home state of Cárdenas, and the border states of Baja California Norte and Chihuahua. Soon after the elections, the PRI acknowledged defeat by the PAN in Baja California Norte, the first time it had lost a governorship

S. DORANTES—SYGMA

Joaquín Hernández Galicia, leader of Mexico's oil workers' union, looks out from behind prison bars after his arrest by Mexican troops. The arrest of Hernández was part of a massive sweep directed by Pres. Carlos Salinas de Gortari to clean up Mexico's unions.

since taking power in 1929, and the PAN also officially secured a majority in the state legislature. The PRD disputed the results in Michoacán, but while the PRI was prepared to concede in 6 of the 18 districts, control of the state legislature remained in PRI hands. The Baja California Norte result was generally perceived as a presidential decision to lose in a state where the victorious party was not a threat, whereas a defeat in Michoacán could have started mass defection from the PRI.

In August the PRI proposed doubling to 128 the number of senators, 4 for each state, with 3 to be elected by direct majority and one on the basis of proportional representation. It also recommended that a party obtaining 35% of the vote in a general election should be assured of 251 seats out of 500 in the Chamber of Deputies, but no party would be allowed to have more than a two-thirds majority. It proposed to strengthen the powers of the Federal Electoral Tribunal as an independent arbiter, but it did not meet opposition demands that the tribunal should be an autonomous body where a ruling party would not have an automatic majority. Initially the PAN and PRD both opposed the PRI proposals, but at the last minute the PAN aligned itself with the PRI to approve the recommendations by 364 votes to 70 in the Chamber of Deputies.

The PAN suffered a serious blow when its former presidential candidate, Manuel Clouthier, died in a car crash on his way to celebrate the PAN gubernatorial victory in Baja California Norte.

Mexico was the first country to seek special treatment from its bank creditors under the debt-reduction initiative of U.S. Treasury Secretary Nicholas Brady. A package was agreed to in principle in July which offered three alternatives. Banks could opt to swap their existing Mexican debt for new bonds, at a discount of 35%, which would pay market rate interest and be guaranteed by U.S. Treasury zero coupon bonds; they could exchange their debt for bonds issued at par but bearing a fixed, below-market rate of interest, also guaranteed; or they could provide new loans to Mexico equivalent to 25% of their existing exposure over a four-year period. Individual banks were slow to agree to the proposals, so that by year's end the package had not been formalized. According to the Mexican government, however, some 90% of the banks had opted for principal or interest rate reduction, while only about 10% were choosing to lend fresh money to Mexico.

Although debt reduction was primarily aimed at improving the external accounts, there were immediate benefits in the domestic economy. Greater confidence brought inflows of flight capital. The Bank of Mexico was able to lower internal interest rates by 20 percentage points in July, thus cutting domestic debt servicing, but the rates had increased again by 12 percentage points by year's end. Although the government forecast a GDP growth of only 1.5% for the year, third-quarter figures already showed a 4% expansion in comparison with the same period of 1988. While export volume increased by 7.5% annually, imports grew by 30%. The prices and incomes pact, which had proved so successful in reducing inflation, was renewed until June 1990. Inflation was down to 1% a month in July–September, but it picked up afterward. The year's rate was estimated at 20%, slightly higher than the government's forecast of 18% but a marked improvement over 50.7% in 1988. The government made further progress toward privatization and deregulation. Foreign investment was encouraged with new regulations allowing greater foreign participation in Mexican companies. President Salinas visited the U.S. and signed seven agreements, including one to increase trade between the two countries.   (SARAH CAMERON)

Violeta Barrios de Chamorro, Nicaragua's opposition candidate for the presidency, registers to vote in Managua. Chamorro, owner of *La Prensa,* Nicaragua's opposition newspaper, took a strong stand against the Sandinista government of Pres. Daniel Ortega.
BLEIBTREU—SYGMA

NICARAGUA

A republic of Central America, Nicaragua has coastlines on the Caribbean Sea and the Pacific Ocean. Area: 130,700 sq km (50,464 sq mi). Pop. (1989 est.): 3,745,000. Cap.: Managua. Monetary unit: new córdoba, with (Oct. 2, 1989) an official rate of 22,000 new córdobas to U.S. $1 (35,596 new córdobas = £1 sterling). President in 1989, Daniel Ortega Saavedra.

Positive signs of a resolution to the eight-year-old civil war between the U.S.-backed Nicaraguan Resistance, or *contras,* and the Sandinista government were seen in 1989. At a meeting of Central American presidents at Tesoro Beach, El Salvador, in February, an accord was reached to disband the *contras* in return for the advancement of presidential, legislative, and municipal elections in Nicaragua to Feb. 25, 1990; the promulgation of laws on press freedom and electoral reforms; and the release of some 1,900 prisoners who had been in the National Guard of former dictator Anastasio Somoza. These last were freed in March; the electoral reforms and press laws were introduced in April (although not without criticism).

The Tela (Honduras) agreement of August 7 specified the terms of the voluntary *contra* disbandment. An international commission would collect the rebels' weapons, monitor their return to Nicaragua or relocation to other countries, and verify the dismantling of their bases in Honduras and Costa Rica by December 5. While some *contras* sought asylum in the U.S. and others returned to join legitimate political parties in Nicaragua, many of the 10,000–12,000 fighters felt that the agreement gave them no guarantees. Foreseeing an end to U.S. support and the dismantling of the bases in Honduras, some expected to carry on fighting within Nicaragua. With the December 5 deadline unmet, the Central American summit in San José, Costa Rica, December 10–12, was largely devoted to an attempt to restart the peace process.

Pres. Daniel Ortega and Vice Pres. Sergio Ramírez were declared to be the Sandinista candidates for their present posts in the 1990 elections, while Violeta Barrios de Chamorro (*see* BIOGRAPHIES), owner of the opposition newspaper *La Prensa,* was chosen as the presidential candidate and Virgilio Godoy Reyes as her running mate for the 14-party coalition, the National Opposition Union (UNO). In August the government satisfied opposition

parties (about 20 in all) that sufficient guarantees would be given for free elections.

The *contra* war, years of U.S. trade sanctions, and the devastation of Hurricane Joan in late 1988 caused economic hardships, which greatly reduced the popularity of the Sandinistas and cast doubt on an assured victory in 1990. Living standards were lower than before the revolution, with Nicaragua reportedly becoming the poorest country in the Western Hemisphere. The córdoba was devalued constantly, causing large hikes in the cost of fuel and food, while attempts to reduce inflation (11,445% for the annual rate to August 1989) were never more than short-lived. The prospect of peace encouraged the government to plan the diversion of funds from defense into production, but substantial foreign assistance could not be expected until after the elections.   (BEN BOX)

This article updates the *Macropædia* article CENTRAL AMERICA: *Nicaragua.*

PANAMA

A republic of Central America, Panama lies between the Caribbean Sea and the Pacific Ocean on the Isthmus of Panama. Area: 77,802 sq km (29,762 sq mi). Pop. (1989 est.): 2,370,000. Cap.: Panama City. Monetary unit: balboa, at par with the U.S. dollar, with a free rate (Oct. 2, 1989) of 1.62 balboas to £1 sterling. Commander of the Panama Defense Forces (de facto ruler) to Dec. 20, 1989, Gen. Manuel Antonio Noriega Morena; presidents, Manuel Solís Palma, Francisco Rodríguez from September 1, and, from December 20, Guillermo Endara.

Events in 1989 reached a climax in December when U.S. troops invaded Panama and overthrew the country's de facto ruler, Gen. Manuel Antonio Noriega. Through most of the year Noriega had managed to cling to power despite increased domestic unrest and U.S. diplomatic and financial pressures. The expectations of a democratic solution early in the year were dashed with the nullification of the election results of May 7. It was generally believed that the opposition, led by Guillermo Endara, would have won.

The new U.S. administration of Pres. George Bush sustained the financial stranglehold on the Noriega regime that the administration of Ronald Reagan, Bush's predecessor, had begun. Initially, however, the Bush administration relied more on the diplomatic pressures that it could muster with other countries, particularly the Latin-American ones,

An armed guard stands watch over the bullet-scarred headquarters of the Panamanian Defense Forces after a coup attempt by middle-ranking officers. The dissidents were defeated by those loyal to Gen. Manuel Noriega.
AFP PHOTO

to oust Noriega. These, however, turned out to be as ineffectual as any of the unilateral efforts pursued by Reagan. A case in point was the attempt of the Organization of American States (OAS) to mediate in the crisis. After three months of negotiations with all the involved parties, the OAS was nowhere near a broadly based solution by September 1, the constitutional deadline for the transfer of government. The regime instead named its own transitional government led by Francisco Rodríguez and later replaced the Legislative Assembly of elected representatives with an Assembly of Popular Power Representatives. The holding of new elections was made conditional on the end of U.S. aggression and the release of Panamanian funds by the U.S. administration. Since March 1988 the U.S. government had been withholding payments due to the Panamanian government from the operation of the Panama Canal and the transisthmian oil pipeline, totaling about $15 million a month, and had frozen Panama's financial assets deposited in U.S. banks, amounting to about $50 million.

An attempted coup against General Noriega on October 3 failed, adding a further twist to the crisis. The uprising by middle-ranking officers led by Maj. Moisés Giroldi Vega was a bloody one, resulting in the deaths of 10 officers, including the leader himself. A purge of the Panama Defense Forces ensued, with many people being arrested or forced

to go into hiding or to leave the country. It was established that the Panama Canal-based U.S. armed forces had a limited involvement in the failed coup, and the country was declared in a state of war. The government issued a series of emergency measures that included the curtailment of civil rights.

The situation deteriorated on December 15, when the assembly named Noriega head of government and "maximum leader" and declared the U.S. and Panama to be in a state of war. Tension intensified with a series of incidents, including the killing of a U.S. marine by Panamanian soldiers. The invasion, called Operation Just Cause by the U.S. military, began shortly after midnight on December 20 and eventually involved some 14,000 troops, in addition to the 12,700 already stationed in Panama to guard the canal. At about the same time the invasion began, a government headed by Endara was sworn in by a Panamanian judge at the U.S. military base.

The fighting lasted several days as elements of the Defense Forces and the paramilitary "Dignity Battalions" continued to resist. For the first time, the canal was closed for about a day to prevent damage to ships. Large areas of Panama City were badly damaged in the fighting and the looting that took place in the absence of an effective police force. At year's end the U.S. put its own casualties at 23 and Panamanian deaths at over 500, about half of them civilians, although unofficial estimates were much higher. Although one of the chief objectives of the invasion was the capture of Noriega, who was wanted in the U.S. to stand trial on charges related to drug trafficking, he evaded his pursuers and took refuge in the Vatican nunciature. Negotiations between the U.S. and the Vatican were continuing at year's end.   (ALEXANDER JOHNS CAMPBELL)

This article updates the *Macropædia* article CENTRAL AMERICA: *Panama*.

PARAGUAY

Paraguay is a landlocked republic of central South America. Area: 406,752 sq km (157,048 sq mi). Pop. (1989 est.): 4,157,-000. Cap.: Asunción. Monetary unit: guaraní, with (Oct. 2, 1989) a free rate of 1,257 guaraníes to U.S. $1 (2,033 guaraníes = £1 sterling). Presidents in 1989, Gen. Alfredo Stroessner and, from February 3, Gen. Andrés Rodríguez.

On Feb. 3, 1989, Gen. Andrés Rodríguez led a military coup that overthrew the regime of Gen. Alfredo Stroessner, Paraguay's head of state since 1954. Scores of people, both military and civilian, were killed in the coup; Stroessner was allowed to go into exile.

General Rodríguez called for general elections on May 1. His participation and overwhelming victory in the elections were partly a reflection of the continued dominance of the Partido Colorado (PC) and partly a vote of thanks from the electorate for ridding the country of a regime that had long outlived its usefulness. As the presidential candidate of the PC, General Rodríguez (who had assumed the office of president after the coup) obtained 74% of the vote; his immediate rival, Domingo Laíno, the leader of the Partido Liberal Radical Auténtico, gained 20%. Opposition parties complained of some fraudulent practices in the elections but later admitted that these had not been systematic or widespread. Rodríguez was sworn in on May 15 and was to complete the five-year term begun by his predecessor on Aug. 15, 1988. In sharp contrast to the Stroessner era, the presidents of Argentina, Brazil, and Uruguay all attended the inauguration. Because the victorious party automatically got two-thirds of the seats in the two chambers, the PC secured 48 deputies and 24 senators.

The new government embarked on a program of economic liberalization. By unifying and freeing the exchange rate, it tackled the source of one of the worst economic distortions during the Stroessner regime. Following a 5.9% rise in 1988, economic growth remained buoyant in 1989 on the continued strength of agriculture. Inflation, however, started to accelerate with consumer price increases of about 40%.   (ALEXANDER JOHNS CAMPBELL)

PERU

The republic of Peru is located in western South America, on the Pacific Ocean. Area: 1,285,216 sq km (496,225 sq mi). Pop. (1989 est.): 21,792,000. Cap.: Lima. Monetary unit: inti, with (Oct. 5, 1989) an official rate of 4,179 intis to U.S. $1 (6,762 intis = £1 sterling) and a free market rate of 5,725 intis to U.S. $1 (9,263 intis = £1 sterling). President in 1989, Alan García Pérez; prime ministers, Armando Villanueva del Campo, Luis Alberto Sánchez from May 15, and, from September 30, Guillermo Larco Cox.

Municipal and regional elections in November 1989 and the expectation of general and presidential elections in March 1990 brought to prominence a new political group in Peru. Fredemo (the Democratic Front), a right-wing coalition comprising the Popular Action and Popular Christian parties and the Liberty Movement (a group headed by the novelist Mario Vargas Llosa), gained much early ground as Pres. Alan García's popularity slumped in the face of economic and social problems.

The campaigning of the main parties could not allay widespread fear that the Maoist guerrilla group, Sendero Luminoso (Shining Path), would disrupt any election. Known to have killed elected officials and government representatives and to have terrorized peasant communities in a large area of the Andean highlands, Sendero Luminoso initiated a series of "armed strikes" that stopped all work, transportation, and power distribution in the highland regions. This effectively cut off all supplies to Lima, which, together with other major cities, faced the periodic blowing up of power lines. In establishing control of the Upper Huallaga Valley, the main coca-growing and processing area of Peru, Sendero Luminoso greatly increased its finances by extracting "taxes" from the narcotics traders who exported coca paste to their laboratories outside the country. An estimated 15,000 people, including foreign-aid workers and tourists, had died or disappeared since Sendero Luminoso began operations in 1980.

In a backlash against the insurgency, a right-wing death squad, called Comando Rodrigo Franco (named after a victim of Sendero Luminoso) and allegedly linked to right-wing elements in the ruling APRA party and to military intelligence, had begun operating in 1988. It killed, among others, journalists critical of the government and labour union activists, including Saúl Cantoral, leader of the miners' federation. This assassination led to a one-day nationwide mining strike, one of a number of miners' strikes during the year. The perilous state of the government's finances also led to work stoppages in the health, education, and financial sectors and to the nonpayment of government contractors and suppliers. In addition, the military was short of funds and equipment. This, in addition to accusations of human rights abuses, seriously lowered morale. A planned coup at the end of 1988 was aborted after the U.S. ambassador said that any disruption of the constitution would not be supported. To ease tension, military and police wages were tripled, and a new fleet of helicopters was purchased from abroad.

President García found himself even more isolated as members of his own party urged him to take a more realistic approach to economic management and the question of the country's $15.8 billion foreign debt. García refused to modify his stance, causing the Inter-American Development Bank, the only multilateral institution to have maintained support for Peru, to declare the country ineligible for further lending after it failed to keep up with interest payments in March. In July Peru resumed payments to the bank. In December it was announced that some payments to the International Monetary Fund would be resumed. Earlier, the IMF had considered expelling Peru for failing to meet its obligations.

Two Cabinet reshuffles brought no major change in policies to tackle either the social or the economic difficulties. Inflation, which reached 48.6% for the month of April, was expected to hold to a monthly rate of 25–30% (in the 12 months to September 1989, inflation was 3,339.6%). Gross domestic product was expected to fall by 15% in the year, compared with an 8.9% decline in 1988; real wages were estimated to have declined 25% compared with 1988. However, domestic recession curtailed imports, and this, together with high international prices for mineral exports, caused reserves to rise. On the strength of this, García proposed a modest reactivation of the economy through wage increases and credit expansion.   (BEN BOX)

Members of the Maoist guerrilla group Sendero Luminoso (Shining Path) in Peru instruct recruits at a training site in the highland jungle. Having begun as an isolated movement in the Andes, Sendero Luminoso now was disrupting election campaigning in Peru's major coastal cities.

SAINT KITTS AND NEVIS

A constitutional monarchy and member of the Commonwealth, St. Kitts and Nevis comprises the islands of St. Kitts and Nevis in the eastern Caribbean Sea. Area: 269 sq km (104 sq mi). Pop. (1989 est.): 44,100. Cap.: Basseterre. Monetary unit: Eastern Caribbean dollar, with (Oct. 2, 1989) a par value of EC$2.70 to U.S. $1 (free rate of EC$4.37 = £1 sterling). Queen, Elizabeth II; governor-general in 1989, Sir Clement Arrindell; prime minister, Kennedy A. Simmonds.

Severe damage to housing, official and commercial property, agriculture, communications, and public utilities was caused when Hurricane Hugo struck the islands on Sept. 18, 1989. One person was killed, and an estimated 2,000 were made homeless. Before the hurricane, economic growth was expected to be similar to the 1988 figure of 4%, with tourism the leading sector. Agriculture, dominated by the sugar industry, continued to lag behind. The government's 1989 budget projected a slight current deficit. Reconstruction after the hurricane appeared certain to place considerable strain on the government's resources.

On March 21 the People's Action Movement (PAM) won a third term at a general election, winning 6 out of 11 seats in the House of Assembly with 54.7% of the St. Kitts vote. The Labour Party won two seats. Two of the three Nevis seats went to the Nevis Reformation Party and the other to the newly formed Concerned Citizens' Movement. The Labour leader, Lee Moore, failed to win his seat and resigned the leadership in favour of Denzil Douglas, a doctor. (ROD PRINCE)

This article updates the *Macropædia* article The WEST INDIES: *Saint Christopher and Nevis.*

SAINT LUCIA

A constitutional monarchy and member of the Commonwealth, St. Lucia is the second largest of the Windward Islands in the eastern Caribbean Sea. Area: 617 sq km (238 sq mi). Pop. (1989 est.): 150,000. Cap.: Castries. Monetary unit: Eastern Caribbean dollar, with (Oct. 2, 1989) a par value of EC$2.70 to U.S. $1 (free rate of EC$4.37 = £1 sterling). Queen, Elizabeth II; governor-general in 1989, Stanislaus A. James (acting); prime minister, John Compton.

Continued strong economic growth was forecast for 1989, similar to the 6% recorded in 1988. The main growth sectors were expected to be manufacturing, tourism, and construction, stimulated by a 58% increase in the government's capital expenditure program in the 1989–90 fiscal year. A surplus on current account of EC$40 million was forecast, despite a 14% increase in expenditure.

Some 1,900 new jobs were expected to be created in the manufacturing sector, following an increase of 900 jobs in 1988, when manufacturing exports set a record of EC$80 million. In the first half of 1989, banana exports were 61,114 tons, almost unchanged from the same period of 1988, but earnings fell from EC$93 million to EC$83 million because of the falling value of sterling against the EC dollar. Banana production in 1988 had reached a record 133,690 tons.

Development plans in 1989 included new passenger facilities at Hewanorra airport and improvements in the waterfront at Soufrière in the southwest. Extensive development continued in the Castries Harbour area, while a U.S. $35 million hotel and casino was to be constructed in the Rodney Bay area in the north. (ROD PRINCE)

This article updates the *Macropædia* article The WEST INDIES: *Saint Lucia.*

SAINT VINCENT AND THE GRENADINES

A constitutional monarchy within the Commonwealth, St. Vincent and the Grenadines comprises the islands of St. Vincent and the northern Grenadines in the eastern Caribbean Sea. Area: 389 sq km (150 sq mi). Pop. (1989 est.): 114,000. Cap.: Kingstown. Monetary unit: Eastern Caribbean dollar, with (Oct. 2, 1989) a par value of EC$2.70 to U.S. $1 (free rate of EC$4.37 = £1 sterling). Queen, Elizabeth II; governors-general in 1989, Henry Harvey Williams (acting) and, from September 20, David Jack; prime minister, James Fitz-Allen Mitchell.

A general election on May 16, 1989, returned Prime Minister James Mitchell to office for a second five-year term. His New Democratic Party (NDP) won all 15 parliamentary seats and obtained 66.2% of the vote, against 30.4% for the opposition St. Vincent Labour Party. In the outgoing Parliament, the NDP had held 10 out of 13 seats; two new constituencies had been created before the election.

Real growth of gross domestic product in 1989 was expected to be similar to the 1988 result of 3%. Growth in 1988 had been dampened by a poor performance from key sectors, including manufacturing, tourism, and nonbanana agriculture. Banana exports, however, amounted to 61,868 metric tons, against 34,033 in 1987, when production was reduced by storm damage. Unemployment, estimated at 40–45%, remained a severe problem.

In July a large fire in central Kingstown destroyed the offices of the commissioner of police and government immigration department, together with commercial property. Total damage was estimated at several million dollars. The fire started in the police barracks, which housed the fire brigade; the Chamber of Industry and Commerce called for urgent action to improve the efficiency of the fire service. (ROD PRINCE)

This article updates the *Macropædia* article The WEST INDIES: *Saint Vincent and the Grenadines.*

SURINAME

The republic of Suriname is in northeastern South America, on the Atlantic Ocean. Area: 163,820 sq km (63,251 sq mi), not including a 17,635-sq km area disputed with Guyana. Pop. (1989 est.): 405,000. Cap.: Paramaribo. Monetary unit: Suriname guilder, with (Oct. 2, 1989) a par value of 1.79 Suriname guilders to U.S. $1 (free rate of 2.89 Suriname guilders = £1 sterling). President in 1989, Ramsewak Shankar; prime minister, Henck Arron.

On June 8, 1989, Jaggernath Lachmon, the speaker of the National Assembly, and Ronnie Brunswijk, the head of the resistance movement, reached agreement on conditions for a truce. The Army would withdraw from the traditional regions of the Bush Negroes (descendants of runaway slaves), and Brunswijk's troops would police the area. On June 23 the government of Pres. Ramsewak Shankar formally approved the agreement, and a peace treaty was signed in Kourou (in French Guiana) on July 21. However, the Army, headed by Lieut. Col. Dési Bouterse, refused to accept the settlement.

The Kourou agreement was also opposed by many of the country's Indians, who feared that an arrangement between the Bush Negroes and the government threatened their own safety. On September 1 a large group of Indians captured a ferryboat and a small airplane, and two more ferryboats were captured on October 24. One person died in the September 1 action.

On June 7 the country was plunged into mourning when a Suriname Airways (SLM) plane crashed, killing 169 of the 182 persons on board. Among the casualties were 14

members of a Dutch soccer team, all of Suriname origin. The crash cost SLM one of its last two long-distance aircraft.   (KLAAS J. HOEKSEMA)

This article updates the *Macropædia* article The GUIANAS: *Suriname*.

TRINIDAD AND TOBAGO

A republic and member of the Commonwealth, Trinidad and Tobago consists of two islands in the Caribbean Sea off the coast of Venezuela. Area: 5,128 sq km (1,980 sq mi). Pop. (1989 est.): 1,285,000. Cap.: Port-of-Spain. Monetary unit: Trinidad and Tobago dollar, with (Oct. 2, 1989) a par value of TT$4.25 to U.S. $1 (free rate of TT$6.88 = £1 sterling). President in 1989, Noor Mohammad Hassanali; prime minister, A.N.R. Robinson.

Trinidad and Tobago's long economic recession showed signs of ending during 1989, with the first six months showing a decline in the gross domestic product of 3.2%, compared with a fall of 6.2% for the first half of 1988; a return to economic growth was expected in 1990. The 1989 budget reduced government expenditure, cutting civil service pay by 10%, and introduced a shift from direct to indirect taxation. This process was scheduled to continue with the introduction of a value-added tax in January 1990.

Aided by an increase in the price of oil, the nation recorded a trade surplus of TT$750.4 million in the first half of 1989, a 33.8% increase over the same period of 1988, while net foreign exchange reserves rose from TT$95 million to TT$418 million. The overall government deficit, at TT$45 million, was the lowest since 1977. However, unemployment increased slightly to 22.3%.

A strike for higher wages in the oil industry was resolved in mid-October after negotiations involving a team of government ministers. Production losses from the month-long dispute were considerable.

The group of former ministers expelled from the governing National Alliance for Reconstruction in 1988 formed a new party, the United National Congress, in late April. Lengthy discussions took place during the year on the implications for civil liberties of the increased police powers proposed in a bill to combat narcotics trafficking. Security measures were increased in September after shots were fired at the presidential car.   (ROD PRINCE)

This article updates the *Macropædia* article The WEST INDIES: *Trinidad and Tobago*.

URUGUAY

A republic of eastern South America, Uruguay lies on the Atlantic Ocean. Area: 176,215 sq km (68,037 sq mi). Pop. (1989 est.): 3,017,000. Cap.: Montevideo. Monetary unit: Uruguayan new peso, with (Oct. 2, 1989) a free rate of 687 new pesos to U.S. $1 (1,111 new pesos = £1 sterling). President in 1989, Julio María Sanguinetti Cairolo.

On Nov. 26, 1989, presidential and congressional elections were held, marking the end of Uruguay's transition to democracy, which had begun in March 1985. The result was a defeat for the ruling Colorado Party of Pres. Julio Sanguinetti. The National (Blanco) Party returned to power for the first time in 23 years with the victory of its presidential candidate, Sen. Luis Alberto Lacalle, and the largest bloc of seats in the legislature, though it lacked a working majority. (For tabulated results, see *Political Parties,* above.) The Colorados also lost the city government of Montevideo, which went to the left-wing Broad Front.

Although considerable animosity between the main po-

litical parties characterized the campaign, the choice of policies was limited. On April 16 the Sanguinetti administration scored a victory with the referendum on the amnesty law, passed in December 1986 to protect the military against prosecution for human rights violations and financial misconduct during 1973–85. The vote to uphold the law was reported as 55 to 42%. Complaints of police abuses forced Minister of the Interior Antonio Marchesano to resign in late July. His replacement, Francisco Forteza, was close to resignation a month later, following further charges of abuse, but the Senate failed to endorse the House of Representatives' vote of no confidence.

Beginning in late 1988, Uruguay—particularly the north and the northeast—suffered a prolonged drought, which affected not only agriculture but also hydroelectric power generation. Consequently, a series of power cuts took place in April–July. Economic management concentrated on controlling inflation, which was expected to remain at an annual rate above 75%. An environment of recession and labour unrest contributed to economic instability.

                              (ALEXANDER JOHNS CAMPBELL)

VENEZUELA

A republic of northern South America, Venezuela lies on the Caribbean Sea. Area: 912,050 sq km (352,144 sq mi). Pop. (1989 est.): 19,246,000. Cap.: Caracas. Monetary unit: bolívar, with (Oct. 2, 1989) a unified rate of 38.02 bolivares to U.S. $1 (61.52 bolivares = £1 sterling). Presidents in 1989, Jaime Lusinchi and, from February 2, Carlos Andrés Pérez.

In his New Year message, Pres. Jaime Lusinchi announced the suspension of principal repayments on $21.3 billion of commercial bank debt, previously rescheduled in 1986–87.

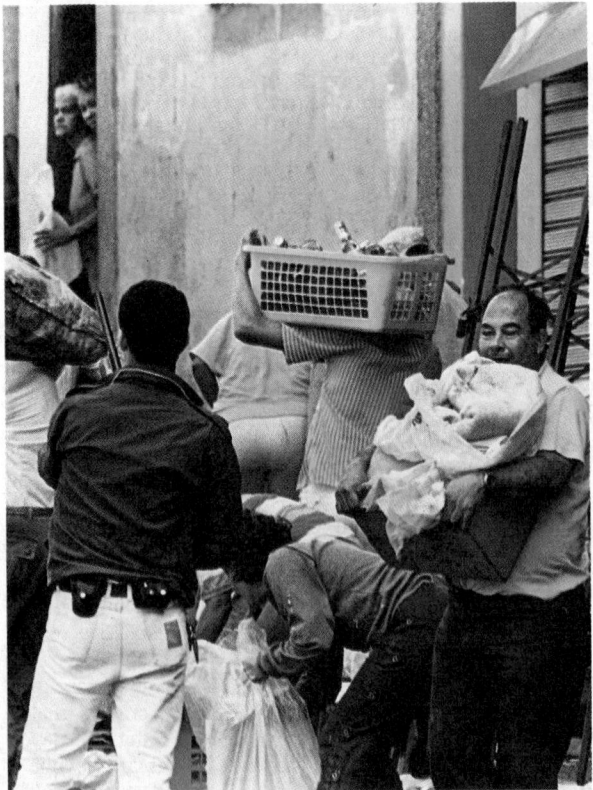

AFP PHOTO

Looters make off with all they can carry in downtown Caracas, where enraged mobs had raided many stores. Violence erupted throughout the nation after an austerity program initiated by Pres. Carlos Andrés Pérez drove up the prices of essential goods.

Low oil prices and rising interest rates had led to a foreign exchange shortage, but while these were contributory factors, the country's overvalued exchange rate, officially at 14.50 bolivares to U.S. $1, compared with the free rate of 38 bolivares to $1, led to a decline in exports, an increase in imports, and capital flight. There was a huge demand for cheap imports in 1988 in anticipation of a devaluation in the currency and a consequent surge in expensive short-term trade financing from banks and suppliers, which the country could ill afford. By January cash reserves at the central bank had been virtually eliminated, and the incoming administration faced a crisis.

Amid increasing uncertainty, Carlos Andrés Pérez (*see* BIOGRAPHIES) took office on February 2, becoming the first president to be sworn in for a second term. He named a Cabinet largely made up of academics and technocrats, with few of the old-guard Acción Democrática (AD) party activists. Two weeks later the president unveiled a bold economic program designed to reduce dependence on oil and pave the way for sustained economic growth. He announced the dismantling of the old exchange-rate and interest-rate systems and the introduction of a freely floating bolívar, the liberalization of controls on interest rates and prices, trade and tariff reform, and the opening up of the economy. The minimum wage was to be raised, and a package of direct subsidies and social welfare benefits was to cushion the effects on the poor.

However, the president's program brought with it massive price increases at a time when supermarket shelves were empty and before wage increases could be implemented. Bus fare price rises of 50% sparked protests on the streets that soon turned into nationwide riots against the government's policies. The authorities were ill-prepared to handle the violence and looting, which left hundreds dead and injured. A curfew was imposed, and constitutional rights were suspended as the armed forces moved in to restore order. During a week of disturbances, more than 300 businesses in Caracas were raided by looters.

The need to gain foreign financing to support the program became urgent. The International Monetary Fund provided a three-year $4.6 billion loan, and the World Bank and Inter-American Development Bank also began lending; the U.S. and Spain arranged short-term financing. Negotiations with commercial banks for new loans were speeded up but later stalled. It was not until October that a short-term loan was agreed upon and that negotiations for a long-term financing package were started.

Meanwhile, the domestic economy went into a tailspin as demand plummeted; gross domestic product was expected to decline by as much as 11%. Importers discovered that the goods they bought on credit in 1988 at the official exchange rate now had to be paid for at the new floating rate, increasing their costs by more than 150%. Those who had borrowed locally when interest rates were heavily subsidized at 12% now found themselves hard-pressed to meet payments with interest rates of about 35%. Discontent was reflected in the low voter turnout in state and local elections December 3 and the AD's loss of the governorships of several important industrial states.

Confidence was also eroded by an investigation into the allocation of $40 billion during the previous administration, which became known as the Recadi scandal after the state agency concerned. The attempted suicide by a former minister, the flight to the U.S. by former president Lusinchi's secretary and companion and by more than 100 local and foreign company executives, and the imprisonment of a prominent businessman for several months kept the case in the public eye.   (SARAH CAMERON)

Oceania

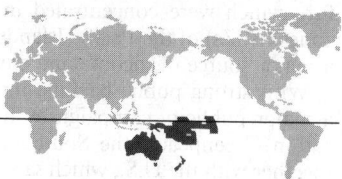

OCEANIAN AFFAIRS

Environmental issues dominated regional affairs in 1989, with particular concern over the implications of the greenhouse effect for small island states and the rapid expansion of gill-net fishing in the international waters of the Pacific.

Greenhouse Effect. Global warming, caused by the buildup of industrial gases in the atmosphere and consequent ozone depletion, would have serious implications for many Pacific Island states if projections of a rise of half a metre (1½ ft) or more in sea levels by the mid-21st century proved accurate. Such a rise would significantly reduce the land area of small, low-lying coral islands and would increase their vulnerability to tropical storms and cyclones. The reduced land area would be further threatened by accelerated coastal erosion, and there would be increasing salinization of the groundwater supplies. The future habitation of such islands could be assured only with engineering measures and financial assistance on a scale well beyond the resources of governments in the region. The options would be limited if current projections could be believed. For countries like the Marshall Islands, Kiribati, Tuvalu, and Tokelau, which had no high islands, forced migration involving their total populations (currently about 100,000 people in all) could not be ruled out.

The broad issues were considered by the 1989 meeting of the South Pacific Forum, held at Tarawa, Kiribati, in July. Australia announced a $A 6,250,000 research program to monitor climatic and sea-level changes throughout the region, and Australia and New Zealand made a commitment to the future resettlement of Pacific peoples whose home islands were rendered uninhabitable as a result of the greenhouse effect. At a subsequent meeting in Majuro, the host, Pres. Amata Kabua of the Marshall Islands, called on the industrial nations to reduce pollution.

Gill Netting. The rapid expansion of gill-net fishing (also called drift-net fishing) brought the small nations of Oceania into an alliance with both their larger neighbours and environmental groups. In 1988 there were some 40 vessels using gill nets in the North Pacific, but with stocks in that area depleted, activity in 1989 was concentrated in the South Pacific between latitudes 38° and 41°, where juvenile tuna are found in large migratory groups close to the surface. The "wall of death" gill nets, which could be up to 50 km (30 mi) or more in length and extend 15 m (9 ft) below the surface, have a mesh of fine monofilament nylon just large enough to catch the young tuna by the gills. The nets are all but invisible to marine creatures and thus kill large numbers of sea birds, dolphins, turtles, small whales, and unwanted fish species as well as tuna. The nets often break, and large sections remain adrift indefinitely, constituting a serious environmental hazard.

By the beginning of the 1989 season there were an estimated 130 vessels from Taiwan, 30 from Japan, and 2 from South Korea using gill nets in the Pacific area. The South Pacific Forum Fisheries Agency estimated that their combined 1989 catch would be 40,000 metric tons, including 30,000 tons of juvenile tuna, or some six times the sustainable yield. If depletion continued at this rate, it would reduce total tuna stocks to one-tenth of current levels within five years. The depletion of juvenile stocks thus posed a serious threat to the longline operations for mature

fish, which were concentrated in the exclusive economic zones (EEZs) of the Pacific Islands nations and represented a major source of income and employment.

With strong public backing throughout the region after a major publicity campaign by the environmental organization Greenpeace, the South Pacific Forum countries—together with the U.S., which saw its own traditional fishing grounds threatened—met in direct negotiations with Taiwan, Japan, and South Korea in Suva, Fiji, in July. South Korea agreed to suspend activities, but it was difficult to apply pressure to Japan, which fished mainly for its own domestic market. The island nations also faced a dilemma because many of them received considerable income from Japan under bilateral arrangements for fishing in their EEZs and because Japan had substantially increased its development aid to the region over the past two years.

In September, under threat of a ban on imports to the U.S., Taiwan signed an agreement that would restrict gill-net fishing by its vessels and make them subject to inspection by U.S. officials. Japan subsequently agreed to monitoring and to undertake research but refused to terminate drift-net fishing until and unless research proved that it was doing serious and permanent damage to the marine environment. In July the South Pacific Forum expressed "profound concern" over the issue, called on nations using gill nets to desist, and in the Tarawa declaration showed strong support for an international ban on gill nets. Most member states then imposed bans on drift nets within their respective EEZs and denied future port access to vessels using gill nets in international waters. An agreement reached at the UN in December provided for an end to gill-net fishing in the South Pacific by July 1991 and a complete ban after June 1992.

Political Developments. Regional governments generally supported French policy for the eventual decolonization of New Caledonia, as proposed in the 1988 Matignon accord. This provided for a decade of intensive political and economic development, followed by a referendum on the future status of the territory. After the assassination in May of Jean-Marie Tjibaou, president of the Kanak Socialist National Liberation Front, there were fears that extremist groups both for and against independence would reemerge. This did not occur, however, and tensions were eased further by the release of Kanak political prisoners in October.

While regional governments continued to see the issue of Fiji's constitutional status as one for Fiji to resolve, concern was expressed by Australia and New Zealand, and by the secretary-general of the Commonwealth, over the delayed return to democracy. The proposed constitution was criticized because it not only would entrench the rights of indigenous Fijians but would discriminate against Indians with regard to political rights and economic opportunities. At the Commonwealth heads of governments meeting in Malaysia in October, U.K. Prime Minister Margaret Thatcher expressed the hope that Fiji would soon return to full Commonwealth membership.　(BARRIE MACDONALD)

AUSTRALIA

A federal parliamentary state (formally a constitutional monarchy) and member of the Commonwealth, Australia occupies the smallest continent and includes the island state of Tasmania. Area: 7,682,300 sq km (2,966,200 sq mi). Pop. (1989 est.): 16,804,000. Cap.: Canberra. Monetary unit: Australian dollar, with (Oct. 2, 1989) a free rate of $A 1.29 to U.S. $1 ($A 2.08 = £1 sterling). Queen, Elizabeth II; governors-general in 1989, Sir Ninian Martin Stephen and, from February 16, William Hayden; prime minister, Robert J. Hawke.

Domestic Affairs. There were several changes at the top of public life in Australia during 1989. The governor-general, Sir Ninian Stephen, was replaced at the end of his tour of duty as the queen's representative in Australia by William ("Bill") Hayden, a former leader of the Australian Labor Party (ALP). Equally significant, the opposition Liberal Party on May 9 changed its leader from John Howard to Andrew Peacock (*see* BIOGRAPHIES). Howard had failed to lift his personal popularity rating to a competitive level, and as a result the Liberals recalled his immediate predecessor, Peacock. This turnabout led Prime Minister Robert ("Bob") Hawke to rub his hands with glee, Peacock having been no match for Hawke in earlier electoral contests. Howard chose to leave quietly, saying that the new leader and his team were entitled to parade their wares unadorned by the ghosts of former chieftains.

While Howard stood aside with dignity and left the conduct of political affairs at the top to Peacock, Hawke was unable to capitalize on splits in the ruling coalition, as one of his own most senior ministers took issue with elements of the prime minister's policy. In July the minister for industry, technology, and commerce, Sen. John Button, said that the government's election victory chances were only 50:50 and that a win would be unlikely, if not impossible, if interest rates did not fall before the next election. This provoked a public counterattack by the prime minister.

There was a new emphasis on environmental issues during 1989 in the political jockeying prior to the general election, scheduled for May 1990. In May a coalition of the ALP and the Green Party won the state election in Tasmania. Opinions varied within the ALP about the strength of the environmentalist ground swell. The minister for the environment, Graham Richardson, thought that the environment would be second only to the economy in voters' minds by the time the next general election was held. Richardson noted that while Tasmanian independents gained 22% of the primary votes in the state election, 80% of Green preferences went to the ALP. Having identified the environment as an election issue, Hawke announced that the government would plant one billion trees over the next 10 years to see a new greening of Australia. He also pledged that $A 320 million of the $A 520 million allocated over the next decade to environmental protection would be used to fight soil degradation. The government postponed the decision over mining in Kakadu National Park until after the next election.

Hawke identified the plight of immigrants as another potential election issue and accordingly announced that his government would spend $A 70 million in a three-year campaign to help remedy what he described as previous grievous injustices. Hawke decided to extend the Special Broadcasting Service, which telecast programs in non-English languages, into new areas. The government also proposed to pass a Multiculturalism Act, which, while recognizing English as the major national language, would also deal with the problem of racial vilification. In addition, the government planned to improve the process of recognizing overseas qualifications and to provide an extra 10% in funding for ethnic schools in Australia. Hawke proposed a package of English-language measures including an extension of the English as a second language program, extra resources for English-language courses for adult immigrants, and a new English-teaching television series.

While Hawke remained Australia's most popular choice as prime minister in Gallup Poll ratings, his international appeal was damaged by a long critical article in the British newspaper *The Sunday Times*. At about the same time, the influential Australian *Bulletin* magazine showed that

in Australia Hawke's personal popularity was 47% and his standing as preferred prime minister was 53%, while Peacock, his nearest political rival, could manage only figures of 31 and 29%, respectively. Despite Hawke's personal charisma, polls showed that the ALP would have lost narrowly had an election been held in June. By October, however, the pendulum had swung back, and polls suggested a narrow ALP victory.

In two sensational cases Australian public leaders fell from grace, albeit temporarily in one of them. The Australian Broadcasting Tribunal ruled after a well-publicized year-long investigation that multimillionaire businessman Alan Bond was unfit to hold a broadcasting license. The tribunal found that Bond had sought to disguise the size of a defamation payout to Sir Johannes Bjelke-Petersen and had indicated that the settlement was necessary for doing business in Queensland. It also found that Bond had threatened to use his television staff to gather information on a business competitor and to expose the competitor by broadcasting the results. Bond rejected the findings and successfully overturned the ruling in a legal appeal. The charismatic and controversial head of the Aboriginal Affairs Department, Charles Perkins, was sacked by the Aboriginal Affairs minister, Gerry Hand. Perkins had refused to drop his support for spending $A 300,000 on poker machines for an Aboriginal social club.

Australia, ordinarily one of the more stable continents, experienced an earthquake measuring 5.5 on the Richter scale on December 28. Worst hit was the city of Newcastle, New South Wales, where 11 people died and more than 120 were injured.

Foreign Affairs. Australia was forced to make a series of adjustments in foreign policy in 1989. Australian diplomats faced major problems emanating from breakdowns in law and order within two of their most important neighbours and trading partners, Papua New Guinea and China. To make matters worse, New Zealand lost its prime minister, David Lange, after five years in office. Lange had always been critical of Australia's government for being "soft" on the nuclear weapons issue and had plunged Australia's defense alliances into chaos in April by threatening to formally abandon the ANZUS security treaty among Australia, New Zealand, and the United States, but he had been in favour of closer defense ties with Australia, if not with

the U.S. The change in leadership threw immediate doubt on whether New Zealand would participate in the planned frigate program, which under Lange's guidance was scheduled to build eight frigates for the Australian Navy and up to four for New Zealand in a joint project. Hawke immediately put pressure on New Zealand's new prime minister, Geoffrey Palmer, threatening him with diplomatic consequences if he ditched the project, which was less popular in New Zealand than in Australia. Although some sections of the New Zealand Labour Party branded the Hawke government as warmongers, New Zealand agreed to purchase at least two ships.

The crisis in China also caused great foreign policy problems for the ALP. Despite the Australian government's vital trade relationship with China, the prime minister was forthright in his condemnation of Chinese behaviour. Hawke wept openly at a memorial service for the victims of the Tiananmen (T'ien-an-men) massacre. The federal foreign affairs, trade, and defense committee of the ALP caucus, unmindful of trade consequences, urged the government to go further and asked Hawke to instruct the Australian ambassador in China to protest the brutal repression of peaceful democratic action.

Australia, the former colonial power that had granted Papua New Guinea its independence, waited on the sidelines during 1989 to support local authorities if conditions deteriorated to the extent that Papua New Guinea was unable to cope with the growing unrest. Australian diplomats were particularly concerned about the closing of the Bougainville copper mine, and the subsequent state of emergency created a series of diplomatic problems. The closure of the mine denied the Papua New Guinea government millions of kina in direct and indirect revenue, leading to an increase in demands for Australian economic assistance. In addition, the rebellion involved a discussion of such issues as the provision of Australian helicopters to use against rebels and to help in the evacuation of casualties. On the positive side, Hawke addressed the Pacific Islands Forum in July and set the banning of deep-sea drift netting as a foremost priority.

Australia forged closer links with France during the year. Despite Australia's vociferous and sustained protests against French nuclear weapons testing in the Pacific, the visit of French Prime Minister Michel Rocard to Australia

Thousands jam the streets in downtown Sydney during a memorial service held for the victims of China's Tiananmen Square massacre. Although the relationship between Australia and China was vital to the Australian economy, Prime Minister Bob Hawke openly condemned China's actions.

was an outstanding diplomatic success. Hawke and Rocard agreed on many matters, including regional economic development and the need to prevent mining in Antarctica.

The Economy. The Australian economy was in bad shape in 1989. High inflation, high interest rates, a poor balance of payments, and corporate collapses among industrial giants painted a bleak picture. The government also faced problems as the influential U.S. rating agency Moody's Investors Service, which had downgraded Australia's credit rating from AAA to AA1 in 1986, threatened in 1989 to lower it still further. In response, Treasurer Paul Keating banned Commonwealth officials from speaking to Moody's representatives. Moody's, however, said that as long as Australian government bonds remained outstanding, Moody's was going to continue to monitor its readings and make judgments if necessary to reflect changes in Australia's financial condition. Moody's, as threatened, downgraded the rating from AA1 to AA2 in August. This coincided with the release of figures showing that Australia's net foreign debt had risen to $A 108 billion in June. The Australian Bureau of Statistics said that the country's net foreign liabilities now amounted to 32.2% of its gross domestic product.

The Australian dollar fluctuated wildly throughout the year. The selling of the dollar was described as "frenzied" in February when the government announced the worst January trade figures on record. In September Australia recorded yet another record $A 2.6 billion deficit. Australian brokers said investors were shocked and were looking at investments in bonds and equities elsewhere.

Australians faced near-record interest rates in 1989 as the nation's foreign debt burden burgeoned and the government used high interest rates to try to dampen domestic demand, which Keating believed was sucking in imports. Home mortgage rates reached 17% in June, and the rates charged by banks to their best corporate business customers reached 20.25%. The banks argued that they would reduce the home loan rate to all their customers if the government would abolish the 13.5% ceiling on 800,000 loans protected by an interest cap. Both Keating and opposition housing spokesman Wilson Tuckey rejected this suggestion. Keating argued that there was no guarantee that general mortgage rates would fall if the ceiling was lifted, and Tuckey agreed that the fortunate minority who contracted loans at a maximum rate of 13.5% were entitled to that contractual right. In September Keating announced a $A 200 million deal with Australia's four major banks, which had agreed to peg mortgage rates at 17% in return for an increase in the yield on bank deposits that the four major banks were required to lodge with the Reserve Bank under Commonwealth law. The shadow treasurer, John Robert Hewson, said the move showed national economic management had been put on hold indefinitely.

High interest rates had a disastrous impact on home loan repayments and, accordingly, Australia entered the 1989 financial year with inflation at a three-year high. The June quarter consumer price index showed an increase of 2.5%, the highest since the last quarter of 1986. The resulting annual inflation rate of 7.6% for 1988–89 represented 70% more than the treasurer's budget forecast of 4.5%.

Australia's largest and hitherto most respectable property company, L.J. Hooker, collapsed in 1989 when the company overextended itself in a failed plan to develop "hypermall" shopping complexes in the U.S. Australian banks, led by Westpac, eventually forced Hooker to appoint a liquidator, signaling the collapse of the business empire of Australia's largest individual property developer, George Herscu.

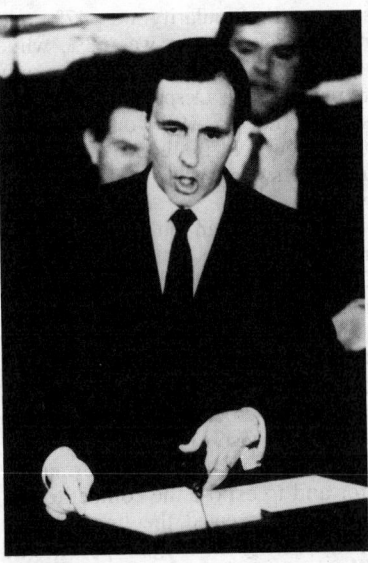

Australia's Treasurer Paul Keating delivers the annual budget to Parliament. He announced a record budget surplus of $A 9.1 billion, which would be used to help pay the national debt.
REUTERS/BETTMANN NEWSPHOTOS

Australia's export income was further damaged by a dispute with Saudi Arabia, which, in a sudden and unexpected move, banned more than 295,000 Australian sheep in August, saying that the sheep were infected by blue tongue virus and sheep pox. The rejected sheep were subsequently accepted by Kuwait and the United Arab Emirates, but the Australian Meat and Livestock Corporation suspended shipments to Saudi Arabia in protest. Australian veterinarians testified that neither disease existed in Australia, and the managing director of the corporation, Bruce Standen, said that supplying Saudi Arabia under current conditions would damage Australia's reputation as the world's foremost supplier of disease-free livestock.

Australia faced a major industrial crisis that lasted more than two months and severely damaged the economy when domestic airline pilots with the major carriers Ansett and Australian Airlines resigned over pay claims. The dispute was inflamed by the prime minister, who compared the pilots to bus drivers and claimed that the Australian economy would be ruined if they were successful in their claim for a 29% wage increase. In response to the pilot resignations, the government waived restrictions on international carriers, allowing them to carry passengers on domestic routes. In addition, suitable aircraft from the Royal Australian Air Force were used to move passengers.

Various solutions to Australia's economic malaise were proposed. Former tourism minister John Brown suggested a tourist-led recovery. He attacked his successors, claiming that although tourism was Australia's best chance for economic recovery, the government had reduced funding for tourism promotion from $A 40 million to $A 1 million, and this had destroyed the capacity to advertise and promote Australia. Hard-line opponents of excessive government expenditure suggested a cut in Australia's welfare spending. Sen. John Owen Stone, a former head of the Treasury, said Australia was a smoking ruin and claimed that the welfare state had significantly eroded Australia's capacity to save and invest.

John Elliott, speaking in his capacity as federal president of the Liberal Party, said that Australians had "a malaise, a handout mentality," and penalized success. He claimed that there were too many people dependent on the welfare system and that would have to be changed. He also said that 30% of Australians received some sort of government handout and that people believed they deserved a piece of the welfare cake. He singled out for special criticism

free health care and unemployment payments without the requirement to work, but he placed his faith in Peacock, who, he said, understood what needed to be done and had the courage to make tough decisions. Elliott believed that Australia should concentrate on agriculture, minerals, and services to Asia rather than high-tech manufacturing.

Hewson claimed that the ALP government was deeply split over how to address Australia's economic woes. Observing that disunity was death in politics, Hewson pointed to criticism of Keating's policies by Prime Minister Hawke and Finance Minister Peter Walsh. Walsh expressed severe reservations about the government's reliance on monetary policy and high interest rates, and Hawke called for a tax on luxuries and for measures to stimulate personal savings. Hewson argued that while Keating rejected criticism from within the ALP as "simplistic nonsense," his economic policies were clearly not working.

Faced with a deteriorating balance of payments position, rising inflation, and unemployment, Keating was in an unenviable position when he announced the nation's annual budget strategy to the Parliament on August 15. Keating announced a record budget surplus of $A 9.1 billion. However, he expected inflation to run at 7.5% over the coming year and to see a repeat of the record current account deficit of $A 18.5 billion in 1989–90. The 1989 budget was the last budget before the general election, and Keating was careful not to appear to be wooing voters with what he called "gimmicks and quick fixes." Accordingly, the budget set out to use its surplus to repay the national debt. Beyond a small increase in the pension and further alterations to the superannuation laws to allow increased tax deductibility for some superannuation contributions, there were almost no concessions.   (A.R.G. GRIFFITHS)

FIJI

The republic of Fiji occupies an island group in the South Pacific Ocean. Area: 18,274 sq km (7,056 sq mi). Pop. (1989 est.): 734,000. Cap.: Suva. Monetary unit: Fiji dollar, with (Oct. 2, 1989) a free rate of F$1.50 to U.S. $1 (F$2.42 = £1 sterling). President in 1989, Ratu Sir Penaia Ganilau; prime minister, Ratu Sir Kamisese Mara.

The interim civilian government appointed after the 1987 coups remained in office in 1989, with few signs of a return to democracy. The prime minister, Ratu Sir Kamisese Mara, agreed to defer retirement, but the coup leader, Maj. Gen. Sitiveni Rabuka, refused to serve as a civilian deputy prime minister, declaring his intention of returning to barracks as commander in chief of Fiji's military forces. A proposed constitution was intended to ensure the paramountcy of the interests of ethnic Fijians, who narrowly outnumbered Indians in the population. In November Timoci Bavadra, the leader of the coalition ousted by Rabuka in the coup of May 1987, died of cancer. Because Bavadra's leadership was a major factor in the creation of the coalition between the multiracial Labour Party and the Indian-dominated National Federation Party, his death aroused renewed uncertainty over Fiji's political future. Later in the month his widow, Adi Kuini Bavadra, agreed to take over the leadership of the opposition.

The government's relaxation of postcoup sabbath-observance laws brought protests from Fijian fundamentalist Methodists, who mounted roadblocks to prevent economic activities on Sundays. In October four Indian places of worship in Lautoka were firebombed by Christian extremists.

The economy continued to recover. A tax-free industrial zone attracted 46 companies employing more than a thousand workers; in January wages and salaries were frozen to control inflation. In an August minibudget, the government tried to stimulate growth further by a policy of deregulation. Australia withheld $A 5.2 million of a $A 10 million aid allocation because of "slow progress in restoring constitutional normality," but other countries continued their programs. French Prime Minister Michel Rocard visited Fiji in August.   (BARRIE MACDONALD)

This article updates the *Macropædia* article PACIFIC ISLANDS: *Fiji.*

KIRIBATI

A republic in the western Pacific Ocean and member of the Commonwealth, Kiribati comprises the former Gilbert Islands, Banaba (Ocean Island), the Line Islands, and the Phoenix Islands. Area: 849 sq km (328 sq mi). Pop. (1989 est.): 69,600. Cap.: Bairiki. Monetary unit: Australian dollar, with (Oct. 2, 1989) a free rate of $A 1.29 to U.S. $1 ($A 2.08 = £1 sterling). President (*berititenti*) in 1989, Ieremia Tabai.

The economy of Kiribati in 1989 continued to be heavily dependent on foreign aid and income from reserves accumulated before the exhaustion of the Banaba phosphate deposits. There was a record balance of payments deficit in 1988, with imports at $A 17.5 million and export income of only $A 2 million. In an attempt to boost employment and foreign earnings through remittances, the government doubled the intake at the marine training school; more than a thousand graduates of the school were currently employed by international shipping lines.

The government announced plans to develop Kiritimati (Christmas) Island. The island, some 3,000 km (1,850 mi) east of the main chain, accounted for about half the country's land area and had potential as a fisheries, aquaculture, and tourism centre. Kiribati was exploring the possibility of regional fishing licensing agreements between South Pacific Forum Fisheries Agency countries and Japan and South Korea. In light of the limited benefits that Kiribati had received under a similar arrangement with the U.S., however, Taomati Iuta, the minister for natural resources, expressed skepticism over the proposals.

Kiribati was host to the 1989 meeting of the South Pacific Forum, which adopted a regional stance on gill-net fishing and initiated further research into global warming. (See *Oceanian Affairs,* above.)   (BARRIE MACDONALD)

This article updates the *Macropædia* article PACIFIC ISLANDS: *Kiribati.*)

NAURU

An island republic within the Commonwealth, Nauru lies in the Pacific Ocean about 1,900 km (1,200 mi) east of New Guinea. Area: 21 sq km (8 sq mi). Pop. (1989 est.): 8,100. Cap.: Yaren. Monetary unit: Australian dollar, with (Oct. 2, 1989) a free rate of $A 1.29 to U.S. $1 ($A 2.08 = £1 sterling). Presidents in 1989, Hammer DeRoburt and, from August 17, Kenos Aroi.

Pres. Hammer DeRoburt had major difficulties in 1989. In January he faced a diplomatic crisis over the behaviour of Australia's high commissioner to Nauru, Beris Gwynne. DeRoburt requested that Gwynne be withdrawn as unsatisfactory because she had released information to New Zealand about the safety record of Nauru's airline. As a result of Gwynne's report, Air Nauru, which provided the island's air service, had its airworthiness certificate suspended by the New Zealand civil aviation administration. In August, DeRoburt was replaced as president by Kenos Aroi. It was the third time since independence that DeRoburt had lost the presidency of the central Pacific island state. DeRoburt remained head chief and in elected

control of the local government council, a power base from which he could contest a new general election scheduled to take place on December 16.   (A.R.G. GRIFFTHS)

This article updates the *Micropædia* article NAURU.

NEW ZEALAND

New Zealand, a constitutional monarchy and member of the Commonwealth in the South Pacific Ocean, consists of North and South islands and Stewart, Chatham, and other minor islands. Area: 267,844 sq km (103,415 sq mi). Pop. (1989 est.): 3,371,000. Cap.: Wellington. Monetary unit: New Zealand dollar, with (Oct. 2, 1989) a free rate of $NZ 1.72 to U.S. $1 ($NZ 2.75 = £1 sterling). Queen, Elizabeth II; governor-general in 1989, Sir Paul Reeves; prime ministers, David Russell Lange and, from August 8, Geoffrey Palmer.

Prime Minister David Lange, nearing the end of the second term of his innovative Labour government, stunned New Zealanders when on Aug. 7, 1989, he announced his resignation. He nominated his deputy, justice minister Geoffrey Palmer (*see* BIOGRAPHIES), to succeed him, and Labour Party members of Parliament on August 8 confirmed his choice. Lange accepted the positions of attorney general and minister of state—outside the Cabinet. He and the party had trailed in public opinion polls for some time, though during the year the polls had reinstated the administration ahead of the National Party opposition. But Labour colleagues had confronted Lange with two motions of no confidence in seven months, and four days before he resigned, the party caucus had voted back to ministerial rank a minister Lange had recently sacked.

Through much of the government's second term, Lange was at odds with his reform-minded finance minister, Roger Douglas. At his departure from office Lange emphasized the social policy changes of the past five years rather than economic change. He claimed that these social changes were now locked in, beyond the reach of any "relentless juggernaut of the New Right." He had resisted Douglas' proposals for a flat-scale tax system, extension of deregulation to labour unions, and increased user-pays privatization of state services.

Lange fired Douglas when the minister accused him of presidential-style leadership that ignored Cabinet prerogatives and made the prime minister impossible to work with. He replaced Douglas in finance with David Caygill. As a former aide to Douglas, Caygill soldiered on in the steps of his predecessor, while Labour MPs lobbied, in the name of government credibility, for the return of Douglas to the Cabinet. Douglas challenged Lange for the party leadership but was defeated by 38 votes to 15. Lange's failure to respond to a caucus demand for peace with Douglas resulted in a no-confidence vote on June 29. He survived this, but the end was in sight.

The new prime minister quickly established himself as firmly in charge. In allocating ministerial responsibilities, Palmer—a former law professor—restricted himself to environment and the Security Intelligence Service; he added labour to Helen Clark's health portfolio and also appointed her deputy prime minister, raising her rank in the Cabinet to second. Mike Moore (external relations and trade), who contested the leadership, remained third in command. Douglas, who withdrew from the leadership race and unsuccessfully ran for deputy, dropped from 4th to 15th, with police, immigration, audit, and special strategic projects as portfolios. Caygill moved up from seventh to fourth. Stan Rodger (state-owned enterprises) moved from 13th to 5th. By year's end, however, five ministers, including Douglas and Rodger, had announced plans to resign, raising speculation that a reshuffle might be imminent.

The government had been united in fighting inflation, achieving a 20-year low of 4% in the year to March. The figure rose to 4.4% in the year to June. The goods and services tax rose from 10 to 12.5% on July 1, causing prices to increase. Unemployment climbed above 11% during the year. While Douglas was being accused of taking Labour to the right, a back-bench Labour MP, Jim Anderton, was directing a splinter group of pensioners and low-paid workers to the left, an additional complication for the party in the 1990 general elections.

New Zealand's balance of payments in trade with other countries registered a surplus, of $NZ 48 million, in the year to June for the first time in 14 years. Caygill's budget of July 27, providing for a deficit of $NZ 729 million (1.06% of gross domestic product), was well received. Also, by mid-August the stock exchange was bullish. One property businessman who survived the 1987 crash, Robert Jones, was knighted; another, already knighted, Sir Ron Brierley, signaled his intention to step down from the chairmanship of the international investment company he had established. Plans were launched for a 150th national birthday celebration in 1990.   (JOHN A. KELLEHER)

Geoffrey Palmer (far left) of New Zealand's Labour Party replaced fellow party member David Lange (left) as New Zealand's prime minister. Although Lange had suffered a decline in public approval, his resignation took many by surprise.

PAPUA NEW GUINEA

A constitutional monarchy and member of the Commonwealth, Papua New Guinea is situated in the southwestern Pacific Ocean and comprises the eastern part of the island of New Guinea, the islands of the Bismarck, Trobriand, Woodlark, Louisiade, and D'Entrecasteaux groups, and parts of the Solomon Islands, including Bougainville. Area: 462,840 sq km (178,704 sq mi). Pop. (1989 est.): 3,593,000. Cap.: Port Moresby. Monetary unit: kina, with (Oct. 2, 1989) a free rate of 0.86 kina to U.S. $1 (1.39 kinas = £1 sterling). Queen, Elizabeth II; governor-general in 1989, Sir Kingsford Dibela; prime minister, Rabbie Namaliu.

In May 1989 the prime minister of Papua New Guinea, Rabbie Namaliu, visited Australia, where he signed a co-operation agreement with the Australian government. Australia pledged to help Papua New Guinea's development and, at the same time, offered help to the Papua New Guinea government, which faced severe difficulties with secessionist unrest on Bougainville Island. Namaliu took charge of the crisis and ordered the nation's security forces to act with caution, understanding, and patience under a state of emergency designed to cope with the secessionist-inclined landowners led by Francis Ona. The rebels closed the giant Bougainville copper mine for months, cutting off vital revenue and undermining the government's budget strategy. Namaliu's plan for ending the rebellion included evacuating people from the villages in the neighbourhood of the mine and placing them in camps. The police and military authorities were given power to search, seize, arrest, and evacuate people from designated areas. In an unrelated incident, Communications Minister Malipu Balakau was assassinated outside his Mt. Hagen home.

(A.R.G. GRIFFTHS)

This article updates the *Macropædia* article EAST INDIES: *Papua New Guinea.*

SOLOMON ISLANDS

A constitutional monarchy and member of the Commonwealth, the Solomon Islands comprises a 1,450-km (900-mi) chain of islands and atolls in the western Pacific Ocean. Area: 28,370 sq km (10,954 sq mi). Pop. (1989 est.): 308,000. Cap.: Honiara. Monetary unit: Solomon Islands dollar, with (Oct. 2, 1989) a free rate of SI$2.37 to U.S. $1 (SI$3.84 = £1 sterling). Queen, Elizabeth II; governor-general in 1989, Sir George Lepping; prime ministers, Ezekiel Alebua and, from March 28, Solomon Mamaloni.

Following elections in February 1989, Solomon Mamaloni (People's Alliance Party) was elected prime minister, defeating Bartholomew Ulufa'alu (Liberal Party). The new prime minister immediately suspended all aid programs pending an investigation of the country's economic situation. He called for trade rather than aid and, in a comment directed at the U.S., for bilateral rather than multilateral aid agreements.

The new government faced a serious economic situation. Export receipts and gross domestic product rose in 1988, but inflation reached nearly 20%, and the currency was devalued by 12% against major world currencies and 27% against the Australian dollar. The Mamaloni government placed a new emphasis on trade in foreign relations, reached an agreement to raise public service salaries by 17.5% on condition there were no more increases before 1991, and embarked on a policy of divesting itself of public holdings in joint ventures. Price controls were removed to encourage competition.

The government announced plans to close its diplomatic mission to the UN in favour of an office in Australia.

Meanwhile, the U.S. announced the establishment of diplomatic representation in Honiara. (BARRIE MACDONALD)

This article updates the *Macropædia* article PACIFIC ISLANDS: *Solomon Islands.*

TONGA

A constitutional monarchy and member of the Commonwealth, Tonga is an island group in the Pacific Ocean east of Fiji. Area: 780 sq km (301 sq mi). Pop. (1989 est.): 95,900. Cap.: Nuku'alofa. Monetary unit: pa'anga, with (Oct. 2, 1989) a free rate of 1.29 pa'anga to U.S. $1 (2.08 pa'anga = £1 sterling). King, Taufa'ahau Tupou IV; prime minister in 1989, Prince Fatafehi Tu'ipelehake.

During 1989 there were signs of popular discontent. Under the 1875 constitution, Parliament was dominated by nominees of the king and representatives of the nation's 33 nobles. A majority of the commoners' representatives continued to attack alleged misuse of public funds, and in August they boycotted Parliament for two weeks to protest the Cabinet's unilateral overturning of legislation granting salary increases to public servants. There were also calls for more members of Parliament to be elected by popular suffrage. In response to these implicit challenges, the police reminded citizens of their legal obligation to show "due respect" to the king.

The country continued to face economic difficulties; inflation stood at 8% in 1988, and gross domestic product fell by 1.9%. Tonga remained dependent on aid for capital development. Japan provided assistance for the establishment of a national shipping line and fisheries development, and a soft loan for the development of market centres and small industries was granted by the Asian Development Bank. Upgrading of the airport to Boeing 747 standard was begun with assistance from Australia, the European Communities, and Japan. Tonga was host to the 1989 South Pacific Mini Games in major new facilities constructed with aid from France and Taiwan. (BARRIE MACDONALD)

This article updates the *Macropædia* article PACIFIC ISLANDS: *Tonga.*

TUVALU

A constitutional monarchy within the Commonwealth, Tuvalu comprises nine main islands and their associated islets and reefs in the western Pacific Ocean. Area: 24 sq km (9 sq mi). Pop. (1989): 8,900. Cap.: Fongafale. Monetary unit: Tuvalu dollar, at par with the Australian dollar (also a legal currency), with (Oct. 2, 1989) a free rate of $T 1.29 to U.S. $1 ($T 2.08 = £1 sterling). Queen, Elizabeth II; governor-general in 1989, Tupua Leupena; prime ministers, Tomasi Puapua and, from October 16, Bikenibeu Paeniu.

Elections in October 1989 were followed by a change of government with Bikenibeu Paeniu, a new member of Parliament, as prime minister. There were no political parties in Tuvalu; Paeniu's government was dominated by new members including Alesana Seluka, the deputy prime minister, and Naama Latasi, the first woman to be elected to Tuvalu's Parliament. Latasi's husband was also elected to Parliament. The new government was expected to raise Tuvalu's profile in regional affairs.

In recognition of the 10th anniversary of Tuvalu's independence, in October 1988, Britain provided a replacement for Tuvalu's only ship. The 1,000-ton *Nivaga II* was purpose-built for the interisland passenger and cargo trade. In an attempt to reduce imports, the government placed renewed emphasis on food production in the outer islands for consumption on Funafuti, seat of the capital. Other development projects focused on the improvement of water

supplies, fisheries development, and the fostering of small businesses.

The Philatelic Bureau, a major source of foreign exchange, continued to operate despite heavy losses resulting from declining international interest and management difficulties. Tuvalu terminated the agreement under which 42 Japanese tuna-fishing vessels worked in its exclusive economic zone when their owners refused to pay increased license fees. (BARRIE MACDONALD)

This article updates the *Macropædia* article PACIFIC ISLANDS: *Tuvalu.*

VANUATU

The republic of Vanuatu, a member of the Commonwealth, comprises 12 main islands and some 60 smaller ones in the southwestern Pacific Ocean. Area: 12,190 sq km (4,707 sq mi). Pop. (1989 est.): 154,000. Cap.: Vila. Monetary unit: vatu, with (Oct. 2, 1989) a free rate of 119.04 vatu to U.S. $1 (192.60 vatu = £1 sterling). Presidents in 1989, Ati George Sokomanu to January 12 and, from January 30, Fred Timakata; prime minister, the Rev. Walter Lini.

The political crisis of late 1988 spilled over into 1989. Barak Sope, formerly a prominent member of the Vanuaaku Party, split with the party and was dismissed from Parliament by the government but was returned on appeal by the courts. Eighteen opposition members of Parliament, dismissed for missing three consecutive sittings, boycotted the subsequent by-elections, as did Sope and his supporters. The 40% turnout prompted the president, Ati George Sokomanu, to declare Parliament dissolved on the grounds that it was unrepresentative and to appoint Sope as interim prime minister. Police and paramilitary forces remained loyal to the government; Sokomanu and Sope were charged with seditious conspiracy and incitement to mutiny and were sentenced to imprisonment for six and five years, respectively. Both convictions were overturned on appeal and, though out of Parliament, Sope retained his power base among the landowners of the capital, Vila, where his Melanesian Progressive Party easily won municipal elections in May.

A number of steps were taken to boost the economy, including tentative agreement to renew the controversial fishing arrangement with the Soviet Union, an agreement with Taiwanese interests on the logging of rain forest on Malakula, and plans for a factory estate at Luganville on Espíritu Santo. A major tourism promotion was mounted in Australia. (BARRIE MACDONALD)

This article updates the *Macropædia* article PACIFIC ISLANDS: *Vanuatu.*

WESTERN SAMOA

A constitutional monarchy and member of the Commonwealth, Western Samoa occupies an island group in the South Pacific Ocean. Area: 2,831 sq km (1,093 sq mi). Pop. (1989 est.): 164,000. Cap.: Apia. Monetary unit: Western Samoa tala, with (Oct. 2, 1989) a free rate of 2.23 tala to U.S. $1 (3.61 tala = £1 sterling). Head of state (*O le Ao o le Malo*) in 1989, Malietoa Tanumafili II; prime minister, Tofilau Eti Alesana.

Western Samoa's 1989 budget provided for revenue of 102 million tala against current expenditure of 82 million tala. Together with aid and soft loans, the resulting 20 million tala operating surplus contributed toward development expenditure of 64.5 million tala. The balance of payments surplus had improved in 1988, but production fell in 1989, partly because of damage from Cyclone Gina in February.

Remittances from Western Samoans overseas, amount-

ing to approximately 75 million tala a year, had considerable economic importance, so a review by New Zealand of immigration procedures affecting Samoans inevitably caused tensions between the two governments. It was shown that the annual quota of 1,100 permanent migrants was being exceeded through a relaxation of family reunification rules and loopholes in the law on adoptions. Some procedures were tightened, but the basic quota remained unchanged.

It was alleged within the region that Japanese aid to Western Samoa was intended to reduce opposition to gillnet fishing by Japanese vessels. When villagers of Falealupa contemplated logging their rain forest to pay for a new school, U.S. conservationists raised $55,000 to ensure preservation of the forest.

As part of its policy of raising its profile in the region, the U.S. based a diplomatic representative in Apia. (BARRIE MACDONALD)

This article updates the *Macropædia* article PACIFIC ISLANDS: *Samoa.*

Dependent States

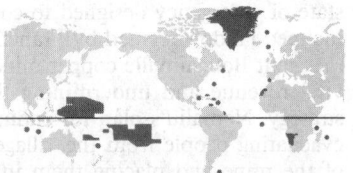

Europe and the Atlantic. In late 1989 Argentina and the U.K. held a series of meetings on the possible renewal of diplomatic relations and on Argentine fishing rights near the Falkland Islands/Islas Malvinas. In the first formal talks since the 1982 armed conflict, both sides agreed to postpone a discussion of sovereignty over the Falklands. In October islanders rejected a new pro-Argentina political party and elected all pro-Britain candidates to the eight-seat Legislative Council. The U.K. announced that it would reduce the number of British troops stationed in Gibraltar, but relations with Spain remained strained. Continuing negotiations between Canada and France led to an agreement to increase the French cod catch in the disputed waters around St. Pierre and Miquelon islands and to the reopening of Canadian ports to French vessels.

In Bermuda the ruling United Bermuda Party (UBP) held a reduced majority of 23 seats (down from 31) after February elections to the House of Assembly. Voter support for the UBP declined from 62% in the 1985 general election to barely 50%. The pro-independence Progressive Labour Party increased its bloc to 15 seats, while the remaining two seats were won by a National Liberal Party candidate and an independent Green.

In September 1989 the Danish government acknowledged that it had received an offer by an unidentified Japanese buyer to purchase the semiautonomous Faeroe Islands. Danish and Canadian geologists reported in November that they had found one of the world's largest gold deposits in Greenland.

Caribbean. Several of the dependent territories in the Caribbean were devastated or severely damaged by Hurricane Hugo on September 17–19. The worst affected were St. Croix in the U.S. Virgin Islands (extensive damage to the oil refinery and 90% destruction of other property), Puerto Rico (6 people killed and up to 50,000 made homeless), Guadeloupe (5 dead, 60 injured, and some 12,000 left homeless), and Montserrat (4 killed and an estimated 95% of buildings destroyed or damaged).

A new executive council in the Cayman Islands, formed after a general election in November 1988, contained two new and two incumbent members. In Anguilla the government of Chief Minister Emile Gumbs was returned to power in a general election on Feb. 27, 1989. The British governor sparked protests in March, however, when he named a member of the opposition party to one of two appointed seats and dismissed a senior nurse at the island's hospital.

Referenda were planned in Puerto Rico and the U.S. Virgin Islands on their future status, with voters being offered a range of options from statehood to independence.

In the British Virgin Islands work started early in 1989 at Pockwood Pond on the new electric power station, construction of which had been delayed by financing difficulties. The government of Montserrat called in British and U.S. fraud investigators in March to assist the police with inquiries into irregularities in the offshore banking sector. Three offshore banks were closed, and a number of U.S. citizens were charged with conspiracy to defraud. In June the French National Assembly approved an amnesty for persons imprisoned or charged in politically motivated cases in Guadeloupe. The amnesty brought the release of Luc Reinette, head of the Alliance Révolutionnaire Caraibe.

In the Netherlands Antilles the head of the St. Maarten Democratic Party, Claude Wathey, continued to press for the islands' independence, a step that would be likely to lead Curaçao to seek separate status. The Dutch government stated in May that it would not press the five-member federation toward independence if referenda indicated that the population did not want it. In Aruba the People's Electoral Movement, led by Nelson Oduber, won a general election on January 6, and in June talks were held with The Netherlands on the transition to independence in 1996.

Africa. Despite initial skepticism, the agreement reached in 1988 between South Africa, the U.S., Angola, and Cuba on independence for South West Africa/Namibia and the withdrawal of Cuban troops from Angola was implemented during 1989. Cuban forces began to leave Angola in January. On April 1 an incursion of guerrilla forces of the South West Africa People's Organization (SWAPO) from Angola into Namibia was ruthlessly repulsed by South

Hong Kong residents protest during the visit of Sir Geoffrey Howe, Britain's foreign secretary. Following the imposition of martial law in China, Hong Kong's Chinese demanded the right to live in Britain after 1997, when the colony would return to Chinese rule.
REUTERS/BETTMANN NEWSPHOTOS

African troops, who were by then supposed to be confined to barracks. Several hundred guerrillas were killed in this operation. In the following months thousands of refugees and exiled SWAPO members returned to Namibia. SWAPO president Sam Nujoma (*see* BIOGRAPHIES) returned in September, two days after Anton Lubowski, a senior official of the organization and its first white member, was assassinated in Windhoek.

UN officials, 1,695 UN-trained supervisors, and South African observers supervised the voting on November 7–11 for a constituent assembly to draft a Namibian constitution. Thousands stood for hours in extreme heat at polling places as more than 90% of the approximately 700,-000 registered voters participated. SWAPO won a majority (57.3%), but it did not receive the expected two-thirds that would have given it sole power to frame the constitution. The previous governing party, the Democratic Turnhalle Alliance, obtained 28.6% of the votes; the United Democratic Front won 5.6%; and the white National Christian Action got 3.5%. SWAPO's shortfall was partly the result of revelations that it had detained and tortured hundreds of its guerrillas in Angola during the war, mainly members of the non-Ovambo minority tribes, suspected of being South African spies.

Fighting again broke out in Western Sahara in October 1989, ending the yearlong informal cease-fire between Morocco and the Popular Front for the Liberation of Saguia el Hamra and Río de Oro (Polisario Front).

Pacific. The fragile peace achieved in New Caledonia in 1988 by the negotiation of the Matignon accord between pro- and anti-independence groups was shattered in May 1989 with the assassination of Jean-Marie Tjibaou, president of the pro-independence Kanak Socialist National Liberation Front (FLNKS), and his deputy, Yeiwene Yei-

Dependent States[1]

Australia	**South Africa**
Christmas Island	South West Africa/Namibia
Cocos (Keeling) Islands	**United Kingdom**
Norfolk Island	Anguilla
Denmark	Bermuda
Faeroe Islands	British Virgin Islands
Greenland	Cayman Islands
France	Falkland Islands
French Guiana	Gibraltar
French Polynesia	Guernsey
Guadeloupe	Hong Kong
Martinique	Isle of Man
Mayotte	Jersey
New Caledonia	Montserrat
Réunion	Pitcairn Island
Saint Pierre and Miquelon	Saint Helena
Wallis and Futuna	Turks and Caicos Islands
Netherlands, The	**United States**
Aruba	American Samoa
Netherlands Antilles	Guam
New Zealand	Puerto Rico
Cook Islands	Trust Territory of the Pacific Islands
Niue	Marshall Islands
Tokelau	Federated States of Micronesia
Norway	Northern Marianas
Jan Mayen	Palau
Svalbard	Virgin Islands (of the U.S.)
Portugal	
Macau	

[1]Excludes territories (1) to which Antarctic Treaty is applicable in whole or in part, (2) without permanent civilian population, (3) without internationally recognized civilian government (Western Sahara, Gaza Strip), or (4) representing unadjudicated unilateral or multilateral territorial claims.

wene, by pro-independence extremists who rejected the accord as a sellout of Kanak interests. The assassination was followed by an uneasy calm, with some easing of tension in October when French Prime Minister Michel Rocard released Kanaks imprisoned for kidnapping and the murder of gendarmes that preceded the Ouvéa massacre of May 1988. In provincial elections the anti-independence Rally for Caledonia in the Republic (RPCR) won 27 of the 54 seats, while the FLNKS took 19.

In French Polynesia the chief justice ruled in April that the government had operated illegally since June 1988 because of procedural errors in the appointment of ministers. The issue was later resolved by the Territorial Assembly. In August, in response to mounting public pressure—heightened by a hunger strike by local antinuclear protesters—there was a special sitting of the Assembly to debate the nuclear-testing issue, the future of Mururoa, and related environmental issues. Concern was not allayed by the announcement that only six tests, rather than the usual eight, would take place in 1990. Local elections in midyear saw some gains for groups seeking independence from France but no serious challenge to candidates associated with the territorial government.

In 1989 Niue celebrated 15 years of internal self-government in free association with New Zealand. The occasion was not without tension because of a concurrent constitutional review in which Niueans sought to establish independent citizenship while maintaining the privileges of free entry into New Zealand, where 10,000 Niueans lived, compared with only 2,000 resident in Niue. In June the government of Sir Robert Rex easily survived a no-confidence motion arising out of alleged misuse of aid funds.

Following a general election in February, the Cook Islands had a new Cook Islands Party government led by Geoffrey Henry. It inherited serious financial difficulties, which it attributed to the previous government's misuse of funds and extravagant spending by ministers on overseas trips. In September Henry visited Tahiti to hold talks with French Prime Minister Rocard on fisheries agreements and economic cooperation and assistance.

American Samoa's long-serving congressional representative, Fofo I.F. Sunia, resigned at the end of 1988 during a fraud investigation over "ghost" employees on his payroll. Peter Coleman, who had been ineligible for a consecutive third term as governor in 1984, was reelected to office in 1989.

Elections in Palau at the end of 1988 returned Pres. Ngiratkel Etpison, who favoured removing the antinuclear clauses of Palau's constitution and thus reaching an accommodation with the U.S. The vice president and the legislature, however, were generally opposed to the Compact of Free Association. Despite the continuing stalemate, the U.S. Congress moved to implement some of the financial provisions of the compact to ease Palau's precarious economic situation.

East Asia. Political turmoil in China brought Hong Kong into sharper international focus. The suppression of the democracy movement in Beijing (Peking) triggered massive protests in Hong Kong and ended a perception that China would exert only minimal authority after Britain transferred sovereignty in 1997. In January 1989 the Basic Law Drafting Committee, appointed by China with representatives from Hong Kong, issued an extremely conservative blueprint for a post-1997 political system. This would include a chief executive chosen by a Beijing-appointed electoral college and a legislature partly appointed and partly chosen by "functional constituencies" representing industry, the professions, and labour. The plan was to be submitted to the National Peoples' Congress in Beijing early in 1990. In September Hong Kong declined to send back a defecting mainland athlete and instead allowed him to leave for political asylum in the U.S. In retaliation, China refused to accept back apprehended illegal immigrants in Hong Kong until November, when more than 1,000 had accumulated. Voluntary repatriation of Vietnamese refugees in Hong Kong began during the year, and in December 51 Vietnamese were forcibly repatriated. Also in December, Britain announced it would grant full passports to 50,000 Hong Kong families.

In Macau, due to revert to China in December 1999, some 4,000 public servants were offered jobs in Portugal and 130,000 people, or 28% of the population, were to get right of abode (the unrestricted right to immigrate to Europe with an authorized Portuguese passport). The British government, however, touched off protests when it refused to grant the right of abode to British nationals in Hong Kong. Both Hong Kong and Macau announced major public works programs, including land reclamation and a new harbour in Macau. In July work began on a $450 million airport designed to lessen Macau's dependence on Hong Kong.   (MARTIN LEGASSICK; BARRIE MacDONALD; ROD PRINCE; MELINDA SHEPHERD; ROBERT WOODROW)

This article updates the *Macropædia* articles HONG KONG; INDIAN OCEAN ISLANDS; PACIFIC ISLANDS; SOUTHERN AFRICA: *South West Africa/Namibia;* THE WEST INDIES.

AFP PHOTO

Sam Nujoma, the exiled leader of the South West Africa People's Organization, kisses the ground upon his return to South West Africa/Namibia. Nujoma arrived in time to register to vote in elections for an assembly that would draft a new constitution.

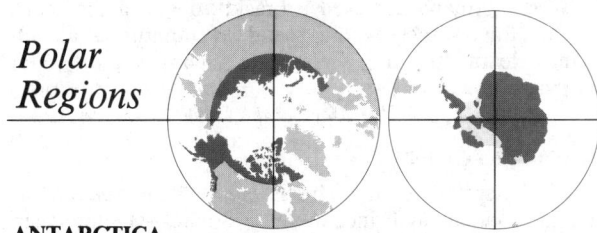

Polar Regions

ANTARCTICA

In Antarctica in 1989, scientific research continued as the dominant activity, with new insights achieved in important areas, particularly Antarctica's influences on and responses to global change.

Minerals Convention. Outside Antarctica the dominant topic was debate about the continent's future. In 1988, following six years of negotiations, representatives of 20 nations had finished writing a Convention on the Regulation of Antarctic Mineral Resource Activities. The document addresses a subject not considered by the 1959 Antarctic Treaty, which reserves the region for peaceful purposes, defers territorial claims, and allows treaty nations to inspect each others' facilities there. The Antarctic Treaty also prohibits nuclear explosions and wastes and encourages environmental preservation and international scientific cooperation.

The new minerals convention is a complex document, with 67 main articles and 12 annex articles. It creates the means for determining the acceptability of mineral resource activities and for regulating any activities deemed acceptable. It acknowledges strong international interest in preserving Antarctica's largely undisturbed environment; it says, in effect, that in some circumstances Antarctica's resources may be developed, but only if significant environmental effects are unlikely to result and only if established uses of Antarctica are not jeopardized. The convention does not automatically open Antarctica to resource-development activities.

The convention would enter into force only if 16 of the 20 participating Antarctic Treaty consultative parties ratified it. For the U.S., ratification would require a presidential decision following concurrence by two-thirds of the Senate. At the end of 1989 this procedure was incomplete. Public scrutiny of the convention, and events taking place after its completion, resulted in vigorous debate. At first all the involved governments appeared to favour ratifica-

tion. Some environmental groups opposed to any minerals development opposed it, while others favoured ratification because of the convention's strong protective provisions.

In January the Argentine government ship *Bahía Paraíso,* carrying 316 people, including 81 tourists, and supplies for its Antarctic stations, hit bottom a mile from the U.S. Palmer Station and lost more than 40,000 bbl of fuel to the sea. The effect on local biota was significant: an entire generation of skua chicks was wiped out, and the 24-year U.S. research baseline in the area was jeopardized. About two months later the tanker *Exxon Valdez* lost a far larger amount of crude oil off the south coast of Alaska. The two events called attention to the potential for environmental degradation by petroleum in cold regions. Two nations—Australia and France—that had participated in negotiation of the convention decided to oppose it. "Mining in Antarctica is not compatible with protection of the fragile antarctic environment," they said in a joint statement in August. The failure of either to ratify would doom the minerals convention.

In September the U.S. Congress' Office of Technology Assessment stated that ratification would further U.S. Antarctic interests: "The environmental provisions of the convention are among the strongest ever developed for any international agreement, but they appear to provide an acceptable balance between U.S. development and environmental protection interests. . . . If a major minerals discovery is made in the absence of an international agreement about antarctic minerals, an unregulated 'gold rush' could follow, . . . damaging all U.S. antarctic interests." The 15th Antarctic Treaty consultative meeting, held in Paris in October, did not schedule debate on the minerals convention, but informal discussions suggested that ultimately the regime would be approved.

Environmental Preservation. At the Paris meeting, a major issue was the question of comprehensive protection of the Antarctic environment. The representatives discussed a recommendation that their governments require environmental impact statements for a wide variety of planned activities, and they passed recommendations for stricter limits on waste disposal and marine pollution. These measures furthered numerous environmental protection standards developed under the treaty since its entry into force nearly three decades earlier. It was agreed to hold a special meeting in 1990 to develop additional comprehensive environmental protection measures.

GREENPEACE; PHOTOGRAPH, STEVE MORGAN

An excavator clears away blasted rock from a construction site behind a seemingly oblivious group of penguins. The construction of a French airstrip on Terre Adelie, Antarctica, prompted members of Greenpeace to occupy the site, claiming that the airstrip would disrupt the region's ecological balance.

Other recommendations at the Paris meeting dealt with air safety and a new category of special areas—multiple-use protected areas—to complement the existing specially protected areas and sites of special scientific interest. More than 100 special areas in Antarctica were now protected by environmental standards even stricter than those in effect for the rest of the continent. Newly approved historic sites included East Base on Stonington Island, site of the oldest U.S. structures in Antarctica.

Three nations that had acceded to the Antarctic Treaty—South Korea, Finland, and Peru—achieved consultative (voting) status, joining 20 others. Colombia acceded, bringing the total number of treaty adherents to 39.

Research Results. Study of deep-sea cores collected at Prydz Bay during leg 119 (1988) of the Ocean Drilling Program extended the known onset of large-scale glaciation of Antarctica back to about 36 million–40 million years ago. The sedimentary record suggests that a fully developed east Antarctic ice sheet reached the coast at Prydz Bay then and was more extensive than the present sheet. While Antarctica's complex glacial history was still incompletely understood, the record was being revealed by a number of methods, including study of offshore glacial deposition made possible by the deep-sea cores. Antarctica's ice sheet is the world's largest remnant of the Ice Age, and comparison of its history to past climates provides powerful clues as to what can be expected in future climatic changes.

A study by French, Soviet, and U.S. scientists confirmed Antarctica's value for global environmental record keeping. Working in an ultraclean laboratory, the investigators proved that the amounts of lead found in layers of snow and ice core from Antarctica do indeed reflect an enormous increase of world industrial lead emissions during the last century, initially from smelters and later from auto exhausts. High lead values from earlier ice core work had been thought to result from contamination during sample collection and analysis. The new study also illustrated just how clean Antarctica is: lead concentrations in Antarctic air 3,000 to 12,000 years ago were one-fifth of those existing there today and about one-millionth of those existing in the air of most modern cities. Soil dust and volcanic eruptions supplied most of the lead in the air during ancient times.

Study of Antarctica's springtime ozone hole continued. By October 1989, following a smaller than usual ozone reduction in 1988, observations from a National Aeronautics and Space Administration satellite and from stations in Antarctica showed the amount of stratospheric ozone had dropped to levels matching the record lows of 1987. Chlorofluorocarbons were the major cause. Scientists now projected that even if all CFC production were halted, the Antarctic ozone hole would continue for at least a century because of CFCs already released throughout the world. Nevertheless, CFC production restraints were still seen as necessary because of the chemicals' threat to stratospheric ozone levels outside the Antarctic.

Ozone-related work in Antarctica included measurement of the increase in ultraviolet radiation (UV) that reaches the Antarctic surface and study of its effect on Antarctic organisms. During the 1988 ozone hole, UV levels at Palmer Station were found to be significantly higher than normal for the time of year. Marine biologists found reduced photosynthesis in the upper few metres of seawater. Longer-term effects were not known, but destruction of the Antarctic food chain seemed unlikely. A more probable effect would be a change in the composition of the marine population, with sensitive species dying out, to be replaced by organisms more tolerant of increased UV.

West Germany achieved a breakthrough on the social front. Nine women would spend 14 months as an all-female team operating Georg von Neumeyer, the West German base camp. (GUY G. GUTHRIDGE)

This article updates the *Macropædia* article ANTARCTICA.

ARCTIC REGIONS

In the aftermath of the March 24, 1989, *Exxon Valdez* tanker accident in Prince William Sound—at more than 200,000 bbl, the largest oil spill in U.S. history—many Alaskans began to question how hard they could bite the hand that fed them economically. Alaska had reaped enormous financial benefits since 1977, thanks largely to the production of oil and its shipment via the Trans-Alaska Pipeline from Prudhoe Bay on Alaska's North Slope to Valdez. Alaska's residents paid no state income or sales tax, and more than 80% of the state's projected 1988–89 revenues of $2.2 billion were derived from oil taxes and royalties. In addition, the Alaska Permanent Fund, established in 1976 from oil royalties, had reached $10 billion and was yielding an annual dividend exceeding $800 per resident of the state. As a reflection of heightened public concern about the environmental consequences of oil and gas development, the state invoked emergency safety regulations for the operations of the pipeline and the marine transportation system, ended a significant tax break for the oil industry, and created a new $50 million hazardous waste emergency fund, to be funded by a five-cent levy on every barrel of crude oil that flowed through the pipeline. (*See* ENVIRONMENT.)

The disastrous spill demonstrated the perils accompanying efforts to extract the last dwindling supplies of untapped oil and gas from ever more inaccessible and environmentally sensitive areas, such as the North Slope of Alaska and the Beaufort Sea. The position of industry and many senior U.S. government officials, including Pres. George Bush, was that the U.S. had no choice but to meet as much of its energy needs as possible within the country, for economic and security reasons. In April L.G. Rawl (*see* BIOGRAPHIES), the head of Exxon, stated that known U.S. oil reserves would last nine years at current rates of production and that shortly after the turn of the century the country would be virtually a captive of foreign producers.

President Bush was reported as saying that despite the *Exxon Valdez* incident, he intended to continue to press Congress to open the Arctic National Wildlife Refuge, near the Alaska-Yukon border, for exploration. The *New York*

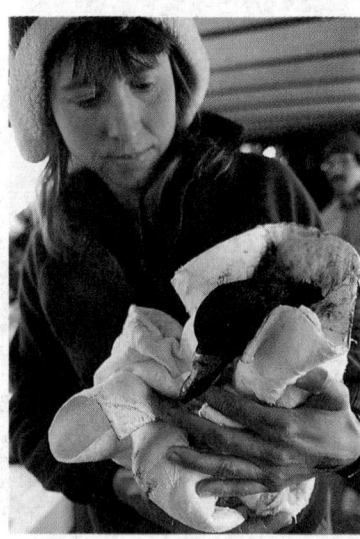

BOB HALLINEN—ANCHORAGE DAILY NEWS/GAMMA/LIAISON

A woman on a bird rescue boat tends to one of the thousands of victims of the *Exxon Valdez* oil spill off Alaska. Oil-soaked birds were cleaned and cared for until they were able to be moved to the Bird Rescue Center in Valdez.

Passengers from the Soviet cruise liner *Maxim Gorky* await rescue in a crowded lifeboat amid ice floes in the North Atlantic. The *Gorky*, much like the *Titanic*, was torn open by partly submerged ice.

NORWEGIAN ARMED FORCES/SCAN FOTO

Times reported that an unpublished Environmental Protection Agency study indicated that improper management practices on the part of the oil industry were seriously damaging the environment in the Prudhoe Bay area, and environmentalists used this to support their contention that oil operations ought to be prohibited on the coastal plain of the refuge. Industry sources had referred to the coastal plain as the most promising area in the U.S. for a major new oil find. The industry also contended it would like to explore and develop less than 1% of the 200-km (124-mi) coastal plain. Opponents countered that the "sphere of influence" caused by development would be 30 to 40 times larger than the development itself. The refuge was the breeding ground for North America's largest remaining herd of migratory caribou, as well as the habitat of polar bears, musk oxen, wolves, arctic foxes, and a rich variety of waterfowl and fish.

With projects to ship petroleum products from the north expected to face stiffer environmental opposition in the future, it was predicted in Canada that some long-stalled northern pipeline projects might be revived. Throughout the year there was increasing evidence of improved energy resource development possibilities in northern Canada. In September the *Toronto Globe and Mail* reported that for the first time in 20 years the federal government had begun selling offshore exploration leases in the Beaufort Sea. Major oil companies, such as Amoco, Gulf, and Chevron, were spending $1 million a day on exploratory drilling in order to evaluate the resource values of their leases before the leases expired in 1991–92.

There was growing optimism that billions of cubic metres of gas from the Mackenzie River Delta could be delivered to customers in the U.S. before the end of the century. By the end of 1989 Canada's National Energy Board (NEB) was expected to decide on an application by a group of energy companies to export 260 billion cu m (9.2 trillion cu ft) of Mackenzie Delta gas to the U.S. over a 20-year period, beginning in 1996. Polar Gas, a consortium led by a group of Canadian companies, was gearing up to seek NEB approval to build the long-awaited Mackenzie Valley pipeline, at an estimated cost of Can$4.4 billion. Late in the year an economic study done by the project sponsors estimated that in all but the least favourable of economic conditions, the megaproject could provide net benefits to the Canadian economy of up to $2.5 billion during the

first 20 years of operation. The study was questioned by native peoples' organizations in the Northwest Territories for failing to take into account the likely environmental and sociological effects.

In September the *Vancouver* (B.C.) *Sun* reported that the Inuit and Dene would sign land claims agreements providing them with billions of dollars in compensation and control over 1,295,000 sq km (500,000 sq mi) of land. Although negotiations were still incomplete, a study presented to the Northwest Territories Legislative Assembly outlined the probable components of what could be the biggest geographic land claim ever dealt with by Canada. The agreements were being negotiated on behalf of 12,-000 Indians and Métis from the Mackenzie Valley and Great Slave Lake and 17,000 Inuit of Nunavut in the northeastern half of the Northwest Territories. In total, the agreements were expected to include multibillion-dollar cash payments, large tracts of land, resource royalties, employment opportunities, exclusive and preferential uses of certain renewable and unrenewable resources, and a variety of tax benefits.

The study also reported on the problems of financial management that native peoples involved in previous settlements had encountered. In Alaska, where native peoples had received close to $1 billion in compensation, most of their development corporations were struggling to survive with average returns on assets of only 1%. For the Cree Indians of James Bay and Northern Quebec, the return on a 1975 settlement of $225 million had improved to about 9% in 1988. Inuit from the U.S.S.R., Canada, the U.S., and Greenland, meeting at the Inuit Circumpolar Conference in Greenland in July, adopted a comprehensive strategy designed to encourage native peoples to become more self-sufficient. The 500 delegates compiled a guide for use at the local and regional levels that spelled out Inuit values on matters such as education and self-government.

In January it was reported that dense stratospheric ice clouds similar to those that had helped human-released chlorine compounds produce a huge hole in the atmospheric ozone over Antarctica had been found over Alert, on the northern tip of Ellesmere Island. Scientists from six nations were probing the Arctic atmosphere to determine the severity of the ozone problem over the north polar ice cap. In Antarctica, where the ozone hole had reached alarming proportions, studies had indicated that when sunlight returned after winter darkness, ice clouds mediated chemical changes that generated large amounts of chlorine in an active form capable of destroying ozone.

In April the Canadian government announced its intention to establish a wide-ranging environmental program to protect the delicate ecology of the North. The first step, in the summer of 1989, was to remove thousands of oil drums that had piled up on Ellesmere Island since World War II. The environmental code would include strict environmental assessments of any proposed development activities or policies affecting the Arctic. Canada's minister of the environment applauded an initiative by Finland to establish an international convention for protection of the Arctic. In November Canada signed an agreement with the Soviet Union covering cooperation in scientific research, the environment, and native peoples.

Continued progress was reported by the U.S.S.R., the U.S., and Canada toward agreement on an Arctic "peace zone." In September the U.S. and the Soviet Union reached an agreement allowing Eskimos to travel across the frontiers of both countries in the Bering Strait area.

(KENNETH DE LA BARRE)

This article updates the *Macropædia* article The ARCTIC.

CONTRIBUTORS

Abdoolcarim, Zoher F. Senior Editor, *Asiaweek,* Hong Kong.
WORLD AFFAIRS: *Indonesia; Malaysia*

Aers, Vivianne L. Editor and Publisher. Editor, *World Fishing.*
AGRICULTURE AND FOOD SUPPLIES: *Fisheries*

Allaby, Michael. Free-lance Writer and Lecturer. Author of *Ecology Facts; A Guide to Gaia.*
ENVIRONMENT *(in part)*

Allan, J.A. Professor of Geography, School of Oriental and African Studies, University of London.
WORLD AFFAIRS: *Libya*

Aloff, Mindy. Dance Writer, *The New Yorker* and *The Threepenny Review;* Senior Critic, *Dance Magazine.*
DANCE *(in part)*

Amedeo, Michael. Writer, Encyclopædia Britannica Educational Corp.; Film Critic, *New City.*
BIOGRAPHIES *(in part)*

Archibald, John J. Feature Writer, *St. Louis Post-Dispatch;* Adjunct Professor, Washington University, St. Louis, Mo. Member of Professional Bowlers Association Hall of Fame.
SPORTS AND GAMES: *Bowling (in part)*

Armstrong, George. Rome Correspondent, *The Guardian.*
WORLD AFFAIRS: *Italy*

Arnold, Darrell. Associate Editor, *The Western Horseman* magazine, Colorado Springs, Colo.
SPORTS AND GAMES: *Rodeo*

Arnold, Guy. Free-lance Writer. Author of *Modern Nigeria; Aid in Africa;* and others.
WORLD AFFAIRS: *Botswana; Burundi; Cape Verde; Equatorial Guinea; Gambia, The; Ghana; Guinea-Bissau; Lesotho; Liberia; Maldives; Mauritius; Nigeria; Rwanda; São Tomé and Príncipe; Seychelles; Sierra Leone; Swaziland*

Arnold, Mavis. Free-lance Journalist, Dublin.
WORLD AFFAIRS: *Ireland*

Arrington, Leonard J. Formerly Church Historian, Church of Jesus Christ of Latter-day Saints.
RELIGION: *Church of Jesus Christ of Latter-day Saints*

Artisien, Patrick. Lecturer in Business and Economics, University of Wales, Cardiff. Author of *Joint Ventures in Yugoslav Industry; North-South Direct Investment in the European Communities; Yugoslavia to 1993: Back from the Brink?*
WORLD AFFAIRS: *Albania*

Baptist, Ines T. Free-lance Writer.
WORLD AFFAIRS: *Belize*

Barford, Michael F. Editor and Director, *Tabacosmos,* London.
INDUSTRIAL REVIEW: *Tobacco*

Bargad, Warren. Samuel M. Melton Professor of Jewish Studies and Director, Center for Jewish Studies, University of Florida.
LITERATURE: *Hebrew*

Barrett, David B. Missions Researcher, Foreign Mission Board, U.S. Southern Baptist Convention.
RELIGION: *World Religious Statistics*

Barrett, John C.A. Headmaster, Kent College, Pembury, England; Secretary, British Committee, World Methodist Council. Author of *Family Worship in Theory and Practice.*
RELIGION: *Methodist Churches*

Bass, Howard. Journalist and Broadcaster. Editor, *Winter Sports,* 1948–69; author of 16 books on winter sports.
SPORTS AND GAMES: *Ice Hockey (in part); Ice Skating; Skiing*

Bergerre, Max. Vatican Affairs Correspondent, *La Vie,* Paris.
WORLD AFFAIRS: *Vatican City State*

Beyer, Reginald Ian. Deputy Curator, Royal Botanic Gardens, Kew, England.
BOTANICAL GARDENS AND ZOOS *(in part)*

Bickelhaupt, David L. Professor Emeritus, Faculty of Finance, College of Business, Ohio State University, Columbus.
INDUSTRIAL REVIEW: *Insurance*

Bird, Thomas E. Director, Council for the Study of Ethics and Public Policy, Queens College, City University of New York.
LITERATURE: *Yiddish*

Bisman, Ronald W. North Island Editor, *New Zealand Harness Racing Weekly.* Author of *Cardigan Bay; Salute to Trotting; Globetrotting Simpson.*
SPORTS AND GAMES: *Horse Racing (in part)*

Boddy, William C. Editor, *Motor Sport.* Full Member, Guild of Motoring Writers.
SPORTS AND GAMES: *Automobile Racing (in part)*

Boden, Edward. Editor, *Veterinary Record.*
HEALTH AND DISEASE: *Veterinary Medicine*

Booth, John Nicholls. Lecturer and Writer. Author of *The Quest for Preaching Power.*
RELIGION: *Unitarian (Universalist) Churches*

Boswall, Jeffery. Head of Film and Video, Royal Society for the Protection of Birds, Bedfordshire, England.
LIFE SCIENCES: *Ornithology*

Box, Ben. Free-lance Writer and Researcher.
WORLD AFFAIRS: *Costa Rica; El Salvador; Guatemala; Honduras; Nicaragua; Peru*

Boye, Roger. Coin columnist, *Chicago Tribune.*
PHILATELY AND NUMISMATICS: *Coins and Paper Money*

Bradsher, Henry S. Foreign Affairs Writer.
WORLD AFFAIRS: *Philippines*

Braidwood, Robert J. Professor Emeritus of Old World Prehistory, Oriental Institute and Department of Anthropology, University of Chicago. Author of *Prehistoric Men.*
ARCHAEOLOGY: *Eastern Hemisphere*

Brazee, Rutlage J. Geophysical Consultant.
EARTH SCIENCES: *Geophysics*

Brecher, Kenneth. Professor of Astronomy and Physics, Boston University. Coauthor and coeditor of *Astronomy of the Ancients.*
ASTRONOMY

Brokopp, John G. Specialist in publicity, public relations, and free-lance writing involving the sport of horse racing.
SPORTS AND GAMES: *Horse Racing (in part)*

Brown, Maggie. Media Editor, The Independent Newspapers, London.
PUBLISHING: *Magazines (in part); Newspapers (in part)*

Burdin, Joel L. Professor of Educational Administration, City College of the City University of New York.
EDUCATION *(in part)*

Burks, Ardath W. Emeritus Professor of Asian Studies, Rutgers University, New Brunswick, N.J.
WORLD AFFAIRS: *Japan*

Butler, Frank. Former Sports Editor, *News of the World,* London. Author of *The Good, the Bad and the Ugly: A Story of Boxing.*
SPORTS AND GAMES: *Boxing*

Cafferty, Bernard. Editor, *British Chess Magazine;* Chess Columnist, *The Sunday Times,* London.
SPORTS AND GAMES: *Chess*

Cameron, Sarah. Economic Advisor, Latin America and the Caribbean, Economics Department, Lloyds Bank PLC, London.

BIOGRAPHIES *(in part);* WORLD AFFAIRS: *Ecuador; Mexico; Venezuela*

Campbell, Alexander Johns. Lloyds Bank PLC, London.
BIOGRAPHIES *(in part);* WORLD AFFAIRS: *Chile; Colombia; Panama; Paraguay; Uruguay*

Cantrell, Scott. Music Critic, *Times–Union,* Rochester, N.Y.
MUSIC: *Classical*

Carter, Robert W. Journalist, London.
SPORTS AND GAMES: *Horse Racing (in part)*

Caswell, Nim. Subeditor, *Financial Times,* international edition, London.
WORLD AFFAIRS: *Benin; Burkina Faso; Chad; Guinea; Mali; Mauritania; Niger; Senegal; Togo*

Chapman, Kenneth F. Former Editor, *Stamp Collecting* and *Philatelic Magazine.*
PHILATELY AND NUMISMATICS: *Stamps*

Chapman, Robin. Senior Economist, Economics Department, Lloyds Bank PLC, London.
WORLD AFFAIRS: *Cuba; Dominican Republic; Haiti*

Chappell, Duncan. Director, Australian Institute of Criminology.
CRIME, LAW ENFORCEMENT, AND PENOLOGY: *Crime; Law Enforcement*

Chapple, Abby. Writer and Consumer Consultant, Consumer Communications, Annapolis, Md.
INDUSTRIAL REVIEW: *Furniture*

Cheuse, Alan. Writing Faculty, English Department, George Mason University, Fairfax, Va. Author of *The Grandmothers' Club; Candace; Fall Out of Heaven; The Bohemians.*
LITERATURE: *English (in part)*

Chuprinin, Sergey. Journalist, Novosti Press Agency, Moscow.
LITERATURE: *Russian (in part)*

Clark, Kenneth R. National Media Writer, *Chicago Tribune.*
TELEVISION AND RADIO: Special Report

Clarke, Judith L. Senior Editor, *Asiaweek,* Hong Kong.
WORLD AFFAIRS: *Kampuchea (Cambodia); Laos; Thailand; Vietnam*

Clarke, R.O. Visiting Professor, Michigan State University.
LABOUR–MANAGEMENT RELATIONS

Cleaveland, Timothy D. Graduate Student, African History, Northwestern University, Evanston, Ill.
WORLD AFFAIRS: *Cameroon; Central African Republic; Comoros; Congo; Côte d'Ivoire; Djibouti; Gabon; Madagascar*

Cleveland, William A. Editor, Britannica World Data and Britannica Atlas.
MINING

Cogle, T.C.J. Editor, *Electrical Review,* London.
INDUSTRIAL REVIEW: *Electrical*

Cook, Kevin G. Publications Officer, Central Office, International Organization of Consumers Unions (IOCU).
CONSUMER AFFAIRS *(in part)*

Cooper, Melanie A. Senior Editorial Assistant, *Newsweek* magazine.
WORLD AFFAIRS: *United States:* Developments in the States in 1989

Cosgrove, Holli Rae. Researcher, Encyclopædia Britannica, Inc.
BIOGRAPHIES *(in part)*

Costin, Stanley H. British Correspondent, *Nykytekstiili,* Finland, and others.
FASHION AND DRESS *(in part)*

Crampton, Richard J. Professor of East European History, University of Kent at Canterbury. Author of *A Short History of Modern*

Bulgaria; Bulgaria 1878–1918: A History.
WORLD AFFAIRS: *Bulgaria*
Cromie, William J. Science Writer, Harvard University News Office.
INDUSTRIAL REVIEW: *Microelectronics; Telecommunications*
Cross, Colin J. Chairman, European Polo Academy.
SPORTS AND GAMES: *Polo*
Crowley, Edward. Technical Journalist; Editor, *100A1* magazine and *Lloyd's Register of Shipping.*
INDUSTRIAL REVIEW: *Shipbuilding;* TRANSPORTATION *(in part)*
Cunningham, Susan. Researcher and Writer on Latin America. Author of *Latin America: A Crisis of Development* (in preparation).
BIOGRAPHIES *(in part);* WORLD AFFAIRS: *Argentina; Brazil; Latin-American Affairs*
Curwen, Peter J. Principal Lecturer in Economics, Sheffield City Polytechnic, England. Author of *The U.K. Publishing Industry; The World Book Industry.*
PUBLISHING: *Books (in part)*
Cviic, K.F. East European Specialist, *The Economist,* London.
WORLD AFFAIRS: *Yugoslavia*
Czerwinski, Edward J. Chairman, Germanic and Slavic Languages and Literature, State University of New York at Stony Brook.
LITERATURE: *Eastern European (in part); Russian (in part)*
Davis, Donald A. Editor, *Drug & Cosmetic Industry* and *Cosmetic Insider's Report.*
INDUSTRIAL REVIEW: *Pharmaceuticals*
Deam, John B. Technical Director, NMTBA—The Association for Manufacturing Technology, McLean, Va.
INDUSTRIAL REVIEW: *Machinery and Machine Tools*
de la Barre, Kenneth. Director, Katimavik, Montreal.
WORLD AFFAIRS: *Arctic Regions*
Deletant, Dennis J. Senior Lecturer in Romanian Studies, University of London. Author of *Colloquial Romanian; Romania* (World Bibliographical Series).
WORLD AFFAIRS: *Romania*
Denselow, Robin. Rock Music Critic, *The Guardian,* London; Current Affairs Reporter, BBC Television.
MUSIC: *Popular*
De Puy, Norman R. Minister, First Baptist Church, Newton Centre, Mass.; Editor and Publisher, *Cabbages and Kings* newsletter.
RELIGION: *Baptist Churches*
Deshayes, Marie-Jose. Head of Documentation Service, International Vine and Wine Office, Paris.
INDUSTRIAL REVIEW: *Beverages (in part)*
Dicks, Geoffrey R. Senior Research Fellow, London Business School. Author of *Sources of World Financial and Banking Information.*
INDUSTRIAL REVIEW: *Introduction*
Dirnbacher, Elfriede. Austrian Civil Servant.
WORLD AFFAIRS: *Austria*
Dixon, Bernard. Science Writer and Consultant. European Editor, *Bio/Technology.* Author of *Magnificent Microbes; Health and the Human Body.*
HEALTH AND DISEASE: *Mental Health; Overview (in part)*
Dooling, Dave. Consultant and Writer, D² Associates, Huntsville, Ala.
SPACE EXPLORATION
Dorris, Thomas Hartley. Editor, Ecumenical Press Service, Geneva.
RELIGION: *Lutheran Communion*
Doyle, Peter J. Information Officer, British Glass. Author of *Glass Making Today.*
INDUSTRIAL REVIEW: *Glass*
Earp, John H. Director, Halcrow Fox and Associates, Bristol, England.
TRANSPORTATION *(in part)*

Emerson, Warren K. Editor, *Badminton USA* magazine.
SPORTS AND GAMES: *Badminton*
Engels, Jan R. Director, Centre Paul Hymans; Editor, *Vooruitgang-Progrès* magazine.
WORLD AFFAIRS: *Belgium*
Ewing, John. Professor, Department of Mathematics, Indiana University. Author of *Puzzle It Out.*
MATHEMATICS
Farr, D.M.L. Professor Emeritus of History, Carleton University, Ottawa.
WORLD AFFAIRS: *Canada*
Faust, Joan Lee. Garden Editor, *New York Times.*
GARDENING *(in part)*
Fendell, Robert J. Author of *The New Era Car Book and Auto Survival Guide; Encyclopedia of Auto Racing Greats; How to Make Your Car Last.*
SPORTS AND GAMES: *Automobile Racing (in part)*
Finkelstein, Ellen. Copy Editor, Encyclopædia Britannica, Inc.
BIOGRAPHIES *(in part);* PUBLISHING: Sidebar
Firth, David. Editor, *The Friend,* London; formerly Editor, *Quaker Monthly,* London.
RELIGION: *Religious Society of Friends*
Follett, Christopher. Denmark Correspondent, *The Times,* London; Newscaster, Radio Denmark, English service. Author of *Fodspor paa Cypern.*
WORLD AFFAIRS: *Denmark*
Fought, Stephen Oliver. Professor, U.S. Naval War College, Newport, R.I. Author of *SDI: A Policy Analysis.*
Macropædia: WAR, THE TECHNOLOGY OF
Franklin, Harold. Bridge Correspondent, *Yorkshire Post.*
SPORTS AND GAMES: *Contract Bridge*
Franz, Frederick W. President, Watch Tower Bible and Tract Society of Pennsylvania.
RELIGION: *Jehovah's Witnesses*
Freedman, Lawrence D. Professor and Head, Department of War Studies, King's College, University of London. Author of *The Evolution of Nuclear Strategy* and others.
Macropædia: WAR, THE THEORY AND CONDUCT OF
Friday, Elbert W., Jr. Assistant Administrator for Weather Services, National Oceanic and Atmospheric Administration.
EARTH SCIENCES: *Meteorology*
Fridovich, Irwin. James B. Duke Professor of Biochemistry, Duke University Medical Center, Durham, N.C.
LIFE SCIENCES: *Molecular Biology (in part)*
Fridovich-Keil, Judith L. Postdoctoral Fellow, Department of Pharmacology, Harvard Medical School, Dana Farber Cancer Institute.
LIFE SCIENCES: *Molecular Biology (in part)*
Friskin, Sydney E. Hockey Correspondent, *The Times,* London.
SPORTS AND GAMES: *Billiard Games (in part); Field Hockey*
Frost, David. Rugby Union Writer, *The Guardian,* London.
SPORTS AND GAMES: *Football (in part)*
Gaddum, Anthony H. Chairman, H. T. Gaddum and Company Ltd., Silk Merchants, Macclesfield, Cheshire, England.
INDUSTRIAL REVIEW: *Textiles (in part)*
Ganado, Albert. Lawyer, Malta.
WORLD AFFAIRS: *Malta*
Ganguly, Dilip. Senior Correspondent, The Associated Press (USA), South Asia Bureau, New Delhi, India.
WORLD AFFAIRS: *Afghanistan; Bangladesh; Bhutan; Myanmar; Nepal; Pakistan; Sri Lanka*
Gibbons, Anne R. Free-lance Writer.
LIFE SCIENCES: *Entomology*
Gibbons, J. Whitfield. Senior Research Ecologist, Savannah River Ecology Laboratory, Aiken, S.C.

LIFE SCIENCES: *Zoology*
Gillespie, Hugh M. Director of Communications, International Road Federation, Washington, D.C.
ENGINEERING PROJECTS: *Roads*
Gjester, Fay. Free-lance Journalist and Editor; formerly Oslo Correspondent, *Financial Times,* London.
WORLD AFFAIRS: *Norway*
Goldblatt, Howard C. Professor of Chinese, University of Colorado, Boulder. Author of *Hsian Hung; Chinese Literature for the 1980s.*
LITERATURE: *Chinese*
Goldsmith, Arthur. Editor-at-Large, *Popular Photography,* New York City.
PHOTOGRAPHY
Goldstein, William W. Free-lance Writer.
PUBLISHING: *Books (in part)*
Golob, Richard Stephen. President, World Information Systems; Publisher, *Golob's Oil Pollution Bulletin* and *Hazardous Materials Intelligence Report.* Editor of *Almanac of Science and Technology.*
ENVIRONMENT: Special Report
Goodwin, Noël. Free-lance Writer and Broadcaster. Associate Editor and Music Editor, *Dance & Dancers.*
DANCE *(in part)*
Gottfried, Martin. Drama Critic, New York City. Author of *Broadway Musicals; Jed Harris: The Curse of Genius; In Person: The Great Entertainers.*
THEATRE *(in part)*
Greeman, Adrian. Editor, *Construction Today.*
ENGINEERING PROJECTS: *Bridges*
Green, Anthony L. Copy Editor, Encyclopædia Britannica, Inc.
BIOGRAPHIES *(in part)*
Griffiths, A.R.G. Senior Lecturer in History, Flinders University of South Australia. Author of *Contemporary Australia.*
BIOGRAPHIES *(in part);* WORLD AFFAIRS: *Australia; Nauru; Papua New Guinea*
Grossman, Joel W. Archaeologist.
ARCHAEOLOGY: *Western Hemisphere*
Grumet, Robert S. Anthropologist, New Hope, Pa.
ANTHROPOLOGY
Guthridge, Guy G. Manager, Polar Information Program, U.S. National Science Foundation.
WORLD AFFAIRS: *Antarctica*
Handelman, Howard. Professor and Chairman, Department of Political Science, University of Wisconsin, Milwaukee.
ECONOMIC AFFAIRS: Special Report
Havard-Williams, P. Professor of Library and Information Studies, University of Botswana. Emeritus Professor, Loughborough University, Leicestershire, England.
LIBRARIES *(in part)*
Hawkland, William D. Chancellor and Professor of Law, Louisiana State University.
LAW: *Court Decisions*
Hebblethwaite, Peter. Vatican Affairs Writer, *National Catholic Reporter,* Kansas City, Mo.
BIOGRAPHIES *(in part);* RELIGION: *Roman Catholic Church*
Hébert, Pierre. Associate Professor, University of Toronto.
LITERATURE: *French (in part)*
Heilbroner, Robert L. Norman Thomas Professor Emeritus of Economics, New School for Social Research, New York City. Author of *The Worldly Philosophers; The Nature and Logic of Capitalism,* and others.
Macropædia: ECONOMIC SYSTEMS
Hendershott, Myrl C. Professor of Oceanography, Scripps Institution of Oceanography, La Jolla, Calif.
EARTH SCIENCES: *Oceanography*
Hess, Marvin G. Executive Vice-President, National Wrestling Coaches Association.
SPORTS AND GAMES: *Wrestling*

Hoeksema, Klaas J. Assistant Professor, Department of Political Science, Free University, Amsterdam.
WORLD AFFAIRS: *Netherlands, The; Suriname*
Hope, Thomas W. Chairman, Hope Reports, Inc., Rochester, N.Y.
MOTION PICTURES *(in part)*
Hunnings, Neville March. Editorial Director, European Law Centre, London. Editor, *Common Market Law Reports.*
LAW: *International Law*
IEIS. International Economic Information Services, London.
ECONOMIC AFFAIRS: *World Economy; Stock Exchanges (in part)*
Ingham, Kenneth. Emeritus Professor of History, University of Bristol, England. Author of *Jan Christian Smuts: The Conscience of a South African.*
WORLD AFFAIRS: *Angola; Kenya; Malawi; Mozambique; Somalia; Sudan, The; Tanzania; Uganda; Zaire; Zambia; Zimbabwe*
Ingram, Derek. Editor, Gemini News Service, London. Author of *Commonwealth for a Colour-Blind World; The Imperfect Commonwealth.*
WORLD AFFAIRS: *Commonwealth of Nations*
Jackson, Martin. Publisher and Editor in Chief, *Broadcast* magazine, London.
TELEVISION AND RADIO *(in part)*
Jacquet, Constant H. Staff Associate, Discipleship and Communication Unit, National Council of Churches. Editor of *Yearbook of American and Canadian Churches.*
WORLD AFFAIRS: *United States (table)*
Jardine, Adrian. Company Director. Member, Guild of Yachting Writers.
SPORTS AND GAMES: *Sailing*
Jaspert, W. Pincus. Technical and Editorial Consultant. International Editor, *American Printer* and *World-Wide Printer.* Author of *Encyclopaedia of Typefaces* (7th ed.); *State of the Art* (4th ed.).
INDUSTRIAL REVIEW: *Printing*
Joffé, George. Journalist and Writer on North African and Middle Eastern Affairs.
WORLD AFFAIRS: *Algeria; Morocco; Tunisia*
Johnsson, William G. Editor, *Adventist Review.* Author of *Behold His Glory; In Absolute Confidence.*
RELIGION: *Seventh-day Adventist Church*
Jones, Alun. University Lecturer.
WORLD AFFAIRS: *Andorra; Liechtenstein; Luxembourg; Monaco; San Marino*
Jones, D.A.N. Novelist and Critic. Author of *Parade in Pairs; Never Had It So Good.*
LITERATURE: *Introduction; United Kingdom*
Jones, W. Glyn. Professor of European Literature, University of East Anglia, Norwich, England.
LITERATURE: *Danish*
Joseph, Lou. Senior Science Writer, Hill and Knowlton, Chicago.
HEALTH AND DISEASE: *Dentistry*
Jotischky, Helma. Principal Research Officer, Paint Research Association, London.
INDUSTRIAL REVIEW: *Paints and Varnishes*
Katz, William A. Professor, School of Library Science, State University of New York, Albany.
PUBLISHING: *Magazines (in part)*
Kelleher, John A. New Zealand Journalist. Former Editor, *The Dominion* and *Dominion Sunday Times,* Wellington, New Zealand. President, National Press Club of New Zealand.
BIOGRAPHIES *(in part);* WORLD AFFAIRS: *New Zealand*
Kellner, Peter. Political Columnist, *The Independent,* London. Author of *The Civil Servants: An Inquiry into Britain's Ruling Class; Callaghan: The Road to Number Ten.*
BIOGRAPHIES *(in part);* WORLD AFFAIRS: *United Kingdom*

Kennedy, Richard M. Agricultural Economist, Agriculture and Trade Analysis Division of the Economic Research Service, U.S. Department of Agriculture.
AGRICULTURE AND FOOD SUPPLIES *(in part)*
Kilian, Michael D. Washington Columnist, *Chicago Tribune.* Author of *Flying Can Be Fun; Heavy Losses.*
SPORTS AND GAMES: *Aerial Sports*
Kimche, Jon. Formerly Editor, *New Middle East; Afro-Asian Affairs,* London. Author of *Second Arab Awakening; Palestine or Israel.*
WORLD AFFAIRS: *Israel*
Kind, Joshua B. Professor of Art History, Northern Illinois University, De Kalb. Author of *Rouault; Geometry as Abstract Art.*
MUSEUMS *(in part)*
King, Charles. Director of Media Relations, International Headquarters, Salvation Army.
RELIGION: *Salvation Army*
Kloos, Jean Clark Cameron. Publisher, *Timber Trades Journal.*
INDUSTRIAL REVIEW: *Wood Products*
Knecht, Jean. Formerly Assistant Foreign Editor, *Le Monde,* Paris.
WORLD AFFAIRS: *France; France:* Sidebar
Knox, Richard A. Managing Editor, *Power Technology International* and *Power Generation Technology.*
INDUSTRIAL REVIEW: *Nuclear Industry*
Kolankiewicz, George. Lecturer in Sociology, University of Essex, England. Coauthor of *Social Groups in Polish Society; Poland: Politics, Economics and Society.*
BIOGRAPHIES *(in part);* WORLD AFFAIRS: *Poland*
Kushnick, Louis. Lecturer, Department of American Studies, University of Manchester, England.
POPULATIONS AND POPULATION MOVEMENTS: *International Migration;* RACE RELATIONS
LaFleur, Virginia M. Advertising Manager, Training and Development, Encyclopædia Britannica Educational Corp.; Freelance Writer.
BIOGRAPHIES *(in part)*
Lamb, Kevin M. Sportswriter, *Chicago Sun-Times.* Author of *Quarterbacks, Nickelbacks & Other Loose Change.*
BIOGRAPHIES *(in part);* SPORTS AND GAMES: *Football (in part)*
Laqueur, Walter. Codirector, Institute of Contemporary History and Wiener Library, London. Author of *Europe Since Hitler.*
WORLD AFFAIRS: *Introduction*
Larsson, Gerd. Japan Correspondent, *Dagens Industri.*
BIOGRAPHIES *(in part)*
Laskey, Elizabeth. Copy Editor, Encyclopædia Britannica, Inc.
BIOGRAPHIES *(in part)*
Lee, Audrey Bertina. Director of News and Information, Office of Communication, Christian Church (Disciples of Christ).
RELIGION: *Christian Church (Disciples of Christ)*
Legassick, Martin. Coordinator (honorary), Southern Africa Labour Education Project; formerly Senior Lecturer in Sociology, University of Warwick, Coventry, England.
WORLD AFFAIRS: *Dependent States (in part); South Africa*
Legum, Colin. Associate Editor (1947–81), *The Observer;* Editor, *Africa Contemporary Record* and *Third World Reports,* London.
BIOGRAPHIES *(in part);* WORLD AFFAIRS: *African Affairs*
Lennox-Kerr, Peter. Editor, *High Performance Textiles* and *OE Report;* European Editor, *Textile World.* Author of *The World Fibers Book.*
INDUSTRIAL REVIEW: *Textiles (in part)*
Levine, Steven I. Visiting Professor in Political Science, Duke University, Durham, N.C.

Author of *Anvil of Victory: The Communist Revolution in Manchuria;* Coeditor of *China's Bitter Victory: The War with Japan, 1937–45.*
BIOGRAPHIES *(in part);* WORLD AFFAIRS: *China; Taiwan*
Litsky, Frank. Sportswriter, *New York Times.*
SPORTS AND GAMES: *Ice Hockey (in part)*
Litweiler, John. Jazz Critic; Contributor to *Down Beat, Chicago Tribune,* and other publications. Author of *The Freedom Principle: Jazz after 1958.*
MUSIC: *Jazz*
Logan, Robert G. Sportswriter, *Daily Herald,* Arlington Heights, Ill. Author of *Cubs Win!; So You Think You're a Diehard Cub Fan.*
SPORTS AND GAMES: *Basketball (in part)*
Longmore, Andrew. Free-lance Sportswriter, *The Times,* London; former Assistant Editor, *The Cricketer.*
BIOGRAPHIES *(in part);* SPORTS AND GAMES: *Cricket*
Lyles, Jean Caffey. Senior News Editor, *The Lutheran;* Editor-at-Large, *The Christian Century.*
RELIGION: *Introduction*
McBride, Gail W. Free-lance Medical Writer and Editor; formerly Medical News Editor, *Journal of the American Medical Association.*
HEALTH AND DISEASE: *Overview (in part)*
McCauley, Martin. Senior Lecturer in Soviet and East European Studies, School of Slavonic and East European Studies, University of London.
BIOGRAPHIES *(in part);* WORLD AFFAIRS: *Union of Soviet Socialist Republics*
Macdonald, Barrie. Reader in History, Massey University, Palmerston North, N.Z.
WORLD AFFAIRS: *Dependent States (in part); Fiji; Kiribati; Oceanian Affairs; Solomon Islands; Tonga; Tuvalu; Vanuatu; Western Samoa*
McGregor, Alan. Geneva Correspondent, *The Times,* London; Swiss Radio International, Bern; ABC, Australia; and RNZ, New Zealand.
WORLD AFFAIRS: *Switzerland*
McLachlan, Keith S. Senior Lecturer, School of Oriental and African Studies, University of London.
WORLD AFFAIRS: *Iran*
Mallett, H.M.F. Editor, *Wool Record Weekly Market Report,* Bradford, England.
INDUSTRIAL REVIEW: *Textiles (in part)*
Mango, Andrew. Foreign Affairs Analyst.
WORLD AFFAIRS: *Turkey*
Martin, David V. Editor, *Tunnels & Tunnelling* magazine, London.
ENGINEERING PROJECTS: *Tunnels*
Marty, Martin E. Fairfax M. Cone Distinguished Service Professor of the History of Modern Christianity, University of Chicago.
RELIGION: Special Report
Mateja, James L. Auto Editor, Columnist, and Financial Reporter, *Chicago Tribune.* Author of *Used Cars: Finding the Best Buy.*
INDUSTRIAL REVIEW: *Automobiles (in part)*
Matthews, Ian D. Manager, International Affairs, British Steel PLC.
INDUSTRIAL REVIEW: *Iron and Steel*
Matthíasson, Björn. Economist, Ministry of Finance, Iceland.
WORLD AFFAIRS: *Iceland*
Mazie, David M. Associate of Carl T. Rowan, syndicated columnist. Free-lance Writer.
SOCIAL SECURITY AND WELFARE SERVICES *(in part)*
Mazze, Edward Mark. Professor of Marketing, School of Business Administration, Temple University, Philadelphia.
CONSUMER AFFAIRS *(in part);* INDUSTRIAL REVIEW: *Advertising*
Mermel, T.W. Consultant; formerly Chairman, Committee on World Register of Dams of the International Commission on Large Dams.

ENGINEERING PROJECTS: *Dams; Dams table*
Meyendorff, John. Professor, Dean of St. Vladimir's Orthodox Theological Seminary; Professor of History, Fordham University, New York City.
RELIGION: *The Orthodox Church; Eastern Non-Chalcedonian Churches*
Millikin, Sandra. Architectural Historian.
ARCHITECTURE; ART EXHIBITIONS AND ART SALES: *Art Exhibitions;* MUSEUMS *(in part)*
Miyahara, Masato. Free-lance Industrial Reporter and Technical Writer. Author of *The Recent Trends in the American Specialty Steel Industry.*
INDUSTRIAL REVIEW: *Automobiles (in part)*
Modiano, Mario. Athens Correspondent, *The Times,* London.
WORLD AFFAIRS: *Greece*
Moragne, Edward Paul. Senior Index Editor, Encyclopædia Britannica, Inc.
BIOGRAPHIES *(in part)*
Morris, Jacqui M. Editor, *Oryx* magazine.
ENVIRONMENT *(in part)*
Morrison, Donald. Special Projects Editor, *Time* magazine.
PUBLISHING: *Newspapers (in part);* WORLD AFFAIRS: *United States*
Mosey, Chris. Nordic Correspondent, *The Observer;* Swedish Correspondent, *The Times* and *Daily Mail.*
WORLD AFFAIRS: *Sweden*
Mulroney, The Right Honourable Brian. Prime Minister of Canada.
Feature Article: THE FUTURE HAS STARTED
Murray, Ian. Bonn Correspondent, *The Times,* London.
WORLD AFFAIRS: *German Democratic Republic; Germany, Federal Republic of*
Murray, Lorraine. Copy Editor, Encyclopædia Britannica, Inc.
BIOGRAPHIES *(in part)*
Myers, D.G. Assistant Professor of English, Texas A&M University, College Station.
SPORTING RECORD: Special Report
Myers, Susan Marts. Index Editor, Encyclopædia Britannica, Inc.
BIOGRAPHIES *(in part)*
Nagy, Joseph L. Senior Editor, *Asiaweek* magazine, Hong Kong.
WORLD AFFAIRS: *Korea*
Naylor, Ernest. Lloyd Roberts Professor of Marine Zoology, University College of North Wales.
LIFE SCIENCES: *Marine Biology*
Nelson, Bert. Editor, *Track and Field News.* Author of *Olympic Track and Field.*
SPORTS AND GAMES: *Track and Field Sports*
Netschert, Bruce C. Vice-President, National Economic Research Associates, Inc., Washington, D.C.
ENERGY
Neusner, Jacob. University Professor, Brown University, Providence, R.I. Author of *Judaism, The Evidence of the Mishnah.*
RELIGION: *Judaism*
Newby, Donald J. Bowls Correspondent, *Daily Telegraph,* London; former Editor, *World Bowls.* Editor, *Bowls Year Book 1990.*
SPORTS AND GAMES: *Lawn Bowls*
Newton, Carolyn D. Free-lance Writer and Editor.
BIOGRAPHIES *(in part)*
Niesz, Dale E. Director, Center for Ceramic Research, Rutgers, The State University of New Jersey.
INDUSTRIAL REVIEW: *Ceramics*
Norman, Geraldine. Art Market Correspondent, *The Independent,* London. Author of *The Sale of Works of Art; Nineteenth Century Painters and Painting; Biedermeier Painting;* Coauthor of *The Fake's Progress.*
ART EXHIBITIONS AND ART SALES: *Art Sales*
Oberman, Bonnie. Writer and Editor.
BIOGRAPHIES *(in part)*

O'Donoghue, Michael. Curator, Science Reference Library, London; Lecturer in Gemmology, City of London Polytechnic.
INDUSTRIAL REVIEW: *Gemstones*
O'Dwyer, Thomas. Director, Levant Bureau; formerly Reuters Bureau Chief, Cyprus; Writer on East Mediterranean and Arab Affairs, Nicosia, Cyprus.
WORLD AFFAIRS: *Cyprus*
Olejnik, Renee Mahn. Executive Editor, American Power Boat Association.
SPORTS AND GAMES: *Motorboating*
Olney, P.J.S. Curator of Birds and Reptiles, Zoological Society of London. Editor, *International Zoo Yearbook.*
BOTANICAL GARDENS AND ZOOS *(in part)*
Osborne, Keith. Editor, *British Rowing Almanack.* Author of *Boat Racing in Britain, 1715–1975.*
SPORTS AND GAMES: *Rowing*
Osterbind, Carter C. Associate, Gerontology Center, and Professor Emeritus of Economics, University of Florida.
INDUSTRIAL REVIEW: *Building and Construction*
Palmer, John. European Editor, *The Guardian,* Brussels.
WORLD AFFAIRS: *Western European Affairs*
Palmer, S.B. Professor of Experimental Physics, Department of Physics, University of Warwick, England.
PHYSICS
Parker, Sandy. Publisher of weekly international newsletter on fur industry; Copublisher, *Fur World.*
INDUSTRIAL REVIEW: *Furs*
Parkes, Christopher. Consumer Industries Editor, *Financial Times,* London.
AGRICULTURE AND FOOD SUPPLIES: Special Report
Pasco, Adam Gerhold. Editor, *Garden News;* Consultant Editor, *Garden Answers.*
GARDENING *(in part)*
Paul, Charles Robert, Jr. Archivist, U.S. Olympic Committee, Colorado Springs, Colo.
SPORTS AND GAMES: *Gymnastics; Weight Lifting*
Penfold, Robin C. Free-lance Writer on industrial topics. Formerly Editor, *Shell Petrochemicals.* Author of *A Journalist's Guide to Plastics.*
INDUSTRIAL REVIEW: *Plastics*
Pertile, Lino. Professor of Italian, University of Edinburgh, Scotland.
LITERATURE: *Italian*
Petherick, Karin. Reader in Swedish, University of London.
LITERATURE: Swedish
Pfeffer, Irving. Attorney. Author of *The Financing of Small Business.*
ECONOMIC AFFAIRS: *Stock Exchanges (in part)*
Pinfold, Geoffrey M. Director, NCL Stewart Scott Ltd., London. Author of *Reinforced Concrete Chimneys and Towers.*
ENGINEERING PROJECTS: *Buildings*
Plotnik, Arthur. Associate Publisher, New Products, American Library Association; Executive Producer, *Library Video Magazine.* Editor, *American Libraries* magazine (1975–89).
LIBRARIES *(in part)*
Poirié, François. Writer and Critic. Author of *La Passade légendaire.*
LITERATURE: *French (in part)*
Post, Avery D. President, United Church of Christ, New York City.
RELIGION: *United Church of Christ*
Prasad, H.Y. Sharada. Secretary, Indira Gandhi Memorial Trust, New Delhi, India.
WORLD AFFAIRS: *India*
Prince, Rod. Journalist specializing in Caribbean matters. Editor, *Caribbean Insight.*
WORLD AFFAIRS: *Antigua and Barbuda; Bahamas, The; Barbados; Dependent States (in*

part); Dominica; Grenada; Guyana; Jamaica; Saint Kitts and Nevis; Saint Lucia; Saint Vincent and the Grenadines; Trinidad and Tobago
Ranger, Robin. Peace Fellow, U.S. Institute of Peace, Washington, D.C. Author of *Arms and Politics 1958–1978; Arms Control in a Changing Political Context.*
MILITARY AFFAIRS
Rebelo, L. S. Reader Emeritus, Department of Portuguese Studies, King's College, University of London.
LITERATURE: *Portuguese (in part)*
Reed, Arthur. Senior Editor, Europe, *Air Transport World.* Author of *Britain's Aircraft Industry;* Coauthor of *RAE Farnborough.*
TRANSPORTATION *(in part)*
Reed, Dwight C. President, National Soft Drink Association, Washington, D.C.
INDUSTRIAL REVIEW: *Beverages (in part)*
Reid, J.H. Reader in German, University of Nottingham, England. Author of *Heinrich Böll: A German for His Time; Writing Without Taboos: The New East German Literature.*
LITERATURE: *German*
Reid, Philip D. Professor of Biological Sciences, Smith College, Northampton, Mass.
LIFE SCIENCES: *Botany*
Reynolds, Frank E. Professor of the History of Religions and Buddhist Studies, Divinity School, University of Chicago.
RELIGION: *Buddhism (in part)*
Riggs, Thomas J. Researcher, Encyclopædia Britannica, Inc.
BIOGRAPHIES *(in part)*
Ripley, Michael D. Senior Public Relations Officer, Brewers' Society, U.K.
INDUSTRIAL REVIEW: *Beverages (in part)*
Robinson, David. Film Critic, *The Times,* London. Author of *A History of World Cinema; Chaplin: His Life and Art.*
MOTION PICTURES *(in part);* MOTION PICTURES: Sidebar
Rollin, Jack. Association Football Columnist, *Sunday Telegraph,* London. Editor, *Rothmans Football Yearbook.* Author of *England's World Cup Triumph; Guinness Book of Soccer Facts and Feats.*
SPORTS AND GAMES: *Football (in part);* Football: Sidebar
Rutherford, Andrew. Senior Lecturer, Faculty of Law, University of Southampton, England. Author of *Prisons and the Process of Justice; Growing out of Crime.*
CRIME, LAW ENFORCEMENT, AND PENOLOGY: Prisons and Penology
Sadie, Stanley. Editor, *The New Grove Dictionary of Music and Musicians.* Editor, *The Musical Times* (1967–87); Music Critic, *The Times,* London (1964–81).
Macropædia: MOZART
Saeki, Shoichi. Professor of Literature, Chuo University, Tokyo. Author of *Japanese Autobiographies.*
LITERATURE: *Japanese*
Salisbury, Jonathan M. Publisher and Editor, *Toy Trader,* Watford, England.
INDUSTRIAL REVIEW: *Games and Toys*
Sanders, Alan J.K. Editor, U.S.S.R. edition, *Summary of World Broadcasts,* BBC. Author of *Mongolia: Politics, Economics and Society.*
WORLD AFFAIRS: *Mongolia*
Sarahete, Yrjö. General Secretary, Fédération Internationale des Quilleurs, Helsinki.
SPORTS AND GAMES: *Bowling (in part)*
Sarmiento, Sergio. Editor in Chief, Spanish-language publications, Encyclopædia Britannica Publishers, Inc.
SPORTS AND GAMES: *Baseball (in part);* Football *(in part)*
Schaeffer, Reverend Jill. Secretary, Department of Cooperation and Witness, World Alliance of Reformed Churches, Geneva.
RELIGION: *Reformed, Presbyterian, and Congregational Churches*

Schoenfield, Albert. Formerly Publisher, *Swimming World;* Vice-Chairman, U.S. Olympic Swimming Committee (1976–88). Honouree, International Swimming Hall of Fame; Honorary Member, American Swimming Coaches of America.
SPORTS AND GAMES: *Swimming*

Schöpflin, George. Lecturer in East European Political Institutions, London School of Economics and School of Slavonic and East European Studies, University of London.
WORLD AFFAIRS: *Czechoslovakia; Eastern European Affairs; Hungary*

Shackleford, Peter. Chief of Research, World Tourism Organization, Madrid.
INDUSTRIAL REVIEW: *Tourism*

Shelley, Andrew. Squash Manager, Squash Rackets Association, England.
SPORTS AND GAMES: *Squash Rackets*

Shepherd, Melinda. Associate Editor, Encyclopædia Britannica Yearbooks.
WORLD AFFAIRS: *Dependent States (in part)*

Sherman, Francine Shonfeld. Assistant Editor, Compton's Encyclopedia.
BIOGRAPHIES *(in part)*

Smith, Donald. Editor, *Rubber World* magazine, Akron, Ohio.
INDUSTRIAL REVIEW: *Rubber*

Smith, Reuben W. Dean, Graduate School, and Professor of History, University of the Pacific, Stockton, Calif.
RELIGION: *Islam*

Smogorzewski, K.M. Writer on contemporary history. Founder and Editor, *Free Europe,* London.
WORLD AFFAIRS: *Political Parties (in part)*

Stern, Irwin. Senior Lecturer in Portuguese, Columbia University, New York City.
LITERATURE: *Portuguese (in part)*

Støverud, Torbjørn. Honorary Research Fellow, University College, London.
LITERATURE: *Norwegian*

Sullivan, H. Patrick. Dean of the College and Professor of Religion, Vassar College, Poughkeepsie, N.Y.
RELIGION: *Hinduism*

Summerhill, Edward M. Staff Member, Reuters; Free-lance Writer, Finnish News Agency.
WORLD AFFAIRS: *Finland*

Sumner, David E. Author of *The Episcopal Church's History: 1945–1985.* Contributor to Episcopal Church periodicals.
RELIGION: *Anglican Communion*

Suzuki, Toshihiko. Associate Editor, *Newsweek Japan,* TBS-Britannica Co., Ltd., Tokyo.
SPORTS AND GAMES: *Baseball (in part)*

Sweetinburgh, Thelma. Fashion Writer, Paris.
FASHION AND DRESS *(in part)*

Swift, Richard N. Professor Emeritus of Politics, New York University, New York City.
WORLD AFFAIRS: *United Nations*

Synan, Vinson. Chairman, North American Renewal Service Committee. Author of *The Holiness-Pentecostal Movement.*
RELIGION: *Pentecostal Churches*

Taggart, Charles Johnson. Free-lance Writer.
BIOGRAPHIES *(in part)*

Taishoff, Lawrence B. President, Broadcasting Publications, Inc., and Publisher, *Broadcasting* magazine and others.
TELEVISION AND RADIO *(in part)*

Tak, Jean van der. Formerly Senior Editor, Population Reference Bureau, Inc.
POPULATIONS AND POPULATION MOVEMENTS: *Demography*

Talbot, Nathan A. Manager, Committees on

Publication, The First Church of Christ, Scientist, Boston.
RELIGION: *Church of Christ, Scientist*

Tateishi, Kay K. Free-lance Writer and Translator.
BIOGRAPHIES *(in part)*

Thomas, Robert Murray. Professor of Education and Head, Program in International Education, University of California at Santa Barbara. Author of *A Chronicle of Indonesian Higher Education; Oriental Theories of Human Development; Comparing Theories of Child Development.*
EDUCATION *(in part)*

Tingay, Lance. Former Tennis Correspondent, *Daily Telegraph,* London. Author of *100 Years of Wimbledon; Tennis Facts and Feats.*
SPORTS AND GAMES: *Tennis*

Trilling, Ossia. Coeditor and Contributor, *International Theatre.* Contributor, BBC, *The Times,* London, and other media.
BIOGRAPHIES *(in part);* THEATRE *(in part)*

UNHCR. The Office of the United Nations High Commissioner for Refugees.
POPULATIONS AND POPULATION MOVEMENTS: *Refugees*

Utt, Roger L. Editor, *Puerta del Sol;* formerly Assistant Professor of Spanish, Department of Romance Languages and Literatures, University of Chicago.
LITERATURE: *Spanish (in part)*

Vale, Norman K. Retired Director of News Services, The United Church of Canada.
RELIGION: *The United Church of Canada*

Van Haveren, Bruce P. Adjunct Professor, Department of Environmental Sciences, Colorado School of Mines, Golden. Author of *Water Resource Measurements: A Handbook.*
EARTH SCIENCES: *Hydrology*

Venzke, Bruce H. Associate Editor, *Pool & Billiard Magazine.* Member, Statistics and Records Committee, Billiard Congress of America; President, Billiard Congress of Wisconsin; Coordinator, Modern Specialty Pool Leagues.
SPORTS AND GAMES: *Billiard Games (in part)*

Verdi, Robert William. Sports Columnist, *Chicago Tribune.*
SPORTS AND GAMES: *Baseball (in part)*

Villacorta, Lynn. Social Security Specialist, International Labour Office, Geneva.
SOCIAL SECURITY AND WELFARE SERVICES *(in part)*

Vint, Arthur Kingsley. Counselor, International Table Tennis Federation.
SPORTS AND GAMES: *Table Tennis*

Walsh, Jennifer. Coordinator, Publications, United States Volleyball Association.
SPORTS AND GAMES: *Volleyball*

Walters, Jonathan S. Ph.D. Candidate, Divinity School, University of Chicago.
RELIGION: *Buddhism (in part)*

Warner, Antony C. Managing Director, Warner, Robinson and Associates, London.
INDUSTRIAL REVIEW: *Beverages (in part)*

Warner, Edward S. Senior Editor, *High Technology Business* magazine.
INFORMATION PROCESSING AND INFORMATION SYSTEMS *(in part)*

Warren, J. Robert. Editor in Chief, *Chemical Business.*
INDUSTRIAL REVIEW: *Chemicals*

Warren, Kenneth S. Director for Science, Maxwell Communication Corp., New York City. Author of *Tropical and Geographical Medicine* (2nd ed.); *Scientific Information Systems and the Principle of Selectivity.*

Feature Article: THE ALMA-ATA DECLARATION: HEALTH FOR ALL BY THE YEAR 2000?

Way, Diane Lois. Historical Researcher.
BIOGRAPHIES *(in part)*

Weinthal, John R. Writer on the automotive industry.
INDUSTRIAL REVIEW: *Automobiles (in part)*

Welch, Melvin D. Secretary, English Basket Ball Association; Editor (1971–78), *Basketball Magazine.*
SPORTS AND GAMES: *Basketball (in part)*

Whelan, John. Associate Editor, Redwood Publishing.
WORLD AFFAIRS: *Bahrain; Egypt; Iraq; Jordan; Kuwait; Lebanon; Middle Eastern and North African Affairs; Oman; Qatar; Saudi Arabia; Syria; United Arab Emirates; Yemen, People's Democratic Republic of; Yemen Arab Republic*

Whitney, Barbara. Senior Copy Editor, Encyclopædia Britannica, Inc.; Contributing Editor, *Medical and Health Annual.*
AGRICULTURE AND FOOD SUPPLIES: Sidebar; BIOGRAPHIES *(in part)*

Wilkinson, John R. Sportswriter, East Midland Provincial Newspapers Ltd., U.K.
SPORTS AND GAMES: *Cycling*

Williams, Michael. Golf Correspondent, *Daily Telegraph,* London.
SPORTS AND GAMES: *Golf*

Williams, Raymond Leslie. Professor of Spanish, University of Colorado, Boulder.
LITERATURE: *Spanish (in part)*

Wilson, Michael. Free-lance Aviation Writer and Consultant; Associate Editor, *Prophecy Today.*
INDUSTRIAL REVIEW: *Aerospace*

Woodrow, Robert. Assistant Managing Editor, *Asiaweek,* Hong Kong.
WORLD AFFAIRS: *Brunei; Dependent States (in part); Singapore; Southeast Asian Affairs*

Woods, Elizabeth. Writer. Author of *The Yellow Volkswagen; Gone; Men; The Amateur.*
LITERATURE: *English (in part)*

Woods, Michael. Science Editor, *Toledo (Ohio) Blade.*
CHEMISTRY

Woollen, Anthony. Editor (1959–79), *Food Manufacture,* London. Editor, *Food Industries Manual* (20th ed.).
AGRICULTURE AND FOOD SUPPLIES: *Food Processing*

Wooller, Michael. Economist, Economics Dept., Lloyds Bank PLC, London.
WORLD AFFAIRS: *Bolivia; Portugal; Spain*

Wyllie, Peter John. Division of Geological and Planetary Sciences, California Institute of Technology.
EARTH SCIENCES: *Geology and Geochemistry*

Yamadori, Yuji. Director, Research and International Affairs, Japan Information Processing Development Center. Editor, *Japan Computer Quarterly.*
INFORMATION PROCESSING AND INFORMATION SYSTEMS *(in part)*

Young, M. Norvel. Chancellor Emeritus, Pepperdine University, Malibu, Calif. Author of *Preachers of Today.*
RELIGION: *Churches of Christ*

Yurieff, Agnieszka. Graduate Research Assistant, Germanic and Slavic Languages and Literatures, State University of New York at Stony Brook.
LITERATURE: *Eastern European (in part); Russian (in part)*

Zeidenberg, Leonard. Chief Correspondent, *Broadcasting* magazine, Washington, D.C.
TELEVISION AND RADIO *(in part)*

1990
Britannica
World Data

Encyclopædia Britannica, Inc.
Chicago
Auckland/Geneva/London/Madrid/Manila/Paris/Rome
Seoul/Sydney/Tokyo/Toronto

CONTENTS

INTRODUCTION

Britannica World Data provides a statistical portrait of some 220 countries and dependencies of the world, at a level appropriate to the size and importance of each. It contains 186 country statements, ranging in length from one to four pages, for the largest and most significant of these, and permits, in the development of more than a score of major thematic subject areas (employment, agriculture, trade), simultaneous comparison among all of these larger countries and 34 additional smaller dependent states.

Updated annually, *Britannica World Data* can be consulted as a separate work of reference developing a particular body of subject matter, but it is particularly intended as direct, structured support for many of Britannica's other reference works—encyclopedias, yearbooks, atlases—at a level of detail that their editorial style or space requirements do not permit.

Like the textual, graphic, or cartographic modes of expression of these other products, statistics possess their own inherent editorial virtues and weaknesses. Two principal goals in the creation of *Britannica World Data* were up-to-dateness and comparability, each possible separately, but not always possible to combine. If, for example, research on some subject (say, registered motor vehicles) is completed during a particular year (x), figures may be available for 100 countries for the preceding year ($x-1$), for 140 countries for the year before that ($x-2$), and for 180 countries for the year before that ($x-3$).

Which year should be the basis of a thematic compilation for 220 countries so as to give the best combination of up-to-dateness and comparability? And, should $x-1$ be adopted for the thematic table, ought up-to-dateness in the country table (for which year x is already available) be sacrificed for agreement with the thematic table? In general, the editors have opted for maximum up-to-dateness in the country statistical boxes and maximum comparability in the thematic tables, so as to take the best advantage of late information, published and unpublished.

Comparability, however, also resides in the meaning of the numbers compiled, which may differ greatly from country to country. The headnotes to the thematic tables explain many of these definitional problems; the Glossary serves the same purpose for the country statistical pages. Since the researcher or editor does not always find a neat, unambiguous choice between a datum compiled on two different bases (say, railroad track length, or route length), one of which is wanted and the other not, a choice must be made between the latest official national data (which may be incomplete, published only after a delay of several years, politically suspect, compiled on the wrong basis [for international comparability], or may refer to some time period other than a standard Gregorian calendar year) and some external figure, often only an estimate, compiled by an international organization (such as the UN, FAO, or IMF), on the desired basis, but often at a considerable remove from the country's own most recent data, both in time and distance. Every effort has been made to obtain the best combination of comparability and up-to-dateness from available sources, and, when the completeness of a country's published data permitted, to analyze it further for better agreement in coverage, scope, and datedness, For certain subjects, especially population, the editors have prepared their own estimates.

The published basis of the information compiled is the statistical collections of Encyclopædia Britannica, Inc., some of the principal elements of which are enumerated in the Bibliography. All of these sources are held, and updated continuously for editorial use, in Britannica's editorial offices. The publications themselves are issued in some 75 languages in common use among the countries of the world; the information contained in them is supplemented by unpublished data received in correspondence from the countries concerned. Usual holdings for a country with a well-developed statistical and publishing program may include any of the following kinds of documents: the national statistical abstract; the most recent censuses of population; periodic or occasional reports on vital statistics, social indicators, agriculture, mining, labour, manufacturing, wholesale and retail trade, finance and banking, development planning, foreign trade, transportation, and communication. These primarily statistical sources are supplemented by other kinds of national reference works, such as gazetteers (of place names), national atlases, constitutions, and monographs by domestic or external analysts.

No reference work on the countries of the world can, or should, be used in isolation. To say that the population density of Hungary is about 300 persons per square mile will not be misleading, because the population is rather evenly distributed across the landscape outside the cities. To give a density for Greenland calculated on the same basis (total population ÷ total area) *would* be misleading (and would amount to only 0.06 person per square mile) because much of Greenland is uninhabitable ice cap. Similarly, the great majority of the social, economic, and financial data contained in this work should not be interpreted in isolation. Interpretive text of long perspective, such as that of the *Encyclopædia Britannica* itself; political, geographic, and topical maps; and recent analysis of political events and economic trends, such as that contained in the articles of the *Book of the Year,* will all help to supply balance, physical framework, and analytical focus that numbers alone cannot provide. By the same token, study of those sources will be amplified and made more concrete by use of the *Britannica World Data* to supply up-to-date geographic, demographic, economic, and financial data to illuminate the generalized and more impressionistic methodology of those works.

GLOSSARY

A number of terms that are used to classify and report data in the "Nations of the World" section require some explanation.

Those italicized terms that are used regularly in the country compilations to introduce specific categories of information (*e.g., birth rate, budget*) appear in this glossary in italic boldface type, followed by a description of the precise kind of information being offered and how it has been edited and presented.

All other terms are printed here in roman boldface type. Many terms have quite specific meanings in statistical reporting, and they are so defined here. Other terms have less specific application as they are used by different countries or organizations. Data in the country compilations based on definitions markedly different from those below will usually be footnoted.

Terms that appear in small capitals in certain definitions are themselves defined at their respective alphabetical locations.

Terms whose definitions are marked by an asterisk (*) refer to data supplied only in the larger two- to four-page country compilations.

access to services, a group of measures indicating a population's level of access to public services, including electrical power, treated public drinking water, sewage removal, and fire protection.*

activity rate, *see* participation rate.

age breakdown, the distribution of a given population by age, usually reported here as percentages of total population in each of six 15-year age brackets. When substantial numbers of persons do not know, or state, their exact age, distributions may not total 100.0%.

area, the total surface area of a country or its administrative subdivisions, including both land and inland (nontidal) water area. Land area is usually calculated from "mean low water" on a "plane table," or "flat," basis.

area and population, a tabulation usually including the first-order administrative subdivisions of the country (such as the states of the United States), with capital (headquarters, or administrative seat), area, and population. When these subdivisions are especially numerous or, occasionally, nonexistent, a regional, electoral, census, or other nonadministrative scheme of subdivisions has been substituted.

associated state, *see* (free) association; *see* state.

atheist, in statements of religious affiliation, one who professes active opposition to religion; "nonreligious" refers to those professing only no religion, nonbelief, or doubt.

balance of payments, a financial statement for a country for a given period showing the balance among: (1) transactions in goods, services, and income between that country and the rest of the world, (2) changes in ownership or valuation of that country's monetary gold, SPECIAL DRAWING RIGHTS, and claims on and liabilities to the rest of the world, and (3) unrequited transfers and counterpart entries needed (in an accounting sense) to balance transactions and changes among any of the foregoing types of exchange that are not mutually offsetting. The United Nations *System of National Accounts* (SNA) provides a framework for international comparability in classifying such transactions, but detail of local law as to what constitutes a transaction, the basis of its valuation, and the size of a transaction visible to fiscal authorities all result in differences in the meaning of a particular national statement.*

balance of trade, the net value of all international goods trade of a country, usually excluding reexports (goods received only for transshipment), and the percentage that this net represents of total trade.

Balance of trade refers only to the "visible" international trade of goods as recorded by customs authorities and is thus a segment of a country's BALANCE OF PAYMENTS, which takes all visible and invisible trade with other countries into account. (Invisible trade refers to imports and exports of money, financial instruments, and services such as transport, tourism, and insurance.) A country has a favourable balance of trade when the value of exports exceeds that of imports.

barrel (bbl), a unit of liquid measure. The barrel conventionally used for reporting crude petroleum and petroleum products is equal to 42 U.S. gallons, or 159 litres. The number of barrels of crude petroleum per metric ton, ranging typically from 6.45 to 8.13, depends upon the specific gravity of the petroleum. The world average is roughly 7.33 barrels per ton.

birth rate, the number of live births annually per 1,000 of midyear population. Birth rates for individual countries may be compared with the world annual average of 27 births per 1,000 population between 1985 and 1990.

budget, the annual receipts and expenditures of the central government for its activities only; does not include state, provincial, or local governments or semipublic (parastatal, quasi-nongovernmental) corporations unless otherwise specified. Figures for budgets are limited to ordinary (recurrent) receipts and expenditures, wherever possible, and exclude capital expenditures, *i.e.,* funds for development and other special projects originating as foreign-aid grants or loans.

When both a recurrent and a capital budget exist for a single country, the former is the budget funded entirely from national resources (taxes, duties, excises, etc.) that would recur (be generated by economic activity) every year. It funds the most basic governmental

---

Abbreviations

Measurements

cu m	cubic metre(s)
kg	kilogram(s)
km	kilometre(s)
kW	kilowatt(s)
kW-hr	kilowatt-hour(s)
metric ton-km	metric ton-kilometre(s)
mi	mile(s)
passenger-km	passenger-kilometre(s)
passenger-mi	passenger-mile(s)
short ton-mi	short ton-mile(s)
sq km	square kilometre(s)
sq m	square metre(s)
sq mi	square mile(s)
troy oz	troy ounce(s)
yr	year(s)

Political Units and International Organizations

CACM	Central American Common Market
CARICOM	Caribbean Community and Common Market
CUSA	Customs Union of Southern Africa
E.Ger.	East Germany
EEC	European Economic Community
FAO	United Nations Food and Agriculture Organization
IMF	International Monetary Fund
OECS	Organization of Eastern Caribbean States
U.A.E.	United Arab Emirates
U.K.	United Kingdom
U.S.	United States
U.S.S.R.	Union of Soviet Socialist Republics
W.Ger.	West Germany

Months

Jan.	January	Oct.	October
Feb.	February	Nov.	November
Aug.	August	Dec.	December
Sept.	September		

Miscellaneous

avg.	average
c.i.f.	cost, insurance, and freight
commun.	communications
CPI	consumer price index
est.	estimate(d)
excl.	excluding
f.o.b.	free on board
GDP	gross domestic product
GNP	gross national product
govt.	government
incl.	including
mo.	month(s)
n.a.	not available (in text)
n.e.s.	not elsewhere specified
NMP	net material product
no.	number
pl.	plural
pos.	position
pub. admin.	public administration
SDR	Special Drawing Right
SITC	Standard International Trade Classification
svcs.	services
teacher tr.	teacher training
transp.	transportation
voc.	vocational
$	dollar (of any currency area)
£	pound (of any currency area)
...	not available (in tables)
—	none, less than half the smallest unit shown, or not applicable (in tables)

services, those least able to stand interruption. The capital budget is usually funded by external aid and may change its size considerably from year to year.

capital, usually, the actual seat of administration and government of a state. When more than one capital exists, each is identified by kind; when interim arrangements exist during the creation or movement of a national capital, the de facto situation is described.

Anomalous cases are footnoted, such as those in which (1) the de jure designation under the country's laws differs from actual local practice (*e.g.,* Benin's designation of one capital in constitutional law, but another in actual practice), (2) international recognition does not support a country's claim (as with the proclamation by Israel of a capital on territory not fully recognized as part of Israel), or (3) both a state and a capital have been proclaimed on territory recognized as part of another state (as with the Turkish Republic of Northern Cyprus).

capital budget, *see* budget.

causes of death, as defined by the World Health Organization, "the disease or injury which initiated the train of morbid events leading directly to death, or the circumstances of accident or violence which produced the fatal injury." This principle, the "underlying cause of death," is the basis of the medical judgment as to cause; the statistical classification system according to which these causes are grouped and named is the *International List of Causes of Death,* the latest revision of which is the Ninth. Reporting is usually in terms of events per 100,000 population. When data on actual causes of death are unavailable, information on morbidity, or illness rate, usually given as reported cases per 100,000 of infectious diseases (notifiable to WHO as a matter of international agreement), may be substituted.

chief of state/head of government, paramount national governmental officer(s) exercising the highest executive and/or ceremonial roles of a country's government. In general usage, the chief of state is the formal head of a national state. The primary responsibilities of the chief of state may range from the purely ceremonial—convening legislatures and greeting foreign officials—to the exercise of complete national executive authority. The head of government, when this function exists separately, is the officer nominally charged (by the constitution) with the majority of actual executive powers, though they may not in practice be exercised, especially in military or single-party regimes in which effective power may reside entirely outside the executive governmental machinery provided by the constitution. A prime minister, for example, usually understood to be the head of government, may in practice exercise only cabinet-level authority.

In communist countries the official identified as the chief of state is the chairman of the policy-making organ, and the official given as the head of government is the chairman of the nominal administrative/executive organ.

c.i.f. (trade valuation): *see* imports.

colony, an area annexed to, or controlled by, an independent state but not an integral part of it; a non-self-governing territory. A colony has a charter and may have a degree of self-government. A crown colony is a colony originally chartered by the British government.

commonwealth (U.S.), a self-governing political entity associated with the United States; examples are Puerto Rico since 1952, or the Northern Marianas since 1979.

communications, collectively, the means available for the public transmission of information within a country. Data are provided for daily newspapers, their number and total circulation, and the per capita rate of circulation implied by that total; for radio, television, and telephone receivers, total numbers and rates of availability are supplied. Telephone receiver data refer to the number of sets (stations) having access to the public switched network. Data for a few countries refer to the number of "main lines" through which subscribers' equipment is connected to the network.

constant prices, an adjustment to the members of a time series (of values) to eliminate the effect of inflation year by year. It consists of referring all data in the series to a single year so that "real" change may be seen.

constitutional monarchy, *see* monarchy.

consumer price index (CPI), also known as the retail price index, or the cost-of-living index, a series of index numbers assigned to the price of a selected "basket," or assortment, of basic consumer goods and services in a country or region to measure changes over time in prices paid by a typical household for those goods and services. Items included in the CPI are ordinarily determined by governmental surveys of typical household expenditures and are assigned weights relative to their proportion of those expenditures. Index values are period averages unless otherwise noted.

coprincipality, *see* monarchy.

current prices, the valuation of a financial aggregate as of the year reported, without adjustment for inflation.

daily per capita caloric intake (supply), the calories equivalent to the known average daily supply of foodstuffs for human consumption in a given country divided by the population of the country (and the proportion of that supply provided, respectively, by vegetable and animal sources). The daily per capita caloric intake of a country may be compared with the corresponding recommended daily per capita caloric requirement. The latter is calculated by the Food and Agriculture Organization of the United Nations from the age and sex distributions, average body weights, and environmental temperatures in a given region to determine the calories needed to sustain a person there at normal levels of activity and health. The daily per capita caloric requirement ranges from 2,200 to 2,500.

de facto population, for a given area, the population composed of those actually present at a particular time, including temporary residents and visitors (such as immigrants not yet granted permanent status, "guest" or expatriate workers, refugees, or tourists), but excluding legal residents temporarily absent.

de jure population, for a given area, the population composed only of those legally resident at a particular time, excluding temporary residents and visitors (such as "guest" or expatriate workers, refugees, or tourists), but including legal residents temporarily absent.

deadweight tonnage, the maximum weight of cargo, fuel, fresh water, stores, and persons that may safely be carried by a ship. It is customarily measured in long tons of 2,240 pounds each, equivalent to 1.016 metric tons. Deadweight tonnage is the difference between the tonnage of a fully loaded ship and the fully unloaded tonnage of that ship.

See also gross (register) ton.

death rate, the number of deaths annually per 1,000 of midyear population. Death rates for individual countries may be compared with the world annual average of 10 deaths per 1,000 population between 1985 and 1990.

density (of population), usually, the DE FACTO POPULATION of a country divided by its total area. Special adjustment is made for inland water or other uninhabitable areas, *e.g.,* excluding the lake area of Finland.

department, a first-order civil administrative subdivision. The *overseas department* (France) is an overseas subdivision of the French Republic, almost equivalent to a department of metropolitan France, with elected representation in the French Parliament.

dependent state, constitutionally or statutorially organized political entity outside of and under the jurisdiction of an independent state (or a federal element of such a state) but not formally annexed to it (*see* Table).

direct taxes, taxes levied directly on firms and individuals, such as taxes on income, profits, and capital gains. The immediate incidence, or burden, of direct taxes is on the firms and individuals thus taxed; direct taxes on firms

---

Dependent states[1]

Australia
- Christmas Island
- Cocos (Keeling) Islands
- Norfolk Island

Denmark
- Faeroe Islands
- Greenland

France
- French Guiana
- French Polynesia
- Guadeloupe
- Martinique
- Mayotte
- New Caledonia
- Réunion
- Saint Pierre and Miquelon
- Wallis and Futuna

Netherlands, The
- Aruba
- Netherlands Antilles

New Zealand
- Cook Islands
- Niue
- Tokelau

Norway
- Jan Mayen
- Svalbard

Portugal
- Macau

South Africa
- South West Africa/Namibia

United Kingdom
- Anguilla
- Bermuda
- British Virgin Islands
- Cayman Islands
- Falkland Islands
- Gibraltar
- Guernsey
- Hong Kong
- Isle of Man
- Jersey
- Montserrat
- Pitcairn Island
- Saint Helena and Dependencies
- Turks and Caicos Islands

United States
- American Samoa
- Guam
- Puerto Rico
- Trust Territory of the Pacific Islands
  - Marshall Islands
  - Federated States of Micronesia
  - Northern Mariana Islands
  - Palau
- Virgin Islands (of the U.S.)

[1]Excludes territories (1) to which Antarctic Treaty is applicable in whole or in part, (2) without permanent civilian population, (3) without internationally recognized civilian government (Western Sahara, Gaza Strip), or (4) representing unadjudicated unilateral or multilateral territorial claims.

may, however, be passed on to consumers and other economic units in the form of higher prices for goods and services, with the result that the distinction between direct and indirect taxation may be unclear.

distribution of income/wealth, the portion of personal income or wealth accruing to households or individuals comprising each respective decile (tenth) or quintile (fifth) of a country's households or individuals.*

divorce rate, the number of legal, civilly recognized divorces annually per 1,000 population.

doubling time, the number of complete years required for a country to double its population at its current rate of natural increase.

earnings index, a series of index numbers comparing average wages for a country or region with the same industries at a previous period to measure changes over time in those wages. It is most commonly reported for wages paid on a daily, weekly, or monthly basis; annual figures represent averages of these shorter periods. The scope of the earnings index varies from country to country; the index is often limited to earnings in manufacturing industries. The index for each country applies to all wage earners in a designated group and ordinarily takes into account basic wages (overtime is normally distinguished), bonuses, cost-of-living allowances, and contributions toward social security. Some countries include payments in kind. Contributions toward social security by employers are usually excluded, as are social security benefits received by wage earners.

economically active population, see population economically active.

education, tabulation of the principal elements of a country's educational establishment, classified as far as possible according to the country's own system of primary, secondary, and higher levels (the usual age limits for these levels being identified in parentheses), with total number of schools (physical facilities) and of teachers and students (whether full- or part-time). The student–teacher ratio is calculated whenever available data permit.

educational attainment, the distribution of the population age 25 and over with completed educations by the highest level of formal education attained or completed; it is often reported, however, for age groups still in school or for the economically active only.

emirate, empire, see monarchy.

enterprise, a legal entity formed to conduct a business, which it may do from more than one establishment (place of business or service point).

ethnic/linguistic composition, ethnic, racial, or linguistic composition of a national population, reported here according to the most reliable breakdown available, whether published in official sources (such as a census) or in external analysis (when the subject is not addressed in national sources [usually because of social or political sensitivities]).

exchange rate, the value of one currency compared with another, or with a standardized unit of account such as the SPECIAL DRAWING RIGHT, or as mandated by local statute when one currency is "tied" by a par value to another. Rates given usually refer to free market values when the currency itself is traded.

exports, material goods legally leaving a country (or customs area) and subject to customs regulations. The total value and distribution by percentage of the major items (in preference to groups of goods) exported are given, together with the distribution of trade among major trading partners (usually single countries or trading blocs). Valuation of goods exported is free on board (f.o.b.) unless otherwise specified. The value of goods exported and imported f.o.b. is calculated from the cost of production and excludes the cost of transport.

external debt, public and publicly guaranteed debt with a maturity of more than one year owed to nonnationals of a country and repayable in foreign currency, goods, or services. The debt may be an obligation of a national or subnational governmental body (or an agency of either), of an autonomous public body, or of a private debtor that is guaranteed by a public entity. The debt is usually either outstanding (contracted) or disbursed (drawn).

external territory (Australia), see territory.

federal, consisting of first-order political subdivisions that are prior to and independent of the central government in certain functions.

federal republic, see republic.

federation, a union of coequal political entities that retain some degree of autonomy within the union.

fertility rate, see total fertility rate.

financial aggregates, tabulation of seven-year time series, providing principal measures of the financial condition of a country, including: (1) the exchange rate of the national currency against the U.S. dollar, the pound sterling, and the International Monetary Fund's SPECIAL DRAWING RIGHT (SDR), (2) the amount and kind of international reserves (holdings of SDRs, gold, and foreign currencies) and reserve position of the country in the IMF, and (3) principal economic rates and prices (central bank discount rate, government bond yields, and industrial stock [share] prices). For BALANCE OF PAYMENTS, the origin in terms of component balance of trade items and balance of invisibles (net) is given.*

fish catch, the live-weight equivalent of the aquatic animals (including fish, crustaceans, mollusks, etc., but excluding whales, seals, and other aquatic mammals) caught in freshwater or marine areas by national fleets and landed in domestic or foreign harbours for commercial, industrial, or subsistence purposes.

f.o.b. (trade valuation): see exports.

food, see daily per capita caloric intake.

form of government/political status, the structure of a country's administration provided for in normal constitutional operation—whether or not suspended by extralegal military or civil action, although such de facto administrations are identified—together with the number of members (elected, appointed, and ex officio) for each legislative house, named according to its English rendering. Dependent states (see Table) are classified according to the status of their political association with the administering country.

(free) association, late stage in the process by which U.K. and U.S. dependencies achieve independence; it usually implies a relation between a largely self-governing dependency and its administering power that is capable of termination in full independence at the instance of the dependent state, though always in consultation with the administering power.

global social product, see material product.

gross domestic product (GDP), the total value of the final goods and services produced by residents and nonresidents within a given country during a given year. The GDP excludes the value of net income earned abroad, which is included in the GROSS NATIONAL PRODUCT (GNP). Unless otherwise noted, the value is given in current prices of the year indicated.

gross national product (GNP), the total value of final goods and services produced both from within a given country *and* from external (foreign) transactions in a given year. Unless otherwise noted, the value is given in current prices of the year indicated. GNP is equal to GROSS DOMESTIC PRODUCT adjusted by net factor income from abroad, which is the income residents receive from abroad for factor services (labour, investment, and interest) less similar payments made to nonresidents who contribute to the domestic economy.

gross (register) ton, unit of measure of the permanently enclosed volume of a ship, less certain exempted spaces such as those devoted to machinery, bunkers, crew accommodations, and so on; the gross register tonnage of a ship is thus a rough estimation of its volumetric cargo capacity. The gross register ton is equivalent to 100 cubic feet, or 2.83 cubic metres. See also deadweight tonnage.

head of government, see chief of state/head of government.

health, a group of measures including number of accredited physicians (according to World Health Organization criteria) currently practicing or employed and their ratio to the total population; total hospital beds and their ratio; and INFANT MORTALITY RATE.

household income and expenditure, data for average size of a HOUSEHOLD (by number of individuals) and average household income. Sources of income and expenditures for major items of consumption are reported as percentages.

In general, household income is the amount of funds, usually measured in monetary units, received by the members (generally those 14 years old and over) of a household in a given time period. The income can be derived from (1) wages or salaries, (2) nonfarm or farm SELF-EMPLOYMENT, (3) transfer payments, such as pensions, public assistance, unemployment benefits, etc., and (4) other income, including interest and dividends, rent, royalties, etc. The income of a household is expressed as a gross amount before deductions for taxes. Data on expenditure refer to consumption of personal or household goods and services; they normally exclude savings, taxes, and insurance; practice with regard to inclusion of credit purchases differs markedly.

household, economically autonomous individual or group of individuals living in a single dwelling unit. A family household is one composed principally of individuals related by blood or marriage.

immigration, usually, the number and origin of those immigrants admitted to a nation in a legal status that would eventually permit the granting of the right to settle permanently or to acquire citizenship.*

imports, material goods legally entering a country (or customs area) and subject to customs regulations; excludes financial movements. The total value and distribution by percentage of the major items (in preference to groups of goods) imported are given, together with the direction of trade among major trading partners (usually single countries), trading blocs (such as the European Economic Community), or customs areas (such as Belgium-Luxembourg). The value of goods imported is given free on board (f.o.b.) unless otherwise specified; f.o.b. is defined above under EXPORTS.

The principal alternate basis for valuation of goods in international trade is that of cost, insurance, and freight (c.i.f.); its use is restricted to imports, as it comprises the principal charges needed to bring the goods to the customs house in the country of destination. Because it inflates the value of imports relative to exports, more countries have, latterly, been estimating imports on an f.o.b. basis as well.

incorporated territory (U.S.), see territory.

independent, of a state, autonomous and controlling both its internal and external affairs.

indirect taxes, taxes levied on sales or transfers of selected intermediate goods and services, including excises, value-added taxes, and tariffs, that are ordinarily passed on to the ultimate consumers of the goods and services. Figures given for individual countries are limited to indirect taxes levied by their respective central governments unless otherwise specified.

infant mortality rate, the number of children per 1,000 live births who die before their

first birthday. Total infant mortality includes neonatal mortality, which is deaths of children within one month of birth.

invisibles (invisible trade), *see* balance of trade.

kingdom, *see* monarchy.

labour force, portion of the POPULATION ECONOMICALLY ACTIVE comprising those most fully employed or attached to the labour market (the unemployed are considered to be "attached" in that they usually represent persons previously employed seeking to be reemployed), particularly as viewed from a short-term perspective. It normally includes those who are self-employed, employed by others (whether full-time, part-time, seasonally, or on some other less than full-time basis), and, as noted above, the unemployed (both those previously employed and those seeking work for the first time). In the "gross domestic product and labour force" table, the majority of the labour data provided refer to population economically active, since PEA represents the longer-term view of working population and, thus, subsumes more of the marginal workers who are often missed by shorter-term surveys.

land use, distribution by classes of vegetational cover or economic use of the land area only (excluding inland water, for example, but not marshland), reported as percentages.

leisure, the principal uses or reported preferences in the use of the individual's free time for recreation, rest, or self-improvement.*

life expectancy, the number of years a person born within a particular population group (age cohort) would be expected to live, based on actuarial calculations.

literacy, the ability to read and write a language with some degree of competence; the precise degree constituting the basis of a particular national statement is usually defined by the national census and is often tested by the census enumerator. Elsewhere, particularly where much adult literacy may be the result of literacy campaigns rather than passage through a formal educational system, definition and testing of literacy may be better standardized.

major cities, usually the five largest cities proper whose population is at least one-tenth that of the primate (largest) city; fewer will be listed if the size disparity is very great or there are fewer urban localities in the country. For multipage tables, 10 or more will be listed without regard for the size of the primate city.* All populations will refer to the most specific administrative or demographically defined city proper, unless a municipality or METROPOLITAN AREA is specified.

manufacturing, mining, and construction enterprises/retail sales and service enterprises, a detailed tabulation of the principal industries in these sectors, showing for each industry the number of enterprises and employees, wages in that industry as a percentage of the general average wage, and the value of that industry's output in terms of value added or turnover.*

marriage rate, the number of legal, civilly recognized marriages annually per 1,000 population.

material (or social) product, in the national accounting systems of the socialist countries, the aggregate (sometimes "global") value of all "productive" economic activity, generally omitting personal (nonpublic) services, financial activities, and the like that in conventional Western national accounts would contribute to the GROSS DOMESTIC PRODUCT, a more comprehensive measure that includes not only material output but also every identifiable service element of a national economy. Socialist countries that are members of the International Monetary Fund have begun, however, to report gross domestic, and national, product according to the *System of National Accounts*

that forms the basis of international standardization of national accounts.

material well-being, a group of measures indicating the percentage of households or dwellings possessing certain goods or appliances, including automobiles, telephones, television receivers, refrigerators, air conditioners, and washing machines.*

merchant marine, the privately or publicly owned ships registered with the maritime authority of a nation (limited to those in Lloyd's of London statistical reporting of 100 or more GROSS REGISTER TONS) that are employed in commerce, whether or not owned or operated by nationals of the country.

metropolitan area, a city and the region of dense, predominantly urban, settlement around the city; the population of the whole is usually economically dependent upon the central city for employment, shopping, transportation services, and the like.

military expenditure, the apparent value of all identifiable military expenditure by the central government on hardware, personnel, pensions, research and development, etc., reported here both as a percentage of the GNP, with a comparison to the world average, and as a per capita value in U.S. dollars.

military personnel, *see* total active duty personnel.

mobility, the rate at which individuals or households change dwellings, usually measured between censuses and including international as well as domestic migration.*

monarchy, a government in which the CHIEF OF STATE holds office, usually hereditarily and for life, but sometimes electively for a term. The state may be a coprincipality, emirate, empire, kingdom, principality, sheikhdom, or sultanate. The powers of the monarch may range from absolute (*i.e.,* he or she both reigns and rules) through various degrees of limitation of authority to merely nominal, as in a constitutional monarchy, in which the titular monarch reigns but others, as elected officials, participate in the ruling.

monetary unit, currency of issue, or that in official use in a given country; name, spelling, and abbreviation in English according to International Monetary Fund recommendations or local practice; name of the lesser, usually decimal, monetary unit comprising the main currency; and valuation in U.S. dollars and U.K. pounds sterling, usually according to market or commercial rates.

See also exchange rate.

natural increase, also called natural growth, or the balance of births and deaths, the excess of births over deaths in a population; the rate of natural increase is the difference between the BIRTH RATE and the DEATH RATE of a given population. Natural increase is added to the balance of migration to calculate the total growth of that population.

net material product, *see* material product.

nonreligious, *see* atheist.

official language(s), that (or those) prescribed for actual day-to-day conduct and publication of a country's official business. Other languages may have local protection, may be permitted in legal action (such as a trial), or may be "national languages," for the protection of which special provisions have been made, but these are not deemed official.

official name, the local official form(s), short or long, of a country's legal name(s) taken from the country's constitution or from other official documents. The English-language form is usually the protocol form in use by the country, the U.S. Department of State, and the United Nations.

official religion, generally, any religion prescribed or given special status or protection by the constitution or legal system of a country. Identification as such is not confined to

constitutional documents utilizing the term explicitly.

organized territory (U.S.), *see* territory.

overseas department (France), *see* department.

overseas territory (France), *see* territory.

parliamentary state, *see* state.

part of a realm, a dependent political entity with some degree of self-government and having a special status above that of a colony (*e.g.,* the prerogative of rejecting for local application any law enacted by the motherland).

participation/activity rates, measures defining differential rates of economic activity within a population. Participation rate refers to the percentage of those employed or economically active who possess a particular characteristic (sex, age, etc.); activity rate refers to the fraction of the total population who *are* economically active.

passenger-miles, or **passenger-kilometres,** aggregate measure of passenger carriage by a specified means of transportation, equal to the number of passengers carried multiplied by the number of kilometres each is transported. Figures given for countries are often calculated from ticket sales and ordinarily exclude passengers carried free of charge.

people's republic, *see* republic.

place of birth/national origin, if the former, numbers of native- and foreign-born population of a country by actual place of birth; if the latter, any of several classifications, including those based on origin of passport at original admission to country, on cultural heritage of family name, on self-designated (often multiple) origin of (some) ancestors, and on other systems for assigning national origin.*

political status, *see* form of government/political status.

population, the number of persons present within a country or other civil entity at the date of a census of population, survey, cumulation of a civil register, or other enumeration. Unless otherwise specified, populations given are DE FACTO, referring to those actually present, rather than DE JURE, those legally resident but not necessarily present on the referent date. If a time series, noncensus year, or per capita ratio referring to a country's total population is cited, it will usually refer to midyear of the calendar year indicated. Populations for cities will usually refer to the city proper, *i.e.,* the legally bounded corporate entity, or the most compact, contiguous, demographically urban portion of the entity defined by the local authorities. Occasionally it has been necessary to provide city figures for METROPOLITAN AREAS when the relevant civil entity at the core of a major agglomeration had an unrepresentatively small population.

population economically active, the total number of persons (above a set age for economic labour, usually 10–15 years) in all employment statuses—self-employed, wage- or salary-earning, part-time, seasonal, unemployed, etc. The International Labour Organisation defines the economically active as "all persons of either sex who furnish the supply of labour for the production of economic goods and services." National practices vary as regards the treatment of such groups as armed forces, inmates of institutions, persons seeking their first job, seasonal workers and persons engaged in part-time economic activities. In some countries, all or part of these groups may be included among the economically active, while in other countries the same groups may be treated as inactive. In general, however, the data on economically active population do not include students, women occupied solely in domestic duties, retired persons, persons living entirely on their own means, and persons wholly dependent upon others.

See also labour force.

population projection, the expected population in the years 2000 and 2010, embodying the country's own projections wherever possible. Estimates of the future size of a population are usually based on assumed levels of fertility, mortality, and migration. Projections in the tables, unless otherwise specified, are medium (*i.e.,* most likely) variants, whether based on external estimates by the United Nations, World Bank, or U.S. Department of Commerce or on those of the country itself.

price and earnings indexes, tabulation comparing the change in the CONSUMER PRICE INDEX over a period of seven years with the change in the general labour force's EARNINGS INDEX for the same period.

principality, *see* monarchy.

production, the physical quantity or monetary value of the output of an industry, usually tabulated here as the most important items or groups of items (depending on the available detail) of primary (extractive) and secondary (manufactured) production. When a single consistent measure of value, such as "value added," can be obtained, this is given, ranked by value; otherwise, and more usually, quantity of production is given.

public debt, the current outstanding debt of all periods of maturity for which the central government and its organs are obligated. Publicly guaranteed private debt is excluded. For many developing countries, only figures for long-term EXTERNAL DEBT are available.

quality of working life, a group of measures including weekly hours of work (including overtime); rates per 100,000 for job-connected injury, illness, and mortality; coverage of labour force by insurance for injury, permanent disability, and death; workdays lost to labour strikes and stoppages; and commuting patterns (length of journey to work in minutes and usual method of transportation).*

railroads, mode of transportation by self-driven or locomotive-drawn cars over fixed rails. Length-of-track figures ordinarily include the total length of all mainline and spurline running track and exclude switching sidings and yard track. Route length, when given, does not compound multiple running tracks laid on the same trackbed.

recurrent budget, *see* budget.

religious affiliation, distribution of practicing or nominal religionists, as a percentage of total population. This usually assigns to children the religion of their parents.

republic, a state with elected leaders and a centralized presidential form of government, local subdivisions being subordinate to the national government. A *federal republic* (as distinguished from a unitary republic) is a republic in which power is divided between the central government and the constituent subnational administrative divisions (*e.g.,* states, provinces, or cantons) in whom the central government itself is held to originate, the division of power being defined in a written constitution and jurisdictional disputes usually being settled in a court; sovereignty usually rests with the authority that has the power to amend the constitution. A *people's republic,* in the dialectics of Communism, is the first stage of development toward a communist state, the second stage being a *socialist republic.* A *soviet republic* is a republic governed by an elected soviet (council). A *unitary republic* (as distinguished from a federal republic) is a republic in which power is held by a central authority and not derived from constituent subdivisions.

retail price index, *see* consumer price index.

retail sales and service enterprises, *see* manufacturing, mining, and construction enterprises/retail sales and service enterprises.

roundwood, wood obtained from removals from forests, felled or harvested (with or without bark), in all forms.

rural, see urban–rural.

self-employment, work in which income derives from direct employment in one's own business, trade, or profession, as opposed to work in which salary or wages are earned from an employer.

self-governing, of a state, in control of its internal affairs in degrees ranging from control of most internal affairs (though perhaps not of public order or of internal security) to complete control of all internal affairs (*i.e.,* the state is autonomous) but having no control of external affairs or defense. In this work the term self-governing refers to the final stage in the successive stages of increasing self-government that generally precede independence.

service/trade enterprises, see manufacturing, mining, and construction enterprises/retail sales and service enterprises.

sex distribution, ratios, calculated as percentages, of male and female population to total population.

sheikhdom, *see* monarchy.

social deviance, a group of measures, usually reported as rates per 100,000, for principal categories of socially deviant behaviour, including specified crimes, alcoholism, drug abuse, and suicide.*

social participation, a group of measures indicative of the degree of social engagement displayed by a particular population, including rates of participation in such activities as elections, voluntary work or memberships, trade unions, and religion.*

social security, public programs designed to protect individuals and families from loss of income owing to unemployment, old age, sickness or disability, or death and to provide other services such as medical care, health and welfare programs, or income maintenance.

socialist republic, *see* republic.

sources of income, *see* household income and expenditure.

soviet republic, *see* republic.

Special Drawing Right (SDR), a unit of account utilized by the International Monetary Fund (IMF) to denominate monetary reserves available under a quota system to IMF members to maintain the value of their national currency unit in international transactions.

state, in international law, a political entity possessing the attributes of: territory, permanent civilian population, government, and the capacity to conduct relations with other states. Though the term is sometimes limited in meaning to fully independent and internationally recognized states, the more general sense of an entity possessing a *preponderance* of these characteristics is intended here. It is, thus, also a first-order civil administrative subdivision, especially of a federated union. An *associated state* is an autonomous state in free association with another that conducts its external affairs and defense. A *parliamentary state* is an independent state in the Commonwealth that is governed by a parliament and that may recognize the British monarch as its titular head.

structure of gross domestic product and labour force, tabulation of the principal elements of the national economy, according to standard industrial categories, together with the distribution of the labour force (when possible POPULATION ECONOMICALLY ACTIVE) that generates the GROSS DOMESTIC PRODUCT.

sultanate, *see* monarchy.

territory, a noncategorized political dependency; a first-order administrative subdivision; a dependent political entity with some degree of self-government, but with fewer rights and less autonomy than a colony since there is no charter. An *external territory* (Australia) is a territory situated outside the area of the country. An *incorporated territory* (U.S.) is a part of the United States with nonvoting represen-

tation in the Congress but with most constitutional provisions extended to its inhabitants (*e.g.,* Alaska until 1959). An *organized territory* (U.S.) is a territory for which a system of laws and a settled government have been provided by an act of the United States Congress. An *overseas territory* (France) is an overseas subdivision of the French Republic with elected representation in the French Parliament, having individual statutes, laws, and internal organization adapted to local conditions. A *trust territory* is a non-self-governing former mandate of the League of Nations, administered by an independent state under trust arrangements with the United Nations, with the goal of eventual self-government. An *unincorporated territory* (U.S.) is a dependency of the United States with limited self-government, whose inhabitants can claim the fundamental but not all of the procedural rights (*e.g.,* trial by jury) guaranteed by the United States Constitution.

ton-miles, or **ton-kilometres,** aggregate measure of freight hauled by a specified means of transportation, equal to tons of freight multiplied by the miles (or kilometres) each ton is transported. Figures are compiled from waybills (nationally) and ordinarily exclude mail, specie, passengers' baggage, the fuel and stores of the conveyance, and goods carried free.

total active duty personnel, full-time active duty military personnel (excluding militias and part-time, informal, or other paramilitary elements), with their distribution by percentages among the major services.

total fertility rate, the sum of the current age-specific birth rates for each of the childbearing years (usually 15–49). It is the probable number of births, given present fertility data, that would occur during the lifetime of each woman should she live to the end of her childbearing years.

tourism, service industry comprising activities connected with domestic and international travel for pleasure or recreation; confined here to international travel and reported as expenditures in U.S.\$ by tourists of all nationalities visiting a particular country and, conversely, the estimated expenditures of that country's nationals in all countries of destination.

transfer payments, *see* household income and expenditure.

transport, all mechanical methods of moving persons or goods. Data reported for national establishments include: for railroads, length of track and volume of traffic for passengers and cargo (but excluding mail, etc.); for roads, length of network and numbers of passenger cars and of commercial vehicles, *i.e.,* trucks and buses; for merchant marine, the number of vessels of more than 100 gross tons and their total deadweight tonnage; for air transport, traffic data for passengers and cargo, and the number of airports with scheduled flights.

trust territory, *see* territory.

unincorporated territory (U.S.), *see* territory.

unitary republic, *see* republic.

urban–rural, social characteristic of local or national populations, defined by predominant economic activities, "urban" referring to a group of largely nonagricultural pursuits, "rural" to agriculturally oriented employment patterns. The distinction is usually based on the country's own definition of urban, which may depend only upon the size (population) of a place or upon factors like employment, administrative status, density of housing, etc.

value added, also called value added by manufacture, the gross output value of a firm or industry minus the cost of inputs—raw materials, supplies, and payments to other firms—required to produce it. Value added is the portion of the sales value or gross output value that is actually created by the firm or industry. Value added generally includes labour costs, administrative costs, and operating profits.

The Nations of the World

Afghanistan

Official name: Da Afghānestān Jamhawrīyat (Pashto); Jomhūrī-ye Afghānestān (Dari) (Republic of Afghanistan).
Form of government: unitary single-party people's republic with two legislative houses (Council of Representatives [234]; Council of Elders [128[1]]).
Chief of state: President.
Head of government: Prime Minister.
Capital: Kābul.
Official languages: Pashto; Dari Persian.
Official religion: Islam.
Monetary unit: 1 afghani (AF) = 100 puls (puli); valuation (Oct. 2, 1989) 1 U.S.\$ = AF 50.60; 1 £ = AF 81.87.

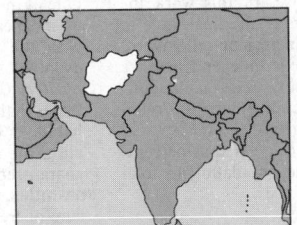

Area and population	area		population
	sq mi	sq km	1984 estimate
Regions			
Eastern	28,664	74,240	1,923,081
North-central	20,461	52,994	2,062,677
North-east	29,911	77,468	1,442,099
North-west	50,581	131,005	2,368,323
South-central	32,963	85,375	1,140,390
South-east	12,546	32,494	3,875,364
Western	76,699	198,649	1,554,500
TOTAL	251,825	652,225	14,366,434[2]

Demography
Population (1989): 14,825,000[2].
Density (1989): persons per sq mi 58.9, persons per sq km 22.7.
Urban–rural (1987): urban 18.1%; rural 81.9%.
Sex distribution[3] (1986): male 51.45%; female 48.55%.
Age breakdown[3] (1986): under 15, 46.1%; 15–29, 24.2%; 30–44, 14.8%; 45–59, 9.3%; 60–74, 4.3%; 75 and over, 1.3%.
Population projection: (2000) 24,501,000; (2010) 31,736,000.
Doubling time: 23 years.
Ethnic composition (1983): Pashtun 52.3%; Tadzhik 20.3%; Uzbek 8.7%; Hazāra 8.7%; Chahar Aimak 2.9%; Turkmen 2.0%; Baluchi 1.0%; other 4.1%.
Religious affiliation (1987): Sunnī Muslim 74%; Shī'ī Muslim 25%; other 1%.
Major cities (1988): Kābul 1,424,400; Qandahār 225,500; Herāt 177,300; Mazār-e Sharīf 130,600.

Vital statistics
Birth rate per 1,000 population (1987): 47.5 (world avg. 27.1).
Death rate per 1,000 population (1987): 22.5 (world avg. 9.9).
Natural increase rate per 1,000 population (1987): 25.0 (world avg. 17.2).
Total fertility rate (avg. births per childbearing woman; 1987): 6.7.
Life expectancy at birth (1987): male 40.6 years; female 41.6 years.
Major reported illness (1981–82): tuberculosis 17,499 cases.

National economy
Budget (1984–85). Revenue: AF 37,615,000,000 (tax revenue 45.4%, nontax revenue 54.6%). Expenditures: AF 51,177,000,000 (1981–82; governmental ministries 50.0%, developmental budget 31.9%, foreign debt service 13.9%, surplus 1.6%).
Public debt (external, outstanding; 1988): U.S.\$1,800,000,000.
Production (metric tons except as noted). Agriculture, forestry, fishing (1988): wheat 2,800,000, corn (maize) 815,000, grapes 510,000, rice 482,-000, barley 300,000; livestock (number of live animals) 17,000,000 sheep, 3,600,000 cattle, 2,800,000 goats, 1,300,000 asses, 410,000 horses, 265,000 camels; roundwood (1987) 7,021,000 cu m; fish catch (1987) 1,500. Mining and quarrying (1986): copper 20,000; salt 10,000; gypsum 3,000; barite 2,000. Manufacturing (by production value in afghanis; 1981–82): food products 3,762,000,000; textiles (all forms) 2,770,000,000; industrial chemicals (including fertilizers) 751,000,000; printing and publishing 539,000,000; cement (1988) 77,100 tons. Construction (AF '000,000; 1985): 1,094. Energy production (consumption): electricity (kW-hr; 1987) 1,257,000,000 (1,257,-000,000); coal (metric tons; 1987) 167,000 (167,000); petroleum products (metric tons; 1987) 6,000 (653,000); natural gas (cu m; 1987) 2,989,000,-000 (630,600,000).
Household size. Average household size[3] (1979): 6.2.
Population economically active[3] (1985–86): total 5,560,000; activity rate of total population 39.9% (participation rates [1985]: ages 10–59, 43.1%; female 7.9%; unemployed 3.0%).

Price indexes (1985 = 100)
	1980	1981	1982	1983	1984	1985	1986
Consumer price index	79.0	82.9	87.6	85.0	91.6	100.0	106.3

Tourism: receipts from visitors (1986) U.S.\$1,000,000; expenditures by nationals abroad (1987) U.S.\$1,000,000.
Gross national product (1985): U.S.\$3,520,000,000 (U.S.\$230 per capita).

Structure of net material product and labour force
	1985–86		1981–82	
	in value AF '000,000[4]	% of total value	labour force	% of labour force
Agriculture	65,100	64.8	2,194,770	57.3
Manufacturing, mining, and public utilities	16,300	16.2	466,860	12.2
Construction	4,000	4.0	48,880	1.3
Transp. and commun.	3,100	3.1	65,650	1.7
Trade	10,200	10.2	126,100	3.3
Public administration			79,260	2.1
Public services	1,700	1.7	204,940	5.3
Other			642,360	16.8
TOTAL	100,400	100.0	3,828,820	100.0

Land use (1987): forested 2.9%; meadows and pastures 46.3%; agricultural and under permanent cultivation 12.4%; other 38.4%.

Foreign trade

Balance of trade (current prices)
	1982	1983	1984	1985	1986	1987
AF '000,000	629	−5,941	−4,569	−32,252	−29,998	−17,917
% of total	0.9%	7.5%	5.4%	36.4%	30.8%	25.7%

Imports (1987): U.S.\$866,000,000 ([1981–82] vehicles 22.7%, petroleum products 18.0%, sugar 8.1%, woven fabrics of flax or ramie 7.9%, processed animal and vegetable oils 4.2%, tea 4.0%). *Major import sources* (1987): U.S.S.R. 38.9%; Japan 13.1%; China 6.8%; South Korea 6.7%; West Germany 2.7%; Pakistan 2.3%; Hong Kong 1.8%; U.K. 1.6%.
Exports (1987): U.S.\$511,900,000 (natural gas 39.9%, dried fruit and nuts 25.1%, carpets and rugs 9.6%, wool and hides 2.4%, cotton 1.7%). *Major export destinations:* U.S.S.R. 68.0%; India 6.9%; West Germany 4.5%; U.K. 2.1%; East Germany 1.9%; Pakistan 1.3%.

Transport and communications
Transport. Railroads (1984): length 6 mi, 10 km. Roads (1986): total length 13,670 mi, 22,000 km (paved, n.a.). Vehicles (1982–83): passenger cars 31,000; trucks and buses 31,700. Merchant marine: none. Air transport (1987): passenger-mi 108,538,000, passenger-km 174,676,000; short ton-mi cargo 5,543,000, metric ton-km cargo 8,093,000; airports (1989) 2.
Communications. Daily newspapers (1988): total number 14; total circulation 150,800; circulation per 1,000 population 10.4. Radio (1986): 150,000 receivers (1 per 93 persons). Television (1987): 20,000 receivers (1 per 709 persons). Telephones (1984): 31,200 (1 per 443 persons).

Education and health

Education (1988–89)
	schools	teachers	students	student/teacher ratio
Primary	553	16,756	586,014	35.0
Secondary	819	5,715	271,000	47.4
Voc., teacher tr.	33	556	8,537	15.4
Higher	5	198	1,491	7.5

Educational attainment (1980). Percent of population age 25 and over having: no formal schooling 88.5%; some primary education 6.8%; complete primary 0.3%; some secondary 1.2%; postsecondary 3.2%. *Literacy* (1985): total population age 15 and over literate 23.7%; males 38.9%; females 7.8%.
Health: physicians (1987) 2,957 (1 per 4,797 persons); hospital beds (1981–82) 6,875 (1 per 2,054 persons); infant mortality rate per 1,000 live births (1987) 175.
Food (1979–81): daily per capita caloric intake 2,055 (vegetable products 90%, animal products 10%); (1984) 91% of FAO recommended minimum.

Military
Total active duty personnel (1989): 55,000 (army 90.9%, air force 9.1%). *Military expenditure as percent of GNP* (1984): 9.1% (world 5.7%); per capita expenditure U.S.\$23.

[1]Includes 64 nonelective seats. [2]Total includes 2,615,000 nomads not distributed by region. Afghan refugees in Pakistan and Iran numbered more than 5.6 million in 1988. [3]Based on settled population only. [4]At prices of 1978.

Albania

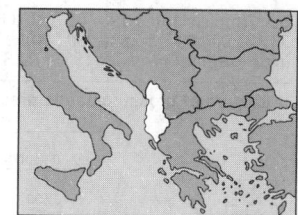

Official name: Republika Popullore Socialiste e Shqipërisë (People's Socialist Republic of Albania).
Form of government: unitary single-party socialist republic with one legislative house (People's Assembly [250]).
Chief of state: President (Chairman of the Presidium of the People's Assembly).
Head of government: Premier (Chairman of the Council of Ministers).
Capital: Tiranë.
Official language: Albanian.
Official religion: none.
Monetary unit: 1 lek = 100 qindars; valuation (Oct. 2, 1989) 1 U.S.$ = 6.20 leks; 1 £ = 10.03 leks.

Area and population

Provinces	Capitals	area sq mi	area sq km	population 1987 estimate
Berat	Berat	396	1,027	171,000
Dibër	Peshkopi	605	1,568	150,300
Durrës	Durrës	327	848	237,900
Elbasan	Elbasan	572	1,481	234,500
Fier	Fier	454	1,175	235,200
Gjirokastër	Gjirokastër	439	1,137	64,800
Gramsh	Gramsh	268	695	43,100
Kolonjë	Ersekë	311	805	24,000
Korçë	Korçë	842	2,181	212,500
Krujë	Krujë	234	607	103,700
Kukës	Kukës	514	1,330	99,100
Lezhë	Lezhë	185	479	58,900
Librazhd	Librazhd	391	1,013	70,800
Lushnjë	Lushnjë	275	712	127,700
Mat	Burrel	397	1,028	75,100
Mirditë	Rrëshen	335	867	50,100
Përmet	Përmet	359	929	39,600
Pogradec	Pogradec	280	725	68,500
Pukë	Pukë	399	1,034	51,000
Sarandë	Sarandë	424	1,097	83,800
Shkodër	Shkodër	976	2,528	225,800
Skrapar	Çorovoda	299	775	45,900
Tepelenë	Tepelenë	315	817	50,000
Tiranë	Tiranë	478	1,238	343,500
Tropojë	Bajram	403	1,043	44,500
Vlorë	Vlorë	621	1,609	171,400
TOTAL		11,100[1]	28,748	3,082,700

Demography

Population (1989): 3,197,000.
Density (1989): persons per sq mi 289.3, persons per sq km 111.7.
Urban–rural (1989): urban 35.5%; rural 64.5%.
Sex distribution (1989): male 51.50%; female 48.50%.
Age breakdown (1985): under 15, 35.8%; 15–29, 29.3%; 30–44, 17.0%; 45–59, 11.1%; 60–74, 5.3%; 75 and over, 1.5%.
Population projection: (2000) 3,987,000; (2010) 4,873,000.
Doubling time: 34 years.
Ethnic composition (1989): Albanian 98.0%; Greek 1.8%; other 0.2%.
Religious affiliation (1980): nonreligious 55.4%; Muslim 20.5%; atheist 18.7%; Christian 5.4%.
Major cities (1987): Tiranë 225,700; Durrës 78,700; Elbasan 78,300; Shkodër 76,300; Vlorë 67,600.

Vital statistics

Birth rate per 1,000 population (1987): 25.9 (world avg. 27.1).
Death rate per 1,000 population (1987): 5.6 (world avg. 9.9).
Natural increase rate per 1,000 population (1987): 20.3 (world avg. 17.2).
Total fertility rate (avg. births per childbearing woman; 1980): 3.6.
Marriage rate per 1,000 population (1987): 8.9.
Divorce rate per 1,000 population (1987): 0.8.
Life expectancy at birth (1986–87): male 68.7 years; female 74.3 years.
Major causes of death per 100,000 population: n.a.; however, major health problems include tuberculosis, hypertension, liver and stomach disorders; malaria and syphilis, formerly widespread, are now practically nonexistent.

National economy

Budget (1988). Revenue: 9,500,000,000 leks (surplus from state enterprises 96.2%, other 3.8%). Expenditures: 9,450,000,000 leks (national economy 52.3%, social and cultural services 29.1%, defense 16.9%, administration 1.7%).
Public debt (1985): U.S.$5,600,000,000[2].
Tourism (1986): number of tourists 8,000; receipts from visitors, n.a.; expenditures by nationals abroad, n.a.
Production (metric tons except as noted). Agriculture, forestry, fishing (1987): wheat 550,000, corn (maize) 410,000, vegetables and fruit except grapes 396,000, sugar beets 338,000, potatoes 142,000, grapes 87,000, sunflower seeds 58,000, barley 38,000, oats 30,000, olives 30,000, tobacco 20,000; livestock (number of live animals) 1,432,300 sheep, 979,100 goats, 671,900 cattle, 214,400 pigs, 113,200 mules and asses, 56,400 horses; roundwood 2,330,000 cu m; fish catch 12,468. Mining and quarrying (1986): ferronickel ores 1,200,000; chromite ore 1,200,000; salt 70,000; copper (metal content) 17,600; nickel 9,700. Manufacturing (1985): cement 848,000; distillate fuel oils 390,000; nitrogenous and phosphate fertilizers 93,000; raw sugar 33,000; paper and paperboard 22,000; olive oil 7,000; wine 230,000 hectolitres; beer 140,000 hectolitres; cigarettes 6,000,000,000 units; cotton and woolen fabrics 60,900,000 m3. Construction (1987): 13,863 units. Energy production (consumption): electricity (kW-hr; 1987) 3,840,000,000 (3,190,000,000); coal (metric tons; 1987) 2,530,000 (2,530,000); crude petroleum (barrels; 1987) 19,782,000 (19,782,000); petroleum products (metric tons; 1987) 1,205,000 (1,205,000); natural gas (cu m; 1987) 384,405,000 (384,405,000).
Gross national product (at current market prices; 1986): U.S.$2,800,000,000 (U.S.$930 per capita).

Structure of net material product and labour force

	1987 value	1987 % of total value	1987 labour force[4]	1987 % of labour force
Agriculture	...	33.3	190,300	24.1
Manufacturing, mining, public utilities	...	45.8	287,000	36.4
Construction	...	6.4	77,800	9.9
Transportation and communications			39,600	5.0
Trade			56,400	7.2
Pub. admin., defense	...	14.5	95,300	12.1
Services				
Other			41,800	5.3
TOTAL	...	100.0	788,200	100.0

Population economically active (1985): total 1,398,000; activity rate of total population 45.8% (participation rates: ages 15–64, 74.5%; female 41.0%; unemployed, n.a.).
Price and earnings indexes: n.a.
Household income and expenditure. Average household size (1984) 5.5; income per household: n.a.; sources of income: n.a.; expenditure: n.a.
Land use (1986): forested 37.9%; meadows and pastures 14.6%; agricultural and under permanent cultivation 26.0%; other 21.5%.

Foreign trade

Balance of trade (current prices)

	1981	1982	1983	1984	1985	1986
'000,000 leks	...	...	...	...	...	65
% of total	...	...	...	...	...	8.2

Imports (1986): U.S.$363,000,000 (1987; mineral fuels and lubricants 28.2%, machinery and transport equipment 26.2%, chemicals and related products 14.2%, food and live animals 12.7%, consumer goods 6.5%). *Major import sources* (1982): U.S.S.R. and Eastern European countries 35.6%; European Economic Community countries 28.7%; United States 4.6%; Japan 2.8%.
Exports (1986): U.S.$428,000,000 (1987; crude minerals and metalliferous ores 29.3%, food and food preparations 17.3%, electricity 13.1%, fuel 11.0%). *Major export destinations* (1987): Czechoslovakia 12.4%; Yugoslavia 11.1%; Romania 9.3%; Bulgaria 7.5%; East Germany 6.8%; Hungary 6.2%; China 6.1%; Greece 5.5%; Italy 4.4%; West Germany 4.0%; Austria 3.5%; Japan 1.6%; Egypt 1.5%.

Transport and communications

Transport. Railroads (1988): length 316 mi, 509 km; passenger-mi 411,098,-000[3], passenger-km 661,600,000[3]; short ton-mi cargo 430,870,000[3], metric ton-km cargo 629,100,000[3]. Roads (1988): total length 10,377 mi, 16,700 km (paved 40%). Vehicles[5] (1970): passenger cars 3,500; trucks and buses 11,200. Merchant marine (1988): vessels (100 gross tons and over) 20; total deadweight tonnage 79,940. Air transport: passengers, n.a.; cargo, n.a.; airports (1989) with scheduled flights 1.
Communications. Daily newspapers (1987): total number 2; total circulation 135,000; circulation per 1,000 population 48. Radio (1987): total number of receivers 500,000 (1 per 6.2 persons). Television (1988): total number of receivers 246,220 (1 per 9.9 persons). Telephones, n.a.

Education and health

Education (1987)

	schools	teachers	students	student/ teacher ratio
Primary (age 6–13)	1,668	27,297	543,000	19.9
Secondary (age 14–17)	446	8,442	124,000	14.7
Voc., teacher tr.	406	6,640	82,000	12.3
Higher	8	1,625	19,000	11.7

Educational attainment (1979). Percent of population age 25 and over having: primary education 74.7%; secondary 20.9%; higher 4.4%. *Literacy* (1989): virtually 100%.
Health (1987): physicians 6,308 (1 per 489 persons); hospital beds 16,943 (1 per 182 persons); infant mortality rate per 1,000 live births 28.2.
Food (1980–82): daily per capita caloric intake 3,060 (vegetable products 87%, animal products 13%); 127% of FAO recommended minimum requirement.

Military

Total active duty personnel (1988): 42,000 (army 75.0%, navy 7.9%, air force 17.1%). *Military expenditure as percent of GNP* (1987): 5.1% (world 5.4%); per capita expenditure U.S.$49.

---

[1]Detail does not add to total given because of rounding. [2]Estimated total since 1949. [3]1987. [4]State sector only. [5]Private cars are banned.

Algeria

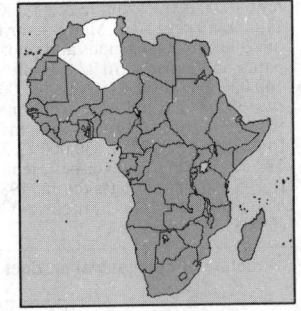

Official name: al-Jumhūrīyah
al-Jazā'irīyah ad-Dīmuqrāṭīyah
ash-Sha'bīyah (Arabic) (Democratic
and Popular Republic of Algeria).
Form of government: multiparty
republic with one legislative house
(The National People's Assembly
[295]).
Chief of state: President.
Head of government: Prime Minister.
Capital: Algiers.
Official language: Arabic.
Official religion: Islam.
Monetary unit: 1 Algerian dinar
(DA) = 100 centimes; valuation (Oct.
2, 1989) 1 U.S.$ = DA 8.10;
1 £ = DA 13.11.

Population (1987 Census[1])

Wilāyat	population	Wilāyat	population
Adrar	217,678	Médéa	652,863
Ain Defla	537,256	Mila	511,605
Ain Temouchent	274,990	Mostaganem	505,932
Alger	1,690,191	M'Sila	604,693
Annaba	455,888	Naâma	113,700
Batna	752,617	Oran	932,473
el-Bayadh	153,254	Ouargla	284,454
Béchar	185,346	el-Oued	376,909
Bejaia	700,952	Oum el-Bouaghi	403,936
Biskra	430,202	Relizane	544,877
Blida	702,188	Saïda	235,494
Bordj Bou Arreridj	424,828	Sétif	1,000,694
Bouira	526,900	Sidi bel-Abbès	446,277
Boumerdes	650,975	Skikda	622,510
ech-Chleff	684,192	Souk Ahras	296,077
Constantine	664,303	Tamanrasset	95,822
Djelfa	494,494	el-Tarf	275,315
Guelma	353,309	Tébessa	410,233
Ghardaïa	216,140	Tiaret	575,794
Illizi	18,930	Tindouf	16,428
Jijel	472,312	Tipaza	620,151
Khenchela	246,541	Tissemsilt	228,120
Laghouat	212,388	Tizi Ouzou	936,948
Mascara	566,901	Tlemcen	714,862
		TOTAL	23,038,942

Demography

Area: 919,595 sq mi, 2,381,741 sq km.
Population (1989): 24,579,000.
Density (1989): persons per sq mi 26.7, persons per sq km 10.3.
Urban-rural (1987): urban 49.7%; rural 50.3%.
Sex distribution (1986): male 49.64%; female 50.36%.
Age breakdown (1987): under 15, 43.9%; 15–29, 28.0%; 30–44, 13.9%; 45–59,
8.4%; 60–74, 4.2%; 75 and over, 1.6%.
Population projection: (2000) 33,088,000; (2010) 40,413,000.
Doubling time: 25 years.
Ethnic composition (1983): Arab 82.6%; Berber 17.0%; French 0.1%; other
0.3%.
Religious affiliation (1980): Sunnī Muslim 99.1%; Roman Catholic 0.5%;
other 0.4%.
Major cities (1987): Algiers 1,483,000; Oran 590,000; Constantine 438,000;
Annaba 310,000; Batna 182,000.

Vital statistics

Birth rate per 1,000 population (1987): 34.6 (world avg. 27.1); legitimacy
rate, n.a.; marriage, however, is nearly universal.
Death rate per 1,000 population (1987): 7.0 (world avg. 9.9).
Natural increase rate per 1,000 population (1987): 27.6 (world avg. 17.2).
Total fertility rate (avg. births per childbearing woman; 1987): 5.9.
Marriage rate per 1,000 population (1985): 5.7[2].
Divorce rate per 1,000 population (1985): 2.1[2].
Life expectancy at birth (1985): male 61.0 years; female 64.1 years.
Notified cases of infectious diseases per 100,000 population (1986): measles
15.2; typhoid fever 12.5; dysentery 11.8.

National economy

Budget (1988–89). Revenue: DA 114,700,000,000 (ordinary receipts 75.4%,
hydrocarbons 24.6%). Expenditures: DA 121,400,000,000 (current expenditures 59.2%, investment 40.3%).
Public debt (external, outstanding; 1987): U.S.$19,240,000,000.
Production (metric tons except as noted). Agriculture, forestry, fishing (1988):
wheat 1,150,000, potatoes 950,000, barley 556,000, tomatoes 490,000, grapes
460,000, oranges 190,000, dates 182,000; livestock (number of live animals)
14,325,000 sheep, 3,570,000 goats, 1,523,000 cattle[3]; roundwood (1987)
2,008,000 cu m; fish catch (1987) 70,258. Mining and quarrying (1987):
iron ore 3,382,000; phosphates 1,209,000; gypsum (1986) 303,000; barite
(1986) 66,000; zinc 17,000; silver (1986) 120,000 troy oz. Manufacturing
(1987): cement 7,541,000; flour and semolina 2,487,000; bricks 1,701,000;
pig iron and ferroalloys 1,677,000; crude steel 1,477,000; edible oils 304,-
000; sugar 205,200; trucks 5,785 units. Construction (1981): residential
28,000 units. Energy production (consumption): electricity (kW-hr; 1987)
13,400,000,000 (13,350,000,000); coal (metric tons; 1987) 8,000 (1,108,000);
crude petroleum (barrels; 1987) 262,600,000 (176,970,000); petroleum prod-

ucts (metric tons; 1987) 37,378,000 (6,317,000); natural gas (cu m; 1987)
33,183,000,000 (16,874,000,000).
Gross national product (1987): U.S.$63,560,000,000 (U.S.$2,760 per capita).

Structure of gross domestic product and labour force

	1986		1985	
	in value DA '000,000	% of total value	labour force[4]	% of labour force[4]
Agriculture	33,270	13.9	999,000	25.7
Crude pet., nat. gas	40,890	17.0		
Other mining	1,020	0.4	595,000	15.3
Manufacturing	34,770	14.5		
Public utilities	3,260	1.4		
Construction	41,225	17.2	670,000	17.3
Transp. and commun.	12,465	5.2	202,000	5.2
Trade	37,615	15.7	311,000	8.0
Services	11,570	4.8	1,107,000[5]	28.5[5]
Customs duties, production taxes	23,750	9.9	—	—
TOTAL	239,835	100.0	3,884,000	100.0

Tourism (1986): receipts from visitors U.S.$137,000,000; expenditures by
nationals abroad U.S.$446,000,000.
Population economically active (1987): total 4,204,460[4]; activity rate of population 18.3%[4] (participation rates [1985]: ages 15–64, 40.0%; female 11.6%).

Price and earnings indexes (1985 = 100)

	1982	1983	1984	1985	1986	1987	1988
Consumer price index	79.0	85.1	90.5	100.0	112.4	120.7	127.9
Earnings index	...	...	...	...	...	...	...

Household income and expenditure. Average household size (1987) 6.9; income per household: n.a.; sources of income: n.a.; expenditure (1979–80):
food and beverages 55.7%, housing and household durable goods 18.1%,
clothing and footwear 9.2%, transport and communications 6.7%, recreation 3.4%, medical care and health 3.1%.
Land use (1987): forested 2.0%; meadows and pastures 12.9%; agricultural
and under permanent cultivation 3.1%; other (mostly desert) 82.0%.

Foreign trade

Balance of trade (current prices)

	1983	1984	1985	1986	1987	1988
DA '000,000	+14,686	+18,672	+15,073	−6,567	+4,959	+4,115
% of total	13.9%	17.2%	13.3%	8.2%	6.8%	4.5%

Imports (1988): DA 43,961,000,000 (industrial equipment 26.9%, food and
beverages 24.1%, consumer products 11.8%, raw materials 8.4%). *Major
import sources (1987):* European Economic Community 54.7%; North
America 8.9%; Japan 7.3%; Eastern Europe 5.2%; Arab countries 2.5%.
Exports (1988): DA 48,075,000,000 (mineral fuels and lubricants 94.8%, crude
materials 2.3%). *Major export destinations (1987):* European Economic
Community 64.8%; North America 19.4%; Japan 1.7%; Arab countries
1.7%; Eastern Europe 1.2%.

Transport and communications

Transport. Railroads (1987): route length 2,337 mi, 3,761 km; passenger-
mi 1,225,000,000, passenger-km 1,972,000,000; short ton-mi cargo 2,012,-
000,000, metric ton-km cargo 2,937,000,000. Roads (1986): total length
50,734 mi, 81,648 km (paved 59%). Vehicles (1985): passenger cars 712,-
700; trucks and buses 471,500. Merchant marine (1988): vessels (100 gross
tons and over) 148; total deadweight tonnage 1,052,551. Air transport[6]
(1987): passenger-mi 1,397,000,000, passenger-km 2,248,000,000; short ton-
mi cargo 7,275,000, metric ton-km cargo 10,622,000; airports (1989) with
scheduled flights 24.
Communications. Daily newspapers (1987): total number 6; total circulation
1,082,000; circulation per 1,000 population 47. Radio (1987): 5,436,395
receivers (1 per 4.2 persons). Television (1987): 1,550,000 receivers (1 per
15 persons). Telephones (1987): 888,539 (1 per 26 persons).

Education and health

Education (1987–88)

	schools	teachers	students	student/ teacher ratio
Primary (age 6–11)	11,843	139,875	3,801,651	27.2
Secondary (age 12–18)	2,479	110,738	2,082,646	18.8
Voc., teacher tr.[7]	71[8]	2,528	98,000	38.8
Higher	15[8]	17,581	160,195	12.3

Educational attainment (1971). Percent of population age 25 and over
having: no formal schooling 84.4%; primary education 13.0%; secondary
education 2.2%; higher 0.3%; unknown 0.4%. *Literacy (1982):* total population age 15 and over literate 4,753,000 (44.7%); males literate 3,087,400
(57.3%); females literate 1,666,000 (31.7%).
Health (1987): physicians 17,760 (1 per 1,302 persons); hospital beds 63,000
(1 per 367 persons); infant mortality rate (1985) 64.1.
Food (1984–86): daily per capita caloric intake 2,687 (vegetable products 88%,
animal products 12%); 112% of FAO recommended minimum requirement.

Military

Total active duty personnel (1989): 138,500 (army 86.6%, navy 4.7%, air force
8.7%). *Military expenditure as percent of GNP (1987):* 3.0% (world 5.4%);
per capita expenditure U.S.$82.

[1]March 20. [2]Algerian population only. [3]1987. [4]Employed persons only. [5]Excludes
military. [6]Air Algérie international traffic only. [7]1986–87. [8]1981–82.

Andorra

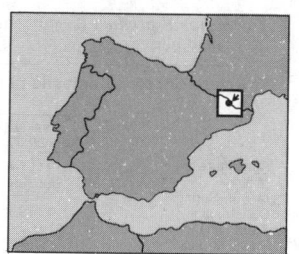

Official name: Principat (Co-Principat)
or Senyoriu (Co-Senyoriu) d'Andorra;
les Valls d'Andorra (Principality
[or Co-Principality] of Andorra; the
Valleys of Andorra).
Form of government: co-principality
with one nonpartisan legislative house
(General Council of the Valleys [28]).
Chiefs of state: President of France;
Bishop of Urgel, Spain.
Head of government: Chief executive.
Capital: Andorra la Vella.
Official language: Catalan.
Official religion: Roman Catholicism.
Monetary unit: There is no local
currency of issue; the French franc
and Spanish peseta are both in
circulation. 1 franc (F) = 100 centimes;
1 peseta (Pta) = 100 céntimos.
Valuation (Oct. 2, 1989)
1 U.S.\$ = F 6.36, 1 £ = F 10.29;
1 U.S.\$ = Ptas 119.00,
1 £ = Ptas 192.55.

Area and population

Parishes	Capitals	area sq mi	area sq km	population 1986 census
Andorra la Vella	Andorra la Vella	49[1]	127[1]	18,463
Canillo	Canillo	74	191	1,153
Encamp	Encamp	74	191	5,766
La Massana	La Massana	25	65	3,229
Les Escaldes–Engordany		[1]	[1]	11,734
Ordino	Ordino	33	85	1,096
Sant Julià de Lòria	Sant Julià de Lòria	[1]	[1]	5,535
TOTAL		181	468	46,976

Demography

Population (1989): 50,000.
Density (1989): persons per sq mi 276.2, persons per sq km 106.8.
Urban–rural (1986): urban 64.7%; rural 35.3%.
Sex distribution (1986): male 53.12%; female 46.88%.
Age breakdown (1986): under 15, 19.0%; 15–29, 27.3%; 30–44, 26.4%; 45–59,
14.8%; 60–74, 9.4%; 75 and over, 3.1%.
Population projection: (2000) 62,000; (2010) 75,000.
Doubling time: 96 years.
Ethnic composition (1986): Spanish 55.1%; Andorran 27.5%; French 7.4%;
Portuguese 4.1%; British 1.5%; other 4.4%.
Religious affiliation (1980): Roman Catholic 94.2%; Jewish 0.4%; Jehovah's
Witnesses 0.3%; Protestant 0.2%; other 4.9%.
Major cities (1986): Andorra la Vella 15,639; Les Escaldes 11,955; Encamp
3,535.

Vital statistics

Birth rate per 1,000 population (1988): 11.7 (world avg. 27.1).
Death rate per 1,000 population (1988): 4.2 (world avg. 9.9).
Natural increase rate per 1,000 population (1988): 7.5 (world avg. 17.2).
Total fertility rate (avg. births per childbearing woman): n.a.
Marriage rate per 1,000 population (1986): 2.8.
Divorce rate per 1,000 population: n.a.
Life expectancy at birth: (1980; both sexes) 70 years.
Major causes of death per 100,000 population: n.a.; however, health problems
are those of a developed country—cardiovascular disease, hypertension,
malignant neoplasms (cancers).

National economy

Budget (1986). Revenue: Ptas 6,655,098,711 ([1983] excise taxes on imported consumer goods and gasoline 93.9%; additional revenue is derived
from a 3% tax on alcoholic beverages). Expenditures: Ptas 6,655,098,711
(primarily administrative services and education; Andorra has virtually no
military expenditures).
Public debt: n.a.
Production. Agriculture, forestry, fishing (1981): potatoes 472 metric tons,
tobacco 264 metric tons, and unknown amounts of hay, rye, buckwheat,
olives, and grapes; livestock (number of live animals; 1982) 9,000 sheep,
1,115 cattle, 217 horses. Mining and quarrying: building stone, alum, iron,
and lead. Manufacturing: ceramics, cigars and cigarettes, alcoholic beverages (including anisette and brandy), clothing, jewelry, textiles (including
woolen blankets and scarves), and wooden furniture. Construction (1984):
90 buildings totaling 83,834 sq m were authorized for construction. Energy
production (consumption): electricity (kW-hr; 1988) 140,000,000 (340,000,-
000[2]); coal, none (n.a.); crude petroleum, none (n.a.); petroleum products
(metric tons; 1986) none (95,349); natural gas, none (n.a.).
Population economically active (1986): total 21,484; activity rate of total
population 46.8% (participation rates: ages 15–64, n.a.; female, n.a.; unemployed, n.a.).

Price and earnings indexes (1985 = 100)[3]

	1982	1983	1984	1985	1986	1987	1988
Consumer price index	73.6	82.6	91.9	100.0	108.8	114.5	120.0
Earnings index	...	...	...	...	...	...	...

Gross national product (at current market prices; 1982): U.S.\$340,000,000
(U.S.\$9,000 per capita)[4].

Structure of labour force

	1986 labour force	1986 % of labour force
Agriculture and forestry	132	0.6
Mining	571	2.7
Manufacturing	957	4.5
Construction	1,754	8.2
Public utilities	1,266	5.9
Transportation and communications	1,832	8.5
Trade	5,777	26.9
Finance	1,281	6.0
Pub. admin., defense	650	3.0
Services and hotel	5,209	24.3
Other	2,025	9.4
TOTAL	21,454	100.0

Household income and expenditure. Average household size: n.a.; income
per household: n.a.; sources of income: n.a.; expenditure: n.a.
Land use (1987): forested 23.7%; meadows and pastures 44.2%; agricultural
and under permanent cultivation 4.0%; other 28.1%.
Tourism (1983): receipts from tourist arrivals, n.a.; expenditures by nationals abroad, n.a.; number of tourist arrivals, approximately 10,000,000
annually, most of whom do not stay overnight; number of hotels 235;
number of hotel rooms (1987) 35,000.

Foreign trade

Balance of trade (current prices)

	1981	1982	1983	1984	1985	1986
Ptas '000,000	−28,090	−30,197	−32,011	−35,795	...	−71,871
% of total	94.8%	91.5%	91.6%	92.1%	...	96.9%

Imports (1986): Ptas 74,312,755,085, of which from France Ptas 31,525,-
222,000, from Spain Ptas 20,036,199,000 (includes fuels, food, perfumes,
clothing, and radio and television sets)[5].
Exports (1986): Ptas 2,325,252,000, of which to France Ptas 1,261,917,000, to
Spain Ptas 762,196,000 (includes wooden furniture, handicrafts, cigarettes,
cigars, leather goods, and electricity).

Transport and communications

Transport. Railroads: none; however, both French and Spanish railways stop
near the border. Roads (1981): total length 138 mi, 220 km (paved 55%).
Vehicles (1986): passenger cars 25,000; trucks and buses 6,250. Merchant
marine: vessels (100 gross tons and over) none. Airports with scheduled
flights: none; the airport at nearby Seo de Urgel, Spain, has scheduled
daily flights to Barcelona and Palma (on Majorca).
Communications. Weekly newspapers (1988): total number 1; circulation
4,000; circulation per 1,000 population 81. Radio (1987): total number
of receivers 8,000 (1 per 5.8 persons). Television (1987): total number of
receivers 4,000 (1 per 12 persons). Telephones (1982): 17,719 (1 per 2.1
persons).

Education and health

Education (1986–87)

	schools	teachers[6]	students	student/ teacher ratio
Primary (age 6–12)	13	214	5,344	...
Secondary (age 12–18)	10	53	2,253	...
Voc., teacher tr.	5	37	1,248	...
Higher	...	...	...	...

Educational attainment, n.a.; education is compulsory to age 16, however.
Literacy (1987): total population literate (virtually 100%).
Health (1988): physicians 112 (1 per 441 persons); hospital beds 113 (1 per
437 persons); infant mortality rate per 1,000 live births (1987) 13.3.
Food (1984–86)[7]: daily per capita caloric intake 3,320 (vegetable products 67%, animal products 33%); 135% of FAO recommended minimum
requirement.

Military

Total active duty personnel (1982): none. France and Spain are responsible
for Andorra's external security; a 100-man police force maintains domestic
security. *Military expenditure as a percent of central government expenditure* (1981): 0.0001% (world 18.5%).

[1]Andorra la Vella includes Les Escaldes-Engordany and Sant Julià de Lòria.
[2]Approximately 200,000,000 kilowatt-hours of electricity are imported from Spain.
[3]In Spanish pesetas. [4]Trade, tourism (including winter-season sports, fairs, and festivals), and the banking system (of some importance as a tax haven for foreign
financial investment and transactions) are the primary sources of GNP. [5]Imported
manufactured items are less expensive in Andorra than in neighbouring countries
because they are duty free. As a result, smuggling remains a profitable sideline for
some. [6]1985–86. [7]Composite values derived from Spanish and French food data.

Angola

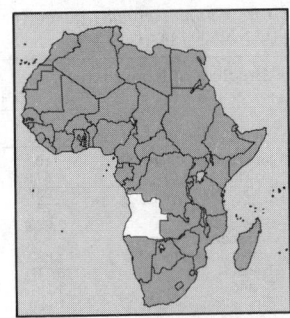

Official name: República Popular de Angola (People's Republic of Angola).
Form of government: people's republic with one legislative house (People's Assembly [290[1]]).
Head of state and government: President.
Capital: Luanda.
Official language: Portuguese.
Official religion: none.
Monetary unit: 1 kwanza (Kz) = 100 lwei; valuation (Oct. 2, 1989) 1 U.S.$ = Kz 29.38; 1 £ = Kz 47.53.

Area and population

Provinces	Capitals	area sq mi	area sq km	population 1989 estimate[2]
Bengo	Caxito	12,112	31,371	162,000
Benguela	Benguela	12,273	31,788	735,000
Bié	Kuito	27,148	70,314	986,000
Cabinda	Cabinda	2,807	7,270	116,000
Cunene	N'Giva	34,495	89,342	258,000
Huambo	Huambo	13,233	34,274	1,333,000
Huila	Lubango	28,958	75,002	857,000
Kuando Kubango	Menongue	76,853	199,049	178,000
Kuanza Norte	N'Dalatando	9,340	24,190	487,000
Kuanza Sul	Sumbe	21,490	55,660	728,000
Luanda	Luanda	934	2,418	1,252,000
Lunda Norte	Lucapa	39,685	102,783	319,000
Lunda Sul	Saurimo	17,625	45,649	153,000
Malanje	Malanje	37,684	97,602	873,000
Moxico	Lwena	86,110	223,023	291,000
Namibe	Namibe	22,447	58,137	81,000
Uíge	Uíge	22,663	58,698	619,000
Zaire	M'Banza Kongo	15,494	40,130	247,000
TOTAL		481,354[3]	1,246,700	9,677,000[3]

Demography

Population (1989): 9,739,000.
Density (1989): persons per sq mi 20.2, persons per sq km 7.8.
Urban–rural (1986): urban 30.8%; rural 69.2%.
Sex distribution (1989): male 51.11%; female 48.89%.
Age breakdown (1989): under 15, 42.2%; 15–29, 27.5%; 30–44, 16.5%; 45–59, 9.5%; 60 and over, 4.3%.
Population projection: (2000) 13,207,000; (2010) 17,437,000.
Doubling time: 26 years.
Ethnic composition (1983): Ovimbundu 37.2%; Mbundu 21.6%; Kongo 13.2%; Luimbe-Nganguela 5.4%; Humbe and Nyaneka 5.4%; Chokwe 4.2%; Luvale (Luena) 3.4%; Luchazi 2.4%; Ambo (Ovambo) 2.4%; Lunda 1.2%; Mbunda 1.2%; Portuguese 0.5%; mestizo 0.5%; other 0.2%.
Religious affiliation (1980): affiliated Christian 65.7%, of which Roman Catholic 55.1%, Protestant 9.2%; nominal Christian 24.3%; traditional beliefs 9.5%; other 0.5%.
Major cities: Luanda (1988) 1,134,000; Huambo (1983) 203,000; Benguela (1983) 155,000; Lobito (1983) 150,000; Lubango (1984) 105,000.

Vital statistics

Birth rate per 1,000 population (1985–90): 47.2 (world avg. 27.1).
Death rate per 1,000 population (1985–90): 20.2 (world avg. 9.9).
Natural increase rate per 1,000 population (1985–90): 27.0 (world avg. 17.2).
Total fertility rate (avg. births per childbearing woman; 1985–90): 6.4.
Marriage rate per 1,000 population (1972): 4.5.
Divorce rate per 1,000 population: n.a.
Life expectancy at birth (1985–90): male 42.9 years; female 46.1 years.
Major causes of death per 100,000 population (1973): accidents, poisonings, and violence 89.0; infectious and parasitic diseases 73.2; diseases of the respiratory system 24.6; diseases of the circulatory system 19.2; neoplasms 6.5.

National economy

Budget (1986). Revenue: Kz 86,205,000,000 (taxes 41.2%, revenues from mixed enterprises 21.3%, loans 17.4%, other 20.1%). Expenditures: Kz 86,205,000,000 (defense[4] and social welfare 37.9%, social services 24.9%, economic and social development 15.9%, administration 12.5%, other 8.8%).
Public debt (external, outstanding; 1987): U.S.$1,849,000,000.
Tourism: receipts from visitors, n.a.; expenditures by nationals abroad, n.a.
Production (metric tons except as noted). Agriculture, forestry, fishing (1988): cassava 1,980,000, sugarcane 330,000, bananas 280,000, corn (maize) 270,000, sweet potatoes 180,000, millet 60,000, dry beans 40,000, palm oil 40,000, peanuts (groundnuts) 20,000, coffee 15,000; livestock (number of live animals) 3,400,000 cattle, 975,000 goats, 480,000 pigs, 265,000 sheep, 6,000,000 chickens; roundwood (1987) 5,139,000 cu m; fish catch (1987) 81,339. Mining and quarrying (1988): diamonds 240,000 carats. Manufacturing (1986): bricks 297,700; fresh meat 87,000; bread 52,500; corn flour 41,700; wheat flour 25,200; refined sugar 20,300; soaps 11,000; molasses 11,000; crude steel 7,000; leather shoes 295,000 pairs; beer 5,830,000 hectolitres; matches 28,000,000 boxes. Construction (value in '000,000 Kz; 1986): residential 608; nonresidential 1,977. Energy production (consumption): electricity (kW-hr; 1987) 1,800,000,000 (1,800,000,000); coal, none (none); crude petroleum (barrels; 1987) 126,148,000 (10,582,000); petroleum products (metric tons; 1987) 1,260,000 (313,000); natural gas (cu m; 1987) 154,000,000 (154,000,000).

Gross national product (at current market prices; 1984): U.S.$6,930,000,000 (U.S. $830 per capita).

Structure of gross domestic product and labour force

	1986 in value Kz '000,000	1986 % of total value	1985 labour force	1985 % of labour force
Agriculture	16,408.2	13.9	2,672,000	71.8
Mining				
Manufacturing	36,933.7	31.2		
Construction	4,979.1	4.2		
Trade, finance	15,022.4	12.7	361,000	9.7
Public utilities	685.1	0.6		
Transportation and communications	8,546.8	7.2		
Pub. admin., defense	37,292.0	31.5	686,000	18.5
Services				
Other	–1,588.8[5]	–1.3[5]		
TOTAL	118,278.5	100.0	3,719,000	100.0

Population economically active (1985): total 3,719,000; activity rate of total population 42.5% (participation rates: ages 15–64, 71.8%; female 39.7%; unemployed, n.a.).
Price and earnings indexes: n.a.
Household income and expenditure. Average household size (1980) 4.8; annual income per household: n.a.; sources of income: n.a.; expenditure: n.a.
Land use (1986): forested 42.7%; meadows and pastures 23.3%; agricultural and under permanent cultivation 2.8%; other 31.2%.

Foreign trade

Balance of trade (current prices)

	1981	1982	1983	1984	1985	1986
Kz '000,000	+5,807	+22,217	+34,007	+39,453	+47,274	+23,265
% of total	5.5%	29.5%	45.3%	48.0%	54.5%	42.5%

Imports (1986): Kz 15,708,000,000 (electrical machinery and equipment 25.6%, transport equipment 16.6%, industrial chemicals 8.0%, vegetable products 7.4%, food and beverages 7.0%). *Major import sources:* France 12.1%; Brazil 11.5%; Portugal 9.9%; United States 9.2%; West Germany 7.8%; The Netherlands 7.6%.
Exports (1986): Kz 38,973,000,000 (mineral fuels 93.4%, vegetable products 4.0%, animal products 1.7%). *Major export destinations:* United States 38.3%; Spain 10.9%; Brazil 8.1%; The Netherlands 5.8%; Portugal 4.1%; United Kingdom 2.7%.

Transport and communications

Transport. Railroads (1988): route length 1,739 mi, 2,798 km; passenger-mi 203,000,000, passenger-km 326,000,000; short ton-mi cargo 1,178,000,000, metric ton-km cargo 1,720,000,000. Roads (1986): total length 45,877 mi, 73,830 km (paved 51%). Vehicles (1984): passenger cars 56,625; trucks and buses 29,000. Merchant marine (1988): vessels (100 gross tons and over) 110; total deadweight tonnage 121,912. Air transport (1985)[6]: passenger-mi 606,000,000, passenger-km 975,000,000; short ton-mi cargo 23,200,000, metric ton-km cargo 33,900,000; airports (1989) with scheduled flights 18.
Communications. Daily newspapers (1984): total number 4; total circulation 111,500; circulation per 1,000 population 13.5. Radio (1988): total number of receivers 435,000 (1 per 22 persons). Television (1988): total number of receivers 40,541 (1 per 228 persons). Telephones (1987): 77,000 (1 per 122 persons).

Education and health

Education (1985–86)

	schools	teachers	students	student/teacher ratio
Primary (age 7–10)	6,308	32,004	930,000	29.1
Secondary (age 11–16)	5,276	3,870[7]	157,000	...
Voc., teacher tr.	...	539[8]	8,123	...
Higher	1	316	4,965	15.7

Educational attainment, n.a. *Literacy* (1980): total population age 15 and over literate 1,196,000 (about 28%); males literate 771,000 (36.2%); females literate 425,000 (19.3%).
Health (1986): physicians 655 (1 per 13,489 persons); hospital beds 13,145 (1 per 672 persons); infant mortality rate per 1,000 live births (1985–90) 137.0.
Food (1985): daily per capita caloric intake 1,969 ([1979–81] vegetable products 92%, animal products 8%); (1984) 84% of FAO recommended minimum requirement.

Military

Total active duty personnel (1989): 100,000[9] (army 91.5%, navy 1.5%, air force 7.0%). *Military expenditure as percent of GNP* (1984): 14.3% (world 5.7%); per capita expenditure U.S.$119.

---

[1]Excluding substitute members. [2]Unified national estimates and projections based on sample surveys, partial censuses, and analysis of provincial vital statistics. [3]Detail does not add to total given because of rounding. [4]According to unofficial estimates, defense consumed more than 60% of the budget in 1983. [5]Net of subsidies. [6]TAAG airline only. [7]1981–82. [8]1984–85. [9]In 1988, about 52,000 Cuban troops and other Soviet-bloc advisers and technicians were assisting government forces. On July 20, 1988, an agreement was reached between South Africa, Cuba, Angola, and the United States calling for the withdrawal of all foreign troops over a period of 27 months.

Antigua and Barbuda

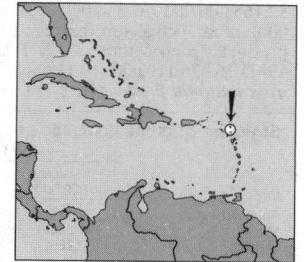

Official name: Antigua and Barbuda.
Form of government: constitutional monarchy with two legislative houses (Senate [17]; House of Representatives [17]).
Chief of state: British Monarch represented by governor-general.
Head of government: Prime Minister.
Capital: Saint John's.
Official language: English.
Official religion: none.
Monetary unit: 1 East Caribbean dollar (EC$) = 100 cents; valuation (Oct. 2, 1989) 1 U.S.$ = EC$2.70; 1 £ = EC$4.37.

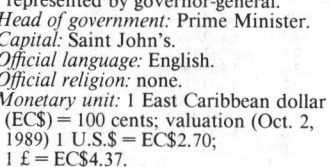

Area and population	area		population
Parishes[1]	sq mi	sq km	1986 estimate
Saint George	10.2	26.4	
Saint John's	26.2	67.9	
Saint Mary	25.1	65.0	
Saint Paul	17.7	45.8	80,000
Saint Peter	12.8	33.2	
Saint Phillip	16.0	41.4	
Islands[1]			
Barbuda	62.0	160.6	1,500
Redonda	0.5	1.3	2
TOTAL	170.5	441.6	81,500[3]

Demography

Population (1989): 78,400.
Density (1989): persons per sq mi 459.8, persons per sq km 177.5.
Urban–rural (1985): urban 30.8%; rural 69.2%.
Sex distribution (1985): male 48.00%; female 52.00%.
Age breakdown (1985): under 15, 37.2%; 15–29, 30.8%; 30–44, 12.8%; 45–59 11.5%; 60–74, 6.4%; 75 and over, 1.3%.
Population projection: (2000) 86,000; (2010) 93,000.
Doubling time: 76 years.
Ethnic composition (1980): black 94.4%; mulatto 3.5%; white 1.3%; other 0.8%.
Religious affiliation (1980): Anglican 44.5%; other Protestant (largely Moravian, Methodist, and Seventh-day Adventist) 41.6%; Roman Catholic 10.2%; Rastafarian 0.7%; other 3.0%.
Major cities (1982): Saint John's 30,000; Codrington 1,200.

Vital statistics

Birth rate per 1,000 population (1987): 14.3 (world avg. 27.1); legitimate 21.2%; illegitimate 78.8%.
Death rate per 1,000 population (1987): 5.1 (world avg. 9.9).
Natural increase rate per 1,000 population (1987): 9.2 (world avg. 17.2).
Total fertility rate (avg. births per childbearing woman; 1987): 1.7.
Marriage rate per 1,000 population (1986): 4.1.
Divorce rate per 1,000 population (1986): 0.3.
Life expectancy at birth (1987): male 70.0 years; female 74.0 years.
Major causes of death per 100,000 population (1985): malignant neoplasms (cancers) 83.3; hypertensive disease 68.8; acute myocardial infarction 38.3; diabetes mellitus 27.8; pneumonia 26.4; diseases of pulmonary circulation and other forms of heart disease 22.5.

National economy

Budget (1987)[4]. Revenue: EC$165,900,000 (tax revenue 85.0%, of which consumer taxes 28.0%, import duties 21.0%, income taxes 11.9%, hotel taxes 6.9%; nontax revenue 15.0%). Expenditure: EC$160,900,000 (personal emoluments 24.9%; public debt charges 20.2%; wages 18.3%).
Public debt (external, outstanding; 1987): U.S.$245,400,000.
Production (metric tons except as noted). Agriculture, forestry, fishing (1986): mangoes (1988) 1,000, cucumbers 329, limes 189, eggplant 186, pumpkins 177, sweet potatoes 166, carrots 135, ginger 32, sea island cotton lint 30; livestock (number of live animals; 1988): 18,000 cattle, 13,000 sheep; roundwood, n.a.; fish catch (1987) 2,400, of which spiny lobster 120. Mining and quarrying (1985): crushed stone 82,500. Manufacturing (value of production in EC$; 1983): clothing 24,000,000; mattresses 4,500,000; stoves 3,300,000; refrigerators 1,700,000; rum 1,200,000; electronic components are assembled for reexport. Construction (1986): total building applications 879; gross value EC$80,700,000. Energy production (consumption): electricity (kW-hr; 1987) 91,000,000 (91,000,000); coal, none (none); crude petroleum, none (none); petroleum products (metric tons; 1987) negligible (88,000); natural gas, none (none).
Tourism: receipts from visitors (1988) U.S.$221,900,000; expenditures by nationals abroad (1987) U.S.$14,800,000.
Population economically active (1985): total 32,254; activity rate of total population 42.6% (participation rates: over age 16 [1983] 56.2%; female 40.1%; unemployed 21.1%).

Price and earnings indexes (1985 = 100)							
	1981	1982	1983	1984	1985	1986	1987
Consumer price index	89.4	93.1	95.3	99.0	100.0	102.0	103.3
Weekly earnings index[5]	...	76.0	88.0	94.0	100.0	107.1	...

Household income and expenditure. Average household size (1970) 4.2; income per household: n.a.; sources of income: n.a.; expenditure (1974)[6]: food and nonalcoholic beverages 42.9%, housing 23.3%, transportation 10.0%, clothing and footwear 7.5%, energy 5.5%, alcoholic beverages and tobacco 3.6%, other 7.2%.
Gross national product (at current market prices; 1987): U.S.$211,000,000 (U.S.$2,570 per capita).

Structure of gross domestic product and labour force				
	1987[7]		1982	
	in value EC$'000,000	% of total value	labour force[8]	% of labour force[8]
Agriculture, fishing	29.3	4.7	2,090	9.0
Quarrying	14.4	2.3	60	0.3
Manufacturing	23.0	3.7	1,718	7.4
Construction	73.1	11.7	2,577	11.1
Public utilities	22.4	3.6	340	1.5
Transportation and communications	100.9	16.2	2,575	11.1
Trade, restaurants, and hotels	156.3	25.0	5,201	22.4
Finance, real estate	94.2	15.1	778	3.3
Pub. admin., defense	97.1	15.5 }		
Services	46.6	7.5 }	7,883	33.9
Other	−32.7[9]	−5.2[9]	—	—
TOTAL	624.7[10]	100.0[10]	23,222	100.0

Land use (1986): forested 11.0%; meadows and pastures 9.0%; agricultural and under permanent cultivation 18.0%; other 62.0%.

Foreign trade[11]

Balance of trade (current prices)						
	1982	1983	1984	1985	1986	1987
EC$'000,000	−243	−266	−310	−395	−701	−573
% of total	56.8%	57.5%	62.0%	72.1%	82.3%	77.5%

Imports (1984): EC$356,100,000 (crude petroleum and petroleum products 24.1%, of which petroleum spirits and kerosene 11.8%; machinery and transport equipment 21.8%, of which motor vehicle parts 6.0%; food and live animals 19.1%, of which meat 5.4%; chemical products 6.4%). *Major import sources:* United States 37.8%; United Kingdom 10.6%; Caricom 7.4%; Yugoslavia 3.9%; Canada 3.4%.
Exports (1984): EC$47,500,000 (miscellaneous manufactured articles 37.8%; machinery and transport equipment 30.1%; mineral fuels 11.5%; chemical products 7.5%). *Major export destinations:* Caricom 38.2%; United States 17.9%; United Kingdom 3.4%; other Western Hemisphere 22.7%.

Transport and communications

Transport. Railroads[12]. Roads (1986): total length 724 mi, 1,161 km (paved 33%). Vehicles (1986): passenger cars 11,188; trucks and buses 3,321. Merchant marine (1988): vessels (100 gross tons and over) 190; total deadweight tonnage 555,070. Air transport (1986)[13]: passenger arrivals 276,568, passenger departures 267,406; short ton-mi cargo, n.a., metric ton-km cargo, n.a.; airports (1989) with scheduled flights 2.
Communications. Daily newspapers (1988): total number 1; total circulation 6,000; circulation per 1,000 population 77. Radio (1988): total number of receivers 22,618 (1 per 3.4 persons). Television (1988): total number of receivers 27,000 (1 per 2.9 persons). Telephones (1984): 11,000 (1 per 6.8 persons).

Education and health

Education (1987–88)				
	schools	teachers	students	student/ teacher ratio
Primary (age 5–10)	43	446	9,097	20.4
Secondary (age 11–16)	15	319	4,413	13.8
Voc., teacher tr.[14]	2	56	631	11.3

Educational attainment (1970). Percent of total population having: no schooling 15.0%; primary education 79.2%; secondary 4.5%; higher 1.3%.
Literacy (1985): total population age 15 and over literate 45,000 (90.0%).
Health (1987): physicians 48 (1 per 1,606 persons); hospital beds (1986) 389 (1 per 196 persons); infant mortality rate per 1,000 live births 21.2.
Food (1984–86): daily per capita caloric intake 2,089 (vegetable products 75%, animal products 25%); 86% of FAO recommended minimum requirement.

Military

Total active duty personnel (1986): 90-member defense force is part of the Eastern Caribbean regional security system. *Military expenditure as percent of central government expenditure:* 1.7%[15].

[1]Community councils on Antigua and the local government council on Barbuda are the actual organs of local government. [2]Uninhabited. [3]Unofficial estimate. 1986 official estimate (without separate island populations) totals 76,296. [4]Current revenue and current expenditures only. 1988 budget: current revenue (actual) EC$203,700,000; current expenditures EC$231,800,000, of which public debt charges (excluding significant debt owed by state corporations) EC$35,900,000. [5]Employees of deluxe hotels only. [6]Weights of consumer price index components. [7]At factor cost. [8]Wage earners and self-employed only. [9]Less imputed bank service charges. [10]Detail does not add to total given because of rounding. [11]Imports c.i.f.; exports f.o.b. [12]48 mi (78 km) of privately owned track are mostly nonoperative. [13]Vere Bird Airport. [14]1986–87; includes higher education. [15]May not agree with military expenditure as percent of GNP because of different bases used.

Argentina

Official name: República Argentina
(Argentine Republic).
Form of government: federal republic
with two legislative houses (Senate
[46]; Chamber of Deputies [254]).
Head of state and government:
President.
Capital: Buenos Aires[1].
Official language: Spanish.
Official religion: Roman Catholicism.
Monetary unit: 1 austral (pl. australes)[2]
(₳) = 1,000 pesos ($a 1,000); valuation
(Oct. 2, 1989) 1 U.S.$ = ₳653.00;
1 £ = ₳1,056.00.

Area and population		area		population
				1986
Provinces	**Capitals**	sq mi	sq km	estimate
Buenos Aires	La Plata	118,754	307,571	12,226,000
Catamarca	San Fernando del Valle de Catamarca	38,984	100,967	230,000
Chaco	Resistencia	38,469	99,633	791,000
Chubut	Rawson	86,752	224,686	316,000
Córdoba	Córdoba	65,161	168,766	2,629,000
Corrientes	Corrientes	34,054	88,199	724,000
Entre Ríos	Paraná	30,418	78,781	968,000
Formosa	Formosa	27,825	72,066	338,000
Jujuy	San Salvador de Jujuy	20,548	53,219	487,000
La Pampa	Santa Rosa	55,382	143,440	231,000
La Rioja	La Rioja	34,626	89,680	183,000
Mendoza	Mendoza	57,462	148,827	1,344,000
Misiones	Posadas	11,506	29,801	690,000
Neuquén	Neuquén	36,324	94,078	315,000
Río Negro	Viedma	78,384	203,013	477,000
Salta	Salta	59,759	154,775	768,000
San Juan	San Juan	34,614	89,651	520,000
San Luis	San Luis	29,633	76,748	234,000
Santa Cruz	Río Gallegos	94,187	243,943	138,000
Santa Fe	Santa Fe	51,354	133,007	2,675,000
Santiago del Estero	Santiago del Estero	52,222	135,254	660,000
Tucumán	San Miguel de Tucumán	8,697	22,524	1,112,000
Other federal entities				
Distrito Federal	Buenos Aires	77	200	2,924,000
Tierra del Fuego	Ushuaia	8,210	21,263	50,000
TOTAL		1,073,399[3]	2,780,092	31,030,000

Demography

Population (1989): 32,425,000.
Density (1989): persons per sq mi 30.2, persons per sq km 11.7.
Urban-rural (1987): urban 85.3%; rural 14.7%.
Sex distribution (1985): male 49.61%; female 50.39%.
Age breakdown (1985): under 15, 31.1%; 15–29, 23.0%; 30–44, 19.1%; 45–59, 14.5%; 60–74, 9.5%; 75 and over, 2.8%.
Population projection: (2000) 37,197,000; (2010) 41,507,000.
Doubling time: 63 years.
Ethnic composition (1986): European 85%; mestizo, Amerindian, and other 15%.
Religious affiliation (1984): Roman Catholic 92.8%; other 7.2%.
Major cities (1980): Buenos Aires 2,922,829 (Greater Buenos Aires 9,967,826); Córdoba 968,829; Rosario 875,664; La Plata 454,884.

Vital statistics

Birth rate per 1,000 population (1989): 20.0 (world avg. 27.1); (1982) legitimate 67.5%; illegitimate 29.8%; unknown 2.7%.
Death rate per 1,000 population (1989): 9.0 (world avg. 9.9).
Natural increase rate per 1,000 population (1989): 11.0 (world avg. 17.2).
Total fertility rate (avg. births per childbearing woman; 1989): 2.8.
Marriage rate per 1,000 population (1983): 6.0.
Life expectancy at birth (1989): male 67.0 years; female 74.0 years.
Major causes of death per 100,000 population (1982): circulatory diseases 361.4; cancers 141.2; respiratory diseases 43.7; accidents 38.2.

National economy

Budget (1986). Revenue: ₳15,179,000,000 (social security taxes 25.2%, excise taxes 20.8%, general sales tax 15.2%, property tax 6.7%, income taxes 6.2%, import duties 5.3%, export duties 5.3%). Expenditures: ₳15,995,000,000 (social security and welfare 32.3%, economic service 18.1%, debt service 7.8%, transportation and communications 7.8%, education 6.0%, defense 6.0%, health 1.9%).
Public debt (external, outstanding; 1987): U.S.$47,451,000,000.
Tourism (1987): receipts from visitors U.S.$614,000,000; expenditures by nationals abroad U.S.$894,000,000.
Production (metric tons except as noted). Agriculture, forestry, fishing (1988): sugarcane 14,773,000, soybeans 9,900,000, corn (maize) 9,200,000, wheat 7,800,000, grapes 3,304,000, sorghum 3,204,000, sunflower seeds 2,915,000, potatoes 2,190,000, tomatoes 780,000; livestock (number of live animals) 50,782,000 cattle, 29,202,000 sheep; roundwood (1987) 11,177,000 cu m; fish catch (1987) 559,394. Mining and quarrying (1988): uranium 208; silver 1,607,700 troy oz; gold 31,508 troy oz. Manufacturing (by value of production in ₳'000; 1987): iron and steel 5,710,721; iron and steel pipes and tubes 5,489,267; motor vehicles 3,905,353; paper and paper products 1,384,180; refined sugar 466,481; beer 312,653. Construction (authorized; 1984): 10,606,800 sq m. Energy production (consumption): electricity (kW-hr; 1987)

52,165,000,000 (52,338,000,000); coal (metric tons; 1987) 373,000 (1,707,000); crude petroleum (barrels; 1987) 157,270,000 (156,184,000); petroleum products (metric tons; 1987) 19,525,000 (19,935,000); natural gas (cu m; 1987) 16,836,119,000 (19,118,665,000).
Gross national product (1987): U.S.$74,490,000,000 (U.S.$2,370 per capita).

Structure of gross domestic product and labour force				
	1987[4]		1980	
	in value ₳'000,000	% of total value	labour force	% of labour force
Agriculture	1,423	14.8	1,200,992	12.0
Mining	233	2.4	47,171	0.5
Manufacturing	2,265	23.5	1,985,995	19.9
Construction	357	3.7	1,003,175	10.1
Public utilities	476	4.9	103,256	1.0
Transp. and commun.	1,131	11.7	460,476	4.6
Trade	1,392	14.5	1,702,080	17.0
Finance	768	8.0	395,704	4.0
Pub. admin., defense } Services	1,587	16.5	2,399,039	24.0
Other	...	...	691,302	6.9
TOTAL	9,632[3]	100.0	9,989,190	100.0

Population economically active (1987): total 11,793,000; activity rate of total population 37.4% (participation rates: ages 15–64, 59.3%; female 27.0%; unemployed 5.2%).

Price and earnings indexes (1985 = 100)							
	1982	1983	1984	1985	1986	1987	1988
Consumer price index	—	1.8	13.0	100.0	210.3	468.7	1,948
Monthly earnings index[5]	—	1.8	15.9	100.0	...	...	...

Land use (1986): forested 21.8%; meadows and pastures 52.1%; agricultural and under permanent cultivation 13.2%; other 12.9%.

Foreign trade

Balance of trade (current prices)						
	1983	1984	1985	1986	1987	1988
U.S.$'000,000	+3,716	+3,982	+4,878	+2,446	+1,000	+4,051
% of total	34.5%	32.6%	29.5%	21.7%	8.5%	29.3%

Imports (1987)[6]: ₳12,929,238,000 (machinery and transport equipment 32.7%, of which electrical machinery 10.0%, transport equipment 5.7%; chemicals 24.0%; petroleum and products 9.0%; iron and steel products 4.9%; plastics 4.2%). *Major import sources:* U.S. 16.4%; Brazil 14.1%; W.Ger. 13.2%; Japan 7.6%.
Exports (1987)[6]: ₳13,580,254,000 (cereals 18.4%; animal feed 12.0%; vegetable oils 9.6%; machinery and transport equipment 7.2%; iron and steel 4.7%; meat 4.2%). *Major export destinations:* U.S. 14.6%; U.S.S.R. 10.1%; The Netherlands 9.7%; Brazil 8.5%; W.Ger. 6.0%; China 4.2%; Italy 3.7%.

Transport and communications

Transport. Railroads (1986): route length 21,233 mi, 34,172 km; passenger-km 12,456,000,000; metric ton-km cargo 8,760,000,000. Roads (1986): total length 131,338 mi, 211,369 km (paved 27%). Vehicles (1986): passenger cars 3,898,000; commercial vehicles and buses 1,434,700. Merchant marine (1988): vessels (100 gross tons and over) 451; total deadweight tonnage 2,834,008. Air transport (1988)[7]: passenger-km 7,785,000,000; metric ton-km cargo 185,704,000; airports (1989) 66.
Communications. Daily newspapers (1986): total number 227; total circulation 2,748,400[8]; circulation per 1,000 population 88[8]. Radio (1988): 21,582,000 receivers (1 per 1.5 persons). Television (1988): 7,165,000 receivers (1 per 4.5 persons). Telephones (1987): 3,654,702 (1 per 8.7 persons).

Education and health

Education (1986)				
	schools	teachers	students	student/teacher ratio
Primary (age 6–12)	20,865	238,818	4,778,264	20.0
Secondary (age 13–17)[9]	1,987[10]	95,869	761,601	7.9
Vocational	3,117[10]	142,342	1,167,969	8.2
Higher	1,251[10]	69,985	902,882	12.9

Educational attainment (1980). Percent of population age 25 and over having: no formal schooling 6.0%; less than primary education 32.0%; primary 34.6%; secondary 20.5%; higher 6.9%. *Literacy* (1980): total population age 15 and over literate 94.9%; males literate 95.5%; females literate 94.4%.
Health: physicians (1984) 81,260 (1 per 370 persons); hospital beds (1980) 151,568 (1 per 186 persons); infant mortality rate per 1,000 live births (1989) 32.0.
Food (1984–86): daily per capita caloric intake 3,191 (vegetable products 68%; animal products 32%); 136% of FAO recommended minimum requirement.

Military

Total active duty personnel (1988): 95,000 (army 57.9%, navy 26.3%, air force 15.8%). *Military expenditure as percent of GNP* (1987): 1.4% (world 5.4%); per capita expenditure: U.S.$35.

[1]Legislation has been enacted to move the capital from Buenos Aires to Viedma in northern Patagonia. [2]Introduced June 14, 1985, at the rate of 1 austral (₳) = 1,000 pesos ($a). [3]Detail does not add to total given because of rounding. [4]At 1970 prices. [5]Skilled workers in manufacturing only. [6]Commodities breakdown is for 1986. [7]Aerolineas Argentina only. [8]For 109 newspapers only. [9]Teacher training included with secondary. [10]1984.

Aruba

Official name: Aruba.
Political status: nonmetropolitan part of The Netherlands realm with one legislative house (States of Aruba [21])[1].
Chief of state: Dutch Monarch represented by governor.
Head of government: Prime Minister.
Capital: Oranjestad.
Official language: Dutch.
Official religion: none.
Monetary unit: 1 Aruban florin[2] (Af.) = 100 cents; valuation (Oct. 2, 1989) 1 U.S.$ = Af. 1.79; 1 £ = Af. 2.90.

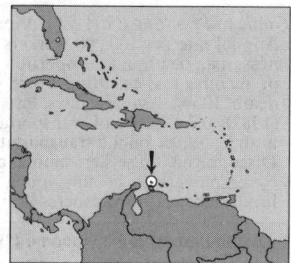

Area and population		area		population
				1981
Island	Capital	sq mi	sq km	census
Aruba	Oranjestad	75	193	60,312
TOTAL		75	193	60,312

Demography

Population (1989): 61,300.
Density (1989): persons per sq mi 817.3, persons per sq km 317.6.
Urban–rural: n.a.
Sex distribution (1989): male 48.38%; female 51.62%.
Age breakdown (1981): under 15, 25.9%; 15–29, 30.6%; 30–44, 21.3%; 45–59, 12.7%; 60–74, 7.4%; 75 and over, 2.1%.
Population projection: (2000) 66,200; (2010) 67,500.
Doubling time: 82 years.
Ethnic composition (1980): mostly Netherlands Antillean (Dutch/Spanish/black/Amerindian) creole[3].
Religious affiliation (1981): Roman Catholic 88.5%; Protestant 7.4%, of which Lutheran/Reformed tradition 2.5%, Methodist 2.4%; other Christian (Jehovah's Witness) 1.1%; Jewish 0.2%; nonreligious 1.6%; other 1.2%.
Major cities (1986): Oranjestad 19,800; San Nicolas 17,000.

Vital statistics

Birth rate per 1,000 population (1988): 14.0 (world avg. 27.1); (1987) legitimate 64.3%; illegitimate 35.7%.
Death rate per 1,000 population (1988): 5.2 (world avg. 9.9).
Natural increase rate per 1,000 population (1988): 8.8 (world avg. 17.2).
Total fertility rate (avg. births per childbearing woman; 1987): 1.8.
Marriage rate per 1,000 population (1988): 5.2.
Divorce rate per 1,000 population (1988): 3.0.
Life expectancy at birth (1981): male 71.6 years; female 76.8 years.
Major causes of death per 100,000 population: (1988): diseases of the circulatory system 210.5, of which ischemic heart disease 82.9, cerebrovascular disease 58.0; malignant neoplasms (cancers) 121.0; accidents, poisonings, and violence 69.7; endocrine and metabolic diseases 44.7.

National economy

Budget (1988). Revenue: Af. 346,749,500 (direct taxes 46.2%, of which income taxes 24.8%, taxes on profits 5.9%; nontax revenues 29.2%, of which water and energy 17.3%, telecommunications services 8.3%; indirect taxes 24.6%, of which import duties 18.6%, excise taxes 5.3%). Expenditures: Af. 364,750,000[4].
Production (metric tons except as noted). Agriculture, forestry, fishing (1987): aloes are cultivated for export; small amounts of tomatoes, beans, cucumbers, gherkins, watermelons, and lettuce are grown on hydroponic farms; divi-divi pods, sour orange fruit, sorghum, and peanuts (groundnuts) are nonhydroponic crops of limited value; livestock (number of live animals; 1987[5]) 21,000 goats, 10,000 sheep, 8,000 cattle, 6,000 pigs; roundwood, n.a.; fish catch 780. Mining and quarrying: excavation of sand for local use. Manufacturing: rum, cigarettes, paints, pharmaceuticals, motor-vehicle parts, furniture, and soft drinks[6]. Construction (number of buildings completed; 1988): residential 175; nonresidential 111. Energy production (consumption): electricity (kW-hr; 1987) 310,000,000 (310,000,000); coal, none (none); crude petroleum (barrels; 1986[5, 7]) none (60,800,000); petroleum products (metric tons; 1987[7]) none (33,000); natural gas, none (none).
Gross national product (at current market prices; 1985[5]): U.S.$1,610,000,000 (U.S.$6,810 per capita).

Structure of gross domestic product and labour force				
	1987		1981[8]	
	in value Af. '000,000	% of total value	labour force	% of labour force
Agriculture	...	...	40	0.2
Mining	...	...	4	—
Manufacturing	...	...	2,020	8.6
Construction	...	...	1,882	8.0
Public utilities	...	...	484	2.1
Transportation and communications	...	...	1,277	5.4
Trade, restaurants, hotels	...	...	7,720	32.7
Finance	...	...	1,045	4.4
Pub. admin., defense	...	...}	9,082	38.5
Services	...	...		
Other	...	...	23	0.1
TOTAL	786	100.0	23,577	100.0

Population economically active (1981): total 26,031; activity rate of total population 43.2% (participation rates: ages 15–64, 62.0%; female 36.7%; unemployed [1988] virtually nil).

Price and earnings indexes (1985 = 100)					
	1984	1985	1986	1987	1988
Consumer price index	96.5	100.0	101.8	105.4	110.0
Monthly earnings index	...	...	...	...	...

Public debt (funded debt to The Netherlands; end of 1987): U.S.$81,000,000.
Household income and expenditure (1981): average household size 3.6; income per household: n.a.; sources of income: n.a.; expenditure[9]: food 24.5%, housing 18.4%, transportation and communications 17.4%, household furnishings 9.1%, clothing and footwear 8.4%, recreation and education 5.0%, health 2.9%, beverages and tobacco 2.9%, other 11.4%.
Tourism (1987): receipts from visitors U.S.$202,500,000; expenditures by nationals abroad U.S.$16,500,000.
Land use (1985): forest, negligible; meadows and pastures, negligible; agricultural and under permanent cultivation 5.0%; other (dry savanna and built-up) 95.0%.

Foreign trade[7, 10]

Balance of trade (current prices)					
	1982	1983	1984	1985	1986	1987
NA f. '000,000	+91	−32	−68	+190	−301	−368
% of total	0.9%	0.4%	0.9%	22.2%	78.0%	78.2%

Imports (1987): Af. 422,600,000 (food and other agricultural products 52.5%, of which cattle and meat products 11.4%, fruit and vegetables 8.2%, cereal and cereal products 3.5%; machinery and transport equipment 28.0%, of which road motor vehicles 8.0%; chemical products 17.6%; crude petroleum and petroleum products 15.3%). *Major import sources* (1983): Venezuela 83.0%; United States 9.4%; Saudi Arabia 2.2%; The Netherlands 1.5%.
Exports (1987): Af. 46,500,000 (food and other agricultural products 58.3%, of which beverages and tobacco 50.3%; machinery and transport equipment 13.1%; chemical products 5.2%). *Major export destinations* (1983): United States 55.5%; Puerto Rico 9.7%; United Kingdom 4.5%; Chile 2.7%; Colombia 2.6%.

Transport and communications

Transport. Railroads: none. Roads (1984): total length 236 mi, 380 km (paved 100%). Vehicles (1988): passenger cars 23,568; trucks and buses 537. Merchant marine: vessels (100 gross tons and over) n.a. Air transport (1987): passenger arrivals 322,714, passenger departures 322,349; cargo unloaded 2,056 metric tons[11], cargo loaded 893 metric tons[11]; airports (1989) with scheduled flights 1.
Communications. Daily newspapers (1988): total number 5; total circulation 19,228[12]; circulation per 1,000 population 319[12]. Radio (1988): total number of receivers 40,000 (1 per 1.5 persons). Television (1988): total number of receivers 19,000 (1 per 3.2 persons). Telephones (1987): 23,103 (1 per 2.6 persons).

Education and health

Education (1987–88)				
	schools	teachers	students	student/ teacher ratio
Primary (age 6–12)	30	323	6,303	19.5
Secondary (age 12–17)	10	166	2,976	17.9
Voc., teacher tr.	15	225	2,807	12.5
Higher	1	20	180	9.0

Educational attainment (1981). Percent of population age 25 and over having: no formal schooling or incomplete primary education 34.9%; completed primary 28.6%; completed secondary/vocational 36.1%; completed higher 0.4%. *Literacy* (1985): total population age 15 and over literate 95.0%.
Health: physicians (1988) 64 (1 per 949 persons); hospital beds (1989) 332 (1 per 183 persons); infant mortality rate per 1,000 live births (1987) 6.0.
Food (1984–86)[5]: daily per capita caloric intake 2,925 (vegetable products 65%; animal products 35%); (1983) 116% of FAO recommended minimum requirement.

Military

Total active duty personnel (1988): A small Dutch naval contingent is stationed permanently in the Netherlands Antilles and Aruba.

[1]Aruba withdrew from the Netherlands Antilles on Jan. 1, 1986, becoming an autonomous member of the Kingdom of The Netherlands, the same status as that of the whole of the Netherlands Antilles. [2]The Aruban florin (Af.), introduced Jan. 1, 1986, is pegged to the U.S. dollar at a fixed rate of Af. 1.79 = 1 U.S.$ and is at near parity with the Netherlands Antillean guilder (NA f., Aruba's currency until 1986), which has had an official exchange rate of NA f. 1.80 = 1 U.S.$ since 1971. [3]Nationality (1981): Dutch 93.8%, of which born in Aruba or the Netherlands Antilles 88.3%, born in The Netherlands 2.3%, born elsewhere 3.2%; citizen of the United Kingdom 1.3%; Colombian 0.8%; Venezuelan 0.7%; citizen of the Dominican Republic 0.7%; citizen of the United States 0.6%; other 2.1%. [4]Equal to the sum of the estimated deficit (Afl. 18,000,000) and total revenue. [5]Includes the Netherlands Antilles. [6]Servicing facilities, including a petroleum transshipment terminal and two ship repair and bunkering facilities, are underutilized. [7]Aruba's oil refinery was closed in March 1985. [8]Employed persons only. [9]Weights of consumer price index components. [10]Imports c.i.f.; exports f.o.b. [11]1985. [12]For 2 newspapers only.

Australia

Official name: Commonwealth of
Australia.
Form of government: federal
parliamentary state (formally a
constitutional monarchy) with two
legislative houses (Senate [76]; House
of Representatives [148]).
Chief of state: British Monarch
represented by governor-general.
Head of government: Prime Minister.
Capital: Canberra.
Official language: English.
Official religion: none.
Monetary unit: 1 Australian dollar
($A) = 100 cents; valuation (Oct. 2,
1989) 1 U.S.$ = $A 1.29;
1 £ = $A 2.08.

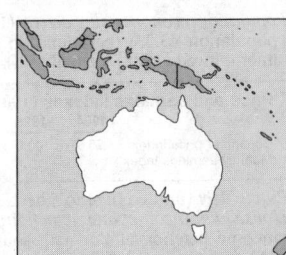

Area and population

| | | area | | population |
States	Capitals	sq mi	sq km	1988 estimate
New South Wales	Sydney	309,500	801,600	5,699,300
Queensland	Brisbane	666,900	1,727,200	2,742,900
South Australia	Adelaide	379,900	984,000	1,408,000
Tasmania	Hobart	26,200	67,800	448,400
Victoria	Melbourne	87,900	227,600	4,260,300
Western Australia	Perth	975,100	2,525,500	1,543,900
Territories				
Australian Capital Territory	Canberra	900	2,400	273,300
Northern Territory	Darwin	519,800	1,346,200	155,800
TOTAL		2,966,200	7,682,300	16,531,900

Demography

Population (1989): 16,804,000.
Density (1989): persons per sq mi 5.7, persons per sq km 2.2.
Urban–rural (1981): urban 85.7%; rural 14.3%.
Sex distribution (1989): male 49.93%; female 50.07%.
Age breakdown (1989): under 15, 22.1%; 15–29, 24.8%; 30–44, 23.0%; 45–59, 14.7%; 60–74, 11.1%; 75 and over, 4.3%.
Population projection: (2000) 19,476,000; (2010) 21,947,000.
Doubling time: 92 years.
Ethnic composition (1983): white 94.4%; Asian 2.1%; aboriginal 1.1%; other 2.4%.
Religious affiliation (1981): Christian 76.4%, of which Anglican Church of Australia 26.1%, Roman Catholic 26.0%, other Protestant 20.8% (Uniting Church 4.9%, Presbyterian 4.4%, Methodist 3.4%), Orthodox 2.9%; Muslim 0.5%; Jewish 0.4%; Buddhist 0.2%; no religion 10.8%; other 11.7%.
Major cities (1987): Sydney 3,531,000; Melbourne 2,964,800; Brisbane 1,215,300; Perth 1,083,400; Adelaide 1,013,000; Newcastle 419,200; Canberra 289,000[1]; Wollongong 233,800; Gold Coast 219,700[2]; Hobart 180,000.
Place of birth (1989): 78.2% native-born; 21.8% foreign-born, of which Europe 14.3% (United Kingdom 7.2%[3], Italy 1.6%, Yugoslavia 1.0%, Greece 1.0%, East and West Germany 0.7%, other Europe 2.8%); Asia and Middle East 3.9%; New Zealand 1.9%; Africa and the Americas 1.5%; other 0.2%.
Mobility (1987). Population age 15 and over living in the same residence as in 1986: 88.2%; different residence, same state 10.6%; different state or territory 1.2%.
Households (1987). Total number of households 5,881,500. Average household size 2.8; (1981) 1 person 18.0%, 2 persons 29.2%, 3 persons 16.9%, 4 persons 19.1%, 5 persons 10.5%, 6 persons 4.1%, 7 or more persons 2.2%. Family households (1987): 4,145,500 (70.5%), nonfamily 1,736,000 (29.5%).
Immigration (1987): permanent immigrants admitted 128,290, from United Kingdom and Ireland 18.7%[3], New Zealand 12.0%, Philippines 7.0%, Vietnam 4.9%, Malaysia 4.0%, Hong Kong 3.3%, South Africa 3.2%, Lebanon 3.0%, Yugoslavia 2.6%, China 2.4%, India 2.2%, Poland 1.5%, United States 1.5%, Kampuchea 1.2%, East and West Germany 1.1%. Refugee arrivals (1986–87) 12,000.

Vital statistics

Birth rate per 1,000 population (1988): 14.9 (world avg. 27.1); (1987) legitimate 82.2%; illegitimate 17.8%.
Death rate per 1,000 population (1988): 7.3 (world avg. 9.9).
Natural increase rate per 1,000 population (1988): 7.6 (world avg. 17.2).
Total fertility rate (avg. births per childbearing woman; 1989): 1.9.
Marriage rate per 1,000 population (1988): 6.9.
Divorce rate per 1,000 population (1988): 2.4.
Life expectancy at birth (1987): male 73.0 years; female 79.5 years.
Major causes of death per 100,000 population (1987): diseases of the circulatory system 342.4; malignant neoplasms (cancers) 174.0; diseases of the respiratory system 52.2; accidents, poisonings, and violence 33.1; chronic liver diseases 7.3; nephritis and nephrosis 6.9.

Social indicators

Educational attainment (1987). Percent of population age 15 and over having: no formal schooling 0.4%; primary and secondary education 63.4%, of which completed secondary 11.3%; postsecondary, technical, or other certificate/diploma 29.7%; university 6.5%.
Leisure, n.a.

Quality of working life (1987). Average workweek: 35.6 hours (19% overtime). Annual rate per 100,000 workers for: injury or accident, n.a.; industrial illness, n.a.; death, n.a. Proportion of employed persons insured for damages or income loss resulting from: injury 100%; permanent disability 100%; death 100%. Average days lost to labour stoppages per 1,000 workdays (1987): 0.7. Means of transportation to work (1981): 62.2% private automobile; 13.9% public transportation; 1.3% bicycle; 5.4% foot; 17.2% other. Discouraged job seekers among persons not in the labour force (considered by employers to be too young or too old, having language or training limitations, or no vacancies in line of work; 1987): 1.5% of labour force.

Distribution of family income (1985–86)

percent of family income by quintile

1	2	3	4	5 (highest)
4.7%	9.5%	15.8%	24.6%	45.4%

Access to services (1976). Proportion of dwellings having access to: electricity 99.5%; bathroom 96.0%; flush toilet 92.2%; kitchen 97.9%; public sewer 73.4%.
Social participation. Eligible voters participating in last national election (1987): 88.0%. Population age 16 and over participating in voluntary work: n.a. Trade union membership in total work force (1987): 42%. Practicing religious population in total affiliated population: n.a.
Social deviance (1985). Offense rate per 100,000 population for: murder 4.2; rape 15.2; serious assault 81.3; auto theft 838.8; burglary and housebreaking 1,856.3; fraud and forgery 1,324.8. Incidence per 100,000 in general population of: alcoholism, n.a.; drug offenses 388.2; suicides (1987) 13.8.
Material well-being (1983). Households possessing: automobile 86%; telephone 85%; refrigerator 99.6%; air conditioner 32.3%; washing machine 91.7%; hot water 98.7%; central heating 3.9%; swimming pool 10.1%.

National economy

Gross national product (at current market prices; 1987): U.S.$176,301,000,-000 (U.S.$10,900 per capita).

Structure of gross domestic product and labour force

| | 1987–88 | | 1987 | |
	in value $A '000,000	% of total value	labour force	% of labour force
Agriculture	12,244	4.7	404,000	5.3
Mining	12,658	4.9	99,400	1.3
Manufacturing	45,437	17.6	1,151,400	15.0
Construction	20,417	7.9	485,700	6.3
Public utilities	9,893	3.8	119,600	1.6
Transportation and communications	22,969	8.9	512,300	6.7
Trade	36,115	14.0	1,408,000	18.3
Finance	51,023	19.8	766,700	10.0
Pub. admin., defense	11,678	4.5	350,900	4.6
Services	43,503	16.9	1,775,200	23.1
Other	−7,769[4]	−3.0[4]	601,900[5]	7.8[5]
TOTAL	258,168	100.0	7,675,100	100.0

Budget (1988–89). Revenue: $A 87,481,000,000 (1986–87; income tax 62.9%, of which individual 51.6%, corporate 11.3%; excise duties and sales tax 27.1%). Expenditures: $A 82,013,000,000 (1985–86; social security and welfare 27.6%; transfers to state governments 19.6%; health 9.7%; interest on public debt 9.7%; defense 9.5%; education 7.2%; general public services 6.9%; economic services 6.3%; housing 2.0%; culture and recreation 1.2%).
Public debt (1988): $A 88,700,000,000[6].
Tourism (1988): receipts from visitors U.S.$2,801,000,000; expenditures by nationals abroad U.S.$2,965,000,000.

Manufacturing, mining, and construction enterprises (1986–87)[7]

	no. of establishments	no. of employees	Avg. annual wages[8] as a % of all wages	annual value added ($A '000,000)
Manufacturing				
Food, beverages, and tobacco	3,598	167,700	96.3	8,511
Paper, printing, and publishing	3,111	104,900	106.7	5,102
Basic metal products	572	75,200	128.9	4,498
Chemical, petroleum, and coal products	865	52,600	124.2	4,140
Transport equipment	1,381	108,900	103.6	3,975
Fabricated metal products	4,396	93,300	95.0	3,431
Wood, wood products, and furniture	4,331	72,000	81.8	2,402
Nonmetallic mineral products	1,797	38,700	112.2	2,314
Clothing and footwear	2,121	72,400	72.0	2,006
Textiles	664	34,300	93.2	1,503
Mining[9]				
Coal, oil, and gas	146	36,045 }	150.5[10]	7,575
Metallic minerals	280	31,380 }		4,958
Nonmetallic minerals	1,047	9,157	...	989
Construction[11]	51,351	246,510	104.0	3,925

Production (gross value in $A '000 except as noted). Agriculture, forestry, fishing (1987–88): livestock slaughtered—cattle 3,054,200, sheep and lambs 786,100, poultry 629,800, pigs 522,600; wool 5,537,300, wheat 2,039,100, sugarcane 633,600, barley 455,100, cotton 437,100, grapes 337,900, oats 216,900, potatoes 198,700, apples 198,700, sorghum 183,100, oranges 147,-900, bananas 123,400, tomatoes 121,500, rice 118,500, pears 72,000, onions 62,300, mushrooms 51,500, carrots 47,800, sunflower seeds 45,200, peaches 43,700, pineapples 38,000, peanuts (groundnuts) 32,800; livestock (number of live animals; 1989) 162,639,000 sheep, 22,223,000 cattle, 2,595,000 pigs, 55,000,000 poultry; roundwood (1987) 1,999,000 cu m; fish catch (1987) 157,100 metric tons. Mining and quarrying (metric tons; 1987–88): iron

ore 101,987,000; bauxite 34,207,000; refined metals, of which aluminum 1,004,000, zinc 310,189, lead 201,317, copper 182,446, tin 563, gold 97,453 kg; diamonds 30,331,000 carats. Manufacturing (metric tons; 1987–88): cement 6,150,000; raw steel 6,093,000; pig iron 5,455,000; superphosphate 3,194,000; iron and steel slabs 2,660,000; sulfuric acid 1,816,000; beef and veal 1,570,200; wheat flour 1,265,000; refined sugar 718,000; plastics and resins 716,000; newsprint 401,066; lamb 294,400; mutton 293,200; pork 285,800; plaster sheets 72,520,000 sq m; textile floor coverings 41,099,000 sq m; woven cotton cloth 39,410,000 sq m; woven woolen cloth 10,633,-000 sq m; concrete roofing tiles 16,344,000 cu m; automotive gasoline 159,950,000 hectolitres; furnace fuel 20,780,000 hectolitres; beer 18,930,-000 hectolitres; finished and partly finished motor vehicles 336,982 units. Construction (buildings completed, by value in $A '000; 1987–88): new dwellings 9,511,800,000; alterations and additions to dwellings 1,395,800,-000; nonresidential 8,962,400.

Retail sales and service enterprises (1979–80)

	no. of establishments	no. of employees	total wages and salaries ($A '000,000)	annual turnover ($A '000,000)
Motor vehicle dealers, gasoline and tire dealers	26,516	175,995	1,319	18,203
Food stores	39,416	260,266	1,131	12,747
Department and general stores	857	99,569	717	4,254
Clothing, fabrics, and furniture stores	17,908	81,797	519	4,143
Household appliances and hardware stores	8,196	43,542	320	2,966
Restaurants, hotels and accommodations	17,702	183,310	1,022	4,670
Licensed clubs	3,243	52,297	697	1,515
Laundries and dry cleaners	1,365	12,106	91	224
Motion picture theatres	577	6,777	45	178
Hairdressers and beauty salons	2,265	12,282	78	173

Energy production (consumption): electricity (kW-hr; 1987) 132,172,000,000 (132,172,000,000); coal (metric tons; 1987) 189,569,000 (85,079,000); crude petroleum (barrels; 1987) 197,380,000 (189,777,000); petroleum products (metric tons; 1987) 26,912,000 (27,636,000); natural gas (cu m; 1987) 15,-806,000,000 (15,806,000,000).

Population economically active (1987): total 7,675,100; activity rate of total population 47.2% (participation rates: ages 15–64, 71.2%; female 39.9%; unemployed 7.8%).

Price and earnings indexes (1985 = 100)

	1983	1984	1985	1986	1987	1988	1989[12]
Consumer price index	90.1	93.7	100.0	108.7	118.1	127.0	135.0
Weekly earnings index	86.9	95.2	100.0	107.8	113.6	121.2	132.3

Household income and expenditure. Average household size (1987): 2.8; average annual income per household (1985–86) $A 21,390 (U.S.$14,219); sources of income (1985–86): wages and salaries 60.3%, transfer payments 25.7%, self-employment 7.4%, other 6.6%; expenditure (1985–86): housing 21.9%, food and nonalcoholic beverages 20.8%, transportation and communications 13.4%, household durable goods 6.7%, health 6.4%, clothing and footwear 6.2%, recreation 3.9%, energy 2.4%.

Financial aggregates

	1982	1983	1984	1985	1986	1987	1988
Exchange Rate, $A 1.00 per:							
U.S. Dollar	1.02	0.90	0.88	0.70	0.67	0.70	0.78
£	0.50	0.59	0.64	0.54	0.46	0.43	0.44
SDR	0.89	0.86	0.84	0.62	0.54	0.51	0.64
International reserves (U.S.$)							
Total (excl. gold; '000,000)	6,371	8,962	7,441	5,768	7,246	8,744	13,598
SDRs ('000,000)	86	81	209	310	332	369	334
Reserve pos. in IMF ('000,000)	...	114	183	207	231	268	275
Foreign exchange ('000,000)	6,285	8,768	7,049	5,250	6,684	8,107	12,989
Gold ('000,000 fine troy oz)	7.93	7.93	7.93	7.93	7.93	7.93	7.93
% world reserves	0.8	0.8	0.8	0.8	0.8	0.8	0.8
Interest and prices							
Central bank discount (%)	15.76	12.14	12.03	15.98	16.93	14.95	13.10
Gov't. Bond yield (%)	15.2	12.8	12.2	14.0	14.0	13.17	12.18
Industrial share prices (1985 = 100)	55.4	70.0	81.6	100.0	134.8	193.4	164.6
Balance of payments (U.S.$'000,000)							
Balance of visible trade	−2,613	30	−884	−1,284	−2,071	−480	−1,136
Imports, f.o.b.	23,406	19,470	23,653	23,559	24,292	26,827	33,896
Exports, f.o.b.	20,793	19,500	22,769	22,275	22,189	26,316	32,760
Balance of invisibles	−5,810	−6,057	−7,751	−7,952	−8,379	−9,207	−11,625
Balance of payments, current account	−8,514	−5,969	−8,549	−8,717	−9,726	−8,725	−11,218

Land use (1987): meadows and pastures 59.0%; agricultural and under permanent cultivation 4.3%; other 36.7%[13].

Foreign trade

Balance of trade (current prices)

	1982–83	1983–84	1984–85	1985–86	1986–87	1987–88
$A '000,000	+1,331	+720	+614	−1,872	−1,736	+234
% of total	3.0%	1.5%	1.0%	2.8%	2.4%	0.3%

Imports (1987–88): $A 40,591,300,000 (1986–87; machinery 29.9%, of which office machines and automatic data-processing equipment 6.9%; basic manufactures 16.4%, of which textile yarn and fabrics 4.9%, nonferrous metals 2.7%, paper and paperboard 2.7%; transport equipment 11.0%, of which road motor vehicles 7.3%; chemicals and related products 9.2%; mineral fuels and lubricants 4.6%; food and live animals 4.3%; crude materials [inedible] excluding fuels 2.9%; beverages and tobacco 0.9%). Major import sources: U.S. 21.0%; Japan 19.3%; U.K. 7.4%; W.Ger. 7.2%; New Zealand

4.3%; Taiwan 4.3%; Italy 3.3%; South Korea 2.5%; France 2.2%; Singapore 2.2%; Hong Kong 2.1%; China 2.1%.

Exports (1987–88): $A 40,825,400,000 (crude materials excluding fuels 27.7%, of which metalliferous ores and metal scrap 13.6%; food and live animals 22.3%, of which cereals 7.8%, meat 6.3%; mineral fuels and lubricants 20.4%, of which coal, coke, and briquettes 15.2%; textile fibres and their waste 10.8%; petroleum, petroleum gases, and petroleum products 5.2%; machinery and transport equipment 7.3%). Major export destinations: Japan 26.1%; U.S. 11.3%; New Zealand 5.3%; Hong Kong 4.7%; South Korea 4.3%; U.K. 4.3%; Taiwan 3.4%; China 3.1%; Singapore 2.9%; Italy 2.7%; W.Ger. 2.6%; France 2.4%; Papua New Guinea 1.8%; U.S.S.R. 1.5%.

Trade by commodity group (1986–87)

SITC Group	imports $A '000,000	%	exports $A '000,000	%
00 Food and live animals	1,612.0	4.3	7,993.5	22.3
01 Beverages and tobacco	326.8	0.9	151.6	0.4
02 Crude materials, excluding fuels	1,083.3	2.9	9,904.0	27.7
03 Mineral fuels, lubricants, and related materials	1,749.2	4.6	7,309.1	20.4
04 Animal and vegetable oils, fat and waxes	91.4	0.2	123.3	0.3
05 Chemicals and related products, n.e.s.	3,472.0	9.2	663.4	1.9
06 Basic manufactures	6,185.8	16.4	3,834.7	10.7
07 Machinery and transport equipment	15,422.6	40.9	2,612.2	7.3
08 Miscellaneous manufactured articles	5,184.8	13.8	853.7	2.4
09 Goods not classified by kind	2,563.3	6.8	2,337.1	6.5
TOTAL	37,691.2	100.0	35,782.6	100.0[14]

Direction of trade (1987–88)

	imports $A '000,000	%	exports $A '000,000	%
Africa	369.0	0.9	609.5	1.5
Asia	16,282.5	40.1	22,224.5	55.4
Japan	7,816.6	19.3	10,644.1	26.1
South America	416.8	1.0	254.3	0.6
North and Central America	9,460.1	23.3	5,391.7	13.2
United States	8,529.9	21.0	4,631.2	11.3
Europe	11,920.3	29.4	8,298.8	20.3
EEC	9,745.7	24.0	6,406.4	15.7
U.S.S.R.	21.7	0.1	631.8	1.5
Other Europe	2,152.9	5.3	1,260.6	3.1
Oceania	1,983.8	4.9	3,408.9	8.4
New Zealand	1,732.7	4.3	2,408.9	5.9
Other countries, including destinations unknown	158.8	0.4	637.7	0.6
TOTAL	40,591.3	100.0	40,825.4	100.0

Transport and communications

Transport. Railroads[15] (1986): route length 24,084 mi, 38,760 km; passenger-mi 1,359,051,000[16], passenger-km 2,187,120,000[16]; short ton-mi cargo 33,-120,000,000, metric ton-km cargo 48,357,000,000. Roads (1988): total length 500,016 mi, 804,700 km (paved 50%). Vehicles (1986): passenger cars 8,770,899; trucks and buses 1,231,359. Merchant marine (1988): vessels (100 gross tons and over) 709; total deadweight tonnage 3,648,909. Air transport (1988): passenger-mi 16,285,000,000, passenger-km 26,208,000,-000; short ton-mi cargo 2,640,000,000, metric ton-km cargo 3,855,000,000; airports (1989) with scheduled flights 441.

Communications. Daily newspapers (1983): total number 61; total circulation 4,739,500; circulation per 1,000 population 308. Radio (1988): 7,168,-558 receivers (1 per 2.3 persons). Television (1985): 6,000,000 receivers (1 per 2.8 persons). Telephones (1985): 8,727,000 (1 per 1.8 persons).

Education and health

Education (1987)

	schools	teachers	students	student/teacher ratio
Primary (age 6–12)	8,442[17]	108,253	1,687,390	15.6
Secondary (age 13–17)	1,637	123,489	1,295,337	10.5
Vocational[17]	234[18]	52,587[18]	886,679	16.9
Higher	95	26,385	393,734	14.9

Literacy (1980): total population age 15 and over literate 99.5%.

Health (1987): physicians (1986) 36,610 (1 per 438 persons); hospital beds 87,586 (1 per 186 persons); infant mortality rate per 1,000 live births 8.7.

Food (1984–86): daily per capita caloric intake 3,326 (vegetable products 65%, animal products 35%); 125% of FAO recommended minimum requirement.

Military

Total active duty personnel (1989): 69,600 (army 45.0%, navy 22.6%, air force 32.4%). Military expenditure as percent of GNP (1987): 2.5% (world 5.4%); per capita expenditure U.S.$310.

---

[1]Includes Queanbeyan. [2]Includes part of Tweed Shire. [3]Includes both Northern Ireland and Republic of Ireland. [4]Less imputed bank service charges. [5]Unemployed. [6]Net foreign debt. [7]Excludes operations of single-establishment enterprises employing fewer than four persons. [8]Excludes the drawings of working proprietors. [9]1987–88. [10]1986–87. [11]1985. [12]Second quarter. [13]Urban areas, state forests and mining leases, unoccupied land (mainly desert). [14]Detail does not add to total given because of rounding. [15]Government railways only. [16]1978–79. [17]Includes special education. [18]1986.

Austria

Official name: Republik Österreich
(Republic of Austria).
Form of government: federal multi-
party republic with two legislative
houses (Federal Council [63]; National
Council [183]).
Chief of state: President.
Head of government: Chancellor.
Capital: Vienna.
Official language: German.
Official religion: none.
Monetary unit: 1 Schilling (S) = 100
Groschen; valuation (Oct. 2, 1989)
1 U.S.$ = S 13.18; 1 £ = S 21.33.

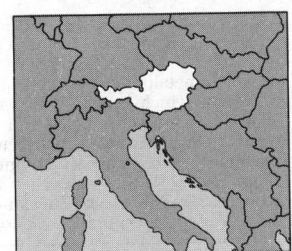

Area and population		area		population
				1987
States	Capitals	sq mi	sq km	estimate
Burgenland	Eisenstadt	1,531	3,966	266,909
Kärnten	Klagenfurt	3,681	9,533	541,876
Niederösterreich	Sankt Pölten	7,403	19,174	1,425,842
Oberösterreich	Linz	4,626	11,980	1,294,220
Salzburg	Salzburg	2,762	7,154	461,879
Steiermark	Graz	6,327	16,387	1,180,967
Tirol	Innsbruck	4,883	12,647	609,754
Vorarlberg	Bregenz	1,004	2,601	314,444
Wien (Vienna)	—	160	415	1,479,841
TOTAL		32,377	83,857	7,575,732

Demography

Population (1989): 7,603,000.
Density (1989): persons per sq mi 234.8, persons per sq km 90.7.
Urban–rural (1981): urban 55.0%; rural 45.0%.
Sex distribution (1988): male 47.60%; female 52.40%.
Age breakdown (1988): under 15, 17.5%; 15–29, 24.3%; 30–44, 20.2%; 45–59,
17.6%; 60–74, 13.4%; 75 and over, 7.0%.
Population projection: (2000) 7,676,000; (2010) 7,583,000.
Doubling time: not applicable; population is stable.
Ethnic composition (national origin; 1981): Austrian 96.1%; Yugoslav 1.7%;
Turkish 0.8%; German 0.5%; other 0.9%.
Religious affiliation (1981): Roman Catholic 84.3%; nonreligious and athe-
ist 6.0%; Evangelical (Lutheran) 5.6%; Muslim 1.0%; Jewish 0.1%; other
(mostly Christian) 1.9%; unknown 1.1%.
Major cities (1986): Vienna 1,479,841[1]; Graz 241,437; Linz 204,799; Salzburg
137,833; Innsbruck 117,011.

Vital statistics

Birth rate per 1,000 population (1987): 11.4 (world avg. 27.1); legitimate
76.6%; illegitimate 23.4%.
Death rate per 1,000 population (1987): 11.2 (world avg. 9.9).
Natural increase rate per 1,000 population (1987): 0.2 (world avg. 17.2).
Total fertility rate (avg. births per childbearing woman; 1987): 1.4.
Marriage rate per 1,000 population (1987): 10.1.
Divorce rate per 1,000 population (1987): 1.9.
Life expectancy at birth (1987): male 71.5 years; female 78.1 years.
Major causes of death per 100,000 population (1987): diseases of the circula-
tory system 592.1, of which ischemic heart disease 204.7, cerebrovascular
disease 176.9; malignant neoplasms (cancers) 251.9.

National economy

Budget (1987). Revenue: S 516,850,000,000 (tax revenue 90.6%, of which
social security contributions 36.8%, domestic taxes on goods and services
26.6%; nontax revenue 8.6%). Expenditures: S 593,950,000,000 (social security and welfare 46.5%; health 12.5%; education 9.7%; transportation and
communications 6.8%; defense 2.8%).
National debt (end of year 1987): S 698,550,000,000.
Production (metric tons except as noted). Agriculture, forestry, fishing
(1987): sugar beets 2,128,000, corn (maize) 1,685,000, wheat 1,451,000,
barley 1,179,000, potatoes 879,000, grapes 310,000, rye 309,000, apples
264,000, pears 106,000; livestock (number of live animals) 3,947,000 pigs,
2,589,000 cattle, 14,504,000 chickens; roundwood 14,118,000 cu m. Mining
and quarrying (value added in S '000,000,000; 1985) petroleum and natural gas 9.0; coal 1.5; metal ores 1.0; earth and stone 0.8. Manufacturing
(value added in S '000,000,000; 1985): machinery and equipment 54.4, of
which electrical 28.0; base metals 26.6; beverages and tobacco 22.2; chemicals and chemical products 19.2; transport equipment 17.1. Construction
(dwellings completed; 1987): residential 3,720,000 sq m; nonresidential,
n.a. Energy production (consumption): electricity (kW-hr; 1987) 50,518,-
000,000 (44,908,000,000); coal (metric tons; 1986) 2,969,000 (7,850,000);
crude petroleum (barrels; 1986) 7,904,000 (53,531,000); petroleum products
(metric tons; 1986) 7,764,000 (10,216,000); natural gas (cu m; 1986) 1,114,-
660,000 (4,795,000,000).
Population economically active (1987): total 3,430,000; activity rate of total
population 45.3% (participation rates: ages 15–64, 66.7%; female 40.1%;
unemployed 5.6%).

Price and earnings indexes (1985 = 100)							
	1982	1983	1984	1985	1986	1987	1988
Consumer price index	88.8	91.7	96.9	100.0	101.7	103.1	105.1
Monthly earnings index	85.9	89.8	94.3	100.0	104.5	107.8	...

Gross national product (at current market prices; 1987): U.S.$90,484,000,000
(U.S.$11,970 per capita).

Structure of gross domestic product and labour force				
	1987			
	in value S '000,000	% of total value	labour force	% of labour force
Agriculture	48,600	3.3	286,900	8.4
Mining	396,760	26.8	14,700	0.4
Manufacturing }			964,400	28.1
Construction	99,650	6.7	281,500	8.2
Public utilities	49,240	3.3	40,600	1.2
Transportation and communications	86,280	5.8	221,900	6.5
Trade	230,910	15.6	607,700	17.7
Finance, real estate	235,050	15.9	196,300	5.7
Pub. admin., defense	217,260	14.7 }	779,300	22.7
Services	54,640	3.7		
Other	63,170[2]	4.2[2]	36,700[3]	1.1[3]
TOTAL	1,481,560	100.0	3,430,000	100.0

Household income and expenditure. Average household size (1987) 2.6; net
income per household[4] (1987) S 208,440 (U.S.$16,870); sources of income
(1985): wages and salaries 56.0%, transfer payments 24.6%, self-employment 19.4%; expenditure (1985): food 17.1%, transportation 16.3%, housing
13.1%, cafe and hotel expenditures 10.5%.
Land use (1986): forested 38.9%; meadows and pastures 24.0%; agricultural
and under permanent cultivation 18.3%; other 18.8%.
Tourism (1987): receipts from visitors U.S.$7,604,000,000; expenditures by
nationals abroad U.S.$4,516,000,000.

Foreign trade[5]

Balance of trade (current prices)						
	1982	1983	1984	1985	1986	1987
S '000,000	−53,460	−55,940	−55,950	−57,570	−47,480	−51,520
% of total	9.1%	9.2%	8.7%	7.5%	6.5%	7.0%

Imports (1987): S 411,860,000,000 (machinery and transport equipment
34.7%, of which road vehicles 9.8%, electrical machinery and apparatus
6.3%; chemicals and related products 10.3%; clothing and wearing apparel
5.2%; textiles 4.6%; petroleum [all forms] 4.5%). *Major import sources:*
West Germany 44.2%; Italy 9.4%; Switzerland 4.7%; Japan 4.4%; France
4.1%; United States 3.5%.
Exports (1987): S 342,430,000,000 (machinery and transport equipment
33.4%, of which electrical machinery and apparatus 7.0%, industrial and
agricultural machinery 5.9%; chemicals and related products 9.0%; iron and
steel 7.4%). *Major export destinations:* West Germany 34.8%; Italy 10.4%;
Switzerland 7.4%; United Kingdom 4.6%; France 4.5%; United States 3.6%.

Transport and communications

Transport. Railroads (1987): length 4,125 mi, 6,638 km; passenger-mi 4,575,-
100,000[6], passenger-km 7,362,900,000[6]; short ton-mi cargo 7,537,000,000[6],
metric ton-km cargo 11,004,000,000[6]. Roads (1987): total length 66,799
mi, 107,503 km (paved 100%). Vehicles (1987): passenger cars 2,684,780;
trucks and buses 221,139. Merchant marine (1988): vessels (100 gross tons
and over) 32; total deadweight tonnage 350,617. Air transport (1987): passenger-mi 1,022,000,000, passenger-km 1,644,000,000; short ton-mi cargo
16,044,000, metric ton-km cargo 23,424,000; airports (1989) with scheduled
flights 6.
Communications. Daily newspapers (1986): total number 33; total circulation, 2,574,000[7]; circulation per 1,000 population 340[7]. Radio (1988):
total number of receivers 4,698,980 (1 per 1.6 persons). Television (1988):
total number of receivers 2,688,000 (1 per 2.8 persons). Telephones (1988):
3,979,000 (1 per 1.9 persons).

Education and health

Education (1987–88)				student/
	schools	teachers	students	teacher ratio
Primary (age 6–9)	3,394	28,652	350,907	12.2
Secondary (age 10–18)	2,048	57,233	462,975	8.1
Voc., teacher tr.[8]	1,392	22,662	364,264	16.1
Higher	18	10,517	183,795	17.5

Educational attainment (1987). Percent of population age 25 and over having: primary education 42.0%; lower secondary 33.8%; higher secondary
14.9%; postsecondary 4.1%; university 5.2%. *Literacy* (1986): virtually 100%.
Health (1988): physicians 20,502 (1 per 370 persons); hospital beds 82,606
(1 per 92 persons); infant mortality rate per 1,000 live births (1987) 9.8.
Food (1984–86): daily per capita caloric intake 3,416 (vegetable products
62%, animal products 38%); (1984) 134% of FAO recommended minimum requirement.

Military

Total active duty personnel (1988): 54,700 (army 91.4%; navy, none; air force
8.6%). *Military expenditure as percent of GNP* (1987): 1.2% (world 5.4%);
per capita expenditure U.S.$191.

[1]1987. [2]Value-added tax plus import duties (S 143,630,000,000) less imputed bank
service charges (S 80,460,000,000). [3]Includes 14,400 not adequately defined and 22,-
300 unemployed not previously employed. [4]Two-person households without children
only. [5]Import figures are f.o.b. in balance of trade and c.i.f. in commodities and
trading partners. [6]Federal railways only. [7]For 28 newspapers only. [8]1986–87.

Bahamas, The

Official name: The Commonwealth of
The Bahamas.
Form of government: constitutional
monarchy with two legislative houses
(Senate [16]; House of Assembly [49]).
Chief of state: British Monarch
represented by governor-general.
Head of government: Prime Minister.
Capital: Nassau.
Official language: English.
Official religion: none.
Monetary unit: 1 Bahamian dollar
(B$) = 100 cents; valuation
(Oct. 2, 1989) 1 Bahamian
dollar = U.S.$1.00 = £1.62.

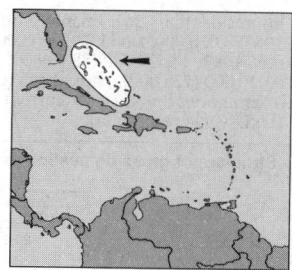

Structure of gross domestic product and labour force

	1986		1980	
	in value B$'000,000	% of total value	labour force	% of labour force
Agriculture	90	4.5	4,554	5.2
Mining			346	0.4
Manufacturing }	206	10.3	4,957	5.7
Public utilities }			1,271	1.5
Construction	61	3.1	6,675	7.7
Transportation and communications	219	10.9	6,176	7.1
Trade	524	26.2	24,474	28.1
Finance	245	12.2	6,441	7.4
Pub. admin., defense	342	17.1 }	32,158[6]	36.9[6]
Services	315	15.7 }		
TOTAL	2,003[7]	100.0	87,052	100.0

Population economically active (1980): total 87,052; activity rate of total population 41.6% (participation rates: ages 15–64, 70.5%; female 44.5%; unemployed [1987] 18.0%).

Price and earnings indexes (1985 = 100)

	1982	1983	1984	1985	1986	1987	1988
Consumer price index	88.4	91.9	95.6	100.0	105.4	111.7	116.4
Annual earnings index	...	...	...	...	...	...	...

Household income and expenditure. Average household size (1986) 4.3; income per household (1986) B$15,400 (U.S.$15,400); sources of income: n.a.; expenditure (1984)[8]: food and beverages 17.1%, transport and communications 15.9%, housing and energy 15.1%, recreation and education 6.3%, household furnishings 5.2%.
Tourism: receipts from visitors (1988) U.S.$1,136,000,000; expenditures by nationals abroad (1987) U.S.$152,000,000.
Land use (1986): forested 32.2%; meadows and pastures 0.2%; agricultural and under permanent cultivation 0.9%; other 66.7%.

Foreign trade[9]

Balance of trade (current prices)

	1982	1983	1984	1985	1986	1987
B$'000,000	−1,814	−646	−705	−353	−591	−502
% of total	16.7%	7.5%	9.4%	6.1%	9.9%	8.4%

Imports (1987): B$3,231,000,000 (crude petroleum 58.2%, petroleum products 9.5%; road motor vehicles 2.9%; inorganic chemicals 1.7%). *Major import sources:* United States 35.9%; Saudi Arabia 24.2%; Nigeria 15.2%; Indonesia 4.9%; United Kingdom 3.4%.
Exports (1987): B$2,729,000,000 (reexports 75.8%, of which crude petroleum 73.7%; domestic exports 24.2%, of which refined petroleum 9.5%, chemicals 8.4%, hormones 1.1%, crayfish 0.8%, rum 0.5%). *Major export destinations:* United States 83.3%; Puerto Rico 7.0%; Japan 2.2%; United Kingdom 1.8%.

Transport and communications

Transport. Railroads: none. Roads (1984): total length 2,548 mi, 4,100 km (paved 40%). Vehicles (1984): passenger cars 88,000; trucks and buses 5,600. Merchant marine (1988): vessels (100 gross tons and over) 572; total deadweight tonnage 15,020,793. Air transport (1985)[10]: passenger-mi 135,200,000, passenger-km 217,600,000; short ton-mi cargo 148,600, metric ton-km cargo 217,000; airports (1989) with scheduled flights 21.
Communications. Daily newspapers (1988): total number 3; total circulation 35,000; circulation per 1,000 population 143. Radio (1988): total receivers 124,407 (1 per 2.0 persons). Television (1988): total receivers 53,724 (1 per 4.6 persons). Telephones (1987): 119,061 (1 per 2.0 persons).

Area and population

		area[1]		population
Islands and Island Groups[2]	Principal Centres	sq mi	sq km	1980 census[3]
Abaco, Great and Little, and Mores Island and cays	Marsh Harbour	649	1,681	7,324
Acklins Island	Pompey Bay	192	497	616
Andros Island	Kemps Bay	2,300	5,957	8,397
Berry Islands	Nicolls Town	12	31	509
Biminis, North and South, Cay Lobos, and Cay Sal	Alice Town	11	28	1,432
Cat Island	Arthur's Town	150	388	2,143
Crooked Island	Colonel Hill	84	218	517
Eleuthera, Harbour Island, and Spanish Wells	Rock Sound	200	518	10,600
Exuma, Great and Little, and cays	George Town	112	290	3,672
Grand Bahama	Freeport	530	1,373	33,102
Inagua, Great and Little	Matthew Town	599	1,551	939
Long Cay	...	9	23	33
Long Island	Clarence Town	230	596	3,358
Mayaguana	Abraham's Bay	110	285	476
New Providence	Nassau	80	207	135,437
Ragged Island and cays	Duncan Town	14	36	146
San Salvador and Rum Cay	Cockburn Town	90	233	804
TOTAL		5,382[4]	13,939[4]	209,505

Demography

Population (1989)[3]: 249,000.
Density (1989): persons per sq mi 46.3, persons per sq km 17.9.
Urban–rural (1987): urban 61.9%; rural 38.1%.
Sex distribution (1985): male 49.80%; female 50.20%.
Age breakdown (1985): under 15, 38.0%; 15–29, 27.9%; 30–44, 17.9%; 45–59, 10.5%; 60–74, 4.8%; 75 and over, 0.9%.
Population projection: (2000) 301,000; (2010) 357,000.
Doubling time: 60 years.
Ethnic composition (1980): black 72.3%; mixed 14.2%; white 12.9%; other 0.6%.
Religious affiliation (1980): non-Anglican Protestant 55.2%, of which Baptist 32.1%, Methodist 6.1%, Church of God (Anderson Ind.) 5.7%; Anglican 20.1%; Roman Catholic 18.8%; other 5.9%.
Major cities (1980): Nassau 110,000; Freeport 25,423; Marsh Harbour 4,000.

Vital statistics

Birth rate per 1,000 population (1987): 16.7 (world avg. 27.1); (1986) legitimate 42.4%, illegitimate 57.6%.
Death rate per 1,000 population (1987): 5.0 (world avg. 9.9).
Natural increase rate per 1,000 population (1987): 11.7 (world avg. 17.2).
Total fertility rate (avg. births per childbearing woman; 1987): 2.6.
Marriage rate per 1,000 population (1987): 7.6.
Divorce rate per 1,000 population (1986): 1.6.
Life expectancy at birth (1987): male 67.0 years; female 74.0 years.
Major causes of death per 100,000 population (1986): diseases of the circulatory system 170.3, of which heart disease 114.9, cerebrovascular disease 45.6; malignant neoplasms (cancers) 120.4; accidents and violence 68.4.

National economy

Budget (1988). Revenue: B$432,579,000 (customs receipts 63.4%, stamp taxes 6.9%, fines and forfeits 6.4%, taxes on services 5.4%, business and professional licenses 4.8%). Expenditures: B$513,841,000 (education 20.1%, health 16.0%, interest on public debt 10.7%, general administration 10.1%, public order 9.8%, tourism 7.8%, defense 3.2%).
Public debt (external, outstanding; 1987): U.S.$174,700,000.
Production (value of production in B$'000 except as noted). Agriculture, forestry, fishing (1988): marine products landed at Nassau (mostly crayfish, groupers, conchs; 1987) 20,400, poultry products 19,900, fruits and vegetables 8,600, beef and mutton 300; roundwood 115,000 cu m. Mining and quarrying (1988): salt 8,000; aragonite 2,900. Manufacturing (1988): pharmaceuticals 99,500; rum 24,100. Construction (gross value of buildings completed in B$'000,000; 1988)[5]: residential 91; nonresidential 34. Energy production (consumption): electricity (kW-hr; 1987) 965,000,000 (965,000,-000); coal, none (none); crude petroleum, none (negligible); petroleum products (metric tons; 1987) negligible (345,000); natural gas, none (none).
Gross national product (at current market prices; 1987): U.S.$2,488,000,000 (U.S.$10,320 per capita).

Education and health

Education (1986–87)

	schools	teachers	students	student/ teacher ratio
Primary (age 5–11)	183	1,677	36,003	21.5
Secondary (age 11–17)	39	1,285	23,280	18.1
Higher	1	127	4,932	38.8

Educational attainment (1970). Percent of population age 25 and over having: no formal schooling 6.7%; primary education only 15.4%; secondary 63.0%; postsecondary or higher 14.9%. *Literacy* (1984): total population age 15 and over literate 125,000 (89.0%).
Health (1986): physicians 296 (1 per 799 persons); hospital beds 999[11] (1 per 236 persons); infant mortality rate per 1,000 live births (1985–87 avg.) 29.8.
Food (1984–86): daily per capita caloric intake 2,699 (vegetable products 69%, animal products 31%); 94% of FAO recommended minimum requirement.

Military

Total active duty personnel (1988): 600[12]. *Military expenditure as percent of GNP* (1984): 0.5% (world 5.7%); per capita expenditure U.S.$40.

[1]Land area only of individual islands or island groups. [2]Out Islands (all islands and island groups other than New Providence) are governed by 20 commissioners assigned by the central government. List of islands is not the same as the administrative organization of the commissioners. [3]De jure. [4]Total includes 10-sq mi (27-sq km) area of small, isolated cays. [5]New Providence and Grand Bahama islands only. [6]Includes 1,705 not adequately defined and 6,359 unemployed persons not previously employed. [7]Detail does not add to total given because of rounding. [8]Domestic purchases by resident households only. [9]Imports c.i.f.; exports f.o.b. [10]Bahamasair only. [11]Excludes two private hospitals. [12]All paramilitary (coast guard) personnel.

Bahrain

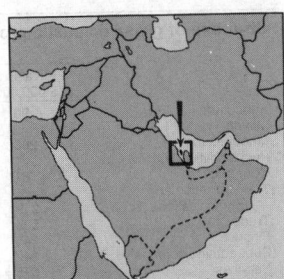

Official name: Dawlat al-Baḥrayn (State of Bahrain).
Form of government: monarchy (emirate) with a cabinet appointed by the Emir.
Chief of state: Emir.
Head of government: Prime Minister.
Capital: Manama.
Official language: Arabic.
Official religion: Islam.
Monetary unit: 1 Bahrain dinar (BD) = 1,000 fils; valuation (Oct. 2, 1989) 1 BD = U.S.$2.65 = £1.64.

Area and population

Regions	area[1] sq mi	area[1] sq km	population 1981 census
al-Gharbiyah	60.2	156.0	14,503
al-Ḥadd	2.2	5.6	7,111
Jidd (Judd) Ḥafṣ	8.3	21.6	33,693
al-Manāmah	9.9	25.6	121,986
al-Muḥarraq	5.9	15.2	61,853
ar-Rifāʿ	112.6	291.6	28,150
ash-Shamāliyah	14.2	36.8	22,117
Sitrah	11.0	28.6	22,993
al-Wusṭā	13.6	35.2	16,776
Towns with special status			
Ḥammād	5.1	13.1	...
Madīnat ʿĪsā	4.8	12.4	21,275
Islands			
Ḥawār and other	19.5	50.6	341
TOTAL	267.3	692.4[2]	350,798

Demography

Population (1989): 488,500.
Density (1989): persons per sq mi 1,827.5, persons per sq km 705.5.
Urban–rural (1986): urban 82.7%; rural 17.3%.
Sex distribution (1988): male 58.00%; female 42.00%.
Age breakdown (1988): under 15, 34.7%; 15–29, 25.6%; 30–44, 26.1%; 45–59, 9.8%; 60 and over, 3.8%.
Population projection: (2000) 503,000; (2010) 825,000.
Doubling time: 23 years.
Ethnic composition (1981): Bahraini Arab 68.0%; Persian, Indian, and Pakistani 24.7%; other Arab 4.1%; European 2.5%; other 0.7%.
Religious affiliation (1981): Muslim 85.0%; (Shīʿī 60.0% and Sunnī 40.0%); Christian 7.3%; other 7.7%.
Major cities (1987): al-Manāmah 146,994; al-Muḥarraq 75,579; Jidd Ḥafṣ 46,741; ar-Rifāʿ 45,530; Madīnat ʿĪsā 39,783.

Vital statistics

Birth rate per 1,000 population (1986): 36.8 (world avg. 27.1); legitimate, n.a.; illegitimate, n.a.
Death rate per 1,000 population (1986): 5.8 (world avg. 9.9).
Natural increase rate per 1,000 population (1986): 31.0 (world avg. 17.2).
Total fertility rate (avg. births per childbearing woman; 1987): 4.1.
Marriage rate per 1,000 population (1986): 6.4.
Divorce rate per 1,000 population (1986): 1.4.
Life expectancy at birth (1986): male 65.0 years; female 68.4 years.
Major causes of death per 100,000 population (1987): diseases of the circulatory system 112.5; accidents and violence 29.8; malignant neoplasms (cancers) 29.8; diseases of the respiratory system 19.7; endocrine, nutritional, and metabolic diseases 16.6; diseases of the digestive system 8.4; infectious and parasitic diseases 5.0; diseases of the nervous system 2.6.

National economy

Budget (1988). Revenue: BD 430,000,000 (petroleum company dividends and oil field receipts 58.6%, tax revenue 27.0%, other income 11.2%). Expenditures: BD 490,000,000 (1984: public utilities 12.9%, defense 10.2%, education 10.2%, health 6.4%, roads 6.3%, social security and welfare 2.3%).
Public debt (external, outstanding; 1987): U.S.$325,000,000.
Population economically active (1986): total 183,179; activity rate of total population 42.1% (participation rates: ages 15–64, 65.3%; female 14.2%; unemployed [1987] 10.0%).

Price and earnings indexes (1985 = 100)

	1982	1983	1984	1985	1986	1987	1988
Consumer price index	99.4	102.4	102.7	100.0	97.7	96.0	96.3
Monthly earnings index	...	...	...	...	...	...	...

Production (metric tons except as noted). Agriculture, forestry, fishing (1988): fruit excluding melons 49,000, dates 41,000, tomatoes 5,000, cow's milk 5,000, hen's eggs 4,750, eggplants 3,000, onions 3,000, cucumbers 1,000, watermelons 1,000; livestock (number of live animals) 16,000 goats, 8,000 sheep, 6,000 cattle, 1,000,000 chickens; fish catch (1987) 7,842. Manufacturing (barrels; 1987): fuel oil 21,225,000; aviation gasoline 19,418,000; naphtha 12,785,000; kerosene 2,681,000; heavy lubricant distillate 1,161,000; petroleum bitumen 967,000; liquefied petroleum gas 296,000; aluminum metal 180,300; other manufactures include methanol, plastics, and paper products. Construction (permits issued; 1987): residential 7,207;

nonresidential 1,367. Energy production (consumption): electricity (kW-hr; 1987) 3,020,000,000 (3,020,000,000); coal, none (n.a.); crude petroleum (barrels; 1987) 14,537,000 (88,499,000); petroleum products (metric tons; 1987) 9,020,000 (725,000); natural gas (cu m; 1987) 4,310,461,000 (4,310,461,000).
Gross national product (at current market prices; 1987): U.S.$4,160,000,000 (U.S.$9,994 per capita).

Structure of gross domestic product and labour force

	1986 value in BD '000,000	1986 % of total value	1986 labour force	1986 % of labour force
Agriculture	20.6	1.5	3,654	2.0
Mining	226.4	16.4	6,374	3.5
Manufacturing	170.8	12.3	14,364	7.8
Construction	104.0	7.5	38,444	21.0
Public utilities	22.9	1.7	3,869	2.1
Transp. and commun.	150.4	10.9	17,236	9.4
Trade	103.4	7.5	24,634	13.5
Finance	282.3	20.4	7,693	4.2
Pub. admin., defense	250.8	18.1	...	...
Services	51.4	3.7	66,911	36.5
Other	—	—	...	...
TOTAL	1,383.0	100.0	183,179	100.0

Households. Average household size (1986) 6.5; income per household: n.a.; sources of income: n.a.; expenditure (1984): food and tobacco 33.3%, housing 21.2%, household durable goods 9.8%, transportation and communications 8.5%, recreation 6.4%, clothing and footwear 5.9%, education 2.7%, health 2.3%, energy and water 2.2%.
Land use (1987): meadows and pastures 6.5%; agricultural and under permanent cultivation 3.2%; built-on and wasteland (mostly sand plains and salt marshes) 90.3%.
Tourism (1987): receipts from visitors U.S.$94,000,000; expenditures by nationals abroad U.S.$66,000,000.

Foreign trade[3]

Balance of trade (current prices)

	1982	1983	1984	1985	1986	1987
BD '000,000	+201	+71	−16	−129	+59.3	−101.0
% of total	7.6%	3.0%	0.7%	5.8%	3.5%	5.4%

Imports (1987): BD 885,000,000 (nonpetroleum products 53.8%, petroleum products 46.2%). Major import sources: Japan 14.1%; United States 7.0%; Singapore 6.0%; Canada 5.1%; United Arab Emirates 4.9%; Thailand 3.4%; United Kingdom 3.2%; Hong Kong 3.2%; West Germany 3.1%; China 3.0%; South Korea 2.8%; India 2.7%; Saudi Arabia 2.3%; The Netherlands 2.3%.
Exports (1987): BD 881,300,000 (petroleum products 82.6%, aluminum products 6.8%). Major export destinations: India 17.4%; United Arab Emirates 16.5%; Japan 11.9%; Singapore 9.6%; United Kingdom 3.9%; United States 2.6%; Saudi Arabia 2.2%; Réunion 2.1%; Djibouti 1.9%.

Transport and communications

Transport. Railroads: none. Roads (1987): total length 182 mi, 293 km (paved n.a.). Vehicles (1986): passenger cars 81,872; trucks and buses 25,479. Merchant marine (1988): vessels (100 gross tons and over) 89; total deadweight tonnage 67,891. Air transport (1988)[4]: passenger-mi 814,000,000, passenger-km 1,418,000,000; short ton-mi cargo 24,700,000, metric ton-km cargo 36,000,000; airports (1989) with scheduled flights 1.
Communications. Daily newspapers (1987): total number 5; total circulation 21,000[5]; circulation per 1,000 population 50[5]. Radio (1988): total number of receivers 248,251 (1 per 1.7 persons). Television (1988): total number of receivers 185,952 (1 per 2.3 persons). Telephones (1987): 121,578 (1 per 3.4 persons).

Education and health

Education (1987–88)

	schools	teachers	students	student/ teacher ratio
Primary (age 6–11)	131	3,673	60,519	16.5
Secondary (age 12–17)	35	1,563	33,148	21.2
Voc., teacher tr.	9	707	7,478	10.6
Higher	4	539	5,529	10.3

Educational attainment (1981). Percent of population age 10 and over having: no formal education 27.2%; knowledge of reading and writing 26.3%; primary education 24.9%; secondary 13.3%; higher 8.3%. *Literacy* (1986): total population age 15 and over literate 213,693 (75.1%); males literate 145,761 (82.0%); females literate 67,932 (63.5%).
Health (1987): physicians (1985) 518 (1 per 819 persons); hospital beds 1,612 (1 per 283 persons); infant mortality rate per 1,000 live births 56.6.

Military

Total active duty personnel (1988): 2,850 (army 80.7%, navy 12.3%, air force 7.0%). Military expenditure as percent of GNP (1987): 4.1% (world 5.4%); per capita expenditure U.S.$346.

[1]Total area includes numerous small uninhabited islands and dependencies of Bahrain. [2]Detail does not add to total given because of rounding. [3]Import figures are f.o.b. in balance of trade and c.i.f. for commodities and trading partners. [4]One-fourth apportionment of international flights of Gulf Air (jointly administered by the governments of Bahrain, Oman, Qatar, and the United Arab Emirates). [5]Circulation based on three dailies only.

Bangladesh

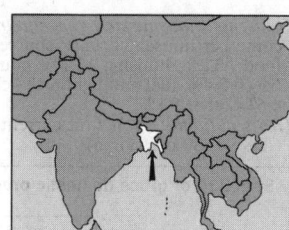

Official name: Gana Prajātantrī Bangladesh (People's Republic of Bangladesh).
Form of government: unitary multiparty republic with one legislative house (Parliament [330[1]]).
Head of state and government: President.
Capital: Dhākā.
Official language: Bengali.
Official religion: Islam.
Monetary unit: 1 Bangladesh taka (Tk) = 100 paisa; valuation (Oct. 2, 1989) 1 U.S.$ = Tk 31.52; 1 £ = Tk 51.00.

Area and population

		area		population
				1989
Divisions[2]	Administrative centres	sq mi	sq km	estimate
Chittagong	Chittagong	17,535	45,415	28,607,000
Dhākā	Dhākā	11,881	30,772	33,217,000
Khulna	Khulna	12,963	33,574	21,713,000
Rājshāhi	Rājshāhi	13,219	34,237	26,753,000
TOTAL		55,598	143,998	110,290,000

Demography

Population (1989): 110,290,000.
Density (1989): persons per sq mi 1,983.7, persons per sq km 765.9.
Urban–rural (1987): urban 22.3%; rural 77.7%.
Sex distribution (1987): male 51.47%; female 48.53%.
Age breakdown (1985): under 15, 44.3%; 15–29, 26.6%; 30–44, 15.2%; 45–59, 8.6%; 60 and over, 5.3%.
Population projection: (2000) 139,693,000; (2010) 167,633,000.
Doubling time: 26 years.
Ethnic composition (1983): Bengali 97.7%; Bihārī 1.3%; tribal (Chakmā, Gāro, Khāsi, Santāl, etc.) 1.0%.
Religious affiliation (1981): Muslim 86.6%; Hindu 12.1%; Buddhist 0.6%; Christian 0.3%; other 0.4%.
Major cities (1987)[3]: Dhākā 4,770,000; Chittagong 1,840,000; Khulna 860,000; Rajshahi 430,000; Mymensingh 191,000[4].

Vital statistics

Birth rate per 1,000 population (1988): 42.0 (world avg. 27.1).
Death rate per 1,000 population (1988): 15.3 (world avg. 9.9).
Natural increase rate per 1,000 population (1988): 26.7 (world avg. 17.2).
Total fertility rate (avg. births per childbearing woman; 1988): 5.5.
Marriage rate per 1,000 population (1987): 11.6.
Divorce rate per 1,000 population: n.a.
Life expectancy at birth (1988): male 51.3 years; female 50.6 years.
Major causes of death per 100 deaths (1976): diseases of the respiratory system 25.7, of which tuberculosis 4.8; malignant neoplasms (cancers) 19.8; infectious intestinal diseases 15.5; diseases of the liver and kidney 11.4; diseases of the circulatory system 5.9; virus fevers 4.5; childbirth related causes 4.4.; diabetes 3.6.

National economy

Budget (1987–88). Revenue: Tk 49,150,000,000 (tax receipts 82.9%, of which customs duties 33.1%, excise duties 20.3%, sales tax 11.0%, income taxes 3.5%, stamps [nonjudicial] 3.1%; dividends and profits from public enterprises 9.4%; land revenue 1.4%). Expenditures: Tk 45,693,000,000 (education 20.3%; general administration 19.9%; defense 16.8%; debt service 11.3%; justice and police 8.7%; health and population control 6.3%; civil works 4.0%; agriculture 3.1%).
Production (metric tons except as noted). Agriculture, forestry, fishing (1987–88): paddy rice 15,738,000, sugarcane 7,093,000, wheat 1,031,000, jute 839,000, bananas 673,000, pulses 530,000, oilseeds 442,000, condiments and spices 343,000, jackfruit 250,000, mangoes 158,000, pineapples 143,000, tobacco leaf 41,000; tea 41,000; livestock (number of live animals; 1987) 23,500,000 cattle, 10,800,000 goats, 1,900,000 buffalo, 1,130,000 sheep, 22,000,000 ducks, 69,000,000 chickens; roundwood (1987) 28,562,000 cu m; fish catch 837,000. Mining and quarrying (1986): marine salt 500,000; industrial limestone 22,082. Manufacturing (1987–88): chemical fertilizers 1,408,000; jute manufactures 529,000; cement 310,000; iron and steel 212,067[5]; sugar 175,000; newsprint 49,000; cotton yarn 47,000; tea 41,000; soaps and detergents 40,000; glass sheet 1,120,000 sq m[5]; matches 13,703,000 gross boxes; television sets 14,991,000 units; electric fans 145,000 units. Construction: n.a. Energy production (consumption): electricity (kW-hr; 1987) 5,895,000,000 (5,895,000,000); coal (metric tons; 1987) none (65,000); crude petroleum (barrels; 1987) 183,000 (9,331,000); petroleum products (metric tons; 1987) 848,000 (1,444,000); natural gas (cu m; 1987) 3,907,141,000 (3,907,141,000).
Land use (1986): forested 15.8%; meadows and pastures 4.5%; agricultural and under permanent cultivation 68.4%; other 11.3%.
Household income. Average household size (1984–85) 5.4; average annual income per household (1985–86) Tk 30,933 (U.S.$1,035); sources of income (1985–86): wages and salaries 26.1%, self-employment 50.8%, transfer payments 0.5%, other 22.6%; expenditure (1985–86): food and drink 63.3%, housing and rent 8.8%, fuel and light 8.4%, clothing and footwear 5.9%, other 13.6%.

Gross national product (at current market prices; 1987): U.S.$17,408,000,000 (U.S.$160 per capita).

Structure of gross domestic product and labour force

	1987–88		1985–86	
	in value Tk '000,000	% of total value	labour force	% of labour force
Agriculture	228,403	38.8	17,685,000	57.2
Mining	} 50,040	8.5	5,000	
Manufacturing			3,059,000	9.9
Construction	34,602	5.9	649,000	2.1
Public utilities	4,995	0.8	45,000	0.1
Transp. and commun.	61,971	10.5	1,329,000	4.3
Trade	48,655	8.3	3,894,000	12.6
Finance	11,435	1.9	371,000	1.2
Public admin., defense	25,756	4.4	} 3,863,000	12.5
Services and other	123,363	20.9		
TOTAL	589,220	100.0	30,900,000	100.0[6]

Population economically active (1985–86): total 30,900,000; activity rate of total population 30.4% (participation rates: over age 10, 45.6%; female 8.2%; unemployed 1.1%[7]).

Price and earnings indexes (1985 = 100)

	1982	1983	1984	1985	1986	1987	1988
Consumer price index	74.7	81.7	90.3	100.0	111.0	121.6	133.0
Daily earnings index[8]	75.5	84.5	94.4	100.0	125.8	148.4	158.1

Public debt (external, outstanding; 1987): U.S.$8,851,000,000.
Tourism (1987): receipts from visitors U.S.$13,000,000; expenditures by nationals abroad U.S.$52,000,000.

Foreign trade

Balance of trade (current prices)

	1983	1984	1985	1986	1987	1988
Tk '000,000	−30,138	−40,882	−41,543	−47,222	−47,948	−39,386
% of total	45.8%	46.4%	42.6%	46.9%	46.6%	32.5%

Imports (1987–88): Tk 91,588,200,000 (machineries 12.4%, wheat 10.6%, drugs and medicines 8.5%, crude oil 7.6%, nonfuel, inedible oils 5.9%, refined petroleum 4.6%, soybean oil 4.2%, transport equipment 3.8%, rice 3.7%). *Major import sources:* Japan 11.0%; United States 8.9%; Singapore 6.9%; Hong Kong 4.7%; United Kingdom 4.6%; India 4.5%; France 3.9%.
Exports (1987–88): Tk 41,161,100,000 (ready-made garments 36.1%, leather and leather products 11.1%, prawn and shrimps 10.7%, raw jute 6.0%, jute burlap 5.5%, jute carpet backing 3.7%, tea 3.1%, jute yarn 2.9%). *Major export destinations:* United States 29.3%; Italy 8.9%; United Kingdom 5.9%; Japan 5.6%; West Germany 5.6%; Singapore 4.0%; Belgium 3.5%.

Transport and communications

Transport. Railroads (1986–87): route length 1,785 mi, 2,872 km; passenger-mi 3,825,000,000, passenger-km 6,155,000,000; short ton-mi cargo 351,000,000, metric ton-km cargo 512,000,000. Roads (1986): total length 63,730 mi, 102,564 km (paved 10%). Vehicles (1987): passenger cars 41,894; trucks and buses 25,202. Merchant marine (1988): vessels (100 gross tons and over) 289; total deadweight tonnage 611,905. Air transport (1988)[9]: passenger-mi 1,235,000,000, passenger-km 1,987,000,000; short ton-mi cargo 50,867,000, metric ton-km cargo 74,265,000; airports with scheduled flights (1989) 7.
Communications. Daily newspapers (1987): total number 59; total circulation 848,000; circulation per 1,000 population 8.1. Radio (1988): 4,448,649 receivers (1 per 24 persons). Television (1986–87): 426,000 receivers (1 per 244 persons). Telephones (1988): 187,650 (1 per 568 persons).

Education and health

Education (1986–87)

	schools	teachers	students	student/ teacher ratio
Primary (age 5–9)	43,992	188,369	11,263,000	59.8
Secondary (age 10–14)	8,983	100,865	2,962,000	29.4
Voc., teacher tr.	157[10]	8,952	277,000	30.9
Higher	854	22,309	709,055	31.8

Educational attainment (1981). Percent of population age 25 and over having: no formal schooling 70.4%; primary education 24.1%; secondary 4.2%; postsecondary 1.3%. *Literacy* (1985): total population age 15 and over literate 18,166,000 (33.1%); males literate 12,272,000 (43.3%); females literate 5,894,000 (22.2%).
Health (1987): physicians 16,929 (1 per 6,219 persons); hospital beds 33,038 (1 per 3,187 persons); infant mortality rate (1988) 118.0.
Food (1984–86): daily per capita caloric intake 1,922 (vegetable products 96%, animal products 4%); (1984) 86% of FAO recommended minimum.

Military

Total active duty personnel (1988): 101,500 (army 88.7%, navy 7.4%, air force 3.9%). *Military expenditure as percent of GNP* (1987): 1.8% (world 5.4%); per capita expenditure U.S.$3.

[1]Includes 30 seats reserved for women. [2]Geographic reorganization at the district level took place in 1984; each division is now divided into the following number of new districts: Chittagong 15, Dhākā 17, Khulna 16, and Rājshāhi 16. [3]Metropolitan population. [4]1986. [5]1986–87. [6]Detail does not add to total given because of rounding. [7]Excluding underemployment. [8]Skilled wage earnings in manufacturing. [9]Bangladesh Biman only. [10]1985–86.

Barbados

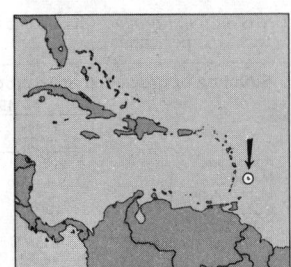

Official name: Barbados.
Form of government: constitutional monarchy with two legislative houses (Senate [21]; House of Assembly [27]).
Chief of state: British Monarch represented by governor-general.
Head of government: Prime Minister.
Capital: Bridgetown.
Official language: English.
Official religion: none.
Monetary unit: 1 Barbados dollar (BDS$) = 100 cents; valuation (Oct. 2, 1989) 1 U.S.$ = BDS$2.01; 1 £ = BDS$3.25.

Area and population

Parishes[1]	area		population
	sq mi	sq km	1980 census
Christ Church	22	57	40,790
St. Andrew	14	36	6,731
St. George	17	44	17,361
St. James	12	31	17,255
St. John	13	34	10,330
St. Joseph	10	26	7,211
St. Lucy	14	36	9,264
St. Michael[2]	15	39	99,953
St. Peter	13	34	10,717
St. Philip	23	60	18,662
St. Thomas	13	34	10,709
TOTAL	166	430[3]	248,983

Demography

Population (1989): 255,000.
Density (1989): persons per sq mi 1,536, persons per sq km 593.
Urban–rural (1986): urban 40.3%; rural 59.7%.
Sex distribution (1987): male 47.85%; female 52.15%.
Age breakdown (1987): under 15, 25.1%; 15–29, 29.3%; 30–44, 20.1%; 45–59, 10.9%; 60 and over, 14.6%.
Population projection: (2000) 262,000; (2010) 268,000.
Doubling time: not applicable; doubling time exceeds 100 years.
Ethnic composition (1980): black 91.9%; white 3.3%; mulatto 2.6%; East Indian 0.5%; other 1.7%.
Religious affiliation (1980): Anglican 39.7%; other Protestant 25.6%, of which Pentecostal 7.6%, Methodist 7.1%; nonreligious 17.5%; Roman Catholic 4.4%; not stated 2.7%; other 10.1%.
Major cities (1985): Bridgetown 7,466 (urban area [1986] 102,000); other cities cannot be identified because no other bounded localities exist.

Vital statistics

Birth rate per 1,000 population (1988): 14.7 (world avg. 27.1); (1979) legitimate 26.9%; illegitimate 73.1%.
Death rate per 1,000 population (1988): 8.7 (world avg. 9.9).
Natural increase rate per 1,000 population (1988): 6.0 (world avg. 17.2).
Total fertility rate (avg. births per childbearing woman; 1987): 1.8.
Marriage rate per 1,000 population (1984): 4.6.
Divorce rate per 1,000 population (1984): 1.2.
Life expectancy at birth (1987): male 72.0 years; female 76.0 years.
Major causes of death per 100,000 population (1984): diseases of the circulatory system 364.7, of which cerebrovascular disease 129.0, diseases of pulmonary circulation and other forms of heart disease 101.2; malignant neoplasms (cancers) 142.1; diabetes mellitus 51.2.

National economy

Budget (1988–89). Revenue: BDS$882,400,000 (tax revenue 84.3%, of which consumption taxes 20.8%, import duties 13.6%, personal income taxes 13.0%, company taxes 11.5%; nontax revenue 16.5%). Expenditures: BDS$972,400,000 (current expenditure 80.3%, of which education 17.5%, general public services 13.3%, economic services 12.0%, health 11.6%, debt charges 11.3%, defense 1.8%; development expenditure 19.7%).
Production (metric tons except as noted). Agriculture, forestry, fishing (1988): sugar 80,300, carrots 2,908, sweet potatoes 2,478, yams 1,365, cabbages 684, tomatoes 595, cotton lint 102[4]; livestock (number of live animals; 1987) 56,000 sheep, 49,000 pigs, 33,000 goats, 17,000 cattle; roundwood, n.a.; fish catch (1987) 3,702. Manufacturing (value added in BDS$'000; 1988): food, beverages, and tobacco (mostly sugar, molasses, rum, cigarettes, and beer) 102,800; metal products and assembly-type goods (mostly electronic components) 31,800; textiles and wearing apparel 31,700; paper products, printing, and publishing 25,700. Construction (value of construction; 1985): BDS$282,400,000. Energy production (consumption): electricity (kW-hr; 1988) 450,000,000 (356,000,000[5]); coal, none (none); crude petroleum (barrels; 1988) 427,000 (1,819,000[5]); petroleum products (metric tons; 1986) 228,000 (222,000[5]); natural gas (cu m; 1988) 35,000,000 (26,300,000[5]).
Population economically active (1987): total 119,300; activity rate of total population 47.1% (participation rates: ages 15–64, 76.2%; female 47.2%; unemployed [1988] 17.8%).

Price and earnings indexes (1985 = 100)

	1982	1983	1984	1985	1986	1987	1988
Consumer price index	87.4	92.0	96.2	100.0	101.3	104.7	109.7
Hourly earnings index	82.6	87.4	95.4	100.0	104.2	105.9	...

Household income and expenditure. Average household size (1980) 3.7; income per household: n.a.; sources of income: n.a.; expenditure (1978–79): food 43.2%, housing 13.1%, household operations 9.6%, alcohol and tobacco 8.4%, fuel and light 6.2%, clothing and footwear 5.1%, transportation 4.6%, other 9.8%.
Gross national product (at current market prices; 1987): U.S.$1,358,000,000 (U.S.$5,330 per capita).

Structure of gross domestic product and labour force

	1988		1987	
	in value BDS$'000,000	% of total value	labour force	% of labour force
Agriculture, fishing	171.9	5.6	9,200	7.7
Mining[6]	17.1	0.6 }	16,200	13.6
Manufacturing	240.2	7.8 }		
Construction	170.3	5.5	9,300	7.8
Public utilities[6]	84.8	2.7	2,100	1.8
Transportation and communications	226.6	7.3	6,800	5.7
Trade, restaurants	861.5	27.8	26,400	22.1
Finance, real estate	358.5	11.6	3,900	3.3
Pub. admin., defense	435.1	14.0 }	41,000	34.4
Services	99.2	3.2 }		
Other	431.8[7]	13.9[7]	4,400	3.7
TOTAL	3,097.0	100.0	119,300	100.0[3]

Public debt (external, outstanding; 1987): U.S.$501,000,000.
Tourism (1988): receipts from visitors U.S.$460,500,000; expenditures by nationals abroad U.S.$37,200,000.
Land use (1986): forested, negligible; meadows and pastures 9.0%; agricultural and under permanent cultivation 77.0%; other 14.0%.

Foreign trade[8]

Balance of trade (current prices)

	1983	1984	1985	1986	1987	1988
BDS$'000,000	−499.0	−431.3	−402.7	−521.0	−628.2	−715.1
% of total	27.9%	21.5%	22.1%	32.0%	50.0%	50.6%

Imports (1988): BDS$1,163,800,000 (machinery, transport equipment, and electrical goods 23.1%, food and beverages 15.6%, chemicals and related products 10.8%, mineral fuels and lubricants 9.5%). *Major import sources:* United States 34.5%; United Kingdom 11.5%; Trinidad and Tobago 9.0%; other EEC 7.6%; Canada 7.1%.
Exports (1988): BDS$354,200,000 (domestic exports 70.0%, of which sugar 16.3%, electrical components 12.1%, clothing 8.6%, chemicals 8.1%; re-exports 30.0%). *Major export destinations:* United States 21.4%; United Kingdom 18.7%; Caricom 15.8%; Canada 3.5%.

Transport and communications

Transport. Railroads: none. Roads (1986): total length 1,020 mi, 1,642 km (paved 79%). Vehicles (1987): passenger cars 34,740; trucks and buses 7,332[9]. Merchant marine (1988): vessels (100 gross tons and over) 38; total deadweight tonnage 8,839. Air transport (1988): passenger arrivals 634,200, passenger departures 629,500; cargo unloaded 8,832 metric tons, cargo loaded 5,190 metric tons; airports (1989) with scheduled flights 1.
Communications. Daily newspapers (1988): total number 2; total circulation 39,004; circulation per 1,000 population 154. Radio (1988): total number of receivers 222,700 (1 per 1.1 persons). Television (1988): total number of receivers 65,800 (1 per 3.9 persons). Telephones (1986): 90,708 (1 per 2.8 persons).

Education and health

Education (1987–88)

	schools	teachers	students	student/ teacher ratio
Primary (age 5–11)	126	1,548[10]	31,661	18.6[10]
Secondary (age 12–16)	36	1,401	25,254	18.0
Vocational	8	79	996	12.6
Higher[11, 12]	1	106	1,389	13.1

Educational attainment (1980). Percent of population age 25 and over having: no formal schooling 0.8%; primary education 63.5%; secondary 32.3%; higher 3.3%. *Literacy* (1980): total population age 15 and over literate[13] 169,894 (98.0%); males literate 78,022 (98.3%); females literate 91,872 (97.7%).
Health (1984): physicians 213 (1 per 1,183 persons); hospital beds 2,143 (1 per 118 persons); infant mortality rate per 1,000 live births (1987–88) 19.4.
Food (1984–86): daily per capita caloric intake 3,181 (vegetable products 72%, animal products 28%); (1984) 129% of FAO recommended minimum requirement.

Military

Total active duty personnel (1988): 154 (paramilitary marine and coast guard components only). *Military expenditure as percent of GNP* (1986): 0.6% (world 5.5%); per capita expenditure U.S.$32.

---

[1]Parishes have no local administrative function. [2]Includes Bridgetown. [3]Detail does not add to total given because of rounding. [4]1989. [5]1986. [6]Mining excludes natural gas; public utilities includes natural gas. [7]Net indirect taxes. [8]Import figures are f.o.b. in balance of trade and c.i.f. in commodities and trading partners. [9]Includes taxis. [10]Public schools only. [11]1986–87. [12]University of the West Indies, Cave Hill campus. [13]National literacy standard based solely on school attendance. Functional literacy may be appreciably lower.

Belgium

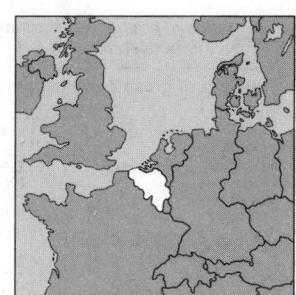

Official name: Koninkrijk België
(Dutch); Royaume de Belgique
(French) (Kingdom of Belgium).
Form of government: constitutional
monarchy with two legislative
houses (Senate [184[1]]; House of
Representatives [212]).
Chief of state: Monarch.
Head of government: Prime Minister.
Capital: Brussels.
Official languages: Dutch; French;
German.
Official religion: none.
Monetary unit: 1 Belgian franc
(BF) = 100 centimes; valuation (Oct.
2, 1989) 1 U.S.$ = BF 39.34;
1 £ = BF 63.65.

Area and population		area		population
		sq mi	sq km	1988 estimate[2]
Provinces	**Capitals**			
Antwerp	Antwerp	1,107	2,867	1,587,450
Brabant	Brussels	1,297	3,358	2,221,818
East Flanders	Ghent	1,151	2,982	1,328,779
Hainaut	Mons	1,462	3,787	1,271,649
Liège	Liège	1,491	3,862	992,068
Limburg	Hasselt	935	2,422	736,982
Luxembourg	Arlon	1,715	4,441	226,452
Namur	Namur	1,415	3,665	415,326
West Flanders	Brugge	1,210	3,134	1,095,193
TOTAL		11,783	30,518	9,875,717

Demography

Population (1989): 9,878,000.
Density (1989): persons per sq mi 838.3, persons per sq km 323.7.
Urban–rural (1985): urban 96.3%; rural 3.7%.
Sex distribution (1987): male 48.82%; female 51.18%.
Age breakdown (1986): under 15, 18.4%; 15–29, 23.1%; 30–44, 21.1%; 45–59, 17.5%; 60–74, 13.5%; 75 and over, 6.4%.
Population projection: (2000) 9,918,000; (2010) 9,955,000.
Doubling time: n.a.; doubling time exceeds 100 years.
Nationality (1981): Belgian 91.1%; Italian 2.8%; Moroccan 1.1%; French 1.1%; Dutch 0.7%; Turkish 0.6%; other 2.6%.
Religious affiliation (1980): Roman Catholic 90.0%; Muslim 1.1%; Protestant 0.4%; nonreligious and atheist 7.5%; other 1.0%.
Major cities (1982[2]): Brussels 136,920[3] (970,346[4]); Antwerp 476,044; Ghent 232,620; Charleroi 208,938; Liège 200,312.

Vital statistics

Birth rate per 1,000 population (1987): 11.9 (world avg. 27.1); (1984) legitimate 93.7%; illegitimate 6.3%.
Death rate per 1,000 population (1987): 10.7 (world avg. 9.9).
Natural increase rate per 1,000 population (1987): 1.2 (world avg. 17.2).
Total fertility rate (avg. births per childbearing woman; 1985–90): 1.6.
Marriage rate per 1,000 population (1987): 5.7.
Divorce rate per 1,000 population (1987): 1.9.
Life expectancy at birth (1979–82): male 70.0 years; female 76.8 years.
Major causes of death per 100,000 population (1986): diseases of the circulatory system 464.3, of which cerebrovascular disease 116.6; malignant neoplasms (cancers) 275.9.

National economy

Budget (1988). Revenue: BF 1,491,124,000,000 (direct taxes 62.4%; value-added, stamp, and similar duties 26.1%; customs and excise duties 7.1%). Expenditures: BF 1,892,341,000,000 (government departments 39.4%; public debt 21.6%; education and culture 15.1%; pension 10.3%; defense 5.4%).
Production (metric tons except as noted). Agriculture, forestry, fishing (1987): sugar beets 5,425,200, potatoes 1,620,300, wheat 1,046,500, barley 678,100, apples 245,000[5], tomatoes 179,000[5], oats 60,400, corn (maize) 40,300, milk 3,777,000; livestock (number of live animals) 5,880,800 pigs, 2,950,200 cattle, 133,100 sheep, 23,100 horses; roundwood[5] 3,528,000 cu m; fish catch 40,374, of which European plaice (flounder) 12,336, Atlantic cod 8,792, common sole 4,606. Mining and quarrying (1986): quartz 275,000; barite 40,000. Manufacturing (value added in BF '000,000; 1986): metal products and machinery 316,700; food, beverages, and tobacco 235,800; chemicals and chemical products 137,400; pig iron, steel, and nonferrous metals 64,-800; paper, printing, and publishing 59,200; furniture and fixtures 50,200; textiles 46,000; building materials 40,800; clothing and footwear 34,400. Construction (1985): residential 17,776,000 cu m; nonresidential 22,422,000 cu m. Energy production (consumption): electricity (kW-hr; 1987) 62,375,-000,000 (60,257,000,000); coal (metric tons; 1987) 4,386,000 (13,086,000); petroleum (barrels; 1987) none (174,659,000); petroleum products (metric tons; 1987) 24,189,000 (18,840,000); natural gas (cu m; 1987) 31,300,000 (7,865,000,000).
Public debt (1988): U.S.$170,366,000,000.
Household income and expenditure. Average household size (1981) 2.7; sources of income (1986): wages and salaries 51.9%, transfer payments 20.7%, property income 17.0%, self-employment 10.4%; expenditure (1986): food 23.5%, housing 16.7%, transportation and communications 12.8%, personal care and health 11.6%, recreation 9.8%, household durable goods 9.3%, clothing and footwear 8.4%, energy 6.3%, other 1.6%.

Gross national product (at current market prices; 1987): U.S.$112,009,000,-000 (U.S.$11,360 per capita).

Structure of gross domestic product and labour force				
	1987			
	in value BF '000,000	% of total value	labour force	% of labour force
Agriculture	110,643	2.1	100,384	2.4
Mining	20,380	0.4 }	781,772	19.0
Manufacturing	1,175,498	22.1 }		
Construction	279,750	5.2	205,495	5.0
Public utilities	166,794	3.1	52,266	1.3
Transp. and commun.	414,915	7.8	257,419	6.2
Trade }	1,788,651	33.6	730,092	17.7
Finance }			321,461	7.8
Pub. admin., defense }	1,555,011	29.2	1,262,823	30.6
Services }				
Other	−188,638[6]	−3.5[6]	414,334[7]	10.0[7]
TOTAL	5,323,004	100.0	4,126,046	100.0

Population economically active (1987): total 4,126,046; activity rate of total population 41.8% (participation rates: ages 15–64, n.a.; female 41.0%; unemployed 10.0%).

Price and earnings indexes (1985 = 100)							
	1982	1983	1984	1985	1986	1987	1988
Consumer price index	83.3	89.7	95.4	100.0	101.3	102.9	104.1
Hourly earnings index	88.2	92.0	96.5	100.0	102.8	104.8	105.6

Land use[5] (1987): forested 21.2%; meadows and pastures 21.3%; agricultural and under permanent cultivation 24.9%; other 32.6%.
Tourism (1987): receipts from visitors U.S.$2,980,000,000; expenditures by nationals abroad U.S.$3,886,000,000.

Foreign trade[5]

Balance of trade (current prices)						
	1983	1984	1985	1986	1987	1988
BF '000,000	−84,800	−107,600	−50,300	+96,800	+124,300	+96,400
% of total	1.6%	1.8%	0.8%	1.6%	2.0%	1.4%

Imports (1987): BF 3,099,209,000,000 (machinery and transport equipment 29.4%, of which road vehicles and parts 13.5%; chemicals and chemical products 10.4%; mineral fuels and lubricants 9.3%, of which petroleum and petroleum products 6.6%, natural gas 1.1%; food and live animals 8.8%; nonindustrial [gem] diamonds 5.6%). *Major import sources:* West Germany 24.3%; The Netherlands 17.2%; France 15.7%; U.K. 7.8%; U.S. 4.7%.
Exports (1987): BF 3,093,069,000,000 (machinery and transport equipment 27.0%, of which passenger cars 11.5%; chemicals and chemical products 12.6%, of which plastics 4.8%; food and live animals 9.0%; iron and steel 7.2%; nonindustrial [gem] diamonds 5.8%; textile yarns and fabrics 5.6%; petroleum and petroleum products 3.4%). *Major export destinations:* France 20.5%; West Germany 19.8%; The Netherlands 15.0%; U.K. 8.4%; Italy 6.4%; U.S. 5.2%.

Transport and communications

Transport. Railroads (1988): route length[8] 2,248 mi, 3,959 km; passenger-mi 3,959,000,000, passenger-km 6,372,000,000; short ton-mi cargo 5,269,000,-000, metric ton-km cargo 7,692,000,000. Roads (1987): total length 79,622 mi, 128,139 km (paved 96%). Vehicles (1987): passenger cars 3,497,818; trucks and buses 312,510. Merchant marine (1988): vessels (100 gross tons and over) 344; total deadweight tonnage 3,400,961. Air transport (1987): passenger-mi 3,713,676,000, passenger-km 5,976,593,000; short ton-mi cargo 368,000,000; metric ton-km cargo 538,000,000; airports (1989) with scheduled flights 4.
Communications. Daily newspapers (1988): total number 39; total circulation 1,930,000[9]; circulation per 1,000 population 195[9]. Radio (1987): 4,520,590 receivers (1 per 2.2 persons). Television (1987): 3,050,000 receivers (1 per 3.2 persons). Telephones (1987): 4,719,273 (1 per 2.1 persons).

Education and health

Education (1986–87)				
	schools	teachers	students	student/ teacher ratio
Primary (age 6–12)	4,294	45,261[10]	727,647	...
Secondary (age 12–18)	2,272[11]	56,719[12]	441,879	...
Voc., teacher tr.	209[12]	6,864[12]	371,112	...
Higher	17[11]	5,349	103,505	19.4

Educational attainment (1977). Percent of population age 25 and over having: less than secondary education 64.4%; lower secondary 16.0%; upper secondary 10.0%; vocational 3.7%; teacher's college 2.1%; university 3.8%.
Literacy (1988): virtually 100% literate.
Health (1986): physicians 29,776 (1 per 331 persons); hospital beds 90,720 (1 per 109 persons); infant mortality rate per 1,000 live births (1987) 9.7.
Food[5] (1984–86): daily per capita caloric intake 3,850 (vegetable products 58%, animal products 42%); 140% of FAO recommended minimum.

Military

Total active duty personnel (1989): 92,400 (army 73.4%, navy 5.1%, air force 21.5%). *Military expenditure as percent of GNP* (1987): 3.0% (world 5.4%); per capita expenditure U.S.$422.

[1]Includes one ex officio member from the royal family. [2]January 1. [3]1987. [4]Région Bruxelloise. [5]Includes Luxembourg. [6]Includes imputed bank service charges. [7]Unemployed. [8]1986. [9]For 35 newspapers only. [10]1983–84. [11]1984–85. [12]1982–83.

Belize

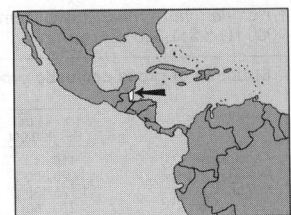

Official name: Belize.
Form of government: constitutional monarchy with two legislative houses (Senate [8][1]; House of Representatives [28][2]).
Chief of state: British Monarch represented by governor-general.
Head of government: Prime Minister.
Capital: Belmopan.
Official language: English.
Official religion: none.
Monetary unit: 1 Belize dollar (BZ$) = 100 cents; valuation (Oct. 2, 1989) 1 U.S.$ = BZ$2.00[3]; 1 £ = BZ$3.24.

Area and population		area		population
		sq mi	sq km	1987 estimate
Districts	**Capitals**			
Belize	Belize City	1,624	4,206	58,300
Cayo	San Ignacio	2,061	5,338	28,800
Corozal	Corozal	718	1,860	29,100
Orange Walk	Orange Walk	1,829	4,737	28,200
Stann Creek	Dangriga	840	2,176	17,300
Toledo	Punta Gorda	1,795	4,649	14,400
TOTAL		8,867	22,965[4]	176,100

Demography

Population (1989): 185,000.
Density (1989): persons per sq mi 20.9, persons per sq km 8.1.
Urban–rural (1985): urban 50.0%; rural 50.0%.
Sex distribution (1987): male 50.66%; female 49.34%.
Age breakdown (1987): under 15, 44.5%; 15–29, 27.9%; 30–44, 12.4%; 45–59, 7.5%; 60–74, 5.1%; 75 and over, 2.6%.
Population projection: (2000) 230,000; (2010) 270,000.
Doubling time: 20 years.
Ethnic composition (1980): Creole (predominantly black) 39.7%; mestizo (Spanish-Indian) 33.1%; Mayan Indian 9.5%; Garifuna (black-Carib Indian) 7.6%; white 4.2%; East Indian 2.1%; other or not stated 3.8%.
Religious affiliation (1980): Roman Catholic 61.7%; Protestant 28.9%, of which Anglican 11.8%, Methodist 6.0%, Mennonite 3.9%, Seventh-day Adventist 3.0%; Baha'i 2.5%; Jewish 1.2%; other Christian 1.0%; other 4.7%.
Major cities (1986): Belize City 47,000; Orange Walk 9,900; Corozal 8,100; Dangriga 7,700; Belmopan 3,500.

Vital statistics

Birth rate per 1,000 population (1987): 38.7 (world avg. 27.1); legitimate 45.2%; illegitimate 54.8%.
Death rate per 1,000 population (1987): 3.9 (world avg. 9.9).
Natural increase rate per 1,000 population (1987): 34.8 (world avg. 17.2).
Total fertility rate (avg. births per childbearing woman; 1987): 5.4.
Marriage rate per 1,000 population (1987): 6.3.
Divorce rate per 1,000 population (1987): 0.5.
Life expectancy at birth (1987): male 66.0 years; female 71.0 years.
Major causes of death per 100,000 population (1986): ischemic heart disease and diseases of pulmonary circulation 113.9; diseases of the respiratory system 71.0; accidents 33.5; diabetes mellitus 25.8.

National economy

Budget (1988–89). Revenue: BZ$201,200,000 (tax revenue 78.7%, of which customs duties 47.8%, income taxes 16.4%; sale of telephone company shares 17.1%). Expenditures: BZ$162,800,000 (current expenditure 81.1%; development expenditure 18.7%).
Public debt (external, outstanding; 1987): U.S.$113,000,000.
Tourism (1987): receipts from visitors U.S.$24,000,000; expenditures by nationals abroad, U.S.$5,000,000.
Production (metric tons except as noted). Agriculture, forestry, fishing (1988): sugarcane 789,000, oranges 54,600, grapefruits 30,500, bananas 26,-600, corn (maize) 23,100, rice 5,500, coconuts 4,000, red kidney beans 2,300, honey 220, cocoa 57; livestock (number of live animals) 50,000 cattle, 26,000 pigs, 1,000,000 chickens; roundwood (1987) 155,000 cu m; fish catch (1987) 1,501, of which marine fishes 545, spiny lobster 530, shrimps 274, conchs 149. Mining and quarrying (1986): limestone 600,000; sand and gravel 500,000. Manufacturing (1988): sugar 83,100; flour 44,500; molasses 23,500; fertilizer 7,800; orange concentrate 42,500 hectolitres; beer 24,200 hectolitres; grapefruit concentrate 20,100 hectolitres; cigarettes 94,400,000 units; garments (mostly overalls and shirts) 3,696,000 units. Construction (1984): residential 6,185 sq m; nonresidential, n.a. Energy production (consumption): electricity (kW-hr; 1987–88) 80,300,000 (65,700,000); coal, none (none); crude petroleum, none (none); petroleum products (metric tons; 1987) none (56,000); natural gas, none (none).
Population economically active (1983–84): total 47,325; activity rate of total population 29.6% (participation rates: ages 15–64 [1980] 63.0%; female 32.5%; unemployed [1987] 14.0%).

Price and earnings indexes (1985 = 100)							
	1983	1984	1985	1986	1987	1988	1989
Consumer price index	93.0	96.5	100.0	101.0	103.3	106.1	107.6[5]
Earnings index	...	...	...	...	...	...	...

Gross national product (at current market prices; 1987): U.S.$219,000,000 (U.S.$1,250 per capita).

Structure of gross domestic product and labour force				
	1987		1983–84	
	in value BZ$'000	% of total value	labour force	% of labour force
Agriculture, fishing, forestry	95,220	22.0	13,065	27.6
Mining	800	0.2	81	0.2
Manufacturing	52,895	12.2	4,192	8.9
Construction	26,810	6.2	1,994	4.2
Public utilities	13,693	3.2	611	1.3
Transportation and communications	46,254	10.7	2,035	4.3
Trade	72,322	16.7	4,558	9.6
Finance, real estate, insurance	40,229	9.3	570	1.2
Pub. admin., defense	53,068	12.3	6,268	13.2
Services	45,910	10.6	7,326	15.5
Other	−14,754[6]	−3.4[6]	6,625[7]	14.0[7]
TOTAL	432,447	100.0	47,325	100.0

Household income and expenditure. Average household size (1986) 5.2; income per household: n.a.; sources of income: n.a.; expenditure (1980): food and beverages 51.5%, clothing and footwear 11.1%, household furnishings 10.1%, transportation and communications 6.5%, energy and water 6.0%, health care 3.4%, housing 2.3%, other 9.1%.
Land use (1986): forested 44.4%; meadows and pastures 2.1%; agricultural and under permanent cultivation 2.4%; other 51.1%.

Foreign trade[8]

Balance of trade (current prices)						
	1983	1984	1985	1986	1987	1988
BZ$'000,000	−47.8	−50.2	−51.8	−37.5	−62.3	−80.8
% of total	13.3%	11.9%	11.9%	9.2%	13.6%	14.4%

Imports (1987): BZ$287,150,000 (manufactured goods 29.3%; food 22.1%; machinery and transport 21.0%; fuels 13.2%; chemicals and chemical products 11.0%). *Major import sources:* United States 58.2%; Mexico 8.9%; United Kingdom 8.2%; The Netherlands 4.4%; Canada 3.9%.
Exports (1987): BZ$198,720,000 (domestic exports 87.5%, of which sugar 31.5%, garments 15.7%, orange concentrate 12.4%, bananas 7.5%; grapefruit concentrate 3.2%; reexports 12.5%). *Major export destinations:* United States 46.7%; United Kingdom 31.5%; Mexico 9.7%; Canada 3.5%; Jamaica 3.3%.

Transport and communications

Transport. Railroads: none. Roads (1985): total length 1,865 mi, 3,001 km (paved 13%). Vehicles (1984): passenger cars 3,707; trucks and buses 1,855. Merchant marine (1988): vessels (100 gross tons and over) 3; total deadweight tonnage 805. Air transport (1987)[9]: passenger arrivals 59,432, passenger departures 63,476; cargo loaded 483 metric tons, cargo unloaded 833 metric tons. Airports (1989) with scheduled flights 8.
Communications. Daily newspapers: none. Radio (1988): total number of receivers 94,923 (1 per 1.9 persons). Television (1988): total number of receivers, 12,000 (1 per 15 persons). Telephones (1988): 9,674[10] (1 per 19 persons).

Education and health

Education (1987–88)	schools	teachers	students	student/ teacher ratio
Primary (age 5–14)	226	1,578	39,779	25.2
Secondary (age, n.a.)	24[11]	297	7,326	24.7
Voc., teacher tr. } Higher	5[11]	...	834[11]	...

Educational attainment (1980). Percent of population age 25 and over having: no formal schooling 10.7%; primary education 75.3%; secondary 11.7%; higher 2.3%. *Literacy* (1985): total population age 15 and over literate 85,000 (93%).
Health (1987): physicians 85 (1 per 2,061 persons); hospital beds 583 (1 per 300 persons); infant mortality rate per 1,000 live births (1985–87 avg.) 21.0.
Food (1984–86): daily per capita caloric intake 2,585 (vegetable products 74%, animal products 26%); 114% of FAO recommended minimum requirement.

Military

Total active duty personnel (1988): 715 (army 90.9%, maritime wing 7.0%, air wing 2.1%); British troops 1,500. *Military expenditure as percent of GNP* (1986): 1.8% (world 5.5%); per capita expenditure U.S.$21.

[1]Excludes president of the Senate, who *may* be elected by the Senate from outside its appointive membership. [2]Excludes speaker of House of Representatives, who *may* be elected by the House from outside its elected membership. [3]The Belize dollar is officially pegged to the U.S. dollar. [4]Detail does not add to total given because of rounding. [5]May. [6]Less imputed bank service charges. [7]Unemployed. [8]Imports are f.o.b. in balance of trade and c.i.f. in commodities and trading partners. [9]Belize International Airport only. [10]Number of subscribers. [11]1986–87.

Benin

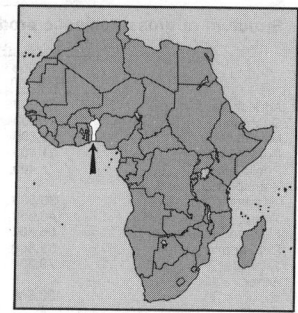

Official name: République Populaire du
Bénin (People's Republic of Benin).
Form of government: unitary
single-party people's republic with
one legislative house (National
Revolutionary Assembly [206]).
Head of state and government:
President.
Capitals[1]: Porto-Novo (official);
Cotonou (de facto).
Official language: French.
Official religion: none.
Monetary unit: 1 CFA franc
(CFAF) = 100 centimes; valuation
(Oct. 2, 1989) 1 U.S.\$ = CFAF 317.90;
1 £ = CFAF 514.37.

Area and population

Provinces	Capitals	area sq mi	area sq km	population 1987 estimate
Atacora	Natitingou	12,050	31,200	622,000
Atlantique	Cotonou	1,250	3,200	909,000
Borgou	Parakou	19,700	51,000	630,000
Mono	Lokossa	1,450	3,800	610,000
Ouémé	Porto-Novo	1,800	4,700	806,000
Zou	Abomey	7,200	18,700	731,000
TOTAL		43,450	112,600	4,308,000

Demography

Population (1989): 4,592,000.
Density (1989): persons per sq mi 105.7, persons per sq km 40.8.
Urban-rural (1985): urban 19.0%; rural 81.0%.
Sex distribution (1985): male 49.11%; female 50.89%.
Age breakdown (1985): under 15, 46.5%; 15–29, 25.7%; 30–44, 14.8%; 45–59,
8.5%; 60 and over, 4.5%.
Population projection: (2000) 6,561,000; (2010) 8,987,000.
Doubling time: 22 years.
Ethnic composition (1983): Fon 65.6%; Bariba 9.7%; Yoruba 8.9%; Somba
5.4%; Fulani 4.0%; other 6.4%.
Religious affiliation (1980): traditional beliefs 61.4%; Christian 23.1%, of
which Roman Catholic 18.5%, Protestant 2.8%; Muslim 15.2%; other 0.3%.
Major cities (1982): Cotonou 487,000; Porto-Novo 208,000; Parakou 66,000;
Abomey 54,000; Kandi 53,000.

Vital statistics

Birth rate per 1,000 population (1985–90): 50.5 (world avg. 27.1).
Death rate per 1,000 population (1985–90): 19.0 (world avg. 9.9).
Natural increase rate per 1,000 population (1985–90): 31.5 (world avg. 17.2).
Total fertility rate (avg. births per childbearing woman; 1985–90): 7.0.
Marriage rate per 1,000 population (1980–85): 12.8.
Divorce rate per 1,000 population (1980–85): 0.8.
Life expectancy at birth (1985–90): male 44.9 years; female 48.1 years.
Major causes of death per 100,000 population (1977): malaria 227.7; diseases
of the respiratory system 206.5; diseases of the digestive system 200.7.

National economy

Budget (1989). Revenue: CFAF 75,266,000,000 (tax revenue 49.4%, of which
import duties 30.5%, income taxes 8.9%; aid, gifts, and subsidies 19.5%;
external loans 16.6%; nontax revenue 14.5%). Expenditures: CFAF 103,-
646,000,000 (debt service 15.5%; education 15.5%; defense 8.8%; general
administration 6.1%; social security and welfare 4.8%; health 2.4%; unspecified expenditures 38.1%).
Production (metric tons except as noted). Agriculture, forestry, fishing
(1987–88): yams 834,900, cassava 570,000, corn (maize) 267,300, millet
and sorghum 114,800, seeed cotton 70,200, peanuts (groundnuts) 51,000,
dry beans 40,000, tomatoes 39,000, sweet potatoes 31,000, coconuts 20,-
000, bananas 13,000, oranges 12,000, mangoes 12,000, palm kernels 9,000,
paddy rice 8,200, coffee beans 4,000, pineapples 3,000, cacao beans 1,000[2],
tobacco 300; livestock (number of live animals; 1987) 1,200,000 sheep,
1,120,000 goats, 950,000 cattle, 620,000 pigs, 23,000,000 chickens; roundwood 4,691,000 cu m; fish catch 41,903. Mining and quarrying (1986):
marine salt 100. Manufacturing (1986): cement 321,000; meat 58,000; sugar
52,000; cotton fibre 37,456[3]; palm oil and palm kernel oil 7,850[3]. Construction: n.a. Energy production (consumption): electricity (kW-hr; 1988)
200,200,000 ([1987] 137,700,000); coal, none (none); crude petroleum (barrels; 1987) 2,565,000 (negligible); petroleum products (metric tons; 1987)
none (118,000); natural gas, none (none).
Land use (1986): forested 33.2%; meadows and pastures 4.0%; agricultural
and under permanent cultivation 16.6%; other 46.2%.
Tourism (1987): receipts from visitors U.S.\$8,000,000; expenditures by na-
tionals abroad U.S.\$3,000,000.
Population economically active (1986): total 1,447,000; activity rate of total
population 34.5% (participation rates: ages 15–64, 60.2%; female 35.6%;
unemployed, n.a.).

Price and earnings indexes (1985 = 100)

	1982	1983	1984	1985	1986	1987
Consumer price index	...	...	...	...	...	...
Hourly earnings index[4]	63.7	100.0	100.0	100.0	100.0	100.0

Gross national product (at current market prices; 1987): U.S.\$1,315,000,000
(U.S.\$300 per capita).

Structure of gross domestic product and labour force

	1985 in value CFAF '000,000	1985 % of total value	1986 labour force	1986 % of labour force
Agriculture	179,571	35.9	980,000	67.7
Mining and manufacturing	46,699	9.3		
Public utilities	3,556	0.7	108,000	7.5
Construction	23,423	4.7		
Trade	96,500	19.3		
Transportation and communications	46,014	9.2		
Finance and services	38,293	7.7	359,000	24.8
Pub. admin., defense	38,841	7.8		
Other	26,951	5.4		
TOTAL	499,848	100.0	1,447,000	100.0

Public debt (external, outstanding; 1987): U.S.\$929,000,000.
Household income and expenditure. Average household size (1979) 5.4; income per household (1983): U.S.\$240; sources of income: n.a.; expenditure:
n.a.

Foreign trade[5]

Balance of trade (current prices)

	1983	1984	1985	1986	1987	1988
CFAF '000,000	−86,681	−81,830	−100.47	−98.23	−61.23	−80.84
% of total	63.1%	46.2%	42.9%	55.5%	13.3%	14.5%

Imports (1984): CFAF 125,903,000,000 (manufactured goods 29.9%, of which
cotton yarn and fabric 8.2%, chemical products 7.4%; food products 17.2%,
of which cereals 6.9%; beverages and tobacco 14.8%; machinery and transport equipment 14.1%, of which electrical equipment 5.8%, nonelectrical
equipment 4.6%, transport equipment 3.7%). *Major import sources* (1987):
France 19.1%; Thailand 13.0%; Korea 6.3%; Japan 5.7%; The Netherlands
5.4%; India 4.5%; Italy 4.0%; Germany 3.7%; Côte d'Ivoire 3.0%; Hong
Kong 2.7%.
Exports (1984): CFAF 72,822,000,000 (energy 44.7%; cotton 19.9%; food
products 17.8%, of which cocoa beans 13.2%, coffee 3.3%; palm kernel oil
and palm oil 7.1%; manufactured goods 3.1%). *Major export destinations*
(1987): Portugal 21.8%; United States 12.6%; Germany 10.5%; Italy 10.2%;
France 8.7%; Romania 4.8%; United Kingdom 3.9%.

Transport and communications

Transport. Railroads (1985): length 360 mi, 580 km; passenger-mi 85,500,-
000[6], passenger-km 137,600,000[6]; short ton-mi cargo 121,100,000[6], metric
ton-km cargo 176,800,000[6]. Roads (1986): total length 4,626 mi, 7,445
km (paved 11%). Vehicles (1985): passenger cars 2,740; trucks and buses
567. Merchant marine (1988): vessels (100 gross tons and over) 13; total
deadweight tonnage 4,760. Air transport[7] (1988): passenger-mi 129,597,000,
passenger-km 208,567,000; short ton-mi cargo 24,126,000, metric ton-km
cargo 35,223,000; airports (1989) with scheduled flights 1.
Communications. Daily newspapers (1988): total number 1; total circulation
10,000; circulation per 1,000 population 2.3. Radio (1988): total number
of receivers 326,900 (1 per 14 persons). Television (1988): total number
of receivers 16,350 (1 per 272 persons). Telephones (1986): 15,492 (1
per 274 persons).

Education and health

Education (1987–88)

	schools	teachers	students	student/teacher ratio
Primary	2,850	15,319	471,016	30.8
Secondary	151	2,711	90,184	33.3
Voc., teacher tr.	13	687	6,879	10.0
Higher	13	1,110	10,112	9.1

Educational attainment (1979). Percent of population age 25 and over having: no formal schooling 89.2%; primary education 8.3%; some secondary
1.4%; secondary 0.8%; postsecondary 0.3%. *Literacy* (1980): total population
age 15 and over literate 530,000 (27.9%); males literate 368,000 (39.8%);
females literate 162,000 (16.6%).
Health: physicians (1983) 238 (1 per 16,025 persons); hospital beds (1982)
4,902 (1 per 749 persons); infant mortality rate per 1,000 live births
(1985–90) 110.0.
Food (1987): daily per capita caloric intake 2,415 ([1984–86] vegetable
products 95%, animal products 5%); (1984) 94% of FAO recommended
minimum requirement.

Military

Total active duty personnel (1988): 4,350 (army 87.4%, navy 4.6%, air force
8.0%). *Military expenditure as percent of GNP* (1986): 2.1% (world 5.5%);
per capita expenditure U.S.\$8.

---

[1]Porto-Novo is the official capital established under the constitution, but Cotonou,
where the president and most government ministers reside, is de facto capital. [2]1986–
87. [3]Export figures. [4]January. [5]Figures do not include unaccountable reexports of
black market goods, which originate mainly in Nigeria and amounted to an estimated
90% of Benin's actual exports in 1981. [6]1984–85. [7]Air Afrique only.

Bermuda

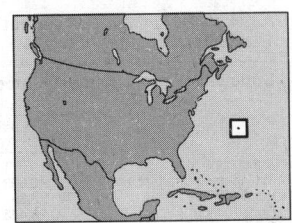

Official name: Bermuda.
Political status: colony (United Kingdom) with two legislative houses (Senate [11]; House of Assembly [40]).
Chief of state: British Monarch, represented by Governor.
Head of government: Premier.
Capital: Hamilton.
Official language: English.
Official religion: none.
Monetary unit: 1 Bermuda dollar (Bd$) = 100 cents; valuation (Oct. 2, 1989) 1 U.S.$ = Bd$1.00[1]; 1 £ = Bd$1.62.

Area and population	area		population
	sq mi	sq km	1980 census
Municipalities			
Hamilton	0.3	0.8	1,617
St. George	0.5	1.3	1,647
Parishes			
Devonshire	1.9	4.9	6,843
Hamilton	2.0	5.2	3,784
Paget	2.0	5.2	4,497
Pembroke[2]	1.8	4.7	10,443
St. George's[3]	1.7	4.4	2,940
Sandys	1.9	4.9	6,255
Smith's	1.9	4.9	4,463
Southampton	2.2	5.7	4,613
Warwick	2.2	5.7	6,948
TOTAL	21.0[4,5]	54.0[4,5]	54,050[6]

Demography

Population (1989): 58,800.
Density (1989): persons per sq mi 2,800, persons per sq km 1,089.
Urban-rural (1987): urban 100.0%; rural, none.
Sex distribution (1987): male 48.72%; female 51.28%.
Age breakdown (1985): under 15, 21.3%; 15-29, 24.6%; 30-44, 25.0%; 45-59, 16.1%; 60-74, 9.7%; 75 and over, 3.3%.
Population projection: (2000) 65,000; (2010) 70,000.
Doubling time: 75 years.
Ethnic composition (1980): black 61.3%; white 37.3%; other 1.4%.
Religious affiliation (1980): Protestant 72.5%, of which Anglican 37.3%, Methodist 16.3%; Roman Catholic 13.8%; nonreligious 7.8%; other 5.9%.
Major cities (1985): St. George 1,707; Hamilton 1,676.

Vital statistics

Birth rate per 1,000 population (1988): 16.0 (world avg. 27.1); legitimate 67.9%; illegitimate 32.1%.
Death rate per 1,000 population (1988): 6.8 (world avg. 9.9).
Natural increase rate per 1,000 population (1988): 9.2 (world avg. 17.2).
Total fertility rate (avg. births per childbearing woman; 1987): 1.7.
Marriage rate per 1,000 population (1988): 14.9.
Divorce rate per 1,000 population (1986): 2.9.
Life expectancy at birth (1987): male 69.0 years; female 77.0 years.
Major causes of death per 100,000 population (1986): diseases of the circulatory system 354.0; malignant neoplasms (cancers) 192.0; accidents and violence 42.0; diseases of the respiratory system 35.0.

National economy

Budget (1988-89). Revenue: Bd$300,900,000 (customs duty 40.1%, hospital levy 10.5%, employment tax 8.4%, land tax 4.2%, hotel occupancy tax 3.7%). Expenditures: Bd$302,600,000 (economic services 17.4%, education 14.7%, health 12.9%, public order 12.3%, general administration 11.7%).
Tourism: receipts from visitors (1988) U.S.$436,600,000; expenditures by nationals abroad (1986) U.S.$81,000,000[7].
Production (value in Bd$ except as noted). Agriculture, forestry, fishing (1987): fish 4,727,000, vegetables 3,900,000, milk 1,209,000, spiny lobsters 795,000, fruits 500,000, eggs 399,000, meat 100,000; livestock (number of live animals) 2,000 pigs, 1,000 cattle; roundwood, n.a. Quarrying (1986-87): crushed stone 13,300 metric tons. Manufacturing: major industries include pharmaceuticals, electronics wares, fish processing, handicrafts, woodworking, small boat building, and textiles. Construction (value in Bd$; 1988)[8]: residential 22,300,000; nonresidential 62,500,000. Energy production (consumption): electricity (kW·hr; 1987) 435,000,000 (435,000,000); coal, none (none); crude petroleum, none (none); petroleum products (metric tons; 1987) none (185,000); natural gas, none (none).
Land use (1987): forested 20.0%; meadows and pastures 1.0%; agricultural and under permanent cultivation 3.9%; built-on, wasteland, and other 75.1%.
Population economically active (1987): total 35,244; activity rate of total population 60.4% (participation rates: ages 16-64 [1980] 82.1%; female 47.3%; registered unemployed [1987] 0.2%).

Price and earnings indexes (1985 = 100)							
	1982	1983	1984	1985	1986	1987	1988
Consumer price index	86.6	91.8	96.6	100.0	104.1	108.7	114.1
Weekly earnings index	77.0	86.2	92.9	100.0	106.2	114.6	...

Gross national product (at current market prices; 1986-87): U.S.$1,328,100,000 (U.S.$23,100 per capita).

Structure of gross domestic product and labour force

	1978-79		1988	
	in value Bd$'000	% of total value	labour force	% of labour force
Agriculture, fishing	2,900	0.7	522	1.4
Quarrying	1,300	0.3		
Manufacturing	19,500	4.4	1,033	2.8
Construction	21,400	4.9	2,895	8.0
Public utilities	7,400	1.7	492	1.4
Transportation and communications	30,500	6.9	2,465	6.8
Trade, restaurants	143,900	32.8	12,545	34.4
Finance, real estate	96,600	22.0	4,826	13.3
Pub. admin., defense	35,800	8.2	9,668	26.5
Services	79,200	18.1		
Other	...	...	1,974[9]	5.4
TOTAL	438,500	100.0	36,420	100.0

Public debt (external, outstanding; 1986-87): none.
Household income and expenditure. Average household size (1982) 2.7; income per household Bd$34,944 (U.S.$34,944); sources of income (1982): wages and salaries 72.2%, imputed income from owner occupancy 9.7%, investments including rents 8.0%, self-employment 6.7%; expenditure (1982): housing 20.8%, food and nonalcoholic beverages 17.3%, household furnishings 11.9%, transportation 10.6%, gifts, contributions, and life insurance 8.2%, foreign travel 6.4%, recreation 5.4%, clothing and footwear 5.3%.

Foreign trade

Balance of trade (current prices)						
	1981	1982	1983	1984	1985	1986
Bd$'000,000	−293.4	−334.1	−355.0	−373.5	−379.4	−382.3
% of total	83.3%	90.8%	88.6%	80.4%	89.2%	74.7%

Imports (1985): Bd$402,491,000 (food 16.0%, of which meat and meat preparations 4.9%; petroleum and petroleum products 14.1%; electrical machinery, including apparatus and appliances 8.4%; clothing 7.4%; transport equipment 6.0%; nonelectrical machinery 4.7%; pharmaceutical products 4.4%). *Major import sources* (1986): United States 52.9%; Japan 9.5%; Netherlands Antilles 9.5%; United Kingdom 8.6%; France 5.1%.
Exports (1985): Bd$23,054,000 (reexports 98.4%, of which drugs and medicine 57.1%, personal effects 8.0%, electrical supplies 5.2%, books and papers 4.6%, electronic supplies 4.0%; Bermuda-originated exports 1.6%). *Major export destinations* (1986): Canada 31.9%; Sweden 29.6%; Colombia 10.8%; United States 8.3%; Brazil 6.0%.

Transport and communications

Transport. Railroads: none. Roads (1986): total length 150 mi, 240 km (paved 100%). Vehicles (1987): passenger cars 17,644; trucks and buses 3,507. Merchant marine (1988): vessels (100 gross tons and over) 116; total deadweight tonnage 6,874,182. Air transport (passengers; 1987): arrivals 518,030, departures 521,948; metric tons cargo unloaded 7,701, metric tons cargo loaded 550; airports (1989) with scheduled flights 1.
Communications. Daily newspapers (1988): total number 1; total circulation 16,000; circulation per 1,000 population 274. Radio (1986): total number of receivers 100,000 (1 per 0.6 person). Television (1988): total number of receivers 67,000 (1 per 0.9 person). Telephones (1987): 83,782 (1 per 0.7 persons).

Education and health

Education (1987-88)	schools	teachers	students	student/ teacher ratio
Primary (age 5-11)	18	252	5,334	21.2
Secondary (age 11-16)[10]	18	293	3,949	13.5
Vocational Higher	1	68[11]	561	...

Educational attainment (1980). Percent of total population age 25 and over having: no formal schooling, primary education, or incomplete secondary 57.4%; completed secondary 19.5%; completed higher 18.5%; other 4.6%.
Literacy (1980): total population age 15 and over literate 39,577 (96.9%); males literate 19,026 (96.7%); females literate 20,551 (97.0%).
Health (1987): physicians 77 (1 per 751 persons); hospital beds 399 (1 per 145 persons); infant mortality rate per 1,000 live births (1986-88 avg.) 7.0.
Food (1984-86): daily per capita caloric intake 2,545 (vegetable products 61%, animal products 39%); (1983) 107% of FAO recommended minimum requirement.

Military

Total active duty personnel: British (1987) 734; U.S. (1987) 1,620.

[1]The Bermuda dollar is at par with the U.S. dollar. [2]Excludes the area and population of the city of Hamilton. [3]Excludes the area and population of the town of St. George. [4]Grand total includes 2.3 sq mi (5.4 sq km) leased to the United States for military bases. [5]Detail does not add to total given (less area for the military bases) because of rounding. [6]Excludes 10,918 short-term visitors, 2,173 on-base military personnel, 620 institutionalized persons, and Bermudians residing abroad. [7]Excludes accommodations. [8]Excludes developments valued below Bd$500,000. [9]Includes 1,972 employees of international companies. [10]Includes 4 special schools for primary and secondary students. [11]1985-86.

Bhutan

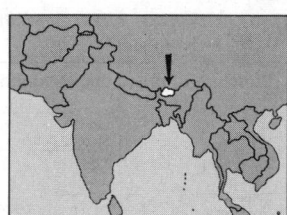

Official name: Druk-Yul (Kingdom of Bhutan).
Form of government: constitutional[1] monarchy with one legislative house (National Assembly [151][2]).
Head of state and government: Monarch (*druk gyalpo*).
Capital: Thimphu.
Official language: Dzongkha (a Tibetan dialect).
Official religion: Mahāyāna Buddhism.
Monetary unit: 1 Ngultrum[3] (Nu) = 100 chetrum; valuation (Oct. 2, 1989) 1 U.S.$ = Nu 17.00; 1 £ = Nu 27.50.

Area and population

Districts	Capitals	area[4] sq mi	area[4] sq km	population[5] 1985 estimate
Bumthang	Jakar	1,150	2,990	23,900
Chirang	Damphu	310	800	108,800
Chhukha	Chhukha	...	...	...
Dagana	Dagana	540	1,400	28,400
Geylegphug	Geylegphug	1,020	2,640	111,300
Ha	Ha	830	2,140	16,700
Lhuntshi	Lhuntshi	1,120	2,910	39,600
Mongar	Mongar	710	1,830	73,200
Paro	Paro	580	1,500	45,600
Pema Gatsel	Pema Gatsel	150	380	37,100
Punakha	Punakha	2,330	6,040	33,600
Samchi	Samchi	830	2,140	172,100
Samdrup Jongkhar	Samdrup Jongkhar	900	2,340	73,100
Shemgang	Shemgang	980	2,540	44,500
Tashigang	Tashigang	1,640	4,260	177,700
Thimphu	Thimphu	630	1,620	58,700
Tongsa	Tongsa	570	1,470	26,000
Wangdi Phodrang	Wangdi Phodrang	1,160	3,000	47,200
TOTAL		18,150[6]	47,000[6]	1,285,300[7]

Demography

Population (1989): 1,408,000.
Density (1989): persons per sq mi 77.6, persons per sq km 30.0.
Urban–rural (1985): urban 13.1%; rural 86.9%.
Sex distribution (1985): male 50.98%; female 49.02%.
Age breakdown (1987): under 15, 40.0%; 15–29, 26.6%; 30–44, 16.5%; 45–59, 10.6%; 60–74, 5.2%; 75 and over, 1.1%.
Population projection: (2000) 1,812,000; (2010) 2,266,000.
Doubling time: 32 years.
Ethnic composition (1983): Bhutia 62.5%; Gurung 15.5%; Assamese 13.2%; other 8.8%.
Religious affiliation (1980): Buddhist 69.6%; Hindu 24.6%; Muslim 5.0%; other 0.8%.
Major cities (1985): Thimphu 20,000; Phuntsholing 10,000[8].

Vital statistics

Birth rate per 1,000 population (1988): 38.3 (world avg. 27.1); legitimate, n.a.; illegitimate, n.a.
Death rate per 1,000 population (1988): 16.7 (world avg. 9.9).
Natural increase rate per 1,000 population (1988): 21.6 (world avg. 17.2).
Total fertility rate (avg. births per childbearing woman; 1988): 5.5.
Marital status of population 15 years and over (1985): married 71.2%; single 19.7%; widowed 7.5%; divorced 1.6%.
Divorce rate per 1,000 population: n.a.
Life expectancy at birth (1988): male 48.8 years; female 47.3 years.
Major causes of death per 100,000 population (1987): n.a.; however, major health problems include diarrhea and dysentery, respiratory tract infections, parasitic worms, skin infections, malaria, and nutritional deficiencies.

National economy

Budget (1987–88). Revenue: Nu 1,698,113,000 (grants from government of India 49.3%, internal revenue 24.2%, grants from UN and other international agencies 20.0%, internal borrowing 5.9%). Expenditures: Nu 2,019,567,000 (industries and mines 16.5%, public works 13.9%, power 13.5%, education 9.1%, agriculture 6.1%, finance 5.4%, post and telecommunications 4.0%, health 3.9%.
Tourism (1987): receipts from visitors U.S.$2,400,000; expenditures by nationals abroad, n.a.
Production (metric tons except as noted). Agriculture, forestry, fishing (1987): corn (maize) 85,000, rice 85,000, oranges 53,000, potatoes 50,000, wheat 19,000, sugarcane 12,000, green peppers and chilies 8,000, millet 7,000, barley 4,000, pulses 4,000, apples 4,000; livestock (number of live animals) 357,000 cattle, 70,300 pigs, 40,900 goats, 36,400 sheep, 218,000 puultry; roundwood 3,224,000 cu m; fish catch 1,000. Mining and quarrying (1986): dolomite 217,400; limestone 172,000; gypsum 24,800; slate 57,100 sq m. Manufacturing (value in Nu; 1980–81): distillery products 47,000,000; cement 36,000,000; chemical products 19,000,000; processed food 14,000,000; forest products 3,000,000. Construction (number of buildings completed; 1977–78): residential 10; nonresidential (guest house) 1. Energy production (consumption): electricity (kW-hr; 1986) 21,000,000 (31,000,000); coal (metric tons; 1986), none (1,000); crude petroleum, none (n.a.); petroleum products (metric tons; 1986) none (10,000); natural gas, none (n.a.).
Household income and expenditure. Average household size (1980): 5.4; income per household: n.a.; sources of income: n.a.; expenditure (1979):

food 72.3%, clothing 21.2%, energy 3.7%, household durable goods 0.7%, personal effects and other 2.1%.
Gross national product (at current market prices; 1987): U.S.$201,000,000 (U.S.$150 per capita).

Structure of gross domestic product and labour force

	1986 in value Nu '000,000	1986 % of total value	1984 labour force	1984 % of labour force
Agriculture	1,373.8	51.3	580,000[9]	87.2
Mining	14.8	0.5	}	
Manufacturing	96.0	3.6	}	
Construction	234.4	8.7	}	
Trade	290.1	10.8	} 6,000[9]	0.9
Public utilities	96.0	3.6	}	
Transportation and communications	68.8	2.6	}	
Finance	192.6	7.2	}	
Pub. admin., defense	355.1	13.3	23,000[9]	3.4
Other	−43.3[10]	−1.6[10]	56,000[9]	8.5[11]
TOTAL	2,678.3	100.0	664,000	100.0

Public debt (external, outstanding; 1987): U.S.$40,700,000.
Population economically active (1984): total 664,000; activity rate of total population 52.7% (participation rates: ages 15–64, 94.8; female 55.0; unemployed 6.5).

Price and earnings indexes (1985 = 100)

	1982	1983	1984	1985	1986	1987	1988
Consumer price index	81.0	93.6	99.3	100.0	110.0	115.3	127.5
Earnings index	...	...	...	...	...	...	...

Land use (1986): forested 70.1%; meadows and pastures 4.6%; agricultural and under permanent cultivation 2.2%; other 23.1%.

Foreign trade

Balance of trade (current prices)

	1982–83	1983–84	1984–85	1985–86	1986–87	1987–88
Nu '000,000	−487.1	−662.6	−644.8	−654.9	−802.5	−641
% of total	60.4%	67.3%	64.1%	54.6%	55.4%	28.9%

Imports (1986)[12]: Nu 814,022,300 (petroleum products 12.6%, cereals 9.1%, iron and steel 8.2%, electrical machinery 6.1%, road vehicles 5.9%, textiles 4.7%, sugar and sugar preparations 4.3%, electricity 4.3%, rubber products 3.7%). *Major import source* (1987–88): India 72.0%.
Exports (1986)[12]: Nu 380,006,100 (wood and wood manufactures 22.2%, nonmetallic mineral manufactures 21.3%, fruit and vegetables 18.2%, electricity 11.0%, coffee, tea, and spices 10.7%, crude fertilizers 4.4%). *Major export destination* (1987–88): India 98.9%.

Transport and communications

Transport. Railroads: none. Roads (1988): total length 1,412 mi, 2,273 km (paved about 76%). Vehicles (1986): passenger cars 1,587; trucks and buses 916. Merchant marine: none. Air transport (1986): passenger-mi 2,722,000, passenger-km 4,381,000; metric ton-km cargo, n.a.; airports (1989) with scheduled flights 1.
Communications. Daily newspapers: none[13]. Radio (1988): total number of receivers 21,555 (1 per 64 persons). Television (1983): total number of receivers 200 (1 per 6,180 persons). Telephones (1986): 1,945 (1 per 675 persons).

Education and health

Education (1987)

	schools	teachers	students	student/ teacher ratio
Primary (age 7–11)	148	1,398	39,628	28.3
Secondary (age 12–16)	30	640	15,299	23.9
Voc., teacher tr.	8 }	145	604	4.2
Higher	2 }			

Educational attainment, n.a. *Literacy* (1977): total population age 15 and over literate 124,000 (18.0%); males literate 98,000 (31.0%); females literate 26,000 (9.0%).
Health (1987): physicians 138 (1 per 9,736 persons); hospital beds 922 (1 per 1,457 persons); infant mortality rate per 1,000 live births (1988) 127.0.
Food (1975–77): daily per capita caloric intake 2,058 (vegetable products 98%, animal products 2%); 89% of FAO recommended minimum requirement.

Military

Total active duty personnel (1988): about 5,000 (army 100%).

---

[1]There is no formal constitution, but a form of constitutional monarchy is in place. [2]Includes 46 nonelective seats. [3]Indian currency is also accepted legal tender; the Ngultrum is at par with the Indian rupee. [4]2,700 sq mi (7,000 sq km) are not included in the district area totals. [5]Rural only. [6]Includes Chhukha area. [7]Includes urban population; includes Chhukha population. [8]1982. [9]Derived value. [10]Imputed bank service charges. [11]Includes 6.5% with no occupation. [12]Trade data with India only. [13]A weekly newspaper is published from Thimphu in Dzongkha, Nepalese, and English, circulation (1989) 10,500.

Bolivia

Official name: República de Bolivia (Republic of Bolivia).
Form of government: unitary, multiparty republic with two legislative houses (Chamber of Senators [27]; Chamber of Deputies [130]).
Head of state and government: President.
Capital: La Paz (administrative); Sucre (judicial).
Official languages: Spanish, Aymara, Quechua.
Official religion: Roman Catholicism.
Monetary unit: 1 boliviano[1] (Bs) = 100 centavos; valuation (Oct. 2, 1989) 1 U.S.$ = Bs 2.85; 1 £ = Bs 4.61.

Area and population		area		population
				1989
Departments	Capitals	sq mi	sq km	estimate
Beni	Trinidad	82,458	213,564	273,000
Chuquisaca	Sucre	19,893	51,524	489,000
Cochabamba	Cochabamba	21,479	55,631	1,079,000
La Paz	La Paz	51,732	133,985	2,367,000
Oruro	Oruro	20,690	53,588	453,000
Pando	Cobija	24,644	63,827	58,000
Potosí	Potosí	45,644	118,218	949,000
Santa Cruz	Santa Cruz	143,098	370,621	1,216,000
Tarija	Tarija	14,526	37,623	309,000
TOTAL		424,164	1,098,581	7,193,000

Demography

Population (1989): 7,193,000.
Density (1989): persons per sq mi 17.0, persons per sq km 6.5.
Urban–rural (1987): urban 49.0%; rural 51.0%.
Sex distribution (1985): male 49.25%; female 50.75%.
Age breakdown (1985): under 15, 43.4%; 15–29, 26.4%; 30–44, 15.7%; 45–59, 9.3%; 60–74, 4.4%; 75 and over, 0.8%.
Population projection: (2000) 9,837,000; (2010) 12,922,000.
Doubling time: 24 years.
Ethnic composition (1982): mestizo 31.2%; Quechua 25.4%; Aymara 16.9%; white 14.5%; other 12.0%.
Religious affiliation (1980): Roman Catholic 92.5%; Baha'i 2.6%; other 4.9%.
Major cities (1986): La Paz 1,033,288; Santa Cruz 457,619; Cochabamba 329,941; Oruro 184,101; Sucre 88,774.

Vital statistics

Birth rate per 1,000 population (1985–90): 43.5 (world avg. 27.1).
Death rate per 1,000 population (1985–90): 14.2 (world avg. 9.9).
Natural increase rate per 1,000 population (1985–90): 29.3 (world avg. 17.2).
Total fertility rate (avg. births per childbearing woman; 1985–90): 6.2.
Marriage rate per 1,000 population (1980): 4.8.
Divorce rate per 1,000 population: n.a.
Life expectancy at birth (1985–90): male 50.9 years; female 55.4 years.
Major causes of death per 100,000 population: n.a.; however, major health problems include diseases of the respiratory system, gastrointestinal infections, measles, diphtheria, malaria, and tetanus.

National economy

Budget (1987). Revenue: $b 1,026,878,000,000,000 (royalties on petroleum 36.1%, internal taxes 22.8%, customs duties 14.2%, royalties on natural gas 13.2%). Expenditures: $b 1,039,402,000,000,000 (public services 43.7%, transfers and contributions 14.0%, public debt service 12.0%, materials and equipment 11.8%, economic and social welfare 11.3%).
Public debt (external, outstanding; 1987): U.S.$4,599,000,000.
Production (metric tons except as noted). Agriculture, forestry, fishing (1987): sugarcane 2,730,000, potatoes 598,000, corn (maize) 543,000, bananas and plantains 450,000, cassava 425,000, rice 130,000, soybeans 112,000, wheat 80,000, barley 67,000, sorghum 62,000; livestock (number of live animals) 9,500,000 sheep, 5,380,000 cattle, 2,300,000 goats, 1,690,000 pigs, 600,000 asses, 311,000 horses; roundwood 1,379,000 cu m; fish catch 4,800. Mining and quarrying (metric tons of pure metal; 1987): zinc 36,300; lead 8,200; antimony 8,165; tin 7,000; tungsten 500; silver 118,193 kilograms; gold 1,213 kilograms. Manufacturing[2] (value added in $b '000,000; 1984): food products 997,100; nonferrous metals 472,100; beverages 268,300; textiles 131,900; chemicals 120,000; petroleum refining 105,700; footwear 67,900; printing and publishing 45,900. Construction[3] (1985): residential dwellings 226. Energy production (consumption): electricity (kW-hr; 1987) 1,520,000,000 (1,522,000,000); coal (metric tons; 1987) none (none); crude petroleum (barrels; 1987) 6,589,000 (7,400,000); petroleum products (metric tons; 1987) 1,030,000 (1,021,000); natural gas (cu m; 1987) 2,443,800,000 (323,200,000).
Population economically active (1987): total 2,101,052; activity rate of total population 31.2% (participation rates: ages 15–64, 54.5%; female 23.6%; unemployed 21.5%).

Price and earnings indexes (1985 = 100)							
	1982	1983	1984	1985	1986	1987	1988
Consumer price index	0.4	1.8	13.0	100.0	376.0	431.0	500.0
Monthly earnings index[4]	265.6	1,102.7	9,060.7	...	...	...	...

Gross national product (at current market prices; 1987): U.S.$4,150,000,000 (U.S.$570 per capita).

Structure of gross domestic product and labour force				
	1987		1986	
	in value[5] $b '000,000	% of total value	labour force[6]	% of labour force
Agriculture	25,489	23.3	841,903	49.0
Mining	11,013	10.1	61,256	3.6
Manufacturing	11,837	10.8	150,146	8.7
Construction	3,080	2.8	43,889	2.5
Public utilities	981	0.9	8,252	0.5
Transportation and communications	8,008	7.3	95,456	5.6
Trade	13,805	12.6	132,241	7.7
Finance	15,179	13.9	15,077	0.9
Pub. admin., defense	15,056	13.7	} 369,682	21.5
Services	4,609	4.2		
Other	467[7]	0.4[7]		
TOTAL	109,524	100.0	1,717,902	100.0

Household income and expenditure. Average household size (1976): 4.3; average annual income per household: n.a.; sources of income: n.a.; expenditure (1979): food 41.7%, housing 12.6%, transportation and communications 12.6%, clothing and footwear 9.8%, household durable goods 8.9%, health 4.6%, recreation 3.1%, education 1.2%.
Tourism (1987): receipts from visitors U.S.$40,000,000; expenditures by nationals abroad U.S.$28,000,000.
Land use (1986): forested 51.5%; meadows and pastures 24.7%; agricultural and under permanent cultivation 3.1%; other 20.7%.

Foreign trade[8]

Balance of trade (current prices)						
	1983	1984	1985	1986	1987	1988
U.S.$'000,000	+282.0	+311.9	+160.5	−36.9	−85.4	+99.2
% of total	23.0%	27.4%	14.8%	3.2%	7.0%	9.0%

Imports (1987): U.S.$776,000,000 (capital goods 41.6%, of which capital goods for industry 23.2%, transport equipment 13.5%; raw materials 40.5%, of which raw materials for industry 31.6%; consumer goods 16.1%, of which durable consumer goods 9.4%, nondurable consumer goods 6.7%). Major import sources: Brazil 9.5%; United States 8.2%; Argentina 5.9%; Japan 3.9%; Chile 3.0%; West Germany 2.6%; Peru 0.7%.
Exports (1987): U.S.$569,793,000 (natural gas 26.1%; tin 12.0%; zinc 5.7%; silver 5.6%; antimony 4.0%; coffee 2.0%; sugar 1.5%; hides 1.4%). Major export destinations: Argentina 45.6%; United States 16.9%; United Kingdom 10.7%; West Germany 5.9%; Peru 4.2%; Brazil 3.4%; Belgium 3.1%; Chile 2.9%; Switzerland 1.2%.

Transport and communications

Transport. Railroads (1987): route length 2,264 mi, 3,643 km; passenger-mi 312,900,000, passenger-km 503,500,000; short ton-mi cargo 344,600,000, metric ton-km cargo 503,100,000. Roads (1984): total length 25,468 mi, 40,987 km (paved 4%). Vehicles (1987): passenger cars 78,160; trucks and buses 142,976. Merchant marine (1988): vessels (100 gross tons and over) 1; total deadweight tonnage 15,765. Air transport (1988): passenger-mi 628,000,000, passenger-km 1,011,000,000; short ton-mi cargo 16,229,000, metric ton-km cargo 23,694,000; airports (1989) with scheduled flights 19.
Communications. Daily newspapers (1984): total number 13; total circulation 311,000; circulation per 1,000 population 50. Radio (1988): total number of receivers 3,939,068 (1 per 1.8 persons). Television (1988): total number of receivers 447,467 (1 per 16 persons). Telephones (1986): 182,433 (1 per 37 persons).

Education and health

Education (1986–87)	schools	teachers	students	student/ teacher ratio
Primary (age 6–13)	9,758	51,376	888,182	17.3
Secondary (age 14–17)	724	8,258	211,519	25.6
Voc. teacher tr.	47	1,805	15,947	8.8
Higher	10	3,555	97,153	27.3

Educational attainment (1976). Percent of population age 25 and over having: no formal schooling 48.6%; primary education 28.5%; secondary 17.9%; higher 5.0%. Literacy (1987): total population age 15 and over literate 2,540,593 (65.8%); males literate 1,195,383 (65.9%); females literate 1,345,210 (65.8%).
Health (1985): physicians 4,032 (1 per 1,595 persons); hospital beds (1984) 13,247 (1 per 472 persons); infant mortality rate per 1,000 live births 110.0.
Food (1984–86): daily per capita caloric intake 2,128 (vegetable products 84%, animal products 16%); 89% of FAO recommended minimum requirement.

Military

Total active duty personnel (1988): 27,600 (army 72.5%, navy 13.0%, air force 14.5%). Military expenditure as percent of GNP (1987): 3.0% (world 5.4%); per capita expenditure U.S.$19.

---

[1]Effective Jan. 1, 1987, a new currency, the boliviano, was introduced at a rate of one boliviano = 1,000,000 old Bolivian pesos ($b). [2]Establishments with 20 or more employees. [3]National government sponsored only. [4]1980 = 100. [5]In 1980 prices. [6]Employed persons only. [7]Includes imputed bank service charges. [8]Import figures are f.o.b. in balance of trade and c.i.f. for commodities and trading partners.

Botswana

Official name: Botswana (Tswana);
Republic of Botswana (English).
Form of government: multiparty
republic with one legislative body
(National Assembly [40[1]]).
Head of state and government:
President.
Capital: Gaborone.
Official languages: Tswana; English.
Official religion: none.
Monetary unit: 1 pula (P) = 100 thebe;
valuation (Oct. 2, 1989)
1 U.S.$ = P 2.00; 1 £ = P 3.24.

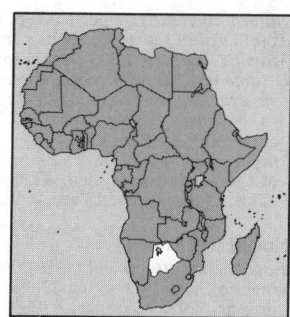

Area and population		area		population
Districts	**Capitals**	sq mi	sq km	1988 estimate
Barolong	...	425	1,100	19,100
Central	Serowe	57,039	147,730	379,500
Ghanzi	Ghanzi	45,525	117,910	23,900
Kgalagadi	Tsabong	41,290	106,940	30,400
Kgatleng	Mochudi	3,073	7,960	51,400
Kweneng	Molepolole	13,857	35,890	148,600
North East	Masunga	1,977	5,120	44,100
North West				
Chobe	Kasane	8,031	20,800	10,300
Ngamiland	Maun	42,135	109,130	79,100
Ngwaketse	Kanye	10,568	27,370	123,400
South East	Ramotswa	687	1,780	42,000
Towns[2]				
Francistown	—	31	79	49,400
Gaborone	—	37	97	111,000
Jwaneng	—	39	100	12,600
Lobatse	—	12	30	25,700
Orapa	—	4	10	8,300
Palapye	—	10	26	...
Selebi-Pikwe	—	19	50	46,500
Tlokweng	—	8	21	...
TOTAL		224,607	581,730	1,205,300

Demography

Population (1989): 1,250,000.
Density (1989): persons per sq mi 5.6, persons per sq km 2.1.
Urban–rural (1986): urban 21.7%; rural 78.3%.
Sex distribution (1986): male 47.60%; female 52.40%.
Age breakdown (1986): under 15, 48.2%; 15–29, 25.9%; 30–44, 13.2%; 45–59,
7.4%; 60–74, 4.0%; 75 and over, 1.3%.
Population projection: (2000) 1,821,000; (2010) 2,536,000.
Doubling time: 21 years.
Ethnic composition (1983): Tswana 75.5%; Shona 12.4%; San (Bushman)
3.4%; Khoikhoin (Hottentot) 2.5%; Ndebele 1.3%; other 4.9%.
Religious affiliation (1980): traditional beliefs 49.2%; Protestant 29.0%;
African Christian 11.8%; Roman Catholic 9.4%; other 0.6%.
Major cities (1988): Gaborone 111,000; Francistown 49,400; Selebi-Pikwe
46,500; Molepolole 29,200; Serowe 28,300.

Vital statistics

Birth rate per 1,000 population (1985–90): 47.3 (world avg. 27.1); legitimate,
n.a.; illegitimate, n.a.
Death rate per 1,000 population (1985–90): 11.7 (world avg. 9.9).
Natural increase rate per 1,000 population (1985–90): 35.6 (world avg. 17.2).
Total fertility rate (avg. births per childbearing woman; 1986): 6.7.
Life expectancy at birth (1985–90): male 55.5 years; female 61.5 years.
Major causes of death (as percent of total deaths; 1977): measles 16.3%;
heart disease 8.4%; influenza and pneumonia 7.6%; diarrheal diseases 7.5%;
malignant neoplasms (cancers) 6.0%.

National economy

Budget (1988–89). Revenue: P 1,825,030,000 (mineral royalties and dividends 59.7%, nontax revenue 15.6%, customs and excise taxes 13.1%, other
[nonmineral] income taxes 7.1%; foreign-aid grants 3.5%). Expenditures:
P 1,800,420,000 (recurrent expenditure 48.2%; development expenditure
51.3% [consolidated expenditure: economic services 36.2%, social services
25.7%, general services including defense 25.1%]).
Population economically active (1984–85): total 367,949; activity rate of total
population 37.0% (participation rates: ages 15–64, 72.7%; female 54.6%;
unemployed [1986] 19.2%).

Price and earnings indexes (1985 = 100)							
	1982	1983	1984	1985	1986	1987	1988
Consumer price index	77.1	85.2	92.5	100.0	110.0	120.8	131.0
Earnings index[3]	78.6	85.7	94.6	100.0	114.3	...	...

Production (metric tons except as noted). Agriculture, forestry, fishing
(1988): cereals 68,700[4] (of which sorghum 62,200, corn [maize] 4,500, millet
2,000), vegetables and melons 16,000, pulses 14,000, fruit 11,000, roots and
tubers 7,000, seed cotton 3,000, cotton seed 2,000, peanuts (groundnuts)
1,000; livestock (number of live animals) 2,350,000 cattle, 1,100,000 goats,
215,000 sheep, 149,000 mules and asses, 25,000 horses; roundwood (1987)
1,270,000 cu m; fish catch (1987) 1,350. Mining and quarrying (1988):
diamonds 15,229,359 carats; nickel–copper matte 46,967. Manufacturing
(1984): beer 155,000 hectolitres. Construction (1985): residential 70,200 sq
m; nonresidential 80,700 sq m. Energy production (consumption): elec-

tricity (kW-hr; 1986) 725,000,000 (621,000,000[5]); coal (metric tons; 1987)
599,000 (n.a.); crude petroleum, none (n.a.); petroleum products, n.a. (n.a.);
natural gas, none (n.a.).
Public debt (external, outstanding; 1988): U.S.$493,800,000.
Tourism: receipts from visitors (1987) U.S.$49,000,000; expenditures by na-
tionals abroad (1986) U.S.$21,000,000.
Gross national product (1987): U.S.$1,175,000,000 (U.S.$1,030 per capita).

Structure of gross domestic product and labour force				
	1987–88		1984–85	
	in value P '000,000	% of total value	labour force	% of labour force
Agriculture	95.6	2.9	159,134	43.2
Mining	1,435.0	43.9	8,999[6]	2.5
Manufacturing	163.3	5.0	8,954	2.4
Construction	109.3	3.3	9,280	2.5
Public utilities	82.4	2.5	1,988	0.5
Transp. and commun.	64.4	2.0	2,573	0.7
Trade	624.2	19.1	15,670	4.3
Finance	200.1	6.1	3,038	0.8
Pub. admin., defense	478.9	14.7 }	65,153	17.7
Services	82.0	2.5 }		
Other	−66.7	−2.0	93,160[7]	25.3[6]
TOTAL	3,268.5	100.0	367,949	100.0[2]

Household income and expenditure. Average household size (1981) 5.7; average annual income per household, n.a.; sources of income (1981): wages
and salaries 65.6%, transfers 19.6%, self-employment 14.8%; expenditure
(1985)[8]: food, beverages, and tobacco 40.1%, rent and services 13.6%,
clothing 10.8%, transportation 10.5%, health 1.3%.
Land use (1987): forested 1.7%; meadows and pastures 77.6%; agricultural
and under permanent cultivation 2.4%; other 18.3%.

Foreign trade[9]

Balance of trade (current prices)						
	1983	1984	1985	1986	1987	1988
P '000,000	+11.6	+93.6	+469.5	+483.3	+1,326.8	+984.1
% of total	0.8%	5.7%	20.0%	17.6%	33.2%	23.6%

Imports (1988): P 1,888,000,000 (food, beverages, and tobacco 16.6%; machinery and electrical goods 16.2%; vehicles and transport equipment
15.6%; chemical and rubber products 9.8%; metal and metal products 9.3%;
textiles and footwear 8.9%; mineral fuels 7.3%; wood and paper 4.5%).
Major import sources (1987): CUSA (Customs Union of Southern Africa,
which includes Botswana, Lesotho, South West Africa/Namibia, South
Africa, and Swaziland) 78.8%; European countries 9.4%, of which United
Kingdom 2.2%; United States 2.0%.
Exports (1988): P 2,703,000,000 (diamonds 72.6%; copper–nickel matte
15.6%; meat and meat products 3.6%; other 8.2%). *Major export destina-
tions* (1987): European countries 90.5%, of which United Kingdom 1.4%;
African countries 8.8%, of which CUSA 4.4%; United States 0.3%.

Transport and communications

Transport. Railroads (1986–87): length 440 mi, 708 km; passenger-mi 160,-
000,000, passenger-km 257,000,000; short ton-mi cargo 764,000, metric ton-
km cargo 1,116,000. Roads (1986): total length 8,389 mi, 13,500 km (paved
15%). Vehicles (1987): passenger cars 17,131; trucks and buses 26,515.
Merchant marine: none. Air transport (1988)[10]: passenger-mi 15,500,000,
passenger-km 25,000,000; short ton-mi cargo 83,000, metric ton-km cargo
121,000; airports (1989) with scheduled flights 8.
Communications. Daily newspapers (1989): total number 1; total circulation
30,000; circulation per 1,000 population 24. Radio (1988): total number of
receivers 149,031 (1 per 8.1 persons). Television (1988): none. Telephones
(1987): 40,197 (1 per 29 persons).

Education and health

Education (1986)	schools	teachers	students	student/ teacher ratio
Primary (age 7–13)	537	7,324	235,941	32.2
Secondary (age 14–19)	73	1,619	35,966	22.2
Voc., teacher tr.	22	317	3,217	10.1
Higher	1	249	1,700	6.8

Educational attainment (1981). Percent of population age 25 and over having: no formal schooling 54.7%; some primary education 31.0%; complete
primary 9.4%; some secondary 3.1%; complete secondary 1.3%; postsecondary 0.5%. *Literacy* (1985): total population over age 15 literate 385,000
(70.8%); males literate 179,000 (72.6%); females literate 206,000 (69.5%).
Health: physicians (1986) 156 (1 per 7,194 persons); hospital beds (1984)
2,367 (1 per 442 persons); infant mortality rate per 1,000 live births (1985–
90) 67.
Food (1984–86): daily per capita caloric intake 2,230 (vegetable products 85%,
animal products 15%); 93% of FAO recommended minimum requirement.

Military

Total active duty personnel (1989): 4,500 (army 100%; navy, none [land-
locked]; air force is part of army). *Military expenditure as percent of GNP*
(1987): 2.2% (world 5.4%); per capita expenditure U.S.$21.

[1]Including 6 nonelective seats. [2]Areas included with respective district area totals.
[3]Excludes government sector. [4]1987–88. [5]1985. [6]20,112 Batswana were employed in
South African mines in 1987. [7]Mostly unemployed. [8]Weights of consumer price index
components. [9]Import figures are f.o.b. in balance of trade and c.i.f. in commodities
and trading partners. [10]Air Botswana only.

Brazil

Official name: República Federativa do Brasil (Federative Republic of Brazil).
Form of government: multiparty federal republic with 2 legislative houses (Federal Senate [72]; Chamber of Deputies [487]).
Chief of state and government: President.
Capital: Brasília.
Official language: Portuguese.
Official religion: none.
Monetary unit: 1 new[1] cruzado (NCz$) = 100 centavos; valuation (Oct. 2, 1989) 1 U.S.$ = NCz$3.79; 1 £ = NCz$6.13.

Area and population

States	Capitals	area sq mi	area sq km	population 1989 estimate
Acre	Rio Branco	58,915	152,589	406,800
Alagoas	Maceió	10,707	27,731	2,381,500
Amapá	Macapá	54,161	140,276	248,100
Amazonas	Manaus	604,036	1,564,445	1,948,500
Bahia	Salvador	216,613	561,026	11,522,000
Ceará	Fortaleza	57,150	148,016	6,356,100
Espírito Santo	Vitória	17,605	45,597	2,476,800
Goiás[2]	Goiânia	137,215	355,386	3,882,100
Maranhão	São Luís	126,897	328,663	5,076,300
Mato Grosso	Cuiabá	340,156	881,001	1,678,100
Mato Grosso do Sul	Campo Grande	135,347	350,548	1,755,700
Minas Gerais	Belo Horizonte	226,708	587,172	15,590,300
Pará	Belém	481,871	1,248,042	4,862,800
Paraíba	João Pessoa	21,765	56,372	3,200,400
Paraná	Curitiba	77,048	199,554	8,935,200
Pernambuco[3]	Recife	37,957	98,307	7,238,300
Piauí	Teresina	96,886	250,934	2,616,900
Rio Grande do Norte	Natal	20,469	53,015	2,277,700
Rio Grande do Sul	Pôrto Alegre	108,952	282,184	9,026,700
Rio de Janeiro	Rio de Janeiro	17,092	44,268	13,845,200
Rondônia	Pôrto Velho	93,840	243,044	1,057,200
Roraima	Boa Vista	88,844	230,104	116,800
Santa Catarina	Florianópolis	37,060	95,985	4,386,700
São Paulo	São Paulo	95,714	247,898	32,361,700
Sergipe	Aracaju	8,492	21,994	1,392,900
Tocantins[2]	Miracema do Tocantins	110,698	286,706	960,000
Federal District				
Distrito Federal	Brasília	2,245	5,814	1,803,500
Disputed areas[4]		2,044	5,294	—
TOTAL		3,286,488[5,6]	8,511,965[6]	147,404,300

Demography

Population (1989): 147,404,000.
Density (1989): persons per sq mi 44.9, persons per sq km 17.3.
Urban–rural (1989): urban 74.4%; rural 25.6%.
Sex distribution (1989): male 49.90%; female 50.10%.
Age breakdown (1985): under 15, 36.4%; 15–29, 28.9%; 30–44, 17.8%; 45–59, 10.3%; 60–74, 5.2%; 75 and over, 1.4%.
Population projection: (2000) 179,487,000; (2010) 207,454,000.
Doubling time: 34 years.
Ethnic composition (1980): Brazilian white 53.0%, of which Portuguese 15.0%, Italian 11.0%, Spanish 10.0%, German 3.0%; mulatto 22.0%; mestizo 12.0%; black 11.0%; Japanese 0.8%; Amerindian 0.1%; other 1.1%.
Religious affiliation (1980): Roman Catholic 87.8%, of which Spiritist Catholic 15.7%[7], Evangelical Catholic 9.0%[8]; Protestant (mostly Assemblies of God, other Pentecostal, and Baptist) 6.1%; Afro-American Spiritist 2.0%[9]; Spiritist 1.7%[10]; nonreligious 1.0%; atheist 0.4%; Buddhist 0.3%; Jewish 0.2%; other 0.5%.
Major cities (*municipio;* 1985)[11]: São Paulo 10,063,110 (15,221,267); Rio de Janeiro 5,603,388 (10,190,384); Belo Horizonte 2,114,429 (3,056,498); Salvador 1,804,438 (2,093,856); Fortaleza 1,582,414 (1,934,581); Brasília 1,567,709; Nova Iguaçu[12] 1,319,491; Recife 1,287,623 (2,494,744); Curitiba 1,279,205 (1,767,720); Porto Alegre 1,272,121.

Other principal *municipios* (1985)

	population		population		population
Belém	1,116,578	Maceió	482,195	São Bernardo do Campo	562,845
Campinas	841,016	Manaus	809,914		
Duque de Caxias[12]	664,105	Natal	510,106	São Gonçalo	728,469
Goiânia	923,333	Niterói[12]	441,684	São João de Meriti[12]	457,753
Guarulhos[13]	713,582	Osasco[13]	591,568		
Jaboatão	409,528	Santo André[13]	635,129	São Luís	561,859
João Pessoa	396,197	Santos	460,100	Teresina	473,901

Place of birth/national origin (1980): 99.07% native-born; 0.93% foreign-born, of which Portugal 0.33%, Japan 0.12%, Italy 0.09%, Spain 0.08%.
Mobility (1980). Population living in same residence: less than 1 year 19.3%, 1–3 years 19.5%, 3–6 years 22.1%.
Families (1986). Average family size 4.1; 1–2 persons 24.3%, 3 persons 20.1%, 4 persons 20.5%, 5–6 persons 23.2%, 7 or more persons 11.9%.
Immigration (1982–84): permanent immigrants admitted 7,673, from Portugal 28.4%, Uruguay 8.7%, Argentina 8.2%.

Vital statistics

Birth rate per 1,000 population (1985–90): 28.6 (world avg. 27.1).
Death rate per 1,000 population (1985–90): 7.9 (world avg. 9.9).

Natural increase rate per 1,000 population (1985–90): 20.7 (world avg. 17.2).
Total fertility rate (avg. births per childbearing woman; 1985–90): 3.5.
Marriage rate per 1,000 population (1986): 7.3.
Divorce rate per 1,000 population (1986): 0.6.
Life expectancy at birth (1985–90): male 62.3 years; female 67.6 years.
Major causes of death per 100,000 population (1984[14]): diseases of the circulatory system 157.7, of which cerebrovascular disease 54.1, acute myocardial infarction 32.2; malignant neoplasms (cancers) 51.1; diseases of the respiratory system 47.9, of which pneumonia 26.3; infectious and parasitic diseases 45.8; accidents 34.0; homicides and other violence 27.9.

Social indicators

Educational attainment (1980). Percent of population age 25 and over having: no formal schooling 32.9%; some primary education 50.3%; complete primary 4.9%; secondary 6.9%; higher 5.0%.

Distribution of income (1986)[15]

	percent of national income by decile								
1	2	3	4	5	6	7	8	9	10 (highest)
1.0	2.2	2.6	3.6	4.1	5.6	7.4	10.1	15.9	47.5

Quality of working life. Average workweek (1986): 79.9% of the labour force works 40 or more hours per week. Annual estimated rate per 100,000 insured urban workers (1986) for: injury or accident 4,460; industrial illness, n.a.; death 20. Proportion of labour force participating in national social insurance system (1986): 49.6%. Proportion of employed population receiving minimum wage (1987): 52.0%.
Access to services (1986). Proportion of households having access to: electricity 83.2%, of which urban households having access 96.0%, rural households having access 43.4%; safe public (piped) water supply 69.9%, of which urban households having access 88.7%, rural households having access 11.6%; public sewage collection 58.5%, of which urban households having access 75.2%, rural households having access 6.5%; public fire protection, n.a.
Social participation. Eligible voters participating in last (November 1989) national election: n.a., voting mandatory. Trade union membership in total work force (1980): 10–15%. Practicing religious population in total affiliated population: most men, and in particular Portuguese-Brazilian men, attend Mass only on special occasions. They believe religion is the domain and duty of women.
Social deviance. The incidence of crime is not accurately reported. Crimes resulting in imprisonment (1985): 253,151, of which murder 4.1%; rape 1.0%, assault 14.0%; theft, burglary, and housebreaking 22.4%, robbery and extortion 8.7%; narcotics trafficking 4.2%; narcotics usage 5.9%. Suicides (1986): 4,754.
Leisure. Favourite leisure activities: n.a.
Material well-being (1980). Households possessing: automobile 22.4% (urban 28.3%, rural 9.5%); telephone 12.4% (urban 17.5%, rural 0.9%); television receiver 56.1% (urban 73.0%, rural 15.7%); refrigerator 63.1%[16] (urban 75.4%, rural 25.1%); air conditioner, n.a.; washing machine, n.a.

National economy

Gross national product (at current market prices; 1987): U.S.$314,642,000,-000 (U.S.$2,020 per capita).

Structure of gross domestic product and labour force

	1986 in value U.S.$'000,000[17]	% of total value	labour force[15, 18]	% of labour force
Agriculture	31,793	9.3	14,330,630	25.9
Mining	2,846	0.8	8,986,445	16.2
Manufacturing	90,355	26.5 }		
Construction	20,032	5.9	3,588,651	6.5
Public utilities	8,164	2.4	820,609	1.5
Transportation and communications	17,504	5.1	1,988,692	3.6
Trade	47,132	13.8	6,252,111	11.3
Pub. admin., defense	21,084	6.2	2,584,511	4.7
Finance, real estate	56,563	16.6 }	15,322,203	27.6
Services	45,125	13.2 }		
Other	—	—	1,562,121	2.8
TOTAL	340,598	100.0[5]	55,435,973	100.0[5]

Budget (1988). Revenue: NCz$4,667,963,808 (taxes 52.9%, principally property taxes and taxes on goods and services; other 47.1%). Expenditures: NCz$4,667,963,808 (unspecified items 72.1%; military 5.9%, of which air force 2.5%, navy 1.7%, army 1.6%; transportation 4.8%; education and culture 2.5%; office of the president [including planning] 1.8%; health 1.6%; mines and energy 1.6%).
Public debt (external, outstanding; 1987): U.S.$91,653,000,000.
Population economically active (1986)[15]: total 56,810,000; activity rate of total population 41.9% (participation rates: over age 15, 62.4%; female 33.8%; unemployed [1987] 9.7%[19]).

Price and earnings indexes (1985 = 100)

	1983	1984	1985	1986	1987	1988	1989 (7 mo.)
Consumer price index	10.3	30.6	100.0	245.2	808.5	6,325	55,754
Earnings index[20]	10.8	29.6	100.0	...	...	...	...

Production. Agriculture, forestry, fishing ('000 metric tons; 1988): sugarcane 258,560, corn (maize) 24,701, cassava 21,603, soybeans 18,049, oranges 13,321, rice 11,807, bananas 7,563, wheat 5,549, dry beans 2,884, coffee 2,642, seed cotton 2,506, tomatoes 2,407, potatoes 2,306, cocoa 343, peanuts (groundnuts) 170; livestock (number of live animals) 134,133,000 cattle, 33,000,000 pigs, 18,473,000 sheep, 5,500,000 horses, 2,000,000 mules;

roundwood (1987) 241,748,000 cu m; fish catch 793, of which crustaceans 99. Mining and quarrying (value of production in '000s of new cruzados; 1986): iron ore 12,591; granite 6,122; limestone 5,855; gold 5,275[21]; clay 3,974; bauxite 2,511; sand 2,489; tin 2,353; titanium 2,202; phosphate fertilizers 2,061; manganese 1,158. Manufacturing (value added, in '000s of new cruzados; 1984): chemicals 22,450; food products 15,228; iron and steel and other worked metals 12,569; electric and nonelectric machinery 9,892; transport equipment 8,158; textiles 6,675; electrical goods (including computers, televisions, and radios) 6,650; clothing and footwear 5,708; cement and other worked nonmetals 4,952; paper and paper products 4,234; plastic products 2,243; drugs and pharmaceuticals 1,930; lumber 1,874. Construction (new buildings completed; 1984) residential 14,304,000 sq m; nonresidential 3,698,000 sq m.

Manufacturing enterprises (1980)

	no. of enter-prises	number of labourers	wages of labourers as a % of avg. of all wages	value added in producer's prices (in new cruzados)
Chemicals	3,419	163,227	169.9	577,003
Metallurgy	14,407	531,729	116.5	452,469
Mechanical products	9,748	538,146	161.5	398,678
Food products	49,366	622,062	62.2	394,759
Transportation equipment	3,983	281,272	141.2	297,171
Textiles	6,062	377,600	80.6	251,520
Electric and communications equipment	3,337	243,494	121.3	249,754
Mineral products (not metals)	43,170	437,405	67.7	228,555
Clothing and footwear	15,338	459,869	59.5	190,255
Paper and paper products	1,704	107,433	109.1	118,980
Lumber	21,018	263,004	57.7	105,715
Publishing and printing	8,328	142,078	118.8	102,055
Plastics	2,651	118,852	90.2	95,711
Furniture	12,667	174,685	69.1	70,200
Pharmaceutical products	492	34,008	128.5	64,516

Land use (1987): forested 66.3%; meadows and pastures 19.7%; agricultural and under permanent cultivation 9.1%; other 4.9%.
Tourism (1987): receipts from visitors U.S.$1,502,000,000; expenditures by nationals abroad U.S.$1,249,000,000.

Retail trade enterprises (1980)

	no. of enterprises	total no. of employees	annual wage as a % of all wages	annual value of sales (in new cruzados)
General merchandise stores (including food products)	16,186	274,379	145.5	658,096
Gasoline stations	21,588	140,865	127.6	594,063
Food, beverages, and tobacco stores	538,638	963,106	16.5	586,249
Automobile dealers and auto parts stores	25,284	157,285	205.4	581,354
Stores selling clothing, fabrics, and textiles	117,595	452,641	102.3	434,793
Hardware stores	37,396	208,783	134.5	407,266
Stores selling radios, televisions, and related electronic goods	26,114	168,431	180.1	353,169
Drugstores	33,631	142,030	118.0	217,781
Agricultural machinery and heavy equipment dealers	6,565	59,244	329.5	204,332
General merchandise stores (excluding food products)	3,367	58,729	239.9	124,359
Book, magazine, and office supply stores	20,192	63,529	123.1	60,327

Energy production (consumption): electricity (kW-hr; 1987) 202,287,000,000 (219,090,000,000); coal (metric tons; 1987) 6,884,000 (16,969,000); crude petroleum (barrels; 1987) 206,720,000 (396,893,000); petroleum products (metric tons; 1987) 50,982,000 (45,071,000); natural gas (cu m; 1987) 2,770,000,000 (2,770,000,000); alcohol[22] (hectolitres; 1986) 102,000,000 (84,600,000).
Household income and expenditure. Average household size (1985) 4.3; income per household of families having income (1986)[15, 23, 24] 21,802 cruzados (U.S.$2,922); sources of income: n.a.; expenditure (1971)[25]: food 43.6%, energy and water 11.7%, housing 8.6%, clothing and footwear 6.4%, transportation 6.3%, beverages and tobacco 5.4%, health care 5.3%, other 12.6%.

Financial aggregates[26]

	1984	1985	1986	1987	1988	1989 (9 mos.)
Exchange rate, new cruzados per:						
U.S. dollar	0.00318	0.01049	0.01490	.0722	0.7653	3.7970
£	0.00368	0.01515	0.01547	0.1352	1.3848	5.9636
SDR	0.0312	0.0152	0.01283	0.1025	1.0299	4.8594
International reserves (U.S.$)						
Total (excl. gold; '000,000)	11,507	10,604	5,803	6,299	...	...
SDRs ('000,000)	1	1	—	—	...	...
Reserve pos. in IMF ('000,000)	—	—	—	—	...	...
Foreign exchange ('000,000)	11,508	10,605	5,803	6,299	...	...
Gold ('000,000 fine troy oz)	1.47	3.10	2.43	2.43	2.73	2.92[27]
% world reserves	0.16	0.33	0.26	0.26	0.29	0.31[27]
Interest and prices						
Central bank discount (%)	215.3	219.4	50.7	391.5	816.1	286.0[27]
Gov't. bond yield (%)	...	...	...	...	...	...
Industrial share prices	...	...	...	...	...	...
Balance of payments (U.S.$'000,000)						
Balance of visible trade	+13,086	+12,466	+8,305	+11,173	+19,182	+7,857[28]
Imports, f.o.b.	13,916	13,153	14,044	15,052	14,601	3,547[28]
Exports, f.o.b.	27,005	25,639	22,349	26,225	33,783	4,310[28]
Balance of invisibles	−13,215	−12,894	−13,695	−12,678	...	...
Balance of payments, current account	+42	−273	−5,304	−1,450	...	...

Foreign trade[29]

Balance of trade (current prices)

	1983	1984	1985	1986	1987	1988
U.S.$'000,000	+6,470	+13,089	+12,486	+8,349	+11,161	+19,182
% of total	17.3%	32.0%	32.2%	22.9%	27.0%	39.6%

Imports (1988): U.S.$16,047,000,000 (1987; minerals, including crude petroleum 35.1%; chemicals 14.7%, of which organic chemicals 6.7%, fertilizers 2.3%; nonelectrical machinery 11.9%; vegetable and animal products 7.8%, of which cereals 2.6%; electrical and electronic goods 7.4%; transport equipment 5.9%, of which airplanes 3.0%, road vehicles 2.0%; metals [all forms] 4.6%, of which iron and steel 1.9%; photographic, surgical, and scientific instruments and apparatus 3.3%; plastics 1.7%; natural and synthetic rubber materials 1.5%). *Major import sources:* United States 20.7%; Iraq 9.9%; West Germany 9.5%; Japan 5.7%; France 3.9%; Argentina 3.7%; Canada 2.8%; China 2.3%; Chile 2.3%; Iran 2.2%; Switzerland 2.2%; Italy 2.2%.
Exports (1988): U.S.$33,783,000,000 (1987; processed foods 17.2%, of which processed vegetables and fruits 3.5%, cocoa beans and cocoa 2.3%, seeds, juice, and industrial products of diverse fruits 2.2%, fresh and frozen meat 1.8%, animal and vegetable fats and oils 1.7%; metals [all forms] 11.8%, of which iron and steel 8.1%; road motor vehicles 8.4%; nonelectrical machinery 6.2%; animal feedstuffs 6.1%; textiles 4.6%; footwear 4.5%; crude petroleum and petroleum products 3.6%; electrical and electronic goods 3.4%; paper and paper products 1.4%. *Major export destinations:* United States 27.9%; Japan 6.4%; The Netherlands 6.1%; Italy 4.8%; West Germany 4.7%; Argentina 3.2%; United Kingdom 2.9%; France 2.6%; Belgium–Luxembourg 2.3%; Canada 2.1%.

Transport and communications

Transport. Railroads (1986): route length 18,526 mi, 29,814 km; passenger-mi 9,807,000,000, passenger-km 15,782,000,000; short ton-mi cargo 71,137,-000,000, metric ton-km cargo 103,860,000,000. Roads (1987): total length 932,280 mi, 1,500,319 km (paved 9%). Vehicles (1986): passenger cars 10,516,000; trucks and buses 1,067,000. Merchant marine (1988): vessels (100 gross tons and over) 719; total deadweight tonnage 10,103,844. Air transport (1987): passenger-km 23,517,000,000; metric ton-km cargo 1,215,-797,000; airports (1989) with scheduled flights 126.
Communications. Daily newspapers (1988): total number 288; total circulation 7,896,600[30]; circulation per 1,000 population 55[30]. Radio (1988): total number of receivers 58,867,032 (1 per 2.5 persons). Television (1988): total number of receivers 36,000,000 (1 per 4.0 persons). Telephones (1987): 13,162,000 (1 per 11 persons).

Education and health

Education (1988)

	schools	teachers	students	student/teacher ratio
Primary (age 7–14)	201,541	1,055,170[31]	26,821,134	24.9[31]
Secondary (age 15–17)	10,244	206,111[32]	3,339,090	14.6[32]
Higher[33]	855	118,870	1,418,196	11.9

Literacy (1986)[15, 34]: total population age 15 and over literate 66,873,-000 (79.3%); males literate 33,067,000 (80.4%); females literate 33,807,000 (78.3%).
Health: physicians (1985) 198,329 (1 per 684 persons); hospital beds (1987) 501,660 (1 per 282 persons); infant mortality rate per 1,000 live births (1985–90) 63.2.
Food (1984–86): daily per capita caloric intake 2,644 (vegetable products 86%, animal products 14%); 106% of FAO recommended minimum requirement.

Military

Total active duty personnel (1989): 324,000 (army 68.8%, navy 15.5%, air force 15.6%). *Military expenditure as percent of GNP* (1987): 0.8% (world 5.4%); per capita expenditure U.S.$15.

[1]The new cruzado, replacing the original at a rate of 1,000 old to one new, was introduced on Jan. 15, 1989. [2]Tocantins was created from northern Goiás as of promulgation of new national constitution on Oct. 5, 1988. [3]Includes former federal territory of Fernando de Noronha. [4]Includes 1,035 sq mi (2,680 sq km) in dispute between Amazonas and Pará and 1,009 sq mi (2,614 sq km) in dispute between Ceará and Piauí. [5]Detail does not add to total given because of rounding. [6]Land area excluding inland water is 3,265,076 sq mi (8,456,508 sq km). [7]Spiritist Catholics are actively and regularly involved in the practice of medium religions; about 60,000,000 Roman Catholics defer to spiritist dogma and participate in organized spiritism occasionally. [8]Evangelical Catholics are persons who are officially regarded as Roman Catholic but who are affiliated to Protestant churches. [9]Non-Christian followers of Afro-Brazilian syncretistic religions ("low spiritism"). [10]Non-Christian followers of Kardecism ("high spiritism"). [11]First population cited refers to the *municipio*, an officially delimited area including a central city and adjacent urban and rural districts; second (parenthetical) figure refers to the metropolitan area, defined as the adjoining predominantly urban *municipios* that are economically dependent on the central city. [12]*Municipio* within Rio de Janeiro metropolitan area. [13]*Municipio* within São Paulo metropolitan area. [14]For population in specified "zones of notification." [15]Of economically active, excludes rural population of Acre, Amazonas, Pará, Rondônia, Amapá, and Roraima. [16]1985. [17]At factor cost. [18]Excludes persons not employed regularly on a weekly basis. [19]Metropolitan São Paulo only. [20]Minimum wages paid in the *municipio* of São Paulo. [21]Official sources estimate 65% of all locally mined gold and 97% of all locally mined precious stones were smuggled out of the country in 1987. [22]Fuel produced from sugarcane used in the operation of locally produced automobiles as either hydrous alcohol or gasohol. [23]Prices of September 1985. [24]Excludes pensioners, domestic servants, and relatives of domestic servants. [25]Weights of CPI components for middle-income families in São Paulo. [26]End-of-year figures. [27]7 months. [28]First quarter. [29]Import figures are f.o.b. in balance of trade and c.i.f. in commodities and trading partners. [30]194 newspapers only. [31]1986–87. [32]1985–86. [33]1986. [34]By official estimate, 1986 functional literacy may be as low as 42.0% of total population over age 15.

Brunei

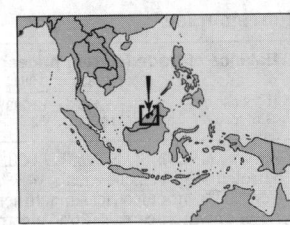

Official name: Negara Brunei Darussalam (State of Brunei, Abode of Peace).
Form of government: monarchy (sultanate)[1].
Head of state and government: Sultan.
Capital: Bandar Seri Begawan.
Official language: Malay.
Official religion: Islam.
Monetary unit: 1 Brunei dollar (B$) = 100 cents; valuation (Oct. 2, 1989) 1 U.S.$ = B$1.96; 1 £ = B$3.18.

Area and population

Districts	Capitals	area sq mi	area sq km	population 1986 estimate
Belait	Kuala Belait	1,052	2,724	53,600
Brunei and Muara	Bandar Seri Begawan	220	571	136,100
Temburong	Bangar	504	1,304	8,500
Tutong	Tutong	450	1,166	28,100
TOTAL		2,226	5,765	226,300

Demography

Population (1989): 251,000.
Density (1989): persons per sq mi 112.8, persons per sq km 43.5.
Urban–rural (1981): urban 59.4%; rural 40.6%.
Sex distribution (1986): male 51.61%; female 48.39%.
Age breakdown (1986): under 15, 36.7%; 15–29, 33.3%; 30–44, 18.3%; 45–59, 7.4%; 60–69, 2.3%; 70 and over, 2.0%.
Population projection: (2000) 341,000; (2010) 451,000.
Doubling time: 29 years.
Ethnic composition (1986): Malay 68.8%; Chinese 18.3%; other indigenous 5.0%; Indian and other 7.9%.
Religious affiliation (1982): Muslim 63.4%; Buddhist 14.0%; Christian 9.7%; other 12.9%.
Major cities (1981): Bandar Seri Begawan 52,300[2]; Seria 23,511; Kuala Belait 19,281; Tutong 6,161.

Vital statistics

Birth rate per 1,000 population (1988): 28.3 (world avg. 27.1); (1982) legitimate 99.6%; illegitimate 0.4%.
Death rate per 1,000 population (1988): 3.9 (world avg. 9.9).
Natural increase rate per 1,000 population (1988): 24.4 (world avg. 17.2).
Total fertility rate (avg. births per childbearing woman; 1988): 4.1.
Marriage rate per 1,000 population (1986): 7.4.
Divorce rate per 1,000 population (1985): 0.73[3].
Life expectancy at birth (1986): male 70.1 years; female 72.7 years.
Major causes of death per 100,000 population (1986): cardiovascular disease 32.7; malignant neoplasms (cancers) 27.0; cerebrovascular disease 19.4; conditions originating from perinatal period 15.9; pneumonia 12.4; bronchitis, emphysema, and asthma 11.0; motor vehicle accidents 11.0; tuberculosis 4.9; signs, symptoms, and other ill-defined conditions 99.4.

National economy

Budget (1986). Revenue: B$3,331,530,000 (indirect taxes 59.4%, government property 36.7%[4]). Expenditures: B$2,720,370,000 (development expenditure 13.9%, defense 8.8%, education 7.6%, public works 5.7%, health 3.4%).
Public debt (external, outstanding; 1988): none.
Tourism (1986): number of tourist arrivals 6,578.
Production (metric tons except as noted). Agriculture, forestry, fishing (1988): 1,045,000 coconuts[5], vegetables and melons 9,000, fruits excluding melons 6,000, eggs 2,270, rice 2,000, cassava 1,000, pineapples 1,000; livestock (number of live animals) 14,000 pigs, 10,000 buffalo, 3,000 cattle, 1,000 goats, 2,000,000 chickens; roundwood (1987) 294,000 cu m; fish catch (1987) 2,652. Mining and quarrying (1988): other than petroleum and natural gas (see below), none except sand and gravel for construction. Manufacturing (1986): gasoline 125,000; diesel oils 58,000; liquid petroleum gas 40,000; jet fuels 18,000; naphtha 4,000; kerosene 3,000. Construction (number of buildings completed; 1984): residential 195; nonresidential 5. Energy production (consumption): electricity (kW-hr; 1987) 998,000,000 (998,000,000); coal, none (none); crude petroleum (barrels; 1987) 51,013,000 (n.a.); petroleum products (metric tons; 1987) 623,000 (649,000); natural gas (cu m; 1987) 8,211,646,000 (934,007,000).
Population economically active (1986): total 86,395; activity rate of total population 37.8% (participation rates: ages 15–64 [1981] 61.1%; female [1981] 23.8%; unemployed 6.1%).

Price and earnings indexes (1985 = 100)

	1980	1981	1982	1983	1984	1985	1986
Consumer price index	80.7	88.1	93.7	94.8	97.7	100.0	101.8
Monthly earnings index[6]	77.5	83.3	86.6	108.0	99.1	100.0	87.9

Household income and expenditure. Average household size (1981) 5.8; income per household: n.a.; sources of income: n.a.; expenditure (1977): food 45.1%, transportation and communications 17.2%, recreation, education, and cultural services 8.9%, household furnishings 8.3%, clothing and footwear 6.1%, rent and utilities 5.0%.

Gross national product (at current market prices; 1986): U.S.$3,570,000,000[7] (U.S.$15,400 per capita).

Structure of gross domestic product and labour force

	1986 in value B$'000,000	1986 % of total value	1986 labour force	1986 % of labour force
Agriculture	107.7	1.9	3,059	3.5
Mining	} 2,920.2	50.6	6,006	7.0
Manufacturing				
Construction	233.5	4.0	9,424	10.9
Public utilities	17.7	0.3	2,042	2.4
Transportation and communications	139.0	2.4	6,883	8.0
Trade	666.8	11.5	8,022	9.3
Finance	379.5	6.6	4,330	5.0
Services	1,451.7	25.1	38,557	44.6
Other	−142.7[8]	−2.5[8]	8,072[9]	9.3[9]
TOTAL	5,773.3[10]	100.0[10]	86,395	100.0

Land use (1987): forested 48.4%; meadows and pastures 1.1%; agricultural and under permanent cultivation 1.3%; other 49.2%.

Foreign trade

Balance of trade (current prices)

	1981	1982	1983	1984	1985	1986
B$'000,000	+7,327	+6,582	+5,629	+5,482	+5,184	+2,540
% of total	74.3%	67.7%	64.6%	67.3%	65.8%	46.7%

Imports (1986): B$1,450,410,000 (machinery and transport equipment 38.0%, manufactured goods 21.1%, food and live animals 14.4%, miscellaneous manufactured articles 10.6%, chemicals 7.0%, beverages and tobacco 5.9%, crude materials 1.2%, mineral fuels 1.0%). *Major import sources:* Singapore 25.7%; Japan 17.7%; United States 12.2%; United Kingdom 7.9%; West Germany 6.0%; Malaysia 5.2%[11]; The Netherlands 3.3%; Thailand 3.1%; Australia 2.6%.
Exports (1986): B$3,990,100,000 (natural gas 52.9%, crude oil 40.6%, petroleum products 3.7%, other 2.8%). *Major export destinations:* Japan 66.9%; Thailand 8.1%; South Korea 7.4%; Singapore 6.7%; United States 6.1%; Taiwan 1.7%.

Transport and communications

Transport. Railroads[12] (1988): length 12 mi, 19 km. Roads (1986): total length 1,156 mi, 1,860 km (paved 50%). Vehicles (1986): passenger cars 84,527; trucks and buses 11,051. Merchant marine (1988): vessels (100 gross tons and over) 34; total deadweight tonnage 345,001. Marine transport (1986): cargo loaded 18,627,000 metric tons, cargo unloaded 671,700 metric tons. Air transport (1988): passenger-mi 207,000,000, passenger-km 333,000,000; short ton-mi cargo 4,095,000, metric ton-km cargo 5,978,000; airports (1989) with scheduled flights 1.
Communications. Daily newspapers (1987): none. Radio (1986): total number of receivers 78,000 (1 per 3.0 persons). Television (1986): total number of receivers 49,500[13] (1 per 4.7 persons). Telephones (1987): 39,534 (1 per 6.1 persons).

Education and health

Education (1986)

	schools	teachers	students	student/ teacher ratio
Primary (age 5–11)	146	2,225	36,983	16.6
Secondary (age 12–20)	29	1,636	18,714	11.4
Voc., teacher tr.	8	414[14]	1,688	4.1
Higher	1	33	176	5.3

Educational attainment (1981). Percent of population age 25 and over having: no formal schooling 32.1%; primary education 28.3%; secondary 30.1%; postsecondary and higher 9.4%. *Literacy* (1984): total population age 15 and over literate 108,900 (80.3%); males literate 64,300 (86.5%); females literate 44,600 (72.8%).
Health (1986): physicians 171 (1 per 1,323 persons); hospital beds 876 (1 per 258 persons); infant mortality rate per 1,000 live births (1988) 16.0.
Food (1984–86): daily per capita caloric intake 2,850 (vegetable products 80%, animal products 20%); 126% of FAO recommended minimum requirement.

Military

Total active duty personnel (1989): 4,200[15] (army 80.9%, navy 11.9%, air force 7.2%). *Military expenditure as percent of GNP* (1983): 5.8% (world 6.1%); per capita expenditure U.S.$1,200.

[1]A nonelective 21-member body advises the Sultan on legislative matters. [2]1988 estimate. [3]For Muslim population only. [4]In 1983 more than 98% of state revenue was derived from exports of oil and gas. [5]1985. [6]Nonagricultural sectors only. [7]GDP data. [8]Imputed bank service charge. [9]Includes unemployed. [10]Detail does not add to total given because of rounding. [11]Peninsular Malaysia only. [12]Privately owned. [13]Colour receivers only. [14]Vocational and teacher training includes higher. [15]All services form part of the army.

Bulgaria

Official name: Narodna Republika Bŭlgaria (People's Republic of Bulgaria).
Form of government: unitary single-party socialist republic with one legislative house (National Assembly [400]).
Chief of state: Chairman of the State Council (president).
Head of government: Chairman of the Council of Ministers (premier).
Capital: Sofia.
Official language: Bulgarian.
Official religion: none.
Monetary unit: 1 lev (leva) = 100 stotinki; valuation (Oct. 2, 1989) 1 lev = U.S.$0.82; 1 £ = 1.33 leva.

Area and population		area		population
				1988[1]
Provinces	**Capitals**	sq mi	sq km	estimate
Burgas	Burgas	5,659	14,657	873,905
Khaskovo	Khaskovo	5,364	13,892	1,047,189
Lovech	Lovech	5,849	15,150	1,068,097
Mikhaylovgrad	Mikhaylovgrad	4,095	10,607	666,277
Plovdiv	Plovdiv	5,262	13,628	1,261,875
Razgrad	Razgrad	4,186	10,842	850,862
Sofiya	Sofia (Sofiya)	7,328	18,978	1,017,214
Varna	Varna	4,606	11,929	981,274
City Commune				
Sofiya	Sofia (Sofiya)	506	1,311	1,209,562
TOTAL		42,855	110,994	8,976,255

Demography

Population (1989): 8,987,000.
Density (1989): persons per sq mi 209.7, persons per sq km 81.0.
Urban–rural (1988): urban 66.4%; rural 33.6%.
Sex distribution (1988): male 49.44%; female 50.56%.
Age breakdown (1988): under 15, 21.2%; 15–29, 20.4%; 30–44, 21.3%; 45–59, 18.8%; 60–74, 13.7%; 75 and over, 4.6%.
Population projection: (2000) 9,075,000; (2010) 9,155,000.
Doubling time: not applicable; population stable.
Ethnic composition (1988): Bulgarian 85.3%; Turkish 8.5%; Gypsy 2.6%; Macedonian 2.5%; Armenian 0.3%; Russian 0.2%; other 0.6%.
Religious affiliation (1982): atheist 64.5%; Eastern Orthodox 26.7%; Muslim 7.5%; Protestant 0.7%; Roman Catholic 0.5%; other 0.1%.
Major cities (1987): Sofia 1,128,859; Plovdiv 356,596; Varna 305,891; Burgas 197,555; Ruse 190,450.

Vital statistics

Birth rate per 1,000 population (1987): 13.0 (world avg. 27.1); legitimate 89.8%; illegitimate 10.2%.
Death rate per 1,000 population (1987): 12.0 (world avg. 9.9).
Natural increase rate per 1,000 population (1987): 1.0 (world avg. 17.2).
Total fertility rate (avg. births per childbearing woman; 1985): 2.0.
Marriage rate per 1,000 population (1987): 7.2.
Divorce rate per 1,000 population (1987): 1.3.
Life expectancy at birth (1984–86): male 68.2 years; female 74.4 years.
Major causes of death per 100,000 population (1986): diseases of the circulatory system 714.1; malignant neoplasms (cancers) 164.5; diseases of the respiratory system 81.7; accidents, poisoning, and violence 60.6; diseases of the digestive system 36.6; endocrine and metabolic disorders 17.9.

National economy

Budget (1987). Revenue: 20,672,800,000 leva (national economy 92.0%, other 8.0%). Expenditures: 20,662,800,000 leva (economy 46.4%, education and health 18.8%, social security 18.0%, administration 15.1%).
Public debt (external, outstanding; 1987): U.S.$6,100,000,000.
Tourism (1987): number of tourist arrivals 7,593,637; receipts from visitors U.S.$354,000,000; expenditures by nationals abroad, n.a.
Production (metric tons except as noted). Agriculture, forestry, fishing (1987): wheat 4,148,650, corn (maize) 1,857,621, barley 1,091,450, grapes 942,643, tomatoes 827,505, sugar beets 736,472; melons and watermelons 361,964, apples 339,177, potatoes 315,727, green peppers 224,219, tobacco 127,174, plums 102,671, cherries 86,194, onions 81,194, pears 74,322, rye 48,699, oats 41,377, green beans 30,380; livestock (number of live animals; 1988) 8,885,863 sheep, 4,034,098 pigs, 1,648,605 cattle; roundwood 3,667,000 cu m; fish catch 110,543. Mining and quarrying (1987): iron ore 1,850,000; lead 95,000; copper 75,000; zinc 68,000; manganese 38,000. Manufacturing (1987): cement 5,494,000; crude steel 3,045,000; pig iron 1,706,000; nitrogenous and phosphate fertilizers 889,700; sulfuric acid 688,500; wood pulp and paper 540,500; plastics and synthetic resins 322,114; lavender oil 157,-986; tobacco 129,858; cotton fabrics 353,418,000 m; woven woolen fabric 43,773,000 m; leather footwear 25,041,000 pairs; rubber footwear 8,725,000 pairs; beverages 6,596,500 hectolitres; wine 3,495,400 hectolitres; automobile tires 1,856,600; clay building bricks 1,051,000,000 pieces; television receivers 198,592 units; motor pumps 98,261 units; bicycles 92,853 units; passenger cars 20,009 units; metal-working lathes 4,886 units; tractors 4,751 units; cranes 1,351 units. Construction (1987): residential 4,330,790 sq m. Energy production (consumption): electricity (kW-hr; 1987) 43,470,000,000 (47,844,000,000); coal (metric tons; 1987) 43,868,000 (43,848,000); crude petroleum (barrels; 1987) 2,126,000 (97,442,000); petroleum products (metric tons; 1987) 11,360,000 (12,943,000); natural gas (cu m; 1987) 122,830,000 (5,592,734,000).
Gross national product (1988): U.S.$67,590,000,000 (U.S.$7,510 per capita).

Structure of net material product and labour force				
	1987			
	in value '000,000 leva	% of total value	labour force[2]	% of labour force
Agriculture	3,712.1	13.1	824,255	20.1
Mining	107.9	0.4	25,846	0.6
Manufacturing	16,649.7	58.8	1,437,507	35.0
Public utilities			58,495	1.4
Construction	2,674.7	9.4	362,884	8.8
Transp. and commun.	2,058.2	7.3	304,084	7.4
Trade	2,499.8	8.8	367,653	8.9
Finance	—	—	23,222	0.6
Pub. admin., defense	—	—	57,874	1.4
Services	—	—	607,152	14.8
Other	635.6[3]	2.2[3]	39,487	1.0
TOTAL	28,338.0	100.0	4,108,459	100.0

Population economically active (1985): total 4,686,140; activity rate of total population 52.4% (participation rates: ages 15–64, 75.7%; female 47.7%).

Price and earnings indexes (1985 = 100)							
	1981	1982	1983	1984	1985	1986	1987
Consumer price index	96.1	96.4	97.7	98.4	100.0	103.5	103.6
Monthly earnings index	89.7	92.2	93.4	97.1	100.0	105.2	109.1

Household income and expenditure. Average household size (1982) 3.3; income per household (1987) 7,627 leva (U.S.$8,973); sources of income (1987): wages and salaries 54.3%, transfer payments 18.3%; self-employment 11.1%; expenditure (1987): food 43.5%, clothing 9.8%, housing 7.4%, recreation 7.4%, transportation 6.8%, household durable goods 4.3%, education and culture 3.4%, tobacco 2.5%, health care 2.1%.
Land use (1986): forested 34.9%; meadows and pastures 18.4%; agricultural and under permanent cultivation 37.5%; other 9.2%.

Foreign trade

Balance of trade (current prices)						
	1982	1983	1984	1985	1986	1987
'000,000 leva	+95.9	−148.5	−145.0	−327.1	−1,022.6	−265.3
% of total	0.4%	0.6%	0.6%	1.2%	3.6%	1.0%

Imports (1987): 14,067,000,000 leva (machinery and equipment 43.5%; fuels, mineral raw materials, and metals 32.4%; chemical products and rubber 6.4%; consumer goods 5.4%; food products 5.2%). *Major import sources:* U.S.S.R. 57.3%; East Germany 5.7%; Czechoslovakia 5.0%; West Germany 4.9%; Poland 4.8%; Cuba 1.8%; Switzerland 1.4%; Italy 1.2%; Japan 1.0%.
Exports (1987): 13,802,000,000 leva (machinery and equipment 60.2%, of which machinery 29.3%; consumer goods 10.2%; fuels, minerals, and metals 8.8%; food and beverages 6.6%; tobacco 6.6%; chemicals 3.7%; building materials 1.9%). *Major export destinations:* U.S.S.R. 61.1%; East Germany 5.5%; Czechoslovakia 4.9%; Poland 4.3%; Libya 3.4%; Iran 2.9%; Romania 2.1%; Hungary 1.8%; Cuba 1.4%.

Transport and communications

Transport. Railroads (1987): length 2,672 mi, 4,300 km; passenger-mi 5,018,-000,000, passenger-km 8,075,000,000; short ton-mi cargo 12,220,000,000, metric ton-km cargo 17,842,000,000. Roads (1987): total length 23,555 mi, 37,908 km (paved 91%). Vehicles (1987): passenger cars 1,138,433; trucks and buses 588,600. Merchant marine (1988): vessels (100 gross tons and over) 201; total deadweight tonnage 1,984,308. Air transport (1987): passenger-mi 2,223,000,000, passenger-km 3,577,600,000; short ton-mi cargo 28,584,000, metric ton-km cargo 41,735,000; airports (1989) 13.
Communications. Daily newspapers (1987): total number 17; total circulation 2,834,000; circulation per 1,000 population 316. Radio (1987): 1,982,-929 receivers (1 per 4.5 persons). Television (1987): 1,692,411 receivers (1 per 5.3 persons). Telephones (1987): 2,073,271 (1 per 4.3 persons).

Education and health

Education (1987–88)				student/
	schools	teachers	students	teacher ratio
Primary (age 6–14)	2,935	62,054	1,091,089	17.6
Secondary (age 15–17)	554	9,837	164,157	16.7
Voc., teacher tr.	537	19,035	238,633	12.5
Higher	30	15,941	116,407	7.3

Educational attainment (1983): Percent of employed population having: postsecondary vocational certificate 15.6%; 4-year college 7.5%. *Literacy* (1980): total population age 15 and over literate 95.5%.
Health (1987): physicians 27,107 (1 per 331 persons); hospital beds 85,804 (1 per 105 persons); infant mortality rate per 1,000 live births 14.7.
Food (1984–86): daily per capita caloric intake 3,634 (vegetable products 76%, animal products 24%); (1984) 99% of FAO minimum requirement.

Military

Total active duty personnel (1988): 157,800 (army 72.9%, navy 5.6%, air force 21.5%). *Military expenditure as percent of GNP* (1987): 10.3% (world 5.4%); per capita expenditure U.S.$743.

[1]January 1. [2]Socialized sector only. [3]Includes other material activities.

Burkina Faso[1]

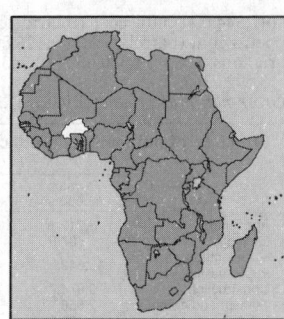

Official name: Burkina Faso
(Burkina Faso).
Form of government: military
regime.
Head of state and government:
Chairman of the Popular Front[2].
Capital: Ouagadougou.
Official language: French.
Official religion: none.
Monetary unit: 1 CFA franc
(CFAF) = 100 centimes; valuation
(Oct. 2, 1989) 1 U.S.$ = CFAF 317.90;
1 £ = CFAF 514.37.

Area and population		area		population
Provinces	**Capitals**	sq mi	sq km	1985 census
Bam	Kongoussi	1,551	4,017	162,575
Bazéga	Kombissiri	2,051	5,313	303,941
Bougouriba	Diébougou	2,736	7,087	220,895
Boulgou	Tenkodogo	3,488	9,033	402,236
Boulkiemde	Koudougou	1,598	4,138	365,223
Comoé	Banfora	7,102	18,393	249,967
Ganzourgou	Zorgho	1,578	4,087	195,652
Gnagna	Bogandé	3,320	8,600	229,152
Gourma	Fada N'Gourma	10,275	26,613	294,235
Houet	Bobo-Dioulasso	6,360	16,472	581,722
Kadiogo	Ouagadougou	451	1,169	459,826
Kénédougou	Orodara	3,207	8,307	139,973
Kossi	Nouna	5,088	13,177	332,960
Kouritenga	Koupéla	628	1,627	198,486
Mouhoun	Dédougou	4,032	10,442	288,735
Nahouri	Pô	1,484	3,843	105,509
Namentenga	Boulsa	2,994	7,755	198,890
Oubritenga	Ziniaré	1,812	4,693	304,265
Oudalan	Gorom Gorom	3,879	10,046	106,194
Passoré	Yako	1,575	4,078	223,830
Poni	Gaoua	4,000	10,361	235,480
Sanguie	Réo	1,994	5,165	217,277
Sanmatenga	Kaya	3,557	9,213	367,724
Sèno	Dori	5,202	13,473	228,905
Sissili	Léo	5,303	13,736	244,919
Soum	Djibo	5,154	13,350	186,812
Sourou	Tougan	3,663	9,487	268,108
Tapoa	Diapaga	5,707	14,780	158,859
Yatenga	Ouahigouya	4,746	12,292	536,578
Zoundwéogo	Manga	1,333	3,453	155,777
TOTAL		105,869[3]	274,200	7,964,705

Demography

Population (1989): 8,714,000.
Density (1989): persons per sq mi 82.3, persons per sq km 31.8.
Urban–rural (1986): urban 8.1%; rural 91.9%.
Sex distribution (1985): male 48.13%; female 51.87%.
Age breakdown (1985): under 15, 48.3%; 15–29, 23.4%; 30–44, 13.4%; 45–59, 8.7%; 60–74, 4.7%; 75 and over, 1.5%.
Population projection: (2000) 11,657,000; (2010) 15,186,000.
Doubling time: 24 years.
Ethnic composition (1983): Mossi 47.9%; Mande 8.8%; Fulani 8.3%; Lobi 6.9%; Bobo 6.8%; Senufo 5.3%; Grosi 5.1%; Gurma 4.8%; Tuareg 3.3%; other 2.8%.
Religious affiliation (1980): traditional beliefs 44.8%; Muslim 43.0%; Christian 12.2%, of which Roman Catholic 9.8%, Protestant 2.4%.
Major cities (1985): Ouagadougou 442,223; Bobo-Dioulasso 231,162; Koudougou 59,644; Ouahigouya 41,595; Banfora 16,843.

Vital statistics

Birth rate per 1,000 population (1985–90): 47.2 (world avg. 27.1).
Death rate per 1,000 population (1985–90): 18.5 (world avg. 9.9).
Natural increase rate per 1,000 population (1985–90): 28.7 (world avg. 17.2).
Total fertility rate (avg. births per childbearing woman; 1985–90): 6.5.
Marriage rate per 1,000 population (1975): 9.4.
Divorce rate per 1,000 population (1975): 1.3.
Life expectancy at birth (1985–90): male 45.6 years; female 48.9 years.
Morbidity (percent of reported cases of illness; 1984): measles 39.6%; malaria 12.4%; tetanus 5.7%; diarrheal diseases 5.3%.

National economy

Budget (1989). Revenue: CFAF 100,533,000,000 (import duties 30.5%, value-added taxes 17.4%, personal income taxes 13.0%, excise taxes 10.8%, other 9.6%). *Expenditures:* CFAF 107,214,000,000 (recurrent expenditures 88.6%, of which education 18.4%, defense 16.8%, debt service 8.7%, health 6.9%, social security and welfare 4.1%; capital expenditures 11.4%).
Public debt (external, outstanding; 1987): U.S.$794,000,000.
Tourism (1987): receipts U.S.$7,000,000; expenditures U.S.$30,000,000.
Production (metric tons except as noted). Agriculture, forestry, fishing (1988): sorghum 1,009,000, millet 817,000, sugarcane 340,000, corn (maize) 227,000, seed cotton 179,000, pulses 174,000, peanuts (groundnuts) 161,000, rice 39,000, sweet potatoes 39,000, sesame 9,000, cassava 8,000; livestock (number of live animals) 5,198,000 goats, 2,972,000 sheep, 2,809,000 cattle, 21,000,000 chickens; roundwood (1987) 7,114,000 cu m; fish catch (1987) 7,000. Mining and quarrying (1988): manganese 15,000; phosphates 3,000[3]; gold 3,049 kg[4]. Manufacturing (1986): flour 25,518; soap 13,835; cotton yarn 238; bicycle and motorcycle tires 526,100 units; motorcycles and scooters 52,800 units; footwear 890,000 pairs; beer 389,269 hectolitres;

soft drinks 128,644 hectolitres. Construction (value added in CFAF; 1983): 7,749,300,000. Energy production (consumption): electricity (kW-hr; 1988) 144,700,000 (130,000,000); coal, none (n.a.); crude petroleum, none (n.a.); petroleum products (metric tons; 1987) none (149,000).
Gross national product (1987): U.S.$1,426,000,000 (U.S.$170 per capita).

Structure of gross domestic product and labour force				
	1986		1985	
	in value CFAF '000,000	% of total value	labour force	% of labour force
Agriculture	186,840	47.2	3,480,000	85.9
Mining	90	0.1		
Manufacturing	56,900	14.4	182,000	4.5
Construction	4,800	1.2		
Public utilities	5,560	1.4		
Transp. and commun.	19,780	5.0		
Finance	17,370	4.4		
Trade	49,560	12.5	389,000	9.6
Pub. admin., defense	59,270	15.0		
Services				
Other	5,890	1.5	...	...
TOTAL	395,580[5]	100.0[5]	4,051,000	100.0

Population economically active: total (1985) 4,051,000; activity rate 51.0% (participation rates: over age 15, 83.0%; female 49.1%; unemployed, n.a.).

Price and earnings indexes (1985 = 100)						
	1983	1984	1985	1986	1987	1988
Consumer price index	89.3	91.2	100.0	97.4	94.8	98.6
Hourly earnings index	100.0	100.0	100.0	100.0	115.0	...

Household income and expenditure. Average household size (1984) 4.9; average annual income per household CFAF 303,000 (U.S.$640); sources of income: n.a.; expenditure (1985)[6]: food 38.7%; transportation 18.6%; electricity and fuel 13.7%; beverages 9.0%; health 5.2%; housing 5.1%.
Land use (1986): forested 25.0%; meadows and pastures 36.5%; agricultural and under permanent cultivation 9.7%; other 28.8%.

Foreign trade

Balance of trade (current prices)						
	1982	1983	1984	1985	1986	1987
CFAF '000,000	−70.82	−63.76	−51.92	−82.91	−80.25	−55.23
% of total	66.2%	59.5%	42.7%	57.1%	58.3%	37.2%

Imports (1987): CFAF 130,527,000,000 (machinery and transport equipment 27.2%, of which road transport equipment 10.5%, electrical machinery 4.7%; manufactured goods 26.1%; chemicals 13.5%; petroleum products 7.7%; cereals 5.7%; dairy products 3.8%; raw materials 3.4%; grease and lubricants 1.4%). *Major import sources:* France 32.2%; Côte d'Ivoire 25.9%; Italy 5.1%; Japan 4.1%; The Netherlands 4.0%; West Germany 3.9%.
Exports (1987): CFAF 46,593,000,000 (raw cotton 43.2%; manufactured goods 32.2%; machinery and equipment 9.7%; live animals 5.4%; vegetable food products 2.7%). *Major export destinations:* France 39.8%; Tunisia 3.8%; Spain 3.3%; Portugal 3.0%; Italy 3.0%; Belgium 2.3%; Egypt 2.0%.

Transport and communications

Transport. Railroads (1984)[7]: length 342 mi, 550 km; passenger-km 679,790,000; metric ton-km cargo 469,675,000. Roads (1986): total length 6,979 mi, 11,231 km (paved 12%). Vehicles (1983): passenger cars 21,182; trucks and buses 5,729. Merchant marine: none. Air transport (1987): passenger-km 213,706,000; metric ton-mi cargo 36,119,000; airports (1989) 3.
Communications. Daily newspapers (1988): total number 2; total circulation 6,500; circulation per 1,000 population 0.8. Radio (1986): 311,000 receivers (1 per 26 persons). Television (1988): 41,500 receivers (1 per 205 persons). Telephones (1986): 16,769 (1 per 482 persons).

Education and health

Education (1987–88)				
	schools	teachers	students	student/ teacher ratio
Primary	1,958	7,096	411,907	58.0
Secondary	113	1,700	57,240	33.7
Vocational[3]	18	421	4,808	11.4
Higher[3]	1	325	3,869	11.9

Educational attainment, n.a. *Literacy* (1985): total population age 15 and over literate 509,700 (13.2%); males 392,100 (20.7%); females 119,900 (6.1%).
Health: physicians (1988) 280 (1 per 29,914 persons); hospital beds (1984) 5,580 (1 per 1,359 persons); infant mortality rate (1985) 137.0.
Food (1984–86): daily per capita caloric intake 2,047 (vegetable products 95%, animal products 5%); (1984) 86% of FAO recommended minimum.

Military

Total active duty personnel (1989): 8,700 (army 97.7%; navy, none; air force 2.3%). *Military expenditure as percent of GNP* (1987): 3.1% (world 5.4%); per capita expenditure U.S.$6.

---

[1]Known as Upper Volta before Aug. 4, 1984. [2]On Oct. 15, 1987, a coup took place changing the leadership of the country from the President and the National Recovery Council, to the Chairman of the Popular Front and the Military Council (formed later in the month). [3]1986. [4]Officially marketed gold only; does not include substantial illegal production. [5]Detail does not add to total given because of rounding. [6]Weights of consumer price index components; Ouagadougou only. [7]Passenger-mi and short ton-mi cargo figures are based on traffic between Abidjan, Côte d'Ivoire, and Ouagadougou.

Burundi

Official name: Republika y'u Burundi
(Rundi); République du Burundi
(French) (Republic of Burundi).
Form of government: military regime[1].
Head of state and government:
President (and Chairman of the
Military Committee for National
Salvation).
Capital: Bujumbura.
Official languages: Rundi; French.
Official religion: none.
Monetary unit: 1 Burundi franc
(FBu) = 100 centimes; valuation (Oct.
2, 1989) 1 U.S.$ = FBu 156.67;
1 £ = FBu 253.50.

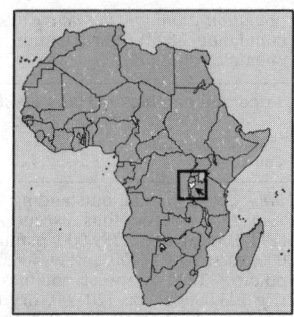

Area and population

Provinces	Capitals	area sq mi	area sq km	population 1987 estimate[2]
Bubanza	Bubanza	422	1,093	200,420
Bujumbura	Bujumbura	515	1,334	584,812
Bururi	Bururi	971	2,515	374,660
Cankuzo	Cankuzo	749	1,940	129,275
Cibitoke	Cibitoke	633	1,639	235,279
Gitega	Gitega	768	1,989	561,950
Karuzi	Karuzi	563	1,459	258,811
Kayanza	Kayanza	475	1,229	446,219
Kirundo	Kirundo	661	1,711	359,485
Makamba	Makamba	761	1,972	155,676
Muramvya	Muramvya	591	1,530	437,846
Muyinga	Muyinga	705	1,825	315,008
Ngozi	Ngozi	567	1,468	476,408
Rutana	Rutana	733	1,898	179,302
Ruyigi	Ruyigi	913	2,365	206,933
TOTAL LAND AREA		10,026[3]	25,967	4,922,084
INLAND WATER		721	1,867	
TOTAL AREA		10,747	27,834	

Demography

Population (1989): 5,287,000.
Density[4] (1988): persons per sq mi 527.3, persons per sq km 203.6.
Urban–rural (1986): urban 7.5%; rural 92.5%.
Sex distribution (1986): male 48.60%; female 51.40%.
Age breakdown (1986): under 15, 44.3%; 15–29, 28.2%; 30–44, 14.5%; 45–59,
7.9%; 60–74, 4.0%; 75 and over, 1.1%.
Population projection: (2000) 7,235,000; (2010) 9,500,000.
Doubling time: 25 years.
Ethnic composition (1983): Rundi 97.4%, of which Hutu 81.9%, Tutsi 13.5%;
Twa Pygmy 1.0%; other 1.6%.
Religious affiliation (1980): Christian 85.5%, of which Roman Catholic
78.3%, Protestant 7.1%; traditional beliefs 13.5%; Muslim 0.9%; other 0.1%.
Major cities (1986): Bujumbura 272,600; Gitega 95,300; Ngozi 20,000[5].

Vital statistics

Birth rate per 1,000 population (1986–87): 45.7 (world avg. 27.1).
Death rate per 1,000 population (1986–87): 17.4 (world avg. 9.9).
Natural increase rate per 1,000 population (1986–87): 28.4 (world avg. 17.2).
Total fertility rate (avg. births per childbearing woman; 1986–87): 6.3.
Marriage rate per 1,000 population: n.a.
Divorce rate per 1,000 population: n.a.
Life expectancy at birth (1986–87): male 46.9 years; female 50.2 years.
Major causes of death per 100,000 population (1983)[6]: measles 45.1; bacil-
lary dysentery 26.2; other diarrheal diseases 7.9; malaria 7.4; pulmonary
tuberculosis 2.6.

National economy

Budget (1989). Revenue: FBu 29,678,900,000 (customs duties 27.5%, excise
duties 16.7%, property tax 8.3%, administrative receipts 7.7%, income tax
7.1%). Expenditures: FBu 34,789,600,000 (goods and services 49.0%, subsidies and transfers 19.7%, public debt 12.5%).
Public debt (external, outstanding; 1987): U.S.$718,000,000.
Tourism (1987): receipts from visitors U.S.$35,000,000; expenditures by na-
tionals abroad U.S.$18,000,000.
Production (metric tons except as noted). Agriculture, forestry, fishing (1987):
bananas 1,440,000, sweet potatoes 615,000, cassava 555,000, pulses 353,000,
sorghum 220,000, corn (maize) 165,000, yams and taros 129,000, peanuts
(groundnuts) 80,000, millet 52,000, coffee 34,000, rice 20,000, wheat 15,000,
sugarcane 7,000, palm kernels 2,000, cotton lint 2,000; livestock (number
of live animals) 865,000 goats, 390,000 sheep, 360,000 cattle, 4,000,000
chickens; roundwood 3,849,000 cu m; fish catch (1986) 6,840. Mining and
quarrying (1986): peat 12,455; kaolin clay 5,113; lime 160; gold 980 troy
oz. Manufacturing (1987): beer 939,000 hectolitres; carbonated beverages
130,000 hectolitres; 271,000,000 cigarettes; blankets 342,000 units; footwear
398,000 pairs. Construction: n.a. Energy production (consumption): electricity (kW-hr; 1987) 54,000,000 (129,000,000); coal, none (n.a.); crude
petroleum, none (n.a.); petroleum products (metric tons; 1987) none (49,-
000); natural gas, none (n.a.); peat (metric tons; 1987) 10,000 (10,000).
Land use (1986): forested 2.5%; meadows and pastures 35.6%; agricultural
and under permanent cultivation 51.8%; other 10.1%.
Gross national product (at current market prices; 1987): U.S.$1,205,000,000
(U.S.$240 per capita).

Structure of gross domestic product and labour force

	1988 in value FBu '000,000[7]	1988 % of total value	1979 labour force	1979 % of labour force
Agriculture	77,786.9	51.9	2,246,200	93.1
Mining	} 1,194.3	0.8	1,400	0.1
Public utilities			1,700	0.1
Manufacturing	13,812.0	9.2	36,700	1.5
Construction	5,458.1	3.6	14,700	0.6
Transportation and communications	3,972.5	2.6	6,400	0.2
Trade	12,205.8	8.1	20,900	0.9
Finance	...	...	1,300	0.1
Pub. admin., defense	18,800.0	12.5	5,700	0.2
Services	2,071.8	1.4	75,000	3.1
Other	15,148.0	10.1	3,100	0.1
TOTAL	149,963.3[3]	100.0[3]	2,413,100	100.0

Population economically active (1986): total 2,653,951; activity rate of total
population 55.5% (participation rates: ages 15–64, 88.7%; female 52.7%;
unemployed, n.a.).

Price and earnings indexes (1985 = 100)

	1982	1983	1984	1985	1986	1987	1988
Consumer price index	77.8	84.4	96.4	100.0	101.8	109.3	114.0
Monthly earnings index[8]	103.0	143.4	170.0	...	...	...	...

Household income and expenditure. Average household size (1980) 4.9;
income per household: n.a.; sources of income: n.a.; expenditure[9]: food
59.6%, clothing and footwear 11.1%, furniture and household goods 6.0%,
energy and water 5.8%, housing 4.4%, other 13.1%.

Foreign trade[10]

Balance of trade (current prices)

	1983	1984	1985	1986	1987	1988
FBu '000,000	−7,326	−5,930	−6,001	−864	−12,273	−7,136
% of total	32.7%	18.0%	18.0%	2.2%	37.0%	16.6%

Imports (1987): FBu 25,465,000,000 (intermediate goods 37.3%, capital goods
35.6%, consumer goods 27.1%). *Major import sources:* Belgium–Luxembourg 17.7%; West Germany 17.6%; Iran 11.4%; France 10.4%; Japan
6.1%; Zambia 4.8%.
Exports (1987): FBu 8,870,000,000 (coffee 80.9%, tea 6.9%, raw cotton 5.7%,
animal hides and skins 2.0%). *Major export destinations:* West Germany
31.6%; Belgium–Luxembourg 20.8%; Finland 7.3%; The Netherlands 5.8%;
France 4.8%; United States 3.5%; Italy 3.2%.

Transport and communications

Transport. Railroads: none. Roads (1988): total length 3,666 mi, 5,900 km
(paved 7%). Vehicles (1987): passenger cars 9,892; trucks and other vehicles
8,685. Merchant marine (1979): vessels (100 gross tons and over) 1; total
gross tonnage 385. Air transport (1986): passenger arrivals 23,711, departures 24,947; cargo loaded 2,390 short tons (2,168 metric tons), unloaded
4,661 short tons (4,228 metric tons); airports (1989) with scheduled flights 2.
Communications. Daily newspapers (1988): total number 1; total circulation
20,000; circulation per 1,000 population 3.9. Radio (1986): total number
of receivers 230,000 (1 per 21 persons). Television (1988): total number of
receivers 4,500 (1 per 1,180 persons). Telephones (1986): 7,910 (1 per 622
persons).

Education and health

Education (1986)

	schools	teachers	students	student/ teacher ratio
Primary (age 6–11)	1,171	7,256	452,424	62.3
Secondary (age 12–18)	62[11]	857	16,798	19.6
Voc., teacher tr.	47[11]	1,051	13,280	12.6
Higher[11]	8	468	2,783	5.9

Educational attainment, n.a. *Literacy* (1982): total population age 10 and
over literate 991,600 (33.8%); males literate 601,500 (42.8%); females literate 390,100 (25.7%).
Health (1985): physicians 178 (1 per 26,494 persons); hospital beds 5,506 (1
per 857 persons); infant mortality rate per 1,000 live births (1986–87) 114.
Food (1984–86): daily per capita caloric intake 2,270 (vegetable products 98%,
animal products 2%); 91% of FAO recommended minimum requirement.

Military

Total active duty personnel (1989): 5,700 (army 96.5%, navy 0.9%, air force
2.6%). *Military expenditure as percent of GNP* (1987): 3.1% (world 5.4%);
per capita expenditure U.S.$7.

[1]Constitution suspended on Sept. 3, 1987. [2]January 1. [3]Detail does not add to total
given because of rounding. [4]Based on land area. [5]1982. [6]Data shown is for four
provinces only. [7]At prices of 1986. [8]Nonagricultural activities in Bujumbura only;
includes family allowances, base year 1980 = 100. [9]Weights of consumer price index
components. [10]Import figures are f.o.b. in balance of trade and c.i.f. in commodities
and trading partners. [11]1985–86.

Cameroon

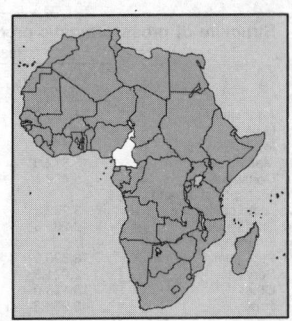

Official name: République du Cameroun (French); Republic of Cameroon (English).
Form of government: unitary single-party republic with one legislative house (National Assembly [180]).
Head of state and government: President.
Capital: Yaoundé.
Official languages: French; English.
Official religion: none.
Monetary unit: 1 CFA franc (CFAF) = 100 centimes; valuation (Oct. 2, 1989) 1 U.S.$ = CFAF 317.90; 1 £ = CFAF 514.37.

Area and population		area		population
				1984
Provinces	Capitals	sq mi	sq km	estimate
Adamaoua	Ngaoundéré	23,979	62,105	355,800
Centre	Yaoundé	26,655	69,035	1,764,400
Est	Bertoua	42,086	109,002	420,000
Extrême-Nord	Maroua	12,477	32,316	1,400,000
Littoral	Douala	7,810	20,229	1,829,900
Nord	Garoua	26,134	67,686	508,200
Nord-Ouest	Bamenda	6,722	17,409	1,009,100
Ouest	Bafoussam	5,360	13,883	1,197,700
Sud	Ebolowa	18,200	47,137	356,400
Sud-Ouest	Buea	9,540	24,709	700,900
LAND AREA		178,963	463,511	9,542,400
INLAND WATER		751	1,947	
TOTAL AREA		179,714	465,458	

Demography

Population (1989): 11,407,000.
Density (1989)[1]: persons per sq mi 63.7, persons per sq km 24.6.
Urban–rural (1985): urban 43.8%; rural 56.2%.
Sex distribution (1986): male 49.90%; female 50.10%.
Age breakdown (1986): under 15, 45.2%; 15–29, 24.9%; 30–44, 15.4%; 45–59, 8.9%; 60 and over, 5.6%.
Population projection: (2000) 15,387,000; (2010) 19,997,000.
Doubling time: 27 years.
Ethnic composition (1983): Fang 19.6%; Bamileke and Bamum 18.5%; Duala, Luanda, and Basa 14.7%; Fulani 9.6%; Tikar 7.4%; Mandara 5.7%; Maka 4.9%; Chamba 2.4%; Mbum 1.3%; Hausa 1.2%; French 0.2%; other 14.5%.
Religious affiliation (1980): Roman Catholic 35%; Protestant 18%; animist 25%; Muslim 22%.
Major cities (1985): Douala 852,700; Yaoundé 583,500; Nkongsamba 105,200; Maroua 100,200; Garoua 96,200.

Vital statistics

Birth rate per 1,000 population (1985–90): 41.6 (world avg. 27.1).
Death rate per 1,000 population (1985–90): 15.6 (world avg. 9.9).
Natural increase rate per 1,000 population (1985–90): 26.0 (world avg. 17.2).
Total fertility rate (avg. births per childbearing woman; 1985–90): 5.8.
Life expectancy at birth (1985–90): male 49.0 years; female 53.0 years.
Major causes of death per 100,000 population: n.a.; however, major health problems include measles, malaria, tuberculosis of respiratory system, anemias, meningitis, intestinal obstruction and hernia, avitaminoses and other nutritional deficiency diseases.

National economy

Budget (1988–89). Revenue: CFAF 600,000,000,000 (direct taxes 31.9%; indirect taxes 29.0%; petroleum royalties 25.0%; customs duties 21.4%; registration and stamp duties 6.0%; receipts for services 4.3%). Expenditures: CFAF 600,000,000,000 (current expenditure 50.0%, of which education 11.1%, defense 7.6%, health 4.0%, administration 4.0%, finance 2.9%).
Gross national product (1987): U.S.$10,441,000,000 (U.S.$960 per capita).

Structure of gross domestic product and labour force				
	1984–85		1985	
	in value CFAF '000,000,000	% of total value	labour force	% of labour force
Agriculture	790.4	20.6	2,900,871	74.0
Mining	629.7	16.4	1,793	0.1
Manufacturing	422.4	11.0	174,498	4.5
Construction	227.6	5.9	66,684	1.7
Public utilities	37.7	1.0	3,522	0.1
Transp. and commun.	230.7	6.0	51,688	1.3
Trade	564.6	14.7	154,014	3.9
Finance	455.3	11.9	8,009	0.2
Public admin., defense	248.8	6.5 }	292,922	7.5
Services	89.6	2.3 }		
Other	142.1[2]	3.7[2]	263,634	6.7
TOTAL	3,838.9	100.0	3,917,635	100.0

Household income and expenditure. Average household size (1980) 5.2; average annual income per household[3] (1983): U.S.$420; sources of income: n.a.; expenditure[3] (1983): food 33.6%, clothing and footwear 16.3%, housing 14.6%, transport and communications 10.5%, recreation 5.1%, health 5.0%.
Tourism (1987): receipts from visitors U.S.$47,000,000; expenditures by nationals abroad U.S.$150,000,000.

Population economically active (1985): total 3,917,635; activity rate of total population 38.5% (participation rates: ages 15–69, 66.3%; female 38.5%; unemployed, n.a.).

Price and earnings indexes (1985 = 100)							
	1982	1983	1984	1985	1986	1987	1988
Consumer price index	76.0	88.7	98.7	100.0	103.2	113.2	122.9
Earnings index	...	...	...	...	...	...	...

Public debt (external, outstanding; 1987): U.S.$2,785,000,000.
Production (metric tons except as noted). Agriculture, forestry, fishing (1987): sugarcane 1,289,000, plantains 986,000, vegetables and melons 429,000, cassava 420,000, millet 400,000, yams 400,000, corn (maize) 380,000, potatoes 172,000, sweet potatoes 150,000, peanuts (groundnuts) 140,000, rice 123,000, cocoa 120,000, dry beans 116,000, palm oil 98,000, bananas 67,000, palm kernels 35,000; livestock (number of live animals) 4,400,000 cattle, 2,500,000 sheep, 2,450,000 goats, 1,200,000 pigs; roundwood 12,447,000 cu m; fish catch 82,529. Mining and quarrying (1986): marble 331,000; pozzolana 168,435; aluminum 83,810; limestone 78,260; tin ore and concentrate 13.0. Manufacturing (1986): cement 779,328; palm oil 87,497; soap 30,630; footwear 3,500,910 pairs; sawnwood 774,540 cu m; shrimp 245,886 kg; beer 4,314,000 hectolitres; soft drinks 859,463 hectolitres. Construction (1983): residential 230,400 sq m; nonresidential 51,100 sq m. Energy production (consumption): electricity (kW-hr; 1987) 2,392,000,000 (2,392,000,000); coal (metric tons; 1987) 1,000 (1,000); petroleum (barrels; 1987) 64,567,000 (16,137,000); petroleum products (metric tons; 1987) 1,865,000 (1,805,000); natural gas, none (n.a.).
Land use (1987): forested 53.5%; meadows and pastures 17.8%; agricultural and under permanent cultivation 15.0%; other 13.7%.

Foreign trade[4]

Balance of trade (current prices)						
	1982	1983	1984	1985	1986	1987
CFAF '000,000,000	−65.7	−94.8	−44.2	−140.8	−265.1	−228.3
% of total	9.2%	11.3%	4.8%	17.9%	32.8%	32.1%

Imports (1986): CFAF 590,439,000,000 (machinery and transport equipment 32.8%, of which road transport equipment and parts 13.5%; iron and steel 6.0%; chemical and pharmaceutical products 4.1%; textile yarn 3.5%; malt 2.5%; cement 0.9%). *Major import sources:* France 42.2%; West Germany 9.1%; Japan 7.6%; United States 4.9%; Italy 4.7%; United Kingdom 3.7%; Belgium–Luxembourg 3.4%; The Netherlands 2.7%.
Exports (1986): CFAF 541,728,000,000 (crude petroleum 35.6%; coffee 21.5%; cacao 16.1%; aluminum and aluminum products 4.1%; sawnwood and logs 3.4%; cotton yarn and fabrics 3.0%; cocoa pulp and butter 2.6%; rubber 1.1%; bananas 1.0%). *Major export destinations:* The Netherlands 27.5%; France 20.6%; United States 16.4%; West Germany 7.3%; Italy 5.7%; Nigeria 2.6%; Belgium–Luxembourg 2.2%; Japan 0.9%; United Kingdom 0.8%.

Transport and communications

Transport. Railroads (1986): route length 729 mi, 1,173 km; passenger-mi 268,000,000, passenger-km 432,000,000; short ton-mi cargo 518,000,000, metric ton-km cargo 756,000,000. Roads (1987): total length 32,444 mi, 52,214 km (paved 6%). Vehicles (1986): passenger cars 86,800; trucks and buses 32,700. Merchant marine (1988): vessels (100 gross tons and over) 46; total deadweight tonnage 71,802. Air transport (1985): passenger-mi 360,000,000, passenger-km 580,000,000; short ton-mi cargo 76,000,000, metric ton-km cargo 111,000,000; airports (1989) with scheduled flights 10.
Communications. Daily newspapers (1988): 1; total circulation 66,000; circulation per 1,000 population 6.0. Radio (1988): total number of receivers 1,006,581 (1 per 11 persons). Television (1988): total number of receivers 5,000 (1 per 2,216 persons). Telephones (1987): 61,567 (1 per 179 persons).

Education and health

Education (1986–87)	schools	teachers	students	student/ teacher ratio
Primary (age 6–14)	5,920	35,431	1,723,024	48.6
Secondary (age 15–24)	388	9,289	288,515	31.1
Voc., teacher tr.	220	4,449	93,857	21.1
Higher	5	975	19,586	20.1

Educational attainment (1976). Percent of population age 15 and over having: no schooling 51.1%; primary education 41.7%; some postprimary 0.2%; secondary 5.7%; some postsecondary 0.3%; higher 0.2%; other 0.8%.
Literacy (1980): total population age 15 and over literate 2,344,100 (55.2%); males literate 1,453,200 (70.2%); females literate 890,900 (41.0%).
Health: physicians (1982) 604 (1 per 14,800 persons); hospital beds (1984–85) 26,832 (1 per 377 persons); infant mortality rate per 1,000 live births (1985–90) 94.0.
Food (1987): daily per capita caloric intake 2,068 ([1984–86] vegetable products 95%, animal products 5%); (1984) 90% of FAO recommended minimum.

Military

Total active duty personnel (1989): 1,600 (army 86.8%, navy 9.2%, air force 4.0%). *Military expenditure as percent of GNP* (1987): 1.9% (world 5.4%); per capita expenditure U.S.$24.

---

[1]Based on land area. [2]Includes import duties less imputed bank service charges. [3]Capital city only. [4]Import figures are f.o.b. in balance of trade and c.i.f. for commodities and trading partners.

Canada

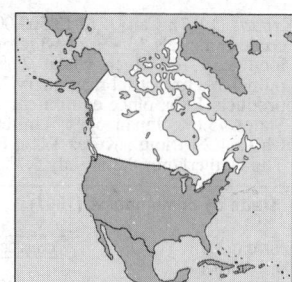

Official name: Canada.
Form of government: federal multiparty parliamentary state with two legislative houses (Senate [104]; House of Commons [295]).
Chief of state: British Monarch represented by governor-general.
Head of government: Prime Minister.
Capital: Ottawa.
Official languages: English; French.
Official religion: none.
Monetary unit: 1 Canadian dollar (Can$) = 100 cents; valuation (Oct. 2, 1989) 1 U.S.$ = Can$1.18; 1 £ = Can$1.91.

Area and population		area		population
				1989
Provinces	**Capitals**	sq mi	sq km	estimate[1]
Alberta	Edmonton	248,800	644,390	2,423,200
British Columbia	Victoria	358,971	929,730	3,044,200
Manitoba	Winnipeg	211,723	548,360	1,083,300
New Brunswick	Fredericton	27,834	72,090	717,600
Newfoundland	Saint John's	143,510	371,690	569,200
Nova Scotia	Halifax	20,402	52,840	885,700
Ontario	Toronto	344,090	891,190	9,546,200
Prince Edward Island	Charlottetown	2,185	5,660	130,000
Quebec	Quebec	523,859	1,356,790	6,679,000
Saskatchewan	Regina	220,348	570,700	1,007,100
Territories				
Northwest Territories	Yellowknife	1,271,442	3,293,020	53,100
Yukon Territory	Whitehorse	184,931	478,970	25,700
TOTAL LAND AREA		3,558,096	9,215,430	26,164,200[2]
INLAND WATER		291,579	755,180	
TOTAL AREA		3,849,675	9,970,610	

Demography

Population (1989): 26,189,000.
Density[3] (1989): persons per sq mi 7.4, persons per sq km 2.8.
Urban-rural (1985): urban 75.9%; rural 24.1%.
Sex distribution (1988): male 49.32%; female 50.68%.
Age breakdown[4] (1986): under 15, 21.4%; 15–29, 25.8%; 30–44, 22.9%; 45–59, 14.9%; 60–74, 10.9%; 75 and over, 4.1%.
Population projection: (2000) 29,110,000; (2010) 32,047,000.
Doubling time: 99 years.
Ethnic origin (1986): British 34.4%; French 25.7%; German 3.6%; Italian 2.8%; Ukrainian 1.7%; Amerindian and Inuktitut (Eskimo) 1.5%; Chinese 1.4%; Dutch 1.4%; multiple origin and other 27.5%[5].
Religious affiliation (1981): Roman Catholic 46.5%; Protestant 41.2%; Eastern Orthodox 1.5%; Jewish 1.2%; Muslim 0.4%; Hindu 0.3%; Sikh 0.3%; nonreligious 7.4%; other 1.2%.
Major metropolitan areas (1986): Toronto 3,427,168; Montreal 2,921,357; Vancouver 1,380,729; Ottawa–Hull 819,263; Edmonton 785,465; Calgary 671,326; Winnipeg 625,304; Quebec 603,267; Hamilton 557,029; Saint Catharines–Niagara 343,258.

Other metropolitan areas (1986)					
	population		population		population
Chicoutimi–		London	342,302	Sherbrooke	129,960
Jonquière	158,458	Oshawa	203,543	Sudbury	148,877
Halifax	295,990	Regina	186,521	Trois Rivières	128,888
Kingston	122,350	Saint John's	161,901	Victoria	255,547
Kitchener	311,195	Saskatoon	200,665	Windsor	253,988

Place of birth (1986): 84.2% native-born; 15.8% foreign-born, of which United Kingdom 3.2%, other European 6.6%, Asian countries 3.2%, other 2.8%.
Mobility (1986). Population living in the same residence as in 1981: 56.3%; different residence, same municipality 24.2%; same province, different municipality 13.5%; different province 4.0%.
Households (1986). Total number of households 8,991,670. Average household size 2.8; (1985) 1 person 20.5%, 2 persons 30.8%, 3 persons 18.0%, 4 persons 18.8%, 5 persons 8.1%, 6 or more persons 3.8%. Family households: 6,635,000 (73.8%), nonfamily 2,356,670 (26.2%, of which 1 person 21.5%).
Immigration (1988): permanent immigrants admitted 159,437, from Asia 50.1%, Europe 25.0%, Central and South America 13.9%, Africa 5.8%, United States 4.0%, other 1.2%; refugee arrivals (1986) 18,282.

Vital statistics

Birth rate per 1,000 population (1987): 14.4 (world avg. 27.1); (1985) legitimate 83.8%; illegitimate 16.2%.
Death rate per 1,000 population (1987): 7.2 (world avg. 9.9).
Natural increase rate per 1,000 population (1987): 7.2 (world avg. 17.2).
Total fertility rate (avg. births per childbearing woman; 1985): 1.7.
Marriage rate per 1,000 population (1986): 7.4.
Divorce rate per 1,000 population (1985): 2.4.
Life expectancy at birth (1983–85): male 72.9 years; female 79.8 years.
Major causes of death per 100,000 population (1986): diseases of the circulatory system 313.2; malignant neoplasms (cancers) 187.5; diseases of the respiratory system 59.0; accidents and violence 54.3.

Social indicators

Educational attainment (1986). Percent of population age 25 and over having: no formal schooling, negligible; less than complete primary edu-

---

cation or complete primary 20.6%; secondary 35.0%; postsecondary vocational 25.1%; university without degree 8.3%; completed university 11.0%; graduates by level (1987): 4-year higher degree 101,960, master's 15,790, doctorate 2,385.

Distribution of income (1986)				
percent of national income by quintile				
1	2	3	4	5 (highest)
4.7%	10.4%	17.0%	24.9%	43.0%

Quality of working life (1986). Average workweek: 38.8 hours (3.1% overtime). Annual rate per 100,000 workers for (1985): injury, accident, or industrial illness 4,501; death 4.8[6]. Proportion of labour force insured for damages or income loss resulting from (1984): injury 99%; permanent disability 99%; death 99%. Average days lost to labour stoppages per 1,000 employee-workdays (1988): 1.5. Average duration of journey to work (1983): 23 minutes[7] (17.3% public transportation, 72.8% automobile, 9.9% other). Rate per 1,000 workers of discouraged (unemployed no longer seeking work; 1983): 10.5.
Access to services (1985). Proportion of households having access to: electricity 100.0%; public water supply 99.7%; public sewage collection 99.3%; public fire protection (1978) 90.4%.
Social participation. Eligible voters participating in last national election (1988): *c.* 77%. Population over 18 years of age participating in voluntary work (1980): 15.0%. Union membership in total work force (1988): 29.6%. Practicing religious population in total affiliated population: 92.7%.
Social deviance (1987). Offense rate per 100,000 population for: violent crime 856; property crime 5,731, of which auto theft 340, burglary and housebreaking 1,421. Incidence per 100,000 in general population of: alcoholism (1981) 2,405; drug and substance abuse 322.4; suicide (1986) 14.5.
Leisure (1985). Favourite leisure activities (hours weekly): television 23.5; social time 10.7[8]; reading 3.5[8]; recreation and culture 2.7[8].
Material well-being (1986). Households possessing: automobile 81.9%; telephone 98.1%; radio 99.1%; television receiver 98.6%; refrigerator 99.2%; central air conditioner 17.8%; automatic washing machine 77.4%; cable television 62.4%[9]; videocassette recorders 35.1%.

National economy

Gross national product (1987): U.S.$390,052,000,000 (U.S.$15,080 per capita).

Structure of gross domestic product and labour force				
	1988		1987	
	in value Can$'000,000	% of total value	labour force	% of labour force
Agriculture	13,885	3.5	644,000	4.9
Mining	23,751	6.0	201,000	1.5
Manufacturing	78,117	19.7	2,231,000	17.0
Construction	28,182	7.1	800,000	6.1
Public utilities	11,993	3.0	126,000	1.0
Transportation and communications	31,771	8.0	838,000	6.4
Trade	48,109	12.2	2,292,000	17.5
Finance	58,387	14.8	1,338,000	10.2
Pub. admin., defense	23,794	6.0 }	4,556,000	34.7
Services	77,907	19.7 }		
Other	—	—	96,000[10]	0.7[10]
TOTAL	395,896[11]	100.0	13,121,000[2]	100.0

Budget (1988–89). Revenue: Can$103,305,000,000 (personal income tax 44.0%; sales tax 16.2%; corporation income tax 11.6%; excise taxes and import duties 7.3%). Expenditures: Can$132,250,000,000 (education, health, and welfare 44.9%; public debt interest 24.2%; economic development 10.1%; defense 8.4%).
National debt (1988): Can$269,224,000,000.
Tourism (1988): receipts from visitors U.S.$4,655,000,000; expenditures by nationals abroad U.S.$6,316,000,000.

Manufacturing, mining, and construction enterprises (1987)			
	no. of enterprises[9]	no. of employees[6]	hourly wages as a % of avg. of all wages[6]	annual shipments (Can$'000,000)
Manufacturing				
Food and beverages	3,532	220,168	90.3	42,384.1
Transport equipment	1,471	187,088	119.4	41,644.2
Paper and related products	688	121,426	125.3	23,305.4
Chemicals and related products	1,256	92,048	114.8	20,157.0
Primary metals	435	99,667	127.1	18,884.2
Metal fabricating	5,537	149,490	96.5	16,332.6
Electrical and electronics products	1,471	112,564	105.0	15,775.2
Wood	3,476	95,822	93.8	14,882.1
Printing, publishing, and related products	5,443	179,480	105.4	11,238.5
Machinery	1,815	81,749	101.3	8,972.2
Nonmetallic mineral products	1,532	38,763[7]	...	7,511.5
Rubber and plastic	1,239	66,761	91.8	7,174.5
Clothing	2,497	88,840	56.5	6,336.2
Furniture and fixtures	1,727	57,960	73.5	3,988.6
Textile	1,017	62,330	82.3	3,100.8
Tobacco products industries	25	8,711	90.5	1,813.6
Leather industries	384	20,632	58.4	1,353.4
Mining	121	145,994	149.3	20,545.0[6]
Construction	...	395,676	112.3	21,428.0[6]

Production (metric tons except as noted). Agriculture, forestry, fishing (1987): wheat 26,342,100, barley 14,382,100, corn (maize) 7,007,500, rapeseed 3,851,500, oats 2,995,200, potatoes 2,972,900, vegetables 1,903,000 (of which tomatoes 575,000, carrots 262,000, cabbage 155,000, onions 130,-000), soybeans 1,266,500, sugar beets 959,000, linseed 787,600, rye 492,600, apples 477,000, dry peas 465,000, hops 450,000, lentils 328,000; livestock (number of live animals; 1988) 12,061,000 cattle, 10,847,000 pigs, 679,000

sheep, 116,000,000[12] poultry; roundwood 191,224,000 cu m; pelts 4,661,-945 units; fish catch 1,571,603. Mining and quarrying (1988): iron ore 38,742,000; zinc 1,254,000; copper 722,000; lead 334,000; nickel 214,000; uranium 13,233; molybdenum 12,388; silver 1,527; gold 4,110,660 troy oz. Manufacturing (1988): wood pulp 24,935,000[12]; crude steel 15,180,000; cement 11,928,000; newsprint 9,969,600; pig iron 9,492,000; sulfuric acid 3,898,000[6]; caustic soda 1,769,000[6]; synthetic rubber 179,800[12]; road motor vehicles 1,635,014 units[12], of which passenger cars 809,887 units, truck and buses 825,127 units; washing machines and dryers 830,520 units[6]; refrigerators 568,960 units[6]; footwear 38,774,000 pairs[12]; beer 235,470,000 hectolitres[6]. Construction (building permits; 1987): residential Can$18,-647,000,000; nonresidential Can$11,899,000,000.

Service enterprises (1988)

	no. of enterprises	no. of employees[13]	weekly wages as a % of all wages	annual sales (Can$'000,000)
Retail trade				
Motor vehicle dealers	...	79,800	...	35,917
Food stores	...	213,400	...	35,187
Service stations	...	63,700	...	14,612
Department stores	...	14	...	13,271
Clothing stores	...	50,200	...	7,486
Pharmacies	...	52,400	...	7,459
Furniture and appliance stores	...	62,100	...	4,447
Automotive stores	...	31,500	...	3,767
General merchandise	...	231,700[14]	...	3,109
Sporting goods	...	...	...	2,669
General stores	...	14	...	2,415
Hardware stores	...	17,300	...	1,824
Shoe stores	...	18,400	...	1,599
Jewelry stores	...	14,000	...	1,215
Variety stores	...	45,100	...	1,057

Energy production (consumption): electricity (kW-hr; 1987) 496,335,000,000 (452,379,000,000); coal (metric tons; 1987) 61,207,000 (50,670,000); crude petroleum (barrels; 1987) 560,510,000 (475,114,000); petroleum products (metric tons; 1987) 78,395,000 (69,732,000); natural gas (cu m; 1987) 85,-391,000,000 (57,558,000,000).

Population economically active (1987): total 13,121,000; activity rate of total population 51.2% (participation rates: ages 15–64, 75.1%; female 43.4%; unemployed 8.8%).

Price and earnings indexes (1985 = 100)

	1982	1983	1984	1985	1986	1987	1988
Consumer price index	87.1	92.2	96.2	100.0	104.2	108.7	113.1
Monthly earnings index	85.0	90.9	96.3	100.0	103.1	105.8	110.7

Household income and expenditure. Average household size (1986) 2.8; average annual income per family (1985) Can$38,100 (U.S.$27,400); sources of income (1985): wages and salaries 64.2%, transfer payments 15.0%, self-employment 8.2%, other 12.6%; expenditure (1985): housing 23.1%, food 17.9%, transportation and communications 15.9%, household durable goods 8.8%, recreation 7.6%, clothing 6.3%, health 3.8%, education 2.9%.

Financial aggregates

	1983	1984	1985	1986	1987	1988	1989[15]
Exchange rate, Can$ per:							
U.S. dollar	1.23	1.29	1.37	1.39	1.33	1.23	1.18
£	1.88	1.50	1.78	2.04	2.18	2.19	1.91
SDR	1.30	1.30	1.54	1.69	1.84	1.60	1.51
International reserves (U.S.$)							
Total (excl. gold; '000,000)	3,465	2,491	2,503	3,251	7,277	15,391	15,694
SDRs ('000,000)	21	72	218	247	399	1,369	1,332
Reserve pos. in IMF ('000,000)	703	678	711	686	661	505	471
Foreign exchange ('000,000)	2,741	1,741	1,574	2,318	6,218	13,517	13,890
Gold ('000,000 fine troy oz)	20.17	20.14	20.11	19.72	18.52	17.14	16.72
% world reserves	2.13	2.13	2.13	2.12	2.12	1.81	1.77
Interest and prices							
Central bank discount (%)	10.04	10.16	9.49	8.49	8.66	11.17	12.40[16]
Gov't. bond yield (%)	11.79	12.75	11.04	9.52	9.95	10.22	9.90[16]
Industrial share prices (1980 = 100)	85.4	84.5	100.0	110.3	128.8	116.4[17]	...
Balance of payments (U.S.$'000,000)							
Balance of visible trade,	14,959	16,558	13,287	8,078	8,755	8,479	
of which:							
Imports, f.o.b.	60,672	72,328	79,917	81,079	88,854	106,153	
Exports, f.o.b.	75,631	88,986	90,204	89,157	97,609	114,632	
Balance of invisibles	−13,429	−14,768	−14,033	−15,800	−17,555	−12,639	
Balance of payments, current account	2,487	2,569	−877	−6,657	−7,235	−9,114	

Land use (1987): forested 38.4%; meadows and pastures 3.5%; agricultural and under permanent cultivation 5.0%; built-on, wasteland, and other 53.1%.

Foreign trade

Balance of trade (current prices)

	1983	1984	1985	1986	1987	1988
Can$'000,000,000	19.4	16.6	14.3	7.8	10.1	5.4
% of total	11.8%	8.0%	6.4%	3.3%	4.1%	1.9%

Imports (1987): Can$116,424,500,000 (road motor vehicles and parts 25.5%; food, feed, beverages, and tobacco 5.7%; chemicals 5.4%; crude petroleum 2.7%; nonferrous metals 2.1%; iron and steel 1.8%). *Major import sources:* United States 68.0%; Japan 6.7%; United Kingdom 3.7%; West Germany 3.0%; Taiwan 1.7%; South Korea 1.6%; France 1.3%; Hong Kong 1.0%; Mexico 1.0%.

Exports (1987): Can$121,413,500,000 (road motor vehicles and parts 26.1%; crude materials 13.8%, of which crude petroleum 4.0%, natural gas 2.0%; food 8.5%, of which wheat 2.6%; newsprint 5.0%; lumber 4.7%; wood pulp 4.5%; industrial machinery 2.8%; aluminum 2.3%; petroleum and coal products 1.8%; office equipment 1.7%). *Major export destinations:* United States 75.6%; Japan 5.8%; United Kingdom 2.3%; West Germany 1.2%; China 1.2%; South Korea 1.0%; Belgium–Luxembourg 0.9%; France 0.8%; The Netherlands 0.8%; Italy 0.7%; U.S.S.R. 0.7%.

Trade by commodities (1987)

SITC Group	imports Can$'000,000	%	exports Can$'000,000	%
00 Food and live animals	6,158.2	5.3	9,881.9	7.9
01 Beverages and tobacco	580.9	0.5	375.3	0.3
02 Crude materials, excluding fuels	4,415.3	3.8	19,888.8	15.9
03 Mineral fuels, lubricants, and related materials	5,693.4	4.9	13,009.0	10.4
04 Animal and vegetable oils, fat, and waxes	...	...	...	...
05 Chemicals and related products, n.e.s.	7,087.7	6.1	6,254.4	5.0
06 Basic manufactures	13,478.3	11.6	20,889.5	16.7
07 Machinery and transport equipment	63,548.1	54.7	47,658.2	38.1
08 Miscellaneous manufactured articles	11,735.4	10.1	4,628.2	3.7
09 Goods not classified by kind	3,369.6	2.9	2,501.7	2.0
TOTAL	116,076.0[2]	100.0[2]	125,087.0	100.0

Direction of trade (1987)[18]

	imports Can$'000,000	%	exports Can$'000,000	%
Africa	779.9	0.7	982.6	0.8
Asia	13,011.0	11.1	12,443.0	9.8
Americas	81,316.8	69.2	95,917.4	75.2
United States	77,504.5	65.9	92,877.2	72.8
South America	2,103.1	1.8	1,705.3	1.3
Central America	1,709.2	1.4	1,334.9	1.0
Europe	15,866.7	13.5	11,543.5	9.0
EEC	13,239.8	11.3	9,327.4	7.3
U.S.S.R. and Eastern Europe	308.1	0.3	969.6	0.8
Other Europe	2,318.8	2.0	1,246.5	1.1
Oceania	756.6	0.6	815.0	0.6
TOTAL	117,552.6	100.0	127,515.6	100.0

Transport and communications

Transport. Railroads (1987): length 58,125 mi, 93,544 km; passenger-mi 1,193,000,000, passenger-km 1,920,000,000; short ton-mi cargo 174,264,-000,000, metric ton-km cargo 255,264,000,000. Roads (1986): total length 174,140 mi, 280,251 km (paved 57%). Vehicles (1986): passenger cars 11,-477,314; trucks and buses 3,212,132. Merchant marine (1988): vessels (100 gross tons and over) 1,225; total deadweight tonnage 3,379,396. Air transport (1988): passenger-mi 32,709,400,000, passenger-km 52,640,700,000; short ton-mi cargo 838,649,700[19], metric ton-km cargo 1,224,400,000[19]; airports (1989) with scheduled flights 61.
Communications. Daily newspapers (1988): total number 109; total circulation 5,520,000; circulation per 1,000 population 213. Radio (1988): total number of receivers 22,577,806 (1 per 1.2 persons). Television (1988): total number of receivers 15,709,000 (1 per 1.7 persons). Telephones (1987): 20,126,000 (1 per 1.3 persons).

Education and health

Education (1987–88)

	schools	teachers	students	student/ teacher ratio
Primary (age 6–14)	15,512	273,190	3,017,900	18.1
Secondary (age 14–18)			1,501,900	
Postsecondary and higher	266	59,300	795,730	13.4

Literacy (1975): total population age 14 and over literate 16,185,000 (95.6%); males literate 8,003,000 (95.6%); females literate 8,182,000 (95.7%).
Health (1987): physicians 51,275 (1 per 467 persons); hospital beds 171,928[20] (1 per 148 persons); infant mortality rate per 1,000 live births 7.3.
Food (1984–86): daily per capita caloric intake 3,425 (vegetable products 66%; animal products 34%); 129% of FAO recommended minimum requirement.

Military

Total active duty personnel (1989): 89,000 (army 26.4%, navy 19.2%, air force 27.2%, not identified by service 27.2%). *Military expenditure as percent of GNP* (1987): 2.2% (world 5.4%); per capita expenditure U.S.$342.

[1]April 1. [2]Detail does not add to total given because of rounding. [3]Based on land area. [4]Excludes 45,000 population in Indian reserves and settlements. [5]Includes 4.6% who are of both French and British origin. [6]1986. [7]Urban areas. [8]1981. [9]1985. [10]Includes 46,000 unemployed persons previously unemployed. [11]At factor cost in 1981 prices; GDP at current prices is Can$484,620,000,000. [12]1987. [13]1984. [14]Department and general stores included with general merchandise. [15]September. [16]August. [17]July. [18]Totals include Can$5,821,600,000 in imports and Can$5,814,100,000 in exports (4.7% of all foreign trade; mostly special transactions) not distributable by region. [19]Air Canada and Canadian Airlines only. [20]Excludes federal and private hospitals.

Cape Verde

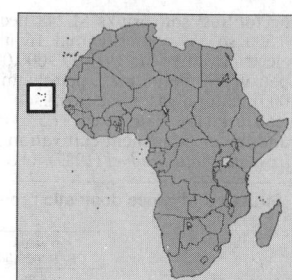

Official name: República de Cabo Verde (Republic of Cape Verde).
Form of government: unitary single-party republic with one legislative house (People's National Assembly [83]).
Chief of state: President.
Head of government: Prime Minister.
Capital: Praia.
Official language: Portuguese.
Official religion: none.
Monetary unit: 1 escudo (C.V. Esc) = 100 centavos; valuation (Oct. 2, 1989) 1 U.S.\$ = C.V. Esc 82.21; 1 £ = C.V. Esc 133.02.

Area and population

Island Groups Islands/Counties[1] Counties	Capitals	area sq mi	area sq km	population 1980 census
Leeward Islands		696[2]	1,803	182,890
Brava	Nova Sintra	26	67	6,869
Fogo	São Filipe	184	476	30,194
Maio	Porto Inglês	104	269	4,076
Santiago		383	991	141,751
Praia	Praia	153	396	56,133
Santa Catarina	Assomada	94	243	39,672
Santa Cruz	Pedra Badejo	58	149	22,212
Tarrafal	Tarrafal	78	203	23,734
Windward Islands		861[2]	2,230	106,137
Boavista	Sal Rei	239	620	3,379
Sal	Santa Maria	83	216	5,836
Santo Antão		300	779	42,367
Paúl	Pombas	21	54	7,863
Porto Novo	Porto Novo	215	558	12,771
Ribeira Grande	Ponta do Sol	64	167	21,733
São Nicolau	Ribeira Brava	150	388	13,121
São Vicente	Mindelo	88	227	41,434
TOTAL		1,557	4,033	289,027

Demography

Population (1989): 337,000.
Density (1989): persons per sq mi 216.4, persons per sq km 83.6.
Urban–rural (1980): urban 35.1%; rural 64.9%.
Sex distribution (1985): male 46.32%; female 53.68%.
Age breakdown (1985): under 15, 45.6%; 15–29, 31.8%; 30–44, 7.9%; 45–59, 8.0%; 60–74, 4.6%; 75 and over, 2.1%.
Population projection: (2000) 412,000; (2010) 489,000.
Doubling time: 29 years.
Ethnic composition (1986): mixed 71%; black 28%; white 1%.
Religious affiliation (1985): Roman Catholic 97.8%; Protestant and other 2.2%.
Major cities (1980): Praia 49,500[3]; Mindelo 36,746; São Filipe 4,370.

Vital statistics

Birth rate per 1,000 population (1987): 32.1 (world avg. 27.1); (1975) legitimate 55.2%; illegitimate 44.8%.
Death rate per 1,000 population (1987): 7.7 (world avg. 9.9).
Natural increase rate per 1,000 population (1987): 24.4 (world avg. 17.2).
Total fertility rate (avg. births per childbearing woman; 1980–85): 2.6.
Marriage rate per 1,000 population (1975): 5.4.
Divorce rate per 1,000 population: n.a.
Life expectancy at birth (1987): male 63.0 years; female 67.0 years.
Major causes of death per 100,000 population (1980): enteritis and other diarrheal diseases 85.5; heart disease 51.9; cerebrovascular disease 45.7; malignant neoplasms (cancers) 43.8; measles and other infectious and parasitic diseases 34.6; pneumonia 27.2; bronchitis, emphysema, and asthma 20.4; avitaminoses and other nutritional deficiencies 14.5.

National economy

Budget. Revenue (1987): C.V. Esc 3,428,939,000 (indirect taxes 38.2%, of which import duties 15.4%; direct taxes 21.2%, of which taxes from industry 7.2%; receipts from petroleum 3.1%). Expenditures (1984): C.V. Esc 2,134,500,000 (no breakdown available).
Public debt (external, outstanding; 1987): U.S.\$120,000,000.
Tourism: n.a.
Production (metric tons except as noted). Agriculture, forestry, fishing (1988): sugarcane 16,000, pulses 13,000, coconuts 10,000, fruit except melons 10,000, corn (maize) 8,000, sweet potatoes 6,000, vegetables including melons 6,000, bananas 5,000, cassava 4,000, potatoes 3,000, dates 2,000; livestock (number of live animals) 80,000 goats, 70,000 pigs, 13,000 cattle; roundwood, n.a.; fish catch (1987) 6,941, of which tuna 4,813. Mining and quarrying (1986): salt C.V. Esc 9,710,000. Manufacturing (C.V. Esc; 1987): cigars 232,253,000; flour 176,677,000; cacao powder 94,439,000[4]; canned fish 78,401,000; bread 35,530,000[4]; alcoholic beverages 25,972,000; soft drinks 7,419,000 litres. Construction (1982): residential C.V. Esc 365,800,000; nonresidential C.V. Esc 1,700,000. Energy production (consumption): electricity (kW-hr; 1987) 30,890,482 (30,876,142); coal, none (none); crude petroleum, none (none); petroleum products (metric tons; 1987) none (11,-000); natural gas, none (none).

Gross national product (at current market prices; 1987): U.S.\$170,000,000 (U.S.\$500 per capita).

Structure of gross domestic product and labour force

	1986 in value C.V. Esc '000,000	1986 % of total value	1980 labour force	1980 % of labour force
Agriculture	2,151	20.6	22,144	33.2
Manufacturing	552	5.3	1,871	2.8
Public utilities	294	2.8	336	0.5
Mining	50	0.5	535	0.8
Construction	2,125	20.4	18,873	28.3
Transportation and communications	1,289	12.4	3,411	5.1
Pub. admin., defense	924	8.9	2,128	3.2
Trade	2,568	24.6	3,930	5.9
Finance	369	3.5	226	0.4
Other	101	1.0	13,156	19.8
TOTAL	10,423	100.0	66,610	100.0

Population economically active (1980): total 66,610; activity rate of total population 22.5% (participation rates: ages 15–64, 42.9%; female 30.5%; unemployed, n.a.).

Price and earnings indexes (1975 = 100)

	1976	1977	1978	1979	1980	1981
Consumer price index	101.2	108.3	122.7	131.2	150.4	167.7
Monthly earnings index	...	...	...	...	...	...

Household income and expenditure. Average household size (1980) 4.3; income per household: n.a.; sources of income: n.a.; expenditure (1986)[5]: food 63.4%, clothing and footwear 9.2%, beverages and tobacco 6.7%, other 20.7%.
Land use (1986): forested 0.2%; meadows and pastures 6.2%; agricultural and under permanent cultivation 9.9%; other 83.7%.

Foreign trade

Balance of trade (current prices)

	1983	1984	1985	1986	1987	1988
C.V. Esc '000,000	−5,971	−6,799	−7,081	−8,240	−6,714	−7,416
% of total	92.1%	94.1%	87.1%	92.1%	85.6%	93.8%

Imports (1988): C.V. Esc 7,652,000,000 (foodstuffs and beverages 27.2%, machinery and apparatus 16.0%, transport equipment 12.4%; nonmetallic mineral products 11.5%; metal products 8.5%). *Major import sources:* Portugal 33.7%; The Netherlands 10.8%; Japan 5.8%; West Germany 5.2%; Brazil 5.0%; Sweden 4.9%.
Exports (1988): C.V. Esc 236,000,000 (bananas 36.7%, frozen tuna 30.5%, spiny lobster 9.4%, canned tuna 3.1%, refined sugar 3.0%). *Major export destinations:* Portugal 41.5%; Spain 30.3%; France 7.3%; The Netherlands 4.8%; Italy 4.3%.

Transport and communications

Transport. Railroads: none. Roads (1984): total length 1,398 mi, 2,250 km (paved 29%). Vehicles (1981): passenger cars 3,000[6], trucks and buses 1,343. Merchant marine (1988): vessels (100 gross tons and over) 35; total deadweight tonnage 25,864. Air transport (1985): passenger-mi 16,148,000, passenger-km 25,987,000; short ton-mi cargo 1,606,000, metric ton-km cargo 2,345,000; airports (1989) with scheduled flights 3.
Communications. Daily newspapers: none. Radio (1986): total number of receivers 50,000 (1 per 6.8 persons). Television: (1985): total number of receivers 500 (1 per 668 persons). Telephones (1985): 4,379 (1 per 76 persons).

Education and health

Education (1986–87)

	schools	teachers	students	student/ teacher ratio
Primary (age 7–10)	347	1,464	49,703	34.0
Secondary (age 10–17)	16	321	10,304	32.1
Voc., teacher tr.	3	53	211	4.0
Higher	...	...	...	...

Educational attainment (1980). Percent of population age 25 and over having: no formal schooling or incomplete primary education 84.2%; complete primary 12.4%; secondary 1.7%; higher 0.5%; unknown 1.2%. *Literacy* (1985): total population age 15 and over literate 73,500 (47.4%); males literate 42,500 (61.4%); females literate 31,000 (38.6%).
Health: physicians (1984) 60 (1 per 5,440 persons); hospital beds (1980) 632 (1 per 470 persons); infant mortality rate per 1,000 live births (1985) 76.5.
Food (1984–86): daily per capita caloric intake 2,729 (vegetable products 88%, animal products 12%); 116% of FAO recommended minimum requirement.

Military

Total active duty personnel (1989): 1,250 (army 80.0%, navy 16.0%, air force 4.0%). *Military expenditure as percent of GNP* (1981): 12.1% (world 5.5%); per capita expenditure U.S.\$43.

---

[1]Island/county areas are coterminous except Santiago and Santo Antão islands. [2]Detail does not add to total given because of rounding. [3]1985. [4]1986. [5]Praia only. [6]1984.

Central African Republic

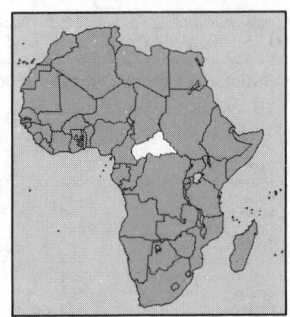

Official name: République Centrafricaine (Central African Republic).
Form of government: unitary single-party republic with one legislative house (National Assembly [52]).
Head of state and government: President.
Capital: Bangui.
Official language: French.
Official religion: none.
Monetary unit: 1 CFA franc (CFAF) = 100 centimes; valuation (Oct. 2, 1989) 1 U.S.$ = CFAF 317.90; 1 £ = CFAF 514.37.

Area and population

Prefectures	Capitals	area sq mi	area sq km	population 1987[1] estimate
Bamingui-Bangoran	Ndélé	22,471	58,200	30,230
Bangui[2]	Bangui	26	67	430,727
Basse-Kotto	Mobaye	6,797	17,604	193,368
Gribingui-Économique	Kaga-Bandoro	7,720	19,996	89,071
Haut-Mbomou	Obo	21,440	55,530	38,475
Haute-Kotto	Bria	33,456	86,650	54,821
Haute-Sangha	Berbérati	11,661	30,203	243,149
Kemo-Gribingui	Sibut	6,642	17,204	81,490
Lobaye	Mbaïki	7,427	19,235	167,241
Mbomou	Bangassou	23,610	61,150	138,283
Nana-Mambere	Bouar	10,270	26,600	205,410
Ombella-Mpoko	Bimbo	12,292	31,835	132,568
Ouaka	Bambari	19,266	49,900	225,460
Ouham	Bossangoa	19,402	50,250	280,397
Ouham-Pendé	Bozoum	12,394	32,100	250,001
Sangha-Économique	Nola	7,495	19,412	61,250
Vakaga	Birao	17,954	46,500	24,926
TOTAL		240,324[3]	622,436	2,646,867

Demography

Population (1989): 2,813,000.
Density (1989): persons per sq mi 11.7, persons per sq km 4.5.
Urban–rural (1987): urban 33.2%; rural 66.8%.
Sex distribution (1986): male 47.84%; female 52.16%.
Age breakdown (1986): under 15, 41.5%; 15–29, 25.8%; 30–44, 16.0%; 45–59, 10.4%; 60 and over, 6.3%.
Population projection: (2000) 3,566,000; (2010) 4,424,000.
Doubling time: 28 years.
Ethnic composition (1983): Banda 28.6%; Baya (Gbaya) 24.5%; Ngbandi 10.6%; Azande 9.8%; Sara 6.9%; Mbaka 4.3%; Mbum 4.1%; Kare 2.4%; French 0.1%; other 8.7%.
Religious affiliation (1980): Protestant 50.0%; Roman Catholic 33.1%; traditional 12.0%; Muslim 3.2%; Bahá'í 0.3%; other 1.4%.
Major cities (1988): Bangui 596,776; Bambari 52,092; Bouar 49,166; Berbérati 45,432; Bossangoa 41,877.

Vital statistics

Birth rate per 1,000 population (1985–90): 44.3 (world avg. 27.1); legitimate, n.a.; illegitimate, n.a.
Death rate per 1,000 population (1985–90): 19.7 (world avg. 9.9).
Natural increase rate per 1,000 population (1985–90): 24.6 (world avg. 17.2).
Total fertility rate (avg. births per childbearing woman; 1985–90): 5.9.
Marriage rate per 1,000 population: n.a.
Divorce rate per 1,000 population: n.a.
Life expectancy at birth (1985–90): male 43.9 years; female 47.1 years.
Morbidity (as percent of reported cases of illness; 1984): malaria 13.3%; dysentery, enteritis, and other intestinal diseases 12.5%; respiratory diseases 9.9%, of which pneumonia 2.7%.

National economy

Budget (1988). Revenue: CFAF 43,400,000,000 (1982; indirect taxes 52.4%, nonfiscal receipts 21.1%, direct taxes 20.3%). Expenditures: CFAF 58,150,-000,000 (1982; education and culture 13.9%, defense 8.3%, repayment of public debt 8.1%).
Public debt (external, outstanding; 1987): U.S.$520,000,000.
Tourism (1987): receipts from visitors U.S.$5,000,000; expenditures by nationals abroad U.S.$33,000,000.
Production (metric tons except as noted). Agriculture, forestry, fishing (1988): cassava 400,000, yams 202,000, peanuts (groundnuts) in shell 87,-000, bananas 86,000, plantains 66,000, corn (maize) 64,000, taro 60,000, millet 50,000, seed cotton 43,000, cotton seed 21,000, coffee 12,000, rice 12,000, cotton lint 11,000, pulses 7,000; livestock (number of live animals) 2,224,000 cattle, 1,135,000 goats, 371,000 pigs, 116,000 sheep, 3,000,000 chickens; roundwood (1987) 3,443,000 cu m; fish catch (1987) 13,000. Mining and quarrying (1988): diamonds 360,000 carats, of which 259,200 gem quality and 100,800 industrial; gold 382 kg. Manufacturing (1986): beauty products 87,119; ice cream 2,753; paints 541; leather goods 452; household aluminum articles 348; coffee 233; printed cloth 5,515,000 m; footwear 321,209 pairs; cigarettes and cigars 52,400,000 units; motorcycles 3,167 units; bicycles 2,924 units; assembled vehicles 72 units; beer 318,706

hectolitres; soft drinks 61,248 hectolitres. Construction (1984): residential 6,500 sq m; nonresidential 16 units. Energy production (consumption): electricity (kW-hr; 1987) 92,000,000 (92,000,000); coal, none (n.a.); crude petroleum, none (n.a.); petroleum products (metric tons; 1987) none (85,-000); natural gas, none (n.a.).
Land use (1987): forested 57.5%; meadows and pastures 4.8%; agricultural and under permanent cultivation 3.2%; other 34.5%.
Gross national product (1987): U.S.$912,000,000 (U.S.$330 per capita).

Structure of gross domestic product and labour force

	1986 in value CFAF '000,000	1986 % of total value	1985 labour force	1985 % of labour force
Agriculture	148,350	43.8	869,000	67.8
Mining	8,000	2.3		
Manufacturing	24,440	7.2	54,000	4.2
Construction	9,080	2.7		
Public utilities	2,610	0.8		
Transp. and commun.	14,210	4.2		
Trade	73,110	21.6		
Finance	11,900	3.5	359,000	28.0
Pub. admin., defense	45,320	13.4		
Other	1,730	0.5		
TOTAL	338,750	100.0	1,282,000	100.0

Population economically active (1985): total 1,282,000; activity rate of total population 49.8% (participation rates: over ages 15–64, 81.6%; female 47.0%; unemployed, n.a.).

Price and earnings indexes (1985 = 100)

	1982	1983	1984	1985	1986	1987	1988
Consumer price index	77.1	88.3	90.6	100.0	102.2	95.1	105.5
Earnings index	...	...	...	...	...	...	...

Household income and expenditure. Average household size (1980) 4.3; average annual income per household CFAF 91,985 (U.S.$435); sources of income: n.a.; expenditure[4] (1983): food 70.5%, clothing 9.5%, energy 6.5%, transportation and communications 4.1%, recreation 1.3%, health 1.0%, housing 0.6%.

Foreign trade

Balance of trade (current prices)

	1982	1983	1984	1985	1986	1987
U.S.$'000,000	−16.1	−11.9	−9.4	−41.7	−40.4	−31.9
% of total	7.0%	6.2%	4.9%	31.4%	25.6%	14.7%

Imports (1988–89): CFAF 38,746,000,000 (food 20.5%, chemicals and plastics 15.6%, fuels and lubricants 12.9%, machinery and transport equipment 12.7%, building materials 6.0%). *Major import sources:* France 44.1%; Cameroon 7.2%; West Germany 5.9%; Japan 5.2%; Congo 2.7%; The Netherlands 2.5%; Belgium–Luxembourg 2.3%; United States 2.0%; Zaire 1.6%.
Exports (1988–89): CFAF 20,262,000,000 (coffee 47.9%, diamonds 25.2%, wood 13.6%, tobacco 3.1%, cotton 1.2%). *Major export destinations:* France 53.3%; Belgium–Luxembourg 23.5%; Switzerland 7.2%; The Sudan 5.4%; Spain 3.0%; Zaire 1.6%; United States 1.4%; Congo 1.0%; Italy 0.9%.

Transport and communications

Transport. Railroads: none. Roads (1986): total length 12,600 mi, 20,278 km (paved 2%). Vehicles (1986): passenger cars 1,035; trucks and buses 20,000. Merchant marine: vessels (100 gross tons and over) none. Air transport (1987)[5]: passenger-mi 132,791,000, passenger-km 213,706,000; short ton-mi cargo 24,739,000, metric ton-km cargo 36,119,000; airports (1989) with scheduled flights 1.
Communications. Daily newspapers (1988): total number 1; total circulation 200; circulation per 1,000 population 0.1. Radio (1986): total number of receivers 125,000 (1 per 22 persons). Television (1983): total number of receivers 1,400 (1 per 1,817 persons). Telephones (1985): 6,952 (1 per 380 persons).

Education and health

Education (1986)

	schools	teachers	students	student/ teacher ratio
Primary (age 6–11)	1,004	4,544	274,179	60.3
Secondary (age 12–18)	41[6]	790	48,558	61.5
Voc., teacher tr.	4[6]	133	2,132	16.0
Higher[6]	...	489	2,651	5.4

Educational attainment (1975). Percent of population age 15 and over having: no formal schooling 73.5%; primary education 22.8%; lower secondary 3.0%; upper secondary 0.6%; higher 0.1%. *Literacy* (1985): total population age 15 and over literate 40.2%; males literate 53.3%; females literate 28.6%.
Health (1984): physicians 112 (1 per 21,900 persons); hospital beds 3,774 (1 per 650 persons); infant mortality rate per 1,000 live births (1985–90) 132.
Food (1984–86): daily per capita caloric intake 1,940 (vegetable products 90%, animal products 10%); 91% of FAO recommended minimum requirement.

Military

Total active duty personnel (1989): 3,800 (army 92.1%; navy, none; air force 7.9%). *Military expenditure as percent of GNP* (1983): 1.9% (world 5.8%); per capita expenditure U.S.$7.

[1]Beginning of year. [2]Autonomous commune. [3]Detail does not add to total given because of rounding. [4]Capital city only. [5]Air Afrique only. [6]1985.

Chad

Official name: République du Tchad (Republic of Chad).
Form of government: pending adoption of a constitution, republican in form with a single political party and a single advisory organ (National Consultative Assembly [30]).
Head of state and government: President.
Capital: N'Djamena.
Official languages: Arabic; French.
Official religion: none.
Monetary unit: 1 CFA franc (CFAF) = 100 centimes; valuation (Oct. 2, 1989) 1 U.S.$ = CFAF 317.90; 1 £ = CFAF 514.37.

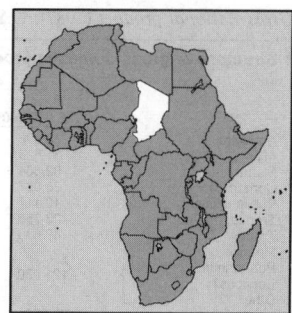

Area and population		area		population
				1984
Préfectures	Capitals	sq mi	sq km	estimate
Batha	Ati	34,285	88,800	410,000
Biltine	Biltine	18,090	46,850	200,000
Borkou-Ennedi-Tibesti	Faya	231,795	600,350	103,000
Chari-Baguirmi	N'Djamena	32,010	82,910	719,000
Guéra	Mongo	22,760	58,950	234,000
Kanem	Mao	44,215	114,520	234,000
Lac	Bol	8,620	22,320	158,000
Logone Occidental	Moundou	3,355	8,695	324,000
Logone Oriental	Doba	10,825	28,035	350,000
Mayo-Kebbi	Bongor	11,625	30,105	757,000
Moyen-Chari	Sarh	17,445	45,180	582,000
Ouaddai	Abéché	29,435	76,240	411,000
Salamat	Am Timan	24,325	63,000	121,000
Tandjilé	Laï	6,965	18,045	341,000
TOTAL		495,755[1]	1,284,000	4,944,000

Demography

Population (1989): 5,538,000.
Density (1989): persons per sq mi 11.2, persons per sq km 4.3.
Urban–rural (1986): urban 23.9%; rural 76.1%.
Sex distribution (1985): male 49.24%; female 50.76%.
Age breakdown (1985): under 15, 42.5%; 15–29, 26.0%; 30–44, 15.8%; 45–59, 9.9%; 60–74, 4.9%; 75 and over, 0.9%.
Population projection: (2000) 7,337,000; (2010) 9,491,000.
Doubling time: 28 years.
Ethnic composition (1983): Sara, Bagirmi, and Kreish 30.5%; Sudanic Arab 26.1%; Teda (Tubu) 7.3%; Mbum 6.5%; Masalit, Maba, and Mimi 6.3%; Tama 6.3%; Mubi 4.2%; Kanuri 2.3%; Hausa 2.3%; Masa 2.3%; Kotoko 2.1%; other 3.8%.
Religious affiliation (1980): Muslim 44.0%; Christian 33.0%, of which Roman Catholic 21.0%, Protestant 11.6%; traditional beliefs 22.8%; other 0.2%.
Major cities (1986): N'Djamena 511,700; Sarh 100,000; Moundou 90,000; Abéché 71,000; Kélo 27,000[2].

Vital statistics

Birth rate per 1,000 population (1985–90): 44.2 (world avg. 27.1); legitimate, n.a.; illegitimate, n.a.
Death rate per 1,000 population (1985–90): 19.5 (world avg. 9.9).
Natural increase rate per 1,000 population (1985–90): 24.7 (world avg. 17.2).
Total fertility rate (avg. births per childbearing woman; 1985–90): 5.9.
Marriage rate per 1,000 population: n.a.
Divorce rate per 1,000 population: n.a.
Life expectancy at birth (1985–90): male 43.9 years; female 47.1 years.
Major causes of death per 100,000 population: n.a.; however, major diseases include malaria, sleeping sickness, leprosy, venereal diseases, and tuberculosis.

National economy

Budget (1988). Revenue: CFAF 17,900,000,000 (1984; indirect taxes 73.2%, of which customs receipts 60.1%; direct taxes 21.7%). Expenditures: CFAF 25,600,000,000 (1984; defense 46.5%; education 10.9%; community projects 9.1%; health 3.8%).
Public debt (external, outstanding; 1987): U.S.$498,500,000.
Tourism (1987): receipts from visitors U.S.$5,000,000; expenditures by nationals abroad U.S.$35,000,000.
Production (metric tons except as noted). Agriculture, forestry, fishing (1988): millet 690,000, cassava 330,000, sugarcane 290,000, yams 240,000, seed cotton 112,000, peanuts (groundnuts) 78,000, pulses 60,000, rice 52,000, corn (maize) 47,000, sweet potatoes 46,000, dates 33,000, mangoes 33,000, potatoes 18,000, onions 14,000, sesame seed 12,000; livestock (number of live animals) 4,060,000 cattle, 2,245,000 goats, 2,200,000 sheep, 509,000 camels, 4,000,000 chickens; roundwood (1987) 3,746,000 cu m; fish catch (1987) 110,000. Mining and quarrying: clay, natron, tungsten, bauxite, and gold. Manufacturing (1988): beef and veal 53,000; refined sugar 27,000; salted, dried, or smoked fish 20,000[3]; goat meat 8,000; cattle hides 7,500; sheepskins and goatskins 3,318; mutton and lamb 1,000; wheat flour 1,000[3]; woven cotton fabrics 13,075,000 metres[3]; beer 130,000 hectolitres[3]; cigarettes 259,000,000 units[3]. Construction: n.a. Energy production (consumption): electricity (kW-hr; 1987) 51,000,000 (51,000,000); coal, none (n.a.); crude petroleum, none (n.a.); petroleum products (metric tons; 1987) none (67,000); natural gas, none (n.a.).

Household income and expenditure. Average household size (1980) 3.9; average annual income per household CFAF 96,806 (U.S.$458); sources of income: n.a.; expenditure[4] (1983): food 45.3%, health 11.9%, energy 5.8%, clothing 3.3%.
Gross domestic product (at current market prices; 1987): U.S.$805,000,000 (U.S.$150 per capita).

Structure of gross domestic product and labour force				
	1986		1985	
	in value CFAF '000,000	% of total value	labour force	% of labour force
Agriculture	133,880	46.0	1,454,000	81.2
Mining	1,350	0.5		
Manufacturing	25,220	8.7		
Construction	4,870	1.7		
Public utilities	1,370	0.5	93,000	5.2
Transportation and communications	5,570	1.9		
Trade	75,270	25.9		
Pub. admin., defense	38,380	13.2		
Finance	1,940	0.6	243,000	13.6
Other services	2,940	1.0		
TOTAL	290,790	100.0	1,790,000	100.0

Population economically active (1985): total 1,790,000; activity rate of total population 35.7% (participation rates: ages 15–64, 57.4%; female 21.7%; unemployed, n.a.).

Price and earnings indexes (1985 = 100)							
	1983	1984	1985	1986	1987	1988	1989[5]
Consumer price index	79.1	95.2	100.0	87.0	84.6	95.4	87.6
Monthly earnings index	...	...	...	...	...	...	...

Land use (1987): forested 10.4%; meadows and pastures 35.7%; agricultural and under permanent cultivation 2.5%; built-on, wasteland, and other 51.4%.

Foreign trade

Balance of trade (current prices)						
	1983	1984	1985	1986	1987	1988
CFAF '000,000	−5,068	−2,219	−41,205	−39,713	−48,277	−50,646
% of total	6.0%	1.9%	34.3%	36.8%	42.1%	37.7%

Imports (1988): CFAF 92,513,000,000 ([1983] petroleum products 16.8%; cereal products 16.8%; pharmaceutical products and chemicals 11.5%; machinery and transport equipment 8.5%, of which transport equipment 7.3%; electrical equipment 5.7%; textiles 2.9%; raw and refined sugar 2.3%). *Major import sources* (1987): France 25.6%; Cameroon 11.9%; Italy 5.3%; United States 4.2%; The Netherlands 3.9%; West Germany 2.7%; United Kingdom 0.8%.
Exports (1988): CFAF 41,867,000,000 ([1983] raw cotton 91.1%; live cattle and frozen bovine meat 1.8%; hides and skins 0.4%). *Major export destinations* (1987): France 9.3%; West Germany 8.1%; Cameroon 4.3%; Belgium–Luxembourg 3.4%; United Kingdom 1.2%; Spain 1.1%; Italy 0.8%.

Transport and communications

Transport. Railroads: none. Roads (1983): total length 24,855 mi, 40,000 km (paved 1%). Vehicles (1985): passenger cars 2,741; trucks and buses 4,000. Merchant marine vessels (100 gross tons and over) none. Air transport[6] (1987): passenger-mi 132,791,000, passenger-km 213,706,000; short ton-mi cargo 24,739,000, metric ton-km cargo 36,119,000; airports (1989) with scheduled flights 1.
Communications. Daily newspapers (1987): total number 1; total circulation 1,500; circulation per 1,000 population 0.3. Radio (1988): total number of receivers 1,268,000 (1 per 4.3 persons). Television: none. Telephones (1987): 4,668 (1 per 1,114 persons).

Education and health

Education (1987)				
	schools	teachers	students	student/ teacher ratio
Primary (age 6–12)	1,139	4,288	300,110	70.0
Secondary (age 13–19)	48	1,204	42,066	34.9
Voc., teacher tr.	25	149	3,976	26.7
Higher	4	26	2,038	78.4

Educational attainment, n.a. *Literacy* (1980): total population age 15 and over literate 466,500 (17.8%); males literate 459,700 (35.6%); females literate 6,800 (0.5%).
Health: physicians (1980) 94 (1 per 47,640 persons); hospital beds (1978) 3,553 (1 per 1,190 persons); infant mortality rate per 1,000 live births (1985–90) 132.
Food (1980–82): daily per capita caloric intake 1,821 (vegetable products 92%, animal products 8%); 63% of FAO recommended minimum requirement.

Military

Total active duty personnel (1989): 17,000 (army 98.8%; navy, none; air force 1.2%). *Military expenditure as percent of GNP* (1987): 3.5% (world 5.4%); per capita expenditure U.S.$6.

[1]Detail does not add to total given because of rounding. [2]1979. [3]1983. [4]Capital city only. [5]June. [6]The airport at N'Djamena is underutilized because of the political and military unrest in Chad.

Chile

Official name: República de Chile
(Republic of Chile).
Form of government: military regime.
Head of state and government:
President (general) assisted by a four-
member junta.
Capital: Santiago.
Official language: Spanish.
Official religion: none.
Monetary unit: 1 peso (Ch$) = 100
centavos; valuation (Oct. 2, 1989)
1 U.S.$ = Ch$268.71;
1 £ = Ch$434.78.

Area and population

Regions	Capitals	area[1] sq mi	sq km	population 1989 estimate
Aisén del General Carlos				
Ibáñez del Campo	Coihaique	42,095	109,025	78,500
Antofagasta	Antofagasta	48,820	126,444	382,300
Araucania	Temuco	12,300	31,858	782,600
Atacama	Copiapó	29,179	75,573	196,800
Bío-Bío	Concepción	14,258	36,929	1,656,800
Coquimbo	La Serena	15,697	40,656	477,700
Libertador General				
Bernardo O'Higgins	Rancagua	6,319	16,365	641,100
Los Lagos	Puerto Montt	25,868	66,997	914,300
Magallanes y de la				
Antártica Chilena	Punta Arenas	50,932	132,034	155,300
Maule	Talca	11,700	30,302	827,400
Santiago,				
Región Metropolitana de	Santiago	5,926	15,349	5,133,700
Tarapacá	Iquique	22,663	58,698	347,200
Valparaíso	Valparaíso	6,331	16,365	1,367,300
TOTAL		292,135[2]	756,626[2]	12,961,000

Demography

Population (1989): 12,961,000.
Density (1989): persons per sq mi 44.4, persons per sq km 17.1.
Urban–rural (1987)[3]: urban 80.8%; rural 19.2%.
Sex distribution (1988)[4]: male 49.55%; female 50.45%.
Age breakdown (1986): under 15, 31.1%; 15–29, 28.6%; 30–44, 19.9%; 45–59, 12.1%; 60–74, 6.4%; 75 and over, 2.0%[2].
Population projection: (2000) 15,272,000; (2010) 17,182,000.
Doubling time: 44 years.
Ethnic composition (1983): mestizo 91.6%; Indian (mostly Araucanian) 6.8%; others (mainly European) 1.6%.
Religious affiliation (1982): Roman Catholic 80.7%; Protestant 6.1%; Jewish 0.2%; atheist and nonreligious 12.8%; other 0.2%.
Major cities (1987): Greater Santiago 4,858,300; Viña del Mar 297,300; Concepción 294,400; Valparaíso 278,800; Talcahuano 231,400.

Vital statistics

Birth rate per 1,000 population (1986): 22.1 (world avg. 27.1); (1985) legitimate 68.2%; illegitimate 31.8%.
Death rate per 1,000 population (1986): 5.9 (world avg. 9.9).
Natural increase rate per 1,000 population (1986): 16.2 (world avg. 17.2).
Total fertility rate (avg. births per childbearing woman; 1985–90): 2.7.
Marriage rate per 1,000 population (1986): 7.6.
Divorce rate per 1,000 population (1985): 0.4.
Life expectancy at birth (1985–90): male 68.1 years; female 75.1 years.
Major causes of death per 100,000 population (1985): diseases of the circulatory system 168.5; malignant neoplasms (cancers) 104.4; diseases of the respiratory system 66.6; accidents and adverse effects 24.3.

National economy

Budget (1986)[4]. Revenue: Ch$929,960,000,000 (excise taxes 43.3%, nontax revenue 20.6%, income taxes 11.6%, import and export duties 8.8%, social security contributions 7.5%, stamp taxes 4.6%). Expenditures: Ch$969,300,-000,000 (social security and welfare 38.0%, education 12.5%, public services 12.5%, defense 10.7%, economic services 9.2%, health 6.0%).
Public debt (external, outstanding; 1987): U.S.$15,536,000,000.
Tourism (1987): receipts from visitors U.S.$173,000,000; expenditures by nationals abroad U.S.$351,000,000.
Production (metric tons except as noted). Agriculture, forestry, fishing (1988): sugar beets 2,487,000, wheat 1,734,000, potatoes 928,000, corn (maize) 661,-000, rice 162,000, oats 157,000, rapeseed 123,000, barley 82,000; livestock (number of live animals) 6,540,000 sheep, 3,371,000 cattle, 1,360,000 pigs; roundwood (1987) 16,488,000 cu m; fish catch (1987) 4,814,000. Mining (1987): iron ore 6,822,536; copper 1,418,000; manganese 31,800; zinc 19,-500; molybdenum 16,900; silver 448,500 kilograms; gold 18,100 kilograms. Manufacturing (1987): cement 1,500,300; cellulose 673,100; fish meal 469,-400; iron or steel plates 259,100; newsprint 184,500; carbonated drinks 3,954,000 hectolitres; tires 1,222,800 units; pressed fibre panels 14,578,500 sq m; flat glass 2,310,500 sq m. Construction[5] (1985) residential 29,900 sq m; nonresidential 93,800 sq m. Energy production (consumption): electricity (kW-hr; 1987) 14,821,400,000 (14,821,400,000); coal (metric tons; 1987) 1,562,000 (1,802,000); crude petroleum (barrels; 1987) 9,893,000 (39,857,-000); petroleum products (metric tons; 1987) 4,413,000 (4,964,000); natural gas (cu m; 1987) 861,939,000 (861,939,000).
Land use (1987): forested 11.6%; meadows and pastures 15.9%; agricultural and under permanent cultivation 7.4%; other 65.1%.

Gross national product (1987): U.S.$16,468,000,000 (U.S.$1,310 per capita).

Structure of gross domestic product and labour force

	1987 in value Ch$'000,000[6]	% of total value	1988[3] labour force	% of labour force
Agriculture	38,308	9.6	682,700	14.8
Mining	31,525	7.9	129,800	2.8
Manufacturing	82,804	20.8	758,400	16.4
Construction	23,057	5.8	268,300	5.8
Public utilities	10,117	2.5	263,000	5.7
Transp. and commun.	23,755	6.0		
Trade	67,635	17.0	665,700	14.4
Finance			313,200	6.8
Pub. admin., defense	121,030	30.4		
Services[7]			1,000,400	21.6
Other			543,500[8]	11.7[8]
TOTAL	398,231	100.0	4,625,000	100.0

Population economically active (1988): total 4,625,000; activity rate of total population 36.3% (participation rates: ages 15–64 [1986] 54.8%; female [1986] 30.0%; unemployed 11.4%[9]).

Price and earnings indexes (1985 = 100)

	1982	1983	1984	1985	1986	1987	1988
Consumer price index	50.2	63.8	76.5	100.0	119.5	143.2	164.3
Monthly earnings index	58.7	66.7	80.0	100.0	122.5	146.1	178.6

Household income and expenditure. Average household size (1982) 4.5; average annual income per family (household) (1985)[10] Ch$440,738 at June prices (U.S.$2,840); sources of income (1976) wages and salaries 40.8%, transfer payments 8.0%, self-employment and other 51.2%; expenditure (1978): food 41.9%, housing 13.3%, transportation and communications 11.8%, recreation and education 8.2%, household goods 7.8%, clothing and footwear 7.6%.

Foreign trade[11]

Balance of trade (current prices)						
	1983	1984	1985	1986	1987	1988
U.S.$'000,000	+1,320	+953	+1,473	+1,620	+1,704	+2,822
% of total	20.8%	15.0%	24.1%	23.7%	20.1%	25.0%

Imports (1987): U.S.$4,023,300,000 (intermediate goods 55.4%; capital goods 24.4%; consumer goods 14.5%). *Major import sources* (1987): U.S. 19.2%; Japan 9.6%; Brazil 9.4%; West Germany 8.3%; Argentina 4.0%; Venezuela 3.6%; U.K. 3.2%; Spain 2.9%.
Exports (1987): U.S.$5,101,900,000 (mining 53.8%, of which copper 41.2%; industrial products 31.6%; fruits and vegetables 11.8%; paper and paper products 7.2%; chemical and petroleum products 2.0%). *Major export destinations* (1987): U.S. 22.4%; Japan 11.0%; West Germany 9.5%; Brazil 6.8%; U.K. 6.2%; Italy 5.4%; France 3.5%; Argentina 3.4%.

Transport and communications

Transport. Railroads (1987): route length 5,037 mi, 8,107 km; passenger-mi 729,000,000, passenger-km 1,174,000,000; short ton-mi cargo 1,097,000,000, metric ton-km cargo 1,601,000,000. Roads (1987): total length 49,227 mi, 79,223 km (paved 13%). Vehicles (1987) passenger cars 660,000; trucks and buses 278,000. Merchant marine (1988): vessels (100 gross tons and over) 287; total deadweight tonnage 912,717. Air transport (1988): passenger-mi 1,516,000,000, passenger-km 2,440,000,000; short ton-mi cargo 318,386,000, metric ton-km cargo 464,836,000; airports (1989) with scheduled flights 18.
Communications. Daily newspapers (1987): total number 33[12]; total circulation 1,145,000; circulation per 1,000 population 91. Radio (1988): 4,219,000 receivers (1 per 3.0 persons). Television (1988): 2,330,500 receivers (1 per 5.5 persons). Telephones (1987): 815,086 (1 per 16 persons).

Education and health

Education (1988)	schools	teachers	students	student/ teacher ratio
Primary (age 6–13)	8,767	62,746[13]	2,004,710	...
Secondary (age 14–17)	1,694	...	601,760	...
Vocational	1,262	...	133,941	...
Higher	201	15,131[14]	233,148	...

Educational attainment (1982). Percent of population age 25 and over having: no formal schooling 9.4%; primary education 56.6%; secondary 26.9%; higher 7.1%. *Literacy* (1988): total population age 15 and over literate 8,308,000 (94.3%); males, n.a.; females, n.a.
Health: physicians (1985) 12,334 (1 per 983 persons); hospital beds (1986) 33,136 (1 per 372 persons); infant mortality rate (1987) 18.7.
Food (1984–86): daily per capita caloric intake 2,573 (vegetable products 85%, animal products 15%); 107% of FAO recommended minimum requirement.

Military

Total active duty personnel (1989): 101,000 (army 56.4%, navy 28.7%, air force 14.9%). *Military expenditure as percent of GNP* (1987): 4.0% (world 5.4%); per capita expenditure: U.S.$55.

[1]Excludes the territory of Antártica Chilena and "inland" (actually tidal) water areas. [2]Detail does not add to total given because of rounding. [3]September. [4]Preliminary. [5]Private new construction only. [6]In constant 1977 pesos. [7]Services includes restaurants and hotels. [8]Includes 528,700 unemployed persons not previously employed. [9]Fourth quarter. [10]Greater Santiago area. [11]Import figures are f.o.b. in balance of trade and c.i.f. for commodities and trading partners. [12]In September 1986 several opposition publications were banned by the government. [13]1982. [14]1984.

China

Official name: Chung-hua Jen-min Kung-ho-kuo (People's Republic of China).
Form of government: single-party people's republic with one legislative house (National People's Congress [2,978]).
Chief of state: President.
Head of government: Premier.
Capital: Peking (Beijing).
Official language: Mandarin Chinese.
Official religion: none.
Monetary unit: 1 Renminbi (yuan) (Y) = 10 jiao = 100 fen; valuation (Oct. 2, 1989) 1 U.S.$ = Y 3.72; 1 £ = Y 6.02.

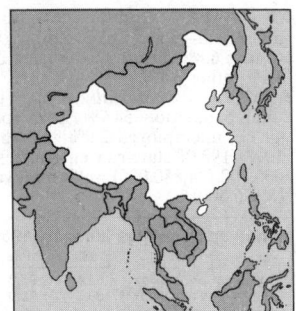

Area and population[1, 2]

Provinces	Capitals	area sq mi	area sq km	population 1988[3] estimate
Anhwei (Anhui)	Ho-fei (Hefei)	54,000	139,900	52,866,000
Chekiang (Zhejiang)	Hangchow (Hangzhou)	39,300	101,800	41,212,000
Fukien (Fujian)	Foochow (Fuzhou)	47,500	123,100	28,005,000
Hainan (Hainan)	Hai-k'ou (Haikou)	13,200	34,300	6,151,000
Heilungkiang (Heilongjiang)	Harbin (Harbin)	179,000	463,600	33,640,000
Honan (Henan)	Cheng-chou (Zhengzhou)	64,500	167,000	79,335,000
Hopeh (Hebei)	Shih-chia-chuang (Shijiazhuang)	78,200	202,700	56,958,000
Hunan (Hunan)	Ch'ang-sha (Changsha)	81,300	210,500	57,826,000
Hupeh (Hubei)	Wu-han (Wuhan)	72,400	187,500	50,581,000
Kansu (Gansu)	Lan-chou (Lanzhou)	141,500	366,500	21,034,000
Kiangsi (Jiangxi)	Nan-ch'ang (Nanchang)	63,600	164,800	35,590,000
Kiangsu (Jiangsu)	Nanking (Nanjing)	39,600	102,600	63,480,000
Kirin (Jilin)	Ch'ang-ch'un (Changchun)	72,200	187,000	23,364,000
Kwangtung (Guangdong)	Canton (Guangzhou)	76,100	197,100	58,321,000
Kweichow (Guizhou)	Kuei-yang (Guiyang)	67,200	174,000	30,514,000
Liaoning (Liaoning)	Shen-yang (Shenyang)	58,300	151,000	37,774,000
Shansi (Shanxi)	T'ai-yüan (Taiyuan)	60,700	157,100	26,908,000
Shantung (Shandong)	Tsinan (Jinan)	59,200	153,300	78,895,000
Shensi (Shaanxi)	Sian (Xi'an)	75,600	195,800	30,882,000
Szechwan (Sichuan)	Ch'eng-tu (Chengdu)	219,700	569,000	104,584,000
Tsinghai (Qinghai)	Hsi-ning (Xining)	278,400	721,000	4,175,000
Yunnan (Yunnan)	K'un-ming (Kunming)	168,400	436,200	35,130,000
Autonomous regions				
Inner Mongolia (Nei Monggol)	Hu-ho-hao-t'e (Hohhot)	454,600	1,177,500	20,536,000
Kwangsi Chuang (Guangxi Zhuang)	Nan-ning (Nanning)	85,100	220,400	40,164,000
Ningsia Hui (Ningxia Hui)	Yin-ch'uan (Yinchuan)	25,600	66,400	4,352,000
Sinkiang Uighur (Xinjiang Uygur)	Urumchi (Urumqi)	635,900	1,646,900	14,063,000
Tibet (Xizang)	Lhasa (Lhasa)	471,700	1,221,600	2,079,000
Municipalities				
Peking (Beijing)	—	6,500	16,800	9,926,000
Shanghai (Shanghai)	—	2,400	6,200	12,495,000
Tientsin (Tianjin)	—	4,400	11,300	8,324,000
TOTAL		3,696,100[4]	9,572,900[4]	1,069,164,000[5]

Demography

Population (1989): 1,104,275,000.
Density (1989): persons per sq mi 298.8, persons per sq km 115.4.
Urban–rural (1988[3]): urban 46.6%; rural 53.4%.
Sex distribution (1988[3]): male 51.50%; female 48.50%.
Age breakdown (1987): under 15, 28.8%; 15–29, 30.3%; 30–44, 20.0%; 45–59, 12.4%; 60–74, 6.9%; 75 and over, 1.6%.
Population projection: (2000) 1,309,799,000; (2010) 1,407,918,000.
Doubling time: 50 years.
Ethnic composition (1982): Han (Chinese) 93.30%; Chuang 1.33%; Hui 0.72%; Uighur 0.59%; Yi 0.54%; Miao 0.50%; Manchu 0.43%; Tibetan 0.39%; Mongolian 0.34%; Tuchia 0.28%; Puyi 0.21%; Korean 0.18%; Tung 0.14%; Yao 0.14%; Pai 0.11%; Hani 0.11%; Kazakh 0.09%; Tai 0.08%; Li 0.08%; other 0.44%.
Religious affiliation (1980): nonreligious 59.2%; Chinese folk-religionist 20.1%; atheist 12.0%; Buddhist 6.0%; Muslim 2.4%; Christian 0.2%; other 0.1%.
Major cities (1988[3]): Shanghai 7,220,000; Peking 6,710,000; Tientsin 5,540,-000; Shen-yang 4,370,000; Wu-han 3,570,000; Canton 3,420,000; Chung-king (Chongqing) 2,890,000; Harbin 2,710,000; Ch'eng-tu 2,690,000; Sian 2,580,000; Nanking 2,390,000; Talien (Dalian) 2,280,000; Tsinan 2,140,000; Ch'ang-ch'un 2,000,000; T'ai-yüan 1,980,000; Cheng-chou 1,580,000; K'un-ming 1,550,000; Lan-chou 1,420,000; An-shan (Anshan) 1,330,000; Qiqihar 1,330,000; Ch'ing-tao (Qingdao) 1,300,000; Hangchow 1,290,000.
Households (1987). Average rural household size 5.0; urban household size 3.7. Family households (1987): 248,383,100 (97.8%); collective 5,698,000 (2.2%).

Vital statistics

Birth rate per 1,000 population (1988): 21.0 (world avg. 27.1).
Death rate per 1,000 population (1988): 6.6 (world avg. 9.9).
Natural increase rate per 1,000 population (1988): 14.4 (world avg. 17.2).
Total fertility rate (avg. births per childbearing woman; 1988): 2.4.
Marriage rate per 1,000 population (1987): 8.6.
Divorce rate per 1,000 population (1987): 0.5.

Life expectancy at birth (1988): male 68.1 years; female 71.0 years.
Major causes of death per 100,000 population (percent distribution; 1987)[6]: diseases of the respiratory system 20.8%; diseases of the circulatory system 14.8%; malignant neoplasms (cancers) 14.2%; diseases of the heart 13.1%; injuries and poisonings 10.4%; digestive diseases 5.0%.

Social indicators

Educational attainment (1982). Percent of population age 25 and over having: no schooling and incomplete primary 44.5%; completed primary 32.7%; completed junior secondary 16.1%; completed senior secondary 5.6%; postsecondary 1.1%.

Distribution of rural household income (1987)

by per capita income group (avg. Y 463)

Y 150 and under	Y 151–Y 300	Y 301–Y 500	over Y 500
3.2%	22.5%	38.6%	35.7%

Quality of working life (1989). Average workweek: 48 hours. Annual rate per 100,000 workers for: injury or accident, n.a.; industrial illness, n.a.; death, n.a. Expenditure on pensions and social welfare relief (1985): Y 3,115,000,-000. Average days lost to labour stoppages per 1,000 workdays: n.a. Average duration of journey to work: n.a. Method of transport: n.a. Rate per 1,000 workers of discouraged (unemployed no longer seeking work): n.a.
Access to services. Proportion of communes having access to electricity (1979) 87.1%. Percent of urban population with: safe public water supply (1987) 86.6%; public sewage collection, n.a.; public fire protection, n.a.
Social participation. Eligible voters participating in last national election: n.a. Population participating in voluntary work: n.a. Trade union membership in total labour force (1988): 18.9%. Practicing religious population in total affiliated population: n.a.
Social deviance. Annual reported arrest rate per 100,000 population (1986) for: property violation 20.7; infringing personal rights 7.2; disruption of social administration 3.3; endangering public security[7] 1.0.
Leisure. Favourite leisure activities: n.a.
Material well-being (1988[3]). Urban families possessing (number per family): wristwatches 3.1; bicycles 1.8; sewing machines 0.7; radios 0.7; televisions 0.6. Rural families possessing (number per family): wristwatches 1.6; bicycles 1.0; sewing machines 0.5; radios 0.5; televisions 0.2.

National economy

Gross national product (at current market prices; 1987): U.S.$319,780,000,-000 (U.S.$300 per capita).

Structure of national income[8] and labour force

	1987 in value Y '000,000,000	1987 % of total value	1988[3] labour force ('000)[9]	1988[3] % of labour force
Agriculture	315.4	33.8	317,200	60.1
Mining	...	...	1,070	0.2
Manufacturing	426.2	45.7	93,420	17.7
Construction	61.7	6.6	24,190	4.6
Public utilities	...	...	5,400	1.0
Transp. and commun.	34.9	3.7	13,730	2.6
Trade	93.9	10.1	26,560	5.0
Finance	—	—	1,700	0.3
Pub. admin.	—	—	9,250	1.8
Services	—	—	20,290	3.8
Other	...	...	15,020	2.8
TOTAL	932.1	100.0[10]	527,830	100.0[10]

Budget (1989). Revenue: Y 285,608,000,000 (1987; taxes 92.2%; funds collected for energy and transport projects 7.4%). Expenditures: Y 293,-080,000,000 (capital construction 21.4%; culture, education, public health 17.5%; subsidies 14.0%; defense 8.4%).
Public debt (external, outstanding; 1987): U.S.$23,659,000,000.
Tourism: receipts from visitors (1988) U.S.$2,247,000,000; expenditures by nationals abroad (1987) U.S.$387,000,000.

Retail and service enterprises (1988[3])

	no. of enterprises	no. of employees	annual wage as a % of all wages	annual gross output value (Y '000,000)
Retail trade	8,814,000	20,125,000	...	...
Grocery stores	170,000	1,182,000	...	...
Department stores	161,000	1,603,000	...	...
Other food shops	113,000	760,000	...	...
Agricultural supplies stores	79,000	368,000	...	...
Household supplies stores	66,000	343,000	...	...
Electrical appliances stores	59,000	583,000	...	...
Grain and oil shops	54,000	550,000	...	...
Textile stores	36,000	222,000	...	...
Drug stores	25,000	194,000	...	...
Book stores	25,000	115,000	...	...
Coal stores	13,000	152,000	...	...
Service trade	1,694,000	3,922,000	...	...
Repair shops	772,000	1,119,000	...	...
Barber shops	317,000	553,000	...	...
Hotels	171,000	1,112,000	...	...
Photo studios	96,000	216,000	...	...

Production (metric tons except as noted). Agriculture, forestry, fishing (1988): grains—rice 172,365,000, wheat 87,505,000, corn (maize) 73,820,-000, sorghum 6,115,000, millet 5,501,000, barley 3,000,000; oilseeds—peanuts (groundnuts) 5,855,000, rapeseed 5,040,000, sunflower seed 1,150,-000; fruits and nuts—watermelons 5,977,000, apples 4,268,000, pears 2,580,000, oranges 3,272,000; cantaloupes 2,378,000; others—sweet potatoes 110,660,000, sugarcane 54,580,000, potatoes 29,550,000, soybeans 10,918,-000, sugar beets 13,290,000, seed cotton 12,600,000, cabbage 7,750,000,

pulses 5,679,000, tomatoes 5,474,000, cucumbers 3,818,000, tobacco leaves 2,353,000, tea 566,000; livestock (number of live animals) 334,862,000 pigs, 102,655,000 sheep, 73,963,000 cattle, 77,894,000 goats, 20,858,000 water buffalo, 10,846,000 asses, 10,691,000 horses, 325,000,000 ducks, 1,849,000,000 chickens; roundwood (1987) 276,518,000 cu m; fish catch (1987) 9,346,222, of which 3,937,870 freshwater fish, 5,408,352 marine fish. Mining and quarrying (1987): metals (metal content of ores)—zinc 425,000, copper 300,000, lead 252,000, tungsten 18,000, tin 15,000, molybdenum 2,000; other metals—iron ore 49,990,000, bauxite 2,400,000, manganese 481,000, silver 3,000,000 troy oz, gold 2,300,000 troy oz; nonmetals—salt 17,962,000, gypsum 7,200,000, phosphates 2,700,000, barite 998,000, talc 998,000, fluorspar 650,000, graphite 185,000, asbestos 150,000. Manufacturing (1988): cement 203,000,000; steel 59,180,000; chemical fertilizer 17,-670,000; paper and paperboard 12,100,000; sulfuric acid 10,980,000; sugar 4,550,000; cotton yarn 4,540,000; woolen fabrics 265,000,000 metres; bicycles 41,220,000 units; television sets 24,850,000 units; household washing machines 10,460,000 units; household refrigerators 7,400,000 units; motor vehicles 646,700 units. Construction (1987): residential 919,765,000 sq m; nonresidential 188,596,000 sq m. Distribution of industrial production (percent of total value of output by sector; 1978 [1987]): state-operated enterprises 80.6% (69.7%); collectives 19.2% (27.9%); privately operated enterprises 0.2% (2.4%). Retail sales (percent of total sales by sector; 1978 [1987]): state-operated enterprises 90.5% (38.6%); collectives 7.4% (35.7%); privately operated enterprises 2.1% (25.7%).

Manufacturing and mining enterprises (1987)

	no. of enterprises	no. of employees[11]	annual wages as a % of avg. of all wages[12]	annual gross output value (Y '000,000)
Manufacturing				
Machinery, transport equipment, and basic manufactures,	118,134	14,948,000	96.7	298,233
of which,				
Industrial equipment	6,580	8,663,000	...	25,194
Transport equipment	12,643	...	...	44,189
Electronic goods	4,524	1,043,000[13]	...	35,828
Metalware for daily use	6,820	...	...	9,609
Textiles,	25,505	6,411,000	95.5	141,066
of which,				
Cotton	8,221	...	...	75,452
Foodstuffs,	61,655	3,840,000	87.5	92,502
of which,				
Grains and edible oils	20,187	...	...	28,865
Processed meat	...	...	...	...
Tobacco manufactures	413	...	...	27,997
Chemicals,	40,926	5,480,000	92.1	156,053
of which,				
Organic chemicals	6,007	...	...	27,169
Plastics	15,336	720,000	...	21,563
Building materials,	63,674	3,377,000	93.0	62,953
of which,				
Brick, tile, other	...	...	...	...
Cement (all forms)	5,452	856,000[13]	...	18,525
Secondary forest products (including paper and stationery)	37,806	1,734,000	96.1	41,356
Primary forest products	2,242	1,115,000	114.3	9,576
Mining				
Nonferrous and ferrous metals	3,864	780,000	107.6	8,105
Crude petroleum	38	529,000	...	29,143
Coal	10,553	4,471,000	119.8	25,698

Energy production (consumption): electricity (kW-hr; 1987) 497,267,000,000 (497,267,000,000); coal (metric tons; 1987) 927,965,000 (916,376,000); crude petroleum (barrels; 1987) 979,222,000 (782,487,000); petroleum products (metric tons; 1987) 78,739,000 (76,883,000); natural gas (cu m; 1987) 14,-014,992,000 (14,014,992,000).

Financial aggregates[14]

	1983	1984	1985	1986	1987	1988	July 1989[15]
Exchange rate, Y per:							
U.S. dollar	1.98	2.80	3.20	3.72	3.72	3.72	3.72
£	2.87	3.23	4.62	5.49	6.96	6.73	6.18
SDR	2.07	2.74	3.52	4.55	5.28	5.01	4.79
International reserves (U.S.$)							
Total (excl. gold; '000,000)	14,853	15,081	12,728	11,453	16,305	18,541	14,522
SDRs ('000,000)	335	406	483	569	640	586	546
Reserve pos. in IMF ('000,000)	176	223	332	370	429	407	377
Foreign exchange	14,342	14,420	11,913	10,514	15,236	17,548	13,586
Gold ('000,000 fine troy oz)	12.7	12.7	12.7	12.7	12.7	12.7	12.7
% world reserves	1.3	1.3	1.3	1.3	1.3	2.5	1.9
Interest and prices							
Central bank discount (%)	...	...	...	...	...	...	...
Gov't bond yield (%)	...	...	...	...	...	...	...
Industrial share prices	...	...	...	...	...	...	...
Balance of payments (Y '000,000)							
Balance of visible trade,	5,130	1,590	−54,310	−28,930		−990	7,00[16]
of which:							
Imports, f.o.b.	38,700	56,370	176,820	137,510	148,170	32,540[16]	
Exports, f.o.b.	43,830	57,960	122,510	108,580	147,180	33,240[16]	
Balance of invisibles	...	...	...	...	...	...	...
Balance of payments, current account	...	...	...	...	...	...	...

Household income and expenditure. Average household size (1987) 4.3; rural household 5.0, urban household 3.7. Average annual income per household, Y 3,002; rural household Y 2,317, urban household Y 3,786. Sources of income (1987): rural household—income from the collective[17] and nonproductive sources 9.1%, sideline production 82.9%, of which farming 48.2%, livestock raising 11.2%, labour service 6.7%; urban household[11]—time wages 56.5%, subsidies 15.5%, bonuses 15.4%, piece-rate wages 9.6%. Expenditure (1987): rural household—food 55.2%, housing 14.5%, personal

effects 11.8%, clothing 8.6%, fuel 4.8%, cultural activities 5.2%; urban household—food 53.5%, clothing 13.7%, personal effects 11.4%, cultural activities 6.8%, fuel 2.7%, housing 2.6%, transportation and communications 1.1%, other 8.2%.

Population economically active (1987): total 584,569,200; activity rate of total population 54.7% (participation rates: over age 15, 76.8%; female 49.7%; unemployed 2.0%[18]). Urban work force by sector of employment, 1978 (1987): state-run enterprises 74,500,000 (96,540,000); collectives 20,-000,000 (34,880,000); self-employment or privately run enterprises 150,000 (5,690,000).

Price and earnings indexes (1985 = 100)

	1982	1983	1984	1985	1986	1987	1988
Consumer price index	85.4	87.0	89.4	100.0	107.0	116.4	140.5
Annual earnings index[19]	69.5	72.0	84.8	100.0	115.8	127.1	150.8

Land use (1987): forested 12.5%; meadows and pastures 34.2%; agricultural and under permanent cultivation 10.4%; other 42.9%.

Foreign trade[20]

Balance of trade (current prices)

	1983	1984	1985	1986	1987	1988
Y '000,000	+1,650	−3,480	−45,050	−41,310	−14,330	−11,470
% of total	1.9%	2.9%	21.8%	16.0%	4.6%	3.1%

Imports (1987): U.S.$43,240,000,000 (machinery and transportation equipment 33.8%; products of textile industries, rubber and metal products 22.5%; chemical and related products 11.6%; inedible raw materials 7.7%; food and live animals 5.6%; light industrial products 4.3%). *Major import sources:* Japan 23.3%; Hong Kong 19.5%; United States 11.2%; West Germany 7.2%; Canada 3.2%; Australia 3.1%; U.S.S.R. 2.9%; Italy 2.9%; United Kingdom 2.1%; France 2.1%; Singapore 1.4%.
Exports (1987): U.S.$39,486,000,000 (products of textile industries, rubber and metal products 21.7%; light industrial products 15.9%; food and live animals 12.1%; mineral fuels and lubricants 11.5%; inedible raw materials 9.2%; chemical and related products 5.7%). *Major export destinations:* Hong Kong 34.9%; Japan 16.2%; United States 7.7%; Singapore 3.4%; Jordan 3.4%; U.S.S.R. 3.2%; West Germany 3.1%; Zaire 1.8%; The Netherlands 1.5%; Italy 1.4%; United Kingdom 1.3%; France 1.1%.

Transport and communications

Transport. Railroads (1988): length[3] 40,364 mi, 64,960 km; passenger-mi 203,000,000,000, passenger-km 326,000,000,000; short ton-mi cargo 676,-400,000,000, metric ton-km cargo 987,600,000,000. Roads (1988[3]): total length 610,336 mi, 982,243 km (paved 83%). Vehicles (1987): passenger cars and buses 1,114,622; trucks 2,812,068. Merchant marine (1988): vessels (100 gross tons and over) 1,841; total deadweight tonnage 19,359,663. Air transport (1988): passenger-mi 13,300,000,000, passenger-km 21,400,-000,000; short ton-mi cargo 507,000,000, metric ton-km cargo 740,000,000; airports (1989) with scheduled flights 80.
Communications. Daily newspapers (1986[3]): total number 222; total circulation, n.a.; circulation per 1,000 population 50. Radio (1988): total number of receivers 121,211,690 (1 per 8.9 persons). Television (1987[3]): total number of receivers 92,140,000 (1 per 12 persons). Telephones (1987): 8,057,000 (1 per 134 persons).

Education and health

Education (1987)

	schools	teachers	students	student/ teacher ratio
Primary (age 7–13)	984,181	6,085,000	146,437,000	24.1
Secondary (age 13–17)	92,857	2,870,000	49,481,000	17.2
Secondary specialized	12,294	395,000	4,550,000	11.5
Higher	1,063	385,000	1,959,000	5.1

Literacy (1982): total population age 15 and over literate 609,283,011 (72.6%); males literate 358,744,834 (83.5%); females literate 250,538,177 (61.2%).
Health (1988): physicians 1,618,000 (1 per 668 persons); hospital beds 2,503,-000 (1 per 432 persons); infant mortality rate per 1,000 live births 32.0.
Food (1984–86): daily per capita caloric intake 2,628 (vegetable products 91%, animal products 9%); 111% of FAO recommended minimum requirement.

Military

Total active duty personnel (1989): 3,030,000 (army 75.9%, navy 8.6%, air force 15.5%). *Military expenditure as percent of GNP* (1987): 4.4% (world 5.4%); per capita expenditure U.S.$19.

[1]Names of the provinces, autonomous regions, and municipalities are stated in conventional form, followed by Pinyin transliteration; names of capitals are stated in conventional form or Wade–Giles transliteration, followed by Pinyin transliteration. [2]Data for Taiwan, Quemoy, and Matsu are excluded. [3]January 1. [4]Includes 4,600 sq mi (11,900 sq km) not shown separately. [5]Total includes servicemen not assigned to any political division. [6]Based on rural sample population. [7]Excludes arrests for anti-Communist activities. [8]Application of term differs from functional definition in a market economy. [9]Employed only. [10]Detail does not add to total given because of rounding. [11]In state-owned and collective-owned industries only. [12]1979. [13]1984. [14]Exchange rates and international reserves are based on end-of-year figures. [15]End-of-month figures for exchange rates and international reserves. [16]January to March total. [17]Breakdown of sideline production is for 1985. [18]Rate of waiting for employment in cities and towns. [19]Average annual wage in industrial establishments in urban areas. [20]Imports, c.i.f.; exports, f.o.b.

Colombia

Official name: República de Colombia (Republic of Colombia).
Form of government: unitary, multiparty republic with two legislative houses (Senate [114]; House of Representatives [199]).
Head of state and government: President.
Capital: Bogotá.
Official language: Spanish.
Official religion: none.
Monetary unit: 1 peso (Col$) = 100 centavos; valuation (Oct. 2, 1989) 1 U.S.$ = Col$406.29; 1 £ = Col$657.38.

Area and population

Commissariats	Capitals	area sq mi	area sq km	population 1985 census
Amazonas	Leticia	42,342	109,665	30,327
Guainía	Puerto Inírida	27,891	72,238	9,214
Guaviare	Guaviare	16,342	42,327	35,305
Vaupés	Mitú	25,200	65,268	18,935
Vichada	Puerto Carreño	38,703	100,242	13,770
Departments				
Antioquia	Medellín	24,561	63,612	3,888,067
Atlántico	Barranquilla	1,308	3,388	1,428,601
Bolívar	Cartagena	10,030	25,978	1,197,623
Boyacá	Tunja	8,953	23,189	1,097,618
Caldas	Manizales	3,046	7,888	838,094
Caquetá	Florencia	34,349	88,965	214,473
Cauca	Popayán	11,316	29,308	795,838
Cesar	Valledupar	8,844	22,905	584,631
Chocó	Quibdó	17,965	46,530	242,768
Córdoba	Montería	9,660	25,020	913,636
Cundinamarca	Bogotá	8,735	22,623	1,382,360
Huila	Neiva	7,680	19,890	647,756
La Guajira	Riohacha	8,049	20,848	255,310
Magdalena	Santander	8,953	23,188	769,141
Meta	Villavicencio	33,064	85,635	412,312
Nariño	Pasto	12,845	33,268	1,019,098
Norte de Santander	Cúcuta	8,362	21,658	883,884
Quindío	Armenia	712	1,845	377,860
Risaralda	Pereira	1,598	4,140	625,451
Santander	Bucaramanga	11,790	30,537	1,438,226
Sucre	Sincelejo	4,215	10,917	529,059
Tolima	Ibagué	9,097	23,562	1,051,852
Valle	Cali	8,548	22,140	2,847,087
Intendancies				
Arauca	Arauca	9,196	23,818	70,085
Casanare	Yopal	17,236	44,640	110,253
Putumayo	Mocoa	9,608	24,885	119,815
San Andrés y Providencia	San Andrés	17	44	35,936
Special District				
Bogotá		613	1,587	3,982,941
TOTAL		440,831[1]	1,141,748	27,867,326[2]

Demography

Population (1989): 32,317,000.
Density (1989): persons per sq mi 73.3, persons per sq km 28.3.
Urban–rural (1985): urban 67.2%; rural 32.8%.
Sex distribution (1989): male 49.65%; female 50.35%.
Age breakdown (1989): under 15, 36.4%; 15–29, 30.4%; 30–44, 18.3%; 45–59, 8.8%; 60–74, 4.7%; 75 and over, 1.4%.
Population projection: (2000) 39,302,000; (2010) 45,298,000.
Doubling time: 34 years.
Ethnic composition (1985): mestizo 58.0%; white 20.0%; mulatto 14.0%; black 4.0%; mixed black-Indian 3.0%; Amerindian 1.0%.
Religious affiliation (1987): Roman Catholic 95.0%; other 5.0%.
Major cities (1985): Bogotá 3,974,813; Medellín 1,418,554; Cali 1,323,944; Barranquilla 896,649; Cartagena 491,368.

Vital statistics

Birth rate per 1,000 population (1983–88): 27.9 (world avg. 27.1); (1982) legitimate 75.2%; illegitimate 24.8%.
Death rate per 1,000 population (1983–88): 7.4 (world avg. 9.9).
Natural increase rate per 1,000 population (1983–88): 20.5 (world avg. 17.2).
Total fertility rate (avg. births per childbearing woman; 1981–86): 3.4.
Marriage rate per 1,000 population (1977): 3.5.
Life expectancy at birth (1986): male 63.0 years; female 67.0 years.
Major causes of death per 100,000 population (1986 est.): acute myocardial infarction 57.9; homicide with firearms 52.2; cardiac insufficiency 27.7.

National economy

Budget (1987). Revenue: Col$1,208,960,000,000 (indirect taxes 49.1%, direct taxes 21.2%, credit resources 17.3%). Expenditures: Col$853,386,000,000 (transfer payments 36.6%, debt service 22.8%, capital investments 15.3%).
Public debt (external, outstanding; 1987): U.S.$13,828,000,000.
Tourism (1987): receipts U.S.$213,000,000; expenditures U.S.$455,000,000.
Production (metric tons except as noted). Agriculture (1988): sugarcane 24,560,000, potatoes 2,520,000, plantains 2,191,000, rice 1,775,000, bananas 1,300,000, cassava 1,222,000, corn (maize) 908,000, coffee (green) 780,000; roundwood (1987) 17,831,000 cu m; fish catch (1987) 58,662; livestock (number of live animals) 24,307,000 cattle, 2,652,000 sheep, 2,586,000 pigs. Mining and quarrying (1988): iron ore 614,727; gold 933,008 troy oz; silver 210,959 troy oz. Manufacturing (value added in Col$'000,000; 1987): processed food 261,048; beverages 211,737; textiles 146,168; chemical products

111,493; machinery and electrical apparatus 91,045; transport equipment 65,279; basic steel 63,146; metal products 53,578. Construction (1988)[3]: residential 6,063,739 sq m; nonresidential 2,040,559 sq m. Energy production (consumption): electricity (kW-hr; 1987) 35,368,000,000 (35,368,000,000); coal (metric tons; 1987) 14,594,000 (5,089,000); crude petroleum (barrels; 1987) 137,536,000 (85,369,000); petroleum products (metric tons; 1987) 10,559,000 (7,286,000); natural gas (cu m; 1987) 4,369,455,000 (4,369,455,000).
Gross national product (1987): U.S.$36,027,000,000 (U.S.$1,220 per capita).

Structure of gross domestic product and labour force

	1988 in value Col$'000,000	1988 % of total value	1980 labour force	1980 % of labour force
Agriculture	2,203,174	18.8	2,412,413	28.5
Mining	744,378	6.4	49,740	0.6
Manufacturing	2,338,758	20.0	1,136,735	13.4
Construction	675,924	5.8	242,191	2.9
Public utilities	273,914	2.3	44,233	0.5
Transp. and commun.	958,684	8.2	352,623	4.2
Trade	1,633,984	14.0	1,261,633	14.9
Finance	1,225,558	10.5	278,210	3.2
Pub. admin., defense	945,302	8.1 }		
Services	503,254	4.3 }	1,998,460	23.6
Other	191,677	1.6	690,762[4]	8.2[4]
TOTAL	11,694,607	100.0	8,467,000	100.0

Population economically active (1985): total 9,558,000; activity rate 34.3% (participation rates: over age 12, 49.4%; female 32.8%; unemployed 4.3%).

Price and earnings indexes (1985 = 100)

	1982	1983	1984	1985	1986	1987	1988
Consumer price index	58.0	69.4	80.6	100.0	118.9	146.6	187.8
Monthly earnings index[5]	91.0	96.1	102.2	100.0	104.0	...	...

Household income and expenditure. Average household size (1985) 4.7; sources of income (1984): wages 49.3%, self-employment 36.6%, transfer payments 6.2%; expenditure (1984–85): food 38.4%, housing 20.0%, clothing and footwear 9.2%, household durable goods 7.5%, transportation and communications 6.8%.
Land use (1986): forested 49.6%; pastures 38.3%; agricultural 5.1%; other 7.0%.

Foreign trade

Balance of trade (current prices)

	1983	1984	1985	1986	1987	1988
U.S.$'000,000	−1,390.7	−590.4	−179.9	+1,537.6	+735.0	+505.4
% of total	18.4%	7.9%	2.5%	17.7%	8.6%	5.3%

Imports (1988): U.S.$5,005,260,000 (machinery 24.0%, chemicals 11.8%, transport equipment 10.6%, steel products 7.5%, plastic products 4.8%, crude petroleum 3.7%). *Major import sources:* U.S. 36.2%; W.Ger. 6.8%; Brazil 4.6%; Mexico 4.1%; France 3.7%; Canada 3.6%; Venezuela 3.5%.
Exports (1988): U.S.$5,026,227,000 (coffee 32.7%, petroleum and petroleum products 25.7%, fruits 5.1%, flowers 3.8%, iron and steel 3.5%, textile apparel 3.4%). *Major export destinations:* U.S. 39.3%; W.Ger. 10.4%; The Netherlands 5.0%; Venezuela 4.4%; France 2.6%; Chile 2.4%.

Transport and communications

Transport. Railroads (1988): route length (1987) 3,236 km; passenger-km 147,962,000; metric ton-km cargo 464,333,000. Roads (1986): total length 106,218 km (paved 10%). Vehicles (1986): cars 840,776; trucks and buses 391,433. Merchant marine (1988): vessels (100 gross tons and over) 97; deadweight tonnage 584,586. Air transport (1987): passenger-km 3,946,731,000; metric ton-km cargo 358,198,000; airports (1989) 69.
Communications. Daily newspapers (1987): 30; circulation 1,861,500; circulation per 1,000 population 61. Radio (1988): 4,364,000 receivers (1 per 7.3 persons). Television (1988): 5,500,000 receivers (1 per 5.6 persons). Telephones (1987): 2,438,201 (1 per 12 persons).

Education and health

Education (1987)

	schools	teachers	students	student/ teacher ratio
Primary	36,109	130,375	3,903,019	29.9
Secondary[6]	5,884	95,077	1,973,025	20.8
Higher	235	47,990	457,680	9.5

Educational attainment (1985). Percent of population age 25 and over having: no schooling 15.3%; primary education 50.1%; secondary 25.4%; higher 6.8%; not stated 2.4%. *Literacy* (1985): population age 18 and over literate 10,714,936 (69.1%).
Health: physicians (1984) 23,250 (1 per 1,229 persons); hospital beds (1983) 46,651 (1 per 612 persons); infant mortality rate (1986) 46.0.
Food (1984–86): daily per capita caloric intake 2,550 (vegetable products 85%, animal products 15%); (1984) 111% of FAO minimum requirement.

Military

Total active duty personnel (1988): 86,300 (army 79.9%, navy 12.3%, air force 7.8%). *Military expenditure as percent of GNP* (1987): 1.1% (world 5.4%); per capita expenditure U.S.$12.

[1]Detail does not add to total given because of rounding. [2]Census total adjusted for underenumeration is 29,265,499. [3]Construction permits issued for 11 urban centres. [4]Includes unemployed not previously employed. [5]Real wages in the industrial sector. [6]Secondary includes vocational and teacher training.

Comoros[1]

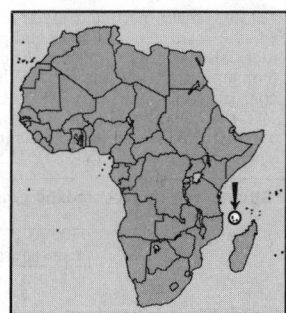

Official name: Jumhurīyat al-Qumur al-Ittihādīyah al-Islāmīyah (Arabic); République Fédéral Islamique des Comores (French) (Federal Islamic Republic of the Comoros).
Form of government: federal Islamic single-party republic with one legislative house (Federal Assembly [42]).
Head of state and government: President.
Capital: Moroni.
Official languages: Arabic; French.
Official religion: Islam.
Monetary unit: 1 Comorian franc (CF) = 100 centimes; valuation (Oct. 2, 1989) 1 U.S.\$ = CF 317.90; 1 £ = CF 514.37.

Area and population		area		population
		sq mi	sq km	1989 estimate[3]
Governorates/Islands[2]	Capitals			
Moili (Mohéli)	Fomboni	112	290	23,584
Ngazidja (Grande Comore)	Moroni	443	1,148	241,259
Ndzouani (Anjouan)	Mutsamudu	164	424	185,920
TOTAL		719	1,862	450,763

Demography

Population (1989): 448,000.
Density (1989): persons per sq mi 623.1, persons per sq km 240.6.
Urban-rural (1986): urban 25.7%; rural 74.3%.
Sex distribution (1986): male 50.47%; female 49.53%.
Age breakdown (1986): under 15, 46.0%; 15–29, 24.3%; 30–44, 14.8%; 45–59, 9.2%; 60 and over, 5.7%.
Population projection: (2000) 630,000; (2010) 841,000.
Doubling time: 21 years.
Ethnic composition (1980): Comorian (a mixture of Bantu, Arab, and Malagasy peoples) 96.9%; Makua (a Bantu people from East Africa) 1.6%; French 0.4%; other 1.1%.
Religious affiliation (1980): Sunnī Muslim 99.7%; Christian 0.2%; Bahā'ī 0.1%.
Major cities (1980): Moroni 21,000[4]; Mutsamudu 16,883; Domoni 7,147; Ouani 6,936; Tsembehou 6,578.

Vital statistics

Birth rate per 1,000 population (1987): 47.0 (world avg. 27.1).
Death rate per 1,000 population (1987): 14.0 (world avg. 9.9).
Natural increase rate per 1,000 population (1987): 33.0 (world avg. 17.2).
Total fertility rate (avg. births per childbearing woman; 1987): 7.0.
Marriage rate per 1,000 population: n.a.
Divorce rate per 1,000 population: n.a.
Life expectancy at birth (1987): male 53.0 years; female 57.0 years.
Major causes of death per 100,000 population: n.a.; however, major diseases (1980) include malaria (afflicts 80% of the adult population), tuberculosis, leprosy, and kwashiorkor (a nutritional deficiency disease).

National economy

Budget (1987). Revenue: CF 13,709,000,000 (tax revenue 38.7%, of which consumption tax on imported items 17.3%, taxes on goods and services 5.2%; external grants applied to development 35.0%; external grants applied to current revenue 15.2%; nontax revenue 11.1%). Expenditures: CF 21,037,000,000[5] (education 25.1%; agriculture, forestry, fishing 18.0%; general public service 12.4%; transportation and communications 11.6%; health 7.3%; defense 4.3%).
Tourism (1988): receipts from visitors U.S.\$3,500,000; expenditures by nationals abroad U.S.\$4,100,000.
Production (metric tons except as noted). Agriculture, forestry, fishing (1987): roots and tubers 60,200, of which cassava 45,200; bananas 51,800; coconuts 47,000; pulses 6,800; corn (maize) 3,400; rice 3,000; copra 1,000; cloves 669[6,7], vanilla 247[6,7], ylang-ylang 67[6,7]; livestock (number of live animals) 96,000 goats, 88,000 cattle, 9,000 sheep; roundwood, n.a.; fish catch 5,250. Mining and quarrying: sand and gravel for local construction. Manufacturing (1987): products include processed vanilla and ylang-ylang, cement, handicrafts, soaps, soft drinks, aluminum kitchen utensils, and clothing. Construction: n.a. Energy production (consumption): electricity (kW-hr; 1987) 14,000,000 (14,000,000); coal, none (none); crude petroleum, none (none); petroleum products (metric tons; 1987) none (16,000); natural gas, none (none).
Population economically active (1985): total 117,216; activity rate of total population 29.6% (participation rates: ages 15–64, 53.1%; female 26.2%; unemployed [1986] 36.0%).

Price and earnings indexes (1979 = 100)							
	1977	1978	1979	1980	1981	1982	1983
Consumer price index	75.5	87.9	100.0	111.2	131.9	177.2	188.5
Daily earnings index[8]	...	...	100.0	...	...	...	133.3

Household income and expenditure. Average household size (1985) 5.6; income per household: n.a.; sources of income: n.a.; expenditure (1983)[9]:

food and beverages 56.0%, energy 14.4%, clothing and footwear 10.0%, transportation and communications 6.6%, health care 5.0%, recreation 3.0%, tobacco 3.0%, other 2.0%.
Gross national product (at current market prices; 1987): U.S.\$160,000,000 (U.S.\$380 per capita).

Structure of gross domestic product and labour force				
	1987		1980	
	in value CF '000,000	% of total value	labour force	% of labour force
Agriculture	18,745	33.8	53,063	53.3
Mining	...	...	62	0.1
Manufacturing	6,518	11.8	3,946	4.0
Construction	5,386	9.7	3,267	3.3
Public utilities	1,581	2.9	129	0.1
Transportation and communications	2,292	4.1	2,118	2.1
Trade, restaurants, hotels	11,735[10]	21.2[10]	1,873	1.9
Finance, insurance	10	10	237	0.2
Public admin., defense	9,121	16.5	2,435	2.5
Services	10	10	4,646	4.7
Other	—	—	27,687[11]	27.8[11]
TOTAL	55,378	100.0	99,463	100.0

Public debt (external, outstanding; 1987): U.S.\$187,700,000.
Land use (1986)[12]: forested 16.0%; meadows and pastures 7.0%; agricultural and under permanent cultivation 45.0%; other 32.0%.

Foreign trade[13]

Balance of trade (current prices)						
	1983	1984	1985	1986	1987	1988
CF '000,000	−5,680	−15,700	−9,433	−5,796	−12,075	−9,245
% of total	27.7%	71.7%	40.1%	29.1%	63.4%	41.9%

Imports (1988): CF 15,645,000,000 (rice 15.6%, vehicles 7.9%, petroleum products 6.8%, iron and steel 4.9%, cement 4.5%, unspecified commodities 60.3%). *Major import sources* (1987): France 55.4%, Botswana 6.5%, Bahrain 6.4%, Réunion 5.6%, Kenya 4.2%.
Exports (1988): CF 6,400,000,000 (vanilla 77.7%, ylang-ylang 11.6%, cloves 7.3%). *Major export destinations* (1987): France 35.0%; United States 18.0%; West Germany 18.0%; Mauritius 12.0%.

Transport and communications

Transport. Railroads: none. Roads (1985): total length 466 mi, 750 km (paved 53%). Vehicles (1983): passenger cars, 3,600; trucks and buses, 2,000. Merchant marine (1988): vessels (100 gross tons and over) 4; total deadweight tonnage 1,456.' Air transport[14]: passenger arrivals and departures (1985) 33,000; cargo loaded and unloaded (1983) 172 metric tons; airports (1989) with scheduled flights 3.
Communications. Daily newspapers: none. Radio (1987): total number of receivers 100,000 (1 per 4.2 persons). Television: total number of receivers, none. Telephones (1983): 496 (1 per 740 persons).

Education and health

Education (1985–86)	schools	teachers	students	student/ teacher ratio
Primary (age 7–13)	257	1,901	66,084	34.8
Secondary	32[15]	432[15]	20,541	...
Voc., teacher tr.	4[15]	41[16]	334[16]	14.6[16]

Educational attainment (1980). Percent of population age 25 and over having: no formal schooling 56.7%; Qur'anic school education 8.3%; primary 3.6%; secondary 2.0%; higher 0.2%; not specified 29.2%. *Literacy* (1980): total population age 15 and over literate 82,053 (46.3%); males literate 46,586 (54.2%); females literate 35,467 (39.0%).
Health: physicians (1984) 31 (1 per 12,237 persons); hospital beds (1982) 813 (1 per 437 persons); infant mortality rate per 1,000 live births (1987) 96.0.
Food (1984–86)[12]: daily per capita caloric intake 2,110 (vegetable products 95%, animal products 5%); 90% of FAO recommended minimum requirement.

Military

Total active duty personnel (1988): 700–800 (army 100%). *Military expenditure as percent of GNP* (1986): 1.9% (world 5.5%); per capita expenditure U.S.\$6.

[1]Excludes Mayotte, a *collectivité territoriale* ("territorial collectivity") of France, unless otherwise indicated. [2]Island names in Comorian Swahili and French, respectively. [3]Mid-September. [4]1986. [5]Of which extrabudgetary accounts CF 10,748,000,000. [6]Export only. [7]1988. [8]Construction sector only. [9]Weights of consumer price index components. [10]Trade, restaurants, hotels includes Finance, insurance and Services. [11]Not adequately defined. [12]Includes Mayotte. [13]Import figures c.i.f.; export figures f.o.b. [14]Air Comores only. [15]1980–81. [16]1986–87.

Congo

Official name: République Populaire du Congo (People's Republic of the Congo).
Form of government: people's republic with one legislative body (People's National Assembly [133]).
Head of state and government: President (Chairman of the Central Committee).
Capital: Brazzaville.
Official language: French.
Official religion: none.
Monetary unit: 1 CFA franc (CFAF) = 100 centimes; valuation (Oct. 2, 1989) 1 U.S.$ = CFAF 317.90; 1 £ = CFAF 514.37.

Area and population

Regions	Capitals	area sq mi	area sq km	population 1984 census
Bouenza	Madingou	4,734	12,260	150,603
Cuvette	Owando	28,900	74,850	135,744
Kouilou	Pointe-Noire	5,274	13,660	74,870
Lékoumou	Sibiti	8,089	20,950	68,287
Likouala	Impfondo	25,500	66,044	49,505
Niari	Loubomo	10,011[1]	25,930[1]	110,003
Plateaux	Djambala	14,826	38,400	109,663
Pool	Kinkala	13,124	33,990	184,263
Sangha	Ouesso	21,544[2]	55,800[2]	34,213
Communes				
Brazzaville	—	25	65	585,812
Loubomo	—	5	12	49,134
Mossendjo	—	1	1	14,469
Nkayi	—	2	5	36,540
Ouesso	—	2	2	11,939
Pointe-Noire	—	13	34	294,203
TOTAL		132,047	342,000	1,909,248

Demography

Population (1989): 2,245,000.
Density (1989): persons per sq mi 17.0, persons per sq km 6.6.
Urban–rural (1984): urban 51.1%; rural 48.9%.
Sex distribution (1985): male 49.31%; female 50.69%.
Age breakdown (1985): under 15, 43.6%; 15–29, 25.8%; 30–44, 15.6%; 45–59, 9.5%; 60–74, 4.6%; 75 and over, 0.9%.
Population projection: (2000) 3,318,000; (2010) 4,732,000.
Doubling time: 26 years.
Ethnic composition (1983): Kongo 51.5%; Teke 17.3%; Mboshi 11.5%; Mbete 4.8%; Punu 3.0%; Sanga 2.7%; Maka 1.8%; Pygmy 1.5%; other 5.9%.
Religious affiliation (1980): Roman Catholic 53.9%; Protestant 24.9%; African Christian 14.2%; traditional beliefs 4.8%; other 2.2%.
Major cities (1984): Brazzaville 596,200[3]; Pointe-Noire 298,014[3]; Loubomo 49,134; Nkayi 36,540; Owando 16,021.

Vital statistics

Birth rate per 1,000 population (1985–90): 44.4 (world avg. 27.1); legitimate, n.a.; illegitimate, n.a.
Death rate per 1,000 population (1985–90): 17.2 (world avg. 9.9).
Natural increase rate per 1,000 population (1985–90): 27.2 (world avg. 17.2).
Total fertility rate (avg. births per childbearing woman; 1985–90): 6.0.
Marriage rate per 1,000 population: n.a.
Divorce rate per 1,000 population: n.a.
Life expectancy at birth (1985–90): male 46.9 years; female 50.2 years.
Morbidity (reported cases per 100,000 population; 1986): malaria 2,823; diarrhea 779; measles 443; hookworm 298; gonorrhea 244.

National economy

Budget (1988). Revenue: CFAF 284,000,000,000 (external financing 44.7%, petroleum revenue 24.7%, taxes and duties 16.4%, customs duties 12.0%). Expenditures: CFAF 284,000,000,000 (public debt 44.7%, administrative staff 27.6%, transfers 13.2%, investment 11.3%).
Public debt (external, outstanding; 1987): U.S.$3,679,000,000.
Tourism (1987): receipts from visitors U.S.$6,000,000; expenditures by nationals abroad U.S.$67,000,000.
Production (metric tons except as noted). Agriculture, forestry, fishing (1988): cassava 700,000, sugarcane 400,000, pineapples 114,000, plantains 65,000, bananas 32,000, avocados 22,000, peanuts (groundnuts) 17,000, palm oil 16,000, yams 15,000, corn (maize) 9,000, coffee 2,000, cacao beans 2,000, natural rubber 2,000; livestock (number of live animals) 186,000 goats, 70,000 cattle, 64,000 sheep; roundwood (1987) 2,614,000 cu m; fish catch (1987) 31,013. Mining and quarrying (1987): zinc concentrate 2,300; lead 1,400; gold 500 troy oz. Manufacturing (1985): raw sugar 51,010; cement 50,895; soap 2,146; wheat flour 1,048; cigarettes 1,027; peanut oil 1,000; beer 881,667 hectolitres; soft drinks 279,000 hectolitres; wine 58,150 hectolitres; veneer sheets 61,807 cu m; footwear 1,121,000 pairs. Construction: n.a. Energy production (consumption): electricity (kW-hr; 1987) 235,000,000 (288,000,000); coal, none (none); crude petroleum (barrels; 1988) 49,355,-000 ([1987] 3,813,000); petroleum products (metric tons; 1987) 506,000 (500,000); natural gas (cu m; 1987) 2,200,000 (2,200,000).
Land use (1986): forested 62.2%; meadows and pastures 29.3%; agricultural and under permanent cultivation 2.0%; other 6.5%.

Gross national product (at current market prices; 1987): U.S.$1,761,000,000 (U.S.$880 per capita).

Structure of gross domestic product and labour force

	1986 in value CFAF '000,000	1986 % of total value	1985 labour force	1985 % of labour force
Agriculture	77,424	12.1	434,000	61.2
Mining	99,444	15.5		
Manufacturing	61,277	9.6		
Construction	38,806	6.1		
Public utilities	9,054	1.4	86,000	12.1
Transportation and communications	71,067	11.1		
Trade, finance	104,377	16.3		
Pub. admin., defense				
Services	178,958	27.9	190,000	26.7
Other				
TOTAL	640,407	100.0	710,000	100.0

Population economically active (1985): total 710,000; activity rate of total population 40.8% (participation rates: ages 15–64, 69.4%; female 39.3%; unemployed, n.a.).

Price and earnings indexes (1985 = 100)

	1983	1984	1985	1986	1987	1988	1989
Consumer price index	83.6	94.2	100.0	102.5	104.8	108.6	113.2[4]
Earnings index	...	...	...	...	...	...	...

Household income and expenditure. Average household size (1980) 4.7; income per household, n.a.; sources of income: n.a.; expenditure: n.a.

Foreign trade[5]

Balance of trade (current prices)

	1981	1982	1983	1984	1985	1986
CFAF '000,000,000	+73.1	+55.8	+99.1	+246.8	+146.3	+50.2
% of total	14.3%	9.5%	13.9%	31.4%	17.8%	12.1%

Imports (1985): CFAF 337,600,000,000 (machinery and transport equipment 35.4%, of which general industrial machinery 8.1%, machinery for special industries 6.0%; basic manufactures 26.0%; food and live animals 16.4%, of which fish and fish preparations 5.5%, cereals 4.7%; metal manufactures 10.7%; chemicals and chemical products 8.4%). *Major import sources* (1987)[6]: France 52.6%; United Kingdom 6.9%; Italy 6.8%; West Germany 3.7%; Belgium–Luxembourg 3.6%.
Exports (1985): CFAF 483,900,000,000 (crude petroleum 90.1%; refined petroleum 3.2%; nonconiferous rough wood and shaped lumber 1.7%; diamonds 1.0%; sugar 0.8%). *Major export destinations* (1987)[7]: United States 45.0%; France 14.5%; Italy 8.8%; West Germany 7.6%; Spain 7.1%.

Transport and communications

Transport. Railroads (1986): length[3] 498 mi, 802 km; passenger-mi 283,-000,000, passenger-km 456,000,000; short ton-mi cargo 367,000,000, metric ton-km cargo 536,000,000. Roads (1985): total length 6,835 mi, 11,000 km (paved 5%). Vehicles (1982): passenger cars 30,500; trucks and buses 18,600. Merchant marine (1988): vessels (100 gross tons and over) 21; total deadweight tonnage 10,840. Air transport[8] (1987): passenger-mi 132,790,-000, passenger-km 213,706,000; short ton-mi cargo 24,739,000, metric ton-km cargo 36,119,000; airports (1989) with scheduled flights 6.
Communications. Daily newspapers (1986): total number 3; total circulation 24,000; circulation per 1,000 population 11. Radio (1988): total number of receivers 229,437 (1 per 9.4 persons). Television (1988): total number of receivers 5,786 (1 per 375 persons). Telephones (1987): 19,239 (1 per 111 persons).

Education and health

Education (1984–85)

	schools	teachers	students	student/teacher ratio
Primary (age 6–13)	1,522	7,612	458,338	60.2
Secondary (age 14–18)	247	5,188	199,073	38.4
Voc., teacher tr.	19	1,073	5,477	22.2
Higher	1	...	9,385	...

Educational attainment[9] (1974). Percent of population age 15 and over having: secondary education 30%, of which males 37%, females 23%. *Literacy* (1985): total population age 15 and over literate 620,000 (62.9%); males literate 332,000 (71.4%); females literate 288,000 (55.4%).
Health (1988): physicians 500 (1 per 4,334 persons); hospital beds 3,787 (1 per 572 persons); infant mortality rate per 1,000 live births (1985–90) 73.
Food (1987): daily per capita caloric intake 2,441 ([1984–86] vegetable products 93%, animal products 7%); (1984–86) 117% of FAO recommended minimum requirement.

Military

Total active duty personnel (1989): 8,800 (army 90.9%, navy 3.4%, air force 5.7%). *Military expenditure as percent of GNP* (1987): 4.6% (world 5.4%); per capita expenditure U.S.$51.

[1]Mossendjo is included with Niari. [2]Ouesso is included with Sangha. [3]1985. [4]June. [5]Import figures c.i.f.; export figures f.o.b. [6]Based on incomplete figures totaling CFAF 144,600,000,000. [7]Based on incomplete figures totaling CFAF 277,100,000,000. [8]Air Afrique only. [9]For the commune of Brazzaville only.

Costa Rica

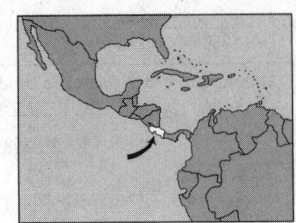

Official name: República de Costa Rica
(Republic of Costa Rica).
Form of government: unitary multiparty
republic with one legislative house
(Legislative Assembly [57]).
Head of state and government:
President.
Capital: San José.
Official language: Spanish.
Official religion: Roman Catholicism.
Monetary unit: 1 Costa Rican colón
(₡) = 100 céntimos; valuation (Oct. 2,
1989) 1 U.S.$ = ₡82.45;
1 £ = ₡133.40.

Area and population

Provinces	Capitals	area		population 1988 estimate[1]
		sq mi	sq km	
Alajuela	Alajuela	3,766	9,753	499,623
Cartago	Cartago	1,206	3,125	316,379
Guanacaste	Liberia	3,915	10,141	227,325
Heredia	Heredia	1,026	2,656	227,950
Limón	Limón	3,548	9,188	200,638
Puntarenas	Puntarenas	4,354	11,277	313,541
San José	San José	1,915	4,960	1,031,102
TOTAL		19,730	51,100	2,816,558

Demography

Population (1989): 2,941,000.
Density (1989): persons per sq mi 149.1, persons per sq km 57.8.
Urban–rural (1987): urban 49.6%; rural 50.4%.
Sex distribution (1988): male 50.52%; female 49.48%.
Age breakdown (1988): under 15, 36.5%; 15–29, 29.4%; 30–44, 18.5%; 45–59, 9.4%; 60–74, 4.9%; 75 and over, 1.3%.
Population projection: (2000) 3,711,000; (2010) 4,366,000.
Doubling time: 28 years.
Ethnic composition (1985): European 87.0%; mestizo 7.0%; black/mulatto 3.0%; East Asian (mostly Chinese) 2.0%; Amerindian 1.0%.
Religious affiliation (1987): Roman Catholic 88.6%; other (mostly Protestant) 11.4%.
Major cities (1984): San José 241,464 (metropolitan area [1988] 692,448); Limón 33,925; Alajuela 29,273; Puntarenas 28,390; Cartago 23,928.

Vital statistics

Birth rate per 1,000 population (1987): 28.9 (world avg. 27.1); (1984) legitimate 62.8%; illegitimate 37.2%.
Death rate per 1,000 population (1987): 3.8 (world avg. 9.9).
Natural increase rate per 1,000 population (1987): 25.1 (world avg. 17.2).
Total fertility rate (avg. births per childbearing woman; 1987): 3.3.
Marriage rate per 1,000 population (1985): 7.8.
Divorce rate per 1,000 population (1983): 1.0.
Life expectancy at birth (1985–90): male 72.4 years; female 77.0 years.
Major causes of death per 100,000 population (1986): diseases of the circulatory system 109.2, of which ischemic heart disease 55.6, cerebrovascular disease 28.4; malignant neoplasms (cancers) 79.2, of which stomach cancer 19.3; diseases of the respiratory system 40.1; accidents 30.9.

National economy

Budget (1988)[2]. Revenue: ₡53,435,000,000 (import duties and import surtaxes on nonessential and luxury goods 37.0%, income taxes 14.0%, general sales taxes 13.4%, export duties 9.1%, consumption taxes 7.0%). Expenditures: ₡58,864,900,000 (wages and salaries 67.8%, public-sector transfers 14.8%, internal debt 8.3%, external debt 4.1%).
Public debt (external, outstanding; 1987): U.S.$3,629,000,000.
Gross national product (at current market prices; 1987): U.S.$4,299,000,000 (U.S.$1,590 per capita).

Structure of gross domestic product and labour force

	1988[3]		1987	
	in value ₡'000,000	% of total value	labour force	% of labour force
Agriculture, fishing	2,161.3	19.3	268,653	27.5
Mining	} 2,475.9	} 22.1	2,596	0.3
Manufacturing			167,641	17.1
Construction	461.2	4.1	58,665	6.0
Public utilities	339.8	3.0	11,599	1.2
Transp. and commun.	873.8	7.8	39,667	4.1
Trade, restaurants	1,963.0	17.5	154,362	15.8
Finance, real estate	1,439.7	12.9	27,649	2.8
Public admin. and defense	1,028.1	9.2 }	226,229	23.1
Services	461.6	4.1 }		
Other	—	—	20,786	2.1
TOTAL	11,204.4	100.0	977,847	100.0

Production (metric tons except as noted). Agriculture, forestry, fishing (1988): sugarcane 2,730,000, bananas 1,050,000, rice 194,000, coffee 145,000, plantains 120,000, corn (maize) 105,000, oranges 82,000, pineapples 65,000, palm oil 58,000, cocoa beans 4,000, other products include cut flowers and ornamental plants grown for export; livestock (number of live animals) 2,360,000 cattle, 238,000 pigs, 6,000,000 chickens; roundwood (1987) 3,191,000 cu m; fish catch (1987) 20,000, of which shrimps 8,670. Mining and quarrying (1987): gold 13,000 troy oz. Manufacturing (value

added in ₡'000,000; 1984): food products 9,836; alcoholic and nonalcoholic beverages 3,734; petroleum products 1,622; wearing apparel 1,418; drugs and medicines 1,225; textiles 1,129; wood products 1,075. Construction (buildings authorized; 1985): residential 760,000 sq m; nonresidential 178,000 sq m. Energy production (consumption): electricity (kW-hr; 1987) 2,930,000,000 (3,005,000,000); coal, none (none); crude petroleum (barrels; 1987) none (4,754,000); petroleum products (metric tons; 1987) 557,000 (705,000); natural gas, none (none).
Population economically active (1987): total 977,847; activity rate of total population 37.5% (participation rates: ages 15–69, 59.5%; female 27.6%; unemployed [1988] 5.6%).

Price index (1985 = 100)

	1983	1984	1985	1986	1987	1988	1989
Consumer price index	77.6	86.9	100.0	111.8	130.7	157.9	177.6[4]
Monthly earnings index[5]	66.2	79.5	100.0	111.9	134.6	...	...

Tourism (1988): receipts from visitors U.S.$164,000,000; expenditures by nationals abroad U.S.$72,000,000.
Family income and expenditure: average household size (1984) 4.8[6]; income per urban family (1983) ₡181,416 (U.S.$4,415), income per rural family ₡98,328 (U.S.$2,393); sources of income: n.a.; expenditure (1974)[7]: food 40.8%, housing 12.3%, clothing and footwear 10.0%, education and recreation 9.2%, household furnishings 8.2%, energy 6.6%, other 12.9%.
Land use (1986): forested 32.4%; meadows and pastures 45.4%; agricultural and under permanent cultivation 10.4%; other 11.8%.

Foreign trade[8]

Balance of trade (current prices)

	1983	1984	1985	1986	1987	1988
₡'000,000	−411	+814	−810	+4,698	−5,685	+3,541
% of total	0.6%	0.9%	0.8%	3.9%	3.8%	1.8%

Imports (1988): ₡106,832,000,000 (primary and intermediate goods 48.9%; consumer goods 22.3%; capital goods 20.5%; fuels and lubricants 4.4%). *Major import sources* (1986): United States 35.8%; Japan 10.6%; West Germany 5.6%; Guatemala 5.4%; Venezuela 5.1%.
Exports (1988): ₡100,047,000,000 (nontraditional exports 46.3%, of which textiles [mostly assembled garments] 20.9%; coffee 24.9%; bananas 19.7%). *Major export destinations* (1986): United States 42.8%; West Germany 14.7%; Panama 4.0%; United Kingdom 3.9%; Guatemala 3.4%.

Transport and communications

Transport. Railroads (1987): route length 435 mi, 700 km; passenger-mi 56,000,000, passenger-km 90,000,000; short ton-mi cargo 102,700,000, metric ton-km cargo 150,000,000. Roads (1988): total length 21,970 mi, 35,357 km (paved 15%). Vehicles (1988): passenger cars 134,954; trucks and buses 89,641. Merchant marine (1988): vessels (100 gross tons and over) 25; total deadweight tonnage 13,980. Air transport (1988)[9]: passenger-mi 489,000,000, passenger-km 787,000,000; short-ton mi cargo 22,724,000, metric ton-km cargo 33,176,000; airports (1989) with scheduled flights 8.
Communications. Daily newspapers (1987): total number 6; total circulation 307,800; circulation per 1,000 population 110. Radio (1988): total number of receivers 253,171 (1 per 11 persons). Television (1988): total number of receivers 470,000 (1 per 6.1 persons). Telephones (1987): 408,755 (1 per 6.9 persons).

Education and health

Education (1988)

	schools	teachers	students	student/ teacher ratio
Primary (age 5–11)	3,207	11,113	409,621	36.9
Secondary (age 12–17)	169	6,052	116,488	19.2
Vocational	76	2,260	26,576	11.8
Higher[10]	8	5,211	50,033	9.6

Educational attainment (1984). Percent of economically active population age 25 and over having: no formal schooling 8.3%; incomplete primary education 28.6%; complete primary 26.3%; secondary 22.6%; postsecondary and higher 14.2%. *Literacy* (1984): total population age 15 and over literate 1,419,365 (92.6%); males literate 702,045 (92.6%); females literate 717,320 (92.6%).
Health: physicians (1984) 2,539 (1 per 1,011 persons); hospital beds (1986) 7,382 (1 per 368 persons); infant mortality per 1,000 live births (1988) 14.7.
Food (1984–86): daily per capita caloric intake 2,781 (vegetable products 83%, animal products 17%); (124% of FAO recommended minimum requirement).

Military

Military expenditure as percent of GNP (1987): 0.6% (world 5.4%); per capita expenditure U.S.$9. The army was officially abolished in 1948. Paramilitary and police forces had 9,500 members in 1988.

[1]January 1. [2]Excludes social-security revenue and contributions. [3]At prices of 1966. [4]March. [5]Wages of insured persons in nonagricultural activities. [6]Average urban household size (1984) 4.5, rural 5.1. [7]Based on survey of selected low- and middle-income families in San José only. [8]Import figures are f.o.b. in balance of trade and c.i.f. for commodities and trading partners. [9]Lacsa (Costa Rican Airlines). [10]1986; excludes correspondence schools.

Côte d'Ivoire

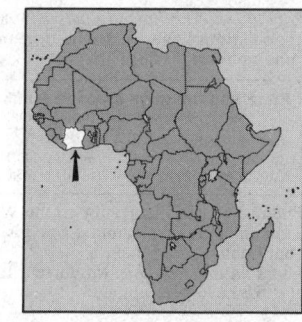

Official name: République de Côte d'Ivoire (Republic of Côte d'Ivoire [Ivory Coast])[1].
Form of government: single-party republic with one legislative house (National Assembly [175]).
Head of state and government: President.
Capital[2]*:* Abidjan (de facto; legislative).
  Capital designate: Yamoussoukro (de jure; administrative).
Official language: French.
Official religion: none.
Monetary unit: 1 CFA franc (CFAF) = 100 centimes; valuation (Oct. 2, 1989) 1 U.S.$ = CFAF 317.90; 1 £ = CFAF 514.37.

Area and population

Departments[3]	Capitals	area sq mi	area sq km	population 1975 census
Abengourou	Abengourou	2,664	6,900	177,692
Abidjan	Abidjan	5,483	14,200	1,389,141
Aboisso	Aboisso	2,413	6,250	148,823
Adzopé	Adzopé	2,019	5,230	162,837
Agboville	Agboville	1,486	3,850	141,970
Biankouma	Biankouma	1,911	4,950	75,711
Bondoukou	Bondoukou	6,382	16,530	296,551
Bongouanou	Bongouanou	2,151	5,570	216,907
Bouaflé	Bouaflé	2,189	5,670	164,817
Bouaké	Bouaké	9,189	23,800	808,048
Bouna	Bouna	8,290	21,470	84,290
Boundiali	Boundiali	3,048	7,895	96,449
Dabakala	Dabakala	3,734	9,670	56,230
Daloa	Daloa	4,483	11,610	265,529
Danané	Danané	1,776	4,600	170,249
Dimbokro	Dimbokro	3,293	8,530	258,116
Divo	Divo	3,058	7,920	202,511
Ferkessedougou	Ferkessedougou	6,845	17,728	90,423
Gagnoa	Gagnoa	1,737	4,500	174,018
Guiglo	Guiglo	5,463	14,150	137,672
Issia	Issia	1,386	3,590	104,081
Katiola	Katiola	3,637	9,420	77,875
Korhogo	Korhogo	4,826	12,500	276,816
Lakota	Lakota	1,054	2,730	76,105
Man	Man	2,722	7,050	278,659
Mankono	Mankono	4,116	10,660	82,358
Odienné	Odienné	7,954	20,600	124,010
Oumé	Oumé	927	2,400	85,486
Sassandra	Sassandra	6,768	17,530	116,644
Séguéla	Séguéla	4,340	11,240	75,181
Soubré	Soubré	3,193	8,270	75,350
Tingréla	Tingréla	849	2,200	35,829
Touba	Touba	3,367	8,720	77,786
Zuénoula	Zuénoula	1,093	2,830	98,792
TOTAL		123,847[4]	320,763	6,702,866

Demography

Population (1989): 12,135,000.
Density (1989): persons per sq mi 98.0, persons per sq km 37.8.
Urban–rural (1986): urban 47.0%; rural 53.0%.
Sex distribution (1985): male 51.09%; female 48.91%.
Age breakdown (1985): under 15, 45.1%; 15–29, 25.4%; 30–44, 15.6%; 45–59, 9.2%; 60–74, 4.0%; 75 and over 0.7%.
Population projection: (2000) 19,289,000; (2010) 29,398,000.
Doubling time: 21 years.
Ethnic composition (1975): Akan 41.4%; Kru 16.7%; Voltaic 15.7%; Malinke 14.9%; Southern Mande 10.2%; other 1.1%.
Religious affiliation (1989): animist 60.0%; Muslim 20.0%; Catholic 15.0%; Protestant 5.0%.
Major cities (1984): Abidjan 1,850,000; Bouaké 220,000; Yamoussoukro 120,000; Gagnoa 93,500[5]; Daloa 59,500.

Vital statistics

Birth rate per 1,000 population (1989): 46.0 (world avg. 27.1).
Death rate per 1,000 population (1989): 13.0 (world avg. 9.9).
Natural increase rate per 1,000 population (1989): 33.0 (world avg. 17.2).
Total fertility rate (avg. births per childbearing woman; 1989): 6.7.
Life expectancy at birth (1989): male 52.0 years; female 55.0 years.
Major causes of death per 100,000 population: n.a.; however, the major infectious diseases include malaria, dysentery, yaws, pneumonia, leprosy.

National economy

Budget (1989). Revenue: CFAF 645,304,000,000 (import taxes and duties 27.9%, income taxes 14.9%, export taxes and duties 13.1%, sales tax 8.6%). Expenditures: CFAF 645,304,000,000 (education 29.8%, public services 21.3%, agriculture 11.5%).
Public debt (external, outstanding; 1987): U.S.$8,450,000,000.
Tourism (1987): receipts U.S.$53,000,000; expenditures U.S.$163,000,000.
Production (metric tons except as noted). Agriculture (1988): yams 2,452,000, sugarcane 1,500,000, cassava 1,333,000, plantains 1,076,000, cacao beans 680,000, rice 597,000, coconuts 500,000, corn (maize) 448,000, pineapples 265,000, palm oil 235,000, coffee 187,000, cotton 114,000; livestock (number of live animals) 1,500,000 sheep, 1,500,000 goats, 960,000 cattle; roundwood (1987) 11,792,000 cu m; fish catch (1987) 102,453. Mining and quarrying (1988): diamonds 600,000 carats. Manufacturing (1986):

cement 770,000; beer 1,300,000 hectolitres; carbonated beverages 495,000 hectolitres; synthetic fibres 5,000,000 metres; other principal industries include food processing, cotton fibre and textiles, and chemicals (fertilizers, insecticides, paints). Construction (in CFAF; 1984): 62,000,000,000. Energy production (consumption): electricity (kW-hr; 1987) 2,200,000,000 (2,200,000,000); coal, none (n.a.); crude petroleum (barrels; 1987) 6,412,000 (13,077,000); petroleum products (metric tons; 1987) 1,709,000 (1,530,000).
Gross national product (1987): U.S.$8,262,000,000 (U.S.$750 per capita).

Structure of gross domestic product and labour force

	1988 in value CFAF '000,000,000	1988 % of total value	1985 labour force	1985 % of labour force
Agriculture	921[6]	31.1	2,452,000	60.5
Manufacturing, construction, mining, and public utilities	599[6]	20.2	409,000	10.1
Trade, finance, transp. and commun., pub. admin., defense, and services	1,443[6]	48.7	1,192,000	29.4
TOTAL	2,963	100.0	4,053,000	100.0

Population economically active (1985): total 4,053,000; activity rate of total population 41.3% (participation rates: ages 15–64, 71.4%; female 34.7%).

Price and earnings indexes (1985 = 100)

	1982	1983	1984	1985	1986	1987	1988
Consumer price index	88.9	94.2	98.2	100.0	107.3	107.7	115.2
Annual wage index	100.0	100.0	100.0	100.0	100.0	100.0	100.0

Household income and expenditure. Average household size (1980) 4.5; average annual income per household CFAF 500,000; sources of income: self-employment 49.9%, wages 44.9%, transfers and other resources 5.2%; expenditure (1985)[7]: food 48.0%, household goods 13.5%, transportation 12.2%, energy and water 8.5%.
Land use (1987): forested 20.1%; meadows and pastures 9.4%; agricultural and under permanent cultivation 11.4%; other 59.1%.

Foreign trade[8]

Balance of trade (current prices)

	1982	1983	1984	1985	1986	1987
CFAF '000,000,000	+36.8	+92.5	+525.8	+545.0	+451.4	+255.2
% of total	2.0%	6.2%	28.5%	26.1%	24.1%	15.9%

Imports (1987): CFAF 673,899,000,000 (machinery and transport equipment 21.3%, of which nonelectrical machinery 9.0%, transport equipment 8.5%, electrical machinery 3.8%; food products 20.2%; crude petroleum 15.0%; chemicals 13.8%). *Major import sources:* France 31.7%; Nigeria 10.9%; Japan 5.5%; Italy 5.4%; W.Ger. 5.2%.
Exports (1987): CFAF 929,143,000,000 (cacao beans 33.6%; coffee 12.7%; energy products 10.9%; cacao butter 5.9%; cotton 2.8%; fish products 2.4%; chemicals 2.3%; pineapples 2.3%). *Major export destinations:* The Netherlands 16.9%; France 15.2%; U.S. 10.5%; Italy 7.3%; W.Ger. 6.1%.

Transport and communications

Transport. Railroads (1987): length 549 km; passenger-km 857,800,000[8]; metric ton-km cargo 530,200,000[9]. Roads (1986): total length 55,000 km (paved 9%). Vehicles (1984): passenger cars 182,956; trucks and buses 52,491. Merchant marine (1988): vessels (100 gross tons and over) 56; total deadweight tonnage 149,337. Air transport[10] (1988): passenger-km 458,354,000; metric ton-km cargo 44,670,000; airports (1989) with scheduled flights 15.
Communications. Daily newspapers (1988): total number 2; total circulation 130,000; circulation per 1,000 population 11. Radio (1988): 1,477,736 receivers (1 per 7.9 persons). Television (1988): 625,000 receivers (1 per 19 persons). Telephones (1980): 88,000 (1 per 97 persons).

Education and health

Education (1984)

	schools	teachers	students	student/ teacher ratio
Primary (age 7–12)	5,976	28,561	1,179,456	41.3
Secondary (age 13–19)	218[11]	4,569[11]	245,043	...
Voc., teacher tr.	38[11]	1,947[12]	21,758	...
Higher	1[11]	1,204[13]	19,660	...

Educational attainment (1975). Percent of population age 6 and over having: no formal schooling 75.3%; primary education 17.3%; secondary 5.1%; higher 0.5%. *Literacy* (1985): population age 15 and over literate 57.3%.
Health (1982): physicians 502 (1 per 17,847 persons); hospital beds 10,062 (1 per 891 persons); infant mortality rate per 1,000 live births (1989) 102.
Food (1984–86): daily per capita caloric intake 2,550 (vegetable products 94%, animal products 6%); 110% of FAO recommended minimum.

Military

Total active duty personnel (1989): 7,100 (army 77.5%, navy 9.8%, air force 12.7%). *Military expenditure as percent of GNP* (1987): 1.9% (world 5.4%); per capita expenditure U.S.$17.

[1]From 1986, Côte d'Ivoire has requested that the French version of the country's name be utilized as the official protocol version in all languages. [2]Yamoussoukro officially named capital in 1983, but transfer of government functions remains incomplete. [3]Fifteen additional departments were created in 1985, for which separate data are not available. [4]Detail does not add to total given because of rounding. [5]1986. [6]Value is derived from given GDP total and corresponding percentage. [7]Weights of consumer price index components. [8]Imports c.i.f.; exports f.o.b. [9]1984; traffic includes Burkina Faso. [10]Air Afrique only. [11]1979–80. [12]1981. [13]1982.

Cuba

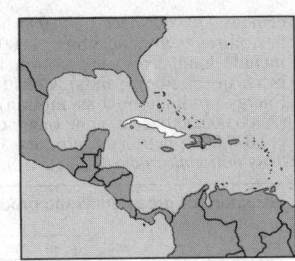

Official name: República de Cuba (Republic of Cuba).
Form of government: unitary socialist republic with one legislative house (National Assembly of the People's Power [510]).
Head of state and government: President.
Capital: Havana.
Official language: Spanish.
Official religion: none.
Monetary unit: 1 Cuban peso (CUP) = 100 centavos; valuation (Oct. 2, 1989) 1 CUP = U.S.$1.31 = £0.81.

Area and population

Provinces	Capitals	area sq mi	area sq km	population 1988 estimate[1]
Camagüey	Camagüey	6,174	15,990	723,437
Ciego de Ávila	Ciego de Ávila	2,668	6,910	352,896
Cienfuegos	Cienfuegos	1,613	4,178	353,540
Ciudad de la Habana[2]	—	281	727	2,059,223
Granma	Bayamo	3,232	8,372	773,247
Guantánamo	Guantánamo	2,388	6,186	484,464
Holguín	Holguín	3,591	9,301	972,047
La Habana[3]	Havana	2,213	5,731	629,972
Las Tunas	Las Tunas	2,544	6,589	477,943
Matanzas	Matanzas	4,625	11,978	595,938
Pinar del Río	Pinar del Río	4,218	10,925	678,197
Sancti Spíritus	Sancti Spíritus	2,604	6,744	420,312
Santiago de Cuba	Santiago de Cuba	2,382	6,170	968,191
Villa Clara	Santa Clara	3,345	8,662	796,148
Special municipality				
Isla de la Juventud	Nueva Gerona	926	2,398	70,646
TOTAL		42,804	110,861	10,356,201

Demography

Population (1989): 10,540,000.
Density (1989): persons per sq mi 246.2, persons per sq km 95.1.
Urban–rural (1988): urban 72.3%; rural 27.7%.
Sex distribution (1988): male 50.35%; female 49.65%.
Age breakdown (1988): under 15, 23.9%; 15–29, 31.4%; 30–44, 19.6%; 45–59, 13.5%; 60 and over, 11.6%.
Population projection: (2000) 11,844,000; (2010) 12,394,000.
Doubling time: 61 years.
Ethnic composition (1981): white 66.0%; mulatto 21.9%; black 12.0%.
Religious affiliation (1980): nonreligious 48.7%; Roman Catholic 39.6%; atheist 6.4%; Protestant 3.3%; Afro-Cuban syncretist 1.6%; other 0.4%.
Major cities (1988): Havana 2,059,223; Santiago de Cuba 389,654; Camagüey 274,974; Holguín 218,148; Guantánamo 192,590.

Vital statistics

Birth rate per 1,000 population (1988): 17.9 (world avg. 27.1).
Death rate per 1,000 population (1988): 6.5 (world avg. 9.9).
Natural increase rate per 1,000 population (1988): 11.4 (world avg. 17.2).
Total fertility rate (avg. births per childbearing woman; 1987): 1.8.
Marriage rate per 1,000 population (1988): 7.9.
Divorce rate per 1,000 population (1988): 3.4.
Life expectancy at birth (1983–84): male 72.7 years; female 76.1 years.
Major causes of death per 100,000 population (1986): diseases of the circulatory system 272.6, of which ischemic heart diseases 149.7, cerebrovascular disease 63.6; malignant neoplasms (cancers) 119.1; accidents, violence, and suicide 73.8.

National economy

Budget (1987). Revenue: CUP 11,574,600,000. Expenditures: CUP 11,689,600,000 (production capital 32.0%; education and public health 23.6%; social, cultural, and scientific activities 15.7%; defense, internal security 11.1%; housing, community services 7.5%).
Production (value of production in CUP '000,000 except as noted). Agriculture, forestry, fishing (1987[4]): sugarcane 741, milk 319, forage and silage 249, beef 244, eggs 134, pork 114, cereals 114, citrus fruits 101, tobacco 73, roots and tubers 71, vegetables 62, coffee 55, bananas 44; roundwood 3,251,000 cu m; fish catch 214,407 metric tons, of which crustaceans 19,994. Mining and quarrying (metric tons; 1987): chromite 60,000; nickel (metal content of ores) 34,000. Manufacturing (1988): processed food (excluding fish and refined sugar) 1,871; refined sugar 1,671; nonelectrical machinery 731; fuels 619; beverages and tobacco products 450; chemicals and chemical products 439; construction materials 390; textiles (excluding ready-made clothing) 343. Construction (1985): residential 4,819,000 sq m; nonresidential 1,803,000 sq m. Energy production (consumption): electricity (kW-hr; 1988) 14,541,000,000 (14,541,000,000); coal (metric tons; 1986) none (100,000); crude petroleum (barrels; 1988) 4,623,000 (46,817,000[5]); petroleum products (metric tons; 1986) 6,111,000 (9,886,000); natural gas (cu m; 1988) 21,900,000 (26,191,000[6]).
Household income and expenditure. Average household size (1981) 4.2; average annual income per household (1982) CUP 3,680 (U.S.$4,330); sources of income (1982): wages and salaries 57.3%, bonuses and other payments 42.7%; personal consumption (1987): food 25.6%, other retail purchases 61.8%, transportation services 5.7%, energy 2.4%, value of self-produced and consumed food 1.5%, other 3.0%.

Population economically active (1986): total 4,342,280; activity rate of total population 42.4% (participation rates: over age 15, 56.4%; female 35.8%; unemployed [1988] 6.0%).

Price and earnings indexes (1985 = 100)

	1981	1982	1983	1984	1985	1986	1987
Consumer implicit deflator index	84.1	90.1	94.9	98.0	100.0	101.4	103.0
Monthly earnings index[7]	90.4	93.8	95.9	99.0	100.0	100.1	98.1

Public debt (hard currency to the West; 1988): U.S.$6,400,000,000.
Tourism (1987): receipts from visitors U.S.$101,000,000; expenditures by nationals abroad, n.a.
Gross national product (at current market prices; 1984): U.S.$26,920,000,000 (U.S.$2,690 per capita).

Structure of global social product and labour force

	1987 in value CUP '000,000[8]	1987 % of total value	1987 labour force[7]	1987 % of labour force
Agriculture	4,080	16.0	632,800	19.2
Manufacturing[9]	11,286	44.1	726,900	22.1
Public utilities	660	2.6		
Construction	2,136	8.3	314,100	9.5
Transp. and commun.	2,045	8.0	225,300	6.8
Finance, insurance	—	—	20,600	0.6
Trade	5,129	20.1	376,200	11.4
Public administration	—	—	161,400	4.9
Services	—	—	792,800	24.0
Other	220	0.9	49,100	1.5
TOTAL	25,556	100.0	3,299,200	100.0

Land use (1986): forested 24.6%; meadows and pastures 24.0%; agricultural and under permanent cultivation 29.9%; other 21.5%.

Foreign trade[10]

Balance of trade (current prices)

	1982	1983	1984	1985	1986	1987
CUP '000,000	−597	−687	−1,751	−2,043	−2,275	−2,210
% of total	5.7%	5.9%	13.8%	14.6%	17.6%	17.0%

Imports (1987): CUP 7,611,000,000 (mineral fuels and lubricants 34.7%, nonelectrical machinery and apparatuses 18.4%, transport equipment 7.8%, electrical machinery and apparatuses 4.6%, cereals 4.1%). *Major import sources:* U.S.S.R. 72.2%; E.Ger. 4.5%; Czechoslovakia 2.5%; Bulgaria 2.4%; Romania 2.4%.
Exports (1987): CUP 5,401,000,000 (sugar 73.8%, petroleum products 6.7%, nickel ore 6.5%, citrus fruits 3.0%, fish products 2.6%). *Major export destinations:* U.S.S.R. 71.6%; E.Ger. 5.2%; Bulgaria 3.1%; Czech. 2.7%.

Transport and communications

Transport. Railroads (1988): route length (1987)[11] 3,140 mi, 5,053 km; passenger-km 2,621,700,000; metric ton-km cargo 2,444,700,000. Roads (1985): total length 21,100 mi, 34,000 km (paved 30%). Vehicles (1984): passenger cars 200,100; trucks and buses 164,500. Merchant marine (1988): vessels (100 gross tons and over) 412, total deadweight tonnage 1,218,841. Air transport: passenger-km (1988) 2,729,000,000; metric ton-km cargo (1987) 39,200,000; airports with scheduled flights (1989) 12.
Communications. Daily newspapers (1986): total number 17; total circulation 1,290,000; circulation per 1,000 population 126. Radio (1988): 3,434,903 receivers (1 per 3.0 persons). Television (1988): 2,069,345 receivers (1 per 5.0 persons). Telephones (1987): 564,212 (1 per 18 persons).

Education and health

Education (1987–88)

	schools	teachers	students	student/ teacher ratio
Primary (age 6–11)	9,617	59,819	936,914	15.7
Secondary (age 12–17)	1,321	65,796	775,345	11.8
Voc., teacher tr.	791	35,912	367,792	10.2
Higher	35	22,492	262,225	11.7

Educational attainment (1981). Percent of population age 25 and over having: no formal schooling or some primary education 39.6%; completed primary 26.6%; secondary 29.6%; higher 4.2%. *Literacy* (1985): total population age 15 and over literate 7,200,000 (96.0%).
Health (1987): physicians 28,060 (1 per 369 persons); hospital beds 58,695 (1 per 176 persons); infant mortality rate per 1,000 live births (1988) 11.9.
Food (1984–86): daily per capita caloric intake 3,107 (vegetable products 78%, animal products 22%); (1986) 128% of FAO recommended minimum requirement.

Military

Total active duty personnel (1988): 180,500 (army 80.3%, navy 7.5%, air force 12.2%)[12]. *Military expenditure as percent of GNP* (1985): 5.4% (world 5.7%); per capita expenditure: U.S.$158.

---

[1]January 1. [2]Province coextensive with the city of Havana. [3]Province bordering the city of Havana on the east, south, and west. [4]At constant prices of 1981. [5]1986. [6]1987. [7]State sector only; excludes military and unemployed. [8]At current prices of producers. [9]Includes mining. [10]Imports c.i.f.; exports f.o.b. [11]Figures exclude 4,785 mi (7,700 km) of nonpublic railways serving mostly sugar plantations or sugar factories. [12]Additional Soviet forces total 8,000.

Cyprus

Island of Cyprus

Area: 3,572 sq mi, 9,251 sq km.
Population (1989): 733,000.

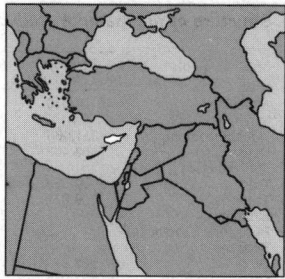

Two states currently exist de facto on the island of Cyprus: the Republic of Cyprus, predominantly Greek in character, occupying the southern two-thirds of the island, which is the original and still the internationally recognized de jure government of the whole island; and the Turkish Republic of Northern Cyprus (TRNC), proclaimed unilaterally Nov. 15, 1983, on territory originally secured for the Turkish Cypriot population by the July 20, 1974, intervention of Turkey, one of the guarantor powers entitled by Cyprus' 1960 independence treaties to act unilaterally "with the sole aim of reestablishing the state of affairs created by the . . . treaty." The TRNC has received no international recognition and the two ethnic communities have been unable to negotiate the reestablishment of a single state. Provision of separate data below is necessitated by the decade-long lack of unified data.

Republic of Cyprus

Official name: Kipriakí Demokratía (Greek); Kıbrıs Cumhuriyeti (Turkish) (Republic of Cyprus).
Form of government: unitary multiparty republic with a unicameral legislature (House of Representatives [80[1]]).
Head of state and government: President.
Capital: Nicosia.
Official languages: Greek; Turkish.
Monetary unit: 1 Cyprus pound (£C) = 100 cents; valuation (Oct. 2, 1989) 1£C = U.S.$2.03 = £1.25.

Area and population[2]

Districts	Capitals	area sq mi	area sq km	population 1989 estimate[3]
Famagusta	Famagusta	...	...	29,100
Larnaca	Larnaca	433	1,121	91,500
Limassol	Limassol	538	1,393	158,400
Nicosia	Nicosia	...	...	234,200
Paphos	Paphos	539	1,396	49,500
TOTAL		2,276	5,896	562,700

Demography

Population (1989): 564,000.
Urban–rural (1982): urban 63.6%; rural 36.4%.
Age breakdown (1987[4]): under 15, 25.4%; 15–29, 24.9%; 30–44, 21.3%; 45–64, 18.0%; 65 and over, 10.4%.
Ethnic composition (1982): Greek 99.2%; other 0.8%.
Religious affiliation (1989): predominantly Greek Orthodox.
Major urban areas (1989): Nicosia 166,900; Limassol 120,000; Larnaca 53,600.

Vital statistics

Birth rate per 1,000 population (1988): 19.2 (world avg. 27.1).
Death rate per 1,000 population (1988): 8.8 (world avg. 9.9).
Natural increase rate per 1,000 population (1988): 10.4 (world avg. 17.2).
Life expectancy at birth (1983–87): male 73.9 years; female 77.8 years.

National economy

Budget (1988): Revenue: £C 377,300,000 (indirect taxes 48.0%, direct taxes 35.3%). Expenditures: £C 406,000,000 (wages and salaries 45.2%, debt service 19.2%).
Tourism (1988): receipts U.S.$782,000,000; expenditures U.S.$136,000,000.
Household expenditure (1987): food and beverages 30.5%, transportation and communications 15.1%, household goods and operations 11.1%, clothing and footwear 9.5%, housing 6.2%.
Gross national product (1987): U.S.$3,532,000,000 (U.S.$5,210 per capita).

Structure of gross domestic product and labour force

	1988 in value £C '000,000	% of total value	labour force	% of labour force
Agriculture	144.2	7.3	36,000	13.8
Mining	6.9	0.3	900	0.3
Manufacturing	306.5	15.5	46,500	17.8
Construction	186.8	9.5	22,500	8.6
Public utilities	41.1	2.1	1,400	0.5
Transp. and commun.	178.0	9.0	14,200	5.4
Trade	391.9	19.8	53,300	20.4
Finance	272.3	13.8	12,900	4.9
Pub. admin., defense	239.2	12.1 }	45,200	17.3
Services	103.3	5.2 }		
Other	106.3[5]	5.4[5]	28,100[6]	10.8[6]
TOTAL	1,976.5	100.0	261,000	100.0[7]

Production

Production (metric tons except as noted). Agriculture (1988): grapes 200,000, potatoes 163,000, barley 144,000, citrus fruit (mainly grapefruit) 122,000; livestock (head; 1986) 500,000 sheep, 360,000 goats, 221,000 pigs. Manufacturing (1988): cement 867,000; wine 244,000 hectolitres; footwear 8,000,000 pairs. Energy production: electricity (kW-hr; 1988) 1,667,000,000.

Foreign trade

Imports (1988): £C 866,800,000 (consumer goods 20.4%, transport equipment 12.6%, petroleum and petroleum products 9.0%). *Major import sources:* United Kingdom 13.9%; Japan 11.6%; Italy 10.3%.
Exports (1988): £C 330,900,000 (clothing 22.5%, chemical and toiletries 5.5%, footwear 5.0%, potatoes 4.9%). *Major export destinations:* United Kingdom 21.6%; Libya 8.7%; Greece 8.3%.

Transport and communications

Transport. Roads (1988): total length 9,186 km. Vehicles (1987): passenger cars 142,569; trucks and buses 56,500. Merchant marine (1988): vessels (100 gross tons and over) 1,352; total deadweight tonnage 32,810,581. Air transport (1987): passenger-km 2,150,607,000; metric ton-km cargo 225,-981,000; airports (1989) 1.
Communications. Daily newspapers (1987): 10; total circulation 85,550; circulation per 1,000 population 157. Radio (1987): 197,932 receivers (1 per 2.7 persons). Television (1988): 165,000 receivers (1 per 3.4 persons). Telephones (1987): 272,200 (1 per 2.0 persons).

Education and health

Education (1987–88)

	schools	teachers	students	student/ teacher ratio
Primary (age 5–12)	379	2,562	56,530	22.1
Secondary (age 12–18)	95	2,886	38,785	13.4
Vocational	10	444	3,406	7.7
Higher	19	359	4,247	11.8

Literacy (1987): population age 15 and over literate 94.5%.
Health (1987): physicians 1,195 (1 per 570 persons); hospital beds 4,256 (1 per 160 persons); infant mortality rate per 1,000 live births (1988) 11.0.

Turkish Republic of Northern Cyprus

Official name: Kuzey Kıbrıs Türk Cumhuriyeti (Turkish) (Turkish Republic of Northern Cyprus).
Capital: Lefkoşa (Nicosia).
Official language: Turkish.
Monetary unit: 1 Turkish lira (LT) = 100 kurush; valuation (Oct. 2, 1989) 1 U.S.$ = LT 2,230; 1£ = LT 3,609.

Area and population

Districts	Administrative centres	area sq mi	area sq km	population 1987 estimate
Lefkoşa (Nicosia)	Lefkoşa	...	...	76,800
Gazimagosa (Famagusta)	Gazimagosa	...	...	62,584
Girne (Kyrenia)	Girne	247	640	25,651
TOTAL		1,295	3,355	165,035

Population (1989): 169,000 (Lefkoşa [1987]: 38,507).
Ethnic composition (1985): Turkish 98.7%, other 1.3%.

Structure of gross domestic product and labour force

	1987 in value LT '000,000	1987 % of total value	1985 labour force	1985 % of labour force
Agriculture	36,081	12.7	20,595	33.6
Manufacturing	32,572	11.5	6,213	10.1
Construction	22,686	8.0	4,454	7.3
Transp. and commun.	20,450	7.2	4,004	6.5
Trade	66,584	23.5	5,386	8.8
Finance	13,199	4.7	1,531	2.5
Real estate	8,171	2.9	...	...
Pub. admin.	47,161	16.6	14,475	23.6
Services	15,319	5.4	4,641	7.6
Other (customs duties)	21,627	7.6	—	—
TOTAL	283,848[7]	100.0[7]	61,299[8]	100.0

Budget (1987). Revenue: LT 106,067,500,000 (aid grants 25.4%, direct taxes 24.7%, indirect taxes 20.6%). Expenditures: LT 106,067,500,000 (current expenditures 79.1%, of which personnel 36.8%; defense 5.6%).
Imports (1987): U.S.$221,042,900 (machinery and transport equipment 29.7%). *Major import sources:* Turkey 42.7%; U.K. 14.2%; W.Ger. 5.9%.
Exports (1987): U.S.$55,119,900 (food and live animals 61.6%). *Major export destinations:* U.K. 66.5%; Turkey 14.3%.

Education (1987–88)

	schools	teachers	students	student/ teacher ratio
Primary (age 7–12)	158	758	17,963	23.7
Secondary (age 13–18)	35	719	14,393	20.0
Vocational	9	225	1,958	8.7
Higher	4	153	3,311	21.6

Health (1987): physicians 219 (1 per 754 persons); hospital beds 761 (1 per 217 persons); infant mortality rate per 1,000 live births 10.3.

[1]24 seats reserved for Turkish Cypriots not occupied. [2]Areas under government control; includes UN Buffer Zone and U.K. Sovereign Base Areas. [3]January 1. [4]Includes imputed adjustment for de jure population of Turkish sector. [5]Less bank service charges plus import duties and other. [6]Includes 7,400 unemployed and 7,700 working abroad. [7]Detail does not add to total given because of rounding. [8]Total of available detail.

Czechoslovakia

Official name: Československá
Socialistická Republika (Czechoslovak
Socialist Republic).
Form of government: federal republic
with one legislative house (Federal
Assembly [350][1]).
Chief of state: interim President.
Head of government: Premier.
Capital: Prague.
Official languages: Czech; Slovak.
Official religion: none.
Monetary unit: 1 koruna (Kčs) = 100
halura; valuation (Oct. 2, 1989)
1 U.S.$ = Kčs 15.05; 1 £ = Kčs 24.35.

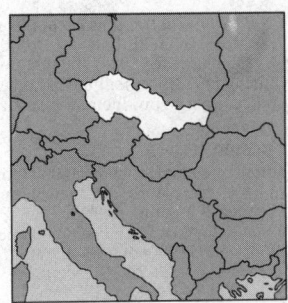

Structure of net material product and labour force

	1987			
	in value Kčs '000,000	% of total value	labour force[2]	% of labour force[2]
Agriculture	44,616	7.6	978,600	12.6
Mining and manufacturing	351,060	59.8	2,913,609	37.4
Construction	63,402	10.8	796,271	10.2
Public utilities	—	—	137,706	1.8
Transp. and commun.	29,353	5.0	507,595	6.5
Trade	96,277	16.4	906,655	11.6
Finance	—	—	[3]	[3]
Pub. admin., defense	—	—	177,393	2.3
Services	—	—	1,358,593[3]	17.4[3]
Other	2,348[4]	0.4[4]	20,100[4]	0.3[4]
TOTAL	587,056	100.0	7,796,522	100.0[5]

Population economically active[2, 6] (1987): total 7,796,522; activity rate of total population 50.1% (participation rates: working age 88.2%; female 46.1%; unemployed, n.a.).

Price and earnings indexes (1985 = 100)

	1981	1982	1983	1984	1985	1986	1987
Consumer price index	91.3	95.9	96.9	97.8	100.0	100.7	100.8
Monthly earnings index	92.7	94.8	96.6	98.3	100.0	102.9	103.0

Household income and expenditure. Average household size (1987) 2.9; income per household (1987) Kčs 82,750 (U.S.$15,240); sources of income: wages and salaries 61.5%, transfer payments 19.7%, other 18.8%; expenditure (1987): food 26.1%, services 11.7%, clothing and footwear 8.7%.

Area and population

Republics Regions	Capitals	area sq mi	area sq km	population 1988[2] estimate
Czech Socialist Republic	Prague			
Jihočeský	České Budějovice	4,380	11,345	696,097
Jihomoravský	Brno	5,802	15,028	2,057,645
Severočeský	Ústí nad Labem	3,019	7,819	1,188,452
Severomoravský	Ostrava	4,273	11,067	1,965,024
Středočeský	Prague	4,245	10,994	1,126,255
Východočeský	Hradec Králové	4,340	11,240	1,241,249
Západočeský	Plzeň	4,199	10,875	869,996
Slovak Socialist Republic	Bratislava			
Středoslovenský	Banská Bystrica	6,944	17,986	1,599,772
Východoslovenský	Košice	6,251	16,191	1,484,130
Západoslovenský	Bratislava	5,595	14,492	1,722,616
Capital Cities				
Prague	—	192	496	1,206,098
Bratislava	—	142	367	429,734
TOTAL		49,382	127,900	15,587,068

Demography

Population (1989): 15,636,000.
Density (1989): persons per sq mi 316.6, persons per sq km 122.3.
Urban–rural (1988): urban 75.7%; rural 24.3%.
Sex distribution (1988): male 48.71%; female 51.29%.
Age breakdown (1988): under 15, 23.9%; 15–29, 21.0%; 30–44, 22.9%; 45–59, 15.7%; 60–74, 11.7%; 75 and over, 4.8%.
Population projection: (2000) 16,086,000; (2010) 16,456,000.
Doubling time: n.a.; population growth is negligible.
Ethnic composition (1987): Czech 63.0%; Slovak 31.6%; Hungarian 3.8%; Polish 0.5%; German 0.4%; Ukrainian 0.3%; Russian 0.1%; other 0.3%.
Religious affiliation (1980): Roman Catholic 65.6%; atheist 20.1%; Czechoslovak Church (non-Roman Catholic) 4.4%; Evangelist Church of Czech Brethren 1.4%; other 8.5%.
Major cities (1989): Prague 1,211,106; Bratislava 435,499; Brno 389,892; Ostrava 330,614; Košice 232,253.

Vital statistics

Birth rate per 1,000 population (1987): 13.8 (world avg. 27.1); legitimate 92.9%; illegitimate 7.1%.
Death rate per 1,000 population (1987): 11.5 (world avg. 9.9).
Natural increase rate per 1,000 population (1987): 2.3 (world avg. 17.2).
Total fertility rate (avg. births per childbearing woman; 1987): 2.0.
Marriage rate per 1,000 population (1987): 7.8.
Divorce rate per 1,000 population (1987): 2.5.
Life expectancy at birth (1987): male 67.5 years; female 75.0 years.
Major causes of death per 100,000 population (1987): diseases of the circulatory system 546.8; malignant neoplasms (cancers) 208.0; bronchitis, emphysema, and asthma 60.9; accidents, poisonings, and violence 66.6, of which suicides 15.4; diseases of the digestive system 47.0.

National economy

Budget (1987). Revenue: Kčs 383,732,000,000 (receipts from enterprises 72.1%; taxes 9.1%). Expenditures: Kčs 382,151,000,000 (education, health, social welfare, and culture 26.5%; national economy 24.8%; defense 7.5%).
Public debt (external, outstanding; 1987): U.S.$5,900,000,000.
Tourism (1987): receipts from visitors U.S.$402,000,000; expenditures by nationals abroad U.S.$229,000,000.
Production (metric tons except as noted). Agriculture, forestry, fishing (1987): sugar beets 6,697,000, wheat 6,154,000, barley 3,551,000, potatoes 3,072,000, corn (maize) 1,160,000; livestock (number of live animals; 1988) 7,235,000 pigs, 5,044,000 cattle, 1,075,000 sheep, 47,984,000 chickens; roundwood 18,526,000 cu m; fish catch 20,736. Mining and quarrying (1987): iron ore 1,798,000; copper 24,762; zinc 20,736; lead 19,800. Manufacturing (1988): crude steel 15,380,000; rolled steel 11,420,000; cement 10,974,000; sulfuric acid 1,249,000; plastic and resins 1,191,900; chemical fertilizers 873,450; cotton fabrics 591,240,000 m; beer 22,670,000 hectolitres; other alcoholic beverages 1,227,000 hectolitres; road motor vehicles 214,332 units. Construction (1987): 4,223,000 sq m. Energy production (consumption): electricity (kW-hr; 1987) 85,825,000,000 (89,246,000,000); coal (metric tons; 1987) 126,072,000 (124,647,000); crude petroleum (barrels; 1987) 997,000 (116,189,000); petroleum products (metric tons; 1987) 13,284,000 (12,691,000); natural gas (cu m; 1987) 783,000,000 (11,632,000,000).
Land use (1987): agricultural 40.1%; forested 36.0%; meadows and pastures 12.9%; other 11.0%.
Gross national product (at current market prices; 1988): U.S.$158,168,000,000 (U.S.$10,140 per capita).

Foreign trade

Balance of trade (current prices)

	1982	1983	1984	1985	1986	1987	1988
Kčs '000,000	+5,681	+8,115	+9,661	+6,137	−1,974	−2,192	+3,978
% of total	1.8%	2.4%	2.6%	1.6%	0.5%	0.5%	0.9%

Imports (1988): Kčs 209,199,000,000 (1987; machinery and transport equipment 35.7%, of which industrial machinery 9.3%, agricultural and construction machinery 8.4%, transport equipment 8.2%; fuels and other energy 27.9%; consumer goods 8.4%; chemicals 6.7%; food and tobacco 5.9%). *Major import sources:* U.S.S.R. 31.1%; E.Ger. 9.4%; Poland 8.2%; W.Ger. 8.1%; Austria 5.3%; Hungary 4.3%; Yugoslavia 3.3%; Bulgaria 2.5%.
Exports (1988): Kčs 213,177,000,000 (1987; machinery and transport equipment 58.1%, of which industrial machinery 12.1%, road vehicles and parts 8.1%; consumer goods 15.8%; chemicals 5.9%; mineral fuels and lubricants 3.3%). *Major export destinations:* U.S.S.R. 33.5%; Poland 8.1%; W.Ger. 7.7%; E.Ger. 6.9%; Hungary 4.2%; Austria 4.1%; Yugoslavia 3.2%; Bulgaria 2.7%; Romania 1.5%; Switzerland 1.5%.

Transport and communications

Transport. Railroads (1987): length 8,141 mi, 13,102 km; passenger-mi 12,445,000,000, passenger-km 20,029,000,000; short ton-mi cargo 46,563,000,000, metric ton-km cargo 67,985,000,000. Roads (1988): total length 45,733 mi, 73,601 km (paved 100%). Vehicles (1985): passenger cars 2,694,994; trucks and buses 425,174. Merchant marine (1988): vessels (100 gross tons and over) 18; total deadweight tonnage 231,720. Air transport (1987): passenger-mi 1,518,111,000, passenger-km 2,443,167,000; short ton-mi cargo 43,132,000, metric ton-km cargo 62,975,000; airports (1989) 14.
Communications. Daily newspapers (1987): total number 30; total circulation 4,372,000; circulation per 1,000 population 280. Radio (1988): 4,257,556 receivers (1 per 3.7 persons). Television (1988): 4,387,144 receivers (1 per 3.6 persons). Telephones (1987): 3,838,000 (1 per 4.1 persons).

Education and health

Education (1986–87)

	schools	teachers	students	student/ teacher ratio
Primary (age 6–14)	6,274	97,385	2,088,750	21.4
Secondary (age 15–18)	343	9,723	134,103	13.8
Voc., teacher tr.	561	17,044	257,968	15.1
Higher	36	19,459	169,011	8.7

Educational attainment (1980). Percent of adult population having: less than full primary education 1.2%; primary and less than full secondary 52.6%; full secondary 41.2%; higher 5.0%. *Literacy* (1987): total population age 15 and over literate 11,856,000 (100%); males literate 5,684,000 (100%); females literate 6,172,000 (100%).
Health (1988): physicians 48,711 (1 per 312 persons); hospital beds 155,082 (1 per 99 persons); infant mortality rate per 1,000 live births (1987) 13.1.
Food (1984–86): daily per capita caloric intake 3,473 (vegetable products 66%, animal products 34%); (1984) 132% of FAO recommended minimum requirement.

Military

Total active duty personnel (1988): 197,000 (army 73.6%; navy, none; air force 26.4%). *Military expenditure as percent of GNP* (1987): 6.8% (world 5.4%); per capita expenditure U.S.$662.

---

[1]Usually meets in two separate bodies (Chamber of Nations [150]; Chamber of the People [200]. [2]End of 1987. [3]Services include finance. [4]Includes other activities of the material sphere. [5]Detail does not add to total given because of rounding. [6]Excludes women on maternity leave and includes workers of working age, which is 15–59 for men and 15–54 for women.

Denmark

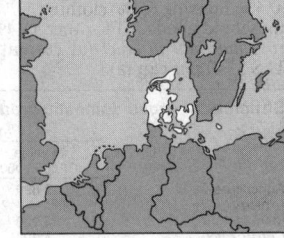

Official name: Kongeriget Danmark (Kingdom of Denmark).
Form of government: parliamentary state and constitutional monarchy with one legislative house (Folketing [179]).
Chief of state: Danish Monarch.
Head of government: Prime Minister.
Capital: Copenhagen.
Official language: Danish.
Official religion: Evangelical Lutheran.
Monetary unit: 1 krone (Dkr; plural kroner) = 100 øre; valuation (Oct. 2, 1989) 1 U.S.$ = Dkr 7.30; 1 £ = Dkr 11.81.

Area and population[1]		area		population
		sq mi	sq km	1988 estimate
Counties	Capitals			
Århus	Århus	1,761	4,561	592,878
Bornholm	Rønne	227	588	46,526
Frederiksborg	Hillerød	520	1,347	340,218
Fyn	Odense	1,346	3,486	457,365
København	—	203	526	603,176
Nordjylland	Ålborg	2,383	6,173	483,724
Ribe	Ribe	1,209	3,131	218,347
Ringkøbing	Ringkøbing	1,874	4,853	266,960
Roskilde	Roskilde	344	891	215,605
Sønderjylland	Åbenrå	1,520	3,938	250,303
Storstrøm	Nykøbing	1,312	3,398	257,280
Vejle	Vejle	1,157	2,997	329,949
Vestjælland	Sorø	1,152	2,984	283,142
Viborg	Viborg	1,592	4,122	231,028
Cities				
Copenhagen (København)	—	34	88	467,810
Frederiksberg	—	3	9	85,404
TOTAL		16,638[2]	43,093[2]	5,129,715

Demography

Population (1989): 5,135,000.
Density (1989): persons per sq mi 308.6, persons per sq km 119.2.
Urban-rural (1986): urban 84.4%; rural 15.6%.
Sex distribution (1989): male 49.28%; female 50.72%.
Age breakdown (1989): under 15, 17.3%; 15–29, 22.7%; 30–44, 22.7%; 45–59, 16.8%; 60–74, 13.6%; 75 and over, 6.9%.
Population projection: (2000) 5,176,000; (2010) 5,065,000.
Doubling time: not applicable; population is stable.
Ethnic composition (1989): Danish 97.2%; Turkish 0.5%; other Scandinavian 0.4%; British 0.2%; Yugoslav 0.2%; other 1.5%.
Religious affiliation (1987): Evangelical Lutheran 90.6%; Roman Catholic 0.5%; Jewish 0.1%; other 8.8%.
Major cities (1986): Greater Copenhagen 1,340,618[3]; Århus 195,152; Odense 137,286; Ålborg 113,650; Frederiksberg 85,404[3, 4].

Vital statistics

Birth rate per 1,000 population (1988): 11.5 (world avg. 27.1); (1987) legitimate 55.5%; illegitimate 44.5%.
Death rate per 1,000 population (1988): 11.5 (world avg. 9.9).
Natural increase rate per 1,000 population (1988): 0.0 (world avg. 17.2).
Total fertility rate (avg. births per childbearing woman; 1987): 1.5.
Marriage rate per 1,000 population (1987): 6.1.
Divorce rate per 1,000 population (1987): 2.8.
Life expectancy at birth (1986–87): male 71.8 years; female 77.6 years.
Major causes of death per 100,000 population (1987): ischemic heart disease 319.8; malignant neoplasms (cancers) 286.5; cerebrovascular disease 101.0.

National economy

Budget (1988). Revenue: Dkr 258,113,000,000 (customs and excise taxes 47.4%, income and property taxes 41.3%, other 11.3%). Expenditures: Dkr 257,596,000,000 (social services 26.3%, interest payments 18.9%, education 7.5%, defense 5.2%, other 42.1%).
National debt (end of year 1987): Dkr 412,856,000,000.
Tourism (1988): receipts from visitors U.S.$2,423,000,000; expenditures by nationals abroad U.S.$3,087,000,000.
Population economically active (1986): total 2,816,069; activity rate of total population 55.0% (participation rates: ages 15–64, 80.7%; female 45.8%; unemployed [1988] 8.7%).

Price and earnings indexes (1985 = 100)						
	1983	1984	1985	1986	1987	1988	1989
Consumer price index	89.9	95.5	100.0	103.6	107.8	112.7	117.5[5]
Hourly earnings index[6]	91.6	95.6	100.0	105.1	115.2	122.8	...

Household income and expenditure. Average household size (1989) 2.2; income per household (1986) Dkr 222,800 (U.S.$27,500); principal sources of income (1981): wages and salaries 67.6%, transfers 17.5%, self-employment 9.3%, interest 5.6%; expenditure (1987): housing and energy 25.7%; food, beverages, and tobacco 22.7%; transportation 16.4%; recreation and education 9.9%.
Production (in Dkr '000,000 except as noted). Agriculture, forestry, fishing (value added; 1988): pork 13,512, milk 12,233, beef 4,935, barley 3,977, flowers and plants 2,279, wheat 2,199, mink furs 1,886, sugar beets 1,176;

roundwood (1987) 2,203,000 cu m; fish catch (1987) 1,695,718 metric tons. Mining and quarrying (1988): sand and gravel 35,900,000 cu m; white chalk 2,300,000 cu m. Manufacturing (value added; 1987): nonelectrical machinery and apparatus 15,454; food other than meat 14,322; industrial chemicals and other chemical products 12,854; metal products 9,693; processed meat 7,929; electrical machinery and apparatus 7,709; bricks, cement, and tiles 5,895. Construction (1987): residential 2,932,000 sq m; nonresidential 5,962,000 sq m. Energy production (consumption): electricity (kW-hr; 1988) 25,788,000,000 ([1987] 31,812,000,000); coal (metric tons; 1987) none (11,921,000); crude petroleum (barrels; 1988) 36,315,000 ([1987] 52,453,000); petroleum products (metric tons; 1987) 7,325,000 (9,149,000); natural gas (cu m; 1988) 2,271,000,000 ([1987] 1,544,000,000).
Gross national product (1987): U.S.$76,640,000,000 (U.S.$15,010 per capita).

Structure of gross domestic product and labour force				
	1988		1986	
	in value Dkr '000,000	% of total value	labour force	% of labour force
Agriculture	27,474	4.5	160,333	5.7
Mining	2,768	0.5	3,746	0.2
Manufacturing	123,703	20.3	560,791	19.9
Construction	37,751	6.2	197,367	7.0
Public utilities	10,006	1.6	17,475	0.6
Transp. and commun.	51,192	8.4	194,046	6.9
Trade	84,056	13.8	402,512	14.3
Finance, real estate	116,015	19.0	228,786	8.1
Pub. admin., defense	141,623	23.2	189,000	6.7
Services	33,308	5.5	817,191	29.0
Other	−18,471[7]	−3.0[7]	44,822	1.6
TOTAL	609,425	100.0	2,816,069	100.0

Land use (1986): forested 11.6%; meadows and pastures 5.1%; agricultural and under permanent cultivation 61.6%; other 21.7%.

Foreign trade[8]

Balance of trade (current prices)					
	1983	1984	1985	1986	1987	1988
Dkr '000,000	−4,371	+1,076	−3,560	−4,830	+8,891	+16,952
% of total	1.5%	0.3%	1.0%	1.4%	2.6%	4.7%

Imports (1988): Dkr 178,269,000,000 (consumer goods 24.1%; machinery and capital equipment 11.5%, chemicals and related products 9.0%; machinery parts 6.2%; fuels and lubricants 6.1%). *Major import sources:* West Germany 23.2%; Sweden 12.3%; U.K. 7.1%; U.S. 6.0%; The Netherlands 6.0%.
Exports (1988): Dkr 187,381,000,000 (machinery and instruments 23.4%; agricultural products 15.5%, of which live swine or pork 5.9%; chemicals and related products 9.8%; transport equipment 4.9%; fish, crustaceans, and mollusks 4.8%). *Major export destinations:* West Germany 17.6%; U.K. 11.7%; Sweden 11.5%; Norway 7.0%; U.S. 5.8%.

Transport and communications

Transport. Railroads (1987): length 1,539 mi, 2,476 km; passenger-mi 2,974,-000,000, passenger-km 4,787,000,000; short ton-mi cargo 1,151,000,000, metric ton-km cargo 1,680,000,000. Roads (1987): total length 43,614 mi, 70,190 km (paved 100%). Vehicles (1987): passenger cars 1,587,419; trucks and buses 287,532. Merchant marine (1988): vessels (100 gross tons and over) 944; total deadweight tonnage 6,332,880[9]. Air transport (1988)[10]: passenger-mi 2,210,000,000, passenger-km 3,556,000,000; short ton-mi cargo 88,490,000, metric ton-km cargo 129,193,000; airports (1989) with scheduled flights 12.
Communications. Daily newspapers (1988): total number 48; total circulation 1,881,000; circulation per 1,000 population 366. Radio (1988): 2,118,-232 receivers (1 per 2.4 persons). Television (1988): 1,932,336 receivers (1 per 2.7 persons). Telephones (1987): 4,434,000 (1 per 1.2 persons).

Education and health

Education (1987–88)	schools	teachers	students	student/ teacher ratio
Primary (age 7–12)	2,523	34,744[11]	380,049	11.6[11]
Secondary (age 13–18)	3,218	38,821[11]	319,034	8.7[11]
Vocational	340	...	181,682	...
Higher	96	...	109,504	...

Educational attainment (1987). Percent of population age 25–66 having: primary education 2.7%; completed lower secondary 25.9%; completed upper secondary or vocational 45.3%; advanced vocational 6.7%; undergraduate 5.7%; graduate 3.8%; unknown 9.9%. *Literacy* (1986): virtually 100%.
Health (1987): physicians 13,144 (1 per 390 persons); hospital beds 32,325 (1 per 159 persons); infant mortality rate per 1,000 live births 8.3.
Food (1984–86): daily per capita caloric intake 3,512 (vegetable products 56%, animal products 44%); 131% of FAO recommended minimum requirement.

Military

Total active duty personnel (1989): 31,600 (army 53.8%, navy 24.4%, air force 21.8%). *Military expenditure as percent of GNP* (1987): 2.2% (world 5.4%); per capita expenditure U.S.$418.

---

[1]Excludes Greenland and the Faeroe Islands. [2]Detail does not add to total given because of rounding. [3]1988. [4]Within Greater Copenhagen. [5]April. [6]Industrial workers. [7]Imputed bank service charges. (Dkr 23,093,000,000) less other producers (Dkr 4,622,000,000). [8]Import figures are f.o.b. in balance of trade and c.i.f. in commodities and trading partners. [9]Includes Greenland and the Faeroe Islands. [10]Danish part of Scandinavian Airlines System. [11]1985–86.

Djibouti

Official name: Jumhūrīyah Jībūtī (Arabic); République de Djibouti (French) (Republic of Djibouti).
Form of government: unitary single-party republic with one legislative house (National Assembly [65]).
Chief of state: President.
Head of government: Prime Minister.
Capital: Djibouti.
Official languages: Arabic; French.
Official religion: none.
Monetary unit: 1 Djibouti franc (DF) = 100 centimes; valuation (Oct. 2, 1989) 1 U.S.$ = DF 177.72; 1 £ = DF 287.55.

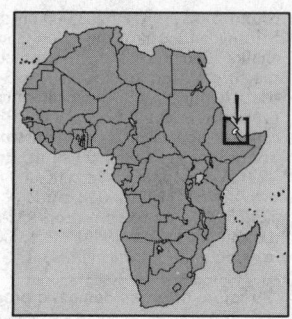

Area and population

Districts	Capitals	area[1] sq mi	area[1] sq km	population 1982 estimate
'Alī Sabīh (Ali-Sabieh)	'Alī Sabīh	925	2,400	15,000
Dikhil	Dikhil	2,775	7,200	30,000
Djibouti	Djibouti	225	600	200,000
Obock	Obock	2,200	5,700	15,000
Tadjoura (Tadjourah)	Tadjoura	2,825	7,300	30,000
TOTAL		8,950	23,200	335,000[2]

Demography

Population (1989): 512,000.
Density (1989): persons per sq mi 57.2, persons per sq km 22.1.
Urban–rural (1983): urban 75.0%; rural 25.0%.
Sex distribution (1983): male 51.80%; female 48.20%.
Age breakdown (1983): under 15, 38.4%; 15–29, 33.5%; 30–44, 16.9%; 45–50, 3.0%; 51 and over, 8.2%.
Population projection: (2000) 709,000; (2010) 953,000.
Doubling time: 23 years.
Ethnic composition (1983): Somali 61.7%, of which Issa 33.4%, Gadaboursi 15.0%, Issaq 13.3%; Afar 20.0%; Arab (mostly Yemeni) 6.0%; European 4.0%; other (refugees) 8.3%.
Religious affiliation (1983): Sunnī Muslim 94%; Christian 6%, of which Roman Catholic 4%, Protestant 1%, Orthodox 1%.
Major city and towns (1982): Djibouti 220,000[3]; 'Alī Sabīh 4,000; Tadjoura 3,500; Dikhil 3,000.

Vital statistics

Birth rate per 1,000 population (1985–90): 47.3 (world avg. 27.1).
Death rate per 1,000 population (1985–90): 17.7 (world avg. 9.9).
Natural increase rate per 1,000 population (1985–90): 29.6 (world avg. 17.2).
Total fertility rate (avg. births per childbearing woman; 1985–90): 6.6.
Marriage rate per 1,000 population (1982): 6.7.
Divorce rate per 1,000 population (1982): 1.9.
Life expectancy at birth (1985–90): male 45.4 years; female 48.7 years.
Major causes of death[4] (percentage of total deaths; 1984): diarrhea and acute dehydration 16.0%; malnutrition 16.0%; poisonings 11.0%; tuberculosis 6.0%; acute respiratory disease 6.0%; malaria 6.0%; anemia 6.0%; heart disease 2.0%; kidney disease 1.0%; other ailments 19.0%; no diagnosis 11.0%.

National economy

Budget (1988). Revenue: DF 23,267,000,000 (current receipts 93.3%, of which indirect taxes 60.6%, direct taxes 21.5%, nontax revenue 11.2%; external development receipts 6.0%). Expenditures: DF 23,266,000,000 (wages and salaries 57.7%; goods and services 27.9%; development expenditures 3.9%).
Public debt (external, outstanding; 1988): U.S.$157,000,000.
Tourism: receipts from visitors (1987) U.S.$6,000,000; expenditures by nationals abroad, n.a.
Production (metric tons except as noted). Agriculture, forestry, fishing (1988): vegetables and melons 16,000, of which tomatoes (1985–86) 1,225, eggplant (1985–86) 66; livestock (number of live animals) 500,000 goats, 412,000 sheep, 70,000 cattle, 58,000 camels, 8,000 asses; fish catch (1987) 440. Mining and quarrying: mineral production limited to locally used construction material and evaporated salt. Manufacturing (1984): detail n.a.; main items produced are furniture, nonalcoholic beverages, light electromechanical goods, and mineral water. Construction (1985): residential 32,214 sq m; nonresidential 21,722 sq m. Energy production (consumption): electricity (kW-hr; 1987) 172,000,000 (172,000,000); coal, none (n.a.); crude petroleum, none (n.a.); petroleum products (metric tons; 1987) none (86,000); natural gas, none (n.a.).
Population economically active (1985): total 161,000; activity rate of total population 44.5% (participation rates: over age 10, 65.2%; female 39.1%; unemployed [1987] c. 40–50%).

Price and earnings indexes (October 1978 = 100)

	1980	1981	1982	1983	1984	1985	1986
Consumer price index[5]	123.6	130.7	127.5	128.7	130.9	129.4[6]	158.5[6]
Monthly earnings index[7]	...	...	...	...	...	...	...

Household income and expenditure. Average household size[8] (1982) 5.6; income per household: n.a.; sources of income (1976): wages and salaries 51.6%, self-employment 36.0%, transfer payments 10.5%, other 1.9%; expen-

diture (expatriate households; 1984): food 50.3%, energy 13.1%, recreation 10.4%, housing 6.4%, clothing 1.7%, personal effects 1.4%, health care 1.0%, household goods 0.3%, other 15.4%.
Gross national product (at current market prices; 1984): U.S.$301,540,000 (U.S.$740 per capita).

Structure of gross domestic product and labour force

	1984 in value DF '000,000	1984 % of total value	1985 labour force	1985 % of labour force
Agriculture	2,690	4.5	125,000	77.5
Mining	—	—		
Manufacturing	4,920	8.2	12,000	7.3
Construction	4,490	7.5		
Public utilities	1,942	3.2		
Transportation and communications	6,010	10.0		
Trade	9,400	15.6		
Finance	6,530	10.8	24,000	15.2
Pub. admin., defense	16,170	26.8		
Services	950	1.6		
Other	7,132[9]	11.8[9]		
TOTAL	60,234	100.0	161,000	100.0

Land use (1986): forested 0.3%; meadows and pastures 9.1%; agricultural and under permanent cultivation[10]; built-on, wasteland, and other 90.6%.

Foreign trade[11]

Balance of trade (current prices)

	1981	1982	1983	1984	1985	1986
DF '000,000	−38,311	−37,965	−37,388	−37,063	−33,182	−29,847
% of total	92.5%	89.5%	90.7%	88.7%	87.0%	80.4%

Imports (1986): U.S.$188,357,000 (food and beverages 27.9%; machinery and electrical machinery 10.8%; textiles and footwear 10.3%; khat [a narcotic leaf] 9.0%; fossil fuels 7.0%; metals and metal products 5.9%; transport equipment and vehicles 5.6%). *Major import sources* (1987): France 19.9%; Bahrain 17.1%; United Kingdom 8.7%; Japan 8.4%; Korea 5.8%; Ethiopia 5.3%.
Exports (1987): U.S.$39,000,000 ([1983] unspecified special transactions 89.6%, of which live animals [including camels] 30.8%, food and food products 18.6%). *Major export destinations:* Yemen (Şanʻaʼ) 34.9%; Yemen (Aden) 26.4%; Somalia 10.8%; Seychelles 6.4%; Ethiopia 4.8%; Italy 4.4%; France 3.6%.

Transport and communications

Transport. Railroads (1984): length 66 mi, 106 km; short ton-mile cargo 90,140,000, metric ton-km cargo 131,600,000[12]. Roads (1988): total length 1,805 mi, 2,905 km (paved 10%). Vehicles (1985): passenger cars 12,049; trucks and buses 951. Merchant marine (1988): vessels (100 gross tons and over) 7; total deadweight tonnage 2,650. Air transport[13] (1987): passenger arrivals 67,856, passenger departures 61,518; cargo loaded 1,612 metric tons, cargo unloaded 6,036 metric tons; airports (1989) with scheduled flights 3.
Communications. Weekly newspapers (1987): total number 1; total circulation 4,000; circulation per 1,000 population 8.5. Radio (1987): total number of receivers 30,000 (1 per 16 persons). Television (1988): total number of receivers 14,000 (1 per 35 persons). Telephone subscribers (1987): 8,699 (1 per 55 persons).

Education and health

Education (1987–88)

	schools	teachers	students	student/ teacher ratio
Primary (age 6–11)	61	655	28,924	44.2
Secondary (age 12–18) }	19	307[14]	8,046	...
Voc., teacher tr.				
Higher[15]	—	—	161	—

Educational attainment, n.a. *Literacy* (1987): population age 20 and over literate 33.7%.
Health (1987): physicians 89 (1 per 5,427 persons); hospital beds 1,185[16] (1 per 408 persons); infant mortality rate per 1,000 live births (1985–90) 122.
Food: n.a.

Military

Total active duty personnel (1989): 3,030[17] (army 94.7%, navy 2.0%, air force 3.3%). *Military expenditure as percent of GNP* (1984): 9.0% (world 5.7%); per capita expenditure U.S.$67.

[1]Original figures are those given in sq km; sq mi equivalent is rounded to appropriate level of generality. [2]Including 45,000 not distributed by district. [3]1987. [4]Infants and children to age 10, district of Djibouti only. [5]European expatriate community only. [6]June only. [7]Minimum monthly wage remained constant between 1980 and 1986. [8]City of Djibouti only. [9]Import duties, less imputed bank service charge. [10]In 1987 only 947 acres (383 hectares) of land were cultivated. [11]The value of imports includes merchandise destined for Ethiopia and northern Somalia; that of exports excludes reexports coming from those areas. In 1980 the value of reexports from Ethiopia and northern Somalia was approximately five times greater than the value of domestic exports. Import figures are c.i.f. [12]Based on total weight of Ethiopian exports and imports transported to and from the port of Djibouti. [13]Djibouti International Airport only. [14]Public schools only. [15]1983–84. [16]Public health only. [17]Excludes 3,650 French troops.

Dominica

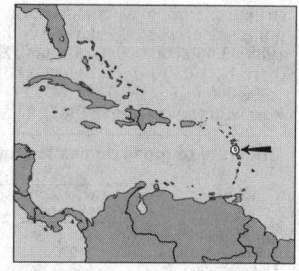

Official name: Commonwealth of Dominica.
Form of government: multiparty republic with one legislative house (House of Assembly [31][1]).
Chief of state: President.
Head of government: Prime Minister.
Capital: Roseau.
Official language: English.
Official religion: none.
Monetary unit: 1 East Caribbean dollar (EC$) = 100 cents; valuation (Oct. 2, 1989) 1 U.S.$ = EC$2.70; 1 £ = EC$4.37.

Area and population

Parishes[2]	area		population 1981
	sq mi	sq km	census
St. Andrew	69	179	12,748
St. David	49	127	7,337
St. George	21	54	20,501
St. John	23	60	5,412
St. Joseph	46	119	6,606
St. Luke	4	10	1,503
St. Mark	4	10	1,921
St. Patrick	32	83	9,780
St. Paul	26	67	6,386
St. Peter	11	29	1,601
TOTAL	290[3, 4]	750[3, 4]	73,795[5, 6]

Demography

Population (1989): 82,800.
Density (1989): persons per sq mi 285.5, persons per sq km 110.4.
Urban–rural: n.a.
Sex distribution[5] (1981): male 49.81%; female 50.19%.
Age breakdown[5] (1981): under 15, 39.8%; 15–29, 28.6%; 30–44, 11.9%; 45–59, 9.2%; 60–74, 7.4%; 75 and over, 3.1%.
Population projection: (2000) 92,000; (2010) 102,000.
Doubling time: 52 years.
Ethnic composition (1981): black 91.2%; mixed race 6.0%; Amerindian 1.5%; white 0.5%; not stated 0.6%; other 0.2%.
Religious affiliation (1981): Roman Catholic 76.9%; Protestant 15.5%, of which Methodist 5.0%, Seventh-day Adventist 3.2%, Pentecostal 2.9%; other 7.6%.
Major towns (1987): Roseau (urban area) 22,000; Portsmouth (urban area) 5,000; Marigot 3,554[7]; St. Joseph 2,665[7].

Vital statistics

Birth rate per 1,000 population (1987): 19.1 (world avg. 27.1); (1980) legitimate 35.0%; illegitimate 65.0%.
Death rate per 1,000 population (1987): 5.6 (world avg. 9.9).
Natural increase rate per 1,000 population (1987): 13.5 (world avg. 17.2).
Total fertility rate (avg. births per childbearing woman; 1987): 3.1.
Marriage rate per 1,000 population: n.a.
Divorce rate per 1,000 population: n.a.
Life expectancy at birth (1985–90)[8]: male 64.3 years; female 68.6 years.
Major causes of death per 100,000 population (1984): diseases of the circulatory system 197.8; malignant neoplasms (cancers) 88.6; diseases of the respiratory system 27.9; endocrine and metabolic disorders 26.7; ill-defined conditions 44.9.

National economy

Budget (1986–87). Revenue: EC$112,400,000 (tax revenues 75.4%, of which consumption taxes on international trade 26.8%, income taxes 21.1%, import duties 9.3%, consumption taxes on domestic production 9.0%; foreign grants 15.6%). Expenditures: EC$116,200,000 (current expenditures 73.1%, of which public debt charges 5.9%; development expenditures 26.9%).
Gross national product (1987): U.S.$115,000,000 (U.S.$1,440 per capita).

Structure of gross domestic product and labour force

	1987		1981	
	in value EC$'000,000[9]	% of total value	labour force	% of labour force
Agriculture	82.8	29.9	7,843[8]	31.0[8]
Mining	1.9	0.7	8	—
Manufacturing	18.2	6.6	1,417	5.6
Construction	14.8	5.4	2,306	9.1
Public utilities	7.5	2.7	245	1.0
Transportation and communications	38.4	13.9	914	3.6
Trade, hotels, restaurants	31.8	11.5	1,613	6.3
Finance, real estate, insurance	32.2	11.6	257	1.0
Pub. admin., defense	57.1	20.6	4,980	19.7
Services	2.8	1.0		
Other	−10.8[10]	−3.9[10]	5,750[11]	22.7
TOTAL	276.7	100.0	25,333	100.0

Public debt (external, outstanding; end of 1987): U.S.$66,000,000.
Population economically active (1981): total 25,333; activity rate of total population 34.3% (participation rates: ages 15–64, 61.7%; female 34.1%; unemployed [1988] 10.0%).

Price and earnings indexes (1985 = 100)

	1982	1983	1984	1985	1986	1987	1988
Consumer price index	92.1	95.9	98.0	100.0	103.0	108.0	109.4[12]
Earnings index	...	...	...	...	...	...	...

Household income and expenditure. Average household size (1981) 4.3; income per household: n.a.; expenditure (1984)[13]: food and nonalcoholic beverages 43.1%, housing and utilities 16.1%, clothing and footwear 6.5%, alcoholic beverages and tobacco 2.0%, other 32.3%.
Production (metric tons except as noted). Agriculture, forestry, fishing (1987): bananas 70,400[14], root crops (mostly dasheens and tanias) 26,000, coconuts 15,000, grapefruits 8,000, limes 6,000, oranges 3,000, cucumbers and gherkins 3,000, cocoa 429[15], coffee 366[15], cut flowers 20[15], bay oil 18[15]; livestock (number of live animals) 9,000 pigs, 6,000 goats, 4,000 cattle; roundwood, n.a.; fish catch 366. Mining and quarrying (1987): pumice and volcanic ash 100,000. Manufacturing (1984): coconut-based soaps 6,571[16, 17]; galvanized sheets 2,739; coconut meal 789; edible coconut oil 6,600 hectolitres; other products include paint, cigarettes, and bottled spring water. Construction (value of starts[18]; 1988): U.S.$12,300,000. Energy production (consumption): electricity (kW-hr; 1987) 19,000,000 (19,000,000); coal, none (none); crude petroleum, none (none); petroleum products (metric tons; 1987) none (13,000); natural gas, none (none).
Tourism (1987): receipts from visitors U.S.$11,000,000; expenditures by nationals abroad U.S.$3,000,000.
Land use (1986): forested 41.0%; meadows and pastures 3.0%; agricultural and under permanent cultivation 23.0%; other 33.0%.

Foreign trade[19]

Balance of trade (current prices)

	1982	1983	1984	1985	1986	1987
EC$'000,000	−62.2	−53.5	−81.6	−72.6	−33.5	−50.6
% of total	32.0%	28.2%	37.1%	32.1%	12.5%	16.3%

Imports (1985): EC$149,400,000 (machinery and transport equipment 22.5%, of which road vehicles and parts 8.4%; food 19.3%, of which cereals and cereal preparations 5.9%; crude petroleum and petroleum products 10.1%; paper and paper products 6.9%). *Major import sources:* United States 27.2%; United Kingdom 16.7%; Trinidad and Tobago 9.8%; Japan 7.4%; St. Lucia 5.7%.
Exports (1985): EC$76,800,000 (food 54.3%, of which bananas 48.2%; coconut-based soaps 25.0%). *Major export destinations:* United Kingdom 50.1%; Jamaica 14.7%; United States 4.4%; Trinidad and Tobago 4.3%; Barbados 4.3%.

Transport and communications

Transport. Railroads: none. Roads (1984): total length 489 mi, 787 km (paved 60%). Vehicles (1983): passenger cars 2,713; trucks and buses 1,250. Merchant marine (1988): vessels (100 gross tons and over) 6; total deadweight tonnage 4,218. Air transport (1984): passenger arrivals 33,954, passenger departures 34,381; cargo unloaded 196 metric tons, cargo loaded 271 metric tons; airports (1989) with scheduled flights 2.
Communications. Daily newspapers: none. Radio (1988): total number of receivers 34,575 (1 per 2.4 persons). Television: [20]. Telephones (1985): 6,882 (1 per 11 persons).

Education and health

Education (1987–88)

	schools	teachers	students	student/teacher ratio
Primary	66	646	16,105	24.9
Secondary	9	171	3,264	19.1
Vocational[21]	...	27	259	9.6
Higher	2	...	...	...

Educational attainment (1981). Percent of population age 25 and over having: no formal schooling 6.6%; primary education 80.6%; secondary 11.1%; higher 1.7%. *Literacy* (1981): total population age 15 and over literate 42,100 (94.9%).
Health (1987): physicians 25 (1 per 3,248 persons); hospital beds 189[18] (1 per 430 persons); infant mortality rate per 1,000 live births (1982–84 avg.) 16.3.
Food (1984–86): daily per capita caloric intake 2,649 (vegetable products 84%, animal products 16%); 109% of FAO recommended minimum requirement.

Military

Total active duty personnel (1987): none[22].

---

[1]Includes 10 nonelective seats. Nine of the 10 nonelective seats are potentially elective according to the constitution. [2]Dominica is divided into 10 parishes for statistical purposes only. Local government is based on village or town councils. [3]Includes inland water area. [4]Detail does not add to total given because of rounding. [5]Excludes institutionalized population. [6]Total population including institutionalized residents equals 74,785. [7]1981. [8]UN estimated average for English-speaking Caribbean countries. [9]At factor cost. [10]Less imputed service charges. [11]Includes 4,746 unemployed. [12]Average of second and third quarters. [13]Weights of consumer price index components. [14]1988. [15]1984. [16]1987. [17]Coconut-based soap products accounted for 75% of total value added of manufacturing sector in 1986. [18]Roseau only. [19]Imports c.i.f.; exports f.o.b. [20]Cable service is provided to part of Dominica. [21]1985–86. [22]300-member police force has residual responsibilities for defense.

Dominican Republic

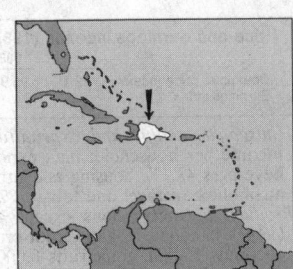

Official name: República Dominicana (Dominican Republic).
Form of government: multiparty republic with two legislative houses (Senate [30]; Chamber of Deputies [120]).
Head of state and government: President.
Capital: Santo Domingo.
Official language: Spanish.
Official religion: none[1].
Monetary unit: 1 Dominican peso (RD$) = 100 centavos; valuation (Oct. 2, 1989) 1 U.S.$ = RD$6.41; 1 £ = RD$10.37.

Area and population

Provinces	Capitals	area sq mi	area sq km	population 1989 estimate
Azua	Azua	938	2,430	189,742
Bahoruco (Baoruco)	Neiba	531	1,376	86,739
Barahona	Barahona	976	2,528	151,294
Dajabón	Dajabón	344	890	63,656
Duarte	San Francisco de Macorís	499	1,292	259,817
El Seibo	El Seibo	641	1,659	96,879
Espaillat	Moca	386	1,000	180,919
Hato Mayor	Hato Mayor	514	1,330	77,255
Independencia	Jimaní	719	1,861	42,763
La Altagracia	Higüey	1,191	3,084	110,431
La Estrelleta	Elías Piña	690	1,788	72,122
La Romana	La Romana	209	541	162,430
La Vega	La Vega	916	2,373	300,838
María Trinidad Sánchez	Nagua	506	1,310	124,235
Monseñor Nouel	Bonao	388	1,004	123,884
Monte Cristi	Monte Cristi	768	1,989	92,002
Monte Plata	Monte Plata	841	2,179	173,525
Pedernales	Pedernales	373	967	18,758
Peravia	Baní	626	1,622	185,448
Puerto Plata	Puerto Plata	726	1,881	228,063
Salcedo	Salcedo	206	533	109,413
Samaná	Samaná	382	989	72,469
San Cristóbal	San Cristóbal	604	1,564	318,581
San Juan	San Juan	1,375	3,561	264,685
San Pedro de Macorís	San Pedro de Macorís	450	1,166	193,157
Sánchez Ramírez	Cotuí	453	1,174	139,610
Santiago	Santiago de los Caballeros	1,205	3,122	688,770
Santiago Rodríguez	Sabaneta	394	1,020	61,121
Santo Domingo[2]	—	570	1,477	2,313,104
Valverde	Mao	220	570	110,657
TOTAL		18,704[3]	48,443[3]	7,012,367

Demography

Population (1989): 7,012,000.
Density (1989): persons per sq mi 374.9, persons per sq km 144.7.
Urban–rural (1986): urban 54.6%; rural 45.4%.
Sex distribution (1989): male 50.82%; female 49.18%.
Age breakdown (1989): under 15, 38.2%; 15–29, 30.1%; 30–44, 17.3%; 45–59, 9.1%; 60–74, 4.3%; 75 and over, 1.0%.
Population projection: (2000) 8,621,000; (2010) 9,904,000.
Doubling time: 28 years.
Ethnic composition (1983): mulatto 73%; white 16%; black 11%.
Religious affiliation (1987): Roman Catholic 91.9%; other (mostly evangelical Protestant and followers of voodoo) 8.1%.
Major cities (1986): Santo Domingo 1,600,000; Santiago de los Caballeros 308,400; La Romana 101,350; San Pedro de Macorís 86,950.

Vital statistics

Birth rate per 1,000 population (1985–90): 31.3 (world avg. 27.1); (1976) legitimate 32.8%; illegitimate 67.2%.
Death rate per 1,000 population (1985–90): 6.8 (world avg. 9.9).
Natural increase rate per 1,000 population (1985–90): 24.5 (world avg. 17.2).
Total fertility rate (avg. births per childbearing woman; 1985–90): 3.8.
Marriage rate per 1,000 population (1986): 2.9.
Divorce rate per 1,000 population (1986): 1.2.
Life expectancy at birth (1985–90): male 63.9 years; female 68.1 years.
Major causes of death per 100,000 population (1982): infectious and parasitic diseases 47.0; diseases of pulmonary circulation 31.6%; diseases of the respiratory system 29.4; ill-defined conditions 96.3.

National economy

Budget (1988). Revenue: RD$4,780,700,000 (tax revenue 81.4%, of which import duties 34.5%, income taxes 17.6%, taxes on goods 15.7%; nontax revenue 10.5%). Expenditures: RD$4,834,200,000 (administration 52.6%; education 7.0%; defense 5.8%; health and welfare 5.4%).
Public debt (external, outstanding; 1987): U.S.$2,938,000,000.
Tourism (1987): receipts from visitors U.S.$500,000,000; expenditures by nationals abroad U.S.$90,000,000.
Production (metric tons except as noted). Agriculture (1987): sugarcane 8,772,000, unhusked rice 514,700, bananas 400,000, tomatoes 173,100, coffee cherries 134,300, beans 52,200, cacao 38,700, raw tobacco 28,700, raw cotton 7,400; livestock (number of live animals) 2,637,000 pigs; 2,058,000 cattle; roundwood 982,000 cu m; fish catch 20,325. Mining (value of production in RD$'000,000; 1986): gold 277; ferronickel 253. Manufacturing (value of production in RD$'000,000; 1986): food products 1,515; alcoholic beverages 558; refined petroleum 505; cigarettes 215; cement 158. Con-struction (value of construction in RD$'000,000; 1986): residential 288; nonresidential 198. Energy production (consumption): electricity (kW-hr; 1988) 3,460,000,000 (2,618,000,000); coal, none (none); crude petroleum (barrels; 1987) none (10,628,000); petroleum products (metric tons; 1987) 1,382,000 (1,864,000).
Gross national product (1987): U.S.$4,930,000,000 (U.S.$730 per capita).

Structure of gross domestic product and labour force

	1986 in value U.S.$'000,000[4]	1986 % of total value	1981 labour force	1981 % of labour force
Agriculture	513.4	16.0	420,463	22.0
Mining	119.8	3.7	4,743	0.2
Manufacturing	544.3	16.9	224,437	11.7
Construction	221.8	6.9	80,850	4.3
Public utilities	62.1	1.9	13,891	0.7
Transp. and commun.	257.4	8.0	40,470	2.1
Trade	497.1	15.5	192,181	10.0
Finance, real estate	351.2	10.9	22,369	1.2
Pub. admin., defense	335.3	10.4	363,125	18.9
Services	313.9	9.8		
Other	—	—	552,859[5]	28.9[5]
TOTAL	3,216.3	100.0	1,915,388	100.0

Population economically active (1981): total 1,915,388; activity rate of total population 33.9% (participation rates: ages 15–64, 53.6%; female 28.9%; unemployed [1987] 27.0%).

Price and earnings indexes (1985 = 100)

	1982	1983	1984	1985	1986	1987	1988
Consumer price index	54.6	57.2	72.7	100.0	109.7	127.2	188.0[6]
Monthly earnings index	...	...	...	...	...	...	...

Household income and expenditure. Average household size (1981) 5.1; average annual income per family (1975) urban family RD$2,299, rural family RD$654; sources of income: n.a.; expenditure (1976–77)[7]: food, beverages, and tobacco 51.7%, housing 23.9%, clothing and footwear 6.0%.
Land use (1986): forested 12.9%; meadows and pastures 43.2%; agricultural and under permanent cultivation 30.5%; other 13.4%.

Foreign trade

Balance of trade (current prices)

	1983	1984	1985	1986	1987	1988
RD$'000,000	−493.8	−389.0	−547.4	−544.1	−880.2	−717.9
% of total	23.9%	18.3%	27.0%	27.4%	38.2%	28.7%

Imports (1985): RD$1,293,000,000 (crude petroleum and petroleum products 33.2%, foodstuffs 13.4%, machinery 9.3%). *Major import sources:* U.S. 35.2%; Venezuela 25.8%; Mexico 7.9%; Japan 6.1%.
Exports (1985): RD$735,200,000 (raw sugar 21.5%, ferronickel 16.3%, gold alloy 15.4%, coffee 11.7%, cacao 7.9%, raw tobacco 2.4%). *Major export destinations:* U.S. 68.9%; The Netherlands 7.2%; Puerto Rico 7.1%.

Transport and communications

Transport. Railroads (1987)[8]: length 1,654 km. Roads (1986): total length 11,400 km (paved 49%). Vehicles (1985): passenger cars 99,952; trucks and buses 59,892. Merchant marine (1988): vessels (100 gross tons and over) 36; total deadweight tonnage 78,081. Air transport (1987)[9]: passenger-km 206,124,000; metric ton-km cargo 3,020,000; airports (1989) 5.
Communications. Daily newspapers (1988): total number 8; total circulation 250,924; circulation per 1,000 population 37. Radio (1988): 1,141,000 receivers (1 per 6.0 persons). Television (1988): 556,000 receivers (1 per 12 persons). Telephones (1987): 311,119 (1 per 22 persons).

Education and health

Education (1986–87)

	schools	teachers	students	student/ teacher ratio
Primary (age 7–14)	6,299[10]	31,275	1,296,366	41.5
Secondary (age 15–18)	...	9,963	426,962	42.9
Vocational, teacher tr.	...	...	24,758	...
Higher[10]	...	6,539	123,748	18.9

Educational attainment (1981). Percent of population age 25 and over having: no formal schooling 48.0%; incomplete primary education 31.7%; complete primary 4.0%; secondary 14.0%; higher 2.3%. *Literacy* (1985): total population age 15 and over literate 2,860,000 (77.3%); males literate 1,447,000 (77.7%); females literate 1,413,000 (76.8%).
Health (1985): physicians 3,056 (1 per 2,100 persons); hospital beds 6,511 (1 per 985 persons); infant mortality rate per 1,000 live births (1987) 70.0.
Food (1984–86): daily per capita caloric intake 2,464 (vegetable products 87%, animal products 13%); (1984) 109% of FAO recommended minimum.

Military

Total active duty personnel (1988): 20,800 (army 62.5%, navy 19.2%, air force 18.3%). *Military expenditure as percent of GNP* (1987): 1.4% (world 5.4%); per capita expenditure U.S.$10.

---

[1]Roman Catholicism is the state religion per concordat with Vatican City. [2]National district. [3]Total includes 63 sq mi (163 sq km) of offshore islands not shown separately. [4]At prices of 1970. [5]Not adequately defined (421,628) and those seeking work for first time (131,231). [6]July. [7]Weights of consumer price index components. [8]Most track serves the sugar industry only except for 88 mi (142 km) for public transport. [9]CDA (Dominicana) airlines only. [10]1985–86.

Ecuador

Official name: República del Ecuador (Republic of Ecuador).
Form of government: unitary multiparty republic with one legislative house (National Congress [71]).
Head of state and government: President.
Capital: Quito.
Official language: Spanish.
Official religion: none.
Monetary unit: 1 Sucre (S/.) = 100 centavos; valuation (Oct. 2, 1989) 1 U.S.$ = S/. 584.86; 1 £ = S/. 946.30.

Area and population

Regions Provinces	Capitals	area sq mi	area sq km	population 1989 estimate
Coastal				
El Oro	Machala	2,281	5,908	449,835
Esmeraldas	Esmeraldas	5,854	15,162	325,472
Guayas	Guayaquil	8,256	21,382	2,750,976
Los Rios	Babahoyo	2,459	6,370	576,596
Manabi	Portoviejo	6,990	18,105	979,221
Eastern				
Morona-Santiago	Macas	10,200	26,418	95,753
Napo	Tena	20,200	52,318	181,160
Pastaza	Puyo	11,687	30,269	36,511
Zamora-Chinchipe	Zamora	7,102	18,394	68,164
Sierra				
Azuay	Cuenca	3,124	8,092	550,086
Bolívar	Guaranda	1,599	4,142	167,204
Cañar	Azogues	1,344	3,481	209,505
Carchi	Tulcán	1,446	3,744	148,922
Chimborazo	Riobamba	2,338	6,056	379,997
Cotopaxi	Latacunga	2,007	5,198	327,777
Imbabura	Ibarra	1,921	4,976	295,470
Loja	Loja	4,429	11,472	421,017
Pichincha	Quito	6,404	16,587	1,914,235
Tungurahua	Ambato	1,201	3,110	272,769
Island territory				
Galápagos Islands	Puerto Baquerizo Moreno	3,086	7,994	9,243
TOTAL		103,930[1]	269,178	10,490,249[2]

Demography

Population (1989): 10,490,000.
Density (1989): persons per sq mi 100.9, persons per sq km 39.0.
Urban–rural (1988): urban 54.2%; rural 45.8%.
Sex distribution (1988): male 50.30%; female 49.70%.
Age breakdown (1988): under 15, 41.1%; 15–29, 28.3%; 30–44, 16.4%; 45–64, 10.5%; 65 and over, 3.7%.
Population projection: (2000) 13,939,000; (2010) 17,403,000.
Doubling time: 25 years.
Ethnic composition (1980): Quechua 49.9%; mestizo 40.0%; white 8.5%; other Amerindian 1.6%.
Religious affiliation (1986): Roman Catholic 93.5%; other 6.5%.
Major cities (1989): Guayaquil 1,699,375; Quito 1,233,865; Cuenca 218,490; Machala 158,798; Portoviejo 156,250.

Vital statistics

Birth rate per 1,000 population: (1987) 35.4[3] (world avg. 27.1); (1982) legitimate 67.9%; illegitimate 32.1%.
Death rate per 1,000 population (1987): 7.6[3] (world avg. 9.9).
Natural increase rate per 1,000 population (1987): 27.8[3] (world avg. 17.2).
Total fertility rate (avg. births per childbearing woman; 1985): 4.8.
Marriage rate per 1,000 population (1986): 6.2[3, 4].
Divorce rate per 1,000 population (1984): 0.4.
Life expectancy at birth (1981): male 59.8 years; female 63.6 years.
Major causes of death per 100,000 population (1986): circulatory diseases 83.1; infectious and parasitic diseases 66.1; respiratory diseases 63.6; accidents, poisonings, and violence 63.1; neoplasms (cancers) 46.2.

National economy

Budget (1988). Revenue: S/. 402,604,000,000 (income from petroleum 40.3%, production and sales tax 20.4%, import duties 16.5%, income taxes 9.1%). Expenditures: S/. 468,334,400,000 (public services 24.0%, debt service 21.0%, education 20.9%, transport and communications 6.9%).
Public debt (external, outstanding; 1987): U.S.$9,026,000,000.
Production (metric tons except as noted). Agriculture, forestry, fishing (1987): sugarcane 3,000,733, bananas 2,386,503, rice 780,776, palm nut 657,740[5], corn (maize) 394,233, coffee 372,615, potatoes 353,920, cacao 57,529; livestock (number of live animals) 4,160,000 pigs, 3,847,000 cattle, 2,100,000 sheep, 42,000,000 chickens; roundwood 8,753,000 cu m; fish catch 679,048. Mining and quarrying (1988): limestone 4,200,000[5]; gold 96,500 troy oz. Manufacturing (value added in S/. '000,000; 1987): food products 177,634, of which beverages (including liquors) 29,284; petroleum products 147,509; textiles and clothing 57,189. Construction (in S/.[6]; 1985): residential 31,391,900,000; nonresidential 2,916,100,000. Energy production (consumption): electricity (kW·hr; 1986) 5,301,000,000 (5,311,000,000); crude petroleum (barrels; 1986) 103,749,000 (34,481,000); petroleum products (metric tons; 1986) 4,541,000 (3,855,000); natural gas (cu m; 1986) 87,405,000 (87,405,000).
Gross national product (1987): U.S.$10,333,000,000 (U.S.$1,040 per capita).

Structure of gross domestic product and labour force

	1987 in value S/. '000,000	% of total value	labour force	% of labour force
Agriculture	290,937	16.1	1,154,941	34.6
Mining	132,995	7.4	21,100	0.6
Manufacturing	337,975	18.7	353,713	10.6
Construction	88,959	4.9	238,118	7.1
Public utilities	7,416	0.4	18,204	0.6
Transp. and commun.	176,259	9.7	154,314	4.6
Trade	380,292	21.0	355,060	10.6
Finance	64,735	3.6	74,349	2.2
Pub. admin., defense	142,779	7.9	788,504	23.6
Services	138,857	7.7		
Other	47,171	2.6	181,815[7]	5.5[7]
TOTAL	1,808,375	100.0	3,340,118	100.0

Tourism (1987): receipts from visitors U.S.$167,000,000; expenditures by nationals abroad U.S.$165,000,000.
Population economically active (1988): total 3,444,368; activity rate of total population 33.8% (participation rates: ages 15–64, 56.6%; female 30.1%; unemployed [1982] 4.6%).

Price and earnings indexes (1985 = 100)

	1982	1983	1984	1985	1986	1987	1988
Consumer price index	40.1	59.5	78.1	100.0	123.0	159.3	252.1
Hourly earnings index[8]	54.1	65.9	77.6	100.0	141.2	170.6	223.5

Household income and expenditure. Average household size (1982) 5.1; average annual income per household (1982) S/. 28,747 (U.S.$956); sources of income (1982): self-employment 53.6%, wages 38.0%, interest, dividends, and rent 2.9%, social security 2.9%; expenditure (1987): food and tobacco 33.4%, housing and utilities 11.6%, transportation and communications 11.5%, clothing 10.2%, household furnishings 5.8%, health care 4.5%.
Land use (1986): forested 43.7%; meadows and pastures 17.7%; agricultural and under permanent cultivation 9.4%; other 29.2%.

Foreign trade[9]

Balance of trade (current prices)

	1983	1984	1985	1986	1987	1988
U.S.$'000,000	+971.6	+1,124.3	+1,285.9	+603.4	+232.2	+674.8
% of total	28.0%	27.8%	30.4%	16.0%	5.5%	16.0%

Imports (1988): U.S.$1,713,525,000 (industrial raw materials 41.3%, industrial capital goods 23.6%, transport equipment 14.5%, consumer goods 5.9%, fuels and lubricants 3.4%). *Major import sources* (1987): United States 25.9%; Japan 13.1%; Venezuela 8.1%; West Germany 8.0%; Brazil 5.4%; Mexico 4.3%; Italy 3.7%.
Exports (1988): U.S.$2,192,898,000 (crude petroleum 39.9%, shrimp 17.7%, bananas 13.6%, coffee 6.9%, petroleum products 4.6%, cacao 3.5%). *Major export destinations* (1987): United States 54.8%; West Germany 3.5%; Singapore 3.0%; Panama 2.8%; Peru 2.7%; Japan 2.4%; Taiwan 2.3%.

Transport and communications

Transport. Railroads (1987): route length 965 km; passenger-km 20,901,000; metric ton-km cargo 5,597,000. Roads (1986): total length 36,187 km (paved 16%). Vehicles (1986): passenger cars 256,812; trucks and buses 36,691. Merchant marine (1988): vessels (100 gross tons and over) 154; deadweight tonnage 608,977. Air transport (1984): passenger-km 893,000,000; metric ton-km cargo 42,600,000; airports (1989) 16.
Communications. Daily newspapers (1985): total number 7; total circulation 538,000; circulation per 1,000 population 57. Radio (1988): 2,987,341 receivers (1 per 3.4 persons). Television (1988): 600,000 receivers (1 per 17 persons). Telephones (1987): 355,377 (1 per 28 persons).

Education and health

Education (1986–87)

	schools	teachers	students	student/ teacher ratio
Primary (age 4–12)	16,146	59,820	1,871,287	31.3
Secondary (age 12–18) Vocational[10]	2,207	49,749	744,373	15.0
Higher	21	12,647	261,913	20.7

Educational attainment (1982). Percent of population age 25 and over having: no schooling 25.4%; incomplete primary 17.0%; complete primary 34.1%; some secondary 8.1%; secondary 7.9%; postsecondary 7.6%[1]. *Literacy* (1982): total population age 15 and over literate 3,914,694 (69.1%); males 2,005,455 (86.8%); females 1,909,239 (56.9%).
Health (1984): physicians 11,033 (1 per 826 persons); hospital beds 15,455 (1 per 590 persons); infant mortality rate per 1,000 live births (1987) 63.0.
Food (1984–86): daily per capita caloric intake 2,058 (vegetable products 82%, animal products 18%); (1984) 90% of FAO minimum requirement.

Military

Total active duty personnel (1988): 40,000 (army 82.5%, navy 10.0%, air force 7.5%). *Military expenditure as percent of GNP* (1987): 2.6% (world 5.4%); per capita expenditure U.S.$25.

[1]Detail does not add to total given because of rounding. [2]Total includes 330,336 persons not shown separately. [3]Excluding nomadic Indian tribes. [4]Based on incomplete registration. [5]1986. [6]Authorized construction. [7]Includes 155,323 unemployed persons not previously employed. [8]General minimum wage. [9]Import figures are f.o.b. in balance of trade and c.i.f. for commodities and trading partners. [10]Includes teacher training.

Egypt

Official name: Jumhūrīyah Miṣr
al-'Arabīyah (Arab Republic of Egypt).
Form of government: republic with
one legislative house (People's
Assembly [458[1]]).
Chief of state: President.
Head of government: Prime Minister.
Capital: Cairo.
Official language: Arabic.
Official religion: Islam.
Monetary unit: 1 Egyptian pound
(LE) = 100 piastres = 1,000 millièmes;
valuation (Oct. 2, 1989)
1 U.S.$ = LE 2.57;
1 £ = LE 4.16.

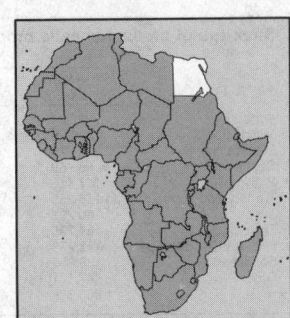

Area and population

Regions Governorates	Capitals	area sq mi	area sq km	population 1986 census
Desert				
al-Baḥr al-Aḥmar	al-Ghurdaqah	78,643	203,685	90,491
Maṭrūḥ	Marsā Maṭrūḥ	81,897	212,112	160,567
Sīnā' al-Janūbīyah	aṭ-Ṭūr	12,796	33,140	28,988
Sīnā' ash-Shamālīyah	al-'Arīsh	10,646	27,574	171,505
al-Wādī al-Jadīd	al-Khārijah	145,369	376,505	113,838
Lower Egypt				
al-Buḥayrah	Damanhūr	3,911	10,130	3,257,168
ad-Daqahlīyah	al-Manṣūrah	1,340	3,471	3,500,470
Dumyāṭ	Dumyāṭ	227	589	741,264
al-Gharbīyah	Ṭanṭā	750	1,942	2,870,960
al-Ismā'īlīyah (Ismailia)	—	557	1,442	544,427
Kafr ash-Shaykh	Kafr ash-Shaykh	1,327	3,437	1,800,129
al-Minūfīyah	Shibīn al-Kawm	592	1,532	2,227,087
al-Qalyūbīyah	Banhā	387	1,001	2,514,244
ash-Sharqīyah	az-Zaqāzīq	1,614	4,180	3,420,119
Upper Egypt				
Aswān	Aswān	262	679	801,408
Asyūṭ	Asyūṭ	600	1,553	2,223,034
Banī Suwayf	Banī Suwayf	510	1,322	1,442,981
al-Fayyūm	al-Fayyūm	705	1,827	1,544,047
al-Jīzah	al-Jīzah	32,878	85,153	3,700,054
al-Minyā	al-Minyā	873	2,262	2,648,043
Qinā	Qinā	715	1,851	2,252,315
Sawhāj	Sawhāj	597	1,547	2,455,134
Urban				
Būr Sa'īd (Port Said)	—	—	28	72	399,793
al-Iskandarīyah (Alexandria)	—	1,034	2,679	2,917,327
al-Qāhirah (Cairo)	—	83	214	6,052,836
as-Suways (Suez)	—	6,888	17,840	326,820
TOTAL		385,229	997,739	48,205,049

Demography

Population (1989): 51,748,000.
Density (1989): persons per sq mi 134.3, persons per sq km 51.9.
Urban–rural (1986): urban 43.9%; rural 56.1%.
Sex distribution (1989): male 51.09%; female 48.91%.
Age breakdown (1986): under 15, 41.8%; 15–29, 26.1%; 30–44, 16.2%; 45–59, 10.4%; 60–74, 4.7%; 75 and over, 0.8%.
Population projection: (2000) 65,452,000; (2010) 76,900,000.
Doubling time: 23 years.
Ethnic composition (1983): Egyptian 99.8%; other 0.2%.
Religious affiliation (1986): Sunnī Muslim 94.1%; Christian 5.9%.
Major cities (1986): Cairo 6,052,836; Alexandria 2,917,327; al-Jīzah 1,670,-800; Shubrā al-Khaymah 533,300; al-Maḥallah al-Kubrā 385,300.

Vital statistics

Birth rate per 1,000 population (1986): 39.3 (world avg. 27.1).
Death rate per 1,000 population (1986): 8.7 (world avg. 9.9).
Natural increase rate per 1,000 population (1986): 30.6 (world avg. 17.2).
Total fertility rate (avg. births per childbearing woman; 1987): 5.4.
Marriage rate per 1,000 population (1986): 9.1.
Divorce rate per 1,000 population (1986): 1.7.
Life expectancy at birth (1986): male 59.0 years; female 62.1 years.
Major causes of death per 100,000 population (1982): diseases of the circulatory system 186.3; infectious and parasitic diseases 168.9; diseases of the respiratory system 106.3; malignant neoplasms (cancers) 21.8.

National economy

Budget (1988–89). Revenue: LE 17,272,000,000 (sovereign tax 71.4%, of which customs duties 18.5%, excise taxes 18.3%; oil revenue and Suez Canal fees 6.3%). Expenditures: LE 24,192,000,000 (debt servicing 12.7%; administration 11.5%; defense 10.2%; pensions 4.9%).
Public debt (external, outstanding; 1987): U.S.$34,515,000,000.
Tourism (1987): receipts from visitors U.S.$1,586,000,000; expenditures by nationals abroad U.S.$52,000,000.
Production (metric tons except as noted). Agriculture, forestry, fishing (1988): sugarcane 9,750,000, tomatoes 5,000,000, corn (maize) 4,088,000, wheat 2,839,000, rice 1,900,000, watermelons 1,390,000, dry onions 650,000, millet 578,000, dates 545,000, cotton (lint) 348,000; livestock (number of live animals) 2,600,000 buffalo, 1,950,000 asses, 1,920,000 cattle, 1,620,000 goats, 1,165,000 sheep, 70,000 camels, 30,000,000 chickens; roundwood (1987) 2,105,000 cu m; fish catch (1987) 250,000. Mining and quarrying (1986): iron ore 2,135,000; phosphate rock 1,162,000; salt 1,040,000. Manufacturing (1985–86): cement 7,612,000; nitrate fertilizers 4,482,000; phosphate fertilizers 934,000; sugar 773,000; steel 281,000[2]; aluminum 175,000[2]; cotton

yarn 225,000; pig iron 241,000[2]; jute yarn and fabrics 48,000. Construction (1985): urban residential units 148,266. Energy production (consumption): electricity (kW-hr; 1987) 32,500,000,000 (32,500,000,000); coal (metric tons; 1987) n.a. (1,250,000); crude petroleum (barrels; 1987) 327,800,000 (162,-750,000); petroleum products (metric tons; 1987) 21,382,000 (18,094,000); natural gas (cu m; 1987) 4,342,000,000 (4,342,000,000).
Gross national product (1987): U.S.$36,028,000,000 (U.S.$710 per capita).

Structure of gross domestic product and labour force

	1987–88[3] in value LE '000,000	1987–88[3] % of total value	1986 labour force	1986 % of labour force
Agriculture	8,903.0	20.7	5,160,500	42.7
Mining	9,303.1	21.6	37,000	0.3
Manufacturing			1,872,400	15.5
Construction	2,117.4	4.9	571,200	4.7
Public utilities	1,455.3[4]	3.3[4]	92,400	0.8
Transp. and commun.	3,977.1	9.2	595,900	4.9
Trade	10,497.6	24.4	1,027,300	8.5
Finance			121,900	1.0
Pub. admin., defense	4,893.7	11.4	2,616,000	21.6
Services	1,921.6	4.5		
TOTAL	43,068.8	100.0	12,094,600	100.0

Population economically active (1986): total 12,094,600; activity rate of total population 25.3% (participation rates: ages 15–64, 45.1%; female 14.6%).

Price and earnings indexes (1985 = 100)

	1982	1983	1984	1985	1986	1987	1988
Consumer price index	65.7	76.2	89.2	100.0	123.9	148.3	174.4
Earnings index	...	...	...	...	...	...	...

Household income and expenditure. Average household size (1986): 4.9; income per household: n.a.; sources of income: n.a.; expenditure[5] (1974–75): food 49.7%, clothing and footwear 14.2%, housing 12.4%, transportation 5.2%, tobacco 4.9%, recreation 1.3%.
Land use (1986): meadows and pastures 0.6%; agricultural and under permanent cultivation 2.5%; built-on, wasteland, and other 96.9%.

Foreign trade

Balance of trade (current prices)

	1982	1983	1984	1985	1986	1987
LE '000,000	−3,535.0	−4,223.4	−4,584.6	−3,676.3	−5,193.2	−4,477.7
% of total	44.7%	48.4%	51.0%	41.4%	55.8%	42.4%

Imports (1986–87): LE 8,051,432,000 (foodstuffs 30.2%; machinery and transport equipment 25.2%; lubricants, fuel, and minerals 8.0%; chemical products 7.4%). *Major import sources:* U.S. 17.9%; W.Ger. 10.4%; France 8.4%; Italy 7.5%; Japan 5.1%.
Exports (1986–87): LE 2,053,959,000 (petroleum and petroleum products 50.7%; raw cotton 15.0%; cotton yarn, textiles, and fabrics 14.1%). *Major export destinations:* Italy 19.0%; Romania 12.0%; U.K. 10.7%; Japan 6.2%; France 6.0%; U.S.S.R. 4.9%; West Germany 4.7%.

Transport and communications

Transport. Railroads (1985–86): length 3,327 mi, 5,355 km; passenger-mi 17,616,000,000, passenger-km 28,350,000,000; short ton-mi cargo 2,005,-000,000, metric ton-km cargo 2,927,000,000. Roads (1987): total length 20,034 mi, 32,241 km (paved 52%). Vehicles (1987): passenger cars 783,306; trucks and buses 371,699. Merchant marine (1988): vessels (100 gross tons and over) 431; total deadweight tonnage 1,821,298. Inland water (1987): Suez Canal, number of transits 17,541; metric ton cargo 347,038,000. Air transport (1987): passenger-km 4,464,000,000; metric ton-km cargo 114,-576,000; airports (1989) 10.
Communications. Daily newspapers (1986): total number 17; total circulation 3,116,268[6]; circulation per 1,000 population 65[6]. Radio (1987): 13,-669,209 receivers (1 per 3.6 persons). Television (1987): 3,860,000 receivers (1 per 13 persons). Telephones (1987): 1,455,000 (1 per 34 persons).

Education and health

Education (1985–86)

	schools	teachers	students	student/ teacher ratio
Primary (age 6–11)	13,233	194,929	6,002,850	30.8
Secondary (age 12–17)	20,106	128,616	2,704,371	21.0
Voc., teacher tr.	5197	48,605[7]	951,986	...
Higher	12	33,200[7]	659,945	...

Educational attainment (1986). Percent of population age 10 and over having: no formal education 73.8%; primary and secondary 21.8%; higher 4.4%. *Literacy* (1986): total population age 15 and over literate 12,447,057 (44.9%); males 8,101,831 (57.6%); females 4,345,226 (31.8%).
Health: physicians (1984) 73,300 (1 per 616 persons); hospital beds (1986) 94,534 (1 per 505 persons); infant mortality rate per 1,000 live births (1985) 70.5.
Food (1984–86): daily per capita caloric intake 3,313 (vegetable products 92%, animal products 8%); 130% of FAO recommended minimum.

Military

Total active duty personnel (1988): 445,000 (army 71.9%, navy 4.5%, air force 23.6%). *Military expenditure as percent of GNP* (1987): 9.2% (world 5.4%); per capita expenditure U.S.$133.

[1]Includes 10 nonelective seats. [2]1984–85. [3]At prices of 1986–87. [4]Includes housing. [5]Urban only. [6]Based on 12 dailies only. [7]1983.

El Salvador

Official name: República de El Salvador (Republic of El Salvador).
Form of government: republic with one legislative house (Legislative Assembly [60]).
Chief of state and government: President.
Capital: San Salvador.
Official language: Spanish.
Official religion: none[1].
Monetary unit: 1 colón (₡) = 100 centavos; valuation (Oct. 2, 1989) 1 U.S.$ = ₡5.00[2]; 1 £ = ₡8.10.

Area and population

Departments	Capitals	area sq mi	area sq km	population 1985 estimate
Ahuachapán	Ahuachapán	479	1,240	271,990
Cabañas	Sensuntepeque	426	1,104	199,229
Chalatenango	Chalatenango	779	2,017	256,688
Cuscatlán	Cojutepeque	292	756	222,389
La Libertad	Nueva San Salvador	638	1,653	440,030
La Paz	Zacatecoluca	473	1,224	278,719
La Unión	La Unión	801	2,074	346,087
Morazán	San Francisco (Gotera)	559	1,447	235,632
San Miguel	San Miguel	802	2,077	480,486
San Salvador	San Salvador	342	886	1,094,249
Santa Ana	Santa Ana	781	2,023	490,367
San Vicente	San Vicente	457	1,184	220,630
Sonsonate	Sonsonate	473	1,226	364,075
Usulután	Usulután	822	2,130	437,325
TOTAL		8,124	21,041	5,337,896[3]

Demography

Population (1989): 5,138,000.
Density (1989): persons per sq mi 632.4, persons per sq km 244.2.
Urban–rural (1987): urban 47.7%; rural 52.3%.
Sex distribution (1986): male 49.31%; female 50.69%.
Age breakdown (1986): under 15, 45.8%; 15–29, 26.2%; 30–44, 13.8%; 45–59, 8.8%; 60–74, 4.4%; 75 and over, 1.0%.
Population projection: (2000) 6,739,000; (2010) 8,491,000.
Doubling time: 26 years.
Ethnic composition (1986): mestizo (white and Indian) 90.0%; Indian (mostly Pipil) 5.0%; white 5.0%.
Religious affiliation (1987): Roman Catholic 92.6%; other 7.4%.
Major cities (1985): San Salvador 462,652; Santa Ana 137,879; Mejicanos 91,465; San Miguel 88,520; Delgado 67,684.

Vital statistics

Birth rate per 1,000 population (1987): 37.0 (world avg. 27.1); (1984) legitimate 32.6%; illegitimate 67.4%.
Death rate per 1,000 population (1987): 10.0 (world avg. 9.9).
Natural increase rate per 1,000 population (1987): 27.0 (world avg. 17.2).
Total fertility rate (avg. births per childbearing woman; 1987): 4.9.
Marriage rate per 1,000 population (1985): 4.0.
Divorce rate per 1,000 population (1985): 0.4.
Life expectancy at birth (1987): male 56.0 years; female 61.0 years.
Major causes of death per 100,000 population (1984): homicide and other violence 67.3; diseases of the circulatory system 63.9; infectious and parasitic diseases 60.0; accidents 45.0; ill-defined conditions 115.9.

National economy

Budget (1988)[4]. Revenue: ₡3,176,000,000 (indirect taxes 56.7%, of which general sales taxes 22.3%, taxes on particular consumer products 13.6%; direct taxes 23.3%, of which income taxes 17.7%; development income 11.5%). Expenditures: ₡3,428,000,000 (current expenditure 81.2%; development expenditure 9.9%; debt amortization 8.9%).
Public debt (external, outstanding; 1987): U.S.$1,597,000,000.
Tourism: receipts from visitors (1987) U.S.$20,000,000; expenditures by nationals abroad (1985) U.S.$89,000,000.
Production (value added in ₡'000,000 except as noted). Agriculture, forestry, fishing (1988): coffee 1,656, corn (maize) 354, aviculture 190, beans 153, sugarcane 139, *maicillo* (variety of millet) 97, cotton 57, rice 54, bananas 36,000 metric tons; livestock (number of live animals) 1,144,000 cattle, 442,000 pigs, 3,000,000 chickens; forestry 66; fishing 120. Mining and quarrying (1987): very limited amounts of gold, silver, and limestone. Manufacturing (1988): food products 1,700; beverages 710; petroleum products 357; textiles 286; chemical products 261; nonmetallic mineral products 235; tobacco products 202; clothing and footwear 176. Construction (1988): private residential 255; private nonresidential 191; total public 270. Energy production (consumption): electricity (kW-hr; 1987) 1,971,000,000 (1,672,-000,000); coal, none (none); petroleum (barrels; 1987), none (4,618,000); petroleum products (metric tons; 1987) 539,000 (490,000); natural gas, none (none).
Household income and expenditure. Average household size (1978) 5.1; income per household ₡8,650 (U.S.$3,460); sources of income: n.a.; expenditure (1978): food and beverages 42.7%, household furnishings 13.2%, transportation 11.2%, clothing and footwear 9.8%.
Population economically active (1980): total 1,593,353; activity rate of total population 35.4% (participation rates: ages 15–64, 62.4%; female 34.8%; unemployed [1987] 33%).

Price and earnings indexes (1985 = 100)

	1982	1983	1984	1985	1986	1987	1988
Consumer price index	64.7	73.3	81.8	100.0	131.9	164.8	199.7[5]
Hourly earnings index[6]	78.7	91.7	93.0	100.0	100.6	...	...

Gross national product (at current market prices; 1987): U.S.$4,220,000,000 (U.S.$850 per capita).

Structure of gross domestic product and labour force

	1988 in value ₡'000,000	1988 % of total value	1980 labour force	1980 % of labour force
Agriculture	3,572	13.1	636,617	40.0
Mining	46	0.2	4,394	0.3
Manufacturing	4,695	17.3	247,621	15.5
Construction	715	2.6	80,089	5.0
Public utilities	562	2.1	9,681	0.6
Transportation and communications	1,197	4.4	65,593	4.1
Trade	8,856	32.5	256,086	16.1
Finance, real estate	2,252	8.3	15,863	1.0
Public admin., defense	2,506	9.2 }	250,158	15.7
Services	2,799	10.3 }		
Other	—	—	27,251[7]	1.7[7]
TOTAL	27,200	100.0	1,593,353	100.0

Land use (1986): forested 5.0%; meadows and pastures 29.4%; agricultural and under permanent cultivation 35.4%; other 30.2%.

Foreign trade[8]

Balance of trade (current prices)

	1983	1984	1985	1986	1987	1988
₡'000,000	−337.4	−650.2	−665.5	−899.8	−2,015.6	−2,052.8
% of total	8.2%	15.3%	16.1%	10.6%	25.4%	25.6%

Imports (1988): ₡5,034,900,000 (chemical products 16.1%, transport equipment 10.8%, nonelectrical machinery and equipment 10.0%, metal products 8.8%, crude petroleum 8.0%). *Major import sources* (1987): United States 36.4%; Guatemala 12.9%; Mexico 9.1%; Venezuela 6.8%; Japan 6.3%.
Exports (1988): ₡2,982,000,000 (coffee 58.4%, raw sugar 3.2%, pharmaceuticals 2.9%, shrimps 2.7%, cardboard boxes 2.0%). *Major export destinations* (1987): United States 44.7%; West Germany 17.2%; Guatemala 12.3%; Costa Rica 5.4%; Japan 4.3%.

Transport and communications

Transport. Railroads (1986): route length 374 mi, 602 km; passenger-mi 3,104,000, passenger-km 4,996,000; short ton-mi cargo 16,701,500, metric ton-km cargo 24,385,300. Roads (1987): total length 7,558 mi, 12,164 km (paved 14%). Vehicles (1987): passenger cars 138,276; trucks and buses 23,381. Merchant marine (1988): vessels (100 gross tons and over) 14; total deadweight tonnage 3,318. Air transport (1988)[9]: passenger-mi 521,000,000, passenger-km 838,000,000; short ton-mi cargo 4,423,000, metric ton-km cargo 6,457,000; airports (1989) with scheduled flights 1.
Communications. Daily newspapers (1988): total number 6; total circulation 327,000; circulation per 1,000 population 65. Radio (1988): total number of receivers 1,936,789 (1 per 2.6 persons). Television (1988): total number of receivers 425,000 (1 per 12 persons). Telephones (1987): 136,185 (1 per 36 persons).

Education and health

Education (1985)

	schools	teachers	students	student/ teacher ratio
Primary (age 7–15)	2,883	24,295	1,049,100[10]	38.7
Secondary (age 16–18)	285	3,880	90,900[10]	23.3
Vocational	17[11]	667[11]	9,505	...
Higher	34	4,789[10]	74,024[10]	15.5[10]

Educational attainment (1980). Percent of population over age 10 having: no formal schooling 30.2%; primary education 60.7%; secondary 6.9%; higher 2.3%. *Literacy* (1980): total population age 15 and over literate 1,771,431 (69.0%); males literate 880,908 (73.2%); females literate 890,523 (65.3%).
Health (1985): physicians 1,649 (1 per 2,891 persons); hospital beds 4,224 (1 per 1,129 persons); infant mortality rate per 1,000 live births (1987) 88.0.
Food (1979–81): daily per capita caloric intake 2,155 (vegetable products 88%, animal products 12%); (1984) 94% of FAO recommended minimum requirement.

Military

Total active duty personnel (1989): 56,000 (army 71.5%, navy 2.3%, air force 3.9%, paramilitary 22.3%). *Military expenditure as percent of GNP* (1987): 3.9% (world 5.4%); per capita expenditure U.S.$36.

---

[1]Roman Catholicism, although not official, enjoys special recognition in the constitution. [2]Official rate; in late 1989 most trade transactions were conducted at a new floating parallel rate (Oct. 2, 1989 [1U.S.$ = ₡6.40; 1£ = ₡10.36]). [3]De jure population. [4]Excludes U.S. foreign aid. [5]Average of 2nd and 3rd quarters. [6]Wages in manufacturing for males in San Salvador department. [7]Mostly unemployed not previously employed. [8]Import c.i.f., exports f.o.b. [9]TACA airlines (scheduled traffic only). [10]1986. [11]1983.

Equatorial Guinea

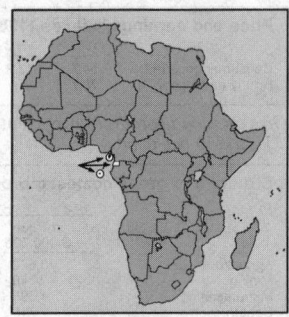

Official name: República de Guinea
Ecuatorial (Republic of Equatorial
Guinea).
Form of government: unitary
single-party republic with one
legislative house (House of
Representatives of the People [60[1]]).
Head of state and government:
President.
Capital: Malabo.
Official language: Spanish.
Official religion: none.
Monetary unit[2]: 1 CFA franc
(CFAF) = 100 centimes; valuation
(Oct. 2, 1989) 1 U.S.$ = CFAF 317.90;
1 £ = CFAF 514.37.

Area and population	area		population
			1983
Regions			
Provinces	sq mi	sq km	census
Insular	785[3]	2,034	59,196
Annobón	7	17	2,006
Bioko Norte	300	776	46,221
Bioko Sur	479	1,241	10,969
Continental	10,045[3]	26,017	240,804
Centro-Sur	3,834	9,931	52,393
Kie-Ntem	1,522	3,943	70,202
Litoral	2,573	6,665	66,370
Wele-Nzas	2,115	5,478	51,839
TOTAL	10,830	28,051	300,000

Demography

Population (1989): 343,000.
Density (1989): persons per sq mi 31.7, persons per sq km 12.2.
Urban-rural (1986): urban 60.7%; rural 39.3%.
Sex distribution (1985): male 48.98%; female 51.02%.
Age breakdown (1985): under 15, 38.1%; 15–29, 26.0%; 30–44, 17.7%; 45–59, 11.5%; 60–74, 5.6%; 75 and over, 1.1%.
Population projection: (2000) 447,000; (2010) 567,000.
Doubling time: 30 years.
Ethnic composition (1983): Fang 72.0%; Bubi 14.7%; Duala 2.7%; Ibibio 1.3%; Maka 1.3%; other 8.0%.
Religious affiliation (1980): Christian (mostly Roman Catholic) 88.8%; traditional beliefs 4.6%; atheist 1.4%; Muslim 0.5%; other 0.2%; none 4.5%.
Major cities (1983): Malabo 15,253; Ela-Nguema 6,179; Bata 5,633; Campo Yaunde 5,199; Los Angeles 4,079.

Vital statistics

Birth rate per 1,000 population (1985–90): 42.4 (world avg. 27.1); legitimate, n.a.; illegitimate, n.a.
Death rate per 1,000 population (1985–90): 19.0 (world avg. 9.9).
Natural increase rate per 1,000 population (1985–90): 23.4 (world avg. 17.2).
Total fertility rate (avg. births per childbearing woman; 1985–90): 5.7.
Marriage rate per 1,000 population: n.a.
Divorce rate per 1,000 population: n.a.
Life expectancy at birth (1985–90): male 44.9 years; female 48.1 years.
Major causes of death per 100,000 population: n.a.; however, major diseases include malaria (affecting about 60% of the population), cholera, leprosy, trypanosomiasis (sleeping sickness), and waterborne (especially gastrointestinal) diseases.

National economy

Budget (1988). Revenue: CFAF 7,147,000,000 (fiscal receipts 77.1%, other receipts 22.9%). Expenditures: CFAF 7,894,000,000 (current expenditure 76.4%, capital expenditure 23.6%).
Public debt (external, outstanding; 1987): U.S.$174,900,000.
Gross domestic product (at current market prices; 1988): U.S.$145,000,000 (U.S.$430 per capita).

Structure of gross domestic product and labour force	1986		1983	
	in value CFAF '000,000	% of total value	labour force	% of labour force
Agriculture, forestry	20,548	59.5	86,500	85.7
Manufacturing	326	0.9	900	0.9
Construction	3,126	9.1	1,000	1.0
Public utilities	728	2.1	...	...
Transportation and communications	897	2.6	...	...
Trade	1,740	5.0	2,600	2.6
Finance			...	...
Pub. admin., defense	7,175	20.8	7,400	7.3
Services			2,500	2.5
Other			...	...
TOTAL	34,540	100.0	100,900	100.0

Production (metric tons except as noted). Agriculture, forestry, fishing (1987): roots and tubers 91,000 (of which cassava 56,000, sweet potatoes 35,000), bananas 19,000, fruit excluding melons 19,000, coconuts 8,000, coffee 7,000, cacao beans 7,000, palm oil 5,200, palm kernels 3,000; livestock (number of live animals) 36,000 sheep, 8,000 goats, 5,000 pigs, 4,000 cattle, 160,000 chickens; roundwood 607,000 cu m; fish catch 4,000. Mining and quarrying:

details n.a.; however, in addition to quarrying for construction materials, unexploited deposits of iron ore, lead, zinc, manganese, and molybdenum are present; traces of gold, diamonds, and radioactive ores have also been located. Manufacturing (1986): palm oil 5,100. Construction: n.a. Energy production (consumption): electricity (kW-hr; 1987) 17,000,000 (17,000,-000); coal, none (n.a.); crude petroleum[4], none (n.a.); petroleum products (metric tons; 1987) none (23,000); natural gas, none (n.a.).
Population economically active (1983): total 100,900; activity rate of total population 34.0% (participation rates: ages 15–64 n.a.; female, n.a.; unemployed, n.a.).

Price and earnings indexes (1985 = 100)					
	1984	1985	1986	1987	1988[5]
Consumer price index	54.1	100.0	82.0	72.0	78.0
Earnings index	...	...	...	...	...

Household income and expenditure. Average household size (1980) 4.5; income per household: n.a.; sources of income: n.a.; expenditure: n.a.
Tourism (1989): Tourism is a government priority but remains undeveloped.
Land use (1987): forested 46.2%; meadows and pastures 3.7%; agricultural and under permanent cultivation 8.2%; built-on, wasteland, and other 41.9%.

Foreign trade

Balance of trade (current prices)				
	1985	1986	1987	1988
CFAF '000,000	−3,825	−6,823	−3,435	−3,166
% of total	15.6%	22.2%	12.9%	11.7%

Imports (1984): EK 8,048,000,000 (machinery and transport equipment 25.4%, of which motor vehicles and parts 16.7%; fuels and lubricants 20.1%; food and live animals 19.4%, of which fish 5.1%; manufactured goods 11.0%, of which electrical machinery and apparatus 6.2%; beverages and tobacco products 4.9%). *Major import sources* (1985): Spain 30.2%; France 23.6%; Italy 14.6%; The Netherlands 4.8%; West Germany 4.1%; Belgium–Luxembourg 3.0%; China 2.4%; United States 1.9%; Japan 1.7%; Norway 1.5%; United Kingdom 1.1%; Switzerland 0.9%.
Exports (1984): EK 7,546,000,000 (food and live animals 57.0%, of which cacao 42.4%, wood 19.4%; fuels and lubricants 19.5%; manufactured goods 2.8%). *Major export destinations* (1985): The Netherlands 37.6%; Spain 31.5%; West Germany 16.4%; Italy 5.0%; France 2.2%; Switzerland 1.4%; Portugal 1.3%; Belgium–Luxembourg 0.7%; Greece 0.3%.

Transport and communications

Transport. Railroads: none. Roads (1986): total length 1,691 mi, 2,721 km (paved [1982] 12%). Vehicles (1979): passenger cars 4,000; trucks and buses 3,000. Merchant marine (1988): vessels (100 gross tons and over) 2; total deadweight tonnage 6,700. Air transport (1985): passenger-mi 4,000,000, passenger-km 7,000,000; short ton-mi cargo 700,000, metric ton-km cargo 1,000,000; airports (1989) with scheduled flights 2.
Communications. Daily newspapers (1986): total number 2; total circulation 1,000; circulation per 1,000 population 3.1. Radio (1988): total number of receivers 96,541 (1 per 3.5 persons). Television (1988): total number of receivers 2,500 (1 per 134 persons). Telephones (1982): 1,366 (1 per 209 persons).

Education and health

Education (1980–81[6])	schools	teachers	students	student/ teacher ratio
Primary (age 6–11)	511	647	40,110	62.0
Secondary (age 12–17)	14	288	3,013	10.5
Voc., teacher tr.[7]	...	...	...	...
Higher[8]	...	60	1,140	19.0

Educational attainment, n.a. *Literacy* (c. 1985): total population literate, about 31%; males literate 46%; females literate 17%.
Health: physicians (mid-1980s) 5 (1 per 61,000 persons); hospital beds (1982) 3,200 (1 per 89 persons); infant mortality rate per 1,000 live births (1985–90) 127.
Food (latest): daily per capita caloric intake 2,230; 68% of FAO recommended minimum requirement.

Military

Total active duty personnel (1989): 1,400 (army 84.6%, navy 7.7%, air force 7.7%). *Military expenditure as percent of GNP* (1981): 1.8% (world 5.8%); per capita expenditure U.S.$9.

---

[1]Number of seats increased from 41 to 60 with the July 10, 1988, elections. [2]As of Jan. 1, 1985, Equatorial Guinea became a member of the franc zone, substituting the CFA franc for the previous monetary unit, the ekwele (EK, plural bipkwele), effectively devaluing the latter by 82%. [3]Detail does not add to total given because of rounding. [4]Equatorial Guinea's offshore prospective oil-lease areas totaled about 13,450 sq km. [5]October. [6]In 1983–84 there were 61,532 students in primary; in 1982–83, 4,368 students in secondary; and in 1980–81, 175 students in higher education studying abroad. [7]Efforts are being undertaken to provide the training necessary to qualify nondegree teachers for service. Also, teacher-training schools are to be expanded in order to increase the number of primary-school teachers. [8]1981–82.

Ethiopia

Official name: YeĒtiyop'iya Hezbawi
 Dimokrasiyawī Republēk (People's
 Democratic Republic of Ethiopia).
Form of government: unitary
 single-party people's republic with one
 legislative house (Shengo [835][1]).
Chief of state and government:
 President.
Capital: Addis Ababa.
Official language: Amharic.
Official religion: none.
Monetary unit: 1 Ethiopian Birr
 (Br) = 100 cents; valuation (Oct. 2,
 1989) 1 U.S.$ = Br 2.07;
 1 £ = Br 3.35.

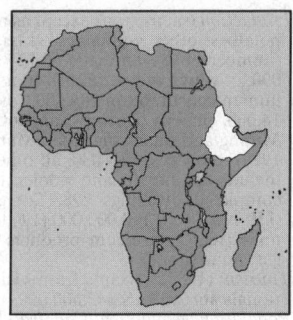

Area and population

Regions	Capitals	area sq mi	area sq km	population 1989 estimate
Arsi	Asela	9,500	24,600	1,914,387
Bale	Goba	49,500	128,300	1,159,289
Eritrea[2]	Asmera	45,300	117,400	3,127,492
Gemu Gofa	Arba Minch	15,400	40,100	1,435,214
Gojam	Debre Markos	24,900	64,400	3,737,306
Gonder	Gonder	28,300	73,400	3,365,163
Hararge	Harer	98,400	254,800	4,792,517
Ilubabor	Metu	19,600	50,800	1,109,288
Kefa	Jima	20,500	53,000	2,819,441
Shewa[2]	Addis Ababa	33,000	85,500	11,044,928
Sidamo	Awasa	45,100	116,700	4,364,128
Tigray	Mekele	25,400	65,700	2,779,984
Welega	Nekemte	27,000	69,800	2,850,048
Welo	Dese	30,500	79,000	4,193,583
TOTAL		472,400	1,223,500	48,696,078[3]

Demography

Population (1989): 48,898,000.
Density (1989): persons per sq mi 103.5, persons per sq km 40.0.
Urban–rural (1989): urban 10.8%; rural 89.2%.
Sex distribution (1989): male 49.95%; female 50.05%.
Age breakdown (1989): under 15, 46.5%; 15–29, 22.8%; 30–44, 15.6%; 45–59,
 8.9%; 60–74, 4.5%; 75 and over, 1.7%.
Population projection: (2000) 67,523,000; (2010) 90,570,000.
Doubling time: 35 years.
Ethnolinguistic composition (1983): Amhara 37.7%; Galla 35.3%; Tigrinya
 8.6%; Gurage 3.3%; Ometo (Omotic) 2.7%; Sidamo 2.4%; Tigre 1.9%; Afar
 1.8%; Somali 1.7%; other 4.6%.
Religious affiliation (1980): Ethiopian Orthodox 52.5%; Muslim 31.4%; tra-
 ditional beliefs 11.4%; other Christian 4.5%; other 0.2%.
Major cities (1985): Addis Ababa 1,495,266; Asmera 295,689; Dire Dawa
 107,287; Gonder 88,344; Dese 77,459.

Vital statistics

Birth rate per 1,000 population (1985–90): 43.7 (world avg. 27.1).
Death rate per 1,000 population (1985–90): 23.6 (world avg. 9.9).
Natural increase rate per 1,000 population (1985): 20.1 (world avg. 17.2).
Total fertility rate (avg. births per childbearing woman; 1985–90): 6.7.
Life expectancy at birth (1985): male 39.5 years; female 42.6 years.
Major causes of death (1977–78)[4]: infectious and parasitic diseases 24.0%;
 digestive system diseases 17.6%; allergy, endocrine, metabolic, nutritional,
 and circulatory diseases 14.9%; respiratory diseases 9.9%.

National economy

Budget (1987–88). Revenue: Br 2,920,000,000 ([1984–85] taxes 71.3%, of
 which income and profit tax 27.3%, excise tax 14.6%, import duties 12.2%,
 export duties 7.4%; nontax revenue 28.7%). Expenditures: Br 4,881,000,000
 (1984–85; general services 35.9%; economic development 31.3%, of which
 agriculture and settlement 11.8%; social services 15.6%, of which education
 8.5%, public health 3.1%; debt service 5.6%).
Tourism (1987): receipts from visitors U.S.$7,000,000; expenditures by na-
 tionals abroad U.S.$4,000,000.
Production (metric tons except as noted). Agriculture, forestry, fishing (1988):
 sugarcane 1,700,000, corn (maize) 1,650,000, sorghum 1,100,000, barley
 1,050,000, pulses 987,000, wheat 825,000, yams 240,000, potatoes 230,000,
 millet 200,000, coffee 180,000, seed cotton 67,000; livestock (number of live
 animals) 31,000,000 cattle, 23,400,000 sheep, 17,500,000 goats, 7,040,000
 horses, mules, and asses, 1,060,000 camels; roundwood (1987) 39,968,000
 cu m; fish catch (1987) 4,000. Mining and quarrying (1987): cement 250,-
 000; salt 135,000; limestone 125,000; gold 21,000 troy oz; platinum 150
 troy oz. Manufacturing (gross value in Br '000[5]; 1985–86): food and beverages 796,300; textiles 376,200; leather and shoes 181,200; metal products
 120,200; cigarettes 107,800; chemicals 103,000; paper and printing 91,600;
 nonmetallic mineral products 69,400. Construction (authorized; 1981): residential 162,000 sq m; nonresidential 32,300 sq m, of which commercial
 24,800 sq m. Energy production (consumption): electricity (kW-hr; 1987)
 810,000,000 (810,000,000); coal, none (n.a.); crude petroleum (barrels; 1987)
 n.a. (5,981,000); petroleum products (metric tons; 1987) 761,000 (797,000);
 natural gas, n.a. (n.a.).
Land use (1987): forested 24.9%; meadows and pastures 40.9%; agricultural
 and under permanent cultivation 12.7%; other 21.5%.
Gross national product (1987): U.S.$5,537,000,000 (U.S.$120 per capita).

Structure of gross domestic product and labour force

	1985–86 in value Br '000,000	1985–86 % of total value	1985 labour force	1985 % of labour force
Agriculture	4,354.5	44.8	14,982,000	78.1
Mining	15.3	0.2		
Manufacturing	1,072.9	11.1		
Construction	387.6	4.0	1,630,000	8.5
Public utilities	109.9	1.1		
Transportation and communications	718.1	7.4		
Trade	1,036.3	10.7		
Finance	339.2	3.5		
Pub. admin., defense	781.6	8.0	2,570,000	13.4
Services	687.3	7.1		
Other	205.1	2.1		
TOTAL	9,707.6[3]	100.0	19,182,000	100.0

Public debt (external, outstanding; 1987): U.S.$2,434,000,000.
Population economically active (1987): total 19,814,900; activity rate of total
 population 43.1% (participation rates: ages 15–64 [1985] 73.5%; female
 35.2%; unemployed, n.a.).

Price and earnings indexes (1985 = 100)

	1982	1983	1984	1985	1986	1987	1988
Consumer price index	77.0	77.4	84.0	100.0	90.2	88.0	94.2
Monthly earnings index	...	...	...	...	...	...	...

Household income and expenditure. Average household size (1984) 4.5;
 income per household c. U.S.$600; sources of income: n.a.; expenditure[6]
 (1963): food 49.0%, energy and household utilities 14.6%, clothing and
 footwear 6.7%, miscellaneous goods and services 5.4%, transportation 4.5%,
 recreation and reading 2.6%, medical care 1.8%, personal care 0.8%.

Foreign trade

Balance of trade (current prices)

	1982	1983	1984	1985	1986	1987
Br '000,000	−775.6	−980.4	−1,086.7	−1,367.0	−981.2	−1,124.7
% of total	31.7%	37.0%	38.6%	49.8%	34.3%	43.3%

Imports (1985–86): Br 2,211,000,000 (food and beverages 24.0%, road transport equipment 13.0%, machinery including aircraft 12.4%, petroleum and
 petroleum products 10.0%, chemicals 3.9%). *Major import sources:* United
 States 17.0%; U.S.S.R. 16.1%; West Germany 10.7%; Italy 9.7%.
Exports (1985–86): Br 924,000,000 (coffee 72.0%, hides 11.9%, live animals
 1.9%, pulses 1.4%, oil seeds 0.9%). *Major export destinations:* West Germany 29.1%; United States 12.8%; The Netherlands 8.8%; Japan 8.6%.

Transport and communications

Transport. Railroads[7] (1986): length 485 mi, 781 km; passenger-mi 217,-
 000,000, passenger-km 350,000,000; short ton-mi cargo 86,000,000, metric
 ton-km cargo 125,000,000. Roads (1988): total length 24,533 mi, 39,482
 km (paved 20%). Vehicles (1988): passenger cars 41,512; trucks and buses
 17,084. Merchant marine (1988): vessels (100 gross tons and over) 26; total
 deadweight tonnage 94,142. Air transport (1987): passenger-mi 346,931,000,
 passenger-km 558,333,000; short ton-mi cargo 71,130,000, metric ton-km
 cargo 103,848,000; airports (1989) with scheduled flights 37.
Communications. Daily newspapers (1988): total number 3; total circulation 47,000; circulation per 1,000 population 1.0. Radio (1988): 8,700,258
 receivers (1 per 5.5 persons). Television (1988): 70,000 receivers (1 per 679
 persons). Telephones (1987): 137,289 (1 per 341 persons).

Education and health

Education (1985–86)

	schools	teachers	students	student/ teacher ratio
Primary (age 7–12)	7,900	50,922	2,448,778	48.1
Secondary (age 13–18)	1,209	15,218	655,517	43.1
Voc., teacher tr.[8]	...	390	4,969	12.7
Higher	11[9]	1,314[8]	18,436	...

Educational attainment, n.a. *Literacy* (1980)[10]: total population age 15 and
 over literate 1,000,000 (4.8%); males (9.3%); females (0.5%).
Health (1986–87): physicians 1,241 (1 per 36,660 persons); hospital beds
 11,745 (1 per 3,873 persons); infant mortality rate (1985–90) 154.0.
Food (1979–81): daily per capita caloric intake 2,149 (vegetable products
 93%, animal products 7%); (1984) 72% of FAO recommended minimum
 requirement.

Military

Total active duty personnel (1989): 318,800[11] (army 98.2%, navy 0.6%, air
 force 1.2%). *Military expenditure as percent of GNP* (1987): 8.5% (world
 5.4%); per capita expenditure U.S.$10.

[1]On Feb. 1, 1987, a referendum approved a constitution providing for civilian rule.
A National Assembly (Shengo) was elected on June 14, 1987. [2]Eritrea includes Aseb
Administration, and Shewa includes Addis Ababa region. [3]Detail does not add to
total given because of rounding. [4]Percentage of deaths in a sample population of
hospital inpatients. [5]At constant prices of 1978–79. [6]Weights of consumer price
index components; excludes rent. Addis Ababa only. [7]Includes 62 mi (100 km) of the
Chemin de Fer Djibouti–Ethiopien (CDE) in Djibouti; excludes 190 mi (306 km) of
Northern Ethiopia Railway, not in use since 1978. [8]1985. [9]1983–84. [10]Adult illiteracy
is reported to have been reduced to about 37% in 1987. [11]About 2,200 Cuban and
other Soviet-bloc advisers are assisting government forces.

Faeroe Islands

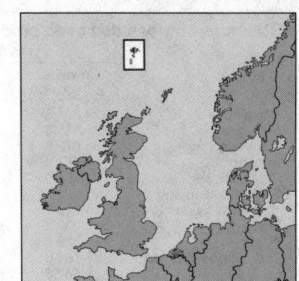

Official name: Færøerne (Danish);
Føroyar (Faeroese) (Faeroe Islands).
Political status: self-governing region
of the Danish realm with a single
legislative body (Lagting [32]).
Chief of state: Danish Monarch
represented by state commissioner.
Head of home government: chairman
of Landsstyre (executive body), also
formally titled Head of the Home
Government.
Capital: Tórshavn (Thorshavn).
Official languages: Faeroese; Danish.
Official religion: Evangelical Lutheran.
Monetary unit: 1 Faeroese krone (FKr)
= 100 øre; valuation (Oct. 2, 1989)
1 U.S.$ = Fkr 7.30; 1£ = FKr 11.81.

Area and population

Districts	Capitals	area sq mi	area sq km	population 1989[1] estimate
Eysturoyar (Østerø)	—	110	286	10,542
Nordhoya (Norderøernes)	—	93	241	6,128
Sandoyar (Sandø)	—	48	125	1,776
Streymoyar (Strømø)	—	151	392	20,383
Sudhuroyar Nordhara (Suderø Nordre)	—	38	97	3,089
Sudhuroyar Sunnara (Suderø Søndre)	—	27	70	2,786
Våga (Vågø)	—	73	188	2,949
TOTAL		540	1,399	47,653

Demography

Population (1989): 47,800.
Density (1989): persons per sq mi 88.5, persons per sq km 34.2.
Urban–rural (1988): urban (Tórshavn only) 30.4%; rural 69.6%.
Sex distribution (1988): male 52.27%; female 47.73%.
Age breakdown (1988): under 15, 24.5%; 15–29, 25.1%; 30–44, 20.8%; 45–59, 13.9%; 60–74, 11.3%; 75 and over, 4.4%.
Population projection: (2000) 54,000; (2010) 61,000.
Doubling time: 77 years.
Ethnic composition (by place of birth; 1970): born in Faeroe Islands 95.3%; born elsewhere 4.7%.
Religious affiliation (1980): Evangelical Lutheran Church of Denmark 74.4%; Plymouth Brethren 19.8%; Roman Catholic 0.1%; other 5.2%.
Major cities (1988): Tórshavn 14,547.

Vital statistics

Birth rate per 1,000 population (1987): 16.6 (world avg. 27.1); legitimate 63.3%; illegitimate 36.7%.
Death rate per 1,000 population (1987): 7.9 (world avg. 9.9).
Natural increase rate per 1,000 population (1987): 8.7 (world avg. 17.2).
Total fertility rate (avg. births per childbearing woman; 1987): 2.3.
Marriage rate per 1,000 population (1987): 4.4.
Divorce rate per 1,000 population (1987): 1.0.
Life expectancy at birth (1981–85): male 73.3 years; female 79.6 years.
Major causes of death per 100,000 population (1987): diseases of the circulatory system 372.9, of which ischemic heart disease 267.9, cerebrovascular disease 81.4; malignant neoplasms (cancers) 177.9; diseases of the respiratory system 49.3, of which pneumonia 27.9, bronchitis, emphysema, and asthma 21.4; automobile accidents 19.3; suicides 4.3.

National economy

Budget (1989). Revenue: FKr 3,231,348,000 (taxes 39.7%; customs and excise duties 35.2%; payments from the Danish government 23.6%). Expenditures: FKr 3,231,348,000 (social welfare 25.6%; agriculture, fishing, and commerce 18.1%; education 13.1%; medical services 12.4%; roads and bridges 9.7%; administration 5.3%).
Public debt: n.a.
Gross national product (at current market prices; 1988): U.S.$894,000,000 (U.S.$18,890 per capita).

Structure of gross domestic product and labour force

	1988 in value FKr '000,000	1988 % of total value	1977 labour force	1977 % of labour force
Agriculture	65	1.1	282	1.6
Fishing	921	15.7	3,032	17.2
Manufacturing and mining	1,262	21.5	3,854	21.9
Construction	530	9.0	1,952	11.1
Public utilities	161	2.7	[2]	[2]
Transportation and communications	523	8.9	1,944	11.1
Trade	936	16.0	2,237[2]	12.7[2]
Finance and real estate	577	9.8	[2]	[2]
Pub. admin.	1,142	19.5	2,927	16.6
Services	265	4.5	796	4.5
Other[3]	−523	−8.9	561	3.2
TOTAL	5,859	100.0[4]	17,585	100.0[4]

Production (metric tons except as noted). Agriculture, forestry, fishing (1987): potatoes, other vegetables, grass, hay, and silage are produced; livestock (number of live animals) 66,125 sheep, 2,228 cattle; fish catch (1988) 357,000, of which industrial fish (not for human consumption) 173,000, fish for human consumption 184,000, (of which cod 46,000, saithe 40,000, rose fish 14,000, prawns, shrimps, and other crustaceans 14,000, haddock 13,000). Mining and quarrying: coal. Manufacturing (value added in FKr '000,000; 1988): processed fish 630; all other manufacturing 351; important products include handicrafts and woolen textiles and clothing. Construction (1987): completed dwellings 298. Energy production (consumption): electricity (kW-hr; 1986[5]) 190,000,000 (190,000,000); coal, n.a. (n.a.); crude petroleum, none (n.a.); petroleum products (metric tons; 1987) none (5,444); natural gas, none (none).
Tourism (1987): receipts from visitors U.S.$10,000,000; expenditures by nationals abroad U.S.$42,600,000.
Population economically active (1977): total 17,585; activity rate of total population 41.9% (participation rates: age 14–64, 64.2%; female 27.2%; unemployed, n.a.).

Price and earnings indexes (Jan. 1, 1983 = 100)

	1983	1984	1985	1986	1987	1988	1989
Consumer price index	100.0	105.4	112.8	117.6	112.4	117.1	121.3
Earnings index	...	...	...	...	...	...	...

Household income and expenditure. Average household size (1977) 3.7; average annual income per household: n.a.; sources of income[6]: self-employment 11.7%, wages and salaries 88.3%; expenditure (1980): food and beverages 40.9%, fuel and energy 18.9%, housing 17.5%, clothing and footwear 11.3%, other 11.4%.
Land use (1986): agricultural and under permanent cultivation 2.1%; other 97.9%.

Foreign trade

Balance of trade (current prices)

	1983	1984	1985	1986	1987	1988
FKr '000,000	−587	−1,039	−688	−838	−838	−732
% of total	15.5%	23.6%	15.0%	17.1%	14.9%	13.5%

Imports (1988): FKr 3,220,689,000 (machinery and transport equipment 41.9%, of which transport equipment [including ships and aircraft 17.5%, motor vehicles 2.4%] 22.4%; goods for household consumption 25.1%; petroleum products 6.3%). *Major import sources:* Denmark 39.6%; Norway 21.1%; United Kingdom 8.2%; Sweden 6.3%; West Germany 5.8%; Japan 3.5%; Iceland 2.4%; U.S.S.R. 1.7%; The Netherlands 1.6%.
Exports (1988): FKr 2,344,657,000 (1987: fishery products 79.9%, of which frozen fish fillets 21.7%, salted, dried, and smoked fish 19.7%, fresh or chilled fish 11.5%, frozen fish except fillets 9.2%, crustaceans and mollusks 7.6%; ships 19.9%). *Major export destinations:* Denmark 18.6%; United Kingdom 11.5%; West Germany 9.7%; United States 9.1%; Norway 8.0%; France 7.6%; Italy 7.2%; Spain 6.7%.

Transport and communications

Transport. Railroads: none. Roads (1987): total length 269 mi, 433 km (paved, n.a.). Vehicles (1987): passenger cars 14,179; trucks and buses 3,462. Merchant marine (1988): vessels (100 gross tons and over) 214; total gross tonnage 129,931. Air transport (1989): airports with scheduled flights 1.
Communications. Daily newspapers: none; one newspaper is published 3 times weekly (circulation [1987] 12,700; circulation per 1,000 population 272). Radio (1987): total number of receivers 18,000 (1 per 2.6 persons). Television (1988): total number of receivers 10,000 (1 per 4.7 persons). Telephones (1987): 19,441 (1 per 2.4 persons).

Education and health

Education (1987–88)

	schools	teachers	students	student/ teacher ratio
Primary (first 7 grades)	67	592	5,536	14.4
Secondary (8th through 10 grades)			2,995	
Vocational, teacher training	9		1,387	...
Higher	1		94	...

Educational attainment (1977). Percent of population age 14–49 having: primary education 45.2%; secondary education 34.2%. *Literacy* (1984): 99%.
Health (1987): physicians 82 (1 per 569 persons); hospital beds 370 (1 per 126 persons); infant mortality rate per 1,000 live births (1981–85) 10.6.
Food (1979–81): daily per capita caloric intake 3,195 (vegetable products 68%, animal products 32%); 120% of FAO recommended minimum requirement.

Military

Defense responsibility lies with Denmark.

[1]January 1. [2]Trade includes Public utilities and Finance and real estate. [3]Imputed bank service charges and nature of employment not stated, respectively. [4]Detail does not add to total given because of rounding. [5]Estimated, based on 9 months' production. [6]Percentages refer to principal sources of income of economically active population.

Fiji

Official name: Republic of Fiji.
Form of government: republic[1].
Chief of state: President[2].
Head of government: Prime Minister[2].
Capital: Suva.
Official language: English.
Official religion: none.
Monetary unit: 1 Fiji dollar
(F$) = 100 cents; valuation (Oct. 2,
1989) 1 U.S.$ = F$1.50; 1£ = F$2.42.

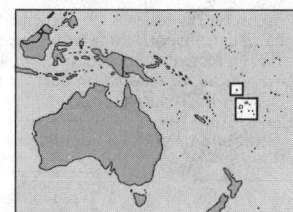

Area and population

Divisions Provinces[3]	Capitals	area sq mi	area sq km	population 1986 census
Central	Suva			
Naitasiri		643	1,666	100,227
Namosi		220	570	4,836
Rewa		105	272	97,442
Serua		320	830	13,356
Tailevu		369	955	44,249
Eastern	Levuka			
Kandavu		185	478	9,805
Lau		188	487	14,203
Lomaiviti		159	411	16,066
Rotuma		18	46	2,688
Northern	Labasa			
Mathuata		774	2,004	74,735
Mbua		532	1,379	13,986
Thakaundrove		1,087	2,816	40,433
Western	Lautoka			
Mba		1,017	2,634	197,633
Nandronga-Navosa		921	2,385	54,431
Ra		518	1,341	31,285
TOTAL		7,056	18,274	715,375

Demography

Population (1989): 734,000.
Density (1989): persons per sq mi 104.0, persons per sq km 40.2.
Urban–rural (1986): urban 38.7%; rural 61.3%.
Sex distribution (1986): male 50.68%; female 49.32%.
Age breakdown (1986): under 15, 38.2%; 15–29, 29.5%; 30–44, 17.8%; 45–59, 9.6%; 60–74, 3.8%; 75 and over, 1.1%.
Population projection: (2000) 837,000; (2010) 931,000.
Doubling time: 32 years.
Ethnic composition (1986): Indian 48.6%; Fijian 46.3%; other 5.1%.
Religious affiliation (1986): Christian 52.9%; Hindu 38.1%; Muslim 7.8%; Sikh 0.7%; other 0.5%.
Major cities (1986): Suva 69,665; Lautoka 28,728; Lami 8,601; Nadi 7,679; Ba 6,518.

Vital statistics

Birth rate per 1,000 population (1988): 26.8 (world avg. 27.1); (1978) legitimate 82.7%; illegitimate 17.3%.
Death rate per 1,000 population (1988): 5.0 (world avg. 9.9).
Natural increase rate per 1,000 population (1988): 21.8 (world avg. 17.2).
Total fertility rate (avg. births per childbearing woman; 1988): 3.1.
Marriage rate per 1,000 population (1985): 9.4.
Divorce rate per 1,000 population (1979): 0.7.
Life expectancy at birth (1988): male 68.3 years; female 72.8 years.
Major causes of death per 100,000 population (1985): diseases of the circulatory system 190.8; birth trauma 169.5; malignant neoplasms (cancers) 53.3; accidents, poisonings, and violence 48.5; diseases of the respiratory system 43.1; infectious and parasitic diseases 31.3; diabetes mellitus 29.1; diseases of the digestive system 13.3.

National economy

Budget (1987). Revenue: F$341,247,000 (income taxes, estate taxes, and gift duties 39.6%; customs duties and port dues 36.9%; fees, royalties and sales 11.1%). Expenditures: F$393,903,000 (departmental expenditure 71.3%; public debt charges 22.8%; pensions and gratuities 5.9%).
Public debt (external, outstanding; 1987): U.S.$334,200,000.
Production (metric tons except as noted). Agriculture, forestry, fishing (1987): sugarcane 2,960,000, paddy rice 23,477, copra 12,999, ginger 4,865; livestock (number of live animals) 159,000 cattle, 59,000 goats, 29,000 pigs; roundwood 249,000 cu m; fish catch 35,266. Mining and quarrying (1987): gold 2,647 kilograms; silver (1986) 774 kilograms. Manufacturing (1987): refined sugar 401,000; cement 58,700; flour 25,720; stock feed 16,-145; coconut oil 8,417; soap 7,406; beer 147,400 hectolitres; paint 16,430 hectolitres. Construction (1987): residential 60,000 sq m; nonresidential 60,000 sq m. Energy production (consumption): electricity (kW-hr; 1987) 430,000,000 (430,000,000); coal (metric tons; 1987) none (16,000); crude petroleum, none (n.a.); petroleum products (metric tons; 1987) none (152,-000); natural gas, none (n.a.).
Population economically active (1986): total 241,160; activity rate of total population 33.7% (participation rates: ages 15–64, 56.0%; female 21.2%; unemployed [1987] 10.2%).

Price and earnings indexes (1985 = 100)

	1982	1983	1984	1985	1986	1987	1988
Consumer price index	85.2	90.9	95.8	100.0	101.8	107.6	120.2
Hourly earnings index	91.3	97.4	98.7	100.0	100.0	...	...

Household income and expenditure. Average household size (1986) 5.7; income per household (1980) F$2,837 (U.S.$3,546); sources of income (1973): wages and salaries 81.5%, self-employment 9.1%, other 9.4%; expenditure (1985): food 33.9%, housing 18.6%, transportation 11.3%, household furnishings 7.6%, clothing and footwear 6.3%, energy 4.9%.
Gross national product (at current market prices; 1987): U.S.$1,091,000,000 (U.S.$1,510 per capita).

Structure of gross domestic product and labour force

	1987 in value F$'000,000	1987 % of total value	1986 labour force	1986 % of labour force
Agriculture	303.0	21.3	106,305	44.1
Mining	29.0	2.0	1,345	0.5
Manufacturing	130.0	9.2	18,106	7.5
Construction	62.0	4.4	11,786	4.9
Public utilities	54.0	3.8	2,154	0.9
Transportation and communications	133.0	9.4	13,151	5.4
Trade	207.0	14.6	26,010	10.8
Finance			6,016	2.5
Pub. admin., defense, services	502.0	35.3	36,619	15.2
Other			19,668[4]	8.2[4]
TOTAL	1,420.0	100.0	241,160	100.0

Land use (1986): forested 64.9%; agricultural and under permanent cultivation 13.1%; meadows and pastures 3.3%; other 18.7%.
Tourism: receipts from visitors (1988) U.S.$180,600,000; expenditures by nationals abroad (1987) U.S.$24,000,000.

Foreign trade

Balance of trade (current prices)

	1983	1984	1985	1986	1987	1988
F$'000,000	−189.0	−148.4	−183.2	−124.7	−131.4	−61.76
% of total	27.8%	20.9%	25.8%	16.6%	16.4%	5.6%

Imports (1988): F$658,744,000 (machinery and transport equipment 21.1%; food, beverages, and tobacco 17.6%; mineral fuels and related materials 13.5%; chemicals 10.0%; miscellaneous manufactured consumer articles 8.7%). *Major import sources:* Australia 29.4%; New Zealand 18.9%; Japan 10.2%; Taiwan 5.3%; United States 4.9%; France 4.3%; Singapore 4.2%; United Kingdom 3.7%; South Korea 3.5%.
Exports (1988)[5]: F$434,883,000 (sugar 45.6%; gold 18.7%; fish 9.2%; timber 5.8%; garments 4.2%; molasses 2.6%; coconut oil 0.8%). *Major export destinations*[6]: United Kingdom 34.9%; Australia 25.6%; New Zealand 7.7%; Japan 5.5%; Canada 4.4%; China 3.9%; United States 3.3%; Taiwan 2.5%.

Transport and communications

Transport. Railroads[7] (1986): length 660 mi, 1,062 km. Roads (1988): total length 2,996 mi, 4,821 km (paved 13%). Vehicles (1987): passenger cars 34,380; trucks and buses 24,318. Merchant marine (1988): vessels (100 gross tons and over) 57; total deadweight tonnage 36,752. Air transport (1988)[8]: passenger-mi 336,000,000, passenger-km 540,000,000; short ton-mi cargo 13,093,000, metric ton-km cargo 19,115,000; airports (1989) with scheduled flights 18.
Communications. Daily newspapers (1985): total number 2; total circulation 53,000; circulation per 1,000 population 74. Radio (1988): total number of receivers 431,355 (1 per 1.7 persons). Television: n.a. Telephones (1987): 60,017 (1 per 12 persons).

Education and health

Education (1987)

	schools	teachers	students	student/teacher ratio
Primary (age 5–15)	672[9]	4,436	136,567	30.8
Secondary (age 16–19)	140[9]	2,646	43,942	16.6
Voc., teacher tr.	44[9]	246	2,723	11.1
Higher	5[10]	320[9]	2,211[9]	6.9[9]

Educational attainment (1986). Percent of population age 25 and over having: no formal schooling 28.3%; primary only 19.1%; some secondary 44.1%; secondary 4.1%; postsecondary 3.3%; other 1.1%. *Literacy* (1985): total population age 15 and over literate 374,300 (85.5%); males literate 197,300 (90.2%); females literate 177,000 (80.9%).
Health (1987): physicians 271 (1 per 2,649 persons); hospital beds 1,721 (1 per 417 persons); infant mortality rate per 1,000 live births (1988) 27.0.
Food (1984–86): daily per capita caloric intake 2,901 (vegetable products 87%, animal products 13%); (1984) 110% of FAO recommended minimum requirement.

Military

Total active duty personnel (1988): 3,500 (army 91.4%; navy 8.6%; air force, none). *Military expenditure as percent of GNP* (1986): 1.2% (world 5.5%); per capita expenditure: U.S.$20.

[1]In late 1988 a new constitution was drafted proposing a unicameral legislative body. By late 1989 this constitution had yet to go into effect. [2]Fiji's first civilian president was appointed Dec. 5, 1987, as was the prime minister, formally returning the nation to civilian rule. [3]The provinces are autonomous only with respect to local affairs. [4]Not stated and unemployed. [5]Excludes reexports, valued at F$83,235,000. [6]Based on exports of local products only. [7]Owned by the Fiji Sugar Corporation. [8]Air Pacific only. [9]1986. [10]1983.

Finland

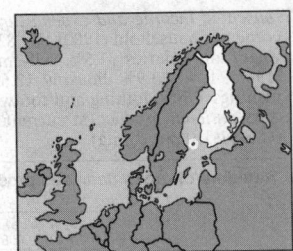

Official name: Suomen Tasavalta
(Finnish); Republiken Finland
(Swedish) (Republic of Finland).
Form of government: multiparty
republic with one legislative house
(Parliament [200]).
Chief of state: President.
Head of government: Prime Minister.
Capital: Helsinki.
Official languages: Finnish; Swedish.
Official religion: none[1].
Monetary unit: 1 markka (Fmk) = 100
pennia; valuation (Oct. 2, 1989)
1 U.S.$ = Fmk 4.27; 1 £ = Fmk 6.91.

Area and population		land area		population
		sq mi	sq km	1989 estimate[2]
Provinces	**Capitals**			
Häme	Hämeenlinna	6,568	17,010	683,728
Keski-Suomi	Jyväskylä	6,266	16,230	249,240
Kuopio	Kuopio	6,375	16,511	256,095
Kymi	Kouvola	4,163	10,783	336,076
Lappi	Rovaniemi	35,930	93,057	200,024
Mikkeli	Mikkeli	6,310	16,342	207,685
Oulu	Oulu	21,956	56,866	434,999
Pohjois-Karjala	Joensuu	6,866	17,782	176,367
Turku ja Pori	Turku	8,559	22,170	715,782
Uusimaa	Helsinki	3,822	9,898	1,226,365
Vaasa	Vaasa	10,211	26,447	444,315
Autonomous Province				
Åland (Ahvenanmaa)	Mariehamn (Maarianhamina)	590	1,527	23,908
TOTAL LAND AREA		117,616	304,623	4,954,584
INLAND WATER		12,943	33,522	
TOTAL		130,559	338,145	

Demography

Population (1989): 4,960,000.
Density[3] (1989): persons per sq mi 42.2, persons per sq km 16.3.
Urban–rural (1989): urban 61.8%; rural 38.2%.
Sex distribution (1988): male 48.45%; female 51.55%.
Age breakdown (1987): under 15, 19.3%; 15–29, 22.0%; 30–44, 24.1%; 45–59, 16.8%; 60–74, 12.5%; 75 and over, 5.3%.
Population projection: (2000) 5,017,000; (2010) 4,982,000.
Doubling time: n.a.; population is stable.
Ethnolinguistic composition (1987): Finnish 93.6%; Swedish 6.1%; other 0.3%.
Religious affiliation (1987): Evangelical Lutheran 88.9%; Finnish (Greek) Orthodox 1.1%; nonaffiliated 9.1%; other 0.9%.
Major cities (1989)[4]: Helsinki 491,182 (metropolitan area 990,189); Tampere 171,027; Espoo 168,349[5]; Turku 159,533; Vantaa 151,726[5].

Vital statistics

Birth rate per 1,000 population (1988): 12.8 (world avg. 27.1); (1986) legitimate 82.0%; illegitimate 18.0%.
Death rate per 1,000 population (1988): 9.9 (world avg. 9.9).
Natural increase rate per 1,000 population (1988): 2.9 (world avg. 17.2).
Total fertility rate (avg. births per childbearing woman; 1987): 1.7.
Marriage rate per 1,000 population (1988): 5.3.
Divorce rate per 1,000 population (1986): 2.0.
Life expectancy at birth (1987): male 70.7 years; female 78.7 years.
Major causes of death per 100,000 population (1986): ischemic heart disease 285.5; malignant neoplasms (cancers) 193.9; cerebrovascular diseases 116.8; accidents 47.0; pneumonia 36.9; suicide and self-inflicted injuries 26.6.

National economy

Budget (1988). Revenue: Fmk 113,817,000,000 (tax revenue 81.4%, of which sales tax 30.0%, income and property taxes 28.5%, excise duties 11.2%, vehicle taxes 3.5%; nontax revenue 18.6%). Expenditures: Fmk 113,816,-000,000 (social security 19.3%; education 15.2%; transportation 8.8%; health 8.6%; agriculture 7.3%; administration 6.5%; defense 5.4%).
National debt (end of February 1989): Fmk 56,675,000,000.
Tourism (1988): receipts from visitors U.S.$1,018,000,000; expenditures by nationals abroad U.S.$1,892,000,000.
Production (metric tons except as noted). Agriculture, forestry, fishing (1988): silage 3,580,000[6], barley 1,612,000, sugar beets 944,000, oats 857,000, potatoes 855,000, strawberries 9,200; livestock (number of live animals) 1,434,000 cattle, 1,291,000 pigs, 366,000 reindeer[6]; roundwood 46,600,000 cu m; fish catch (1987) 159,300. Mining and quarrying (1988): iron ore 556,000; zinc concentrate 124,000. Manufacturing (value added, in Fmk '000,000; 1986): paper and paper products 10,565; food, beverages, and tobacco 10,470; nonelectrical machinery 8,527; chemicals and rubber and plastic products 7,857; graphic arts 6,257; wood products including furniture 5,088. Construction (1988): residential 16,030,000 cu m; nonresidential 26,-220,000 cu m. Energy production (consumption): electricity (kW-hr; 1988) 51,664,000,000 (59,061,000,000[6]); coal (metric tons; 1987) none (5,239,000); crude petroleum (barrels; 1987) none (78,438,000); petroleum products (metric tons; 1988) 9,523,000 (10,180,000[6]); natural gas (cu m; 1987) none (1,561,000,000).
Household income and expenditure. Average household size (1986) 2.6; income per household (1984) Fmk 103,500 (U.S.$17,247); sources of income (1988): wages and salaries 62.6%, transfer payments 18.7%, self-employ-

ment 14.0%, other 4.7%; expenditure (1987): food, beverages, and tobacco 25.2%, transportation and communications 18.0%, housing and energy 17.7%, recreation and education 10.3%.
Gross national product (at current market prices; 1987): U.S.$71,084,000,000 (U.S.$14,370 per capita).

Structure of gross domestic product and labour force				
	1988		1987	
	in value Fmk '000,000	% of total value	labour force	% of labour force
Agriculture, fishing	11,530	3.0	218,000	8.4
Forestry	12,765	3.3	45,000	1.7
Mining	1,324	0.4	8,000	0.3
Manufacturing	92,773	24.2	559,000	21.6
Public utilities	10,300	2.7	29,000	1.1
Construction	33,659	8.8	206,000	8.0
Transp. and commun.	30,764	8.0	187,000	7.2
Trade	45,088	11.8	363,000	14.1
Finance, real estate	68,280	17.8	180,000	7.0
Pub. admin., defense	65,402	17.1	129,000	5.0
Services	16,451	4.3	634,000	24.6
Other	−5,414[7]	−1.4[7]	25,000[8]	1.0[8]
TOTAL	382,922	100.0	2,583,000	100.0

Population economically active (1987): total 2,583,000; activity rate of total population 52.4% (participation rates: ages 15–64, 76.5%; female 47.1%; unemployed [1988] 4.5%).

Price and earnings indexes (1985 = 100)							
	1983	1984	1985	1986	1987	1988	1989
Consumer price index	88.2	94.5	100.0	102.9	107.1	112.6	120.4[9]
Hourly earnings index	84.2	92.2	100.0	106.9	114.4	124.7	...

Land use (1986): forested 76.0%; meadows and pastures 0.4%; agricultural and under permanent cultivation 7.9%; other 15.7%.

Foreign trade[10]

Balance of trade (current prices)						
	1983	1984	1985	1986	1987	1988
Fmk '000,000	+1,667	+9,498	+6,160	+8,411	+4,749	+6,895
% of total	1.2%	6.2%	3.8%	5.4%	2.8%	3.9%

Imports (1988): Fmk 88,192,000,000 (raw materials and producer goods 54.4%; consumer goods 22.8%; investment goods 18.8%). *Major import sources:* West Germany 16.9%; Sweden 13.3%; U.S.S.R. 12.1%; Japan 7.4%; United Kingdom 6.8%.
Exports (1988): Fmk 90,861,000,000 (paper, paper products, and graphic arts 33.4%; metal products and machinery 31.0%; wood products including furniture 8.2%). *Major export destinations:* U.S.S.R. 14.9%; Sweden 14.1%; United Kingdom 13.0%; West Germany 10.8%; United States 5.8%.

Transport and communications

Transport. Railroads (1988): length (1987) 5,553 mi, 8,936 km; passenger-mi 1,988,900,000, passenger-km 3,200,900,000; short ton-mi cargo 5,354,000,-000, metric ton-km cargo 7,816,000,000. Roads (1987): total length 47,453 mi, 76,369 km (paved 54%). Vehicles (1989): passenger cars 1,795,908; trucks and buses 238,258. Merchant marine (1988): vessels (100 gross tons and over) 259; total deadweight tonnage 810,888. Air transport (1988): passenger-mi 2,470,000,000, passenger-km 4,034,000,000; short ton-mi cargo 73,922,000, metric ton-km cargo 107,924,000; airports (1989) 21.
Communications. Daily newspapers (1988): total number 103; total circulation 3,300,000; circulation per 1,000 population 667. Radio (1988): 4,922,-000 receivers (1 per 1.0 persons). Television (1988): 1,851,000 receivers (1 per 2.7 persons). Telephones (1987)[11]: 2,365,000 (1 per 2.1 persons).

Education and health

Education (1985–86)	schools	teachers	students	student/ teacher ratio
Primary (age 7–12)	4,233	25,140	380,509	15.1
Secondary (age 13–19)	1,093	22,360	300,748	13.4
Voc., teacher tr.	574[12]	22,869[12]	113,117[12]	10.8[12]
Higher			133,933[12]	

Educational attainment (1986). Percent of population age 15 and over having: incomplete upper secondary education 54.3%; complete upper secondary or vocational 37.4%; some postsecondary 3.4%; undergraduate 1.6%; graduate 2.9%; postgraduate 0.3%; unknown 0.1%. *Literacy* (1987): virtually 100%.
Health (1986): physicians (1987) 10,889 (1 per 453 persons); hospital beds 60,448 (1 per 81 persons); infant mortality rate per 1,000 live births 5.8.
Food (1984–86): daily per capita caloric intake 3,080 (vegetable products 57%, animal products 43%); 114% of FAO recommended minimum requirement.

Military

Total active duty personnel (1989): 31,000 (army 89.7%, navy 4.5%, air force 5.8%). *Military expenditure as percent of GNP* (1986): 1.7% (world 5.5%); per capita expenditure U.S.$269.

---

[1]The Evangelical Lutheran and Finnish (Greek) Orthodox churches have special recognition. [2]January 1. [3]Based on land area only. [4]April 1. [5]Within metropolitan Helsinki. [6]1987. [7]Imputed bank service charges (Fmk 13,251,000,000) less other producers (Fmk 7,837,000,000). [8]Unemployed not previously employed. [9]July. [10]Import figures are f.o.b. in balance of trade and c.i.f. in commodities and trading partners. [11]Main lines. [12]1986–87.

France

Official name: République Française (French Republic).
Form of government: republic with two legislative houses (Parliament; Senate [321], National Assembly [577]).
Chief of state: President.
Head of government: Prime Minister.
Capital: Paris.
Official language: French.
Official religion: none.
Monetary unit: 1 Franc (F) = 100 centimes; valuation (Oct. 2, 1989) 1 U.S.$ = F 6.36; 1 £ = F 10.29.

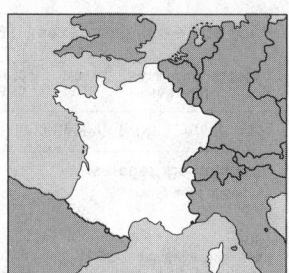

Area and population

Regions Departments	Capitals	area sq mi	area sq km	population 1988 estimate[1]
Alsace				
Bas-Rhin	Strasbourg	1,836	4,755	945,800
Haut-Rhin	Colmar	1,361	3,525	668,100
Aquitaine				
Dordogne	Périgueux	3,498	9,060	378,800
Gironde	Bordeaux	3,861	10,000	1,168,400
Landes	Mont-de-Marsan	3,569	9,243	309,800
Lot-et-Garonne	Agen	2,070	5,361	306,300
Pyrénées-Atlantiques	Pau	2,952	7,645	573,900
Auvergne				
Allier	Moulins	2,834	7,340	361,500
Cantal	Aurillac	2,211	5,726	159,200
Haute-Loire	Le Puy	1,922	4,977	209,600
Puy-de-Dôme	Clermont-Ferrand	3,077	7,970	598,000
Basse Normandie				
Calvados	Caen	2,142	5,548	611,800
Manche	Saint-Lô	2,293	5,938	479,700
Orne	Alen	2,356	6,103	293,800
Bretagne				
Côtes-du-Nord	Saint-Brieuc	2,656	6,878	541,000
Finistère	Quimper	2,600	6,733	833,200
Ille-et-Vilaine	Rennes	2,616	6,775	784,500
Morbihan	Vannes	2,634	6,823	614,200
Bourgogne				
Côte-d'Or	Dijon	3,383	8,763	487,300
Nièvre	Nevers	2,632	6,817	234,500
Saône-et-Loire	Mâcon	3,311	8,575	572,100
Yonne	Auxerre	2,868	7,427	320,000
Centre				
Cher	Bourges	2,793	7,235	323,200
Eure-et-Loire	Chartres	2,270	5,880	382,400
Indre	Châteauroux	2,622	6,791	237,400
Indre-et-Loire	Tours	2,366	6,127	526,000
Loiret	Orléans	2,616	6,775	576,800
Loir-et-Cher	Blois	2,449	6,343	301,700
Champagne-Ardenne				
Ardennes	Charleville-Mézières	2,019	5,229	296,400
Aube	Troyes	2,318	6,004	294,100
Haute-Marne	Chaumont	2,398	6,211	207,200
Marne	Châlons-sur-Marne	3,151	8,162	562,300
Corse				
Corse-du-Sud	Ajaccio	1,550	4,014	112,100
Haute-Corse	Bastia	1,802	4,666	135,200
Franche-Comté				
Doubs	Besançon	2,021	5,234	479,900
Haute-Saône	Vesoul	2,070	5,360	233,800
Jura	Lons-le-Saunier	1,930	4,999	244,200
Territoire de Belfort	Belfort	235	609	130,300
Haute-Normandie				
Eure	Évreux	2,332	6,040	498,700
Seine-Maritime	Rouen	2,424	6,278	1,211,800
Île-de-France				
Essonne	Évry	696	1,804	1,062,300
Hauts-de-Seine	Nanterre	68	176	1,368,900
Paris	Paris	40	105	2,057,000
Seine-et-Marne	Melun	2,284	5,915	1,001,200
Seine-Saint-Denis	Bobigny	91	236	1,345,700
Val-de-Marne	Créteil	95	245	1,202,300
Val-d'Oise	Pontoise	481	1,246	1,003,700
Yvelines	Versailles	882	2,284	1,278,600
Languedoc-Roussillon				
Aude	Carcassonne	2,370	6,139	293,100
Gard	Nîmes	2,260	5,853	573,000
Hérault	Montpellier	2,356	6,101	777,600
Lozère	Mende	1,995	5,167	72,200
Pyrénées-Orientales	Perpignan	1,589	4,116	364,000
Limousin				
Corrèze	Tulle	2,261	5,857	237,900
Creuse	Guéret	2,149	5,565	134,600
Haute-Vienne	Limoges	2,131	5,520	359,500
Lorraine				
Meurthe-et-Moselle	Nancy	2,024	5,241	705,000
Meuse	Bar-le-Duc	2,400	6,216	196,400
Moselle	Metz	2,400	6,216	1,029,300
Vosges	Épinal	2,268	5,874	390,000
Midi-Pyrénées				
Ariège	Foix	1,888	4,890	135,800
Aveyron	Rodez	3,373	8,736	275,600
Gers	Auch	2,416	6,257	175,200
Haute-Garonne	Toulouse	2,436	6,309	865,900
Haute-Pyrénées	Tarbes	1,724	4,464	232,100
Lot	Cahors	2,014	5,217	155,200
Tarn	Albi	2,223	5,758	341,500
Tarn-et-Garonne	Montauban	1,435	3,718	196,000
Nord-Pas-de-Calais				
Nord	Lille	2,217	5,742	2,502,200
Pas-de-Calais	Arras	2,576	6,671	1,422,800

Area and population (continued)

	Capitals	sq mi	sq km	population 1988 estimate[1]
Pays de la Loire				
Loire-Atlantique	Nantes	2,631	6,815	1,037,000
Maine-et Loire	Angers	2,767	7,166	711,000
Mayenne	Laval	1,998	5,175	282,400
Sarthe	Le Mans	2,396	6,206	515,000
Vendée	La Roche-sur-Yon	2,595	6,720	509,100
Picardie				
Aisne	Laon	2,845	7,369	532,100
Oise	Beauvais	2,263	5,860	702,500
Somme	Amiens	2,382	6,170	548,800
Poitou-Charentes				
Charente	Angoulême	2,300	5,956	343,800
Charente-Maritime	La Rochelle	2,650	6,864	525,400
Deux-Sèvres	Niort	2,316	5,999	347,700
Vienne	Poitiers	2,699	6,990	382,700
Provence–Alpes-Côte d'Azur				
Alpes-Maritimes	Nice	1,660	4,299	913,000
Alpes-de-Haute-Provence	Digne	2,674	6,925	126,300
Bouches-du-Rhône	Marseille	1,964	5,087	1,765,900
Hautes-Alpes	Gap	2,142	5,549	109,100
Var	Toulon	2,306	5,973	766,100
Vaucluse	Avignon	1,377	3,567	467,800
Rhône-Alpes				
Ain	Bourg-en-Bresse	2,225	5,762	457,000
Ardèche	Privas	2,135	5,529	276,000
Drôme	Valence	2,521	6,530	406,000
Haute-Savoie	Annecy	1,694	4,388	539,000
Isère	Grenoble	2,869	7,431	992,000
Loire	Saint-Étienne	1,846	4,781	738,000
Rhône	Lyon	1,254	3,249	1,462,000
Savoie	Chambéry	2,327	6,028	335,000
TOTAL		210,026	543,965	55,750,300

Demography

Population (1989): 56,107,000.
Density (1989): persons per sq mi 267.1, persons per sq km 103.1.
Urban–rural (1985): urban 73.4%; rural 26.6%.
Sex distribution (1988): male 48.72%; female 51.28%.
Age breakdown (1988): under 15, 20.5%; 15–29, 23.0%; 30–44, 21.8%; 45–59, 16.0%; 60–74, 12.1%; 75 and over, 6.6%.
Population projection: (2000) 58,748,000; (2010) 61,256,000.
Doubling time: n.a.; doubling time exceeds 100 years.
Ethnolinguistic composition (1982): French (mother tongue) 93.2%, of which fully or substantially bilingual in Occitan 2.7%, German (mostly Alsatian) 2.3%, Breton 1.0%, Catalan 0.4%; Arabic 2.6%; other 4.2%.
Religious affiliation (1980): Roman Catholic 76.4%; other Christian 3.7%; atheist 3.4%; Muslim 3.0%; other 13.5%.
Major cities (1982): Paris 2,165,892 (metropolitan area 10,210,059); Marseille 868,435 (1,227,901); Lyon 410,455 (1,533,305); Toulouse 344,917 (648,267); Nice 331,165 (865,492); Strasbourg 247,068 (613,380); Nantes 237,789 (558,-814); Bordeaux 201,965 (843,411); Saint-Étienne 193,938 (547,729).
National origin (1982): French 90.6%; Algerian 1.5%; Portuguese 1.4%; Moroccan 0.8%; Spanish 0.6%; Italian 0.6%; other 4.5%[2].
Mobility (1982). Population living in same residence as in 1975: n.a.; same region 91.7%; different region 5.8%; different country 2.5%.
Households (1982). Average household size 2.7; 1 person 24.6%, 2 persons 28.5%, 3 persons 18.8%, 4 persons 16.1%, 5 persons 7.4%, 6 persons or more 4.6%. Family households: 14,118,940 (72.1%); nonfamily 5,471,460 (27.9%, of which 1-person 24.6%).
Immigration (1987): permanent immigrants admitted 39,000, from Morocco 21.9%, Turkey 11.9%, Tunisia 6.6%, Italy 3.0%, West Germany 2.7%.

Vital statistics

Birth rate per 1,000 population (1988): 13.8 (world avg. 27.1); (1987) legitimate 75.9%; illegitimate 24.1%.
Death rate per 1,000 population (1988): 9.4 (world avg. 9.9).
Natural increase rate per 1,000 population (1988): 4.4 (world avg. 17.2).
Total fertility rate (avg. births per childbearing woman; 1987): 1.8.
Marriage rate per 1,000 population (1988): 4.9.
Divorce rate per 1,000 population (1987): 1.9.
Life expectancy at birth (1985–87): male 71.6 years; female 79.8 years.
Major causes of death per 100,000 population (1987): malignant neoplasms (cancers) 250.2; heart disease 192.6; other circulatory diseases 142.8.

Social indicators

Educational attainment (1974). Percent of adult employed population having: less than full primary education 36.2%; primary 30.4%; secondary 21.0%; some postsecondary 7.0%; 4-year degree 2.4%; postgraduate 2.8%.

Distribution of income (1975)

percent of household income by quintile

1	2	3	4	5 (highest)
5.5%	11.5%	17.1%	23.7%	42.2%

Quality of working life. Average workweek (1988): 38.9 hours. Annual rate per 100,000 workers (1986) for: injury or accident 2,907; industrial illness 15.9; death 4.1. Proportion of labour force insured for damages or income loss resulting from: injury, permanent disability, or death, n.a. Average days lost to labour stoppages per 1,000 workers (1987): 19.7. Average duration of journey to work (1974): 53 minutes.
Access to services (1984). Proportion of dwellings having: central heating 69.6%; piped water 99.6%; indoor plumbing 85.3%; natural gas (1982) 48.9%.
Social participation. Eligible voters participating in last national election: 78.0%. Population over 15 years of age participating in voluntary associations: 28.0%.

Social deviance. Offense rate per 100,000 population (1987) for: murder 3.9; rape 5.7; other assault 64.3; theft, including burglary and housebreaking 3,650.9. Incidence per 100,000 in general population of: alcoholism[3] (late 1970s) 3,500–4,000; drug and substance abuse, n.a.; suicides (1986) 22.5.

Leisure (1987–88). Favourite leisure activities: watching television 82%; reading magazines 79%; listening to radio 75%; entertaining relatives 64%; visiting relatives 61%; attending fairs/expositions 56%.

Material well-being (1987). Households possessing: automobile 74.6%; television receiver 94.0%, of which colour 78.1%; refrigerator 97.0%; washing machine 86.2%.

National economy

Gross national product (at current market prices; 1987): U.S.$714,994,000,-000 (U.S.$12,860 per capita).

Structure of gross domestic product and labour force

	1987			
	in value F '000,000	% of total value	labour force	% of labour force
Agriculture	332,441	6.3	1,650,900	6.8
Mining	} 915,831	17.3	68,300	0.3
Manufacturing			4,420,200	18.4
Construction	287,096	5.4	1,521,900	6.3
Public utilities	245,586	4.7	210,000	0.9
Transp. and commun.	315,948	6.0	1,371,200	5.7
Trade	567,976	10.7	3,691,100	15.3
Finance	260,643	4.9	673,100	2.8
Pub. admin., defense	873,588	16.5	4,228,700	17.6
Services	1,258,149	23.8	3,394,800	14.1
Other	231,441[4]	4.4[4]	2,854,100[5]	11.8[5]
TOTAL	5,288,699[6]	100.0	24,084,300	100.0

Budget (1989). Revenue: F 1,193,000,000,000 (value-added taxes 47.3%, income tax 22.5%, customs taxes 10.5%). Expenditure: F 1,177,200,000,000 (educ. 23.6%, health and soc. services 19.0%, defense 16.2%, admin. 12.6%).

Manufacturing and mining enterprises (1985)

	no. of enterprises	no. of employees	hourly wages as a % of avg. of all wages[7]	annual value added (F '000,000)
Food products	...	548,000	100	160,500
Transport equipment	671	560,000	115	141,200
Electrical machinery	704	479,000	101	89,300
Petroleum refineries	49	26,000	...	89,100
Industrial chemicals	291	126,000	117	66,100
Iron and steel	134	206,000	...	56,800
Metal products	3,284	234,000	109	52,100
Textiles	1,877	237,000	83	39,100
Printing, publishing	1,779	214,000	117	31,600
Paper and products	638	106,000	109	31,200
Beverages	...	52,000	100	31,200
Wearing apparel	2,464	217,000	79	26,400
Rubber products	169	89,000	97	16,800
Tobacco	...	8,000	100	14,700
Glass products	144	58,000	112	12,000

Production (metric tons except as noted). Agriculture, forestry, fishing (1988): wheat 29,677,000, sugar beets 28,606,000, corn (maize) 13,996,000, barley 10,086,000, grapes 7,419,000, potatoes 6,344,000, rapeseed 2,469,000, sunflower seeds 2,457,000, apples 2,357,000, oats 1,074,000, tomatoes 743,000, cauliflower 568,000, carrots 515,000, peaches 472,000, pears 355,000, rye 276,000; livestock (number of live animals) 21,100,000 cattle, 12,577,000 pigs, 10,360,000 sheep, 1,150,000 goats; roundwood (1987) 40,901,000 cu m; fish catch (1987) 843,714. Mining and quarrying (1988): iron ore 2,927,-000[8]; potash salts 1,500,000; bauxite 877,200; zinc 31,320[8]; lead 2,520[8]; gold 75,618 troy oz[8]. Manufacturing (1988): cement 25,272,000; crude steel 18,900,000; pig iron 13,440,000[9]; sulfuric acid 3,957,600; rubber products 558,900, of which tires 54,924,000 units[9]; aluminum 536,400; automobiles 3,138,000 units. Construction (dwelling units completed; 1987) 254,000.

Retail trade enterprises (1986)

	no. of enterprises	no. of employees	weekly wages as a % of all wages	annual turnover (F '000,000)
Large food stores	3,263	335,478	...	397,744
Small food stores	125,102	335,252	...	176,024
butcher shops	47,494	145,121	...	66,955
Clothing stores	70,854	188,174	...	82,463
Pharmacies	21,661	116,195	...	68,542
Department stores	2,454	66,075	...	48,005
Furniture stores	7,029	48,011	...	39,393
Electrical and electronics stores	10,266	47,641	...	29,693
Gas, coal, and other energy products	4,769	18,550	...	28,152
Publishing and paper	19,544	52,169	...	21,680

Energy production (consumption)[10]: electricity (kW-hr; 1987) 356,200,000,-000 (326,500,000,000); coal (metric tons; 1987) 19,077,000 (31,747,000); crude petroleum (barrels; 1987) 23,719,000 (478,060,000); petroleum products (metric tons; 1987) 62,043,000 (72,185,000); natural gas (cu m; 1987) 3,662,400,000 (26,933,300,000).

Household income and expenditure. Average household size (1987) 2.7; average annual income per household (1985) F 165,200 (U.S.$18,385). Sources of income (1985): wages and salaries 50.4%, social security 28.9%, self-employment 20.7%; expenditure (1985): food 19.6%, housing 18.2%, health 13.9%, transportation 13.8%, clothing 6.3%, recreation 6.3%.

Tourism (1987): receipts from visitors U.S.$12,008,000,000; expenditures by nationals abroad U.S.$8,618,000,000.

Population economically active (1987): total 24,084,300; activity rate of total population 43.3% (participation rates: ages 15–64, 65.4%[10]; female 42.4%; unemployed 10.5%).

Price and earnings indexes (1985 = 100)

	1982	1983	1984	1985	1986	1987	1988
Consumer price index	80.3	88.0	94.6	100.0	102.5	105.9	108.8
Hourly earnings index	77.1	86.9	94.8	100.0	104.5	109.4	...

Public debt (1988): F 988,800,000,000 (U.S.$243,600,000,000).

Financial aggregates

	1984	1985	1986	1987	1988	1989[11]
Exchange rate, F per:						
U.S. dollar	9.59	7.56	6.46	5.34	6.06	6.34
£	11.09	10.92	9.52	9.99	10.96	10.30
SDR	9.40	8.30	7.90	7.58	8.15	8.11
International reserves (U.S.$)						
Total (excl. gold; '000,000)	20,940	26,589	31,454	33,049	25,364	25,753[12]
SDRs ('000,000)	572	900	1,290	1,502	1,390	1,221
Reserve pos. in IMF ('000,000)	1,265	1,370	1,736	1,914	1,615	1,406
Foreign exchange	19,102	24,319	28,428	29,634	22,359	23,222[12]
Gold ('000,000 fine troy oz)	81.85	81.85	81.85	81.85	81.85	81.85[12]
% world reserves	8.6	8.6	8.6	8.7	8.7	8.7[12]
Interest and prices						
Central bank discount (%)	9.50	9.50	9.50	9.50	9.50	9.50
Gov't. bond yield (%)	12.41	10.94	8.44	9.43	9.06	8.39[12]
Industrial share prices (1985 = 100)	85.6	100.0	153.3	177.6	162.1	245.2[12]
Balance of payments (U.S.$'000,000)						
Balance of visible trade	−4,651	−5,276	−2,354	−9,821	−8,089	...
Imports, f.o.b.	96,865	101,203	120,343	148,713	168,727	...
Exports, f.o.b.	92,214	95,927	117,988	138,893	160,638	...
Balance of invisibles	6,673	7,868	9,671	9,558	11,274	...
Balance of payments, current account	−876	−35	3,002	−5,091	−3,547	...

Land use (1987): forested 26.7%; meadows and pastures 21.6%; agricultural and under permanent cultivation 35.4%; other 16.3%.

Foreign trade

Balance of trade (current prices)

	1983	1984	1985	1986	1987	1988
F '000,000,000	−34.5	−19.7	−24.2	−3.0	−30.7	−32.8
% of total	2.3%	3.0%	1.3%	0.2%	1.7%	1.6%

Imports (1988): F 1,053,406,000,000 (machinery 26.3%; chemicals and chemical products 16.0%; agricultural products 12.3%; fuels 8.1%, of which petroleum and petroleum products 7.5%; transport equipment 9.9%, of which automobiles 5.3%). *Major import sources:* West Germany 19.7%; Italy 11.6%; Belgium–Luxembourg 9.1%; U.S. 7.7%; U.K. 7.3%; The Netherlands 5.3%.

Exports (1988): F 963,262,000,000 (machinery 24.5%; agricultural products 17.5%; chemicals 16.3%; transport equipment 13.3%, of which automobiles 6.6%). *Major export destinations:* West Germany 16.4%; Italy 12.2%; U.K. 9.8%; Belgium–Luxembourg 9.0%; U.S. 7.3%; The Netherlands 5.6%.

Transport and communications

Transport. Railroads (1988): route length[9] 21,528 mi, 34,647 km; passenger-mi 39,302,000,000, passenger-km 63,250,000,000; short ton-mi cargo 35,-814,000,000, metric ton-km cargo 52,287,000,000. Roads (1987): total length 500,165 mi, 804,940 km (paved [1985] 92%). Vehicles (1987): passenger cars 21,970,000; trucks and buses 3,982,000. Merchant marine (1988): vessels (100 gross tons and over) 930; total deadweight tonnage 6,854,064. Air transport[13] (1988): passenger-mi 24,857,000,000, passenger-km 40,004,000,-000; short ton-mi cargo 2,514,000,000, metric ton-km cargo 3,670,000,000; airports (1989) with scheduled flights 69.

Communications. Daily newspapers (1988): number 112; circulation 9,453,-800[14]; circulation per 1,000 population 169[14]. Radio (1988): 49,008,761 receivers (1 per 1.1 persons). Television (1988): 21,967,522 receivers (1 per 2.5 persons). Telephones (1987): 33,357,900[15] (1 per 1.7 persons).

Education and health

Education (1987–88)

	schools	teachers	students	student/ teacher ratio
Primary (age 6–10)	47,047	343,664	4,118,403	12.0
Secondary (age 11–18)	} 11,207	408,263	5,377,725	13.2
Voc., teacher tr.				
Higher	1,062	45,797	1,208,783	26.4

Literacy (1980): total population literate 41,112,000 (98.8%); males literate 19,933,000 (98.9%); females literate 21,179,000 (98.7%).

Health (1986): physicians 138,825 (1 per 399 persons); hospital beds 722,378 (1 per 80 persons); infant mortality rate per 1,000 live births (1988) 7.7.

Food (1984–86): daily per capita caloric intake 3,273 (vegetable products 63%, animal products 37%); 130% of FAO recommended minimum requirement.

Military

Total active duty personnel (1989): 466,300 (army 62.7%, navy 14.0%, air force 20.2%, other 3.1%). *Military expenditure as percent of GNP* (1987): 4.0% (world 5.4%); per capita expenditure U.S.$626.

[1]January 1. [2]Includes 2.6% naturalized citizens not identified by national origin. [3]Estimated according to a narrow definition of alcoholism. [4]Includes value-added taxes, customs duties, and imputed bank service charges. [5]Includes 2,545,800 unemployed persons and 250,800 members of the armed forces. [6]At 1980 prices. [7]1982. [8]Metal content of ores. [9]1987. [10]All energy statistics include Monaco. [11]September. [12]August. [13]Air France, UTA, and Air Inter only. [14]80 newspapers only. [15]Does not include public telephones.

French Guiana

Official name: Département de la Guyane française (Department of French Guiana).
Political status: overseas department of France with two legislative houses (General Council [19]; Regional Council [31]).
Chief of state: President of France.
Heads of government: Commissioner of the Republic (for France); President of the General Council (for French Guiana); President of the Regional Council (for French Guiana).
Capital: Cayenne.
Official language: French.
Official religion: none.
Monetary unit: 1 franc (F) = 100 centimes; valuation (Oct. 2, 1989) 1 U.S.$ = F 6.36; 1 £ = F 10.29.

Area and population		area		population
				1982
Arrondissements	Capitals	sq mi	sq km	census
Cayenne	Cayenne	17,590	45,559	61,587
Saint-Laurent-du-Maroni	Saint-Laurent-du-Maroni	15,809	40,945	11,435
TOTAL		33,399	86,504	73,022

Demography

Population (1989): 95,000.
Density (1989): persons per sq mi 2.8, persons per sq km 1.1.
Urban–rural (1982): urban 73.4%; rural 26.6%.
Sex distribution (1982): male 52.66%; female 47.34%.
Age breakdown (1982): under 15, 34.2%; 15–29, 29.2%; 30–44, 19.9%; 45–59, 9.8%; 60–74, 5.1%; 75 and over, 1.8%.
Population projection: (2000) 132,000; (2010) 178,000.
Doubling time: 27 years.
Ethnic composition (1980): Guianese (mixed) Creole 72.3%, of which French (metropolitan) 45.7%, Haitian 17.0%, French West Indian 5.3%; Bush Negro 6.4%; Brazilian 5.9%; Amerindian 4.2%; other (other West Indian, Surinamese, Hmong, other Southeast Asian, and other European) 11.2%.
Religious affiliation (1980)[1]: Roman Catholic 87.0%; Protestant 3.9%; nonreligious 2.5%; Afro-American spiritist 2.0%; traditional beliefs 1.5%; Chinese folk-religionist 1.3%; Muslim 1.0%; Baha'i 0.7%; other 0.1%.
Major cities (1982): Cayenne 37,097; Kourou 6,465; Rémire-Montjoly 5,921; Saint-Laurent-du-Maroni 5,042.

Vital statistics

Birth rate per 1,000 population (1988): 31.4 (world avg. 27.1); legitimate 18.4%; illegitimate 81.6%.
Death rate per 1,000 population (1988): 5.7 (world avg. 9.9).
Natural increase rate per 1,000 population (1988): 25.7 (world avg. 17.2).
Total fertility rate (avg. births per childbearing woman; 1975–79): 3.1.
Marriage rate per 1,000 population (1988): 3.5.
Divorce rate per 1,000 population (1988): 0.5.
Life expectancy at birth (1975–79): male 63.4 years; female 69.7 years.
Major causes of death per 100,000 population (1984): diseases of the circulatory system 152.9, of which hypertensive disease 51.4, cerebrovascular disease 40.1; accidents 76.5; malignant neoplasms (cancers) 62.7; infectious and parasitic diseases 55.2.

National economy

Budget (1989). Revenue: F 1,137,000,000 (internal loans and ordered advancements 49.3%, receipts from French central government 23.2%). Expenditures: F 1,137,000,000 (current expenditures 86.6%, of which debt payments 2.7%, investment 13.1%).
Production. Agriculture, forestry, fishing (value of production in F '000 except as noted; 1986): market-garden vegetables 103,800, roots and tubers 46,600, cereals (mostly rice) 20,900, pork 19,500, beef 10,000, poultry 9,900, fruits (mostly limes, other citrus, and bananas) 9,800, eggs 4,700, milk 2,700, sugarcane 667; roundwood (1987) 254,000 cu m; fish catch (metric tons; 1988) 7,619, of which shrimps and prawns caught by foreign vessels 1,816, local catch of shrimps and prawns 2,432, local fish catch 2,532. Mining and quarrying (1988): gold 530 kg; stone, sand, and gravel 1,000,000 metric tons. Manufacturing (1988): yogurt 3,700,500 cups; flans 197,746 units; sawnwood and veneer sheets 42,683 cu m; finished wood products 3,184 cu m; pasteurized milk 1,281 hectolitres; rum 756 hectolitres; other products include leather goods, clothing, rosewood essence, and beer. Construction (1988): residential 64,050 sq m; nonresidential authorized 24,579 sq m. Energy production (consumption): electricity (kW-hr; 1988) 282,200,000 (282,200,000); coal, none (none); crude petroleum, none (none); petroleum products (metric tons; 1987) none (121,000); natural gas, none (none).
Household income and expenditure. Average household size (1982) 3.3; income per household (1980) F 75,762 (U.S.$16,776); sources of income (1980): wages and salaries 76.4%, industrial and commercial profits 12.3%, pensions and rents 3.8%, noncommercial profits 2.5%, income from stocks and bonds 1.6%, other 3.4%; expenditure (1984–85)[2]: food and beverages 31.9%, housing 18.4%, transportation and communications 10.7%, recreation and education 9.2%, clothing and footwear 5.8%, household furnishings 5.3%, health 4.3%, other 14.4%.

Gross national product (at current market prices; 1985): U.S.$176,000,000 (U.S.$2,130 per capita).

Structure of gross domestic product and labour force				
	1979		1982	
	in value F 000,000	% of total value	labour force	% of labour force
Agriculture, forestry fishing	53.4	5.3	3,706	11.4
Mining	...	...	163	0.6
Manufacturing	36.6	3.7	1,359	4.1
Construction	82.5	8.2	2,837	8.8
Public utilities	−6.4	−0.6	380	1.2
Transp. and commun.	65.1	6.5	1,347	4.2
Trade	123.2	12.3	2,025	6.2
Finance, real estate	89.5	8.9	3,662	11.3
Pub. admin., defense, services	557.1	55.7	10,123	31.3
Other	—	—	6,773[3]	20.9[3]
TOTAL	1,001.0	100.0	32,375	100.0

Public debt (external, outstanding; 1985)[4]: U.S.$18,000,000.
Population economically active (1986): total 37,600; activity rate of total population 43.9% (participation rates: ages 15 and over, 65.0%; female 45.5%; unemployed 19.3%).

Price and earnings indexes (December 1985 = 100)[5]							
	1982	1983	1984	1985	1986	1987	1988
Consumer price index	75.4	87.7	94.3	100.0	102.2	106.3	108.8
Monthly earnings index[6]	77.4	83.6	95.0	100.0	102.1	104.9	106.6[7]

Tourism (1988): number of tourist arrivals 141,382.
Land use (1987): forested 82.8%; meadows and pastures 0.1%; agricultural and under permanent cultivation 0.1%; other 17.0%.

Foreign trade

Balance of trade (current prices)					
	1982	1983	1984	1985	1986	1987
F '000,000	−1,431	−1,843	−1,831	−1,956	−1,801	−2,048
% of total	77.1%	75.8%	73.7%	74.7%	77.9%	76.0%

Imports (1987): F 2,371,847,000 (food products 22.3%; electrical and non-electrical machinery 20.9%; consumer goods 15.8%; mineral fuels 10.1%; metals and metal products 8.1%; chemicals and chemical products 8.0%). *Major import sources:* France 62.1%; other EEC 11.6%; Trinidad and Tobago 9.3%; United States 4.3%; Japan 3.2%.
Exports (1987): F 323,730,000 (agricultural products [mostly shrimps, prawns, and rice] 70.2%; consumer goods [mostly wood and wood products] 12.7%; professional and scientific goods 8.3%; base-metal products 7.7%). *Major export destinations:* France 38.4%; United States 21.9%; Guadeloupe 14.2%; Japan 10.7%; Martinique 10.3%.

Transport and communications

Transport. Railroads (1988): none. Roads (1988): total length 706 mi, 1,137 km (paved 74%). Vehicles (1987): passenger cars 27,010; trucks and buses 1,120. Merchant marine: n.a. Air transport (1988): passenger arrivals 123,-792, passenger departures 121,575; cargo unloaded 3,632 metric tons, cargo loaded 1,572 metric tons; airports (1989): with scheduled flights 8.
Communications. Daily newspapers (1987): total number 2; total circulation 17,000; circulation per 1,000 population 191. Radio (1986): 44,000 receivers (1 per 1.9 persons). Television (1987): 6,500 receivers (1 per 14 persons). Telephones (1987): 27,776 (1 per 3.2 persons).

Education and health

Education (1987–88)	schools	teachers	students	student/ teacher ratio
Primary (age 6–11)	84	...	11,342	...
Secondary (age 12–18)	11	...	6,541	...
Vocational	8	...	3,778	...
Higher	...	...	...	...

Educational attainment (1982). Percent of population age 25 and over having: no formal schooling 20.8%; some primary education 40.4%; some secondary 32.4%; completed secondary and higher 6.4%. *Literacy* (1982): total population age 16 and over literate 38,964 (82.0%); males literate 21,021 (82.5%); females literate 17,943 (81.3%).
Health (1987): physicians 237 (1 per 374 persons); hospital beds 861 (1 per 103 persons); infant mortality rate per 1,000 live births (1985–88 avg.) 22.7.
Food (1984–86): daily per capita caloric intake 2,747 (vegetable products 71%, animal products 29%); 121% of FAO recommended minimum requirement.

Military

Total active duty personnel (1984): 2,700[8].

[1]*Religious affiliation* (1986): Roman Catholic 74.7%; other 25.3%. [2]Weights of consumer price index components based on households in Cayenne. [3]Includes 2,013 in categories not clearly defined and 4,760 unemployed. [4]Includes external long-term private debt not guaranteed by the government. [5]Indexes based on end-of-year figures. [6]Based on minimum-level wage in public administration. [7]March. [8]Includes French Foreign Legion troops assigned to guard the Kourou Space Centre.

French Polynesia

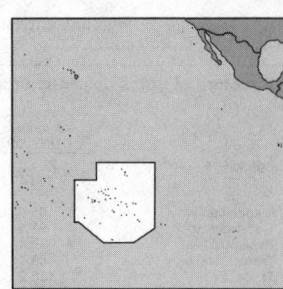

Official name: Territoire de la
Polynésie française (French);
Polynesia Farani (Tahitian) (Territory
of French Polynesia).
Political status: overseas territory
(France) with one legislative house
(Territorial Assembly [41]).
Chief of state: President of France.
Head of government: High
Commissioner (for France); President
of the Council of Ministers (for
French Polynesia).
Capital: Papeete.
Official languages: French; Tahitian.
Official religion: none.
Monetary unit: 1 Franc de la Comptoirs
française du pacifique (CFPF) = 100
centimes; valuation (Oct. 2,
1989) 1 U.S.$ = CFPF 114.91;
1 £ = CFPF 185.92.

Area and population

		area		population
Circumscriptions	Capitals	sq mi	sq km	1988 census
Îles Australes	Mataura	57	148	6,509
Îles Marquises	Taiohae	405	1,049	7,358
Îles sous le Vent	Uturoa	156	404	22,232
Îles Tuamotu et Gambier	Papeete	280	726	12,374
Îles du Vent	Papeete	461	1,194	140,341
TOTAL		1,544[1]	4,000[1]	188,814

Demography

Population (1989): 192,000.
Density (1988)[2]: persons per sq mi 141.3, persons per sq km 54.5.
Urban–rural (1985): urban 62.2%; rural 37.8%.
Sex distribution (1988): male 52.32%; female 47.68%.
Age breakdown (1985): under 15, 37.9%; 15–29, 30.0%; 30–44, 16.5%; 45–59, 10.5%; 60–74, 4.3%; 75 and over, 0.8%.
Population projection: (2000) 236,000; (2010) 269,000.
Doubling time: 29 years.
Ethnic composition (1988): Polynesian 66.8%; mixed 18.6%, of which Polynesian-European 16.8%, Polynesian-Chinese 1.3%, European-Chinese 0.5%; European (mostly French) 10.2%; Chinese 3.8%; other 0.6%.
Religious affiliation (1980): Protestant 46.6%, of which Evangelical Church of French Polynesia 32.8%; Roman Catholic 39.4%; other Christian 8.2%, of which Mormon 3.5%; nonreligious 5.0%; other 0.8%.
Major cities (1988)[3]: Papeete 23,555 (urban agglomeration 103,857); Faaa 24,048[4]; Punaauia 15,781[4]; Pirae 13,366[4]; Mahina 10,323[4].

Vital statistics

Birth rate per 1,000 population (1988): 29.3 (world avg. 27.1); (1983) legitimate 41.1%; illegitimate 58.9%.
Death rate per 1,000 population (1988): 5.1 (world avg. 9.9).
Natural increase rate per 1,000 population (1988): 24.2 (world avg. 17.2).
Total fertility rate (avg. births per childbearing woman; 1987): 3.5.
Marriage rate per 1,000 population (1987): 5.3.
Divorce rate per 1,000 population (1983): 0.8.
Life expectancy at birth (1986–87): male 65.3 years; female 69.9 years.
Major causes of death per 100,000 population (1984): diseases of the circulatory system 120.1; malignant neoplasms (cancers) 67.7; accidents, suicide, and violence 58.9; ill-defined conditions 94.2.

National economy

Budget (1989). Revenue: CFPF 70,355,000,000 (indirect taxes 58.6%; extraordinary receipts 16.3%; nontax revenue 14.6%; direct taxes 10.5%). Expenditures: CFPF 70,355,000,000 (operating expenses 83.7%; extraordinary expenses 16.3%).
Public debt (external, outstanding; 1987)[5]: U.S.$242,000,000.
Tourism (1988): receipts from visitors U.S.$145,000,000; expenditures by nationals abroad, n.a.
Production (metric tons except as noted). Agriculture, forestry, fishing (1988): coconuts 150,000, copra 15,000, cassava 5,000, pineapples 3,000, sugarcane 3,000, potatoes 3,000, watermelon 3,000, sweet potatoes 1,000, bananas 1,000, tomatoes 300, cucumbers 290, flowers (value of production; 1984) CFPF 655,000,000[6]; livestock (number of live animals) 54,000 pigs, 10,000 cattle, 5,000 sheep and goats, 1,000,000 chickens; roundwood, n.a.; fish catch 1,964[7], of which skipjack tuna 398[7], black cultured pearls (1986) *c.* 350 kg. Mining and quarrying: none. Manufacturing (1987): refined coconut oil 191; other manufactures include *monoï* oil (primarily refined coconut and sandalwood oils), beer, printed cloth, and sandals. Construction (buildings completed; 1988): 110,000 sq m. Energy production (consumption): electricity (kW-hr; 1988) 256,400,000 (230,700,000); coal, none (none); crude petroleum, none (none); petroleum products (metric tons; 1987) none (195,000); natural gas, none (none).
Household income and expenditure. Average household size (1983) 5.0; average annual income per household (1977) CFPF 2,118,161 (U.S.$23,624); sources of income (1982): salaries 48.0%, self-employment 40.9%, transfer payments 9.4%, other 1.7%; expenditure (1979)[8]: food and beverages

36.5%, household furnishings 14.4%, transportation 13.1%, clothing 9.0%, recreation and education 8.7%, energy 8.6%, other 9.7%.
Gross domestic product (at current market prices; 1985): U.S.$1,370,000,000 (U.S.$7,830 per capita).

Structure of gross domestic product and labour force

	1984		1988	
	in value CFPF '000,000	% of total value	labour force	% of labour force
Agriculture	8,142	4.6	7,350	11.3
Manufacturing[9]	16,779	9.5	3,563	5.5
Construction	20,222	11.5	5,920	9.1
Public utilities	1,544	0.9		
Transp. and commun.	11,729	6.7	3,850	5.9
Trade	24,585	14.0	12,117	18.6
Finance, real estate			1,272	1.9
Pub. admin., defense	92,883[10]	52.8	22,420	34.4
Services			5,433	8.3
Other	—	—	3,275[11]	5.0
TOTAL	175,884	100.0	65,200	100.0

Population economically active (1988): total 76,630; activity rate of total population 40.6% (participation rates: ages 15–64, 65.7%; female 36.6%; unemployed 14.9%).

Price and earnings indexes (1985 = 100)[12]

	1982	1983	1984	1985	1986	1987	1988
Consumer price index	73.8	83.9	92.8	100.0	99.4	101.4	104.0
Monthly earnings index[13]	65.7	78.5	89.1	100.0	101.1	105.7	109.3

Land use (1987): forested 31.4%; meadows and pastures 5.5%; agricultural and under permanent cultivation 20.5%; other 42.6%.

Foreign trade[14]

Balance of trade (current prices)

	1983	1984	1985	1986	1987	1988
CFPF '000,000	−69,399	−80,392	−82,300	−87,555	−81,493	−507,397
% of total	87.0%	88.1%	85.7%	89.0%	81.8%	83.8%

Imports (1988): CFPF 556,492,000,000 (machinery and appliances 23.5%; food products 18.6%; transport equipment 11.9%; metal manufactures 9.4%; mineral products 6.7%; industrial chemical products 6.0%). *Major import sources:* France 53.4%; other EEC 11.5%; United States 11.3%; Australia 6.3%; New Zealand 5.0%.
Exports (1988): CFPF 49,095,000,000 (reexports 70.5%, of which petroleum products 44.8%; fish 7.9%; black cultured pearls 22.2%; coconut oil 3.9%; mother-of-pearl 0.9%; vanilla 0.5%). *Major export destinations*[15]: France 43.7%; United States 20.9%; Japan 11.8%; New Caledonia 10.4%.

Transport and communications

Transport. Railroads: none. Roads (1988): total length 492 mi, 792 km (paved 33%). Motor vehicles (1987): 54,979. Merchant marine: vessels (100 gross tons and over), n.a. Air transport (1988): passenger arrivals 383,988, passenger departures 368,118; cargo unloaded 6,918 metric tons[16], cargo loaded 910 metric tons[16]; airports (1989) with scheduled flights 31.
Communications. Daily newspapers (1987): total number 3; total circulation 23,000; circulation per 1,000 population 126. Radio (1988): total number of receivers 90,000 (1 per 2.1 persons). Television (1987): total number of receivers 26,500 (1 per 6.9 persons). Telephones (1986): 41,210 (1 per 4.4 persons).

Education and health

Education (1988–89)

	schools	teachers	students	student/ teacher ratio
Primary (age 6–10)	270	1,337[17]	43,300	20.5[17]
Secondary (age 11–17)	24	804[17]	18,610	16.9[17]
Vocational	17	362[17]		9.5[17]
Higher	1	...	180[18]	...

Educational attainment (1983). Percent of population age 25 and over having: no formal schooling 9.3%; primary education 58.7%; secondary 25.7%; higher 6.3%. *Literacy* (1983): total population age 15 and over literate 98,314 (95.0%); males literate 51,910 (94.9%); females literate 46,404 (95.0%).
Health: physicians (1985) 214 (1 per 815 persons); hospital beds (1983) 903 (1 per 183 persons); infant mortality rate per 1,000 live births (1985–88 avg.) 19.3[19].
Food (1984–86): daily per capita caloric intake 2,896 (vegetable products 78%, animal products 22%); 109% of FAO recommended minimum requirement.

Military

Total active duty personnel (1988): 5,000 French military personnel. *Military expenditure as percent of GNP:* n.a.

[1]Approximate total area including inland water; total land area is 1,359 sq mi (3,521 sq km). [2]Based on land area. [3]Populations cited are for communes unless otherwise noted. [4]Part of Papeete urban agglomeration. [5]Includes external long-term private debt not guaranteed by the government. [6]Excludes flowers processed for perfume. [7]Commercial production only. [8]Weights of consumer price index components. [9]Includes mining. [10]Includes nonmarket services with an imputed value of CFPF 56,479,000,000. [11]Includes 1,339 not adequately defined and 3,258 unemployed. [12]All end-of-year. [13]Manufacturing sector. [14]Imports c.i.f.; exports f.o.b. [15]1985. [16]Excludes local interisland traffic. [17]1984–85. [18]1983–84. [19]Through September 1988.

Gabon

Official name: République Gabonaise (Gabonese Republic).
Form of government: unitary single-party republic with one legislative house (National Assembly [120[1]]).
Chief of state: President.
Head of government: Prime Minister.
Capital: Libreville.
Official language: French.
Official religion: none.
Monetary unit: 1 CFA franc (CFAF) = 100 centimes; valuation (Oct. 2, 1989) 1 U.S.$ = CFAF 317.90; 1 £ = CFAF 514.37.

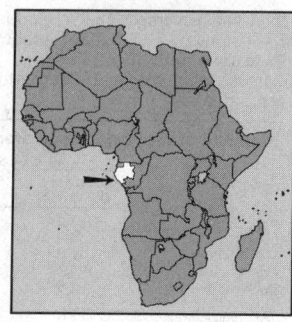

Area and population

Provinces	Capitals	area		population 1978 estimate[2]
		sq mi	sq km	
Estuaire	Libreville	8,008	20,740	359,000
Haut-Ogooué	Franceville	14,111	36,547	213,000
Moyen-Ogooué	Lambaréné	7,156	18,535	49,000
Ngounié	Mouila	14,575	37,750	118,000
Nyanga	Tchibanga	8,218	21,285	98,000
Ogooué-Ivindo	Makokou	17,790	46,075	53,000
Ogooué-Lolo	Koulamoutou	9,799	25,380	49,000
Ogooué-Maritime	Port-Gentil	8,838	22,890	194,000
Woleu-Ntem	Oyem	14,851	38,465	166,000
TOTAL		103,347[3]	267,667	1,300,000[3]

Demography

Population (1989)[2]: 1,245,000.
Density (1989): persons per sq mi 12.0, persons per sq km 4.7.
Urban–rural (1985): urban 40.9%; rural 59.1%.
Sex distribution (1985): male 49.14%; female 50.86%.
Age breakdown (1985): under 15, 34.6%; 15–29, 24.4%; 30–44, 18.3%; 45–59, 13.3%; 60–74, 7.6%; 75 and over, 1.8%.
Population projection: (2000) 1,603,000; (2010) 1,978,000.
Doubling time: 32 years.
Ethnic composition (1983): Fang 35.5%; Mpongwe 15.1%; Mbete 14.2%; Punu 11.5%; other 23.7%.
Religious affiliation (1980): Christian 96.2%, of which Roman Catholic 65.2%, Protestant 18.8%, African indigenous 12.1%; traditional religion 2.9%; Muslim 0.8%; other 0.1%.
Major cities (1987): Libreville 352,000; Port-Gentil 164,000; Franceville 75,000.

Vital statistics

Birth rate per 1,000 population (1985–90): 38.8 (world avg. 27.1).
Death rate per 1,000 population (1985–90): 16.4 (world avg. 9.9).
Natural increase rate per 1,000 population (1985–90): 22.4 (world avg. 17.2).
Total fertility rate (avg. births per childbearing woman; 1989): 4.0.
Marriage rate per 1,000 population: n.a.
Divorce rate per 1,000 population: n.a.
Life expectancy at birth (1985–90): male 49.9 years; female 53.2 years.
Major causes of death per 100,000 population: n.a.; however, major diseases include malaria, measles, shigellosis (infection with dysentery), trypanosomiasis, and tuberculosis.

National economy

Budget (1988). Revenue: CFAF 325,000,000,000 (indirect taxes 39.5%, of which customs duties 26.8%; taxes on petroleum organizations and petroleum fees 20.9%; direct taxes 17.5%). Expenditures: CFAF 325,000,000,000 (personnel costs 30.5%; goods and services 20.6%; public debt 18.5%).
Tourism (1987): receipts from visitors U.S.$5,000,000; expenditures by nationals abroad U.S.$133,000,000.
Production (metric tons except as noted). Agriculture, forestry, fishing (1988): roots and tubers 415,000, cassava 265,000, plantains 180,000, sugarcane 155,000, corn (maize) 10,000, peanuts (groundnuts) 9,000, bananas 8,000, palm oil 3,800, cacao beans 2,000, coffee 2,000; livestock (number of live animals) 154,000 pigs, 84,000 sheep, 63,000 goats, 9,000 cattle, 2,000,000 chickens; roundwood (1987) 3,847,000 cu m; fish catch (1987) 20,900. Mining and quarrying (1988): manganese 2,250,000; uranium 904. Manufacturing (1986): cement 210,000; flour 28,240; raw sugar 18,000; beer 820,000 hectolitres; soft drinks 480,000 hectolitres; cigarettes 17,800,000 packs[4]; textiles CFAF 2,420,000,000[4]. Construction: n.a. Energy production (consumption): electricity (kW-hr; 1987) 876,000,000 (876,000,000); crude petroleum (barrels; 1987) 56,840,000 (7,800,000); petroleum products (metric tons; 1987) 833,000 (642,000); natural gas (cu m; 1987) 171,957,000 (171,957,000); fuelwood and bagasse (cu m; 1985) 1,310,000 (1,310,000).
Population economically active (1985): total 518,000; activity rate of total population 45.0% (participation rates: ages 15–64, 68.2%; female 38.4%; unemployed, n.a.).

Price and earnings indexes (1985 = 100)

	1982	1983	1984	1985	1986	1987	1988[5]
Consumer price index	79.7	88.0	93.2	100.0	106.3	105.3	92.7
Earnings index[6]	126.6	156.3	...	...	...	...	...

Gross national product (at current market prices; 1987): U.S.$2,890,000,000 (U.S.$2,750 per capita).

Structure of gross domestic product and labour force

	1986		1983	
	in value CFAF '000,000	% of total value	labour force[7]	% of labour force[7]
Agriculture, forestry, fishing	80,000	7.0	14,118	10.2
Mining	276,000	24.0	3,919	2.9
Manufacturing	55,700	4.9	4,123	3.0
Construction	103,000	9.0	13,154	9.5
Public utilities	26,200	2.3	8	8
Transportation and communications	60,000	5.2	8	8
Trade	154,000	13.4	3,732	2.7
Finance	12,800	1.1	8	8
Pub. admin., defense	157,300	13.7	42,678	31.0
Services	131,000	11.4	8	8
Other, including taxes on imports	92,000	8.0	56,143[8]	40.7[8]
TOTAL	1,148,000	100.0	137,867	100.0

Household income and expenditure. Average household size (1980) 4.0; income per household: n.a.; sources of income (1983): private sector 73.4%, public sector 26.6%; expenditure[9] (1983): food and tobacco 54.7%, clothing and footwear 17.5%, housing 13.0%, transportation and communications 6.3%.
Public debt (external, outstanding; 1987): U.S.$1,605,000,000.
Land use (1987): forested 77.6%; meadows and pastures 18.2%; agricultural and under permanent cultivation 1.8%; other 2.4%.

Foreign trade

Balance of trade (current prices)

	1982	1983	1984	1985	1986	1987
CFAF '000,000	+252,100	+421,700	+492,600	+500,000	+140,000	+170,000
% of total	32.4%	39.4%	40.8%	39.2%	18.9%	28.2%

Imports (1987): CFAF 216,600,000,000 (machinery and mechanical equipment 22.2%, food and agricultural products 21.4%, transport equipment 16.2%, manufactured products 12.0%, metal and metal products 11.2%, construction materials 4.2%, chemical products 3.7%, mining products 1.6%). Major import sources: France 53.5%; United States 7.7%; West Germany 4.7%; Japan 4.5%; The Netherlands 3.6%; Italy 3.0%; United Kingdom 2.9%; Belgium–Luxembourg 2.6%; Thailand 1.7%.
Exports (1987): CFAF 386,600,000,000 (crude petroleum and petroleum products 68.9%, wood 12.1%, manganese ore and concentrate 8.4%, uranium ore and concentrate 6.2%). Major export destinations: France 36.4%; United States 27.0%; Spain 11.4%; The Netherlands 4.5%; Japan 3.1%; West Germany 2.7%.

Transport and communications

Transport. Railroads (1987): length 416 mi, 670 km; passenger-mi 12,000,000[10], passenger-km 19,000,000[10]; short ton-mi cargo 71,000,000[10], metric ton-km cargo 103,000,000[10]. Roads (1986): total length 4,682 mi, 7,535 km (paved 8%). Vehicles (1985): passenger cars 16,093; trucks and buses 10,503. Merchant marine (1988): vessels (100 gross tons and over) 27; total deadweight tonnage 29,276. Air transport (1988)[11]: passenger-mi 259,455,000, passenger-km 417,553,000; short ton-mi cargo 18,626,000, metric ton-km cargo 27,193,000; airports (1989) with scheduled flights 23.
Communications. Daily newspapers (1984): total number 2; total circulation 33,000; circulation per 1,000 population 35. Radio (1988): total number of receivers 103,326 (1 per 12 persons). Television (1988): total number of receivers 37,200 (1 per 33 persons). Telephones (1983): 13,800 (1 per 81 persons).

Education and health

Education (1984–85)

	schools	teachers	students	student/ teacher ratio
Primary	940	3,837	178,811	46.6
Secondary	51	1,894	25,815	13.6
Voc., teacher tr.	29	720	13,529	18.8
Higher[12]	1	616	3,228	5.2

Educational attainment, n.a. Literacy (1978): total population age 15 and over literate 800,000 (77%); males literate, n.a.; females literate, n.a.
Health (1984): physicians 565 (1 per 2,000 persons); hospital beds 10,980 (1 per 103 persons); infant mortality rate per 1,000 live births (1985–90) 103.0.
Food (1984–86): daily per capita caloric intake 2,700 (vegetable products 88%, animal products 12%); (1984) 104% of FAO recommended minimum requirement.

Military

Total active duty personnel (1988): 3,000 (army 63.3%, navy 16.7%, air force 20.0%), not including 600 French troops. Military expenditure as percent of GNP (1986): 4.8% (world 5.5%); per capita expenditure U.S.$141.

[1]Including 9 nonelective seats. [2]Population distribution is based on country estimate, which is substantially higher than estimates from external sources (such as the United Nations and the World Bank), which form the basis of the 1989 estimate. [3]Detail does not add to total given because of rounding. [4]1984. [5]Third quarter. [6]1980 = 100. [7]Official government figures for salaried workers only, not including traditional agricultural workers; agricultural workers (FAO estimate, 1986) totaled 370,000 (71.0% of the labour force). [8]Public utilities, transportation and communications, finance, and service employees included with other. [9]Libreville only. [10]1986. [11]Air Gabon only. [12]1983–84.

Gambia, The

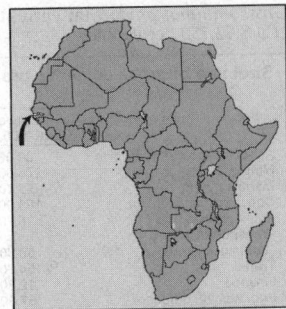

Official name: Republic of The Gambia.
Form of government: multiparty republic with one legislative house (House of Representatives [50])[1].
Head of state and government: President.
Capital: Banjul.
Official language: English.
Official religion: none.
Monetary unit: 1 dalasi (D) = 100 butut; valuation (Oct. 2, 1989) 1 U.S.$ = D 7.75; 1 £ = D 12.54.

Area and population		area		population
		sq mi	sq km	1983 census[2]
Divisions	Capitals			
Kombo St. Mary[3]	Kanifing	29	76	101,504[4]
Lower River	Mansakonko	625	1,618	55,263
MacCarthy Island	Kuntaur/Georgetown	1,117	2,894	126,004
North Bank	Kerewan	871	2,256	112,225
Upper River	Basse	799	2,069	111,388
Western	Brikama	681	1,764	137,245
City				
Banjul	—	5	12	44,188[4]
TOTAL		4,127	10,689	687,817

Demography

Population (1989): 835,000.
Density[5] (1988): persons per sq mi 251.1, persons per sq km 96.9.
Urban–rural (1985): urban 20.1%; rural 79.9%.
Sex distribution (1985): male 49.40%; female 50.60%.
Age breakdown (1986): under 15, 44.6%; 15–29, 26.4%; 30–44, 15.2%; 45–59, 8.8%; 60 and over, 5.0%.
Population projection: (2000) 1,156,000; (2010) 1,554,000.
Doubling time: 27 years.
Ethnic composition (1983): Malinke 40.4%; Fulani 18.7%; Wolof 14.6%; Dyola 10.3%; Soninke 8.2%; other 7.8%.
Religious affiliation (1983): Muslim 95.4%; Christian 3.7%; traditional beliefs and other 0.9%.
Major cities/urban areas (1986): Serekunda 102,600[3]; Banjul 44,188[4, 6] (Greater Banjul 145,692[4, 6]); Brikama 24,300; Bakau 23,600[3]; Farafenni 10,168[6].

Vital statistics

Birth rate per 1,000 population (1985–90): 46.8 (world avg. 27.1); legitimate, n.a.; illegitimate, n.a.
Death rate per 1,000 population (1985–90): 21.3 (world avg. 9.9).
Natural increase rate per 1,000 population (1985–90): 25.5 (world avg. 17.2).
Total fertility rate (avg. births per childbearing woman; 1985–90): 6.4.
Marriage rate per 1,000 population: n.a.
Divorce rate per 1,000 population: n.a.
Life expectancy at birth (1985–90): male 41.4 years; female 44.6 years.
Major causes of death per 100,000 population: n.a.; however, major infectious diseases include malaria, gonococcal infections and syphilis, leprosy (Hansen's disease), chicken pox, schistosomiasis, tetanus, tuberculosis, and trypanosomiasis (sleeping sickness).

National economy

Budget (1988–89)[7]. Revenue: D 405,170,000 (tax revenue 92.1%, of which import duties and excises 65.6%, income taxes 10.4%; nontax revenue and grants 7.9%). Expenditures: D 404,611,000 (education and culture 8.7%; health and social welfare 5.7%; public works and communications 3.4%; agriculture 2.7%; unspecified expenditures 79.5%).
Public debt (external, outstanding; 1987): U.S.$272,900,000.
Production (metric tons except as noted). Agriculture, forestry, fishing (1988): peanuts (groundnuts) 110,000, millet 74,000, paddy rice 30,000, corn (maize) 16,000, cassava 6,000, pulses (mostly beans) 4,000, palm oil 2,500, palm kernels 2,000, seed cotton 1,000; livestock (number of live animals) 300,000 cattle, 200,000 goats, 200,000 sheep; roundwood (1987) 862,000 cu m; fish catch (1987) 14,376, of which inland water 2,700, Atlantic Ocean 11,676. Mining and quarrying: sand and gravel are excavated for local use. Manufacturing (value of production in D '000; 1982): processed food, including peanut and palm kernel oil 62,878; beverages 10,546; textiles 3,253; chemicals and related products 1,031; nonmetals 922; printing and publishing 358; leather 150. Construction: n.a. Energy production (consumption): electricity (kW-hr; 1987) 44,000,000 (44,000,000); coal, none (none); crude petroleum, none (none); petroleum products (metric tons; 1987) none (59,000); natural gas, none (none).
Population economically active (1983): total 325,623; activity rate of total population 47.3% (participation rates: ages 15–64 78.2%; female 46.3%; unemployed, n.a.).

Price and earnings indexes (1985 = 100)							
	1982	1983	1984	1985	1986	1987	1988
Consumer price index	62.6	69.2	84.5	100.0	156.6	193.4	216.0
Earnings index	...	...	...	...	...	...	...

Household income and expenditure. Average household size (1980) 4.9; income per household: n.a., sources of income: n.a., expenditure[8] (1986):

food and beverages 58.0%, clothing and footwear 17.5%, energy and water 5.4%, housing 5.1%, education, health, transportation and communications, recreation, and other 14.0%.
Gross national product (at current prices; 1987): U.S.$177,000,000 (U.S.$220 per capita).

Structure of gross domestic product and labour force				
	1987–88[9]		1983	
	in value D'000,000	% of total value	labour force	% of labour force
Agriculture	153.2	30.2	239,940	73.7
Mining			66	0.0
Manufacturing	27.8	5.5	8,144	2.5
Construction	17.7	3.5	4,373	1.3
Public utilities	1.6	0.3	1,233	0.4
Transportation and communications	44.5	8.8	8,014	2.5
Trade	135.3	26.6	16,551	5.1
Finance	27.7	5.4	4,577	1.4
Public administration	50.3	9.9	8,295	2.5
Services	7.4	1.5	9,381	2.9
Other	42.3[10]	8.3[10]	25,049[11]	7.7[11]
TOTAL	507.8[8]	100.0	325,623	100.0

Tourism (1987): receipts from visitors U.S.$36,000,000; expenditures by nationals abroad U.S.$3,000,000.
Land use (1986): forested 18.0%; meadows and pastures 9.0%; agricultural and under permanent cultivation 16.7%; built-on area, wasteland, and other 56.3%.

Foreign trade[12]

Balance of trade (current prices)						
	1982	1983	1984	1985	1986	1987
D '000,000	−122.7	−177.7	−191.6	−189.2	−497.0	−615.9
% of total	38.4%	41.2%	37.1%	35.3%	51.3%	52.3%

Imports (1987): D 897,300,000 (food 28.1%; machinery and transport equipment 22.4%; basic manufactures 20.9%; mineral fuels and lubricants 7.3%; chemicals and related products 6.4%). *Major import sources:* EEC countries 52.9%, of which United Kingdom 19.0%, Italy 9.2%, West Germany 7.5%; United States and Canada 6.2%; China 5.5%; U.S.S.R. and eastern European countries 4.8%.
Exports (1987): D 281,400,000 (reexports 58.1%[13]; domestic exports 41.9%, of which peanut oil 16.8%, shelled peanuts 14.3%, fish and fish preparations 5.3%). *Major export destinations:* EEC countries 44.3%, of which United Kingdom 25.4%; other western European countries 25.8%.

Transport and communications

Transport. Railroads: none. Roads (1986): total length 1,484 mi, 2,388 km (paved 21%). Vehicles (1986): passenger cars 5,200; trucks and buses 720. Merchant marine (1988): vessels (100 gross tons and over) 7; total deadweight tonnage 5,098. Air transport (1986): passenger arrivals and departures 905,072; cargo 39,351 metric tons; airports (1989) with scheduled flights 1.
Communications. Daily newspapers (1988): total number 1; total circulation 1,000; circulation per 1,000 population 1.2. Radio (1988): total number of receivers 110,000 (1 per 6.1 persons). Television: none. Telephones (1986): 3,600 (1 per 216 persons).

Education and health

Education (1984–85)				
	schools	teachers	students	student/ teacher ratio
Primary (age 8–14)	189	2,640	66,257	25.1
Secondary (age 15–21)	8	235	4,348	18.5
Secondary vocational	16	502	10,102	20.1
Postsecondary	9	177	1,489	8.4

Educational attainment (1973). Percent of population age 20 and over having: no formal schooling 90.8%; primary education 6.2%; secondary 2.6%; higher 0.4%. *Literacy* (1985): total population age 15 and over literate 24.9%; males literate 35.6%; females literate 15.1%.
Health (1981): physicians 66 (1 per 9,900 persons); hospital beds 756 (1 per 865 persons); infant mortality rate per 1,000 live births (1985–90) 143.
Food (1987): daily per capita caloric intake 2,317 ([1984–86] vegetable products 93%, animal products 7%); (1984–86) 99% of FAO recommended minimum requirement.

Military

Total active duty personnel (1989): 900. *Military expenditure as percent of GNP* (1987): n.a. (world 5.4%).

[1]Includes 5 indirectly elected chiefs and 9 nonelective seats. [2]Preliminary. [3]Kombo St. Mary includes the fast-growing urban areas of Serekunda and Bakau. [4]Kombo St. Mary and Banjul city comprise Greater Banjul. [5]Based on land area, which is 8,613 sq km (3,325 sq mi). [6]1983. [7]Excludes development revenue and expenditure. In 1986–87 development revenue of D 201,000,000 was mostly provided by external loan (68.0%) and external grants (25.0%). [8]Low-income population in Banjul and Kombo St. Mary only; weights of consumer price index components. [9]At factor cost in constant prices of 1977–78. [10]Indirect taxes less subsidies. [11]Not adequately defined. [12]Imports c.i.f.; exports f.o.b. [13]Mostly unofficial trade with Senegal.

German Democratic Republic

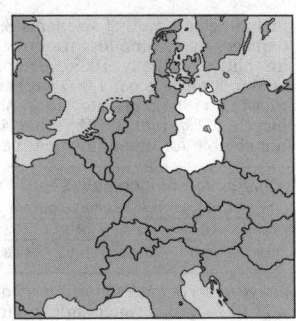

Official name: Deutsche Demokratische Republik (German Democratic Republic).
Form of government: unitary republic with one legislative house (People's Chamber [500]).
Chief of state: interim President.
Head of government: Prime Minister.
Capital: Berlin.
Official language: German.
Official religion: none.
Monetary unit: 1 Mark of Deutsche Demokratische Republik (M) = 100 Pfennige; valuation (Oct. 2, 1989) 1 U.S.$ = M 1.87; 1 £ = M 3.03.

Area and population		area		population
				1988[1]
Districts	Capitals	sq mi	sq km	estimate
Berlin, capital city	—	156	403	1,260,921
Cottbus	Cottbus	3,190	8,262	884,942
Dresden	Dresden	2,602	6,738	1,766,654
Erfurt	Erfurt	2,837	7,349	1,238,137
Frankfurt	Frankfurt	2,774	7,186	712,146
Gera	Gera	1,546	4,004	741,171
Halle	Halle	3,386	8,771	1,779,424
Karl-Marx-Stadt	Karl-Marx-Stadt	2,320	6,009	1,863,279
Leipzig	Leipzig	1,917	4,966	1,366,017
Magdeburg	Magdeburg	4,450	11,526	1,249,384
Neubrandenburg	Neubrandenburg	4,227	10,948	620,389
Potsdam	Potsdam	4,853	12,568	1,122,759
Rostock	Rostock	2,732	7,075	913,632
Schwerin	Schwerin	3,348	8,672	593,627
Suhl	Suhl	1,489	3,856	548,941
TOTAL		41,827	108,333	16,661,423

Demography
Population (1989): 16,613,000.
Density (1989): persons per sq mi 397.2, persons per sq km 153.3.
Urban–rural (1987): urban 76.8%; rural 23.2%.
Sex distribution (1987): male 47.63%; female 52.37%.
Age breakdown (1987): under 15, 19.3%; 15–29, 22.1%; 30–44, 19.7%; 45–59, 19.7%; 60–74, 10.9%; 75 and over, 8.3%.
Population projection: (2000) 16,457,000; (2010) 16,316,000.
Doubling time: not applicable; population is declining.
Ethnic composition (1987): German 99.7%; other 0.3%.
Religious affiliation (1987): Protestant 47.0%; Roman Catholic 7.0%; unaffiliated and other 46.0%.
Major cities (1988): Berlin (East) 1,260,921; Leipzig 549,230; Dresden 521,205; Karl-Marx-Stadt 313,238; Magdeburg 289,778; Rostock 251,894.

Vital statistics
Birth rate per 1,000 population (1987): 13.6 (world avg. 27.1); (1986) legitimate 65.5%; illegitimate 34.5%.
Death rate per 1,000 population (1987): 12.9 (world avg. 9.9).
Natural increase rate per 1,000 population (1987): 0.7 (world avg. 17.2).
Total fertility rate (avg. births per childbearing woman; 1986): 1.6.
Marriage rate per 1,000 population (1987): 8.5.
Divorce rate per 1,000 population (1987): 3.0.
Life expectancy at birth (1986): male 69.5 years; female 75.5 years.
Major causes of death per 100,000 population (1987): circulatory diseases 750.2; malignant neoplasms (cancers) 209.2; diseases of the respiratory system 70.5; accidents 42.0; endocrine and metabolic diseases 39.2.

National economy
Budget (1988). Revenue: M 291,180,400,000 (revenue from state-owned enterprises 69.0%, taxes and dues 7.1%, social insurance contributions 6.4%, health care contributions 3.2%). Expenditures: M 291,005,400,000 (economic development 33.8%, social welfare and health 18.2%, economic subsidies and price supports 17.0%, housing construction 5.6%, defense 5.4%, education 3.6%).
Production (metric tons except as noted). Agriculture, forestry, fishing (1987): potatoes 12,227,617, sugar beets 7,683,281, barley 6,118,222, wheat 4,039,613, rye 2,282,957, oats 636,771; livestock (number of live animals; 1988) 12,502,600 pigs, 5,720,500 cattle, 2,655,900 sheep, 50,719,300 chickens; commercial timber 10,605,000 cu m; fish catch 193,622. Mining and quarrying (1987): potash (K$_2$O content) 3,510,000; copper ore 10,000; tin 2,500; silver 1,200,000 troy oz. Manufacturing (1987): cement 12,430,000; steel 8,243,000; fertilizer 5,119,000; pig iron 2,755,000; plastics and synthetic resins 1,061,000; paper 944,000; sugar 895,000; sulfuric acid 867,000; caustic soda 577,000; consumer goods: 1,479,000 vacuum cleaners; 1,240,000 radios; 1,075,000 refrigerators; 723,000 television receivers; 497,000 washing machines. Construction (sq m; 1987): residential 6,957,000; nonresidential, n.a. Energy production (consumption): electricity (kW-hr; 1987) 114,180,000,000 (117,967,000,000); coal (metric tons; 1987) 302,976,000 (310,390,000); crude petroleum (barrels; 1987) 301,000 (154,067,000); petroleum products (metric tons; 1987) 18,933,000 (14,383,000); natural gas (cu m; 1987) 2,351,533,000 (8,165,249,000).
Gross national product (at current market prices; 1988): U.S.$207,648,000,000 (U.S.$12,430 per capita).

Structure of net material product and labour force				
	1987			
	in value M '000,000	% of total value	labour force[2]	% of labour force
Agriculture	29,966	11.0	928,500	10.8
Mining, manufacturing	174,360[3]	64.2[3]	3,479,400	40.6
Construction	19,690	7.3	568,900	6.6
Transp. and commun.	14,300	5.3	632,700	7.4
Trade	23,594	8.7	881,000	10.3
Services	—	—	2,080,200[4]	24.3[4]
Other	9,500[5]	3.5[5]	—	—
TOTAL	271,410[6]	100.0	8,570,700	100.0

Public debt (external, outstanding; 1987): U.S.$20,400,000,000.
Population economically active (1987): total 8,570,700[2]; activity rate of total population 51.4% (participation rates: ages 15–64, n.a.; female 49.0%).

Price and earnings indexes (1980 = 100)							
	1980	1981	1982	1983	1984	1985	1986
Consumer price index	100.0	100.3	100.3	100.3	100.3	100.3	100.3
Monthly earnings index	100.0	102.4	105.2	106.6	107.4	...	...

Household income and expenditure. Average household size (1986) 2.9; average annual income per household (1985) M 21,000 (U.S.$10,340); sources of income: wages and salaries 68.3%, social welfare 31.7%; expenditure (1987): food and beverages 42.9%, clothing and footwear 14.6%, household durable goods 4.8%, housing 3.3%, energy 2.1%.
Tourism (1986): total tourist arrivals 1,038,866.
Land use (1986): forested 27.3%; meadows and pastures 11.8%; agricultural and under permanent cultivation 47.3%; other 13.6%.

Foreign trade

Balance of trade (current prices)						
	1982	1983	1984	1985	1986	1987
M '000,000	+5,353	+8,031	+6,901	+6,789	+1,040	+3,264
% of total	3.7%	5.0%	4.0%	3.8%	0.6%	1.8%

Imports (1987): M 86,646,300,000 (fuels, minerals, and unfabricated metals 38.0%; machinery, equipment, and transportation equipment 34.1%; fabricated and partially fabricated industrial materials 13.1%; chemicals and related products 9.1%; consumer goods 5.7%).
Exports (1987): M 89,910,000,000 (machinery, equipment, and transportation equipment 48.0%; fuels, minerals, and unfabricated metals 16.7%; consumer goods 16.0%; chemical products 12.5%; fabricated industrial materials 6.8%). *Direction of total trade*[7]: U.S.S.R. 38.8%; Czechoslovakia 8.1%; West Germany 7.1%; Poland 5.6%; Hungary 5.2%; Bulgaria 3.2%; Romania 2.9%.

Transport and communications
Transport. Railroads (1987): length 8,704 mi, 14,008 km; passenger-mi 14,020,000,000, passenger-km 22,563,000,000; short ton-mi cargo 40,288,000,000, metric ton-km cargo 58,823,000,000. Roads (1987): total length 75,940 mi, 122,214 km (paved n.a.). Vehicles (1987): passenger cars 3,600,450; trucks and buses 434,864. Merchant marine (1988): vessels (100 gross tons and over) 369; total deadweight tonnage 1,800,325. Air transport (1987): passenger-mi 1,768,000,000, passenger-km 2,846,000,000; short ton-mi cargo 54,000,000, metric ton-km cargo 78,800,000; airports (1989) with scheduled flights 4.
Communications. Daily newspapers (1987): total number 39; total circulation 9,070,000; circulation per 1,000 population 545. Radio (1988): 6,758,500 receivers (1 per 2.5 persons). Television (1988): 6,199,300 receivers (1 per 2.7 persons). Telephones (1987): 3,875,278 (1 per 4.3 persons).

Education and health

Education (1987)				
	schools	teachers	students	student/ teacher ratio
Primary (age 6–10) Secondary (age 10–18) }	5,898	167,230	2,047,275	12.2
Vocational	957	55,234[8]	366,279	...
Higher	53	30,500	132,602	4.4

Educational attainment (1987). Percent of employed population age 20 and over having: primary education, virtually 100%; academic secondary 16.0%; vocational 75.0%; higher 9.0%. *Literacy* (1988): total population age 15 and over literate, virtually 100%.
Health (1987): physicians 40,516 (1 per 411 persons); hospital beds 167,612 (1 per 99 persons); infant mortality rate per 1,000 live births 8.7.
Food (1984–86): daily per capita caloric intake 3,800 (vegetable products 64%, animal products 36%); (1984) 145% of FAO recommended minimum requirement.

Military
Total active duty personnel (1988): 172,000 (army 69.8%, navy 8.7%, air force 21.5%). *Military expenditure as percent of GNP* (1987): 7.3% (world 5.4%); per capita expenditure U.S.$870.

[1]January 1. [2]Employed only. [3]Includes public utilities. [4]Includes finance, public administration, and defense. [5]Other material activities. [6]At 1985 prices. [7]Separate figures are not available for import sources and export destinations. [8]1985.

Germany, Federal Republic of

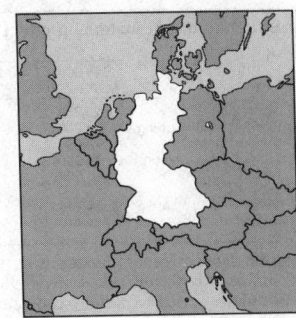

Official name: Bundesrepublik Deutschland (Federal Republic of Germany).
Form of government: federal multiparty republic with two legislative houses (Federal Council [45]; Federal Diet [519]).
Chief of state: President.
Head of government: Chancellor.
Capital: Bonn (provisional).
Official language: German.
Official religion: none.
Monetary unit: 1 Deutsche Mark (DM) = 100 Pfennige; valuation (Oct. 2, 1989) 1 U.S.$ = DM 1.87; 1 £ = DM 3.03.

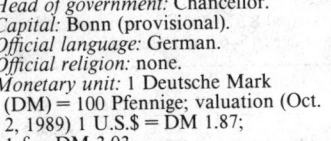

Area and population		area		population
				1988
States	**Capitals**	sq mi	sq km	estimate
Baden–Württemberg	Stuttgart	13,804	35,751	9,374,000
Bayern	Munich	27,241	70,553	10,989,600
Bremen	Bremen	156	404	660,400
Hamburg	Hamburg	292	755	1,595,300
Hessen	Wiesbaden	8,152	21,114	5,541,200
Niedersachsen	Hannover	18,316	47,439	7,169,200
Nordrhein–Westfalen	Düsseldorf	13,153	34,068	16,789,700
Rheinland–Pfalz	Mainz	7,663	19,848	3,640,100
Saarland	Saarbrücken	992	2,569	1,053,100
Schleswig–Holstein	Kiel	6,073	15,728	2,559,300
Berlin (West)[1]	Berlin (West)	185	480	2,046,100
TOTAL		96,027	248,709	61,418,000

Demography

Population (1989): 61,131,000[2].
Density (1989): persons per sq mi 636.6, persons per sq km 245.8.
Urban–rural (1985): urban 85.5%; rural 14.5%.
Sex distribution (1988): male 48.10%; female 51.90%.
Age breakdown (1987): under 15, 14.6%; 15–29, 24.0%; 30–44, 20.1%; 45–59, 20.6%; 60–74, 13.6%; 75 and over, 7.2%.
Population projection: (2000) 61,409,000; (2010) 61,663,000.
Doubling time: not applicable; population has been in approximate demographic balance since about 1980.
Ethnic composition (by nationality; 1987): German 93.2%; Turk 2.3%; Yugoslav 0.9%; Italian 0.8%; other European Community 0.8%; Greek 0.4%; other 1.6%.
Religious affiliation (1980): Christian 92.8%, of which Protestant 47.3% (including Lutheran-Reformed tradition 23.5%, Lutheran tradition 21.7%, Reformed tradition 0.7%, other 1.4%), Roman Catholic 43.8%, New Apostolic (non-Roman) Catholic 0.6%, Orthodox 1.0%, other Christian 0.1%; nonreligious 3.7%; Muslim 2.4%; atheist 0.9%; Jewish 0.1%; other 0.1%.
Major cities (1987): Berlin (West) 2,016,100; Hamburg 1,593,600; Munich 1,188,800; Cologne 927,500; Essen 623,000; Frankfurt am Main 618,500; Dortmund 583,600; Düsseldorf 563,400; Stuttgart 552,300; Bonn 276,500.
Place of birth: n.a.
Mobility: n.a.
Households (1987). Number of households 26,216,000; average household size 2.4; 1 person 33.4%, 2 persons 28.4%, 3 persons 17.7%, 4 persons 13.7%, 5 or more persons 6.7%. Family (multiperson) households (1988) 17,840,000 (65.1%); nonfamily (single-person) 9,563,000.
Immigration (1987): immigrants admitted 614,609, from Poland 25.7%, Turkey 10.9%, Italy 7.8%, Yugoslavia 5.6%, United States 4.3%, German Democratic Republic 3.7%, Romania 3.2%, U.S.S.R. 2.8%, Greece 2.7%, United Kingdom 2.6%, France 2.5%.

Vital statistics

Birth rate per 1,000 population (1988): 11.0 (world avg. 27.1); legitimate (1988) 90.0%; illegitimate 10.0%.
Death rate per 1,000 population (1988): 11.2 (world avg. 9.9).
Natural increase rate per 1,000 population (1988): −0.2 (world avg. 17.2).
Total fertility rate (avg. births per childbearing woman; 1987): 1.3.
Marriage rate per 1,000 population (1988): 6.3.
Divorce rate per 1,000 population (1987): 2.1.
Life expectancy at birth (1985–87): male 71.8 years; female 78.4 years.
Major causes of death per 100,000 population (1987): diseases of the circulatory system 560.4, of which acute myocardial infarction 130.4; cerebrovascular disease 142.4; malignant neoplasms (cancers) 272.3, of which stomach, colon, and rectum 62.9, bronchial, lung, and tracheal 38.8, breast 23.7; pulmonary diseases 64.9, of which pneumonia 21.0, chronic bronchitis 20.6; chronic liver disease and cirrhosis 22.6; suicides 19.0.

Social indicators

Educational attainment (1987). Percent of population age 25 and over having: less than full primary education, 1.3%; primary and lower (junior) secondary 69.8%; primary and intermediate secondary 16.4%; vocational postsecondary and certification for higher education 12.5%, of which postsecondary vocational degree 2.8%, university graduates (all levels) 5.3%.
Quality of working life. Average workweek (1987): 40.2 hours. Annual rate per 100,000 workers (1986) for: injuries or accidents at work 5,911; deaths,

including commuting accidents 8.0. Proportion of labour force insured for damages or income loss resulting from: injury, virtually 100%; permanent disability, virtually 100%; death, virtually 100%. Average days lost to labour stoppages per 1,000 workers (1988): 1.8. Principal means of journey to work (1986): private automobile 32.4%; public transportation 19.2%; bicycle 6.2%; foot 37.5%; other 4.7%. Percentage of unemployed workers not eligible for unemployment benefits (1988): 31.4%.

Distribution of income (1978)				
percent of household income by quintile				
1	2	3	4	5 (highest)
6.9	11.0	15.9	21.9	44.8

Access to services. Proportion of dwellings (1987) having: electricity, virtually 100%; piped water supply, virtually 100%; flush sewage disposal 98.3%; public fire protection, virtually 100%.
Social participation. Eligible voters participating in last (January 1987) national election 84.3%. Population participating in voluntary work: n.a. Trade union membership in total work force (1988): 42%. Practicing religious population in total affiliated population (1989): 5% of Protestants and 25% of Catholics "regularly" attend religious services.
Social deviance (1987). Offense rate per 100,000 population for: murder and manslaughter 4; sexual abuse 56, of which child molestation 16, rape and forcible sexual assault 15; assault and battery 104; larceny 4,562, of which burglary 339, auto theft 121. Incidence per 100,000 in general population (late 1970s) of: alcoholism 2,500 to 3,000; drug and substance abuse 650; suicide 19.0[3].
Leisure (1981). Favourite leisure activities: hiking and walking 27%; reading 27%; yard work 16%; swimming 14%; watching television 14%.
Material well-being (1988). Households possessing: automobile 67.8%; telephone 93.2%; colour television receiver 87.4%; refrigerator, virtually 100%; washing machine 85.7%; home freezer 51.7%.

National economy

Gross national product (at current market prices; 1987): U.S.$879,630,000,-000 (U.S.$14,460 per capita).

Structure of gross domestic product and labour force

	1988			
	in value DM '000,000	% of total value	labour force	% of labour force
Agriculture	31,980	1.5	1,283,000	4.2
Mining	62,750	3.0	[4]	[4]
Manufacturing	683,290	32.4	8,268,000[4]	27.0[4]
Construction	110,370	5.2	1,712,000	5.6
Public utilities	...	...	479,000	1.6
Transp. and commun. }	302,700	14.3	1,468,000	4.8
Trade			3,386,000	11.0
Finance }	599,050	28.4	837,700	2.7
Services }			4,426,000	14.4
Pub. admin., defense	276,600	13.1	4,202,000	13.7
Other	44,200	2.1	4,582,300	15.0
TOTAL	2,110,940	100.0	30,644,000	100.0

Budget (1988). Revenue: DM 924,490,000,000 (social security contributions 39.6%, indirect taxes 27.8%, direct taxes 27.6%, other current transfers received 2.7%, income from self-employed property and entrepreneurship 2.2%). Expenditures: DM 907,900,000,000 (current transfers paid 43.0%, wages and salaries 23.9%, goods and services 21.2%, debt interest payments 6.6%, subsidies 5.3%).
Total national debt (1989[5]) DM 483,720,000,000.
Tourism (1988)[6]: receipts from visitors U.S.$15,054,000,000; expenditures by nationals abroad U.S.$44,311,000,000.

Manufacturing, mining, and construction enterprises (1987)

	no. of enterprises	no. of tradesmen and professionals	wages as a % of avg. of all wages	annual gross production value (DM '000,000)
Manufacturing	35,871	6,863,000	101.5	1,457,367
of which				
Road motor vehicle	1,727	844,000	112.1	207,607
Chemical	1,153	589,000	125.2	170,237
Machinery and appliances (electric)	2,511	1,033,000	103.7	166,865
Machinery (nonelectric)	4,762	997,000	106.2	166,527
Food and beverage	3,676	445,000	85.7	148,997
Petroleum and natural gas	48	31,000	164.4	72,613
Calculator, computer	2,052	290,000	90.3	44,894
Iron and steel	104	205,000	100.9	43,827
Plastics	1,772	219,000	89.3	38,778
Textile	1,315	223,000	76.9	35,239
Cement, sand, and gravel	1,915	146,000	101.0	29,728
Wood and wood products	1,966	182,000	82.2	28,759
Metalware	1,294	151,000	97.6	24,467
Mining	79	206,000	108.8	32,259
Construction	14,275	909,000	81.8	105,784

Production (value of production in DM; 1987–88). Agriculture, forestry, fishing: cereal grains 4,979,000,000, flowers and ornamental plants 2,440,-000,000, fruits 2,178,000,000, sugar beets 2,019,000, grapes for wine 1,786,-000,000, oilseed crops 951,000,000, potatoes 916,000,000; livestock (number of live animals) 22,589,000 pigs, 15,023,000 cattle, 72,035,000 poultry; roundwood (1987) 28,693,000 cu m; fish catch 142,207, of which Atlantic cod 37,766, blue mussel 30,866, salmon and pollack 23,139. Mining and quarrying (metric tons; 1988): potash 27,000,000; iron ore 68,900; zinc 61,-600; lead 14,300. Manufacturing (value added at factor cost in DM; 1987): capital equipment 243,720,000,000, of which electrical equipment 67,649,-000,000, machinery 61,766,000,000, transport equipment 59,068,000,000; chemicals (including medicinal products) 51,374,000,000; food and bev-

erages 26,047,000,000; calculators and computers 16,759,000,000; plastics and other synthetic products 12,889,000,000; semiprocessed iron and steel 11,308,000,000; textiles 10,999,000,000; stone and ceramic products 9,799,-000,000; furniture and other wood products 9,759,000,000; printed matter 9,247,000,000; metalware 9,152,000,000; office machines 8,191,000,000; precision mechanical and optical products 7,991,000,000; clothing 6,842,-000,000; rubber products 6,579,000,000. Construction (1988): residential 2,978,000 sq m; nonresidential 23,773,000 sq m; restoration and conversion 3,699,000 sq m.

Service enterprises (1987)

	no. of enterprises	no. of employees	weekly wage as a % of all wages	annual turnover (DM '000,000)
Gas	136	28,000	113.8	23,506
Water	144	15,000	99.8	3,053
Electrical power	459	237,000	116.3	116,944
Transport				
air	188	44,794	...	13,844
buses[7]	5,717	137,039	...	10,238
Rail[7]	1	9,394	...	1,361
shipping	1,810	10,445	...	...
Communications				
press[8]	2,223	213,193	...	28,575
film[9]	615	3,000	...	836
Postal services	17,616	515,190	...	52,050
Hotels and restaurants[8]	114,167	651,600	...	42,736
Wholesale trade[8]	41,909	990,800	...	793,111
Retail trade[8]	168,230	2,099,600	...	482,797

Energy production (consumption): electricity (kW-hr; 1987) 415,812,000,000 (419,619,000,000); hard coal (metric tons; 1987) 82,380,000 (85,062,000); lignite-brown coal (metric tons; 1988) 108,852,000 (110,697,000); crude petroleum (barrels; 1987) 27,765,000 (489,730,000); petroleum products (metric tons; 1987) 68,153,000 (102,472,000); natural gas (cu m; 1987) 15,871,000,000.

Population economically active (1988): total 30,644,000; activity rate of total population (1986) 48.5% (participation rates: ages 15–64, 67.2%[10]; female 39.7%; unemployed [1989] 7.5%).

Price and earnings indexes (1985 = 100)

	1983	1984	1985	1986	1987	1988	1989[5]
Consumer price index	95.6	97.9	100.0	99.8	100.1	101.2	104.5
Hourly earnings index	94.1	96.3	100.0	103.5	107.6	112.1	116.3

Household income and expenditure. Average household size (1988) 2.4; average annual income per household (1988) DM 49,711 (U.S.$27,923); sources of take-home income (1988): wages 82.1%, self-employment 7.9%, transfer payments 9.9%, transfers 3.9%; expenditure (1988): food 23.2%, rent 20.1%, transportation 17.4%, entertainment and education 10.4%, clothing and footwear 8.2%, household operations and maintenance 8.3%, electricity and gas 5.7%, other 6.8%.

Financial aggregates

	1983	1984	1985	1986	1987	1988	1989 (9 mo.)
Exchange rate, DM per:							
U.S. dollar	2.7238	3.1480	2.9440	2.1715	1.7974	1.7562	1.9526
£	3.9511	3.6407	3.8163	3.1856	2.9458	3.1825	3.0668
SDR	2.8517	3.0857	2.7035	2.3740	2.2436	2.3957	2.3911
International reserves (U.S.$)							
Total (excl. gold; '000,000)	42,674	40,141	44.380	51,734	78,756	58,528	57,698
SDRs ('000,000)	1,613	1,362	1,547	2,020	1,964	1,857	1,719
Reserve pos. in IMF ('000,000)	3,748	3,750	3,808	3,848	3,900	3,346	2,986
Foreign exchange	37,313	35,028	39,025	45,866	72,893	56,324	52,993
Gold ('000,000 fine troy oz)	95.18	95.18	95.18	95.18	95.18	95.18	95.18
% world reserves	10.06	10.06	10.03	10.03	10.07	10.02	10.11
Interest and prices							
Central bank discount (%)	4.0	4.5	4.0	3.5	2.5	3.5	5.0
Gov't. bond yield (%)	7.9	7.8	6.9	5.9	5.8	6.1	7.2
Industrial share prices (1985 = 100)	66.8	75.2	100.0	135.2	124.5	104.0	144.9
Balance of payments (U.S.$ '000,000)							
Balance of visible trade	21.42	22.29	28.51	55.74	69.88	78.70	19.00[11]
Imports, f.o.b.	138.48	139.09	145.15	175.30	208.22	230.11	62.23[11]
Exports, f.o.b.	159.90	161.38	173.66	231.03	278.09	308.80	81.22[11]
Balance of invisibles	−6.15	−2.15	−1.61	−3.34	−7.97	−11.90	−0.95[11]
Balance of payments, current account	5.40	9.75	16.98	39.85	46.63	48.64	13.75[11]

Land use (1987): forested 30.0%; meadows and pastures 18.3%; agricultural and under permanent cultivation 30.6%; other 21.1%.

Foreign trade

Balance of trade (current prices)

	1983	1984	1985	1986	1987	1988
DM '000,000	+19,840	+20,340	+26,950	+53,630	+70,160	+78,690
% of total	6.7%	6.8%	8.5%	13.3%	14.4%	14.6%

Imports (1988): DM 439,768,000,000 (machinery and transport equipment 29.2%, of which transport equipment 7.1%, electrical machinery other than office equipment 7.8%, office equipment 4.2%; food and beverages 10.4%, of which fruits and vegetables 3.2%, meat and meat products 1.3%, coffee, tea, and spices 1.3%; chemicals and chemical products 9.7%, of which organic chemical products 2.5%, medical and pharmaceutical products 1.0%; mineral fuels 7.6%, of which crude petroleum and petroleum products 5.9%, natural gas 1.3%; clothing and wearing apparel 5.8%; iron and steel 3.7%; textiles and yarn 3.5%; paper and paper products 2.3%; metallic ores and scrap metal 1.7%). *Major import sources:* France 12.1%; The Netherlands 10.3%; Italy 9.1%; Belgium–Luxembourg 7.1%; United Kingdom 6.9%; United States 6.6%; Japan 6.5%.

Exports (1988): DM 567,750,000,000 (machinery and transport equipment 48.1%, of which transport equipment 16.9%, electrical machinery other than office equipment 8.4%; chemicals and chemical products 13.6%, of which organic chemical products 3.2%, medical and pharmaceutical products 1.4%, dyes and dye products 1.4%; iron and steel 4.2%; food and beverages 4.2%, of which dairy products 1.3%, meat and meat products 0.6%; textiles and yarn 3.3%; paper and paper products 2.1%). *Major export destinations:* France 12.6%; United Kingdom 9.3%; Italy 9.1%; The Netherlands 8.7%; United States 8.0%; Belgium–Luxembourg 7.4%; Switzerland 6.1%; Austria 5.6%.

Trade by commodity group (1988)

SITC Group	imports DM '000,000	%	exports DM '000,000	%
00 Food and live animals	41,450	9.4	23,650	4.2
01 Beverages and tobacco	4,380	1.0	3,250	0.6
02 Crude materials, excluding fuels	28,510	6.5	10,640	1.9
03 Mineral fuels, lubricants, and related materials	33,560	7.6	6,920	1.2
04 Animal and vegetable oils, fat, and waxes	1,450	0.3	1,600	0.3
05 Chemicals and related products, n.e.s.	42,620	9.7	78,950	13.9
06 Basic manufactures	80,480	18.3	102,560	18.1
07 Machinery and transport equipment	128,200	29.2	272,860	48.1
08 Miscellaneous manufactured articles	65,720	14.9	62,370	11.0
09 Goods not classified by kind	13,380	3.0	6,960	1.2
TOTAL	439,770	100.0	567,750	100.0

Direction of trade (1988)

	imports DM '000,000	%	exports DM '000,000	%
Africa	14,288	3.2	15,891	2.8
Asia	62,199	14.1	52,069	9.2
Middle East	4,992	1.1	13,137	2.3
Japan	28,388	6.5	13,118	2.3
other Asia	28,819	6.6	25,814	4.5
South America	10,995	2.5	7,191	1.3
North and Central America	35,199	8.0	53,271	9.4
United States	29,119	6.6	45,679	8.0
other North and Central Am.	6,080	1.4	7,592	1.3
Europe	313,528	71.3	434,232	76.4
EEC	227,449	51.7	308,232	54.3
U.S.S.R.	6,878	1.8	9,424	1.7
other Europe	79,201	18.0	116,576	20.5
Oceania	3,278	0.7	4,274	0.8
TOTAL	439,768	100.0	567,750	100.0

Transport and communications

Transport. Railroads (1988): length 41,522 mi, 66,821 km; passenger-mi 27,470,000,000, passenger-km 44,208,000,000; short ton-mi cargo 41,907,-000,000, metric ton-km cargo 61,180,000,000. Roads (1987): total length 305,242 mi, 491,240 km (paved 99%). Vehicles (1988): passenger cars 28,878,200; trucks and buses 1,392,000. Merchant marine (1988): vessels (100 gross tons and over) 1,233; total deadweight tonnage 4,994,457. Air transport (1988): passenger-mi 21,131,000,000, passenger-km 34,006,300,-000; short ton-mi cargo 2,376,500,000, metric ton-km cargo 3,469,500,000; airports (1989) with scheduled flights 27.

Communications. Daily newspapers (1987): total number 356; total circulation 25,255,000; circulation per 1,000 population 413. Radio (1988): total number of receivers 26,892,000 (1 per 2.3 persons). Television (1988): total number of receivers 23,742,000 (1 per 2.6 persons). Telephones (1988): 41,735,000 (1 per 1.5 persons).

Education and health

Education (1987–88)

	schools	teachers	students	student/ teacher ratio
Primary (age 6–10)	27,421	301,644	4,225,047	14.0
Secondary (age 10–19)	5,284	186,390	2,552,731	13.7
Voc., teacher tr.	7,546	90,343	2,508,515	27.8
Higher	111	341,149	1,470,738	4.3

Literacy (1989): about 99%.
Health (1988): physicians 171,487 (1 per 357 persons); hospital beds 673,687 (1 per 91 persons); infant mortality rate per 1,000 live births 8.3.
Food (1984–86): daily per capita caloric intake 3,475 (vegetable products 62%, animal products 38%); 129% of FAO recommended minimum requirement.

Military

Total active duty personnel (1989): 494,300 (army 68.9%, navy 7.3%, air force 21.4%; interservice personnel 2.3%). *Military expenditure as percent of GNP* (1987): 3.0% (world 5.4%); per capita expenditure U.S.$560.

---

[1]Berlin (West) is under tripartite (France, United Kingdom, United States) jurisdiction and is only administratively a part of West Germany. [2]Excluding some 600,000 immigrants and refugees admitted in various statuses, mostly from eastern Europe, during 1989. [3]1987. [4]Manufacturing includes mining. [5]September. [6]Includes West Berlin. [7]1988. [8]1986. [9]1984. [10]1985. [11]6 months.

Ghana

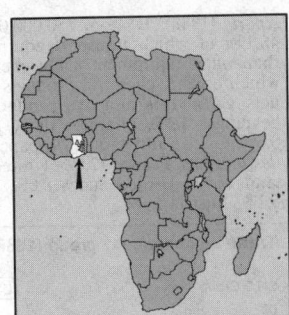

Official name: Republic of Ghana.
Form of government: military regime.
Head of state and government: Chairman of the Provisional National Defense Council.
Capital: Accra.
Official language: English.
Official religion: none.
Monetary unit: 1 cedi (₡) = 100 pesewas; valuation (Oct. 2, 1989) 1 U.S.$ = ₡321.38; 1 £ = ₡520.00.

Area and population

Regions	Capitals	area sq mi	area sq km	population 1988 estimate[1]
Ashanti	Kumasi	9,417	24,389	2,308,100
Brong-Ahafo	Sunyani	15,273	39,557	1,332,200
Central	Cape Coast	3,794	9,826	1,262,200
Eastern	Koforidua	7,461	19,323	1,855,800
Greater Accra	Accra	1,253	3,245	1,580,000
Northern	Tamale	27,175	70,384	1,285,900
Upper East	Bolgatanga	3,414	8,842	853,200
Upper West	Wa	7,134	18,476	483,600
Volta	Ho	7,942	20,570	1,338,200
Western	Sekondi-Takoradi	9,236	23,921	1,278,300
TOTAL		92,098[2]	238,533	13,577,500

Demography

Population (1989): 14,566,000.
Density (1988): persons per sq mi 158.2, persons per sq km 61.1.
Urban–rural (1985): urban 31.5%; rural 68.5%.
Sex distribution (1985): male 49.61%; female 50.39%.
Age breakdown (1984): under 15, 45.0%; 15–29, 26.4%; 30–44, 14.6%; 45–59, 8.1%; 60–74, 4.1%; 75 and over, 1.8%.
Population projection: (2000) 20,418,000; (2010) 27,071,000.
Doubling time: 23 years.
Ethno-linguistic composition (1983): Akan 52.4%; Mossi 15.8%; Ewe 11.9%; Ga-Adangme 7.8%; Gurma 3.3%; Yoruba 1.3%; other 7.5%.
Religious affiliation (1980): Christian 62.6%, of which Protestant 27.9%, Roman Catholic 18.7%, African indigenous 16.0%; traditional beliefs 21.4%; Muslim 15.7%, of which Aḥmadīyah 7.9%; other 0.3%.
Major cities (1988): Accra 949,100; Kumasi 385,200; Tamale 151,100; Tema 110,000; Sekondi-Takoradi 103,600.

Vital statistics

Birth rate per 1,000 population (1985–90): 44.3 (world avg. 27.1); legitimate, n.a.; illegitimate, n.a.
Death rate per 1,000 population (1985–90): 13.1 (world avg. 9.9).
Natural increase rate per 1,000 population (1985–90): 31.2 (world avg. 17.2).
Total fertility rate (avg. births per childbearing woman; 1985–90): 6.4.
Life expectancy at birth (1985–89): male 55.2 years; female 55.8 years.
Major causes of death per 100,000 population: n.a.; however, major infectious diseases include malaria, tuberculosis, leprosy, trypanosomiasis (sleeping sickness), and onchocerciasis (river blindness).

National economy

Budget (1987–88). Revenue: ₡111,046,000,000 (export duty on cocoa 24.3%; income taxes 20.3%, of which corporate 13.0%, personal 7.3%; import duties 11.5%; excise taxes 7.5%; grants and loans 5.4%). Expenditures: ₡102,125,600,000 (education 26.5%; debt service 10.4%; health 9.3%; social security and welfare 6.4%; defense 4.2%).
Public debt (external, outstanding; 1987): U.S.$2,237,000,000.
Tourism (1987): receipts from visitors U.S.$2,000,000; expenditures by nationals abroad U.S.$12,000,000.
Production (metric tons except as noted). Agriculture, forestry, fishing (1988): roots and tubers 6,815,000 (of which cassava 3,300,000, yams 1,200,000, taro 1,116,000), cereals 995,000 (of which corn [maize] 600,000, sorghum 175,000, millet 300,000, rice 95,000), bananas and plantains 722,000, cocoa 288,800, peanuts (groundnuts) 128,000, sugarcane 110,000, coconuts 110,000, green peppers 75,000, oranges 35,000, lemons and limes 30,000, palm kernels 30,000, pulses 11,000; livestock (number of live animals) 3,000,000 goats, 2,500,000 sheep, 1,300,000 cattle, 750,000 pigs, 12,000,000 chickens; roundwood (1987) 9,884,000 cu m; fish catch (1987) 371,817 (of which anchovies 87,984). Mining and quarrying (1988): bauxite 287,300; manganese ore 230,900; gold 11,631.2 kg; diamonds 215,900 carats. Manufacturing (1988): kerosene, gasoline, and diesel fuel 542,600; cement 412,100; wheat flour 95,215; soap 36,053; cocoa cake, cocoa butter, and cocoa liquor 19,327; margarine 3,205; iron rods 1,336; toothpaste 158; textiles 22,700,000 metres; soft drinks 658,000 hectolitres[3]; beer 614,000 hectolitres; evaporated milk 275,000 hectolitres; ice cream 6,280 hectolitres; cigarettes 1,831,000,000 units. Construction (value added in ₡'000; 1985): 9,779,200. Energy production (consumption): electricity (kW-hr; 1987) 4,758,000,000 (4,477,000,000); coal (metric tons; 1987) none (3,000); crude petroleum (barrels; 1987) none (7,000,000); petroleum products (metric tons; 1987) 888,000 (899,000); natural gas, none (n.a.).
Household income and expenditure. Average household size (1983) 4.9; average annual income per household (1978) ₡9,600 (U.S.$[4]); sources of income: n.a.; expenditure (1978): food and beverages 57.4%, housing and

energy 11.5%, clothing and footwear 14.3%, transport and communications 3.3%, health care 1.3%.
Gross national product (at current market prices; 1987): U.S.$5,328,000,000 (U.S.$390 per capita).

Structure of gross domestic product and labour force

	1987 in value ₡'000,000	1987 % of total value	1984 labour force	1984 % of labour force
Agriculture	377,480.9	50.6	3,310,967	59.4
Mining	13,629.6	1.8	26,828	0.5
Manufacturing	73,719.9	9.9	588,418	10.5
Construction	18,318.5	2.5	64,686	1.2
Public utilities	13,278.7	1.8	15,437	0.3
Transp. and commun.	27,524.2	3.7	122,806	2.2
Trade	137,962.7	18.5	792,147	14.2
Finance	19,249.5	2.5	27,475	0.5
Pub. admin., defense	54,122.6	7.3	97,548	1.7
Services	6,398.6	0.8	376,168	6.7
Other	4,314.6[5]	0.6[5]	157,624[6]	2.8[6]
TOTAL	745,999.8	100.00	5,580,104	100.0

Population economically active (1984): total 5,580,104; activity rate of total population 45.4% (participation rates: over age 15, 82.5%; female 51.2%; unemployed 2.8%).

Price and earnings indexes (1985 = 100)

	1982	1983	1984	1985	1986	1987	1988
Consumer price index	29.1	64.9	90.7	100.0	124.6	174.2	228.8
Earnings index	13.9	33.2	68.3	100.0	...	...	...

Land use (1987): forested 36.0%; meadows and pastures 14.8%; agricultural and under permanent cultivation 12.5%; other 36.7%.

Foreign trade

Balance of trade (current prices)

	1982	1983	1984	1985	1986	1987
₡'000,000	+588.0	−85.0	+637.1	−4,070.0	+11,578.0	+7,594.0
% of total	13.9%	0.4%	1.6%	5.8%	8.1%	2.6%

Imports (1985): ₡47,155,286,000 (mineral fuels and lubricants 29.1%; machinery and transport equipment 26.4%; chemicals 12.5%; basic manufactures 10.7%; food and live animals 4.0%; beverages and tobacco 1.6%). *Major import sources:* United Kingdom 25.1%; Nigeria 22.5%; West Germany 11.4%; Japan 6.0%; United States 5.8%; Italy 3.3%.
Exports (1985): ₡33,489,805,000 (food and live animals 67.3%, of which cocoa 59.4%; gold 15.0%; logs and sawn timber 4.2%; manganese ore 1.5%; industrial diamonds 0.8%). *Major export destinations:* United Kingdom 20.3%; The Netherlands 10.2%; Japan 9.7%; United States 8.2%; U.S.S.R. 6.4%; West Germany 6.1%.

Transport and communications

Transport. Railroads (1988): route length[3] 592 mi, 953 km; passenger-mi 241,900,000, passenger-km 389,300,000; short ton-mi cargo 85,960,000, metric ton-km cargo 125,500,000. Roads (1985): total length 17,600 mi, 28,300 km (paved 20%). Vehicles (1984): passenger cars 52,864; trucks and buses 23,375. Merchant marine (1988): vessels (100 gross tons and over) 136; total deadweight tonnage 122,465. Air transport (1986): passenger-mi 168,404,000, passenger-km 271,021,000; short ton-mi cargo 23,084,000, metric ton-km cargo 33,703,000; airports (1989) with scheduled flights 4.
Communications. Daily newspapers (1987): total number 4; total circulation 460,000; circulation per 1,000 population 33. Radio (1988): 2,920,088 receivers (1 per 4.7 persons). Television (1987): 175,000 receivers (1 per 77 persons). Telephones (1987): 74,932 (1 per 179 persons).

Education and health

Education (1985–86)

	schools	teachers	students	student/ teacher ratio
Primary (6–12)	9,180	67,261	1,567,778	23.3
Secondary (13–20)	5,702	44,578	768,347	17.2
Voc., teacher tr.	137	2,887	40,485	14.0
Higher	9	1,316	10,225	7.8

Educational attainment (1984). Percent of population age 25 and over having: no formal schooling 60.4%; primary education 7.1%; middle school 25.4%; secondary 3.5%; vocational and other postsecondary 2.9%; higher 0.6%. *Literacy* (1985): total population age 15 and over literate 3,835,000 (53.2%); males literate 2,261,000 (64.1%); females literate 1,574,000 (42.8%).
Health: physicians (1984) 1,900 (1 per 6,640 persons); hospital beds (1981) 20,582 (1 per 563 persons); infant mortality rate per 1,000 live births (1985–90) 90.
Food (1984–86): daily per capita caloric intake 1,733 (vegetable products 95%, animal products 5%); 75% of FAO minimum recommended requirement.

Military

Total active duty personnel (1989): 11,600 (army 86.2%, navy 6.9%, air force 6.9%). *Military expenditure as percent of GNP* (1987): 0.9% (world 5.4%); per capita expenditure U.S.$3.

[1]January 1. [2]Detail does not add to total given because of rounding. [3]1986. [4]Unofficial exchange rate (7.5 to 9.9 times the official rate) does not permit meaningful conversion into other currencies. [5]Import duties less imputed bank service charges. [6]Unemployed only.

Greece

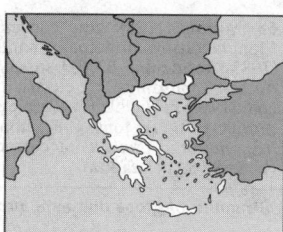

Official name: Ellinikí Dimokratía (Hellenic Republic).
Form of government: unitary multiparty republic with one legislative house (Greek Chamber of Deputies [300]).
Chief of state: President.
Head of government: Prime Minister.
Capital: Athens.
Official language: Greek.
Official religion: Eastern Orthodox.
Monetary unit: 1 drachma (Dr) = 100 lepta; valuation (Oct. 2, 1989)
1 U.S.$ = Dr 164.49; 1 £ = Dr 266.15.

Area and population		area		population
Regions[1]		sq mi	sq km	1981 census
Anatolikí Makedonía kaí Thráki	(Eastern Macedonia and Thrace)	5,466	14,157	575,210
Attikí	(Attica)	1,470	3,808	3,369,424
Dhytikí Ellás	(Western Greece)	4,382	11,350	655,262
Dhytikí Makedonía	(Western Macedonia)	3,649	9,451	289,071
Iónioi Nísoi	(Ionian Islands)	891	2,307	182,651
Ípiros	(Epirus)	3,553	9,203	324,541
Kedrikí Makedonía	(Central Macedonia)	7,393	19,147	1,602,892
Kríti	(Crete)	3,218	8,336	502,165
Nótion Aiyaíon	(Southern Aegean)	2,041	5,286	233,529
Pelopónnisos	(Peloponnesos)	5,981	15,490	577,030
Stereá Ellás	(Central Greece)	6,004	15,549	537,984
Thessalía	(Thessaly)	5,420	14,037	695,654
Vóreion Aiyaíon	(Northern Aegean)	1,481	3,836	195,004
TOTAL		50,949	131,957	9,740,417

Demography

Population (1989): 10,096,000.
Density (1989): persons per sq mi 198.2, persons per sq km 76.5.
Urban–rural (1985): urban 57.7%; rural 42.3%.
Sex distribution (1986): male 49.20%; female 50.80%.
Age breakdown (1986): under 15, 20.5%; 15–29, 22.1%; 30–44, 19.3%; 45–59, 19.7%; 60–74, 12.7%; 75 and over, 5.7%.
Population projection: (2000) 10,289,000; (2010) 10,346,000.
Doubling time: n.a.; doubling time exceeds 100 years.
Ethnic composition (1983): Greek 95.5%; Macedonian 1.5%; Turkish 0.9%; Albanian 0.6%; other 1.5%.
Religious affiliation (1980): Christian 98.1%, of which Greek Orthodox 97.6%, Roman Catholic 0.4%, Protestant 0.1%; Muslim 1.5%; other 0.4%.
Major cities (1981): Athens 885,737; Thessaloníki 406,413; Piraiévs 196,389; Pátrai 142,163; Peristérion 140,858.

Vital statistics

Birth rate per 1,000 population (1987): 10.6 (world avg. 27.1); legitimate 97.9%; illegitimate 2.1%.
Death rate per 1,000 population (1987): 9.5 (world avg. 9.9).
Natural increase rate per 1,000 population (1987): 1.1 (world avg. 17.2).
Total fertility rate (avg. births per childbearing woman; 1986): 2.2.
Marriage rate per 1,000 population (1987): 6.3.
Divorce rate per 1,000 population (1985): 0.8.
Life expectancy at birth (1980): male 72.2 years; female 76.4 years.
Major causes of death per 100,000 population (1987): malignant neoplasms (cancers) 185.1; cerebrovascular disease 177.6; diseases of pulmonary circulation and other forms of heart disease 176.4; ischemic heart disease 108.9.

National economy

Budget (1988). Revenue: Dr 2,801,530,000,000 (indirect and excise taxes 48.9%, direct taxes 22.0%, European Community 1.9%). Expenditures: Dr 2,756,530,000,000 (government ministries 82.0%, defense 12.6%, European Community 2.9%, police and other sectors 2.6%).
Tourism (1987): receipts from visitors U.S.$2,192,000,000; expenditures by nationals abroad U.S.$507,000,000.
Production (metric tons except as noted). Agriculture, forestry, fishing (1987): corn (maize) 2,370,000, wheat 2,147,000, tomatoes 1,921,000, sugarbeets 1,700,000, grapes 1,500,000, olives 1,100,000, potatoes 905,000, barley 626,000, oranges 461,000, cotton 168,000, onions 154,000, tobacco 145,000, rice 114,000; livestock (number of live animals) 11,412,000 sheep, 5,000,000 goats, 1,226,000 pigs, 743,000 cattle, 185,000 asses, 31,000,000 chickens; roundwood 2,945,000 cu m; fish catch 135,072. Mining and quarrying (1987)[2]: bauxite 2,476,800; iron ore 900,000[3]; zinc ore 22,500[3]; lead ore 21,000[3]; nickel 9,200. Manufacturing (value added in Dr; 1987): food, beverages, and tobacco 190,160,000,000; textiles 177,440,000,000; chemicals 117,620,000,000; clothing and footwear 72,190,000,000; paper and printing 75,460,000,000; transport equipment 64,560,000,000. Construction (cu m authorized; 1987): residential 44,423,000; nonresidential 68,349,000. Energy production (consumption): electricity (kW-hr; 1987) 30,087,000,000 (30,702,000,000); coal (metric tons; 1987) 44,612,000 (44,425,000); crude petroleum (barrels; 1987) 8,248,000 (110,170,000); petroleum products (metric tons; 1987) 15,144,000 (9,792,000); natural gas (cu m; 1987) 133,-260,000 (133,260,000).
Household income and expenditure. Average household size (1982) 3.3; income per household (1982) Dr 252,300 (U.S.$3,777); sources of income (1985): wages and salaries 43.0%, transfer payments 17.5%, other 39.5%; expenditure (1985): food, beverages, and tobacco 40.3%, transportation 14.9%, housing 8.5%, clothing and footwear 8.6%, other 27.7%.

Gross national product (1987): U.S.$43,557,000,000 (U.S.$4,350 per capita).

Structure of gross domestic product and labour force				
	1987			
	in value Dr '000,000	% of total value	labour force	% of labour force
Agriculture	875,000	15.8	975,700	24.1
Mining	100,400	1.8	26,100	0.6
Manufacturing	971,000	17.5	750,100	18.5
Construction	341,100	6.2	249,100	6.2
Public utilities	167,900	3.0	36,400	0.9
Transp. and commun.	444,300	8.0	261,300	6.5
Trade	893,100[4]	16.1[4]	612,400	15.1
Finance		[4]	149,700	3.7
Pub. admin., defense	985,200	17.8	648,300	16.0
Services	447,800	8.1 }		
Other	313,300[5]	5.7[5]	337,400[6]	8.3[6]
TOTAL	5,539,100	100.0	4,046,400	100.0[7]

Public debt (1985): U.S.$14,632,600,000.
Population economically active (1987): total 4,046,400; activity rate of total population 40.5% (participation rates: ages [1985] 15–64, 57.5%; female 36.3%; unemployed 7.1%).

Price and earnings indexes (1985 = 100)							
	1982	1983	1984	1985	1986	1987	1988
Consumer price index	58.9	70.8	83.8	100.0	112.7	123.0	143.2
Hourly earnings index	55.3	66.1	83.4	100.0	112.7	123.5	146.3

Land use (1986): forested 20.0%; meadows and pastures 40.3%; agricultural and under permanent cultivation 30.1%; other 9.6%.

Foreign trade

Balance of trade (current prices)							
	1982	1983	1984	1985	1986	1987	1988
Dr '000,000	−303.0	−356.6	−416.6	−621.2	−614.8	−688.4	−861.4
% of total	34.6%	31.2%	27.7%	33.0%	28.0%	28.1%	33.8%

Imports (1988): Dr 1,924,292,300,000 (machinery and transport equipment 23.0%, of which electrical equipment 1.8%; food, beverages, and tobacco 16.8%, of which meat products 6.3%, milk and cream 2.6%, fish 1.0%; crude petroleum 9.2%; chemical products 9.3%, of which plastics and resins 2.9%, medicinal and pharmaceutical products 1.2%). Major import sources: West Germany 19.3%; Italy 12.9%; United States 10.0%; France 8.1%; The Netherlands 7.2%; United Kingdom 5.8%; Japan 3.3%; U.S.S.R. 3.0%.
Exports (1988): Dr 841,739,800,000 (food, beverages, and tobacco 27.8%, of which tobacco 3.0%, olive oil 3.0%, olives 1.4%; textiles 23.0%; petroleum products 8.2%; furs 1.9%). Major export destinations: West Germany 21.2%; United States 14.1%; Italy 13.8%; United Kingdom 8.6%; France 7.4%; The Netherlands 2.5%.

Transport and communications

Transport. Railroads (1987): route length 1,540 mi, 2,479 km; passenger-mi 1,204,000,000, passenger-km 1,938,000,000; short ton-mi cargo 410,000,-000, metric ton-km cargo 599,000,000. Roads (1985): total length 64,191 mi, 103,306 km (paved 83%). Vehicles (1989): passenger cars 1,526,863; trucks and buses 717,448. Merchant marine (1988): vessels (100 gross tons and over) 1,874; total deadweight tonnage 39,718,620. Air transport (1987): passenger-mi 4,437,000,000, passenger-km 7,140,000,000; short ton-mi cargo 78,149,000, metric ton-km cargo 114,096,000; airports (1989) with scheduled flights 29.
Communications. Daily newspapers (1987): total number 142; total circulation 1,236,277[8]; circulation per 1,000 population, n.a. Radio (1987): 4,085,-492 receivers (1 per 2.4 persons). Television (1987): 1,754,818 receivers (1 per 5.7 persons). Telephones (1987): 4,122,300 (1 per 2.4 persons).

Education and health

Education (1985–86)	schools	teachers	students	student/ teacher ratio
Primary (age 6–12)	8,657	37,994	887,735	23.4
Secondary (age 12–18)	2,654	41,782	704,119	16.8
Voc., teacher tr.	480	8,138	109,415	13.4
Higher	89	11,878	181,901	15.3

Educational attainment (1981). Percent of population age 25 and over having: no formal schooling (illiterate) 11.4%; some primary education 16.8%; completed primary 44.1%; lower secondary 6.0%; higher secondary 13.5%; some postsecondary 2.5%; a degree from institution of higher education 4.9%. Literacy (1985): total population age 14 and over literate 7,209,500 (93.8%); males literate 3,555,000 (97.3%); females literate 3,654,500 (90.6%).
Health (1987): physicians (1985) 29,103 (1 per 341 persons); hospital beds 51,745 (1 per 193 persons); infant mortality rate per 1,000 live births 12.6.
Food (1984–86): daily per capita caloric intake 3,688 (vegetable products 75%, animal products 25%); (1984) 149% of FAO minimum.

Military

Total active duty personnel (1988): 214,000 (army 79.7%, navy 9.1%, air force 11.2%). Military expenditure as percent of GNP (1987): 6.2% (world 5.4%); per capita expenditure U.S.$290.

[1]New administrative regions approved by the Greek Cabinet on Jan. 19, 1987. [2]Metal content of ore. [3]1986. [4]Trade includes finance. [5]Income from ownership of buildings. [6]Includes 286,200 unemployed. [7]Detail does not add to total given because of rounding. [8]For 24 dailies only.

Greenland

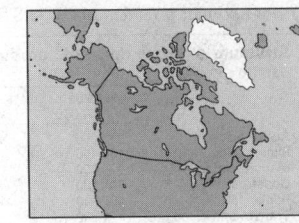

Official name: Kalaallit Nunaat
(Greenlandic); Grønland (Danish)
(Greenland).
Political status: integral part of the
Danish realm with one legislative
house (Parliament [27]).
Chief of state: Danish Monarch.
Heads of government: High Commissioner (for Denmark); Prime Minister
(for Greenland).
Capital: Nuuk (Godthåb).
Official languages: Greenlandic;
Danish.
Official religion: Lutheran Church of
Greenland (Evangelical Lutheran).
Monetary unit: 1 Danish krone
(Dkr) = 100 øre; valuation (Oct. 2,
1989) 1 U.S.$ = Dkr 7.30;
1 £ = Dkr 11.81.

Area and population

Counties	area sq mi	area sq km	population 1989 estimate[1]
Communes			
Avanersuaq (Nordgrønland)	41,200	106,700	
Qaanaaq (Thule)	...	...	849
Kitaa (Vestgrønland)	46,000	119,100	
Aasiaat (Egedesminde)	...	...	3,601
Ilulissat (Jakobshavn)	...	...	4,609
Ivittuut (Ivigtut)	...	...	3
Kangaatsiaq (Kangåtsiaq)	...	...	1,297
Maniitsoq (Sukkertoppen)	...	...	4,024
Nanortalik	...	...	2,662
Narsaq (Narssaq)	...	...	2,169
Nuuk (Godthåb)	...	...	12,426
Paamiut (Frederikshåb)	...	...	2,582
Qaqortoq (Julianehåb)	...	...	3,514
Qasigiannguit (Christianshåb)	...	...	1,715
Qeqertarsuaq (Godhavn)	...	...	1,143
Sisimiut (Holsteinsborg)	...	...	5,024
Upernavik	...	...	2,369
Uummannaq (Umanaq)	...	...	2,637
Tunu (Østgrønland)	44,700	115,900	
Illoqqortoormiut (Scoresbysund)	...	...	564
Tasiilaq (Angmagssalik)	...	...	2,861
TOTAL (ICE-FREE)	131,900	341,700	55,171[2]
PERMANENT ICE[3]	708,100	1,833,900	
TOTAL	840,000	2,175,600	

Demography

Population (1989): 55,400.
Density[3] (1989): persons per sq mi 0.42, persons per sq km 0.16.
Urban–rural (1989): urban (town) 79.6%; rural (settlement) 20.4%.
Sex distribution (1989): male 54.29%; female 45.71%.
Age breakdown (1989): under 15, 25.0%; 15–29, 31.2%; 30–44, 24.0%; 45–59, 13.6%; 60–74, 5.0%; 75 and over, 1.2%.
Population projection: (2000) 62,000; (2010) 69,000.
Doubling time: 50 years.
Ethnic composition (by place of birth; 1989): born in Greenland 82.7%; born elsewhere 17.3%.
Religious affiliation (1980): Protestant 98.3%, of which Evangelical Lutheran 95.7%, Pentecostal 1.4%; other 1.7%.
Major towns (1989): Nuuk (Godthåb) 11,957; Sisimiut (Holsteinsborg) 4,814; Ilulissat (Jakobshavn) 4,239; Aasiaat (Egedesminde) 3,304; Qaqortoq (Julianehåb) 3,115.

Vital statistics

Birth rate per 1,000 population (1988): 22.2 (world avg. 27.1); (1987) legitimate 29.4%; illegitimate 70.6%.
Death rate per 1,000 population (1988): 8.1 (world avg. 9.9).
Natural increase rate per 1,000 population (1988): 14.1 (world avg. 17.2).
Total fertility rate (avg. births per childbearing woman; 1987): 2.1.
Marriage rate per 1,000 population (1987): 7.1.
Divorce rate per 1,000 population (1985): 2.7.
Life expectancy at birth (1981–85): male 60.4 years; female 66.3 years.
Major causes of death per 100,000 population (1987): malignant neoplasms (cancers) 146.0; suicides 127.5; accidents 99.8; cerebrovascular disease 81.3; heart disease 81.3.

National economy

Budget (1987). Revenue: Dkr 3,350,100,000 (block grant from Danish government 40.0%; taxes and royalties for Greenland treasury 11.9%; import duties 9.5%; EEC fishery license fees 6.2%). Expenditures: Dkr 3,350,100,000 (current expenditure 45.1%, of which social welfare 13.3%, education 9.4%; development expenditure 44.7%; other expenditure 10.2%).
Public debt (external, outstanding): n.a.
Tourism: receipts from visitors, n.a.; expenditures by nationals abroad, n.a.
Production (metric tons except as noted). Fishing, agriculture, hunting: fish catch (1988) 222,500 (by local boats 133,500, of which shrimps 65,100, cod 55,300; by foreign boats 89,000); livestock (number of live animals; 1985) 21,443 sheep, 5,980 reindeer; hunting (value of sales in Dkr '000; 1985) sealskins 10,860, reindeer skins and antlers 1,668, whale meat and blubber 1,602, seal meat and blubber 236, fox skins 190, polar bear skins

65. Mining (1988): zinc concentrates 135,000; lead concentrates 34,300. Manufacturing: principally handicrafts and fish processing. Construction (1985): residential 33,100 sq m; nonresidential 12,300 sq m. Energy production (consumption): electricity (kW-hr; 1987) 172,000,000 (172,000,000); coal (1987) negligible (negligible); crude petroleum, none (none); petroleum products (metric tons; 1987) none (109,000); natural gas, none (none).
Gross national product (at current market prices; 1986): U.S.$465,000,000 (U.S.$8,780 per capita).

Structure of gross domestic product[4] and labour force

	1979 in value Dkr '000,000	1979 % of total value	1976 labour force	1976 % of labour force
Fishing, hunting, and sheep farming	231.8	20.8	3,222	15.1
Mining	327.0 }	29.4	318	1.5
Manufacturing			2,887	13.5
Construction	259.8	23.3	3,112	14.6
Transportation and communications	42.5	3.8	1,842	8.6
Trade, restaurants	172.5	15.5	2,153	10.1
Public utilities	—	—	293	1.4
Public administration[5]	—	—	5,374	25.1
Private services	80.5	7.2	1,589	7.4
Other	—	—	588	2.7
TOTAL	1,114.1	100.0	21,378	100.0

Population economically active (1976): total 21,378; activity rate of total population 43.1% (participation rates: ages 15–64, n.a.; female 33.4%; unemployed, n.a.).

Price and earnings indexes (January 1985 = 100)[6]

	1983	1984	1985	1986	1987	1988	1989
Consumer price index	84.6	91.4	100.0	105.4	108.4	116.7	121.8
Monthly earnings index	83.2	91.8	100.0	104.6	107.4	113.3	118.6

Household income and expenditure. Average household size (1976) 3.9[7]; taxable income per taxpayer (1984) Dkr 93,920 (U.S.$9,070); sources of income: n.a.; expenditure (1987)[8]: food 20.9%, household furnishings 13.3%, alcoholic beverages 10.0%, housing 10.0%, clothing 7.7%.
Land use (1986): forested 0.03%; meadows and pastures 0.69%; agricultural and under permanent cultivation, none; other (principally ice cap) 99.28%.

Foreign trade[9]

Balance of trade (current prices)

	1983	1984	1985	1986	1987	1988
DKr '000,000	−779	−1,085	−1,303	−834	−1,101	−790
% of total	19.2%	23.6%	26.3%	16.7%	18.9%	13.1%

Imports (1988): Dkr 3,420,000,000 (goods for household consumption 35.8%; intermediate goods for construction industry 13.6%; transport equipment 11.9%, of which ships and aircraft 9.2%, machinery and capital equipment 9.0%). *Major import sources:* Denmark 66.0%; Norway 5.2%; West Germany 4.0%; Japan 3.8%; Sweden 3.6%.
Exports (1988): Dkr 2,630,000,000 (shrimps, prawns, and mollusks 63.8%; zinc 14.9%; fish and fish products 14.8%; lead 3.1%). *Major export destinations:* Denmark 76.8%; West Germany 7.2%; Sweden 5.1%; Finland 2.4%; Norway 2.4%.

Transport and communications

Transport. Railroads: none. Roads (1987): total length 50 mi, 80 km (paved, n.a.). Vehicles (1987): passenger cars 2,009; trucks and buses 1,591. Merchant marine (1988): vessels (100 gross tons and over) 82; total deadweight tonnage, n.a. Air transport (1985)[10]: passenger-mi 16,318,000, passenger-km 26,262,000; short ton-mi cargo 232,000, metric ton-km cargo 339,000; airports (1989) with scheduled flights 19.
Communications. Daily newspapers: none. Radio (1988): total number of receivers 15,000 (1 per 3.7 persons). Television (1988): total number of receivers 12,000 (1 per 4.6 persons). Telephone subscribers (1987): 17,900 (1 per 3.0 persons).

Education and health

Education (1988–89)

	schools	teachers	students	student/teacher ratio
Primary (age 6–15)	90 }	1,110	7,435 }	8.1
Secondary (age 15–19)			1,508	
Voc., teacher tr.[11]	8	110	650	5.9
Higher[11]	2	35	200	5.7

Educational attainment (1970). Percent of adult population ages 14 through 39 having: primary education 61.7%; secondary 25.9%. *Literacy* (1986): total population age 15 and over literate 40,218 (virtually 100%).
Health (1987): physicians 65 (1 per 833 persons); hospital beds 556 (1 per 97 persons); infant mortality rate per 1,000 live births 26.6.
Food: daily per capita caloric intake, n.a.

Military

Total active duty personnel[12] (1987): 290.

---

[1]January 1. [2]Includes 1,122 people not distributed by county. [3]Area of permanent ice not distributable by county; population density calculated with reference to ice-free area only. [4]Breakdown is for value-added of private enterprises only. [5]Includes public services (education and social and health services). [6]All January. [7]Average family size (1988) 1.9. [8]Weights of consumer price index components. [9]Imports c.i.f.; exports f.o.b. [10]Greenlandair only. [11]1986–87. [12]Data for U.S. Air Force personnel only.

Grenada

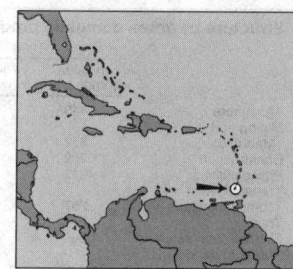

Official name: Grenada.
Form of government: constitutional monarchy with two legislative houses (Senate [13]; House of Representatives [15]).
Chief of state: British Monarch represented by governor-general.
Head of government: Prime Minister.
Capital: St. George's.
Official language: English.
Official religion: none.
Monetary unit: 1 East Caribbean dollar (EC$) = 100 cents; valuation (Oct. 2, 1989) 1 U.S.$ = EC$2.70; 1 £ = EC$4.37.

Area and population[1]

Parishes	Capitals	area sq mi	area sq km	population 1981 census
Carriacou	—	13	34	4,671
St. Andrew	—	35	91	22,425
St. David	—	18	47	10,195
St. George's	—	26	67	29,369
St. John	—	15	39	8,328
St. Mark	—	9	23	3,968
St. Patrick	—	17	44	10,132
TOTAL		133	345	89,088

Demography

Population (1989): 96,600.
Density (1989): persons per sq mi 726.3, persons per sq km 280.0.
Urban–rural: n.a.
Sex distribution (1981): male 48.20%; female 51.80%.
Age breakdown (1985): under 15, 35.1%; 15–29, 35.1%; 30–44, 12.4%; 45–59, 9.3%; 60–74, 6.2%; 75 and over, 2.1%.
Population projection: (2000) 112,000; (2010) 128,000.
Doubling time: 28 years.
Ethnic composition (1983): black 84%; mixed 12%; East Indian 3%; white 1%.
Religious affiliation (1980): Roman Catholic 64.4%; Protestant 34.5%, of which Anglican 20.7%, Seventh-day Adventist 3.1%, Methodist 2.1%; other 1.1%.
Major localities (1986): St. George's 7,500; Gouyave 2,980[2]; Grenville 2,100[2]; Victoria 2,000[2].

Vital statistics

Birth rate per 1,000 population (1986): 32.5 (world avg. 27.1); (1979) legitimate 22.5%; illegitimate 77.5%.
Death rate per 1,000 population (1986): 7.2 (world avg. 9.9).
Natural increase rate per 1,000 population (1986): 25.3 (world avg. 17.2).
Total fertility rate (avg. births per childbearing woman; 1987): 3.1.
Marriage rate per 1,000 population (1979): 3.9.
Divorce rate per 1,000 population (1979): 0.2.
Life expectancy at birth (1980–85): male 65.4 years; female 69.4 years.
Major causes of death per 100,000 population (1981): diseases of the circulatory system 186.3; malignant neoplasms (cancers) 90.9; endocrine, nutritional, and metabolic diseases 48.3; diseases of the respiratory system 41.5; diseases of the digestive system 31.4; ill-defined conditions 158.3.

National economy

Budget (1987). Revenue: EC$226,300,000 (internal sources 56.2%; external loans and grants 43.8%). Expenditures: EC$226,300,000 (current expenditure 64.6%, of which debt service 15.1%, education 9.5%, health and housing 7.4%; development expenditure 35.4%, of which road and bridge improvement 10.5%).
Public debt (external, outstanding; 1987): U.S.$66,800,000.
Tourism: receipts from visitors (1988) U.S.$28,200,000; expenditures by nationals abroad (1987) U.S.$4,000,000.
Gross national product (at current market prices; 1987): U.S.$134,000,000 (U.S.$1,340 per capita).

Structure of gross domestic product and labour force

	1987 in value EC$'000,000	1987 % of total value	1981[3] labour force	1981[3] % of labour force
Agriculture	56.8	18.8	7,987	28.7
Quarrying	1.1	0.4	75	0.3
Manufacturing	16.2	5.4	1,566	5.6
Construction	28.3	9.4	2,863	10.3
Public utilities	8.7	2.9	371	1.3
Transportation and communications	39.3	13.0	1,689	6.1
Trade, restaurants	60.9	20.2	3,902	14.0
Finance, real estate	36.1	12.0	367	1.3
Pub. admin., defense	56.0	18.6	1,682	6.0
Services	12.0	4.0	2,566	9.2
Other	−14.0[4]	−4.7[4]	4,779	17.2
TOTAL	301.4	100.0	27,847	100.0

Production (metric tons except as noted). Agriculture, forestry, fishing (1988): bananas 9,344, coconuts 8,000, sugarcane 8,000, citrus fruits 4,000, roots and tubers 4,000, nutmeg 2,879, mangoes 2,000, avocados 2,000, cacao 1,402, soursop 709[5], sapodilla plums 456[5], mace 332; livestock (number of live animals) 17,000 sheep, 11,000 goats, 11,000 pigs, 4,000 cattle; roundwood, n.a.; fish catch (1987) 4,881. Mining and quarrying: excavation of gravel for local use. Manufacturing (1984): flour 4,770; clothing EC$1,400,000 in export sales; beer 9,400 hectolitres; malt 2,500 hectolitres; edible coconut oil 5,000 hectolitres; rum 1,900 hectolitres; other products include paints, retread tires, and aerated beverages. Construction:[6]. Energy production (consumption): electricity (kW-hr; 1987) 25,000,000 (25,000,000); coal, none (none); crude petroleum, none (none); petroleum products (metric tons; 1987) none (22,000); natural gas, none (none).
Household income and expenditure. Average household size (1970) 4.7; income per household: n.a.; sources of income: n.a.; expenditure (weights of current price index components): food 59.0%, clothing and footwear 8.0%, housing 6.5%, household furnishings 6.5%, fuel and light 6.0%, transportation 4.0%, alcohol and tobacco 2.5%, other 7.5%.
Population economically active (1984): total 43,300; activity rate of total population c. 47.0% (participation rates: ages 15–64, n.a.; female, n.a.; unemployed [1987] 20–30%).

Price and earnings indexes (1985 = 100)

	1982	1983	1984	1985	1986	1987	1988
Consumer price index	87.0	92.3	97.5	100.0	100.5	99.7	105.8[7]
Earnings index[8]	...	...	...	...	...	...	...

Land use (1986): forested 9.0%; meadows and pastures 3.0%; agricultural and under permanent cultivation 41.0%; other 47.0%.

Foreign trade[9]

Balance of trade (current prices)

	1983	1984	1985	1986	1987	1988
U.S.$'000,000	−36.7	−37.8	−46.9	−54.4	−56.7	−59.6
% of total	49.2%	51.0%	51.2%	48.8%	47.1%	47.8%

Imports (1983): U.S.$55,600,000 (basic manufactures 25.4%; food 22.9%; machinery and transportation equipment 11.1%; mineral fuels 11.1%; chemicals 7.8%). *Major import sources* (1986): United States 25.6%; United Kingdom 16.9%; Trinidad and Tobago 13.4%; Canada 7.9%; Japan 7.1%.
Exports (1983): U.S.$18,920,000[10] (domestic exports 97.4%, of which fresh fruit 21.9%, cocoa beans 21.4%, nutmeg 17.2%, bananas 17.1%, clothing 9.4%, mace 4.0%; reexports 2.6%). *Major export destinations* (1986): United Kingdom 28.8%; Trinidad and Tobago 22.7%; The Netherlands 18.4%; West Germany 15.7%; United States 4.0%.

Transport and communications

Transport. Railroads: none. Roads (1986): total length 621 mi, 1,000 km (paved 66%). Vehicles (1981): passenger cars 4,784; trucks and buses 981. Merchant marine (1988): vessels (100 gross tons and over) 2; total deadweight tonnage 484. Air transport (1982): passenger arrivals and departures, n.a.; cargo loaded 59 metric tons, cargo unloaded 116 metric tons; airports (1989) with scheduled flights 2.
Communications. Daily newspapers: none. Radio (1988): total number of receivers 44,600 (1 per 2.4 persons). Television: total number of receivers, n.a. Telephones (1988): 6,000 (1 per 18 persons).

Education and health

Education (1987–88)

	schools	teachers	students	student/ teacher ratio
Primary (age 5–11)	58	761	19,963	26.2
Secondary (age 12–16)	18	297	6,437	21.7
Vocational	...	...	...	...
Higher	2	195	850	4.4

Educational attainment (1981). Percent of population age 25 and over having: no formal schooling 2.2%; primary education 87.8%; secondary 8.5%; higher 1.5%. *Literacy* (1981): total population age 15 and over literate 46,000 (85.0%).
Health (1987): physicians 42 (1 per 2,462 persons); hospital beds 360 (1 per 287 persons); infant mortality rate per 1,000 live births 15.9.
Food (1984–86): daily per capita caloric intake 2,409 (vegetable products 81%, animal products 19%); (1984) 98% of FAO recommended minimum requirement.

Military

Total active duty personnel (1987):[11]. *Military expenditure as percent of GNP:* n.a.; per capita expenditure, n.a.

[1]Grenada is divided into seven parishes for statistical purposes only. [2]1979. [3]Employed labour force only, including 5,932 self-employed. [4]Less imputed bank charges. [5]1984. [6]Only 260 houses were built by public authorities between 1978 and 1987. [7]August. [8]Grenada does not have a systematically computed index of wage rates. [9]Imports c.i.f.; exports f.o.b. [10]*Exports* (1988): U.S.$32,500,000 (nutmeg 35.7%, bananas 14.5%, cocoa beans 9.8%, mace 8.3%). [11]The police force includes an 80-member paramilitary unit.

Guadeloupe

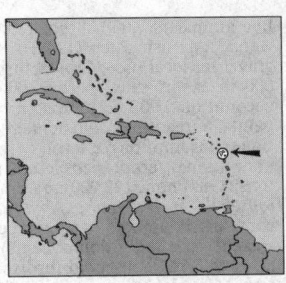

Official name: Département de la Guadeloupe (Department of Guadeloupe).
Political status: overseas department (France) with two legislative houses (General Council [42]; Regional Council [41]).
Chief of state: President of France.
Heads of government: Commissioner of the Republic (for France); President of the General Council (for Guadeloupe); President of the Regional Council (for Guadeloupe).
Capital: Basse-Terre.
Official language: French.
Official religion: none.
Monetary unit: 1 Franc (F) = 100 centimes; valuation (Oct. 2, 1989) 1 U.S.$ = F 6.36; 1 £ = F 10.29.

Area and population

Arrondissements	Capitals	area sq mi	area sq km	population 1982 census
Basse-Terre[1]	Basse-Terre	332	861	138,242
Pointe-à-Pitre[2]	Pointe-à-Pitre	297	769	179,027
Saint-Martin–Saint-Barthélemy[3]	Marigot	29	75	11,131
TOTAL		687[4]	1,780[4]	328,400

Demography

Population (1989): 341,000.
Density (1989): persons per sq mi 496.4, persons per sq km 191.6.
Urban–rural (1985): urban 45.7%; rural 54.3%.
Sex distribution (1985): male 48.8%; female 51.2%.
Age breakdown (1982): under 15, 31.1%; 15–29, 29.2%; 30–44, 16.6%; 45–59, 12.0%; 60–74, 7.8%; 75 and over, 2.8%; not specified 0.5%.
Population projection: (2000) 368,000; (2010) 391,000.
Doubling time: 49 years[5].
Ethnic composition (1980): Creole (mulatto) 77.0%; black 10.0%; Guadeloupe mestizo (French–East Asian) 10.0%; white 2.0%; other 1.0%.
Religious affiliation (1987): Roman Catholic 90.7%; other 9.3%.
Major cities (1982): Les Abymes 51,837 (agglomeration 121,157[6]); Pointe-à-Pitre 25,151; Le Gosier 13,741; Basse-Terre 13,397; Le Moule 9,800.

Vital statistics

Birth rate per 1,000 population (1988): 21.0 (world avg. 27.1); legitimate 39.9%; illegitimate 60.1%.
Death rate per 1,000 population (1988): 6.6 (world avg. 9.9).
Natural increase rate per 1,000 population (1988): 14.4 (world avg. 17.2).
Total fertility rate (avg. births per childbearing woman; 1987): 2.2.
Marriage rate per 1,000 population (1988): 5.5.
Divorce rate per 1,000 population (1988): 1.1.
Life expectancy at birth (1987): male 69.0 years; female 76.0 years.
Major causes of death per 100,000 population (1987): diseases of the circulatory system 216.0; malignant neoplasms (cancers) 118.0; accidents and violence 74.6; diseases of the digestive system 40.7; diseases of the respiratory system 29.1.

National economy

Budget (1989). Revenue: F 1,623,000,000 (receipts from French central government and local administrative bodies 44.5%, new loans 15.6%, investments 8.9%, taxes on motor fuels 8.1%). Expenditures: F 1,623,000,000 (health and social services 32.6%, capital investments and works 30.9%, debt amortization 4.7%).
Public debt (external, outstanding; 1987[7]): U.S.$57,000,000.
Tourism (1987): receipts from visitors U.S.$100,000,000; expenditures by nationals abroad, n.a.
Production (metric tons except as noted). Agriculture, forestry, fishing (1988): bananas 120,000, raw sugar 70,900, roots and tubers 25,000, pineapples 3,684[8], eggplant 3,290[8], coconuts 3,000, limes 1,668[8], cut flowers 629, foliage and plants 26[9]; livestock (number of live animals) 74,000 cattle, 43,000 pigs; roundwood (1987) 17,000 cu m; fish catch 8,150 metric tons. Mining and quarrying (1987): pozzolan 220,000. Manufacturing (1988): cement 241,400; rum 74,600 hectolitres; other products include clothing, wooden furniture and posts, and metalware. Construction (buildings authorized): residential (1985) 239,000 sq m; nonresidential (1987) 105,000 sq m. Energy production (consumption): electricity (kW-hr; 1988) 640,000,000 (565,000,000); coal, none (none); crude petroleum, none (none); petroleum products (metric tons; 1987) none (242,000); natural gas, none (none).
Household income and expenditure. Average household size (1984–85) 3.7; income per household (1980) F 72,898 (U.S.$16,142); sources of income (1980): wages and salaries 76.8%, rent 4.0%, other 19.2%; expenditure (1984–85): food and beverages 29.8%, of which poultry and meat 7.4%; housing, household furnishings, and energy 26.3%; transportation and communications 13.3%; clothing and footwear 8.2%; other 22.4%.
Gross national product (at current market prices; 1985): U.S.$1,170,000,000 (U.S.$3,490 per capita).

Structure of gross domestic product and labour force

	1980 in value F '000,000	1980 % of total value	1986 labour force	1986 % of labour force
Agriculture	449	7.7	9,379	7.2
Mining and Manufacturing	372	6.3	6,072	4.7
Construction	259	4.4	8,825	6.8
Public utilities	12	0.2	763	0.6
Transportation and communications	267	4.6	4,006	3.1
Trade	1,071	18.3	9,561	7.4
Finance, real estate	1,560	26.6	18,736	14.5
Pub. admin., defense, services, and other	1,870	31.9	31,388	24.3
Unemployed	—	—	40,641	31.4
TOTAL	5,860	100.0	129,371	100.0

Population economically active (1986): total 129,371; activity rate of total population 38.6% (participation rates: ages 15–64, 66.1%; female 46.6%; unemployed [1988] 38.0%).

Price and earnings indexes (1985 = 100)[10]

	1983	1984	1985	1986	1987	1988	1989[11]
Consumer price index	88.2	95.0	100.0	101.3	104.9	106.9	106.7
Earnings index[12]	90.2	93.9	100.0	100.4	102.0	105.0	104.7

Land use (1986): forested 40.0%; meadows and pastures 16.0%; agricultural and under permanent cultivation 23.0%; other 21.0%.

Foreign trade

Balance of trade (current prices)

	1983	1984	1985	1986	1987	1988
F '000,000	−4,412	−4,480	−5,076	−4,709	−5,665	−6,246
% of total	77.9%	74.9%	79.1%	75.9%	83.4%	73.0%

Imports (1987): F 6,229,000,000 (food 22.8%, electrical machinery and apparatuses 14.7%, transport vehicles 14.2%, chemical products 8.9%, metal manufactures 7.0%, petroleum products 5.7%). *Major import sources:* France 76.9%; Martinique 6.8%; Italy 3.1%; Netherlands Antilles 2.8%.
Exports (1987): F 564,000,000 (bananas 50.2%, wheat flour 8.2%, rum 7.8%, sugar 3.3%). *Major export destinations:* France 82.4%; Martinique 10.3%; Dominica 1.7%.

Transport and communications

Transport. Railroads: none. Roads (1987): total length 1,314 mi, 2,115 km (paved [1986] 80%). Vehicles (1985): passenger cars 95,962; trucks and buses 28,134. Merchant marine (1988): vessels (100 gross tons and over) 11; deadweight tonnage, n.a. Air transport (1988)[13]: passenger arrivals 586,901, passenger departures 595,690; cargo loaded 4,212 metric tons, cargo unloaded 7,219 metric tons; airports (1989) with scheduled flights 7.
Communications. Daily newspapers (1988): total number 1; total circulation 19,500; circulation per 1,000 population 58. Radio (1987): total number of receivers 100,000 (1 per 3.4 persons). Television (1988): total number of receivers 150,000 (1 per 2.3 persons). Telephones (1989): 103,103 (1 per 3.3 persons).

Education and health

Education (1987–88)

	schools	teachers	students	student/teacher ratio
Primary (age 6–10)	333[14]	1,927[15]	39,991	22.2[15]
Secondary (age 11–17)	50	} 3,015[16]	34,360	...
Vocational	49		17,757	...
Higher	2		5,835	...

Educational attainment (1982). Percent of population age 25 and over having: no formal schooling 10.7%; primary education 54.6%; secondary 29.5%; higher 5.2%. *Literacy* (1982): total population age 15 and over literate 225,400 (90.1%); males literate 108,700 (89.7%); females literate 116,700 (90.5%).
Health: physicians (1986) 491 (1 per 682 persons); hospital beds (1987) 3,391 (1 per 99 persons); infant mortality rate per 1,000 live births (1988) 12.9.
Food (1984–86): daily per capita caloric intake 2,674 (vegetable products 73%, animal products 27%); 110% of FAO recommended minimum requirement.

Military

Total active duty personnel (1989): 8,200 French troops[17].

[1]Comprises Basse-Terre 327 sq mi (848 sq km) and Îles des Saintes 5 sq mi (13 sq km), pop. 2,901. [2]Comprises Grande-Terre 228 sq mi (590 sq km); Marie-Galante 61 sq mi (158 sq km), pop. 13,757; La Désirade 8 sq mi (20 sq km), pop. 1,602; and the small, uninhabited Îles de la Petite-Terre. [3]Comprises the French part of Saint-Martin 20 sq mi (52 sq km), pop. 8,072; Saint-Barthélemy 8 sq mi (21 sq km), pop. 3,059; and the small, uninhabited island of Tintamarre. [4]Total area includes 29 sq mi (75 sq km) not allocated by arrondissement. [5]Net migration to metropolitan France nearly outweighs natural increase rate. [6]Includes Pointe-à-Pitre. [7]Includes external long-term private debt not guaranteed by the government. [8]1987. [9]Export only. [10]Base and indexes are end of year unless footnoted. [11]End of March. [12]Based on minimum-level wage in public administration. [13]Raizet international airport only. [14]Includes preprimary schools. [15]1985–86. [16]1983–84. [17]Includes Martinique and French Guiana.

Guam

Official name: Guam.
Political status: self-governing organized unincorporated territory of the United States with one legislative house (21).
Chief of state: President of the United States.
Head of government: Governor.
Capital: Agana.
Official language: English.
Official religion: none.
Monetary unit: 1 United States dollar (U.S.$) = 100 cents; valuation (Oct. 2, 1989) 1 U.S.$ = £0.62.

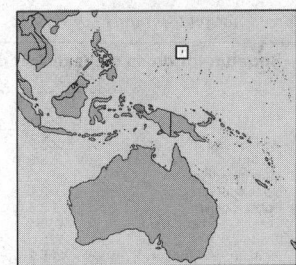

Area and population

Election Districts	area sq mi	area sq km	population[1] 1989 estimate
Agana	1	3	1,100
Agana Heights	1	3	4,000
Agat	10	26	4,900
Asan	6	16	2,500
Barrigada	9	23	9,500
Chalan Pago-Ordot	6	16	3,800
Dededo	30	78	28,800
Inarajan	19	49	2,500
Mangilao	10	26	8,300
Merizo	6	16	2,000
Mongmong-Toto-Maite	2	5	6,400
Piti	7	18	3,500
Santa Rita	17	44	11,200
Sinajana	1	3	3,000
Talofofo	17	44	2,400
Tamuning	6	16	16,600
Umatac	6	16	900
Yigo	35	91	12,600
Yona	20	52	5,200
TOTAL	209	541[2]	129,300[2]

Demography

Population (1989): 129,000.
Density (1989): persons per sq mi 617.2, persons per sq km 238.4.
Urban-rural (1980): urban[3] 39.5%; rural 60.5%.
Sex distribution (1985): male 54.31%; female 45.69%.
Age breakdown (1980): under 15, 34.9%; 15–29, 30.6%; 30–44, 19.4%; 45–59, 10.5%; 60–74, 3.9%; 75 and over, 0.7%.
Population projection: (2000) 165,000; (2010) 205,000.
Doubling time: 32 years.
Ethnic composition (1980): Chamorro 41.8%; Filipino 21.2%; German 2.1%; Korean 1.8%; Japanese 1.8%; other[4] 31.3%.
Religious affiliation (1980): Roman Catholic 79.5%; Protestant 17.3%; other 3.2%.
Major populated places (1980): Tamuning 8,862; Apra Harbor 5,633; Andersen Air Force Base 4,892; Mangilao 4,029.

Vital statistics

Birth rate per 1,000 population (1988): 26.5 (world avg. 27.1); (1986) legitimate 68.6%; illegitimate 31.4%.
Death rate per 1,000 population (1988): 4.2 (world avg. 9.9).
Natural increase rate per 1,000 population (1988): 22.3 (world avg. 17.2).
Total fertility rate (avg. births per childbearing woman; 1988): 3.1.
Marriage rate per 1,000 population (1987): 12.2.
Divorce rate per 1,000 population (1987): 10.2.
Life expectancy at birth (1988): male 71.7 years; female 71.7 years.
Major causes of death per 100,000 population (1986): diseases of the circulatory system 143.7; accidents, poisonings, and violence 58.1; malignant neoplasms (cancers) 46.0; diseases of the respiratory system 36.3; endocrinal and metabolic disorders 17.0; diseases of the digestive system 13.7.

National economy

Budget (1986). Revenue: U.S.$257,033,935 (local income taxes 40.0%, gross business receipt taxes 19.6%, special revenue funds 19.4%, revenue from United States agencies[5] 11.5%, other local taxes 3.8%). Expenditures: U.S.$219,845,645 (public education 30.1%, special projects 24.9%, general government 15.7%, law and public safety 12.5%, public health and community services 9.5%).
Tourism (1987): receipts from visitors U.S.$364,000,000; expenditures by nationals abroad, U.S.$304,000,000.
Land use (1987): forested 18.2%; meadows and pastures 14.5%; agricultural and under permanent cultivation 21.8%; other 45.5%.
Production. Agriculture, forestry, fishing (value of production in U.S.$ except as noted; 1986): watermelons 1,368,900, pineapples 628,102, cucumbers 591,300, bananas 371,565, cantaloupes 248,520, pepino melons 217,404, long beans 210,375, tomatoes 202,406, bitter melon 144,900, eggs 2,053,965; livestock (number of live animals) 2,845 pigs, 262 cattle, 173 goats; fish catch (metric tons; 1986) 650. Mining and quarrying (1983): sand and gravel. Manufacturing (value of gross business receipts in U.S.$; 1980): petroleum refining and related products 322,083,000; food processing 11,-742,000; printing and publishing 6,039,000; industrial and medical goods and materials 412,000. Construction (gross value of building and construction permits in U.S.$; 1988): residential 108,056,000; nonresidential 119,477,000. Energy production (consumption): electricity (kW-hr; 1986) 1,100,000,000 (1,100,000,000); coal, none (n.a.); crude petroleum (barrels; 1986) none (10,995,000); petroleum products (metric tons; 1986) 1,400,000 (820,000); natural gas, none (n.a.).
Public debt (external, outstanding): n.a.
Gross national product (at current market prices; 1985): U.S.$670,000,000 (U.S.$5,660 per capita).

Structure of gross business income and labour force

	1982 in value U.S.$'000,000	1982 % of total value	1988 labour force[6]	1988 % of labour force
Agriculture	1.4	0.2	150	0.3
Manufacturing	107.3	13.1	1,820	3.9
Construction	64.6	7.9	4,630	9.9
Trade	422.3	51.5	9,460	20.3
Transp. and commun.	45.3	5.5	2,900[7]	6.2
Finance	80.8	9.9	2,180	4.7
Pub. admin., defense	...	...	16,760	36.0
Services	99.6	12.2	8,720	18.7
TOTAL	819.2[2]	100.0[2]	46,620	100.0

Population economically active (1988): total 38,280[8]; activity rate of total population 30.3% (participation rates: over age 16, 63.8%; female 42.4%; unemployed 5.3%).

Price and earnings indexes (1985 = 100)

	1982	1983	1984	1985	1986	1987	1988
Consumer price index	85.5	88.5	96.3	100.0	102.4	107.2	112.8
Hourly earnings index	...	97.9	94.9	100.0	106.9	103.0	113.5

Household income and expenditure. Average household size (1980) 3.7; median annual income per household (1979) U.S.$16,203; sources of income: n.a.; expenditure (1978): housing 28.6%, food 24.1%, transportation 18.0%, clothing 10.6%, entertainment 5.1%, medical care 4.7%.

Foreign trade

Balance of trade (current prices)

	1978	1979	1980	1981	1982	1983
U.S.$'000	−236,227	−403,144	−483,141	...	...	−571,519
% of total	76.7%	82.5%	79.8%	...	...	87.9%

Imports (1983): U.S.$610,743,985 (mineral fuels 46.9%, of which crude petroleum 28.8%; machinery and transport equipment 19.1%, of which passenger cars 12.4%; food and live animals 12.0%, of which beef and veal 1.5%; beverages and tobacco 4.5%, of which cigarettes 1.3%; manufactured goods 4.4%; chemicals 2.3%). *Major import sources* (1984): United States 37.5%; Japan 24.7%; Hong Kong 4.6%; Taiwan 1.9%; Philippines 1.4%.
Exports (1983): U.S.$39,224,728 (clothing 16.9%; beverages and tobacco 12.0%, of which alcoholic beverages 4.4%, cigarettes 3.5%, nonalcoholic beverages 1.9%; machinery and transport equipment 11.4%; travel goods 3.0%; lubricating oils and greases 2.7%; fish and fish products 2.6%; cosmetics 2.6%; watches and watch cases 1.5%; cement 1.5%). *Major export destinations* (1984): Micronesia[9] 79.2%; Japan 9.9%; United States 7.2%.

Transport and communications

Transport. Railroads: none. Roads (1988): total length 419 mi, 674 km (paved 100%). Vehicles[10] (1986): passenger cars 55,147; trucks and buses 16,828. Merchant marine (1988): vessels (100 gross tons and over) 5, total deadweight tonnage, n.a.; surface cargo loaded, unloaded, or transshipped (1987) 1,138,400 metric tons. Air transport (1987): passenger arrivals 477,-491; passenger departures, n.a.; cargo loaded 6,898 metric tons; cargo unloaded 8,190 metric tons; airports (1989) with scheduled flights 1.
Communications. Daily newspapers (1986): total number 1; total circulation 18,076; circulation per 1,000 population 149. Radio (1988): total receivers 105,000 (1 per 1.2 persons). Television (1988): total receivers 83,000 (1 per 1.5 persons). Telephones (1987): 25,496[11] (1 per 4.9 persons).

Education and health

Education (1986–87)

	schools	teachers	students	student/teacher ratio
Primary (age 5–10)	31	822	14,471	17.6
Secondary (age 11–18)	24	944	15,281	16.2
Vocational	3	117	2,410	20.6
Higher	1	206	2,208	10.7

Educational attainment (1980). Percent of population age 25 and over having: primary education 21.3%; some secondary 13.1%; secondary 31.2%; college 34.4%. *Literacy* (1980): total population age 15 and over literate 66,-537 (96.4%); males literate 35,091 (96.4%); females literate 31,446 (96.5%).
Health (1986): physicians 147 (1 per 823 persons); hospital beds (1979) 223 (1 per 470 persons); infant mortality rate per 1,000 live births 9.4.
Food: daily per capita caloric intake, n.a.

Military

Total active duty U.S. personnel (1987): 11,768 (navy 65.2%, air force 33.6%, other 1.2%).

[1] Includes active-duty military personnel, U.S. Department of Defense employees, and dependents. [2] Detail does not add to total given because of rounding. [3] Places of 2,500 or more. [4] Includes various Pacific Island groups (mostly Micronesian) and persons of multiple ethnic origin. [5] Consists largely of federal income tax. [6] Employed persons only. [7] Includes public utilities. [8] Excludes nonimmigrant aliens and civilians living on military reservations. [9] Includes Commonwealth of Northern Marianas Islands, Federated States of Micronesia, Republic of Palau, and Marshall Islands. [10] Excludes military vehicles. [11] Number of primary lines.

Guatemala

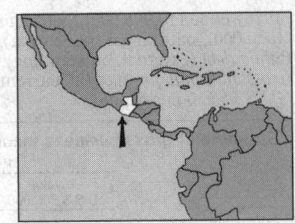

Official name: República de Guatemala (Republic of Guatemala).
Form of government: republic with one legislative house (Congress of the Republic [100]).
Head of state and government: President.
Capital: Guatemala City.
Official language: Spanish.
Official religion: none.
Monetary unit: 1 Guatemalan quetzal (Q) = 100 centavos; valuation (Oct. 2, 1989) 1 U.S.$ = Q 2.78; 1 £ = Q 4.50.

Area and population

Departments	Capitals	area sq mi	area sq km	population 1989 estimate
Alta Verapaz	Cobán	3,354	8,686	556,282
Baja Verapaz	Salamá	1,206	3,124	174,892
Chimaltenango	Chimaltenango	764	1,979	324,651
Chiquimula	Chiquimula	917	2,376	241,895
El Progreso	Progreso	742	1,922	104,057
Escuintla	Escuintla	1,693	4,384	510,733
Guatemala	Guatemala City	821	2,126	1,908,085
Huehuetenango	Huehuetenango	2,857	7,400	671,441
Izabal	Puerto Barrios	3,490	9,038	306,244
Jalapa	Jalapa	797	2,063	181,383
Jutiapa	Jutiapa	1,243	3,219	339,293
Petén	Ciudad Flores	13,843	35,854	227,481
Quetzaltenango	Quetzaltenango	753	1,951	527,501
Quiché	Santa Cruz	3,235	8,378	539,669
Retalhuleu	Retalhuleu	717	1,856	225,241
Sacatepéquez	Antigua Guatemala	180	465	169,833
San Marcos	San Marcos	1,464	3,791	663,074
Santa Rosa	Cuilapa	1,141	2,955	256,850
Sololá	Sololá	410	1,061	227,406
Suchitepéquez	Mazatenango	969	2,510	342,765
Totonicapán	Totonicapán	410	1,061	280,908
Zacapa	Zacapa	1,039	2,690	155,711
TOTAL		42,042[1]	108,889	8,935,395

Demography

Population (1989): 8,935,000.
Density (1989): persons per sq mi 212.5, persons per sq km 82.1.
Urban-rural (1987): urban 36.4%; rural 63.6%.
Sex distribution (1987): male 50.54%; female 49.46%.
Age breakdown (1985): under 15, 45.9%; 15–29, 26.5%; 30–44, 14.3%; 45–59, 8.6%; 60–74, 3.8%; 75 and over, 0.9%.
Population projection: (2000) 12,222,000; (2010) 15,827,000.
Doubling time: 26 years.
Ethnic composition (1983): Amerindian 55%; Ladino (Hispanic/Amerindian) 42%; white or black 3%.
Religious affiliation (1986): Roman Catholic c. 75%, of which Catholic/traditional syncretist c. 25%; Protestant (mostly fundamentalist) c. 25%.
Major cities (1989): Guatemala City 1,057,210; Quetzaltenango 88,769; Escuintla 60,673; Mazatenango 37,837; Puerto Barrios 37,766.

Vital statistics

Birth rate per 1,000 population (1987): 36.5 (world avg. 27.1).
Death rate per 1,000 population (1987): 9.5 (world avg. 9.9).
Natural increase rate per 1,000 population (1987): 27.0 (world avg. 17.2).
Total fertility rate (avg. births per childbearing woman; 1987): 5.1.
Marriage rate per 1,000 population (1985): 4.8.
Divorce rate per 1,000 population (1985): 0.2.
Life expectancy at birth (1987): male 58.0 years; female 62.0 years.
Major causes of death per 100,000 population (1984): infectious and parasitic diseases 211.5; diseases of the respiratory system 145.7, of which pneumonia 112.4; diseases of the circulatory system 57.2; malnutrition 45.3; homicide and other violence 35.1; ill-defined conditions 72.6.

National economy

Budget (1988). Revenue: Q 2,299,100,000 (tax revenue 78.0%, of which value-added taxes 21.6%, income taxes 18.0%, import duties 16.9%; non-tax revenue 12.5%; grants 9.4%). Expenditures: Q 2,584,000,000 (current expenditures 80.3%; development expenditures 19.7%).
Public debt (external, outstanding; 1987): U.S.$2,345,000,000.
Tourism: receipts from visitors (1988) U.S.$124,000,000; expenditures by nationals abroad (1987) U.S.$33,000,000.
Production (metric tons except as noted). Agriculture, forestry, fishing (1988): sugarcane 7,000,000, corn (maize) 1,217,000, bananas 470,000, coffee 162,000, seed cotton 125,000, dry beans 86,000, cardamom 12,800[2], lemongrass oil 987 hectolitres[3]; livestock (number of live animals) 2,140,-000 cattle, 875,000 pigs, 660,000 sheep; roundwood (1987) 7,184,000 cu m; fish catch (1987) 2,425, of which shrimps 1,145. Mining and quarrying: limestone (1986) 900,000; antimony (metal content; 1987) 1,900. Manufacturing (value added in Q '000,000; 1986): food products 334; drugs and medicines 138; beverages 106; textiles 78; rubber products 47. Construction (tender value in Q '000,000; 1985)[4]: residential 37.6; nonresidential 13.8. Energy production (consumption): electricity (kW-hr; 1987) 1,770,000,000 (1,770,000,000); coal, none (none); crude petroleum (barrels; 1987) 1,319,-000 (4,464,000); petroleum products (metric tons; 1987) 557,000 (864,000); natural gas, none (none).

Gross national product (1987): U.S.$6,839,000,000 (U.S.$810 per capita).

Structure of gross domestic product and labour force

	1988 in value[5] Q '000,000	1988 % of total value	1986–87 labour force	1986–87 % of labour force
Agriculture	803.2	25.6	1,365,251	49.8
Mining	8.8	0.3	2,735	0.1
Manufacturing	487.5	15.5	334,107	12.2
Construction	67.0	2.1	94,672	3.5
Public utilities	73.0	2.3	10,556	0.4
Transp. and commun.	230.5	7.3	51,904	1.9
Trade	772.5	24.6	357,279	13.0
Finance, real estate	285.9	9.1	30,699	1.1
Pub. admin., defense	215.4	6.9 }	394,807	14.4
Services	195.7	6.2 }		
Other	—	—[1]	98,051	3.6
TOTAL	3,139.5	100.0[1]	2,740,061	100.0

Population economically active (1986–87): total 2,740,061; activity rate of total population 33.6% (participation rates: age 15–64, 59.2%; female 24.5%; unemployed [1987] 11.7%[6]).

Price and earnings indexes (1985 = 100)

	1982	1983	1984	1985	1986	1987	1988
Consumer price index	77.9	81.5	84.3	100.0	136.9	153.8	170.5
Annual earnings index[7]	98.0	103.8	97.6	100.0	112.1	134.4	154.1

Household income and expenditure. Average household size (1981) 5.5[8]; income per household: n.a.; sources of income: n.a.; expenditure (1981): food 64.4%, housing and energy 16.0%, transportation and communications 7.0%, household furnishings 5.0%, clothing 3.1%.
Land use (1986): forested 37.5%; meadows and pastures 12.3%; agricultural and under permanent cultivation 17.0%; other 33.2%.

Foreign trade[9]

Balance of trade (current prices)

	1983	1984	1985	1986	1987	1988
Q '000,000	+134.9	−43.8	−22.5	+227.8	−355.2	−339.8
% of total	6.0%	1.9%	1.1%	11.5%	15.4%	13.7%

Imports (1988): Q 1,557,000,000 (machinery, equipment, and tools 22.2%, consumer goods 18.1%, petroleum 7.1%, construction materials 5.9%). Major import sources (1987): United States 40.5%; Japan 6.6%; West Germany 5.9%; Mexico 5.8%; El Salvador 5.0%.
Exports (1988): Q 1,073,400,000 (coffee 36.0%, sugar 7.3%, bananas 7.1%, chemical products 6.9%, cardamom 3.5%). Major export destinations (1987): United States 50.7%; West Germany 6.6%; El Salvador 6.2%; Italy 4.8%; Costa Rica 3.3%.

Transport and communications

Transport. Railroads (1987)[10]: route length 561 mi, 903 km; passenger-mi 31,015,000, passenger-km 49,914,000; short ton-mi cargo 51,039,000, metric ton-km cargo 74,517,000. Roads (1986): total length 10,700 mi, 17,300 km (paved 17%). Vehicles (1983): passenger cars 188,100; trucks and buses 58,500. Merchant marine (1988): vessels (100 gross tons and over) 5; total deadweight tonnage 6,450. Air transport (1987)[11]: passenger-mi 102,300,-000, passenger-km 164,700,000; short ton-mi cargo 7,800,000, metric ton-km cargo 11,388,000; airports (1989) with scheduled flights 3.
Communications. Daily newspapers (1986): total number 9; total circulation 225,500[12]; circulation per 1,000 population 28. Radio (1988): 407,473 receivers (1 per 21 persons). Television (1988): 475,000 receivers (1 per 18 persons). Telephones (1985): 128,179 (1 per 63 persons).

Education and health

Education (1987)

	schools	teachers	students	student/teacher ratio
Primary (age 7–12)	8,481	31,441	1,097,851	34.9
Secondary (age 13–18) } Voc., teacher tr. }	...	16,332	241,053	14.8
Higher[13]	1	3,007	50,000	16.6

Educational attainment (1981). Percent of population age 25 and over having: no formal schooling 52.9%; primary education 34.5%; incomplete secondary 7.1%; complete secondary and higher 2.1%; unknown 3.4%. Literacy (1985): total population age 15 and over literate 3,079,000 (55.0%); males literate 1,790,000 (62.6%); females literate 1,289,000 (47.1%).
Health: physicians (1984) 3,544 (1 per 2,256 persons); hospital beds (1985) 9,575 (1 per 832 persons); infant mortality rate per 1,000 live births (1988) 65.0.
Food (1984–86): daily per capita caloric intake 2,297 (vegetable products 92%, animal products 8%); (1984) 105% of FAO recommended minimum.

Military

Total active duty personnel (1988): 42,050 (army 95.1%, navy 2.9%, air force 2.0%). Military expenditure as percent of GNP (1987): 1.5% (world 5.4%); per capita expenditure U.S.$12.

[1]Detail does not add to total given because of rounding. [2]Export only. [3]1985. [4]Authorized construction in Guatemala City metropolitan area. [5]At 1958 prices. [6]Excludes underemployed (1987) 34.0%. [7]Based on employees entitled to social security. [8]Excludes vacant households. [9]Import figures are f.o.b. in balance of trade and c.i.f. for commodities and trading partners. [10]Guatemala Railways only. [11]Aviateca Airlines only. [12]Five newspapers only. [13]University of San Carlos only.

Guinea

Official name: République de Guinée
(Republic of Guinea).
Form of government: interim military
regime ruling through the Military
Committee for National Recovery
(CMRN [20]).
Head of state and government:
President (and Head of Military
Committee for National Recovery).
Capital: Conakry.
Official language: French.
Official religion: none.
Monetary unit: 1 Guinean franc[1]
(GF) = 100 cauris; valuation (Sept. 30,
1989) 1 U.S.$ = GF 615.00;
1 £ = GF 999.50.

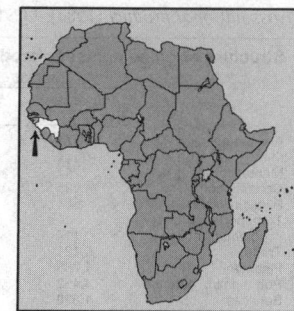

Area and population

Regions	Capitals	area sq mi	area sq km	population 1983 census
Beyla	Beyla	6,738	17,452	161,347
Boffa	Boffa	1,932	5,003	141,719
Boké[2]	Boké	3,881	10,053	225,207
Conakry	Conakry	119	308	705,280
Coyah (Dubréka)	Coyah	2,153	5,576	134,190
Dabola	Dabola	2,317	6,000	97,986
Dalaba	Dalaba	1,313	3,400	132,802
Dinguiraye	Dinguiraye	4,247	11,000	133,502
Faranah[2]	Faranah	4,788	12,400	142,923
Forécariah	Forécariah	1,647	4,265	116,464
Fria	Fria	840	2,175	70,413
Gaoual	Gaoual	4,440	11,500	135,657
Guéckédou	Guéckédou	1,605	4,157	204,757
Kankan	Kankan	7,104	18,400	229,861
Kérouané	Kérouané	3,070	7,950	106,872
Kindia	Kindia	3,409	8,828	216,052
Kissidougou	Kissidougou	3,425	8,872	183,236
Koubia	Koubia	571	1,480	98,053
Koundara	Koundara	2,124	5,500	94,216
Kouroussa	Kouroussa	4,647	12,035	136,926
Labé	Labé	973	2,520	253,214
Lélouma	Lélouma	830	2,150	138,467
Lola	Lola	1,629	4,219	106,654
Macenta	Macenta	3,363	8,710	193,109
Mali	Mali	3,398	8,800	210,889
Mamou	Mamou	2,378	6,160	190,525
Mandiana	Mandiana	5,000	12,950	136,317
Nzérékoré	Nzérékoré	1,460	3,781	216,355
Pita	Pita	1,544	4,000	227,912
Siguiri	Siguiri	7,626	19,750	209,164
Télimélé	Télimélé	3,119	8,080	243,256
Tougué	Tougué	2,394	6,200	113,272
Yomou	Yomou	843	2,183	74,417
TOTAL		94,926[3]	245,857	5,781,014

Demography

Population (1989): 6,705,000.
Density (1989): persons per sq mi 70.6, persons per sq km 27.3.
Urban–rural (1986): urban 22.9%; rural 77.1%.
Sex distribution (1986): male 49.51%; female 50.49%.
Age breakdown (1985): under 15, 43.1%; 15–29, 26.2%; 30–44, 16.2%; 45–59, 9.6%; 60–74, 4.2%; 75 and over, 0.7%.
Population projection: (2000) 8,879,000; (2010) 11,451,000.
Doubling time: 28 years.
Ethnic composition (1983): Fulani 38.6%; Malinke 23.2%; Susu 11.0%; Kissi 6.0%; Kpelle 4.6%; other 16.6%.
Religious affiliation (1988): Muslim 85.0%; traditional beliefs 5.0%; Christian 1.5%, other 8.5%.
Major cities (1983): Conakry 705,280; Kankan 88,760; Labé 65,439; Kindia 55,904.

Vital statistics

Birth rate per 1,000 population (1985–90): 46.6 (world avg. 27.1).
Death rate per 1,000 population (1985–90): 21.9 (world avg. 9.9).
Natural increase rate per 1,000 population (1985–90): 24.7 (world avg. 17.2).
Total fertility rate (avg. births per childbearing woman; 1985–90): 6.2.
Life expectancy at birth (1985–90): male 40.6 years; female 43.8 years.
Major causes of death per 100,000 population: n.a.; however, major diseases include malaria, venereal disease, tuberculosis, intestinal infections, measles, and schistosomiasis.

National economy

Budget (1989). Revenue: GF 377,100,000,000 (domestic receipts 51.7%, of which mineral sector 28.8%; external receipts 48.3%, of which investment borrowing 24.0%, investment grants 11.9%, deficit borrowing 9.9%, deficit grants 2.5%). Expenditures: GF 381,000,000,000 (capital spending 43.8%; public debt 24.3%; personnel 16.2%; provision of services 13.2%; subsidies 2.2%).
Public debt (external, outstanding; 1987): U.S.$1,616,000,000.
Tourism: n.a.
Production (metric tons except as noted). Agriculture, forestry, fishing (1987): roots and tubers 663,000 (of which cassava 500,000, yams 61,000), rice 480,000, vegetables and melons 420,000, plantains 350,000, sugarcane 200,000, citrus fruit 163,000, bananas 107,000, peanuts (groundnuts) 75,000, pulses 50,000, corn (maize) 45,000, palm kernels 40,000, pineapples 20,-

000, coconuts 15,000, coffee 15,000, eggs 13,860; livestock (number of live animals) 1,800,000 cattle, 460,000 goats, 460,000 sheep, 50,000 pigs, 13,000,-000 chickens; roundwood 4,455,000 cu m; fish catch 30,000. Mining and quarrying (1988): bauxite 16,300,000; alumina 570,000; diamonds 200,000 carats. Manufacturing (value of production in GS '000; 1985): corrugated and sheet iron 571,081; plastics 462,242; tobacco products 375,154; cement 326,138; printed matter 216,511; fruit juice 75,763; beer 69,934; matches 22,449. Construction: n.a. Energy production (consumption): electricity (kW-hr; 1987) 500,000,000 (500,000,000); coal, none (n.a.); crude petroleum, none (n.a.); petroleum products (metric tons; 1987) none (314,000); natural gas, none (n.a.).
Gross national product (1986): U.S.$1,523,000,000 (U.S.$240 per capita).

Structure of gross domestic product and labour force

	1986 in value U.S.$'000,000	1986 % of total value	1985 labour force	1985 % of labour force
Agriculture	745	44.7	2,236,000	78.6
Mining	376	22.6		
Manufacturing	21	1.3	268,000	9.4
Construction	51	3.1		
Public utilities	13	0.8		
Transp. and commun.	30	1.8		
Trade	310	18.6		
Finance	77	4.6	342,000	12.0
Pub. admin., defense				
Services	42	2.5		
TOTAL	1,665	100.0	2,846,000	100.0

Population economically active (1985): total 2,846,000; activity rate of total population 46.8% (participation rates: ages 15–64, 76.2%; female 40.8%; unemployed, n.a.).
Household income and expenditure. Average household size (1980) 4.7; average annual income per capita (1984) GS 7,660 (U.S.$305); sources of income: n.a.; expenditure (1985): food 61.5%, health care 11.2%, clothing and footwear 7.9%, housing and energy 7.3%, transportation 5.1%, recreation 4.2%, durable goods 2.9%.
Land use (1987): forested 40.5%; meadows and pastures 12.2%; agricultural and under permanent cultivation 6.4%; other 40.9%.

Foreign trade[4]

Balance of trade (current prices)

	1983	1984	1985	1986	1987	1988
U.S.$'000,000	+123	+94	+111	+104	+116	+57
% of total	13.9%	9.7%	11.0%	10.3%	11.0%	5.5%

Imports (1988): U.S.$491,200,000 (intermediate goods 43.9%, capital goods 17.0%, petroleum products 13.7%, food products 12.8%, consumer goods 12.6%). *Major import sources* (1987)[5]: France 31.4%; United States 8.4%; Belgium–Luxembourg 7.9%; West Germany 5.7%; Italy 5.1%; Spain 4.8%.
Exports (1988): U.S.$548,100,000 (bauxite and alumina 78.1%, diamonds 10.8%, gold 4.5%, coffee 3.1%, fish 0.6%). *Major export destinations* (1987)[5]: United States 18.8%; Spain 10.4%; West Germany 9.5%; Italy 9.1%; Belgium–Luxembourg 8.4%; Cameroon 6.4%.

Transport and communications

Transport. Railroads (1986): route length 584 mi, 940 km. Roads (1988): total length 17,600 mi, 28,400 km (paved 4%). Vehicles (1982): passenger cars 9,948; trucks and buses 9,992. Merchant marine (1988): vessels (100 gross tons and over) 19; total deadweight tonnage 2,927. Air transport (1986): passenger-mi 17,873,000, passenger-km 28,764,000; short ton-mi cargo 1,684,000, metric ton-km cargo 2,458,000; airports (1989) with scheduled flights 2.
Communications. Daily newspapers (1988): none. Radio (1986): 200,000 receivers (1 per 31 persons). Television (1988): 50,000 receivers (1 per 131 persons). Telephones (1981): 15,800 (1 per 310 persons).

Education and health

Education (1986–87)

	schools	teachers	students	student/ teacher ratio
Primary (age 7–12)	2,204	7,493	270,140	36.0
Secondary (age 13–18)	225	3,577	76,493	21.4
Voc., teacher tr.	31	758	4,929	6.5
Higher	23	946	7,470	7.9

Educational attainment, n.a. *Literacy* (1985): total population age 15 and over literate 874,000 (28.3%); males literate 603,000 (39.7%); females literate 271,000 (17.2%).
Health (1988): physicians 672 (1 per 9,732 persons); hospital beds 3,382 (1 per 1,934 persons); infant mortality rate per 1,000 live births (1985–90) 147.
Food (1984–86): daily per capita caloric intake 1,782 (vegetable products 96%, animal products 4%); 77% of FAO recommended minimum.

Military

Total active duty personnel (1989): 9,900 (army 85.9%, navy 6.0%, air force 8.1%). *Military expenditure as percent of GNP* (1984): 3.1% (world 5.7%); per capita expenditure U.S.$7.

[1]In January 1986 the Guinean syli (GS) was replaced at par by the Guinean franc (GF), and its value was depreciated by 92.5% in terms of foreign currency. [2]The provinces of Boké and Faranah were abolished by presidential decree in January 1988. [3]Detail does not add to total given because of rounding. [4]Imports c.i.f.; exports f.o.b. [5]Detail excludes trade with the Eastern bloc (mostly with the U.S.S.R.) and most oil imports.

Guinea-Bissau

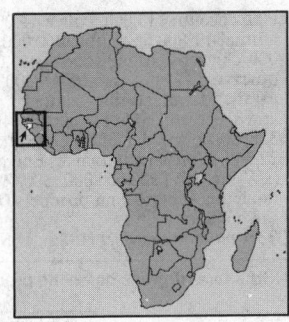

Official name: Républica da Guiné-Bissau (Republic of Guinea-Bissau).
Form of government: single-party republic with one legislative house (National People's Assembly [150]).
Head of state and government: President.
Capital: Bissau.
Official language: Portuguese.
Official religion: none.
Monetary unit: 1 Guinea-Bissau peso (PG) = 100 centavos; valuation (Oct. 2, 1989) 1 U.S.$ = PG 650; 1 £ = PG 1,052.

Area and population

Regions	Capitals	area sq mi	area sq km	population 1979 census[1]
Bafatá	Bafatá	2,309	5,981	115,656
Biombo[2]	Bissau	324	840	51,796
Bolama	Bolama	1,013	2,624	25,449
Cacheu	Cacheu	1,998	5,175	127,514
Gabú	Gabú	3,533	9,150	103,683
Oio	Farim	2,086	5,403	131,271
Quinara	Fulacunda	1,212	3,138	35,567
Tombali	Catió	1,443	3,736	55,088
Autonomous Sector				
Bissau[2]		30	78	107,281
TOTAL		13,948	36,125	753,305

Demography

Population (1989): 953,000.
Density (1989): persons per sq mi 68.3, persons per sq km 26.4.
Urban–rural (1986): urban 27.8%; rural 72.2%.
Sex distribution (1986): male 48.34%; female 51.66%.
Age breakdown (1985): under 15, 42.9%; 15–29, 25.6%; 30–44, 15.7%; 45–59, 10.2%; 60–74, 4.7%; 75 and over, 0.9%.
Population projection: (2000) 1,200,000; (2010) 1,480,000.
Doubling time: 33 years.
Ethnic composition (1979): Balante 27.2%; Fulani 22.9%; Malinke 12.2%; Mandyako 10.6%; Pepel 10.0%; other 17.1%.
Religious affiliation (1986): traditional beliefs 65%; Muslim 30%; Christian 5%.
Major cities (1979): Bissau (1988) 125,000; Bafatá 13,429; Gabú 7,803; Mansôa 5,390; Catió 5,179.

Vital statistics

Birth rate per 1,000 population (1985–90): 40.8 (world avg. 27.1); legitimate, n.a.; illegitimate, n.a.
Death rate per 1,000 population (1985–90): 20.0 (world avg. 9.9).
Natural increase rate per 1,000 population (1985–90): 20.8 (world avg. 17.2).
Total fertility rate (avg. births per childbearing woman; 1985–90): 5.4.
Marriage rate per 1,000 population: n.a.
Divorce rate per 1,000 population: n.a.
Life expectancy at birth (1985–90): male 43.4 years; female 46.6 years.
Major causes of death per 100,000 population: n.a.; however, major diseases include tuberculosis of the respiratory system, whooping cough, typhoid fever, bacillary dysentery and amebiasis, malaria, pneumonia, and meningococcal infections.

National economy

Budget (1987). Revenue: PG 34,596,000,000 (grants from abroad 64.9%; tax revenue 22.6%, of which excise tax 10.6%, export duties 9.8%; nontax revenue 12.5%). Expenditures: PG 48,822,000,000 (economic affairs 40.0%, of which agriculture, forestry, and fishing 20.1%; general public services 25.5%; health 5.4%; education 5.2%; defense 4.4%).
Public debt (external, outstanding; 1987): U.S.$390,700,000.
Tourism: n.a.; however, the island of Bubaque is being developed as a tourist resort, with 110 rooms in 1979; work began in 1985 on a 180-room hotel in Bissau.
Land use (1987): forested 38.1%; meadows and pastures 38.4%; agricultural and under permanent cultivation 11.9%; other 11.6%.
Production (metric tons except as noted). Agriculture, forestry, fishing (1988): rice 145,000, fruit 42,000, roots and tubers (sweet potatoes and cassava) 40,000, sorghum 35,000, peanuts (groundnuts) 30,000, coconuts 25,000, plantains 25,000, millet 25,000, vegetables 20,000, cashews (1989) 18,000, corn (maize) 15,000, palm kernels 14,000, sugarcane 6,000, copra 5,000, seed cotton 5,000; livestock (number of live animals) 340,000 cattle, 290,000 pigs, 210,000 goats, 205,000 sheep, 1,000,000 chickens; roundwood (1987) 563,000 cu m; fish catch (1987) 3,500, of which crustaceans 947. Mining and quarrying: n.a.; however, prospecting for bauxite, petroleum, and phosphates was being carried out in the late-1980s. Manufacturing (in PG '000,000; 1982): beverages 143.7, of which beer 122.3, orangeade and lemonade 16.5; clothing 14.0[3]; peanut oil 7.0; palm oil 2.4. Construction (in PG '000,000; 1982): total buildings 2.5. Energy production (consumption): electricity (kW-hr; 1987) 14,000,000 (14,000,000); coal, none (none); crude petroleum, none (none); petroleum products (metric tons; 1987) none (39,-000); natural gas, none (none).

Gross national product (1987): U.S.$152,000,000 (U.S.$170 per capita).

Structure of gross domestic product and labour force

	1986 in value Esc '000,000[4]	1986 % of total value	1979 labour force	1979 % of labour force
Agriculture	14,774	51.5	153,069	71.9
Mining	416	1.4	162	0.1
Manufacturing			2,905	1.4
Construction	525	1.8	1,667	0.8
Public utilities	624	2.2	162	0.1
Transportation and communications	117	0.4	2,372	1.1
Trade	5,121	17.8	5,085	2.4
Finance	1,288	4.5	162	0.1
Pub. admin., defense	4,452	15.5	26,194	12.3
Services	1,398	4.9	21,232[5]	10.0[5]
Other	—		—	
TOTAL	28,715	100.0	213,010	100.0[6]

Population economically active (1988): total 279,081; activity rate of total population 30.0% (participation rates: ages 15–64 [1979] 41.0%; female 3.6%; unemployed, n.a.).

Price and earnings indexes (1985 = 100)

	1980	1981	1982	1983	1984	1985	1986
Consumer price index[7]	...	...	...	35.4	60.4	100.0	145.8
Annual earnings index	...	...	...	50.8	75.6	100.0	129.9

Household income and expenditure. Average household size (1981) 4.1; income per household: n.a.; sources of income: n.a.; expenditure: n.a.

Foreign trade

Balance of trade (current prices)

	1981	1982	1983	1984	1985	1986
U.S.$'000,000	−38.1	−49.7	−49.8	−42.7	−51.4	−43.1
% of total	57.8%	67.8%	74.0%	55.1%	68.9%	69.2%

Imports (1985): U.S.$63,000,000 (food, beverages, and tobacco 23.3%; crude petroleum and petroleum products 12.5%; other 64.2%). *Major import sources* (1987): Portugal 20.1%; Italy 14.1%; The Netherlands 9.6%; Thailand 6.8%; Sweden 6.2%; France 5.0%; Japan 5.0%.
Exports (1985): PG 11,600,000 (cashews 41.4%; fish and crustaceans 27.6%; peanuts [groundnuts] 16.4%; palm kernels 8.6%; wood products 3.4%). *Major export destinations* (1987): Portugal 42.2%; France 17.2%; Belgium–Luxembourg 8.7%; The Netherlands 7.8%; West Germany 7.4%; Italy 4.1%; Spain 3.9%.

Transport and communications

Transport. Railroads: none. Roads (1983): total length 3,143 mi, 5,058 km (paved, 8%). Vehicles (1982): private motor vehicles 4,100. Merchant marine (1988): vessels (100 gross tons and over) 17; total deadweight tonnage 2,846. Air transport (1985): passenger-mi 6,000,000, passenger-km 9,000,-000; short ton-mi cargo 700,000, metric ton-km cargo 1,000,000; airports (1989) with scheduled flights 1.
Communications. Daily newspapers (1986): total number 1; total circulation 6,000; circulation per 1,000 population 7.0. Radio (1988): total number of receivers 31,200 (1 per 30 persons). Television: none. Telephones (1986): 3,000 (1 per 297 persons).

Education and health

Education (1984–85)

	schools	teachers	students	student/ teacher ratio
Primary (age 7–13)	668	3,153	81,444	25.8
Secondary (age 13–18)	12	650	11,710	18.0
Voc., teacher tr.	4	107	1,027	9.6

Educational attainment (1979). Percent of population age 7 and over having: no formal schooling or knowledge of reading and writing 90.4%; primary education 7.9%; secondary 1.0%; technical 0.5%; higher 0.2%. *Literacy* (1985): total population age 15 and over literate, c. 157,000 (31.4%); males literate, c. 112,000 (46.2%); females literate, c. 45,000 (17.3%).
Health: physicians (1985) 122 (1 per 7,164 persons); hospital beds (1983) 1,593 (1 per 526 persons); infant mortality rate per 1,000 live births (1985–90) 132.
Food (1984–86): daily per capita caloric intake 2,278 (vegetable products 93%, animal products 7%); 84% of FAO recommended minimum requirement.

Military

Total active duty personnel (1989): 7,200 (army 94.4%, navy 4.2%, air force 1.4%). *Military expenditure as percent of GNP* (1987): 3.3% (world 5.4%); per capita expenditure U.S.$4.

[1]Preliminary. [2]Biombo region excludes Bissau city. [3]Production figure for first three quarters only. [4]Esc is the abbreviation for Portuguese escudo. [5]Not adequately defined. [6]Detail does not add to total given because of rounding. [7]Guinea-Bissau has no official consumer price index. Index cited is based on the price of rice, the main staple.

Guyana

Official name: Co-operative Republic of Guyana.
Form of government: unitary multiparty republic with one legislative house (National Assembly [65[1]]).
Head of state and government: President assisted by Prime Minister.
Capital: Georgetown.
Official language: English.
Official religion: none.
Monetary unit: 1 Guyana dollar (G$) = 100 cents; valuation (Oct. 2, 1989) 1 U.S.$ = G$30.00; 1 £ = G$48.54.

Area and population

Administrative Regions	Capitals	area sq mi	area sq km	population 1986 estimate[2]
Region 1 (Barima/Waini)	Mabaruma	7,853	20,339	18,516
Region 2 (Pomeroon/Supenaam)	Anna Regina	2,392	6,195	41,966
Region 3 (Essequibo Islands/West Demerara)	Vreed-en-Hoop	1,450	3,755	102,760
Region 4 (Demerara/Mahaica)	Paradise	862	2,233	310,758
Region 5 (Mahaica/Berbice)	Fort Wellington	1,610	4,170	55,556
Region 6 (East Berbice/Corentyne)	New Amsterdam	13,998	36,255	148,967
Region 7 (Cuyuni/Mazaruni)	Bartica	18,229	47,213	17,941
Region 8 (Potaro/Siparuni)	Mahdia	7,742	20,052	5,672
Region 9 (Upper Takutu/Upper Essequibo)	Lethem	22,313	57,790	15,338
Region 10 (Upper Demerara/Berbice)	Linden	6,595	17,081	38,598
TOTAL		83,044	215,083	756,072

Demography

Population (1989): 754,000.
Density (1989): persons per sq mi 9.1, persons per sq km 3.5.
Urban–rural (1987): urban 31.1%; rural 68.9%.
Sex distribution (1985): male 50.16%; female 49.84%.
Age breakdown (1985): under 15, 37.5%; 15–29, 31.9%; 30–44, 15.8%; 45–59, 8.8%; 60–74, 4.8%; 75 and over, 1.2%.
Population projection: (2000) 809,000; (2010) 868,000.
Doubling time: 35 years[3].
Ethnic composition (1980): East Indian 51.4%; black (African Negro and Bush Negro) 30.5%; mixed 11.0%; Amerindian 5.3%, of which Carib 3.7%, Arawak 1.4%; Chinese 0.2%; white, mostly Portuguese, 0.1%; other 1.5%.
Religious affiliation (1980): Christian 42.4%, of which Protestant 30.5% (including Anglican 14.3%), Roman Catholic 11.4%; Hindu 37.1%; Muslim 8.7%; nonreligious 3.7%; other and not stated 8.1%.
Major cities (1985): Georgetown 200,000; Linden 35,000; New Amsterdam 25,000; Corriverton 13,718[4]; Bartica 6,223[4].

Vital statistics

Birth rate per 1,000 population (1985–90): 25.0 (world avg. 27.1); legitimate, n.a.; illegitimate, n.a.
Death rate per 1,000 population (1985–90): 5.0 (world avg. 9.9).
Natural increase rate per 1,000 population (1985–90): 20.0 (world avg. 17.2).
Total fertility rate (avg. births per childbearing woman; 1985–90): 2.8.
Marriage rate per 1,000 population: n.a.
Divorce rate per 1,000 population: n.a.
Life expectancy at birth (1985–90): male 67.3 years; female 72.3 years.
Major causes of death per 100,000 population (1984): diseases of the circulatory system 163.5, of which cerebrovascular disease 63.8; diseases of the digestive system 59.7; accidents and violence 45.6; diseases of the respiratory sytem 32.2.

National economy

Budget (1988). Revenue: G$1,844,400,000 (tax revenue 79.5%, of which consumption taxes 18.4%, taxes on companies 14.1%, personal income taxes 8.0%; external grants 10.9%; nontax revenue 9.5%). Expenditures: G$3,919,100,000 (current expenditure 72.6%, of which debt amortization 41.8%; development expenditure 27.4%).
Production (metric tons except as noted). Agriculture, forestry, fishing (1988): raw sugar 172,700, rice 132,100, coconuts 45,000, roots and tubers 31,000, plantains 25,000, bananas 18,000, oranges 14,000, pineapples 6,000; livestock (number of live animals) 210,000 cattle, 185,000 pigs, 120,000 sheep, 15,000,000 chickens; roundwood 125,000 cu m; fish catch 41,617[5], of which shrimps 1,643[5]. Mining and quarrying (1988): bauxite 1,300,000, of which calcined bauxite 400,800; gold 18,800 troy oz; diamonds 4,200 carats. Manufacturing (1985): rum 179,000 hectolitres; beer 80,000 hectolitres; cigarettes 467,000,000 units; other products include clothing and pharmaceuticals. Construction: n.a. Energy production (consumption): electricity (kW-hr; 1987) 385,000,000 (385,000,000); coal, none (none); crude petroleum, none (none); petroleum products (metric tons; 1987) none (330,000); natural gas, none (none).
Household income and expenditure. Average household size (1980) 5.1; income per household: n.a.; sources of income (1974): wages and salaries 73.0%, transfer payments 6.3%, other 20.7%; expenditure (1970)[6]: food, beverages, and tobacco 42.5%, rent and water 21.4%, clothing and footwear 8.6%, education and recreation 6.4%, fuel and light 5.2%, other 15.9%.
Gross national product (at current market prices; 1987): U.S.$310,000,000 (U.S.$380 per capita).

Structure of gross domestic product and labour force

	1988 in value G$'000,000	1988 % of total value	1980 labour force	1980 % of labour force
Agriculture, fishing	1,085	26.2	50,316	20.4
Mining	360	8.7	9,669	3.9
Manufacturing	312[7]	7.5[7]	28,980	11.8
Construction	246	6.0	7,024	2.8
Public utilities	[7]	[7]	2,850	1.2
Transportation and communications	299	7.2	9,412	3.8
Trade	290	7.0	15,231	6.2
Finance	250	6.1	2,944	1.2
Pub. admin., defense	633	15.3	29,948	12.1
Services	125	3.0	29,295	11.9
Other	538[8]	13.0[8]	61,002[9]	24.7[9]
TOTAL	4,138	100.0	246,671	100.0

Population economically active (1987): total 270,074; activity rate of total population 35.7% (participation rates: ages 15–64, 60.4%; female 29.9%; unemployed [1986] 29.9%).

Price and earnings indexes (1985 = 100)

	1982	1983	1984	1985	1986	1987	1988
Consumer price index	61.3	69.4	86.9	100.0	107.9	138.9	200.2[10]
Weekly earnings index	...	...	...	...	...	...	...

Public debt (external, outstanding; 1987): U.S.$874,000,000.
Tourism: receipts from visitors (1987) U.S.$24,000,000; expenditures by nationals abroad (1983) U.S.$11,000,000.
Land use (1986): forested 83.2%; meadows and pastures 6.2%; agricultural and under permanent cultivation 2.5%; other 8.1%.

Foreign trade[11, 12]

Balance of trade (current prices)						
	1983	1984	1985	1986	1987	1988
G$'000,000	−170.8	−13.6	−178.1	−49.8	−218.6	+157.4
% of total	13.1%	0.8%	9.2%	2.5%	4.4%	3.5%

Imports (1985): G$1,053,500,000 (fuels and lubricants 44.3%, capital goods 17.8%, consumer goods 10.3%). *Major import sources* (1987): United States 29.9%; United Kingdom 12.6%; Japan 4.5%; Trinidad and Tobago 3.4%; not specified Western Hemisphere 21.9%.
Exports (1985[13]): G$875,400,000 (calcined bauxite 34.4%, sugar 31.2%, dried bauxite 11.6%, rice 6.3%, rum 3.2%, shrimps 2.0%, timber 2.0%). *Major export destinations* (1987): United Kingdom 34.5%; United States 22.9%; Canada 9.7%; West Germany 5.0%; East Germany 3.8%.

Transport and communications

Transport. Railroads: length (1985) 65 mi, 109 km; passenger-mi, none; short ton-mi cargo, n.a. Roads (1985): total length 5,524 mi, 8,890 km (paved 9%). Vehicles (1985): passenger cars 25,541; trucks and buses 7,648. Merchant marine (1988): vessels (100 gross tons and over) 75; total deadweight tonnage 13,261. Air transport (1985): passenger-mi 104,000,000, passenger-km 168,000,000; short ton-mi cargo 12,000,000, metric ton-km cargo 18,000,000; airports (1989) with scheduled flights 1.
Communications. Daily newspapers (1988): total number 1; total circulation 58,000; circulation per 1,000 population 77. Radio (1988): total number of receivers 307,500 (1 per 2.5 persons). Television (1988): total number of receivers 40,000 (1 per 19 persons). Telephones (1987): 30,311 (1 per 25 persons).

Education and health

Education (1986–87)	schools	teachers	students	student/ teacher ratio
Primary (age 6–11)	425	3,948[14]	134,679	...
Secondary (age 12–17)	93	2,087	73,418	...
Voc., teacher tr.	5	...	...	...
Higher	1	401	1,796	4.5

Educational attainment (1980). Percent of population age 25 and over having: no formal schooling 8.1%; primary education 72.8%; secondary 17.3%; higher 1.8%. *Literacy* (1985): total population age 15 and over literate, c. 453,000 (95.9%); males literate, c. 230,000 (97.0%); females literate, c. 223,000 (94.8%).
Health (1987): physicians 142 (1 per 5,307 persons); hospital beds (1985) 3,666 (1 per 206 persons); infant mortality rate per 1,000 live births 44.0.
Food (1984–86): daily per capita caloric intake 2,456 (vegetable products 89%, animal products 11%); 108% of FAO recommended minimum requirement.

Military

Total active duty personnel (1989): 5,450 (army 91.7%, navy 2.8%, air force 5.5%). *Military expenditure as percent of GNP* (1985): 9.3% (world 5.7%); per capita expenditure U.S.$32.

[1]Includes 12 seats not popularly elected.   [2]Sample survey.   [3]Net migration nearly equals natural-increase rate.   [4]1980.   [5]1987.   [6]Weights of consumer price index components for Georgetown, New Amsterdam, and Linden only.   [7]Manufacturing includes Public utilities.   [8]Indirect taxes less subsidies.   [9]Represents not stated.   [10]Average of 2nd and 3rd quarters.   [11]Imports c.i.f.; exports f.o.b.   [12]Trade statistics are difficult to evaluate because of widespread smuggling.   [13]Domestic exports (1988): G$2,436,400,000 (bauxite 32.8%, sugar 27.8%, shrimps 9.4%, gold 7.5%, rice 5.7%).   [14]1985–86.

Haiti

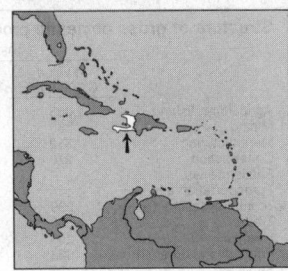

Official name: Repiblik Dayti (Haitian Creole): République d'Haïti (French) (Republic of Haiti).
Form of government: military regime.
Head of state and government: President.
Capital: Port-au-Prince.
Official languages: Haitian Creole; French.
Official religion: none[1].
Monetary unit: 1 gourde (G) = 100 centimes; valuation (Oct. 2, 1989) 1 U.S.$ = G 5.00; 1 £ = G 8.09.

Area and population

Departements	Capitals	area sq mi	area sq km	population 1987 estimate
Artibonite	Gonaïves	1,750	4,532	789,019
Centre	Hinche	1,429	3,700	393,217
Grande Anse	Jérémie	1,268	3,284	514,962
Nord	Cap-Haïtien	790	2,045	602,336
Nord-Est	Fort-Liberté	676	1,752	197,669
Nord-Ouest	Port-de-Paix	899	2,330	320,632
Ouest	Port-au-Prince	1,795	4,649	1,808,274
Sud	Les Cayes	1,117	2,894	526,420
Sud-Est	Jacmel	855	2,215	379,273
TOTAL		10,579[2]	27,400[2, 3]	5,531,802[4]

Demography

Population (1989): 5,520,000.
Density (1989): persons per sq mi 521.8, persons per sq km 201.5.
Urban–rural (1987): urban 26.0%; rural 74.0%.
Sex distribution (1982): male 48.48%; female 51.52%.
Age breakdown (1982): under 15, 39.2%; 15–29, 26.9%; 30–44, 15.6%; 45–59, 10.0%; 60–74, 5.4%; 75 and over, 2.9%.
Population projection: (2000) 6,338,000; (2010) 7,187,000.
Doubling time: 33 years.
Ethnic composition (1985): black 95.0%; mulatto 4.9%; white 0.1%.
Religious affiliation (1982): Roman Catholic 80.3%[5]; Protestant 15.8%, of which Baptist 9.7%, Pentecostal 3.6%; nonreligious 1.2%; other 2.7%.
Major cities (1987): Port-au-Prince 472,895; Cap-Haïtien 72,161; Gonaïves 37,034; Les Cayes 35,829; Pétionville 35,333[6].

Vital statistics

Birth rate per 1,000 population (1987): 34.0 (world avg. 27.1).
Death rate per 1,000 population (1987): 13.0 (world avg. 9.9).
Natural increase rate per 1,000 population (1987): 21.0 (world avg. 17.2).
Total fertility rate (avg. births per childbearing woman; 1987): 4.6.
Marriage rate per 1,000 population (1980): 0.7[7].
Divorce rate per 1,000 population (1980): 0.1[7].
Life expectancy at birth (1987): male 54.0 years; female 56.0 years.
Major causes of death per 100,000 population (1982)[8]: infectious and parasitic diseases 46.0, of which tuberculosis 13.1; diseases of the circulatory system 11.9; diseases associated with malnutrition 8.5; diseases of the respiratory system 8.3; endocrine and metabolic disorders 8.0; ill-defined conditions 115.2.

National economy

Budget (1986–87). Revenue: G 1,262,300,000 (tax revenue 78.8%, of which excises 21.8%, import duties 18.2%, general sales taxes 14.1%; nontax revenue 13.2%; foreign grants 8.0%). Expenditures: G 1,959,300,000[9, 10] (goods and services 48.0%; wages and salaries 35.7%).
Production (metric tons except as noted). Agriculture, forestry, fishing (1988): sugarcane 3,000,000, mangoes 355,000, sweet potatoes 300,000, plantains 275,000, bananas 230,000, corn (maize) 145,000, rice 103,000, sorghum 90,000, dry beans 48,000, oranges 31,000, coffee 31,000, sisal 5,000, cacao 5,000; livestock (number of live animals) 1,549,000 cattle, 1,200,000 goats, 900,000 pigs; roundwood (1987) 6,207,000 cu m; fish catch (1987) 8,050. Mining and quarrying (1986–87): limestone 246,000. Manufacturing (1988–89): cement 271,000; flour 104,900; essential oils (mostly amyris, neroli, and vetiver) 167; cigarettes 957,000,000 units; articles assembled for re-export (value of production in G '000,000) 1,478, of which garments 591, transformers and switches 281, sports equipment and toys 225, electrical goods 60. Construction: n.a. Energy production (consumption): electricity (kW-hr; 1988–89) 557,000,000 (339,000,000); coal, none (none); crude petroleum, none (none); petroleum products (metric tons; 1987) none (191,000); natural gas, none (none).
Household income and expenditure. Average household size (1982) 4.4; sources of income: n.a.; expenditure (1976): food and beverages 77.9%[11], housing 8.3%, household furnishings 4.0%, clothing and footwear 3.2%, other 6.6%.
Public debt (external, outstanding; 1987): U.S.$673,000,000.
Population economically active (1988): total 2,350,302; activity rate of total population 42.2% (participation rates: ages 15–64, 66.3%; female 40.9% (unemployed [1987] unofficially 60.0%).

Price and earnings indexes (1985 = 100)

	1983	1984	1985	1986	1987	1988	1989
Consumer price index	84.9	90.4	100.0	103.3	91.5	98.4	99.2[12]
Daily earnings index[13]	88.0	88.0	100.0	...	...	...	...

Gross national product (at current market prices; 1987): U.S.$2,221,000,000 (U.S.$360 per capita).

Structure of gross domestic product and labour force

	1986 in value U.S.$'000,000	1986 % of total value	1988 labour force	1988 % of labour force
Agriculture	606	32.7	1,184,804	50.4
Mining	2	0.1	17,635	0.8
Manufacturing	286	15.4	115,498	4.9
Construction	112	6.0	22,423	1.0
Public utilities	17	0.9	2,912	0.1
Transp. and commun.	32	1.7	16,599	0.8
Trade	324	17.5	260,708	11.0
Finance, real estate	187	10.1	3,577	0.1
Pub. admin., defense	73	3.9	115,453	4.9
Services	216	11.6		
Other			610,693[14]	26.0[14]
TOTAL	1,856[3]	100.0[3]	2,350,302	100.0

Tourism (1987): receipts from visitors U.S.$93,000,000; expenditures by nationals abroad U.S.$47,000,000.
Land use (1986): forested 1.9%; meadows and pastures 18.0%; agricultural and under permanent cultivation 32.8%; other 47.3%.

Foreign trade[15, 16]

Balance of trade (current prices)

	1983–84	1984–85	1985–86	1986–87	1987–88	1988–89
G '000,000	−1,080.2	−1,113.2	−866.9	−808.4	−755.1	−544.4
% of total	33.0%	33.0%	30.9%	27.3%	28.1%	18.5%

Imports (1988–89): G 1,742,000,000 (food and live animals 20.2%; machinery and transport equipment 19.0%; basic manufactures 15.2%; petroleum products 14.0%; chemical products 9.3%). *Major import sources* (1986–87): United States 45.6%; Caribbean area 13.6%; Japan 6.9%; Canada 6.0%; France 4.9%.
Exports (1988–89): G 1,197,600,000 (assembled manufactured goods for reexport [including electronics, sports equipment, and garments] 54.5%; coffee 17.2%; sisal and twine 2.0%; essential oils 2.0%; cocoa 1.6%). *Major export destinations* (1986–87): United States 52.7%; Italy 12.2%; France 11.0%; Belgium 8.1%; Caribbean area 5.0%.

Transport and communications

Transport. Railroads (1986)[17]. Roads (1985): total length 2,299 mi, 3,700 km (paved 17%). Vehicles (1985): passenger cars 34,669; trucks and buses 11,658. Merchant marine (1988): vessels (100 gross tons and over) 2; total deadweight tonnage 170. Air transport (1987)[18]: passenger arrivals 248,444, passenger departures 265,226; cargo unloaded 12,819 metric tons, cargo loaded 14,496 metric tons; airports (1989) with scheduled flights 2.
Communications. Daily newspapers (1988): total number 4; total circulation 44,500; circulation per 1,000 population 8.2. Radio (1988): total number of receivers 131,900 (1 per 41 persons). Television (1988): total number of receivers 25,000 (1 per 218 persons). Telephones (1986): 82,000 (1 per 65 persons).

Education and health

Education (1985–86)

	schools	teachers	students	student/ teacher ratio
Primary (age 6–12)	3,734	23,200	872,500	37.6
Secondary (age 13–18)	376	6,978	139,422	20.0
Voc., teacher tr.	36	...	14,437	...
Higher	16	818[19]	6,288	6.7[19]

Educational attainment (1982). Percent of population age 25 and over having: no formal schooling 76.9%; primary education 15.2%; secondary 7.2%; higher 0.7%. *Literacy* (1986): total population age 15 and over literate 1,365,200 (41.5%); males literate 699,800 (44.0%); females literate 665,400 (39.2%).
Health (1985): physicians 803 (1 per 6,539 persons); hospital beds 4,956 (1 per 1,060 persons); infant mortality rate per 1,000 live births (1987) 108.0.
Food (1984–86): daily per capita caloric intake 1,902 (vegetable products 94%, animal products 6%); 84% of FAO recommended minimum requirement.

Military

Total active duty personnel (1989): 7,400 (army 94.6%, navy 3.4%, air force 2.0%). *Military expenditure as percent of GNP* (1987): 1.8% (world 5.4%); per capita expenditure U.S.$7.

[1]Roman Catholicism has special recognition per 1984 concordat with Vatican City. [2]Per 1982 census; other official surveys cite different figures. [3]Detail does not add to total given because of rounding. [4]Preliminary estimate; total revised downward to 5,382,800. [5]About 90% of all Roman Catholics also practice voodoo. [6]1982 preliminary census figure. [7]Registered only. [8]Public health facilities only. [9]Current expenditure only. [10]Haiti is a major beneficiary of international aid organizations. Up to 75% of its budget is financed by foreign donors. [11]Excludes alcoholic beverages. [12]Average of first quarter. [13]Minimum wage in industrial enterprises. [14]Includes 48,909 not adequately defined and 561,784 officially unemployed. [15]Import figures c.i.f.; export figures f.o.b. [16]Figures exclude large-scale smuggling from the United States and the Dominican Republic. [17]The only railway is privately owned and used to transport sugarcane. [18]Port-au-Prince airport only. [19]1984–85.

Honduras

Official name: República de Honduras (Republic of Honduras).
Form of government: multiparty republic with one legislative house (Congress [134]).
Head of state and government: President.
Capital: Tegucigalpa[1].
Official language: Spanish.
Official religion: none.
Monetary unit: 1 Honduran lempira (L) = 100 centavos; valuation (Oct. 2, 1989) 1 U.S.$ = L 2.00; 1 £ = L 3.24.

Area and population

Departments	Administrative centres	area sq mi	area sq km	population 1988 census
Atlántida	La Ceiba	1,641	4,251	237,180
Choluteca	Choluteca	1,626	4,211	293,260
Colón	Trujillo	3,427	8,875	146,224
Comayagua	Comayagua	2,006	5,196	238,790
Copán	Santa Rosa de Copán	1,237	3,203	218,864
Cortés	San Pedro Sula	1,527	3,954	644,807
El Paraíso	Yuscarán	2,787	7,218	255,400
Francisco Morazán	Tegucigalpa	3,068	7,946	797,611
Gracias a Dios	Puerto Lempira	6,421	16,630	34,159
Intibucá	La Esperanza	1,186	3,072	123,512
Islas de la Bahía	Roatán	100	261	21,553
La Paz	La Paz	900	2,331	105,996
Lempira	Gracias	1,656	4,290	175,450
Ocotepeque	Nueva Ocotepeque	649	1,680	74,286
Olancho	Juticalpa	9,402	24,351	282,018
Santa Bárbara	Santa Bárbara	1,975	5,115	277,995
Valle	Nacaome	604	1,565	119,889
Yoro	Yoro	3,065	7,939	329,845
TOTAL		43,277	112,088	4,376,839

Demography

Population (1989): 4,530,000.
Density (1989): persons per sq mi 104.7, persons per sq km 40.4.
Urban–rural (1988): urban 40.0%; rural 60.0%.
Sex distribution (1988): male 49.59%; female 50.41%.
Age breakdown (1986): under 15, 46.0%; 15–29, 27.2%; 30–44, 14.0%; 45–59, 7.9%; 60–74, 3.9%; 75 and over 1.0%.
Population projection: (2000) 6,203,000; (2010) 7,828,000.
Doubling time: 23 years.
Ethnic composition (1987): mestizo 89.9%; Amerindian 6.7%; black (including Black Carib) 2.1%; white 1.3%.
Religious affiliation (1987): Roman Catholic 94.6%; other (mostly Protestant) 5.4%.
Major cities (1988): Tegucigalpa 551,606[2]; San Pedro Sula 279,356; La Ceiba 68,289; El Progreso 55,523; Choluteca 53,799.

Vital statistics

Birth rate per 1,000 population (1987): 39.0 (world avg. 27.1); legitimate, n.a.; illegitimate, n.a.
Death rate per 1,000 population (1987): 8.0 (world avg. 9.9).
Natural increase rate per 1,000 population (1987): 31.0 (world avg. 17.2).
Total fertility rate (avg. births per childbearing woman; 1987): 5.6.
Marriage rate per 1,000 population (1983): 4.9.
Divorce rate per 1,000 population (1983): 0.4.
Life expectancy at birth (1985–90): male 61.9 years; female 66.1 years.
Major causes of death per 100,000 population (1982): infectious and parasitic diseases 71.4; accidents and violence 55.3; diseases of the circulatory system 53.8; diseases of the respiratory system 29.1; ill-defined conditions 161.8.

National economy

Budget (1987). Revenue: L 3,448,800,000 (current revenue 64.1%, of which nontax revenue 22.6%, tax on production and internal trade 11.3%, import duties 10.0%, income tax 8.6%; development revenue 35.9%, of which internal credit 18.2%). Expenditures: L 3,448,800,000 (current expenditure 65.5%; public debt service 16.1%; development expenditure 15.4%).
Tourism (1987): receipts from visitors U.S.$26,000,000; expenditures by nationals abroad U.S.$30,000,000.
Production (metric tons except as noted). Agriculture, forestry, fishing (1988): sugarcane 2,800,000, bananas 1,030,000, corn (maize) 505,000, plantains 180,000, coffee 90,000, palm oil 72,000, rice 57,000, dry beans 46,000; livestock (number of live animals) 2,824,000 cattle, 600,000 pigs; roundwood (1987) 5,637,000 cu m; fish catch (1987) 13,500, of which spiny lobster 5,330, peneus shrimp 3,240. Mining and quarrying (1987): limestone 500,-000[3]; lead 20,000; silver 2,000,000 troy oz. Manufacturing (1987): cement 445,800; raw sugar 189,600; steel rods 16,600; beer 544,600 hectolitres; rum 189,600 hectolitres; cigarettes 2,091,000,000 units. Construction (1987–88)[4]: residential 236,000 sq m; nonresidential 128,000 sq m. Energy production (consumption): electricity (kW-hr; 1987) 1,779,100,000 (1,466,700,000); coal, none (none); crude petroleum (barrels; 1987) none (1,906,000); petroleum products (metric tons; 1987) 237,000 (522,000); natural gas, none (none).
Land use (1986): forested 32.0%; meadows and pastures 30.4%; agricultural and under permanent cultivation 15.9%; other 21.7%.
Gross national product (at current market prices; 1987): U.S.$3,627,000,000 (U.S.$780 per capita).

Structure of gross domestic product and labour force

	1987 in value L '000,000	% of total value	labour force[5]	% of labour force
Agriculture	1,529	19.0	624,200	52.5
Mining	118	1.5	3,800	0.3
Manufacturing	1,030	12.8	163,100	13.7
Construction	383	4.8	51,800	4.4
Public utilities	133	1.6	4,400	0.4
Transportation and communications	483	6.0	46,700	3.9
Trade	952	11.8	114,300	9.6
Finance, real estate	1,069	13.3	13,500	1.1
Public admin., defense	433	5.4		
Services	930	11.6	168,100	14.1
Other	983[6]	12.2		
TOTAL	8,043	100.0	1,189,900	100.0

Public debt (external, outstanding; 1987): U.S.$2,681,000,000.
Population economically active (1984): total 1,256,349; activity rate of total population 29.7% (participation rates: ages 15–64, 53.6%; female 16.7%; unemployed [1987] 27.0%).

Price and earnings indexes (1985 = 100)

	1982	1983	1984	1985	1986	1987	1988
Consumer price index	85.3	92.4	96.7	100.0	104.4	106.9	111.8
Weekly earnings index[7]	86.8	61.4	73.5	100.0	...	...	...

Household income and expenditure: Average household size (1988) 5.4; income per household: n.a.; sources of income (1983): wages and salaries 52.7%, transfer payments 1.7%, other 45.6%; expenditure (1983): food 44.4%, utilities and housing 22.3%, clothing and footwear 9.1%, household furnishings 8.3%, health care 6.9%, other 9.0%.

Foreign trade[8]

Balance of trade (current prices)

	1982	1983	1984	1985	1986	1987
L '000,000	+77.8	−101.7	−170.7	−78.2	+124.7	−10.4
% of total	3.0%	3.6%	5.6%	2.5%	3.8%	0.3%

Imports (1987): L 1,797,300,000 (machinery and transport equipment 23.1%, chemical products 22.6%, basic manufactures 21.1%, mineral fuels 11.6%, food products 9.9%). Major import sources: U.S. 39.0%; Japan 11.4%; Venezuela 5.9%; Mexico 3.9%; The Netherlands 3.6%.
Exports (1987): L 1,616,100,000 (coffee 39.8%, bananas 24.7%, shrimp and lobsters 5.6%, roundwood 4.3%, frozen meat 2.8%). Major export destinations: U.S. 54.0%; West Germany 11.5%; Japan 6.0%; Italy 5.9%; Belgium 3.7%.

Transport and communications

Transport. Railroads (1987): route length 624 mi, 1,004 km; passengers, n.a.; cargo, n.a. Roads (1987): total length 11,152 mi, 17,947 km (paved 12%). Vehicles (1987): passenger cars 77,556; trucks and buses 17,078. Merchant marine (1988): vessels (100 gross tons and over) 587; total deadweight tonnage 873,015. Air transport (1985)[9]: passenger-mi 242,600,000, passenger-km 390,500,000; short ton-mi cargo 9,784,000, metric ton-km cargo 14,-285,000; airports (1989) with scheduled flights 9.
Communications. Daily newspapers (1987): total number 7; total circulation 218,000; circulation per 1,000 population 51. Radio (1988): total number of receivers 1,847,000 (1 per 2.4 persons). Television (1988): total number of receivers 140,000 (1 per 31 persons). Telephones (1987): 53,858 (1 per 79 persons).

Education and health

Education (1987)

	schools	teachers	students	student/teacher ratio
Primary (age 7–13)	7,054	21,476	840,057	39.1
Secondary (age 14–19)	438	7,618	142,679	18.7
Voc., teacher tr.	...	...	95,956	...
Higher[10]	7	2,692	34,478	14.0

Educational attainment (1983). Percentage of population age 25 and over having: no formal schooling 33.5%; incomplete primary education 51.3%; incomplete secondary 4.3%; complete secondary 7.6%; higher 3.3%. Literacy (1985): total population age 15 and over literate 1,381,000 (59.5%); males literate 706,000 (60.7%); females literate 675,000 (58.4%).
Health: physicians 2,228 (1 per 2,100 persons); hospital beds 5,708 (1 per 820 persons); infant mortality rate per 1,000 live births 69.0.
Food (1984–86): daily per capita caloric intake 2,078 (vegetable products 87%, animal products 13%); (1984) 98% of FAO recommended minimum.

Military

Total active duty personnel (1988): 18,700 (army 81.9%, navy 6.4%, air force 11.7%). Military expenditure as percent of GNP (1987): 3.7% (world 5.4%); per capita expenditure U.S.$28.

---

[1]Tegucigalpa and adjacent city of Comayagüela jointly form the capital according to the constitution. [2]Population cited is for Central District (Tegucigalpa and Comayagüela). [3]1986. [4]Data is for 9 months of private construction in Tegucigalpa, San Pedro Sula, and La Ceiba only. [5]Employed labour force only. [6]Includes net indirect taxes. [7]Wages in nonagricultural activities for establishments employing 10 or more persons. [8]Import figures are f.o.b. in balance of trade and c.i.f. for commodities and trading partners. [9]TAN and SAHSA airlines only. [10]1985.

Hong Kong

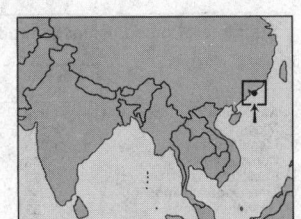

Official name: Hsiang Kang (Chinese);
Hong Kong (English).
Political status: colony (United
Kingdom)[1] with three nominated
advisory councils (Executive Council
[15]; Legislative Council [57[2]]; Urban
Council [30]).
Chief of state: British Monarch.
Head of government: Governor.
Capital: none[3].
Official languages: Chinese; English.
Official religion: none.
Monetary unit: 1 HK dollar
(HK$) = 100 cents; valuation (Oct. 2,
1989) 1 U.S.$ = HK$7.80;
1 £ = HK$12.63.

Area and population	area[4]		population[5]
Area	sq mi	sq km	1986 census
Hong Kong Island	30.4	78.7	1,175,860
Kowloon	16.3	42.2	2,301,691
New Territories	356.6	923.7	1,881,166
Marine	—	—	37,280
TOTAL	403.3	1,044.6	5,395,997

Demography

Population (1989): 5,754,000.
Density (1989): persons per sq mi 14,267.3, persons per sq km 5,508.3.
Urban-rural (1988): urban 100.0%.
Sex distribution (1988): male 51.33%; female 48.67%.
Age breakdown[5] (1988): under 15, 22.1%; 15–29, 28.1%; 30–44, 23.8%; 45–59, 13.7%; 60–74, 9.5%; 75 and over, 2.8%.
Population projection: (2000) 6,624,000; (2010) 7,528,000.
Doubling time: 82 years.
Ethnic composition (1987): Chinese 97.0%; Filipino 0.7%; British 0.3%; other 2.0%.
Religious affiliation (1988): predominantly Buddhist and Taoist; however, there are about 500,000 Christians, 50,000 Muslims, and 12,000 Hindus.
Major cities: no bounded localities exist within Hong Kong.

Vital statistics

Birth rate per 1,000 population (1988): 13.4 (world avg. 27.1); legitimate (1985) 94.5%; illegitimate 5.5%.
Death rate per 1,000 population (1988): 4.9 (world avg. 9.9).
Natural increase rate per 1,000 population (1988): 8.5 (world avg. 17.2).
Total fertility rate (avg. births per childbearing woman; 1988): 1.4.
Marriage rate per 1,000 population (1988): 8.0.
Divorce rate per 1,000 population (1987): 1.0.
Life expectancy at birth (1988): male 74.0 years; female 80.0 years.
Major causes of death per 100,000 population (1988): malignant neoplasms (cancers) 143.1; diseases of circulatory system 141.3; diseases of respiratory system 82.9; accidents and poisonings 28.1; diseases of the genitourinary system 22.1; diseases of digestive system 19.5.

National economy

Budget (1988–89 est.). Revenue: HK$61,070,000,000 (earnings and profit taxes 38.9%; indirect taxes 26.5%, of which entertainment and stamp duties 13.4%, duties 7.1%; capital revenue 13.3%). Expenditures: HK$62,590,600,-000 (education 17.6%; transport and public works 13.7%; general services support 13.1%; housing 12.3%; law and order 11.7%; health 9.3%; culture and recreation 6.1%; social welfare 5.8%).
Public debt: n.a.
Gross domestic product (at current market prices; 1988): U.S.$54,567,000,000 (U.S.$9,600 per capita).

Structure of gross domestic product and labour force	1987			
	in value HK$'000,000	% of total value	labour force	% of labour force
Agriculture	1,358	0.4	41,700	1.5
Mining	273	0.1	1,000	0.1
Manufacturing	76,615	21.0	932,000	34.0
Construction	16,015	4.4	220,500	8.0
Public utilities	9,667	2.6	18,100	0.7
Transp. and commun.	30,052	8.2	233,300	8.5
Trade	80,489	22.0	639,000	23.4
Finance	80,446	22.0	172,500	6.3
Pub. admin., defense, and services	51,764	14.2	470,800	17.2
Other	18,649[6]	5.1[6]	7,300	0.3
TOTAL	365,328	100.0	2,736,200	100.0

Production (metric tons except as noted). Agriculture, forestry, fishing (1988): vegetables 132,000, fruits and nuts 2,020, milk 2,000, field crops 1,590, eggs 180,000,000 units; livestock (number of live animals) 630,000[7] pigs, 740 cattle, 7,000,000 chickens; roundwood (1987) 186,000 cu m; fish catch (1987) 228,094. Mining and quarrying (1988): clay and kaolin 61,888; feldspar 11,050. Manufacturing (value added in HK$; 1986): wearing apparel 14,540,000,000; textile 10,990,000,000; plastic products 6,196,000,000; electrical and electronic machinery 4,489,000,000; consumer electrical appliances and products 4,290,000,000; fabricated metal products 4,221,000,000;

publishing and printed material 2,735,000,000. Construction (1988): residential 1,260,000 sq m; nonresidential 2,400,000 sq m. Energy production (consumption): electricity (kW-hr; 1987) 23,753,000,000 (22,391,000,000); coal (metric tons; 1987) none (8,010,000); petroleum products (metric tons; 1987) none (3,220,000); natural gas (cu m; 1986) none (271,239,000).
Population economically active (1988): total 2,772,600; activity rate of total population 48.8% (participation rates: over age 15, 64.4%; female 48.0%; unemployed 1.7%).

Price and earnings indexes (1985 = 100)							
	1982	1983	1984	1985	1986	1987	1988
Consumer price index	81.6	89.6	97.0	100.0	102.9	108.6	116.6
Daily earnings index[8]	74.5	82.6	92.8	100.0	110.2	123.5	...

Household income and expenditure. Average household size (1986) 3.7; income per household (1983) HK$92,000 (U.S.$11,800); sources of income: n.a.; expenditure (1985): food 18.3%, housing 15.6%, clothing and footwear 20.0%, transportation and vehicles 8.1%, durable goods 12.6%.
Tourism (1988): receipts from visitors U.S.$4,273,000,000; expenditures by nationals abroad, n.a.
Land use (1988): forested 20.5%; agricultural and under permanent cultivation 6.7%; fish ponds 2.5%; built-on, scrublands, and other 70.3%.

Foreign trade

Balance of trade (current prices)						
	1983	1984	1985	1986	1987	1988
HK$'000,000	−14,743	−1,929	+3,733	+575	+86	−5,717
% of total	4.4%	0.4%	0.8%	0.1%		0.6%

Imports (1988): HK$498,797,940,845 (machinery and transport equipment 28.8%, of which electrical machinery 10.5%, telecommunications equipment 6.6%; textile yarn and fabrics 12.6%; chemicals and related products 9.0%; apparel and accessories 6.4%; food and live animals 6.3%; photographic apparatus, watches, and clocks 5.5%). *Major import sources:* China 31.2%; Japan 18.6%; Taiwan 8.9%; United States 8.3%; South Korea 5.3%; Singapore 3.7%; United Kingdom 2.6%; West Germany 2.6%.
Exports (1988): HK$217,663,882,242[9] (clothing accessories and apparel 30.9%; machinery and transport equipment 25.3%, of which telecommunications equipment 8.0%, electrical machinery 8.0%; photographic apparatus, watches, and clocks 8.9%; textile yarn and fabrics 7.1%). *Major export destinations:* United States 33.4%; China 17.5%; West Germany 7.4%; United Kingdom 7.1%; Japan 5.3%; Canada 2.7%; Singapore 2.4%.

Transport and communications

Transport. Railroads (1988): length 21 mi, 34 km; passenger-mi 1,469,000,-000, passenger-km 2,364,000,000; short ton-mi cargo 49,000,000, metric ton-km cargo 72,000,000. Roads (1988): total length 891 mi, 1,434 km (paved 100%). Vehicles (1988): passenger cars 182,621; trucks and buses 118,405. Merchant marine (1988): vessels (100 gross tons and over) 394; total deadweight tonnage 12,352,110. Air transport (1988): passenger arrivals 6,623,231, passenger departures 6,812,109; airports (1989) with scheduled flights 1.
Communications. Daily newspapers (1987): total number 68; total circulation 3,189,000[10]; circulation per 1,000 population 602[10]. Radio (1988): total number of receivers 2,750,000 (1 per 2.1 persons). Television (1987): total number of receivers 1,357,000 (1 per 4.1 persons). Telephones (1988): 2,893,000 (1 per 2.0 persons).

Education and health

Education (1986–87)	schools	teachers	students	student/ teacher ratio
Primary (age 6–11)	714	19,368	531,993	27.5
Secondary (age 12–18)	397	18,323	434,145	23.7
Vocational	27	1,174	21,593	18.4
Higher	11	3,530	34,434	9.8

Educational attainment (1986). Percent of population age 25 and over having: no formal schooling 18.4%; primary education 35.6%; lower secondary 15.5%; upper secondary 18.4%; matriculation 4.4%; nondegree tertiary 2.7%; degreed tertiary 5.0%. *Literacy* (1985): total population age 15 and over literate 3,668,000 (88.1%); males literate 2,040,000 (94.7%); females literate 1,628,000 (80.9%).
Health (1988): physicians 5,380 (1 per 1,056 persons); hospital beds 24,560 (1 per 231 persons); infant mortality rate per 1,000 live births 7.4.
Food (1984–86): daily per capita caloric intake 2,779 (vegetable products 70%, animal products 30%); (1984) 118% of FAO recommended minimum requirement.

Military

Total active duty personnel (1988): 8,500[11] (army 88.7%; navy 8.2%; air force 3.1%). *Military expenditure as percent of GNP* (1984): 0.6% (world 5.9%); per capita expenditure U.S.$39.

---

[1]On July 1, 1997, Hong Kong will revert to China as a Special Administrative Region where the existing socioeconomic system will remain unchanged for another 50 years. [2]Includes 31 nonelective seats. [3]Victoria, for some time, had been regarded as the capital because it is the seat of the British administration of the Crown Colony. [4]Excludes the surface areas of reservoirs. [5]Excludes transients and Vietnamese refugees. [6]Indirect taxes less subsidies. [7]Excludes local pigs not slaughtered in abattoirs. [8]In manufacturing. [9]Excludes reexports valued at HK$275,405,293,406. [10]Thirty-five newspapers only. [11]British forces with a few locally enlisted personnel.

Hungary

Official name: Magyar Köztársaság (Hungarian Republic; or Republic of Hungary).
Form of government: unitary multi-party republic with one legislative house (National Assembly [387]).
Chief of state: interim President.
Head of government: Prime Minister.
Capital: Budapest.
Official language: Hungarian.
Official religion: none.
Monetary unit: 1 forint (Ft) = 100 filler; valuation (Oct. 2, 1989) 1 U.S.$ = Ft 59.89; 1 £ = Ft 96.90.

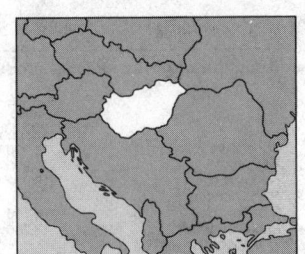

Area and population		area		population
				1989[1]
Counties	Capitals	sq mi	sq km	estimate
Baranya	Pécs	1,732	4,487	434,000
Bács-Kiskun	Kecskemét	3,229	8,362	552,000
Békés	Békéscsaba	2,175	5,632	413,000
Borsod-Abaúj-Zemplén	Miskolc	2,798	7,247	772,000
Csongrád	Szeged	1,646	4,263	456,000
Fejér	Székesfehérvár	1,688	4,373	426,000
Győr-Sopron	Győr	1,549	4,012	426,000
Hajdú-Bihar	Debrecen	2,398	6,211	550,000
Heves	Eger	1,404	3,637	336,000
Komárom	Tatabánya	869	2,251	320,000
Nógrád	Salgótarján	982	2,544	227,000
Pest	Budapest[2]	2,469	6,394	989,000
Somogy	Kaposvár	2,331	6,036	348,000
Szabolcs-Szatmár	Nyíregyháza	2,293	5,938	564,000
Szolnok	Szolnok	2,165	5,607	427,000
Tolna	Szekszárd	1,430	3,704	262,000
Vas	Szombathely	1,288	3,337	276,000
Veszprém	Veszprém	1,810	4,689	387,000
Zala	Zalaegerszeg	1,461	3,784	310,000
Capital City				
Budapest[2]		203	525	2,115,000
TOTAL		35,920	93,033	10,590,000

Demography

Population (1989): 10,580,000.
Density (1989): persons per sq mi 294.8, persons per sq km 113.8.
Urban-rural (1989): urban 59.5%; rural 40.5%.
Sex distribution (1989): male 48.22%; female 51.78%.
Age breakdown (1989): under 15, 20.8%; 15–29, 19.6%; 30–49, 29.2%; 50–59, 11.7%; 60 and over, 18.7%.
Population projection: (2000) 10,396,000; (2010) 10,231,000. During the intercensal period 1970–80, the average annual growth rate was 0.2%; since 1980, however, the population has been decreasing.
Ethnic composition (nationality; 1987): Magyar 96.6%; German 1.6%; Slovak 1.1%; other 0.7%.
Religious affiliation (1986): Christian 86.3%, of which Roman Catholic 62.4%, Protestant 23.4%; Orthodox 0.5%; Jewish 0.8%; atheist and non-religious 12.9%.
Major cities (1989)[1]: Budapest 2,115,000; Debrecen 220,000; Miskolc 208,000; Szeged 189,000; Pécs 183,000.

Vital statistics

Birth rate per 1,000 population (1988): 11.7 (world avg. 27.1); (1985) legitimate 90.8%; illegitimate 9.2%.
Death rate per 1,000 population (1988): 13.1 (world avg. 9.9).
Natural increase rate per 1,000 population (1988): −1.4 (world avg. 17.2).
Total fertility rate (avg. births per childbearing woman; 1985): 1.7.
Marriage rate per 1,000 population (1988): 6.2.
Divorce rate per 1,000 population (1988): 2.4.
Life expectancy at birth (1987): male 65.7 years; female 73.7 years.
Major causes of death per 100,000 population (1988): diseases of the circulatory system 653.1; malignant neoplasms (cancers) 273.6.

National economy

Budget (1987). Revenue: Ft 760,600,000,000 (payments by enterprises 61.7%, turnover tax 16.1%, personal income tax 10.4%). Expenditures: Ft 795,000,000,000 (expenditure of budgetary organs 30.5%, social welfare and health 19.5%, economic tasks 19.0%, supplement to consumer prices 8.4%).
Public debt (external, outstanding; 1989): U.S.$17,500,000,000.
Production (metric tons except as noted). Agriculture, forestry, fishing (1988): wheat 6,962,000, corn (maize) 6,027,000, sugar beets 4,504,000, barley 1,168,000, potatoes 887,000, sunflower seeds 705,000, rye 245,000; livestock (number of live animals) 8,327,000 pigs, 2,216,000 sheep, 1,690,000 cattle, 64,000,000 poultry; roundwood 6,665,000 cu m; fish catch 36,759. Mining and quarrying (1988): bauxite 2,906,404; dolomite 1,200,000; manganese ore 110,803. Manufacturing (1988): cement 3,873,000; crude steel 3,583,000; rolled steel 2,790,000; pig iron 2,093,000; chemical fertilizers 922,000; alumina 873,232; cotton fabrics 311,000,000 sq m; leather footwear 32,600,000 pairs; diesel motors 22,505 units; buses and trucks 13,043 units. Construction (1987): residential 4,643,000 sq m. Energy production (consumption): electricity (kW-hr; 1987) 29,749,000,000 (40,362,000,000); coal (metric tons; 1987) 22,844,000 (25,515,000); crude petroleum (barrels; 1987) 12,805,000 (55,775,000); petroleum products (metric tons; 1987) 8,253,000 (8,428,000); natural gas (cu m; 1987) 6,506,000,000 (10,969,000,000).
Gross national product (1988): U.S.$91,648,000,000 (U.S.$8,650 per capita).

Structure of gross domestic product and labour force				
	1987[3]		1988	
	in value Ft '000,000,000	% of total value	labour force	% of labour force
Agriculture	162.1	19.5	911,500	18.8
Mining and manufacturing	305.0	36.7	1,497,200	30.9
Construction	57.3	6.9	345,400	7.1
Public utilities	11.6	1.4	79,600	1.6
Transp. and commun.	74.8	9.0	400,000	8.3
Trade	79.8	9.6	519,700	10.7
Services	128.8	15.5	1,041,900	21.5
Other[4]	11.6	1.4	49,500	1.0
TOTAL	831.0	100.0	4,844,800	100.0[5]

Population economically active (1988): total 4,844,800; activity rate of total population 45.7% (participation rates: working age [1986] 78.4%; female 45.8%; unemployed, n.a.).

Price and earnings indexes (1985 = 100)							
	1983	1984	1985	1986	1987	1988	1989[6]
Consumer price index	86.3	93.4	100.0	105.3	114.4	132.3	151.0
Monthly earnings index	86.6	91.2	100.0	107.4	117.0	129.9	148.0

Household income and expenditure. Average household size (1986) 2.7; income per household Ft 194,700 (U.S.$4,200); sources of income: (1988) wages 61.8%, social income 37.0%; expenditure (1985): food 31.4%, clothing and footwear 10.5%, transportation 10.3%, housing 8.7%, beverages and tobacco 8.1%, culture and recreation 8.0%.
Land use (1988): forested 18.0%; meadows and pastures 13.8%; agricultural and under permanent cultivation 56.8%; other 11.4%.
Tourism (1988): receipts from visitors U.S.$913,670,000; expenditures by nationals abroad U.S.$742,900,000.

Foreign trade

Balance of trade (current prices)						
	1983	1984	1985	1986	1987	1988
Ft '000,000,000	+15.0	+30.0	+14.5	−19.4	−11.8	+31.6
% of total	2.0%	3.8%	1.7%	2.3%	1.2%	3.2%

Imports (1988): Ft 472,500,000,000 (machinery and transport equipment 28.8%; semifinished products 25.5%; raw and basic materials 13.4%; fuel and electric energy 13.1%; industrial consumer goods 11.7%; agricultural and food products 7.5%). *Major import sources:* U.S.S.R. 25.0%; West Germany 13.9%; Austria 7.2%; East Germany 6.4%; Czechoslovakia 5.1%; Poland 4.1%; Italy 3.2%; Yugoslavia 2.9%.
Exports (1988): Ft 504,100,000,000 (machinery and transport equipment 33.4%, of which spare parts 6.5%; food and agricultural products 20.7%; semifinished products 19.4%; industrial consumer goods 15.9%). *Major export destinations:* U.S.S.R. 27.6%; West Germany 11.0%; Austria 5.7%; Czechoslovakia 5.4%; East Germany 5.3%; Italy 4.2%; Poland 3.3%; United States 3.0%; Yugoslavia 2.8%.

Transport and communications

Transport. Railroads (1988): length 8,171 mi, 13,150 km; passenger-mi 7,153,000,000, passenger-km 11,512,000,000; short ton-mi cargo 14,423,000,000, metric ton-km cargo 21,057,000,000. Roads (1988): total length 18,455 mi, 29,701 km (paved 99%). Vehicles (1988): passenger cars 1,789,600; trucks and buses 218,744. Merchant marine (1988): vessels (100 gross tons and over) 15; total deadweight tonnage 108,015. Air transport[7] (1988): passenger-mi 835,000,000, passenger-km 1,344,000,000; short ton-mi cargo 7,971,000, metric ton-km cargo 11,638,000; airports (1989) 4.
Communications. Daily newspapers (1987): total number 29; total circulation 3,078,731; circulation per 1,000 population 290. Radio (1987): 6,092,939 (1 per 1.7 persons). Television (1987): 4,214,949 (1 per 2.5 persons). Telephones (1987): 1,609,465 (1 per 6.6 persons).

Education and health

Education (1988–89)	schools	teachers	students	student/ teacher ratio
Primary (age 6–13)	3,526	90,620	1,242,700	13.7
Secondary (age 14–18)	186	8,368	127,679	15.3
Vocational	758	22,467	398,488	17.7
Higher	58	16,242	103,041	6.3

Educational attainment (1984). Percent of population age 7 and over having: no formal schooling 1.3%; primary education 65.5%; secondary 27.1%; higher 6.1%. *Literacy* (1984): total population age 15 and over literate 8,269,850 (98.9%); males literate 3,934,250 (99.2%); females literate 4,335,600 (98.6%).
Health (1988): physicians (1987) 30,924 (1 per 343 persons); hospital beds 104,832 (1 per 101 persons); infant mortality rate per 1,000 live births 15.8.
Food (1984–86): daily per capita caloric intake 3,540 (vegetable products 64%; animal products 36%); (1984) 132% of FAO recommended minimum.

Military

Total active duty personnel (1988): 99,000 (army 77.8%, air force 22.2%). *Military expenditure as percent of GNP* (1987): 5.2% (world 5.4%); per capita expenditure U.S.$427.

[1]January 1. [2]Budapest has separate county status. The area and population of the city are excluded from the larger county (Pest), which it administers. [3]At constant prices of 1980. [4]Other material activities. [5]Detail does not add to total given because of rounding. [6]March. [7]Malev airline only.

Iceland

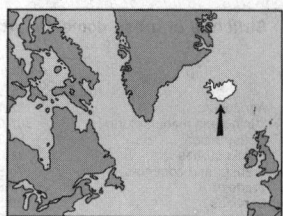

Official name: Lýdhveldidh Ísland (Republic of Iceland).
Form of government: unitary multiparty republic with one legislative house (Althing [63[1]]).
Chief of state: President.
Head of government: Prime minister.
Capital: Reykjavík.
Official language: Icelandic.
Official religion: Evangelical Lutheran.
Monetary unit: 1 króna (ISK) = 100 aurar; valuation (Oct. 2, 1989)
1 U.S.$ = ISK 60.96; 1 £ = ISK 98.63.

Area and population		area		population
Regions[2]	Administrative centres	sq mi	sq km	1988 estimate[3]
Austurland	Egilsstadhir	8,683	22,490	13,167
Höfudhborgarsvædhi	Reykjavík	741[4]	1,920[4]	141.938
Nordhurland eystra	Akureyri	8,371	21,680	26,075
Nordhurland vestra	Saudhárkrókur	4,973	12,880	10,551
Sudhurland	Selfoss	9,649	24,990	20,096
Sudhurnes	Keflavík	4	4	14,949
Vestfirdhir	Ísafjördhur	3,676	9,520	10,097
Vesturland	Borgarnes	3,676	9,520	14,817
TOTAL		39,769	103,000	251,690

Demography

Population (1989): 252,000.
Density (1989): persons per sq mi 6.3, persons per sq km 2.4.
Urban–rural (1988): urban 90.3%; rural 9.7%.
Sex distribution (1988): male 50.24%; female 49.76%.
Age breakdown (1988): under 15, 25.0%; 15–29, 25.9%; 30–44, 21.6%; 45–59, 13.1%; 60–74, 9.9%; 75 and over, 4.5%.
Population projection: (2000) 268,000; (2010) 277,000.
Doubling time: 69 years.
Ethnic composition (place of birth; 1988): Iceland 96.3%; Denmark 0.9%; United States 0.5%; Sweden 0.4%; West Germany 0.3%; other 1.6%.
Religious affiliation (1988): Protestant 97.0%, of which Evangelical Lutheran 92.9%, other Lutheran 3.4%; nonreligious 1.3%; Roman Catholic 0.9%; other 0.8%.
Major cities (1988): Reykjavík 95,799 (urban area 140,265); Kópavogur 15,-535[5]; Hafnarfjördhur 14,197[5]; Akureyri 13,969; Keflavík 7,322.

Vital statistics

Birth rate per 1,000 population (1987): 17.1 (world avg. 27.1); legitimate 49.9%; illegitimate 50.1%.
Death rate per 1,000 population (1987): 7.0 (world avg. 9.9).
Natural increase rate per 1,000 population (1987): 10.1 (world avg. 17.2).
Total fertility rate (avg. births per childbearing woman; 1987): 2.1.
Marriage rate per 1,000 population (1987): 4.7.
Divorce rate per 1,000 population (1987): 1.9.
Life expectancy at birth (1986–87): male 75.0 years; female 80.1 years.
Major causes of death per 100,000 population (1987): diseases of the circulatory system 324.8, of which ischemic heart disease 197.4, cerebrovascular disease 71.6; malignant neoplasms (cancers) 178.0; diseases of the respiratory system 71.1.

National economy

Budget (1988). Revenue: ISK 64,590,000,000 (indirect taxes 79.6%, of which sales tax 46.1%, import duties 9.8%; direct taxes 14.6%). Expenditures: ISK 71,970,000,000 (health, social security, and welfare 42.0%; economic services 19.4%; education and culture 16.6%).
Production (metric tons except as noted). Agriculture, forestry, fishing (1988): fodder crops 3,643,000[6], milk 103,000, potatoes 17,000; livestock (number of live animals) 586,900 sheep, 70,800 cattle, 63,500 horses; fish catch (1988) 1,703,200, of which capelin 916,100, cod 360,600, herring 87,600, lobster and shrimp 27,900. Mining and quarrying (1988): diatomite 25,000. Manufacturing (value added, in ISK '000,000; 1986): food, beverages, and tobacco 11,774; fabricated metal products 2,609; graphic arts 2,140; wood products including furniture 1,558; nonmetallic mineral products 1,418. Construction (new buildings completed, in ISK '000,000; 1987): residential 7,230; nonresidential 10,850. Energy production (consumption): electricity (kW-hr; 1988) 4,417,000,000 (3,781,000,000[6]); coal (metric tons; 1987) none (60,000); crude petroleum none (none); petroleum products (metric tons; 1987) none (527,000); natural gas, none (none).
Household income and expenditure. Average household size (1985) 2.9; disposable income per person (1982) ISK 82,240 (U.S.$6,660); sources of income (1982): wages, salaries, and self-employment 80.0%, other 20%; expenditure (April 1989): food and beverages 22.6%, transportation and communications 19.8%, housing 12.3%, education and recreation 11.3%, clothing and footwear 7.6%, household furnishings 7.4%; other 19.0%.
Population economically active (1987): total 132,259; activity rate of total population 53.8% (participation rates: 15–64, n.a.; female [1984] 39.5%; unemployed [1988] 0.7%).

Price and earnings indexes (1985 = 100)							
	1983	1984	1985	1986	1987	1988	1989
Consumer price index	57.8	75.4	100.0	120.6	143.4	181.3	225.7[7]
Hourly wages index	61.1	74.7	100.0	132.6	188.3	235.3	...

Gross national product (1987): U.S.$4,083,000,000 (U.S.$16,670 per capita).

Structure of gross national product and labour force				
	1988		1987	
	in value ISK '000,000[8]	% of total value	labour force	% of labour force
Agriculture	13,300[9]	5.4[9]	7,013	5.3
Fishing	20,900	8.5	6,838	5.2
Fish processing	18,900	7.7	9,950	7.5
Manufacturing	29,500[9]	12.0[9]	18,479	14.0
Construction	18,700	7.6	12,338	9.3
Public utilities	16,200	6.6	1,146	0.9
Transportation and communications	20,900	8.5	8,591	6.5
Trade	33,000	13.4	20,752	15.7
Finance, real estate	} 97,200	} 39.5	9,760	7.4
Pub. admin., defense,			23,355	17.6
Services			8,194	6.2
Other	−22,400[10]	−9.1[10]	5,843[11]	4.4
TOTAL	245,971[12]	100.0[12]	132,259	100.0

Public debt (external, outstanding; end of 1988): U.S.$1,434,000,000.
Tourism (1988): receipts from visitors U.S.$108,800,000; expenditures by nationals abroad U.S.$230,200,000.
Land use (1986): forested 1.2%; meadows and pastures 22.7%; agricultural and under permanent cultivation 0.1%; other 76.0%.

Foreign trade[13]

Balance of trade (current prices)						
	1983	1984	1985	1986	1987	1988
ISK '000,000	−90	−789	−356	+3,356	−2,617	−1,050
% of total	0.2%	1.6%	0.5%	3.9%	2.4%	0.8%

Imports (1988): ISK 68,971,000,000 (ships and aircraft 8.5%; motor vehicles 8.4%; fuels and lubricants 5.8%; clothing 5.4%; electrical machinery and equipment 5.3%; general industrial machinery 4.8%; metal manufactures 4.3%). *Major import sources:* West Germany 14.2%; Denmark 9.2%; Norway 9.1%; Sweden 8.7%; U.K. 8.2%.
Exports (1988): ISK 61,674,000,000 (marine products 71.1%, of which frozen fish 26.3%, salted fish 16.4%, lobster, shrimp, and scallops 7.8%; aluminum 10.7%; ferrosilicon 3.9%). *Major export destinations:* U.K. 23.3%; U.S. 13.6%; West Germany 10.3%; Portugal 8.5%; Japan 7.6%.

Transport and communications

Transport. Railroads: none. Roads (1987): total length 7,067 mi, 11,373 km (paved 15%). Vehicles (1987): passenger cars 120,456; trucks and buses 13,102. Merchant marine (1988): vessels (100 gross tons and over) 396; total deadweight tonnage 148,307. Air transport (1988)[14]: passenger-mi 1,462,000,000, passenger-km 2,353,000,000; short ton-mi cargo 19,230,000, metric ton-km cargo 28,070,000; airports (1989) with scheduled flights 31.
Communications. Daily newspapers (1987): total number 6; total circulation 126,900; circulation per 1,000 population 516. Radio (1988): 153,264 receivers (1 per 1.6 persons). Television (1988): 76,250 receivers (1 per 3.3 persons). Telephones (1987): 113,000[15] (1 per 2.2 persons).

Education and health

Education (1986–87)				
	schools	teachers	students	student/ teacher ratio
Primary (age 7–12)	187	2,600[16]	25,108	9.6[16]
Secondary (age 12–20)	122	...	20,664	...
Voc., teacher tr.	43	...	7,491	...
Higher	4	280[16]	4,744	17.1[16]

Educational attainment, n.a. *Literacy* (1985): 99.9%.
Health (1986): physicians 632 (1 per 385 persons); hospital beds 2,835 (1 per 86 persons); infant mortality rate per 1,000 live births (1985–87 avg.) 6.1.
Food (1984–86): daily per capita caloric intake 3,146 (vegetable products 54%, animal products 46%); (1984) 116% of FAO recommended minimum.

Military

Total active duty personnel (1986): *c.* 125 coast guard personnel; NATO-sponsored U.S.-manned Iceland Defense Force (1988): 3,100 (navy 58.1%, air force 41.9%).

[1]Usually meets as two separate bodies (Upper House [21]; Lower House [42]). [2]Regions have limited administrative authority. Counties, the former local administrative bodies, ceased to exist at the end of 1988. [3]December 1. [4]Höfudhborgarsvædhi includes Sudhurnes. [5]Within Reykjavík urban area. [6]1987. [7]August. [8]Data estimated from percentage distribution of sectors. [9]Agriculture includes nonfish food processing. [10]Net of imputed bank service charges and changes in value of stock. [11]Includes 588 unemployed. [12]Detail does not add to total given because of rounding. [13]Import figures are f.o.b. in balance of trade and c.i.f. in commodities and trading partners. [14]Icelandair only. [15]Number of subscribers. [16]1982–83.

India

Official name: Bhārat (Hindī); Republic of India (English).
Form of government: multiparty federal republic with two legislative houses (Council of States [244][1], House of the People [546][2]).
Chief of state: President.
Head of government: Prime Minister.
Capital: New Delhi.
Official languages: Hindī; English.
Official religion: none.
Monetary unit: 1 Indian rupee (Rs) = 100 paisa; valuation (Oct. 2, 1989) 1 U.S.$ = Rs 17.00; 1 £ = Rs 27.50.

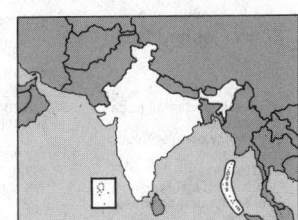

Area and population

States	Capitals	area sq mi	area sq km	population 1981 census
Andhra Pradesh	Hyderābād	106,204	275,068	53,549,673
Arunāchal Pradesh	Itānagar	32,333	83,743	631,839
Assam	Dispur	30,285	78,438	19,896,843[3]
Bihār	Patna	67,134	173,877	69,914,734
Goa	Panaji	1,430	3,702	1,007,749
Gujarāt	Gāndhinagar	75,685	196,024	34,085,799
Haryāna	Chandīgarh	17,070	44,212	12,922,618
Himāchal Pradesh	Shimla	21,495	55,673	4,280,818
Jammu and Kashmir	Srinagar	39,145[4]	101,387[4]	5,987,389
Karnātaka	Bangalore	74,051	191,791	37,135,714
Kerala	Trivandrum	15,005	38,863	25,453,680
Madhya Pradesh	Bhopāl	171,215	443,446	52,178,844
Mahārāshtra	Bombay	118,800	307,690	62,784,171
Manipur	Imphāl	8,621	22,327	1,420,953
Meghālaya	Shillong	8,660	22,429	1,335,819
Mizorām	Āizawl	8,140	21,081	493,757
Nāgāland	Kohima	6,401	16,579	774,930
Orissa	Bubaneshwar	60,119	155,707	26,370,271
Punjab	Chandīgarh	19,445	50,362	16,788,915
Rājasthān	Jaipur	132,140	342,239	34,261,862
Sikkim	Gangtok	2,740	7,096	316,385
Tamil Nādu	Madras	50,216	130,058	48,408,077
Tripura	Agartala	4,049	10,486	2,053,058
Uttar Pradesh	Lucknow	113,673	294,411	110,862,013
West Bengal	Calcutta	34,267	88,752	54,580,647
Union Territories				
Andaman and Nicobar Islands	Port Blair	3,185	8,249	188,741
Chandīgarh	Chandīgarh	44	114	451,610
Dādra and Nagar Haveli	Silvassa	190	491	103,676
Daman and Diu	Daman	43	112	78,981
Delhi	Delhi	572	1,483	6,220,406
Lakshadweep	Kavaratti	12	32	40,249
Pondicherry	Pondicherry	190	492	604,471
TOTAL		1,222,559[4]	3,166,414[4]	685,184,692

Demography

Population (1989): 835,812,000.
Density (1988)[4]: persons per sq mi 683.7, persons per sq km 264.0.
Urban–rural (1986–91): urban 27.5%; rural 72.5%.
Sex distribution (1985): male 51.74%; female 48.26%.
Age breakdown (1985): under 15, 36.8%; 15–29, 27.8%; 30–44, 17.2%; 45–59, 11.4%; 60–74, 5.7%; 75 and over, 1.1%.
Population projection: (2000) 1,042,530,000; (2010) 1,225,305,000.
Doubling time: 33 years.
Linguistic composition (1971): Hindī 28.1%; Telugu 8.2%; Bengali 8.1%; Marāṭhī 7.6%; Tamil 6.9%; Urdū 5.2%; Gujarāti 4.7%; Malayālam 4.0%; Kannaḍa 3.9%; Oriyā 3.6%; Bhojpurī 2.6%; Punjābī 2.5%; Assamese 1.6%; Chhattisgarhī 1.2%; Magadhī 1.2%; Maithilī 1.1%; other 9.5%.
Religious affiliation (1981)[5]: Hindu 82.64%; Muslim 11.35%; Christian 2.43%; Sikh 1.97%; Buddhist 0.71%; Jain 0.48%; Zoroastrian 0.01%; other 0.41%.
Major cities (1981): Greater Bombay 8,243,405 (10,137,000[6]); Delhi 4,884,234 (6,993,000[6]); Calcutta 3,305,006 (10,462,000[6]); Madras 3,276,622 (4,983,000[6]); Bangalore 2,476,355 (3,685,000[6]); Hyderābād 2,150,058 (3,022,000[6]); Ahmadābād 2,059,725 (3,037,000[6]); Kānpur 1,481,789; Nāgpur 1,219,461; Pune 1,203,351; New Delhi 273,036.

Other principal cities (1981)

	population		population		population
Āgra	694,191	Jaipur	977,165	Rānchi	489,626
Ajmer	375,593	Jabalpur	614,162	Solāpur	
Allahābād	616,051	Jalandhar (Jullundur)	408,196	(Sholāpur)	514,860
Amritsar	594,844	Jamshedpur	438,385	South Suburban	378,765
Bareilly	386,734	Jodhpur	506,345	Srinagar	586,038
Bhopāl	671,018	Kozhikode		Sūrat	776,563
Chandīgarh	373,789	(Calicut)	394,447	Tiruchchirāppalli	362,045
Cochin	513,249	Lucknow	895,721	Trivandrum	483,086
Coimbatore	704,514	Ludhiāna	607,052	Vadodara	
Guntūr	367,699	Madurai	820,891	(Baroda)	734,473
Gwalior	539,015	Meerut	417,395	Vārānasi	
Howrah (Hāora)	744,429	Mysore	441,754	(Benares)	708,647
Hubli-Dhārwād	527,108	Patna	776,371	Vijayawāda	454,577
Indore	829,327	Rājkot	445,076	Vishākhapatnam	565,321

Place of birth (foreign born; 1981): other Asia 7,875,399, of which Bangladesh 4,170,524, Pakistan 2,736,038, Nepal 501,292, Sri Lanka 211,514, Burma 134,783; Africa 42,726; Europe 13,046; United States and Canada 5,923.

Mobility (1981). Population living in same district but at different residence as in 1971: 47,604,000; different district, same state 22,557,000; different state 10,860,000; moved outside the country 1,179,000.
Households[5] (1981). Total households 119,230,710. Average household size 5.6; 1 person 5.6%, 2 persons 8.3%, 3 persons 11.0%, 4 persons 14.6%, 5 persons 15.9%, 6 or more persons 44.6%. Average number of rooms per household 2.0; no exclusive room 6.6%, 1 room 44.7%, 2 rooms 28.6%, 3 rooms 12.2%, 4 rooms 6.3%, 5 rooms 2.7%, 6 or more rooms 3.1%, unspecified number of rooms 1.8%. Average number of persons per room 2.8. Shelterless population (1987) estimated at more than 100,000,000.
Emigration (1987 approximation): persons living abroad 12,697,000 (accepting foreign citizenship, 8,200,000), of which in Nepal (1980) 3,800,000 (2,388,000); Malaysia 1,170,000 (1,029,000); Sri Lanka 1,028,000 (457,000); Middle Eastern countries 1,064,000 (102,000); South Africa 850,000 (850,-000); United Kingdom 789,000 (395,000); Mauritius 701,000 (700,000); United States 500,000 (287,000); Trinidad and Tobago 430,000 (430,000); Fiji 339,000 (339,000); Burma 330,000 (50,000); Canada 229,000 (129,000).

Vital statistics

Birth rate per 1,000 population (1987): 32.0 (world avg. 27.1); legitimate, n.a.; illegitimate, n.a.
Death rate per 1,000 population (1987): 10.8 (world avg. 9.9).
Natural increase rate per 1,000 population (1987): 21.2 (world avg. 17.2).
Total fertility rate (avg. births per childbearing woman; 1987): 4.1.
Marriage rate per 1,000 population: n.a.
Divorce rate per 1,000 population: n.a.
Life expectancy at birth (1986–91): male 58.1 years; female 59.1 years.
Major causes of death (rural areas only; 1986)[7]: senility 22.4%; infectious and parasitic diseases 15.8%, of which tuberculosis 5.3%; diseases of the respiratory system 14.3%, of which bronchitis and asthma 8.5%; all causes peculiar to infancy 10.5%; diseases of the circulatory system 9.0%; diseases of the digestive system 7.7%; accidents, violence, and suicides 7.0%; diseases of the nervous system 3.7%.

Social indicators

Educational attainment (1981). Percent of population age 25 and over having: no formal schooling (illiterate) 64.8%; literate population with no formal schooling 0.9%; some primary education only 11.2%; some secondary only 6.2%; completed secondary 7.1%; higher 2.5%; other 7.3%.

Distribution of income (1975–76)

percent of household income by quintile:

1	2	3	4	5 (highest)
7.0%	9.2%	13.9%	20.5%	49.4%

Quality of working life (1981). Average workweek: 45 hours. Rate of fatal (nonfatal) injuries per 100,000 workers (1981–82): industrial workers 16 (7,657); miners 34 (371); railway workers 20 (1,531). Employees covered under Employee's State Insurance Scheme (1984–85) 7,011,500, number of beneficiaries 27,204,600. Average days lost to labour stoppages per 1,000 workdays (1986–87): 0.4. Average duration of journey to work: n.a. Rate per 1,000 workers of discouraged (unemployed no longer seeking work): n.a.
Access to services. Proportion of villages having access to electricity (1988–89) 77.1%; proportion of population having access to safe water supply (1986) 56%.
Social participation. Eligible voters participating in last (November 1989) national election: n.a. Verified trade union membership in total workforce (1986): less than 5% (about 10,000,000 workers). Practicing religious population in total affiliated population: n.a.
Social deviance (1984). Offense rate per 100,000 population for: murder 3.4; dacoity (gang robbery) 1.4; theft and housebreaking 43.7; rape 0.8. Incidence in general population of: alcoholism, n.a.; drug and substance abuse, n.a. Rate per 100,000 population of suicide (1983): 6.4.
Leisure (1987). Favourite leisure activities in urban areas: listening to the radio, watching television, reading periodicals, and attending the cinema.
Material well-being (1983). Households possessing: automobile 0.8%; telephone 2.3%; television receiver 1.6%; radio receiver 17.2%.

National economy

Gross national product (at current market prices; 1987): U.S.$241,305,000,-000 (U.S.$300 per capita).

Structure of gross domestic product and labour force

	1987–88[8] in value Rs '000,000,000	1987–88[8] % of total value	1981[5] labour force	1981[5] % of labour force
Agriculture	836.2	32.2	153,015,000	62.5
Mining	61.7	2.4	1,264,000	0.5
Manufacturing	487.0	18.8	25,143,000	10.3
Construction	161.5	6.2	3,565,000	1.5
Public utilities	25.5	1.0	974,000	0.4
Transp. and commun.	138.1	5.3	6,069,000	2.5
Trade	355.5	13.7	12,165,000	5.0
Finance, real estate	199.8	7.7	1,764,000	0.7
Pub. admin., defense	162.2	6.2	...	...
Services	168.7	6.5	18,557,000	7.6
Other	—	—	22,089,000[9]	9.0
TOTAL	2,596.2	100.0	244,605,000	100.0

Budget (1989–90). Revenue: Rs 748,240,000,000 (tax revenue 68.0%, of which excise taxes 30.3%, customs duties 23.9%, taxes on corporations 6.4%; nontax revenue 32.0%, of which interest receipts 10.7%). Expenditures: Rs 821,610,000,000 (interest payments 20.7%; economic services 19.4%; defense 15.8%; social services 5.7%).

Public debt (external, outstanding; 1987): U.S.$37,325,000,000.

Production (gross value of production in Rs '000,000 except as noted). Agriculture, forestry, fishing (1985–86): grains 290,840, of which rice 161,600, wheat 83,300, jowar (variety of sorghum) 17,910, bajra (variety of millet) 6,780; oilseeds 56,830, of which peanuts (groundnuts) 23,210, rapeseed and mustard 12,040; fruits and vegetables 87,930; pulses 50,660, of which gram (mostly chick-peas) 22,280; sugarcane 44,660; condiments and spices 27,460; cotton 21,200; tea 9,700; jute 9,010; tobacco 4,280; rubber 2,440; coffee 2,120; livestock (number of live animals; 1988) 193,000,000 cattle, 105,000,000 goats, 72,000,000 water buffalo, 51,684,000 sheep, 1,390,000 camels; roundwood (1987) 254,263,000 cu m; fish catch (metric tons; 1987) 2,893,436, of which freshwater fishes 1,211,951. Mining and quarrying (metric tons; 1988): coal 188,000,000; limestone 61,000,000; iron ore 54,000,000; crude petroleum 30,800,000; copper 5,326,000; bauxite 3,011,000; manganese 1,324,000; chromite 759,000; zinc 111,400; lead 39,900; mica 3,600; gold 1,900 kg. Manufacturing (metric tons; 1987–88): cement 37,300,000; steel ingots 13,100,000; pig iron 10,900,000; finished steel 10,700,000; refined sugar 9,100,000; nitrogenous fertilizers 5,466,000; paper and paperboard 1,662,000; jute manufactures 1,200,000; vanaspati (hydrogenated vegetable fat) 980,000; soda ash 956,000; aluminum 278,000; refrigerators 680,000 units; bicycles 6,700,000 units; electric motors 3,900,000 horsepower; motorcycles and scooters 1,541,000 units; power-driven pumps 516,000 units; sewing machines 327,000 units; passenger cars and jeeps 171,500 units; commercial vehicles 119,600 units; tractors 83,200 units; cotton cloth 10,-700,000,000 metres. Construction (value in Rs; 1984) residential 87,010,-000,000; nonresidential 40,730,000,000.

Manufacturing enterprises (1984–85)[10]

	no. of factories	no. of persons engaged	avg. wages as a % of avg. of all wages[11]	annual value added (Rs '000,000)
Textiles	11,802	1,583,000	88.8	25,935
Chemicals and chemical products,	6,032	517,000	144.6	25,695
of which drugs and medicines	1,265	123,000	171.7	5,716
Electrical machinery	3,831	356,000	145.9	17,107
Iron and steel	5,023	620,000	144.7	16,975
Food products	17,459	1,027,000	53.1	16,473
Nonelectrical machinery	7,168	438,000	129.6	16,089
Transport equipment,	3,041	525,000	138.2	15,356
of which motor vehicles	1,529	174,000	164.9	7,842
Nonmetal products,	7,841	420,000	68.8	9,959
of which pottery, china, and glass	1,063	85,000	73.6	1,316
Rubber and plastic products	3,476	145,000	104.0	6,220
Metal products	6,078	204,00	102.2	4,906
Beverages and tobacco	7,093	357,000	37.5	4,604
Petroleum and coal products	424	45,000	187.8	4,109
Printing and publishing	3,292	162,000	106.5	3,743
Paper and pulp products	1,516	133,000	95.2	3,622
Clothing, leather, and footwear	2,120	129,000	66.1	2,410
Nonferrous metals	878	56,000	143.1	1,645
Professional goods	671	41,000	111.2	1,237
Furniture and wood products	3,647	79,000	52.8	1,051
Other industries	838	29,000	93.0	1,253

Energy production (consumption): electricity (kW-hr; 1987) 217,500,000,000 (217,486,000,000); coal (metric tons; 1987) 185,355,000 (183,301,000); crude petroleum (barrels; 1987) 229,079,000 (360,544,000); petroleum products (metric tons; 1987) 37,134,000 (38,893,000); natural gas (cu m; 1987) 6,241,-000,000 (6,241,000,000).

Financial aggregates[12]

	1983	1984	1985	1986	1987	1988	1989 (Sept.)
Exchange rate, Rs per:							
U.S. dollar	10.49	12.45	12.17	13.12	12.88	14.95	16.68
£	15.22	14.40	17.57	19.35	24.10	27.05	27.10
SDR	10.99	12.20	13.36	16.05	18.27	20.12	21.34
International reserves (U.S.$)							
Total (excl. gold; '000,000)	4,937	5,842	6,420	6,396	6,454	4,899	3,664
SDRs ('000,000)	110	331	336	356	159	96	114
Reserve pos. in IMF ('000,000)	510	477	535	596	691	656	624
Foreign exchange ('000,000)	4,318	5,034	5,549	5,444	5,603	4,148	2,927
Gold ('000,000 fine troy oz)	8.594	8.737	9.397	10.449	10.449	10.449	10.449
% world reserves	0.9	0.9	1.0	1.1	1.1	1.1	1.1
Interest and prices							
Central bank discount (%)	10.0	10.0	10.0	10.0	10.0	10.0	10.0
Advance (prime) rate (%)	16.5	16.5	16.5	16.5	16.5	16.5	16.5
Industrial share prices (1985 = 100)	62.9	67.4	100.0	122.1	111.9	115.0	...
Balance of payments (U.S.$'000,000)							
Balance of visible trade	−4,098	−4,024	−5,616	−5,438	−5,777	...	...
Imports, f.o.b.	13,868	14,216	15,081	15,686	17,661	...	...
Exports, f.o.b.	9,770	10,192	9,465	10,248	11,884	...	...
Balance of invisibles	2,145	1,681	1,438	841	585	...	...
Balance of payments, current account	−1,953	−2,343	−4,178	−4,597	−5,192	...	...

Population economically active (1981)[5]: total 244,605,000; activity rate of total population 36.8% (participation rates: over age 15, 57.4%; female 26.0%; unemployed [1987] 10.7%).

Price and earnings indexes (1985 = 100)

	1983	1984	1985	1986	1987	1988	1989
Consumer price index	87.5	94.7	100.0	108.7	118.3	129.4	135.4[13]
Earnings index	...	...	...	...	...	...	...

Household income and expenditure. Average household size[14] (1981) 5.5; income per household: n.a.; sources of income (1984–85): salaries and wages 42.2%, self-employed 39.7%, interest 8.6%, profits and dividends 6.0%, rent 3.5%; expenditure (1985–86): food and beverages 56.1%, transportation and communications 11.8%, clothing and footwear 10.1%, energy 4.6%, household furnishings 4.2%, housing 2.7%, education 2.6%, other 7.9%.

Service enterprises (1980)

	no. of enterprises	no. of employees	annual wage as a % of all wages	annual value added (Rs '000,000)[15]
Wholesale and retail trade	6,046,200	10,228,700	...	262,270
Transportation	307,400	1,194,300	...	110,246
Community and personal services	3,177,700	13,128,800	...	108,670
Construction	152,000	451,200	...	96,290
Finance and insurance	273,500	1,570,800	...	73,970
Real estate and business services	...	...	86.4[16]	71,180
Electricity, gas, and steam	33,700	363,500	...	35,580
Restaurants and hotels	807,000	2,080,500	...	19,120
Communications	98,900	530,900	...	14,580
Storage and warehousing	122,400	356,900	...	34
Water works and supply	208[17]	14,607[17]	108.7[16]	1,840

Tourism (1987): receipts from visitors U.S.$1,455,000,000; expenditures by nationals abroad U.S.$302,000,000.

Land use (1987): forested 22.6%; meadows and pastures 4.0%; agricultural and under permanent cultivation 56.8%; other 16.6%.

Foreign trade[18]

Balance of trade (current prices)

	1983	1984	1985	1986	1987	1988
Rs '000,000	−34,733	−47,235	−63,693	−54,149	−47,352	−53,696
% of total	15.8%	18.0%	21.8%	18.4%	13.9%	12.7%

Imports (1987–88): Rs 223,990,000,000 (crude petroleum and petroleum products 18.2%; nonelectrical machinery 12.9%; pearls, precious and semiprecious stones [mostly diamonds] 8.9%; iron and steel 5.7%; electrical machinery 5.0%; chemical elements and compounds 4.7%; edible oils 4.1%). *Major import sources:* West Germany 9.7%; Japan 9.5%; United States 9.0%; United Kingdom 8.1%; Belgium 6.3%; Saudi Arabia 6.2%; U.S.S.R. 5.7%; France 3.6%.

Exports (1987–88): Rs 157,412,000,000 (pearls, precious and semiprecious stones [mostly diamonds], and jewelry 16.6%; ready-made garments 11.4%; machinery, transport equipment, and metal manufactures including iron and steel 9.1%; leather and leather manufactures 7.3%; cotton fabrics 6.8%; chemicals 5.2%; tea and maté 3.5%; iron ore 3.4%). *Major export destinations:* United States 18.5%; U.S.S.R. 12.5%; Japan 10.3%; West Germany 6.7%; United Kingdom 6.6%; Belgium 3.1%; France 2.4%; Saudi Arabia 1.9%.

Transport and communications

Transport. Railroads (1988): route length 38,500 mi, 62,000 km; passenger-mi 167,000,000,000, passenger-km 269,000,000,000; short ton-mi cargo 158,-000,000,000, metric ton-km cargo 231,000,000,000. Roads (1984–85): total length 1,101,000 mi, 1,772,000 km (paved 47%). Vehicles (1987): passenger cars 1,628,000; trucks and buses 1,214,000. Merchant marine (1988): vessels (100 gross tons and over) 797; total deadweight tonnage 9,922,847. Air transport (1987): passenger-mi 10,658,000,000, passenger-km 17,153,-000,000; short ton-mi cargo 442,100,000, metric ton-km cargo 645,400,000; airports (1989) with scheduled flights 95.
Communications. Daily newspapers (1986): total number 1,802; total circulation 16,731,000[19]; circulation per 1,000 population 23[19]. Radio (1988): total number of receivers 53,937,000 (1 per 15 persons). Television (1988): total number of receivers 13,200,000 (1 per 62 persons). Telephones (1987): 4,420,000 (1 per 180 persons).

Education and health

Education (1986–87)

	schools	teachers	students	student/teacher ratio
Primary (age 6–10)	537,399	1,522,108	89,993,046	59.1
Secondary (age 11–17)	201,436	2,178,440	44,281,298	20.3
Voc., teacher tr.	...	...	...	...
Higher	...	...	...	...

Literacy (1981): total population age 15 and over literate 168,900,000 (40.8%); males literate 117,600,000 (54.8%); females literate 51,300,000 (25.7%).
Health (1986): physicians 318,000 (1 per 2,471 persons); hospital beds 695,000 (1 per 1,130 persons); infant mortality rate per 1,000 live births (1987) 95.0.
Food (1984–86): daily per capita caloric intake 2,204 (vegetable products 94%, animal products 6%); 100% of FAO recommended minimum requirement.

Military

Total active duty personnel (1989): 1,260,000 (army 87.3%, navy 3.7%, air force 8.8%, coast guard 0.2%). *Military expenditure as percent of GNP* (1987): 3.9% (world 5.4%); per capita expenditure U.S.$12.

[1]Includes 13 nonelective seats. [2]Includes 2 nonelective seats. [3]Estimate; state not censused. [4]Excludes 46,660 sq mi (120,849 sq km) of territory claimed by India as part of Jammu and Kashmir but occupied by Pakistan or China. Final status of these claims is not determined. [5]Excludes Assam. [6]Population of urban agglomeration; 1985 est. [7]Percentage breakdown based on 18,262 deaths recorded at 1,160 nationally dispersed, primary health centre villages. [8]At current factor cost. [9]Includes not adequately defined and unemployed. [10]Establishments with 10 or more workers using electrical power, or 20 or more workers not using electrical power. [11]Excludes working proprietors. [12]End of period. [13]May. [14]Excludes shelterless population. [15]1984. [16]1983. [17]1983–84. [18]Import figures are f.o.b. in balance of trade and c.i.f. in commodities and trading partners. [19]1983.

Indonesia

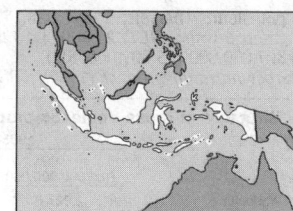

Official name: Republik Indonesia (Republic of Indonesia).
Form of government: unitary multiparty republic with two legislative houses (House of People's Representatives [500[1]]; People's Consultative Assembly [1,000[2]]).
Head of state and government: President.
Capital: Jakarta.
Official language: Bahasa Indonesia.
Official religion: monotheism.
Monetary unit: 1 Indonesian rupiah (Rp) = 100 sen; valuation (Oct. 2, 1989) 1 U.S.$ = Rp 1,788; 1 £ = Rp 2,892.

Area and population

Metropolitan district	Capitals	area sq mi	area sq km	population 1988 estimate
Jakarta Raya	Jakarta	228	590	8,860,600
Provinces				
Bali	Denpasar	2,147	5,561	2,766,000
Bengkulu	Bengkulu	8,173	21,168	1,068,000
Irian Jaya	Jayapura	162,928	421,981	1,506,200
Jambi	Jambi	17,345	44,924	1,954,600
Jawa Barat	Bandung	17,877	46,300	33,084,700
Jawa Tengah	Semarang	13,207	34,206	27,961,700
Jawa Timur	Surabaya	18,503	47,922	32,606,700
Kalimantan Barat	Pontianak	56,664	146,760	3,043,600
Kalimantan Selatan	Banjarmasin	14,541	37,660	2,409,700
Kalimantan Tengah	Palangkaraya	58,919	152,600	1,230,300
Kalimantan Timur	Samarinda	78,162	202,440	1,722,500
Lampung	Tanjung Karang	12,860	33,307	6,845,100
Maluku	Ambon	28,767	74,505	1,741,800
Nusa Tenggara Barat	Mataram	7,790	20,177	3,172,500
Nusa Tenggara Timur	Kupang	18,485	47,876	3,277,000
Riau	Pakanbaru	36,511	94,562	2,810,000
Sulawesi Selatan	Ujung Pandang	28,101	72,781	6,968,200
Sulawesi Tengah	Palu	26,921	69,726	1,663,200
Sulawesi Tenggara	Kendari	10,690	27,686	1,243,000
Sulawesi Utara	Menado	7,345	19,023	2,442,100
Sumatera Barat	Padang	19,219	49,778	3,888,500
Sumatera Selatan	Palembang	40,034	103,688	5,875,200
Sumatera Utara	Medan	27,331	70,787	10,132,300
Timor Timur	Dili	5,743	14,874	681,300
Special autonomous districts				
Aceh	Banda Aceh	21,387	55,392	3,215,400
Yogyakarta	Yogyakarta	1,224	3,169	3,046,500
TOTAL		741,101[3]	1,919,443	175,216,700

Demography

Population (1989): 177,046,000.
Density (1989): persons per sq mi 238.9, persons per sq km 92.2.
Urban–rural (1985): urban 26.2%; rural 73.8%.
Sex distribution (1985): male 49.77%; female 50.23%.
Age breakdown (1985): under 15, 39.4%; 15–29, 27.2%; 30–44, 16.9%; 45–59, 10.8%; 60–74, 4.7%; 75 and over, 1.0%.
Population projection: (2000) 214,410,000; (2010) 246,102,000.
Doubling time: 44 years.
Ethnolinguistic composition (1980): Javanese 40.1%; Sundanese 15.3%; Bahasa Indonesian 12.0%; Madurese 4.8%; other 27.8%.
Religious affiliation (1985): Muslim 86.9%; Christian 9.6%, of which Roman Catholic 3.1%; Hindu 1.9%; Buddhist 1.0%; other 0.6%.
Major cities (1985): Jakarta 7,829,000; Surabaya 2,345,000; Medan 2,110,000; Bandung 1,633,000; Semarang (1984) 1,077,000.

Vital statistics

Birth rate per 1,000 population (1988): 27.2 (world avg. 27.1).
Death rate per 1,000 population (1988): 11.1 (world avg. 9.9).
Natural increase rate per 1,000 population (1988): 16.1 (world avg. 17.2).
Total fertility rate (avg. births per childbearing woman; 1988): 3.3.
Marriage rate per 1,000 population (1985–86): 7.6.
Divorce rate per 1,000 population (1985–86): 0.8.
Life expectancy at birth (1988): male 54.9 years; female 57.7 years.
Major causes of death: n.a.; however, major diseases include tuberculosis, malaria, dysentery, cholera, and plague.

National economy

Budget (1988–89 est.). Revenue: Rp 28,963,600,000,000 (royalties from energy production 30.6%, aid for development 24.7%, value-added tax 16.5%, income tax 13.0%, excise tax 4.6%, nontax revenues 4.3%). Expenditures: Rp 28,963,600,000,000 (debt service 36.8%, development 30.7%, civil service 16.6%, subsidies for autonomous regions 10.0%).
Public debt (external, outstanding; 1987): U.S.$41,284,000,000.
Tourism (1987): receipts from visitors: U.S.$803,000,000; expenditures by nationals abroad U.S.$494,000,000.
Production (metric tons except as noted). Agriculture, forestry, fishing (1987): rice 38,676,000, sugarcane 21,764,000, cassava 13,700,000, corn 4,800,000, sweet potatoes 2,200,000, palm oil 1,698,000, copra 1,400,000, rubber 1,000,000; livestock (number of live animals) 12,900,000 goats, 6,470,000 cattle, 5,300,000 sheep, 2,994,000 buffalo; roundwood 160,085,000 cu m; fish catch 2,609,700. Mining and quarrying (1987): nickel ore 1,936,576; bauxite 612,670; copper ore[4] 243,246; iron ore[4] 148,958; tin ore[4] 25,889;

silver 2,635,000 kg. Manufacturing (1987): cement 11,860,607; fertilizer 6,476,425; paper 121,489; cotton yarn 162,069 bales; beer 827,870 hectolitres; cigarettes 14,186,129,000 units. Energy production (consumption): electricity (kW-hr; 1987) 34,810,000,000 (34,810,000,000); coal (metric tons; 1987) 1,730,000 (2,914,000); crude petroleum (barrels; 1987) 488,436,000 (240,027,000); petroleum products (metric tons; 1987) 28,566,000 (23,792,000); natural gas (cu m; 1987) 27,669,700,000 (6,493,000,000).
Gross national product (1987): U.S.$76,766,000,000 (U.S.$450 per capita).

Structure of gross domestic product and labour force

	1987 in value Rp '000,000,000	1987 % of total value	1986 labour force	1986 % of labour force
Agriculture	29,208.2	25.5	37,644,472	53.6
Mining	15,044.6	13.1	[5]	[5]
Manufacturing	15,952.0	13.9	5,605,971	8.0
Construction	6,087.4	5.3	[5]	[5]
Public utilities	1,018.5	0.9	[5]	[5]
Transp. and commun.	7,405.4	6.5	[5]	[5]
Trade	19,251.8	16.8	9,756,404	13.9
Finance, real estate	6,901.8	6.0	5,182,039[5]	7.4[5]
Pub. admin., defense	8,911.8	7.8 }	10,018,096	14.3
Services	4,737.0	4.1 }		
Other	...	...	1,985,930[6]	2.8[6]
TOTAL	114,518.5	100.0[3]	70,192,912	100.0

Population economically active: total (1986) 70,192,912; activity rate 41.6% (participation rates: ages 15–64, 68.1%; female 39.4%; unemployed 2.6%).

Price and earnings indexes (1980 = 100)

	1983	1984	1985	1986	1987	1988	1989[7]
Consumer price index	86.4	95.5	100.0	105.8	115.6	124.9	133.3
Monthly earnings index[8]	80.1	90.7	100.0	108.4	...	...	...

Household income and expenditure (1986). Average household size 4.9; income per household: n.a.; sources of income (1976): wages 42.1%, self-employment 41.5%, transfer payments 2.5%; expenditure: food 61.2%, housing and utilities 17.4%, clothing 4.9%, durable goods 2.9%.
Land use (1987): forested 67.1%; meadows and pastures 6.5%; agricultural and under permanent cultivation 11.7%; other 14.7%.

Foreign trade

Balance of trade (current prices)

	1983	1984	1985	1986	1987	1988
U.S.$'000,000	+6,545	+9,508	+9,430	+5,249	+5,625	+7,419
% of total	18.3%	27.7%	34.0%	21.5%	19.6%	23.5%

Imports (1988): U.S.$13,248,500,000 (machinery and transport equipment 38.5%, chemicals 19.2%, mineral fuels 9.1%, crude materials 7.2%). *Major import sources:* Japan 25.6%; U.S. 13.1%; Singapore 6.8%.
Exports (1988): U.S.$19,218,500,000 (crude petroleum 21.3%, natural gas 13.7%, plywood 10.8%, preparation rubber 5.9%, petroleum products 5.0%). *Major export destinations:* Japan 41.7%; U.S. 16.0%; Singapore 8.6%.

Transport and communications

Transport. Railroads: (1988) length 6,583 km; (1986) passenger-km 7,332,000,000; (1986) metric ton-km cargo 1,452,000,000. Roads (1986): length 219,791 km (paved 39%). Vehicles (1988): passenger cars 1,191,231; trucks and buses 1,284,278. Merchant marine (1988): vessels (100 gross tons and over) 1,736; deadweight tonnage 2,956,574. Air transport (1988): passenger-km 13,824,000,000; metric ton-km cargo 463,176,000; airports (1989) 134.
Communications. Daily newspapers (1986): total number 97; total circulation 3,048,635; circulation per 1,000 population 18. Radio (1988): 21,785,492 receivers (1 per 8.0 persons). Television (1988): 7,112,469 receivers (1 per 24 persons). Telephones (1987): 890,117 (1 per 193 persons).

Education and health

Education (1987–88)[9]

	schools	teachers	students	student/teacher ratio
Primary (age 7–12)	144,561	1,107,100	26,649,890	24.1
Secondary (age 13–18)	26,367	583,527	8,793,056	15.1
Voc., teacher tr.	3,460	95,777	1,447,278	15.1
Higher	792	115,359	1,179,489	10.2

Educational attainment (1985). Percent of population age 25 and over having: no schooling 30.3%; less than complete primary 32.2%; primary 22.8%; some secondary 6.4%; secondary 7.1%; higher 1.2%. *Literacy* (1985): total population age 15 and over literate 79,197,000 (74.1%); males literate 41,450,000 (83.0%); females literate 33,708,000 (65.4%).
Health (1986): physicians 20,768 (1 per 8,010 persons); hospital beds 111,300 (1 per 1,495 persons); infant mortality rate per 1,000 live births (1988) 83.0.
Food (1984–86): daily per capita caloric intake 2,513 (vegetable products 97%, animal products 3%); 117% of FAO recommended minimum.

Military

Total active duty personnel (1989): 285,000 (army 75.4%, navy 15.8%, air force 8.8%). *Military expenditure as percent of GNP* (1987): 2.1% (world 5.4%); per capita expenditure U.S.$8.

[1]Includes 100 nonelective seats reserved for the military. [2]Includes the 500 members of the House of People's Representatives plus 500 other delegates. [3]Detail does not add to total given because of rounding. [4]Concentrates. [5]Included in finance and real estate. [6]Mostly unemployed. [7]May. [8]Based on daily average wages of agricultural estate workers. [9]Refers to schools under the Department of Education and Culture only.

Iran

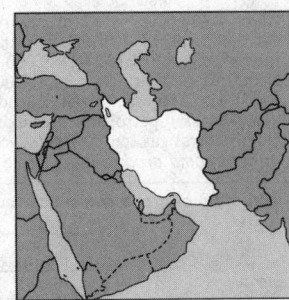

Official name: Jomhūrī-ye Eslāmī-ye Īrān (Islamic Republic of Iran).
Form of government: unitary Islamic republic with a single legislative house (Islamic Consultative Assembly [270]).
Chief of state: Rahbar (religious guide, or leader).
Head of state and government: President.
Capital: Tehrān.
Official language: Farsī (Persian).
Official religion: Islam.
Monetary unit: 1 rial (Rls) = 100 dinars; valuation (Oct. 2, 1989)
1 U.S.$ = Rls 72.25; 1£ = Rls 116.90.

Area and population

Provinces	Capitals	area sq mi	area sq km	population 1986 census
Āzarbāījān-e Gharbī	Orūmīyeh	15,000	38,850	1,971,677
Āzarbāījān-e Sharqī	Tabrīz	25,908	67,102	4,114,084
Bakhtarān	Bakhtarān	9,138	23,667	1,462,965
Boyer Ahmadī va Kohkīlūyeh	Yāsūj	5,506	14,261	411,828
Būshehr	Būshehr	10,677	27,653	612,183
Chahār Mahāll va Bakhtīārī	Shahr Kord	5,741	14,870	631,179
Esfahān	Esfahān	40,405	104,650	3,294,916
Fārs	Shīrāz	51,467	133,298	3,193,769
Gīlān	Rasht	5,679	14,709	2,081,037
Hamadān	Hamadān	7,639	19,784	1,505,826
Hormozgān	Bandar 'Abbās	25,819	66,871	762,206
Īlām	Īlām	7,353	19,044	382,091
Kermān	Kermān	69,466	179,916	1,622,958
Khorāsān	Mashhad	120,980	313,337	5,280,605
Khūzestān	Ahvāz	25,978	67,282	2,681,978
Kordestān	Sanandaj	9,652	24,998	1,078,415
Lorestān	Khorramābād	11,121	28,803	1,367,029
Markazī	Arāk	11,591	30,020	1,082,109
Māzandarān	Sārī	18,291	47,375	3,419,346
Semnān	Semnān	34,764	90,039	417,035
Sīstān va Balūchestān	Zāhedān	70,108	181,578	1,197,059
Tehrān	Tehrān	11,195	28,994	8,712,087
Yazd	Yazd	27,031	70,011	574,028
Zanjān	Zanjān	14,053	36,398	1,588,600
TOTAL LAND AREA		634,562	1,643,510	49,445,010
INLAND WATER		1,809	4,686	
TOTAL AREA		636,372[1]	1,648,196	

Demography

Population (1989): 54,333,000.
Density (1989): persons per sq mi 85.6, persons per sq km 33.1.
Urban–rural (1986): urban 54.3%; rural 45.7%.
Sex distribution (1986): male 51.13%; female 48.87%.
Age breakdown (1985–86): under 15, 43.5%; 15–29, 25.9%; 30–44, 15.9%; 45–59, 9.3%; 60–74, 4.4%; 75 and over, 1.1%.
Population projection: (2000) 73,801,000; (2010) 93,553,000.
Doubling time: 21 years.
Ethnic composition (1983): Persian 45.6%; Azerbaijani 16.8%; Kurdish 9.1%; Gīlakī 5.3%; Luri 4.3%; Māzandarānī 3.6%; Baluchi 2.3%; Arab 2.2%; Bakhtiari 1.7%; Turkmen 1.5%; Armenian 0.5%; other 7.1%.
Religious affiliation (1987): Muslim 98.8% (Shī'ī 91.0%, Sunnī 7.8%); Christians 0.7%; Jews 0.3%; other 0.2%.
Major cities (1986): Tehrān 6,042,584; Mashhad 1,463,508; Esfahān 986,753; Tabrīz 971,472; Shīrāz 848,289.

Vital statistics

Birth rate per 1,000 population (1985–90): 42.4 (world avg. 27.1).
Death rate per 1,000 population (1985–90): 8.0 (world avg. 9.9).
Natural increase rate per 1,000 population (1985–90): 34.4 (world avg. 17.2).
Total fertility rate (avg. births per childbearing woman; 1985–90): 5.6.
Marriage rate per 1,000 population (1984–85): 8.9.
Life expectancy at birth (1985–90): male 65.0 years; female 65.5 years.
Major causes of death per 100,000 population (1985–86): diseases of the circulatory system 223.7; accidents 134.6; diseases of early infancy 73.8; malignant neoplasms 62.8; diseases of the respiratory system 56.9; diseases of the digestive system 30.6; diseases of the nervous system 28.1.

National economy

Budget (1987–88). Revenue: Rls 3,970,800,000,000 (oil and gas 46.1%, taxes 28.7%). Expenditures: Rls 3,970,800,000,000 (current expenditure 74.7%, of which war expenditures 17.6%).
Tourism (1987): receipts U.S.$26,000,000; expenditures U.S.$400,000,000.
Production (metric tons except as noted). Agriculture, forestry, fishing (1988): wheat 8,200,000, sugar beets 3,500,000, barley 2,500,000, potatoes 2,200,000, sugarcane 2,035,000, rice (paddy) 1,757,000, grapes 1,350,000; livestock (number of live animals) 34,500,000 sheep, 13,620,000 goats, 8,350,000 cattle; roundwood (1987) 6,789,000 cu m; fish catch (1987) 150,000. Mining and quarrying (1988): iron ore 2,800,000[2]; copper 420,000; chromium ore (oxide content) 65,000; manganese 60,000; zinc and lead 60,000. Manufacturing (value added, in Rls; 1984–85): machinery 281,345,000,000; textiles, clothing, and leather 219,724,000,000; nonmetallic mineral products (except energy) 139,466,000,000; food processing 131,058,000,000; chemicals 123,065,000,000. Construction (1985–86): 25,769,000 sq m. Energy production (consumption): electricity (kW-hr; 1987) 37,910,000,000 (37,910,000,000); coal (metric tons; 1987) 1,240,000 (1,440,000); crude petroleum (barrels; 1987) 828,175,000 (212,137,000); petroleum products (metric tons; 1987) 25,600,000 (29,195,000); natural gas (cu m; 1987) 15,807,000,000 (15,807,000,000).
Gross national product (1987): U.S.$93,500,000,000 (U.S.$1,800 per capita).

Structure of gross domestic product and labour force

	1985–86 in value Rls '000,000,000	1985–86 % of total value	1986 labour force	1986 % of labour force
Agriculture	2,927.6	19.5	3,190,761	24.5
Mining	1,493.6	10.0	32,370	0.2
Manufacturing	1,174.3	7.8	1,451,330	11.1
Construction	1,020.2	6.8	1,206,264	9.2
Public utilities	113.7	0.8	91,044	0.7
Transp. and commun.	1,138.1	7.6	630,546	4.8
Trade	3,040.5	20.3	[3]	[3]
Finance	273.3	1.8	114,288	0.9
Services	2,724.8	18.2 }	3,049,753[3]	23.4[3]
Pub. admin., defense	1,355.2	9.0 }		
Other	−269.8	−1.8	3,274,644[4]	25.1
TOTAL	14,991.5	100.0	13,041,000	100.0[1]

Population economically active (1986): total 13,041,000; activity rate of total population 26.4% (participation rates: ages 15–64, 51.3%; female *c.* 20%; unemployed 25.1%).

Price and earnings indexes (1985 = 100)

	1980	1981	1982	1983	1984	1985	1986[5]
Consumer price index	48.2	59.9	71.1	85.1	95.8	100.0	109.5
Monthly earnings index[6]	55.4	59.3	64.2	76.6	88.1	100.0	...

Household income and expenditure. Average household size (1986) 5.1; income per household (1975) Rls 298,761 (U.S.$4,235); sources of income: wages 40.8%, self-employment 28.2%, assistance 4.5%; expenditure (1984): food and tobacco 43.3%, housing and energy 22.8%, clothing and footwear 9.6%, household goods 6.3%, transportation 6.0%, health care 4.6%.
Land use (1987): forested 10.9%; meadows and pastures 26.9%; agricultural and under permanent cultivation 9.4%; other 52.8%.

Foreign trade

Balance of trade (current prices)

	1982	1983	1984	1985	1986	1987
U.S.$000,000	+4,964	+218	+812	+2,066	−1,425	+1,919
% of total	18.2%	0.6%	2.7%	8.2%	8.1%	9.7%

Imports (1987): U.S.$8,981,000,000 (1985–86; machinery and transport equipment 32.5%, iron and steel 14.7%, food and live animals 12.8%, chemicals 9.7%). *Major import sources:* W.Ger. 19.4%; Japan 12.9%; U.K. 6.2%; Italy 6.2%; Turkey 5.3%; U.S.S.R. 4.4%; The Netherlands 3.5%; Australia 3.1%.
Exports (1987): U.S.$10,900,000,000 (petroleum and petroleum products 98.4%). *Major export destinations:* United States 14.6%; Japan 13.1%; Italy 8.8%; The Netherlands 8.1%; India 6.0%; Turkey 5.8%; Spain 5.6%; Romania 5.5%; France 5.3%; W.Ger. 4.2%.

Transport and communications

Transport. Railroads (1984–85): route length 2,837 mi, 4,567 km; passenger-km 2,526,000,000; metric ton-km cargo 3,861,000,000. Roads (1987): length 86,599 mi, 139,368 km (paved 48%). Vehicles: passenger cars (1984) 2,246,143; trucks and buses (1987) 440,000. Merchant marine (1988): vessels (100 gross tons and over) 375; total deadweight tonnage 7,939,315. Air transport (1986): passenger-km 5,411,666,000; metric ton-km cargo 685,860,000; airports (1989) 17.
Communications. Daily newspapers (1987): 17; circulation 640,000[7]; circulation per 1,000 population 12.6[7]. Radio (1988): 11,093,164 receivers (1 per 4.7 persons). Television (1988): 2,250,000 receivers (1 per 23 persons). Telephones (1987): 2,078,593 (1 per 25 persons).

Education and health

Education (1986–87)

	schools	teachers	students	student/ teacher ratio
Primary (age 7–11)	53,039	282,296	7,356,257	26.1
Secondary[8] (age 12–18)	14,894	206,345[9]	3,376,272	...
Voc., teacher tr.	1,045	[9]	252,620	...
Higher	116	14,341	167,971	11.7

Educational attainment (1976). Percent of population age 10 and over having: no formal schooling 16.1%; Qur'anic education 10.7%; primary education 43.0%; secondary 23.7%; higher 6.4%; certificate not reported 0.1%. *Literacy* (1986): percent of total population age 15 and over literate 61.8%; males literate 71.0%; females literate 52.1%.
Health (1987): physicians 16,918 (1 per 2,992 persons); hospital beds (1986) 70,184 (1 per 704 persons); infant mortality rate 108.1.
Food (1978–80): daily per capita caloric intake 2,912 (vegetable products 90%, animal products 10%); 130% of FAO minimum requirement.

Military

Total active duty personnel (1989): 604,500 (revolutionary guard corps 41.4%, army 50.5%, navy 2.4%, air force 5.8%). *Military expenditure as percent of GNP* (1985): 7.9% (world 5.7%); per capita expenditure U.S.$477.

[1]Detail does not add to total given because of rounding. [2]1986. [3]Services include trade. [4]Unemployed. [5]Second quarter. [6]Large establishments only. [7]Circulation based on three dailies only. [8]Includes intermediate pre-secondary: "guidance," or "orientation" schools. [9]Includes vocational and teacher training.

Iraq

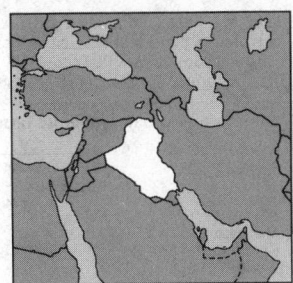

Official name: al-Jumhūrīyah al-'Irāqīyah (Republic of Iraq).
Form of government: unitary single-party republic with one legislative house (National Assembly [250]).
Head of state and government: President.
Capital: Baghdād.
Official language: Arabic.
Official religion: Islam.
Monetary unit: 1 Iraqi dinar (ID) = 20 dirhams = 1,000 fils; valuation (Oct. 2, 1989) 1 ID = U.S.$3.23; 1 ID = £2.00.

Area and population		area[1]		population
				1987
Governorates	Capitals	sq mi	sq km	census
al-Anbār	ar-Ramādī	53,476	138,501	820,690
Bābil	al-Ḥillah	2,497	6,468	1,109,574
Baghdād	Baghdād	283	734	3,841,268
al-Baṣrah	Basra	7,363	19,070	872,176
Dhī Qār	an-Nāṣirīyah	4,981	12,900	921,066
Diyālā	Ba'qūbah	7,365	19,076	961,073
Karbalā'	Karbalā'	1,944	5,034	469,282
Maysān	al-'Amārah	6,205	16,072	487,448
al-Muthannā	as-Samāwah	19,977	51,740	315,815
an-Najaf	an-Najaf	11,129	28,824	590,078
Ninawā	Mosul	14,410	37,323	1,479,430
al-Qādisiyah	ad-Dīwānīyah	3,148	8,153	559,805
Ṣalāḥ ad-Dīn	Tikrīt	9,556	24,751	726,138
at-Ta'mīm	Kirkūk	3,970	10,282	601,219
Wasiṭ	al-Kūt	6,623	17,153	564,670
Kurdish Autonomous Region				
Dahūk	Dahūk	2,530	6,553	293,304
Irbil	Irbil	5,587	14,471	770,439
as-Sulaymānīyah	as-Sulaymānīyah	6,573	17,023	951,723
LAND AREA		167,618[2]	434,128	16,335,198
INLAND WATER		357	924	
TOTAL AREA		167,975[2]	435,052	

Demography

Population (1989): 17,215,000.
Density[3] (1989): persons per sq mi 102.7; persons per sq km 39.7.
Urban–rural (1987): urban 70.2%; rural 29.8%.
Sex distribution (1987): male 51.40%; female 48.60%.
Age breakdown (1986): under 15, 45.3%; 15–29, 28.4%; 30–44, 13.6%; 45–59, 7.6%; 60–74, 3.8%; 75 and over, 1.3%.
Population projection: (2000) 24,023,000; (2010) 30,932,000.
Doubling time: 23 years.
Ethnic composition (1983): Arab 77.1%; Kurd 19.0%; Turkmen 1.4%; Persian 0.8%; Assyrian 0.8%; other 0.9%.
Religious affiliation (1980): Muslim 95.8% (of which Shī'ī 53.5%, Sunnī 42.3%); Christian 3.5%; other 0.7%.
Major cities (1985): Baghdād 3,844,600[4]; Basra 616,700; Mosul 570,926; Irbīl 333,903; as-Sulaymānīyah 279,424.

Vital statistics

Birth rate per 1,000 population (1986): 45.1 (world avg. 27.1).
Death rate per 1,000 population (1986): 8.6 (world avg. 9.9).
Natural increase rate per 1,000 population (1986): 36.5 (world avg. 17.2).
Total fertility rate (avg. births per childbearing woman; 1987): 6.7.
Marriage rate per 1,000 population (1982): 4.0.
Divorce rate per 1,000 population (1981): 0.1.
Life expectancy at birth (1986): male 61.0 years; female 64.5 years.
Major causes of death per 100,000 population (1975): heart disease (except ischemic) 69.9; accidents (all types) 27.6; pneumonia 27.2; malignant neoplasms (cancers) 19.6; during the 1980s, however, there were high war casualties and high incidence of trachoma, influenza, measles, whooping cough, and tuberculosis.

National economy

Budget (1987). Revenue: ID 8,170,000,000 (1981; revenue from oil and public enterprises 88.5%, sales tax 7.7%, income tax 1.3%). Expenditures: ID 9,970,000,000 (1981; economic services 44.9%, defense 24.0%, local government 8.3%, internal security 5.2%, health 4.6%, education 2.9%.
Public debt (external, outstanding; 1987): U.S.$60,000,000,000.
Production (metric tons except as noted). Agriculture, forestry, fishing (1987): barley 743,000, wheat 722,000, tomatoes 675,000, watermelons 520,000, grapes 450,000, cucumbers and gherkins 350,000, melons 350,000, dates 344,000, oranges 175,000, eggplants 170,000, potatoes 120,000; livestock (number of live animals) 8,700,000 sheep, 1,500,000 cattle, 1,400,000 goats, 425,000 mules and asses, 140,000 buffalo, 55,000 camels, 75,000,000 chickens; roundwood 143,000 cu m; fish catch 20,500. Mining and quarrying (1986): elemental sulfur 600,000; gypsum 300,000. Manufacturing (value added in ID '000,000; 1986): industrial chemicals 541.1; pottery and glass products 193.1; machinery and transport equipment 118.9, of which electrical machinery 54.6, transport equipment 17.6; food products 99.6; textiles 76.0; tobacco 38.9; beverages 36.8; metal products 23.3. Construction (1985): authorized residential 11,521,000 sq m; authorized nonresidential 1,176,000 sq m. Energy production (consumption): electricity (kW-hr; 1987)

22,860,000,000 (22,860,000,000); coal, none (n.a.); crude petroleum (barrels; 1987) 743,300,000 (124,100,000); petroleum products (metric tons; 1987) 13,420,000 (7,620,000); natural gas (cu m; 1987) 3,716,000,000 (991,000).
Tourism (1987): receipts U.S.$40,000,000; expenditures, n.a.
Gross national product (1987): U.S.$40,700,000,000 (U.S.$2,420 per capita).

Structure of gross domestic product and labour force				
	1987		1986	
	in value ID '000,000	% of total value	labour force	% of labour force
Agriculture	2,208.0	17.9	1,193,170	27.7
Mining	3,453.1	28.1	62,096	1.4
Manufacturing	1,215.1	9.9	386,809	9.0
Construction	1,056.7	8.6	521,013	12.1
Public utilities	237.5	1.9	34,179	0.8
Transp. and commun.	941.8	7.7	260,237	6.0
Trade	1,667.2	13.5	329,704	7.7
Finance	1,527.3	12.4	50,043	1.2
Pub. admin., defense	...	...	} 1,470,090	34.1
Services	...	...		
Other	—	—	—	—
TOTAL	12,306.7	100.0	4,307,341	100.0

Population economically active (1986): total 4,307,341; activity rate of total population 26.9% (participation rates: over age 15, 50.6%; female 18.2%; unemployed [1984] 0.9%).

Price and earnings indexes (1980 = 100)					
	1980	1981	1982	1983	1984
Consumer price index	100.0	110.6	135.2	151.4	168.5
Earnings index	...	...	...	...	...

Household income and expenditure. Average household size (1986) 7.8; income per household: n.a.; sources of income: n.a.; expenditure (1971–72): food 55.4%, clothing 10.3%, housing 7.9%, household goods 6.2%, transp. and commun. 5.3%, energy 4.1%, medical care 2.4%, recreation 1.2%.
Land use (1986): forested 4.4%; meadows and pastures 9.2%; agricultural and under permanent cultivation 12.5%; built-on, wasteland, and other 73.9%.

Foreign trade[5]

Balance of trade (current prices)					
	1982	1983	1984	1985	1986	1987
ID '000,000	−11,304	−2,381	+282	+966	−1,124	+2,006
% of total	35.6%	10.8%	1.3%	4.4%	6.9%	12.5%

Imports (1987): U.S.$7,015,000,000 ([1986] machinery and transport equipment 39.8%, manufactured goods 27.1%, food and agricultural raw materials 15.5%, chemical and pharmaceutical products 7.5%). *Major import sources:* Turkey 14.8%; U.S. 10.7%; W.Ger. 7.3%; U.K. 7.0%; Japan 6.2%; France 5.8%; Brazil 5.2%; Yugoslavia 4.6%; Romania 4.6%; Italy 4.1%.
Exports (1987): U.S.$9,021,000,000 (fuels and other energy 99.0%, food and agricultural raw materials 1.0%). *Major export destinations:* Brazil 16.5%; Italy 12.2%; France 10.2%; Turkey 7.5%; Japan 6.9%; Spain 6.7%; Yugoslavia 6.4%; U.S. 5.3%; W.Ger. 4.1%.

Transport and communications

Transport. Railroads (1986): route length (1987) 1,516 mi, 2,439 km; passenger-mi 624,000,000, passenger-km 1,005,000,000; short ton-mi cargo 886,000,000, metric ton-km cargo 1,294,000,000. Roads (1986): total length 20,653 mi, 33,238 km (paved 72%). Vehicles (1986): passenger cars 491,800; trucks and buses 246,700. Merchant marine (1988): vessels (100 gross tons and over) 135; total deadweight tonnage 1,675,923. Air transport (1984): passenger-mi 746,000,000, passenger-km 1,200,000,000; short ton-mi cargo 36,000,000, metric ton-km cargo 52,000,000; airports (1989) 3.
Communications. Daily newspapers (1987): total number 6; total circulation 328,000; circulation per 1,000 population 21. Radio (1987): 3,222,300 receivers (1 per 5.3 persons). Television (1987): 972,000 receivers (1 per 18 persons). Telephones (1985): 886,133 (1 per 17 persons).

Education and health

Education (1988–89)				student/
	schools	teachers	students	teacher ratio
Primary (age 6–11)	7,930	122,089	3,012,028	24.7
Secondary (age 12–17)	2,387	42,829	981,409	22.9
Voc., teacher tr.	258	9,323	153,647	16.5
Higher[6]	25	8,327	142,495	17.1

Educational attainment, n.a. *Literacy* (1984): total population age 15 and over literate 2,815,895 (45.9%); males literate 2,034,011 (65.9%); females literate 781,884 (26.0%).
Health: physicians (1984) 4,428 (1 per 3,324 persons); hospital beds (1985) 27,756 (1 per 552 persons); infant mortality rate per 1,000 live births (1986) 63.3.
Food (1984–86): daily per capita caloric intake 2,907 (vegetable products 88%, animal products 12%); (1984) 121% of FAO recommended minimum.

Military

Total active duty personnel (1989): 1,000,000 (army 95.5%, navy 0.5%, air force 4.0%). *Military expenditure as percent of GNP* (1986): 32.0% (world 5.4%); per capita expenditure U.S.$1,060.

[1]Excluding Iraq–Saudi Arabia Neutral Zone. [2]Detail does not add to total given because of rounding. [3]Based on the land area only. [4]1987. [5]Import figures are f.o.b. in balance of trade and c.i.f. for commodities and trading partners. [6]1986–87.

Ireland

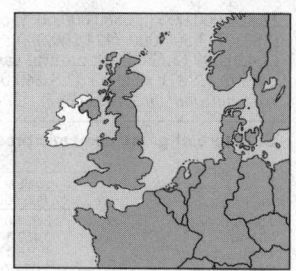

Official name: Éire (Irish); Ireland[1] (English).
Form of government: unitary multiparty republic with two legislative houses (Senate [60[2]]; House of Representatives [166]).
Chief of state: President.
Head of government: Prime Minister.
Capital: Dublin.
Official languages: Irish; English.
Official religion: [3].
Monetary unit: 1 Irish pound (I£) = 100 new pence; valuation (Oct. 2, 1989) 1 Ir£ = U.S.$1.43 = £0.88.

Area and population	area		population
Provinces **Counties**	sq mi	sq km	1986 census
Connacht	6,611	17,122	431,409
Galway[4]	2,293	5,940	178,552
Leitrim	581	1,525	27,035
Mayo	2,084	5,398	115,184
Roscommon	951	2,463	54,592
Sligo	693	1,796	56,046
Leinster	7,580	19,633	1,852,649
Carlow	346	896	40,988
Dublin[4]	356	922	1,021,449
Kildare	654	1,694	116,247
Kilkenny	796	2,062	73,186
Laoighis	664	1,719	53,284
Longford	403	1,044	31,496
Louth	318	823	91,810
Meath	902	2,336	103,881
Offaly	771	1,998	59,835
Westmeath	681	1,763	63,379
Wexford	908	2,351	102,552
Wicklow	782	2,025	94,542
Munster	9,315	24,127	1,020,577
Clare	1,231	3,188	91,344
Cork[4]	2,880	7,460	412,735
Kerry	1,815	4,701	124,159
Limerick[4]	1,037	2,686	164,569
Tipperary North Riding	771	1,996	59,522
Tipperary South Riding	872	2,258	77,097
Waterford[4]	710	1,838	91,151
Ulster	3,093	8,012	236,008
Cavan	730	1,891	53,965
Donegal	1,865	4,830	129,664
Monaghan	498	1,291	52,379
TOTAL LAND AREA	26,600	68,895[5]	3,540,643
INLAND WATER	537	1,390	
TOTAL AREA	27,137	70,285	

Demography

Population (1989): 3,515,000.
Density (1989): persons per sq mi 132.1, persons per sq km 51.0.
Urban–rural (1985): urban 57.0%; rural 43.0%.
Sex distribution (1986): male 49.97%; female 50.03%.
Age breakdown (1986): under 15, 28.9%; 15–29, 24.7%; 30–44, 18.8%; 45–59, 12.8%; 60–74, 10.7%; 75 and over, 4.1%.
Population projection: (2000) 3,447,000; (2010) 3,387,000.
Doubling time: 92 years.
Ethnic composition (1981): more than 94% Irish nationality.
Religious affiliation (1981): Roman Catholic 93.1%; Church of Ireland (Anglican) 2.8%; Presbyterian 0.4%; other 3.7%.
Major cities[6] (1986): Dublin 502,749; Cork 133,271; Limerick 56,279; Galway 47,104; Waterford 39,529.

Vital statistics

Birth rate per 1,000 population (1988): 15.3 (world avg. 27.1); (1987) legitimate 89.2%; illegitimate 10.8%.
Death rate per 1,000 population (1988): 8.9 (world avg. 9.9).
Natural increase rate per 1,000 population (1988): 6.4 (world avg. 17.2).
Total fertility rate (avg. births per childbearing woman; 1985–90): 2.5.
Life expectancy at birth (1985–90): male 71.5 years; female 76.9 years.
Major causes of death per 100,000 population (1987): heart and circulatory diseases 424.8, of which ischemic heart disease 293.3; malignant neoplasms (cancers) 195.3; respiratory disease 67.7, of which pneumonia 48.6.

National economy

Budget (1988). Revenue: Ir£7,035,000,000 (income taxes 38.5%, value-added tax 23.7%, excise taxes 20.1%). Expenditures: Ir£8,183,000,000 (debt service 30.9%, social welfare 24.1%, education 15.2%, health 14.5%, defense 4.2%).
Public debt (Dec. 31, 1987): U.S.$40,960,800,000.
Tourism (1987): receipts U.S.$811,000,000; expenditures U.S.$814,000,000.
Production (metric tons except as noted). Agriculture, forestry, fishing (1987): sugar beets 1,623,000, barley 974,000, potatoes 424,000, wheat 266,000, oats 45,000, milk 53,620,000 hectolitres; livestock (number of live animals; 1988) 5,636,700 cattle, 4,991,200 sheep, 961,200 pigs; roundwood 1,245,000 cu m; fish catch 247,430. Mining and quarrying (1987): gypsum 284,200; zinc ore 177,000[7]; lead ore 33,800[7]. Manufacturing (value added in Ir£; 1986): metals and engineering goods 1,984,700,000; food products 1,624,800,000; chemical products 891,800,000; nonmetallic mineral products 341,500,000; paper, printing, and publishing 305,200,000; textiles 154,300,000. Construction (1985): residential 2,265,000 sq m. Energy production (consumption): electricity (kW-hr; 1986) 12,307,000,000 (12,307,000,000); coal (metric tons;

1986) 54,000 (2,307,000); crude petroleum (barrels; 1986) none (10,880,000); petroleum products (metric tons; 1986) 1,431,000 (4,325,000); natural gas (cu m; 1986) 1,590,600,000 (1,589,600,000).
Gross national product (1987): U.S.$21,761,000,000 (U.S.$6,030 per capita).

Structure of gross domestic product and labour force				
	1987			
	in value Ir£'000,000	% of total value	labour force	% of labour force
Agriculture	1,874	10.6	168,000	12.7
Mining			8,800	0.7
Manufacturing	6,584	37.3	235,600	17.9
Construction			98,100	7.4
Public utilities			15,000	1.1
Transp. and commun.	3,250	18.4	71,200	5.4
Trade			212,200	16.1
Pub. admin., defense	1,185	6.7	...[8]	...[8]
Services			298,600[8]	22.6[8]
Finance	4,774	27.0	85,100	6.4
Other			126,800[9]	9.6[9]
TOTAL	17,667	100.0	1,319,200[5]	100.0[5]

Population economically active (1987): total 1,319,200; activity rate of total population 37.2% (participation rates: ages 15–64, 59.9%; female 30.9%; unemployed 19.0%).

Price and earnings indexes (1985 = 100)							
	1982	1983	1984	1985	1986	1987	1988
Consumer price index	79.0	87.3	94.8	100.0	103.8	107.1	109.4
Weekly earnings index	74.3	83.0	93.1	100.0	108.1	113.6	119.2

Household income and expenditure. Average household size (1983) 3.9; income per household: n.a.; sources of income (1986): wages and salaries 59.8%, self-employment 12.7%, interest and dividends 7.2%; expenditure (1986): food 37.1%, rent and household goods 12.4%, transportation 12.1%.
Land use (1986): forest 4.8%; pasture 71.4%; agricultural 11.3%; other 12.5%.

Foreign trade[10]

Balance of trade (current prices)						
	1983	1984	1985	1986	1987	1988
Ir£'000,000	−420	−15.3	+312	1,164	2,004	2,576
% of total	2.9%	0.1%	1.6%	6.6%	10.6%	11.7%

Imports (1987): Ir£9,155,207,000 (machinery and transport equipment 33.5%; chemicals 12.3%; petroleum and petroleum products 5.6%; food 5.6%; textiles 3.7%; paper 3.3%; iron and steel 1.7%). *Major import sources:* U.K. 41.6%; U.S. 17.0%; W.Ger. 8.4%; France 4.4%; Japan 4.3%.
Exports (1987): Ir£10,723,498,000 (machinery and transport equipment 31.4%, of which office machinery 20.9%, electrical machinery 4.3%; food 15.8%, of which meat 7.1%, dairy products 5.8%). *Major export destinations:* U.K. 28.4%; W.Ger. 11.2%; France 9.3%; U.S. 7.8%.

Transport and communications

Transport. Railroads (1987): length 2,953 km; passenger-km 1,201,900,000; metric ton-km cargo 563,100,000. Roads (1987): length 92,303 km (paved 94%). Vehicles (1986): passenger cars 711,087; trucks and buses 106,285. Merchant marine (1988): vessels (100 gross tons and over) 169; total deadweight tonnage 172,821. Air transport (1987): passenger-km 2,736,000,000; metric ton-km cargo 84,120,000; airports (1989) 6.
Communications (1988). Daily newspapers (1987): 7; circ. 712,000; circ. per 1,000 population 200. Radios: 2,112,863 (1 per 1.7 persons). Televisions: 937,397 (1 per 3.8 persons). Telephones (1985): 942,000 (1 per 3.8 persons).

Education and health

Education (1986–87)	schools	teachers	students	student/ teacher ratio
Primary (age 6–11)	3,450	21,611	576,197	26.7
Secondary (age 12–18)	596	14,546	257,959	17.7
Voc., teacher tr.	260	6,572	85,814	13.1
Higher	51	4,396	56,579	12.9

Educational attainment (1981). Percent of population age 25 and over having: primary education 52.3%; secondary 23.3%; some postsecondary 16.5%; university or like institution 7.9%. *Literacy* (1987): virtually 100% literate.
Health: physicians (1984) 5,180 (1 per 681 persons); hospital beds (1986) 27,634[11] (1 per 128 persons); infant mortality rate per 1,000 live births (1987) 7.4.
Food (1984–86): daily per capita caloric intake 3,692 (vegetable products 62%, animal products 38%); (1984) 153% of FAO recommended minimum.

Military

Total active duty personnel (1988): 13,200 (army 87.8%, navy 6.1%, air force 6.1%). *Military expenditure as percent of GNP* (1986): 1.9% (world 5.5%); per capita expenditure U.S.$130.

[1]As provided by the constitution; the 1948 Republic of Ireland Act provides precedent for this longer formulation of the official name but, per official sources, "has not changed the usage *Ireland* as the name of the state in the English language." [2]Includes 11 nonelective seats. [3]Though a 1973 amendment to the Irish constitution deleted sections that had given "special position" to the Roman Catholic Church, much doctrinal language remains. [4]Includes county borough(s). [5]Detail does not add to total given because of rounding. [6]County boroughs. [7]Metal content of ores. [8]Services include Pub. admin., defense. [9]Includes 40,400 unemployed persons not previously employed. [10]Import figures are f.o.b. in balance of trade and c.i.f. in commodities and trading partners. [11]Includes 10,758 beds used by long-term resident psychiatric patients.

Israel

Official name: Medinat Yisra'el (Hebrew); Isrā'īl (Arabic) (State of Israel).
Form of government: multiparty republic with one legislative house (Knesset [120]).
Chief of state: President.
Head of government: Prime Minister.
Capital: Jerusalem is the proclaimed capital of Israel (from Jan. 23, 1950) and the actual seat of government, but recognition of its status as capital by the international community has largely been withheld pending final settlement of territorial and other issues through peace talks between Israel and the Arab parties concerned.
Official languages: Hebrew; Arabic.
Official religion: none.
Monetary unit: 1 New (Israeli) sheqel (NIS) = 100 agorot; valuation (Oct. 2, 1989) 1 U.S.$ = NIS 2.00; 1 £ = NIS 3.24.

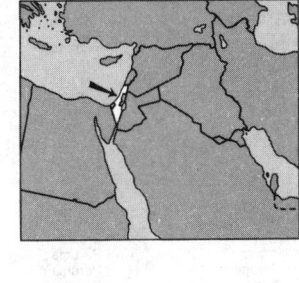

Area and population

Districts	Capitals	area[1] sq mi	area[1] sq km	population 1988 estimate
Central (Ha Merkaz)	Ramla	479	1,242	927,900
Haifa (Ḥefa)	Haifa	330	854	600,600
Jerusalem (Yerushalayim)	Jerusalem	215	557	532,500
Northern (Ha Ẕafon)	Tiberias	1,347	3,490	732,400
Southern (Ha Darom)	Beersheba	5,555	14,387	525,700
Tel Aviv	Tel Aviv–Yafo	66	170	1,027,200
TOTAL		7,992	20,700	4,346,300

Demography[2]

Population (1989): 4,563,000.
Density[1] (1989): persons per sq mi 570.9, persons per sq km 220.4.
Urban–rural (1986): urban 89.4%; rural 10.6%.
Sex distribution (1986): male 49.89%; female 50.11%.
Age breakdown (1986): under 15, 32.4%; 15–29, 24.6%; 30–44, 19.1%; 45–59, 11.6%; 60–74, 8.9%; 75 and over, 3.4%.
Population projection: (2000) 5,490,000; (2010) 6,508,000.
Doubling time: 44 years.
Ethnic composition (1983): Jewish 83.0%; Arab 16.8%; other 0.2%.
Religious affiliation (1988): Jewish 82.0%; Muslim (mostly Sunnī) 13.9%; Christian 2.3%; Druze and other 1.8%.
Major cities (1986): Jerusalem 457,700; Tel Aviv–Yafo 322,800; Haifa 224,600; Ḥolon 138,800; Bat Yam 131,200.

Vital statistics[2]

Birth rate per 1,000 population (1988): 22.6 (world avg. 27.1); (1984) legitimate 99.0%; illegitimate 1.0%.
Death rate per 1,000 population (1988): 6.6 (world avg. 9.9).
Natural increase rate per 1,000 population (1988): 16.0 (world avg. 17.2).
Total fertility rate (avg. births per childbearing woman; 1987): 2.8.
Marriage rate per 1,000 population (1988): 7.0.
Divorce rate per 1,000 population (1988): 1.2.
Life expectancy at birth (1985): male 73.5 years; female 77.0 years.
Major causes of death per 100,000 population (1985): diseases of the circulatory system 273.5; malignant neoplasms (cancers) 118.5; diseases of the respiratory system 46.2.

National economy

Budget (1988–89). Revenue: NIS 53,088,000,000 (1987–88; internal loans 25.1%, income tax and property tax 22.7%, foreign loans 18.0%, value-added tax 13.1%, sales tax 5.3%). Expenditures: NIS 53,088,000,000 (1987–88; debt 27.8%, defense 20.9%, interest on loans 16.6%, health 13.7%).
Public debt (external, outstanding; 1987): U.S.$16,767,000,000.
Production (metric tons except as noted). Agriculture, forestry, fishing (1988): citrus fruits 1,060,700 (of which oranges 700,000), vegetables 760,000 (of which tomatoes 236,000, potatoes 199,300), fruit excluding citrus and olives 346,400 (of which apples 107,000, bananas 82,000, grapes 82,000, avocados 55,000), wheat 211,000, cotton lint and seed 186,700, olives 122,000; livestock (number of live animals) 321,000 cattle, 280,000 sheep, 128,000 goats, 23,000,000 chickens; roundwood (1987) 118,000 cu m; fish catch (1987) 28,922. Mining and quarrying (1988): phosphate rock 2,548,000; potash 2,070,000; phosphoric acid 175,000; bromine compounds 120,000; periclase 44,000. Manufacturing (1988): cement 2,326,000; wheat flour 528,000; sulfuric acid 163,600; polyethylene 94,305; cardboard 71,087; paper 60,257; ammonium sulfate 40,855; cotton yarn 13,543; wine 1,699,500 hectolitres. Construction (1988): residential 2,778,000 sq m; nonresidential 1,337,000 sq m. Energy production (consumption): electricity (kW-hr; 1987) 17,491,000,000 (17,132,000,000); coal (metric tons; 1987) none (3,397,000); crude petroleum (barrels; 1987) 102,000 (51,700,000); petroleum products (metric tons; 1987) 6,477,000 (6,084,000); natural gas (cu m; 1987) 41,003,000 (41,003,000).
Population economically active (1988)[3]: total 1,553,000; activity rate of total population 34.4% (participation rates: over age 15, 51.4%; female 39.6%; unemployed 6.4%).

Price and earnings indexes (1985 = 100)

	1983	1984	1985	1986	1987	1988	1989
Consumer price index	5	25	100	148	178	207	249[4]
Monthly earnings index	6	28	100	161	212	258	292[5]

Tourism (1987): receipts from visitors U.S.$1,347,000,000; expenditures by nationals abroad U.S.$998,000,000.
Gross national product (1987): U.S.$29,803,000,000 (U.S.$4,370 per capita).

Structure of gross domestic product and labour force

	1987 in value NIS '000,000	1987 % of total value	1988 labour force	1988 % of labour force
Agriculture	2,020	5.0	66,800	4.3
Manufacturing, mining	8,661	21.4	321,500	20.7
Construction	2,153	5.3	73,800	4.8
Public utilities	953	2.4	14,500	0.9
Transp. and commun.	3,191	7.9	94,800	6.1
Trade	5,284	13.1	206,700	13.3
Finance			146,600	9.4
Public and community services	18,228	45.0	421,400	27.1
Services			97,400	6.2
Other			109,500[6]	7.1[6]
TOTAL	40,490	100.0[7]	1,553,000	100.0[7]

Household income and expenditure (1986). Average urban household size 3.6; monthly income per household NIS 1,667 (U.S.$1,120); sources of income (1984): wages 90.8%, transfer payments and other 8.4%, self-employment 0.8%; expenditure (1988): food, beverages, and tobacco 27.4%, housing 18.0%, clothing 8.0%, household durable goods 6.4%, transportation 4.0%, energy 3.3%.
Land use (1987): forested 5.5%; meadows and pastures 40.2%; agricultural and under permanent cultivation 21.5%; other 32.8%.

Foreign trade

Balance of trade (current prices)

	1983	1984	1985	1986	1987	1988
U.S.$'000,000	–3,210	–2,600	–2,426	–1,939	–3,441	–3,220
% of total	22.5%	17.4%	15.5%	11.2%	16.9%	14.2%

Imports (1988): U.S.$12,959,700,000 (diamonds 20.3%; investment goods 15.2%; consumer goods 11.3%; fuel and lubricants 8.2%). *Major import sources:* U.S. 16.6%; Belgium and Luxembourg 15.2%; W.Ger. 11.3%; U.K. 9.3%; Switzerland 9.0%; Ireland 6.1%; France 4.2%.
Exports (1988): U.S.$9,739,300,000 (machinery 29.1%; diamonds 29.0%; chemicals 21.7%; textiles 7.6%; food, beverages, and tobacco 5.4%; rubber and plastic 2.8%; ore and minerals 2.7%). *Major export destinations:* U.S. 30.7%; U.K. 7.9%; Japan 6.7%; W.Ger. 5.4%; Hong Kong 5.2%; The Netherlands 4.7%; Belgium and Luxembourg 4.0%; France 3.9%.

Transport and communications

Transport. Railroads (1986–87): route length 328 mi, 528 km; passenger-mi 107,700,000, passenger-km 173,400,000; short ton-mi cargo 673,700,000, metric ton-km cargo 983,600,000. Roads (1987): total length 7,968 mi, 12,823 km (paved 100%). Vehicles (1987): passenger cars 696,712; trucks and buses 140,352. Merchant marine (1988): vessels (100 gross tons and over) 66; total deadweight tonnage 655,627. Air transport[8] (1987): passenger-mi 4,526,000,000, passenger-km 7,284,000,000; short ton-mi cargo 443,900,000, metric ton-km cargo 648,000,000; airports (1989) with scheduled flights 5.
Communications. Daily newspapers (1988): total number 28; total circulation 1,611,000; circulation per 1,000 population 357. Radio (1988): 2,054,610 receivers (1 per 2.2 persons). Television (1988): 655,000 receivers (1 per 6.9 persons). Telephones (1988): 2,065,000 (1 per 2.2 persons).

Education and health

Education (1987–88)

	schools	teachers	students	student/teacher ratio
Primary (age 6–13)	2,004	45,351	761,385	16.8
Secondary (age 14–17)	609	26,378	236,358	9.0
Vocational	378	...	105,324	...
Higher	7[9]	8,112[10]	98,821	...

Educational attainment (1982). Percent of population age 25 and over having: no formal schooling 9.7%; primary education 30.6%; secondary 36.6%; postsecondary, vocational, and higher 23.1%. *Literacy* (1983): total population age 15 and over literate 2,542,403 (91.8%); males literate 1,312,258 (95.0%); females literate 1,230,145 (88.7%).
Health (1986): physicians[11] 11,895 (1 per 345 persons); hospital beds 27,399 (1 per 159 persons); infant mortality rate per 1,000 live births (1988) 10.
Food (1984–86): daily per capita caloric intake 3,037 (vegetable products 79%, animal products 21%); 119% of FAO recommended minimum.

Military

Total active duty personnel (1989): 141,000 (army 73.7%, navy 6.4%, air force 19.9%). *Military expenditure as percent of GNP* (1987): 16.6% (world 5.4%); per capita expenditure U.S.$1,247.

---

[1]Excluding West Bank, Gaza Strip, Golan Heights, and East Jerusalem. [2]De jure; includes population of East Jerusalem and about 25,000 Israeli residents living in occupied territories. [3]Excludes armed forces; includes Israelis in occupied territories. [4]June. [5]March. [6]Mostly unemployed. [7]Detail does not add to total given because of rounding. [8]El Al only. [9]Universities only. [10]1985–86. [11]1983.

Italy

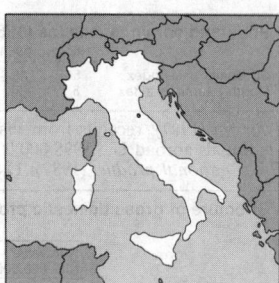

Official name: Repubblica Italiana (Italian Republic).
Form of government: republic with two legislative houses (Senate [322[1]]; Chamber of Deputies [630]).
Chief of state: President.
Head of government: Prime Minister.
Capital: Rome.
Official language: Italian.
Official religion: none.
Monetary unit: 1 lira (Lit, plural lire) = 100 centesimi; valuation (Oct. 2, 1989) 1 U.S.$ = Lit 1,372; 1 £ = Lit 2,220.

Area and population

Regions Provinces	Capitals	area sq mi	area sq km	population 1988 estimate[2]
Abruzzi	L'Aquila	4,168	10,794	1,257,988
Chieti	Chieti	999	2,587	384,268
L'Aquila	L'Aquila	1,944	5,034	298,530
Pescara	Pescara	473	1,225	294,792
Teramo	Teramo	752	1,948	280,398
Basilicata	Potenza	3,858	9,992	621,506
Matera	Matera	1,331	3,447	208,695
Potenza	Potenza	2,527	6,545	412,811
Calabria	Catanzaro	5,823	15,080	2,146,724
Catanzaro	Catanzaro	2,026	5,247	774,450
Cosenza	Cosenza	2,568	6,650	780,122
Reggio di Calabria	Reggio di Calabria	1,229	3,183	592,152
Campania	Naples	5,249	13,595	5,731,426
Avellino	Avellino	1,078	2,792	449,301
Benevento	Benevento	800	2,071	298,884
Caserta	Caserta	1,019	2,639	812,442
Napoli	Naples	452	1,171	3,111,410
Salerno	Salerno	1,900	4,922	1,059,389
Emilia-Romagna	Bologna	8,542	22,123	3,924,199
Bologna	Bologna	1,429	3,702	914,471
Ferrara	Ferrara	1,016	2,632	370,382
Forlì	Forlì	1,123	2,910	608,428
Modena	Modena	1,039	2,690	595,892
Parma	Parma	1,332	3,449	395,424
Piacenza	Piacenza	1,000	2,589	272,246
Ravenna	Ravenna	718	1,859	352,819
Reggio nell'Emilia	Reggio nell'Emilia	885	2,292	414,537
Friuli-Venezia Giulia	Trieste	3,029	7,845	1,210,242
Gorizia	Gorizia	180	467	140,481
Pordenone	Pordenone	878	2,273	275,839
Trieste	Trieste	82	212	268,032
Udine	Udine	1,889	4,893	525,890
Lazio	Rome	6,642	17,203	5,137,270
Frosinone	Frosinone	1,251	3,239	480,915
Latina	Latina	869	2,251	467,257
Rieti	Rieti	1,061	2,749	145,716
Roma	Rome	2,066	5,352	3,766,050
Viterbo	Viterbo	1,395	3,612	277,332
Liguria	Genoa	2,092	5,418	1,749,572
Genova	Genoa	709	1,836	1,000,571
Imperia	Imperia	446	1,155	221,449
La Spezia	La Spezia	341	882	235,176
Savona	Savona	596	1,545	292,376
Lombardia	Milan	9,211	23,857	8,886,402
Bergamo	Bergamo	1,066	2,760	916,001
Brescia	Brescia	1,846	4,782	1,033,527
Como	Como	798	2,067	785,821
Cremona	Cremona	684	1,771	328,155
Mantova	Mantova	903	2,339	371,805
Milano	Milan	1,066	2,762	3,981,398
Pavia	Pavia	1,145	2,965	499,626
Sondrio	Sondrio	1,240	3,212	176,209
Varese	Varese	463	1,199	793,860
Marche	Ancona	3,743	9,693	1,428,557
Ancona	Ancona	749	1,940	438,223
Ascoli Piceno	Ascoli Piceno	806	2,087	359,807
Macerata	Macerata	1,071	2,774	294,979
Pesaro e Urbino	Pesaro	1,117	2,892	335,548
Molise	Campobasso	1,713	4,438	334,680
Campobasso	Campobasso	1,123	2,909	240,952
Isernia	Isernia	590	1,529	93,728
Piemonte	Turin	9,807	25,399	4,377,229
Alessandria	Alessandria	1,375	3,560	449,776
Asti	Asti	583	1,511	210,367
Cuneo	Cuneo	2,665	6,903	546,437
Novara	Novara	1,388	3,594	501,122
Torino	Turin	2,637	6,830	2,286,208
Vercelli	Vercelli	1,159	3,001	383,319
Puglia	Bari	7,470	19,348	4,042,996
Bari	Bari	1,980	5,129	1,522,602
Brindisi	Brindisi	710	1,838	408,291
Foggia	Foggia	2,774	7,185	701,648
Lecce	Lecce	1,065	2,759	811,746
Taranto	Taranto	941	2,437	598,709
Sardegna	Cagliari	9,301	24,090	1,651,218
Cagliari	Cagliari	2,662	6,895	763,920
Nuoro	Nuoro	2,720	7,044	277,447
Oristano	Oristano	1,016	2,631	159,900
Sassari	Sassari	2,903	7,520	449,951
Sicilia (Sicily)	Palermo	9,926	25,709	5,141,343
Agrigento	Agrigento	1,175	3,042	490,848
Caltanissetta	Caltanissetta	822	2,128	294,282
Catania	Catania	1,371	3,552	1,069,740
Enna	Enna	989	2,562	198,046
Messina	Messina	1,254	3,248	690,952
Palermo	Palermo	1,927	4,992	1,258,119
Ragusa	Ragusa	623	1,614	290,036
Siracusa	Siracusa	814	2,109	411,148
Trapani	Trapani	951	2,462	438,172

Area and population (continued)

		area sq mi	area sq km	population 1988 estimate[2]
Toscana	Florence	8,877	22,992	3,568,308
Arezzo	Arezzo	1,248	3,232	313,760
Firenze	Florence	1,498	3,879	1,196,181
Grosseto	Grosseto	1,739	4,504	220,374
Livorno	Livorno	468	1,213	344,142
Lucca	Lucca	684	1,773	382,422
Massa-Carrara	Massa-Carrara	447	1,157	205,066
Pisa	Pisa	945	2,448	388,108
Pistoia	Pistoia	373	965	265,540
Siena	Siena	1,475	3,821	252,715
Trentino-Alto Adige	Bolzano	5,258	13,618	881,986
Bolzano-Bozen	Bolzano	2,857	7,400	436,604
Trento	Trento	2,401	6,218	445,382
Umbria	Perugia	3,265	8,456	818,226
Perugia	Perugia	2,446	6,334	592,161
Terni	Terni	819	2,122	226,065
Valle d'Aosta	Aosta	1,259	3,262	114,325
Veneto	Venice	7,090	18,364	4,374,911
Belluno	Belluno	1,420	3,678	215,766
Padova	Padova	827	2,142	817,196
Rovigo	Rovigo	691	1,789	249,944
Treviso	Treviso	956	2,477	733,867
Venezia	Venice	950	2,460	835,255
Verona	Verona	1,195	3,096	783,886
Vicenza	Vicenza	1,051	2,722	738,997
TOTAL		116,324	301,277	57,399,108

Demography

Population (1989): 57,436,000.
Density (1989): persons per sq mi 493.8, persons per sq km 190.6.
Urban–rural (1988): urban 67.0%; rural 33.0%.
Sex distribution (1988): male 48.58%; female 51.42%.
Age breakdown (1988): under 15, 17.8%; 15–29, 24.1%; 30–44, 20.1%; 45–59, 18.6%; 60–74, 13.5%; 75 and over 5.9%.
Population projection: (2000) 57,554,000; (2010) 56,489,000.
Doubling time: n.a.; population stable.
Ethnolinguistic composition (1983): Italian 94.1%; Sardinian 2.7%; Rhaetian 1.3%; other 1.9%.
Religious affiliation (1980): Roman Catholic 83.2%; nonreligious 13.6%; atheist 2.6%; other 0.6%.
Major cities (1988): Rome 2,817,227; Milan 1,478,505; Naples 1,200,958; Turin 1,025,390; Genoa 722,026; Palermo 728,843; Bologna 427,240; Florence 421,299; Catania 372,212; Bari 358,906; Venice 327,700.
National origin (1980): Italian 98.8%; foreign-born 1.2%, of which Austrian 0.4%, French 0.2%, Slovene 0.2%, Albanian 0.1%, other 0.3%.
Mobility (1981). Population living in the same residence as in 1976: 92.4%.
Households. Average household size (1986) 2.9; composition of households (1981) 1 person 17.9%, 2 persons 23.6%, 3 persons 22.1%, 4 persons 21.5%, 5 persons 9.5%, 6 or more persons 5.4%. Family households (1983): 15,205,000 (85.3%); nonfamily 2,617,000 (14.7%), of which 1-person 13.0%.
Immigration (1986): immigrants admitted 75,725, from Europe 59.3%, of which West Germany 20.6%, Switzerland 11.0%, France 8.1%; Africa 9.7%; United States 7.5%; Asia 7.1%.

Vital statistics

Birth rate per 1,000 population (1987): 9.6 (world avg. 27.1); legitimate 94.2%; illegitimate 5.8%.
Death rate per 1,000 population (1987): 9.3 (world avg. 9.9).
Natural increase rate per 1,000 population (1987): 0.3 (world avg. 17.2).
Total fertility rate (avg. births per childbearing woman; 1985–90): 1.4.
Marriage rate per 1,000 population (1987): 5.3.
Divorce rate per 1,000 population: (1987): 0.4.
Life expectancy at birth (1983): male 71.4 years; female 78.1 years.
Major causes of death per 100,000 population (1986): diseases of the circulatory system 421.4; malignant neoplasms (cancers) 236.7; diseases of the respiratory system 66.9; diseases of the digestive system 52.4.

Social indicators

Educational attainment (1981). Percent of population age 25 and over having: no formal schooling 19.3%[3]; primary education 47.4%; lower secondary 18.0%; upper secondary 11.2%; higher 4.1%.

Distribution of income (1980) percent of household income by quintile				
1	2	3	4	5 (highest)
7.0	11.0	16.0	22.0	45.0

Quality of working life. Average workweek (1985): 36.6 hours. Annual rate per 100,000 workers (1984) for: injury or accident 3,702; industrial illness 4054; death 6.7. Proportion of labour force insured for damages or income loss (1982) resulting from: injury 100%; permanent disability 100%; death 100%. Number of working days lost to labour stoppages (1987): 32,240,000. Average duration of journey to work: n.a. Rate per 1,000 workers of discouraged (unemployed no longer seeking work; 1982): 0.9.
Material well-being. Rate per 1,000 of population possessing (1987): telephone 437; automobile 407; television 255 (colour 141). Households possessing (1979): television 72%; refrigerator 91%; washing machine 88%.
Social participation. Eligible voters participating in last national election (1987): 88.5%. Population participating in voluntary work: n.a. Trade union membership in total workforce (1984): c. 70%. Practicing religious population in total affiliated population (1980): 65.7%, of which weekly 28.0%.
Social deviance (1987). Offense rate per 100,000 population for: murder 1.7; rape 2.1; other assault 23.6; theft, including burglary and housebreaking 2,293. Incidence per 100,000 in general population of: alcoholism (1978) 2.0; drug and substance abuse (1978) 25.1; suicide (1987) 7.1.

Access to services (1981). Proportion of dwellings having access to: electricity 99.5%; safe water supply 98.7%; toilet facilities 98.5%; bath facilities 86.4%.
Leisure (1985). Favourite leisure activities (as percent of public spending on culture): cinema 24.4%; sporting events 18.9%; theatre 11.3%.

National economy
Gross national product (1987): U.S.$596,995,000,000 (U.S.$10,420 per capita).

Structure of gross domestic product and labour force

	1987			
	in value 000,000,000 lire	% of total value	labour force	% of labour force
Agriculture	39,448	4.0	2,169,000	9.1
Mining	26,369	2.7	227,000	1.0
Manufacturing	201,265	20.5	4,639,000	19.5
Construction	53,465	5.4	1,849,000	7.8
Public utilities	49,875	5.1	...	...
Transp. and commun.	58,976	6.0	1,148,000	4.8
Trade	190,491	19.4	4,465,000	18.7
Finance	110,112	11.2	793,000	3.3
Pub. admin., defense	118,048	12.0 }	5,696,000	23.9
Services	120,997	12.3 }		
Other	13,549[5]	1.4[5]	2,833,000[6]	11.9[6]
TOTAL	982,595	100.0	23,819,000	100.0

Budget (1987). Revenue: Lit 394,034,000,000,000 (social security taxes 35.9%; income taxes 33.4%, of which individual 26.5%, corporate 6.9%; value-added and excise taxes 20.7%; property taxes 1.5%). Expenditures: Lit 438,323,000,000,000 (social security and welfare 40.2%; debt service 24.4%; health 11.0%; education and culture 9.3%; transportation and communications 7.3%; national defense 3.7%).
Tourism (1987): receipts from visitors U.S.$12,174,000,000; expenditures by nationals abroad U.S.$4,536,000,000.

Manufacturing, mining, and construction enterprises (1984)

	no. of enter- prises[7]	no. of employees[8]	hourly wages as a % of avg. of all wages[9]	annual value added (Lit '000,000,000)
Manufacturing				
Transport equipment	924	354,161	117.7	11,839
Industrial chemicals	1,184	205,789	119.7	11,570
Electrical machinery	1,559	296,320	112.1	10,483
Metal products	4,232	280,627	86.7	9,553
Machinery, nonelectrical	3,043	252,798	98.0	9,531
Textiles	3,393	253,598	84.4	8,360
Iron and steel	409	143,115	122.6	4,938
Food products	1,631	112,780	92.2	4,655
Printing, publishing	1,022	92,031	103.2	4,017
Wearing apparel	2,475	162,991	75.0	3,849
Pottery, ceramics, and glass	950	98,964	...	3,502
Plastic products	1,236	81,796	84.4	3,159
Paper and paper products	689	65,519	102.2	2,830
Petroleum and gas	17	6,590	138.6	2,702
Mining and quarrying	...	206,000	...	20,060
Construction	326,000[10]	1,645,000	...	46,686

Production (metric tons except as noted). Agriculture, forestry, fishing (1987): sugar beets 14,951,700, grapes 11,650,000, wheat 9,359,100, corn (maize) 5,761,900, tomatoes 4,766,300, potatoes 2,463,100, olives 2,902,500, apples 2,143,000, barley 1,707,900, soybeans 1,588,400, oranges 1,415,000, peaches 1,191,600, rice 1,043,000; livestock (number of live animals) 9,799,-000 sheep, 9,278,000 pigs, 8,819,000 cattle, 112,000,000 chickens; round-wood 9,122,000 cu m; fish catch 554,464. Mining and quarrying (1988): rock salt 3,601,381; potash 1,576,616; feldspar 1,363,700; asbestos 94,549; barite 77,061; zinc 72,107; magnesium 62,525; lead 28,259. Manufacturing (1987): cement 38,220,000[11]; crude steel 23,664,000[11]; pig iron 11,568,000; chemical fertilizers 6,764,285; sulfuric acid 4,358,692; plastics and resins 2,662,000; caustic soda 1,216,200; textiles and cloth 224,311; wine 76,987,-000 hectolitres[12]; beer 11,502,571 hectolitres; olive oil 6,428,000 hectolitres; 3,141,102 motorized road vehicles, of which 1,912,230 automobiles, 1,033,-890 motorcycles, scooters, and mopeds, 194,980 trucks and buses; 4,140,481 washing machines; 3,767,006 refrigerators; 2,232,947 television receivers, of which 2,054,887 colour. Construction (1986): residential 64,068,212 cu m; commercial, industrial, and other 58,809,987 cu m.

Service enterprises (1986)

	no. of enter- prises[9]	no. of employees	hourly wage as a % of all wages	annual value added (Lit '000,000,000)
Public utilities	1,398	...	...	47,730
Transportation }	132,164	1,120,000	...	51,138
Communications }			...	5,842
Finance	89,092	749,000	...	105,439
Wholesale and retail trade	1,495,702	4,407,000	...	171,955
Pub. admin., services	...	5,668,000	...	210,960

Energy production (consumption): electricity (kW-hr; 1987) 198,292,000,000 (221,438,000,000); coal (metric tons; 1987) 22,927,000 (22,916,000); crude petroleum (barrels; 1987) 26,782,000 (516,120,000); petroleum products (metric tons; 1987) 75,901,000 (88,421,000); natural gas (cu m; 1987) 14,-597,600,000 (35,437,200,000).
Population economically active (1987): total 23,819,000; activity rate of total population 41.5% (participation rates: ages 14–64, 59.1%; female 36.3%; unemployed 11.9%).

Price and earnings indexes (1985 = 100)

	1982	1983	1984	1985	1986	1987	1988
Consumer price index	72.1	82.7	91.6	100.0	105.9	110.9	116.5
Earnings index	71.6	...	91.4	100.0	104.4	111.7	...

Land use (1986): forested 22.9%; meadows and pastures 16.8%; agricultural and under permanent cultivation 41.4%; other 18.9%.
Public debt (1987): U.S.$678,200,000,000.

Financial aggregates

	1984	1985	1986	1987	1988	1989[13]
Exchange rate, Lit per:						
U.S. dollar	1,757.0	1,909.4	1,490.8	1,296.1	1,301.6	1,371.0
£	2,347.9	2,759.1	2,187.0	2,124.2	2,318.7	2,224.0
SDR	1,897.6	1,843.7	1,661.3	1,658.8	1,757.2	1,731.0
International reserves (U.S.$)						
Total (excl. gold; '000,000)	20,795	15,595	19,987	30,214	34,715	40,996
SDRs ('000,000)	633	326	587	948	949	939
Reserve pos. in IMF ('000,000)	1,074	1,160	1,268	1,447	1,266	1,366
Foreign exchange ('000,000)	19,089	14,029	18,116	27,765	32,500	38,691
Gold ('000,000 fine troy oz)	66.67	66.67	66.67	66.67	66.67	66.67
% world reserves	7.1	7.0	7.0	7.1	7.1	7.1
Interest and prices						
Central bank discount (%)	16.50	15.00	12.00	12.00	12.50	13.50[14]
Gov't. bond yield (%)	14.95	13.00	10.52	9.65	10.16	10.46[15]
Industrial share prices						
(1985 = 100)	60.0	100.0	232.8	224.6	185.1	198.8[15]
Balance of payments (U.S.$'000,000)						
Balance of visible trade	−5,818	−6,083	4,525	−72	−767	...
Imports, f.o.b.	−79,654	−82,157	−92,194	−115,867	−128,816	...
Exports, f.o.b.	73,836	76,073	96,719	115,939	128,048	...
Balance of invisibles	1,696	1,516	18	−481	−3,440	...
Balance of payments, current account	−2,501	−3,540	2,912	−1,510	−4,636	...

Household income and expenditure (1987). Average household size 2.9; average annual income per household (1984) Lit 19,692,000 (U.S.$11,208); sources of income: salaries and wages 49.5%, transfer payments 20.6%, self-employment 19.9%; expenditure: food and beverages 25.5%, transport and communications 16.1%, housing 15.2%, recreation and education 5.7%.

Foreign trade

Balance of trade (current prices)

	1983	1984	1985	1986	1987	1988
Lit '000,000,000	−2,689	−10,807	−6,614	+6,592	−6,533	−1,012
% of total	2.4%	4.0%	2.2%	2.3%	2.2%	0.3%

Imports (1987): Lit 161,596,642,000,000 (machinery and transport equipment 29.4%, of which transport equipment 11.1%, precision machinery 6.2%; chemicals and chemical products 16.1%; food and live animals 8.4%; metal and semiprocessed metal 8.0%; crude petroleum 7.1%; refined petroleum products 4.0%). *Major import sources:* W.Ger. 21.1%; France 14.6%; The Netherlands 5.6%; U.S. 5.3%; U.K. 5.2%; Switzerland 4.8%.
Exports (1987): Lit 150,454,325,000,000 (nontransport machinery 28.6%; textiles 10.9%; chemicals and chemical products 10.8%; transport equipment 10.8%, of which automobiles 4.4%, tractors and construction equipment 0.7%; wearing apparel 7.5%, of which shoes 3.9%; metal and processed metal 6.8%; petroleum products 3.9%). *Major export destinations:* W.Ger. 18.6%; France 16.3%; U.S. 9.6%; U.K. 7.4%; Switzerland 4.7%.

Transport and communications
Transport. Railroads (1987): length 12,156[12] mi, 19,563[12] km; passenger-mi 25,721,000,000, passenger-km 41,395,000,000; short ton-mi cargo 12,621,-000,000, metric ton-km cargo 18,427,000,000. Roads (1985): total length 187,391 mi, 301,577 km (paved 100%). Vehicles (1986): passenger cars 23,342,000; trucks and buses 1,918,800. Merchant marine (1988): vessels (100 gross tons and over) 1,583; total deadweight tonnage 11,867,321. Air transport (1988)[16]: passenger-mi 9,715,000,000, passenger-km 15,636,000,-000; short ton-mi cargo 715,639,000, metric ton-km cargo 1,044,800,000; airports (1989) 36.
Communications. Daily newspapers (1987): total number 99; total circulation 6,931,500[17]; circulation per 1,000 population 121[17]. Radio (1988): 14,817,-197 receivers (1 per 3.9 persons). Television (1988): 14,605,448 receivers (1 per 3.9 persons). Telephones (1987): 28,052,228 (1 per 2.0 persons).

Education and health

Education (1987–88)

	schools	teachers	students	student/ teacher ratio
Primary (age 6–10)	26,643	215,039	3,370,709	15.7
Secondary (age 11–18)	10,032	127,274	2,618,679	20.6
Voc., teacher tr.	7,702	125,054	2,719,334	21.7
Higher[18]	47	51,264	1,004,509	19.6

Literacy (1985): total population age 15 and over literate 38,421,342 (97.0%); males literate 18,767,897 (97.9%); females literate 19,653,445 (96.3%).
Health (1986): physicians 245,116 (1 per 233 persons); hospital beds 450,377 (1 per 127 persons); infant mortality rate per 1,000 live births 9.8.
Food (1984–86): daily per capita caloric intake 3,494 (vegetable products 73%, animal products 27%); (1984) 140% of FAO recommended minimum requirement.

Military
Total active duty personnel (1988): 386,000 (army 68.7%, navy 12.4%, air force 18.9%). *Military expenditure as percent of GNP* (1987): 2.5% (world 5.4%); per capita expenditure U.S.$320.

[1]Includes 7 nonelective seats. [2]January 1. [3]More than two-thirds are age 55 and over. [4]1978. [5]Imputed bank charges less duties on imports. [6]Unemployed. [7]Enterprises with 20 or more persons engaged. [8]Total number of persons engaged. [9]1981. [10]All enterprises (1982). [11]1988. [12]1986. [13]July. [14]May. [15]April. [16]Alitalia only. [17]For 66 newspapers only. [18]1986–87.

Jamaica

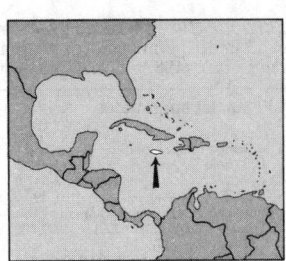

Official name: Jamaica.
Form of government: constitutional monarchy with two legislative houses (Senate [21]; House of Representatives [60]).
Chief of state: British Monarch represented by governor-general.
Head of government: Prime Minister.
Capital: Kingston.
Official language: English.
Official religion: none.
Monetary unit: 1 Jamaica dollar (J$) = 100 cents; valuation (Oct. 2, 1989) 1 U.S.$ = J$5.48; 1 £ = J$8.87.

Area and population

Parishes	Capitals	area sq mi	area sq km	population 1988 estimate[1]
Clarendon	May Pen	462	1,196	214,600
Hanover	Lucea	174	450	65,100
Kingston	[2]	8	22	[3]
Manchester	Mandeville	321	830	158,200
Portland	Port Antonio	314	814	77,100
Saint Andrew	[2]	166	431	646,400[3]
Saint Ann	Saint Ann's Bay	468	1,213	147,200
Saint Catherine	Spanish Town	460	1,192	354,000
Saint Elizabeth	Black River	468	1,212	144,500
Saint James	Montego Bay	230	595	150,900
Saint Mary	Port Maria	236	611	111,700
Saint Thomas	Morant Bay	287	743	85,400
Trelawny	Falmouth	338	875	73,200
Westmoreland	Savanna-la-Mar	312	807	126,800
TOTAL		4,244	10,991	2,355,100

Demography

Population (1989): 2,376,000.
Density (1989): persons per sq mi 559.8, persons per sq km 216.2.
Urban-rural (1987): urban 49.6%; rural 50.4%.
Sex distribution (1988): male 49.75%; female 50.25%.
Age breakdown (1988): under 15, 34.9%; 15–29, 31.5%; 30–44, 14.8%; 45–59, 9.2%; 60–74, 6.2%; 75 and over, 3.4%.
Population projection: (2000) 2,602,000; (2010) 2,826,000.
Doubling time: 40 years[4].
Ethnic composition (1983): black 76.3%; Afro-European 15.1%; East Indian and Afro-East Indian 3.4%; white 3.2%; other 2.0%.
Religious affiliation (1982): Protestant 55.9%, of which Church of God 18.4%, Baptist 10.0%, Anglican 7.1%, Seventh-day Adventist 6.9%, Pentecostal 5.2%; Roman Catholic 5.0%; nonreligious or atheist 17.7%; religion not stated 11.2%; other 10.2%.
Major cities (1982): Kingston 104,041[5] (metropolitan area 524,638); Spanish Town 89,097; Portmore 73,400; Montego Bay 70,265; May Pen 40,962.

Vital statistics

Birth rate per 1,000 population (1988): 22.7 (world avg. 27.1); (1985) legitimate 15.4%, illegitimate 84.6%.
Death rate per 1,000 population (1988): 5.2 (world avg. 9.9).
Natural increase rate per 1,000 population (1988): 17.5 (world avg. 17.2).
Total fertility rate (avg. births per childbearing woman; 1987): 2.9.
Marriage rate per 1,000 population (1987): 4.5.
Divorce rate per 1,000 population (1987): 0.4.
Life expectancy at birth (1985): male 68.1 years; female 72.6 years.
Major causes of death per 100,000 population (1982): cerebrovascular disease 80.5; ischemic heart diseases 77.4; malignant neoplasms (cancers) 75.3; hypertensive disease 29.7; diabetes mellitus 23.5.

National economy

Budget (1988–89). Revenue J$6,020,300,000 (tax revenue 81.2%, of which income taxes 33.6%, consumption taxes 20.2%, stamp duties 10.9%; nontax revenue 9.8%; grants 7.3%). Expenditures: J$8,199,000,000 (current expenditure 60.9%, of which debt interest 21.8%; development expenditure 39.1%).
Public debt (external, outstanding; 1987): U.S.$3,511,000,000.
Tourism: receipts from visitors (1988) U.S.$525,000,000; expenditures by nationals abroad (1987) U.S.$32,000,000.
Production (metric tons except as noted). Agriculture, forestry, fishing (1987): sugarcane 1,982,000, coconuts 180,000, yams 176,000, bananas 50,900, oranges 42,000, plantains 28,200, tomatoes 16,000, cocoa 8,060, pimientos 2,390, tobacco 2,000, coffee 1,660; livestock (number of live animals) 440,000 goats, 290,000 cattle, 246,000 pigs; roundwood 153,000 cu m; fish catch 10,621. Mining and quarrying (value of production in J$'000,000; 1987): bauxite 1,274; alumina 1,274; gypsum 8. Manufacturing (value of production in J$'000,000; 1987): beer and stout 431; sugar 427; cigarettes 334; carbonated beverages 259; poultry meat 254; flour 180. Construction (private sector only): residential completions (1983) 54,500 sq m; nonresidential starts (1986) 16,300 sq m. Energy production (consumption): electricity (kW-hr; 1987) 2,385,000,000 (2,385,000,000); coal, none (none); crude petroleum (barrels; 1987) none (6,964,000); petroleum products (metric tons; 1987) 820,000 (1,763,000); natural gas, none (none).
Land use (1986): forested 17.5%; meadows and pastures 18.0%; agricultural and under permanent cultivation 24.8%; other 39.7%.
Gross national product (at current market prices; 1987): U.S.$2,256,000,000 (U.S.$960 per capita).

Structure of gross domestic product and labour force

	1988 in value J$'000,000	% of total value	labour force	% of labour force
Agriculture	988	5.7	261,100	24.3
Mining	1,567	9.0	6,200	0.6
Manufacturing	3,741	21.4	131,100	12.2
Construction	1,618	9.3	48,900	4.5
Public utilities	486	2.8 }	40,700	3.8
Transp. and commun.	1,426	8.2 }		
Trade	3,739	21.4	135,000	12.6
Pub. admin., defense	1,529	8.7	74,100	6.9
Finance, real estate	3,065	17.5 }	167,800	15.6
Services	809	4.6 }		
Other	−1,496[6]	−8.6[6]	210,200[7]	19.5[7]
TOTAL	17,472	100.0	1,075,100	100.0

Population economically active (1987): total 1,079,200; activity rate of total population 46.1% (participation rates: ages 14–64, 75.2%; female 45.3%; unemployed [1988] 18.9%).

Price and earnings indexes (1985 = 100)

	1983	1984	1985	1986	1987	1988	1989
Consumer price index	62.2	79.6	100.0	115.1	122.8	132.9	149.5[8]
Monthly earnings index	...	...	...	...	...	...	...

Household income and expenditure. Average household size (1982) 4.3; income per household, n.a.; sources of income (1985): wages and salaries 60.7%, transfers 15.2%, self-employment 14.3%; expenditure (1987)[9]: food 30.0%, cafés, restaurants, and hotels 12.4%, transportation 10.9%, energy and water 6.1%, rent 5.6%, beverages 5.2%, household furnishings 5.2%.

Foreign trade[10]

Balance of trade (current prices)

	1983	1984	1985	1986	1987	1988
J$'000,000	−1,071.2	−1,103.8	−2,417.5	−1,370.6	−2,254.2	−2,837.6
% of total	27.8%	16.5%	28.4%	17.3%	24.0%	25.5%

Imports (1988): J$7,852,000,000 (raw materials 48.9%, of which fuels 13.5%; capital goods 31.7%, of which machinery 13.6%, construction materials 9.5%; consumer goods 19.4%). *Major import sources:* United States 48.0%; Canada 7.3%; United Kingdom 6.9%; Venezuela 4.6%; Japan 3.5%.
Exports (1988): J$4,519,000,000 (alumina 37.8%; garments 15.4%; bauxite 12.9%; raw sugar 10.9%; bananas 1.9%; rum 1.7%; coffee 1.3%). *Major export destinations:* United States 35.5%; United Kingdom 14.3%; Canada 13.1%; The Netherlands 7.6%; Trinidad and Tobago 3.1%.

Transport and communications

Transport. Railroads (1986): length 183 mi, 294 km; passenger-mi 41,861,000, passenger-km 67,368,000; short ton-mi cargo 116,784,000, metric ton-km cargo 170,502,000. Roads (1985): total length 7,680 mi, 12,360 km (paved 39%). Vehicles (1988)[11]: passenger cars 52,886; trucks and buses 23,032[12]. Merchant marine (1988): vessels (100 gross tons and over) 12; total deadweight tonnage 21,317. Air transport (1988)[13]: passenger-mi 1,202,000,000, passenger-km 1,935,000,000; short ton-mi cargo 15,510,000, metric ton-km cargo 22,645,000; airports (1989) with scheduled flights 6.
Communications. Daily newspapers (1988): total number 2; total circulation 89,400; circulation per 1,000 population 38. Radio (1988): 907,060 receivers (1 per 2.6 persons). Television (1988): 387,000 receivers (1 per 6.1 persons). Telephones (1988): 170,410 (1 per 14 persons).

Education and health

Education (1986–87)[14]

	schools	teachers	students	student/teacher ratio
Primary (age 6–11)	787	9,419	332,636	35.3
Secondary (age 12–16)	131	7,447	226,288	30.4
Voc., teacher tr.	10	501	8,778	17.5
Higher	17	...	17,791	...

Educational attainment (1982). Percent of population age 25 and over having: no formal schooling 3.2%; some primary education 79.8%; some secondary 15.0%; complete secondary and higher 2.0%. *Literacy* (1980): total population age 14 and over literate 1,100,600 (88.6%); males literate 542,600 (88.2%); females literate 558,000 (89.1%).
Health (1988): physicians 367[15] (1 per 6,421 persons); hospital beds 5,698 (1 per 414 persons); infant mortality rate per 1,000 live births (1987) 18.0.
Food (1984–86): daily per capita caloric intake 2,581 (vegetable products 86%, animal products 14%); (1984) 115% of FAO recommended minimum requirement.

Military

Total active duty personnel (1988): 2,500 (army 88.0%; navy 6.0%; air force 6.0%). *Military expenditure as percent of GNP* (1987): 1.1% (world 5.4%); per capita expenditure U.S.$12.

---

[1]January 1. [2]The parishes of Kingston and Saint Andrew are jointly administered from the Half Way Tree section of Saint Andrew. [3]Kingston included with Saint Andrew. [4]Net migration abroad in 1988 was equal to 94% of natural-increase rate. [5]City of Kingston is coextensive with Kingston parish. [6]Less imputed service charges. [7]Includes 203,300 unemployed. [8]May. [9]Includes expenditure in domestic market by nonresidents equaling 26.1% of total expenditure. [10]Import figures are f.o.b. in balance of trade and c.i.f. in commodities and trading partners. [11]Vehicles passing road-fitness test only. [12]Includes tractors. [13]Air Jamaica only. [14]Public schools only. [15]Government-employed only.

Japan

Official name: Nihon (Japan).
Form of government: constitutional monarchy with a National Diet consisting of two legislative houses (House of Councillors [252]; House of Representatives [512]).
Chief of state: Emperor.
Head of government: Prime Minister.
Capital: Tōkyō.
Official language: Japanese.
Official religion: none.
Monetary unit: 1 yen (¥) = 100 sen; valuation (Oct. 2, 1989) 1 U.S.$ = ¥139.52; 1 £ = ¥225.75.

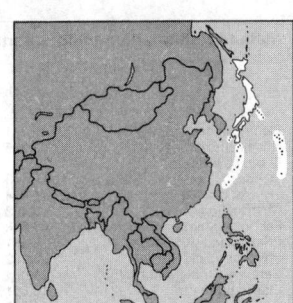

Other principal cities (1988)

	population		population		population
Akashi	264,274	Kanazawa	437,202	Ōmiya	390,765
Akita	299,683	Kashiwa	296,154	Otsu	247,609
Amagasaki	502,974	Kasugai	263,961	Sagamihara	510,757
Aomori	293,020	Kawagoe	298,715	Sakai	815,946
Asahikawa	364,401	Kawaguchi	426,435	Sasebo	248,382
Chiba	815,238	Kōchi	316,826	Sendai	884,087
Fujisawa	341,505	Koriyama	308,807	Shimizu	242,110
Fukushima	275,009	Koshigaya	275,820	Shimonoseki	266,062
Fukuyama	364,065	Kumamoto	570,791	Shizuoka	472,829
Fukui	253,234	Kurashiki	414,801	Suita	350,262
Funabashi	527,367	Machida	340,756	Takamatsu	330,252
Gifu	409,054	Maebashi	283,567	Takatsuki	358,380
Hachinohe	243,083	Matsudo	448,533	Tokorozawa	293,858
Hachiōji	446,970	Matsuyama	437,829	Tokushima	261,831
Hakodate	312,771	Miyazaki	285,427	Toyama	318,812
Hamamatsu	527,564	Nagano	343,200	Toyohashi	330,918
Higashi–Ōsaka	522,661	Nagasaki	447,535	Toyonaka	414,922
Himeji	453,276	Naha	305,987	Toyota	322,112
Hirakata	391,340	Nara	344,970	Urawa	400,803
Ibaraki	255,118	Neyagawa	258,448	Utsunomiya	419,578
Ichihara	248,534	Niigata	482,700	Wakayama	399,240
Ichikawa	422,577	Nishinomiya	424,283	Yamagata	248,421
Ichinomiya	261,460	Ōita	402,718	Yao	276,591
Iwaki	353,246	Okayama	587,408	Yokkaichi	269,857
Kagoshima	535,202	Okazaki	298,477	Yokosuka	431,192

Mobility (1980). Population living in same residence from birth 24.0%; different residence established prior to October 1975, 44.0%; different residence established after October 1975, 32.0%, of which: same prefecture 24.1%; different prefecture 7.7%.
Households (1987). Total households 39,536,000; average household size 3.2; composition of households (1985) 1 person 20.8%, 2 persons 18.4%, 3 persons 17.9%, 4 persons 23.6%, 5 persons 11.0%, 6 persons 5.2%, 7 or more persons 2.9%. Family households (1985) 30,021,000 (79.0%); nonfamily 7,967,000 (21.0%), of which 1-person 7,900,000 (20.8%).

Type of household (1988)

Total number of dwelling units: 37,454,000

	number of dwellings	percent of total
by kind of dwelling		
exclusive entry (do not share bathroom or kitchen)	34,708,000	92.7
combined with nondwelling	2,746,000	7.3
detached house	23,377,000	62.4
apartment building	11,344,000	30.3
tenement (substandard or overcrowded building)	2,535,000	6.8
other	197,000	0.5
by legal tenure of householder		
owned	22,981,000	61.4
rented	13,950,000	37.2
other	523,000	1.4
by kind of amenities		
flush toilet	24,642,000	65.8
bathroom	34,068,000	91.0
by year of construction		
prior to 1945	2,705,000	7.3
1945–70	11,495,000	31.2
1971–80	13,469,000	36.6
1981–83	3,566,000	9.7
1984–88	5,580,000	15.2

Immigration (1987): permanent immigrants/registered aliens admitted 884,000, from North and South Korea 76.2%, Taiwan, Hong Kong, and China 10.8%, United States 3.5%, Philippines 2.8%, United Kingdom 0.9%, West Germany 0.4%, Canada 0.3%, France 0.3%, Malaysia 0.3%, Australia 0.2%.

Area and population

Regions Prefectures	Capitals	area sq mi	area sq km	population 1988 estimate[1]
Chūbu				
Aichi	Nagoya	1,984	5,139	6,590,000
Fukui	Fukui	1,619	4,192	822,000
Gifu	Gifu	4,091	10,596	2,052,000
Ishikawa	Kanazawa	1,621	4,198	1,159,000
Nagano	Nagano	5,245	13,585	2,152,000
Niigata	Niigata	4,857	12,579	2,480,000
Shizuoka	Shizuoka	3,001	7,773	3,636,000
Toyama	Toyama	1,642	4,252	1,121,000
Yamanashi	Kōfu	1,723	4,463	846,000
Chūgoku				
Hiroshima	Hiroshima	3,269	8,467	2,846,000
Okayama	Okayama	2,738	7,092	1,929,000
Shimane	Matsue	2,559[2]	6,629[2]	791,000
Tottori	Tottori	1,349[2]	3,494[2]	618,000
Yamaguchi	Yamaguchi	2,358	6,107	1,592,000
Hokkaidō				
Hokkaidō (Territory)	Sapporo	32,247	83,520	5,671,000
Kantō				
Chiba	Chiba	1,989	5,151	5,392,000
Gumma	Maebashi	2,454	6,356	1,946,000
Ibaraki	Mito	2,353	6,094	2,794,000
Kanagawa	Yokohama	928	2,403	7,760,000
Saitama	Urawa	1,467	3,799	6,181,000
Tochigi	Utsunomiya	2,476	6,414	1,903,000
Kinki				
Hyōgo	Kōbe	3,236	8,381	5,349,000
Mie	Tsu	2,231	5,778	1,773,000
Nara	Nara	1,425	3,692	1,352,000
Shiga	Ōtsu	1,551	4,016	1,193,000
Wakayama	Wakayama	1,824	4,725	1,081,000
Kyūshū				
Fukuoka	Fukuoka	1,916	4,963	4,771,000
Kagoshima	Kagoshima	3,539	9,167	1,815,000
Kumamoto	Kumamoto	2,860	7,408	1,847,000
Miyazaki	Miyazaki	2,986	7,735	1,176,000
Nagasaki	Nagasaki	1,588	4,113	1,583,000
Ōita	Ōita	2,447	6,338	1,245,000
Saga	Saga	942	2,440	881,000
Ryukyu				
Okinawa	Naha	871	2,255	1,213,000
Shikoku				
Ehime	Matsuyama	2,190	5,672	1,527,000
Kagawa	Takamatsu	727	1,883	1,026,000
Kōchi	Kōchi	2,744	7,107	835,000
Tokushima	Tokushima	1,601	4,146	835,000
Tohoku				
Akita	Akita	4,484[3]	11,613[3]	1,239,000
Aomori	Aomori	3,714[3]	9,619[3]	1,509,000
Fukushima	Fukushima	5,322	13,784	2,095,000
Iwate	Morioka	5,898	15,277	1,423,000
Miyagi	Sendai	2,815	7,292	2,221,000
Yamagata	Yamagata	3,601	9,327	1,262,000
Metropolis				
Tōkyō[4]	Tōkyō	836	2,166	11,890,000
Urban prefectures				
Kyōto[5]	Kyōto	1,781	4,613	2,605,000
Ōsaka[5]	Ōsaka	722	1,869	8,751,000
TOTAL		145,883[6,7]	377,835[6,7]	122,783,000[7]

Demography

Population (1989): 123,120,000.
Density (1989): persons per sq mi 843.9, persons per sq km 325.8.
Urban–rural (1985): urban 76.7%; rural 23.3%.
Sex distribution (1989): male 49.16%; female 50.84%.
Age breakdown (1989): under 15, 19.0%; 15–29, 21.6%; 30–44, 22.4%; 45–59, 20.1%; 60–69, 9.2%; 70 and over, 7.7%.
Population projection: (2000) 129,380,000; (2010) 131,990,000.
Doubling time: n.a.; doubling time exceeds 100 years.
Composition by nationality (1988): Japanese 99.4%; Korean 0.5%; Chinese and other 0.1%.
Place of birth (1989): 99.4% native-born; 0.6% foreign-born (mainly Korean).
Religious affiliation (1987): most Japanese consider themselves to be adherents of both Shintō (89.5%), a body of indigenous beliefs and practices, and Buddhism (76.4%). A small proportion of the population is Christian (1.2%). Most of the others (9.3%) are members of the "new religions," which incorporate to varying degrees Shintō, Buddhist, Taoist, and Christian beliefs.
Major cities (1988): Tōkyō 8,323,699; Yokohama 3,151,087; Ōsaka 2,644,691; Nagoya 2,147,677; Sapporo 1,621,418; Kyōto 1,474,507; Kōbe 1,447,547; Fukuoka 1,203,729; Kawasaki 1,142,953; Hiroshima 1,073,194; Kita-Kyūshū 1,039,482.

Vital statistics

Birth rate per 1,000 population (1989): 11.0 (world avg. 27.1); (1985) legitimate 99.0%; illegitimate 1.0%.
Death rate per 1,000 population (1989): 6.0 (world avg. 9.9).
Natural increase rate per 1,000 population (1989): 4.0 (world avg. 17.2).
Total fertility rate (avg. births per childbearing woman; 1988): 1.7.
Marriage rate per 1,000 population[8] (1987): 5.7; median age at first marriage, men 28.3 years, women 25.6 years.
Divorce rate per 1,000 population[8] (1987): 1.3.
Life expectancy at birth (1988): male 75.9 years; female 82.1 years.
Major causes of death per 100,000 population (1987): malignant neoplasms (cancers) 163.5; heart diseases 117.9; cerebrovascular diseases 101.2; pneumonia and bronchitis 44.6; accidents and adverse effects 23.2; senility without mention of psychosis 20.7; suicide 19.5; cirrhosis of the liver 13.7; nephritis, nephrotic syndrome, and nephrosis 11.7; hypertensive diseases 8.8.

Social indicators

Educational attainment (1980). Percent of population aged 15 years and over having: no schooling 0.3%; primary and lower secondary education 38.5%; higher secondary 38.0%; junior college and technical college 5.7%; university and postgraduate 8.0%; still in school 9.5%.

Distribution of income (1986)

percent of average household income by decile

1	2	3	4	5	6	7	8	9	10 (highest)
33.0	49.8	61.1	71.6	81.8	92.8	105.8	122.6	148.2	232.9

Quality of working life. Average workweek (1987): 44.3 hours. Annual rate of industrial deaths per 100,000 workers (1987): 3.1. Proportion of labour force insured for damages or income loss resulting from injury, permanent disability, and death (1988): 47.7%. Average man-days lost to labour

stoppages per 1,000 workdays (1987): 0.1. Average duration of journey to work[9] (1988): 26.8 minutes ([1983] 26.7% private automobile, 67.4% public transportation, 5.5% taxi, 0.4% other). Rate per 1,000 workers of discouraged (unemployed no longer seeking work; 1982): 69.7.

Access to services (1983). Proportion of households having access to: gas supply (1980) 63.0%; safe public water supply 93.7%; public sewage collection 89.4%.

Social participation. Eligible voters participating in last national election (1986): 69.9%. Population 15 years and over participating in social service activities on a voluntary basis (1987): 26.0%. Trade union membership in total work force (1987): 27.6%.

Social deviance (1987). Offense rate per 100,000 population for: homicide 1.4; rape 1.4; robbery 1.6; larceny and theft 1,130.2. Incidence in general population of: alcoholism, n.a.; drug and substance abuse, n.a. Rate of suicide per 100,000 population 19.5.

Leisure/use of personal time

Discretionary daily activities (1986)
(Population age 15 years and over)

	weekly average hrs./min.
Total discretionary daily time	5:47
of which	
Hobbies and amusements	0:31
Sports	0:10
Learning (except schoolwork)	0:12
Social service	0:02
Voluntary social organizations and associations	0:28
Radio, television, newspapers, and magazines	2:18
Rest and relaxation	1:21
Other activities	0:45

Major leisure activities (1986)
(Population age 15 years and over)

	Percentage of participation		
	Male	Female	Total
Hobbies and amusements	89.4	86.8	88.0
Sports	84.0	69.1	76.3
Light exercises	30.4	32.9	31.6
Swimming	31.5	21.0	26.1
Bowling	29.6	18.8	24.0
Learning (except schoolwork)	37.0	34.1	35.5
Travel			
Domestic	76.1	70.4	73.1
Foreign	5.8	3.7	4.7

Material well-being (1988). Households possessing: automobile 71.9%; telephone, virtually 100%; colour television receiver 99.0%; refrigerator 98.3%; air conditioner 59.3%; washing machine 99.0%; vacuum cleaner 98.2%; videocassette recorder 53.0%; camera 85.3%; microwave oven 57.0%.

National economy

Gross national product (at current market prices; 1989): U.S.$1,843,000,000,-000 (U.S.$15,030 per capita).

Structure of gross domestic product and labour force

	1987		1988	
	in value ¥'000,000,000	% of total value	labour force	% of labour force
Agriculture, fishing	9,335.2	3.0	4,740,000	7.7
Mining	1,184.3	0.4	70,000	0.1
Manufacturing	107,927.8	34.8	14,540,000	23.6
Construction	21,986.4	7.1	5,600,000	9.1
Public utilities	8,734.7	2.8	310,000	0.5
Transp. and commun.	18,150.5	5.8	3,530,000	5.7
Trade	46,608.5	15.0	13,890,000	22.5
Finance	49,434.9	15.9	2,360,000	3.8
Pub. admin., defense	12,675.8	4.1	1,940,000	3.1
Services	52,062.3	16.8	12,840,000	20.8
Other	−17,588.0[10]	−5.7[10]	1,840,000[11]	3.0[11]
TOTAL	310,512.4	100.0[7]	61,660,000	100.0[7]

Budget (1989)[12]. Revenue: ¥60,414,194,000,000 (income tax 30.1%; corporation tax 23.3%; public bonds 11.8%; inheritance tax 4.6%; liquor and tobacco tax 4.5%; stamp duties 3.1%; securities transaction tax 1.8%; customs duties 1.3%). Expenditures: ¥60,414,194,000,000 (transfers to local governments 22.2%; social security 19.8%; national debt 19.3%; public works 10.3%; culture, education, and science promotion 8.2%; national defense 6.5%; pensions 3.1%; economic cooperation 1.2%; foodstuff control 0.7%; measures for energy 0.9%; small-enterprise assistance 0.3%).

Public debt (1988): U.S.$1,240,700,000,000.

Population economically active (1988): total 61,660,000; activity rate of total population 50.2% (participation rates: ages 15–64, 72.5%; female 40.1%; unemployed 2.5%).

Price and earnings indexes (1985 = 100)

	1983	1984	1985	1986	1987	1988	1989
Consumer price index	95.8	98.0	100.0	100.6	100.7	101.4	104.0[13]
Monthly earnings index	93.7	96.9	100.0	102.8	105.0	108.9	114.0[14]

Household income and expenditure[15] (1988). Average household size 3.2; average annual income per household ¥5,775,600 (U.S.$45,000); sources of income: wages and salaries 94.2%, of which (1987) regular income of household head 64.4%, temporary income and bonuses of household head 17.3%, income of other household members 12.0%; expenditure (1988): food 24.4%, transportation 10.2%, reading and recreation 9.1%, clothing and footwear 7.1%, fuel, light, and water charges 5.1%, housing 5.1%, education 4.7%, furniture and household utensils 4.0%, medical care 2.4%.

Tourism (1988): receipts from visitors U.S.$2,893,000,000; expenditures by nationals abroad U.S.$18,682,000,000.

Manufacturing and mining enterprises (1986)

	no. of establishments	avg. no. of persons engaged	monthly avg. as a % of contract wages	annual value added (¥'000,000,000)
Electrical machinery	35,171	1,867,000	88.1	14,723
Nonelectrical machinery	43,225	1,117,000	101.5	9,513
Food, beverages, and tobacco	52,143	1,188,000	77.4	8,977
Transport equipment	14,964	916,000	104.8	8,649
Chemical products	5,462	396,000	124.7	8,532
Fabricated metal products	49,388	782,000	90.2	5,541
Printing and publishing	29,581	527,000	125.3	4,853
Iron and steel	6,482	369,000	114.6	4,269
Ceramic, stone, and clay	21,004	460,000	91.7	3,987
Plastic products	18,861	397,000	83.6	2,984
Textiles	34,515	591,000	66.7	2,886
Paper and paper products	11,808	277,000	98.8	2,440
Apparel products	31,585	559,000	50.9	1,800
Precision instruments	7,603	259,000	80.4	1,764
Nonferrous metal products	4,194	162,000	105.7	1,495
Lumber and wood products	21,602	265,000	75.0	1,399
Furniture and fixtures	17,589	224,000	81.5	1,265
Rubber products	5,862	168,000	94.6	1,220
Petroleum and coal products	1,063	37,000	144.7	927
Leather products	5,996	79,000	70.2	398
Mining[16]	848	40,982	103.0	293

Energy production (consumption): electricity (kW-hr; 1987) 698,970,000,000 (698,970,000,000); coal (metric tons; 1987) 13,049,000 (102,512,000); crude petroleum (barrels; 1987) 4,500,000 (1,147,000,000); petroleum products (metric tons; 1987) 134,820,000, of which (by volume) heavy fuel oil 38.7%, gasoline 21.7%, kerosene and jet fuel 16.6%, diesel 14.5%, naphtha 5.9% (165,300,000); natural gas (cu m; 1987) 2,092,000,000 (41,865,000,000). Composition of energy supply by source (1986): crude oil and petroleum products 55.2%, coal 19.1%, nuclear power 10.3%, natural gas 9.6%, hydroelectric power 5.3%, other 0.5%. Domestic energy demand by end use (1986): mining and manufacturing 37.3%, residential and commercial 27.9%, transportation 15.6%, agriculture, forestry, and fisheries 2.5%, other 16.7%.

Financial aggregates

	1982	1983	1984	1985	1986	1987	1988
Exchange rate[16] ¥ per:							
U.S. dollar	249.08	237.51	237.52	238.54	168.52	144.64	128.15
£	379.41	336.83	290.40	289.62	247.2	237.0	210.0
SDR	259.23	243.10	246.13	220.23	194.61	175.2	169.4
International reserves (U.S.$)[17]							
Total (excl. gold; '000,000)	23,334	24,602	26,429	26,719	42,257	80,973	96,728
SDRs ('000,000)	2,091	1,935	1,927	2,116	2,218	2,463	2,936
Reserve pos. in IMF ('000,000)	2,071	2,303	2,219	2,275	2,382	2,853	3,278
Foreign exchange ('000,000)	19,172	20,364	22,283	22,328	37,657	75,657	90,514
Gold ('000,000 fine troy oz)	24.23	24.23	24.23	24.23	24.23	24.23	24.23
% world reserves	2.6	2.6	2.6	2.6	2.6	2.6	2.6
Interest and prices							
Central bank discount (%)	5.50	5.00	5.00	5.00	3.00	2.50	2.50
Gov't. bond yield (%)	8.06	7.42	6.81	6.34	4.94	4.94	4.27
Industrial share prices (1985 = 100)	55.1	64.9	81.9	100.0	132.9	196.4	213.9
Balance of payments (U.S.$'000,000,000)							
Balance of visible trade	18.1	31.5	44.3	56.0	92.8	96.4	95.0
Imports, f.o.b.	119.6	114.0	124.0	118.0	112.8	128.2	164.8
Exports, f.o.b.	137.7	145.5	168.3	174.0	205.6	224.6	259.8
Balance of invisibles	−9.9	−9.1	−7.8	−5.2	−4.9	−5.8	−11.3
Balance of payments, current account	6.9	20.8	35.0	49.2	85.8	87.0	79.6

Production (metric tons except as noted). Agriculture, forestry, fishing (1988): rice 12,419,000, potatoes 4,000,000, sugar beets 3,760,000, sugarcane 2,900,-000, mandarin oranges 2,800,000, radishes 2,655,000, cabbages 1,650,000, Chinese cabbages 1,420,000, sweet potatoes 1,400,000, onions 1,294,000, cucumbers 1,050,000, apples 998,000, wheat 860,000, watermelons 855,000, tomatoes 840,000, carrots 660,000, eggplants 605,000, Welsh onions 564,-000[17], Japanese pears 497,000, lettuce 490,000, spinach 387,000, taro 360,-000, soybeans 320,000, grapes 312,000, persimmons 290,000[17], pumpkins 273,000, peaches 213,000, turnips 212,000, strawberries 208,300, cauliflowers 145,000, tobacco 104,000, tea 96,000, cow's milk 7,608,000 (of which marketed as fluid milk 4,324,000), hen's eggs 2,409,000; livestock (number of live animals) 11,725,000 pigs, 4,667,000 cattle (of which 2,017,000 dairy cows), 41,000 goats, 29,000 sheep, 22,000 horses, 334,000,000 poultry; roundwood (1987) 66,767,000 cu m, of which coniferous species 20,292,000 cu m, broadleaved species 10,601,000 cu m; fish catch (1987) 12,465,000, of which sardines 4,362,000, Alaska pollack 1,313,000, mackerel 1,032,000, oysters 259,000, squid 183,000, yellowtails 159,000, eel and trout 57,000. Mining and quarrying (1986): limestone 162,368,000; quicklime 6,617,000; gypsum 6,400,000; dolomite 3,953,000; fire clay 1,004,150; pyrophyllite clay 310,300[17]; zinc 147,211[17]; iron ore 131,400[17]; talc 84,522; barite 66,018; lead 22,899[17]; copper 16,666[17]; chromium 7,420; silver 339,659 kg; gold 3,100 kg. Manufacturing (1987): crude steel 98,513,000; semifinished steel 92,440,000; hot-rolled steel products 77,597,000; pig iron 73,418,000; cement 71,551,-000; cold-rolled steel strips 19,850,000; paper pulp 9,733,000; sulfuric acid 6,541,000; plastic products 5,020,000; compound fertilizers 3,469,000; spun yarn 1,036,000; cotton fabrics 1,837,000,000 sq m; finished products (in number of units) 314,979,000 fluorescent lamps, 285,072,000 watches, 53,-776,000 electronic desk calculators, 29,319,000 stereo recorders, 27,489,000 videocassette recorders, 16,399,000 35-mm cameras, 14,286,000 colour television receivers, 12,603,000 air conditioners, 8,654,000 microwave ovens, 7,891,000 passenger cars, 7,311,000 trucks and buses, 5,008,000 electric refrigerators, 4,772,000 automatic washing machines, 2,631,000 motorcycles, 2,411,000 facsimile machines, 2,111,000 digital computers, 2,209,000 copying machines, 45,050 industrial robots. Construction (floor area started; 1987): residential 123,703,000 sq m; nonresidential 237,226,000 sq m, of

which government and public owned 21,040,000 sq m, private owned 216,186,000 sq m.

Retail and wholesale trade and services (1985)

	no. of establish-ments	avg. no. of em-ployees	annual sales (¥'000,000,000)
Retail trade	1,628,644	6,329,000	101,719
Food and beverages	671,190	2,351,000	31,818
Grocery	92,602	622,000	12,846
Liquors	106,693	294,000	5,045
General merchandise	3,531	389,000	13,855
Department stores	1,827	381,000	13,694
Gasoline service stations	74,470	357,000	11,109
Apparel and accessories	229,634	755,000	10,721
Motor vehicles and bicycles	83,931	464,000	10,271
Furniture and home furnishings	172,686	586,000	8,767
Eating and drinking places	838,449	1,965,000	8,686
Wholesale trade	413,016	3,998,000	428,291
General merchandise	985	58,000	84,080
Machinery and equipment	85,072	960,000	76,666
General machinery except electrical	40,389	393,000	23,836
Motor vehicles and parts	13,745	195,000	19,575
Minerals and metals	21,017	245,000	59,775
Farm, livestock, and fishery products	39,193	380,000	53,359
Food and beverages	54,082	496,000	34,866
Textiles, apparel, and accessories	41,004	461,000	30,781
Building materials	56,029	355,000	20,534
Chemicals	15,546	149,000	17,742
Drugs and toilet goods	16,809	238,000	12,665
Medical services	171,986	2,026,000	...
Educational services	84,512	2,065,000	...

Land use (1986): forested 66.7%; meadows and pastures 1.7%; agricultural and under permanent cultivation 13.0%; other 18.6%.

Foreign trade[18]

Balance of trade (current prices)

	1983	1984	1985	1986	1987	1988
¥'000,000,000	+7,373	+10,674	+13,238	+15,519	+12,174	+11,903
% of total	11.8%	20.9%	18.7%	28.2%	22.4%	21.3%

Imports (1988): ¥24,007,000,000,000 (food 15.5%, of which fish 5.6%; machinery and equipment 14.2%; crude petroleum and petroleum products 13.8%; chemicals 7.9%; textiles 5.7%; nonferrous metals 5.0%; metal ores and scrap 4.5%, of which iron ore 1.5%; wood 3.8%; coal 2.9%). *Major import sources:* United States 22.4%; South Korea 6.3%; Australia 5.5%; China 5.3%; Indonesia 5.1%; Taiwan 4.7%; Canada 4.4%; West Germany 4.3%; Saudi Arabia 3.4%; Malaysia 2.5%; U.S.S.R. 1.5%.
Exports (1988): ¥33,928,000,000,000 (motor vehicles 18.4%; office machinery 6.9%; iron and steel 5.8%; chemicals 5.3%, of which plastic materials 1.5%; scientific and optical equipment 4.1%; tape recorders 2.9%; textiles and allied products 2.6%; power-generating machinery 2.5%; metalworking machinery 1.5%; vessels 1.5%; radio receivers 0.8%; televison receivers 0.7%). *Major export destinations:* United States 33.8%; West Germany 6.0%; South Korea 5.8%; Taiwan 5.4%; Hong Kong 4.4%; United Kingdom 3.9%; China 3.6%; Canada 2.5%; Australia 2.5%.

Trade by commodity group (1988)

SITC group	imports U.S.$'000,000	%	exports U.S.$'000,000	%
00 Food and live animals / 01 Beverages and tobacco	30,190	16.1	1,665	0.6
02 Crude materials, excluding fuels	25,415[19]	13.6[19]	1,746[19]	0.7[19]
03 Mineral fuels, lubricants, and related materials	38,356	20.5	642	0.2
04 Animal and vegetable oils, fats, and waxes	[19]	[19]	[19]	[19]
05 Chemicals and related products, n.e.s.	14,540	7.8	13,780	5.2
06 Basic manufactures	17,330	9.2	22,778	8.6
07 Machinery and transport equipment	20,771	11.1	127,386	48.1
08 Miscellaneous manufactured articles	22,644	12.1	70,350	26.6
09 Goods not classified by kind	18,108	9.6	26,570	10.0
TOTAL	187,354	100.0	264,917	100.0

Direction of trade (1988)

	imports U.S.$'000,000	%	exports U.S.$'000,000	%
Africa	4,304	2.3	6,058	2.3
Asia	77,444	41.3	84,985	32.1
South America	5,856	3.1	3,162	1.2
North America and Central America	52,930	28.3	102,194	38.6
United States	42,037	22.4	89,634	33.8
other North and Central Am.	10,893	5.9	12,560	4.8
Europe	34,041	18.2	60,152	22.7
EEC	24,071	12.9	46,873	17.7
U.S.S.R.	2,766	1.5	3,130	1.2
other Europe	7,204	3.8	10,149	3.8
Oceania	12,779	6.8	8,366	3.1
TOTAL	187,354	100.0	264,917	100.0

Transport and communications

Transport. Railroads (1987): length 16,016 mi, 25,776 km; rolling stock (1985) locomotives 3,177, passenger cars 46,192, freight cars 40,951; passengers carried 19,414,000,000; passenger-mi 211,972,000,000, passenger-km 341,136,000,000; short ton-mi cargo 13,907,000,000, metric ton-km cargo 20,304,000,000. Roads (1987): total length 682,800 mi, 1,098,900 km (paved 65%). Vehicles (1987): passenger cars 28,653,692; trucks 19,091,587; buses 232,516. Merchant marine (1988): vessels (100 gross tons and over) 9,804; total deadweight tonnage 48,413,587. Air transport (1988): passengers carried 58,516,000; passenger-mi 52,024,000,000, passenger-km 83,724,000,000; short ton-mi cargo 2,865,000,000, metric ton-km cargo 4,182,000,000; airports (1989) with scheduled flights 65. Shares of domestic passenger traffic by mode of transportation (1987): automobiles 47.1%; railway 37.1%; buses 11.1%; airplanes 4.1%; ships 0.6%.

Distribution of traffic (1987)

	cargo carried ('000,000 tons)	% of nat'l total	passengers carried ('000,000)	% of nat'l total
Road	5,046.0	90.2	37,085.0	48.7
Rail (intercity)	82.0	1.5	19,978.0	26.2
Urban transport	—	—	18,920.0	24.8
road	—	—	8,200.0	10.8
rail	—	—	10,720.0	14.0
Inland water	463.0	8.3	155.0	0.2
Air	0.7	0.0	50.0	0.1
TOTAL	5,591.7	100.0	76,188.0	100.0

Communications. Daily newspapers (1988): total number 124; total circulation 71,172,000; circulation per 1,000 population 584. Radio (1988): 96,702,506 receivers (1 per 1.3 persons). Television (1988): 30,250,000 receivers (1 per 4.1 persons). Telephones (1985): 66,636,000 (1 per 1.8 persons).

Other communications media (1987)

Print	titles	Electronic	traffic ('000)
Books (new)	37,010	Telegram	41,038
of which		Domestic	40,087
Social sciences	9,162	International	951
Fiction	6,993	Telex	50,000[20]
Engineering	3,357		
Art	3,063		
Natural sciences	2,954		
History	2,275	Post	
Philosophy	1,869	Mail	19,324,000
Magazines/journals	3,780	Domestic	19,072,000
Weekly	104	International	252,000
Monthly	2,527	Parcels	196,000
		Domestic	191,700
Cinema		International	4,300
Feature films (greater than 1,600 m)	386		

Radio and television broadcasting (1988): total radio stations 1,164, of which commercial 837; total television stations 13,425, of which commercial 6,910. Commercial broadcasters' broadcasting hours (by percentage of programs; 1986): reports—radio 12.6%, television 17.2%; education—radio 5.7%, television 11.9%; culture—radio 17.5%, television 23.9%; entertainment—radio 29.6%, television 42.1%; music—radio 28.6%, television 0%; sports—radio 4.8%, television 3.4%; other—radio 1.1%, television 1.6%. Advertisements (daily avg.; 1986): radio 156, television 254.

Education and health

Education (1988)

	schools	teachers	students	student/teacher ratio
Primary (age 6–11)	24,901	445,000	9,872,000	22.2
Secondary (age 12–17)	16,778	569,000	11,430,000	20.1
Higher	1,123	142,000	2,496,000	17.6

Literacy (1989): total population age 15 and over literate, virtually 100%.
Health (1987): physicians 183,129 (1 per 668 persons); dentists 66,797 (1 per 1,830 persons); nurses[21] 333,040 (1 per 367 persons); pharmacists 135,990 (1 per 899 persons); midwives 24,056 (1 per 5,082 persons); hospital beds 1,582,000 (1 per 77 persons), of which general 72.9%, mental 22.2%, tuberculosis 3.3%, other 1.6%; infant mortality rate per 1,000 live births (1989) 5.0.
Food (1984–86): daily per capita caloric intake 2,858 (vegetable products 79%, animal products 21%); 122% of FAO recommended minimum.

Military

Total active duty personnel (1989): 247,000 (army 63.6%, navy 17.8%, air force 18.6%). *Military expenditure as percent of GNP* (1987): 1.0% (world 5.4%); per capita expenditure U.S.$198.

[1]Oct. 1, 1987. [2]Excludes Lake Naka (38 sq mi [98 sq km]), which is part of both Tottori and Shimane prefectures. [3]Excludes Lake Towada (23 sq mi [60 sq km]), which is part of both Akita and Aomori prefectures. [4]Part of Kanto geographical region. [5]Part of Kinki geographical region. [6]1987 survey; includes Lake Naka and Lake Towada. [7]Detail does not add to total given because of rounding. [8]Figures relate only to Japanese nationals in Japan. [9]Applies to passengers carried within metropolitan areas only. [10]Import duties and statistical discrepancy less imputed bank service charge. [11]Includes 1,730,000 unemployed. [12]Initial budget. [13]July. [14]June. [15]Worker's household. [16]End of period. [17]1987. [18]Import figures are f.o.b. in balance of trade and c.i.f. in commodities and trading partners. [19]Crude materials includes animal and vegetable oils, fats, and waxes. [20]1985. [21]Clinical nurses only.

Jordan

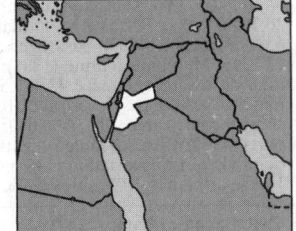

Official name: al-Mamlakah
al-Urdunnīyah al-Hāshimīyah
(al-Urdun) (Hashemite Kingdom of
Jordan).
Form of government: constitutional
monarchy with two legislative houses
(Senate [30 appointed by king]; House
of Deputies [80][1]).
Chief of state: Monarch.
Head of government: Prime Minister
(on King's authority).
Capital: Amman.
Official language: Arabic.
Official religion: Islam.
Monetary unit: 1 Jordan Dinar
(JD) = 1,000 fils; valuation (Oct. 2,
1989) JD 1.00 = U.S.$1.49 = £0.92.

Area and population

Governorates	Capitals	area sq mi	area sq km	population 1988 estimate[2]
'Ammān	Amman	...	...	1,248,580
al-Balqā'	aṣ-Ṣalt	...	...	207,500
Irbid	Irbid	...	...	728,200
al-Karak	al-Karak	...	...	128,450
Ma'ān	Ma'ān	...	...	104,550
al-Mafraq	al-Mafraq	...	...	105,450
aṭ-Ṭafīlah	aṭ-Ṭafīlah	...	...	44,270
az-Zarqā'	az-Zarqā'	...	...	434,000
TOTAL		34,343	88,947	3,001,000

Demography

Population (1989): 3,059,000.
Density (1989): persons per sq mi 89.1, persons per sq km 34.4.
Urban–rural (1986): urban 69.6%; rural 30.4%.
Sex distribution (1986): male 52.31%; female 47.69%.
Age breakdown (1986): under 15, 48.1%; 15–29, 27.4%; 30–44, 12.5%; 45–59, 8.0%; 60–74, 3.1%; 75 and over, 0.9%.
Population projection: (2000) 4,583,000; (2010) 6,620,000.
Doubling time: 19 years.
Ethnic composition (1983): Arab 99.2%; Circassian 0.5%; Armenian 0.1%; Turk 0.1%; Kurd 0.1%.
Religious affiliation (1980): Sunnī Muslim 93.0%; Christian 4.9%; other 2.1%.
Major cities (1988[2]): Amman 900,000; az-Zarqā' 306,500; Irbid 161,690; ar-Ruṣayfah 65,560[3]; aṣ-Ṣalt 42,690[3].

Vital statistics

Birth rate per 1,000 population (1986): 34.7 (world avg. 27.1).
Death rate per 1,000 population (1986): 5.8 (world avg. 9.9).
Natural increase rate per 1,000 population (1986): 28.9 (world avg. 17.2).
Total fertility rate (avg. births per childbearing woman; 1986): 7.4.
Marriage rate per 1,000 population (1986): 6.9.
Divorce rate per 1,000 population (1986): 1.2.
Life expectancy at birth (1986): male 65.0 years; female 68.8 years.
Major causes of death per 100,000 population: n.a.; however, major diseases include tuberculosis, typhoid, and paratyphoid fevers, salmonella, hepatitis, and dysentery; nonvenereal syphilis is widespread in the southern desert region.

National economy

Budget (1989). Revenue: JD 913,100,000 (1986; foreign grants and loans 37.0%; indirect taxes 31.2%, of which import duties 13.8%, excise taxes 6.6%, fees 5.3%; direct taxes 7.2%. Expenditures: JD 1,035,400,000 (1986; finance administration 26.6%; defense 20.8%; economic development 19.8%; social welfare 11.3%; internal security 5.5%; communications and transport 2.3%).
Production (metric tons except as noted). Agriculture, forestry, fishing (1988): tomatoes 200,000, citrus fruit 121,000, wheat 80,000, cucumbers 68,000, potatoes 62,000, watermelons 60,000, eggplants 57,000, barley 40,000, squash 34,000, olives 30,000, green pepper 28,000, grapes 22,000, cauliflower 20,000, pulses 15,000; livestock (number of live animals) 1,220,000 sheep, 460,000 goats, 29,000 cattle, 14,000 camels; roundwood (1987) 10,000 cu m; fish catch (1987) 70. Mining and quarrying (1988): phosphate ore 5,666,000; potash 1,203,200. Manufacturing (1987): cement 2,371,600; chemical acids 1,400,000; fertilizer 604,000; steel 217,000; fodder 44,600[3]; detergents 27,600[3]; metallic pipes 12,500[3]; cigarettes 4,000,400,000 units; liquid batteries 55,400 units[3]; alcoholic beverages 5,320,000 litres. Construction (1986): residential 1,709,300 sq m; nonresidential 557,300 sq m. Energy production (consumption): electricity (kW-hr; 1987) 3,486,000,000 (3,122,000,000); coal, none (n.a.); crude petroleum (barrels; 1987) 183,000 (18,287,000); petroleum products (metric tons; 1987) 2,307,000 (2,793,000); natural gas, none (n.a.).
Population economically active (1986): total 524,200; activity rate of total population 19.6% (participation rates: over age 15, 39.0%; female 10.9%; unemployed 4.5%).

Price and earnings indexes (1985 = 100)

	1983	1984	1985	1986	1987	1988	1989
Consumer price index	93.5	97.1	100.0	100.0	99.7	102.9	125.7[4]
Daily earnings index	...	...	...	...	...	...	...

Household income and expenditure. Average household size (1984) 6.9; income per household (1979)[5] JD 1,820 (U.S.$6,055); sources of income: n.a.; expenditure (1985): food and beverages 37.5%; housing 6.3%; transportation 5.8%; clothing and footwear 5.5%; household durable goods 4.7%; health care 4.0%; education 3.3%; other goods and services 32.9%.
Public debt (external, outstanding; 1987): U.S.$3,518,000,000.
Gross national product (at current market prices; 1987): U.S.$4,370,000,000 (U.S.$1,540 per capita).

Structure of gross domestic product and labour force

	1987 in value JD '000,000	1987 % of total value	1986 labour force	1986 % of labour force
Agriculture	123.2	7.3	32,666	6.2
Mining	64.4	3.8	5,944	1.1
Manufacturing	246.9	14.6	31,438	6.0
Construction	101.3	6.0	56,070	10.7
Public utilities	48.1	2.9	2,858	0.5
Transportation and communications	188.6	11.2	44,880	8.6
Trade	269.8	16.0	54,933	10.5
Finance			17,257	3.3
Pub. admin., defense	} 644.0	} 38.2	} 278,147	53.1
Services				
TOTAL	1,686.3	100.0	524,193	100.0

Land use (1987): forested 0.4%; meadows and pastures 1.0%; agricultural and under permanent cultivation 4.2%; wasteland (mostly desert), built-on, and other 94.4%.
Tourism (1988): receipts from visitors U.S.$621,000,000; expenditures by nationals abroad U.S.$480,000,000.

Foreign trade

Balance of trade (current prices)[6]

	1982	1983	1984	1985	1986	1987
JD '000,000	−878	−893	−781	−763	−594	−667
% of total	52.9%	61.0%	45.7%	55.1%	53.7%	57.3%

Imports (1987): JD 915,545,000 (machinery and transport equipment 20.3%; basic manufactures 18.5%; mineral fuels and lubricants 17.1%, of which crude petroleum 13.0%; food and live animals 17.0%; chemicals 10.0%; miscellaneous manufactured articles 9.6%). *Major import sources:* Iraq 10.8%; United States 10.2%; Saudi Arabia 8.4%; West Germany 7.7%; United Kingdom 6.4%; Japan 6.1%; Italy 5.1%; Turkey 3.8%; France 3.7%; The Netherlands 3.0%; Belgium 2.5%.
Exports (1987): JD 248,773,000 (chemicals 28.1%; phosphate fertilizers 24.5%; potash 11.3%; basic manufactures 10.8%; vegetables, fruit, and nuts 8.0%). *Major export destinations:* Iraq 24.1%; Saudi Arabia 10.5%; India 8.9%; Egypt 5.4%; Pakistan 4.1%; Italy 3.7%; Kuwait 3.5%; Indonesia 3.2%; Japan 3.0%; Syria 2.9%; Poland 2.8%; Romania 2.6%.

Transport and communications

Transport. Railroads (1987): route length 409 mi, 658 km; passengers, 31,304; short ton-mi cargo 864,000,000[7], metric ton-km cargo 1,262,000,000[7]. Roads (1987): total length 3,495 mi, 5,625 km (paved 73%). Vehicles (1986): passenger cars 158,892; trucks and buses 73,469. Merchant marine (1988): vessels (100 gross tons and over) 4; total deadweight tonnage 47,710. Air transport (1988): passenger-mi 2,440,000,000, passenger-km 3,926,835,000; short ton-mi cargo 138,034,000, metric ton-km cargo 201,539,000; airports (1989) with scheduled flights 3.
Communications. Daily newspapers (1987): total number 5; total circulation 185,000; circulation per 1,000 population 65.0. Radio (1988): 1,100,000 receivers (1 per 2.7 persons). Television (1988): 250,000 receivers (1 per 12 persons). Telephones (1987): 343,743[8] (1 per 10 persons).

Education and health

Education (1987–88)

	schools	teachers	students	student/ teacher ratio
Primary[9] (age 4–11)	1,884	19,133	605,777	31.7
Secondary (age 12–17)	1,681	21,729	357,475	16.5
Voc., teacher tr.[10]	52	1,152	50,138	43.5
Higher	3	1,430	36,149	25.3

Educational attainment (1979). Percent of population age 14 and over having: no formal schooling 47.9%; primary education 19.8%; secondary 26.4%; higher 5.9%. *Literacy* (1986): total population age 15 and over literate 1,451,100 (79.4%); males literate 761,900 (81.7%); females literate 689,200 (73.9%).
Health (1986): physicians 3,114 (1 per 881 persons); hospital beds 5,246 (1 per 523 persons); infant mortality rate per 1,000 live births 48.6.
Food (1984–86): daily per capita caloric intake 2,498 (vegetable products 89%, animal products 11%); 120% of FAO recommended minimum requirement.

Military

Total active duty personnel (1988): 82,250 (army 86.8%, navy 0.3%, air force 12.9%). *Military expenditure as percent of GNP* (1987): 13.9% (world 5.4%); per capita expenditure U.S.$235.

[1]A 60-member House of Deputies (142 members according to a never-implemented 1986 law), including 30 representatives from the Israeli-occupied West Bank, was dissolved July 30, 1988, pending Nov. 8, 1989, elections for an 80-seat House that excluded representation for the West Bank. [2]End of year. [3]1986. [4]June. [5]Households involved in nonagricultural activities only. [6]Includes reexports. [7]1985. [8]Main lines. [9]Includes kindergarten. [10]1986–87.

Kampuchea

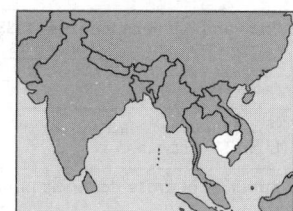

Official name: Roat Kampuchea (State of Kampuchea)[1].
Form of government: single-party people's republic with one legislative house (National Assembly [123]).
Chief of state: President, Council of State.
Head of government: Chairman, Council of Ministers (Prime Minister).
Capital: Phnom Penh.
Official language: Khmer.
Official religion: Buddhism.
Monetary unit: 1 riel = 100 sen; valuation (Oct. 2, 1989)
1 U.S.$ = 150.00 riels; 1 £ = 242.70 riels.

Area and population

Provinces	Capitals	area sq mi	area sq km	population 1981 census
Bătdâmbâng	Bătdâmbâng	7,407	19,184	719,000
Kâmpóng Cham	Kâmpóng Cham	3,783	9,799	1,070,000
Kâmpóng Chhnăng	Kâmpóng Chhnăng	2,132	5,521	221,000
Kâmpóng Saôm	Kâmpóng Saôm	26	68	53,000
Kâmpóng Spoe	Kâmpóng Spoe	2,709	7,017	340,000
Kâmpóng Thum	Kâmpóng Thum	10,657[2]	27,602[2]	379,000
Kâmpôt	Kâmpôt	2,320	6,008	354,000
Kândal	...	1,472	3,812	720,000
Kaôh Kŏng	Krŏng Kaôh Kŏng	4,309	11,161	25,000
Krâchéh	Krâchéh	4,283	11,094	157,000
Môndól Kiri	Senmonorom	5,517	14,288	16,000
Phnom Penh	Phnom Penh	18	46	329,000
Poŭthisăt	Poŭthisăt	4,900	12,692	175,000
Preăh Vihéar	Phnum Tbéng Meanchey	2	2	70,000
Prey Vêng	Prey Vêng	1,885	4,883	672,000
Rôtânôkiri	Lumphăt	4,163	10,782	45,000
Siĕmréab	Siĕmréab	6,354	16,457	477,000
Stŏeng Trêng	Stŏeng Trêng	4,283	11,092	39,000
Svay Riĕng	Svay Riĕng	1,145	2,966	292,000
Takêv	Takêv	1,376	3,563	531,000
TOTAL LAND AREA		68,721	177,987	6,684,000
INLAND WATER		1,177	3,048	
TOTAL AREA		69,898	181,035	

Demography

Population (1989): 8,055,000.
Density[3] (1989): persons per sq mi 115.3, persons per sq km 44.5.
Urban-rural (1985): urban 10.8%; rural 89.2%.
Sex distribution (1985): male 49.73%; female 50.27%.
Age breakdown (1985): under 15, 32.5%; 15–29, 33.5%; 30–44, 19.6%; 45–59, 9.8%; 60–74, 4.0%; 75 and over 0.6%.
Population projection: (2000) 10,046,000; (2010) 11,539,000.
Doubling time: 28 years.
Ethnic composition (1983): Khmer 88.1%; Chinese 4.6%; Vietnamese 4.6%; (although recent Vietnamese immigration may have raised their proportion to as much as 8%); other 2.7%.
Religious affiliation (1980): Buddhist 88.4%; Muslim 2.4%; other 9.2%.
Major cities (1971): Phnom Penh 750,000[4]; Kâmpóng Cham 34,706; Kâmpóng Chhnăng 15,813; Kratié 14,765; Pursat 14,736; Svay Riĕng 13,766.

Vital statistics

Birth rate per 1,000 population (1988): 40.9 (world avg. 27.1); legitimate, n.a.; illegitimate, n.a.
Death rate per 1,000 population (1988): 16.4 (world avg. 9.9).
Natural increase rate per 1,000 population (1988): 24.5 (world avg. 17.2).
Total fertility rate (avg. births per childbearing woman; 1988): 4.7.
Marriage rate per 1,000 population: n.a.
Divorce rate per 1,000 population: n.a.
Life expectancy at birth (1988): male 47.3 years; female 50.2 years.
Major causes of death per 100,000 population (registered deaths only; 1966): tuberculosis of the respiratory system 154; all accidents other than vehicle accidents 111; malaria 55; pneumonia 51.

National economy

Budget. The lack, since the mid-1970s, of a taxable domestic economic base or of much income-earning exports has left Kampuchea without a central governmental budget other than the dispersal of foreign aid and the management of development grants.
Production (metric tons except as noted). Agriculture, forestry, fishing (1988): rice 1,600,000, roots and tubers 169,000 (of which cassava 112,000, sweet potatoes 42,000), corn (maize) 100,000, beans 40,000, rubber 24,500[5]; tobacco 10,000; livestock (number of live animals) 1,950,000 cattle, 1,500,000 pigs, 700,000 buffalo, 6,000,000 chickens; roundwood (1987) 5,545,000 cu m; fish catch (1987) 74,000. Mining and quarrying (1986): salt 40,000. Manufacturing (1987): cement 50,000; rubber 28,000; pork 24,000; beef and veal 17,000; sawn wood 47,000 cu m; plywood 2,000 cu m; cigarettes 4,100,000,000 units. Construction: n.a. Energy production (consumption): electricity (kW-hr; 1987) 162,800,000 (162,800,000); coal, n.a. (n.a.); crude petroleum, n.a. (n.a.); petroleum products (metric tons; 1987) none (160,000); natural gas, n.a. (n.a.).
Household income and expenditure. Average household size (1980) 5.6; income per household: n.a.; sources of income: n.a.; expenditure: n.a.

Gross national product (at current market prices; 1981): U.S.$600,000,000 (U.S.$90 per capita).

Structure of gross domestic product and labour force

	1966 in value '000,000 riels	1966 % of total value	1985 labour force	1985 % of labour force
Agriculture	13,100	40.9	2,613,000	72.5
Mining and manufacturing	3,300	10.3		
Construction	1,700	5.3		
Public utilities	400	1.3		
Transportation and communications	700	2.2	989,000	27.5
Trade	7,300	22.8		
Public admin., defense	3,900	12.2		
Services	1,600	5.0		
TOTAL	32,000	100.0	3,602,000	100.0

Public debt (1985): U.S.$508,000,000.
Population economically active (1985): total 3,602,000; activity rate of total population 49.5% (participation rates: ages 15–64, 71.4%; female 40.5%; unemployed, n.a.).

Price and earnings indexes (1970 = 100)

	1967	1968	1969	1970	1971	1972	1973
Consumer price index[6]	79.5	84.1	89.4	100.0	172.0	215.2	556.1
Earnings index	...	...	...	...	...	...	...

Land use (1987): forested 75.8%; meadows and pastures 3.3%; agricultural and under permanent cultivation 17.2%; other 3.7%.
Tourism: none.

Foreign trade

Balance of trade (current prices)

	1980	1981	1982	1983	1984	1985
U.S.$'000,000	...	−60	...	−96	−98	−105
% of total	...	41.1%	...	88.2%	87.1%	80.9%

Imports (1985): U.S.$117,176,000 (machinery and transport equipment 36.9%, of which transport equipment 10.9%; petroleum and petroleum products 30.2%; woven cotton fabrics 3.6%; synthetic fabrics 2.5%; cotton yarn 2.3%; basic manufactures 1.5%; chemicals 1.2%). *Major import sources:* U.S.S.R. 93.5%; Japan 1.5%; France 1.1%; Australia 1.1%; United Kingdom 0.6%.
Exports (1985): U.S.$12,355,000 (rubber 82.9%; basic manufactures 5.1%; miscellaneous manufactured articles 3.0%). *Major export destinations:* U.S.S.R. 88.2%; United States 2.9%; Japan 2.9%.

Transport and communications

Transport. Railroads (1986): length 380 mi, 612 km; passenger-mi 33,554,000[6], passenger-km 54,000,000[6]; short ton-mi cargo 6,850,000[6], metric ton-km cargo 10,000,000[6]. Roads (1986): total length 8,296 mi, 13,351 km (paved 20%). Vehicles (1981): passenger cars 700; trucks 1,800. Merchant marine (1988): vessels (100 gross tons and over) 3; total deadweight tonnage 3,558. Air transport (1977): passenger-mi 26,098,800, passenger-km 42,000,000; short ton-mi cargo 274,000, metric ton-km cargo 400,000; airports (1989) with scheduled flights 1.
Communications. Daily newspapers (1984): total number 10; total circulation, n.a. Radio (1988): total number of receivers 753,038 (1 per 10 persons). Television (1988): total number of receivers 48,605 (1 per 141 persons). Telephones (1981): 7,315 (1 per 790 persons).

Education and health

Education (1983–84)

	schools	teachers	students	student/teacher ratio
Primary (age 6–11)[7]	3,629[8]	45,000	1,900,000	42.2
Secondary	207	4,494	145,730	32.4
Voc., teacher tr.	13	278	7,334	26.4
Higher	2	...	586[9]	...

Educational attainment, n.a. *Literacy* (1980): total population age 15 and over literate 48%.
Health (1984): physicians 200 (1 per 36,000 persons); hospital beds 16,200 (1 per 441 persons); infant mortality rate per 1,000 live births (1988) 129.
Food (1984–86): daily per capita caloric intake 2,170 (vegetable products 95%, animal products 5%); (1984) 95% of FAO recommended minimum requirement.

Military

Total active duty personnel (1989): 49,300[10] (army 96.4%, navy 2.0%, air force 1.6%). *Military expenditure as percent of GNP:* n.a.; per capita expenditure, n.a.

---

[1]The UN continues to seat Democratic Kampuchea (DK), whose present leadership calls itself the Coalition Government of Democratic Kampuchea and is composed of Khmer People's National Liberation Front, the DK (Khmer Rouge), and the organization of Norodom Sihanouk. [2]Area of Preăh Vihéar included with Kâmpóng Thum. [3]Based on land area. [4]1987. [5]1986. [6]1981. [7]1986–87. [8]1981–82. [9]1982–83. [10]Excludes about 65,000 Vietnamese troops and about 55,000 opposition forces in June 1989.

Kenya

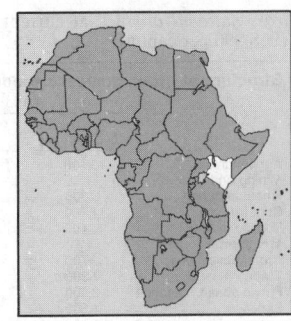

Official name: Jamhuri ya Kenya (Swahili); Republic of Kenya (English).
Form of government: unitary single-party republic with one legislative house (National Assembly [202[1]]).
Head of state and government: President.
Capital: Nairobi.
Official languages: Swahili; English.
Official religion: none.
Monetary unit: 1 Kenya shilling (K Sh) = 100 cents; valuation (Oct. 2, 1989) 1 U.S.$ = K Sh 21.51; 1 £ = K Sh 34.80.

Area and population		area		population
		sq mi	sq km	1989 estimate
Provinces	**Provincial headquarters**			
Central	Nyeri	5,087	13,176	3,550,300
Coast	Mombasa	32,279	83,603	2,064,600
Eastern	Embu	61,734	159,891	4,192,700
North Eastern	Garissa	48,997	126,902	611,400
Nyanza	Kisumu	6,240	16,162	4,173,800
Rift Valley	Nakuru	67,131	173,868	5,128,500
Western	Kakamega	3,228	8,360	2,732,300
Special area				
Nairobi	—	264	684	1,429,000
TOTAL LAND AREA		220,625	571,416	23,882,600
INLAND WATER		4,336	11,230	
TOTAL AREA		224,961	582,646	

Demography

Population (1989): 23,883,000.
Density[2] (1989): persons per sq mi 108.3, persons per sq km 41.8.
Urban-rural (1985): urban 19.7%; rural 80.3%.
Sex distribution (1989): male 49.88%; female 50.12%.
Age breakdown (1989): under 15, 51.2%; 15–29, 26.1%; 30–44, 12.7%; 45–59, 6.6%; 60–74, 2.9%; 75 and over, 0.5%.
Population projection: (2000) 37,505,000; (2010) 56,629,000.
Doubling time: 17 years.
Ethnic composition (1979): Kenyan 98.8% (Kikuyu 20.9%, Luhya 13.8%, Luo 12.8%, Kamba 11.3%, Kalenjin 10.8%, other Kenyan 29.2%); other 1.2%.
Religious affiliation (1980): Christian 73.0%, of which Protestant 26.5% Roman Catholic 26.4%; African Indigenous 17.6%, Orthodox 2.5%; traditional beliefs 18.9%; Muslim 6.0%; other 2.1%.
Major cities (1984): Nairobi 1,429,000[3]; Mombasa 425,600; Kisumu 167,100; Nakuru 101,700; Machakos 92,300[4].

Vital statistics

Birth rate per 1,000 population (1985–90): 53.9 (world avg. 27.1).
Death rate per 1,000 population (1985–90): 11.9 (world avg. 9.9).
Natural increase rate per 1,000 population (1985–90): 42.0 (world avg. 17.2).
Total fertility rate (avg. births per childbearing woman; 1985–90): 8.1.
Life expectancy at birth (1985–90): male 56.5 years; female 60.5 years.
Major causes of death per 100,000 population: n.a.; however, major infectious diseases include malaria, gastroenteritis, venereal diseases, diarrhea and dysentery, trachoma, amebiasis, and schistosomiasis.

National economy

Budget (1988–89). Revenue: K Sh 36,860,000,000 (indirect taxes 58.9%, of which sales tax 30.6%, custom and excise duties 23.4%; direct taxes 28.0%; grants 18.5%; nontax revenue 7.8%). Expenditures: K Sh 49,166,000,000 (recurrent expenditure 71.4%; development expenditure 28.6%).
Production (metric tons except as noted). Agriculture, forestry, fishing (1987): sugarcane 4,000,000, corn (maize) 1,900,000, potatoes 730,000, cassava 540,000, pulses 460,000, sweet potatoes 380,000, plantains 286,000, pineapples 203,000, wheat 185,000, tea 160,000, bananas 146,000, sorghum 130,000, coffee 109,000, coconuts 72,000, millet 50,000, sisal 40,000, seed cotton 36,000, cottonseed 24,000, tomatoes 22,000, barley 18,000, cashew nuts 12,000, copra 5,000, sunflower seeds 5,000; livestock (number of live animals) 9,500,000 cattle, 8,300,000 goats, 7,200,000 sheep; roundwood 35,180,000 cu m; total fish catch 131,181, of which freshwater fish 94.8%. Mining and quarrying (1986): limestone 2,069,020; soda ash 237,650; salt 100,379; fluorspar 50,851; corundum (ruby) 66 kilograms. Manufacturing (1986): cement 1,178,000; sugar 368,836; wheat flour 303,800; soap 29,257; fabrics 81,597,000 sq m; beer and stout 2,926,330 hectolitres; mineral water 1,759,620 hectolitres; paint 5,701 hectolitres; alcoholic beverages 5,509 hectolitres. Construction (1986): residential 136,000 sq m; nonresidential 180,000 sq m. Energy production (consumption): electricity (kW-hr; 1987) 2,629,000,000 (2,805,000,000); coal (metric tons; 1987) 92,000 (91,000); crude petroleum (barrels; 1986) none (15,360,000); petroleum products (metric tons; 1987) 1,989,000 (1,287,000).
Public debt (external, outstanding; 1987): U.S.$4,482,000,000.
Household income and expenditure. Average household size (1980) 6.2; average annual income per household: n.a.; sources of income: n.a.; expenditure (1980): food 46.5%, housing 10.0%, furniture and utensils 9.4%, transportation 8.4%, clothing and footwear 7.7%, health 2.2%, education 1.0%.
Population economically active (1985): total 8,389,000; activity rate of total population 40.7% (participation rates: ages 15–64, 76.2%; female 40.9%; unemployed, n.a.).

Price and earnings indexes (1985 = 100)							
	1982	1983	1984	1985	1986	1987	1988
Consumer price index	72.0	80.3	88.5	100.0	104.0	109.4	118.4
Annual earnings index	79.1	84.3	92.3	100.0	...	...	...

Gross national product (at current market prices; 1987): U.S.$7,500,000,000 (U.S.$340 per capita).

Structure of gross domestic product and labour force	1987		1985	
	in value K Sh '000,000	% of total value	labour force[5]	% of labour force
Agriculture	35,210.2	26.6	240,900	20.5
Mining	265.4	0.2	4,800	0.4
Manufacturing	13,111.2	9.9	158,800	13.5
Construction	6,265.4	4.7	49,900	4.3
Public utilities	2,049.8	1.6	17,700	1.5
Transp. and commun.	7,036.0	5.3	55,700	4.7
Trade	15,536.4	11.7	89,700	7.6
Finance	16,235.6	12.3	53,400	4.6
Pub. admin., defense	17,083.4	12.9	158,600	13.5
Services	4,167.6	3.2	344,900	29.4
Other	15,333.0[6]	11.6[6]	—	—
TOTAL	132,294.0	100.0	1,174,400	100.0

Tourism (1987): receipts from visitors U.S.$355,000,000; expenditures by nationals abroad U.S.$21,000,000.
Land use (1986): forested 6.5%; meadows and pastures 6.6%; agricultural and under permanent cultivation 4.1%; other 82.8%.

Foreign trade[7]

Balance of trade (current prices)						
	1983	1984	1985	1986	1987	1988
K Sh '000,000	−2,514	−3,511	−4,609	−3,271	−9,063	−11,137
% of total	8.8%	10.2%	12.6%	7.7%	22.3%	22.6%

Imports (1987): K Sh 28,635,870,000 (machinery and transport equipment 34.4%, crude petroleum 19.8%, chemicals 17.8%, manufactured goods 14.1%, food and live animals 4.0%). *Major import sources:* U.K. 17.1%; Japan 10.9%; West Germany 8.2%; U.S. 7.1%; France 6.8%; Italy 3.4%; The Netherlands 2.9%; India 1.3%.
Exports (1987): K Sh 15,787,850,000[8] (coffee [not roasted] 25.8%, tea 21.7%, petroleum products 13.3%, vegetables and fruit 10.2%, corn [maize] 2.6%, hides and skins 2.2%). *Major export destinations:* U.K. 16.9%; West Germany 9.7%; Uganda 8.8%; The Netherlands 7.2%; U.S. 5.4%.

Transport and communications

Transport. Railroads (1986): route length 1,649 mi, 2,654 km; passenger-mi 422,507,000, passenger-km 679,960,000; short ton-mi cargo 1,252,007,000, metric ton-km cargo 1,827,900,000. Roads (1986): total length 33,700 mi, 54,300 km (paved 12%). Vehicles (1987): passenger cars 133,335; trucks and buses 110,806. Merchant marine (1988): vessels (100 gross tons and over) 28; total deadweight tonnage 4,841. Air transport[9] (1988): passenger-mi 468,498,000, passenger-km 753,976,000; short ton-mi cargo 68,440,000, metric ton-km cargo 99,921,000; airports (1989) with scheduled flights 16.
Communications. Daily newspapers: total number (1986) 5; total circulation 280,000; circulation per 1,000 population 13. Radio (1988): 1,815,000 receivers (1 per 12 persons). Television (1988): 192,000 receivers (1 per 118 persons). Telephones (1987): 316,050 (1 per 70 persons).

Education and health

Education (1986–87)	schools	teachers	students	student/ teacher ratio
Primary (age 5–11)	13,392	142,807	4,843,432	33.9
Secondary (age 12–17)	2,417	22,296	458,712	20.6
Voc., teacher tr.	44	1,734	23,496	13.6
Higher	4[10]	...	9,888[10]	...

Educational attainment (1979). Percent of population over age 25 having: no formal schooling 58.6%; primary education 32.2%; some secondary 7.9%; complete secondary and higher 1.3%. *Literacy* (1985): total population over age 15 literate 5,758,000 (59.2%); males literate 3,311,000 (69.6%); females literate 2,447,000 (49.2%).
Health (1985): physicians 2,842 (1 per 7,122 persons); hospital beds 30,936 (1 per 657 persons); infant mortality rate per 1,000 live births (1984) 92.
Food (1984–86): daily per capita caloric intake 2,140 (vegetable products 92%, animal products 8%); (1984–86) 93% of FAO recommended minimum requirement.

Military

Total active duty personnel (1989): 23,600 (army 80.5%; navy 4.7%; air force 14.8%). *Military expenditure as percent of GNP* (1987): 2.4% (world 5.4%); per capita expenditure U.S.$8.

[1]Includes 14 nonelective seats. [2]Land area only. [3]1989. [4]1983. [5]Employed persons only. [6]Indirect taxes less subsidies and imputed bank service charges. [7]Import figures are f.o.b. in balance of trade and c.i.f. in commodities and trading partners. [8]Includes K Sh 629,670,000 reexports. [9]Kenya Airways only. [10]Universities only.

Kiribati

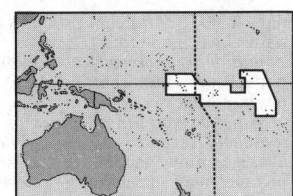

Official name: Republic of Kiribati.
Form of government: unitary republic with one legislature (House of Assembly [41[1]]).
Head of state and government: President.
Capital: Bairiki, on Tarawa Atoll.
Official language: English.
Official religion: none.
Monetary unit: 1 Australian Dollar ($A) = 100 cents; valuation (Oct. 2, 1989) 1 U.S.$ = $A 1.29; 1 £ = $A 2.08.

Area and population

Island Groups Islands	Capitals	area[2] sq mi	area[2] sq km	population 1988 estimate
Gilberts Group	Bairiki Islet	110	285	65,366
Abaiang	Tuarabu	7	17	4,689
Abemama	Kariatebike	11	27	3,170
Aranuka	Takaeang	4	12	1,050
Arorae	Roreti	4	9	1,563
Banaba	Anteeren	2	6	50
Beru	Taubukinberu	7	18	2,887
Butaritari	Butaritari	5	13	3,866
Kuria	Tabontebike	6	15	1,126
Maiana	Tebangetua	6	17	2,287
Makin	Makin	3	8	1,900
Marakei	Rawannawi	5	14	2,873
Nikunau	Rungata	7	19	2,199
Nonouti	Teuabu	8	20	3,133
Onotoa	Buariki	6	16	2,048
Tabiteuea North	Utiroa	10	26	3,378
Tabiteuea South	Buariki	5	12	1,409
Tamana	Bakaka	2	5	1,468
Tarawa North	Abaokoro	6	15	3,437
Tarawa South	Bairiki	6	16	22,833
Line Group	Kiritimati	207	535	2,815
Northern		167	432	—
Kiritimati (Christmas)	London	150	388	1,861
Tabuaeran (Fanning)	Paelau	13	34	473
Teraina (Washington)	Washington	4	10	481
Southern (Caroline, Flint, Malden, Starbuck, Vostok)		40	103	—
Phoenix Group (Birnie, Enderbury, Kanton [Canton], McKean, Manra [Sydney], Nikumaroro [Gardner], Orona [Hull], Rawaki [Phoenix])	Kanton	11	29	26
TOTAL		328	849	68,207

Demography

Population (1989): 69,600.
Density[3] (1989): persons per sq mi 248.6, persons per sq km 95.9.
Urban–rural (1985): urban 33.4%; rural 66.6%.
Sex distribution (1985): male 49.56%; female 50.44%.
Age breakdown (1985)[4]: under 15, 38.9%; 15–29, 29.9%; 30–44, 16.1%; 45–59, 9.3%; 60–74, 4.9%; 75 and over, 0.9%.
Population projection: (2000) 87,000; (2010) 108,000.
Doubling time: 30 years.
Ethnic composition (1985): I-Kiribati 96.1%; mixed (part I-Kiribati and other) 2.6%; Tuvaluan 0.7%; European 0.4%; other 0.2%.
Religious affiliation (1985)[4]: Roman Catholic 52.6%; Kiribati Protestant (Congregational) 40.9%; Bahā'ī 2.4%; Seventh-day Adventist 1.4%; other 2.7%.
Major cities (1988): Urban Tarawa 22,833.

Vital statistics

Birth rate per 1,000 population (1988): 31.3 (world avg. 27.1); legitimate, n.a.; illegitimate, n.a.
Death rate per 1,000 population (1988): 8.1 (world avg. 9.9).
Natural increase rate per 1,000 population (1988): 23.2 (world avg. 17.2).
Total fertility rate (avg. births per childbearing woman; 1988): 4.1.
Marriage rate per 1,000 population (1988): 5.2.
Divorce rate per 1,000 population: n.a.
Life expectancy at birth (1981–85): male 50.6 years; female 55.6 years.
Major causes of death per 100,000 population: n.a.; however, the leading causes of morbidity include influenza, diarrhea, sores and skin diseases, conjuctivitis, dental disorders, ear diseases, parasitic infestations, and chicken pox.

National economy

Budget (1988). Revenue: $A 24,947,000 (nontax revenue 46.0%, of which reserve fund drawdown 32.1%, fish licenses 9.8%; tax revenue 28.4%, of which import duties 9.4%, income tax 4.9%; development revenue 25.6%). Expenditures: $A 21,434,000 (education 16.1%; development 15.9%; health 13.0%; natural resources 7.3%; communications 7.0%; public works 6.6%).
Public debt (external, outstanding; 1985): U.S.$10,000,000.
Tourism (1987): receipts from visitors U.S.$1,000,000; expenditures by nationals abroad, n.a.
Production (metric tons except as noted). Agriculture, forestry, fishing (1987): coconuts 90,000, roots and tubers 13,000 (of which taro 3,000), copra 12,000, vegetables and melons 5,000, bananas 4,000; livestock (number

of live animals) 10,000 pigs, 191,000 chickens[5]; fish catch 43,868. Mining and quarrying: none[6]. Manufacturing (1988): copra 14,406; other important products are processed fish, baked goods, clothing, and handicrafts. Energy production (consumption): electricity (kW-hr; 1988) 6,740,000 (6,647,000) coal: none (n.a.); crude petroleum: none (n.a.); petroleum products (metric tons; 1986) none (6,000); natural gas: none (n.a.).
Gross national product (at current market prices; 1987): U.S.$32,000,000 (U.S.$480 per capita).

Structure of gross domestic product and labour force

	1988 in value $A '000	1988 % of total value	1985 labour force	1985 % of labour force
Agriculture, fishing	13,320	29.6	19,200[7]	72.9
Mining	—	—	14	0.1
Manufacturing	762	1.7	132	0.5
Construction	2,200	4.9	440	1.7
Public utilities	770	1.7	232	0.9
Transportation and communications	6,100	13.6	1,050	4.0
Trade	5,500	12.2	1,127	4.3
Finance	2,990	6.7	93	0.4
Pub. admin., defense	9,840	21.9	1,601	6.1
Services	1,148	2.6	1,802	6.8
Other	2,300	5.1	646[8]	2.5
TOTAL	44,930	100.0	26,337	100.0[9]

Population economically active (1985): total 26,337; activity rate of total population 41.2% (participation rates: over age 15, 67.8%; female 36.1%; unemployed 2.4%).

Price and earnings indexes (1985 = 100)

	1982	1983	1984	1985	1986	1987	1988
Consumer price index	85.4	90.8	95.7	100.0	106.5	113.4	116.9
Monthly earnings index	...	...	...	...	...	...	...

Household income and expenditure. Average household size (1985) 6.1; income per household: n.a.; sources of income (1978): agriculture 35.9%, wages only 27.5%, wages and other 19.3%, agriculture and other 12.6%, other 4.7%; expenditure (1982): food 50.0%, tobacco and alcohol 14.0%, clothing 8.0%, transportation 8.0%, housing, energy, and household operation 7.5%.
Land use (1986): forested 2.8%; agricultural and under permanent cultivation 52.1%; other 45.1%.

Foreign trade

Balance of trade (current prices)

	1983	1984	1985	1986	1987	1988
$A '000	−15,603	−8,421	−15,525	−18,956	−22,274	−21,515
% of total	66.1%	25.3%	56.2%	79.2%	79.5%	61.7%

Imports (1988): $A 28,185,000 (food 28.7%, machinery and transport equipment 27.2%, manufactured goods 20.2%, mineral fuels 10.5%, beverages and tobacco 5.6%, chemicals 4.9%, crude materials 2.0%). *Major import sources:* Australia 43.8%; Fiji 15.3%; Japan 10.9%; China 5.2%; New Zealand 4.9%; United States 4.8%; Hong Kong 2.9%.
Exports (1988): $A 6,670,000 (copra 63.0%, fish and fish preparations 24.3%, reexports 12.3%). *Major export destinations:* The Netherlands 69.3%; Fiji 23.2%; United States 4.2%; Tonga 2.5%.

Transport and communications

Transport. Roads (1988): total length 398 mi, 640 km (paved, 5%). Vehicles (1985): passenger cars 307; trucks and buses 130. Merchant marine (1988): vessels (100 gross tons and over) 7; total deadweight tonnage 2,841. Air transport (1986): passenger-mi 6,184,000, passenger-km 9,953,000; short ton-mi cargo 32,000, metric ton-km cargo 47,000; airports (1989) with scheduled flights 17.
Communications. Daily newspapers: none. Radio (1988): total number of receivers 10,000 (1 per 6.8 persons). Television: none. Telephones (1987): 1,400 (1 per 48 persons).

Education and health

Education (1988)

	schools	teachers	students	student/ teacher ratio
Primary (age 6–13)	112	458	13,868	30.3
Secondary (age 14–18)	8	140	2,437	17.4
Voc., teacher tr.	6	52	568	10.9
Higher[10]	—	—	—	—

Educational attainment (1985)[4]. Percent of population age 25 and over having: no schooling 5.8%; less than full primary education 56.1%; primary 22.3%; some secondary 15.3%; secondary 0.5%. *Literacy* (1985): total population age 15 and over literate 90%.
Health (1986): physicians 16 (1 per 4,094 persons); hospital beds 283 (1 per 231 persons); infant mortality rate per 1,000 live births (1988) 110.
Food (1984–86): daily per capita caloric intake 2,936 (vegetable products 91%, animal products 9%); (1983) 117% of FAO recommended minimum requirement.

[1]Includes 2 nonelective members. [2]Includes uninhabited islands. [3]Density based on inhabited island areas (280 sq mi, 726 sq km) only. [4]Indigenous population only, who constitute 98.7% of the total population. [5]1982. [6]Mining of phosphates on Banaba (Ocean Island) ceased in 1979. [7]Includes 18,719 persons engaged in "village work" (subsistence agriculture or fishing). [8]Includes 627 unemployed. [9]Detail does not add to total given because of rounding. [10]85 students overseas.

Korea, North

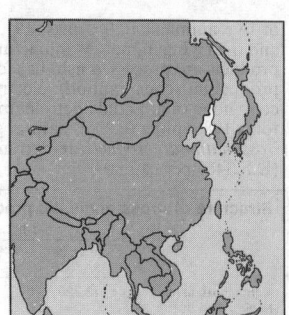

Official name: Chosŏn Minjujuŭi
In'min Konghwaguk (Democratic
People's Republic of Korea).
Form of government: unitary
single-party republic with one
legislative house (Supreme People's
Assembly [655]).
Chief of state: President.
Head of government: Premier.
Capital: P'yŏngyang.
Official language: Korean.
Official religion: none.
Monetary unit: 1 won = 100
chon; valuation (Oct. 2, 1989)
1 U.S.$ = 0.97 won; 1 £ = 1.57 won.

Area and population

Provinces	Capitals	area[1] sq mi	sq km	population 1968 estimate
Chagang-do	Kanggye	6,300	16,200	780,000
Hamgyŏng-namdo	Hamhŭng	7,400	19,200	1,315,000
Hamgyŏng-pukto	Ch'ŏngjin	6,100	15,900	1,110,000
Hwanghae-namdo	Haeju	2,900	7,600	1,340,000
Hwanghae-pukto	Sariwŏn	3,300	8,600	1,060,000
Kangwŏn-do	Wŏnsan	4,100	10,700	1,030,000
P'yŏngan-namdo	P'yŏngsan	4,700	12,300	2,250,000
P'yŏngan-pukto	Sinŭiju	4,600	12,000	1,760,000
Yanggang-do	Hyesan	5,400	14,100	435,000
Special cities				
Ch'ŏngjin-si	—	700	1,900	385,000
Hamhŭng-si	—	300	800	530,000
P'yŏngyang-si	P'yŏngyang	700	1,800	1,275,000
Special district				
Kaesŏng-chigu	Kaesŏng	500	1,200	289,000
TOTAL		47,300[2]	122,400[2]	13,559,000

Demography

Population (1989): 22,418,000.
Density (1989): persons per sq mi 474.0, persons per sq km 183.2.
Urban–rural (1985): urban 63.8%; rural 36.2%.
Sex distribution (1985): male 49.55%; female 50.45%.
Age breakdown (1985): under 15, 38.7%; 15–29, 29.2%; 30–44, 16.6%; 45–59, 9.8%; 60–74, 4.7%; 75 and over, 1.0%.
Population projection: (2000) 28,165,000; (2010) 33,115,000.
Doubling time: 28 years.
Ethnic composition (1983): Korean 99.8%; Chinese 0.2%.
Religious affiliation (1980): atheist or nonreligious 67.9%; traditional beliefs 15.6%; Ch'ŏndogyo 13.9%; Buddhist 1.7%; Christian 0.9%.
Major cities (1981): P'yŏngyang 1,283,000; Hamhŭng-Hŭngnam 775,000; Ch'ŏngjin 490,000; Wŏnsan 398,000; Kaesŏng 259,000.

Vital statistics

Birth rate per 1,000 population (1985–90): 28.9 (world avg. 27.1).
Death rate per 1,000 population (1985–90): 5.4 (world avg. 9.9).
Natural increase rate per 1,000 population (1985–90): 23.5 (world avg. 17.2).
Total fertility rate (avg. births per childbearing woman; 1987): 3.6.
Marriage rate per 1,000 population: n.a.
Divorce rate per 1,000 population: n.a.
Life expectancy at birth (1985–90): male 66.2 years; female 72.7 years.
Major causes of death: n.a.; however, major diseases include endemic diseases (typhoid fever, dysentery, clonorchiasis [liver fluke], paragonimiasis [lung fluke], encephalitis, poliomyelitis, diphtheria, measles, tuberculosis of respiratory system, bronchitis, malignant neoplasms (cancers), hypertensive and ischemic heart diseases, and intestinal obstruction and hernia.

National economy

Budget (1988). Revenue: 31,852,000,000 won (1984; turnover tax 55.0%, payments by state enterprises 30%). Expenditures: 31,852,000,000 won (1984; national economy 63.3%, social and cultural affairs 20.0%, defense 14.6%, other 2.1%).
Public debt (external, outstanding; 1988): U.S.$2,500,000,000.
Production (metric tons except as noted). Agriculture, forestry, fishing (1988): rice 6,200,000, vegetables 3,094,000, corn (maize) 2,950,000, potatoes 1,975,-000, wheat 880,000, barley 630,000, millet 575,000, sweet potatoes 497,000, soybeans 445,000, pulses 310,000, sorghum 201,000, pears 106,000, peaches 95,000, tobacco 62,000, dry onions 44,000, seed cotton 16,000; livestock (number of live animals) 3,100,000 pigs, 1,250,000 cattle, 372,000 sheep, 285,000 goats, 19,000,000 chickens; roundwood (1987) 4,649,000 cu m; fish catch (1987) 1,800,000. Mining and quarrying (1986): iron ore 8,500,000; magnesite (metal content) 882,000; phosphate rock 500,000; sulfur 230,-000; zinc 180,000; lead (metal content) 110,000; gypsum 82,000; fluorspar 40,000; graphite 25,000; silver 1,600,000 troy oz; gold 160,000 troy oz. Manufacturing (1987): cement 7,800,000; pig iron 5,800,000; crude steel 4,300,000; chemical fertilizers 4,000,000; steel semimanufactures 3,400,-000[3]; meat 235,000; television sets 240,000 units[4]; machine tools 29,000 units[3]; tractors 24,000 units[3]; cars 20,000 units[4]; refrigerators 10,000 units[3]; textile fabrics 600,000,000 m. Construction: n.a. Energy production (consumption): electricity (kW-hr; 1987) 50,200,000 (50,200,000); coal (metric tons; 1987) 52,500,000 (54,450,000); crude petroleum (barrels; 1987) none

(20,440,000); petroleum products (metric tons; 1987) 2,650,000 (3,170,000); natural gas, none (n.a.).
Population economically active (1985): total 9,084,000; activity rate of total population 44.6% (participation rates: ages 15–64, 75.3%; female 46.0%; unemployed, n.a.).
Price and earnings indexes: n.a.
Household income and expenditure. Average household size (1980) 5.7; average annual income per household 3,677 won (U.S.$4,275); sources of income: n.a.; expenditure[5] (1984): food 46.5%; clothing 29.9%; furniture 3.8%; energy 3.3%; housing 0.6%.
Gross national product (1988): U.S.$20,000,000,000 (U.S.$910 per capita).

Structure of gross domestic product and labour force

	1982 in value '000,000 won	% of total value	labour force	% of labour force
Agriculture	...	...	3,276,000	44.1
Mining and manufacturing	...	...		
Construction	...	...	2,790,000	33.0
Public utilities	...	...		
Transp. and commun.	...	...	418,000	4.9
Trade	...	...		
Finance	...	...		
Pub. admin., defense	...	...	1,521,000	18.0
Services	· ...	...		
Other	...	...		
TOTAL	11,800	100.0	8,455,000	100.0

Land use (1987): forested 74.5%; meadows and pastures 0.4%; agricultural and under permanent cultivation 19.2%; other 5.9%.
Tourism: n.a.

Foreign trade

Balance of trade (current prices)

	1974	1976	1978	1979	1980	1981
'000,000 won	−601	−176	−53	+165	−256	−285
% of total	31.6%	11.5%	3.3%	6.3%	9.4%	10.3%

Imports (1987): U.S.$2,500,000,000 (crude petroleum, coal and coke, industrial machinery and transport equipment [including trucks], industrial chemicals, textile yarn and fabrics, and grain are among the major imports). *Major import sources* (1985): U.S.S.R. 36.1%; China 18.8%; Japan 13.2%; West European countries 4.0%; Hong Kong 3.5%.
Exports (1987): U.S.$1,800,000,000 (minerals [including lead, magnesite, and zinc], metallurgical products [iron and steel, nonferrous metals], cement, agricultural products [including fish, grain, fruit and vegetables, tobacco], and manufactured goods [textile fabrics, clothing] are among the major exports). *Major export destinations* (1985): U.S.S.R. 43.6%; Japan 15.1%; China 13.4%; West European countries 4.3%; Australia 3.3%; Hong Kong 3.1%.

Transport and communications

Transport. Railroads (1987): length 5,280 mi, 8,500 km; passengers, n.a.; cargo, n.a. Roads (1987): total length 13,670 mi, 22,000 km (paved 2%). Vehicles (1982): passenger cars 180,000. Merchant marine (1988): vessels (100 gross tons and over) 77; total deadweight tonnage 581,714. Air transport (1979): passenger-mi 52,200,000, passenger-km 84,000,000; short ton-mi cargo 1,370,000, metric ton-km cargo 2,000,000; airports (1989) with scheduled flights 3.
Communications. Daily newspapers (1987): total number 16; total circulation 3,000,000[6]; circulation per 1,000 population 140[6]. Radio (1987): total number of receivers 3,697,153 (1 per 5.8 persons). Television (1987): total number of receivers 214,983 (1 per 99 persons). Telephones (1983): 10,000 (1 per 2,000 persons).

Education and health

Education (1982)

	schools	teachers	students	student/ teacher ratio
Primary (age 5–9)	4,700[7]		c. 2,500,000	...
Secondary (age 10–15) Voc., teacher tr.	600[8]	c. 100,000	c. 2,500,000[9]	...
Higher	245[8]	9,244	200,000	21.6

Educational attainment, n.a. *Literacy* (1979): 90%.
Health (1987): physicians 57,800 (1 per 370 persons); hospital beds 289,000 (1 per 74 persons); infant mortality rate per 1,000 live births (1985–90) 24.0.
Food (1984–86): daily per capita caloric intake 3,199 (vegetable products 92%, animal products 8%); 128% of FAO recommended minimum requirement.

Military

Total active duty personnel (1989): 1,040,000 (army 89.5%, navy 3.8%, air force 6.7%). *Military expenditure as percent of GNP* (1987): 22.4% (world 5.4%); per capita expenditure U.S.$270.

---

[1]Areas approximate. [2]Detail does not add to total given because of rounding. [3]1984. [4]1986. [5]Workers and clerical workers only. [6]Four dailies only. [7]1976. [8]1987. [9]Includes vocational students.

Korea, South

Official name: Taehan Min'guk
(Republic of Korea).
Form of government: unitary multiparty
republic with a National Assembly
(299 members).
Chief of state: President.
Head of government: Prime Minister.
Capital: Seoul.
Official language: Korean.
Official religion: none.
Monetary unit: 1 won (W) = 100 chon;
valuation (Oct. 2, 1989)
1 U.S.$ = W 670; 1 £ = W 1,085.

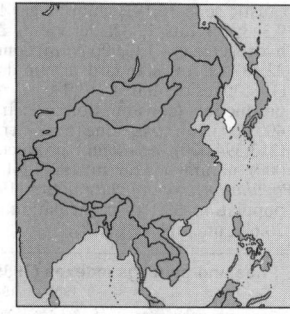

Area and population		area		population
Provinces	Capitals	sq mi	sq km	1989 estimate
Cheju-do	Cheju	705	1,825	505,000
Chŏlla-namdo	Kwangju	4,556	11,799	2,540,000
Chŏlla-pukto	Chŏnju	3,109	8,052	2,118,000
Ch'ungch'ŏng-namdo	Taejŏn	3,417	8,851	3,008,000
Ch'ungch'ŏng-pukto	Ch'ŏngju	2,871	7,437	1,356,000
Kangwŏn-do	Ch'unch'ŏn'	6,525	16,899	1,663,000
Kyŏnggi-do	Suwŏn¹	4,196	10,867	5,466,000
Kyŏngsang-namdo	Masan	4,579	11,859	3,636,000
Kyŏngsang-pukto	Taegu	7,507	19,442	2,846,000
Special cities				
Inch'ŏn-si	Inch'ŏn	80	208	1,604,000
Kwangju-si	Kwangju	193	501	1,165,000
Pusan-si	Pusan	168	436	3,754,000
Sŏul-t'ŭkpyŏlsi	Seoul	234	605	10,513,000
Taegu-si	Taegu	176	456	2,206,000
TOTAL		38,316	99,237	42,380,000

Demography

Population (1989): 42,380,000.
Density (1989): persons per sq mi 1,106.1, persons per sq km 427.1.
Urban–rural (1987): urban 68.9%; rural 31.1%.
Sex distribution (1989): male 50.40%; female 49.60%.
Age breakdown (1985): under 15, 29.9%; 15–29, 31.3%; 30–44, 19.5%; 45–59, 12.5%; 60–74, 5.5%; 75 and over, 1.3%.
Population projection: (2000) 46,617,000; (2010) 48,372,000.
Doubling time: 56 years.
Ethnic composition (1985): Korean 99.9%; other 0.1%.
Religious affiliation (1985)²: Buddhist 19.9%; Protestant 16.1%; Roman Catholic 4.6%; Confucian 1.2%; Wonbulgyo 0.2%; Ch'ondogyo 0.1%; other 0.5%; none 57.4%.
Major cities (1989): Seoul 10,513,000; Pusan 3,754,000; Taegu 2,206,000; Inch'ŏn 1,604,000; Kwangju 1,165,000.

Vital statistics

Birth rate per 1,000 population (1988): 18.6 (world avg. 27.1).
Death rate per 1,000 population (1988): 6.2 (world avg. 9.9).
Natural increase rate per 1,000 population (1988): 12.4 (world avg. 17.2).
Total fertility rate (avg. births per childbearing woman; 1988): 2.0.
Marriage rate per 1,000 population (1983): 8.9.
Divorce rate per 1,000 population (1985): 0.7.
Life expectancy at birth (1988): male 66.4 years; female 72.6 years.
Major causes of death per 100,000 population (1985): diseases of the circulatory system 155.0; malignant neoplasms (cancers) 73.5; accidents, poisonings, and violence 56.5; diseases of the digestive system 43.9; diseases of the respiratory system 22.6.

National economy

Budget (1988). Revenue: W 17,541,900,000,000 (internal tax 61.7%, defense surtax 13.9%, customs duties 12.4%, monopoly profits 4.2%). Expenditures: W 17,541,900,000,000 (defense 32.8%, education 20.6%, economic development 14.4%, administration 10.2%, supports to provinces 8.7%).
Production (metric tons except as noted). Agriculture, forestry, fishing (1987): rice 7,596,000, cabbages 2,600,000, sweet potatoes 744,000, potatoes 647,000, apples 572,000, barley 516,000, dry onions 400,000, tangerines 350,000, garlic 280,000, soybeans 257,000; livestock (number of live animals) 4,281,000 pigs, 2,386,000 cattle, 166,000 goats, 59,324,000 chickens; roundwood 6,849,000 cu m; fish catch 3,331,800. Mining and quarrying (1987): iron ore 565,000; graphite 99,765; zinc ore 47,004; lead ore 26,-316; tungsten ore 3,956. Manufacturing (1987): cement 25,946,000; crude steel 16,722,662; pig iron 10,868,949; chemical fertilizers 2,877,683; man-made fabrics 2,624,355,000 sq m; steel cargo ships 1,318,835 gross tons; television receivers 14,664,621 units; passenger cars 777,894 units. Construction (1987): residential 21,639,000 sq m; nonresidential 26,344,000 sq m. Energy production (consumption): electricity (kW-hr; 1987) 80,250,-000,000 (80,250,000,000); coal (metric tons; 1987) 24,274,000 (41,911,000); crude petroleum (barrels; 1987) none (211,207,000); petroleum products (metric tons; 1987) 24,186,000 (23,598,000); natural gas (cu m; 1987) none (2,256,000,000).
Household income and expenditure (1987)³. Average household size 4.0; income per household W 6,740,100 (U.S.$8,510); sources of income: wages and salaries 85.9%, other 14.1%; expenditure: food and beverages 34.8%, education and recreation 10.7%, clothing and footwear 7.8%, health care 7.5%, transportation and communications 6.6%, energy 6.2%, household durable goods 5.3%, housing 4.3%, other 16.8%.

Gross national product (1987): U.S.$112,947,000,000 (U.S.$2,690 per capita).

Structure of gross domestic product and labour force				
	1987			
	in value W '000,000,000	% of total value	labour force	% of labour force
Agriculture	11,365.5	11.4	3,580,000	21.2
Mining	1,189.2	1.2	186,000	1.1
Manufacturing	30,261.6	30.3	4,416,000	26.2
Construction	8,158.2	8.2	920,000	5.4
Public utilities	3,212.6	3.2	44,000	0.3
Transp. and commun.	8,168.4	8.2	763,000	4.5
Trade	13,153.2	13.2	3,611,000	21.4
Finance	10,810.6	10.8	680,000	4.0
Pub. admin., defense	4,116.3	4.1	2,153,000 }	12.8
Services	3,423.1	3.4		
Other	5,931.3	6.0	519,000⁴	3.1⁴
TOTAL	99,790.0	100.0	16,872,000	100.0

Population economically active (1989): total 18,471,000; activity rate 43.6% (participation rates: ages 15 and over, 61.0%; female 41.1%; unemployed 2.3%).

Price and earnings indexes (1985 = 100)							
	1983	1984	1985	1986	1987	1988	1989⁵
Consumer price index	95.4	97.6	100.0	102.8	105.9	113.4	120.8
Monthly earnings index	84.0	91.0	100.0	109.2	121.9	145.9	...

Public debt (external, outstanding; 1987): U.S.$24,541,000,000.
Tourism (1988): receipts from visitors U.S.$3,265,000,000; expenditures by nationals abroad U.S.$1,354,000,000.
Land use (1987): forested 65.8%; meadows and pastureland 0.9%; agricultural and under permanent cultivation 21.7%; other 11.6%.

Foreign trade

Balance of trade (current prices)						
	1983	1984	1985	1986	1987	1988
US$'000,000	−1,970	−1,386	−853	4,236	−6,940	+8,510
% of total	3.9%	2.3%	1.4%	7.4%	9.8%	10.6%

Imports (1987): U.S.$41,019,812,000 (petroleum and petroleum products 11.3%, electronic components 6.2%, organic chemicals 5.1%, power-generating machinery 2.3%, plastic materials 2.2%, electric power machinery 2.2%). *Major import sources:* Japan 33.3%; United States 21.4%; West Germany 4.4%; Australia 3.1%; Malaysia 2.6%; Saudi Arabia 2.6%; Canada 2.3%; Indonesia 2.0%.
Exports (1987): U.S.$47,280,928,000 (transport equipment 10.8%, electrical machinery 8.9%, footwear 5.8%, textile fabrics 5.1%, iron and steel sheets 1.6%, fish 1.6%). *Major export destinations:* United States 38.7%; Japan 17.8%; Hong Kong 4.7%; West Germany 4.2%; United Kingdom 3.2%; Canada 3.1%; Saudi Arabia 2.2%; Singapore 2.0%.

Transport and communications

Transport. Railroads (1987): length 3,939 mi, 6,340 km; passenger-km 24,-457,000,000; metric ton-km cargo 13,061,000,000. Roads (1987): total length 33,982 mi, 54,689 km (paved 57%). Vehicles (1987): passenger cars 844,350; trucks and buses 746,906. Merchant marine (1988): vessels (100 gross tons and over) 1,930; total deadweight tonnage 11,524,125. Air transport (1987): passenger-km 14,496,000,000; metric ton-km cargo 1,654,200,000; airports (1989) with scheduled flights 6.
Communications. Daily newspapers (1986): total number 26; total circulation 11,000,000; circulation per 1,000 population 265. Radio (1988): 41,-958,516 receivers (1 per 1.0 persons). Television (1987): 8,643,235 receivers (1 per 4.9 persons). Telephones (1988): 10,306,000 (1 per 4.1 persons).

Education and health

Education (1987–88)	schools	teachers	students	student/ teacher ratio
Primary (age 6–13)	6,531	130,142	4,771,722	36.7
Secondary (age 14–19)	3,454	120,834	4,055,089	33.6
Vocational	688	32,016	857,624	26.8
Higher	442	35,753	1,340,381	37.5

Educational attainment (1985). Percent of population age 25 and over having: no formal schooling 14.3%; primary education 46.2%; some secondary 3.8%; secondary 24.8%; postsecondary 10.9%. *Literacy* (1981): total population age 15 and over literate 13,191,432 (92.7%); males literate 6,937,242 (97.5%); females literate 6,254,190 (87.9%).
Health (1987): physicians 34,185 (1 per 1,216 persons); hospital beds 85,327 (1 per 487 persons); infant mortality rate per 1,000 live births (1988): 25.0.
Food (1984–86): daily per capita caloric intake 2,876 (vegetable products 88%, animal products 12%); 121% of FAO recommended minimum requirement.

Military

Total active duty personnel (1989): 650,000 (army 84.6%, navy 9.2%, air force 6.2%). *Military expenditure as percent of GNP* (1987): 5.8% (world 5.4%); per capita expenditure: U.S.$133.

---

¹The capital of Kyŏnggi province was changed from Inchŏn to Suwŏn in 1981. ²Refers to persons who have received commandments, accepted baptism, or entered a faith and who participate in a religious function regularly or put the religious idea into practice. ³Excludes farm households. ⁴Unemployed. ⁵August.

Kuwait

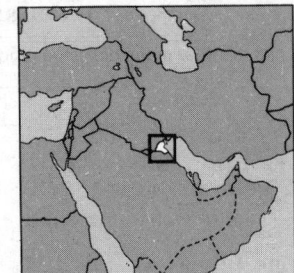

Official name: Dawlat al-Kuwayt (State of Kuwait).
Form of government: Constitutional monarchy with a single parliamentary house (National Assembly [64])[1].
Head of state and government: Emir, assisted by Prime Minister.
Capital: Kuwait City.
Official language: Arabic.
Official religion: Islam.
Monetary unit: 1 Kuwaiti dinar (KD) = 1,000 fils; valuation (Oct. 2, 1989) 1 KD = U.S.$3.38 = £2.09.

Area and population

Governorates	Capitals	area		population
		sq mi	sq km	1987 estimate
al-Aḥmadī	al-Aḥmadī	1,984	5,138	345,783
al-Jahrā'	al-Jahrā'	4,372	11,324	329,588
Capital	Kuwait City	38	98	160,860
Ḥawallī	Ḥawallī	138	358	1,036,337
Islands[2]	—	347	900	...
TOTAL		6,880[3]	17,818	1,872,568

Demography

Population (1989): 2,048,000.
Density (1989): persons per sq mi 297.7, persons per sq km 114.9.
Urban–rural (1986): urban 90.1%; rural 9.9%.
Sex distribution (1988): male 56.65%; female 43.35%.
Age breakdown (1986): under 15, 37.4%; 15–29, 27.9%; 30–44, 23.9%; 45–59, 8.6%; 60–74, 1.8%; 75 and over, 0.4%.
Population projection: (2000) 2,841,000; (2010) 3,516,000.
Doubling time: 24 years.
Ethnic composition (1985): Kuwaiti Arab 40.1%; non-Kuwaiti Arab 37.9%; Asian 21.0%; European 0.7%; other 0.3%.
Religious affiliation (1980): Muslim 91.5% (Sunnī about 80%, Shī'ah about 20%); Christian 6.4%; other 2.1%.
Major cities (1985): as-Sālimīyah 153,220; Ḥawallī 145,215; al-Jahrā' 111,165; al-Farwānīyah 68,665; Kuwait City 44,224.

Vital statistics

Birth rate per 1,000 population (1988): 26.2 (world avg. 27.1); legitimate, n.a.; illegitimate, n.a.
Death rate per 1,000 population (1988): 2.2 (world avg. 9.9).
Natural increase rate per 1,000 population (1988): 24.0 (world avg. 17.2).
Total fertility rate (avg. births per childbearing woman; 1987): 4.7.
Marriage rate per 1,000 population (1987): 5.3.
Divorce rate per 1,000 population (1987): 1.4.
Life expectancy at birth (1986): male 70.3 years; female 73.0 years.
Major causes of death per 100,000 population (1987): circulatory diseases 73.6; accidents, poisonings, and violence 31.4; malignant neoplasms (cancers) 25.5; respiratory diseases 16.5; endocrine, nutritional, and metabolic diseases 6.9; infectious and parasitic diseases 6.7; diseases of the digestive system 4.9; diseases of the nervous system 1.3.

National economy

Budget (1988–89). Revenue: KD 2,054,000,000 (oil revenue 87.1%, service charges 9.2%, custom duties 3.0%). Expenditures: KD 3,194,800,000 (wages and salaries 27.7%, construction projects 23.7%, education 9.6%, defense 9.5%, goods and services 8.3%, public works 7.5%, health 6.8%).
Public debt: none.
Tourism (1987): receipts from visitors U.S.$100,000,000; expenditures by nationals abroad U.S.$2,505,000,000.
Gross national product (at current market prices; 1987): U.S.$29,472,000,000 (U.S.$14,870 per capita).

Structure of gross domestic product and labour force

	1987		1986	
	in value KD '000,000	% of total value	labour force	% of labour force
Agriculture	62.4	1.1	13,718	1.9
Mining (oil sector)	2,233.2	40.8	7,544	1.1
Manufacturing	792.1	14.5	53,613	7.5
Construction	166.8	3.0	130,471	18.3
Public utilities	−58.4	−1.1	7,819	1.1
Transportation and communications	257.9	4.7	39,401	5.5
Trade	386.4	7.1	80,141	11.3
Finance	419.5	7.7	22,252	3.1
Pub. admin., defense, Services	517.0 } 701.3	9.4 } 12.8	356,640	50.1
TOTAL	5,478.2	100.0	711,599	100.0[3]

Production (metric tons except as noted). Agriculture, forestry, fishing (1988): tomatoes 39,000, cucumbers and gherkins 24,000, eggplants 19,000, onions 2,000, pumpkins and squash 1,000, garlic 1,000; livestock (number of live animals) 300,000 sheep, 26,000 cattle, 20,000 goats, 8,000 camels, 8,000,000 chickens; fish catch 6,384. Mining and quarrying (1985): sulfur 202,377; asphalt 945,000 barrels. Manufacturing (1988): urea 832,000; flour 135,101; bread 78,878; bran 37,085; salt 31,753; cattle feed 17,188; liquefied

caustic soda 16,191; chlorine gas 14,352; fats and oil 12,367; asbestos pipes 9,323; biscuits 2,332; detergents 2,018; hydrochloric acid 778,400 gallons; hydrogen gas 4,170,000 cu m; concrete 91,516 cu m; sodium hydrochloride 22,687 cu m; standard accumulators (batteries) 959 units. Construction (1988): residential 4,717,000 sq m; nonresidential 279,000 sq m. Energy production (consumption): electricity (kW-hr; 1987) 18,400,000,000 (18,-400,000,000); coal, none (none); crude petroleum (barrels; 1987) 445,126,000 (213,394,000); petroleum products (metric tons; 1987) 27,913,000 (4,561,-000); natural gas (cu m; 1987) 5,122,837,000 (9,871,000,000).
Population economically active (1988[4]): total 698,918; activity rate of total population 38.1% (participation rates [1986]: ages 15–64, 63.5%; female 20.6%; unemployed 1.9%).

Price and earnings indexes (1985 = 100)

	1983	1984	1985	1986	1987	1988	1989[4]
Consumer price index	97.4	98.5	100.0	101.0	101.6	103.4	105.8
Monthly earnings index	...	...	...	...	...	...	...

Household income and expenditure. Average household size (1986) 7.4; annual income per household (1973)[5] KD 4,246 (U.S.$12,907); sources of income: wages and salaries 53.8%, self-employment 20.8%, other 25.4%; expenditure (1986): food, beverages, and tobacco 27.5%, housing and energy 26.1%, transportation 12.7%, household appliances 11.3%, clothing and footwear 8.3%, education and recreation 3.9%, health 0.5%.
Land use (1987): forested 0.1%; meadows and pastures 7.5%; agricultural and under permanent cultivation 0.2%; other, built-up, and wasteland 92.2%.

Foreign trade

Balance of trade (current prices)

	1983	1984	1985	1986	1987	1988
KD '000,000	+1,224.5	+1,590.7	+1,367.2	+389.9	+854.0	+505.4
% of total	22.2%	28.0%	27.7%	10.2%	22.4%	14.5%

Imports (1988): KD 1,492,300,000 (1986; machinery and transport equipment 38.6%, manufactured goods 19.1%, food and live animals 16.7%, miscellaneous manufactured articles 15.9%, chemicals 5.9%). *Major import sources:* Japan 14.4%; United States 14.3%; West Germany 8.9%; United Kingdom 8.2%; Italy 6.4%; France 6.0%.
Exports (1988): KD 1,997,700,000 (crude petroleum and petroleum products 87.9%). *Major export destinations:* Japan 18.3%; Italy 9.6%; The Netherlands 8.5%; Taiwan 7.0%; Pakistan 5.0%; United States 4.6%; Singapore 3.4%; France 2.7%.

Transport and communications

Transport. Railroads: none. Roads (1988): total length 2,405 mi, 3,871 km (paved 100%). Vehicles (1988): passenger cars 424,554; trucks and buses 115,361. Merchant marine (1988): vessels (100 gross tons and over) 206; total deadweight tonnage 1,010,974. Air transport (1988): passenger-mi 2,093,955,000, passenger-km 3,369,901,000; short ton-mi cargo 231,657,000, metric ton-km cargo 338,235,000; airports (1989) with scheduled flights 1.
Communications. Daily newspapers (1987): total number 7; total circulation 418,000; circulation per 1,000 population 223. Radio (1988): total number of receivers 1,100,000 (1 per 1.8 persons). Television (1988): total number of receivers 800,000 (1 per 2.4 persons). Telephones (1986): 310,132 (1 per 5.9 persons).

Education and health

Education (1987–88)

	schools	teachers	students	student/ teacher ratio
Primary (age 6–10)	295	10,125	181,844	18.0
Secondary (age 11–18)	431	19,996	255,566	12.8
Voc., teacher tr.	...	586	11,388	19.4
Higher	1	863	15,751	18.2

Educational attainment (1985). Percent of population age 15 and over having: no formal schooling 44.4%; primary education 9.2%; some secondary 19.6%; complete secondary 18.2%; higher 8.6%. *Literacy* (1986): total population age 15 and over literate 856,146 (75.1%); males literate 539,058 (78.7%); females literate 317,088 (69.6%).
Health (1987): physicians 2,799 (1 per 669 persons); hospital beds 5,503[6] (1 per 340 persons); infant mortality rate per 1,000 live births (1986) 34.2.
Food (1984–86): daily per capita caloric intake 3,076 (vegetable products 75%, animal products 25%); 127% of FAO recommended minimum requirement.

Military

Total active duty personnel (1988): 20,300 (army 78.8%, navy 10.3%, air force 10.9%). *Military expenditure as percent of GNP* (1987): 5.2% (world 5.4%); per capita expenditure U.S.$714.

[1]Parliament was suspended on July 3, 1986; its membership includes 50 elected and (at its most recent sitting) 14 ex officio members of the Cabinet. [2]Bubian Island 333 sq mi (863 sq km) and Warba Island 14 sq mi (37 sq km). [3]Detail does not add to total given because of rounding. [4]March. [5]Kuwaiti households only. [6]Government hospitals only.

Laos

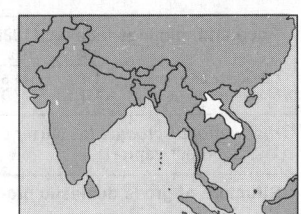

Official name: Sathalanalat Paxathipatai Paxaxôn Lao (Lao People's Democratic Republic).
Form of government: unitary single-party people's republic with one legislative house (Supreme People's Assembly [79]).
Chief of state: President.
Head of government: Prime Minister.
Capital: Vientiane.
Official language: Lao.
Official religion: none.
Monetary unit: 1 new kip (KN) = 100 at; valuation (Oct. 2, 1989)
1 U.S.$ = KN 583.00;
1 £ = KN 943.29.

Area and population

Provinces	Capitals	area sq mi	area sq km	population 1985 census
Attapu	Attapu	...	...	69,631
Bokeo	Houayxay	...	...	54,925
Bolikhamxay	Pakxan	...	...	122,300
Champasak	Pakxé	...	...	403,041
Houaphan	Xam Nua	...	...	209,921
Khammouan	Thakhek	...	...	213,462
Louang Namtha	Louang Namtha	...	...	97,028
Louangphrabang	Louangphrabang	...	...	295,475
Oudomxay	Xay	...	...	187,115
Phôngsali	Phôngsali	...	...	122,984
Saravan	Saravan	...	...	187,515
Savannakhét	Savannakhét	...	...	543,611
Vientiane	Vientiane	...	...	264,277
Xaignabouri	Xaignabouri	...	...	223,611
Xékong	Thong	...	...	50,909
Xiangkhoang	Phônsavan	...	...	161,589
Municipalities				
Vientiane	—	...	...	377,409
TOTAL		91,400	236,800	3,584,803

Demography

Population (1989): 3,936,000.
Density (1989): persons per sq mi 43.1, persons per sq km 16.6.
Urban–rural (1987): urban 16.0%; rural 84.0%.
Sex distribution (1987): male 49.02%; female 50.98%.
Age breakdown (1985): under 15, 42.8%; 15–29, 26.4%; 30–44, 16.2%; 45–59, 9.6%; 60–74, 4.3%; 75 and over, 0.7%.
Population projection: (2000) 4,964,000; (2010) 6,016,000.
Doubling time: 33 years.
Ethnic composition (1983): Lao 67.1%; Paiaung-Wa 11.9%; Tai 7.9%; Miao (Hmong) and Man (Yao) 5.2%; Mon-Khmer 4.6%; other 3.3%.
Religious affiliation (1980): Buddhist 57.8%; tribal religionist 33.6%; Christian 1.8%, of which Roman Catholic 0.8%; Protestant 0.2%; Muslim 1.0%; atheist 1.0%; Chinese folk-religionist 0.9%; none 3.8%; other 0.1%.
Major cities (1975): Vientiane 377,409[1]; Savannakhét 53,000; Pakxé 47,000; Louangphrabang 46,000.

Vital statistics

Birth rate per 1,000 population (1988): 41.0 (world avg. 27.1).
Death rate per 1,000 population (1988): 16.2 (world avg. 9.9).
Natural increase rate per 1,000 population (1988): 24.8 (world avg. 17.2).
Total fertility rate (avg. births per childbearing woman; 1988): 5.7.
Marriage rate per 1,000 population: n.a.
Divorce rate per 1,000 population: n.a.
Life expectancy at birth (1988): male 47.3 years; female 50.3 years.
Major causes of death per 100,000 population: n.a; however, during the 1970s malaria, influenza, dysentery, and pneumonia were among the country's major health problems.

National economy

Budget (1986). Revenue: KN 14,127,000,000 (state enterprises 87.3%; private-sector taxes 12.7%). Expenditures: KN 24,979,000,000 (current expenditure 48.7%, of which wages and salaries 18.6%; capital expenditure 51.3%, of which transport and communications 21.4%).
Public debt (external, outstanding; 1987): U.S.$736,000,000.
Tourism (1982): total number of tourist arrivals 29,000.
Population economically active (1985): total 2,014,000; activity rate of total population 48.9% (participation rates: ages 15–64, 84.2%; female 45.3%; unemployed, n.a.).

Price and earnings indexes (1979 = 100)

	1980	1981	1982	1983	1984	1985
Consumer price index	170	209	296	467	594	982
Monthly earnings index	...	...	...	...	...	...

Production (metric tons except as noted). Agriculture, forestry, fishing (1988): rice 1,400,000, sweet potatoes 118,000, sugarcane 105,000, cassava 88,000, potatoes 53,000, pineapples 45,000, onions 45,000, melons 37,000, corn (maize) 36,000, oranges 33,000; livestock (number of live animals) 1,520,000 pigs, 1,050,000 water buffalo, 590,000 cattle, 74,000 goats, 6,000,000 chickens; roundwood 4,313,000 cu m; fish catch 20,000. Mining and

quarrying (1988): gypsum 100,000; rock salt 10,000; tin (metal content) 502. Manufacturing (1986): domestic animal feed 5,000; cement 5,000; washing powder 2,500; plastic products 191; textiles 97,900 sq m; clothing 883,000 pieces; ceramic articles 87,000; cigarettes 16,000,000 packets; rubber tires and tubes 883,000 units; beer and soft drinks 26,000 hectolitres; fish sauce 2,300 hectolitres. Construction: n.a. Energy production (consumption): electricity (kW-hr; 1987) 1,100,000,000 (365,000,000); coal (metric tons; 1981) 1,000 (1,000); crude petroleum, n.a. (n.a.); petroleum products (metric tons; 1987) none (69,000); natural gas, n.a. (n.a.).
Gross domestic product (at current market prices; 1987): U.S.$551,000,000 (U.S.$140 per capita).

Structure of gross domestic product and labour force

	1987 in value KN '000,000	1987 % of total value	1985 labour force	1985 % of labour force
Agriculture	49,216	67.7	1,491,000	74.0
Manufacturing	7,743[2]	10.6[2]		
Mining				
Construction	2,804	3.9		
Public utilities	[2]	[2]		
Transportation and communications	1,460	2.0	523,000	26.0
Trade	6,675	9.2		
Finance				
Pub. admin., defense	4,826	6.6		
Services				
TOTAL	72,724	100.0	2,014,000	100.0

Household income and expenditure. Average household size (1980) 5.3; average annual income per household KN 3,710 (U.S.$371); sources of income: n.a.; expenditure: n.a.
Land use (1987): forested 56.7%; meadows and pastures 3.5%; agricultural and under permanent cultivation 3.9%; other 35.9%.

Foreign trade

Balance of trade (current prices)

	1983	1984	1985	1986	1987	1988
U.S.$'000,000	−66.8	−36.7	−45.0	−55.9	−170	−188
% of total	56.7%	61.9%	54.2%	66.0%	63.4%	64.4%

Imports (1988): U.S.$240,000,000 (important imports include cereals, other food products, petroleum products, agricultural and general machinery, and transport equipment). *Major import sources* (1987): Thailand 45.7%; Japan 19.2%; United Kingdom 3.5%; Sweden 2.7%; Indonesia 2.3%; West Germany 2.2%; Switzerland 2.1%; Italy 1.3%.
Exports (1988): U.S.$52,000,000 (1985: electricity 50.1%, wood 29.3%, coffee 17.2%, tin 3.4%). *Major export destinations* (1987): China 40.8%; Thailand 22.7%; France 8.7%; Japan 5.9%; United Kingdom 4.7%; United States 3.8%; Sweden 2.1%; Denmark 1.7%; Hong Kong 1.3%.

Transport and communications

Transport. Railroads: none. Roads (1987): total length 17,105 mi, 27,527 km (paved 31%). Vehicles: passenger cars (1987) 15,800; trucks and buses (1984) 5,068. Merchant marine: none. Air transport (1985): passenger-mi 6,000,000, passenger-km 9,000,000; short ton-mi cargo 685,000, metric ton-km cargo 1,000,000; airports (1989) with scheduled flights 7.
Communications. Daily newspapers (1985): total number 3; total circulation (1983) 12,500; circulation per 1,000 population (1983) 3.6. Radio (1987): total number of receivers 367,000 (1 per 10 persons). Television (1987): total number of receivers 32,000 (1 per 118 persons). Telephones (1985): 8,136 (1 per 450 persons).

Education and health

Education (1984–85)

	schools	teachers	students	student/ teacher ratio
Primary (age 6–10)	7,470	18,070	584,000	27.4
Secondary (age 11–16)	563	5,815	91,356	15.7
Voc., teacher tr.	117	2,326	19,358	8.3
Higher	6	452	2,399	5.3

Educational attainment, n.a. *Literacy* (1985): total population age 15 and over literate 83.9%; males literate 92.0%; females literate 75.8%.
Health (1985): physicians 558 (1 per 6,495 persons); hospital beds 9,815 (1 per 369 persons); infant mortality rate per 1,000 live births (1988) 109.0.
Food (1984–86): daily per capita caloric intake 2,190 (vegetable products 90%, animal products 10%); (1984) 100% of FAO recommended minimum requirement.

Military

Total active duty personnel (1989): 55,500 (army 94.6%, navy 1.8%, air force 3.6%). *Military expenditure as percent of GNP* (1984): 10.5% (world 5.7%); per capita expenditure U.S.$16.

---

[1]1985. [2]Manufacturing includes Public utilities.

Lebanon

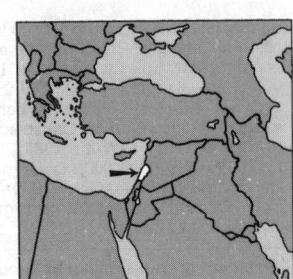

Official name: al-Jumhūrīyah al-Lubnānīyah (Republic of Lebanon).
Form of government: multiparty republic with one legislative house (National Assembly [99[1]]).
Chief of state: President[1].
Head of government: Prime Minister.
Capital: Beirut.
Official language: Arabic.
Official religion: none.
Monetary unit: 1 Lebanese pound (LL) = 100 piastres; valuation (Oct. 2, 1989) 1 U.S.$ = LL 459.15; 1 £ = LL 742.90.

Area and population

Governorates	Capitals	area sq mi	area sq km	population 1970 estimate
Bayrūt	Beirut (Bayrūt)	7	18	474,870
al-Biqā'	Zaḥlah	1,653	4,280	203,520
Jabal Lubnān	B'abdā	753	1,950	833,055
al-Janūb	Sidon (Ṣaydā)	772	2,001	249,945
ash-Shamāl	Tripoli (Ṭarābulus)	765	1,981	364,935
TOTAL		3,950	10,230	2,126,325

Demography

Population (1989): 2,897,000.
Density (1989): persons per sq mi 733.5, persons per sq km 283.2.
Urban–rural (1986): urban 80.8%; rural 19.2%.
Sex distribution (1986): male 48.36%; female 51.64%.
Age breakdown (1986): under 15, 37.0%; 15–29, 29.5%; 30–44, 14.7%; 45–59, 10.9%; 60–74, 6.1%; 75 and over, 1.8%.
Population projection: (2000) 3,603,000; (2010) 4,170,000.
Doubling time: during the 1970–75 prewar period the average growth rate was 2.6%; however, since 1976 continuing dislocation of the population by the civil war has rendered both the absolute size and principal components of population change (births, deaths, migration) highly problematic.
Ethnic composition (1983): Lebanese 82.6%; Palestinian 9.6%; Armenian 4.9%; Syrian, Kurd, and other 2.9%.
Religious affiliation (1983): no official data exist subsequent to the 1932 census, when Christians (predominantly Maronite Roman Catholic) were a slight majority; it is thought that Muslims today constitute the majority but by what margin is highly uncertain. Unofficial and CIA estimates (1984/1986) indicated that the main religious groups were distributed as follows: Shī'ī Muslim 32/41%; Maronite Christian 24.5/16%; Sunnī Muslim 21/27%; Druze 7/7%; Greek Orthodox 6.5/5%; Greek Catholic 4/3%; Armenian Christian 4%/n.a.; other 1.0%.
Major cities (1985): Beirut 200,000[2]; Tripoli 500,000; Zaḥlah 200,000; Sidon (Ṣaydā) 100,000; an-Nabaṭīyah 100,000.

Vital statistics

Birth rate per 1,000 population (1989): 28 (world avg. 27.1); legitimate, n.a.; illegitimate, n.a.
Death rate per 1,000 population (1989): 7 (world avg. 9.9).
Natural increase rate per 1,000 population (1989): 21 (world avg. 17.2).
Total fertility rate (avg. births per childbearing woman; 1989): 3.8.
Life expectancy at birth (1986): male 64.7 years; female 68.8 years.
Major causes of death: normally, heart ailments and gastrointestinal diseases, including typhoid fever and dysentery; but, with the continuing civil war, violence and acts of war are now among the principal causes of mortality.

National economy

Budget (1989). Revenue: LL 130,000,000,000 (1986; income taxes 49.6%, customs duties 31.5%). Expenditure: LL 219,500,000,000 (1986; internal debt service 30.2%, defense 20.7%).
Public debt (external, outstanding; 1987): U.S.$236,200,000.
Production (metric tons except as noted). Agriculture, forestry, fishing (1988): fruits and vegetables 1,172,000 (of which oranges 248,000, potatoes 210,000, grapes 159,000, tomatoes 132,000, apples 80,000, cucumbers 77,-000, lemons and limes 36,000, watermelons 32,000, onions 29,000, bananas 23,000, cabbages 22,000, eggplants 19,000, cantaloupes 14,000, green beans 10,000, carrots 9,000, green peas 9,000, cauliflowers 8,000), wheat 19,000, sugar beets 4,000; livestock (number of live animals) 470,000 goats, 141,000 sheep, 52,000 cattle, 12,000,000 chickens; roundwood (1987) 493,000 cu m; fish catch (1987) 1,800. Mining and quarrying (1985): salt 6,000; gypsum 3,000. Manufacturing (1984): cement 800,000; wheat flour 190,000[3]; paper and paperboard 45,000; quicklime 20,000. Construction (1981): 5,863,000 sq m. Energy production (consumption): electricity (kW-hr; 1987) 4,600,-000,000 (4,630,000,000); coal, n.a. (none); crude petroleum (barrels; 1987) n.a. (9,160,000); petroleum products (metric tons; 1987) 1,150,000 (2,495,-000); natural gas, none (n.a.).
Household income and expenditure. Average household size (1980) 5.3; income per household: n.a.; sources of income (1974): wages and salaries 27.9%, transfers 3.0%, other 69.1%; expenditure[4, 5]: food 42.8%, housing 16.8%, clothing 8.6%, health care 7.2%.
Tourism (1980): number of tourist arrivals 135,548[6].
Population economically active (1986): total 693,812; activity rate of total population 25.1% (participation rates: over age 15, 39.9%; female 21.7%; unemployed [1987] 25–50%).

Price and earnings indexes (1980 = 100)

	1981	1982	1983	1984	1985	1986	1987
Consumer price index	119.4	141.5	149.9	164.4	180.8	c. 518	c. 2,700
Monthly earnings index[7]	118.5	137.0	...	...	...	...	...

Gross national product (at current market prices; 1985): U.S.$1,800,000,000 (U.S.$690 per capita).

Structure of gross domestic product and labour force

	1984 in value LL '000,000	1984 % of total value	1986 labour force	1986 % of labour force
Agriculture	814.0	8.4	132,211	19.1
Mining	...	...	694	0.1
Manufacturing	1,277.0	13.2	123,647	17.8
Construction	331.2	3.4	43,357	6.2
Public utilities	516.4	5.3	6,668	1.0
Transp. and commun.	741.4	7.6	48,242	7.0
Finance	1,218.0	12.5	24,224	3.5
Trade	2,722.6	28.0	114,706	16.5
Pub. admin., defense	1,060.2	10.9 }	200,063	28.8
Services	1,036.5	10.7 }		
TOTAL	9,717.3	100.0	693,812	100.0

Land use (1987): forested 7.8%; meadows and pastures 1.0%; agricultural and under permanent cultivation 29.4%; wasteland and other areas 61.8%.

Foreign trade

Balance of trade (current prices)

	1982	1983	1984	1985	1986	1987
LL '000,000	−9,890	−12,461	−13,987	−25,581	−59,090	−269,311
% of total	48.5%	69.0%	64.9%	61.8%	60.6%	50.4%

Imports (1987): LL 402,027,000,000 (1982; consumer goods 40%, machinery and transport equipment 35%, petroleum products 20%). *Major import sources:* Italy 10.7%; Turkey 8.5%; France 8.1%; West Germany 5.9%; United States 5.5%; Romania 4.7%; Saudi Arabia 4.5%.
Exports (1987): LL 132,716,000,000 (1985; jewelry 10.2%, clothing 5.2%, pharmaceutical products 4.9%, metal products 4.8%). *Major export destinations:* Saudi Arabia 8.7%; Switzerland 7.6%; Jordan 6.0%; Kuwait 5.4%; United States 5.2%.

Transport and communications

Transport. Railroads (1982)[8]: length (1986) 259 mi, 417 km; passenger-mi 5,325,000, passenger-km 8,570,000; short ton-mi cargo 28,770,000, metric ton-km cargo 42,010,000. Roads (1987): total length 4,580 mi, 7,370 km (paved 85%). Vehicles (1982): passenger cars 473,372; trucks and buses 49,560. Merchant marine (1988): vessels (100 gross tons and over) 201; total deadweight tonnage 634,525. Air transport[9] (1988): passenger-mi 554,-154,000, passenger-km 891,854,000; short ton-mi cargo 16,942,000, metric ton-km cargo 24,735,000; airports (1989) with scheduled flights 1 (intermittently closed).
Communications. Daily newspapers (1986): total number 39; total circulation 572,734[10]; circulation per 1,000 population 211.6[10]. Radio (1988): 2,198,450 receivers (1 per 1.3 persons). Television (1988): 838,037 receivers (1 per 3.4 persons). Telephones (1987): 150,400 (1 per 18.4 persons).

Education and health

Education (1984–85)

	schools[11]	teachers	students	student/ teacher ratio
Primary (age 5–9)	2,130	22,810[11]	329,340	...
Secondary (age 10–16)	1,405	21,344[12]	230,934	...
Voc., teacher tr.	181	3,506	37,036	10.6
Higher	18	7,460	70,510	9.5

Educational attainment (1970). Percent of population age 25 and over having: no formal schooling 45.6%; ability to read and write 35.6%; incomplete primary education 28.5%, complete primary 10.8%; incomplete secondary 7.1%, complete secondary 4.9%; higher 3.1%. *Literacy* (1985): total population age 15 and over literate, c. 1,325,000 (77.0%); males literate, c. 715,000 (85.7%); females literate, c. 610,000 (68.9%).
Health (1986): physicians 3,509 (1 per 771 persons); hospital beds (1982) 11,400 (1 per 263 persons); infant mortality rate per 1,000 live births 49.2.
Food (1979–81): daily per capita caloric intake 2,995 (vegetable products 84%, animal products 16%); 120% of FAO recommended minimum.

Military

Total active duty personnel (1989): Lebanese national armed forces 22,300 (army 94.2%, navy 2.2%, air force 3.6%); external regular military forces include: UN peacekeeping force in Lebanon 5,500; Syrian army 30,000. Principal armed civilian factions include[13]: Maronite Christian (Lebanese Forces [Phalange]) 35,000; Shī'ī Muslim (pro-Syrian Amal) 15,000; Druze (Progressive Socialist Party) 12,000; Palestine Liberation Organization 9,800; Shī'ī Muslim (pro-Iran Hezbollah [Party of God]) 15,000. *Military expenditure as percent of GNP* (1983): 8.2% (world 5.8%); per capita expenditure: U.S.$161[14].

[1]Assembly elected 1972; surviving members named two new presidents in 1989. [2]1989. [3]1983. [4]Weights based on consumer price index components. [5]For capital city only. [6]Approximately one-fourth the annual prewar rates of the early 1970s. [7]Excludes banking sector. [8]No track is currently in use. [9]MEA-Airliban international flights only. [10]For 20 newspapers only. [11]1981–82. [12]1980–81. [13]Total personnel. [14]Constant prices of 1987. A defense buget of US$26,000,000 (c. $9 per capita) was announced in 1988.

Lesotho

Official name: Lesotho (Sotho); King-
dom of Lesotho (English).
Form of government: monarchy assisted
by a Military Council[1].
Chief of state: King[1].
Head of government: Chairman of the
Military Council[1].
Capital: Maseru.
Official languages: Sotho; English.
Official religion: Christianity.
Monetary unit: 1 loti (plural maloti
[M]) = 100 lisente; valuation (Oct. 2,
1989) 1 U.S.$ = M 2.69; 1 £ = M 4.35.

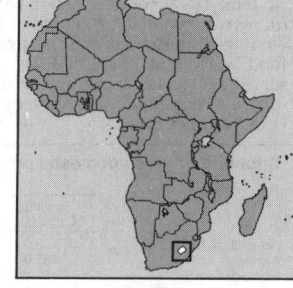

Area and population		area		population
Districts	Capitals	sq mi	sq km	1987 estimate
Berea	Teyateyaneng	858	2,222	199,600
Butha-Buthe	Butha-Buthe	682	1,767	103,000
Leribe	Hlotse	1,092	2,828	264,600
Mafeteng	Mafeteng	818	2,119	200,600
Maseru	Maseru	1,652	4,279	319,100
Mohale's Hoek	Mohale's Hoek	1,363	3,530	168,600
Mokhotlong	Mokhotlong	1,573	4,075	76,600
Qacha's Nek	Qacha's Nek	907	2,349	65,600
Quthing	Quthing	1,126	2,916	113,200
Thaba-Tseka	Thaba-Tseka	1,649	4,270	106,800
TOTAL		11,720	30,355	1,617,700

Demography

Population (1989): 1,715,000.
Density (1989): persons per sq mi 146.3, persons per sq km 56.5.
Urban–rural (1986): urban 16.0%; rural 84.0%.
Sex distribution (1986): male 48.57%; female 51.43%.
Age breakdown (1985): under 15, 42.3%; 15–29, 25.9%; 30–44, 16.2%; 45–59,
9.9%; 60–74, 4.7%; 75 and over, 1.0%.
Population projection: (2000) 2,282,000; (2010) 2,958,000.
Doubling time: 27 years.
Ethnic composition (1983): Sotho 99.7%; other 0.3%.
Religious affiliation (1980): Roman Catholic 43.5%; Protestant (mostly
Lesotho Evangelical) 29.8%; Anglican 11.5%; other Christian 8.0%; tribal
6.2%; other 1.0%.
Major urban centres (1986): Maseru 106,000; Maputsoe 15,823[2]; Teyateya-
neng 8,589[2].

Vital statistics

Birth rate per 1,000 population (1985–90): 40.8 (world avg. 27.1); legitimate,
n.a.; illegitimate, n.a.
Death rate per 1,000 population (1985–90): 12.4 (world avg. 9.9).
Natural increase rate per 1,000 population (1985–90): 28.4 (world avg. 17.2).
Total fertility rate (avg. births per childbearing woman; 1985–90): 5.8.
Marriage rate per 1,000 population (1987): n.a.
Divorce rate per 1,000 population (1987): n.a.
Life expectancy at birth (1985–90): male 48.3 years; female 54.3 years.
Major causes of death per 100,000 population: n.a.; however, major diseases
include malaria, typhoid fever, and infectious and parasitic diseases.

National economy

Budget (1988–89). Revenue: M 385,000,000 (tax revenue 92.7%, of which customs receipts 50.2%, sales tax 16.9%, company tax 8.1%, income tax 3.6%;
grants 7.3%). Expenditures: M 482,700,000 (recurrent expenditure 66.0%, of
which personal emoluments 28.8%, interest payments 7.6%, subsidies and
transfers 5.4%, other goods and services 24.2%; capital expenditure 34.0%).
Production (metric tons except as noted). Agriculture, forestry, fishing
(1988): corn (maize) 95,000, sorghum 31,000, vegetables and melons 26,-
000, wheat 19,000, pulses 15,000, fruit 15,000, roots and tubers 6,000, peas
3,779[3], beans 1,502[3]; livestock (number of live animals) 1,440,000 sheep,
1,030,000 goats, 525,000 cattle, 126,000 mules and asses, 119,000 horses,
72,000 pigs, 1,000,000 chickens; roundwood (1987) 553,000 cu m; fish catch
(1987) 17. Mining and quarrying (1986): diamonds M 2,100,000[4]. Manufacturing (total value added; 1986): M 59,200,000; food and beverages 60.7%;
textiles, apparel, and leather 14.7%; iron and steel products 5.3%; chemical
products 4.8%; printing and publishing 4.5%; furniture and fixtures 3.4%.
Construction (total value added; 1986): M 57,500,000. Energy production
(consumption): electricity (kW-hr; 1987) 1,000,000 (n.a.); coal, none (n.a.);
petroleum, none (n.a.); natural gas, none (n.a.).
Public debt (external, outstanding; 1987): U.S.$237,000,000.
Tourism (1987): receipts from visitors U.S.$10,400,000; expenditures by na-
tionals abroad U.S.$6,000,000.
Population economically active (1985): total 716,270; activity rate of total
population 45.7% (participation rates: ages 15–64, 79.8%; female 45.5%;
unemployed, n.a.).

Price and earnings indexes (1985 = 100)							
	1982	1983	1984	1985	1986	1987	1988
Consumer price index	66.9	78.2	87.1	100.0	117.2	131.5	147.3
Annual earnings index	...	...	...	...	...	...	...

Household income and expenditure. Average household size (1980) 4.4;
average annual income per household (1985–86) M 3,110 (U.S.$1,400);
sources of income (1978–79): self-employment 51.6%, wages and salaries

42.0% (of which migrant workers' remittances 32.4%), transfer payments
and other 6.4%; expenditure (1975)[5]: food 34.0%, clothing 19.3%, housing
16.7%, transportation 9.5%, education 4.1%, health 1.8%.
Gross national product (at current market prices; 1987): U.S.$591,000,000
(U.S.$360 per capita).

Structure of gross domestic product and labour force				
	1987		1985–86	
	in value M '000,000	% of total value	labour force	% of labour force
Agriculture	118.3	16.3	474,171	66.2
Mining	1.9	0.3	6,446	0.9
Manufacturing	78.3[6]	10.8[6]	19,339	2.7
Construction	65.9	9.1	31,516	4.4
Public utilities	6.0	0.8	1,433	0.2
Transp. and commun.	14.6	2.0	5,014	0.7
Trade	105.6	14.5	22,204	3.1
Finance	83.4	11.5	3,581	0.5
Pub. admin., defense	82.5	11.3	17,907	2.5
Services	61.3	8.4	126,780	17.7
Other	109.1[7]	15.0[7]	7,879	1.1
TOTAL	726.9	100.0	716,270	100.0

Land use (1987): meadows and pastures 65.9%; agricultural and under permanent cultivation 9.9%; other 24.2%.

Foreign trade[8]

Balance of trade (current prices)							
	1981	1982	1983	1984	1985	1986	1987
M '000,000	−405.9	−528.1	−594.0	−684.5	−746.9	−834.6	−830.5
% of total	82.5%	87.1%	89.9%	89.5%	88.2%	87.8%	81.4%

Imports (1987): M 1,053,790,000 (1981; manufactured goods [excluding
chemicals, machinery, and transport equipment] 37.4%, of which clothing 8.4%, blankets and traveling rugs 3.6%, footwear 3.3%; food and live
animals 18.9%, of which cereals [all forms] 5.9%, sugar [all forms] 2.6%;
machinery and transport equipment 17.0%, of which trucks and vans 3.5%;
petroleum products 8.6%). *Major import sources* (1981): Customs Union
of Southern Africa 97.1%; European Economic Community 1.5%.
Exports (1987): M 94,660,000 (1981; diamonds 42.1%; food and live animals
10.3%; umbrellas, brooms, brushes, and basketwork 8.1%; mohair 8.0%;
road vehicles 3.1%; footwear 3.0%). *Major export destinations* (1981): Customs Union of Southern Africa 46.7%; Switzerland 41.8%; West Germany
7.0%.

Transport and communications

Transport. Railroads (1987): length 1 mi, 2 km. Roads (1987): total length
2,640 mi, 4,250 km (paved 12%). Vehicles (1982): passenger cars 5,129;
trucks and buses 11,962. Merchant marine: vessels (100 gross tons and
over) none. Air transport (1987): passenger-mi 6,810,000, passenger-km
10,960,000; short ton-mi cargo 860,000, metric ton-km cargo 1,255,000;
airports (1988) with scheduled flights 14.
Communications. Daily newspapers (1985): total number 3; total circulation
44,000; circulation per 1,000 population 28. Radio (1988): total number
of receivers 45,821 (1 per 36 persons). Television (1987): total number
of receivers 1,500 (1 per 1,085 persons). Telephones (1985): 13,738 (1
per 117 persons).

Education and health

Education (1986–87)				
	schools	teachers	students	student/ teacher ratio
Primary (age 6–12)	1,174	5,880	331,858	56.4
Secondary (age 13–17)	164	1,891	41,138	21.8
Voc., teacher tr.	10	183	2,567	14.0
Higher	1	132	1,081	8.2

Educational attainment (1976). Percent of population age 10 and over having: no formal education 28.8%; primary 64.6%; secondary 2.3%; higher
0.6%. *Literacy* (1985): total population age 15 and over literate 655,400
(73.6%); males literate 273,800 (62.4%); females literate 381,600 (84.5%).
Health (1982): physicians 114 (1 per 12,265 persons); hospital beds 2,300 (1
per 608 persons); infant mortality rate per 1,000 live births (1985–90) 100.
Food (1984–86): daily per capita caloric intake 2,296 (vegetable products
93%, animal products 7%); (1984) 103% of FAO recommended minimum
requirement.

Military

Total active duty personnel (1988): 2,000[9]. *Military expenditure as percent
of GNP* (1986): 2.4% (world 5.4%); per capita expenditure U.S.$15.

[1]Following a military coup in January 1986, executive and legislative powers were
nominally vested in the King, though effectively exercised by a six-member Military
Council and a Council of Ministers. The 1966 independence constitution, suspended
in 1970 and reinstated in 1983, was again suspended in 1986 following the coup,
dissolving Lesotho's legislative organs. [2]1976. [3]1986. [4]Individual diamond diggers.
[5]Weights of consumer price index components. [6]Includes handicrafts. [7]Indirect taxes
less imputed bank service charges. [8]Import figures are f.o.b. in balance of trade and
c.i.f. in commodities and trading partners. [9]Royal Lesotho Defence Force.

Liberia

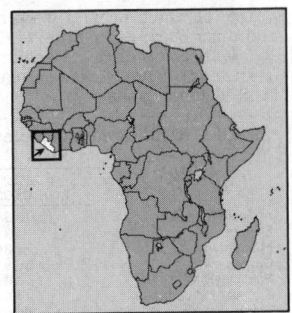

Official name: Republic of Liberia.
Form of government: multiparty republic with two legislative houses (Senate [26]; House of Representatives [64]).
Head of state and government: President.
Capital: Monrovia.
Official language: English.
Official religion: none.
Monetary unit: 1 Liberian dollar (L$) = 100 cents; valuation (Oct. 2, 1989) 1 U.S.$ = L$1.00; 1 £ = L$1.62.

Area and population

Counties	Capitals	area sq mi	area sq km	population 1986 estimate
Bong	Gbarnga	3,127	8,099	268,100
Grand Bassa	Buchanan	3,382	8,759	166,900
Grand Cape Mount	Robertsport	2,250	5,827	83,900
Grand Gedeh	Zwedru	6,575	17,029	109,000
Grand Kru[1]	Barclayville	[2]	[2]	[2]
Lofa	Voinjama	7,475	19,360	261,000
Margibi[3]	Kakata	1,260	3,263	104,000
Maryland	Harper	2,066[2]	5,351[2]	137,700[2]
Montserrado	Bensonville	1,058	2,740	582,400
Nimba	Sanniquellie	4,650	12,043	325,700
Sinoe	Greenville	3,959	10,254	65,400
Territories				
Bomi	Tubmanburg	755	1,955	67,300
Rivercess	Rivercess City	1,693	4,385	39,900
TOTAL		38,250	99,067[4]	2,221,300[5]

Demography

Population (1989): 2,508,000.
Density (1989): persons per sq mi 65.6, persons per sq km 25.3.
Urban–rural (1985): urban 39.5%; rural 60.5%.
Sex distribution (1985): male 50.69%; female 49.31%.
Age breakdown (1984): under 15, 43.2%; 15–29, 28.2%; 30–44, 14.7%; 45–59, 7.7%; 60–74, 4.4%; 75 and over, 1.8%.
Population projection: (2000) 3,596,000; (2010) 4,989,000.
Doubling time: 22 years.
Ethnic composition (1984): Kpelle 19.4%; Bassa 13.8%; Grebo 9.0%; Gio 7.8%; Kru 7.3%; Mano 7.1%; other 35.6%.
Religious affiliation (1984): Christian 67.7%; Muslim 13.8%[6]; traditional beliefs and other 18.5%.
Major cities (1974): Monrovia 421,058[7]; Buchanan 23,999; Congo Town 21,495; Yekepa 14,189; Tubmanburg 14,089.

Vital statistics

Birth rate per 1,000 population (1985–90): 45.0 (world avg. 27.1).
Death rate per 1,000 population (1985–90): 13.3 (world avg. 9.9).
Natural increase rate per 1,000 population (1985–90): 31.7 (world avg. 17.2).
Total fertility rate (avg. births per childbearing woman; 1985–90): 6.5.
Marriage rate per 1,000 population: n.a.
Divorce rate per 1,000 population: n.a.
Life expectancy at birth (1985–90): male 53.0 years; female 56.0 years.
Major causes of death per 100,000 population[8] (1985): complications during pregnancy 632.6[7]; malaria 79.8; pneumonia 64.2; anemia 50.2; malnutrition 23.4; measles 12.7.

National economy

Budget (1988). Revenue: L$208,200,000 (import duties and consular fees 33.9%; income and profits taxes 28.9%; excise tax 13.5%; nontax revenue 12.2%). Expenditures: L$330,800,000 (current expenditure 91.1%, of which wages and salaries 34.1%, interest on public debt 13.1%, goods and services 7.8%, subsidies and grants 5.1%; development expenditure 8.9%).
Public debt (external, outstanding; 1987): U.S.$1,152,000,000.
Tourism: receipts from visitors (1986) U.S.$6,000,000; expenditures by nationals abroad, n.a.
Population economically active (1984): total 669,330; activity rate of total population 31.8% (participation rates: ages 15–64, 64.7%[9]; female 31.2%[9]; unemployed 12.5%).

Price and earnings indexes (1985 = 100)

	1982	1983	1984	1985	1986	1987	1988
Consumer price index	96.7	99.4	100.6	100.0	103.6	108.8	119.3
Monthly earnings index	...	...	...	...	...	...	...

Production (metric tons except as noted). Agriculture, forestry, fishing (1988): cassava 310,000, rice 279,000, sugarcane 225,000, natural rubber 85,000, bananas 80,000, plantains 33,000, green coffee 20,000, sweet potatoes 18,000, yams 18,000, oranges 7,000, pineapples 7,000, cocoa beans 5,000; livestock (number of live animals) 240,000 sheep, 235,000 goats, 140,000 pigs, 42,000 cattle, 4,000,000 chickens; roundwood (1987) 5,640,000 cu m; fish catch (1987) 18,731. Mining and quarrying (1988): iron ore 12,770,000; diamonds 350,000 carats; gold 20,229 troy oz[10]. Manufacturing (1986): cement 96,350; palm oil 35,000; cigarettes 91,235,200 units; soft drinks 115,092 hectolitres; beer 105,547 hectolitres. Construction: n.a. Energy production (consumption): electricity (kW-hr; 1987) 825,000,000 (825,000,000); coal, none (n.a.);

crude petroleum (barrels; 1985) none (4,764,000); petroleum products (metric tons; 1987) none (207,000); natural gas, none (n.a.).
Household income and expenditure. Average household size (1983) 4.3; income per household: n.a.; sources of income: n.a.; expenditure (1963)[11]: food 34.4%, rent 14.9%, clothing and footwear 13.8%, household goods and services 6.1%, beverages and tobacco 5.7%, fuel and light 5.0%.
Gross national product (at current market prices; 1987): U.S.$1,030,000,000 (U.S.$440 per capita).

Structure of gross domestic product and labour force

	1985 in value L$'000,000[12]	1985 % of total value	1984 labour force	1984 % of labour force
Agriculture	138.9	19.4	481,177	71.9
Mining	137.0	19.2	17,500	2.6
Manufacturing	58.7	8.2	10,699	1.6
Construction	26.9	3.8	4,072	0.6
Public utilities	16.5	2.3	2,878	0.4
Transportation and communications	50.9	7.1	13,986	2.1
Trade	51.4	7.2	46,850	7.0
Finance	105.9	14.8	2,117	0.3
Pub. admin., defense	115.3	16.1	61,168	9.2
Services	34.0	4.7		
Other	−20.3[13]	−2.8[13]	28,883	4.3
TOTAL	715.2	100.0	669,330	100.0

Land use (1987): forested 21.8%; meadows and pastures 2.5%; agricultural and under permanent cultivation 3.9%; other 71.8%.

Foreign trade

Balance of trade (current prices)

	1982	1983	1984	1985	1986	1987
L$'000,000	+107.4	+73.8	+137.6	+189.4	+201.1	+115.9
% of total	12.7%	9.4%	17.1%	27.8%	33.1%	17.9%

Imports (1987): L$490,900,000 (petroleum and petroleum products 17.3%, basic manufactures 17.0%, machinery and transportation equipment 16.9%, food and live animals 15.2%, chemicals 5.5%). *Major import sources* (1985): United States 25.9%; West Germany 9.8%; Japan 8.4%; United Kingdom 7.4%; The Netherlands 6.5%; Spain 2.5%; Belgium–Luxembourg 2.5%; China 2.3%; Denmark 2.1%.
Exports (1987): L$375,000,000 (iron ore 58.1%, rubber 23.8%, logs and timber 9.5%, diamonds 2.9%, coffee 2.6%, cocoa 1.6%). *Major export destinations* (1985): West Germany 32.3%; United States 19.2%; Italy 15.8%; France 8.9%; Belgium–Luxembourg 5.9%; The Netherlands 4.4%; Spain 4.0%; United Kingdom 1.0%; Japan 0.5%.

Transport and communications

Transport. Railroads[14] (1987): route length 304 mi, 490 km; short ton-mi cargo 1,746,000,000[15], metric ton-km cargo 2,549,000,000[15]. Roads (1987): total length 5,011 mi, 8,064 km (paved 9%). Vehicles (1984): passenger cars 12,747; trucks and buses 8,288. Merchant marine (1988): vessels (100 gross tons and over) 1,507; total deadweight tonnage 93,987,093. Air transport (1980): passenger-mi 10,600,000, passenger-km 17,000,000; short ton-mi cargo 68,000, metric ton-km cargo 100,000; airports (1989) with scheduled flights 2.
Communications. Daily newspapers (1987): total number 7; total circulation 23,000[16]; circulation per 1,000 population 9.8[16]. Radio (1988): total number of receivers 565,964 (1 per 4.4 persons). Television (1988): total number of receivers 43,000 (1 per 55 persons). Telephones (1988): 8,736 (1 per 278 persons).

Education and health

Education (1980)

	schools	teachers	students	student/ teacher ratio
Primary (age 6–12)	1,651	9,099	227,431	25.0
Secondary (age 13–18)	419	1,129	51,666	45.8
Voc., teacher tr.	6	63	2,322	36.9
Higher	3	190	3,955[9]	...

Educational attainment (1974). Percent of population age 25 and over having: no grade completed 87.1%; some primary education 4.8%; complete primary 1.5%; some secondary 5.1%; higher 1.5%. *Literacy* (1984): total population age 15 and over literate 273,670 (22.4%); males literate 164,059 (27.4%); females literate 109,611 (18.4%).
Health: physicians (1983) 221 (1 per 9,324 persons); hospital beds (1981) 3,000 (1 per 653 persons); infant mortality rate per 1,000 live births (1985–90) 87.0.
Food (1984–86): daily per capita caloric intake 2,357 (vegetable products 93%, animal products 7%); 100% of FAO recommended minimum.

Military

Total active duty personnel (1989): 5,800 (army 91.4%[17], navy 8.6%). *Military expenditure as percent of GNP* (1987): 3.8% (world 5.4%); per capita expenditure U.S.$17.

[1]New county created from Kru Coast and Sasstown territories and part of Maryland County. [2]Figures for Grand Kru included in Maryland. [3]New county created from Marshall and Gibi territories. [4]Detail does not add to total given because of rounding. [5]Includes 10,000 persons not accounted for. [6]Some external sources estimate the Muslim population to exceed 30%. [7]1984. [8]Hospital inpatient morbidity rates. [9]1985. [10]1986. [11]Monrovia only. [12]At current factor cost. [13]Imputed bank service charges. [14]For iron-ore transport only. [15]Lamco and Bong Mining Company railroads only. [16]For 4 newspapers only. [17]Army includes air force personnel.

Libya

Official name: al-Jamāhīrīyah
al-'Arabīyah al-Lībīyah ash-Sha'bīyah
al-Ishtirākīyah (Socialist People's
Libyan Arab Jamahiriya).
Form of government: socialist state
with one policy-making body (General
People's Congress [1,112]).
Chief of state: Mu'ammar al-Qadhdhafi
(de facto)[1]; Secretary of General
People's Congress (de jure).
Head of government: Secretary of the
General People's Committee (prime
minister).
Capital: Tripoli[2].
Official language: Arabic.
Official religion: Islam.
Monetary unit: 1 Libyan dinar
(LD) = 1,000 dirhams; valuation
(Oct. 2, 1989) 1 Libyan
dinar = U.S.$3.33 = £2.08.

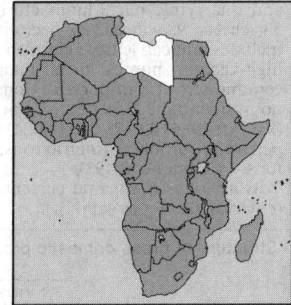

Area and population

Baladīyāt	Capitals	area sq mi	area sq km	population 1988 estimate
Banghāzī	Banghāzī	5,800	15,000	512,200
al-Jabal al-Akhḍar	al-Bayḍā'	14,300	37,000	308,300
al-Jabal al-Gharbī	Gharyān	33,600	87,000	204,300
Khalīj Surt	Surt	145,200	376,000	382,100
al-Kufrah	al-Kufrah	186,900	484,000	23,800
Margib	al-Khums	11,200	29,000	408,900
Marzūq	Marzūq	135,100	350,000	45,200
Nikāt al-Khums	Zuwārah	39,000	101,000	196,000
Sabhā	Sabhā	31,700	82,000	121,700
Ṭarābulus	Tripoli (Ṭarābulus)	1,200	3,000	1,083,100
Ṭubruq	Ṭubruq	32,400	84,000	110,900
Wādī al-Ḥa'iṭ	Awbārī	40,500	105,000	49,600
az-Zāwiyah	az-Zāwiyah	1,500	4,000	326,500
TOTAL		678,400	1,757,000	3,772,600

Demography

Population (1989): 4,080,000.
Density (1989): persons per sq mi 6.0, persons per sq km 2.3.
Urban–rural (1984): urban 75.8%; rural 24.2%.
Sex distribution (1984): male 51.07%; female 48.93%.
Age breakdown (1984): under 15, 49.7%; 15–29, 25.3%; 30–44, 13.7%; 45–59, 7.4%; 60–74, 3.2%; 75 and over, 0.6%.
Population projection: (2000) 5,559,000; (2010) 6,517,000.
Doubling time: 20 years.
Ethnic composition (1984): Libyan Arab and Berber 89.0%; other 11.0%.
Religious affiliation (1982): Sunnī Muslim 97.0%; other 3.0%.
Major cities (1988): Tripoli 591,100; Banghāzī 446,250; Miṣrātah 121,700.

Vital statistics

Birth rate per 1,000 population (1985–90): 43.9 (world avg. 27.1).
Death rate per 1,000 population (1985–90): 9.4 (world avg. 9.9).
Natural increase rate per 1,000 population (1985–90): 34.5 (world avg. 17.2).
Total fertility rate (avg. births per childbearing woman; 1985–90): 6.9.
Marriage rate per 1,000 population (1981): 4.3.
Divorce rate per 1,000 population (1981): 1.1.
Life expectancy at birth (1985–90): male 59.1 years; female 62.5 years.
Major causes of death per 100,000 population: n.a.; however, major diseases include trachoma, tuberculosis, malaria, and dysentery.

National economy

Budget (1989). Revenue and expenditure: LD 1,174,000,000 ([1987] development expenditures 34.5%, trade 33.7%, current spending 30.5%).
Production (metric tons except as noted). Agriculture, forestry, fishing (1988): tomatoes 212,000, wheat 193,000, watermelons 147,000, olives 120,000, potatoes 115,000, dates 102,000, barley 99,000, onions 91,000, oranges 76,000, almonds 12,600; livestock (number of live animals) 5,750,000 sheep, 965,000 goats, 215,000 cattle, 185,000 camels; roundwood (1987) 637,000 cu m; fish catch (1987) 8,000. Mining and quarrying (1987): gypsum 180,000; salt 12,000. Manufacturing (1985): cement (1987) 2,700,000; urea 668,300; ammonia 495,000; methanol 495,000; ethylene 247,500; asphalt 150,000; crude steel 10,000. Construction (gross value in LD; 1982): residential 127,051,000; nonresidential 200,877,000. Energy production (consumption): electricity (kW-hr; 1987) 14,260,000,000 (14,260,000,000); coal (metric tons; 1987) none (2,000); crude petroleum (barrels; 1988) 370,099,000 ([1987] 55,649,000); petroleum products (metric tons; 1987) 6,200,000 (4,687,000); natural gas (cu m; 1987) 4,428,000,000 (3,564,000,000).
Tourism: receipts from visitors (1984) U.S.$4,000,000; expenditures by nationals abroad (1986) U.S.$213,000,000.
Population economically active (1984[3]): total 664,000; activity rate of total population 20.5% (participation rates: ages 15–59, 44.1%; female (1985) 8.1%; unemployed, n.a.).

Price and earnings indexes (1975 = 100)

	1973	1974	1975	1976	1977	1978	1979
Consumer price index	85.3	91.6	100.0	105.4	112.1	145.0	137.1
Monthly earnings index	...	...	...	...	...	...	...

Gross national product (at current market prices; 1987): U.S.$22,326,000,000 (U.S.$5,500 per capita).

Structure of gross domestic product and labour force

	1986 in value LD '000,000	1986 % of total value	1984 labour force[3]	1984 % of labour force
Agriculture	338	3.9	149,000	22.4
Mining and quarrying	3,287	38.3	16,000	2.4
Manufacturing	456	5.3	55,000	8.3
Construction	973	11.3	41,000	6.2
Public utilities	111	1.3	20,000	3.0
Transportation and communications	446	5.2	65,000	9.8
Trade	516	6.0	45,000	6.8
Finance, insurance	573	6.7	12,000	1.8
Pub. admin., defense	1,232	14.4 }	261,000	39.3
Services } Other }	650	7.6 }	—	—
TOTAL	8,582	100.0	664,000	100.0

Public debt (external, outstanding; 1985): U.S.$1,177,000,000.
Household income and expenditure. Average household size (1980) 5.1; income per household: n.a.; sources of income: n.a.; expenditure (1977): food 37.2%, housing and energy 32.2%, transportation 9.4%, education and recreation 8.5%, clothing 6.9%, health care 3.3%.
Land use (1987): forested 0.4%; meadows and pastures 7.6%; agricultural and under permanent cultivation 1.2%; desert and built-up areas 90.8%.

Foreign trade

Balance of trade (current prices)

	1983	1984	1985	1986	1987	1988
U.S.$'000,000	+4,881	+2,564	+4,591	+1,253	+398	+22
% of total	24.6%	13.2%	28.5%	12.3%	3.4%	0.2%

Imports (1982): U.S.$7,175,000,000 (machinery and transport equipment 36.8%, consumer goods 27.1%, food and live animals 14.2%). *Major import sources* (1987)[4]: Italy 19.3%; West Germany 8.9%; United Kingdom 6.3%; France 4.2%; unspecified 56.8%.
Exports (1987): U.S.$6,148,000,000 (crude petroleum 95.8%). *Major export destinations:* Italy 38.7%; West Germany 18.8%; Spain 13.3%; U.S.S.R. 7.7%; France 7.0%.

Transport and communications

Transport. Railroads: none. Roads (1987): total length 11,992 mi, 19,300 km (paved 56%). Vehicles (1986): passenger cars 428,000; trucks and buses 216,000. Merchant marine (1988): vessels (100 gross tons and over) 107; total deadweight tonnage 1,463,243. Air transport[5] (1987): passenger-mi 900,000,000, passenger-km 1,447,000,000; short ton-mi cargo 2,398,000, metric ton-km cargo 3,501,000; airports (1989) with scheduled flights 11.
Communications. Daily newspapers (1988): total number 1; circulation 40,000; circulation per 1,000 population 10. Radio (1988): total number of receivers 1,007,141 (1 per 3.9 persons). Television (1988): total number of receivers 294,884 (1 per 13 persons). Telephones (1987): 500,000 (1 per 7.8 persons).

Education and health

Education (1984–85)

	schools	teachers	students	student/ teacher ratio
Primary (age 6–12)	2,744[6]	41,515	788,780	19.0
Secondary (age 13–18)	1,555[6]	30,524	373,374	12.2
Teacher tr.	195[6, 7]	3,051	30,511	10.0
Higher	8[8]	...	30,000	...

Educational attainment (1973). Percent of population age 25 and over having: no formal schooling (illiterate) 72.7%; incomplete primary education 18.8%; complete primary 3.5%; secondary 4.0%; higher 1.0%. *Literacy* (1985): total population age 10 and over literate 2,701,446 (74.4%); males literate 1,666,170 (85.0%); females literate 1,035,276 (62.0%).
Health: physicians (1984) 5,272 (1 per 690 persons); hospital beds (1982) 16,051 (1 per 207 persons); infant mortality rate per 1,000 live births (1986) 85.0.
Food (1984–86): daily per capita caloric intake 3,611 (vegetable products 83%, animal products 17%); 153% of FAO recommended minimum requirement.

Military

Total active duty personnel (1989): 85,000 (army 64.7%, navy 9.4%, air force 25.9%). *Military expenditure as percent of GNP* (1987): 11.1% (world 5.4%); per capita expenditure U.S.$799.

---

[1]No formal titled office exists. [2]Hūn, near the al-Jufrah oasis, about 650 km south of Tripoli was designated future capital in 1986; after an unsuccessful program to fully accomplish this move, a second city, Surt (Sidra), on the Gulf of Sidra, was named future capital in September 1988, to be ready by Sept. 1, 1989, the 20th anniversary of the Revolution. Ministries would be located in all three cities, effectively decentralizing government. [3]Libyan nationals only; foreign contract labour, predominantly (c. 60%) in construction, numbered a further 263,000. [4]1987 imports equal U.S.$5,750,000,000. [5]Libyan Arab Airlines; international flights only. [6]1982–83. [7]Includes vocational. [8]1981–82.

Liechtenstein

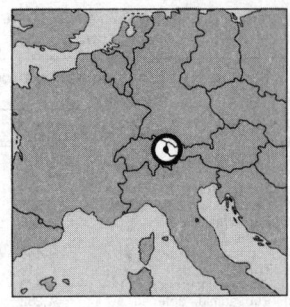

Official name: Fürstentum Liechtenstein (Principality of Liechtenstein).
Form of government: constitutional monarchy with one legislative house (Diet [25[1]]).
Chief of state: Prince.
Head of government: Head of the Government.
Capital: Vaduz.
Official language: German.
Official religion: none.
Monetary unit: 1 Swiss franc (Sw F) = 100 centimes; valuation (Oct. 2, 1989) 1 U.S.$ = Sw F 1.62; 1 £ = Sw F 2.63;

Area and population

Communes	area		population
	sq mi	sq km	1989 estimate[2]
Balzers	7.6	19.6	3,581
Eschen	4.0	10.3	2,933
Gamprin	2.4	6.1	934
Mauren	2.9	7.5	2,767
Planken	2.0	5.3	299
Ruggell	2.9	7.4	1,443
Schaan	10.4	26.8	4,883
Schellenberg	1.4	3.5	745
Triesen	10.2	26.4	3,329
Triesenberg	11.5	29.8	2,348
Vaduz	6.7	17.3	4,919
TOTAL	61.8[3]	160.0	28,181

Demography

Population (1989): 28,300.
Density (1989): persons per sq mi 458.1, persons per sq km 176.9.
Urban–rural: n.a.
Sex distribution (1989): male 48.94%; female 51.06%.
Age breakdown (1989): under 15, 19.5%; 15–29, 26.3%; 30–44, 25.3%; 45–59, 15.3%; 60–74, 9.6%; 75 and over, 4.0%.
Population projection: (2000) 32,400; (2010) 36,700.
Doubling time: not applicable; doubling time exceeds 100 years.
National composition (1989): Liechtensteiner 63.9%; Swiss 15.7%; Austrian 7.7%; German 3.7%; other 9.0%.
Religious affiliation (1989): Roman Catholic 87.3%; Protestant 8.1%; other 4.6%.
Major cities (1989): Vaduz 4,919; Schaan 4,883.

Vital statistics

Birth rate per 1,000 population (1988): 14.8 (world avg. 27.1); legitimate 95.1%; illegitimate 4.9%.
Death rate per 1,000 population (1988): 6.9 (world avg. 9.9).
Natural increase rate per 1,000 population (1988): 7.9 (world avg. 17.2).
Total fertility rate: n.a.
Marriage rate per 1,000 population (1988): 6.4.
Divorce rate per 1,000 population (1984): 7.3.
Life expectancy at birth (1980–84): male 77.6 years; female 82.6 years.
Major causes of death per 100,000 population (1987): diseases of the circulatory system 221.4, of which heart disease 174.2 (including ischemic heart disease 65.3); malignant neoplasms (cancers) 152.4; accidents, poisonings, and acts of violence 40.0 (including suicide 18.1); diseases of the respiratory system 18.1.

National economy

Budget (1987). Revenue: Sw F 338,215,000 (taxes and interest 70.5%; post, telephone, and telegraph 18.1%; other revenue sources include real estate capital-gains taxes and death and estate taxes). Expenditures: Sw F 323,077,000 (financial affairs 44.2%; education 14.0%; post, telephone, and telegraph 13.1%; social affairs 9.7%).
Public debt: none.
Tourism (1988): 71,633 tourist arrivals; receipts from visitors, n.a.; expenditures by nationals abroad, n.a.
Population economically active (1988[4]): total 13,658; activity rate of total population 48.5% (participation rates: ages 15–64, 68.5%; female 34.4%; unemployed 0.2%).

Price and earnings indexes (December 1982 = 100)

	1982	1983	1984	1985	1986	1987	1988[5]
Consumer price index[6]	98.0	100.9	103.8	107.4	108.2	109.7	112.0
Monthly earnings index	...	...	...	...	...	...	...

Household income and expenditure. Average household size (1980) 3.0; income per household: n.a.; sources of earned income (1987): wages and salaries 92.9%, self-employment 7.1%; expenditure (1986)[7]: food 21.3%, rent 18.0%, education and self-improvement 16.3%, transportation 13.3%, health 7.7%, clothing 6.6%.
Production (metric tons except as noted). Agriculture, forestry, fishing (1986): silo corn (maize) 29,400, milk 13,339, potatoes 1,194, barley 480, wheat 360; livestock (number of live animals; 1988) 6,029 cattle, 3,119 pigs, 2,328 sheep; commercial timber (1986–7) 13,194 cu m. Mining

and quarrying: n.a. Manufacturing (1987): whipped cream 1,573; yogurt 53; cheese 9; wine 539.7 hectolitres; small-scale precision manufacturing includes optical lenses, electron microscopes, electronic equipment, and high-vacuum pumps; metal manufacturing, construction machinery, and ceramics are also important. Construction (1987): residential 193,510 cu m; nonresidential 328,797 cu m. Energy production (consumption): electricity (kW-hr; 1986) 43,371,000 (182,414,000); coal (metric tons; 1986) none (86); petroleum products (metric tons; 1986) none (51,457); natural gas (metric tons; 1986) none (2,493).
Gross national product (at current market prices; 1985): c. U.S.$450,000,000 (c. U.S.$16,500 per capita).

Structure of gross domestic product and labour force

	1980		1988	
	in value Sw F '000	% of total value	labour force	% of labour force
Agriculture	...	...	338	2.5
Mining	...	...	70	0.5
Manufacturing	...	...	4,618	33.8
Construction	...	...	1,128	8.3
Public utilities	...	...	163	1.2
Transportation and communications	...	...	408	3.0
Trade	...	...	1,606	11.8
Finance, insurance, real estate	...	...	923	6.8
Pub. admin., defense	...	...	639	4.7
Services	...	...	3,666	26.8
Other	...	...	99[8]	0.7[8]
TOTAL	876,000	100.0	13,658	100.0[3]

Land use (latest): forested 34.8%; meadows and pastures 15.7%; agricultural and under permanent cultivation 24.3%; other 25.2%.

Foreign trade

Balance of trade (current prices)

	1982	1983	1984	1985	1986	1987
Sw F '000,000	+523.5	+560.7	+625.4	+755.6	+761.6	+737.6
% of total	39.3%	41.6%	41.8%	46.4%	44.4%	42.0%

Imports (1987): Sw F 509,071,000 (machinery and transport equipment 32.2%; metal products 14.5%; limestone, cement, and other building materials 8.7%; chemical products 5.7%; unrefined and semifabricated metal 5.4%; food, beverages, and tobacco 1.9%, of which fruits and vegetables 0.5%; wood and cork 1.1%). *Major import sources:* n.a.
Exports (1987): Sw F 1,246,651,000 (machinery and transport equipment 48.3%; metal products 19.9%; other finished goods 18.9%; chemical products 6.4%; limestone, cement, and other building materials 4.5%). *Major export destinations:* European Economic Community countries 38.2%; Switzerland 22.4%; other European Free Trade Association countries 6.5%.

Transport and communications

Transport. Railroads (1987): length 11.5 mi, 18.5 km; passenger and cargo traffic, n.a. Roads (1986): total length 201 mi, 323 km. Vehicles (1988): passenger cars 15,889; trucks and buses 1,801. Merchant marine: none. Air transport: none.
Communications. Daily newspapers (1987): total number 2; total circulation 15,000; circulation per 1,000 population 546. Radio (1987): total number of receivers 9,381 (1 per 2.9 persons). Television (1987): total number of receivers 8,875 (1 per 3.1 persons). Telephones (1986): 26,529 (1 per 1.0 persons).

Education and health

Education (1988–89)

	schools	teachers	students	student/ teacher ratio
Primary (age 7–12)	14[9]	102	1,807	17.7
Secondary (age 13–19)	9[9]	107	1,686	15.8
Vocational	1	74[10]	147	...

Educational attainment (1980). Percent of population age 25 and over having: no formal schooling 0.2%; primary and lower secondary education 47.6%; higher secondary and vocational 41.0%; some postsecondary 6.6%; university 4.6%. *Literacy:* virtually 100%.
Health: physicians (1987) 29 (1 per 950 persons); hospital beds (1985) 100 (1 per 269 persons); infant mortality rate per 1,000 live births (1982–86) 15.4.
Food (1984–86)[11]: daily per capita caloric intake 3,425 (vegetable products 61%, animal products 39%); (1983) 129% of FAO recommended minimum requirement.

Military

Total active duty personnel: none. *Military expenditure as percent of GNP:* none.

---

[1]From March 5, 1989, increased from 15 to 25 seats. [2]January 1. [3]Detail does not add to total given because of rounding. [4]December 31. [5]September. [6]The index is for Switzerland, which is united with Liechtenstein in a customs and monetary union. [7]Household expenditures are taken from a 1986 Swiss sample survey; a similarity of consumption patterns is assumed. [8]Includes 74 unclassifiable and 25 unemployed persons. [9]1987–88. [10]Includes part-time teachers. [11]Figures are derived from statistics for Switzerland and Austria.

Luxembourg

Official name: Grand-Duché
de Luxembourg (French);
Grossherzogtum Luxemburg
(German) (Grand Duchy of
Luxembourg).
Form of government: constitutional
monarchy with two legislative houses
(Council of State [21]; Chamber of
Deputies [60]).
Chief of state: Grand Duke.
Head of government: Prime Minister.
Capital: Luxembourg.
Official languages: French; German.
Official religion: none.
Monetary unit: 1 Luxembourg franc
(Lux F) = 100 centimes; valuation
(Oct. 2, 1989) 1 U.S.$ =
Lux F 39.34; 1 £ = Lux F 63.65.

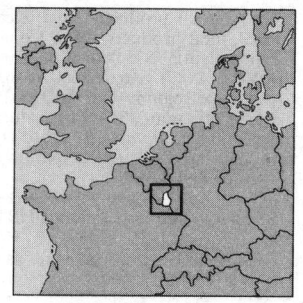

Area and population	area		population
Districts **Cantons**	sq mi	sq km	1986 estimate[1]
Diekirch	447	1,157	54,420
Clervaux	128	332	9,710
Diekirch	92	239	22,390
Redange	103	267	10,500
Vianden	21	54	2,790
Wiltz	102	265	9,030
Grevenmacher	203	525	40,030
Echternach	72	186	10,990
Grevenmacher	82	211	16,910
Remich	49	128	12,130
Luxembourg	349	904	272,250
Capellen	77	199	28,790
Esch	94	243	112,250
Luxembourg (Ville et Campagne)	92	238	113,570
Mersch	86	224	17,640
TOTAL	999	2,586	366,700

Demography

Population (1989): 377,000.
Density (1989): persons per sq mi 377.4, persons per sq km 145.8.
Urban–rural (1985): urban 77.6%; rural 22.4%.
Sex distribution (1987): male 48.61%; female 51.39%.
Age breakdown (1985): under 15, 17.3%; 15–29, 23.6%; 30–44, 21.9%; 45–59, 19.0%; 60–74, 12.6%; 75 and over, 5.6%.
Population projection: (2000) 378,000; (2010) 376,000.
Doubling time: n.a.; population stable.
Ethnic composition (nationality; 1987): Luxemburger 73.8%; Portuguese 8.1%; Italian 5.4%; French 3.3%; German 2.3%; Belgian 2.3%; other 4.8%.
Religious affiliation (1980): Roman Catholic 93.0%; Protestant 1.3%; other 5.7%.
Major cities[2] (1987): Luxembourg 76,640; Esch-sur-Alzette 23,720; Differdange 16,000; Dudelange 14,060; Pétange 11,590.

Vital statistics

Birth rate per 1,000 population (1988): 12.2 (world avg. 27.1); (1987) legitimate 89.2%; illegitimate 10.8%.
Death rate per 1,000 population (1988): 10.2 (world avg. 9.9).
Natural increase rate per 1,000 population (1988): 2.0 (world avg. 17.2).
Total fertility rate (avg. births per childbearing woman; 1987): 1.4.
Marriage rate per 1,000 population (1988): 5.5.
Divorce rate per 1,000 population (1988): 2.1.
Life expectancy at birth (1985–87): male 70.6 years; female 77.9 years.
Major causes of death per 100,000 population (1987): circulatory diseases 518.5, of which cerebrovascular disease 175.6, ischemic heart disease 169.4; malignant neoplasms (cancers) 275.8; accidents and suicides 70.7, of which suicide 20.0.

National economy

Budget (1989). Revenue: Lux F 89,319,047,000 (income and excise taxes 55.5%, customs taxes 12.1%). Expenditures: Lux F 89,249,900,000 (social security 17.3%, education 10.8%, transportation 9.3%, administration 7.5%, debt service 3.2%, defense 2.8%).
Public debt (1988): U.S.$415,000,000.
Production (metric tons except as noted). Agriculture, forestry, fishing (1987): barley 60,208, wheat 31,711, potatoes 22,522, oats 21,656; livestock (number of live animals) 217,254 cattle, 74,944 pigs; roundwood (1986) 326,500 cu m. Mining and quarrying (1986): metal ores, none; sand and gravel 677,058, crushed stone 546,670, gypsum 420,000. Manufacturing (1987): finished rolled steel products 3,480,731; steel ingots and castings 3,301,860; pig iron 2,305,100; meat products 21,869, of which beef and veal 14,189, pork 7,680; wine 142,643 hectolitres. Construction (1985): residential and semiresidential 309,979 sq m; nonresidential 234,554 sq m. Energy production (consumption): electricity (kW-hr; 1987) 1,036,332,000 (3,968,-635,000); coal (metric tons; 1987) none (197,724); crude petroleum, none (n.a.); petroleum products (metric tons; 1987) none (1,321,704); natural gas (cu m; 1987) none (407,726,000).
Gross national product (at current market prices; 1987): U.S.$5,805,000,000 (U.S.$15,860 per capita).

Structure of gross domestic product and labour force	1986		1987	
	in value Lux F '000,000	% of total value	labour force	% of labour force
Agriculture	6,570	2.6	5,137	3.2
Mining	250	0.1	62	0.1
Manufacturing	70,220	27.8	29,638	18.7
Construction	14,150	5.6	13,931	8.8
Public utilities	5,300	2.1	933	0.6
Transp. and commun.	14,400	5.7	10,515	6.6
Trade	38,900	15.4	32,702	20.7
Finance	34,100	13.5	15,977	10.1
Pub. admin., defense	30,820	12.2 }	42,317	26.8
Services	37,890	15.0 }		
Other	...	...	6,888[4]	4.4[4]
TOTAL	252,600	100.0	158,100	100.0

Population economically active (1987): total 158,100; activity rate of total population 42.6% (participation rates: ages 15–64, 61.0%; female 35.3%; unemployed 2.5%).

Price and earnings indexes (1985 = 100)							
	1982	1983	1984	1985	1986	1987	1988
Consumer price index	83.7	90.9	96.1	100.0	100.3	100.7	101.7
Hourly earnings index	...	...	...	...	...	...	...

Household income and expenditure. Average household size (1982) 2.8; income per household Lux F 751,800 (U.S.$16,455); sources of income (1987): wages and salaries 88.6%, self-employment 9.1%, transfer payments 2.3%; expenditure (1986): food and beverages 16.6%, transportation and communications 16.8%, housing 12.6%, household goods and furniture 9.3%, health 6.9%, clothing and footwear 6.7%.
Tourism (1988): Number of tourist arrivals 682,801[3].
Land use (1988): forested 34.3%; meadows and pastures 27.3%; agricultural and under permanent cultivation 21.5%; other 16.9%.

Foreign trade

Balance of trade (current prices)						
	1983	1984	1985	1986	1987	1988
Lux F '000,000	−16,492	−14,503	−9,093	−13,390	−24,530	−20,549
% of total	6.9%	4.7%	2.6%	3.9%	7.0%	5.2%

Imports (1988): Lux F 206,905,000,000 (metal products, machinery, and transport equipment 46.0%, of which electrical machinery 17.2%, transport equipment 10.1%; mineral products 9.8%; chemical products 8.9%; food, beverages, and tobacco 8.4%). *Major import sources:* Belgium 37.3%; West Germany 31.5%; France 11.9%; The Netherlands 4.7%; United States 2.3%; Italy 2.1%.
Exports (1988): Lux F 186,356,000,000 (metal products, machinery, and transport equipment 58.6%, of which electrical machinery 10.8%; plastic materials and rubber manufactures 13.9%; food, beverages, and tobacco 5.4%; textile yarn, fabrics, and related products 5.2%; chemical products 4.9%). *Major export destinations:* West Germany 27.2%; Belgium 17.6%; France 16.5%; United Kingdom 6.0%; The Netherlands 5.6%; United States 4.8%; Italy 4.8%.

Transport and communications

Transport. Railroads (1988): route length 169 mi, 272 km; passenger-mi 172,000,000, passenger-km 276,000,000; short ton-mi cargo 436,000,000, metric ton-km cargo 636,000,000. Roads (1988): total length 3,160 mi, 5,085 km (paved 99%). Vehicles (1988): passenger cars 177,011; trucks and buses 16,776. Merchant marine: vessels (100 gross tons and over) 1; total deadweight tonnage 1,731. Air transport (1987): passenger arrivals 459,714, departures 466,622; short ton-mi cargo 606,902,000, metric ton-km cargo 886,062,000; airports (1989) with scheduled flights 1.
Communications. Daily newspapers (1987): total number 6; total circulation 130,000; circulation per 1,000 population 365. Radio (1988): 229,375 receivers (1 per 1.6 persons). Television (1987): 91,500 receivers (1 per 4.0 persons). Telephones (1987): 161,682 (1 per 2.3 persons).

Education and health

Education (1986–87)	schools	teachers	students	student/ teacher ratio
Primary (age 6–11)	...	1,745[5]	24,381	...
Secondary (age 12–18)	... }		7,772	...
Voc., teacher tr.	... }	3,482[6,7]	15,217	...
Higher	...		795	...

Educational attainment, n.a. *Literacy* (1988): virtually 100% literate.
Health (1987): physicians 666 (1 per 557 persons); hospital beds 4,661 (1 per 80 persons); infant mortality rate per 1,000 live births 9.4.
Food (1984–86): daily per capita caloric intake[8] 3,850 (vegetable products 58%, animal products 42%); (1984) 140% of FAO recommended minimum requirement.

Military

Total active duty personnel (1988): 800 (army 100.0%). *Military expenditure as percent of GNP* (1987): 0.8% (world 5.4%); per capita expenditure U.S.$200.

[1]January 1. [2]From country register. [3]Hotel, camping, and free lodging arrivals. [4]Includes 3,600 unemployed. [5]1985–86. [6]1982–83. [7]Includes part-time teachers. [8]Figures for Belgium–Luxembourg.

Macau

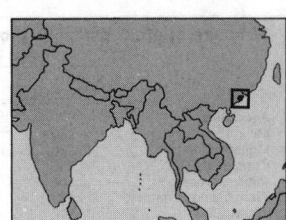

Official name: Macau.
Political status: overseas territory (Portugal) with one legislative house (Legislative Assembly [171]).
Head of state and government: Governor.
Capital: Macau.
Official language: Portuguese.
Official religion: Roman Catholicism.
Monetary unit: 1 pataca[2] = 100 avos; valuation (Oct. 2, 1989)
1 U.S.$ = 8.06 patacas; 1 £ = 13.04 patacas.

Area and population

Districts	Capital	area		population 1986 estimate
		sq mi	sq km	
Parishes				
Islands		4.2	10.9	10,200
Nossa Senhora Carmo (Taipa)	—	1.5	3.8	6,500
São Francisco Xavier (Coloane)	—	2.7	7.1	3,700
Macau	Macau	2.4	6.1	416,200
Nossa Senhora Fátima	—	...	...	...
Santo António	—	...	...	...
São Lázaro	—	...	...	...
São Lourenço	—	...	...	...
Sé	—	...	...	...
Marine Area	—	—	—	...
TOTAL		6.5[3]	16.9[3]	426,400

Demography

Population (1989): 484,000.
Density (1989): persons per sq mi 74,462, persons per sq km 28,639.
Urban–rural (1981): urban 94.9%[4].
Sex distribution (1987): male 51.78%; female 48.22%.
Age breakdown (1987): under 15, 22.0%; 15–29, 35.2%; 30–44, 25.4%; 45–59, 8.9%; 60–74, 6.3%; 75 and over, 2.2%.
Population projection: (2000) 819,000; (2010) 1,169,000.
Doubling time: 49 years.
Nationality (1981): Chinese 73.5%; Portuguese 20.3%; English 0.9%; other 5.3%.
Religious affiliation (1981): Buddhist 45.1%; Christian 8.7%, of which Roman Catholic 7.4%, Protestant 1.3%; nonreligious 45.8%; other 0.4%.
Major city (1986): Macau 416,200.

Vital statistics

Birth rate per 1,000 population (1987): 17.6 (world avg. 27.1); legitimate, n.a.; illegitimate, n.a.
Death rate per 1,000 population (1987): 3.1 (world avg. 9.9).
Natural increase rate per 1,000 population (1987): 14.5 (world avg. 17.2).
Total fertility rate (avg. births per childbearing woman; 1985–90): 3.4.
Marriage rate per 1,000 population (1987): 5.8.
Divorce rate per 1,000 population (1987): 0.1.
Life expectancy at birth (1985–87): male 75.0 years; female 80.0 years.
Major causes of death per 100,000 population (1987): diseases of the circulatory system 113.6; malignant neoplasms (cancers) 63.0; diseases of the respiratory system 34.2; injuries and poisonings 20.2; diseases of the digestive system 13.5; endocrine and metabolic disorders 11.2; infectious and parasitic diseases 10.5; diseases of the genito-urinary system 10.2.

National economy

Budget (1987). Revenue: 2,339,290,000 patacas (gambling revenue 29.9%, direct taxes 19.8%, indirect taxes 18.1%, capital receipts 12.9%). Expenditures: 2,339,290,000 patacas (recurrent payments 56.8%, capital payments 31.7%, autonomous-agency expenditures 11.5%).
Gross domestic product (at current market prices; 1987): U.S.$2,262,000,000 (U.S.$5,210 per capita).

Structure of labour force

	labour force	% of labour force
	1981	
Agriculture	7,551	5.9
Mining	71	0.1
Manufacturing	56,304	44.2
Construction	9,937	7.8
Public utilities	876	0.7
Transportation and communications	5,776	4.5
Trade	23,102	18.1
Finance	2,191	1.7
Public administration	4,056	3.2
Services	15,190	11.9
Other	2,305[5]	1.8[5]
TOTAL	127,359	100.0[3]

Production (metric tons except as noted). Agriculture, forestry, and fishing (1987): grapes 5,000, eggs 618; livestock (number of live animals) 3,000 cattle, 6,000 pigs, 1,000,000 ducks; fish catch 3,517. Mining and quarrying (1982): granite 656,920. Manufacturing (output in '000,000 patacas; 1985): wearing apparel 2,836.8; textiles 1,330.6; miscellaneous plastic products

523.1; metal products 306.5; electrical appliances 159.0; leather products 118.0; food products 108.9. Construction (1986): residential 294,300 sq m; nonresidential 375,000 sq m. Energy production (consumption): electricity (kW-hr; 1987) 616,000,000 (656,000,000); coal (metric tons; 1987) none (none); petroleum (barrels; 1981) none (2,559); petroleum products (metric tons; 1987) none (314,000); natural gas, none (n.a.).
Population economically active (1981): total 127,359; activity rate of total population 48.6% (participation rates: over age 10, 61.5%; female 37.1%; unemployed 3.9%).

Price and earnings indexes (1985 = 100)

	1983	1984	1985	1986	1987
Consumer price index[6]	86.0	96.5	100.0	101.9	106.6
Earnings index	...	...	...	...	...

Public debt (long-term, external, 1985): U.S.$91,000,000.
Tourism (1987): number of tourist arrivals 5,100,461.
Household income and expenditure. Average household size (1980): 4.8; income per household: n.a.; sources of income: n.a.; expenditure (1981–82): food 42.0%, housing 22.8%, education, health, and other services 8.1%, clothing and footwear 7.3%, transportation 4.9%, energy 4.9%, household durable goods 2.9%.
Land use (1979): forested 50.0%; agricultural and under permanent cultivation 4.0%; built-on area, wasteland, and other 46.0%.

Foreign trade

Balance of trade (current prices)

	1982	1983	1984	1985	1986	1987
'000,000 patacas	+38.5	+250.3	+919.4	+1,002	+1,312	+2,216.4
% of total	0.4%	2.3%	6.7%	7.5%	8.2%	10.9%

Imports (1987): 9,017,166,000 patacas (industrial raw materials 66.8%, nonedible consumer goods 12.4%, capital goods 10.6%, food and beverages 5.9%, fuels and lubricants 4.3%). *Major import sources:* Hong Kong 38.9%; China 21.3%; Japan 9.9%; European Economic Community 6.9%; United States 4.9%.
Exports (1987): 11,233,528,000 patacas (textiles and garments 73.5%, toys 9.9%, artificial flowers 2.4%, electronics 2.3%, leather articles 1.9%). *Major export destinations:* United States 33.4%; Hong Kong 15.5%; West Germany 12.5%; France 9.6%; United Kingdom 7.0%; China 3.8%; Japan 2.2%; Australia 1.7%.

Transport and communications

Transport. Railroads: none. Roads (1984): total length 56 mi, 90 km (paved 100%). Vehicles (1987): passenger cars 20,391; trucks and buses 4,099. Merchant marine (1986): vessels 581[7]; total gross tonnage 22,689. Air transport: none.
Communications. Daily newspapers (1986): total number 14; total circulation 242,000; circulation per 1,000 population 568. Radio (1988): total number of receivers 150,000 (1 per 3.0 persons). Television (1988): total number of receivers 80,000 (1 per 5.6 persons). Telephones (1987): 68,956 (1 per 6.3 persons).

Education and health

Education (1986–87)

	schools	teachers	students	student/ teacher ratio
Primary (age 6–11)	74	1,118	31,914	28.5
Secondary (age 12–18)	30	851	14,913	17.5
Teacher tr.	2	26	61	2.3
Higher	5	70	6,891	98.4

Educational attainment (1981). Percent of economically active population age 10 and over having: no formal schooling 13.8%; primary education 22.6%; some secondary 27.2%; complete secondary 20.5%; some postsecondary 13.0%; higher 2.9%. *Literacy* (1981): total population age 10 and over literate 127,359 (61.3%); males literate 80,102 (76.4%); females literate 47,257 (46.2%).
Health (1987): physicians 518 (1 per 831 persons); hospital beds 1,242 (1 per 350 persons); infant mortality rate per 1,000 live births 6.9.
Food (1984–86): daily per capita caloric intake 2,205 (vegetable products 73%, animal products 27%); 96% of FAO recommended minimum requirement.

Military

Total active duty personnel (1988): the Portuguese garrison has been replaced by a paramilitary force of 1,800 men drawn from the Chinese residents only.

---

[1]Includes six directly elected; six indirectly elected by social, cultural, and economic functional constituencies; and five appointed by the governor. [2]The pataca free floats with the Hong Kong dollar and has a parity of 1.03 patacas = HK$1.00. [3]Detail does not add to total given because of rounding. [4]5.1% of Macau's population live on sampans and other vessels. [5]Mostly unemployed not previously employed. [6]Excluding rent. [7]All registered vessels including barges, tugboats, floating casinos, sampans, dredgers, but excluding barges used for restaurants and recreation.

Madagascar

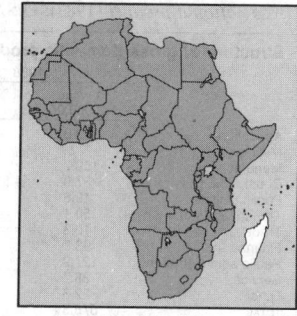

Official name: Repoblika Demokratika Malagasy (Malagasy); République Démocratique de Madagascar (French) (Democratic Republic of Madagascar).
Form of government: multiparty[1] republic with one legislative house (National People's Assembly [137]).
Chief of state: President.
Head of government: Prime Minister.
Capital: Antananarivo.
Official languages: Malagasy; French.
Official religion: none.
Monetary unit: 1 franc (FMG) = 100 centimes; valuation (Oct. 2, 1989) 1 U.S.$ = FMG 1,458; 1 £ = FMG 2,359.

Area and population

Provinces	Capitals	area sq mi	area sq km	population 1985 estimate
Antananarivo	Antananarivo	22,503	58,283	3,195,800
Antsiranana	Antsiranana	16,620	43,046	689,800
Fianarantsoa	Fianarantsoa	39,526	102,373	2,209,700
Mahajanga	Mahajanga	57,924	150,023	1,075,300
Toamasina	Toamasina	27,765	71,911	1,444,700
Toliara	Toliara	62,319	161,405	1,396,700
TOTAL		226,658	587,041	10,012,000

Demography

Population (1989): 11,602,000.
Density (1989): persons per sq mi 51.2, persons per sq km 19.8.
Urban–rural (1986): urban 22.4%; rural 77.6%.
Sex distribution (1986): male 49.31%; female 50.69%.
Age breakdown: under 15, 44.2%; 15–29, 25.3%; 30–44, 15.5%; 45–59, 9.5%; 60–74, 4.6%; 75 and over, 0.9%.
Population projection: (2000) 16,562,000; (2010) 22,594,000.
Doubling time: 22 years.
Ethnic composition (1983): Malagasy 98.9%, of which Merina 26.6%, Betsimisaraka 14.9%, Betsileo 11.7%, Tsimihety 7.4%, Sakalava 6.4%; Antandroy 5.3%; Comorian 0.3%; Indian and Pakistani 0.2%; French 0.2%; Chinese 0.1%; other 0.3%.
Religious affiliation (1980): Christian 51.0%, of which Roman Catholic 26.0%, Protestant 22.8%; traditional beliefs 47.0%; Muslim 1.7%; other 0.3%.
Major cities (1980): Antananarivo 662,600[2]; Toamasina 95,505; Fianarantsoa 83,250; Mahajanga 80,881.

Vital statistics

Birth rate per 1,000 population (1985–90): 45.7 (world avg. 27.1); legitimate, n.a.; illegitimate, n.a.
Death rate per 1,000 population (1985–90): 14.0 (world avg. 9.9).
Natural increase rate per 1,000 population (1985–90): 31.7 (world avg. 17.2).
Total fertility rate (avg. births per childbearing woman; 1985–90): 6.6.
Marriage rate per 1,000 population: n.a.
Divorce rate per 1,000 population: n.a.
Life expectancy at birth (1985–90): male 52.0 years; female 55.0 years.
Major causes of death per 100,000 population: n.a.; however, major diseases include malaria, leprosy, and tuberculosis.

National economy

Budget (1988). Revenue: FMG 497,919,516,000 ([1987] taxes 80.2%, of which import duties 14.9%, excises 14.8%, income tax 12.5%; other receipts 19.8%). Expenditures: FMG 577,002,323,000 ([1987] current expenditure 77.3%, of which education 12.3%, defense 7.5%, health 4.2%, agriculture 1.8%; public works 0.7%).
Public debt (external, outstanding; 1987): U.S.$3,113,000,000.
Tourism (1987): receipts from visitors U.S.$10,000,000; expenditures by nationals abroad U.S.$21,000,000.
Production (metric tons except as noted). Agriculture, forestry, fishing (1988): cassava 2,200,000, rice 2,100,000, sugarcane 2,000,000, sweet potatoes 472,000, potatoes 268,000, bananas 260,000, mangoes 193,000, corn (maize) 150,000, oranges 83,000, coconuts 82,000, coffee 81,000, pineapples 52,000, seed cotton 46,000, peanuts (groundnuts) 32,000, sisal 20,000, livestock (number of live animals) 10,600,000 cattle, 1,400,000 pigs, 1,080,000 goats, 611,000 sheep, 21,000,000 chickens; roundwood (1987) 7,250,000 cu m; fish catch (1987) 63,589. Mining and quarrying (1987): chromite concentrate 99,800; salt 30,000; graphite 16,300; mica 3,300 lbs; gold 130 troy oz. Manufacturing (1987): raw sugar 101,216; cement 44,490; soap 14,563; vegetable oils 7,956; cigarettes 2,669; chewing tobacco 878; beer 240,257 hectolitres. Construction (1986)[3]: residential 19,700 sq m; nonresidential 5,700 sq m. Energy production (consumption): electricity (kW-hr; 1987) 504,000,000 (504,000,000); coal (metric tons; 1987) none (17,000); crude petroleum (barrels; 1987) none (1,833,000); petroleum products (metric tons; 1987) 230,000 (255,000); natural gas, none (n.a.).
Household income and expenditure. Average household size (1980) 4.7; average annual income per household (1981) FMG 4,485 (U.S.$1,650); sources of income[4] (1975): wages and salaries 58.8%, self-employment 14.1%, other 27.1%; expenditure[5]: food 60.4%, fuel and light 9.1%, clothing and footwear 8.6%, household goods and utensils 2.4%.

Gross national product (at current market prices; 1987): U.S.$2,172,000,000 (U.S.$200 per capita).

Structure of gross domestic product and labour force

	1986 in value U.S.$'000,000	1986 % of total value	1985 labour force	1985 % of labour force
Agriculture	966	42.3	3,125,000	79.5
Manufacturing	278	12.2		
Mining				
Construction	117	5.1	248,000	6.3
Public utilities				
Transportation and communications				
Trade				
Finance	922	40.4	556,000	14.2
Services				
Pub. admin., defense				
TOTAL	2,283[6]	100.0	3,929,000	100.0

Population economically active (1985): total 3,929,000; activity rate of total population 39.3% (participation rates: ages 15–64, 74.9%; female 44.2%; unemployed [1982] 0.6%).

Price and earnings indexes (1985 = 100)

	1982	1983	1984	1985	1986	1987	1988[7]
Consumer price index	69.0	82.4	90.5	100.0	114.5	131.7	163.0
Earnings index	...	...	...	...	...	...	...

Land use (1987): forested 25.3%; meadows and pastures 58.5%; agricultural and under permanent cultivation 5.3%; other 10.9%.

Foreign trade[8]

Balance of trade

	1981	1982	1983	1984	1985	1986
FMG '000,000,000	−37.8	−19.3	−25.0	+15.1	−39.1	+26.7
% of total	18.1%	8.2%	9.9%	4.1%	9.7%	6.7%

Imports (1987): FMG 413,377,400,000[9] (chemical products 14.9%, machinery 14.2%, crude petroleum 9.9%, vehicles and parts 8.7%, metal products 7.3%, electrical equipment 4.2%, textiles 2.2%). *Major import sources:* France 30.6%; United States 9.0%; West Germany 8.7%; Japan 3.5%; Italy 3.1%; United Kingdom 3.0%; The Netherlands 3.0%.
Exports (1987): FMG 348,025,000,000 (coffee 27.9%, vanilla 25.6%, sugar 5.4%, cloves and clove oil 4.0%, petroleum products 1.5%). *Major export destinations:* France 32.4%; United States 20.2%; Japan 10.7%; West Germany 8.7%; Reunion 3.8%; Italy 3.6%; The Netherlands 2.6%; United Kingdom 2.6%.

Transport and communications

Transport. Railroads (1987): route length 549 mi, 883 km; passenger-mi 127,-000,000, passenger-km 205,000,000; short ton-mi cargo 138,000,000, metric ton-km cargo 201,000,000. Roads (1987): total length 11,560 mi, 18,610 km (paved 30%). Vehicles (1986): passenger cars 21,860; trucks and buses 14,542. Merchant marine (1988): vessels (100 gross tons and over) 77; total deadweight tonnage 117,212. Air transport (1987): passenger-mi 262,570,-000, passenger-km 422,566,000; short ton-mi cargo 26,049,000, metric ton-km cargo 38,031,000; airports (1989) with scheduled flights 51.
Communications. Daily newspapers (1988): total number 5; total circulation 138,000; circulation per 1,000 population 12. Radio (1988): total number of receivers 2,108,000 (1 per 5.3 persons). Television (1988): total number of receivers 100,000 (1 per 112 persons). Telephones (1987): 46,377 (1 per 239 persons).

Education and health

Education (1987–88)

	schools	teachers	students	student/ teacher ratio
Primary (age 6–13)	13,404	38,361	1,487,726	38.8
Secondary (14–18)	1,367	12,473	350,024	28.1
Voc., teacher tr.	61	1,172	15,526	13.2
Higher	5	613	27,294	44.5

Educational attainment, n.a. *Literacy* (1985): total population age 15 and over literate 3,778,000 (67.5%); males literate 2,004,000 (73.7%); females literate 1,774,000 (61.6%).
Health (1982): physicians 1,233 (1 per 7,451 persons); hospital beds 20,800 (1 per 442 persons); infant mortality rate per 1,000 live births (1985–90) 120.
Food (1987): daily per capita caloric intake 2,417 ([1984–86] vegetable products 92%, animal products 8%); (1984) 106% of FAO recommended minimum requirement.

Military

Total active duty personnel (1989): 21,000 (army 95.2%, navy 2.4%, air force 2.4%). *Military expenditure as percent of GNP* (1987): 2.4% (world 5.4%); per capita expenditure U.S.$4.

[1]Parties ideologically compatible with socialist outlook of 1975 constitution only. [2]1985. [3]Capital city only. [4]Malagasy households only. [5]Weights of consumer price index components in Antananarivo only; housing not included. [6]At factor cost. [7]January. [8]Import figures are f.o.b. in balance of trade and c.i.f. in commodities and trading partners. [9]Excludes gold and military equipment.

Malawi

Official name: Republic of Malaŵi (English).
Form of government: single-party republic with one legislative house (National Assembly [123[1]]).
Head of state and government: President.
Capital: Lilongwe.
Official language: English.
Official religion: none.
Monetary unit: 1 Malaŵi kwacha (MK) = 100 Tambala; valuation (Oct. 2, 1989) 1 U.S.$ = MK 2.74; 1 £ = MK 4.43.

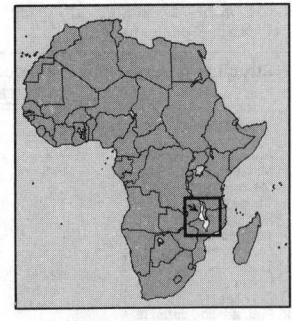

Area and population		area		population
Regions				1987
Districts	**Capitals**	sq mi	sq km	census[2]
Central	Lilongwe	13,742	35,592	3,116,038
Dedza	Dedza	1,399	3,624	410,847
Dowa	Dowa	1,174	3,041	322,112
Kasungu	Kasungu	3,042	7,878	322,854
Lilongwe	Lilongwe	2,378	6,159	986,411
Mchinji	Mchinji	1,296	3,356	248,161
Nkhotakota	Nkhotakota	1,644	4,259	157,083
Ntcheu	Ntcheu	1,322	3,424	359,618
Ntchisi	Ntchisi	639	1,655	120,697
Salima	Salima	848	2,196	188,255
Northern	Mzuzu	10,398	26,931	907,121
Chitipa	Chitipa	1,353	3,504	96,842
Karonga	Karonga	1,141	2,955	147,096
Mzimba	Mzimba	4,027	10,430	432,437
Nkhata Bay	Nkhata Bay	1,579	4,090	136,044
Rumphi	Rumphi	2,298	5,952	94,702
Southern	Blantyre	12,260	31,753	3,959,448
Blantyre	Blantyre	777	2,012	587,893
Chikwawa	Chikwawa	1,836	4,755	319,781
Chiradzulu	Chiradzulu	296	767	210,736
Machinga	Machinga	2,303	5,964	514,569
Mangochi	Mangochi	2,422	6,272	495,876
Mulanje	Mulanje	1,332	3,450	638,326
Mwanza	Mwanza	886	2,295	121,267
Nsanje	Nsanje	750	1,942	201,311
Thyolo	Thyolo	662	1,715	431,549
Zomba	Zomba	996	2,580	438,150
TOTAL LAND AREA		36,400	94,276[3]	7,982,607
INLAND WATER		9,347	24,208	
TOTAL		45,747	118,484	

Demography

Population (1989): 8,515,000[4].
Density[5] (1989): persons per sq mi 233.9, persons per sq km 90.3.
Urban-rural (1987): urban 11.0%; rural 89.0%.
Sex distribution (1987): male 48.61%; female 51.39%.
Age breakdown (1987): under 15, 47.8%; 15–29, 25.6%; 30–44, 14.4%; 45–59, 8.1%; 60–74, 3.5%; 75 and over, 0.6%.
Population projection: (2000) 12,201,000; (2010) 16,573,000.
Doubling time: 21 years.
Ethnic composition (1983): Maravi (including Nyanja, Chewa, Tonga, and Tumbuka) 58.3%; Lomwe 18.4%; Yao 13.2%; Ngoni 6.7%; other 3.4%.
Religious affiliation (1980): Christian 64.5%, of which Protestant 33.7%, Roman Catholic 27.6%; traditional beliefs 19.0%; Muslim 16.2%; other 0.3%.
Major cities (1987): Blantyre 402,500; Lilongwe 220,300; Mzuzu 115,000.

Vital statistics

Birth rate per 1,000 population (1985–90): 53.0 (world avg. 27.1).
Death rate per 1,000 population (1985–90): 20.0 (world avg. 9.9).
Natural increase rate per 1,000 population (1985–90): 33.0 (world avg. 17.2).
Total fertility rate (avg. births per childbearing woman; 1985–90): 7.0.
Marriage rate per 1,000 population (1977): 7.8.
Divorce rate per 1,000 population (1977): 1.4.
Life expectancy at birth (1985–90): male 46.3 years; female 47.7 years.
Major causes of death per 100,000 population[6] (1983): infectious and parasitic diseases 56.0, of which measles 17.4, malaria 13.7, diarrheal diseases 11.4; pneumonia 17.5; malnutrition 15.9; anemia 12.1.

National economy

Budget (1988–89). Revenue: MK 681,750,000 (recurrent revenue 85.0%, of which surtax 30.5%, import duties 12.0%). Expenditures: MK 967,510,000 (recurrent expenditures 72.4%, of which debt payment 18.0%, wages and salaries 17.1%; development expenditure 27.6%).
Tourism (1987): receipts from visitors U.S.$7,000,000; expenditures by nationals abroad U.S.$7,000,000.
Production (metric tons except as noted). Agriculture (1988): sugarcane 1,700,000, corn (maize) 1,455,000, potatoes 278,000, peanuts (groundnuts) 192,000, cassava 135,000, plantains 114,000, bananas 81,000, dry beans 77,000, tobacco 56,000, tea 35,000, sorghum 22,000; livestock (number of live animals) 1,000,000 cattle, 950,000 goats, 210,000 pigs, 210,000 sheep; roundwood (1987) 6,946,000 cu m; fish catch (1987) 88,588. Mining and quarrying (1986): limestone 110,000; cement 69,000. Manufacturing (1986): raw sugar 163,800; tea 31,900; beer 627,000 hectolitres; cigarettes 874,-000,000 units; blankets 616,000 units. Construction (value in MK; 1988): 5,740,000. Energy production (consumption): electricity (kW-hr; 1987) 578,-000,000 (527,000,000); coal (metric tons; 1987) none (26,000); petroleum products (metric tons; 1987) none (134,000).

Gross national product (1987): U.S.$1,223,000,000 (U.S.$160 per capita).

Structure of gross domestic product and labour force				
	1988		1985	
	in value MK '000,000	% of total value	labour force	% of labour force
Agriculture	319.9	36.4	2,502,000	81.4
Mining	...	...		
Manufacturing	102.7	11.7		
Construction	37.9	4.3	206,000	6.7
Public utilities	19.6	2.2		
Transp. and commun.	50.1	5.7		
Trade	110.3	12.5		
Finance	93.7	10.7		
Public administration	127.9	14.6	366,000	11.9
Services	38.7	4.4		
Other	−22.3[7]	−2.5[7]		
TOTAL	878.5[8]	100.0	3,074,000	100.0

Public debt (external, outstanding; 1987): U.S.$1,155,000,000.
Population economically active (1985): total 3,074,000; activity rate of total population 44.3% (participation rates: ages 15–64, 74.3%; female 42.6%; unemployed 1.0%[9]).

Price and earnings indexes (1985 = 100)							
	1982	1983	1984	1985	1986	1987	1988
Consumer price index	66.4	75.4	90.5	100.0	114.0	142.7	191.1
Monthly earnings index	131.9	124.3	125.1	...	...	...	...

Household income and expenditure (1979–80). Average household size[10] 4.5; income per household MK 1,934 (U.S.$2,419); sources of income: wages 83.3%, household enterprise 6.0%; expenditure (1985)[11]: food 32.9%, transportation 17.6%, housing 13.3%, clothing and footwear 10.7%.
Land use (1987): forested 45.7%; meadows and pastures 19.6%; agricultural and under permanent cultivation 25.2%; other 9.5%.

Foreign trade[12]

Balance of trade (current prices)						
	1983	1984	1985	1986	1987	1988
MK '000,000	−30.5	+211.7	+118.3	+175.5	+222.7	+139.4
% of total	3.7%	34.2%	16.3%	23.4%	22.1%	10.1%

Imports (1987): MK 655,900,000 (basic manufactures 41.0%, machinery and equipment 18.9%, consumer goods 10.5%, transport equipment 9.2%, building and construction materials 4.8%). *Major import sources:* South Africa 34.6%; U.K. 20.1%; Japan 5.6%; Zimbabwe 5.6%; West Germany 5.6%.
Exports (1987): MK 617,151,000 (tobacco 62.1%, sugar 10.5%, tea 10.1%, peanuts [groundnuts] 2.2%). *Major export destinations:* U.K. 23.5%; South Africa 10.5%; The Netherlands 10.2%; West Germany 9.4%.

Transport and communications

Transport. Railroads (1987): route length 515 mi, 829 km; passenger-mi 63,963,000, passenger-km 102,939,000; short ton-mi cargo 67,441,000, metric ton-km cargo 98,469,000. Roads (1985): total length 7,590 mi, 12,215 km (paved 21%). Vehicles (1986): passenger cars 15,339; trucks and buses 15,755. Merchant marine (1987): vessels (100 gross tons and over) 1; total deadweight tonnage 300. Air transport (1988): passenger-mi 53,995,000, passenger-km 86,896,000; short ton-mi cargo 6,568,000, metric ton-km cargo 9,616,000; airports (1989) with scheduled flights 4.
Communications. Daily newspapers (1985): total number 2; total circulation 32,000; circulation per 1,000 population 4.5. Radio (1988): total number of receivers 1,907,200 (1 per 4.3 persons). Television (1988): total number of receivers, n.a. Telephones (1987): 46,879 (1 per 172 persons).

Education and health

Education (1987–88)				
	schools	teachers	students	student/ teacher ratio
Primary (age 6–13)	2,660	16,885	1,066,642	63.1
Secondary (age 14–18)	79	1,258	26,396	21.0
Teacher tr., voc.	12	234	3,634	15.5
Higher	4	306	2,330	7.6

Educational attainment (1987). Percent of population age 5 and over having no formal education 54.9%; primary education 41.7%; secondary and higher 3.4%. *Literacy* (1985): total population age 15 and over literate 1,555,000 (41.2%).
Health: physicians (1984) 262 (1 per 27,094 persons); hospital beds (1986) 12,119 (1 per 600 persons); infant mortality rate per 1,000 live births (1985–90) 150.0.
Food (1984–86): daily per capita caloric intake 2,372 (vegetable products 96%, animal products 4%); (1984–86) 102% of FAO recommended minimum.

Military

Total active duty personnel (1989): 7,250 (army 96.5%, marines 1.4%, air force 2.1%). *Military expenditure as percent of GNP* (1987): 1.4% (world 5.4%); per capita expenditure U.S.$2.

[1]Includes 11 nonelective members. [2]Preliminary. [3]Detail does not add to total given because of rounding. [4]Excludes refugees estimated to number between 700,000 and 840,000. [5]Based on land area. [6]Reported inpatient deaths in hospitals. [7]Less imputed bank service charges. [8]At constant prices of 1978. [9]Registered. [10]Based on sample survey of the city of Blantyre. [11]Weights of consumer price index components, cities of Blantyre and Lilongwe only. [12]Import figures are f.o.b. in balance of trade and c.i.f. in commodities and trading partners. Reexports included in balance of trade, excluded from commodities and trading partners.

Malaysia

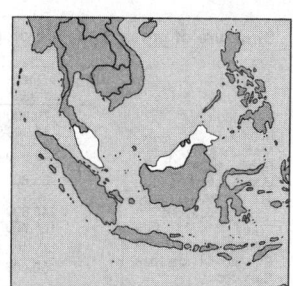

Official name: Malaysia.
Form of government: federal constitutional monarchy with two legislative houses (Senate [69[1]]; House of Representatives [177]).
Chief of state: Yang di-Pertuan Agong (Paramount Ruler).
Head of government: Prime Minister.
Capital: Kuala Lumpur.
Official language: Malay.
Official religion: Islam.
Monetary unit: 1 ringgit, or Malaysian dollar (M$) = 100 cents; valuation (Oct. 2, 1989) 1 U.S.$ = M$2.69; 1 £ = M$4.35.

Area and population		area		population
Regions **States**	**Capitals**	**sq mi**	**sq km**	**1987 estimate**
East Malaysia				
Sabah	Kota Kinabalu	28,425	73,620	1,322,900[2]
Sarawak	Kuching	48,050	124,449	1,550,000
West Malaysia				
Johor	Johor Baharu	7,331	18,986	1,963,600
Kedah	Alor Setar	3,639	9,426	1,325,700
Kelantan	Kota Baharu	5,769	14,943	1,116,400
Melaka	Melaka	637	1,650	548,800
Negeri Sembilan	Seremban	2,565	6,643	679,000
Pahang Darul Makmur	Kuantan	13,886	35,965	978,100
Perak	Ipoh	8,110	21,005	2,107,800
Perlis	Kangar	307	795	175,600
Pulau Pinang	Pinang	398	1,031	1,087,000
Selangor Darul Ehsan	Shah Alam	3,072	7,956	1,830,800
Terengganu	Kuala Terengganu	5,002	12,955	683,900
Federal Territories				
Kuala Lumpur	—	94	243	1,158,200
Labuan	—	35	91	[2]
TOTAL LAND AREA		127,320	329,758	16,527,800
INLAND WATER		264	684	
TOTAL AREA		127,584	330,442	

Demography

Population (1989): 17,421,000.
Density (1989): persons per sq mi 136.8, persons per sq km 52.8.
Urban–rural (1985): urban 38.2%; rural 61.8%.
Sex distribution (1987): male 50.39%; female 49.61%.
Age breakdown (1986): under 15, 37.8%; 15–29, 29.2%; 30–44, 17.5%; 45–59, 9.8%; 60–74, 4.5%; 75 and over, 1.2%.
Population projection: (2000) 21,485,000; (2010) 24,363,000.
Doubling time: 29 years.
Ethnic composition (1987): Malay and other indigenous (Orang Asli, or Bumiputera) 60.9%; Chinese 30.4%; Indian 8.2%; other nonindigenous 0.5%.
Religious affiliation (1980): Muslim 52.9%; Buddhist 17.3%; Chinese folk-religionist 11.6%; Hindu 7.0%; Christian 6.4%; other 4.8%.
Major cities (1980): Kuala Lumpur 1,103,200[3]; Ipoh 293,849; Pinang 248,241; Johor Baharu 246,395; Petaling Jaya 207,805.

Vital statistics

Birth rate per 1,000 population (1988): 29.3 (world avg. 27.1).
Death rate per 1,000 population (1988): 4.9 (world avg. 9.9).
Natural increase rate per 1,000 population (1988): 24.4 (world avg. 17.2).
Total fertility rate (avg. births per childbearing woman; 1988): 3.6.
Marriage rate per 1,000 population (1979): 1.7.
Divorce rate per 1,000 population (1979): 0.02.
Life expectancy at birth (1988): male 68.9 years; female 72.7 years.
Major causes of death per 100,000 population (1981)[4]: heart disease 29.1; infectious and parasitic diseases 19.2; malignant neoplasms (cancers) 18.6; cerebrovascular diseases 14.4; pneumonia 10.6.

National economy

Budget (1989). Revenue: M$22,742,000,000 (nontax revenue 33.8%, income tax 31.5%, import duties 11.8%, excise taxes 7.0%). Expenditures: M$22,286,000,000 (social services 28.6%, debt service 26.9%, security 16.2%, administration 10.8%, economic services 8.8%, transfer payments 4.7%).
Tourism (1987): receipts from visitors U.S.$717,000,000; expenditures by nationals abroad U.S.$1,272,000,000.
Production (metric tons except as noted). Agriculture (1988): palm oil 5,000,000, rice 1,725,000, rubber 1,610,000, cocoa beans 204,000, pineapples 143,600, peppers 17,500; livestock (number of live animals) 2,258,000 pigs, 625,000 cattle, 347,000 goats, 220,000 buffalo, 99,000 sheep, 57,000,000 chickens; roundwood 33,600,000 cu m; fish catch 932,500. Mining and quarrying (1988): bauxite 360,798; iron ore 131,821; copper concentrates 91,500; tin concentrates 28,866. Manufacturing (1986): cement 3,176,000; processed palm oil 2,255,000; iron and steel products 362,000; paints 37,062,000 litres; plywood 503,000 cu m; tires 3,846,000 units; television receivers 863,000 units; air conditioners 337,000 units; road motor vehicles 153,000 units. Construction (buildings completed; 1986)[5]: residential 8,809,100 sq m; nonresidential 959,900 sq m. Energy production (consumption): electricity (kW-hr; 1987) 17,387,000,000 (17,364,000,000); coal (metric tons; 1987) none (475,000); petroleum (barrels; 1987) 185,348,000 (55,176,000); petroleum products (metric tons; 1987) 7,064,000 (9,407,000); natural gas (cu m; 1987) 12,227,000,000 (4,479,000,000).
Gross national product (1987): U.S.$29,556,000,000 (U.S.$1,800 per capita).

Structure of gross domestic product and labour force				
	1988			
	in value[6] **M$'000,000**	**% of total value**	**labour force[7]**	**% of labour force**
Agriculture	13,790	21.1	1,899,800	31.2
Mining	6,944	10.6	37,200	0.6
Manufacturing	15,781	24.2	999,200	16.4
Construction	2,098	3.2	356,400	5.9
Public utilities	1,203	1.8	[8]	[8]
Transp. and commun.	4,311	6.6	261,200	4.3
Trade	6,905	10.6	[8]	[8]
Finance	5,678	8.7	211,600	3.5
Pub. admin., defense	7,845	12.0	844,300	13.9
Services	1,442	2.2	1,473,200[8]	24.2[8]
Other	−659[9]	−1.0[9]	...	...
TOTAL	65,338	100.0	6,082,900	100.0

Public debt (external, outstanding; 1987): U.S.$19,065,000,000.
Population economically active (1988): total 6,622,200; activity rate of total population 39.0% (participation rates: over age 15 [1985] 58.8%; female [1980] 33.6%; unemployed 8.1%).

Price index (1985 = 100)							
	1982	**1983**	**1984**	**1985**	**1986**	**1987**	**1988**
Consumer price index	92.5	95.9	99.7	100.0	100.7	101.6	103.6

Household income and expenditure. Average household size (1980) 5.2; annual income per household (1984): M$13,140; sources of income: n.a.; expenditure (1978): food 37.1%, transportation 18.0%, housing 10.6%, household durable goods 7.7%, recreation 6.0%, clothing and footwear 5.7%, health 2.2%.
Land use (1987): forested 59.6%; meadows and pastures 0.1%; agricultural and under permanent cultivation 13.3%; other 27.0%.

Foreign trade[10]

Balance of trade (current prices)					
	1983	**1984**	**1985**	**1986**	**1987**	**1988**
M$'000,000	+5,028	+8,954	+10,664	+10,480	+11,864	+16,048
% of total	8.3%	13.1%	16.2%	17.1%	17.1%	17.0%

Imports (1987): M$31,983,000,000 (thermionic valves and tubes 17.8%, petroleum products 5.0%, steel plates and sheets 2.4%, grain 2.1%, crude petroleum 1.5%, raw beet and cane sugar 1.0%). *Major import sources:* Japan 21.7%; U.S. 18.7%; Singapore 14.8%; U.K. 4.3%; West Germany 4.2%; Australia 4.1%.
Exports (1987): M$45,176,000,000 (thermionic valves and tubes 15.3%, crude petroleum 13.9%, sawn logs and timber 13.0%, natural rubber 8.7%, palm oil 7.2%, liquefied natural gas 3.9%). *Major export destinations:* Japan 19.5%; Singapore 18.2%; U.S. 16.6%; South Korea 5.3%; The Netherlands 3.5%; West Germany 3.4%.

Transport and communications

Transport. Railroads: track length (1986) 1,381 mi, 2,222 km; passenger-mi 947,000,000[11], passenger-km 1,524,000,000[11]; short ton-mi cargo 912,000,000[11], metric ton-km cargo 1,332,000,000[11]. Roads (1987): total length 24,276 mi, 39,069 km (paved 80%). Vehicles (1987): passenger cars 1,504,208; trucks and buses 338,980. Merchant marine (1988): vessels (100 gross tons and over) 499; total deadweight tonnage 2,265,811. Air transport (1988): passenger-km 8,592,000,000; metric ton-km cargo 385,944,000; airports (1989) with scheduled flights 38.
Communications. Daily newspapers (1985): total number 42; circulation 1,670,000[12]; circulation per 1,000 population 109[12]. Radio (1988): 7,090,979 receivers (1 per 2.4 persons). Television (1987): 1,658,566 receivers[13] (1 per 10 persons). Telephones (1987): 1,500,507 (1 per 11 persons).

Education and health

Education (1987)	schools	teachers	students	student/ teacher ratio
Primary (age 7–12)	6,691	102,356	2,274,452	22.2
Secondary (age 13–19)	1,165	60,390	1,302,048	21.6
Voc., teacher tr.	54	1,969	23,145	11.8
Higher[14]	42	10,347	109,545	10.6

Educational attainment (1980). Percent of population age 25 and over having: no formal schooling 36.6%; primary education 42.1%; secondary 19.4%; higher 1.9%. *Literacy* (1980): total population age 15 and over literate 5,719,358 (72.6%); males 3,195,031 (82.2%); females 2,524,327 (63.2%).
Health: physicians (1987) 5,794 (1 per 2,853 persons); hospital beds (1986) 32,960 (1 per 489 persons); infant mortality rate (1988) 24.0.
Food (1984–86): daily per capita caloric intake 2,723 (vegetable products 84%, animal products 16%); 121% of FAO minimum.

Military

Total active duty personnel (1989): 114,500 (army 78.6%, navy 10.9%, air force 10.5%). *Military expenditure as percent of GNP* (1987): 3.2% (world 5.4%); per capita expenditure U.S.$57.

[1]Includes 43 nonelective seats. [2]Includes Labuan federal territory. [3]1985. [4]Medically certified deaths only. [5]Results of the Central Bank Survey of four major towns: Kuala Lumpur, Shah Alam, Kelang, and Seberang Prai. [6]At constant prices of 1978. [7]Employed only. [8]Services includes public utilities and trade. [9]Includes import duties and bank service charges. [10]Import figures are f.o.b. in balance of trade and c.i.f. for commodities and trading partners. [11]Peninsular Malaysia and Singapore; 1988. [12]1984. [13]Licenses. [14]1986.

Maldives

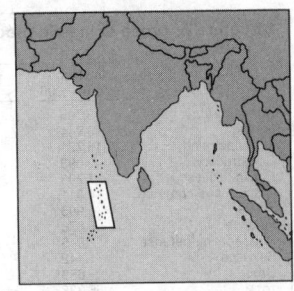

Official name: Divehi Jumhuriyya
(Republic of Maldives).
Form of government: republic with
one legislative house (People's
Council [48[1]]).
Head of state and government:
President.
Capital: Male.
Official language: Divehi.
Official religion: Islam.
Monetary unit: 1 Maldivian Rufiyaa
(Rf) = 100 laaris; valuation (Oct. 2,
1989) 1 U.S.$ = Rf 9.01;
1 £ = Rf 14.58.

Area and population[2]		area		population
				1985
Administrative atolls	Capitals	sq mi	sq km	census
Haa-Alifu	Dhidhdhoo	...	...	9,891
Haa-Dhaalu	Nolhivaranfaru	...	...	10,848
Shaviyani	Farukolhu Funadhoo	...	...	7,529
Noonu	Manadhoo	...	...	6,874
Raa	Ugoofaaru	...	...	9,516
Baa	Eydhafushi	...	...	6,945
Lhaviyani	Naifaru	...	...	6,402
Kaafu	Male	...	...	54,908
Alifu	Mahibadhoo	...	...	7,695
Vaavu	Felidhoo	...	...	1,423
Meemu	Muli	...	...	3,493
Faafu	Magoodhoo	...	...	2,148
Dhaalu	Kudahuvadhoo	...	...	3,576
Thaa	Veymandhoo	...	...	6,942
Laamu	Hithadhoo	...	...	7,158
Gaafu-Alifu	Viligili	...	...	6,081
Gaafu-Dhaalu	Thinadhoo	...	...	8,870
Gnyaviyani	Foah Mulah	...	...	6,189
Seenu	Hithadhoo	...	...	14,965
TOTAL		115	298	181,453

Demography

Population (1989): 209,000.
Density (1989): persons per sq mi 1,817.4, persons per sq km 701.3.
Urban–rural (1985): urban 25.5%; rural 74.5%.
Sex distribution (1986): male 51.84%; female 48.16%.
Age breakdown (1985): under 15, 44.4%; 15–29, 27.0%; 30–44, 13.5%; 45–59, 11.2%; 60 and over, 3.9%.
Population projection: (2000) 300,000; (2010) 350,000.
Doubling time: 23 years.
Ethnic composition: the majority is principally of Sinhalese and Dravidian extraction; Arab, African, and Negrito influences are also present.
Religious affiliation: virtually 100% Sunni Muslim.
Major cities (1985): Male 46,334.

Vital statistics

Birth rate per 1,000 population (1988): 44.1 (world avg. 27.1); legitimate, n.a.; illegitimate, n.a.
Death rate per 1,000 population (1988): 12.8 (world avg. 9.9).
Natural increase rate per 1,000 population (1988): 31.3 (world avg. 17.2).
Total fertility rate (avg. births per childbearing woman; 1988): 6.4.
Marriage rate per 1,000 population: n.a.
Divorce rate per 1,000 population: n.a.
Life expectancy at birth (1987): male 58.0 years; female 59.0 years.
Major causes of death per 100,000 population: n.a.; however, waterborne diseases (including gastroenteritis, cholera, and typhoid fever) are principal health problems, as are malaria, shigellosis, filariasis, leprosy, and tuberculosis.

National economy

Budget (1988). Revenue: Rf 355,700,000 (nontax revenue 33.1%, import duties 24.6%, foreign grants 20.3%, sales and excise taxes 14.1%). Expenditures: Rf 470,600,000 (transport and communications 21.9%, housing and community amenities 17.3%, general public services 14.9%, education 11.4%, public order and safety 7.6%, agriculture 5.7%, fuel and energy 4.3%, health 3.5%).
Public debt (external, outstanding; 1987) U.S.$61,800,000.
Production (metric tons except as noted). Agriculture, forestry, fishing (1988): vegetables and melons 18,000, coconuts 12,000, roots and tubers 9,000 (including cassava, sweet potatoes, and yams), fruits excluding melons 8,000, copra 2,000; fish catch (1987) 46,880, of which skipjack tuna 32,049, yellow-fin tuna 7,123. Mining and quarrying: coral for construction materials. Manufacturing: details n.a.; however, major industries include boat building and repairing, coir yarn and mat weaving, coconut and fish processing, lacquer work, garment manufacturing, and handicrafts. Construction: n.a. Energy production (consumption): electricity (kW-hr; 1987) 13,000,000 (13,000,000); coal, none (n.a.); petroleum products (metric tons; 1987) none (26,000); natural gas, none (n.a.).
Tourism (1987): receipts from visitors U.S.$39,000,000; expenditures by nationals abroad U.S.$5,000,000.
Household income and expenditure. Average household size (1985) 6.1; income per household: n.a.; sources of income: n.a.; expenditure: n.a.
Gross national product (at current market prices; 1987): U.S.$58,000,000 (U.S.$300 per capita).

Structure of gross domestic product and labour force

	1988		1985	
	in value Rf '000[3]	% of total value	labour force	% of labour force
Agriculture[4]	79,800	10.3	15,443	29.5
Mining	13,900	1.8	643	1.3
Manufacturing	43,600	5.7	11,559	22.1
Public utilities			504	1.0
Construction	63,800	8.3	2,563	4.9
Transportation and communications	40,800	5.3	3,327	6.3
Trade	128,700	16.7	5,434	10.4
Finance			418	0.8
Pub. admin., defense	400,600	51.9	10,431	20.0
Services				
Other			1,941	3.7
TOTAL	771,200	100.0	52,263	100.0

Population economically active (1985): total 52,263; activity rate of total population 28.8% (participation rates: ages 15–64 [1977] 78.3%; female 21.7%; unemployed, n.a.).
Land use (1987): forested 3.3%; meadows and pastures 3.3%; agricultural and under permanent cultivation 10.0%; built-on, wasteland, and other 83.4%.

Foreign trade[5]

Balance of trade (current prices)						
	1983	1984	1985	1986	1987	1988
U.S.$'000,000	−38,283	−30,850	−24,864	−33,459	−47,932	−54,977
% of total	58.7%	46.7%	35.1%	40.5%	43.8%	40.7%

Imports (1987): U.S.$86,570,000 (food, beverages, and tobacco 14.3%; basic manufactures 9.7%; machinery and transport equipment 9.1%; mineral fuels 5.9%; miscellaneous manufactured goods 4.6%; chemicals 3.2%). *Major import sources:* Japan 16.5%; United Kingdom 5.8%; West Germany 3.9%.
Exports (1987): U.S.$30,768,000 (fresh skipjack tuna 32.3%; dried skipjack 7.4%; dried salted fish 3.2%). *Major export destinations:* Japan 3.6%; United Kingdom 2.0%; Switzerland 1.0%.

Transport and communications

Transport. Railroads: none. Roads: total length, n.a. Vehicles (1987): passenger cars 401; trucks 234. Merchant marine (1988): vessels (100 gross tons and over) 41; total deadweight tonnage 165,425. Air transport (1985): passenger arrivals 123,609, passenger departures 122,315; cargo loaded 343 metric tons, cargo unloaded 2,391 metric tons; airports (1989) with scheduled flights 2.
Communications. Daily newspapers (1987): total number 2; total circulation 1,500[6]; circulation per 1,000 population 7.7[6]. Radio (1988): total number of receivers 22,044 (1 per 9.2 persons). Television (1988): total number of receivers 4,640 (1 per 44 persons). Telephones (1985): 2,485 (1 per 75 persons).

Education and health

Education (1986)	schools	teachers	students	student/ teacher ratio
Primary (age 6–11)	243	1,138	41,812	36.7
Secondary (age 11–18)	9	291	3,581	12.3
Voc., teacher tr.	10	52	462	8.9
Higher	—	—	—	—

Educational attainment (1977). Percent of population age 25 and over having: no formal schooling or no standard passed 80.2%; primary standard 15.1%; secondary standard 3.9%; postsecondary 0.1%; higher 0.1%; not stated 0.6%. *Literacy* (1982): total population age 15 and over literate 62,365 (81.1%); males literate 31,896 (80.2%); females literate 30,469 (82.0%).
Health (1985): physicians 23 (1 per 7,957 persons); hospital beds[7] 121 (1 per 1,512 persons); infant mortality rate per 1,000 live births (1987) 49.9.
Food: daily per capita caloric intake (1979–81) 1,983 (vegetable products 91%, animal products 9%); (1984) 92% of FAO recommended minimum requirement.

Military

Total active duty personnel: Maldives maintains a single security force numbering about 700–1,000; it performs both army and police functions.

---

[1]Includes eight nonelective seats. [2]Maldives is divided into 19 administrative districts corresponding to atoll groups; arrangement shown here is from north to south; total area excludes 34,634 sq mi (89,702 sq km) of tidal waters. [3]At 1985 prices. [4]Primarily fishing. [5]Import figures are f.o.b. in balance of trade and c.i.f. for commodities and trading partners. [6]For one daily newspaper only. [7]In government establishments only.

Mali

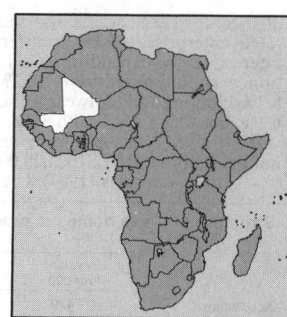

Official name: République du Mali (Republic of Mali).
Form of government: unitary single-party republic with one legislative house (National Assembly [82]).
Head of state and government: President.
Capital: Bamako.
Official language: French.
Official religion: none.
Monetary unit: 1 CFA franc (CFAF) = 100 centimes; valuation (Oct. 2, 1989) 1 U.S.$ = CFAF 317.90; 1 £ = CFAF 514.37.

Area and population

Regions	Capitals	area sq mi	area sq km	population 1987 census
Gao	Gao	124,323	321,996	383,734
Kayes	Kayes	76,356	197,760	1,058,575
Koulikoro	Koulikoro	34,685	89,833	1,180,260
Mopti	Mopti	34,257	88,752	1,261,383
Ségou	Ségou	21,671	56,127	1,328,250
Sikasso	Sikasso	29,529	76,480	1,308,828
Tombouctou[1]	Tombouctou	157,907	408,977	453,032
District				
Bamako	Bamako	103	267	646,163
TOTAL		478,841	1,240,192	7,620,225

Demography

Population (1989): 7,911,000.
Density (1989): persons per sq mi 16.5, persons per sq km 6.4.
Urban-rural (1987): urban 20.3%; rural 79.7%.
Sex distribution (1987): male 48.99%; female 51.01%.
Age breakdown (1985): under 15, 46.2%; 15–29, 25.7%; 30–44, 14.9%; 45–59, 8.6%; 60–74, 3.9%; 75 and over, 0.7%.
Population projection: (2000) 9,535,000; (2010) 11,299,000.
Doubling time: 24 years.
Ethnic composition (1983): Bambara 31.9%; Fulani 13.9%; Senufo 12.0%; Soninke 8.8%; Tuareg 7.3%; Songhai 7.2%; Malinke 6.6%; Dogon 4.0%; Dyula 2.9%; Bobo 2.4%; Arab 1.2%; other 1.8%.
Religious affiliation (1983): Muslim 90%; traditional beliefs 9%; Christian 1%.
Major cities (1987): Bamako 646,163; Ségou 88,877; Mopti 73,979; Sikasso 73,050; Gao 54,874.

Vital statistics

Birth rate per 1,000 population (1989): 49.0 (world avg. 27.1); legitimate, n.a.; illegitimate, n.a.
Death rate per 1,000 population (1989): 20.0 (world avg. 9.9).
Natural increase rate per 1,000 population (1989): 29.0 (world avg. 17.2).
Total fertility rate (avg. births per childbearing woman; 1989): 6.6.
Marriage rate per 1,000 population (1983): 2.8.
Divorce rate per 1,000 population: n.a.
Life expectancy at birth (1989): male 44.0 years; female 47.0 years.
Major causes of death per 100,000 population: n.a.; morbidity ([notified cases of illness] percent of all reported illness; 1985): malaria 62.1%; measles 10.3%; amebiasis 10.3%; syphilis and gonococcal infections 6.0%; influenza 4.9%.

National economy

Budget (1989). Revenue: CFAF 218,357,000,000 ([1986] indirect taxes 35.8%, of which customs duties 15.4%; direct taxes 16.3%; carryover revenue from previous fiscal years 9.7%). Expenditures: CFAF 275,491,000,000 ([1986] defense 18.7%; education 12.6%; foreign affairs 3.3%; commerce and finance 2.9%).
Tourism (1987): receipts from visitors U.S.$16,000,000; expenditures by nationals abroad U.S.$25,000,000.
Population economically active (1985): total 2,598,000; activity rate of total population 32.1% (participation rates: ages 15–64, 42.6%; female 16.8%; unemployed 1.3%[2]).

Price and earnings indexes (1985 = 100)

	1981	1982	1983	1984	1985	1986	1987
Consumer price index[3]	73.5	75.2	82.6	92.8	100.0	96.1	82.4
Hourly earnings index[4]	88.4	100.0	100.0	100.0	100.0	134.6	...

Production (metric tons except as noted). Agriculture, forestry, fishing (1988): millet 1,276,000, vegetables (including melons) 245,000, sugarcane 220,000, corn (maize) 211,000, rice 190,000, seed cotton 187,000, cottonseed 142,000, cassava 73,000, cotton lint 71,000, peanuts (groundnuts) 60,000, pulses 57,000, sweet potatoes 57,000, yams 13,000, fruit (excluding melons) 12,000, wheat 2,000, tobacco 1,000; livestock (number of live animals) 5,500,000 sheep, 5,500,000 goats, 4,738,000 cattle, 550,000 asses, 241,000 camels, 62,000 horses, 60,000 pigs, 15,000,000 chickens; roundwood (1987) 5,201,000 cu m; fish catch (1987) 55,702. Mining and quarrying (1987): limestone 25,000, salt 3,000, gold 700 kg. Manufacturing (1988): cotton fibre 70,000[5]; beef and veal 65,000; soft drinks 43,700[6]; goat, mutton, and lamb meat 26,000; cement 26,000[5]; sugar 20,000; cattle hides 10,000; molasses 8,400[6];

sheepskins 4,930; goatskins 3,570; beer 9,500 hectolitres[7]. Construction: n.a.
Energy production (consumption): electricity (kW-hr; 1987) 204,000,000 (204,000,000); coal, none (n.a.); crude petroleum, none (n.a.); petroleum products (metric tons; 1987) none (121,000); natural gas, none (n.a.).
Gross national product (at current market prices; 1987): U.S.$1,576,000,000 (U.S.$200 per capita).

Structure of gross domestic product and labour force

	1986 in value CFAF '000,000,000	1986 % of total value	1985 labour force	1985 % of labour force
Agriculture	281.5	55.3	2,174,000	83.7
Mining	7.7	1.5	}	
Manufacturing	40.1	7.9		
Construction	22.8	4.5	60,000	2.3
Public utilities	6.7	1.3	}	
Transp. and commun.	24.0	4.7		
Trade	66.4	13.0		
Finance	8.2	1.6	364,000	14.0
Pub. admin., defense	42.1	8.3		
Services	...	...		
Other	9.6	1.9		
TOTAL	509.1	100.0	2,598,000	100.0

Public debt (external, outstanding; 1988): U.S.$2,100,000,000.
Household income and expenditure. Average household size (1980) 5.1; average annual income per household: n.a.; sources of income: n.a.; expenditure: n.a.
Land use (1987): forested 7.0%; meadows and pastures 24.6%; agricultural and under permanent cultivation 1.7%; other 66.7%.

Foreign trade[8]

Balance of trade (current prices)

	1983	1984	1985	1986	1987	1988
CFAF '000,000,000	−71.7	−71.5	−131.7	−100.5	−70.2	−79.0
% of total	36.3%	28.6%	45.4%	41.4%	31.0%	33.0%

Imports (1988): CFAF 159,000,000,000 ([1986] machinery, appliances, and transportation equipment 26.8%; petroleum products 16.5%; food products 13.1%, of which cereals 7.2%; construction materials 9.4%; chemicals and pharmaceutical products 8.2%). *Major import sources* (1987): France 24.7%; Côte d'Ivoire 21.8%; West Germany 7.7%; Italy 5.0%; Senegal 4.2%; Spain 3.6%; The Netherlands 3.5%; Belgium–Luxembourg 2.7%; United States 2.3%; Hong Kong 2.3%; United Kingdom 2.0%; Japan 1.8%; China 1.3%; Switzerland 0.6%.
Exports (1988): CFAF 80,100,000,000 ([1986] raw cotton and cotton products 36.8%; live animals 25.0%; nuts 3.8%; salted, dried, or smoked fish 1.7%). *Major export destinations* (1987): France 11.2%; United Kingdom 9.5%; West Germany 7.7%; Morocco 7.6%; Belgium–Luxembourg 5.7%; Algeria 5.7%; Portugal 5.6%; Spain 5.0%; The Netherlands 4.4%; Réunion 4.1%; Tunisia 3.1%.

Transport and communications

Transport. Railroads (1987): route length 401 mi, 646 km; passenger-mi 480,173,000, passenger-km 772,765,000; short ton-mi cargo 213,293,000, metric ton-km cargo 429,334,000. Roads (1987): total length 11,185 mi, 18,000 km (paved 8%). Vehicles (1987): passenger cars 29,436; trucks and buses 7,556. Merchant marine: vessels (100 gross tons and over) none. Air transport (1983): passenger-mi 68,000,000; passenger-km 110,000,000; short ton-mi cargo 411,000, metric ton-km cargo 600,000; airports (1989) with scheduled flights 2.
Communications. Daily newspapers (1988): total number 1; total circulation (1985) 40,000; circulation per 1,000 population (1985) 4.9. Radio (1988): total number of receivers 132,515 (1 per 59 persons). Television (1988): total number of receivers 900 (1 per 8,642 persons). Telephones (1986): 13,000 (1 per 580 persons).

Education and health

Education (1985–86)

	schools	teachers	students	student/teacher ratio
Primary (age 6–14)	1,348	8,597	292,395	34.0
Secondary (age 15–17)[9]	277	4,024	50,596	12.3
Higher	7	499	5,792	11.6

Educational attainment (1976). Percent of adult population age 25 and over having: no formal schooling 95.4%; primary education 3.8%; secondary 0.6%; postsecondary and higher 0.2%. *Literacy* (1980): total population age 15 and over literate 361,800 (10.1%); males literate 329,200 (18.6%); females literate 32,600 (1.8%).
Health (1983): physicians 349 (1 per 20,474 persons); hospital beds 4,215 (1 per 1,695 persons); infant mortality rate per 1,000 live births (1989) 159.
Food (1984–86): daily per capita caloric intake 2,021 (vegetable products 93%, animal products 7%); 68% of FAO recommended minimum.

Military

Total active duty personnel (1989): 7,300 (army 94.5%, air force 5.5%). *Military expenditure as percent of GNP* (1985): 2.5% (world 5.7%); per capita expenditure U.S.$5.

---

[1]Area for Tombouctou region is estimated as a residue between total reported area and the remainder of the regions. [2]Urban areas, estimated. [3]Food index for Bamako only. [4]Minimum hourly wages of industrial workers. [5]1986. [6]1985. [7]1983. [8]Imports c.i.f. [9]Includes vocational and teacher training.

Malta

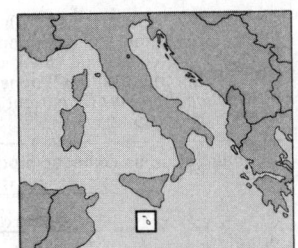

Official name: Repubblika ta' Malta
(Maltese); Republic of Malta (English).
Form of government: unitary multiparty
republic with one legislative house
(House of Representatives [69[1]]).
Chief of state: President.
Head of government: Prime Minister.
Capital: Valletta.
Official languages: Maltese; English.
Official religion: Roman Catholicism.
Monetary unit: 1 Maltese lira
(Lm) = 100 cents = 1,000 mils;
valuation[2] (Oct. 2, 1989)
1 Lm = U.S.$2.86 = £1.79.

Area and population

Census regions[3]	area		population
	sq mi	sq km	1988 estimate[4]
Gozo and Comino	27	70	25,162
Inner Harbour	6	15	101,043
Northern	30	78	32,083
Outer Harbour	12	32	99,320
South Eastern	20	53	43,179
Western	27	69	44,849
TOTAL	122	316[5]	345,636

Demography

Population (1989): 349,000.
Density (1989): persons per sq mi 2,860.7, persons per sq km 1,104.4.
Urban-rural (1985): urban 85.3%; rural 14.7%.
Sex distribution (1989): male 49.29%; female 50.71%.
Age breakdown (1988): under 15, 23.9%; 15–29, 22.5%; 30–44, 24.2%; 45–59, 14.9%; 60–74, 10.6%; 75 and over, 3.9%.
Population projection: (2000) 368,000; (2010) 380,000.
Doubling time: 98 years.
Ethnic composition (1980): Maltese 95.7%; British 2.1%; other 2.2%.
Religious affiliation (1980): Roman Catholic 97.3%; Anglican 1.2%; other 1.5%.
Major cities (1988): Birkirkara 20,490; Qormi 18,586; Hamrun 13,632; Sliema 13,604; Valletta 9,239.

Vital statistics

Birth rate per 1,000 population (1987): 15.4 (world avg. 27.1); legitimate 98.8%; illegitimate 1.2%.
Death rate per 1,000 population (1987): 8.4 (world avg. 9.9).
Natural increase rate per 1,000 population (1987): 7.0 (world avg. 17.2).
Total fertility rate (avg. births per childbearing woman; 1985–90): 1.9.
Marriage rate per 1,000 population (1987): 7.1.
Divorce rate per 1,000 population: n.a.
Life expectancy at birth (1987): male 72.5 years; female 77.0 years.
Major causes of death per 100,000 population (1987): diseases of the circulatory system 533.2; malignant neoplasms (cancers) 155.8; diseases of the respiratory system 46.8%; endocrine, nutritional, and metabolic diseases of the blood and blood-forming organs 21.5; accidents, poisonings, and violence 18.0; diseases of the digestive system 16.8.

National economy

Budget (1988). Revenue: Lm 254,492,000 (national insurance and Central Bank contributions 53.2%, customs and excise taxes 21.5%, income tax 18.4%, licenses and fees 4.8%). Expenditures: Lm 223,540,000 (national insurance benefits 32.1%, health 11.8%, education 9.9%, defense 4.0%, debt service 3.1%).
Public debt (1986): U.S.$164,138,000.
Production (value added in Lm except where noted). Agriculture, forestry, fishing (1983): vegetables 7,912,000 (of which tomatoes 2,751,000, melons 387,000, onions 223,000), cereals 2,417,000 (of which wheat 929,000, barley 333,000), fruits 1,900,000 (of which citrus fruits 731,000, strawberries 553,-000), potatoes 1,617,000; livestock (number of live animals; 1988) 95,000 pigs, 9,000 cattle, 5,000 sheep, 1,000,000 chickens; fish catch (metric tons; 1987) 1,003. Mining and quarrying (1986): quarrying 869,400. Manufacturing (1986): textiles and wearing apparel 38,973,000, of which clothing 30,319,200, footwear 4,689,300, textiles 3,964,600; machinery and transport equipment 25,902,900; food and beverages 24,949,800; printing and publishing 8,539,500; wood, cork, and furniture 5,364,000; tobacco and tobacco products 3,727,800; plastics 2,141,500; chemicals 1,873,100. Construction (1986): 13,549,300. Energy production (consumption): electricity (kW-hr; 1987) 944,000,000 (944,000,000); coal (metric tons; 1987) none (182,000); crude petroleum, none (n.a.); petroleum products (metric tons; 1987) none (301,000); natural gas, none (n.a.).
Population economically active (1987): total 127,551; activity rate of total population 37.0% (participation rates: ages 15–64, n.a.; female 24.9%; unemployed 4.4%).

Price and earnings indexes (1985 = 100)

	1982	1983	1984	1985	1986	1987	1988
Consumer price index	101.5	100.7	100.2	100.0	102.0	102.5	103.4
Annual earnings index	...	...	...	...	...	...	...

Household income and expenditure. Average household size (1985) 3.3; average annual income per household (1982) Lm 4,736 (U.S.$11,399); sources

of income (1987): wages and salaries 49.9%, professional and unincorporated enterprises 17.4%, transfer payments 14.2%, rents, dividends, and interest 11.7%; expenditure (1987): food and beverages 31.5%, transportation and communications 15.2%, household furnishings and operations 8.7%, clothing and footwear 8.5%, recreation, entertainment, and education 6.1%, housing 5.9%, health 3.5%, tobacco 3.0%.
Tourism (1987): receipts from visitors U.S.$363,000,000; expenditures by nationals abroad U.S.$102,000,000.
Gross national product (1987): U.S.$1,444,000,000 (U.S.$4,010 per capita).

Structure of gross domestic product and labour force

	1987			
	in value Lm '000	% of total value	labour force	% of labour force
Agriculture	21,429	4.3	3,203	2.5
Manufacturing	136,427	27.5	35,857	28.1
Mining	21,051	4.3	887	0.7
Construction			5,849	4.6
Public utilities	6	6	1,866	1.5
Transportation and communications	30,204	6.1	8,952	7.0
Trade	70,847	14.3	11,984	9.4
Finance	62,782[7]	12.7[7]	4,229	3.3
Pub. admin., defense	110,981[6]	22.4[6]	49,094	38.5
Services	41,729	8.4		
Other	...	...	5,630[8]	4.4[8]
TOTAL	495,450	100.0	127,551	100.0

Land use (1983): agricultural and under permanent cultivation 41.2%; other (infertile clay soil with underlying limestone) 58.8%.

Foreign trade[9]

Balance of trade (current prices)

	1983	1984	1985	1986	1987	1988
Lm '000,000	−128.1	−149.1	−114.1	−167.6	−184.3	−168.1
% of total	28.9%	29.1%	21.8%	31.7%	30.6%	26.3%

Imports (1988): Lm 447,247,000 (manufactured articles, machinery, and transport equipment 47.3%, of which machinery and transport equipment 37.2%; semimanufactured goods 23.4%; food and live animals 10.4%; chemicals and chemical products 7.8%; mineral fuels 4.5%; nonfuel materials 2.0%; beverages and tobacco 2.0%). *Major import sources:* Italy 22.3%; United Kingdom 17.9%; West Germany 14.8%; United States 9.5%; France 5.0%; The Netherlands 2.9%; Australia 0.4%.
Exports (1988): Lm 235,921,000 (manufactured articles, machinery, and transport equipment 76.2%, of which machinery and transport equipment 35.5%; semimanufactured goods 10.6%; reexports 7.9%; food and live animals 2.1%; beverages and tobacco 1.1%; chemicals and chemical products 1.1%; nonfuel materials 0.8%). *Major export destinations:* West Germany 27.1%; Italy 17.4%; United Kingdom 13.2%; United States 11.2%; Libya 6.2%; Belgium 3.1%.

Transport and communications

Transport. Railroads: none. Roads (1987): total length 860 mi, 1,385 km (paved 93%). Vehicles (1987): passenger cars 86,298; trucks and buses 18,-546. Merchant marine (1988): vessels (100 gross tons and over) 356; total deadweight tonnage 4,518,532. Air transport (1987): passenger-mi 395,000,-000, passenger-km 636,000,000; short ton-mi cargo 3,551,000, metric ton-km cargo 5,184,000; airports (1989) with scheduled flights 1.
Communications. Daily newspapers (1989): total number 3; total circulation 67,000; circulation per 1,000 population 192. Radio (1988): 106,704 receivers (1 per 3.2 persons). Television (1988): 131,957 receivers (1 per 2.6 persons). Telephones (1988): 162,770 (1 per 2.1 persons).

Education and health

Education (1987–88)

	schools	teachers	students	student/ teacher ratio
Primary (age 5–10)	125	1,603	36,564	22.8
Secondary (age 11–17)	42	1,762	22,341	12.7
Voc., teacher tr.	26	690	6,465	9.4
Higher	1	147	1,447	9.8

Educational attainment (1967). Percent of economically active population having: no formal schooling 10.8%; primary education 60.4%; lower secondary 3.4%; upper secondary 17.6%; technical secondary 3.9%; postsecondary and higher 3.9%. *Literacy* (1985): total population age 15 and over literate 250,419 (96.0%); males literate 121,899 (96.2%); females literate 128,520 (95.9%).
Health (1988): physicians 710 (1 per 489 persons); hospital beds 3,217 (1 per 108 persons); infant mortality rate per 1,000 live births (1987) 7.3.
Food (1984–86): daily per capita caloric intake 2,878 (vegetable products 72%, animal products 28%); 103% of FAO recommended minimum requirement.

Military

Total active duty personnel (1988): 751 (army 100%). *Military expenditure as percent of GNP* (1987): 1.5% (world 5.4%); per capita expenditure U.S.$70.

[1]Normally a 65-member body; however, in the elections of May 9, 1987, 4 additional seats were awarded to the minority party (by seats won), which had obtained a majority of the popular vote. [2]The Maltese lira is tied to the currencies of several principal trading partners. [3]Malta has no first-order administrative subdivisions; data are reported according to census regions. [4]January 1. [5]Detail does not add to total given because of rounding. [6]Pub. admin., defense includes public utilities. [7]Finance includes income from property. [8]Unemployed only. [9]Import figures are f.o.b. in balance of trade and c.i.f. for commodities and trading partners.

Martinique

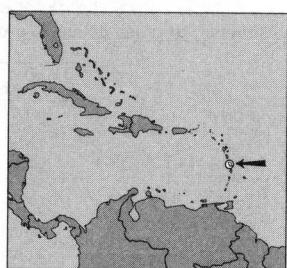

Official name: Département de la Martinique (Department of Martinique).
Political status: overseas department (France) with two legislative houses (General Council [45]; Regional Council [41]).
Chief of state: President of France.
Heads of government: Commissioner of the Republic (for France); President of the General Council (for Martinique); President of the Regional Council (for Martinique).
Capital: Fort-de-France.
Official language: French.
Official religion: none.
Monetary unit: 1 Franc (F) = 100 centimes; valuation (Oct. 2, 1989) 1 U.S.$ = F 6.36; 1 £ = F 10.29.

Area and population

Arrondissements	Capitals	area		population
		sq mi	sq km	1982 census
Fort-de-France	Fort-de-France	141	365	176,749
Le Marin	Le Marin	154	399	78,329
La Trinité	La Trinité	126	327	73,488
TOTAL		421	1,091	328,566[1]

Demography

Population (1989): 337,000.
Density (1989): persons per sq mi 800.5, persons per sq km 308.9.
Urban–rural (1985): urban 71.1%; rural 28.9%.
Sex distribution (1985): male 48.48%; female 51.52%.
Age breakdown (1982): under 15, 28.3%; 15–29, 30.3%; 30–44, 16.2%; 45–59, 13.2%; 60–74, 8.5%; 75 and over, 3.3%; not specified, 0.2%.
Population projection: (2000) 346,000; (2010) 349,000.
Doubling time: 55 years.
Ethnic composition (1983): mulatto 93.7%; French (metropolitan and Martinique white) 2.6%; East Indian 1.7%; other 2.0%.
Religious affiliation (1987): Roman Catholic 87.9%; other (mostly Seventh-day Adventist, Jehovah's Witness, syncretist, and nonreligious) 12.1%.
Major cities (1982): Fort-de-France 96,649; Schoelcher 16,412; Le Lamentin 6,872; Saint-Pierre 4,923; Ducos 4,429.

Vital statistics

Birth rate per 1,000 population (1988): 19.0 (world avg. 27.1); legitimate 34.0%; illegitimate 66.0%.
Death rate per 1,000 population (1988): 6.2 (world avg. 9.9).
Natural increase rate per 1,000 population (1988): 12.8 (world avg. 17.2).
Total fertility rate (avg. births per childbearing woman; 1987): 2.1.
Marriage rate per 1,000 population (1988): 4.6.
Divorce rate per 1,000 population (1988): 1.1.
Life expectancy at birth (1987): male 71.0 years; female 77.0 years.
Major causes of death per 100,000 population (1985): diseases of the circulatory system 234.8, of which cerebrovascular disease 110.4, diseases of pulmonary circulation and other forms of heart disease 74.7; malignant neoplasms (cancers) 129.6; diseases of the digestive system 36.3; diseases of the respiratory system 35.1.

National economy

Budget (1989). Revenue: F 1,442,000,000 (general receipts from French central government and local administrative bodies 36.4%, new loans 15.9%, public-works subsidies 12.2%, particular health and social service receipts from local administrative bodies 3.1%). Expenditures: F 1,693,000,000 (improvements to public works and property 38.2%, health and social assistance 35.9%, other administrative services 14.8%, debt amortization 3.3%).
Public debt (external, outstanding; 1987[2]): U.S.$30,000,000.
Production (metric tons except as noted). Agriculture, forestry, fishing (1988): bananas 205,200, sugarcane 104,800, pineapples 24,000, yams 14,000, plantains 8,000, sweet potatoes 6,000, tomatoes 5,000, cucumbers 4,000, avocados 2,580, limes 800, flowers and foliage 143[3], pimientos 142[3]; livestock (number of live animals) 90,000 sheep, 48,000 pigs, 46,000 goats, 43,000 cattle; roundwood (1987) 13,000 cu m; fish catch (1987) 4,554. Mining and quarrying (1987): pumice 132,000; sand and gravel for local construction. Manufacturing (1988): cement 246,800; sugar 7,500; pineapple juice 2,052; pineapple compote 1,022; rum 85,500 hectolitres; other products include clothing, fabricated metals, and yawls and sails. Construction (buildings authorized; 1988): residential, n.a.; nonresidential 225,000 sq m. Energy production (consumption): electricity (kW-hr; 1988) 559,000,000 (501,000,000); coal, none (none); crude petroleum (barrels; 1988) none (4,133,000); petroleum products (metric tons; 1987) 552,000 (238,000); natural gas, none (none).
Household income and expenditure. Average household size (1984–85) 3.7; income per household (1979) F 70,009 (U.S.$17,415); sources of income (1979): wages and salaries 74.2%, rent 4.8%, other 21.0%; expenditure (1984–85): food and beverages 31.9%, of which poultry and meat 7.9%; housing, household furnishings, and energy 24.7%; transportation and communications 14.2%; clothing and footwear 7.2%; other 22.0%.

Gross domestic product (at current market prices; 1985): U.S.$1,400,000,000 (U.S.$4,280 per capita).

Structure of gross domestic product and labour force

	1982		1986	
	in value F '000,000	% of total value	labour force	% of labour force
Agriculture, fishing	720	8.1	10,364	7.1
Mining, manufacturing	552	6.2	5,769	4.0
Construction	324	3.6	6,894	4.7
Public utilities	96	1.1	1,303	0.9
Transportation and communications	390	4.4	5,870	4.0
Trade, restaurants, hotels	1,541	17.4	12,399	8.5
Finance, real estate, insurance	630	7.1	19,296	13.2
Pub. admin., defense, services	4,267	48.1	32,894	22.6
Other	354	4.0	51,135[4]	35.0[4]
TOTAL	8,874	100.0	145,924	100.0

Population economically active (1986): total 145,924; activity rate of total population 44.5% (participation rates: ages 15–64, 67.4%; female 50.6%; unemployed [1986] 35.0%).

Price and earnings indexes (1985 = 100)[5]

	1983	1984	1985	1986	1987	1988	1989[6]
Consumer price index	87.3	94.2	100.0	102.6	105.3	108.8	109.9
Monthly earnings index[7]	82.7	93.9	100.0	101.0	103.1	106.1	106.1

Land use (1986): forested 25%; meadows and pastures 32%; agricultural and under permanent cultivation 18%; other 25%.
Tourism (1987): receipts from visitors U.S.$100,000,000; expenditures by nationals abroad, n.a.

Foreign trade

Balance of trade (current prices)

	1983	1984	1985	1986	1987	1988
F '000,000	–4,359	–4,632	–4,593	–4,569	–5,544	–6,551
% of total	62.4%	63.2%	61.2%	60.4%	70.4%	73.7%

Imports (1987): F 6,707,700,000 (transport equipment 22.2%, food products 19.0%, electrical machinery and equipment 13.4%, mineral fuels 9.4%, chemical products 8.3%, metal manufactures 5.6%). *Major import sources:* France 65.2%; United Kingdom 6.2%; Italy 3.7%; West Germany 3.0%; Japan 2.5%.
Exports (1987): F 1,163,300,000 (bananas 48.0%, petroleum products 14.0%, rum 13.4%, fertilizer 2.1%). *Major export destinations:* France 64.6%; Guadeloupe 24.1%; West Germany 5.6%; French Guiana 2.9%.

Transport and communications

Transport. Railroads: none. Roads (1987): total length 1,185 mi, 1,907 km (paved [1985] 85%). Vehicles (1985): passenger cars 135,269; trucks and buses 7,328. Merchant marine (1988): vessels (100 gross tons and over) 6; total deadweight tonnage, n.a. Air transport (1988): passenger arrivals 542,180, passenger departures 532,928; cargo unloaded 7,060 metric tons, cargo loaded 5,243 metric tons; airports (1989) with scheduled flights 1.
Communications. Daily newspapers (1988): total number 1; total circulation 31,500; circulation per 1,000 population 94. Radio (1986): total number of receivers 55,000 (1 per 6.0 persons). Television (1988): total number of receivers 45,000 (1 per 7.5 persons). Telephones (1987): 106,940 (1 per 3.1 persons).

Education and health

Education (1986–87)

	schools	teachers	students	student/ teacher ratio
Primary (age 6–11)	218	2,024[8]	39,492	19.3[8]
Secondary (age 12–18)	}	2,745	45,247	16.5
Vocational	...			
Higher[8]	1	40	1,220	30

Educational attainment (1982). Percent of population age 25 and over having: no formal schooling 9.8%; primary education 62.7%; secondary 21.2%; higher 6.3%. *Literacy* (1982): total population age 15 and over literate 206,807 (92.5%); males literate 97,538 (91.8%); females literate 109,269 (93.2%).
Health (1986): physicians 519 (1 per 641 persons); hospital beds 3,070 (1 per 108 persons); infant mortality rate per 1,000 live births (1986–88) 10.2.
Food (1984–86): daily per capita caloric intake 2,780 (vegetable products 80%, animal products 20%); (1984) 116% of FAO recommended minimum requirement.

Military

Total active duty personnel (1984): 2,800 French troops[9].

[1]De jure (legally resident, but not necessarily present) census result 326,717. [2]Includes external long-term private debt not guaranteed by the government. [3]Production for export only. [4]All unemployed. [5]All figures are end of year unless otherwise footnoted. [6]End of March. [7]Based on minimum-level wage in public administration. [8]1983–84. [9]Includes police.

Mauritania

Official name: al-Jumhūrīyah al-Islāmīyah al-Mūrītānīyah (Arabic), République Islamique de Mauritanie (French) (Islamic Republic of Mauritania).
Form of government: military regime.
Head of state and government: President heads Military Committee for National Salvation (membership varies).
Capital: Nouakchott.
Official languages: Arabic; French.
Official religion: Islam.
Monetary unit: 1 Mauritanian Ouguiya (UM) = 5 khoums; valuation (Oct. 2, 1989) 1 U.S.$ = UM 83.62; 1 £ = UM 135.30.

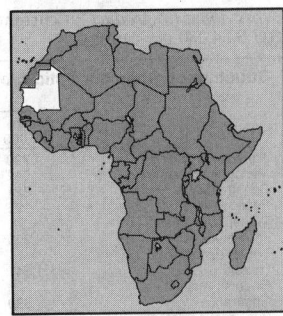

Area and population

Regions	Capitals	area sq mi	area sq km	population 1987 estimate[1]
el-'Açâba	Kiffa	13,900	36,000	160,000
Adrar	Atar	83,100	215,300	70,000
Brakna	Aleg	14,000	37,100	169,000
Dakhlet Nouadhibou	Nouadhibou	11,600	30,000	33,000
Gorgol	Kaédi	5,400	14,000	188,000
Guidimaka	Sélibaby	4,000	10,000	115,000
Hodh ech-Chargui	Néma	64,000	166,000	267,000
Hodh el-Gharbi	'Ayoûn el-'Atroûs	22,000	57,000	140,000
Inchiri	Akjoujt	19,000	49,000	26,000
Tagant	Tidjikdja	36,000	93,000	80,000
Tiris Zemmour	Fdérik	98,600	255,300	37,000
Trarza	Rosso	26,000	67,000	249,000
District				
Nouakchott	Nouakchott	400	1,000	285,000
TOTAL		398,000	1,030,700	1,819,000

Demography

Population (1989): 1,946,000.
Density (1989): persons per sq mi 4.9, persons per sq km 1.9.
Urban–rural (1987): urban 34.0%; rural 66.0%.
Sex distribution (1985): male 49.48%; female 50.52%.
Age breakdown (1985): under 15, 46.4%; 15–29, 26.0%; 30–44, 14.6%; 45–59, 8.4%; 60–74, 3.9%; 75 and over, 0.7%.
Population projection: (2000) 2,673,000; (2010) 3,616,000.
Doubling time: 26 years.
Ethnic composition (1983): Moor 81.5% (about half Arab–Berber and half African Sudanic); Wolof 6.8%; Tukulor 5.3%; Soninke 2.8%; Fulani 1.1%; other 2.5%.
Religious affiliation (1980): Muslim 99.4%; Christian 0.4%; other 0.2%.
Major cities (1987): Nouakchott 600,000; Kaédi 32,000; Nouadhibou 30,000; Zouérate (Zouîrât) 17,500[2].

Vital statistics

Birth rate per 1,000 population (1985–90): 46.2 (world avg. 27.1); legitimate, n.a.; illegitimate, n.a.
Death rate per 1,000 population (1985–90): 19.0 (world avg. 9.9).
Natural increase rate per 1,000 population (1985–90): 27.2 (world avg. 17.2).
Total fertility rate (avg. births per childbearing woman; 1985–90): 6.5.
Marriage rate per 1,000 population: n.a.
Divorce rate per 1,000 population: n.a.
Life expectancy at birth (1989): male 43.0 years; female 48.0 years.
Morbidity (notified cases of infectious disease per 100,000 population; 1984): enteritis and diarrhea 10,566; conjunctivitis 7,080; malaria 2,897; scarlet fever 2,476; measles 714.0; chicken pox 306.4.

National economy

Budget (1989). Revenue: UM 22,000,000,000 (tax revenue 59.1%, grants and loans 40.9%). Expenditures: UM 22,000,000,000 (rural development 37.0%, mining 20.0%, land development 18.0%, industrial development 8.5%).
Public debt (external, outstanding; 1987): U.S.$1,868,000,000.
Tourism: receipts from visitors (1986) U.S.$7,000,000; expenditures by nationals abroad (1983) U.S.$22,000,000.
Land use (1987): forested 14.6%; meadows and pastures 38.1%; agricultural and under permanent cultivation 0.2%; desert 47.1%.
Production (metric tons except as noted). Agriculture, forestry, fishing (1988): millet 89,000, pulses 28,000, rice 15,000, vegetables (including melons) 15,000, dates 13,000, corn (maize) 8,000, roots and tubers 6,000 (of which sweet potatoes 2,000, peanuts [groundnuts] 2,000); livestock (number of live animals) 4,100,000 sheep, 3,200,000 goats, 1,250,000 cattle, 810,000 camels, 166,000 horses and asses, 4,000,000 chickens; roundwood (1987) 12,000 cu m; fish catch (1987) 99,300. Mining and quarrying (1987): iron ore (gross weight) 9,108,000; gypsum 19,422. Manufacturing (1988): milk 96,000; meat 41,000, of which fresh beef and veal 19,000, fresh mutton and lamb 6,000, goat meat 5,000; hides and skins 4,308; cheese 1,754; butter 647. Construction (1984): 42,478 sq m. Energy production (consumption): electricity (kW-hr; 1987) 120,000,000 (120,000,000); coal (metric tons; 1987) none (6,000); crude petroleum, none (n.a.); petroleum products (metric tons; 1987) 832,000 (938,000); natural gas, none (n.a.).
Gross national product (at current market prices; 1987): U.S.$816,000,000 (U.S.$440 per capita).

Structure of gross domestic product and labour force

	1986[3] in value UM '000,000	1986[3] % of total value	1985 labour force	1985 % of labour force
Agriculture	13,001	35.3	389,000	66.0
Mining	5,402	14.7		
Manufacturing	1,475	4.0	59,000	10.0
Public utilities	2,575	7.0		
Construction				
Transportation and communications	3,273	8.9		
Trade and finance	6,618	17.9	142,000	24.0
Services				
Pub. admin., defense	4,518	12.2		
Other (indirect taxes net of subsidies)	—	—	—	—
TOTAL	36,862	100.0	590,000	100.0

Population economically active (1985): total 590,000; activity rate of total population 31.2% (participation rates: ages 15–64, 55.7%; female 21.0%; unemployed [1988] 50.0%).

Price and earnings indexes (1985 = 100)

	1983	1984	1985	1986	1987	1988	1989[4]
Consumer price index	82.1	88.0	100.0	107.8	116.2	117.8	130.1
Earnings index	...	...	...	...	...	...	...

Household income and expenditure. Average household size (1980) 5.0; income per household: n.a.; sources of income: n.a.; expenditure[5] (1983): food and beverages 61.0%; housing 24.0%; clothing and footwear 5.2%.

Foreign trade

Balance of trade (current prices)

	1981	1982	1983	1984	1985	1986
UM '000,000	+1,178	−530	+4,969	+7,877	+13,129	+11,581
% of total	4.9%	2.1%	18.4%	27.0%	29.4%	29.2%

Imports (1986): UM 14,009,000,000 ([1983] food 22.9%, crude petroleum and petroleum products 18.7%, machinery 9.1%, consumer goods 7.9%, transport 2.6%). *Major import sources* (1987): France 34.5%; Algeria 15.3%; Spain 12.1%; West Germany 8.3%; China 6.3%; United States 3.4%; The Netherlands 3.3%; Italy 2.7%; Senegal 2.3%; Côte d'Ivoire 1.8%; Japan 1.5%; Thailand 1.1%; United Kingdom 0.9%; Sweden 0.8%; India 0.5%.
Exports (1986): UM 25,950,000,000 (fish 59.2%, iron ore 40.8%). *Major export destinations* (1987): Japan 31.3%; Italy 14.4%; France 12.5%; Belgium 10.9%; Spain 6.1%; Romania 4.1%; United Kingdom 3.8%; Côte d'Ivoire 3.5%; Algeria 2.1%; West Germany 1.9%; Cameroon 1.8%; United States 1.4%; Portugal 1.1%; Senegal 0.6%.

Transport and communications

Transport. Railroads (1988): route length 429 mi, 690 km; passenger-mi 4,350,000[6], passenger-km 7,000,000[6]; short ton-mi cargo 4,207,000,000[6], metric ton-km cargo 6,142,000,000[6]. Roads (1988): total length 5,064 mi, 8,150 km (paved 17%). Vehicles (1985): passenger cars 15,017; trucks and buses 2,188. Merchant marine (1988): vessels (100 gross tons and over) 112; total deadweight tonnage 19,617. Air transport[7] (1988): passenger-mi 129,597,000, passenger-km 208,567,000; short ton-mi cargo 24,126,000, metric ton-km cargo 35,223,000; airports (1989) with scheduled flights 12.
Communications. Daily newspapers (1988): total number 1; total circulation, n.a. Radio (1988): total number of receivers 233,196 (1 per 8.1 persons). Television (1988): total number of receivers 1,100 (1 per 1,722 persons). Telephones (1985): 5,200 (1 per 337 persons).

Education and health

Education (1986)

	schools	teachers	students	student/ teacher ratio
Primary (age 6–11)	947	3,023	150,605	49.8
Secondary (age 12–17)	44	1,501	35,129	23.4
Voc., teacher tr.	6	186	2,808	15.1
Higher	7	250	4,830	19.3

Educational attainment, n.a. *Literacy* (1985): total population age 15 and over literate 28.0%; males literate 38.0%; females literate 17.0%.
Health (1984): physicians 170 (1 per 9,547 persons); hospital beds 1,325 (1 per 1,225 persons); infant mortality rate per 1,000 live births (1985–90) 127.
Food (1984–86): daily per capita caloric intake 2,283 (vegetable products 68%, animal products 32%); 99% of FAO recommended minimum requirement.

Military

Total active duty personnel (1989): 11,000 (army 94.5%, navy 3.2%, air force 2.3%). *Military expenditure as percent of GNP* (1987): 4.2% (world 5.4%); per capita expenditure U.S.$20.

---

[1]January 1. [2]1977. [3]At constant 1982 prices. [4]April. [5]Nouakchott only. [6]1984. [7]Includes part of Air Afrique traffic.

Mauritius

Official name: Mauritius.
Form of government: constitutional
  monarchy with one legislative house
  (Legislative Assembly [70[1]]).
Chief of state: British Monarch
  represented by governor-general.
Head of government: Prime Minister.
Capital: Port Louis.
Official language: English.
Official religion: none.
Monetary unit: 1 Mauritian Rupee
  (Mau Re; plural Mau Rs) = 100
  cents; valuation (Oct. 2, 1989) 1
  U.S.$ = Mau Rs 15.53; 1 £ = Mau
  Rs 25.13.

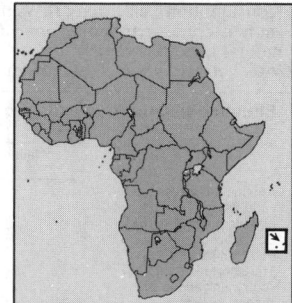

Area and population	area		population
Islands			1988
Districts	sq mi	sq km	estimate[2]
Mauritius	720	1,865	1,019,624
Black River	100	259	40,124
Flacq	115	298	115,842
Grand Port	100	260	98,915
Moka	89	231	65,021
Pamplemousses	69	179	96,834
Plaines Wilhems	78	203	314,111
Port Louis	17	43	139,038
Rivière du Rempart	57	148	87,050
Savanne	95	245	62,689
Rodrigues	40	104	36,743
Agalega | Saint Brandon ∫	27	71	500
TOTAL	788[3]	2,040[3]	1,056,867

Demography

Population (1989): 1,061,000.
Density (1989): persons per sq mi 1,346.4, persons per sq km 520.1.
Urban–rural (1988)[4]: urban 41.2%; rural 58.8%.
Sex distribution (1988): male 50.09%; female 49.91%.
Age breakdown (1987)[4]: under 15, 30.6%; 15–29, 30.3%; 30–44, 20.8%; 45–
  59, 10.6%; 60–74, 6.3%; 75 and over, 1.4%.
Population projection: (2000) 1,177,000; (2010) 1,294,000.
Doubling time: 60 years.
Ethnolinguistic composition (1983): Creole 55.5%; Indian 39.6%; European
  3.8%; Chinese 0.6%; other 0.5%.
Religious affiliation (1983)[4]: Hindu 52.5%; Roman Catholic 25.7%; Muslim
  12.9%; Protestant 4.4%; Buddhist 0.4%; other 4.1%.
Major cities (1988): Port Louis 139,038; Beau Bassin–Rose Hill 93,016;
  Curepipe 64,687; Quatre Bornes 64,668; Vacoas–Phoenix 55,464.

Vital statistics

Birth rate per 1,000 population (1987): 18.2 (world avg. 27.1); (1985) legiti-
  mate 72.8%, illegitimate 27.2%.
Death rate per 1,000 population (1987): 6.6 (world avg. 9.9).
Natural increase rate per 1,000 population (1987): 11.6 (world avg. 17.2).
Total fertility rate (avg. births per childbearing woman; 1986)[4]: 1.9.
Marriage rate per 1,000 population (1987)[4]: 10.8.
Divorce rate per 1,000 population (1986)[4]: 0.6.
Life expectancy at birth (1982–84): male 64.4 years; female 71.2 years.
Major causes of death per 100,000 population (1987): diseases of the cir-
  culatory system 289.7; diseases of the respiratory system 54.4; malignant
  neoplasms (cancers) 53.8; injuries and poisonings 48.6.

National economy

Budget (1987–88). Revenue: Mau Rs 6,120,000,000 (tax revenue 72.8%, of
  which import and stamp duties 43.8%, export duties 9.9%; income tax
  11.2%). Expenditures: Mau Rs 5,745,000,000 (public debt service 40.7%;
  social services 29.5%, of which education, art and culture 12.5%, social
  security 8.7%, health 7.3%).
Tourism (1987): receipts from visitors U.S.$138,000,000; expenditures by
  nationals abroad U.S.$51,000,000.
Land use (1986): forested 31.2%; meadows and pastures 3.8%; agricultural
  and under permanent cultivation 51.5%; other 7.5%.
Gross national product (at current market prices; 1987): U.S.$1,524,000,000
  (U.S.$1,470 per capita).

Structure of gross domestic product and labour force				
	1988			
	in value Mau Rs '000,000[5]	% of total value	labour force[6]	% of labour force
Agriculture	2,852	13.6	44,800	17.1
Mining	27	0.1	200	0.1
Manufacturing	5,533	26.3	104,600	40.0
Construction	1,080	5.1	9,000	3.5
Public utilities	510	2.4	3,600	1.4
Transportation and communications	2,280	10.8	10,500	4.0
Trade	3,120	14.8	12,700	4.9
Finance	2,648	12.6	...	...
Pub. admin., defense	2,125	10.1 }	55,200	21.1
Services	890	4.2 }		
Other	...	...	20,700	7.9
TOTAL	21,065	100.0	261,300	100.0

Production (metric tons except as noted). Agriculture, forestry, fishing
  (1987): sugarcane 6,231,000, green tea 39,917, potatoes 15,535, bananas
  7,920, black tea 7,000, tomatoes 6,825, corn (maize) 3,865, cabbages 3,000,
  onions 2,000, peanuts (groundnuts) 2,000, tobacco 903; livestock (number of live animals) 95,000 goats, 38,000 cattle, 10,000 pigs, 7,000 sheep;
  roundwood 33,000 cu m; fish catch 18,004. Manufacturing (value added,
  Mau Rs '000,000; 1986): textiles, wearing apparel, and footwear 1,241; processed food (including sugar) 665; alcoholic, nonalcoholic beverages and
  tobacco 162; chemicals and chemical products 144; metal products 109.
  Construction (1987): residential 363,000 sq m; nonresidential 205,000 sq
  m. Energy production (consumption): electricity (kW-hr; 1986) 518,000,000
  (518,000,000); coal (metric tons; 1986) none (56,000); crude petroleum,
  none (none); petroleum products (metric tons; 1986) none (232,000); natural gas, none (none).
Public debt (external, outstanding; 1987): U.S.$545,000,000.
Population economically active (1987): total 426,400; activity rate of total
  population 42.9% (participation rates: ages 15–64, 69.8%; female 34.2%;
  unemployed 11.0%).

Price and earnings indexes (1985 = 100)							
	1982	1983	1984	1985	1986	1987	1988
Consumer price index	82.6	87.3	93.7	100.0	101.6	102.2	111.5
Monthly earnings index	83.1	91.6	97.8	100.0	101.9	105.87	...

Household income and expenditure. Average household size (1983)[4] 4.7;
  income per household (1979) Mau Rs 15,540 (U.S.$2,430); sources of
  income (1984): salaries and wages 53.1%, entrepreneurial income 32.4%,
  transfer payments 7.3%, interest and dividends 4.3%, other 2.9%; expenditure (1980–81)[8]: food, beverages, and tobacco 50.4, clothing and footwear
  10.5%, housing 10.4%, transportation 10.0%, energy 6.4%, health care 3.0%,
  other 9.3%.

Foreign trade[9]

Balance of trade (current prices)						
	1982	1983	1984	1985	1986	1987
Mau Rs '000,000	−330.0	−161.6	−482.8	−1,101.8	+310.5	−1,438.0
% of total	4.0%	1.8%	4.5%	7.3%	1.7%	6.2%

Imports (1987): Mau Rs 13,042,000,000 (manufactured goods classified
  chiefly by material 40.0%, machinery and transport equipment 22.1%, food
  11.3%, mineral fuels and lubricants 7.5%, chemicals 6.4%, inedible crude
  materials excluding fuels 3.1%, animal and vegetable oils and fats 1.1%).
  Major import sources: France 13.0%; Japan 9.8%; South Africa 8.5%; United
  Kingdom 8.1%; Hong Kong 6.3%; West Germany 5.6%; China 5.3%.
Exports (1987): Mau Rs 11,604,000,000 (clothing 48.1%, sugar 37.1%, watches
  and clocks 2.9%, processed diamonds and synthetic stones 1.6%, textile
  yarn and fabric 1.2%, fish and fish preparations 1.1%, tea 0.8%). *Major
  export destinations:* United Kingdom 35.0%; France 26.5%; United States
  14.6%; West Germany 7.8%; Italy 2.5%; Canada 2.4%; Réunion 2.3%.

Transport and communications

Transport. Railroads: none. Roads (1986): total length 1,108 mi, 1,783 km
  (paved 92%). Vehicles (1987): passenger cars 24,365; trucks and buses 6,178.
  Merchant marine (1988): vessels (100 gross tons and over) 33; total deadweight tonnage 223,422. Air transport (1987)[10]: passenger-mi 732,821,400,
  passenger-km 1,179,364,000; short ton-mi cargo 96,961,000, metric ton-km
  cargo 141,560,000; airports (avg. 1989) with scheduled flights 2.
Communications. Daily newspapers (1988): total number 8; total circulation
  90,000; circulation per 1,000 population 86. Radio (1988): 250,948 receivers
  (1 per 4.2 persons). Television (1988): 128,111 receivers (1 per 8.2 persons).
  Telephones (1987): 66,883[4] (1 per 15 persons).

Education and health

Education (1987)				
	schools	teachers	students	student/ teacher ratio
Primary (age 5–12)	277	6,504	144,130	22.2
Secondary (age 12–20)	127	3,683	71,059	19.3
Voc., teacher tr.[11]	7	69[12]	444	...
Higher[11]	2	184[12]	344	...

Educational attainment (1983). Percent of population age 25 and over having: no formal education 24.2%; incomplete primary 28.1%; primary 23.2%;
  incomplete secondary 13.1%; secondary 7.7%; higher 3.6%; other 0.1%.
Literacy (1983)[4]: total population age 15 and over literate 501,262 (81.8%);
  males literate 267,835 (89.0%); females literate 233,427 (74.8%).
Health (1987): physicians 801 (1 per 784 persons); hospital beds 2,857 (1 per
  364 persons); infant mortality rate per 1,000 live births 23.7.
Food (1987): daily per capita caloric intake 2,680 ([1984–86] vegetable
  products 89%, animal products 11%); (1984) 121% of FAO recommended
  minimum requirement.

Military

Total active duty personnel: none; however, a special 800-man police mobile unit ensures internal security. *Military expenditure as percent of GNP*
  (1987): 0.8% (world 5.4%); per capita expenditure U.S.$3.

[1]Includes 8 nonelective seats. [2]January 1. [3]Detail does not add to total given because of rounding. [4]Island of Mauritius only. [5]At factor cost. [6]Employed persons
in establishments employing 10 or more persons. [7]March. [8]Current weights of CPI
components; Island of Mauritius only. [9]Import figures are f.o.b. in balance of trade
and c.i.f. for commodities and trading partners. [10]Air Mauritius only. [11]1984. [12]1982.

Mayotte

Official name: Collectivité Territoriale de Mayotte (Territorial Collectivity of Mayotte).
Political status: overseas dependency of France[1] with one legislative house (General Council [17]).
Chief of state: President of France.
Head of government: Commissioner of the Republic (for France); President of the General Council (for Mayotte).
Capital: Dzaoudzi (Capital designate, Mamoudzou).
Official language: French.
Official religion: none.
Monetary unit: 1 French (metropolitan) franc (F) = 100 centimes; valuation (Oct. 2, 1989) 1 U.S.$ = F 6.36; 1 £ = F 10.29.

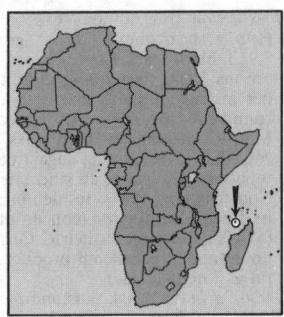

Area and population

Islands Communes	Capitals	area		population
		sq mi	sq km	1985 census
Grande Terre				
Acoua	Acoua	4.9	12.6	2,708
Bandraboua	Bandraboua	12.5	32.4	3,533
Bandrele	Bandrele	14.1	36.5	2,974
Boueni	Boueni	5.4	14.1	3,004
Chiconi	Chiconi	3.2	8.3	4,025
Chirongui	Chirongui	10.9	28.3	3,387
Dembeni	Dembeni	15.0	38.8	2,322
Kani-Keli	Kani-Keli	7.9	20.5	2,792
Koungou	Koungou	11.0	28.4	3,479
Mamoudzou	Mamoudzou	16.2	41.9	12,086
Mtsamboro	Mtsamboro	5.3	13.7	3,918
M'tsangamouji	M'tsangamouji	8.4	21.8	3,249
Ouangani	Ouangani	7.3	19.0	2,575
Sada	Sada	4.3	11.2	4,137
Tsingoni	Tsingoni	13.4	34.8	3,007
Petite Terre				
Dzaoudzi-Labattoir	Dzaoudzi	2.6	6.7	5,865
Pamandzi	Pamandzi	1.7	4.3	4,106
TOTAL		144.1	373.2[2]	67,167

Demography

Population (1989): 78,000.
Density (1989): persons per sq mi 541.3, persons per sq km 209.0.
Urban–rural (1985): urban 59.7%; rural 40.3%.
Sex distribution (1985): male 51.26%; female 48.74%.
Age breakdown (1985): under 15, 50.2%; 15–29, 24.7%; 30–44, 13.4%; 45–59, 6.9%; 60–74, 3.4%; 75 and over, 1.4%.
Population projection: (2000) 119,000; (2010) 175,000.
Doubling time: 20 years.
Ethnic composition (1985): Comorian (a mixture of Bantu, Arab, and Malagasy peoples) 96.9%; Europeans 2.5%; other 0.5%.
Religious affiliation (1985): Sunnī Muslim 96.9%; Christian, principally Roman Catholic, 3.0%; other 0.1%.
Major towns (1985): Mamoudzou 7,325; Dzaoudzi 5,425; Pamandzi 4,106; Sada 3,718; Chiconi 3,152.

Vital statistics

Birth rate per 1,000 population (1985): 42.3 (world avg. 27.1); (1978) legitimate (monogamous marriage) 70.8%, legitimate (polygamous marriage) 18.4%, illegitimate 10.8%.
Death rate per 1,000 population (1985): 6.2 (world avg. 9.9).
Natural increase rate per 1,000 population (1985): 36.1 (world avg. 17.2).
Total fertility rate (avg. births per childbearing woman; 1985): 6.7.
Marriage rate per 1,000 population: n.a.; *marital status of adult population* (1985): monogamous marriage 49.1%; unmarried 32.9%; polygamous marriage 10.3%; divorced 4.4%; widowed 3.3%.
Divorce rate per 1,000 population: n.a.
Life expectancy at birth (1987): male 53.0; female 57.0.
Morbidity (number of reported cases of infectious diseases; 1985): malaria 73; syphilis 63; gonorrhea 61; tuberculosis 14; typhoid 14; leprosy 12.

National economy

Budget (1989). Revenue: F 371,606,000 (subsidies 51.5%, indirect taxes 14.6%, returns on investments 11.5%, loans 6.7%, direct taxes 4.2%). Expenditures: F 371,606,000 (investments 56.9%, general administrative services 31.9%, debt service 1.5%).
Public debt: n.a.
Tourism (number of visitors; 1988): 3,030, of which tourists 2,100.
Production (metric tons except as noted). Agriculture, forestry, fishing (1988): rice 2,300[3], mangoes 1,500[4], bananas 1,300[4], citrus fruit 600[4], cassava 500[4], corn (maize) 173[3], ylang-ylang 25,900 kilograms[5], coffee 18,200 kilograms[5], coconut products 11,300 kilograms[5], vanilla 5,300 kilograms[5], pepper and pimento 1,093 kilograms[3, 5], cloves 1,050 kilograms[5, 6], cinnamon 750 kilograms[3, 5]; livestock (number of live animals) 30,000 goats, 4,000 cattle, 2,000 sheep; roundwood, n.a.; fish catch (1987) 1,200. Mining and quarrying: negligible. Manufacturing (1987): mostly involves processing of agricultural products for export. Construction (public works authorized in F '000; 1988): residential 55,000; nonresidential 129,700. Energy production

(consumption): electricity (kW-hr; 1988) 10,500,000 (9,300,000); coal, none (none); crude petroleum, none (none); petroleum products, none (n.a.); natural gas, none (none).
Gross national product (at current market prices): n.a.

Structure of gross domestic product and labour force

	1985			
	in value	% of total value	labour force	% of labour force
Agriculture, forestry, and fishing	...	...	12,285	55.0
Manufacturing	...	...	713	3.2
Construction	...	...	1,982	8.9
Public utilities	...	...	137	0.6
Transportation and communications	...	...	570	2.6
Trade	...	...	597	2.7
Finance, insurance, real estate	...	...	895	4.0
Pub. admin., defense, services	...	...	2,900	13.0
Other	...	...	2,251[7]	10.1
TOTAL	...	...	22,330	100.0[2]

Population economically active (1985): total 22,330; activity rate of total population 33.4% (participation rates: ages 15–64, 68.9%; female 40.1%; unemployed 8.8%).

Price and earnings indexes (1985 = 100[8])

	1982	1983	1984	1985	1986	1987	1988
Consumer price index[9]	82.3	88.1	93.1	100.0	102.8	103.7	105.0
Monthly earnings index[10]	75.3	83.0	92.3	100.0	115.6	121.0	131.5

Household income and expenditure. Average household size (1985) 5.1; income per household: n.a.; sources of income: n.a.; expenditure: n.a.
Land use (1987): agricultural and under permanent cultivation 29.0%; other 71.0%.

Foreign trade

Balance of trade (current prices)

	1983	1984	1985	1986	1987	1988
F '000,000	−140	−173	−185	−188	−233	−242
% of total	90.1%	89.6%	89.1%	85.5%	86.7%	69.5%

Imports (1988): F 294,981,000 (food products 22.0%; machinery and apparatus 20.7%; transport equipment 17.0%; metals and metal products 10.5%; chemical products 6.3%; wood and wood products 5.9%). *Major import sources:* France 65.8%; South Africa 9.1%; Thailand 4.3%; Singapore 3.2%.
Exports (1988): F 53,126,000 (reexports [including rice products, clothing, cigarettes, and chemical products] 80.8%; domestic exports 19.2%, of which ylang-ylang 15.4%, vanilla 3.4%, coffee 0.3%). *Major export destinations* (1987; domestic exports only)[11]: France 99.0%.

Transport and communications

Transport. Railroads: none. Roads (1984): total length 143 mi, 230 km (paved 49%). Vehicles (1984): 1,528. Merchant marine: n.a. Air transport (1988): passenger arrivals 15,566, passenger departures 15,068; cargo unloaded 447 metric tons, cargo loaded 219 metric tons; airports (1989) with scheduled flights 1.
Communications. Daily newspapers (1987): total number 1; total circulation, n.a. Radio (1986): total number of receivers 30,000 (1 per 2.3 persons). Television: total number of receivers, n.a.[12] Telephones: (1987)[13]: 1,573 (1 per 46 persons).

Education and health

Education (1986–87)

	schools	teachers	students	student/teacher ratio
Primary (age 6–11)	28	366	15,632	42.7
Secondary (age 12–18) Voc., teacher tr. }	2	65	1,392	21.4
Higher	—	—	—	—

Educational attainment (1985). Percent of population age 20 and over having: no formal education 77.3%; some primary 13.3%; lower secondary 5.7%; higher secondary 2.7%; postsecondary and higher 1.0%. *Literacy* (1985): total population age 15 and over literate 10,542 (31.8%).
Health: physicians (1980) 9 (1 per 5,797 persons); hospital beds (1982) 112 (1 per 514 persons); infant mortality rate per 1,000 live births (1984–85) 81.0.
Food: daily per capita caloric intake, n.a.

Military

Total active duty personnel (1985): 300 French troops.

---

[1]Final status of Mayotte is not yet determined; it is claimed by the Comoros as an integral part of that country. [2]Detail does not add to total given because of rounding. [3]1987. [4]1983. [5]Export production only. [6]1986. [7]Includes 1,966 unemployed. [8]All indexes are for December. [9]Limited to 17 (mostly food) items. [10]Skilled workers. [11]Most reexports are sent to the Comoros. [12]Television transmission began in 1986. [13]Number of subscribers.

Mexico

Official name: Estados Unidos
Mexicanos (United Mexican States).
Form of government: federal republic
with two legislative houses (Senate
[64]; Chamber of Deputies [500]).
Chief of state and head of government:
President.
Capital: Mexico City.
Official language: Spanish.
Official religion: none.
Monetary unit: 1 peso (Mex$) = 100
centavos; valuation (Oct. 2, 1989)
1 U.S.$ = Mex$2,598;
1 £ = Mex$4,204.

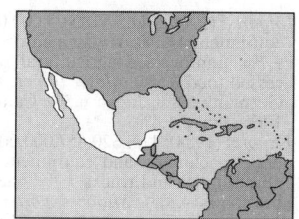

Area and population

States	Capitals	area sq mi	area sq km	population 1989 estimate
Aguascalientes	Aguascalientes	2,112	5,471	702,615
Baja California Norte	Mexicali	26,997	69,921	1,408,774
Baja California Sur	La Paz	28,369	73,475	327,389
Campeche	Campeche	19,619	50,812	613,133
Chiapas	Tuxtla Gutiérrez	28,653	74,211	2,559,463
Chihuahua	Chihuahua	94,571	244,938	2,253,975
Coahuila	Saltillo	57,908	149,982	1,937,209
Colima	Colima	2,004	5,191	426,225
Durango	Durango	47,560	123,181	1,402,782
Guanajuato	Guanajuato	11,773	30,491	3,593,210
Guerrero	Chilpancingo	24,819	64,281	2,604,947
Hidalgo	Pachuca	8,036	20,813	1,847,259
Jalisco	Guadalajara	31,211	80,836	5,269,826
México	Toluca	8,245	21,355	12,013,044
Michoacán	Morelia	23,138	59,928	3,424,235
Morelos	Cuernavaca	1,911	4,950	1,288,875
Nayarit	Tepic	10,417	26,979	857,359
Nuevo León	Monterrey	25,067	64,924	3,202,434
Oaxaca	Oaxaca	36,275	93,952	2,669,120
Puebla	Puebla	13,090	33,902	4,139,609
Querétaro	Querétaro	4,420	11,449	976,548
Quintana Roo	Chetumal	19,387	50,212	414,301
San Luis Potosí	San Luis Potosí	24,351	63,068	2,055,364
Sinaloa	Culiacán	22,521	58,328	2,425,006
Sonora	Hermosillo	70,291	182,052	1,828,390
Tabasco	Villahermosa	9,756	25,267	1,322,613
Tamaulipas	Ciudad Victoria	30,650	79,384	2,294,680
Tlaxcala	Tlaxcala	1,551	4,016	676,446
Veracruz	Jalapa	27,683	71,699	6,798,109
Yucatán	Mérida	14,827	38,402	1,327,298
Zacatecas	Zacatecas	28,283	73,252	1,259,407
Federal District				
Distrito Federal	—	571	1,479	10,355,347
TOTAL		756,066	1,958,201	84,274,992

Demography

Population (1989): 84,275,000.
Density (1989): persons per sq mi 111.5, persons per sq km 43.0.
Urban–rural (1987): urban 69.6%; rural 30.4%.
Sex distribution (1989): male 50.13%; female 49.87%.
Age breakdown (1989): under 15, 36.5%; 15–29, 31.5%; 30–44, 17.2%; 45–59, 9.1%; 60–74, 4.4%; 75 and over, 1.3%.
Population projection: (2000) 100,039,000; (2010) 116,663,000.
Doubling time: 26 years.
Ethnic composition (1981): mestizo 55.0%; Amerindian 29.0%; Caucasian 15.0%; black 0.5%; other 0.5%.
Religious affiliation (1980): Roman Catholic 92.6%; Protestant (including Evangelical) 3.3%; Jewish 0.1%; other 0.9%; none 3.1%.
Major cities (1980): Mexico City 8,831,079; Guadalajara 1,626,152; Ciudad Netzahualcóyotl 1,341,230; Monterrey 1,090,009; Puebla 835,759; León 593,002; Juárez 544,496; Tijuana 429,500; Mérida 400,142; Chihuahua 385,603.
Place of birth (1980): 98.4% native-born; 1.6% foreign-born and unknown.
Mobility (1970). Population living in the same state as in 1960: 87.2%; different state 12.8%.
Households. Total households (1983) 14,795,600; distribution by size (1980): 1 person 5.4%, 2 persons 10.2%, 3 persons 12.4%, 4 persons 14.3%, 5 persons 13.5%, 6 persons 11.7%, 7 or more persons 32.5%. Family households (1983): 13,996,700 (94.6%); nonfamily 798,900 (5.4%).
Immigration (1986): permanent immigrants admitted 63,054.
Emigration (1987): legal immigrants to the United States 72,351.

Vital statistics

Birth rate per 1,000 population (1987): 34.3 (world avg. 27.1); (1983) legitimate 72.5%, illegitimate 27.5%.
Death rate per 1,000 population (1987): 5.1 (world avg. 9.9).
Natural increase rate per 1,000 population (1987): 29.2 (world avg. 17.2).
Total fertility rate (avg. births per childbearing woman; 1988): 3.2.
Marriage rate per 1,000 population (1985): 7.1.
Divorce rate per 1,000 population (1984): 0.4.
Life expectancy at birth (1988): male 67.8 years; female 73.9 years.
Major causes of death per 100,000 population (1984): diseases of the circulatory system 95.7; accidents 79.8; diseases of the respiratory system 65.6; infectious and parasitic diseases 63.8; malignant neoplasms (cancers) and nonmalignant tumours 43.8; diseases of the digestive system 43.3; conditions originating in the perinatal period 30.7; ill-defined conditions 23.6.

Social indicators

Educational attainment (1980). Percent of population age 25 and over having: no primary education 38.0%; some primary 31.7%; completed primary 17.3%; some secondary 8.1%; some postsecondary 4.9%.

Distribution of income (1983)

percent of household income by quintile

1	2	3	4	5 (highest)
4.0	8.8	14.2	22.4	50.6

Quality of working life. Average workweek (1984): 45.8 hours. Annual rate (1986) per 100,000 insured workers for: temporary disability 9,077; indemnification for permanent injury 281; death 23. Labour stoppages (1988): 68, involving 4,750 workers. Average duration of journey to work: n.a. Method of transport: n.a. Rate per 1,000 workers of discouraged (unemployed no longer seeking work): n.a.
Access to services (1989). Proportion of dwellings having: electricity 85.4%; piped water supply 79.2%; drained sewage 60.0%.
Social participation. Eligible voters participating in national election (1988): c. 50%. Population participating in voluntary work: n.a. Trade union membership in total work force: n.a. Practicing religious population in total affiliated population (1970): weekly 10% of urban dwellers, 25% of rural dwellers; yearly 55% of urban dwellers, 73% of rural dwellers.
Social deviance (1986). Criminal cases tried by local authorities per 100,-000 population for: murder 7.4; rape 2.8; other assault 30.5; theft 28.4. Incidence per 100,000 in general population of: alcoholism, n.a.; drug and substance abuse, n.a.[1]; suicide 1.47[2].
Leisure (1984). Favourite leisure activities (average daily paid attendance): cinema 691,047; sporting events 18,825; live theatre 18,825; museums and archaeological sites 8,772; bullfights 2,175.
Material well-being (1985). Households possessing: radio 96%; television 73%; washing machine 33%; automobile 29%; telephone 27%; refrigerator 23%.

National economy

Gross national product (1987): U.S.$149,395,000,000 (U.S.$1,820 per capita).

Structure of gross domestic product and labour force

	1988 in value Mex$'000,000,000	1988 % of total value	1987 labour force	1987 % of labour force
Agriculture	35,905.5	9.0	7,060,500	25.8
Mining	15,442.8	3.9	636,600	2.3
Manufacturing	104,809.9	26.4	3,194,200	11.7
Construction	15,967.4	4.0	1,620,300	5.9
Public utilities	4,607.0	1.2	144,800	0.5
Transp. and commun.	30,052.5	7.6	847,000	3.1
Trade	108,778.1	27.4	2,166,800	7.9
Finance	28,355.8	7.1	511,000	1.9
Pub. admin., defense } Services	59,323.5	14.9	3,035,700	11.1
Other	−5,668.9[3]	−1.5[3]	8,107,100[4]	29.8[4]
TOTAL	397,573.6	100.0	27,324,000	100.0

Budget (1989). Revenue: Mex$81,787,500,000,000 (income taxes 31.7%, petroleum revenues 26.8%, value-added taxes 17.2%, import duties 6.9%, use taxes 5.9%, excise taxes 5.5%). Expenditures: Mex$207,806,200,000,000 (amortization and interest on public debt 70.1%, public education 6.4%, commercial and industrial development 1.9%).
Public debt (external, outstanding; 1987): U.S.$82,771,000,000.
Tourism (1987): receipts from visitors U.S.$3,497,000,000; expenditures by nationals abroad U.S.$2,361,000,000.

Manufacturing, mining, and construction enterprises (1985)

	no. of enterprises	no. of employees ('000)	yearly wages as a % of avg. of all wages[2]	annual income (Mex$'000,000)
Manufacturing	127,539	2,303.6	166.2	16,492,900
Food, beverages, and tobacco	46,260	476.2	130.0	4,281,300
Chemicals	4,476	264.8	...	2,777,800
Nonelectrical machinery and transport equipment	6,879	264.9	...	2,456,200
Textiles and apparel	15,753	399.9	122.8	1,462,700
Iron and steel	1,013	113.0	...	1,364,200
Electrical machinery	2,084	220.3	...	1,066,600
Nonmetallic mineral products	9,173	127.7	...	903,000
Paper and printing	6,750	118.7	...	871,100
Metal products	18,750	173.5	...	830,800
Wood and wood products	14,852	108.6	...	297,800
Other manufactures	1,549	36.0	...	181,400
Mining	466	59.5	198.2	374,700
Construction	4,648	336.4	131.8	1,449,100

Production (metric tons except as noted). Agriculture, forestry, fishing (1988): sugarcane 41,500,000, corn (maize) 11,800,000, sorghum 5,500,000, wheat 3,700,000, oranges 1,942,000, tomatoes 1,494,000, bananas 1,080,000, dry beans 1,075,000, coconuts 1,006,000, potatoes 960,000, mangoes 780,-000, lemons and limes 681,000, grapes 560,000, chilies and green peppers 560,000, apples 535,000, watermelons 470,000, barley 465,000, cottonseed 450,000, rice 420,000, soybeans 400,000, cantaloupes 370,000, pineapples 293,000, avocados 293,000, coffee 283,000, cucumbers 270,000, cotton lint 253,000, safflower seed 252,000, chick-peas 150,000, pumpkins 145,000; livestock (number of live animals) 31,200,000 cattle, 16,500,000 pigs, 10,-500,000 goats, 6,160,000 horses, 6,000,000 sheep, 3,183,000 asses, 3,130,000 mules, 224,000,000 chickens; roundwood (1987) 21,947,000 cu m; fish catch (1987) 1,419,168, of which sardines 477,076, anchovies 161,268. Mining and quarrying (metal content of ores; 1988): iron ore 5,599,310; zinc 288,150; copper 250,030; lead 175,650; manganese 150,400; silver 2,548; gold 8.09;

(nonmetals; 1988) salt 6,393,220; gypsum 2,457,810; sulfur 2,389,730; fluorite 723,590; phosphorite (phosphate rock) 670,950. Manufacturing (value added Mex$'000,000; 1986): machinery and transport equipment 952,700, of which transport equipment 396,600, electrical machinery 334,600; food and beverages 838,000; chemical products 538,200; printed and published materials 274,000; textiles 268,400; metal products 251,500; iron and steel products 228,400; paper and paper products 210,100; wearing apparel and footwear 151,000; rubber products 67,500. Construction (gross value of new construction, in Mex$'000,000; 1985): residential 154,835; nonresidential 168,096.

Trade and service enterprises (1985)

	no. of establish-ments	no. of employees	yearly wage as a % of avg. of all wages[2]	annual income (Mex$'000,000)
Trade	618,059	1,780,700	...	14,348,200
Wholesale	30,264	329,100	...	5,205,700
Retail	587,795	1,451,600	...	9,142,500
Boutiques (excluding food products)	223,601	600,200	...	3,022,900
Food and tobacco speciality stores	339,736	588,500	...	2,050,800
Automobile, tire, and auto parts dealers	16,768	104,400	...	1,737,600
Small supermarkets and grocery stores	4,512	96,400	...	1,227,300
Gasoline stations	2,395	23,900	...	708,700
Other	783	38,200	...	395,200
Services	341,436	1,401,500	85.2	3,476,900
Professional services	21,040	193,000	77.9	645,700
Food and beverages services	109,108	341,400	...	620,600
Transp. and travel agencies	3,058	41,000	133.4	353,400
Lodging	7,819	111,500	...	283,900
Automotive repair	55,850	148,500	...	209,800
Educational services (private)	8,227	124,200	134.3	166,000
Medical and social assistance	38,606	101,000	206.4	151,700
Amusement services (cinemas and theatres)	2,915	29,500	148.9	144,500
Recreation	8,323	41,000	...	139,500
Other repair	36,031	64,200	...	86,500
Commercial and professional organizations	3,209	41,900	77.9	67,400
Other	47,250	164,300	49.9	607,900

Energy production (consumption): electricity (kW-hr; 1987) 104,791,000,000 (102,866,000,000); coal (metric tons; 1987) 11,137,000 (10,528,000); crude petroleum (barrels; 1987) 919,979,000 (429,713,000); petroleum products (metric tons; 1987) 66,533,000 (65,530,000); natural gas (cu m; 1987) 22,-849,000,000 (22,895,000,000).
Population economically active (1987): total 27,324,000; activity rate of total population 33.7% (participation rates: ages 15–64, 57.2%[5]; female 27.8%[5]; unemployed 9.7%[2]).

Price and earnings indexes (1985 = 100)

	1982	1983	1984	1985	1986	1987	1988
Consumer price index	19.0	38.3	63.4	100.0	186.2	431.7	924.6
Daily earnings index	27.1	39.6	63.3	100.0	212.7	617.9	816.3

Household income and expenditure. Average household size (1986) 5.3; income per household (1983) Mex$442,000 (U.S.$3,680); sources of income (1983): wages and salaries 52.4%, property and entrepreneurship 23.6%, transfer payments 5.6%, other 18.4%; expenditure (1984): food, beverages, and tobacco 35.8%, housing (includes household furnishings) 20.2%, transportation and communications 12.4%, clothing and footwear 10.3%, recreation and entertainment 4.9%, health and medical services 5.0%.
Land use (1987): forested 23.1%; meadows and pastures 39.0%; agricultural and under permanent cultivation 12.9%; other 25.0%.

Financial aggregates[6]

	1984	1985	1986	1987	1988	1989 (9 mo.)
Exchange Rate, Mex$ per:						
U.S. Dollar	167.8	256.9	611.8	1,378.2	2,273.1	2,415.6
£	224.2	333.0	897.5	2,258.7	4,049.3	4,004.5
SDR	172.0	260.8	717.7	1,782.1	3,054.9	3,095.2
International reserves (U.S.$)						
Total (excl. gold; '000,000)	7,272	4,906	5,670	12,464	5,279	4,846[7]
SDRs ('000,000)	3	—	9	706	394	533
Reserve pos. in IMF ('000,000)	—	—	—	—	—	—
Foreign exchange	7,269	4,906	5,661	11,758	4,885	4,404[7]
Gold ('000,000 fine troy oz)	2.42	2.36	2.57	2.54	2.56	1.16[7]
% world reserves	0.26	0.25	0.27	0.27	0.27	0.12[7]
Interest and prices						
Treasury bill rate	49.47	63.36	88.57	103.07	61.95	51.51[8]
Balance of payments (U.S.$'000,000)						
Balance of visible trade,	+12,941	+8,451	+4,599	+8,433	+1,752	...
of which:						
Imports, f.o.b.	11,255	13,212	11,432	12,222	18,905	...
Exports, f.o.b.	24,196	21,663	16,031	20,655	20,657	...
Balance of invisibles	−8,747	−7,321	−6,272	−4,475	−4,657	...
Balance of payments, current account	+4,194	+1,130	−1,673	+3,968	−2,905	...

Foreign trade

Balance of trade (current prices)

	1983	1984	1985	1986	1987	1988
Mex$'000,000,000	+1,708.6	+2,162.2	+2,249.1	+3,178.3	+11,794.1	+4,635.0
% of total	48.1%	36.0%	24.6%	18.7%	25.6%	5.2%

Imports (1988): U.S.$18,905,000,000 (metallic products, machinery, and equipment 44.1%, of which automotive equipment 8.6%; chemical products 9.7%; unprocessed agricultural products 6.5%; iron and steel 5.5%; processed food 3.5%). *Major import sources* (1987): United States 64.4%; West Germany 6.8%; Japan 6.5%; Canada 2.9%; France 2.8%; United Kingdom 1.8%; Brazil 1.4%.
Exports (1988): U.S.$20,657,000,000 (crude petroleum 28.5%; metallic products, machinery, and equipment 25.7%, of which automobile parts 9.5%, automobiles and trucks 7.2%; chemical products 6.8%; processed food and beverages 4.8%). *Major export destinations* (1987): United States 64.5%; Japan 6.5%; France 2.8%; West Germany 1.6%; Canada 1.5%; United Kingdom 1.5%; Israel 1.1%.

Trade by commodity group (1985)

SITC group	imports U.S.$'000,000	%	exports U.S.$'000,000	%
00 Food and live animals	1,619	12.0	1,323	6.2
01 Beverages and tobacco	—	—	747	3.5
02 Crude materials, excluding fuels	209	1.6	514	2.4
03 Mineral fuels, lubricants, and related materials	1,341	10.0	15,281	71.7
04 Animal and vegetable oils, fats, and waxes	—	—	—	—
05 Chemicals and related products, n.e.s.	1,373	10.2	676	3.2
06 Basic manufactures	4,726	35.4	1,118	5.2
07 Machinery and transport equipment	1,404	10.5	1,564	7.3
08 Miscellaneous manufactured articles	2,581	19.2	91	0.4
09 Goods not classified by kind	151	1.1	6	0.1
TOTAL[9]	13,440	100.0	21,320	100.0

Direction of trade (1987)

	imports U.S.$'000,000	%	exports U.S.$'000,000	%
Western Hemisphere	8,626	70.5	15,365	74.4
United States	7,876	64.4	13,322	64.5
Latin America and the Caribbean	395	3.2	1,727	8.4
Canada	355	2.9	316	1.5
Europe	2,360	19.4	3,186	15.4
EEC	1,980	16.2	3,008	14.6
EFTA	346	2.8	113	0.5
U.S.S.R.	10	0.1	—	—
Other Europe	24	0.3	65	0.3
Asia	975	8.0	1,759	8.5
Japan	795	6.5	1,349	6.5
Africa	55	0.4	62	0.3
Other	207	1.7	284	1.4
TOTAL	12,223	100.0	20,656	100.0

Transport and communications

Transport. Railroads (1989): route length 16,341 mi, 26,299 km; passenger-mi 3,666,000,000, passenger-km 5,900,000,000; short ton-mi cargo 28,262,-000,000, metric ton-km cargo 41,700,000,000. Roads (1989): total length 146,290 mi, 235,431 km (paved[10] 45.2%). Vehicles (1985): passenger cars 5,195,273; trucks and buses 2,167,000. Merchant marine (1988): vessels (100 gross tons and over) 659; total deadweight tonnage 1,985,347. Air transport[11] (1988): passenger-mi 9,239,000,000, passenger-km 14,868,000,-000; short ton-mi cargo 85,654,000, metric ton-km cargo 125,052,000; airports (1989) 78.
Communications. Daily newspapers (1986): total number 392; total circulation 11,256,000; circulation per 1,000 population 142. Radio (1988): 16,-311,000 receivers (1 per 5.1 persons). Television (1988): 9,500,000 receivers (1 per 8.7 persons). Telephones (1989): 9,579,000 (1 per 8.8 persons).

Education and health

Education (1989–90)

	schools	teachers	students	student/teacher ratio
Primary (age 6–12)	82,137	471,033	14,675,300	31.2
Secondary (age 12–18)	19,098	234,600	4,400,400	18.8
Voc., teacher tr.	6,507	176,232	2,167,300	12.3
Higher	...	121,896	1,786,200	14.7

Literacy (1988): total population age 15 and over literate 49,318,000 (92.2%); males literate[12] 20,400,000 (92.3%); females literate[12] 20,400,000 (88.3%).
Health: physicians (1983) 74,640 (1 per 1,001 persons); hospital beds (1984) 72,000 (1 per 1,060 persons); infant mortality rate per 1,000 live births (1988) 46.6.
Food (1984–86): daily per capita caloric intake 3,148 (vegetable products 83%, animal products 17%); 135% of FAO recommended minimum.

Military

Total active duty personnel (1989): 141,500 (army 74.6%, navy 19.8%, air force 5.6%). *Military expenditure as percent of GNP* (1987): 0.5% (world 5.4%); per capita expenditure U.S.$9.

[1]Through 1982, cannabis remained the most abused drug. [2]1984. [3]Imputed bank service charge. [4]Includes 153,000 unemployed not previously employed and 7,954,100 not adequately defined. [5]1980. [6]Exchange rates and treasury bill rates are expressed in period averages; international reserves are expressed in end-of-period rates. [7]End of June. [8]Average of first six months. [9]Totals include adjustments of unspecified nature. [10]1986. [11]All scheduled traffic of Mexicana and AeroMexico airlines. [12]1985.

Micronesia, Federated States of

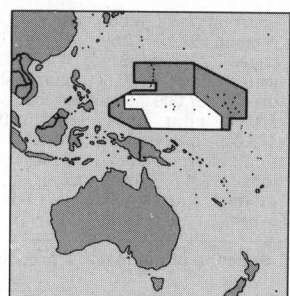

Official name: Federated States of Micronesia.
Political status: federal republic in free association with the United States with one legislative house (National Congress [14])[1].
Head of state and government: President.
Capital: Kolonia.
Official language: none.
Official religion: none.
Monetary unit: 1 U.S. dollar (U.S.$) = 100 cents; valuation (Oct. 2, 1989) 1£ = U.S.$1.62.

Area and population

States Major Islands	area sq mi	area sq km	population 1985 estimate
Kosrae	42.3	109.6	6,462
Kosrae Island	42.3	109.6	6,462
Pohnpei	133.3	345.2	27,871
Pohnpei Island	129.0	334.1	24,788
Truk	49.1	127.2	46,159
Moen Islands	7.0	18.1	14,218
Yap	45.9	118.9	10,948
Yap Island	38.7	100.2	6,951
TOTAL	270.8[2]	701.4[2]	91,440

Demography

Population (1989): 105,000.
Density (1989): persons per sq mi 387.7, persons per sq km 149.7.
Urban–rural (1980): urban 19.4%; rural 80.6%.
Sex distribution (1980): male 51.12%; female 48.88%.
Age breakdown (1980): under 15, 46.4%; 15–29, 26.8%; 30–44, 12.6%; 45–59, 8.5%; 60–74, 4.5%; 75 and over, 1.2%.
Population projection: (2000) 128,000; (2010) 146,000.
Doubling time: 26 years.
Ethnic composition (1980): Trukese 41.1%; Pohnpeian 25.9%; Mortlockese 8.3%; Kosraean 7.4%; Yapese 6.0%; Ulithian, or Woleaian, 4.0%; Pingelapese, or Mokilese, 1.2%; Western Trukese 1.0%; Palauan 0.4%; Filipino 0.2%; other 4.5%.
Religious affiliation: Christianity is the predominant religious tradition, with the Kosraeans, Pohnpeians, and Trukese being mostly Protestant and the Yapese mostly Roman Catholic.
Major cities (1980): Moen 10,351; Tol 6,705; Kolonia 6,306[3].

Vital statistics

Birth rate per 1,000 population (1985): 30.6 (world avg. 27.1); legitimate, n.a.; illegitimate, n.a.
Death rate per 1,000 population (1985)[4]: 3.6 (world avg. 9.9).
Natural increase rate per 1,000 population (1985): 27.0 (world avg. 17.2).
Total fertility rate (avg. births per childbearing woman; 1985)[5]: 5.3.
Marriage rate per 1,000 population: n.a.
Divorce rate per 1,000 population: n.a.
Life expectancy at birth (1985)[4]: male 64.0 years; female 68.1 years.
Major causes of death per 100,000 population (1985)[4]: diseases of the cerebrovascular system 85.7; major infectious diseases 39.6, of which intestinal diseases 14.3, septicemia 8.9; pneumonia, influenza, and tuberculosis 29.7; malignant and benign neoplasms (cancers) 23.1; homicides, suicides, and accidents 22.0.

National economy

Budget (1986). Revenue: U.S.$51,189,000 (U.S. Department of the Interior 75.7%, domestic taxes and other local revenue sources 19.5%, other U.S. government grants and federal program funds 4.8%). Expenditures: U.S. $13,208,000.
Public debt (external, outstanding): n.a.
Tourism (1986): number of visitors 6,538.
Production (metric tons except as noted). Agriculture, forestry, fishing (1987): n.a.; however, Micronesia's major crops include coconuts (from which more than 4,000 tons of copra is produced), breadfruit, cassava, sweet potatoes, and a variety of tropical fruits (including bananas); livestock comprises mostly pigs and poultry; fish catch, 3,634, of which skipjack tuna 600. Mining and quarrying: quarrying of sand and aggregate for local construction only. Manufacturing: n.a.; however, copra is the most important product, and the manufacture of handicrafts and personal items (clothing, mats, boats, etc.) by individuals is also important. Construction: n.a. Energy production (consumption): electricity[6] (kW-hr; 1987) 169,000,000 (169,000,000); coal, none (n.a.); crude petroleum, none (n.a.); petroleum products (metric tons; 1984) none (50,000[6]); natural gas, none (n.a.).
Household income and expenditure (1980). Average household size (1980) 7.0; average annual income per household, n.a.; sources of income (as percent of workers over age 16): wage and salary workers (private) 22.8%, wage and salary workers (government) 51.5%, self-employed persons 2.7%, primarily subsistence workers 5.7%; expenditure (1985): food and beverages 73.5%.
Land use (1984)[6]: forested 22.5%; meadows and pastures 13.5%; agricultural and under permanent cultivation 33.5%; other 30.5%.

Gross national product (at current market prices; 1988): U.S.$130,000,000 (U.S.$1,500 per capita).

Structure of gross domestic product and labour force

	1983 in value U.S.$'000,000	1983 % of total value	1980 labour force	1980 % of labour force
Agriculture and Fishing	44.9	42.2	197	2.0
Trade	12.7	11.9	864	8.8
Public administration	31.5	29.6	1,765	18.0
Manufacturing			115	1.2
Construction			945	9.6
Transportation, communications, and public utilities	17.4	16.3	472	4.8
Finance			121	1.2
Services			3,086	31.5
Other			2,233[7]	22.8[7]
TOTAL	106.5	100.0	9,798	100.0[2]

Population economically active (1982): total 9,798; activity rate of total population 13.4% (participation rates: over age 16, 26.1%; female 29.8%; unemployed 17.1%).
Price and earnings indexes: n.a.

Foreign trade

Balance of trade (current prices)

	1981	1982	1983	1984	1985	1986
U.S.$'000,000	...	...	−54.94	−35.1	−37.5	−41.9
% of total	...	...	88.4%	90.1%	89.9%	90.2%

Imports (1986): U.S.$44,199,000 (food, beverages, and tobacco 45.7%; manufactured goods 30.3%; machinery and transport equipment 14.2%; chemicals 8.2%). *Major import sources:* United States 41.2%; Japan 30.1%; South Pacific Region 16.0%; Australia 9.2%.
Exports (1986): U.S.$2,300,000 (primarily from copra, but black pepper, handicrafts, and a few marine products are also exported). *Major export destinations:* United States; Japan.

Transport and communications

Transport. Railroads: none. Roads (1987): total length 140 mi, 226 km (paved 17%). Vehicles: passenger cars, trucks, and buses, n.a. Merchant marine: n.a. Air transport: n.a.; airports (1989) with scheduled flights 4.
Communications. Daily newspapers (1985): there are no private newspapers. Radios (1988): total number of receivers 17,500 (1 per 5.8 persons). Television (1987): total number of receivers 1,125 (1 per 87 persons). Telephones: (1986): 1,556 (1 per 61 persons).

Education and health

Education (1983–84)

	schools	teachers	students	student/ teacher ratio
Elementary (age 6–13)	151	1,051	23,345	22.2
Secondary (age 12–18)	14	314	4,159	13.2
College[8]	...	...	920	...

Educational attainment (1980). Percent of population age 25 and over having: no formal schooling 24.8%; some primary education 38.2%; primary 11.7%; some secondary 7.7%; secondary 9.6%; higher 8.0%. *Literacy* (1980): total population age 15 and over literate 30,074 (76.7%); males literate 13,710 (67.0%); females literate 16,364 (87.2%).
Health (1985): physicians 36[9] (1 per 2,540 persons); hospital beds 325 (1 per 280 persons); infant mortality rate per 1,000 live births (1987) 23.3[4].
Food: daily per capita caloric intake, n.a.

Military

External security is provided by the United States.

[1]On Nov. 3, 1986, the United States unilaterally terminated the UN trusteeship it held over the Federated States of Micronesia, thus formally initiating their free-association political status. The United Nations Trusteeship Council has recognized the termination of the trusteeship, but the Security Council, which also participated in the creation of the trusteeship, has not. [2]Detail does not add to total given because of rounding. [3]1985. [4]Registered deaths only. [5]Includes other islands in geographic Micronesia. [6]Includes all areas formerly comprising the U.S. Trust Territory of the Pacific Islands. [7]Includes 1,673 unemployed. [8]In 1985, 1,200 students were enrolled in colleges and universities in the United States. [9]Excludes medical officers.

Mongolia

Official name: Bügd Nayramdah
Mongol Ard Uls (Mongolian People's
Republic).
Form of government: unitary
single-party republic with one
legislative house (People's Great
Khural [370]).
Chief of state: Chairman of
the Presidium of the People's
Great Khural.
Head of government: Premier.
Capital: Ulaanbaatar (Ulan Bator).
Official language: Khalkha Mongolian.
Official religion: none.
Monetary unit: 1 tugrik = 100 möngös;
valuation (Oct 2, 1989) 1 U.S.$ = 3.35
tugriks; 1 £ = 5.43 tugriks.

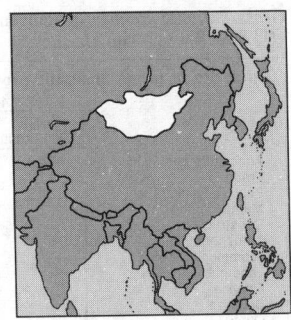

Area and population		area		population
		sq mi	sq km	1986 estimate
Provinces	**Capitals**			
Arhangay	Tsetserleg	21,000	55,000	85,800
Bayanhongor	Bayanhongor	45,000	116,000	87,900
Bayan-Ölgiy	Ölgiy	18,000	46,000	71,100
Bulgan	Bulgan	19,000	49,000	48,000
Dornod	Choybalsan	47,700	123,500	70,800
Dornogovi	Saynshand	43,000	111,000	49,600
Dundgovi	Mandalgov	30,000	78,000	45,400
Dzavhan	Uliastay	32,000	82,000	91,500
Govi-Altay	Altay	55,000	142,000	64,000
Hentiy	Öndörhaan	32,000	82,000	63,000
Hovd	Hovd	29,000	76,000	76,000
Hövsgöl	Mörön	39,000	101,000	99,900
Ömnögovi	Dalandzadgad	64,000	165,000	36,900
Övörhangay	Arvayheer	24,000	63,000	95,600
Selenge	Sühbaatar	16,000	42,000	81,500
Sühbaatar	Baruun-urt	32,000	82,000	49,300
Töv	Dzuunmod	31,000	81,000	94,700
Uvs	Ulaangom	27,000	69,000	84,100
Autonomous municipalities				
Darhan	—	100	200	74,000
Erdenet	—	300	800	45,400
Ulaanbaatar	—	800	2,000	500,200
TOTAL		604,800[1]	1,566,500	1,914,700

Demography

Population (1989): 2,096,000.
Density (1989): persons per sq mi 3.5, persons per sq km 1.3.
Urban–rural (1987): urban 52.0%; rural 48.0%.
Sex distribution (1987): male 50.05%; female 49.95%.
Age breakdown (1985): under 15, 42.7%; 15–29, 26.2%; 30–44, 16.1%; 45–59, 9.7%; 60–74, 4.4%; 75 and over, 0.9%.
Population projection: (2000) 2,778,000; (2010) 3,590,000.
Doubling time: 23 years.
Ethnic composition (1979): Khalkha Mongol 77.5%; Kazakh 5.3%; Dörbed Mongol 2.8%; Bayad 2.0%; Buryat Mongol 1.9%; Dariganga Mongol 1.5%; other 9.0%.
Religious affiliation: Although formal freedom of worship, or of propagandization against religion, exists, all traditional religious practice (lamaistic Buddhism, shamanism, Islam, and others) has been greatly reduced during the 20th century; reliable data on the current situation do not exist.
Major cities (1986): Ulaanbaatar (Ulan Bator) 528,000[2]; Darhan 74,000; Erdenet 45,400.

Vital statistics

Birth rate per 1,000 population (1988): 38.8 (world avg. 27.1); legitimate, n.a.; illegitimate, n.a.
Death rate per 1,000 population (1988): 7.9 (world avg. 9.9).
Natural increase rate per 1,000 population (1988): 30.9 (world avg. 17.2).
Total fertility rate (avg. births per childbearing woman; 1988): 5.4.
Marriage rate per 1,000 population (1987): 8.6.
Divorce rate per 1,000 population (1987): 0.5.
Life expectancy at birth (1988): male 61.7 years; female 65.8 years.
Major causes of death per 100,000 population: n.a.; however, major diseases include brucellosis, helminthiasis (an infection with worms), bacillary dysentery and amoebiasis, enteritis and other diarrheal diseases, cerebrospinal meningitis, trachoma, and tuberculosis of the respiratory system. Typhus, diphtheria, and acute poliomyelitis, formerly widespread, have reportedly been eliminated.

National economy

Budget (1989). Revenue: 6,970,000,000 tugriks (turnover tax 63.5%, deductions from profits 29.3%, social insurance contributions 3.5%, income tax 0.7%). Expenditures: 6,970,000,000 tugriks (economy 45.2%, social and cultural services 39.6%, defense 12.2%, administration and other 3.0%).
Public debt (1985): U.S.$4,396,000,000.
Tourism (1983): number of tourists 170,000; receipts from visitors, n.a.; expenditures by nationals abroad, n.a.
Production (metric tons except as noted). Agriculture, forestry, fishing (1988): wheat 672,000, potatoes 102,700, barley 100,000, vegetables 55,000, oats 50,000; livestock (number of live animals) 13,234,000 sheep, 4,388,000 goats, 2,526,000 cattle, 2,047,000 horses, 550,000 camels, 120,000 pigs; roundwood (1987) 2,390,000 cu m; fish catch (1987) 380. Mining and

quarrying (1985): fluorspar 787,000; copper 120,000. Manufacturing (1988): cement 502,100; flour 196,300; bread 70,000; meat 59,500; wool 10,400[3]; paper 1,200[3]; furniture 31,600,000 tugriks[3]; woolen cloth 2,200,000 sq m; leather shoes 3,500,000 pairs[3]; sheep and goat skins 2,840,000 sq m[3]; soft drinks 207,000 hectolitres; beer 50,400 hectolitres[3]; sheepskin coats 185,300,000 units; bricks 180,200,000 units. Construction (1987): residential 373,000 sq m; nonresidential 174,000 sq m. Energy production (consumption): electricity (kW-hr; 1987) 3,153,000,000 (3,223,000,000); coal (metric tons; 1987) 7,765,000 (7,224,000); crude petroleum, none (n.a.); petroleum products (metric tons; 1987) none (803,000); natural gas, none (n.a.).
Gross national product (1986): U.S.$3,620,000,000 (U.S.$1,820 per capita).

Structure of net material product and labour force				
	1987			
	value	% of total value	labour force	% of labour force
Agriculture	...	18.8	561,200	59.3
Mining and manufacturing	...	33.7	101,000	10.7
Construction	...⎱	6.7	30,700	3.2
Public utilities	...⎰		20,500	2.2
Transportation and communications	...	11.5	41,500	4.4
Trade	...	27.2	45,300	4.8
Services[4]	...	...	115,200	12.2
Other	...	2.1[5]	30,600	3.2
TOTAL	...	100.0	946,000	100.0

Population economically active (1987): total 946,000; activity rate of total population 47.5% (participation rates [1985] ages 15–64, 82.2%; female 45.5%; unemployed, n.a.).

Price and earnings indexes (1985 = 100)						
	1980	1981	1982	1983	1984	1985
Consumer price index	...	...	...	...	...	...
Monthly earnings index	95.4	...	...	...	96.8	100.0

Household income and expenditure. Average household size (1980) 5.0; income per household: n.a.; sources of income: n.a.; expenditure: n.a.
Land use (1987): forested 9.7%; meadows and pastures 78.8%; agricultural and under permanent cultivation 0.8%; other 10.7%.

Foreign trade

Balance of trade (current prices)						
	1982	1983	1984	1985	1986	1987
U.S.$'000,000	−220	−305	−230	−388	−452	−445
% of total	17.0%	20.7%	18.1%	22.7%	22.8%	22.5%

Imports (1987): U.S.$1,213,000,000 (machinery and equipment 32.2%; fuels, minerals, and metals 30.8%; consumer goods 18.4%; food products 10.4%; chemical products, fertilizers, and rubber 8.2%). *Major import sources:* U.S.S.R. and socialist countries 98.3%; capitalist countries 1.7%.
Exports (1987): U.S.$768,000,000 (raw materials and food products 40.2%; minerals and metals 39.5%; consumer goods 15.8%; chemicals and related products 4.5%). *Major export destinations:* U.S.S.R. and socialist countries 95.9%; capitalist countries 4.1%.

Transport and communications

Transport. Railroads (1987): length 1,128 mi, 1,815 km; passenger-mi 303,000,000, passenger-km 487,000,000; short ton-mi cargo 4,233,000,000, metric ton-km cargo 6,180,000,000. Roads (1987): total length 30,600 mi, 49,200 km (paved 2%). Vehicles: n.a. Merchant marine: vessels (100 gross tons and over) none. Air transport (1987): passenger-mi 229,000,000, passenger-km 368,000,000; short ton-mi cargo 5,548,000, metric ton-km cargo 8,100,000; airports (1989) with scheduled flights 1.
Communications. Daily newspapers (1987): total number 2; total circulation 179,000; circulation per 1,000 population 90.0. Radio (1987): total receivers 212,000 (1 per 9.4 persons). Television (1987): total receivers 111,000 (1 per 18 persons). Telephones (1987): 55,000 (1 per 36 persons).

Education and health

Education (1987–88)	schools	teachers	students	student/teacher ratio
Primary and secondary (age 8–18)	712	18,400	443,000	24.1
Voc., teacher tr.	28	1,300	22,200	17.1
Higher	8	1,500	22,600	15.1

Educational attainment (1979). Percent of population age 10 and over having: primary education 48.0%; some secondary 29.7%; complete secondary 9.5%; vocational secondary 7.0%; some higher and complete higher 5.8%.
Literacy (1980): total population age 15 and over literate 849,000 (89.5%); males literate 443,000 (93.4%); females literate 406,000 (85.5%).
Health (1987): physicians 5,000 (1 per 403 persons); hospital beds 22,600 (1 per 88 persons); infant mortality rate per 1,000 live births (1988) 65–75.
Food (1984–86): daily per capita caloric intake 2,830 (vegetable products 70%, animal products 30%); 116% of FAO recommended minimum requirement.

Military

Total active duty personnel (1989): 21,500 (army 97.7%; navy, none; air force 2.3%). *Military expenditure as percent of GNP,* n.a.; estimated foreign military assistance (1986) $600,000,000; per capita expenditure, n.a.

[1]Detail does not add to total given because of rounding. [2]1988. [3]1987. [4]Services includes finance, public administration, and defense. [5]Other material activities.

Morocco

Official name: al-Mamlakah al-Maghribīyah (Kingdom of Morocco).
Form of government: constitutional monarchy with one legislative house (House of Representatives [306[1]]).
Head of state and government: King.
Capital: Rabat.
Official language: Arabic.
Official religion: Islam.
Monetary unit: 1 Moroccan dirham (DH) = 100 Moroccan francs; valuation (Oct. 2, 1989) 1 U.S.$ = DH 8.46; 1 £ = DH 13.69.

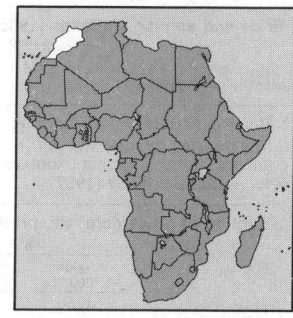

Area and population[2]		area		population
				1987
Provinces	Capitals	sq mi	sq km	estimate
Agadir	Agadir	2,282	5,910	700,000
Azilal	Azilal	3,880	10,050	412,000
Béni Mellal	Béni Mellal	2,732	7,075	812,000
Ben Slimane	Ben Slimane	1,066	2,760	193,000
Boulemane	Boulemane	5,558	14,395	145,000
Chaouen (Chefchaouen)	Chaouen (Chefchaouen)	1,680	4,350	343,000
Essaouira	Essaouira	2,446	6,335	421,000
Fès	Fès	2,085	5,400	933,000
Figuig	Figuig	21,618	55,990	108,000
Guelmim	Guelmim	11,100	28,750	150,000
al-Hoceima	al-Hoceima	1,371	3,550	347,000
Ifrane	Ifrane	1,278	3,310	111,000
el-Jadida	el-Jadida	2,317	6,000	863,000
el-Kelaa des Srarhna	el-Kelaa des Srarhna	3,888	10,070	644,000
Kénitra	Kénitra	1,832	4,745	833,000
Khémisset	Khémisset	3,207	8,305	447,000
Khénifra	Khénifra	4,757	12,320	411,000
Khouribga	Khouribga	1,641	4,250	501,000
Marrakech	Marrakech	5,697	14,755	1,425,000
Meknès	Meknès	1,542	3,995	704,000
Nador	Nador	2,367	6,130	704,000
Ouarzazate	Ouarzazate	16,043	41,550	603,000
Oujda	Oujda	7,992	20,700	895,000
er-Rachidia	er-Rachidia	23,006	59,585	472,000
Safi	Safi	2,813	7,285	793,000
Settat	Settat	3,764	9,750	757,000
Sidi Kacem	Sidi Kacem	1,568	4,060	569,000
Tangier	Tangier	461	1,195	509,000
Tan-Tan	Tan-Tan	6,678	17,295	54,000
Taounate	Taounate	2,156	5,585	581,000
Taroudannt	Taroudannt	6,355	16,460	621,000
Tata	Tata	10,010	25,925	107,000
Taza	Taza	5,799	15,020	679,000
Tétouan	Tétouan	2,326	6,025	800,000
Tiznit	Tiznit	2,687	6,960	353,000
Prefectures				
Ain Chok–Hay Hassani	—			375,000
Ain Sebaa–Hay Mohammadi	—			509,000
Ben Msik–Sidi Othmane	—	623	1,615	813,000
Casablanca–Anfa	—			1,019,000
Mohammadia–Znata	—			188,000
Rabat	—			610,000
Salé	—	492	1,275	513,000
Skhirate-Temara	—			164,000
TOTAL		177,117	458,730	23,191,000

Demography

Population (1989): 24,530,000[2].
Density (1989)[2]: persons per sq mi 138.5, persons per sq km 53.5.
Urban–rural (1987)[2]: urban 44.8%; rural 55.2%.
Sex distribution (1987)[3]: male 50.10%; female 49.90%.
Age breakdown (1987): under 15, 41.2%; 15–29, 28.6%; 30–44, 14.8%; 45–59, 9.4%; 60–74, 4.3%; 75 and over, 1.7%.
Population projection: (2000) 31,407,000; (2010) 36,973,000.
Doubling time: 27 years.
Ethnic composition (1983): Arab–Berber 99.5%; other 0.5%.
Religious affiliation (1982): Muslim (mostly Sunnī) 98.7%; Christian 1.1%.
Major cities (1982): Casablanca 2,139,204; Rabat 518,616; Fès 448,823.

Vital statistics

Birth rate per 1,000 population (1985–90): 35.3 (world avg. 27.1).
Death rate per 1,000 population (1985–90): 9.7 (world avg. 9.9).
Natural increase rate per 1,000 population (1985–90): 25.6 (world avg. 17.2).
Total fertility rate (avg. births per childbearing woman; 1985–90): 4.8.
Life expectancy at birth (1985–90): male 59.1 years; female 62.5 years.
Major causes of death (percentage of total deaths; 1985)[4]: circulatory diseases 16.1%; infectious and parasitic diseases 11.2%; accidents 9.6%; childhood diseases 8.1%; malignant neoplasms 4.8%.

National economy

Budget (1989). Revenue: DH 67,662,000,000 (indirect taxes 43.7%, direct taxes 29.4%, customs duties 21.8%). Expenditures: DH 74,627,000,000 (administration 46.0%, debt service 26.7%, investment 18.6%).
Public debt (external, outstanding; 1987): U.S.$18,468,000,000.
Tourism (1987): receipts U.S.$1,000,000,000; expenditures U.S.$100,000,000.
Production (metric tons except as noted). Agriculture, forestry, fishing (1987): sugar beets 2,750,000, wheat 2,427,000, barley 1,543,000, oranges 656,000, potatoes 560,000; livestock (number of live animals) 16,135,660 sheep, 5,806,900 goats, 3,177,540 cattle; roundwood 2,030,000 cu m; fish catch 491,000. Mining and quarrying (1987): phosphate rock 21,300,000;

iron ore 210,200; barite 143,500; salt 118,800; lead 105,100; fluorspar 78,500; manganese 42,500; copper 42,100. Manufacturing (1987): cement 3,982,000; wheat products 2,202,900; refined sugar 685,880; carpets 1,666,036 sq m; tires and tire tubes 1,622,508 units; pasteurized milk 2,737,510 hectolitres. Construction (value added in DH; 1987): 6,853,547,000. Energy production (consumption): electricity (kW-hr; 1987) 7,120,000,000 (7,120,000,000); coal (metric tons; 1987) 760,000 (1,570,000); crude petroleum (barrels; 1987) 182,400 (33,894,000); petroleum products (metric tons; 1987) 3,976,000 (4,177,000); natural gas (cu m; 1987) 86,107,000 (86,107,000).
Gross national product (1987): U.S.$14,213,000,000 (U.S.$620 per capita).

Structure of gross domestic product and labour force				
	1987		1982	
	in value DH '000,000	% of total value	labour force	% of labour force
Agriculture	23,991.6	16.5	2,351,629	39.2
Mining	4,812.3	3.3	63,360	1.1
Manufacturing	35,662.7	24.5	930,615	15.5
Construction	7,370.4	5.1	437,464	7.3
Public utilities	4,270.8	2.9	22,465	0.4
Transp. and commun.	10,352.9	7.1	140,981	2.3
Trade	24,448.0	16.8 }	498.130	8.3
Finance	4,808.0	3.3 }		
Pub. admin., defense	17,711.0	12.2	532,803	8.9
Services	16,658.0	11.4	474,109	7.9
Other	–4,533.0	–3.1	547,704[5]	9.1[5]
TOTAL	145,552.7	100.0	5,999,260	100.0

Population economically active (1982): total 5,999,260; activity rate 29.3% (participation rates: ages 15–64, 48.9%; female 19.7%; unemployed 10.7%).

Price and earnings indexes (1985 = 100)							
	1982	1983	1984	1985	1986	1987	1988
Consumer price index	77.7	82.6	92.8	100.0	108.7	111.7	114.3
Hourly earnings index	...	...	...	...	...	...	...

Household income and expenditure. Average household size (1982) 5.8; income per household: n.a.; sources of income: n.a.; expenditure (1972–73)[6]: food 54.0%, clothing 8.5%, housing 7.0%, transportation 6.9%.
Land use (1986): forested 11.6%; meadows and pastures 46.8%; agricultural and under permanent cultivation 19.0%; other 22.6%.

Foreign trade[7]

Balance of trade (current prices)						
	1983	1984	1985	1986	1987	1988
DH '000,000	–8,173	–12,190	–13,454	–9,201	–8,707	–6,035
% of total	22.2%	24.2%	23.6%	17.1%	15.7%	9.3%

Imports (1987): DH 35,270,700,000 (capital goods 20.9%; crude oil 15.1%; consumer goods 11.6%; food, beverages, and tobacco 11.3%; sulfur 5.9%). *Major import sources:* France 21.8%; U.S. 9.1%; Spain 8.8%.
Exports (1987): DH 23,390,000,000 (food, beverages, and tobacco 27.1%; phosphates 13.2%; phosphoric acid 15.3%; clothing 10.0%). *Major export destinations:* France 29.5%; Spain 6.8%; West Germany 6.2%; Italy 5.5%.

Transport and communications

Transport. Railroads (1987): route length 1,893 km; passenger-km 2,069,-000,000; metric ton-km cargo 4,725,000,000. Roads (1987): total length 59,171 km (paved 47%). Vehicles (1987): passenger cars 554,059; trucks and buses 255,149. Merchant marine (1988): vessels (100 gross tons and over) 335; total deadweight tonnage 593,015. Air transport (1987): passenger-km 2,218,181,000; metric ton-km cargo 50,931,000; airports (1989) 15.
Communications. Daily newspapers (1987): total number 11; total circulation 305,000[8]; circulation per 1,000 population 13[8]. Radio (1988): 4,395,059 receivers (1 per 5.4 persons). Television (1987): 1,206,000 receivers (1 per 19.2 persons). Telephones (1987): 342,740 (1 per 68 persons).

Education and health

Education (1987–88)	schools	teachers	students	student/ teacher ratio
Primary (age 7–12)	3,752	80,833[9]	2,182,348	26.0[9]
Secondary (age 13–17)	1,241	63,478[9]	1,348,670	20.2[9]
Vocational[10]	696	5,705	70,075	12.3
Higher	29	6,320	189,422	30.0

Educational attainment (1982). Percent of population age 25 and over having: no formal education 47.8%; some primary education 47.8%; some secondary 3.8%; higher 0.6%; not specified 2.3%. *Literacy* (1980): total population over age 15 literate 70.7%; males 82.4%; females literate 58.7%.
Health (1987): physicians 4,908 (1 per 4,725 persons); hospital beds 25,254[11] (1 per 918 persons); infant mortality rate (1985–90) 82.0.
Food (1984–86): daily per capita caloric intake 2,863 (vegetable products 93%, animal products 7%); (1984) 118% of FAO recommended minimum.

Military

Total active duty personnel (1989): 192,500 (army 88.3%, navy 3.4%, air force 8.3%). *Military expenditure as percent of GNP* (1987): 7.1% (world 5.4%); per capita expenditure U.S.$46.

[1]Includes 100 nonelected members. [2]Excludes Western Sahara. [3]Includes Western Sahara. [4]Urban population only. [5]Unemployed, not previously employed only. [6]Weights of consumer price index components. [7]Import figures are f.o.b. in balance of trade and c.i.f. in commodities and trading partners. [8]For 8 newspapers only. [9]Public schools only. [10]Public institutions only; excludes teacher training, which is conducted entirely at the third level. [11]Public only.

Mozambique

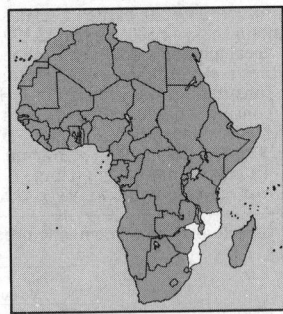

Official name: República Popular de Moçambique (People's Republic of Mozambique).
Form of government: single-party republic with a single legislative house (People's Assembly [249]).
Chief of state and head of government: President.
Capital: Maputo.
Official language: Portuguese.
Official religion: none.
Monetary unit: 1 metical (Mt., plural meticais) = 100 centavos; valuation (Oct. 2, 1989) 1 U.S.$ = Mt. 808.00; 1 £ = Mt. 1,307.00.

Area and population

| | | area[1] | | population |
Provinces	Capitals	sq mi	sq km	1989 estimate[2]
Cabo Delgado	Pemba	31,902	82,625	1,189,920
Gaza	Xai-Xai	29,231	75,709	1,221,841
Inhambane	Inhambane	26,492	68,615	1,254,379
Manica	Chimoio	23,807	61,661	800,704
Maputo	Maputo	9,944	25,756	583,926
Nampula	Nampula	31,508	81,606	3,027,916
Niassa	Lichinga	49,828	129,055	651,259
Sofala	Beira	26,262	68,018	1,337,723
Tete	Tete	38,890	100,724	1,052,175
Zambézia	Quelimane	40,544	105,008	3,137,229
City				
Maputo	—	232	602	1,069,727
TOTAL LAND AREA		308,642[3]	799,379	15,326,799
INLAND WATER		5,019	13,000	
TOTAL AREA		313,661[3]	812,379	

Demography

Population (1989): 15,293,000.
Density[4] (1989): persons per sq mi 50.4, persons per sq km 19.1.
Urban–rural (1980): urban 13.2%; rural 86.8%.
Sex distribution (1986): male 48.81%; female 51.19%.
Age breakdown (1980): under 15, 44.4%; 15–29, 26.7%; 30–44, 15.9%; 45–59, 8.7%; 60–74, 3.6%; 75 and over, 0.7%.
Population projection: (2000) 20,463,000; (2010) 26,131,000.
Doubling time: 26 years.
Ethnolinguistic composition (1983): Makua 47.3%; Tsonga 23.3%; Malawi 12.0%; Shona 11.3%; Yao 3.8%; Swahili 0.8%; Makonde 0.6%; Portuguese 0.2%; other 0.7%.
Religious affiliation (1980): traditional beliefs 47.8%; Christian 38.9%, of which Roman Catholic 31.4%; Muslim 13.0%; other 0.3%.
Major cities (1989): Maputo 1,069,727; Beira 291,604; Nampula 197,379.

Vital statistics

Birth rate per 1,000 population (1985–90): 45.0 (world avg. 27.1); (1974) legitimate 73.1%; illegitimate 26.9%.
Death rate per 1,000 population (1985–90): 18.5 (world avg. 9.9).
Natural increase rate per 1,000 population (1985–90): 26.5 (world avg. 17.2).
Total fertility rate (avg. births per childbearing woman; 1985–90): 6.4.
Marriage rate per 1,000 population (1974): 0.7.
Divorce rate per 1,000 population (1973): 0.01.
Life expectancy at birth (1985–90): male 44.9 years; female 48.1 years.
Major infectious diseases (certified cases per 100,000 population; 1980): measles 227.4; pulmonary tuberculosis 55.9; viral hepatitis 19.2; leprosy 13.8; cholera 4.6; tetanus 4.5.

National economy

Budget (1987). Revenue: Mt. 68,601,000,000 (1986; indirect taxes 42.8%, of which excise taxes 27.7%, customs taxes 7.3%; direct taxes 31.0%, of which corporate income tax 22.3%, individual income tax 8.2%; profits from state enterprises 10.8%). Expenditures: Mt. 84,795,000,000 (1986; education 16.8%, health 6.6%).
Production (metric tons except as noted). Agriculture, forestry, fishing (1988): cassava 3,370,000, sugarcane 570,000, coconut 420,000, corn (maize) 334,000, sorghum 131,000, bananas 82,000, peanuts (groundnuts) 65,000; livestock (number of live animals) 1,360,000 cattle, 375,000 goats, 119,000 pigs, 160,000 sheep, 21,000,000 chickens; roundwood (1987) 15,279,000 cu m; fish catch (1987) 36,117. Mining and quarrying (1985): marine salt 28,000; hydraulic lime 10,000; bauxite 5,037; bentonite 361; copper 118[5]; garnet 1,500 kg. Manufacturing (value added in '000 Mt.[6]; 1987): food products 13,088,600; processed fish products 12,436,300; textiles 10,471,-900; tobacco 8,479,900; machinery and transport equipment 6,992,100, of which electrical equipment 3,289,400; footwear and clothing 5,888,700; alcoholic beverages 3,689,000; chemical products 2,521,800. Construction (1974): residential 247,000 sq m; nonresidential 121,000. Energy production (consumption): electricity (kW-hr; 1987) 500,000,000 (830,000,000); coal (metric tons; 1987) 43,000 (63,000); crude petroleum (1987) none (none[7]); petroleum products (metric tons; 1987) none[7] (254,000); natural gas, none (none).
Population economically active (1980): total 5,671,290; activity rate of total population 48.6% (participation rates: over age 15, 87.3%; female 52.4%; unemployed 1.7%).

Price and earnings indexes (1985 = 100)

	1981	1982	1983	1984	1985	1986	1987
Consumer price index	39.1	46.0	59.4	77.4	100.0	138.7	365.2
Monthly earnings index	...	...	...	...	...	...	...

Public debt (external, outstanding; 1985)[8]: U.S.$1,224,000,000.
Household income and expenditure. Average household size (1980) 4.2; income per household: n.a.; sources of income: n.a.; expenditure: n.a.
Gross national product (1987): U.S.$2,135,000,000 (U.S.$150 per capita).

Structure of gross domestic product and labour force

| | 1986[6] | | 1980 | |
	in value Mt. '000,000	% of total value	labour force	% of labour force
Agriculture	25,000	44.5	4,754,831	83.8
Mining	} 14,800	26.3	73,425	1.3
Manufacturing			273,369	4.8
Construction	6,200	11.0	42,121	0.7
Public utilities	...	...	9	9
Transportation and communications	4,600	8.2	77,025	1.4
Trade and finance			112,244	2.0
Pub. admin., defense	} 5,600	10.0	} 243,449[9]	4.3[9]
Services				
Other			94,826[10]	1.7[10]
TOTAL	56,200	100.0	5,671,290	100.0

Tourism: n.a.
Land use (1987): forested 18.9%; meadows and pastures 56.1%; agricultural and under permanent cultivation 4.0%; other 21.0%.

Foreign trade

Balance of trade (current prices)

	1981	1982	1983	1984	1985	1986
Mt. '000,000	−18,392	−22,918	−20,286	−18,843	−18,989	−18,739
% of total	48.1%	57.0%	65.7%	70.6%	69.4%	74.6%

Imports (1987): U.S.$625,073,000[11] (foodstuffs 37.6%, capital equipment 18.9%, machinery and spare parts 14.7%, crude petroleum and derivatives 10.0%, chemicals 4.9%, metals 4.4%). *Major import sources:* Italy 13.6%; South Africa 12.1%; United States 10.1%; U.S.S.R. 8.8%; France 5.7%; Japan 5.5%.
Exports (1987): U.S.$97,025,000 (shrimps 38.7%, cashew nuts 32.0%, cotton 7.0%, sugar 3.1%, copra 3.0%, citrus fruit 2.6%, lobster 2.0%). *Major export destinations:* United States 16.6%; Japan 15.4%; East Germany 8.7%; Spain 7.0%; U.S.S.R. 6.2%.

Transport and communications

Transport. Railroads (1987): length (1986) 2,182 mi, 3,512 km; passenger-mi 64,995,000, passenger-km 104,600,000; short ton-mi cargo 170,483,000, metric ton-km cargo 248,900,000. Roads (1986): total length 16,215 mi, 26,095 km (paved 20%). Vehicles (1981): passenger cars 99,400; trucks and buses 24,700. Merchant marine (1988): vessels (100 gross tons and over) 106; total deadweight tonnage 27,810. Air transport (1988): passenger-mi 242,110,000, passenger-km 389,639,000; short ton-mi cargo 30,779,000, metric ton-km cargo 44,937,000; airports (1989) with scheduled flights 2.
Communications. Daily newspapers (1988): total number 2; total circulation 81,000; circulation per 1,000 population 5.4. Radio (1988): total number of receivers 479,361 (1 per 31 persons). Television (1988): total number of receivers 35,000 (1 per 425 persons). Telephones (1987): 62,615 (1 per 235 persons).

Education and health

Education (1987)

	schools	teachers	students	student/ teacher ratio
Primary (age 5–9)[12]	3,927	20,884	1,286,961	61.6
Secondary (age 10–16)	198	3,163	103,322	32.7
Voc., teacher tr.	30	852	9,066	10.6
Higher	3	354	1,862	5.3

Educational attainment (1980). Percent of population age 25 and over having: no formal schooling 80.7%; primary education 18.2%; secondary 0.9%; higher 0.2%. *Literacy* (1985): total population age 15 and over literate 1,270,389 (16.6%); males literate 743,101 (20.0%); females literate 527,288 (13.3%).
Health (1987): physicians 327 (1 per 44,392 persons); hospital beds 11,671 (1 per 1,244 persons); infant mortality rate per 1,000 live births (1985–90) 141.0.
Food (1984–86): daily per capita caloric intake 1,607 (vegetable products 96%, animal products 4%); 69% of FAO recommended minimum requirement.

Military

Total active duty personnel (1989): 65,000 (army 92.3%, navy 1.2%, air force 6.5%). *Military expenditure as percent of GNP* (1987): 8.4% (world 5.4%); per capita expenditure U.S.$7.

[1]Total area is shown for the provinces. [2]January 1. [3]Detail does not add to total given because of rounding. [4]Density is based on land area. [5]Metal content only. [6]At prices of 1980. [7]Internal disorder and a lack of foreign exchange have brought the production of refined petroleum products and importation of crude petroleum practically to a halt. [8]Includes external long-term private debt not guaranteed by the government. [9]Services includes public utilities. [10]Unemployed. [11]Imports figures are in f.o.b. in balance of trade and c.i.f. in commodities and trading partners. [12]Includes initiation classes in which pupils learn Portuguese.

Myanmar (Burma)

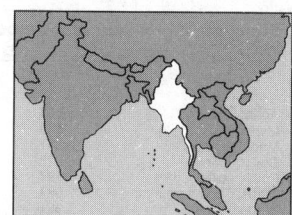

Official name: Pyeidaungzu Myanma Naingngandaw (Union of Myanmar).
Form of government: military regime[1].
Head of state and government:
Chairman of the State Law and Order Restoration Council.
Capital: Yangon (Rangoon).
Official language: Burmese.
Official religion: none.
Monetary unit: 1 Myanmar kyat (K) = 100 pyas; valuation (Oct. 2, 1989) 1 U.S.$ = K 6.66; 1 £ = K 10.78.

Area and population

Divisions	Capitals	area sq mi	area sq km	population 1983 census
Irrawaddy (Ayeyarwady)	Bassein (Pathein)	13,567	35,138	4,994,061
Magwe (Magway)	Magwe (Magway)	17,305	44,820	3,243,166
Mandalay	Mandalay	14,295	37,024	4,577,762
Pegu (Bago)	Pegu (Bago)	15,214	39,404	3,799,791
Sagaing	Sagaing	36,535	94,625	3,862,172
Tenasserim (Tanintharyi)	Tavoy (Dawei)	16,735	43,343	917,247
Yangon	Yangon (Rangoon)	3,927	10,171	3,965,916
States				
Chin	Hakha	13,907	36,019	368,949
Kachin	Myitkyinā	34,379	89,041	904,794
Karen	Pa-an (Hpa-an)	11,731	30,383	1,055,359
Kayah	Loi-kaw	4,530	11,733	168,429
Mon	Moulmein (Mawlamyine)	4,748	12,297	1,680,157
Rakhine (Arakan)	Sittwe (Akyab)	14,200	36,778	2,045,559
Shan	Taunggyi	60,155	155,801	3,716,841
TOTAL		261,228	676,577	35,307,913[2]

Demography

Population (1989): 40,810,000.
Density (1988): persons per sq mi 156.2, persons per sq km 60.3.
Urban–rural (1985): urban 23.9%; rural 76.1%.
Sex distribution (1987–88): male 49.59%; female 50.41%.
Age breakdown (1985): under 15, 41.2%; 15–29, 27.2%; 30–44, 15.3%; 45–59, 10.3%; 60–74, 5.0%; 75 and over, 1.0%.
Population projection: (2000) 51,129,000; (2010) 60,567,000.
Doubling time: 33 years.
Ethnic composition (1983): Burman 69.0%; Shan 8.5%; Karen 6.2%; Rakhine 4.5%; Mon 2.4%; Chin 2.2%; Kachin 1.4%; other 5.8%.
Religious affiliation (1983): Buddhist 89.4%; Christian 4.9%; Muslim 3.8%; tribal religions 1.1%; Hindu 0.5%; other 0.3%.
Major cities (1983): Yangon (Rangoon) 2,458,712; Mandalay 532,895; Moulmein (Mawlamyine) 219,991; Pegu (Bago) 150,447; Bassein (Pathein) 144,092.

Vital statistics

Birth rate per 1,000 population (1988): 30.5 (world avg. 27.1).
Death rate per 1,000 population (1988): 9.6 (world avg. 9.9).
Natural increase rate per 1,000 population (1988): 20.9 (world avg. 17.2).
Total fertility rate (avg. births per childbearing woman; 1988): 4.0.
Marriage rate per 1,000 population, n.a.
Divorce rate per 1,000 population, n.a.
Life expectancy at birth (1988): male 58.6 years; female 62.1 years.
Major causes of death per 100,000 population (1978): pneumonia 16.1; heart diseases 10.5; enteritis and other diarrheal diseases 10.0; tuberculosis 9.4; malignant neoplasms (cancers) 6.5; cerebrovascular disease 4.1; malaria 3.5.

National economy

Budget (1988–89). Revenue: K 7,331,400,000 (commodities and services tax 34.0%, receipts from state economic enterprises 24.6%, customs duties 13.6%, taxes on income and property 6.3%, taxes on the use of state properties 6.1%, interest income 3.8%). Expenditures: K 6,461,800,000 (manufacturing 19.8%, transport and communications 17.0%, agriculture 16.9%, mining 13.7%, power 10.9%, administration 7.0%, social services 6.6%).
Tourism (1987): receipts from visitors U.S.$14,000,000; expenditures by nationals abroad U.S.$1,000,000.
Land use (1987): forested 49.3%; meadows and pastures 0.6%; agricultural and under permanent cultivation 15.3%; other 34.8%.
Production (metric tons except as noted). Agriculture, forestry, fishing (1988): rice 14,000,000, sugarcane 3,072,000, pulses 732,000, peanuts (groundnuts) 559,000, corn (maize) 300,000, millet 250,000, wheat 241,000, plantains 220,000, onions 192,000, sesame seeds 190,000, potatoes 133,000, cassava 90,000, seed cotton 82,000, tobacco leaves 56,000, garlic 42,000, jute 41,-000; livestock (number of live animals) 10,000,000 cattle, 3,000,000 pigs, 2,200,000 buffalo, 1,395,000 sheep and goats, 6,000,000 ducks, 34,000,000 chickens; roundwood (1987) 19,427,000 cu m; fish catch (1987) 685,858, of which marine fishing areas 540,873. Mining and quarrying (1987–88): copper concentrates 50,800; gypsum 22,700; barites 17,000; jade 13,500; zinc concentrates 10,160; refined lead 6,000; tin concentrates 868; tungsten concentrates 496; refined silver 450,000 troy oz. Manufacturing (value of production in '000,000 kyats; 1987–88): food and beverages 23,549.8; clothing and wearing apparel 1,606.6; industrial raw materials 1,468.9; construction materials 1,120.9; transport vehicles 719.0; personal goods 327.8. Construction[3] (units; 1987–88): residential 1,193; nonresidential 1,483. Energy production (consumption): electricity (kW-hr; 1987–88) 2,279,000,000 (1,664,000,000); coal (metric tons; 1987) 81,000 (202,000); crude petroleum

(barrels; 1987) 7,141,000 (7,141,000); petroleum products (metric tons; 1987) 614,000 (614,000); natural gas (cu m; 1987) 1,136,400,000 (1,136,400,000).
Gross national product (1986): U.S.$7,450,000,000 (U.S.$200 per capita).

Structure of gross domestic product and labour force

	1987–88 in value K '000,000	% of total value	labour force	% of labour force
Agriculture	30,668.6	50.5	10,289,000	65.1
Mining	532.7	0.9	91,000	0.6
Manufacturing	5,597.2	9.2	1,369,000	8.7
Construction	977.2	1.6	265,000	1.7
Public utilities	281.6	0.5	20,000	0.1
Transp. and commun.	2,438.7	4.0	518,000	3.3
Trade	13,468.6	22.2	1,556,000	9.8
Finance	1,499.3	2.5	} 1,047,000	6.6
Public admin., services	5,196.4	8.6		
Other	...	...	658,000	4.1
TOTAL	60,660.3	100.0	15,813,000	100.0

Public debt (external, outstanding; 1987): U.S.$4,257,000,000.
Population economically active (1987–88): total 15,813,000; activity rate of total population 41.0% (participation rates [1983]: ages 15–64, 64.2%; female 35.3%; unemployed 4.3%).

Price and earnings indexes (1985 = 100)

	1983	1984	1985	1986	1987	1988	1989[4]
Consumer price index	89.3	93.6	100.0	109.3	136.4	158.3	207.8
Monthly earnings index[5]	111.7	108.5	...	...	...	...	...

Household income and expenditure. Average household size (1983) 5.2; average annual income per household: n.a.; sources of income: n.a.; expenditure (1978)[6]: food and beverages 64.4%, clothing and footwear 8.0%, fuel and light 7.8%, household rent and repairs 3.8%, tobacco 3.7%, other 12.3%.

Foreign trade[7]

Balance of trade (current prices)

	1983	1984	1985	1986	1987	1988
K '000,000	+1,084.1	+1,338.1	+393.2	+160.0	−173.5	−346.8
% of total	21.7%	26.7%	8.3%	3.8%	5.6%	14.2%

Imports (1987–88): K 3,936,100,000 (industrial raw materials 45.8%, machinery and equipment 37.7%, construction materials 14.8%, tools and spare parts 13.1%, transport equipment 8.5%, consumer goods 5.9%). Major import sources: Japan 50.4%; EEC 19.5%; Southeast Asian countries 8.0%; eastern European countries 6.8%; China 2.4%.
Exports (1987–88): K 2,528,200,000 (forest products 43.2%, agricultural products 31.8%, minerals and gems 11.2%, animal and marine products 5.0%). Major export destinations: Southeast Asian countries 29.6%; EEC 12.4%; Japan 10.6%; India 6.8%; African countries 5.7%; China 4.8%.

Transport and communications

Transport. Railroads (1987): route length 1,949 mi, 3,137 km; passenger-mi 2,707,000,000, passenger-km 4,356,000,000; short ton-mi cargo 378,000,000, metric ton-mi cargo 552,000,000. Roads (1985–86): total length 14,416 mi, 23,200 km (paved 17%). Vehicles (1985): passenger cars 35,000; trucks and buses 50,000. Merchant marine (1988): vessels (100 gross tons and over) 120; total deadweight tonnage 412,508. Air transport (1987–88): passenger-mi 133,270,000, passenger-km 214,471,000; short ton-mi cargo 1,470,000, metric ton-km cargo 2,146,000; airports (1989) with scheduled flights 21.
Communications. Daily newspapers (1987): total number 6; total circulation 533,000; circulation per 1,000 population 14. Radio (1985): total receivers 3,173,517 (1 per 13 persons). Television (1988): total receivers 67,500 (1 per 592 persons). Telephones (1987–88): 61,872 (1 per 624 persons).

Education and health

Education (1987–88)

	schools	teachers	students	student/ teacher ratio
Primary (age 5–9)	31,499	188,417	5,369,641	28.5
Secondary (age 10–15)	2,429	61,556	1,591,927	25.9
Voc., teacher tr.	146	1,536	17,000	11.1
Higher	35	7,191	255,866	35.6

Educational attainment (1983). Percent of population age 25 and over having: no formal schooling 55.8%; primary education 39.4%; secondary 4.6%; religious 0.1%; postsecondary 0.1%. *Literacy* (1983): total population age 15 and over literate 16,472,494 (78.5%); males literate 8,816,031 (85.8%); females literate 7,656,463 (71.6%).
Health (1987–88): physicians 11,076 (1 per 3,485 persons); hospital beds 25,759 (1 per 1,498 persons); infant mortality rate per 1,000 live births (1988) 69.
Food (1984–86): daily per capita caloric intake 2,592 (vegetable products 95%, animal products 5%); 120% of FAO recommended minimum.

Military

Total active duty personnel (1989): 200,000 (army 91.0%, navy 4.5%, air force 4.5%). *Military expenditure as percent of GNP* (1987): 3.0% (world 5.4%); per capita expenditure U.S.$7.

---

[1]National elections are scheduled in May 1990. [2]Includes 7,710 persons not distributed by area. [3]Construction Corporation activity only. [4]June. [5]Males in manufacturing only; 1980 = 100. [6]Based on 24 rural townships. [7]Import figures are f.o.b. in balance of trade and c.i.f. in commodities and trading partners.

Nepal

Official name: Nepāl Adhirājya
(Kingdom of Nepal).
Form of government: constitutional
monarchy with one legislative house
(National Panchayat [140[1]]).
Chief of state: King.
Head of government: Prime Minister.
Capital: Kāthmāndu.
Official language: Nepālī.
Official religion: Hinduism.
Monetary unit: 1 Nepalese rupee
(NRs) = 100 paisa (pice); valuation
(Oct. 2, 1989) 1 U.S.$ = NRs 24.00;
1 £ = NRs 38.83.

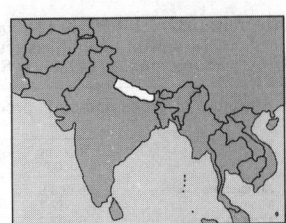

Area and population

Development regions Zones	Capitals	area sq mi	area sq km	population 1981 census
Eastern	Dhankūtā	10,987	28,456	3,708,923
Koshi		3,733	9,669	1,423,624
Mechi		3,165	8,196	932,625
Sāgarmāthā		4,089	10,591	1,352,674
Central	Kāthmāndu	10,583	27,410	4,909,357
Bāgmati		3,640	9,428	1,782,439
Janakpur		3,733	9,669	1,688,115
Nārāyani		3,210	8,313	1,438,803
Western	Pokharā	11,351	29,398	3,128,859
Dhawalāgiri		3,146	8,148	453,462
Gandaki		4,740	12,275	1,107,569
Lumbini		3,465	8,975	1,567,828
Mid-western	Surkhet	16,362	42,378	1,955,611
Bheri		4,071	10,545	836,402
Karnāli		8,244	21,351	242,486
Rāpti		4,047	10,482	876,723
Far-western	Dipāyal	7,544	19,539	1,320,089
Mahākāli		2,698	6,989	525,178
Seti		4,846	12,550	794,911
TOTAL		56,827	147,181	15,022,839

Demography

Population (1989): 18,452,000.
Density (1989): persons per sq mi 324.7, persons per sq km 125.4.
Urban-rural (1987): urban 8.3%; rural 91.7%.
Sex distribution (1988): male 51.52%; female 48.48%.
Age breakdown (1986): under 15, 42.2%; 15-29, 25.6%; 30-44, 17.3%; 45-59,
10.0%; 60-74, 4.2%; 75 and over, 0.7%.
Population projection: (2000) 23,176,000; (2010) 27,807,000.
Doubling time: 28 years.
Ethnic composition (1981): Nepalese 58.4%; Bihārī (including Maithilī and
Bhojpurī) 18.7%; Tharu 3.6%; Tamang 3.5%; Newār 3.0%; other 12.8%.
Religious affiliation (1981): Hindu 89.5%; Buddhist 5.3%; Muslim 2.7%; Jain
0.1%; other 2.4%.
Major cities (1981): Kāthmāndu 235,160; Birātnagar 93,544; Lalitpur 79,875;
Bhaktapur 48,472; Pokhara 46,642.

Vital statistics

Birth rate per 1,000 population (1988): 39.3 (world avg. 27.1).
Death rate per 1,000 population (1988): 14.6 (world avg. 9.9).
Natural increase rate per 1,000 population (1988): 24.7 (world avg. 17.2).
Total fertility rate (avg. births per childbearing woman; 1988): 5.8.
Marriage rate per 1,000 population: n.a.
Divorce rate per 1,000 population: n.a.
Life expectancy at birth (1988): male 54.4 years; female 51.6 years.
Major causes of death per 100,000 population: n.a.; however, major diseases
include malaria, tuberculosis, cholera, and typhoid.

National economy

Budget (1987-88). Revenue: NRs 9,848,000,000 (1985-86; taxes on goods
and services 38.7%, customs duties 21.0%, income tax 9.9%, interest on
loans 9.0%, registration taxes 6.5%, land revenue 6.6%, government services 5.2%). Expenditures: NRs 15,187,700,000 (economic services 47.9%,
social services 23.6%, loan repayment 9.9%, defense 5.4%, general administration 4.8%).
Public debt (external, outstanding; 1987): U.S.$902,000,000.
Tourism: receipts from visitors (1988) U.S.$28,000,000; expenditures by na-
tionals abroad (1987) U.S.$35,000,000.
Production (metric tons except as noted). Agriculture, forestry, fishing
(1988): rice 2,787,000, corn (maize) 890,000, sugarcane 816,000, wheat
745,000, potatoes 566,000, millet 160,000, pulses 153,000, barley 24,000,
jute 16,000, tobacco 5,000; livestock (number of live animals) 6,374,000
cattle, 5,125,000 goats, 2,900,000 buffalo, 833,000 sheep, 479,000 pigs;
roundwood (1987) 16,479,000 cu m; fish catch (1987) 10,716. Mining and
quarrying (1985-86): limestone 167,789; magnesite 63,190; talc 8,780; garnet (1984-85) 27,300 kg. Manufacturing (1986-87): cement 151,631; sugar
24,565; jute goods 18,239; soap 11,460; tea 1,112; plywood 2,438,000 square
feet; cigarettes 5,600,000,000 units; shoes 121,000 pairs. Construction: n.a.
Energy production (consumption): electricity (kW-hr; 1987) 538,000,000
(549,000,000); coal (metric tons; 1987) none (85,000); petroleum products
(metric tons; 1987) none (178,000); natural gas, none (none).
Gross national product (at current market prices; 1987): U.S.$2,836,000,000
(U.S.$160 per capita).

Structure of gross domestic product and labour force

	1985-86 in value NRs '000,000	1985-86 % of total value	1981 labour force	1981 % of labour force
Agriculture	29,603	58.0	6,244,289	91.1
Mining	139	0.3	971	[2]
Manufacturing	2,271	4.4	33,029	0.5
Construction	3,223	6.3	2,022	[2]
Public utilities	197	0.4	3,013	[2]
Transp. and commun.	3,087	6.0	7,424	0.1
Trade	1,901	3.7	109,446	1.6
Finance	3,674	7.2	9,850	0.1
Services	3,562	7.0	313,570	4.6
Other	3,421[3]	6.7[3]	127,272[4]	1.9[4]
TOTAL	51,078	100.0	6,850,886	100.0[5]

Population economically active (1986): total 7,760,155; activity rate of total
population 45.5% (participation rates: ages 15-64, 82.5%; female 34.7%;
unemployed [1980] 5.5%).

Price and earnings indexes (1985 = 100)

	1982	1983	1984	1985	1986	1987	1988
Consumer price index	80.1	90.0	92.5	100.0	119.0	131.8	143.6
Monthly earnings index	...	...	...	...	...	...	...

Household income and expenditure. Average family size (1981) 5.8; income
per family (1976-77) NRs 5,914 (U.S.$473); sources of income (1973-
74)[6]: wages and salaries 39.2%, self-employment 33.6%, owner-occupied
dwellings 17.5%; expenditure (1973-75)[6]: food and beverages 57.4%, housing 11.4%, clothing 10.5%, recreation 7.9%, health care 4.2%, transport and
communications 2.1%, personal effects and other 6.5%.
Land use (1987): forested 16.9%; meadows and pastures 14.5%; agricultural
and under permanent cultivation 17.1%; other 51.5%.

Foreign trade[7]

Balance of trade (current prices)

	1983	1984	1985	1986	1987	1988
NRs '000,000	−5,064.2	−4,411.4	−5,048.0	−6,275.7	−7,659.6	−10,780
% of total	65.0%	51.1%	46.3%	51.0%	52.8%	54.6%

Imports (1986-87): NRs 11,020,300,000 (1985-86; basic manufactured goods
29.5%; machinery and transport equipment 22.9%; chemicals 12.5%; mineral fuels 11.3%; food and live animals, chiefly for food 10.4%; miscellaneous manufactured articles 6.8%; crude materials except fuels 4.2%).
Major import sources (1985-86): India 42.5%; Japan 16.5%; South Korea
5.1%; Singapore 3.7%; China 3.3%; West Germany 3.0%.
Exports (1986-87): NRs 3,059,700,000 (basic manufactures 34.5%; food and
live animals, chiefly for food 22.7%; machinery, transport equipment, and
other manufactured articles 22.3%; crude materials except fuels 16.6%; animal and vegetable oils 3.9%). *Major export destinations* (1985-86): India
40.3%; United States 27.3%; West Germany 7.6%; Singapore 7.3%; United
Kingdom 3.6%; Soviet Union 2.3%.

Transport and communications

Transport. Railroads (1986-87): route length 33 mi, 53 km; passengers carried 1,673,000; freight handled 19,000 metric tons. Roads (1986-87): total
length 3,918 mi, 6,306 km (paved 44%). Vehicles (1978): passenger cars
14,201; trucks and buses 9,988. Merchant marine: none. Air transport[8]
(1987): passenger-mi 209,000,000, passenger-km 336,000,000; short ton-
mi cargo 4,036,000, metric ton-km cargo 5,892,000; airports (1989) with
scheduled flights 5.
Communications. Daily newspapers (1986-87): total number 59; total circulation, n.a.; circulation per 1,000 population, n.a. Radio (1986): 2,012,000
receivers (1 per 8.5 persons). Television (1988): 27,000 receivers (1 per 667
persons). Telephones (1987): 25,606 (1 per 686 persons).

Education and health

Education (1986-87)

	schools	teachers	students	student/ teacher ratio
Primary (age 6-11)	12,186	53,405	1,857,658	34.8
Secondary (age 12-17)	5,140	21,785	540,049	24.8
Vocational[9]	5	117	648	5.5
Higher[9]	116	4,165	67,555	16.2

Educational attainment (1981). Percent of population age 25 and over
having: no formal schooling 41.2%; primary education 29.4%; secondary
22.7%; higher 6.8%. *Literacy* (1981): total population age 15 and over
literate 1,822,718 (20.7%); males literate 1,425,241 (31.9%); females literate
397,477 (9.2%).
Health (1987): physicians 863 (1 per 20,356 persons); hospital beds 3,842 (1
per 4,572 persons); infant mortality rate per 1,000 live births (1988) 127.
Food (1984-86): daily per capita caloric intake 2,050 (vegetable products
93%, animal products 7%); 92% of FAO recommended minimum.

Military

Total active duty personnel (1989): 35,000 (army 100.0%). *Military expenditure as percent of GNP* (1987): 1.2% (world 5.4%); per capita expenditure
U.S.$2.

[1]Includes 28 members appointed by the King. [2]Less than 0.05%. [3]Includes indirect
taxes. [4]Activities not adequately defined. [5]Detail does not add to total given because
of rounding. [6]For Kāthmāndu only. [7]Import figures are f.o.b. in balance of trade and
c.i.f. for commodities and trading partners. [8]International flights only. [9]1985-86.

Netherlands, The

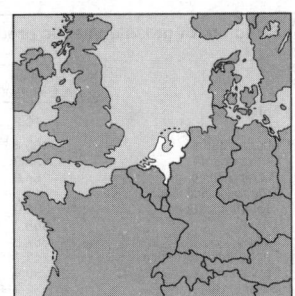

Official name: Koninkrijk der Nederlanden (Kingdom of The Netherlands).
Form of government: constitutional monarchy with a parliament (States General) comprising two legislative houses (First Chamber [75]; Second Chamber [150]).
Chief of state: Monarch.
Head of government: Prime Minister.
Seat of government: The Hague.
Capital: Amsterdam.
Official language: Dutch.
Official religion: none.
Monetary unit: 1 Netherlands guilder (f.) = 100 cents; valuation (Oct. 2, 1989) 1 U.S.$ = f. 2.12; 1 £ = f. 3.43.

Area and population		area		population
				1988
Provinces	Capitals	sq mi	sq km	estimate[1]
Drenthe	Assen	1,025	2,654	436,586
Flevoland	Lelystad	549	1,422	193,739
Friesland	Leeuwarden	1,295	3,353	599,104
Gelderland	Arnhem	1,935	5,011	1,783,610
Groningen	Groningen	906	2,346	556,757
Limburg	Maastricht	838	2,170	1,095,424
Noord-Brabant	's-Hertogenbosch	1,910	4,946	2,156,280
Noord-Holland	Haarlem	1,029	2,665	2,352,888
Overijssel	Zwolle	1,289	3,339	1,009,997
Utrecht	Utrecht	514	1,331	965,229
Zeeland	Middelburg	692	1,792	355,501
Zuid-Holland	The Hague	1,123	2,908	3,208,414
TOTAL LAND AREA		13,103[2]	33,937	14,714,948
INLAND WATER		3,060	7,926	
TOTAL AREA		16,163	41,863	

Demography

Population (1989): 14,846,000.
Density[3] (1989): persons per sq mi 1,125.0, persons per sq km 434.4.
Urban–rural (1988): urban 88.5%; rural 11.5%.
Sex distribution (1988): male 49.43%; female 50.57%.
Age breakdown (1988): under 15, 18.5%; 15–29, 25.4%; 30–44, 23.3%; 45–59, 15.8%; 60–74, 11.8%; 75 and over, 5.2%.
Population projection: (2000) 15,719,000; (2010) 15,743,000.
Doubling time: n.a.; vital rates and net migration in near balance.
Ethnic composition (by nationality; 1988): Netherlander 96.0%; Turkish 1.1%; Moroccan 0.9%; German 0.3%; other 1.7%.
Religious affiliation (1986): Roman Catholic 36.0%; Dutch Reformed Church 18.5%; Reformed Churches 8.4%; other 4.5%; no religion 32.6%.
Major cities (1988): Amsterdam 691,738; Rotterdam 574,299; The Hague 444,312; Utrecht 230,373; Eindhoven 191,002.

Vital statistics

Birth rate per 1,000 population (1988): 12.6 (world avg. 27.1); legitimate 89.8%; illegitimate 10.2%.
Death rate per 1,000 population (1988): 8.4 (world avg. 9.9).
Natural increase rate per 1,000 population (1988): 4.2 (world avg. 17.2).
Total fertility rate (avg. births per childbearing woman; 1987): 1.6.
Marriage rate per 1,000 population (1988): 6.0.
Divorce rate per 1,000 population (1987): 1.9.
Life expectancy at birth (1987): male 73.5 years; female 80.1 years.
Major causes of death per 100,000 population (1987): malignant neoplasms (cancers) 236.4, of which lung cancer 56.9; ischemic heart diseases 163.3; cerebrovascular diseases 78.7; accidents, poisonings, and violence 36.9.

National economy

Budget (1988). Revenue: f. 156,834,000,000 (income and corporate taxes 38.3%, value-added taxes 23.2%, excise and import taxes 7.1%, natural gas royalties 2.9%). Expenditures: f. 179,266,000,000 (education and culture 18.8%, social security and public health 16.3%, debt service 12.4%, defense 7.8%, transportation 7.4%).
Public debt (1987): U.S.$131,049,000,000.
Tourism (1987): receipts from visitors U.S.$2,666,000,000; expenditures by nationals abroad U.S.$6,362,000,000.
Production (metric tons except as noted). Agriculture, forestry, fishing (1988): sugar beets 6,923,000, potatoes 6,742,000, vegetables and melons 3,011,000, wheat 827,000; livestock (number of live animals) 13,934,000 pigs, 4,710,000 cattle, 1,169,000 sheep; roundwood (1987) 1,156,000 cu m; fish catch (1987) 435,209. Manufacturing (value of sales in f. '000,000; 1986): foodstuffs 70,000; synthetic fibres 36,300; electrical machinery 24,-000; petroleum products 14,600; transport equipment 12,500. Construction (1985): residential 35,616,000 cu m; nonresidential 49,968,000 cu m. Energy production (consumption): electricity (kW-hr; 1987) 68,411,000,000 (72,-034,000,000); coal (metric tons; 1987) none (11,455,000); crude petroleum (barrels; 1987) 29,406,000 (350,600,000); petroleum products (metric tons; 1987) 54,448,000 (28,277,000); natural gas (cu m; 1987) 82,499,000,000 (49,438,000,000).
Household income and expenditure. Average household size (1987) 2.5; income per household (1985) f. 80,000 (U.S.$24,000); sources of income (1987): wages 40.0%, transfer payments 24.7%, self-employment 20.8%, other 14.5%; expenditure (1987): food, beverages, and tobacco 18.7%, rent

and utilities 18.5%, medical care 12.6%, transportation and communications 11.5%, education and recreation 9.6%, household furnishings and appliances 7.9%, clothing and footwear 7.5%, other 13.7%.
Gross national product (at current market prices; 1987): U.S.$173,357,000,-000 (U.S.$11,860 per capita).

Structure of gross domestic product and labour force				
	1987			
	in value f. '000,000	% of total value	labour force	% of labour force
Agriculture	17,130	4.3	292,300	4.5
Mining	15,440	3.8	12,900	0.2
Manufacturing	80,540	20.0	1,107,300	16.9
Construction	24,310	6.0	380,400	5.8
Public utilities	8,700	2.2	51,100	0.8
Transp. and commun.	28,430	7.1	354,200	5.4
Trade	70,140	17.4	1,073,400	16.4
Finance	174,260	43.3	557,200	8.5
Pub. admin., defense	...	...	2,023,600	30.8
Services	...	...		
Other	−16,550[4]	−4.1[4]	706,800[5]	10.8[5]
TOTAL	402,400	100.0	6,559,100[2]	100.0[2]

Population economically active (1987): total 6,559,100; activity rate of total population 44.7% (participation rates: ages 15–64, 64.4%; female 37.4%; unemployed 9.6%).

Price and earnings indexes (1985 = 100)							
	1982	1983	1984	1985	1986	1987	1988
Consumer price index	92.1	94.7	97.8	100.0	100.1	99.4	100.1
Hourly earnings index	92.0	94.0	95.5	100.0	102.0	103.0	104.0

Land use (1986): forested 8.8%; meadows and pastures 32.7%; agricultural and under permanent cultivation 26.7%; other 31.8%.

Foreign trade

Balance of trade (current prices)						
	1983	1984	1985	1986	1987	1988
f. '000,000	16,076	20,978	21,469	20,386	13,201	17,647
% of total	4.6%	5.3%	5.0%	5.5%	3.6%	4.5%

Imports (1988): f. 196,349,000,000 (machinery and transport equipment 27.8%, of which transport equipment 7.6%; foodstuffs, beverages, and tobacco 13.6%; chemicals and chemical products 10.8%; mineral fuels 9.3%; metals and metal products 7.6%; textiles 6.7%; raw materials, oils, and fats 6.3%). *Major import sources:* West Germany 26.3%; Belgium–Luxembourg 14.7%; U.K. 7.7%; U.S. 7.6%; France 7.6%.
Exports (1988): f. 203,729,000,000 (machinery and transport equipment 20.9%, of which transport equipment 5.4%; foodstuffs, beverages, and tobacco 20.0%; chemicals and chemical products 18.9%; mineral fuels 8.5%; metals and metal products 6.7%; textiles 4.5%). *Major export destinations:* West Germany 26.2%; Belgium–Luxembourg 14.7%; France 10.8%; U.K. 10.8%; Italy 6.4%.

Transport and communications

Transport. Railroads (1988): length 2,809 km; passenger-km 9,396,000,000[6]; metric ton-km cargo 3,000,000,000[6]. Roads (1988): total length 115,413 km (paved 87%). Vehicles (1987): passenger cars 5,118,000; trucks and buses 477,000. Merchant marine[7] (1988): vessels (100 gross tons and over) 1,265; total deadweight tonnage 4,698,468. Air transport (1987): passenger-km 22,027,396,000; metric ton-km cargo 1,731,064,000; airports (1989) 4.
Communications. Daily newspapers (1986): total number 43; total circulation 4,579,000; circulation per 1,000 population 315. Radio (1987): total number of receivers 12,146,299 (1 per 1.2 persons). Television (1987): total number of receivers 4,703,000 (1 per 3.2 persons). Telephones (1986): 9,080,000 (1 per 1.6 persons).

Education and health

Education (1987–88)				
	schools	teachers[8]	students	student/ teacher ratio
Primary (age 6–12)	9,502	102,388[9]	1,536,000	...
Secondary (age 12–18)	1,338	53,361	747,000	...
Voc., teacher tr.	1,693	55,931	594,000	...
Higher[8]	453	30,952	307,537	9.9

Educational attainment (1985). Percent of population[10] ages 25–64 having: primary education 16.7%; secondary 61.8%; higher 20.0%; other 1.5%. *Literacy* (1988): virtually 100% literate.
Health (1988): physicians 37,144 (1 per 396 persons); hospital beds 94,000 (1 per 157 persons); infant mortality rate per 1,000 live births (1988) 6.8.
Food (1984–86): daily per capita caloric intake 3,258 (vegetable products 62%, animal products 38%); (1983) 129% of FAO recommended minimum requirement.

Military

Total active duty personnel (1988): 106,100 (army 62.2%, navy 16.1%, air force 17.1%, other[11] 4.6%). *Military expenditure as percent of GNP* (1987): 3.1% (world 5.4%); per capita expenditure U.S.$447.

[1]January 1; includes 1,419 persons having no fixed municipality of residence. [2]Detail does not add to total given because of rounding. [3]Based on land area only. [4]Imputed bank service charge. [5]Includes 631,200 unemployed persons. [6]1987. [7]Includes Netherlands Antilles and Aruba. [8]1985–86. [9]Includes special subject teachers. [10]Economically active population (4,612,000) only. [11]Includes 3,900 military police.

Netherlands Antilles

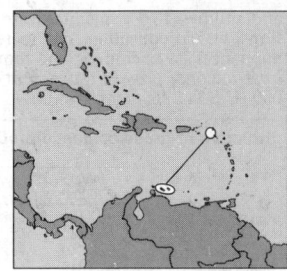

Official name: Nederlandse Antillen
(Netherlands Antilles).
Political status: nonmetropolitan
territory of The Netherlands with
one legislative house (States of the
Netherlands Antilles [22])[1].
Chief of state: Dutch Monarch
represented by governor.
Head of government: Prime Minister.
Capital: Willemstad.
Official language: Dutch.
Official religion: none.
Monetary unit: 1 Netherlands Antillean
guilder (NA f.) = 100 cents; valuation
(Oct. 2, 1989) 1 U.S.$ = NA f. 1.80;
1 £ = NA f. 2.91.

Area and population		area		population
Island councils	Capitals	sq mi	sq km	1987 estimate[2]
Leeward Islands				
Bonaire	Kralendijk	111	288	10,625
Curaçao	Willemstad	171	444	153,736
Windward Islands				
Saba	The Bottom	5	13	983
Sint Eustatius or Statia	Oranjestad	8	21	1,838
Sint Maarten (Dutch part only)	Philipsburg	13	34	21,319
TOTAL		308	800	188,501

Demography

Population (1989): 183,000.
Density (1989): persons per sq mi 592.2, persons per sq km 228.8.
Urban–rural (1985)[3]: urban 92.4%; rural 7.6%.
Sex distribution (1987): male 48.68%; female 51.32%.
Age breakdown (1981): under 15, 30.0%; 15–29, 29.9%; 30–44, 19.5%; 45–59, 11.3%; 60–74, 6.7%; 75 and over, 2.6%.
Population projection: (2000) 188,000; (2010) 192,000.
Doubling time: 45 years.
Ethnic composition (1980)[3]: Netherlands Antillean (Dutch/Spanish/black/Amerindian) creole 84.0%; white 6.1%; other West Indian 4.9%; Suriname creole 2.9%; other 2.1%.
Religious affiliation (1981): Roman Catholic 83.8%; Protestant 10.2%, of which Lutheran/Reformed tradition 3.3%, Methodist 3.2%, Seventh-day Adventist 1.5%; Jewish 0.3%; nonreligious 2.6%; other 3.1%.
Major cities (1985): Willemstad (urban area) 125,000; Philipsburg 10,000[4].

Vital statistics

Birth rate per 1,000 population (1985)[5]: 21.7 (world avg. 27.1); legitimate 50.7%; illegitimate 49.3%[5].
Death rate per 1,000 population (1985)[5]: 6.2 (world avg. 9.9).
Natural increase rate per 1,000 population (1985)[5]: 15.5 (world avg. 17.2).
Total fertility rate (avg. births per childbearing woman; 1984)[3]: 3.4.
Marriage rate per 1,000 population (1985)[5]: 6.1.
Divorce rate per 1,000 population (1985)[5]: 2.8.
Life expectancy at birth (1981)[6]: male 71.1 years; female 75.8 years.
Major causes of death per 100,000 population (1985): diseases of the circulatory system 247.2; malignant neoplasms (cancers) 113.9; respiratory diseases 45.8; accidents 43.5; conditions originating in the perinatal period 33.8; endocrinal and metabolic diseases 24.6.

National economy

Budget (1988). Revenue: NA f. 993,600,000 (revenue from local sources 87.0%[7], of which profit taxes from offshore sector 34.4%, taxes on wages 17.3%, taxes on goods and services 11.3%; development revenue from The Netherlands 13.0%[8]). Expenditures[7]: NA f. 1,007,900,000 (tranfer payments 23.2%, of which other government levels 12.8%, households 10.1%; goods and services 23.0%; debt service 4.4%).
Tourism: receipts from visitors (1988) U.S.$319,800,000, of which Sint Maarten U.S.$225,300,000, Curaçao U.S.$80,600,000, Bonaire U.S.$13,900,000; expenditures by nationals abroad (1983)[3] U.S.$107,000,000.
Production (metric tons except as noted). Agriculture, forestry, fishing (value of production in NA f. '000; 1982): eggs 3,863, fruits and vegetables 2,850[9], pork 1,250, goat meat 555; livestock (number of live animals; 1988)[3] 23,000 goats, 10,000 sheep, 8,000 cattle, 6,000 pigs; roundwood, n.a.; fish catch (1987) 1,000. Mining and quarrying (1986): unrefined salt 380,000. Manufacturing (1985): residual fuel oil 6,800,000[3, 10]; ship repair NA f. 48,000,000[11]; curaçao liqueur 780 hectolitres; other manufactures include electronic parts, cigarettes, textiles, and rum. Construction (gross value of construction; 1986[6]): NA f. 57,700,000. Energy production (consumption): electricity (kW-hr; 1987) 625,000,000 (625,000,000); coal, none (none); crude petroleum (barrels; 1987) none (71,100,000); petroleum products (metric tons; 1987) 8,965,000 (1,406,000); natural gas, none (none).
Household income and expenditure. Average household size (1981) 3.7; income per household: n.a.; sources of income: n.a.; expenditure (1986)[12, 13]: transportation and communications 23.6%, food 19.0%, housing 16.8%, household furnishings 10.2%, clothing and footwear 8.4%, recreation and education 6.6%, health 2.3%, beverages and tobacco 2.2%, other 10.9%.
Gross national product (at current market prices; 1985)[3]: U.S.$1,610,000,000 (U.S.$6,810 per capita).

Structure of gross domestic product and labour force				
	1982		1986	
	in value NA f. '000,000	% of total value	labour force	% of labour force
Agriculture	10.8	0.4	426	0.6
Mining			187	0.2
Manufacturing	185.6	7.3	5,297	6.9
Construction	198.3	7.8	5,484	7.1
Public utilities	54.9	2.2	1,370	1.8
Transportation and communications	336.0	13.1	3,832	5.0
Trade	668.7	26.1	16,390	21.2
Finance	387.3	15.1	5,207	6.7
Pub. admin., defense	548.1	21.4	21,085	27.3
Services	250.4	9.8		
Other	−82.2[14]	−3.2[14]	17,932[15]	23.2[15]
TOTAL	2,557.9	100.0	77,210	100.0

Population economically active (1986): total 77,210; activity rate of total population 44.0% (participation rates [1981]: ages 15–64, 63.5%; female 40.6%; unemployed 23.2%, of which Curaçao 28.9%, Bonaire 15.2%, Windward Islands, negligible).

Price and earnings indexes (1985 = 100)						
	1983	1984	1985	1986	1987	1988
Consumer price index[13]	97.5	99.6	100.0	101.3	105.1	107.8
Monthly earnings index[16]	94.5	95.5	100.0	89.3	...	...

Public debt (external, outstanding; end of 1987): U.S.$389,600,000.
Land use (1988): forested, negligible; meadows and pastures, negligible; agricultural and under permanent cultivation 8.0%; other (dry savanna) 92.0%.

Foreign trade[17]

Balance of trade (current prices)						
	1982	1983	1984	1985	1986	1987
NA f. '000,000	+637	−7	−368	−1,038	−1,206	−1,411
% of total	3.8%	0.1%	2.6%	14.7%	82.5%	83.7%

Imports (1987)[13]: NA f. 2,703,292,000 (crude petroleum and petroleum products 69.9%, machinery and transport equipment 8.1%, food and live animals 6.8%, chemicals 3.1%). *Major import sources* (1984)[3]: Venezuela 50.0%; Mexico 15.4%; United States 10.3%; Libya 3.9%; The Netherlands 3.4%.
Exports (1987)[13]: NA f. 2,353,634,000 (crude petroleum and petroleum products 95.2%, machinery and transport equipment 0.9%). *Major export destinations* (1984)[3]: United States 17.4%; Jamaica 9.3%; Puerto Rico 8.7%; Cuba 8.4%; The Netherlands 6.0%; Colombia 5.3%.

Transport and communications

Transport. Railroads: none. Roads (1984): total length 510 mi, 820 km (paved, n.a.). Vehicles (1986): passenger cars 54,140; trucks and buses 10,174. Merchant marine (1987): vessels (100 gross tons and over) 793; total deadweight tonnage, n.a. Air transport (1982)[18]: passenger-mi 234,000,000, passenger-km 377,000,000; short ton-mi cargo 1,243,000, metric ton-km cargo 1,815,000; airports (1989) with scheduled flights 5.
Communications. Daily newspapers (1988): total number 6; total circulation 42,900[19]; circulation per 1,000 population 236[19]. Radio (1988): 150,000 receivers (1 per 1.2 persons). Television (1988): 32,000 receivers (1 per 5.7 persons). Telephones (1986): 40,301 (1 per 4.6 persons).

Education and health

Education (1986)				
	schools	teachers	students	student/ teacher ratio
Primary (age 6–12)	91	1,145	24,600	21.5
Secondary (age 12–17)	22	630	8,600	13.7
Voc., teacher tr.	3	50	650	13.0
Higher	2	80	700	8.8

Educational attainment (1981). Percent of population age 25 and over having: no formal schooling or some primary education 29.7%; completed primary 31.5%; completed vocational or secondary 37.6%; completed higher 1.2%. *Literacy* (1985): total population age 15 and over literate 95.0%.
Health (1985): physicians (1987) 232 (1 per 760 persons); hospital beds 1,779 (1 per 98 persons); infant mortality rate per 1,000 live births 18.25.
Food (1984–86)[3]: daily per capita caloric intake 2,925 (vegetable products 65%, animal products 35%); 121% of FAO recommended minimum requirement.

Military

Total active duty personnel (1989): A small Dutch naval contingent is stationed permanently in the Netherlands Antilles.

---

[1]Aruba withdrew from the Netherlands Antilles on Jan. 1, 1986, becoming an autonomous member of the Kingdom of The Netherlands, the same status as the whole of the Netherlands Antilles. [2]January 1. [3]Includes Aruba. [4]1980. [5]Excludes Sint Eustatius. [6]Curaçao only. [7]For central government and island government of Curaçao. [8]For central government and all island governments. [9]Mostly tomatoes, beans, cucumbers, gherkins, melons, and lettuce grown on hydroponic farms; aloes grown for export, divi-divi pods, and sour orange fruit are non-hydroponic crops. [10]Curaçao's oil refinery was operational in early 1988, but the oil refinery on Aruba was closed in March 1985. [11]Foreign income in 1986. [12]Weights of consumer price index components. [13]Curaçao and Bonaire only. [14]Less imputed bank service charges. [15]Unemployed. [16]Average nonagricultural wage. [17]Imports c.i.f.; exports f.o.b. [18]ALM airlines only. [19]For 4 newspapers only.

New Caledonia

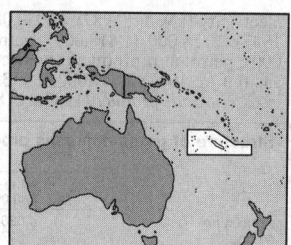

Official name: Territoire de la Nouvelle-Calédonie et Dépendances (Territory of New Caledonia and Dependencies).
Political status: overseas territory (France) under interim direct rule pending the establishment of a Territorial Congress.
Chief of state: President of France.
Head of government: High Commissioner.
Capital: Nouméa.
Official language: French.
Official religion: none.
Monetary unit: 1 franc of the Comptoirs français du Pacifique (CFPF) = 100 centimes; valuation (Oct. 2, 1989) 1 U.S.$ = CFPF 114.91; 1 £ = CFPF 185.92.

Area and population

		area		population
Regions[1]	Capitals	sq mi	sq km	1983 census
Loyauté	...	765	1,981	15,510
Nord	...	2,837	7,348	21,512
Nouméa	Nouméa	637	1,650	85,098
Sud	...	2,995	7,757	23,248
TOTAL		7,233[2,3]	18,734[2,3]	145,368

Demography

Population (1989): 158,000.
Density (1989): persons per sq mi 21.8, persons per sq km 8.4.
Urban–rural (1983): urban 58.5%; rural 41.5%.
Sex distribution (1983): male 51.10%; female 48.90%.
Age breakdown (1983): under 15, 36.2%; 15–29, 26.9%; 30–44, 19.5%; 45–59, 11.2%; 60–74, 5.1%; 75 and over, 1.1%.
Population projection: (2000) 183,000; (2010) 209,000.
Doubling time: 38 years.
Ethnic composition (1983): Melanesian 43.4%, of which local Melanesian 42.6%; European 37.1%; Polynesian 12.2%, of which Wallisian 8.4%, Tahitian 3.8%; Indonesian 3.7%; Vietnamese 1.6%; other 2.0%.
Religious affiliation (1984): Roman Catholic 62.7%; Sunnī Muslim 4.0%; other (mostly Protestant) 33.3%.
Major cities (1983)[4]: Nouméa 60,112; Mont-Doré 14,614; Dumbéa 5,538.

Vital statistics

Birth rate per 1,000 population (1987): 23.8 (world avg. 27.1); legitimate 48.1%; illegitimate 51.9%.
Death rate per 1,000 population (1987): 5.3 (world avg. 9.9).
Natural increase rate per 1,000 population (1987): 18.5 (world avg. 17.2).
Total fertility rate (avg. births per childbearing woman; 1987): 3.3.
Marriage rate per 1,000 population (1987): 4.5.
Divorce rate per 1,000 population (1987): 1.1.
Life expectancy at birth (1980–85): male 64.6 years; female 68.5.
Major causes of death per 100,000 population (1981)[5]: diseases of the circulatory system 45.0; traumas 31.6; malignant neoplasms (cancers) 23.5; infectious and parasitic diseases 10.9; ill-defined conditions 94.2.

National economy

Budget (1989). Revenue: CFPF 51,787,000,000 (current revenue 84.4%, of which indirect taxes 33.8%, French government grants 18.5%; direct taxes 15.8%; development revenue 15.6%). Expenditures: CFPF 51,787,000,000 (current expenditure 84.4%, of which contributions to assistance funds 40.6%, social and cultural services 32.2%, public debt 7.3%; development expenditure 15.6%).
Public debt (external, outstanding; 1985[6]): U.S.$126,000,000.
Production (metric tons except as noted). Agriculture, forestry, fishing (1987): yams 15,000, coconuts 11,000, fruits 4,360, sweet potatoes 4,000, pulses 3,620 cassava 3,000, potatoes 2,150, bananas and plantains 2,000, copra 688, coffee 471; livestock (number of live animals; 1988) 120,824 cattle, 35,265 pigs, 17,584 goats, 469,698 poultry; roundwood 11,607 cu m; fish catch 6,338. Mining and quarrying (metric tons; 1988): nickel ore 3,380,000 (ferronickel [metal content] 37,300, nickel matte [metal content] 10,500); chromite ore 112,000 (concentrate 70,000). Manufacturing (metric tons; 1988): cement 63,343; soap 381; crude vegetable oil 164; copra cake 108; beer 65,141 hectolitres. Construction (dwellings authorized; 1984): residential 45,900 sq m; nonresidential, n.a. Energy production (consumption): electricity (kW-hr; 1988) 1,180,000,000 (1,173,000,000); coal (metric tons; 1987) none (155,000); crude petroleum, none (none); petroleum products (metric tons; 1987) none (350,000); natural gas, none (none).
Population economically active (1983): total 44,842; activity rate of total population 30.8% (participation rates: over age 20, 46.4%; female 17.4%; unemployed [1987] 7.0%).

Price and earnings indexes (1985 = 100)[7]

	1982	1983	1984	1985	1986	1987	1988
Consumer price index	79.9	88.7	95.1	100.0	99.5	100.9	104.4
Earnings index[8]	80.3	88.9	95.3	100.0	100.6	101.5	104.6

Land use (1986): forested 37.7%; meadows and pastures 14.8%; agricultural and under permanent cultivation 1.1%; other 46.4%.
Gross national product (at current market prices; 1985): U.S.$856,000,000 (U.S.$5,720 per capita).

Structure of gross domestic product and labour force

	1986		1983	
	in value CFPF '000,000	% of total value	labour force	% of labour force
Agriculture	2,831	1.9	9,888	22.1
Mining	5,324	3.5	3,121	7.0
Manufacturing	14,368	9.5	1,426	3.2
Construction	6,698	4.4	2,725	6.1
Public utilities	3,789	2.5	565	1.3
Transportation and communications	6,969	4.6	2,659	5.9
Trade	40,496	26.8	4,370	9.7
Finance } Services }	24,729	16.3	1,025 / 6,021	2.3 / 13.4
Pub. admin., defense	46,077	30.5	12,901	28.8
Other	...	...	141	0.3
TOTAL	151,281	100.0	44,842	100.0[2]

Household income and expenditure. Average household size (1983) 4.1; average annual income per household (1980–81) CFPF 1,627,000 (U.S.$18,-598)[9]; sources of income (1986): wages and salaries 59.0%, self-employment 19.6%, transfer payments 21.4%; expenditure (1981): food 27.5%, transportation 15.1%, housing 13.3%, household furnishings 11.4%, recreation 6.4%, other 26.3%.
Tourism (1986): receipts from visitors U.S.$40,000,000; expenditures by nationals abroad, n.a.

Foreign trade

Balance of trade (current prices)

	1983	1984	1985	1986	1987	1988
CFPF '000,000	−18,971	−12,902	−11,109	−36,164	−34,691	+496
% of total	28.4%	14.9%	11.0%	40.3%	37.7%	0.4%

Imports (1988): CFPF 65,386,000,000 (food 20.1%, transportation equipment 18.1%, machinery and electrical goods 16.3%, mineral products 9.2%, chemicals and chemical products 6.8%). *Major import sources:* France 47.9%; Australia 10.3%; United States 6.6%; Japan 5.2%; New Zealand 3.6%.
Exports (1988): CFPF 65,882,000,000 (ferronickel and nickel matte 83.5%, nickel ore 9.7%, copra 5.3%, chromite 1.5%). *Major export destinations* (1987): France 44.0%; Japan 19.1%; West Germany 8.6%; United States 7.5%; India 4.5%.

Transport and communications

Transport. Railroads: none. Roads (1987): total length 4,037 mi, 6,497 km (paved 18%). Vehicles (1985): passenger cars 42,000; trucks and buses 2,500. Merchant marine: vessels (100 gross tons and over) n.a. Air transport (1988)[10]: passenger-mi 53,000,000, passenger-km 112,000,000; short ton-mi cargo 332,000, metric ton-km cargo 485,000; airports (1989) with scheduled flights 9.
Communications. Daily newspapers (1987): total number 2; total circulation 24,000; circulation per 1,000 population 158. Radio (1988): total number of receivers 90,000 (1 per 1.7 persons). Television (1987): total number of receivers 35,500 (1 per 4.3 persons). Telephones (1987): 21,915[11] (1 per 7.0 persons).

Education and health

Education (1987)

	schools	teachers	students	student/teacher ratio
Primary (age 6–10)	276	1,564	32,205	20.6
Secondary (age 11–17)	47	1,179	13,540	11.5
Vocational	28	200	5,887	29.4
Higher	6	40	853	21.3

Educational attainment (1983). Percent of population age 20 and over having: no formal schooling 17.4%; primary education 51.8%; secondary 25.9%; higher 4.8%. *Literacy* (1976): total population age 14 and over literate 75,-819 (89.4%); males literate 40,296 (90.1%); females literate 35,523 (88.7%).
Health (1988): physicians 173 (1 per 901 persons); hospital beds 1,081 (1 per 144 persons); infant mortality rate per 1,000 live births (1987) 15.0.
Food (1984–86): daily per capita caloric intake 2,984 (vegetable products 78%, animal products 22%); (1984) 110% of FAO recommended minimum requirement.

Military

Total active duty personnel (1988): 9,500 French troops. *Military expenditure as percent of GNP:* n.a.

[1]Breakdown reflects administrative organization between November 1985 and July 1988. In a November 1988 plebiscite, New Caledonia was reorganized into three autonomous provinces. [2]Detail does not add to total given because of rounding. [3]Total area per new survey equals 7,172 sq mi (18,576 sq km); regional areas are not available. [4]Populations cited are for communes. [5]Public health facilities only. [6]Includes external long-term private debt not guaranteed by the government. [7]All figures are end-of-year. [8]Based on minimum hourly wage. [9]Average European household CFPF 2,243,000 (U.S.$25,640); Melanesian CFPF 777,000 (U.S.$8,882). [10]Air Calédonie only. [11]Subscribers.

New Zealand

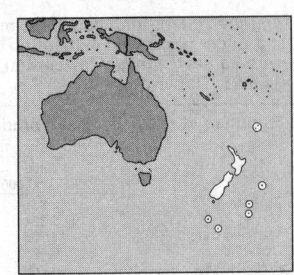

Official name: New Zealand (English);
Aotearoa (Maori).
Form of government: constitutional
monarchy with one legislative house
(House of Representatives [97]).
Chief of state: British Monarch,
represented by governor-general.
Head of government: Prime Minister.
Capital: Wellington.
Official language: English; Maori.
Official religion: none.
Monetary unit: 1 New Zealand
dollar ($NZ) = 100 cents; valuation
(Oct. 2, 1989) 1 U.S.$ = $NZ 1.72;
1 £ = $NZ 2.75.

Area and population		area		population
		sq mi	sq km	1988 estimate[2]
Local Government Regions	**Centres[1]**			
North Island				
Auckland[3]	Auckland	2,008	5,201	911,700
Bay of Plenty	Tauranga	3,523	9,126	192,700
East Cape	Gisborne	4,425	11,461	53,800
Hawke's Bay	Napier	4,786	12,396	141,200
Horowhenua	Levin	623	1,614	55,400
Manawatu	Palmerston North	2,575	6,669	116,200
Northland	Whangarei	4,866	12,604	128,900
Taranaki	New Plymouth	3,040	7,876	108,300
Thames Valley	Thames-Coromandel	1,802	4,666	60,000
Tongariro	Taupo	4,666	12,085	41,600
Waikato	Hamilton	5,112	13,241	230,600
Wairarapa	Masterton	2,661	6,894	39,600
Wanganui	Wanganui	3,541	9,171	69,400
Wellington	Wellington	532	1,379	327,700
South Island				
Aorangi	Timaru	7,687	19,910	80,400
Canterbury	Christchurch	6,743	17,465	350,700
Clutha-Central Otago	...	11,190	28,982	49,500
Coastal-North Otago	Dunedin	4,088	10,590	136,900
Marlborough	Blenheim	4,973	12,882	38,100
Nelson Bays	Nelson	3,937	10,197	71,000
Southland	Invercargill	10,701	27,716	103,200
West Coast	Greymouth	8,839	22,893	35,100
Remainder		1,097	2,826	5,400
TOTAL		103,415	267,844	3,347,300[4]

Demography

Population (1989): 3,371,000.
Density (1989): persons per sq mi 32.6, persons per sq km 12.6.
Urban-rural (1987): urban 83.7%; rural 16.3%.
Sex distribution (1989): male 49.44%; female 50.56%.
Age breakdown (1989): under 15, 23.1%; 15–29, 25.9%; 30–44, 21.7%; 45–59,
14.3%; 60–74, 10.7%; 75 and over, 4.3%.
Population projection: (2000) 3,584,000; (2010) 3,789,000.
Doubling time: 89 years.
Ethnic composition (1986): European 82.2%; New Zealand Maori 9.2%; Pa-
cific Island Polynesian 2.9%; other and not specified 5.7%.
Religious affiliation (1986): Anglican 24.3%; Presbyterian 18.0%; Roman
Catholic 15.2%; Methodist 4.7%; nonreligious 16.4%; other 21.4%.
Major cities (1988): Manukau 185,800; Christchurch 167,700; Auckland
149,500; Wellington 136,000; Waitemata 100,700.

Vital statistics

Birth rate per 1,000 population (1988): 17.3 (world avg. 27.1); legitimate
(1987) 71.4%; illegitimate 28.6%.
Death rate per 1,000 population (1988): 8.2 (world avg. 9.9).
Natural increase rate per 1,000 population (1988): 9.1 (world avg. 17.2).
Total fertility rate (avg. births per childbearing woman; 1988): 2.1.
Marriage rate per 1,000 population (1987): 7.4.
Divorce rate per 1,000 population (1988): 0.4.
Life expectancy at birth (1987): male 71.8 years; female 77.8 years.
Major causes of death per 100,000 population (1986): diseases of the cir-
culatory system 381.6, of which ischemic heart disease 223.9; malignant
neoplasms 189.8; diseases of the respiratory system 86.7; accidents 62.2;
diseases of the digestive system 23.0; metabolic diseases 16.3.

National economy

Budget (1988–89). Revenue: $NZ 25,529,100,000 (income tax 59.9%, goods
and services tax 16.5%, interest and profits 9.8%, sales tax 7.0%). Expenditures: $NZ 25,568,500,000 (social services 35.4%, debt service and
investment 17.9%, health 14.2%, education 13.6%, administration 10.3%).
Public debt (external, outstanding; 1988): U.S.$19,200,000,000.
Tourism (1987): receipts U.S.$934,000,000; expenditures U.S.$734,000,000.
Production (metric tons except as noted). Agriculture, forestry, fishing
(1988): fruits 691,000, barley 356,100, potatoes 290,000, wheat 206,000, corn
136,900, oats 64,000; livestock (number of live animals) 64,600,000 sheep,
8,058,000 cattle, 1,301,000 goats, 414,000 pigs; roundwood (1987) 9,341,000
cu m; fish catch (1987) 430,705. Mining and quarrying (1986): limestone
2,422,800; serpentine 22,362; lead 5,000; iron ore and sand concentrate
4,685; gold 1,265. Manufacturing (value added, $NZ '000; 1985–86): food
2,170,135; machinery 1,618,825; paper 1,207,880; textiles 911,462; fabricated metal products 811,017; wood products 707,513; chemicals 569,468;
rubber and plastic 418,268. Construction ($NZ '000; 1988–89): residen-
tial 2,088,600; nonresidential 1,443,800. Energy production (consumption):

electricity (kW-hr; 1987) 27,030,000,000 (27,030,000,000); coal (metric tons;
1987) 2,118,000 (1,818,000); petroleum (barrels; 1987) 9,286,000 (24,243,-
000); petroleum products (metric tons; 1987) 2,724,000 (2,635,000); natural
gas (cu m; 1987) 3,547,000,000 (3,547,000,000).
Gross national product (1987): U.S.$27,131,000,000 (U.S.$8,230 per capita).

Structure of gross domestic product and labour force				
	1986–87		1986	
	in value $NZ '000,000	% of total value	labour force	% of labour force
Agriculture	4,328	8.1	161,640	10.0
Mining	527	1.0	5,997	0.4
Manufacturing	11,192	21.0	316,206	19.7
Construction	2,682	5.0	102,039	6.3
Public utilities	1,882	3.5	15,732	1.0
Transp. and commun.	4,122	7.7	110,982	6.9
Trade	9,437	19.0	292,131	18.2
Finance	10,126	17.7	122,943	7.6
Pub. admin., defense } Services	8,619	16.1	357,735	22.2
Other	467[5]	0.9[5]	123,207[6]	7.7[6]
TOTAL	53,382	100.0	1,608,612	100.0

Population economically active (1986): total 1,608,612; activity rate 49.3%
(participation rates: ages 15–64, 74.6%; female 41.7%; unemployed 3.6%).

Price and earnings indexes (1985 = 100)							
	1982	1983	1984	1985	1986	1987	1988
Consumer price index	76.0	81.6	86.6	100.0	113.2	131.0	139.4
Weekly earnings index	90.4	90.7	92.8	100.0	116.4	125.7	133.2[7]

Household income and expenditure. Average household size (1986) 2.9; annual income per household (1986–87) $NZ 31,400 (U.S.$16,400); sources
of income (1986): wages and salaries 68.1%, transfer payments 12.7%, self-
employment 9.1%; expenditure (1986–87): housing 22.4%, transportation
17.6%, food 17.4%, household durable goods 11.6%, clothing 5.9%, recreation 5.2%, energy 2.7%, health 1.8%, education 0.6%.
Land use (1987): forested 38.3%; meadows and pastures 52.5%; agricultural
and under permanent cultivation 1.7%; other 7.5%.

Foreign trade

Balance of trade (current prices)						
	1983	1984	1985	1986	1987	1988
$NZ '000,000	+1,181.8	+1,386.2	+636.4	+578.6	+927.9	+3,114.0
% of total	7.9%	7.8%	2.8%	2.6%	4.0%	13.2%

Imports (1988–89): $NZ 11,402,400,000 (machinery 29.8%; transport equip-
ment 9.9%; chemicals 8.4%; fuels 5.6%; iron, steel, and nonferrous metals
5.5%; textiles, clothing, and footwear 4.0%; crude petroleum 3.9%). *Major
import sources:* Australia 21.4%; Japan 17.6%; U.S. 16.0%; U.K. 9.5%;
W.Ger. 5.6%.
Exports (1988–89): $NZ 14,907,200,000 (food and live animals 40.4%; wool
13.0%; wood 7.7%; skins and leather 5.5%; aluminum 5.2%; machinery
3.7%; chemicals 3.3%). *Major export destinations:* Japan 16.7%; Australia
16.7%; U.S. 14.7%; U.K. 8.5%; China 3.5%; W.Ger. 2.4%; S.Korea 2.3%.

Transport and communications

Transport. Railroads (1987): length 4,332 km; passenger-km (1984) 458,-
160,000; metric ton-km cargo (1985–86) 3,192,000,000. Roads (1987): total
length 93,130 km (paved 55%). Vehicles (1988): passenger cars 1,393,326;
trucks and buses 305,208. Merchant marine (1988): vessels (100 gross tons
and over) 133; total deadweight tonnage 378,113. Air transport (1988):
passenger-km 10,728,000,000; metric ton-km cargo 334,800,000; airports
(1989) 36.
Communications. Daily newspapers (1986): total number 32; total circulation 1,055,000; circulation per 1,000 population 324. Radio (1987): 3,053,-
146 receivers (1 per 1.1 persons). Television (1987): 978,460 receivers (1
per 3.5 persons). Telephones (1987): 2,315,000 (1 per 1.4 persons).

Education and health

Education (1987)				
	schools	teachers	students	student/ teacher ratio
Primary (age 5–12)	2,575	19,113	432,972	22.7
Secondary (age 13–17)	396	13,490	232,307	17.2
Voc., teacher tr.	28	3,130[8]	130,483[9]	...
Higher[10]	7	2,775	37,074	13.4

Educational attainment (1987). Percent of population age 25 and over
having: primary and some secondary education 51.9%; secondary 35.8%;
higher 6.9%; not specified 5.4%. *Literacy* (1987): virtually 100.0%.
Health (1987): physicians 6,390 (1 per 522 persons); hospital beds 30,645 (1
per 111 persons); infant mortality rate per 1,000 live births 10.0.
Food (1984–86): daily per capita caloric intake 3,405 (vegetable products
56%, animal products 44%); 129% of FAO recommended minimum.

Military

Total active duty personnel (1988): 12,800 (army 46.9%, navy 20.3%, air force
32.8%). *Military expenditure as percent of GNP* (1987): 2.2% (world 5.4%);
per capita expenditure U.S.$228.

[1]Principal centres have no administrative significance. [2]March 31. [3]Excludes Great
Barrier Island and Chatham Island counties. [4]Detail does not add to total given
because of rounding. [5]Includes import duties less imputed bank service charges.
[6]Includes 109,191 unemployed. [7]Third quarter. [8]1986. [9]Includes part-time students.
[10]Universities only.

Nicaragua

Official name: República de Nicaragua (Republic of Nicaragua).
Form of government: unitary multiparty republic with one legislative house (National Assembly [96[1]]).
Head of state and government: President.
Capital: Managua.
Official language: Spanish.
Official religion: none.
Monetary unit: 1 Nicaraguan new córdoba[2] (C$) = 100 centavos; valuation ([official rate] Oct. 2, 1989) 1 U.S.$ = C$22,000; 1 £ = C$35,596.

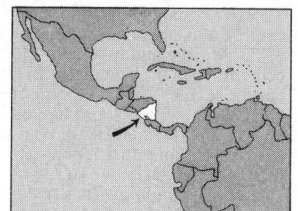

Area and population		area[3]		population
				1988
Regions	**Capitals**	**sq mi**	**sq km**	**estimate**
Región I	Estelí	2,915	7,549	389,768
Región II	León	3,808	9,862	631,977
Región III	Managua	1,325	3,432	979,363
Región IV	Jinotepe	1,894	4,905	609,024
Región V	Juigalpa	9,316	24,129	337,304
Región VI	Matagalpa	6,397	16,569	465,555
Special Zones				
Región Autónoma del Atlántico Norte	Rosita	12,409	32,139	116,384
Región Autónoma del Atlántico Sur	Bluefields	5,925	15,346	60,702
Zona Especial III	San Carlos	2,478	6,418	31,517
TOTAL LAND AREA		46,467	120,349	3,621,594
INLAND WATER		3,997	10,351	
TOTAL		50,464	130,700	

Demography

Population (1989): 3,745,000.
Density (1989)[4]: persons per sq mi 80.6, persons per sq km 31.1.
Urban-rural (1988): urban 59.2%; rural 40.8%.
Sex distribution (1988): male 50.07%; female 49.93%.
Age breakdown (1988): under 15, 46.2%; 15–29, 27.5%; 30–44, 14.7%; 45–59, 7.3%; 60–74, 3.5%; 75 and over, 0.8%.
Population projection: (2000) 5,261,000; (2010) 6,824,000.
Doubling time: 21 years.
Ethnic composition (1985): mestizo (Spanish/Indian) 77.0%; white 10.0%; black 9.0%; Amerindian 4.0%.
Religious affiliation (1987): Roman Catholic 88.3%; other (mostly Baptist, Moravian, and Pentecostal) 11.7%.
Major cities (1985): Managua 682,111; León 100,982; Granada 88,636; Masaya 74,946; Chinandega 67,792.

Vital statistics

Birth rate per 1,000 population (1988): 41.8 (world avg. 27.1).
Death rate per 1,000 population (1988): 8.0 (world avg. 9.9).
Natural increase rate per 1,000 population (1988): 33.8 (world avg. 17.2).
Total fertility rate (avg. births per childbearing woman; 1987): 5.2.
Marriage rate per 1,000 population (1988): 2.1.
Divorce rate per 1,000 population (1988): 0.4.
Life expectancy at birth (1987): male 60.0 years; female 62.0 years.
Major causes of death per 100,000 population (1984): accidents, poisonings, and violence 81.9; diseases of the circulatory system 54.3; infectious and parasitic diseases 43.9; malignant neoplasms (cancers) 28.5.

National economy

Budget (1986). Revenue: C$163,900,000,000 (revenue 82.9%, of which excises 30.1%, income taxes 14.1%, general sales taxes 9.0%; nontax revenue 8.7%). Expenditures: C$228,037,000,000 (current expenditures 91.8%, development expenditures 8.2%).
Public debt (external, outstanding; 1987): U.S.$6,150,000,000.
Production (metric tons except as noted). Agriculture, forestry, fishing (1988): sugarcane 2,233,000, corn (maize) 278,000, sorghum 250,000, bananas 110,000, rice 104,000[5], plantains 85,000[5], cottonseed 82,000, dry beans 67,000, oranges 56,000, coffee 41,000, sesame 3,100, tobacco 2,100; livestock (number of live animals) 1,700,000 cattle, 745,000 pigs; roundwood (1987) 3,770,000 cu m; fish catch (1987) 4,983, of which crustaceans 2,907. Mining and quarrying (1988): gold 28,300 troy oz. Manufacturing (value of production in C$'000,000; 1988[6]): processed foods 1,556; beverages 1,204; metal products 694; textiles 640; chemicals and chemical products 572; nonmetal mineral products 361; clothing 285; tobacco products 247. Construction (buildings completed; 1988): 41,600 cu m. Energy production (consumption): electricity (kW-hr; 1988) 1,120,000,000 (952,000,000); coal, none (none); crude petroleum (barrels; 1987) none (3,665,000); petroleum products (metric tons; 1987) 479,000 (650,000); natural gas, none (none).
Population economically active (1987): total 1,126,300; activity rate of total population 32.2% (participation rates: ages 15–64 [1980] 54.0%; female [1980] 21.6%; unemployed 25.0%).

Price and earnings indexes (1985 = 100)							
	1982	1983	1984	1985	1986	1987	1988
Consumer price index	17.6	23.1	31.3	100.0	781.4	7,907.3	815,000
Weekly earnings index[7]	27.2	30.7	39.7	100.0	286.7	...	...

Gross national product (at current market prices; 1987): U.S.$2,959,000,000 (U.S.$830 per capita).

Structure of gross domestic product and labour force				
	1988		1987	
	in value C$'000,000[8]	% of total value	labour force	% of labour force
Agriculture	4,580	23.6	365,200	32.4
Mining	96	0.5	3,000	0.3
Manufacturing	4,106	21.1	90,500	8.0
Construction	694	3.6	16,800	1.5
Public utilities	477	2.5	7,800	0.7
Transportation and communications	1,154	5.9	20,900	1.8
Trade	3,503	18.0	94,600	8.4
Finance, real estate	1,432	7.4	18,700	1.7
Pub. admin., defense	2,496	12.9	77,400	6.9
Services	876	4.5	148,500	13.2
Other	—	—	282,900[9]	25.1[9]
TOTAL	19,414	100.0	1,126,300	100.0

Household income and expenditure. Average household size (1980) 6.9; income per household: n.a.; sources of income: n.a.; expenditure (1986)[10, 11]: food, beverages, and tobacco 68.4%, housing, energy, and household furnishings 12.2%, clothing and footwear 11.6%, other 7.8%.
Tourism (1988): receipts from visitors U.S.$1,800,000; expenditures by nationals abroad U.S.$5,400,000.
Land use (1986): forested 32.2%; meadows and pastures 43.8%; agricultural and under permanent cultivation 10.7%; other 13.3%.

Foreign trade[12]

Balance of trade (current prices)						
	1983	1984	1985	1986	1987	1988
U.S.$'000,000	−349.3	−413.9	−576.7	−534.8	−538.0	−482.6
% of total	28.9%	34.9%	48.9%	52.0%	47.3%	50.6%

Imports (1988): U.S.$807,100,000 (primary and intermediate goods for industry 20.1%, crude petroleum and petroleum products 15.0%, capital goods for industry 14.1%, transport equipment 13.8%, nondurable consumer goods 12.8%). *Major import sources:* Socialist bloc 39.5%; EEC 19.5%; CACM 5.4%.
Exports (1988): U.S.$235,700,000 (coffee 35.9%, cotton 22.5%, beef 8.2%, bananas 6.2%, gold 5.6%). *Major export destinations:* EEC 42.4%; Socialist bloc 12.8%; CACM 7.6%.

Transport and communications

Transport. Railroads (1985): length (1986) 214 mi, 344 km; passenger-mi 15,845,000, passenger-km 25,500,000; short ton-mi cargo 47,000,000, metric ton-km cargo 68,000,000. Roads (1988): total length 9,319 mi, 14,997 km (paved 10%). Vehicles (1986): passenger cars 46,184; trucks and buses 30,535. Merchant marine (1988): vessels (100 gross tons and over) 23; total deadweight tonnage 18,191. Air transport (1985)[10]: passenger arrivals 126,972, passenger departures 134,471; cargo unloaded 3,384, metric tons, cargo loaded 2,595 metric tons; airports (1989) with scheduled flights, n.a.
Communications. Daily newspapers (1987): total number 4; total circulation 218,500; circulation per 1,000 population 62. Radio (1988): 883,400 receivers (1 per 4.1 persons). Television (1988): 210,000 receivers (1 per 17 persons). Telephones (1986): 43,900 (1 per 77 persons).

Education and health

Education (1988)	schools	teachers	students	student/ teacher ratio
Primary (age 7–12)[13]	4,624	24,127	678,937	28.1
Secondary (age 13–18) Voc., teacher tr.	328	7,167	172,108	24.0
Higher	13	1,484	25,478	17.2

Educational attainment (1971). Percent of population age 25 and over having: no formal schooling 53.9%; some primary and complete primary education 41.7%; some secondary and complete secondary education 4.4%.
Literacy (1986): total population age 15 and over literate 74.0%.
Health (1988): physicians (1987) 2,086 (1 per 1,678 persons); hospital beds 4,762 (1 per 761 persons); infant mortality rate per 1,000 live births 61.7.
Food (1979–81): daily per capita caloric intake 2,188 (vegetable products 84%, animal products 16%); (1984) 108% of FAO recommended minimum requirement.

Military

Total active duty personnel (1989): 80,000 (army 91.9%, navy 4.4%, air force 3.7%). *Military expenditure as percent of GNP* (1985): 17.2% (world 5.7%); per capita expenditure U.S.$1,597.

[1]Includes 6 nonelective seats. [2]Introduced February 1988 at the rate of 1 new córdoba = 1,000 old córdobas. [3]Total land area only is shown for the regions and special zones; the total area (both land and water) is shown only in the grand total. [4]Based on land area. [5]1987. [6]At prices of 1983. [7]Registrants of Nicaraguan Institute of Social Security and Welfare. [8]At prices of 1980. [9]Mostly underemployed informal workers. [10]Managua only. [11]Weights of consumer price index components. [12]Import figures are f.o.b. in balance of trade and c.i.f. in commodities and trading partners. [13]Includes preschool.

Niger

Official name: République du Niger (Republic of Niger).
Form of government: single-party republic with a single legislative house (National Assembly [93])[1].
Head of state and government: President[1].
Capital: Niamey.
Official language: French.
Official religion: none.
Monetary unit: 1 CFA franc (CFAF) = 100 centimes; valuation (Oct. 2, 1989) 1 U.S.$ = CFAF 317.90; 1 £ = CFAF 514.37.

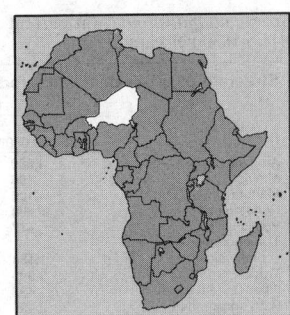

Area and population

		area		population
				1988
Departments	Capitals	sq mi	sq km	census[2]
Agadez	Agadez	244,869	634,209	203,959
Diffa	Diffa	54,138	140,216	189,316
Dosso	Dosso	11,970	31,002	1,019,997
Maradi	Maradi	14,896	38,581	1,388,999
Tahoua	Tahoua	41,188	106,677	1,306,652
Tillabéry	Tillabéry	34,604	89,623	1,331,611
Zinder	Zinder	56,151	145,430	1,410,797
Commune				
Niamey	Niamey	259	670	398,265
TOTAL		458,075	1,186,408	7,249,596

Demography

Population (1989): 7,523,000.
Density (1989): persons per sq mi 16.4, persons per sq km 6.3.
Urban–rural (1988): urban 21.1%; rural 78.9%.
Sex distribution (1985): male 49.53%; female 50.47%.
Age breakdown (1985): under 15, 46.7%; 15–29, 25.6%; 30–44, 14.9%; 45–59, 8.0%; 60–74, 3.9%; 75 and over, 0.9%.
Population projection: (2000) 10,656,000; (2010) 14,484,000.
Doubling time: 23 years.
Ethnic composition (1977): Hausa 54.1%; Songhai, Zerma, and Dendi 21.7%; Fulani 10.1%; Tuareg 8.4%; Kanuri 4.2%; Teda 0.2%; other 1.3%.
Religious affiliation (1988): Sunnī Muslim 80%; traditional beliefs 20%.
Major cities (1983): Niamey 399,100; Zinder 82,800; Maradi 65,100; Tahoua 41,900; Agadez 30,800.

Vital statistics

Birth rate per 1,000 population (1985–90): 50.9 (world avg. 27.1).
Death rate per 1,000 population (1985–90): 20.9 (world avg. 9.9).
Natural increase rate per 1,000 population (1985–90): 30.0 (world avg. 17.2).
Total fertility rate (avg. births per childbearing woman; 1985–90): 7.1.
Marriage rate per 1,000 population: n.a.
Divorce rate per 1,000 population: n.a.
Life expectancy at birth (1985–90): male 42.9 years; female 46.1 years.
Major causes of death (1984): n.a.; however, among selected major causes registered at medical facilities are measles, diarrhea, meningitis, malaria, pneumonia, tetanus, viral hepatitis, and poliomyelitis.

National economy

Budget (1989). Revenue: CFAF 215,309,000,000 (foreign loans 34.6%, external aid and gifts 25.4%, import duties 8.7%, sales taxes 3.8%, personal income taxes 3.8%, excise taxes 3.7%, corporate and business taxes 3.7%). Expenditures: CFAF 215,309,000,000 (agriculture 20.4%, amortization of public debt 17.3%, education 11.5%, housing 10.0%, transportation and communications 9.6%, health 5.3%, defense 2.7%).
Public debt (external, outstanding; 1987): U.S.$1,259,000,000.
Tourism (1987): receipts from visitors U.S.$7,000,000; expenditures by nationals abroad U.S.$13,000,000.
Gross national product (at current market prices; 1987): U.S.$1,898,000,000 (U.S.$280 per capita).

Structure of gross domestic product and labour force

	1987		1985	
	in value CFAF '000,000	% of total value	labour force	% of labour force
Agriculture	351,100	45.5	2,870,000	89.6
Mining	52,000	6.7		
Manufacturing	31,500	4.1	64,000	2.0
Construction	23,500	2.1		
Public utilities	16,200	3.0		
Transportation and communications	31,800	4.1		
Trade and finance	101,200	13.2	269,000	8.4
Pub. admin., defense	60,900	7.9		
Services	130,000	16.8		
Other	−26,600	−3.4	—	—
TOTAL	771,900[3]	100.0	3,203,000	100.0

Production (metric tons except as noted). Agriculture, forestry, fishing (1988): millet 1,783,000, sorghum 603,000, pulses 373,000, roots and tubers 246,000, vegetables and melons 166,000, onions 126,000, sugarcane 112,000, rice 50,000, peanuts (groundnuts) 41,000, corn (maize) 9,000, wheat 8,000, cotton 4,000, tobacco leaf 1,000; livestock (number of live animals)

7,550,000 goats, 3,500,000 sheep, 3,500,000 cattle, 512,000 asses, 417,000 camels, 296,000 horses; roundwood (1987) 4,163,000 cu m; fish catch (1987) 2,400. Mining and quarrying (1988): uranium 2,964. Manufacturing (1983): cement 30,000; beverages 108,000 hectolitres; beer 100,000 hectolitres; cotton textiles 7,000,000 square metres. Construction (1980): CFAF 75,-937,000,000. Energy production (consumption): electricity (kW-hr; 1987) 157,000,000 (292,000,000); coal (metric tons; 1987) 65,000 (65,000); crude petroleum, none (n.a.); petroleum products (metric tons; 1987) none (179,-000); natural gas, none (n.a.).
Population economically active (1985): total 3,203,000; activity rate of total population 52.4% (participation rates: ages 15–64, 89.7%; female 47.4%; unemployed, n.a.).

Price and earnings indexes (1985 = 100)

	1982	1983	1984	1985	1986	1987	1988
Consumer price index	95.5	93.1	100.9	100.0	96.8	90.3	89.0
Hourly earnings index[4]	100.0	100.0	100.0	100.0	100.0	100.0	100.0

Household income and expenditure. Average household size (1980) 5.2; income per household: n.a.; sources of income (1977): self-employment 59.5%, family 30.1%, salary or wages 4.8%, employer 0.7%; expenditure (1983): food and beverages 50.5%, household expenses 19.1%, clothing 7.3%.
Land use (1987): forested 2.0%; meadows and pastures 7.3%; agricultural and under permanent cultivation 2.8%; other 87.9%.

Foreign trade[5]

Balance of trade (current prices)

	1980	1981	1982	1983	1984	1985
CFAF '000,000	+18,860	+2,087	−30,161	+1,816	+6,204	−38,057
% of total	8.6%	0.9%	12.1%	0.8%	2.7%	16.8%

Imports (1985): CFAF 154,787,100,000 (food products 34.8%, of which cereals 23.3%; sugar 3.1%; petroleum products 10.9%; nonelectrical machinery 8.8%; transportation equipment 8.5%; chemical products 8.1%; cotton thread and fabrics 4.2%). *Major import sources:* France 27.7%; United States 11.4%; Côte d'Ivoire 7.2%; Nigeria 6.7%; West Germany 5.5%; Japan 3.8%; China 3.2%.
Exports (1985): CFAF 93,900,900,000 (uranium 78.9%; foodstuffs 14.5%, of which live animals 11.6%, vegetables 2.2%). *Major export destinations:* France 65.6%; Nigeria 13.7%; Japan 6.0%; Spain 5.8%; Algeria 3.4%; Côte d'Ivoire 1.7%.

Transport and communications

Transport. Railroads (1988): none[6]. Roads (1988): total length 24,836 mi, 39,970 km (paved 8%). Vehicles (1988): passenger cars 27,254; trucks and buses 25,248. Air transport (1986)[7]: passenger-mi 147,619,000, passenger-km 237,571,000; short ton-mi cargo 26,340,000, metric ton-km cargo 38,-455,000; airports (1989) with scheduled flights 1.
Communications. Daily newspapers (1988): total number 1; total circulation 5,000; circulation per 1,000 population 0.7. Radio (1988): total number of receivers 357,000 (1 per 19 persons). Television (1988): total number of receivers 25,000 (1 per 277 persons). Telephones (1985): 11,824 (1 per 563 persons).

Education and health

Education (1986)

	schools	teachers	students	student/teacher ratio
Primary (age 7–12)	1,976	7,690	293,512	38.2
Secondary (age 13–19)	64[8]	1,963[9]	51,448[9]	26.2[9]
Voc., teacher tr.	8[10]	120[10]	2,208[9]	19.6[10]
Higher[11]	3	310[12]	4,101[12]	13.2[12]

Educational attainment (1977). Percent of population age 25 and over having: no formal schooling 91.1%; primary education 8.4%; secondary 0.3%; higher 0.2%. *Literacy* (1980): total population age 15 and over literate 278,-000 (9.8%); males literate 195,000 (14.0%); females literate 83,000 (5.8%).
Health: physicians (1985) 160 (1 per 38,500 persons); hospital beds (1979) 3,261 (1 per 1,633 persons); infant mortality rate per 1,000 live births (1985–90) 135.0.
Food (1984–86): daily per capita caloric intake 2,349 (vegetable products 93%, animal products 7%); 100% of FAO recommended minimum requirement.

Military

Total active duty personnel (1989): 3,300 (army 97.0%, air force 3.0%). *Military expenditure as percent of GNP* (1986): 0.7% (world 5.5%); per capita expenditure U.S.$3.

---

[1]A new constitution was approved by referendum on Sept. 24, 1989, providing for the Dec. 10, 1989, election of a 93-seat National Assembly and the president of the republic. The new civilian government took office December 20. Until this election, the head of state had been the president of the Supreme Council of National Orientation, a military-dominated policy organ that had directed the later stages of the restoration of civilian government. [2]De jure. [3]Detail does not add to total given because of rounding. [4]Guaranteed minimum wage for professionals. [5]Import figures are f.o.b. in balance of trade and c.i.f. for commodities and trading partners. [6]Niger is a cofounder of the Common Benin–Niger Organization for Railroads and Transport, currently maintaining rail operations only in Benin but having the purpose of extending rail services from the sea at Cotonou, Benin, to Dosso and, ultimately, Niamey, Niger. [7]Air Afrique. [8]1980–81. [9]1985. [10]1980. [11]1988. [12]Université de Niamey and École Nationale d'Administration du Niger only.

Nigeria

Official name: Federal Republic of
Nigeria.
Form of government: federal republic;
temporarily governed (pending
restoration of civilian governmental
apparatus by 1992) under emergency
powers by Armed Forces Ruling
Council (AFRC).
Head of state and government:
President of FRN/Chairman
of AFRC.
Capital: Lagos (Capital
designate: Abuja[1]).
Official language: English.
Official religion: none.
Monetary unit: 1 Nigerian naira
(₦) = 100 kobo; valuation (Oct. 2,
1989) 1 U.S.$ = ₦7.33; 1 £ = ₦11.86.

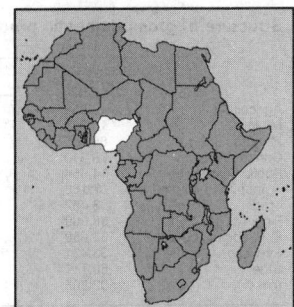

Area and population		area		population
States	Capitals	sq mi	sq km	1989 estimate
Akwa Ibom	Uyo	2	2	5,215,200
Anambra	Enugu	6,824	17,675	7,403,800
Bauchi	Bauchi	24,944	64,605	5,004,900
Bendel	Benin City	13,707	35,500	5,066,000
Benue	Makurdi	17,442	45,174	4,996,100
Borno	Maiduguri	44,942	116,400	6,170,500
Cross River	Calabar	10,516[2]	27,237[2]	1,944,700
Gongola	Yola	35,286	91,390	5,363,100
Imo	Owerri	4,575	11,850	7,560,300
Kaduna	Kaduna	27,122[3]	70,245[3]	3,403,400
Kano	Kano	16,712	43,285	11,887,800
Katsina	Katsina	3	3	5,033,200
Kwara	Ilorin	25,818	66,869	3,512,800
Lagos	Ikeja	1,292	3,345	4,345,400
Niger	Minna	25,111	65,037	2,222,700
Ogun	Abeokuta	6,472	16,762	3,192,700
Ondo	Akure	8,092	20,959	5,619,200
Oyo	Ibadan	14,558	37,705	10,722,700
Plateau	Jos	22,405	58,030	4,144,900
Rivers	Port-Harcourt	8,436	21,850	3,540,500
Sokoto	Sokoto	39,589	102,535	9,343,300
Federal Capital Territory		2,824	7,315	279,800
TOTAL		356,669[4]	923,768	115,973,000

Demography

Population (1989): 115,973,000.
Density (1989): persons per sq mi 325.2, persons per sq km 125.5.
Urban–rural (1985): urban 31.0%; rural 69.0%.
Sex distribution (1986): male 49.46%; female 50.54%.
Age breakdown (1986): under 15, 46.7%; 15–29, 26.1%; 30–44, 14.9%; 45–59,
8.2%; 60 and over, 4.1%.
Population projection: (2000) 166,012,000; (2010) 224,314,000.
Doubling time: 21 years.
Ethnic composition (1983): Hausa 21.3%; Yoruba 21.3%; Igbo (Ibo) 18.0%;
Fulani 11.2%; Ibibio 5.6%; Kanuri 4.2%; Edo 3.4%; Tiv 2.2%; Ijaw 1.8%;
Bura 1.7%; Nupe 1.2%; other 8.1%.
Religious affiliation (1980): Muslim 45.0%; Protestant 26.3%; Roman Catholic
12.1%; African indigenous 10.6%; traditional beliefs 5.6%; other 0.4%.
Major cities (1989): Lagos 1,274,000; Ibadan 1,201,000; Ogbomosho 612,800;
Kano 565,800; Oshogbo 400,300; Ilorin 399,500.

Vital statistics

Birth rate per 1,000 population (1985–90): 49.8 (world avg. 27.1).
Death rate per 1,000 population (1985–90): 15.6 (world avg. 9.9).
Natural increase rate per 1,000 population (1985–90): 34.2 (world avg. 17.2).
Total fertility rate (avg. births per childbearing woman; 1985–90): 7.0.
Life expectancy at birth (1985–90): male 48.8 years; female 52.2 years.
Major causes of death per 100,000 population: n.a.; major diseases include
malaria, tuberculosis, trypanosomiasis, onchocerciasis, and leprosy.

National economy

Budget (1986)[5]. Revenue: ₦14,189,900,000 (petroleum revenues 58.1%; import duties 12.2%; special funds 10.6%). Expenditures: ₦12,524,100,000
(recurrent expenditure 61.0%, of which debt service 40.8%, defense 9.0%,
education 7.8%, police 5.4%, health 3.3%; capital expenditure 39.0%).
Public debt (external, outstanding; 1987): U.S.$26,057,000,000.
Production (metric tons except as noted). Agriculture, forestry, fishing (1987):
sorghum 5,182,000, yams 4,951,000, millet 3,905,000, cassava 1,486,000,
corn (maize) 1,202,000, plantains 1,071,000, sugarcane 852,000, palm oil
840,000, beans 688,000, palm kernel 353,000, rubber 180,000, melon 145,-
000, cocoa 141,000, wheat 139,000, soybeans 107,000; livestock (number of
live animals) 26,328,000 goats, 13,160,000 sheep, 12,169,000 cattle; roundwood 95,524,000 cu m; fish catch 248,964. Mining and quarrying (1986):
limestone 1,850,000; marble 1,482,000; tin metal 1,000,000. Manufacturing
(value added in producers' prices ₦'000,000; 1983): beverages and tobacco
768.2; transport equipment 754.2, of which motor vehicles 734.4; food
products 654.5; textiles 538.6; chemical products 465.0, of which drugs and
medicines 95.0; rubber products 62.5. Construction (dwellings completed;
1982): 31,038. Energy production (consumption): electricity (kW-hr; 1987)
9,905,000,000 (9,805,000,000); coal (metric tons; 1987) 145,000 (100,000);
crude petroleum (barrels; 1987) 454,240,000 (50,313,000); petroleum prod-

ucts (metric tons; 1987) 6,450,000 (7,867,000); natural gas (cu m; 1987)
3,700,000,000 (3,700,000,000).
Tourism (1986): receipts U.S.$78,000,000; expenditures U.S.$38,000,000.
Gross national product (1987): U.S.$39,533,000,000 (U.S.$370 per capita).

Structure of gross domestic product and labour force				
	1985			
	in value ₦'000,000	% of total value	labour force	% of labour force
Agriculture	24,379.1	37.2	20,866,000	57.8
Mining	13,026.2	19.9	144,000	0.4
Manufacturing	4,216.2	6.4	6,570,000	18.2
Construction	1,995.6	3.1	433,000	1.2
Public utilities	395.7	0.6	72,000	0.2
Transp. and commun.	1,880.7	2.9	217,000	0.6
Trade	12,595.8	19.2	5,776,000	16.0
Finance	1,562.2	2.4		
Pub. admin., defense	2,929.0	4.5	2,022,000	5.6
Services	2,486.5	3.8		
TOTAL	65,467.0	100.0	36,100,000	100.0

Population economically active (1984): total 33,708,000; activity rate of total
population 36.1% (participation rates: ages 15–64, 58.2%; female [1983]
31.9%; unemployed [registered] 0.5%).

Price and earnings indexes (1985 = 100)							
	1982	1983	1984	1985	1986	1987	1988
Consumer price index	55.1	67.9	94.8	100.0	105.4	116.1	160.5
Earnings index	...	...	...	...	...	...	...

Household income and expenditure. Average household size (1983) 5.0; average annual income per household (1981) ₦2,300 (U.S.$3,745)[6]; sources of
income (1979): self-employment 49.4%, wages and salaries 36.2%, interest
5.4%, rent 4.7%, transfer payments 4.3%; expenditures (1979): food 53.0%
(of which beverages and tobacco 4.9%), fuel and light 11.4%, clothing 6.0%,
transportation 4.7%, household goods 3.8%, other 21.1%.
Land use (1986): forested 16.0%; meadows and pastures 23.0%; agricultural
and under permanent cultivation 34.4%; other 26.6%.

Foreign trade

Balance of trade (current prices)						
	1982	1983	1984	1985	1986	1987
₦'000,000	−1,523	−540	+2,604	+4,049	+3,043	+15,401
% of total	8.5%	3.5%	16.7%	22.0%	21.8%	35.2%

Imports (1986): ₦5,469,700,000 (machinery and transport equipment 46.0%;
manufactured goods 19.3% [mostly iron and steel products, textiles, and
paper products]; chemicals 13.2%; food 9.8%; mineral fuels 0.6%). *Major
import sources* (1985): U.K. 19.8%; U.S. 13.4%; West Germany 11.8%;
France 8.3%; Japan 7.4%; Italy 3.8%.
Exports (1986): ₦8,513,000,000 (crude petroleum 97.2%; other significant exports include cocoa, rubber, and palm kernels). *Major export destinations*
(1985): U.S. 18.1%; Italy 16.4%; France 16.2%; The Netherlands 12.2%;
West Germany 7.4%; Spain 5.7%.

Transport and communications

Transport. Railroads (1987): length 3,505 km; passenger-km 2,717,632,000[7];
metric ton-km cargo 827,400,000[7]. Roads (1984): total length 124,000 km
(paved 48%). Vehicles (1981): passenger cars 262,550; trucks 90,731. Merchant marine (1988): vessels (100 gross tons and over) 220; total deadweight
tonnage 851,930. Air transport[8] (1987): passenger-km 1,631,613,000; metric
ton-km cargo 37,232,000; airports (1989) 14.
Communications. Daily newspapers (1988): total number 26; total circulation
1,704,000[9]; circulation per 1,000 population 15.2[9]. Radio (1988): 9,557,866
receivers (1 per 12 persons). Television (1988): 5,600,000 receivers (1 per
20 persons). Telephones (1986): 265,000 (1 per 397 persons).

Education and health

Education (1984–85)				
	schools	teachers[10]	students	student/ teacher ratio
Primary (age 6–12)	35,181	359,701	13,612,765	...
Secondary (age 12–17)	5,826	82,749	3,169,624[10]	38.3[10]
Voc., teacher tr.	479	15,738	336,868	...
Higher	80[10]	10,038	126,285	12.6

Educational attainment, n.a. *Literacy* (1985): total population age 15 and
over literate 20,208,000 (42.4%); males literate 12,551,000 (53.8%); females
literate 7,657,000 (31.5%).
Health (1985): physicians 14,757 (1 per 6,900 persons); hospital beds 89,177
(1 per 1,142 persons); infant mortality rate (1985–90) 105.0.
Food (1984–86): daily per capita caloric intake 2,114 (vegetable products
97%, animal products 3%); (1984) 86% of FAO recommended minimum.

Military

Total active duty personnel (1989): 94,500 (army 84.7%, navy 5.3%, air force
10.0%). *Military expenditure as percent of GNP* (1987): 0.8% (world 5.4%);
per capita expenditure U.S.$2.

[1]It is presently planned to move the capital from Lagos to Abuja in the Federal
Capital Territory in 1990. [2]Area of Akwa Ibom is included in Cross River. [3]Area
of Katsina is included in Kaduna. [4]Detail does not add to total given because of
rounding. [5]Budget (1989). Revenue: ₦29,414,000,000. Expenditures: ₦30,107,000,-
000 (recurrent expenditure 69.1%; capital expenditure 30.9%). [6]Urban households
only. [7]1985. [8]Nigeria Airways only. [9]For 17 newspapers only. [10]1983–84.

Norway

Official name: Kongeriket Norge (Kingdom of Norway).
Form of government: constitutional monarchy with one legislative house (Parliament [165]).
Chief of state: King.
Head of government: Prime Minister.
Capital: Oslo.
Official language: Norwegian.
Official religion: Evangelical Lutheran.
Monetary unit: 1 Norwegian krone (NKr) = 100 øre; valuation (Oct. 2, 1989) 1 U.S.$ = NKr 6.92; 1 £ = NKr 11.19.

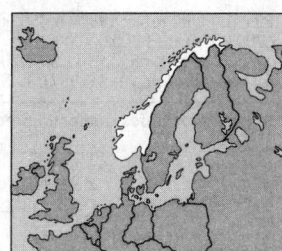

Area and population		area[1]		population
Counties	Capitals	sq mi	sq km	1989 estimate[2]
Akershus	—	1,898	4,917	410,671
Aust-Agder	Arendal	3,557	9,212	96,660
Buskerud	Drammen	5,763	14,927	224,457
Finnmark	Vardø	18,779	48,637	74,045
Hedmark	Hamar	10,575	27,388	186,870
Hordaland	Bergen	6,036	15,634	408,106
Møre og Romsdal	Molde	5,832	15,104	238,422
Nordland	Bodø	14,798	38,327	239,975
Nord-Trøndelag	Steinkjer	8,673	22,463	126,905
Oppland	Lillehammer	9,753	25,260	182,603
Oslo	Oslo	175	454	455,632
Østfold	Moss	1,615	4,183	237,992
Rogaland	Stavanger	3,529	9,141	333,392
Sogn og Fjordane	Leikanger	7,195	18,634	106,408
Sør-Trøndelag	Trondheim	7,271	18,831	249,731
Telemark	Skien	5,913	15,315	163,395
Troms	Tromsø	10,021	25,954	146,804
Vest-Agder	Kristiansand	2,811	7,281	143,424
Vestfold	Tønsberg	856	2,216	196,046
TOTAL		125,050	323,878	4,221,538[3]

Demography

Population (1989): 4,228,000.
Density (1989): persons per sq mi 33.8, persons per sq km 13.0.
Urban-rural (1985): urban 72.8%; rural 27.2%.
Sex distribution (1988): male 49.45%; female 50.55%.
Age breakdown (1988): under 15, 19.1%; 15–29, 23.4%; 30–44, 22.0%; 45–59, 14.3%; 60–74, 14.4%; 75 and over, 6.8%.
Population projection: (2000) 4,427,000; (2010) 4,615,000.
Doubling time: n.a.; doubling time exceeds 100 years.
Ethnic composition (by country of citizenship; 1988): Norway 97.0%; Denmark 0.4%; United Kingdom 0.3%; Sweden 0.3%; Pakistan 0.2%; United States 0.2%; Vietnam 0.1%; other 1.5%.
Religious affiliation (1980): Lutheran 87.9%; nonreligious 3.2%; other 8.9%.
Major cities (1989[4]): Oslo 455,632; Bergen 211,214; Trondheim 136,629; Stavanger 97,093; Baerum 88,752.

Vital statistics

Birth rate per 1,000 population (1988): 13.7 (world avg. 27.1); (1987) legitimate 69.1%; illegitimate 30.9%.
Death rate per 1,000 population (1988): 10.7 (world avg. 9.9).
Natural increase rate per 1,000 population (1988): 3.0 (world avg. 17.2).
Total fertility rate (avg. births per childbearing woman; 1987): 1.7.
Marriage rate per 1,000 population (1987): 5.0.
Divorce rate per 1,000 population (1987): 2.0.
Life expectancy at birth (1987): male 72.8 years; female 79.6 years.
Major causes of death per 100,000 population (1987): ischemic heart disease 280.6; malignant neoplasms (cancers) 230.2; cerebrovascular disease 129.9.

National economy

Budget (1989). Revenue: NKr 272,296,000,000 (social security taxes 27.1%, value-added taxes 24.3%, taxes on interest and dividends 14.3%, ordinary income tax 7.8%, taxes on petroleum income and activity 3.1%). Expenditures: NKr 255,257,000,000 (social security and welfare 25.7%, debt service 6.7%, health 7.7%).
Public debt (1987): U.S.$26,525,000,000.
Tourism (1988): receipts from visitors U.S.$1,444,000,000; expenditures by nationals abroad U.S.$3,406,000,000.
Production (metric tons except as noted). Agriculture, forestry, fishing (1987): barley 500,000, oats 400,000, potatoes 360,000; livestock (number of live animals) 2,350,000 sheep, 965,000 cattle, 742,000 pigs; roundwood 10,540,000 cu m; fish catch 1,869,388, of which herring 343,506, cod 269,775, blue whiting 193,647, capelin 143,388, prawns and shrimps 41,-000. Mining and quarrying (1987)[5]: iron ore 2,044,000, titanium 27,000[6], zinc 22,200, copper 21,960. Manufacturing (value added in NKr '000,000; 1987): machinery and equipment 26,426, of which electrical equipment 5,613, transport equipment 5,175; paper and paper products 11,785; food products 10,120; chemical products 9,594; wood and wood products 5,588. Construction (1985): residential 4,408,000 sq m; nonresidential 2,709,000 sq m. Energy production (consumption): electricity (kW-hr; 1987) 103,-810,000,000 (103,431,000,000); coal (metric tons; 1987) 399,000 (870,000); crude petroleum (barrels; 1987) 372,990,000 (70,813,000); petroleum products (metric tons; 1987) 9,179,000 (8,424,000); natural gas (cu m; 1987) 29,462,000,000 (1,561,000,000).
Gross national product (1987): U.S.$71,420,000,000 (U.S.$17,110 per capita).

Structure of gross domestic product and labour force				
	1988			
	in value NKr '000,000	% of total value	labour force	% of labour force
Agriculture	18,558	3.7	134,000	6.1
Mining	19,938	4.0	24,000	1.1
Manufacturing	85,905	17.1	337,000	15.4
Construction	33,610	6.7	166,000	7.6
Public utilities	14,654	2.9	21,000	1.0
Transp. and commun.	37,188	7.4	176,000	8.1
Trade	53,452	10.6	376,000	17.2
Finance	58,009	11.5	166,000	7.6
Pub. admin., defense	86,850	17.3		
Services	33,421	6.7	783,000[7]	35.9[7]
Other	60,717[8]	12.1[8]		
TOTAL	502,302	100.0	2,183,000	100.0

Population economically active (1988): total 2,183,000; activity rate of total population 51.8% (participation rates: ages 16–64 [1987] 79.1%; female 44.5%; unemployed 3.2%).

Price and earnings indexes (1985 = 100)							
	1982	1983	1984	1985	1986	1987	1988
Consumer price index	82.1	89.0	94.6	100.0	107.2	116.5	124.3
Hourly earnings index	79.0	85.0	92.0	100.0	110.0	128.0	135.0

Household income and expenditure. Average household size (1982) 2.7; consumption expenditure per household NKr 88,000 (U.S.$13,600); sources of income (1985): wages and salaries 62.0%, social security 19.1%, self-employment and property income 17.7%, other 1.2%; expenditure (1986): food 19.7%, transportation 17.6%, housing 17.1%, recreation 8.7%, clothing 8.2%, household furniture and equipment 8.1%.
Land use (1987): forested 27.1%; meadows and pastures 0.3%; agricultural and under permanent cultivation 2.8%; built-up and other 69.8%.

Foreign trade

Balance of trade (current prices)						
	1983	1984	1985	1986	1987	1988
NKr '000,000	35,569	43,764	41,498	−12,403	−3,645	−2,976
% of total	15.6%	16.6%	13.8%	4.4%	1.2%	1.0%

Imports (1988): NKr 151,107,000,000 (machinery and transport equipment 28.3%, of which road vehicles 5.8%; metals and metal products 11.8%, of which iron and steel 3.5%; raw materials 11.3%, of which fuels 3.6%; food products 5.5%, of which fruits and vegetables 1.6%). *Major import sources* (1987): Sweden 18.8%; West Germany 15.5%; U.K. 9.0%; Denmark 7.7%.
Exports (1988): NKr 146,652,000,000 (fuels and fuel products 36.5%, of which crude petroleum 22.7%, natural gas 10.7%; metals and metal products 18.1%, of which iron and steel 4.0%; machinery and transport equipment 10.1%; food products 8.1%, of which fish and fish products 6.9%). *Major export destinations* (1987): U.K. 26.6%; West Germany 15.3%; Sweden 11.0%; The Netherlands 7.3%.

Transport and communications

Transport. Railroads (1987): route length 2,622 mi, 4,219 km; passenger-mi 1,358,700,000, passenger-km 2,186,700,000; short ton-mi cargo 1,933,000,-000, metric ton-km cargo 2,822,000,000. Roads (1987): total length 53,938 mi, 86,805 km (paved 68%). Vehicles (1987): passenger cars 1,623,137; trucks and buses 280,070. Merchant marine (1988): vessels (100 gross tons and over) 2,078; total deadweight tonnage 15,235,060. Air transport (1987): passenger-mi 5,485,359,000, passenger-km 8,827,846,000; short ton-mi cargo 622,351,000, metric ton-km cargo 908,617,000; airports (1989) 49.
Communications. Daily newspapers (1987): total number 84; total circulation 2,268,000; circulation per 1,000 population 540. Radio (1988): 3,285,-188 receivers (1 per 1.3 persons). Television (1988): 1,465,858 receivers (1 per 2.9 persons). Telephones (1984): 2,578,812 (1 per 1.6 persons).

Education and health

Education (1986–87)	schools	teachers	students	student/ teacher ratio
Primary (age 7–12)	3,500	33,005	593,767	18.0
Secondary (age 13–18) and vocational	940	18,135	206,086	11.4
Higher	227	7,002	103,111	14.7

Educational attainment (1985). Percent of population age 16 and over having: lower secondary education 49.8%; higher secondary 37.2%; higher 13.0%. *Literacy* (1988): virtually 100% literate.
Health (1987): physicians (1986) 9,443 (1 per 441 persons); hospital beds 24,442 (1 per 171 persons); infant mortality rate per 1,000 live births 8.4.
Food (1984–86): daily per capita caloric intake 3,219 (vegetable products 63%, animal products 37%); (1984) 121% of FAO recommended minimum.

Military

Total active duty personnel (1988): 35,800 (army 53.1%, navy 19.6%, air force 25.4%, joint service personnel 1.9%). *Military expenditure as percent of GNP* (1987): 3.4% (world avg. 5.4%); per capita expenditure U.S.$664.

---

[1]Excludes Svalbard and Jan Mayen (24,360 sq mi [63,080 sq km]). [2]January 1. [3]Includes the Norwegian population of Svalbard and Jan Mayen registered as residents in municipalities on the mainland. [4]Population of communes. [5]Metal content of ore. [6]1986. [7]Includes 49,336 unemployed. [8]Includes imputed bank service charge and various excise and import taxes.

Oman

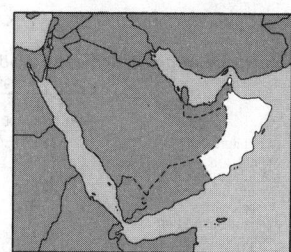

Official name: Saltanat 'Umān
(Sultanate of Oman).
Form of government: monarchy with a
consultative council (55) appointed by
the Sultan.
Head of state and government: Sultan.
Capital: Muscat.
Official language: Arabic.
Official religion: Islam.
Monetary unit: 1 rial Omani
(RO) = 1,000 baizas; valuation (Oct. 2,
1989) 1 RO = U.S.$2.63 = £1.61.

Area and population

Administrative Areas[3]	Centres[4]	area[1] sq mi	area[1] sq km	population[2] 1989 estimate
al-Bāṭinah	ar-Rustāq Ṣuḥār	...	...	...
al-Dākhilīyah	Nizwā, Samā'il	...	...	...
al-Janūbīyah	Salālah	40,000	100,000	...
Masqaṭ	Muscat	...	...	...
Musandam	Khaṣab	800	2,000	...
ash-Sharqīyah	Ibrā, Sūr	...	...	...
aẓ-Ẓāhirah	al-Buraymī, 'Ibrī	...	...	...
TOTAL		120,000	300,000	1,413,000

Demography

Population (1989): 1,422,000.
Density (1989): persons per sq mi 11.8, persons per sq km 4.7.
Urban–rural (1986): urban 9.2%; rural 90.8%.
Sex distribution (1986): male 57.31%; female 42.69%.
Age breakdown (1986): under 15, 39.8%; 15–29, 22.2%; 30–44, 25.7%; 45–59, 8.5%; 60–74, 2.9%; 75 and over, 0.9%.
Population projection: (2000) 2,057,000; (2010) 2,882,000.
Doubling time: 33 years.
Ethnic composition (1984): Omani Arab 77%; Indian 15%; Pakistani (mostly Baluchi) 3.5%; Bengali 2.5%; other 2%.
Religious affiliation (1984): Muslim 86%; Hindu 13%; other 1%.
Major cities (1982): Muscat 85,000; Nizwā 10,000; Salālah 10,000.

Vital statistics

Birth rate per 1,000 population (1986): 44.2 (world avg. 27.1).
Death rate per 1,000 population (1986): 13.0 (world avg. 9.9).
Natural increase rate per 1,000 population (1986): 31.2 (world avg. 17.2).
Total fertility rate (avg. births per childbearing woman; 1986): 7.0.
Marriage rate per 1,000 population: n.a.
Divorce rate per 1,000 population: n.a.
Life expectancy at birth (1986): male 53.7 years; female 56.0 years.
Morbidity (reported cases of illness per 100,000 population; 1987): influenza 7,615; malaria 1,160; chicken pox 1,098; mumps 390; dysentery 288; bacillary dysentery 185; tuberculosis 46; measles 24; brucellosis 17; food poisoning 17.

National economy

Budget (1989): Revenue: RO 1,162,700,000 (oil revenue 77.8%, gas revenue 4.2%, other 18.0%). Expenditures: RO 1,570,300,000 (1988; defense 36.3%, economic services 22.4%, general public services 13.6%, education 10.1%, health 5.0%).
Public debt (external, outstanding; 1987): U.S.$2,474,000,000.
Gross national product (at current market prices; 1987): U.S.$7,668,000,000 (U.S.$5,760 per capita).

Structure of gross domestic product and labour force

	1987 in value RO '000,000	1987 % of total value	1986 labour force	1986 % of labour force
Agriculture	105.4	3.5	108,800	23.3
Mining	1,413.0	47.4	9,700	2.1
Manufacturing	111.5	3.7	5,100	1.1
Construction	137.0	4.6	128,500	27.5
Public utilities	43.5	1.5	500	0.1
Transportation and communications	97.7	3.3	6,300	1.3
Trade	327.3	11.0	123,600	26.4
Finance	267.1	8.9	7,800	1.7
Pub. admin., defense	509.9	17.1 }	77,400	16.5
Services	40.4	1.4 }		
Other	−70.3[5]	−2.4[5]	—	—
TOTAL	2,982.5	100.0	467,700	100.0

Tourism (1987): receipts from visitors, U.S. $44,000,000[6]; expenditures by nationals abroad, n.a.
Household income and expenditure. Average household size (1986) 3.7; income per household: n.a.; sources of income: n.a.; food expenditure (1978): meat and eggs 20.6%, cereals 15.2%, fruits and nuts 12.4%, vegetables 11.9%, dairy products 10.3%, other foods 29.6%.
Production (metric tons except as noted). Agriculture, forestry, fishing (1988): vegetables and melons 226,000, dates 80,000, bananas 30,000, mangoes 16,000, watermelons 12,000, onions 10,000, tobacco leaf 2,000, wheat 1,000, potatoes 1,000; livestock (number of live animals) 712,000 goats, 218,000 sheep, 136,000 cattle, 2,000,000 chickens; fish catch 115,011. Mining and quarrying (1986): sand and gravel 7,514,000; stone 2,875,000; marble 44,000;

copper 18,000. Manufacturing: major products include cement blocks and floors, furniture, aluminum products, electric wire and cable, spark plugs, household utensils, fertilizers, and fibreglass products. Construction (1987): number of residential permits 3,025; nonresidential permits 328. Energy production (consumption): electricity (kW-hr; 1987) 3,793,000,000 (3,793,-000,000); coal, none (none); crude petroleum (barrels; 1987) 212,500,000 (15,400,000); petroleum products (metric tons; 1987) 6,883,000 (5,363,000); natural gas (cu m; 1987) 2,178,000,000 (2,178,000,000).
Population economically active (1986): total 467,700; activity rate of total population 35.7% (participation rates: ages 15–64, 60.9%; female 7.5%; unemployed, n.a.).

Price and earnings indexes (1978 = 100)

	1982	1983	1984	1985	1986	1987	1988
Consumer price index[7]	124.0	118.6	108.8	107.8	118.5	118.3	120.6
Annual earnings index	521.1	788.0	681.8	704.3	...	...	...

Land use (1987): meadows and pastures 4.7%; agricultural and under permanent cultivation 0.2%; other (mostly desert and developed area) 95.1%.

Foreign trade

Balance of trade (current prices)

	1983	1984	1985	1986	1987	1988
RO '000,000	+606.4	+578.3	+628.3	+175.9	+751.2	+396.0
% of total	26.0%	23.3%	22.4%	8.8%	34.0%	18.0%

Imports (1988): RO 900,000,000 (machinery and transport equipment 33.5%, manufacture goods 21.6%, food and live animals 17.4%; miscellaneous manufactured articles 10.9%; chemicals 5.6%; beverages and tobacco 1.9%).
Major import sources: United Arab Emirates 21.0%; Japan 16.8%; United Kingdom 13.3%; United States 8.8%; West Germany 5.2%; Italy 4.1%.
Exports (1988): RO 1,296,000,000[8] (crude petroleum 88.0%, food and live animals 1.9%, of which fish 1.5%; copper cathodes 1.3%; fruits and vegetables 0.3%). *Major export destinations:* United Arab Emirates 46.4%; Taiwan 7.7%; United Kingdom 5.8%; Saudi Arabia 4.6%; United States 4.6%; Australia 3.6%.

Transport and communications

Transport. Railroads: none. Roads (1987): total length 12,893 mi, 20,749 km (paved 20%). Vehicles (1987): private vehicles 120,368, commercial vehicles 106,096. Merchant marine (1988): vessels (100 gross tons and over) 32; total deadweight tonnage 16,399. Air transport (1988)[9]: passenger-mi 814,000,000, passenger-km 1,418,000,000; short ton-mi cargo 24,700,000, metric ton-km cargo 36,000,000; airports (1989) with scheduled flights 6.
Communications. Daily newspapers (1987): total number 3; total circulation 30,000; circulation per 1,000 population 22. Radio (1988): total number of receivers 888,300 (1 per 1.6 persons). Television (1988): total number of receivers 1,000,033 (1 per 1.4 persons). Telephones (1987): 79,929 (1 per 17 persons).

Education and health

Education (1987–88)

	schools	teachers	students	student/ teacher ratio
Primary (age 6–12)	367	8,080	212,328	26.3
Secondary (age 13–18)	311	4,332	56,394	13.0
Voc., teacher tr.	23	702	5,922	8.4
Higher	1	203	1,138	5.6

Educational attainment, n.a. *Literacy* (1979): total population age 6 and over literate 38%; males literate 55%; females literate 20%.
Health (1987): physicians 1,243 (1 per 1,071 persons); hospital beds 4,016 (1 per 331 persons); infant mortality rate per 1,000 live births (1986) 110.5.
Food: daily capita caloric intake, n.a.

Military

Total active duty personnel (1989): 25,500 (army 78.4%, navy 9.8%, air force 11.8%); foreign troops 3,700. *Military expenditure as percent of GNP* (1987): 23.3% (world 5.4%); per capita expenditure U.S.$1,235.

---

[1]No detailed area survey has been carried out thus far in the Sultanate of Queen. [2]No census has ever been taken in Oman; the total given is an unofficial estimate. For planning purposes the Omani government uses a 1985 estimate of 2,000,000. [3]Administrative areas are divided into 50 wilāyat (governorates). [4]Centres of the areas are not administrative capitals. [5]Less imputed bank service charges. [6]Hotel revenues. [7]Applies to food and beverages in the capital area only. [8]Includes reexports of RO 92,000,000. [9]One-fourth apportionment of international flights of Gulf Air.

Pakistan

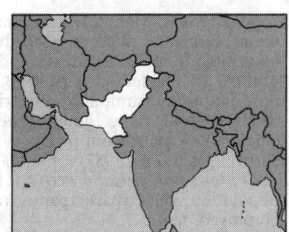

Official name: Islām-ī Jamhūrīya-e Pākistān (Islamic Republic of Pakistan).
Form of government: multiparty, federal Islamic republic with two legislative houses (Senate [87]; National Assembly [237]).
Chief of state: President.
Chief of government: Prime Minister.
Capital: Islāmābād.
Official language: Urdū.
Official religion: Islam.
Monetary unit: 1 Pakistan Rupee (PRs) = 100 paisa; valuation (Oct. 2, 1989) 1 U.S.$ = PRs 21.32; 1 £ = PRs 34.50.

Area and population		area[1]		population
				1983
Provinces	Capitals	sq mi	sq km	estimate[2]
Baluchistān	Quetta	134,050	347,188	4,611,000
North–West Frontier	Peshāwar	28,773	74,522	11,658,000
Punjab	Lahore	79,284	205,345	50,460,000
Sind	Karāchi	54,407	140,913	20,312,000
Federally Administered Tribal Areas	...	10,510	27,221	2,329,000
Federal Capital Area Islāmābād	...	350	906	359,000
TOTAL		307,374	796,095	89,729,000

Demography

Population (1989): 118,820,000[2].
Density (1989): persons per sq mi 386.6, persons per sq km 149.3.
Urban–rural (1987): urban 32.0%; rural 68.0%.
Sex distribution (1987): male 51.37%; female 48.63%.
Age breakdown (1987): under 15, 46.0%; 15–29, 24.6%; 30–44, 14.0%; 45–59, 9.3%; 60–74, 4.8%; 75 and over, 1.3%.
Population projection: (2000) 162,467,000; (2010) 205,472,000.
Doubling time: 21 years.
Linguistic composition (1981): Punjabī 48.2%; Pashto 13.1%; Sindhī 11.8%; Saraiki 9.8%; Urdū 7.6%; other 9.5%.
Religious affiliation (1981): Muslim 96.7%; Christian 1.6%; Hindu 1.5%; other 0.2%.
Major cities (1981): Karāchi 5,208,132; Lahore 2,952,689; Faisalābād 1,104,209; Rāwalpindi 794,843; Islāmābād 204,364.

Vital statistics

Birth rate per 1,000 population (1988): 46.5 (world avg. 27.1).
Death rate per 1,000 population (1988): 12.4 (world avg. 9.9).
Natural increase rate per 1,000 population (1988): 34.1 (world avg. 17.2).
Total fertility rate (avg. births per childbearing woman; 1988): 6.4.
Marriage rate per 1,000 population (1975–80): 10.7.
Divorce rate per 1,000 population (1975–80): 0.3.
Life expectancy at birth (1988): male 56.8 years; female 56.8 years.
Major causes of death (percent distribution; 1987): malaria 18.2%; childhood diseases 12.1%; diseases of digestive system 9.8%; diseases of respiratory system 9.2%; infection of intestinal tract 7.7%.

National economy

Budget (1988–89). Revenue: PRs 134,993,900,000 (indirect taxes 63.3, income from property and enterprises 18.3%, direct taxes 9.7%, receipts from civil administration 3.4%). Expenditures: PRs 165,558,700,000 (defense 30.0%, public debt service 28.7%, development fund 13.5%, grants to provinces 11.0%, administration 3.6%, social services 3.5%, subsidies 2.5%).
Production (metric tons except as noted). Agriculture, forestry, fishing (1987–88): sugarcane 31,239,000, wheat 12,926,000, rice 3,271,000, cottonseed (1986–87) 2,639,800, corn (maize) 1,513,000, cotton 1,128,000, tobacco 69,000; livestock (number of live animals) 33,000,000 goats, 27,500,000 sheep, 17,200,000 cattle, 14,000,000 buffalo, 1,000,000 camels, 150,400,000 poultry; roundwood (1987) 21,855,000 cu m; fish catch (1987) 427,760. Mining and quarrying (1987–88): limestone 5,705,000; rock salt 321,000; gypsum 320,000; aragonite/marble 168,000; silica sand 128,000; fire clay 99,000; china clay 32,000; barite 12,000; chromite 8,000. Manufacturing (1987–88): cement 5,219,000; chemical fertilizers 2,156,300, of which urea 1,491,600; refined sugar 1,541,000; chemicals 214,300; paper and paperboard 75,300; jute textiles 53,500; cotton textiles 202,671,000 sq m; beverages 419,592,000 bottles; cigarettes 31,592,000,000 units; bicycles 502,000 units; electric fans 75,600 units; sewing machines 63,300 units. Construction (value in PRs; 1984): residential 8,490,000,000; nonresidential 14,579,000,000. Energy production (consumption): electricity (kW-hr; 1987) 33,475,000,000 (33,475,000,000); coal (metric tons; 1987) 2,419,000 (3,218,000); crude petroleum (barrels; 1987) 15,098,000 (42,510,000); petroleum products (metric tons; 1987) 4,943,000 (7,838,000); natural gas (cu m; 1987) 10,121,000,000 (10,121,000,000).
Public debt (external, outstanding; 1987): U.S.$13,150,000,000.
Household income and expenditure. Average household size (1987) 6.5; income per household (1981) PRs 20,530 (U.S.$2,075); sources of income (1984–85): self-employment 49.1%, wages and salaries 28.9%, transfer payments 1.6%, other 20.4%; expenditure (1984–85): food 48.6%, housing 11.2%, clothing and footwear 7.5%, energy 5.6%, transport 4.5%, other 22.6%.

Gross national product (1987): U.S.$36,211,000,000 (U.S.$350 per capita).

Structure of gross domestic product and labour force				
	1987–88		1984–85	
	in value PRs '000,000	% of total value	labour force	% of labour force
Agriculture	135,991	22.3	14,054,000	48.7
Mining	14,029	2.3	47,000	0.1
Manufacturing	108,060	17.7	3,800,000	13.2
Construction	39,242	6.4	1,556,000	5.4
Public utilities	13,974	2.3	192,000	0.7
Transportation and communication	48,504	8.0	1,445,000	5.0
Trade	98,611	16.2	3,207,000	11.1
Finance	40,473	6.7	245,000	0.8
Pub. admin., defense	58,565	9.6 }	3,077,000	10.7
Services	51,923	8.5 }		
Other	...	...	1,249,000[3]	4.3[3]
TOTAL	609,372[4]	100.0	28,872,000	100.0

Population economically active (1987–88): total 30,520,000; activity rate of total population 29.4% (participation rates [1984–85]: ages 15–64, 50.6%; female 9.4%; unemployed [1987–88] 3.0%).

Price and earnings indexes (1985 = 100)							
	1983	1984	1985	1986	1987	1988	1989[5]
Consumer price index	89.3	94.7	100.0	103.5	108.4	117.9	127.2
Monthly earnings index	...	...	...	...	...	...	...

Land use (1987): forested 4.1%; meadows and pastures 6.5%; agricultural and under permanent cultivation 26.9%; built-on, wasteland, and other 62.5%.
Tourism (1987): receipts from visitors U.S.$171,000,000; expenditures by nationals abroad U.S.$248,000,000.

Foreign trade[6]

Balance of trade (current prices)						
	1983	1984	1985	1986	1987	1988
PRs '000,000	−23,475	−38,927	−42,029	−25,214	−19,938	−27,036
% of total	22.5%	35.1%	32.5%	18.3%	12.1%	14.2%

Imports (1987–88): PRs 111,382,000,000 (nonelectric machinery 17.6%, mineral oils 16.2%, chemicals 9.3%, transport equipment 8.6%, edible oils 7.0%, iron and steel 3.5%, electric machinery and appliances 3.3%). Major import sources: Japan 15.2%; U.S. 11.2%; W.Ger. 7.9%; Kuwait 7.2%; U.K. 6.8%; Saudi Arabia 5.0%; France 4.4%; China 3.5%; Malaysia 3.4%; South Korea 3.0%.
Exports (1987–88): PRs 78,445,000,000 (raw cotton 13.7%, cotton yarn 12.2%, cotton fabrics 10.9%, rice 8.2%, leather 6.4%, woolen carpets 5.7%, synthetic textiles 4.4%, fish and fish preparations 2.8%, sporting goods 1.5%). Major export destinations: Japan 11.3%, U.S. 11.0%; W.Ger. 7.0%; U.K. 6.8%; Italy 5.8%; Saudi Arabia 5.0%; Hong Kong 3.5%; France 3.2%.

Transport and communications

Transport. Railroads (1987–88): length 7,842 mi, 12,620 km; passenger-mi 11,000,000,000, passenger-km 17,000,000,000; short ton-mi cargo 5,300,000,000, metric ton-km cargo 7,800,000,000. Roads (1987–88): total length 68,430 mi, 110,128 km (paved 52%). Vehicles (1987): passenger cars 540,835; trucks and buses 158,895. Merchant marine (1988): vessels (100 gross tons and over) 73; total deadweight tonnage 526,234. Air transport (1987–88): passenger-km 7,707,486,000; metric ton-km cargo 360,191,000; airports (1989) with scheduled flights 32.
Communications. Daily newspapers (1987): total number 125; total circulation 1,321,331; circulation per 1,000 population 12. Radio (1988): total number of receivers 9,775,297 (1 per 11 persons). Television (1988): total number of receivers 1,508,657 (1 per 73 persons). Telephones (1987): 679,370 (1 per 159 persons).

Education and health

Education (1987–88)	schools	teachers	students	student/ teacher ratio
Primary (age 5–9)	84,307	194,200	7,687,000	39.6
Secondary (age 10–14)	11,361	147,300	2,809,000	19.1
Voc., teacher tr.	299	4,502	63,000	14.0
Higher	705	39,233	567,805	14.5

Educational attainment (1981). Percent of population age 25 and over having: no formal schooling 78.9%; some primary education 8.7%; some secondary 10.5%; postsecondary 1.9%. Literacy (1981): total population age 15 and over literate 11,938,790 (25.6%); males literate 8,709,162 (36.0%); females literate 3,229,628 (15.2%).
Health (1988): physicians (1987) 51,020 (1 per 2,176 persons); hospital beds 64,471 (1 per 1,783 persons); infant mortality rate per 1,000 live births 108.0.
Food (1984–88): daily per capita caloric intake 2,244 (vegetable products 89%, animal products 11%); 93% of FAO recommended minimum requirement.

Military

Total active duty personnel (1989): 520,000 (army 92.3%, navy 2.9%, air force 4.8%). Military expenditure as percent of GNP (1987): 6.5% (world 5.4%); per capita expenditure U.S.$20.

[1]Excludes the Pakistani-occupied part of Jammu and Kashmir. [2]Provincial estimates exclude and 1989 estimate includes Afghan refugees and residents of Pakistani-occupied Jammu and Kashmir. [3]Includes unemployed. [4]At factor cost. [5]July. [6]Import figures are f.o.b. in balance of trade and c.i.f. for commodities and trading partners.

Panama

Official name: República de Panamá (Republic of Panama).
Form of government: military regime.
Head of state and government: Provisional President[1].
Capital: Panama City.
Official language: Spanish.
Official religion: none.
Monetary unit: 1 balboa (B) = 100 cents; valuation (Oct. 2, 1989) 1 U.S.$ = B 1.00; 1 £ = B 1.62.

Area and population		area		population
		sq mi	sq km	1988 estimate
Provinces	**Capitals**			
Bocas del Toro	Bocas del Toro	3,443	8,917	79,596
Chiriquí	David	3,381	8,758	367,664
Coclé	Penonomé	1,944	5,035	167,312
Colón	Colón	1,915	4,961	165,995
Darién	La Palma	6,488	16,803	39,633
Herrera	Chitré	937	2,427	102,856
Los Santos	Las Tablas	1,493	3,867	81,688
Panamá	Panama City	4,642	12,022	1,062,887
Veraguas	Santiago	4,280	11,086	212,951
Special territory				
Comarca de San Blas	El Porvenir	1,238	3,206	41,419
TOTAL AREA		29,762[2]	77,082	2,322,001

Demography

Population (1989): 2,370,000.
Density (1989): persons per sq mi 79.6, persons per sq km 30.7.
Urban–rural (1987): urban 51.9%; rural 48.1%.
Sex distribution (1985): male 50.97%; female 49.03%.
Age breakdown (1986): under 15, 37.0%; 15–29, 29.5%; 30–44, 17.2%; 45–59, 9.6%; 60–74, 5.2%; 75 and over, 1.5%.
Population projection: (2000) 2,893,000; (2010) 3,324,000.
Doubling time: 32 years.
Ethnic composition (1985): mestizo 62.0%; black 14.0%; white 10.0%; Amerindian 6.0%; mulatto 5.0%; other 3.0%.
Religious affiliation (1985): Roman Catholic 84.0%; Protestant 4.8%; Muslim 4.5%; Baha'ī 1.1%; Hindu 0.3%; other 5.3%.
Major cities (1989): Panama City 435,458; San Miguelito 252,560; Colón 58,479; David 49,472[3]; La Chorrera 37,566[3].

Vital statistics

Birth rate per 1,000 population (1987): 27.0 (world avg. 27.1); (1985) legitimate 28.1%; illegitimate 71.9%.
Death rate per 1,000 population (1987): 5.0 (world avg. 9.9).
Natural increase rate per 1,000 population (1987): 22.0 (world avg. 17.2).
Total fertility rate (avg. births per childbearing woman; 1987): 3.2.
Marriage rate per 1,000 population (1987): 4.5.
Divorce rate per 1,000 population (1987): 0.5.
Life expectancy at birth (1985–90): male 70.2 years; female 74.1 years.
Major causes of death per 100,000 population (1986): diseases of the circulatory system 115.3, of which ischemic heart disease 46.0, cerebrovascular disease 39.5; malignant neoplasms (cancers) 52.1; accidents 35.0; diseases of the respiratory system 33.9.

National economy

Budget (1988). Revenue: B 610,500,000 (direct taxes 38.0%, of which income taxes 32.2%; indirect taxes 34.5%, of which sales taxes 14.3%). Expenditures: B 875,600,000 (education 28.8%; payments on internal debt 18.3%; home affairs and justice 14.6%; health 9.8%; payments on external debt 4.4%).
Public debt (external, outstanding; 1987): U.S.$3,722,000,000.
Tourism: receipts from visitors (1988) U.S.$168,000,000; expenditures by nationals abroad (1987) U.S.$65,000,000.
Production (metric tons except as noted). Agriculture, forestry, fishing (1988): sugarcane 1,600,000, bananas 900,000, rice 166,000, corn (maize) 97,000, oranges 36,000, tomatoes 32,000, plantains 30,000, coffee 13,000; livestock (number of live animals) 1,502,000 cattle, 240,000 pigs; roundwood (1987) 2,047,000 cu m; fish catch (value of production in B; 1986): shrimps 47,895,000, lobster 6,241,000, fish 4,216,000. Mining and quarrying (1987): limestone 294,000[4]; salt 17,100. Manufacturing (value of production in B '000,000; 1987): processed food and beverages 809, of which prepared meat 159, marine products 95, milk products 94, milled grains 67, products of bakeries 60; refined petroleum 236; paper and paper products 167. Construction (value of construction in B '000,000; 1986): residential 118; nonresidential 34. Energy production (consumption): electricity (kW-hr; 1987) 2,902,000,000 (2,902,000,000); coal (metric tons; 1987) none (5,000); crude petroleum (barrels; 1987) none (9,529,000); petroleum products (metric tons; 1987) 1,159,000 (735,000); natural gas, none (none).
Population economically active (1987): total 770,472[5]; activity rate of total population 32.3% (participation rates: ages 15–69 [1986] 57.6%; female [1986] 31.5%; unemployed 11.6%).

Price and earnings indexes (1985 = 100)							
	1982	1983	1984	1985	1986	1987	1988
Consumer price index	95.4	97.4	99.0	100.0	99.9	100.9	101.2
Monthly earnings index[6]	84.3	92.2	95.3	100.0	100.7	...	...

Household income and expenditure. Average household size (1980) 4.8; median income per household (1980) B 2,950 (U.S.$2,950); sources of income (1979): wages and salaries 85.3%, transfers 9.2%, other 5.5%; expenditure (1978): food 47.3%, housing and energy 12.7%, household furnishings 8.5%, transportation 6.8%, health care 4.9%, other 19.8%.
Gross national product (at current market prices; 1987): U.S.$5,128,000,000 (U.S.$2,240 per capita).

Structure of gross domestic product and labour force				
	1988			
	in value B '000,000[7]	% of total value	labour force[8]	% of labour force
Agriculture	196.9	11.2	199,200	30.4
Mining	1.9	0.1	400	0.1
Manufacturing	141.3	8.0	62,200	9.5
Construction	36.3	2.1	22,400	3.4
Public utilities	73.5	4.2	9,400	1.4
Transportation and communications	503.7[9]	28.6[9]	37,200	5.7
Trade	174.2	9.9	97,400	14.8
Finance, real estate	270.4	15.3	23,700	3.6
Pub. admin., defense	262.6	14.9 }	187,300	28.5
Services	151.5	8.6 }		
Other	−50.1[10]	−2.8[10]	17,000	2.6
TOTAL	1,762.2	100.0[2]	656,200	100.0

Land use (1986): forested 52.5%; meadows and pastures 15.3%; agricultural and under permanent cultivation 7.5%; other 24.7%.

Foreign trade[11, 12]

Balance of trade (current prices)						
	1983	1984	1985	1986	1987	1988
B '000,000	−946.2	−1,000.3	−903.4	−754.2	−784.7	−393.6
% of total	59.6%	64.4%	57.4%	51.9%	53.6%	41.3%

Imports (1987): B 1,211,100,000 (capital goods 16.3%, crude petroleum 14.4%, food products 9.3%, unspecified 60.0%). *Major import sources:* U.S. 33.5%; Colón Free Zone 11.8%; Mexico 8.5%; Japan 7.4%; Venezuela 4.0%.
Exports (1987): B 339,000,000 (bananas 25.3%, shrimps 19.2%, coffee 5.3%, sugar 5.0%, clothing 4.7%). *Major export destinations:* U.S. 64.5%; West Germany 5.9%; Costa Rica 5.7%; Puerto Rico 2.6%; Italy 2.5%.

Transport and communications

Transport. Railroads: route length (1988) 149 mi, 240 km; passengers carried 46,895[13]; short ton-mi cargo 7,165,000[14], metric ton-km cargo 10,460,-000[14]. Roads (1986): total length 6,039 mi, 9,719 km (paved 33%). Vehicles (1986): passenger cars 134,339; trucks and buses 46,545. Merchant marine (1988): vessels (100 gross tons and over) 5,022; total deadweight tonnage 71,476,002. Panama Canal traffic (1988): oceangoing transits 12,234; cargo 154,011,780 metric tons. Air transport (1986)[15]: passenger-mi 313,900,000, passenger-km 505,174,000; short ton-mi cargo 6,343,000, metric ton-km cargo 9,261,000; airports (1989) with scheduled flights 6.
Communications. Daily newspapers (1988): total number 4; total circulation 99,000; circulation per 1,000 population 43. Radio (1986): 900,000 receivers (1 per 2.5 persons). Television (1988): 476,000 receivers (1 per 4.9 persons). Telephones (1987): 239,995 (1 per 9.3 persons).

Education and health

Education (1987)	schools	teachers	students	student/ teacher ratio
Primary (age 6–11)	2,617	13,698	346,137	25.3
Secondary (age 12–17)	341	10,068	189,771	18.8
Voc., teacher tr.	50	624	9,853	15.8
Higher	8	3,317	55,633	16.8

Educational attainment (1980). Percent of population age 25 and over having: no formal schooling 17.4%; incomplete primary education 27.3%; complete primary education 23.4%; secondary 23.5%; higher 8.4%. *Literacy* (1985): total population age 15 and over literate 1,204,000 (88.2%); males literate 618,000 (89.0%); females literate 586,000 (87.7%).
Health (1987): physicians 2,722 (1 per 836 persons); hospital beds 7,798 (1 per 292 persons); infant mortality rate per 1,000 live births 23.2.
Food (1984–86): daily per capita caloric intake 2,439 (vegetable products 81%, animal products 19%); 106% of FAO recommended minimum requirement.

Military

Total active duty personnel (1989): 4,400 (army 79.5%, navy 9.1%, air force 11.4%). U.S. forces in former Canal Zone 10,700. *Military expenditure as percent of GNP* (1987): 2.0% (world 5.4%); per capita expenditure U.S.$46.

[1]The commander of the National Defense Forces was the de facto executive in October 1989. [2]Detail does not add to total given because of rounding. [3]1980. [4]1985. [5]Excludes indigenous areas, former Canal Zone, and institutional households. [6]Median figure of public sector. [7]At prices of 1970. [8]Employed only, excluding not adequately defined. [9]Includes trans-Panamanian oil pipeline, commission of Panama Canal, and all activities of Colón Free Zone. [10]Net of imputed bank service charges and import fees. [11]Import figures are f.o.b. in balance of trade and c.i.f. in commodities and trading partners. [12]Excludes Colón Free Zone (1987 imports c.i.f. B 2,043,700,000; 1987 reexports f.o.b. B 2,285,800,000) and transshipped oil. [13]Chiriqui National Railroad; 1987. [14]Chiriqui Land Company Railways; 1987. [15]COPA and Air Panama only.

Papua New Guinea

Official name: Papua New Guinea.
Form of government: constitutional
monarchy with one legislative house
(National Parliament [109]).
Chief of state: British Monarch
represented by governor-general.
Head of government: Prime Minister.
Capital: Port Moresby.
Official language: English.
Official religion: none.
Monetary unit: 1 Papua New Guinea
kina (K) = 100 toea; valuation
(Oct. 2, 1989) 1 U.S.$ = K 0.86;
1 £ = K 1.39.

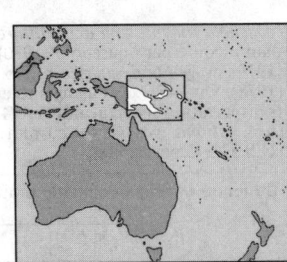

Area and population

Provinces	Administrative centres	area		population
		sq mi	sq km	1989 estimate[1]
Central	Central	11,400	29,500	132,200
Chimbu	Kundiawa	2,350	6,100	191,100
Eastern Highlands	Goroka	4,300	11,200	326,800
East New Britain	Rabaul	6,000	15,500	149,100
East Sepik	Wewak	16,550	42,800	269,800
Enga	Wabag	4,950	12,800	190,300
Gulf	Kerema	13,300	34,500	72,900
Madang	Madang	11,200	29,000	256,200
Manus	Lorengau	800	2,100	29,700
Milne Bay	Samarai	5,400	14,000	152,200
Morobe	Lae	13,300	34,500	392,900
National Capital District	Port Moresby	100	240	166,100
New Ireland	Kavieng	3,700	9,600	78,200
Northern	Popondetta	8,800	22,800	93,500
North Solomons	Buka	3,600	9,300	155,600
Southern Highlands	Mendi	9,200	23,800	273,000
Western	Daru	38,350	99,300	97,600
Western Highlands	Mount Hagen	3,300	8,500	322,500
West New Britain	Kimbe	8,100	21,000	114,400
West Sepik	Vanimo	14,000	36,300	128,800
TOTAL		178,704[2]	462,840	3,592,900[3]

Demography

Population (1989): 3,592,900.
Density (1989): persons per sq mi 20.1, persons per sq km 7.8.
Urban–rural (1985): urban 14.3%; rural 85.7%.
Sex distribution (1985): male 52.09%; female 47.91%.
Age breakdown (1985): under 15, 41.6%; 15–29, 27.5%; 30–44, 16.0%; 45–59, 9.3%; 60–74, 4.5%; 75 and over, 1.0%[2].
Population projection: (2000) 4,568,000; (2010) 5,692,000.
Doubling time: 27 years.
Ethnic composition (1983): New Guinea Papuan 84.0%; New Guinea Melanesian 15.0%; other 1.0%.
Religious affiliation (1980): Protestant 58.4%; Roman Catholic 32.8%; Anglican 5.4%; traditional beliefs 2.5%; Bahā'ī 0.6%; other 0.3%.
Major cities (1987): Port Moresby 152,100; Lae 79,600; Madang 24,700; Wewak 23,200; Goroka 21,800.

Vital statistics

Birth rate per 1,000 population (1988): 38.0 (world avg. 27.1); legitimate, n.a.; illegitimate, n.a.
Death rate per 1,000 population (1988): 11.9 (world avg. 9.9).
Natural increase rate per 1,000 population (1988): 26.1 (world avg. 17.2).
Total fertility rate (avg. births per childbearing woman; 1988): 5.5.
Marriage rate per 1,000 population: n.a.
Divorce rate per 1,000 population: n.a.
Life expectancy at birth (1988): male 53.4 years; female 55.0 years.
Major causes of death per 100,000 population: (1984): pneumonia 27.6; conditions originating from perinatal period 10.9; malaria 9.3; diarrheal diseases 9.0; meningitis 7.7; tuberculosis 6.7.

National economy

Budget (1989). Revenue: K 963,400,000 (foreign grants 20.9%, import duties 19.5%, personal income tax 16.6%, nontax revenue 12.3%, excise duties 9.8%). Expenditures: K 1,016,300,000 (administrative 43.0%, transfers to provincial governments 25.8%, interest payments 6.9%, capital works 6.8%).
Public debt (external, outstanding; 1987): U.S.$1,471,000,000.
Tourism (1987): receipts from visitors U.S.$17,000,000; expenditures by nationals abroad U.S.$32,000,000.
Land use (1986): forested 84.7%; agricultural and under permanent cultivation 0.9%; meadows and pastures 0.2%; other 14.2%.
Production (metric tons except as noted). Agriculture, forestry, fishing (1987): bananas 967,000, coconuts 900,000, sweet potatoes 476,000, sugarcane 232,000, taro 187,000, yams 177,000, copra 150,000, palm oil 139,000, cassava 107,000, palm kernels 58,400, coffee 52,000, cocoa 34,000, pineapples 11,000, tea 9,000; livestock (number of live animals) 1,500,000 pigs, 123,000 cattle, 17,000 goats, 3,000,000 chickens; roundwood 8,231,000 cu m; fish catch 15,563. Mining and quarrying (1987): copper 217,700; silver 61,056 kg; gold 33,250 kg. Manufacturing (value added, in K; 1985): food, beverages, and tobacco 162,558,000; metals, metal products, machinery, and equipment 47,493,000; wood and wood products 29,807,000. Construction (value[4]; 1986): residential K 19,369,000; nonresidential K 55,675,000. Energy production (consumption): electricity (kW-hr; 1987) 1,797,000,000 (1,797,000,000); coal (metric tons; 1987) none K (1,000); crude petroleum

(barrels; 1987) none (n.a.); petroleum products (metric tons; 1987) none (760,000); natural gas, none (n.a.).
Gross national product (1987): U.S.$2,555,000,000 (U.S.$730 per capita).

Structure of gross domestic product and labour force

	1986		1980	
	in value K '000,000	% of total value	labour force[5]	% of labour force[5]
Agriculture	833.7	33.9	564,500	77.0
Mining	294.4	12.0	4,300	0.6
Manufacturing	221.3	9.0	14,000	1.9
Construction	87.1	3.5	21,600	2.9
Public utilities	35.6	1.4	2,800	0.4
Transp. and commun.	84.5	3.4	17,400	2.4
Trade	193.8	7.9	25,100	3.4
Finance	165.8	6.7	4,500	0.6
Pub. admin., defense	170.6	6.9	77,100	10.5
Services	262.0	10.6		
Other	112.8	4.6	1,500	0.2
TOTAL	2,461.6	100.0[2]	732,800	100.0[2]

Population economically active (1980)[5]: total 732,800; activity rate of total population 24.6% (participation rates: over age 10, 35.2%; female 39.8%; unemployed 12.8%[6]).

Price and earnings indexes (1985 = 100)

	1982	1983	1984	1985	1986	1987	1988
Consumer price index	83.2	89.8	96.4	100.0	105.5	109.0	114.9
Daily earnings index[7]	86.3	91.2	95.8	100.0	104.5	109.5	112.8

Household income and expenditure. Average household size (1980) 4.6; income per household (1975–76) K 2,771 (U.S.$3,483); sources of income: n.a.; expenditure (1987)[8]: food and beverages 40.9%, transportation and communications 13.0%, housing 12.5%, clothing and footwear 6.2%, heating and lighting 4.9%, services and other 22.5%.

Foreign trade[9]

Balance of trade (current prices)

	1983	1984	1985	1986	1987	1988
K '000,000	−138.0	−64.7	+35.9	−45.0	+174.4	+214.7
% of total	9.2%	3.9%	2.0%	2.7%	8.3%	9.4%

Imports (1986): K 902,069,000 (machinery and transport equipment 34.1%; food and live animals 18.0%; basic manufactures 16.5%; mineral fuels, lubricants, and related materials 10.4%). *Major import sources:* Australia 40.4%; Japan 17.7%; U.S. 9.5%; Singapore 6.2%; U.K. 3.4%; West Germany 2.8%.
Exports (1986): K 1,013,776,000 (gold 39.8%; copper ore and concentrates 15.6%; coffee 13.5%; timber 10.3%; cocoa beans 5.6%; palm oil 2.4%; copra 1.5%). *Major export destinations:* West Germany 34.4%; Japan 25.6%; Australia 14.9%; South Korea 6.1%; U.K. 4.5%; U.S. 3.3%; Spain 2.1%.

Transport and communications

Transport. Railroads: none. Roads (1986): total length 12,263 mi, 19,736 km (paved 6%). Vehicles (1986): passenger cars 18,748; trucks and buses 30,497. Merchant marine (1988): vessels (100 gross tons and over) 82; total deadweight tonnage 46,259. Air transport (1987): passenger-mi 306,000,000, passenger-km 492,000,000; short ton-mi cargo 6,633,000, metric ton-km cargo 9,684,000; airports (1989) with scheduled flights 177.
Communications. Daily newspapers (1988): total number 1; total circulation 32,000; circulation per 1,000 population 9.1. Radio (1988): total number of receivers 229,504 (1 per 15 persons). Television (1985): total number of receivers 230,000 (1 per 14 persons). Telephones (1987): 72,104 (1 per 48 persons).

Education and health

Education (1986)

	schools	teachers	students	student/ teacher ratio
Primary (age 7–12)	2,461	12,318	374,950	30.4
Secondary (age 13–16)	122	2,025	49,974	24.7
Voc., teacher tr.	112	745	10,078	13.5
Higher	2	400	3,029	7.6

Educational attainment (1980). Percent of population age 25 and over having: no formal schooling 82.6%; some primary education 8.2%; completed primary 5.0%; some secondary 4.2%. *Literacy* (1980): total population age 15 and over literate 757,500 (42.3%); males literate 490,100 (52.4%); females literate 267,400 (31.3%).
Health: physicians (1987) 283 (1 per 11,904 persons); hospital beds ((1984) 14,661 (1 per 222 persons); infant mortality rate per 1,000 live births (1988) 60.0.
Food (1980–82): daily per capita caloric intake 2,074 (vegetable products 90%, animal products 10%); (1984) 82% of FAO recommended minimum.

Military

Total active duty personnel (1988): 3,200 (army 90.6%, navy 6.3%, air force 3.1%). *Military expenditure as percent of GNP* (1986): 1.5% (world 5.5%); per capita expenditure U.S.$12.

[1]De jure. [2]Detail does not add to total given because of rounding. [3]Includes non-citizens. [4]Completed new buildings. [5]Citizens of Papua New Guinea over age 10 involved in "money-raising activities" only. [6]1977; in six urban centres. [7]Minimum wage of urban labourers. [8]Weights of retail price index components. [9]Import figures are f.o.b. in balance of trade and c.i.f. for commodities and trading partners.

Paraguay

Official name: República del Paraguay (Republic of Paraguay).
Form of government: republic with two legislative houses (Senate [36]; Chamber of Deputies [72]).
Head of state and government: President.
Capital: Asunción.
Official language: Spanish.
Official religion: Roman Catholicism.
Monetary unit: 1 Paraguayan Guaraní (₲) = 100 céntimos; valuation[1] (Oct. 2, 1989) 1 U.S.$ = ₲1,257; 1 £ = ₲2,033.

Area and population

Regions Departments	Capitals	area sq mi	area sq km	population 1989 estimate
Occidental		95,338	246,925	71,500
Alto Paraguay	Fuerte Olimpio	17,754	45,982	11,000
Boquerón	Dr. Pedro P. Peña	18,034	46,708	18,300
Chaco	Mayor Pablo Lagerenza	14,041	36,367	400
Nueva Asunción	General Eugenio A. Garay	17,359	44,961	300
Presidente Hayes	Pozo Colorado	28,150	72,907	41,500
Oriental		61,710	159,827	4,085,800
Alto Paraná	Ciudad del Este	5,751	14,895	358,700
Amambay	Pedro Juan Caballero	4,994	12,933	83,800
Asunción	Asunción	45	117	567,700
Caaguazú	Coronel Oviedo	4,430	11,474	427,000
Caazapá	Caazapá	3,666	9,496	134,700
Canendiyú	Salto del Guairá	5,663	14,667	108,700
Central	Asunción	952	2,465	751,300
Concepción	Concepción	6,970	18,051	178,500
Cordillera	Caacupé	1,910	4,948	233,600
Guairá	Villarrica	1,485	3,846	183,800
Itapúa	Encarnación	6,380	16,525	358,600
Misiones	San Juan Bautista	3,690	9,556	97,800
Ñeembucú	Pilar	4,690	12,147	88,500
Paraguarí	Paraguarí	3,361	8,705	244,700
San Pedro	San Pedro	7,723	20,002	268,400
TOTAL		157,048	406,752	4,157,300

Demography

Population (1989): 4,157,000.
Density (1989): persons per sq mi 26.5; persons per sq km 10.2.
Urban–rural (1986): urban 43.9%; rural 56.1%.
Sex distribution (1987): male 50.62%; female 49.38%.
Age breakdown (1987): under 15, 40.7%; 15–29, 28.7%; 30–44, 17.1%; 45–59, 8.1%; 60–74, 4.3%; 75 and over, 1.1%.
Population projection: (2000) 5,538,000; (2010) 6,928,000.
Doubling time: 25 years.
Ethnic composition (1980): mestizo (Spanish–Guaraní) 90.8%; Amerindian 3.0%; German 1.7%; other 4.5%.
Religious affiliation (1980): Roman Catholic 96.0%; Protestant 2.1%; other 1.9%.
Major cities (1985): Asunción 567,678; San Lorenzo 123,737; Ciudad del Este 116,758; Encarnación 64,324; Concepción 62,577.

Vital statistics

Birth rate per 1,000 population (1985–90): 34.9 (world avg. 27.1); (1985) legitimate 68.7%[2]; illegitimate 31.3%[2].
Death rate per 1,000 population (1985–90): 6.6 (world avg. 9.9).
Natural increase rate per 1,000 population (1985–90): 28.3 (world avg. 17.2).
Total fertility rate (avg. births per childbearing woman; 1985–90): 4.6.
Marriage rate per 1,000 population (1987): 4.3[2].
Divorce rate per 1,000 population: n.a.
Life expectancy at birth (1985–90): male 63.7 years; female 68.6 years.
Major causes of death per 100,000 population (1984): diseases of the circulatory system 95.7; infectious and parasitic diseases 40.5; diseases of the respiratory system 31.4; malignant neoplasms (cancers) 25.6.

National economy

Budget (1988). Revenue: ₲255,465,100,000 (domestic taxes on goods and services 36.7%, income tax 16.2%, sales tax 10.5%, customs duties 7.5%, pension funds 4.4%, alcohol tax 3.5%, real estate taxes 3.1%). Expenditures: ₲228,586,700,000 (public debt 21.8%, defense 14.3%, education 13.7%, ministry of interior 9.0%, public health 3.7%, public works 3.2%).
Public debt (external, outstanding; 1987): U.S.$2,218,000,000.
Production (metric tons except as noted). Agriculture, forestry, fishing (1988): cassava 3,891,000, sugarcane 3,382,000, soybeans 1,407,000, corn (maize) 1,200,000, seed cotton 537,000, bananas 420,000, oranges 360,000, lint cotton 150,000, sweet potatoes 113,000; livestock (number of live animals) 7,780,000 cattle, 2,108,000 pigs, 16,000,000 chickens; roundwood (1987) 8,439,000 cu m; fish catch (1987) 10,000. Mining and quarrying (1986): limestone 180,000; kaolin 55,000; gypsum 6,000. Manufacturing (1987): cement 269,200; beef and veal 118,000[3]; sugar 104,236; hides 13,863; tung oil 8,128; edible coconut oil 3,619; coconut pulp 2,040; woven cotton fabrics 6,175,000 metres; nonalcoholic beverages 1,292,100 hectolitres; beer 917,980 hectolitres; alcohol 39,410 hectolitres[4]; cigarettes 56,711,000 cases; matches 9,159,000 boxes[4]. Construction (1985): residential 60,800 sq m; nonresidential 163,200 sq m. Energy production (consumption): electricity (kW-hr; 1987) 2,825,000,000 (2,835,000,000); coal, none (none); crude petroleum (barrels; 1987) none (1,534,000); petroleum products (metric tons; 1987) 199,000 (507,000); natural gas, none (none).

Tourism (1987): receipts from visitors U.S.$121,000,000; expenditures by nationals abroad U.S.$50,000,000.
Gross national product (1987): U.S.$3,923,000,000 (U.S.$1,000 per capita).

Structure of gross domestic product and labour force

	1986 in value ₲'000,000	1986 % of total value	1982 labour force	1982 % of labour force
Agriculture	498,900	27.2	445,518	42.9
Mining	8,300	0.5	1,406	0.1
Manufacturing	296,000	16.1	124,658	12.0
Construction	110,100	6.0	69,900	6.7
Public utilities	44,800	2.4	2,605	0.3
Transp. and commun.	80,100	4.4	30,524	2.9
Trade	489,800	26.7	85,961	8.3
Finance			18,019	1.7
Pub. admin., defense	305,700	16.7	174,228	16.8
Services				
Other			86,444	8.3
TOTAL	1,833,800[5]	100.0	1,039,258[5]	100.0

Population economically active (1982): total 1,039,258; activity rate of total population 51.5% (participation rates: ages 15–64, 57.5%; female 19.7%; unemployed 4.6%).

Price and earnings indexes (1985 = 100)

	1982	1983	1984	1985	1986	1987	1988
Consumer price index	58.5	66.4	79.9	100.0	131.7	160.5	124.1
Monthly earnings index	...	...	...	...	...	...	...

Household income and expenditure: average household size (1982) 5.2; sources of income (1985): wages and salaries 37.5%, transfer payments 2.5%, other 60.0%; expenditure (1980): food 48.7%, housing 16.4%, clothing 9.7%, household durable goods 6.2%, transportation and communications 4.5%.
Land use (1987): forested 50.2%; meadows and pastures 39.3%; agricultural and under permanent cultivation 5.5%; other 5.0%.

Foreign trade

Balance of trade (current prices)

	1983	1984	1985	1986	1987	1988
₲'000,000	−26,519	−42,316	−75,892	−150,210	−115,975	+28,520
% of total	23.5%	21.7%	28.2%	44.9%	21.8%	4.5%

Imports (1988): U.S.$494,749,000 (machinery and transport equipment 40.4%, of which transport equipment 9.7%; fuels and lubricants 18.6%; tobacco and beverages 10.1%; chemicals and pharmaceuticals 8.0%; iron and steel 4.0%). *Major import sources:* Brazil 30.4%; Argentina 11.9%; United States 10.1%; Algeria 7.5%; Japan 7.4%; United Kingdom 7.0%.
Exports (1988): U.S.$509,843,000 (cotton fibres 41.1%; soybeans 30.2%; processed meat 7.9%; timber 3.1%; vegetable oil 1.8%, of which coconut oil 0.7%; tobacco 1.2%; perfume oils 0.9%). *Major export destinations:* Brazil 22.9%; The Netherlands 13.3%; Switzerland 7.6%; Argentina 6.6%; West Germany 3.8%; United States 3.7%; Spain 3.0%.

Transport and communications

Transport. Railroads (1980): route length (1987) 274 mi, 441 km; passenger-mi 13,900,000, passenger-km 22,400,000; short ton-mi cargo 23,600,000, metric ton-km cargo 34,400,000. Roads (1985): total length 9,186 mi, 14,783 km (paved 13%). Vehicles (1985): passenger cars 84,986; trucks and buses 41,986. Merchant marine (1988): vessels (100 gross tons and over) 39; total deadweight tonnage 44,272. Air transport (1988): passenger-mi 542,261,000, passenger-km 872,687,000; short ton-mi cargo 4,214,000, metric ton-km cargo 6,153,000; airports (1989) with scheduled flights 1.
Communications. Daily newspapers (1987): total number 4; total circulation 123,000; circulation per 1,000 population 32. Radio (1988): 752,852 receivers (1 per 5.4 persons). Television (1988): 350,000 receivers (1 per 12 persons). Telephones (1987): 100,120 (1 per 42 persons).

Education and health

Education (1988)

	schools	teachers	students	student/ teacher ratio
Primary (age 7–12)	4,318	24,729	627,190	25.4
Secondary (age 13–18)[6]	780	9,444	164,086	17.4
Higher	2	2,694[7]	28,737	...

Educational attainment (1982). Percent of population age 25 and over having: no formal schooling 13.6%; primary education 64.7%; secondary 15.5%; higher 3.4%; not stated 2.8%. *Literacy* (1982): total population age 15 and over literate 1,534,810 (85.7%); males literate 782,560 (88.7%); females literate 752,250 (82.9%).
Health: physicians (1984) 2,453 (1 per 1,458 persons); hospital beds (1987) 2,850 (1 per 1,459 persons); infant mortality rate per 1,000 live births (1985–90) 48.9.
Food (1984–86): daily per capita caloric intake 2,843 (vegetable products 81%, animal products 19%); 123% of FAO recommended minimum requirement.

Military

Total active duty personnel (1989): 16,000 (army 78.1%, navy 15.6%, air force 6.3%). *Military expenditure as percent of GNP* (1987): 1.0% (world 5.4%); per capita expenditure U.S.$11.

---

[1]Free rate. [2]Civil Registry records only. [3]1986. [4]1984. [5]Detail does not add to total given because of rounding. [6]Includes vocational education and teacher training. [7]1985.

Peru

Official name: República del Perú (Spanish) (Republic of Peru).
Form of government: unitary multiparty republic with two legislative houses (Senate [60]; Chamber of Deputies [180]).
Head of state and government: President.
Capital: Lima.
Official languages: Spanish; Quechua.
Official religion: Roman Catholicism.
Monetary unit: 1 Inti (I/.) = 100 céntimos = 1,000 soles; valuation (Oct. 5, 1989) 1 U.S.$ = I/. 5,725; 1 £ = I/. 9,263.

Area and population		area		population
		sq mi	sq km	1989 estimate
Departments	**Capitals**			
Amazonas	Chachapoyas	15,945	41,297	327,000
Ancash	Huaraz	14,158	36,669	967,000
Apurímac	Abancay	7,934	20,550	368,000
Arequipa	Arequipa	24,528	63,528	937,000
Ayacucho	Ayacucho	17,058	44,181	562,000
Cajamarca	Cajamarca	13,486	34,930	1,246,000
Cuzco	Cuzco	29,471	76,329	1,021,000
Huancavelica	Huancavelica	8,139	21,079	374,000
Huánuco	Huánuco	13,088	33,897	596,000
Ica	Ica	8,205	21,251	531,000
Junín	Huancayo	15,944	41,296	1,088,000
La Libertad	Trujillo	8,973	23,241	1,212,000
Lambayeque	Chiclayo	5,304	13,737	908,000
Lima	Lima	13,058	33,821	6,511,000
Loreto	Iquitos	146,342	379,025	638,000
Madre de Dios	Puerto Maldonado	30,271	78,403	48,000
Moquegua	Moquegua	6,065	15,709	131,000
Pasco	Cerro de Pasco	9,356	24,233	277,000
Piura	Piura	14,055	36,403	1,454,000
Puno	Puno	27,947	72,382	1,010,000
San Martín	Moyobamba	20,197	52,309	445,000
Tacna	Tacna	5,881	15,232	203,000
Tumbes	Tumbes	1,827	4,732	140,900
Ucayali	Pucallpa	38,931	100,831	224,000
Constitutional Province				
Callao	Callao	57	148	575,000
TOTAL		496,225[1]	1,285,216[1]	21,792,000[1]

Demography

Population (1989): 21,792,000.
Density (1989): persons per sq mi 43.9, persons per sq km 17.0.
Urban-rural (1988): urban 68.8%; rural 31.2%.
Sex distribution (1988): male 50.37%; female 49.63%.
Age breakdown (1985): under 15, 40.5%; 15–29, 28.2%; 30–44, 16.3%; 45–59, 9.5%; 60–74, 4.5%; 75 and over, 1.0%.
Population projection: (2000) 27,952,000; (2010) 33,479,000.
Doubling time: 28 years.
Ethnic composition (1981): Quechua 47.1%; mestizo 32.0%; white 12.0%; Aymara 5.4%; jungle Amerindian 1.7%; other 1.8%.
Religious affiliation (1984): Roman Catholic 92.4%; other 7.6%.
Major cities (1988): Lima 5,493,900; Arequipa 591,700; Callao 560,000; Trujillo 491,000; Chiclayo 394,800; Piura 297,200.

Vital statistics

Birth rate per 1,000 population (1989): 33.5 (world avg. 27.1); (1977) legitimate 57.8%; illegitimate 42.2%.
Death rate per 1,000 population (1989): 8.7 (world avg. 9.9).
Natural increase rate per 1,000 population (1989): 24.8 (world avg. 17.2).
Total fertility rate (avg. births per childbearing woman; 1989): 4.3.
Marriage rate per 1,000 population (1982): 6.0[2].
Life expectancy at birth (1989): male 60.8 years; female 64.7 years.
Major causes of death per 100,000 population (1983): respiratory diseases 111.0, infectious and parasitic diseases 101.1; diseases of the circulatory system 59.7; accidents, poisonings, and violence 30.7; malignant neoplasms (cancers) 30.3.

National economy

Budget (1987). Revenue: I/. 66,788,000,000 (tax on fuel 38.9%; tax on external trade 21.4%; income taxes 19.7%; tax on goods and services 11.9%; nontax revenues 6.7%). Expenditures: I/. 133,896,000,000 (current expenditure 69.1%, of which wages 23.1%, transfer payments 16.3%, defense 15.9%, interest payments 9.8%; public debt amortization 16.9%).
Public debt (external, outstanding; 1987): U.S.$12,485,000,000.
Tourism (1987): receipts from visitors U.S.$393,000,000; expenditures by nationals abroad U.S.$383,000,000.
Production (metric tons except as noted). Agriculture, forestry, fishing (1988): sugarcane 6,200,000, potatoes 1,960,000, rice 1,080,000, corn (maize) 880,000, cassava 441,000, plantains 415,000, seed cotton 280,400, coffee 103,000; livestock (number of live animals) 13,300,000 sheep, 3,900,000 cattle, 2,400,000 pigs, 52,000,000 chickens; roundwood (1987) 7,735,000 cu m; fish catch (1987) 4,583,600. Mining and quarrying (1988): iron ore 2,750,000; zinc 485,429; copper 298,332; lead 149,037; silver 1,551. Manufacturing (1987): cement 2,584,000; wheat flour 890,828; animal feed 674,525; refined sugar 560,000; sulfuric acid 211,780; cooking oil 154,980; urea 99,148; motor vehicles 13,088 units. Construction (value added in I/. '000;

1985): buildings 9,753,500[3]. Energy production (consumption): electricity (kW-hr; 1987) 14,195,000,000 (14,195,000,000); coal (metric tons; 1987) 150,000 (140,000); crude petroleum (barrels; 1987) 64,841,000 (64,908,000); petroleum products (metric tons; 1987) 8,340,000 (6,348,000); natural gas (cu m; 1987) 734,146,000 (734,146,000).
Gross national product (1987): U.S.$29,682,000,000 (U.S.$1,430 per capita).

Structure of gross domestic product and labour force				
	1987		1988	
	in value I/. '000	% of total value	labour force	% of labour force
Agriculture	80,359.7	10.6	2,507,500	34.8
Mining	20,540.4	2.7	172,900	2.4
Manufacturing	171,143.0	22.5	742,200	10.3
Construction	54,438.6	7.2	259,400	3.6
Public utilities	7,432.0	1.0	21,600	0.3
Transp. and commun.	40,412.2	5.3	317,100	4.4
Trade	153,525.3	20.2	1,080,800	15.0
Finance	86,278.6	11.3	180,100	2.5
Services[4]	146,036.4	19.2	1,923,900	26.7
TOTAL	760,166.2	100.0	7,205,500	100.0

Population economically active (1988): total 7,205,500; activity rate of total population 33.9% (participation rates: over age 15, 56.2%; female [1981] 25.4%; unemployed [1986] 8.2%).

Price and earnings indexes (1985 = 100)						
	1982	1983	1984	1985	1986	1987
Consumer price index	8.6	20.8	38.0	100.0	177.9	330.7
Monthly earnings index[5]	13.0	22.6	43.3	100.0	225.1	332.5

Household income and expenditure (1986). Average household size 5.2; income per household I/. 39,392 (U.S.$2,824); sources of income: n.a.; expenditure: food and beverages 55.4%, rent and utilities 10.4%, transportation 8.6%, clothing 7.5%, recreation and education 6.9%, household durables 4.6%, health care 4.6%, other 2.0%.
Land use (1987): forest 54.0%; pasture 21.2%; agricultural 2.9%; other 21.9%.

Foreign trade

Balance of trade (current prices)						
	1982	1983	1984	1985	1986	1987
I/. '000,000	+457.8	+1,845.0	+5,206.6	+17,914.2	+6,439	+2,161
% of total	11.0%	22.7%	31.2%	37.5%	10.2%	2.5%

Imports (1987): U.S.$3,068,000,000 (raw and intermediate materials 45.9%, industrial capital goods 19.8%, consumer goods 13.0%, machinery and transport equipment 8.9%). *Major import sources:* U.S. 18.4%; West Germany 7.6%; Japan 6.8%; Brazil 5.3%; Argentina 4.9%; Colombia 2.9%; Canada 2.7%.
Exports (1987): U.S.$2,605,000,000 (copper 19.8%, petroleum and derivatives 10.5%, lead 9.6%, zinc 9.0%, fish flour 8.8%, textiles 8.0%, coffee 5.5%). *Major destinations:* U.S. 20.8%; Japan 6.2%; United Kingdom 3.3%; Brazil 3.2%; W.Ger. 2.7%; U.S.S.R. 2.5%; Venezuela 2.2%.

Transport and communications

Transport. Railroads (1987): route length 2,144 mi, 3,451 km; passenger-km 517,030,000; metric ton-km cargo 1,018,414,000. Roads (1986): total length 43,460 mi, 69,942 km (paved 11%). Vehicles (1987): passenger cars 377,424; trucks and buses 233,389. Merchant marine (1988): vessels (100 gross tons and over) 621; total deadweight tonnage 896,866. Air transport (1987): passenger-km 2,543,809,000; metric ton-km cargo 306,761,000; airports (1989) 24.
Communications. Daily newspapers (1985): total number 66; total circulation 1,121,900[6]; circulation per 1,000 population 57[6]. Radio (1988): 4,374,255 receivers (1 per 4.9 persons). Television (1987): 1,600,000 receivers (1 per 13 persons). Telephones (1986): 628,643 (1 per 32 persons).

Education and health

Education (1987)	schools	teachers	students	student/ teacher ratio
Primary (age 6–11)	23,486	119,750	3,763,730	31.4
Secondary (age 12–16)	4,189	76,373	1,732,466	22.7
Voc., teacher tr.	1,071	7,995	206,137	25.8
Higher	46	23,480	409,654	17.4

Educational attainment (1981). Percent of population age 25 and over having: no formal schooling 20.1%; less than primary education 33.2%; primary 21.1%; secondary 20.8%; higher 4.8%. *Literacy* (1988): total population age 15 and over literate (87.0%); males (93.5%); females (79.9%).
Health: physicians (1987) 20,198 (1 per 1,026 persons); hospital beds (1986) 32,326 (1 per 625 persons); infant mortality rate per 1,000 live births (1989) 83.3.
Food (1984–86): daily per capita caloric intake 2,192 (vegetable products 88%, animal products 12%); 92% of FAO recommended minimum.

Military

Total active duty personnel (1989): 120,000 (army 66.7%, navy 20.8%, air force 12.5%). *Military expenditure as percent of GNP* (1987): 4.9% (world 5.4%); per capita expenditure U.S.$106.

[1]Detail does not add to total given because of rounding. [2]Excludes Indian jungle population; based on incomplete information. [3]Includes new construction and capital repairs. [4]Services includes public administration and defense and other. [5]Estimate for Lima metropolitan area only. [6]Partial circulation.

Philippines

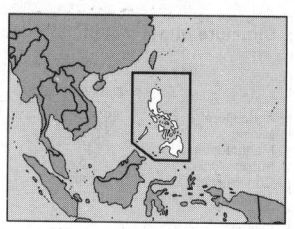

Official name: Republika ñg Pilipinas (Pilipino); Republic of the Philippines (English).
Form of government: unitary republic with two legislative houses (Senate [24]; House of Representatives [204[1]]).
Chief of state and head of government: President.
Capital: Manila.
Official languages: Pilipino; English.
Official religion: none.
Monetary unit: 1 Philippine peso (₱) = 100 centavos; valuation (Oct. 2, 1989) 1 U.S.$ = ₱ 21.76; 1 £ = ₱ 35.20.

Area and population

Regions	area		population
	sq mi	sq km	1989 estimate
Bicol	6,808	17,633	4,293,000
Cagayan Valley	14,055	36,403	2,778,000
Central Luzon	7,039	18,231	6,002,000
Central Mindanao	8,994	23,293	2,872,000
Central Visayas	5,773	14,951	4,531,000
Eastern Visayas	8,275	21,432	3,301,000
Ilocos	8,328	21,568	4,212,000
National Capital Region	246	636	7,768,000
Northern Mindanao	10,937	28,328	3,526,000
Southern Mindanao	12,237	31,693	4,232,000
Southern Tagalog	18,117	46,924	7,797,000
Western Mindanao	7,214	18,685	3,128,000
Western Visayas	7,808	20,223	5,466,000
TOTAL	115,800[2]	300,000	59,906,000

Demography

Population (1989): 59,906,000.
Density (1989): persons per sq mi 517.3, persons per sq km 199.7.
Urban–rural (1987): urban 41.0%; rural 59.0%.
Sex distribution (1989): male 50.38%; female 49.62%.
Age breakdown (1984): under 15, 39.0%; 15–29, 30.5%; 30–44, 17.0%; 45–59, 8.7%; 60–74, 4.0%; 75 and over, 0.8%.
Population projection: (2000) 76,094,000; (2010) 90,288,000.
Doubling time: 25 years.
Ethnic composition (by mother tongue of households; 1980): Tagalog 29.7%; Cebuano 24.2%; Ilocano 10.3%; Hiligaynon Ilongo 9.2%; Bicol 5.6%; Samar-Leyte 4.0%; Pampango 2.8%; Pangasinan 1.8%; other 12.5%[2].
Religious affiliation (1980): Roman Catholic 84.1%; Aglipayan (Philippine Independent Church) 6.2%; Muslim 4.3%; Protestant 3.9%; other 1.5%.
Major cities (1984): Manila 1,728,400; Quezon City 1,326,000; Cebu 552,200; Caloocan 524,600; Makati 409,000.

Vital statistics

Birth rate per 1,000 population (1988): 35.9 (world avg. 27.1); (1982) legitimate 93.9%; illegitimate 6.1%.
Death rate per 1,000 population (1988): 7.8 (world avg. 9.9).
Natural increase rate per 1,000 population (1988): 28.1 (world avg. 17.2).
Total fertility rate (avg. births per childbearing woman; 1988): 4.7.
Marriage rate per 1,000 population (1986): 7.0.
Life expectancy at birth (1988): male 61.8 years; female 65.5 years.
Major causes of death per 100,000 population (1984): pneumonia 89.3; heart diseases 61.0; tuberculosis 52.9; vascular diseases 39.6; malignant neoplasms (cancers) 30.2; diarrhea 27.8; accidents 16.8; malnutrition 13.4.

National economy

Budget (1987). Revenue: ₱ 103,097,000,000 (tax revenue 83.2%, nontax revenue 16.8%). Expenditures: ₱ 122,682,000,000 (current expenditures 80.4%, capital expenditures 10.2%, net lending/equity 9.3%).
Tourism (1987): receipts from visitors U.S.$459,000,000; expenditures by nationals abroad U.S.$88,000,000.
Production (metric tons except as noted). Agriculture, forestry, fishing (1988): sugarcane 15,664,000, rice 8,971,000, coconuts 8,640,000, corn (maize) 4,428,000, bananas and plantains 3,645,000, pineapples 2,250,000, cassava 1,785,000, copra 1,700,000, centrifugal sugar 1,369,000, sweet potatoes 778,000; livestock (number of live animals) 2,890,000 buffalo, 1,700,000 cattle, 2,120,000 goats, 7,580,000 pigs, 60,000,000 chickens; roundwood (1987) 36,701,000 cu m; fish catch (1987) 1,988,718. Mining and quarrying (1988): nickel ore 532,898; copper 218,202; chromite 182,242; silver 54,727 kilograms; gold 32,486 kilograms. Manufacturing (value added in producers' prices ₱ '000,000; 1986)[3]: food items 20,052; petroleum products 14,173; beverages 8,342; tobacco 6,250; industrial chemicals 3,956; electrical machinery 3,896; paper and products 3,238; textiles 2,924; drugs and medicines 2,803. Construction (authorized; 1985): residential 2,124,000 sq m; nonresidential 2,170,000 sq m. Energy production (consumption): electricity (kW-hr; 1987) 23,852,000,000 (23,852,000,000); coal (metric tons; 1987) 1,171,000 (2,094,000); petroleum (barrels; 1987) 2,105,000 (69,011,-000); petroleum products (metric tons; 1987) 7,938,000 (8,618,000); natural gas, n.a. (n.a.).
Land use (1987): forested 36.7%; meadows and pastures 4.0%; agricultural and under permanent cultivation 26.6%; other 32.7%.
Gross national product (1987): U.S.$34,638,000,000 (U.S.$590 per capita).

Structure of gross domestic product and labour force

	1987			
	in value ₱ '000,000	% of total value	labour force	% of labour force
Agriculture	177,017	24.9	9,940,000	43.4
Mining	10,757	1.5	146,000	0.7
Manufacturing	174,000	24.5	2,059,000	9.0
Construction	28,092	3.9	759,000	3.3
Public utilities	17,333	2.4	81,000	0.4
Transp. and commun.	42,027	5.9	946,000	4.1
Trade	137,355	19.3	2,857,000	12.5
Finance			386,000	1.7
Services	124,955	17.6	3,621,000	15.8
Other			2,086,000[4]	9.1[4]
TOTAL	711,536	100.0	22,881,000	100.0

Population economically active (1987): total 22,881,000; activity rate 39.9% (participation rates: ages 15–64, 67.1%; female 37.0%; unemployed 9.1%).

Price and earnings indexes (1985 = 100)

	1983	1984	1985	1986	1987	1988	1989[5]
Consumer price index	54.0	81.2	100.0	100.8	104.6	113.7	124.6

Public debt (external, outstanding; 1987): U.S.$22,321,000,000.
Household income and expenditure. Average household size (1985) 5.7; income per family (1985) ₱ 30,748 (U.S.$1,616); sources of income (1985): wages and self-employment 95.7%, pensions, social security, and related benefits 4.3%; expenditure (1985): food, beverages, and tobacco 56.0%, household furnishings and operations 13.9%, clothing 6.5%, fuel and power 4.7%, transport and communications 3.1%.

Foreign trade[6]

Balance of trade (current prices)

	1983	1984	1985	1986	1987	1988
₱ '000,000	−28,566	−10,907	−8,113	−2,974	−22,368	−24,023
% of total	20.7%	5.8%	4.5%	1.5%	8.8%	7.5%

Imports (1987): U.S.$6,737,000,000 (mineral fuels and lubricants 18.5%, materials and accessories for the manufacture of electrical equipment 11.4%, nonelectrical machinery 8.0%, electrical machinery 6.7%, base metals 6.3%, inorganic chemicals 4.9%, transport equipment 2.2%, cereals 2.0%). *Major import sources:* United States 22.0%; Japan 16.6%; Taiwan 5.5%; Kuwait 4.7%; Hong Kong 4.6%; West Germany 4.2%; Singapore 3.4%; Saudi Arabia 3.2%; China 3.1%; Australia 3.0%.
Exports (1987): U.S.$5,720,000,000 (semiconductor devices 10.2%, ready-made apparel 9.9%, coconut oil 6.7%, electronic microcircuits 5.6%; copper metal 2.8%, shrimps and prawns 2.7%, lumber 2.7%). *Major export destinations:* United States 34.5%; Japan 17.2%; The Netherlands 5.4%; West Germany 5.1%; Hong Kong 4.9%; United Kingdom 4.3%; Singapore 3.4%; Taiwan 2.5%.

Transport and communications

Transport. Railroads (1987): route length 658 mi, 1,059 km; passenger-mi 142,000,000, passenger-km 228,000,000; short ton-mi cargo 41,000,000, metric ton-km cargo 60,000,000. Roads (1987): total length 98,058 mi, 157,810 km (paved 14%). Vehicles (1986): passenger cars 773,242; trucks and buses 110,192. Merchant marine (1988): vessels (100 gross tons and over) 1,483; total deadweight tonnage 15,485,093. Air transport[7] (1988): passenger-mi 5,377,000,000, passenger-km 8,653,000,000; short ton-mi cargo 187,739,000, metric ton-km cargo 274,095,000; airports (1989) with scheduled flights 18.
Communications. Daily newspapers (1984): total number 25; circulation 2,379,145; circulation per 1,000 population 44. Radio (1986): 7,500,000 receivers (1 per 7.5 persons). Television (1988): 6,700,000 receivers (1 per 8.8 persons). Telephones (1986): 856,014 (1 per 65 persons).

Education and health

Education (1986–87)

	schools	teachers	students	student/teacher ratio
Primary (age 7–12)	33,607	292,602	9,204,168	31.5
Secondary (age 13–16)	5,388[8]	101,082	3,420,921	33.8
Voc., teacher tr.[8] Higher[8]	1,178	33,935	1,127,968	33.2

Educational attainment (1980). Percent of population age 25 and over having: no grade completed 11.7%; elementary education 53.8%; secondary 18.8%; college 15.2%; not stated 0.5%. *Literacy* (1980): total population age 15 and over literate 25,139,700 (88.7%); males literate 12,772,200 (89.9%); females literate 12,367,500 (87.5%).
Health: physicians (1982) 46,579 (1 per 1,090 persons); hospital beds (1986) 89,171 (1 per 628 persons); infant mortality rate (1988) 45.0.
Food (1984–86): daily per capita caloric intake 2,354 (vegetable products 90%, animal products 10%); (1984) 104% of FAO recommended minimum requirement.

Military

Total active duty personnel (1989): 112,000 (army 60.7%, navy 25.0%, air force 14.3%). *Military expenditure as percent of GNP* (1987): 1.3% (world 5.4%); per capita expenditure U.S.$7.

[1]Includes four nonelective seats allotted for indigenous minorities. [2]Detail does not add to total given because of rounding. [3]Manufacturing establishments with 10 or more workers. [4]Includes unemployed. [5]June. [6]Import figures are f.o.b. in balance of trade and c.i.f. for commodities and trading partners. [7]Philippines Airlines only. [8]1984–85.

Poland

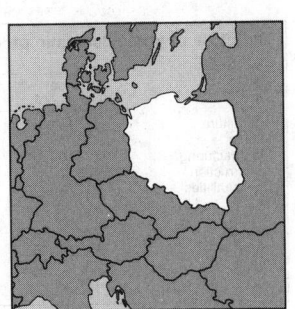

Official name: Polska Rzeczpospolita
(Republic of Poland).
Form of government: unitary multiparty
republic with two legislative houses
(Senate [100]; Diet [460]).
Chief of state: President.
Head of government: Prime Minister.
Capital: Warsaw.
Official language: Polish.
Official religion: none.
Monetary unit: 1 złoty (Zl) = 100
groszy; valuation (Oct. 2, 1989)
1 U.S.$ = Zl 1,395; 1 £ = Zl 2,258.

Area and population

Provinces	Capitals	area sq mi	area sq km	population 1988[1] estimate
Biała Podlaska	Biała Podlaska	2,065	5,348	301,100
Białystok	Białystok	3,882	10,055	679,900
Bielsko	Bielsko Biala	1,430	3,704	884,700
Bydgoszcz	Bydgoszcz	3,996	10,349	1,096,600
Chełm	Chełm	1,493	3,866	243,500
Ciechanów	Ciechanów	2,456	6,362	422,200
Częstochowa	Częstochowa	2,387	6,182	771,300
Elbląg	Elbląg	2,356	6,103	472,200
Gdańsk	Gdańsk	2,855	7,394	1,419,800
Gorzów	Gorzów Wielkopolski	3,276	8,484	490,700
Jelenia Góra	Jelenia Góra	1,690	4,378	513,800
Kalisz	Kalisz	2,514	6,512	703,700
Katowice	Katowice	2,568	6,650	3,970,800
Kielce	Kielce	3,556	9,211	1,115,600
Konin	Konin	1,984	5,139	463,400
Koszalin	Koszalin	3,270	8,470	498,400
Kraków	Kraków	1,256	3,254	1,216,600
Krosno	Krosno	2,202	5,702	483,700
Legnica	Legnica	1,559	4,037	502,700
Leszno	Leszno	1,604	4,154	380,400
Łódź	Łódź	588	1,523	1,148,400
Łomża	Łomża	2,581	6,684	342,200
Lublin	Lublin	2,622	6,792	997,300
Nowy Sącz	Nowy Sącz	2,153	5,576	679,400
Olsztyn	Olsztyn	4,759	12,327	738,600
Opole	Opole	3,295	8,535	1,022,700
Ostrołęka	Ostrołęka	2,509	6,498	389,500
Piła	Piła	3,168	8,205	472,600
Piotrków	Piotrków Trybunalski	2,419	6,266	639,200
Płock	Płock	1,976	5,117	512,800
Poznań	Poznań	3,147	8,151	1,316,100
Przemyśl	Przemyśl	1,713	4,437	400,500
Radom	Radom	2,816	7,294	736,500
Rzeszów	Rzeszów	1,698	4,397	703,700
Siedlce	Siedlce	3,281	8,499	642,000
Sieradz	Sieradz	1,880	4,869	403,700
Skierniewice	Skierniewice	1,529	3,960	413,200
Słupsk	Słupsk	2,878	7,453	403,900
Suwałki	Suwałki	4,050	10,490	458,900
Szczecin	Szczecin	3,854	9,981	958,700
Tarnobrzeg	Tarnobrzeg	2,426	6,283	586,900
Tarnów	Tarnów	1,603	4,151	651,800
Toruń	Toruń	2,065	5,348	649,600
Wałbrzych	Wałbrzych	1,609	4,168	739,300
Warszawa	Warszawa	1,463	3,788	2,431,800
Włocławek	Włocławek	1,700	4,402	428,000
Wrocław	Wrocław	2,427	6,287	1,121,100
Zamość	Zamość	2,695	6,980	489,900
Zielona Góra	Zielona Góra	3,424	8,868	654,900
TOTAL		**120,727**	**312,683**	**37,764,300**

Demography

Population (1989): 37,875,000.
Density (1989): persons per sq mi 313.7, persons per sq km 121.1.
Urban–rural (1988): urban 61.2%; rural 38.8%.
Sex distribution (1988): male 48.77%; female 51.23%.
Age breakdown (1988): under 15, 25.6%; 15–29, 21.7%; 30–44, 22.7%; 45–59, 15.8%; 60–74, 10.2%; 75 and over, 4.0%.
Population projection: (2000) 39,643,000; (2010) 41,289,000.
Ethnic composition (1987): Polish 98.7%; Ukrainian 0.6%; other 0.7%.
Religious affiliation (1987): Roman Catholic 95.0%; other 5.0%.
Major cities (1988): Warsaw 1,651,000; Łódź 852,000; Kraków 744,000.

Vital statistics

Birth rate per 1,000 population (1987): 16.1 (world avg. 27.1); (1985) legitimate 95.0%, illegitimate 5.0%.
Death rate per 1,000 population (1987): 10.1 (world avg. 9.9).
Natural increase rate per 1,000 population (1987): 6.0 (world avg. 17.2).
Total fertility rate (avg. births per childbearing woman; 1986): 2.3.
Marriage rate per 1,000 population (1987): 6.7.
Divorce rate per 1,000 population (1987): 1.3.
Life expectancy at birth (1987): male 66.8 years; female 75.2 years.
Major causes of death per 100,000 population (1987): diseases of the circulatory system 525.4; malignant neoplasms (cancers) 184.2.

National economy

Budget (1987). Revenue: Zl 5,850,500,000,000 (turnover tax 32.8%, tax on state enterprises 34.4%). Expenditures: Zl 5,973,200,000,000 (economy 42.3%, education and culture 11.6%, health 10.8%, defense 7.8%).
Public debt (external, outstanding; 1987): U.S.$35,569,000,000.
Tourism (1987): receipts U.S.$184,000,000; expenditures U.S.$203,000,000.
Gross national product (1988): U.S.$272,842,000,000 (U.S.$7,200 per capita).

Structure of net material product and labour force

	1987 in value Zl '000,000,000	1987 % of total value	1988 labour force	1988 % of labour force
Agriculture	2,089.5	13.9	4,873,000	28.4
Mining	} 7,283.3	} 48.4	569,000	3.3
Manufacturing			4,177,300	24.4
Public utilities	228.3	1.5	185,300	1.1
Construction	1,848.9	12.3	1,352,600	7.9
Transp. and commun.	1,031.8	6.9	1,279,800	7.5
Trade	2,412.8	16.0	1,531,700	8.9
Finance	—	—	386,000	2.3
Public administration	—	— }	2,716,700	15.9
Services	—	—		
Other	147.1[2]	1.0[2]	57,400	0.3
TOTAL	**15,041.7**	**100.0**	**17,128,800**	**100.0**

Production (metric tons except as noted). Agriculture (value added in Zl '000,000; 1987): potatoes 331,000, wheat 233,300, industrial crops 205,300, rye 152,000, barley 115,000; livestock (live animals; 1988) 18,546,000 pigs, 10,523,000 cattle; roundwood 22,498,000 cu m; fish catch 670,908. Mining and quarrying (1987): copper 390,000; zinc 177,000; lead 89,800; iron ore 6,300; silver 831. Manufacturing (value added in Zl '000,000,000; 1987): machinery and transport equipment 2,038.1; food 791.4; textiles 543.6; chemicals 501.4. Construction (1987): 13,856,000 sq m. Energy production (consumption): electricity ('000,000 kW-hr; 1987) 145,835 (147,455); coal ('000 metric tons; 1987) 266,207 (266,176); crude petroleum (barrels; 1987) 1,105,000 (1,210,600); petroleum products ('000 metric tons; 1987) 14,306 (17,655); natural gas ('000,000 cu m; 1987) 5,781 (13,324).
Population economically active (1988): total 17,128,800; activity rate of total population 45.4% (participation rates: ages 18–64 [male], 18–59 [female] 82.4%; female [18–59] 45.4%).

Price and earnings indexes (1985 = 100)

	1982	1983	1984	1985	1986	1987	1988[3]
Consumer price index	61.9	75.5	86.9	100.0	117.7	147.4	245.8
Monthly earnings index	57.5	73.4	83.4	100.0	121.1	147.0	229.7

Household income and expenditure. Average household size (1986) 2.9; average annual income (1987) Zl 652,000 (U.S.$2,460[4]); sources of income: wages 74.3%, other 25.7%; expenditure (1987): food and beverages 43.5%, clothing 13.8%, housing 10.3%, recreation 9.7%, transportation 5.5%.
Land use (1987): forest 27.7%; meadow 13.0%; agriculture 47.3%; other 12.0%.

Foreign trade

Balance of trade (current prices)

	1983	1984	1985	1986	1987	1988
Zl '000,000,000	+90.0	+126.2	+96.1	+151.6	+360.9	+775.1
% of total	4.4%	5.0%	2.9%	7.2%	5.9%	6.9%

Imports (1988): Zl 5,236,233,000,000 (machinery and transport equipment 35.7%, chemicals 15.9%, fuel and power 15.0%, consumer goods 8.9%, iron and steel products 8.0%). *Major import sources:* U.S.S.R. 23.4%; W.Ger. 13.0%; Czechoslovakia 6.4%; E.Ger. 5.1%; U.K. 4.2%; Yugoslavia 3.3%.
Exports (1988): Zl 6,011,310,000,000 (machinery and transport equipment 39.2%, chemicals 10.9%, fuel and power 10.2%, metals 10.0%, textiles and clothing 6.6%). *Major export destinations:* U.S.S.R. 24.5%; W.Ger. 12.4%; Czechoslovakia 6.0%; U.K. 5.0%; E.Ger. 4.4%; Yugoslavia 2.7%.

Transport and communications

Transport. Railroads (1987): length 26,637 km; passenger-km 48,284,800,000; metric ton-km cargo 121,381,300,000. Roads (1988): total length 340,191 km (paved 63%). Vehicles (1987): passenger cars 4,231,700; trucks and buses 953,668. Merchant marine (1988): vessels (100 gross tons and over) 714; total deadweight tonnage 4,666,786. Air transport (1987): passenger-km 3,340,200,000; metric ton-km cargo 19,500,000; airports (1988) 12.
Communications. Daily newspapers (1987): 45; circulation 7,250,000. Radio (1988): 10,845,000 (1 per 3.5 persons). Television (1988): 9,868,000 (1 per 3.8 persons). Telephones (1988): 4,618,000 (1 per 8.2 persons).

Education and health

Education (1988–89)

	schools	teachers	students	student/ teacher ratio
Primary (age 7–14)	17,264	263,026	5,087,005	19.3
Secondary (age 15–18)	903	21,912	393,532	18.0
Voc., teacher tr.	6,224	73,071	1,357,579	18.6
Higher	92	59,142	272,531	4.6

Educational attainment (1978). Percent of population age 25 and over having: no formal schooling 2.8%; less than full primary education 12.7%; primary 44.9%; secondary 33.9%; higher 5.7%. *Literacy* (1983): total population age 15 and over literate 27,352,000 (99.2%).
Health (1988): physicians 77,496 (1 per 487 persons); hospital beds 202,188 (1 per 187 persons); infant mortality rate per 1,000 live births (1987) 17.4.
Food (1984–86): daily per capita caloric intake 3,298 (vegetable products 67%, animal products 33%); 126% of FAO recommended minimum.

Military

Total active duty personnel (1989): 412,000 (army 68.4%, navy 6.1%, air force 25.5%). *Military expenditure as percent of GNP* (1987): 6.9% (world 5.4%); per capita expenditure U.S.$476.

[1]January 1. [2]Other material activities. [3]Third quarter average. [4]At official exchange rate; actual purchasing power substantially higher.

Portugal

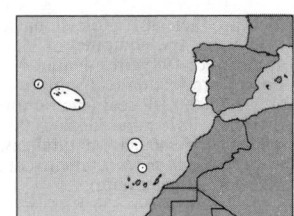

Official name: República Portuguesa
(Republic of Portugal).
Form of government: parliamentary
state with one legislative house
(Assembly of the Republic [250]).
Chief of state: President.
Head of government: Prime Minister.
Capital: Lisbon.
Official language: Portuguese.
Official religion: none.
Monetary unit: 1 Escudo (Esc) = 100
centavos; valuation (Oct. 2, 1989)
1 U.S.$ = Esc 158.96; 1 £ =
Esc 257.20.

Area and population		area		population
Continental Portugal				1988
Districts	Capitals	sq mi	sq km	estimate[1]
Aveiro	Aveiro	1,084	2,808	665,500
Beja	Beja	3,948	10,225	177,700
Braga	Braga	1,032	2,673	771,400
Bragança	Bragança	2,551	6,608	184,700
Castelo Branco	Castelo Branco	2,577	6,675	223,700
Coimbra	Coimbra	1,524	3,947	446,500
Évora	Évora	2,854	7,393	174,300
Faro	Faro	1,915	4,960	341,200
Guarda	Guarda	2,131	5,518	196,200
Leiria	Leiria	1,357	3,515	435,900
Lisboa	Lisbon (Lisboa)	1,066	2,761	2,126,400
Portalegre	Portalegre	2,342	6,065	137,500
Porto	Porto	925	2,395	1,670,600
Santarém	Santarém	2,605	6,747	460,600
Setúbal	Setúbal	1,955	5,064	779,600
Viana do Castelo	Viana do Castelo	871	2,255	266,400
Vila Real	Vila Real	1,671	4,328	262,900
Viseu	Viseu	1,933	5,007	423,300
Azores (Açores)				
Autonomous Region[2]	Ponta Delgada	868	2,247	254,200
Madeira Autonomous				
Region	Funchal	306	794	271,400
TOTAL		35,672[3]	92,389[3]	10,270,000

Demography

Population (1989): 10,372,000.
Density (1989): persons per sq mi 290.8, persons per sq km 112.3.
Urban-rural (1981): urban 29.6%; rural 70.4%.
Sex distribution (1988): male 48.30%; female 51.70%.
Age breakdown (1987): under 15, 22.7%; 15–29, 24.6%; 30–44, 18.8%; 45–59,
16.5%; 60–74, 12.6%; 75 and over, 4.8%.
Population projection: (2000) 10,773,000; (2010) 11,123,000.
Nationality (1988): Portuguese 99.1%; Cape Verdean 0.3%; Brazilian 0.1%;
Spanish 0.1%; American 0.1%; British 0.1%; other 0.2%.
Religious affiliation (1981): Christian 96.0%, of which Roman Catholic
94.5%, Protestant 0.6%, other Christian (mostly Apostolic Catholic and
Jehovah's Witness) 0.9%; nonreligious 3.8%; Jewish 0.1%; Muslim 0.1%.
Major cities (1986): Lisbon 829,600; Porto 347,300; Amadora 95,518[4].

Vital statistics

Birth rate per 1,000 population (1987): 11.5 (world avg. 27.1); legitimate
86.8%; illegitimate 13.2%.
Death rate per 1,000 population (1987): 8.4 (world avg. 9.9).
Natural increase rate per 1,000 population (1987): 3.1 (world avg. 17.2).
Total fertility rate (avg. births per childbearing woman; 1985–90): 1.8.
Marriage rate per 1,000 population (1987): 7.0.
Divorce rate per 1,000 population (1987): 0.9.
Life expectancy at birth (1984–87): male 70.0 years; female 76.9 years.
Major causes of death per 100,000 population (1988): circulatory diseases
386.1, of which cerebrovascular diseases 217.1, ischemic heart disease 74.2;
malignant neoplasms (cancers) 155.7; respiratory diseases 35.5.

National economy

Budget (1987). Revenue: Esc 1,119,115,000,000 (indirect taxes 64.1%, direct
taxes 26.0%, property income 5.2%). Expenditures: Esc 1,835,526,000,000
(education 13.1%, health 10.2%, defense 6.8%, administration 6.2%, public works 4.0%).
Public debt (1987): U.S.$29,028,500,000.
Production (metric tons except as noted). Agriculture, forestry, fishing
(1988): grapes 1,400,000, tomatoes 865,000, potatoes 795,000, corn (maize)
663,000, wheat 401,000, rice 151,000, olives 149,000, oats 76,000, cork
109,262[5]; livestock (number of live animals) 5,220,000 sheep, 2,800,000
pigs, 1,387,000 cattle; roundwood 9,420,000 cu m; fish catch 395,250. Mining and quarrying (1987): copper pyrites 279,061; kaolin 56,992; tungsten
2,011. Manufacturing (value of production in Esc '000,000; 1988): cotton
and synthetic fibres 225,387; refined petroleum 163,986; clothing 117,154;
knitted fabrics 95,792; motor vehicles 95,738; dairy products 77,599; iron
and steel 62,398; cement 51,927; alcoholic beverages 42,601. Construction
(1987): residential 5,896,276 sq m; nonresidential 1,596,816 sq m. Energy
production (consumption): electricity (kW-hr; 1987) 20,101,000,000 (23,-
126,000,000); coal (metric tons; 1987) 254,000 (2,759,000); crude petroleum
(barrels; 1987) none (58,017,000); petroleum products (metric tons; 1987)
6,485,000 (6,566,000); natural gas, none (n.a.).
Gross national product (1987): U.S.$29,555,000,000 (U.S.$2,890 per capita).

Structure of gross domestic product and labour force				
	1987			
	in value Esc '000,000	% of total value	labour force	% of labour force
Agriculture	427,700	8.2	975,500	20.6
Mining			26,900	0.6
Manufacturing }	1,496,800	28.8	1,081,000	22.8
Construction	300,600	5.8	377,000	8.0
Public utilities	178,700	3.4	35,400	0.8
Trade	1,019,000	19.6	615,100	13.0
Pub. admin., defense	558,800	10.8		
Services		}	976,000	20.6
Transp. and commun.			179,900	3.8
Finance	1,218,500	23.4	135,300	2.8
Other			329,600[6]	7.0
TOTAL	5,200,100	100.0	4,731,700	100.0

Population economically active (1987): total 4,731,700; activity rate of total
population 46.0% (participation rates: ages 15–64, 67.4%; female 42.0%;
unemployed 7.0%).

Price and earnings indexes (1985 = 100)							
	1982	1983	1984	1985	1986	1987	1988
Consumer price index	51.8	64.9	83.6	100.0	111.8	122.2	134.0
Daily earnings index	60.6	70.7	83.4	100.0	122.1	...	...

Household income and expenditure. Average household size (1981) 3.8;
income per household: n.a.; sources of income (1986): wages and salaries
42.4%, property and entrepreneurial income 35.8%, transfer payments
21.8%; expenditure (1981): food 34.8%, transportation and communications
14.6%, clothing and footwear 11.2%, cafes and hotels 8.8%, health 4.3%,
recreation 3.9%, housing 3.2%, other 9.2%.
Tourism (1987): receipts from visitors U.S.$2,148,000,000; expenditures by
nationals abroad U.S.$421,000,000.
Land use (1986): forested 39.7%; meadows and pastures 5.8%; agricultural
and under permanent cultivation 30.1%; other 24.4%.

Foreign trade

Balance of trade (current prices)						
	1983	1984	1985	1986	1987	1988
Esc '000,000	−308,700	−291,700	−213,700	−255,500	−457,800	−580,000
% of total	23.3%	16.1%	9.9%	9.4%	15.2%	16.0%

Imports (1988): Esc 2,414,592,000,000 (machinery and transport equipment
37.0%, of which road vehicles 15.2%; crude petroleum 8.5%; iron and
steel products 4.3%; chemicals 3.8%). *Major import sources:* W.Ger. 13.7%;
Spain 13.5%; France 11.5%; Italy 9.3%; U.K. 8.2%; The Netherlands 4.8%.
Exports (1988): Esc 1,531,728,000,000 (clothing and wearing apparel 26.3%;
machinery and transport equipment 20.1%, of which road vehicles 4.8%;
footwear 8.0%; paper and paper products 7.6%; wood and wood products
7.0%[7]; chemicals and chemical products 1.8%). *Major export destinations:*
France 15.4%; W.Ger. 14.7%; U.K. 14.2%; Spain 11.4%.

Transport and communications

Transport. Railroads (1987): route length 2,241 mi, 3,607 km; passenger-
km 5,907,065,000; metric ton-km cargo 1,614,742,000. Roads (1981): total
length 32,282 mi, 51,953 km (paved 86%). Vehicles (1987): passenger cars
2,571,457[8]; trucks and buses 189,822. Merchant marine (1988): vessels (100
gross tons and over) 306; total deadweight tonnage 1,581,646. Air transport
(1987)[9]: passenger-km 4,980,000,000; metric ton-km cargo 136,044,000; airports (1989) 20.
Communications. Daily newspapers (1986): total number 30; total circulation 859,315[10]; circulation per 1,000 population 84[10]. Radio (1987): 2,172,-
573 receivers (1 per 4.7 persons). Television (1987): 1,618,000 receivers (1
per 6.4 persons). Telephones (1987): 2,089,684 (1 per 4.9 persons).

Education and health

Education (1986–87)				
	schools	teachers	students	student/ teacher ratio
Primary (age 5–11)	12,692	75,456	1,234,293	16.4
Secondary (age 12–19)[11]	1,509	53,881	647,391	12.0
Voc., teacher tr.[12]	345	2,971	27,946	9.4
Higher	221	10,179	109,190	10.7

Educational attainment (1981). Percent of population age 25 and over
having: no formal schooling 4.4%; primary education 76.2%; secondary
19.0%; postsecondary 0.1%; higher 0.3%. *Literacy* (1985): total population
age 15 and over literate 6,567,000 (84.0%); males literate 3,288,000 (88.8%);
females literate 3,279,000 (79.7%).
Health (1988): physicians 26,381 (1 per 388 persons); hospital beds 48,838
(1 per 209 persons); infant mortality rate per 1,000 live births (1987) 10.0.
Food (1984–86): daily per capita caloric intake 3,134 (vegetable products
80%, animal products 20%); (1983) 124% of FAO recommended minimum requirement.

Military

Total active duty personnel (1988): 73,900 (army 59.5%, navy 22.1%, air force
18.4%). *Military expenditure as percent of GNP* (1987): 3.2% (world 5.4%);
per capita expenditure U.S.$110.

[1]January 1. [2]Comprises 3 districts not shown separately. [3]Includes 156 sq mi (404
sq km) of inland water. [4]1981. [5]1986. [6]Mostly unemployed. [7]More than one-half is
composed of cork products. [8]Includes minibuses. [9]TAP (Air Portugal) only. [10]For 28
newspapers only. [11]1985–86. [12]1983–84.

Puerto Rico

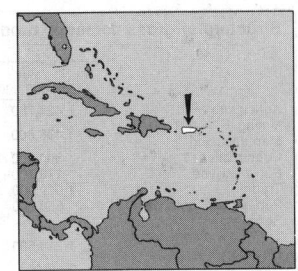

Official name: Estado Libre
Asociado de Puerto Rico (Spanish);
Commonwealth of Puerto Rico
(English).
Political status: self-governing
commonwealth associated with the
United States, having two legislative
houses (Senate [27]; House of
Representatives [51]).
Chief of state: President of the
United States.
Head of government: Governor.
Capital: San Juan.
Official languages: Spanish; English.
Official religion: none.
Monetary unit: 1 U.S. dollar
(U.S.$) = 100 cents; valuation (Oct. 2,
1989) 1 U.S.$ = £0.62.

Population (1984 estimate)

Municipio	population	Municipio	population	Municipio	population
Adjuntas	18,900	Fajardo	33,200	Naguabo	21,300
Aguada	32,400	Florida	7,600	Naranjito	25,100
Aguadilla	55,000	Guánica	18,800	Orocovis	20,900
Agunas Buenas	23,000	Guayama	40,300	Patillas	17,900
Aibonito	22,500	Guayanilla	21,000	Peñuelas	20,200
Añasco	24,400	Guaynabo	85,100	Ponce	190,900
Arecibo	87,000	Gurabo	25,000	Quebradillas	19,700
Arroyo	18,200	Hatillo	30,400	Rincón	12,400
Barceloneta	19,600	Hormigueros	15,200	Río Grande	37,700
Barranquitas	22,800	Humacao	52,400	Sabana Grande	21,100
Bayamón	202,500	Isabela	38,200	Salinas	26,600
Cabo Rojo	35,000	Jayuya	15,000	San Germán	34,200
Caguas	121,100	Juana Díaz	43,600	San Juan	428,900
Camuy	26,200	Juncos	27,000	San Lorenzo	33,300
Canóvanas	32,400	Lajas	21,300	San Sebastián	36,100
Carolina	165,700	Lares	28,000	Santa Isabel	19,500
Cataño	25,900	Las Marías	8,600	Toa Alta	33,400
Cayey	43,300	Las Piedras	23,100	Toa Baja	77,700
Ceiba	15,100	Loíza	24,600	Trujillo Alto	50,800
Ciales	17,200	Luquillo	15,400	Utuado	34,600
Cidra	29,600	Manatí	38,000	Vega Alta	30,000
Coamo	32,200	Maricao	6,700	Vega Baja	48,800
Comerío	18,400	Maunabo	11,800	Vieques	7,800
Corozal	29,600	Mayagüez	101,000	Villalba	22,500
Culebra	1,300	Moca	29,900	Yabucoa	31,400
Dorado	26,700	Morovis	21,900	Yauco	39,200
				TOTAL	3,270,000

Demography

Area: 3,515 sq mi, 9,104 sq km.
Population (1989): 3,308,000.
Density (1989): persons per sq mi 941.1, persons per sq km 363.4.
Urban–rural (1985): urban 70.7%; rural 29.3%.
Sex distribution (1985): male 48.68%; female 51.32%.
Age breakdown (1980): under 15, 31.6%; 15–29, 26.5%; 30–44, 18.4%; 45–59,
12.3%; 60–74, 8.3%; 75 and over, 2.9%.
Population projection: (2000) 3,389,000; (2010) 3,465,000.
Doubling time: 57 years.
Ethnic composition (1980): white 80.0%; black 20.0%.
Religious affiliation (1984): Roman Catholic 85.3%; Protestant 4.7%; other
10.0%.
Major cities (municipio; 1986): San Juan 431,227; Bayamón 211,616; Ponce
190,679; Carolina 162,888; Caguas 126,298.

Vital statistics

Birth rate per 1,000 population (1986): 19.4 (world avg. 27.1); (1983) legiti-
mate 75.6%; illegitimate 24.4%.
Death rate per 1,000 population (1986): 7.1 (world avg. 9.9).
Natural increase rate per 1,000 population (1986): 12.3 (world avg. 17.2).
Total fertility rate (avg. births per childbearing woman; 1986): 2.4.
Marriage rate per 1,000 population (1986): 9.9.
Divorce rate per 1,000 population (1985): 4.5.
Life expectancy at birth (1985–90): male 71.5 years; female 78.4 years.
Major causes of death per 100,000 population (1985): diseases of the cir-
culatory system 262.5, of which ischemic heart disease 102.1, diseases of
pulmonary circulation 64.2; malignant neoplasms (cancers) 106.1; diseases
of the respiratory system 78.6.

National economy

Budget (1985–86). Revenue: U.S.$4,624,000,000 (income taxes 34.9%, excise
taxes 20.1%, property taxes 3.2%, other receipts 41.8%). Expenditures:
U.S.$4,288,000,000 (grants and subsidies 51.0%, personal services 28.3%,
debt service 6.4%, other 14.3%).
Public debt (outstanding; 1987): U.S.$10,030,000,000.
Tourism (1987): receipts from visitors U.S.$866,000,000; expenditures by
nationals abroad U.S.$591,000,000.
Production (in U.S.$'000,000 except as noted). Agriculture, forestry, fishing
(gross farm income; 1987): milk 182, poultry 65, coffee 65, starchy vegetables 55, beef 52, pork 47, fruit 38, eggs 25, sugar 23; livestock (number
of live animals) 583,000 cattle, 210,000 pigs; roundwood, n.a.; fish catch
(1987) 1,191 metric tons. Mining (value of production; 1984): stone 28.
Manufacturing (net income in U.S.$'000,000; 1987): chemicals, pharmaceu-
ticals, and allied products 3,758; electrical machinery and equipment 1,330;

food products 981; professional and scientific equipment 670; nonelectrical
machinery and equipment 435; clothing 422. Construction (new buildings
authorized; 1985): residential 1,798,000 sq m; nonresidential 41,000 sq m.
Energy production (consumption): electricity (kW-hr; 1987) 13,757,000,000
(13,757,000,000); coal (metric tons; 1987) none (200,000); crude petroleum
(barrels; 1987) none (35,200,000); petroleum products (metric tons; 1987)
4,800,000 (5,940,000); natural gas, none (none).
Gross national product (at current market prices; 1987): U.S.$18,472,000,000
(U.S.$5,520 per capita).

Structure of gross domestic product and labour force

	1987		1988	
	in value US$'000,000	% of total value	labour force	% of labour force
Agriculture	372.1	1.6	33,000	3.2
Manufacturing	9,388.5	39.7 }	157,000	15.0
Mining	408.3	1.7 }	49,000	4.7
Construction }				
Public utilities	1,872.4	7.9	12,000	1.2
Transp. and commun. }			36,000	3.4
Trade	3,503.0	14.8	169,000	16.1
Finance, real estate	3,090.6	13.1	33,000	3.2
Pub. admin., defense	2,629.4	11.1 }	396,000	37.8
Services	2,154.7	9.1 }		
Other	226.5	1.0	161,000[1]	15.4[1]
TOTAL	23,645.5	100.0	1,046,000	100.0

Population economically active (1988): total 1,046,000; activity rate of total
population 31.7% (participation rates: ages 16–64, 51.3%; female 37.5%;
unemployed 15.4%).

Price and earnings indexes (1985 = 100)

	1982	1983	1984	1985	1986	1987	1988
Consumer price index	96.2	97.2	98.7	100.0	99.2	100.7	104.0
Hourly earnings index[2]	94.8	94.2	96.8	100.0	103.5	...	...

Household income and expenditure. Average family size (1987) 4.1; income
per family U.S.$20,016; sources of income (1987): wages and salaries 56.0%,
transfers 28.0%, rent 6.6%, self-employment 6.4%, other 3.0%; expenditure
(1985): food and beverages 28.8%, transportation 16.8%, housing and energy 15.9%, clothing 8.4%, household furnishings 6.3%, health care 6.0%,
recreation 4.3%, education 2.2%, other 11.3%.
Land use (1987): forested 20.0%; meadows and pastures 37.7%; agricultural
and under permanent cultivation 14.4%; other 27.9%.

Foreign trade

Balance of trade (current prices)

	1983	1984	1985	1986	1987	1988
U.S.$'000,000	−466	−690	+925	+1,472	+1,354	+1,327
% of total	2.7%	3.3%	4.4%	6.8%	5.9%	5.3%

Imports (1988): U.S.$11,859,106,000 (metals and metal products 20.3%; food
13.2%; chemicals [all forms] 12.9%; textile fibre and textile products 4.7%;
wood, paper, and printed products 3.6%). *Major import sources:* United
States 66.8%; Japan 4.9%; Venezuela 3.0%; Brazil 1.7%.
Exports (1988): U.S.$13,185,929,000 (chemicals and chemical products
36.7%; metals and metal products 17.7%; food 16.1%; textile fibre and
textile products 4.7%). *Major export destinations:* United States 88.1%;
Dominican Republic 2.4%; U.S. Virgin Islands 1.2%; Venezuela 0.8%.

Transport and communications

Transport. Railroads (1988)[3]: length 59 mi, 96 km. Roads (1986): total length
5,810 mi, 9,351 km (paved 87%). Vehicles (1987): passenger cars 1,297,098;
trucks and buses 257,554. Merchant marine: n.a. Air transport (1987–88):
passenger arrivals 3,830,693, passenger departures 3,868,674; cargo loaded
and unloaded 166,411 metric tons; airports (1989) with scheduled flights 8.
Communications. Daily newspapers (1988): total number 4; total circulation
473,000; circulation per 1,000 population 143. Radio (1988): 2,000,000 receivers (1 per 1.6 persons). Television (1987): 830,000 receivers (1 per 4.0
persons). Telephones (1985): 772,006 (1 per 4.3 persons).

Education and health

Education (1985–86)

	schools	teachers	students	student/ teacher ratio
Primary (age 5–12)	1,542	18,359	427,582	23.3
Secondary (age 13–18)	395	13,612	334,661	24.6
Voc., teacher tr.	52	...	149,191	...
Higher	45	9,045	156,818	17.3

Educational attainment (1987). Percent of population age 25 and over
having: some primary education 47.8%; some secondary 12.7%; complete
secondary 21.1%; higher 18.4%. *Literacy* (1980): total population age 15
and over literate 1,948,151 (89.1%); males literate 935,553 (89.7%); females
literate 1,012,598 (88.5%).
Health (1984): physicians 7,560 (1 per 433 persons); hospital beds 12,493 (1
per 262 persons); infant mortality rate per 1,000 live births (1986) 13.7.
Food: daily per capita caloric intake, n.a.

Military

Total active duty personnel (1986): 3,600 U.S. personnel.

---

[1]Unemployed. [2]Manufacturing sector only. [3]Privately owned railway for sugarcane
transport only.

Qatar

Official name: Dawlat Qaṭar (State of Qatar).
Form of government: constitutional monarchy; Islamic law is the basis of legislation in the state.
Head of state and government: Emir.
Capital: Doha.
Official language: Arabic.
Official religion: Islam.
Monetary unit: 1 riyal (QR) = 100 dirhams; valuation (Oct. 2, 1989) 1 U.S.$ = QR 3.64; 1 £ = QR 5.89.

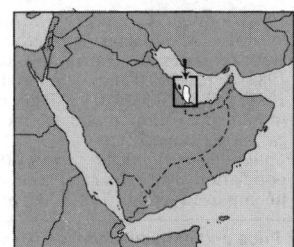

Area and population

Municipalities	Capitals	area sq mi	area sq km	population[1] 1986 census
ad-Dawḥah (Doha)	—	51	132	217,294
al-Ghuwayriyah	al-Ghuwayriyah	238	616	1,629
Jarayān al-Bāṭinah	Jarayān al-Bāṭinah	1,447	3,748	2,727
al-Jumayliyah	al-Jumayliyah	921	2,386	7,217
al-Khawr	al-Khawr	399	1,033	8,993
ar-Rayyān	ar-Rayyān	343	888	91,996
ash-Shamāl	Madinat ash-Shamāl	362	937	4,380
Umm Ṣalāl	Umm Ṣalāl Muḥammad	191	494	11,161
al-Wakrah	al-Wakrah	426	1,103	23,682
TOTAL		4,377[2]	11,337	369,079

Demography

Population (1989): 427,000.
Density (1989): persons per sq mi 97.5, persons per sq km 37.7.
Urban–rural (1986): urban 88.3%; rural 11.7%.
Sex distribution (1986): male 67.15%; female 32.85%.
Age breakdown (1986): under 15, 27.8%; 15–29, 29.3%; 30–44, 32.3%; 45–59, 8.6%; 60 and over, 2.0%.
Population projection: (2000) 600,000; (2010) 758,000.
Doubling time: 29 years.
Ethnic composition (1983): South Asian 34%; Qatari 20%; other Arab 25%; Iranian 16%; other 5%.
Religious affiliation (1980): Muslim 92.4% (mostly Sunnī); Christian 5.9%; Hindu 1.1%; Bahā'ī 0.2%; other 0.4%.
Major cities (1986): Doha 217,294; Umm Sa'īd 40,000[3].

Vital statistics

Birth rate per 1,000 population (1987): 30.4 (world avg. 27.1); legitimate, n.a.; illegitimate, n.a.
Death rate per 1,000 population (1987): 2.4 (world avg. 9.9).
Natural increase rate per 1,000 population (1987): 28.0 (world avg. 17.2).
Total fertility rate (avg. births per childbearing woman; 1986): 4.9.
Marriage rate per 1,000 population (1986): 3.1.
Divorce rate per 1,000 population (1986): 0.8.
Life expectancy at birth (1986): male 65.2 years; female 67.6 years.
Major causes of death per 100,000 population (1986): diseases of the circulatory system 50.0; injuries and poisonings 41.0; neoplasms (including benign neoplasms) 20.4; certain conditions originating in the perinatal period 14.0; diseases of the respiratory system 10.6; endocrine, metabolic, and nutritional diseases and immunity disorders 6.9; diseases of the digestive system 6.1; signs, symptoms, and ill-defined conditions 29.4.

National economy

Budget (1988–89). Revenue: QR 6,335,800,000 (crude oil 85.0%). Expenditures: QR 12,242,500,000 (1987–88): wages and salaries 34.3%; state capital development projects 22.6%, of which electricity and water 4.6%; housing and public buildings 4.4%, education 2.2%, transport and communications 2.1%, social services 0.9%, health 0.8%).
Public debt: none.
Production (metric tons except as noted). Agriculture, forestry, fishing (value of production in QR '000; 1986): vegetables and other crops except cereals 74,237, forage 68,144, fruits and dates 21,116, cereals 1,455; livestock (number of live animals) 118,692 sheep, 68,000 goats, 18,637 camels, 7,713 cattle, 2,415 deer; roundwood, n.a.; fish catch (1987) 2,678. Mining and quarrying (1986): limestone 1,300,000; clay, sand, and gypsum are also mined for local use. Manufacturing (1986): urea 746,892; ammonia 658,328; steel reinforcing bars 493,000; cement 324,000; clinker 308,155; ethylene 258,349; sulfur 44,734; organic fertilizers 21,000. Construction (1986): residential 391,400 sq m; nonresidential 167,600 sq m. Energy production (consumption): electricity (kW-hr; 1987) 4,420,000,000 (4,420,000,000); coal, none (n.a.); crude petroleum (barrels; 1987) 102,700,000 (10,700,000); petroleum products (metric tons; 1987) 2,104,000 (544,000); natural gas (cu m; 1987) 4,724,000,000 (4,724,000,000).
Tourism (1986): receipts and expenditures, n.a.; total number of tourists staying in hotels 106,730.
Population economically active (1986): total 201,800; activity rate of total population 54.7% (participation rates: over age 15, 75.5%; female 9.8%; unemployed, 1.0%).

Price and earnings indexes (1985 = 100)

	1981	1982	1983	1984	1985	1986
Consumer price index	89.4	94.5	97.1	98.1	100.0	101.6
Earnings index	...	...	...	...	...	...

Household income and expenditure. Average household size (1986) 6.4; income per household: n.a.; sources of income: n.a.; expenditure (1982–83): food 39.1%, household durable goods 24.4%, recreation and personal effects 15.1%, housing 10.7%, clothing 4.4%, transportation and communications 3.7%, education 1.6%, energy and water 0.8%, health 0.2%.
Gross national product (at current market prices; 1987): U.S.$4,129,000,000 (U.S.$12,360 per capita).

Structure of gross domestic product and labour force

	1987 in value QR '000,000	1987 % of total value	1986 labour force	1986 % of labour force
Agriculture	241	1.3	6,283	3.1
Mining	5,630	30.3	4,807	2.4
Manufacturing	1,847	9.9	13,914	6.9
Construction	1,086	5.9	40,523	20.1
Public utilities	359	1.9	5,266	2.6
Transportation	412	2.2	7,357	3.6
Trade	1,172	6.3	21,964	10.9
Finance	1,958	10.6	3,157	1.6
Pub. admin., defense } Services	5,875	31.6	96,466	47.8
Other	...	...	2,040[4]	1.0[4]
TOTAL	18,580	100.0	201,777	100.0

Land use (1987): meadows and pastures 4.5%; agricultural and under permanent cultivation 0.3%; built-up, desert, and other 95.2%.

Foreign trade

Balance of trade (current prices)

	1982	1983	1984	1985	1986	1987
QR '000,000	+9,307	+6,703	+8,015	+7,130	+2,730	+3,224
% of total	39.6%	38.7%	48.6%	46.2%	25.4%	28.7%

Imports (1987): QR 4,127,900,000 (machinery and transport equipment 40.4%, manufactured goods 17.2%, food and live animals 17.1%, chemicals and chemical products 6.3%, beverages and tobacco 1.9%). *Major import sources:* Japan 16.3%; United Kingdom 16.0%; United States 11.9%; West Germany 7.2%; Italy 4.9%; France 4.3%; Saudi Arabia 2.7%; The Netherlands 2.5%.
Exports (1987): QR 7,224,000,000 (1985; crude petroleum 91.1%, liquefied gas and other nonpetroleum exports 8.9%). *Major export destinations* (1987): Japan 38.5%; Singapore 13.1%; Italy 8.4%; Brazil 4.6%; Australia 2.8%; The Netherlands 2.0%; United Kingdom 1.1%; China 0.9%.

Transport and communications

Transport. Railroads: none. Roads (1986): total length 671 mi, 1,080 km (paved, n.a.). Vehicles (1986): passenger cars 131,044; trucks and buses 3,710. Merchant marine (1988): vessels (100 gross tons and over) 65; total deadweight tonnage 463,385. Air transport[5] (1988): passenger-mi 814,000,000, passenger-km 1,418,000,000; short ton-mi cargo 24,700,000, metric ton-km cargo 36,000,000; airports (1989) with scheduled flights 1.
Communications. Daily newspapers (1986): total number 5; total circulation 51,500; circulation per 1,000 population 147. Radio (1988): total number of receivers 160,205 (1 per 2.5 persons). Television (1988): total number of receivers 160,000 (1 per 2.5 persons). Telephones (1986): 115,471 (1 per 3.4 persons).

Education and health

Education (1986–87)

	schools	teachers	students	student/ teacher ratio
Primary (age 6–11)	122	3,141	42,502	14.0
Secondary (age 12–17)	69	2,801	22,518	8.0
Vocational	3	113	856	7.6
Higher	1	452	4,931	10.9

Educational attainment (1986). Percent of population age 25 and over having: no formal education 53.2%, of which illiterates 27.9%; primary 9.9%; preparatory (lower secondary) 10.1%; secondary 13.3%; postsecondary 13.3%; other 0.2%. *Literacy* (1986): total population age 15 and over literate 201,743 (74.7%); males literate 149,980 (76.8%); females literate 51,753 (72.5%).
Health (1986): physicians 543 (1 per 679 persons); hospital beds 915 (1 per 403 persons); infant mortality rate per 1,000 live births 37.4.
Food: daily per capita caloric intake, n.a.

Military

Total active duty personnel (1989): 7,000 (army 85.7%, navy 10.0%, air force 4.3%). *Military expenditure as percent of GNP* (1985): 46.9% (world 5.7%); per capita expenditure U.S.$6,700.

[1]Total population excludes 2,784 Qataris residing abroad. [2]Detail does not add to total given because of rounding. [3]1983. [4]Unemployed. [5]One-fourth apportionment of international flights of Gulf Air.

Réunion

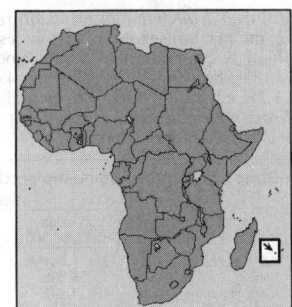

Official name: Département de la Réunion (Department of Reunion).
Political status: overseas department (France) with two legislative houses (General Council [44]; Regional Council [45]).
Chief of state: President of France.
Heads of government: Commissioner of the Republic (for France); President of General Council (for Réunion); President of Regional Council (for Réunion).
Capital: Saint-Denis.
Official language: French.
Official religion: none.
Monetary unit: 1 Franc (F) = 100 centimes; valuation (Oct. 2, 1989) 1 U.S.$ = F 6.36; 1 £ = F 10.29.

Area and population

Arrondissements	Capitals	area sq mi	area sq km	population 1988 estimate[1]
Saint-Benoît	Saint-Benoît	284	736	82,663
Saint-Denis	Saint-Denis	164	423	200,855
Saint-Paul	Saint-Paul	180	467	104,651
Saint-Pierre	Saint-Pierre	339	878	183,451
TOTAL		969[2, 3]	2,510[2, 3]	571,620

Demography

Population (1989): 584,000.
Density (1989): persons per sq mi 602.7, persons per sq km 232.7.
Urban–rural (1982): urban 52.8%; rural 47.2%.
Sex distribution (1982): male 49.05%; female 50.95%.
Age breakdown (1982): under 15, 35.6%; 15–29, 29.8%; 30–44, 17.2%; 45–59, 11.1%; 60–74, 4.6%; 75 and over, 1.7%.
Population projection: (2000) 689,000; (2010) 785,000.
Doubling time: 39 years.
Ethnic composition (1983): mixed race 63.5%; East Indian 28.2%; Chinese 2.2%; French 1.9%; East African 1.1%; other 3.1%.
Religious affiliation (1986): Roman Catholic 90.3%; Muslim 1.2%; other (includes Bahā'ī, Hindu, atheist, and other Christian) 8.5%.
Major cities (1989)[1, 4]: Saint-Denis 122,584; Saint-Paul 66,546; Saint-Pierre 56,563; Tampon 44,665[5]; Saint-Louis 35,390[5].

Vital statistics

Birth rate per 1,000 population (1988): 23.6 (world avg. 27.1); legitimate 47.8%; illegitimate 52.2%.
Death rate per 1,000 population (1988): 5.7 (world avg. 9.9).
Natural increase rate per 1,000 population (1988): 17.9 (world avg. 17.2).
Total fertility rate (avg. births per childbearing woman; 1988): 2.7.
Marriage rate per 1,000 population (1988): 5.8.
Divorce rate per 1,000 population (1988): 1.1.
Life expectancy at birth (1987): male 68.0 years; female 74.0 years.
Major causes of death per 100,000 population (1985): diseases of the circulatory system 164.0; malignant neoplasms (cancers) 82.4; diseases of the digestive system 49.1; diseases of the respiratory system 45.0; ill-defined conditions 52.7.

National economy

Budget (1989). Revenue: F 3,287,000,000 (receipts from the French central government and local administrative bodies 58.1%, new loans 12.0%, taxes [including taxes on fuel, motor vehicles, and cigarettes] 10.2%). Expenditures: F 3,287,000,000 (health and social services 42.9%, other administrative and operational services 37.5%, investment 19.6%).
Public debt (external, outstanding; 1987)[6]: U.S.$60,000,000.
Tourism (1988): number of tourist arrivals 182,723.
Gross national product (at current market prices; 1985): U.S.$1,830,000,000 (U.S.$3,350 per capita).

Structure of gross domestic product and labour force

	1983 in value F '000,000	1983 % of total value	1982 labour force	1982 % of labour force
Agriculture	841	6.1	17,390	9.9
Manufacturing	1,247	9.1	7,369	4.2
Construction	699	5.1	11,176	6.4
Public utilities	255	1.9	697	0.4
Transportation and communications	709	5.2	5,871	3.3
Trade	2,135	15.6	14,328	8.1
Finance, real estate, insurance	624	4.6	16,297	9.3
Pub. admin., defense, and services	6,797	49.7	47,343	27.0
Other	368	2.7	55,124[7]	31.4[7]
TOTAL	13,675[8]	100.0	175,595	100.0

Production (value of production in F '000,000; 1987): export crops (sugar, tobacco, vanilla, geranium extract, khuskus [vetiver] extract) 825, vegetables 361, fruits 299, pigs 149, chickens 133, flowers and plants 102, eggs 61, cereals 36; roundwood 33,000 cu m; fish (value of catch in F '000,000;

1988) lobster 36, other 15. Mining and quarrying: gravel and sand for local use. Manufacturing (metric tons; 1988): sugar 252,100; cement 172,-800[9]; molasses 76,000; rum 60,400 hectolitres. Construction (value added; 1983): F 655,000,000. Energy production (consumption): electricity (kW-hr; 1988) 762,800,000 (680,000,000); coal, none (none); crude petroleum, none (none); petroleum products (metric tons; 1987) none (235,000); natural gas, none (none).
Population economically active (1982): total 175,595; activity rate of total population 34.0% (participation rates: ages 16–64, 57.5%; female 35.3%; unemployed [end of 1988] 33.0%).

Price and earnings indexes (December 1985 = 100)[10]

	1983	1984	1985	1986	1987	1988	1989[11]
Consumer price index	87.9	94.2	100.0	101.9	104.8	106.4	107.9
Hourly earnings index[12]	90.3	93.9	100.0	100.1	102.0	105.0	105.6

Household income and expenditure. Average household size (1989) 4.3; income per household (1985) F 190,800 (U.S.$20,914); sources of income (1982): wages and salaries 65.4%, self-employment 18.1%, transfer payments 12.9%, other 3.6%; expenditure (1976–77)[13]: food and beverages 38.8%, clothing and footwear 11.5%, energy 7.4%, transportation 7.2%, housing 7.1%, household furnishings 6.2%, food away from home 2.7%, other 19.1%.
Land use (1986): forested 35.2%; meadows and pastures 4.0%; agricultural and under permanent cultivation 22.0%; other 38.8%.

Foreign trade

Balance of trade (current prices)

	1982	1983	1984	1985	1986	1987
F '000,000	−4,616	−5,748	−6,199	−6,589	−6,930	−7,865
% of total	77.0%	79.3%	79.8%	76.7%	78.8%	81.6%

Imports (1987): F 8,751,200,000 (food and agricultural products 20.7%, electrical and nonelectrical machinery 15.5%, transport equipment 14.0%, metals and metal products 10.5%, chemical products 8.8%). *Major import sources:* France 67.9%; Italy 3.5%; Bahrain 3.0%; West Germany 2.9%.
Exports (1987): F 886,600,000 (sugar 74.9%, rum 3.2%, lobster 2.9%, geranium extract 1.1%, vanilla 0.7%). *Major export destinations:* France 71.4%; Portugal 15.3%; Mayotte 3.1%; Japan 2.7%.

Transport and communications

Transport. Railroads (1984): route length 384 mi, 614 km[14]; traffic, n.a. Roads (1985): total length 1,684 mi, 2,710 km (paved 81%). Vehicles (1985): passenger cars 138,081; trucks and buses 45,017. Merchant marine (1985): vessels (100 gross tons and over) 6; total deadweight tonnage, n.a. Air transport (1988): passenger arrivals 321,216, passenger departures 324,888; cargo unloaded 9,916 metric tons, cargo loaded 3,480 metric tons; airports (1989) with scheduled flights 1.
Communications. Daily newspapers (1986): total number 3; total circulation 55,000; circulation per 1,000 population 99. Radio (1988): total number of receivers 150,000 (1 per 3.8 persons). Television (1988): total number of receivers 90,000 (1 per 6.4 persons). Telephones (1987): 132,565 (1 per 4.3 persons).

Education and health

Education (1986–87)

	schools	teachers	students	student/ teacher ratio
Primary (age 6–11)	351	3,917	73,526	18.8
Secondary (age 12–18)	...	3,263	57,699	17.7
Voc., teacher tr.	...	719	11,903	16.6
Higher	...	...	4,135	...

Educational attainment (1974). Percent of population age 20 and over having: no formal schooling 30.1%; primary education 30.2%; secondary 36.5%; higher 2.5%; not specified 0.7%. *Literacy* (1982): total population age 15 and over literate 268,300 (78.6%); males literate 126,500 (76.5%); females literate 141,800 (80.5%).
Health: physicians (1988) 959 (1 per 599 persons); hospital beds (1987) 3,874 (1 per 146 persons); infant mortality rate per 1,000 live births (1986–88[15]) 8.9[16].
Food (1984–86): daily per capita caloric intake 3,011 (vegetable products 81%, animal products 19%); (1984) 129% of FAO recommended minimum requirement.

Military

Total active duty personnel (1988): 3,300 French troops[17].

[1]January 1. [2]Includes 2 sq mi (6 sq km) not distributed by arrondissement. [3]Indian Ocean islets administered by France from Réunion are excluded from total. Areas of these islets, which have no permanent population, are: Îles Glorieuses 1.7 sq mi (4.3 sq km), Île Juan de Nova 1.9 sq mi (4.8 sq km), Île Tromelin 0.3 sq mi (0.8 sq km), Bassas da India 0.1 sq mi (0.2 sq km), Île Europa 7.8 sq mi (20.2 sq km). [4]Populations cited are for communes. [5]1988. [6]Includes long-term private debt not guaranteed by the government. [7]Includes 54,338 unemployed. [8]1988 GDP estimate equals F 22,754,000,000. [9]1984. [10]Unless footnoted, indexes refer to December. [11]March. [12]Based on minimum-level wage in public administration. [13]Based on urban households whose head is a wage earner. [14]For sugar industry only. [15]Through November 1988. [16]Excludes live-born infants dying before registration of birth. [17]Includes troops stationed on Mayotte.

Romania

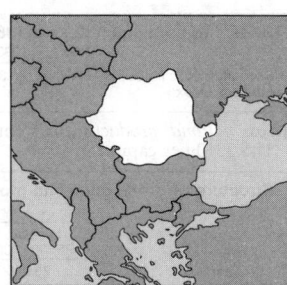

Official name: România (Romania)[1].
Form of government: unitary republic[2] with one legislative house (Grand National Assembly [369]).
Chief of state: interim[2] President.
Head of government: interim[2] Prime Minister.
Capital: Bucharest.
Official language: Romanian.
Official religion: none.
Monetary unit: 1 Romanian leu (plural lei) = 100 bani; valuation (Oct. 2, 1989) 1 U.S.$ = 8.79[3] lei; 1 £ = 14.22[3] lei.

Area and population

Districts	Capitals	area sq mi	area sq km	population 1987 estimate
Alba	Alba Iulia	2,406	6,231	425,903
Arad	Arad	2,954	7,652	504,556
Argeș	Pitești	2,626	6,801	671,954
Bacău	Bacău	2,551	6,606	717,946
Bihor	Oradea	2,909	7,535	657,707
Bistrița-Năsăud	Bistrița	2,048	5,305	322,501
Botoșani	Botoșani	1,917	4,965	460,211
Brăila	Brăila	1,824	4,724	400,832
Brașov	Brașov	2,066	5,351	695,160
Buzău	Buzău	2,344	6,072	522,685
Caraș-Severin	Reșița	3,283	8,503	407,402
Călărași	Călărași	1,959	5,074	347,312
Cluj	Cluj-Napoca	2,568	6,650	740,929
Constanța	Constanța	2,724	7,055	726,059
Covasna	Sfîntu Gheorghe	1,431	3,705	233,049
Dîmbovița	Tîrgoviște	1,559	4,036	563,621
Dolj	Craiova	2,862	7,413	771,971
Galați	Galați	1,708	4,425	635,425
Giurgiu	Giurgiu	1,404	3,636	325,150
Gorj	Tîrgu Jiu	2,178	5,641	380,582
Harghita	Miercurea-Ciuc	2,552	6,610	359,205
Hunedoara	Deva	2,709	7,016	559,619
Ialomița	Slobozia	1,718	4,449	304,809
Iași	Iași	2,112	5,469	793,369
Maramureș	Baia Mare	2,400	6,215	546,035
Mehedinți	Drobeta-Turnu-Severin	1,892	4,900	327,309
Mureș	Tîrgu Mureș	2,585	6,696	616,401
Neamț	Piatra Neamț	2,274	5,890	570,204
Olt	Slatina	2,126	5,507	531,323
Prahova	Ploiești	1,812	4,694	868,779
Sălaj	Zalău	1,486	3,850	412,227
Satu Mare	Satu Mare	1,701	4,405	267,517
Sibiu	Sibiu	2,093	5,422	507,850
Suceava	Suceava	3,303	8,555	685,661
Teleorman	Alexandria	2,224	5,760	504,623
Timiș	Timișoara	3,356	8,692	731,667
Tulcea	Tulcea	3,255	8,430	269,808
Vaslui	Vaslui	2,045	5,297	457,699
Vîlcea	Rîmnicu Vîlcea	2,203	5,705	427,059
Vrancea	Focșani	1,878	4,863	390,055
Muncipality				
Bucharest	Bucharest	654	1,695	2,298,256
TOTAL		91,699	237,500	22,940,430

Demography

Population (1989): 23,168,000.
Density (1989): persons per sq mi 252.7, persons per sq km 97.5.
Urban–rural (1986): urban 50.6%; rural 49.4%.
Sex distribution (1987): male 49.34%; female 50.66%.
Age breakdown (1985): under 15, 24.6%; 15–29, 22.6%; 30–44, 19.6%; 45–59, 18.8%; 60–74, 10.7%; 75 and over, 3.7%.
Population projection: (2000) 24,409,000; (2010) 25,595,000.
Ethnic composition (1987): Romanian 89.1%; Hungarian 7.8%; other 3.1%.
Religious affiliation (1980): Romanian Orthodox 70.0%; Greek Orthodox 10.0%; Muslim 1.0%; atheist 7.0%; other 3.0%; none 9.0%.
Major cities (1986): Bucharest 2,014,400[4]; Brașov 351,500; Constanța 327,700; Timișoara 325,300; Iași 313,000.

Vital statistics

Birth rate per 1,000 population (1985): 15.8 (world avg. 29.0).
Death rate per 1,000 population (1985): 10.9 (world avg. 11.0).
Natural increase rate per 1,000 population (1985): 4.9 (world avg. 18.0).
Total fertility rate (avg. births per childbearing woman; 1985): 2.1.
Marriage rate per 1,000 population (1985): 7.1.
Divorce rate per 1,000 population (1985): 1.4.
Life expectancy at birth (1982–84): male 67.0 years; female 72.6 years.
Major causes of death per 100,000 population (1984): diseases of the circulatory system 603.7; malignant neoplasms (cancers) 128.4.

National economy

Budget (1989): Revenue: 423,473,500,000 lei (turnover tax 55.1%, state social insurance 13.4%, share in profit of state enterprises 13.0%, income tax 12.0%). Expenditures: 423,473,500,000 lei (national economy 43.3%, social services 25.3%, defense 2.8%).
Tourism (1986): receipts U.S.$178,000,000; expenditures U.S.$57,000,000.
Production (metric tons except as noted). Agriculture (1987): corn (maize) 18,377,600, wheat and rye 9,726,700, potatoes 7,571,900, sugar beets 7,149,100, vegetables 6,718,800; livestock (number of live animals) 18,793,000

sheep, 15,224,000 pigs, 7,182,000 cattle; roundwood 24,629,000 cu m; fish catch 264,371. Mining and quarrying (1987): iron ore 2,281,000; bauxite 555,000; lead and zinc 74,000[5]. Manufacturing (1987): crude steel 13,885,000; cement 12,435,000; rolled steel 9,675,000; fertilizers 3,198,000. Construction (1985): 8,591,000 sq m. Energy production (consumption): electricity (kW-hr; 1987) 73,090,000,000 (76,190,000,000); coal (metric tons; 1987) 47,300,000 (52,600,000); crude petroleum (barrels, 1987) 76,561,000 (196,657,000); petroleum products (metric tons; 1987) 22,909,000 (14,109,000); natural gas (cu m; 1987) 38,919,000,000 (40,952,000,000).
Public debt (external, outstanding; 1989): none.
Gross national product (1988): U.S.$148,048,000,000 (U.S.$6,400 per capita).

Structure of net material product and labour force

	1987 in value '000,000 lei	% of total value	labour force	% of labour force
Agriculture	127,100	15.9	3,065,500	28.6
Mining, manufacturing, and public utilities	499,500	62.5	4,008,800	37.4
Construction	59,100	7.4	793,200	7.4
Transp. and commun.	48,000	6.0	739,600	6.9
Trade	6	6	632,400	5.9
Pub. admin., defense	—	—	53,600	0.5
Services	—	—	1,275,500	11.9
Other	65,500[6]	8.2[6]	150,000	1.4
TOTAL	799,200	100.0	10,718,600	100.0

Population economically active (1987): total 10,718,600; activity rate 46.7% (participation rates [1985]: over age 15, 61.8%; female 45.9%).

Price and earnings indexes (1985 = 100)

	1980	1981	1982	1983	1984	1985	1986
Consumer price index	79.0	80.7	99.4	99.3	100.4	100.0	99.9
Monthly earnings index	81.1	84.1	89.8	92.4	99.4	100.0	100.2

Household income and expenditure. Average household size (1984) 3.1; income per household 62,310 lei (U.S.$3,500); sources of income (1982): wages 62.6%, other 37.4%; expenditure (1980): food 62.7%, clothing 13.8%.
Land use (1986): forested 26.7%; meadows and pastures 18.5%; agricultural and under permanent cultivation 43.3%; other 11.5%.

Foreign trade

Balance of trade (current prices)

	1981	1982	1983	1984	1985	1986	1987
'000,000 lei	+3,031	+26,987	+34,379	+67,300	+43,934	+31,550	+44,700
% of total	0.9%	9.8%	12.4%	17.3%	12.9%	8.4%	14.4%

Imports (1987): 133,000,000,000 lei (mineral fuels 53.5%, machinery 28.4%, chemicals 5.0%). *Major import sources:* U.S.S.R. 25.9%; Egypt 12.0%; Iran 6.9%; E.Ger. 6.7%; Poland 6.3%; China 4.4%; W.Ger. 3.8%.
Exports (1987): 177,700,000,000 lei (machinery and transport equipment 37.6%, fuels 23.2%, chemicals 8.6%). *Major export destinations:* U.S.S.R. 24.2%; Italy 6.9%; W.Ger. 6.3%; United States 6.2%; E.Ger. 4.8%; France 4.3%; Egypt 4.0%; Poland 4.0%; China 3.5%.

Transport and communications

Transport. Railroads (1987): length 7,006 mi, 11,275 km; passenger-km 33,506,000,000; metric ton-km cargo 78,074,000,000. Roads (1986): length 72,799 km (paved 64%). Vehicles (1980): cars 250,000; trucks and buses 130,000. Merchant marine (1988): vessels (100 gross tons and over) 462; total deadweight tonnage 5,356,547. Air transport (1988): passenger-km 3,852,000,000; metric ton-km cargo 63,000,000; airports (1989) 15.
Communications. Daily newspapers (1987): total number 36; total circulation 3,133,400; circulation per 1,000 population 137. Radios (1987): 3,150,000 (1 per 7.3 persons). Televisions (1987): 3,801,000 (1 per 6.0 persons). Telephones (1985): 1,962,681 subscribers (1 per 11 persons).

Education and health

Education (1987–88)

	schools	teachers	students	student/ teacher ratio
Primary (age 6–13)	13,895	141,609	3,027,196	21.4
Secondary (age 14–17)	981	43,805	1,228,490	28.0
Vocational	764	12,419	278,003	22.4
Higher	44	12,036	157,041	13.0

Educational attainment (1977). Percent of population age 25 and over having: primary education 55.6%; secondary 39.8%; postsecondary 4.6%.
Literacy (1983) 95.8%.
Health (1987): physicians 41,059 (1 per 559 persons); hospital beds 214,253 (1 per 107 persons); infant mortality rate per 1,000 live births (1986) 25.6.
Food (1984–86): daily per capita caloric intake 3,358 (vegetable products 76%, animal products 24%); 127% of FAO recommended minimum.

Military

Total active duty personnel (1988): 179,500 (army 78.0%, navy 4.2%, air force 17.8%). *Military expenditure as percent of GNP* (1987): 5.2% (world 5.4%); per capita expenditure U.S.$332.

[1]Until Dec. 29, 1989, called the Socialist Republic of Romania. [2]Governed from Dec. 26, 1989, by a Council of National Salvation pending national elections in April 1990. The CNS named an interim president and prime minister to serve for the same period. [3]Noncommercial rate. [4]1987. [5]1986. [6]Includes trade and other material activities.

Rwanda

Official name: Repubulika y'u Rwanda (Rwanda); République Rwandaise (French) (Republic of Rwanda).
Form of government: single-party republic with one legislative house (National Development Council [70]).
Head of state and government: President.
Capital: Kigali.
Official languages: Rwanda; French.
Official religion: none.
Monetary unit: 1 Rwanda franc (RF); valuation (Oct. 2, 1989) 1 U.S.$ = RF 80.25; 1 £ = RF 129.85.

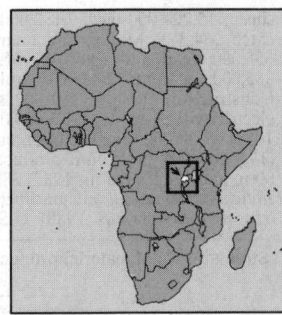

Area and population		area		population
		sq mi	sq km	1983 estimate
Prefectures	**Capitals**			
Butare	Butare	707	1,830	682,500
Byumba	Byumba	1,925	4,987	623,600
Cyangugu	Cyangugu	859	2,226	343,500
Gikongoro	Gikongoro	846	2,192	401,900
Gisenyi	Gisenyi	925	2,395	566,400
Gitarama	Gitarama	865	2,241	706,200
Kibungo	Kibungo	1,596	4,134	420,200
Kibuye	Kibuye	510	1,320	500,600
Kigali	Kigali	1,255	3,251	835,400
Ruhengeri	Ruhengeri	680	1,762	581,200
TOTAL		10,169[1]	26,338	5,661,400[1]

Demography

Population (1989): 6,989,000.
Density (1989): persons per sq mi 687.3, persons per sq km 265.4.
Urban–rural (1985): urban 6.2%; rural 93.8%.
Sex distribution (1985): male 49.41%; female 50.59%.
Age breakdown (1985): under 15, 48.4%; 15–29, 26.3%; 30–44, 13.6%; 45–59, 8.0%; 60–74, 3.5%; 75 and over, 0.2%.
Population projection: (2000) 10,144,000; (2010) 13,556,000.
Doubling time: 21 years.
Ethnic composition (1983): Hutu 90%; Tutsi 9%; Twa 1%.
Religious affiliation (1988): Roman Catholic 65%; Protestant 9%; Muslim 9%; traditional beliefs 17%.
Major cities (1978): Kigali 156,700[2]; Butare 21,691; Ruhengeri 16,025; Gisenyi 12,436.

Vital statistics

Birth rate per 1,000 population (1985–90): 51.0 (world avg. 27.1); legitimate (1978) 94.9%; illegitimate 5.1%.
Death rate per 1,000 population (1985–90): 17.1 (world avg. 9.9).
Natural increase rate per 1,000 population (1985–90): 33.9 (world avg. 17.2).
Total fertility rate (avg. births per childbearing woman; 1985–90): 8.3.
Marriage rate per 1,000 population (1984): 2.5[3].
Divorce rate per 1,000 population: n.a.
Life expectancy at birth (1985–90): male 46.9 years; female 50.2 years.
Major causes of death per 100,000 population[4] (1984): complications of pregnancy, childbirth, and birth injury 192.4; infectious and parasitic diseases (including malaria, typhoid fever, trypanosomiasis [sleeping sickness], pneumonia, tuberculosis of the respiratory system, bacillary dysentery and amoebiasis, diphtheria, meningococcal infection, and acute poliomyelitis) 11.8; diseases of the digestive system 10.3; diseases of the nervous system 10.1; accidents, poisonings, and violence 5.2.

National economy

Budget (1988–89). Revenue: RF 27,500,000,000 (1984; import and export duties 39.6%, taxes on goods and services 25.3%, income tax 18.1%, property taxes 1.9%). Expenditures: RF 27,500,000,000 (1987; education 19.9%, debt repayment 16.6%, defense 9.9%, infrastructure 6.6%, health 4.6%, agriculture 1.1%).
Public debt (external, outstanding; 1987): U.S.$544,400,000.
Production (metric tons except as noted). Agriculture, forestry, fishing (1988): plantains 2,140,000, roots and tubers 1,435,000 (of which sweet potatoes 800,000, cassava 390,000, potatoes 183,000), cereals 279,000 (of which sorghum 177,000, corn [maize] 88,000), coffee 42,000, tea 8,000, tobacco 3,000; livestock (number of live animals) 1,200,000 goats, 660,000 cattle, 360,000 sheep, 92,000 pigs; roundwood (1987) 5,842,000 cu m; fish catch (1987) 1,630. Mining and quarrying (1986): cassiterite (tin ore) 1,158; wolframite (tungsten ore) 280; gold 220 troy oz. Manufacturing (1987): cement 57,073; sheet metal 9,598; lye soap 5,354; sugar 3,368; beer 91,767,000 bottles; lemonade 63,452,000 bottles; footwear 327,000 pairs. Construction (1981): residential 59,600 sq m; nonresidential 34,400 sq m. Energy production (consumption): electricity (kW-hr; 1987) 108,470,000 (105,250,000); coal, none (n.a.); petroleum products (metric tons; 1987) none (118,000); natural gas (cu m; 1987) 897,000 (897,000).
Tourism (1987): receipts from visitors U.S.$7,000,000; expenditures by nationals abroad U.S.$15,000,000.
Land use (1986): forested 20.2%; meadows and pastures 16.4%; agricultural and under permanent cultivation 44.6%; other 18.8%.
Population economically active (1985): total 3,063,000; activity rate of total population 50.5% (participation rates: ages 15–64 89.4%; female 48.6%; unemployed, n.a.).

Price and earnings indexes (1985 = 100)							
	1982	1983	1984	1985	1986	1987	1988
Consumer price index	87.5	93.3	98.3	100.0	98.9	103.0	106.0
Earnings index	...	...	...	...	...	...	...

Gross national product (at current market prices; 1987): U.S.$2,008,000,000 (U.S.$310 per capita).

Structure of gross domestic product and labour force	1986		1985	
	in value RF '000,000	% of total value	labour force	% of labour force
Agriculture	79,090	44.6	2,827,000	92.3
Mining	620	0.4	}	
Manufacturing	32,090	18.1		
Construction	7,460	4.2	} 95,000	3.1
Public utilities	430	0.2		
Transportation and communications	2,840	1.6		
Trade	27,140	15.3		
Finance	6,560	3.7	} 141,000	4.6
Pub. admin., defense } Services	20,370	11.5		
Other	790	0.4		
TOTAL	177,390	100.0	3,063,000	100.0

Household income and expenditure. Average household size (1983) 5.2; average annual income per household RF 122,870 (U.S.$1,300); sources of income (1977): self-employment (profits, interest, etc.) 71.0%, salaries and wages 16.5%, transfers 9.5%; expenditure: n.a.

Foreign trade[5]

Balance of trade (current prices)						
	1983	1984	1985	1986	1987	1988
RF '000,000	−6,542	−4,912	−7,840	−4,860	−10,562	−11,403
% of total	22.3%	14.5%	22.9%	12.9%	37.1%	40.7%

Imports (1988): RF 28,280,000,000 (1985; machinery and transport equipment 21.6%, of which transport equipment 11.4%, electrical equipment 4.8%; mineral fuels and lubricants 15.2%; food, beverages, and tobacco 15.2%; textiles, clothing, and footwear 7.4%). *Major import sources* (1987): Kenya 22.3%; Japan 13.9%; France 13.1%; Belgium–Luxembourg 11.0%; West Germany 9.8%; The Netherlands 4.9%; Italy 3.8%; China 2.2%; India 1.9%; United Kingdom 1.5%.
Exports (1988): RF 8,291,000,000 (coffee 78.9%; tea 13.1%). *Major export destinations* (1987): West Germany 50.6%; The Netherlands 8.4%; France 8.3%; United Kingdom 5.1%; Italy 3.6%; Belgium–Luxembourg 3.5%; Kenya 3.3%.

Transport and communications

Transport. Railroads: none. Roads (1987): total length 7,500 mi, 12,070 km (paved 7%). Vehicles (1987): passenger cars 7,109; trucks and buses 10,026. Merchant marine: none. Air transport (1984): passenger arrivals 46,029, passenger departures 46,586; metric ton cargo loaded 13,120; metric ton cargo unloaded 11,864; airports (1989) with scheduled flights 2.
Communications. Daily newspapers (1984): total number 1; total circulation per 1,000 population, n.a. Radio (1988): total number of receivers 411,735 (1 per 16 persons). Television: none. Telephones (1987): 10,181 (1 per 652 persons).

Education and health

Education (1986)	schools	teachers	students	student/ teacher ratio
Primary (age 7–15)	1,612	16,003	904,378	56.5
Secondary (age 16–19)	...	1,479[6]	8,577	...
Voc., teacher tr.	...	...	12,295	...
Higher[7]	3	331	1,987	6.0

Educational attainment (1978). Percent of population age 25 and over having: no formal schooling 76.9%; some primary education 16.8%; complete primary education 4.0%; some secondary and complete secondary education 2.0%; some postsecondary vocational and higher education 0.3%.
Literacy (1980): total population age 15 and over literate 1,295,900 (49.4%); males literate 798,800 (62.2%); females literate 497,100 (37.2%).
Health (1984): physicians 177[8] (1 per 33,170 persons); hospital beds 9,046 (1 per 649 persons); infant mortality rate per 1,000 live births (1985–90) 122.0.
Food (1984–86): daily per capita caloric intake 1,881 (vegetable products 97%, animal products 3%); 80% of FAO recommended minimum requirement.

Military

Total active duty personnel (1989): 5,200 (army 96.2%; navy, none; air force 3.8%). *Military expenditure as percent of GNP* (1987): 2.0% (world 5.4%); per capita expenditure U.S.$6.

---

[1]Detail does not add to total given because of rounding. [2]1981. [3]Excludes marriages not registered in court. [4]In hospitals only. [5]Imports f.o.b. in balance of trade and c.i.f. in commodities and trading partners. [6]Includes vocational and teacher training. [7]1985. [8]Excludes foreign physicians.

Saint Kitts and Nevis

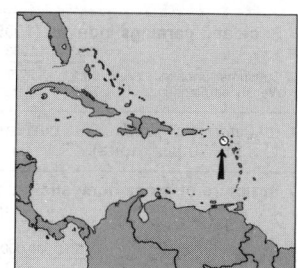

Official name: Federation of Saint Kitts and Nevis[1].
Form of government: constitutional monarchy with one legislative house (National Assembly [15][2]).
Chief of state: British Monarch represented by governor-general.
Head of government: Prime Minister.
Capital: Basseterre.
Official language: English.
Official religion: none.
Monetary unit: 1 Eastern Caribbean dollar (EC$) = 100 cents; valuation (Oct. 2, 1989) 1 U.S.$ = EC$2.70; 1 £ = EC$4.37.

Area and population

Islands[3]	Capitals	area sq mi	area sq km	population 1986 estimate
Nevis	Charlestown	36.0	93.2	9,600
St. Kitts	Basseterre	68.0	176.2	34,100
TOTAL		104.0	269.4	43,700

Demography

Population (1989): 44,100.
Density (1989): persons per sq mi 424.0, persons per sq km 163.7.
Urban–rural (1985): urban 45.0%; rural 55.0%.
Sex distribution (1986): male 50.34%; female 49.66%.
Age breakdown (1984): under 15, 34.3%; 15–29, 30.3%; 30–44, 13.7%; 45–59, 9.1%; 60–74, 9.1%; 75 and over, 3.5%.
Population projection: (2000) 44,000; (2010) 45,000.
Doubling time: 54 years.
Ethnic composition (1985): black 90.5%; mixed 5.0%; Indo-Pakistani 3.0%; white 1.5%.
Religious affiliation (1980): Protestant 82.7%, of which Anglican 32.6%, Methodist 28.8%, Moravian 8.7%; Roman Catholic 7.2%; other 10.1%.
Major towns (1985): Basseterre 18,500; Charlestown 1,700.

Vital statistics

Birth rate per 1,000 population (1987): 23.2 (world avg. 27.1); (1983) legitimate 19.2%; illegitimate 80.8%.
Death rate per 1,000 population (1987): 10.3 (world avg. 9.9).
Natural increase rate per 1,000 population (1987): 12.9 (world avg. 17.2).
Total fertility rate (avg. births per childbearing woman; 1987): 3.0.
Marriage rate per 1,000 population (1977): 3.5.
Divorce rate per 1,000 population (1977): 0.2.
Life expectancy at birth (1987): male 63.0 years; female 67.0 years.
Major causes of death per 100,000 population (1984): diseases of the circulatory system 462.7, of which cerebrovascular disease 175.4; malignant neoplasms (cancers) 114.0; diseases of the respiratory system 41.7; infectious and parasitic diseases 35.1; ill-defined conditions 142.5.

National economy

Budget (1987). Revenue: EC$138,200,000 (current revenue 52.8%, of which tax revenue 31.6%, nontax revenue 21.2%; development revenue 47.2%). Expenditures: EC$138,200,000 (current expenditure 50.3%; development expenditure 49.7%).
Public debt (external, outstanding; end of 1987): U.S.$22,000,000.
Production (metric tons except as noted). Agriculture, forestry, fishing (1988): sugarcane 300,000, coconuts 2,000, fruits 2,000, vegetables 1,000, peanuts (groundnuts) 234, cotton 164; livestock (number of live animals) 15,000 sheep, 10,000 pigs, 10,000 goats, 7,000 cattle; roundwood, n.a.; fish catch 1,500[4]. Mining and quarrying: excavation of sand for local use. Manufacturing (1987): raw sugar (1988) 25,600; molasses 8,800; aerated beverages 37,100 hectolitres; alcoholic beverages 13,790 hectolitres; shoes 23,800 pairs[5]; other manufactures include garments and electronic components. Construction: n.a. Energy production (consumption): electricity (kW-hr; 1987) 42,500,000 (36,000,000); coal, none (none); crude petroleum, none (none); petroleum products (metric tons; 1987) none (18,000); natural gas, none (none).
Gross national product (at current market prices; 1987): U.S.$80,000,000 (U.S.$1,700 per capita).

Structure of gross domestic product and labour force

	1987 in value EC$'000,000	1987 % of total value	1984 labour force[6]	1984 % of labour force
Agriculture	21.9	9.4	4,380	29.6
Mining	0.5	0.2	—	—
Manufacturing	33.4	14.4	2,170	14.7
Construction	18.0	7.7	400	2.7
Public utilities	4.6	2.0	1,030	7.0
Transportation and communications	29.2	12.5	450	3.0
Trade, restaurants	53.4	23.0	940	6.3
Finance, real estate	31.1	13.4	280	1.9
Pub. admin., defense	44.6	19.2 }	4,700	31.7
Services	10.2	4.4 }		
Other	−14.4[7]	−6.2[7]	460	3.1
TOTAL	232.5	100.0	14,810	100.0

Household income and expenditure. Average household size (1980) 3.7; income per household: n.a.; sources of income: n.a.; expenditure (1978)[8]: food, beverages, and tobacco 55.6%, household furnishings 9.4%, housing 7.6%, clothing and footwear 7.5%, fuel and light 6.6%, transportation 4.3%, other 9.0%.
Population economically active (1980): total 17,125; activity rate of total population 39.5% (participation rates: ages 15–64, 69.5%; female 41.0%; unemployed[9]).

Price and earnings indexes (1984 = 100)

	1981	1982	1983	1984	1985	1986	1987
Consumer price index	93.3	95.1	97.4	100.0	102.2	101.9	102.8
Annual earnings index[10]	93.8	96.6	98.0	100.0	...	...	...

Tourism (1987): receipts from visitors U.S.$47,000,000; expenditures by nationals abroad U.S.$3,000,000.
Land use (1986): forested 17.0%; meadows and pastures 3.0%; agricultural and under permanent cultivation 39.0%; other 41.0%.

Foreign trade[11]

Balance of trade (current prices)

	1982	1983	1984	1985	1986	1987
EC$'000,000	−69.0	−88.9	−85.7	−85.9	−110.7	−141.4
% of total	40.4%	47.2%	44.1%	42.2%	46.5%	48.8%

Imports (1984): EC$140,100,000 (food 19.7%, of which cereals and cereal preparations 4.7%; crude petroleum and petroleum products 9.9%; electrical machinery and apparatus 9.6%; clothing 7.1%; transport equipment 5.5%). *Major import sources* (1987): United States 39.4%; EEC countries 18.1%; Caricom countries 16.4%.
Exports (1984): EC$54,400,000 (sugar 56.8%; electrical machinery and apparatus 10.9%; clothing 10.3%; footwear 6.5%; beverages 4.9%). *Major export destinations* (1987)[12]: United States 44.0%; EEC countries 20.4%; Caricom countries 9.2%.

Transport and communications

Transport. Railroads (1987): length 36 mi, 58 km[13]. Roads (1987): total length 190 mi, 305 km (paved 41%). Vehicles (1985): passenger cars 3,540; trucks and buses 690. Merchant marine (1988): vessels (100 gross tons and over) 1; total deadweight tonnage 550. Air transport: passenger arrivals (1987) 98,263; passenger departures (1982) 52,410; cargo handled, n.a.; airports (1989) with scheduled flights 2.
Communications. Daily newspapers (1988): none. Radio (1988): total number of receivers 22,800 (1 per 1.9 persons). Television (1988): total number of receivers 7,000 (1 per 6.3 persons). Telephones (1988): 4,000 (1 per 11 persons).

Education and health

Education (1987–88)

	schools	teachers	students	student/ teacher ratio
Primary (age 5–12)[14]	27	263	6,457	24.6
Secondary (age 13–17)	6	273	4,115	15.1
Voc., teacher tr.[15]	1	18	166	9.2
Higher[14, 15]	1	9	55	6.1

Educational attainment (1980). Percent of population age 25 and over having: no formal schooling 1.1%; primary education 29.6%; secondary 67.2%; higher 2.1%. *Literacy* (1985): 90.0%.
Health (1987): physicians 22 (1 per 2,000 persons); hospital beds 258 (1 per 171 persons); infant mortality rate per 1,000 live births (1987) 35.0[16].
Food (1984–86): daily per capita caloric intake 2,349 (vegetable products 75%, animal products 25%); 97% of FAO recommended minimum requirement.

Military

Total active duty personnel (1987): the country maintains a police force and a small defense force of volunteers.

---

[1]Saint Christopher and Nevis and Federation of Saint Christopher and Nevis are both officially acceptable, variant, short- and long-form names of the country. [2]Includes 4 nonelective seats. [3]Parish subdivisions of both islands are for statistical purposes only. [4]1987. [5]1986. [6]Employed persons only. [7]Less imputed bank service charges. [8]Weights of consumer price index components. [9]Unemployment in 1988 was very low because of increased construction in tourism sector. [10]Average wages paid sugar-industry employees. [11]Imports c.i.f.; exports f.o.b. including reexports. [12]Based on domestic exports only equaling 92.9% of total exports. [13]Light railway serving the sugar industry on Saint Kitts. [14]Public institution(s) only. [15]1986–87. [16]Estimate.

Saint Lucia

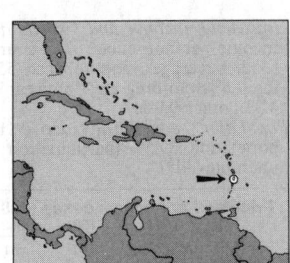

Official name: Saint Lucia.
Form of government: constitutional
  monarchy with two legislative houses
  (Senate [11]; House of Assembly [17]).
Chief of state: British Monarch
  represented by governor-general.
Head of government: Prime Minister.
Capital: Castries.
Official language: English.
Official religion: none.
Monetary unit: 1 Eastern Caribbean
  Dollar (EC$) = 100 cents; valuation
  (Oct. 2, 1989) 1 U.S.$ = EC$2.70;
  1 £ = EC$4.37.

Area and population

Quarters[1]	Capitals	area sq mi	area sq km	population 1986 estimate
Anse-la-Raye	Anse-la-Raye	} 18.1	46.9	6,111
Canaries	Canaries		2,567
Castries	Castries	30.7	79.5	52,868
Choiseul	Choiseul	12.1	31.3	7,995
Dennery	Dennery	26.9	69.7	11,874
Gros Islet	Gros Islet	39.2	101.5	12,502
Laborie	Laborie	14.6	37.8	8,483
Micoud	Micoud	30.9	80.0	14,678
Soufrière	Soufrière	19.5	50.5	8,972
Vieux Fort	Vieux Fort	16.9	43.8	13,479
TOTAL		238.4[2]	617.4[2]	139,529

Demography

Population (1989): 150,000.
Density (1989): persons per sq mi 629.2, persons per sq km 243.0.
Urban–rural (1982): urban 52.1%; rural 47.9%.
Sex distribution (1986): male 48.54%; female 51.46%.
Age breakdown (1986): under 15, 44.5%; 15–29, 27.7%; 30–44, 11.3%; 45–59,
  8.5%; 60–74, 5.8%; 75 and over, 2.2%.
Population projection: (2000) 175,000; (2010) 201,000.
Doubling time: 34 years.
Ethnic composition (1985): black 87.0%; mixed 9.1%; East Indian 2.6%;
  white 1.3%.
Religious affiliation (1980): Roman Catholic 85.6%; Protestant 11.4%, of
  which Seventh-day Adventist 4.3%, Anglican 2.7%; other 3.0%.
Major cities (1986)[3]: Castries 52,868; Vieux Fort 13,479.

Vital statistics

Birth rate per 1,000 population (1987): 26.9 (world avg. 27.1); legitimate
  15.0%; illegitimate 85.0%.
Death rate per 1,000 population (1987): 6.6 (world avg. 9.9).
Natural increase rate per 1,000 population (1987): 20.3 (world avg. 17.2).
Total fertility rate (avg. births per childbearing woman; 1987): 3.8.
Marriage rate per 1,000 population (1986): 3.1.
Divorce rate per 1,000 population (1986): 0.4.
Life expectancy at birth (1986): male 68.0 years; female 74.8 years.
Major causes of death per 100,000 population (1986): diseases of the circula-
  tory system 203.5, of which ischemic heart diseases 111.1, cerebrovascular
  disease 50.9, hypertensive disease 38.0; malignant neoplasms (cancers) 65.2;
  diseases of the respiratory system 55.9; ill-defined conditions 84.6.

National economy

Budget (1987–88). Revenue: EC$220,800,000 (taxes on international trade
  34.1%, taxes on goods and services 22.6%, taxes on income 21.2%, grants
  12.7%, nontax revenue 8.3%). Expenditures: EC$219,000,000 (current ex-
  penditures 72.1%, development expenditures 27.9%).
Public debt (external, outstanding; end of 1987): U.S.$37,200,000.
Tourism (1987): receipts from visitors U.S.$78,400,000; expenditures by na-
  tionals abroad U.S.$52,000,000.
Production (metric tons except as noted). Agriculture, forestry, fishing (1988):
  bananas 133,700, mangoes 46,000, coconuts 31,000, plantains 2,000, sweet
  potatoes 1,000, tomatoes 305[4], oranges 282[4], cabbages 183[4], ginger 127[4],
  cocoa beans 52[5]; livestock (number of live animals) 15,000 sheep, 13,000
  cattle, 12,000 pigs, 12,000 goats; roundwood, n.a.; fish catch 900[6]. Mining
  and quarrying: excavation of sand for local construction and pumice.
  Manufacturing (value of production in EC$'000; 1986): paper products and
  cardboard boxes 41,210[7]; alcoholic beverages and tobacco 14,483; garments
  13,477; nonalcoholic beverages 8,468; electrical components 5,730[7]; copra
  5,566; petroleum storage and transshipment is also important. Construction (buildings authorized; 1986): residential 17,300 sq m; nonresidential
  10,140 sq m. Energy production (consumption): electricity (kW-hr; 1987)
  74,000,000 (74,000,000); coal, none (none); crude petroleum, none (none);
  petroleum products (metric tons; 1987) none (41,000); natural gas, none
  (none).
Household income and expenditure. Average household size (1980) 4.6;
  income per household: n.a.; sources of income: n.a.; expenditure (1984)[8]:
  food 46.8%, housing 13.5%, clothing and footwear 6.5%, transportation and
  communications 6.3%, household furnishings 5.8%, fuel and light 4.5%,
  recreation and education 3.2%, beverages and tobacco 2.8%, health care
  2.3%, other 8.3%.
Population economically active (1980): total 42,200; activity rate of total
  population 37.2% (participation rates: ages 15–64, 69.9%; female 39.1%;
  unemployed [1989] 20.0%).

Price and earnings indexes (1985 = 100)

	1982	1983	1984	1985	1986	1987	1988
Consumer price index	96.1	97.5	98.7	100.0	102.3	109.6	109.7[9]
Weekly earnings index[10]	70.9	...	...	100.0	...	...	...

Gross national product (at current market prices; 1987): U.S.$196,000,000
  (U.S.$1,370 per capita).

Structure of gross domestic product and labour force

	1987[11] in value EC$'000,000	1987[11] % of total value	1983[12] labour force	1983[12] % of labour force
Agriculture	64.1	14.4	13,000	29.7
Mining	2.7	0.6 }		
Manufacturing	35.0	7.9	2,600	5.9
Construction	36.1	8.1	1,500	3.4
Public utilities	18.5	4.2 }		
Transportation and communications	42.7	9.6		
Trade	104.4	23.4	15,800	36.1
Finance, real estate	46.0	10.3		
Pub. admin., defense	98.4	22.1		
Services	20.7	4.6 }		
Other	−23.1[13]	−5.2[13]	10,900[14]	24.9[14]
TOTAL	445.5	100.0	43,800	100.0

Land use (1986): forested 13.0%; meadows and pastures 5.0%; agricultural
  and under permanent cultivation 28.0%; other 54.0%.

Foreign trade[15]

Balance of trade (current prices)

	1982	1983	1984	1985	1986	1987
EC$'000,000	−206.0	−160.2	−190.9	−197.0	−194.0	−272.2
% of total	47.8%	38.4%	42.5%	41.2%	30.2%	39.5%

Imports (1987): EC$480,800,000 (basic and miscellaneous manufactures
  35.4%, food products 20.3%, mineral fuels 6.2%). *Major import sources*
  (1986): United States 34.1%; United Kingdom 15.9%; Trinidad and Tobago
  7.8%; Japan 6.9%; Canada 3.1%.
Exports (1987): EC$208,600,000 (bananas 71.2%; clothing 14.0%; paper prod-
  ucts 9.1%). *Major export destinations*[16] (1986): United Kingdom 70.5%;
  United States 11.3%; Trinidad and Tobago 2.9%; Barbados 2.7%.

Transport and communications

Transport. Railroads: none. Roads (1986): total length 464 mi, 747 km (paved
  79%). Vehicles (1984): passenger cars 7,049; trucks and buses 2,084. Merchant marine (1988): vessels (100 gross tons and over) 7; total deadweight
  tonnage 2,070. Air transport (1987): passenger arrivals 161,253, passenger
  departures 163,029; cargo unloaded 1,591 metric tons, cargo loaded 2,593
  metric tons; airports (1989) with scheduled flights 2.
Communications. Daily newspapers: none. Radio (1988): total number of
  receivers 99,100 (1 per 1.5 persons). Television (1986): total number of
  receivers 5,000 (1 per 28 persons). Telephones (1986): 14,104 (1 per 10
  persons).

Education and health

Education (1987–88)

	schools	teachers	students	student/ teacher ratio
Primary (age 5–11)	81	1,060	32,809	31.0
Secondary (age 12–16)	12	351	6,284	17.9
Voc., teacher tr.[17]	4	...	817	...
Higher[17]	1	16	123	7.7

Educational attainment (1980). Percent of population age 25 and over having: no formal schooling 17.5%; primary education 74.4%; secondary 6.8%;
  higher 1.3%. *Literacy* (1985): more than 90%.
Health (1987): physicians 54 (1 per 2,636 persons); hospital beds 501 (1 per
  284 persons); infant mortality rate per 1,000 live births 20.4.
Food (1984–86): daily per capita caloric intake 2,499 (vegetable products 77%,
  animal products 23%); 103% of FAO recommended minimum requirement.

Military

Total active duty personnel (1987):[18].

---

[1]Saint Lucia is divided into 10 quarters for statistical purposes only. Local government is based on town or village councils. [2]Total includes the uninhabited 29.5-sq
mi (76.4-sq km) Central Forest Reserve. [3]Populations cited are for quarters. [4]1983.
[5]1986. [6]1987. [7]1985. [8]Weights of consumer price index components. [9]Average of
2nd and 3rd quarters. [10]Wages in nonagricultural activities excluding mining. [11]At
factor cost. [12]Wage earners and self-employed. [13]Less imputed bank service charges.
[14]Unemployed. [15]Imports c.i.f.; exports f.o.b. and c.i.f. in commodities and trading
partners. [16]Based on domestic exports only. [17]1986–87. [18]The 489-member police
force includes a specially trained paramilitary unit.

Saint Vincent and the Grenadines

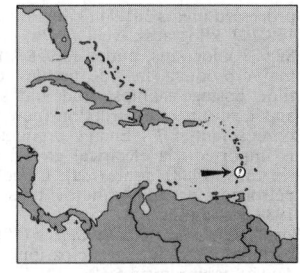

Official name: Saint Vincent and the Grenadines.
Form of government: constitutional monarchy with one legislative house (House of Assembly [21][1]).
Chief of state: British Monarch represented by governor-general.
Head of government: Prime Minister.
Capital: Kingstown.
Official language: English.
Official religion: none.
Monetary unit: 1 Eastern Caribbean Dollar (EC$) = 100 cents; valuation (Oct. 2, 1989) 1 U.S.$ = EC$2.70; 1 £ = EC$4.37.

Area and population

Constituencies[2]	area		population
	sq mi	sq km	1988 estimate[3]
Island of Saint Vincent			
Barrouallie	14.2	36.8	5,370
Bridgetown	7.2	18.6	7,780
Calliaqua	11.8	30.6	20,063
Chateaubelair	30.9	80.0	7,026
Colonarie	13.4	34.7	8,298
Georgetown	22.2	57.5	7,476
Kingstown (city)	1.9	4.9	19,028
Kingstown (suburbs)	6.4	16.6	9,908
Layou	11.1	28.7	6,339
Marriaqua	9.4	24.3	9,671
Sandy Bay	5.3	13.7	3,299
Saint Vincent Grenadines			
Northern Grenadines	9.0	23.3	5,449
Southern Grenadines	7.5	19.4	2,882
TOTAL	150.3	389.3[4]	112,589

Demography

Population (1989): 114,000.
Density (1989): persons per sq mi 758.5, persons per sq km 292.8.
Urban–rural[5] (1988): urban 25.7%; rural 74.3%.
Sex distribution (1988): male 48.44%; female 51.56%.
Age breakdown (1985): under 15, 37.4%; 15–29, 32.7%; 30–44, 14.9%; 45–59, 7.5%; 60–74, 5.6%; 75 and over, 1.9%.
Population projection: (2000) 129,000; (2010) 145,000.
Doubling time: 37 years.
Ethnic composition (1983): black 74.0%; mulatto 19.0%; white 3.0%; Amerindian/black 2.0%; East Indian 2.0%.
Religious affiliation (1980): Protestant 77.3%, of which Anglican 36.0%, Methodist 20.4%, Seventh-day Adventist 4.1%, Plymouth Brethren 3.9%; Roman Catholic 19.3%; other 3.4%.
Major city (1987): Kingstown 18,830.

Vital statistics

Birth rate per 1,000 population (1987): 25.0 (world avg. 27.1); legitimate, n.a.; illegitimate, n.a.
Death rate per 1,000 population (1987): 6.0 (world avg. 9.9).
Natural increase rate per 1,000 population (1987): 19.0 (world avg. 17.2).
Total fertility rate (avg. births per childbearing woman; 1987): 3.0.
Marriage rate per 1,000 population (1987): 3.7.
Divorce rate per 1,000 population (1980): 0.2.
Life expectancy at birth (1987): male 68.0 years; female 74.0 years.
Major causes of death per 100,000 population (1987): diseases of the circulatory system 236.1, of which heart disease 85.8, hypertensive disease 76.0, cerebrovascular disease 66.2; malignant neoplasms (cancers) 50.1; violence 35.8; endocrine and metabolic disorders 32.2.

National economy

Budget (1987). Revenue: EC$113,400,000 (tax revenue 77.7%, of which import duties 40.7%, taxes on income, profits, and capital gains 21.3%; nontax revenue 16.9%; grants 5.2%). Expenditures: EC$108,200,000 (economic services 22.6%; education 18.2%; general public services 17.7%; health 12.8%; police and defense 6.7%).
Public debt (external, outstanding; 1987): U.S.$36,000,000.
Tourism: receipts from visitors (1987) U.S.$35,000,000[6]; expenditures by nationals abroad (1986) U.S.$8,000,000.
Production (metric tons except as noted). Agriculture, forestry, fishing (1987): bananas 63,600[7], coconuts 20,000, eddoes and dasheens[8] 7,500, sweet potatoes 4,600, tanias[8] 2,900, plantains 2,800, ginger 668, arrowroot starch 161, soursops, guavas, and papaws are other important fruits; livestock (number of live animals) 14,000 sheep, 8,000 cattle, 7,000 pigs; roundwood, n.a.; fish catch 129. Mining and quarrying: sand and gravel for local use. Manufacturing (1984): flour 24,100; cigarettes 20,000,000 units; rum 4,960 hectolitres[9]; other products include carbonated drinks, beer, garments, yachts, and electronic components. Construction (gross floor area planned; 1987): 87,400 sq m. Energy production (consumption): electricity (kW-hr; 1987) 43,300,000 (35,000,000); coal, none (none); crude petroleum, none (none); petroleum products (metric tons; 1987) none (14,000); natural gas, none (none).
Gross national product (1987): U.S.$121,000,000 (U.S.$1,070 per capita).

Structure of gross domestic product and labour force

	1987[10]		1980	
	in value EC$'000,000	% of total value	labour force	% of labour force
Agriculture	63.3	20.8	8,928	25.7
Mining	0.9	0.3	108	0.3
Manufacturing	25.2	8.3	1,781	5.1
Construction	31.8	10.5	3,549	10.2
Public utilities	12.7	4.2	402	1.2
Transportation and communications	56.5	18.6	1,882	5.4
Trade	40.0	13.2	2,566	7.4
Finance	32.4	10.7	351	1.0
Pub. admin., defense	47.3	15.6 }	7,579	21.8
Services	7.3	2.4 }		
Other	−13.6[11]	−4.5[11]	7,593[12]	21.9[12]
TOTAL	303.7[4]	100.0[4]	34,739	100.0

Population economically active (1980): total 34,739; activity rate of total population 35.5% (participation rates: over age 15, 60.9%; female 36.1%; unemployed [1988] 30.0%).

Price and earnings indexes (1985 = 100)

	1982	1983	1984	1985	1986	1987	1988
Consumer price index	90.4	95.4	98.0	100.0	101.2	104.1	103.9[13]
Annual earnings index	...	...	92.6	100.0	107.0	...	...

Household income and expenditure. Average household size (1978) 5.0; income per household: n.a.; sources of income: n.a.; expenditure (1981)[14]: food, beverages, and tobacco 62.6%, clothing 7.7%, household furnishings 6.6%, housing 6.3%, energy 6.2%, other 10.6%.
Land use (1986): forested 41.0%; meadows and pastures 6.0%; agricultural and under permanent cultivation 50.0%; other 3.0%.

Foreign trade[15]

Balance of trade (current prices)

	1982	1983	1984	1985	1986	1987
EC$'000,000	−88.8	−79.1	−62.2	−43.1	−63.2	−125.1
% of total	33.8%	26.3%	17.7%	11.2%	15.5%	30.7%

Imports (1987): EC$264,600,000 (basic and miscellaneous manufactures 35.3%, machinery and transport equipment 19.7%, food 19.0%, chemicals and chemical products 13.3%, mineral fuels 6.2%). *Major import sources:* United States 35.5%; United Kingdom 17.8%; Trinidad and Tobago 11.1%; Canada 4.7%; Barbados 3.8%.
Exports (1987): EC$139,500,000 (bananas 38.0%, flour 12.0%, eddoes and dasheens[8] 8.1%, sweet potatoes 4.3%, tanias[8] 3.2%). *Major export destinations:* United Kingdom 39.1%; Trinidad and Tobago 21.8%; United States 15.0%; Saint Lucia 5.5%; Antigua and Barbuda 3.5%.

Transport and communications

Transport. Railroads: none. Roads (1986): total length 463 mi, 745 km (paved 58%). Vehicles (1987): passenger cars 4,946; trucks and buses 2,407. Merchant marine (1988): vessels (100 gross tons and over) 237; total deadweight tonnage 1,420,136. Air transport (1987): passenger arrivals 81,635, passenger departures 82,396; airports (1989) with scheduled flights 4.
Communications. Daily newspapers: none. Radio (1988): total number of receivers 58,190 (1 per 2.0 persons). Television (1988): total number of receivers 10,000 (1 per 11 persons). Telephones (1985): 8,520 (1 per 13 persons).

Education and health

Education (1987–88)

	schools	teachers	students	student/ teacher ratio
Primary (age 5–11)	61	1,261	24,541	19.5
Secondary (age 12–18)	21	371	6,447	17.4
Voc., teacher tr.	...	...	...	...
Higher	...	...	...	...

Educational attainment (1980). Percent of population age 25 and over having: no formal schooling 2.4%; primary education 88.0%; secondary 8.2%; higher 1.4%. *Literacy* (1983): total population age 15 and over literate 54,000 (85.0%).
Health (1987): physicians 39 (1 per 2,874 persons); hospital beds *c.* 350 (1 per 320 persons); infant mortality rate per 1,000 live births (1985–87 avg.) 22.7.
Food (1984–86): daily per capita caloric intake 2,776 (vegetable products 87%, animal products 13%); 115% of FAO recommended minimum requirement.

Military

Total active duty personnel (1987): part of the 489-member police force is trained for defense purposes. *Military expenditure as percent of GNP:* n.a.

[1]Includes six nonelective seats. [2]For statistical purposes and the election of legislative represenatives; no civil administrative subdivisions exist. [3]January 1. [4]Detail does not add to total given because of rounding. [5]Urban defined as Kingstown and suburbs. [6]Number of the tourist arrivals (1987): St. Vincent 50,494, the Grenadines 67,176. [7]1988. [8]Varieties of taro roots. [9]1986. [10]At factor cost. [11]Less imputed service charges. [12]Not adequately defined. [13]Average of second and third quarters. [14]Weights of consumer price index components. [15]Imports c.i.f; exports f.o.b.

San Marino

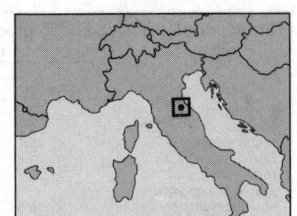

Official name: Serenissima Repubblica
di San Marino (Most Serene Republic
of San Marino).
Form of government: unitary multiparty
republic with one legislative house
(Great and General Council [60]).
Head of state and government:
Captains-Regent (2).
Capital: San Marino.
Official language: Italian.
Official religion: none.
Monetary unit: 1 Italian lira (Lit; plural
lire) = 100 centesimi; valuation (Oct.
2, 1989) 1 U.S.$ = Lit 1,372;
1 £ = Lit 2,220.

Area and population

Castles	Capitals	area sq mi	area sq km	population 1989 estimate[1]
Acquaviva	Acquaviva	1.88	4.86	1,167
Borgo Maggiore	Borgo	3.48	9.01	4,602
Citta	San Marino	2.74	7.09	4,178
Chiesanuova	Chiesanuova	2.11	5.46	729
Domagnano	Domagnano	2.56	6.62	1,914
Faetano	Faetano	2.99	7.75	736
Fiorentino	Fiorentino	2.53	6.56	1,529
Montegiardino	Montegiardino	1.28	3.31	581
Serravalle/Dogano	Serravalle	4.07	10.53	7,107
TOTAL		23.63[2]	61.19	22,543

Demography

Population (1989): 22,860.
Density (1989): persons per sq mi 967.4, persons per sq km 373.6.
Urban–rural (1989): urban 90.1%; rural 9.9%.
Sex distribution (1989): male 49.86%; female 50.14%.
Age breakdown (1989): under 15, 17.0%; 15–29, 25.5%; 30–44, 21.8%; 45–59,
18.4%; 60–74, 12.5%; 75 and over, 4.8%.
Population projection: (2000) 24,200; (2010) 25,500.
Doubling time: not applicable; natural population growth is negligible, av-
eraging only 0.2% during 1984–88.
Ethnic composition (1989[1]): Sammarinesi 85.8%; Italian 13.8%; other 0.4%.
Religious affiliation (1980): Roman Catholic 95.2%; no religion 3.0%; other
1.8%.
Major cities (1989): Serravalle/Dogano 4,638; San Marino 2,371; Borgo
Maggiore 2,135; Murata 1,346; Domagnano 945.

Vital statistics

Birth rate per 1,000 population (1984–88): 9.5 (world avg. 27.1); (1985)
legitimate 95.2%; illegitimate 4.8%.
Death rate per 1,000 population (1984–88): 7.6 (world avg. 9.9).
Natural increase rate per 1,000 population (1984–88): 1.9 (world avg. 17.2).
Total fertility rate (avg. births per childbearing woman; 1984): 1.3.
Marriage rate per 1,000 population (1986): 6.8.
Divorce rate per 1,000 population (1988): 0.9.
Life expectancy at birth (1980–85): male 70.7 years; female 76.2 years.
Major causes of death per 100,000 population (1984–88): diseases of the
circulatory system 318.8; malignant neoplasms (cancers) 262.0; accidents,
violence, and suicide 53.3.

National economy

Budget (1989). Revenue: Lit 259,275,000,000 (mainly receipts from postage
stamp sales, tourism, and customs duties [collected by Italy and paid
as a subsidy]). Expenditures: Lit 259,275,000,000 ([3]finance and economic
planning 31.0%, internal affairs 11.3%, health and social security 9.0%,
education and culture 7.1%, public works 6.3%).
Public debt: n.a.
Tourism: number of tourist arrivals (1988) 2,917,061; receipts from visitors
(1983) U.S.$56,454,000; expenditures by nationals abroad, n.a.
Gross national product (at current market prices; 1987): U.S.$188,000,000
(U.S.$8,590 per capita).

Structure of labour force (1989[1])

	labour force	% of labour force
Agriculture	335	2.8
Manufacturing	4,257	35.1
Construction and public utilities	891	7.4
Transportation and communications	165	1.4
Trade	1,823	15.0
Finance and insurance	239	2.0
Services	741	6.1
Public administration and defense	1,957	16.1
Other	1,715[4]	14.1[4]
TOTAL	12,123	100.0

Production (metric tons except as noted). Agriculture, forestry, fishing[3]:
wheat *c.* 4,400, grapes *c.* 700, barley *c.* 500; livestock (number of live
animals; 1988) 1,441 cattle, 1,326 pigs, 610 sheep. Manufacturing (1988):

processed meats 581,945 kilograms, of which beef 346,125 kilograms, swine
158,242 kilograms, veal 69,765 kilograms; milk 1,292,171 litres; cheese
82,683 kilograms; butter 14,958 kilograms; yogurt 11,198 kilograms; other
major products include textiles, cement, paper, leather, bricks, pottery,
tiles, postage stamps, gold and silver jewelry, paints, synthetic rubber,
and furniture. Construction (new units completed; 1988): residential 134;
nonresidential 77. Energy production (consumption): all electrical power
is imported via electrical grid from Italy, consumption n.a.; coal (metric tons; 1988) none (n.a); crude petroleum (barrels; 1987) none (n.a.);
petroleum products (metric tons; 1988) none (n.a.); natural gas (cu m;
1988) none (n.a.).
Population economically active (1989[1]): total 12,123; activity rate of total
population 53.3% (participation rates: ages 15–64 [1986] 71.2%; female
41.4%; unemployed 5.5%).

Price and earnings indexes (1980 = 100)

	1982	1983	1984	1985	1986	1987	1988
Consumer price index	76.5	84.2	89.1	100.0	107.9	114.6	120.7
Monthly earnings index	...	...	...	...	...	...	...

Household income and expenditure. Total number of households (1989[1]):
7,916; average household size (1989[1]) 2.8; income per household: n.a.;
sources of income: n.a.; expenditure[5] (1985): food, beverages, and tobacco
30.4%; transportation and communications 14.5%; housing, fuel, and electrical energy 9.7%; clothing and footwear 8.8%; recreation, entertainment,
education, and culture 8.1%; furniture, appliances, and goods and services
for the home 7.5%; health and sanitary services 5.1%; other goods and
services 15.9%.
Land use (1985): agricultural and under permanent cultivation 74%; meadows and pastures 22%; forested, built-on, wasteland, and other 4%.

Foreign trade

Balance of trade: n.a. San Marino and Italy form a single customs area;
separate figures for San Marino are not available.
Imports (1988): manufactured goods of all kinds, oil, and gold. *Major import source:* Italy.
Exports (1988): wine, wheat, woolen goods, furniture, wood, ceramics,
building stone, dairy products, meat, and postage stamps. *Major export
destination:* Italy.

Transport and communications

Transport. Railroads: none (nearest rail terminal is at Rimini, Italy, 17 mi
[27 km] northeast). Roads (1987): total length 147 mi, 237 km. Vehicles
(1989[1]): passenger cars 18,304; trucks and buses 1,851. Merchant marine:
vessels (100 gross tons and over) none. Air transport: airports with scheduled flights, none; however, there is a heliport that provides passenger
and cargo service between San Marino and Rimini, Italy, during the
summer months.
Communications. Daily newspapers (1989): none; however, there are several
journals of lesser frequency; total circulation of the oldest of these, *Il Nuovo
Titano,* 1,300; circulation per 1,000 population 57.1. Radio (1988): total
number of receivers 12,535 (1 per 1.8 persons). Television (1987): total
number of receivers 6,608 (1 per 3.4 persons). Telephones (1987): 14,200 (1
per 1.6 persons).

Education and health

Education (1986–87)

	schools	teachers	students	student/ teacher ratio
Primary (age 6–10)	13	171	1,363	8.0
Secondary (age 11–18)	5	179	1,222	6.8
Vocational	...	...	697[6]	...
Teacher tr.	...	...	47[6]	...
Higher	...	...	332[6]	...

Educational attainment (1989[1]). Percent of the adult labour force having:
basic literacy or primary education 32.4%; secondary 34.3%; some postsecondary 27.5%; higher degree 5.8%. *Literacy* (1986): total population age
15 and over literate 18,135 (98.0%); males literate 8,957 (98.2%); females
literate 9,178 (97.7%).
Health (1987): physicians 60 (1 per 375 persons); hospital beds 149 (1 per
151 persons); infant mortality rate per 1,000 live births (1984–88) 13.0.
Food (1984–86): daily per capita caloric intake 3,494 (vegetable products
73%, animal products 27%); (1984) 139% of FAO recommended minimum requirement.

Military

Total active duty personnel (1987): none[7]. *Military expenditure as a percent of national budget* (1987): 0.9% (world 5.4%); per capita expenditure
(1987) U.S.$82.

---

[1]January 1. [2]Detail does not add to total given because of rounding. [3]Early 1980s.
[4]Includes 661 unemployed persons. [5]Weighting coefficients for component expenditures are those of the 1985 official Italian consumer price index. [6]In Italy. [7]Defense is
provided by a public security force of about 50; all fit males 16–55 constitute a militia.

São Tomé and Príncipe

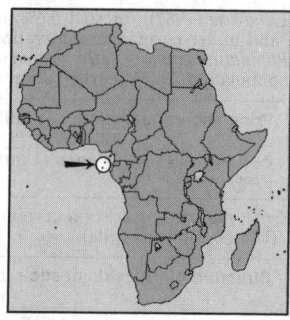

Official name: República democrática de São Tomé e Príncipe (Democratic Republic of São Tomé and Príncipe).
Form of government: single-party republic with one legislative house (National People's Assembly [51]).
Head of state and government: President assisted by Prime Minister[1].
Capital: São Tomé.
Official language: Portuguese.
Official religion: Roman Catholicism.
Monetary unit: 1 dobra (Db) = 100 cêntimos; valuation (Oct. 2, 1989) 1 U.S.$ = Db 106.35; 1 £ = Db 172.07.

Area and population

		area		population
Islands Districts	Capitals	sq mi	sq km	1984 estimate
Príncipe	São António	55	142	5,671
Paguê	Príncipe	55	142	5,671
São Tomé		332	859	98,693
Aqua Grande	São Tomé	7	17	34,997
Cantagalo	Santana	46	119	11,270
Caué	São João Angolares	103	267	4,972
Lemba	Neves	88	229	8,537
Lobata	Guadalupe	41	105	12,717
Mé-zóchi	Trinidade	47	122	26,200
TOTAL		386	1,001	104,364

Demography

Population (1989): 118,000.
Density (1989): persons per sq mi 305.7, persons per sq km 117.9.
Urban–rural (1985): urban 37.6%; rural 62.4%.
Sex distribution (1981): male 49.72%; female 50.28%.
Age breakdown (1981): under 15, 46.3%; 15–29, 25.0%; 30–44, 11.6%; 45–59, 10.0%; 60–74, 5.3%; 75 and over, 1.8%.
Population projection: (2000) 157,000; (2010) 203,000.
Doubling time: 23 years.
Ethnic composition: mestiços, angolares (descendants of Angolan slaves), forros (descendants of freed slaves), serviçais (alien contract labourers), tongas (children of serviçais), and Europeans.
Religious affiliation (1986): Roman Catholic, about 84%; remainder mostly Protestant, predominantly Seventh-day Adventist and an indigenous Evangelical Church.
Major city (1984): São Tomé 34,997.

Vital statistics

Birth rate per 1,000 population (1989): 38.0 (world avg. 27.1); (1977) legitimate 9.8%; illegitimate 90.2%.
Death rate per 1,000 population (1989): 7.0 (world avg. 9.9).
Natural increase rate per 1,000 population (1989): 31.0 (world avg. 17.2).
Total fertility rate (avg. births per childbearing woman; 1987): 5.3.
Marriage rate per 1,000 population: n.a.
Divorce rate per 1,000 population: n.a.
Life expectancy at birth (1987): male 63.0 years; female 67.0 years.
Major causes of death per 100,000 population (1984–85) infectious and parasitic diseases 318.5; diseases of the respiratory system 138.0; diseases of the circulatory system 95.4; diseases of the digestive system 52.0; accidents, poisonings, and violence 48.1; malignant neoplasms (cancers) 36.1; diseases of the nervous system 18.5; endocrine and metabolic disorders 5.6.

National economy

Budget (1987). Revenue: Db 673,100,000 (indirect taxes 36.3%, direct taxes 18.4%, other sources 45.3%). Expenditures: Db 1,832,200,000 (current expenditure 53.4%, of which wages and salaries 24.7%; capital expenditure 45.3%; net lending 1.3%).
Tourism (1986): receipts from visitors U.S.$1,000,000; expenditures by nationals abroad U.S.$1,000,000.
Public debt (external, outstanding; 1987): U.S.$83,900,000.
Production (metric tons except as noted). Agriculture, forestry, fishing (1988): coconuts 37,000, cacao 5,000, copra 4,000, fruit other than melons 4,000, cassava 4,000, bananas 3,000, palmetto 3,000, vegetables and melons 3,000, cereals 1,000; taro 742[2], palm kernel 500; livestock (number of live animals) 4,000 goats, 3,000 cattle, 3,000 pigs, 2,000 sheep; roundwood (1987) 6,000 cu m; fish catch (1987) 2,982, principally marine fish and shellfish. Mining and quarrying: some quarrying to support local construction industry. Manufacturing (1987): bread 2,459; soap 604; coconut oil 330; palm oil 177; ice 191[3]; limes 22[3]; corn (maize) flour 18[3]; sawn wood 3,272 cu m; beer 28,540 hectolitres; bottled water 13,750 hectolitres; soft drinks 10,460 hectolitres; other products include clothing, bricks, and clay products. Construction: (1972) buildings authorized 44 (5,561 sq m, of which residential 3,698, mixed residential–commercial 1,361, commercial 502). Energy production (consumption): electricity (kW-hr; 1987) 15,000,000 (15,000,000); coal, none (n.a.); crude petroleum, none (n.a.); petroleum products (metric tons; 1987) none (11,000); natural gas, none (n.a.).
Household income and expenditure: average household size: n.a.; income per household: n.a.; sources of income: n.a.; expenditure: n.a.
Gross national product (at current market prices; 1987): U.S.$32,000,000 (U.S.$280 per capita).

Structure of gross domestic product and labour force

	1986		1987	
	in value Db '000,000	% of total value	labour force	% of labour force
Agriculture	451	26.8	8,448	40.4
Mining	4	0.2		
Manufacturing	159	9.5	1,129[4]	5.4[4]
Public utilities	44	2.6		
Construction	149	8.9	742	3.5
Transportation and communications	196	11.7	455	2.2
Trade	168	10.0	4	4
Finance	21	1.2	4	4
Pub. admin., defense	489	29.1	3,708	17.7
Services	—	0.0		
Other	...	...	6,430[5]	30.7[5]
TOTAL	1,681	100.0	20,912	100.0[6]

Population economically active (1987): total 20,912; activity rate of total population 18.5% (participation rates [1981]: ages 15–64, 61.1%; female 32.4%; unemployed 30.7%[2]).

Earnings indexes (1981 = 100)

	1981	1982	1983	1984	1985	1986
Agricultural sector	100.0	93.6	98.5	103.0	97.2	96.3
Nonagricultural sectors	100.0	101.4	100.7	107.7	107.7	123.8

Land use (1987): meadows and pastures 1.0%; agricultural and under permanent cultivation 38.5%; forest, built-on, wasteland, and other 60.5%.

Foreign trade[7]

Balance of trade (current prices)

	1983	1984	1985	1986	1987	1988
Db '000,000	−543.6	−732.1	−765.2	−252.6	−268.4	−127.4
% of total	42.6%	40.4%	54.8%	26.9%	25.8%	8.3%

Imports (1988): Db 831,400,000 (1987; machinery and electrical equipment 59.0%, food and other agricultural products 32.0%, mineral fuels and lubricants 9.0%). *Major import sources* (1987): Portugal 33.7%; East Germany 12.1%; Spain 11.3%; Angola 8.8%; West Germany 8.4%; France 6.5%; The Netherlands 5.4%; Norway 4.2%; Belgium–Luxembourg 3.5%.
Exports (1988): Db 704,000,000 (1984; cacao 80.0%, copra 15.0%, coffee 1.0%, palm kernels 0.4%). *Major export destinations:* West Germany 52.3%; East Germany 20.2%; The Netherlands, 12.7%.

Transport and communications

Transport. Railroads: none. Roads (1988): total length 236 mi, 380 km (paved 66%). Vehicles (1975): passenger cars 1,774; trucks and buses 265. Merchant marine (1988): vessels (100 gross tons and over) 3; total deadweight tonnage 1,172. Air transport (1985): passenger-mi 3,800,000, passenger-km 6,100,000; short ton-mi cargo 70,000, short ton-km cargo 100,000; airports (1989) with scheduled flights 1.
Communications. Daily newspapers: none; 3 government weeklies (circulation, n.a.). Radio (1988): total number of receivers 30,343 (1 per 3.9 persons). Television: none. Telephones (1987): 2,616 (1 per 44 persons).

Education and health

Education (1984–85)

	schools	teachers	students	student/ teacher ratio
Primary (age 6–13)	63	517	16,013	31.0
Secondary (age 14–18)	11	300	6,186	20.6
Voc., teacher tr.	2	35	370	10.6
Higher	...	...	700[8]	...

Educational attainment (1981). Percent of population age 25 and over having: no formal schooling 56.6%; incomplete primary education 18.0%; primary 19.2%; incomplete secondary 4.6%; complete secondary 1.3%; postsecondary 0.3%. *Literacy* (1981): total population age 15 and over literate 28,114 (54.2%); males literate 17,689 (70.2%); females literate 10,425 (39.1%).
Health (1987): physicians 40 (1 per 2,819 persons); hospital beds (1983) 640 (1 per 158 persons); infant mortality rate per 1,000 live births 70.
Food (1984–86): daily per capita caloric intake 2,385 (vegetable products 93%, animal products 7%); 100% of FAO recommended minimum requirement.

Military

Total active duty personnel (1988): 1,000, of which 300 are Angolan troops (distribution by branch of service, n.a.). *Military expenditure as percent of GNP* (1980): 1.6% (world 5.4%); per capita expenditure U.S.$6.

[1]Position of prime minister reintroduced January 1988, but not as effective head of government. [2]1987. [3]1983. [4]Includes Trade and Finance. [5]Unemployed. [6]Detail does not add to total given because of rounding. [7]Import figures are c.i.f. [8]Students abroad, 1982–83.

Saudi Arabia

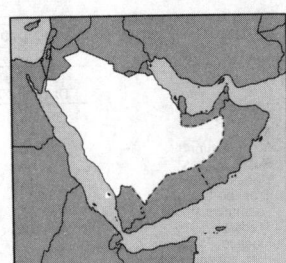

Official name: al-Mamlakah
al-ʿArabīyah as-Saʿūdīyah (Kingdom of
Saudi Arabia).
Form of government: monarchy.
Head of state and government: King.
Capital: Riyadh.
Official language: Arabic.
Official religion: Islam.
Monetary unit: 1 Saudi riyal
(SRls) = 100 halalah; valuation (Oct.
2, 1989) 1 U.S.$ = SRls 3.75;
1 £ = SRls 6.07.

Area and population

Regions		area		population
				1985
Administrative Districts	**Capitals**	sq mi	sq km	estimate
al-Gharbīyah (Western)	—	...	...	3,043,189
al-Bāḥah	al-Bāḥah	...	...	...
al-Madīnah	Medina (al-Madīnah)	...	...	...
Makkah	Mecca (Makkah)	...	...	...
al-Janūbīyah (Southern)	—	...	...	625,017
ʿAsīr	Abha	...	...	...
Jīzān	Jīzān	...	...	...
Najrān	Najrān	...	...	...
ash-Shamālīyah (Northern)	—	...	...	679,476
al-Ḥudūd ash-Shamālīyah (Northern Borders)	ʿArʿar	...	...	...
al-Jawf	Sakākah	...	...	...
al-Qurayyāt	an-Nabk	...	...	...
Tabūk	Tabūk	...	...	3,030,765
ash-Sharqīyah (Eastern)	—	...	...	...
ash-Sharqīyah (Eastern)	ad-Dammām	...	...	3,632,092
al-Wūsṭā (Central)	—	...	...	...
Ḥāʾil	Ḥāʾil	...	...	...
al-Qaṣim	Buraydah	...	...	...
ar-Riyāḍ	Riyadh (ar-Riyāḍ)	...	...	...
TOTAL		865,000	2,240,000	11,010,539

Demography

Population (1989): 13,592,000.
Density (1989): persons per sq mi 15.7, persons per sq km 6.1.
Urban–rural (1986): urban 73.3%; rural 26.7%.
Sex distribution (1986): male 59.71%; female 40.29%.
Age breakdown (1986): under 15, 40.0%; 15–29, 26.2%; 30–44, 19.9%; 45–59, 8.6%; 60–74, 3.9%; 75 and over, 1.4%.
Population projection: (2000) 20,686,000; (2010) 29,551,000.
Doubling time: 21 years.
Ethnic composition (1983): Saudi 82.0%; Yemeni 9.6%; other Arab 3.4%; other 5.0%.
Religious affiliation (1980): Muslim (mostly Sunnī) 98.8%; Christian 0.8%; other 0.4%.
Major cities (1980): Riyadh 1,308,000[1]; Jidda (Jiddah) 1,500,000[2]; Mecca 550,000; aṭ-Ṭāʾif 300,000.

Vital statistics

Birth rate per 1,000 population (1986): 37.3 (world avg. 27.1).
Death rate per 1,000 population (1986): 12.8 (world avg. 9.9).
Natural increase rate per 1,000 population (1986): 24.5 (world avg. 17.2).
Total fertility rate (avg. births per childbearing woman; 1987): 7.1.
Marriage rate per 1,000 population: n.a.
Divorce rate per 1,000 population: n.a.
Life expectancy at birth (1986): male 54.8 years; female 57.7 years.
Major causes of death per 100,000 population: n.a.; however, major diseases include cholera, cerebrospinal meningitis, yellow fever, typhoid, tuberculosis, lung infections, and asphyxia.

National economy

Budget (1988–89). Revenue: SRls 105,300,000,000 (oil revenues 69.8%). Expenditures: SRls 141,200,000,000 (defense and security 35.5%, public administration and other government spending 17.7%, human resources development 16.6%, health and social development 7.6%, transport and communications 6.7%).
Public debt: none.
Production (metric tons except as noted). Agriculture, forestry, fishing (1986–87): wheat 2,653,000, dates 484,225, tomatoes 346,000, watermelons 323,000, barley 162,000, grapes 100,000, onions 78,000, pumpkins, squash, and gourds 55,816, sorghum and millet 48,000, eggplants 21,432, potatoes 16,045, cucumbers and gherkins 15,000, pulses 7,000; livestock (number of live animals; 1988) 7,466,000 sheep, 3,600,000 goats, 417,000 camels, 325,000 cattle, 110,000 asses, 69,000,000 poultry; fish catch 45,500. Mining and quarrying (1986): gypsum 300,000; lime 12,000. Manufacturing (1985): cement 10,633,500; methanol 1,287,000; steel rods and bars 948,000; ethylene 927,900; urea 825,000; ethylene glycol 310,000; industrial ethanol 200,000; ethylene dichloride 190,000; styrene 125,000; caustic soda 125,000; nitrogen 82,000; citric acid 75,000; oxygen 55,000; melamine 14,000. Construction (value added in SRls; 1987): 33,003,000,000. Energy production (consumption): electricity (kW-hr; 1987) 37,100,000,000 (37,100,000,000); coal, n.a. (n.a.); crude petroleum (barrels; 1987) 1,440,060,000 (444,139,000); petroleum products (metric tons; 1987) 62,124,000 (33,451,000); natural gas (cu m; 1987) 23,239,000,000 (23,239,000,000).
Tourism (1987): receipts from visitors U.S.$2,600,000,000; expenditures by nationals abroad U.S.$2,000,000,000.

Land use (1987): forested 0.6%; meadows and pastures 39.5%; agricultural and under permanent cultivation 0.5%; other, built-on, and waste 59.4%.
Population economically active (1986): total 3,032,000; activity rate of total population 29.8% (participation rates: ages 15–64, 51.5%; female 3.2%).

Price and earnings indexes (1985 = 100)

	1983	1984	1985	1986	1987	1988	1989[3]
Consumer price index	104.6	103.4	100.0	97.0	96.1	97.1	98.6
Monthly earnings index	...	...	...	...	...	...	...

Gross national product (at current market prices; 1986): U.S.$83,270,000,000 (U.S.$6,930 per capita).

Structure of gross domestic product and labour force

	1987		1986	
	in value SRls '000,000	% of total value	labour force	% of labour force
Agriculture	18,312	6.6	432,082	14.3
Mining	1,723	0.6 }	48,514	1.6
Oil sector	63,393	23.0 }		
Manufacturing	22,790	8.3	301,699	9.9
Construction	35,600	12.9	567,619	18.7
Public utilities	681	0.2	101,577	3.3
Transp. and commun.	22,087	8.0	210,128	6.9
Trade	27,797	10.1	374,168	12.3
Finance	20,572	7.5	94,300	3.1
Pub. admin., defense	26,792	9.7 }	902,066	29.8
Services and other	36,426	13.2 }		
Other	−679[4]	−0.24	—	—
TOTAL	275,494	100.0[5]	3,032,153	100.0[5]

Pilgrims to Mecca from abroad (1988): 762,755.
Household income and expenditure. Average household size (1986) 6.6; income per household: n.a.; sources of income: n.a.; expenditure[6] (1980): food 52.2%, housing 17.2%, clothing 6.6%, furniture and utensils 5.9%, transport and communications 4.5%, health care 2.1%.

Foreign trade

Balance of trade (current prices)

	1982	1983	1984	1985	1986	1987
SRls '000,000	+152.0	+42.7	+30.1	+20.2	+8.2	+11.6
% of total	25.6%	15.6%	12.8%	11.3%	5.9%	7.1%

Imports (1987): SRls 75,312,600,000 (machinery and appliances 19.1%, foodstuffs and tobacco 16.5%, transport equipment 13.5%, textiles and clothing 13.2%, metals and metal articles 8.4%, chemicals 4.2%, scientific instruments 4.1%). *Major import sources:* Japan 17.3%; U.S. 15.3%; U.K. 7.8%; W.Ger. 7.7%; Italy 6.8%; France 5.3%; South Korea 4.9%; Taiwan 3.9%; Switzerland 2.4%; The Netherlands 2.2%; Belgium 1.7%; Spain 1.5%.
Exports (1987): SRls 86,879,000,000 (crude petroleum 94.3%, other 5.7%). *Major export destinations:* Japan 22.1%; U.S. 19.3%; The Netherlands 6.1%; Bahrain 4.9%; Singapore 4.9%; Taiwan 4.2%; Italy 4.0%; Brazil 3.5%; South Korea 3.1%; France 2.6%; Spain 2.4%; U.K. 1.5%; W.Ger. 1.3%.

Transport and communications

Transport. Railroads (1988): route length 544 mi, 875 km; passenger-mi 57,-352,000, passenger-km 92,300,000; short ton-mi cargo 321,960,000, metric ton-km cargo 470,080,000. Roads (1988): total length 57,664 mi, 92,802 km (paved 36%). Vehicles (1987): passenger cars 2,245,042; trucks and buses 2,023,365. Merchant marine (1988): vessels (100 gross tons and over) 320; total deadweight tonnage 3,802,471. Air transport (1988): passenger-mi 9,280,000,000, passenger-km 14,935,000,000; short ton-mi cargo 335,533,-000, metric ton-km cargo 489,900,000; airports (1989) 23.
Communications. Daily newspapers (1987): total number 11; total circulation 587,300; circulation per 1,000 population 47. Radio (1988): 3,997,459 receivers (1 per 3.3 persons). Television (1988): 3,750,000 receivers (1 per 3.5 persons). Telephones (1988): 1,013,963 (1 per 13 persons).

Education and health

Education (1987–88)

	schools	teachers	students	student/teacher ratio
Primary (age 6–12)	7,682	88,314	1,484,663	16.8
Secondary (age 13–18)	3,031	43,358	620,238	14.3
Voc., teacher tr.	32	3,295	31,354	9.5
Higher	78	9,950	114,516	11.5

Educational attainment (1986). Percent of population age 25 and over having: no formal schooling 31.8%; primary, secondary, or higher education 68.2%. *Literacy* (1986): total population age 12 and over literate 3,862,439 (57.2%); males literate 3,006,249 (69.7%); females literate 856,190 (35.1%).
Health (1987): physicians 12,907 (1 per 973 persons); hospital beds 30,921 (1 per 406 persons); infant mortality rate per 1,000 live births 108.6.
Food (1984–86): daily per capita caloric intake 3,031 (vegetable products 80%, animal products 20%); 129% of FAO recommended minimum.

Military

Total active duty personnel (1989): 65,700 (army 57.8%, navy 11.0%, air force 25.1%, air defense forces 6.1%). *Military expenditure as percent of GNP* (1987): 12.8% (world 5.4%); per capita expenditure U.S.$710.

[1]1981 estimate. [2]1983 estimate. [3]January. [4]Import duties less imputed bank service charges. [5]Detail does not add to total given because of rounding. [6]Urban middle-income households only.

Senegal

Official name: République du Sénégal (Republic of Senegal).
Form of government: multiparty republic with one legislative house (National Assembly [120]).
Head of state and government: President.
Capital: Dakar.
Official language: French.
Official religion: none.
Monetary unit: 1 CFA franc (CFAF) = 100 centimes; valuation (Oct. 2, 1989) 1 U.S.$ = CFAF 317.90; 1 £ = CFAF 514.37.

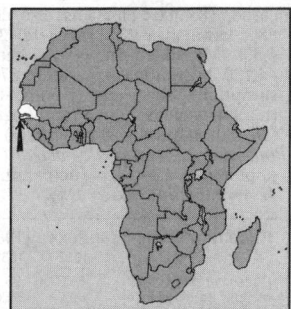

Area and population		area		population
Regions	Capitals	sq mi	sq km	1988 estimate
Dakar	Dakar	212	550	1,608,700
Diourbel	Diourbel	1,683	4,359	558,700
Fatick	Fatick	3,064	7,935	577,600
Kaolack	Kaolack	6,181	16,010	842,100
Kolda	Kolda	8,112	21,011	601,300
Louga	Louga	11,270	29,188	541,900
Saint-Louis	Saint-Louis	17,038	44,127	686,100
Tambacounda	Tambacounda	23,012	59,602	421,800
Thiès	Thiès	2,549	6,601	949,300
Ziguinchor	Ziguinchor	2,834	7,339	399,700
TOTAL		75,955	196,722	7,187,200

Demography

Population (1989): 7,400,000.
Density (1989): persons per sq mi 97.4 persons per sq km 37.6.
Urban–rural (1986): urban 40.0%; rural 60.0%.
Sex distribution (1986): male 49.61%; female 50.39%.
Age breakdown (1986): under 15, 46.5%; 15–29, 25.6%; 30–44, 14.9%; 45–59, 8.4%; 60 and over, 4.6%.
Population projection: (2000) 10,193,000; (2010) 13,639,000.
Doubling time: 26 years.
Ethnic composition (1983): Wolof 36.2%; Fulani (Peul) 17.8%; Serer 17.0%; Tukulor 9.7%; Diola (Jola) 8.1%; Mandingo 6.5%; Soninke 2.1%; Arabs 1.0%; other 1.6%.
Religious affiliation (1980): Sunnī Muslim 91.0%; Roman Catholic 5.6%; traditional beliefs 3.2%; other 0.2%.
Major cities (1985): Dakar 1,382,000; Thiès 156,200; Kaolack 132,400; Ziguinchor 106,500; Saint-Louis 91,500.

Vital statistics

Birth rate per 1,000 population (1985–90): 45.7 (world avg. 27.1).
Death rate per 1,000 population (1985–90): 18.9 (world avg. 9.9).
Natural increase rate per 1,000 population (1985–90): 26.8 (world avg. 17.2).
Total fertility rate (avg. births per childbearing woman; 1985–90): 6.4.
Marriage rate per 1,000 population: n.a.
Divorce rate per 1,000 population: n.a.
Life expectancy at birth (1985–90): male 44.2 years; female 47.4 years.
Major causes of death per 100,000 population (officially confirmed transmissible diseases only; 1983): malaria 5.9; meningitis 5.5; tetanus 3.7; tuberculosis of respiratory system 1.9; measles 1.7.

National economy

Budget (1989). Revenue: CFAF 350,095,000,000 (current revenue 67.9%, of which import duties 26.1%, value-added taxes 15.4%, personal income taxes 14.8%, excise taxes 1.9%, personal property taxes 1.9%; new debt 32.1%, of which foreign 27.4%, domestic 4.7%). Expenditures: CFAF 350,095,000,000 (recurrent expenditures 64.8%, of which education 14.7%, defense 8.6%, health 3.1%, social security and welfare 0.8%; capital expenditures 35.2%).
Public debt (external, outstanding; 1987): U.S.$3,068,000,000.
Production (metric tons except as noted). Agriculture, forestry, fishing (1988–89): sugarcane 700,000, peanuts (groundnuts) 604,504, millet and sorghum 594,200, paddy rice 134,100, beans 130,000[1], corn (maize) 123,300, cotton seed 38,000, cotton 36,000[1]; livestock (number of live animals; 1988) 3,792,000 sheep, 2,608,000 cattle, 1,150,000 goats, 470,000 pigs; roundwood (1987) 4,196,000 cu m; fish catch (1987) 299,000. Mining and quarrying (1988): calcium phosphate 2,326,600; cement 389,000; aluminum phosphate 119,300. Manufacturing (1986): peanut oil 300,000; wheat flour 86,400; nitrogenous fertilizers 62,400; sugar 50,700; soap 29,700; canned fish 26,705; cotton fibres 16,100; carbonated beverages 261,200 hectolitres; beer 197,100 hectolitres; footwear 2,659,900 pairs. Construction (authorized; 1985): residential 228,000 sq m; nonresidential 37,000 sq m. Energy production (consumption): electricity (kW-hr; 1987) 752,000,000 (752,000,000); coal, none (n.a.); crude petroleum (barrels; 1987) none (3,872,000); petroleum products (metric tons; 1987) 488,000 (654,000); natural gas, none (n.a.).
Population economically active (1985): total 3,095,000; activity rate of total population 47.1% (participation rates: ages 15–64, 78.1%; female 41.8%; unemployed [1984] 12.8%[2]).

Price and earnings indexes (1985 = 100)							
	1982	1983	1984	1985	1986	1987	1988
Consumer price index	70.9	79.7	88.5	100.0	106.4	101.8	99.9
Hourly earnings index[3]	76.5	82.7	95.3	100.0	100.0	100.0	100.0

Household income and expenditure[4]. Average household size (1980) 4.8; average annual income per household (1975) CFAF 1,105,800 (U.S.$5,160); sources of income: wages and salaries 51.6%, remittances and gifts 17.5%, pensions, social security, and related benefits 12.5%, other 18.4%; expenditure (1979): food and tobacco 57.5%, housing, maintenance, and utilities 18.4%, clothing 11.9%, transport 5.4%, other 6.8%.
Gross national product (1987): U.S.$3,545,000,000 (U.S.$510 per capita).

Structure of gross domestic product and labour force				
	1986		1982	
	in value CFAF '000,000,000	% of total value	labour force[5]	% of labour force
Agriculture	232.6	21.5	10,654	9.1
Mining	14.9	1.4	1,918	1.6
Manufacturing	205.9	19.0	30,736	26.4
Public utilities	21.9	2.0	3,221	2.8
Construction	77.2	7.1	8,402	7.2
Transp. and commun.	96.5	8.9	24,789	21.2
Trade	156.9	14.5	14,648	12.6
Finance	42.6	4.0	7,921	6.8
Services	69.0	6.4	14,339	12.3
Pub. admin., defense	164.1	15.2		
Other	...	...	...	...
TOTAL	1,081.6	100.0	116,628	100.0

Tourism (1987): receipts from visitors U.S.$123,000,000; expenditures by nationals abroad U.S.$42,000,000.
Land use (1987): forested 30.8%; meadows and pastures 29.6%; agricultural and under permanent cultivation 27.2%; other 12.4%.

Foreign trade

Balance of trade (current prices)						
	1982	1983	1984	1985	1986	1987
CFAF '000,000,000	−145.9	−174.4	−203.1	−100.1	−93.0	−130.3
% of total	28.8%	27.5%	30.3%	21.4%	18.7%	28.8%

Imports (1986): CFAF 295,179,000,000 (crude petroleum and petroleum products 18.1%, agricultural and industrial equipment 16.3%, pharmaceutical and chemical products 4.9%, cereals 4.4%, edible oils 3.3%, milk products 2.9%). Major import sources: France 34.2%; Nigeria 9.5%; Italy 6.4%; West Germany 6.2%; United States 4.9%; Côte d'Ivoire 4.9%; The Netherlands 4.2%; Spain 3.9%; Japan 3.4%.
Exports (1986): CFAF 202,166,000,000 (petroleum products 16.8%, crustaceans, mollusks, and shellfish 10.5%, fresh fish 8.9%, phosphates 8.9%, canned fish 7.4%, cotton and cotton fabrics 5.0%, peanut oil cake 2.3%, fresh vegetables 1.4%, fertilizers 0.7%). Major export destinations: France 30.8%; The Netherlands 4.5%; Côte d'Ivoire 4.2%; Mauritania 3.7%; Japan 3.1%; Mali 2.9%; Italy 2.9%; United Kingdom 2.7%; Spain 2.5%.

Transport and communications

Transport. Railroads (1984–85): route length (1987–88) 572 mi, 905 km; passenger-mi 18,929,836[6], passenger-km 30,482,827[6]; short ton-mi cargo 316,000,000, metric ton-km cargo 462,000,000. Roads (1987): total length 9,315 mi, 15,000 km (paved 30%). Vehicles (1985): passenger cars 76,142; trucks and buses 37,105. Merchant marine (1988): vessels (100 gross tons and over) 155; total deadweight tonnage 37,561. Air transport[7] (1988): passenger-mi 129,597,000, passenger-km 208,567,000; short ton-mi cargo 24,126,000, metric ton-km cargo 35,223,000; airports (1989) with scheduled flights 10.
Communications. Daily newspapers (1984): total number 1; total circulation 31,000; circulation per 1,000 population 4.9. Radio (1987): total number of receivers 824,210 (1 per 8.7 persons). Television (1988): total number of receivers 234,408 (1 per 31 persons). Telephones (1985): 33,633 (1 per 192 persons).

Education and health

Education (1985–86)	schools	teachers	students	student/ teacher ratio
Primary (age 6–11)	2,171	11,513	583,507	41.2
Secondary (age 12–18)	162	2,346[8]	113,653	...
Voc., teacher tr.	5	...	3,515	...
Higher	7	497[8]	13,450	...

Educational attainment (1970). Percent of population age 6 and over having: no formal schooling 95.3%; primary education 3.9%; secondary 0.7%; higher 0.1%. *Literacy* (1980): total population age 15 and over literate 1,274,000 (22.5%); males literate 1,755,000 (31.0%); females literate 804,000 (14.2%).
Health[9]: physicians (1984) 311 (1 per 20,569 persons); hospital beds (1982) 6,200 (1 per 973 persons); infant mortality rate per 1,000 live births (1986) 110.0.
Food (1987): daily per capita caloric intake 2,577 ([1984–86] vegetable products 93%, animal products 7%); (1984–86) 103% of FAO recommended minimum requirement.

Military

Total active duty personnel (1988)[10]: 9,700 (army 87.6%, navy 7.2%, air force 5.2%). *Military expenditure as percent of GNP* (1987): 2.2% (world 5.4%); per capita expenditure U.S.$14.

[1]1987–88. [2]Dakar only. [3]January 1; index refers to the *S.M.I.G.* (*salaire minimum interprofessionnel guaranti*), a form of minimum professional wage. [4]Traditional African households in Dakar. [5]Wage earners, excluding armed forces only. [6]Excludes international travelers. [7]International flights only. [8]1983–84. [9]Public sector only. [10]Confederal armed forces of Senegal and The Gambia.

Seychelles

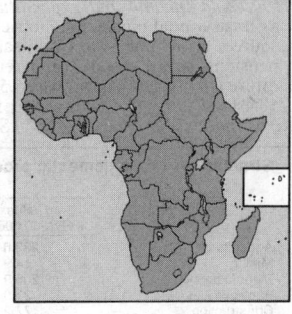

Official name: Repiblik Sesel (Creole);
Republic of Seychelles (English);
République des Seychelles (French).
Form of government: unitary
single-party republic with one
legislative house (People's Assembly
[25[1]]).
Head of state and government:
President.
Capital: Victoria.
Official languages[2]: Creole; English;
French.
Official religion: none.
Monetary unit: 1 Seychelles rupee
(SR) = 100 cents; valuation (Oct. 2,
1989) 1 U.S.$ = SR 5.75;
1 £ = SR 9.30.

Area and population		area		population
				1984
Island Groups	Capital	sq mi	sq km	estimate
Central (Granitic) group				
La Digue and satellites	—	6	15	2,000
Mahé and satellites	Victoria	61	158	57,400
Praslin and satellites	—	16	42	4,650
Silhouette	—	8	20	200
Other islands	—	2	4	50
Outer (Coralline) islands	—	83	214	400
TOTAL		175[3]	453	64,700

Demography

Population (1989): 67,100.
Density (1989): persons per sq mi 383.4, persons per sq km 148.1.
Urban–rural (1986): urban 47.2%; rural 52.8%.
Sex distribution (1986): male 50.15%; female 49.85%.
Age breakdown (1986): under 15, 38.8%; 15–29, 26.9%; 30–44, 16.4%; 45–59, 10.4%; 60 and over 7.5%.
Population projection: (2000) 73,000; (2010) 78,000.
Doubling time: 39 years.
Ethnic composition (1983): Seychellois Creole (mixture of Asian, African, and European) 89.1%; Indian 4.7%; Malagasy 3.1%; Chinese 1.6%; English 1.5%.
Religious affiliation (1977): Roman Catholic 90.9%; other Christian (mostly Anglican) 7.5%; Hindu 0.7%; other 0.9%.
Major city (1977): Victoria 23,012.

Vital statistics

Birth rate per 1,000 population (1987): 25.4 (world avg. 27.1); (1985) legitimate 29.8%; illegitimate 70.2%.
Death rate per 1,000 population (1987): 7.6 (world avg. 9.9).
Natural increase rate per 1,000 population (1987): 17.8 (world avg. 17.2).
Total fertility rate (avg. births per childbearing woman; 1985): 3.3.
Marriage rate per 1,000 population (1984): 6.0.
Divorce rate per 1,000 population (1985): 0.7.
Life expectancy at birth (1980–85): male 66.2 years; female 73.5 years.
Major causes of death per 100,000 population (1985–87): diseases of the circulatory system 236.4, of which cerebrovascular disease 59.1; malignant neoplasms (cancers) 110.6; diseases of the respiratory system 78.8, of which pneumonia 42.4; accidents and adverse effects 66.7; diseases of the digestive system 24.2.

National economy

Budget (1989). Revenue: SR 750,100,000 (customs taxes and duties 53.6%, dividends and interest 13.0%, companies 7.4%, administrative fees 7.1%, fees and fines 5.6%, rents and royalties 2.8%). Expenditures: SR 735,100,- 000 (education and information 20.6%, debt service 20.0%, defense 10.1%, health 6.6%, tourism and transport 4.6%, national development 4.1%).
Public debt (external, outstanding; 1987): U.S.$84,200,000.
Gross national product (at current market prices; 1987): U.S.$210,000,000 (U.S.$3,180 per capita).

Structure of gross domestic product and labour force					
	1987			1985	
	in value SR '000,000	% of total value	labour force[4]	% of labour force	
Agriculture	64.5	4.7	2,282	9.5	
Mining and manufacturing	132.5	9.6	1,672	7.0	
Construction	61.7	4.5	1,063	4.4	
Public utilities	19.3	1.4	633	2.6	
Transportation and communications	592.4[5]	43.1[5]	2,256	9.4	
Trade	127.6	9.3	3,054	12.8	
Finance	118.9	8.6	814	3.4	
Public admin., defense	223.5	16.2 }	3,587	15.0	
Services	35.8	2.6 }			
Other	...	...	8,582[6]	35.8[6]	
TOTAL	1,376.2	100.0	23,943	100.0[3]	

Production (metric tons except as noted). Agriculture, forestry, fishing (1987): coconuts 21,000, copra 2,866, bananas 2,000, cinnamon bark 847, tea 109; livestock (number of live animals) 15,000 pigs, 4,000 goats, 2,000

cattle, 185,200[7] chickens; fish catch 3,953, of which jack 1,240, snapper 889, kawakawa 287, mackerel 247. Mining and quarrying (1985): guano 4,500. Manufacturing (1987): beer and stout 46,500 hectolitres; soft drinks 44,120 hectolitres; cigarettes 67,800,000 units. Energy production (consumption): electricity (kW-hr; 1987) 70,400,000 (70,400,000); coal, none (n.a.); petroleum, none (n.a.); petroleum products (metric tons; 1987) none (36,000); natural gas, none (n.a.).
Population economically active (1985): total 27,700; activity rate of total population 42.4% (participation rates: ages 15 and over 66.8%; female 42.4%; unemployed 20.6%).

Price and earnings indexes (1985 = 100)							
	1982	1983	1984	1985	1986	1987	1988
Consumer price index	89.9	95.3	99.2	100.0	100.3	102.9	104.7
Monthly earnings index	89.6	96.5	98.6	100.0	...	...	...

Household income and expenditure. Average household size (1982) 4.8; average annual income per household (1978) SR 18,480 (U.S.$2,658); sources of income: wages and salaries 77.2%, self-employment 3.8%, transfer payments 3.2%; expenditure (1983–84): food and beverages 53.9%, housing 13.6%, energy and water 9.1%, household and personal goods 6.6%, transportation 6.4%, clothing and footwear 4.2%, recreation 1.4%.
Tourism (1988): receipts from visitors U.S.$80,450,000; expenditures by nationals abroad U.S.$13,100,000.
Land use (1986): forested 18.5%; agricultural and under permanent cultivation 22.2%; built-on, wasteland, and other 59.3%.

Foreign trade

Balance of trade (current prices)						
	1983	1984	1985	1986	1987	1988
SR '000,000	−379.3	−356.6	−422.1	−447.2	−511.6	−546.4
% of total	58.0%	49.6%	52.0%	66.1%	67.3%	61.7%

Imports (1988): SR 823,012,000 (machinery and transport equipment 32.0%, of which transport equipment 13.8%, telecommunications equipment 4.6%; manufactured goods 27.3%, of which textile yarn, fabrics, and finished articles 2.9%, nonmetallic mineral products 2.7%; food, beverages, and tobacco 21.3%; petroleum and petroleum products 10.6%; chemicals and related products 6.1%). *Major import sources:* United Kingdom 15.3%; South Africa 11.0%; United States 11.0%; France 10.8%; Singapore 10.7%; Japan 6.8%; West Germany 3.8%; Hong Kong 2.4%; Italy 2.4%; The Netherlands 2.2%.
Exports (1988): SR 169,217,000[8] (petroleum products 43.1%[9]; canned tuna 33.4%; fish 6.1%; food, beverages, and tobacco 1.8%[9]; copra 1.7%; cinnamon bark 0.6%). *Major export destinations*[10] (1987): Italy 33.6%; Thailand 22.5%; United States 16.1%; United Kingdom 2.0%; Australia 1.5%; Pakistan 1.4%.

Transport and communications

Transport. Railroads: none. Roads (1987): total length 164 mi, 269 km (paved 61%). Vehicles (1985): passenger cars 3,531; trucks and buses 1,277. Merchant marine (1988): vessels (100 gross tons and over) 6; total deadweight tonnage 2,491. Air transport (1987): passenger arrivals 78,000, passenger departures 77,000; metric ton cargo unloaded 1,149, metric ton cargo loaded 417; airports (1989) with scheduled flights 6.
Communications. Daily newspapers (1987): total number 1; total circulation 4,000; circulation per 1,000 population 60. Radio (1988): total number of receivers 22,255 (1 per 3 persons). Television (1988): total number of receivers 5,500 (1 per 12 persons). Telephones (1987): 13,200 (1 per 5 persons).

Education and health

Education (1988)	schools[7]	teachers	students	student/ teacher ratio
Primary (age 6–15)	25[11]	702	14,522	20.7
Secondary (age 16–18)	4	162	2,643	16.3
Voc., teacher tr.	1	147	1,405	9.6

Educational attainment (1977). Percent of population age 15 and over having: no formal schooling 13.7%; primary education 50.1%; some secondary 32.4%; complete secondary 1.4%; postsecondary 1.8%. *Literacy* (1971): total population age 15 and over literate 17,066 (57.3%); males literate 8,103 (54.9%); females literate 8,963 (59.6%).
Health (1988): physicians[12] 68 (1 per 980 persons); hospital beds 353 (1 per 189 persons); infant mortality rate per 1,000 live births (1987) 18.4.
Food (1984–86): daily per capita caloric intake, 2,261 (vegetable products 83%, animal products 17%); FAO recommended minimum requirement, n.a.

Military

Total active duty personnel (1989): 1,300 (army 76.9%, navy 15.4%, air force 7.7%). *Military expenditure as percent of GNP* (1984): 5.6% (world 5.7%); per capita expenditure U.S.$206[13].

---

[1]Includes 2 nonelected members. [2]As of July 1981, Creole replaced English and French as the prescribed national language, but, per official source, "all are still considered official languages." [3]Detail does not add to total given because of rounding. [4]Excludes self-employed and domestic workers. [5]Includes import duties. [6]Includes 5,713 unemployed. [7]1986. [8]Includes SR 95,290,000 of reexports. [9]Items reexported [10]Domestic export only. [11]1987. [12]Includes dentists. [13]At prices of 1987.

Sierra Leone

Official name: Republic of Sierra Leone.
Form of government: a unitary single-party republic with one legislative house (House of Representatives [127[1]]).
Head of state and government: President.
Capital: Freetown.
Official language: English.
Official religion: none.
Monetary unit: 1 leone (Le) = 100 cents; valuation (Oct. 2, 1989) 1 U.S.$ = Le 65.36; 1 £ = Le 105.75.

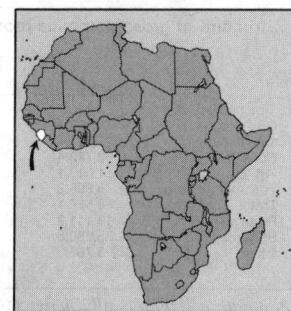

Area and population

Provinces Districts	Capitals	area sq mi	area sq km	population 1985 census[2]
Eastern Province	Kenema	6,005	15,553	960,551
Kailahun	Kailahun	1,490	3,859	233,839
Kenema	Kenema	2,337	6,053	337,055
Kono	Sefadu	2,178	5,641	389,657
Northern Province	Makeni	13,875	35,936	1,262,226
Bombali	Makeni	3,083	7,985	315,914
Kambia	Kambia	1,200	3,108	186,231
Koinaduga	Kabala	4,680	12,121	183,286
Port Loko	Port Loko	2,208	5,719	329,344
Tonkolili	Magburaka	2,704	7,003	247,451
Southern Province	Bo	7,604	19,694	740,510
Bo	Bo	2,015	5,219	268,671
Bonthe (incl. Sherbro)	Bonthe	1,339	3,468	105,007
Moyamba	Moyamba	2,665	6,902	250,514
Pujehun	Pujehun	1,585	4,105	116,318
Western Area[3]	Freetown	215	557	554,243
TOTAL		27,699	71,740	3,517,530

Demography

Population (1989): 3,957,000.
Density (1989): persons per sq mi 142.9, persons per sq km 55.2.
Urban–rural (1985): urban 28.3%; rural 71.7%.
Sex distribution (1985): male 49.06%; female 50.94%.
Age breakdown (1985): under 15, 41.4%; 15–29, 26.1%; 30–44, 17.1%; 45–59, 10.3%; 60–74, 4.5%; 75 and over, 0.6%.
Population projection: (2000) 4,874,000; (2010) 5,892,000.
Doubling time: 28 years.
Ethnic composition (1983): Mende 34.6%; Temne 31.7%; Limba 8.4%; Kono 5.2%; Bullom 3.7%; Fulani 3.7%; Koranko 3.5%; Yalunka 3.5%; Kissi 2.3%; other 3.4%.
Religious affiliation (1980): traditional beliefs 51.5%; Sunnī Muslim 39.4%; Protestant 4.7%; Roman Catholic 2.2%; Anglican 1.2%; other 1.0%.
Major cities (1985): Freetown 469,776; Koidu-New Sembehun 80,000; Bo 26,000; Kenema 13,000; Makeni 12,000.

Vital statistics

Birth rate per 1,000 population (1985–90): 48.2 (world avg. 27.1); legitimate, n.a.; illegitimate, n.a.
Death rate per 1,000 population (1985–90): 23.4 (world avg. 9.9).
Natural increase rate per 1,000 population (1985–90): 24.8 (world avg. 17.2).
Total fertility rate (avg. births per childbearing woman; 1985–90): 6.5.
Marriage rate per 1,000 population: n.a.
Divorce rate per 1,000 population: n.a.
Life expectancy at birth (1985–90): male 39.4 years; female 42.6 years.
Major causes of death per 100,000 population: n.a.; however, the major diseases are malaria, tuberculosis, leprosy, whooping cough, measles, tetanus, and diarrhea.

National economy

Budget (1989–90). Revenue: Le 5,618,000,000 (taxes 83.5%, grants 10.5%, nontax revenue 6.0%). Expenditures: Le 8,350,000,000 (recurrent expenditure 86.8%, development expenditure 13.2%).
Production (metric tons except as noted). Agriculture, forestry, fishing (1988): rice 430,000, cassava 116,000, sugarcane 70,000, palm oil 44,000, pulses 35,000, palm kernels 30,000, millet 22,000, taros 22,000, sorghum 19,000, peanuts (groundnuts) 19,000, sweet potatoes 14,000, corn (maize) 13,000, cocoa beans 11,000, coffee 9,000; livestock (number of live animals) 333,000 cattle, 330,000 sheep, 180,000 goats, 50,000 pigs, 6,000,000 chickens; roundwood (1987) 8,071,000 cu m; fish catch (1987) 53,000. Mining and quarrying (1988): bauxite 1,379,000; rutile (a titanium ore) 126,331; iron ore 70,000[4]; diamonds 17,492 carats[5]. Manufacturing (1984): salt 19,-200; nails 2,300; paint 1,140 hectolitres; beer and stout 35,670 hectolitres; plastic footwear 497,000 pairs[6]; cigarettes 1,346,000 units. Construction (value added in Le; 1981): 56,000,000. Energy production (consumption): electricity (kW-hr; 1987) 196,000,000 (196,000,000); coal, none (n.a.); crude petroleum (barrels; 1987) none (1,722,000); petroleum products (metric tons; 1987) 233,000 (196,000); natural gas, none (n.a.).
Household income and expenditure. Average household size (1983) 4.7; average annual income per household (1984): U.S.$320; sources of income (1984): self-employment 61.6%, wages and salaries 27.9%, other 10.5%; expenditure (1984): food, beverages, and tobacco 55.1%, clothing and footwear 12.9%, transportation and communications 9.2%, furniture, furnishings, and household durable goods 8.0%, housing 7.4%, recreation, entertainment, and education 3.8%, health 1.3%.

Tourism (1987): receipts from visitors U.S.$10,000,000; expenditures by nationals abroad U.S.$6,000,000.
Public debt (external, outstanding; 1987): U.S.$513,000,000.
Gross national product (at current market prices; 1987): U.S.$1,172,000,000 (U.S.$300 per capita).

Structure of gross domestic product and labour force

	1985 in value Le '000,000	1985 % of total value	1986 labour force[7]	1986 % of labour force
Agriculture	2,777.4	43.7	7,051	9.6
Mining	787.2	12.4	6,357	8.6
Manufacturing	312.0	4.9	8,314	11.3
Construction	112.0	1.8	9,181	12.4
Public utilities	20.1	0.3	2,182	3.0
Transportation and communications	601.3	9.5	8,019	10.9
Trade	803.7	12.6	4,685	6.4
Finance			2,297	3.1
Pub. admin., defense	939.0	14.8	25,626	34.7
Services				
Other			...	...
TOTAL	6,352.7	100.0	73,712	100.0

Population economically active (1985): total 1,352,000; activity rate of total population 36.9% (participation rates: ages 15–64 62.9%; female 33.7%; unemployed [registered; 1984] 7.6%).

Price index (1985 = 100)

	1982	1983	1984	1985	1986	1987	1988
Consumer price index	20.2	34.0	56.6	100.0	180.9	504.1	676.9

Land use (1987): forested 29.0%; meadows and pastures 30.8%; agricultural and under permanent cultivation 25.1%; other 15.1%.

Foreign trade

Balance of trade (current prices)

	1983	1984	1985	1986	1987	1988
Le '000,000	−85.0	−46.7	−249.0	+172.4	+962.5	−981.2
% of total	17.4%	5.9%	18.7%	4.6%	11.5%	12.4%

Imports (1985): Le 788,654,000 (food and live animals 29.8%; machinery and transport equipment 23.3%; minerals, fuels, and lubricants 21.3%; basic manufactured goods 13.4%; chemicals 4.2%). *Major import sources* (1984): United Kingdom 11.4%; West Germany 11.0%; Japan 6.1%; The Netherlands 5.0%; France 4.9%; United States 4.6%; China 2.3%.
Exports (1985): Le 649,266,000 (rutile 21.8%; coffee 20.3%; diamonds 18.8%; bauxite 17.4%; cacao 15.6%; gold 4.2%). *Major export destinations:* The Netherlands 30.9%; United Kingdom 14.6%; West Germany 11.2%; United States 9.5%.

Transport and communications

Transport. Railroads (1985): length 52 mi, 84 km. Roads (1986): total length 5,200 mi, 8,300 km (paved 17%). Vehicles (1985): passenger cars 23,500; trucks and buses 6,763[8]. Merchant marine (1988): vessels (100 gross tons and over) 40; total deadweight tonnage 8,690. Air transport[9] (1985): passenger-mi 68,290,000, passenger-km 109,903,000; short ton-mi cargo 1,400,-000, metric ton-km cargo 2,044,000; airports (1989) with scheduled flights 1.
Communications. Daily newspapers (1987): total number 1; total circulation 10,000; circulation per 1,000 population 2.6. Radio (1988): total number of receivers 935,915 (1 per 4.2 persons). Television (1988): total number of receivers 34,104 (1 per 114 persons). Telephones (1986): 14,900 (1 per 251 persons).

Education and health

Education (1984–85)

	schools	teachers	students	student/teacher ratio
Primary (age 5–11)	1,219	10,451	350,160	33.5
Secondary (age 12–18)	171	3,829	81,879	21.4
Voc., teacher tr.	12	406	4,774	11.8
Higher	2	296	2,445	8.3

Educational attainment (1974). Percent of population age 5 and over having: no formal schooling 81.3%; primary education 12.1%; secondary 5.9%; higher 0.7%. *Literacy* (1980): total population age 15 and over literate 460,-300 (23.6%); males literate 294,500 (31.2%); females literate 165,800 (16.5%).
Health: physicians (1984) 262 (1 per 13,736 persons); hospital beds (1983) 4,754 (1 per 742 persons); infant mortality rate per 1,000 live births (1985–90) 154.
Food (1984–86): daily per capita caloric intake 1,868 (vegetable products 96%, animal products 4%); 90% of FAO recommended minimum requirement.

Military

Total active duty personnel (1988): 3,150 (army 95.2%, navy 4.8%, air force, none). *Military expenditure as percent of GNP* (1986): 0.5% (world 5.5%); per capita expenditure U.S.$1.

[1]Maximum; includes up to 22 nonelective seats. [2]Preliminary figures exclude adjustment for underenumeration; adjusted total is 3,700,000. [3]Officially not a province; the administration of the Western Area is split among Greater Freetown (the city and its suburbs) and other administrative bodies. [4]1985; iron-ore mines have been inactive since 1985 owing to a lack of financing. [5]Official production, estimated to be less than 10% of total output; the remainder is lost to smuggling. [6]1983. [7]Registered employment only. [8]1984. [9]International flights only.

Singapore

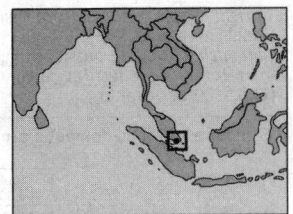

Official name: Hsin-chia-p'o
 Kung-ho-kuo (Mandarin Chinese);
 Republik Singapura (Malay);
 Singapore Kudiyarasu (Tamil);
 Republic of Singapore (English).
Form of government: unitary multiparty
 republic with one legislative house
 (Parliament [81][1]).
Chief of state: President.
Head of government: Prime Minister.
Capital: Singapore.
Official languages: Chinese; Malay;
 Tamil; English.
Official religion: none.
Monetary unit: 1 Singapore dollar
 (S$) = 100 cents; valuation (Oct. 2,
 1989) 1 U.S.$ = S$1.96; 1 £ = S$3.18.

Area and population	area		population
Census areas[2]	sq mi	sq km	1984 estimate
Central city area	3	8	157,000
City periphery	17	46	942,800
North	7	19	228,100
Northeast	3	9	301,500
West	7	18	413,200
Suburbs	49	127	754,700
East	7	19	195,000
North	13	34	309,900
West	29	74	249,800
Outlying areas	169	437	674,600
East	46	118	301,100
North	53	137	177,500
West	70	182	196,000
TOTAL	240[3]	622[3]	2,529,100

Demography

Population (1989): 2,674,000.
Density (1989): persons per sq mi 11,141.7, persons per sq km 4,299.0.
Urban–rural (1989): urban 100.0%.
Sex distribution (1988): male 50.90%; female 49.10%.
Age breakdown (1988): under 15, 23.1%; 15–29, 29.5%; 30–44, 25.9%; 45–59, 13.2%; 60 and over, 8.3%.
Population projection: (2000) 2,950,000; (2010) 3,117,000.
Doubling time: 47 years.
Ethnic composition (1988): Chinese 76.0%; Malay 15.2%; Indian[4] 6.5%; other 2.3%.
Religious affiliation (1988): Buddhist 28.3%; Christian 18.7%; Muslim 16.0%; Taoist 13.4%; Hindu 4.9%; nonreligious 17.6%; other 1.1%.
Major cities: Singapore is a unitary city-state having no separately defined cities within its borders.

Vital statistics

Birth rate per 1,000 population (1988): 20.0 (world avg. 27.1).
Death rate per 1,000 population (1988): 5.2 (world avg. 9.9).
Natural increase rate per 1,000 population (1988): 14.8 (world avg. 17.2).
Total fertility rate (avg. births per childbearing woman; 1988): 1.9.
Marriage rate per 1,000 population (1988): 9.4.
Divorce rate per 1,000 population (1988): 1.0.
Life expectancy at birth (1988): male 70.3 years; female 75.8 years.
Major causes of death per 100,000 population (1987): diseases of the circulatory system 178.9; malignant neoplasms (cancers) 119.8; diseases of the respiratory system 74.3; accidents, poisonings, and violence 35.6; endocrine and metabolic disorders 19.8.

National economy

Budget (1988–89). Revenue: S$11,555,900,000 (tax revenue 49.6%, nontax revenue 28.5%, development fund account 13.3%, sinking fund account 8.5%). Expenditures: S$12,466,100,000 (public services 26.3%, defense 21.1%, government development 16.3%, personnel 13.6%, debt servicing 13.1%, grants 6.8%).
Public debt (external, outstanding; 1987): U.S.$2,543,000,000.
Tourism (1987): receipts from visitors U.S.$2,216,000,000; expenditures by nationals abroad U.S.$791,000,000.
Production (metric tons except as noted). Agriculture, forestry, fishing (1987): vegetables 17,000, fruits 5,000; livestock (number of live animals) 459,000 pigs, 2,000 goats, 1,000,000 ducks, 7,000,000 chickens; fish catch (1988) 13,-152. Mining and quarrying (value added in S$; 1988): granite 55,900,000. Manufacturing (value added in S$; 1988): electronic products and components 6,547,900,000; transport equipment 1,365,400,000; industrial chemicals and gases 1,194,500,000; fabricated metal products except machinery and equipment 1,007,500,000; nonelectrical machinery 902,100,000; paints, pharmaceuticals, and chemical products 875,600,000; petroleum refining and petroleum products 743,500,000. Construction (1988): residential 30,-853 units; nonresidential 1,518,830 sq m. Energy production (consumption): electricity (kW-hr; 1988) 13,017,500,000 (11,734,800,000); coal, none (none); crude petroleum (barrels; 1987) none (254,248,000); petroleum products (metric tons; 1987) 30,341,000 (8,697,000); natural gas, none (none).
Land use (1986): forested 5.3%; agricultural and under permanent cultivation 7.0%; built-up area and other 87.7%.
Gross national product (1987): U.S.$20,717,000,000 (U.S.$7,940 per capita).

Structure of gross domestic product and labour force				
	1988			
	in value S$'000,000[5]	% of total value	labour force[6]	% of labour force
Agriculture	206.7	0.4	5,416	0.5
Quarrying	88.1	0.2	778	0.1
Manufacturing	13,821.1	28.9	352,594	28.5
Construction	2,742.4	5.7	83,302	6.7
Public utilities	1,012.1	2.1	7,802	0.6
Transp. and commun.	6,806.2	14.2	120,195	9.7
Trade	8,566.1	17.9	283,582	22.9
Finance	13,151.2	27.5	111,427	9.0
Services	5,280.8	11.0	271,597	21.9
Other	–3,766.3[7]	–7.97	1,770	0.1
TOTAL	47,908.4	100.0	1,238,463	100.0

Population economically active (1987): total 1,251,723; activity rate of total population 47.9% (participation rates: ages 15–64, 66.2%; female 37.8%; unemployed 4.7%).

Price and earnings indexes (1985 = 100)							
	1982	1983	1984	1985	1986	1987	1988
Consumer price index	95.8	97.0	99.5	100.0	98.6	99.1	100.6
Weekly earnings index	81.8	87.4	95.0	100.0	...	...	...

Household income and expenditure. Average household size (1984) 3.9; income per household S$20,800 (U.S.$9,700); sources of income (1977–78): wages and salaries 75.4%, self-employment 18.7%, transfer payments 2.0%, other 3.9%; expenditure (1987): food 23.0%, recreation and education 13.7%, transportation and communications 12.2%, housing (rent and utilities) 10.3%, furniture and household equipment 9.3%, clothing and footwear 8.7%, health 3.7%.

Foreign trade[8]

Balance of trade (current prices)						
	1983	1984	1985	1986	1987	1988
S$'000,000	–10,140	–6,497	–4,521	–3,384	–4,265	–4,159
% of total	9.9%	6.0%	4.3%	3.3%	3.4%	2.6%

Imports (1988): S$88,226,700,000 (crude petroleum 9.4%, office machines 5.4%, telecommunications apparatus 5.2%, petroleum products 4.7%, electric power machinery 4.1%, scientific and optical instruments 2.7%, musical instruments 2.5%, woven textile fabrics 2.4%). *Major import sources:* Japan 21.9%; United States 15.5%; Malaysia 14.7%; Taiwan 4.5%; Saudi Arabia 4.4%; China 3.8%; West Germany 3.7%; United Kingdom 2.9%.
Exports (1988): S$79,051,300,000 (office machines 13.8%, petroleum products 12.2%, telecommunications apparatus 9.6%, clothing 3.2%, crude rubber 2.9%, electrical circuit apparatus 2.3%, scientific and optical instruments 2.0%). *Major export destinations:* United States 23.8%; Malaysia 13.6%; Japan 8.6%; Hong Kong 6.3%; Thailand 5.5%; West Germany 3.5%; China 3.0%; United Kingdom 2.9%; Taiwan 2.8%.

Transport and communications

Transport. Railroads (1988): length 16 mi, 26 km. Roads (1988): total length 1,669 mi, 2,686 km (paved 96%). Vehicles (1988): passenger cars 251,414; trucks and buses 117,401. Merchant marine (1988): vessels (100 gross tons and over) 715; total deadweight tonnage 11,793,498. Air transport (1987): passenger-mi 15,502,000,000, passenger-km 24,948,000,000; short ton-mi cargo 889,478,000, metric ton-km cargo 1,298,616,000; airports (1989) 1.
Communications. Daily newspapers (1987): total number 7; total circulation 700,900; circulation per 1,000 population 268. Radio (1988): 745,907 receivers (1 per 3.5 persons). Television (1988): 538,196 receivers (1 per 4.9 persons). Telephones (1988): 1,271,000 (1 per 2.1 persons).

Education and health

Education (1988)	schools	teachers	students	student/ teacher ratio
Primary (age 6–11)	288	10,795	278,348	25.8
Secondary (age 12–18)	157	8,967	200,185	22.3
Voc., teacher tr.	17	1,565	26,911	17.2
Higher	6	4,018	46,904	11.7

Educational attainment (1980). Percent of population age 25 and over having: no schooling or without primary six certificate 43.7%; primary education 38.3%; secondary 14.6%; postsecondary 3.4%. *Literacy* (1980): total population age 15 and over literate 1,459,828 (82.9%); males literate 818,864 (91.6%); females literate 640,964 (74.0%).
Health (1987): physicians 2,941 (1 per 888 persons); hospital beds 9,793 (1 per 267 persons); infant mortality rate per 1,000 live births (1988) 7.0.
Food (1984–86): daily per capita caloric intake 2,854 (vegetable products 73%, animal products 27%); (1984) 120% of FAO recommended minimum requirement.

Military

Total active duty personnel (1988): 55,500 (army 81.1%, navy 8.1%, air force 10.8%). *Military expenditure as percent of GNP* (1986)[9]: 5.5% (world 5.5%); per capita expenditure U.S.$402.

[1]Excludes nonvoting, nonconstituency members of parliament. [2]The census areas have no administrative function. [3]Includes 2 sq mi (4 sq km) not distributable by census areas. [4]Includes Sri Lankan. [5]At prices of 1985. [6]Employed only. [7]Imputed bank service charges. [8]Import figures are f.o.b. in balance trade and c.i.f. for commodities and trading partners. [9]Constant 1987 dollars.

Solomon Islands

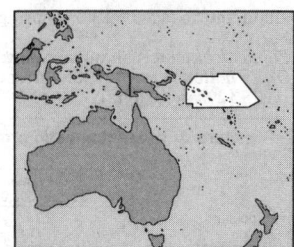

Official name: Solomon Islands.
Form of government: constitutional monarchy with one legislative house (National Parliament [38]).
Chief of state: British Monarch represented by governor-general.
Head of government: Prime Minister.
Capital: Honiara.
Official language: English.
Official religion: none.
Monetary unit: 1 Solomon Islands dollar (SI$) = 100 cents; valuation (Oct. 2, 1989) 1 U.S.$ = SI$2.37; 1 £ = SI$3.84.

Area and population

| | | area | | population |
| | | | | 1989 |
Provinces	Capitals	sq mi	sq km	estimate
Central Islands	Tulagi	497	1,286	22,233
Guadalcanal	Honiara	2,060	5,336	46,550
Isabel	Buala	1,597	4,136	16,749
Makira	Kira Kira	1,231	3,188	22,152
Malaita	Auki	1,631	4,225	84,410
Temotu	Santa Cruz	334	865	16,303
Western	Gizo	3,595	9,312	68,140
Capital Territory				
Honiara	—	8	22	31,060
TOTAL		10,954[1]	28,370	307,597

Demography

Population (1989): 308,000.
Density (1989): persons per sq mi 28.1, persons per sq km 10.9.
Urban–rural (1986): urban 15.7%; rural 84.3%.
Sex distribution (1986): male 51.76%; female 48.24%.
Age breakdown (1986): under 15, 47.3%; 15–29, 25.7%; 30–44, 13.9%; 45–59, 8.1%; 60 and over, 4.9%[1].
Population projection: (2000) 448,000; (2010) 595,000.
Doubling time: 20 years.
Ethnic composition (1986): Melanesian 94.2%; Polynesian 3.7%; other Pacific Islanders 1.4%; European 0.4%; Asian 0.2%; other 0.1%.
Religious affiliation (1986): Christian 96.7%, of which Protestant 77.5%, Roman Catholic 19.2%; Baha'i 0.4%; traditional beliefs 0.2%; other and no religion 2.7%.
Major cities (1986)[2]: Honiara 30,499; Gizo 3,727; Auki 3,262; Kira Kira 2,585; Buala 1,913.

Vital statistics

Birth rate per 1,000 population (1988): 44.5 (world avg. 27.1).
Death rate per 1,000 population (1988): 9.9 (world avg. 9.9).
Natural increase rate per 1,000 population (1988): 34.6 (world avg. 17.2).
Total fertility rate (avg. births per childbearing woman; 1988): 7.2.
Marriage rate per 1,000 population: n.a.
Divorce rate per 1,000 population: n.a.
Life expectancy at birth (1988): male 59.3 years; female 59.3 years.
Major causes of death per 100,000 population: n.a.; however, major diseases include malaria, tuberculosis, and leprosy[3].

National economy

Budget (1988). Revenue: SI$120,000,000 (foreign grants 31.3%, import duties 29.2%, income taxes 19.6%, export duties 9.7%, nontax revenue 7.8%). Expenditures: SI$138,260,000 (education 22.4%, agriculture 17.2%, transportation and communications 12.9%, transfers to provinces 9.7%, general public services 8.3%, public order 7.2%, health 6.2%).
Public debt (external, outstanding; 1987): U.S.$85,000,000.
Tourism (1987): receipts from visitors U.S.$2,000,000; expenditures by nationals abroad U.S.$3,000,000.
Gross national product (at current market prices; 1987): U.S.$123,000,000 (U.S.$420 per capita).

Structure of gross domestic product and labour force

| | 1986 | | | |
	in value SI$'000,000	% of total value	labour force[4]	% of labour force
Agriculture	108.3	43.3	18,031	46.0
Mining	−2.6	−1.0	703	1.8
Manufacturing	10.1	4.0	2,273	5.8
Construction	11.4	4.6	2,206	5.6
Public utilities	2.6	1.0	426	1.1
Transportation and communications	13.0	5.2	2,014	5.1
Trade	18.9	7.5	3,300	8.4
Finance	14.6	5.8	550	1.4
Pub. admin., defense } Services	48.0	19.2	9,378	23.9
Other	26.1	10.4	329	0.8
TOTAL	250.4[6]	100.0	39,210	250.4[1]

Household income and expenditure. Average household size (1986) 6.4; average annual income per household (1983) SI$1,010[5] (U.S.$1,160); sources of income (1983): wages and salaries 74.1%, self-employment, remittances, gifts, and other assistance 25.9%; expenditure (1987)[6]: food 51.0%, housing 12.5%, transportation 6.6%, clothing 4.9%.

Population economically active (1986): total 39,210[4]; activity rate of total population 13.7% (participation rates: over age 14, 24.9%; female 25.6%; unemployed, n.a.).

Price and earnings indexes (1985 = 100)

	1982	1983	1984	1985	1986	1987	1988
Consumer price index	77.4	82.2	91.3	100.0	113.6	126.1	147.8
Annual earnings index[5]	72.4	81.5	92.6	100.0	106.5	114.7	...

Production (metric tons except as noted). Agriculture, forestry, fishing (1988): coconuts 200,000, sweet potatoes 51,000, copra 29,272, taro 25,000, yams 20,000, palm oil 15,227, rice 6,000, palm kernels 3,172, cocoa beans 2,639; livestock (number of live animals) 52,000 pigs, 13,927 cattle; roundwood 290,500 cu m; fish catch 41,913. Mining and quarrying (1987): gold 4,000 troy oz. Manufacturing (1986): processed fish 44,042; milled rice 2,282; sawn timber 37,400 cu m; other major industries include soap and tobacco manufacturing, weaving, wood carving, fibreglass products, boatbuilding, and leather working. Construction (gross value in SI$; 1980): residential 1,858,000; nonresidential 693,000. Energy production (consumption): electricity (kW-hr; 1987) 30,000,000 (30,000,000); coal, none (n.a.); petroleum products (metric tons; 1987) none (44,000); natural gas, none (n.a.).
Land use (1987): forested 91.5%; meadows and pastures 1.4%; agricultural and under permanent cultivation 2.0%; other 5.1%.

Foreign trade

Balance of trade (current prices)

	1982	1983	1984	1985	1986	1987
SI$'000	−929	+592	+34,725	+1,142	+10,562	−6,646
% of total	0.8%	0.4%	17.2%	0.6%	4.8%	2.5%

Imports (1987): SI$134,944,000 (machinery and transport equipment 29.1%, manufactured goods 20.5%, food 15.0%, mineral fuels and lubricants 14.7%, chemicals 6.7%). *Major import sources:* Australia 41.4%; Japan 19.1%; Singapore 9.2%; New Zealand 7.9%; United Kingdom 4.4%; China 3.5%; United States 2.9%; Hong Kong 2.4%; Papua New Guinea 1.9%.
Exports (1987): SI$128,298,000 (fish products 41.0%, wood products 29.0%, copra 8.0%, cocoa beans 7.4%, palm oil products 5.9%). *Major export destinations:* Japan 35.6%; United Kingdom 13.8%; Thailand 12.2%; South Korea 6.0%; United States 5.3%; West Germany 4.2%; Australia 3.7%; Fiji 2.7%; Belgium 2.2%; The Netherlands 2.0%; Puerto Rico 2.0%.

Transport and communications

Transport. Railroads: none. Roads[7] (1987): total length 1,300 mi, 2,100 km (paved 2%). Vehicles (1986): passenger cars 1,350; trucks and buses 1,708. Merchant marine (1988): vessels (100 gross tons and over) 36; total deadweight tonnage 6,797. Air transport (1984)[8]: passenger-mi 6,852,000, passenger-km 11,027,000; short ton-mi cargo 25,000, metric ton-km cargo 37,000; airports (1989) with scheduled flights 17.
Communications. Daily newspapers[9] (1987): none. Radio (1988): total number of receivers 65,000 (1 per 4.6 persons). Television (1986): none. Telephones (1987): 4,983 (1 per 58 persons).

Education and health

Education (1987)

	schools	teachers	students	student/ teacher ratio
Primary (age 7–12)	462	2,124	42,374	20.0
Secondary (age 13–18)	20	300	5,604	18.7
Voc., teacher tr.[10]	2	63	1,142	18.1
Higher	—	—	—	—

Educational attainment (1986)[11]. Percent of population age 25 and over having: no schooling 44.4%; primary education 46.2%; secondary 6.8%; higher 2.6%. *Literacy* (1976): total population age 15 and over literate 55,500 (54.1%); males 33,600 (62.4%); females 21,900 (44.9%).
Health (1986): physicians 38 (1 per 7,402 persons); hospital beds 1,479 (1 per 190 persons); infant mortality rate per 1,000 live births (1988) 74.0.
Food (1984–86): daily per capita caloric intake 2,163 (vegetable products 89%, animal products 11%); 80% of FAO recommended minimum requirement.

Military

Total active duty personnel: no military forces are maintained, but a police force of 475 provides internal security.

---

[1]Detail does not add to total given because of rounding. [2]Ward populations. [3]Reported cases of these diseases in 1986 were: malaria 72,108, tuberculosis 337, and leprosy 260. [4]Population working for money only. [5]Public service earnings. [6]Retail price index components. [7]Includes 500 mi (800 km) of privately maintained roads mainly for plantation use. [8]Solair only. [9]In 1985 there were two weekly newspapers with a combined circulation of 6,700. [10]1984. [11]Indigenous population only.

Somalia

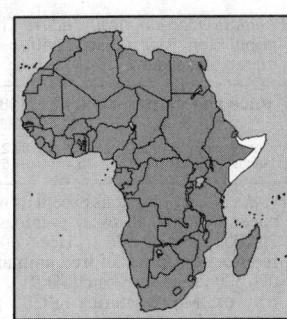

Official name: Jamhuuriyadda
Dimuqraadiga Soomaaliya
(Somali); Jumhūriyah aṣ-Ṣūmāl
ad-Dīmuqrāṭīyah (Arabic) (Somali
Democratic Republic).
Form of government:
military-dominated, single-party
republic with one legislative house
(People's Assembly [177][1]).
Head of state and government:
President.
Capital: Mogadishu.
Official languages: Somali; Arabic.
Official religion: Islam.
Monetary unit: 1 Somali shilling
(So.Sh.) = 100 cents; valuation (Oct. 2,
1989) 1 U.S.$ = So.Sh. 410.00;
1 £ = So.Sh. 663.38.

Area and population

Regions	Capitals	area sq mi	area sq km	population 1980 estimate
Bakool	Oddur (Xuddur)	10,000	27,000	148,700
Banaadir	Mogadishu (Muqdisho)	400	1,000	520,100
Bari	Bender Cassim (Boosaaso)	27,000	70,000	222,300
Bay	Baidoa (Baydhabo)	15,000	39,000	451,000
Galguduud	Dusa Marreb (Dhuusamarreeb)	17,000	43,000	255,900
Gedo	Garbahaarrey	12,000	32,000	235,000
Hiiraan	Beledweyne	13,000	34,000	219,300
Jubbada Dhexe	Bu'aale	9,000	23,000	147,800
Jubbada Hoose	Chisimayu (Kismaayo)	24,000	61,000	272,400
Mudug	Galcaio (Gaalkacyo)	27,000	70,000	311,200
Nugaal	Garoowe	19,000	50,000	112,200
Sanaag	Erigavo (Ceerigaabo)	21,000	54,000	216,500
Shabeellaha Dhexe	Giohar (Jawhar)	8,000	22,000	352,000
Shabeellaha Hoose	Merca (Marka)	10,000	25,000	570,700
Togdheer	Burao (Burco)	16,000	41,000	383,900
Woqooyi Galbeed	Hargeysa	17,000	45,000	655,000
TOTAL		246,000[2]	637,000	5,074,000

Demography

Population (1989): 7,339,000.
Density (1989): persons per sq mi 29.8, persons per sq km 11.5.
Urban–rural (1985): urban 32.5%; rural 67.5%.
Sex distribution (1985): male 47.53%; female 52.47%.
Age breakdown (1985): under 15, 43.7%; 15–29, 25.0%; 30–44, 14.7%; 45–59, 10.1%; 60–74, 5.9%; 75 and over, 0.6%.
Population projection: (2000) 9,803,000; (2010) 13,247,000.
Doubling time: 23 years.
Ethnic composition (1983): Somali 98.3%; Arab 1.2%; Bantu 0.4%; other 0.1%.
Religious affiliation (1980): Sunnī Muslim 99.8%; Christian 0.1%; other 0.1%.
Major cities (1981): Mogadishu 500,000; Hargeysa 70,000; Chisimayu 70,000; Berbera 65,000; Merca 60,000.

Vital statistics

Birth rate per 1,000 population (1985–90): 50.2 (world avg. 27.1); legitimate, n.a.; illegitimate, n.a.
Death rate per 1,000 population (1985–90): 20.1 (world avg. 9.9).
Natural increase rate per 1,000 population (1985–90): 30.1 (world avg. 17.2).
Total fertility rate (avg. births per childbearing woman; 1985–90): 6.5.
Marriage rate per 1,000 population: n.a.
Divorce rate per 1,000 population: n.a.
Life expectancy at birth (1985–90): male 43.4 years; female 46.6 years.
Major causes of death per 100,000 population: n.a.; however, major diseases include leprosy, malaria, tetanus, and tuberculosis.

National economy

Budget (1988). Revenue: So.Sh. 17,807,000,000 (domestic revenue sources, principally indirect taxes and import duties 67.0%; external grants and transfers 33.0%). Expenditures: So.Sh. 17,807,000,000 (equipment and services 67.5%, of which debt service 21.5%; investments 19.3%; wages and salaries 13.2%).
Tourism: receipts from visitors (1986) U.S.$8,000,000; expenditures by nationals abroad (1983) U.S.$13,000,000.
Production (metric tons except as noted). Agriculture, forestry, fishing (1988): sugarcane 370,000, corn (maize) 282,000, sorghum 220,000, bananas 120,000, vegetables 55,000, sesame seed 50,000, roots and tubers 48,000, citrus fruits 27,000, rice 12,000, dates 7,000, seed cotton 3,000, peanuts (groundnuts) 1,000; livestock (number of live animals) 20,000,000 goats, 13,195,000 sheep, 6,680,000 camels, 5,000,000 cattle; roundwood (1987) 4,625,000 cu m; fish catch (1987) 17,000. Mining and quarrying (1986): salt 30,000. Manufacturing (value added in So.Sh. '000,000; 1986)[3]: food 79; paper and printing 42; beverages 38; tobacco 31; textiles 20; clothing and footwear 14; petroleum products 11; metal fittings 6. Construction (value added in So.Sh.; 1982): 1,687,200,000. Energy production (consumption): electricity (kW-hr; 1987) 255,000,000 (255,000,000); coal, none (n.a.); crude petroleum (barrels; 1987) n.a. (1,810,000); petroleum products (metric tons; 1987) 211,000 (280,000); natural gas, none (n.a.).
Household income and expenditure. Average household size (1980) 4.9; income per household: n.a.; sources of income: n.a.; expenditure[4] (1983):

food and tobacco 62.3%, housing 15.3%, clothing 5.6%, energy 4.3%, other 12.1%.
Public debt (external, outstanding; 1988): U.S.$1,762,000,000.
Gross national product (at current market prices; 1987): U.S.$1,657,000,000 (U.S.$290 per capita).

Structure of gross domestic product and labour force

	1986 in value So.Sh. '000,000	1986 % of total value	1985 labour force	1985 % of labour force
Agriculture	3,707	54.9	1,475,000	73.8
Mining	21	0.3		
Manufacturing	334	4.9	176,000	8.8
Construction	318	4.7		
Public utilities	62	0.9		
Transportation and communications	427	6.3		
Trade	580	8.6		
Finance	349	5.2	348,000	17.4
Pub. admin., defense	461	6.8		
Services	194	2.9		
Other	302	4.5		
TOTAL	6,755	100.0	1,999,000	100.0

Population economically active (1985): total 1,999,000; activity rate of total population 43.0% (participation rates: ages 15–64, 72.8%; female 39.7%; unemployed, n.a.).

Price and earnings indexes (1985 = 100)

	1982	1983	1984	1985	1986	1987	1988[5]
Consumer price index	27.9	38.0	72.6	100.0	135.8	174.0	282.2
Earnings index	...	...	...	...	...	...	...

Land use (1987): forested 14.2%; meadows and pastures 46.0%; agricultural and under permanent cultivation 1.7%; other 38.1%.

Foreign trade

Balance of trade (current prices)

	1982	1983	1984	1985	1986	1987
So.Sh. '000,000	−74.5	−1,421.4	−793.4	−275.0	−1,446.6	−1,209.5
% of total	1.8%	33.3%	26.6%	3.7%	10.2%	5.3%

Imports (1987): So.Sh. 12,109,400,000 ([1984] food 25.5%; machinery and transport equipment 22.0%, of which transport equipment 15.1%, electrical equipment 2.5%; construction materials 20.4%; mineral fuels 7.8%; manufacturing raw materials 5.6%; beverages and tobacco 2.0%; chemical products 1.72%; clothing and footwear 1.5%). *Major import sources* (1987): Italy 35.7%; United States 10.5%; West Germany 8.5%; France 4.7%; United Kingdom 4.6%; Thailand 3.3%; Kenya 2.9%; Japan 2.6%; Singapore 1.0%; China 0.8%.
Exports (1987): So.Sh. 10,899,900,000 (live animals 67.0%; bananas 22.6%; undressed hides, skins, furs, and fish 10.4%). *Major export destinations:* Italy 27.7%; United States 3.2%; China 1.1%.

Transport and communications

Transport. Railroads: none. Roads (1985): total length 10,697 mi, 17,215 km (paved 15%). Vehicles (1985): passenger cars 17,754; trucks and buses 9,533. Merchant marine (1988): vessels (100 gross tons and over) 26; total deadweight tonnage 15,860. Air transport (1988): passenger-mi 84,592,000, passenger-km 136,138,000; short ton-mi cargo 1,355,000, metric ton-km cargo 1,978,000; airports (1989) with scheduled flights 14.
Communications. Daily newspapers (1988): total number 1; total circulation, n.a. Radio (1988): total number of receivers 362,292 (1 per 20 persons). Television[6]: total number of receivers, n.a. Telephones (1985): 6,000 (1 per 1,066 persons).

Education and health

Education (1984–85)

	schools	teachers	students	student/teacher ratio
Primary (age 6–14)	1,121	14,521	274,610	18.9
Secondary (age 15–18)	80	2,522	65,186	25.8
Voc., teacher tr.	23	725	10,203	14.1
Higher	1	262[7]	3,405	...

Educational attainment, n.a. *Literacy* (1975): total population age 10 and over literate 54.8%; males literate 60.9%; females literate 47.9%.
Health: physicians (1986) 450 (1 per 13,315 persons); hospital beds (1985) 5,536 (1 per 1,053 persons); infant mortality rate per 1,000 live births (1985–90) 132.
Food (1984–86): daily per capita caloric intake 2,088 (vegetable products 69%, animal products 31%); 90% of FAO recommended minimum requirement.

Military

Total active duty personnel (1989): 65,000 (army 94.3%, navy 1.8%, air force 3.9%). *Military expenditure as percent of GNP* (1984): 3.0% (world 5.7%); per capita expenditure U.S.$5.

---

[1]Including 6 nonelective seats. [2]Detail does not add to total given because of rounding. [3]At 1977 prices. [4]Capital city only. [5]Second quarter. [6]Since the end of 1983 television service covers Mogadishu area and Hargeysa. [7]1980–81.

South Africa

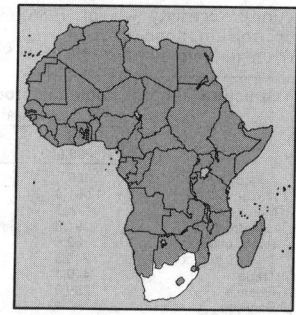

Official name: Republiek van Suid-Afrika (Afrikaans); Republic of South Africa (English).
Form of government: multiparty republic with three legislative houses (House of Assembly [178]; House of Representatives [85]; House of Delegates [42])[1, 2].
Head of state and government: State President.
Capitals: Pretoria (executive); Bloemfontein (judicial); Cape Town (legislative).
Official languages: Afrikaans; English.
Official religion: none.
Monetary unit: 1 rand (R) = 100 cents; valuation (Oct. 2, 1989) 1 U.S.\$ = R 2.69; 1 £ = R 4.35.

Area and population[3]

Provinces	Capitals	area sq mi	area sq km	population[4] 1983 estimate	population[4] 1985 census
Cape	Cape Town	247,638	641,379	5,374,000	5,041,137
Natal	Pietermaritzburg	21,344	55,281	2,842,000	2,145,018
Orange Free State	Bloemfontein	49,166	127,338	2,080,000	1,776,903
Transvaal	Pretoria	87,658	227,034	8,950,000	7,532,179
National states					
Gazankulu	Giyani	2,535	6,565	585,000	497,213
KaNgwane	Louieville	1,476	3,823	184,000	392,782
KwaNdebele	Siyabuswa	1,253	3,244	200,000	235,855
KwaZulu	Ulundi	13,928	36,074	3,792,000	3,747,015
Lebowa	Lebowakgomo	8,430	21,833	1,869,000	1,835,984
Qwaqwa	Phuthaditjhaba	253	655	306,000	181,559
TOTAL		433,680[5]	1,123,226	26,182,000	23,385,645

Demography

Population (1989): 30,224,000[6].
Density (1989): persons per sq mi 69.7, persons per sq km 26.9.
Urban–rural (1985)[7]: urban 55.9%; rural 44.1%.
Sex distribution (1985): male 49.37%; female 50.63%.
Age breakdown (1985)[7]: under 15, 41.0%; 15–29, 26.9%; 30–44, 16.1%; 45–59, 9.8%; 60–74, 5.0%; 75 and over, 1.2%.
Population projection: (2000) 37,783,000; (2010) 46,283,000.
Doubling time: 30 years.
Ethnic composition (1984): black 68.2%, of which Zulu 23.8%, North Sotho 9.8%, Xhosa 9.7%, South Sotho 7.3%, Tswana 5.7%, other 11.9%; white 18.0%; Coloured 10.5%; Asian 3.3%.
Religious affiliation (1980): Christian 78.1%, of which black independent churches 20.8%, Afrikaans Reformed 15.5%, Roman Catholic 9.6%; Hindu 2.1%; Muslim 1.4%; other 18.4%.
Major cities (municipality; 1985): Cape Town 1,911,521; Johannesburg 1,609,408; Durban 982,075; Pretoria 822,925.

Vital statistics

Birth rate per 1,000 population (1985): 33.4 (world avg. 27.1); (1978) legitimate 75.9%[8]; illegitimate 24.1%[8].
Death rate per 1,000 population (1985): 10.4 (world avg. 9.9).
Natural increase rate per 1,000 population (1985): 23.0 (world avg. 17.2).
Total fertility rate (avg. births per childbearing woman; 1985–90)[8]: 4.5.
Life expectancy at birth (1985–90)[7]: male 57.5 years; female 63.5 years.
Major causes of death per 100,000 population (1977)[8]: heart disease 215.3; malignant neoplasms 107.3; cerebrovascular disease 90.2; pneumonia 75.2.

National economy

Budget (1988–89). Revenue: R 42,840,000,000 (income tax 57.7%, sales tax 27.1%, customs duty and excise tax 9.7%). Expenditures: R 52,933,000,000 (education 18.7%, defense 16.2%, debt service 14.1%, health 9.4%, social services 9.2%).
Production (metric tons except as noted). Agriculture, forestry, fishing (1988): sugarcane 20,332,000, corn (maize) 6,900,000, wheat 3,400,000; livestock (number of live animals) 29,800,000 sheep, 11,820,000 cattle; roundwood (1987) 27,000,000 cu m; fish catch (1987) 902,079. Mining and quarrying (1988): iron ore 24,676,069; chrome 3,749,285; manganese ore 3,480,659; gold 617,900 kg; silver 179,100 kg; platinum 131,240 kg[9]; diamonds 8,382,257 carats. Manufacturing (value added in R '000,000; 1985): metal products 5,553, of which iron and steel 2,435; chemicals 5,198; food and beverages 3,770; machinery and transport equipment 3,726, of which electrical machinery 1,461, transport equipment 939; textiles 980; printing and publishing 795; wearing apparel 622. Construction (1987): residential 4,905,088 sq m; nonresidential 1,150,496 sq m. Energy production (consumption)[10]: electricity (kW-hr; 1987) 122,465,000,000 (122,165,000,000); coal (metric tons; 1987) 177,282,000 (134,532,000); petroleum (barrels; 1987) none (117,000,000); petroleum products (metric tons; 1987) 13,690,000 (10,492,000).
Household income and expenditure. Average household size (1983) 4.5; average annual income per household (1980) R 8,829 (U.S.\$11,349); sources of income (1984): wages and salaries 82.9%, transfer payments 4.8%, other 12.3%; expenditure (1987): food and beverages 35.9%, transp. and commun. 9.4%, housing and energy 9.1%; wearing apparel 7.4%, health 4.3%.
Tourism (1987): receipts from visitors U.S.\$587,000,000; expenditures by nationals abroad U.S.\$835,000,000.

Gross national product (1987): U.S.\$62,926,000,000 (U.S.\$1,890 per capita).

Structure of gross domestic product and labour force

	1987 in value R '000,000	1987 % of total value	1985 labour force	1985 % of labour force
Agriculture	8,831	5.5	1,179,590	13.6
Mining	21,321	13.2	743,065	8.6
Manufacturing	37,302	23.2	1,379,518	15.8
Construction	4,925	3.0	556,339	6.4
Public utilities	7,152	4.4	92,720	1.1
Transp. and commun.	13,486	8.4	418,156	4.8
Trade	19,270	12.0	941,867	10.8
Finance	24,544	15.2	339,204	3.9
Pub. admin., defense	22,370	13.9	1,965,040	22.6
Services	2,851	1.8	1,076,864	12.4
Other	−1,021[11]	−0.6[11]		
TOTAL	161,031	100.0	8,692,363	100.0

Population economically active (1985): total 8,692,363; activity rate of total population 37.2% (participation rates: ages 20–64 [1980] 65.4%; female 36.4%; unemployed 8.4%).

Price and earnings indexes (1985 = 100)

	1982	1983	1984	1985	1986	1987	1988
Consumer price index	68.7	77.1	86.0	100.0	118.7	136.7	155.4
Monthly earnings index	70.7	76.2	89.2	100.0	114.7	131.7	...

Public debt (1989[12]): U.S.\$29,000,000,000.
Land use (1987): forested 3.7%; meadows and pastures 66.6%; agricultural and under permanent cultivation 10.8%; other 18.9%.

Foreign trade

Balance of trade (current prices)

	1983	1984	1985	1986	1987	1988
R '000,000	+4,479	+3,705	+13,748	+15,246	+15,167	+9,643
% of total	12.1%	7.9%	23.0%	22.1%	20.9%	10.9%

Imports (1988): R 39,528,300,000 (machinery and transport equipment 45.5%, of which motor vehicles 14.2%; chemicals 10.6%; metal products 4.9%; plastics and rubber products 4.8%). *Major import sources* (1987): U.S. 68.6%; W.Ger. 18.2%; Japan 13.5%; U.K. 11.1%.
Exports (1988): R 48,800,700,000 (gold 39.2%; metals and metal products 13.8%; precious stones 8.2%; food and tobacco 5.4%; chemicals 3.3%). *Major export destinations* (1987): U.S. 43.6%; Japan 10.6%; Italy 7.7%; W.Ger. 6.4%; Canada 6.0%; U.K. 4.6%.

Transport and communications

Transport. Railroads (1987): route length 14,669 mi, 23,607 km; passenger-km 15,195,600,000; metric ton-km cargo 91,690,592,000. Roads (1987): length 113,691 mi, 182,968 km (paved 29%). Vehicles (1987): passenger cars 3,107,031; trucks and buses 1,217,214. Merchant marine (1988): vessels 241; total deadweight tonnage 522,723. Air transport (1986[13]): passenger-km 4,508,783,000; metric ton-km cargo 189,264,000; airports (1989) 39.
Communications. Daily newspapers (1987): total number 23; total circulation 1,445,000; circulation per 1,000 population 41. Radio (1988): 10,000,000 receivers (1 per 3.6 persons). Television (1986): 2,629,000 receivers (1 per 13 persons). Telephones (1987): 4,235,022 (1 per 8.5 persons).

Education and health

Education (1988)

	schools	teachers	students	student/teacher ratio
Primary (age 6–12) } Secondary (age 13–17)	19,310[9]	286,228	7,163,987	25.0
Voc., teacher tr.	132[14]	19,219	170,656	8.9
Higher	84[14]	28,478	267,608	9.4

Educational attainment (1985). Percent of economically active population having: no formal schooling or incomplete primary 49.4%; complete primary education 9.1%; some secondary 27.5%; complete secondary 12.4%; postsecondary degree 1.6%. *Literacy*[7] (1984): percent of adult population literate 50%; white 93%; Asians 69%; Coloured 62%; black 32%.
Health: physicians (1986) 22,525 (1 per 1,510 persons); hospital beds (1980) 98,308 (1 per 246 persons); infant mortality rate (1985) 59.2.
Food (1984–86): daily per capita caloric intake 2,941 (vegetable products 86%, animal products 14%); 120% of FAO recommended minimum.

Military

Total active duty personnel (1989): 103,000 (army 75.2%, navy 6.3%, air force 10.7%, intraservice medical service 7.8%). *Military expenditure as percent of GNP* (1987): 4.4% (world 5.4%); per capita expenditure U.S.\$99.

[1]For representation of whites, Coloureds, and Asians (mainly Indians), respectively. [2]Including 4, 1, and 0 nonelective seats, respectively. [3]Data exclude Bophuthatswana, Ciskei, Transkei, and Venda, which the South African government recognizes as sovereign nations. Together they had (1986) an area of 39,610 sq mi (102,589 sq km) and a population of 6,724,000. [4]1985 census data represented an estimated undercount of 4,336,455. Some indication of its extent and distribution may be seen by comparing the 1983 estimates (based on the more accurate 1980 census) with the 1985 figures. [5]Detail does not add to total given because of rounding. [6]The 1989 estimate is a continuation of a series incorporating the 1980 census, the 1983 estimates, and the corrected 1985 census. [7]Includes Bophuthatswana, Ciskei, Transkei, and Venda. [8]Whites, Asians, and Coloureds only. [9]1987. [10]Data refer to the Customs Union of Southern Africa, comprising South Africa, Botswana, Lesotho, South West Africa/Namibia, and Swaziland. [11]Includes imputed finance charges. [12]May 1. [13]Through July only. [14]1985.

South West Africa/ Namibia

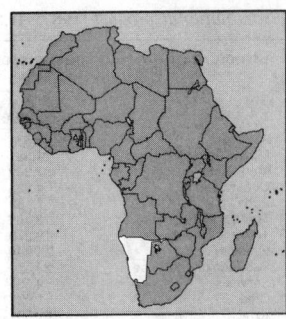

Official name: Suidwes-Afrika/Namibië (Afrikaans); South West Africa/ Namibia (English).
Political status: dependency of South Africa with no legislative body[1].
Head of state and government: Administrator-General[1].
Capital: Windhoek.
Official languages: Afrikaans; English.
Official religion: none.
Monetary unit: 1 South African rand (R) = 100 cents; valuation (Oct. 2, 1989) 1 U.S.$ = R 2.69; 1 £ = R 4.35.

Area and population[2]		area		population
Magisterial Districts	Capitals	sq mi	sq km	1987 estimate[3]
Bethanien	Bethanien	6,951	18,004	3,000
Boesmanland	Tsumkwe	7,131	18,468	3,000
Caprivi Oos	Katima Mulilo	4,453	11,533	44,000
Damaraland	Khorixas	17,977	46,560	28,000
Gobabis	Gobabis	16,003	41,447	25,000
Grootfontein	Grootfontein	10,239	26,520	25,000
Hereroland-Oos	Otjinene	20,058	51,949	22,000
Hereroland-Wes	Okakarara	6,371	16,500	18,000
Kaokoland	Opuwo	22,467	58,190	20,000
Karasburg	Karasburg	14,717	38,116	11,000
Karibib	Karibib	5,108	13,230	10,000
Kavango	Rundu	19,674	50,955	122,000
Keetmanshoop	Keetmanshoop	14,788	38,302	20,000
Lüderitz	Lüderitz	20,488	53,063	16,000
Maltahöhe	Maltahöhe	9,874	25,573	6,000
Mariental	Mariental	18,413	47,689	24,000
Namaland	Gibeon	8,154	21,120	15,000
Okahandja	Okahandja	6,811	17,640	15,000
Omaruru	Omaruru	3,253	8,425	6,000
Otjiwarongo	Otjiwarongo	7,934	20,550	19,000
Outjo	Outjo	14,951	38,722	10,000
Owambo	Ondangwa	20,000	51,800	520,000
Rehoboth	Rehoboth	5,476	14,182	33,000
Swakopmund	Swakopmund	17,258	44,697	18,000
Tsumeb	Tsumeb	6,340	16,420	22,000
Windhoek	Windhoek	12,930	33,489	129,000
TOTAL		317,818	823,144	1,184,000

Demography

Population (1989): 1,270,000.
Density (1989): persons per sq mi 4.0, persons per sq km 1.5.
Urban–rural (1987): urban *c.* 26%; rural 74%.
Sex distribution (1985): male 49.35%; female 50.65%.
Age breakdown (1985): under 15, 45.1%; 15–29, 25.9%; 30–44, 15.3%; 45–59, 8.7%; 60–74, 4.1%; 75 and over, 0.9%.
Population projection: (2000) 1,667,000; (2010) 2,134,000.
Doubling time: 23 years.
Ethnic composition (1989): Ovambo 49.8%; Kavango 9.3%; Herero 7.5%; Damara 7.5%; white 6.4%; Nama 4.8%; other 14.7%.
Religious affiliation (1981): Lutheran 51.2%; Roman Catholic 19.8%; Dutch Reformed 6.1%; Anglican 5.0%; other 17.9%.
Major cities (1988): Windhoek 114,500; Swakopmund 15,500; Rundu 15,000; Rehoboth 15,000; Keetmanshoop 14,000.

Vital statistics

Birth rate per 1,000 population (1985–90): 44.0 (world avg. 27.1).
Death rate per 1,000 population (1985–90): 12.2 (world avg. 9.9).
Natural increase rate per 1,000 population (1985–90): 31.8 (world avg. 17.2).
Total fertility rate (avg. births per childbearing woman; 1985–90): 6.1.
Marriage rate per 1,000 population: n.a.
Life expectancy at birth (1985–90): male 55.0 years; female 57.5 years.
Major causes of death per 100,000 population: n.a.; however, major diseases include malaria, tuberculosis, and trypanosomiasis (sleeping sickness).

National economy

Budget (1988–89). Revenue: R 1,865,400,000 (customs and excise taxes 21.0%, grants from South Africa 16.5%, general sales tax 11.0%). Expenditures: R 1,945,300,000 (finance 14.7%, national defense 11.3%, transportation 7.4%, education 6.3%, health and welfare 4.9%).
Public debt (external, outstanding; 1984): U.S.$352,000,000.
Tourism (1981): receipts from visitors U.S.$45,960,000; expenditures by nationals abroad, n.a.
Production (metric tons except as noted). Agriculture, forestry, fishing (1988): roots and tubers 245,000, corn [maize] 48,000, millet 43,000, fruit other than melons 33,000, vegetables and melons 28,000, sorghum 7,000; pulses 7,000, wool 1,848[4], karakul pelts 770,627 units[5]; livestock (number of live animals) 2,050,000 cattle, 6,400,000 sheep, 2,500,000 goats; fish catch (1987) 519,518, of which anchovies 376,627, South African pilchard 65,336, mackerel 34,068, Cape hake 30,531. Mining and quarrying (1988): diamonds 938,000 carats, mostly gem quality; copper 42,200; lead 44,400; zinc 65,200; uranium 3,600; gold 195 kg; silver 108 kg. Manufacturing (gross output in R '000,000; 1976): food and beverages 140.8; metal products 34.2; wood products 6.6; chemical products 3.6; printing and publishing 2.4; other 12.4. Construction (value of buildings completed in R '000,000; 1984): residential 19.4; nonresidential 11.5. Energy production (consump-

tion): electricity (kW-hr; 1986) 692,000,000 (n.a.); coal, none (n.a.); crude petroleum, none (n.a.).
Gross national product (1988): U.S.$1,600,000,000 (U.S.$1,300 per capita).

Structure of gross domestic product and labour force

	1988		1981	
	in value R '000,000	% of total value	labour force	% of labour force
Agriculture	469.3	12.5	71,402	35.0
Mining	1,051.8	28.1	15,515	7.6
Manufacturing	174.3	4.7	8,017	3.9
Construction	94.8	2.5	17,654	8.6
Public utilities	82.8	2.2	1,922	0.9
Transp. and commun.	249.5	6.7	9,615	4.7
Trade	449.4	12.0	22,253	10.9
Finance	250.8	6.7	3,764	1.8
Services	6	6	22,417	11.0
Public admin., defense	745.9	19.9	31,079	15.2
Other	174.7[6]	4.7[6]	360	0.2
TOTAL	3,743.3	100.0	203,998	100.0[7]

Population economically active: total (1984) 310,000; activity rate of total population, *c.* 27% (participation rates: ages 15–64, *c.* 56%; female 20.4%[8]; unemployed, *c.* 15%).

Price and earnings indexes (1985 = 100)[9]

	1981	1982	1983	1984	1985	1986	1987
Consumer price index	62.8	75.6	81.2	90.5	100.0	113.0	126.7
Earnings index	...	...	...	...	...	...	...

Household income and expenditure. Average household size (1981) 4.8; average annual income per household (1980) R 3,223 (U.S.$4,143); sources of income (1987): wages and salaries 72.8%, income from property 23.9%, transfer payments 3.3%; expenditure: n.a.
Land use (1987): forested 22.4%; meadows and pastures 64.3%; agricultural and under permanent cultivation 0.8%; other 12.6%.

Foreign trade

Balance of trade (current prices)

	1982	1983	1984	1985	1986	1987
R '000,000	−97.4	−68.1	−82.9	324.2	511.7	97.0
% of total	4.6%	3.5%	3.6%	11.3%	14.8%	2.8%

Imports (1986): R 1,479,300,000 (1983 est.; food and other consumer goods 33.5%; fuel 27.5%; transport equipment and other capital goods 25.5%). *Major import sources:* South Africa (75–100%).
Exports (1986): R 1,991,000,000 (minerals 82.6%, of which diamonds 30.9%; agricultural products 7.7%, of which cattle 4.1%, karakul pelts 0.9%). *Major export destinations:* United States 25%; South Africa 19%; Japan 15%.

Transport and communications

Transport. Railroads[10]: length (1988) 1,481 mi, 2,383 km; (1983) metric ton-km cargo 4,900,000,000. Roads (1986): total length 34,230 mi, 55,088 km (paved 9%[11]). Number of registered motor vehicles (1986): 103,715. Merchant marine: vessels (100 gross tons and over), none. Air transport (1987–88)[12]: passengers handled 318,222; cargo handled 2,200 metric tons[4]; airports (1989) with scheduled flights 7.
Communications. Daily newspapers (1988): total number 3; total circulation 8,700; circulation per 1,000 population 7.0. Radio (1987): 220,000 receivers (1 per 5.8 persons). Television (1987–88): 29,072 receivers (1 per 42 persons). Telephones (1986): 69,273 (1 per 17 persons).

Education and health

Education (1987)

	schools	teachers	students	student/ teacher ratio
Primary (age 6–12) } Secondary (age 13–19)	1,122	11,945	281,000 } 83,000	30.5
Voc., teacher tr.	5	81[13]	1,200[13]	14.8[13]
Higher	1	170	4,200	24.7

Educational attainment (1977). Percent of labour force having: no formal schooling 59.8%; primary education 33.2%; secondary 5.0%; higher 2.0%.
Literacy (1985): total population age 15 and over literate 474,000 (72.5%); males literate 239,000 (74.2%); females literate 235,000 (70.8%).
Health (1988): physicians 281 (1 per 4,450 persons); hospital beds 7,540 (1 per 166 persons); infant mortality rate per 1,000 live births (1985–90) 106.
Food (1979–81): daily per capita caloric intake 2,197 (vegetable products 77%, animal products 23%); 96% of FAO recommended minimum requirement.

Military

Total active duty personnel[14] (1989): none. *Military expenditure as percent of GNP* (1984): 7.7% (world 5.9%); per capita expenditure U.S.$113.

[1]The former (1985–89) National Assembly dissolved itself Feb. 24, 1989, and transferred its responsibilities to the South African-appointed administrator-general for the duration of the independence transition period. The 72-member Constituent Assembly elected Nov. 7–11, 1989, has the sole responsibility of drafting the independence constitution. [2]Excludes area and population of Walvis Bay (part of South Africa), administered as part of South West Africa/Namibia until 1977. [3]January 1. [4]1984. [5]1987. [6]Other includes services. [7]Detail does not add to total given because of rounding. [8]Formal sector only. [9]Windhoek only. [10]Transferred from South African administration to Namibian National Transport Corp., July 1988. [11]1985. [12]Two largest airports only. [13]1982. [14]The South West Africa Territory Force (SWATF) is allegedly disbanded; during the transition period, 1,500 South African and 4,470 United Nations troops will remain in the country.

Spain

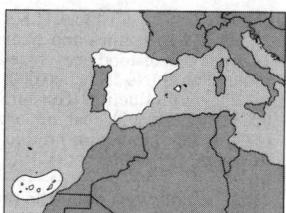

Official name: Reino de España (Kingdom of Spain).
Form of government: constitutional monarchy with two legislative houses (Senate [257[1]]; Congress of Deputies [350]).
Chief of state: King.
Head of government: Prime Minister.
Capital: Madrid.
Official language: Spanish.
Official religion: none.
Monetary unit: 1 peseta (Pta) = 100 céntimos; valuation (Oct. 2, 1989)
1 U.S.$ = Ptas 119.00;
1 £ = Ptas 192.55.

Area and population

Autonomous communities	Capitals	area sq mi	area sq km	population 1988 estimate
Andalucía	Seville	33,694	87,268	6,823,517
Aragón	Zaragoza	18,398	47,650	1,208,474
Asturias	Oviedo	4,079	10,565	1,134,772
Baleares	Palma de Mallorca	1,936	5,014	673,351
Canarias	Santa Cruz de Tenerife	2,796	7,242	1,453,330
Cantabria	Santander	2,042	5,289	527,887
Castilla-La Mancha	Toledo	30,591	79,230	1,693,068
Castilla-León	Valladolid	36,368	94,193	2,625,027
Cataluña	Barcelona	12,328	31,930	6,099,319
Extremadura	Mérida	16,063	41,602	1,097,801
Galicia	Santiago de Compostela	11,365	29,434	2,848,358
La Rioja	Logroño	1,944	5,034	258,805
Madrid	Madrid	3,087	7,995	4,925,005
Murcia	Murcia	4,370	11,317	1,015,187
Navarra	Pamplona	4,023	10,421	520,124
País Vasco	Vitoria	2,803	7,261	2,195,919
Valencia	Valencia	8,998	23,305	3,769,428
TOTAL SPAIN		**194,885**	**504,750**	**38,869,372**
Enclaves in Northern Morocco				
Ceuta	—	7.1	18.5	}126,784
Melilla	—	5.4	14.0	
Other enclaves	(*plazas de soberanía*)	0.26	0.66	...
TOTAL		**194,897.79[2]**	**504,783.16**	**38,996,156**

Demography

Population (1989): 39,159,000.
Density (1989): persons per sq mi 200.9, persons per sq km 77.6.
Urban–rural (1985): urban 75.8%; rural 24.2%.
Sex distribution (1988): male 49.10%; female 50.90%.
Age breakdown (1985): under 15, 24.6%; 15–29, 24.2%; 30–44, 18.5%; 45–59, 16.8%; 60–74, 11.6%; 75 and over, 4.3%.
Population projection: (2000) 40,746,000; (2010) 41,194,000.
Doubling time: n.a.; doubling time exceeds 100 years.
Ethnolinguistic composition (1980): Spanish 72.8%; Catalan 16.4%; Galician 8.2%; Basque 2.3%; other 0.3%.
Religious affiliation (1980): Roman Catholic 97.0%; Protestant 0.4%; nonreligious and atheist 2.6%.
Major cities (1987)[3]: Madrid 3,100,507; Barcelona 1,703,744; Valencia 732,491; Sevilla 655,435; Zaragoza 575,317.

Vital statistics

Birth rate per 1,000 population (1986): 11.2 (world avg. 27.1).
Death rate per 1,000 population (1986): 7.9 (world avg. 9.9).
Natural increase rate per 1,000 population (1986): 3.3 (world avg. 17.2).
Total fertility rate (avg. births per childbearing woman; 1985–90): 1.7.
Marriage rate per 1,000 population (1986): 5.3.
Life expectancy at birth (1985–90): male 73.6 years; female 79.7 years.
Major causes of death per 100,000 population (1985): circulatory diseases 363.3; malignant neoplasms (cancers) 178.6; respiratory diseases 74.8.

National economy

Budget (1989). Revenue: Ptas 8,737,000,000,000 (indirect taxes 42.9%, personal income taxes 34.4%, direct taxes on enterprises 11.4%). Expenditures: Ptas 8,064,000,000,000 (current transfers 58.7%, wages and salaries 23.5%).
Production (metric tons except as noted). Agriculture, forestry, fishing (1987): barley 9,602,000, sugar beets 7,908,000, grapes 6,181,000, wheat 5,768,000, potatoes 5,379,000, corn (maize) 3,555,000, oranges 2,359,000, tomatoes 2,347,000, onions 1,104,000, apples 1,039,000, oats 503,000; livestock (number of live animals) 17,177,000 sheep, 14,000,000 pigs, 4,954,000 cattle, 2,800,000 goats; roundwood 17,539,000 cu m; fish catch 1,393,362. Mining and quarrying (metal content in metric tons; 1987): iron ore 2,244,000, zinc 231,600, lead 78,840, copper 11,160. Manufacturing (value added, in Ptas '000,000; 1985): machinery and transport equipment 1,673,999, of which electrical equipment 354,144, transport equipment 350,144; food and beverage products 1,061,024; chemicals and chemical products 618,325; paper and paper products 364,622; textiles 246,202; wood and cork products 228,207, of which furniture 106,375; clothing and footwear 226,018. Construction (1987): dwellings 200,775. Energy production (consumption): electricity (kW-hr; 1987) 133,168,000,000 (131,635,000,000); coal (metric tons; 1987) 34,953,000 (45,452,000); crude petroleum (barrels; 1987) 12,310,000 (336,858,000); petroleum products (metric tons; 1987) 41,426,000 (31,376,000); natural gas (cu m; 1987) 687,009,000 (3,024,600,000).
Gross national product (1987): U.S.$233,417,000,000 (U.S.$6,010 per capita).

Structure of gross domestic product and labour force

	1987 in value Ptas '000,000	1987 % of total value	1987 labour force	1987 % of labour force
Agriculture	1,941,000	5.4	1,979,900	13.8
Mining	} 11,034,000	} 30.9	88,000	0.6
Manufacturing			2,908,500	20.3
Public utilities	...	...	80,800	0.6
Construction	2,860,000	8.0	1,187,400	8.3
Transp. and commun.			673,000	4.7
Trade	} 16,303,000	} 45.6	2,497,200	17.5
Finance			567,900	4.0
Services				
Pub. admin., defense	5,142,000	14.4 }	2,836,400	19.8
Other	−1,567,000[4]	−4.4[4]	1,487,000[5]	10.4[5]
TOTAL	35,714,000[2]	100.0[2]	14,306,600[2]	100.0

Public debt (1986): Ptas 12,611,300,000,000 (U.S.$95,253,000,000).
Tourism (1987): receipts from visitors U.S.$14,760,000,000; expenditures by nationals abroad U.S.$1,938,000,000.
Population economically active (1987): total 14,306,600; activity rate of total population 36.8% (participation rates: ages 16–64, 58.6%; female 33.0%; unemployed 20.5%).

Price and earnings indexes (1985 = 100)

	1982	1983	1984	1985	1986	1987	1988
Consumer price index	73.6	82.6	91.9	100.0	108.8	114.5	120.0
Monthly earnings index	70.0	80.5	90.6	100.0	110.1	119.7	129.1

Household income and expenditure. Average household size (1983) 2.8; income per household Ptas 1,250,000 (U.S.$8,700); sources of income (1984): wages and salaries 52.3%, profits and self-employment 28.6%, social security 16.8%; expenditure (1986): food 27.2%, housing 15.2%, transportation 13.8%, clothing and footwear 7.2%, household goods and services 7.0%.
Land use (1986): forested 31.3%; meadows and pastures 20.6%; agricultural and under permanent cultivation 40.9%; other 7.2%.

Foreign trade

Balance of trade (current prices)

Ptas '000,000	1983	1984	1985	1986	1987	1988
	−1,105.5	−588.3	−686.9	−814.5	−1,493.0	−1,954.7
% of total	16.3%	7.2%	7.7%	9.7%	15.1%	17.2%

Imports (1988): Ptas 7,039,512,000,000 (transport equipment 11.7%, agricultural and food products 10.1%, chemicals and chemical products 3.7%, optical instruments 3.0%). *Major import sources* (1987): West Germany 16.1%; France 12.8%; Italy 8.8%; U.S. 8.3%; U.K. 7.0%.
Exports (1988): Ptas 4,686,312,000,000 (transport equipment 17.2%, agricultural and food products 15.6%, chemicals and chemical products 3.0%). *Major export destinations* (1987): France 18.8%; West Germany 12.0%; U.K. 9.5%; Italy 8.9%; U.S. 8.2%.

Transport and communications

Transport. Railroads (1988): route length (1987) 7,898 mi, 12,710 km; passenger-km 15,720,000,000; metric ton-km cargo 11,724,000,000. Roads (1987): total length 197,609 mi, 318,022 km (paved 56%). Vehicles (1987): passenger cars 10,318,526; trucks and buses 1,864,475. Merchant marine (1988): vessels (100 gross tons and over) 2,343; total deadweight tonnage 7,263,227. Air transport (1987): passenger-km 22,212,000,000; metric ton-km cargo 630,000,000; airports (1989) with scheduled flights 30.
Communications. Daily newspapers (1987): total number 106; total circulation 2,970,000[6]; circulation per 1,000 population 76[6]. Radio (1988): 11,819,741 receivers (1 per 3.4 persons). Television (1988): 14,870,518 receivers (1 per 2.6 persons). Telephones (1987): 15,476,776 (1 per 2.5 persons).

Education and health

Education (1986–87)

	schools	teachers	students	student/ teacher ratio
Primary (age 6–13)	23,105[7]	220,980	5,575,519	25.2
Secondary (age 14–17)	2,632	74,918	1,278,206	17.1
Vocational	2,184	50,933	751,995	14.8
Higher[8]	33	34,378[9]	826,306	...

Educational attainment (1981). Percent of population age 25 and over having: less than primary education 46.1%, of which illiterate or no formal schooling 34.5%; primary 34.0%; lower secondary 9.3%; upper secondary 3.3%; higher 7.1%. *Literacy* (1983): total population age 15 and over literate 26,004,225 (92.8%); males literate 12,950,282 (95.9%); females literate 13,053,943 (89.9%).
Health: physicians (1987) 135,406 (1 per 287 persons); hospital beds (1986) 181,794 (1 per 213 persons); infant mortality rate per 1,000 live births (1985) 8.5.
Food (1984–86): daily per capita caloric intake 3,365 (vegetable products 72%, animal products 28%); 136% of FAO recommended minimum.

Military

Total active duty personnel (1988): 309,500 (army 75.0%, navy 14.5%, air force 10.5%). *Military expenditure as percent of GNP* (1987): 2.4% (world 5.4%); per capita expenditure U.S.$177.

[1]Includes 49 nonelective seats. [2]Detail does not add to total given because of rounding. [3]For *municipios*, which may contain rural. [4]Import taxes and imputed bank service charges. [5]Includes 1,113,700 unemployed persons not previously employed. [6]For 77 newspapers only. [7]1982–83. [8]1984–85. [9]1985–86.

Sri Lanka

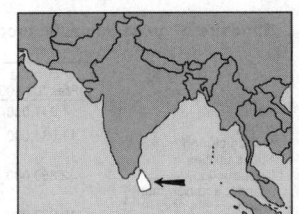

Official name: Sri Lankā Praja-thanthrika Samajavadi Janarajaya (Sinhalese); Ilangai Jananayaka Social-isa Kudiarasu (Tamil) (Democratic Socialist Republic of Sri Lanka).
Form of government: unitary multiparty republic with one legislative house (Parliament [225]).
Head of state and government: President.
Capitals: Colombo (administrative); Sri Jayawardenapura Kotte (legislative and judicial).
Official languages: Sinhalese; Tamil.
Official religion: none.
Monetary unit: 1 Sri Lanka rupee (SL Rs) = 100 cents; valuation (Oct. 2, 1989) 1 U.S.$ = SL Rs 40.17; 1 £ = SL Rs 65.00.

Area and population		area		population
				1988
Districts	**Capitals**	sq mi	sq km	estimate
Amparai	Amparai	1,705	4,415	456,000
Anuradhapura	Anuradhapura	2,772	7,179	682,000
Badulla	Badulla	1,104	2,861	689,000
Batticaloa	Batticaloa	1,102	2,854	393,000
Colombo	Colombo	270	699	1,886,000
Galle	Galle	638	1,652	907,000
Gampaha	Gampaha	536	1,387	1,493,000
Hambantota	Hambantota	1,007	2,609	494,000
Jaffna	Jaffna	396	1,025	846,000
Kalutara	Kalutara	617	1,598	915,000
Kandy	Kandy	749	1,940	1,217,000
Kegalle	Kegalle	654	1,693	733,000
Kilinochchi	Kilinochchi	494	1,279	95,000
Kurunegala	Kurunegala	1,859	4,816	1,373,000
Mannar	Mannar	771	1,996	125,000
Matale	Matale	770	1,993	405,000
Matara	Matara	495	1,283	743,000
Monaragala	Monaragala	2,177	5,639	333,000
Mullaitivu	Mullaitivu	1,010	2,617	90,000
Nuwara Eliya	Nuwara Eliya	672	1,741	526,000
Polonnaruwa	Polonnaruwa	1,271	3,293	305,000
Puttalam	Puttalam	1,186	3,072	571,000
Ratnapura	Ratnapura	1,264	3,275	896,000
Trincomalee	Trincomalee	1,053	2,727	302,000
Vavuniya	Vavuniya	759	1,967	111,000
TOTAL		25,332	65,610	16,586,000

Demography

Population (1989): 16,855,000.
Density (1989): persons per sq mi 665.4, persons per sq km 256.9.
Urban–rural (1985): urban 21.1%; rural 78.9%.
Sex distribution (1987): male 50.97%; female 49.03%.
Age breakdown (1987): under 15, 35.3%; 15–24, 21.0%; 25–44, 26.5%; 45–59, 10.6%; 60–69, 4.0%; 70 and over, 2.6%.
Population projection: (2000) 19,256,000; (2010) 21,303,000.
Doubling time: 44 years.
Ethnic composition (1981): Sinhalese 74.0%; Tamil 18.2%; Sri Lankan Moor 7.1%; other 0.7%.
Religious affiliation (1981): Buddhist 69.3%; Hindu 15.5%; Muslim 7.6%; Christian 7.5%; other 0.1%.
Major cities (1986): Colombo 683,000; Dehiwala–Mount Lavinia 191,000; Moratuwa 143,000; Jaffna 138,000; Sri Jayawardenepura Kotte 104,000.

Vital statistics

Birth rate per 1,000 population (1988): 22.3 (world avg. 27.1); (1982) legitimate 94.6%; illegitimate 5.4%.
Death rate per 1,000 population (1988): 6.0 (world avg. 9.9).
Natural increase rate per 1,000 population (1988): 16.3 (world avg. 17.2).
Total fertility rate (avg. births per childbearing woman; 1988): 2.7.
Marriage rate per 1,000 population (1986): 7.9.
Divorce rate per 1,000 population (1983): 0.1.
Life expectancy at birth (1988): male 68.4 years; female 72.6 years.
Major causes of death per 100,000 population (1982): diseases of the circulatory system 84.7; injury and poisoning 64.9%; infectious and parasitic diseases 50.4; respiratory diseases 43.2[1]; malignant neoplasms (cancers) 24.6.

National economy

Budget (1988). Revenue: SL Rs 51,225,000,000 (general sales and turnover tax 24.6%, import duties 24.4%, nontax revenue 12.6%, excise taxes 11.1%, grants 9.8%, income taxes 9.5%). Expenditures: SL Rs 72,534,000,000 (public-debt service 16.5%, general public services 15.0%, social security 8.4%, civil administration 6.3%, defense 6.2%, education 5.9%, economic services 4.1%, health 3.5%).
Public debt (external, outstanding; 1987): U.S.$4,109,000,000.
Tourism (1987): receipts U.S.$82,000,000; expenditures U.S.$44,000,000.
Production (metric tons except as noted). Agriculture, forestry, fishing (1988): rice 2,466,000, coconuts 1,440,000, sugarcane 720,000, cassava 420,000, tea 225,000, rubber 125,000, sweet potatoes 75,000, copra 65,000; livestock (number of live animals) 1,820,000 cattle, 1,050,000 buffalo, 503,000 goats; roundwood (1987) 8,814,000 cu m; fish catch (1987) 190,002. Mining and quarrying (1986): ilmenite 129,907; clays 110,322; salt 104,278; rutile 8,443;

graphite 7,453; gemstones U.S.$23,304,000. Manufacturing (value added, in SL Rs; 1987): textiles and wearing apparel 15,428,000,000; petrochemicals 13,477,000,000; food, beverages, and tobacco 12,962,000,000; nonmetallic mineral products 2,156,000,000. Construction (1985): residential 833,200 sq m. Energy production (consumption): electricity (kW-hr; 1987) 2,707,000,-000 (2,707,000,000); coal, none (none); crude petroleum (barrels; 1987) none (12,484,000); petroleum products (metric tons; 1987) 1,536,000 (1,235,000).
Gross national product (1987): U.S.$6,560,000,000 (U.S.$400 per capita).

Structure of gross domestic product and labour force				
	1987		1985	
	in value SL Rs '000,000	% of total value	labour force	% of labour force
Agriculture	43,067.2	22.6	2,530,967	42.4
Mining	2,120.4	1.1	66,726	1.1
Manufacturing	29,937.3	15.7	648,469	10.9
Construction	14,304.8	7.5	226,913	3.8
Public utilities	3,007.5	1.6	21,484	0.3
Transp. and commun.	20,293.6	10.7	220,025	3.7
Trade	37,072.7	19.5	513,872	8.6
Finance	11,295.3	6.0	65,094	1.1
Pub. admin., defense	12,689.7	6.7 }	631,408	10.6
Services	5,012.5	2.6 }		
Other	11,394.0	6.0	1,047,043[3]	17.5[3]
TOTAL	190,197.0[2]	100.0	5,972,001	100.0

Population economically active: total (1985) 5,972,001; activity rate 37.7% (participation rates: ages 15–64, 61.0%; female 32.8%; unemployed 14.1%).

Price and earnings indexes (1985 = 100)						
	1982	1983	1984	1985	1986	1987	1988
Consumer price index	74.1	84.5	98.5	100.0	108.0	116.3	132.6
Average wage index[4]	66.3	72.6	91.5	100.0	105.3	110.5	138.3

Household income and expenditure. Average household size (1981) 5.2; income per household (1973) SL Rs 3,936 (U.S.$611); sources of income (1985): wages 54.1%, property income 34.3%, government transfers 11.6%; expenditure (1985): food and beverages 47.9%, transportation 15.8%, clothing 6.8%, housing and energy 5.7%, recreation 3.5%, health 1.5%.
Land use (1987): forested 27.0%; meadows and pastures 6.8%; agricultural and under permanent cultivation 29.1%; other 37.1%.

Foreign trade

Balance of trade (current prices)						
	1983	1984	1985	1986	1987	1988
SL Rs '000,000	−14,519	−3,933	−9,890	−12,773	−13,146	−17,058
% of total	22.4%	5.1%	12.0%	15.8%	13.8%	15.4%

Imports (1987): SL Rs 60,304,000,000 (petroleum 14.5%, machinery and transport equipment 13.4%, sugar 4.0%, cars and cycles 3.7%, paper and paperboard 2.6%). *Major import sources:* Japan 15.0%; U.K. 6.9%; U.S. 5.6%; Iran 5.1%; India 4.1%; China 3.1%.
Exports (1987): SL Rs 39,861,000,000 (tea 26.6%, rubber 7.4%, precious and semiprecious stones 5.7%, desiccated coconut 2.8%, coconut oil 0.6%). *Major export destinations:* U.S. 26.6%; W.Ger. 7.5%; U.K. 5.5%; Japan 5.0%; Pakistan 2.4%.

Transport and communications

Transport. Railroads (1988): route length (1987) 1,453 km; passenger-km 2,069,000,000; metric ton-km cargo 228,000,000. Roads (1985): total length 20,693 km (paved 41%). Vehicles (1987): passenger cars 147,837; trucks and buses 243,913. Merchant marine (1988): vessels (100 gross tons and over) 111; total deadweight tonnage 557,603. Air transport (1988): passenger-km 2,431,350,000; metric ton-km cargo 282,869,000; airports (1989) 1.
Communications. Daily newspapers (1988): total number 14; total circulation 783,900; circulation per 1,000 population 47. Radio (1988): 3,200,000 receivers (1 per 5.1 persons). Television (1988): 500,000 receivers (1 per 33 persons). Telephones (1987): 125,250 (1 per 130 persons).

Education and health

Education (1986)	schools	teachers	students	student/ teacher ratio
Primary (age 5–10)	9,325	146,356	2,304,499	15.7
Secondary (age 11–17)[5]	5,629	113,148	2,930,070	25.9
Voc., teacher tr.	28	1,101[6]	21,771	...
Higher	9[7]	2,549	59,377	23.3

Educational attainment (1981). Percent of population age 25 and over having: no schooling 15.5%; less than complete primary education 12.1%; complete primary 52.3%; postprimary 14.7%; secondary 3.0%; higher 1.1%; unspecified 1.3%. *Literacy (1981):* population age 15 and over literate 86.1%; males literate 90.8%; females literate 81.2%.
Health (1987): physicians 2,341 (1 per 6,989 persons); hospital beds 45,776 (1 per 357 persons); infant mortality rate per 1,000 live births (1988) 33.
Food (1984–86): daily per capita caloric intake 2,436 (vegetable products 96%, animal products 4%); 110% of FAO recommended minimum.

Military

Total active duty personnel (1988): 49,200 (army 81.3%, navy 11.2%, air force 7.5%). *Military expenditure as percent of GNP (1987):* 3.1% (world 5.4%); per capita expenditure U.S.$12.

[1]1981. [2]Detail does not add to total given because of rounding. [3]Includes unemployed. [4]Agricultural minimum rates. [5]1983. [6]1985. [7]Universities only.

Sudan, The

Official name: Jumhūrīyat as-Sūdān (Republic of the Sudan).
Form of government: military regime.
Head of state and government:
President, Command Council of the National Salvation Revolution.
Capital: Khartoum.
Official language: Arabic.
Official religion: situation indeterminate while constitution and Sharī'ah law are in suspension.
Monetary unit: 1 Sudanese pound (LSd) = 100 piastres; valuation (Oct. 2, 1989) 1 U.S.$ = LSd 4.50; 1 £ = LSd 7.28.

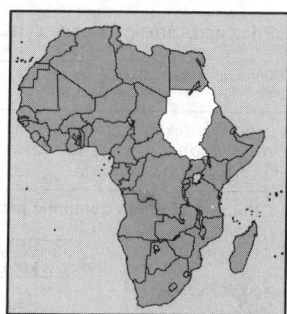

Area and population

Regions Provinces	Capitals	area sq mi	area sq km	population 1983 census
A'ālī an-Nīl (Upper Nile)	Malakāl	92,198	238,792	1,599,605
A'ālī an-Nīl (Upper Nile)	Nāṣir	45,231	117,148	802,354
Junqulī (Jongley)	Bor	46,781	121,164	797,251
Baḥr al-Ghazāl (Bahr el-Ghazal)	Wāu	77,566	200,894	2,265,510
Baḥr al-Ghazāl al-Gharbiyah (Western Bahr el-Ghazal)	Raga			
Baḥr al-Ghazāl ash-Sharqiyah (Eastern Bahr el-Ghazal)	Uwayl	51,960	134,576	1,492,597
al-Buḥayrāh (El Buheyrah)	Rumbek	25,606	66,318	772,913
Dārfūr (Darfur)	al-Fāshir	196,404	508,684	3,093,699
Dārfūr al-Janūbīyah (Southern Darfur)	Nyala	62,753	162,529	1,765,752
Dārfūr ash-Shamālīyah (Northern Darfur)	al-Fāshir	133,651	346,155	1,327,947
al-Istiwā'īyah (Equatoria)	Jūbā	76,436	197,969	1,406,181
al-Istiwā'īyah al-Gharbiyah (Western Equatoria)	Yambio	30,398	78,732	359,056
al-Istiwā'īyah ash-Sharqiyah (Eastern Equatoria)	Jūbā	46,038	119,237	1,047,125
Kurdufān (Kordofan)	al-Ubayyiḍ	146,817	380,255	3,093,294
Kurdufān al-Janūbīyah (Southern Kordofan)	Kāduqlī	61,141	158,355	1,287,525
Kurdufān ash-Shamālīyah (Northern Kordofan)	al-Ubayyiḍ	85,676	221,900	1,805,769
ash-Shamālīyah (Northern)	ad-Dāmir	183,800	476,040	1,083,024
an-Nīl (Nile)	ad-Dāmir	49,167	127,343	649,633
ash-Shamālīyah (Northern)	Dunqulah	134,633	348,697	433,391
ash-Sharqīyah (Eastern)	Kassalā	128,987	334,074	2,208,209
al-Baḥr al-Aḥmar (Red Sea)	Port Sudan	84,912	219,920	695,874
Kassalā (Kassala)	Kassalā	44,075	114,154	1,512,335
al-Wasṭā (Central)	Wad Madanī	53,675	139,017	4,012,543
an-Nīl al-Abyaḍ (White Nile)	ad-Duwaym	16,149	41,825	933,136
al-Jazīrah (El-Gezira)	Wad Madanī	13,536	35,057	2,023,094
an-Nīl al-Azraq (Blue Nile)	ad-Damazin	23,990	62,135	1,056,313
National Capital				
Kharṭūm (Khartoum)	Khartoum	10,875	28,165	1,802,299
TOTAL		966,757[1]	2,503,890	20,564,364

Demography

Population (1989): 27,268,000.
Density (1989): persons per sq mi 28.2, persons per sq km 10.9.
Urban–rural (1985): urban 29.4%; rural 70.6%.
Sex distribution (1985): male 50.13%; female 49.87%.
Age breakdown (1985): under 15, 44.6%; 15–29, 26.0%; 30–44, 15.7%; 45–59, 8.9%; 60–74, 4.0%; 75 and over, 0.8%.
Population projection: (2000) 37,607,000; (2010) 49,063,000.
Doubling time: 24 years.
Ethnic composition (1983): Sudanese Arab 49.1%; Dinka 11.5%; Nuba 8.1%; Beja 6.4%; Nuer 4.9%; Azande 2.7%; Bari 2.5%; Fur 2.1%; Shilluk 1.7%; Lotuko 1.5%; other 9.5%.
Religious affiliation (1980): Sunnī Muslim 73.0%; traditional beliefs 16.7%; Roman Catholic 5.6%; Anglican 2.3%; other 2.4%.
Major cities (1983): Omdurman 526,287; Khartoum 476,218; Khartoum North 341,146; Port Sudan 206,727; Wad Madanī 141,065.

Vital statistics

Birth rate per 1,000 population (1985–90): 44.6 (world avg. 27.1).
Death rate per 1,000 population (1985–90): 15.8 (world avg. 9.9).
Natural increase rate per 1,000 population (1985–90): 28.8 (world avg. 17.2).
Total fertility rate (avg. births per childbearing woman; 1985–90): 6.4.
Life expectancy at birth (1985–90): male 48.6 years; female 51.0 years.
Major causes of death per 100,000 population (1979)[2]: pneumonia 26.4; tuberculosis 1.8; meningitis 1.3; infectious hepatitis 1.1.

National economy

Budget (1988–89). Revenue: LSd 5,885,000,000 (1987–88; tax revenue 60.9%; nontax revenue 34.5%). Expenditures: LSd 9,767,000,000 (current expenditures 77.1%; development budget 22.6%, of which agriculture 6.2%, transport and communications 3.5%, energy and mining 0.5%).
Public debt (external, outstanding; 1987): U.S.$8,248,000,000.
Tourism (1987): receipts from visitors U.S.$14,000,000; expenditures by nationals abroad U.S.$51,000,000.
Production (metric tons except as noted). Agriculture, forestry, fishing (1988): sorghum 4,640,000, sugarcane 4,500,000, millet 550,000, peanuts (groundnuts) 527,000, seed cotton 394,000, sesame seeds 278,000, cotton lint 130,000, yams 120,000, cassava 65,000; livestock (number of live animals)

22,500,000 cattle, 19,000,000 sheep, 13,500,000 goats, 2,850,000 camels; roundwood (1987) 20,678,000 cu m; fish catch (1987) 24,000. Mining and quarrying (1987): salt 40,000; chromite concentrate 20,000; gypsum and anhydrite 7,000. Manufacturing (1986–87): refined sugar 471,889; wheat flour 342,800; cement 198,800; plastics 12,195, yarn 9,700, perfumes 2,500; textiles 58,600,000 metres; shoes 9,000,000 pairs[3]; cigarettes 1,700,000,000 units[3]; tires and tubes 695,600 units. Construction: n.a. Energy production (consumption): electricity (kW-hr; 1987) 1,055,000,000 (1,055,000,000); crude petroleum (barrels; 1987) none (7,370,000); petroleum products (metric tons; 1987) 832,000 (975,000).
Gross national product (1987): U.S.$7,746,000,000 (U.S.$330 per capita).

Structure of gross domestic product and labour force

	1986–87 in value LSd '000,000	1986–87 % of total value	1985 labour force	1985 % of labour force
Agriculture	7,138.3	34.4	4,786,000	68.5
Mining				
Manufacturing }	1,475.8	7.1		
Construction	1,130.0	5.4	587,000	8.4
Public utilities	420.8	2.0		
Transp. and commun.	2,212.0	10.7		
Trade and finance	3,038.2	14.6		
Pub. admin., defense }	5,348.7	25.8	1,618,000	23.1
Services				
TOTAL	20,763.8	100.0	6,991,000	100.0

Population economically active (1985): total 6,991,000; activity rate of total population 32.4% (participation rates: over age 15–64, 55.6%; female 20.8%; unemployed, n.a.).

Price indexes (1985 = 100)

	1982	1983	1984	1985	1986	1987	1988[4]
Consumer price index	39.3	51.3	68.8	100.0	124.4	150.7	190.8

Household income and expenditure. Average household size (1980) 5.3; income per household: n.a.; sources of income: n.a.; expenditure (1981): food, beverages, and tobacco 62.9%, housing 9.8%, clothing 5.7%, health 5.3%, household goods 4.7%, energy 4.4%, education 0.8%.
Land use (1987): forested 19.9%; meadows and pastures 23.6%; agricultural and under permanent cultivation 5.3%; desert and other 51.2%.

Foreign trade

Balance of trade (current prices)

	1982	1983	1984	1985	1986	1987
LSd '000,000	−621.3	−791.6	−550.6	−786.5	−1,420.3	−1,115.9
% of total	36.8%	32.8%	25.2%	31.8%	46.0%	27.2%

Imports (1987): LSd 2,612,900,000 (machinery and transport equipment 32.7%, of which transport equipment 14.1%; manufactured goods 19.2%; petroleum products 18.5%; food and tobacco 15.8%; chemicals 9.5%; textiles 3.2%). *Major import sources:* Saudi Arabia 21.0%; U.K. 10.4%; U.S. 10.4%; Japan 7.4%; West Germany 7.3%; Egypt 6.5%.
Exports (1987): LSd 1,497,100,000 (cotton 30.4%; gum arabic 17.8%; sesame seeds 9.0%; sheep and lambs 2.6%). *Major export destinations:* Italy 10.8%; The Netherlands 10.4%; Saudi Arabia 9.5%; United Kingdom 8.2%; West Germany 7.3%; Japan 6.3%; Belgium 5.1%; U.S. 4.7%; France 4.0%.

Transport and communications

Transport. Railroads (1987–88): route length, 5,503 km; passenger-km 357,000,000[5]; metric ton-km cargo 699,000,000[5]. Roads (1985): total length 6,599 km (paved 59%). Vehicles (1985): passenger cars 99,400; trucks and buses 17,211. Merchant marine (1988): vessels (100 gross tons and over) 25; total deadweight tonnage 127,655. Air transport (1988)[6]: passenger-km 671,963,000; metric ton-km cargo 11,757,000; airports (1989) with scheduled flights 10.
Communications. Daily newspapers (1984): total number 6; total circulation 105,000; circulation per 1,000 population 4.6. Radio (1988): 5,737,465 receivers (1 per 4.6 persons). Television (1988): 1,165,780 receivers (1 per 23 persons). Telephones (1988): 76,347 (1 per 338 persons).

Education and health

Education (1985)

	schools	teachers	students	student/ teacher ratio
Primary (age 7–12)	6,675	50,089	1,738,341	34.7
Secondary (age 13–18)	2,167	21,342	525,533	24.6
Voc., teacher tr.	98	1,693	31,054	18.3
Higher	16	2,165	37,367	17.3

Educational attainment, n.a. *Literacy* (1980): total population age 15 and over literate 2,507,200 (21.6%); males 36.5%; females 6.5%.
Health (1981): physicians[7] 2,169 (1 per 9,369 persons); hospital beds 17,328 (1 per 1,110 persons); infant mortality rate (1985–90) 108.
Food (1984–86): daily per capita caloric intake 2,074 (vegetable products 78%, animal products 22%); 88% of FAO recommended minimum.

Military

Total active duty personnel (1989): 72,800 (army 89.3%, navy 2.5%, air force 8.2%). *Military expenditure as percent of GNP* (1987): 2.7% (world 5.4%); per capita expenditure U.S.$10.

[1]Detail does not add to total given because of rounding. [2]Reported by hospitals and dispensaries. [3]1985–86. [4]First quarter. [5]1987. [6]Sudan Airways only. [7]Includes dentists.

Suriname

Official name: Republiek Suriname (Republic of Suriname).
Form of government: multiparty republic with one legislative house (National Assembly [51])[1].
Head of state and government: President[1].
Capital: Paramaribo.
Official language: Dutch.
Official religion: none.
Monetary unit: 1 Suriname guilder (Sf) = 100 cents; valuation (Oct. 2, 1989) 1 U.S.$ = Sf 1.79; 1 £ = Sf 2.89.

Area and population

Districts	Capitals	area[2] sq mi	sq km	population 1980 census[3]
Brokopondo	Brokopondo	8,278	21,440	20,249
Commewijne	Nieuw Amsterdam	1,587	4,110	14,351
Coronie	Totness	626	1,620	2,777
Marowijne	Albina	17,753	45,980	23,402
Nickerie	Nieuw Nickerie	24,946	64,610	34,480
Para	Onverwacht	378	980	14,867
Saramacca	Groningen	9,042	23,420	10,335
Suriname	...	629	1,628	166,494
Town district				
Paramaribo	Paramaribo	12	32	67,905
TOTAL		63,251	163,820	354,860

Demography

Population (1989): 405,000.
Density (1989): persons per sq mi 6.4, persons per sq km 2.5.
Urban–rural (1987): urban 64.7%; rural 35.3%.
Sex distribution (1985): male 49.60%; female 50.40%.
Age breakdown (1985): under 15, 40.2%; 15–29, 36.1%; 30–44, 9.2%; 45–59, 8.4%; 60–74, 4.6%; 75 and over, 1.5%.
Population projection: (2000) 469,000; (2010) 535,000.
Doubling time: 36 years.
Ethnic composition (1983): Indo-Pakistani 37.0%; Suriname Creole 31.3%; Javanese 14.2%; Bush Negro 8.5%; Amerindian 3.1%; Chinese 2.8%; Dutch 1.4%; other 1.7%.
Religious affiliation (1980): Hindu 27.4%; Roman Catholic 22.8%; Muslim 19.6%; Protestant (mostly Moravian) 18.8%; other 11.4%.
Major cities (1980): Paramaribo 67,905[4]; Nieuw Nickerie 6,078; Meerzorg 5,355; Marienburg 3,633.

Vital statistics

Birth rate per 1,000 population (1985–90): 25.9 (world avg. 27.1); legitimate, n.a.; illegitimate, n.a.
Death rate per 1,000 population (1985–89): 6.1 (world avg. 9.9).
Natural increase rate per 1,000 population (1985–89): 19.8 (world avg. 17.2).
Total fertility rate (avg. births per childbearing woman; 1985–90): 3.0.
Marriage rate per 1,000 population (1985): 6.1.
Divorce rate per 1,000 population (1985): 1.5.
Life expectancy at birth (1985–90): male 67.1 years; female 72.1 years.
Major causes of death per 100,000 population (1985): diseases of the circulatory system 149.1, of which ischemic heart disease 51.6, diseases of pulmonary circulation and other forms of heart disease 41.9; malignant neoplasms (cancers) 48.0; diseases of the respiratory system 42.2; ill-defined conditions 67.6.

National economy

Budget (1988). Revenue: Sf 713,000,000 ([1986[5]] tax revenue 75.4%, of which individual income tax 20.9%, import duties 20.0%, corporate tax 14.4%; nontax revenue 24.0%, of which property income 10.5%). Expenditures: Sf 1,124,000,000 ([1986[5]] general public services 30.6%; economic services 25.2%; education 17.6%; social security 6.2%; defense 4.4%; health 3.7%).
Production (metric tons except as noted). Agriculture, forestry, fishing (1988): rice 300,000, sugarcane 45,000, bananas 45,000, coconuts 11,000, oranges 9,000, palm oil 6,800, plantains 5,000, cassava 3,000, tomatoes 1,000, cucumbers 1,000; livestock (number of live animals) 74,000 cattle, 20,000 pigs; roundwood (1987) 196,000 cu m; fish catch (1987) 5,187, of which shrimps 1,107. Mining and quarrying (1987): bauxite 2,522,000; gold 100 troy oz[6]. Manufacturing (1987): cement 40,478; aluminum 1,913[7]; alumina 1,363[7]; sugar 1,210; plywood 1,043 cu m; shoes 206,591 pairs; soft drinks 287,060 hectolitres; beer 123,350 hectolitres; cigarettes 492,000,000 units. Construction (buildings authorized; 1985): residential Sf 46,500,000; nonresidential Sf 8,100,000. Energy production (consumption): electricity (kW-hr; 1987) 1,330,000,000 (1,330,000,000); hard coal (metric tons; 1987) none (1,000); crude petroleum (barrels; 1987) 967,000 (893,000); petroleum products (metric tons; 1987) none (254,000); natural gas, none (none).
Tourism (1987): receipts from visitors U.S.$4,000,000; expenditures by nationals abroad U.S.$8,000,000.
Land use (1987): forested 92.0%; meadows and pastures 0.1%; agricultural and under permanent cultivation 0.4%; other 7.5%.
Population economically active (1985): total 99,240; activity rate of total population 25.9% (participation rates [1980]: ages 10–64, 38.7%; female 27.2%; unemployed [1986] 25.0%).

Price and earnings indexes (1985 = 100)

	1982	1983	1984	1985	1986	1987	1988
Consumer price index[8]	83.3	87.0	90.1	100.0	118.7	182.0	195.4
Earnings index	...	...	...	...	...	...	...

Public debt (external, outstanding; 1986): U.S.$69,600,000.
Gross national product (at current market prices; 1987): U.S.$972,000,000 (U.S.$2,360 per capita).

Structure of gross domestic product and labour force

	1987 in value U.S.$'000,000[9]	1987 % of total value	1985 labour force	1985 % of labour force
Agriculture, forestry	97	10.4	16,700	16.8
Mining	40	4.3	4,600	4.7
Manufacturing	124	13.3	10,960	11.1
Construction	55	5.9	2,800	2.8
Public utilities	33	3.6	1,420	1.4
Transportation and communications	85	9.2	3,830	3.9
Trade	106	11.4	12,840	12.9
Finance, real estate	98	10.5	2,100	2.1
Pub. admin., defense	279	30.0	40,190	40.5
Services	13	1.4	3,800	3.8
TOTAL	930	100.0	99,240	100.0

Household income and expenditure. Average household size (1980) 3.9; income per household: n.a.; sources of income (1975): wages and salaries 74.6%, transfer payments 3.2%, other 22.2%; expenditure[8] (1968–69): food and beverages 40.0%, household furnishings 12.3%, clothing and footwear 11.0%, transport and communications 9.5%, recreation and education 8.4%, energy 6.9%, housing 4.4%, other 7.5%.

Foreign trade

Balance of trade (current prices)

	1982	1983	1984	1985	1986	1987
Sf '000,000	−147.7	−153.8	+17.7	+54.1	−5.0	+17.3
% of total	8.8%	10.5%	1.4%	4.8%	0.6%	1.6%

Imports (1987): Sf 525,400,000 (fuels and lubricants 21.5%, machinery and transport equipment 17.4%). Major import sources: United States 31.2%; The Netherlands 19.7%; Trinidad and Tobago 9.7%; Brazil 8.9%.
Exports (1987): Sf 542,700,000 (alumina 62.4%, shrimps 14.6%, rice 13.0%, bauxite 3.5%, bananas 3.3%, aluminum 1.2%). Major export destinations: The Netherlands 24.7%; Norway 21.8%; United States 20.1%; Japan 13.0%; Brazil 6.9%.

Transport and communications

Transport. Railroads (1987): length[11] 54 mi, 87 km; passengers, n.a.; cargo, n.a. Roads (1985): total length 5,541 mi, 8,917 km (paved 26%). Vehicles (1987): passenger cars 32,102; trucks and buses 12,137. Merchant marine (1988): vessels (100 gross tons and over) 23; total deadweight tonnage 13,706. Air transport (1987)[10]: passenger-mi 231,642,000, passenger-km 372,793,000; short ton-mi cargo 8,211,000, metric ton-km cargo 11,988,000; airports (1989) with scheduled flights 5.
Communications. Daily newspapers (1988): total number 2; total circulation, 23,000; circulation per 1,000 population 58. Radio (1988): total number of receivers 247,741 (1 per 1.6 persons). Television (1988): total number of receivers 40,000 (1 per 10 persons). Telephones (1987): 38,146 (1 per 10 persons).

Education and health

Education (1986–87)

	schools	teachers	students	student/ teacher ratio
Primary (age 6–11)	301	3,984	59,633	14.9
Secondary (age 12–18)	89	1,588	23,217	14.6
Voc., teacher tr.[11]	64	1,283	15,996	12.5
Higher[11]	...	373	2,914	7.8

Educational attainment, n.a. Literacy (1980): total population age 15 and over literate 170,817 (79.2%); males literate 88,351 (83.8%); females literate 82,466 (74.8%).
Health (1985): physicians 219 (1 per 1,798 persons); hospital beds 1,964 (1 per 200 persons); infant mortality rate per 1,000 live births 27.6.
Food (1984–86): daily per capita caloric intake 2,713 (vegetable products 86%, animal products 14%); 120% of FAO recommended minimum requirement.

Military

Total active duty personnel (1989): 3,050[12] (army 88.5%, navy 8.2%, air force 3.3%). Military expenditure as percent of GNP (1986): 2.6% (world 5.5%); per capita expenditure U.S.$81.

[1]Military-influenced Council of State has constitutional powers, in the event of "exceptional circumstances," to annul laws passed by National Assembly. [2]Area excludes 6,809 sq mi (17,635 sq km) of territory disputed with Guyana. [3]Preliminary. [4]1988 metropolitan area 246,000. [5]Revenues and expenditures in 1986 were Sf 498,000,000 and Sf 926,000,000, respectively. [6]1986. [7]Production severely curtailed in 1987 because of civil war. [8]For Paramaribo and environs. [9]At factor cost. [10]SLM (Suriname Airways) only. [11]1984–85. [12]All services are part of the army.

Swaziland

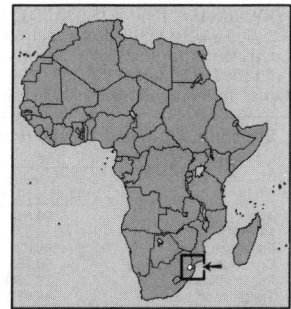

Official name: Umbuso weSwatini (Swazi); Kingdom of Swaziland (English).
Form of government: monarchy with two legislative houses (Senate [20[1]]; House of Assembly [50[1]]).
Head of state and government: King, assisted by Prime Minister.
Capitals: Mbabane (administrative); Lobamba (royal and legislative).
Official languages: Swazi; English.
Official religion: none.
Monetary unit: 1 lilangeni (plural emalangeni [E]) = 100 cents; valuation (Oct. 2, 1989) 1 U.S.$ = E 2.69[2]; 1 £ = E 4.35.

Area and population

Districts	Capitals	area sq mi	area sq km	population 1986 census[3]
Hhohho	Mbabane	1,378	3,569	178,936
Lubombo	Siteki	2,296	5,947	153,958
Manzini	Manzini	1,571	4,068	192,596
Shiselweni	Nhlangano	1,459	3,780	155,569
TOTAL		6,704	17,364	681,059

Demography

Population (1989): 746,000.
Density (1989): persons per sq mi 111.3, persons per sq km 42.9.
Urban-rural (1986): urban 22.8%; rural 77.2%.
Sex distribution (1986): male 47.22%; female 52.78%.
Age breakdown (1986): under 15, 47.3%; 15–29, 26.6%; 30–44, 13.4%; 45–59, 7.4%; 60–74, 3.4%; 75 and over, 1.3%; unknown 0.6%.
Population projection: (2000) 1,082,000; (2010) 1,488,000.
Doubling time: 21 years.
Ethnic composition (1983): Swazi 84.3%; Zulu 9.9%; Tsonga 2.5%; Indian 0.8%; Pakistani 0.8%; Portuguese 0.2%; other 1.5%.
Religious affiliation (1980): Christian 77.0%, of which Protestant 37.3%, Roman Catholic 10.8%; African indigenous 28.9%; traditional beliefs 20.9%; other 2.1%.
Major cities (1986): Manzini 52,000; Mbabane 38,290; Nhlangano 4,108; Piggs Peak 3,223; Siteki 2,271.

Vital statistics

Birth rate per 1,000 population (1985–90): 46.8 (world avg. 27.1); legitimate, n.a.; illegitimate, n.a.
Death rate per 1,000 population (1985–90): 12.5 (world avg. 9.9).
Natural increase rate per 1,000 population (1985–90): 34.3 (world avg. 17.2).
Total fertility rate (avg. births per childbearing woman; 1985–90): 6.4.
Marriage rate per 1,000 population: n.a.
Divorce rate per 1,000 population: n.a.
Life expectancy at birth (1985–90): male 53.7 years; female 57.3 years.
Major causes of death (1985)[4]: respiratory diseases 11.3%; infectious intestinal diseases 10.4%; circulatory diseases 7.5%; tuberculosis 7.1%; malnutrition 6.5%; accidents and injuries 6.0%; perinatal conditions 5.6%.

National economy

Budget (1988–89). Revenue: E 359,700,000 (receipts from Customs Union of Southern Africa 45.1%; tax on income and profits 27.9%; sales tax 10.4%; foreign aid grants 6.4%; property income 3.5%; fees, services, and fines 1.3%). Expenditures: E 369,200,000 (recurrent expenditure 74.0%, of which education 20.8%, general administration 12.1%, economic services 11.5%, justice and police 7.5%, health 7.3%, defense 5.1%, public debt payments 5.0%).
Land use (1986): forested 6.0%; meadows and pastures 63.4%; agricultural and under permanent cultivation 10.5%; other 20.1%.
Tourism (1987): receipts from visitors U.S.$19,000,000; expenditures by nationals abroad U.S.$14,000,000.
Gross national product (at current market prices; 1987): U.S.$496,000,000 (U.S.$700 per capita).

Structure of gross domestic product and labour force

	1986 in value E '000	% of total value	labour force[5]	% of labour force
Agriculture	201,698	21.1	23,072	30.2
Mining	21,477	2.3	2,455	3.2
Manufacturing	166,337	17.4	10,944	14.3
Construction	33,205	3.5	5,210	6.8
Public utilities	26,762	2.8	1,426	1.9
Transp. and commun.	54,882	5.7	5,643	7.4
Trade	99,646	10.4	7,479	9.8
Finance	127,633	13.4	3,469	4.5
Pub. admin., defense	130,156	13.6	} 16,707	} 21.9
Services	24,248	2.5		
Other	69,908[6]	7.3[6]		
TOTAL	955,952	100.0	76,405	100.0

Population economically active (1985): total 273,000; activity rate of total population 42.0% (participation rates: ages 15–64, 72.1%; female 39.9%; unemployed [1983] 4.0%).

Price and earnings indexes (1985 = 100)

	1982	1983	1984	1985	1986	1987	1988
Consumer price index	66.6	73.9	83.5	100.0	111.8	125.7	140.4
Monthly earnings index[7]	172.1	181.3	...	...	...	...	...

Public debt (external, outstanding; 1987): U.S.$272,700,000.
Production (metric tons except as noted). Agriculture, forestry, fishing (1987): sugarcane 4,000,000, corn (maize) 92,000, citrus fruits 82,700, seed cotton 32,000, lint cotton 11,000, roots and tubers 9,000 (of which potatoes 7,000, sweet potatoes 2,000), pulses 3,000; livestock (number of live animals) 655,000 cattle, 275,000 goats, 35,000 sheep, 18,000 pigs, 1,000,000 chickens; roundwood 2,223,000 cu m; fish catch 44. Mining and quarrying (1986): asbestos (1987) 27,929; diamonds 39,144 carats. Manufacturing (value added in E; 1983): paper products 65,068,000; food products and beverages 57,520,000; industrial chemicals 46,043,000; wood products, furniture, and fixtures 18,477,000; metal products 13,452,000; textiles 10,097,000. Construction (value in E; 1986)[8]: residential 11,000,000; nonresidential 5,000,000. Energy production (consumption): electricity (kW-hr; 1986) 149,300,000 (650,000,000); coal (metric tons; 1986) 172,199 (23,408); crude petroleum, n.a. (n.a.); petroleum products, n.a. (n.a.); natural gas, n.a. (n.a.).
Household income and expenditure. Average household size (1980) 5.0; income per household: n.a.; sources of income: n.a.; expenditure[9]: food, beverages, and tobacco 39.3%, transportation and communications 15.3%, clothing and footwear 10.0%, furniture and utensils 9.0%, health and education 8.0%, energy and water 6.5%.

Foreign trade[10]

Balance of trade (current prices)

	1982	1983	1984	1985	1986	1987
E '000,000	−123.6	−177.4	−205.2	−229.2	−198.3	−232.4
% of total	14.9%	20.7%	23.1%	22.9%	15.5%	15.5%

Imports (1986): E 809,204,000 (machinery and transport equipment 15.4%; minerals, fuels, and lubricants 15.4%; manufactured items 11.8%; food and live animals 9.3%; chemicals 6.5%; crude inedible materials 1.6%). *Major import sources* (1986–87): South Africa 90.1%; United Kingdom 3.6%; Australia 1.3%; Japan 1.3%; United States 0.8%.
Exports (1986): E 610,000,000[11] (sugar 33.7%; wood and wood products 20.0%, of which wood pulp 17.1%; minerals, fuels, and lubricants 6.6%; canned fruit and juices 5.0%; manufactured goods 4.5%; beverages and tobacco 0.7%; machinery and transport equipment 0.6%). *Major export destinations:* South Africa 37.8%; United Kingdom 1.1%.

Transport and communications

Transport. Railroads (1987): length 320 mi, 515 km; passengers, n.a.; short ton-mi cargo 73,300,000[12], metric ton-km cargo 107,000,000[12]. Roads (1986): total length 1,773 mi, 2,853 km (paved 18%). Vehicles (1986): passenger cars 20,883; trucks and buses 7,271. Merchant marine: none; landlocked state. Air transport (1984)[13]: passenger-mi 13,977,000, passenger-km 22,494,000; short ton-mi cargo 1,508,000, metric ton-km cargo 2,201,000; airports (1989) with scheduled flights 1.
Communications. Daily newspapers (1986): total number 2; total circulation 16,000; circulation per 1,000 population 24. Radio (1988): total number of receivers 114,682 (1 per 6.3 persons). Television (1988): total number of receivers 12,500 (1 per 58 persons). Telephones (1987): 20,667 (1 per 34 persons).

Education and health

Education (1986–87)

	schools	teachers	students	student/ teacher ratio
Primary (age 6–13)	477	4,462	147,743	33.1
Secondary (age 14–18)	113	1,760	32,942	18.7
Voc., teacher tr.	7	181	1,280	7.1
Higher	1	178	1,270	7.1

Educational attainment (1976). Percent of population age 25 and over having: no formal schooling 53.6%; some primary education 25.4%; complete primary 9.2%; some secondary 7.9%; secondary and higher 3.9%. *Literacy* (1986): total population age 15 and over literate 240,171 (67.0%); males literate 112,578 (69.0%); females literate 127,593 (65.0%).
Health (1984): physicians 80 (1 per 7,971 persons); hospital beds 1,608 (1 per 396 persons); infant mortality rate per 1,000 live births (1985–90) 118.0.
Food (1987): daily per capita caloric intake 2,520 ([1984–86] vegetable products 89%, animal products 11%); (1984) 111% of FAO recommended minimum requirement.

Military

Total active duty personnel (1983): 2,657. *Military expenditure as percent of GNP* (1987): 1.3% (world 5.4%); per capita expenditure U.S.$11.

---

[1]Includes 10 nonelective seats. [2]The lilangeni is at par with the South African rand. [3]Preliminary. [4]Percentage of deaths of known cause at government, mission, and private hospitals. [5]Wage earners only. [6]Includes imputed bank service charges and indirect taxes. [7]Based on earnings of skilled male workers in manufacturing; 1980 = 100. [8]Urban areas under the jurisdiction of the Manzini and Mbabane town councils only. [9]Weights of consumer price index components. [10]Import figures are f.o.b. in balance of trade and c.i.f. in commodities and trading partners. [11]Reexports accounted for 5.6% of all exports. [12]1984. [13]Royal Swazi National Airways only.

Sweden

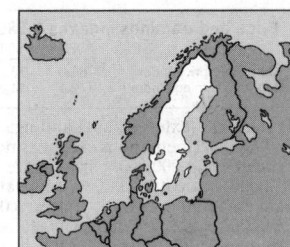

Official name: Konungariket Sverige (Kingdom of Sweden).
Form of government: constitutional monarchy and parliamentary state with one legislative house (Parliament [349]).
Chief of state: King.
Head of government: Prime Minister.
Capital: Stockholm.
Official language: Swedish.
Official religion: Church of Sweden (Lutheran).
Monetary unit: 1 Swedish krona (SKr) = 100 ore; valuation (Oct. 2, 1989) 1 U.S.$ = SKr 6.43; 1 £ = SKr 10.41.

Area and population		area		population
		sq mi	sq km	1989 estimate[1]
Counties	Capitals			
Älvsborg	Vänersborg	4,400	11,395	433,417
Blekinge	Karlskrona	1,136	2,941	149,544
Gävleborg	Gävle	7,024	18,191	287,004
Göteborg och Bohus	Göteborg	1,985	5,141	729,629
Gotland	Visby	1,212	3,140	56,383
Halland	Halmstad	2,106	5,454	247,417
Jämtland	Östersund	19,090	49,443	134,116
Jönköping	Jönköping	3,839	9,944	304,021
Kalmar	Kalmar	4,313	11,170	237,781
Kopparberg	Falun	10,886	28,194	284,407
Kristianstad	Kristianstad	2,350	6,087	283,818
Kronoberg	Växjö	3,266	8,458	175,427
Malmöhus	Malmö	1,907	4,938	763,349
Norrbotten	Luleå	38,191	98,913	261,536
Örebro	Örebro	3,289	8,519	270,031
Östergötland	Linköping	4,078	10,562	396,919
Skaraborg	Mariestad	3,065	7,937	272,126
Södermanland	Nyköping	2,340	6,060	251,423
Stockholm	Stockholm	2,505	6,488	1,617,038
Uppsala	Uppsala	2,698	6,989	260,476
Värmland	Karlstad	6,789	17,584	280,694
Västerbotten	Umeå	21,390	55,401	247,521
Västernorrland	Härnösand	8,370	21,678	259,964
Västmanland	Västerås	2,433	6,302	254,847
TOTAL LAND AREA		158,661[2]	410,929	8,458,888
INLAND WATER		15,071	39,035	
TOTAL		173,732[2]	449,964	

Demography

Population (1989): 8,498,000.
Density (1989)[3]: persons per sq mi 53.3, persons per sq km 20.7.
Urban–rural (1985): urban 83.4%; rural 16.6%.
Sex distribution (1989): male 49.37%; female 50.63%.
Age breakdown (1989): under 15, 17.8%; 15–29, 20.7%; 30–44, 21.8%; 45–59, 16.6%; 60–74, 15.1%; 75 and over, 8.0%.
Population projection: (2000) 8,780,000; (2010) 9,046,000.
Ethnic composition (1988): Swedish 90.8%; Finnish 3.1%; other 6.1%.
Religious affiliation (1987): Church of Sweden 88.9% (nominally; about 30% nonpracticing); Roman Catholic 1.5%; Pentecostal 1.2%; other 8.4%.
Major cities (1989): Stockholm 669,485; Göteborg 430,763; Malmö 231,575; Uppsala 161,828; Örebro 119,824; Norrköping 119,370.

Vital statistics

Birth rate per 1,000 population (1988): 13.3 (world avg. 27.1); (1987) legitimate 50.1%; illegitimate 49.9%.
Death rate per 1,000 population (1988): 9.0 (world avg. 9.9).
Natural increase rate per 1,000 population (1988): 4.3 (world avg. 17.2).
Total fertility rate (avg. births per childbearing woman; 1987): 1.8.
Marriage rate per 1,000 population (1987): 4.9.
Divorce rate per 1,000 population (1987): 2.2.
Life expectancy at birth (1987): male 74.2 years; female 80.2 years.
Major causes of death per 100,000 population (1986): heart disease 424.2; malignant neoplasms (cancers) 231.2; cerebrovascular disease 116.7.

National economy

Budget (1987–88). Revenue: SKr 347,092,000,000 (value-added and excise taxes 42.2%, income and capital gains taxes 25.9%, social-security contributions 15.7%, property taxes 5.0%, nontax revenue 11.2%). Expenditures: SKr 353,567,000,000 (health and social affairs 27.3%, interest on national debt 15.3%, education and culture 13.1%, defense 8.5%).
Public debt (1988): U.S.$81,607,000,000.
Tourism (1987): receipts from visitors U.S.$2,033,000,000; expenditures by nationals abroad U.S.$3,781,000,000.
Production (metric tons except as noted). Agriculture, forestry, fishing (1988): sugar beets 2,353,000, barley 1,942,000, oats 1,402,000, wheat 1,357,000, potatoes 1,241,000; livestock (number of live animals) 2,217,-000 pigs, 1,667,000 cattle, 402,000 sheep; roundwood 53,374,000 cu m; fish catch 214,538, of which Atlantic herring 119,871. Mining and quarrying (1988): iron ore 13,290,000[4], zinc 344,000[5], copper 311,000[5], lead 122,000[5]. Manufacturing (value added, in SKr '000,000; 1986): machinery and transport equipment 102,150, of which automobiles 23,250; food and beverages 23,110, of which meat and dairy products 7,597; paper and paper products 20,099; printing and publishing 14,308. Construction (1987): 30,884 dwellings completed. Energy production (consumption): electricity

(kW-hr; 1987) 146,625,000,000 (142,609,000,000); coal (metric tons; 1987) 25,000 (4,168,000); crude petroleum (barrels; 1987) 21,700 (118,200,000); petroleum products (metric tons; 1987) 14,367,000 (14,136,000); natural gas (cu m; 1987) none (283,300,000).
Gross national product (1987): U.S.$131,142,000,000 (U.S.$15,690 per capita).

Structure of gross domestic product and labour force				
	1987			
	in value SKr '000,000	% of total value	labour force	% of labour force
Agriculture	28,314	3.2	171,000	3.9
Mining	3,375	0.4	12,000	0.3
Manufacturing	206,021	23.5	960,000	21.7
Construction	60,163	6.9	278,000	6.3
Public utilities	28,985	3.3	40,000	0.9
Transp. and commun.	64,682	7.4	310,000	7.0
Trade	110,971	12.7	606,000	13.7
Finance	128,377	14.6	330,000	7.5
Pub. admin., defense } Services	235,601	26.9	204,000 1,423,000	4.6 32.2
Other	9,955[6]	1.1[6]	88,000[7]	2.0[7]
TOTAL	876,444	100.0	4,421,000[2]	100.0[2]

Population economically active (1987): total 4,421,000; activity rate of total population 52.6% (participation rates: ages 16–64, 83.4%; female 48.0%; unemployed 1.9%).

Price and earnings indexes (1985 = 100)							
	1982	1983	1984	1985	1986	1987	1988
Consumer price index	79.2	86.2	93.1	100.0	104.2	108.6	114.9
Hourly earnings index	76.7	82.7	91.7	100.0	107.2	115.1	123.1

Household income and expenditure. Average household size (1985) 2.2; income per household (1983) SKr 98,400 (U.S.$15,165); sources of income (1985): wages and salaries 60.7%, transfer payments 22.0% (includes social security 15.3%), self-employment 17.3%; expenditure (1986): housing 25.8%, food 24.0%, transportation 16.4%, education and recreation 9.9%.
Land use (1987): forested 68.1%; meadows and pastures 1.4%; agricultural and under permanent cultivation 7.2%; other 23.4%.

Foreign trade

Balance of trade (current prices)						
	1983	1984	1985	1986	1987	1988
SKr '000,000	10,150	24,710	16,080	37,910	29,827	31,208
% of total	2.5%	5.4%	3.2%	7.7%	5.6%	5.4%

Imports (1988): SKr 280,200,000,000 (machinery and transport equipment 35.9%, of which transport equipment 12.8%, electrical machinery 9.3%; chemicals 10.2%; food and tobacco products 6.3%; clothing and footwear 5.5%). *Major import sources:* W.Ger. 21.2%; U.K. 8.6%; U.S. 7.5%; Finland 7.0%; Denmark 6.6%; Norway 6.0%.
Exports (1988): SKr 304,970,000,000 (machinery and transport equipment 42.8%, of which transport equipment 15.8%, electrical machinery 8.3%; paper products 11.1%; wood and wood pulp 7.2%; chemicals 7.1%; iron and steel products 6.3%). *Major export destinations:* W.Ger. 12.1%; U.K. 11.2%; U.S. 9.9%; Norway 9.3%; Denmark 6.9%; Finland 6.6%.

Transport and communications

Transport. Railroads (1988): length (1987) 7,279 mi, 11,715 km; passenger-mi 3,706,000,000, passenger-km 5,964,000,000; short ton-mi cargo 12,444,-000,000, metric ton-km cargo 18,168,000,000. Roads (1987): total length 80,897 mi, 130,191 km (paved 70%). Vehicles (1987): passenger cars 3,366,-570; trucks and buses 259,576. Merchant marine (1988): vessels (100 gross tons and over) 633; total deadweight tonnage 1,926,589. Air transport (1987): passenger-mi 3,549,000,000, passenger-km 5,712,000,000; short ton-mi cargo 120,873,000, metric ton-km cargo 176,472,000; airports (1989) 43.
Communications. Daily newspapers (1986): total number 186; total circulation 4,902,000; circulation per 1,000 population 586. Radio (1987): 7,271,-556 receivers (1 per 1.2 persons). Television (1987): 3,292,126 receivers (1 per 2.5 persons). Telephones (1983): 7,410,000 (1 per 1.1 persons).

Education and health

Education (1987–88)				
	schools	teachers	students	student/ teacher ratio
Primary (age 7–9)	4,674	99,030	928,009	9.4
Secondary (age 10–18)	484	29,080	285,116	9.8
Higher	...	25,400	336,995	13.3

Educational attainment (1979). Percent of population age 25 and over having: lower secondary education 7.3%; higher secondary 35.7%; some postsecondary 15.4%. *Literacy* (1988): virtually 100%.
Health (1987): physicians 22,485 (1 per 373 persons); hospital beds 56,848 (1 per 148 persons); infant mortality rate per 1,000 live births (1988) 5.8.
Food (1984–86): daily per capita caloric intake 3,049 (vegetable products 61%, animal products 39%); (1984) 115% of FAO requirement.

Military

Total active duty personnel (1988): 67,000 (army 70.2%, navy 17.9%, air force 11.9%). *Military expenditure as percent of GNP* (1987): 2.9% (world 5.4%); per capita expenditure U.S.$529.

[1]January 1. [2]Detail does not add to total given because of rounding. [3]Density based on land area only. [4]Metal content of ore. [5]Ore concentrates. [6]Includes statistical discrepancies and unallocated indirect taxes. [7]Includes 85,000 unemployed.

Switzerland

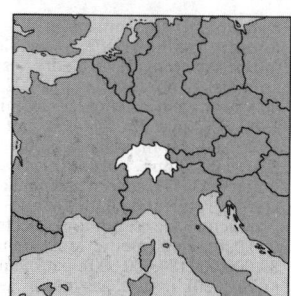

Official name: Confédération Suisse (French); Schweizerische Eidgenossenschaft (German); Confederazione Svizzera (Italian) (Swiss Confederation).
Form of government: federal state with two legislative houses (Council of States [46]; National Council [200]).
Head of state and government: President.
Capital: Bern.
Official languages: French; German; Italian.
Official religion: none.
Monetary unit: 1 Swiss Franc (Sw F) = 100 centimes; valuation (Oct. 2, 1989) 1 U.S.$ = Sw F 1.62; 1 £ = Sw F 2.63.

Area and population

Cantons	Capitals	area sq mi	area sq km	population 1988[1] estimate
Aargau	Aarau	542	1,405	478,511
Appenzell Ausser-Rhoden[2]	Herisau	94	243	49,782
Appenzell Inner-Rhoden[2]	Appenzell	66	172	13,140
Basel-Landschaft[2]	Liestal	165	428	227,126
Basel-Stadt[2]	Basel	14	37	192,559
Bern	Bern	2,335	6,049	928,758
Fribourg	Fribourg	645	1,670	197,175
Genève	Geneva	109	282	365,525
Glarus	Glarus	264	684	36,674
Graubünden	Chur	2,744	7,106	167,143
Jura	Delémont	323	837	64,645
Luzern	Luzern	576	1,492	308,741
Neuchâtel	Neuchâtel	308	797	156,943
Nidwalden[2]	Stans	107	276	31,347
Obwalden[2]	Sarnen	189	491	27,749
Sankt Gallen	Sankt Gallen	778	2,014	407,012
Schaffhausen	Schaffhausen	115	298	70,094
Schwyz	Schwyz	351	908	104,634
Solothurn	Solothurn	305	791	220,252
Thurgau	Frauenfeld	391	1,013	195,219
Ticino	Bellinzona	1,085	2,811	278,647
Uri	Altdorf	416	1,076	33,435
Valais	Sion	2,018	5,226	235,390
Vaud	Lausanne	1,243	3,219	556,942
Zug	Zug	92	239	82,790
Zürich	Zürich	668	1,729	1,136,566
TOTAL		15,943	41,293	6,566,799[3]

Demography

Population (1989): 6,689,000.
Density (1989): persons per sq mi 419.6, persons per sq km 162.0.
Urban-rural (1987): urban 60.4%; rural 39.6%.
Sex distribution (1987): male 49.13%; female 50.87%.
Age breakdown (1988): under 15, 17.1%; 15–29, 22.9%; 30–44, 22.8%; 45–59, 17.8%; 60–74, 12.8%; 75 and over, 6.6%.
Population projection: (2000) 6,911,000; (2010) 6,932,000.
Ethnolinguistic composition (1980): German 65.0%; French 18.4%; Italian 9.8%; Spanish 1.6%; Turkish 0.6%; other 3.8%.
Religious affiliation (1980): Roman Catholic 47.6%; Protestant 44.3%; Jewish 0.3%; other 7.8%.
Major cities (1988): Zürich 346,879 (840,313[4]); Basel 171,574 (363,029[4]); Geneva 161,473 (384,507[4]); Bern 136,292; Lausanne 124,022.

Vital statistics

Birth rate per 1,000 population (1988): 12.3 (world avg. 27.1; 1987); legitimate 94.1%; illegitimate 5.9%.
Death rate per 1,000 population (1988): 9.2 (world avg. 9.9).
Natural increase rate per 1,000 population (1988): 3.1 (world avg. 17.2).
Total fertility rate (avg. births per childbearing woman; 1987): 1.5.
Marriage rate per 1,000 population (1988): 6.8.
Life expectancy at birth (1986–87): male 73.8 years; female 80.5 years.
Major causes of death per 100,000 population (1987): heart disease 265.4, of which ischemic 148.1, other 117.3; malignant neoplasms (cancers) 243.4.

National economy

Budget (1987). Revenue: Sw F 24,902,000,000 (indirect taxes 54.7%, of which sales taxes 31.8%; income and property taxes 38.9%, of which direct federal taxes 21.4%). Expenditures: Sw F 23,846,000,000 (social welfare 22.3%; defense 19.8%; transportation 14.1%; education 9.1%).
National debt (end of year 1987): SwF 27,671,000,000.
Tourism (1988): receipts from visitors U.S.$5,615,000,000; expenditures by nationals abroad U.S.$5,019,000,000.
Production (metric tons except as noted). Agriculture, forestry, fishing (1987): milk 3,700,000, sugar beets 800,000, potatoes 720,000, wheat 460,000, apples 350,000, barley 250,000, grapes 165,000; livestock (number of live animals) 1,973,000 pigs, 1,880,000 cattle; roundwood 4,885,000 cu m; fish catch 4,807. Mining (1987): salt 400,000. Manufacturing (value added in Sw F '000,000; 1985): machinery and transport equipment 10,364; electrical goods, electronics, and optics 8,764; chemicals (all forms) 7,969; metal products 5,711; graphic arts 4,058; food products 3,806; wood products 3,172; watches and jewelry 2,469. Construction (in Sw F '000,000; 1986): residential 14,663; nonresidential 20,151.

Energy production (consumption)[5]: electricity (kW-hr; 1987) 56,976,000,000 (47,521,000,000); coal (metric tons; 1987) none (521,000); crude petroleum (barrels; 1987) none (28,330,000); petroleum products (metric tons; 1987) 3,998,000 (11,076,000); natural gas (cu m; 1987) 8,585,000 (1,659,169,000).
Gross national product (1987): U.S.$138,163,000,000 (U.S.$21,250 per capita).

Structure of gross domestic product and labour force

	1985 in value Sw F '000,000	1985 % of total value	1986 labour force	1986 % of labour force
Agriculture	8,180	3.6	209,200	6.4
Manufacturing, mining	58,625	25.7	966,200	29.8
Construction	17,325	7.6	225,900	7.0
Public utilities	5,023	2.2	21,300	0.7
Transp. and commun.	14,763	6.5	198,500	6.1
Trade	39,742	17.4	603,300	18.6
Finance, insurance[6]	36,994	16.2	303,300	9.3
Pub. admin., defense	26,065	11.4	271,400	8.4
Services	27,933	12.3	419,600	12.9
Other	−6,700[7]	−2.9[7]	25,700[8]	0.8[8]
TOTAL	227,950	100.0	3,244,400	100.0

Population economically active (1986): total 3,244,400; activity rate of total population 49.4% (participation rates: age 15 and over [1984] 58.9%; female 37.2%; unemployed [1988] 0.7%).

Price and earnings indexes (1985 = 100)

	1982	1983	1984	1985	1986	1987	1988
Consumer price index	91.2	93.9	96.7	100.0	100.8	102.2	104.1
Hourly earnings index	90.3	93.8	96.3	100.0	103.6	...	...

Household income and expenditure. Average household size (1981) 2.5; average income per household (1982) Sw F 61,000 (U.S.$30,045); sources of income (1985): wages 64.0%, social security 11.8%, other 24.2%. Expenditure (1987): food 20.8%, housing 18.0%, education and recreation 16.0%, transportation 13.8%, health 7.6%.
Land use (1986): forested 26.4%; meadows and pastures 40.5%; agricultural and under permanent cultivation 10.4%; other 22.7%.

Foreign trade[9]

Balance of trade (current prices)

	1983	1984	1985	1986	1987	1988
Sw F '000,000	−6,871	−7,852	−7,359	−5,781	−6,933	−7,834
% of total	6.0%	6.1%	5.2%	4.1%	4.9%	5.0%

Imports (1987): Sw F 75,171,000,000 (machinery 20.3%, chemical products 11.0%, clothing and textiles 10.1%, precious metals and jewelry 7.4%, tourism vehicles 6.6%). *Major import sources:* W.Ger. 34.3%; France 10.8%; Italy 10.2%; U.K. 6.1%; U.S. 5.3%; Japan 4.6%.
Exports (1987): Sw F 67,477,000,000 (nonelectrical machinery 20.3%, electrical machinery 11.9%, pharmaceuticals 8.1%, precious-metal articles and jewelry 6.9%, watches 6.4%). *Major export destinations:* W.Ger. 21.3%; France 9.1%; U.S. 8.8%; Italy 8.3%; U.K. 7.5%; Japan 3.8%.

Transport and communications

Transport. Railroads (1988): length[10] 3,117 mi, 5,016 km; passenger-km 10,853,000,000[11]; metric ton-km cargo 7,500,000,000[11]. Roads (1987): total length 44,128 mi, 71,018 km. Vehicles (1987): passenger cars 2,732,720; trucks and buses 228,757. Merchant marine (1988): vessels (100 gross tons and over) 25; total deadweight tonnage 434,041. Air transport (1988)[12]: passenger-km 14,325,000,000; metric ton-km cargo 813,400,000; airports (1989) with scheduled flights 5.
Communications. Daily newspapers (1988): total number 96; total circulation 2,869,518; circulation per 1,000 population 429. Radio (1988): 2,553,701 receivers (1 per 2.6 persons). Television (1988): 2,316,413 receivers (1 per 2.9 persons). Telephones (1986): 5,622,976 (1 per 1.2 persons).

Education and health

Education (1987–88)

	schools	teachers	students	student/ teacher ratio
Primary (age 7–12)	...	...	375,300	...
Secondary (age 13–19)	...	...	362,900	...
Voc., teacher tr.	...	...	240,600	...
Higher	...	...	121,700	...

Educational attainment (1970). Percent of population age 25 and over having: no formal schooling 0.4%; primary and lower-secondary education 73.1%; higher-secondary 7.2%; some postsecondary 10.2%; university degree 3.1%. *Literacy:* virtually 100.0%.
Health: physicians (1986) 10,602 (1 per 620 persons); hospital beds (1983) 66,192 (1 per 98 persons); infant mortality rate (1987) 6.8.
Food (1984–86): daily per capita caloric intake 3,432 (vegetable products 59%, animal products 41%); (1984) 128% of FAO recommended minimum.

Military

Total active duty personnel[13] (1988): 605,000 (army 89.6%, air force 10.4%).
Military expenditure as percent of GNP (1987): 2.1% (world 5.4%); per capita expenditure U.S.$563.

[1]January 1. [2]Demicanton; functions as a full canton. [3]Includes 999,688 resident aliens. [4]Population of urban agglomeration; 1986. [5]Includes Liechtenstein. [6]Includes consulting services. [7]Imputed bank charges less import duties. [8]Unemployed. [9]Import figures are f.o.b. in balance of trade and c.i.f. in commodities and trading partners. [10]1986. [11]Swiss Federal Railways. [12]Swissair only. [13]Mobilized personnel.

Syria

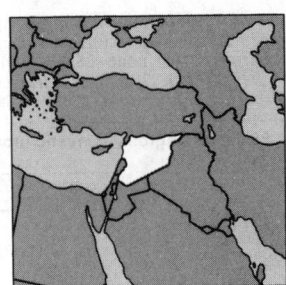

Official name: al-Jumhūrīyah al-'Arabīyah as-Sūrīyah (Syrian Arab Republic).
Form of government: unitary multiparty[1] republic with one legislative house (People's Council [195]).
Head of state and government: President.
Capital: Damascus.
Official language: Arabic.
Official religion: none[2].
Monetary unit: 1 Syrian Pound (LS) = 100 piastres; valuation (Oct. 2, 1989) 1 U.S.$ = LS 11.225; 1£ = LS 18.16.

Area and population

Governorates	Capitals	area sq mi	area sq km	population 1989 estimate
Dar'ā	Dar'ā	1,440	3,730	499,000
Dayr az-Zawr	Dayr az-Zawr	12,765	33,060	517,000
Dimashq	Damascus	6,962	18,032	1,216,000
Ḥalab	Aleppo	7,143	18,500	2,421,000
Ḥamāh	Ḥamāh	3,430	8,883	943,000
al-Ḥasakah	al-Ḥasakah	9,009	23,334	865,000
Ḥimṣ	Homs	16,302	42,223	1,084,000
Idlib	Idlib	2,354	6,097	777,000
al-Lādhiqiyah	Latakia	887	2,297	712,000
al-Qunayṭirah	al-Qunayṭirah	719[3]	1,861[3]	37,000
ar-Raqqah	ar-Raqqah	7,574	19,616	450,000
as-Suwaydā'	as-Suwaydā'	2,143	5,550	256,000
Ṭarṭūs	Ṭarṭūs	730	1,892	581,000
Municipality				
Dimashq	—	41	105	1,361,000
TOTAL		71,498[3]	185,180[3]	11,719,000

Demography

Population (1989): 11,719,000.
Density (1989): persons per sq mi 163.9, persons per sq km 63.3.
Urban–rural (1988): urban 50.0%; rural 50.0%.
Sex distribution (1988): male 51.09%; female 48.91%.
Age breakdown (1988): under 15, 49.3%; 15–29, 22.4%; 30–44, 14.3%; 45–59, 7.5%; 60–74, 4.8%; 75 and over, 1.7%.
Population projection: (2000) 16,857,000; (2010) 22,533,000.
Doubling time: 21 years.
Ethnic composition (1981): Arab 88.8%; Kurdish 6.3%; other 4.9%.
Religious affiliation (1980): Muslim (mostly Sunnī) 89.6%; Christian 8.9%; other 1.5%.
Major cities (1989): Damascus 1,361,000; Aleppo 1,308,000; Homs 464,000; Latakia 258,000; Ḥamāh 214,000[4].

Vital statistics

Birth rate per 1,000 population (1985–90): 44.1 (world avg. 27.1).
Death rate per 1,000 population (1985–90): 7.0 (world avg. 9.9).
Natural increase rate per 1,000 population (1985–90): 37.1 (world avg. 17.2).
Total fertility rate (avg. births per childbearing woman; 1985–90): 6.8.
Marriage rate per 1,000 population (1987)[5]: 8.0.
Divorce rate per 1,000 population (1987)[5]: 0.7.
Life expectancy at birth (1985–90): male 63.2 years; female 66.9 years.
Major causes of death per 100,000 population (1981): signs, symptoms, and ill-defined conditions 207.3; diseases of the circulatory system 60.7; infectious and parasitic diseases 15.1.

National economy

Budget (1988). Revenue: LS 51,545,000,000 (taxes and duties 32.6%, of which direct taxes 24.0%; budget surplus carryover 23.4%; loans and assistances 12.1%; special revenues 3.2%). Expenditures: LS 51,545,000,000 (defense 28.2%; administration 14.6%; agriculture 9.0%; education 8.1%; transport and communications 3.3%).
Public debt (external, outstanding; 1987): U.S.$3,648,000,000.
Tourism (1987): receipts from visitors U.S.$477,000,000; expenditures by nationals abroad U.S.$250,000,000.
Gross national product (at current market prices; 1987): U.S.$20,421,000,000 (U.S.$1,820 per capita).

Structure of gross domestic product and labour force

	1987 in value LS '000,000	1987 % of total value	1986 labour force	1986 % of labour force
Agriculture	34,369	27.2	745,550	30.0
Mining	17,099	13.5	3,936	0.2
Manufacturing			330,223	13.3
Construction	6,772	5.3	385,967	15.5
Public utilities	...	...	25,966	1.0
Transportation and communications	11,793	9.3	157,595	6.3
Trade	29,719	23.5	257,887	10.4
Finance	5,545	4.4	22,572	0.9
Pub. admin.	17,808	14.1	558,510	22.4
Services	3,220	2.6		
TOTAL	126,325	100.0[6]	2,488,206	100.0

Production (value added in LS '000,000 except as noted). Agriculture, forestry, fishing (1987): vegetables 8,290.7, fruits 7,625.1, cereals 7,569.0, industrial crops 3,696.0, dry legumes 1,441.8; livestock (number of live animals) 12,669,000 sheep, 1,002,000 goats, 710,000 cattle; roundwood 48,000 cu m; fish catch 4,850. Mining and quarrying (1987): phosphate rock 1,985,000; gypsum 248,000; salt 81,000; asphalt 54,000; sand and gravel 13,122,000 cu m; stone 608,000 cu m. Manufacturing (tons; 1987): cement 3,870,000; flour 1,016,000; sugar 108,000; fertilizers 101,000; glass and pottery 43,000; soap 41,000; silk and cotton textiles 25,000. Construction (1987): residential 3,912,000 sq m; nonresidential 382,000 sq m. Energy production (consumption): electricity (kW-hr; 1987) 7,161,000,000 (7,031,000,000); coal (metric tons) none (none); crude petroleum (barrels; 1987) 89,000,000 (84,000,000); petroleum products (metric tons; 1987) 10,086,000 (7,769,000); natural gas (cu m; 1987) 189,640,000 (189,640,000).
Population economically active (1986): total 2,488,000; activity rate of total population 23.2% (participation rates: ages 15–64, 46.7%; female 12.8%; unemployed [1987] 13.3%).

Price and earnings indexes (1985 = 100)

	1982	1983	1984	1985	1986	1987	1988[7]
Consumer price index	73.6	78.1	85.3	100.0	136.1	217.0	272.2
Annual earnings index[8]	75.5	85.3	89.0	100.0	132.7		

Average household size (1986): 5.7.
Land use (1987): steppe and pasture 44.7%; cultivable 30.4%; forested 2.9%; other 22.0%.

Foreign trade

Balance of trade (current prices)

	1983	1984	1985	1986	1987	1988
LS '000,000	−10,281	−8,879	−7,857	−5,510	−12,723	−7,798
% of total	40.5%	37.9%	37.9%	34.6%	29.5%	20.5%

Imports (1987): LS 27,915,000,000 (machinery and equipment 30.2%; chemicals and chemical products 21.2%; food, beverages, and tobacco 11.5%; basic metals industries 7.9%; textiles 3.2%; paper and paper products 1.9%). *Major import sources:* France 9.8%; U.S.S.R. 8.3%; Iran 8.2%; West Germany 8.2%; Italy 6.7%; Libya 5.6%; United States 5.3%; Switzerland 3.3%.
Exports (1987): LS 15,192,000,000 (crude petroleum and natural gas 33.2%; chemicals and chemical products 29.4%; textiles, wearing apparel, and leather 25.5%; food, beverages, and tobacco 3.6%). *Major export destinations:* Italy 31.1%; U.S.S.R. 20.8%; France 9.9%; Romania 8.6%; Iran 5.0%; West Germany 5.0%; United Kingdom 1.2%.

Transport and communications

Transport. Railroads (1987): route length 1,275 mi, 2,052 km; passenger-mi 559,000,000, passenger-km 900,000,000; short ton-mi cargo 970,000,000, metric ton-km cargo 1,416,000,000. Roads (1987): total length 18,770 mi, 30,208 km (paved 94%). Vehicles (1987): passenger cars 112,595; trucks and buses 127,420. Merchant marine (1988): vessels (100 gross tons and over) 59; total deadweight tonnage 97,380. Air transport (1987): passenger-mi 526,820,000, passenger-km 847,836,000; short ton-mi cargo 61,520,000, metric ton-km cargo 89,817,000; airports (1989) with scheduled flights 5.
Communications. Daily newspapers (1986): total number 9; total circulation 201,400; circulation per 1,000 population 19.0. Radio (1986): total number of receivers 2,000,000 (1 per 5.3 persons). Television (1986): total number of receivers 400,000 (1 per 26.5 persons). Telephones (1987): 653,000 (1 per 17 persons).

Education and health

Education (1987–88)

	schools	teachers	students	student/ teacher ratio
Primary (age 6–11)	9,231	82,753	2,182,000	26.4
Secondary (age 12–18)	1,983	51,395	852,605	16.6
Voc., teacher tr.	257	9,883	78,012	7.9
Higher	...	...	192,977	...

Educational attainment (1984). Percent of population age 10 and over having: no schooling 32.0%; knowledge of reading and writing 28.4%; primary education 31.3%; secondary 4.9%; certificate 2.0%; higher 1.9%. *Literacy* (1986): total population age 15 and over literate 3,393,164 (61.1%); males literate 2,144,085 (76.5%); females literate 1,249,079 (45.5%).
Health (1987): physicians 8,146 (1 per 1,347 persons); hospital beds 12,606 (1 per 870 persons); infant mortality rate per 1,000 live births (1985–90) 48.0.
Food (1984–86): daily per capita caloric intake 3,259 (vegetable products 86%, animal products 14%); (1984) 128% of FAO recommended minimum requirement.

Military

Total active duty personnel (1988): 404,000 (army 74.3%, navy 1.0%, air force 24.7%). *Military expenditure as percent of GNP* (1987): 11.9% (world 5.4%); per capita expenditure U.S.$302.

[1]Parties other than the Communist Party form a coalition (National Progressive Front). [2]Islam is required to be the religion of the head of state and is the basis of the legal system. [3]Includes territory in the Golan Heights recognized internationally as part of Syria (located between the 1949 Israel–Syria Armistice line [west] and the 1974 UN Disengagement of Forces zone [east]) that has been occupied by Israel since 1967. Israel's unilateral annexation of this territory in December 1981 has received no international recognition. [4]1987. [5]Syrian Arabs only. [6]Detail does not add to total given because of rounding. [7]First quarter. [8]Public sector only.

Taiwan

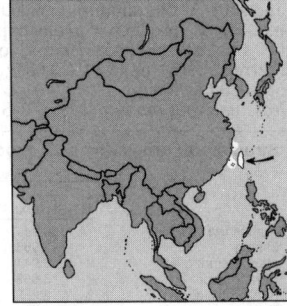

Official name: Chung-hua Min-kuo (Republic of China).
Form of government: unitary republic with a National Assembly (946)[1].
Chief of state: President.
Head of government: Premier.
Capital: Taipei.
Official language: Mandarin Chinese.
Official religion: none.
Monetary unit: 1 New Taiwan dollar (NT$) = 100 cents; valuation (Oct. 2, 1989) 1 U.S.$ = NT$25.53; 1 £ = NT$41.30.

Area and population		area		population
				1989
Counties	Capitals	sq mi	sq km	estimate[2, 3]
Chang-hua	Chang-hua	415	1,074	1,231,848
Chia-i	Chia-i	734	1,902	552,946
Hsin-chu	Hsin-chu	551	1,428	368,249
Hua-lien	Hua-lien	1,787	4,629	351,849
I-lan	I-lan	825	2,137	447,232
Kao-hsiung	Feng-shan	1,078	2,793	1,095,790
Miao-li	Miao-li	703	1,820	545,452
Nan-t'ou	Nan-t'ou	1,585	4,106	533,128
P'eng-hu	Ma-kung	49	127	97,327
P'ing-tung	P'ing-tung	1,072	2,776	890,730
T'ai-chung	Feng-yuan	792	2,051	1,213,382
T'ai-nan	Hsin-ying	778	2,016	1,009,036
T'ai-pei	Pan-ch'iao	792	2,052	2,903,199
T'ai-tung	T'ai-tung	1,357	3,515	258,953
T'ao-yüan	T'ao-yüan	471	1,221	1,292,888
Yün-lin	Tou-liu	498	1,291	762,705
Municipalities				
Chia-i	—	23	60	255,800
Chi-lung	—	51	133	348,685
Hsin-chu	—	40	104	315,414
Kao-hsiung	—	59	154	1,364,356
T'ai-chung	—	63	163	732,974
T'ai-nan	—	68	176	668,867
Taipei	—	105	272	2,687,352
TOTAL		13,900[4]	36,000	19,928,162

Demography

Population (1989): 20,024,000.
Density (1988): persons per sq mi 1,440.6, persons per sq km 556.2.
Urban–rural[3] (1987): urban 73.1%; rural 26.9%.
Sex distribution[3] (1988): male 51.80%; female 48.20%.
Age breakdown[3] (1987): under 15, 28.7%; 15–29, 29.5%; 30–44, 20.5%; 45–59, 12.6%; 60–74, 7.1%; 75 and over, 1.6%.
Population projection: (2000) 22,810,000; (2010) 25,677,000.
Doubling time: 58 years.
Ethnic composition (1986): Taiwanese 84.0%; mainland Chinese 14.0%; aborigine 2.0%.
Religious affiliation (1980): Chinese folk-religionist 48.5%; Buddhist 43.0%; Christian 7.4%; Muslim 0.5%; other 0.6%.
Major cities (1988): Taipei 2,637,100; Kao-hsiung 1,342,797; T'ai-chung 715,107; T'ai-nan 656,927; Chi-lung 348,541; Hsin-chu 309,899.

Vital statistics

Birth rate per 1,000 population (1988): 17.2 (world avg. 27.1); (1987) legitimate 98.0%; illegitimate 2.0%.
Death rate per 1,000 population (1988): 5.1 (world avg. 9.9).
Natural increase rate per 1,000 population (1988): 12.1 (world avg. 17.2).
Total fertility rate[3] (avg. births per childbearing woman; 1987): 1.7.
Marriage rate per 1,000 population (1988): 7.9.
Divorce rate per 1,000 population (1988): 1.3.
Life expectancy at birth (1987): male 71.1 years; female 76.3 years.
Major causes of death per 100,000 population (1987): malignant neoplasms 88.6; cerebrovascular diseases 74.0; accidents and suicide 66.6; heart disease 57.3; diabetes 16.8; liver diseases 16.7; hypertensive disease 15.8.

National economy

Budget (1987)[5]. Revenue: NT$707,843,000,000 (surplus of public enterprises 14.5%, income taxes 12.9%, customs duties 10.8%, land tax 9.2%, business tax 8.8%). Expenditures: NT$662,135,000,000 (administration and defense 33.4%, education 20.3%, communications 17.3%, social welfare 15.5%).
Public debt (foreign; 1987): U.S.$2,845,000,000.
Production (metric tons except as noted). Agriculture, forestry, fishing (1987): sugarcane 5,162,920, vegetables 3,283,889, rice 1,900,475, citrus fruits 522,865, sweet potatoes 344,816, corn (maize) 306,906, bananas 204,486, pineapple 193,337, peanuts 111,700; livestock (number of live animals) 7,129,034 pigs, 245,369 cattle, 207,024 goats; timber 422,644 cu m; fish catch 1,236,170. Mining and quarrying (1987): silver 9,856 kilograms; gold 536 kilograms. Manufacturing (1988): cement 17,280,809; steel ingots 2,533,855; paperboard 2,161,478; man-made fibre 1,339,608; fertilizers 1,269,136; PVC plastics 779,342; electronic calculators 68,263,519 units; television receivers 5,030,722 units; microcomputer systems 3,067,702 units; sewing machines 2,272,651 units; video tape recorders 1,784,381 units. Construction (1988): total residential and nonresidential 29,766,000 sq m. Energy production (consumption): electricity (kW-hr; 1988) 71,643,000,000 (45,221,434,000[6]); coal (metric tons; 1988) 1,225,487 (3,202,000[7]); petroleum (barrels; 1986) 704,700 (n.a.); natural gas (cu m; 1988) 1,157,495,000 (n.a.).

Gross national product (1988)[8]: U.S.$119,135,000,000 (U.S.$6,020 per capita).

Structure of gross domestic product and labour force[3]				
	1988			
	in value NT$'000,000	% of total value	labour force[9]	% of labour force
Agriculture	169,262	5.1	1,113,000	15.3
Mining	16,336	0.5	28,000	0.4
Manufacturing	1,276,648	38.4	2,798,000	35.0
Construction	142,386	4.3	588,000	6.9
Public utilities	107,794	3.2	35,000	0.4
Transportation and communications	201,019	6.0	431,000	5.3
Trade	471,908	14.2	1,539,000	17.9
Finance	386,020	11.6	269,000	2.9
Pub. admin., defense	319,987	9.6		
Services	189,447	5.7 }	1,308,000	15.9
Other	44,645[10]	1.3[10]	...	...
TOTAL	3,325,452	100.0[4]	8,108,000[4]	100.0[4]

Tourism (1987): receipts from visitors U.S.$1,619,000,000.
Population economically active (1987): total 9,640,318; activity rate 49.0% (participation rates: age 15–64, 71.6%; female 37.2%; unemployed 2.0%).

Price and earnings indexes (1985 = 100)[3]							
	1982	1983	1984	1985	1986	1987	1988
Consumer price index	98.8	100.2	100.1	100.0	100.7	101.2	102.5
Monthly earnings index[11]	83.0	88.2	101.8	100.0	110.0	120.7	133.6

Household income and expenditure (1987). Average household size 4.2; income per household NT$428,931 (U.S.$13,561[8]); sources of income: wages 59.4%, self-employment 22.6%, transfer payments 6.1%, other 11.9%; expenditure: food and tobacco 36.5%, rent, fuel, and power 23.0%, recreation and education 10.6%, transport and communications 8.5%, clothing and footwear 6.0%, health care 5.4%, household furnishings 4.4%, other 5.6%.
Land use (1980): forested 55.0%; agricultural and under permanent cultivation 25.2%; other 19.8%.

Foreign trade

Balance of trade (current prices)						
	1983	1984	1985	1986	1987	1988
NT$'000,000	191,518	333,836	421,057	590,181	592,545	306,852
% of total	10.5%	16.1%	20.8%	24.4%	21.0%	9.7%

Imports (1988): NT$1,422,614,000,000 (electronic components 7.9%, crude petroleum 4.5%, iron and steel 2.3%, nonelectrical machinery 2.2%, telecommunications equipment 1.9%, motor-vehicle parts 1.9%, raw cotton 1.0%). *Major import sources:* Japan 29.8%; U.S. 26.2%; W.Ger. 4.3%; Australia 2.7%; Saudi Arabia 2.5%; U.K. 2.2%.
Exports (1988): NT$1,729,466,000,000 (electronic products and appliances 11.6%, articles of plastic 8.2%, apparel and clothing 6.2%, textile yarns and fabrics 3.8%, wood, bamboo, and rattan manufactures 2.4%, processed food 2.0%, dolls and toys 1.1%). *Major export destinations:* U.S. 38.7%; Japan 14.4%; Hong Kong 9.2%; W.Ger. 3.9%; U.K. 3.1%; Canada 2.6%.

Transport and communications

Transport. Railroads (1988): track length 4,800 km; passenger-km 8,233,000,000; metric ton-km cargo 2,278,000,000. Roads (1987): total length 19,945 km (paved 85%). Vehicles (1988): passenger cars 1,579,121; trucks and buses 524,144. Merchant marine (1988): vessels (100 gross tons and over) 617; total deadweight tonnage 6,810,588. Air transport (1988): passenger-km 17,609,482,000; metric ton-km cargo 3,218,500,000; airports (1989) 9.
Communications. Daily newspapers (1987): total number 31; total circulation 3,500,000; circulation per 1,000 population 179. Radio (1988): 13,593,818 receivers (1 per 1.5 persons). Television (1987): 6,085,000 receivers (1 per 3.2 persons). Telephones (1987): 6,549,000 (1 per 3.0 persons).

Education and health

Education (1987–88)				
	schools	teachers	students	student/ teacher ratio
Primary (age 6–12)	2,447	75,826	2,392,750	31.6
Secondary (age 13–18)	838	61,034	1,254,460	20.6
Vocational	208	17,259	445,747	25.8
Higher	107	22,924	464,664	20.3

Educational attainment (1987). Percent of population age 25 and over having: no formal schooling 3.2%; less than complete primary education 8.0%; primary 35.9%; incomplete secondary 19.5%; secondary 20.7%; some college 6.8%; higher 5.9%. *Literacy* (1987): population age 15 and over literate 12,886,638 (91.2%); males 7,042,812 (96.0%); females 5,843,826 (86.0%).
Health (1987): physicians 19,369 (1 per 1,010 persons); hospital beds 86,328 (1 per 227 persons); infant mortality rate per 1,000 live births 5.1.
Food (1983): daily per capita caloric intake (1987) 2,999 (vegetable products 77%, animal products 23%); 118% of FAO recommended minimum.

Military

Total active duty personnel (1988): 405,500 (army 66.6%, navy 16.1%, air force 17.3%). *Military expenditure as percent of GNP* (1987): 4.6% (world 5.4%); per capita expenditure U.S.$238.

[1]As of Sept. 4, 1987. [2]End of February. [3]For Taiwan area only, excluding Quemoy and Matsu. [4]Detail does not add to total given because of rounding. [5]General government. [6]By industry only. [7]1986. [8]Based on the average exchange rate. [9]Civilian employed persons only. [10]Import duties less imputed bank service charge. [11]In manufacturing.

Tanzania

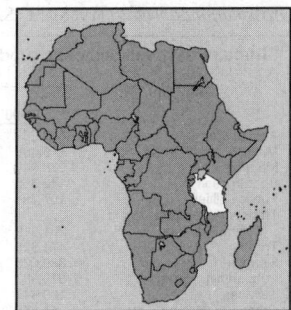

Official name: Jamhuri ya Mwungano wa Tanzania (Swahili); United Republic of Tanzania (English).
Form of government: unitary single-party republic with one legislative house (National Assembly [244[1]]).
Head of state and government: President.
Seat of government: Dar es Salaam (Capital designate, Dodoma).
Official languages: Swahili; English.
Official religion: none.
Monetary unit: 1 Tanzanian shilling (T Sh) = 100 cents; valuation (Oct. 2, 1989) 1 U.S.$ = T Sh 144.25; 1 £ = T Sh 233.40.

Area and population		area		population
		sq mi	sq km	1987 estimate
Regions	Capitals			
Arusha	Arusha	31,698	82,098	1,274,000
Bukoba	Bukoba	10,987	28,456	1,397,000
Dar es Salaam	Dar es Salaam	538	1,393	1,605,000
Dodoma	Dodoma	15,950	41,311	1,239,000
Iringa	Iringa	21,950	56,850	1,167,000
Kigoma	Kigoma	14,301	37,040	828,000
Kilimanjaro	Moshi	5,116	13,250	1,159,000
Lindi	Lindi	25,498	66,040	631,000
Mara	Musoma	8,402	21,760	908,000
Mbeya	Mbeya	23,301	60,350	1,421,000
Morogoro	Morogoro	27,268	70,624	1,202,000
Mtwara	Mtwara	6,452	16,710	916,000
Mwanza	Mwanza	7,600	19,683	1,836,000
Pemba North	Wete	} 380	} 984	}[2]
Pemba South	Chake Chake			
Pwani	Dar es Salaam	12,566	32,547	600,000
Rukwa	Sumbawanga	26,500	68,635	656,000
Ruvuma	Songea	24,583	63,669	725,000
Shinyanga	Shinyanga	19,598	50,760	1,779,000
Singida	Singida	19,050	49,340	770,000
Tabora	Tabora	29,402	76,150	1,185,000
Tanga	Tanga	10,300	26,677	1,305,000
Zanzibar North	Mkokotoni			
Zanzibar South and Central	Koani	} 641	} 1,660	} 605,000[2]
Zanzibar West	Zanzibar			
TOTAL LAND AREA		342,081	885,987	23,208,000
INLAND WATER		22,800	59,050	
TOTAL		364,881	945,037	

Demography

Population (1989): 23,729,000.
Density[3] (1989): persons per sq mi 69.4, persons per sq km 26.8.
Urban–rural (1987): urban 17.9%; rural 82.1%.
Sex distribution (1985): male 49.32%; female 50.68%.
Age breakdown (1985): under 15, 48.8%; 15–29, 25.5%; 30–44, 14.2%; 45–59, 7.7%; 60–74, 3.2%; 75 and over, 0.6%.
Population projection: (2000) 32,292,000; (2010) 42,732,000.
Doubling time: 19 years.
Ethnic composition (1983): Nyamwezi and Sukuma 21.1%; Swahili 8.8%; Hehet and Bena 6.9%; Makonde 5.9%; Haya 5.9%; other 51.4%.
Religious affiliation (1984): Christian 34%; Muslim 33%; traditional beliefs and other 33%.
Major cities (1985): Dar es Salaam 1,100,000; Mwanza 252,000; Tabora 214,000; Mbeya 194,000; Tanga 172,000.

Vital statistics

Birth rate per 1,000 population (1985–90): 50.5 (world avg. 27.1).
Death rate per 1,000 population (1985–90): 14.0 (world avg. 9.9).
Natural increase rate per 1,000 population (1985–90): 36.5 (world avg. 17.2).
Total fertility rate (avg. births per childbearing woman; 1985–90): 7.1.
Marriage rate per 1,000 population (1967): 9.8.
Life expectancy at birth (1985–90): male 51.3 years; female 54.7 years.
Major causes of death per 100,000 population: n.a.; however, the major diseases include malaria, bilharziasis, tuberculosis, and sleeping sickness.

National economy

Budget (1988–89). Revenue: T Sh 115,572,000,000[4] ([1986–87] sales tax 46.4%, income tax 21.2%, customs and excise tax 11.7%). Expenditures: T Sh 118,672,000,000 ([1986–87] public administration 25.5%, defense 20.1%, economic services 16.4%, education 6.4%, health 3.7%).
Public debt (external, outstanding; 1987): U.S.$4,068,000,000.
Tourism: receipts from visitors (1986) U.S.$15,000,000; expenditures by nationals abroad (1983) U.S.$12,000,000.
Production (metric tons except as noted). Agriculture (1988): cassava 5,000,-000, corn (maize) 2,339,000, bananas 1,300,000, plantains 1,300,000, sugarcane 1,190,000, rice 628,000, sorghum 420,000, coconuts 350,000, sweet potatoes 340,000, millet 280,000, seed cotton 245,000, dry beans 240,000, potatoes 230,000, mangoes 184,000, cottonseed 159,000, unshelled peanuts (groundnuts) 60,000; livestock (number of live animals) 13,500,000 cattle, 6,600,000 goats, 4,700,000 sheep, 30,000,000 chickens; roundwood (1987) 24,754,000 cu m; fish catch (1987) 313,545. Mining and quarrying (1987): phosphate minerals 18,400; diamonds 150,000 carats. Manufacturing (1987): cement 410,000; meats 220,000; fertilizer 47,032[5]; iron sheets 8,557[5]; hides

and skins 39,500; aluminum 6,000[6]; textiles 55,770,000 sq m[5]. Construction: n.a. Energy production (consumption): electricity (kW-hr; 1987) 874,000,-000 (874,000,000); coal (metric tons; 1987) 3,000 (3,000); crude petroleum (barrels; 1987) none (4,008,000); petroleum products (metric tons; 1987) 511,000 (589,000).
Gross national product (1987): U.S.$5,202,000,000 (U.S.$220 per capita).

Structure of gross domestic product and labour force				
	1987		1985	
	in value T SH '000,000	% of total value	labour force	% of labour force
Agriculture	120,941	53.1	9,091,000	83.3
Mining	563	0.2		
Manufacturing	9,044	4.0	469,000	4.3
Construction	3,658	1.6		
Public utilities	2,259	1.0		
Transp. and commun.	16,794	7.4		
Trade	27,453	12.0	} 1,353,000	} 12.4
Finance				
Pub. admin., defense	} 47,167	} 20.7		
Services				
Other			...	...
TOTAL	227,879	100.0	10,913,000	100.0

Population economically active (1985): total 10,913,000; activity rate of total population 48.5% (participation rates: ages 15–64, 85.7%; female 48.9%; unemployed, n.a.).

Price and earnings indexes (1985 = 100)							
	1983	1984	1985	1986	1987	1988	1989[7]
Consumer price index	55.1	74.6	100.0	132.4	172.1	225.8	268.7
Monthly earnings index	...	90.0	100.0	...	...	...	...

Household income and expenditure. Average household size (1980) 5.1; income per household: n.a.; sources of income: n.a.; expenditures (1981): food, beverages, and tobacco 54.3%, housing 8.6%, clothing 10.8%, energy 6.6%, transportation 6.4%.
Land use (1987): forested 48.0%; meadows and pastures 39.5%; agricultural and under permanent cultivation 5.9%; other 6.6%.

Foreign trade

Balance of trade (current prices)						
	1983	1984	1985	1986	1987	1988
T Sh '000,000	−3,384.0	−5,506.0	−10,314	−12,505	−31,947	−41,463
% of total	29.5%	32.3%	51.0%	36.0%	46.3%	43.2%

Imports (1988): T Sh 68,731,000,000 ([1986] machinery, transport equipment, and industrial goods 73.2%; consumer goods 7.1%; construction materials 6.9%). *Major import sources* (1987): United Kingdom 14.4%; Japan 8.6%; Italy 7.4%; West Germany 6.3%; Iran 5.2%; Denmark 4.4%; The Netherlands 3.7%; United States 3.3%; Yugoslavia 1.7%.
Exports (1988): T Sh 27,268,000,000 (coffee 25.9%; cotton 23.6%; sisal 1.4%). *Major export destinations* (1987): West Germany 19.3%, United Kingdom 11.6%; The Netherlands 10.1%; Japan 4.9%; Finland 4.3%; Italy 4.1%; France 4.1%; United States 3.8%; Singapore 3.7%; Portugal 3.2%.

Transport and communications

Transport. Railroads (1988): length 1,603 mi, 2,580 km; passenger-mi 2,125,-000,000, passenger-km 3,420,000,000; short ton-mi cargo 857,000,000, metric ton-km cargo 1,248,000,000. Roads (1986): length 51,025 mi, 82,114 km (paved 4.2%). Vehicles (1986): passenger cars 49,000; trucks and buses 33,000. Merchant marine (1988): vessels (100 gross tons and over) 39; deadweight tonnage 33,638. Air transport (1988): passenger-km 237,295,-000; metric ton-km 2,706,000; airports (1989) 19.
Communications. Daily newspapers: total number (1988) 2; total circulation 180,000; circulation per 1,000 population 7.8. Radio (1988): 2,000,000 receivers (1 per 12 persons). Television (1988): 10,000 receivers (1 per 2,300 persons). Telephones (1987): 122,600 (1 per 186 persons).

Education and health

Education (1986–87)				
	schools	teachers	students	student/ teacher ratio
Primary (age 7–13)	10,255	94,928	3,158,839	33.3
Secondary (age 14–19)	288	4,869	91,643	18.8
Voc., teacher tr.	63	1,278	12,077	9.4
Higher[8]	2	1,198	3,437	2.9

Educational attainment (1978). Percent of population age 10 and over having: no schooling 48.6%; some primary education 40.7%; completed primary 8.7%; secondary and higher 1.9%. *Literacy* (1987): 85%.
Health (1984): physicians 1,065 (1 per 19,775 persons); hospital beds 22,800 (1 per 924 persons); infant mortality rate per 1,000 live births (1985–90) 106.
Food (1984–86): daily per capita caloric intake 2,214 (vegetable products 93%, animal products 7%); 95% of FAO recommended minimum.

Military

Total active duty personnel (1989): 45,300 (army 96.3%, navy 1.5%, air force 2.2%). *Military expenditure as percent of GNP* (1985): 3.3% (world 5.4%); per capita expenditure U.S.$9.

[1]Includes 169 directly elected, 35 indirectly elected, 15 presidential nominees, and 25 ex officio members. [2]Pemba North and Pemba South are included with Zanzibar. [3]Based on land area. [4]Includes T Sh 45,360,000,000 foreign grants and loans. [5]1986. [6]1984. [7]First quarter. [8]University-equivalent institutions only.

Thailand

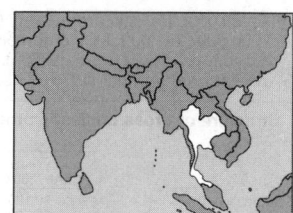

Official name: Muang Thai, or Prathet Thai (Kingdom of Thailand).
Form of government: constitutional monarchy with a multiparty National Assembly (Senate [268]; House of Representatives [357]).
Chief of state: King.
Head of government: Prime Minister.
Capital: Bangkok.
Official language: Thai.
Official religion: Buddhism.
Monetary unit: 1 Thai Baht (B) = 100 stangs; valuation (Oct. 2, 1989) 1 U.S.$ = B 25.96; 1 £ = B 42.00.

Area and population	area		population
Regions	sq mi	sq km	1987 estimate
Bangkok Metropolis	604	1,565	5,972,000
Central[1]	7,236	18,742	5,126,000
Eastern	14,481	37,507	3,232,000
Northeastern	65,195	168,854	18,622,000
Northern	65,500	169,644	10,488,000
Southern	27,303	70,715	6,996,000
Western	17,795	46,088	3,169,000
TOTAL	198,115[2]	513,115	53,605,000

Demography

Population (1989): 55,258,000.
Density (1989): persons per sq mi 278.9, persons per sq km 107.7.
Urban–rural (1985): urban 19.8%; rural 80.2%.
Sex distribution (1988): male 50.06%; female 49.94%.
Age breakdown (1985): under 15, 36.2%; 15–29, 30.7%; 30–44, 17.2%; 45–59, 10.2%; 60–69, 3.5%; 70 and over, 2.2%.
Population projection: (2000) 63,402,000; (2010) 71,594,000.
Doubling time: 47 years.
Ethnic composition (1983): Thai 79.5%, of which Siamese 52.6%, Lao 26.9%; Chinese 12.1%; Malay 3.7%; Khmer 2.7%; other 2.0%.
Religious affiliation (1986): Buddhist 95.0%; Muslim 3.8%; Christian 0.5%; other 0.7%.
Major cities (1983): Bangkok 5,363,378[3]; Chiang Mai 150,499; Hat Yai 113,-964; Khon Kaen 115,515; Nakhon Ratchasima 190,692.

Vital statistics

Birth rate per 1,000 population (1988): 22.1 (world avg. 27.1).
Death rate per 1,000 population (1988): 7.0 (world avg. 9.9).
Natural increase rate per 1,000 population (1988): 15.1 (world avg. 17.2).
Total fertility rate (avg. births per childbearing woman; 1988): 2.6.
Marriage rate per 1,000 population (1987): 6.9.
Divorce rate per 1,000 population (1987): 0.6.
Life expectancy at birth (1988): male 63.2 years; female 67.3 years.
Major causes of death per 100,000 population (1986): heart disease 22.8; diseases of digestive system 18.4; malignant neoplasms (cancers) 16.8; diseases of pulmonary circulation 12.4; homicide 10.2; tuberculosis 9.8.

National economy

Budget (1987–88). Revenue: B 243,500,000,000 (taxes 73.3%, borrowing 18.1%, state enterprises 3.6%, sale of property and services 2.2%). Expenditures: B 243,500,000,000 (debt service 24.5%, education 18.0%, defense 17.7%, economic services 15.6%, public utilities and health 11.2%, internal security 4.8%, general administration 2.7%).
Production (metric tons except as noted). Agriculture, forestry, fishing (1987): sugarcane 24,450,000, cassava 19,554,000, rice 17,650,000, corn (maize) 2,736,000, coconuts 1,350,000, rubber 860,000, seed cotton 75,000, tobacco 63,000, coffee 20,000; livestock (number of live animals) 6,350,000 buffalo, 4,931,000 cattle, 4,200,000 pigs, 80,000,000 chickens; roundwood 37,600,000 cu m; fish catch 2,165,100. Mining and quarrying (1987): limestone 11,391,249; gypsum 3,030,919; zinc 341,145; fluorite 104,552; lead ore 55,300; barite 33,370; tin concentrate 20,486. Manufacturing (1986): cement 8,004,726; refined sugar 2,491,343; synthetic detergents 107,308; tin plate 104,438; motorcycles 241,148 units. Construction (1986): residential 5,812,000 sq m; nonresidential 4,356,000 sq m. Energy production (consumption): electricity (kW-hr; 1987) 29,992,000,000 (30,390,000,000); coal (metric tons; 1987) 6,901,000 (7,099,000); crude petroleum (barrels; 1987) 6,461,000 (59,261,000); petroleum products (metric tons; 1987) 9,169,000 (11,851,000); natural gas (cu m; 1987) 4,391,000,000 (4,391,000,000).
Land use (1986): forested 28.9%; meadows and pastures 1.4%; agricultural and under permanent cultivation 38.8%; other 30.9%.
Population economically active (1987): total 28,715,800; activity rate of total population 53.7% (participation rates: over age 15, 79.7%; female 45.6%; unemployed 4.2%).

Price and earnings indexes (1985 = 100)							
	1982	1983	1984	1985	1986	1987	1988
Consumer price index	93.3	96.8	97.6	100.0	101.8	104.4	108.4
Monthly earnings index	...	...	...	...	...	...	...

Public debt (external, outstanding; 1987): U.S.$14,023,000,000.
Gross national product (at current market prices; 1987): U.S.$44,785,000,000 (U.S.$840 per capita).

Structure of gross domestic product and labour force				
	1987			
	in value B '000,000	% of total value	labour force[4]	% of labour force
Agriculture	195,059	15.9	14,924,300	53.9
Mining	37,606	3.1	76,600	0.3
Manufacturing	294,496	24.1	2,832,300	10.2
Construction	62,087	5.1	1,050,800	3.8
Public utilities	31,497	2.6	116,600	0.4
Transportation and communications	96,523	7.9	692,900	2.5
Trade	193,116	15.8	3,065,900	11.1
Finance	91,088	7.4		
Pub. admin., defense	53,127	4.3	2,924,100	10.6
Services	168,619	13.8		
Other	...	...	1,990,600[5]	7.2[5]
TOTAL	1,223,218	100.0	27,674,100	100.0

Tourism (1987): receipts from visitors U.S.$1,947,000,000; expenditures by nationals abroad U.S.$381,000,000.
Household income and expenditure. Average household size (1986) 4.3; average annual income per household (1986) B 44,172 (U.S.$1,680); sources of income (1986): wages and salaries 36.7%, self-employment 29.7%, transfer payments 6.0%, other 27.6%; expenditure (1986): food 37.4%, housing 23.1%, transportation and communications 10.7%, clothing and footwear 6.4%, medical and personal care 5.6%, education and recreation 4.3%, other 12.5%.

Foreign trade[6]

Balance of trade (current prices)						
	1983	1984	1985	1986	1987	1988
B' 000,000	−66,497	−45,425	−33,285	−10,133	−1,900	−59,529
% of total	18.5%	11.5%	7.9%	2.1%	0.3%	6.9%

Imports (1987): B 334,340,000,000 (machinery and transport equipment 32.4%, basic manufactures 19.6%, chemicals 15.2%, mineral fuels and lubricants 13.4%, inedible crude materials 7.8%, food and live animals 4.2%). *Major import sources:* Japan 26.0%; United States 12.4%; Singapore 7.8%; West Germany 5.9%; Malaysia 4.2%; China 3.9%; Taiwan 3.7%; United Kingdom 3.2%; South Korea 2.4%; Australia 1.7%.
Exports (1987): B 299,853,000,000 (food and live animals 36.5%, basic manufactures 19.6%, machinery and transport equipment 11.8%, inedible crude materials 8.9%, chemicals 1.5%). *Major export destinations:* United States 18.6%; Japan 14.9%; Singapore 9.0%; The Netherlands 6.7%; West Germany 4.9%; Hong Kong 4.2%; United Kingdom 3.6%; China 3.3%; Malaysia 3.3%; Saudi Arabia 2.5%.

Transport and communications

Transport. Railroads (1987)[7]: route length 2,321 mi, 3,735 km; passenger-mi 5,954,427,000, passenger-km 9,582,740,000; short ton-mi cargo 1,874,-319,000, metric ton-km cargo 2,736,460,000. Roads (1987): total length 52,670 mi, 84,764 km (paved 40%). Vehicles (1986): passenger cars 572,107; trucks and buses 898,310. Merchant marine (1988): vessels (100 gross tons and over) 258; total deadweight tonnage 776,727. Air transport (1987): passenger-mi 8,359,000,000, passenger-km 13,452,000,000; short ton-mi cargo 358,576,000, metric ton-km cargo 523,512,000; airports (1989) with scheduled flights 23.
Communications. Daily newspapers (1985): total number 31; total circulation 2,564,500[8]; circulation per 1,000 population 50[8]. Radio (1988): 9,567,-402 receivers (1 per 5.7 persons). Television (1986): 4,819,200 receivers (1 per 11 persons). Telephones (1986): 999,678 receivers (1 per 53 persons).

Education and health

Education (1986)	schools	teachers	students	student/teacher ratio
Primary (age 7–12)	32,683	356,844	7,160,494	20.1
Secondary (age 13–18)	1,437[9]	107,493[10]	1,829,559[10]	17.0
Voc., teacher tr.	1,528[9]	17,893[10]	390,640[10]	21.8
Higher	62[9]	30,905[11]	1,026,952[11]	33.2

Educational attainment (1980). Percent of population age 25 and over having: no formal schooling 20.5%; primary education 67.3%; secondary 9.3%; postsecondary 2.9%. *Literacy* (1985): total population age 15 and over literate 28,451,390 (88.8%); males literate 14,877,240 (93.2%); females literate 13,574,150 (84.5%).
Health (1986): physicians 9,464 (1 per 5,564 persons); hospital beds 84,438 (1 per 624 persons); infant mortality rate per 1,000 live births (1988) 38.0.
Food (1984–86): daily per capita caloric intake 2,328 (vegetable products 93%, animal products 7%); 111% of FAO recommended minimum requirement.

Military

Total active duty personnel (1988): 256,000 (army 64.8%, navy 16.4%, air force 18.8%). *Military expenditure as percent of GNP* (1987): 3.7% (world 5.4%); per capita expenditure U.S.$31.

[1]Excluding Bangkok Metropolis. [2]Detail does not add to total given because of rounding. [3]1986. [4]February; economically active persons 11 years and over. [5]Mostly unemployed. [6]Import figures are f.o.b. in balance of trade and c.i.f. for commodities and trading partners. [7]Traffic data refer to fiscal year ending September 30. [8]Excludes circulation for two dailies. [9]1980. [10]1984. [11]1985.

Togo

Official name: République Togolaise (Republic of Togo).
Form of government: single-party republic with one legislative body (National Assembly [77]).
Head of state and government: President.
Capital: Lomé.
Official language: French.
Official religion: none.
Monetary unit: 1 CFA franc (CFAF) = 100 centimes; valuation (Oct. 2, 1989) 1 U.S.$ = CFAF 317.90; 1 £ = CFAF 514.37.

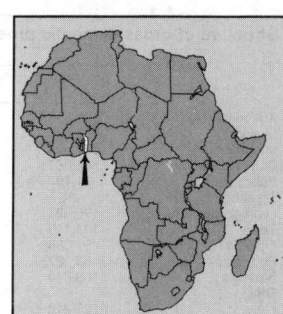

Area and population		area		population
Regions **Prefectures**	**Capitals**	sq mi	sq km	1981 census
Centrale	Sokodé			269,174
Sotouboua	Sotouboua	2,892	7,490	128,617
Tchamba	Tchamba	1	1	44,912
Tchaoudjo	Sokodé	2,198[1]	5,692[1]	95,645
De la Kara	Kara			432,626
Assoli	Bafilo	362	938	32,444
Bassar	Bassar	2,444	6,330	118,345
Binah	Pagouda	180	465	50,077
Doufelgou	Niamtougou	432	1,120	66,120
Kéran	Kandé	653	1,692	44,762
Kozah	Kara	419	1,085	120,878
Des Plateaux	Atakpamé			561,656
Amou	Amlamé	1,692[2]	4,382[2]	72,951
Haho	Notsé	1,412	3,658	109,995
Kloto	Kpalimé	1,077	2,790	106,429
Ogou	Atakpamé	2,372	6,145	163,906
Wawa	Badou	2	2	108,375
Des Savanes	Dapaong			326,826
Oti	Sansanné-Mango	1,453	3,762	77,747
Tône	Dapaong	1,869	4,840	249,079
Maritime	Lomé			1,039,700
Golfe	Lomé	133	345	438,110
Lacs	Aného	275	712	140,006
Vo	Vogan	290	750	150,313
Yoto	Tabligbo	483	1,250	100,387
Zio	Tsévié	1,289	3,339	210,884
TOTAL		21,925	56,785	2,700,982[3]

Demography

Population (1989): 3,622,000.
Density (1989): persons per sq mi 165.2, persons per sq km 63.8.
Urban–rural (1986): urban 22.8%; rural 77.2%.
Sex distribution (1986): male 48.55%; female 51.45%.
Age breakdown (1986): under 15, 43.7%; 15–29, 25.2%; 30–44, 15.8%; 45–59, 9.8%; 60 and over, 5.5%.
Population projection: (2000) 5,125,000; (2010) 6,942,000.
Doubling time: 23 years.
Ethnic composition (1981): Ewe-Adja 43.1%; Tem-Kabre 26.7%; Gurma 16.1%; Kebu-Akposo 3.8%; Ana-Ife (Yoruba) 3.2%; non-African 0.3%; other 6.8%.
Religious affiliation (1981): traditional beliefs 58.8%; Roman Catholic 21.5%; Muslim 12.1%; Protestant 6.8%; other 0.8%.
Major cities (1983): Lomé 366,476; Sokodé 48,098[4]; Kpalimé 27,669[4].

Vital statistics

Birth rate per 1,000 population (1985–90): 44.9 (world avg. 27.1); legitimate, n.a.; illegitimate, n.a.
Death rate per 1,000 population (1985–90): 14.1 (world avg. 9.9).
Natural increase rate per 1,000 population (1985–90): 30.8 (world avg. 17.2).
Total fertility rate (avg. births per childbearing woman; 1985–90): 6.1.
Marriage rate per 1,000 population (1979): 2.3.
Divorce rate per 1,000 population: n.a.
Life expectancy at birth (1985–90): male 51.3 years; female 54.8 years.
Morbidity (reported cases of illness per 100,000 population; 1978): infectious and parasitic diseases 26,926; diseases of the respiratory system 9,296; diseases of the digestive system 8,007; accidents, poisoning, and traumas 7,172.

National economy

Budget (1989). Revenue: CFAF 92,500,000,000 (tax revenue 90.1%, nontax revenue 9.9%). Expenditures: CFAF 92,500,000,000 (administrative 79.0%, debt service 17.2%, equipment and supplies 3.8%).
Public debt (external, outstanding; 1987): U.S.$1,042,000,000.
Tourism (1987): receipts from visitors U.S.$21,000,000; expenditures by nationals abroad U.S.$33,000,000.
Production (metric tons except as noted). Agriculture, forestry, fishing (1988): cassava 410,000, yams 378,000, corn (maize) 296,000, sorghum 120,000, cottonseed 68,000, millet 50,000, cacao beans 36,000, rice 27,000, pulses 25,000, peanuts (groundnuts) 17,000, bananas 16,000, coconuts 14,000, palm oil 14,000, oranges 12,000, coffee 11,000, tomatoes 7,000; livestock (number of live animals) 1,000,000 sheep, 900,000 goats, 300,000 pigs, 290,000 cattle, 3,000,000 chickens; roundwood 813,000 cu m; fish catch 15,176. Mining and quarrying (1988): phosphate rock 3,464,000; salt 600,-000[5]; marble 5,000[6]. Manufacturing (1985): cement 284,000; wheat flour 32,000; beer 423,000 hectolitres; nonalcoholic beverages 68,000 hectolitres[7]; footwear 520,000 pairs[8]. Construction (value added in CFAF; 1981): 11,-

000,000,000. Energy production (consumption): electricity (kW-hr; 1987) 40,000,000 (278,000,000); crude petroleum, none (n.a.); petroleum products (metric tons; 1987) none (92,000).
Gross national product (1986): U.S.$963,000,000 (U.S.$300 per capita).

Structure of gross domestic product and labour force	1983		1985	
	in value CFAF '000,000	% of total value	labour force	% of labour force
Agriculture	90,100	32.0	883,000	71.0
Mining	28,700	10.2		
Manufacturing	20,100	7.1		
Construction	8,100	2.9		
Public utilities	5,700	2.0		
Transp. and commun.	18,100	6.4		
Trade	61,900	22.0	361,000	29.0
Finance	...	...		
Pub. admin., defense	27,800	10.0		
Services	...	...		
Other	20,800	7.4		
TOTAL	281,300	100.0	1,244,000	100.0

Population economically active: total (1985) 1,244,000; activity rate of total population 42.0% (participation rates: ages 15–64, 69.5%; female 37.5%; unemployed [1980] 2.3%).

Price and earnings indexes (1985 = 100)							
	1982	1983	1984	1985	1986	1987	1988
Consumer price index	96.5	105.6	101.8	100.0	104.1	104.2	104.0
Hourly earning index[9]	100.0	100.0	100.0	100.0	100.0	105.5	105.5

Household income and expenditure. Average household size (1980) 5.6; average annual income per household CFAF 102,000 (U.S.$452); sources of income: n.a.; expenditure (1970): food and beverages 60.9%, housing 9.9%, transportation 8.2%, clothing 7.7%, household durable goods 3.9%, other 9.4%.
Land use (1987): forested 24.8%; meadows and pastures 3.7%; agricultural and under permanent cultivation 26.3%; other 45.2%.

Foreign trade

Balance of trade (current prices)						
	1981	1982	1983	1984	1985	1986
CFAF '000,000,000	−60.3	−70.2	−46.2	−34.9	−8.7	−29.7
% of total	34.4%	37.6%	27.2%	17.3%	3.8%	13.2%

Imports (1986): U.S.$300,000,000 (food and animal products 16.6%; tobacco 4.6%; fish and fishery products 2.7%; beverages 1.7%). *Major import sources:* France 29.8%; The Netherlands 8.6%; West Germany 7.7%; Japan 5.4%; Hong Kong 5.1%; United Kingdom 4.9%; Italy 3.9%; United States 3.8%.
Exports (1986): U.S.$235,000,000 (crude fertilizer 32.8%; coffee, tea, cocoa, and spices 22.9%; textile fibres 15.3%; oilseeds 4.8%; fish and fishery products 0.4%). *Major export destinations:* France 11.2%; United States 10.1%; The Netherlands 7.6%; Italy 7.3%; Spain 7.3%; West Germany 5.9%.

Transport and communications

Transport. Railroads (1987): length 250 mi, 403 km; passenger-mi 68,000,-000[6], passenger-km 109,000,000[6]; short ton-mi cargo 8,000,000[6], metric ton-km cargo 11,000,000[6]. Roads (1987): total length 4,689 mi, 7,547 km (paved 22%). Vehicles (1988): passenger cars 47,083; trucks and buses 22,-230. Merchant marine (1988): vessels (100 gross tons and over) 12; total deadweight tonnage 74,682. Air transport (1987): passenger-mi 132,791,000, passenger-km 213,706,000; short ton-mi cargo 24,739,000, metric ton-km cargo 36,119,000; airports (1989) with scheduled flights 1.
Communications. Daily newspapers (1988): total number 2; total circulation 10,000[10]; circulation per 1,000 population 2.9[10]. Radio (1988): 693,000 receivers (1 per 5.0 persons). Television (1988): 23,000 receivers (1 per 152 persons). Telephones (1983): 11,105 (1 per 255 persons).

Education and health

Education (1986–87)	schools	teachers	students	student/ teacher ratio
Primary (age 6–11)	2,345	10,209	474,998	46.5
Secondary (age 12–18)	358[7]	4,098	92,289	22.5
Voc., teacher tr.	18	221	5,688	25.7
Higher	1	308	4,500	14.6

Educational attainment (1981). Percent of population age 15 and over having: no formal schooling 76.5%; primary education 13.5%; secondary 8.7%; higher 1.3%. *Literacy* (1985): total population age 15 and over literate 631,-700 (39.1%); males literate 401,800 (51.7%); females literate 229,900 (27.5%).
Health: physicians (1985) 230 (1 per 12,992 persons); hospital beds (1982) 3,655 (1 per 752 persons); infant mortality rate (1985–90) 94.0.
Food (1984–86): daily per capita caloric intake 2,224 (vegetable products 96%, animal products 4%); 94% of FAO recommended minimum requirement.

Military

Total active duty personnel (1989): 4,350 (army 92.0%, navy 2.3%, air force 5.7%). *Military expenditure as percent of GNP* (1987): 3.3% (world 5.4%); per capita expenditure U.S.$12.

---

[1]Tchaoudjo includes Tchamba. [2]Amou includes Wawa. [3]Total includes 71,000 persons not counted separately. [4]1981. [5]1982. [6]1986. [7]1984. [8]Excludes rubber. [9]January 1 figures. [10]For one daily only.

Tonga

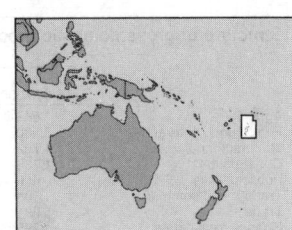

Official name: Pule'anga Fakatu'i 'o Tonga (Tongan); Kingdom of Tonga (English).
Form of government: constitutional monarchy with one legislative house (Legislative Assembly [29][1]).
Head of state and government: King.
Capital: Nuku'alofa.
Official languages: Tongan; English.
Official religion: none.
Monetary unit: 1 pa'anga (T$)[2] = 100 seniti; valuation (Oct. 2, 1989) 1 U.S.$ = T$1.29; 1 £ = T$2.08.

Area and population		area		population
Divisions				1986
Districts	Capitals	sq mi	sq km	census
'Eua	'Ohonua	33.7	87.4	4,393
'Eua Fo'ou		...	...	1,995
'Eua Motu'a		...	...	2,398
Ha'apai	Pangai	42.5	110.0	8,979
Foa		...	...	1,409
Ha'ano		...	...	892
Lulunga		...	...	1,588
Mu'omu'a		...	...	897
Pangai		...	...	2,840
'Uiha		...	...	1,353
Niuas	Hihifo	27.7	71.7	2,379
Niua Fo'ou		...	...	763
Niua Toputapu		...	...	1,616
Tongatapu	Nuku'alofa	100.6	260.5	63,614
Kolofo'ou		...	...	15,782
Kolomotu'a		...	...	13,117
Kolovai		...	...	4,023
Lapaha		...	...	6,992
Nukunuku		...	...	5,790
Tatakamotonga		...	...	6,778
Vaini		...	...	11,132
Vava'u	Neiafu	46.0	119.2	15,170
Hahake		...	...	2,292
Hihifo		...	...	2,095
Leimatu'a		...	...	2,875
Motu		...	...	1,387
Neiafu		...	...	5,273
Pangaimotu		...	...	1,248
TOTAL LAND AREA		289.5[3]	749.9[3]	94,535
INLAND WATER		11.4	29.6	
TOTAL		300.9	779.5	

Demography

Population (1989): 95,900.
Density[4] (1989): persons per sq mi 331.3; persons per sq km 127.9.
Urban–rural (1986): urban 30.7%; rural 69.3%.
Sex distribution (1986): male 50.30%; female 49.70%.
Age breakdown (1986): under 15, 40.6%; 15–29, 29.0%; 30–44, 13.8%; 45–59, 10.2%; 60–74, 5.0%; 75 and over, 1.4%.
Population projection: (2000) 101,000; (2010) 106,000.
Doubling time: 30 years.
Ethnic composition (1986): Tongan 95.5%; part Tongan 2.8%; other 1.7%.
Religious affiliation (1986): Free Wesleyan 43.0%; Roman Catholic 16.0%; Mormon 12.1%; Free Church of Tonga 11.0%; Church of Tonga 7.3%; other 10.6%.
Major city (1986): Nuku'alofa 21,383.

Vital statistics

Birth rate per 1,000 population (1988): 30.4 (world avg. 27.1).
Death rate per 1,000 population (1988): 7.3 (world avg. 9.9).
Natural increase rate per 1,000 population (1988) 23.1 (world avg. 17.2).
Total fertility rate (avg. births per childbearing woman; 1988): 4.0.
Marriage rate per 1,000 population (1985): 6.6.
Divorce rate per 1,000 population (1985): 0.6.
Life expectancy at birth (1980–85): male 61.0 years; female 64.8 years.
Major causes of death per 100,000 population (1985): diseases of the circulatory system 81.9; malignant neoplasms (cancers) 42.6; diseases of the respiratory system 27.7; endocrine and metabolic disorders 14.9.

National economy

Budget (1987). Revenue: T$29,819,000 (nontax revenues 70.3%, tax revenues 29.7%). Expenditures: T$32,018,000 (public services 33.8%, transport and communications 17.3%, education 13.2%, health 10.4%, agriculture 5.0%, defense 3.6%).
Tourism (1987): receipts from visitors U.S.$9,000,000; expenditures by nationals abroad U.S.$3,000,000.
Production (metric tons except as noted). Agriculture, forestry, fishing (1988): coconuts 53,000, yams 35,000, taro 30,000, sweet potatoes 18,000, cassava 17,000, fruits excluding melons 14,000, vegetables including melons 7,000, copra 6,000; livestock (number of live animals) 65,000 pigs, 11,000 goats, 9,000 horses, 8,000 cattle; roundwood (1987) 5,000 cu m; fish catch (1987) 2,800. Mining and quarrying (1982): coral 150,000; sand 25,000. Manufacturing (value added in T$; 1983): food products and beverages 2,623,000; furniture, fixtures, and wood products 328,000; metal products 252,000; glass and china products 203,000; paper and products 26,000. Construction (value in T$; 1984): residential 9,552,300; nonresidential 11,377,100. Energy production (consumption): electricity (kW-hr; 1987) 16,000,000 (16,000,-000); coal, none (n.a.); petroleum, none (n.a.); petroleum products (metric tons; 1987) n.a. (22,000); natural gas, none (n.a.).
Gross national product (at current market prices; 1987): U.S.$72,000,000 (U.S.$720 per capita).

Structure of gross domestic product and labour force				
	1983		1986	
	in value T$'000	% of total value	labour force	% of labour force
Agriculture	35,790	41.5	10,429	42.9
Mining	394	0.5	27	0.1
Manufacturing	4,271	4.9	622	2.6
Construction	3,354	3.9	1,741	7.2
Public utilities	404	0.5	326	1.3
Transportation and communications	4,950	5.7	1,176	4.8
Trade	12,774	14.8	1,612	6.6
Finance	5,189	6.0	465	1.9
Pub. admin., defense	...	...	5,492	22.6
Services	...	...		
Other	19,149[5]	22.2[5]	2,434	10.0
TOTAL	86,275	100.0	24,324	100.0

Public debt (external, outstanding; 1985): U.S.$24,180,000.
Population economically active (1986): total 24,324; activity rate of total population 25.8% (participation rates: ages 15–64, 44.7%; female 21.5%; unemployed 9.1%).

Price and earnings indexes (1985 = 100)							
	1982	1983	1984	1985	1986	1987	1988
Consumer price index	76.1	83.5	83.6	100.0	121.8	127.4	136.7
Earnings index	...	...	...	...	...	...	...

Household income and expenditure. Average household size (1986) 6.3; income per household: n.a.; sources of income: n.a.; expenditure (1984)[6]: food 49.3%, household operations 13.3%, housing 10.5%, tobacco and beverages 7.0%, transportation 5.8%, clothing and footwear 5.6%.
Land use (1987): forested 11.1%; meadows and pastures 5.6%; agricultural and under permanent cultivation 66.7%; other 16.6%.

Foreign trade

Balance of trade (current prices)						
	1982	1983	1984	1985	1986	1987
T$'000,000	−37.0	−35.2	−36.6	−51.8	−47.7	−58.0
% of total	81.5%	73.2%	64.7%	78.3%	72.7%	74.4%

Imports (1987): T$68,460,000 (basic manufactures 18.3%, food and live animals 21.6%, machinery and transport equipment 23.6%, mineral fuels 10.2%, chemicals 6.5%, beverages and tobacco 5.3%). *Major import sources:* New Zealand 45.8%; United Kingdom 9.1%; Japan 7.6%.
Exports (1988): T$9,553,000 (coconut oil products 16.9%, bananas 15.4%, vanilla beans 12.7%, desiccated coconut 5.8%). *Major export destinations:* New Zealand 56.4%; Australia 29.1%.

Transport and communications

Transport. Railroads: none. Roads (1988): total length 269 mi, 433 km (paved 65%). Vehicles (1984): passenger cars 1,561, commercial vehicles 3,397. Merchant marine (1988): vessels (100 gross tons and over) 16; total deadweight tonnage 17,991. Air transport (1988): passenger-mi 3,446,000, passenger-km 5,546,000; short ton-mi cargo 11,000, metric ton-km cargo 16,000; airports (1989) with scheduled flights 6.
Communications. Daily newspapers: none. Radio (1988): total number of receivers 79,716 (1 per 1.2 persons). Television: total number of receivers, n.a.[7] Telephones (1984): 3,996 (1 per 24 persons).

Education and health

Education (1986)	schools	teachers	students	student/ teacher ratio
Primary (age 6–11)	111	758	16,912	22.3
Secondary (age 12–18)	51	745	13,120	17.6
Voc., teacher tr.	12	54	407	7.5
Higher	1	...	705[8]	

Educational attainment (1976). Percent of population age 25 and over having: no formal schooling 0.4%; incomplete primary education 37.3%; complete primary 12.4%; lower secondary 45.6%; secondary 0.1%; postsecondary 0.1%; higher 0.6%; other education 2.4%; other 1.1%. *Literacy* (1976): total population age 15 and over literate 46,456 (92.8%); males 23,372 (92.9%); females 23,084 (92.8%).
Health (1987): physicians 47 (1 per 2,020 persons); hospital beds 307 (1 per 309 persons); infant mortality rate per 1,000 live births (1988) 49.0.
Food (1984–86): daily per capita caloric intake 2,942 (vegetable products 85%, animal products 15%); 108% of FAO recommended minimum.

Military

Total active duty personnel: Tonga had a national defense force of about 250 in the early 1980s.

---

[1]Includes 11 nonelective seats. [2]The pa'anga is at par with the Australian dollar. [3]Also includes 39.0 sq mi (101.1 sq km) of uninhabited islands. [4]Density is based on land area. [5]Includes indirect taxes less subsidies. [6]Current weight of consumer price index components. [7]Tonga has no authorized television service, but a "pirate" station began transmitting in mid-1984. [8]1982.

Trinidad and Tobago

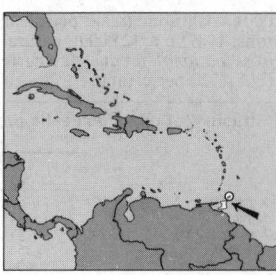

Official name: Republic of Trinidad and Tobago.
Form of government: multiparty republic with two legislative houses (Senate [31]; House of Representatives [36]).
Chief of state: President.
Head of government: Prime Minister.
Capital: Port-of-Spain.
Official language: English.
Official religion: none.
Monetary unit: 1 Trinidad and Tobago dollar (TT$) = 100 cents; valuation (Oct. 2, 1989) 1 U.S.$ = TT$4.25; 1 £ = TT$6.88.

Area and population		area		population
		sq mi	sq km	1987 estimate
Counties	**Capitals**			
Caroni	Chaguanas	214.0	554.3	167,300
Nariva/Mayaro	Rio Claro	352.0	911.7	33,200
St. Andrew/St. David	Sangre Grande	361.7	936.8	57,800
St. George	...	350.4	907.5	435,800
St. Patrick	Siparia	251.0	650.1	122,800
Tobago[1]	Scarborough	116.2	301.0	44,300
Victoria	Princes Town	314.1	813.5	218,700
Cities				
Port-of-Spain	—	3.7	9.6	58,300
San Fernando	—	2.5	6.5	33,100
Boroughs				
Arima	—	4.7	12.2	28,500
Point Fortin	—	9.8	25.4	17,300
TOTAL		1,980.1	5,128.4[2]	1,217,100

Demography

Population (1989): 1,285,000.
Density (1989): persons per sq mi 649.0, persons per sq km 250.6.
Urban–rural (1987): urban 54.0%; rural 46.0%.
Sex distribution (1986): male 50.05%; female 49.95%.
Age breakdown (1985): under 15, 34.0%; 15–29, 30.2%; 30–44, 17.9%; 45–59, 10.0%; 60–74, 6.1%; 75 and over, 1.8%.
Population projection: (2000) 1,608,000; (2010) 1,931,000.
Doubling time: 35 years.
Ethnic composition (1980): black 40.8%; East Indian 40.7%; mixed 16.3%; white 0.9%; Chinese 0.5%; Arab 0.1%; other 0.7%.
Religious affiliation (1980): Roman Catholic 32.2%; Protestant 27.6% (including Anglican 14.4%, Presbyterian 3.7%, Pentecostal 3.4%); Hindu 24.3%; Muslim 5.9%; nonreligious 1.0%; unknown 6.0%; other 3.0%.
Major cities (1987): Port-of-Spain 58,300; San Fernando 33,100; Arima 28,500; Point Fortin 17,300; Scarborough 6,089[3].

Vital statistics

Birth rate per 1,000 population (1986): 27.0 (world avg. 27.1); (1979) legitimate 56.9%; illegitimate 43.1%.
Death rate per 1,000 population (1986): 7.0 (world avg. 9.9).
Natural increase rate per 1,000 population (1986): 20.0 (world avg. 17.2).
Total fertility rate (avg. births per childbearing woman; 1987): 2.8.
Marriage rate per 1,000 population (1988): 5.9.
Divorce rate per 1,000 population (1988): 0.9.
Life expectancy at birth (1987): male 68.0 years; female 72.0 years.
Major causes of death per 100,000 population (1986): diseases of the circulatory system 253.9; malignant neoplasms (cancers) 83.6; endocrine and metabolic disorders 76.6; accidents and violence 56.8.

National economy

Budget (1988): Revenue: TT$4,775,500,000 (current revenue 99.6%, of which tax revenue 83.2%, nontax revenue 16.4%; development revenue 0.4%). Expenditures: TT$5,977,300,000 (current expenditures 80.6%, of which interest payments 8.7%; development expenditures 19.4%).
Tourism (1988): receipts from visitors U.S.$89,000,000; expenditures by nationals abroad U.S.$173,000,000.
Production (metric tons except as noted). Agriculture, forestry, fishing (1988): sugarcane 1,100,000, coconuts 62,000, oranges 7,000, rice 7,000, corn (maize) 3,000, coffee 1,824[4], cocoa 1,501[4]; livestock (number of live animals) 84,000 pigs, 78,000 cattle, 50,000 goats; roundwood (1987) 65,000 cu m; fish catch (1987) 3,200. Mining and quarrying (1987): natural asphalt 26,000. Manufacturing (1987): anhydrous ammonia 1,363,400; urea 473,400; methanol 424,300; iron and steel billets 375,500; cement 326,000; sugar 85,500; television receivers 9,200 units; motor vehicles 5,900 units; rum 137,500 hectolitres. Construction (new building authorized; 1987): residential 320,800 sq m; nonresidential 27,700 sq m. Energy production (consumption): electricity (kW-hr; 1987) 3,315,000,000 (3,315,000,000); coal, none (none); crude petroleum (barrels; 1988) 54,130,000 (34,442,000[5]); petroleum products (metric tons; 1987) 5,143,000 (1,136,000); natural gas (cu m; 1987) 4,066,000,000 (4,066,000,000).
Public debt (external, outstanding; 1987): U.S.$1,635,000,000.
Land use (1986): forested 43.7%; meadows and pastures 2.1%; agricultural and under permanent cultivation 23.0%; other 31.2%.
Gross national product (at current market prices; 1987): U.S.$5,130,000,000 (U.S.$4,220 per capita).

Structure of gross domestic product and labour force				
	1987			
	in value TT$'000,000[6]	% of total value	labour force[7]	% of labour force
Agriculture	547	3.4	47,000[8]	9.8[8]
Petroleum[9], natural gas	3,580	22.1	20,300	4.2
Manufacturing	1,702	10.5	46,000[10]	9.6[10]
Construction[11]	1,736	10.7	82,700	17.2
Public utilities	406	2.5	8,600	1.8
Transp. and commun.	1,894	11.7	33,100	6.9
Trade	1,091	6.7	78,200	16.2
Finance, real estate	1,895	11.7	30,000	6.2
Pub. admin., defense	2,653	16.4 }	134,100	27.9
Services	1,302	8.1 }		
Other	−617[12]	−3.8[12]	800	0.2
TOTAL	16,189	100.0	480,800	100.0

Population economically active (1987): total 478,850; activity rate of total population 39.3% (participation rates: ages 15–64, 63.0%; female 33.8%; unemployed [1987] 22.3%).

Price and earnings indexes (1985 = 100)							
	1983	1984	1985	1986	1987	1988	1989
Consumer price index	82.0	92.9	100.0	107.7	119.3	128.5	140.0[13]
Weekly earnings index[14]	80.8	93.1	100.0	101.8	106.2	...	...

Household income and expenditure. Average household size (1980) 4.2; income per household: n.a.; sources of income: n.a.; expenditure (1981–82): food and beverages 27.7%, housing 22.7%, clothing and footwear 15.5%, transportation 13.2%, household furnishings 8.8%, other 12.1%.

Foreign trade[15]

Balance of trade (current prices)						
	1983	1984	1985	1986	1987	1988
TT$'000,000	+77	+1,079	+1,882	+615	+1,316	+1,545
% of total	0.7%	11.5%	21.9%	6.6%	14.3%	16.6%

Imports (1987): TT$4,387,500,000 (machinery and transport equipment 29.2%, of which mining and industrial machinery 11.3%; food 19.0%; chemical products 12.2%). *Major import sources:* United States 41.0%; United Kingdom 9.2%; Canada 6.7%; West Germany 5.8%; Japan 5.3%.
Exports (1987): TT$5,264,600,000 (domestic exports 98.4%, of which crude petroleum 35.5%, petroleum products 35.3%, anhydrous ammonia 7.7%, iron and steel bar rods 5.0%, manufactured fertilizers 2.8%, methanol 2.8%; reexports 1.6%). *Major export destinations:* United States 56.4%; Barbados 3.1%; United Kingdom 3.1%; Jamaica 2.5%; Japan 2.4%.

Transport and communications

Transport. Railroads: none. Roads (1985): total length 4,909 mi, 7,900 km (paved 46%). Vehicles (1985): passenger cars 241,595; trucks and buses 82,361. Merchant marine (1988): vessels (100 gross tons and over) 51; total deadweight tonnage 13,715. Air transport (1986)[16]: passenger-mi 1,339,000,000, passenger-km 2,155,000,000; short ton-mi cargo 8,605,000, metric ton-km cargo 12,563,000; airports (1989) with scheduled flights 2.
Communications. Daily newspapers (1988): total number 4; total circulation 172,634; circulation per 1,000 population 138. Radio (1988): 401,078 receivers (1 per 3.1 persons). Television (1988): 345,000 receivers (1 per 3.6 persons). Telephones (1987): 199,840 (1 per 6.2 persons).

Education and health

Education (1988–89)	schools	teachers	students	student/ teacher ratio
Primary (age 5–11)	469	7,686	182,764	23.8
Secondary (age 12–16)[17]	89	4,878	91,808	18.8
Voc., teacher tr.	10	...	7,103	...
Higher[18]	1	241	2,488	10.3

Educational attainment (1980). Percent of population age 25 and over having: no formal schooling 7.1%; primary education 66.5%; secondary 21.7%; higher 2.7%; other 2.0%. *Literacy* (1980): total population age 15 and over literate 653,122 (95.1%); males literate 328,645 (96.7%); females literate 324,477 (93.6%).
Health (1987): physicians 1,164 (1 per 1,055 persons); hospital beds 4,241[19] (1 per 290 persons); infant mortality rate per 1,000 live births (1984) 13.7.
Food (1984–86): daily per capita caloric intake 3,058 (vegetable products 79%, animal products 21%); (1984) 124% of FAO recommended minimum requirement.

Military

Total active duty personnel (1988): 2,750 (army 100.0%). *Military expenditure as percent of GNP* (1984): 2.7% (world 5.7%); per capita expenditure U.S.$93.

[1]Attained full internal self-government in 1987. [2]Detail does not add to total given because of rounding. [3]1980. [4]Production for export only. [5]1987. [6]At factor cost. [7]Fourth-quarter average. [8]Includes sugar industry. [9]Includes refined petroleum. [10]Excludes sugar industry. [11]Includes quarrying. [12]Less imputed bank service charges. [13]April. [14]Manufacturing sector only. [15]Import figures are f.o.b. in balance of trade and c.i.f. in commodities and trading partners. [16]BWIA International airways only. [17]1986–87. [18]University of the West Indies, St. Augustine campus. [19]Includes nursing homes.

Tunisia

Official name: al-Jumhūrīyah at-Tūnisīyah (Republic of Tunisia).
Form of government: multiparty republic with one legislative house (Chamber of Deputies [141]).
Chief of state: President.
Head of government: Prime Minister.
Capital: Tunis.
Official language: Arabic.
Official religion: Islam.
Monetary unit: 1 dinar (D) = 1,000 millimes; valuation (Oct. 2, 1989) D 1.00 = U.S.$1.05 = £0.65.

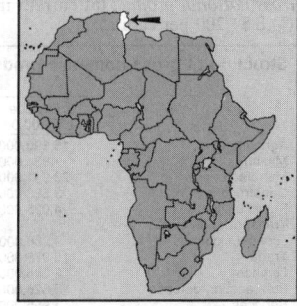

Area and population

Governorates	Capitals	area sq mi	area sq km	population 1988 estimate
Aryānah	Aryānah	602	1,558	455,800
Bājah	Bājah	1,374	3,558	290,400
Banzart	Banzart	1,423	3,685	426,200
Bin 'Arūs	Bin 'Arūs	294	761	296,200
Jundūbah	Jundūbah	1,198	3,102	390,600
al-Kāf	al-Kāf	1,917	4,965	261,200
Madaniyin	Madaniyin	3,316	8,588	336,800
al-Mahdīyah	al-Mahdīyah	1,145	2,966	300,300
al-Munastir	al-Munastir	393	1,019	309,800
Nābul	Nābul	1,076	2,788	510,000
Qābis	Qābis	2,770	7,175	276,200
Qafṣah	Qafṣah	3,471	8,990	265,700
al-Qaṣrayn	al-Qaṣrayn	3,114	8,066	338,200
al-Qayrawān	al-Qayrawān	2,591	6,712	469,000
Qibilī	Qibilī	8,527	22,084	109,100
Ṣafāqis	Ṣafāqis	2,913	7,545	650,700
Sīdī Bū Zayd	Sīdī Bū Zayd	2,700	6,994	329,100
Silyānah	Silyānah	1,788	4,631	236,900
Sūsah	Sūsah	1,012	2,621	364,300
Taṭāwīn	Taṭāwīn	15,015	38,889	114,200
Tawzar	Tawzar	1,822	4,719	77,600
Tūnis	Tunis (Tūnis)	134	346	831,200
Zaghwān	Zaghwān	1,069	2,768	130,400
TOTAL		**59,664**	**154,530**	**7,769,900**

Demography

Population (1989): 7,973,000.
Density (1989): persons per sq mi 133.6, persons per sq km 51.6.
Urban–rural (1985): urban 53.0%; rural 47.0%.
Sex distribution (1988): male 51.07%; female 48.93%.
Age breakdown (1988): under 15, 38.1%; 15–29, 29.4%; 30–44, 15.4%; 45–59, 10.2%; 60–74, 5.5%; 75 and over, 1.4%.
Population projection: (2000) 10,594,000; (2010) 13,099,000.
Doubling time: 34 years.
Ethnic composition (1983): Arab 98.2%; Berber 1.2%; French 0.2%; Italian 0.1%; other 0.3%.
Religious affiliation (1980): Sunnī Muslim 99.4%; Christian 0.3%; Jewish 0.1%; other 0.2%.
Major cities (commune; 1984): Tunis 596,654; Ṣafāqis 231,911; Aryānah 98,655; Banzart 94,509; Sūsah 83,509.

Vital statistics

Birth rate per 1,000 population (1988): 27.6 (world avg. 27.1); (1974) legitimate 99.8%; illegitimate 0.2%.
Death rate per 1,000 population (1988): 6.1 (world avg. 9.9).
Natural increase rate per 1,000 population (1988): 21.5 (world avg. 17.2).
Total fertility rate (avg. births per childbearing woman; 1985–90): 4.1.
Marriage rate per 1,000 population (1988): 6.1.
Divorce rate per 1,000 population (1988): 1.3.
Life expectancy at birth (1985–90): male 64.6 years; female 66.1 years.
Major causes of death per 100,000 population: n.a.; however, of approximately 7,000 deaths[1] for which a cause was reported in 1986, diseases of the circulatory system 20.1%; infectious and parasitic diseases 17.1%; complications of pregnancy and childbirth 14.0%; accidents and poisonings 11.0%.

National economy

Budget (1987). Revenue: D 2,235,600,000 (indirect taxes 54.8%, investment 19.6%, direct taxes 14.6%). Expenditures: D 1,696,600,000 (education 19.9%, finance 19.0%, interior affairs 11.2%, health 9.3%, defense 6.7%, agriculture 4.2%).
Tourism (1987): receipts from visitors U.S.$672,000,000; expenditures by nationals abroad U.S.$94,000,000.
Land use (1986): forested 3.6%; meadows and pastures 19.5%; agricultural and under permanent cultivation 30.2%; other 46.7%.
Production (metric tons except as noted). Agriculture, forestry, fishing (1988): olives 500,000, tomatoes 400,000, watermelons 270,000, sugar beets 256,000, wheat 220,000, potatoes 180,000, oranges 120,000, barley 70,000, dates 70,000, alfalfa 70,000, grapes 45,000, almonds 30,000, tobacco 5,000; livestock (number of live animals) 5,900,000 sheep, 1,115,000 goats, 612,000 cattle; roundwood (1987) 2,914,000 cu m; fish catch (1987) 99,169. Mining and quarrying (1988): phosphate rock 6,026,400; iron ore 325,200; zinc 16,270; lead 3,540. Manufacturing (1988): cement 3,600,000; phosphoric acid 855,600; flour 532,800; crude steel 274,800; mineral water 496,800 hectolitres. Construction (1982): residential building authorized 2,679,000 sq m. Energy production (consumption): electricity (kW-hr; 1987) 4,549,000,000 (4,549,000,000); coal (metric tons; 1987) none (16,000); crude petroleum (barrels;

1987) 38,449,613 (12,300,000); petroleum products (metric tons; 1987) 1,452,000 (2,653,000); natural gas (cu m; 1987) 366,950,000 (649,200,000).
Gross national product (1987): U.S.$9,019,000,000 (U.S.$1,210 per capita).

Structure of gross domestic product and labour force

	1986 in value D '000,000	1986 % of total value	1984 labour force	1984 % of labour force
Agriculture	960.0	13.5	475,370	22.2
Mining	608.0	8.6	22,500	1.1
Manufacturing	924.1	13.0	345,120	16.1
Construction	403.0	5.7	237,490	11.1
Public utilities	115.4	1.6	15,530	0.7
Transp. and commun.	390.5	5.5	86,700	4.1
Trade	1,614.2	22.7	153,860	7.2
Finance	301.4	4.2	13,060	0.6
Pub. admin., defense	865.0	12.2	129,510	6.1
Services	924.4	13.0	212,200	9.9
Other	...	...	445,870[2]	20.9[2]
TOTAL	7,106.8[3]	100.0	2,137,210	100.0

Public debt (external, outstanding; 1987): U.S.$6,415,000,000.
Population economically active (1984): total 2,137,210, activity rate of total population 30.6% (participation rates: ages 15–64, 52.9%; female 21.3%; unemployed 16.4%).

Price and earnings indexes (1985 = 100)

	1982	1983	1984	1985	1986	1987	1988
Consumer price index	78.4	85.4	92.6	100.0	105.8	113.4	120.6
Monthly earnings index	...	...	...	...	...	...	...

Household income and expenditure. Average household size (1984) 5.5; income per household: n.a.; sources of income: n.a.; expenditure (1985): food and beverages 39.0%, household durable goods 11.2%, housing 10.7%, transportation 9.0%, recreation 7.1%, clothing and footwear 6.0%, energy 5.1%, health care 3.0%, education 1.8%, other 7.1%.

Foreign trade

Balance of trade (current prices)

	1983	1984	1985	1986	1987	1988
D '000,000	−704.2	−909.6	−690.4	−737.3	−569.9	−898.9
% of total	21.8%	24.6%	19.3%	20.8%	13.9%	17.9%

Imports (1988): D 3,167,018,000 (textiles 8.2%, wheat 5.4%, plastic materials 2.8%, pharmaceutical products 2.2%, iron and steel products 2.0%). *Major import sources:* France 24.8%; Italy 13.1%; West Germany 12.6%; United States 7.1%; Belgium–Luxembourg 4.8%; Spain 4.4%; The Netherlands 2.4%.
Exports (1988): D 2,055,474,000 (clothing and accessories 16.8%, petroleum and petroleum products 16.1%, phosphates 11.1%, phosphoric acid 6.9%, olive oil 3.4%, fish and crustaceans 3.1%). *Major export destinations:* France 25.9%; Italy 19.2%; West Germany 14.0%; Belgium–Luxembourg 5.9%; Spain 3.4%.

Transport and communications

Transport. Railroads (1988): route length (1987) 1,314 mi, 2,115 km; passenger-mi 630,000,000, passenger-km 1,014,000,000; short ton-mi cargo 1,477,000,000, metric ton-km cargo 2,156,000,000. Roads (1987): total length 17,008 mi, 27,371 km (paved 57%). Vehicles (1987): passenger cars 281,201; trucks and buses 193,963. Merchant marine (1988): vessels (100 gross tons and over) 72; total deadweight tonnage 447,420. Air transport (1987): passenger-mi 1,475,493,000, passenger-km 2,374,581,000; short ton-mi cargo 14,757,125, metric ton-km cargo 21,545,010; airports (1989) 6.
Communications. Daily newspapers (1987): total number 6; total circulation 230,000[4]; circulation per 1,000 population 33[4]. Radio (1988): 1,693,527 receivers (1 per 4.7 persons). Television (1987): 500,000 receivers (1 per 15 persons). Telephones (1987): 312,029 (1 per 24 persons).

Education and health

Education (1988–89)

	schools	teachers	students	student/ teacher ratio
Primary (age 6–11)	3,676	43,921	1,326,150	30.2
Secondary (age 12–18)	485	23,300	447,795	19.2
Voc., teacher tr.[5]	...	229[6]	4,183	18.3
Higher	...	3,901	54,466	14.0

Educational attainment (1984). Percent of population age 25 and over having: no formal schooling 65.8%; Qur'anic education 1.2%; primary 17.5%; secondary 11.2%; vocational 0.8%; higher 1.7%; unspecified 1.8%. *Literacy* (1984): total population age 15 and over literate 2,023,500 (48.2%); males literate 1,282,700 (60.4%); females literate 740,800 (35.7%).
Health (1987): physicians 3,474 (1 per 2,198 persons); hospital beds 15,838 (1 per 482 persons); infant mortality rate per 1,000 live births (1985–90) 59.0.
Food (1984–86): daily per capita caloric intake 2,942 (vegetable products 91%, animal products 9%); (1984) 119% of FAO recommended minimum.

Military

Total active duty personnel (1988): 38,000 (army 79.0%, navy 11.8%, air force 9.2%). *Military expenditure as percent of GNP* (1987): 3.1% (world 5.4%); per capita expenditure U.S.$38.

[1]Urban areas only. [2]Includes 95,080 undefined and 350,790 unemployed. [3]Detail does not add to total given because of rounding. [4]Circulation for 4 dailies only. [5]1986–87. [6]Teacher training only.

Turkey

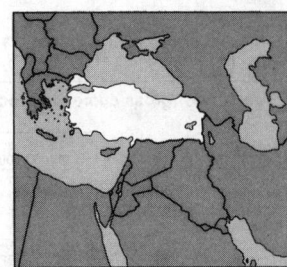

Official name: Türkiye Cumhuriyeti
 (Republic of Turkey).
Form of government: multiparty
 republic with one legislative house
 (Turkish Grand National Assembly
 [450]).
Chief of state: President.
Head of government: Prime Minister.
Capital: Ankara.
Official language: Turkish.
Official religion: none.
Monetary unit: 1 Turkish lira
 (LT) = 100 kurush; valuation (Oct. 2,
 1989) 1 U.S.$ = LT 2,230;
 1 £ = LT 3,609.

Area and population

Geographic regions[1]	area		population 1985 census
	sq mi	sq km	
Akdeniz kıyısı (Mediterranean Coast)	22,933	59,395	4,653,426
Batı Anadolu (West Anatolia)	29,742	77,031	3,538,253
Doğu Anadolu (East Anatolia)	68,074	176,311	6,290,086
Güneydoğu Anadolu (Southeast Anatolia)	15,347	39,749	2,413,593
İç Anadolu (Central Anatolia)	91,254	236,347	12,193,155
Karadeniz kıyısı (Black Sea Coast)	31,388	81,295	6,652,172
Marmara ve Ege kıyıları (Marmara and Aegean coasts)	33,035	85,560	9,834,576
Trakya (Thrace)	9,175	23,764	5,089,197
TOTAL	300,948	779,452	50,664,458

Demography

Population (1989): 55,541,000.
Density (1989): persons per sq mi 184.6, persons per sq km 71.3.
Urban–rural (1985): urban 45.9%; rural 54.1%.
Sex distribution (1985): male 50.40%; female 49.60%.
Age breakdown (1985): under 15, 37.1%; 15–29, 26.3%; 30–44, 17.1%; 45–59, 12.6%; 60 and over, 6.9%.
Population projection: (2000) 73,029,000; (2010) 83,963,000.
Doubling time: 35 years.
Ethnic composition (1983): Turkish 85.7%; Kurdish 10.6%; Arab 1.6%; other 2.1%.
Religious affiliation (1980): Sunnī Muslim 99.2%; Eastern Orthodox 0.3%; other 0.5%.
Major cities (1985): Istanbul 5,475,982; Ankara 2,235,035; İzmir 1,489,772; Adana 777,554; Bursa 612,510.

Vital statistics

Birth rate per 1,000 population (1985–90): 28.4 (world avg. 27.1).
Death rate per 1,000 population (1985–90): 8.4 (world avg. 9.9).
Natural increase rate per 1,000 population (1985–90): 20.0 (world avg. 17.2).
Total fertility rate (avg. births per childbearing woman; 1985): 3.9.
Marriage rate per 1,000 population (1986): 7.5.
Divorce rate per 1,000 population (1986): 1.4.
Life expectancy at birth (1980–85): male 62.5 years; female 65.8 years.
Major causes of death per 100,000 population: n.a.; however, of the 134,025 deaths (approximately 30% of total deaths[2]) for which a cause was reported in 1987 include diseases of the circulatory system 41.6%; malignant neoplasms (cancers) 9.5%; complications of pregnancy and childbirth 9.3%; accidental death 3.4%.

National economy

Budget (1988). Revenue: LT 17,831,000,000,000 (indirect taxes 40.4%, direct taxes 39.7%, nontax revenue 15.2%). Expenditures: LT 21,271,000,000,000 (personnel 23.6%, investment 16.6%, debt service 14.8%).
Tourism (1987): receipts from visitors U.S.$1,721,000,000; expenditures by nationals abroad U.S.$448,000,000.
Production (metric tons except as noted). Agriculture, forestry, fishing (1988): wheat 20,500,000, sugar beets 11,534,000, barley 7,500,000, potatoes 4,350,000, grapes 3,350,000, corn (maize) 2,000,000, apples 1,950,000, dry onions 1,345,000, sunflower seeds 1,150,000, olives 1,100,000, lentils 1,040,000, chick-peas 778,000, tea leaves 756,000, oranges 740,000, rye 280,000, oats 276,000, rice 158,000; livestock (number of live animals; 1987) 40,400,000 sheep, 12,400,000 cattle, 13,100,000 goats; roundwood (1987) 16,171,000 cu m; fish catch (1987) 625,722. Mining and quarrying (1988): iron ore 5,597,000; chrome ore 1,227,000. Manufacturing (1988): cement 22,675,000; steel ingot 8,009,000; commercial fertilizers 7,840,000; crude iron 4,462,000; rolled steel 2,614,000; iron and steel bars 1,033,000; pig iron 454,000; beer 237,483,000 litres; wine 22,624,000 litres; cotton fabric 202,931,000 m. Construction (building permits issued; 1987): residential 57,535,000 sq m; nonresidential 13,377,000 sq m. Energy production (consumption): electricity (kW-hr; 1987) 44,353,000,000 (44,925,000,000); coal (metric tons; 1987) 46,988,000 (48,504,000); crude petroleum (barrels; 1987) 18,804,000 (166,538,000); petroleum products (metric tons; 1987) 19,066,000 (17,605,000); natural gas (cu m; 1987) 283,563,000 (283,563,000).
Household income and expenditure[3]. Average household size (1980) 5.2; income per household (1978–79) LT 11,880 (U.S.$471); sources of income: self-employment 46.8%, wages and salaries 38.9%, transfer grants 9.4%, other 4.9%; expenditure (1978–79): food 41.2%, housing 25.2%, clothing 14.8%, recreation and entertainment 6.1%, transportation 5.5%, health 3.3%, other 3.9%.

Gross national product (at current market prices; 1987): U.S.$63,643,000,000 (U.S.$1,200 per capita).

Structure of gross domestic product and labour force

	1988			
	in value LT '000,000	% of total value	labour force	% of labour force
Agriculture	15,690,000	17.2	9,300,000	47.4
Mining	1,834,000	2.0	123,000	0.6
Manufacturing	23,961,000	26.2	2,116,000	10.8
Construction	3,563,000	3.9	721,000	3.7
Public utilities	4,025,000	4.4	153,000	0.8
Transportation and communications	9,286,000	10.2	614,000	3.1
Trade	16,075,000	17.6	928,000	4.7
Finance	2,596,000	2.8	258,000	1.3
Pub. admin., defense	5,326,000	5.8 }	2,653,000	13.5
Services	4,955,000	5.4 }		
Other	4,074,000[4]	4.5[4]	2,748,000[5]	14.0[5]
TOTAL	91,385,000	100.0	19,615,000[6]	100.0[6]

Public debt (external, outstanding; 1987): U.S.$30,490,000,000.
Population economically active (1988): total 19,615,000; activity rate of total population 36.2% (participation rates: ages 15–64, 58.5%[7]; female 30.1%[7]; unemployed 14.0%).

Price and earnings indexes (1985 = 100)

	1982	1983	1984	1985	1986	1987	1988
Consumer price index	35.0	46.5	69.0	100.0	134.6	186.9	327.8
Daily earnings index[8]	38.7	52.9	73.2	100.0	132.7	169.9	...

Land use (1986): forested 26.2%; meadows and pastures 11.4%; agricultural and under permanent cultivation 35.7%; other 26.7%.

Foreign trade

Balance of trade (current prices)

	1983	1984	1985	1986	1987	1988
U.S.$'000,000	−3,507	−3,624	−3,386	−3,648	−3,973	−1,800
% of total	23.4%	20.3%	17.5%	19.7%	16.3%	7.1%

Imports (1988): U.S.$14,340,000,000 (fuels 18.9%, machinery 16.7%, chemicals 13.8%, iron and steel 11.5%, pharmaceutical products 7.1%). Major import sources: West Germany 14.3%; United States 10.6%; Iraq 10.0%; Italy 7.0%; United Kingdom 5.8%; France 5.2%; Iran 4.6%; Japan 3.9%.
Exports (1988): U.S.$11,662,000,000 (textiles 27.4%, agricultural products 20.1%, iron and nonferrous metals 14.4%, food 6.6%, chemical products 6.3%, leather and hides 4.4%, machinery 2.9%). Major export destinations: West Germany 18.4%; Iraq 8.4%; Italy 8.2%; United States 6.5%; United Kingdom 4.9%; Iran 4.7%; France 4.3%; Saudi Arabia 3.1%.

Transport and communications

Transport. Railroads (1987): route length 5,076 mi, 8,169 km; passenger-mi 3,833,000,000, passenger-km 6,168,000,000; short ton-mi cargo 4,973,000,000, metric ton-km cargo 7,260,000,000. Roads (1986): total length 198,293 mi, 319,133 km (paved 19%). Vehicles (1987): passenger cars 1,193,121; trucks and buses 559,220. Merchant marine (1988): vessels (100 gross tons and over) 872; total deadweight tonnage 5,441,307. Air transport (1986): passenger-mi 1,626,598,000, passenger-km 2,617,761,000; short ton-mi cargo 31,144,000, metric ton-km cargo 45,469,000; airports (1989) with scheduled flights 14.
Communications. Daily newspapers (1986)[9]: total number 338; total circulation 4,188,262; circulation per 1,000 population 81.3. Radio (1988): total number of receivers 7,092,693 (1 per 7.8 persons). Television (1988): total number of receivers 8,074,758 (1 per 6.8 persons). Telephones (1987): 3,703,000 (1 per 14 persons).

Education and health

Education (1986–87)

	schools	teachers	students	student/ teacher ratio
Primary (age 5–12)	49,714	216,859	6,703,528	30.9
Secondary (age 13–18)	5,734[10]	100,431	2,412,347	24.0
Voc., teacher tr.	2,075[10]	46,368	676,136	14.6
Higher	310[10]	24,382	505,091	20.7

Educational attainment (1980). Percent of population age 25 and over having: no formal schooling 52.4%; primary education 35.3%; secondary 8.7%; higher 3.6%. *Literacy* (1980): total population age 15 and over literate 8,561,370 (65.6%); males literate 6,530,035 (81.3%); females literate 2,031,335 (49.8%).
Health (1987): physicians 38,829 (1 per 1,360 persons); hospital beds 111,135 (1 per 476 persons); infant mortality rate per 1,000 live births (1986) 84.0.
Food (1984–86): daily per capita caloric intake 3,146 (vegetable products 91%, animal products 9%); (1984) 126% of FAO recommended minimum requirement.

Military

Total active duty personnel (1988): 635,300 (army 82.3%, navy 8.7%, air force 9.0%). *Military expenditure as percent of GNP* (1987): 4.4% (world 5.4%); per capita expenditure U.S.$55.

---

[1]Administratively divided into 67 provinces. [2]Province and district centres only. [3]Urban areas only. [4]Ownership of dwellings. [5]Unemployed. [6]Detail does not add to total given because of rounding. [7]1985. [8]Insured workers only. [9]Principal daily newspapers only. [10]1985–86.

Tuvalu

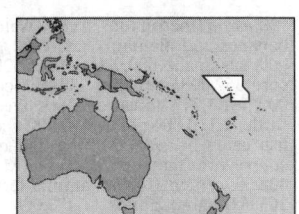

Official name: Tuvalu.
Form of government: constitutional monarchy with one legislative house (Parliament [12]).
Chief of state: British Monarch, represented by governor-general.
Head of government: Prime Minister.
Capital: Fongafale, on Funafuti atoll.
Official language: none.
Official religion: none.
Monetary unit[1]: 1 Tuvalu Dollar = 1 Australian Dollar ($T = $A) = 100 Tuvalu and Australian cents; valuation (Oct. 2, 1989) 1 U.S.$ = $A 1.29; 1 £ = $A 2.08.

Area and population

Islands[2]	area sq mi	area sq km	population 1985 census
Funafuti	0.91	2.36	2,810
Nanumaga	1.00	2.59	672
Nanumea	1.38	3.57	879
Niulakita	0.16	0.41	74
Niutao	0.82	2.12	904
Nui	1.27	3.29	604
Nukufetau	1.18	3.06	694
Nukulaelae	0.64	1.66	315
Vaitupu	1.89	4.90	1,231
TOTAL	9.25	23.96	8,229[3,4]

Demography

Population (1989): 8,900.
Density (1989): persons per sq mi 962.2, persons per sq km 371.5.
Urban–rural (1985): urban 34.2%; rural 65.8%.
Sex distribution (1985): male 47.42%; female 52.58%.
Age breakdown (1979): under 15, 33.8%; 15–29, 31.0%; 30–44, 14.3%; 45–59, 13.2%; 60–74, 6.1%; 75 and over, 1.6%.
Population projection: (2000) 11,000; (2010) 14,000.
Doubling time: 41 years.
Ethnic composition (1979): Tuvaluan (Polynesian) 91.2%; mixed (Polynesian/Micronesian/other) 7.2%; European 1.0%; other 0.6%.
Religious affiliation (1979): Church of Tuvalu (Congregational) 96.9%; Seventh-day Adventist 1.4%; Bahā'ī 1.0%; Roman Catholic 0.2%; other 0.5%.
Major locality (1985): Fongafale, on Funafuti atoll 2,810.

Vital statistics

Birth rate per 1,000 population (1989): 27.0 (world avg. 27.1); legitimate 82.2%; illegitimate 17.8%.
Death rate per 1,000 population (1989): 10.0 (world avg. 9.9).
Natural increase rate per 1,000 population (1989): 17.0 (world avg. 17.2).
Total fertility rate (avg. births per childbearing woman; 1989): 2.8.
Marriage rate per 1,000 population: n.a.
Divorce rate per 1,000 population: n.a.
Life expectancy at birth (1989): male 60.0 years; female 63.0 years.
Major causes of death per 100,000 population (1985): diseases of the digestive system 170.0; diseases of the circulatory system 150.0; diseases of the respiratory system 120.0; diseases of the nervous system 120.0; malignant neoplasms (cancers) 70.0; infectious and parasitic diseases 40.0; endocrine and metabolic disorders 20.0; ill-defined conditions 430.0.

National economy

Budget (1987). Revenue: $A 13,498,000 (current revenue 31.1%, of which local sources 25.4%, British grants 5.7%; capital [development] revenue 68.9%, all from foreign grants and loans). Expenditures: $A 13,498,000 (current expenditures 31.1%; capital [development] expenditures 68.9%, of which marine transport 20.7%, education 13.0%, fisheries 5.6%, health 3.1%).
Gross domestic product (at current market prices; 1985): U.S.$3,427,000 (U.S.$420 per capita).

Structure of gross domestic product and labour force

	1985 in value $A	1985 % of total value	1979 labour force[5]	1979 % of labour force
Agriculture, fishing	549,000	10.9	38	1.0
Mining	—	—	1	—
Manufacturing	106,000	2.1	62	1.6
Construction	483,000	9.6	224	5.6
Public utilities	90,000	1.8	14	0.3
Transportation and communications	40,000	0.8	107	2.7
Trade	559,000	11.1	98	2.4
Finance	} 3,207,000	} 63.7	11	0.3
Pub. admin., defense			177	4.4
Services			170	4.2
Unemployed	—	—	162	4.0
Noncash economy	—	—	2,946[6]	73.5
TOTAL	5,034,000	100.0	4,010	100.0

Production (metric tons except as noted). Agriculture[7], forestry, fishing (1988): coconuts 3,000, hens' eggs 16, other agricultural products include breadfruit, pulaka (taro), bananas, pandanus fruit, and pawpaws; livestock (number of live animals) 10,000 pigs[8]; forestry, n.a.; fish catch (1987) 736. Mining and quarrying: n.a. Manufacturing (1984): copra 840 metric tons; handicrafts; baked goods. Construction: n.a. Energy production (consumption): electricity (kW-hr; 1987) 3,000,000 (3,000,000); coal, none (none); crude petroleum, none (none); petroleum products, none (n.a.); natural gas, none (none).
Public debt: n.a.
Tourism (1987): number of visitors 258.
Population economically active (1979)[5]: total 4,010; activity rate of total population 55.2% (participation rates: over age 15, 81.1%; female 51.3%; unemployed 4.0%).

Price and earnings indexes (1985 = 100)

	1981	1982	1983	1984	1985	1986	1987
Consumer price index	77.3	84.5	90.2	93.4	100.0	107.5	109.2[9]
Monthly earnings index	...	...	...	...	...	...	...

Household income and expenditure. Average household size (1979) 6.4; average annual income per household: $A 2,575; sources of income: agriculture and other 61.2%, cash economy only 17.9%, agriculture only 14.9%, other 6.0%; expenditure (1987)[10]: food 45.5%, housing and household operations 11.5%, transportation 10.5%, alcohol and tobacco 10.5%, clothing 7.5%, other 14.5%.
Land use (1983): agricultural and under permanent cultivation 75%[11]; other 25%.

Foreign trade

Balance of trade (current prices)

	1981	1982	1983	1984	1985	1986
$A '000	−2,556	−2,853	−2,877	−3,637	−3,969	−4,034
% of total	98.6%	97.5%	95.0%	85.4%	92.7%	98.9%

Imports (1986): $A 4,056,000 (food and live animals 29.5%, manufactured goods 25.2%, machinery and transport equipment 15.1%, petroleum and petroleum products 13.8%, beverages and tobacco 7.0%, chemicals 6.6%). *Major import sources:* Australia 40.6%; New Zealand 10.9%; United Kingdom 5.1%; Japan 3.0%; United States 1.0%.
Exports (1986): $A 22,000 (copra 86.4%). *Major export destinations:* n.a.

Transport and communications

Transport. Railroads: none. Roads (1985): total length 5 mi, 8 km (paved, none). Vehicles: passenger cars, n.a.; trucks and buses, n.a.[12]. Merchant marine (1988): vessels (100 gross tons and over) 2; total deadweight tonnage 458. Air transport (1977): passenger arrivals (Funafuti) 1,443; cargo, n.a.; airports (1989) with scheduled flights 1.
Communications. Daily newspapers: none. Radio (1988): total number of receivers 4,000 (1 per 2.2 persons). Television: none. Telephones (1987): 160 (1 per 54 persons).

Education and health

Education (1984)

	schools	teachers	students	student/ teacher ratio
Primary (age 5–11)	11	61	1,349	22.1
Secondary (age 12–18)	1	15[13]	243	...
Vocational[13]	8	16	354	22.1
Higher	—	—	—	—

Educational attainment (1979). Percent of population age 25 and over having: no formal schooling 0.4%; primary education 93.0%; secondary 6.1%; higher 0.5%. *Literacy* (1983): total population literate 5,509 (95.5%); males literate 2,443 (95.5%); females literate 3,066 (95.5%).
Health: physicians (1986) 3 (1 per 2,798 persons); hospital beds (1987) 36 (1 per 238 persons); infant mortality rate per 1,000 live births (1989) 30.
Food: daily per capita caloric intake, n.a.

Military

Total active duty personnel (1987): There is a police force of 32 men.

[1]The value of the Tuvalu Dollar is pegged to the value of the Australian Dollar, which is also legal currency in Tuvalu. [2]Local government councils have been established on all islands except Niulakita. [3]Total includes 46 persons unaccounted for in island populations. [4]De facto population; about 1,500 Tuvaluans live abroad, mainly in Nauru or on foreign fishing vessels. [5]Based on indigenous de facto population only. [6]Mostly subsistence fishermen and handicraft workers. [7]Because of poor soil quality, only limited subsistence agriculture is possible on the islands. [8]Other livestock include goats. [9]Average of first three quarters. [10]Weights of consumer price index components. [11]Capable of supporting coconut palms, pandanus, and breadfruit. [12]There are several cars, tractors, trailers, and light trucks on Funafuti; a few motorcycles are in use on most islands. [13]1982–83.

Uganda

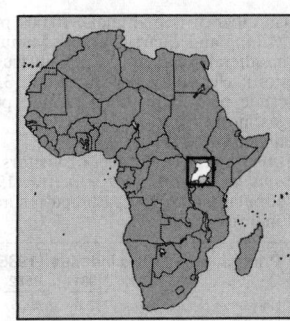

Official name: Republic of Uganda.
Form of government: military regime
  with one interim legislative body
  (National Resistance Council [278[1]])[2].
Head of state and government:
  President.
Capital: Kampala.
Official language: English; Swahili.
Official religion: none.
Monetary unit: 1 Uganda
  shilling (U Sh) = 100 cents;
  valuation (Oct. 2, 1989)
  1 U.S.$ = U Sh 200.00[3];
  1 £ = U Sh 323.60.

Area and population		area		population
		sq mi	sq km	1985 estimate
Districts	**Capitals**			
Apac	Apac	2,510	6,490	369,000
Arua	Olaki	3,020	7,830	543,300
Bundibugyo	Busaru	900	2,340	134,500
Bushenyi	Bumbaire	2,080	5,400	600,300
Gulu	Bungatira	4,530	11,740	305,500
Hoima	Hoima	3,820	9,900	358,400
Iganga	Bulamogi	5,060	13,110	755,100
Jinja	Jinja	280	730	253,400
Kabale	Rubale	960	2,490	503,700
Kabarole	Karambe	3,230	8,360	630,500
Kampala	Kampala	70	180	560,800
Kamuli	Namwendwa	1,680	4,350	400,100
Kapchorwa	Kaptanya	670	1,740	83,100
Kasese	Rukoki	1,240	3,200	342,400
Kitgum	Labongo	6,230	16,140	354,100
Kotido	Kotido	5,100	13,210	194,700
Kumi	Kumi	1,100	2,860	273,100
Lira	Lira	2,800	7,250	430,600
Luwero	Luwero	3,550	9,200	477,800
Masaka	Kaswa Bukoto	6,310	16,330	741,600
Masindi	Nyangeya	3,720	9,640	259,800
Mbale	Bunkoko	980	2,550	647,400
Mbarara	Kakika	4,190	10,840	829,100
Moroto	Katikekile	5,450	14,110	210,900
Moyo	Moyo	1,930	5,010	119,600
Mpigi	Mpigi	2,400	6,220	738,000
Mubende	Bageza	3,980	10,310	616,500
Mukono	Kawuga Mukono	5,500	14,240	708,500
Nebbi	Nebbi	1,120	2,890	258,600
Rakai	Byakabanda	1,920	4,970	329,600
Rukungiri	Kagunga	1,060	2,750	337,400
Soroti	Soroti	3,880	10,060	545,300
Tororo	Sukulu	1,760	4,550	767,100
TOTAL LAND AREA		76,080	197,040	14,679,800
INLAND WATER[4]		16,990	44,000	
TOTAL		93,070[5]	241,040[5]	

Demography

Population (1989): 16,452,000.
Density[6] (1989): persons per sq mi 216.2, persons per sq km 83.5.
Urban–rural (1986): urban 9.7%; rural 90.3%.
Sex distribution (1986): male 46.70%; female 53.30%.
Age breakdown (1985): under 15, 48.5%; 15–29, 25.8%; 30–44, 14.1%; 45–59, 7.4%; 60–74, 3.6%; 75 and over, 0.6%.
Population projection: (2000) 22,399,000; (2010) 29,638,000.
Doubling time: 20 years.
Ethnic composition (1983): Ganda 17.8%; Teso 8.9%; Nkole 8.2%; Soga 8.2%; Gisu 7.2%; Chiga 6.8%; Lango 6.0%; Rwanda 5.8%; Acholi 4.6%; other 26.5%.
Religious affiliation (1980): Roman Catholic 49.6%; Protestant 28.7%; Muslim 6.6%; other 15.1%.
Major cities (1980): Kampala 458,503; Jinja 45,060; Masaka 29,123; Mbale 28,039; Mbarara 23,160.

Vital statistics

Birth rate per 1,000 population (1985–90): 50.1 (world avg. 27.1).
Death rate per 1,000 population (1985–90): 15.4 (world avg. 9.9).
Natural increase rate per 1,000 population (1985–90): 34.7 (world avg. 17.2).
Total fertility rate (avg. births per childbearing woman; 1985–90): 6.9.
Life expectancy at birth (1985–90): male 49.4 years; female 52.7 years.
Major causes of death per 100,000 population: n.a.; however, major diseases include malaria, measles, venereal diseases, and dysentery.

National economy

Budget (1988–89). Revenue: U Sh 45,290,000,000 (sales tax 39.0%, customs duties 17.0%, other 44.0%). Expenditures: U Sh 58,351,000,000 ([1985–86] defense 26.3%, public services 21.7%, education 15.0%, economic services 14.8%).
Public debt (external, outstanding; 1987): U.S.$1,116,000,000.
Tourism (1987): receipts from visitors U.S.$8,000,000; expenditures by nationals abroad U.S.$10,000,000.
Population economically active (1985): total 7,054,000; activity rate of total population 45.6% (participation rates: ages 15–64, 78.9%; female 41.9%).

Price index (1985 = 100)							
	1983	1984	1985	1986	1987	1988	1989[7]
Consumer price index	30.1	43.0	100.0	268.5	908.0	2,576.0	4,467.0

Production (metric tons except as noted). Agriculture, forestry, fishing (1988): bananas and plantains 8,450,000, cassava 4,500,000, sweet potatoes 2,540,000, sugarcane 600,000, pulses 528,000, millet 490,000, dry beans 400,000, corn 357,000, sorghum 330,000, coffee 205,000, peanuts (groundnuts) 120,000, tea 3,747, tobacco 2,500; livestock (number of live animals) 4,260,000 cattle, 2,110,000 goats, 690,000 sheep; roundwood (1987) 13,385,000 cu m; fish catch 214,700. Mining and quarrying (1988): tungsten (wolfram) 75; copper ore (metal content) 64. Manufacturing (1988): meat 107,000; sugar 40,000; cement 14,960; animal feed 10,996; metal products 3,000; footwear 363,000 pairs; fabrics 11,472,000 sq m; cigarettes 1,638,000,000 units; beer 214,930 hectolitres. Construction: n.a. Energy production (consumption): electricity (kW-hr; 1987) 655,000,000 (548,000,000); petroleum products (metric tons; 1987) none (231,000).
Gross national product (at current market prices; 1987): U.S.$4,086,000,000 (U.S.$260 per capita).

Structure of gross domestic product and labour force				
	1988		1985	
	in value U Sh '000,000[8]	% of total value	labour force	% of labour force
Agriculture	3,952	49.9	5,940,000	84.2
Manufacturing and mining	366	4.6		
Construction	219	2.8	317,000	4.5
Public utilities	99	1.2		
Transp. and commun.	328	4.1		
Trade	743	9.4		
Finance	780	9.8	797,000	11.3
Pub. admin., defense	959	12.1		
Services	481	6.1		
TOTAL	7,927	100.0	7,054,000	100.0

Household size. Average household size (1983) 4.8; income per household: n.a.; expenditure[9] (1981): food 58.0%, clothing 14.0%, transportation 10.0%, fuel and lighting 6.0%.
Land use (1987): forested 28.8%; meadows and pastures 25.0%; agricultural and under permanent cultivation 33.6%; other 12.6%.

Foreign trade

Balance of trade (current prices)						
	1983	1984	1985	1986	1987	1988
U.S.$'000,000	+25.2	+120.5	+109.5	+85.4	−170.8	−226.3
% of total	3.5%	17.4%	18.7%	12.1%	20.4%	29.3%

Imports (1988): U.S.$499,200,000 ([1984] sugar 16.0%, motor vehicles 10.8%, clothing and fabrics 9.6%, construction materials 8.0%, food 5.4%). *Major import sources* (1987): Kenya 24.7%; United Kingdom 13.6%; Italy 12.7%; West Germany 9.5%; Japan 7.1%.
Exports (1988): U.S.$272,900,000 (unroasted coffee 96.8%). *Major export destinations* (1987): United States 25.1%; United Kingdom 17.8%; France 11.3%; Spain 9.7%; The Netherlands 9.0%; West Germany 5.7%.

Transport and communications

Transport. Railroads (1988): route length 1,300 km; passenger-km 118,000,000; metric ton-km cargo 83,000,000. Roads (1986): total length 28,332 km (paved 22%). Vehicles (1988): passenger cars 32,913; trucks and buses 5,646[10]. Merchant marine (1988): vessels (100 gross tons and over) 3; total deadweight tonnage 8,600. Air transport[11] (1988): passenger-km 130,000,000; metric ton-km cargo 16,000,000; airports (1989) 5.
Communications. Daily newspapers (1988): total number 6; total circulation 100,000; circulation per 1,000 population 6.3. Radio (1988): 345,114 receivers (1 per 46 persons). Television (1988): 90,000 receivers (1 per 178 persons). Telephones (1983): 54,439 (1 per 255 persons).

Education and health

Education (1984)	schools	teachers	students	student/teacher ratio
Primary (age 5–11)	6,420	58,377	1,908,564	32.7
Secondary (age 12–15)	297	5,603	114,828	20.5
Voc., teacher tr.	118	1,039	23,335	22.5
Higher	14	934	8,216	8.8

Educational attainment (1969). Percent of population age 25 and over having: no formal schooling, or less than one full year 58.2%; primary education 33.9%; lower secondary 5.0%; upper secondary 2.5%; higher 0.4%.
Literacy (1985): population age 15 and over literate 4,822,000 (57.0%); males literate 2,880,000 (69.7%); females literate 1,942,000 (45.3%).
Health: physicians (1984) 700 (1 per 20,300 persons); hospital beds (1983) 20,343 (1 per 683 persons); infant mortality rate per 1,000 live births (1985–90) 103.0.
Food (1984–86): daily per capita caloric intake 2,225 (vegetable products 94%, animal products 6%); 95% of FAO recommended minimum requirement.

Military

Total active duty personnel (1989): 70,000 (army 100%). *Military expenditure as percent of GNP* (1985): 1.4% (world 5.7%); per capita expenditure U.S.$4.

---

[1]Includes 68 nonelective seats. [2]Constitution of 1967 suspended July 1985. [3]On Oct. 24, 1989, the Uganda shilling was devalued by about 41%. [4]Includes swamps. [5]Detail does not add to total given because of rounding. [6]Based on land area. [7]April. [8]At 1966 prices. [9]Middle-income families only. [10]1986. [11]Uganda Airlines only.

Union of Soviet Socialist Republics

Official name: Soyuz Sovetskykh Sotsialisticheskikh Respublik (Sovetsky Soyuz) (Union of Soviet Socialist Republics [Soviet Union]).
Form of government: federal socialist republic with two legislative houses (Congress of People's Deputies [2,250]; Supreme Soviet [542], comprising two chambers, Soviet of the Union [271] and Soviet of the Nationalities [271]).
Chief of state: President (Chairman of the Supreme Soviet).
Head of government: Premier (Chairman of the Council of Ministers).
Capital: Moscow.
Official language: Russian.
Official religion: none.
Monetary unit: 1 ruble = 100 kopecks; valuation[1] (Oct. 2, 1989) 1 ruble = U.S.$1.59 = £0.98.

Area and population		area		population
				1989[2]
Soviet Federated Socialist Republic	Capitals	sq mi	sq km	census
Russian S.F.S.R.	Moscow	6,592,800	17,075,400	147,386,000
Soviet Socialist Republics				
Armenian	Yerevan	11,500	29,800	3,283,000
Azerbaijan	Baku	33,400	86,600	7,029,000
Belorussian	Minsk	80,200	207,600	10,200,000
Estonian	Tallinn	17,400	45,100	1,573,000
Georgian	Tbilisi	26,900	69,700	5,449,000
Kazakh	Alma-Ata	1,049,200	2,717,300	16,538,000
Kirgiz	Frunze	76,600	198,500	4,291,000
Latvian	Riga	24,900	64,500	2,681,000
Lithuanian	Vilnius	25,200	65,200	3,690,000
Moldavian	Kishinyov	13,000	33,700	4,341,000
Tadzhik	Dushanbe	55,300	143,100	5,112,000
Turkmen	Ashkhabad	188,500	488,100	3,534,000
Ukrainian	Kiev	233,100	603,700	51,704,000
Uzbek	Tashkent	172,700	447,400	19,906,000
TOTAL LAND AREA		8,600,700	22,275,700	286,717,000
INLAND WATER		49,100	127,300	
TOTAL		8,649,800	22,403,000	

Demography

Population (1989): 287,800,000.
Density (1989): persons per sq mi 33.2, persons per sq km 12.8.
Urban–rural (1989): urban 65.9%; rural 34.1%.
Sex distribution (1989): male 47.26%; female 52.74%.
Age breakdown (1987): under 15, 25.5%; 15–29, 24.0%; 30–44, 18.7%; 45–59, 18.3%; 60–69, 7.1%; 70 and over, 6.4%.
Population projection: (2000) 311,078,000; (2010) 333,404,000.
Doubling time: 70 years.
Ethnic composition (1983): Russian 51.9%; Ukrainian 15.8%; Uzbek 5.1%; Belorussian 3.6%; Kazakh 2.6%; Tatar 2.4%; Azerbaijani 2.2%; Armenian 1.7%; Georgian 1.4%; Tadzhik 1.2%; Moldavian 1.1%; Lithuanian 1.1%; other 9.9%.
Religious affiliation (1989): Christian 36.7%, of which Orthodox 31.5%, Protestant 3.3%, Roman Catholic 1.9%; Muslim 11.9%; Jewish 1.1%; nonreligious 29.7%; atheist 20.5%; other 0.1%.
Major cities (1989): Moscow 8,769,000; Leningrad 4,456,000; Kiev 2,587,000; Tashkent 2,073,000; Baku 1,757,000; Kharkov 1,611,000; Minsk 1,589,000; Novosibirsk 1,436,000; Gorky 1,438,000; Sverdlovsk 1,367,000; Tbilisi 1,260,000; Kuybyshev 1,257,000; Dnepropetrovsk 1,179,000.

Other principal cities (1989)					
	population		population		population
Alma-Ata	1,128,000	Krasnodar	620,000	Samarkand	366,000
Barnaul	602,000	Krasnoyarsk	912,000	Saratov	905,000
Chelyabinsk	1,143,000	Krivoy Rog	713,000	Tolyatti	630,000
Donetsk	1,110,000	Lvov	790,000	Tula	540,000
Dushanbe	595,000	Mariupol	517,000	Ufa	1,083,000
Frunze	616,000	Novokuznetsk	600,000	Ulyanovsk	625,000
Irkutsk	626,000	Odessa	1,115,000	Vilnius	582,000
Izhevsk	635,000	Omsk	1,148,000	Vladivostok	648,000
Karaganda	614,000	Orenburg	547,000	Volgograd	999,000
Kazan	1,094,000	Penza	543,000	Voronezh	887,000
Kemerovo	520,000	Perm	1,091,000	Yaroslavl	633,000
Khabarovsk	601,000	Riga	915,000	Yerevan	1,199,000
Kishinyov	665,000	Rostov-na-Donu	1,020,000	Zaporozhye	884,000

Place of birth (1983): 99.9% native-born; 0.1% foreign-born.
Mobility (1985). Population living in the same residence from birth: 57.0%; 15 years and more 20.1%; 14–10 years 5.7%; 9–6 years 5.1%; 5–2 years 7.2%; less than 2 years 4.9%.
Households[3] (1979). Average household size 3.5; 2 persons 29.7%, 3 persons 28.8%, 4 persons 23.0%, 5 persons 9.5%, 6 persons 4.1%, 7 or more persons 4.9%. Family households population: 232,075,245 (86.9%), nonfamily population 30,360,755 (13.1%).
Emigration (1988): 106,000.

Vital statistics

Birth rate per 1,000 population (1987): 19.8 (world avg. 27.1); legitimate, 90.2%; illegitimate, 9.8%.
Death rate per 1,000 population (1987): 9.9 (world avg. 9.9).
Natural increase rate per 1,000 population (1987): 9.9 (world avg. 17.2).
Total fertility rate (avg. births per childbearing woman; 1987): 2.4.
Marriage rate per 1,000 population (1987): 9.8.
Divorce rate per 1,000 population (1987): 3.4.
Life expectancy at birth (1987): male 65.1 years; female 73.8 years.
Major causes of death per 100,000 population (1986): diseases of the circulatory system 544.3; malignant neoplasms (cancers) 155.2; accidents, poisonings, and violence 88.6; diseases of the respiratory system 81.3; diseases of the digestive system 28.4; infectious and parasitic diseases 21.2.

Social indicators

Educational attainment (1987). Percent of population age 10 and over having: primary education 29.2%; some secondary 18.8%; secondary 41.5%; some postsecondary 1.5%; higher and postgraduate 9.0%.
Distribution of income: n.a.
Quality of working life (1988). Average workweek: 39.0 hours (5.0% overtime). Annual rate per 100,000 workers for: injury or accident, 582; industrial illness, n.a.; death, 12.1. Proportion of labour force insured for damages or income loss resulting from: injury 100.0%; permanent disability 100.0%; death 100.0%. Average days lost to labour stoppages per 1,000 workdays: (1989) 6.2. Average duration of journey to work: 58–68 minutes (mostly by public transportation and foot). Rate per 1,000 workers of discouraged (unemployed no longer seeking work): n.a.
Access to services[4] (1987). Proportion of dwellings having access to: electricity, virtually 100%; safe public water supply 92.5%; public sewage collection 90.5%; central heating 89.7%; gas 77.9%; hot water 73.7%; bathroom 84.7%.
Social participation. Eligible voters participating in last national election (1989): 98%. Population participating in voluntary work (1986): 75.1%. Trade union membership in total work force: 100.0%. Practicing religious population in total affiliated population: n.a; estimated at 10%.
Social deviance. Offense rate per 100,000 population (1989)[5] for: murder 7.7; rape 7.9; serious body injuries 21.6; burglary and housebreaking 196.6. Incidence per 100,000 in general population (1988) of: alcoholism 1,598; drug and substance abuse 24.3; suicide, n.a.
Leisure (1987). Favourite leisure activities (annual attendance): movies 3,775,000,000; lectures 301,800,000; museums 199,000,000; concerts 142,100,000; theatre 122,800,000.
Material well-being (1987). Households possessing: automobile 16.0%; telephone 28.5%; television receiver virtually 100%; refrigerator 93.0%; air conditioner, virtually none; washing machine 70.0%; motorcycle 14.0%; bicycle 58.0%; tape recorder 41.0%.

National economy

Gross national product[6] (at current market prices; 1987): U.S.$2,310,000,000,000 (U.S.$8,160 per capita).

Structure of net material product and labour force				
	1987			
	in value '000,000,000 rubles	% of total value	labour force	% of labour force
Agriculture	122.9	20.5	24,840,000	19.0
Mining and manufacturing	268.6	44.8	38,139,000	29.1
Public utilities			5,057,000	3.9
Construction	75.0	12.5	11,955,000	9.1
Transportation and communications	36.6	6.1	12,048,000	9.2
Trade	96.5	16.1	10,334,000	7.9
Finance	—	—	674,000	0.5
Pub. admin., defense	—	—	1,987,000	1.5
Services	—	—	23,812,000	18.2
Other	—	—	2,106,000	1.6
TOTAL	599.6	100.0	130,952,000	100.0

Public debt (1989): U.S.$55,800,000,000[7].
Land use (1987): forested 35.7%; meadows and pastures 16.8%; agricultural and under permanent cultivation 10.2%; other 37.3%.

Manufacturing, mining, and construction enterprises (1987)				
	no. of enterprises	no. of employees	monthly wages as a % of avg. of all wages	value added ('000,000 rubles)
Manufacturing				
Machinery and metal products	9,238	16,500,000	110.4	34,678
Fuel and energy	2,603	2,600,000	145.2	21,841
Metallurgy	711	2,200,000	133.6	14,431
Chemicals and chemical products	6,619	4,700,000	110.5	12,192
Textiles, clothing, and footwear	7,960	5,100,000	86.0	11,769
Food, beverages, and tobacco	9,554	3,000,000	101.7	9,415
Building materials	4,336	2,300,000	108.0	3,026

Budget (1989). Revenue: 459,814,445,000 rubles (share in profits of state and cooperative enterprises 91.4%). Expenditures: 494,797,545,000 rubles (national economy 51.4%, social welfare, education, and culture 33.0%, defense 15.6%).
Tourism (1987): receipts from visitors U.S.$198,000,000; expenditures by nationals abroad U.S.$175,000,000.
Production (metric tons except as noted). Agriculture, forestry, fishing (1988): sugar beets 87,855,000, wheat 84,445,000, potatoes 62,705,000, barley 44,463,000, vegetables 29,330,000, rye 18,715,000, corn (maize) 16,030,000, oats 15,287,000, raw cotton 8,689,000, grapes 6,500,000, sunflower seeds 6,157,000, rice 2,866,000, tobacco 490,000; live-

stock (number of live animals) 140,500,000 sheep, 120,500,000 cattle, 77,300,000 pigs, 6,700,000 horses, 6,500,000 goats, 1,168,300,000 poultry; roundwood (1987) 297,000,000 cu m; fish catch 10,900,000. Mining and quarrying (1988): iron ore 248,000,000; phosphate rock 94,000,000; salt 15,500,000; potash salts 11,000,000; bauxite 4,600,000; chromium ore 3,700,000; manganese (metal content) 2,700,000; asbestos 2,600,000; magnesite 2,500,000; zinc 810,000; copper 640,000; lead 440,000; nickel 190,000; molybdenum 11,500; tungsten 9,200; silver 1,550; gold 280; mercury 67,000 flasks; diamonds 11,000,000 carats. Manufacturing (1988): crude steel 163,000,000; cement 139,000,000; rolled steel 116,000,000; pig iron 112,000,000; mineral fertilizers 37,100,000; sulfuric acid 29,000,000; steel pipes 21,400,000; meat 19,300,000; sugar 12,100,000; paper and paperboard 6,300,000; canned fish 4,600,000; resins and plastics 5,488,800[8]; soda ash 5,100,000; caustic soda 3,288,000[8]; vegetable oil 2,950,000[8]; cotton fibre 2,840,000; cotton yarn 1,747,000[8]; man-made fibres 2,055,000; butter 1,672,000[8]; margarine 1,500,000; synthetic detergents 1,200,000[9]; soap 1,100,000[8]; insecticides 600,000[9]; woolen yarn 465,000; woolen fibre 421,000[11]; flax fibre 217,000[8]; leather 124,000; cotton fabrics 8,114,000,000 sq m; silk fabrics 2,123,000,000 sq m; linen fabrics 1,158,000,000 sq m; woolen fabrics 708,000,000 sq m; agricultural equipment 4,213,000,000 rubles[9]; machine tools 2,838,000,000 rubles[8]; food-processing equipment 1,800,000,000 rubles[8]; chemical equipment 966,000,000 rubles[8]; forge press machines 643,000,000 rubles[8]; oil equipment 241,000,000 rubles[8]; leather footwear 820,000,000 pairs; tires 67,800,000 units[8]; television receivers 9,628,000 units; radio receivers 8,026,000 units; refrigerators 6,231,000 units; bicycles 5,637,000 units; washing machines 6,103,000 units; passenger cars 1,300,000 units; motorcycles 1,068,000 units; buses 85,315 units[9]; railroad freight cars 58,433 units[10]; railroad passenger cars 1,814 units[10]; beer 51,200,000 hectolitres; wine 29,200,000 hectolitres. Construction (1987): residential 131,500,000 sq m, of which urban 90,400,000 sq m, rural 41,100,000 sq m.

Service enterprises (1987)

	no. of enterprises	no. of employees	monthly wages as a % of all wages
Public utilities	...	4,104,000	76.1
Electrical power	1,424	953,000	108.0
Transport: rail	...	2,402,000	116.8
Transport: road	...	7,606,000	117.1
Transport: water	...	434,000	140.2
Communications	91,016	1,606,000	86.3
Finance	...	674,000	97.9
Wholesale trade	...	} 10,334,000	81.6
Retail trade	727,600		76.7
Tourism	...	...	...
Education	183,806	10,420,000	81.6
Public services and administration	...	1,987,000	92.6
Other services	...	13,392,000	...

Energy production (consumption): electricity (kW-hr; 1988) 1,705,000,-000,000 (1,630,300,000,000[8]); coal (metric tons; 1988) 772,000,000 (694,-897,000[8]); crude petroleum (barrels; 1988) 4,477,000,000 (3,676,000,000[8]); petroleum products (metric tons; 1987) 436,453,000 (373,593,000); natural gas (cu m; 1988) 770,000,000,000 (568,000,000,000). Production of energy by source (1988): thermal power 73.9%; hydroelectric power 13.5%; nuclear power 12.6%.
Population economically active (1987): total 130,952,000; activity rate of total population 46.3% (participation rates: ages 16–59 [male], 16–54 [female] 82.9%; female 49.9%; unemployed, n.a.).

Price and earnings indexes (1985 = 100)

	1981	1982	1983	1984	1985	1986	1987
Consumer price index	96.4	99.5	100.2	99.0	100.0	102.0	103.0
Monthly earnings index	93.7	96.5	98.3	99.6	100.0	105.9	109.2

Household income and expenditure. Average household size (1985) 3.2; average annual income per household 6,100 rubles (U.S.$8,700); sources of income (1987): wages and salaries 79.1%, transfer payments 9.3%, self-employment 3.3%, other 8.3%; expenditure (1987): food 40.6%, clothing 20.8%, household durable goods 11.6%, recreation and culture 8.6%.

Foreign trade

Balance of trade (current prices)

	1981	1982	1983	1984	1985	1986	1987
'000,000,000 rubles	4.5	6.7	8.3	9.1	3.2	5.7	7.4
% of total	4.1%	5.6%	6.5%	6.5%	2.3%	4.4%	5.8%

Imports (1987): 60,741,000,000 rubles (machinery and transport equipment 41.4%; cereals and food products 16.1%; consumer goods 13.0%; raw materials 8.1%; mineral fuels and lubricants 5.2%; chemicals and related products 5.3%; textiles and clothing 1.5%). *Major import sources* (1987): East Germany 11.7%; Czechoslovakia 11.4%; Bulgaria 10.8%; Poland 10.4%; Hungary 8.4%; Japan 7.8%; Cuba 6.3%; West Germany 4.3%; Romania 3.8%; Yugoslavia 3.4%; Finland 3.3%; Italy 2.7%; India 1.8%; France 1.8%; United States 1.5%; Iraq 1.3%; China 1.2%; Mongolia 0.7%.
Exports (1987): 68,142,000,000 rubles (crude petroleum and petroleum products 35.7%; machinery and transport equipment 15.5%; mineral fuels and natural gas 10.8%; raw materials 8.5%; chemicals, fertilizers, and resins 3.4%; wood and paper products 3.3%). *Major export destinations* (1987): East Germany 11.2%; Czechoslovakia 9.9%; Poland 9.6%; Bulgaria 9.2%; Hungary 6.8%; Cuba 5.5%; Romania 3.7%; West Germany 3.4%; Yugoslavia 2.8%; Italy 2.6%; Finland 2.5%; France 2.2%; United Kingdom 2.3%; Vietnam 2.1%; Mongolia 1.7%; India 1.6%; Japan 1.4%; North Korea 1.2%.

Trade by commodity group (1987)

SITC Group	imports '000 rubles	%	exports '000 rubles	%
00 Food and live animals	9,779,000	16.1	1,090,000	1.6
02 Raw materials, excluding fuels	4,920,000	8.1	5,792,000	8.5
03 Mineral fuels, lubricants, and related materials	2,369,000	3.9	31,686,000	46.5
05 Chemicals and related products	3,219,000	5.3	2,317,000	3.4
65 Textile yarn, fabrics and related materials	911,000	1.5	1,022,000	1.5
07 Machinery and transport equipment	25,147,000	41.4	10,562,000	15.5
08 Miscellaneous manufactured articles	7,896,000	13.0	1,772,000	2.6
09 Goods not classified by kind	6,500,000	10.7	13,901,000	20.4
TOTAL	60,741,000	100.0	68,142,000	100.0

Direction of trade (1987)

	imports '000 rubles	%	exports '000 rubles	%
Communist				
Comecon	38,856,000	64.0	40,696,000	59.7
Other	3,265,000	5.4	3,504,000	5.1
Market Economy				
Industrial countries	13,873,000	22.8	14,186,000	20.8
Developing countries	4,747,000	7.8	9,756,000	14.4
TOTAL	60,741,000	100.0	68,142,000	100.0

Transport and communications

Transport. Railroads (1987): length 90,809 mi, 146,144 km; passenger-mi 250,000,000,000, passenger-km 402,300,000,000; short ton-mi cargo 2,619,-500,000,000, metric ton-km cargo 3,824,700,000,000. Roads (1988): total length 603,500 mi, 971,200 km (paved 74%). Vehicles (1980): passenger cars 8,255,000; trucks and buses 7,254,000. Inland waterways (1987): length 76,550 mi, 123,200 km; passenger-mi 3,542,000,000, passenger-km 5,700,-000,000; short ton-mi cargo 172,900,000,000, metric ton-km cargo 252,500,-000,000. Merchant marine (1988): vessels (100 gross tons and over) 6,741; total deadweight tonnage 29,199,278. Air transport (1988): passenger-mi 132,458,000,000, passenger-km 213,171,000,000; short ton-mi cargo 1,865,-000,000, metric ton-km cargo 2,722,800,000; airports (1989) with scheduled flights 52. Shares of domestic passenger traffic by mode of transportation (1987): buses 43.4%; railway 37.1%; ships and airplanes 19.5%. Oil and gas pipelines (1988): length 176,100 mi, 283,400 km; short ton-mi cargo 1,735,800,000,000[8]; metric ton-km cargo 2,793,500,000,000[8].

Distribution of traffic (1987)

	cargo carried ('000,000 tons)	% of nat'l total	passengers carried ('000,000)	% of nat'l total
Road	6,853.0	52.5	49,983.0	43.2
Rail	4,067.0	31.1	4,360.0	3.8
Urban transport			60,997.0	52.7
road	—	—	36,100.0	31.2
rail	—	—	24,897.0	21.5
Sea and river	925.0	7.1	178.0	0.2
Air	3.2	0.0	119.0	0.1
Pipeline	1,212.0	9.3	—	—
TOTAL	13,060.2	100.0	115,637.0	100.0

Communications. Daily newspapers (1987): total number 726; total circulation 105,900,000; circulation per 1,000 population 374. Radio (1987): 191,-547,000 receivers (1 per 1.5 persons). Television (1987): 88,000,000 receivers (1 per 3.2 persons). Telephones (1987): 42,100,000 (1 per 6.7 persons).

Education and health

Education (1987–88)

	schools	teachers	students	student/teacher ratio
Primary (age 6–13)	67,100 }	2,807,000	37,900,000 }	15.2
Secondary (age 14–17)	63,200		4,700,000	
Vocational	4,508	251,800	2,911,000	11.6
Higher	898	370,000	2,675,000	7.2

Literacy (1984): total population age 15 and over literate 99.0%.
Health (1988): physicians 1,098,100 (1 per 259 persons); hospital beds 3,965,-000 (1 per 72 persons); infant mortality rate per 1,000 live births (1987) 25.4.
Food (1984–86): daily per capita caloric intake 3,205 (vegetable products 74%, animal products 26%); (1984) 105% of FAO recommended minimum.

Military

Total active duty personnel (1988): 5,096,600 (army 37.3%, command and general support troops 29.1%, air defense forces 10.2%, navy 9.0%, air force 8.6%, strategic rocket forces 5.8%). *Military expenditure as percent of GNP* (1987): 12.3%[6] (world 5.4%); per capita expenditure U.S.$1,067.

[1]Official rate only; the black market rate is 10 rubles per U.S.$. [2]Preliminary. [3]Family households only. [4]Urban dwellings only. [5]Annualized rates based on first six months. [6]Estimated by Western sources. [7]Foreign debt at the beginning of the year; 33,600,000,000 rubles converted at the official rate of 1 ruble = U.S.$1.66. [8]1987. [9]1986. [10]1985.

United Arab Emirates

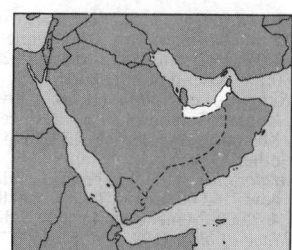

Official name: Ittiḥād al-Imārāt al-ʿArabīyah (United Arab Emirates).
Form of government: monarchy; federal union of seven emirates with one appointive advisory body (Federal National Council [40][1]).
Chief of state: President.
Head of government: Prime Minister.
Capital: Abu Dhabi[2].
Official language: Arabic.
Official religion: Islam.
Monetary unit: 1 U.A.E. Dirham (Dh) = 100 fils; valuation (Oct. 2, 1989) 1 U.S.$ = Dh 3.67; 1 £ = Dh 5.94.

Area and population

Emirates	Capitals	area sq mi	area sq km	population 1985 census
Abu Dhabi (Abū Ẓaby)	Abu Dhabi	26,000	67,350	670,125
ʿAjmān (Ajman)	ʿAjmān	100	250	64,318
Dubayy (Dubai)	Dubayy	1,510	3,900	419,104
Al-Fujayrah (Fujairah)	Al-Fujayrah	440	1,150	54,425
Ra's al-Khaymah (Ras al-Khaimah)	Ra's al-Khaymah	660	1,700	116,470
Ash-Shāriqah (Sharjah)	Ash-Shāriqah	1,000	2,600	268,722
Umm al-Qaywayn (Umm al-Qaiwain)	Umm al-Qaywayn	290	750	29,229
TOTAL		30,000	77,700	1,622,393

Demography

Population (1989): 1,827,000.
Density (1989): persons per sq mi 60.9, persons per sq km 23.5.
Urban–rural (1986): urban 86.6%; rural 13.4%.
Sex distribution (1986): male 67%; female 33%.
Age breakdown (1986): under 15, 29.8%; 15–29, 25.1%; 30–44, 35.9%; 45–59, 7.6%; 60–74, 1.3%; 75 and over, 0.3%.
Population projection: (2000) 2,518,000; (2010) 3,371,000.
Doubling time: 23 years.
Ethnic composition (1983): Arab 87.1%, of which Arab from United Arab Emirates 30.7%; Pakistani and Indian 9.1%; Persian 1.7%; Baluchi 0.8%; African 0.8%; British 0.2%; American 0.1%; other 0.2%.
Religious affiliation (1980): Muslim 94.9% (Sunnī 80%, Shīʿī 20%); Christian 3.8%; other 1.3%.
Major cities (1980): Dubayy 266,000; Abu Dhabi 243,000; ash-Shāriqah 125,000; al-ʿAyn 102,000; Ra's al-Khaymah 42,000.

Vital statistics

Birth rate per 1,000 population (1986): 33.5 (world avg. 27.1); legitimate, n.a.; illegitimate, n.a.
Death rate per 1,000 population (1986): 3.9 (world avg. 9.9).
Natural increase rate per 1,000 population (1986): 29.6 (world avg. 17.2).
Total fertility rate (avg. births per childbearing woman; 1987): 5.7.
Marriage rate per 1,000 population (1986): 2.9[3].
Divorce rate per 1,000 population (1986): 1.3[3].
Life expectancy at birth (1986): male 68.4 years; female 71.7 years.
Major causes of death per 100,000 population (1986)[3]: cardiovascular diseases 68.0; accidents and poisonings 29.1; malignant neoplasms (cancers) 22.5; congenital anomalies 21.5; respiratory diseases 14.6.

National economy

Budget (1987). Revenue: U.S.$7,250,000,000 (oil revenue 85.5%). Expenditures: U.S.$9,000,000,000 (current expenditure 64.4%, development 16.7%).
Gross national product (at current market prices; 1987): U.S.$22,827,000,000 (U.S.$15,680 per capita).

Structure of gross domestic product and labour force

	1987 in value Dh '000,000	1987 % of total value	1986 labour force	1986 % of labour force
Agriculture	1,435	1.7	44,124	5.0
Mining	32,473	38.0	18,100	2.0
Manufacturing	7,904	9.2	57,029	6.4
Construction	7,435	8.7	221,003	24.8
Public utilities	−376	−0.4	17,233	1.9
Transportation and communications	4,400	5.1	65,896	7.4
Trade	9,614	11.2	121,278	13.6
Finance	9,812	11.5	27,831	3.1
Pub. admin., defense } Services	13,979	16.3	318,447	35.7
Other	−1,136	−1.3	—	—
TOTAL	85,540	100.0	890,941	100.0[4]

Public debt (external, outstanding; 1982): U.S.$1,117,000,000.
Production (metric tons except as noted). Agriculture, forestry, fishing (1988): watermelons and melons 73,000, tomatoes 65,000, dates 65,000, cabbages 27,000, pumpkins and squash 19,000, eggplants 16,000, cauliflowers 13,000, cucumbers 9,000, lemons and limes 7,000, mangoes 3,000, green peppers 3,000; livestock (number of live animals) 825,000 goats, 400,000 sheep, 121,000 camels, 48,000 cattle, 5,000,000 chickens; fish catch 85,410. Mining and quarrying (1986): lime 45,000; also marble, shale for ceramic applications, and aggregate for cement. Manufacturing (1987): cement 5,100,000;

aluminum 154,000; cow's milk 12,000; mutton and lamb meat 7,000; goat meat 5,000; beef and veal 3,000; sulfur 1,460; butter and ghee 299. Construction (value added in Dh; 1987): 7,435,000,000. Energy production (consumption): electricity (kW-hr; 1987) 13,100,000,000 (13,100,000,000); coal, none (n.a.); crude petroleum (barrels; 1987) 526,388,000 (54,020,000); petroleum products (metric tons; 1987) 12,026,000 (6,436,000); natural gas (cu m; 1987) 16,404,000,000 (13,529,000,000).
Tourism (1983): 16,351 rooms for tourists.
Population economically active (1986): total 891,000; activity rate of total population 53.2% (participation rates: ages 15–64, 76.7%; female 6.6%; unemployed, n.a.).
Price and earnings indexes: n.a.
Household income and expenditure: Average household size (1986) 6.8; income per household: n.a.; sources of income: n.a.; expenditure: n.a.
Land use (1986): forested, none; meadows and pastures 2.4%; agricultural and under permanent cultivation 0.2%; built-up, wasteland, and other 97.4%.

Foreign trade

Balance of trade (current prices)

	1982	1983	1984	1985	1986
Dh '000,000	+18,187	+24,430	+27,238	+23,249	+36,707
% of total	31.6%	28.5%	36.7%	31.8%	46.1%

Imports (1986): Dh 21,432,000,000 (machinery and transport equipment 31.0%, basic manufactures 21.1%, food and live animals 16.0%, chemicals 6.7%, mineral fuels 4.9%, crude minerals 1.8%). *Major import sources* (1987): Japan 15.7%; United Kingdom 10.9%; West Germany 10.4%; United States 8.6%; France 5.8%; Italy 5.3%; Bahrain 3.2%; The Netherlands 2.5%; Australia 2.4%; Singapore 1.7%; China 1.6%; Belgium-Luxembourg 1.5%; Switzerland 1.4%; Saudi Arabia 1.0%; Thailand 0.9%; Turkey 0.6%.
Exports (1986): Dh 58,139,000,000 (crude petroleum 89.6%, nonpetroleum exports 10.4%). *Major export destinations* (1987): Japan 37.7%; United States 5.0%; Oman 4.4%; Singapore 3.7%; Italy 3.4%; South Korea 3.4%; France 2.0%; West Germany 1.6%; Pakistan 1.2%; United Kingdom 1.1%; Australia 0.9%; Bangladesh 0.9%; The Netherlands 0.9%; Belgium-Luxembourg 0.3%; Bahrain 0.2%.

Transport and communications

Transport. Railroads: none. Roads (1984): total length 2,709 mi, 4,360 km (paved [1981] 61%). Vehicles (1984): passenger cars 61,146; trucks and buses 16,618. Merchant marine (1988): vessels (100 gross tons and over) 241; total deadweight tonnage 1,311,865. Air transport[5] (1988): passenger-mi 1,881,915,000, passenger-km 3,028,654,000; short ton-mi cargo 65,903,000, metric ton-km cargo 96,223,000; airports (1989) with scheduled flights 5.
Communications. Daily newspapers (1986): total number 12; total circulation 291,000; circulation per 1,000 population 174. Radio (1988): total number of receivers 377,791 (1 per 4.7 persons). Television (1988): total number of receivers 150,000 (1 per 12 persons). Telephones (1987): 403,601 (1 per 4.3 persons).

Education and health

Education (1986–87)

	schools	teachers	students	student/ teacher ratio
Primary (age 6–11) }	354	6,793	165,463	24.4
Secondary (age 12–18) }		4,464	67,621	15.1
Vocational[6]	9	372	2,614	7.0
Higher	...	449[7]	7,640	...

Educational attainment (1975). Percent of population age 25 and over having: no formal schooling 72.2%; primary education 5.2%; secondary 16.6%; higher 6.0%. *Literacy* (1986): total population age 15 and over literate 858,149 (73.0%); males literate 657,579 (74.5%); females literate 200,570 (68.4%).
Health (1985): physicians 2,361 (1 per 659 persons); hospital beds 5,817 (1 per 267 persons); infant mortality rate per 1,000 live births (1986) 39.9.
Food (1984–86): daily per capita caloric intake 3,714 (vegetable products 80%, animal products 20%); 154% of FAO recommended minimum requirement.

Military

Total active duty personnel (1988): 43,000 (army 93.0%, navy 3.5%, air force 3.5%). *Military expenditure as percent of GNP* (1986): 7.4% (world 5.5%); per capita expenditure U.S.$929.

[1]All appointed seats. [2]Provisional. [3]Registered; Abu Dhabi Emirate only. [4]Detail does not add to total given because of rounding. [5]Emirates (airline) and one-fourth apportionment of international flights of Gulf Air only. [6]1985–86. [7]1984–85.

United Kingdom

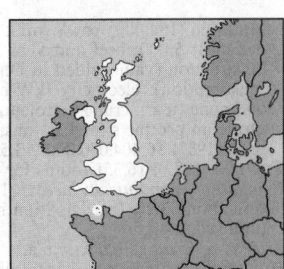

Official name: United Kingdom of
Great Britain and Northern Ireland.
Form of government: constitutional
monarchy with two legislative houses
(House of Lords [1,190]; House of
Commons [650]).
Chief of state: Sovereign.
Head of government: Prime Minister.
Capital: London.
Official language: English.
Official religion: Churches of England
and Scotland "established" (protected
by the state, but not "official") in their
respective countries; no established
church in Northern Ireland or Wales.
Monetary unit: 1 pound sterling
(£) = 100 new pence; valuation (Oct.
2, 1989) 1 £ = U.S.$1.62.

Area and population

Countries	Capitals	area sq mi	area sq km	population 1987 estimate
England	London	50,363	130,439	47,406,700
Counties				
Avon		520	1,346	951,200
Bedfordshire		477	1,235	525,900
Berkshire		486	1,259	740,600
Buckinghamshire		727	1,883	621,300
Cambridgeshire		1,316	3,409	642,400
Cheshire		899	2,329	951,900
Cleveland		225	583	554,500
Cornwall[1]		1,376	3,564	453,100
Cumbria		2,629	6,810	486,900
Derbyshire		1,016	2,631	918,700
Devon		2,591	6,711	1,010,000
Dorset		1,025	2,654	648,600
Durham		941	2,436	598,700
East Sussex		693	1,795	698,000
Essex		1,418	3,672	1,521,800
Gloucestershire		1,020	2,643	522,200
Greater London[2]		610	1,579	6,770,400
Greater Manchester[2]		497	1,287	2,580,100
Hampshire		1,458	3,777	1,537,000
Hereford & Worcester		1,516	3,927	665,100
Hertfordshire		631	1,634	986,800
Humberside		1,356	3,512	846,500
Isle of Wight		147	381	126,900
Kent		1,441	3,731	1,510,500
Lancashire		1,183	3,064	1,381,300
Leicestershire		986	2,553	879,400
Lincolnshire		2,284	5,915	574,600
Merseyside[2]		252	652	1,456,800
Norfolk		2,073	5,368	736,200
Northamptonshire		914	2,367	561,800
Northumberland		1,943	5,032	300,900
North Yorkshire		3,208	8,309	705,800
Nottinghamshire		836	2,164	1,007,800
Oxfordshire		1,007	2,608	578,000
Shropshire		1,347	3,490	396,500
Somerset		1,332	3,451	452,300
South Yorkshire[2]		602	1,560	1,295,600
Staffordshire		1,049	2,716	1,027,500
Suffolk		1,466	3,797	635,100
Surrey		648	1,679	1,000,400
Tyne and Wear[2]		208	540	1,135,800
Warwickshire		765	1,981	484,200
West Midlands[2]		347	899	2,624,300
West Sussex		768	1,989	700,000
West Yorkshire[2]		787	2,039	2,052,400
Wiltshire		1,344	3,480	550,900
Northern Ireland[3]	Belfast	5,452	14,120	1,575,200
Scotland	Edinburgh	30,418[4]	78,783	5,112,100[4]
Regions				
Borders		1,814	4,698	102,100
Central		1,042	2,700	272,100
Dumfries and Galloway		2,481	6,425	147,000
Fife		509	1,319	344,600
Grampian		3,379	8,752	502,900
Highland		10,092	26,137	200,600
Lothian		683	1,770	743,700
Strathclyde		5,318	13,773	2,332,500
Tayside		2,951	7,643	393,800
Island areas[5] (TOTAL)		2,149	5,566	72,700
Wales	Cardiff	8,019	20,768	2,836,200[4]
Counties				
Clwyd		937	2,427	402,800
Dyfed		2,227	5,768	343,200
Gwent		531	1,376	443,100
Gwynedd		1,494	3,869	236,300
Mid Glamorgan		393	1,018	534,700
Powys		1,960	5,077	113,300
South Glamorgan		161	416	399,500
West Glamorgan		316	817	363,200
TOTAL		94,251	244,110	56,930,200

Demography

Population (1989): 57,218,000.
Density (1989): persons per sq mi 607.1, persons per sq km 234.4.
Urban–rural (1985): urban 91.5%; rural 8.5%.
Sex distribution (1989): male 48.77%; female 51.23%.
Age breakdown (1989): under 15, 18.9%; 15–29, 23.4%; 30–44, 20.7%; 45–59, 16.4%; 60–74, 13.8%; 75 and over, 6.8%.
Population projection: (2000) 58,958,000; (2010) 59,778,000.

Doubling time: more than 100 years.
Ethnic composition (1986): white 94.2%; Asian Indian 1.4%; West Indian 1.0%; Pakistani 0.8%; African 0.2%; Chinese 0.2%; Bangladeshi 0.2%; Arab 0.1%; other and not stated 1.9%.
Religious affiliation (1980): Christian 86.9%, of which Anglican 56.8%, Roman Catholic 13.1%, Presbyterian 7.0%, Methodist 4.3%, Baptist 1.4%; Muslim 1.4%; Jewish 0.8%; Hindu 0.7%; Sikh 0.4%; nonreligious 8.8%; other 1.0%.
Major cities (1987): Greater London 6,770,000; Birmingham 998,000; Glasgow 716,000; Leeds 709,000; Sheffield 532,000; Liverpool 476,000; Bradford 462,000; Manchester 450,000; Edinburgh 439,000; Bristol 384,000.
Place of birth (1985): 93.5% (50,720,000) native-born; 5.9% foreign-born, of which Ireland 1.0%, India 0.7%, Caribbean 0.5%, Pakistan 0.4%; not stated 0.6%.
Mobility (1981). Population living in the same residence as 1980: 90.9%; different residence, same country (of the U.K.) 8.2%; different residence, different country within the U.K. 0.4%; from outside the U.K. 0.5%.
Households[6] (1985). Average household size 2.7 (3.1); 1 person 24% (20%), 2 persons 33% (26%), 3 persons 17% (16%), 4 persons 18% (17%), 5 persons 6% (10%), 6 or more persons 3% (11%). Family households (1984): 16,079,-300 (74.3%), nonfamily 5,593,100 (25.7%, of which 1-person 22.5%).
Immigration (1987): permanent residents 212,000, from EEC 25.9%, Australia, New Zealand, and Canada 15.1%, United States 13.2%, Bangladesh, India, and Sri Lanka 6.6%, Pakistan 4.7%, South Africa 2.4%.

Vital statistics

Birth rate per 1,000 population (1988): 13.8 (world avg. 27.1); legitimate (1987) 77.1%; illegitimate 22.9%.
Death rate per 1,000 population (1988): 11.1 (world avg. 9.9).
Natural increase rate per 1,000 population (1988): 2.7 (world avg. 17.2).
Total fertility rate (avg. births per childbearing woman; 1987): 1.8.
Marriage rate per 1,000 population (1987): 7.0.
Divorce rate per 1,000 population (1987): 2.9.
Life expectancy at birth (1984–86): male 71.7 years; female 77.5 years.
Major causes of death per 100,000 population (1987): diseases of the circulatory system 544.1, of which ischemic heart disease 313.0, cerebrovascular disease 139.6; malignant neoplasms (cancers) 278.9; diseases of the respiratory system 116.3, of which pneumonia 52.5; diseases of the digestive system 35.1; accidents 37.4; diseases of the endocrine system 18.5, of which diabetes mellitus 14.5; diseases of the genitourinary system 15.4.

Social indicators

Educational attainment (1981): Percent of population age 25 and over having: primary or secondary education only 89.7%; some postsecondary 4.8%; bachelor's or equivalent degree 4.9%; higher university degree 0.6%.

Distribution of disposable income (1986)

percent of household income by quintile

1	2	3	4	5 (highest)
5.9	11.0	16.4	24.1	42.2

Quality of working life (1986). Average workweek (hours): male 41.8, female 37.3 (overtime male 8.6%, female 2.1%). Annual rate per 100,000 workers for: injury or accident 63.1; industrial diseases 0.5[7]; death 2.3. Proportion of labour force (employed persons) insured for damages or income loss resulting from: injury 100%; permanent disability 100%; death 100%. Average days lost to labour stoppages per 1,000 employee workdays: 0.3. Principal means of transport to work (1985–86): 67% private automobile, 17% public transportation, 6% foot, 6% bicycle, 4% other.
Access to services (1987). Proportion of households having access to: bath or shower 98%; toilet 98%; central heating 73%.
Social participation. Eligible voters participating in last national election: 74.6%. Population age 16 and over participating in voluntary work (1986): 20%. Trade union membership in total work force (1986) 37.6%.
Social deviance (1987)[8]. Offense rate per 100,000 population for: theft and handling stolen goods 4,084.2; burglary 1,791.5; fraud and forgery 264.7; violence against the person 280.6; robbery 64.9; sexual offense 50.2. Incidence per 100,000 population of: notified drug addicts 9.6[9]; suicide 8.1.
Leisure (1986). Favourite leisure activities (hours weekly): watching television 28.0; listening to radio 8.7; reading 2.6[9]; cultural activities 1.5[9].
Material well-being (1987). Households possessing: automobile 64%, telephone 83%, television receiver 98% (colour 86%), refrigerator 95%, central heating 73%, washing machine 83%, videocassette recorder 46%.

National economy

Gross national product (at current market prices; 1987): U.S.$592,946,000,-000 (U.S.$10,430 per capita).

Structure of gross domestic product and labour force

	1988 in value £'000,000	1988 % of total value	1987 labour force	1987 % of labour force
Agriculture	5,625	1.4	592,000	2.1
Mining	21,845[10]	5.5[10]	208,000	0.8
Manufacturing	93,433	23.7	5,398,000	19.4
Construction	25,745	6.5	1,559,000	5.6
Public utilities	[10]	[10]	285,000	1.0
Transp. and commun.	28,657	7.3	1,503,000	5.4
Trade	55,131	14.0	5,061,000	18.1
Finance	76,992	19.5	2,610,000	9.4
Pub. admin., defense	62,260	15.8	2,358,000	8.4
Services	25,785	6.5	5,417,000	19.4
Other	−867[11]	−0.2[11]	2,905,000[12]	10.4[12]
TOTAL	394,606	100.0	27,896,000	100.0

Budget (1988–89). Revenue: £128,200,000,000 (taxes on expenditures 37.4%, income tax 32.8%, corporation tax 15.4%). Expenditures: £114,225,000,-000 (social security benefits 38.9%, defense 16.8%, national health service 15.4%, debt interest 16.0%, education and science 2.6%).
Total national debt (March 1987): £190,650,000,000.

Financial aggregates

	1983	1984	1985	1986	1987	1988	1989[13]
Exchange rate:							
U.S. Dollar per £	1.52	1.34	1.30	1.47	1.64	1.78	1.57
SDRs per £	1.39	1.18	1.32	1.20	1.32	1.34	1.27
International reserves (U.S.$)							
Total (excl. gold; '000,000,000)	11.34	9.44	12.86	18.42	41.72	44.10	37.48
SDRs ('000,000,000)	0.52	0.50	1.13	1.55	1.38	1.32	1.20
Reserve pos. in IMF ('000,000,000)	2.10	1.97	1.99	1.98	1.78	1.67	1.59
Foreign exchange ('000,000,000)	8.72	6.97	9.74	14.89	38.56	41.12	34.69
Gold ('000,000 fine troy oz)	19.01	19.03	19.03	19.01	19.01	19.00	19.00
% world reserves	2.0	2.0	2.0	2.0	2.0	2.0	2.0
Interest and prices							
Central bank discount (%)	...	...	...	...	...	...	...
Gov't. Bond yield (%) long term	10.81	10.69	10.62	9.87	9.48	9.36	9.37[14]
Industrial share prices (1985 = 100)	68.1	81.0	100.0	124.1	163.8	147.6	167.4[15]
Balance of payments (U.S.$'000,000)							
Balance of visible trade,	−1,676	−6,109	−2,653	−12,801	−17,962	−36,994	...
Imports, f.o.b.	93,636	99,593	103,511	119,272	148,247	180,527	...
Exports, f.o.b.	91,960	93,484	100,858	106,472	130,285	143,534	...
Balance of invisibles	9,948	11,802	11,248	16,104	17,354	17,417	...
Balance of payments, current account	5,831	2,608	4,765	158	−6,712	−26,015	...

Tourism (1987): receipts from visitors U.S.$10,229,000,000; expenditures by nationals abroad U.S.$11,898,000,000.

Manufacturing, mining, and construction enterprises (1985)

	no. of enter-prises[8]	no. of employees	annual wages as a % of avg. of all wages[9]	annual value added (£'000,000)
Manufacturing				
Food, beverages, and tobacco	3,282	582,000	103.0	10,801.5
Mechanical engineering	3,023	615,000	108.4	9,651.3
Transport equipment	1,671	545,000	...	9,058.0
Paper and paper products; printing and publishing	3,237	439,000	133.8	8,364.1
Electrical and electronic engineering	2,412	590,000	96.8	8,281.7
Chemical engineering	1,354	281,000	118.1	8,220.5
Rubber and plastic	1,529	204,000	118.1	3,273.6
Metal manufacturing	901	153,000	102.8	2,955.7
Clothing and footwear	2,727	341,000	85.6	2,645.5
Textiles	1,883	229,000	79.2	2,502.8
Timber and wood products	2,091	193,000	98.1	2,393.1
Mining				
Extraction of coal, mineral oil, and natural gas		188,000	118.1	12,807.6
Extraction of minerals other than fuels	1,649	11,000	103.1	689.7
Mineral oil processing		14,000	118.1	1,336.6
Construction	166,184	1,122,000	...	13,183.2

Production (metric tons except as noted). Agriculture, forestry, fishing (1987): wheat 11,800,000, barley 9,100,000, sugar beets 7,467,000, potatoes 6,788,000, turnips and rutabagas 3,855,000[16, 17], rapeseed 1,300,000, corn (maize) 915,000[16, 17], cabbage 853,000, oats 557,000; livestock (number of live animals) 38,701,000 sheep, 12,158,000 cattle, 7,942,000 pigs; roundwood 5,204,000 cu m; fish catch 954,730. Mining (metric tons; 1987): iron ore 262,700; zinc 5,600; tin 3,900; lead 4,300. Manufacturing (total sales in £'000,000; 1987): motor vehicles and parts 13,970; aerospace equipment 8,305; electronic data processing and telecommunications equipment 4,314; radios and electronic goods 3,146; mechanical lifting and handling equipment 1,825; boilers 1,814; constructional steelwork 1,784; telephone and telegraph equipment 1,673. Construction (value in £; 1987): residential 6,745,000,000; nonresidential 12,321,000,000, of which public 3,870,000,-000, industrial 3,204,000,000, commercial 5,247,000,000.

Retail trade enterprises (1986)

	no. of enter-prises	no. of employees	weekly wage as a % of all wages	annual turnover (£'000,000)[18]
Food and grocery, of which	77,137	818,000	...	33,386
large grocery	94	457,000	...	23,546
other grocery	30,116	128,000	...	3,919
meats	15,833	84,000	...	2,680
Household goods, of which	43,000	305,000	...	14,670
electrical and musical goods	9,476	89,000	...	5,402
furniture	10,950	73,000	...	3,789
Drink, confectionery, and tobacco, of which	44,344	268,000	...	9,704
tobacco and confectionery	39,633	234,000	...	7,557
Clothing and footwear, of which	32,655	294,000	...	9,347
women's, girls', and infants' wear	17,791	27,135	...	2,974
footwear	3,790	80,000	...	2,065
men's and boys' wear	3,836	34,000	...	1,307
Mail order	14	32,000	...	3,165
Pharmaceuticals	8,535	77,000	...	3,005

Energy production (consumption): electricity (kW-hr; 1987) 300,247,000,000 (311,882,000,000); coal (metric tons; 1987) 104,435,000 (117,187,000); crude petroleum (barrels; 1987) 878,100,000 (511,200,000); petroleum products (metric tons; 1987) 75,060,000 (72,001,000); natural gas (cu m; 1987) 52,-082,000,000 (63,973,000,000).

Population economically active (1988): total 28,164,000; activity rate of total population 49.4% (participation rates: ages 15–64, 75.6%[19]; female 52.1%[19]; unemployed 8.3%).

Price and earnings indexes (1985 = 100)

	1983	1984	1985	1986	1987	1988	1989[20]
Consumer price index	89.7	94.3	100.0	103.4	107.0	113.0	122.2
Monthly earnings index	85.1	89.9	100.0	108.3	116.9	...	...

Household income and expenditure (1987). Average household size 2.5; average annual income per household (1985) £8,133 (U.S.$10,868); sources of income (1986): wages and salaries 64.3%, social security benefits 13.0%, rent, dividends, and interest 9.6%, income from self-employment 7.7%; expenditure (1986): food and beverages 24.2%, housing 16.8%, transport and vehicles 14.3%, services 12.7%, household goods 7.8%, clothing and footwear 7.5%, energy 5.9%.
Land use (1987): forested 9.6%; meadows and pastures 47.9%; agricultural and under permanent cultivation 28.9%; other 13.6%.

Foreign trade

Balance of trade (current prices)

	1983	1984	1985	1986	1987	1988
£'000,000	−5,403	−8,594	−6,527	−13,255	−14,177	−24,937
% of total	4.3%	5.8%	4.0%	8.3%	8.2%	13.3%

Imports (1988): £106,412,900,000 (machinery and transport equipment 37.6%, of which road vehicles 10.6%, data-processing equipment 5.9%; chemicals and chemical products 8.8%, of which organic chemicals 2.2%; food and live animals 8.5%, of which vegetables and fruits 2.3%, meat and meat preparations 1.6%; textile yarn and fabrics 3.4%; paper and paperboard 3.4%; petroleum and petroleum products 3.3%; nonferrous metals 2.4%; iron and steel products 2.2%). *Major import sources:* W.Ger. 16.6%; U.S. 10.1%; France 8.8%; The Netherlands 7.8%; Japan 6.1%; Italy 5.5%; Belgium–Luxembourg 4.7%; Ireland 3.6%; Switzerland 3.6%; Sweden 3.2%.
Exports (1988): £81,476,200,000 (machinery and transport equipment 39.1%, of which data-processing equipment 6.5%, road vehicles 6.1%, power-generating machinery and equipment 4.8%, machinery specialized for particular industries 4.0%; chemicals and chemical products 13.9%, of which organic chemicals 3.8%; petroleum and petroleum products 10.6%; nonmetallic mineral manufactures 3.6%; professional, scientific, and controlling instruments 3.1%; iron and steel products 2.9%). *Major export destinations:* U.S. 12.9%; W.Ger. 11.7%; France 10.2%; The Netherlands 6.8%; Belgium–Luxembourg 5.2%; Italy 5.0%; Ireland 5.0%; Spain 3.3%; Sweden 2.7%; Canada 2.5%; Saudi Arabia 2.1%.

Transport and communications

Transport. Railroads[21] (1987): length 23,900 mi, 38,464 km; passenger-mi 19,983,000,000, passenger-km 32,160,000,000; short ton-mi cargo 9,912,-000,000, metric ton-km cargo 14,472,000,000. Roads (1987): total length 218,906 mi, 352,295 km (paved 100%). Vehicles (1988): passenger cars 18,432,000; trucks and buses 2,731,000. Merchant marine (1988): vessels (100 gross tons and over) 2,142; total deadweight tonnage 11,113,525. Air transport (1987): passenger-mi 36,783,000,000, passenger-km 59,196,000,-000; short ton-mi cargo 1,416,616,000, metric ton-km cargo 2,068,224,000; airports (1989) with scheduled flights 47.
Communications. Daily newspapers (1989): total number 124; total circulation 25,159,000[17]; circulation per 1,000 population 443[17]. Radio (1987): total number receivers 57,456,832 (1 per 1.0 person). Television (1987): total number of licenses 18,953,000 (1 per 3.0 persons). Telephones (1984): 29,517,991 (1 per 1.9 persons).

Education and health

Education (1986–87)[22]

	schools	teachers	students	student/ teacher ratio
Primary (age 5–10)	24,609	208,700	4,550,800	21.8
Secondary (age 11–19)	5,091	253,800	3,902,400	15.4
Voc., teacher tr.[23]	729	93,000[24]	529,791	...
Higher[25]	46	31,432	360,809	11.5

Literacy (1987): total population literate, virtually 100%.
Health (1981): physicians 92,172 (1 per 611 persons); hospital beds (1986) 410,000 (1 per 138 persons); infant mortality rate per 1,000 live births (1988) 8.8.
Food (1984–86): daily per capita caloric intake 3,218 (vegetable products 65%, animal products 35%); 128% of FAO recommended minimum requirement.

Military

Total active duty personnel (1989): 311,650 (army 49.9%, navy 20.7%, air force 29.4%). *Military expenditure as percent of GNP* (1987): 4.7% (world 5.4%); per capita expenditure U.S.$556.

[1]Includes separately administered Isles of Scilly (area 6 sq mi [16 sq km]; pop. 1,900). [2]Geographical entity only; since April 1, 1986, the administrative functions of the former metropolitan county councils have been dispersed among other local authorities. [3]Comprises 26 local government districts not shown separately. [4]Detail does not add to total given because of rounding. [5]Includes three separately administered island groups (Orkney 377 sq mi, pop. 19,300; Shetland 553 sq mi, pop. 22,400; Western Isles 1,119 sq mi, pop. 31,000). [6]Figures in parentheses are for Northern Ireland (1984). [7]1982. [8]England and Wales only. [9]1984. [10]Mining includes Public utilities. [11]Plus rent; less imputed bank service charges. [12]Unemployed. [13]September. [14]August. [15]February. [16]Primarily for fodder. [17]1986. [18]Includes value-added taxes. [19]1987. [20]July. [21]British Rail only. [22]Public sector only. [23]Third level. [24]1984–85. [25]Universities only.

United States

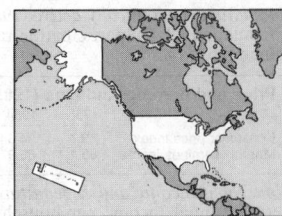

Official name: United States of America.
Form of government: federal republic with two legislative houses (Senate [100]; House of Representatives [435]).
Head of state and government: President.
Capital: Washington, D.C.
Official language: English.
Official religion: none.
Monetary unit: 1 dollar (U.S.$) = 100 cents; valuation (Oct. 2, 1989)
1 U.S.$ = £0.62; 1 £ = U.S.$1.62.

Area and population

States	Capitals	area[1] sq mi	area[1] sq km	population 1989 estimate[2]
Alabama	Montgomery	51,705	133,915	4,150,000
Alaska	Juneau	591,004	1,530,693	565,000
Arizona	Phoenix	114,000	295,259	3,649,000
Arkansas	Little Rock	53,187	137,754	2,414,000
California	Sacramento	158,706	411,047	28,607,000
Colorado	Denver	104,091	269,594	3,393,000
Connecticut	Hartford	5,018	12,997	3,257,000
Delaware	Dover	2,044	5,294	658,000
Florida	Tallahassee	58,664	151,939	12,535,000
Georgia	Atlanta	58,910	152,576	6,524,000
Hawaii	Honolulu	6,471	16,760	1,121,000
Idaho	Boise	83,564	216,430	1,013,000
Illinois	Springfield	57,871	149,885	11,599,000
Indiana	Indianapolis	36,413	94,309	5,542,000
Iowa	Des Moines	56,275	145,752	2,780,000
Kansas	Topeka	82,277	213,096	2,485,000
Kentucky	Frankfort	40,409	104,659	3,742,000
Louisiana	Baton Rouge	47,752	123,677	4,510,000
Maine	Augusta	33,265	86,156	1,203,000
Maryland	Annapolis	10,460	27,091	4,665,000
Massachusetts	Boston	8,284	21,455	5,863,000
Michigan	Lansing	97,102	251,493	9,266,000
Minnesota	St. Paul	86,614	224,329	4,298,000
Mississippi	Jackson	47,689	123,514	2,680,000
Missouri	Jefferson City	69,697	180,514	5,163,000
Montana	Helena	147,046	380,847	808,000
Nebraska	Lincoln	77,355	200,349	1,590,000
Nevada	Carson City	110,561	286,352	1,049,000
New Hampshire	Concord	9,279	24,032	1,116,000
New Jersey	Trenton	7,787	20,168	7,827,000
New Mexico	Santa Fe	121,593	314,924	1,595,000
New York	Albany	52,735	136,583	17,761,000
North Carolina	Raleigh	52,669	136,412	6,602,000
North Dakota	Bismarck	70,702	183,117	664,000
Ohio	Columbus	44,787	115,998	10,787,000
Oklahoma	Oklahoma City	69,956	181,185	3,285,000
Oregon	Salem	97,073	251,418	2,750,000
Pennsylvania	Harrisburg	46,043	119,251	11,844,000
Rhode Island	Providence	1,212	3,139	996,000
South Carolina	Columbia	31,113	80,582	3,507,000
South Dakota	Pierre	77,116	199,730	708,000
Tennessee	Nashville	42,144	109,152	4,933,000
Texas	Austin	266,807	691,027	17,451,000
Utah	Salt Lake City	84,899	219,887	1,750,000
Vermont	Montpelier	9,614	24,900	557,000
Virginia	Richmond	40,767	105,586	6,068,000
Washington	Olympia	68,139	176,479	4,612,000
West Virginia	Charleston	24,231	62,758	1,871,000
Wisconsin	Madison	66,215	171,496	4,803,000
Wyoming	Cheyenne	97,809	253,324	503,000
District				
Dist. of Columbia	—	69	179	615,000
TOTAL		3,679,192[3]	9,529,063	247,732,000[3]

Demography

Population (1989): 248,777,000.
Density (1989): persons per sq mi 67.6, persons per sq km 26.1.
Urban–rural (1987): urban 76.7%; rural 23.3%.
Sex distribution (1988): male 48.71%; female 51.29%.
Age breakdown (1988): under 15, 21.5%; 15–29, 24.2%; 30–44, 23.2%; 45–59, 14.2%; 60–74, 11.7%; 75 and over, 5.1%.
Population projection: (2000) 268,834,000; (2010) 283,174,000.
Doubling time: 95 years.
Composition by race (1988): white 84.3%; black 12.5%; other races 3.2%.
Religious affiliation (1987): Christian 87.1%, of which Protestant 49.1%, Roman Catholic 29.6%, other Christian 8.4%; Jewish 2.7%; Muslim 1.9%; Hindu 0.2%; nonreligious 6.6%; atheist 0.2%; other 1.3%.
Place of birth (1980): native-born 212,465,899 (93.8%); foreign-born 14,079,906 (6.2%), of which Mexico 2,199,221; Germany (East and West) 849,384; Canada 842,859; Italy 831,922; United Kingdom 669,149; Cuba 607,814; Philippines 501,440; Poland 418,128; U.S.S.R. 406,022; South Korea 289,885; China 286,120; Vietnam (South) 231,120; Japan 221,794; Portugal 211,614; Greece 210,998; India 206,087; others 5,096,349.
Mobility (1987). Population living in the same residence as in 1986: 81.4%; different residence, same county 11.6%; different county, same state 3.7%; different state 2.8%; moved from abroad 0.5%.
Immigration (1987[4]): permanent immigrants admitted 601,516, from Mexico 12.0%, Philippines 8.3%, South Korea 6.0%, Cuba 4.8%, India 4.6%, China 4.3%, Dominican Republic 4.1%, Vietnam 4.0%, Jamaica 3.8%, African countries 2.9%, Haiti 2.5%, Iran 2.4%, United Kingdom 2.2%. Refugee arrivals (1987): 70,000.

Major cities (1988): New York 7,346,352; Los Angeles 3,402,342; Chicago 2,994,100; Houston 1,725,421; Philadelphia 1,657,285; Detroit 1,086,714; San Diego 1,073,466; Dallas 1,017,818; Phoenix 951,717; San Antonio 935,729.

Other principal cities (1988)

	population		population		population
Akron	227,158	Fort Worth	432,889	Omaha	377,958
Albuquerque	378,176	Fresno	294,695	Pittsburgh	387,190
Anaheim	251,045	Honolulu	838,656	Portland (Ore.)	387,659
Anchorage	217,429	Indianapolis	783,187	Richmond	219,979
Arlington (Tex.)	251,712	Jacksonville	635,430	Rochester (N.Y.)	235,877
Atlanta	444,995	Jersey City	218,492	Sacramento	340,483
Aurora (Colo.)	219,440	Kansas City (Mo.)	447,461	St. Louis	425,187
Austin	467,423	Lexington (Ky.)	225,700	St. Paul	267,945
Baltimore	763,880	Long Beach	413,670	St. Petersburg	235,450
Baton Rouge	238,297	Louisville	281,880	San Francisco	753,927
Birmingham	283,237	Memphis	668,935	San Jose	732,022
Boston	579,921	Mesa	267,642	Santa Ana	246,925
Buffalo	323,714	Miami	371,100	Seattle	505,380
Charlotte	370,492	Milwaukee	611,140	Shreveport	217,495
Cincinnati	377,783	Minneapolis	364,750	Tampa	281,790
Cleveland	544,515	Nashville	502,759	Toledo	344,960
Colorado Springs	278,944	Newark	319,191	Tucson	383,174
Columbus	588,428	New Orleans	538,047	Tulsa	373,600
Corpus Christi	261,984	Norfolk	285,180	Virginia Beach	355,560
Denver	500,555	Oakland	367,782	Washington, D.C.	620,000
El Paso	501,544	Oklahoma City	440,136	Wichita	292,733

Households (1988). Total households 91,066,000 (married-couple families 51,809,000 [56.9%]). Average household size 2.6; 1 person 24.0%, 2 persons 32.2%, 3 persons 17.7%, 4 persons 15.5%, 5 or more persons 10.6%. Family households: 65,132,000 (71.5%); nonfamily 25,934,000 (28.5%, of which 1-person 24.0%).

Vital statistics

Birth rate per 1,000 population (1989[5]): 16.0 (world avg. 27.1); (1987) legitimate 75.5%; illegitimate 24.5%.
Death rate per 1,000 population (1989[5]): 8.7 (world avg. 9.9).
Natural increase rate per 1,000 population (1989[5]): 7.3 (world avg. 17.2).
Total fertility rate (avg. births per childbearing woman; 1987): 1.8.
Marriage rate per 1,000 population (1989[5]): 9.6; median age at first marriage (1988): men 25.9 years, women 23.6 years.
Divorce rate per 1,000 population (1989[5]): 4.7.
Life expectancy at birth (1987): white male 72.0 years, black and other male 67.6 years; white female 78.8 years, black and other female 75.4 years.
Major causes of death per 100,000 population (12 months ending June 1989): cardiovascular diseases 381.1, of which ischemic heart disease 201.2, other forms of heart disease 83.5, cerebrovascular diseases 59.3, atherosclerosis 8.6, other cardiovascular diseases 9.3; malignant neoplasms (cancers) 198.6; diseases of the respiratory system 64.5, of which pneumonia 30.5; accidents and adverse effects 38.0, of which motor-vehicle accidents 19.2; diabetes mellitus 17.2; suicide 11.8; chronic liver disease and cirrhosis 10.3; nephritis and nephrosis 9.0; homicide 8.7.
Morbidity rates of infectious diseases per 100,000 population (1987): gonorrhea 320.8; chicken pox 87.6; syphilis 35.6; salmonellosis 20.9; hepatitis B (serum) 10.6; hepatitis A (infectious) 10.4; shigellosis 9.8; tuberculosis 9.3; acquired immune deficiency syndrome (AIDS) 8.7; mumps 5.3; aseptic meningitis 4.7.
Incidence of chronic health conditions per 1,000 population (1986): chronic sinusitis 145.5; arthritis 130.8; hypertension 122.6; deformities or orthopedic impairments 115.9; hay fever 91.8; hearing impairment 87.7; heart conditions 78.1; chronic bronchitis 48.1; hemorrhoids 41.9; asthma 41.0.

Social indicators

Educational attainment (1987). Percent of population age 25 and over having: less than full primary education 6.9%; primary 5.8%; less than full secondary 11.7%; secondary 38.7%; some postsecondary 17.1%; 4-year higher degree and more 19.8%, of which postgraduate 8.5%. Number of earned degrees (1987–88): bachelor's degree 989,000; master's degree 290,000; doctor's degree 33,600; first-professional degrees (in fields such as medicine, theology, and law) 74,400.

Distribution of income (1986)

percent of national household income by quintile

1	2	3	4	5 (highest)
3.7	9.7	16.2	24.3	46.1

Quality of working life (1988). Average workweek: 41.1 hours (9.5% overtime). Annual rate per 100,000 workers for (1987): injury or accident 1,800; death 10.0. Proportion of labour force insured for damages or income loss resulting from: injury, permanent disability, and death (1986) 49.0%. Average days lost to labour stoppages per 1,000 workdays (1988): 0.8. Average duration of journey to work (1979): 22.5 minutes (85.7% private automobile, 5.9% public transportation, 1.3% bicycle or motorcycle, 3.9% foot, 2.3% work at home, 0.9% other). Rate per 1,000 workers of discouraged (unemployed no longer seeking work; 1983): 53.5.
Access to services (1985). Proportion of dwellings having access to: electricity virtually 100.0%; safe public water supply 98.6%; public sewage collection 99.2%; public fire protection, n.a.
Social participation. Eligible voters participating in last national election (1988): 57.0%. Population age 18 and over participating in voluntary work (1987): 45.0%. Trade union membership in total work force (1987): 17.0%. Practicing religious population in total affiliated population (church attendance; 1987): once a week 47%; once in six months 67%; once a year 74%.
Social deviance (1988). Offense rate per 100,000 population for: murder 8.4; rape 37.6; robbery 220.9; aggravated assault 370.2; motor-vehicle theft

582.9; burglary and housebreaking 1,309.2; larceny-theft 3,134.9; drug abuse violation 420.6; drunkenness 382.8. Drug and substance users (population age 26 and over; 1985): alcohol 60.7%; marijuana 6.2%; cocaine 2.1%; tranquilizers 1.0%; analgesics 0.9%; stimulants 0.7%; hallucinogens 0.5%; heroin 0.5%. Rate per 100,000 population of suicide (1988) 11.8.

Crime rates per 100,000 population in metropolitan areas (1988)

	violent crime				
	total	murder	rape	robbery	assault
Atlanta	959.5	14.3	60.9	383.5	500.7
Baltimore	1,041.0	12.4	38.1	414.1	576.4
Boston	720.2	4.5	33.6	252.3	429.9
Chicago	...	12.1	...	517.7	650.3
Dallas	1,093.5	18.3	72.4	466.2	536.7
Detroit	945.1	17.4	62.6	392.4	472.8
Houston	813.8	17.5	51.8	375.8	368.7
Los Angeles	1,393.3	15.5	45.9	531.3	800.8
Miami[6]	1,814.2	20.1	50.2	797.7	946.2
Minneapolis	435.4	3.8	41.9	164.5	225.2
New York	1,949.5	22.7	41.8	1,032.7	852.3
Philadelphia	605.2	10.2	33.5	254.1	307.4
Pittsburgh	341.2	2.5	24.7	152.5	161.5
St. Louis	720.3	11.3	23.1	209.7	476.2
San Francisco	873.5	7.9	43.1	355.4	467.1
Washington, D.C.	685.3	14.8	29.3	299.8	341.4

	property crime				
	total	burglary	larceny	auto theft	arson
Atlanta	7,532.1	1,933.0	4,670.1	929.0	63.8
Baltimore	5,422.5	1,324.4	3,410.8	687.2	91.8
Boston	4,466.5	915.0	2,467.4	1,084.1	30.0[6]
Chicago	5,778.6	1,259.2	3,539.6	979.8	92.9
Dallas	10,098.7	2,840.1	5,921.4	1,337.3	134.6
Detroit	6,194.8	1,491.9	3,454.8	1,248.0	155.3
Houston	7,484.9	2,410.8	3,776.7	1,297.4	103.3
Los Angeles	5,467.4	1,366.0	2,808.2	1,293.2	163.1
Miami[6]	10,572.6	2,886.9	5,986.4	1,699.2	49.3
Minneapolis	5,060.6	1,165.4	3,400.4	494.8	74.0
New York	7,032.2	1,597.5	3,962.4	1,472.3	89.8
Philadelphia	3,769.8	866.0	2,200.1	703.7	82.2[6]
Pittsburgh	2,800.3	738.9	1,389.3	672.1	106.7[6]
St. Louis	4,843.5	1,311.7	3,014.9	516.9	131.1[6]
San Francisco	5,706.9	1,069.9	3,809.1	827.8	49.8
Washington, D.C.	5,001.8	1,046.6	3,185.4	769.8	51.8

Leisure (1976). Favourite leisure activities (weekly hours): watching television 9.6; social time 7.6; reading 3.7; cultural activities 1.5; recreation 1.2. *Material well-being* (1988). Occupied dwellings with householder possessing: automobile 77.7%[5]; telephone 92.9%; radio receiver 99.0%; television receiver 98.0%; refrigerator 99.7%; air conditioner 59.5%; washing machine 72.8%; videocassette recorder 58.1%; cable television 51.1%. *Recreational expenditures* (1987): U.S.$223,300,000,000 (television and radio receivers 18.5%; durable toys and sport equipment 15.0%; nondurable toys and sport supplies 12.0%; golfing, bowling, and other participatory activities 7.8%; magazines and newspapers 7.1%; spectator amusements 5.0%, of which movies 1.8%, theatre and opera 1.7%; books and maps 4.3%; clubs and fraternal organizations 2.4%; spectator sports 1.5%).

National economy

Budget (1989). Revenue: U.S.$973,510,000,000 (individual income tax 43.6%, social insurance taxes and contributions 36.8%, corporation income tax 11.4%, excise taxes 3.5%, customs duties 1.8%). Expenditures: U.S.$1,118,-964,000,000 (social security and medicare 28.5%, defense 26.2%, interest on debt 14.1%, income security 12.1%, health 4.4%, education 3.2%, veteran benefits and services 2.6%).
Total national debt (1989[7]): U.S.$2,884,080,000,000.

Manufacturing, mining, and construction enterprises (1988)

	no. of enter-prises[8]	no. of employees	weekly wage as a % of all wages	value added (U.S.$'000,000)[9]
Manufacturing				
Transportation equipment	8,466	2,051,300	125.8	125,670.6
Electric and electronic machinery	15,116	2,070,200	91.9	112,322.8
Food and related products	20,208	1,635,800	81.1	112,237.7
Machinery, except electrical	48,947	2,081,800	103.8	108,401.2
Chemical and related products	11,363	1,064,500	118.6	100,069.3
Fabricated metal products	32,793	1,431,100	95.1	68,675.0
Paper and related products	6,160	692,600	111.4	43,935.9
Instruments and related products	7,661	748,500	91.6	40,000.2
Primary metals	7,048	592,100	117.2	38,159.4
Rubber and plastic products	12,348	829,400	84.3	37,243.5
Stone, clay, and glass products	15,591	599,900	98.0	30,697.6
Apparel and related products	21,367	1,092,300	50.1	28,450.7
Lumber and wood	28,293	764,800	76.8	23,268.1
Textile-mill products	6,192	729,100	67.1	22,225.0
Petroleum and coal products	2,165	161,800	147.2	17,695.9
Furniture and fixtures	9,160	529,700	69.2	17,639.0
Miscellaneous manufacturing industries	14,352	385,700	69.5	14,619.6
Tobacco products	117	55,800	129.3	12,727.9
Leather and leather products	2,558	144,300	52.0	3,593.5
Mining				
Oil and gas extraction	23,577	405,900	132.9	
Coal mining	4,133	150,800	148.8	122,300[10]
Metal mining	985	51,400	123.9	
Nonmetallic, except fuels	5,126	112,900	110.0	
Construction				
General contractors and operative builders	112,963	1,367,800	100.9	
Heavy construction contractors	29,055	769,000	115.2	152,500[10]
Special trade contractors	243,729	2,987,800	110.9	

Gross national product (at current market prices; 1988): U.S.$4,880,600,000,-000 (U.S.$19,860 per capita).

Gross national product and national income
in U.S.$000,000,000

	1984	1985	1986	1987	1988
Gross national product	3,772.2	4,014.9	4,240.3	4,524.3	4,880.6
By type of expenditure					
Personal consumption expenditures	2,430.5	2,629.4	2,807.5	3,010.8	3,235.1
Durable goods	335.5	372.2	406.5	421.0	455.2
Nondurable goods	867.3	911.2	943.6	998.1	1,052.3
Services	1,345.6	1,457.3	1,457.3	1,591.7	1,727.6
Gross private domestic investment	664.8	643.1	665.9	699.9	750.3
Fixed investment	597.1	631.8	650.4	670.6	719.6
Changes in business inventories	67.7	11.3	15.5	29.3	30.6
Net exports of goods and services	−58.9	−78.0	−104.4	−112.6	−73.7
Exports	383.5	370.9	378.4	448.6	547.7
Imports	442.4	448.9	428.2	561.2	621.3
Government purchases of goods and services	735.9	820.8	871.2	926.1	968.9
Federal	310.5	355.2	366.2	381.6	381.3
State and local	425.4	465.6	505.0	544.5	587.6
By major type of product					
Goods output	1,581.4	1,641.2	1,697.9	1,785.2	1,931.9
Durable goods	681.5	706.6	725.3	777.5	863.7
Nondurable goods	899.9	934.6	972.6	1,007.6	1,068.3
Services	1,813.9	1,968.3	2,118.4	2,304.5	2,499.2
Structures	377.0	405.4	424.0	434.6	449.5
National income (incl. capital consumption adjustment)	3,028.6	3,234.0	3,437.1	3,665.4	3,972.6
By type of income					
Compensation of employees	2,213.9	2,367.5	2,507.1	2,690.0	2,907.6
Proprietors' income	234.5	255.9	286.7	311.6	327.8
Rental income of persons	8.5	9.2	12.4	13.4	15.7
Corporate profits	266.9	282.3	298.9	298.7	328.6
Net interest	304.8	319.0	331.9	351.7	392.9
By industry division (excl. capital consumption adjustment)					
Agriculture, forestry, fishing	79.5	77.0	81.5	90.8	90.4
Mining and construction	198.3	209.1	215.5	227.7	245.6
Manufacturing	660.3	671.2	686.4	718.7	788.6
Durable	392.4	395.8	405.7	422.9	455.0
Nondurable	267.9	275.4	280.7	295.8	333.6
Transportation	106.4	105.9	112.8	120.0	131.1
Communications	65.7	68.9	73.6	80.6	83.6
Public utilities	75.9	77.2	80.2	78.1	85.5
Wholesale and retail trade	455.0	475.0	502.2	528.2	570.1
Finance, insurance, real estate	381.7	425.9	475.5	520.0	568.8
Services	519.6	576.8	639.8	714.4	789.0
Government and government enterprise	436.6	468.9	495.7	529.3	566.9
Other	47.4	40.7	34.9	30.5	33.3

Structure of gross domestic product and labour force

	1987		1988	
	in value U.S.$'000,000,000	% of total value	labour force	% of labour force
Agriculture	94.9	2.1	3,546,000	2.9
Mining	85.4	1.9	721,000	0.6
Manufacturing	853.6	18.9	19,403,000	15.7
Construction	218.5	4.9	5,125,000	4.2
Public utilities	136.4	3.0		
Transportation and communications	271.8	6.0	5,548,000[11]	4.5[11]
Trade	740.4	16.5	25,139,000	20.4
Finance	775.4	17.2	6,676,000	5.4
Public administration, defense	535.3	11.9	17,373,000	14.1
Services	793.5	17.6	25,600,000	20.7
Other	−8.0[12]	−0.2[12]	14,247,000[13]	11.5[13]
TOTAL	4,497.2	100.0	123,378,000	100.0

Business activity (1985): number of businesses 16,920,000 (sole proprietorships 70.5%, active corporations 19.4%, active partnerships 10.1%), of which services 6,812,000, wholesaling and retailing 3,407,000; business receipts $9,306,000,000,000 (active corporations 90.2%, sole proprietorships 5.8%, active partnerships 4.0%), of which wholesaling and retailing $2,682,-600,000,000, services $759,400,000,000; net profit $310,000,000,000 (active corporations 77.4%, sole proprietorships 25.4%, partnerships −2.8%), of which services $65,400,000,000, wholesaling and retailing $43,400,000,000. New business concerns and business failures (1988): total number of new incorporations 684,109; total failures 57,093; failure rate per 10,000 concerns 83; current liabilities of failed concerns $35,892,700,000, average liability $628,700. Business expenditures for new plant and equipment (1987): total $388,600,000,000, of which trade, services, and communications $168,200,-000,000, manufacturing businesses $145,500,000,000 (nondurable goods 51.3%, durable 48.7%), public utilities $44,800,000,000, transportation $18,-800,000,000, mining $11,300,000,000.
Production (metric tons except as noted). Agriculture, forestry, fishing (1988): corn (maize) 125,004,010, milk 66,010,000, wheat 49,294,440, soybeans 41,875,630, sugarcane 27,530,340, sugar beets 22,492,740, potatoes 15,874,520, sorghum 14,670,470, oranges 7,751,000, rice 7,236,930, barley 6,325,000, cottonseed 5,492,100, grapes 5,111,000, apples 4,700,000, cotton 3,362,860, oats 3,175,000, grapefruit 2,523,000, peaches and pears 2,160,000, peanuts (groundnuts) 1,819,390, onions 1,541,000, dry beans 872,260, sunflower seeds 765,890, lemons 764,000, pineapples 598,000, tobacco 611,500, sweet potatoes 536,690, almonds 439,000, rye 382,210; livestock (number of live animals) 98,994,000 cattle, 42,845,000 pigs, 10,-774,000 sheep, 10,720,000 horses, 1,650,000 goats, 1,540,000,000 poultry; roundwood (1987) 524,282,000 cu m; fish catch 3,235,000. Mining and quarrying (1988): iron ore 51,347,000; phosphate rock 40,000,000; copper 1,437,100; bauxite 560,000; lead 385,000; zinc 242,100; nickel 45,000; molybdenum 34,000; tin 15,087; uranium 5,900; silver 1,395; tungsten 230; gold 205. Manufacturing (1988): crude steel 99,924,000; paper and

paper products 76,403,000; cement 71,544,000; wood pulp 61,161,000; pig iron 55,745,000; sulfuric acid 42,775,000; nitrogenous and phosphate fertilizers 16,858,000; gypsum and gypsum products 16,390,000; plastic and resins 15,526,000; caustic soda 11,983,000; newsprint 5,427,000; man-made fibre 4,103,900; aluminum 3,944,000; cheese 2,507,000; synthetic rubber 2,234,860; butter 547,700; machine tools U.S.$2,399,000,000; cotton fabric 3,778,000,000 sq m; footwear 217,636,000 pairs; motor-vehicle tires 211,351,000 units; radio receivers 23,623,000 units; television receivers 20,170,000 units; major household appliances 47,070,000 units, of which 10,988,000 microwave ovens, 7,227,000 refrigerators, 6,190,000 washing machines, 4,637,000 air conditioners, 4,601,000 clothes dryers, 3,956,-000 water heaters, 3,907,000 dishwashers. Construction (1988): private U.S.$328,700,000,000, of which residential U.S.$198,100,000,000, commercial and industrial U.S.$79,800,000,000, other U.S.$50,800,000,000; federal, state, and local U.S.$80,900,000,000.

Retail and wholesale trade and services (1987)

	no. of establishments	no. of employees	weekly wage as a % of all wages	annual sales (U.S.$'000,000)
Retail trade	1,441,200	18,483,000	57.1	1,493,309
Automotive dealers	102,704	2,003,700	91.1	333,420
Building materials, hardware, garden supply, and mobile home dealers	73,805	744,100	81.7	81,487
Furniture, home furnishings, equipment stores	109,653	792,100	78.3	74,783
Food stores	190,706	2,961,800	66.5	301,847
General merchandise group stores	35,434	2,411,800	58.6	181,147
Eating and drinking places	391,303	6,105,800	...	148,776
Gasoline service stations	114,748	608,000	59.9	101,997
Apparel and accessory stores	149,435	1,125,500	47.4	77,391
Drugstores and proprietary stores	52,181	580,700	52.2	53,825
Liquor stores	35,194	123,100	...	18,597
Wholesale trade[14]	415,829	5,844,000	117.3	1,482,975
Durable goods	256,103	3,427,000	119.9	725,683
Machinery, equipment, and supplies	99,250	1,450,300	128.9	187,737
Motor vehicles, automotive equipment	39,460	429,600	105.5	152,231
Electrical goods	29,170	491,800	124.0	97,686
Metals and minerals, except petroleum	10,121	133,200	133.1	57,756
Lumber and other construction materials	17,041	225,500	116.5	57,286
Hardware, plumbing, heating equipment and supplies	20,815	278,100	113.0	44,225
Furniture and home furnishings	12,498	144,800	78.3	25,187
Sporting, recreational, photographic, and hobby goods	7,266	85,100	112.0	22,135
Miscellaneous durable goods	20,482	201,500	93.5	81,440
Nondurable goods	159,726	2,417,000	113.6	757,292
Groceries and related products	38,516	792,200	115.7	222,377
Farm-products raw materials	13,872	150,100	...	102,200
Apparel and accessories	14,289	196,200	107.5	45,413
Beer, wine, and distilled alcoholic beverages	6,378	150,000	127.4	43,357
Paper and paper products	13,967	204,700	121.3	44,251
Chemicals and allied products	10,724	127,700	149.8	25,198
Drugs, drug proprietaries, and druggists' sundries	3,851	180,700	129.3	32,788
Miscellaneous nondurable goods	39,434	451,100	92.3	106,477
Services[15]	1,711,800	21,543,000	87.3	751,055
Business	258,400	4,777,300	92.1	216,306
Health, except hospitals	390,200	7,144,200	68.6	189,520
Legal	125,700	712,300	129.3	64,510
Engineering, architectural, and surveying	53,200	724,400	162.8	50,468
Hotels, motels, and other lodging places	48,000	1,550,300	60.3	51,097
Amusement and recreation, including motion pictures	60,200	918,300	63.4	29,407
Automotive repair, services, garages	127,600	836,700	92.1	57,837
Personal	175,200	1,174,500	67.9	42,363
Accounting, auditing, and bookkeeping	58,100	498,100	119.7	27,949
Miscellaneous repair services	56,700	385,300	109.0	21,598

Energy production (consumption): electricity (kW-hr; 1988) 2,701,000,000,-000 (2,566,000,000,000); coal (metric tons; 1988) 870,200,000 (799,800,000); crude petroleum (barrels; 1988) 2,979,120,000 (4,920,000,000); petroleum products (metric tons; 1988) 752,696,000 (865,987,000); natural gas (cu m; 1988) 491,270,000,000 (510,840,000,000). Domestic production of energy by source (1988): coal 31.7%, crude oil 26.3%, natural gas 26.1%, nuclear power 8.6%, hydroelectric power 3.5%, other 3.8%.

Energy consumption by end use ('000,000,000 kW-hr; 1988): total 2,566, of which industrial 884, residential 890, commercial 710, other 82; by source: coal 56.9%, nuclear 19.5%, natural gas 9.3%, hydroelectric power 8.3%, crude oil 5.5%, other 0.5%.

Household income and expenditure. Average household size (1988) 2.6; average annual income per household (1987) U.S.$32,144; sources of income: wages and salaries 68.7%, transfer payments 15.1%, self-employment 8.5%, other 7.7%; expenditure (1988)[16]: food 17.3%, housing 15.5%, health 13.7%, transportation 12.6%, household durable goods 7.7%, recreation 7.7%, clothing 7.2%, energy 4.2%, education 1.2%.

Selected household characteristics (1988). Total number of households 91,-066,000, of which (by race and Spanish origin[17]) white 86.2%, black 11.2%, other 2.6%, Spanish origin 6.3%; (by location) in metropolitan areas 77.6%, outside metropolitan areas 22.4% (farms 1.8%); (by tenure) owned 58,-214,000 (63.9%), rented 32,852,000 (36.1%); family households 65,132,000,

of which married couple 79.5%, female head with children under age 18, 11.6%, other 8.9%; nonfamily households 25,934,000, of which female householder 56.4%, male 43.6%. Work disability status of householder (1988): having no work disability 91.4%, having work disability 8.6%.

Financial aggregates

	1983	1984	1985	1986	1987	1988	1989[18]
Exchange rate, U.S.$ per:							
£[19]	1.52	1.34	1.30	1.47	1.63	1.81	1.63
SDR[19]	1.07	1.03	1.02	1.17	1.29	1.35	1.23
International reserves (U.S.$)[20]							
Total (excl. gold; '000,000,000)	22.63	23.84	32.10	37.45	34.72	36.7	57.4
SDRs ('000,000,000)	5.03	5.64	7.29	8.39	10.28	9.64	9.49
Reserve pos. in IMF ('000,000,000)	11.31	11.54	11.95	11.73	11.35	9.75	8.79
Foreign exchange ('000,000,000)	6.29	6.66	12.86	17.33	13.09	17.36	39.08
Gold ('000,000 fine troy oz)	263.39	262.79	262.65	262.04	262.38	261.87	262.06
% world reserves	27.80	27.77	27.68	27.63	27.74	27.69	...
Interest and prices							
Central bank discount (%)[19]	8.50	8.00	7.50	5.5	6.0	6.5	7.0
Gov't. bond yield (%)[19]	10.45	11.89	9.64	7.06	7.67	8.24	8.26
Industrial share prices[19] (1985 = 100)	86.9	87.2	100.0	126.2	159.2	147.6	191.1
Balance of payments ($'000,000,000)							
Balance of visible trade	−67.08	−112.51	−122.15	−144.54	−160.28	−150.88	−26.75[21]
Imports, f.o.b.	268.89	332.41	338.09	368.52	409.85	409.77	119.95[21]
Exports, f.o.b.	201.81	219.90	215.94	223.98	249.57	250.89	93.20[21]
Balance of invisibles	29.88	18.19	21.65	21.02	19.74	15.3	−1.11[21]
Balance of payments, current account	−46.28	−107.09	−116.43	−138.84	−153.95	−126.18	−30.75[21]

Population economically active (1988): total 123,378,000; activity rate of total population 50.1% (participation rates: ages 16 and over 65.2%; female 44.5%; unemployed 5.4%).

Price and earnings indexes (1985 = 100)

	1983	1984	1985	1986	1987	1988	1989[18]
Consumer price index	92.6	96.4	100.0	101.9	105.7	109.9	115.3
Hourly earnings index	87.7	97.8	100.0	102.1	104.0	106.7	109.5

Average employee earnings

	average hourly earnings in U.S.$		average weekly earnings in U.S.$	
	July 1988	July 1989	July 1988	July 1989
Manufacturing				
Durable goods	10.67	11.00	439.60	449.90
Lumber and wood products	8.66	8.93	349.00	352.74
Furniture and fixtures	7.99	8.25	310.81	318.45
Stone, clay, and glass products	10.53	10.74	446.47	457.52
Primary metal industries	12.22	12.41	526.68	528.67
Fabricated metal products	10.20	10.51	419.22	428.81
Machinery, except electrical	10.98	11.36	464.45	474.85
Electrical and electronic equipment	10.13	10.43	409.25	418.24
Transportation equipment	13.19	13.72	550.02	570.75
Instruments and related products	9.96	10.29	409.36	418.80
Miscellaneous manufacturing	7.98	8.30	308.03	320.38
Nondurable goods	9.46	9.76	377.45	390.40
Food and kindred products	9.12	9.35	367.54	383.35
Tobacco manufactures	15.78	16.31	620.15	616.52
Textile mill products	7.31	7.65	295.32	310.59
Apparel and other textile products	6.03	6.28	221.30	230.48
Paper and allied products	11.72	12.05	502.79	515.74
Printing and publishing	10.48	10.87	396.14	404.67
Chemicals and allied products	12.70	13.11	533.40	553.24
Petroleum and coal products	14.93	15.31	676.33	678.23
Rubber and miscellaneous plastics products	9.15	9.45	376.07	385.56
Leather and leather products	6.19	6.53	230.89	246.83
Nonmanufacturing				
Metal mining	13.37	13.74	546.83	599.06
Coal mining	16.02	15.86	643.92	659.60
Oil and gas extraction	11.92	12.44	497.06	516.26
Nonmetallic minerals, except fuels	10.97	11.32	510.11	533.17
Construction	12.96	13.33	500.26	518.54
Transportation and public utilities	12.32	12.57	490.34	500.29
Wholesale trade	9.95	10.40	381.09	398.32
Retail trade	6.28	6.49	188.40	194.05
Finance, insurance, and real estate	9.03	9.58	325.98	347.75
Hotels, motels, and tourist courts	6.32	6.53	203.50	210.27
Health services	9.23	9.84	301.82	323.74
Legal services	12.75	13.65	446.25	483.21
Miscellaneous services	12.60	13.42	480.06	507.28

Tourism (1987): receipts from visitors U.S.$14,778,000,000; expenditures by nationals abroad U.S.$20,496,000,000; number of foreign visitors 10,434,-000 (4,663,000 from western Europe, 1,241,000 from Central America and the Caribbean, 935,000 from South America); number of nationals traveling abroad 13,248,000 (6,175,000 to Europe and the Mediterranean, 4,118,000 to Central America and the Caribbean, 768,000 to South America).

Land use (1987): forested 33.1%; meadows and pastures 26.2%; agricultural and under permanent cultivation 20.9%; other 19.8%.

Foreign trade

Balance of trade (current prices)

	1983	1984	1985	1986	1987	1988
U.S.$'000,000,000	−67.1	−112.5	−122.1	−144.5	−152.1	−138.4
% of total	14.3%	20.4%	22.0%	24.3%	23.0%	17.7%

Imports (1988): U.S.$460,209,000,000 (machinery and transport equipment 42.8%, of which new passenger cars 10.3%, telecommunications and sound

recording and reproducing apparatus 6.2%, office machinery and automatic data-processing machines 5.2%, transport-equipment parts 3.2%; basic and miscellaneous manufactures 28.7%, of which clothing 4.0%; mineral fuels and lubricants 8.9%, of which crude petroleum 5.6%, petroleum products 3.3%; food 4.4%. *Major import sources:* Japan 20.2%; Canada 17.7%; West Germany 5.8%; Taiwan 5.4%; Mexico 5.1%; South Korea 4.4%; United Kingdom 3.9%; France 2.7%; Italy 2.5%; Hong Kong 2.2%.

Exports (1988): U.S.$321,813,106,000 (machinery 29.7%, of which office machinery and computers 7.5%, power-generating machinery 4.1%, special-purpose machinery 2.4%, telecommunications equipment 1.9%; transport equipment 14.6%, of which motor vehicles and parts 7.8%, aircraft and parts 6.3%; basic and miscellaneous manufactures 15.7%, of which professional, scientific, and controlling instruments and apparatus 2.4%; chemicals and related products 10.1%; food 8.4%, of which grain and cereal preparations 3.1%). *Major export destinations:* Canada 21.5%; Japan 11.7%; Mexico 6.4%; United Kingdom 5.7%; West Germany 4.4%; Taiwan 3.8%; South Korea 3.5%; The Netherlands 3.2%; France 3.1%; Belgium–Luxembourg 2.3%.

Trade by commodity group (1988)

SITC Group	imports (c.i.f.) U.S.$'000,000	%	exports (f.a.s.) U.S.$'000,000	%
00 Food and live animals	20,106.6	4.4	26,931.8	8.4
01 Beverages and tobacco	4,139.0	0.9	4,602.0	1.4
02 Crude materials, excluding fuels	13,397.5	2.9	25,508.7	7.9
03 Mineral fuels, lubricants, and related materials	41,087.8	8.9	8,229.5	2.6
04 Animal and vegetable oils, fat, and waxes	849.0	0.2	1,470.0	0.5
05 Chemicals and related products, n.e.s.	19,875.6	4.3	32,663.6	10.1
06 Basic manufactures	61,636.0	13.4	23,758.1	7.4
07 Machinery and transport equipment	197,053.3	42.8	142,433.9	44.3
08 Miscellaneous manufactured articles	70,465.3	15.3	26,654.6	8.3
09 Goods not classified by kind	31,598.9	6.9	29,560.9	9.2
TOTAL	460,209.0	100.0	321,813.1	100.0[3]

Direction of trade (1988)

	imports (c.i.f.) U.S.$'000,000	%	exports (f.a.s.) U.S.$'000,000	%
Africa	11,709.8	2.5	7,430.9	2.3
South Africa	1,529.6	0.3	1,690.3	0.5
Other	10,180.2	2.2	5,740.6	1.8
Americas	135,135.3	29.4	113,154.8	35.2
Canada	81,434.0	17.7	69,232.8	21.5
Caribbean countries and Central America	6,836.7	1.5	8,576.4	2.7
Mexico	23,544.7	5.1	20,643.4	6.4
South America	23,319.9	5.1	14,702.2	4.6
Asia	200,359.8	43.5	99,704.6	31.0
Japan	93,168.1	20.2	37,732.1	11.7
Other Asia	107,191.7	23.3	61,972.5	19.3
Europe	107,192.6	23.3	91,644.9	28.5
EEC	88,697.0	19.3	75,926.0	23.6
Other Western Europe	16,338.0	3.6	12,068.9	3.7
U.S.S.R.	578.0	0.1	2,767.6	0.9
Eastern Europe	1,579.6	0.3	882.4	0.3
Oceania	5,299.4	1.1	8,242.2	2.6
Australia	3,856.0	0.8	6,980.7	2.2
Other Oceania	1,443.4	0.3	1,261.5	0.4
Other	512.1	0.1	1,635.6	0.5
TOTAL	460,209.0	100.0[3]	321,813.0	100.0[3]

Transport and communications

Transport. Railroads (1987): length 184,235 mi, 296,497 km; passenger-mi 12,000,000,000, passenger-km 19,200,000,000; short ton-mi cargo 976,000,000,000, metric ton-km cargo 1,424,900,000,000. Roads (1987): total length 3,879,538 mi, 6,243,340 km (paved 88%). Vehicles (1987): passenger cars 139,041,000; trucks and buses 41,948,000. Merchant marine (1988): vessels (100 gross tons and over) 6,442; total deadweight tonnage 29,920,374. Air transport (1988)[23]: passenger-mi 390,934,000,000, passenger-km 629,148,000,000; short ton-mi cargo 11,065,500,000, metric ton-km cargo 16,156,300,000; airports (1989) with scheduled flights 834. Certified route passenger/cargo air carriers (1987) 93; operating revenue (U.S. $'000,000; 1987) 56,129, of which domestic 45,339, international 10,790; operating expenses 53,726, of which domestic 43,605, international 10,121; net operating income 2,403, of which domestic 1,734, international 669.

Intercity passenger and freight traffic by mode of transportation (1987)

	cargo traffic ('000,000,000 ton-mi)	% of nat'l total	passenger traffic ('000,000,000 passenger-mi)	% of nat'l total
Rail	976	36.5	12	0.7
Road	666	24.9	1,517	81.1
Inland water	435	16.3	—	—
Air	8.7	0.3	341	18.2
Pipeline	587	22.0	—	—
TOTAL	2,672.7	100.0	1,870	100.0

Communications. Daily newspapers (1989): total number 1,643; total circulation (1988) 62,694,816; circulation per 1,000 population 255. Radio (1988): total number of receivers 515,496,140 (1 per 0.5 persons). Television (1988): total number of receivers 195,795,300 (1 per 1.3 persons). Telephones (1987; access lines): 126,700,000 (1 per 1.9 persons).

Other communication media (1987)

Print	titles		titles
Books (new)	47,489	Home economics	90
of which		Industrial arts	106
Agriculture	575	Journalism and	
Art	1,338	communication	90
Biography	1,994	Labour and industrial	
Business	1,375	relations	70
Education	979	Law	273
Fiction	5,144	Library and information	
General works	2,083	sciences	118
History	2,550	Literature and language	158
Home economics	929	Mathematics and science	238
Juvenile	4,212	Medicine	182
Language	534	Philosophy and religion	130
Law	1,129	Physical education and	
Literature	1,982	recreation	151
Medicine	3,376	Political science	136
Music	273	Psychology	138
Philosophy, psychology	1,656	Sociology and anthropology	149
Poetry, drama	1,106	Zoology	94
Religion	2,306		
Science	3,118	**Cinema**[6]	
Sociology, economics	7,119	Feature films	511
Sports, recreation	941		
Technology	2,216		traffic
Travel	554		(units, '000)
Periodicals	3,371	**Electronic**[9]	
of which		Telegrams	53,000
Agriculture	153	Domestic	42,000
Business and economics	262	International	11,000
Chemistry and physics	170	Telex	69,559
Children's periodicals	78		
Education	203		(pieces of mail)
Engineering	265	**Post**[6]	
Fine and applied arts	145	Mail	153,931,000
General interest	181	Domestic	153,153,000
History	151	International	778,000

Education and health

Education (1988–89)

	schools	teachers	students	student/ teacher ratio
Primary (age 6–13)		1,306,001	25,506,170	19.5
Secondary and vocational (age 14–17)	101,050	977,079	14,786,138	15.1
Higher, including teacher-training colleges[24]	3,406	722,000	7,117,000	9.9

Literacy (1980): total population age 15 and over literate 166,497,565 (95.5%); males literate 79,161,126 (95.7%); females literate 87,336,439 (95.3%); other studies indicate adult "functional" literacy may not exceed 85%.

Health: physicians (1987) 594,700 (1 per 410 persons), specialties (1986) internal medicine 16.0%, general practice 11.9%, general surgery 6.5%, pediatrics 6.4%, psychiatry 5.7%, obstetrics and gynecology 5.5%, anesthesiology 4.1%, orthopedics 3.1%, pathology 2.7%, ophthalmology 2.7%, radiology 1.5%, other 33.9%; hospital beds (1986) 1,283,000 (1 per 188 persons), of which nonfederal 91.3% (short-term general and special 76.1%, psychiatric 12.9%, long-term general and special 2.3%, tuberculosis 0.1%), federal 8.7%; infant mortality rate per 1,000 live births (1989[5]) 9.9.

Food (1984–86): daily per capita caloric intake 3,642 (vegetable products 66%, animal products 34%); 138% of FAO recommended minimum requirement. Per capita consumption of major food groups (pounds annually; 1987): dairy products 598.2; sweeteners 151.4; red meat 144.0; grains 128.0; fresh fruits 98.6; fresh vegetables 78.6; fats and oils 62.7; poultry products 62.7; citrus fruit juices 46.5; fish 15.4.

Military

Total active duty personnel (1989): 2,124,900 (army 36.1%, navy 27.5%, air force 27.3%, marines 9.2%). *Military expenditure as percent of GNP* (1987): 6.5% (world 5.4%); per capita expenditure U.S.$1,215. *Military aid* (1987): total $5,102,000,000 (Middle East and South Asia 84.3%, of which Israel 35.3%, Egypt 25.5%, Turkey 9.7%, Greece 6.7%, Pakistan 6.2%, Jordan 0.8%; Latin America 4.2%, of which El Salvador 2.2%, Honduras 1.2%; Europe 3.7%, of which Spain 2.1%, Portugal 1.6%; East Asia 3.4%, of which Philippines 2.0%, Thailand 1.0%; Africa 2.7%, of which Tunisia 1.1%, Morocco 0.6%; international organizations 1.1%).

[1]Total area excluding U.S. share of Great Lakes is 3,618,770 sq mi (9,372,571 sq km). [2]Excludes armed forces overseas. [3]Detail does not add to total given because of rounding. [4]Fiscal year ending September 30. [5]First seven months only. [6]1987. [7]November 22. [8]1984. [9]1986. [10]Annual value of shipments. [11]Includes public utilities. [12]Statistical discrepancy. [13]Includes 6,662,000 unemployed. [14]Number of establishments is for 1982. [15]Number of establishment is for 1985. [16]Personal consumption expenditure. [17]Persons of Spanish origin may be of any race. [18]September. [19]Annual average. [20]End of year. [21]Second quarter. [22]Includes reexports valued at U.S.$12,985,200,000. [23]Major carriers only. [24]1987–88.

Uruguay

Official name: República Oriental del Uruguay (Oriental Republic of Uruguay).
Form of government: republic with two legislative houses (Senate [31][1]; Chamber of Representatives [99]).
Head of state and government: President.
Capital: Montevideo.
Official language: Spanish.
Official religion: none.
Monetary unit: 1 Uruguayan new peso (NUr$) = 100 centésimos; valuation (Oct. 2, 1989) 1 U.S.$ = NUr$687; 1 £ = NUr$1,111.

Area and population

Departments	Capitals	area sq mi	area sq km	population 1985 census[2]
Artigas	Artigas	4,605	11,928	68,400
Canelones	Canelones	1,751	4,536	359,700
Cerro Largo	Melo	5,270	13,648	78,000
Colonia	Colonia del Sacramento	2,358	6,106	112,100
Durazno	Durazno	4,495	11,643	54,700
Flores	Trinidad	1,986	5,144	24,400
Florida	Florida	4,022	10,417	65,400
Lavalleja	Minas	3,867	10,016	61,700
Maldonado	Maldonado	1,851	4,793	93,000
Montevideo	Montevideo	205	530	1,309,100
Paysandú	Paysandú	5,375	13,922	104,500
Río Negro	Fray Bentos	3,584	9,282	47,500
Rivera	Rivera	3,618	9,370	88,400
Rocha	Rocha	4,074	10,551	68,500
Salto	Salto	5,468	14,163	107,300
San José	San José de Mayo	1,927	4,992	91,900
Soriano	Mercedes	3,478	9,008	77,500
Tacuarembó	Tacuarembó	5,961	15,438	82,600
Treinta y Tres	Treinta y Tres	3,679	9,529	45,500
TOTAL LAND AREA		67,574	175,016	2,940,200
INLAND WATER		463	1,199	
TOTAL AREA		68,037	176,215	

Demography

Population (1989): 3,017,000.
Density (1989): persons per sq mi 44.6, persons per sq km 17.2.
Urban–rural (1985): urban 86.2%; rural 13.8%.
Sex distribution (1985): male 48.68%; female 51.32%.
Age breakdown (1985): under 15, 26.6%; 15–29, 22.9%; 30–44, 18.3%; 45–59, 16.5%; 60–74, 11.4%; 75 and over, 4.3%.
Population projection: (2000) 3,207,000; (2010) 3,391,000.
Doubling time: 87 years.
Ethnic composition (1980): mixed Spanish–Italian 85.9%; mestizo 3.0%; Italian 2.6%; Jewish 1.7%; mulatto 1.2%; other 5.6%.
Religious affiliation (1980): Christian 62.9%, of which Roman Catholic 59.5%; nonreligious and atheist 35.1%; Jewish 1.7%; other 0.3%.
Major cities (1985): Montevideo 1,246,500; Salto 77,400; Paysandú 75,200; Las Piedras 61,300; Rivera 55,400.

Vital statistics

Birth rate per 1,000 population (1987): 17.9 (world avg. 27.1); (1983) legitimate 73.8%; illegitimate 26.2%.
Death rate per 1,000 population (1987): 9.8 (world avg. 9.9).
Natural increase rate per 1,000 population (1987): 8.1 (world avg. 17.2).
Total fertility rate (avg. births per childbearing woman; 1985–90): 2.4.
Marriage rate per 1,000 population (1986): 8.0.
Divorce rate per 1,000 population (1986): 1.4.
Life expectancy at birth (1985–90): male 67.8 years; female 74.4 years.
Major causes of death per 100,000 population (1987): diseases of the circulatory system 401.3; malignant neoplasms (cancers) 216.2; accidents 46.9; respiratory diseases 38.6; diabetes 21.2; perinatal causes 20.3.

National economy

Budget (1988). Revenue: NUr$456,675,200,000 (direct taxes 77.1%, receipts from foreign trade 13.8%). Expenditures: NUr$510,651,400,000 (social security and welfare 57.9%, general public services 13.6%, capital investments 11.1%, interest on public debt 8.7%, subsidies 6.0%).
Public debt (external, outstanding; 1987): U.S.$3,048,000,000.
Production (metric tons except as noted). Agriculture, forestry, fishing (1988) sugarcane 494,700, rice 380,600, wheat 307,800, sugar beets 256,100, sorghum 121,200, corn (maize) 118,300; livestock (number of live animals; 1987) 25,560,000 sheep, 10,323,000 cattle, 500,000 horses; roundwood (1987) 3,289,000 cu m; fish catch 107,348. Mining and quarrying (1987): hydraulic cement 401,000; gypsum 110,000. Manufacturing (value added in NUr$'000,000; 1987): food products excluding beverages 73,085; textiles 47,375, petroleum products 47,053; chemicals and chemical products 40,322; beverages 33,906; transport equipment 32,641, tobacco products 19,829; leather products 17,540; paper and paper products 15,729. Construction (approvals; 1987): residential 479,845 sq m; nonresidential 127,188 sq m. Energy production (consumption): electricity (kW-hr; 1987) 4,526,000,000 (4,520,000,000); coal, none (none); crude petroleum (barrels; 1987) none (9,492,000); petroleum products (metric tons; 1987) 1,147,000 (1,025,000); natural gas, none (n.a.).
Gross national product (1987): U.S.$6,556,000,000 (U.S.$2,180 per capita).

Structure of gross domestic product and labour force

	1988 in value NUr$'000,000	1988 % of total value	1985 labour force	1985 % of labour force
Agriculture	267,457	9.4	179,200	15.3
Mining	3	3	1,900	0.2
Manufacturing	566,651	19.8	211,600	18.0
Construction	62,635	2.2	63,300	5.4
Public utilities	74,485	2.6	17,100	1.5
Transp. and commun.	176,354	6.2	59,100	5.0
Trade	279,509	9.8	136,800	11.7
Finance	363,162	12.7	42,100	3.6
Pub. admin., defense	289,263	10.1	361,000	30.8
Services	323,084[3]	11.33[3]		
Other	452,724[4]	15.94	99,400[5]	8.55
TOTAL	2,855,324	100.0	1,171,500	100.0

Tourism (1987): receipts U.S.$208,000,000; expenditures U.S.$129,000,000.
Population economically active (1985): total 1,171,500; activity rate 39.9% (participation rates: ages 20–64, 71.3%; female 33.1%; unemployed [1987] 9.1%).

Price and earnings indexes (1985 = 100)

	1983	1984	1985	1986	1987	1988	1989
Consumer price index	37.4	58.1	100.0	176.4	288.5	467.9	754.6[6]
Monthly earnings index[7]	42.4	59.8	100.0	186.7	319.8	524.8	...

Household income and expenditure. Avg. household size (1985) 3.3; avg. annual income per household (1985): NUr$266,261 (U.S.$2,625); sources of income: wages 53.5%, self-employment 17.0%, transfer payments and other 29.5%[8]; expenditure (1982–83)[9]: food 39.9%, housing 17.6%, transport and communications 10.4%, health care 9.3%, clothing 7.0%, durable goods 6.3%, recreation 3.1%, education 1.3%, personal effects and other 5.1%.
Land use (1986): forested 3.6%; meadows and pastures 78.0%; agricultural and under permanent cultivation 8.3%; other 10.1%.

Foreign trade[10]

Balance of trade (current prices)

	1983	1984	1985	1986	1987	1988
U.S.$'000,000	+305.4	+183.6	+179.1	+305.2	+99.6	+300.3
% of total	17.1%	11.0%	11.7%	16.3%	4.4%	12.0%

Imports (1988): U.S.$1,176,949,000 (machinery and appliances 17.1%; chemical products 16.1%; mineral products 15.1%; transport equipment 15.0%; synthetic plastic, resins, and rubber 8.3%; base metals and products 6.5%; vegetable products 4.2%). *Major import sources* (1987): Brazil 24.4%; Argentina 13.7%; West Germany 8.1%; United States 7.9%; Mexico 7.5%.
Exports (1988): U.S.$1,404,527,000 (textiles and textile products 35.1%; live animals and live-animal products 19.5%; hides and skins 15.0%; vegetable products 11.3%; food, beverages, and tobacco 2.7%; synthetic plastics, resins, and rubber 2.2%). *Major export destinations* (1987): Brazil 17.2%; United States 14.8%; West Germany 10.3%; Argentina 9.5%; Italy 5.0%.

Transport and communications

Transport. Railroads (1987): route length (1988) 2,991 km; passenger-km 140,600,000; metric ton-km cargo 212,000,000. Roads (1984): length 52,000 km (paved 23%). Vehicles (1981): passenger cars 281,275; trucks and buses 49,813. Merchant marine (1988): vessels (100 gross tons and over) 87; deadweight tonnage 282,234. Air transport (1985): passenger-km 389,326,000; metric ton-km cargo 37,037,000; airports (1989) 7.
Communications. Daily newspapers (1985): total number 21; total circulation 556,100[11]; circulation per 1,000 population 185[11]. Radio (1988): total receivers 1,780,162 (1 per 1.7 persons). Television (1987): total receivers 500,000 (1 per 5.9 persons). Telephones (1987): 437,035 (1 per 6.8 persons).

Education and health

Education (1987)

	schools	teachers	students	student/ teacher ratio
Primary (age 6–12)	2,382	16,568	354,177	21.4
Secondary	276	12,244	175,710	14.4
Vocational	94	...	52,766	...
Higher	1	5,490	61,367	11.2

Educational attainment (1985). Percent of population age 25 and over having: no formal schooling 7.5%; less than primary education 26.6%; primary 31.2%; secondary 19.9%; higher 14.8%. *Literacy* (1985): Population age 15 and over literate 95.0%; males 975,200 (94.5%); females 1,074,300 (95.4%).
Health (1987): physicians 6,679 (1 per 447 persons); hospital beds (1983) 23,400 (1 per 127 persons); infant mortality rate per 1,000 live births 23.8.
Food (1984–86): daily per capita caloric intake 2,676 (vegetable products 64%, animal products 36%); 100% of FAO recommended minimum.

Military

Total active duty personnel (1988): 24,400 (army 70.5%, navy 17.2%, air force 12.3%). *Military expenditure as percent of GNP* (1986): 2.5% (world 5.5%); per capita expenditure U.S.$55.

---

[1]Includes the vice president who serves as ex officio presiding officer. [2]Preliminary. [3]Mining is included with Services. [4]Includes indirect taxes less subsidies. [5]Includes unemployed not previously employed. [6]May. [7]Salaried employees only. [8]Urban only. [9]Weights of consumer price index components in Montevideo. [10]Import figures are f.o.b. in balance of trade and c.i.f. for commodities and trading partners. [11]Partial circulation only.

Vanuatu

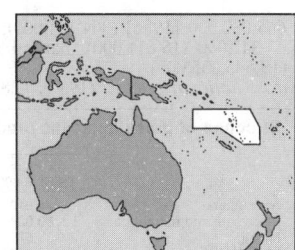

Official name: Ripablik blong Vanuatu (Bislama); République de Vanuatu (French); Republic of Vanuatu (English).
Form of government: republic with a single legislative house (Parliament [46]).
Chief of state: President.
Head of government: Prime Minister.
Capital: Vila.
Official languages: Bislama; French; English.
Official religion: none.
Monetary unit: vatu (VT); valuation (Oct. 2, 1989) 1 U.S.$ = VT 119.04; 1 £ = VT 192.60.

Area and population

Local Government Regions	Capitals	area sq mi	area sq km	population 1987 estimate
Ambrym	Eas	257	666	8,100
Ambae/Maéwo	Longana	270	699	11,780
Banks/Torres	Sola	341	882	6,400
Éfaté	Vila	356	923	28,590
Épi	Ringdove	172	446	3,090
Malekula	Lakatoro	793	2,053	18,850
Paama	Liro	23	60	2,420
Pentecost	Loltong	193	499	11,780
Santo/Malo	Luganville	1,640	4,248	26,310
Shepherd	Morua	33	86	5,160
Taféa	Isangel	629	1,628	22,400
TOTAL		4,707	12,190	144,880

Demography

Population (1989): 154,000.
Density (1989): persons per sq mi 32.7, persons per sq km 12.6.
Urban–rural (1987): urban[1] 14.5%; rural 85.5%.
Sex distribution (1979): male 53.10%; female 46.90%.
Age breakdown (1985): under 15, 45.1%; 15–29, 26.3%; 30–44, 16.5%; 45–59, 8.3%; 60–74, 3.0%; 75 and over, 0.8%.
Population projection: (2000) 217,000; (2010) 296,000.
Doubling time: 21 years.
Ethnic composition (1988): Ni-Vanuatu 97.0%; non-Ni-Vanuatu 3.0%.
Religious affiliation (1979): Christian 81.5%, of which Presbyterian 36.7%, Anglican 15.1%, Roman Catholic 14.8%, Seventh-day Adventist 6.2%; traditional beliefs (mostly followers of cargo cults) 7.6%; nonreligious 1.1%; unknown 9.8%.
Major towns (1987): Vila (Port-Vila) 15,100; Luganville (Santo) 5,900; Port Olry 884[2]; Isangel 752[2].

Vital statistics

Birth rate per 1,000 population (1988): 40.7 (world avg. 27.1).
Death rate per 1,000 population (1988): 7.8 (world avg. 9.9).
Natural increase rate per 1,000 population (1988): 32.9 (world avg. 17.2).
Total fertility rate (avg. births per childbearing woman; 1988): 6.2.
Marriage rate per 1,000 population (1985): c. 7.4.
Divorce rate per 1,000 population (1985): less than 0.7.
Life expectancy at birth (1985): male 61.1 years; female 59.3 years.
Major causes of death per 100,000 population (1985)[3]: infectious and parasitic diseases 69.3; diseases of the respiratory system 60.5; diseases of the circulatory system 37.6; accidents and violence 23.6; malignant neoplasms (cancers) 22.9; ill-defined conditions 117.3.

National economy

Budget (1986). Revenue: VT 3,321,600,000 (import duties 45.5%, domestic excise taxes 19.6%, foreign grants 16.4%, local nontax revenue 16.3%). Expenditures: VT 4,131,800,000 (education 27.1%, public services 19.4%, health 12.4%, transport and communications 12.3%, agriculture 9.6%, public order 7.6%).
Public debt (external, outstanding; 1987): U.S.$14,600,000.
Tourism (1987): receipts from visitors U.S.$4,000,000; expenditures by nationals abroad, U.S.$2,000,000.
Production (metric tons except as noted). Agriculture, forestry, fishing (1987): coconuts 330,000, copra 40,000, roots and tubers 30,000, vegetables and melons 8,000, bananas 1,000, cocoa beans 1,000, corn (maize) 1,000; livestock (number of live animals) 103,000 cattle, 73,000 pigs, 12,000 goats; roundwood 38,000 cu m; fish catch 3,249. Mining and quarrying (1985): small quantities of coral reef limestone, crushed stone, sand, and gravel. Manufacturing (value added in '000 VT; 1984): food, beverages, and tobacco 358,000; wood products 96,000; fabricated metal products 60,000; paper products, including printing and publishing 48,800; nonmetallic mineral products 24,600; handicrafts 14,600; textiles, clothing, and leather 12,900. Construction (approvals in Vila and Luganville; 1988): residential 14,969 sq m; nonresidential 14,520 sq m. Energy production (consumption): electricity (kW-hr; 1987) 26,000,000 (26,000,000); coal, none (none); crude petroleum, none (none); petroleum products (metric tons; 1987) none (17,000); natural gas, none (none).
Population economically active (1979): total 51,130; activity rate of total population 46.0% (participation rates: ages 15–64, 84.3%; female 43.4%; unemployed, n.a.).

[1]Vila and Luganville only. [2]1979. [3]Deaths reported to the Ministry of Health only. [4]Second quarter. [5]Weights of consumer price index components. [6]Imports c.i.f.; exports f.o.b. [7]Included with Secondary. [8]A centre of the University of the South Pacific in Vila was completed in 1988.

Price and earnings indexes (1985 = 100)

	1982	1983	1984	1985	1986	1987	1988
Consumer price index	92.2	93.8	99.0	100.0	104.8	120.3	129.4[4]
Monthly earnings index	...	...	...	...	...	...	...

Land use (1986): forested 1.1%; meadows and pastures 1.7%; agricultural 9.8%; limestones, volcanic rock, and other 87.4%.
Gross national product (at current market prices; 1985): U.S.$116,700,000 (U.S.$860 per capita).

Structure of gross domestic product and labour force

	1985 in value VT '000,000	1985 % of total value	1979 labour force	1979 % of labour force
Agriculture	4,335	33.8	39,276	76.8
Mining	...	...	76	0.1
Manufacturing	491	3.8	990	1.9
Construction	239	1.9	1,103	2.2
Public utilities	202	1.6	62	0.1
Transportation and communications	4,219	32.9	1,323	2.6
Trade			2,176	4.3
Finance	76	0.6	326	0.6
Pub. admin., defense	1,893	14.8	5,492	10.8
Services	1,355	10.6		
Other			306	0.6
TOTAL	12,810	100.0	51,130	100.0

Household income and expenditure (1985)[1]. Average household size 4.8; income per household: U.S.$11,299; sources of income: wages and salaries 59.0%, self-employment 33.7%; expenditure[5] (1987): food and beverages 45.5%, clothing and footwear 14.1%, housing 10.2%, transportation 9.8%.

Foreign trade[6]

Balance of trade (current prices)

	1983	1984	1985	1986	1987	1988
VT '000,000	−3,352	−2,416	−4,115	−4,264	−5,696	−5,247
% of total	36.3%	21.6%	38.7%	53.7%	59.5%	55.4%

Imports (1988): VT 7,361,000,000 (basic and miscellaneous manufactures 31.0%; machinery and transport equipment 24.4%; food and live animals 17.2%; mineral fuels 7.9%; chemical products 5.7%; beverages and tobacco 5.0%). *Major import sources:* Australia 41.7%; New Zealand 10.1%; Japan 9.0%; Fiji 6.6%; France 4.7%; New Caledonia 3.9%; Hong Kong 3.8%; Singapore 3.6%.
Exports (1988): VT 2,114,000,000 (domestic exports 76.0%, of which copra 45.1%, beef and veal 11.4%, cocoa 5.5%, timber 5.0%; reexports 24.0%). *Major export destinations:* The Netherlands 39.3%; Japan 11.6%; France 4.7%; Belgium 3.1%; New Caledonia 2.6%; Singapore 1.4%.

Transport and communications

Transport. Railroads: none. Roads (1984): total length 660 mi, 1,062 km; (paved 24%). Vehicles (1984): passenger cars 3,087; trucks and buses, n.a. Merchant marine (1988): vessels (100 gross tons and over) 127; total deadweight tonnage 1,429,699. Air transport (1987), domestic passenger arrivals 91,378, international passenger arrivals 20,131, international cargo unloaded 432 metric tons, international cargo loaded 133 metric tons; airports (1989) with scheduled flights 27.
Communications. Daily newspapers: none. Radio (1988): total number of receivers 20,000 (1 per 7.5 persons). Television: none. Telephones (1986): 3,240 (1 per 44 persons).

Education and health

Education (1986)

	schools	teachers	students	student/ teacher ratio
Primary (age 6–11)	265	1,036	23,856	23.0
Secondary (age 11–18)	21	133	2,904	21.8
Voc., teacher tr.[7]	...	...	...	...
Higher[8]	...	...	...	...

Educational attainment (1979). Percent of population age 25 and over having: no formal schooling 37.2%; some primary education 34.3%; complete primary 6.5%, lower-level secondary 14.7%, upper-level secondary and higher 7.3%. *Literacy* (1979): total population age 15 and over literate 32,120 (52.9%); males 18,550 (57.3%); females 13,570 (47.8%).
Health: physicians (1986) 27 (1 per 5,191 persons); hospital beds (1983) 437 (1 per 294 persons); infant mortality rate per 1,000 live births (1988) 55.
Food (1984–86): daily per capita caloric intake 2,344 (vegetable products 79%, animal products 21%); 103% of FAO recommended minimum requirement.

Military

Total active duty personnel: Vanuatu has a paramilitary force of about 300.

Venezuela

Official name: República de Venezuela
(Republic of Venezuela).
Form of government: federal multiparty
republic with two legislative
houses (Senate [49][1]; Chamber of
Deputies [201]).
Head of state and government:
President.
Capital: Caracas.
Official language: Spanish.
Official religion: none.
Monetary unit: 1 bolívar (B, plural
Bs) = 100 céntimos; valuation[2] (Oct.
2, 1989) 1 U.S.$ = Bs 38.02;
1 £ = Bs 61.52.

Area and population		area		population
States	**Capitals**	**sq mi**	**sq km**	**1989 estimate**
Anzoátegui	Barcelona	16,700	43,300	857,058
Apure	San Fernando de Apure	29,500	76,500	247,874
Aragua	Maracay	2,700	7,014	1,287,424
Barinas	Barinas	13,600	35,200	454,500
Bolívar	Ciudad Bolívar	91,900	238,000	969,916
Carabobo	Valencia	1,795	4,650	1,550,235
Cojedes	San Carlos	5,700	14,800	191,012
Falcón	Coro	9,600	24,800	622,576
Guárico	San Juan de Los Morros	25,091	64,986	474,041
Lara	Barquisimeto	7,600	19,800	1,214,590
Mérida	Mérida	4,400	11,300	608,408
Miranda	Los Teques	3,070	7,950	1,966,467
Monagas	Maturín	11,200	28,900	499,117
Nueva Esparta	La Asunción	440	1,150	273,811
Portuguesa	Guanare	5,900	15,200	589,421
Sucre	Cumaná	4,600	11,800	735,048
Táchira	San Cristóbal	4,300	11,100	837,293
Trujillo	Trujillo	2,900	7,400	543,869
Yaracuy	San Felipe	2,700	7,100	372,555
Zulia	Maracaibo	24,400	63,100	2,160,149
Other federal entities				
Amazonas	Puerto Ayacucho	67,900	175,750	83,160
Delta Amacuro	Tucupita	15,500	40,200	95,788
Dependencias Federales	—	50	120	[3]
Distrito Federal	Caracas	745	1,930	2,611,209
TOTAL		352,144[2]	912,050	19,245,521

Demography

Population (1989): 19,246,000.
Density (1989): persons per sq mi 54.7, persons per sq km 21.1.
Urban–rural (1989): urban 83.6%; rural 16.4%.
Sex distribution (1989): male 50.46%; female 49.54%.
Age breakdown (1989): under 15, 38.5%; 15–29, 28.2%; 30–44, 18.4%; 45–59, 9.2%; 60–74, 4.5%; 75 and over, 1.2%.
Population projection: (2000) 24,715,000; (2010) 30,006,000.
Doubling time: 29 years.
Ethnic composition (1981): mestizo 69%; white 20%; black 9%; Indian 2%.
Religious affiliation (1987): Roman Catholic 91.7%; other 8.3%.
Major cities (1989): Caracas 1,275,591; Maracaibo 1,179,384; Valencia 922,-138; Barquisimeto 702,764; Maracay 524,952; Petare 519,866.

Vital statistics

Birth rate per 1,000 population (1987): 28.3 (world avg. 27.1); (1974) legitimate 47.0%; illegitimate 53.0%.
Death rate per 1,000 population (1987): 4.4 (world avg. 9.9).
Natural increase rate per 1,000 population (1987): 23.9 (world avg. 17.2).
Total fertility rate (avg. births per childbearing woman; 1987): 3.4.
Marriage rate per 1,000 population (1987): 5.7.
Life expectancy at birth (1985–90): male 66.7 years; female 72.8 years.
Major causes of death per 100,000 population (1987): heart diseases 64.8; malignant neoplasms (cancers) 46.4; accidents 45.4; perinatal problems 31.1; infectious and parasitic diseases 29.2; cerebrovascular diseases 25.9.

National economy

Budget (1988). Revenue: Bs 175,172,000,000 (oil revenues 38.2%, nontax revenues 22.4%, indirect taxes 16.2%, direct taxes 14.5%, internal borrowing 8.0%). Expenditures: Bs 188,334,000,000 (operating expenses 93.0%, public debt service 7.0%).
Public debt (external, outstanding; 1987): U.S.$25,245,000,000.
Tourism (1987): receipts from visitors U.S.$409,000,000; expenditures by nationals abroad U.S.$521,000,000.
Production (metric tons except as noted). Agriculture, forestry, fishing (1987): sugarcane 7,000,000, corn (maize) 1,200,000, bananas 1,000,000, sorghum 850,000, oranges 392,000, rice 300,000, sesame seed 80,000, coffee 66,000, cacao 14,000; livestock (number of live animals) 12,654,000 cattle; roundwood 1,328,000 cu m; fish catch 290,562. Mining and quarrying (1987): iron ore 10,973,000; aluminum ore 427,363; gold 107,030 troy ounces; diamonds 106,000 carats. Manufacturing (value added in Bs '000; 1987): base metals 18,452,468; chemicals 18,187,493; food products 17,053,850; beverages 9,647,189; nonmetallic minerals 7,167,588; textiles 6,356,088; metal products 6,329,515; tobacco 5,606,202; electrical machinery and equipment 5,200,809; transport equipment 5,160,961. Construction (in Bs; 1987): residential 12,945,000,000; nonresidential 42,466,000,000. Energy production (consumption): electricity (kW-hr; 1986) 46,724,000,000 (46,716,000,000); coal (metric tons; 1986) 57,000 (307,000); crude petroleum (barrels; 1987)

665,030,000 [1986] (304,151,000); petroleum products (metric tons; 1986) 43,347,000 (18,671,000); natural gas (cu m; 1987) 36,350,000,000 [1986] (19,545,335,000).
Gross national product (1987): U.S.$48,241,000,000 (U.S.$3,230 per capita).

Structure of gross domestic product and labour force				
	1987			
	in value Bs '000,000	% of total value	labour force	% of labour force
Agriculture	42,616	5.9	857,141	13.6
Petroleum and natural gas	63,004	8.8	62,126	1.0
Mining	5,579	0.8		
Manufacturing	158,859	22.1	1,072,785	17.0
Construction	34,624	4.8	589,928	9.3
Public utilities	11,035	1.5	70,489	1.1
Transp. and commun.	49,132	6.8	396,204	6.3
Trade	131,542	18.3	1,210,416	19.1
Finance	88,083	12.2	320,712	5.1
Pub. admin., defense	55,858	7.8	1,646,928	26.0
Services	57,599	8.0		
Other	21,492	3.0	94,837[4]	1.5[4]
TOTAL	719,423	100.0	6,321,566	100.0

Population economically active (1987): total 6,321,566; activity rate 34.4% (participation rates: ages 15–64, 58.1%; female 27.7%; unemployed 9.1%).

Price and earnings indexes (1985 = 100)							
	1981	1982	1983	1984	1985	1986	1987
Consumer price index	68.7	75.3	80.0	89.8	100.0	111.5	142.9
Monthly earnings index[5]	89.6	...	93.4	105.7	100.0	108.3	141.8

Household income and expenditure: average household size (1981) 5.3; average annual income per household (1981) Bs 42,492 (U.S.$9,899); sources of income: n.a.; expenditure (1985): food 51.8%, transport and communications 10.8%, rent and utilities 8.5%, education and recreation 6.8%, household furnishings and maintenance 6.3%, medical care 4.9%, clothing 4.7%.
Land use (1986): forested 35.5%; meadows and pastures 19.8%; agricultural and under permanent cultivation 4.3%; other 40.4%.

Foreign trade

Balance of trade (current prices)						
	1982	1983	1984	1985	1986	1987
Bs '000,000	+20,765	+31,427	+49,665	+36,786	+11,429	+7,510
% of total	26.0%	31.8%	34.3%	25.0%	7.8%	3.2%

Imports (1987): Bs 115,135,549,400 (machinery and transport equipment 43.7%, chemicals 16.6%, food and live animals 11.2%, base metals and metal products 7.4%, paper products 4.1%). *Major import sources:* U.S. 44.2%; W.Ger. 8.6%; Japan 6.4%; Italy 5.1%; Brazil 4.4%; France 3.6%; U.K. 3.5%.
Exports (1987): Bs 122,553,000,000 (crude petroleum and petroleum products 82.3%, base metals 10.4%). *Major export destinations* (1986): U.S. 35.8%; Japan 14.6%; Colombia 7.9%; The Netherlands 3.4%; Puerto Rico 2.6%; W.Ger. 2.0%.

Transport and communications

Transport. Railroads (1987): route length 273 mi, 439 km; passenger-km 22,-239,031; metric ton-km cargo 17,821,351. Roads (1986): total length 62,492 mi, 100,571 km (paved 33%). Vehicles (1986): passenger cars 2,300,000; trucks and buses 1,248,000. Merchant marine (1988): vessels (100 gross tons and over) 286; total deadweight tonnage 1,428,629. Air transport (1987): passenger-km 3,540,000,000; metric ton-km cargo 113,208,000; airports (1989) with scheduled flights 29.
Communications. Daily newspapers (1984): total number 61; total circulation 2,739,000; circulation per 1,000 population 163. Radio (1988): 8,025,-590 receivers (1 per 2.3 persons). Television (1987): 2,760,000 receivers (1 per 6.6 persons). Telephones (1987): 1,581,063 (1 per 11 persons).

Education and health

Education (1986–87)				
	schools[6]	teachers	students	student/ teacher ratio
Primary (age 7–12)	19,868	112,157	2,880,333	25.7
Secondary (age 13–17)[7]	2,277	61,671	1,058,058	17.2
Higher	82	32,404	441,734	13.6

Educational attainment (1987). Percent of population age 15 and over having: no formal schooling 12.4%; primary education 41.2%; secondary 37.5%; higher 8.9%. *Literacy* (1987): total population age 15 and over literate 10,055,776 (89.6%); males 5,146,691 (91.4%); females 4,909,085 (87.8%).
Health: physicians 28,400 (1 per 643 persons); hospital beds 47,535 (1 per 384 persons); infant mortality rate 25.1.
Food (1984–86): daily per capita caloric intake 2,532 (vegetable products 80%, animal products 20%); (1984) 105% of FAO recommended minimum.

Military

Total active duty personnel (1988): 69,000 (army 78.3%, navy 14.5%, air force 7.2%). *Military expenditure as percent of GNP* (1987): 3.6% (world 5.4%); per capita expenditure U.S.$75.

---

[1]In addition, three former Presidents hold lifetime membership. [2]Venezuela's three-tiered system of official exchange rates was replaced on March 14, 1989, by a unified market-determined exchange rate. The free-market rate governs, and is sometimes identified as, a luxury goods rate. [3]Population not estimated separately by source. [4]Mostly unemployed persons not previously employed. [5]In nonagricultural activities. [6]1985–86. [7]Includes vocational and teacher training.

Vietnam

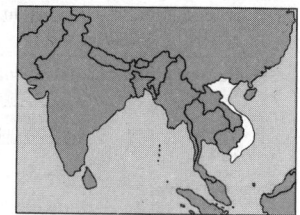

Official name: Cong Hoa Xa Hoi Chu Nghia Viet Nam (Socialist Republic of Vietnam).
Form of government: unitary single-party socialist republic with one legislative house (National Assembly [496]).
Chief of state: Chairman of the State Council (President).
Head of government: Chairman of the Council of Ministers (Premier).
Capital: Hanoi.
Official language: Vietnamese.
Official religion: none.
Monetary unit: 1 dong (D) = 10 hao = 100 xu; valuation (Oct. 2, 1989) 1 U.S.$ = D 4,500; 1 £ = D 7,281.

Area and population

Provinces	Capitals	area sq mi	area sq km	population 1984 estimate
An Giang	Long Xuyen	1,349	3,493	1,764,500
Bac Thai	Thai Nguyen	2,507	6,494	903,000
Ben Tre	Ben Tre	859	2,225	1,163,600
Binh Tri Thien	Hue	7,081	18,340	2,020,500
Cao Bang	Cao Bang	3,261	8,445	540,400
Cuu Long	Vinh Long	1,488	3,854	1,685,600
Dac Lac	Buon Me Thuot	7,645	19,800	611,100
Dong Nai	Bien Hoa	2,926	7,578	1,314,400
Dong Thap	Cao Lamh	1,309	3,391	1,501,700
Gia Lai-Kon Tum	Kon Tum	9,860	25,536	692,400
Ha Bac	Bac Giang	1,780	4,609	1,891,700
Ha Nam Ninh	Nam Dinh	1,453	3,763	3,060,900
Ha Son Binh	Hanoi	2,308	5,978	1,704,800
Ha Tuyen	Ha Giang	5,263	13,631	880,800
Hai Hung	Hai Duong	986	2,555	2,396,300
Hau Giang	Can Tho	2,365	6,126	2,495,200
Hoang Lien Son	Lao Cai	5,734	14,852	865,600
Kien Giang	Rach Gia	2,455	6,358	1,122,900
Lai Chau	Lai Chau	6,586	17,068	378,200
Lam Dong	Da Lat	3,835	9,933	487,300
Lang Son	Lang Son	3,161	8,187	534,000
Long An	Tan An	1,681	4,355	1,081,200
Minh Hai	Bac Lieu	2,972	7,697	1,549,500
Nghe Tinh	Vinh	8,688	22,502	3,397,700
Nghia Binh	Qui Nhon	4,595	11,900	2,355,000
Phu Khanh	Nha Trang	3,785	9,804	1,332,300
Quang Nam-Da Nang	Da Nang	4,629	11,989	1,678,300
Quang Ninh	Hai Duong	2,293	5,938	811,500
Son La	Son La	5,586	14,468	562,100
Song Be	Thu Dau Mot	3,807	9,859	734,200
Tay Ninh	Ho Chi Minh City	1,556	4,030	758,100
Thai Binh	Thai Binh	577	1,495	1,652,900
Thanh Hoa	Thanh Hoa	4,300	11,138	2,779,500
Thuan Hai	Phan Thiet	4,392	11,374	1,084,600
Tien Giang	My Tho	918	2,377	1,388,300
Vinh Phu	Viet Tri	1,786	4,626	1,656,300
Municipalities				
Haiphong	—	580	1,503	1,397,400
Hanoi	—	826	2,139	2,878,300
Ho Chi Minh City	—	787	2,029	3,563,900
Special zone				
Vung Tau-Con Dao	—	96	249	94,300
TOTAL		128,065	331,688	58,770,300

Demography

Population (1989): 64,747,000.
Density (1989): persons per sq mi 505.5; persons per sq km 195.2.
Urban–rural (1988): urban 19.8%; rural 80.2%.
Sex distribution (1989): male 48.62%; female 51.38%.
Age breakdown (1985): under 15, 39.3%; 15–29, 31.3%; 30–44, 13.7%; 45–59, 9.4%; 60–74, 5.1%; 75 and over, 1.2%.
Population projection: (2000) 81,542,000; (2010) 96,183,000.
Doubling time: 33 years.
Ethnic composition (1979): Vietnamese 87.3%; Chinese (Hoa) 1.8%; Tai 1.7%; Thai 1.5%; Khmer 1.4%; Muong 1.3%; Nung 1.1%; other 4.0%.
Religious affiliation (1980): Buddhist 55.3%; Roman Catholic 7.0%; Muslim 1.0%; other 36.7%.
Major cities (1989): Ho Chi Minh City 3,900,000; Hanoi 3,100,000; Haiphong 330,755[1]; Da Nang 318,655[1]; Bien Hoa 190,086[1].

Vital statistics

Birth rate per 1,000 population (1988): 31.7 (world avg. 27.1).
Death rate per 1,000 population (1988): 9.4 (world avg. 9.9).
Natural increase rate per 1,000 population (1988): 22.3 (world avg. 17.2).
Total fertility rate (avg. births per childbearing woman; 1988): 4.1.
Life expectancy at birth (1988): male 59.4 years; female 63.8 years.
Major causes of death per 100,000 population (1979): diseases of the circulatory system 123.8; malignant neoplasms (cancers) 54.0; infectious and parasitic diseases 48.0.

National economy

Budget (1987). Revenue: U.S.$3,200,000,000 (transfers from state enterprises 72.0%, tax revenue 20.0%, other 8.0%). Expenditures: U.S.$4,300,000,000 (current expenditures 87.7%, capital expenditures 12.3%).
Gross national product (1987): U.S.$12,600,000,000 (U.S.$198 per capita).

Structure of net material product and labour force

	1987 by value	% of total value	labour force	% of labour force
Agriculture	...	41.6	19,015,000	62.6
Mining and manufacturing	...	33.1[2]	964,000	3.2
Construction	...	2.6	545,000	1.8
Public utilities	...	2	33,000	0.1
Transp. and commun.	...	0.7	188,000	0.7
Trade	...	18.5	483,000	1.6
Services	...		950,000	3.1
Other	...	3.5[3]	8,174,000[4]	26.9[4]
TOTAL		100.0	30,352,000	100.0

Public debt (external, outstanding; 1987): U.S.$10,700,000,000.
Tourism: receipts from visitors (1987 est.) U.S.$15,000,000; expenditures by nationals abroad, n.a.
Production (metric tons except as noted). Agriculture, forestry, fishing (1988): rice 15,300,000, sugarcane 6,600,000, fruits 3,828,000, vegetables 3,096,000, cassava 2,950,000, sweet potatoes 2,150,000, coconuts 605,000, corn (maize) 550,000, peanuts (groundnuts) 278,000, potatoes 255,000; livestock (number of live animals) 12,051,000 pigs, 5,732,000 cattle, 414,000 sheep and goats, 95,900,000 poultry; roundwood 25,844,000 cu m; fish catch 871,404. Mining and quarrying (1986): phosphate rock 530,000; salt 450,000; chromite 15,000; bauxite 6,000; zinc ore 5,000. Manufacturing (1987): cement 1,635,000; fertilizers 484,000; sugar 340,000; paper and paperboard 87,600; crude steel 69,100; soap 51,300; natural rubber 26,000; textiles 357,000,000 sq m; beer 872,000 hectolitres; leather footwear 3,200,000 pairs. Construction: n.a. Energy production (consumption): electricity (kW-hr; 1987) 6,194,000,000 (6,194,000,000); coal (metric tons; 1987) 6,777,000 (6,277,000); crude petroleum, none (n.a.); petroleum products (metric tons; 1987) none (1,406,000); natural gas, none (n.a.).
Population economically active (1987): total 30,352,000; activity rate of total population 48.6% (participation rates [1985]: ages 15–64, 80.1%; female 47.2%; unemployed [1987] 30%).
Land use (1987): forested 40.4%; meadows and pastures 0.8%; agricultural and under permanent cultivation 23.3%; other 35.5%.

Foreign trade

Balance of trade (current prices)

	1982	1983	1984	1985	1986	1987
U.S.$'000,000	−1,199	−1,112	−1,345	−1,498	−2,115	−2,467
% of total	51.5%	48.9%	50.5%	50.5%	44.7%	46.5%

Imports (1987): U.S.$3,884,900,000 ([1985] fuel and raw materials 44.7%, machinery 23.2%, wheat flour and food products 17.2%). *Major import sources* (1985): U.S.S.R. 69.2%; Japan 8.2%; Singapore 7.0%; Hong Kong 3.0%; EEC countries 3.0%; Czechoslovakia 3.0%; Hungary 1.0%.
Exports (1987): U.S.$1,418,400,000 ([1985] raw materials 46.0%, handicrafts 24.1%, agricultural products 9.5%). *Major export destinations* (1985): U.S.S.R. 51.1%; Hong Kong 13.8%; Japan 9.1%; Singapore 8.6%; Czechoslovakia 4.6%; EEC countries 3.1%; Poland 2.3%; Hungary 1.5%.

Transport and communications

Transport. Railroads (1987): length 2,000 mi, 3,218 km; passenger-mi 3,016,000,000, passenger-km 4,854,000,000; short ton-mi cargo 686,000,000, metric ton-km cargo 1,001,000,000. Roads (1988): total length 53,250 mi, 85,700 km (paved 11%). Vehicles (1976): passenger cars 100,000; trucks and buses 200,000. Merchant marine (1988): vessels (100 gross tons and over) 164; total deadweight tonnage 501,493. Air transport (1987): passenger-mi 6,454,000,000, passenger-km 10,387,000,000; short ton-mi cargo 4,100,000[5], metric ton-km cargo 6,000,000[5]; airports (1989) with scheduled flights 3.
Communications. Daily newspapers (1987): 4; total circulation 2,250,000; circulation per 1,000 population 38.3. Radio (1988): 6,600,000 receivers (1 per 10 persons). Television (1988): 2,200,000 receivers (1 per 30.0 persons). Telephones (1988): 116,000 (1 per 544 persons).

Education and health

Education (1986–87)

	schools	teachers	students	student/teacher ratio
Primary and secondary (age 7–18)	13,731	426,000	12,483,000	29.3
Vocational	292	11,300	156,000	13.8
Higher	96	19,200	127,000	6.6

Educational attainment (1979). Percent of population age 25 and over having: no formal education (illiterate) 22.5%, some primary 5.9%, complete primary 42.8%, secondary 20.0%, post-secondary and higher 7.7%. *Literacy* (1979): total population age 15 and over literate 28,903,500 (94.0%).
Health (1988): physicians 20,100[6] (1 per 3,140 persons); hospital beds 216,000 (1 per 292 persons); infant mortality rate per 1,000 live births (1988) 63.
Food (1984–86): daily per capita caloric intake 2,290 (vegetable products 94%, animal products 6%); (1984) 104% of FAO recommended minimum.

Military

Total active duty personnel (1989): 1,249,000 (army 96.1%, navy 3.0%, air force 0.9%). *Military expenditure as percent of GNP* (1986): 19.4% (world 5.5%); per capita expenditure U.S.$39.

[1]1979. [2]Mining and manufacturing includes public utilities. [3]Other material activities. [4]Includes finance and public administration and defense. [5]1985. [6]Includes dentists.

Virgin Islands (U.S.)

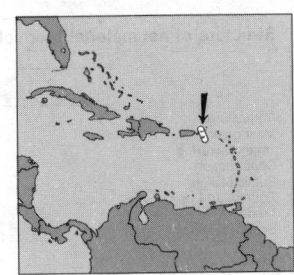

Official name: Virgin Islands of the United States.
Political status: organized unincorporated territory of the United States with one legislative house (Senate [15]).
Chief of state: President of the United States.
Head of government: Governor.
Capital: Charlotte Amalie.
Official language: English.
Official religion: none.
Monetary unit: 1 U.S. dollar (U.S.$) = 100 cents; valuation (Oct. 2, 1989) 1 U.S.$ = £0.62.

Area and population

Municipal Councils	Capitals	area sq mi	area sq km	population 1986 estimate
St. Croix	Christiansted	84	217	54,300
St. Thomas/St. John[1]	Charlotte Amalie	52	135	55,200
TOTAL		136	352	109,500

Demography

Population (1989): 107,000.
Density (1989): persons per sq mi 786.8, persons per sq km 304.0.
Urban–rural (1985): urban 45.2%; rural 54.8%.
Sex distribution (1980): male 47.85%; female 52.15%.
Age breakdown (1980): under 15, 36.0%; 15–29, 24.2%; 30–44, 21.5%; 45–59, 11.1%; 60–74, 5.8%; 75 and over, 1.4%.
Population projection: (2000) 114,000; (2010) 121,000.
Doubling time: 42 years.
Ethnic composition (1980)[2]: black 79.7%, of which Spanish or Hispanic origin 10.3%; white 14.8%, of which Spanish or Hispanic origin 2.3%; other 5.5%, of which Spanish or Hispanic origin 3.7%.
Religious affiliation (1980): Christian 98.0%, of which Protestant 63.2% (Anglican 17.4%, Pentecostal *c.* 12.0%, Moravian *c.* 9.0%, Methodist *c.* 8.0%, Lutheran *c.* 3.0%), Roman Catholic 33.6%; Baha'i 0.5%; Jewish 0.3%; nonreligious 1.2%.
Major cities (1980): Charlotte Amalie 11,842; Christiansted 2,914; Cruz Bay 1,928; Frederiksted 1,046.

Vital statistics

Birth rate per 1,000 population (1987): 22.4 (world avg. 27.1); (1981) legitimate 48.7%; illegitimate 51.3%.
Death rate per 1,000 population (1987): 5.3 (world avg. 9.9).
Natural increase rate per 1,000 population (1987): 17.1 (world avg. 17.2).
Total fertility rate (avg. births per childbearing woman; 1987): 2.6.
Marriage rate per 1,000 population (1987): 18.0.
Divorce rate per 1,000 population (1987): 3.4.
Life expectancy at birth (1980–85): male 66.7 years; female 70.7 years.
Major causes of death per 100,000 population (1987): diseases of the circulatory system 177.4, of which cerebrovascular diseases 37.7, hypertensive heart disease 24.5; malignant neoplasms (cancers) 91.5, of which lung cancer 14.2, prostate cancer 13.2; accidents, homicides, and suicides 64.2.

National economy

Budget. Revenue (1985): U.S.$263,347,000 (1983; personal income tax 38.6%, gross receipts tax 13.8%, corporate income tax 11.1%, property tax 9.3%, excise tax 3.5%). Expenditures (1983): U.S.$231,000,000 (education 25.4%, health 15.7%, executive branch 12.5%, public works 7.7%, public safety 5.7%, College of the Virgin Islands 3.8%, Territorial Court 2.7%).
Public debt (1985): U.S.$172,000,000.
Production (value of sales in U.S.$ except as noted). Agriculture, forestry, fishing (1987): milk 1,042,698, livestock and livestock products 838,554 (of which cattle and calves 613,392, hogs and pigs 125,226), ornamental plants and other nursery products 241,230, tomatoes 113,664, lettuce 49,513, mangoes 44,007, bananas 38,891, cucumbers 29,771, spinach 25,026; livestock (number of live animals) 4,035 goats; 3,762 cattle; 2,889 sheep, 18,345 chickens; roundwood, n.a.; fish catch 549 metric tons. Mining and quarrying (1985): sand and crushed stone for local use. Manufacturing (1986): food and related products 28,771,000[3]; watches, clocks, and watchcases 13,845,000[3]; printing, publishing, and allied industries 5,206,000[3]; heavy oils 9,900,000 metric tons; gasoline 1,425,000 metric tons; jet fuel 730,000 metric tons; kerosene 550,000 metric tons; liquefied petroleum gas 40,000 metric tons; rum 88,100 hectolitres[4]. Construction (1982): general building 64,775,000; heavy construction 52,414,000; special trade construction 24,776,000. Energy production (consumption): electricity (kW-hr; 1987) 963,000,000 (963,000,000); coal, none (none); crude petroleum (barrels; 1987) none (71,028,000); petroleum products (metric tons; 1987) 9,146,000 (620,000); natural gas, none (none).
Household income and expenditure: average household size (1980) 3.4; average annual income per household (1979) U.S.$14,453; sources of income (1984): wages and salaries 65.7%, transfer payments 13.0%, interest, dividends, and rent 12.7%, self-employment 2.6%; expenditure (1976)[5]: food and beverages 25.3%, housing 24.9%, transportation and communications 11.7%, energy 6.5%, clothing and footwear 5.4%, household furnishings 4.3%, other 21.9%.

Gross domestic product (at current market prices; 1986): U.S.$1,070,000,000 (U.S.$10,050 per capita).

Structure of gross domestic product and labour force

	1986 in value U.S.$'000,000	1986 % of total value	1987 labour force	1987 % of labour force
Agriculture	...	...	150	0.4
Manufacturing	...	...	2,350	5.4
Construction and mining	...	...	2,330	5.4
Transportation and public utilities	...	...	2,570	5.9
Trade, hotels, restaurants	...	...	13,950	32.2
Finance, insurance, real estate	...	...	1,940	4.5
Pub. admin., defense	...	...	13,200	30.4
Services	...	...	2,300	5.3
Other	...	...	4,550[6]	10.5[6]
TOTAL	1,070[7]	100.0[7]	43,340	100.0

Population economically active (1987): total 43,340; activity rate of total population 40.8% (participation rates [1980]: ages 15–64, 65.1%; female 45.5%; unemployed [1987] 2.8%).

Price and earnings indexes (1985 = 100)

	1983	1984	1985	1986	1987	1988	1989
Consumer price index[8]	92.6	96.6	100.0	101.9	105.7	109.9	116.2[9]
Annual earnings index[10]	89.4	95.2	100.0	...	...	...	...

Tourism (1987): receipts from visitors U.S.$623,000,000; expenditures by nationals abroad, n.a.
Land use (1985): forested 6.0%; meadows and pastures 26.0%; agricultural and under permanent cultivation 21.0%; other 47.0%.

Foreign trade

Balance of trade (current prices)

	1981	1982	1983	1984	1985	1986	1987
U.S.$'000,000	+54.6	−300.2	−1,019.5	−786.4	−383.5	−523.8	−1,312
% of total	0.5%	2.9%	12.2%	9.0%	5.4%	11.0%	24.2%

Imports (1986): U.S.$2,642,800,000 (of which U.S.$1,444,600,000 [crude petroleum 66.8%, food 8.2%, xylenes 4.1%, passenger cars 3.3%]). *Major import sources:* United States 54.7%; other countries 45.3%.
Exports (1986): U.S.$2,119,000,000 (of which U.S.$2,051,800,000 [petroleum products 88.2%, chemical products 8.8%, watches 0.6%, watch movements 0.2%, rum 0.2%]). *Major export destinations:* United States 96.8%; other countries 3.2%.

Transport and communications

Transport. Railroads: none. Roads (1987): total length 531.6 mi, 855.5 km. Registered motor vehicles (1987): 52,922. Shipping (1987): cruise ship arrivals 1,064, passenger arrivals 955,918. Air transport (1986)[11]: passenger arrivals 761,672, passenger departures 770,696; cargo unloaded 4,165 metric tons, cargo loaded 703 metric tons; airports (1989) with scheduled flights 6[12].
Communications. Daily newspapers (1987): total number 2; total circulation 19,200; circulation per 1,000 population 181. Radio (1988): total number of receivers 103,500 (1 per 1.0 persons). Television (1988): total number of receivers 64,400 (1 per 1.7 persons). Telephones (1987): 55,400 (1 per 1.9 persons).

Education and health

Education (1986–87)[13]

	schools	teachers	students	student/teacher ratio
Primary (age 4.5–12)	41	781[14]	14,723	17.2[14]
Secondary (age 12–18)	10	506[14]	10,903	21.0[14]
Voc., teacher tr.[15]	3	27	775	28.7
Higher	1	97	757	8.3

Educational attainment (1980): Percent of population age 25 and over having: no formal schooling 1.5%; primary education 34.1%; secondary 40.0%; higher 24.4%. *Literacy* (1982): total population age 15 and over literate 90%.
Health (1985): physicians 167 (1 per 622 persons); hospital beds 507 (1 per 205 persons); infant mortality rate per 1,000 live births (1984–86) 17.8.
Food: daily per capita caloric intake, n.a.

Military

Total active duty personnel: No domestic military force is maintained; the United States is responsible for defense and external security.

---

[1]Comprises St. Thomas 32 sq mi (83 sq km), pop. 52,260, and St. John 20 sq mi (52 sq km), pop. 2,940. [2]*Place of birth:* U.S. Virgin Islands 44.8%; United States 12.4%; Puerto Rico 5.2%; other West Indies 29.2%, of which St. Kitts and Nevis 6.8%, Antigua and Barbuda 5.1%, British Virgin Islands 3.4%; not reported 5.6%. [3]1982. [4]1984. [5]St. Thomas only. [6]Includes 3,550 self-employed and unpaid family workers. [7]Tourism accounts for about 70% of GDP. [8]U.S. mainland. [9]September. [10]Annual average gross pay. [11]St. Croix and St. Thomas airports. [12]Scheduled services at 2 airports, 3 seaplane bases, and 1 heliport. [13]Excludes 19 combined primary–secondary schools. [14]Private school teachers not included in total. [15]1983–84.

Western Samoa

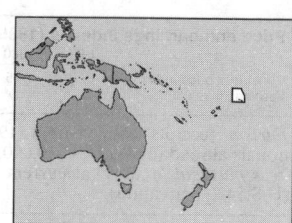

Official name: Malo Sa'oloto Tuto'atasi o Samoa i Sisifo (Samoan); Independent State of Western Samoa (English).
Form of government: constitutional monarchy[1] with one legislative house (Legislative Assembly [48][2]).
Chief of state: Head of State.
Head of government: Prime Minister.
Capital: Apia.
Official languages: Samoan; English.
Official religion: none.
Monetary unit: 1 tala (WS$, plural tala) = 100 sene; valuation (Oct. 2, 1989) 1 U.S.$ = WS$2.23; 1 £ = WS$3.61.

Area and population

Islands	area		population
Political Districts	sq mi	sq km	1981 census
Savaii	659	1,707	45,900
Fa'aseleleaga			11,876
Gaga'emauga			6,643
Gaga'ifomauga			5,304
Palauli			9,234
Satupa'itea			5,391
Vaisigano			7,452
Upolu	432	1,119	110,449
A'ana			20,288
Aiga-i-le-Tai			3,960
Atua			19,837
Tuamasaga			64,845
Vaa-o-Fonoti			1,519
TOTAL	1,093[3]	2,831[3]	156,349[4]

Demography

Population (1989): 163,000.
Density (1989): persons per sq mi 149.1, persons per sq km 57.6.
Urban-rural (1981): urban 21.2%; rural 78.8%.
Sex distribution (1986): male 52.00%; female 48.00%.
Age breakdown (1981): under 15, 44.3%; 15–29, 29.1%; 30–44, 12.2%; 45–59, 9.0%; 60–74, 3.8%; 75 and over, 1.6%.
Population projection: (2000) 173,000; (2010) 183,000.
Doubling time: 27 years.
Ethnic composition (1982): Samoan (Polynesian) *c.* 88%; Euronesian *c.* 10%; European *c.* 2%.
Religious affiliation (1981): Congregational 47.3%; Roman Catholic 21.7%; Methodist 16.2%; Mormon 8.3%; other 6.5%.
Major city (1981): Apia 33,170.

Vital statistics

Birth rate per 1,000 population (1988): 33.1 (world avg. 27.1); (1978) legitimate 43.5%; illegitimate 56.5%.
Death rate per 1,000 population (1985): 7.1 (world avg. 9.9).
Natural increase rate per 1,000 population (1985): 26.0 (world avg. 17.2).
Total fertility rate (avg. births per childbearing woman; 1988): 4.8.
Marriage rate per 1,000 population (1985): 5.7[5].
Divorce rate per 1,000 population (1985): 0.3[5].
Life expectancy at birth (1986): male 62.6 years; female 65.6 years.
Major causes of death per 100,000 population[5] (1985): diseases of the circulatory system 42.0; malignant neoplasms (cancers) 18.2; diseases of the respiratory system 13.2; infectious and parasitic diseases 8.8; diabetes mellitus 5.6.

National economy

Budget (1987). Revenue: WS$145,100,000 (current revenue 58.1%, of which taxes 47.4%, nontax revenue 10.7%; foreign aid grants 28.5%; domestic borrowing 13.4%). Expenditures: WS$100,300,000 (capital expenditure 53.3%; current expenditure 46.7%, of which education 9.7%, economic services 9.1%; health 7.1%).
Public debt (external, outstanding; 1987): U.S.$71,800,000.
Tourism (1987): receipts from visitors U.S.$9,000,000; expenditures by nationals abroad U.S.$2,000,000.
Land use (1987): forested 47.3%; meadows and pastures 0.4%; agricultural and under permanent cultivation 43.1%; other 9.2%.
Production (metric tons except as noted). Agriculture, forestry, fishing (1988): coconuts 200,000, taro 40,000, bananas 23,000, copra 14,000, papayas 12,000, mangoes 6,000, pineapples 6,000, avocados 2,000, cacao 1,000, milk 1,000; livestock (number of live animals) 65,000 pigs, 27,000 cattle, 1,000,000 chickens; roundwood (1987) 131,000 cu m; fish catch (1987) 3,400. Mining and quarrying: n.a. Manufacturing (1985): coconut oil 11,766, copra meal 6,098, copra 2,731, sawn wood 21,000 cu m[6], veneer sheets 1,061 cu m[7]; other products include coconut cream, beverages, tobacco products, aluminum products, concrete blocks, handicrafts, and kava. Construction (permits issued in WS$; 1985): residential 2,114,400; commercial, industrial, and other 5,430,500. Energy production (consumption): electricity (kW-hr; 1987) 46,000,000 (46,000,000.); coal, none (n.a.); crude petroleum, none (n.a.); petroleum products (metric tons; 1987) none (37,000).
Gross national product (at current market prices; 1987): U.S.$93,000,000 (U.S.$560 per capita).

Structure of gross domestic product and labour force

	1986[8]		1981	
	in value WS$'000	% of total value	labour force	% of labour force
Agriculture	66,200	31.2	25,050	60.4
Mining	9,400[9]	4.4[9]	9	—
Manufacturing	31,400	14.8	757	1.8
Construction	4,000	1.9	2,279	5.5
Public utilities	3,000	1.4	447	1.1
Transp. and commun.	11,800	5.6	1,353	3.3
Trade	39,000	18.4	1,821	4.4
Finance	20,600	9.7	1,305	3.1
Pub. admin., defense, government services	18,900	8.9	1,842	4.4
Other services	7,900	3.7	6,374	15.4
Other			269	0.6
TOTAL	212,200	100.0	41,506	100.0

Population economically active (1981): total 41,506; activity rate of total population 26.5% (participation rates: ages 15–64, 48.6%; female 15.0%).

Price and earnings indexes (1985 = 100)

	1982	1983	1984	1985	1986	1987	1988
Consumer price index	70.4	81.9	91.7	100.0	107.2	110.6	120.0
Monthly earnings index[10, 11]	130.0	146.6	163.0	...	...	...	...

Household income and expenditure. Average household size (1981) 5.1; income per household (1972) WS$1,518 (U.S.$2,200); sources of income (1972): wages 49.4%, self-employment 22.8%, remittances, gifts, and other assistance 18.0%, land rent 8.7%, other 1.1%; expenditure (1987)[12]: food 58.8%, transportation 9.0%, housing and furnishings 5.1%, fuel and light 5.0%, clothing 4.2%, other goods and services 1.9%, other 16.0%.

Foreign trade[13]

Balance of trade (current prices)

	1983	1984	1985	1986	1987	1988
WS$'000	−45,719	−48,024	−66,772	−72,388	−94,240	−111,729
% of total	45.5%	39.5%	46.9%	60.6%	65.4%	64.0%

Imports (1987): WS$131,010,000 (1983; food 21.3%, machinery 21.0%, petroleum products 18.4%, miscellaneous manufactured articles 7.4%, chemicals 5.9%, animal oils and fats 0.5%). *Major import sources:* New Zealand 33.8%; Australia 16.2%; Japan 10.5%; U.K. 4.9%; U.S. 4.7%; Singapore 2.9%.
Exports (1987): WS$24,968,000 (1986; coconut oil 29.3%, taro 19.4%, cocoa 14.3%, coconut cream 12.6%, copra and copra meal 7.6%, cigarettes 3.1%, timber 2.7%). *Major export destinations:* New Zealand 54.2%; U.S. 15.3%; Australia 13.6%; West Germany 9.3%; Japan 5.1%.

Transport and communications

Transport. Railroads: none. Roads (1987): total length[14] 1,296 mi, 2,085 km (paved 19%). Vehicles (1985): passenger cars 1,757; trucks and buses 2,593. Merchant marine (1988): vessels (100 gross tons and over) 6; total deadweight tonnage 34,751. Air transport: passengers, n.a.; cargo, n.a.; airports (1989) with scheduled flights 3.
Communications. Daily newspapers: none. Radio (1988): 71,854 receivers (1 per 2.3 persons). Television (1985): 5,000 receivers (1 per 32 persons). Telephones (1987): 7,000 (1 per 23 persons).

Education and health

Education (1986)

	schools	teachers	students	student/teacher ratio
Primary (age 5–11)	164[15]	1,511[16]	31,412	20.8
Secondary (age 12–18)	38[7]	513	20,168	39.3
Voc., teacher tr.	4[15]	53	436	8.2
Higher[15]	6	37	562	15.2

Educational attainment (1981). Percent of population age 25 and over having: some primary education 16.5%; complete primary 24.5%; some secondary 52.1%; complete secondary 3.1%; higher 2.0%; unknown 1.8%.
Literacy (1981): virtually 100%.
Health (1988): physicians 44 (1 per 3,685 persons); hospital beds (1987) 682 (1 per 236 persons); infant mortality rate per 1,000 live births 50.
Food (1984–86): daily per capita caloric intake 2,463 (vegetable products 81%, animal products 19%); 108% of FAO recommended minimum requirement.

Military

No military forces are maintained; New Zealand is responsible for defense.

---

[1]According to the constitution, the current Head of State, paramount chief HH Malietoa Tanumafili II, will hold office for life. Upon his death, the monarchy will functionally cease, and future Heads of State will be elected by the Legislative Assembly. [2]Includes the Head of State as an ex officio member. [3]Total includes 2 sq mi (5 sq km) of uninhabited islands. [4]The provisional total for the 1986 census is 158,940. [5]Registered only. [6]1984. [7]1982. [8]At prices of 1984. [9]Includes forestry and fishing. [10]Government employees only. [11]1980 = 100. [12]Consumer price index components. [13]Import figures are f.o.b. in balance of trade and c.i.f. in commodities and trading partners. [14]Total length includes 733 mi (1,180 km) of plantation roads. [15]1983. [16]Includes some secondary teachers.

Yemen (Aden)

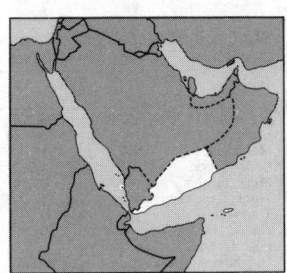

Official name: Jumhūrīyat al-Yaman ad-Dimuqrātīyah ash-Sha'bīyah (People's Democratic Republic of Yemen).
Form of government: single-party socialist republic with one legislative house (Supreme People's Council [111]).
Head of state: Chairman of the Presidium of the Supreme People's Council.
Head of government: Prime Minister.
Capital: Aden.
Official language: Arabic.
Official religion: Islam.
Monetary unit: 1 Yemeni dinar (YD) = 1,000 fils; valuation (Oct. 2, 1989) 1 YD = U.S.$2.86 = £1.79.

Area and population

Governorates	Capitals	area		population 1986 estimate
		sq mi	sq km	
Abyān	Zinjibār	8,297	21,489	434,000
'Adan	Aden	2,695	6,980	407,000
Hadramawt	al-Mukallā	59,991	155,376	686,000
Lahij	Lahij	4,928	12,766	382,000
al-Mahrah	al-Ghaydah	25,618	66,350	85,000
Shabwah	'Atāq	28,536	73,908	226,000
TOTAL		130,066[1]	336,869	2,220,000[2]

Demography

Population (1989): 2,406,000[2].
Density (1989): persons per sq mi 18.5, persons per sq km 7.1.
Urban–rural (1986): urban 40.6%; rural 59.4%.
Sex distribution (1987): male 49.47%; female 50.53%.
Age breakdown (1986): under 15, 47.8%; 15–29, 21.0%; 30–44, 15.9%; 45–59, 8.8%; 60–74, 5.5%; 75 and over, 1.0%.
Population projection: (2000) 3,191,000; (2010) 4,124,000.
Doubling time: 21 years.
Ethnic composition (1983): Arab 95.7%; Indo-Pakistani 1.8%; Somali 1.4%; Amhara and Swahili 0.7%; Jews 0.1%; Persian 0.1%; other 0.2%.
Religious affiliation (1980): predominantly Sunnī Muslim 99.5%; Hindu 0.2%; Christian 0.1%; nonreligious 0.1%; other 0.1%.
Major cities (1984): Aden 318,000; al-Mukalla 59,100; Saywūn 25,400; ash-Shiḥr 23,000; Tarīm 22,500.

Vital statistics

Birth rate per 1,000 population (1989): 48.0 (world avg. 27.1); legitimate, n.a.; illegitimate, n.a.
Death rate per 1,000 population (1989): 15.0 (world avg. 9.9).
Natural increase rate per 1,000 population (1989): 33.0 (world avg. 17.2).
Total fertility rate (avg. births per childbearing woman; 1989): 7.1.
Marriage rate per 1,000 population: n.a.
Divorce rate per 1,000 population: n.a.
Life expectancy at birth (1989): male 50.0 years; female 53.0 years.
Major causes of death per 100,000 population: n.a.; however, major diseases include poliomyelitis, diphtheria, schistosomiasis, typhoid and paratyphoid fevers, yellow fever, hepatitis, asphyxia, trachoma, heart ailments, gastrointestinal diseases, respiratory diseases, salmonella, leprosy, measles, whooping cough, cholera, pulmonary tuberculosis, intestinal bilharzia, influenza, anemia and malnutrition, shigellosis, and malaria.

National economy

Budget (1986). Revenue: YD 7,200,000,000 (custom duties and indirect taxes 83.3%). Expenditures: YD 9,900,000,000 (ordinary expenditures 60.6%, development 39.4%).
Production (metric tons except as noted). Agriculture, forestry, fishing (1988): millet 85,000, watermelons 56,000, bananas 24,000, corn (maize) 16,000, wheat 15,000, seed cotton 15,000, tomatoes 13,000, dates 12,000, onions 10,000, potatoes 8,000, lint cotton 5,000, sesame seed 3,000; livestock (number of live animals) 1,427,000 goats, 938,000 sheep, 171,000 asses, 97,000 cattle, 81,000 camels, 2,000,000 chickens; roundwood (1987) 306,000 cu m; fish catch (1987) 48,492. Mining and quarrying (1987): salt 80,000. Manufacturing (value added in YD '000; 1984): food, beverages, and tobacco 61,586; electricity 14,100; chemicals, petroleum, coal, rubber, and plastic products 9,469; clothing and apparel industries 5,164; fabricated metal products, machinery, and equipment 5,097; nonmetallic mineral products except petroleum and coal 2,918; paper and paper products, printing, and publishing 2,022; wood and wood products including furniture 1,950. Construction (value of total output; 1984): YD 93,400,000. Energy production (consumption): electricity (kW-hr; 1987) 465,000,000 (465,000,000); coal, none (n.a.); crude petroleum (barrels; 1987) none (24,922,000); petroleum products (metric tons; 1987) 3,101,000 (1,437,000); natural gas, none (n.a.).
Public debt (external, outstanding; 1987): U.S.$1,669,000,000.
Household income and expenditure. Average household size (1986) 5.6; income per household: n.a.; sources of income: n.a.; expenditure: n.a.
Population economically active (1986): total 550,843; activity rate of total population 24.7% (participation rates: ages 15–64, 50.8%; female 10.9%; unemployed, n.a.).

Price and earnings indexes (1985 = 100)

	1979	1980	1981	1982	1983	1984	1985
Consumer price index	67.7	74.5	77.3	84.7	94.1	95.2	100.0
Earnings index	...	...	...	...	...	...	...

Tourism: receipts from visitors (1986) U.S.$7,000,000; expenditures by nationals abroad (1981) U.S.$10,000,000.
Gross national product (at current market prices; 1987): U.S.$956,000,000[3] (U.S.$420 per capita).

Structure of gross domestic product and labour force

	1986			
	in value US$'000,000	% of total value	labour force	% of labour force
Agriculture	120.9	24.0	256,693	46.6
Mining	1.4	0.3	10,466	1.9
Manufacturing	64.6	12.8	48,474	8.8
Construction	82.3	16.4	38,614	7.0
Public utilities	12.5	2.5	10,466	1.9
Transportation and communications	79.4	15.8	31,894	5.8
Trade	102.0	20.3	47,373	8.6
Finance	11.6	2.3	551	0.1
Pub. admin., defense	28.4	5.6	106,312	19.3
Services			...	...
Other			...	...
TOTAL	503.2[1]	100.0	550,843	100.0

Land use (1987): forested 4.6%; meadows and pastures 27.2%; agricultural 0.4%; built-up, wasteland, and other 67.8%.

Foreign trade

Balance of trade (current prices)

	1982	1983	1984	1985	1986	1987
YD '000,000	−248.3	−250.4	−278.7	−106.0	−66.7	+49.5
% of total	31.1%	35.0%	38.5%	32.7%	27.5%	13.7%

Imports (1986): YD 154,357,000 (food and live animals 31.9%, machinery and transport equipment 20.5%, manufactured goods 19.5%, petroleum products 15.3%, chemicals 6.2%, animal and vegetable oils and fats 4.1%, crude minerals 1.7%, beverages and tobacco 0.8%. *Major import sources:* U.S.S.R. 16.4%; United Kingdom 7.4%; Japan 5.6%; China 5.5%; Denmark 5.5%; Singapore 4.9%; The Netherlands 4.8%; Saudi Arabia 3.7%; West Germany 3.5%; United Arab Emirates 3.3%; Iran 2.9%; France 2.8%.
Exports (1986): YD 10,021,000 (food and live animals 70.2%, petroleum products 12.1%, crude materials 8.5%, beverages and tobacco 6.2%). *Major export destinations:* Japan 27.3%; France 23.2%; Saudi Arabia 12.9%; United Arab Emirates 11.2%; Yemen Arab Republic 10.2%; Italy 4.3%; Singapore 1.6%.

Transport and communications

Transport. Railroads: none. Roads (1984): total length 6,793 mi, 10,932 km (paved 18%). Vehicles (1986): passenger cars 26,500; commercial vehicles 43,500. Merchant marine (1988): vessels (100 gross tons and over) 22; total deadweight tonnage 12,353. Air transport (1982): passenger-km 100,000,000; metric ton-km cargo 1,700,000; airports (1989) with scheduled flights 9.
Communications. Daily newspapers (1988): total number 2; total circulation 49,000; circulation per 1,000 population 21. Radio (1988): total number of receivers 171,143 (1 per 14 persons). Television (1987): total number of receivers 47,000 (1 per 49 persons). Telephones (1985): 31,000 (1 per 70 persons).

Education and health

Education (1986–87)

	schools	teachers	students	student/ teacher ratio[4]
Primary (age 7–12)	998	11,281[4]	301,669	26.1
Secondary (age 13–18)	63	1,493[4]	32,796	19.6
Voc., teacher tr.	29	453[4]	4,612	12.4
Higher	1	486[5]	4,386	...

Educational attainment, n.a. *Literacy* (1980): total population age 15 and over literate 411,900 (38.9%); males literate 354,700 (66.6%); females literate 57,200 (10.9%).
Health (1986): physicians 652 (1 per 3,416 persons); hospital beds 4,499 (1 per 495 persons); infant mortality rate per 1,000 live births (1989) 113.0.
Food (1984–86): daily per capita caloric intake 2,331 (vegetable products 88%, animal products 12%); 97% of FAO recommended minimum requirement.

Military

Total active duty personnel (1989): 27,500 (army 87.3%, navy 3.6%, air force 9.1%). *Military expenditure as percent of GNP* (1986): 22.0% (world 5.5%); per capita expenditure U.S.$88.

---

[1]Detail does not add to total given because of rounding. [2]Preliminary total of the March 1988 census of population: 2,345,266. [3]According to estimates by the Arab Labour Organization, remittances by expatriate workers constituted about 70% of Yemen's gross national product between 1975 and 1987. [4]1983–84. [5]1982–83.

Yemen (Ṣanʿāʾ)

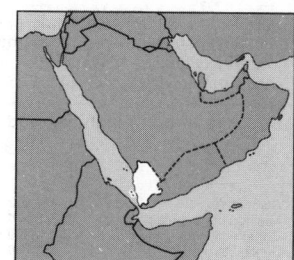

Official name: al-Jumhūrīyah al-ʿArabīyah al-Yamanīyah (Yemen Arab Republic).
Form of government: unitary single-party republic with one legislative house (Consultative Council [159¹]).
Head of state and government: President.
Capital: Ṣanʿāʾ.
Official language: Arabic.
Official religion: Islam.
Monetary unit: 1 Yemen Rial (YRl) = 100 fils; valuation (Oct. 2, 1989) 1 U.S.$ = YRls 9.76; 1 £ = YRls 15.79.

Area and population

Governorates	Capitals	area sq mi	area sq km	population 1986 census
al-Bayḍāʾ	al-Bayḍāʾ	4,310	11,170	381,249
Dhamār	Dhamār	3,430	8,870	812,981
Ḥajjah	Ḥajjah	3,700	9,590	897,814
al-Ḥudaydah	al-Ḥudaydah	5,240	13,580	1,294,359
Ibb	Ibb	2,480	6,430	1,511,879
al-Jawf	al-Jawf	...	...	87,299
al-Maḥwīt	al-Maḥwīt	830	2,160	322,226
Maʾrib	Maʾrib	15,400	39,890	121,437
Saʿdah	Saʿdah	4,950	12,810	344,152
Ṣanʿāʾ	Ṣanʿāʾ	7,840	20,310	1,856,876
Taʿizz	Taʿizz	4,020	10,420	1,643,901
TOTAL		52,210²,³	135,230³	9,274,173⁴

Demography

Population (1989)⁵: 8,834,000.
Density (1989): persons per sq mi 169.2, persons per sq km 65.3.
Urban–rural (1986): urban 21.0%; rural 79.0%.
Sex distribution (1986): male 50.11%; female 49.89%.
Age breakdown (1986): under 15, 50.4%; 15–29, 20.3%; 30–44, 14.5%; 45–59, 9.1%; 60–74, 4.3%; 75 and over, 1.4%.
*Population projection*⁵: (2000) 11,660,000; (2010) 15,006,000.
Doubling time: 25 years.
Ethnic composition (1984): predominantly Arab.
Religious affiliation (1980): Shīʿī Muslim 60%; Sunnī Muslim 40%.
Major cities (1986): Ṣanʿāʾ 427,150; Taʿizz 178,043; al-Ḥudaydah 155,110.

Vital statistics

Birth rate per 1,000 population (1986): 49.1 (world avg. 27.1); legitimate, n.a.; illegitimate, n.a.
Death rate per 1,000 population (1986): 20.8 (world avg. 9.9).
Natural increase rate per 1,000 population (1986): 28.3 (world avg. 17.2).
Total fertility rate (avg. births per childbearing woman; 1986): 7.5.
Marriage rate per 1,000 population: n.a.
Divorce rate per 1,000 population: n.a.
Life expectancy at birth (1986): male 45.6 years; female 48.9 years.
Major causes of death per 100,000 population: n.a.; however, major infectious diseases include malaria, tuberculosis, intestinal infections, leprosy, schistosomiasis, typhoid and paratyphoid fevers, viral hepatitis, and filarial infections.

National economy

Budget (1987–88). Revenue: YRls 9,069,500,000 (import duties 24.6%, nontax revenues 24.1%, foreign grants 16.1%, income taxes 11.2%, excise taxes 9.2%). Expenditures: YRls 15,052,600,000 (defense 22.2%, general public services 21.1%, education 16.5%, economic services 6.3%, transport and communications 3.9%).
Public debt (external, outstanding; 1987): U.S.$2,155,000,000.
Production (metric tons except as noted). Agriculture, forestry, fishing (1987): sorghum 477,000, vegetables and melons 455,000, grapes 129,000, potatoes 110,000, wheat 100,000, goat's milk 76,000, corn (maize) 48,000, barley 40,000, pulses 39,000, dates 15,000, hen's eggs 12,500; livestock (number of live animals) 2,604,000 sheep, 1,594,000 goats, 1,023,000 cattle, 520,000 asses, 61,000 camels; fish catch 22,254. Mining and quarrying (1987): salt 163,000; gypsum 53,000. Manufacturing (1987): flour 129,700; biscuits 56,400; soaps and detergents 20,468; canned beans 5,398; fruit syrup 72,026,000 litres; soft drinks 48,000,000 litres; cigarettes 467,500 cartons; woven textiles 9,088,000 yards. Construction (value added in '000,000 YRls; 1985): 1,550. Energy production (consumption): electricity (kW-hr; 1987) 718,000,000 (718,000,000); coal, none (n.a.); crude petroleum (barrels; 1987) 6,597,000 (2,932,000); petroleum products (metric tons; 1987) 350,000 (920,000); natural gas, none (n.a.).
Population economically active (1986): total 1,492,394; activity rate of total population 18.2% (participation rates: ages 15–64, 38.5%; female 12.5%; unemployed, n.a.).

Price and earnings indexes (1980 = 100)

	1980	1981	1982	1983	1984	1985	1986
Consumer price index	100.0	105.0	108.0	114.0	148.2	188.2	244.7
Earnings index	...	...	...	...	...	...	...

Household income and expenditure. Average household size (1986) 5.6; income per household: n.a.; sources of income: n.a.; expenditure (1972): food, beverages, and tobacco 65.0%, household durable goods 7.8%, energy 7.2%, housing 6.1%, clothing and footwear 5.8%, medical care, health, and hygiene 4.0%, transportation 3.2%, education 0.9%.
Gross national product (1987): U.S.$4,918,000,000 (U.S.$580 per capita).

Structure of gross domestic product and labour force

	1987 in value YRls '000,000	1987 % of total value	1986 labour force	1986 % of labour force
Agriculture	12,153	27.9	894,655	59.9
Mining	697	1.6	1,305	0.1
Manufacturing	4,835	11.1	46,439	3.1
Construction	1,437	3.3	122,338	8.2
Public utilities	479	1.1	22,386	1.5
Transp. and commun.	4,748	10.9	75,717	5.1
Trade	5,184	11.9	201,606	13.5
Finance	...	...	8,206	0.5
Pub. admin., defense	5,314	12.2	...	...
Services	5,271	12.1	119,742	8.0
Other	3,441⁶	7.9	...	...
TOTAL	43,559	100.0	1,492,394	100.0²

Land use (1987): forested 8.2%; meadows and pastures 35.9%; agricultural and under permanent cultivation 7.0%; other 48.9%.
Tourism (1987): receipts from visitors U.S.$48,000,000; expenditures by nationals abroad U.S.$37,000,000.

Foreign trade

Balance of trade (current prices)

	1982	1983	1984	1985	1986	1987
YRls '000,000	−8,235	−9,439	−8,449	−7,782	−8,466	−13,460
% of total	78.4%	83.1%	79.0%	77.2%	78.4%	90.4%

Imports (1987): U.S.$1,370,700,000 (food and live animals 31.6%, basic manufactured goods 28.6%, machinery and transport equipment 21.9%, chemical products 9.3%, raw materials 5.8%, beverages and tobacco 2.4%). *Major import sources:* Japan 12.0%; United States 10.8%; The Netherlands 10.0%; West Germany 7.1%; France 6.3%; Italy 5.3%; Saudi Arabia 5.3%.
Exports (1987): U.S.$69,000,000 (coffee 16.6%, cigarettes 15.6%, biscuits 13.6%, leather 12.5%, grapes 8.6%, sesame seeds 4.2%, sugar and honey 1.6%). *Major export destinations:* Saudi Arabia 53.6%; Yemen (Aden) 24.0%; Italy 8.2%; Japan 4.0%.

Transport and communications

Transport. Railroads: none. Roads (1987): total length 23,168 mi, 37,285 km (paved 6%). Vehicles (1987): passenger cars 125,464; trucks and buses 183,582. Merchant marine (1988): vessels (100 gross tons and over) 11; total deadweight tonnage 408,490. Air transport (1987)⁷: passenger-mi 363,167,000, passenger-km 584,461,000; short ton-mi cargo 41,279,000, metric ton-km cargo 60,267,000; airports (1989) with scheduled flights 5.
Communications. Daily newspapers (1986): total number 2; total circulation, n.a.; circulation per 1,000 population, n.a. Radio (1988): total number of receivers 149,886 (1 per 57 persons). Television (1987): total number of receivers 150,000 (1 per 56 persons). Telephones (1984): 63,255 (1 per 104 persons).

Education and health

Education (1985–86)

	schools	teachers	students	student/teacher ratio
Primary (age 7–12)	5,814	16,115	907,480	56.3
Secondary (age 13–18)	942	5,988	122,022	20.4
Voc., teacher tr.	73	736	12,507	17.0
Higher	1	245	9,024	36.8

Educational attainment (1975). Percent of population age 10 and over having: no formal schooling, 82.6%; reading ability only 5.3%; reading and writing ability 10.6%; primary education, 0.8%; secondary education 0.2%; higher 0.1%; not specified 0.4%. *Literacy* (1986): total population age 15 and over literate 768,200 (18.9%); males literate 698,021 (38.5%); females literate 70,179 (3.1%).
Health (1986): physicians 1,234 (1 per 6,637 persons); hospital beds 5,986 (1 per 1,367 persons); infant mortality rate per 1,000 live births 164.0.
Food (1984–86): daily per capita caloric intake 2,275 (vegetable products 90%, animal products 10%); 93% of FAO recommended minimum.

Military

Total active duty personnel (1989): 36,500 (army 95.9%, navy 1.4%, air force 2.7%). *Military expenditure as percent of GNP* (1987): 7.2% (world 5.4%); per capita expenditure U.S.$39.

---

¹Includes 31 nonelective members. ²Detail does not add to total given because of rounding. ³Area shown is according to the Swiss Technical Co-operation Service. The major part of the eastern boundary with Saudi Arabia and Yemen (Aden) is not officially delimited or demarcated; however, the government of Yemen (Ṣanʿāʾ) uses a higher estimate of 77,200 sq mi (200,000 sq km). ⁴Includes nationals abroad. ⁵Based on reported 1986 census result of 8,105,974 resident population. ⁶Includes import duties and indirect taxes. ⁷Yemen Airways only.

Yugoslavia

Official name: Socijalistička Federativna
Republika Jugoslavija (Macedonian,
Serbo-Croatian); Socijalistična
Federativna Republika Jugoslavija
(Slovene); (Socialist Federal
Republic of Yugoslavia).
Form of government: single-party
federal socialist republic with two
legislative houses (Chamber of
Republics and Provinces [88] and
Federal Chamber [220]).
Chief of state: President of Collective
Presidency.
Head of government: Prime Minister.
Capital: Belgrade.
Official languages: Macedonian;
Serbo-Croatian; Slovene.
Official religion: none.
Monetary unit: 1 Yugoslav dinar
(Din) = 100 paras; valuation
(Oct. 2, 1989) 1 U.S.$ = Din 37,050;
1 £ = Din 59,947.

Area and population		area		population
Socialist republics	Capitals	sq mi	sq km	1988 estimate
Bosnia and Hercegovina	Sarajevo	19,741	51,129	4,441,000
Croatia	Zagreb	21,829	56,538	4,679,000
Macedonia	Skopje	9,928	25,713	2,088,000
Montenegro	Titograd	5,333	13,812	632,000
Serbia	Belgrade	21,609	55,968	5,831,000
Slovenia	Ljubljana	7,819	20,251	1,943,000
Autonomous provinces[1]				
Kosovo	Priština	4,203	10,887	1,893,000
Vojvodina	Novi Sad	8,304	21,506	2,052,000
TOTAL		98,766	255,804	23,559,000

Demography

Population (1989): 23,710,000.
Density (1989): persons per sq mi 240.1, persons per sq km 92.7.
Urban–rural (1985): urban 46.5%; rural 53.5%.
Sex distribution (1985): male 49.36%; female 50.64%.
Age breakdown (1985): under 15, 23.5%; 15–29, 23.9%; 30–44, 21.0%; 45–59,
18.8%; 60–74, 9.4%; 75 and over, 3.4%.
Population projection: (2000) 25,431,000; (2010) 27,105,000.
Doubling time: 99 years.
Ethnic composition (1981): Serb 36.3%; Croat 19.7%; Bosnian Muslim 8.9%;
Slovene 7.8%; Albanian 7.7%; Macedonian 6.0%; Montenegrin 2.6%; other
11.0%.
Religious affiliation (1980): Serbian Orthodox 34.6%; Roman Catholic 26.0%;
Crypto-Christian 11.3%; Muslim 10.4%; other 17.7%.
Major cities (1981): Belgrade 1,087,915; Zagreb 649,586; Skopje 408,143;
Sarajevo 319,017; Ljubljana 224,817.

Vital statistics

Birth rate per 1,000 population (1987): 15.3 (world avg. 27.1); (1986) legiti-
mate 90.6%; illegitimate 9.4%.
Death rate per 1,000 population (1987): 9.2 (world avg. 9.9).
Natural increase rate per 1,000 population (1987): 6.1 (world avg. 17.2).
Total fertility rate (avg. births per childbearing woman; 1987): 1.9.
Marriage rate per 1,000 population (1987): 7.0.
Divorce rate per 1,000 population (1986): 1.0.
Life expectancy at birth (1982–83): male 66.0 years; female 74.0 years.
Major causes of death per 100,000 population (1985): diseases of the cir-
culatory system 463.7; neoplasms 141.6; diseases of the respiratory system
53.3; diseases of the digestive system 35.3.

National economy

Budget (1987). Revenue: Din 3,008,605,700,000 (share in profit of state
enterprises 71.8%, import duties 26.2%, other revenue 2.0%). Expenditures:
Din 3,008,605,700,000 (defense 65.5%, social welfare and health 21.8%).
Public debt (external, outstanding; 1987): U.S.$14,446,000,000.
Tourism (1986): receipts from visitors U.S.$1,337,000,000; expenditures by
nationals abroad U.S.$132,000,000.
Production (metric tons except as noted). Agriculture (1987): corn (maize)
8,863,000, sugar beets 6,238,000, wheat 5,272,000, potatoes 2,210,000,
grapes 1,255,000, plums 757,000, barley 504,000, sunflower seeds 486,000,
tomatoes 480,000, melons 436,000, apples 423,000, oats 232,000, rye 69,-
000, tobacco 61,204, rice 49,000; livestock (number of live animals; 1988)
8,323,000 pigs, 7,824,000 sheep, 4,881,000 cattle, 78,589,000 poultry; roundwood 22,263,000 cu m; fish catch 81,332. Mining and quarrying (1988):
copper ore 30,056,000; iron ore 5,545,000; lead and zinc ore 3,847,000;
bauxite 3,034,000; antimony 38,000; manganese 25,000; silver (refined)
139. Manufacturing (1988): cement 8,840,000; crude steel 4,487,000; rolled
steel 4,120,000; pulp and paper 2,860,600; pig iron 2,787,000; sulfuric acid
1,731,000; automobile tires 13,747,000 units; radio and television receivers
678,443 units; leather 23,079,000 sq m; cotton fabrics 350,964 sq m. Construction (1987): residential 13,137,000 sq m; industrial 1,694,000 sq m;
commercial 855,000 sq m. Energy production (consumption): electricity
(kW-hr; 1987) 80,792,000,000 (81,167,000,000); coal (metric tons; 1987)

71,133,000 (75,080,000); crude petroleum (barrels; 1987) 28,819,000 (107,-
835,000); petroleum products (metric tons; 1987) 12,467,000 (12,716,000);
natural gas (cu m; 1987) 2,179,905,000 (5,738,852,000).
Gross national product (1988): U.S.$153,573,000,000 (U.S.$6,540 per capita).

Structure of gross material product and labour force				
	1987		1981	
	in value Din '000,000	% of total value	labour force	% of labour force
Agriculture	5,815,962	11.8	2,682,828	28.7
Mining and manufacturing	24,272,978	49.3	2,209,693[2]	23.6[2]
Construction	3,299,509	6.7	689,291	7.4
Public utilities	538,770	1.1	[2]	[2]
Transp. and commun.	3,496,777	7.1	445,362	4.8
Trade	10,000,130	20.3	827,575	8.8
Finance	...	...	204,866	2.2
Pub. admin., defense, and services	...	...	1,585,205	16.9
Other	1,788,301[3]	3.6[3]	713,851[4]	7.6[4]
TOTAL	49,212,427	100.0[5]	9,358,671	100.0

Population economically active (1981): total 9,358,671; activity rate of total
population 43.4% (participation rates: ages 20–64, 68.7%; female 38.7%;
unemployed [1986] 10.6%).

Price and earnings indexes (1985 = 100)							
	1983	1984	1985	1986	1987	1988	1989[6]
Consumer price index	37.5	58.0	100.0	189.8	419.0	1,232.3	3,108.7
Monthly earnings index	39.0	56.0	100.0	205.0	420.0	1,139.0	...

Household income and expenditure. Average household size (1983) 3.6; income per household (1986) Din 1,621,374 (U.S.$4,300); sources of income
(1985): wages 56.9%, receipts from abroad and interest 12.9%, welfare
11.6%, other 18.6%; expenditure (1986): food 38.3%, transportation 11.8%,
beverages and tobacco 11.1%, clothing and footwear 10.2%, housing 8.5%,
household utilities 8.2%, recreation 4.0%, health 3.4%.
Land use (1987): forested 36.6%; meadows and pastures 24.9%; agricultural
and under permanent cultivation 30.5%; other 8.0%.

Foreign trade

Balance of trade (current prices)							
	1982	1983	1984	1985	1986	1987	1988
Din '000,000,000	−98.2	−119.2	−114.4	−114.8	−135.9	+127.0	+1,370.5
% of total	8.5%	5.9%	3.4%	1.9%	1.7%	0.7%	2.0%

Imports (1988): Din 34,150,200,000,000 (machinery and transport equipment
27.2%; mineral fuels 17.6%; chemicals 17.3%; manufactured goods 16.0%;
raw materials 11.0%; food and tobacco 6.4%). *Major import sources* (1987):
West Germany 18.3%; U.S.S.R. 15.3%; Italy 10.3%; United States 5.7%;
Austria 4.5%; France 4.5%; Czechoslovakia 4.3%; Iraq 3.4%.
Exports (1988): Din 32,779,700,000,000 (machinery and transport equipment
30.8%; manufactured goods 28.6%; chemicals 9.1%; food products 7.5%;
raw materials 5.5%; mineral fuels 1.6%). *Major export destinations* (1987):
U.S.S.R. 19.4%; Italy 13.0%; West Germany 11.6%; Czechoslovakia 3.7%.

Transport and communications

Transport. Railroads (1988): length 5,760 mi, 9,270 km; passenger-km
11,542,000,000; metric ton-km cargo 25,413,000,000. Roads (1988): total
length 120,747 km (paved 59%). Vehicles (1987): passenger cars 3,023,693;
trucks and buses 290,466. Merchant marine (1988): vessels (100 gross
tons and over) 499; total deadweight tonnage 5,487,671. Air transport
(1988): passenger-km 8,869,000,000; metric ton-km cargo 138,853,000; airports (1989) 17.
Communications. Daily newspapers (1987): 28; total circulation 2,585,800;
circulation per 1,000 population 110. Radio (1987): 4,772,000 receivers (1
per 4.9 persons). Television (1987): 4,089,000 receivers (1 per 5.7 persons).
Telephones (1987): 3,909,000 (1 per 6.0 persons).

Education and health

Education (1988–89)	schools	teachers	students	student/ teacher ratio
Primary (age 7–14)	12,069	138,459	2,361,532	17.1
Secondary (age 15–18)	1,248	62,534	1,422,162	22.7
Higher	91	26,238	340,844	13.0

Educational attainment (1981). Percent of population age 15 and over
having: less than full primary education 44.7%; primary 24.2%; secondary
25.5%; higher 5.6%. *Literacy* (1981): total population age 15 and over
literate 15,172,877 (89.6%); males 95.5%; females 83.9%.
Health (1986): physicians 32,691 (1 per 712 persons); hospital beds 142,597
(1 per 163 persons); infant mortality rate per 1,000 live births 26.2.
Food (1984–86): daily per capita caloric intake 3,599 (vegetable products
77%, animal products 23%); 139% of FAO minimum requirement.

Military

Total active duty personnel (1988): 188,000 (army 76.6%, navy 5.9%, air force
17.5%). *Military expenditure as percent of GNP* (1987): 2.2% (world 5.4%);
per capita expenditure U.S.$56.

[1]The autonomous provinces are administratively part of the Socialist Republic of
Serbia. [2]Public utilities included with mining and manufacturing. [3]Other material
activities. [4]Includes unemployed. [5]Detail does not add to total given because of
rounding. [6]February.

Zaïre

Official name: République du Zaïre
(Republic of Zaire).
Form of government: single party
republic with one legislative house
(Legislative Council [210]).
Head of state and government:
President.
Capital: Kinshasa.
Official language: French.
Official religion: none.
Monetary unit: 1 zaïre (Z) = 100
makuta (singular likuta) = 10,000
sengi; valuation (Oct. 2, 1989)
1 U.S.$ = Z 418.23; 1 £ = Z 676.70.

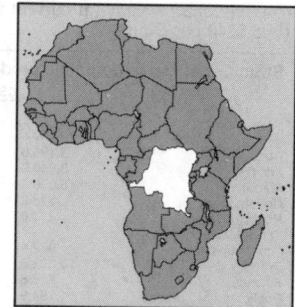

Area and population

Regions	Capitals	area sq mi	area sq km	population 1989 estimate
Bandundu	Bandundu	114,154	295,658	4,078,978
Bas-Zaire	Matadi	20,880	54,078	2,163,817
Equateur	Mbandaka	155,712	403,292	3,705,769
Haute-Zaïre	Kisangani	194,302	503,239	4,609,795
Kasai-Occidental	Kananga	60,605	156,967	2,355,696
Kasai-Oriental	Mbuji-Mayi	64,949	168,216	2,622,808
Kinshasa	—	3,848	9,965	3,391,628
Maniema	Kindu	50,916[1]	131,871[1]	860,299
Nord-Kivu	Goma	23,188[1]	60,057[1]	2,771,876
Shaba	Lubumbashi	191,845	496,877	4,342,394
Sud-Kivu	Bukavu	25,048[1]	64,875[1]	2,433,275
TOTAL		905,446[2]	2,345,095	33,336,235[2]

Demography

Population (1989): 33,336,235.
Density (1989): persons per sq mi 36.8, persons per sq km 14.2.
Urban–rural (1985): urban 44.2%; rural 55.8%.
Sex distribution (1984): male 49.18%; female 50.82%.
Age breakdown (1985): under 15, 45.2%; 15–29, 26.0%; 30–44, 15.5%; 45–59, 8.7%; 60–74, 3.9%; 75 and over, 0.7%.
Population projection: (2000) 42,980,000; (2010) 54,112,000.
Doubling time: 24 years.
Ethnic composition (1983): Luba 18.0%; Kongo 16.1%; Mongo 13.5%; Rwanda 10.3%; Azande 6.1%; Bangi and Ngale 5.8%; Rundi 3.8%; Teke 2.7%; Boa 2.3%; Chokwe 1.8%; Lugbara 1.6%; Banda 1.4%; other 16.6%.
Religious affiliation (1980): Roman Catholic 48.4%; Protestant 29.0%; indigenous Christian 17.1%; traditional beliefs 3.4%; Muslim 1.4%; other 0.7%.
Major cities (1984): Kinshasa 2,653,558; Lubumbashi 543,268; Mbuji-Mayi 423,363; Kananga 290,898; Kisangani 282,650.

Vital statistics

Birth rate per 1,000 population (1985–90): 45.6 (world avg. 27.1).
Death rate per 1,000 population (1985–90): 13.9 (world avg. 9.9).
Natural increase rate per 1,000 population (1985–90): 31.7 (world avg. 17.2).
Total fertility rate (avg. births per childbearing woman; 1985–90): 6.1.
Marriage rate per 1,000 population (1977): 0.07[3].
Divorce rate per 1,000 population (1977): 0.02.
Life expectancy at birth (1985–90): male 50.8 years; female 54.2 years.
Major causes of death per 100,000 population[4] (1977): measles 9.6; meningitis 1.1; influenza 0.4; whooping cough 0.3.

National economy

Budget (1988). Revenue: Z 147,777,000,000 (1986; direct and indirect taxes 91.4%, of which external trade taxes 33.7%, income tax 31.4%, sales tax 22.8%; other revenue 8.6%. Expenditures: Z 152,777,000,000 (service of external and internal debt 26.4%; government salaries 22.4%; capital expenditure 11.5%; defense 8.4%; education 5.2%).
Tourism (1987): receipts from visitors U.S.$14,000,000; expenditures by nationals abroad U.S.$22,000,000.
Production (metric tons except as noted). Agriculture, forestry, fishing (1988): cassava 16,254,000, plantains 1,520,000, sugarcane 1,200,000, corn (maize) 730,000, peanuts (groundnuts) 400,000, sweet potatoes 372,000, bananas 345,000, rice 300,000, yams 264,000, papayas 180,000, pineapples 180,000, mangoes 155,000, oranges 150,000, pulses 131,000, coffee 97,000, dry beans 80,000, seed cotton 77,000, palm kernels 70,000, tomatoes 38,000, natural rubber 21,000; livestock (number of live animals) 3,040,000 goats, 1,400,000 cattle, 880,000 sheep, 800,000 pigs, 18,000,000 chickens; roundwood (1987) 32,304,000 cu m; fish catch (1987) 166,000. Mining and quarrying (1988): copper 438,570; lime 102,600; zinc 61,000; cobalt 10,032; cassiterite 2,687; wolframite 20; gold 3,533 kg; diamonds 18,318,639 carats. Manufacturing (1987): cement 491,600; sulphuric acid 140,255; corn flour 89,685; sugar 69,410; soap 67,946; animal feedstuff 15,436; explosives 12,909; plastics 7,586; iron and steel products 3,694; paint 3,060; medicines 45; cotton textiles 43,732,000 sq m; cigarettes 5,141,000,000 units; tires 117,733 units; bicycles 9,997 units; trucks 85 units; beer 4,378,000 hectolitres; carbonated beverages 815,000 hectolitres; leather shoes 2,951,000 pairs. Construction (1985): residential 20,000 sq m; nonresidential 39,000 sq m. Energy production (consumption): electricity (kW-hr; 1987) 5,295,000,000 (5,188,000,000); coal (metric tons; 1987) 95,000 (136,000); crude petroleum (barrels; 1987) 9,453,000 (2,263,000); petroleum products (metric tons; 1987) 287,000 (808,-000); natural gas, none (n.a.).
Household income and expenditure. Average household size (1982) 6.0; average annual income per household Z 1,200 (U.S.$209); sources of income: wages and salaries, small-scale trading; expenditure (1985): food 61.7%, housing and energy 11.5%, clothing and footwear 9.7%, transportation 5.9%, furniture and utensils 4.9%, medical care 2.6%, recreation and education 2.0%.
Gross national product (1987): U.S.$5,287,000,000 (U.S.$160 per capita).

Structure of gross domestic product and labour force

	1987 in value Z '000,000	1987 % of total value	1985 labour force	1985 % of labour force
Agriculture	102,444.5[5]	31.3[5]	8,844,000	68.0
Mining	78,792.8	24.1		
Manufacturing	4,409.7	1.3		
Construction	18,061.5[6]	5.5[6]	1,886,000	14.5
Public utilities	179.4	[7]		
Transp. and commun.	2,528.9	0.8		
Trade	58,076.2	17.8		
Finance				
Pub. admin., defense	53,460.0	16.4	2,276,000	17.5
Services				
Other	8,993.3[8]	2.8[8]		
TOTAL	326,946.3	100.0	13,006,000	100.0

Public debt (external, outstanding; 1987): U.S.$7,334,000,000.
Population economically active (1985): total 13,006,000; activity rate of total population 40.7% (participation rates; age 15–64, 75.1%; female 33.4%; unemployed, n.a.).

Price and earnings indexes (1985 = 100)

	1982	1983	1984	1985	1986	1987	1988[9]
Consumer price index	30.0	53.1	80.8	100.0	144.4	258.0	479.1
Annual earnings index	11.6	29.5	80.0	100.0	...	...	...

Land use (1987): forested 77.3%; meadows and pastures 4.1%; agricultural and under permanent cultivation 2.9%; other 15.7%.

Foreign trade

Balance of trade (current prices)

	1983	1984	1985	1986	1987	1988
Z '000,000	+7,102.7	+11,554.3	+13,339.7	+13,228	+36,258	+86,582
% of total	34.2%	18.9%	16.4%	11.3%	19.8%	26.0%

Imports (1988): Z 123,016,000,000 (1987; machinery and transport equipment 45.5%, of which mining equipment 32.0%, transport equipment 7.8%; food, beverages, and tobacco 14.6%; energy 13.8%; consumer goods 7.4%; minerals 5.4%; chemical products 4.4%; textiles and clothing 3.7%). *Major import sources* (1987): China 37.4%; Belgium–Luxembourg 15.6%; France 7.9%; West Germany 7.2%; U.S. 5.5%; Japan 2.5%.
Exports (1988): Z 209,598,000,000 (1987; copper 51.5%; coffee 16.0%; diamonds 10.5%; crude petroleum 8.4%; cobalt 4.6%; zinc 0.8%). *Major export destinations* (1987): Belgium–Luxembourg 39.1%; U.S. 19.5%; West Germany 11.9%; Italy 11.4%; France 6.8%; Japan 3.9%.

Transport and communications

Transport. Railroads (1988)[10]: length 3,265 mi, 5,254 km; passenger 223,300,000, passenger-km 359,400,000; short ton-mi cargo 1,277,000,000, metric ton-km cargo 1,864,000,000. Roads (1988): total length 90,000 mi, 146,500 km (paved 12%). Vehicles (1985): passenger cars 24,253; trucks and buses 60,528. Merchant marine (1988): vessels (100 gross tons and over) 30; total deadweight tonnage 75,932. Air transport (1988)[11]: passenger-mi 314,546,000, passenger-km 506,214,000; short ton-mi cargo 37,885,000, metric ton-km cargo 55,315,000; airports (1989) with scheduled flights 22.
Communications. Daily newspapers (1988): total number 7; total circulation 45,000; circulation per 1,000 population 1.4. Radio (1988): 3,349,356 receivers (1 per 9.7 persons). Television (1988): 16,000 receivers (1 per 2,035 persons). Telephones (1986): 38,845 (1 per 800 persons).

Education and health

Education (1985–86)

	schools[12]	teachers	students	student/ teacher ratio
Primary (age 6–11)	149,753	161,925	4,993,523	30.8
Secondary (age 12–17)	29,213	47,952	2,334,578	48.7
Voc., teacher tr.	...	...	862,873	...
Higher	35	3,803	40,878	10.7

Educational attainment, n.a. *Literacy* (1985): total population age 15 and over literate 11,004,000 (61.2%); males literate 6,872,000 (78.6%); females literate 4,132,000 (44.7%).
Health (1985): physicians 1,318 (1 per 23,193 persons); hospital beds 64,071 (1 per 476 persons); infant mortality rate per 1,000 live births (1985–90) 98.
Food (1984–86): daily per capita caloric intake 2,160 (vegetable products 97%, animal products 3%); 97% of FAO recommended minimum.

Military

Total active duty personnel (1989): 26,000 (army 84.6%, navy 5.8%, air force 9.6%). *Military expenditure as percent of GNP* (1986): 3.0% (world 5.5%); per capita expenditure U.S.$5.

[1]Estimate. [2]Detail does not add to total given because of rounding. [3]Registered marriages only. [4]Infectious diseases only. [5]Includes Z 58,591,700,000 in the subsistence sector. [6]Includes Z 6,020,500,000 in the subsistence sector. [7]Less than 0.1%. [8]Import taxes and duties less imputed bank service charge. [9]Third quarter. [10]Traffic statistics are for 1987 and for services operated by the Zaire National Railways (SNCZ), which controls more than 90% of the country's total rail facility. [11]Air Zaire only. [12]Number of classes.

Zambia

Official name: Republic of Zambia.
Form of government: republic with
one legislative house (National
Assembly [136[1]]).
Head of state and government:
President.
Capital: Lusaka.
Official language: English.
Official religion: none.
Monetary unit: 1 Zambian kwacha
(K) = 100 ngwee; valuation (Oct.
2, 1989) 1 U.S.$ = K 16.07;
1 £ = K 26.00.

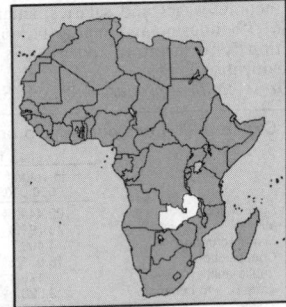

Area and population		area		population
		sq mi	sq km	1987 estimate[2]
Provinces	Capitals			
Central	Kabwe	36,446	94,395	669,432
Copperbelt	Ndola	12,096	31,328	1,707,559
Eastern	Chipata	26,682	69,106	783,398
Luapula	Mansa	19,524	50,567	500,833
Lusaka	Lusaka	8,454	21,896	1,030,615
Northern	Kasama	57,076	147,826	795,003
North-Western	Solwezi	48,582	125,827	376,480
Southern	Livingstone	32,928	85,283	849,103
Western	Mongu	48,798	126,386	555,104
TOTAL		290,586	752,614	7,267,527

Demography

Population (1989): 8,148,000[3].
Density (1989): persons per sq mi 28.0, persons per sq km 10.8.
Urban–rural (1986): urban 50.7%; rural 49.3%.
Sex distribution (1986): male 49.11%; female 50.89%.
Age breakdown (1986): under 15, 47.0%; 15–29, 25.8%; 30–44, 14.6%; 45–59,
8.3%; 60 and over, 4.3%.
Population projection: (2000) 12,197,000; (2010) 17,152,000.
Doubling time: 19 years.
Ethnolinguistic composition (1980): Bemba tribes 36.2%; Maravi (Nyanja)
tribes 17.6%; Tonga tribes 15.1%; North-Western tribes 10.1%; Barotze
tribes 8.2%; Mambwe tribes 4.6%; Tumbuka tribes 4.6%; other 3.6%.
Religious affiliation (1980): Christian 72.0%, of whom Protestant 34.2%,
Roman Catholic 26.2%, African Christian 8.3%; traditional beliefs 27.0%;
Muslim 0.3%; other 0.7%.
Major cities (1988): Lusaka 870,030; Kitwe 472,255; Ndola 442,666; Mufulira
199,368.

Vital statistics

Birth rate per 1,000 population (1985–90): 51.2 (world avg. 27.1); legitimate,
n.a.; however, marriage is both early and universal, suggesting that legiti-
mate births are a relatively high proportion of all births.
Death rate per 1,000 population (1985–90): 13.7 (world avg. 9.9).
Natural increase rate per 1,000 population (1985–90): 37.5 (world avg. 17.2).
Total fertility rate (avg. births per childbearing woman; 1985–90): 7.2.
Marriage rate per 1,000 population: n.a.
Divorce rate per 1,000 population: n.a.
Life expectancy at birth (1985–90): male 52.4 years; female 54.5 years.
Major causes of death per 100,000 population: n.a.; however, among the
nearly 7,000,000 visits to outpatient clinics in 1982, nearly two-thirds of
the reported illnesses were related to nutritional deficiencies and infectious
and parasitic diseases.

National economy

Budget (1988). Revenue: K 5,552,000,000 (customs duties and excise taxes
44.5%; income tax 33.1%; mineral revenue 0.2%). Expenditures: K 6,350,-
000,000 (constitutional and statutory expenditures 36.6%; other, including
education, health, land development, and police 63.4%).
Production (metric tons except as noted). Agriculture, forestry, fishing (1987):
sugarcane 1,250,000, corn (maize) 954,000, fruits and vegetables 347,000
(of which tomatoes 28,000, onions 26,000, oranges 4,000), cassava 230,000,
sunflower seeds 43,000, millet 30,000, sorghum 26,000, sweet potatoes 23,-
000, lint cotton 21,000, peanuts (groundnuts) 14,000, pulses 6,000, tobacco
4,000; livestock (number of live animals) 2,850,000 cattle, 420,000 goats,
221,000 pigs, 80,000 sheep, 14,000,000 chickens; roundwood 9,960,000; fish
catch 68,000. Mining and quarrying (production year ending March 31,
1988): copper 422,224; lead 38,153; zinc 26,078; cobalt 6,580; gold 11,445
oz. Manufacturing (1984): sulfuric acid 276,900; raw sugar 141,000; nitrogen
fertilizer 86,013[4]; cement 75,000 cu m. Construction (value in K; 1985):
buildings 151,100,000; other construction 43,200,000. Energy production
(consumption): electricity (kW-hr; 1987) 8,479,000,000 (6,999,000,000); coal
(metric tons; 1987) 495,000 (490,000); crude petroleum (barrels; 1987) none
(4,215,000); petroleum products (metric tons; 1987) 495,000 (434,000); natural gas, none (n.a.).
Population economically active (1987): total 2,644,268; activity rate of total
population 35.0% (participation rates: ages 15–64, 60.1%[5]; female 28.2%[5];
unemployed 17.4%).

Price and earnings indexes (1985 = 100)							
	1982	1983	1984	1985	1986	1987	1988
Consumer price index	128.2	153.4	184.1	100.0	151.6	216.9	337.8
Monthly earnings index	...	...	...	...	...	...	...

Gross national product (at current market prices; 1987): U.S.$1,696,000,000
(U.S.$240 per capita).

Structure of gross domestic product and labour force				
	1988		1987	
	in value K '000,000	% of total value	labour force	% of labour force
Agriculture	3,196.6	15.1	1,859,794	70.3
Mining	3,359.6	15.9	56,050	2.1
Manufacturing	5,576.9	26.4	49,190	1.9
Construction	515.2	2.5	29,320	1.1
Public utilities	213.0	1.0	8,810	0.3
Transportation and communications	962.4	4.6	23,460	0.9
Trade	3,392.8	16.1	29,320	1.1
Finance	866.6	4.1	22,110	0.8
Public admin., defense,	1,794.9	8.5 }	104,800	4.0
Services	1,230.2	5.8 }		
Other	...	...	461,414	17.5
TOTAL	21,108.2	100.0	2,644,268	100.0

Household income and expenditure. Average household size (1981) 5.8; average annual income per household (1981) K 1,041 (U.S.$908); sources of
income (1981): wages and salaries 94.0%, other 6.0%; expenditure (1977):
food 37.7%, housing 11.0%, clothing 8.3%, transportation 4.3%, education
2.1%, health 1.0%.
Public debt (external, outstanding; 1987): U.S.$4,354,000,000.
Tourism (1987): receipts from visitors U.S.$6,000,000; expenditures by na-
tionals abroad U.S.$46,000,000.
Land use (1986): forested 39.6%; meadows and pastures 47.2%; agricultural
and under permanent cultivation 7.0%; other 6.2%.

Foreign trade

Balance of trade (current prices)						
	1982	1983	1984	1985	1986	1987
K '000,000	20.5	154.4	80.4	−124.0	−1,373.3	+1,431.1
% of total	1.1%	8.0%	3.5%	4.0%	18.2%	10.2%

Imports (1984): K 1,107,866,000 (machinery and transport equipment 28.7%;
basic manufactures 16.3%; chemicals 14.5%; food 4.6%; mineral fuels, lubricants, and electricity 4.5%). *Major import sources:* South Africa 21.1%;
United Kingdom 12.5%; United States 6.4%; West Germany 5.4%; Japan
3.3%; China 0.2%.
Exports (1984): K 1,188,098,000 (copper 86.8%; zinc 4.3%; cobalt 1.6%;
lead 0.5%; tobacco 0.4%). *Major export destinations:* Japan 23.4%; United
States 9.5%; China 9.4%; United Kingdom 5.8%; West Germany 3.6%;
South Africa 0.8%.

Transport and communications

Transport. Railroads (1985): length[6] 1,340 mi, 2,157 km; passenger-mi
346,834,000, passenger-km 558,176,000; short ton-mi cargo 1,072,208,000,
metric ton-km cargo 1,565,496,000. Roads (1987): total length 23,214 mi,
37,359 km (paved 19%). Vehicles (1982): passenger cars 105,783; trucks and
buses 94,780. Merchant marine: vessels (100 gross tons and over) none.
Air transport (1987): passenger-mi 378,440,000, passenger-km 609,040,000;
short ton-mi cargo 17,577,000, metric ton-km cargo 25,662,000; airports
(1989) with scheduled flights 9.
Communications. Daily newspapers (1987): total number 2; total circulation
88,954; circulation per 1,000 population 12. Radio (1986): total number
of receivers 1,000,000 (1 per 7.3 persons). Television (1988): total number of receivers 200,000 (1 per 39 persons). Telephones (1987): 80,865 (1
per 94 persons).

Education and health

Education (1986)				
	schools	teachers	students	student/ teacher ratio
Primary (age 7–13)	3,164	29,841	1,365,926	45.8
Secondary (age 14–18)	276	5,627	150,298	26.8
Voc., teacher tr.	28	1,055	9,687	9.2
Higher	2	575	3,831	6.7

Educational attainment (1980). Percent of population age 25 and over
having: no formal schooling 54.7%; some primary education 34.4%; some
secondary 10.5%; higher 0.4%. *Literacy* (1980): total population literate
2,128,500 (68.6%); males literate 1,207,300 (79.3%); females literate 921,200
(58.3%).
Health (1984): physicians 798 (1 per 10,008 persons); hospital beds 21,668 (1
per 297 persons); infant mortality rate per 1,000 live births (1985–90) 80.0.
Food (1984–86): daily per capita caloric intake 2,126 (vegetable products
95%, animal products 5%); (1984) 93% of FAO recommended minimum
requirement.

Military

Total active duty personnel (1988): 16,200 (army 92.6%; navy, none; air force
7.4%). *Military expenditure as percent of GNP* (1985): 6.8% (world 5.7%);
per capita expenditure U.S.$24.

[1]Includes 11 nonelected members. [2]Central Statistical Office estimate based on the
1980 census. [3]United Nations estimate. [4]1983. [5]1985. [6]1986.

Zimbabwe

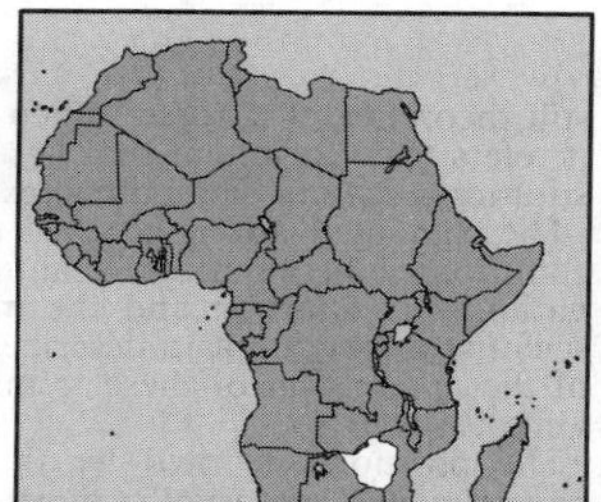

Official name: Republic of Zimbabwe.
Form of government: unitary single-party republic with two legislative houses (Senate [40[1]]; House of Assembly [100]).
Head of state and government[2]: President.
Capital: Harare.
Official language: English.
Official religion: none.
Monetary unit: 1 Zimbabwe Dollar (Z$) = 100 cents; valuation (Oct. 2, 1989) 1 U.S.$ = Z$2.21; 1 £ = Z$3.57.

Area and population		area		population
				1982
Provinces	Capitals	sq mi	sq km	census
Manicaland	Mutare	13,463	34,870	1,103,837
Mashonaland Central	Bindura	10,534	27,284	560,847
Mashonaland East	Marondera	9,627	24,934	1,496,500
Mashonaland West	Chinhoyi	23,346	60,467	854,098
Masvingo (Victoria)	Masvingo	17,108	44,310	1,029,504
Matabeleland North	Bulawayo	28,393	73,537	962,064
Matabeleland South	Gwanda	25,633	66,390	515,298
Midlands	Gweru	22,767	58,967	1,086,284
TOTAL		150,873[3]	390,759	7,608,432

Demography

Population (1989): 9,122,000.
Density (1989): persons per sq mi 60.5, persons per sq km 23.3.
Urban-rural (1982): urban 25.7%; rural 74.3%.
Sex distribution (1987): male 49.07%; female 50.93%.
Age breakdown (1987): under 15, 44.9%; 15–29, 29.2%; 30–44, 14.6%; 45–59, 7.3%; 60–74, 3.1%; 75 and over, 0.9%.
Population projection: (2000) 11,943,000; (2010) 14,739,000.
Doubling time: 20 years.
Ethnolinguistic composition (1982): African 97.6%, of which Shona-speaking Bantu 70.8%; Ndebele-speaking Bantu 15.8%; European 2.0%; Asian 0.1%; other 0.3%.
Religious affiliation (1980): Christian 44.8%, of which Protestant (including Anglican) 17.5%, African indigenous 13.6%, Roman Catholic 11.7%; animist 40.4%; other 14.8%.
Major cities (1987): Harare 863,000; Bulawayo 495,317[4]; Chitungwiza 229,000; Gweru 78,940[4]; Mutare 75,358[4].

Vital statistics

Birth rate per 1,000 population (1982–87): 37.9 (world avg. 26.0).
Death rate per 1,000 population (1982–87): 11.2 (world avg. 9.9).
Natural increase rate per 1,000 population (1982–87): 26.7 (world avg. 16.1).
Total fertility rate (avg. births per childbearing woman; 1987): 4.9.
Marriage rate per 1,000 population: n.a.
Divorce rate per 1,000 population: n.a.
Life expectancy at birth (1987): male 57.9 years; female 61.4 years.
Major causes of death per 100,000 population[5] (1982): accidents and violence 46.6; infectious and parasitic diseases 32.2; diseases of the respiratory system 25.4; diseases of the circulatory system 24.5; malnutrition 15.5.

National economy

Budget (1988–89). Revenue: Z$3,235,032,000 (income tax 57.7%, sales tax 22.1%, customs duties 21.6%, excise tax 11.4%, revenue from investments and property 6.2%, pension contributions 3.7%, international grants 2.8%). Expenditures: Z$6,127,219,000 (recurrent expenditures 74.3%, of which education 16.5%, defense 12.7%, housing 6.1%, health 4.8%, transportation 4.3%, social security and welfare 0.5%).
Tourism (1987): receipts from visitors U.S.$32,000,000; expenditures by nationals abroad U.S.$38,000,000.
Population economically active (1982): total 2,484,070; activity rate of total population 33.1% (participation rates: over age 15, 63.5%; female 39.2%; unemployed 27.0%[6]).

Price and earnings indexes (1985 = 100)	1983	1984	1985	1986	1987	1988[7]
Consumer price index	76.7	92.2	100.0	114.3	128.6	142.2
Monthly earnings index	99.1	99.2	100.0	...	...	...

Production (value of production in Z$ except as noted). Agriculture, forestry, fishing (1986–87): tobacco 365,035,000, corn (maize) 283,586,000, cotton 183,919,000, beef 148,908,000, sugar 146,940,000, milk and dairy products 86,882,000, wheat 74,107,000, coffee 73,890,000, soybeans 28,059,000; livestock (number of live animals; 1987) 5,500,000 cattle, 1,600,000 goats, 570,000 sheep, 180,000 pigs, 10,000,000 chickens; roundwood 7,634,000[6] cu m; fish catch 17,500[6] metric tons. Mining and quarrying (1987): gold 349,800,000; coal 103,400,000; asbestos 97,000,000; nickel 73,400,000; copper 45,900,000; chrome 44,100,000; iron ore 27,171,000; silver 10,812,000; tin 10,767,000. Manufacturing (1985–86): foodstuffs 1,057,000,000; metals and metal products 910,700,000; chemicals and petroleum products 786,800,000; beverages and tobacco 574,900,000; textiles, canvas, and yarns 551,200,000; clothing and footwear 306,800,000; paper, printing, and publishing 251,400,000; transport equipment 143,500,000; nonmetallic mineral products 120,800,000; wood and furniture 111,400,000; other manufactured goods 54,000,000. Construction (Z$; 1987): residential 140,552,000; commercial 80,212,000; industrial 32,957,000. Energy production (consumption): electricity (kW-hr; 1987) 7,645,000,000 (8,995,000,000); coal (metric tons; 1987) 4,843,000 (4,818,000); crude petroleum, none (none); petroleum products (metric tons; 1987) none (705,000); natural gas, none (none).
Public debt (external, outstanding; 1987): U.S.$2,044,000,000.
Household income and expenditure. Average household size (1980) 5.8; income per household Z$1,689 (U.S.$2,628); sources of income: n.a.; expenditure (1986): food, beverages, and tobacco 33.4%, clothing, footwear, and textiles 18.8%, household durable goods 14.8%, energy 7.6%, housing 6.3%, transportation 4.0%, education 3.7%, health service 1.8%, recreation 0.6%.
Gross national product (1987): U.S.$5,265,000,000 (U.S.$590 per capita).

Structure of gross domestic product and labour force	1987		1985	
	in value Z$'000,000	% of total value	labour force[8]	% of labour force
Agriculture	947	10.9	276,800	26.1
Mining	476	5.5	54,100	5.1
Manufacturing	2,720	31.3	171,400	16.2
Construction	213	2.4	45,700	4.3
Public utilities	364	4.2	7,800	0.7
Transp. and commun.	416	4.8	50,400	4.8
Trade	1,118	12.8	78,800	7.4
Finance	475	5.4	15,500	1.5
Pub. admin., defense	590	6.8	91,800	8.7
Services	1,615	18.6	266,400	25.2
Other	−233[9]	−2.7[9]	—	—
TOTAL	8,701	100.0	1,058,700	100.0

Land use (1986): forested 61.6%; meadows and pastures 12.6%; agricultural and under permanent cultivation 6.9%; other 18.9%.

Foreign trade

Balance of trade (current prices)	1982	1983	1984	1985	1986	1987
Z$'000,000	160.0	84.0	185.0	349.0	529.9	590.3
% of total	5.7%	3.8%	8.6%	10.8%	13.9%	14.5%

Imports (1987): Z$1,741,763,000 (machinery and transport equipment 34.7%, of which transport equipment 13.9%; chemicals 17.8%; manufactured goods 16.1%, of which textile yarns and fabrics 4.0%, iron and steel plates 3.0%; fuels 15.0%, of which petroleum products 12.2%). *Major import sources:* South Africa 20.8%; United Kingdom 11.5%; United States 9.4%; West Germany 8.7%; Botswana 5.7%; Japan 3.9%; France 3.7%; Italy 3.0%; The Netherlands 2.8%; Switzerland 2.2%; Zambia 1.5%.
Exports (1987): Z$2,332,100,000 (domestic exports 81.1%, of which tobacco 19.0%; gold sales 18.9%; ferroalloys 10.7%; cotton 5.2%; nickel metal 4.0%; asbestos 3.9%; corn [maize] 3.7%; sugar 2.2%; copper 2.1%). *Major export destinations*[10]: United Kingdom 12.9%; West Germany 10.2%; South Africa 9.8%; United States 6.8%; Botswana 5.5%; Japan 5.0%; Italy 4.4%; Belgium 3.7%; The Netherlands 3.7%; Mozambique 3.7%; Zambia 2.8%.

Transport and communications

Transport. Railroads (1987): route length 2,109 mi, 3,394 km; number of passengers 2,650,000; short ton-mi cargo 7,698,000,000, metric ton-km cargo 11,239,000,000. Roads (1985): total length 48,421 mi, 77,927 km (paved 17%). Vehicles (1985): passenger cars 253,470; trucks and buses 28,839. Merchant marine: none. Air transport (1987): passenger-mi 403,000,000[11], passenger-km 648,000,000[11]; short ton-mi cargo 6,262,000, metric ton-km cargo 9,142,400; airports (1988) with scheduled flights 8.
Communications. Daily newspapers (1985): total number 3; total circulation 191,000; circulation per 1,000 population 23. Radio (1988): 421,062 receivers (1 per 23 persons). Television (1988): 137,090 receivers (1 per 71 persons). Telephones (1986): 256,369 (1 per 33 persons).

Education and health

Education (1988)	schools	teachers	students	student/ teacher ratio
Primary (age 7–13)	4,471	57,566	2,220,967	38.6
Secondary (age 14–19)	1,484	23,899	653,353	27.3
Voc., teacher tr.	21	1,224	40,854	33.4
Higher	1	561	7,699	13.7

Educational attainment (1969). Percent of population age 17 and over having: no formal schooling 41.6%; some primary education 36.5%; primary 13.6%; secondary 3.3%; other 5.0%. *Literacy* (1985): total population age 15 and over literate 3,413,000 (76.0%); males literate 1,846,000 (81.5%); females literate 1,567,000 (66.8%).
Health: physicians (1986) 1,257 (1 per 6,687 persons); hospital beds (1984) 19,407 (1 per 433 persons); infant mortality rate per 1,000 live births (1985) 61.0.
Food (1984–86): daily per capita caloric intake 2,120 (vegetable products 93%, animal products 7%); (1984) 86% of FAO minimum requirement.

Military

Total active duty personnel (1988): 47,000 (army 97.9%, air force 2.1%). *Military expenditure as percent of GNP* (1987): 5.0% (world 5.4%); per capita expenditure U.S.$30.

[1]Includes six nonelective seats. [2]In October 1987, Parliament passed a constitutional amendment whereby the presidency became an executive post, incorporating the former post of prime minister. [3]Detail does not add to total given because of rounding. [4]1982. [5]Registered deaths. [6]1987. [7]November. [8]Wage-earning workers only. [9]Imputed bank service charges. [10]Excludes gold sales and reexports. [11]1986.

Government and international organizations

This table summarizes principal facts about the governments of the countries of the world, their branches and organs, the topmost layers of local government comprising each country's chief administrative subdivisions, and the participation of their central governments in the principal intergovernmental organizations of the world.

In this table "date of independence" may refer to a variety of circumstances. In the case of the newest countries, those that attained full independence after World War II, the date given is usually just what is implied by the heading—the date when the country, within its present borders, attained full sovereignty over both its internal and external affairs. In the case of longer established countries, the choice of a single date may be somewhat more complicated, and grounds for the use of several different dates often exist. The reader interested in this subject should refer to relevant Macropædia and Micropædia articles on national histories and relevant historical acts. In cases of territorial annexation or dissolution, the date given here refers either to the final act of union of a state composed of smaller entities or to the final act of separation from a larger whole (e.g., the separation of Bangladesh from Pakistan in 1971).

The date of the current, or last, constitution is in some ways a less complicated question, but governments sometimes do not, upon taking power, either adhere to existing constitutional forms or trouble to terminate the previous document and legitimize themselves by the installation of new constitutional forms. Often, however, the desire to legitimize extraconstitutional political activity by associating it with existing forms of long precedent leads to partial or incomplete modification, suspension, or abrogation of a constitution, so that the actual day-to-day conduct of government may be largely unrelated to the provisions of a constitution still theoretically in force. When a date in this column is given in italics, it refers to a document that has been suspended, abolished by extraconstitutional action, or modified extensively.

The characterizations adopted under "type of government" represent a compromise between the ideal forms provided for by the language of the national constitution and the more pragmatic language that a political scientist might adopt to describe these same systems. For an explanation of the application of these terms in the Britannica World Data, see the Glossary at p. 549.

The positions denoted by the terms "chief of state" and "head of government" are usually those identified with those functions by the constitution. The duties of the chief of state may range from largely ceremonial responsibilities, with little or no authority over the day-to-day conduct of government, to complete executive authority as the effective head of government. In certain countries, an official of a political party or a revolutionary figure entirely outside the constitutional structure may effectively exercise the powers of both positions.

Membership in the legislative house(s) of each country as given here includes all elected or appointed members, as well as ex officio members (those who by virtue of some other office or title are members of the body), whether voting or nonvoting. The legislature of a country with a unicameral system is shown as the upper house in this table.

The number of administrative subdivisions for each country is listed down to the second level. A single country may, depending on its size, complexity, and historical antecedents, have as many as five levels of administrative subordination (as does the U.S.S.R.) or it may have none at all. Each level of subordination may have several kinds of subdivisions.

Government and international organizations

country	date of independence[a]	date of current or last constitution[b]	type of government	executive branch[c] chief of state	executive branch[c] head of government	legislative branch[d] upper house (members)	legislative branch[d] lower house (members)	admin. subdivisions first-order (number)	admin. subdivisions second-order (number)	seaward claims territorial (nautical miles)	seaward claims fishing/economic (nautical miles)
Afghanistan	Aug. 19, 1919	Nov. 30, 1987	people's republic	chairman PPA	chairman CM	192	234	30	185	—	—
Albania	Nov. 28, 1912	Dec. 27, 1976	socialist republic	president	president	250	—	27	3,315	15	15
Algeria	July 5, 1962	Feb. 23, 1989	republic	president	prime minister	295	—	48	1,541	12	12
American Samoa		July 1, 1967	territory (U.S.)	U.S. president[2]	governor	18	20	3	15	12	200
Andorra	Dec. 6, 1288		coprincipality		chief executive	28	—	7	...		
Angola	Nov. 11, 1975	Nov. 11, 1975	people's republic	president[3]		290	—	18	157	20	200
Anguilla		April 1, 1982	territory (U.K.)	British monarch		12	—		...	3	200
Antigua and Barbuda	Nov. 1, 1981	Nov. 1, 1981	constitutional monarchy	British monarch	prime minister	17	17	30	...	12	200
Argentina	July 9, 1816	July 9, 1853	federal republic	president[5]		46	254	24	...	200	4
Aruba		Dec. 29, 1954	integral part of Neth.	Dutch monarch		21	—		...	12	
Australia	Jan. 1, 1901	July 1, 1900	federal parl. state[7]	British monarch	prime minister	76	148	8	866	3	200
Austria		Oct. 1, 1920	federal republic	president	chancellor	63	183	9	99	—	
Bahamas, The	July 10, 1973	July 10, 1973	constitutional monarchy	British monarch	prime minister	16	49		20	3	200
Bahrain	Aug. 15, 1971	Dec. 6, 1973	monarchy (emirate)	emir	prime minister	x	—	6		3	8
Bangladesh	March 26, 1971	Dec. 16, 1972	republic	president[9]		330	—	4	64	12	200
Barbados	Nov. 30, 1966	Nov. 30, 1966	constitutional monarchy	British monarch	prime minister	21	27			12	200
Belgium	Oct. 4, 1830	Feb. 7, 1831	constitutional monarchy	monarch	prime minister	184	212	9	589	12	—
Belize	Sept. 21, 1981	Sept. 21, 1981	constitutional monarchy	British monarch	prime minister	8	28	6		3	200
Benin	Aug. 1, 1960	Aug. 26, 1977	people's republic	president		206	—	6	84	200	200
Bermuda		June 8, 1968	colony (U.K.)	British monarch[9]		11	40	11		12	200
Bhutan	March 24, 1910		[10]	king		151	—	18	36	—	—
Bolivia	Aug. 6, 1825	Feb. 2, 1967	republic	president	president	27	130	9	108	—	—
Botswana	Sept. 30, 1966	Sept. 30, 1966	republic	president	president	15[11]	40	19		—	—
Brazil	Sept. 7, 1822	Oct. 5, 1988	federal republic	president		72	487	27	4,114	200	200
British Virgin Islands		June 1, 1977	colony (U.K.)	British monarch		12	—			3	200
Brunei	Jan. 1, 1984	Sept. 29, 1959	monarchy (sultanate)	sultan		21	—	4	300	12	200
Bulgaria	Oct. 5, 1908	May 18, 1971	socialist republic	chairman SC	chairman CM	400	x	9	300	12	200
Burkina Faso	Aug. 5, 1960	Nov. 27, 1977	state	chairman PF		(65)	—	30	114	—	—
Burundi	July 1, 1962	Nov. 20, 1981	republic	president CMSN			—	15	114	—	—
Cameroon	Jan. 1, 1960	June 2, 1972	republic	president		180	—	10	49	50	4
Canada	July 1, 1867	April 17, 1982	federal parl. state[7]	British monarch	prime minister	104	295	12	4,172	12	200
Cape Verde	July 5, 1975	Feb. 12, 1981	republic	president	prime minister	83	—	14	31	12[12]	200[12]
Cayman Islands		Aug. 22, 1972	colony (U.K.)	British monarch	governor	16	—			3	200
Central African Republic	Aug. 13, 1960	Nov. 21, 1986	republic	president		52	—	17	50	—	—
Chad	Aug. 11, 1960	April 1962	republic	president		x	—	14	53	—	—
Chile	Sept. 18, 1810	March 11, 1981[13]	republic	president		2,978	—	13	52	12	200
China	1523 BC	Dec. 4, 1982	people's republic	president	premier SC	9	—	30	325	12	4
Christmas Island		Oct. 1, 1958	external territory (Aust.)	Australian GG	administrator		—			3	200
Cocos (Keeling) Islands		Nov. 23, 1955	external territory (Aust.)	Australian GG	administrator	7	—			3	200
Colombia	July 20, 1810	Aug. 5, 1886	republic	president		114	199	33	1,015	12	200
Comoros	July 6, 1975	Oct. 1, 1978	federal Islamic republic	president		42	—	3	7	12	200
Congo	Aug. 15, 1960	July 8, 1979	people's republic	president		133	—	15	47	200	4
Cook Islands		Aug. 4, 1965	territory (N.Z.)[14]	British monarch	prime minister		24			—	200
Costa Rica	Sept. 15, 1821	Nov. 9, 1949	republic	president		57	—	7	81	12	200
Côte d'Ivoire	Aug. 7, 1960	Oct. 31, 1960	republic	president		175	—	49	163	12	200
Cuba	May 20, 1902	Feb. 24, 1976	socialist republic	president		510	—	15	169	12	200
Cyprus[15]	Aug. 16, 1960	Aug. 16, 1960	republic	president		80[16]	—	5		12	4
Czechoslovakia	Oct. 28, 1918	July 11, 1960	federal socialist republic	president	premier	150	200	2	12	—	—
Denmark	c. 800	June 5, 1953	constitutional monarchy	monarch	prime minister	179	—	16	276	3	200
Djibouti	June 27, 1977	January 1981[17]	republic	president	prime minister	65	—	5	13	12	200
Dominica	Nov. 3, 1978	Nov. 3, 1978	republic	president	prime minister	31	—			—	200
Dominican Republic	Feb. 27, 1844	Nov. 28, 1966	republic	president		30	120	27	129	6	200
Ecuador	May 24, 1822	Aug. 10, 1979	republic	president		71	—	20	147	200	200
Egypt	Feb. 28, 1922	Sept. 11, 1971	republic	president	prime minister	458	—	26	176	12	200
El Salvador	Jan. 30, 1841	Dec. 20, 1983	republic	president		60	—	14	262	200	200

Finally, in the second half of the table are listed the memberships each country maintains in the principal international intergovernmental organizations of the world. This part of the table may also be utilized to provide a complete membership list for each of these organizations as of Dec. 1, 1989.

Notes for the column headings

a. The date may also be either that of the organization of the present form of government or the inception of the present administrative structure (federation, confederation, union, etc.).
b. Constitutions whose dates are in italic type had been wholly or substantially suspended or abolished as of late 1989.
c. For abbreviations used in this column see the list on the facing page.
d. When a legislative body has been adjourned or otherwise suspended, figures in parentheses indicate the number of members in the legislative body as provided for in constitution or law. If the provision for the legislative body in the constitution has been abrogated then the space has been marked with an "X".
e. Vatican City also a member.
f. States contributing funds to or receiving aid from UNICEF in 1988.
g. Palestine (Liberation Organization) also a member.

International organizations, conventions

ACP	African, Caribbean, and Pacific (Lomé III) convention
ASEAN	Association of South East Asian Nations
COMECON	Council for Mutual Economic Assistance
EC	The European Communities
ECOWAS	Economic Community of West African States
EEC	European Economic Community
FAO	Food and Agriculture Organization
GATT	General Agreement on Tariffs and Trade
I-ADB	Inter-American Development Bank
IAEA	International Atomic Energy Agency
IBRD	International Bank for Reconstruction and Development
ICAO	International Civil Aviation Organization
ICJ	International Court of Justice
IDA	International Development Association
IDB	Islamic Development Bank
IFC	International Finance Corporation
ILO	International Labour Organisation
IMF	International Monetary Fund
IMO	International Maritime Organization
ITU	International Telecommunication Union
LAS	League of Arab States
NATO	North Atlantic Treaty Organization
OAS	Organization of American States
OAU	Organization of African Unity
OPEC	Organization of Petroleum Exporting Countries
SPC	South Pacific Commission
UNCTAD	United Nations Conference on Trade and Development
UNESCO	United Nations Educational Scientific and Cultural Organization
UNICEF	United Nations Children's Fund
UNIDO	United Nations Industrial Development Organization
UPU	Universal Postal Union
WHO	World Health Organization
WIPO	World Intellectual Property Organization
WMO	World Meteorological Organization
WTO	Warsaw Treaty of Friendship, Co-operation and Mutual Assistance (The Warsaw Pact)

Abbreviations used in the executive-branch column

CCRNS	Command Council of the National Salvation Revolution
CM	Council of Ministers
CMRN	Military Committee for National Recovery
CMSN	Military Committee for National Salvation
CP	Collective Presidency
CS	Council of State
CSON	Supreme Council of National Orientation
FC	Federal Council
FEC	Federal Executive Council
GG	Governor-general
GPC	General People's Committee
MC	Military Council
PF	Popular Front
PNDC	Provisional National Defense Council
PPA	Presidium, People's Assembly
PPGK	Presidium, People's Great Khural
PSPC	Presidium, Supreme People's Council
SC	State Council
SLORC	State Law and Order Restoration Council
SS	Supreme Soviet

membership in international organizations																																								country
United Nations (date of admission)	UN organs★ and affiliated intergovernmental organizations																				Commonwealth of Nations	regional multi-purpose						economic							military			
	UNCTAD★▪	UNICEF★f	ICJ★	FAO	GATT	IAEA▪	IBRD	ICAO	IDA	IFC	ILO	IMF	IMO	ITU▪	UNESCO	UNIDO	UPU▪	WHO	WIPO▪	WMO		ASEAN	EC	LASg	OAS	OAU	SPC	ACP	COMECON	ECOWAS	EEC	I-ADB	IDBg	OPEC	NATO	WTO	
1946	●	●	●	●		●	●	●	●		●	●		●	●	●	●	●		●																	Afghanistan
1955	●	●	●	●			●	●	●		●			●	●	●	●	●		●														●			Albania
1962	●	●	●	●	●1	●	●	●	●	●	●	●	●	●	●	●	●	●	●	●						●		●						●			Algeria
—														●			●																	●	●		American Samoa
—																																					Andorra
1976	●	●	●	●	●1		●	●	●		●	●	●	●	●	●	●	●		●						●		●									Angola
—	●	●	●	●							●			●	●			●			●				●												Anguilla
1981	●	●	●	●			●	●	●		●	●	●	●	●1	●	●	●			●				●			●				●					Antigua and Barbuda
—	●	●	●	●	●	●	●	●	●	●	●	●	●	●6	●	●	●	●	●	●					●							●					Argentina
—																																					Aruba
1945	●	●	●	●	●	●	●	●	●	●	●	●	●	●	●	●	●	●	●	●	●						●										Australia
1955	●	●	●	●	●	●	●	●	●	●	●	●	●	●	●	●	●	●	●	●																	Austria
1973	●	●	●	●	●1	●	●	●	●	●	●	●	●	●	●	●	●	●	●	●	●																Bahamas, The
1971	●	●	●	●	●1		●	●	●	●	●	●	●	●	●	●	●	●		●	●			●									●				Bahrain
1974	●	●	●	●			●	●	●	●	●	●	●	●	●	●	●	●		●	●												●				Bangladesh
1966	●	●	●	●	●	●	●	●	●	●	●	●	●	●	●	●	●	●	●		●				●			●				●					Barbados
1945	●	●	●	●	●	●	●	●	●	●	●	●	●	●	●	●	●	●	●	●			●								●				●		Belgium
1981	●	●	●	●			●	●	●		●	●	●	●	●	●	●	●			●				●			●				●					Belize
1960	●	●	●	●			●	●	●	●	●	●		●	●	●	●	●		●						●		●		●							Benin
—																																					Bermuda
1971	●	●	●	●			●		●			●		●	●	●	●	●		●																	Bhutan
1945	●	●	●	●		●	●	●	●	●	●	●		●	●	●	●	●	●	●					●							●					Bolivia
1966	●	●	●	●			●	●	●	●	●	●		●	●	●	●	●		●	●					●		●									Botswana
1945	●	●	●	●	●	●	●	●	●	●	●	●	●	●6	●	●	●	●	●	●					●							●					Brazil
—																		●																			British Virgin Islands
1984	●							●					●	●	●		●	●			●	●												●			Brunei
1955	●	●	●	●		●		●			●		●	●	●	●	●	●	●	●									●							●	Bulgaria
1960	●	●	●	●	●		●	●	●	●	●	●	●	●	●	●	●	●		●						●		●		●			●				Burkina Faso
1962	●	●	●	●			●	●	●	●	●	●		●	●	●	●	●		●						●		●									Burundi
1960	●	●	●	●	●		●	●	●	●	●	●	●	●	●	●	●	●		●						●		●					●				Cameroon
1945	●	●	●	●	●	●	●	●	●	●	●	●	●	●	●	●	●	●	●	●	●				●							●				●	Canada
1975	●	●	●	●	●1		●	●	●		●	●		●	●	●	●	●								●		●									Cape Verde
—																		●																			Cayman Islands
1960	●	●	●	●			●	●	●	●	●	●		●	●	●	●	●		●						●		●									Central African Republic
1960	●	●	●	●			●	●	●	●	●	●		●	●	●	●	●		●						●		●					●				Chad
1945	●	●	●	●	●	●	●	●	●	●	●	●	●	●	●	●	●	●	●	●					●							●					Chile
1945	●	●	●	●		●	●	●	●	●	●	●	●	●	●	●	●	●	●	●																	China
—																		●									●										Christmas Island
—																											●										Cocos (Keeling) Islands
1945	●	●	●	●		●	●	●	●	●	●	●	●	●	●	●	●	●	●	●					●							●					Colombia
1975	●	●	●	●			●	●	●	●	●	●		●	●	●	●	●							●			●					●				Comoros
1960	●	●	●	●			●	●	●	●	●	●		●	●	●	●	●		●						●		●									Congo
—																											●										Cook Islands
1945	●	●	●	●		●	●	●	●	●	●	●	●	●	●	●	●	●	●	●					●							●					Costa Rica
1960	●	●	●	●	●		●	●	●	●	●	●	●	●	●	●	●	●		●						●		●		●							Côte d'Ivoire
1945	●	●	●	●				●			●		●	●	●	●	●	●	●	●								●	●							●	Cuba
1960	●	●	●	●	●	●	●	●	●	●	●	●	●	●	●	●	●	●	●	●	●								●6			●					Cyprus15
1945	●	●	●	●	●	●		●			●		●	●	●	●	●	●	●	●									●							●	Czechoslovakia
1945	●	●	●	●	●	●	●	●	●	●	●	●	●	●	●	●	●	●	●	●											●				●		Denmark
1977	●	●	●	●			●	●	●		●	●		●	●	●	●	●						●		●		●					●				Djibouti
1978	●	●	●	●	●1		●	●	●		●	●	●	●	●	●	●	●			●				●			●				●					Dominica
1945	●	●	●	●	●		●	●	●	●	●	●	●	●	●	●	●	●	●	●					●							●					Dominican Republic
1945	●	●	●	●		●	●	●	●	●	●	●	●	●	●	●	●	●	●	●					●							●		●			Ecuador
1945	●	●	●	●		●	●	●	●	●	●	●	●	●	●	●	●	●	●	●				●		●							●				Egypt
1945	●	●	●	●			●	●	●	●	●	●	●	●	●	●	●	●	●	●					●							●					El Salvador

Government and international organizations (continued)

country	date of independence[a]	date of current or last constitution[b]	type of government	executive branch[c] chief of state	head of government	legislative branch[d] upper house (members)	lower house (members)	admin. subdivisions first-order (number)	second-order (number)	seaward claims territorial (nautical miles)	fishing/ economic (nautical miles)
Equatorial Guinea	Oct. 12, 1968	Oct. 12, 1982	republic	—— president ——		41	—	7	...	12	200
Ethiopia	c. 1000 BC	Sept. 12, 1987	people's republic	—— president ——		835	—	15	103	12	4
Faeroe Islands	—	March 23, 1948	part of Danish realm	Danish monarch[18]		32	—	7	51	3	200
Falkland Islands	—	Oct. 3, 1985	colony (U.K.)	British monarch[3]		10	—	—	15	3	150
Fiji	Oct. 10, 1970	Oct. 10, 1970	republic	president	prime minister	(22)	(52)	4	15	12[12]	200[12]
Finland	Dec. 6, 1917	July 17, 1919	republic	president	prime minister	200	—	12	461	4	12
France	August 843	Oct. 4, 1958	republic	president	prime minister	321	577	22	96	12	200
French Guiana	—	March 19, 1946	overseas dept. (Fr.)	French president[19]		19	31	2	20	12	200
French Polynesia	—	Sept. 6, 1984	overseas territory (Fr.)	French president[20]		41	—	5	48	12	200
Gabon	Aug. 17, 1960	May 1975	republic	president	prime minister	120	—	9	37	12	200
Gambia, The	Feb. 18, 1965	April 24, 1970	republic	—— president ——		50	—	7	35	12	200
Gaza Strip	—	—	Israeli military	—— area commander		—	—	3	—	—	—
Germany, East	Oct. 7, 1949	April 9, 1968	socialist republic	chairman CS	chairman CM	500	—	15	229	12	200
Germany, West	May 5, 1955	May 23, 1949	federal republic	president	chancellor	45	519	11	30	3	200
Ghana	March 6, 1957	Sept. 24, 1979	republic	—— chairman PNDC ——		(...)	—	10	110	12	200
Gibraltar	—	Aug. 11, 1969	colony (U.K.)	British monarch	governor	18	—	—	—	3	200
Greece	Feb. 3, 1830	June 11, 1975	republic	president	prime minister[21]	300	—	14	51	6	4
Greenland	—	May 1, 1979	part of Danish realm	Danish monarch		27	—	3	18	3	200
Grenada	Feb. 7, 1974	March 3, 1967	constitutional monarchy	British monarch	prime minister[19]	13	15	6	—	12	200
Guadeloupe	—	March 19, 1946	overseas dept. (Fr.)	French president		42	41	3	34	12	200
Guam	—	Aug. 1, 1950	territory (U.S.)	U.S. president	governor	21	—	—	—	12	200
Guatemala	Sept. 15, 1821	Jan. 14, 1986	republic	—— president ——		100	—	22	328	12	200
Guernsey	—	Jan. 1, 1949	crown dependency (U.K.)	British monarch[22]	bailiff	60	—	1	2	3	200
Guinea	Oct. 2, 1958	May 14, 1982	republic	—— president CMRN ——		x	—	31	175	12	200
Guinea-Bissau	Sept. 10, 1974	May 16, 1984	republic	—— president ——		150	—	9	37	12	200
Guyana	May 26, 1966	Oct. 6, 1980	cooperative republic	—— president[23] ——		65	—	10	26	12	200
Haiti	Jan. 1, 1804	March 29, 1987[24]	republic	—— president ——		(27)	(77)	9	130	12	200
Honduras	Nov. 5, 1838	Jan. 20, 1982	republic	—— president ——		134	—	18	289	12	200
Hong Kong	—	—	colony (U.K.)	British monarch	governor	57	—	...	19	3	4
Hungary	Nov. 16, 1918	Aug. 20, 1949[25]	republic	interim president	prime minister	387	—	20	125	—	—
Iceland	June 17, 1944	June 17, 1944	republic	president	prime minister	21	42	...	...	12	200
India	Aug. 15, 1947	Jan. 26, 1950	federal republic	president	prime minister	244	546	32	439	12[12]	200[12]
Indonesia	Aug. 17, 1945	Aug. 17, 1945	republic	—— president[26] ——		1,000	500	27	281	12	50[27]
Iran	Oct. 7, 1906	Dec. 2–3, 1979	Islamic republic	—— president ——		270	—	24	195	12	4
Iraq	Oct. 3, 1932	Sept. 22, 1968[28]	republic	—— president ——		250	—	18	...	12	4
Ireland	Dec. 6, 1921	Dec. 29, 1937	republic	president	prime minister	60	166	32	80	3	200
Isle of Man	—	1961	crown dependency (U.K.)	British monarch[22]	chief minister	10	24	26	—	3	200
Israel	May 14, 1948	June 1950[29]	republic	president	prime minister	120	—	6	15	6	4
Italy	March 17, 1861	Jan. 1, 1948	republic	president	prime minister	322	630	20	94	12	4
Jamaica	Aug. 6, 1962	Aug. 6, 1962	constitutional monarchy	British monarch	prime minister	21	60	13	—	12	4
Japan	c. 660 BC	May 3, 1947	constitutional monarchy	emperor	prime minister	252	512	47	3,246	12[30]	200
Jersey	—	Jan. 1, 1949	crown dependency (U.K.)	British monarch[22]	bailiff	58	—	12	...	3	200
Jordan	May 25, 1946	Jan. 8, 1952	constitutional monarchy	—— king[23] ——		40	80	9	...	3	4
Kampuchea (Cambodia)	Nov. 9, 1953	May 5, 1989[13]	people's republic	chairman CS	chairman CM	117	—	21	...	12	200
Kenya	Dec. 12, 1963	Dec. 12, 1963	republic	—— president ——		202	—	8	40	12	200
Kiribati	July 12, 1979	July 12, 1979	republic	—— president ——		41	—	6	23	12	200
Korea, North	Sept. 9, 1948	Dec. 27, 1972	socialist republic	president	premier	655	—	13	172	12[31]	12
Korea, South	Aug. 15, 1948	Feb. 25, 1988	republic	president	prime minister	299	—	14	194	12	4
Kuwait	June 19, 1961	Nov. 16, 1962	const. mon. (emirate)	—— emir[23] ——		(64)	—	—	—	12	4
Laos	Oct. 23, 1953	May 11, 1947	people's republic	president	chairman CM	79	—	17	...	12	4
Lebanon	Nov. 26, 1941	May 23, 1926[32]	republic	president	prime minister	99[33]	—	...	...	12	4
Lesotho	Oct. 4, 1966	Oct. 4, 1966	monarchy	king	chairman MC	(33)	(60)	10	...	—	—
Liberia	July 26, 1847	Jan. 6, 1986	republic	—— president ——		26	64	13	...	200	4
Libya	Dec. 24, 1951	March 2, 1977	socialist state[34]	rev. leader	sec. GPC	1,112	—	24	...	12[35]	1
Liechtenstein	July 12, 1806	Oct. 5, 1921	constitutional monarchy	prince	head of gov't.	25	—	11	—	—	—
Luxembourg	May 10, 1867	Oct. 17, 1868	constitutional monarchy	grand duke	prime minister	21[11]	60	3	12	—	—
Macau	—	August 1976	overseas terr. (Port.)	Port. president	governor	17	—	2	5	6	12
Madagascar	June 26, 1960	Dec. 30, 1975	republic	president	prime minister	137	—	6	18	12	200
Malawi	July 6, 1964	July 6, 1966	republic	—— president ——		123	—	3	24	—	—
Malaysia	Aug. 31, 1957	Aug. 31, 1957	fed. const. monarchy	paramount ruler	prime minister	69	177	15	134	12	200
Maldives	July 26, 1965	Nov. 11, 1968	republic	—— president ——		48	—	19	202	12, 36	36
Mali	Sept. 22, 1960	June 19, 1979	republic	—— president ——		82	—	8	46	12	25
Malta	Sept. 21, 1964	Dec. 13, 1974	republic	president	prime minister	69	—	3	34	12	200
Martinique	—	March 19, 1946	overseas dept. (Fr.)	French president[19]		45	41	13	49	70	200
Mauritania	Nov. 28, 1960	May 20, 1961	republic	—— president CMSN ——		x	—	...	...	12	200
Mauritius	March 12, 1968	March 12, 1968	constitutional monarchy	British monarch	prime minister	70	—	8	103	12	200
Mayotte	—	Dec. 24, 1976	terr. collectivity (Fr.)	French president[37]		17	—	17	—	12	200
Mexico	Sept. 16, 1810	Feb. 5, 1917	federal republic	—— president ——		64	500	32	2,359	12	4
Monaco	Feb. 2, 1861	Dec. 17, 1962	constitutional monarchy	prince	min. of state	18	—	—	—	12	4
Mongolia	March 13, 1921	July 6, 1960	people's republic	chairman PPGK	premier	370	—	21	299	—	—
Montserrat	—	Jan. 1, 1960	colony (U.K.)	British monarch	governor	12	—	—	—	3	200
Morocco	March 2, 1956	March 10, 1972	constitutional monarchy	—— king[23] ——		306	—	43[38]	125[38]	12	200
Mozambique	June 25, 1975	June 25, 1975	people's republic	—— president ——		249	—	11	124	12	200
Myanmar (Burma)	Jan. 4, 1948	Jan. 4, 1974	republic	—— chairman SLORC ——		(489)	—	14	314	12	200
Nauru	Jan. 31, 1968	Jan. 31, 1968	republic	—— president ——		18	—	—	—	12	200
Nepal	Nov. 13, 1769	Dec. 16, 1962	constitutional monarchy	king	prime minister	140	—	14	75	—	—
Netherlands, The	March 30, 1814	Feb. 17, 1983	constitutional monarchy	monarch	prime minister	75	150	12	714	12	200
Netherlands Antilles	—	Dec. 29, 1954	integral part of Neth.	Dutch monarch[5]		22	—	5	—	12	200
New Caledonia	—	—	overseas territory (Fr.)	French president[40]		54	—	3	...	12	200
New Zealand	Sept. 26, 1907	June 30, 1852[29]	constitutional monarchy	British monarch	prime minister	97	—	22	...	12	200
Nicaragua	April 30, 1838	Jan. 9, 1987	republic	—— president ——		(96)	—	9	—	200	200
Niger	Aug. 3, 1960	Sept. 24, 1989[41]	republic	—— president CSON ——		...	—	8	...	30	200
Nigeria	Oct. 1, 1960	Oct. 1, 1979	federal republic	—— president ——		x	x	22	—	12	200
Niue	—	Oct. 19, 1974	territory (N.Z.)[14]	British monarch	premier	20	—	14	—	3	200
Norfolk Island	—	May 30, 1979	external territory (Aust.)	Australian GG	administrator	9	—	—	—	3	200

membership in international organizations

United Nations (date of admission)	UN organs★ and affiliated intergovernmental organizations																				Commonwealth of Nations	regional multi-purpose						economic							military		country
	UNCTAD★●	UNICEF★⁴	ICJ★	FAO	GATT	IAEA●	IBRD●	ICAO	IDA	IFC	ILO	IMF	IMO	ITU●	UNESCO	UNIDO	UPU●	WHO	WIPO●	WMO		ASEAN	EC	LAS⁹	OAS	OAU	SPC	ACP	COMECON	ECOWAS	EEC	I-ADB	IDB⁹	OPEC	NATO	WTO	
1968	●	●	●	●	●¹		●	●	●		●	●	●	●	●	●	●	●		●						●		●									Equatorial Guinea
1945	●	●	●	●	●	●	●	●	●		●	●	●	●	●	●	●	●		●						●		●									Ethiopia
—														●			●	●																			Faeroe Islands
1970	●	●	●	●	●¹		●	●	●	●	●	●	●	●	●	●	●	●	●	●	●						●										Falkland Islands
																	●	●									●	●									Fiji
1955	●	●	●	●	●	●	●	●	●	●	●	●	●	●	●	●	●	●	●	●			●				●										Finland
1945	●	●	●	●	●	●	●	●	●	●	●	●	●	●	●	●	●	●	●	●			●				●				●	●			●		France
—	●													●			●	●		●																	French Guiana
1960	●													●			●	●		●			●			●		●				●	●				French Polynesia
1965	●	●	●	●			●	●	●	●	●	●	●	●	●	●	●	●		●	●		●			●		●		●		●					Gabon
																		●																			Gambia, The
1973	●	●	●	●			●	●	●	●	●	●	●	●	●	●	●	●	●	●									●							●	Gaza Strip
1973	●	●	●	●	●¹	●	●	●	●	●	●	●	●	●	●	●	●	●	●	●			●					●			●	●			●	●	Germany, East
1957	●	●	●	●	●	●	●	●	●	●	●	●	●	●	●	●	●	●	●	●	●							●							●		Germany, West
1945	●	●	●	●			●	●	●	●	●	●	●	●	●	●	●	●		●			●				●					●			●		Ghana
—	●																●	●										●					●			●	Gibraltar
1974	●	●	●	●	●¹		●	●		●	●	●	●	●	●	●	●	●		●	●				●			●									Greece
—														●			●																				Greenland
—																	●				●																Grenada
1945	●	●	●	●			●	●	●	●	●	●	●	●	●	●	●			●								●				●					Guadeloupe
1958	●	●	●	●			●	●	●	●	●	●	●	●	●	●	●	●		●	●				●			●				●					Guam
1974	●	●	●	●	●¹		●	●	●	●	●	●	●	●	●	●	●	●	●	●						●		●		●		●					Guatemala
																		●								●		●									Guernsey
1966	●	●	●	●			●	●	●	●	●	●	●	●	●	●	●	●		●	●							●				●					Guinea
1945	●	●	●	●			●	●	●	●	●	●	●	●	●	●	●	●		●			●					●									Guinea-Bissau
1945	●	●	●	●			●	●	●	●	●	●	●	●	●	●	●			●								●				●					Guyana
—		●	●	●			●	●			●	●⁶		●	●		●	●		●												●					Haiti
1955	●	●	●	●			●	●	●	●	●	●	●	●	●	●	●	●		●	●											●				●	Honduras
1946	●	●	●	●			●	●	●	●	●	●	●	●	●	●	●	●	●	●															●		Hong Kong
1945	●	●	●	●			●	●	●	●	●	●	●	●	●	●	●	●	●	●		●											●	●			Hungary
1950	●	●	●	●			●	●	●	●	●	●	●	●	●	●	●	●	●	●		●											●	●			Iceland
1945	●	●	●	●			●	●	●	●	●	●	●	●	●	●	●	●	●	●			●					●									India
1955	●	●	●	●			●	●	●	●	●	●	●	●	●	●	●	●		●																	Indonesia
—																	●															●					Ireland
1949	●	●	●	●			●	●	●	●	●	●	●	●	●	●	●	●		●	●							●				●					Isle of Man
1955	●	●	●	●			●	●	●	●	●	●	●	●	●	●	●	●	●	●			●								●	●					Israel
1962	●	●	●	●			●	●	●	●	●	●	●	●	●	●	●	●	●	●								●							●		Italy
1956	●	●	●	●			●	●	●	●	●	●	●	●	●	●	●	●		●																	Jamaica
1955	●	●	●	●			●	●	●	●	●	●	●	●	●	●	●	●	●	●			●														Japan
1955	●	●	●	●	●¹		●	●	●	●	●	●	●	●	●	●	●	●	●	●								●				●					Jersey
1963	●	●	●	●			●	●	●	●	●	●	●	●	●	●	●	●		●					●												Jordan
																		●								●		●									Kampuchea (Cambodia)
—		●			●¹		●	●	●	●	●	●	●	●	●	●	●	●	●	●	●						●	●									Kenya
—		●												●			●	●		●												●					Kiribati
1963	●	●	●	●			●	●	●	●	●	●	●	●	●	●	●	●		●																	Korea, North
1955	●	●	●	●			●	●	●	●	●	●	●	●	●	●	●	●		●			●					●				●	●				Korea, South
																		●																			Kuwait
1945	●	●	●	●			●	●	●	●	●	●	●	●	●	●	●	●	●	●		●											●				Laos
1966	●	●	●	●			●	●	●	●	●	●	●	●	●	●	●	●		●	●					●		●		●							Lebanon
1945	●	●	●	●			●	●	●	●	●	●	●	●	●	●	●	●		●	●					●		●									Lesotho
1955	●	●	●	●			●	●	●	●	●	●	●	●	●	●	●	●		●			●					●		●							Liberia
—		●												●			●	●															●	●			Libya
1945	●	●	●	●										●	●		●			●			●								●				●		Liechtenstein
1960	●	●	●	●			●	●	●	●	●	●	●	●	●	●	●	●		●			●					●									Luxembourg
1964	●	●	●	●			●	●	●	●	●	●	●	●	●	●	●	●		●					●			●				●					Macau
1957	●	●	●	●			●	●	●	●	●	●	●	●	●	●	●	●		●	●	●				●		●									Madagascar
																		●																			Malawi
1965	●	●	●	●			●	●	●	●	●	●	●	●	●	●	●	●		●	●							●									Malaysia
1960	●	●	●	●	●¹		●	●	●	●	●	●	●	●	●	●	●	●		●	●					●		●		●		●					Maldives
1964	●	●	●	●			●	●	●	●	●	●	●	●	●	●	●	●		●								●					●⁶				Mali
1961	●	●	●	●			●	●	●	●	●	●	●	●	●	●	●	●		●	●							●									Malta
1968	●	●	●	●			●	●	●	●	●	●	●	●	●	●	●	●		●			●					●				●					Martinique
1945	●	●	●	●			●	●	●	●	●	●	●	●	●	●	●	●		●	●				●	●		●		●							Mauritania
1961	●	●	●	●			●	●	●	●	●	●	●	●	●	●	●	●		●						●		●				●					Mauritius
																		●																			Mayotte
1956	●	●	●	●	●¹		●	●	●	●	●	●	●	●	●	●	●	●		●					●							●					Mexico
1975	●	●	●	●			●	●	●	●	●	●	●	●	●	●	●	●		●												●					Monaco
1948	●			●							●			●	●		●	●		●																	Mongolia
																		●			●																Montserrat
—	●	●	●	●			●	●	●	●	●	●	●	●	●	●	●	●		●	●³⁹						●										Morocco
1955	●	●	●	●			●	●	●	●	●	●	●	●	●	●	●	●	●	●		●						●				●	●		●		Mozambique
1945	●	●	●	●			●	●	●	●	●⁶	●	●	●	●	●	●	●		●							●										Myanmar (Burma)
																		●										●									Nauru
1945	●	●	●	●			●	●	●	●	●	●	●	●	●	●	●	●		●			●					●							●		Nepal
1960	●	●	●	●			●	●	●	●	●	●	●	●	●	●	●	●		●						●		●									Netherlands, The
1960	●	●												●	●		●	●		●						●		●					●				New Zealand

Government and international organizations (continued)

country	date of independence[a]	date of current or last constitution[b]	type of government	executive branch[c] chief of state	head of government	legislative branch[d] upper house (members)	lower house (members)	admin. subdivisions first-order (number)	second-order (number)	seaward claims territorial (nautical miles)	fishing/economic (nautical miles)
Norway	June 7, 1905	May 17, 1814	constitutional monarchy	king	prime minister	165	—	19	451	4	200
Oman	Dec. 20, 1951	—	monarchy (sultanate)	— sultan —		55[11]	—	41	...	12	200
Pacific Is., Trust Terr. of											
Marshall Islands	—	May 1, 1979	republic	— president —		12[11]	33	26	—	12	200
Micronesia, F.S. of	—	May 10, 1979	federal republic	— president —		14	—	4	...	12	200
Northern Mariana Is.	—	Jan. 9, 1978	commonwealth (U.S.)	U.S. president	governor	9	15	4	—	3	200
Palau	—	Jan. 1, 1981	republic	— president —		18	16	16	—	3	200
Pakistan	Aug. 14, 1947	Aug. 14, 1973	federal Islamic republic	president	prime minister	87	237	...	...	12	200
Panama	Nov. 3, 1903	Oct. 11, 1972	republic	— provisional president[42] —		(67)	—	10	65	200	4
Papua New Guinea	Sept. 16, 1975	Sept. 16, 1975	constitutional monarchy	British monarch	prime minister	109	—	20	160	12[12]	200[12]
Paraguay	May 14, 1811	Aug. 25, 1967	republic	— president —		36	72	20	196	—	—
Peru	July 28, 1821	July 28, 1980	republic	— president —		60[43]	180	25	180	200	200
Philippines	July 4, 1946	Feb. 11, 1987	republic	— president —		24	204	75	1,591	36	200[12]
Pitcairn Island	—	Nov. 30, 1838	colony (U.K.)	British monarch [44]		10	—	—	—	3	200
Poland	Nov. 10, 1918	July 22, 1952	socialist republic	president	chairman CM	100	460	49	2,904	12	200
Portugal	c. 1140	April 25, 1976[45]	parliamentary state	president	prime minister	250	—	22	305	12	200
Puerto Rico	—	July 25, 1952	commonwealth (U.S.)	U.S. president	governor	27	51	78	...	12	200
Qatar	Sept. 3, 1971	July 1970[28]	monarchy	— emir —		30[11]	—	9	—	3	46
Réunion	—	March 19, 1946	overseas dept. (Fr.)	French president [19]		44	45	4	24	12	200
Romania	May 21, 1877	Aug. 21, 1965	socialist republic	president	prime minister	369	—	41	237	12	200
Rwanda	July 1, 1962	Dec. 20, 1978	republic	— president —		70	—	11	143	—	—
St. Helena and Ascension	—	Jan. 1, 1967	colony (U.K.)	British monarch	governor	15	—	3	—	3	200
St. Kitts and Nevis	Sept. 19, 1983	Sept. 19, 1983	constitutional monarchy	British monarch	prime minister	15	—	1	—	12	200
St. Lucia	Feb. 22, 1979	Feb. 22, 1979	constitutional monarchy	British monarch	prime minister	11	17	2	—	12	200
St. Pierre and Miquelon	—	June 1985	terr. collectivity (Fr.)	French president [37]		14	—	—	—	12	200
St. Vincent	Oct. 27, 1979	Oct. 27, 1979	constitutional monarchy	British monarch	prime minister	21	—	—	—	12	200
San Marino	855	Oct. 8, 1600	republic	— captains-regent (2) —		60	—	9	—	12[12]	200[12]
São Tomé and Príncipe	July 12, 1975	Dec. 15, 1982	republic	— president[23] —		51	—	2	7	12	4
Saudi Arabia	Sept. 23, 1932	—	monarchy	— king —		—	—	14	...	12	200
Senegal	Aug. 20, 1960	March 7, 1963	republic	— president —		120	—	10	30	12	200
Seychelles	June 29, 1976	June 5, 1979	republic	— president —		25	—	—	—	12	200
Sierra Leone	April 27, 1961	June 14, 1978	republic	— president —		127	—	...	...	200	4
Singapore	Aug. 9, 1965	June 3, 1959	republic	president	prime minister	84	—	—	—	3	12
Solomon Islands	July 7, 1978	July 7, 1978	constitutional monarchy	British monarch	prime minister	38	—	8	—	12[12]	200[12]
Somalia	July 1, 1960	Aug. 25, 1979	republic	— president —		177	—	18	87	200	200
South Africa	May 31, 1910	Sept. 3, 1984	republic	— state president —		305[47]	—	4[48]	508[48]	12	200
Bophuthatswana	Dec. 6, 1977[49]	Dec. 6, 1977	republic	— president —		108	—	12	76	—	—
Ciskei	Dec. 4, 1981[49]	Dec. 4, 1981	republic	— president —		55	—	7	42	—	—
Transkei	Oct. 26, 1976[49]	Dec. 1963	republic	— head of military council —		(150)	—	28	123	—	—
Venda	Sept. 13, 1979[49]	Sept. 13, 1979	republic	— president —		92	—	4	28	—	—
South West Africa/Namibia	—	—	dependency of S.Af.[50]	— administrator-general —		72	—	26	—	12	200
Spain	1492	Dec. 29, 1978	constitutional monarchy	king	prime minister	257	350	17	50	12	200
Sri Lanka	Feb. 4, 1948	Sept. 7, 1978	republic	— president —		225	—	8	68	12	200
Sudan, The	Jan. 1, 1956	Oct. 10, 1985	republic	— president CCRNS —		(301)	—	7	...	12	4
Suriname	Nov. 25, 1975	Nov. 25, 1987	republic	— president —		51	—	9	—	12	200
Swaziland	Sept. 6, 1968	Sept. 6, 1968	monarchy	— king[23] —		20	50	4	40	—	—
Sweden	before 836	Jan. 1, 1975	constitutional monarchy	king	prime minister	349	—	24	284	12	200
Switzerland	Sept. 22, 1499	May 29, 1874	federal state	— president FC —		46	200	26	3,028	—	—
Syria	April 17, 1946	March 14, 1973	republic	— president —		195	—	14	60	35	4
Taiwan	Oct. 25, 1945	Dec. 25, 1947	republic	president	premier	79[51]	261[51]	3	21	12	200
Tanzania	Dec. 9, 1961	April 25, 1977	republic	president	prime minister	244	—	25	99	50	4
Thailand	1350	Dec. 22, 1978	constitutional monarchy	king	prime minister	268	357	73	650	12	200
Togo	April 27, 1960	Dec. 30, 1979	republic	— president —		77	—	5	21	30	200
Tokelau	—	1948	territory (N.Z.)	New Zealand GG [52]		—	—	3	—	12	200
Tonga	June 4, 1970	Nov. 4, 1875	constitutional monarchy	— monarch[23] —		29	—	6	23	12	200
Trinidad and Tobago	Aug. 31, 1962	July 27, 1976	republic	president	prime minister	31	36	11	...	12	200
Tunisia	March 20, 1956	June 1, 1959	republic	president	prime minister	141	—	23	245	12	4
Turkey	Oct. 29, 1923	Nov. 7, 1982	republic	president	prime minister	450	—	67	580	12[53]	200[54]
Turks and Caicos Islands	—	Aug. 30, 1976	colony (U.K.)	British monarch	governor	16	—	6	—	3	200
Tuvalu	Oct. 1, 1978	Oct. 1, 1978	constitutional monarchy	British monarch	prime minister	12	—	9	—	12	200
Uganda	Oct. 9, 1962	Sept. 8, 1967	republic	— president —		278[55]	—	33	—	12	200
U.S.S.R.	c. 900	Oct. 7, 1977	fed. socialist republic	chairman SS	chairman CM	2,250	542	15	167	12	200
United Arab Emirates	Dec. 2, 1971	Dec. 2, 1971[28]	federation of emirates	president	prime minister	40	—	7	—	3	200
United Kingdom	Oct. 14, 1066	[57]	constitutional monarchy	monarch	prime minister	1,190	650	4	154	3	200
United States	July 4, 1776	March 4, 1789	federal republic	— president —		100	435	51	3,140	12	200
Uruguay	Aug. 25, 1828	Feb. 15, 1967	republic	— president —		31	99	19	...	200	200
Vanuatu	July 30, 1980	July 30, 1980	republic	president	prime minister	46	—	11	...	12[12]	200[12]
Venezuela	July 5, 1811	Jan. 23, 1961	federal republic	— president —		52	201	24	—	12	200
Vietnam	Sept. 2, 1954	Dec. 18, 1980	socialist republic	chairman CS	chairman CM	496	—	40	...	12	200
Virgin Islands (U.S.)	—	—	territory (U.S.)	U.S. president	governor	15	—	2	—	12	200
Wallis and Futuna	—	July 29, 1961	overseas territory (Fr.)	French president [58]		20	—	3	5	12	200
West Bank	—	—	Israeli military	— area commander —		—	—	7	—	12	—
Western Sahara	—	—	annexture of Morocco [60]			—	—	4	8	12	200
Western Samoa	Jan. 1, 1962	Oct. 28, 1960		head of state	prime minister	48	—	21	—	12	200
Yemen (Aden)	Nov. 30, 1967	Dec. 27, 1978	socialist republic	chairman PSPC	prime minister	111	—	6	...	12	200
Yemen (Ṣan'ā')	December 1918	June 19, 1974[28]	republic	— president —		159	—	11	...	12	12
Yugoslavia	Dec. 1, 1918	Feb. 21, 1974	federal socialist republic	president CP	president FEC	88	220	8	527	12	12
Zaire	June 30, 1960	Feb. 15, 1978	republic	— president —		210	—	9	41	12	200
Zambia	Oct. 24, 1964	Aug. 25, 1973	republic	— president —		136	—	9	53	—	—
Zimbabwe	April 18, 1980	April 18, 1980	republic	— president —		40	100	8	—	—	—

[1]Full membership pending. [2]President of France and Bishop of Urgel, Spain. [3]Executive responsibilities divided between (for the U.K.) the governor and (locally) the chief officer of the Executive Council. [4]Territorial sea claim assumed to claim fishing/economic rights within the same zone. [5]Executive responsibilities divided between (for The Netherlands) the governor and (locally) the prime minister. [6]Associate member. [7]Formally a constitutional monarchy. [8]Defined by equidistant line. [9]Executive responsibilities divided between (for the U.K.) the governor and (locally) the premier of the Cabinet. [10]Resembles a constitutional monarchy without a formal constitution. [11]Body with limited legislative authority. [12]Measured from claimed archipelagic baselines. [13]Transitional constitution. [14]Self-governing state in free association with New Zealand. [15]Republic of Cyprus only. [16]56 seats occupied. [17]Partial constitution. [18]Executive responsibilities divided between (for Denmark) the state commissioner and (locally) the head of the home government. [19]Executive responsibilities divided among (for France) the commissioner and (locally) the president of the Council of Ministers. [21]Executive responsibilities divided between (for France) the high commissioner and (locally) the president of the Regional Council. [20]Executive responsibilities divided between (for France) the high commissioner and (locally) the president of the Council of Ministers. [21]Executive responsibilities divided between (for Denmark) the high commissioner and (locally) the prime minister. [22]Represented by the lieutenant-governor. [23]Assisted by the prime minister. [24]Referendum date; constitution pending implementation. [25]Significantly amended by transitional constitution of Oct. 18, 1989. [26]Shares coexecutive authority with spiritual leader. [27]Sea of Oman only; median line boundaries in the Persian Gulf. [28]Provisional constitution. [29]Evolving body of constitutional law. [30]3 nm in 5 straits. [31]3 nm in Korean Strait. [32]Charter of national reconciliation effective

membership in international organizations

United Nations (date of admission)	UN organs★ and affiliated intergovernmental organizations (UNCTAD★°, UNICEF★¹, ICJ★, FAO, GATT, IAEA°, IBRD, ICAO, IDA, IFC, ILO, IMF, IMO, ITU°, UNESCO, UNIDO, UPU°, WHO, WIPO°, WMO)	Commonwealth of Nations	regional multi-purpose (ASEAN, EC, LAS⁹, OAS, OAU, SPC)	economic (ACP, COMECON, ECOWAS, EEC, I-ADB, IDB⁹, OPEC)	military (NATO, WTO)	country
1945						Norway
1971						Oman
—						Pacific Is., Trust Terr. of
—						Marshall Islands
—						Micronesia, F.S. of
—						Northern Mariana Is.
—						Palau
1947						Pakistan
1945						Panama
1975						Papua New Guinea
1945						Paraguay
1945						Peru
1945						Philippines
—						Pitcairn Island
1945						Poland
1955						Portugal
1971						Puerto Rico
—						Qatar
—						Réunion
1955						Romania
1962						Rwanda
—						St. Helena and Ascension
1983						St. Kitts and Nevis
1979						St. Lucia
—						St. Pierre and Miquelon
1980						St. Vincent
1975						San Marino
1945						São Tomé and Príncipe
1960						Saudi Arabia
						Senegal
1976						Seychelles
1961						Sierra Leone
1965						Singapore
1978						Solomon Islands
1960						Somalia
1945						South Africa
—						Bophuthatswana
—						Ciskei
—						Transkei
—						Venda
—						South West Africa/Namibia
1955						Spain
1955						Sri Lanka
1956						Sudan, The
1975						Suriname
1968						Swaziland
1946						Sweden
—						Switzerland
1945						Syria
—						Taiwan
1961						Tanzania
1946						Thailand
1960						Togo
—						Tokelau
—						Tonga
1962						Trinidad and Tobago
1956						Tunisia
1945						Turkey
—						Turks and Caicos Islands
—		(●³⁹)				Tuvalu
1962						Uganda
1945⁵⁶	(●⁵⁶ markers)					U.S.S.R.
1971						United Arab Emirates
1945						United Kingdom
1945						United States
1945						Uruguay
1981						Vanuatu
1945						Venezuela
1977						Vietnam
—						Virgin Islands (U.S.)
—						Wallis and Futuna
—						West Bank
—			(●⁵⁹)			Western Sahara
1976						Western Samoa
1967						Yemen (Aden)
1947						Yemen (Şan'ā')
1945						Yugoslavia
1960						Zaire
1964						Zambia
1980						Zimbabwe

Nov. 4, 1989.   [33]73 seats occupied Nov. 4, 1989.   [34]Formally a *jamahiriya*, translated as "the masses of people."   [35]Based on Gulf of Sidra closing line (32° 30′ N), in part.   [36]Zone defined by geographic coordinates.   [37]Executive responsibilities divided between (for France) the commissioner and (locally) the president of the General Council.   [38]Excludes Western Sahara.   [39]Special member.   [40]Executive responsibilities divided between (for France) the high commissioner and (locally) the president of the Territorial Congress.   [41]Date of referendum approving new constitution.   [42]Military commander is de facto executive.   [43]Elective seats only.   [44]Executive responsibilities divided between (for the U.K.) the High Commissioner to New Zealand and (locally) the island magistrate.   [45]Amendments to constitution (effective Aug. 8, 1989) removed Marxist elements.   [46]Limits of continental shelf or median line boundaries.   [47]Total of 3 legislative houses.   [48]Excludes national states.   [49]Recognized by South Africa and each other only.   [50]Interim status pending independence in 1990.   [51]As of Nov. 12, 1989.   [52]Executive responsibilities divided among (for New Zealand) the Deputy Secretary of Foreign Affairs assisted by the Official Secretary based in Western Samoa and (locally) village councils.   [53]Black Sea and Mediterranean Sea; six nautical miles in Aegean Sea.   [54]Black Sea only.   [55]Interim legislature.   [56]Belorussian and Ukrainian S.S.R.'s are also members.   [57]Based on evolving body of statutes and common law.   [58]Executive responsibilities divided between (for France) the superior administrator and (locally) the president of the Territorial Assembly.   [59]Membership held by the Sahrawi Arab Democratic Republic.   [60]Mixed political system approximating a constitutional monarchy.

Area and population

This table provides the area and population for each of the countries of the world and for all political dependencies with a permanent civilian population. Only countries such as the Vatican City State, the British Indian Ocean Territory, and similar anomalous cases are omitted. The data represent the latest published and unpublished data for both the surveyed area of the countries and their populations, the latter both as of a single year (1989) to provide the best comparability and as of the most recent census to provide the fullest comparison of certain demographic measures that are not always available in estimated form between successive national censuses. The 1989 mid-year estimates represent a combination of national, United Nations (UN) or other international organization, and *Encyclopædia Britannica* estimates so as to give the best fit to available published series, to take account of unpublished information received in correspondence, and to incorporate the results of very recent censuses for which published analyses are not yet available.

One principal point to bear in mind when studying these statistics is that all of them, whatever degree of precision may be implied by the exactness of the numbers, are estimates—all of varying, and some of suspect accuracy. Even a country like the United States—which has a long tradition both of census taking and of the use of the most sophisticated analytical tools in processing the data—is unable to determine within 2.5% its total population nationally. And that is an average underenumeration. In larger cities, where enumeration of certain populations, both legal and illegal, is most difficult, the accuracy of the enumerated count may be off considerably more than 5%. When a country like Nigeria, the most populous in Africa, does not know within 20% its real population and is

delayed or prevented from measuring it by political circumstances, both the amount and the margin of error are likely to increase. The editors have tried to take account of the range of variation and accuracy in published data, but it is difficult to establish a value for many sources of inaccuracy unless some country or agency has made a conscientious effort to establish both the relative accuracy (precision) of its estimate and the absolute magnitude of the quantity it is trying to measure—for example, the number of people in Kampuchea (Cambodia) who died at the hands of the Khmer Rouge. Was it 1,000,000, 2,000,000, 3,000,000? If a figure of 1,000,000 is adopted, what is its accuracy: ± 1%, 10%, 50%? Are the original data complete or incomplete, analytically biased or unbiased, in good agreement with other published data, or isolated and inferential?

Many similar problems exist and in endless variations: What is the extent of southern European immigration to western Europe in search of jobs? How many refugees from Afghanistan, Ethiopia, or the Sudan are there in surrounding countries? How many undocumented aliens are there in the United States? How many Palestinians are there in the Middle East (they are politically inconvenient to enumerate everywhere)? How many Amerindians exist (remain, preserve their original language and a mode of life unassimilated by the larger national culture) in the countries of South America? How many people have died or emigrated as a result of the civil violence in Central America?

Still, much information is accurate, well founded, and updated regularly. The sources of these data are censuses; national population registers (cumulated periodically); registration of migration, births, and deaths, and so on; sample surveys to establish demographic conditions; and the like.

Area and population

country	area			population (latest estimate)					population (most recent census)				
	square miles	square kilometres	rank	total midyear 1989	rank	density		% annual growth rate 1984–89	census year	total	male (%)	female (%)	urban (%)
						per sq mi	per sq km						
Afghanistan	251,825	652,225	40	14,825,000	53	58.9	22.7	1.4	1979	13,051,358[1]	51.4	48.6	15.1
Albania	11,100	28,748	126	3,197,000	109	288.0	111.2	2.0	1989	3,182,417	51.5	48.5	35.5
Algeria	919,595	2,381,741	10	24,579,000	33	26.7	10.3	3.1	1987[3]	23,038,942	49.7[2]	50.3[2]	49.7
American Samoa	77	199	195	38,200	191	496.1	192.0	1.8	1980	32,297	50.7	49.3	17.5
Andorra	181	468	177	50,000	187	276.2	106.8	3.8	1986	45,877	53.1	46.9	64.7
Angola	481,354	1,246,700	21	9,739,000	67	20.2	7.8	2.7	1970	5,673,046	52.1	47.9	14.2
Anguilla	35	91	203	7,300	206	208.6	80.2	0.8	1984	6,987	49.1	50.9	—
Antigua and Barbuda	171	442	179	78,400	178	458.5	177.4	0.9	1970	65,525	47.23	52.8[3]	30.8[2]
Argentina	1,073,399	2,780,092	8	32,425,000	29	30.2	11.7	1.5	1980	27,947,446	49.2	50.8	86.3
Aruba	75	193	196	61,300	183	817.3	317.6	−0.7	1981	60,312	48.6	51.4	...
Australia	2,966,200	7,682,300	6	16,804,000	47	5.7	2.2	1.5	1986	16,018,350	49.9	50.1	85.5[2]
Austria	32,377	83,857	109	7,603,000	79	234.8	90.7	0.1	1981	7,555,338	47.4	52.6	55.1
Bahamas, The	5,382	13,939	140	249,000	158	46.3	17.9	1.7	1980	209,505[4]	48.8	51.2	54.4
Bahrain	267	691	169	489,000	143	1,831.5	707.7	3.7	1981	350,798	58.4	41.6	80.7
Bangladesh	55,598	143,998	90	110,290,000	10	1,983.7	765.9	2.4	1981	89,912,000	51.5	48.5	15.7
Barbados	166	430	180	255,000	155	1,536.1	593.0	0.3	1980	248,983	47.6	52.4	40.1[5]
Belgium	11,783	30,518	124	9,878,000	66	838.3	323.7	0.0	1981	9,848,647	48.7	51.3	72.4[5]
Belize	8,867	22,965	133	185,000	162	20.9	8.1	2.6	1980	145,353	50.6	49.4	52.0
Benin	43,450	112,600	96	4,592,000	95	105.7	40.8	3.2	1979	3,331,210	47.9	52.1	26.5
Bermuda	21	54	206	58,800	185	2,800.0	1,088.9	0.8	1980[6]	54,050	48.9	51.1	100.0
Bhutan	18,150	47,000	118	1,408,000	127	77.6	30.0	2.2	1980	1,165,000	51.4[5]	48.6[5]	3.9[7]
Bolivia	424,164	1,098,581	27	7,193,000	83	17.0	6.5	2.8	1976	4,613,486	49.1	50.9	41.7
Botswana	224,607	581,730	45	1,250,000	130	5.6	2.1	3.7	1981	941,027	47.1	52.9	15.9
Brazil	3,286,488	8,511,965	5	147,404,000	6	44.9	17.3	2.1	1980[3]	119,002,706	49.7	50.3	67.6
British Virgin Islands	59	153	199	12,500	202	211.9	81.7	1.3	1980[9]	10,985	51.1	49.9	12.0
Brunei	2,226	5,765	150	251,000	157	112.8	43.5	2.8	1981	192,832	53.4	46.6	59.4
Bulgaria	42,855	110,994	98	8,987,000	69	209.7	81.9	0.1	1985	8,942,976	49.5	50.5	58.0[10]
Burkina Faso	105,869	274,200	68	8,714,000	72	82.3	31.8	2.8	1985[3]	7,964,705	48.1	51.9	11.7
Burundi	10,747	27,834	129	5,287,000	91	492.0	189.9	2.9	1979[11]	4,114,135	48.3	51.7	8.2[2]
Cameroon	179,714	465,458	49	11,407,000	60	63.5	24.5	2.9	1976	7,663,246	49.0	51.0	28.5
Canada	3,849,675	9,970,610	2	26,189,000	32	6.8	2.6	1.0	1986	25,354,064	49.3	50.7	75.9[2]
Cape Verde	1,557	4,033	152	337,000	153	216.4	83.6	1.0	1980[3]	295,073	46.3	53.7	35.1
Cayman Islands	102	264	191	25,300	195	248.0	95.8	4.9	1979	16,677[12]	48.6	51.4	100.0
Central African Republic	240,324	622,436	42	2,813,000	114	11.7	4.5	1.8	1975	2,088,000	48.5[3]	51.5[3]	27.4
Chad	495,755	1,284,000	20	5,538,000	89	11.2	4.3	2.5	1975	4,029,917	47.7	52.3	16.0
Chile	292,135	756,626	37	12,961,000	56	44.4	17.1	1.7	1982	11,329,736	49.0	51.0	82.2
China	3,696,100	9,572,900	3	1,104,275,000	1	298.8	115.4	1.4	1982	1,008,175,288	51.5	48.5	21.2
Christmas Island	52	135	200	1,200	213	23.1	8.9	−13.5	1988	1,229	55.1	44.9	—
Cocos (Keeling) Islands	5.6	14.4	211	600	214	107.1	41.7	2.0	1986	616	53.7[13]	46.3[13]	—
Colombia	440,831	1,141,748	26	32,317,000	30	73.3	28.3	2.1	1985	30,062,193	49.5	50.5	63.6[14]
Comoros	719	1,862	158	448,000	145	623.1	240.6	3.4	1980	335,150	49.9	50.1	23.2
Congo	132,047	342,000	57	2,245,000	120	17.0	6.6	3.6	1984	1,912,429	48.5[15]	51.5[15]	51.1
Cook Islands	91	236	194	16,900	198	185.7	71.6	−0.3	1986	19,369	52.2	47.8	...
Costa Rica	19,730	51,100	116	2,941,000	112	149.1	57.6	2.8	1984	2,416,809	50.0	50.0	43.9
Côte d'Ivoire	123,847	320,763	63	12,135,000	57	98.0	37.8	4.3	1975	6,702,866	51.8	48.2	32.0
Cuba	42,804	110,861	99	10,540,000	62	246.2	95.1	1.1	1981	9,723,605	50.6	49.4	69.0
Cyprus	3,572	9,251	147	733,000	139	205.2	79.2	1.1	1982[3]	642,731	49.7	50.3	63.5
Czechoslovakia	49,382	127,900	93	15,636,000	50	316.6	122.3	0.2	1980	15,283,095	48.7	51.3	65.5
Denmark	16,638	43,092	119	5,135,000	93	308.6	119.2	0.1	1989[16]	5,129,254	49.3	50.7	84.4[17]
Djibouti	8,950	23,200	132	512,000	142	57.2	22.1	4.8	1960–61	81,200	...	...	75.0[18]
Dominica	290	750	167	82,800	176	285.5	110.4	1.4	1981[6]	73,795	49.8	50.2	...
Dominican Republic	18,704	48,443	117	7,012,000	84	374.9	144.7	2.0	1981	5,647,977	50.1	49.9	52.0
Ecuador	103,930	269,178	69	10,490,000	63	100.9	39.0	2.9	1982	8,060,712	49.9	50.1	49.2
Egypt	385,229	997,739	29	51,748,000	21	134.3	51.9	2.7	1986	48,205,049	51.1	48.9	43.9
El Salvador	8,124	21,041	134	5,138,000	92	632.4	244.2	1.5	1971	3,554,648	49.6	50.4	39.4

The statistics provided for area and population by country are ranked, and the population densities based on those values are also provided. The population densities, for purposes of comparison within this table, are calculated on the bases of the 1989 mid-year population estimate as shown and of total area of the country. Elsewhere in individual country presentations the reader may find densities calculated on more specific population figures and more specialized area bases: land area for Finland (because of its many lakes), or ice-free area for Greenland (most of which is ice cap). The data in this section conclude with the estimated average annual growth rate for the country (including both natural growth and net migration) during the five-year period, 1984–89.

In the section containing census data, information supplied includes the census total (usually de facto, the population actually present, rather than de jure, the population legally resident, who might be anywhere); the male–female breakdown; the proportion that is urban (according to the country's own definition of the term "urban," which differs very much from country to country); and finally an analysis of the age structure of the population by 15-year age groups. This last analysis may be particularly useful in distinguishing the general type of population being recorded—young, fast-growing nations show a high proportion of people under 30 (some countries like Jordan or Mayotte have more than 50% of their population under 15 years), while other nations (for example Sweden, which suffered no age-group losses in World War II) exhibit quite uniform proportions among age groups.

Finally, a section is provided giving the population of each country at 10-year intervals from 1940 to 2010. The data for years past represent the best available analysis of the published data by the country itself, by the demographers of the United Nations, or by the editors of Britannica. The projections for 1990, 2000, and 2010 similarly, represent the best fit of available data through the late-1980s with projected population structure and growth rates during the next 21 years. The evidence of the last 20 years with respect to similar estimates published around 1970, however, shows how cloudy is the glass through which these numbers are read. In 1970 no respectable Western analyst would have imagined proposing that mainland China could achieve the degree of birth control that it has since then (as evidenced in the 1982 census); on the other hand, even the Chinese admit that their methods have been somewhat Draconian and that they expect some backlash in terms of higher birth-rates among those who have so far postponed larger families. How much is "some" by 2000? Compound that problem with all the social, economic, political, and biological factors that can affect 200 countries' populations, and the difficulty facing the prospective compiler of such projections may be appreciated.

Specific data about the vital rates affecting the data in this table may be found in great detail in both the country statistical boxes in "The Nations of the World" section and in the *Vital statistics, marriage, family* table, beginning at page 780.

Percentages in this table for male and female population will always total 100.0, but percentages by age group may not for reasons such as nonresponse on census forms, "don't know" responses, which are common in countries with poor birth registration systems, and the like.

age distribution (%)						population (by decade, '000s)								country
0–14	15–29	30–44	45–59	60–74	75 and older	1940	1950	1960	1970	1980	1990 projection	2000 projection	2010 projection	
44.5	26.9	15.8	8.6	3.6	0.6	...	8,150	9,829	12,431	14,985	15,592	24,501	31,736	Afghanistan
35.4[2]	29.3[2]	17.0[2]	11.3[2]	5.4[2]	1.6[2]	1,088	1,215	1,607	2,136	2,671	3,278	4,020	4,930	Albania
46.0[2]	27.2[2]	12.8[2]	8.3[2]	4.4[2]	1.4[2]	7,688	8,956	10,800	14,330	18,666	25,337	33,088	40,413	Algeria
40.9	28.8	16.0	9.4	4.0	0.9	13	19	20	27	32	40	48	58	American Samoa
19.0	27.3	26.4	14.8	9.4	3.1	5	6	8	19	33	51	62	75	Andorra
41.7	23.2	17.0	7.4	3.8	1.0	3,738	4,131	4,816	5,588	7,722	10,002	13,207	17,437	Angola
34.9	28.5	13.6	8.9	10.1	4.0	...		6	6	7	7	8	8	Anguilla
44.0	24.2	12.0	11.7	—8.0—		34	45	55	66	73	79	86	93	Antigua and Barbuda
30.4	23.9	18.8	15.1	9.0	2.8	14,169	17,150	20,611	23,788	28,237	32,880	37,197	41,507	Argentina
25.9	30.6	21.3	12.7	7.4	2.1	31	51	57	61	60	62	66	68	Aruba
23.1	25.2	22.1	14.6	11.0	4.0	7,079	8,219	10,315	12,552	14,741	17,076	19,787	22,218	Australia
19.9	23.6	20.1	17.1	13.2	6.1	6,684	6,935	7,048	7,447	7,549	7,614	7,676	7,583	Austria
38.1	27.8	17.9	9.8	5.1	1.3	70	79	113	169	210	253	301	357	Bahamas, The
32.9	34.5	20.0	8.8	3.1	0.7	90	127	162	215	337	503	654	825	Bahrain
46.6	24.6	14.9	8.2	—5.7—		41,259	45,482	54,699	68,171	88,507	113,005	139,693	167,633	Bangladesh
28.9	32.3	14.2	11.2	—13.3—		179	209	232	235	249	256	262	268	Barbados
20.0	23.7	19.1	18.6	12.8	5.8	8,301	8,639	9,153	9,690	9,859	9,881	9,918	9,955	Belgium
46.2	27.1	11.8	8.4	4.7	1.8	56	68	90	120	145	190	230	270	Belize
45.9[5]	25.4[5]	15.1[5]	8.6[5]	3.9[5]	0.9[5]	1,375	1,528	2,025	2,718	3,494	4,741	6,561	8,987	Benin
22.7	27.5	22.2	15.7	9.0	2.9	31	37	43	53	55	59	65	70	Bermuda
39.2[8]	26.5[8]	16.3[8]	10.9[8]	—7.1—		500	726	853	1,045	1,165	1,442	1,812	2,266	Bhutan
41.5	27.0	15.4	9.8	4.6	1.7	2,508	2,765	3,405	4,265	5,600	7,400	9,837	12,922	Bolivia
56.5	19.9	10.2	6.6	3.4	3.4	278	407	490	590	795	1,295	1,821	2,536	Botswana
39.1	28.6	16.4	10.0	—5.9—		41,525	52,901	71,539	93,139	121,286	150,368	179,487	207,454	Brazil
34.0	29.0	18.7	9.7	6.3	2.3	7	7	7	10	11	13	14	16	British Virgin Islands
38.5	32.7	16.4	7.9	—4.5—		36	48	84	129	187	258	341	451	Brunei
22.2	20.4[2]	20.4[2]	19.4[2]	13.1[2]	4.5[2]	6,344	7,251	7,867	8,490	8,862	8,995	9,075	9,155	Bulgaria
48.3	23.4	13.4	8.7	4.7	1.4	3,036	3,584	4,350	5,412	6,599	8,948	11,657	15,186	Burkina Faso
42.4	29.4	13.4	8.2	4.8	1.8	1,887	2,435	2,908	3,350	4,120	5,439	7,235	9,500	Burundi
43.4	24.3	16.6	9.9	4.3	1.5	...	4,888	5,609	6,727	8,700	11,742	15,387	19,997	Cameroon
21.4	25.8	23.0	14.9	10.9	4.1	11,693	13,737	17,909	21,324	24,067	26,442	29,110	32,047	Canada
46.0	27.6	9.1	9.0	6.3	2.0	181	148	199	272	295	339	412	489	Cape Verde
29.1	25.8	22.1	13.1	7.3	2.6	7	7	8	11	17	26	30	34	Cayman Islands
43.5	23.5	17.1	12.4	2.7	0.8	991	1,311	1,500	1,793	2,333	2,875	3,566	4,424	Central African Republic
40.6	28.3	17.2	9.5	—4.4—		2,351	2,658	3,064	3,652	4,477	5,678	7,337	9,491	Chad
31.9	29.1	19.1	11.7	6.3	1.9	5,063	6,091	7,585	9,368	11,104	13,173	15,272	17,182	Chile
33.6	29.1	17.5	12.2	6.3	1.3	530,000	556,613	667,070	818,316	981,242	1,121,544	1,309,799	1,407,918	China[1]
35.8	—64.2—					...	1	3	3	3	1	1	1	Christmas Island
27.4[13]	28.3[13]	27.2[13]	11.2[13]	—5.9[13]—			1	1	1	1	1	1	1	Cocos (Keeling) Islands
36.1	31.2	17.2	9.5	4.6	1.4	9,097	11,268	15,321	20,884	26,670	32,961	39,302	45,298	Colombia
47.2	23.2	14.8	7.6	5.1	1.8	119	148	177	245	333	463	630	841	Comoros
45.6[15]	22.2[15]	15.5[15]	11.3[15]	4.7[15]	0.7[15]	...	815	960	1,182	1,631	2,326	3,318	4,732	Congo
37.8	29.1	14.1	11.6	5.7	1.2	13	15	18	18	18	17	16	15	Cook Islands
37.9	31.5	15.8	9.2	4.4	1.2	619	862	1,236	1,731	2,285	3,015	3,711	4,366	Costa Rica
44.5	27.0	16.7	7.8	2.8	1.2	2,350	2,775	3,865	5,550	8,320	12,657	19,289	29,398	Côte d'Ivoire
30.3	27.6	19.1	12.1	8.2	2.7	4,566	5,752	7,019	8,565	9,724	10,683	11,844	12,394	Cuba
25.0	26.6	20.1	13.8	—14.5—		413	494	573	615	628	742	828	925	Cyprus
24.3	22.9	19.8	17.2	11.5	4.3	14,713	12,389	13,654	14,334	15,265	15,664	16,086	16,456	Czechoslovakia
17.6	22.8	22.8	16.4	13.7	6.7	3,832	4,271	4,581	4,929	5,123	5,141	5,176	5,065	Denmark
38.0[18]	34.0[18]	17.0[18]	—11.0[18]—			44	60	78	158	355	528	709	953	Djibouti
39.8	28.6	11.9	9.2	7.4	3.1	45	51	60	70	74	84	92	102	Dominica
43.9[5]	29.3[5]	14.2[5]	8.2[5]	3.5[5]	1.0[5]	1,759	2,313	3,160	4,343	5,622	7,170	8,621	9,904	Dominican Republic
41.9	28.1	15.4	8.6	4.5	1.5	2,546	3,307	4,421	5,958	8,123	10,782	13,939	17,403	Ecuador
39.9[19,20]	26.7[19,20]	16.6[19,20]	10.6[19,20]	5.2[19,20]	1.0[19,20]	16,942	20,461	26,085	33,329	40,546	53,170	65,452	76,900	Egypt
46.2	25.1	15.2	8.2	4.3	1.0	1,550	1,931	2,527	3,534	4,508	5,252	6,739	8,491	El Salvador

Area and population (continued)

country	area square miles	area square kilometres	rank	population (latest estimate) total midyear 1989	rank	density per sq mi	density per sq km	% annual growth rate 1984–89	census year	total	male (%)	female (%)	urban (%)
Equatorial Guinea	10,831	28,051	128	343,000	150	31.7	12.2	2.3	1983	300,000	48.1	51.9	27.6
Ethiopia	472,400	1,223,500	24	48,898,000	22	103.5	40.0	2.9	1984	42,184,966	49.8	50.2	10.2
Faeroe Islands	540	1,399	160	47,800	188	88.5	34.2	1.2	1987	46,369	52.3	47.7	96.2
Falkland Islands	4,700	12,173	142	2,000	210	0.4	0.2	1.0	1986	1,885	54.7[21]	45.3[21]	56.8[21]
Fiji	7,056	18,274	137	734,000	138	104.0	40.2	1.4	1986	715,375	50.7	49.3	38.7
Finland	130,559	338,145	58	4,960,000	94	38.0	14.7	0.3	1980	4,784,710	48.3	51.7	59.9
France	210,026	543,965	46	56,107,000	17	267.1	103.1	0.4	1982	54,334,871	49.0	51.0	73.2[5]
French Guiana	33,399	86,504	108	95,000	175	2.8	1.1	3.6	1982	73,022	52.7	47.3	73.4
French Polynesia	1,544	4,000	153	192,000	161	124.4	48.0	2.5	1983	166,753	51.1	48.9	39.7
Gabon	103,347	267,667	71	1,245,000	131	12.0	4.7	1.9	1960–61	448,564	49.1[2]	50.9[2]	40.9[2]
Gambia, The	4,127	10,689	145	835,000	135	202.3	78.1	3.0	1983	695,886	50.7[14]	49.3[14]	21.2
Gaza Strip	140	363	184	588,000	140	4,200.0	1,619.8	3.2	1986[16]	527,000	49.9	50.1	...
Germany, East	41,827	108,333	101	16,613,000	48	397.2	153.4	–0.1	1981	16,705,635	47.0	53.0	76.4
Germany, West	96,027	248,709	74	61,131,000	13	636.6	245.8	–0.0	1987	61,077,042	48.0	52.0	85.5[2]
Ghana	92,098	238,533	78	14,566,000	54	158.2	61.1	3.3	1984	12,296,081	49.3	50.7	32.0
Gibraltar	2.3	5.8	213	30,200	192	13,727.3	5,206.9	1.0	1981[22]	26,479	52.2	47.8	...
Greece	50,949	131,957	91	10,096,000	65	198.2	76.5	0.4	1981	9,740,417	49.1	50.9	58.1
Greenland	840,000	2,175,600	13	55,400	186	0.1	0.0	1.0	1988[16]	54,524	54.4	45.6	79.3
Grenada	133	345	186	96,600	173	726.3	280.0	0.9	1981	89,088	47.1[5]	52.9[5]	25.3[23]
Guadeloupe	687	1,780	159	341,000	151	496.4	191.6	0.6	1982[3]	327,002	49.0	51.0	43.5[5]
Guam	209	541	173	129,000	168	617.2	238.4	2.2	1980	105,979	52.2	47.8	39.5
Guatemala	42,042	108,889	100	8,935,000	70	212.5	82.1	2.9	1981[3]	6,043,559	49.8	50.2	34.3
Guernsey	30	78	204	59,800	184	1,993.3	766.7	0.8	1986[24]	55,482	48.4	51.6	...
Guinea	94,926	245,857	75	6,705,000	86	70.6	27.3	2.5	1983	5,781,014	48.6	51.4	26.0
Guinea-Bissau	13,948	36,125	122	953,000	133	68.3	26.4	2.2	1979	767,739	48.2	51.8	14.0
Guyana	83,000	215,000	81	754,000	136	9.1	3.5	–0.1	1980	758,619	49.5	50.5	30.5[5]
Haiti	10,579	27,400	130	5,520,000	90	521.8	201.5	1.3	1982	5,053,792	48.5	51.5	20.6
Honduras	43,277	112,088	97	4,530,000	97	104.7	40.4	3.5	1974	2,656,948	49.5	50.5	37.5
Hong Kong	403	1,045	162	5,754,000	88	14,277.9	5,506.2	1.3	1986[25]	5,396,000	51.4	48.6	93.1
Hungary	35,920	93,033	105	10,580,000	61	294.5	113.7	–0.2	1980	10,709,463	48.4	51.6	53.2
Iceland	39,769	103,000	102	252,000	156	6.3	2.4	1.1	1988[16]	251,743	50.2	49.8	90.3
India	1,222,559	3,166,414	7	835,812,000	2	683.7	264.0	2.1	1981	685,184,692	50.3	49.7	23.7
Indonesia	741,101	1,919,443	15	177,046,000	5	238.9	92.2	2.1	1980	147,490,298	49.7	50.3	22.3
Iran	636,372	1,648,196	17	54,333,000	20	85.4	33.0	3.7	1986	49,445,010	51.1	48.9	54.3
Iraq	167,975	435,052	53	17,215,000	45	102.5	39.6	3.1	1987	16,335,199	51.4	48.6	70.2
Ireland	27,137	70,285	113	3,515,000	106	129.5	50.0	–0.1	1986	3,540,643	50.0	50.0	55.6[13]
Isle of Man	221	572	172	64,000	182	289.6	111.9	–0.1	1986[3]	64,282	47.9	52.1	51.1
Israel[27]	7,992	20,700	135	4,563,000	96	570.9	220.4	1.7	1983[3, 28]	4,037,620	49.8	50.2	86.9
Italy	116,324	301,277	65	57,436,000	15	493.8	190.6	0.2	1981[3]	56,556,911	48.6	51.4	66.5[5]
Jamaica	4,244	10,991	144	2,376,000	118	559.8	216.2	0.8	1982	2,190,357	49.1	50.9	47.8
Japan	145,883	377,835	56	123,120,000	7	844.0	325.9	0.5	1985	121,047,196	49.2	50.8	76.7
Jersey	45	116	201	82,600	177	1,835.6	712.1	1.1	1986[3]	80,212	48.3	51.7	...
Jordan[29]	34,343	88,947	107	3,059,000	110	89.1	34.4	3.7	1979	2,132,997	52.3	47.7	59.5
Kampuchea (Cambodia)	69,898	181,035	85	8,055,000	76	115.2	44.5	2.4	1981	6,684,000	50.0[30]	50.0[30]	15.1
Kenya	224,961	582,646	44	23,883,000	35	106.2	41.0	4.1	1979	15,327,061	49.7	50.3	15.1
Kiribati	328	849	164	69,600	180	212.2	82.0	2.2	1985	64,026	49.6	50.4	33.5
Korea, North	47,250	122,370	94	22,418,000	39	474.5	183.2	2.4	[31]	[31]	49.6[2]	50.4[2]	63.8[2]
Korea, South	38,316	99,237	103	42,380,000	23	1,106.1	427.1	1.0	1985[3]	40,448,486	50.0	50.0	65.4
Kuwait	6,880	17,818	138	2,048,000	122	297.7	114.9	4.6	1985	1,697,301	56.9	43.1	100.0
Laos	91,400	236,800	80	3,936,000	102	43.1	16.6	2.1	1985	3,584,803	50.4[2]	49.6[2]	15.9[2]
Lebanon	3,950	10,230	146	2,897,000	113	733.4	283.2	1.8	1970	2,126,325	50.8	49.2	60.1
Lesotho	11,720	30,355	125	1,715,000	125	146.3	56.5	2.6	1986[3]	1,577,536	48.2	51.8	16.0
Liberia	38,250	99,067	104	2,508,000	116	65.6	25.3	3.5	1984	2,101,628	50.6	49.4	38.8
Libya	678,400	1,757,000	16	4,080,000	100	6.0	2.3	2.3	1984	3,637,488	51.1[3]	48.9[3]	75.8[3]
Liechtenstein	62	160	198	28,300	194	456.5	176.9	1.2	1980	25,215	49.6	50.4	...
Luxembourg	999	2,586	155	377,000	148	377.4	145.8	0.6	1981	364,602	48.8	51.2	77.6[5]
Macau	6.5	16.9	210	466,000	144	71,692.3	27,574.0	4.9	1981[3]	241,729	50.9	49.1	95.4
Madagascar	226,658	587,041	43	11,602,000	59	51.2	19.8	3.2	1974–75	7,603,790	50.0	50.0	16.3
Malawi	45,747	118,484	95	8,515,000	73	186.1	71.9	3.7	1987	7,982,607	48.6	51.4	8.5[26]
Malaysia	127,584	330,442	61	17,421,000	44	136.5	52.7	2.7	1980	13,136,109	50.2	49.8	34.2
Maldives	115	298	188	209,000	159	1,817.4	701.3	3.4	1985	181,453	51.8	48.2	25.5
Mali	478,841	1,240,192	22	7,911,000	78	16.5	6.4	1.7	1987[3]	7,620,225	49.0	51.0	20.3
Malta	122	316	187	349,000	149	2,860.7	1,104.4	0.7	1985	345,418	49.2	50.8	94.3[32]
Martinique	421	1,091	161	337,000	152	800.5	308.9	0.4	1982[3]	326,717	48.5	51.5	57.1
Mauritania	398,000	1,030,700	28	1,946,000	123	4.9	1.9	2.6	1976–77	1,419,939	50.1	49.9	21.9
Mauritius	788	2,040	157	1,061,000	132	1,346.4	520.1	1.0	1983	1,002,178	49.8	50.2	41.7[33]
Mayotte	144	373	183	78,000	179	541.7	209.1	4.2	1985	67,167	49.9[34]	50.1[34]	53.3[34]
Mexico	756,066	1,958,201	14	84,275,000	11	111.5	43.0	2.0	1980	66,846,833	49.4	50.6	66.3
Monaco	0.7	1.9	215	29,100	193	41,571.4	15,315.8	0.8	1982	27,063	46.6	53.4	100.0
Mongolia	604,800	1,566,500	18	2,096,000	121	3.5	1.3	2.6	1979	1,594,800	50.1	49.9	51.2
Montserrat	40	102	202	12,000	203	300.0	117.6	0.3	1980	11,606	48.1	51.9	13.2
Morocco	177,117	458,730	51	24,530,000	34	138.5	53.5	2.9	1982	20,419,555[35]	50.1	49.9	42.7
Mozambique	308,642	799,380	35	15,293,000	51	49.5	19.1	2.6	1980	12,130,000	48.7	51.3	13.2
Myanmar (Burma)	261,228	676,577	39	40,810,000	24	156.2	60.3	2.1	1983	35,313,905	49.6	50.4	24.0
Nauru	8.2	21.2	209	9,100	204	1,109.8	429.2	2.2	1983	8,042	52.1[26, 36]	47.9[26, 36]	—
Nepal	56,827	147,181	89	18,452,000	43	324.7	125.4	2.6	1981	15,022,839	51.2	48.8	6.4
Netherlands, The	16,163	41,863	120	14,846,000	52	918.5	354.6	0.6	1988[16]	14,714,948	49.4	50.6	88.5
Netherlands Antilles	308	800	165	183,000	163	594.2	228.8	0.0	1981	171,620	48.3	51.7	...
New Caledonia	7,172	18,576	136	166,000	164	23.1	8.9	1.3	1989	164,173	51.1	48.9	58.5[18]
New Zealand	103,415	267,844	70	3,371,000	107	32.6	12.6	0.6	1986	3,307,084	49.5	50.5	83.8
Nicaragua	50,464	130,700	92	3,745,000	103	74.2	28.7	3.4	1971	1,877,952	48.3	51.7	48.0
Niger	458,075	1,186,408	25	7,523,000	80	16.4	6.3	3.4	1988[3]	7,249,596	49.6	50.4	16.2[22]
Nigeria	356,669	923,768	31	115,973,000	9	325.2	125.5	3.3	1963[37]	55,670,055	50.5	49.5	16.1
Niue	100	259	192	2,200	209	22.0	8.5	–4.9	1984	2,887	51.2	48.8	...
Norfolk Island	14	35	207	1,900	211	135.7	54.3	0.2	1986[3]	1,977	50.7	49.3	—

age distribution (%)						population (by decade, '000s)								country
0–14	15–29	30–44	45–59	60–74	75 and older	1940	1950	1960	1970	1980	1990 projection	2000 projection	2010 projection	
38.1[2]	26.0[2]	17.7[2]	11.5[2]	5.6[2]	1.1[2]	...	211	244	291	255	351	447	567	Equatorial Guinea
46.6	22.7	15.6	8.9	4.5	1.7	...	16,675	20,024	24,068	38,457	50,341	67,523	90,570	Ethiopia
24.8	—45.7—		13.8	—15.7—		27	31	35	39	43	48	54	61	Faeroe Islands
25.4[21]	22.6[21]	—38.0[21]—		—14.0[21]—		2	2	2	2	2	2	2	2	Falkland Islands
38.2	29.5	17.8	9.6	3.8	0.8	218	289	394	520	634	741	837	931	Fiji
20.2	24.4	22.1	16.8	12.4	4.1	3,698	4,009	4,430	4,606	4,780	4,971	5,017	4,982	Finland
22.0	23.5	19.6	17.3	11.6	6.0	41,300	41,736	45,684	50,770	53,880	56,342	58,748	61,256	France
34.2	29.2	19.9	9.8	5.1	1.8	30	27	33	49	69	98	132	178	French Guiana
38.5	29.7	16.5	10.3	4.2	0.8	50	62	84	109	151	197	236	269	French Polynesia
35.4[2]	24.1[2]	18.1[2]	13.1[2]	7.5[2]	1.8[2]	442	405	630	950	1,064	1,273	1,603	1,978	Gabon
41.3[14]	26.5[14]	17.6[14]	8.3[14]	4.3[14]	1.7[14]	193	232	357	458	632	860	1,156	1,554	Gambia, The
49.2	—38.9—		—11.9—			...	...	370	451	607	807	1,067		Gaza Strip
19.4	24.2	20.0	17.3	12.8	6.3	16,800	18,387	17,240	17,058	16,737	16,598	16,457	16,316	Germany, East
14.6	24.0	20.1	20.6	13.6	7.2	40,600	49,986	55,433	60,714	61,566	61,156	61,409	61,663	Germany, West
45.0	26.4	14.6	8.1	4.1	1.8	3,636	5,297	6,958	8,789	11,133	15,020	20,418	27,071	Ghana
21.4	22.2	22.3	17.7	12.6	3.8	14	23	24	26	30	30	34	37	Gibraltar
23.7	21.5	19.2	18.7	12.3	4.6	7,319	7,566	8,327	8,793	9,643	10,141	10,289	10,346	Greece
24.6	32.4	23.7	13.4	4.9	1.1	19	23	33	41	50	56	62	69	Greenland
39.4[5]	31.2[5]	10.1[5]	9.2[5]	7.3[5]	2.8[5]	71	76	90	95	91	98	112	128	Grenada
31.1	29.2	16.6	12.0	7.8	2.8	180	206	265	320	327	344	368	391	Guadeloupe
34.9	30.6	19.4	10.5	3.9	0.5	22	59	67	85	107	132	165	205	Guam
44.9	26.8	14.8	8.5	3.9	1.1	2,201	3,024	4,005	5,263	6,917	9,197	12,222	15,827	Guatemala
17.6	22.8	21.0	17.3	14.4	6.9	44	44	45	51	55	60	65	71	Guernsey
43.1[2]	26.2[2]	16.3[2]	9.6[2]	4.2[2]	0.7[2]	...	3,245	3,660	4,388	5,407	6,876	8,879	11,451	Guinea
44.3	25.5	15.1	8.2	4.7	2.2	341	411	520	653	787	973	1,200	1,480	Guinea-Bissau
40.8	30.5	14.0	8.8	4.4	1.2	344	423	560	702	759	754	809	868	Guyana
39.2	26.9	15.6	10.0	5.4	2.9	2,827	3,097	3,723	4,234	4,922	5,590	6,338	7,187	Haiti
48.1	25.8	13.9	7.8	3.6	0.9	1,146	1,390	1,873	2,553	3,316	4,674	6,203	7,828	Honduras
23.1	29.9	21.2	14.3	9.1	2.4	1,786	1,974	3,074	3,942	5,063	5,841	6,449	6,737	Hong Kong
21.8	20.7	—40.6—		—16.9—		9,280	9,338	9,984	10,353	10,708	10,563	10,396	10,231	Hungary
25.0	25.9	21.6	13.1	9.9	4.5	121	143	176	204	228	255	268	277	Iceland
39.5	25.9	17.4	10.7	—6.5—		317,000	352,664	427,802	543,132	687,057	853,373	1,042,530	1,225,305	India
40.8	27.0	16.4	10.2	4.5	1.1	70,500	75,449	92,701	119,467	146,449	180,763	214,410	246,102	Indonesia
44.5[20]	25.2[20]	14.8[20]	10.1[20]	3.8[20]	1.0[20]	14,000	16,913	21,554	28,359	38,783	56,293	73,801	93,553	Iran
48.9[26]	24.5[26]	12.3[26]	8.2[26]	4.2[26]	1.9[26]	3,745	5,180	6,847	9,356	13,043	17,754	24,023	30,932	Iraq
30.3[13]	24.6[13]	17.2[13]	13.1[13]	10.9[13]	3.8[13]	2,958	2,969	2,834	2,954	3,415	3,509	3,447	3,387	Ireland
17.6	20.2	19.0	16.0	17.4	9.2	52	55	49	52	64	64	63	62	Isle of Man
32.6	26.4	18.0	12.3	9.4	3.1	...	2,114	2,958	3,896	4,616	5,490	6,508		Israel[27]
21.4	22.4	20.0	18.7	12.7	4.7	43,840	46,769	50,223	53,565	56,434	57,461	57,544	56,489	Italy
38.4	28.8	13.8	9.4	6.9	2.6	1,212	1,403	1,629	1,891	2,133	2,396	2,602	2,826	Jamaica
21.5	20.7	23.9	19.2	10.8	3.9	73,075	83,200	93,419	103,720	116,807	123,700	129,380	131,990	Japan
15.3	25.8	22.7	16.9	12.8	6.4	51	57	63	71	76	83	92	102	Jersey
51.6	23.4	13.4	7.4	3.1	1.1	...	1,095	1,384	1,795	2,181	3,173	4,583	6,620	Jordan[29]
43.8[30]	24.9[30]	16.8[30]	9.8[30]	4.1[30]	0.6[30]	3,400	4,346	5,433	6,938	6,400	8,246	10,046	11,539	Kampuchea (Cambodia)
51.4	24.8	13.2	7.0	3.0	0.6	4,470	6,018	8,115	11,225	16,667	24,872	37,505	56,629	Kenya
38.9	29.9	16.1	9.3	4.9	0.9	29	33	41	49	57	71	88	108	Kiribati
38.7[2]	29.2[2]	16.6[2]	9.8[2]	4.7[2]	1.0[2]	...	9,740	10,526	13,892	18,025	22,937	28,165	33,115	Korea, North
29.9	31.3	19.5	12.5	5.5	1.3	...	21,147	25,142	32,976	38,124	42,791	46,617	48,372	Korea, South
36.8	28.3	14.1	8.6	1.8	0.4	...	145	292	748	1,370	2,143	2,841	3,516	Kuwait
42.5[2]	26.6[2]	16.2[2]	9.7[2]	4.3[2]	0.7[2]	1,075	1,949	2,382	2,962	3,292	4,024	4,964	6,016	Laos
42.6	23.8	16.7	9.1	—7.7—		965	1,443	1,857	2,469	2,669	2,965	3,603	4,170	Lebanon
39.1[20]	25.5[20]	15.5[20]	10.4[20]	5.2[20]	2.3[20]	566	766	885	1,043	1,358	1,760	2,282	2,958	Lesotho
43.2	28.2	14.7	7.7	4.4	1.8	...	758	1,004	1,393	1,864	2,591	3,596	4,989	Liberia
49.7[3]	25.3[3]	13.7[3]	7.4[3]	3.2[3]	0.6[3]	900	1,029	1,349	1,982	3,054	4,206	5,559	6,517	Libya
23.0	26.5	24.1	14.1	9.2	3.1	11	14	16	21	26	29	32	37	Liechtenstein
18.5	23.7	21.2	18.7	12.8	5.1	296	296	314	339	364	377	378	376	Luxembourg
22.9	36.2	16.7	12.7	8.8	2.6	375	188	169	221	258	514	819	1,169	Macau
44.4	25.7	14.2	10.0	4.6	1.1	4,034	4,230	5,309	6,742	8,777	11,980	16,562	22,594	Madagascar
44.6[26]	25.7[26]	14.2[26]	9.0[26]	4.3[26]	2.0[26]	1,696	3,033	3,481	4,511	6,137	8,831	12,201	16,573	Malawi
39.5	29.1	16.5	9.2	4.6	1.1	...	6,187	7,908	10,466	13,764	17,886	21,485	24,363	Malaysia
44.6[26]	24.8[26]	16.4[26]	9.6[26]	3.5[26]	0.6[26]	81	82	106	128	155	216	300	350	Maldives
44.0[20]	24.9[20]	16.1[20]	8.7[20]	4.8[20]	1.5[20]	3,388	3,426	4,224	5,690	6,791	8,047	9,535	11,299	Mali
24.1	23.2	23.0	15.4	10.5	3.8	270	308	329	326	324	351	368	380	Malta
30.5	29.3	15.9	13.0	8.2	3.0	200	222	252	287	326	338	346	349	Martinique
45.7[5]	26.1[5]	14.8[5]	8.7[5]	4.0[5]	0.6[5]	666	781	970	1,245	1,548	1,999	2,673	3,616	Mauritania
32.6	31.7	17.8	10.9	5.7	1.3	428	479	662	824	957	1,071	1,177	1,294	Mauritius
50.2[34]	23.4[34]	13.9[34]	7.0[34]	3.8[34]	1.7[34]	16	17	25	35	52	81	119	175	Mayotte
43.0	27.8	14.9	8.4	4.0	1.8	19,815	25,828	34,993	48,934	69,655	85,784	100,039	116,663	Mexico
11.9	—38.4—		—49.7—			20	22	23	24	27	29	31	31	Monaco
43.1[5]	26.2[5]	16.3[5]	9.4[5]	4.1[5]	0.9[5]	750	747	931	1,248	1,663	2,150	2,778	3,590	Mongolia
31.5	27.2	13.8	10.7	11.6	5.3	15	14	12	12	12	12	12	13	Montserrat
42.2	28.3	14.1	9.2	4.8	1.5	7,750	8,953	11,640	15,126	19,082	25,228	31,407	36,973	Morocco
44.4	26.7	15.9	8.7	3.6	0.7	...	6,458	7,584	9,390	12,103	15,696	20,463	26,593	Mozambique
37.6[2]	28.4[2]	17.6[2]	9.8[2]	5.6[2]	1.1[2]	16,119	18,489	22,063	26,997	33,116	41,675	51,129	60,567	Myanmar (Burma)
44.1[26,36]	33.1[26,36]	11.4[26,36]	8.5[26,36]	1.9[26,36]	1.0[26,36]	3	4	5	7	8	9	11	14	Nauru
41.4	25.5	17.4	10.0	4.7	1.0	7,000	8,000	9,180	11,232	14,642	18,910	23,176	27,807	Nepal
18.5	25.4	23.3	15.8	11.8	5.2	8,834	10,027	11,417	12,958	14,150	14,927	15,719	15,743	Netherlands, The
30.0	29.9	19.5	11.3	6.7	2.6	77	112	136	163	171	183	188	192	Netherlands Antilles
36.2[18]	26.9[18]	19.5[18]	11.2[18]	5.1[18]	1.1[18]	53	59	79	110	140	169	199	230	New Caledonia
24.4	26.0	20.8	14.1	10.7	4.0	1,636	1,908	2,372	2,820	3,170	3,390	3,584	3,789	New Zealand
48.1	25.6	14.1	7.4	3.8	1.1	825	1,109	1,472	1,972	2,771	3,871	5,261	6,824	Nicaragua
46.7[2]	25.6[2]	14.9[2]	8.0[2]	3.9[2]	0.9[2]	1,700	2,291	2,913	4,016	5,568	7,779	10,656	14,484	Niger
43.0	31.9	16.5	5.1	2.5	1.0	...	33,320	42,366	56,346	87,255	119,812	166,012	224,314	Nigeria
38.2	26.9	14.4	11.3	6.3	2.8	4	4	4	4	3	2	2	2	Niue
24.2	16.5	22.7	20.0	—16.7—		1	1	1	2	2	2	2	2	Norfolk Island

Area and population (continued)

country	area			population (latest estimate)				population (most recent census)				
	square miles	square kilo- metres	rank	total midyear 1989	rank	density		% annual growth rate 1984–89	census year	total	male (%)	female (%)	urban (%)
						per sq mi	per sq km						
Norway	125,050	323,878	62	4,228,000	98	33.8	13.1	0.4	1988[16]	4,198,289	49.5	50.5	70.3[21]
Oman	120,000	300,000	66	1,422,000	126	11.9	4.7	3.6	[31]	[31]	52.9[2]	47.1[2]	8.8[2]
Pacific Is., Trust Territory of the													
Marshall Islands	70	181	197	43,900	190	627.1	242.5	4.0	1980	30,873	51.3	48.7	47.8
Micronesia, Federated States of	271	702	168	105,000	172	387.5	149.6	3.5	1980	73,160	51.1	48.9	19.4
Northern Mariana Islands	184	477	176	22,600	197	122.8	47.4	3.0	1980	16,780	52.5	47.5	16.0
Palau	188	488	175	14,200	200	75.5	29.1	1.3	1986	13,873	53.3	46.7	51.4[21]
Pakistan	339,697	879,811	33	118,820,000	8	349.8	135.1	3.6	1981[38]	84,253,644	52.5	47.5	28.3
Panama	29,762	77,082	111	2,370,000	119	79.6	30.7	2.1	1980	1,831,399	50.7	49.3	49.7
Papua New Guinea	178,704	462,840	50	3,593,000	105	20.1	7.8	2.2	1980	3,010,727	52.3	47.7	13.1
Paraguay	157,048	406,752	54	4,157,000	99	26.5	10.2	3.1	1982	3,035,360	50.1	49.9	42.8
Peru	496,225	1,285,216	19	21,792,000	40	43.9	17.0	2.6	1981	17,005,210	49.7	50.3	64.9
Philippines	115,800	300,000	67	59,906,000	14	517.3	199.7	2.3	1980	48,098,460	50.2	49.8	37.3
Pitcairn Island	1.7	4.5	214	56	215	32.9	12.4	−0.4	1989	56	54.7[13]	45.3[13]	—
Poland	120,727	312,683	64	37,875,000	26	313.7	121.1	0.5	1988	37,769,000	48.7[34]	51.3[34]	61.2
Portugal	35,672	92,389	106	10,372,000	64	290.8	112.3	0.6	1981[3]	9,833,014	48.2	51.8	29.7
Puerto Rico	3,515	9,104	148	3,308,000	108	941.1	363.4	0.2	1980	3,196,520	48.7	51.3	66.8
Qatar	969	2,510	156	427,000	146	97.6	37.7	6.4	1986	369,079	67.2	32.8	88.0[2]
Réunion	4,377	11,337	143	584,000	141	602.7	232.7	1.7	1982[3]	515,798	49.1	50.9	52.8
Romania	91,699	237,500	79	23,168,000	38	252.7	97.5	0.5	1977	21,559,910	49.3	50.7	47.5
Rwanda	10,169	26,338	131	6,989,000	85	687.3	265.4	3.4	1978	4,830,984	48.9	51.1	4.5
St. Helena and Ascension	159	412	181	7,300	207	45.9	17.7	1.0	1987[39]	6,366	51.5	48.5	20.9
St. Kitts and Nevis	104	269	190	44,100	189	424.0	163.9	−0.3	1980	43,309	48.1	51.9	37.1
St. Lucia	238	617	171	150,000	167	630.3	243.1	2.3	1980	120,300	47.2	52.8	...
St. Pierre and Miquelon	93	242	193	6,200	208	66.7	25.6	0.4	1982	6,041	49.4	50.6	...
St. Vincent and the Grenadines	150	389	182	114,000	170	760.0	293.1	1.1	1980	97,845	48.5[5]	51.5[5]	25.7[5]
San Marino	24	61	205	22,900	196	954.2	375.4	0.5	1976	19,149	50.4	49.6	90.1[40]
São Tomé and Príncipe	386	1,001	163	118,000	169	305.7	117.9	2.6	1981	96,611	49.7	50.3	...
Saudi Arabia	865,000	2,240,000	12	13,592,000	55	15.7	6.1	4.1	1974	6,726,466	53.2	46.8	65.9[5]
Senegal	75,955	196,722	82	7,400,000	81	97.4	37.6	3.0	1976	4,907,057	49.5	50.5	26.7
Seychelles	175	453	178	67,100	181	383.4	148.1	0.7	1977	61,898	50.4	49.6	37.2
Sierra Leone	27,699	71,740	112	3,957,000	101	142.9	55.2	1.9	1985	3,517,530	49.6	50.4	28.3[2]
Singapore	240	622	170	2,674,000	115	11,141.7	4,299.0	1.1	1980	2,413,945	51.0	49.0	100.0
Solomon Islands	10,954	28,370	127	308,000	154	28.1	10.9	3.2	1986	285,176	51.9	48.1	9.3[20]
Somalia	246,000	637,000	41	7,339,000	82	29.8	11.5	3.5	1975	3,253,024[1]	49.4[5]	50.6[5]	30.2[5]
South Africa[41]	473,290	1,225,815	23	36,692,000	27	77.5	29.9	2.1	1985[42]	27,722,100	51.2	48.8	55.9[43]
Bophuthatswana	16,988	44,000	—	1,914,000	—	112.7	43.5	2.4	1980	1,287,814	46.9[23]	53.1[23]	14.2[23]
Ciskei	2,996	7,760	—	824,000	—	275.0	106.2	2.4	1985	831,636	47.3	52.7	49.8
Transkei	16,855	43,653	—	3,224,000	—	191.3	73.9	2.4	1980	2,334,946	41.2[23]	58.8[23]	3.2[23]
Venda	2,771	7,176	—	506,000	—	182.6	70.5	2.4	1985	459,986	41.0[21]	59.0[21]	2.1[21]
South West Africa/Namibia	317,818	823,144	34	1,270,000	129	4.0	1.5	2.6	1981	1,033,196	49.2	50.8	26.0
Spain	194,898	504,783	48	39,159,000	25	200.9	77.6	0.4	1981	37,746,260	49.1	50.9	72.8[5]
Sri Lanka	25,332	65,610	114	16,842,000	46	664.9	256.7	1.5	1981	14,848,364	50.8	49.2	21.5
Sudan, The	966,757	2,503,890	9	27,268,000	31	28.2	10.9	3.8	1983	20,564,364	50.8	49.2	20.6[2]
Suriname	63,251	163,820	87	405,000	147	6.4	2.5	1.5	1980	354,860	49.5	50.5	44.8[5]
Swaziland	6,704	17,364	139	746,000	137	111.3	43.0	3.3	1986	681,059	47.2	52.8	22.8
Sweden	173,732	449,964	52	8,498,000	74	48.9	18.9	0.4	1988[16]	8,414,083	49.4	50.6	83.1[21]
Switzerland	15,943	41,293	121	6,689,000	87	419.6	162.0	0.6	1980[44]	6,365,960	48.9	51.1	57.1
Syria	71,498	185,180	84	11,719,000	58	163.9	63.3	3.4	1981	9,052,628	51.1	48.9	47.0
Taiwan	13,900	36,000	123	20,024,000	41	1,440.6	556.2	1.2	1980[3]	17,968,797	52.2	47.8	70.6[5]
Tanzania	364,881	945,037	30	23,729,000	36	65.0	25.1	2.8	1988	23,174,336	48.9	51.1	13.8[34]
Thailand	198,115	513,115	47	55,258,000	19	278.9	107.7	2.0	1980	44,824,540	49.8	50.2	17.0
Togo	21,925	56,785	115	3,622,000	104	165.2	63.8	4.3	1981	2,705,250	48.7	51.3	15.2
Tokelau	4.7	12.2	212	1,700	212	361.7	139.3	1.2	1986	1,690	49.2	50.8	—
Tonga	301	780	166	95,900	174	318.6	122.9	0.5	1986[3]	94,649	50.3	49.7	30.7
Trinidad and Tobago	1,980	5,128	151	1,285,000	128	649.0	250.6	1.9	1980	1,079,791	50.0	50.0	56.9[5]
Tunisia	59,664	154,530	88	7,973,000	77	133.6	51.6	2.5	1984	6,975,450	50.8	49.2	52.8
Turkey	300,948	779,452	36	55,541,000	18	184.6	71.3	2.5	1985	50,664,458	50.4	49.6	45.9
Turks and Caicos Islands	193	500	174	13,500	201	69.9	27.0	7.8	1980	7,413	48.3	51.7	—
Tuvalu	9.3	24.0	208	8,900	205	957.0	370.8	1.4	1985	8,229	47.4	52.6	...
Uganda	93,070	241,040	77	16,452,000	49	176.8	68.3	2.9	1980	12,636,179	49.5	50.5	8.1
U.S.S.R.	8,649,800	22,403,000	1	287,800,000	3	33.3	12.8	0.9	1989	286,717,000	47.3	52.7	65.9
United Arab Emirates	30,000	77,700	110	1,827,000	124	60.9	23.5	5.1	1985	1,622,464	64.9	35.1	80.8[13]
United Kingdom	94,251	244,110	76	57,218,000	16	607.1	234.4	0.3	1981[46]	56,379,000	48.6	51.4	89.6
United States	3,679,192	9,529,063	4	248,777,000	4	67.6	26.1	1.0	1980[47]	226,545,805	48.6	51.4	73.7
Uruguay	68,037	176,215	86	3,017,000	111	44.3	17.1	0.6	1985	2,955,241	48.7	51.3	86.2
Vanuatu	4,707	12,190	141	154,000	166	32.7	12.6	3.1	1979	111,251	53.1	46.9	17.8
Venezuela	352,144	912,050	32	19,246,000	42	54.7	21.1	2.7	1981	14,516,735	50.0	50.0	85.7
Vietnam	128,065	331,688	60	64,747,000	12	505.6	195.2	2.0	1989	64,411,668	48.6	51.4	19.2[45]
Virgin Islands (U.S.)	136	352	185	107,000	171	786.8	304.0	−0.0	1980	96,569	47.8	52.2	29.6
Wallis and Futuna	106	274	189	15,400	199	145.3	56.2	3.5	1983	12,408	50.5	49.5	...
West Bank	2,270	5,900	149	885,000	134	389.9	150.0	2.5	1985[16]	793,400	49.8	50.2	...
Western Sahara	97,344	252,120	73	195,000	160	2.0	0.8	2.5	1970	76,425	...	...	...
Western Samoa	1,093	2,831	154	164,000	165	150.0	57.9	0.7	1981	156,349	51.8	48.2	21.2
Yemen (Aden)	130,066	336,869	59	2,406,000	117	18.5	7.1	2.6	1973	1,590,275	49.5	50.5	33.3
Yemen (San'ā')	75,300	195,000	83	8,834,000	71	117.3	45.3	2.6	1986	9,274,173[48]	47.3[13]	52.7[13]	10.2[13]
Yugoslavia	98,766	255,804	72	23,710,000	37	240.1	92.7	0.6	1981	22,424,711	49.4	50.6	47.3
Zaire	905,446	2,345,095	11	33,336,000	28	36.8	14.2	2.4	1984	29,671,407	49.2	50.8	36.6[2]
Zambia	290,586	752,614	38	8,148,000	75	28.0	10.8	3.9	1980	5,661,801	48.9	51.1	39.9
Zimbabwe	150,873	390,759	55	9,122,000	68	60.5	23.3	2.8	1982	7,532,000	49.3	50.7	23.0

[1]Settled population only. [2]1985 estimate. [3]Data are for de jure population. [4]Includes residents abroad; excludes visitors. [5]1980 estimate. [6]Excludes institutional population. [7]1969 census. [8]1982 estimate. [9]Excludes institutional population, residents abroad, and visitors. [10]1975 census. [11]Includes residents abroad and visitors. [12]Excludes visitors. [13]1981 census. [14]1973 census. [15]1974 census. [16]Civil register; not a census. [17]1986 register. [18]1983 estimate. [19]Excludes the Sinai and residents abroad. [20]1976 census. [21]1980 census. [22]Excludes visitors, transients, and family members of British servicemen. [23]1970 census. [24]Data exclude Alderney (population 2,130) and Sark (population 604). [25]Excludes residents abroad, visitors, and Vietnamese refugees. [26]1977 census. [27]Excluding territory occupied after 1967. [28]Includes East Jerusalem and Israeli residents in the occupied territories. [29]Excluding West Bank. [30]1962 census. [31]No census

age distribution (%)						population (by decade, '000s)								country
0–14	15–29	30–44	45–59	60–74	75 and older	1940	1950	1960	1970	1980	1990 projection	2000 projection	2010 projection	
19.1	23.4	22.0	14.3	14.4	6.8	2,973	3,265	3,581	3,877	4,086	4,245	4,427	4,615	Norway
44.3[2]	24.8[2]	18.0[2]	8.9[2]	3.5[2]	0.6[2]	...	413	505	654	984	1,468	2,057	2,882	Oman
50.5	25.2	12.1	7.0	4.2	1.0	...	11	15	22	31	46	67	99	Pacific Is., Trust Territory of the Marshall Islands
46.4	26.8	12.6	8.5	4.5	1.1	...	30	40	57	76	109	128	146	Micronesia, Federated States of
40.6	27.9	17.8	9.2	3.8	0.8	48	6	9	10	17	23	31	42	Northern Mariana Islands
35.0	29.6	17.9	9.6	6.0	1.9	25	6	9	11	12	14	15	16	Palau
44.5	23.9	15.4	9.3	5.3	1.6	28,300	39,513	49,955	65,706	85,299	122,666	162,467	205,472	Pakistan
39.1	28.1	16.7	9.5	5.1	1.5	620	893	1,148	1,531	1,956	2,418	2,893	3,324	Panama
43.0	25.9	17.0	10.4	3.5	0.2	1,308	1,613	1,920	2,419	2,966	3,671	4,568	5,692	Papua New Guinea
41.1	28.1	15.4	9.1	4.8	1.5	1,111	1,351	1,774	2,351	3,147	4,277	5,538	6,928	Paraguay
41.2	27.9	15.6	9.3	4.4	1.6	6,784	7,632	9,931	13,193	17,295	22,332	27,952	33,479	Peru
42.0	28.5	15.6	8.6	4.3	1.0	16,459	20,988	27,561	36,850	48,316	61,483	76,094	90,288	Philippines
32.1[13]	13.2[13]	18.9[13]	13.2[13]	9.4[13]	13.2[13]	0.20	0.14	0.14	0.09	0.06	0.06	...	...	Pitcairn Island
23.9[34]	27.4[34]	18.5[34]	16.9[34]	9.9[34]	3.4[34]	31,500	24,824	29,561	32,657	35,578	38,064	39,643	41,289	Poland
25.5	23.5	18.0	17.2	11.9	3.9	7,696	8,405	8,826	9,040	9,766	10,434	10,773	11,123	Portugal
31.6	26.4	18.5	12.3	8.3	2.9	1,878	2,218	2,360	2,721	3,297	3,316	3,389	3,465	Puerto Rico
27.8	29.3	32.3	8.6	1.6	0.4	...	47	59	151	229	444	600	758	Qatar
35.6	29.8	——27.6——		——6.9——		221	244	338	447	507	594	689	785	Réunion
25.7	23.7	19.6	17.1	10.9	3.0	15,907	16,311	18,407	20,799	22,201	23,278	24,409	25,595	Romania
47.7[5]	25.7[5]	14.2[5]	8.4[5]	3.4[5]	0.6[5]	1,910	2,120	2,742	3,728	5,163	7,232	10,144	13,556	Rwanda
26.4	28.9	22.0	11.9	7.5	3.4	5	5	5	5	7	7	8	8	St. Helena and Ascension
37.2	30.4	9.5	9.4	10.0	3.5	43	49	51	46	43	44	44	45	St. Kitts and Nevis
49.6	21.3	11.6	9.8	5.5	2.2	70	79	94	100	124	153	175	201	St. Lucia
28.7	26.0	20.4	13.2	8.5	3.2	4	5	5	5	6	6	7	7	St. Pierre and Miquelon
41.7[5]	33.3[5]	11.5[5]	7.3[5]	5.2[5]	1.0[5]	61	67	80	86	103	116	129	145	St. Vincent and the Grenadines
24.4	23.0	19.9	17.4	11.4	3.9	10	13	15	19	21	23	24	25	San Marino
46.3	25.0	11.6	10.0	5.3	1.8	60	60	64	74	94	121	157	203	São Tomé and Príncipe
46.7	23.9	15.2	7.9	——6.3——		...	3,201	4,075	5,745	9,372	14,131	20,686	29,551	Saudi Arabia
43.1	26.2	15.3	9.1	4.6	1.5	1,857	2,600	3,076	4,267	5,711	7,618	10,193	13,639	Senegal
39.6	26.3	14.0	10.8	6.8	2.1	32	34	42	54	63	68	73	78	Seychelles
40.7[15]	24.8[15]	17.4[15]	9.2[15]	——7.9[15]——		1,700	1,809	2,165	2,692	3,336	4,033	4,874	5,892	Sierra Leone
27.0	34.7	19.8	11.3	5.9	1.3	751	1,022	1,639	2,075	2,414	2,702	2,950	3,117	Singapore
47.3	25.7	13.9	8.1	——4.9——		94	104	125	163	229	329	448	595	Solomon Islands
44.1[5]	25.5[5]	15.8[5]	9.5[5]	4.3[5]	0.7[5]	...	2,423	2,935	3,668	5,352	7,555	9,803	13,247	Somalia
37.1	28.5	18.1	10.1	4.7	1.5	10,353	12,458	15,925	22,460	29,799	37,466	46,171	56,905	South Africa[41]
52.6[23]	21.3[23]	10.4[23]	——13.6[23]——		2.1[23]	...	...	...	...	1,335	1,959	2,482	3,143	Bophuthatswana
44.9	26.2	15.0	6.9	5.5	1.5	...	...	...	...	682	844	1,069	1,354	Ciskei
43.7[23]	21.5[23]	13.3[23]	——20.3[23]——		1.2[23]	...	...	...	...	2,336	3,301	4,181	5,295	Transkei
43.3[23]	20.3[23]	12.4[23]	——22.7[23]——		1.3[23]	...	...	...	...	345	518	656	830	Venda
44.0[5]	26.0[5]	15.5[5]	9.3[5]	4.3[5]	0.9[5]	336	405	522	761	1,002	1,302	1,667	2,136	South West Africa/ Namibia
25.6[3]	23.2[3]	17.9[3]	17.6[3]	11.4[3]	4.2[3]	25,757	27,868	30,303	33,779	37,424	39,322	40,747	41,194	Spain
35.3	29.6	17.9	10.6	5.2	1.4	5,972	7,678	9,889	12,514	14,747	17,108	19,256	21,303	Sri Lanka
45.1[2]	26.1[2]	15.6[2]	8.7[2]	3.8[2]	0.7[2]	8,500	9,322	11,256	14,090	19,449	28,311	37,607	49,063	Sudan, The
39.3	29.5	13.8	10.0	4.5	2.8	193	215	247	292	355	411	469	535	Suriname
47.3	26.6	13.4	7.4	3.4	1.3	154	253	320	409	559	770	1,082	1,488	Swaziland
17.8	20.7	22.1	16.3	15.3	7.8	6,371	7,041	7,498	8,081	8,310	8,523	8,780	9,046	Sweden
19.2	23.1	22.0	17.4	12.7	5.6	4,234	4,715	5,429	6,270	6,385	6,724	6,911	6,932	Switzerland
47.5[5]	27.4[5]	12.4[5]	7.9[5]	3.6[5]	1.1[5]	2,597	3,495	4,561	6,305	8,704	12,113	16,857	22,533	Syria
32.1	32.1	16.5	12.6	5.7	1.0	5,987	7,619	10,792	14,676	17,642	20,262	22,810	25,677	Taiwan
46.2[34]	24.9[34]	14.4[34]	8.5[34]	4.5[34]	1.6[34]	...	7,892	10,073	13,273	18,441	24,403	32,292	42,732	Tanzania
38.3	30.1	16.1	10.1	4.3	1.1	15,296	20,010	26,392	35,745	46,538	56,147	63,402	71,594	Thailand
44.4[5]	25.8[5]	15.6[5]	9.1[5]	4.3[5]	0.8[5]	834	1,201	1,465	1,954	2,600	3,764	5,125	6,942	Togo
42.9[13]	22.5[13]	12.7[13]	10.2[13]	7.2[13]	4.5[13]	1.3	1.5	1.8	1.7	1.6	2	2	2	Tokelau
40.6	29.0	13.8	10.1	5.0	1.4	37	50	65	80	92	96	101	106	Tonga
34.2	30.9	16.3	10.0	6.2	1.7	503	668	828	941	1,082	1,321	1,608	1,931	Trinidad and Tobago
39.7	28.8	14.2	10.7	5.4	1.2	2,887	3,530	4,221	5,137	6,392	8,182	10,594	13,099	Tunisia
37.1	26.3	17.1	12.6	——6.9——		17,723	20,809	27,509	35,321	44,438	56,941	73,029	83,963	Turkey
41.4	26.7	11.8	11.0	7.0	2.2	6	6	6	6	7	14	16	19	Turks and Caicos Islands
31.8[45]	31.7[45]	15.2[45]	13.2[45]	6.3[45]	1.7[45]	4	5	5	6	8	9	11	14	Tuvalu
47.8[5]	26.0[5]	14.0[5]	8.0[5]	3.5[5]	0.6[5]	4,233	5,969	7,551	9,806	12,786	16,928	22,399	29,638	Uganda
25.5[40]	24.0[40]	18.7[40]	18.3[40]	7.1[40]	6.4[40]	195,000	180,075	214,335	241,700	265,542	290,417	311,078	333,404	U.S.S.R.
31.9[2]	24.9[2]	32.1[2]	8.7[2]	1.9[2]	0.5[2]	...	70	90	223	980	1,881	2,518	3,371	United Arab Emirates
20.6	22.8	19.4	16.9	14.4	5.8	48,226	50,290	52,372	55,632	56,330	57,376	58,958	59,778	United Kingdom
22.6	27.4	19.1	15.2	11.3	4.4	132,594	152,271	180,671	204,879	227,757	250,941	268,834	283,174	United States
26.6	22.8	18.3	16.5	11.4	4.3	1,974	2,194	2,531	2,824	2,868	3,033	3,207	3,391	Uruguay
45.3	27.5	15.0	7.7	3.4	1.1	43	52	65	86	118	159	207	296	Vanuatu
40.5	29.9	15.8	8.7	4.0	1.1	3,740	5,009	7,502	10,604	15,024	19,735	24,715	30,006	Venezuela
39.3[2]	31.3[2]	13.7[2]	9.4[2]	5.1[2]	1.1[2]	...	24,600	30,200	40,064	53,722	66,111	81,542	96,183	Vietnam
36.0	24.2	21.5	11.1	5.7	1.4	25	27	32	75	98	108	114	121	Virgin Islands (U.S.)
45.8	24.8	13.8	9.0	5.7	0.9	...	7	8	9	11	16	16	16	Wallis and Futuna
46.6	30.1	9.5	8.2	——5.7——		...	...	...	608	721	906	1,142	1,442	West Bank
42.9	27.2	16.3	7.4	4.4	1.8	...	14	32	76	155	200	257	330	Western Sahara
44.3	29.1	12.2	9.0	3.8	1.0	61	82	111	143	155	165	176	188	Western Samoa
47.3	20.8	15.8	8.6	——6.6——		...	907	1,109	1,436	1,910	2,468	3,191	4,124	Yemen (Aden)
45.7[13]	23.2[13]	15.1[13]	10.5[13]	4.7[13]	0.8[13]	...	3,622	4,429	4,840	6,933	9,060	11,660	15,006	Yemen (Şan'ā')
24.5	25.0	19.8	18.3	8.3	3.5	16,425	16,346	18,402	20,371	22,304	23,861	25,431	27,105	Yugoslavia
45.2[2]	25.9[2]	15.5[2]	8.7[2]	3.9[2]	0.7[2]	10,370	13,055	16,151	21,368	27,406	34,138	42,980	54,112	Zaire
49.0	24.8	13.1	7.4	3.5	0.9	1,484	2,440	3,141	4,189	5,738	8,456	12,197	17,152	Zambia
51.0	26.3	13.4	6.5	1.2		1,940	2,730	3,840	5,308	7,100	9,369	11,943	14,739	Zimbabwe

ever taken. [32] 1967 census. [33] Island of Mauritius only. [34] 1978 census. [35] Including 163,868 in Western Sahara. [36] Indigenous population only. [37] A census was taken in 1973, but the results were repudiated. [38] Excludes Afghan refugees and residents of Pakistani-occupied Jammu and Kashmir. [39] St. Helenians only. [40] 1987 estimate. [41] Includes Black states shown separately. [42] Excludes Bophuthatswana, Ciskei, Transkei, and Venda. [43] 1985 estimate; includes Bophuthatswana, Ciskei, Transkei, and Venda. [44] Includes resident aliens; excludes seasonal workers. [45] 1979 census. [46] Includes residents abroad and foreign military personnel; excludes visitors. [47] Excludes 515,000 armed forces overseas. [48] Includes 1,168,199 nationals abroad.

Major cities and national capitals

The following table lists the principal cities or municipalities (those exceeding 100,000 in population) of the countries of the world, together with figures for each national capital (indicated by a ★), regardless of size.

Most of the populations given refer to a so-called city proper, that is, a legally defined, incorporated, or chartered area defined by administrative boundaries and by national or state law. Some data, however, refer to the municipality, or commune, similar to the medieval city-state in that the city is governed together with its immediately adjoining, economically dependent areas, whether urban or rural in nature. Some countries define no other demographic or legal entities within such communes or municipalities, but many identify a centre, seat, head (*cabecera*), or locality that corresponds to the most densely populated, compact, contiguous core of the municipality. Because the amount of work involved in defining these "centres" carefully may be considerable, the necessary resources usually exist only at the time of a national census (generally 5 or 10 years apart). Between censuses, therefore, it may be possible only to track the growth of the municipality as a whole. Thus, in order to provide the most up-to-date data for cities in this table, figures referring to municipalities or communes may be given (identified by the abbreviation "MU"), even though the country itself may define a smaller, more closely knit city proper. Specific identification of municipalities is provided in this table *only* when the country also publishes data for a more narrowly defined city proper; it is *not* provided when the sole published figure is the municipality, whether or not this is the proper local administrative term for the entity.

Problems also exist in the identification of cities in terms of named legal entities. There is, for example, a single municipality (*commune*) named Brussel (Brussels) at the centre of the Brussels agglomeration in Belgium; the *commune* numbers only about 137,000 population, while the agglomeration, which is understood by most people to constitute the city, numbers nearly a million. Both are shown so as to apprise the reader of the existence of a problem.

For certain countries, more than one form of the name of the city is given, usually to permit recognition of recent place name changes or of *forms* of the place name likely to be encountered in press stories if the title of the city's entry in the *Encyclopædia Britannica* is spelled according to a different romanization or spelling policy. Chinese names, *e.g.*, are given first in their Wade-Giles spelling (the scholarly system used by Britannica) and then, parenthetically, in their Pinyin spelling, the official Chinese system now encountered in press reports, official documents, and maps.

Sources for this data were usually the national census and statistical abstracts of the countries concerned, supplemented by correspondence with most national statistical offices to solicit unpublished data.

Major cities and national capitals

country city	population
Afghanistan (1988 est.)	
Herāt	177,300
★ Kābul	1,424,400
Mazār-e Sharif	130,600
Qandahār	225,500
Albania (1987 est.)	
★ Tiranë	225,700
Algeria (1987)	
★ Algiers	1,507,241
Annaba	305,526
Batna	181,601
Béchar	107,311
Bejaïa	114,534
Biskra	128,280
Blida (el-Boulaida)	170,935
ech-Cheliff	129,976
Constantine (Qacentina)	440,842
Mostaganem	114,037
Oran (Wahran)	628,558
Sétif	170,182
Sidi bel Abbès	152,778
Skikda	128,747
Tébessa	107,559
Tlemcen (Tilimsen)	126,882
American Samoa (1985 est.)	
★ Pago Pago	3,400
Andorra (1986)	
★ Andorra la Vella	15,639
Angola (1989 est.)	
★ Luanda	1,459,900
Lubango	105,000[1]
Anguilla (1984)	
★ The Valley	1,042
Antigua and Barbuda (1982 est.)	
★ Saint John's	30,000
Argentina (1980)	
Almirante Brown	332,548
Avellaneda	330,654
Bahía Blanca	220,765
Berazategui	200,926
★ Buenos Aires	2,922,829
Caseros	340,343
Córdoba	968,829
Corrientes	180,612
Esteban Echeverría	187,969
Florencio Varela	172,654
General San Martín	384,306
General Sarmiento	499,648
Godoy Cruz	141,553
Guaymallén	157,334
La Plata	454,884
Lanús	465,891
Lomas de Zamora	508,620
Mar del Plata	407,024
Mendoza	118,427
Merlo	282,828
Moreno	193,626
Morón	596,769
Paraná	161,638
Posadas	143,889
Quilmes	441,780
Resistencia	218,438
Río Cuarto	110,254
Rosario	875,664
Salta	260,744
San Fernando	134,156
San Isidro	287,048
San Juan	117,731
San Justo	946,715
San Miguel de Tucumán	392,888
San Salvador de Jujuy	124,950
Santa Fe	287,240
Santiago del Estero	148,758
Tigre	205,926
Vicente López	289,815
Aruba (1986 est.)	
★ Oranjestad	19,800
Australia (1987 est.)[2, 3]	
Adelaide	1,013,000
Brisbane	1,215,300
★ Canberra	289,000
Geelong	149,300
Gold Coast	219,700
Hobart	180,000
Melbourne	2,964,800
Newcastle	419,200
Perth	1,083,400
Sydney	3,531,000
Townsville	108,300
Wollongong	233,800
Austria (1981)	
Graz	243,166
Innsbruck	117,287
Linz	199,910
Salzburg	139,426
★ Vienna	1,531,346
Bahamas, The (1980)	
★ Nassau	110,000
Bahrain (1988 est.)	
★ al-Manāmah	151,500
Bangladesh (1981)	
Barisāl	172,905
Chittagong	980,000
Comilla	184,132
★ Dhākā (Dacca)	2,365,695
Jessore	148,927
Khulna	646,359
Mymensingh	190,911
Pābna	109,065
Rājshāhi	253,740
Rangpur	153,174
Saidpur	126,608
Sirājganj	106,774
Sylhet	168,371
Barbados (1985 est.)	
★ Bridgetown	7,466
Belgium (1988 est.)	
Antwerp	476,044
Brugge (Bruges)	117,857
★ Brussels	136,920[4]
Agglomeration	970,346
Charleroi	208,938
Ghent	232,620
Liège (Luik)	200,312
Namur	103,104
Schaerbeek	104,919[4]
Belize (1986 est.)	
★ Belmopan	3,500
Benin (1982 est.)	
★ Cotonou (official)	487,020
★ Porto-Novo (de facto)	208,258
Bermuda (1985 est.)	
★ Hamilton	1,676
Bhutan (1985 est.)	
★ Paro (administrative)	3,000
★ Thimphu (official)	20,000
Bolivia (1988 est.)	
Cochabamba	381,393
★ La Paz (administrative)	1,057,079
Oruro	195,525
Potosí	114,105
Santa Cruz	627,920
★ Sucre (judicial)	96,093
Botswana (1988 est.)	
★ Gaborone	110,973
Brazil (1980)	
Americana	121,794
Anápolis	160,520
Aracaju	288,106
Araçatuba	113,486
Barra Mansa	123,421
Bauru	178,861
Belém	758,117
Belo Horizonte	1,442,483
Blumenau	144,819
★ Brasília	411,305
Campina Grande	222,229
Campinas	566,517
Campo Grande	282,844
Campos	174,218
Canoas	214,115
Carapicuiba	185,763
Caruaru	137,636
Cascavel	100,351
Caxias do Sul	198,824
Contagem	111,697
Cuiabá	167,894
Curitiba	843,733
Diadema	228,594
Divinopolis	108,344
Duque de Caxias	306,057
Feira de Santana	225,003
Florianópolis	153,547
Fortaleza	648,815
Franca	143,630
Goiânia	703,263
Governador Valadares	173,699
Guarulhos	395,117
Imperatriz	111,818
Ipatinga	105,083
Itabuna	129,938
Jacareí	103,652
João Pessoa	290,424
Joinville	217,074
Juàzeiro do Norte	125,248
Juiz de Fora	299,728
Jundiaí	210,015
Lages	108,768
Limeira	137,812
Londrina	258,054
Maceió	376,479
Manaus	613,068
Marília	103,904
Maringá	158,047
Mauá	205,817
Mogi das Cruzes	122,265
Montes Claros	151,881
Mossoró	118,007
Natal	376,552
Nilópolis	103,033
Niterói	386,185
Nova Iguaçu	491,802
Novo Hamburgo	132,066
Olinda	266,392
Osasco	473,856
Passo Fundo	103,121
Pelotas	197,092
Petrópolis	149,427
Piracicaba	179,395
Ponta Grossa	171,111
Porto Alegre	1,108,883
Porto Velho	101,644
Presidente Prudente	127,623
Recife	1,184,215
Ribeirão Prêto	300,704
Rio Claro	103,174
Rio de Janeiro	5,090,700
Rio Grande	124,706
Salvador	1,506,602
Santa Maria	151,202
Santarém	101,534
Santo Andre	549,278
Santos	411,023
São Bernardo do Campo	381,261
São Caetano do Sul	163,030
São Carlos	109,231
São Gonçalo	221,278
São João de Meriti	210,548
São José do Rio Prêto	171,982
São José dos Campos	268,073
São Luís	182,466
São Paulo	7,033,529
São Vicente	192,770
Sorocaba	254,718
Taubaté	155,371
Teresina	339,264
Uberaba	180,296
Uberlândia	230,400
Vitória	144,143
Vitória da Conquista	125,717
Volta Redonda	177,772
British Virgin Islands (1980)	
★ Road Town	2,525
Brunei (1988 est.)	
★ Bandar Seri Begawan	52,300
Bulgaria (1988 est.)	
Burgas	197,555
Pleven	133,747
Plovdiv	356,596
Ruse	190,450
Shumen	106,496
★ Sofia	1,128,859
Sliven	106,610
Stara Zagora	156,441
Tolbukhin	111,037
Varna	305,891
Burkina Faso (1985)	
Bobo Dioulasso	231,162
★ Ouagadougou	442,223
Burundi (1986 est.)	
★ Bujumbura	272,622
Cameroon (1987 est.)	
Douala	1,116,872
Garoua	102,057
Maroua	106,242
Nkongsamba	112,454
★ Yaoundé	712,089
Canada (1986)	
Brampton	188,498
Burlington	116,675
Burnaby	145,161
Calgary	636,104
East York	101,085
Edmonton	573,982
Etobicoke	302,973
Halifax	113,577
Hamilton	306,728
Kitchener	150,604
Laval	284,164
London	269,140
Longueuil	125,441
Markham	114,597
Mississauga	374,005
Montreal	1,015,420
North York	556,297
Oshawa	123,651
★ Ottawa	300,763
Quebec	164,580
Regina	175,064
Richmond	108,492
Saint Catharines	123,455
Saskatoon	177,641
Scarborough	484,676
Surrey	181,447
Thunder Bay	112,272
Toronto	612,289
Vancouver	431,137
Windsor	193,111
Winnipeg	594,551
York	135,401
Cape Verde (1985 est.)	
★ Praia	49,500
Cayman Islands (1988 est.)	
★ George Town	13,700
Central African Republic (1988 est.)	
★ Bangui	596,776
Chad (1986 est.)	
★ N'Djamena	511,700
Sarh	100,000
Chile (1987 est.; MU)	
Antofagasta	204,577
Arica	169,774
Calama	109,645
Chillán	148,805
Concepción	294,375
Coquimbo	105,252
Iquique	132,948
La Serena	106,617
Los Angeles	126,122
Osorno	122,462
Puente Alto	165,534
Puerto Montt	113,488
Punta Arenas	111,724
Quilpué	103,004
Rancagua	172,489
San Bernardo	168,534
★ Santiago	421,900
Greater Santiago	4,858,342
Talca	164,482
Talcahuano	231,356
Temuco	217,789
Valdívia	117,205
Valparaíso	278,762
Viña del Mar	297,294
China (1988 est.)[5]	
A-K'o-su (Aksu)	148,000
An-ch'ing (Anqing)	235,000
An-shan (Anshan)	1,148,000
An-shun (Anshun)	132,000
An-ta (Anda)	131,000
An-yang (Anyang)	372,000
Canton (Guangzhou)	2,718,000
Chan-chiang (Zhanjiang)	364,000
Ch'ang-chi (Changji)	117,000
Chang-chia-k'ou (Zhangjiakou)	511,000
Ch'ang-chih (Changzhi)	293,000
Ch'ang-chou (Changzhou)	485,000
Chang-chou (Zhangzhou)	169,000
Ch'ang-ch'un (Changchun)	1,557,000
Ch'ang-sha (Changsha)	1,030,000
Ch'ang-shu (Changshu)	150,000
Ch'ang-te (Changde)	190,000
Chao-ch'ing (Zhaoqing)	156,000
Ch'ao-chou (Chaozhou)	277,000
Ch'ao-hu (Chaohu)	115,000
Chao-tung (Zhaodong)	168,000

country / city	population
Ch'ao-yang (Chaoyang)	202,000
Chen-chiang (Zhenjiang)	339,000
Chen-chou (Chenzhou)	161,000
Cheng-chou (Zhengzhou)	1,065,000
Ch'eng-te (Chengde)	239,000
Ch'eng-tu (Chengdu)	1,614,000
Chi-an (Ji'an)	141,000
Chi-hsi (Jixi)	650,000
Chi-lin (Jilin)	971,000
Chi-nan (Jinan)	1,257,000
Chi-ning (Jining) (Inner Mongolia)	153,000
Chi-ning (Jining) (Shantung)	229,000
Ch'i-t'ai-ho (Qitaihe)	183,000
Chia-hsing (Jiaxing)	206,000
Chia-mu-ssu (Jiamusi)	449,000
Chiang-men (Jiangmen)	193,000
Chiao-tso (Jiaozuo)	364,000
Ch'ih-feng (Chifeng)	316,000
Chin-ch'eng (Jincheng)	119,000
Chin-chou (Jinzhou)	641,000
Ch'in-chou (Qinzhou)	103,000
Chin-hsi (Jinxi)	234,000
Chin-hua (Jinhua)	131,000
Ch'in-huang-tao (Qinhuangdao)	333,000
Ching-men (Jingmen)	188,000
Ch'ing-tao (Qingdao)	1,199,000
Ching-te-chen (Jingdezhen)	315,000
Chiu-chiang (Jiujiang)	268,000
Ch'iung-hai (Qionghai)	111,000
Chou-k'ou (Zhoukou)	123,000
Chou-shan (Zhoushan)	146,000
Ch'ü-ching (Qujing)	160,000
Ch'ü-chou (Quzhou)	103,000
Chu-chou (Zhuzhou)	371,000
Ch'u-hsien (Chuxian)	112,000
Chu-ma-tien (Zhumadian)	112,000
Ch'üan-chou (Quanzhou)	167,000
Chungking (Chongqing)	2,179,000
Chung-shan (Zhongshan)	254,000
Fo-shan (Foshan)	265,000
Fu-chou (Fuzhou) (Kiangsi)	112,000
Fu-chou (Fuzhou)	832,000
Fu-hsin (Fuxin)	608,000
Fu-ling (Fuling)	167,000
Fu-shun (Fushun)	1,151,000
Fu-yang (Fuyang)	164,000
Fu-yü (Fuyu)	173,000
Ha-mi (Hami)	153,000
Hai-ch'eng (Haicheng)	201,000
Hai-k'ou (Haikou)	228,000
Hai-la-erh (Hailar)	166,000
Han-chung (Hanzhong)	156,000
Han-tan (Handan)	778,000
Hang-chou (Hangzhou)	1,049,000
Harbin	2,328,000
Heng-yang (Hengyang)	446,000
Ho-fei (Hefei)	669,000
Ho-kang (Hegang)	492,000
Ho-pi (Hebi)	191,000
Ho-tse (Heze)	148,000
Hsi-ch'ang (Xichang)	124,000
Hsi-ning (Xining)	527,000
Hsia-men (Xiamen)	360,000
Hsiang-fan (Xiangfan)	351,000
Hsiang-t'an (Xiangtan)	411,000
Hsiao-kan (Xiaogan)	140,000
Hsien-ning (Xianning)	121,000
Hsien-t'ao (Xiantao)	207,000
Hsien-yang (Xianyang)	312,000
Hsin-hsiang (Xinxiang)	433,000
Hsin-t'ai (Xintai)	186,000
Hsin-yang (Xinyang)	176,000
Hsin-yu (Xinyu)	149,000
Hsing-t'ai (Xingtai)	283,000
Hsü-ch'ang (Xuchang)	182,000
Hsü-chou (Xuzhou)	753,000
Hsüan-ch'eng (Xuancheng)	111,000
Hu-chou (Huzhou)	214,000
Hu-ho-hao-t'e (Hohhot)	605,000
Huai-hua (Huaihua)	112,000
Huai-nan (Huainan)	655,000
Huai-pei (Huaibei)	325,000
Huai-yin (Huaiyin)	211,000
Huang-shih (Huangshi)	430,000
Hui-chou (Huizhou)	131,000
Hun-chiang (Hunjiang)	458,000

country / city	population
Hung-hu (Honghu)	177,000
I-ch'ang (Yichang)	353,000
I-cheng (Yizheng)	103,000
I-ch'un (Yichun)	770,000
I-ch'un (Yichun) (Kiangsi)	145,000
I-ning (Yining)	162,000
I-pin (Yibin)	227,000
I-yang (Yiyang)	167,000
Juian (Rui'an)	154,000
K'ai-feng (Kaifeng)	473,000
K'ai-li (Kaili)	103,000
Kan-chou (Ganzhou)	356,000
Kashgar (Kashi)	159,000
Ko-chiu (Gejiu)	208,000
K'o-la-ma-i (Karamay)	182,000
K'u-erh-le (Korla)	139,000
Kuang-yüan (Guangyuan)	170,000
Kuei-lin (Guilin)	341,000
K'uei-t'un (Kuytun)	115,000
Kuei-yang (Guiyang)	938,000
K'un-ming (Kunming)	1,144,000
Kung-chu-ling (Gongzhuling)	211,000
Lai-wu (Laiwu)	154,000
Lan-chou (Lanzhou)	1,121,000
Lang-fang (Langfang)	136,000
Lao-ho-k'ou (Laohekou)	110,000
Le-shan (Leshan)	329,000
Lei-yang (Leiyang)	127,000
Leng-shui-chiang (Lengshuijiang)	130,000
Lhasa	106,000
Liao-ch'eng (Liaocheng)	139,000
Liao-yang (Liaoyang)	461,000
Liao-yüan (Liaoyuan)	328,000
Lien-yüan (Lianyuan)	109,000
Lien-yün-kang (Lianyungang)	317,000
Li-ling (Liling)	102,000
Lin-fen (Linfen)	170,000
Lin-ho (Linhe)	111,000
Lin-i (Linyi)	185,000
Liu-chou (Liuzhou)	561,000
Liu-p'an-shui (Liupanshui)	328,000
Lo-ho (Luohe)	110,000
Lo-yang (Luoyang)	697,000
Long-yen (Longyan)	124,000
Lou-ti (Loudi)	111,000
Lu-an (Lu'an)	133,000
Lu-chou (Luzhou)	249,000
Ma-an-shan (Ma'anshan)	279,000
Man-chou-li (Manzhouli)	112,000
Mao-ming (Maoming)	150,000
Mei-ho-k'ou (Meihekou)	192,000
Mei-hsien (Meixian)	186,000
Mien-yang (Mianyang)	243,000
Mu-tan-chiang (Mudanjiang)	531,000
Nan-ch'ang (Nanchang)	1,003,000
Nan-ch'ung (Nanchong)	168,000
Nan-ning (Nanning)	660,000
Nan-p'ing (Nanping)	162,000
Nan-t'ung (Nantong)	306,000
Nan-yang (Nanyang)	208,000
Nanking (Nanjing)	1,972,000
Nei-chiang (Neijiang)	206,000
Ning-po (Ningbo)	520,000
O-ch'eng (Echeng)	175,000
Pai-ch'eng (Baicheng)	206,000
Pai-yin (Baiyin)	188,000
Pang-pu (Bengbu)	419,000
P'an-shan (Panshan)	308,000
Pao-chi (Baoji)	301,000
Pao-ting (Baoding)	467,000
Pao-t'ou (Baotou)	936,000
Pei-an (Bei'an)	204,000
Pei-piao (Beipiao)	186,000
★ Peking (Beijing)	5,468,540
Pen-hsi (Benxi)	726,000
Pin-chou (Binzhou)	108,000
P'ing-hsiang (Pingxiang)	404,000
P'ing-ting-shan (Pingdingshan)	403,000
P'u-ch'i (Puqi)	113,000
San-ming (Sanming)	151,000
Sha-shih (Shashi)	246,000
Shan-t'ou (Shantou)	513,000
Shao-hsing (Shaoxing)	169,000
Shao-kuan (Shaoguan)	324,000
Shao-yang (Shaoyang)	228,000
Shang-ch'iu (Shangqiu)	145,000
Shang-jao (Shangrao)	124,000
Shanghai	7,112,000
Shen-chen (Shenzhen)	245,000
Shen-yang (Shenyang)	3,412,000

country / city	population
Shih-chia-chuang (Shijiazhuang)	987,000
Shih-ho-tzu (Shihezi)	301,000
Shih-tsui-shan (Shizuishan)	243,000
Shih-yen (Shiyan)	252,000
Shuang-ya-shan (Shuangyashan)	362,000
Sian (Xi'an)	1,828,000
Ssu-p'ing (Siping)	293,000
Su-chou (Suzhou) (Anhwei)	131,000
Su-chou (Suzhou)	649,000
Sui-chou (Suizhou)	180,000
Sui-hua (Suihua)	211,000
Sui-ning (Suining)	132,000
Ta-ch'ing (Daqing)	601,000
Ta-hsien (Daxian)	167,000
Ta-li (Dali)	121,000
Ta-lien (Dalian)	1,619,000
Ta-t'ung (Datong)	740,000
T'ai-an (Tai'an)	219,000
T'ai-chou (Taizhou)	141,000
T'ai-yüan (Taiyuan)	1,480,000
Tan-chiang (Danjiang)	103,000
Tan-tung (Dandong)	491,000
T'ang-shan (Tangshan)	980,000
T'ao-nan (Taonan)	139,000
Te-chou (Dezhou)	169,000
Te-yang (Deyang)	186,000
T'ieh-fa (Tiehfa)	120,000
T'ieh-ling (Tieling)	229,000
T'ien-men (Tianmen)	174,000
T'ien-shui (Tianshui)	229,000
Tientsin (Tianjin)	4,314,271
Tsa-lan-t'un (Zalantun)	119,000
Ts'ang-chou (Cangzhou)	219,000
Tsao-chuang (Zaozhuang)	297,000
Tsitsihar (Qiqihar)	1,018,000
Tsun-i (Zunyi)	247,000
Tu-k'ou (Dukou)	384,000
Tu-yün (Duyun)	129,000
Tun-hua (Dunhua)	222,000
T'ung-ch'uan (Tongchuan)	279,000
T'ung-hua (Tonghua)	304,000
Tung-kuan (Dongguan)	277,000
T'ung-liao (Tongliao)	233,000
T'ung-ling (Tongling)	209,000
Tung-t'ai (Dongtai)	157,000
Tung-ying (Dongying)	217,000
Tzu-hsing (Zixing)	104,000
Tzu-kung (Zigong)	376,000
Tzu-po (Zibo)	801,000
Wa-fang-tien (Wafangdian)	237,000
Wan-hsien (Wanxian)	146,000
Wei-fang (Weifang)	332,000
Wei-nan (Weinan)	118,000
Wen-chou (Wenzhou)	383,000
Wu-chou (Wuzhou)	204,000
Wu-hai (Wuhai)	246,000
Wu-han (Wuhan)	3,107,000
Wu-hsi (Wuxi)	752,000
Wu-hu (Wuhu)	409,000
Wu-lan-hao-t'e (Ulanhot)	141,000
Wu-lu-mu-ch'i (Ürümqi)	986,000
Ya-k'o-she (Yakeshi)	355,000
Yang-chou (Yangzhou)	284,000
Yang-ch'üan (Yangquan)	334,000
Yen-ch'eng (Yancheng)	205,000
Yen-chi (Yanji)	195,000
Yen-t'ai (Yantai)	369,000
Yin-ch'uan (Yinchuan)	314,000
Ying-k'ou (Yingkou)	391,000
Yü-lin (Yulin)	132,000
Yü-tz'u (Yuci)	179,000
Yü-yao (Yuyao)	117,000
Yüeh-yang (Yueyang)	264,000
Yung-an (Yong'an)	107,000
Christmas Island (1980 est.)	
★ The Settlement at Flying Fish Cove	1,200
Cocos (Keeling) Islands (1987 est.)	
★ West Island	242
Colombia (1985)	
Armenia	180,221
Barrancabermeja	137,406
Barranquilla	896,649
Bello	206,297
★ Bogotá	3,974,813
Bucaramanga	341,513
Buenaventura	160,342
Cali	1,323,944
Cartagena	491,368

country / city	population
Cúcuta	357,026
Floridablanca	137,975
Ibagué	269,495
Itagüí	135,797
Manizales	275,067
Medellín	1,418,554
Montería	157,466
Neiva	178,130
Palmira	175,186
Pasto	197,407
Pereira	233,271
Popayán	141,964
Santa Marta	177,922
Sincelejo	120,537
Soledad	164,494
Valledupar	142,771
Villavicencio	161,166
Comoros (1986 est.)	
★ Moroni	21,000
Congo (1985 est.)	
★ Brazzaville	596,200
Pointe-Noire	298,014
Cook Islands (1986)	
★ Rarotonga Island	9,678
Costa Rica (1984)	
★ San José	241,464
Côte d'Ivoire (1984 est.)	
★ Abidjan	1,850,000
Bouaké	220,000
Yamoussoukro	120,000
Cuba (1988 est.)	
Bayamo	118,854
Camagüey	274,974
Cienfuegos	115,800
Guantánamo	192,590
Holguín	218,148
★ Havana	2,059,223
Las Tunas	111,196
Matanzas	110,307
Pinar del Río	112,280
Santa Clara	188,392
Santiago de Cuba	389,654
Cyprus (1988 est.)[2]	
Limassol	120,000
★ Nicosia	166,900[6]
Czechoslovakia (1988 est.)	
Bratislava	429,734
Brno	388,084
Košice	229,175
Liberec	103,273
Olomouc	106,435
Ostrava	329,587
Plzen	174,580
★ Prague	1,206,098
Denmark (1986)	
Alborg	113,650
Århus	195,152
★ Copenhagen	1,351,999[2]
Odense	137,286
Djibouti (1988 est.)	
★ Djibouti	290,000
Dominica (1987 est.)	
★ Roseau	22,000
Dominican Republic (1983 est.)	
La Romana	101,000
Santiago de los Caballeros	285,000
★ Santo Domingo	1,410,000
Ecuador (1989 est.)	
Ambato	133,643
Cuenca	218,490
Guayaquil	1,699,375
Machala	158,798
Portoviejo	156,250
★ Quito	1,233,865
Egypt (1986 est.)	
Alexandria	2,917,327[7]
Aswān	195,700
Asyūt	291,300
Banhā	120,200
Bani Suwayf	162,500
Būr Sa'īd (Port Said)	382,000
★ Cairo	6,052,836[7]
Damanhūr	225,900
Damyāt	121,200
al-Fayyūm	227,300
Hulwan (Helwan)	352,300
al-Ismā'īlīyah	236,200
al-Jīzah (Giza)	1,670,800
Kafr ad-Dawwar	160,554[8]
Kafr ash-Shaykh	104,200
al-Maḥallah al-Kubrā	385,300
al-Manṣūrah	357,800
al-Minya	203,300
Qinā	141,700
Sawhāj	141,500
Shibin al-Kawm	135,900
Shubrā al-Khaymah	533,300
as-Suways (Suez)	265,000
Ṭanṭā	373,500
al-Uqsur (Luxor)	147,900
az-Zaqāzīq	274,400
El Salvador (1985 est.)	
★ San Salvador	459,902
Santa Ana	137,879

country / city	population
Equatorial Guinea (1983)	
★ Malabo	30,710
Ethiopia (1986 est.)	
★ Addis Ababa	1,495,266
Asmera	295,689
Faeroe Islands (1989 est.)	
★ Tórshavn	14,547
Falkland Islands (1986)	
★ Stanley	1,232
Fiji (1986)	
★ Suva	69,665
Finland (1989 est.)	
Espoo	168,066
★ Helsinki	491,811
Tampere	171,041
Turku	159,395
Vantaa	151,439
France (1982)	
Aix-en-Provence	100,221
Amiens	130,302
Angers	135,293
Besançon	112,023
Bordeaux	201,965
Boulogne-Billancourt	102,582
Brest	154,110
Caen	112,332
Clermont-Ferrand	145,901
Dijon	139,188
Grenoble	156,437
Le Havre	198,700
Le Mans	145,976
Lille	167,791
Limoges	137,809
Lyon	410,455
Marseille	868,435
Metz	113,236
Montpellier	190,423
Mulhouse	111,742
Nantes	237,789
Nice	331,165
Nîmes	120,515
★ Paris	2,165,892
Perpignan	107,812
Reims	176,419
Rennes	190,861
Roubaix	101,488
Rouen	100,696
Saint-Étienne	193,938
Strasbourg	247,068
Toulon	177,443
Toulouse	344,917
Tours	131,265
Villeurbanne	115,378
French Guiana (1982)	
★ Cayenne	37,097
French Polynesia (1983)	
★ Papeete	23,496
Gabon (1987 est.)	
★ Libreville	352,000
Port Gentil	164,000
Gambia, The (1986 est.)	
★ Banjul	44,188[8]
Serekunda	102,600
Gaza Strip (1979 est.)	
Gaza (Ghazzah)	120,000
Germany, East (1988 est.)	
★ Berlin (East)	1,260,921
Cottbus	128,136
Dessau	103,831
Dresden	521,205
Erfurt	218,701
Gera	133,993
Halle	235,421
Jena	107,774
Karl-Marx-Stadt	313,238
Leipzig	549,230
Magdeburg	289,778
Potsdam	142,191
Rostock	251,894
Schwerin	129,475
Zwickau	121,870
Germany, West (1987 est.)	
Aachen	239,170
Augsburg	245,962
Bergisch Gladbach	101,776
Berlin (West)	1,879,225
Bielefeld	299,360
Bochum	381,216
★ Bonn	291,439
Bottrop	112,256
Braunschweig	247,836
Bremen	521,976
Bremerhaven	132,194
Cologne (Köln)	914,336
Darmstadt	133,572
Dortmund	568,164
Duisburg	514,628
Düsseldorf	560,572
Erlangen	100,200
Essen	615,421
Frankfurt am Main	592,411
Freiburg im Breisgau	186,156
Gelsenkirchen	283,560

Major cities and national capitals (continued)

country city	population
Göttingen	133,796
Hagen	206,070
Hamburg	1,571,267
Hamm	165,957
Hannover	505,718
Heidelberg	136,227
Heilbronn	111,713
Herne	171,274
Hildesheim	100,558
Karlsruhe	268,309
Kassel	184,353
Kiel	243,626
Koblenz	110,277
Krefeld	216,598
Leverkusen	154,703
Lübeck	209,159
Ludwigshafen	152,162
Mainz	189,005
Mannheim	294,648
Mönchengladbach	255,087
Mülheim an der Ruhr	170,392
Munich (München)	1,274,716
Münster	267,628
Neuss	143,832
Nürnberg	467,392
Oberhausen	221,542
Offenbach am Main	107,078
Oldenburg	139,256
Osnabrück	153,776
Paderborn	110,296
Pforzheim	104,452
Recklingshausen	117,585
Regensburg	123,821
Remscheid	121,005
Saarbrücken	184,353
Salzgitter	105,392
Siegen	107,319
Solingen	157,401
Stuttgart	565,486
Ulm	100,745
Wiesbaden	266,542
Witten	102,232
Wolfsburg	121,951
Wuppertal	376,217
Würzburg	127,050
Ghana (1988 est.)	
★ Accra	949,113
Kumasi	385,192
Sekondi-Takoradi	103,653
Tamale	151,069
Tema	109,975
Gibraltar (1989 est.)	
★ Gibraltar	30,077[9]
Greece (1981)	
★ Athens	885,737
Iráklion	102,398
Kallithéa	117,319
Larissa	102,426
Pátrai (Patras)	142,163
Peristérion	140,858
Piraiévs (Piraeus)	196,389
Thessaloníki	406,413
Greenland (1989 est.)	
★ Nuuk (Godthåb)	11,957
Grenada (1986 est.)	
★ Saint George's	7,500
Guadeloupe (1982)	
★ Basse-Terre	13,397
Guam (1980)	
★ Agana	896
Guatemala (1989 est.)	
★ Guatemala City	1,057,210
Guernsey (1986)	
★ St. Peter Port	16,085
Guinea (1983)	
★ Conakry	705,280
Guinea-Bissau (1979)	
★ Bissau	109,214
Guyana (1985 est.)	
★ Georgetown	200,000
Haiti (1987 est.)	
★ Port-au-Prince	472,895
Honduras (1988)	
San Pedro Sula	279,356
★ Tegucigalpa	551,606[10]
Hong Kong (1989 est.)	
Hong Kong	5,736,100[9]
Hungary (1989 est.)	
★ Budapest	2,115,000
Debrecen	220,000
Győr	132,000
Kecskemét	106,000
Miskolc	208,000
Nyíregyháza	119,000
Pécs	183,000
Szeged	189,000
Székesfehérvár	114,000
Iceland (1988 est.)	
★ Reykjavík	95,755
India (1981)	
Ādoni	108,939
Agartala	132,186
Āgra	694,191
Ahmadābād	2,059,725
Ahmadnagar	143,937
Ajmer	375,593
Akola	225,412
Alīgarh	320,861
Allahābād	616,051
Alleppey	169,940
Alwar	145,795
Ambāla	104,565
Ambattur	114,915
Amrāvati	261,404
Amritsar	594,844
Amroha	112,682
Anantapur	119,531
Arrah	125,111
Asansol	183,375
Aurangābād	284,607
Avadi	124,574
Bally	147,735
Bālurghāt	104,648
Bangalore	2,476,355
Baranagar	170,343
Bareilly	386,734
Barrackpur	115,253
Belgaum	274,430
Bellary	201,579
Bhāgalpur	225,062
Bharatpur	105,274
Bharūch	110,070
Bhatinda	124,453
Bhātpāra	260,761
Bhavnagar	307,121
Bhilai (Nagar)	290,090
Bhīlwāra	122,625
Bhimavaram	101,894
Bhiwandi	115,298
Bhiwāni	101,277
Bhopāl	671,018
Bhubaneswar	219,211
Bhusāwal	123,133
Bihār	151,343
Bijāpur	147,313
Bikaner	253,174
Bilāspur	147,218
Bokaro Steel City	224,099
Bombay (Greater)	8,243,405
Brahmapur	162,550
Bulandshahr	103,436
Burdwān	167,364
Burhānpur	140,986
Calcutta	3,305,006
Chandernagore	101,925
Chandīgarh	373,789
Chandrapur	115,777
Chāpra	111,564
Cochin	513,249
Coimbatore	704,514
Cuddalore	127,625
Cuddapah	103,125
Cuttack	269,950
Darbhanga	176,301
Dāvangere	196,621
Dehra Dūn	211,416
Delhi	4,884,234
Dhānbād	120,221
Dhārwār-Hubli	527,108
Dhūlia	210,759
Dindigul	164,103
Dombivli	103,222
Durg	114,637
Durgāpur	311,798
Elūru	168,154
Erode	142,252
Etāwah	212,174
Faizābād	101,873
Farīdābād	330,864
Farrukhābād-Fatehgarh	145,793
Fīrozābād	202,338
Gadag-Betigeri	117,368
Gangānagar	123,692
Garden Reach	191,107
Gaya	247,075
Ghāziābād	271,730
Gondia	100,423
Gorakhpur	290,814
Gulbarga	221,325
Guntūr	367,699
Gwalior	539,015
Hāpur	102,837
Hardwār	114,180
Hissār	131,309
Howrah (Haora)	744,429
Hugli Chinsurah	125,193
Hyderābād	2,150,580
Ichalkaranji	133,751
Imphāl	156,622
Indore	829,327
Jabalpur	614,162
Jadabpur	251,968
Jaipur	977,165
Jālgaon	145,335
Jālna	122,276
Jammu	206,135
Jāmnagar	277,615
Jamshedpur	438,385
Jaunpur	105,140
Jhānsi	246,172
Jodhpur	506,345
Jullundur	408,196
Junāgadh	118,646
Kākināda	226,409
Kalyān	136,052
Kāmārhāti	234,951
Kānchipuram	130,926
Kānpur	1,481,789
Karnāl	132,107
Katihār	104,781
Khandwa	114,725
Kharagpur	150,475
Kolhāpur	340,625
Kota	358,241
Kozhikode (Calicut)	394,447
Kumbakonam	132,832
Kurnool	206,362
Lātūr	111,986
Lucknow	895,721
Ludhiāna	607,052
Madras	3,276,622
Madurai	820,891
Mālegaon	245,883
Mandya	100,285
Mangalore	172,252
Masulipatam	138,530
Mathura	147,493
Meerut	417,395
Miraj	105,455
Mirzāpur-cum-Vindhyachal	127,787
Monghyr	129,260
Morādābād	330,051
Muzaffarnagar	171,816
Muzaffarpur	190,416
Mysore	441,754
Nabadwīp	109,108
Nadiād	142,689
Nāgercoil	171,648
Nāgpur	1,219,461
Naihāti	114,607
Nānded	191,269
Nāsik (Nashik)	262,428
Navsāri	106,793
Nellore	237,065
★ New Delhi	273,036
Nizāmābād	183,061
Pālghāt	111,245
Pānihāti	205,718
Pānīpat	137,927
Parbhani	109,364
Pathānkot	110,039
Patiāla	205,141
Patna	776,371
Pimpri-Chinchwad	220,966
Pondicherry	162,639
Porbandar	115,182
Proddatūr	107,070
Pune	1,203,351
Puri	100,942
Quilon	137,943
Raichūr	124,762
Raipur	338,245
Rājahmundry	203,358
Rājapālaiyam	101,640
Rājkot	445,076
Rāmpur	204,610
Rānchi	489,626
Ratlām	142,319
Raurkela Steel Township	206,821
Rewa	100,641
Rohtak	166,767
Sāgar	160,392
Sahāranpur	295,355
Salem	361,394
Sambalpur	110,282
Sambhal	108,232
Sāngli	152,389
Secunderābād (Cantonment)	135,994
Shāhjahānpur	185,396
Shillong	109,244
Shimoga	151,783
Sholāpur (Solapur)	511,103
Shrīrāmpur	127,304
Sīkar	102,970
Silīguri	154,378
Sītāpur	101,210
Sonepat	109,369
South Dum-Dum	230,266
South Suburban	378,765
Srīnagar	586,038
Surat	776,583
Tamkūr	108,670
Tenāli	119,257
Thāna (Thane)	309,897
Thanjāvūr	184,015
Tiruchchirāppalli	362,045
Tirunelveli	128,850
Tirupati	115,292
Tiruppūr	165,223
Tiruvottiyūr	134,014
Titāgarh	104,534
Trivandrum	483,086
Tumkūr	108,670
Tuticorin	192,949
Udaipur	232,588
Ujjain	278,454
Ulhāsnagar	273,668
Vadodara (Baroda)	734,473
Valparai	115,452
Vārānasi (Benares)	708,647
Vellore	174,247
Vijayawāda	454,577
Vishākhapatnam	565,321
Vizianagaram	114,806
Warangal	335,150
Yamunānagar	109,304
Indonesia (1980)	
Ambon	208,898
Balikpapan	280,675
Bandung	1,462,637
Banjarmasin	381,286
Bogor	247,409
Cirebon	223,776
★ Jakarta	6,503,449
Jambi	230,373
Jember	122,712
Kediri	221,830
Madiun	150,562
Magelang	123,484
Malang	511,780
Manado	217,159
Medan	1,378,955
Padang	480,922
Pakanbaru	186,262
Palembang	787,187
Pekalongan	132,558
Pematangsiantar	150,376
Pontianak	304,778
Probolinggo	100,296
Samarinda	264,718
Semarang	1,026,671
Sukabumi	109,994
Surabaya	2,027,913
Surakarta	469,888
Tanjung Karang-Telukbetung	284,275
Tegal	131,728
Ujung Pandang	709,038
Yogyakarta	398,727
Iran (1986)	
Ahvāz	579,826
Āmol	118,242
Arāk	265,349
Ardabīl	281,973
Bābol	115,320
Bakhtarān	560,514
Bandar 'Abbās	201,642
Borūjerd	183,879
Bushire	120,787
Dezfūl	151,420
Gorgān	139,430
Hamadan	272,499
Isfahan (Eşfahān)	986,753
Karaj	275,100
Kāshān	138,599
Kermān	257,284
Khorramābād	208,592
Khvoy	115,343
Malāyer	103,640
Masjed Suleymān	104,787
Meshed (Mashhad)	1,463,508
Neyshābūr	109,285
Orūmīyeh	300,746
Qazvīn	248,591
Qom	543,139
Rasht	290,897
Sabzevār	129,103
Sanandaj	204,537
Shīrāz	848,289
Tabrīz	971,482
★ Tehrān	6,042,584
Yazd	230,483
Zāhedān	281,923
Zanjān	215,261
Iraq (1985 est.)	
al-Amārah	131,758
★ Baghdad	4,648,609
Ba'qūbah	114,516
Basra	616,700
al-Ḥillah	215,249
Irbīl	333,903
Karbalā'	184,574
Kirkūk	207,900[11]
Mosul	570,926
an-Najaf	242,603
an-Nasiriyah	138,842
ar-Ramādī	137,388
as-Sulaymaniyah	279,424
Ireland (1986)	
Cork	133,271
★ Dublin	502,749
Isle of Man (1986)	
★ Douglas	20,368
Israel (1987 est.)	
Bat Yam	132,000
Beersheba (Be'er Sheva')	115,000
Bene Beraq	104,700
Haifa (Ḥefa)	223,400
Ḥolon	140,000
★ Jerusalem (Yerushalayim, Al-Quds)	468,900
Netanya	112,000
Petaḥ Tiqwa	130,700
Ramat Gan	115,500
Rishon le-Ẓiyyon	116,500
Tel Aviv–Yafo	320,300
Italy (1988 est.; MU)	
Ancona	104,525
Bari	358,906
Bergamo	118,655
Bologna	427,240
Bolzano	101,230
Brescia	198,839
Cagliari	221,790
Catania	372,212
Catanzaro	103,004
Cosenza	105,913
Ferrara	143,046
Florence (Firenze)	421,299
Foggia	159,192
Forlì	110,334
Genoa (Genova)	722,026
La Spezia	107,435
Lecce	101,520
Livorno	173,114
Messina	270,546
Milan (Milano)	1,478,505
Modena	176,556
Monza	122,726
Naples (Napoli)	1,200,958
Novara	102,961
Padua (Padova)	223,907
Palermo	728,843
Parma	175,301
Perugia	147,602
Pescara	130,525
Piacenza	104,976
Pisa	103,527
Prato	164,824
Ravenna	136,324
Reggio di Calabria	178,714
Reggio nell'Emilia	130,015
Rimini	129,506[1]
★ Rome (Roma)	2,817,227
Salerno	153,807
Sassari	120,497
Siracusa	123,706
Taranto	244,845
Terni	110,704
Torre del Greco	104,654[1]
Trento	100,677
Turin (Torino)	1,025,390
Trieste	237,191
Venice (Venezia)	327,700
Verona	258,523
Vicenza	109,932
Jamaica (1982)	
★ Kingston	104,041
Japan (1988 est.)	
Abiko	117,484
Ageo	188,594
Aizuwakamatsu	118,778
Akashi	264,274
Akishima	103,254
Akita	299,683
Amagasaki	502,974
Anjō	138,306
Aomori	293,020
Asahikawa	364,401
Ashikaga	168,163
Atsugi	188,734
Beppu	132,710
Chiba	815,238
Chigasaki	196,487
Chōfu	196,731
Daitō	125,190
Ebina	101,114
Fuchu	207,649
Fuji	219,183
Fujieda	117,106
Fujinomiya	115,393
Fujisawa	341,505
Fukui	253,234
Fukuoka	1,203,729
Fukushima	275,009
Fukuyama	364,065
Funabashi	527,367
Gifu	409,054
Habikino	113,764
Hachinohe	243,083
Hachiōji	446,970
Hadano	151,184
Hakodate	312,771
Hamamatsu	527,564
Higashi-Kurume	111,661
Higashi-Murayama	130,781
Higashi-Ōsaka	522,661
Himeji	453,276
Hino	160,956
Hirakata	391,340
Hiratsuka	238,758
Hirosaki	175,953
Hiroshima	1,073,194
Hitachi	204,269
Hōfu	118,683
Ibaraki	255,118
Ichihara	248,534
Ichikawa	422,577
Ichinomiya	261,460
Ikeda	103,993
Imabari	123,314
Iruma	132,230
Ise	105,026

country city	population
Isesaki	113,849
Ishinomaki	123,352
Itami	186,734
Iwaki	353,246
Iwakuni	111,243
Iwatsuki	104,995
Izumi	144,603
Joetsu	130,863
Kadoma	141,884
Kagoshima	535,802
Kakamigahara	128,600
Kakogawa	235,062
Kamakura	175,995
Kanazawa	437,202
Kariya	116,722
Kashihara	114,413
Kashiwa	296,154
Kasugai	263,961
Kasukabe	182,728
Katsuta	107,161
Kawachi-Nagano	102,304
Kawagoe	298,715
Kawaguchi	426,435
Kawanishi	141,700
Kawasaki	1,142,953
Kiryū	128,502
Kisarazu	121,862
Kishiwada	187,948
Kita-Kyūshū	1,039,482
Kitami	107,439
Kobe	1,447,547
Kochi	316,826
Kodaira	160,541
Kofu	201,576
Koganei	104,948
Komaki	119,584
Komatsu	106,116
Koriyama	308,807
Koshigaya	275,820
Kumagaya	147,916
Kumamoto	570,791
Kurashiki	414,801
Kure	220,743
Kurume	225,737
Kushiro	211,438
Kyōto	1,474,507
Machida	340,756
Maebashi	283,567
Matsubara	136,432
Matsudo	448,533
Matsue	142,792
Matsumoto	199,950
Matsusaka	117,965
Matsuyama	437,829
Minakoyojō	131,621
Minō	120,590
Misato	119,288
Mishima	103,568
Mitaka	167,022
Mito	233,236
Miyazaki	285,427
Moriguchi	158,806
Morioka	231,373
Muroran	129,833
Musashino	139,132
Nagano	343,200
Nagaoka	184,574
Nagareyama	135,058
Nagasaki	447,535
Nagoya	2,147,667
Naha	305,987
Nara	344,970
Narashino	146,775
Neyagawa	258,448
Niigata	482,700
Niihama	130,724
Niiza	135,025
Nishinomiya	424,283
Nobeoka	133,404
Noda	110,638
Numazu	211,223
Obihiro	166,957
Odawara	190,210
Ōgaki	147,749
Ōita	402,718
Okayama	587,408
Okazaki	298,477
Okinawa	104,773
Ōme	119,652
Ōmiya	390,765
Ōmuta	154,314
Ōsaka	2,644,691
Ōta	137,330
Otaru	170,717
Ōtsu	247,609
Oyama	137,893
Saga	169,541
Sagamihara	510,757
Sakai	815,949
Sakata	101,096
Sakura	135,196
Sapporo	1,621,418
Sasebo	248,382
Sayama	154,113
Sendai	884,087
Seto	125,012
Shimizu	242,110
Shimonoseki	266,062

country city	population
Shizuoka	472,829
Sōka	201,312
Suita	350,262
Suzuka	170,734
Tachikawa	151,190
Takamatsu	330,252
Takaoka	176,328
Takarazuka	201,318
Takasaki	234,838
Takatsuki	358,380
Tama	138,558
Tokorozawa	293,858
Tokushima	261,831
Tokuyama	112,025
★ Tokyo	8,323,699
Tomakomai	159,174
Tondabayashi	106,761
Tottori	140,461
Toyama	318,812
Toyohashi	330,918
Toyokawa	109,494
Toyonaka	414,922
Toyota	322,112
Tsu	152,662
Tsuchiura	123,988
Tsukuba	137,007
Ube	175,267
Ueda	117,663
Uji	174,758
Urawa	400,803
Urayasu	106,647
Utsunomiya	419,578
Wakayama	399,240
Yachiyo	146,133
Yaizu	110,829
Yamagata	248,421
Yamaguchi	128,288
Yamato	188,351
Yao	276,591
Yatsushiro	109,080
Yokkaichi	269,857
Yokohama	3,151,087
Yokosuka	431,192
Yonago	131,908
Zama	106,974
Jersey (1986)	
★ St. Helier	27,083
Jordan (1988 est.)	
★ Amman	900,000
az-Zarqā'	306,500
Irbid	161,690
Kampuchea (1988 est.)	
★ Phnom Penh	750,000
Kenya (1984 est.)	
Kisumu	167,100
Mombasa	425,600
★ Nairobi	1,103,600
Nakuru	101,700
Kiribati (1985)	
★ Bairiki	21,393
Korea, North (1981 est.)	
Ch'ŏngjin	490,000
Haeju	213,000[8]
Hamhŭng-Hungnam	775,000
Kaesŏng	240,000
Kimch'aek (Songjin)	490,000[8]
★ P'yŏngyang	1,283,000
Sinŭiju	200,000
Wŏnsan	240,000
Korea, South (1985)	
Andong	114,216
Anyang	361,577
Ch'angwŏn	173,508
Chech'ŏn	102,274
Cheju	202,911
Chinhae	121,341
Chinju	227,309
Ch'ŏnan	170,196
Ch'ŏngju	350,256
Chŏnju	426,473
Ch'unch'ŏn	162,988
Ch'ungju	113,331
Inch'ŏn	1,386,911
Iri	192,269
Kangnŭng	132,897
Kumi	142,094
Kunsan	185,649
Kwangju	905,896
Kwangmyŏng	219,611
Kyŏngju	127,544
Masan	448,746
Mokp'o	236,085
P'ohang	260,691
Puch'ŏn	456,292
Pusan	3,514,798
Sŏngnam	447,692
★ Seoul (Sŏul)	9,639,110
Sunch'ŏn	121,958
Suwŏn	430,752
T'aebaek	113,997
Taegu	2,029,853
Taejŏn	866,148
Ŭijŏngbu	162,700
Ulsan	551,014
Wŏnju	151,165
Yŏsu	171,933

country city	population
Kuwait (1985)	
Ḩawallī	145,215
★ Kuwait (al-Kuwayt)	44,224
as-Sālimīyah	153,220
Laos (1985)	
★ Vientiane	377,410
Lebanon (1985 est.)	
★ Beirut (Bayrūt)	1,500,000
an-Nabaţīyah	100,000
Sidon (Şaydā)	100,000
Tripoli (Ţarābulus)	500,000
Zaḩlah	200,000
Lesotho (1986)[2]	
★ Maseru	109,382
Liberia (1984 est.)	
★ Monrovia	425,000
Libya (1988 est.)	
Banghāzī	446,250
Misrātah	121,669
★ Tripoli (Ţarābulus)	591,062
Liechtenstein (1989 est.)	
★ Vaduz	4,919
Luxembourg (1987 est.)	
★ Luxembourg	76,640
Macau (1986 est.)	
★ Macau (Santo Nome de Deus)	416,200
Madagascar (1985 est.)	
★ Antananarivo	662,600
Malaŵi (1987 est.)	
Blantyre	402,500
★ Lilongwe	220,300
Mzuzu	115,000
Malaysia (1980)	
Ipoh	293,849
Johor Baharu	246,395
Kelang	192,080
Kota Baharu	167,872
★ Kuala Lumpur	565,329
Kuala Terengganu	180,296
Kuantan	131,547
Petaling Jaya	207,805
Pinang (George Town)	248,241
Port Kelang	192,080
Seremban	132,911
Taiping	146,002
Maldives (1985)	
★ Male	46,334
Mali (1987)	
★ Bamako	646,163
Malta (1988 est.)	
★ Valletta	9,239
Martinique (1982)	
★ Fort-de-France	96,649
Mauritania (1984 est.)	
★ Nouakchott	350,000
Mauritius (1988 est.)	
★ Port Louis	139,038
Mayotte (1985)	
★ Dzaoudzi	5,425
Mamoudzou (★ designate)	7,325
Mexico (1980)	
Acapulco	301,902
Aguascalientes	293,152
Atizapán de Zaragoza (Ciudad López Mateos)	188,497
Campeche	128,434
Celaya	141,675
Chihuahua	385,603
Ciudad Madero	132,444
Ciudad Obregón	165,572
Ciudad Victoria	140,161
Coatzacoalcos	127,170
Cuernavaca	192,770
Culiacán	304,826
Ensenada	120,483
Durango	257,915
Gómez Palacio	116,967
Guadalajara	1,626,152
Guadalupe	370,524
Hermosillo	297,175
Irapuato	170,138
Jalapa	204,594
Juárez	544,496
León	593,002
Los Mochis	122,531
Matamoros	188,745
Mazatlán	199,830
Mérida	400,142
Mexicali	341,559
★ Mexico City	8,831,079
Minatitlán	106,765
Monclova	115,786
Monterrey	1,090,009
Morelia	297,544
Nezahualcóyotl	1,341,230
Nuevo Laredo	201,731
Oaxaca	154,223
Orizaba	114,848
Pachuca	110,351
Poza Rica	166,799
Puebla	835,759
Querétaro	215,976
Reynosa	194,693
Saltillo	284,937
San Luis Potosí	362,371

country city	population
San Nicolás de los Garza	280,696
Tampico	267,957
Tepic	145,741
Tijuana	429,500
Tlaquepaque	133,500
Toluca	199,778
Torreón	328,086
Tuxtla	131,096
Uruapan	122,828
Veracruz	284,822
Villahermosa	158,216
Zapopan	345,390
Monaco (1982)	
★ Monaco	27,063[9]
Mongolia (1989)	
★ Ulaanbaatar (Ulan Bator)	548,400
Montserrat (1980)	
★ Plymouth	1,568
Morocco (1982)	
Agadir	110,479
Casablanca (Dar el-Beida)	2,139,204
Fès (Fez)	448,823
Kenitra	188,194
Khouribga	127,181
Marrakech	439,728
Meknès	319,783
Mohammedia	105,120
Oujda	260,082
★ Rabat	518,616
Safi	197,309
Salé	289,391
Tanger	266,346
Tétouan	199,615
Mozambique (1989 est.)	
Beira	291,604
★ Maputo (Lourenço Marques)	1,069,727
Nacala	101,615
Nampula	197,379
Myanmar (Burma) (1983)	
Bassein (Pathein)	144,092
Mandalay	532,895
Monywa	106,873
Moulmein (Mawlamyine)	219,991
Pegu (Bago)	150,447
Sittwe (Akyab)	107,907
Taunggye	107,607
★ Yangon (Rangoon)	2,458,712
Nauru (1983)	
★ Yaren	559
Nepal (1981)	
★ Kāthmāndu	235,160
Netherlands, The (1988 est.)	
★ Amsterdam (capital)	691,738
Apeldoorn	145,696[4]
Arnhem	128,107
Breda	120,212
Dordrecht	107,871
Eindhoven	191,002
Enschede	144,695
Groningen	167,429
Haarlem	148,740
Leiden	107,893
Maastricht	115,782
Nijmegen	145,816
Rotterdam	574,299
★ The Hague (seat of government)	444,313
Tilburg	154,425
Utrecht	230,373
Zaanstad	128,833
Netherland Antilles (1985 est.)[2]	
★ Willemstad	125,000
New Caledonia (1989; MU)	
★ Nouméa	65,110
New Zealand (1988 est.)	
Auckland	149,500
Christchurch	167,700
Manukau	185,800
Waitemata	100,700
★ Wellington	136,000
Nicaragua (1985 est.)	
León	100,982
★ Managua	682,111
Niger (1988; MU)	
★ Niamey	398,265
Nigeria (1989 est.)	
Aba	250,900
Abeokuta	358,800
Ado-Ekiti	301,700
Akure	136,200
Benin City	192,700
Bida	105,400
Calabar	146,400
Deba	116,200
Ede	257,700
Effon-Alaiye	128,500
Enugu	265,400
Gusau	132,600
Ibadan	1,201,000
Ife	249,200
Ijebu-Ode	131,300
Ikare	118,200

country city	population
Ikerre	205,300
Ikire	103,500
Ikirun	152,400
Ikorodu	155,200
Ila	221,600
Ilawe-Ekiti	154,800
Ilesha	317,700
Ilobu	167,000
Ilorin	399,500
Inisa	100,600
Iseyin	182,400
Iwo	303,900
Jos	173,200
Kaduna	287,200
Kano	565,800
Katsina	173,400
Kumo	124,300
Lafia	102,800
★ Lagos	1,274,000
Maiduguri	268,100
Makurdi	103,400
Minna	114,900
Mushin	279,700
Offa	165,000
Ogbomosho	612,800
Oka	120,200
Ondo	142,400
Onitsha	312,300
Oshogbo	400,300
Owo	153,900
Oyo	215,300
Port Harcourt	344,200
Sapele	116,900
Shaki	146,200
Shomolu	124,000
Sokoto	172,100
Warni	105,800
Zaria	318,400
Niue (1984)	
★ Alofi	894
Norfolk Island	
★ Kingston	...
Norway (1989 est.; MU)	
Bergen	211,214
★ Oslo	455,632
Trondheim	136,629
Oman (1981 est.)	
★ Muscat	50,000
Pacific Islands, Trust Territory of the	
Marshall Is. (1985 est.)	
★ Majuro	14,267
Micronesia, Federated States of (1980)	
★ Kolonia	5,549
Northern Mariana Is. (1989 est.)	
★ Saipan	19,440
Palau (1986)	
★ Koror	9,442
Pakistan (1981)	
Bahāwalpur	180,263
Chiniot	105,559
Dera Ghāzi Khān	102,007
Faisalābād (Lyallpur)	1,104,209
Gujrānwāla	658,753
Gujrāt	155,058
Hyderābād	751,529
★ Islamābād	204,364
Jhang	195,558
Jhelum	106,462
Karāchi	5,208,132
Kasūr	155,523
Lahore	2,952,689
Lahore Cantonment	237,000
Lārkāna	123,890
Mardān	147,977
Mīrpur Khās	124,371
Multān	730,070
Nawābshāh	102,139
Okāra	153,483
Peshāwar	566,248
Quetta	285,719
Rahīm Yār Khān	119,036
Rāwalpindi	794,843
Sāhiwāl	150,954
Sargodha	291,362
Sheikhūpura	141,168
Siālkot	302,009
Sukkur	190,551
Wāh Cantonment	122,335
Panama (1989 est.)	
★ Panama City	435,458
San Miguelito	252,560
Papua New Guinea (1987 est.)	
★ Port Moresby	152,100
Paraguay (1985 est.)	
★ Asunción	477,065
Peru (1988 est.)	
Arequipa	591,700
Callao	560,000
Chiclayo	394,800
Chimbote	278,600
Cuzco	255,300
Huancayo	199,200

Major cities and national capitals (continued)

country / city	population
Ica	144,000
Iquitos	247,900
Juliaca	120,900
★ Lima	417,959
Metro Lima-Callao	6,053,900
Piura	297,200
Pucallpa	140,700
Sullana	145,500
Tacna	137,500
Trujillo	491,100
Philippines (1989 est.)	
Angeles	245,896
Bacolod	317,685
Bago	126,436
Baguio	152,193
Batangas	175,533
Butuan	220,231
Cabanatuan	170,911
Cadiz	140,278
Cagayan de Oro	342,629
Calbayog	122,670
Caloocan	593,362[12]
Cebu	623,593
Cotabato	104,172
Dagupan	111,716
Davao	836,400
General Santos	229,668
Gingoog	100,757
Iligan	197,126
Iloilo	284,646
Lapu-Lapu	127,037
Las Piñas	194,064[12]
Legaspi	118,174
Lipa	147,457
Lucena	143,285
Makati	441,411[12]
Malabon	233,469[12]
Mandaluyong	223,084[12]
Mandaue	173,764
★ Manila	1,987,055[12]
Metro Manila	7,211,753[12]
Marikina	318,251[12]
Muntilupa	170,282[12]
Naga	100,691
Navotas	145,050[12]
Olongapo	192,568
Ormoc	129,947
Pagadian	102,256
Parañaque	371,450[12]
Pasay	321,210[12]
Pasig	318,853[13]
Quezon City	1,322,907[12]
Roxas	101,468
San Carlos	116,975
San Juan del Monte	156,568[12]
San Pablo	154,446
Silay	131,351
Tacloban	135,504
Tagig	165,742[12]
Toledo	114,956
Valenzuela	260,450[12]
Zamboanga	422,752
Pitcairn Island (1989 est.)	
★ Adamstown	56[9]
Poland (1988 est.)	
Białystok	259,600
Bielsko-Biała	177,700
Bydgoszcz	372,600
Bytom	239,800
Chorzów	138,200
Czestochowa	252,900
Dąbrovo Górnicza	140,000
Elbląg	121,800
Gdańsk	469,100
Gdynia	249,500
Gliwice	211,300
Gorzów Wielkopolski	119,500
Jastrzębie-Zdrój	102,200
Kalisz	105,300
Katowice	368,600
Kielce	208,100
Koszalin	104,700
Kraków	744,900
Legnica	100,700
Łódź	844,900
Lublin	333,000
Olsztyn	154,900
Opole	128,200
Płock	117,600
Poznań	585,900
Radom	221,800
Ruda Śląska	167,900
Rybnik	141,000
Rzeszów	147,300
Sosnowiec	259,600
Szczecin	396,000
Tarnów	118,400
Toruń	197,000
Tychy	187,800
Wałbrzych	141,100
★ Warsaw (Warszawa)	1,671,400
Włocławek	119,200
Wodzislaw Śląskie	111,500
Wrocław	640,200
Zabrze	199,400
Zielona Góra	113,300
Portugal (1986 est.)	
★ Lisbon	829,600
Porto	347,300
Puerto Rico (1984 est.; MU)	
Bayamón	202,500
Caguas	121,100
Carolina	165,700
Mayagüez	101,000
Ponce	190,900
★ San Juan	428,900
Qatar (1986)	
★ Doha	217,294
Réunion (1982)	
★ Saint-Denis	84,400
Romania (1986 est.)	
Arad	187,744
Bacău	179,877
Baia Mare	139,704
Botoşani	108,775
Brăila	235,620
Braşov	351,493
★ Bucharest	1,989,823
Buzău	136,080
Cluj-Napoca	310,017
Constanţa	327,676
Craiova	281,044
Galaţi	295,372
Iaşi	313,060
Oradea	213,846
Piatra Neamţ	109,393
Piteşti	157,190
Ploieşti	234,886
Reşiţa	105,914
Satu Mare	130,082
Sibiu	177,511
Timişoara	325,272
Tirgu Mureş	158,998
Rwanda (1981 est.)	
★ Kigali	156,700
St. Helena and Ascension (1987)	
★ Jamestown	1,332
St. Kitts and Nevis (1985 est.)	
★ Basseterre	18,500
St. Lucia (1986 est.)	
★ Castries	52,868
St. Pierre and Miquelon (1982)	
★ Saint-Pierre	5,415
St. Vincent and The Grenadines (1987 est.)	
★ Kingstown	18,830
San Marino (1989 est.)	
★ San Marino	2,371
São Tomé and Príncipe (1984 est.)	
★ São Tomé	34,997
Saudi Arabia (1980 est.)	
ad-Dammām	200,000
Jiddah	1,500,000[8]
Mecca (Makkah)	550,000
Medina (al-Madinah)	290,000
★ Riyadh (ar-Riyad)	1,308,000[14]
aṭ-Ṭā'if	300,000
Senegal (1985 est.)	
★ Dakar	1,382,000
Kaolack	132,400
Thiès	156,200
Ziguinchor	106,500
Seychelles (1977)	
★ Victoria	23,012
Sierra Leone (1985)	
★ Freetown	469,776
Singapore (1989 est.)[9]	
★ Singapore	2,674,000
Solomon Islands (1986; MU)	
★ Honiara	30,499
Somalia (1981 est.)	
★ Mogadishu	500,000
South Africa (1985)	
★ Bloemfontein (judicial)	104,381
Boksburg	110,832
★ Cape Town (legislative)	776,617
Metro Cape Town	1,911,521
Durban	634,301
Metro Durban	982,075
Germiston	116,718
Johannesburg	632,369
Metro Johannesburg	1,609,408
Pietermaritzburg	133,809
Port Elizabeth	272,844
★ Pretoria (executive)	443,059
Metro Pretoria	822,925
Roodepoort	141,764
Soweto	864,000[13]
Bophuthatswana	
★ Mmabatho	...
Ciskei (1986 est.)	
★ Bisho	2,850
Mdantsane	242,823
Transkei (1978 est.)	
★ Umtata	30,000
Venda (1985)	
★ Thohoyandou	10,166
South West Africa/Namibia (1988 est.)	
★ Windhoek	114,500
Spain (1986 est.; MU)	
Albacete	126,594
Alcalá de Henares	142,862[14]
Alcorcón	140,657[14]
Alicante	258,707
Almería	154,242
Badajoz	119,220
Badalona	227,744[14]
Barcelona	1,699,231
Bilbao	379,107
Burgos	158,610
Cádiz	155,219
Castellón de la Plana	127,578
Córdoba	296,075
Coruña, La	239,505
Gerona	126,030[14]
Getafe	127,060[14]
Gijón	255,969[14]
Granada	256,528
Hospitalet de Llobregat	294,033[14]
Huelva	135,576
Jaén	103,291
La Laguna	112,635[14]
Leganés	163,426[14]
León	135,014
Lérida	107,787
Logroño	115,922
★ Madrid	3,053,101
Málaga	566,480
Móstoles	149,649[14]
Murcia	304,185
Orense	100,430
Oviedo	185,920
Palma (de Mallorca)	295,351
Palmas de Gran Canaria, Las (Is. Canarias)	356,730
Pamplona	184,340
Sabadell	194,943[14]
Salamanca	152,766
San Sebastián	175,267
Santa Coloma de Gramanet	140,588[14]
Santa Cruz de Tenerife	212,523
Santander	186,456
Sevilla (Seville)	651,299
Tarragona	106,361
Terrassa	155,360[14]
Valencia	728,622
Valladolid	327,786
Vigo	258,724[14]
Vitoria	199,936
Zaragoza (Saragossa)	573,711
Sri Lanka (1986 est.)	
★ Colombo (administrative)	683,000
Dehiwala-Mount Lavinia	191,000
Galle	109,000
Jaffna	143,000
Kandy	130,000
Moratuwa	138,000
★ Sri Jayawardenepura Kotte (legislative and judicial)	104,000[15]
Sudan, The (1983)	
★ Khartoum	476,218
Khartoum North	341,146
Port Sudan	206,727
Omdurman	526,287
al-Ubayyiḍ	140,024
Wad Madanī	141,065
Suriname (1986 est.)	
★ Paramaribo	77,558
Swaziland (1986)	
★ Mbabane	38,290
Sweden (1989 est.; MU)	
Borås	100,795
Göteborg	430,763
Helsingborg	107,443
Jönköping	109,890
Linköping	119,167
Malmö	231,575
Norrköping	119,370
Örebro	119,824
★ Stockholm	669,485
Uppsala	161,828
Västerås	117,717
Switzerland (1988 est.)	
Basel (Bâle)	173,582
★ Bern (Berne)	137,606
Geneva (Genève)	164,423
Lausanne	125,646
Zürich	351,086
Syria (1987 est.)	
Aleppo (Halab)	1,216,000
★ Damascus (Dimashq)	1,292,000
Hamāh	214,000
Homs (Hims)	431,000
Latakia (al-Ladhiqiyah)	241,000
Taiwan (1988 est.)	
Chang-hua	206,603
Chi-lung (Keelung)	348,541
Chia-i	254,875
Chung-ho	343,389
Chung-li	247,639
Feng-shan (Kao-hsiung-hsien)	276,259
Fêng-yüan	144,434
Hsin-chu	309,899
Hsin-chuang	259,001
Hsin-tien	205,094
Hua-lien	106,658
Kao-hsiung	1,342,797
Pan-ch'iao (T'ai-pei-hsien)	506,220
P'ing-tung	204,990
San-chu'ung	362,171
T'ai-chung	715,107
T'ai-nan	656,927
T'ai-tung	109,358
★ Taipei (T'ai-pei)	2,637,100
T'ao-yuan	220,255
Yung-ho	242,252
Tanzania (1978)	
★ Dar es Salaam	769,445
Mwanza	110,553
Tanga	103,399
Zanzibar	110,506
Thailand (1986 est.)	
★ Bangkok	5,468,915
Chiang Mai	157,843
Khon Kaen	130,773
Nakhon Ratchasima	206,758
Nakhon Sawan	101,498
Ubon Ratchathani	100,145
Togo (1983)	
★ Lomé	366,476
Tokelau	
—	—
Tonga (1986)	
★ Nuku'alofa	21,383
Trinidad and Tobago (1987 est.)	
★ Port-of-Spain	58,300
Tunisia (1984)	
Ṣafāqis (Sfax)	231,911
★ Tunis	596,654
Turkey (1985)	
Adana	777,554
Adapazari	155,041
★ Ankara	2,235,000
Antakya	109,233
Antalya	258,139
Balıkesir	152,402
Batman	114,210
Bursa	612,500
Denizli	171,360
Diyarbakır	305,259
Elazığ	181,523
Erzurum	252,648
Eskişehir	367,328
Gaziantep	466,302
İçel	314,105
İskenderun	173,607
Isparta	101,784
İstanbul	5,475,982
İzmir	1,489,772
İzmit	236,144
Kahramanmaraş	212,206
Kayseri	378,458
Konya	438,839
Kütahya	120,354
Malatya	251,257
Manisa	126,319
Osmaniye	107,748
Samsun	280,068
Sivas	197,266
Trabzon	155,960
Urfa (Şanlıurfa)	206,385
Van	121,306
Zonguldak	119,125
Turks and Caicos Islands (1980)	
★ Cockburn Town	3,124
Tuvalu (1985 est.)	
★ Funafuti	2,810
Uganda (1980)	
★ Kampala	458,503
Union of Soviet Socialist Republics (1989)	
Abakan	154,000
Achinsk	122,000
Aleksandriya	103,000
Aktyubinsk	253,000
Alma-Ata	1,128,000
Almalyk	114,000
Almetyevsk	129,000
Andizhan	293,000
Angarsk	266,000
Angren	131,000
Anzhero-Sudzhensk	108,000
Arkhangelsk	416,000
Armavir	161,000
Arzamas	109,000
Ashkhabad	398,000
Astrakhan	509,000
Baku	1,150,000
Balakovo	198,000
Balashikha	136,000
Baranovichi	159,000
Barnaul	602,000
Batumi	136,000
Belaya Tserkov	197,000
Belgorod	300,000
Belovo	118,000[4]
Beltsy	159,000
Bendery	130,000
Berdyansk	132,000
Berezniki	201,000
Biysk	233,000
Blagoveshchensk	206,000
Bobruysk	223,000
Borisov	144,000
Bratsk	255,000
Brest	258,000
Bryansk	452,000
Bukhara	224,000
Chardzhou	161,000
Cheboksary	420,000
Chelyabinsk	1,143,000
Cherepovets	310,000
Cherkassy	290,000
Cherkessk	113,000
Chernigov	296,000
Chernovtsy	257,000
Chimkent	393,000
Chirchik	156,000
Chita	366,000
Daugavpils	127,000
Dimitrovgrad	124,000
Dneprodzerzhinsk	282,000
Dnepropetrovsk	1,179,000
Donetsk	1,110,000
Dushanbe	595,000
Dzerzhinsk	285,000
Dzhambul	307,000
Dzhezkazgan	109,000
Dzhizak	102,000
Ekibastuz	135,000
Elektrostal	153,000
Engels	182,000
Fergana	200,000
Frunze	116,000
Glazov	104,000
Gomel	500,000
Gorky	1,438,000
Gorlovka	337,000
Grodno	270,000
Grozny	401,000
Guryev	149,000
Irkutsk	626,000
Ivano-Frankovsk	214,000
Ivanovo	481,000
Izhevsk	635,000
Kalinin	451,000
Kaliningrad	401,000
Kaliningrad (*Moscow obl.*)	160,000
Kaluga	312,000
Kamensk-Uralsky	209,000
Kamenets-Podolsky	102,000
Kamyshin	122,000
Kansk	110,000
Karaganda	614,000
Karshi	156,000
Kaunas	423,000
Kazan	1,094,000
Kemerovo	520,000
Kerch	174,000
Khabarovsk	601,000
Kharkov	1,611,000
Kherson	355,000
Khimki	133,000
Khmelnitsky	237,000
Kiev	2,587,000
Kineshma	105,000
Kirov	441,000
Kirovabad	278,000
Kirovakan	169,000[4]
Kirovograd	269,000
Kiselevsk	128,000
Kishinyov	665,000
Kislovodsk	114,000
Klaipėda	204,000
Kokand	182,000
Kokchetav	137,000
Kolomna	162,000
Kolpino	142,000
Kommunarsk	126,000
Komsomolsk-na-Amure	315,000
Konstantinovka	108,000
Kostroma	278,000
Kovrov	160,000
Kramatorsk	198,000
Krasnodar	620,000
Krasnoyarsk	912,000
Krasny Luch	113,000
Kremenchug	236,000
Krivoy Rog	713,000
Kurgan	356,000
Kursk	424,000
Kustanay	224,000
Kutaisi	235,000
Kuybyshev	1,257,000
Kzyl-Orda	153,000
Leninabad	160,000
Leninakan	120,000

country / city	population
Leningrad	4,456,000
Leninsk-Kuznetsky	165,000
Liepāja	114,000
Lipetsk	450,000
Lisichansk	127,000
Lutsk	198,000
Lvov	790,000
Lyubertsy	165,000
Magadan	152,000
Magnitogorsk	440,000
Makeyevka	430,000
Makhachkala	315,000
Margilan	125,000
Mariupol	517,000
Maykop	149,000
Melitopol	174,000
Mezhdurechensk	107,000
Miass	168,000
Michurinsk	109,000
Minsk	1,589,000
Mogilyov	356,000
★ Moscow	8,769,000
Mozyr	101,000
Murmansk	468,000
Murom	124,000
Mytishchi	154,000
Naberezhnye Chelny	501,000
Nakhodka	165,000
Nalchik	235,000
Namangan	308,000
Navoi	107,000
Neftekamsk	107,000
Nevinnomyssk	121,000
Nikolayev	503,000
Nikopol	158,000
Nizhnekamsk	191,000
Nizhnevartovsk	242,000
Nizhny Tagil	440,000
Noginsk	123,000
Norilsk	174,000
Novgorod	229,000
Novocheboksarsk	115,000
Novocherkassk	187,000
Novokuybyshevsk	113,000
Novokuznetsk	600,000
Novomoskovsk (*Tula obl.*)	146,000
Novorossiysk	186,000
Novoshakhtinsk	106,000
Novosibirsk	1,436,000
Novotroitsk	106,000
Nukus	169,000
Odessa	1,115,000
Odintsovo	125,000
Oktyabrsky	105,000
Omsk	1,148,000
Ordzhonikidze	300,000
Orekhovo-Zuyevo	137,000
Orenburg	547,000
Orsha	123,000
Orsk	271,000
Oryol	337,000
Osh	213,000
Panevėžys	126,000
Pavlodar	331,000
Pavlograd	131,000
Penza	543,000
Perm	1,091,000
Pervouralsk	142,000
Petropavlovsk	241,000
Petropavlovsk-Kamchatsky	269,000
Petrozavodsk	270,000
Pinsk	119,000
Podolsk	210,000
Poltava	315,000
Prokopyevsk	274,000
Pskov	204,000
Pyatigorsk	129,000
Riga	915,000
Rostov-na-Donu	1,020,000
Rovno	228,000
Rubtsovsk	172,000
Rudny	124,000
Rustavi	159,000
Ryazan	515,000
Rybinsk	252,000
Salavat	150,000
Samarkand	566,000
Saransk	312,000
Sarapul	111,000
Saratov	905,000
Semipalatinsk	334,000
Serov	104,000
Serpukhov	144,000
Sevastopol	356,000
Severodonetsk	131,000
Severodvinsk	249,000
Shakhty	224,000
Shchelkovo	109,000
Shevchenko	159,000
Šiauliai	145,000
Simferopol	344,000
Slavyansk	135,000
Smolensk	341,000
Sochi	337,000
Solikamsk	110,000
Stakhanov	112,000
Stary Oskol	174,000
Stavropol	318,000
Sterlitamak	248,000
Sukhumi	121,000
Sumgait	231,000
Sumy	291,000
Surgut	248,000
Sverdlovsk (*Sverdlovsk obl.*)	1,367,000
Syktyvkar	233,000
Syzran	174,000
Taganrog	291,000
Taldy-Kurgan	119,000
Tallinn	482,000
Tambov	305,000
Tartu	114,000
Tashauz	112,000
Tashkent	2,073,000
Tbilisi	1,260,000
Temirtau	212,000
Ternopol	205,000
Tiraspol	182,000
Tolyatti (Togliatti)	630,000
Tomsk	502,000
Tselinograd	277,000
Tula	540,000
Tyumen	477,000
Ufa	1,083,000
Ukhta	111,000
Ulan-Ude	353,000
Ulyanovsk	625,000
Uralsk	200,000
Urgench	128,000
Usolye-Sibirskoye	107,000
Ussuriysk	162,000
Ust-Ilimsk	109,000
Ust-Kamenogorsk	324,000
Uzhgorod	117,000
Velikiye Luki	114,000
Vilnius	582,000
Vinnitsa	374,000
Vitebsk	350,000
Vladimir	350,000
Vladivostok	648,000
Volgodonsk	176,000
Volgograd	999,000
Vologda	283,000
Volzhsky	269,000
Vorkuta	116,000
Voronezh	887,000
Voroshilovgrad	497,000
Votkinsk	103,000
Yakutsk	187,000
Yaroslavl	633,000
Yelets	112,000
Yenakiyevo	121,000
Yerevan	1,199,000
Yevpatoriya	108,000
Yoshkar-Ola	242,000
Yuzhno-Sakhalinsk	157,000
Zagorsk	115,000
Zaporozhye	884,000
Zelenograd	158,000
Zhitomir	292,000
Zhukovsky	101,000
Zlatoust	208,000
United Arab Emirates (1980)	
★ Abu Dhabi (Abū Ẓaby)	243,000
Al-'Ayn	102,000
Dubai (Dubayy)	266,000
Sharjah (ash-Shāriqah)	125,000
United Kingdom (1981)	
Aberdeen	190,465
Belfast	354,400
Birmingham	1,024,118
Blackburn	110,254
Blackpool	149,012
Bolton	143,921
Bournemouth	148,382
Bradford	295,048
Brighton	137,985
Bristol	420,234
Cardiff	266,267
Coventry	322,573
Derby	220,681
Dudley	187,367
Dundee	174,345
Edinburgh	420,169
Glasgow	765,030
Gloucester	108,150
Huddersfield	148,544
Ipswich	131,131
Kingston upon Hull	325,485
Leeds	451,841
Leicester	328,835
Liverpool	544,861
★ London	6,677,928
Luton	164,743
Manchester	448,604
Middlesbrough	159,421
Newcastle upon Tyne	203,591
Newport	116,658
Northampton	155,694
Norwich	173,286
Nottingham	277,203
Oldbury/Smethwick	153,461
Oldham	107,830
Oxford	119,909
Peterborough	114,733
Plymouth	242,560
Poole	124,974
Portsmouth	177,905
Preston	168,405
Reading	198,341
Rotherham	123,312
St. Helens	114,822
Sheffield	477,257
Slough	106,822
Southampton	214,802
Southend-on-Sea	156,969
Stockport	136,792
Stoke-on-Trent	275,168
Sunderland	195,896
Sutton Coldfield	103,097
Swansea	175,172
Swindon	128,493
Walsall	178,852
West Bromwich	154,531
Wolverhampton	265,631
York	126,377
United States (1988 est.)	
Abilene (*Tex.*)	110,150
Akron (*Ohio*)	227,160
Albuquerque (*N.M.*)	378,180
Alexandria (*Va.*)	109,580
Allentown (*Pa.*)	106,270
Amarillo (*Tex.*)	167,090
Anaheim (*Calif.*)	251,050
Anchorage (*Alsk.*)	217,430
Ann Arbor (*Mich.*)	109,720
Arlington (*Tex.*)	251,710
Arlington (*Va.*)	161,580
Atlanta (*Ga.*)	445,000
Aurora (*Colo.*)	219,400
Austin (*Tex.*)	467,420
Bakersfield (*Calif.*)	156,340
Baltimore (*Md.*)	763,880
Baton Rouge (*La.*)	238,300
Beaumont (*Tex.*)	117,130
Berkeley (*Calif.*)	107,270
Birmingham (*Ala.*)	283,240
Boise City (*Idaho*)	109,480
Boston (*Mass.*)	579,920
Bridgeport (*Conn.*)	142,630
Brownsville (*Tex.*)	104,580
Buffalo (*N.Y.*)	323,710
Cedar Rapids (*Iowa*)	108,860
Charlotte (*N.C.*)	370,490
Chattanooga (*Tenn.*)	166,050
Chesapeake (*Va.*)	143,710
Chicago (*Ill.*)	2,994,100
Chula Vista (*Calif.*)	125,660
Cincinnati (*Ohio*)	377,780
Cleveland (*Ohio*)	544,520
Colorado Springs (*Colo.*)	278,940
Columbus (*Ga.*)	182,280
Columbus (*Ohio*)	588,430
Concord (*Calif.*)	110,880
Corpus Christi (*Tex.*)	261,980
Dallas (*Tex.*)	1,017,820
Dayton (*Ohio*)	184,360
Denver (*Colo.*)	500,560
Des Moines (*Iowa*)	194,150
Detroit (*Mich.*)	1,086,710
Durham (*N.C.*)	117,710
El Monte (*Calif.*)	100,860
El Paso (*Tex.*)	501,540
Elizabeth (*N.J.*)	106,880
Erie (*Pa.*)	115,940
Eugene (*Ore.*)	106,680
Evansville (*Ind.*)	129,800
Flint (*Mich.*)	147,250
Fort Lauderdale (*Fla.*)	145,610
Fort Wayne (*Ind.*)	178,210
Fort Worth (*Tex.*)	432,890
Fremont (*Calif.*)	158,240
Fresno (*Calif.*)	294,700
Fullerton (*Calif.*)	113,410
Garden Grove (*Calif.*)	140,630
Garland (*Tex.*)	179,010
Gary (*Ind.*)	134,920
Glendale (*Ariz.*)	133,930
Glendale (*Calif.*)	160,400
Grand Rapids (*Mich.*)	190,340
Greensboro (*N.C.*)	182,800
Hampton (*Va.*)	130,000
Hartford (*Conn.*)	141,180
Hayward (*Calif.*)	104,600
Hialeah (*Fla.*)	162,080
Hollywood (*Fla.*)	120,140
Honolulu (*Ha.*)	838,660
Houston (*Tex.*)	1,725,420
Huntington Beach (*Calif.*)	191,490
Huntsville (*Ala.*)	163,620
Independence (*Mo.*)	114,040
Indianapolis (*Ind.*)	727,130
Inglewood (*Calif.*)	107,050
Irving (*Tex.*)	130,350
Jackson (*Miss.*)	206,990
Jacksonville (*Fla.*)	635,430
Jersey City (*N.J.*)	218,490
Kansas City (*Kan.*)	162,270
Kansas City (*Mo.*)	447,460
Knoxville (*Tenn.*)	175,440
Lakewood (*Colo.*)	123,620
Lansing (*Mich.*)	131,240
Laredo (*Tex.*)	120,030
Las Vegas (*Nev.*)	210,620
Lexington (*Ky.*)	212,930[4]
Lincoln (*Neb.*)	185,250
Little Rock (*Ark.*)	184,510
Livonia (*Mich.*)	100,590
Long Beach (*Calif.*)	413,670
Los Angeles (*Calif.*)	3,402,342
Louisville (*Ky.*)	281,880
Lubbock (*Tex.*)	188,750
Macon (*Ga.*)	121,820
Madison (*Wis.*)	179,010
Manchester (*N.H.*)	103,660
Memphis (*Tenn.*)	668,940
Mesa (*Ariz.*)	267,640
Miami (*Fla.*)	371,100
Milwaukee (*Wis.*)	611,140
Minneapolis (*Minn.*)	364,750
Mobile (*Ala.*)	211,210
Modesto (*Calif.*)	139,990
Montgomery (*Ala.*)	194,460
Nashville (*Tenn.*)	502,760
New Haven (*Conn.*)	125,890
New Orleans (*La.*)	538,050
New York City (*N.Y.*)	7,346,350
Newark (*N.J.*)	319,190
Newport News (*Va.*)	165,340
Norfolk (*Va.*)	285,180
Oakland (*Calif.*)	367,780
Oceanside (*Calif.*)	104,830
Oklahoma City (*Okla.*)	440,140
Omaha (*Neb.*)	377,960
Ontario (*Calif.*)	123,060
Orange (*Calif.*)	105,060
Orlando (*Fla.*)	155,950
Overland Park (*Kan.*)	101,510
Oxnard (*Calif.*)	132,960
Pasadena (*Calif.*)	135,600
Pasadena (*Tex.*)	117,810
Paterson (*N.J.*)	140,850
Peoria (*Ill.*)	108,840
Philadelphia (*Pa.*)	1,657,290
Phoenix (*Ariz.*)	951,720
Pittsburgh (*Pa.*)	387,190
Plano (*Tex.*)	115,210
Pomona (*Calif.*)	120,610
Portland (*Ore.*)	387,660
Portsmouth (*Va.*)	111,820
Providence (*R.I.*)	161,080
Pueblo (*Colo.*)	101,290
Raleigh (*N.C.*)	188,310
Reno (*Nev.*)	120,080
Richmond (*Va.*)	219,980
Riverside (*Calif.*)	212,620
Roanoke (*Va.*)	101,660
Rochester (*N.Y.*)	235,880
Rockford (*Ill.*)	135,900
Sacramento (*Calif.*)	340,480
St. Louis (*Mo.*)	425,190
St. Paul (*Minn.*)	267,950
St. Petersburg (*Fla.*)	235,450
Salt Lake City (*Utah*)	162,010
San Antonio (*Tex.*)	935,730
San Bernardino (*Calif.*)	149,220
San Diego (*Calif.*)	1,073,470
San Francisco (*Calif.*)	753,930
San Jose (*Calif.*)	732,020
Santa Ana (*Calif.*)	246,930
Santa Rosa (*Calif.*)	102,390
Savannah (*Ga.*)	151,290
Scottsdale (*Ariz.*)	118,310
Seattle (*Wash.*)	505,380
Shreveport (*La.*)	217,500
South Bend (*Ind.*)	108,480
Spokane (*Wash.*)	175,180
Springfield (*Mass.*)	149,840
Springfield (*Ill.*)	100,180
Springfield (*Mo.*)	141,760
Stamford (*Conn.*)	101,630
Sterling Heights (*Mich.*)	114,840
Stockton (*Calif.*)	191,440
Sunnyvale (*Calif.*)	115,270
Syracuse (*N.Y.*)	160,350
Tacoma (*Wash.*)	165,230
Tallahassee (*Fla.*)	125,640
Tampa (*Fla.*)	281,790
Tempe (*Ariz.*)	145,280
Toledo (*Ohio*)	340,760
Topeka (*Kan.*)	120,250
Torrance (*Calif.*)	141,520
Tucson (*Ariz.*)	383,170
Tulsa (*Okla.*)	373,600
Virginia Beach (*Va.*)	355,560
Waco (*Tex.*)	106,200
Warren (*Mich.*)	153,650
★ Washington D.C.	620,000
Waterbury (*Conn.*)	104,320
West Covina (*Calif.*)	101,140
Wichita (*Kan.*)	292,730
Winston-Salem (*N.C.*)	153,430
Worcester (*Mass.*)	159,120
Yonkers (*N.Y.*)	187,110
Youngstown (*Ohio*)	105,740
Uruguay (1985)	
★ Montevideo	1,246,500
Vanuatu (1987 est.)	
★ Vila	15,100
Venezuela (1989 est.)	
Acarigua	126,998
Barcelona	236,714
Barinas	172,626
Barquisimeto	702,764
Baruta	271,934
Cabimas	164,727
★ Caracas	1,275,591
Ciudad Bolívar	258,130
Ciudad Guayana (San Felix de Guayana)	509,963
Coro	131,229
Cumaná	227,411
Guarenas	175,820
Los Teques	159,430
Maracaibo	1,179,384
Maracay	524,952
Maturín	220,636
Mérida	197,541
Petare	519,866
San Cristóbal	242,167
Turmero	199,122
Valencia	922,138
Valera	137,682
Vietnam (1979)	
Bien Hoa	190,086
Can Tho	182,856
Da Nang	318,655
Haiphong	330,755
★ Hanoi	819,913
Ho Chi Minh City (Saigon)	2,441,185
Hon Gai	115,312
Hue	165,865
Long Xuyen	112,488
My Tho	101,496
Nam Dinh	161,180
Nha Trang	172,663
Quy Nhon	130,534
Tha Nguyen	138,023
Thanh Hoa	103,981
Vinh	154,040
Virgin Islands (U.S.) (1980)	
★ Charlotte Amalie	11,842
Wallis and Futuna (1983)	
★ Matautu	815
West Bank	
★ —	—
Western Sahara (1982)	
★ El Aaiún (Laayoune)	93,875
Western Samoa (1981)	
★ Apia	33,170
Yemen (Aden) (1984 est.)	
★ Aden	318,000
Yemen (Ṣan'ā') (1986)	
Al-Ḥudaydah	155,110
★ Ṣan'ā'	427,185
Ta'izz	178,430
Yugoslavia (1981)	
Banja Luka	123,937
★ Belgrade (Beograd)	1,087,915
Ljubljana	224,817
Maribor	106,113
Niš	161,376
Novi Sad	170,020
Osijek	104,775
Priština	108,083
Rijeka	159,433
Sarajevo	319,017
Skopje (Skoplje)	408,143
Split	169,322
Subotica	100,516
Zagreb	649,586
Zaire (1984)	
Bukavu	171,064
Kananga	290,898
Kikwit	146,784
★ Kinshasa	2,653,558
Kisangani	282,650
Likasi	194,465
Lubumbashi	543,268
Matadi	144,742
Mbandaka	125,263
Mbuji-Mayi	423,363
Zambia (1988 est.)	
Chingola	194,350
Kabwe	200,290
Kitwe	472,260
Luanshya	165,850
★ Lusaka	870,030
Mufulira	199,370
Ndola	442,670
Zimbabwe (1983 est.)	
Bulawayo	429,000
Chitungwiza	202,000
★ Harare	681,000

[1]1984. [2]Population refers to widest officially-defined agglomeration or metropolitan area. [3]Population of the statistical division containing the city. [4]1987. [5]Excludes the agricultural population of the named civil division. [6]Excludes population of Lefkoşa (Turkish-occupied Nicosia), estimated at 37,400 in 1985. [7]1986 census. [8]1983. [9]No separate areas within the state are distinguished administratively as cities. [10]Population includes Comayagüela. [11]1970. [12]1986. [13]1988. [14]1981. [15]Population refers to Kotte only.

Language

This table presents data on the principal language communities of each of the countries of the world. The countries, and the principal languages used in each, are listed alphabetically; a bullet (●) indicates those languages that are designated as official by each country. The sum of the estimated populations for each language community and of the "Other" group equals the 1989 estimated de facto population of the country given in the "Area and population" table.

The estimates represent, so far as national data collection systems permit, the distribution of mother tongues (a mother tongue being the language spoken first and, usually, most fluently by an individual). Many countries do not collect data on this basis, however, and for these countries a variety of techniques have been used to approximate mother-tongue distribution. Some countries compile data on ethnic or "national" groups; for such countries ethnic distribution was often assumed to conform roughly to the distribution of language communities. This approach, however, must be used with caution, because a minority population is not always free to educate its children in its own language and because better economic opportunities often draw minority group members into the majority-language community. For some countries, a given individual may only be visible in national statistics as a passport-holder of a foreign nation, however long he may remain resident. Such persons, often guest workers, have sometimes had to be assumed to be speakers of the principal language of their home country. For example, since The Netherlands does not collect language data, holders of Moroccan passports were assumed to be speakers of Arabic (although perhaps a quarter of them might be of Berber heritage). For other countries, the language mosaic may be so complex, the language communities so minute in size, scholarly study so inadequate, and the census base so obsolete that it is possible only to assign percentages to groups of related languages, despite their mutual unintelligibility (Papuan and Melanesian languages in Papua New Guinea, for instance). For some countries in the Americas, so few speakers of any single indigenous language remain that it was necessary to combine these groups as *Amerindian* so as to give a fair impression of their aggregate size within their respective countries.

No systematic attempt has been made to account for populations that may legitimately be described as bilingual, unless the country itself collects data on that basis, as does Bolivia or the Comoros, for example. Where a nonindigenous official or excolonial language constitutes a lingua franca of the country, however, speakers of the language as a second tongue are shown in italics, even though very few may speak it as a mother tongue. No comprehensive attempt has been made to distinguish between degrees of dialectical variance among communities *usually* classified as belonging to the same language though this *was* possible for some countries—*e.g.,* between French and Occitan (the dialect of southern France), or among the various dialects of Chinese.

In giving the names of Bantu languages, grammatical particles specific to a language's autonym (name for itself) have been omitted (the form *Rwanda* is used here, for example, rather than *kinyaRwanda,* and *Tswana* instead of *seTswana*). Parenthetical alternatives are given for a number of languages that differ markedly from the name of the people speaking them (such as Kurukh, spoken by the Oraon tribes of India) or that may be combined with other groups sometimes distinguishable in national data but appearing here under the name of the largest member—*e.g.,* "Tamil (and other Indian languages)" combining data on South Asian Indian populations in Singapore. The term *creole* as used here refers to distinguishable dialectical communities related to a national, official, or former colonial language (such as the French creole that survives in Mauritius from the end of French rule in 1810).

Language

Major languages by country	Number of speakers	Major languages by country	Number of speakers	Major languages by country	Number of speakers	Major languages by country	Number of speakers	Major languages by country	Number of speakers
Afghanistan[1]		**Australia**		**Benin**[1]		**Burkina Faso**[1, 2]		**Cayman Islands**	
● Dari (Persian), of which		Aboriginal and Torres		Bariba	440,000	Bobo	590,000	● English	25,300
Chahar Aimaq	430,000	Strait Islander		Fon	3,010,000	● French	520,000	**Central African Republic**[1]	
Hazāra	1,290,000	languages	180,000	● French	710,000	Fulani	730,000	Banda	800,000
Tadzhik	3,010,000	Chinese languages		Fulani (Peul)	190,000	Grusi	450,000	Baya (Gbaya)	690,000
● Pashto	7,750,000	(Hakka, Hokkien, and		Somba	250,000	Gurma	420,000	● French	320,000
Turkmen	300,000	Cantonese dialects,		Yoruba (Nago)	410,000	Lobi	610,000	Kare	70,000
Uzbek	1,290,000	and Standard Chinese		Other	300,000	Mande	770,000	Mbaka	120,000
Other (including		[Mandarin])	120,000	**Bermuda**		Mossi	4,180,000	Mbum	110,000
other Dari)	750,000	Dutch	120,000	● English	55,000	Senufo	460,000	Ngbandi	300,000
Albania[1]		● English	14,940,000	Other	4,000	Tuareg	290,000	Sango (lingua franca)	...
● Albanian	3,132,000	German	150,000	**Bhutan**[1]		Other	220,000	Sara	200,000
Greek	59,000	Greek	190,000	Assamese	190,000	**Burundi**[1]		Zande (Azande)	280,000
Macedonian	5,000	Italian	320,000	● Dzongkha (Bhutia)	880,000	● French	360,000	Other	250,000
Other	1,000	Yugoslav languages		Gurung	220,000	● Rundi	5,150,000	**Chad**[1]	
Algeria[1]		(Croatian, Macedonian,		Other	120,000	Hutu	4,330,000	● Arabic	1,450,000
● Arabic	20,290,000	Serbian, and		**Bolivia**		Tutsi	710,000	Dagu	130,000
Berber	4,170,000	Slovene)	170,000	● Aymara	550,000	Twa	50,000	● French	330,000
French	30,000	Other	620,000	● Quechua	990,000	Other[3]	140,000	Hausa	130,000
Other	80,000	**Austria**		● Spanish	2,610,000	**Cameroon**[1]		Kanuri	130,000
American Samoa		Czech	1,000	Aymara-Quechua	90,000	Bamileke-Widekum-		Kotoko	120,000
● English	2,000	● German	7,515,000	Spanish-Aymara	1,180,000	Bamum	2,120,000	Masa	130,000
● Samoan	34,000	Hungarian	3,000	Spanish-Quechua	1,500,000	Duala-Lunda-Basa	1,680,000	Masalit, Maba, and	
Other	3,000	Serbo-Croatian	12,000	Spanish-Aymara-		● English	...	Mimi	350,000
Andorra[1]		Slovene	9,000	Quechua	180,000	Fang	2,240,000	Mbum	360,000
● Catalan	14,000	Other	63,000	Spanish-others	90,000	● French	1,720,000	Mubi	230,000
French	4,000	**Bahamas, The**		Other	10,000	Fulani	1,100,000	Sara, Bagirmi,	
Spanish	28,000	● English	...	**Botswana**[1]		Maka	450,000	and Kreish	1,690,000
Other	5,000	English Creole	212,000	● English	...	Mandara	650,000	Tama	350,000
Angola[1]		French (Haitian) Creole	37,000	Khoikhoin (Hottentot)	31,000	Tikar	850,000	Teda (Tubu)	400,000
Ambo (Ovambo)	230,000	**Bahrain**		Ndebele	16,000	Other	2,340,000	Other	90,000
Chokwe	410,000	● Arabic	350,000	San (Bushmen)	44,000	**Canada**		**Chile**[1]	
Herero	70,000	Other	140,000	Shona	155,000	● English	15,839,000	Amerindian languages	
Kongo	1,280,000	**Bangladesh**[1]		Tswana	943,000	● French	6,361,000	(mostly Araucanian)	890,000
Luchazi	230,000	● Bengali	107,790,000	Other	61,000	English-French	343,000	● Spanish	11,870,000
Luimbe-Nganguela	530,000	Chakma	410,000	**Brazil**[1]		English-other	542,000	Other	200,000
Lunda	120,000	Garo	100,000	Amerindian		French-other	37,000	**China**[1]	
Luvale (Luena)	350,000	Khasi	90,000	languages	250,000	English-French-other	47,000	Achang	20,000
Mbunda	120,000	Magh	210,000	German	810,000	Aboriginal (Amerindian		Bulan (Blang)	60,000
Mbundu	2,100,000	Santal	80,000	Italian	620,000	and Eskimo [Inuktitut])		Ch'iang (Qiang)	110,000
Nyaneka-Humbe	530,000	Tippera	80,000	Japanese	710,000	languages	189,000	Chinese (Han)	1,030,320,000
Ovimbundu	3,620,000	Other	1,540,000	● Portuguese	143,650,000	Arabic	42,000	Cantonese	
● Portuguese	...	**Barbados**		Other	1,370,000	Chinese	275,000	(Yüeh [Yue])	51,500,000
Other	150,000	● English	20,000	**British Virgin Islands**		Dutch	128,000	Hakka	38,100,000
Anguilla		English Creole	233,000	● English	...	Filipino (Pilipino)	45,000	Hsiang (Xiang)	49,500,000
● English	...	Other	2,000	English Creole	12,000	Finnish	26,000	Kan (Gan)	24,700,000
English Creole	7,300	**Belgium**[1]		Other	1,000	German	453,000	● Mandarin	736,700,000
Antigua and Barbuda		● Dutch	5,860,000	**Brunei**[1]		Greek	115,000	Min	42,200,000
● English	...	● French	3,250,000	Chinese	46,000	Hungarian	71,000	Wu	87,060,000
English Creole	75,000	● German	90,000	● English	77,000	Italian	471,000	Chingpo (Jingpo)	100,000
Other	3,000	Italian	280,000	Indian	9,000	Polish	128,000	Chuang (Zhuang)	14,720,000
Argentina		Other	390,000	● Malay	173,000	Portuguese	160,000	Daghur (Daur)	100,000
Amerindian		**Belize**		Other indigenous	13,000	Punjābi	65,000	Evenk (Ewenki)	20,000
languages	360,000	Black Carib (Garífuna)	12,000	Other	10,000	Russian	26,000	Gelo	60,000
Italian	570,000	● English	94,000	**Bulgaria**[1]		Spanish	86,000	Hani (Woni)	1,170,000
● Spanish	31,140,000	English Creole (lingua		Armenian	30,000	Ukrainian	215,000	Hui	7,950,000
Other	360,000	franca)	140,000	● Bulgarian	7,670,000	Vietnamese	42,000	Kazakh	1,000,000
Aruba		German	3,000	Macedonian	220,000	Yiddish	24,000	Kirgiz	120,000
● Dutch	...	Mayan (Kekchi)	18,000	Romany	230,000	Other	458,000	Korean	1,940,000
Papiamento	55,000	Spanish	58,000	Russian	20,000	**Cape Verde**		Lahu	330,000
Other	6,000	Spanish (lingua		Turkish	760,000	Crioulo (Portuguese		Li	980,000
		franca)	110,000	Other	50,000	Creole)	368,000	Lisu	530,000
						● Portuguese	...	Manchu	4,740,000
								Maonan	40,000

Major languages by country	Number of speakers
Miao	5,520,000
Mongol	3,750,000
Mulam	100,000
Nakhi (Naxi)	280,000
Nu	30,000
Pai (Bai)	1,250,000
Pumi	30,000
Puyi (Chung-chia)	2,330,000
Salar	80,000
She	410,000
Shui	320,000
Sibo (Xibe)	90,000
Tadzhik	30,000
Tai (Dai)	920,000
Tibetan	4,230,000
Tu	180,000
T'u-chia (Tujia)	3,120,000
T'ung (Dong)	1,570,000
Tung-hsiang (Dongxiang)	310,000
Uighur	6,560,000
Wa (Va)	330,000
Yao	1,550,000
Yi	6,000,000
Other	990,000
Christmas Island	
Chinese	700
• English	300
Malay	300
Other	100
Cocos (Keeling) Islands[1]	
• English	200
Malay	400
Colombia[1]	
Amerindian languages	270,000
Arawakan	30,000
Cariban	20,000
Chibchan	140,000
Other	90,000
English Creole	40,000
• Spanish	32,000,000
Comoros	
• Arabic	...
Comorian	336,000
Comorian-French	58,000
Comorian-Malagasy	25,000
Comorian-Arabic	7,000
Comorian-Swahili	2,000
Comorian-French-other	17,000
• French	*30,000*
Other	2,000
Congo[1]	
Bubangi	30,000
• French	*650,000*
Kongo	1,160,000
Kota	20,000
Lingala (lingua franca)	...
Maka	40,000
Mbete	110,000
Mboshi	260,000
Monokutuba (lingua franca)	...
Punu	70,000
Sanga	60,000
Teke	390,000
Other	120,000
Cook Islands	
• English	...
• Maori	16,000
Other	1,000
Costa Rica	
Chibchan	6,000
Chinese	6,000
English Creole	59,000
• Spanish	2,859,000
Spanish-Chibchan	12,000
Côte d'Ivoire[1]	
Akan	5,020,000
• French	*3,180,000*
Kru	2,020,000
Malinke	1,800,000
Southern Mande	1,240,000
Voltaic (including Senufo)	1,910,000
Other	140,000
Cuba	
• Spanish	10,540,000
Cyprus[1]	
• Greek	540,000
• Turkish	170,000
Other	30,000
Czechoslovakia[1]	
• Czech	9,880,000
German	56,000
Hungarian	597,000
Polish	72,000
Romany	*400,000*
Russian	8,000
• Slovak	4,924,000
Ukrainian	47,000
Other	52,000
Denmark[1]	
• Danish	4,999,000
English	15,000

Major languages by country	Number of speakers
German	9,000
Norwegian	10,000
Swedish	8,000
Turkish	25,000
Yugoslav languages	9,000
Other	60,000
Djibouti[1]	
Afar	160,000
• Arabic	30,000
• French	*40,000*
Issa	190,000
Other	140,000
Dominica	
• English	...
French Creole	58,000
French Creole-English	25,000
Dominican Republic	
French (Haitian) Creole	140,000
• Spanish	6,870,000
Ecuador	
Quechuan (and other Indian languages)	730,000
• Spanish	9,760,000
Egypt[1]	
• Arabic	51,130,000
Other	620,000
El Salvador	
• Spanish	5,138,000
Equatorial Guinea[1]	
Bubi	50,000
Duala	9,000
Fang	247,000
Ibibio	5,000
Maka	5,000
• Spanish	...
Other[4]	27,000
Ethiopia[1]	
• Amharic	18,440,000
Gurage	1,600,000
Oromo (Galla)	17,280,000
Tigrinya	4,210,000
Other	7,370,000
Faeroe Islands	
• Danish	...
• Faeroese	47,800
Falkland Islands	
• English	2,000
Fiji[1]	
• English	...
Fijian	338,000
Hindī	358,000
Other	38,000
Finland	
• Finnish	4,644,000
• Swedish	301,000
Other	15,000
France	
Arabic[5]	1,460,000
• French[5, 6, 7]	52,300,000
Basque	*80,000*
Breton	*560,000*
Catalan (Rousillonais)	*200,000*
Corsican	*160,000*
Dutch (Flemish)	*100,000*
German (Alsatian)	*1,280,000*
Occitan	*1,520,000*
Italian[5]	350,000
Polish[5]	70,000
Portuguese[5]	790,000
Spanish[5]	330,000
Turkish[5]	130,000
Other[5]	680,000
French Guiana	
Amerindian languages	3,000
English Creole	1,000
• French	...
French Creoles	85,000
Other	5,000
French Polynesia	
• French[8]	12,000
Tahitian[8]	133,000
Other[9]	47,000
French speakers	*160,000*
Gabon[1]	
Fang	440,000
• French	*420,000*
Mbete	180,000
Mpongwe	190,000
Punu	140,000
Other	290,000
Gambia, The	
Dyola	90,000
• English	...
Fulani	160,000
Malinke	340,000
Soninke	70,000
Wolof	120,000
Other	60,000

Major languages by country	Number of speakers
Gaza Strip	
Arabic	579,000
Hebrew	...
Other	9,000
Germany, East[1]	
• German	16,560,000
Other	50,000
Germany, West[1]	
Dutch	110,000
• German	56,790,000
Greek	280,000
Italian	540,000
Portuguese	80,000
Spanish	150,000
Turkish	1,440,000
Yugoslav languages	590,00
Other	1,150,000
Ghana[1]	
Akan	7,640,000
• English	...
Ewe	1,730,000
Ga-Adangme	1,130,000
Mossi	2,310,000
Other	1,760,000
Gibraltar	
• English	10,000
Spanish	11,000
Other	9,000
Greece[1]	
Albanian	60,000
• Greek	9,640,000
Macedonian	150,000
Turkish	90,000
Other	140,000
Greenland	
• Danish	8,000
• Greenlandic	48,000
Grenada	
• English	...
English Creole	93,000
Other	3,000
Guadeloupe	
French Creole-French	325,000
• French	...
Other	17,000
Guam	
Chamorro	44,000
• English	46,000
Japanese	2,000
Palauan	1,000
Philippine languages	21,000
Other	13,000
Guatemala	
Black Carib (Garífuna)	20,000
Mayan languages	3,020,000
Cakchiquel	560,000
Kekchí	340,000
Mam	360,000
Quiché	1,190,000
• Spanish	5,900,000
Guernsey	
English	60,000
French	...
Guinea[1]	
• French	*570,000*
Fulani (Peul)	2,590,000
Kissi	400,000
Mande	3,420,000
Malinke	1,550,000
Susu	740,000
Other	1,130,000
Other	290,000
Guinea-Bissau	
Balante	139,000
Crioulo (Portuguese Creole)	41,000
Crioulo-Portuguese	21,000
Crioulo-other (except Portuguese)	285,000
Fulani	158,000
Malinke	66,000
Mandyako	47,000
Pepel	26,000
• Portuguese	—
Portuguese-other (except Crioulo)	77,000
Other	93,000
Guyana	
Amerindian languages	14,000
Arawakan	5,000
Cariban	9,000
• English	...
English Creoles	589,000
Other (includes Caribbean Hindi and English)	151,000
Haiti	
• French	50,000
French-Haitian (French) Creole	670,000
• Haitian (French) Creole	4,810,000

Major languages by country	Number of speakers
Honduras	
Black Carib (Garífuna)	93,000
English Creole	14,000
Miskito	13,000
• Spanish	4,408,000
Other	2,000
Hong Kong[1]	
• Chinese (Cantonese)[10]	5,581,000
• English	...
Filipino (Pilipino)	38,000
Other	135,000
Hungary[1]	
German	170,000
• Hungarian	10,220,000
Romanian	20,000
Slovak	120,000
Southern Slav	30,000
Other	20,000
Iceland[1]	
• Icelandic	244,000
Other	8,000
India	
Anga (Angika)	620,000
Assamese	13,680,000
Baghēlkhaṇḍī	350,000
Bāgṛī	1,610,000
Banjārī	720,000
Barel	350,000
Bengali	67,980,000
Bhīlī (Bhilali)	380,000
Bhīlī (Bhilodi)	1,910,000
Bhojpurī	21,900,000
Boḍo	780,000
Bundēlkhaṇḍī	570,000
Chhattīsgaṛhī	10,220,000
Ḍōgrī	1,980,000
• English (lingua franca)	*21,000,000*
Gaṛhwālī	1,950,000
Gārō	630,000
Gojri	500,000
Gōṇḍī	2,360,000
Gujarātī	39,180,000
Halabī	530,000
Hāṛautī	510,000
• Hindī	234,740,000
Hindī (lingua franca)	*376,000,000*
Hō	1,150,000
Kachchī	720,000
Kannaḍa	32,940,000
Kashmiri	3,700,000
Khāsī	590,000
Khortha (Khotta)	770,000
Kōṅkaṇī	2,330,000
Kōrkū	430,000
Kōyā	320,000
Kui	530,000
Kumaunī	1,890,000
Kurukh (Oraon)	1,890,000
Lamani (Banjārī)	1,840,000
Lushai (Mizo)	410,000
Maghī (Magadhi)	10,140,000
Maithilī	9,350,000
Malayāḷam	33,470,000
Mālvī	980,000
Maṇḍeālī	370,000
Marāṭhī	63,710,000
Mārwāṛī	7,200,000
Meithei (Manipurī)	1,190,000
Mēwāṛī	1,250,000
Mikir	300,000
Muṇḍā	330,000
Muṇḍārī	1,180,000
Nagpurī	510,000
Nepali (Gōrkhālī)	1,960,000
Nimāḍī	1,210,000
Oṛiyā	30,120,000
Pahāṛī	1,940,000
Punjābī	21,230,000
Rajāsthānī	3,200,000
Sadānī (Sadrī)	1,230,000
Santālī	5,640,000
Savara (Sōrā)	340,000
Sindhī	1,840,000
Surgujia	820,000
Tamil	57,400,000
Telugu	68,270,000
Tripuri	410,000
Tuḷu	1,770,000
Urdū	43,670,000
Other	11,820,000
Indonesia	
• Bahasa Indonesia	21,280,000
Balinese	3,610,000
Banjarese	2,370,000
Batak	3,770,000
Bugi	3,400,000
Javanese	71,000,000
Madurese	8,520,000
Minang	4,460,000
Sundanese	27,000,000
Other	31,640,000
Iran[1]	
Armenian	260,000
Iranian languages	40,260,000
Bakhtyārī (Lurī)	910,000

Major languages by country	Number of speakers
Baluchi	1,240,000
• Farsī (Persian)	24,790,000
Gīlakī	2,870,000
Kurdish	4,960,000
Lurī	2,350,000
Māzandarānī	1,960,000
Other	1,180,000
Semitic languages	1,300,000
Arabic	1,170,000
Other	130,000
Turkic languages	12,110,000
Afshari	610,000
Azerbaijani	9,130,000
Qashqa'i	690,000
Shahsavani	330,000
Turkish (mostly Pishagchi, Bayat, and Qajar)	390,000
Turkmen	850,000
Other	110,000
Other	400,000
Iraq[1]	
• Arabic	13,270,000
Assyrian	140,000
Kurdish	3,270,000
Persian	140,000
Turkish	60,000
Turkmen	230,000
Other	100,000
Ireland	
• English	3,340,000
• Irish	180,000
Isle of Man	
• English	64,000
Israel	
• Arabic	839,000
English	55,000
French	37,000
German	30,000
• Hebrew	3,138,000
Hungarian	26,000
Romanian	71,000
Russian	78,000
Spanish	39,000
Yiddish	98,000
Other	152,000
Italy[1]	
Albanian	120,000
Catalan	30,000
French	300,000
German	300,000
Greek	40,000
• Italian	54,020,000
Rhaetian	740,000
Friulian	720,000
Ladin	20,000
Sardinian	1,520,000
Slovene	120,000
Other	240,000
Jamaica	
Chinese	22,000
• English	636,000
English Creoles	1,663,000
Hindi and other Indian languages	49,000
Spanish	5,000
Japan[1]	
Chinese	60,000
• Japanese	122,400,000
Korean	580,000
Other	90,000
Jersey	
English	83,000
• French	...
Jordan[1]	
• Arabic	3,030,000
Other	30,000
Kampuchea (Cambodia)[1]	
Chinese	370,000
• Khmer	7,090,000
Vietnamese	370,000
Other[11]	210,000
Kenya[1]	
Arabic	60,000
Bajun (Rajun)	60,000
Basuba	90,000
Boran	110,000
Degodia	140,000
Embu	280,000
Gabbra	50,000
Gurreh	130,000
Gusii (Kisii)	1,450,000
Kalenjin	2,530,000
Kamba	2,650,000
Kikuyu	4,910,000
Kuria	140,000
Luhya	3,520,000
Luo	3,000,000
Masai	370,000
Mbere	90,000
Meru	1,290,000
Nyika (Mijikenda)	1,120,000
Ogaden	40,000
Orma	50,000

Language (continued)

Major languages by country	Number of speakers
Pokomo	60,000
Sambur	110,000
Somali	240,000
Swahili	10,000
● Swahili (lingua franca)	14,100,000
Taita	240,000
Teso	200,000
Turkana	320,000
Other[12]	530,000
Kiribati[1]	
● English	...
Kiribati (Gilbertese)	68,700
Tuvaluan (Ellice)	500
Other	400
Korea, North[1]	
● Korean	22,370,000
Chinese	40,000
Korea, South[1]	
● Korean	42,340,000
Other	40,000
Kuwait[1]	
● Arabic	1,600,000
Other	450,000
Laos[1]	
● Lao	2,640,000
Miao (Hmong)- Man (Yao)	210,000
Mon-Khmer	180,000
Palaung-Wa	470,000
Tai	310,000
Other[13]	130,000
Lebanon[1]	
● Arabic	2,636,000
Armenian	20,000
French	700,000
Kurdish	14,000
Other	226,000
Lesotho[1]	
● English	...
● Sotho	1,710,000
Other	5,000
Liberia[1]	
● English	370,000
Kwa (Kru)	
Bassa	347,000
Belle	13,000
Dey	9,000
Grebo	225,000
Krahn	95,000
Kru	184,000
Mande (Northern)	
Gbandi	71,000
Kpelle	487,000
Loma	142,000
Mandingo	128,000
Mende	20,000
Vai	90,000
Mande (Southern)	
Gio	197,000
Mano	178,000
West Atlantic (Mel)	
Gola	99,000
Kissi	101,000
Other	124,000
Libya[1]	
● Arabic	3,700,000
Berber	210,000
Other[14]	170,000
Liechtenstein[1]	
● German	25,900
Other	2,400
Luxembourg[1]	
Belgian	9,000
● French	12,000
● German	9,000
Italian	20,000
Luxembourgish	278,000
Portuguese	30,000
Spanish	2,000
Other	16,000
Macau	
Chinese	473,000
● Portuguese	...
Other	11,000
Madagascar[1]	
● French	1,200,000
Malagasy	11,480,000
Other	120,000
Malawi[1]	
● Chewa (Maravi)	4,970,000
● English	...
Lomwe	1,560,000
Ngoni	570,000
Yao	1,130,000
Other	290,000
Malaysia	
Bajau	110,000
Chinese	1,010,000
Chinese and others	570,000
Dusan	180,000
English	90,000
English and others	190,000

Major languages by country	Number of speakers
Iban	410,000
Iban and others	70,000
● Malay	7,510,000
Malay and others	2,670,000
Tamil	680,000
Tamil and others	10,000
Other	3,920,000
Maldives	
● Divehi (Maldivian)	209,000
Mali[1]	
Bambara	2,520,000
Bobo	190,000
Dogon	320,000
Dyula	230,000
● French	630,000
Fulani	1,100,000
Malinke	530,000
Senufo	950,000
Songhai	570,000
Soninke	690,000
Tuareg	580,000
Other	240,000
Malta[1]	
● English	7,000
● Maltese	334,000
Other	8,000
Martinique	
French Creole-French	326,000
● French	...
Other	11,000
Mauritania[1]	
● Arabic	...
● French	110,000
Fulani	20,000
Hassānīyah Arabic	1,590,000
Soninke	50,000
Tukulor	100,000
Wolof	130,000
Other	50,000
Mauritius	
Bhojpuri	209,000
● English	2,000
French	38,000
French Creole	589,000
Hindi	118,000
Tamil	38,000
Urdū	25,000
Other	42,000
Mayotte[15]	
Maharais (local dialect of Comorian Swahili)	70,000
Other Comorian Swahili dialects	29,000
Malagasy	32,000
● French	25,000
Arabic	2,000
Other	3,000
Mexico	
Amerindian languages	7,590,000
Aztec (Nahuatl)	2,020,000
Chinantec	110,000
Chol	140,000
Huastec	150,000
Huichol	80,000
Mazahua	280,000
Mazatec	180,000
Mayo	80,000
Mixe	110,000
Mixtec	470,000
Otomi	450,000
Tarahumara	90,000
Tarasco	170,000
Tlapanec	80,000
Totonac	290,000
Tzeltal	320,000
Tzotzil	200,000
Yucatec (Mayan)	970,000
Zapotec	620,000
Other	770,000
● Spanish	76,650,000
Spanish-Amerindian languages	5,420,000
Monaco[1]	
English	2,000
● French	14,000
Italian	5,000
Monegasque	5,000
Other	4,000
Mongolia[1]	
Bayad	41,000
Buryat	39,000
Dariganga	32,000
Dörbed	59,000
Dzakhchin	26,000
Kazakh	111,000
● Khalkha (Mongolian)	1,625,000
Ould	12,000
Torgut	11,000
Uryankhai	25,000
Other	116,000
Montserrat	
● English	...
English Creole	12,000

Major languages by country	Number of speakers
Morocco[1]	
● Arabic	18,250,000
Berber	6,160,000
Other[11]	130,000
Mozambique[1]	
Makua	7,240,000
Malawi	1,840,000
● Portuguese	...
Shona	1,720,000
Tsonga	3,560,000
Yao	580,000
Other	360,000
Myanmar (Burma)[1]	
● Burmese	27,750,000
Karen	2,690,000
Rakhine (Arakanese)	1,800,000
Shan	3,630,000
Other	4,940,000
Nauru	
Chinese	700
English	600
Kiribati (Gilbertese)	1,400
● Nauruan	4,700
Tuvaluan (Ellice)	700
Nepal	
Bhojpuri	1,400,000
Bhutia (Sherpa)	90,000
Gurung	210,000
Hindī (Awadhi dialect)	290,000
Limbu	160,000
Magar	260,000
Maithili	2,050,000
● Nepāli	10,770,000
Newari	550,000
Rai, Kirati	270,000
Tamang	640,000
Thārū	670,000
Other	1,080,000
Netherlands, The[1]	
Arabic	131,000
● Dutch	14,249,000
Dutch and Frisian	400,000
Turkish	169,000
Other	297,000
Netherlands Antilles	
● Dutch	...
English	15,000
Papiamento	157,000
Other	11,000
New Caledonia	
● French	56,000
Melanesian languages	66,000
Polynesian languages (mostly Wallisian)	26,000
Other	9,000
New Zealand	
● English	3,149,000
● Maori	108,000
Other	115,000
Nicaragua	
English Creole	37,000
Misumalpan languages	
Miskito	148,000
Sumo	9,000
● Spanish	3,548,000
Other	3,000
Niger	
Arabic	30,000
● French	1,100,000
Fulani	720,000
Gurma	10,000
Hausa	3,860,000
Hausa (lingua franca)	6,100,000
Kanuri	300,000
Songhai, Zerma, and Dendi	1,550,000
Tamashek (Tuareg)	600,000
Teda (Tubu)	20,000
Other	60,000
Nigeria[1]	
Arabic	300,000
Bura	1,800,000
Edo	3,900,000
● English (lingua franca)	17,000,000
English Creole (lingua franca)[16]	41,000,000
Fulani	13,000,000
Hausa	24,700,000
Hausa (lingua franca)	37,000,000
Ibibio	6,500,000
Igbo (Ibo)	20,800,000
Ijaw	2,100,000
Kanuri	4,800,000
Nupe	1,400,000
Tiv	2,600,000
Yoruba	24,700,000
Other	9,100,000
Niue	
● English	...
Niuean	2,200

Major languages by country	Number of speakers
Norfolk Island	
● English	1,900
Norway[1]	
Danish	17,000
English	25,000
● Norwegian	4,117,000
Swedish	11,000
Other	58,000
Oman[1]	
● Arabic (Omani)	1,090,000
Bengali	40,000
Indian	210,000
Pakistani (mostly Baluchi)	50,000
Other	30,000
Pacific Islands, Trust Territory of the Marshall Islands	
● English	700
● Marshallese	40,200
Other	3,000
Micronesia, Federated States of	
● English	500
Kosraean	7,700
Mortlockese	8,000
Palauan	400
Pohnpeian	24,900
Trukese	43,700
Woleaian	3,900
Yapese	6,100
Other	9,900
Northern Mariana Islands	
Chamorro	12,400
● English	1,200
Palauan	900
Philippine languages	3,100
Woleaian	2,600
Other	2,500
Palau	
● English	1,100
● Palauan	12,600
Other	2,200
Pakistan	
Baluchi	3,580,000
Brahui	1,430,000
Pashto	15,610,000
Punjābi, of which	
Punjābi	57,240,000
Hindko	2,890,000
Sindhi, of which	
Sindhī	13,990,000
Siraiki	11,680,000
● Urdū	9,030,000
Other[12]	3,390,000
Panama	
Amerindian languages	111,000
Chibchan	99,000
Cuna	43,000
Guaymí	56,000
Choco	12,000
Chinese	7,000
English	...
English Creoles	332,000
● Spanish	1,917,000
Other	3,000
Papua New Guinea[1]	
● English	...
Melanesian languages	540,000
Papuan languages	3,020,000
Other[17]	30,000
Paraguay	
German	36,000
Guarani	1,668,000
Guarani-Spanish	2,022,000
Portuguese	131,000
● Spanish	270,000
Other	30,000
Peru	
Aymara	630,000
● Quechua	5,790,000
● Spanish	14,820,000
Other	550,000
Philippines	
Aklanon	590,000
Bicol	4,170,000
Bolinao (Zambal)	260,000
Cebuano	14,610,000
Chavacano	310,000
Chinese	150,000
Davaweno	180,000
● English	20,000
● Filipino (Pilipino; Tagalog)	14,270,000
Hamtikanon	490,000
Hiligaynon/Ilongo	5,990,000
Ibanag	350,000
Ifugao	190,000
Ilocano	6,670,000
Kangkanai	220,000
Maguindanao	720,000
Manobo	190,000
Maranao	860,000

Major languages by country	Number of speakers
Masbate	440,000
Pampango	2,050,000
Pangasinan	1,350,000
Romblon	250,000
Samal	350,000
Samar-Leyte (Waray-Waray)	2,770,000
Subanon	200,000
Sulu-Moro (Tau Sug)	470,000
Other	1,810,000
Pitcairn Island	
● English	56
Poland	
Belorussian	190,000
● Polish	37,380,000
Ukrainian	230,000
Other	80,000
Portugal[1]	
● Portuguese	10,280,000
Other	90,000
Puerto Rico	
● English	13,000
● Spanish	1,877,000
Spanish-English	1,372,000
Other	46,000
Qatar[1]	
● Arabic	170,000
Other[18]	260,000
Réunion	
● French	180,000
French Creole	530,000
Other[19]	60,000
Romania	
Bulgarian	9,000
German	357,000
Hebrew	25,000
Hungarian	1,796,000
● Romanian	20,640,000
Romany	81,000
Russian	19,000
Serbo-Croatian	42,000
Slovak	21,000
Tatar	23,000
Turkish	23,000
Ukrainian	56,000
Other	76,000
Rwanda	
● French	480,000
● Rwanda	6,990,000
St. Helena and Ascension	
● English	7,300
St. Kitts and Nevis	
● English	...
English Creole	44,000
St. Lucia	
● English	...
French/English Creole	142,000
Other	8,000
St. Pierre and Miquelon[1]	
● French	6,100
Other	100
St. Vincent and the Grenadines	
● English	...
English Creole	113,000
Other	1,000
San Marino[1]	
● Italian	22,900
São Tomé and Príncipe	
Crioulo (Portuguese Creole)	118,000
● Portuguese	...
Saudi Arabia[1]	
● Arabic	12,910,000
Other	680,000
Senegal[1]	
Dyola	500,000
● French	370,000
Fulani (Peul)	920,000
Malinke (Mandingo)	400,000
Maure	90,000
Sarakole (Soninke)	120,000
Serer	1,060,000
Tukulor	780,000
Wolof	3,100,000
Other	410,000
Seychelles	
● English	...
● French	10,000
French Creole	64,000
Other	3,000
Sierra Leone[1]	
Bullom	150,000
● English	...
Fulani	150,000
Kissi	90,000
Kono	200,000
Koranko	140,000

Major languages by country	Number of speakers
Krio (English Creole [lingua franca])	...
Limba	330,000
Mende	1,370,000
Temne	1,250,000
Yalunka	140,000
Other	140,000
Singapore[1]	
● Bahasa Malaysia	405,000
Chinese	2,032,000
● English	...
● Mandarin Chinese	...
● Tamil (and other Indian languages)	174,000
Other	63,000
Solomon Islands[1]	
● English	...
Melanesian languages	272,000
Papuan languages	27,000
Polynesian languages	12,000
Other[20]	7,000
Somalia[1]	
● Arabic	...
English	...
● Somali	7,210,000
Other	120,000
South Africa[21]	
● Afrikaans[22]	6,000,000
● English[22]	3,420,000
Nguni	11,640,000
North Ndebele	200,000
South Ndebele	360,000
Swazi	800,000
Xhosa	2,640,000
Zulu	7,650,000
Sotho	7,100,000
North Sotho	3,040,000
South Sotho	2,390,000
Tswana (Western Sotho)	1,670,000
Tsonga	1,140,000
Venda	200,000
Other	730,000
Bophuthatswana	
● Afrikaans	...
● English	...
Nguni	270,000
North Ndebele	50,000
South Ndebele	40,000
Swazi	30,000
Xhosa	90,000
Zulu	60,000
Sotho	1,480,000
North Sotho	120,000
South Sotho	80,000
● Tswana	1,280,000
Tsonga	130,000
Venda	10,000
Other	20,000
Ciskei	
● English	...
● Xhosa	810,000
Other	20,000
Transkei	
● English	...
● Xhosa	3,040,000
Other	190,000
Venda	
● Afrikaans	...
● English	...
● Venda	450,000
Other	50,000
South West Africa/Namibia[1]	
● Afrikaans	...
Bergdama (Damara)	96,000
East Caprivian (mostly Lozi)	47,000
● English	135,000
German	...
Herero	96,000
Kavango (Okavango)	118,000
Nama	61,000
Ovambo (Ambo [Kwanyama])	632,000
San (Bushmen)	36,000
Other	183,000
Spain	
Basque	900,000
● Castilian Spanish	28,510,000
Catalan	6,420,000
Galician	3,210,000
Other	120,000
Sri Lanka	
English	10,000
English-Sinhalese	930,000
English-Tamil	190,000
English-Sinhalese-Tamil	610,000
● Sinhalese	10,170,000
Sinhalese-Tamil	1,570,000
● Tamil	3,310,000
Other	60,000
Sudan, The[1]	
● Arabic	13,460,000
Azande	740,000
Bari	670,000
Beja	1,740,000
Dinka	3,150,000
Fur	560,000
Lotuko	400,000
Nubian	2,210,000
Nuer	1,340,000
Shilluk	470,000
Other	2,540,000
Suriname	
● Dutch	...
English	...
Sranantonga	170,000
Sranantonga-other	170,000
Other (mostly Hindi, Javanese, and Saramacca)	90,000
Swaziland[1]	
● English	...
● Swazi	630,000
Zulu	70,000
Other[23]	40,000
Sweden[1]	
Finnish	263,000
● Swedish	7,732,000
Other	502,000
Switzerland	
● French	1,232,000
● German	4,351,000
● Italian	654,000
Romansh	54,000
Other	399,000
Syria[1]	
● Arabic	10,410,000
Armenian	330,000
Kurdish	740,000
Other	250,000
Taiwan[1]	
South Fukien Chinese	13,420,000
Hakka and Hokkien Chinese	2,000,000
● Mandarin Chinese	4,190,000
Other	420,000
Tanzania[1]	
Chagga (Chaga), Pare	1,170,000
● English	...
Gogo	930,000
Ha	820,000
Haya	1,400,000
Hehet	1,630,000
Iramba	680,000
Luguru	1,170,000
Luo	200,000
Makonde	1,400,000
Masai	230,000
Ngoni	310,000
Nyakyusa	1,280,000
Nyamwezi (Sukuma)	5,010,000
Shambala	1,010,000
● Swahili	2,100,000
Tatoga	180,000
Yao	580,000
Other	3,650,000
Thailand[1]	
Chinese	6,700,000
Karen	200,000
Malay	2,010,000
Mon-Khmer languages	1,490,000
Khmer	700,000
Kuy	590,000
Other	190,000
Thai languages	44,290,000
Lao	14,860,000
● Thai (Siamese)	29,050,000
Other	380,000
Other	570,000
Togo[1]	
● French	620,000
Gur (Voltaic) languages	
Gurma	580,000
Tem-Kabre	970,000
Kwa languages	
Ana-Ife (Yoruba)	120,000
Ewe-Adja	1,560,000
Kebu-Akposo	140,000
Other	260,000
Tokelau	
● English	...
Tokelauan	1,700
Tonga	
● English	...
● Tongan	94,000
Other	2,000
Trinidad and Tobago	
● English	...
English Creole	1,285,000
French Creole	...
Hindi	...
Spanish	...
Tunisia	
● Arabic	5,580,000
Arabic-French	2,090,000
Arabic-French-English	250,000
Arabic-other	10,000
Other-no Arabic	20,000
Other	20,000
Turkey[1]	
Arabic	880,000
Kurdish	5,880,000
● Turkish	47,580,000
Other	1,210,000
Turks and Caicos Islands	
● English	...
English Creole	10,800
Haitian (French) Creole	2,700
Tuvalu	
● English	...
Kiribati (Gilbertese)	700
Tuvaluan (Ellice)	8,200
Uganda[1]	
Acholi	770,000
Chiga (Kiga)	1,130,000
● English	...
Ganda (Luganda)	2,930,000
Gisu	1,180,000
Gwere	470,000
Karamojong	340,000
Lango	990,000
Lugbara	630,000
Nkole	1,350,000
Nyoro	540,000
Rundi	510,000
Rwanda	960,000
Soga	1,350,000
● Swahili	...
Teso	1,460,000
Toro	530,000
Other	1,330,000
U.S.S.R.	
Armenian	4,130,000
Avar	520,000
Azerbaijani	5,890,000
Bashkir	1,010,000
Belorussian	7,710,000
Bulgarian	270,000
Buryat	350,000
Chechen	820,000
Chuvash	1,570,000
Dargin	310,000
Estonian	1,070,000
Gagauz	170,000
Georgian	3,850,000
German	1,210,000
Greek	140,000
Hebrew	280,000
Hungarian	180,000
Ingush	200,000
Kabardinian	350,000
Kara-Kalpak	320,000
Kazakh	7,020,000
Kirgiz	2,050,000
Komi	270,000
Komi-Permyak	130,000
Korean	240,000
Kumyk	250,000
Lak	100,000
Latvian	1,500,000
Lezgian	380,000
Lithuanian	3,070,000
Mari	590,000
Moldavian	3,040,000
Mordvinian	950,000
Ossetian	520,000
Polish	370,000
● Russian	168,560,000
Tadzhik	3,110,000
Tatar	5,960,000
Turkmenian	2,200,000
Tuvinian	180,000
Udmurt	600,000
Uighur	200,000
Ukrainian	38,500,000
Uzbek	13,470,000
Yakut	340,000
Other	3,840,000
United Arab Emirates[1]	
● Arabic	770,000
Other[18]	1,060,000
United Kingdom	
● English	53,170,000
Scots-Gaelic	70,000
Welsh	530,000
Other	3,440,000
United States	
American Indian or Alaska Native languages	430,000
Arabic	270,000
Armenian	120,000
Asian Indian languages	310,000
Chinese	760,000
Czech	140,000
Dutch	180,000
● English	220,620,000
Finnish	80,000
French	1,870,000
German	1,880,000
Greek	480,000
Hungarian	200,000
Italian	1,870,000
Japanese	400,000
Korean	340,000
Lithuanian	80,000
Norwegian	130,000
Persian	130,000
Philippine languages	600,000
Polish	940,000
Portuguese	420,000
Russian	200,000
Serbo-Croatian	180,000
Slovak	100,000
Spanish	13,910,000
Swedish	120,000
Thai	110,000
Ukrainian	140,000
Vietnamese	240,000
Yiddish	360,000
Other	1,190,000
Uruguay	
● Spanish	2,910,000
Other	110,000
Vanuatu	
● Bislama (English Creole)	130,000
● English	...
● French	50,000
Melanesian languages	145,000
Other	9,000
Venezuela	
● Amerindian languages	190,000
Goajiro (Guajiro)	70,000
Warrau (Waroa)	30,000
Other	90,000
● Spanish	18,640,000
Other	420,000
Vietnam[1]	
Bahnar	100,000
Chinese	1,240,000
Hre	130,000
Jarai	200,000
Khmer	810,000
Miao (Meo or Hmong)	440,000
Muong	760,000
Nung	600,000
Rhadé	180,000
Tai	760,000
Tho (Tay)	960,000
● Vietnamese	57,450,000
Other	1,650,000
Virgin Islands (U.S.)	
● English	87,000
French	3,000
Spanish	14,000
Other	3,000
Wallis and Futuna	
● French	...
Wallisian	15,400
West Bank	
Arabic	854,000
Hebrew	31,000
Western Sahara	
Arabic	195,000
Western Samoa	
● English	1,000
● Samoan	77,000
Samoan-English	85,000
Yemen (Aden)[1]	
● Arabic	2,300,000
Other	100,000
Yemen (Ṣan'ā')[1]	
● Arabic	8,690,000
Other	140,000
Yugoslavia	
Albanian	1,860,000
Hungarian	430,000
● Macedonian	1,450,000
Romany	150,000
● Serbo-Croatian	17,280,000
● Slovene	1,860,000
Vlach	140,000
Other	540,000
Zaire[1]	
Azande	2,030,000
Boa	780,000
Chokwe	610,000
● French	2,590,000
Kongo	5,350,000
Luba	5,990,000
Lugbara	540,000
Mongo	4,490,000
Ngala and Bangi	1,930,000
Rundi	1,280,000
Rwanda	3,420,000
Teke	910,000
Other	5,990,000
Zambia[1]	
Barotze group	670,000
Lozi (Barotze)	490,000
Luyana (Luyi)	120,000
Nkoya	50,000
Other	10,000
Bemba group	2,960,000
Bemba	2,040,000
Bisa	120,000
Lala	230,000
Lamba	190,000
Ushi (Aushi)	140,000
Other	240,000
● English	...
Mambwe group	370,000
Lungu	80,000
Mambwe	130,000
Mwanga (Winamwanga)	150,000
Other	10,000
Maravi (Nyanja) group	1,430,000
Chewa	430,000
Maravi (Nyanja)	420,000
Ngoni	160,000
Nsenga	370,000
Other	50,000
North-Western group	820,000
Chokwe	50,000
Kaonde	220,000
Luchazi	50,000
Lunda	210,000
Luvale (Luena)	160,000
Mbunda	120,000
Tonga (Ila-Tonga) group	1,230,000
Ila	70,000
Lenje	140,000
Soli	60,000
Tonga	890,000
Other	70,000
Tumbuka group	370,000
Senga	70,000
Tumbuka	300,000
Other	290,000
Zimbabwe	
● English	710,000
Ndebele (Nguni)	1,440,000
Nyanja	470,000
Shona	6,460,000
Other	40,000

[1]Figures given represent ethnolinguistic groups. [2]Majority of population speak Moré (language of the Mossi); Dyula is language of commerce. [3]Swahili also spoken. [4]Pidgin English and Portuguese Creole also spoken. [5]Based on "nationality" at 1982 census. [6]Includes naturalized citizens. [7]French is the universal language throughout France; traditional dialects and minority languages are retained regionally in the approximate numbers shown, however. [8]Mother tongue. [9]Mostly non-Tahitian Polynesian and Chinese languages bilingual or multilingual with French or Tahitian. [10]Includes some Kan-Hakka and Mandarin speakers. [11]French also spoken. [12]English also spoken. [13]English and French also spoken. [14]English and Italian also spoken. [15]Data reflect ability to speak the language, not mother tongue. 1989 population estimate is 78,000. [16]Includes speakers of standard English. [17]About half the population also speaks Pisin (Pidgin English); English and Hiri (Police Motu) also spoken. [18]Mostly Pakistanis, Indians, and Iranians. [19]Gujarāti and Chinese also spoken. [20]Solomon Islands Pidgin (English) is the lingua franca. [21]Excludes the Black states shown separately. [22]White, Coloured, and Asian speakers only. [23]Afrikaans and Portuguese also spoken.

Religion

The following table presents statistics on religious affiliation for each of the countries of the world. An assessment was made for each country of the available data on distribution of religious communities within the total population; the best available figures, whether originating as census data, membership figures of the churches concerned, or estimates by external analysts in the absence of reliable local data, were applied as percentages to the estimated 1989 midyear population of the country to obtain the data shown below.

Several concepts govern the nature of the available data, each useful separately but none the basis of any standard of international practice in the collection of such data. The word "affiliation" was used above to describe the nature of the relationship joining the religious bodies named and the populations shown. This term implies some sort of formal, usually documentary, connection between the religion and the individual (a baptismal certificate, a child being assigned the religion of its parents on a census form, maintenance of one's name on the tax rolls of a state religion, etc.) but says nothing about the nature of the individual's personal religious practice, in that the individual may have lapsed, never been confirmed as an adult, joined another religion, or may have joined an organization that is formally atheist.

The user of these statistics should be careful to note that not only does the nature of the affiliation (with an organized religion) differ greatly from country to country, but the social context of religious practice does also. A country in which a single religion has long been predominant will often show more than 90% of its population to be *affiliated,* while in actual fact, no more than 10% may actually *practice* that religion on a regular basis. Such a situation often leads to undercounting of minority religions (where someone [head of household, communicant, child] is counted at all), blurring of distinctions seen to be significant elsewhere (a Hindu country may not distinguish Protestant [or even Christian] denominations; a Christian country may not distinguish among its Muslim or Buddhist citizens), or double-counting in countries where an individual may conscientiously practice more than one "religion" at a time.

Communist countries consciously attempt to ignore, suppress, or render invisible religious practice within their boundaries. Countries with large numbers of adherents of traditional, often animist, religions and belief systems usually have little or no formal methodology for defining the nature of local religious practice. On the other hand, countries with strong missionary traditions, or good census organizations, or few religious sensitivities may have very good, detailed, and meaningful data.

The most authoritative work available is DAVID B. BARRETT (ed.), *World Christian Encyclopedia* (1982); it examines both the theoretical and practical problems of collecting and analyzing religious statistics, assembles a mine of national detail, and establishes a basis for further study.

Religion

Religious affiliation	1989 population
Afghanistan	
Sunnī Muslim	10,970,000
Shī'ī Muslim	2,220,000
other	1,630,000
Albania	
Muslim	660,000
Christian[1]	170,000
atheist	600,000
nonreligious	1,770,000
Algeria	
Sunnī Muslim	24,360,000
other	220,000
American Samoa	
Congregational	22,000
other	17,000
Andorra	
Roman Catholic	50,000
Angola	
Christian[1]	8,770,000
traditional beliefs	930,000
other	50,000
Anguilla	
Anglican	2,900
Methodist	2,400
other	2,000
Antigua and Barbuda	
Anglican	35,000
Protestant	33,000
Roman Catholic	8,000
other	2,000
Argentina	
Roman Catholic	30,150,000
other	2,280,000
Aruba	
Roman Catholic	54,300
other	7,000
Australia[2]	
Anglican	4,390,000
Roman Catholic	4,370,000
Uniting Church	820,000
Presbyterian	740,000
Methodist	570,000
Orthodox	490,000
other Protestant	1,070,000
nonreligious	1,820,000
other	2,530,000
Austria	
Roman Catholic	6,410,000
Protestant	430,000
atheist and nonreligious	450,000
other	320,000
Bahamas, The	
Protestant	137,000
Anglican	50,000
Roman Catholic	47,000
other	15,000
Bahrain	
Shī'ī Muslim	290,000
Sunnī Muslim	120,000
other	80,000
Bangladesh	
Muslim	95,570,000
Hindu	13,380,000
other	1,340,000
Barbados	
Anglican	101,000
Protestant	65,000
other	89,000
Belgium	
Roman Catholic	8,890,000
other	990,000
Belize	
Roman Catholic	114,000
Anglican	22,000
other	49,000
Benin	
traditional beliefs	2,820,000
Roman Catholic	850,000
Muslim	700,000
other	220,000
Bermuda	
Anglican	22,000
Methodist	10,000
Roman Catholic	8,000
other	19,000
Bhutan	
Buddhist	980,000
Hindu	350,000
other	80,000
Bolivia	
Roman Catholic	6,650,000
other	540,000
Botswana	
Christian[1]	630,000
traditional beliefs	620,000
other	10,000
Brazil	
Roman Catholic	129,420,000
Protestant	8,990,000
Afro-American Spiritist	2,950,000
Spiritist	2,510,000
atheist and nonreligious	2,060,000
other	1,470,000
British Virgin Islands	
Methodist	5,700
Anglican	2,600
other	4,200
Brunei	
Muslim	159,000
other	92,000
Bulgaria	
Eastern Orthodox	2,400,000
Muslim	670,000
atheist	5,800,000
other	120,000
Burkina Faso	
traditional beliefs	3,900,000
Muslim	3,750,000
Christian[1]	1,060,000
Burundi	
Roman Catholic	4,140,000
traditional beliefs	710,000
other	450,000
Cameroon	
Roman Catholic	3,990,000
Protestant	2,010,000
traditional beliefs	2,460,000
Muslim	2,510,000
other	430,000
Canada	
Roman Catholic	12,400,000
Protestant	7,680,000
Anglican	2,650,000
Eastern Orthodox	390,000
Jewish	320,000
Muslim	110,000
Sikh	70,000
Hindu	80,000
nonreligious	1,940,000
other	550,000
Cape Verde	
Roman Catholic	360,000
Protestant	8,000
Cayman Islands	
Presbyterian	9,000
Church of God	6,000
other	10,000
Central African Republic	
Protestant	1,390,000
Roman Catholic	930,000
traditional beliefs	340,000
other	160,000
Chad	
Muslim	2,440,000
Christian[1]	1,830,000
traditional beliefs	1,260,000
other	10,000
Chile	
Roman Catholic	10,460,000
other	2,500,000
China	
nonreligious	653,700,000
Chinese folk-religionist	222,000,000
atheist	132,500,000
Buddhist	63,300,000
Muslim	26,500,000
other	3,300,000
Christmas Island	
Buddhist	500
Muslim	400
other	500
Cocos (Keeling) Islands	
Muslim	340
other	260
Colombia	
Roman Catholic	30,700,000
other	1,620,000
Comoros	
Sunnī Muslim	447,000
Christian	1,000
Congo	
Roman Catholic	1,210,000
Protestant	550,000
African Christian	320,000
other	170,000
Cook Islands	
Congregational	11,300
other	5,600
Costa Rica	
Roman Catholic	2,610,000
other	340,000
Côte d'Ivoire	
traditional beliefs	7,300,000
Roman Catholic	1,800,000
Protestant	600,000
Muslim	2,400,000
Cuba	
Roman Catholic	4,170,000
nonreligious	5,130,000
atheist	670,000
other	570,000
Cyprus	
Greek Orthodox	535,000
Muslim	170,000
other	27,000
Czechoslovakia	
Roman Catholic	10,260,000
atheist	3,140,000
Czechoslovak Church	690,000
other	1,550,000
Denmark	
Evangelical Lutheran	4,651,000
other	484,000
Djibouti	
Sunnī Muslim	481,000
Christian[1]	31,000
Dominica	
Roman Catholic	64,000
other	19,000
Dominican Republic	
Roman Catholic	6,450,000
other	570,000
Ecuador	
Roman Catholic	9,810,000
other	680,000
Egypt	
Sunnī Muslim	48,700,000
Christian	3,040,000
other	10,000
El Salvador	
Roman Catholic	4,760,000
other	380,000
Equatorial Guinea	
Roman Catholic	280,000
other	60,000
Ethiopia	
Ethiopian Orthodox	25,670,000
Muslim (mostly Sunnī)	15,350,000
traditional beliefs	5,570,000
other	2,310,000
Faeroe Islands	
Evangelical Lutheran	36,000
other	12,000
Falkland Islands	
Anglican	1,000
other	1,000
Fiji	
Christian	388,000
Hindu	280,000
Muslim	57,000
other	9,000
Finland	
Evangelical Lutheran	4,411,000
other	549,000
France	
Roman Catholic	42,870,000
nonreligious	6,850,000
atheist	1,910,000
Muslim	1,680,000
other	2,800,000
French Guiana	
Roman Catholic	70,000
other	24,000
French Polynesia	
Protestant	89,000
Roman Catholic	76,000
other	27,000
Gabon	
Roman Catholic	810,000
other	440,000
Gambia, The	
Muslim (mostly Sunnī)	797,000
other	38,000
Gaza Strip	
Muslim (mostly Sunnī)	582,000
other	6,000
Germany, East	
Protestant	7,810,000
Roman Catholic	1,160,000
unaffiliated and other	7,640,000
Germany, West	
Protestant	28,550,000
Roman Catholic	26,780,000
other Christian	1,400,000
nonreligious	2,260,000
Muslim	1,470,000
atheist	550,000
other	120,000
Ghana	
Christian[1]	9,120,000
traditional beliefs	3,120,000
Muslim	2,290,000
other	40,000
Gibraltar	
Roman Catholic	23,000
other	7,000
Greece	
Greek Orthodox	9,850,000
Muslim	150,000
other	90,000
Greenland	
Evangelical Lutheran	54,000
other	1,000
Grenada	
Roman Catholic	62,000
Anglican	20,000
other	15,000
Guadeloupe	
Roman Catholic	310,000
other	30,000
Guam	
Roman Catholic	103,000
Protestant	20,000
other	6,000
Guatemala	
Roman Catholic	6,700,000
Protestant	2,230,000
Guernsey	
Anglican	39,000
other	21,000
Guinea	
Muslim	5,700,000
traditional beliefs	340,000
other	670,000
Guinea-Bissau	
traditional beliefs	620,000
Muslim	290,000
Christian	50,000
Guyana	
Hindu	279,000
Protestant	122,000
Anglican	108,000
Muslim	66,000
other	179,000
Haiti	
Roman Catholic	4,430,000
Baptist	540,000
other	550,000
Honduras	
Roman Catholic	4,280,000
other	250,000
Hong Kong	
Buddhist (with Confucianist and Taoist)	4,240,000
Christian	480,000
other	1,030,000
Hungary	
Roman Catholic	6,600,000
Protestant	2,470,000
nonreligious and atheist	1,370,000
other	140,000
Iceland	
Evangelical Lutheran	234,000
other	18,000
India[3]	
Hindu	670,640,000
Muslim	92,110,000
Christian	19,720,000
Sikh	15,950,000
Buddhist	5,750,000
Jain	3,910,000
other	3,450,000
Indonesia	
Muslim	153,890,000
Protestant	11,440,000
Roman Catholic	5,540,000
Hindu	3,430,000
Buddhist	1,740,000
other	1,010,000
Iran	
Shī'ī Muslim	49,440,000
Sunnī Muslim	4,240,000
other	640,000
Iraq	
Shī'ī Muslim	10,760,000

Religious affiliation	1989 population
Sunnī Muslim	5,940,000
other	520,000
Ireland	
Roman Catholic	3,271,000
other	243,000
Isle of Man	
Anglican	40,000
other	24,000
Israel	
Jewish	3,750,000
Muslim (mostly Sunnī)	630,000
other	190,000
Italy	
Roman Catholic	47,730,000
nonreligious	7,810,000
atheist	1,490,000
other	410,000
Jamaica	
Protestant	1,150,000
Anglican	170,000
Roman Catholic	120,000
other	940,000
Japan	
Shintoist[4]	114,700,000
Buddhist[4]	91,020,000
Christian	1,700,000
other	14,710,000
Jersey	
Anglican	51,000
Roman Catholic	19,000
other	13,000
Jordan	
Sunnī Muslim	2,840,000
other	220,000
Kampuchea (Cambodia)	
Buddhist	7,120,000
other	930,000
Kenya	
Roman Catholic	6,210,000
Protestant	4,540,000
Anglican	1,690,000
African Christian	4,140,000
traditional beliefs	4,440,000
Muslim	1,410,000
other	1,080,000
Kiribati	
Roman Catholic	37,000
Congregational	28,000
other	5,000
Korea, North	
atheist and nonreligious	15,220,000
traditional beliefs	3,500,000
Ch'ŏndogyo	3,120,000
other	580,000
Korea, South	
Buddhist	15,390,000
Confucian	10,360,000
Protestant	9,890,000
Roman Catholic	2,190,000
Wonbulgyo	1,100,000
Ch'ŏndogyo	980,000
other	2,470,000
Kuwait	
Sunnī Muslim	920,000
Shī'ī Muslim	610,000
other Muslim	200,000
other	310,000
Laos	
Buddhist	2,280,000
traditional beliefs	1,320,000
other	340,000
Lebanon	
Shī'ī Muslim	930,000
Maronite Christian	710,000
Sunnī Muslim	610,000
Druze	200,000
other	460,000
Lesotho	
Roman Catholic	750,000
Protestant	510,000
other	460,000
Liberia	
Christian	1,700,000
traditional beliefs	460,000
Muslim	350,000
Libya	
Sunnī Muslim	3,960,000
other	120,000
Liechtenstein	
Roman Catholic	24,700
other	3,600
Luxembourg	
Roman Catholic	351,000
other	26,000
Macau	
Buddhist	218,000
nonreligious	222,000
other	44,000
Madagascar	
Christian[1]	5,920,000
traditional beliefs	5,450,000
other	230,000
Malaŵi	
Christian[1]	5,490,000
traditional beliefs	1,620,000
Muslim	1,380,000
other	20,000
Malaysia	
Muslim	9,220,000
Buddhist	3,010,000
Chinese folk-religionist	2,020,000
Hindu	1,220,000
Christian	1,110,000
other	840,000
Maldives	
Sunnī Muslim	209,000
Mali	
Muslim	7,120,000
traditional beliefs	710,000
Christian	80,000
Malta	
Roman Catholic	340,000
other	9,000
Martinique	
Roman Catholic	300,000
other	40,000
Mauritania	
Sunnī Muslim	1,930,000
other	10,000
Mauritius	
Hindu	560,000
Roman Catholic	270,000
Muslim	140,000
other	90,000
Mayotte	
Sunnī Muslim	76,000
Christian	2,000
Mexico	
Roman Catholic	78,030,000
Protestant	2,770,000
nonreligious	2,630,000
other	810,000
Monaco	
Roman Catholic	26,000
other	3,000
Mongolia	
atheist and nonreligious	1,370,000
traditional beliefs	650,000
other	80,000
Montserrat	
Anglican	4,400
Methodist	2,500
other	5,100
Morocco	
Muslim (mostly Sunnī)	24,210,000
other	320,000
Mozambique	
traditional beliefs	7,310,000
Roman Catholic	4,800,000
Muslim	1,990,000
other	1,190,000
Myanmar (Burma)	
Buddhist	36,500,000
Christian	2,000,000
Muslim	1,560,000
other	750,000
Nauru	
Congregational	4,400
other	3,700
Nepal	
Hindu	16,510,000
Buddhist	980,000
Muslim	500,000
other	460,000
Netherlands, The	
Roman Catholic	5,340,000
Dutch Reformed Church	2,750,000
Reformed Churches	1,250,000
nonreligious	4,840,000
other	670,000
Netherlands Antilles	
Roman Catholic	153,000
other	30,000
New Caledonia	
Roman Catholic	102,000
other	56,000
New Zealand	
Anglican	820,000
Presbyterian	610,000
Roman Catholic	510,000
Methodist	160,000
nonreligious	550,000
other	720,000
Nicaragua	
Roman Catholic	3,310,000
other	440,000
Niger	
Sunnī Muslim	5,720,000
traditional beliefs	1,430,000
Nigeria	
Muslim	52,190,000
Protestant	30,500,000
Roman Catholic	14,030,000
African Christian	12,290,000
traditional beliefs	6,490,000
other	460,000
Niue	
Congregational	1,500
other	700
Norfolk Island	
Anglican	700
other	1,200
Norway	
Evangelical Lutheran	3,716,000
other	512,000
Oman	
Muslim	1,220,000
other	190,000
Pacific Islands, Trust Territory of the[5]	
Protestant	92,000
Roman Catholic	85,000
other	9,000
Pakistan	
Muslim (mostly Sunnī)	115,020,000
other	3,800,000
Panama	
Roman Catholic	1,991,000
other	379,000
Papua New Guinea	
Protestant	2,100,000
Roman Catholic	1,180,000
other	310,000
Paraguay	
Roman Catholic	3,991,000
other	166,000
Peru	
Roman Catholic	20,030,000
other	1,760,000
Philippines	
Roman Catholic	50,380,000
Aglipayan	3,710,000
Protestant	2,100,000
Muslim	2,580,000
other	1,140,000
Pitcairn Island	
Seventh-day Adventist	56
Poland	
Roman Catholic	35,990,000
other	1,890,000
Portugal	
Roman Catholic	9,800,000
other	570,000
Puerto Rico	
Roman Catholic	2,820,000
other	490,000
Qatar	
Muslim (mostly Sunnī)	395,000
other	32,000
Réunion	
Roman Catholic	530,000
other	60,000
Romania	
Romanian Orthodox	16,220,000
Greek Orthodox	2,320,000
atheist	1,620,000
nonreligious	2,090,000
other	920,000
Rwanda	
Roman Catholic	4,540,000
Protestant	630,000
Muslim	630,000
traditional beliefs	1,190,000
St. Helena and Ascension	
Anglican	6,400
other	900
St. Kitts and Nevis	
Anglican	14,000
Methodist	13,000
other	17,000
St. Lucia	
Roman Catholic	128,000
other	22,000
St. Pierre and Miquelon	
Roman Catholic	6,100
other	100
St. Vincent and the Grenadines	
Anglican	41,000
Methodist	23,000
Roman Catholic	22,000
other	28,000
San Marino	
Roman Catholic	21,800
other	1,100
São Tomé and Príncipe	
Roman Catholic	100,000
Protestant	20,000
Saudi Arabia	
Muslim (mostly Sunnī)	13,430,000
other	160,000
Senegal	
Sunnī Muslim	6,730,000
other	670,000
Seychelles	
Roman Catholic	61,000
other	6,000
Sierra Leone	
traditional beliefs	2,040,000
Sunnī Muslim	1,560,000
other	357,000
Singapore	
Taoist	358,000
Buddhist	757,000
Muslim	428,000
Christian	500,000
Hindu	131,000
nonreligious	471,000
other	29,000
Solomon Islands	
Protestant	132,000
Anglican	107,000
Roman Catholic	61,000
other	17,000
Somalia	
Sunnī Muslim	7,324,000
other	14,000
South Africa[6]	
Dutch (Afrikaans) Reformed	4,690,000
Roman Catholic	2,910,000
Anglican	1,990,000
Black independent churches	6,290,000
other Christian churches	7,730,000
Hindu	630,000
Muslim	410,000
other[7]	5,590,000
Bophuthatswana	
Christian	1,730,000
traditional beliefs	180,000
Ciskei	
Christian	590,000
traditional beliefs	230,000
Transkei	
Christian[1]	2,260,000
traditional beliefs	960,000
Venda	
traditional beliefs	390,000
Christian	110,000
South West Africa/Namibia	
Lutheran	650,000
Roman Catholic	251,000
other	369,000
Spain	
Roman Catholic	37,750,000
other	1,410,000
Sri Lanka	
Buddhist	11,680,000
Hindu	2,610,000
Muslim	1,270,000
Roman Catholic	1,160,000
other	130,000
Sudan, The	
Sunnī Muslim	19,910,000
traditional beliefs	4,550,000
Christian[1]	2,480,000
other	330,000
Suriname	
Hindu	119,000
Roman Catholic	99,000
Muslim	85,000
Protestant	82,000
other	50,000
Swaziland	
Christian[1]	570,000
traditional beliefs	160,000
other	20,000
Sweden	
Church of Sweden (Lutheran)	7,556,000
other	942,000
Switzerland	
Roman Catholic	3,184,000
Protestant	2,956,000
other	539,000
Syria	
Muslim (mostly Sunnī)	10,500,000
Christian	1,040,000
other	190,000
Taiwan	
Chinese folk-religionist	9,710,000
Buddhist	8,610,000
Christian[1]	1,480,000
other	220,000
Tanzania	
Christian	8,070,000
Muslim	7,830,000
traditional beliefs	7,830,000
Thailand	
Buddhist	52,510,000
Muslim	2,120,000
other	650,000
Togo	
traditional beliefs	2,130,000
Roman Catholic	780,000
Sunnī Muslim	440,000
other	270,000
Tokelau	
Congregational	1,100
Roman Catholic	600
Tonga	
Free Wesleyan	41,000
Roman Catholic	15,000
other	40,000
Trinidad and Tobago	
Roman Catholic	414,000
Anglican	185,000
Protestant	171,000
Hindu	313,000
other	202,000
Tunisia	
Sunnī Muslim	7,930,000
other	50,000
Turkey	
Muslim (mostly Sunnī)	55,100,000
other	440,000
Turks and Caicos Islands	
Baptist	5,600
Methodist	2,600
Anglican	2,500
other	2,800
Tuvalu	
Congregational	8,600
other	300
Uganda	
Roman Catholic	8,160,000
Anglican	4,310,000
traditional beliefs	2,070,000
Muslim (mostly Sunnī)	1,090,000
other	820,000
U.S.S.R.	
Christian	105,510,000
Orthodox	90,710,000
Protestant	9,360,000
Roman Catholic	5,340,000
Muslim	34,330,000
Jewish	3,120,000
nonreligious	85,430,000
atheist	58,900,000
other	510,000
United Arab Emirates	
Sunnī Muslim	1,460,000
Shī'ī Muslim	290,000
other	70,000
United Kingdom	
Christian[1]	49,720,000
Church of England	32,500,000
Protestant	8,580,000
Roman Catholic	7,500,000
nonreligious	5,040,000
Muslim	800,000
Jewish	460,000
other	1,200,000
United States	
Christian[1]	216,640,000
Protestant	122,170,000
Roman Catholic	73,740,000
Anglican	5,900,000
Eastern Orthodox	5,400,000
Jewish	6,770,000
Muslim	4,730,000
Hindu	550,000
atheist and nonreligious	16,840,000
other	3,250,000
Uruguay	
Roman Catholic	1,760,000
other	1,260,000
Vanuatu	
Presbyterian	57,000
Anglican	23,000
Roman Catholic	23,000
other	51,000
Venezuela	
Roman Catholic	17,650,000
other	1,600,000
Vietnam	
Buddhist	36,100,000
atheist and nonreligious	12,080,000
Roman Catholic	4,570,000
other	12,530,000
Virgin Islands (U.S.)	
Protestant	49,000
Roman Catholic	36,000
other	22,000
Wallis and Futuna	
Roman Catholic	15,400
West Bank	
Muslim (mostly Sunnī)	710,000
Jewish	110,000
Christian and other	70,000
Western Sahara	
Sunnī Muslim	195,000
Western Samoa	
Congregational	77,000
Roman Catholic	35,000
other	51,000
Yemen (Aden)	
Muslim (mostly Sunnī)	2,394,000
other	12,000
Yemen (Ṣan'ā')	
Shī'ī Muslim	5,300,000
Sunnī Muslim	3,530,000
Yugoslavia	
Orthodox	8,200,000
Roman Catholic	6,160,000
Crypto-Christian	2,680,000
Muslim	2,470,000
atheist and nonreligious	3,970,000
other	230,000
Zaire	
Roman Catholic	16,130,000
Protestant	9,670,000
African Christian	5,700,000
traditional beliefs	1,130,000
other	710,000
Zambia	
Christian[1]	5,870,000
traditional beliefs	2,200,000
other	80,000
Zimbabwe	
Christian[1]	5,290,000
traditional beliefs	3,690,000
other	130,000

[1]Includes affiliated and nominal Christians. [2]Based on self-identification of respondent at 1981 census. [3]Excludes Assam. [4]Many Japanese adhere to both Shintoism and Buddhism. [5]Includes the Marshall Is., the Fed. States of Micronesia, N. Mariana Is., and Palau. [6]Excludes Black republics listed separately. [7]Includes traditional beliefs, nonreligious, and religion not known.

Vital statistics, marriage, family

This table provides some of the basic measures of the factors that influence the size, direction, and rates of population change within a country. The accuracy of these data depends on the effectiveness of each respective national system for registering vital and civil events (birth, death, marriage, etc.) and on the sophistication of the analysis that can be brought to bear upon the data so compiled.

Data on birth rates, for example, depend not only on the completeness of registration of births in a particular country but also on the conditions under which those data are collected: Do all births take place in a hospital? Are the births reported comparably in all parts of the country? Are the records of the births tabulated at a central location in a timely way with an effort to eliminate inconsistent reporting of birth events, perinatal mortality, etc.? Similar difficulties attach to death rates but with the added need to identify "cause of death." Even in a developed country such identifications are often left to nonmedical personnel, and in a developing country with, say, only one physician for every 10,000 population there will be too few physicians to perform autopsies to assess accurately the cause of death after the fact and also too few to provide ongoing care at a level where records would permit inference about cause of death based on prior condition or diagnosis.

Calculating natural increase, which at its most basic is simply the difference between the birth and death rates, may be affected by the differing degrees of completeness of birth and death registration for a given country. The total fertility rate may be understood as the average number of children that would be borne per woman if all childbearing women lived to the end of their childbearing years and bore children at each age at the

average rate for that age. Calculating a meaningful fertility rate requires analysis of changing age structure of the female population over time, changing mortality rates among mothers and their infants, and changing medical practice at births, each improvement of natural survivorship or medical support leading to greater numbers of live-born children and greater numbers of children who survive their first year (the basis for measurement of infant mortality, another basic indicator of demographic conditions and trends within a population).

As indicated above, data for causes of death are not only particularly difficult to obtain, since many countries are not well equipped to collect the data, but are also difficult to assess, as their accuracy may be suspect and their meaning may be subject to varying interpretation. Take the case of a citizen of a less developed country who dies of what is clearly a lung infection: Was the death complicated by chronic malnutrition, itself complicated by a parasitic infestation, these last two together so weakening the subject that he died of an infection that he might have survived had his general health been better? Similarly, in a developed country: Someone may die from what is identified in an autopsy as a cerebrovascular accident, but if that accident occurred in a vascular system that was weakened by diabetes, what was the actual cause of death? Statistics on causes of death seek to identify the "underlying" cause (that which sets the final train of events leading to death in motion) but often must settle for the most proximate cause or symptom. Even this kind of analysis may be misleading for those charged with interpreting the data with a view to ordering health-care priorities for a particular country. The eight groups of causes of death utilized here include most, but not all, of the

Vital statistics, marriage, family

country	vital rates						causes of death (rate per 100,000 population)								
	year	birth rate per 1,000 population	death rate per 1,000 population	infant mortality rate per 1,000 live births	rate of natural increase per 1,000 population	total fertility rate	year	infectious and parasitic diseases	malignant neoplasms (cancers)	endocrine and metabolic disorders	diseases of the nervous system	diseases of the circulatory system	diseases of the respiratory system	diseases of the digestive system	accidents, poisonings, and violence
Afghanistan	1985–90	49.3	23.0	172.0	26.3	6.9	...	...	...	...	...	...	...	...	...
Albania	1987	25.9	5.6	28.2	20.3	3.6[2]	...	...	...	...	...	...	...	...	...
Algeria	1987	34.6	7.0	64.1[3]	27.6	5.9	1986	2.8[4]	66.2	19.3[5]	...	110.3[6]	44.1[7]	...	38.6[8]
American Samoa	1989	42.0	4.0	11.0	38.0	5.4									
Andorra	1986	11.6	3.8	3.7	7.8	1.1[9]									
Angola	1985–90	47.2	20.2	137.0	27.0	6.4	1973	73.2	6.5	4.9	3.6	19.2	24.6	3.6	89.0
Anguilla	1986	22.2	9.0	19.5	13.2	1.9[10]	1981–85[11]	45.0	111.0	30.0	18.0	414.0	135.0	9.0	...
Antigua and Barbuda	1987	14.3	5.1	21.2	9.2	1.7	1983	21.7	62.6	34.5	26.4[13]	171.3	40.3[13]	18.1[13]	31.1[14]
Argentina	1989	20.0	9.0	35.3[15]	11.0	2.8	1985	24.4	137.9	22.0	8.6	360.8	45.7	36.8	47.9
Aruba	1988	14.0	5.2	8.0	8.8	1.8	1988	13.2	121.0	44.7	3.3	210.5	21.6	16.6	69.7
Australia	1988	14.9	7.3	8.8[16]	7.6	1.9[16]	1986	3.7	174.1	15.6	11.1	345.0	49.4	24.5	48.9
Austria	1987	11.4	11.2	9.8	0.2	1.4	1987	4.0	251.9	21.4	15.6	592.1	54.4	55.0	81.0
Bahamas, The	1987	16.7	5.0	29.8[17]	11.7	2.6	1986	18.6	120.4	41.0	15.2	170.3	42.7	30.8	68.4
Bahrain	1986	36.8	5.8	50.0	31.0	4.1[18]	1987	5.0	29.6	16.6	2.6	112.5	19.7	8.4	29.8
Bangladesh	1988	42.0	15.3	118.0	26.7	5.5	1976	15.5	19.8	...	...	5.9	25.7	...	...
Barbados	1988	14.7	8.7	17.1[19]	6.0	1.8[18]	1985	21.8	143.3	72.9	12.7[20]	381.9	40.4	11.5	44.3
Belgium	1987	11.9	10.7	9.7	1.2	1.6[10]	1986	8.4	275.9	25.6	27.6	464.3	95.4	41.3	71.3
Belize	1987	38.7	3.9	21.0[17]	34.8	5.4	1982–84[11]	42.9	34.0	19.2	8.3	123.1	50.6	15.4	33.3
Benin	1985–90	50.5	19.0	110.0	31.5	7.0	1977	...	...	...	...	206.5	200.7	...	...
Bermuda	1988	16.0	6.8	7.0[19]	9.2	1.7[18]	1986	3.5[20]	192.0	50.0[14]	7.0[14]	354.0	35.0	19.6[13]	42.0
Bhutan	1988	38.3	16.7	127.0	21.6	5.5	...	...	...	...	...	...	...	...	...
Bolivia	1985–90	42.8	14.1	110.0	28.7	6.1	...	...	...	...	...	...	...	...	...
Botswana	1985–90	47.3	11.7	67.0	35.6	6.3	...	...	...	...	...	...	...	...	...
Brazil	1985–90	28.6	7.9	63.2	20.7	3.5	1984[23]	45.8	51.1	11.7	7.2	157.7	47.9	21.3	62.0
British Virgin Islands	1987	21.6	6.8	38.0	14.8	2.2[9]	1987	16.4	24.6	8.2[5]	...	205.0	114.8	65.6	49.2[24]
Brunei	1988	28.3	3.9	16.0	24.4	4.1	1986	5.3	27.0	...	...	80.0	23.4	...	39.8
Bulgaria	1987	13.0	12.0	14.7	1.0	2.0[3]	1986	7.8	164.5	17.9	5.4	714.1	81.7	36.6	60.6
Burkina Faso	1985–90	47.2	18.5	138.0	28.7	6.5	...	...	...	...	...	...	...	...	...
Burundi	1986–87	45.7	17.4	114.0	28.4	6.3	...	...	...	...	...	...	...	...	...
Cameroon	1985–90	41.6	15.6	94.0	26.0	5.8	...	...	...	...	...	...	...	...	...
Canada	1987	14.4	7.2	7.3	7.2	1.7[3]	1986	4.2	187.5	19.9	14.6	313.2	59.0	27.1	54.3
Cape Verde	1987	32.1	7.7	76.5[3]	24.4	2.6[25]	1980	153.7	43.8	20.6	16.5	135.8	72.3	27.1	30.1
Cayman Islands	1988	15.3	4.4	11.1[16]	10.9	1.6[9]	1984–88[11]	9.1	98.5	20.1	3.6	220.8	34.7	11.9	74.8
Central African Republic	1985–90	44.3	19.7	132.0	24.6	5.9	1978	59.0	...	...	...	...	...	...	...
Chad	1985–90	44.2	19.5	132.0	24.7	5.9	...	...	...	...	...	...	...	...	...
Chile	1986	22.1	5.9	19.1	16.2	3.0[26]	1987	20.4	102.6	12.4	8.0	160.6	64.6	43.6	67.0
China	1988	21.0	6.6	32.0	14.0	2.4	1981[27]	23.7	113.0	6.3	9.4	251.1	43.0	25.9	31.3
Christmas Island	1985	15.4	1.8	—	13.6	...	...	...	...	...	...	...	...	...	...
Cocos (Keeling) Islands	1981	14.4	1.8	—	12.6	...	...	...	...	...	...	...	...	...	...
Colombia	1983–88	27.9	7.4	46.0[16]	20.5	3.4[29]	1981	70.5	53.3[13,30]	15.0	6.1[30,31]	160.7	59.2	19.7	97.3
Comoros	1987	47.0	14.0	96.0	33.0	7.0	...	...	...	...	...	...	...	...	...
Congo	1985–90	44.4	17.2	73.0	27.2	6.0	...	...	...	...	...	...	...	...	...
Cook Islands	1986	24.0	5.2	21.7	18.8	4.1[3]	1976–78	54.0	38.0	27.0	0.0	197.0	110.0	18.0	49.0
Costa Rica	1987	28.9	3.8	17.4	25.1	3.3	1988	13.7	77.8	8.4	9.0	107.2	39.4	16.8	42.5
Côte d'Ivoire	1989	46.0	13.0	102.0	33.0	6.7	...	...	...	...	...	...	...	...	...
Cuba	1988	17.9	6.5	11.9	11.4	1.8[18]	1987	9.2	122.2	18.9	9.6	280.9	61.4	23.6	75.6
Cyprus	1988	19.2	8.8	11.0	10.4	2.4[16]	...	...	...	...	...	...	...	...	...
Czechoslovakia	1987	13.8	11.5	13.1	2.3	2.0	1986	4.4	238.8	20.6	8.8	654.7	87.1	45.8	78.5
Denmark	1988	11.5	11.5	8.3[18]	0.0	1.5[18]	1986	5.1	285.7	20.4[32]	10.4	521.6	81.3	38.0	76.6
Djibouti	1985–90	47.3	17.7	122.0	29.6	6.6	...	...	...	...	...	...	...	...	...
Dominica	1987	19.1	5.6	16.3[33]	13.5	3.1	1985	13.2	72.3	18.4	17.1	213.1	46.0	21.0	27.6
Dominican Republic	1985–90	31.3	6.8	70.0	24.5	3.8	1985	51.4	27.4	12.3	8.6	100.3	35.4	22.3	33.7
Ecuador	1987	35.4	7.6	63.0	27.8	4.8[3]	1986	66.1	46.2	9.9	9.8	83.1	63.6	25.4	63.1
Egypt	1986	39.3	8.7	70.5[3]	30.6	5.4[18]	1982	168.9	21.8	7.3[5]	1.7[31]	186.3	106.3	8.8	39.7
El Salvador	1987	37.0	10.0	88.0	27.0	4.9	1984	60.0	21.6	9.0	9.0	63.9	34.8	26.1	124.6

detailed causes classified by the World Health Organization and would not, thus, aggregate to the country's crude death rate for the same year. Among the lesser causes excluded by the present classification are: benign neoplasms; nutritional disorders; anemias; mental disorders; kidney and genitourinary diseases not classifiable under the main groups; maternal deaths (for which data *are* provided, however, in the "Health services" table); diseases of the skin and musculoskeletal systems; congenital and perinatal conditions; and general senility and other ill-defined (ill-diagnosed) conditions, a kind of "other" category.

Expectation of life is probably the most accurate single measure of the quality of life in a given society. It summarizes in a single number all of the natural and social stresses that operate upon individuals in that society. The number may range from as few as 40 years of life in the least developed countries to as much as 80 years for women in the most developed nations. The lost potential in the years separating those two numbers is prodigious, regardless of how the loss arises—wars and civil violence, poor public health services, or poor individual health practice in matters of nutrition, exercise, stress management, and so on.

Data on marriages and marriage rates probably are less meaningful in terms of international comparisons than some of the measures mentioned above because the number, timing, and kinds of social relationships that substitute for marriage depend on many kinds of social variables—income, degree of social control, heterogeneity of the society (race, class, language communities), or level of development of civil administration (if one must travel for a day or more to obtain a legal civil ceremony, one may forgo it). Nevertheless, the data for a single country say specific things about local practice in terms of the age at which a man or woman typically marries, and the overall rate will at least define the number of legal civil marriages, though it cannot say anything about other, less formal arrangements (here the figure for the legitimacy rate for children in the next section may identify some of the societies in which economics or social constraints may operate to limit the number of marriages that are actually confirmed on civil registers). The available data usually include both first marriages and remarriages after annulment, divorce, widowhood, or the like.

The data for families provide information about the average size of a family unit (individuals related by blood or civil register) and the average number of children under a specified age (set here at 15 to provide a consistent measure of social minority internationally, though legal minority depends on the laws of each country). When well-defined family data are not collected as part of a country's national census or vital statistics surveys, data for households are substituted on the assumption that most households worldwide represent families in some conventional sense. In the older countries of Europe and North America increasing numbers of households are composed of unrelated individuals (unmarried heterosexual couples, aged [or younger] groups sharing limited [often fixed] incomes for reasons of economy, or homosexual couples); such arrangements are not yet so common in the rest of the world that they represent great numbers overall. Very few census programs, even in developed countries, make adequate provision for distinguishing these households.

| expectation of life at birth (latest year) | | marriages | | | age at marriage (latest): groom (percent) | | | age at marriage (latest): bride (percent) | | | families (F), households (H) (latest) | | | | | | country |
male	female	year	total number	rate per 1,000 population	19 and under	20–29	30 and over	19 and under	20–29	30 and over	families (households) total ('000)	size	children number under age 15	children percent legitimate	induced abortions number	induced abortions ratio per 100 live births	country
41.0	42.0	1970	6,212	0.4							H 2,110	H 6.2	H 2.8[1]	...			Afghanistan
68.7	74.3	1987	27,370	8.9	1.2	79.3	19.5	20.4	75.0	4.6	F 463	F 5.6	...	...			Albania
61.0	64.1	1985	123,688	5.7	3.4	68.3	28.3	37.7	53.5	8.8	...	H 6.9	...	...			Algeria
69.0	74.0	1982	362	10.7	5.6	65.5	28.8	24.5	60.5	15.0	H 4	H 7.1	H 2.9	86.0			American Samoa
74.0	80.0	1984	130	3.1													Andorra
42.9	46.1	1972	26,278	4.5							...	H 4.8					Angola
68.6	71.9	1986	154	22.2	1.7[12]	56.7[12]	41.6[12]	10.7[12]	58.0[12]	31.3[12]	F 1.6	F 4.1	H 1.8	34.4			Anguilla
70.0	74.0	1986	309	3.8	0.5	41.1	58.5	10.6	54.8	34.6	H 15	H 4.2	H 1.9	21.2			Antigua and Barbuda
67.0	74.0	1983	177,010	6.0	5.6	71.5	22.9	26.0	58.6	15.4	H 7,104	H 3.9	H 1.2	67.5			Argentina
72.0	80.0	1983	490	7.5							...	H 3.6		41.3			Aruba
72.8	79.1	1986	114,900	6.9	1.4	62.6	36.0	9.1	65.4	25.5	F 4,140	F 3.1	F 0.5	83.2			Australia
71.5	78.1	1987	76,205	10.1	2.1	72.6	27.4	10.9	72.8	16.3	F 2,057	F 3.6	F 0.6	76.6			Austria
67.0	74.0	1986	1,784	7.6	1.3	57.0	41.7	7.0	63.2	29.8	H 49	H 4.3	H 1.8	42.4			Bahamas, The
65.0	68.4	1986	2,708	6.6	2.5	72.2	25.3	29.1	60.1	10.8	H 67	H 4.9	H 3.0	...			Bahrain
51.3	50.6	1987	1,150,000	11.6							...	H 6.5					Bangladesh
72.0	76.0	1984	1,163	4.6	0.9	42.2	56.9	4.2	54.9	40.9	H 67	H 3.7	H 1.5	26.9			Barbados
70.0	76.8	1987	56,783	5.7	4.3	79.8	15.9	22.1	67.1	10.8	F 3,613	F 2.7	F 0.5	93.7			Belgium
66.0	71.0	1987	1,103	6.3							H 33	H 5.2	H 2.4	45.2			Belize
44.9	48.1	1980–85		12.8							...	H 5.4					Benin
69.0	77.0	1987	786	13.6	0.8[21]	40.5[22]	58.7	2.9[21]	52.0[22]	45.1	H 18	H 2.7	H 0.7	67.7	92	11.0	Bermuda
48.8	47.3										...	H 5.4					Bhutan
50.9	55.4	1980	26,990	4.8	8.3	75.1	16.6	26.1	55.4	18.5	H 1,050	H 4.4	H 1.8	80.9			Bolivia
55.5	61.5										H 125	H 5.7	H 2.0	28.0	17	0.1	Botswana
62.3	67.6	1985	952,294	7.0	7.5	70.3	22.2	33.8	52.3	13.9	F 31,076	F 4.1	F 1.6	...			Brazil
68.6	71.9	1987	189	15.5	—	37.0	63.0	1.1	51.3	47.6	H 3	H 3.3	H 1.1	24.9			British Virgin Islands
70.1	72.7	1986	1,673	7.4	5.6	72.5	21.9	12.5	58.9	28.6	H 23	H 5.8	H 2.5	99.6			Brunei
68.2	74.4	1987	64,429	7.2	6.3	73.9	19.8	38.3	49.2	12.5	F 2,627	F 3.3	F 0.7	89.8	132,041	111.0	Bulgaria
45.6	48.9	1975		9.4							...	H 4.9					Burkina Faso
46.9	50.2										...	H 4.9					Burundi
49.0	53.0										...	H 5.2					Cameroon
72.9	79.8	1986	190,680	7.4	1.7	64.9	33.4	8.4	68.2	23.4	F 6,735	F 3.1	F 0.8	83.8	60,928	16.2	Canada
60.3	64.0	1975	1,604	5.4							F 59	F 5.1	...	55.2			Cape Verde
—74.5—		1988	252	10.1							H 4	H 3.8	H 1.1	64.5			Cayman Islands
43.9	47.1										...	H 4.3					Central African Republic
43.9	47.1										...	H 3.9					Chad
68.1	75.1	1985	91,099	7.5	6.5	74.4	19.1	26.4	60.7	12.9	H 1,690	H 4.5	H 2.0	68.2	2,346	1.0	Chile
68.1	71.0	1985	8,290,588	8.0							H 241.3[28]	H 4.3			10,500,000	47.7	China
63.0	66.5	1982	25	8.3	—	90.9	9.1	45.5	36.4	18.1	—	H 5.8	H 1.5	97.1			Christmas Island
63.0	66.5	1981	6	10.8	—	100.0	—	—	100.0	—	—	H 6.3	H 2.6	93.3	2	40.0	Cocos (Keeling) Islands
63.0	67.0	1977	88,401	3.5	5.6	69.5	24.9	33.6	55.3	11.1	F 4,772	F 5.4	F 2.5	75.2			Colombia
53.0	57.0	1964	1,959	8.5							...	H 5.6					Comoros
46.9	50.2										H 326	H 4.7	H 2.0	...			Congo
64.0	70.0	1986	105	6.1	1.2	63.4	35.4	22.0	51.2	26.8	H 3	H 5.6	H 2.4	...			Cook Islands
72.4	77.0	1985	19,747	7.8	9.2	69.3	21.5	36.2	51.1	12.7	F 472	F 5.0	F 1.7	62.8			Costa Rica
50.8	54.2										...	H 4.5					Côte d'Ivoire
72.7	76.1	1986	84,274	8.3	10.6	57.9	31.5	29.5	48.3	22.2	F 2,002	F 4.2	H 1.6	...	138,671	76.2	Cuba
73.9	77.8	1986	6,255	9.3	1.3	75.5	23.2	18.2	70.2	11.6	H 160	H 3.5	H 1.1	99.6			Cyprus
67.5	75.0	1987	122,183	7.8	6.6	71.8	21.6	28.0	57.0	15.0	F 5,288	H 2.9	H 0.9	92.9	149,576	67.8	Czechoslovakia
71.8	77.6	1986	30,773	6.0	0.6	47.4	52.0	3.0	60.9	36.1	F 2,675	F 1.9	F 0.3	55.5	20,067	36.3	Denmark
45.4	48.7	1982	2,500	6.7							...	H 5.6		96.8			Djibouti
64.3	68.6	1969	234	3.3							H 18	H 4.3	H 2.2	35.0			Dominica
63.9	66.8	1986	18,974	2.9	8.0[3]	63.0[3]	29.0[3]	29.7[3]	51.0[3]	19.3[3]	H 753		H 2.5	32.8	562	0.5	Dominican Republic
59.8	63.6	1986	60,205	6.2	12.8	65.4	21.8	38.2	49.1	12.7	...	H 5.1		67.9			Ecuador
59.0	62.1	1986	451,000	9.1	8.5[3]	61.5[3]	30.0[3]	46.9[3]	42.3[3]	10.8[3]	H 9,619	H 5.0	H 2.1	100.0			Egypt
56.0	61.0	1984	16,727	3.5	7.2	57.2	35.6	27.1	49.1	23.8	H 686	H 5.4	H 2.4	32.6			El Salvador

Vital statistics, marriage, family (continued)

country	vital rates						causes of death (rate per 100,000 population)								
	year	birth rate per 1,000 population	death rate per 1,000 population	infant mortality rate per 1,000 live births	rate of natural increase per 1,000 population	total fertility rate	year	infectious and parasitic diseases	malignant neoplasms (cancers)	endocrine and metabolic disorders	diseases of the nervous system	diseases of the circulatory system	diseases of the respiratory system	diseases of the digestive system	accidents, poisonings, and violence
Equatorial Guinea	1985–90	42.4	19.0	127.0	23.4	5.7	...	...	...	...	...	...	...	...	...
Ethiopia	1985–90	43.7	23.6	154.0	20.1	6.2	1978	39.5	3.8	24.6	2.7	5.6	16.3	28.9	15.8
Faeroe Islands	1987	16.6	7.9	6.4[16]	8.7	2.3	1987	2.1	177.8	2.1[5]	4.3[31]	372.8	49.3	12.9	53.6
Falkland Islands	1989	10.8	7.0	...	3.8	...	1983	—	200.1	—	—	450.2	—	—	100.1
Fiji	1988	26.8	5.0	27.0	21.8	3.1	1985	31.3	53.3	29.1[5]	2.7[31]	190.8	43.1	13.3	48.5
Finland	1988	12.8	9.9	5.8[16]	2.9	1.7[18]	1986	7.8	193.9	11.8[32]	11.1	505.1	65.9	26.6	80.8
France	1988	13.8	9.4	7.7	4.4	1.8[18]	1986	12.8	240.1	22.0	16.7	352.6	68.3	54.8	89.7
French Guiana	1988	31.4	5.7	22.2[17]	25.7	3.1[34]	1984	55.2	62.7	10.1[5]	3.8[31]	152.9	25.1	33.8	104.0
French Polynesia	1988	29.3	5.1	26.6[18]	24.2	3.5[18]	1984	21.2	67.7	10.0	19.4	120.1	36.5	17.7	58.9
Gabon	1985–90	38.8	16.4	103.0	22.4	5.0	...	...	...	...	...	...	...	...	...
Gambia, The	1985–90	46.8	21.3	143.0	25.5	6.4	...	...	...	...	...	...	...	...	...
Gaza Strip	1989	47.0	7.0	56.0	40.0	7.2	...	...	...	...	...	...	...	...	...
Germany, East	1987	13.6	12.9	8.7	0.7	1.6[16]	1987	4.4	209.2	39.2	9.5	750.2	70.5	31.1[3]	37.9[3]
Germany, West	1987	10.5	11.2	8.6[16]	-0.7	1.3[16]	1987	7.5	272.3	22.6	15.8	560.4	64.9	51.4	54.0
Ghana	1985–90	44.3	13.1	90.0	31.2	6.4	...	...	...	...	...	...	...	...	...
Gibraltar	1988	17.5	9.8	6.0[9]	7.7	2.4[9]	1987	17.0	203.9	—	—	601.4	34.0	23.8	3.4
Greece	1987	10.6	9.5	12.6	1.1	2.2[16]	1986	5.7	184.3	11.5	12.1	460.6	50.6	30.1	46.2
Greenland	1988	22.2	8.1	23.4[16]	14.1	2.1[18]	1987	29.6	146.0	1.8[5]	3.7[31]	170.0	62.8	5.5	245.7
Grenada	1986	32.5	7.2	15.9[18]	25.3	3.1[18]	1984	13.5	90.5	62.9	11.4	290.3	54.1	39.5	47.9
Guadeloupe	1988	21.0	6.6	12.9	14.4	2.2[18]	1987	21.7	118.0	25.9	16.4[35]	216.0	29.1	40.7	74.6
Guam	1988	26.5	4.2	9.4[16]	22.3	3.1	1986	5.7	46.0[36]	17.0[32]	10.5	143.7	36.3	13.7	58.1
Guatemala	1987	36.5	9.5	66.0	27.0	5.1	1984	211.5	29.8	29.6	9.0	57.2	145.7	21.7	52.0
Guernsey	1987	11.6	10.4	5.1[17]	1.2	1.6[9]	1987	3.6	239.7	3.6[32]	21.6	515.5	120.8	39.7	36.0
Guinea	1985–90	46.6	21.9	147.0	24.7	6.2	...	...	...	...	...	...	...	...	...
Guinea-Bissau	1985–90	40.8	20.0	132.0	20.8	5.4	...	...	...	...	...	...	...	...	...
Guyana	1985–90	25.0	5.0	30.0	20.0	2.8	1984	15.6	29.9	26.9	9.4	163.5	32.2	59.7	45.6
Haiti	1987	34.0	13.0	108.0	21.0	4.6	...	...	...	...	...	...	...	...	...
Honduras	1987	39.0	8.0	69.0	31.0	5.6	1983	46.6	12.4	5.3	7.8	48.4	26.3	16.7	42.2
Hong Kong	1988	13.4	4.9	7.4	8.5	1.4	1987	14.7	147.1	4.5	4.2	140.0	78.4	19.4	28.2
Hungary	1988	11.7	13.1	15.8	-1.4	1.7[3]	1987	10.6	281.1	21.4	11.1	711.8	59.7	75.2	120.9
Iceland	1987	17.1	7.0	6.1[17]	10.1	2.1	1987	2.8	178.0	3.3	12.2	324.8	71.1	17.5	49.6
India	1988	31.9	11.2	98.0	20.7	4.3	...	...	...	...	...	...	...	...	...
Indonesia	1988	27.2	11.1	83.0	16.1	3.3	...	...	...	...	...	...	...	...	...
Iran	1985–90	42.4	8.0	63.0	34.4	5.6	...	...	...	...	...	...	...	...	...
Iraq	1986	45.1	8.6	63.3	36.5	6.7[18]	...	...	...	...	...	...	...	...	...
Ireland	1988	15.3	8.9	7.4[18]	6.4	2.5[10]	1986	6.9	194.5	11.6	16.4	463.5	136.2	24.4	43.4
Isle of Man	1987	11.4	14.4	15.5[16]	-3.0	1.8[9]	1987	9.3	348.5	14.0[5]	3.1[31]	749.8	144.7	21.8	77.8
Israel	1988	22.6	6.6	10.0	16.0	2.8[18]	1986	14.0	123.9	13.4	9.0	300.3	23.1	16.9	46.3
Italy	1987	9.6	9.3	9.8	0.3	1.6[25]	1985	4.0	234.4	34.4	15.4	437.3	65.3	56.3	50.3
Jamaica	1988	22.7	5.2	18.0[18]	17.5	2.9[18]	1978	39.3	74.8	40.5[32]	12.0	210.9	41.7	21.4	28.0
Japan	1989	11.0	6.0	5.0	5.0	1.8[15]	1987	9.4	168.4	9.1	5.3	241.0	64.0	31.1	47.0
Jersey	1987	12.5	10.5	6.0[9]	2.0	1.3[9]	...	...	...	...	...	...	...	...	...
Jordan	1986	34.7	5.8	48.6	27.9	7.4	...	...	...	...	...	...	...	...	...
Kampuchea (Cambodia)	1988	40.9	16.4	129.0	24.5	4.7	...	...	...	...	...	...	...	...	...
Kenya	1985–90	53.9	11.9	72.0	42.0	8.1	...	...	...	...	...	...	...	...	...
Kiribati	1988	31.3	8.1	82.0[38]	23.2	4.1	...	...	...	...	...	...	...	...	...
Korea, North	1985–90	28.9	5.4	24.0	23.4	3.6	1982 est.	4	60[36]	3[32]	...	192	39	25	...
Korea, South	1988	18.6	6.2	25.0	12.4	2.0	1985	19.9	73.5	6.4	5.7	155.0	22.6	43.9	56.5
Kuwait	1988	26.2	2.2	16.7	24.0	4.7[18]	1987	6.7	25.5	6.9	1.3	73.6	16.5	4.9	31.4
Laos	1988	41.0	16.2	109.0	24.8	5.7	...	...	...	...	...	...	...	...	...
Lebanon	1989	28.0	7.0	49.2[16]	21.0	3.8	...	...	...	...	...	...	...	...	...
Lesotho	1985–90	40.8	12.4	100.0	28.4	5.8	...	...	...	...	...	...	...	...	...
Liberia	1985–90	45.0	13.3	87.0	31.7	6.5	...	...	...	...	...	...	...	...	...
Libya	1985–90	43.9	9.4	82.0	34.5	6.9	...	...	...	...	...	...	...	...	...
Liechtenstein	1988	14.8	6.9	15.4[39]	7.9	...	1987	7.3	152.4[36]	21.8[5]	...	221.4	18.1	25.4	58.1
Luxembourg	1988	12.2	10.2	9.4[18]	2.0	1.4[18]	1987	7.0	275.8	24.7	15.9	518.5	59.9	51.3	70.7
Macau	1987	17.6	3.1	6.9	14.5	3.4[10]	1987	10.5	63.0[36]	11.2[32]	1.4	113.6	34.2	13.5	20.2
Madagascar	1985–90	45.7	14.0	120.0	31.7	6.6	...	...	...	...	...	...	...	...	...
Malawi	1985–90	53.0	20.0	150.0	33.0	7.0	1982[42]	45.9	3.6	16.0	4.7	3.6	18.6	2.8	6.1
Malaysia	1988	29.3	4.9	24.0	24.4	3.6	1981[43]	19.2	18.6	2.7	1.5	43.5	10.6	3.3	21.0
Maldives	1988	44.1	12.8	49.9[18]	31.3	6.4	...	...	...	...	...	...	...	...	...
Mali	1989	49.0	20.0	159.0	29.0	6.6	...	...	...	...	...	...	...	...	...
Malta	1987	15.4	8.4	7.3	7.0	2.0	1987	4.4	155.6	21.5[44]	5.5	532.7	46.7	16.8	18.0
Martinique	1988	19.0	6.2	10.2[19]	12.8	2.1[18]	1985	11.6	129.6	22.9	10.7	234.8	35.1	36.3	52.4
Mauritania	1985–90	46.2	19.0	127.0	27.2	6.5	...	...	...	...	...	...	...	...	...
Mauritius	1987	18.2	6.6	23.7	11.6	1.9[16]	1987	14.6	54.1	34.1	9.2	298.5	55.3	29.7	50.1
Mayotte	1987	51.0	13.0	96.0	38.0	6.9	...	...	...	...	...	...	...	...	...
Mexico	1987	34.3	5.1	46.6[15]	29.2	3.2[15]	1984	63.8	43.8[36]	39.8[32]	8.5	95.7	65.6	43.3	79.8
Monaco	1989	7.0	7.0	9.0	0.0	1.2	...	...	...	...	...	...	...	...	...
Mongolia	1988	38.8	7.9	44.0	30.9	5.4	...	...	...	...	...	...	...	...	...
Montserrat	1987	16.5	10.5	28.2	6.0	1.9[9]	1985	67.5	75.9	8.4	8.4	615.9	59.1	67.5	33.7
Morocco	1985–90	35.3	9.7	82.0	25.6	4.8	...	...	...	...	...	...	...	...	...
Mozambique	1985–90	45.0	18.5	141.0	26.5	6.4	...	...	...	...	...	...	...	...	...
Myanmar (Burma)	1988	30.5	9.6	69.0	20.9	4.0	1978	32.6	6.5	6.1	...	14.1	19.8	1.7	7.3
Nauru	1989	21.0	5.0	41.0	16.0	2.5	1976–81[11]	33.0	38.0	24.0	13.0	89.0	16.0	53.0	116.0
Nepal	1988	39.3	14.6	127.0	24.7	5.9	...	...	...	...	...	...	...	...	...
Netherlands, The	1988	12.6	8.4	6.8	4.2	1.6	1986	4.9	233.1	27.6	16.2	365.2	67.2	29.6	38.4
Netherlands Antilles	1985	21.7	6.2	18.2	15.5	3.4[20, 46]	1983	20.8	128.6	17.9	5.2	206.0	27.1	31.2	57.1
New Caledonia	1987	23.8	5.3	15.0	18.5	3.3	...	...	...	...	...	...	...	...	...
New Zealand	1988	17.3	8.2	10.0[18]	9.1	2.1	1986	4.9	189.8	16.3	12.2	381.6	86.7	23.0	62.2
Nicaragua	1988	41.8	8.0	61.7	33.8	5.2[18]	1978	52.3	13.5	2.9	4.5	62.1	18.6	14.2	59.2
Niger	1985–90	50.9	20.9	135.0	30.0	7.1	...	...	...	...	...	...	...	...	...
Nigeria	1985–90	49.8	15.6	105.0	34.2	7.0	...	...	...	...	...	...	...	...	...
Niue	1987	20.9	5.4	19.1[38]	15.5	...	...	...	...	...	...	...	...	...	...
Norfolk Island	1987–88	12.4	11.9	...	0.5	...	...	...	...	...	...	...	...	...	...

expectation of life at birth (latest year)		nuptiality, family, and family planning															country
		marriages			age at marriage (latest)						families (F), households (H) (latest)						
		year	total number	rate per 1,000 population	groom (percent)			bride (percent)			families (households)		children		induced abortions		
male	female				19 and under	20–29	30 and over	19 and under	20–29	30 and over	total ('000)	size	number under age 15	percent legitimate	number	ratio per 100 live births	
44.9	48.1	...	...									H 4.5	...	...	...	...	Equatorial Guinea
39.4	42.6	...	...									H 4.5					Ethiopia
73.3	79.6	1986	222	4.8	—	65.3	34.7	8.1	69.4	22.5	F ...	F 3.0	F 0.9	60.0	26	3.3	Faeroe Islands
		1980	11								H 1	H 3.3	H 0.9	75.0			Falkland Islands
68.3	72.8	1985	6,593	9.4	7.3	72.5	20.2	14.4	75.0	10.6	F 97	F 6.0	F 2.5	82.7	...	...	Fiji
70.7	78.7	1986	25,820	5.3	2.5	68.5	29.0	10.6	69.4	20.0	F 1,163	H 2.5	F 0.9	82.0	13,645	21.0	Finland
71.3	79.5	1987	265,400	4.8	0.8	70.0	29.2	7.4	72.0	20.6	H 20,899	H 2.5	H 1.0	78.1	173,300	22.6	France
63.4	69.7	1987	365	4.1							H 12	H 3.3	H 1.4	18.4	388	16.8	French Guiana
70.0	74.0	1987	971	5.3	11.3[12]	75.8[12]	12.9[12]	41.5[12]	52.5[12]	6.0[12]	H 32	H 5.0	H 2.0	41.1	...	...	French Polynesia
49.9	53.2	...									H 136	H 4.0					Gabon
41.4	44.6										H 123	H 4.9	H 3.4				Gambia, The
63.0	66.0																Gaza Strip
69.5	75.5	1986	137,208	7.8	2.9	70.7	26.4	13.9	67.9	18.2	F 4,781	F 3.5	F 0.7	65.5	80,100	35.0	Germany, East
71.5	78.1	1986	371,900	6.1	1.9	63.7	34.4	10.1	69.1	20.8	F 22,882	F 2.7	F 0.5	90.4	85,538	14.6	Germany, West
52.2	55.8										H 2,355	H 4.9	H 2.2				Ghana
72.0	78.0	1988	249	8.3							H 7	H 3.8	H 1.0	97.1			Gibraltar
72.2	76.4	1986	58,933	5.9	1.7	64.5	33.8	25.8	58.6	15.6	H 2,990	H 3.3	H 0.7	97.9	180	0.2	Greece
60.4	66.3	1986	349	6.5	1.4	46.4	52.2	6.0	61.3	32.7	F 28	F 1.9	F 0.5	29.4	539	51.3	Greenland
65.4	69.4	1979	360	3.9							H 20	H 4.7	H 2.2	22.5			Grenada
69.0	76.0	1986	1,709	5.1	0.6	56.8	42.6	8.8	67.5	23.7	H 70	H 3.7	H 1.9	39.9	561	8.7	Guadeloupe
69.6	74.5	1986	1,522	12.3	4.7	62.1	33.2	12.0	65.8	22.2	H 25	H 3.7	H 1.5	68.6			Guam
58.0	62.0	1985	38,489	4.8	15.9	55.8	28.3	41.5	38.0	20.5	H 1,102	H 5.5	H 2.7	34.8			Guatemala
77.4[37]	71.5[37]										H 18	H 2.9		81.7			Guernsey
40.6	43.8	...									H 1,064	H 4.7					Guinea
43.4	46.6	...									H 124	H 4.1	H 2.8	11.3			Guinea-Bissau
67.3	72.3	...									H 150	H 5.1	H 2.1	61.4			Guyana
54.0	56.0										H 1,147	H 4.4	H 1.8				Haiti
61.9	66.1	1983	19,875	4.9	7.7	65.1	27.2	27.9	58.5	13.6	H 463	H 5.7	H 2.8				Honduras
74.0	80.0	1987	48,561	9.0	0.9	59.6	39.5	4.8	73.0	22.2	H 1,453	H 3.7	H 0.9	94.5	10,600	12.0	Hong Kong
65.7	73.7	1988	65,932	6.2	5.7	69.4	25.0	27.4	54.6	17.9	F 3,058	F 2.9	F 0.8	90.8	87,000	70.0	Hungary
75.0	80.1	1987	1,160	4.7	2.6[16]	68.8[16]	28.6[16]	7.6[16]	73.7[16]	18.7[16]	H 85	H 2.9	H 1.3	49.9	687	15.7	Iceland
58.0	58.2	...	...								H 97,093	H 5.6	H 2.4		561,033	2.2	India
54.9	57.7	1985–86	1,249,034	7.6							H 34,507	H 4.9	H 2.0				Indonesia
65.0	65.5	1984–85	384,876	8.9							H 8,125	H 5.0	H 2.2				Iran
61.0	64.5	1982	56,440	4.0	4.0	49.1	46.9	23.9	47.2	28.9	H 2,128	H 6.9	H 3.2				Iraq
70.1	75.6	1987	18,149	5.1	2.2[3]	76.0[3]	21.8[3]	7.6[3]	80.5[3]	11.9[3]	H 726	H 3.9	H 1.3	89.2	...	...	Ireland
		1987	430	6.8	1.2	53.3	45.5	8.1	60.5	31.4				75.9			Isle of Man
73.5	77.0	1987	30,141	6.9	3.3	75.4	21.3	24.0	65.2	10.8	H 1,026	H 3.7	H 1.3	99.0	18,406	18.5	Israel
71.4	78.1	1986	296,539	5.2	1.7	75.2	23.1	18.7	70.1	11.2	F 17,615	F 3.2	F 0.7	94.2	187,618	34.0	Italy
68.1	72.6	1987	10,536	4.5							H 509	H 4.3	H 2.0	15.4	...	...	Jamaica
75.2	80.9	1986	711,000	5.9	1.0[12]	63.5[12]	35.5[12]	3.3[12]	81.7[12]	15.0[12]	F 22,240	F 5.4	F 1.2	99.0	598,100	37.9	Japan
											H 29	H 2.6	H 0.4	88.1			Jersey
65.0	68.8	1984	18,189	7.1	6.0	71.6	22.4	46.7	47.8	5.5	H 375	H 6.9	H 3.4				Jordan
47.3	50.2											H 5.6					Kampuchea (Cambodia)
56.5	60.5	...									H 1,938	H 6.2	H 2.7				Kenya
50.6	55.6	1988	352	5.2							H 10	H 6.1	F 2.0				Kiribati
66.2	72.7											H 5.7					Korea, North
66.4	72.6	1983	355,056	8.9	1.5	83.1	15.4	8.9	85.8	3.8	F 7,969	F 4.8	F 1.6	99.5			Korea, South
70.3	73.0	1986	9,842	5.3	3.8	70.4	22.0	34.9	54.6	10.5	H 246	H 7.4	H 1.6				Kuwait
47.3	50.3											H 5.3			...	...	Laos
64.7	68.8	1973	18,601	7.0							H 405	H 5.3	H 2.2		...	...	Lebanon
48.3	54.3	...									H 330	H 4.8	H 2.0		...	...	Lesotho
53.0	56.0										H 474	H 5.0			...	...	Liberia
59.1	62.5	1979	17,236	6.0							F 383	F 5.4	F 2.9		...	...	Libya
77.6	82.6	1988	178	6.4	1.7[21]	53.4[40]	44.9[41]	2.2[21]	78.7[40]	19.1[41]	H 8	H 3.0	H 0.7	95.1	...	...	Liechtenstein
70.6	77.9	1987	1,958	5.3	1.4	63.6	35.0	8.2	69.2	22.6	H 128	H 2.8	H 0.5	89.2	...	...	Luxembourg
68.0	73.0	1986	2,845	6.8	0.2	53.6	46.2	1.7	75.9	22.4	H 50	H 4.8	H 1.8	99.3	...	...	Macau
52.0	55.0	1975	19,800	2.6	14.5	60.3	25.2	49.5	36.9	13.6	H 1,709	H 4.7	H 2.0		...	...	Madagascar
46.3	47.7	1977	4,300	7.8								H 4.5					Malawi
68.9	72.7											H 5.2					Malaysia
58.0	59.0	...									H 23	H 6.1	H 2.7		...	...	Maldives
42.4	45.6	1983	21,785	2.8							H 1,254	H 5.1			...	...	Mali
72.2	77.0	1986	2,619	7.6	1.5	78.2	20.3	9.7	79.1	11.2	H 76	H 3.6	H 1.2	98.5	...	...	Malta
71.0	77.0	1987	1,537	4.6	0.5	54.7	44.8	5.0	65.1	29.9	H 90	H 3.7	H 1.0	34.0	1,753	30.6	Martinique
44.4	47.6										H 246	H 5.0			...	...	Mauritania
64.4	71.2	1986	10,337	10.3	1.5	58.3	40.2	23.9	59.0	17.1	F 155	F 5.3	F 2.0	72.8	...	...	Mauritius
53.0	57.0	...									H 10	H 4.7	H 2.3	89.2	...	...	Mayotte
67.8	73.9	1985	553,000	7.1	17.3	63.5	19.2	40.7	46.9	12.4	H 14,796	H 5.1	H 2.3	72.5	...	...	Mexico
72.0	80.0	1981	190	7.3							H 10	H 2.3	H 0.3	96.8	...	...	Monaco
61.7	65.8	1985	12,500	6.3							F 311	F 5.1			...	...	Mongolia
68.6	71.9	1985	55	4.6	—	41.8	58.2	9.1	45.5	45.5	H 4	H 3.1		23.4			Montserrat
59.1	62.5										H 2,819	H 5.8	H 2.5		...	...	Morocco
44.9	48.1	1974	6,037	0.7							F 1,860	F 4.4	F 2.0	73.1			Mozambique
58.6	62.1											H 5.2					Myanmar (Burma)
64.0	69.0	1977	43[45]	6.3							H 1	H 8.0	H 2.6				Nauru
51.8	50.6											F 5.8	H 2.2				Nepal
73.5	80.1	1987	87,400	6.0	0.3	64.1	35.6	2.9	73.8	23.3	H 5,565	H 2.6	H 0.6	89.8	18,700	10.7	Netherlands, The
74.0	79.0	1982	959	5.6	4.0	77.0	18.9	22.2	61.1	16.7	H 41	H 3.7	H 2.1	52.3	...	...	Netherlands Antilles
64.6	68.5	1987	729	4.5	0.5	54.5	45.0	10.2	61.9	27.9		H 4.1		48.1	...	...	New Caledonia
71.8	77.8	1986	24,037	7.3	1.3	62.8	35.9	7.7	67.2	25.1	H 1,078	H 3.1	H 0.8	71.4	8,056	21.1	New Zealand
60.0	62.0	1985	11,822	3.6	—18.1[21]—		81.9[47]	—48.2[21]—		51.8[47]		H 6.9					Nicaragua
42.9	46.1										H 1,029	H 5.2	H 2.4				Niger
48.8	52.2										H 14,441	H 5.0					Nigeria
63.0	66.5	1982	12	3.8							F 1	F 4.1	F 1.9	58.2			Niue
58.0	59.9	1987–88	16	7.9	—	56.3[16]	43.7[16]	6.3[16]	50.0[16]	43.7[16]	...	...		100.0			Norfolk Island

Vital statistics, marriage, family (continued)

country	\<vital rates\> year	birth rate per 1,000 population	death rate per 1,000 population	infant mortality rate per 1,000 live births	rate of natural increase per 1,000 population	total fertility rate	\<causes of death (rate per 100,000 population)\> year	infectious and parasitic diseases	malignant neoplasms (cancers)	endocrine and metabolic disorders	diseases of the nervous system	diseases of the circulatory system	diseases of the respiratory system	diseases of the digestive system	accidents, poisonings, and violence
Norway	1988	13.7	10.7	8.4[18]	3.0	1.7[18]	1986	6.7	230.2	13.2	15.8	509.7	90.0	31.0	64.8
Oman	1986	44.2	13.0	110.5	31.2	7.0	...	...	...	...	...	...	...	...	...
Pacific Is., Trust Terr. of the															
Marshall Islands	1985	38.7	5.2	30.3	33.5	5.1[2]	1985	35.5	32.7	38.2	27.3	70.9	109.1	13.6	49.1
Micronesia, Fed. States of	1989	34.0	5.0	26.0	29.0	5.0	1984	20.4	27.1	6.8	4.5	53.2	47.5	5.7	23.8
Northern Mariana Islands	1987	45.6	5.5	4.1	40.1	4.2[48]	1987	18.7	70.2[36]	23.4	14.0	135.7	70.2	9.4	145.1
Palau	1988	24.9	6.5	26.0	18.4	3.2[16]	1985–86	15.3	92.1[36]	19.2[32]	11.5	176.5	99.8	34.5	95.9
Pakistan	1988	46.5	12.4	108.0	34.1	6.4	...	...	...	...	...	...	...	...	...
Panama	1987	27.0	5.0	23.2	22.0	3.2	1987	22.6	54.4	9.5	6.5	113.1	37.5	16.4	50.9
Papua New Guinea	1988	38.0	11.9	60.0	26.1	5.5	...	...	...	...	...	...	...	...	...
Paraguay	1985–90	34.8	6.6	42.0	28.2	4.6	1986[50]	60.7	48.3	20.8	8.8	157.5	43.4	17.9	40.3
Peru	1989	33.5	8.7	83.3	24.8	4.3	1983	101.1	30.3	17.3	11.4	59.7	111.0	24.9	30.7
Philippines	1988	35.9	7.8	45.0	28.1	4.7	1984	179.8	30.2	13.4	...	100.6	...	...	16.8
Pitcairn Island	1982	—	—	—	...	...	...	...	...	...	...	...	...	...	...
Poland	1987	16.1	10.1	17.4	6.0	2.3[16]	1987	8.9	184.2	16.3	9.1	525.4	47.9	31.8	67.9
Portugal	1987	11.5	8.4	10.0	3.1	1.8[10]	1987	7.4	163.7	23.2	7.9	413.5	61.5	46.6	68.6
Puerto Rico	1986	19.4	7.1	14.9[3]	12.3	2.4	1986	11.6	108.2	39.9	10.2	251.6	78.3	43.9	64.5
Qatar	1987	30.4	2.4	37.4[16]	28.0	4.9[16]	1986	9.3	20.4[36]	6.9[32]	2.4	50.0	10.6	6.1	41.0
Réunion	1988	23.6	5.7	8.9[19]	17.9	2.7	1985	12.1	82.4	17.4[32]	...	164.0	45.0	49.1	71.1[20]
Romania	1985	15.8	10.9	25.6	4.9	2.1	1984	8.4	128.4	7.4	8.3	603.7	115.4	50.0	66.3
Rwanda	1985–90	51.0	17.1	122.0	33.9	8.3	...	...	...	...	...	...	...	...	...
St. Helena and Ascension	1986	9.0	3.6	29.7	5.4	1.8[9]	...	...	...	...	...	...	...	...	...
St. Kitts and Nevis	1987	23.2	10.3	35.0	12.9	3.0	1984	35.1	114.0	37.9[35]	6.8[2]	462.7	41.7	6.6	28.5
St. Lucia	1987	26.9	6.6	20.3[51]	20.3	3.8	1986	24.4	65.2	19.4	15.8	203.5	55.9	30.8	39.4
St. Pierre and Miquelon	1984	21.0	9.5	12.3[35]	11.5	2.2[9]	1977	72.9	108.3	102.1	25.0	366.7	45.8	39.6	39.6
St. Vincent and the Grenadines	1987	25.0	6.0	22.7[17]	19.0	3.0	1987	11.6	50.1	32.2	14.3	236.1	25.9	24.1	45.6
San Marino	1984–88	9.5	7.6	13.0	1.9	1.3[20]	1984–88[11]	—	262.0	5.3[5]	0.9[31]	318.8	32.0	18.6	53.3
São Tomé and Príncipe	1985	36.3	8.8	61.7	27.5	5.0	1984–85	318.5	36.1	5.6	18.5	95.4	138.0	52.8	48.1
Saudi Arabia	1986	37.3	12.8	108.6	24.5	7.2	...	...	...	...	...	...	...	...	...
Senegal	1985–90	45.7	18.9	128.0	26.8	6.4	...	...	...	...	...	...	...	...	...
Seychelles	1987	25.4	7.6	18.4	17.8	3.3[3]	1985–87	43.9	110.6	9.1	12.1	236.4	78.8	24.2	66.7
Sierra Leone	1985–90	48.2	23.4	154.0	24.8	6.5	...	...	...	...	...	...	...	...	...
Singapore	1988	20.0	5.2	7.0	14.8	1.5[18]	1987	16.5	119.8	19.8	3.9	178.9	74.3	12.6	35.6
Solomon Islands	1988	44.5	9.9	74.0	34.6	7.2	...	...	...	...	...	...	...	...	...
Somalia	1985–90	50.8	20.2	132.0	30.6	6.6	...	...	...	...	...	...	...	...	...
South Africa	1985–90	31.7	9.8	72.0	21.9	4.5	...	...	...	...	...	...	...	...	...
Bophuthatswana	1982	...	...	89.0	...	...	...	...	...	...	...	...	...	...	...
Ciskei	1982	...	...	89.0	...	...	...	...	...	...	...	...	...	...	...
Transkei	1982	...	...	89.0	...	...	...	...	...	...	...	...	...	...	...
Venda	1982	...	...	89.0	...	...	...	...	...	...	...	...	...	...	...
South West Africa/ Namibia	1985–90	44.0	12.2	106.0	31.8	6.1	...	...	...	...	...	...	...	...	...
Spain	1986	11.2	7.9	8.5[3]	3.3	1.7[10]	1984	8.4	171.6	24.3	8.4	350.1	67.0	45.7	41.2
Sri Lanka	1988	22.3	6.0	33.0	16.3	2.7	1983	47.8	27.8	8.1	43.5	84.2	40.6	14.4	82.8
Sudan, The	1985–90	44.6	15.8	108.0	28.8	6.4	...	...	...	...	...	...	...	...	...
Suriname	1985–90	25.9	6.1	31.0	19.8	3.0	1985	34.5	48.0	25.1	6.3	149.1	42.2	28.2	67.6
Swaziland	1985–90	46.8	12.5	118.0	34.3	6.4	...	...	...	...	...	...	...	...	...
Sweden	1988	13.3	9.0	5.8	4.3	1.8[18]	1986	7.9	231.2	19.1[32]	10.6	609.2	87.8	28.6	59.8
Switzerland	1988	12.3	9.2	6.8[18]	3.1	1.5[18]	1987	7.4	243.4	23.7[32]	16.5	408.1	49.9	29.9	78.8
Syria	1985–90	44.1	7.0	48.0	37.1	6.8	1981	15.1	8.4	5.0	4.0	60.7	13.2	4.5	20.0
Taiwan	1988	17.2	5.1	5.1[18]	12.1	1.7[18]	1987	...	88.6	16.8[5]	...	147.1[53]	25.3[54]	16.7[55]	66.6[8]
Tanzania	1985–90	50.5	14.0	106.0	36.5	7.1	...	...	...	...	...	...	...	...	...
Thailand	1988	22.1	7.0	38.0	15.1	2.6	...	...	...	...	...	...	...	...	...
Togo	1985–90	44.9	14.1	94.0	30.8	6.1	...	...	...	...	...	...	...	...	...
Tokelau	1982	27.7	10.3	—	17.4	4.3	...	...	...	...	...	...	...	...	...
Tonga	1988	30.4	7.3	49.0	23.1	4.0	1980	53.5	46.9	13.1	3.3	61.1	41.5	17.5	14.2
Trinidad and Tobago	1986	27.0	7.0	13.7[20]	20.0	2.8[18]	1986	13.0	83.6	76.6	12.0	253.9	41.9	24.3	56.8
Tunisia	1988	27.6	6.1	59.0[10]	21.5	4.1[10]	1988[50, 57]	13.9	23.4	2.2[5]	0.9[31]	115.3	9.9	4.2	7.6
Turkey	1985–90	28.4	8.4	84.0[16]	20.0	3.9	1987	—	100.1	12.5	—	175.2	—	—	—
Turks and Caicos Islands	1983	27.5	3.9	10.2[59]	23.6	3.8[9]	1985	40.0	70.0	20.0	120.0	150.0	120.0	170.0	...
Tuvalu	1989	27.0	10.0	30.0	17.0	2.8	...	...	...	...	...	...	...	...	...
Uganda	1985–90	50.1	15.4	103.0	34.7	6.9	...	...	...	...	...	...	...	...	...
U.S.S.R.	1987	19.8	9.9	25.4	9.9	2.4	1986	21.2	155.2	4.6[32]	7.4	544.3	81.3	28.4	88.6
United Arab Emirates	1986	33.5	3.9	39.9	29.6	5.7[18]	...	...	...	...	...	...	...	...	...
United Kingdom	1988	13.8	11.1	8.8	2.7	1.8[18]	1987	4.7	278.9	18.5	21.0	544.1	116.3	35.1	37.4
United States	1988–89	16.0	8.7	9.8	7.3	1.8[18]	1988–89	17.6	197.5	16.1[5]	0.5[31]	400.9	63.1[61]	17.2	60.5
Uruguay	1987	17.9	9.8	23.8	8.1	2.4[10]	1986	20.7	219.7	24.6	13.1	380.3	60.4	37.1	56.1
Vanuatu	1988	40.7	7.8	55.0	32.9	6.2	1985[62]	29.9	22.9	16.2	11.8	37.6	60.5	12.5	23.6
Venezuela	1987	28.3	4.4	25.1	23.9	3.4	1983	47.4	54.3	17.4	10.0	132.0	35.6	19.0	71.4
Vietnam	1988	31.7	9.4	63.0	22.3	4.1	1979	48.0	54.0	...	...	123.8	...	...	...
Virgin Islands (U.S.)	1987	22.4	5.3	17.8[51]	17.1	2.6	1986	7.3	74.9	16.4[5]	0.9[31]	179.9	9.1	17.4	48.4
Wallis and Futuna	1989	29.0	6.0	33.0	23.0	3.9	...	...	...	...	...	...	...	...	...
West Bank	1989	38.0	7.0	49.0	31.0	5.1	...	...	...	...	...	...	...	...	...
Western Sahara	1989	48.0	23.0	176.0	25.0	7.2	...	...	...	...	...	...	...	...	...
Western Samoa	1988	33.1	7.1	50.0	26.0	4.8	1985[62]	8.8	18.2	5.6[5]	0.6[31]	42.0	13.2	6.9	8.8
Yemen (Aden)	1989	48.0	15.0	113.0	33.0	7.1	...	...	...	...	...	...	...	...	...
Yemen (Ṣan'ā')	1986	49.1	20.8	164.0	28.3	7.5	...	...	...	...	...	...	...	...	...
Yugoslavia	1987	15.3	9.2	26.2	6.1	1.9	1985	12.1	141.6	11.9	6.2	463.7	53.3	35.3	56.7
Zaire	1985–90	45.6	13.9	98.0	31.7	6.1	...	...	...	...	...	...	...	...	...
Zambia	1985–90	51.2	13.7	80.0	37.5	7.2	...	...	...	...	...	...	...	...	...
Zimbabwe	1982–87	37.9	11.2	61.0[3]	26.7	4.9[18]	1979	7.3	152.9	7.0	1.6	310.6	64.7	6.6	102.4

[1]Excludes nomadic tribes. [2]1980. [3]1985. [4]Septicemia only. [5]Diabetes mellitus only. [6]Diseases of the heart and cerebrovascular disease only. [7]Chronic obstructive pulmonary diseases, pneumonia, and influenza only. [8]Suicide and accidents only. [9]1989. [10]1985–90. [11]Average annual rates for the period. [12]First marriages only. [13]1977. [14]1978. [15]1988. [16]1986. [17]1985–87 average. [18]1987. [19]1980–88 average. [20]1984. [21]Under 21 years of age. [22]21–29 years of age. [23]Data exclude deaths of unknown cause. [24]Motor vehicle accidents and drownings only. [25]1980–85. [26]1981. [27]Estimates based on rural survey. [28]Millions of households. [29]1981–86 average. [30]Based on burial permits. [31]Meningitis only. [32]Includes nutritional disorders. [33]1982–84 average. [34]1975–80. [35]1983. [36]Includes benign neoplasms. [37]Average age at death. [38]1981–85 average. [39]1982–86 average. [40]21–30 years of age. [41]Over 31 years of age.

expectation of life at birth (latest year) male	female	nuptiality — marriages year	total number	rate per 1,000 pop	groom ≤19	groom 20-29	groom 30+	bride ≤19	bride 20-29	bride 30+	families (F), households (H) total ('000)	size	children number under age 15	children percent legitimate	induced abortions number	ratio per 100 live births	country
72.8	79.6	1985	20,221	4.8	1.5	68.0	30.5	9.2	72.2	18.6	F 1,684	F 2.4	F 0.6	69.1	15,422	28.5	Norway
53.7	56.0										H 350	H 3.7					Oman
																	Pacific Is., Trust Terr. of the Marshall Islands
68.0	73.0										H 4	H 8.0					Micronesia, Fed. States of
											H 11	H 7.0					
59.0	64.0	1987	685	31.2	2.5	50.2	47.3	5.7	70.4	23.9	H 3	H 5.4		53.9			Northern Mariana Islands
59.1	62.8										H 2	H 5.9					Palau
56.8	56.8											H 6.5					Pakistan
70.2	74.1	1987	10,186	4.5	4.2[49]	56.1[49]	39.7[49]	18.7[49]	54.0[49]	27.3[49]	F 347	F 4.9		28.1	12	—	Panama
53.4	55.0										H 674	H 4.6					Papua New Guinea
64.8	69.1	1985	18,370	5.8	3.1	62.5	34.4	31.2	46.5	22.3	H 345	H 5.2		68.7			Paraguay
60.8	64.7	1982	109,200	6.0	5.5	60.4	34.1	25.9	51.4	22.6	H 3,099	H 5.2		57.8			Peru
61.8	65.5	1983	351,663	6.8	10.4	70.3	19.3	30.0	58.0	12.0	F 9,566	F 5.7	F 2.4	93.9			Philippines
63.0	66.5											H 6.5					Pitcairn Island
66.8	75.2	1987	252,819	6.7	3.6[16]	78.3[16]	18.1[16]	19.2[16]	67.8[16]	13.0[16]	F 9,435	F 3.6	F 0.9	95.0	135,564	20.0	Poland
70.0	76.9	1987	71,656	7.0	5.0	75.6	19.4	21.7	65.8	12.5	F 2,954	F 3.8	H 0.8	86.8			Portugal
71.0	79.0	1984	29,499	9.1	11.0	57.7	31.3	25.7	51.1	23.2	F 563	F 4.1	F 1.8	75.6			Puerto Rico
65.2	67.6	1986	1,181	3.1	6.4	73.2	20.4	39.5	54.7	5.8	H 61	H 6.4					Qatar
68.0	74.0	1988	3,354	5.8	2.3[3]	73.6[3]	24.1[3]	29.0[3]	56.6[3]	14.4[3]	H 121	H 4.2	H 2.3	47.8	3,838	32.5	Réunion
67.0	72.6	1985	161,094	7.1	3.1	75.1	21.8	34.2	51.0	14.8	H 7,115	H 3.1			404,000	99.0	Romania
46.9	50.2	1982	14,313	2.6							H 894	H 5.2		94.9			Rwanda
		1982	29	5.2	8.3	58.4	33.3	38.9	44.4	16.7	H 1.4	H 3.8	H 1.1	56.4			St. Helena and Ascension
63.0	67.0	1977	150	3.5							H 12	H 3.7	H 1.4	19.2			St. Kitts and Nevis
68.0	74.8	1986	432	3.1	0.7	46.9	52.4	8.8	53.6	37.6	H 25	H 4.6	H 2.0	15.0			St. Lucia
65.8	71.6	1985	32	5.2							H 2	H 3.3	H 0.9	83.0			St. Pierre and Miquelon
68.0	74.0	1987	416	3.7	0.7[20]	44.2[20]	55.1[20]	11.1[20]	57.2[20]	31.7[20]	H 20	H 5.0					St. Vincent and the Grenadines
70.7	76.2	1985	202	9.0	2.8	80.8	16.4	19.9	72.6	7.5	F 8	F 2.9	F 0.8	95.2			San Marino
41.7	44.9													9.8			São Tomé and Príncipe
54.8	57.7										H 1,513	H 6.6					Saudi Arabia
44.2	47.4										H 1,167	H 4.8					Senegal
66.2	73.5	1984	390	6.0	1.8	55.9	42.3	15.6	60.8	23.6	H 13	H 4.8	H 1.9	29.8	188	10.9	Seychelles
39.4	42.6										H 749	H 4.7					Sierra Leone
70.0	76.3	1988	24,853	9.4	0.6[18]	68.6[18]	30.8[18]	7.0[18]	78.3[18]	14.7[18]	H 510	H 3.9	H 1.3		23,512	55.3	Singapore
59.9	61.4										F 41	F 5.6	F 2.3				Solomon Islands
43.4	46.6											H 4.9					Somalia
57.5	63.5	1977	64,979[52]	...	3.5[52]	69.4[52]	27.1[52]	22.1[52]	58.6[52]	19.3[52]	F 1,403	H 5.1		75.9			South Africa
—57.0—											H 144	H 6.2					Bophuthatswana
—57.0—																	Ciskei
—57.0—																	Transkei
—57.0—											H 70	H 5.4					Venda
55.0	57.5											H 4.8					South West Africa/Namibia
73.6	79.7	1983	183,068	4.8	5.7	80.8	13.5	20.8	71.7	7.5	F 10,665	F 3.5		97.9			Spain
68.4	72.6	1985	128,034	7.8	0.5	71.1	28.4	16.9	73.0	10.1	H 2,721	H 5.2	H 1.9	94.6			Sri Lanka
48.6	51.0										H 3,471	H 5.3					Sudan, The
67.1	72.1	1985	2,400	6.1								H 3.9					Suriname
53.7	57.3										H 112	H 5.0			1,145		Swaziland
74.2	80.2	1987	41,064	4.9	0.4	42.7	56.9	2.3	56.4	41.3	H 3,670	H 2.3	H 0.5	50.1	34,707	33.2	Sweden
73.8	80.5	1987	43,063	6.6	0.2	56.0	43.8	3.0	70.1	26.9	H 2,500	H 2.5		94.1			Switzerland
63.2	66.9	1985	96,326	7.7							F 1,151	F 6.2	F 2.4				Syria
71.1	76.3	1987	146,075	7.5	2.4	76.6	21.0	11.2	81.5	7.3	H 4,645	H 4.2	H 1.5	98.0			Taiwan
51.3	54.7	1967	3,475	9.8							H 3,435	H 5.1	H 2.3				Tanzania
63.2	67.3	1987	373,637	6.9							H 9,410	H 4.6	H 2.0				Thailand
51.3	54.8	1979[56]	5,753	2.3							H 479	H 5.6					Togo
63.0	66.5	1981	9	6.0	—	83.3	16.7	—	100.0	—		H 5.5		90.7			Tokelau
61.0	64.8	1985	645	6.6							F 15	F 6.1	F 2.7	80.6			Tonga
68.0	72.0	1988	7,327	5.9	3.0	61.0	36.0	19.0	58.0	23.0	H 193	H 4.2	H 2.1	56.9	9	—	Trinidad and Tobago
64.6	66.1	1986	47,914	6.4	1.4	72.5	26.1	35.9	54.7	9.4	H 1,313	H 5.5		99.8	20,500	9.5	Tunisia
62.5	65.8	1983	308,256	6.4	7.1[58]	74.0[58]	18.9[58]	35.7[58]	53.5[58]	10.8[58]	H 8,601	H 5.2	H 2.0				Turkey
68.6	71.9	1980	27	3.6							H 1	H 4.3	H 2.0	82.4			Turks and Caicos Islands
59.0	62.0										H 1	H 6.4	H 2.2	82.2			Tuvalu
49.4	52.7										H 2,766	H 4.8					Uganda
65.1	73.8	1986	2,753,100	9.8	3.7	73.6	22.7	24.8	56.3	18.9	F 66,307	F 3.9		90.2	10,000,000	230.0	U.S.S.R.
68.4	71.7										H 247	H 6.8					United Arab Emirates
71.7	75.8	1987	397,937	7.0	6.1[21]	59.8[22]	34.1	17.3[21]	58.2[22]	24.5	H 21,672	H 2.7	H 1.7	77.1	180,983[60]	25.0[60]	United Kingdom
71.4	78.3	1988	2,389,000	9.7	5.0[16]	55.3[16]	39.7[16]	13.1[16]	56.1[16]	30.8[16]	F 63,558	F 2.6	F 1.0	76.6	1,588,600	42.5	United States
67.8	74.4	1985	22,336	7.6	8.3	62.7	29.0	28.3	51.7	20.0	H 863	H 3.3		73.8			Uruguay
61.1	59.3										H 23	H 5.0					Vanuatu
66.7	72.8	1987	105,058	5.7	11.1	62.8	26.1	32.8	51.0	16.2	H 2,707	H 5.3		47.0			Venezuela
59.4	63.8																Vietnam
66.7	70.7	1983	1,341	12.9	3.1	44.6	52.3	12.7	50.9	36.4	H 28	H 3.4	H 1.3	48.7			Virgin Islands (U.S.)
69.0	70.0	1980	60	5.6								H 6.6	H 3.0	78.3			Wallis and Futuna
65.0	68.0																West Bank
39.0	41.0	1972	459	4.9													Western Sahara
62.6	65.6	1984	555	5.0	0.9	58.7	40.4	7.2	68.8	24.0	F 20	F 7.8	F 3.8	43.5			Western Samoa
50.0	53.0										H 392	H 5.6					Yemen (Aden)
45.6	48.9										H 1,456	H 5.6					Yemen (San'ā')
66.0	72.0	1986	160,277	7.0	2.5	73.4	24.1	18.6	61.7	19.7	H 6,187	H 3.6	H 0.9	90.6	288,100	74.0	Yugoslavia
50.8	54.2	1975	185,300	7.5								H 6.0					Zaire
52.4	54.5										H 1,370	H 4.4	H 2.1				Zambia
57.9	61.4											H 5.8		95.8			Zimbabwe

[42]Reported inpatient deaths only. [43]Medically certified deaths only. [44]Includes nutritional disorders and diseases of the blood. [45]1973. [46]Includes Aruba. [47]Over 21 years of age. [48]1976–80 average. [49]Excludes tribal Indians. [50]Reporting areas only. [51]1984–86 average. [52]Whites, Asians, and Coloureds only. [53]Cerebrovascular disease, heart disease, and hypertensive disease only. [54]Pneumonia, bronchitis, emphysema, and asthma only. [55]Chronic liver disease and cirrhosis only. [56]African population only. [57]Data are based on about 30 percent of total deaths. [58]Urban areas only. [59]1982. [60]Excludes Northern Ireland. [61]Bronchitis, pneumonia, influenza, and chronic obstructive pulmonary diseases only. [62]Registered events only.

National product and accounts

The national product and accounts table furnishes, for most of the countries of the world, breakdowns of (1) total and per capita gross national product (GNP), (2) nominal and real gross domestic product (GDP), (3) principal accounting and industrial components of national GDP, (4) growth rates of real GDP during the last two decades, and (5) principal elements of each country's balance of payments, including international goods trade, invisibles, and tourism payments.

Measures of national output. The two most commonly used measures of national output (except for certain centrally planned economies) are GDP and GNP. Each of these measures represents an aggregate value of goods and services produced by a specific country. The GDP, the more basic of these, is a measure of the total value of goods and services produced entirely within a given country. The GNP, the more comprehensive value, is composed of both domestic production, GDP, *and* the net income from current (short-term) transactions with other countries. When the income received from other countries is greater than payments to them, a country's GNP is greater than its GDP. In theory, if all national accounts could be equilibrated, the global summation of GDP would equal GNP.

In the first section of the table, data are provided for the nominal GNP (value in current prices for the year indicated), together with the per capita value of this product, both denominated in U.S. dollars for ease of comparison. Beside these are given figures for GDP denominated in the national currency, first as a nominal value, then as a "real" value (adjusted, that is, to eliminate the effect of recent inflation [most often] or, occasionally, of deflation). The real values are obtained by dividing the nominal GDP by a GDP deflator (essentially a consumer price index

that covers price changes in the whole economy) and are adjusted to a common base year of 1980. GNP per capita provides a rough measure of annual national income per person, but values should be compared cautiously, as they are subject to a number of distortions, notably of purchasing power parity (the differing ability [by more than a simple exchange rate] of any two currencies to purchase comparable goods in their respective domestic markets) and in the existence of elements of national production that do not enter the monetary economy in such a way as to be visible to fiscal authorities (*e.g.*, food, clothing, or housing produced and consumed within families or communal groups; services exchanged; criminal transactions; and the like).

In a number of countries with centrally planned economies, the conventional concept for the aggregated national income/product is net material product (NMP), which includes only material goods and "productive" services. These NMP accounts are not directly comparable to the GDP values presented in this table for free market economies. The GDP value is more comprehensive and includes a number of sectors (especially personal and financial services) excluded from the NMP value. Estimated GNPs have been supplied for most countries (including the centrally planned), based either on the country's own, or on external, analysis.

The internal structure of the national product. Even though GDP/GNP values allow comparison of the relative size of national economies, more information is provided when these aggregates are analyzed according to their component kinds of expenditure, cost components, and industrial sectors of origin.

There are three major domestic components of GDP expenditure: pri-

National product and accounts

country	gross national product (GNP), 1987 nominal ('000,000 U.S.$)	gross national product (GNP), 1987 per capita (U.S.$)	gross domestic product (GDP), 1987 nominal ('000,000,000 national currency)	gross domestic product (GDP), 1987 real (constant prices of 1980; '000,000,000 national currency)	GDP by type of expenditure, 1986 (%) consumption private	GDP by type of expenditure, 1986 (%) consumption government	GDP by type of expenditure, 1986 (%) gross domestic investment	GDP by type of expenditure, 1986 (%) foreign trade exports	GDP by type of expenditure, 1986 (%) foreign trade imports	cost components of GDP, 1986 (%) indirect taxes net of subsidies	cost components of GDP, 1986 (%) consumption of fixed capital	cost components of GDP, 1986 (%) compensation of employees	cost components of GDP, 1986 (%) net operating surplus
Afghanistan	3,520[1]	230[1]	...	100.3[2,3]	...	...	...	...	...	...	...	...	...
Albania	2,800[3]	880[3]	...	...	...	...	...	...	...	...	...	...	...
Algeria	63,560	2,760	307.9	...	49	15	41	16	−22	20[8]	8[8]	37[8]	35[8]
American Samoa	190[1]	5,340[1]	...	...	...	...	...	...	...	...	...	...	...
Andorra	360[6]	9,000[6]	...	...	...	...	...	...	...	...	...	...	...
Angola	6,930[10]	830[10]	156.8[3]	124.4[3]	62	27	9	34	−32	16	—	84 —	
Anguilla	...	2,900[13]	0.056	0.041[14]	41[9]	17[9]	29[9]	56[9]	−43[9]	19[9]	—	81[9] —	
Antigua and Barbuda	211	2,570	0.510[3]	0.366[3]	70	19	36	75	−100	8[6]	16	34[6]	57[6,16]
Argentina	74,490	2,370	74.309[3]	0.027[3]	72[10]	14[10]	14[10]	13[10]	−9[10]	13[10]	16	...	...
Aruba	...	8,480[13]	0.917	0.886[17]	66	21	17	— −3 —					
Australia	176,301	10,900	276.2	161.1	60	19	24	16	−19	12[1]	16[1]	50[1]	21[1]
Austria	90,484	11,970	1,487.5	1,101.9	56	19	24	37	−36	14[1]	12[1]	52[1]	21[1]
Bahamas, The	2,488	10,320	2.730	...	53	13	20	72	−58	...	...	...	...
Bahrain	3,670[3]	8,530[3]	1.603[1]	1.511[1]	42	19	41	64	−66	4	15	40	41
Bangladesh	17,408	160	539.2	259.9	89	8	11	5	−14	...	...	...	...
Barbados	1,358	5,330	2.914	...	66	17	16	46	−45	14[8]	6[8]	57[8]	24[8]
Belgium	112,009	11,360	5,323.0	3,830.0	64	17	16	65	−62	10[1]	9[1]	55[1]	26[1]
Belize	219	1,250	0.425[3]	0.409[3]	63	24	20	55	−62	12[10]	9[10]	— 79[10] —	
Benin	1,315	300	502.7[3]	359.5[3]	94	9	21	23	−48	6[6]	10[6]	21[6]	63[6]
Bermuda	1,313	22,790	1.281	0.657	65	11	14	64	−54	...	...	...	...
Bhutan	201	150	2.678[3]	2.452[3,20]	...	...	...	...	...	10[8]	6[8]	36[8]	47[8]
Bolivia	4,150	570	10.559[3]	0.106[3]	77	9	17	24	−26	13[6]	7[6]	38[6]	43[6]
Botswana	1,175	1,030	2.747	1.584	37	24	23	67	−51	10[12]	5[12]	— 85[12] —	
Brazil	314,642	2,020	12,788.6	15.9	69	10	19	8	−4	12[22]	16	53[22]	36[16,22]
British Virgin Islands	...	9,490[13]	0.116	...	43[6]	18[6]	38[6]	114[6]	−115[6]	...	...	...	...
Brunei	...	11,600[3,13]	5.773[3]	...	...	...	...	...	...	...	...	...	...
Bulgaria	67,590[24]	7,510[24]	26.851[2,3]	25.923[2,3]	58[10]	11[10]	24[10]	— 7[10] —		7[10]	6[10]	25[10]	61[10]
Burkina Faso	1,426	170	430.0[3]	307.1[3]	95	16	4	27	−44	9[6]	3[6]	21[6]	68[6]
Burundi	1,205	240	140.480	112.017	74	17	16	11	−18	13[6]	5[6]	27[6]	54[6]
Cameroon	10,441	960	3,838.9[10]	2,398.7[10]	64	10	28	15	−17	...	...	...	...
Canada	390,052	15,080	549.7	382.8	59	20	21	27	−26	10[1]	11[1]	54[1]	24[1]
Cape Verde	170	500	11.2[3]	6.5[3]	100	11	26	8	−44	...	...	...	...
Cayman Islands	...	17,390[13]	0.329	...	...	...	...	22	−33	...	...	...	...
Central African Republic	912	330	323.7	191.9	83	18	9	22	−33	...	...	...	...
Chad	805	150	465.7[1]	...	80	22	7	20	−28	...	...	...	...
Chile	16,468	1,310	4,159.8	502.9	69	13	15	31	−27	14[12]	11[12]	42[12]	34[12]
China	319,780	300	915.3[29]	702.0[29]	60[2]	9[2]	37[2]	— 5[2] —		...	...	...	...
Christmas Island	...	...	...	...	...	...	...	...	...	...	...	...	...
Cocos (Keeling) Islands	...	...	...	...	...	...	...	...	...	9[10]	16	44[10]	47[10,16]
Colombia	36,027	1,220	8,779.4	1,954.0	65	10	18	19	−12	...	...	— 93 —	
Comoros	160	380	56.4[3]	36.7[3]	74	28	24	16	−41	7			
Congo	1,761	880	640.4[3]	...	58	23	26	42	−49	16[10]	18[10]	27[10]	39[10]
Cook Islands	21	1,250	...	...	...	...	...	...	...	...	...	...	...
Costa Rica	4,299	1,590	285.284	46.393	60	15	24	31	−30	14[1]	3[1]	48[1]	36[1]
Côte d'Ivoire	8,262	750	3,244.3[3]	2,421.0[3]	62	15	12	39	−27	19[12]	8[12]	35[12]	38[12]
Cuba	26,920[10]	2,690[10]	12,202.2[2]	13,174.7[2]	90[2]	9[2]	19[2]	— −17[2] —		8[1]	11[1]	— 81[1] —	
Cyprus	3,532	5,210	1.792	1.080	62	14	26	45	−48	...	...	...	...
Czechoslovakia	158,168[24]	10,140[24]	574.2[2]	520.2[2]	69[2]	9[2]	20[2]	— −3[2] —		16[1]	9[1]	54[1]	22[1]
Denmark	76,640	15,010	693.0	435.0	55	24	21	32	−32	— 17[31] —		35[31]	48[31]
Djibouti	330	1,070	63.5[3]	58.2[3]	78	36	23	40	−78	...	...	...	...
Dominica	115	1,440	0.340	...	71[10]	25[10]	39[10]	37[10]	−72[10]	7[10]	6[10]	— 87[10] —	
Dominican Republic	4,930	730	21.710	7.982	76	7	18	8	−9	12[1]	6[1]	18[1]	70[1,16]
Ecuador	10,333	1,040	1,808.4	318.9	67	12	20	23	−23	6[12]	16	36[12]	59[12,16]
Egypt	36,028	710	44.050	...	71	16	21	16	−24	9[1]	4[1]	— 87[1] —	
El Salvador	4,220	850	23.309	8.395	76	14	13	25	−29				

vate consumption (analyzed in greater detail in the "Household budgets and consumption" table), government spending, and gross domestic investment. The fourth, nondomestic, component of GDP expenditure is net foreign trade; values are given for both exports (a positive value) and imports (a negative value, representing obligations to other countries). The sum of these five percentages, excluding statistical discrepancies and rounding, should be 100% of the GDP.

The structure of GDP as accounted by cost components here comprises four general categories: indirect taxes (excise or value-added taxes), net of subsidies; consumption of fixed capital (depreciation); and two income categories: (a) compensation of employees (salaries, wages, etc.) and (b) net operating surplus ("profits," interests, rent, etc.).

The distribution of GDP for ten industrial sectors is aggregated into three major industrial groups:
1. The primary sector, composed of agriculture (including forestry and fishing) and mineral production (including fossil fuels).
2. The secondary sector, composed of manufacturing, construction, and public utilities.
3. The tertiary sector, which includes transportation and communications, trade (wholesale and retail), financial services (including banking, real estate, etc.), other (personal and business) services, and government.

Percentages in this section of the table may not add to 100 because the value of each industry is calculated as a percentage of the total GDP, which may contain significant monetary adjustments that are not distributable to all industries.

Average annual growth rate of real GDP. These columns show average annual growth rates of real product for the decade from 1970 to 1980, as well as for the seven years from 1980 to 1987. Real GDP growth rates indicate the change in total output achieved by each country during the periods indicated excluding inflation.

Balance of payments (external account transactions). The external account records the sum (net) of all economic transactions of a current nature between one country and the rest of the world. The account shows a country's net of overseas receipts and obligations, including not only the trade of goods and services but also such invisible items as interest and dividends, short- and long-term investments, tourism, transfers to or from overseas residents, etc. Each transaction gives rise either to a foreign claim for payment, recorded as a deficit (e.g., from imports, capital outflows), or a foreign obligation to pay, recorded as a surplus (e.g., from exports, capital inflows) or a domestic claim on another country. Any international transaction automatically creates a deficit in the balance of payments of one country and a surplus in that of another. Values are given in U.S. dollars for comparability.

Tourist trade. Net income or expenditure from tourism is often a significant element in a country's balance of payments. Receipts from foreign nationals reflect payments for goods and services from foreign currency resources by tourists in the given country. Expenditures by nationals abroad are also payments for goods and services, but in this case made by the residents of the given country as tourists abroad. The U.S. dollar is used as the common currency for comparability by the World Tourism Organization.

origin of GDP by economic sector, 1986 (%) — avg. annual growth rate of real GDP (%) — balance of payments, 1988 (current external transactions; '000,000 U.S.$) — tourist trade, 1987 ('000,000 U.S.$)

agri-culture	mining	manu-facturing	con-struction	public utilities	transp., communications	trade	financial svcs.	other svcs.	govt.	1970–1980	1980–1987	net transfers goods-merchandise	invisibles	current balance of payments	receipts from foreign nationals	expenditures by nationals abroad	country
65[2]	4	16[2,4]	4[2]		3[2]	10[2]		2[2]		2.1[2]	2.0[2,5]	−278	304	26	1	1	Afghanistan
34[2,6]	4	43[2,4,6]	8[2,6]	4		15[2,6]				6.3[2]	5.7[2,7]						Albania
14	17	14	17	1	5	16		15		7.8	3.6	2,413[9]	−2,272[9]	141[9]	125	450	Algeria
...	...	...	...	...	...	...				...	...	−60[3]	...	...	11	...	American Samoa
...	...	...	...	...	...	...				...	...						Andorra
14	11	31[11]	4	1	7	13		32		−2.2	2.8	−34[12]	−175[12]	−209[12]			Angola
6[9]	·[29]	1[9]	18[9]	2[9]	7	12[9]	34[9]	12[9]	2[9] 18[9]		10.1[15]				22		Anguilla
5	2	4	9	4	16	25	16	8	17	2.3	6.2	−230[9]	147[9]	−83[9]	131	14	Antigua and Barbuda
15	3	24	3	5	11	15	8	17		2.4	−0.6	4,043	−5,289	−1,246	614	894	Argentina
...	...	...	...	...	...	...				...	...				203	17	Aruba
4	6	17	7	4	7	16	20	16	4	3.3	3.2	−1,136	−9,401	−10,537	1,789	2,351	Australia
3	11	28[11]	7	3	6	16	15	3	14	3.7	1.5	−5,828	5,126	−702	7,604	4,516	Austria
4	4	10[4]	3	4	11	26	12	16	17	6.3	3.5	−774	642	−132	1,174	152	Bahamas, The
1	21	10	9	2	10	7	20	4	16	4.6	2.45	−13[9]	−140[9]	−153[9]	94	66	Bahrain
40	—	10	6	1	11	9	10	9	4	4.5	4.0	−1,444	1,157	−287	13	52	Bangladesh
6	1	9	5	3	8	27	12	4	14	4.3	0.4	−327[9]	274[9]	−53[9]	379	29	Barbados
2	—	23	5	4	7	21	6	35		3.3	1.05	−1,569[9,18]	3,076[9,18]	2,920[9,18]	2,980	3,886	Belgium
20	—	11	5	3	9	17	12	12	13	4.9	2.9	−98[9]	−38[9]	−60[9]	24	5	Belize
40	11	6[11]	5	1	10	19	20			3.9	2.8	−71[9]	−49[9]	−75[9]	8	3	Benin
1[19]		4[19]	5[19]	2[19]	7[19]	33[19]	22[19]	18[19]	8[19]	3.0	0.7	−390[9]	487[9]	97[9]	475	81	Bermuda
51	1	4	9	4	3	11	7	...	13	4.1	6.0	−49[21]	−23[21]	−72[21]	2[3]	...	Bhutan
28	5	12	5	—	8	20	12	3	6	4.5	−1.7	57	−255	−198	40	28	Bolivia
4	47	6	3	2	2	18	5	2	13	15.8	12.3	592	−81	511	49	25	Botswana
9	1	27	6	2	5	14	17	13	6	8.6	3.3	11,158[9]	−12,608[9]	−1,450[9]	1,502	1,249	Brazil
4	—	3	7	23		86[23]				3.7	−0.47	...	...	...	140	...	British Virgin Islands
2	11	51[11]	4	—	2	12	7	25		8.9	−4.85	...	...	...	...	...	Brunei
15[2]	—	62[2,25]	10[2]	25	72	52		22,26		6.7[2]	4.0[2,5]	...	...	...	354	...	Bulgaria
47[1]	—	11[1]	11	11	7[1]	10[1]	23[1]			5.3	3.8	−222[1]	153[1]	−69[1]	7	30	Burkina Faso
63	1	10	5	—	2	7	...	1	10	4.0	3.9	−42	−20	−62	35	18	Burundi
25[1]	17[1]	11[1]	6[1]	1[1]	5[1]	28[1]			8[1]	4.5	6.5	440[3]	−1,004[3]	−564[3]	47	150	Cameroon
4	6	20	7	3	8	12	14	20	6	4.1	3.1	8,479	−17,593	−9,114	3,939	5,840	Canada
24[1]	1[1]	5[1]	21[1]			49[1]				−0.2	7.8	−661[19]	641[19]	−219	...	...	Cape Verde
...	...	...	...	...	...	...				10.3[27]	7.6[28]	−172[9]	148[9]	−24[9]	120	...	Cayman Islands
41[1]	2[1]	7[1]	1	1	4[1]	21[1]	20[1]			2.6	2.1	−71[9]	−49[9]	−75[9]	5	33	Central African Republic
46[1]	1[1]	9[1]	2[1]			42[1]				0.5	4.2	−117[9]	91[9]	−26[9]	5	35	Chad
10	8	21	6	3	6	17	30			2.8	1.3	1,230[9]	−2,041[9]	−811[9]	173	351	Chile
41[29]	...	38[29]	6[29]	...	4[29]	10[29]				5.7[29]	9.6[29]	−1,661[9]	1,961[9]	300[9]	1,845	387	China
...	...	...	...	...	...	...				...	...	...	...	...	...	...	Christmas Island
...	...	...	...	...	...	...				...	...	...	...	...	...	...	Cocos (Keeling) Islands
21	3	22	4	1	10	12	7	13	8	5.5	3.1	1,868[9]	−1,532[9]	336[9]	220	340	Colombia
37	...	4	10		4	25	...	16		2.0	−0.7	−35[9]	12[9]	−23[9]	3	5	Comoros
12	16	10	6	1	11	16	28			4.7	6.1	373	−701	−328	6	67	Congo
26[8]	—	11[8]	9[8]	2[8]	7[8]	14[8]	3[8]	...	...	−2.6	3.27	−20[3]	...	...	19	...	Cook Islands
19	11	22[11]	5	3	7	17	13	4	10	5.7	1.6	−141[9]	−239[9]	−380[9]	136	71	Costa Rica
29[9]	30	21[9,30]	30	30	30	51[9]				6.5	1.4	1,546[3]	−1,684[3]	−138[3]	53	163	Côte d'Ivoire
15[2]	4	37[2,4]	9[2]	4	8[2]	31[2]		12,26		5.8[2]	4.7[2]	...	...	...	80[3]	...	Cuba
7	—	15	10	2	10	19	14	10	7	4.2	5.3	−777[9]	869[9]	92[9]	666	118	Cyprus
8[2]	4	60[2,4]	11[2]	4	5[2]	16[2]		12,26		4.8[2]	3.0[2]	...	...	...	402	229	Czechoslovakia
5	1	20	6	1	8	14	4	21	21	2.4	2.2	2,063	−3,865	−1,802	2,219	2,860	Denmark
5	—	9	4	1	11	16	12	2	32	0.9	4.7	−100[12]	75[12]	−25[12]	6	...	Djibouti
29	1	9	7	2	9	14	12		21	2.9	5.3	−149	15[9]	19	11	3	Dominica
16	4	17	7	2	8	15	11	10	10	7.0	2.7	−839[9]	569[9]	−270[9]	500	90	Dominican Republic
15	11	20	5	—	9	18	4	7	8	9.1	1.2	589	−1,186	−597	167	165	Ecuador
16	11	33[11]	5	1	8	13	5	4	15	7.1	5.6	−6,751	5,561	−1,190	1,586	52	Egypt
24	—	17	3	4	6	16	8	7	14	3.4	−0.9	−124[3]	241[3]	117[3]	20	89	El Salvador

National product and accounts (continued)

country	gross national product (GNP), 1987 nominal ('000,000 U.S.$)	per capita (U.S.$)	gross domestic product (GDP), 1987 nominal ('000,000,000 national currency)	real (constant prices of 1980; '000,000,000 national currency)	GDP by type of expenditure, 1986 (%) consumption private	government	gross domestic investment	foreign trade exports	imports	cost components of GDP, 1986 (%) indirect taxes net of subsidies	consumption of fixed capital	compensation of employees	net operating surplus
Equatorial Guinea	...	330[3,13]	34.540[3]	...	57	28	14	35	-35	26	...	—74—	
Ethiopia	5,537	120	11.134	...	80	19	11	13	-23	9	16	62	29[16]
Faeroe Islands	550[3]	12,180[3]	5.250	...	61	20	39	45	-65	...	...	...	...
Falkland Islands	56	30,860	...	...	...	...	...	...	...	...	...	...	...
Fiji	1,091	1,510	1.493[3]	1.113[3]	60	19	19	42	-40	10[1]	7[1]	46[1]	38[1]
Finland	71,084	14,370	393.6	236.9	54	21	24	27	-25	11[1]	14[1]	55[1]	20[1]
France	714,994	12,860	5,279.0	3,154.3	60	19	19	21	-20	13[1]	12[1]	54[1]	21[1]
French Guiana	180[6]	2,340[6]	...	...	68[12]	34[12]	32[12]	12[12]	-45[12]	6[12]	17[12]	46[12]	31[12]
French Polynesia	...	7,490[10,13]	202.4[10]	...	38	23	36	51	-49	22[12]	9[12]	26[12]	42[12]
Gabon	2,890	2,750	1,019.3	...	...	...	...	...	...	...	...	...	...
Gambia, The	177	220	1,078.1	296.5	91	19	19	23	-52	...	...	...	...
Gaza Strip	560	1,030	0.495[3]	0.002[3]	152	14	34	47	-148	...	...	...	...
Germany, East	207,648[24]	12,430[24]	248.8[2]	209.0[2]	57[10]	11[10]	18[10]	—13[10]—		10[2,12]	9[2,12]	40[2,12]	41[2,12]
Germany, West	879,630	14,460	2,009.1	1,834.5	55	20	20	33	-27	10[1]	13[1]	54[1]	23[1]
Ghana	5,328	390	746.0	46.7	82	11	10	19	-22	5[22]	3[22]	—91[22]—	
Gibraltar	130[1]	4,550[1]	0.074[1]	...	...	...	...	...	...	10[1]	9[1]	42[1]	39[1]
Greece	43,557	4,350	6,389.5	1,843.6	69	20	20	23	-32	...	...	...	...
Greenland	470[3]	8,790[3]	...	...	75	23	32	49	-80	...	...	...	...
Grenada	134	1,340	0.376	0.272	...	...	...	...	...	11[8]	16	70[8]	19[8,16]
Guadeloupe	...	3,190[1,13]	9.550[1]	...	97[1]	35[1]	22[1]	8[1]	-61[1]	...	...	...	...
Guam	1,000	7,680	...	...	...	...	...	...	...	...	...	...	...
Guatemala	6,839	940	17.595	7.689	81	7	10	16	-15	...	...	...	...
Guernsey	1,350[1,34]	9,900[1,34]	...	...	...	...	...	...	...	...	...	...	...
Guinea	...	270[3,13]	571.9[3]	244.7[3]	75	8	13	32	-28	...	...	...	...
Guinea-Bissau	152	170	31.8[3]	6.0[3]	134	22	18	11	-85	...	...	...	...
Guyana	310	380	3.357	1.270	45	39	26	49	-60	17[10]	7[10]	—76[10]—	
Haiti	2,221	360	9.752	6.822	—94—		14	18	-26	10[12]	3[12]	—87[12]—	
Honduras	3,627	780	8.020	5.795	72	15	15	27	-29	12[1]	5[1]	—84[1]—	
Hong Kong	...	8,330[13]	363.0	228.3	64	8	24	110	-105	—7[10]—		48[10]	45[10]
Hungary	91,648[24]	8,650[24]	1,226.4	795.1	64	11	27	40	-41	...	...	...	...
Iceland	4,083	16,670	206.346	18.221	62	17	17	40	-35	19	14	47	13
India	241,305	300	3,304.6	1,847.2	67	12	25	—3—		12[1]	7[1]	—81[1]—	
Indonesia	76,766	450	114,519.0	60,909.6	63	12	25	22	-22	3[1]	5[1]	—92[1]—	
Iran	93,500	1,800	14,991.5[1]	9,044.3[1]	57[1]	16[1]	27[1]	8[1]	-7[1]	2[10]	7[10]	—91[10]—	
Iraq	34,000	1,950	13.576[3]	...	—79—		29	20	-28	2[1]	10[1]	32[1]	56[1]
Ireland	21,761	6,030	19.775	10.836	60	19	19	56	-53	10[1]	9[1]	55[1]	26[1]
Isle of Man	340[38]	5,280[38]	0.200[38]	0.156[38]	...	...	...	...	...	...	...	...	...
Israel	29,803	6,810	55.336	0.139	63	32	20	39	-53	14[1]	13[1]	46[1]	27[1]
Italy	596,995	10,420	982,590.0	450,400.0	62	16	21	19	-18	9[1]	10[1]	55[1]	27[1]
Jamaica	2,256	960	15.717	5.110	64	15	19	55	-53	12[1]	9[1]	44[1]	35[1]
Japan	1,925,614	15,770	343,238.0	310,512.0	58	10	28	13	-9	7[1]	14[1]	55[1]	24[1]
Jersey	1,647	20,340	0.825	...	76	27	30	38	-71	14	9	46	31
Jordan	4,370	1,540	1.686	1.301	...	...	...	...	...	...	...	...	...
Kampuchea (Cambodia)	600[31]	90[31]	...	...	59	18	23	26	-26	13[1]	16	37[1]	50[1,16]
Kenya	7,500	340	132.294	67.417	...	...	...	...	...	...	...	...	...
Kiribati	32	480	0.032[3]	0.023[3]	85	56	31	23	-94	12	12	52	25
Korea, North	20,000	910	11.8[12]	...	...	...	...	...	...	...	...	...	...
Korea, South	112,947	2,690	99,790.0	67,820.0	55	11	29	41	-35	12[1]	9[1]	41[1]	38[1]
Kuwait	27,324	14,870	4.816[3]	7.948[3]	50	30	22	50	-51	3[9]	8	—92[39]—	
Laos	590	160	...	...	...	...	...	...	...	...	...	...	...
Lebanon	1,492[10]	560[10]	9.717[10]	7.272[10]	125[10]	38[10]	5[10]	41[10]	-109[10]	2[10]		—98[10]—	
Lesotho	591	360	0.727	...	151	30	38	14	-134	22[6]	3[6]	40[6]	35[6]
Liberia	1,030	440	1.035[3]	0.788[3]	48	18	15	57	-38	14[12]		—86[12]—	
Libya	22,326	5,500	9.562[3]	8.639[3]	39[1]	33[1]	24[1]	46[1]	-42[1]	4[12]	5[12]	30[12]	61[12]
Liechtenstein	450[3]	16,500[3]	...	...	...	...	...	...	...	...	...	...	...
Luxembourg	5,805	15,860	252.6[3]	176.1[3]	52	14	20	96	-83	13[1]	11[1]	58[1]	18[1]
Macau	...	5,280[13]	18.073	12.212[40]	40	6	20	90	-55	12		—88—	
Madagascar	2,172	200	1,761.5	681.1	79	14	14	13	-20	10		—90—	
Malawi	1,223	160	2.720	1.137	72	15	18	25	-30	...	...	...	...
Malaysia	29,556	1,800	80.609	72.869	51	17	25	57	-51	16[22]	16	32[22]	52[16,22]
Maldives	58	300	0.596[1]	...	59[1]	18[1]	33[1]	68[1]	-78[1]	8[12]	7[12]	25[12]	60[12]
Mali	1,576	200	532.8[3]	388.6[3]	88	11	22	16	-37	9[1]	4[1]	47[1]	39[1]
Malta	1,444	4,010	0.549	0.462	68	17	25	71	-82	10[8]	16	66[8]	24[8,16]
Martinique	...	4,230[1,13]	12.577[1]	...	87[1]	33[1]	17[1]	12[1]	-49[1]	...	...	...	...
Mauritania	816	440	57.210[3]	34.658[3]	74	22	22	58	-77	...	...	...	...
Mauritius	1,524	1,470	22.720	12.538	61	11	22	61	-54	16[1]	16	42[1]	42[1,16]
Mayotte	...	...	...	...	...	...	...	...	...	...	...	...	...
Mexico	149,395	1,820	77,778.0[3]	4,460.4[3]	68	9	18	17	-13	10[10]	6[10]	28[10]	56[10]
Monaco	280[12]	10,260[12]	...	...	...	...	...	...	...	...	...	...	...
Mongolia	1,911[1]	1,010[1]	...	...	...	...	...	...	...	...	...	...	...
Montserrat	30[1]	2,530[1]	0.114[3]	0.076[3]	89	19	36	10	-54	...	...	...	...
Morocco	14,213	620	133.590[3]	82.811[3]	70	17	21	24	-34	14[8]	16	33[8]	53[8,16]
Mozambique	2,135	150	126.5[3]	54.3[3]	84	21	6	5	-16	9		—91—	
Myanmar (Burma)	7,450[3]	200[3]	60.660	32.640	—87—		15	5	-8	7[1]	9[1]	38[1]	45[1]
Nauru	160	20,000	...	...	...	...	...	...	...	...	...	...	...
Nepal	2,836	160	58.504	30.086	78	11	21	13	-22	6[10]	5[10]	—89[10]—	
Netherlands, The	173,357	11,860	431.8	367.5	60	16	20	54	-50	9[1]	10[1]	52[1]	29[1]
Netherlands Antilles	860[1]	6,020[1]	...	...	55[8,45]	24[8,45]	21[8,45]	110[8,45]	-109[8,45]	5[12,45]	8[12,45]	73[12,45]	14[12,45]
New Caledonia	1,210[6]	8,300[6]	139.6[1]	...	55[1]	38[1]	14[1]	33[1]	-40[1]	3[6]	9[6]	59[6]	29[6]
New Zealand	27,131	8,230	52.247	...	59	17	24	28	-28	10[1]	8[1]	49[1]	33[1]
Nicaragua	2,959	830	2.390	0.023	56	35	17	13	-21	9[22]	4[22]	56[22]	31[22]
Niger	1,898	280	799.1[3]	554.6[3]	76	11	17	30	-32	9[8]	7[8]	16[8]	68[8]
Nigeria	39,533	370	107.640	35.258	84	7	6	11	-9	4[6]	2[6]	29[6]	65[6]
Niue	3	1,080	...	...	...	...	...	...	...	...	...	...	...
Norfolk Island	...	...	...	...	...	...	...	...	...	...	...	...	...

origin of GDP by economic sector, 1986 (%)										avg. annual growth rate of real GDP (%)		balance of payments, 1988 (current external transactions; '000,000 U.S.$) net transfers		current balance of payments	tourist trade, 1987 ('000,000 U.S.$)		country
primary		secondary			tertiary					1970–1980	1980–1987	goods-merchandise	invisibles		receipts from foreign nationals	expenditures by nationals abroad	
agri-culture	mining	manu-factur-ing	con-struc-tion	public util-ities	transp., commu-nications	trade	finan-cial svcs.	other svcs.	govt.								
59	...	1	9	2	3	5	—21—			-9.4	-3.9	-153[31]	-3[31]	-183[31]	...	...	Equatorial Guinea
45	—	11	4	1	7	11	3	7	8	2.6	1.7	-455[3]	128[3]	-327[3]	7	4	Ethiopia
16	—	24	9	3	11	14	9	—22—		...	...	-107[3]	46[3]	-61[3]	...	...	Faeroe Islands
...	...	...	...	...	...	...	...	...	...	...	...	...	...	...	...	...	Falkland Islands
21	1	11	5	3	10	17	13	—21—		3.9	1.6	-54	84	30	101	24	Fiji
7	...	22	7	3	7	11	15	3	15	3.7	3.0	1,136	-4,134	-2,998	791	1,458	Finland
6[9]	11	17[9,11]	5[9]	5[9]	6[9]	11[9]	5[9]	24[9]	17[9]	3.6	1.7	-8,732	4,941	-3,791	12,008	8,618	France
5[19]	...	4[19]	8[19]	-1[19]	7[19]	12[19]	9[19]	—56[19]—		2.9	-4.8[7]	-341[9]	...	...	...	...	French Guiana
5[10]	—	10[10]	12[10]	71[10]	7[10]	14[10]	—53[10]—			5.4	5.3[7]	-379[12]	337[12]	-421[2]	156	...	French Polynesia
7	24	5	9	2	5	13	1	11	14	7.5	-1.0	404	-1,020	-616	5	133	Gabon
26	—	5	4	1	9	29	6	2	11	2.2	2.5	-26[9]	40[9]	14[9]	36	3	Gambia, The
22	11	13[11]	22	23	—43[23]—					7.13[2]	1.65	-237[3]	295[3]	58[3]	41	8[1]	Gaza Strip
11[2]	4	64[2,4]	7[2]	4	5[2]	9[2]	—32,26—			4.9[2]	1.42				41		Germany, East
2	1	32	5	3	6	10	—41—			2.7	3.2	78,640	-30,060	48,580	7,716	23,551	Germany, West
44	2	11	2	2	5	23	—11—			1.3	1.3	-125[9]	28[9]	-97[9]	2	12	Ghana
17	2	18	6	3	8	—16—		8	17	4.8	1.1			-95[3]	20	...	Gibraltar
16[9]	11	32[11,19]	27[19]	33	33	8[19]		12[19,33]		...	...	-6,072	5,114	-958	2,192	507	Greece
17	...	5	9	2	14	20	—16—		22	3.4	4.4	-103[9]	...		...	...	Greenland
7[8]	11	6[8,11]	4[8]	—	4[8]	18[8]	11[8]	20[8]	29[8]	5.2	1.2[7]	-46[9]	20[9]	-26[9]	30	4	Grenada
												-627[8]	458[8]	-169[8]	100	...	Guadeloupe
—	...	13[12]	8[12]		6[12]	52[12]	10[12]	—12[12]—							364	304	Guam
26	—	16	2	2	7	25	9	6	7	5.7	-0.3	-355[9]	-88[9]	-443[9]	103	24[3]	Guatemala
...	...	...	...	...	1[1]	21[1]	3[1]	—12[1]—		2.7	2.3				...	...	Guernsey
58[1]	...	4[1]	3[1]		—14[1]—		—21—		19[1]	1.4	4.9	-65[1]	15[1]	-50[1]	...	...	Guinea
...	...	...	...	...	...	...	...	...	...								Guinea-Bissau
27	8	11	7	35	7	7	7	2	22[35]	1.8	-2.4	51	-102[1]	-97[1]	24	115	Guyana
32	...	15	6	1	2	18	6	13	7	4.8	-0.7	-128	75	-53	93	47	Haiti
19[9]	19	13[9]	5[9]	29	6[9]	12[9]	13[9]	12[9]	5[9]	4.8	1.9	-319	-234[9]	-265[9]	26	30	Honduras
—	—	22	4	3	8	22	28	—17—		9.6	7.6	-736			3,184		Hong Kong
18[2]	11	47[2,11]	10[2]	12	14[2]	—1[2,26]—				5.0	1.4	166[9]	-746[9]	-580[9]	827	276	Hungary
22	...	13	8	3[6]	10	21[36]	3[6]	—27—		4.9	2.7	-19	-209	-228	86	213	Iceland
31	3	17	5	2	7	15	8	6	5	3.3	5.4	-5,438[3]	841[3]	-4,597[3]	1,455	302	India
26	11	14	5	1	7	17	6	4	9	8.0	4.3	5,726	-6,915	-1,189	803	494	Indonesia
19[1]	10[1]	8[1]	7[1]	1[1]	7[1]	20[1]	—29[1]—			3.6	3.1[5]	2,358[10]	-2,772[10]	-414[10]	26	400	Iran
16	19	9	7	2	7	12	11	1	21	9.3	-5.1[5]				40	...	Iraq
10	3[7]	38[37]	3[7]	3[7]	—18—		—27—		7	4.6	2.1	3,829	-3,178	651	811	814	Ireland
31	...	16[1]	10[1]	3[1]	11[1]	12[1]	30[19]	24[19]	8[1]	3.7	-4.1[5]				36[3]	...	Isle of Man
5	11	22[11]	4	2	8	14	—44—			3.4	3.2	-3,144	2,466	-678	1,347	998	Israel
4	3	21	6	5	6	19	12	12	12	3.2	2.1	-767	-3,869	-4,636	12,174	4,536	Italy
6[9]	7[9]	22[9]	8[9]	3[9]	8[9]	22[9]	15[9]	4[9]	9[9]	-0.7	1.0	-362[9]	271[9]	-91[9]	595	32	Jamaica
3	...	34	7	3	6	15	16	18	4	4.7	3.7	94,990	-15,400	79,590	2,097	10,760	Japan
4	—	—2—			—94—							-328[8]			354		Jersey
7	3	12	7	2	10	15	—4—		17	7.1	4.1	-1,467[9]	1,115[9]	-352[9]	580	445	Jordan
...	...	...	...	...	...	...				-8.8	-2.1[7]						Kampuchea (Cambodia)
26	—	10	5	2	5	11	13	3	13	6.1	3.6	-714[9]	223[9]	-491[9]	344	21	Kenya
29	—	2	5	3	15	12	7	3	28	0.6	0.0[5]	-16	22	6	1	...	Kiribati
...	...	...	...	...	...	...				5.9[2]	8.5[2,7]						Korea, North
12	1	30	8	3	8	13	—24—			8.3	8.7	11,445	2,716	14,161	2,299	704	Korea, South
1	37	11	3	-2	5	9	5	—30—		2.3	-1.6	1,907	2,806	4,713	100	2,505	Kuwait
75[10]	4	5[4,10]	5	4	1[10]	12[10]	—1[10]—			0.8	6.6						Laos
8[10]	—	13[10]	3[10]	5[10]	8[10]	28[10]	13[10]	11[10]	11[10]	1.5	-15.1[7]						Lebanon
17	—	9	9	1	2	14	12	8	12	9.0	1.6	-422	349	-73	10	6	Lesotho
32	13	6	3	2	7	5	—23—			0.6	-1.4	639	-181[9]	-118[9]	63	...	Liberia
4[1]	56[1]	4[1]	—9[1]—		—27[1]—					7.5	-3.4	1,380[3]	-1,536[3]	-156[3]	3	213	Libya
...	...	...	...	...	...	...	...	...	...								Liechtenstein
3	...	29	6	2	6	16	—39—			4.4	2.8[5]	18	18	18	193	...	Luxembourg
...	...	...	...	...	...	...				...	7.74[1]						Macau
42	4[2]	12	5[42]	4[2]	—40—					0.7	-0.3	-23	-134[3]	-136[3]	10	21	Madagascar
38	—	12	4	2	6	13	11	4	12	5.1	1.8	101[9]	-91[9]	10[9]	7	7	Malawi
21	11	21	4	2	7	12	8	2	12	8.1	4.6	5,643	-3,759	-1,884	717	1,272	Malaysia
27	1	4[25]	8	2[5]	6	9	—25—		19	13.2	9.5[7]	-39[9]	39[9]	-9	39	5	Maldives
52[1]	3[1]	7[1]	—6[1]—		—32[1]—					0.3	1.6	-110	4	-106	16	25	Mali
4	43	29	4[43]	35	6	14	13	8	21[35]	10.6	2.4	-393[9]	399[9]	69	363	102	Malta
8[12]	11	6[11,12]	4[12]	1[12]	4[12]	17[12]	—55[12]—			3.9	0.1[7]	-736[8]	581[8]	-155[8]	100	...	Martinique
19[10]	10[10]	8[10]	8[10]	1[10]	7[10]	—13[10]—		18[10]	6[10]	2.2	1.9	43[9]	-191[9]	-148[9]	73	22[6]	Mauritania
14	—	22	6	3	10	13	15	5	11	5.9	5.4	-147[9]	225[9]	78[9]	138	51	Mauritius
...	...	...	...	...	...	...	...	...	...								Mayotte
9	7	26	5	1	7	24	7	—16—		6.6	0.8	1,752	-4,657	-2,905	3,497	2,361	Mexico
...	...	...	...	...	...	...	...	...	...								Monaco
19[2]	11	34[2,11]	—7[2]—		12[2]	27[2]	—2[2,26]—			6.1[2]	6.4[2,5]						Mongolia
4	1	6	7	3	11	18	—50—			4.6	2.6[5]	-8[1]	7[1]	-1[1]	9	...	Montserrat
21	7[44]	17	6	44	5	17	—15—		12	5.6	2.8	-1,069[9]	1,244[9]	175[9]	1,000	100	Morocco
44	11	26[11]	11		8	—10—				-0.6	-1.9	-372[6]	178[6]	-194[6]			Mozambique
51[9]	19	9[9]	2[9]	—	4[9]	22[9]	2[9]	—9[9]—		4.3	4.0	-202[1]	-41	-206[1]	14	1	Myanmar (Burma)
...	...	...	...	...	...	...	...	...	...								Nauru
58	—	4	6	—	6	4	—7—		7	2.1	3.7	-477	197	-280	56	35	Nepal
5	6	21	5	2	7	16	—42—			3.4	1.3	8,171	-2,861	5,310	2,666	6,362	Netherlands, The
1	1	13[1]	10[1]	3[1]	12[1]	18[1]	16[1]	6[1]	24[1]			-690[9]	640[9]	-509[9]	280	107[6]	Netherlands Antilles
2[6]	5[6]	10[6]	5[6]	2[6]	4[6]	27[6]	—17[6]—		28[6]	0.7	-2.0[7]	-106[6]	273[6]	167[6]	30	...	New Caledonia
9	1	22	6	3	8	19	7	5	11	2.4	2.5[5]	2,015	-2,776	-761	934	784	New Zealand
21	1	28	4	2	4	24	6	5	7	1.8	0.6	-479[3]	-214[3]	-693[3]	53	76	Nicaragua
45[9]	7[9]	4[9]	2[9]	3[9]	4[9]	—13[9]—		17[9]	8[9]	3.9	-1.5	-61	-33	-94	7	13	Niger
27[1]	20[1]	9[1]	5[1]	1[1]	3[1]	20[1]	4[1]	4[1]	8[1]	4.9	-4.8	2,419	-3,432	-1,013	78	38	Nigeria
...	...	...	...	...	...	...				...					0.6[3]	...	Niue
...	...	...	...	...	...	...	...	...	...						...	...	Norfolk Island

National product and accounts (continued)

country	gross national product (GNP), 1987 — nominal ('000,000 U.S.$)	per capita (U.S.$)	gross domestic product (GDP), 1987 — nominal ('000,000,000 national currency)	real (constant prices of 1980; '000,000,000 national currency)	GDP by type of expenditure, 1986 (%) — consumption private	government	gross domestic investment	foreign trade exports	imports	cost components of GDP, 1986 (%) — indirect taxes net of subsidies	consumption of fixed capital	compensation of employees	net operating surplus
Norway	71,420	17,110	556.9	353.4	54	20	29	38	-41	13[1]	14[1]	48[1]	25[1]
Oman	7,768	5,780	2.798[3]	2.398[3]	43	31	24	36	-34	1	16	35	64[16]
Pacific Is., Trust Terr. of the													
Marshall Islands	...	1,180[3,13]	0.046[3]	...	...	...	...	...	...	10[10]	4[10]	51[10]	36[10]
Micronesia, F.S. of	...	1,130[3,13]	0.107[3]	...	...	...	...	...	...	...	...	...	...
Northern Mariana Is.	...	12,360[3,13]	0.256[3]	...	...	...	...	...	...	5[1]	5[1]	62[1]	28[1]
Palau	...	2,290[3,13]	0.032[3]	...	...	...	...	...	...	9[1]	6[1]	— 85[1] —	
Pakistan	36,211	350	608.2	369.1	79	12	16	12	-19	8[1]	8[1]	51[1]	33[1]
Panama	5,128	2,240	5.317	4.334	58	22	17	35	-31	8[1]	8[1]	51[1]	33[1]
Papua New Guinea	2,555	730	2.764	1.879	63	22	22	45	-52	8[1]	9[1]	38[1]	45[1]
Paraguay	3,923	1,000	2,493.6	654.3	78	7	25	22	-32	5[1]	10[1]	31[1]	54[1]
Peru	29,862	1,430	157,977[1]	4.842[1]	67	11	24	11	-14	9[6]	7[6]	31[6]	53[6]
Philippines	34,638	590	705.7	272.0	75	8	15	23	-22	8[1]	11[1]	— 81[1] —	
Pitcairn Island	...	...	...	...	...	...	...	...	...	...	...	...	...
Poland	272,842[24]	7,200[24]	16,940.0	...	61	9	29	18	-17	...	...	...	...
Portugal	29,555	2,890	4,418.8[3]	1,310.0[3]	66	14	23	33	-36	10[1]	4[1]	45[1]	41[1]
Puerto Rico	18,472	5,520	23.706	17.681	71	14	12	58	-54	6[1]	6[1]	44[1]	43[1]
Qatar	4,129	12,360	18.580	...	31	47	19	32	-30	1	— 99 —		
Réunion	...	4,900[3,13]	18.857[3]	...	95	17	20	5	-38	10[12]	16	63[12]	27[12,16]
Romania	148,048[24]	6,400[24]	871.8[3]	...	58[1]	6[1]	32[1]	— 41 —		...	...	...	...
Rwanda	2,008	310	166.5	124.9	71	20	19	12	-22	8[10]	4[10]	19[10]	69[10]
St. Helena	...	...	...	...	...	...	...	...	...	...	...	...	...
St. Kitts	80	1,700	0.266	...	78[10]	22[10]	32[10]	56[10]	-87[10]	...	...	...	...
St. Lucia	196	1,370	0.538	...	62[10]	25[10]	35[10]	64[10]	-86[10]	...	...	...	...
St. Pierre and Miquelon	...	...	...	...	...	...	...	...	...	...	...	...	...
St. Vincent	121	1,070	0.367	...	61	20	30	66	-77	17[19]	8[19]	49[19]	26[19]
San Marino	188	8,590	...	...	...	...	...	...	...	...	...	...	...
São Tomé and Príncipe	32	280	1.942[3]	1.290[3]	66	45	24	38	-73	-0.2	— 100.2 —		
Saudi Arabia	74,000	5,480	267.6	350.1	43	40	27	36	-45	17[31]	6[31]	— 77[31] —	
Senegal	3,545	510	1,309.3[3]	762.0[3]	76	17	13	27	-33	18[10]	6[10]	39[10]	37[10]
Seychelles	210	3,180	1.181[3]	0.939[3]	56	38	23	38	-55	4[6]	10[6]	39[6]	60[6]
Sierra Leone	1,172	300	5.902[3]	...	64	8	30	16	-18	...	...	...	...
Singapore	20,717	7,940	41.899	37.502	47	14	38	— 1 —		10[6]	14[6]	29[6]	47[6]
Solomon Islands	123	420	0.283	...	...	...	...	...	...	5	— 95 —		
Somalia	1,656	290	76.0[3]	10.2[3]	66	19	13	9	-7	...	...	...	...
South Africa	62,926	1,890	164.455	67.887	53	18	19	32	-22	8[1]	16[1]	52[1]	23[1]
Bophuthatswana	1,736[10,52]	950[10,52]	1.207[1]	...	...	...	...	...	...	...	...	...	...
Ciskei	377[1]	490[1]	0.397[1]	...	...	...	...	...	...	...	...	...	...
Transkei	1,471[10,52]	470[10,52]	1.458[1]	...	...	...	...	...	...	...	...	...	...
Venda	201[10,52]	490[10,52]	0.245[1]	...	...	...	...	...	...	...	...	...	...
S.W. Africa/Namibia	1,250	1,060	3.131	1.434	53	29	12	63	-57	7	5	46	42
Spain	233,417	6,010	32,085.0[3]	16,845.0[3]	63	14	20	20	-18	7[1]	12[1]	47[1]	34[1]
Sri Lanka	6,560	400	196.723	89.758	78	10	24	24	-35	14[1]	5[1]	45[1]	35[1]
Sudan, The	7,646	330	31.157	...	74	17	16	7	-15	7[31]	9[31]	40[31]	44[31]
Suriname	972	2,360	1.923	1.243	45	38	17	32	-32	12[10]	10[10]	68[10]	9[10]
Swaziland	496	700	0.956	0.551	92	26	31	45	-94	16[12]	7[12]	47[12]	30[12]
Sweden	131,142	15,690	1,005.2	594.2	51	28	18	33	-30	12[1]	11[1]	58[1]	19[1]
Switzerland	138,163	21,250	255.1	183.0	60	13	26	37	-35	6[1]	10[1]	62[1]	22[1]
Syria	20,421	1,820	126.325	52.374	65	21	23	10	-20	4	3	— 93 —	
Taiwan	99,356	5,080	3,098.0	2,968.2	48	15	16	60	-40	10	9	49	31
Tanzania	5,202	220	227.897	47.015	89	8	17	10	-25	10[1]	2[1]	13[1]	75[1]
Thailand	44,785	840	1,212.5	961.3	65	13	21	28	-25	11[1]	9[1]	27[1]	54[1]
Togo	963	300	363.6[3]	235.7[3]	69	14	29	36	-48	14[12]	7[12]	28[12]	51[12]
Tokelau	0.9[8]	560[8]	0.073[6]	0.073[6]	96[6]	18[6]	28[6]	— 41[6] —		11[6]	3[6]	37[6]	48[6]
Tonga	72	720	...	...	...	...	...	...	...	...	...	...	...
Trinidad and Tobago	5,130	4,220	16.572	11.289	60	24	23	33	-40	—	8[1]	61[1]	32[1]
Tunisia	9,019	1,210	8.013	4.508	66	17	23	31	-38	14[10]	10[10]	— 76[10] —	
Turkey	63,643	1,200	39,155.0[3]	5,914.9[3]	69	9	25	— 3 —		7[1]	5[1]	— 88[1] —	
Turks and Caicos Is.	...	4,780[13]	0.049	...	...	...	...	...	...	...	...	...	...
Tuvalu	4[10]	450[10]	0.004[6]	...	...	...	...	...	...	...	...	...	...
Uganda	4,086	260	3,325.6[3]	98.8[3]	78	12	13	13	-16	65	— 35 —		
U.S.S.R.	2,500,000	8,700	585.8[2]	576.7[2]	— 72[2,6] —		26[2,6]	— 22[2,6] —		...	...	...	...
United Arab Emirates	22,827	15,680	87.0	81.6	38	23	29	50	-41	-3	19	31	52
United Kingdom	592,946	10,430	408.6	270.7	63	21	17	26	-27	14[1]	12[1]	56[1]	20[1]
United States	4,486,176	18,430	4,497.2	3,279.1	67	18	18	7	-10	8[1]	13[1]	60[1]	19[1]
Uruguay	6,556	2,180	1,700.6	88.6	74	13	7	23	-18	13[1]	2[1]	— 84[1] —	
Vanuatu	118[1]	880[1]	9.442[12]	...	...	...	...	...	...	...	...	...	...
Venezuela	48,241	3,230	719.4	264.8	69	11	20	21	-21	7[9]	8[9]	36[9]	49[9]
Vietnam	12,600	200	...	...	...	...	...	...	...	...	...	...	...
Virgin Islands (U.S.)	1,068[3]	9,750[3]	1.088[3]	836.5[3]	...	...	...	...	...	...	...	...	...
Wallis and Futuna	10[12]	920[12]	...	...	...	...	...	...	...	...	...	...	...
West Bank	1,500	1,550	1.826[3]	0.005[3]	97	9	31	21	-57	...	...	...	...
Western Sahara	...	...	...	...	...	...	...	...	...	...	...	...	...
Western Samoa	93	560	...	...	...	...	...	...	...	...	...	...	...
Yemen (Aden)	956	420	0.369[1]	0.308[1]	105	58	35	7	-105	9	7	76	8
Yemen (Şan'ā')	4,918	580	43.559	19.319	93	16	13	3	-25	8	3	— 90 —	
Yugoslavia	153,573[24]	6,540[24]	25,083.2[3,55]	1,662.8[3,55]	50	14	38	16	-17	7[1]	11[1]	— 82[1] —	
Zaire	5,287	160	326.946	19.277	59	13	33	59	-64	...	...	...	...
Zambia	1,696	240	18.080	3.204	49	27	24	46	-46	12[1]	13[1]	45[1]	30[1]
Zimbabwe	9,001	590	8.880[3]	4.286[3]	54	19	22	29	-25	12[1]	16	53[10]	31[10,16]

[1]1985. [2]Net material product. [3]1986. [4]Manufacturing includes mining and public utilities. [5]1980–86. [6]1983. [7]1980–84. [8]1980. [9]1987. [10]1984. [11]Manufacturing includes mining. [12]1982. [13]GDP. [14]At prices of 1984. [15]1984–87. [16]Net operating surplus includes consumption of fixed capital. [17]At prices of 1986. [18]Data refer to the Belgium–Luxembourg Economic Union (BLEU) and exclude transactions between the two countries. [19]1979. [20]At prices of 1981. [21]1987–88. [22]1978. [23]Tertiary sector includes public utilities. [24]1988. [25]Manufacturing includes public utilities. [26]Activities in the material sphere not elsewhere specified. [27]1972–83. [28]1983–87. [29]National income. [30]Manufacturing includes mining, construction, public utilities, and transportation and communications. [31]1981. [32]1968–80. [33]Services includes public utilities and transportation and communications. [34]Guernsey and Jersey. [35]Government includes

origin of GDP by economic sector, 1986 (%)										avg. annual growth rate of real GDP (%)		balance of payments, 1988 (current external transactions; '000,000 U.S.$)			tourist trade, 1987 ('000,000 U.S.$)		country
primary		secondary			tertiary					1970–1980	1980–1987	net transfers		current balance of payments	receipts from foreign nationals	expenditures by nationals abroad	
agri-culture	mining	manu-facturing	con-struc-tion	public utilities	transp., commu-nications	trade	finan-cial svcs.	other svcs.	govt.			goods-merchan-dise	invisibles				
4	11	15	6	5	10	13	8	8	19	4.8	3.1	−111	−3,567	−3,678	1,244	3,056	Norway
3	36	6	8	1	4	14	10	1	18	3.6	12.9[5]	2,036[9]	−1,185[9]	851[9]	44	47[3]	Oman
...	...	...	...	...	...	...	...	...	...	...	...	...	...	...	...	...	Pacific Is., Trust. Terr. of Marshall Islands Micronesia, F.S of
16[1]	—	—	11[1]	11	3[1]	19[1]	4[1]	2[1]	36[1]	...	...	−27[1]	...		167	...	Northern Mariana Is. Palau
24	2	18	7	2	8	17	6	8	9	4.7	6.7	−2,316[9]	1,754[9]	−562[9]	171	248	Pakistan
9	—	8	5	4	20	14	19	9	15	5.6	2.9	−177	904	727	208	65	Panama
33[6]	11[6]	9[6]	4[6]	16	4[6]	8[6]	10[6]	13[6]	8[6]	4.0	1.4	238	−399	−161	17	32	Papua New Guinea
27	—	16	6	2	4	27		17		8.6	2.2	69	−194	−125	121	50	Paraguay
15	9	23	5	46	46	41[46]	46	8		3.5	2.1	−56	−1,072	−1,128	393	384	Peru
26	2	25	4	2	6	21		15		6.1	0.4	−1,085	712	−373	459	88	Philippines
...																	Pitcairn Island
16[2]	11	47[2,11]	13[2]	1[2]	6[2]	16[2]		12,26		5.6[2]	4.5[2]	1,021[9]	−1,165[9]	−144[9]	184	203	Poland
9	11	31[11]	6	2	47	20	47	21[47]	11	4.8	1.3	−5,137	4,508	−629	2,148	421	Portugal
29	43	40[9]	29,43	48	8[9,48]	15[9]	13[9]	9[9]	11[9]	4.4	2.9	−720[10]	−1,668[10]	−2,388[10]	866	591	Puerto Rico
1	31	10	7	1	2	6	10	31		4.0	−5.24[9]	1,842[6]	−1,432[6]	410[6]	...	...	Qatar
7[12]	...	10[12]	6[12]	2[12]	5[12]	15[12]	24[12]	32[12]		6.0	4.47	−699[12]	696[12]	−3[12]	...	...	Réunion
16[2]	4	63[2,4]	8[2]	4	6[2]		82			9.2[2]	4.4[2,49]	1,953[3,50]	−464[3,50]	1,489[3,50]	191	60	Romania
40	—	16	6	1	3	14		21		3.0	2.1	−161	42	−119	7	15	Rwanda
...																	St. Helena
11	—	12	10	1	11	18	17		23	3.0	4.5	−28[6]	14[6]	−14[6]	47	3	St. Kitts
17	1	8	7	4	10	22	11	5	22	5.8	3.9	−85[9]	72[9]	−13[9]	78	52	St. Lucia
...																	St. Pierre and Miquelon
17	—	9	11	3	21	15	11		15	2.8	5.6	−37[9]	18[9]	−19[9]	35	8	St. Vincent
...																	San Marino
54[10]	—	10[10]	9[10]	3[10]	11[10]	10[10]	1[10]		29[10]	−1.1	−2.5	−6[6]	−2[6]	−8[6]	...	...	São Tomé and Príncipe
5	30	7	12	—	7	8	7	13	10	11.1	−1.4	5,340[9]	−14,910[9]	−9,570[9]	2,600	2,000	Saudi Arabia
22	4	20[4]	7	4			52			2.0	3.5	−221[10]	−53[10]	−274[10]	123	42	Senegal
6	11	9[11]	6	3	44	8	8	3	14	6.2	0.9	−113	91	−22	72	12	Seychelles
44[1]	12[1]	5[1]	2[1]	—	9[1]	13[1]		15[1]		2.0	0.2	25[9]	49[9]	−24[9]	10	6	Sierra Leone
1	—	25	8	2	14	17	28	12		9.2	5.9	−2,345	4,005	1,660	2,216	791	Singapore
59[51]	4	14,51	25[1]	4	25[1]	8[51]	8[51]		14[51]	8.6	4.77	−22	6	−16	2	3	Solomon Islands
37	5	8	5	2	9	7	7	4	11	1.7	3.4	−382[9]	282[9]	−100[9]	8[3]	13[6]	Somalia
6	16	22	3	4	9	12	12	4	13	3.4	1.3	5,222	−3,950	1,272	587	835	South Africa
6[8]	37	69[8,37]	37	37		25[8]				...	...	...	...	...	...	...	Bophuthatswana
8[10]	37	13[10]	10[10]	37	9[10]	3[10]	7[10]	50[10]		9.1	9.6[49]	...	...	...	...	...	Ciskei
27[8]	37	12[8,37]	37	37		61[8]				...	...	...	...	...	...	...	Transkei
...																	Venda
8	36	5	2	2	7	11	6	2	18	4.8	−0.1	48	29	77	46[31]	...	S.W. Africa/Namibia
6[1]	11	27[1,11]	7[1]	3[1]	6[1]	20[1]		30[1]		3.8	1.7[5]	−12,980[9]	12,845[9]	−135[9]	14,760	1,938	Spain
23	1	17	8	2	11	19	6	2	7	4.7	4.4	−544	140	−404	82	44	Sri Lanka
32	11	10[11]	4	3	10	22		9	11	2.2	0.2	−522	199	−323	14	51	Sudan, The
10	7	15	6	4	8	14	8	2	25	5.2	−2.5	65[9]	10[9]	75[9]	4	8	Suriname
22	2	24	5	1	6	9	10	3	17	6.9	3.9	8	−79	−71	19	14	Swaziland
3	1	24	7	3	7	13	14	4	23	2.0	1.8	4,748	−7,297	−2,549	2,033	3,781	Sweden
4[1]	11	25[1]	8[1]	2[1]	7[1]	17[1]	10[1]	14[1]	11[1]	1.3	1.0	−5,531[9]	11,412[9]	5,881[9]	5,352	4,339	Switzerland
27[9]	11	14,9[11]	5[9]	4	9[9]	24[9]	4[9]	3[9]	14[9]	9.9	0.3	−869[9]	682[9]	−187[9]	477	250	Syria
6	1	43	4	4	6	14	9	7	9	9.7	7.6	13,805	−3,638	10,167	1,619	1,229[6]	Taiwan
55	—	7	2	1	6	15	9	3	4	5.4	1.6	−811	553	−258	25	12	Tanzania
17	2	21	5	3	9	19	9	11	4	6.9	5.0	−2,074	403	−1,671	1,947	381	Thailand
48[1]	—	13[1]		6[1]		35[1]				3.2	−0.2	−18	−32	−50	21	33	Togo
...																	Tokelau
41[6]	—	5[6]	4[6]		6[6]	15[6]	6[6]	22[6]		4.1	8.6[7]	−21[1]	15[1]	−6[1]	9	3	Tonga
3	21	10	9	2	13	7	14	9	17	4.4	−4.2	350[9]	−597[9]	−247[9]	92	158	Trinidad and Tobago
14	9	13	6	2	5	23	4	13	12	7.1	3.6	−1,090	1,302	212	672	94	Tunisia
19	2	26	4	5	10	18	7	5	6	5.2	5.6	−1,800	3,300	1,500	1,721	448	Turkey
...										5.6	−0.2[7]	...			24	...	Turks and Caicos Is.
16[19]	—	1[19]	13[19]	...	4[19]	34[19]		32[19]		...	...	...					Tuvalu
72	—	7	1	—	3	5	6	2	5	−1.6	1.9	−226	32	−194	8	10	Uganda
21[2]	—	44[2,4]	12[2]	4	6[2]	17[2]				5.12	3.5[2]	...	...	...	198	175	U.S.S.R.
2	34	11	11	3	5	11		23		15.1	−4.2	...	...	...	...	...	United Arab Emirates
2	7[44]	24	6	44	7	14	22	15	7	2.0	2.3	−36,514	10,425	−26,089	10,229	11,898	United Kingdom
2	2	20	5	3	6	17	17	17	12	2.5	2.9	−126,780	590	−126,190	15,374	20,785	United States
11[9]	53	23[9]	29	3[9]	5[9]	10[9]	12[9]	11[9,53]	9[9]	3.1	−0.6	292	−279	13	208	129	Uruguay
20[12]	8[12,44]	5[12]	2[12]	44	3[12]	10[12]		52[12]		3.5	7.6[7]	−46	49	3	14	2	Vanuatu
7	7	20	3	4	13	9		22	14	4.1	0.6	1,347	−3,345	−4,692	409	521	Venezuela
42	4	33[2,4]	3[2]	4	1[2]	19[2]		32,26		0.5[2]	10.7[2,7]	...	...	...			Vietnam
...										3.1	0.4[5]	...	...	...	623		Virgin Islands (U.S.)
...																	Wallis and Futuna
33	11	8[11]	14	...			46[23]			10.2[32]	3.6[5]	−269[3]	383[3]	114[3]	71	351[1]	West Bank
...	...	...	...														Western Sahara
31	4	15	2	1	6	18	10	4	9	3.0	−3.2[54]	−53	57	4	9	2	Western Samoa
13	—	7	9	1	9	11	4	1	28	1.2	4.4	−516	133	−383	73	126	Yemen (Aden)
20	2	13	4	1	13	13	13	20		8.0	5.7	−1,141[9]	689[9]	−452[9]	48	37	Yemen (Şan'ā')
13[2]	11	47[2,11]	7[2]	12	7[2]	21[2]		32,26		5.7[55]	1.1[5,55]	83[9]	1,166[9]	1,249[9]	1,668	132	Yugoslavia
32[10]	25[10]	2[10]	5[10]	—	1[10]	19[10]		15[10]		0.5	1.7	563	130	693	14	22	Zaire
13	30	18	3	1	10	9	6	7	5	1.4	0.6	261[9]	−402[9]	−1,419[9]	6	46	Zambia
11	7	30	4	2	9	11	6	2		3.5	4.0	217	−208	9	32	35	Zimbabwe

public utilities. [36]Trade includes public utilities and finance. [37]Manufacturing includes mining, construction, and public utilities. [38]1985–86. [39]Net operating surplus includes indirect taxes net of subsidies. [40]At prices of 1982. [41]1982–87. [42]Construction includes mining and public utilities. [43]Construction includes mining. [44]Mining includes public utilities. [45]Includes Aruba. [46]Trade includes public utilities, transportation and communications, and finance. [47]Services includes transportation and communications and finance. [48]Transportation and communications includes public utilities. [49]1980–85. [50]Transactions in convertible currencies only. [51]1972. [52]At prices of 1978. [53]Services includes mining. [54]1980–83. [55]Gross material product.

Employment and labour

This table provides international comparisons of the world's national labour forces—giving their size; composition by demographic component and employment status; and structure by industry.

The table focuses on the concept of "economically active population," which the International Labour Organisation (ILO) defines as persons of all ages who are either employed or looking for work. In general, "economically active population" does not include students, persons occupied solely in domestic duties, retired persons, persons living entirely on their own means, and persons wholly dependent on others. Persons engaged in illegal economic activities—smugglers, prostitutes, drug dealers, bootleggers, black marketeers, and others—also fall outside the purview of the ILO definition. Countries differ markedly in their treatment, as part of the labour force, of such groups as members of the armed forces, inmates of institutions, the unemployed (both persons seeking their first job and those previously employed), seasonal and international migrant workers, and persons engaged in informal, subsistence, or part-time economic activities. Some countries include all or most of these groups among the economically active, while others may treat the same groups as inactive.

Three principal structural comparisons of the economically active total are given in the first part of the table: (1) participation rate, or the proportion of the economically active who possess some particular char-

acteristic, is given for women and for those of working age (usually ages 15 to 64); (2) activity rate, the proportion of the total population who *are* economically active, is given for both sexes and as a total; and (3) employment status, usually (and here) grouped as employers, self-employed, employees, family workers (usually unpaid), and others.

Each of these measures indicates certain characteristics in a given national labour market; none should be interpreted in isolation, however, as the meaning of each is influenced by a variety of factors—demographic structure and change, social or religious customs, educational opportunity, sexual differentiation in employment patterns, degree of technological development, and the like. Participation and activity rates, for example, may be high in a particular country because it possesses an older population with few children, hence a higher proportion of working age, or because, despite a young population with many below working age, the economy attracts eligible immigrant workers, themselves almost exclusively of working age. At the same time, low activity and participation rates might be characteristic of a country having a young population with poor employment possibilities or of a country with a good job market distorted by the presence of large numbers of "guest" or contract workers who are not part of the domestic labour force. An illiterate woman in a strongly sex-differentiated labour force is likely to begin and end as

Employment and labour

country	year	economically active population							employment status (%)				distribution by economic sector			
		total ('000)	participation rate (%)		activity rate (%)								agriculture, forestry, fishing		manufacturing; mining, quarrying; public utilities	
			female	ages 15–64	total	male	female	employers, self-employed	employees	unpaid family workers	other	number ('000)	% of econ. active	number ('000)	% of econ. active
Afghanistan	1979	3,946	7.9	49.1	30.2	54.1	4.9	...	...	...	...	2,369	60.1	494	12.5
Albania	1985	1,398	41.0	74.5	45.8	53.5	38.1	...	...	...	...	1903[3, 4]	24.1[3, 4]	287[3, 4]	36.43, 4]
Algeria	1985[5]	4,498	11.6	40.0	18.0[6]	33.8[6]	2.4[6]	21.0[7]	72.2[7]	6.4[7]	0.4[7]	999[8]	25.7[8]	595[8]	15.3[8]
American Samoa	1980	9	39.2	46.1	26.4	31.6	21.0	2.4	97.3	0.2	0.1	0.1[9]	1.49	2.69, 10]	31.49, 10]
Andorra	1986	21	...	...	46.8							0.1	0.6	2.8	13.0
Angola	1985	3,719	39.7	71.8	42.5	52.1	33.2	...	...	...	...	2,672	71.8	361[14]	9.7[14]
Anguilla	1984	2.8	40.5	73.6	41.6	50.8	32.9	17.2	56.6	—	26.2	0.2	6.3	0.1	3.4
Antigua and Barbuda	1985	32	40.1	56.2[6, 18]	42.6	53.3	32.9	12.3[19]	69.9[19]	0.6[19]	17.2[19]	2.1[20, 21]	9.0[20, 21]	2.1[20, 21]	9.1[20, 21]
Argentina	1987	11,793	27.0	59.3	37.4	55.1	20.0	25.1[22]	71.2[22]	3.3[22]	0.4[22]	1,201[22]	12.0[22]	2,136[22]	21.3[22]
Aruba	1981	26	36.7	62.0	43.2	56.1	30.9	...	...	...	...	0.04[8]	0.2[8]	2.5[8]	10.6[8]
Australia	1987[5]	7,675	39.9	70.4	47.2	56.8	37.6	14.2	77.2	0.8	7.8	422	5.5	1,449	18.9
Austria	1987	3,430	40.1	66.7	45.3	57.0	34.6	10.0	85.7	4.4	—	287	8.4	1,020	29.7
Bahamas, The	1980	87	44.5	70.5	41.6	47.4	36.0	81.4	3.4	0.5	14.8	4.5	5.2	6.6	7.6
Bahrain	1986	183	14.2	65.3	42.1	61.9	14.4	9.8[25]	88.7[25]	0.1[25]	1.4[25]	4	2.0	25	13.4
Bangladesh	1984–85	29,510	9.1	49.6	30.2	53.8	5.6	39.2	40.0	17.6	3.2	16,707	56.6	3,148	10.7
Barbados	1987	119	47.2	76.2	47.1	51.9	42.6	8.8[20]	76.4[20]	0.2[20]	14.6[20]	9	7.7	18	15.3
Belgium	1986	4,212	40.3	65.4[25, 26]	42.7	52.2	33.6	12.2	72.2	3.3	12.2	103	2.5	853	20.3
Belize	1983–84	47	32.5	63.0[22]	29.6	39.5	19.5	23.4	55.1	7.5	14.0	13.1	27.6	4.9	10.3
Benin	1986	1,447	35.6	60.2	34.5	45.7	23.9	...	...	...	...	980	67.7[21]	108[14]	7.5[14]
Bermuda	1987	35	46.8[27]	82.1[22, 28]	58.3[27]	63.5[27]	53.3[27]	7.7[22]	88.6[22]	0.5[22]	3.2[22]	0.3	0.9	1.5	4.4
Bhutan	1985	632	32.9	69.0	44.6	58.0	30.3	...	...	...	...	531[22]	92.5[22]	16[14, 22]	2.8[14, 22]
Bolivia	1987	2,101	23.6	54.5	31.2	48.4	14.5	48.9[30]	38.2[30]	9.1[30]	3.8[30]	693[30]	46.2[30]	208[30]	13.9[30]
Botswana	1985[5]	368	53.0	72.7	37.0	38.1	36.0	2.1	33.5	39.0	25.3	159	43.2	20	5.4
Brazil	1986[5]	56,816	33.8	62.4[31]	41.9	56.3	27.9	25.7	64.5	7.4	2.4	14,331	25.2	9,807	17.3
British Virgin Islands	1980	5.3	38.8	76.7	48.0	57.5	38.1	12.9	79.7	0.8	6.6	0.3	5.2	0.3	6.1
Brunei	1981	71	23.8	61.1	36.7	52.3	18.7	7.4	88.4	0.6	3.6	3.4	4.9	8.6	12.2
Bulgaria	1985	4,686	47.7	75.7	52.4	55.1	49.6	0.3	98.2	—	1.5	772	16.5	1,778	37.9
Burkina Faso	1985	4,051	49.1	83.0[31]	51.0	53.9	48.2	...	...	...	...	3,480	85.9	182[14]	4.5[14]
Burundi	1986	2,654	52.7	88.7	55.5	54.0	56.9	35.7[34]	5.6[34]	58.5[34]	0.2[34]	2,246[34]	93.1[34]	40[34]	1.7[34]
Cameroon	1985	3,918	38.5	66.3[35]	38.5	47.4	29.6	60.2[20]	14.6[20]	18.0[20]	7.1[20]	2,901	74.0	180	4.6
Canada	1987[5]	13,121	43.4	75.1	51.2	58.7	43.8	8.6	89.9	0.7	0.7	644	4.9	2,558	19.5
Cape Verde	1980	67	30.5	42.9	22.5	34.1	12.7	24.1	65.1	1.1	9.6	22.1	33.2	2.7	4.1
Cayman Islands	1985	10	43.8	...	48.7[34]	58.1[34]	39.8[34]	12.1	87.9	—	—	0.4	3.4	0.3	3.4
Central African Republic	1985	1,282	47.0	81.6	49.8	54.5	45.3	...	...	...	...	869	67.8	54[14]	4.2[14]
Chad	1985	1,790	21.7	57.4	35.7	56.7	15.3	...	...	...	...	1,454	81.2	93[14]	5.2[14]
Chile	1987	4,353	30.0	54.8[27]	35.1[27]	50.2[27]	20.6[27]	23.7[27]	63.7[27]	3.9[27]	8.8[27]	863	19.8	775	17.8
China	1987[5]	584,569	44.5	76.8[31]	54.7	59.6	49.7	...	...	...	...	414,740	71.0	95,977	16.4
Christmas Island	1981	1.6	9.8	75.9[31]	56.3	76.0	16.6	...	...	...	...	0.1	0.1	1.1	68.8
Cocos (Keeling) Islands	1981	0.3	33.5	70.5[31]	51.2	63.4	37.0	...	...	...	...	0.1	21.8	...	3.2
Colombia	1985	9,558	32.8	49.4[36]	34.3	46.6	22.3	...	...	...	...	2,412[22]	28.5[22]	1,231[22]	14.5[22]
Comoros	1985	117	26.2	53.1	29.6	43.5	15.6	47.6[22]	25.6[22]	—26.8[22]—		53[22]	53.3[22]	4.1[22]	4.2[22]
Congo	1985	710	39.3	69.4	40.8	50.2	31.6	...	...	...	...	434	61.2	86[14]	12.1[14]
Cook Islands	1981	5.8	30.3	63.1	33.7	45.6	21.1	11.0	65.7	3.7	19.6	1.7	29.2	5.5	9.5
Costa Rica	1987	978	27.6	59.5[35]	37.5	54.0	20.8	22.9	70.5	5.4	1.2	269	27.5	182	18.6
Côte d'Ivoire	1985	4,053	34.7	71.4	41.3	52.8	29.3	...	...	...	...	2,452	60.5	409[14]	10.1[14]
Cuba	1986	4,342	35.8	56.4[31]	42.4	54.0	30.6	4.8[25]	94.1[25]	0.2[25]	0.9[25]	602[37]	18.4[37]	726[37]	22.2[37]
Cyprus	1987[38]	256	35.8	67.2[22]	46.7	60.2	33.4	24.2[39]	70.6[39]	1.5[39]	3.7[39]	36[39]	14.8[39]	47[39]	19.4[39]
Czechoslovakia	1987	7,797	46.1	78.9[22]	50.1	55.4	45.0	0.1[22]	91.2[22]	8.5[22]	0.2[22]	979	12.6	3,051	39.1
Denmark	1986	2,816	45.8	80.7	55.0	60.3	49.9	8.9	88.8	2.1	0.3	160	5.7	582	20.7
Djibouti	1985	161	39.1	65.2[40]	44.5	52.5	36.0	...	...	...	...	125	77.5	12[14]	7.3[14]
Dominica	1981	25	34.1	61.7	34.3	45.4	23.3	29.4	49.8	1.9	18.9	7.8	31.0	1.7	6.6
Dominican Republic	1981	1,915	28.9	53.6	33.9	48.1	19.7	36.5	51.3	3.3	8.9	420	22.0	243	12.7
Ecuador	1988	3,444	30.1	56.6	33.8	46.9	20.4	37.3[20]	47.6[20]	6.2[20]	9.3[20]	1,155[4]	34.6[4]	393[4]	11.8[4]
Egypt	1986	12,095	14.6	45.1	26.5	42.3	7.6	26.5[7]	50.7[7]	16.8[7]	6.0[7]	5,161	42.7	2,002	16.6
El Salvador	1980[5]	1,593	34.8	62.4	35.4	47.5	24.0	28.2	59.2	10.9	1.7	637	40.0	262	16.4
Equatorial Guinea	1983	101	...	...	34.0			...	...	...	...	86.5	85.7	0.9	0.9
Ethiopia	1985	19,182	38.4	73.5	44.0	54.5	33.7	...	...	...	...	14,982	78.1	1,630[14]	8.5[14]
Faeroe Islands	1977	7.6	27.2	64.2[41]	41.9	58.2	23.9	11.9	86.1		2.0	3.3	18.8	3.9	21.9
Falkland Islands	1986	1.0	30.8	70.3[31]	54.3	70.9	35.5	...	...	...	...	106	44.1	22	9.0
Fiji	1986	241	21.2	56.0	33.7	52.4	14.5	33.6	42.2	16.3	7.9	106	44.1	22	9.0

a family or traditional agricultural worker. Loss of working-age men to war, civil violence, or emigration for job opportunities may also affect the structure of a particular labour market.

The distribution of the economically active population by employment status reveals that a large percentage of economically active persons in some less developed countries falls under the heading "employers, self-employed." This occurs because the countries involved have poor, largely agrarian economies in which the average worker is a farmer who tills his own small plot of land. In countries with well-developed economies, "employees" will usually constitute the largest portion of the economically active.

Caution should be exercised when using the economically active data to make intercountry comparisons, as countries often differ in their choices of classification schemes, definitions, and coverage of groups and in their methods of collection and tabulation of data. The population base containing the economically active population, for example, may range, in developing countries, from age 9 or 10 with no upper limit to, in developed countries, age 18 or 19 upward to a usual retirement age of from 55 to 65, with sometimes a different range for each sex. Data on female labour-force participation, in particular, often lack comparability. In many less developed countries, particularly those dominated by the

Islamic faith, a cultural bias favouring traditional roles for women results in the undercounting of economically active women. In other, less developed countries, particularly those in which subsistence workers are deemed economically active, the role of women may be overstated.

The second major section of the table provides data on the distribution by economic (also conventionally called industrial) sector of the "economically active population." The data usually include such groups as unpaid family workers, members of the armed forces, and the unemployed, the last distributed by industry as far as possible.

The categorization of industrial sectors is based on the divisions listed in the *International Standard Industrial Classification of All Economic Activities.* The "other" category includes persons whose activities were not adequately defined and the unemployed who were not distributable by industrial sector.

A substantial part of the data presented in this table is summarized from various issues of the ILO's *Yearbook of Labour Statistics,* which compiles its statistics both from official publications and from information submitted directly by national census and labour authorities. The editors have supplemented and updated ILO statistical data with information from Britannica's holdings of relevant official publications and from direct correspondence with national authorities.

construction number ('000)	construction % of econ. active	transportation, communications number ('000)	transportation, communications % of econ. active	trade, hotels, restaurants number ('000)	trade, hotels, restaurants % of econ. active	finance, real estate number ('000)	finance, real estate % of econ. active	public administration, defense number ('000)	public administration, defense % of econ. active	services number ('000)	services % of econ. active	other number ('000)	other % of econ. active	country
51	1.3	66	1.6	138	3.5	1	1	1	1	749[1]	19.0[1]	78[2]	2.0[2]	Afghanistan
78[3,4]	9.9[3,4]	40[3,4]	5.0[3,4]	56[3,4]	7.2[3,4]	...	...	...	...	95[3,4]	12.1[3,4]	42[3,4]	5.3[3,4]	Albania
670[8]	17.3[8]	202[8]	5.2[8]	311[8]	8.0[8]	1	1	1	1	1,107[1,8]	28.5[1,8]	—	—	Algeria
0.6	7.4	10	10	0.9	11.2	0.2	2.6	11	11	3.6[11]	43.6[11]	0.2[12]	2.4[12]	American Samoa
1.8	8.2	1.8	8.5	5.8[13]	26.9[13]	1.3	6.0	0.7	3.0	5.2[13]	24.3[13]	2.0	9.4	Andorra
14	14	15	15	15	15	15	15	15	15	686[15]	18.5[15]			Angola
0.4	15.5	0.2	5.8	0.4	14.6			0.6	22.7	0.1[16]	4.6[16]			Anguilla
2.6[20,21]	11.1[20,21]	2.6[20,21]	11.1[20,21]	5.2[20,21]	22.4[20,21]	0.8[20,21]	3.4[20,21]	11	11	7.9[11,20,21]	33.9[11,20,21]	0.8[17]	27.2[17]	Antigua and Barbuda
1,003[22]	10.0[22]	460[22]	4.6[22]	1,702[22]	17.0[22]	396[22]	3.9[22]	11	11	2,399[11,22]	23.9[11,22]	736[23]	7.3[23]	Argentina
1.9[8]	8.0[8]	1.3[8]	5.4[8]	7.7[8]	32.7[8]	1.0[8]	4.4[8]	11	11	9.1[8,11]	38.5[8,11]	0.02[8]	0.1[8]	Aruba
520	6.8	525	6.8	1,490	19.4	787	10.3	351	4.6	1,851	24.1	281[12]	3.7[12]	Australia
282	8.2	222	6.5	608	17.7	196	5.7	11	11	779[11]	22.7[11]	37[24]	1.1[24]	Austria
6.7	7.7	6.2	7.1	24.5	28.1	6.4	7.4	11	11	24.1[11]	27.7[11]	8.1[17]	9.3[17]	Bahamas, The
38	21.0	17	9.4	25	13.4	7	4.2	11	11	67[11]	36.5[11]	—	—	Bahrain
553	1.9	1,172	4.0	3,610	12.2	921	3.1	11	11	1,993[11]	6.8[11]	1,404	4.8	Bangladesh
9	7.8	7	5.7	26	22.1	4	3.3	11	11	41[11]	34.4[11]	42	3.7[2]	Barbados
205	4.9	260	6.2	713	16.9	301	7.2	11	11	1,262[11]	30.0[11]	514[17]	12.2[17]	Belgium
2.0	4.2	2.0	4.3	4.6	9.6	0.6	1.2	6.3	13.2	7.3	15.5	6.6[12]	14.0[12]	Belize
14	14	15	15	15	15	15	15	15	15	359[15]	24.8[15]			Benin
2.2	6.3	2.5	7.0	12.5	35.4	4.8	13.6	11	11	9.5[11]	27.0[11]	1.9[29]	5.5[29]	Bermuda
14	14	15	15	15	15	15	15	15	15	27[15,22]	4.7[15,22]			Bhutan
82[30]	5.5[30]	56[30]	3.7[30]	107[30]	7.1[30]	13[30]	0.9[30]	11	11	282[11,30]	18.8[11,30]	60[23,30]	4.0[23,30]	Bolivia
9	2.5	3	0.7	16	4.3	3	0.8	11	11	65[11]	17.7[11]	93[17]	25.3[17]	Botswana
3,589	6.3	1,989	3.5	6,252[32]	11.0[32]	1,569	2.8	11	11	16,338[11,32]	28.8[11,32]	2,942[33]	5.2[33]	Brazil
0.6	12.0	0.1	2.6	0.4	8.1	0.3	5.5	0.9	17.1	1.9	35.4	0.4[17]	8.0[17]	British Virgin Islands
12.6	17.9	4.5	6.4	7.4	10.4	2.0	2.8	11	11	29.3[11]	41.4[11]	2.8[17]	4.0[17]	Brunei
407	8.7	315	6.7	397	8.5	25	0.5	11	11	993[11]	21.2[11]	1	—	Bulgaria
15[34]	0.6[34]	6[34]	0.3[34]	21[34]	0.9[34]	1.3[34]	0.1[34]	6[34]	0.2[34]	389[15]	9.6[15]	—	—	Burkina Faso
67	1.7	52	1.3	154	3.9	8	0.2	11	11	75[34]	3.1[34]	—	—	Burundi
										293[11]	7.5[11]	228[17]	5.8[17]	Cameroon
800	6.1	838	6.4	2,292	17.5	1,338	10.2	668	5.1	3,888	29.6	96[12]	0.7[12]	Canada
18.9	28.3	3.4	5.1	3.9	5.9	0.2	0.3	2.1	3.2	13.2	19.8	—	—	Cape Verde
1.1	10.7	1.1	10.8	3.6	35.6	1.8	17.7	1.1	11.3	1.0	10.1	—	—	Cayman Islands
14	14	15	15	15	15	15	15	15	15	359[15]	28.0[15]	—	—	Central African Republic
14	14	15	15	15	15	15	15	15	15	243[15]	13.6[15]	—	—	Chad
244	5.6	274	6.3	738	16.9	189	4.3	11	11	1,205[11]	27.7[11]	67[24]	1.5[24]	Chile
13,298	2.3	10,898	1.9	20,785	3.6	1,268	0.2	9,704	1.7	17,414	3.0	487	0.1	China
0.1	3.3	0.1	4.5	0.1	4.0	—	1.5	—	2.0	0.2	9.7	0.1[33]	6.2[33]	Christmas Island
0.1	24.6	—	5.3	—	4.6	—	0.7	—	11.6	0.1	22.2	—	6.0	Cocos (Keeling) Islands
242[22]	2.9[22]	353[22]	4.2[22]	1,262[22]	14.9[22]	278[22]	3.3[22]	11	11	1,998[11,22]	23.6[11,22]	691[22,23]	8.2[22,23]	Colombia
3.3[22]	3.3[22]	2.1[22]	2.1[22]	1.9[22]	1.9[22]	0.2[22]	0.2[22]	2.4[22]	2.4[22]	4.6[22]	4.7[22]	28[22]	27.8[22]	Comoros
14	14	15	15	15	15	15	15	15	15	190[15]	26.7[15]	—	—	Congo
0.3	5.3	0.6	10.0	0.7	12.3	0.1	2.3	11	11	1.6[11]	27.1[11]	0.3	4.3	Cook Islands
59	6.0	40	4.1	154	15.8	28	2.8	11	11	226[11]	23.1[11]	21[24]	2.1[24]	Costa Rica
14	14	15	15	15	15	15	15	15	15	1,192[15]	29.4[15]	—	—	Côte d'Ivoire
322[37]	9.9[37]	224[37]	6.9[37]	371[37]	11.4[37]	21[37]	0.6[37]	169[5,37]	5.2[5,37]	777[37]	23.8[37]	52[37]	1.6[37]	Cuba
21[39]	8.6[39]	12[39]	5.0[39]	44[39]	18.1[39]	11[39]	4.5[39]	11	11	45[11,39]	18.6[11,39]	27[33,39]	10.9[33,39]	Cyprus
796	10.2	508	6.5	907	11.6	16	16	177	2.3	1,359[16]	17.4[16]	20	0.3	Czechoslovakia
197	7.0	197	6.9	403	14.3	228	8.1	189	6.7	817	29.0	45[23]	1.6[23]	Denmark
14	14	15	15	15	15	15	15	15	15	24[15]	15.2[15]	—	—	Djibouti
2.3	9.1	0.9	3.6	1.6	6.4	0.3	1.0	11	11	5.0[11]	19.7[11]	5.8[17]	22.7[17]	Dominica
81	4.3	40	2.1	192	10.0	22	1.2	11	11	363[11]	18.9[11]	553[23]	28.9[23]	Dominican Republic
238[4]	7.1[4]	154[4]	4.6[4]	355[4]	10.6[4]	74[4]	2.2[4]	11	11	789[4,11]	23.6[4,11]	182[4,24]	5.4[4,24]	Ecuador
571	4.7	596	4.9	1,027	8.5	122	1.0	11	11	2,616[11]	21.6[11]	—	—	Egypt
80	5.0	66	4.1	256	16.1	16	1.0	11	11	250[11]	15.7[11]	27[24]	1.7[24]	El Salvador
1.0	1.0	...	...	2.6	2.6	...	...	7.4	7.3	2.5	2.5	—	—	Equatorial Guinea
14	14	15	15	15	15	15	15	15	15	2,570[15]	13.4[15]	—	—	Ethiopia
2.0	11.1	1.9	11.1	2.1	11.9	0.3	1.9	11	11	3.5[11]	20.1[11]	0.6	3.2	Faeroe Islands
...	...	...	...	...	...	...	...	...	...	...	...	—	—	Falkland Islands
12	4.9	13	5.5	26	10.8	6	2.5	11	11	37[11]	15.2[11]	20[17]	8.2[17]	Fiji

Employment and labour (continued)

country	year	economically active population — total ('000)	participation rate (%) — female	participation rate (%) — ages 15–64	activity rate (%) — total	activity rate (%) — male	activity rate (%) — female	employment status (%) — employers, self-employed	employment status (%) — employees	employment status (%) — unpaid family workers	employment status (%) — other	agriculture, forestry, fishing — number ('000)	agriculture, forestry, fishing — % of econ. active	manufacturing; mining, quarrying; public utilities — number ('000)	manufacturing; mining, quarrying; public utilities — % of econ. active
Finland	1987	2,583	47.1	76.5	52.4	57.2	47.8	13.6	84.6	1.1	0.8	263	10.2	596	23.1
France	1987[5]	23,972	43.3	66.1	44.3	51.8	37.3	11.3	74.7	3.3	10.7	1,595	6.7	4,947	20.6
French Guiana	1982	32	35.8	69.8	44.3	54.1	33.5	14.9	65.5	—19.6—		4	11.4	2	5.9
French Polynesia	1983	62	32.0	60.8[42]	37.4	48.9	25.0	15.3	72.0	5.2	7.6	8.0	12.8	4.5	7.3
Gabon	1985	518	38.4	68.2	45.0	56.4	34.0	...	...	...	...	380	73.5	58[14]	11.1[14]
Gambia, The	1983	326	46.3	78.2	47.3	51.1	43.6	...	...	...	...	240	73.7	9	2.9
Gaza Strip	1986	96	4.6	33.4[43]	17.5	...	...	...	...	...	...	17.3	18.8	16.5[44]	17.3[44]
Germany, East	1987	8,571	49.0	...	51.4	55.1	48.1	...	...	...	...	929	10.8	3,479	40.6
Germany, West	1987	28,079	39.4	67.7[27]	47.9[27]	60.6[27]	36.3[27]	8.6	88.4	3.0	...	1,352	4.8	9,140	32.6
Ghana	1984	5,580	51.2	82.5[31]	45.4	44.9	45.8	67.7	15.7	12.2	4.4	3,311	59.3	631	11.3
Gibraltar	1987	13.4	31.3	64.1[25,31]	45.0	59.9	29.2	5.9[25]	93.8[25]	—	0.3[25]	—	—	2.9	21.5
Greece	1987	4,046	36.3	57.5[39]	39.2[39]	51.4[39]	27.3[39]	31.4[27]	43.8[27]	13.7[27]	11.1[27]	976	24.1	813	20.1
Greenland	1976	21.4	33.4	...	45.4	53.0	31.4	12.6	82.5	0.4	4.5	3.2	15.1	3.5	16.4
Grenada	1981[8]	28	...	...	31.3	...	...	21.3	77.7	1.0	—	8.0	28.7	2.0	7.2
Guadeloupe	1986	129	46.6	66.1	38.6	42.1	35.2	19.5[20]	54.5[20]	0.5[20]	25.6[20]	13[20]	10.5[20]	7.3[20]	5.9[20]
Guam	1980	44	34.8	66.6[18]	42.0	52.4	30.6	2.3	96.6	0.1	1.0	0.3	0.7	1.6[45]	3.6[45]
Guatemala	1986–87	2,740	24.5	59.2	33.6	51.3	16.2	30.9	47.2	16.0	5.9	1,365	49.8	347	12.7
Guernsey	1976	25.6	...	...	47.7	62.4	34.0	17.9	82.1	—	—	4.5	17.7	2.2	8.7
Guinea	1985	2,846	40.8	76.2	48.0	56.1	40.0	...	...	...	...	2,236	78.6	268[14]	9.4[14]
Guinea-Bissau	1988	279	3.3	41.0[34]	30.0	60.1	1.9	...	...	...	...	153[34]	71.9[34]	3[34]	1.5[34]
Guyana	1987[46]	270	29.9	60.4	35.7	50.9	21.0	14.3[22]	63.8[22]	1.9[22]	20.0[22]	50[22]	20.4[22]	41[22]	16.8[22]
Haiti	1988	2,350	40.9	66.3	42.2	51.4	33.6	51.6	14.3	9.1	25.1	1,185	50.4	136	5.8
Honduras	1984	1,256	16.7	53.6	29.7	49.3	9.9	11.6	85.1	1.5	1.7	719	57.2	177	14.1
Hong Kong	1987[5]	2,736	36.7	70.6	50.0	61.6	37.8	3.6[4]	81.1[4]	2.4[4]	12.8[4]	42	1.5	951	34.8
Hungary	1988	4,845	45.8	72.5[22]	45.7	51.3	40.5	...	...	...	...	1,022[4]	20.9[4]	1,526[4]	31.2[4]
Iceland	1986[47]	125	31.5[6]	79.1[48]	51.0	...	...	9.3	17.4	3.8	69.5	13	10.8	28	22.1
India	1981[49]	244,605	26.0	57.4[31]	36.8	52.7	19.8	43.7	25.0	28.4	2.8	153,015	62.6	27,381	11.2
Indonesia	1986	70,193	39.4	68.1	41.6	50.7	32.6	30.5	48.4	10.4	10.6	37,644	53.6	5,606[51]	8.0[51]
Iran	1976	9,796	14.8	50.2	29.1	48.1	8.9	25.4[52]	59.5[52]	11.4[52]	3.7[52]	3,615	36.9	1,834	18.7
Iraq	1986	4,307	18.2	50.6	26.9	42.5	10.1	...	...	...	...	1,193	27.7	483	11.2
Ireland	1987	1,319	30.9	59.9	37.2	51.5	23.0	18.2	70.7	1.9	9.2	168	12.7	259	19.7
Isle of Man	1981	27.6	38.2	67.7	42.6	55.1	31.2	14.0	79.8	—	6.2	1.4	5.1	4.0	14.4
Israel	1987[5]	1,494	39.2	56.0	34.2	41.7	26.8	18.2	74.3	1.4	6.1	73	4.9	353	23.7
Italy	1987[5]	23,819	36.4	59.1[41]	41.7	54.6	29.6	21.3	62.4	4.4	11.9	2,169	9.1	4,866	20.4
Jamaica	1987	1,079	45.3	75.2[41]	46.1	51.0	41.2	34.3	41.7	3.2	20.9	279	25.8	166[45]	15.4[45]
Japan	1987	60,840	39.9	68.7	49.8	60.9	39.0	15.0	72.8	9.0	3.2	4,890	8.0	14,640	24.1
Jersey	1986	45	41.6	65.7[31]	55.6	67.2	44.7	13.3	84.1	...	2.6	2.5	5.6	4.3	9.6
Jordan	1986	524	10.9	39.0	19.6	33.6	4.5	22.8[34]	67.2[34]	0.8[34]	9.2[34]	33	6.2	40	7.7
Kampuchea (Cambodia)	1985	3,602	40.5	71.4	49.5	59.2	39.8	...	...	...	...	2,454[22]	74.4[22]	220[14,22]	6.7[14,22]
Kenya	1985	8,389	40.9	76.2	40.7	48.4	33.2	...	...	...	...	6,635	79.1	596[14]	7.1[14]
Kiribati	1985	26	36.1	67.8[31]	41.2	53.1	29.5	71.0	26.5	...	2.5	19.2	72.9	0.4	1.4
Korea, North	1985	9,084	46.0	75.3	44.6	48.6	40.6	...	...	...	...	3,355[22]	42.8[22]	2,373[14,22]	30.3[14,22]
Korea, South	1987[5]	16,872	39.9	58.4	40.1	47.8	32.3	29.6	54.5	12.9	3.1	3,580	21.2	4,646	27.5
Kuwait	1986	712	20.6	63.5	39.0	54.8	18.5	5.9[39]	92.4[39]	0.1[39]	1.5[39]	14	1.9	69	9.7
Laos	1985	2,014	45.3	84.2	48.9	53.1	44.6	...	...	...	...	1,393[22]	75.7[22]	130[14,22]	7.1[14,22]
Lebanon	1986	694	21.7	39.9[31]	25.1	40.7	10.6	...	...	...	...	132	19.1	131	18.9
Lesotho	1976	424	32.3	56.1	34.8	48.9	21.7	7.5	49.9	36.8	5.8	99	23.3	141	33.2
Liberia	1984	669	31.2[39]	64.7[39]	31.8	...	...	...	...	...	...	481	71.9	31	4.6
Libya	1985	1,062	8.1	47.6	24.1[53]	42.3[53]	3.5[53]	23.7[53]	69.6[53]	4.2[53]	2.6[53]	178	16.8	162	15.2
Liechtenstein	1988	14	34.4	68.5	48.5	63.1	34.4	7.8	89.7	2.5	—	0.3	2.5	4.9	35.5
Luxembourg	1987[54]	158	35.3	61.0	42.8	56.9	29.4	8.9	84.9	1.9	4.3	5	3.2	31	19.4
Macau	1981	127	37.1	61.5[40]	48.6	59.0	37.5	9.7	84.9	3.4	2.0	8	5.9	57	45.0
Madagascar	1985	3,929	44.2	74.9	39.3	48.8	31.6	...	...	...	...	3,125	79.6	248[14]	6.3[14]
Malawi	1985	3,074	42.6	74.3	44.3	51.9	36.9	79.9[52]	17.8[52]	0.3[52]	2.0[52]	2,502	81.4	206[14]	6.7[14]
Malaysia	1980	4,924	33.7	62.1	37.5	49.6	25.3	28.7	54.3	10.2	6.7	1,855	37.7	652	13.2
Maldives	1985	52	21.7	78.3[52]	28.7	43.5	13.0	49.4	39.1	6.1	5.4	15	29.5	13	24.3
Mali	1976	2,266	17.0	53.2	35.4	60.2	11.8	45.8	4.1	42.5	7.5	1,862	82.2	27	1.2
Malta	1987	128	24.9	...	36.9	56.2	18.1	14.1[6]	77.4[6]	—	8.5[6]	3	2.5	39	30.3
Martinique	1986	146	50.6	67.4	44.5	45.3	43.8	12.3[20]	57.4[20]	0.3[20]	30.0[20]	10	7.1	7	4.9
Mauritania	1985	590	21.0	55.7	31.2	49.8	13.0	...	...	...	...	389	66.0	59[14]	10.0[14]
Mauritius	1987[55]	426	34.2	69.8	42.9	56.5	29.3	9.0[6]	60.8[6]	0.6[6]	29.6[6]	75	18.5	141	34.7
Mayotte	1978	15.1	35.9	65.0	32.1	41.0	23.1	48.1	26.3	19.8	5.8	9.3	61.6	1.0	6.5
Mexico	1987	27,324	27.8[22]	57.2[22]	33.0[22]	48.2[22]	18.2[22]	27.0	44.3	5.4	23.3	7,061	25.8	3,976	14.5
Monaco	1982	11.7	39.6	64.6[56]	43.3	56.1	32.1	18.6[56]	76.4[56]	1.7[56]	3.3[56]	—	0.2[56]	2.0[14,56]	17.8[14,56]
Mongolia	1987	946	45.5[39]	82.2[39]	46.9[39]	50.9[39]	42.8[39]	...	...	...	...	561	59.3	122	12.9
Montserrat	1980	5.1	41.6	74.1	44.0	53.4	35.3	20.4[19]	78.0[19]	1.6[19]	—	0.5	9.3	0.6	10.9
Morocco	1982	5,999	19.7	48.9	29.3	47.1	11.6	27.1	40.5	17.6	14.8	2,352	39.2	1,016	16.9
Mozambique	1980	5,671	52.4	87.3[31]	48.6	47.6	49.5	44.4[19]	40.0[19]	14.5[19]	1.1[19]	4,755	83.8	347	6.1
Myanmar (Burma)	1987–88	15,847	35.3[6]	64.2[6]	40.2[6]	52.4[6]	28.2[6]	...	...	...	...	10,127[57]	63.9[57]	1,458	9.2
Nauru	1977	2.2	8.8[59]	69.8[59]	30.5	...	...	...	...	...	...				
Nepal	1986	7,760	34.7	82.5	45.5	57.8	32.5	86.2[25]	9.1[25]	2.5[25]	2.2[25]	6,244[25]	91.1[25]	37[25]	0.5[25]
Netherlands, The	1987	6,559	37.4	64.4	44.7	57.1	33.1	9.2	79.2	2.0	9.6	292	4.5	1,171	17.9
Netherlands Antilles	1986[5]	77	41.8	59.5	40.4	48.6	32.8	...	...	...	...	0.4	0.6	6.9	8.9
New Caledonia	1983	58	...	63.6[30]	40.0	...	...	...	...	...	...	20	33.9	8[14]	13.5[14]
New Zealand	1986	1,609	41.7	74.6	49.3	58.1	40.7	16.0	75.7	1.1	7.2	162	10.0	338	21.0
Nicaragua	1987	1,126	21.6[22]	54.0[22]	32.2	...	...	...	...	...	...	365	32.4	101	9.0
Niger	1985	3,203	47.4	89.7	52.4	55.6	49.2	...	...	...	...	2,870	89.6	64[14]	2.0[14]
Nigeria	1983	29,453	31.9	59.4	32.0	43.1	20.6	55.9	28.0	8.9	7.2	9,296	31.6	1,764	6.0
Niue	1984	1.0	35.7	57.3[31]	35.4	44.5	25.9	9.1	71.5	10.9	8.5	0.2	19.5	0.1	11.5
Norfolk Island	1986	1.2	45.3	79.2[31]	61.6	66.5	56.5	...	...	...	...	0.037	3.0	0.048	3.9
Norway	1987	2,171	44.3	79.1[28]	51.9	58.4	45.4	8.7	86.7	2.3	2.3	141	6.5	406	18.7
Oman	1986	468	7.5	60.9	35.7	57.6	6.2	...	...	...	...	109	23.3	15	3.3
Pacific Is., Trust Terr. of the Marshall Islands	1980	4.4	25.2	30.0[18]	14.3	20.8	7.4	3.3	78.1	0.3	18.4	0.1	1.0	0.4[10]	9.4[10]
Micronesia, Fed. States of	1980	9.8	29.8	26.1[18]	13.4	18.4	8.2	2.7	74.4	0.1	22.7	0.2	2.0	0.6[10]	6.0[10]

construction		transportation, communications		trade, hotels, restaurants		finance, real estate		public administration, defense		services		other		country
number ('000)	% of econ. active	number ('000)	% of econ. active	number ('000)	% of econ. active	number ('000)	% of econ. active	number ('000)	% of econ. active	number ('000)	% of econ. active	number ('000)	% of econ. active	
206	8.0	187	7.2	363	14.1	180	7.2	129	5.0	635	24.6	25[24]	1.0[24]	Finland
1,577	6.6	1,297	5.4	3,449	14.4	1,759	7.3	11	11	6,686[11]	27.9[11]	2,663[17]	11.1[17]	France
3	8.8	1.3	4.2	2	6.2	4	11.3	11	11	10[11]	31.3[11]	7[17]	20.9[17]	French Guiana
6.2	10.0	3.4	5.5	9.7	15.5	2.6	4.1	11	11	23.4[11]	37.4[11]	4.6[17]	7.4[17]	French Polynesia
14	14	15	15	15	15	15	15	15	15	80[15]	13.7[15]	—	—	Gabon
4	1.3	8	2.5	17	5.1	1	1	1	1	22[1]	6.8[1]	25	7.7	Gambia, The
23.5	24.6	4.8	5.0	13.3	13.9	16	16	12.0	12.6	5.9[16,44]	6.2[16,44]	1.4[12]	1.5[12]	Gaza Strip
569	6.6	633	7.4	881	10.3	1	1	1	1	2,080[1]	24.3[1]	—	—	Germany, East
1,774	6.3	1,590	5.7	4,176	14.9	1,785	6.4	11	11	7,584[11]	27.0[11]	678[23]	2.4[23]	Germany, West
65	1.2	123	2.2	792	14.2	27	0.5	98	1.7	376	6.7	158[12]	2.8[12]	Ghana
2.7	20.0	0.6	4.4	2.7	20.2	0.9	7.0	11	11	2.5[11]	18.8[11]	1.1[33]	8.0[33]	Gibraltar
249	6.2	249	6.2	612	15.1	150	3.7	11	11	648[11]	16.0[11]	337[17]	8.3[17]	Greece
3.1	14.6	1.8	8.6	2.2	10.1	16	16	1.5	7.1	5.4[16]	25.5[16]	0.6	2.8	Greenland
2.9	10.3	1.7	6.1	3.9	14.0	0.4	1.3	1.7	6.0	2.6	9.2	4.8	17.2	Grenada
10[20]	8.1[20]	4.8[20]	3.9[20]	10[20]	8.1[20]	15[20]	12.2[20]	11	11	28[11,20]	22.7[11,20]	35[17,20]	28.6[17,20]	Guadeloupe
3.0	6.8	3.3[45]	7.5[45]	7.3	16.4	1.6	3.5	16.0	35.9	9.7	21.8	1.7[17]	3.8[17]	Guam
95	3.5	52	1.9	357	13.0	31	1.1	11	11	395[11]	14.4[11]	98[23]	3.6[23]	Guatemala
2.7	10.7	1.3	5.2	5.8	22.5	1.1	4.2	3.0	12.0	4.5	17.5	0.4	1.4	Guernsey
14	14	15	15	15	15	15	15	15	15	342[15]	12.0[15]	—	—	Guinea
2[34]	0.8[34]	2[34]	1.1[34]	5[34]	2.4[34]	0.2[34]	0.1[34]	11	11	26[11,34]	12.3[11,34]	21[34]	10.0[34]	Guinea-Bissau
7[22]	2.8[22]	9[22]	3.8[22]	15[22]	6.2[22]	3[22]	1.2[22]	30[22]	12.1[22]	29[22]	11.9[22]	61[17,22]	24.7[17,22]	Guyana
22	1.0	17	0.7	261	11.1	4	0.2	11	11	115[11]	4.9[11]	611[17]	26.0[17]	Haiti
43	3.5	38	3.0	107	8.5	12	1.0	11	11	160[11]	12.8[11]	—	—	Honduras
221	8.1	233	8.5	639	23.4	173	6.3	11	11	471[11]	17.2[11]	7[24]	0.3[24]	Hong Kong
342[4]	7.0[4]	404[4]	8.3[4]	514[4]	10.5[4]	1	1	1	1	1,077[1,4]	22.0[1,4]	—	—	Hungary
11	9.1	...	...	19	15.3	...	...	...	...	21	16.9	32	25.7	Iceland
3,565	1.5	6,069	2.5	12,165	5.0	1,764	0.7	11	11	18,557[11]	7.6[11]	22,088[50]	9.0[50]	India
51	51	51	51	9,756	13.9	5,182[51]	7.4[51]	11	11	10,018[11]	14.3[11]	1,986[17]	2.8[17]	Indonesia
1,202	12.3	433	4.4	672	6.9	101	1.0	11	11	1,524[11]	15.6[11]	415[24]	4.2[24]	Iran
521	12.1	260	6.0	330	7.0	50	1.2	11	11	1,470[11]	34.1[11]	—	—	Iraq
98	7.4	71	5.4	212	16.1	85	6.5	11	11	299[11]	22.6[11]	127[23]	9.6[23]	Ireland
2.9	10.6	2.3	8.3	5.5	20.1	1.5	5.5	1.6	5.9	6.3	22.7	2.0[17]	7.3[17]	Isle of Man
74	4.9	94	6.3	202	13.5	138	9.2	11	11	504[11]	33.8[11]	55[24]	3.7[24]	Israel
1,849	7.8	1,148	4.8	4,465	18.7	793	3.3	11	11	5,696[11]	23.9[11]	2,833[12]	11.9[12]	Italy
50	4.6	48[45]	4.4[45]	143	13.2	16	16	84	7.8	203[16]	18.8[16]	107[24]	9.9[24]	Jamaica
5,330	8.8	3,480	5.7	13,660	22.5	2,340	3.8	1,980	3.3	12,550	20.6	1,970[17]	3.2[17]	Japan
3.9	8.8	2.6	5.8	10.6	23.9	5.8	12.9	2.9	6.6	10.8	24.1	1.2[17]	2.8[17]	Jersey
56	10.7	45	8.6	55	10.5	17	3.3	11	11	278[11]	53.1[11]	—	—	Jordan
14	14	15	15	15	15	15	15	15	15	625[15,22]	18.9[15,22]	—	—	Kampuchea (Cambodia)
14	14	15	15	15	15	15	15	15	15	1,158[15]	13.8[15]	—	—	Kenya
0.4	1.7	1.1	4.0	1.1	4.3	0.1	0.4	1.6	6.1	1.8	6.8	0.6[17]	2.5[17]	Kiribati
14	14	15	15	15	15	15	15	15	15	2,110[15,22]	26.9[15,22]	—	—	Korea, North
920	5.5	763	4.5	3,611	21.4	680	4.0	11	11	2,153[11]	12.8[11]	519[12]	3.1[12]	Korea, South
130	18.3	39	5.5	80	11.3	22	3.1	11	11	357[11]	50.1[11]	—	—	Kuwait
14	14	15	15	15	15	15	15	15	15	316[15,22]	17.2[15,22]	—	—	Laos
43	6.2	48	7.0	115	16.5	24	3.5	11	11	200[11]	28.8[11]	—	—	Lebanon
12	2.9	4	1.1	8	2.0	0.3	0.1	11	11	74[11]	17.6[11]	84	19.9	Lesotho
4	0.6	14	2.1	47	7.0	2	0.3	11	11	61[11]	9.1[11]	29	4.3	Liberia
257	24.2	93	8.7	41	3.9	13	1.2	69	6.5	184	17.3	66	6.2	Libya
1.1	8.3	0.4	3.0	1.6	11.8	0.9	6.8	0.6	4.7	3.7	26.8	0.1[33]	0.7[33]	Liechtenstein
14	8.8	11	6.7	33	20.7	16	10.1	15	9.4	28	17.4	7[17]	4.4[17]	Luxembourg
10	7.8	6	4.5	23	18.1	2	1.7	5	3.2	15	11.9	2[24]	1.8[24]	Macau
14	14	15	15	15	15	15	15	15	15	556[15]	14.1[15]	—	—	Madagascar
14	14	15	15	15	15	15	15	15	15	366[15]	11.9[15]	—	—	Malawi
208	4.2	161	3.3	560	11.4	80	1.6	306	6.2	666	13.5	438[17]	8.9[17]	Malaysia
2.6	4.9	3.3	6.4	5.4	10.4	0.4	0.8	11	11	10.4[11]	20.0[11]	1.9[33]	3.7[33]	Maldives
8	0.3	12	0.5	45	2.0	0.2	—	49	2.1	124	5.5	139	6.1	Mali
6	4.6	9	7.0	12	9.4	4	3.3	11	11	49[11]	38.5[11]	6[12]	4.4[12]	Malta
7	4.7	6	4.0	12	8.5	19	13.2	11	11	33[11]	22.6[11]	51[12]	35.0[12]	Martinique
14	14	15	15	15	15	15	15	15	15	142[15]	24.0[15]	—	—	Mauritania
21	5.2	25	6.2	45	11.1	7	1.7	55	13.5	37	9.1	—	—	Mauritius
1.4	9.0	0.3	1.9	0.7	4.5	0.2	1.5	0.2	1.4	1.2	7.8	0.9[12]	5.8[12]	Mayotte
1,620	5.9	847	3.1	2,167	7.9	511	1.9	11	11	3,036[11]	11.1[11]	8,107[23]	29.7[23]	Mexico
14	14	0.6[56]	5.4[56]	2.6[56]	23.6[56]	0.9[56]	8.5[56]	2.1[56]	18.8[56]	2.4[56]	21.7[56]	0.5[17,56]	4.1[17,56]	Monaco
31	3.2	42	4.4	45	4.8	1	1	1	1	115[1]	12.2[1]	31	3.2	Mongolia
0.7	13.3	0.2	4.5	0.4	8.1	0.1	1.7	0.8	16.0	1.2	23.8	0.6	12.4	Montserrat
437	7.3	141	2.3	498	8.3	16	16	533	8.9	474[16]	7.9[16]	548[2]	9.1[2]	Morocco
42	0.7	7.7	1.4	112	2.0	1	1	1	1	243[1]	4.3[1]	95[12]	1.7[12]	Mozambique
258	1.6	513	3.2	1,507	9.5	1	1	1	1	994[1]	6.3[1]	990[58]	6.2[58]	Myanmar (Burma)
...	...	...	...	...	...	...	...	...	...	...	...	—	—	Nauru
2[25]	—	7[25]	0.1[25]	109[25]	1.6[25]	10[25]	0.1[25]	11	11	314[11,25]	4.6[11,25]	127	1.9	Nepal
380	5.8	354	5.4	1,073	16.4	557	8.5	11	11	2,024[11]	30.9[11]	707[17]	10.8[17]	Netherlands, The
5.5	7.1	3.8	5.0	16.4	21.2	5.2	6.7	11	11	21.1[11]	27.3[11]	17.9[12]	23.2[12]	Netherlands Antilles
14	14	3	4.6	4[32]	7.5[32]	1	1.8	11	11	19[11,32]	32.5[11,32]	4[17]	6.3[17]	New Caledonia
102	6.3	111	6.9	292	18.2	123	7.6	11	11	358[11]	22.2[11]	123[17]	7.7[17]	New Zealand
17	1.5	21	1.8	95	8.4	19	1.7	77	6.9	149	13.2	283[50]	25.1[50]	Nicaragua
14	14	15	15	15	15	15	15	15	15	269[15]	8.4[15]	—	—	Niger
909	3.1	1,123	3.8	6,534	22.2	204	0.7	11	11	7,081[11]	24.0[11]	2,542[17]	8.6[17]	Nigeria
0.1	9.6	—	4.2	0.1	8.7	—	0.1	11	11	0.4[11]	37.0[11]	0.1[12]	8.5[12]	Niue
0.092	7.6	0.070	5.8	0.275[32]	22.6[32]	0.062	5.1	0.202	16.6	0.325[32]	26.7[32]	0.106	8.7	Norfolk Island
168	7.7	180	8.3	382	17.6	156	7.2	140	6.4	579	26.7	20[23]	0.9[23]	Norway
128	27.5	6	1.4	124	26.4	8	1.7	11	11	77[11]	16.5[11]	—	—	Oman
0.4	8.4	10	10	0.5	12.3	—	0.7	0.6	13.4	1.6	36.4	0.8[17]	18.4[17]	Pacific Is., Trust Terr. of the Marshall Islands
0.9	9.6	10	10	0.9	8.8	0.1	1.2	1.8	18.0	3.1	31.5	2.2[17]	22.8[17]	Micronesia, Fed. States of

Employment and labour (continued)

country	year	economically active population						employment status (%)				distribution by economic sector			
		total ('000)	participation rate (%)		activity rate (%)			employers, self-employed	employees	unpaid family workers	other	agriculture, forestry, fishing		manufacturing; mining, quarrying; public utilities	
			female	ages 15–64	total	male	female					number ('000)	% of econ. active	number ('000)	% of econ. active
Northern Mariana Islands	1980	6.1	34.3	63.6[18]	36.4	45.5	26.3	2.0	95.2	—	2.8	0.1	2.1	0.6[10]	10.3[10]
Palau	1980	2.9	34.3	41.6[18]	23.9	30.3	17.0	3.0	89.1	—	7.9	0.1	2.9	0.3[10]	10.6[10]
Pakistan	1984–85[5]	28,872	9.4	50.6	29.6	51.7	5.8	44.7	26.0	25.6	3.7	14,054	48.7	4,039	14.0
Panama	1986[60]	720	31.5	57.6[35]	32.3	43.4	20.8	26.0	65.5	4.3	4.2	188	26.2	80	11.1
Papua New Guinea	1980[61]	733	39.8	35.2[40]	24.6	28.3	20.5	72.7	26.4	—	0.9	564	77.0	21	2.9
Paraguay	1982	1,039	19.7	57.5	34.3	54.8	13.6	43.1	37.7	9.2	9.9	446	42.9	129	12.4
Peru	1988	7,206	25.4[25]	56.2[31]	33.9	...	...	39.8[25]	41.8[25]	8.4[25]	10.0[25]	2,508	34.8	938	13.0
Philippines	1987[5]	22.881	37.0	67.1	39.9	50.1	29.6	35.6	40.1	15.2	9.1	9,940	43.4	2,286	10.0
Pitcairn Island	1981	0.035	...	...	66.0	...	...	...	...	...	...	0.003	8.6	0.002	5.7
Poland	1987	18,012	45.4	82.4[62]	47.7	53.4	42.3	13.2[48]	74.0[48]	12.1[48]	0.7[48]	5,019	27.9	5,356	29.7
Portugal	1987	4,732	42.0	67.4	46.0	55.3	37.4	24.7	63.6	4.5	7.2	976	20.6	1,143	24.2
Puerto Rico	1988[5]	1,046	37.6	51.3[28]	31.7	40.5	23.2	13.5	84.5	0.8	1.1	33	3.2	169	16.2
Qatar	1986	201	9.8	75.5[31]	47.9	73.3	16.2	...	...	...	...	0.3	0.1	43.3	21.5
Réunion	1982	176	35.3	57.5[28]	34.0	44.9	23.6	10.4	56.3	1.1	32.2	17	10.1	8	4.7
Romania	1987	10,719	45.6[52]	75.6[52]	50.1[52]	55.2[52]	45.1[52]	...	...	...	...	3,065	28.6	4,009	37.4
Rwanda	1978	2,661	51.5	94.3	55.1	54.6	55.8	38.8	7.2	53.8	0.2	2,472	92.9	49	1.8
St. Helena and Ascension	1987[21,64]	2.6	35.8	71.7	46.4	61.3	32.3	4.3	95.7	—	—	4.5	26.1	3.8	22.3
St. Kitts and Nevis	1980	17.1	41.0	69.5	39.5	48.4	31.2	9.7	78.5	0.4	11.4	10.7	25.5	3.7	8.7
St. Lucia	1980	42.2	39.1	69.9	37.2	47.1	28.0	21.0	55.8	1.6	21.6	0.1	4.4	0.4	13.7
St. Pierre and Miquelon	1986	2.7	28.1	60.6[20]	44.4	60.3	28.8	8.5	—80.0—		11.5	8.9	25.7	2.3	6.6
St. Vincent	1980	35	36.1	60.9[31]	35.5	46.6	25.0	18.0[19]	82.5[19]	1.5[19]	—	0.3	2.8	4.3[65]	35.1[65]
San Marino	1989	12.1	41.4	71.2[27]	53.3	63.6	43.4	19.9	73.8	0.8	5.5	16	53.9	1.9	6.2
São Tomé and Príncipe	1981	31	32.4	61.1	31.7	43.1	20.4	15.8	79.4	0.1	4.7	432	14.3	452	14.9
Saudi Arabia	1986	3,032	3.2	51.5	29.8	48.4	2.3	...	...	...	...	2,464	79.6	200[14]	6.5[14]
Senegal	1985	3,095	41.8	78.1	47.1	55.3	39.1	...	...	...	...	2,3[66]	9.5[66]	2.3[66]	9.6[66]
Seychelles	1985	28	42.4	66.8[31]	42.4	49.0	35.9	10.7[25]	76.6[25]	0.3[25]	12.4[25]	904	66.9	204[14]	15.1[14]
Sierra Leone	1985	1,352	33.7	62.9	37.5	50.8	24.8	...	...	...	...	10	0.8	327	26.1
Singapore	1987[5]	1,252	37.8	66.2	47.9	59.5	36.3	13.0	80.2	2.1	4.7	18	46.0	3.4	8.7
Solomon Islands	1986[67]	39	25.6	24.9[43]	13.7	19.7	7.3	29.6	68.6	—	1.8	1,475	73.8	176[14]	8.8[14]
Somalia	1985	1,999	39.7	72.8	43.0	52.5	33.7	...	...	...	...	1,180	13.6	2,215	25.5
South Africa	1985	8,692	36.4	68.3[26]	37.2	47.9	26.7	4.0[22]	89.4[22]	...	6.6[22]	157	47.2	54	16.2
Bophuthatswana	1980[68]	333	...	...	25.2	...	...	...	...	...	...	11	7.9	31	21.9
Ciskei	1980[68]	140	...	...	20.5...	...	...	...	...	...	...	420	75.9	30	5.4
Transkei	1980[68]	554	...	...	23.8	...	...	...	...	...	...	50	84.8	0.8	1.4
Venda	1980[68]	60	...	...	18.9	...	...	...	...	...	...	185[22]	43.4[22]	93[14,22]	21.8[14,22]
South West Africa/Namibia	1985	477	23.9	55.4	30.8	47.3	14.6	...	...	...	...	1,979	13.8	3,077	21.5
Spain	1987	14,306	33.0	58.6[28]	36.8	50.3	23.9	18.4	65.5	5.4	10.7	2,531	42.4	737	12.3
Sri Lanka	1985	5,972	32.8	61.0	37.7	50.1	25.0	24.4	50.1	11.5	14.1	4,786	68.5	587[14]	8.4[14]
Sudan, The	1985	6,991	20.8	55.6	32.4	51.2	13.5	59.2[53]	25.3[53]	9.9[53]	5.6[53]	7.6	7.8	14.1	14.4
Suriname	1980	98	28.1[8]	38.7[69]	27.5	...	...	11.2[8]	78.1[8]	2.1[8]	8.6[8]	194	71.0	25[14]	9.1[14]
Swaziland	1985	273	39.9	72.1	42.0	51.2	33.1	8.6	89.1	0.4	1.9	171	3.9	1,012	22.9
Sweden	1987[5]	4,421	48.0	83.4[28]	52.6	55.5	49.9	9.7[22]	90.3[22]	...	...	209	6.4	988	30.4
Switzerland	1986	3,244	37.2	70.7[22]	49.4	63.2	36.0	34.0[6]	56.2[6]	7.4[6]	2.4[6]	746	30.0	360	14.5
Syria	1986	2,488	12.8	46.7	23.2	39.6	6.1	20.5	67.4	10.1	2.0	2,086	21.6	2,889	30.0
Taiwan	1987	9,640	37.2	71.6	49.0	59.4	37.8					9,091	83.3	469[14]	4.3[14]
Tanzania	1985	10,913	48.9	85.7	48.5	50.2	46.8	30.0	32.9	27.3	9.8	15,321[57]	54.9[57]	3,112	11.1
Thailand	1987[70]	27,928	45.4	78.5[39]	52.5	57.2	47.8	70.3[25]	10.4[25]	11.3[25]	8.0[25]	579[25]	64.3[25]	59[25]	6.6[25]
Togo	1985	1,244	37.5	69.5	42.0	53.3	31.1	...	...	...	...	0.1	16.1	—	—
Tokelau	1981	0.8	51.2	88.3	48.5	47.9	49.2	32.7[30]	33.3[30]	13.1[30]	20.9[30]	10.4	42.9	1.0	4.0
Tonga	1986	24	21.5	44.7	25.8	40.2	11.1	18.7[27]	73.4[27]	5.4[27]	2.5[27]	46[27]	9.7[27]	65[27,65]	13.7[27,65]
Trinidad and Tobago	1987	479	33.8	63.0	39.3	52.0	26.7	21.4	54.9	5.4	18.3	475	22.2	383	17.9
Tunisia	1984	2,137	21.3	52.9	30.6	48.7	13.3	23.2[22]	32.1[22]	40.9[22]	3.8[22]	7,272	39.5	2,494	13.5
Turkey	1985	18,423	30.1	58.5	36.2	50.1	21.9	...	...	...	...	0.4	13.9	—	1.0
Turks and Caicos Islands	1980	2.9	42.8	69.4	39.2	46.5	32.5	0.3	22.2	—77.5—		—	1.0	0.1	1.9
Tuvalu	1979[71]	4.0	51.3	81.1[31]	55.2	57.6	53.1	...	...	...	...	5,940	84.2	317[14]	4.5[14]
Uganda	1985	7,054	41.9	78.9	45.6	53.4	37.9	...	...	...	...	24,840	19.0	43,196	33.0
U.S.S.R.	1987[5]	130,952	49.9	82.9[73]	46.3	49.3	43.6	6.8[22]	92.7[22]	0.1[22]	0.5[22]	44	5.0	92	10.4
United Arab Emirates	1986	891	6.6	76.7	53.2	73.1	11.0	10.3	79.3	...	10.4	592	2.1	5,891	21.1
United Kingdom	1987	27,896	41.4	72.4[27]	49.0	59.0	39.5	8.1	90.8	0.3	0.8	3,622	3.0	24,728	20.3
United States	1987[74]	121,602	44.3	73.5	50.0	57.2	43.1	22.7	70.6	1.7	5.0	179	15.3	231	19.7
Uruguay	1985	1,172	33.1	71.3[26]	39.9	54.8	25.7	...	...	...	...	39.3	76.8	1.1	2.2
Vanuatu	1979	51	43.4	84.3	46.0	49.0	42.5	26.0	62.7	2.8	8.5	857	13.6	1,205	19.1
Venezuela	1987	6,322	27.7	58.1	34.4	49.2	19.3	7.1	86.4	0.3	6.2	19,015	62.6	997	3.3
Vietnam	1987	30,352	47.2[39]	80.1[39]	48.2[39]	52.3[39]	44.2[39]					0.5	1.2	3.8	10.0
Virgin Islands (U.S.)	1980	38	45.5	65.1	39.4	44.9	34.4	42.2	18.3	39.5	—	2.7	79.2	0.2[14]	5.5[14]
Wallis and Futuna	1976	3.4	35.8	65.1[43]	36.5	46.9	26.1	...	...	...	...	38.5	22.2	27.3[44]	15.7[44]
West Bank	1986	174	14.3	37.8[43]	20.8	...	...	...	...	...	...	...	...	...	...
Western Sahara		...	...	...	...	...	...	21.1	43.5	35.0	0.4	25	60.4	1.2	2.9
Western Samoa	1981	42	15.0	48.6	26.5	43.5	8.3	29.8[53]	34.2[53]	15.1[53]	20.9[53]	257	46.6	69	12.6
Yemen (Aden)	1986	551	10.9	50.8	25.0	45.0	5.4	45.2[34]	34.0[34]	19.1[34]	1.7[34]	895	59.9	70	4.7
Yemen (Şan'ā')	1986	1,492	12.5	38.5	18.2	33.6	4.3	17.2	65.7	10.5	6.6	2,683	28.7	2,210	23.6
Yugoslavia	1981	9,359	38.7	68.7[26]	43.4	54.3	32.9	...	...	...	...	7,939	68.1	1,692[14]	14.5[14]
Zaire	1985	11,666	36.6	66.8	39.0	50.2	28.1	...	...	...	...	1,587	71.5	227[14]	10.2[14]
Zambia	1985	2,221	28.2	60.1	33.6	48.6	18.8	...	...	...	...	2,411	70.7	377[14]	11.1[14]
Zimbabwe	1985	3,410	35.7	68.0	38.9	50.3	27.5								

[1]Services includes finance, real estate and public administration, defense. [2]Unemployed, not previously employed only. [3]State sector only, excluding agricultural cooperatives. [4]1987. [5]Excludes armed forces. [6]1983. [7]1984. [8]Employed persons only. [9]Agriculture includes mining, quarrying. [10]Manufacturing; mining, quarrying; public utilities include transportation, communications. [11]Services includes public administration, defense. [12]Unemployed only. [13]Services includes hotels. [14]Manufacturing; mining, quarrying; public utilities include construction. [15]Services includes transportation, communications; trade, hotels, restaurants; finance, real estate; and public administration, defense. [16]Services includes finance, real estate. [17]Mostly unemployed. [18]Over age 16. [19]1970. [20]1982. [21]Wage earners and self-employed only. [22]1980. [23]Includes unemployed, not previously employed. [24]Mostly unemployed, not previously employed. [25]1981. [26]Ages 20–64. [27]1986. [28]Ages 16–64. [29]Mostly employees of international corporations. [30]1976. [31]Over age 15. [32]Services includes hotels and restaurants. [33]Includes unemployed. [34]1979. [35]Ages 15–69. [36]Over age 12. [37]State sector only. [38]Republic of Cyprus only. [39]1985. [40]Over age 10. [41]Ages 14–64. [42]Ages 14–59. [43]Over age 14. [44]Services includes public administration. [45]Transportation, communications includes public utilities. [46]Data are for persons aged 15–64 only. [47]Workers covered by compulsory social insurance only.

construction		transportation, communications		trade, hotels, restaurants		finance, real estate		public administration, defense		services		other		country
number ('000)	% of econ. active	number ('000)	% of econ. active	number ('000)	% of econ. active	number ('000)	% of econ. active	number ('000)	% of econ. active	number ('000)	% of econ. active	number ('000)	% of econ. active	
1.0	16.4	[10]	[10]	0.9	15.1	0.2	2.7	1.3	20.7	1.8	30.1	0.2[17]	2.7[17]	Northern Mariana Islands
0.5	16.4	[10]	[10]	0.3	11.6	—	1.6	0.5	16.2	1.0	32.8	0.2[17]	8.0[17]	Palau
1,556	5.4	1,445	5.0	3,207	11.1	245	0.8	[11]	[11]	3,077[11]	10.7[11]	1,249[33]	4.3[33]	Pakistan
40	5.6	40	5.6	104	14.5	29	4.0	[11]	[11]	193[11]	26.8[11]	46[24]	6.3[24]	Panama
22	2.9	1.7	2.4	25	3.4	4	0.6	[11]	[11]	77[11]	10.5[11]	2	0.2	Papua New Guinea
70	6.7	31	2.9	86	8.3	18	1.7	[11]	[11]	174[11]	16.8[11]	86[23]	8.3[23]	Paraguay
259	3.6	317	4.4	1,081	15.0	180	2.5	[11]	[11]	1,924[11]	26.7[11]			Peru
759	3.3	946	4.1	2,857[32]	12.5[32]	386	1.7	[11]	[11]	3,621[11,32]	15.8[11,32]	2,086[12]	9.1[12]	Philippines
—	—	0.005	14.3	0.002	5.7	0.016	45.7	[11]	[11]	0.007[11]	20.0[11]			Pitcairn Island
1,339	7.4	1,049	5.8	1,486	8.2	162	0.9	270	1.5	2,238	12.4	1,095[63]	6.2[63]	Poland
377	8.0	180	3.8	615	13.0	135	2.9	[11]	[11]	976[11]	20.6[11]	330[17]	7.0[17]	Portugal
49	4.7	36	3.4	169[13]	16.2[13]	33	3.2	[11]	[11]	396[11,13]	37.9[11,13]	161[12]	15.4[12]	Puerto Rico
36.1	17.9	6.1	3.0	30.8	15.3	7.8	3.9	[11]	[11]	74.9[11]	37.1[11]	2.0[12]	1.0[12]	Qatar
11	6.5	6	3.4	14	8.3	16	9.4	[11]	[11]	45[11]	25.8[11]	55[17]	31.9[17]	Réunion
793	7.4	740	6.9	632	5.9	[16]	[16]	54	0.5	1,276[16]	11.9[16]	150	1.4	Romania
25	0.9	7	0.3	26	1.0	1	—	[11]	[11]	74[11]	2.8[11]	8	0.3	Rwanda
...	...	...	...	...	...	...	...	...	...	...	...	...	...	St. Helena and Ascension
0.4	2.5	0.3	1.6	1.3	7.3	0.8	4.7	1.0	5.7	2.9	17.0	2.2[17]	12.8[17]	St. Kitts and Nevis
2.6	6.3	1.5	3.5	2.8	6.5	0.5	1.1	2.4	5.6	7.9	18.8	10.1[17]	24.0[17]	St. Lucia
0.2	6.0	0.1	5.5	0.4	15.0	0.1	3.3	[11]	[11]	1.1[11]	40.3[31]	0.3[17]	11.9[17]	St. Pierre and Miquelon
3.5	10.2	1.9	5.4	2.6	7.4	0.4	1.0	[11]	[11]	7.6[11]	21.8[11]	7.6	21.9	St. Vincent
0.9[65]	7.3[65]	0.2	1.4	1.8	15.0	0.2	2.0	2.0	16.1	0.7	6.1	1.7[33]	14.1[33]	San Marino
1.8	5.9	1.0	3.4	2.0	6.5	0.2	0.5	[11]	[11]	5.8[11]	19.0[11]	1.4[12]	4.6[12]	São Tomé and Príncipe
568	18.7	210	6.9	374	12.3	94	3.1	[11]	[11]	902[11]	29.8[11]	—	—	Saudi Arabia
[14]	[14]	[15]	[15]	[15]	[15]	[15]	[15]	[15]	[15]	431[15]	13.9[15]			Senegal
1.1[66]	4.4[66]	2.3[66]	9.4[66]	3.1[66]	12.8[66]	0.8[66]	3.4[66]	[11]	[11]	3.6[11,66]	15.0[11,66]	8.6[33,66]	35.8[33,66]	Seychelles
[14]	[14]	[15]	[15]	[15]	[15]	[15]	[15]	[15]	[15]	243[15]	18.0[15]			Sierra Leone
91	7.3	121	9.7	279	22.3	106	8.4	[11]	[11]	257[11]	20.5[11]	60[17]	4.8[17]	Singapore
2.2	5.6	2.0	5.1	3.3	8.4	0.6	1.4	[11]	[11]	9.4[11]	23.9[11]	0.3	0.8	Solomon Islands
[14]	[14]	[15]	[15]	[15]	[15]	[15]	[15]	[15]	[15]	348[15]	17.4[15]			Somalia
556	6.4	418	4.8	942	10.8	339	3.9	446	5.1	1,520	17.5	1,077[17]	12.4[17]	South Africa
22	6.6	7	2.2	23	6.8	1.2	0.4	[11]	[11]	52[11]	15.7[11]	17	5.0	Bophuthatswana
6	4.1	5	3.8	14	10.0	1.2	0.9	[11]	[11]	33[11]	23.9[11]	38	27.5	Ciskei
15	2.7	4	0.6	11	2.1	1.1	0.2	[11]	[11]	49[11]	8.9[11]	23	4.2	Transkei
1.3	2.2	0.6	1.0	1.3	2.2	0.1	0.1	[11]	[11]	3.8[11]	6.4[11]	1.2	2.0	Venda
[14]	[14]	[15]	[15]	[15]	[15]	[15]	[15]	[15]	[15]	148[15,22]	34.7[15,22]			South West Africa/Namibia
1,187	8.3	674	4.7	2,497	17.5	568	4.0	[11]	[11]	2,836[11]	19.8[11]	1,487[24]	10.4[24]	Spain
227	3.8	220	3.7	514	8.6	65	1.1	[11]	[11]	631[11]	10.6[11]	1,047[17]	17.5[17]	Sri Lanka
[14]	[14]	[15]	[15]	[15]	[15]	[15]	[15]	[15]	[15]	1,618[15]	23.1[15]			Sudan, The
3.9	4.0	2.9	3.0	11.4	11.7	2.0	2.0	[11]	[11]	38.0[11]	38.9[11]	17.7[17]	18.1[17]	Suriname
[14]	[14]	[15]	[15]	[15]	[15]	[15]	[15]	[15]	[15]	54[15]	19.9[15]			Swaziland
278	6.3	310	7.0	606	13.7	330	7.5	204	4.6	1,423	32.2	88[17]	2.0[17]	Sweden
226	7.0	199	6.1	603	18.6	303	9.3	271	8.4	420	12.9	26[12]	0.8[12]	Switzerland
386	15.5	158	6.3	258	10.4	23	0.9	[11]	[11]	559[11]	24.4[11]			Syria
389	4.0	431	4.5	1,399	14.5	223	2.3	1,410	14.6	616	6.4	196[17]	2.0[17]	Taiwan
[14]	[14]	[15]	[15]	[15]	[15]	[15]	[15]	[15]	[15]	1,353[15]	12.4[15]	1,691[17]	6.1[17]	Tanzania
763	2.7	698	2.5	3,197	11.4	[1]	[1]	[1]	[1]	3,147[1]	11.3[1]			Thailand
21[25]	2.3[25]	21[25]	2.3[25]	105[25]	11.6[25]	2[25]	0.2[25]	[11]	[11]	64[11,25]	7.1[11,25]	50[24,25]	5.6[24,25]	Togo
—	—	—	0.9	—	3.0	—	—	0.1	10.0	0.4	55.2	0.1	14.8	Tokelau
1.7	7.2	1.2	4.8	1.6	6.6	0.5	1.9	[11]	[11]	5.5[11]	22.6[11]	2.4	10.0	Tonga
94[27,65]	19.8[27,65]	31[27]	6.5[27]	95[27]	20.1[27]	[1]	[1]	[1]	[1]	142[1,27]	30.2[1,27]	—	—	Trinidad and Tobago
237	11.1	87	4.1	154	7.2	13	0.6	130	6.1	212	9.9	446[17]	20.9[17]	Tunisia
735	4.0	817	4.4	1,855	10.1	401	2.2	[11]	[11]	2,584[11]	14.0[11]	2,265[17]	12.3[17]	Turkey
0.3	9.7	0.1	3.7	0.1	4.3	—	1.0	0.7	24.8	0.5	17.1	0.7[17]	24.0[17]	Turks and Caicos Islands
0.2	5.6	0.1	2.7	0.1	2.4	—	0.3	0.2	4.4	0.2	4.2	3.1[33,72]	77.5[33,72]	Tuvalu
[14]	[14]	[15]	[15]	[15]	[15]	[15]	[15]	[15]	[15]	797[15]	11.3[15]			Uganda
11,955	9.1	12,048	9.2	10,334	7.9	674	0.5	1,987	1.5	23,812	18.2	2,106	1.6	U.S.S.R.
221	24.8	66	7.4	121	13.6	28	3.1	[11]	[11]	318[11]	35.7[11]			United Arab Emirates
1,559	5.6	1,503	5.4	5,061	18.1	2,610	9.4	2,358	8.5	5,417	19.4	2,905[12]	10.4[12]	United Kingdom
8,256	6.8	6,641	5.5	25,021[13]	20.6[13]	13,039	10.7	18,991[74]	15.6[74]	20,346[13]	16.7[13]	959[75]	0.8[75]	United States
63	5.4	59	5.0	137	11.7	42	3.6	[11]	[11]	362[11]	30.9[11]	99[23]	8.5[23]	Uruguay
1.1	2.2	1.3	2.6	2.2	4.3	0.3	0.6	[11]	[11]	5.5[11]	10.7[11]	0.3	0.6	Vanuatu
590	9.3	396	6.3	1,210	19.1	321	5.1	[11]	[11]	1,647[11]	26.1[11]	95[24]	1.5[24]	Venezuela
545	1.8	188	0.6	483	1.6	[1]	[1]	[1]	[1]	9,124[1]	30.1[1]			Vietnam
3.7	9.7	2.8	7.4	9.0	23.8	2.6	6.7	4.1	10.8	9.2	24.2	2.3[12]	6.2[12]	Virgin Islands (U.S.)
[14]	[14]	—	1.2	0.1	1.5	[1]	[1]	[1]	[1]	0.4[1]	12.5[1]			Wallis and Futuna
40.8	23.5	8.2	4.7	23.1	13.3	[16]	[16]	21.0	12.1	8.2[16,44]	4.7[16,44]	6.6[12]	3.8[12]	West Bank
...	...	...	...	...	...	...	...	...	...	...	...	...	...	Western Sahara
2.3	5.5	1.4	3.3	1.8	4.4	1.3	3.1	1.8	4.4	6.4	15.4	0.3	0.6	Western Samoa
39	7.0	32	5.8	47	8.6	0.6	0.1	[11]	[11]	106[11]	19.3[11]	—	—	Yemen (Aden)
122	8.2	76	5.1	202	13.5	8	0.5	[11]	[11]	120[11]	8.0[11]			Yemen (Şan'ā')
689	7.4	445	4.8	828	8.8	205	2.2	[11]	[11]	1,585[11]	16.9[11]	714[17]	7.6[17]	Yugoslavia
[14]	[14]	[15]	[15]	[15]	[15]	[15]	[15]	[15]	[15]	2,035[15]	17.4[15]			Zaire
[14]	[14]	[15]	[15]	[15]	[15]	[15]	[15]	[15]	[15]	407[15]	18.3[15]			Zambia
[14]	[14]	[15]	[15]	[15]	[15]	[15]	[15]	[15]	[15]	622[15]	18.3[15]			Zimbabwe

[48] 1978. [49] Excludes Assam. [50] Mostly underemployed informal workers. [51] Finance, real estate includes mining, public utilities; construction; and transportation and communications. [52] 1977. [53] 1973. [54] Excludes foreign border workers. [55] Island of Mauritius only. [56] 1975. [57] Includes unemployed seasonal agricultural workers. [58] Includes unemployed seasonal nonagricultural workers. [59] 1966. [60] Excludes indigenous areas, former Canal Zone, and institutional households. [61] Citizens over age 10 involved in money-raising activities only. [62] Ages 18–64 (male) and ages 18–59 (female). [63] Mostly employed abroad. [64] Residents on St. Helena only. [65] Construction includes public utilities. [66] Excludes self-employed and domestic workers. [67] Wage earners only. [68] Excludes migrant workers in South Africa. [69] Ages 10–64. [70] February survey. [71] De facto indigenous population only. [72] Mostly workers in the noncash economy. [73] Ages 16–59 (male) and ages 16–54 (female). [74] Excludes armed forces overseas. [75] Unemployed not previously employed and persons whose last job was in the armed forces only.

Agriculture and land use

This table provides data on the structure of national agricultural sectors from the perspective of farms and farmland use. The data are taken mainly from national agricultural censuses and surveys, supplemented by reports of the United Nations Food and Agriculture Organization's (FAO's) *World Census of Agriculture*. Many of these national censuses, of course, are taken under guidelines established by the FAO for the *World Census of Agriculture* programs (the 1990 census is the fifth and will include national censuses taken during the decade 1986–95). It represents a cooperative effort by FAO member countries to collect agricultural data within a general framework that permits international harmonization of concepts and definitions; transfer of technical expertise; and increased effectiveness in the collection, analysis, publication, and policy-related use of such statistics. Some 92 countries participated in the 1980 round; more than 100 countries were expected to participate in the 1990 round.

All agricultural statistics are subject to quality-control problems, including errors or biases arising from such factors as incomplete or inaccurate lists of holdings, ambiguous questions, respondents who inadvertently or willfully give inaccurate information, failure to record data for all parts of fragmented holdings, respondents' misunderstandings of the definitions of land use and cropping methods, or a failure to report livestock temporarily absent from the holding on public or common pasture land or in transit. Frequently, subjects studied, classificational schemes, and definitions vary from the FAO guidelines (economic planners need different information about a commercial, high-technology, multicrop agricultural sector than they do for a family-subsistence, low-technology, one-crop sector). When a complete census of agriculture is impossible, a sample survey may be taken. This is a limited census of a predetermined number of carefully screened holdings. From these results, nationwide projections may be prepared, but these are often of uncertain reliability.

With respect to the first section of the table, number and size of farms, many countries impose a minimum size limit for holdings that may be covered in their census reports, and this cutoff, if not sufficiently low, can result in a substantial undercount of smaller holdings; conversely Soviet bloc nations often publish statistics only on state collective or cooperative farms and exclude privately held plots of land, even though in some instances these provide a significant fraction of agricultural output.

The land tenure statistics classify farms according to the rights under which the farmer holds the land. Owner-operated includes two types of ownership: outright ownership in which the holder has title and has the right to determine use and transfer of the land; and ownerlike possession in which the holder lacks the legal title but uses it under perpetual lease, hereditary tenure, or leases of 30 years or more with nominal, or no, rent.

Agriculture and land use

country	year	number of farms ('000)	average (ha)	under 1 ha	1–5 ha	5–10 ha	10–20 ha	20–50 ha	50–200 ha	over 200 ha	owner-operated individual/family	owner-operated corporate/state	owner-operated socialized/collective	rented (including share-croppers)	tribal/communal	other[b]
Afghanistan	1981	126[1]	3.5[1]	44.8[1]	35.2[1]	20.0[1]					55.1[1]			25.1[1]		19.8[1]
Albania	1987	0.4	1,205[2]									100.0				
Algeria	1986	899[3]	6.2[3]	1.1[3]	12.7[3]	15.8[3]	21.7[3]	25.6[3]	18.0[3]	5.1[3]	85.9			5.0		9.1
American Samoa	1980	1.3	1.8	49.2[4]	45.5[4]	4.9[6]			0.47							
Andorra																
Angola	1970	1,067	3.9	3.3	13.5	9.3	11.3	13.7	19.2	29.7	80.5	1.1	—		18.2	0.2
Anguilla																
Antigua and Barbuda	1984	2.3	2.1	61.7	33.8	2.9	0.6	0.6	0.4	—	32.1[9]	22.9[9]		40.5[9]		4.5[9]
Argentina	1974	510	399	19.4		8.2	9.5	16.7	25.1	21.1	73.8[9]	—		11.7[9]		14.5[9]
Aruba																
Australia	1985–86	173	2,834	0.7[10]	7.2[10]	5.2[10]	6.3[10]	11.9[10]	26.2[10]	42.6[10]	90.9	6.4	—			2.7
Austria	1980[11]	303	24.2	3.7	31.0	17.3	21.0	21.2	5.2	0.6	59.0	—	—	2.3	—	38.7
Bahamas, The	1978	4.2	8.5	55.2[4]	30.1[5]	12.3[6]		1.1[12]	0.4[13]	1.0[14]	74.9	0.6	—	4.0	—	20.5
Bahrain	1980	0.8	4.4	19.4	52.9	17.4	8.2	2.0	0.1		37.9	0.1	—	62.0	—	—
Bangladesh	1983–84	10,045	0.9	70.3	27.0[15]	2.5[16]	0.2[17]				53.2[18]	—	—	0.5[18]	—	46.3[18]
Barbados	1969	0.2	95.8	37.4		15.3	20.8	19.6	4.5		27.7[9,19]	—	0.8[9,19]	71.5[9,19]	—	—
Belgium	1986	97	14.2	69.4			16.7	8.6	4.4	0.9	43.6	56.4	—	—	—	—
Belize	1974	8.9	26.7													
Benin	1983															
Bermuda	1985	0.08	3.1													
Bhutan	1984	160	0.8	51.3[4,20]	42.9[5,20]	5.8[20,21]					80.0[22]					20.0[22]
Bolivia	1980	700	25.0[22]									0.6			99.4	
Botswana	1985	81.0	3.2	32.1	49.9	12.6	5.4				63.2			17.9		18.4[25]
Brazil	1985	5,835	64.5	11.1	28.6	13.2	14.0	15.6	12.4	4.9						
British Virgin Islands	1981	0.3														
Brunei	1964	6.3	2.6	44.1[4]	40.5[5]	15.5[21]										
Bulgaria	1987	2.2[27,28]	2,467[27,28]									84.6[9,28]		15.4[29]		
Burkina Faso																
Burundi	1983										2.4			5.2	59.5	32.9
Cameroon	1973	926	1.6	42.7	53.8	3.2	0.3	—	—	—						
Canada	1986	293	231	1.6[4]	3.4[5]	12.1[33]	29.7[34]	14.6[35]	38.6[36]		63.7[9]			36.3[9]		
Cape Verde	1979										90.0			10.0		
Cayman Islands	1984	0.2		—	5.0	80.0	—	10.0	3.0	2.0	0.3[9]			0.1[9]	98.6[9]	1.2[9]
Central African Republic	1974	283	1.7	32.2	65.2	2.5	0.8									
Chad	1973	366	2.6	19.7	69.5	10.0					84.0			7.2	8.8	
Chile	1976	306	94.1	16.0	32.5	13.4	12.3	11.8	9.2	4.8	52.3	1.0	—	22.0	—	24.7
China	1987	1,650[39]										10.0[10]	90.0[10]			
Christmas Island																
Cocos (Keeling) Islands																
Colombia	1971	1,177	26.3	22.8	36.7	13.6	10.0	8.5	6.3	2.1	68.7			5.8	4.1	21.4
Comoros	1982										91.7[9]	8.3[9]				
Congo	1986	143[3]	1.4[3]	37.3[3]	62.3[3]	0.5[3]	—									
Cook Islands	1975[40]	1.1	2.3													
Costa Rica	1973	82	38.3	23.3	25.5	11.2	10.8	15.2	10.7	3.3	97.9	1.7	—	0.1	—	0.3
Côte d'Ivoire	1975	550	5.0	9.5	54.4	24.9	9.4	1.7	0.1							
Cuba	1986	1.8[27]	1,047[27]									79.0		9.4		11.6[41]
Cyprus	1985	48.0	3.8	24.4	56.8	15.0	2.9	0.9						0.6		
Czechoslovakia	1980	1,391	8.1	89.9[42]	9.9[43]				0.04[44]	0.2[45]	6.0[9]	30.8[9]	63.2[9]			
Denmark	1987	87	32.2	3.0		16.0	25.0	39.0	17.0							
Djibouti	1979	2.8	0.4	c. 100												
Dominica	1986										53.2	18.5	4.5	1.6	—	17.4
Dominican Republic	1981	385	6.3	16.0	65.7	8.5	5.4	2.6	1.5	0.3	70.3	0.3	—	7.7	7.4	14.3
Ecuador	1974	517	15.4	27.8	38.8	10.6	8.0	8.2	5.6	0.9						
Egypt	1984	3,481	0.7	95.3[46]	2.5[47]	2.2[48]			0.1[49]							
El Salvador	1970–71	271	5.4	48.9	37.9	5.8	3.4	2.6	1.2	0.2	41.5			28.2	6.3	24.1
Equatorial Guinea																
Ethiopia	1976–77	4,893	1.4	49.9	46.5	3.4	0.2				98.4	1.6				
Faeroe Islands									3.2	96.8	80.6		10.8	2.2		
Falkland Islands	1988	0.09	13,089													
Fiji	1978–79	66	4.2	64.3	20.6	8.1	3.7	2.1	1.2			3.5			95.1	1.4	

Farms classed as owner-operated are divided into individual and family, corporate or state, and socialized or collective proprietorships. Rented includes sharecropping; communal/tribal includes types of customary or traditional arrangements in which title or goods do not change hands. "Other" usually includes farms held under multiple forms of tenure.

Statistics on types of farms by commodities produced refer to FAO categories. The terms "mainly crops" and "mainly livestock" indicate that more than half of the for-sale production was that indicated.

The section on technology provides some principal measures of the extent to which modern technology plays a role in the farm activities of each country (although, of course, irrigation may employ technology developed in ancient times). Ratios referred to area mean area of "arable" (cultivated and cultivable) land, roughly "cropland," less area of permanent crops (see below).

The classification of farmland by economic use is also subject to differing treatment internationally. For purposes of this table, "cropland" comprises: (1) land under temporary crops (those requiring replanting after each harvest), (2) land under permanent crops (those *not* requiring replanting, including tree, bush and shrub, and vine crops), and (3) land temporarily (less than five years) fallow (unused, but capable of being returned to cultivation with no special preparation). "Meadows and pas-tures" includes land (both permanent and temporary use) whose principal purpose is the raising of animal fodder or forage. "Woodland and forest" includes both natural and planted tracts of timber, whether harvested or not. "Other" comprises: (1) mixed and multiple use lands, (2) residue of farmland holdings not classifiable according to categories listed above (including areas of farm buildings, roads, ornamental gardens, flooded land, wasteland, etc.), (3) land not classified by respondents in census, or (4) detail not distinguishable as one of categories above by reason of its summarization in a published source.

Measurements of area are given in hectares (1 hectare is equal to 2.471 acres). A kilogram (kg) is equal to 2.205 pounds (1 kg/ha = 0.89 lb/ac). The following notes further define the column headings:
a. All properties used wholly or partly for agricultural production. A property need not have agricultural land to be considered a farm; piggeries, hatcheries, and poultry batteries are farms because they engage in agricultural production, *i.e.*, raise livestock and produce livestock products.
b. All forms of tenure not included in the preceding categories. Includes land operated by schools, religious bodies, squatters, seasonally by nomads, and built-on, waste, and similar types of alienation.
... Not available, or no agricultural census or survey ever taken.
— None, less than half the smallest unit shown, or not applicable.

activity (% of farms)			technology (latest)				farmland use									country
							land in farms		land use (%)							
									cropland				mead-ows and pastures	wood-land and forest	other	
mainly crops	mainly live-stock	mixed/ other	tractors (per 1,000 ha)	electri-city (% of farms having)	irriga-tion (% of land irrig.)	artificial fertilizer (kg/ha)	total ('000 ha)	% of total land area	perma-nent crops	tempo-rary crops	fallow	total crop-land				
...	...	...	0.1	...	33	9	39,810	61.0	1.8	46.3	51.9	19.9	75.4	4.8	—	Afghanistan
...	...	...	18.0	...	69	175	1,111	40.0	17.4	82.6		64.3	35.7	...	...	Albania
...	...	...	12.3	...	5	38	39,663	16.7	7.5	53.9	38.7	18.9	78.5	—	2.5	Algeria
5.6	1.0	93.4	6.0	39.7	...	...	2.4	12.2	89.3		10.7	78.0	5.1	...	16.9	American Samoa
...	...	...	...	...	...	...	...	...	...	...	...	...	...	...	...	Andorra
...	...	...	3.4	...	89[8]	6	4,180	3.4	36.8	63.2	—	1.7	82.0	...	16.2	Angola
32.9	44.1	23.0	29.5	...	...	...	...	...	...	...	...	...	...	...	...	Anguilla
10.6	78.9	10.5	6.6	...	8	4	2.5	5.7	26.0	57.1	16.9	62.6	36.0	1.4		Antigua and Barbuda
...	...	...	...	...	...	...	203,345	73.1	...	...	...	10.6	78.9	4.8	5.7	Argentina
30.5	52.6	16.9	...	...	...	...	...	...	...	...	...	...	...	...	...	Aruba
...	...	...	7.1	...	4	24	485,200	63.2	0.3	99.7		10.0	90.0	...	...	Australia
...	...	...	227	...	—	255	7,326	87.4	6.6	87.4	6.0	21.3	26.0	41.5	11.2	Austria
...	...	...	9.6	...	10[8]	...	36.2	2.6	23.3	59.9	16.8	23.3	6.9	25.7	44.0	Bahamas, The
...	...	...	0.6	21.3	25	59	3.5	5.2	50.7	49.3	—	45.9	...	...	54.1	Bahrain
91.3[18]	8.7[18]	—	0.6	...	25	59	9,117	63.5	2.1[18]	96.3[18]	1.5[18]	88.7[18]	—	11.3[18]		Bangladesh
...	...	...	18.2	...	...	101	19.8	45.9	...	...	...	13.7	86.3			Barbados
...	...	...	150.1	...	—	523	1,383	45.3	0.9	98.8	0.3	52.1	47.8	...	0.1	Belgium
...	...	...	23.2	...	5	46	233	10.0	13.1	81.1	5.8	36.5	15.9	36.1	11.6	Belize
...	...	...	0.1	...	—	7	3,300	29.3	16.4	69.0	14.6	100.0	8.0	...	...	Benin
...	...	...	...	...	...	...	2.4	4.4	16.4	69.0	14.6	92.0	8.0	...	...	Bermuda
...	...	...	0.2	...	24	1	156	3.4	11.7	88.3		100.0	...	...	...	Bhutan
13.6	27.9	58.5	1.6	...	5	1.7[23]	84,060	76.3	19.3	80.7	—	1.4	49.4	49.2	...	Bolivia
80.0[26]	16.2[26]	3.8[26]	11.9	4.1[26]	4	43	343[24]	5.9[24]	—	100.0[24]	—	83.5[24]	...	...	...	Botswana
...	...	...	1.0	...	...	...	376,287	44.5	18.2[24]	66.9[24]	14.9[24]	15.8[24]	47.8[24]	24.2[24]	12.2[24]	Brazil
...	...	...	...	...	...	...	...	...	...	...	...	...	...	...	...	British Virgin Islands
68.5[30]	31.5[30]	—	24.3	...	33	128	16.4	2.8	78.0	22.0	—	54.8	0.1	16.4	28.7	Brunei
...	...	...	14.0	...	33	209	6,165	55.7	6.5	93.5		75.4	24.6	...[31]	...	Bulgaria
...	...	...	0.04	...	1	5	...	...	...	...	...	...	...	...	...	Burkina Faso
...	...	...	0.05	...	6	2	2,388	85.8	73.8		26.2	56.7	37.7	5.6	...	Burundi
...	...	...	0.2	...	—	60.0[32]	1,490	3.3	...	...	...	100.0	...	...	...	Cameroon
52.2	44.4	3.4	16.2	...	1.7	51	67,826	7.4	79.6		20.4	61.5	5.2	33.3		Canada
...	...	...	0.4	...	5	—	25[37]	6.2[37]	20.8[37]	79.1[37]		100.0[37]	...	...	...	Cape Verde
2.4	7.1	90.5	90.0	...	85[8]	1	...	...	...	...	...	...	...	...	...	Cayman Islands
...	...	...	0.1	...	—	2	491	0.8	11.8	88.2	—	100.0	...	...	...	Central African Republic
...	...	...	0.05	...	—	2	23,877[38]	45.8[38]	50.0[38]	50.0[38]		23.7[38]	76.3[38]	...	...	Chad
...	...	...	7.7	...	23	39	28,759	38.0	24.4	36.6	38.9	11.5	42.3	20.7	25.5	Chile
...	...	...	9.5	...	48	169	166,902	17.4	4.1	95.9		100.0	...	...	...	China
...	...	...	...	...	...	...	...	...	...	...	...	...	...	...	...	Christmas Island
...	...	...	...	...	...	...	...	...	...	...	...	...	...	...	...	Cocos (Keeling) Islands
...	...	...	9.0	...	13	69	30,993	27.0	30.6	27.6	41.8	24.7	56.4	...	18.9	Colombia
...	...	...	...	...	...	...	83	44.3	56.4	43.6		100.0	...	...	...	Comoros
...	...	...	1.1	...	1	7	226	0.7	14.8	85.2	—	100.0	...	...	...	Congo
...	...	...	134	...	...	...	...	...	55.9	21.9	22.2	100.0	...	...	...	Cook Islands
...	...	...	22.1	...	40	154	3,122	60.0	42.2	57.8	—	15.7	49.9	22.9	11.4	Costa Rica
...	...	...	1.4	...	2	12	2,753	8.6	65.9	34.1	—	100.0	...	...	...	Côte d'Ivoire
72.7	27.3	—	22.5	...	33	179	8,679	78.3	...	...	...	33.9	32.1	31.9	2.1	Cuba
34.3	24.4	41.3	131	...	30	115	210	35.6	34.7	54.3	11.0	74.9	—	25.1		Cyprus
51.6	23.1	25.3	28.0	100.0	5	337	6,924	54.1	2.6	97.4		75.3	24.7	...	...	Czechoslovakia
...	...	...	63.5	...	16	242	2,798	65.2	1.0	98.9	0.1	92.5	7.5	...	...	Denmark
...	...	...	...	...	...	...	...	...	...	...	...	...	...	...	...	Djibouti
...	...	...	12.9	...	...	159	20	26.3	...	...	...	...	...	...	...	Dominica
44.0	56.0	—	2.0	60.0	18	41	2,412	49.8	38.0	40.2	21.8	34.1	51.6	13.0	0.9	Dominican Republic
67.8	12.4	19.8	4.8	...	32	28	7,955	29.6	32.8	51.5	15.7	75.2	32.2	29.0	6.0	Ecuador
...	...	...	18.8	...	107	347	2,731[50]	3.0[50]	3.5[50]	96.5[50]		100.0[50]	...	...	...	Egypt
95.3	4.7	—	6.0	...	21	116	1,452	69.0	25.1	58.6	16.4	44.9	38.2	11.6	5.3	El Salvador
...	...	...	0.8	...	...	...	...	...	...	...	...	...	...	...	...	Equatorial Guinea
...	...	...	0.3	...	1	5	6,971	5.7	7.4	76.8	15.8	86.9	9.1	...	4.0	Ethiopia
—	100.0		...	...	...	...	1,217	100.0	—	—	—	—	100.0	—	—	Faeroe Islands
—	...	...	...	...	...	...	...	...	...	...	...	...	...	...	...	Falkland Islands
...	...	...	29.6	...	...	72	277	15.2	...	...	...	...	...	...	...	Fiji

Agriculture and land use (continued)

country	farms (latest census of agriculture)[a]														
	year	number of farms ('000)	size of holding									tenure (% of farms)					
			average (ha)	size class (%)							owner-operated			rented (including share-croppers)	tribal/communal	other[b]
				under 1 ha	1–5 ha	5–10 ha	10–20 ha	20–50 ha	50–200 ha	over 200 ha	individual/family	corporate/state	socialized/collective			
Finland	1986	211	60.6	7.3	26.6	25.2	24.7	14.4	—1.7—			—82.6—		17.4	—	—
France	1987	982	26.6[24]	7.1	16.9	10.9	17.8	30.5	—16.8—		65.2[10]			33.5[10]	—	1.2[10]
French Guiana	1986	2.3	5.4[2]	48.9	39.6	4.4	2.7	2.5	—2.0—		...	...	...	...	...	...
French Polynesia	...	...	...	...	...	...	...	...	...		81.8	—	—	0.3	5.3	12.5
Gabon	1975	71	1.0	68.0	—32.0—		—	—	—		...	...	...	...	...	...
Gambia, The	...	...	...	...	...	...	...	...	...		...	...	...	...	...	...
Gaza Strip	1968	...	...	...	...	...	...	...	...		...	...	...	...	...	...
Germany, East	1987[27]	4.3	...	...	...	...	...	...	...		—	10.7	89.3	...	...	...
Germany, West	1983	887	13.6	16.0	26.4	15.4	18.8	19.5	3.9		39.5	—	—	6.7	—	53.8
Ghana	1970	805	3.2	36.6	48.7	9.0	3.9	1.8	—		...	...	...	...	...	...
Gibraltar	...	...	...	...	...	...	...	...	...		...	...	...	...	...	...
Greece	1981	999	3.5	24.7	54.2	15.0	4.7	1.2	—0.2—		...	...	...	...	...	...
Greenland	...	...	...	...	...	...	...	...	...			—73.2—		14.1	—	12.7
Grenada	1981	8	1.7	88.3[51]	6.9[52]	3.3[53]	0.7	0.4[12]	—0.3[54]—		46.6[55]			19.1[55]	—	34.3[55]
Guadeloupe	1986	17	4.0	28.2	60.2	8.7	—2.8—				...	...	...	...	...	...
Guam	1987	0.4	15.1	42.2[4]	33.9[5]	—19.4[6]—		2.0[60]	—4.6[7]—		64.4		—74.0[62]—		4.3	—	31.3
Guatemala	1979	600	6.8	39.7[57]	49.8[58]	8.2[59]	2.0[60]	—0.2[61]—			28.6[9]			71.4[9]	—	6.3[62] 5.8[62] 13.9[62]
Guernsey	1988	0.106	18.0	6.7[63]	24.0[63]	23.1[63]	—46.1[63]—				...	...	...	...	...	...
Guinea	...	...	...	...	...	...	...	...	...		...	...	...	...	...	...
Guinea-Bissau	1961	87	3.0	13.4	73.3	10.0	3.0	0.3	—		...	...	...	...	...	...
Guyana	1964	...	...	...	...	—3.8—	...	...	66.6		...	90.0	...	—	...	10.0
Haiti	1971	617	1.4	58.7	37.5						...	...	25.0	—	8.4	—
Honduras	1974	195	13.5	17.3	46.6	14.5	9.8	7.8	3.3	0.8	99.7	0.1	—	—	0.2	—
Hong Kong	1986	11	0.3	97.5	2.3	0.1	—0.1—					—9.0—		77.0	—	14.0
Hungary	1981	798	8.3	...	...	...	...	...	...		6.8	13.3	74.5	—	—	—
Iceland	1981	7.0	...	15.7	9.3	11.7	23.7	35.8	—3.7—		92.7	—	—	1.2	—	6.1
India	1976–77	81,569	2.0	54.6	35.8	6.6	2.4	0.5	—0.1—		74.8[3]	—3	—3	3.2[3]	—3	22.1[3]
Indonesia	1987	19,501[50]	~1[50]	70.7[50]			—29.3[50]—				...	...	...	...	...	...
Iran	1982	...	...	...	...	...	...	...	...		52.5	—	—	40.9	—	6.6
Iraq	1971	591	9.7	20.2	29.3	21.4	18.5	9.0	1.3	0.3	...	...	...	...	...	...
Ireland	1986	279[26]	25.0[63]	2.7[26]	—37.8[26]—		—52.4[26]—		7.1[26]		72.4	—	—	27.6	—	...
Isle of Man	1987	0.8	59.7		—25.8[65]—		14.0[66]	18.2[12]	23.4[13]	18.5[14]	84.0	—	1.4	—	—	14.6
Israel	1981	52	11.3	26.5	57.6	8.3	4.0	—1.8—			81.5[26]	—	—	6.7[26]	—	11.8[26]
Italy	1982	3,269	7.2	18.0[67]	30.2[67]	37.7[67]	3.1[67]	9.2[67]	1.8[67]		99.5[70]	0.2[70]	—	—	—	0.3[70]
Jamaica	1978–79	184	2.9	32.5[68]	60.7[69]	4.8[53]	0.9	0.4[12]	0.3[13]	0.4[14]	79.4[26]	—	—	—	—	20.6[26]
Japan	1987	4,270	1.2	68.1	29.7	—2.2—					31.4[20]	—	—	68.6[20]	—	—
Jersey	1987	0.7	9.9	—45.0[71]—		17.6[72]	24.7[73]	—19.3[74]—			80.5	—	—	13.1	0.3	6.1
Jordan	1983	57	6.3	25.3	44.6	15.6	8.6	4.5	1.3	0.1	...	...	...	...	...	...
Kampuchea (Cambodia)	1962	840	3.6	30.7	54.9	10.4	—0.6—				...	...	...	...	...	...
Kenya	1976–79	2,750	2.5	65.5	27.3	2.7[76]	3.4	—4.4[77]—			...	...	...	...	...	...
Kiribati	...	...	...	...	...	...	...	...	...		...	...	...	...	...	...
Korea, North	...	...	...	...	...	...	...	...	...		...	...	...	...	...	...
Korea, South	1984	1,974	1.1	66.6	—33.4—						82.5[26]	—	—	17.4[26]	—	0.1[26]
Kuwait	1985–86	1.9	2.4	48.6[26]	25.4[26]	10.2[26]	8.7[26]	4.0[26]	3.1[26]	—	95.3	...	...	...	...	4.7
Laos	1983	...	...	...	...	...	...	...	...		...	...	...	...	...	...
Lebanon	1970	143	4.3	47.7	—44.5—		—6.5—		1.2	0.1	...	...	...	...	...	...
Lesotho	1986	207	2.0[26]	27.0[26]	67.5[26]	—5.5[26]—		—3.7—		—0.5—	40.0[9]	—	—	—	43.3[9]	16.7[9]
Liberia[78]	1971	122	3.0	52.8	31.0	12.0	—42.0[79,80]—		—13.0[79,81]—		...	...	...	...	...	...
Libya	1977	170	11.0	5.0[79]	—40.0[79]—		—42.0[79,80]—		—13.0[79,81]—		85.5	—	—	11.7	—	2.8
Liechtenstein	1985	0.45	8.7	30.8	27.9	13.4	13.2	13.6	—1.1—		...	...	...	...	...	...
Luxembourg	1988	4.1	34	8.6	17.4	8.8	10.8	28.7	—25.7—		50.8[9]		—0.5[9]—		48.7[9]	—	—
Macau	...	...	...	...	...	...	...	...	...		...	...	...	...	...	...
Madagascar	1984–85	1,544	1.3	65.0[10]	35.0[10]	—	—	—	—		...	...	...	...	...	...
Malawi	1980–81	1,136	1.2	54.9	40.1[83]		—5.0[84]—				53.2[26,86]	18.2[26,88]	—	19.6[26,86]	—	9.0[26,86]
Malaysia[85]	1980	920[86]	2.2[86,87]	...	...	...	...	...	...		...	...	...	...	...	...
Maldives	1985	...	...	...	...	...	...	...	...		96.8[90]	3.2	—	—	—	—
Mali	1982–83	562	4.0	20.1	54.1	17.4	—8.4—				16.0	—	—	70.4	—	13.6[41]
Malta	1983	12	1.1	67.8	30.0	2.0	—0.2—				...	...	...	...	...	...
Martinique	1986	12.5	4.9	49.6	38.5	7.3	—3.7—		—10.9—		...	...	...	...	...	...
Mauritania	1985	...	...	...	...	...	...	...	...		...	...	...	...	...	...
Mauritius	1980	32.5	1.1	61.3	36.2	1.9	0.3	0.2	—0.1—		95.8	—	—	4.2	—	—
Mayotte	1987	5.9[50]	1.7[75]	...	...	...	...	...	...		...		—97.6—		1.0	—	1.5
Mexico	1970[91]	2,848	49	23.5	39.4	21.1	8.8	2.7	2.9	1.5	...	...	...	...	...	...
Monaco	...	...	...	...	...	...	...	...	...		—	16.0[92]	84.0[92]	—	—	—
Mongolia	1985	0.3	385,000	...	...	...	...	...	...		...	...	...	...	...	...
Montserrat	1979	0.8	1.2	62.5[68]	28.0[93]	—9.5[94]—					14.6	—	—	84.4	—	1.0
Morocco	1985–86	1,900[75]	3.9[75]	—75.0[75]—		—25.0[75]—					0.2	0.1	—	—	99.7	...
Mozambique	1973	1,605	3.1	—89.7[95]—		—10.0[96]—		—0.3—			...	...	...	...	...	...
Myanmar (Burma)	1987–88	4,308[22]	2.3[22]	61.2[22,97]	24.7[22,98]	11.5[22,99]	2.5[22,66]	—0.8[7,22]—			...	...	...	...	...	...
Nauru	...	...	...	...	...	...	...	...	...		...	...	...	...	...	...
Nepal	1981–82	2,194	1.1	66.7	29.9	2.7	—0.7—				97.5		—		1.6	—	0.9
Netherlands, The	1987	132	15.3	11.2	22.1	16.4	22.2	24.2	—3.9—			—47.4—		11.2	—	41.3[41]
Netherlands Antilles	...	...	...	...	...	...	...	...	...		...	...	...	...	...	...
New Caledonia	1983–84	12.7	23	71.2[97]	13.8[101]	3.7	2.3	2.5	3.8	2.8	...	...	...	...	...	3.4[102]
New Zealand	1987	82.1	216	—12.5[107]—		10.3[102]	8.4[102]	—46.5[102]—		22.3[102]	85.7[102]	10.9[102]	—	—	—	—
Nicaragua	1984	...	...		—26.2—			—30.6[9]—		43.3[9]	62.3[9]	19.3[9]	18.6[9]	—	—	—
Niger	1980[2]	699	4.9	3.8	54.1	37.8	—4.3—				...	...	...	...	...	...
Nigeria	1971	...	...	92	7.8	0.2	—	—	—	—	100.0	—	—	—	—	—
Niue	1985	2.5	...	...	...	...	...	...	...		...	...	...	...	...	...
Norfolk Island	...	...	...	...	...	...	...	...	...		...	...	...	...	...	...
Norway	1987	98	9.4	10.8[97]	24.8[101]	27.9	25.9	9.8	—0.8—		97.4[9,19]	1.8[9,19]	—	—	—	0.8[9,19]
Oman	1978–79	65	1.3	...	...	...	...	...	...		90.8	—	—	1.4	—	7.8
Pacific Is., Trust Terr. of	1970	4.0	10.3	7.4	53.4	22.4	7.8	5.5	3.6	—	...	...	...	...	...	...
Marshall Islands	...	...	...	...	...	...	...	...	...		...	...	...	...	...	...
Micronesia, F.S. of	...	...	...	...	...	...	...	...	...		...	...	...	...	...	...

activity (% of farms)			technology (latest)				land in farms		land use (%) — cropland				land use (%)			
mainly crops	mainly livestock	mixed/ other	tractors (per 1,000 ha)	electricity (% of farms having)	irrigation works (% of land irrig.)	artificial fertilizer (kg/ha)	total ('000 ha)	% of total land area	permanent crops	temporary crops	fallow	total cropland	meadows and pastures	woodland and forest	other	country
52.3	—47.6—		99.5	100.0[26]	3	210	11,849	38.9	0.3[26]	97.6[26]	2.1[26]	20.4	1.1	58.0	20.5	Finland
...	...	...	83.7	...	7	301	33,649	61.8	7.4	90.6	2.0	53.6	34.1	8.2	4.1	France
...	...	...	18.0	...	...	201	13.5	0.2	18.7	69.8	11.5	48.0	52.0	...	...	French Guiana
...	...	...	31.0	...	...	15	...	...	...	...	...	...	...	...	...	French Polynesia
...	...	...	4.8	...	...	6	73.0	0.3	...	...	...	...	...	...	...	Gabon
...	...	...	0.3	...	7	24										Gambia, The
28.4	71.6	—	45.0	...	53	...	19.3	53.2	74.6	25.4	...	100.0	...	...	...	Gaza Strip
...	...	...	35.0	...	3	330	6,187	57.1	...	...	...	75.9	20.3	...	3.8	Germany, East
...	...	...	202	...	4	427	12,026	48.4	1.2[19]	97.8[19]	...	51.7[19]	32.6[19]	11.5[19]	4.2[19]	Germany, West
...	...	...	3.3	...	1	3	2,574	10.8	61.4	38.6	—	100.0	...	...	...	Ghana
...	...	...				4										Gibraltar
...	...	...	63.0	...	40.0	174	3,546	26.9	29.2	61.1	9.7	98.1	1.9	...	...	Greece
...	...	...	5.6	...	...	...	13.9	40.2	...	...	...	...	...	...	...	Greenland
...	...	...	44.2	...	9	231	90	52.8	27.4	68.9	3.6	33.3	32.2	34.5	...	Grenada
																Guadeloupe
72.2[56]	17.2[56]	10.5[56]	13.3	68.7	...	...	5.3	9.8	—51.2[20]—		48.8[20]	17.8[20]	34.3[20]	—47.9[20]—		Guam
...	100.0	—	3.0	...	6	52	4,147	38.1	27.6	—72.4—		42.0	27.3	27.2	3.4	Guatemala
—	100.0	—	0.1	...	5	...	2	30.2	—	100.0	—	5.8	94.2	...	...	Guernsey
...	...	...	0.2	...	...	...	169	4.7	...	...	...	...	...	...	...	Guinea
																Guinea-Bissau
...	...	...	7.4	...	27	25	10,652	26.2	...	...	...	8.4	91.6	...	...	Guyana
...	...	...	1.0	...	13	4	1,579	57.0	...	...	...	54.4	33.3	12.3	...	Haiti
56.3	37.3	6.4	2.2	...	6	13	2,630	23.5	15.4[19]	34.6[19]	50.0[19]	52.0[19]	48.0[19]	...	...	Honduras
...	...	...	1.0	...	43	100.0[23]	7.3	6.8	7.4	37.0	55.6	100.0	...	...	...	Hong Kong
...	...	...	10.6	...	3	254	7,413	79.7	11.8	86.1	2.1	71.7	17.3	...	11.0	Hungary
...	...	...	1,638	87.0[37]	...	3,151	...	...	...	...	...	...	...	...	...	Iceland
86.8[3]	—[3]	13.2[3]	4.2	...	25	51	163,343	49.7	—88.3[64]—		11.7[64]	96.0[64]	1.5[64]	—2.5[64]—		India
...	...	...	0.8	...	47	94	48,583	25.3	27.0	45.2	27.8	60.7	5.1	18.9	15.3	Indonesia
87.9	11.2	0.8	8.2	...	41	61	104,900	63.8	4.9	62.0	33.2	14.2	85.8	...	...	Iran
...	...	...	8.0	...	33	32	5,732	13.1	3.0	62.4	34.6	87.2	0.7	0.2	11.9	Iraq
...	...	...	165	...	...	784	5,692	82.6	0.5	99.5	...	9.5	69.5	—21.0—		Ireland
...	...	...	...	...	...	...	48	83.3	3.5	—96.5—		12.8	87.2	...	...	Isle of Man
...	...	...	73.6	...	81	220	584	28.2	22.0	—78.0—		70.5	19.1	10.4	...	Israel
...	...	...	144	...	33	171	23,632	78.4	26.3[67]	73.7[67]	...	52.4[67]	21.2[67]	17.1[67]	9.3[67]	Italy
...	...	...	14.6	...	16	44	603[70]	54.8[70]	22.2[70]	72.2[70]	5.6[70]	41.3[70]	21.6[70]	13.5[70]	23.6[70]	Jamaica
80.8[24]	—19.2[24]—		455	...	71	427	5,340	14.1	10.3	—89.7—		95.5	—	...	4.5	Japan
85.1[75]	14.9[75]	—	...	...	...	...	6.5	56.2	—98.9—		1.1	63.4		—36.6—		Jersey
58.2[56,67]	14.9[56,67]	26.9[56,67]	13.6	1.5	13	37	364	4.1	13.3	63.0	23.7	87.7	1.0	0.3	11.0	Jordan
...	...	...	0.5	...	3	1	2,984	16.5	94.9	3.5	1.6	96.1	...	...	...	Kampuchea (Cambodia)
...	...	...	4.4	...	2	46	6,922	11.9	11.5	—88.5—		71.0	23.8	1.9	3.3	Kenya
...	...	...	32.6	...	51	342	...	...	...	...	...	...	...	...	...	Kiribati
94.0[70]	0.4[70]	5.6[70]	9.9	10.3[72]	63	376	2,152	21.7	5.9	—94.1—		100.0	...	...	...	Korea, North
36.7	61.8	1.5	25.5	100.0	25	233	44.5	0.3	30.2	69.8	—	100.0	...	...	...	Korea, South
...	...	...	0.9	...	14	2	1,680	7.1	2.3	—97.7—		52.4	47.6	...	...	Kuwait
...	...	...														Laos
77.0[56]	8.1[56]	14.9[56]	14.4	...	41	119	275[24]	27.0[24]	36.7[24]	39.7[24]	23.6[24]	100.0[24]				Lebanon
37.3	—	62.7	5.3	...	...	12	372[26]	12.3[26]	—89.6[26]—		10.4[26]	98.8[26]	...	...	...	Lesotho
...	...	...	2.5	...	2	4	370[32]	3.8[32]	66.2[32]	33.8[32]	...	98.3[32]	...	1.7[32]	1.2[26]	Liberia[78]
...	...	...	17.0	...	13	26	8,800[32]	5.1[32]	—33.3[32]—		66.7[32]	20.5[32]	79.5[32]	...	...	Libya
23.9	61.6	14.5	107	...	...	...	3.7	23.1	1.6	—98.4—		30.4	66.0	2.5	1.1	Liechtenstein
26.4	53.6	20.0	160[82]	...	...	...	138	53.3	2.5	96.8	0.7	41.5	50.1	7.6	0.8	Luxembourg
...	...	...														Macau
22.1	...	77.9	1.1	...	35	3	2,044	3.5	15.4	84.6	—	100.0	...	...	...	Madagascar
...	...	...	0.6	...	0.8	23	1,332	14.1	0.2	99.8	—	94.8	...	5.2	...	Malawi
...	...	...	11.3[89]	...	33[89]	140[89]	4,100[20]	31.2[20]	84.8[20]	15.2[20]	—	100.0[20]	...	...	...	Malaysia[85]
...	...	...					19	63.5	...	...	...	...	...	...	...	Maldives
...	...	...	0.4	...	10	13	2,277	1.8	—	100.0	—	100.0	...	...	...	Mali
...	...	...	37.3	...	8	56	13.0	41.2	5.0	—95.0—		87.5		—12.5—		Malta
...	...	...	66.7	...	50	795	75.4[32]	71.1[32]	39.6[32]	60.0[32]	0.4[32]	36.9[32]	33.6[32]	10.0[32]	19.5[32]	Martinique
...	...	...	1.6	...	6	10	194	0.2	...	56.2	43.8	100.0	...	...	...	Mauritania
...	...	...	3.5	...	17	261	171	91.5	5.9	94.1	...	62.2	4.4	33.4	...	Mauritius
...	...	...	...	...	...	...	11.0	29.4	...	...	...	...	...	...	...	Mayotte
88.8	8.3	2.9	7.0	...	22	69	139,868	72.7	6.3	58.1	35.6	16.5	53.3	14.2	16.0	Mexico
...	...	...														Monaco
...	...	...	8.7	...	3	14	124,587	79.6	...	66.8	33.2	0.9	99.1	...	...	Mongolia
...	...	...	6.0	...	...	...	1.6[39]	15.3[39]	32.1[39]	67.9[39]	...	46.9[39]	53.1[39]	...	...	Montserrat
...	...	...	4.2	...	16	36	8,062	17.6	6.6	72.9	20.5	100.0	...	...	...	Morocco
...	...	...	2.0	...	4	1	13,626	17.8	—44.9—		55.1	55.0	45.0	...	...	Mozambique
...	...	...	1.1	...	11	20	12,560[100]	18.6	3.0	79.5	17.5	97.0	3.0	...	...	Myanmar (Burma)
...	...	...					...	...	...	...	...	...	...	...	...	Nauru
31.8	55.4	12.8	1.2	...	29	19	2,464	16.7	1.3	97.1	1.6	94.0	1.7	0.6	3.7	Nepal
...	...	...	215	...	60	786	2,014	48.1	—98.4—		0.6	45.9	54.1	...	...	Netherlands, The
...	...	...	2.5	...	...	...										Netherlands Antilles
...	...	...	128	...	...	20	293	15.8	51.7	34.8	13.5	6.5	93.5	...	...	New Caledonia
13.1	67.9	19.0	160	...	54	822	17,746	66.3	13.0[103]	87.0[103]	—	1.9[103]	98.1[103]	...	...	New Zealand
...	...	...	2.3	...	8	50	5,651	47.7	...	...	...	...	...	...	...	Nicaragua
...	...	...	0.5	...	1	1	3,407	2.9	...	...	...	...	...	...	...	Niger
...	...	...	0.4	...	3	10	34,290	37.1	—20.0—		80.0	31.4	27.5	41.1	...	Nigeria
96.0	—	4.0	10.0	...	—	80.0[23]	7.5	29.1	43.9	35.1	21.0	98.3	1.7	...	...	Niue
...	...	...					...	...	...	...	...	...	...	...	...	Norfolk Island
...	...	...	176	...	11	278	958	3.0	...	...	...	45.1	54.9	...	...	Norway
...	...	...	8.3	...	87	102	83	0.3	68.6	31.4	...	49.2		—50.8—		Oman
...	...	...	2.1	...	...	...	40	21.1	54.2	9.8	36.0	68.7	17.5	...	13.7	Pacific Is., Trust Terr. of Marshall Islands
...	...	...	...	...	...	...	...	...	...	...	...	...	...	...	...	Micronesia, F.S. of

Agriculture and land use (continued)

farms (latest census of agriculture)[a]; size class and tenure values are percentages (size class %; tenure % of farms).

country	year	number of farms ('000)	average (ha)	under 1 ha	1–5 ha	5–10 ha	10–20 ha	20–50 ha	50–200 ha	over 200 ha	owner-operated individual/family	corporate/state	socialized/collective	rented (incl. sharecroppers)	tribal/communal	other[b]
Northern Mariana Is.	1980	0.3	16.5	32.8[97]	34.1[98]			33.1[21]			75.6	...	—	12.4	...	12.0
Palau											64.1[9]	0.3[9]	—	35.6[9]		
Pakistan	1980	4,070	4.7	17.2	56.2	17.4	6.5	2.7			23.2	...	—	2.0	—	74.8[25]
Panama	1980	153	14.7	41.0	25.0	9.3	9.0	9.0	5.6	1.0	26.9[9,50]	71.0[9,50]	—	2.1[9,50]		
Papua New Guinea[104]	1985	0.8	483	26.8[50]					28.3[50]	44.9[50]	...	...	...	...		
Paraguay	1981	249	88	8.6	27.4	19.9	22.7	14.5	4.4	2.5	54.5	0.4	—	9.2	—	35.9[25]
Peru	1984	1,574	9.5	24.1	47.7	13.2	6.7	5.5	2.8		75.5	—	—	0.8	6.8	16.9
Philippines	1980	3,420	2.6	22.7	63.3	10.5	3.5				58.3	—	—	27.4	—	14.3
Pitcairn Island																
Poland	1986	3,952	4.8	52.0[97]	19.5[101]	17.5		10.9		0.1	76.5[9]	—	23.5[9]			
Portugal	1979	784	6.6	44.5	41.9	7.7	3.3	1.5	0.7	0.4	68.1	—	—	8.7	—	23.2
Puerto Rico	1987	20	17.2	48.7[105]		19.5[106]	16.7[107]	6.7[108]	8.3[54]		77.5			7.1	—	15.4
Qatar	1986	0.8[50]	42.5[50]	79.1[24,109]			20.9[24,110]				46.1[3]			22.5[3]	—	31.4[3]
Réunion	1981	21	3.6	50.9	41.6	5.3	1.8		0.3		...	13.7[9,102]	60.8[9,102]	—		25.5[9,10]
Romania	1987	4.2[27,102]	2,700[27,102]								50.9	—	—	1.4	—	47.7[41]
Rwanda	1984	1,112	1.2	56.8	26.8[111]	16.4[94]						—	—	100.0	—	
St. Helena	1983										46.8[9]	48.0[9]	—	5.2[9]		
St. Kitts and Nevis	1981										69.1	—	—	18.3	—	12.6
St. Lucia	1973–74	11	2.7	47.8[68]	44.9[69]	4.3[53]	1.8	0.5[12]	0.2[13]	0.8[14]						
St. Pierre and Miquelon																
St. Vincent	1985–86	8[55]	1.8[55]	48.0[55,68]	40.7[55,93]	8.5[98,55]	2.4[7,55]	0.5[8,55]			62.0[55]	—	—	8.8[55]	—	19.2[55]
San Marino	1975	0.7	7.0	21.3	47.8	24.7		5.1	1.1		39.9[9]	15.5[9]	—	29.9[9]	—	14.7[9]
São Tomé and Principe	1964	11.1	8.7	88.5	9.8	0.7	0.2	0.2	0.2	0.4	77.2	—	—	20.5	—	2.3
Saudi Arabia	1983	212	10.1	36.6	35.8	11.3	8.2	5.0	2.6	0.5	85.9	—	—	2.6	—	11.5
Senegal	1976	362	7.0	99.4						0.6	...	...	0.6	...	...	99.4
Seychelles	1977	4.9	1.5								93.6	—	—	6.4	...	...
Sierra Leone	1971	286	1.8	38.8	55.0	6.1			0.1		7.4	—	—	88.8	—	3.8
Singapore	1973	16	0.8	77.4	22.2	0.3	0.1								100.0	
Solomon Islands	1975[86]	92	1.0								99.9	0.1				
Somalia	1984	198	3.6													
South Africa	1978	72	1,193													
Bophuthatswana	1976															
Ciskei	1986															
Transkei	1976															
Venda	1976	53.3	9.3													
S.W. Africa/Namibia	1983										75.4			4.0	—	20.6
Spain	1982	2,375	18.7	26.4	37.1	14.0	10.2	7.1	3.9	1.3	77.1[3]	6.4[3]	0.1[3]	14.4[3]	—	2.0[3]
Sri Lanka	1982	1,817	1.1	77.5[4]	22.2[112]		0.1[113]	0.1[12]	0.1[54]		22.3	2.2		28.0	42.0	5.5
Sudan, The	1982			21.9[70]	61.2[70]	11.1[70]	3.6[70]	1.6[70]	0.3[70]	0.3[70]	20.2[70]	0.9[70]		49.5[70]	—	29.4[70]
Suriname	1981	22	7.5							1.4	86.1	—	—	3.4	—	10.5
Swaziland	1972	39	19.5	26.2	60.4	12.0				0.8	47.6	—	—	15.6	—	36.8[41]
Sweden	1988[114]	101	28.5		15.8[2]	19.9	21.7	27.7	14.1	0.9	36.2[24]	—	0.8[24]	58.5[24]	—	4.5[24]
Switzerland	1985	119	9.1	23.1	18.7	14.6	27.5	15.2	0.9		65.8[9,90]	1.8[9]	32.5[9]			
Syria	1987	485[32]	11.5[32]	51.0[32,109]			42.0[32,115]		6.2[32,116]	0.8[32,117]	93.5	—	—	6.5	—	—
Taiwan	1985	897	1.1	67.5[24]	30.3[24]	1.5[24]	0.4[24]	0.1[24]			87.3	—	—	3.6	—	9.1
Tanzania	1972	2,489	3.0	59.7	37.7	2.1	0.4	0.1		0.2	72.4	—	—	5.5	—	22.1
Thailand	1983	4,471	3.6	14.7	70.2[118]	15.1[119]					70.7[9]	—	—	21.1[9]	8.2[9]	—
Togo	1982–83	263	1.5	48.8	38.6[83]	12.7[84]							97.2			
Tokelau	1987	0.2	6.1													2.8
Tonga	1985	10.1	3.3	18.9	67.9	12.7	—	0.5								
Trinidad and Tobago	1982	30.6	4.3	35.1	50.7	9.6	4.1	—	0.4	0.1	52.1	—	—	36.5	—	11.4
Tunisia	1986										88.6	—	—	12.1	—	1.2
Turkey	1980	3,651	6.2	15.8	46.3	20.2	11.6	5.3	0.8						0.1	
Turks and Caicos Is.											99.9	—	—			
Tuvalu	1976	1.5	1.7												—	2.6[122]
Uganda	1964	1,171	3.9	20.7	59.8	11.2	8.3				97.4	—	—			
U.S.S.R.	1987	49.6[27]	12,300[27]	—	—	—	—	—	—	100.0[27]	—	46.2	53.8			
United Arab Emirates	1986–87	5.8[123]	2.5[123]									72.5[124]		27.5[124]		
United Kingdom	1987	254	67.9	5.6[97]	8.0[101]	12.6	16.5	25.2	26.3	5.8	75.2	12.7	—	11.6	—	0.5
United States	1982	2,241	180.0	8.4[68]		20.0[6]		31.8[125]	23.5[126]	16.3[127]	59.1[24]			17.3[24]	—	23.6[24]
Uruguay	1986	57	280.5	—	9.0	13.0	12.8	16.0	22.8	26.3	65.3[24]	34.7[24]	—	—	—	—
Vanuatu	1983–84	27	6.9								61.5[10]	...	...	6.1[10]	—	31.3[10,2]
Venezuela	1984–85	381	82.0	8.3	36.3	15.7	13.0	10.4	9.3	7.1						
Vietnam	1983										75.3	—	—	8.6	—	16.1
Virgin Islands (U.S.)	1987	0.3	27.0	30.0[95]	30.3[128]	12.0	13.9	6.0	3.7[129]	4.1[130]						
Wallis and Futuna	1983										7.1[6]			6.4	—	22.0
West Bank	1965	55	3.4	49.8	34.4	10.6	4.0	1.0	0.2	0.2						
Western Sahara	1983														86.0	14.0
Western Samoa	1975												44.3[27]	55.7[27]		
Yemen (Aden)	1977	0.08[27]	604[27]											9.4[9]	—	0.3[9]
Yemen (Şan'ā')	1977–83	591	2.3	57.5	30.9	7.4	3.3	0.8	0.1		90.3[9]	—	0.1			
Yugoslavia	1981	2,680	4.2	30.4	48.4	16.4	3.8	0.9	0.1		99.9	—	0.1			
Zaire	1970	2,538	2.3	41.6	57.3	1.0	0.2				4.2	0.1	...		95.6	0.1
Zambia	1971	768	3.1	50.5	45.2		3.8		0.5					2.0		
Zimbabwe	1974	765	38.7	16.7[65]				52.8[131]	29.8[132]	0.7[81]					98.0	

[1]1967. [2]Cultivated area only. [3]1973. [4]Less than 1.2 hectares. [5]1.2 to 4.0 hectares. [6]4.0 to 20 hectares. [7]20 hectares or more. [8]Percent of farms having irrigation. [9]Based on area, not number, of holdings. [10]1971. [11]Excludes holdings without land. [12]20 to 40 hectares. [13]40 to 81 hectares. [14]81 hectares or more. [15]1.0 to 4.0 hectares. [16]4.0 to 10.1 hectares. [17]10.1 hectares or more. [18]1977. [19]1979. [20]1982. [21]4.0 hectares or more. [22]Family farms only. [23]Percent of farms using artificial fertilizer. [24]1980. [25]Almost all squatters. [26]1970. [27]State farms and cooperatives only. [28]Agro-Industrial Complexes (state enterprises) only. [29]"Private" plots for which rent is paid. [30]Based on value of output by sector. [31]Forestry enterprises not managed by Agro-Industrial Complexes. [32]1982. [33]4.0 to 28 hectares. [34]28 to 100 hectares. [35]100 to 160 hectares. [36]160 hectares or more. [37]Irrigated land only. [38]1968. [39]1984. [40]Rarotonga only. [41]Owned and rented holdings. [42]Less than 0.5 hectare. [43]0.5 to 50 hectares. [44]50 to 1,000 hectares. [45]1,000 hectares or more. [46]Less than 2.1 hectares. [47]2.1 to 4.2 hectares. [48]4.2 to 21 hectares. [49]21 hectares or more. [50]1983. [51]Less than 2.0 hectares. [52]2.0 to 4.0 hectares. [53]4.0 to 10 hectares. [54]4.0 hectares or more. [55]1972. [56]Commercial farms only. [57]Less than 0.7 hectare. [58]0.7 to 7.1 hectares. [59]7.1 to 45 hectares. [60]45 to 452 hectares. [61]452 hectares or more. [62]Excludes holdings of 0.04 hectare (500 square metres) or less. [63]1974. [64]Excludes state of Punjab. [65]Less than 8.0 hectares. [66]8.0 to 20 hectares. [67]1975. [68]Less than 0.4 hectare. [69]0.4 to 4.0 hectares. [70]1969. [71]Less than 4.5 hectares. [72]4.5 to 9.0 hectares. [73]9.0 to 18 hectares. [74]18 hectares or more. [75]1978. [76]5.0 to 8.0 hectares. [77]8.0 hectares or more. [78]Excludes temporary rangeland available for agricultural use to subsistence

mainly crops	mainly live-stock	mixed/ other	tractors per 1,000 ha	electri-city (% of farms having)	irriga-tion (% of land irrig.)	artificial fertilizer (kg/ha)	total ('000 ha)	% of total land land	perma-nent crops	tempo-rary crops	fallow	total crop-land	mead-ows and pastures	wood-land and forest	other	country
...	...	...											...	...	...	Northern Mariana Is.
...	...	...														Palau
			8.6		79	73	19,109	24.0		—83.7—	16.3	93.8		0.6	5.6	Pakistan
			14.1	0.5[10]	7	45	2,259	29.3	21.6	43.3	35.0	24.6	57.4	15.6	2.4	Panama
			37.1			22	386	0.8	100.0			33.7	26.4		39.9	Papua New Guinea[104]
33.0	—67.0—		5.0		3	5	21,941	53.9	4.2	76.6	19.2	12.6	47.5	38.5	1.4	Paraguay
4.9	93.0	2.1	4.6	6.5	36	20	14,893	11.6	24.1	75.9	—	27.1	47.5	19.8	5.6	Peru
98.2	1.5	0.3	4.4		33	36	9,034	30.1	57.5	42.5	—	86.3	6.8	—6.9—		Philippines
...	...	...														Pitcairn Island
			72.1		1	230	18,804	60.1	1.6	—98.4—		86.7	13.3			Poland
61.0	33.4	5.6	38.4		31	87	5,183	56.1	26.1	44.6	29.3	52.6	3.2	34.5	9.7	Portugal
99.7	0.3	—	30.0		57		349	39.3		—70.4—	29.6	28.0	46.4	19.1	6.6	Puerto Rico
			21.8		100	145	65	5.7	36.1	63.9		6.5			93.5	Qatar
			34.0		10	259	74	29.1	5.0	86.3	8.7	61.2	11.6	13.8	13.4	Réunion
			18.2		33	129	15,094	63.6	4.0	96.0		70.8	29.2			Romania
			0.1		1	1	1,350	51.3		—85.6—	14.4	63.7	10.6	5.2	20.5	Rwanda
			4.0				4.0	12.9		—100.0—		50.0	50.0			St. Helena
			27.0				12	45.3	31.5	—68.5—		58.1		—41.9—		St. Kitts and Nevis
25.0	—75.0—		17.0		6		29	47.3	68.5	—31.5—		57.9	10.2	26.4	5.5	St. Lucia
...	...	...														St. Pierre and Miquelon
			5.9		2		17.9	34.8	64.3	16.1	19.6	84.3	15.7			St. Vincent
			3		6		4.7	76.5	60.9	6.5	32.6	69.2	6	8.2	16.4	San Marino
			1.6		38	293	96	100.0	99.4	—0.6—		38.3		59.7	2.0	São Tomé and Príncipe
			0.1		3	4	2,135	1.0	4.1	18.7	77.2	88.5		—11.5—		Saudi Arabia
							11,338	59.1	0.1	—99.9—		22.4	77.6			Senegal
1.8	32.4	65.8	38.0				7.5	27.8	89.6	—10.4—		100.0				Seychelles
50.3	—49.7—		0.3		2	2	2,732	38.1	20.7	—79.3—		19.3	80.7			Sierra Leone
12.5	6.2	81.3	29.0		100	1,043	5.6[39]	9.0[39]	75.0	25.0		66.7		33.3		Singapore
43.4	—56.6—						93	3.4	40.0	45.2	14.8	100.0				Solomon Islands
20.0	60.0	20.0	2.3		12	4										Somalia
			13.9		9	66	85,447	70.2	5.9	—94.1—		11.9	79.7	1.3	7.1	South Africa
					1		3,839	94.8		87.1		2.4	97.6			Bophuthatswana
					3		770	95.3	9.7	80.3		10.0	90.0			Ciskei
							622	14.9				100.0				Transkei
			0.3		1	4.8	500	64.9	25.4	63.6	11.0	9.2	90.8			Venda
			4.4	0.6			662	0.8	0.3	—99.7—						S.W. Africa/Namibia
			43.6		21	82	44,312	87.8	23.8	55.8	20.4	40.9	12.5	21.7	24.9	Spain
			31.3		58	104	2,009	30.6	56.4	43.6		86.0	1.0	2.7	8.8	Sri Lanka
			1.6		15	7	31,500	13.3	0.8	88.7	10.5	23.8	76.2			Sudan, The
33.0[70]	12.5[70]	54.5[70]	30.7		100	198	165	1.0	15.0	53.0	32.0	40.4	23.1	19.1	17.4	Suriname
39.7	—60.3—		20.6		39	46	766,775	44.6	2.0	81.1	16.9	19.7	60.6	12.0	7.7	Swaziland
25.6[104]	60.6[104]	13.8[104]	62.0		4	141	8,254	20.1		90.2	9.8	34.8	4.0	50.3	10.9	Sweden
35.5[24]	—64.5[24]—		276		6	436	1,203	29.1	6.7	66.2	27.1	36.1	53.4	10.5		Switzerland
			10.5		13	41	6,133	33.1		—71.8—	28.2	91.8			8.2	Syria
					38	400[75]	995	27.7	8.6[75]	91.4[75]		67.0[75]	—33.0[75]—			Taiwan
56.2	—43.8—		4.5		4	8	7,545	8.5	19.1	72.5	8.4	49.8	10.2	24.7	15.3	Tanzania
			7.6		22	21	15,916	31.0	10.6	—89.4—		94.0	—4.3—		1.7	Thailand
95.0	5.0		0.2		1	7	406	7.1	17.3[18]	—82.7[18]—		71.0[18]	29.0[18]			Togo
8.4[120]	—	91.6[120]	1.0	85.0		3.0	1.2	100.0	99.9		0.1	98.4	0.1	1.6		Tokelau
			6.7			2	33	44.5		—62.7—	37.3	81.2	6.7	10.1	1.9	Tonga
63.7[121]	—36.3[121]—		35.4	40.7	30	60	132	25.8	55.9	—44.1—		62.3	4.4	6.1	27.2	Trinidad and Tobago
11.5	2.5	86.0	8.3		9	19	4,696	30.4	38.7	38.0	23.3	100.0				Tunisia
			25.5		9	54	30,732	39.9	17.5	71.0	11.5	85.4	7.3	1.7	5.4	Turkey
...	...	...														Turks and Caicos Is.
...	...	...														Tuvalu
—	—	100.0	0.8				2,262	11.3	29.8	70.2	—	100.0				Uganda
			12.0		9	109	608,000	27.2		—92.2—	7.8	37.5	61.6	—0.9—		U.S.S.R.
					56	221	17.5[75]	0.2[75]	64.8[75]	18.2[75]	17.1[75]	97.6[75]		1.3[75]	1.1[75]	United Arab Emirates
43.4	52.6	4.0	75.0	66.2	2	357	18,619	77.3	0.7	98.7	0.6	37.6	59.4	1.7	1.2	United Kingdom
			24.9		10	94	416,707	43.7	1.5	86.4	12.1	45.1	42.4	8.8	3.7	United States
37.1[24]	58.7[24]	4.2[24]	23.3		7	42	15,882	90.7	3.1	—96.9—		8.8	85.3	4.2	1.7	Uruguay
92.2	7.2	0.6	2.9				183	15.0	62.5	3.0	34.5	84.9	15.1			Vanuatu
27.6	9.0	63.4	14.5		10	127	31,278	34.3	19.0	59.0[10]	22.0[10]	13.2[10]	57.0[10]	22.8[10]	7.0[10]	Venezuela
			6.1		30	55	7,857	24.1	8.4	—91.6—		65.4	34.6			Vietnam
48.3	40.8	10.9	48.0	85.4			7.2	20.9	18.3	13.7	68.0	10.7	75.3	10.3	3.7	Virgin Islands (U.S.)
...	...	...	14.1[20]		5		5.0	25.0	80.0	—20.0—		100.0				Wallis and Futuna
							185[24]	31.4[24]	62.2[24]	37.8[24]	—	100.0[24]				West Bank
			0.6				5,002	18.8					100.0			Western Sahara
			27.4		52	14	70	24.8	71.2	28.8		93.8	6.2			Western Samoa
							108	0.3	3.9	85.1	11.0	95.7	4.3			Yemen (Aden)
35.5[9,120]	56.9[9,120]	7.6[9,120]	1.7		20	12	1,351	0.1	6.7	69.7	23.6	98.8			1.2	Yemen (Ṣan'ā')
12.7[70]	—87.3[70]—		144		2	128	14,208	55.5	7.4	71.6	21.0	69.2	30.2	—	0.6	Yugoslavia
92.3	—9.7—		0.4		—	1	5,897	2.6	7.7	—92.3—		70.6	20.1	2.0	7.3	Zaire
15.8	9.7	74.5	0.9		—	15	938	1.3	4.5	—95.5—		14.2	38.1		47.7	Zambia
1.8[9,75]	26.7[9,75]	71.5[9,75]	7.6		7	62	29,620	76.6	2.5	—97.5—		34.5	65.7			Zimbabwe

farms. [79]Western Libya only. [80]10 to 100 hectares. [81]100 hectares or more. [82]1988. [83]1.0 to 3.0 hectares. [84]3.0 hectares or more. [85]Peninsular Malaysia except as noted; excludes shifting cultivators. [86]Smallholder farms only. [87]Average size of estate farm is 400 hectares. [88]Based on total number of households on estates. [89]All Malaysia. [90]Includes rented farms. [91]Includes 1,828,000 holdings on 22,700 communes (ejidos). [92]In area, state lands constitute 80.6% of Mongolia's farmland, agricultural cooperatives 19.4%. [93]0.4 to 2.0 hectares. [94]2.0 to 8.0 hectares. [95]Less than 3.0 hectares. [96]3.0 to 50 hectares. [97]Less than 2.0 hectares. [98]2.0 to 4.0 hectares. [99]4.0 to 8.0 hectares. [100]Within demarcated cultivation areas only. [101]1.0 to 3.9 hectares. [102]1985. [103]1987. [104]Large holdings only. [105]1.0 to 3.9 hectares. [106]3.9 to 7.9 hectares. [108]9.7 to 40 hectares. [109]Less than 7.0 hectares. [107]7.0 hectares or more. [110]1.0 to 2.0 hectares. [111]1.0 to 2.0 hectares. [121]1.2 to 12 hectares. [112]3 to 20 hectares. [114]Holdings of arable land only. [115]7.0 to 25 hectares. [116]25 to 300 hectares. [117]300 hectares or more. [118]1.0 to 6.4 hectares. [119]6.4 hectares or more. [120]1976. [121]1963. [122]4,600,000 farm households work small plots constituting 8% of total farmland. [123]Abu Dhabi only. [124]Excludes Northern Ireland. [125]20 to 72 hectares. [126]72 to 202 hectares. [127]202 hectares or more. [128]3 to 10 hectares. [129]100 to 260 hectares. [130]260 hectares or more. [131]8.0 to 16 hectares. [132]16 to 100 hectares.

Crops and livestock

This table provides comparative data for selected categories of agricultural production for the countries of the world. The data are taken mainly from the United Nations Food and Agriculture Organization's (FAO) annual *Production Yearbook*.

The FAO depends largely on questionnaires supplied to each country for its statistics, but, where no official or semiofficial responses are returned, the FAO makes estimates, using incomplete, unofficial, or other similarly limited data. And, although the FAO provides standardized guidelines upon which many nations have organized their data collection systems and methods, persistent, often traditional, variations in standards of coverage, methodology, and reporting periods reduce the comparability of statistics that *can* be supplied on such forms. FAO data are based on calendar-year periods; that is, data for any particular crop refer to the calendar year in which the harvest (or the bulk of the harvest) occurred.

In spite of the often tragic food shortages in a number of countries in recent years, worldwide agricultural production is probably more often underreported than overreported. Many countries do not report complete domestic production; the Soviet bloc, for example, excepting Czechoslo-vakia, publishes, initially at least, statistics only for collective or cooperative production and excludes the production of privately held plots of land that in some instances represent a significant part of total agricultural production. Some countries report only crops that are sold commercially and ignore crops produced for family or communal subsistence.

Methodological problems attach to much smaller parts of the agricultural whole, however. The FAO's cereals statistics relate, ideally, to weight or volume of crops harvested for dry grain (excluding cereal crops used for grazing; harvested for hay; or harvested green for food, feed, or silage). Some countries, however, collect the basic data they report to the FAO on sown or cultivated areas instead and calculate production statistics from estimates of yield. Millet and sorghum, which in many European and North American countries are used primarily as livestock or poultry feed, may be reportable by such countries as animal fodder only, while the U.S.S.R. and many African and Asian nations use the same grains for human consumption and report them as cereals. Statistics for tropical fruits are frequently not compiled by producing countries, and coverage is not uniform, with some countries reporting only commercial fruits and others including those consumed for subsistence as well. Figures on

Crops and livestock

country	grains production ('000 metric tons) 1979–81 avg	grains production 1988	grains yield (kg/hectare) 1979–81 avg	grains yield 1988	roots and tubers[a] production ('000 metric tons) 1979–81 avg	roots production 1988	roots yield (kg/hectare) 1979–81 avg	roots yield 1988	pulses[b] production ('000 metric tons) 1979–81 avg	pulses production 1988	pulses yield (kg/hectare) 1979–81 avg	pulses yield 1988	fruits[c] production ('000 metric tons) 1979–81 avg	fruits production 1988	vegetables[d] production ('000 metric tons) 1979–81 avg	vegetables production 1988
Afghanistan	4,360	4,408	1,340	1,350	283	355	14,863	16,136	38	40	1,624	1,633	786	781	704	370
Albania	916	1,024	2,500	2,925	112	137	6,967	9,161	23	25	387	413	156	216	193	155
Algeria	1,958	1,771	656	671	540	950	6,878	8,482	52	70	431	435	1,197	1,190	882	1,595
American Samoa	...	...	...	...	3	4	4,613	5,765	...	...	...	...	2	1	...	...
Andorra	...	...	...	...	...	...	...	...	...	...	...	...	...	...	...	...
Angola	379	352	533	345	2,070	2,200	4,050	4,194	42	40	385	364	432	425	224	227
Anguilla	...	...	...	...	...	...	4,673	5,652	...	...	...	...	9	10	1	3
Antigua and Barbuda	—	—	1,809	2,000	—	—	...	...	...	...	...	...	...	...	...	...
Argentina	24,457	21,597	2,183	2,443	2,328	2,707	14,087	17,476	239	241	918	892	6,259	6,321	2,279	2,675
Aruba[4]	...	...	...	...	...	...	...	...	...	...	...	...	...	...	...	...
Australia	21,139	22,081	1,321	1,559	844	1,065	23,445	27,042	141	855	889	923	2,148	2,281	1,052	1,396
Austria	4,391	4,833	4,130	4,976	1,356	901	25,387	26,416	2	1	1,987	2,270	950	856	666	506
Bahamas, The	1	1	1,142	1,262	2	2	8,998	9,297	1	1	1,238	1,302	13	14	27	27
Bahrain	...	...	...	...	—	—	19,048	13,800	...	...	...	...	44	49	18	12
Bangladesh	20,982	22,989	1,939	2,159	1,705	1,833	10,062	10,510	228	188	686	737	1,304	1,373	1,061	1,212
Barbados	2	2	2,538	2,500	11	8	11,653	8,281	1	1	1,209	1,254	3	3	10	6
Belgium[5]	2,069	2,298	4,861	6,211	1,468	2,000	39,246	40,000	7	16	3,080	3,827	382	409	925	1,400
Belize	27	30	1,928	1,776	3	4	20,000	21,875	1	3	525	743	72	131	3	4
Benin	367	571	697	862	1,363	1,611	7,449	8,636	34	52	445	572	142	158	121	178
Bermuda	...	...	...	...	1	1	9,041	17,672	...	...	...	...	1	—	2	2
Bhutan	159	194	1,439	1,594	40	69	6,767	8,675	2	4	592	722	29	56	11	10
Bolivia	663	801	1,183	1,294	1,059	1,202	5,196	4,703	20	27	1,014	1,117	501	633	276	297
Botswana	35	56	203	621	7	7	5,513	5,385	19	14	622	467	9	11	16	16
Brazil	30,805	42,540	1,496	1,852	27,265	24,792	11,570	12,149	2,206	2,981	464	491	18,607	27,523	4,089	5,527
British Virgin Islands	...	...	...	...	...	...	...	...	...	...	...	...	1	1	...	...
Brunei	3	2	1,640	1,267	1	1	1,470	2,368	...	...	...	...	5	6	8	9
Bulgaria	8,130	7,858	3,853	3,712	376	359	10,175	9,828	68	93	984	961	1,975	1,747	2,021	1,973
Burkina Faso	1,166	2,101	575	727	131	130	8,783	9,288	176	174	372	355	56	70	76	128
Burundi	395	524	1,180	1,246	1,033	1,475	6,877	7,747	325	356	943	870	1,164	1,558	151	190
Cameroon	866	916	849	971	2,030	2,256	2,335	2,395	105	129	542	576	1,233	1,328	307	436
Canada	42,709	35,348	2,174	1,749	2,626	2,785	23,818	25,308	186	518	1,460	1,001	704	700	1,746	1,906
Cape Verde	4	8	365	320	15	15	3,146	2,863	4	13	289	431	12	10	5	6
Cayman Islands	...	...	...	...	...	...	4,345	5,000	...	...	...	...	1	1	...	...
Central African Republic	102	126	525	832	1,164	663	3,334	4,698	6	7	500	493	163	180	44	53
Chad	539	825	615	720	424	643	4,505	5,541	59	60	434	435	97	116	59	74
Chile	1,742	2,800	2,124	3,532	901	935	10,262	14,856	171	146	843	1,071	1,657	2,337	1,743	1,487
China	286,591	352,306	3,029	3,922	144,326	144,926	16,718	15,663	6,648	5,679	1,223	1,286	8,857	18,430	79,989	112,954
Christmas Island	...	...	...	...	...	...	...	...	...	...	...	...	...	...	...	...
Cocos (Keeling) Islands	...	...	...	...	...	...	...	...	...	...	...	...	...	...	...	...
Colombia	3,339	3,554	2,452	2,514	4,144	3,870	11,043	11,506	128	148	604	657	3,905	4,160	1,362	1,526
Comoros	19	24	1,082	1,097	101	114	3,390	3,155	2	7	624	840	36	44	3	4
Congo	13	11	649	700	674	755	6,643	7,167	5	8	705	737	218	252	33	40
Cook Islands	...	...	...	...	12	12	30,990	31,371	...	...	...	...	14	15	2	2
Costa Rica	337	310	2,498	2,454	45	56	5,817	7,179	12	29	498	610	1,362	1,388	52	78
Côte d'Ivoire	856	1,049	858	857	3,429	4,101	5,165	5,672	8	8	667	667	1,549	1,555	324	393
Cuba	551	584	2,458	2,546	1,038	982	6,567	6,409	26	28	738	800	810	1,571	466	676
Cyprus	87	144	1,793	2,550	182	198	23,108	24,915	6	4	1,054	1,201	359	346	101	118
Czechoslovakia	9,762	11,861	3,798	4,804	3,388	3,659	16,730	20,643	137	253	1,692	2,341	645	1,005	1,017	1,129
Denmark	7,346	8,092	4,040	5,091	913	942	26,904	32,483	14	579	3,420	4,827	124	75	263	305
Djibouti	...	...	...	...	...	...	...	...	...	...	...	...	...	...	10	16
Dominica	—	—	1,427	1,444	23	27	9,808	9,839	—	1	502	510	43	99	5	6
Dominican Republic	447	559	3,004	3,591	214	234	5,783	6,602	73	96	958	876	1,333	1,556	209	289
Ecuador	686	891	1,633	1,752	552	454	9,595	6,206	39	51	547	542	3,767	3,470	266	371
Egypt	8,131	9,514	4,052	4,715	1,330	1,882	18,336	22,037	283	616	2,000	3,254	2,310	3,710	7,293	10,818
El Salvador	719	798	1,702	1,979	27	33	12,350	14,145	41	56	850	983	257	254	96	164
Equatorial Guinea	...	...	...	...	86	93	2,556	2,385	...	...	...	...	16	20	...	...
Ethiopia	5,803	5,960	1,186	1,255	1,414	1,370	3,349	2,985	962	987	1,061	1,050	198	218	487	569
Faeroe Islands	...	...	...	...	1	1	13,684	13,462	...	...	...	...	...	...	...	...
Falkland Islands	...	...	...	...	...	...	...	...	...	...	...	...	...	...	...	...
Fiji	19	33	1,983	2,330	25	58	8,104	8,519	1	1	1,709	1,907	16	23	10	10

wild fruits and berries are seldom included in national reports at all. FAO vegetable statistics include vegetables and melons grown for human consumption only. Some countries do not make this distinction in their reports, and some exclude the production of kitchen gardens and small family plots, although in certain countries, such small-scale production may account for 20 to 40 percent of total ouput.

Livestock statistics may be distorted by the timing of country reports. Ireland, for example, takes a livestock enumeration in December that is reported the following year and that appears low against data for otherwise comparable countries because of the slaughter and export of animals at the close of the grazing season. It balances this, however, with a June enumeration, when numbers tend to be high. Milk production as defined by the FAO includes whole fresh milk, excluding milk sucked by young animals but including amounts fed by farmers or ranchers to livestock, but national practices vary. Certain countries do not distinguish between milk cows and other cattle, so that yield per dairy cow must be estimated. Some countries do not report egg production statistics (here given in metric tons), and external estimates must be based on the numbers of chickens and reported or assumed egg-laying rates. Other countries report egg production by number, and this must be converted to weight, using conversion factors specific to the makeup by species of national poultry flocks.

Metric system units used in the table may be converted to English system units as follows:

metric tons × 1.1023 = short tons
kilograms × 2.2046 = pounds
kilograms per hectare × 0.8922 = pounds per acre.

The notes that follow, keyed by references in the table headings, provide further definitional information.
a. Includes such crops as potatoes and cassava.
b. Includes beans and peas harvested for dry grain only. Does not include green beans and green peas.
c. Excludes melons.
d. Includes melons, green beans, and green peas.
e. From milk cows only.
f. From chickens only.

livestock													country
cattle		sheep		hogs		chickens		milk[e]				eggs[f]	
stock ('000 head)		stock ('000 head)		stock ('000 head)		stock ('000 head)		production ('000 metric tons)		yield (kg/animal)		production (metric tons)	
1979–81 average	1988	1979–81 average	1988	1979–81 average	1988	1979–81 average	1988	1979–81 average	1988	1979–81 average	1988	1979–81 average	1988
3,723	3,600	18,667	17,000	...	...	6,000	7,000	552	610	491	521	14,000	14,200	Afghanistan
582	672	1,232	1,432	174	214	4,000	5,000	326	347	1,423	1,412	9,957	14,000	Albania
1,356	361	13,111	14,325	4	5	18,000	23,000	514	585	975	1,026	20,217	124,000	Algeria
...	...	...	...	10	11	491	502	—	—	800	800	34	30	American Samoa
...	13	...	93	...	...	...	...	...	...	...	...	...	...	Andorra
3,117	3,400	225	265	400	480	5,000	6,000	146	148	500	502	...	...	Angola
14	18	12	13	4	4	621	802	6	6	977	1,000	3,650	3,900	Anguilla
55,620	50,782	31,473	29,202	3,751	4,100	38,000	55,000	5,311	6,450	1,746	2,279	138	160	Antigua and Barbuda
...	...	...	...	...	...	...	...	...	...	...	...	253,731	293,000	Argentina
														Aruba[4]
26,161	23,500	134,871	164,000	2,416	2,720	46,000	56,000	5,590	6,298	2,950	2,850	197,870	187,000	Australia
2,553	2,590	193	24	3,906	3,947	15,000	14,000	3,434	3,630	3,509	3,769	96,804	103,000	Austria
4	5	35	40	18	20	1,000	1,000	3	3	1,000	1,000	356	460	Bahamas, The
6	6	7	8	...	...	1,000	1,000	6	6	2,838	2,594	3,238	4,000	Bahrain
21,806	22,789	1,064	1,140	...	...	59,000	81,000	833	728	221	206	39,189	54,000	Bangladesh
18	18	52	56	45	49	1,000	1,000	7	12	1,294	1,306	1,489	1,850	Barbados
3,104	2,950	110	184	5,083	5,881	29,000	34,000	4,042	3,900	3,877	4,114	200,655	160,000	Belgium[5]
50	50	3	4	16	26	—	1,000	4	4	1,017	1,035	883	1,250	Belize
810	914	972	860	455	648	11,000	23,000	12	15	120	130	7,860	17,100	Benin
1	1	...	...	2	2	561	502	2	2	3,003	3,056	435	580	Bermuda
299	409	10	27	55	63	1251		26	28	257	257	159	253	Bhutan
4,570	5,450	9,050	9,600	1,553	1,750	7,000	12,000	71	105	1,396	1,400	22,500	30,000	Bolivia
2,906	2,350	147	220	5	9	1,000	1,000	90	101	350	350	627	738	Botswana
116,645	134,133	18,414	20,000	34,102	32,700	426,000	550,000	11,378	13,200	712	729	765,117	1,280,000	Brazil
2	2	8	6	3	2	...	...	...	...	...	...	...	...	British Virgin Islands
4	3	...	...	11	14	1,000	2,000	...	...	...	...	1,787	2,270	Brunei
1,782	1,649	10,358	8,886	3,803	4,034	39,000	40,000	1,843	2,177	2,675	3,358	131,679	161,008	Bulgaria
2,760	2,809	1,855	2,972	198	500	11,000	21,000	81	81	175	175	7,448	15,050	Burkina Faso
623	340	309	350	46	80	3,000	4,000	37	21	350	350	2,356	3,040	Burundi
3,521	4,471	2,167	2,897	1,139	1,237	8,000	16,000	42	49	500	500	8,400	11,200	Cameroon
13,328	12,060	729	697	9,709	10,847	96,000	107,000	7,830	8,150	4,404	5,674	330,950	323,170	Canada
12	13	1	3	40	70	591	2302	1	1	500	500	65	184	Cape Verde
5	5	...	...	...	...	161	212	...	...	...	...	84	87	Cayman Islands
1,662	2,313	84	120	243	382	2,000	3,000	4	5	110	110	966	1,008	Central African Republic
4,250	4,060	2,620	2,245	9	12	3,000	4,000	115	110	270	270	2,850	3,240	Chad
3,650	3,371	6,059	6,540	1,068	1,360	18,000	21,000	1,078	1,240	1,514	1,938	66,046	85,000	Chile
52,567	73,963	101,864	102,655	313,660	334,862	860,000	1,849,000	1,191	3,845	1,953	1,757	2,882,415	6,685,000	China
...	...	...	...	...	...	...	...	...	...	...	...	...	...	Christmas Island
														Cocos (Keeling) Islands
24,110	24,307	2,399	2,652	2,013	2,586	30,000	39,000	2,187	3,230	965	950	176,972	240,000	Colombia
78	85	8	10	...	...	2431	3622	3	4	500	500	564	616	Comoros
65	70	61	64	29	48	1,000	1,000	3	3	1,500	1,500	825	1,125	Congo
...	...	...	...	17	18	631		...	...	...	...	95	112	Cook Islands
2,183	2,190	5	6	223	223	5,000	5,000	318	415	1,067	1,339	16,760	14,000	Costa Rica
664	960	1,200	1,500	340	450	17,000	16,000	12	19	110	121	10,253	11,500	Côte d'Ivoire
5,166	4,984	356	382	1,950	2,500	24,000	27,000	1,045	1,122	1,579	1,925	99,218	104,857	Cuba
22	45	290	310	162	266	2,000	3,000	33	76	3,601	4,205	5,309	6,600	Cyprus
4,935	5,044	883	1,075	7,694	7,235	46,000	46,000	5,830	6,963	3,140	3,894	243,327	279,823	Czechoslovakia
2,970	2,266	55	128	9,699	9,214	15,000	15,000	5,126	4,728	4,920	5,859	77,130	75,000	Denmark
41	70	423	414	...	...	...	...	...	...	...	...	...	...	Djibouti
7	9	6	9	8	5	981	1172	1	5	1,000	1,000	255	72	Dominica
1,918	2,129	65	100	298	409	12,000	22,000	427	289	1,742	1,284	19,267	18,950	Dominican Republic
2,987	4,007	2,310	1,707	3,417	4,160	33,000	48,000	924	1,290	1,446	1,611	43,056	38,950	Ecuador
1,906	1,920	1,590	1,165	15	15	28,000	30,000	648	980	674	676	78,100	155,000	Egypt
1,234	1,144	4	5	455	442	5,000	3,000	268	250	925	969	36,822	24,500	El Salvador
4	5	33	35	4	5	1201	1952					116	165	Equatorial Guinea
26,000	31,000	23,250	23,400	18	19	53,000	57,000	590	814	215	210	73,140	78,660	Ethiopia
2	2	72	73	...	...	...	...	...	...	...	...	...	...	Faeroe Islands
8	7	658	695	...	...	31	22	2	2	1,000	1,000	...	...	Falkland Islands
153	159	...	...	27	29	1,000	2,000	54	49	1,701	1,700	2,070	2,423	Fiji

Crops and livestock (continued)

country	crops — grains				roots and tubers[a]				pulses[b]				fruits[c]		vegetables[d]	
	production ('000 metric tons)		yield (kg/hectare)		production ('000 metric tons)		yield (kg/hectare)		production ('000 metric tons)		yield (kg/hectare)		production ('000 metric tons)		production ('000 metric tons)	
	1979–81 average	1988	1979–81 average	1988	1979–81 average	1988	1979–81 average	1988	1979–81 average	1988	1979–81 average	1988	1979–81 average	1988	1979–81 average	1988
Finland	2,993	3,520	2,489	2,826	629	855	15,578	19,074	13	4	2,182	1,760	107	98	130	150
France	46,091	56,178	4,700	6,051	6,735	6,344	28,465	34,596	340	2,623	3,304	4,912	14,252	11,145	6,864	7,098
French Guiana	1	15	1,326	4,092	13	15	10,842	11,563	...	...	...	...	2	2	3	12
French Polynesia	...	...	...	...	20	13	12,365	8,333	...	...	528	617	4	5	6	6
Gabon	11	11	1,718	1,459	372	415	6,270	6,709	...	...	...	...	181	197	22	29
Gambia, The	78	122	1,189	1,184	6	6	3,000	3,000	3	4	215	267	4	4	7	8
Gaza Strip	5	5	2,933	2,857	5	18	18,333	20,000	—	—	2,357	2,000	199	195	62	99
Germany, East	9,115	9,816	3,645	4,082	10,612	11,473	27,270	25,923	82	90	1,653	1,725	832	1,096	1,234	1,265
Germany, West	22,928	27,131	4,416	5,720	8,853	7,353	29,359	35,000	34	403	2,965	3,322	3,604	5,399	1,971	2,423
Ghana	726	1,061	807	990	3,045	4,950	6,421	7,355	14	11	101	88	890	838	379	717
Gibraltar	...	...	...	...	...	...	...	...	...	...	...	...	...	...	...	...
Greece	4,951	5,584	3,090	3,917	1,041	852	16,378	15,463	94	54	1,257	1,421	3,437	3,959	3,636	3,894
Greenland	—	—	949	1,000	3	4	4,533	4,819	1	1	1,545	1,379	29	25	2	2
Grenada	—	—	1,200	1,200	22	25	8,459	11,925	—	—	514	552	115	139	17	19
Guadeloupe	...	...	...	...	2	2	13,756	12,831	...	...	...	...	2	1	2	1
Guam	...	...	1,500	1,500	...	...	...	...	...	...	...	...	...	...	...	...
Guatemala	1,122	1,423	1,547	1,614	52	79	4,321	5,490	77	96	844	495	734	769	264	317
Guernsey	...	...	829	792	...	...	...	...	...	...	...	...	...	...	...	...
Guinea	559	599	682	938	644	700	7,116	7,447	44	50	672	769	649	680	410	420
Guinea-Bissau	95	225	...	...	42	40	6,410	6,154	2	2	567	567	41	42	20	20
Guyana	250	228	2,733	2,249	16	31	6,626	7,045	1	2	487	600	41	67	9	12
Haiti	419	338	1,009	1,009	689	667	3,778	4,077	90	92	471	515	1,007	1,051	281	306
Honduras	492	604	1,170	1,451	21	26	4,896	7,551	38	46	518	575	1,675	1,392	95	115
Hong Kong	—	—	1,712	1,250	...	...	25,407	23,791	...	...	...	...	3	3	189	141
Hungary	13,001	14,635	4,519	5,156	1,507	1,132	15,882	16,690	127	270	1,547	2,051	2,389	1,859	1,841	2,041
Iceland	...	...	...	...	11	11	11,858	11,000	...	...	...	...	...	...	1	2
India	138,182	175,638	1,324	1,711	16,777	20,804	12,926	15,626	10,509	11,229	461	498	20,356	24,649	40,585	48,528
Indonesia	33,613	48,441	2,834	3,642	16,278	17,871	9,123	11,339	352	339	882	820	4,103	5,598	2,430	3,180
Iran	9,146	12,562	1,195	1,301	1,269	2,102	14,436	16,357	247	386	1,038	679	2,866	3,692	3,871	4,203
Iraq	1,803	2,768	832	1,013	96	150	18,464	15,789	36	28	802	891	1,161	1,307	1,880	2,870
Ireland	1,967	2,074	4,629	5,835	902	680	22,780	25,000	—	1	3,444	3,500	21	16	288	250
Isle of Man	...	...	...	...	...	...	...	...	...	...	...	...	...	...	...	...
Israel	239	257	1,840	2,259	201	208	36,551	38,304	8	11	956	1,119	1,913	1,738	762	839
Italy	18,025	17,423	3,548	3,796	2,962	2,341	18,274	18,424	321	213	1,335	1,310	20,661	18,846	13,401	13,662
Jamaica	7	7	1,667	1,750	230	255	11,666	12,430	8	8	882	916	332	317	104	120
Japan	14,318	13,870	5,252	5,429	5,342	6,037	22,838	25,922	108	134	1,254	1,543	6,325	5,929	15,230	15,250
Jersey	...	...	...	...	9	62	16,866	26,170	8	15	588	911	90	156	437	583
Jordan	91	124	571	1,231	165	169	6,244	8,244	17	36	635	837	121	224	323	470
Kampuchea (Cambodia)	1,249	2,100	980	1,284	1,390	1,680	8,751	9,282	185	470	430	922	632	730	447	479
Kenya	2,281	3,156	1,364	1,464	...	...	...	...	...	...	...	...	...	...	...	...
Kiribati	...	...	...	...	12	14	8,748	9,013	...	...	...	...	5	5	4	5
Korea, North	8,649	11,872	3,956	4,648	1,909	2,472	12,486	13,290	280	315	849	900	851	1,251	2,222	3,094
Korea, South	8,073	9,287	4,764	5,844	1,655	1,342	17,760	23,767	56	57	946	1,130	1,002	1,777	9,070	8,712
Kuwait	...	...	3,087	5,738	1	2	16,934	17,500	...	...	1,728	2,143	89	172	36	119
Laos	1,056	1,043	1,402	1,648	184	265	10,114	10,115	17	30	...	...	704	751	347	421
Lebanon	41	25	1,307	1,622	130	211	16,923	20,987	10	11	968	1,022	15	15	21	26
Lesotho	198	203	977	759	6	6	15,526	15,000	8	6	536	411	121	130	64	77
Liberia	251	279	1,237	1,139	346	364	6,894	6,744	3	3	500	550	209	284	512	602
Libya	225	299	430	700	11	12	18,742	18,212	9	12	1,111	1,187	...	...	...	...
Liechtenstein	...	...	...	...	...	...	...	...	...	...	...	...	...	...	...	...
Luxembourg[5]	...	...	...	...	3	4	10,058	10,100	...	...	...	...	4	5	2	2
Macau	...	...	...	...	...	...	...	...	...	...	...	...	...	...	...	...
Madagascar	2,178	2,252	1,664	1,677	2,267	3,036	5,704	6,325	53	50	852	807	719	805	272	301
Malawi	1,452	1,523	1,130	1,180	556	413	4,608	2,894	204	236	609	630	371	407	200	225
Malaysia	2,061	1,700	3,137	2,627	468	505	8,895	9,387	...	...	...	...	962	1,179	587	479
Maldives	—	—	806	796	7	9	5,176	5,214	—	—	600	613	7	8	15	18
Mali	1,064	2,432	790	1,222	118	143	9,196	8,938	43	57	1,049	1,036	13	13	173	245
Malta	8	10	3,252	3,834	21	13	8,948	6,842	1	2	2,333	2,471	10	15	47	49
Martinique	...	...	...	...	22	37	6,997	9,221	...	...	...	...	178	240	27	28
Mauritania	57	113	437	746	7	6	2,888	1,905	29	28	407	368	15	15	7	9
Mauritius	1	4	2,536	3,845	12	14	17,368	20,547	1	1	491	650	6	10	26	31
Mayotte	...	...	...	...	...	...	...	...	...	...	...	...	...	...	...	...
Mexico	20,692	21,992	2,152	2,200	1,120	1,095	12,906	13,985	1,311	1,285	719	629	7,316	7,937	3,884	4,675
Monaco	...	...	...	...	...	...	...	...	...	...	...	...	...	...	...	...
Mongolia	320	832	573	1,277	50	103	7,878	7,833	—	3	292	825	3	—	26	55
Montserrat	...	...	1,000	1,786	—	—	2,471	3,302	...	...	...	...	...	...	...	...
Morocco	3,586	8,018	812	1,483	503	550	14,169	13,097	230	450	571	927	1,539	1,787	1,259	1,493
Mozambique	642	530	670	593	3,212	3,490	5,217	5,861	57	60	459	480	327	363	184	198
Myanmar (Burma)	12,984	14,821	2,521	2,794	167	251	8,087	8,433	365	732	588	843	838	920	1,872	2,195
Nauru	...	...	...	...	...	...	...	...	...	...	...	...	...	...	...	...
Nepal	3,640	4,606	1,615	1,591	349	733	5,455	6,560	126	153	419	436	135	159	235	275
Netherlands, The	1,280	1,222	5,696	6,202	6,329	6,742	37,752	41,978	24	106	3,145	3,462	535	535	2,527	2,962
Netherlands Antilles[4]	1[1]	2[2]	653[1]	714[2]	22	23	6,463	5,718	—	—	856	667	9	7	3	4
New Caledonia	3	3	2,134	2,960	...	...	...	...	...	...	576	564	324	341	47	52
New Zealand	785	909	4,077	4,913	220	299	26,301	29,132	62	105	2,965	2,928	363	691	381	431
Nicaragua	394	561	1,480	1,822	28	89	9,107	12,068	39	50	268	188	37	43	142	166
Niger	1,702	2,457	440	491	212	246	7,210	7,548	291	373	512	495	2	2	...	...
Nigeria	7,976	11,975	1,136	1,212	30,072	32,102	9,965	10,117	747	1,050	...	...	2,262	3,200	2,906	3,946
Niue	...	...	...	...	...	...	...	...	...	...	...	...	...	...	...	...
Norfolk Island	...	...	...	...	...	...	...	...	...	...	...	...	117	121	189	160
Norway	1,129	1,285	3,634	3,991	524	414	25,884	23,000	...	...	...	...	109	193	97	226
Oman	2	2	982	1,124	1	1	13,663	13,514	...	...	600	600	3	3	3	3
Pacific Is., Trust Territory of the																
Marshall Islands	—	—	1,167	1,221	13	14	8,420	8,953	...	...	...	...	...	...	...	...
Micronesia, Fed. States of	...	...	...	...	...	...	...	...	...	...	...	...	...	...	...	...

cattle stock ('000 head)		sheep stock ('000 head)		hogs stock ('000 head)		chickens stock ('000 head)		milk[e] production ('000 metric tons)		yield (kg/animal)		eggs[f] production (metric tons)		country
1979–81 average	1988	1979–81 average	1988	1979–81 average	1988	1979–81 average	1988	1979–81 average	1988	1979–81 average	1988	1979–81 average	1988	
1,747	1,434	107	63	1,430	1,291	9,000	6,000	3,236	2,753	4,572	5,149	77,967	76,700	Finland
23,825	21,100	11,452	10,360	11,472	12,577	177,000	189,000	32,088	27,510	3,163	2,978	849,667	912,000	France
6	15	—	—	6	9	121[1]	100[2]	—	1	2,080	1,700	292	250	French Guiana
8	10	2	2	24	54	—	1,000	2	2	2,845	2,547	923	1,340	French Polynesia
5	9	85	84	136	154	2,000	2,000	—	1	250	250	1,050	1,440	Gabon
293	300	158	200	10	13	280[1]	349[2]	5	5	175	175	402	618	Gambia, The
5	4	15	10	...	...	1,000	2,000	11	7	4,185	4,000	2,265	3,750	Gaza Strip
5,630	5,721	1,994	2,656	12,245	12,503	51,000	51,000	8,240	9,204	3,889	4,594	322,587	335,000	Germany, East
15,042	14,887	1,153	1,414	22,523	23,670	86,000	72,000	24,514	23,978	4,479	4,874	800,987	726,000	Germany, West
804	1,300	1,942	2,500	379	750	11,000	12,000	7	11	55	55	12,203	12,720	Ghana
...	...	...	...	...	...	...	...	...	...	...	...	...	...	Gibraltar
929	800	8,040	10,816	944	1,190	30,000	31,000	666	630	1,867	1,826	122,540	124,000	Greece
...	...	20	22	...	...	...	...	...	...	...	...	...	...	Greenland
6	5	14	17	13	11	252[1]	260[2]	2	2	800	800	975	1,000	Grenada
91	74	3	4	45	43	420[1]	390[2]	1	2	507	500	814	1,200	Guadeloupe
1	2	...	...	13	14	127[1]	218[2]	...	...	...	...	1,071	4,000	Guam
1,886	2,140	615	660	737	875	14,000	15,000	318	366	885	915	39,947	42,800	Guatemala
4	4	...	...	...	...	...	...	8	9	3,514	3,872	...	...	Guernsey
1,753	1,800	436	460	39	50	7,000	13,000	41	42	185	185	7,420	13,860	Guinea
290	340	177	205	256	290	—	1,000	9	10	170	170	300	540	Guinea-Bissau
189	210	114	120	135	185	13,000	15,000	13	47	730	901	3,900	4,200	Guyana
1,000	1,545	89	94	1,533	900	5,000	13,000	20	23	229	237	2,943	4,000	Haiti
1,980	2,824	5	7	418	600	5,000	8,000	271	296	652	889	18,947	23,700	Honduras
7	2	...	...	520	353	6,000	7,000	4	2	3,022	2,200	2,737	2,100	Hong Kong
1,936	1,664	2,960	2,333	8,232	8,216	62,000	61,000	2,559	2,825	3,727	4,871	250,000	200,000	Hungary
60	72	838	770	11	14	247[1]	307[2]	121	114	3,635	3,800	3,000	3,700	Iceland
186,500	193,000	44,987	51,684	9,433	10,300	160,000	260,000	13,224	22,500	522	776	682,000	990,000	India
6,505	6,500	4,124	5,415	3,234	6,500	165,000	410,000	79	250	762	1,000	177,767	434,000	Indonesia
7,800	8,350	33,833	34,500	27	...	71,000	110,000	1,567	1,700	776	723	155,333	250,000	Iran
1,650	1,600	10,399	9,200	...	...	23,000	76,000	290	285	750	750	48,362	100,000	Iraq
6,043	5,580	2,374	4,301	1,122	960	8,000	7,000	5,392	5,463	3,623	3,784	35,000	34,000	Ireland
...	32[6]	...	147[6]	...	8[6]	...	71[6]	...	...	...	...	...	...	Isle of Man
299	321	243	280	96	130	25,000	23,000	702	890	6,817	8,396	91,675	101,400	Israel
8,697	8,794	9,120	11,457	8,885	9,383	107,000	120,000	10,546	10,869	3,478	3,599	659,163	705,600	Italy
279	290	4	3	210	250	5,000	6,000	48	49	1,000	1,000	15,500	17,000	Jamaica
4,261	4,667	13	29	9,851	11,725	284,000	334,000	6,526	7,608	4,526	5,320	1,998,041	2,409,000	Japan
7	6[6]	...	...	...	...	...	...	...	...	...	...	...	...	Jersey
29	29	950	1,220	...	...	28,000	60,000	18	31	1,696	1,694	19,000	27,000	Jordan
831	1,950	1	1	205	1,500	3,100	7,000	14	17	170	170	5,400	10,000	Kampuchea (Cambodia)
10,418	9,800	5,100	7,300	89	102	17,000	23,000	938	1,015	450	450	19,968	36,432	Kenya
...	...	...	...	10	10	154[1]	220[2]	...	...	...	...	105	120	Kiribati
945	1,250	292	372	2,100	3,100	18,000	20,000	55	85	2,244	2,429	103,833	137,000	Korea, North
1,728	2,386	7	3	2,115	4,281	41,000	59,000	450	1,561	4,882	5,876	255,786	397,000	Korea, South
16	26	250	300	...	...	9,000	28,000	24	54	2,653	3,375	8,573	17,500	Kuwait
437	590	...	...	1,117	1,520	5,000	9,000	6	8	200	200	22,167	29,500	Laos
64	52	137	141	18	22	8,000	12,000	85	97	2,290	2,366	41,275	59,200	Lebanon
582	525	1,183	1,430	75	72	1,000	1,000	20	23	290	290	789	812	Lesotho
39	42	200	240	103	140	2,000	4,000	1	1	100	100	2,336	3,744	Liberia
164	215	5,046	5,750	...	...	6,000	37,000	63	77	1,499	1,571	16,233	17,200	Libya
8	9	1	3	8	10	43[1]	...	17	20	3,276	3,373	250	250	Liechtenstein
...	...	...	...	...	...	...	...	...	...	...	...	575	630	Luxembourg[5]
1	—	...	...	5	6	353[1]	450[2]	...	...	...	...	575	630	Macau
10,147	10,600	695	611	1,090	1,400	18,000	21,000	36	41	700	700	12,588	11,880	Madagascar
817	1,000	84	210	192	210	8,000	8,000	34	44	457	460	10,725	11,700	Malawi
532	625	66	99	1,871	2,258	51,000	58,000	25	24	550	550	121,067	185,000	Malaysia
...	...	...	...	...	...	...	...	...	...	...	...	...	...	Maldives
5,670	4,736	6,247	5,500	48	60	12,000	19,000	113	95	200	200	6,570	10,080	Mali
13	14	5	5	12	95	1,000	1,000	29	29	4,111	3,973	6,256	6,800	Malta
57	43	57	90	37	48	2,000	2,000	5	3	754	750	1,500	850	Martinique
1,262	1,250	5,098	4,100	...	...	3,000	4,000	85	96	350	353	2,720	3,740	Mauritania
27	30	10	7	7	10	2,000	2,000	25	25	2,500	2,500	2,800	4,200	Mauritius
...	...	...	...	...	...	...	...	...	...	...	...	...	...	Mayotte
27,706	31,200	6,484	6,000	16,895	16,500	177,000	224,000	6,949	7,600	1,284	1,188	636,256	928,000	Mexico
...	...	...	...	...	...	...	...	...	...	...	...	...	...	Monaco
2,452	2,526	14,261	13,234	32	120	165[1]	300[2]	210	269	389	452	983	1,612	Mongolia
9	...	4	4	1	1	30[1]	33[2]	2	2	750	750	42	60	Montserrat
3,362	3,300	15,228	15,700	7	9	24,000	37,000	753	860	640	551	72,900	85,100	Morocco
1,400	1,360	106	119	120	160	17,000	21,000	63	66	170	170	9,400	12,800	Mozambique
8,565	10,000	235	295	2,263	3,000	23,000	34,000	283	585	245	246	31,435	51,000	Myanmar (Burma)
...	...	...	...	2	2	3[1]	...	...	...	...	...	8	11	Nauru
6,893	6,374	730	833	375	479	8,000	10,000	190	220	325	326	14,767	13,100	Nepal
5,071	4,546	856	1,100	10,058	14,226	81,000	98,000	11,832	11,315	5,025	5,832	540,409	599,700	Netherlands, The
8	8	8	10	7	6	100[1]	135[2]	4	4	1,250	1,281	517	560	Netherlands Antilles[4]
113	124	4	3	16	47	—	1,000	3	4	600	600	887	1,550	New Caledonia
8,063	8,062	67,393	64,970	433	428	7,000	9,000	6,586	7,850	3,306	3,578	56,855	50,000	New Zealand
2,373	1,700	3	3	667	745	5,000	5,000	225	100	767	556	28,833	29,500	Nicaragua
3,343	3,500	2,979	3,500	31	37	10,000	17,000	97	106	200	200	6,800	8,160	Niger
12,267	12,200	11,683	13,200	1,100	1,300	120,000	190,000	354	360	288	295	180,000	293,000	Nigeria
1	1	...	...	1	1	15[1]	20[2]	—	—	713	715	20	20	Niue
...	...	...	...	...	...	...	...	...	...	...	...	...	...	Norfolk Island
989	945	2,033	2,306	675	788	4,000	4,000	1,926	1,953	5,125	5,645	44,665	57,000	Norway
141	136	114	218	...	...	—	2,000	16	18	420	420	710	1,600	Oman
8	12	...	...	26	29	164[1]	...	...	...	...	...	147	160	Pacific Is., Trust Territory of the Marshall Islands
...	...	...	...	...	...	...	...	...	...	...	...	...	...	Micronesia, Fed. States of

Crops and livestock (continued)

Production columns are in '000 metric tons; yield columns are in kg/hectare.

country	grains prod. 1979–81 avg	grains prod. 1988	grains yield 1979–81 avg	grains yield 1988	roots & tubers[a] prod. 1979–81 avg	roots & tubers prod. 1988	roots & tubers yield 1979–81 avg	roots & tubers yield 1988	pulses[b] prod. 1979–81 avg	pulses prod. 1988	pulses yield 1979–81 avg	pulses yield 1988	fruits[c] prod. 1979–81 avg	fruits prod. 1988	vegetables[d] prod. 1979–81 avg	vegetables prod. 1988
Northern Mariana Islands	...	...	...	...	...	...	...	...	...	...	...	...	...	...	...	...
Palau	...	...	...	...	...	...	...	...	...	...	...	...	...	...	...	...
Pakistan	17,200	18,849	1,608	1,735	423	581	10,495	9,818	595	552	397	451	2,569	3,993	2,083	2,895
Panama	255	289	1,486	1,546	76	79	8,496	8,693	5	6	412	469	1,211	1,015	44	62
Papua New Guinea	4	3	2,087	1,545	1,102	1,192	6,920	6,952	2	2	500	524	1,054	1,122	248	288
Paraguay	645	1,624	1,530	1,887	2,080	4,014	13,100	16,389	69	62	803	899	827	1,037	218	285
Peru	1,412	2,285	1,945	2,408	2,249	2,740	7,456	8,243	99	134	861	836	1,418	1,154	698	781
Philippines	11,088	13,399	1,633	1,904	3,481	2,768	7,177	6,430	37	35	652	804	5,813	6,778	1,025	853
Pitcairn Island	...	...	...	...	...	...	...	...	...	...	...	...	...	...	...	...
Poland	18,466	24,504	2,345	2,904	39,508	34,707	16,808	18,599	216	565	1,232	1,665	1,584	2,173	4,555	5,505
Portugal	1,220	1,422	1,105	1,566	1,164	827	9,125	6,568	77	78	229	372	2,055	1,836	1,638	1,971
Puerto Rico	6	6	8,925	5,914	39	27	6,470	5,986	6	3	916	525	297	305	28	42
Qatar	1	2	2,623	3,007	—	—	13,367	8,462	...	...	...	...	6	8	18	22
Réunion	12	14	4,954	5,556	11	10	13,133	10,957	1	1	2,626	1,714	27	34	12	13
Romania	19,827	31,090	3,086	4,760	4,381	8,000	14,952	24,242	116	337	261	513	3,004	4,321	4,279	6,839
Rwanda	271	279	1,134	1,071	1,743	1,435	8,809	7,077	221	152	727	532	2,162	2,177	169	194
St. Helena and Ascension	...	...	...	...	3	3	3,393	3,438	—	—	1,000	1,000	2	2	1	1
St. Kitts and Nevis	...	...	703	746	...	...	...	...	...	...	...	...	...	...	...	...
St. Lucia	—	—	...	...	10	11	4,246	4,174	...	...	2,187	2,500	104	175	1	1
St. Pierre and Miquelon	...	...	...	...	...	...	...	...	...	...	...	...	...	...	...	...
St. Vincent and the Grenadines	1	1	3,294	3,095	24	66	8,071	5,919	—	—	913	1,000	36	47	1	1
San Marino	...	...	...	...	...	...	...	...	...	...	...	...	...	...	...	...
São Tomé and Príncipe	1	1	1,538	1,556	14	16	12,701	13,913	...	...	...	...	4	4	3	3
Saudi Arabia	303	3,247	820	4,069	3	35	9,930	15,909	6	7	1,813	1,846	480	624	664	1,171
Senegal	767	919	628	751	43	30	4,344	4,054	21	25	398	347	75	84	82	101
Seychelles	...	...	...	...	—	—	5,000	5,000	...	...	...	...	2	2	1	2
Sierra Leone	541	485	1,248	1,187	126	152	3,673	3,326	31	35	579	633	128	153	153	186
Singapore	...	...	...	...	2	—	11,330	11,190	...	...	...	...	9	5	39	17
Solomon Islands	13	6	3,513	6,000	79	97	13,797	16,247	2	2	740	1,200	11	13	5	6
Somalia	300	493	466	647	39	48	10,863	10,434	10	25	494	503	192	275	27	55
South Africa[7]	13,921	10,981	1,881	1,665	793	1,014	11,435	11,393	108	105	1,034	1,214	3,139	3,499	1,662	1,886
Bophuthatswana[7]	...	...	...	...	...	...	...	...	...	...	...	...	...	...	...	...
Ciskei[7]	...	...	...	...	...	...	...	...	...	...	...	...	...	...	...	...
Transkei[7]	...	...	...	...	...	...	...	...	...	...	...	...	...	...	...	...
Venda[7]	...	...	...	...	...	...	...	...	...	...	...	...	...	...	...	...
South West Africa/Namibia	90	99	468	494	203	245	9,242	9,800	6	7	944	1,000	31	33	28	28
Spain	14,699	23,660	1,987	3,063	5,670	4,628	15,986	16,340	365	319	704	816	12,623	11,024	8,547	9,754
Sri Lanka	2,132	2,516	2,464	2,932	717	575	9,685	8,873	26	39	639	653	1,718	815	535	883
Sudan, The	3,073	5,377	666	643	296	193	3,329	2,473	98	108	1,285	1,108	763	813	795	928
Suriname	258	300	3,972	3,982	3	4	6,205	6,387	—	—	706	800	52	61	6	14
Swaziland	92	92	1,345	1,355	13	9	1,993	1,889	3	3	576	609	121	126	12	13
Sweden	5,407	4,952	3,595	3,884	1,191	1,241	28,914	31,979	32	125	2,248	3,008	207	120	228	243
Switzerland	843	1,159	4,883	6,247	924	748	37,834	38,756	1	1	3,354	3,865	732	1,020	306	273
Syria	3,069	5,031	1,156	1,671	279	353	15,302	15,914	180	282	799	1,010	733	1,427	2,973	2,171
Taiwan	3,565[1]	3,303[2]	4,264[1]	5,272[2]	2,341[1]	5,430[2]	15,146[1]	13,889[2]	32[1]	40[2]	944[1]	1,887[2]	1,639[1]	2,165[2]	2,387[1]	3,531[2]
Tanzania	3,011	3,751	1,061	1,274	6,273	5,580	9,679	6,168	315	380	454	475	2,458	3,136	973	1,074
Thailand	20,314	26,207	1,917	2,086	15,477	22,693	13,975	14,271	304	389	664	622	6,304	5,538	3,005	3,118
Togo	301	499	729	909	922	801	8,914	9,133	23	25	238	386	41	48	65	79
Tokelau	...	...	...	...	...	...	17,286	17,500	...	...	...	...	...	...	...	...
Tonga	...	...	...	...	93	100	6,542	6,868	...	...	...	...	11	14	7	7
Trinidad and Tobago	11	10	3,066	2,533	20	8	12,206	9,674	4	2	1,734	1,299	58	58	30	15
Tunisia	1,146	324	828	632	127	180	12,905	11,180	89	49	560	565	515	607	1,044	1,273
Turkey	25,232	30,985	1,861	2,267	2,957	4,350	16,679	21,748	817	2,298	1,140	1,125	7,682	8,890	13,324	16,889
Turks and Caicos Islands	...	...	...	...	...	...	...	...	...	...	...	...	1	...	...	...
Tuvalu	...	...	...	...	—	—	...	...	...	...	...	...	...	...	...	...
Uganda	1,171	1,063	1,555	1,287	3,563	4,358	5,855	5,682	252	356	698	704	6,299	7,135	270	330
U.S.S.R.	170,456	187,060	1,408	1,724	76,706	62,700	11,082	10,137	5,055	8,735	1,000	1,370	16,038	14,503	30,902	33,781
United Arab Emirates	3	5	6,100	3,784	2	—	14,558	10,698	...	...	...	...	61	107	130	285
United Kingdom	18,840	20,983	4,791	5,351	6,601	6,812	32,891	37,802	240	568	3,168	3,079	526	418	3,762	3,797
United States	301,292	206,467	4,154	3,715	15,441	16,414	28,845	30,439	1,457	1,140	1,633	1,733	26,552	25,735	25,471	27,894
Uruguay	1,012	1,200	1,644	2,293	197	200	5,497	5,882	5	6	909	960	273	346	172	186
Vanuatu	1	1	513	531	32	40	20,000	19,190	...	...	...	...	5	7	6	8
Venezuela	1,550	2,386	1,904	1,986	602	649	7,906	8,257	37	57	509	550	2,031	2,237	401	426
Vietnam	12,135	15,835	2,033	2,623	6,214	5,420	6,603	5,815	115	190	618	945	2,587	3,879	2,515	3,165
Virgin Islands (U.S.)	...	...	...	...	...	...	...	...	...	...	...	...	...	...	...	...
Wallis and Futuna	...	...	...	...	6	6	10,535	10,161	...	...	...	...	9	9	1	1
West Bank	...	...	...	...	...	...	...	...	...	...	...	...	...	...	...	...
Western Sahara	1[1]	2[2]	708[1]	741[2]	...	...	...	...	...	...	...	...	53	59	—	1
Western Samoa	...	...	...	...	40	45	7,119	7,112	...	...	...	...	...	...	...	...
Yemen (Aden)	122	120	1,581	1,734	6	8	10,793	14,953	—	—	...	...	45	52	109	118
Yemen (Şan'ā')	793	808	990	962	127	110	12,062	12,901	80	46	1,087	1,550	139	273	258	465
Yugoslavia	15,521	14,996	3,601	3,580	2,646	1,935	6,869	7,054	204	163	1,146	1,106	2,969	3,078	2,880	2,197
Zaire	891	1,156	806	854	13,532	16,992	6,869	7,286	148	131	567	655	2,432	2,634	483	545
Zambia	1,020	1,564	1,650	1,875	205	267	3,465	3,607	7	11	340	613	76	95	209	260
Zimbabwe	2,259	2,989	1,350	1,537	76	118	3,823	4,828	23	49	566	687	107	135	136	148

livestock

Stock figures in '000 head (cattle, sheep, hogs, chickens); milk production in '000 metric tons; milk yield in kg/animal; eggs production in metric tons.

cattle stock 1979–81 avg	cattle stock 1988	sheep stock 1979–81 avg	sheep stock 1988	hogs stock 1979–81 avg	hogs stock 1988	chickens stock 1979–81 avg	chickens stock 1988	milk[e] prod. 1979–81 avg	milk[e] prod. 1988	yield 1979–81 avg	yield 1988	eggs[f] 1979–81 avg	eggs[f] 1988	country
...	...	...	...	...	...	...	...	...	...	...	...	...	...	Northern Mariana Islands
...	...	...	...	...	...	...	...	...	...	...	...	...	...	Palau
15,268	17,156	24,180	27,479	...	...	54,000	150,000	2,189	3,001	888	1,067	96,367	194,600	Pakistan
1,425	1,502	...	...	205	240	5,000	7,000	94	109	988	1,000	14,553	15,500	Panama
129	101	2	9	1,464	1,700	2,000	3,000	—	—	228	200	1,815	3,000	Papua New Guinea
5,966	7,780	387	430	1,090	2,108	12,000	16,000	163	200	1,903	1,905	26,025	34,000	Paraguay
3,958	3,900	14,565	13,320	2,083	2,400	37,000	52,000	796	850	1,084	1,209	59,700	110,000	Peru
1,885	1,700	30	30	7,712	7,580	53,000	60,000	13	15	994	1,034	201,285	231,000	Philippines
...	...	...	...	...	...	...	...	...	...	...	...	...	...	Pitcairn Island
12,494	10,322	4,105	4,377	20,343	19,605	77,000	57,000	16,250	15,420	2,778	3,121	488,642	445,000	Poland
1,332	1,387	4,440	5,220	3,367	2,800	17,000	18,000	750	909	2,123	2,180	62,008	74,000	Portugal
497	579	6	7	225	195	7,000	11,000	420	346	2,324	3,740	21,904	17,784	Puerto Rico
9	8	48	125	...	...	1,000	1,000	5	9	1,560	1,517	281	1,400	Qatar
20	20	2	3	61	75	3,000	4,000	5	5	526	457	2,413	1,900	Réunion
6,275	7,120	15,766	18,793	10,926	15,224	89,000	136,000	4,038	4,300	1,938	2,150	331,267	400,000	Romania
625	660	303	360	124	92	1,000	1,000	61	77	510	481	860	1,200	Rwanda
1	1	2	1	1	1	12[1]	15[2]	...	...	...	...	...	...	St. Helena and Ascension
6	7	14	15	9	10	74[1]	85[2]	...	...	...	...	297	379	St. Kitts and Nevis
10	13	13	15	10	12	128[1]	250[2]	1	1	1,390	1,360	497	540	St. Lucia
...	...	...	...	...	...	...	...	...	...	...	...	...	...	St. Pierre and Miquelon
8	7	13	15	6	9	139[1]	178[2]	1	2	1,364	1,455	530	590	St. Vincent and the Grenadines
3	3	2	2	2	3	70[1]	100[2]	—	—	170	170	148	172	San Marino
...	...	...	...	...	...	...	...	...	...	...	...	...	...	São Tomé and Príncipe
374	325	2,888	7,466	...	...	19,000	69,000	64	210	443	1,680	41,967	114,100	Saudi Arabia
2,424	2,608	1,966	3,792	176	470	8,000	11,000	87	94	357	360	6,353	10,000	Senegal
3	2	...	...	10	15	109[1]	290[2]	1	—	519	524	855	1,530	Seychelles
349	330	268	330	36	50	4,000	6,000	18	17	350	350	4,669	6,325	Sierra Leone
1	—	...	...	1,017	462	14,000	7,000	...	...	...	...	26,870	16,000	Singapore
23	13	...	...	45	52	133[1]	143[2]	1	1	600	600	284	288	Solomon Islands
3,883	5,000	11,500	13,500	9	10	3,000	3,000	319	550	410	550	2,320	2,720	Somalia
13,647	11,820	31,625	29,800	1,339	1,460	30,000	37,000	2,553	2,600	2,809	2,826	159,952	190,000	South Africa[7]
...	...	...	...	...	...	...	...	...	...	...	...	...	...	Bophuthatswana[7]
...	...	...	...	...	...	...	...	...	...	...	...	...	...	Ciskei[7]
...	...	...	...	...	...	...	...	...	...	...	...	...	...	Transkei[7]
...	...	...	...	...	...	...	...	...	...	...	...	...	...	Venda[7]
2,300	2,050	5,433	6,400	37	48	—	1,000	68	70	412	412	150	175	South West Africa/Namibia
4,608	4,980	14,721	17,894	10,392	16,941	51,000	55,000	5,984	6,620	3,255	3,789	665,560	757,500	Spain
1,662	1,820	27	28	71	101	6,000	9,000	182	170	448	262	28,857	48,300	Sri Lanka
18,376	22,500	17,628	18,500	...	...	27,000	29,000	1,352	1,750	500	507	31,745	39,000	Sudan, The
46	74	3	4	19	20	5,000	6,000	7	13	1,239	1,806	2,638	4,530	Suriname
658	650	32	35	17	19	1,000	1,000	36	39	252	255	272	304	Swaziland
1,928	1,667	392	402	2,711	2,217	13,000	11,000	3,452	3,429	5,257	6,069	113,633	117,000	Sweden
2,008	1,837	350	367	2,113	1,941	6,000	6,000	3,653	3,790	4,194	4,779	43,186	44,000	Switzerland
778	723	9,311	13,304	1	1	15,000	12,000	504	660	1,353	2,276	68,759	64,300	Syria
130[1]	105[2]	...	...	3,267[1]	6,674[2]	24,760[1]	59,313[2]	46[1]	92[2]	3,426[1]	5,000[2]	59,462[1]	178,500[2]	Taiwan
12,616	13,500	3,754	4,700	160	184	18,000	30,000	372	448	160	160	36,021	61,620	Tanzania
4,228	5,000	25	95	3,344	4,260	60,000	85,000	23	108	1,960	1,600	100,600	111,150	Thailand
229	290	592	1,000	231	300	2,000	3,000	7	9	225	225	1,677	2,400	Togo
...	...	...	...	1	1	3[1]	...	...	...	...	...	5	4	Tokelau
9	8	...	...	77	65	121[1]	130[2]	—	...	1,500	1,500	348	420	Tonga
77	78	10	12	59	84	7,000	8,000	6	10	1,712	1,700	7,433	8,000	Trinidad and Tobago
583	612	4,651	5,900	4	4	13,000	17,000	216	363	1,064	1,452	36,383	57,000	Tunisia
15,467	12,000	46,199	40,000	13	10	55,000	58,000	3,449	3,000	579	600	217,164	306,350	Turkey
...	...	...	...	6	10	10[1]	21[2]	...	...	...	...	...	...	Turks and Caicos Islands
...	...	...	...	...	...	...	...	...	...	...	...	11	16	Tuvalu
5,181	3,910	1,152	1,740	242	440	13,000	15,000	363	378	350	350	9,533	18,000	Uganda
114,748	120,593	142,591	140,783	73,588	77,403	927,000	1,129,000	90,557	105,950	2,095	2,523	3,760,300	4,656,000	U.S.S.R.
26	50	132	430	...	...	2,000	10,000	4	12	446	452	2,533	10,000	United Arab Emirates
13,321	11,849	21,643	27,820	7,856	7,915	116,000	127,000	15,917	14,981	4,755	4,909	834,000	790,000	United Kingdom
112,142	98,994	12,667	10,774	64,045	42,845	1,068,000	1,540,000	58,139	66,010	5,377	6,444	4,121,430	4,045,600	United States
10,964	10,408	19,219	26,049	327	215	6,000	8,000	811	947	1,592	1,722	16,903	21,000	Uruguay
93	105	...	...	67	79	131[1]	180[2]	2	2	201	198	224	260	Vanuatu
10,527	12,756	333	425	2,156	2,707	41,000	57,000	1,340	1,545	1,149	1,217	128,745	162,800	Venezuela
1,645	2,923	14	23	9,392	12,051	55,000	69,000	26	36	800	800	55,250	103,000	Vietnam
8	11	4	3	5	3	57[1]	49[2]	3	2	3,477	2,721	196	200	Virgin Islands (U.S.)
...	...	...	...	18	30	20[1]	36[2]	—	—	1,500	1,500	35	46	Wallis and Futuna
...	...	17[1]	25[2]	...	...	...	1,000[2]	...	...	...	...	...	...	West Bank
...	...	...	...	...	...	...	...	...	...	...	...	...	...	Western Sahara
26	27	...	...	59	65	1,000	1,000	1	1	1,000	1,000	152	184	Western Samoa
89	97	892	938	...	...	2,000	2,000	14	16	416	426	1,700	2,300	Yemen (Aden)
884	1,053	2,110	2,674	...	...	4,000	23,000	65	80	213	230	5,520	13,500	Yemen (Şan'ā')
5,467	4,881	7,359	7,824	7,705	8,323	59,000	73,000	4,370	4,700	1,629	1,811	218,030	242,000	Yugoslavia
1,161	1,400	726	880	685	800	15,000	19,000	6	7	827	883	7,247	7,800	Zaire
2,238	2,684	29	80	217	180	18,000	15,000	59	81	300	300	27,893	32,400	Zambia
5,378	5,700	481	580	155	190	9,000	10,000	152	225	1,435	1,573	11,100	12,700	Zimbabwe

[1]1975–77. [2]1986. [3]1982. [4]Netherlands Antilles includes Aruba. [5]Belgium includes Luxembourg. [6]1987. [7]South Africa includes Bophuthatswana, Ciskei, Transkei, and Venda.

Extractive industries

Extractive industries are generally defined as those exploiting *in situ* natural resources and include such activities as mining, forestry, fisheries, and agriculture; the definition is often confined, however, to nonrenewable resources only. For the purposes of this table, agriculture is excluded; it is covered in the two tables immediately preceding.

Extractive industries are divided here into three parts: mining, forestry, and fisheries. These major headings are each divided into two main subheadings, one that treats production and one that treats foreign trade. The production sections are presented in terms of volume except for mining, and the trade sections are presented in terms of U.S. dollars. Volume of production data usually imply output of primary (unprocessed) raw materials only, but, because of the way national statistical information is reported, the data may occasionally include some processed and manufactured materials as well, since these are often indistinguishably associated with the extractive process (sulfur from petroleum extraction, cured or treated lumber, or "processed" fish). This is also the case in the trade sections, where individual national trade nomenclatures may not distinguish some processed and manufactured goods from unprocessed raw materials.

Mining. In the absence of a single international source publication or standard of practice for reporting volume or value of mineral production, single-country sources predominantly have been used to compile mining production figures, supplemented by U.S. Bureau of Mines data and industry sources, especially *Mining Journal*'s *Mining Annual Review*. Each country has its own methods of classifying mining data, which do not always accord with the principal mineral production categories adopted in this table—namely, "metals," "nonmetals," and "energy." The available data have therefore been adjusted to make them accord better with the definition of each group. Included in the "metal" category are all ferrous and nonferrous metallic ores, concentrates, and scrap; the "nonmetal" group includes all nonmetallic minerals (stone, clay, precious gems, etc.) except the mineral fuels; the last group, "energy," is composed predominantly of the natural hydrocarbon fuels, though it may also include manufactured gas.

The contribution (value) of each national mineral sector to its country's gross domestic product is given, as is the distribution by group of that contribution (to gross domestic product and to foreign trade), although statistics regarding the value of mineral production are less readily available in country sources than those regarding trade or volume of minerals produced. Figures for value added by mineral output, though not always available, were sought first, as they provide the most consistent standard to compare the importance of minerals both within a particular national economy and among national mineral sectors worldwide. Where value added to the gross domestic product was not available, gross value of production or sales was substituted and the exception footnoted. Figures for value of production are reported here in millions of U.S. dollars to permit comparisons to be made from country to country. Comparisons can also be made as to the relative importance of each mineral group within a given country.

Since the data for value of mineral production are obtained mostly from

Extractive industries

country	mining % of GDP, 1987	mineral production (value added) year	total ('000,000 U.S.$)	metals[a]	non-metals[b]	energy[c]	trade (value) year	exports total ('000,000 U.S.$)	exports metals[a]	exports non-metals[b]	exports energy[c]	imports total ('000,000 U.S.$)	imports metals[a]	imports non-metals[b]	imports energy[c]
Afghanistan	...	1982–83	283.8[1]	—	0.1[1]	99.9[1]	1986	272.6[2]	—	—	100.0[2]	0.3	—	100.0	—
Albania	17.4[3]	1984	12,722.2	—	1.1	98.9	1986	5,801.0	0.4	0.4	99.2	135.6	23.0	30.4	46.6
Algeria	...	1985	...	—	100.0		1985	—				0.3	—	6.8	93.2
American Samoa	...	1985	...				1987	...			100.0[6]	2.8	—	100.0	—
Andorra	...	...	...												
Angola	17.4[5]	1985	764.0	...	...	...	1987	2,051.6	—	2.8	97.2				
Anguilla	1.6	1987	0.3	—	100.0	—	1981	[8]	—	100.0	—	1.1	...	...	100.0
Antigua and Barbuda	1.8[3]	1984	1.0	—	100.0	—	1984	...				613.3	25.9	6.9	67.2
Argentina	2.5	1986	632.6	3.3	7.2	89.4	1986	57.1	48.1	12.7	39.2	...			
Aruba	...	1986	...	—	100.0		1986	...				836.3	4.2	27.5	68.2
Australia	4.9[12]	1987–88	10,040.8	36.7	7.3	56.0	1987	7,894.4	42.6	2.0	55.4	2,249.9	15.0	7.9	77.1
Austria	0.5[5]	1985	645.7	7.2	14.2	78.6	1987	253.2	45.3	53.8	0.9	83.5	—	—	100.0
Bahamas, The	...	1988	11.3[13]	—	100.0	—	1987	33.5	—	55.0	45.0	116.8	2.8	14.8	82.4
Bahrain	16.4[3]	1986	602.1	—	1.2	98.8	1985	90.1	42.0	4.2	53.8	211.7	0.2	11.5	88.3
Bangladesh	0.2[14]	1986–87	32.5	—	0.3	99.7	1987	...							
Barbados	0.6	1985	12.3	—	100.0		1986	1.0	—	100.0	—	6.8	12.9	32.4	54.7
Belgium	0.4	1987	545.9	—	44.6[5]	55.4[5]	1987[15]	5,610.1	4.9	93.1	2.0	11,991.3	13.4	44.9	41.7
Belize	0.2	1985	0.4	—	100.0	—	1985	0.1	—	100.0	—	1.1	—	—	100.0
Benin	0.2[5]	1985	2.0	—	100.0[16]	—	1986	56.6	—	3.8	96.2	2.0[7]	—	100.0[7]	—
Bermuda	0.3[17]	1978–79	1.3	—	100.0		1985	0.3[6]	73.2[6]	26.8[6]		1.7	—	42.0	58.0[18]
Bhutan	0.5[3]	1986	1.1	—	100.0		1986	1.8	18.2	75.5	6.3[18]	0.3	3.1	26.6	70.3[18]
Bolivia	10.1	1986	268.6	—	35.9	64.1	1986	465.9	16.9	3.3	79.8	1.2	—	100.0	—
Botswana	44.1	1987–88	916.5	12.5[7,13]	86.6[7,13]	0.9[7,13]	[20]								
Brazil	0.8[3]	1985	3,854.8	25.3[6,13]	22.1[6,13]	52.6[6,13]	1987	2,049.5	88.1	11.7	0.2	5,572.2	4.5	4.1	91.4
British Virgin Islands	0.2[21]	1985	0.8	—	100.0	—	1982	0.1	—	65.4	34.6	0.6	—	39.0	61.0
Brunei	54.3[5]	1985	1,918.3	...	...	...	1987	1,758.2	—	—	100.0	13.8	1.7	98.3	—
Bulgaria	0.4	1986	113.3	...	...	...		...				2.3	—	100.0	—
Burkina Faso	0.1[3]	1984	0.7	—	100.0		1983	...				3.3	—	100.0	—
Burundi	0.7	1987	8.0	...	...	...	1987	0.7[5]	—	100.0[5]	—	37.2	76.6	23.4	—
Cameroon	17.2[5]	1983–84	1,247.1[16]				1987	142.1	—	—	100.0				
Canada	5.8	1985	25,294.8	13.0	3.8	83.2	1987	11,660.2	25.5	11.0	63.5	4,802.5	26.0	10.0	64.0
Cape Verde	0.5[3]	1981	0.2	—	100.0	—	1984	0.2	—	100.0	—	0.8[22]	—	—	100.0[22]
Cayman Islands	0.3	1987	1.2	—	100.0	—	1983	3.8[23]	—	14.1[23]	85.9[23]	0.4[22]	—	—	100.0[22]
Central African Republic	2.3[3]	1985	17.4[24]	—	100.0[24]	—	1987	44.5	—	100.0[7]	—	0.8	—	100.0	—
Chad	0.5[5]	1985	3.0	—	100.0		1984					0.8	—	100.0	—
Chile	7.9	1987	2,026.2	...	...	...	1986	854.4	94.4	5.5	0.1	403.8	3.8	6.1	90.1
China	...	1986	11,296.3	8.3	20.0	71.7	1982	3,923.9	4.1	4.2	91.7	773.4	76.4	15.7	7.9
Christmas Island	...	1986	...	—	100.0	—	1987	29.9	—	100.0	—				
Cocos (Keeling) Islands	...	...	...				1987	0.8	—	100.0	—				
Colombia	6.8	1987	2,445.3	...	...	...	1986	433.7	0.6	8.9	90.5	51.7	25.6	57.8	16.7
Comoros	...	1985	...	—	100.0		1983	0.1	—	100.0	—	2.9[5]	—	100.0[5]	—
Congo	15.5[3]	1986	287.2[16]				1986	785.6	1.7	5.9	92.4	0.1[22]	—	42.1[22]	57.9[22]
Cook Islands	—	1979	75.9	23.6[26]	76.4[26]		1984	0.8	100.0	—	—	94.2	—	8.2	91.8
Costa Rica	1.9[6]	1984	192.5[16]				1985	37.2	6.4	0.9	92.7	313.1	0.2	3.6	96.2
Côte d'Ivoire	2.9[27]	1984	...				1985	886.5	40.5	0.7	58.8	41.4	3.4	69.5	27.1
Cuba	0.4	1988	14.8	...	8.7	91.3	1987	9.8	5.0	95.0	—	106.3	0.1	9.9	90.0
Cyprus	...	1986	4,179.1	9.3	8.0	82.7	1987	627.2[28]	2.5	12.1	85.4[28]	7,150.1[18,28]	8.5	3.0	88.5[18,28]
Czechoslovakia	2.3[6]	1986	...	...	9.5[5]	90.5[5]	1987	476.7	19.6	11.9	68.5	1,161.3	4.3	9.7	86.0
Denmark	0.7	1987	738.7	—	—	...	1983	...				22.9[28]	—	6.8	93.2[28]
Djibouti	—[5]	1983	...				1985	...							
Dominica	0.8[5]	1985	0.5	—	100.0	—	1985	...				0.6	—	16.9	83.1
Dominican Republic	3.7[3]	1986	327.0	94.1[6]	5.9[6]		1985	1.3	20.8	79.2		367.2	14.7	—	85.3
Ecuador	7.4	1987	780.2	—	9.3	90.7	1986	838.4	—	—	100.0	10.6	1.4	53.8	44.8
Egypt	18.5[5]	1985	10,311.0	0.3[10]	1.1[10]	98.6[10]	1987	1,132.5	0.6	0.3	99.1	382.5	14.4	17.5	68.1
El Salvador	0.1	1985	8.2	—	100.0	—	1984	1.6	4.6	95.4		490.4	0.2	0.9	98.9

country sources, there is some variation (from a standard calendar year) in the time periods to which the data refer. In addition, the time period for which production data are available does not always correspond with the year for which mineral trade data are available.

The Standard International Trade Classification (SITC), Revision 3, was used to determine the commodity groupings for foreign trade statistics. The actual trade data for these groups is taken largely from the United Nations annual *Yearbook of International Trade Statistics* and national sources.

Forestry. Data for the production and trade sections of forestry are based on the United Nations annual *Yearbook of Forest Products*. Production of roundwood (all wood obtained in removals from forests) is the principal indicator of the volume of each country's forestry sector; this total is broken down further (as percentages of the roundwood total) into its principal components: fuelwood and charcoal, and industrial roundwood. The latter group was further divided to show its principal component, sawlogs and veneer; lesser categories of industrial roundwood could not be shown for reasons of space. These included pitprops (used in mining, a principal consumer of wood) and pulpwood (used in papermaking and plastics). Value of trade in forest products is given for both imports and exports, although exports alone tend to be the significant indicator for producing countries, while imports of wood are rarely a significant fraction of the trade of most importing countries.

Fisheries. Data for nominal (live weight) catches of fish, crustaceans, mollusks, etc., in all fishing areas (marine areas and inland waters) are taken from the United Nations annual *Yearbook of Fishery Statistics* (*Catches and Landings*). Total catch figures are given in metric tons; the catches in inland waters and marine areas are given as percentages of the total catch, as are the main kinds of catch—fish, crustaceans, and mollusks. The total catch figures exclude marine mammals, such as whales and seals; and such aquatic animal products as corals, sponges, and pearls; but include frogs, turtles, and jellyfish. The subtotals by kind of catch, however, exclude the last group, which do not belong taxonomically to the fish, crustaceans, or mollusks.

Figures for trade in fishery products (including processed products and preparations like oils, meals, and animal feeding stuffs) are taken from the United Nations annual *Yearbook of Fishery Statistics* (*Fishery Commodities*). Value figures for trade in fish products are given for both imports and exports.

The following notes further define the column headings:
a. Includes ferrous and nonferrous metallic ores and scraps, such as bauxite, copper, gold (except unwrought or semimanufactured), iron ore, lead, uranium, or zinc.
b. Includes natural fertilizers; stone, sand, and aggregate; and pearls, precious and semiprecious stones, worked and unworked.
c. Includes hydrocarbon solids, liquids, and gases.
1 cubic metre = 35.3147 cubic feet
1 metric ton = 1.1023 short tons

forestry, 1987						fisheries, 1987								country
production of roundwood				trade (value '000 U.S.$)		catch (nominal)						trade (value, '000 U.S.$)		
total ('000 cubic metres)	fuelwood, charcoal (%)	industrial roundwood (%)		exports	imports	total ('000 metric tons)	by source (%)		by kind of catch (%)			exports	imports	
		total	sawlogs, veneer				marine	fresh-water	fish	crusta-ceans	mollusks			
7,021	77.1	22.9	12.2	...	29,018	1.5	—	100.0	100.0	—	—	...	...	Afghanistan
2,330	69.0	31.0	31.0	710	445	12.5	74.4	25.6	88.1	1.2	10.7	...	...	Albania
2,008	87.8	12.2	1.0	...	266,840	70.3	99.6	0.4	95.4	4.6	—	240	36,000	Algeria
...	...	...	...	...	1,801[4, 5]	0.2	100.0	—	100.0	—	—	253,620[3]	1,241[3]	American Samoa
...	...	...	...	...	...	...	—	100.0	100.0	—	—	...	...	Andorra
5,139	80.1	19.9	2.1	98[7]	256	81.3	90.2	9.8	99.8	0.2	—	...	33,690	Angola
...	...	...	...	...	...	—	100.0	—	100.0	—	—	9	9	Anguilla
...	...	...	...	...	2,596[10]	2.4	100.0	—	95.0	5.0	—	...	530	Antigua and Barbuda
11,117	51.5	48.5	16.3	34,360	119,895	559.4	98.6	1.4	89.9	0.6	9.5	262,794	14,307	Argentina
...	...	...	...	...	...	0.8	100.0	—	100.0	—	—	11	11	Aruba
20,018	14.4	85.6	40.8	308,516	858,998	200.0	98.8	1.2	64.7	19.3	16.0	420,982	299,584	Australia
14,118	10.0	90.0	55.7	2,188,157	1,072,501	4.6	—	100.0	100.0	—	—	1,945	117,705	Austria
115	—	100.0	13.0	1,061[5]	17,660	6.0	99.6	0.4	32.0	60.4	7.2	17,910	3,730	Bahamas, The
...	...	...	...	...	40,164	7.8	100.0	—	73.3	26.3	0.4	...	3,840	Bahrain
28,562	97.0	3.0	1.6	7,688	14,916	814.7	28.6	71.4	91.1	8.9	—	143,788	...	Bangladesh
3,528[15]	15.2[15]	84.8[15]	58.7[15]	1,318,112[15]	2,238,828[15]	3.7	100.0	—	100.0	—	—	100	4,240	Barbados
155	81.3	18.7	18.7	657	3,193	40.4	98.5	1.5	93.8	3.4	2.8	167,005[15]	529,941[15]	Belgium
4,691	94.7	5.3	0.7	...	1,869	1.5	99.8	0.2	36.5	53.6	9.9	8,436	742	Belize
...	...	...	...	...	2,434[5, 19]	41.9	23.7	76.3	84.8	15.2	—	1,000	2,180	Benin
...	...	...	...	...	...	0.9	100.0	—	96.0	4.0	—	...	7,717	Bermuda
3,224	91.4	8.6	7.4	286	143[10]	1.0	—	100.0	100.0	—	—	...	...	Bhutan
1,379	89.2	10.8	9.9	18,999	5,100	4.8	—	100.0	100.0	—	—	...	2,000	Bolivia
1,270	93.9	6.1	—	...	9,415	1.9	—	100.0	100.0	—	—	350	1,350	Botswana
241,478	72.6	27.4	16.6	963,373	232,957	793.1	72.9	27.1	85.1	13.9	1.0	178,163	138,391	Brazil
...	...	...	...	...	...	0.3	100.0	—	92.1	7.9	—	...	...	British Virgin Islands
294	26.9	73.1	70.1	30	6,775	2.7	96.1	3.9	86.7	13.1	0.2	275	3,710	Brunei
4,445	39.8	60.2	23.5	24,680	172,700	110.5	88.4	11.6	97.0	—	3.0	14,250	10,490	Bulgaria
7,114	95.5	4.5	—	...	2,427	7.0	—	100.0	100.0	—	—	...	2,380	Burkina Faso
3,849	98.8	1.2	0.2	...	1,342	5.0	—	100.0	100.0	—	—	301	19	Burundi
12,447	77.6	22.4	16.8	73,762	44,019	82.5	75.8	24.2	84.5	15.5	—	7,005	41,210	Cameroon
191,224	3.5	96.5	74.6	15,095,422	1,312,812	1,453.5	97.0	3.0	86.0	6.6	7.4	2,092,170	511,901	Canada
...	...	...	...	...	963	6.9	100.0	—	99.2	0.8	—	2,750	110	Cape Verde
...	...	...	...	...	...	5.9	100.0	—	91.5	8.5	—	18,590	1,290	Cayman Islands
3,443	88.7	11.3	4.5	18,389	280	13.0	—	100.0	100.0	—	—	...	1,600	Central African Republic
3,746	85.9	14.1	0.1	...	591	110.0	—	100.0	100.0	—	—	...	...	Chad
16,488	38.0	62.0	33.8	543,184	45,719	4,814.4	100.0	—	96.6	0.6	2.2	635,583	1,400	Chile
276,518[25]	64.2[25]	35.8[25]	19.7[25]	648,083[25]	3,307,122[25]	9,346.2	57.9	42.1	79.0	8.4	12.3	912,476	113,373	China
...	...	...	...	...	...	—	100.0	—	100.0	—	—	...	...	Christmas Island
...	...	...	...	...	...	—	100.0	—	100.0	—	—	...	...	Cocos (Keeling) Islands
17,831	85.0	15.0	11.0	14,011	110,887	58.7	39.9	60.1	85.6	11.9	2.5	44,531	47,400	Colombia
...	...	...	...	...	...	5.3	100.0	—	99.0	1.0	—	...	460	Comoros
2,614	64.4	35.6	26.5	81,277	2,350	31.0	56.5	43.5	99.7	0.3	—	3,650	34,550	Congo
...	...	...	...	...	...	1.1	100.0	—	68.9	0.5	28.1	...	250	Cook Islands
3,191	84.0	16.0	9.8	12,361	61,103	20.0	98.5	1.5	53.9	44.5	0.7	33,805	5,340	Costa Rica
11,792	72.4	27.6	21.9	245,117	27,200	102.5	72.5	27.5	97.5	2.5	—	97,360	108,125	Côte d'Ivoire
3,251	81.1	18.9	4.8	...	269,591	214.4	92.2	7.8	84.8	9.4	5.3	180,913	60,513	Cuba
76	28.9	71.1	43.4	46	66,381	2.6	98.2	1.8	92.1	0.2	7.7	353	16,980	Cyprus
18,679	7.9	92.1	54.4	417,595	93,390	20.7	—	100.0	100.0	—	—	4,700	94,989	Czechoslovakia
2,203	18.4	81.6	42.7	271,159	1,366,838	1,695.7	98.6	1.4	94.2	1.2	4.6	1,750,652	842,476	Denmark
...	...	...	...	...	1,587	0.4	100.0	—	98.9	1.1	—	...	750	Djibouti
982	99.4	0.6	0.4	17[10]	602	0.4	100.0	—	100.0	—	—	...	740	Dominica
8,753	72.0	28.0	26.1	15,342	51,266	20.3	90.9	9.1	90.6	6.0	3.2	2,340	12,630	Dominican Republic
2,105	95.3	4.7	—	...	107,690	679.0	99.9	0.1	88.1	11.7	0.2	481,039	...	Ecuador
5,053	98.4	1.6	1.1	...	801,671	250.0	19.3	80.7	98.4	1.0	0.6	3,997	123,546	Egypt
				2,597	21,525	18.0	89.4	10.6	37.5	61.8	0.7	20,880	815	El Salvador

Extractive industries (continued)

country	mining % of GDP, 1987	mineral production (value added) year	total ('000,000 U.S.$)	metals[a]	non-metals[b]	energy[c]	trade (value) year	exports total ('000,000 U.S.$)	exports metals[a]	exports non-metals[b]	exports energy[c]	imports total ('000,000 U.S.$)	imports metals[a]	imports non-metals[b]	imports energy[c]
Equatorial Guinea	—	1986	7.4	—	100.0	—	1983	1.3	100.0	—	—	...	...	...	...
Ethiopia	0.2[3]	1986	—	—	—	—	1985	...	...	...	...	136.0	1.4	0.4	98.2
Faeroe Islands	—						1987	—	—	—	...	1.7	—	100.0	—
Falkland Islands							1983	0.2	85.7	13.0	1.3	2.9	0.3	41.3	58.4
Fiji	2.0	1987	25.4	22.0[27]	78.0[27]		1985	74.5	28.5	62.8	8.7	2,271.5	11.8	8.5	79.7
Finland	0.3	1986	205.1	39.4	60.6	—	1987	1,641.7	47.7	35.1	17.2	13,878.7	7.6	7.1	85.3
France	0.6	1985	3,583.7	4.7	30.4	64.9	1987	1.5	100.0	—	—	...	...	...	100.0
French Guiana	...	1986	—	—	100.0	—	1987	21.1	0.3	99.7	—	3.5[6]	...	...	100.0[6]
French Polynesia	...						1986	...	...	...	...	6.5[6]	—	100.0[6]	—
Gabon	24.0[3]	1986	794.1	8.9[6]	0.1[6]	91.0[6]	1986	1,285.1	7.5	—	92.5	...	...	...	...
Gambia, The	—	1986–87	—	—	—	—	1986	3.3	—	100.0	—	...	...	...	...
Gaza Strip	...						[30]	[30]				...	...	...	...
Germany, East	3.1	1986	6,149.2[27]	0.3[13]	18.2[13]	81.5[13]	1987	3,072.8	30.3	35.4	34.3	17,748.4	18.0	7.4	74.6
Germany, West	1.6[3]	1983	547.9	97.7	2.3		1986	51.2	37.8	62.2	—	331.8[7]	4.8[7]	0.5[7]	94.7[7]
Ghana	...	1986	...				1986	1.0	—	100.0	—	0.3	—	100.0	—
Gibraltar	...	1985	...				1986	1.0	—	100.0	—	...	...	...	...
Greece	1.6[3]	1985	576.2	12.9	24.0	63.1	1987	297.8	37.4	35.8	26.8	1,716.3	4.6	5.3	90.1
Greenland	...	1985	...				1987	41.7	95.5	4.5	—	2.0	—	100.0	—
Grenada	0.4[3]	1985	1.1	—	100.0	—	1984	—	...	...	...	0.1[22]	2.7[22]	—	97.3[22]
Guadeloupe	...	1980	...				1987	0.2	100.0	—	—	3.7	—	—	100.0
Guam	...	1984	—	—	100.0	—	1986[31]	—	100.0[31]	—	—	365.5[27]	...	0.7[27]	99.3[27]
Guatemala	0.3	1986	30.0[16]	...			1986	13.6	—	1.3	98.7	...	...	...	...
Guernsey	...							410.9	91.9	8.1	—	0.3[5]	100.0[5]	—	—
Guinea	10.1[3]	1983	299.0[33]	100.0[33]	—		1986	1.0	—	100.0	—	1.3[22]	—	89.5[22]	10.5[22]
Guinea-Bissau	1.3[6]	1983	1.0	—	100.0	—	1986	75.6	98.7	1.3	—	1.1	—	100.0	—
Guyana	5.1	1987	17.5[34]	—	100.0[34]	—	1986	8.5[23]	100.0[23]	—	—	133.3	0.4	1.4	98.2
Haiti	0.1[3]	1986	1.1	100.0	—	—	1983	...	...	...	...	...	...	...	...
Honduras	1.5	1987	59.0	—	100.0	—	1985	30.9	100.0	—	—	1,671.0	3.1	79.6	17.3
Hong Kong	0.1	1985	46.2	4.3	3.0	92.7	1987	685.1	30.8	68.4	0.8	1,632.4[18,28]	4.1	5.7	90.2[18,28]
Hungary	8.1[6]	1986	1,322.7				1987	451.4[28]	16.6	—	83.4[28]	36.0	61.3	27.3	11.4
Iceland	...	1987	...	—	100.0	—	1987	13.6	—	100.0	—	1,873.1	14.3	73.4	12.3
India	3.0[3]	1986–87	5,818.1	7.0	11.0	82.0	1987	2,735.5	23.4	75.8	0.8	856.2	21.6	10.7	67.7
Indonesia	11.1[3]	1986	8,374.3	—	6.8	93.2	1986	7,732.9	4.0	0.3	95.7	23.9	14.9	24.8	60.3
Iran	9.8[5]	1984–85	18,789.3	—	8.2[13,35]	91.8[13,35]	1987	9,417.7	0.1	0.1	99.8	4.6	23.5	74.9	1.6
Iraq	24.7[5]	1985	11,569.3[16]				1986	8,784.3	—	0.4	99.6	608.2	12.6	7.6	79.8
Ireland	1.2[10]	1984	310.8[36]	29.6	69.0	1.4[36]	1987	344.8	65.8	25.0	9.2	3,068.2	0.2	72.8	27.0
Isle of Man	...	1987	—	—	100.0	—	1987	...	...	...	...	...	...	...	...
Israel	0.7[37]	1982–83	195.4	5.7[37,38]	94.3[37]	—[37,38]	1987	2,444.4	0.2	99.8	—	14,596.5	11.0	6.1	82.9
Italy	0.9[3]	1985	1,749.8	4.5	17.8	77.7	1987	571.9	26.8	53.6	19.6	10.0	5.6	22.5	71.9
Jamaica	7.3	1987	161.4	98.5	1.5	—	1987	336.9	99.6	0.4	—	...	...	...	...
Japan	0.3	1987	8,303.4	6.5[3]	26.3[3]	67.2[3]	1987	361.3	33.7	65.6	0.7	41,015.5	14.9	7.5	77.6
Jersey	...	1986	180.7	—	100.0	—	1986	276.2	—	100.0	—	309.3	0.4	8.9	90.7
Jordan	3.3[3]	1985	...	—	100.0	—	1982	3.8	100.0	—	—	...	...	...	...
Kampuchea	...	1987	16.2	0.8[7]	99.2[7]		1987	24.2	8.6	90.0	1.4	310.2	1.0	1.7	97.3
Kenya	0.2		...				1987	0.03	98.6	1.4	—	0.04	—	67.4	32.6
Kiribati	—	1986	...				1987	...	...	...	...	...	...	...	...
Korea, North	...	1985	872.4	5.3	21.2	73.5	1987	133.2	19.1	80.8	0.1	6,833.7	20.7	5.0	74.3
Korea, South	1.2	1987	8,015.6	—	100.0	—	1986	4,048.1	0.5	0.4	99.1	10.5	30.8	68.3	0.9
Kuwait	41.0	1985	...				1983	0.7[23]	100.0[23]	—	—	...	...	...	...
Laos	...	1985	...				1986	45.8	28.3	71.7	—	28.9	2.2	78.3	19.5
Lebanon	...	1987	0.9	—	100.0	—	[20]	...	...	...	...	...	...	...	...
Lesotho	0.3	1986	129.6[40]	—	100.0[40]	—	1986	193.3	86.3	13.7	—	...	...	...	...
Liberia	12.5	1986	...				1986	...	...	...	...	...	...	...	...
Libya	37.5[5]	1985	9,710.0	—	0.7[22]	99.3[22]	1986	6,521.8	—	—	100.0	86.7[6]	80.1[6]	19.9[6]	—
Liechtenstein	...							...	...	...	...	...	...	...	...
Luxembourg	0.1[3]	1986	3.5	—	100.0	—	[15]	1.0	29.6	70.4	—	4.2	17.6	—	82.4
Macau	...	1985	0.1	—	100.0	—	1985	18.0	36.0	64.0	—	2.3	—	58.9	41.1
Madagascar	0.2[5]	1985	7.8	—	100.0	—	1983	...	...	...	...	6.4	—	42.4	57.6
Malawi	...	1984	0.3[7]	—	100.0	—	1986	...	...	...	...	234.9	38.4	29.8	31.8
Malaysia	10.9	1987	2,555.6				1986	3,716.0	2.9	1.1	96.0	...	...	...	...
Maldives	1.7[3]	1986	1.7	—	100.0	—	1985	11.5	—	100.0	—	1.5	—	100.0	—
Mali	1.5[3]	1984	2.6[42]	—	100.0[42]	—	1986	4.1	11.6	88.4	—	4.7	—	98.2	1.8
Malta	...	1986	2.2	—	100.0	—	1987	1.5	39.4	—	60.6	80.3	—	100.0	—
Martinique	...	1984	...	—	100.0	—	1986	...	...	...	...	0.3	—	100.0	—
Mauritania	9.9[27]	1984	69.4	—	100.0	—	1986	150.6	100.0	—	—	...	...	...	...
Mauritius	0.1	1987	1.9	—	100.0	—	1987	14.6	—	100.0	—	18.8	0.8	80.2	19.0
Mayotte	...							...	...	...	...	...	...	...	...
Mexico	7.2[3]	1984	17,160.2	5.6	4.4	90.0	1987	8,471.0	3.0	3.4	93.6	285.1	37.0	34.1	28.9
Monaco	...		...					...	...	...	...	...	...	...	...
Mongolia	...		...					...	...	...	...	...	...	...	...
Montserrat	1.1[3]	1986	0.5	—	100.0	—	1986	0.4	—	—	100.0	5.1	—	100.0	—
Morocco	3.0	1987	575.7	—	92.3	7.7	1986	492.5	10.9	87.8	1.3	831.0	0.2	30.8	69.0
Mozambique	0.3[5]	1985	6.0				1984	1.7	71.6	—	28.4	21.0	—	100.0	—
Myanmar (Burma)	0.9	1987	80.1[43]	—	100.0	—	1987	23.7	52.7	47.3	—	...	...	...	...
Nauru	...	1986	...				1987	90.9	—	100.0	—	2.8	17.7	75.3	7.0
Nepal	0.3[3]	1985–86	7.0				1985	0.2	—	100.0	—	9,045.1	8.6	7.4	84.0
Netherlands, The	3.8	1987	8,456.3	—	2.1[27]	97.9[27]	1987	4,071.6	17.0	10.9	72.1	100.4	—	5.4[6]	94.6[6]
Netherlands Antilles	...	1986	...	—	100.0	—	1987	114.9[3]	2.3[3]	13.8[3]	83.9[3]	9.2[6]	—	5.4[6]	94.6[6]
New Caledonia	6.2[5]	1983	36.0	100.0	—	—	1987	70.4	100.0	—	—	463.5	22.8	14.9	62.3
New Zealand	1.0	1985–86	442.6	—	16.5	83.5	1987	56.3	46.8	14.8	38.4	152.1[7]	—	1.5[7]	98.5[7]
Nicaragua	0.6[3]	1986	16.0	—	100.0	—	1984	3.2	100.0	—	—	9.6[10]	—	100.0[10]	—
Niger	6.7	1985	115.1	97.9[22]	2.9[22]	-0.8[22]	1984	363.2[22,18]	99.3[22,18]	0.4[2]	0.3[22,18]	128.1	14.2	85.8	—
Nigeria	19.8[5]	1985	8,104.2	0.1[44]	7.2[44]	92.7[44]	1984	11,340.4	—	0.1	99.9	—	...	...	...
Niue	...	1983	...	—	100.0	—	1984	—	...	...	...	...	...	...	...
Norfolk Island	...	...	...				1985	...	...	...	...	...	—	100.0[6]	—

forestry, 1987 production of roundwood — total ('000 cubic metres)	fuelwood, charcoal (%)	industrial roundwood (%) total	industrial roundwood (%) sawlogs, veneer	trade (value '000 U.S.$) exports	imports	fisheries, 1987 catch (nominal) total ('000 metric tons)	by source (%) marine	fresh-water	by kind of catch (%) fish	crusta-ceans	mollusks	trade (value, '000 U.S.$) exports	imports	country
607	73.6	26.4	26.4	18,616	...	4.0	90.0	10.0	81.1	11.3	3.8	—	2,800	Equatorial Guinea
39,968	95.5	4.5	0.3	...	15,073	4.0	12.5	87.5	100.0	—	—	—	730	Ethiopia
...	...	...	...	...	...	355.4	100.0	—	96.5	2.9	0.6	270,844	5,724	Faeroe Islands
...	...	...	...	...	...	...	100.0	—	30.4	69.6	—	—		Falkland Islands
249	14.9	85.1	82.3	5,916	8,450	35.3	86.5	13.5	79.6	2.4	14.9	23,185	13,876	Fiji
41,659	7.2	92.8	42.9	7,073,642	438,589	159.3	79.3	20.7	100.0	—	—	8,613	130,177	Finland
40,901	25.5	74.5	49.6	2,762,014	4,987,015	843.7	95.3	4.7	69.6	3.3	27.1	654,464[29]	2,022,470[29]	France
254	26.0	74.0	70.5	2,169	1,087	5.1	100.0	—	45.1	54.9	—	33,507	10,527	French Guiana
...	...	...	...	...	14,695	2.1	100.0	—	98.8	0.9	0.3	—	7,210	French Polynesia
3,847	68.2	31.8	31.8	128,774	3,655	20.9	90.9	9.1	92.0	8.0	—	11,120	8,760	Gabon
862	97.6	2.4	1.6	...	235	14.4	81.2	18.8	68.6	30.1	1.3	1,770	2,850	Gambia, The
...	...	...	...	...	...	0.5	100.0	—	100.0	—	—	...	...	Gaza Strip
10,831	6.6	93.4	38.0	182,700	460,600	193.6	89.6	10.4	97.8	0.4	1.8	1,266	37,944	Germany, East
33,739	10.8	89.2	48.4	4,454,633	8,102,147	201.8	88.1	11.9	76.8	8.4	14.8	439,657	1,270,495	Germany, West
9,884	88.9	11.1	7.3	67,646	4,344	371.8	85.5	14.5	98.7	0.7	0.6	26,725	13,050	Ghana
...	...	...	...	...	...	...	100.0	—	...	...	...	...	...	Gibraltar
2,945	68.4	31.6	19.4	37,101	462,200	135.1	92.4	7.6	86.8	5.6	7.6	59,323	123,587	Greece
—	—	—	—	...	...	101.0	100.0	—	36.2	63.4	0.4	288,854	3,005	Greenland
...	...	...	...	...	...	4.9	100.0	—	98.2	0.3	1.1	2,910	320	Grenada
17	88.2	11.8	11.8	...	15,820	8.6	99.5	0.5	94.4	1.9	3.5	220	14,512	Guadeloupe
...	...	...	...	77[6]	1,935[6]	0.5	82.0	18.0	100.0	—	—	...	...	Guam
7,184	98.4	1.6	1.4	9,458	43,822	2.4	78.4	21.6	52.8	47.2	—	11,850	1,390	Guatemala
...	...	...	...	...	...	[32]	[32]	[32]	[32]	[32]	[32]	...	...	Guernsey
4,455	86.0	14.0	4.0	800	1,056	30.0	93.3	6.7	100.0	—	—	...	3,380	Guinea
563	75.0	25.0	7.1	350	310	3.5	100.0	—	72.3	27.1	0.6	600	370	Guinea-Bissau
227	7.9	92.1	82.8	8,000	2,710	41.6	97.4	2.6	96.1	3.9	—	20,640	...	Guyana
6,207	96.1	3.9	3.6	...	4,584	8.1	96.3	3.7	96.9	3.1	—	750	5,790	Haiti
5,637	85.7	14.3	14.1	28,251	24,076	13.5	98.5	1.5	10.0	85.2	4.8	52,465	1,940	Honduras
186	100.0	—	—	78,239	793,567	228.1	97.2	2.8	84.6	8.1	7.3	501,815	794,280	Hong Kong
6,714	44.4	55.6	29.8	133,585	291,003	36.8	—	100.0	100.0	—	—	17,851	42,779	Hungary
—	—	—	—	...	64,933	1,633.1	100.0	—	96.6	2.5	0.9	1,071,067	3,379	Iceland
254,263	90.5	9.5	7.2	16,337	267,177	2,893.4	58.1	41.9	91.1	8.0	0.9	409,170	...	India
160,085	82.4	17.6	15.8	2,509,487	251,601	2,609.7	75.4	24.6	89.8	7.5	2.2	441,079	26,519	Indonesia
6,769	35.4	64.6	5.5	38[27]	181,006	150.0	80.0	20.0	95.5	3.4	1.1	15,930	24,500	Iran
143	65.0	35.0	14.0	...	117,556	20.5	24.4	75.6	100.0	—	—	...	...	Iraq
1,245	3.7	96.3	52.9	29,591	268,020	247.4	100.0	—	88.2	4.7	7.1	199,083	61,554	Ireland
...	...	...	...	...	...	5.8	100.0	—	18.4	2.7	78.9	...	...	Isle of Man
118	9.3	90.7	22.0	11,134	226,578	26.9	49.9	50.1	99.0	0.6	0.4	2,914	26,510	Israel
9,122	49.4	50.6	28.6	1,097,584	4,518,050	554.5	90.0	10.0	60.6	5.0	34.4	140,270[39]	1,738,226[39]	Italy
153	8.5	91.5	83.0	100	45,968	10.6	86.6	13.4	99.8	0.2	—	2,200	25,760	Jamaica
32,322	1.8	98.2	58.8	863,949	9,912,750	11,841.1	98.1	1.9	83.6	1.8	13.5	889,828	8,308,077	Japan
10	60.0	40.0	—	9,267	60,949	2.4[32]	100.0[32]	—	11.0[32]	82.7[32]	6.3[32]	4,654	...	Jersey
5,545	89.8	10.2	2.0	94	100	0.1	100.0	—	100.0	—	—	...	9,315	Jordan
35,180	95.4	4.6	1.2	786	22,255	70.0	9.3	90.7	99.3	0.7	—	...	...	Kampuchea
...	...	...	...	...	...	131.2	5.2	94.8	99.2	0.7	0.1	4,110	1,320	Kenya
4,649	87.1	12.9	12.9	...	24,750	43.9	100.0	—	91.0	0.3	8.7	760	95	Kiribati
6,849	64.2	35.8	15.6	365,461	1,310,942	1,700.0	94.1	5.9	100.0	—	—	61,552	...	Korea, North
—	—	—	—	20,152	102,443	2,876.4	98.0	2.0	65.3	3.3	30.2	1,505,697	212,497	Korea, South
4,313	92.6	7.4	4.9	10,251	200	8.6	100.0	—	76.0	24.0	—	3,880	24,455	Kuwait
...	...	...	...	...	...	10.6	—	100.0	100.0	—	—	...	...	Laos
493	94.9	5.1	5.1	2,451	70,374	1.8	94.4	5.6	97.2	1.4	1.4	...	2,500	Lebanon
553	100.0	—	—	...	4,588	—	—	100.0	100.0	—	—	...	...	Lesotho
5,640	83.1	16.9	14.4	36,026	1,942	18.7	78.6	21.4	97.3	2.7	—	1,100	8,040	Liberia
637	84.1	15.9	9.9	...	75,754	8.0	100.0	—	100.0	—	—	...	15,710	Libya
8[5]	—	100.0[5]	...	...	...	—	—	100.0	100.0	—	—	41	41	Liechtenstein
15	15	15	15	15	15	—	—	100.0	100.0	—	—	15	15	Luxembourg
...	...	...	...	399	7,981	3.5	100.0	—	29.4	68.1	2.5	7,817	13,558	Macau
7,250	88.9	11.1	6.5	264	4,404	63.6	27.7	72.3	87.8	12.0	0.1	30,540	320	Madagascar
6,946	95.4	4.6	0.7	600[27]	7,595	88.6	—	100.0	100.0	—	—	235	80	Malawi
44,261	17.9	82.1	79.3	2,550,952	264,673	607.5	98.5	1.5	74.9	12.9	10.8	191,577	157,502	Malaysia
5,201	93.6	6.4	0.2	...	1,915	46.9	100.0	—	100.0	—	—	16,530	...	Maldives
...	...	...	...	...	27,605	55.7	—	100.0	100.0	—	—	500	1,950	Mali
13	76.9	23.1	23.1	...	22,846	1.0	100.0	—	96.2	2.4	1.4	481	7,529	Malta
12	58.3	41.7	8.3	...	3,353	4.6	98.8	1.2	95.9	3.2	—	157	21,625	Martinique
...	...	...	...	...	...	99.3	100.0	—	47.6	0.5	51.9	169,100	—	Mauritania
33	63.6	36.4	21.2	...	10,501	18.0	99.7	0.3	96.9	0.6	2.5	10,703	7,328	Mauritius
...	...	...	...	...	...	0.8[3]	...	...	...	...	...	...	...	Mayotte
21,947	66.2	33.8	19.7	13,884	319,305	1,419.2	87.8	12.2	87.0	6.9	5.9	569,914	2,490	Mexico
...	...	...	...	...	1.5[3]	1.5	100.0	—	100.0	—	—	29	29	Monaco
2,390	56.5	43.5	43.5	70[27]	6,800	0.4	—	100.0	100.0	—	—	...	2,480	Mongolia
...	...	...	...	...	367[4,10]	0.1	100.0	—	100.0	—	—	...	...	Montserrat
2,030	64.5	35.5	6.5	17,008	133,932	491.0	99.7	0.3	94.3	0.3	5.4	352,704	1,292	Morocco
15,297	93.4	6.6	0.6	1,299	396	36.1	99.3	0.7	83.6	15.9	0.5	33,600	6,325	Mozambique
19,427	84.8	15.2	9.3	139,672	7,500	685.9	78.9	21.1	99.0	1.0	—	23,760	...	Myanmar (Burma)
...	...	...	...	...	...	—	100.0	—	100.0	—	—	...	...	Nauru
16,479	96.6	3.4	3.4	12,000	7,181	10.7	—	100.0	100.0	—	—	...	...	Nepal
1,156	10.0	90.0	44.1	1,679,844	3,320,604	435.2	98.8	1.2	77.2	—	22.8	953,177	509,430	Netherlands, The
...	...	...	...	...	12,136	1.0	100.0	—	100.0	—	—	145[11]	6,830[11]	Netherlands Antilles
12	—	100.0	91.7	...	5,936	4.4	100.0	—	45.7	3.1	0.7	3,266	4,421	New Caledonia
9,341	0.5	99.5	52.9	400,019	178,199	430.7	100.0	—	82.0	1.2	16.7	402,948	29,868	New Zealand
3,770	76.7	23.3	22.0	2,569	10,566	5.0	96.6	3.4	45.1	54.9	—	10,950	—	Nicaragua
4,163	93.8	6.2	—	...	2,383	2.4	—	100.0	100.0	—	—	...	970	Niger
101,786	92.3	7.7	5.5	6,091	177,376	249.0	58.5	41.5	99.3	0.7	—	7,635	168,046	Nigeria
...	...	...	...	...	...	—	100.0	—	100.0	—	—	...	...	Niue
...	...	...	...	...	...	—	100.0	—	100.0	—	—	...	...	Norfolk Island

Extractive industries (continued)

country	mining % of GDP, 1987	mineral production (value added) year	total ('000,000 U.S.$)	metals[a]	non-metals[b]	energy[c]	trade (value) year	exports total ('000,000 U.S.$)	metals[a]	non-metals[b]	energy[c]	imports total ('000,000 U.S.$)	metals[a]	non-metals[b]	energy[c]
Norway	9.3	1986	7,225.4	0.8	1.6	97.6	1987	8,396.9	2.5	1.3	96.2	1,229.4	43.8	11.4	44.8
Oman	47.4	1986	2,610.4	0.4	0.5	99.1	1987	3,459.0	—	0.1	99.9	17.7	41.2	5.9	52.9
Pacific Is., Trust Terr. of the															
Marshall Islands	...	...	...	...	...	...	1982					3.7	—	—	100.0
Micronesia, Fed. States of	—	...	...	...	...	...	...	...	...	...	...	...	...	...	...
Northern Mariana Islands	—	—	—	—	—	—	1983	...	...	...	—	2.1[6]	—	—	100.0[6]
Palau	—	—	—	—	—	—	1986	17.2	27.4	72.6	—	564.4	11.6	4.0	84.4
Pakistan	2.3	1985–86	674.2	—	22.0[13]	78.0[13]	1985	136.9	18.4	81.6	—	314.9	2.6	11.8	85.6
Panama	0.1	1987	7.3	—	100.0	—	1985	265.1	99.9	0.1	—	0.5	—	100.0	—
Papua New Guinea	10.7[6]	1983	252.7	100.0			1986	...	...	...	...	59.6	—	5.8	94.2
Paraguay	0.5	1987	20.9	—	100.0	—	1986	...	...	...	...	22.8	35.2	55.7	9.1
Peru	2.7	1986	2,320.0	51.5[22]	8.2[22,46]	40.3[22,46]	1986	671.9[27]	71.6[27]	0.6[27]	27.8[27]	888.6	1.9	6.7	91.4
Philippines	1.5	1986	339.4	86.6	2.6	10.8	1986	284.3	93.9	2.1	4.0				
Pitcairn Island	—	—	—	—	—	—									
Poland	5.4[6]	1986	2,895.2	12.3	13.5	74.2	1986	1,752.1	0.4	22.7	76.9	2,217.1	10.4	6.9	82.7
Portugal	0.6[22]	1985	105.9	20.3	74.4	5.3	1987	124.8	19.9	78.3	1.8	1,427.7	2.5	7.1	90.4
Puerto Rico	0.1	1986	13.4	—	100.0	—	1986[31]	50.7	2.4	95.9	1.7	52.1	0.4	28.8	70.8
Qatar	30.3	1987	1,546.7[43]	—	100.0	—	1985	3,034.2	—	—	100.0	4.8	58.3	41.7	—
Réunion	...	1984	...	—	100.0	—	1987	0.1	100.0	—	—	6.2	—	—	100.0
Romania	...	...	...	...	...	...									
Rwanda	0.2[3]	1986	3.5	—	100.0	—	1985	9.8	100.0	—	—	4.3	—	100.0	—
St. Helena and Ascension	...	...	...	...	...	...	1984	1.4	—	—	100.0	0.4[7]	—	100.0[7]	
St. Kitts and Nevis	0.3[3]	1986	0.2	—	100.0	—	1985	12.9	—	—	100.0	...	...	...	...
St. Lucia	0.6[3]	1986	0.9	—	100.0	—	1983	—	—	—	100.0	0.1[27]	—	—	100.0[27]
St. Pierre and Miquelon	...	...	...	...	...	...	1985	1.3	—	—	100.0	0.6[22]	—	—	100.0[22]
St. Vincent	0.3	1986	0.3	—	100.0	—	1983	—	...	...	...	...	...	...	...
San Marino	...	...	...	...	...	...	...	...	...	...	...	...	...	...	...
São Tomé and Príncipe	0.3[27]	1982	0.1	—	100.0	—	1983	...	...	...	...	...	...	...	...
Saudi Arabia	29.6	1986–87	21,215.0	—	2.2	97.8	1986	22,750.0	0.2	0.3	99.5	109.7	32.9	64.4	2.7
Senegal	1.2[5]	1985	25.0	—	100.0	—	1986	66.9	4.0	96.0	—	258.9[27]	0.1[27]	5.4[27]	94.5[27]
Seychelles	...	1985	...	—	100.0	—	1985	0.3[27]	0.4[27]	99.6[27]	—	0.2	1.0	—	99.0
Sierra Leone	5.9[5]	1985	43.0	—	100.0	—	1986	112.6	57.0	43.0	—	0.1	—	100.0	—
Singapore	0.2	1986	32.1	—	100.0	—	1987	233.0	57.6	18.6	23.8	4,253.7	2.0	2.4	95.6
Solomon Islands	0.3[6]	1984	...	—	100.0	—	1987	1.0[49]	100.0[49]	—	—	0.2	—	74.9	25.1
Somalia	0.3[5]	1985	3.3	—	100.0	—	1983	—	...	...	...	0.8[22]	—	74.8[22]	25.2[22]
South Africa	13.2	1987	10,050.6	—	87.3[5]	12.7[5]	1986[20]	2,999.4[50]	30.0	29.8	40.2[50]	224.2[50]	36.2	63.8	—[50]
Bophuthatswana	52.6[22]	...	...	...	...	...	...	...	...	...	...	...	...	...	...
Ciskei	0.1[22]	...	...	...	...	...	...	...	...	...	...	...	...	...	...
Transkei	...	...	...	...	...	...	...	...	...	...	...	...	...	...	...
Venda	...	...	...	...	...	...	...	...	...	...	...	...	...	...	...
South West Africa/Namibia	24.9	1987	382.7	—	100.0	—	1983	593.0	64.0	36.0	—	[20]	[20]	[20]	[20]
Spain	1.4[27]	1984	1,549.5	13.9	18.2	67.9	1987	383.1	42.5	51.4	6.1	8,107.1	11.7	4.4	83.9
Sri Lanka	1.0[3]	1986	59.6[52]	—	100.0[52]	—	1986	84.8	14.2	85.8	—	82.0	1.4	54.8	43.8
Sudan, The	0.1[5]	1985	6.0	—	100.0	—	1981	1.2[2]	100.0[2]	—	—	162.7	—	0.1	99.9
Suriname	3.1	1987	32.9	99.8[13,27]	0.2[13,27]	—	1986	178.3	99.6	—	0.4	4.4	—	—	100.0
Swaziland	2.2[3]	1986	9.5	9.4[22]	77.3[22]	13.3[22]	1986	17.2	—	70.0	30.0	[20]	[20]	[20]	[20]
Sweden	0.3	1986	541.9	85.8	14.2	—	1987	719.7	77.5	16.3	6.2	2,971.8	13.1	8.7	78.2
Switzerland	1.1[5]	1984	...	—	100.0	—	1987	1,992.0	4.0	95.7	0.3	3,231.5	2.2	72.4	25.4
Syria	6.7	1987	2,171.7[16]	—	100.0[16]	—	1986	466.1	—	7.9	92.1	22.1	2.0	1.9	96.1
Taiwan	0.5	1987	479.5	—	65.7	34.3	1987	27.2[18]	—	54.0	46.0[18]	3,563.4[18]	—	11.7	88.3[18]
Tanzania	0.2	1987	8.8	...	...	...	1982	15.3	50.4	49.6	—	159.6[10]	—	3.0[10]	97.0[10]
Thailand	2.1[3]	1986	888.8	18.9[27]	39.6[27]	41.5[27]	1986	434.5	10.7	89.2	0.1	1,124.3	7.3	16.0	76.7
Togo	13.7[27]	1984	92.2	—	100.0	—	1986	208.7	—	100.0	—	83.2[22]	—	1.4[22]	98.6[22]
Tokelau	—	1987	—	—	—	—	1983	—	...	...	...	...	...	...	...
Tonga	0.5[6]	1983	0.4	—	100.0	—	1985	—	—	—	—	0.4	—	73.2	26.8
Trinidad and Tobago	22.1	1986	790.6	—	0.4	99.6	1987	530.2	—	1.3	98.7	62.5	40.3	12.5	47.2
Tunisia	8.3	1987	797.3	—	9.1[3]	90.9[3]	1987	515.1	1.2	8.9	89.9	313.5	1.7	50.4	47.9
Turkey	2.0	1986	1,150.5	22.6[1]	13.7[1]	63.7[1]	1987	816.5	6.6	27.2	66.2	3,145.7	11.7	2.2	86.1
Turks and Caicos Is.	1.4[3]	1987	0.6	—	100.0	—	1987	—	—	100.0	—	2.9[28]	—	—	100.0[28]
Tuvalu	...	1987	...				1983	—	...	...	...	...	—	—	100.0
Uganda	0.1[5]	1985	2.0	...	...	...	1984	1.6	100.0	—	—	...	...	...	...
U.S.S.R.	...	1984	63,099.0	—	31.8[13]	68.2[13]	1984	52,690.0[53]	10.3	1.4	88.3[53]	10,070.0[53]	59.3	2.7	38.0[53]
United Arab Emirates	33.8[3]	1986	7,205.9	...	0.2[5,54]	99.8[5,54]	1986	9,043.3	0.3	0.1	99.6	33.3	19.7	79.5	0.8
United Kingdom	3.4[3]	1986	18,799.6	0.1[6,13]	5.2[6,13]	94.7[6,13]	1987	15,711.7	4.7	21.7	73.6	11,876.6	16.9	27.0	56.1
United States	1.9	1987	86,400.0	2.8[5]	4.9[5]	92.3[5]	1987	9,113.2	34.5	23.2	42.3	41,073.5	6.3	11.9	81.8
Uruguay	1.1	1987	83.3	—	100.0	—	1987	5.6	—	100.0	—	189.3[28]	—	6.5	93.5[28]
Vanuatu	...	1984	...	—	100.0	—	1984	—	...	...	...	0.4	—	—	100.0
Venezuela	9.5	1987	4,729.9	—	8.1	91.9	1986	6,016.3	3.4	0.4	96.2	168.1	65.5	29.0	5.5
Vietnam	...	...	...	...	...	...	1988[31]	0.3	18.3	81.7	—	966.5	...	0.2	99.8
Virgin Islands (U.S.)	...	1985	...	—	100.0	—	...	...	...	...	...	...	...	...	...
Wallis and Futuna	...	...	...	...	...	...	1986[30]	11.8[30,55]	...	...	...	...	...	...	...
West Bank	...	...	...	...	...	56	...	...	...	...	...	...	...	...	...
Western Sahara	...	...	...	...	...	...	1983	—[2]	100.0[2]	—	—	0.2	—	81.6	18.4
Western Samoa	—	1984	—	—	100.0	—	1983	29.2[23]	—	—	100.0[23]	160.2	—	—	100.0
Yemen (Aden)	0.3[3]	1983	1.4	—	100.0	—	1985	0.4	—	100.0	—	86.5[28]	—	—	100.0[28]
Yemen (San'ā')	2.0[3]	1986	53.7	—	100.0	—	1987	273.7[18]	58.2	9.9	31.9[18]	3,809.0[18]	7.0	8.4	84.6[18]
Yugoslavia	2.8[5]	1986	1,453.0	22.5	17.6	59.9	1986	278.0	9.7	45.4	44.9	1.7[22]	4.9[22]	95.1[22]	—
Zaire	24.8[27]	1984	684.0	65.2[57]	27.8[58]	7.0[59]	1986	13.6	40.4	59.6	—	...	...	...	...
Zambia	15.3	1987	311.0	95.9[5]	4.1[5]	—	1986	75.2	20.8	79.2	—	10.3[7]	98.5[7]	1.5[7]	—
Zimbabwe	5.5	1987	286.6	68.8[3,13]	18.5[3,13]	12.7[3,13]									

[1]Gross value of sales. [2]1983–84 average. [3]1986. [4]Lumber only. [5]1985. [6]1983. [7]1982. [8]Salt exports valued at U.S.$33,000. [9]St. Kitts and Nevis includes Anguilla. [10]1981. [11]Netherlands Antilles includes Aruba. [12]1987–88. [13]Gross value of production (output). [14]1986–87. [15]Belgium includes Luxembourg. [16]Mostly crude petroleum. [17]1978–79. [18]Includes coke and briquettes. [19]Wood, lumber, and cork only. [20]South Africa includes Botswana, Lesotho, South West Africa/Namibia, and Swaziland. [21]1984–86 average. [22]1980. [23]1982–83 average. [24]Mostly diamonds; some gold. [25]China includes Taiwan. [26]1978. [27]1984. [28]Includes petroleum products. [29]France includes Monaco. [30]West Bank includes Gaza Strip. [31]Trade with United States only. [32]Jersey includes Guernsey. [33]Mostly bauxite and diamonds. [34]Mostly bauxite. [35]1982–83. [36]Excludes crude petroleum and natural gas. [37]1979–80. [38]Metals

forestry, 1987						fisheries, 1987								country
production of roundwood — total ('000 cubic metres)	fuelwood, charcoal (%)	industrial roundwood (%) total	industrial roundwood (%) sawlogs, veneer	trade exports ('000 U.S.$)	trade imports ('000 U.S.$)	catch total ('000 metric tons)	by source (%) marine	by source (%) fresh-water	by kind (%) fish	by kind (%) crusta-ceans	by kind (%) mollusks	trade exports ('000 U.S.$)	trade imports ('000 U.S.$)	
10,540	8.7	91.3	44.3	1,131,364	761,225	1,929.3	100.0	—	95.3	2.3	2.4	1,474,930	120,748	Norway
...	...	...	...	352[7,19]	52,147	115.0	100.0	—	98.3	1.5	0.2	25,530	3,060	Oman
...	...	...	...			0.2	100.0	—	100.0	—	—		50	Pacific Is., Trust Terr. of the Marshall Islands
						3.6	99.9	0.1	99.2	0.4	0.2	40	...	Micronesia, Fed. States of
						0.4	100.0	—	97.5	1.4	1.1		...	Northern Mariana Islands
						1.4	100.0	—	99.3	0.7	—	137	...	Palau
21,855	93.8	6.2	4.6		131,452	427.8	78.6	22.4	92.9	7.0	0.1	110,907	229	Pakistan
2,047	83.4	16.6	13.6	676	84,885	168.8	99.5	0.5	94.7	5.0	0.3	118,211[45]	6,060[45]	Panama
8,231	67.2	32.8	30.1	124,029	5,504	15.6	67.8	32.2	93.4	6.6	—	12,138	37,400	Papua New Guinea
8,439	60.3	39.7	34.9	111,867	10,464	10.0	—	100.0	100.0	—	—		...	Paraguay
7,735	84.4	15.6	14.4	3,355	57,109	4,583.6	99.2	0.8	99.1	0.2	0.7	290,330	7,400	Peru
36,701	83.6	16.4	9.3	258,015	74,460	1,988.7	71.7	28.3	83.4	4.8	11.6	267,895	31,254	Philippines
							100.0	—	100.0	—	—			Pitcairn Island
23,306	16.1	83.9	43.4	287,936	279,027	670.9	95.4	4.6	85.5	0.3	14.2	166,913	71,086	Poland
9,420	6.3	93.7	40.6	940,332	223,252	395.3	99.4	0.6	95.3	0.6	4.1	153,753	424,716	Portugal
...	...	...	...		18,015	1.2	100.0	—	87.5	6.7	5.8	[47]	[47]	Puerto Rico
33	93.9	6.1	—		28,765	2.7	100.0	—	94.4	2.9	2.7		829	Qatar
...	...	...	...			1.5	100.0	—	66.6	33.4	—	5,127	23,562	Réunion
24,629	18.6	81.4	36.2	284,750	116,610	264.4	74.7	25.3	100.0	—	—		28,950	Romania
5,842	95.9	4.1	0.5		1,362	1.6	—	100.0	100.0	—	—		50	Rwanda
...						0.7	100.0	—	48.7	51.3	—	140	...	St. Helena and Ascension
				11[10]	857[10]	1.5	100.0	—	100.0	—	—	160[9]	550[9]	St. Kitts and Nevis
...	...	...	...	5,227[7,48]	6,385[6]	0.9	100.0	—	99.9	0.1	—		685	St. Lucia
						12.5[27]	100.0[27]	—	100.0[27]	—	—	22,414	140	St. Pierre and Miquelon
...					2,984	0.5	100.0	—	100.0	—	—	385	600	St. Vincent
6	—	100.0	100.0				—	100.0	—	100.0	—	[39]	[39]	San Marino
...						2.5	100.0	—	99.1	0.1	0.8		670	São Tomé and Príncipe
...	...	...	...		312,659	45.5	100.0	—	87.1	12.5	0.4	5,763	58,612	Saudi Arabia
4,196	86.3	13.7	0.5		21,920	299.0	95.0	5.0	91.2	2.7	6.1	264,610	9,178	Senegal
8,071	98.3	1.7	0.2	146	1,028	4.0	100.0	—	98.2	—	1.5	5,438	3,115	Seychelles
...				545,835	462,672	53.0	69.8	30.2	96.5	1.6	1.9	8,600	750	Sierra Leone
589	35.7	64.3	64.3	10,530	2,292	15.3	98.6	1.4	84.4	11.4	4.2	289,354	312,955	Singapore
4,625	98.5	1.5	0.6		2,170	44.5	100.0	—	99.7	—	—	26,733	253	Solomon Islands
						17.0	100.0	—	97.1	2.9	—	4,980	—	Somalia
18,618[51]	38.0[51]	62.0[51]	20.0[51]	324,550[51]	216,234[51]	902.1	99.9	0.1	98.8	0.8	0.4	129,740[20]	69,670[20]	South Africa
...	...	...	...	...	...	...	...	...	...	...	...	...	...	Bophuthatswana
...	...	...	...	...	...	...	...	...	...	...	...	...	...	Ciskei
...	...	...	...	...	...	...	...	...	...	...	...	...	...	Transkei
...	...	...	...	...	...	...	...	...	...	...	...	...	...	Venda
[51]	[51]	[51]	[51]	[51]	[51]	519.5	100.0	—	99.7	0.3	—	20	20	South West Africa/Namibia
17,539	19.3	80.7	23.4	508,814	990,919	1,393.4	97.9	2.1	73.0	2.3	24.7	474,752	1,321,771	Spain
8,814	92.3	7.7	1.5	600	26,179	190.0	80.8	19.2	97.3	2.7	—	14,800	36,125	Sri Lanka
20,678	90.6	9.4	0.2		29,590	24.0	5.0	95.0	100.0	—	—	450	770	Sudan, The
196	7.1	92.9	79.6	2,666	8,310	5.2	97.9	2.1	77.7	22.3	—	5,273	20	Suriname
2,223	25.2	74.8	14.3	83,424	730		—	100.0	100.0	—	—	20	20	Swaziland
53,374	8.3	91.7	42.9	7,287,618	1,086,290	214.5	98.2	1.8	97.6	1.2	1.2	117,792	404,897	Sweden
4,885	18.1	81.9	59.8	873,580	1,324,020	4.8	—	100.0	100.0	—	—	8,907[41]	332,827[41]	Switzerland
48	31.3	68.7	31.3	113	115,100	5.0	14.0	86.0	100.0	—	—	49	6,288	Syria
423	16.0	84.0	...			1,236.2	75.3	24.7	99.7	0.3	—	405,527	85,940	Taiwan
24,754	93.8	6.2	1.4	1,665	15,700	313.5	15.2	84.8	99.6	0.3	0.1	3,560	110	Tanzania
37,600	87.7	12.3	5.7	120,954	381,294	2,165.1	92.4	7.6	76.9	8.8	11.4	1,261,066	267,149	Thailand
813	78.7	21.3	2.2		2,525	15.2	95.3	4.7	100.0	—	—	1,310	11,500	Togo
...		100.0	100.0		2,166	2.8	100.0	—	100.0	—	—			Tokelau
5	—	100.0	100.0									565	133	Tonga
65	33.8	66.2	63.1	25	66,472	3.2	100.0	—	87.5	12.5	—	2,865	14,007	Trinidad and Tobago
2,914	95.6	4.4	0.2		105,268	99.2	100.0	—	79.2	4.5	16.3	81,504	150	Tunisia
16,171	64.9	35.1	22.8	28,066	123,262	625.7	92.8	7.2	96.3	1.0	2.7	64,751	3,445	Turkey
...	...	...	...	...	...	1.7	100.0	—	24.3	12.1	63.6	3,440	—	Turks and Caicos Is.
						0.7	100.0	—	100.0	—	—		...	Tuvalu
13,385	87.0	13.0	0.6	38[22]	1,166	200.0	—	100.0	100.0	—	—		...	Uganda
378,970	22.9	77.1	43.0	3,007,100	658,900	11,159.6	91.1	8.9	92.4	6.4	1.1	637,287	152,122	U.S.S.R.
...						85.4	100.0	—	99.8	0.2	—	3,360	18,580	United Arab Emirates
5,204	2.8	97.2	58.9	1,233,282	8,104,629	954.7	98.4	1.6	88.1	5.1	6.8	717,565	1,386,818	United Kingdom
524,282	21.6	78.4	50.8	8,169,509	12,989,183	5,736.5	98.7	1.3	77.4	6.5	15.7	1,836,451[47]	5,662,329[47]	United States
3,289	92.2	7.8	2.9	7,066	11,358	138.0	99.2	0.8	98.0	—	2.0	82,772	2,746	Uruguay
38	63.2	36.8	36.8	376	380	3.2	100.0	—	66.6	8.2	25.2	2	1,350	Vanuatu
1,328	52.9	47.1	45.2		246,048	303.5	91.0	9.0	89.3	3.4	7.3	25,720	943	Venezuela
25,844	87.2	12.8	6.3		8,707	871.4	71.2	28.8	88.1	8.1	3.8	140,883	—	Vietnam
...						0.5	100.0	—	94.4	3.6	2.0			Virgin Islands (U.S.)
						1.0	100.0	—	100.0	—	—			Wallis and Futuna
...	...	...	...	...	...	...	...	...	...	...	...	...	...	West Bank
...	...	...	...	...	...	—	100.0	—	...	...	...	...	...	Western Sahara
131	53.4	46.6	44.3	1,478	2,369	3.4	100.0	—	97.3	1.2	1.5	5.	950	Western Samoa
306	100.0	—	—	29[3]	10,499	48.5	100.0	—	92.1	3.1	4.6	11,240	325	Yemen (Aden)
15,980	28.0	72.0	52.5	636,756	337,135	22.3	100.0	—	98.4	1.6	—	1,130	1,690	Yemen (Ṣan'ā')
32,304	92.0	8.0	1.2	22,283	4,225	81.3	69.0	31.0	97.1	0.5	2.4	39,030	86,735	Yugoslavia
9,960	94.6	5.4	1.3		7,390	166.0	1.2	98.8	100.0	—	—		55,960	Zaire
7,634	80.4	19.6	5.4	8,059	14,529	68.0	—	100.0	100.0	—	—		400	Zambia
...						17.5	—	100.0	100.0	—	—	30	1,510	Zimbabwe

includes energy.   [39]Italy includes San Marino.   [40]Mostly iron ore.   [41]Switzerland includes Liechtenstein.   [42]Includes cement.   [43]Mostly crude petroleum and natural gas.   [44]1983–84.   [45]Excludes the Free Zone of Colón and the Canal Zone.   [46]Nonmetals includes coal mining.   [47]United States includes Puerto Rico.   [48]Paper and paperboard only.   [49]Gold only.   [50]Excludes crude petroleum.   [51]South Africa includes South West Africa/Namibia.   [52]Mostly precious and semiprecious stones.   [53]Includes refined petroleum and electricity.   [54]Abu Dhabi only.   [55]Exports of stone and marble to Jordan only.   [56]Accounts for 5% to 6% of 1988 phosphate production of Morocco.   [57]Includes coal and nonmetals other than diamonds.   [58]Diamonds only.   [59]Crude petroleum only.

Manufacturing industries

This table summarizes the activity of the manufacturing sectors of the countries of the world, providing figures for value added, number of establishments, and the distribution of value added by size of establishment (as reckoned by number of employees). The data are organized to show the relative importance of six principal sectors for each country and the concentration of activity within each sector. Manufacturing activity is classified according to the scheme outlined in the International Standard Industrial Classification (ISIC), revision 2, published by the United Nations.

The sectors for which data have been provided include: (1) food, beverages, and tobacco, (2) textiles, apparel, and leather, (3) wood, paper, chemicals, and related products, (4) primary and fabricated metals and processed minerals, (5) machinery (except electrical) and transport equipment, (6) electrical and electronic machinery. For each of these sectors (for which ISIC definitions are provided below), data are given for their respective share of total manufacturing value added (or, occasionally, some other measure of value, when value added was not reported); for the number of establishments with fewer than and more than 100 employees, and, where it was known, for the share of the sectoral value added represented by these two groups of establishments; and, finally, for the total value added in U.S.$ by all manufacturing.

The collection and publication of national manufacturing data is usually carried out by one of three methods: a full census of manufacturing (usually done every 5 to 10 years for a given country), a periodic survey of manufacturing (usually taken at annual or other regular intervals between censuses), and the onetime sample survey (often limited in geographical, sectoral, or size-of-enterprise coverage). The full census is, naturally, the most complete, but since up to 10 years may elapse between such censuses, it has often been necessary to substitute a survey of more recent date, but less complete coverage, in order to provide more timely data. For each country the initial date indicates the year of the survey.

To permit international comparisons U.S. dollar figures for total value added by manufacturing have been given, but should be used only with caution, because of inherent uncertainties with respect to national accounting methods, purchasing power parities, price structures and preferments, exchange rates, and so on.

The majority of countries collect data for establishments, generally referring to each separate physical facility, regardless of the number of separately incorporated legal entities (companies, partnerships, parastatal organizations), any of which may operate more than one facility. Other countries collect data only for enterprises, focusing on the corporate legal entity but often combining data for several separate, and smaller, estab-

Manufacturing industries

country	year	food, beverages, and tobacco (group 1) percent of total value added	1–99 employees number	1–99 employees percent of value added	100 or more emp. number	100 or more emp. percent of value added	textiles, apparel, and leather (group 2) percent of total value added	1–99 employees number	1–99 employees percent of value added	100 or more emp. number	100 or more emp. percent of value added	wood, paper, chemicals, and related products (group 3) percent of total value added	1–99 employees number	1–99 employees percent of value added	100 or more emp. number	100 or more emp. percent of value added
Afghanistan[1]	1983	52.0	67	...	...	...	20.2	...	...	78	...	25.5	...	...	55	...
Albania	1984	...	...	...	...	...	16.2	...	...	...	...	14.4	...	...	...	...
Algeria	1986	19.9	...	...	...	...	...	...	...	...	...	...	...	...	...	...
American Samoa	1982[3]	...	...	...	...	...	...	104	...	...	...	...	49	...	...	...
Andorra	1972	...	142	...	...	...	...	...	...	...	...	...	...	...	...	...
Angola[4]	1985	...	...	...	...	...	...	...	...	...	...	...	...	...	...	...
Anguilla	1987	...	14	100.0	—	—	...	12	100.0	—	—	23.7	15	100.0	—	—
Antigua and Barbuda[5]	1987	...	14	100.0	—	—	9.3	1,059	...	75	—	23.7	1,394	...	101	—
Argentina[4, 6]	1986	25.1	1,188	...	92	—	9.3	...	...	...	...	...	...	...	...	...
Aruba	1982	...	...	...	...	...	...	...	...	...	...	...	...	...	...	...
Australia[8, 9]	1986–87	18.5	2,986	32.8	401	67.2	7.8	2,414	44.7	253	55.3	29.9	7,463	55.3	419	44.7
Austria	1985	15.8	728	...	...	...	8.4	927	...	...	...	19.4	3,227	...	...	...
Bahamas, The[11, 12]	1987	11.2	...	...	...	...	—	...	...	...	...	88.4	...	...	...	...
Bahrain	1982	...	...	...	...	...	34.2	...	...	1,776	...	92.5	...	...	...	...
Bangladesh[13]	1984–85	22.8	640	...	...	...	...	...	...	...	...	24.6	768	...	...	...
Barbados	1984	30.8	40	47.2	10	52.8	11.4	37	25.1	7	74.9	20.3	76	80.3	3	19.7
Belgium[4, 14]	1986	20.2	6,964	...	...	...	22.3[15]	3,728	...	...	...	21.2	5,883	...	...	...
Belize	1986	65.0[16]	...	...	...	...	15.0	...	...	...	...	9.9	...	...	...	...
Benin[4]	1985	45.6	...	...	...	...	...	...	...	...	...	...	...	...	...	...
Bermuda	1979	...	...	...	...	...	...	...	...	...	...	...	63	...	4	...
Bhutan	1986	...	246	...	3	...	...	5	...	—	...	13.3	256	...	...	...
Bolivia[17, 18]	1984	52.1	201	...	...	...	9.5	145	...	...	...	10.0	104	...	...	...
Botswana[4]	1984–85	51.5	104	...	...	...	7.2	124	...	...	...	30.8	27,752	30.5	1,925	69.5
Brazil[17]	1980	17.0	26,226	38.6	1,272	61.4	10.9	14,325	23.8	1,913	76.2	...	2	100.0	—	—
British Virgin Islands	1978	...	1	100.0	—	—	...	...	...	...	...	...	60	100.0	—	—
Brunei[21]	1980	...	29	100.0	—	—	...	76	100.0	—	—	28.9	...	...	397	...
Bulgaria[23]	1987	8.5	...	...	318	...	4.2	...	...	272	...	5.5	34	...	4	...
Burkina Faso[24, 25]	1986	60.1	41	...	6	...	21.6	3	...	4	...	10.0	...	...	...	...
Burundi	1985	58.0	...	...	...	...	11.6	...	...	...	...	12.8	...	...	...	...
Cameroon[4]	1985	35.0	...	...	...	...	17.2	...	...	...	...	...	...	...	...	...
Canada	1985	13.9	3,038	27.9	519	72.1	6.0	3,381	37.2	517	62.8	34.6	12,818	28.1	1,132	71.9
Cape Verde	1983	100.0	...	...	...	...	—	...	...	...	...	—	...	...	...	...
Cayman Islands	1986[20]	...	...	...	13	...	...	...	...	4	...	21.3	...	...	19	...
Central African Republic[4, 24]	1986	47.4	...	...	...	...	25.9	...	...	...	...	...	...	...	...	...
Chad[4]	1985	...	...	...	...	...	...	...	...	...	...	...	...	...	...	...
Chile[13, 17, 26]	1985	25.9	1,190	13.5	338	86.5	7.2	583	17.8	207	82.2	28.9	773	11.2	349	88.8
China[24, 27]	1986	12.5	89,584	...	...	...	14.6	55,362	...	...	...	25.3	106,822	...	...	...
Christmas Island		..	...	...	...	...	...	...	...	...	...	—	—	—	—	—
Cocos (Keeling) Islands		...	...	...	...	...	...	...	...	...	...	—	—	—	—	—
Colombia	1985	36.1	1,012	19.6	222	80.4	13.8	1,538	21.6	208	78.4	27.1	1,347	21.9	242	78.1
Comoros	1985	...	...	...	...	...	18.9	...	...	...	...	22.4	...	...	...	...
Congo[4]	1985	47.7	...	...	...	...	28	...	...	...	...	...	...	...	...	...
Cook Islands	1985	28	...	...	...	...	9.8	...	...	...	...	30.6	...	...	...	...
Costa Rica[17]	1984	46.8	...	...	...	...	16.6	...	...	73	...	26.8	164	...	...	...
Côte d'Ivoire[4, 14, 24]	1985	36.1	298	...	...	...	4.5	...	...	45	...	11.6[31]	...	...	85[31]	...
Cuba[24]	1986	61.1[30]	...	...	332[30]	...	24.6	1,737	71.5	25	28.5	26.7	2,133	82.4	6	17.6
Cyprus[17]	1985	27.7	950	46.5	16	53.5	10.3	...	...	86	...	28.8	...	...	178	...
Czechoslovakia[24]	1987	8.7	...	...	125	...	5.2	781[34]	...	...	...	28.4	2,390[34]	...	...	...
Denmark[33]	1986	22.5	860[34]	...	...	...	...	...	...	...	...	...	...	...	...	...
Djibouti	1984	...	...	...	...	...	...	...	...	...	...	...	...	...	...	...
Dominica	1986	...	...	...	...	...	3.3	222	...	...	...	21.0	346	...	...	...
Dominican Republic[35, 36]	1984	65.2	...	...	1,077	...	16.7	258	...	...	...	11.7	450	...	...	...
Ecuador[13]	1986	54.8	368	...	...	...	26.5	...	...	1,309	...	18.4	...	...	643	...
Egypt[4, 6, 37]	1985	39.5	2,521	...	...	...	9.9	80	...	...	...	21.4	108	...	...	...
El Salvador[36, 38]	1986	55.9	66	...	...	...	...	...	...	...	...	...	...	...	...	...
Equatorial Guinea[4]	1985	...	...	...	...	...	...	...	...	...	...	...	...	...	...	...
Ethiopia[13, 17, 26]	1984–85	51.4	76	...	87	...	17.8	34	...	52	...	23.4	43	...	46	...
Faeroe Islands	1987	50.3[39]	...	...	...	...	...	...	...	...	...	...	...	...	...	...
Falkland Islands	1986	28	...	...	...	...	28	...	...	...	...	...	...	...	...	...
Fiji	1985	51.6	95	...	8	...	4.5	125	...	2	...	27.4	161	...	4	...

lishments. When only a single sectoral enterprise or establishment total was available, the *average* size of these establishments was calculated (since the total number of employees in the sector was known), and the figure for number of establishments was placed in the table above or below the 100-employee cutoff accordingly. Such figures are given in italics.

Another impediment to international comparability in terms of size of establishment is the limit each country establishes as the minimum reporting unit for such surveys. "Size" is usually determined either by number of employees or by value of sales. Employees may include owners, partners, or unpaid family workers. For a small country, it may be both feasible and desirable to survey all establishments, however small. For larger countries, the cost to collect and analyze data for all establishments may be prohibitively high, and, moreover, interest from a development point of view may be exclusively in middle- and large-scale industry, that needed to permit replacement of imported goods with domestic manufactures. Thus, when the distributions of number of establishments are examined, it should be noted (and has been footnoted wherever possible) when such limits in coverage may be applicable.

In terms of the industrial groups implied by the names of the manufacturing sectors used here, the content of each sector is usually defined by the two- or three-digit level of classification in the ISIC system:

group	EB category	ISIC code(-s)	remarks
1.	Food, beverages, and tobacco	31	
2.	Textiles, apparel, and leather	32	
3.	Wood, paper, chemicals, and related products	33	wood and furniture
		34	paper and products; printing and publishing
		35	industrial chemicals, pharmaceuticals, petroleum and products, rubber, plastics
4.	Primary and fabricated metals and processed minerals	36	pottery, china, glass
		37	iron; steel; nonferrous metals
		381	metal products
5.	Machinery (except electrical) and transport equipment	382 + 384 minus 3825	machinery and transport equipment minus office equipment and computers
6.	Electrical and electronic machinery	383 + 3825	electrical and electronic equipment, plus office equipment and computers

It should be noted that these groups do not account for ISIC groups 385 and 390 (professional goods and other industries, respectively).

primary and fabricated metals; proc. minerals (group 4)					machinery (except elec.) and transport equip. (group 5)					electrical and electronic machinery (group 6)					total manufacturing value added (U.S.$'000,-000)	country
percent of total value added	establishments				percent of total value added	establishments				percent of total value added	establishments					
	1–99 employees		100 or more emp.			1–99 employees		100 or more emp.			1–99 employees		100 or more emp.			
	number	percent of value added	number	percent of value added		number	percent of value added	number	percent of value added		number	percent of value added	number	percent of value added		
2.3[2]	...	...	17[2]	...	2	...	...	2	...	2	...	...	2	...	202	Afghanistan
...	...	...	...	...	2	...	...	...	...	2	...	...	...	...	1,100	Albania
42.2[2]	...	...	...	...	...	...	...	...	...	...	...	...	...	...	7,394	Algeria
...	38	...	...	...	25	...	...	...	83	...	...	...	...	...	American Samoa
															Andorra
...	...	...	...	...	...	...	...	...	...	...	...	...	...	127	Angola
...	10	100.0	—	—	...	—	—	...	...	...	...	...	...	0.3	Anguilla
10.6	206	...	21	...	24.5[7]	...	...	151	...	7	...	...	29	...	12	Antigua and Barbuda
...	...	...	...	...	...	...	...	...	...	...	...	...	...	15,724	Argentina
...	...	...	...	...	...	...	...	...	...	...	...	...	...	20	Aruba
22.3	6,020	35.0	357	65.0	13.6	6,744[10]	34.1[10]	554[10]	65.9[10]	5.9	10	10	10	10	30,142	Australia
25.2	1,273	...	...	...	17.9	...	...	781	...	11.5	...	...	393	...	11,765	Austria
0.4	...	...	...	...	...	...	...	...	...	...	...	...	...	...	141[11]	Bahamas, The
7.5	...	...	...	...	...	...	...	...	...	...	...	...	73	...	400	Bahrain
6.2	436	...	...	...	8.7	183	...	...	...	3.4	...	...	...	...	841	Bangladesh
36.0[2]	50[2]	62.4[2]	7[2]	37.6[2]	2	2	2	2	2	2	2	2	2	2	116	Barbados
36.3[2]	4,651	...	...	...	2	1,343	...	...	...	2	...	...	628	...	26,068	Belgium
12.6[2]	...	...	...	...	...	...	...	...	...	2	...	...	...	...	19	Belize
...	...	...	...	...	2	...	...	...	...	—	...	...	...	...	53	Benin
...	...	...	...	...	...	...	...	...	...	...	...	...	...	20	Bermuda
24.1	4	...	2	...	...	...	...	...	...	...	...	...	...	...	7.5	Bhutan
	121	...		...	0.3[19]	21	...	...	...	0.4[19]	13	...	...	...		
10.7[2]	108[2]	...	...	...	2	2	...	...	...	2	...	...	...	...	1,068	Bolivia
17.9	25,084	25.3	1,641	74.7	15.6	9,268	18.0	1,651	82.0	5.3	2,245	48.7	558	51.3	58	Botswana
...	4	100.0	—	—	—	—	—	—	—	...	...	...	...	...	77,648	Brazil
	70[2]	100.0[2]	—	—		2	2		—		2	2		—	3.2[20]	British Virgin Islands
10.3	...	...	156	...	29.6	...	...	493	...	18.5	2	2	...	—	382[22]	Brunei
3.0[2]	22	...	3	...	2	...	...	2	...	2	...	...	202	...	1,520	Bulgaria
12.3	...	...	...	...	8.1	...	...	...	...	...	...	...	...	...	116	Burkina Faso
29.6[2]	...	...	...	...	2	...	...	...	...	2	...	...	...	...	151	Burundi
...	...	...	...	...	...	...	...	...	...	...	...	...	...	790	Cameroon
17.4	6,980	31.7	524	68.3	18.5	2,783	13.7	503	86.3	7.0	1,102	15.7	277	84.3	70,213	Canada
—	...	...	...	...	...	...	...	...	...	...	...	...	...	...	5	Cape Verde
3.1[2]	7[2]	...	...	...	2	2	...	...	...	2	2	...	...	...	4.4	Cayman Islands
...	...	...	...	...	...	...	...	...	...	...	...	...	...	50	Central African Republic
...	...	...	...	...	...	...	...	...	...	...	...	...	...	50	Chad
32.9	377	3.5	179	96.5	2.4	158	21.3	55	78.7	1.3	33	11.6	23	88.4	5,302	Chile
21.2	101,972	...	...	...	17.7	59,880	...	...	...	7.6	18,477	...	...	...	72,081	China
—	—	—	—	—	—	—	—	—	—	—	—	—	—	—		Christmas Island
13.2	806	15.9	149	84.1	4.9	439	26.2	60	73.8	3.2	150	20.8	38	79.2	6,711	Cocos (Keeling) Islands
															Colombia
8.1[2]	...	...	...	...	2	...	...	...	...	2	...	...	...	...	5	Comoros
...	...	...	...	...	...	...	...	...	...	...	...	...	...	127	Congo
6.3	...	...	...	...	3.5[19]	...	...	...	...	2.9[19]	...	...	...	...	0.9[29]	Cook Islands
17.4[2]	79[2]	...	...	...	2	2	...	...	...	2	2	...	...	...	701	Costa Rica
...	...	...	...	...	...	...	...	...	...	...	...	...	...	631	Côte d'Ivoire
6.8	...	...	93	...	9.0[19]	...	...	146[19]	...	1.4[19]	...	...	18[19]	...	4,909[32]	Cuba
13.1	1,072	73.9	6	24.1	4.2	300	81.0	2	19.0	1.7	63	65.5	1	34.5	417	Cyprus
11.6	...	...	137	...	32.4[19]	...	...	226[19]	...	7.1[19]	...	...	52[19]	...	41,217[32]	Czechoslovakia
15.1	1,357[34]	...	...	...	17.7[19]	1,269[34]	...	...	...	6.1[19]	343[34]	...	...	...	14,776	Denmark
...	...	...	...	...	...	...	...	...	...	—	—	—	—	—	28	Djibouti
8.5	145	...	...	...	0.5[19]	11[19]	...	...	...	0.6[19]	16[19]	...	...	...	8	Dominica
12.0	263	...	...	...	2.5[7]	51[19]	...	...	...	7	45[19]	...	...	...	4,014	Dominican Republic
15.5[2]	...	...	1,125	...	2	...	...	118	...	2	...	...	48	...	2,193	Ecuador
8.0	40	...	...	...	1.1	11	...	...	...	1.6	8	...	...	...	8,270	Egypt
															617	El Salvador
7.2	27	...	32	...	—	—	...	—	...	0.1	2	...	1	...	2	Equatorial Guinea
...	...	...	...	...	...	...	...	...	...	...	...	...	...	577	Ethiopia
...	...	...	...	...	...	...	...	...	...	...	...	...	...	175	Faeroe Islands
12.5	55	...	1	...	3.1[7]	33[7]	...	1[7]	...	7	7	...	—[7]	...	89	Fiji

Manufacturing industries (continued)

country	year	food, beverages, and tobacco (group 1) percent of total value added	establishments 1–99 employees number	1–99 percent of value added	100 or more emp. number	100+ percent of value added	textiles, apparel, and leather (group 2) percent of total value added	1–99 number	1–99 percent of value added	100 or more number	100+ percent of value added	wood, paper, chemicals, and related products (group 3) percent of total value added	1–99 number	1–99 percent of value added	100 or more number	100+ percent of value added
Finland	1985	12.5	888	...	141	...	6.5	722	...	155	...	40.8	2,087	...	400	...
France	1986	11.5	...	...	...	...	6.7	8[41]	...	1[41]	...	31.4	[41]	...	[41]	...
French Guiana[37]	1982	...	2	...	1	...	...	...	...	...	...	...	...	...	...	...
French Polynesia	1980	20.3	...	...	...	...	2.3	...	...	...	...	55.5	...	...	...	...
Gabon[4]	1985	21.1	...	...	...	...	...	...	...	...	...	...	...	...	...	...
Gambia, The[17,43]	1982	74.4	...	...	13	...	3.6	2	...	...	...	1.7	4	...	...	...
Gaza Strip[44]	1986	15.0	114	...	...	...	32.4	572	...	1,167[45]	...	12.8	348	...	45	...
Germany, East[11,24]	1986	16.9	...	...	558	...	39.5[45]	...	...	1,270	...	21.3	8,302	...	2,655	...
Germany, West	1985	11.3	3,258	...	1,160	...	4.5	3,586	...	55[46]	...	21.9	...	...	164[46]	...
Ghana[14]	1984	63.7	...	...	74[46]	...	7.4	...	...	...	...	...	...	...	...	...
Gibraltar		...	...	...	...	...	...	...	...	...	...	...	...	...	...	...
Greece[9]	1987	19.6	21,925	...	157	...	25.7	30,928	...	206	...	23.5	33,036	...	132	...
Greenland[1]	1986	99.3	...	...	...	...	0.6	...	...	...	...	7.9[48]	11[48]	...	...	...
Grenada[1]	1984	76.2	16	...	...	...	15.9	7	...	...	...	[49]	[49]	...	1	...
Guadeloupe[37]	1982	46.3[35]	17	...	4	...	53.7[49]	29[49]	...	...	...	[49]	[49]	...	...	...
Guam	1982[3]	...	...	...	...	...	...	...	...	...	...	...	...	...	...	...
Guatemala[9,17,43]	1985	40.5	577	...	...	...	11.3	388	...	...	...	32.0	545	...	...	...
Guernsey		...	...	...	...	...	...	...	...	...	...	...	...	...	...	...
Guinea[4]	1985	...	...	...	...	...	...	...	...	...	...	...	...	...	...	...
Guinea-Bissau[4]	1985	...	...	...	...	...	...	...	...	...	...	...	...	...	...	...
Guyana[43,51]	1981	36.7	31	...	...	...	63.3[49]	8	...	...	...	[49]	20	...	...	...
Haiti[17]	1986	40.9	424	...	...	...	14.5	163	...	...	...	17.1[52]	109	...	...	...
Honduras	1986	51.1	...	...	...	...	5.7	...	...	...	...	29.6	...	...	...	...
Hong Kong	1986	4.1	976	...	...	...	41.9	15,842	...	...	...	19.0	13,828	...	...	...
Hungary[24]	1986	5.9	16	...	275	...	11.0	27[45]	...	224[45]	...	22.6	...	...	45	...
Iceland[4]	1985	51.1	911	...	...	...	7.8	285	...	...	...	18.6	798	...	...	...
India[4,53]	1984–85	11.8	24,552	...	...	...	15.9	...	...	13,922	...	24.9	18,387	...	3,353[31]	...
Indonesia[54,55]	1986	11.0	...	...	3,875	...	5.5	2,852	...	208	...	71.6	1,416	...	146	...
Iran	1985	14.8	725	...	151	...	23.1	992	...	115	...	15.9	...	...	223	...
Iraq[46]	1986	14.2	168	...	...	...	9.1	...	...	...	...	47.4	...	...	...	...
Ireland[56]	1984	25.7	773	39.8	131	60.2	5.8	530	48.1	76	51.9	26.6	1,323	36.8	74	63.2
Isle of Man		...	...	...	...	...	...	...	...	...	...	...	...	...	...	...
Israel[4,25,57]	1986	14.0[43]	953	...	...	...	11.2[43]	1,895	...	...	...	23.2[43]	3,419	...	...	...
Italy[9,55]	1987	10.9	2,399	...	...	...	16.5	7,851	...	...	...	23.7	7,207	...	...	...
Jamaica[9]	1986	39.6	325	...	...	...	6.0	135	...	...	...	37.1	329	...	...	...
Japan[8]	1986	10.1	50,149	43.9	1,994	56.1	5.7	70,542	74.5	1,554	25.5	26.5	109,353	41.1	2,475	58.9
Jersey	1986	...	...	...	...	...	...	...	...	...	...	29.4	1,538	...	...	...
Jordan	1986	28.2	976	...	...	...	5.2	1,122	...	9	...	...	...	...	11	...
Kampuchea (Cambodia)[24,27]	1983	...	10	...	...	...	...	...	...	...	...	...	...	...	...	...
Kenya[59]	1986	40.7	239	15.2	159	84.8	10.6	329	15.8	95	84.2	26.5	598	13.9	179	86.1
Kiribati	1984	...	...	...	...	...	...	...	...	...	...	...	...	...	...	...
Korea, North		...	...	...	...	...	...	...	...	...	...	...	...	...	...	...
Korea, South[43]	1987	11.7	4,323	15.3	397	84.7	16.4	12,568	29.5	1,485	70.5	23.3	11,992	24.1	913	75.9
Kuwait[9]	1986	8.0	406	...	...	...	4.5	2,150	...	...	...	74.2	436	...	...	...
Laos		...	...	...	...	...	...	...	...	...	...	...	...	...	...	...
Lebanon	1984	...	...	...	...	...	...	...	...	...	...	...	...	...	...	...
Lesotho[14]	1986	60.7	5	...	6	...	14.7	6	—	4	—	12.7	9	...	2	...
Liberia[11,54,55]	1986	56.7	15	...	...	...	...	...	...	...	...	14.9	19	...	...	...
Libya	1985	38.1	5	...	2	...	26.1	14	—	...	—	26.1	80	...	...	...
Liechtenstein	1985	...	...	...	...	...	...	...	...	...	...	...	...	...	...	...
Luxembourg[9,55]	1986	7.4	30	...	...	...	1.8	...	...	6	...	20.8	...	...	43	63.0
Macau	1984	1.5	95	85.7	1	14.3	67.0	411	27.1	151	72.9	13.4	221	37.0	14	63.0
Madagascar[17]	1985	49.7	...	...	122	...	25.2	...	...	61	...	20.1[61]	127[61]	...	...	...
Malawi[4,62]	1983	49.0	...	...	37	...	13.4	...	...	22	...	27.1	...	...	34	...
Malaysia[4]	1985	21.1	1,324	...	...	...	4.9	...	...	420	...	37.4	2,068	...	...	...
Maldives	1985	...	...	...	...	...	...	...	...	...	...	2.6	17	...	...	...
Mali[24]	1981	24.4	51	...	...	...	57.4	16	...	...	...	18.7	507	...	5	...
Malta	1985	20.7	362	...	6	...	31.0	163	...	36	...	[49]	[49]	...	...	...
Martinique[37]	1982	37.0	22	...	3	...	63.0[49]	20[49]	...	1[49]	...	3.3	...	...	...	...
Mauritania	1984	87.5	...	...	...	...	3.9	...	...	...	...	...	...	...	...	...
Mauritius[4,13]	1985	31.1	198	...	...	...	46.7	...	...	285	...	9.8	113	...	...	...
Mayotte		...	...	...	...	...	...	...	...	...	...	...	...	...	...	...
Mexico	1985	25.4	...	...	...	...	11.6	...	...	...	...	32.8	...	...	...	...
Monaco		...	...	...	...	...	...	...	...	...	...	...	...	...	...	...
Mongolia[11,24]	1986	32.1	...	...	45	...	41.8	...	...	56	...	19.8	...	...	93	...
Montserrat	1980	...	7	...	...	—	...	5	...	...	—	...	7	...	...	—
Morocco[6]	1983	24.3	5,481	...	...	...	14.2	21,312	...	...	...	28.8	9,092	...	...	...
Mozambique[11]	1985	39.1	...	...	...	...	27.1	...	...	...	...	15.9	...	...	...	...
Myanmar (Burma)	1985	38.8	...	...	...	...	9.4	...	...	...	...	8.6	...	...	...	...
Nauru	1985	—	...	—	...	...	...	...	...	—	...	—	...	—	...	...
Nepal	1981–82	69.8	3,715	...	58	...	11.5	256	...	16	...	12.2	477	...	13	...
Netherlands, The[13]	1985	21.2	1,284	24.0[64]	244	76.0[64]	3.3	564	52.3[64]	84	47.7[64]	33.8	2,223	14.7[64]	404	85.3[64]
Netherlands Antilles[65]	1982	...	...	...	...	...	...	...	...	...	...	...	...	...	...	...
New Caledonia	1985	10.8	...	...	...	...	9.8	2,352	...	74	...	31.1	5,586	...	134	...
New Zealand[54]	1987	25.6	1,867	...	147	...	12.9	...	...	59	...	27.8	90	...	...	...
Nicaragua[17,46]	1984	49.8	...	...	84	...	...	...	...	...	...	27.1	11	...	...	...
Niger[24]	1980	32.5	9	...	...	...	...	...	...	152	...	32.7	...	...	737	...
Nigeria[13,17]	1983	27.2	676	...	...	...	11.4	...	...	...	...	...	...	...	...	...
Niue		...	...	...	...	...	...	...	...	...	...	...	...	...	...	...
Norfolk Island		...	...	...	...	...	...	...	...	...	...	...	...	...	...	...
Norway	1986	15.7	2,195	39.4	93	60.6	2.7	758	70.2	27	29.8	32.9	4,451	49.1	182	50.9
Oman	1986	...	...	...	...	...	...	...	...	...	...	47.0[66]	...	...	...	...
Pacific Is., Trust Terr. of the Marshall Islands[1]	1981	39.7	...	...	...	...	...	...	...	...	...	60.3	...	...	...	...
Micronesia, Fed. States of		...	...	...	...	...	...	...	...	...	...	...	...	...	...	...

primary and fabricated metals; proc. minerals (group 4) — percent of total value added	establishments 1–99 employees number	establishments 1–99 employees percent of value added	establishments 100 or more emp. number	establishments 100 or more emp. percent of value added	machinery (except elec.) and transport equip. (group 5) — percent of total value added	establishments 1–99 employees number	establishments 1–99 employees percent of value added	establishments 100 or more emp. number	establishments 100 or more emp. percent of value added	electrical and electronic machinery (group 6) — percent of total value added	establishments 1–99 employees number	establishments 1–99 employees percent of value added	establishments 100 or more emp. number	establishments 100 or more emp. percent of value added	total manufacturing value added (U.S.$'000,000)	country
13.9	1,168	...	151	...	18.6[19]	879[19]	...	184[19]	...	5.6[19]	182[19]	...	58[19]	...	13,593	Finland
13.7	...	...	...	...	16.4[40]	...	...	...	...	9.2[40]	...	...	...	...	186,956	France
...	41	...	41	...	—	...	—	—	—	—	—	—	—	—	9[42]	French Guiana
21.1[2]	...	...	...	...	49.6[7]	...	...	7	...	...	...	...	...	...	107	French Polynesia
...	...	...	...	...	2	...	...	2	...	2	...	...	...	...	175	Gabon
−0.8	2	...	...	...	...	...	...	...	...	...	...	...	...	...	8	Gambia, The
34.0[2]	649[2]	...	...	...	2	2	...	...	...	2	2	...	—	...	36	Gaza Strip
12.4	...	...	186	...	22.2	...	...	1,164	...	9.0	...	...	309	...	234,143[32]	Germany, East
20.7	7,988	...	2,510	...	25.3	5,438	...	2,584	...	14.2	1,918	...	1,496	...	198,376	Germany, West
5.7	...	...	38[46]	...	0.5	...	...	12[46]	...	0.5	...	...	11[46]	...	291	Ghana
...	...	...	...	...	...	...	...	...	...	...	...	...	...	...	...	Gibraltar
28.6[2]	21,655	...	87	...	2	24,821	...	47	...	2	6,887	...	35	...	7,170	Greece
48	48	...	...	...	48	48	...	...	...	48	48	...	...	...	90[47]	Greenland
49	49	...	—	—	49	49	...	...	...	49	49	...	...	...	12[47]	Grenada
...	...	...	...	...	...	...	...	...	...	...	...	...	...	...	51	Guadeloupe
12.8	293	...	...	...	0.7	53	...	...	...	2.3	30	...	...	...	8[50]	Guam
...	...	...	...	...	...	...	...	...	...	...	...	...	...	...	1,009	Guatemala
...	...	...	...	...	...	...	...	...	...	...	...	...	...	...	71	Guernsey
...	...	...	...	...	...	...	...	...	...	...	...	...	...	...	2	Guinea-Bissau
49	...	...	...	...	49	...	...	...	...	49	1	...	...	...	53	Guyana
27.5[2]	59	...	...	...	2	...	...	2[97]	...	2	...	...	7	...	134	Haiti
10.0	...	...	...	...	1.0	...	...	...	...	1.4	...	...	...	...	429	Honduras
8.5	7,806	...	...	...	4.9	4,951	...	...	...	14.0	2,161	...	...	...	8,049	Hong Kong
14.6	171[2]	...	311[2]	...	21.3[19]	2	...	2	...	15.5[19]	2	...	2	...	5,851	Hungary
20.2[2]	667[2]	...	...	...	2	2	...	...	...	2	2	...	...	...	457	Iceland
18.8	19,820	...	...	...	17.4	10,109	...	...	...	9.8	3,931	...	...	...	15,023	India
7.4	1,794	...	...	...	2.7[19]	...	...	487	...	1.6[19]	...	...	231	...	15,275	Indonesia
22.4	2,534	...	343	...	14.7	675	...	143	...	6.7	95	...	49	...	9,873	Iran
18.1	...	...	252	...	5.2	...	...	13	...	4.4	...	...	14	...	3,972	Iraq
10.7	940	39.2	121	60.8	5.3	349	41.1	35	58.9	20.2	228	15.2	59	84.8	5,734	Ireland
...	...	...	...	...	...	...	...	...	...	...	...	...	...	...	...	Isle of Man
21.9[43]	2,923	...	...	...	10.5[43]	356[19]	...	...	...	18.9[43]	502[19]	...	...	...	4,733[43]	Israel
21.2	6,909	...	...	...	16.4[19]	...	...	4,826	...	7.3[19]	...	...	1,621	...	175,630	Italy
16.3[2]	361[2]	...	...	...	2	2	...	...	...	2	2	...	...	...	538	Jamaica
17.1	79,004	47.6	2,084	52.4	20.3	55,499	29.5	2,720	70.5	16.5	32,003	18.2	3,168	81.8	529,872	Japan
...	...	...	...	...	...	...	...	...	...	...	...	...	...	...	20	Jersey
32.5[58]	2,543[58]	...	...	...	58	58	...	...	...	0.4	11	...	...	...	669	Jordan
...	...	...	...	...	...	11	...	...	...	...	...	...	...	...	...	Kampuchea (Cambodia)
8.2	237	20.4	80	79.6	7.3	149	36.7	67	63.3	5.2	27	12.1	9	87.9	750	Kenya
—	...	—	—	—	...	...	...	...	...	—	...	—	—	—	0.5	Kiribati
15.9	7,944	24.6	663	75.4	14.3	5,719	19.5	456	80.5	15.4	4,042	13.3	668	86.7	49,317	Korea, North
13.0[2]	741	...	...	...	2	47	...	...	...	2	25	...	...	...	1,902	Korea, South
...	...	...	...	...	...	...	...	...	...	...	...	...	...	...	...	Kuwait
...	...	...	...	...	...	...	...	...	...	...	...	...	...	...	...	Laos
9.3	11[2]	...	...	...	...	2	...	...	...	...	2	...	...	...	196	Lebanon
22.6	6	...	—	—	0.4	1	...	—	—	0.8	2	...	—	—	31	Lesotho
9.3[2]	...	...	...	...	2	...	...	...	...	2	2	...	...	...	594	Liberia
...	48	...	3	...	...	18	...	4	...	...	17[60]	...	3[60]	...	1,375	Libya
...	...	...	...	...	...	...	...	...	...	...	...	...	...	...	...	Liechtenstein
58.8	...	...	51[52]	...	7.8	...	...	27[60]	...	3.2[60]	5	...	...	...	1,346	Luxembourg
6.2	97	24.5	5	75.5	3.1	48	20.3	3	79.7	2.1	23	49.8	7	50.2	207	Macau
61	61	...	16	...	2.5	9	...	2	...	2.5	10	...	...	...	127	Madagascar
9.0	...	...	...	...	0.8	...	...	...	...	0.7	4	...	...	...	100	Malawi
13.7	1,053	...	...	...	6.4	596	...	...	...	15.1	...	...	225	...	4,879	Malaysia
6.5	...	...	3	...	9.1	19	...	...	...	...	...	...	...	...	4[63]	Maldives
7.0	217	...	1	...	4.3[19]	56[19]	...	2[19]	...	11.8[19]	33[19]	...	5[19]	...	188	Mali
49	49	...	49	...	49	49	...	49	...	49	49	...	49	...	266	Malta
5.0	...	...	...	...	...	...	...	...	...	...	...	...	...	...	68	Martinique
...	...	...	...	...	...	...	...	...	...	...	...	...	...	...	55	Mauritania
5.2	95[2]	...	...	...	1.3	2	...	...	...	1.2	2	...	...	...	172	Mauritius
...	...	...	...	...	...	...	...	...	...	...	...	...	...	...	...	Mayotte
12.9	...	...	...	...	8.8[19]	...	...	...	...	2.2[19]	...	...	...	...	43,183	Mexico
6.3[2,60]	...	...	23[2,60]	...	2	...	...	...	...	2	...	...	2	...	...	Monaco
...	...	...	...	...	...	...	...	...	...	...	...	...	...	...	...	Mongolia
...	4[2]	...	—	...	...	2	...	—	—	...	2	...	2	...	2.5[20]	Montserrat
22.1	5,817[2]	...	...	...	6.4	...	...	...	...	3.8	...	...	...	...	1,626	Morocco
9.5	...	...	...	...	2.4	...	...	...	...	3.6	...	...	...	...	359	Mozambique
31.1	...	...	...	...	6.7	...	...	...	...	1.1	...	...	...	...	731	Myanmar (Burma)
—	—	—	—	—	—	—	—	—	—	—	—	—	—	—	...	Nauru
3.3	201	...	57	...	1.2	42	...	3	...	—	—	...	—	...	178	Nepal
15.0	1,637	...	222	...	12.1	1,376	29.3[64]	240	70.7[64]	13.5	266	...	92	...	20,686	Netherlands, The
...	...	...	...	...	8.6	...	...	...	...	7	...	...	...	...	103	Netherlands Antilles
66.9	...	...	...	...	...	...	...	...	...	...	...	...	...	...	122	New Caledonia
16.2	3,884	...	54	...	11.6[19]	3,719[19]	...	50[19]	...	4.3[19]	694[19]	...	35[19]	...	4,716	New Zealand
1.9	19	...	...	...	1.4	19	...	...	...	0.8	10	...	...	...	1,335	Nicaragua
14.2[2]	12[2]	...	...	...	2	2	...	...	...	2	2	...	...	...	28	Niger
11.2	...	...	459	...	15.6	...	...	40	...	1.8	...	...	33	...	7,223	Nigeria
...	...	...	...	...	...	...	...	...	...	...	...	...	...	...	...	Niue
...	...	...	...	...	...	...	...	...	...	...	...	...	...	...	...	Norfolk Island
20.1	2,291	40.2	101	59.8	20.2[19]	2,086[19]	35.9[19]	135[19]	64.1[19]	7.2[19]	419[19]	28.7[19]	50[19]	71.3[19]	9,975	Norway
...	...	...	...	...	...	...	...	...	...	...	...	...	...	...	464	Oman
...	...	...	...	...	...	...	...	...	...	...	...	...	...	...	0.2	Pacific Is., Trust Terr. of the Marshall Islands
...	...	...	...	...	...	...	...	...	...	...	...	...	...	...	...	Micronesia, Fed. States of

Manufacturing industries (continued)

country	year	food, beverages, and tobacco (group 1) percent of total value added	1–99 employees number	1–99 employees percent of value added	100 or more emp. number	100 or more emp. percent of value added	textiles, apparel, and leather (group 2) percent of total value added	1–99 employees number	1–99 employees percent of value added	100 or more emp. number	100 or more emp. percent of value added	wood, paper, chemicals, and related products (group 3) percent of total value added	1–99 employees number	1–99 employees percent of value added	100 or more emp. number	100 or more emp. percent of value added
Northern Mariana Islands	1982[3]	...	...	...	...	...	...	...	...	...	...	...	...	...	...	...
Palau	1983	...	...	...	...	...	...	...	...	...	...	...	...	...	...	...
Pakistan	1980–81	35.2	380	11.8	169	88.2	21.3	1,067	25.8	244	74.2	23.6	537	13.0	126	87.0
Panama[43]	1982	46.5	270	29.4	34	70.6	8.9	75	49.6	19	50.4	24.9	210	43.8	21	56.2
Papua New Guinea	1985	60.9	147	...	...	...	0.6	16	...	...	...	17.0	157	...	...	...
Paraguay	1985	47.0	...	...	...	...	12.8	...	...	...	...	23.7	...	...	...	...
Peru[17,43]	1984	22.4[68]	2,605[68]	...	...	...	11.8	2,689	...	...	...	40.1	3,186	...	...	...
Philippines	1983	30.0	16,000	14.6	242	85.4	9.8	22,596	14.9	264	85.1	36.1	7,477	10.9	383	89.1
Pitcairn Island		...	...	...	...	...	...	...	...	...	...	...	...	...	...	...
Poland[69]	1987	16.6	1,600	...	880	...	15.1	6,224	...	186	...	18.8	3,977	...	922	...
Portugal	1986	16.6	3,215	...	...	...	25.1	...	...	2,147	...	28.4	4,452	...	...	...
Puerto Rico	1982	11.2	296	22.7	37	77.3	8.4	286	25.6	131	74.4	47.5	578	25.2	68	74.8
Qatar	1985	4.2	104	...	...	...	3.2	536	...	...	...	69.7	278	...	...	...
Réunion[70]	1988	45.8	81	...	...	...	2.2	7	...	...	...	23.3	58	...	...	...
Romania[24,71]	1985	11.0	...	...	301	...	15.0	...	...	227	...	74.0[48]	...	...	196	...
Rwanda[17,24]	1986	65.0	33	...	...	...	2.5	11	...	...	...	11.6	46	...	...	...
St. Helena and Ascension		...	...	...	...	...	...	...	...	...	...	...	...	...	...	...
St. Kitts and Nevis	1984	42.4[72]	...	...	...	...	...	...	...	...	...	...	...	...	...	...
St. Lucia	1986	...	...	...	...	...	...	...	...	...	...	...	...	...	...	...
St. Pierre and Miquelon		...	...	...	...	...	...	...	...	...	...	...	...	...	...	...
St. Vincent	1986	...	...	...	...	...	...	...	...	...	...	...	...	...	...	...
San Marino	1978	7.2	31	100.0	—	—	9.5	3	...	2	...	22.2	112	100.0	—	—
São Tomé and Príncipe[4]	1985	...	...	...	...	...	...	...	...	...	...	...	...	...	...	...
Saudi Arabia[6,73]	1986–87	...	2,145	...	26	...	...	8,019	...	2	...	41.2[66]	2,751	...	37	...
Senegal[17]	1984	48.2[68]	...	...	52[68]	...	16.0	...	...	33	...	15.4	72	...	...	...
Seychelles	1984	79.1	14	...	...	...	2.0	2	...	...	...	12.0	10	...	...	...
Sierra Leone[13]	1985–86	60.4	38	...	...	...	0.5	16	...	...	...	20.3	63	...	...	...
Singapore[4,13]	1987	5.0	310	...	...	...	3.7	536	...	...	...	26.1	1,074	...	...	...
Solomon Islands	1986	...	...	...	...	...	...	...	...	...	...	...	...	...	...	...
Somalia[4,51]	1985	83.0	75	...	...	...	6.1	58	...	...	...	8.3	37	...	...	...
South Africa[4,51]	1985	16.6	1,722	16.5	457	83.5	7.8	1,733	14.9	556	85.1	33.5	3,666	20.7	649	79.3
Bophuthatswana	1985	...	...	...	...	...	...	...	...	...	...	...	...	...	...	...
Ciskei	1984	...	5	...	...	...	...	...	...	30	...	...	...	...	13	...
Transkei		...	8	...	...	...	...	12	...	...	...	4.9	6	...	...	...
Venda[1]	1985	70.7	...	...	...	...	19.4	...	...	...	...	...	...	...	...	...
South West Africa/Namibia	1986	62.2	...	...	...	...	...	...	...	...	...	26.6	...	...	...	...
Spain[9]	1985	19.4	42,822	...	...	...	9.5	14,699	...	...	...	...	43,335	...	...	...
Sri Lanka[36]	1985	45.6	1,248	...	...	...	19.2	776	...	...	...	18.5	525	...	...	...
Sudan, The[4,75]	1980–81	46.2	296	...	...	...	12.0	123	...	...	...	29.0	232	...	...	...
Suriname	1985	...	...	...	...	...	...	...	...	...	...	...	...	...	...	...
Swaziland[4,13,76]	1985	63.4	...	...	11	...	2.9	10	...	61	...	27.4	...	...	43	...
Sweden	1986	10.1	659	...	159	...	2.4	546	...	131	...	34.1	2,748	...	428	...
Switzerland	1985	10.5	3,352	...	149	...	6.2	2,699	...	...	...	30.3	15,395	...	318	...
Syria[4,9,77]	1986	2.1	8,029	...	...	...	13.5	15,126	...	...	...	63.9	12,783	...	...	...
Taiwan[75]	1987	10.7	8,770	...	81	...	15.9	9,583	...	1,066	...	29.1	26,140	...	1,071	...
Tanzania[4,13]	1985	33.3	156	...	...	...	19.9	...	...	163	...	23.6	225	...	...	...
Thailand[13,17]	1984	44.9	3,267	...	...	...	12.6	...	...	1,305	...	22.0	...	...	2,224	...
Togo[17,24]	1979	62.1	...	...	12	...	7.4	3	...	...	...	13.6	26	...	...	...
Tokelau		...	...	...	...	...	...	...	...	...	...	...	...	...	...	...
Tonga	1981	73.8	33	100.0	—	—	1.1	11	100.0	—	—	11.7	23	100.0	—	—
Trinidad and Tobago[37,38]	1987	35.5	230	...	...	...	4.7	152	...	...	...	32.9	361	...	...	...
Tunisia[6]	1987	22.7	283	35.9	35	64.1	27.5	276	26.4	124	73.6	19.9[31]	253	26.8	49	73.2
Turkey[17,78]	1984	20.5	1,595	16.3	304	83.7	15.9	1,521	18.3	326	81.7	29.4	1,432	9.2	242	90.8
Turks and Caicos Islands	1986[20]	...	...	...	...	...	...	...	...	...	...	...	...	...	...	...
Tuvalu	1979	...	...	...	...	...	...	...	...	...	...	...	...	...	...	...
Uganda[4]	1985	50.2	...	...	...	...	24.8	...	...	...	...	7.0	...	...	...	...
U.S.S.R.[24]	1987	9.9	...	...	9,554	...	12.4	...	...	7,960	...	12.9	...	...	6,619	...
United Arab Emirates[37,79,80]	1985	2.5	20	...	3	...	...	13	...	—	—	92.3	29	...	11	...
United Kingdom[4]	1986	13.2	8,815	11.3	1,516	88.7	6.6	14,116	27.8	1,076	72.2	29.2	41,468	21.8	3,920	78.2
United States[4,75]	1986	12.1	18,523	20.3	3,770	79.7	5.3	28,446	33.3	5,310	66.7	30.2	121,107	27.0	9,339	73.0
Uruguay[43,81]	1986	28.9	2,712	36.7	70	63.3	18.4	1,878	37.9	117	62.1	36.7	2,858	33.3	48	66.7
Vanuatu	1984	51.5	...	...	...	...	1.9	...	...	...	...	20.8	...	...	...	...
Venezuela[43]	1986	22.6	2,378	17.8	174	82.2	8.4	1,740	34.3	127	65.7	36.2	2,512	16.0	238	84.0
Vietnam		...	...	...	...	...	...	...	...	...	...	...	...	...	...	...
Virgin Islands (U.S.)	1982[3]	...	...	...	...	...	...	...	...	...	...	...	...	...	...	...
Wallis and Futuna		...	...	...	...	...	...	...	...	...	...	...	...	...	...	...
West Bank[44]	1986	43.5	229	...	...	...	14.3	648	...	...	...	20.3	540	...	...	...
Western Sahara		...	...	...	...	...	...	...	...	...	...	...	...	...	...	...
Western Samoa[51,82]	1983	...	25	...	...	...	...	3	...	...	...	...	31	...	...	...
Yemen (Aden)[51,82]	1984	36.7[43]	488	...	...	...	11.7[43]	...	...	13	...	30.6[43]	...	...	14	...
Yemen (Ṣan'ā')[43]	1980	34.2	442	...	...	...	7.9	536	...	...	...	13.6	659	...	...	...
Yugoslavia[24,83,84]	1986	13.5	...	...	1,317	...	16.6	...	...	1,547	...	22.6	...	...	2,734	...
Zaire	1980	39.5	...	...	...	...	16.0	...	...	...	...	17.3	...	...	...	...
Zambia	1985	41.9	...	...	...	...	14.1	...	...	...	...	17.8	...	...	...	...
Zimbabwe	1983	35.9	...	...	...	...	13.0	...	...	...	...	21.1	...	...	...	...

[1]Percentages in value-added columns are based on gross output in value of sales. [2]Group 4 includes groups 5 and 6. [3]Census data insufficiently detailed. [4]Value added calculated in factor values. [5]Establishments data are for 1980. [6]Establishments data are for 1981. [7]Group 5 includes group 6. [8]Four or more employees only. [9]Establishments data are for 1984. [10]Group 5 includes group 6 and ISIC groups 385 and 390. [11]Data in value-added columns refer to gross output in producer's prices. [12]Data refer to foreign-owned manufactures of rum, pharmaceuticals, and cement only. [13]Ten or more employees only. [14]Establishments data are for 1983. [15]Includes ISIC groups 385 and 390 and diamond industry. [16]Sugar and citrus fruit only. [17]Value added calculated in producer's prices. [18]Twenty or more employees only. [19]Group 5 includes, and group 6 excludes, ISIC 3825. [20]1985–87 average. [21]Establishments data are incomplete. [22]1984. [23]State enterprises only. [24]Establishments data refer to enterprises. [25]Value-added data are for 1984. [26]Establishments data breakdown is for 10–49 employees and 50 or more employees. [27]Average enterprise size not available. [28]Most manufacturing is in food and apparel industries. [29]1978. [30]Includes sugarcane cropping; excludes fish processing. [31]Excludes petroleum refining. [32]Based on official exchange rate. [33]Value-added data are for 20 or more employees. [34]Six or more employees only. [35]Includes sugarcane cropping. [36]Establishments data are for 5 or more employees. [37]Establishments data are for 10 or more employees. [38]Establishments data are for 1985. [39]Fish processing. [40]Group 5 includes ISIC 3825. Group 6 includes ISIC 390. [41]Group 2 includes groups 3 and 4. [42]1979. [43]Five or more employees only. [44]Value-added data are "revenue" (mostly value of sales). [45]Group 2 includes group 3. [46]Thirty or more employees.

primary and fabricated metals; proc. minerals (group 4)					machinery (except elec.) and transport equip. (group 5)					electrical and electronic machinery (group 6)					total manufacturing value added (U.S.$'000,000)	country
percent of total value added	1–99 emp. number	1–99 emp. percent of value added	100+ emp. number	100+ emp. percent of value added	percent of total value added	1–99 emp. number	1–99 emp. percent of value added	100+ emp. number	100+ emp. percent of value added	percent of total value added	1–99 emp. number	1–99 emp. percent of value added	100+ emp. number	100+ emp. percent of value added		
...	...	...	...	...	...	...	...	...	...	...	...	...	...	...	...	Northern Mariana Islands
...	...	...	...	...	...	...	...	...	...	...	...	...	...	...	0.1	Palau
11.5	528	17.2	69	82.8	4.2	358	14.0	37	86.0	3.5	154	15.9	31	84.1	2,898	Pakistan
12.6	112	48.3	13	51.7	1.4	20	100.0	—	—	0.8	12	100.0	—	—	452	Panama
21.5[2,67]	145[2,67]	...	...	...	2	2	...	...	...	2	2	...	...	...	267	Papua New Guinea
6.6[2]	...	...	...	...	2	...	...	...	...	2	...	...	...	...	737	Paraguay
16.5	1,911	...	...	...	5.0	854	...	...	...	3.0	384	...	...	...	3,767[68]	Peru
12.0	5,903	14.1	138	85.9	3.9[19]	1,545[19]	20.9[19]	71[19]	79.1[19]	5.9[19]	144[19]	9.6[19]	75[19]	90.4[19]	5,107	Philippines
...	...	...	...	...	...	...	...	...	...	...	...	...	...	...	...	Pitcairn Island
15.2	4,594	...	877	...	21.7	1,819	...	865	...	7.5	1,065	...	324	...	20,516	Poland
16.0	1,851	...	...	...	7.6	...	...	503	...	5.8	...	...	146	...	4,911	Portugal
3.1	351	53.0	16	47.0	6.7[19]	104[19]	13.9[19]	12[19]	86.1[19]	13.2[19]	112[19]	18.5[19]	69[19]	81.5[19]	8,606	Puerto Rico
22.7[58]	267	...	...	...	...	2	...	—	...	...	2	...	...	...	486	Qatar
25.1[2]	75[2]	...	472[2]	...	...	2	...	...	...	...	2	...	...	...	105	Réunion
48	...	...	...	...	48	...	...	2	...	48	...	...	2	...	...	Romania
20.9[2]	12[2]	...	...	...	2	...	...	...	...	2	...	...	...	...	193	Rwanda
...	...	...	...	...	...	...	...	...	...	...	...	...	...	...	...	St. Helena and Ascension
...	...	...	...	...	...	...	...	...	...	...	...	...	...	...	8	St. Kitts and Nevis
...	...	...	...	...	...	...	...	...	...	...	...	...	...	...	13	St. Lucia
...	...	...	...	...	...	...	...	...	...	...	...	...	...	...	...	St. Pierre and Miquelon
38.5	136	...	4	...	...	...	...	...	...	...	...	...	...	...	9	St. Vincent
...	...	...	...	...	...	...	...	...	...	...	...	...	...	...	47	San Marino
...	...	...	...	...	...	...	...	...	...	...	...	...	...	...	3	São Tomé and Príncipe
20.4[2,67]	6,361	...	...	...	...	609[19]	...	...	...	...	2,287[19]	...	...	...	4,797	Saudi Arabia
...	45[2,67]	...	...	...	2	...	...	...	...	2	...	...	...	...	205[68]	Senegal
6.9	4	...	...	...	—	—	...	...	...	...	—	...	...	...	14	Seychelles
10.8[2]	18[2]	...	...	...	2	2	...	...	...	2	2	...	...	...	43	Sierra Leone
8.3	552	...	...	...	14.0	571	...	...	...	39.1	...	...	327	...	6,801	Singapore
1.5[2]	37	...	...	...	2	2	...	...	...	2	2	...	...	...	6	Solomon Islands
...	...	...	...	...	...	...	...	...	...	...	...	...	...	...	112	Somalia
28.7	3,585	15.9	577	84.1	9.3[19]	2,117	23.5	312	76.5	6.0[19]	638	16.7	117	83.3	11,132	South Africa
...	8[2]	...	...	...	...	2	...	...	...	...	2	...	...	...	120	Bophuthatswana
...	...	...	...	...	...	...	...	...	...	...	...	...	...	...	36[74]	Ciskei
...	...	...	...	...	...	...	...	...	...	...	...	...	...	...	...	Transkei
5.0	9	...	—	...	—	...	...	...	...	...	...	...	...	...	12	Venda
22.5	24,939	...	...	...	14.6	14,701	...	...	...	6.5	2,471	...	...	...	58	South West Africa/Namibia
16.3[2]	438	...	...	...	2	42	...	...	...	2	19	...	...	...	32,124	Spain
12.0[2]	...	...	...	...	2	...	...	...	...	2	...	...	...	...	498	Sri Lanka
...	...	...	...	...	...	...	...	...	...	...	...	...	...	...	905	Sudan, The
...	...	...	...	...	...	...	...	...	...	...	...	...	...	...	115	Suriname
6.1	18	...	...	...	0.2[7]	3[7]	...	...	...	7	7	...	...	...	46	Swaziland
16.6	1,851	...	244	...	25.0	1,284	...	319	...	9.9	352	...	123	...	32,176	Sweden
14.1	7,973	...	228	...	17.7	2,983	...	280	...	14.9	2,676[60]	...	224[60]	...	23,859	Switzerland
19.5	18,254[2]	...	...	...	...	2	...	...	...	...	2	...	...	...	2,762	Syria
37.2[2]	24,861	...	490	...	2	11,552[19]	...	322[19]	...	2	4,597[19]	...	509[19]	...	38,565	Taiwan
10.6	...	...	63	...	7.8	...	...	33	...	2.2	10	...	...	...	284	Tanzania
13.3	1,729	...	...	...	3.9	414	...	...	...	2.6	...	...	214	...	14,177	Thailand
16.5	...	...	9	...	—	—	...	—	—	...	—	...	...	...	52	Togo
...	...	...	...	...	...	...	...	...	...	...	...	...	...	...	...	Tokelau
12.8[2]	19	100.0	—	...	2	7	100.0	—	—	2	2	100.0	—	—	4	Tonga
...	385	...	...	...	...	50	...	...	...	...	45	...	...	...	539	Trinidad and Tobago
16.0	...	...	...	...	13.9[7]	...	...	...	...	7	...	...	...	...	1,248[31]	Tunisia
18.3	1,519	16.0	285	84.0	10.4	835	13.9	165	86.1	5.0	452	10.1	85	89.9	9,706	Turkey
—	...	...	...	...	—	...	...	...	...	—	...	...	...	...	0.4	Turks and Caicos Islands
...	...	...	...	...	...	...	...	...	...	...	...	...	...	...	0.04	Tuvalu
17.9[2]	...	...	...	...	...	2	...	...	...	...	2	...	...	...	165	Uganda
18.4	...	...	5,047	...	36.6[7]	...	...	9,238[7]	...	7	...	...	7	...	149,577[32]	U.S.S.R.
5.2	49	...	4	...	...	...	...	...	...	...	...	...	7	...	2,210	United Arab Emirates
13.5	17,388	24.1	2,318	75.9	22.8	26,252	18.2	2,495	81.8	12.1	9,540	13.0	1,311	87.0	120,213	United Kingdom
12.4	53,491	29.6	5,675	70.4	21.2	55,566	17.0	4,620	83.0	13.6	14,839	9.7	3,783	90.3	1,032,900	United States
7.3	1,504	49.3	37	50.7	5.5	796	55.8	14	44.2	2.7	349	57.1	12	42.9	1,649	Uruguay
13.7	...	...	...	...	—	...	...	...	...	...	—	...	...	...	7	Vanuatu
21.0	1,835	16.6	130	83.4	6.0	422	23.5	66	76.5	2.7	174	31.0	45	69.0	13,764	Venezuela
...	...	...	...	...	...	...	...	...	...	...	...	...	...	...	...	Vietnam
...	...	...	...	...	...	...	...	...	...	...	...	...	...	...	...	Virgin Islands (U.S.)
...	...	...	...	...	...	...	...	...	...	...	...	...	...	...	...	Wallis and Futuna
14.6	785	...	...	...	...	...	...	...	...	...	...	...	...	...	134	West Bank
—	—	—	—	—	—	...	...	—	...	—	...	...	—	...	...	Western Sahara
...	11[2]	...	...	...	2	...	...	...	...	2	...	...	...	...	5	Western Samoa
21.1[2,43]	11[2]	...	...	...	2	2	...	...	...	2	2	...	...	...	127	Yemen (Aden)
27.9[2]	1,324[2]	...	...	...	2	...	...	...	...	2	2	...	...	...	172	Yemen (Șan'ā')
21.2	...	...	1,892	...	16.1[19]	...	...	1,138[19]	...	8.8[19]	...	...	541[19]	...	22,886	Yugoslavia
9.6	...	...	...	...	6.4	...	...	...	...	1.7	...	...	...	...	1,369	Zaire
25.4[2]	...	...	...	...	2	...	...	...	...	...	...	...	...	...	513	Zambia
25.1[58]	...	...	...	...	58	...	...	...	...	3.3	...	...	...	...	1,609	Zimbabwe

[47]Value of sales. [48]Group 3 includes groups 4, 5, and 6. [49]Group 2 includes groups 3, 4, 5, and 6. [50]1985. [51]Establishments data are for 1979. [52]Includes ISIC 390. [53]All data refer to either establishments with electric power and 10 or more employees or establishments without electric power and 20 or more employees. [54]Value-added data are for 1985. [55]Establishments data are for 20 or more employees. [56]Three or more employees only. [57]Excludes diamond industry. [58]Group 4 includes group 5. [59]Breakdown is for 1–49 employees and 50 or more employees. [60]Includes ISIC 385. [61]Group 3 includes group 4. [62]Establishments data refer to establishments with annual sales of 100,000 kwachas or more. [63]Includes electricity. [64]Percentages based on value of sales. [65]Includes Aruba. [66]Petroleum refining. [67]Includes ISIC groups 385 and 390. [68]Excludes fish processing. [69]Establishments data are for 1986. [70]Value-added data are for 1983. [71]Value-added data are for 1982. [72]Sugar only. [73]Privately owned establishments only. [74]1980. [75]Establishments data are for 1982. [76]Based on incomplete figures. [77]Establishments data are for private sector only. [78]Excludes private establishments with fewer than 10 employees. [79]Abu Dhabi only. [80]Value-added data excludes textiles, apparel, and leather. [81]Establishments data are for 1978. [82]Percentages in value-added columns are based on 1984 gross output of production. [83]Socialized sector only. [84]Data in value-added columns refer to social product.

Energy

This table provides data about the commercial energy supplies (reserves, production, consumption, and trade) of the various countries of the world, together with data about oil pipeline networks and traffic. Many of the data and concepts used in this table are adopted from the United Nations' *Energy Statistics Yearbook*.

Electricity. Total installed electrical power capacity comprises the sum of the rated power capacities of all main and auxiliary generators in a country. "Total installed capacity" (kW) is multiplied by 8,760 hours per year to yield "Total production capacity" (kW-hr).

Production of electricity comprises the total gross production of electricity by publicly or privately owned enterprises and also that generated by industrial establishments for their own use, but usually excludes consumption by the utility itself. Measured in 1,000,000s of kilowatt-hours (kW-hr), annual production of electricity ranges generally between 30% and 40% of total production capacity. The data are further analyzed by type of generation: fossil fuels, hydroelectric power, and nuclear fuel.

The great majority of the world's electrical and other energy needs are met by the burning of fossil hydrocarbon solids, liquids, and gases, either for thermal generation of electricity or in internal combustion engines. Many renewable and nontraditional sources of energy are being developed worldwide (wood, biogenic gases and liquids, tidal, wave, and wind power, geothermal and photothermal [solar] energy, and so on), but collectively these sources are still negligible in the world's total energy consumption.

For this reason only hydroelectric and nuclear generation are considered here separately with fossil fuels.

Trade in electrical energy refers to the transfer of generated electrical output via an international grid. Total electricity consumption (residential and nonresidential) is equal to total electricity requirements less transformation and distribution losses.

Coal. The term coal, as used in the table, comprises all grades of anthracite, bituminous, subbituminous, and lignite that have acquired or may in the future, by reason of new technology or changed market prices, acquire an economic value. These types of coal may be differentiated according to heat content (density) and content of impurities. Most coal reserve data are based on proved recoverable reserves only, of all grades of coal. Exceptions are footnoted, with proved in-place reserves reported only when recoverable reserves are unknown. Production figures include deposits removed from both surface and underground workings as well as quantities used by the producers themselves or issued to the miners. Wastes recovered from mines or nearby preparation plants are excluded from production figures.

Natural gas. This term refers to any combustible gas (usually chiefly methane) of natural origin from underground sources. The data for production cover, to the extent possible, gas obtained from gas fields, petroleum fields, or coal mines that is actually collected and marketed. (Much natural gas in Middle Eastern and North African oil fields is

Energy

country	electricity installed capacity, 1987 ('000 kW)	production, 1987 capacity ('000,000 kW-hr)	production, 1987 amount ('000,000 kW-hr)	power source, 1987 fossil fuel (%)	power source, 1987 hydro power (%)	power source, 1987 nuclear fuel (%)	trade, 1987 exports ('000,000 kW-hr)	trade, 1987 imports ('000,000 kW-hr)	consumption amount, 1987 ('000,000 kW-hr)	consumption per capita, 1987 (kW-hr)	consumption residential, 1986 (%)	consumption nonresidential, 1986 (%)	coal reserves, latest ('000,000 metric tons)	coal production, 1987 ('000 metric tons)	coal consumption, 1987 ('000 metric tons)
Afghanistan	470	4,117	1,257	39.2	60.8	—	—	—	1,257	85	...	...	66	167	167
Albania	765	6,701	3,840	12.8	87.2	—	650	—	3,190	1,036	...	...	15[1]	2,300	2,530
Algeria	3,836	33,603	13,400	97.8	2.2	—	170	120	13,350	578	...	...	43	8	1,108
American Samoa	32	280	75	100.0	—	—	—	—	75	2,027	27.5[3]	72.5[3]	—	—	...
Andorra	...	...	...	...	...	...	...	...	...	...	...	...	—	—	—
Angola	605	5,300	1,800	25.8	74.2	—	—	—	1,800	195	27.5[2]	72.5[2]	...	—	—
Anguilla	—	—	—	...	...	...	—	—	—	—	...	...	—	—	...
Antigua and Barbuda	26	228	91	100.0	—	—	—	—	91	1,083	42.4[4]	57.6[4]	—	—	—
Argentina	16,593	145,355	52,165	45.6	42.0	12.4	7	180	52,338	1,681	46.3	53.7	130	373	1,707
Aruba	90	788	310	100.0	—	—	...	...	310	5,160	...	...	...	—	—
Australia	33,849	296,517	132,172	89.2	10.1	0.7[5]	—	—	132,172	8,177	30.1[2]	69.9[2]	72,430	189,569	85,079
Austria	16,045	140,554	50,220	29.2	70.8	—	9,606	3,997	44,611	5,952	23.1[2]	83.4[2]	64	2,786	5,968
Bahamas, The	357	3,127	965	100.0	—	—	—	—	965	3,845	33.6[4]	66.4[4]	...	—	—
Bahrain	1,099	9,627	3,020	100.0	—	—	—	—	3,020	6,495	...	...	...	—	...
Bangladesh	1,925	16,863	5,895	91.0	9.0	—	—	—	5,895	55	43.5	56.5	1,054[1]	—	65
Barbados	100	876	425	100.0	—	—	—	—	425	1,654	29.9	70.1	...	—	1
Belgium	14,058	123,148	62,375	31.9	0.8	67.3	7,778	5,660	60,257	6,075	26.9[7]	73.1[7]	410	4,356	13,086
Belize	22	193	75	100.0	—	—	—	—	75	439	...	...	...	—	...
Benin	15	131	5	100.0	—	—	—	160	165	38	...	...	...	—	...
Bermuda	123	1,077	435	100.0	—	—	—	—	435	7,500	41.4[3]	58.6[3]	—	—	—
Bhutan	19	166	21	61.9	38.1	—	—	10	31	22	29.2[3]	69.8[3]	...	—	1
Bolivia	469	4,108	1,520	25.7	74.3	—	—	2	1,522	226	60.7	39.3	...	—	—
Botswana	[10]	[10]	522[10,11]	[10]	[10]	[10]	[10]	82[10,11]	[10]	[10]	...	...	3,850	400[7,10]	[10]
Brazil	47,244	413,857	202,287	7.8	91.7	0.5	—	16,813	219,090	1,549	42.2	57.8	2,780	6,884	16,969
British Virgin Islands	6	53	32	100.0	—	—	—	—	32	2,286	...	...	...	—	—
Brunei	288	2,523	998	100.0	—	—	—	—	998	4,124	55.3[4]	44.7[4]	...	—	—
Bulgaria	10,743	94,109	43,470	65.6	5.8	28.6	952	5,326	47,844	5,324	41.2[3]	58.8[3]	4,030	36,819	43,848
Burkina Faso	59	517	125	100.0	—	—	—	—	125	15	...	...	...	—	—
Burundi	19	166	54	3.7	96.3	—	—	75	29	26	...	...	...	—	—
Cameroon	605	5,300	2,392	2.8	97.2	—	—	—	2,392	230	...	...	...	1	1
Canada	100,600	881,256	496,335	20.7	63.7	15.6	47,427	3,471	452,379	17,486	28.8[4]	71.2[4]	7,550	61,207	50,670
Cape Verde	5	44	28	100.0	—	—	—	—	28	80	...	...	—	—	—
Cayman Islands	35	307	138	100.0	—	—	—	—	138	6,273	56.7	43.3	—	—	—
Central African Republic	43	377	92	19.6	80.4	—	—	—	92	34	...	...	4	—	—
Chad	31	272	51	100.0	—	—	—	—	51	10	...	...	...	—	—
Chile	4,033	35,329	15,636	22.3	77.7	—	—	—	15,636	1,247	34.1	65.9	1,300	1,598	1,838
China	92,000	805,920	497,267	79.9	20.1	—	—	—	497,267	465	6.1[11]	93.9[11]	108,900	927,965	916,376
Christmas Island	11	96	38	100.0	—	—	—	—	34[3]	16,940[3]	...	...	...	—	—
Cocos (Keeling) Islands	...	...	...	100.0	—	—	—	—	...	...	...	...	...	—	—
Colombia	7,291	63,869	35,368	27.7	72.3	—	—	—	35,368	1,181	66.9	33.1	1,130	14,594	5,089
Comoros	5	44	14	85.7	14.3	—	—	—	14	30	...	...	...	—	—
Congo	149	1,305	235	0.9	99.1	—	—	53	288	157	...	...	...	—	—
Cook Islands	6	53	12	100.0	—	—	—	—	12	571	...	...	—	—	—
Costa Rica	914	8,007	2,308	1.7	98.3	—	100	175	3,005	1,076	71.4	28.6	—	—	—
Côte d'Ivoire	1,163	10,188	2,200	41.4	58.6	—	—	—	2,200	197	33.3	66.7	...	—	—
Cuba	3,532	30,940	13,594	99.7	0.3	—	—	—	13,594	1,349	29.4[4]	70.6[4]	...	—	107
Cyprus	389	3,408	1,512	100.0	—	—	—	—	1,512	2,220	76.7	23.3	...	—	151
Czechoslovakia	21,017	184,109	85,825	68.4	5.7	25.9	8,510	11,931	89,246	5,734	23.6[3]	76.4[3]	6,150	126,072	124,647
Denmark	8,557	74,959	29,398	99.3	0.1	0.6[5]	1,758	4,172	31,812	6,212	32.5[7]	67.5[7]	63[1]	—	11,921
Djibouti	38	333	172	100.0	—	—	—	—	172	461	...	...	...	—	...
Dominica	7	61	19	10.5	89.5	—	—	—	19	241	53.5[4]	46.5[4]	—	—	1[11]
Dominican Republic	1,065	9,329	5,296	82.1	17.9	—	—	—	5,296	788	...	...	...	—	—
Ecuador	1,961	17,178	5,668	19.3	80.7	—	—	—	5,668	571	67.2	32.8	18	—	—
Egypt	6,340	55,538	32,500	81.5	18.5	—	—	—	32,500	648	28.3[4]	71.1[4]	53	—	1,250
El Salvador	500	4,380	1,900	6.8	54.2	39.0[7]	—	—	1,900	386	67.1	32.9	...	—	—

flared [burned] because it is often not economical to capture and market it.) Manufactured gas is generally a by-product of industrial operations such as gasworks, coke ovens, and blast furnaces. It is usually burned at the point of production and rarely enters the marketplace. Production of manufactured gas is, therefore, only reported as a percentage of domestic gas consumption.

Crude petroleum. Crude petroleum is the liquid product obtained from oil wells; the term also includes shale oil, tar sand extract, and field or lease condensate. Production and consumption data in the table refer, so far as possible, to the same year so that the relationship between national production and consumption patterns can be clearly seen; both are given in barrels.

Proved reserves are that oil remaining underground in known fields whose existence has been "proved" by the evaluation of nearby producing wells or by seismic tests in sedimentary strata known to contain crude petroleum, and that is judged recoverable within the limits of present technology and economic conditions (prices). The published proved reserve figures do not necessarily reflect the true reserves of a country, because government authorities or corporations often have political or economic motives for withholding or altering such data.

The estimated exhaustion rate of petroleum reserves is an extrapolated ratio of published proved reserves to the current rate of withdrawal/production. Present world published proved reserves will last about 40 to 45 years at the present rate of withdrawal, but there are large country-to-country variations above or below the average.

Data on petroleum and product pipelines are provided because of the great importance to both domestic and international energy markets of this means of bringing these energy sources from their production or transportation points to refineries, intermediate consumption and distribution points, and final consumers. Their traffic may represent a very significant fraction of the total movement of goods within a country. Available data for petroleum pipelines are often incomplete and their basis varies internationally, some countries reporting only international shipments, others reporting domestic shipments of 50 kilometres or more, and so on.

For data in the hydrocarbons portions of the table (coal, natural gas, and petroleum), extensive use has been made of a variety of international sources, such as those of the United Nations, the International Energy Agency (of the Organization for Economic Cooperation and Development), and the World Energy Conference; of the resources of the U.S. Department of Energy; and of various industry surveys, such as those published by British Petroleum (BP *Statistical Review of World Energy*), the *International Petroleum Encyclopedia,* the *Oil and Gas Journal,* the *Petroleum Economist,* and *World Oil.*

a. Includes refined petroleum products pipelines.

natural gas						crude petroleum							country
published proved reserves, 1989 ('000,000,000 cu m)	production		consumption			reserves, 1989		production, 1988 ('000,000 barrels)	consumption, 1987 ('000,000 barrels)	refining capacity, 1989 ('000 barrels per day)	pipelines (latest)a		
	natural gas, 1988 ('000,000 cu m)	manufactured gas, 1987 (% of total gas consumption)	amount, 1987 ('000,000 cu m)	residential, 1986 (%)	non-residential, 1986 (%)	published proved ('000,000 barrels)	years to exhaust proved reserves				length (km)	traffic ('000,000 metric ton-km)	
100	3,000	...	610	...	...								Afghanistan
10	800	...	384	...	...	193	12	16	22	40	200	—	Albania
3,230	44,900	27.7	16,874	26.8[2]	73.2[2]	8,400	35	243	163	465	6,910	...	Algeria
...	...	...	...	...	...	...	...	—	—	—	—	...	American Samoa
...	...	...	...	...	...	...	...	—	—	—	—	—	Andorra
60	500	10.0	154	...	...	2,024	12	164	11	32	179	...	Angola
...	...	...	...	...	...	...	...	—	—	—	—	—	Anguilla
771	18,960	10.2	21,469	46.2	53.8	2,268	14	164	160	690	6,990	...	Antigua and Barbuda
...	...	...	...	...	...	...	...	—	—	—	—	—	Argentina
										...			Aruba
2,300	14,080	31.0	15,806	...	...	1,673	8	202	177	644	3,000	...	Australia
13	1,260	19.6	4,961	25.7[2]	74.3[2]	100	13	8	53	204	725	5,003	Austria
263	5,500	6.2	4,310	...	...	126	8	15	89	243	72	...	Bahamas, The
350	4,600	0.3	3,907	35.8	64.2	—	—	0.2	9	31	—	—	Bahrain
													Bangladesh
—	22[6]	...	22	61.1	38.9	3.3	8	0.4	2	3	—	—	Barbados
...	29[8]	29.0	9,645	43.4[7]	56.6[7]	...	...	—	175[9]	631	1,328	709	Belgium
—	...	...	...	...	...	...	...	—	—	—	—	—	Belize
...	...	...	...	...	...	100	59	1.7	—	—	—	—	Benin
...	...	...	...	...	...			—	—	—	—	—	Bermuda
147	2,780	41.1	323	—	100.0	176	25	7	7	58	2,380	...	Bhutan
...	...	10	...	...	...	...	...	—	10	—	—	—	Bolivia
109	2,760	71.7	2,770	—	100.0	2,550	13	203	435	1,407	5,804	...	Botswana
...	...	...	...	...	...	...	...	—	—	—	—	—	Brazil
													British Virgin Islands
322	8,520	2.2	934	...	...	1,400	28	50	—	10	553	...	Brunei
5	150	11.1	6,208	...	...	13	43	0.3	97	300	611	...	Bulgaria
...	...	...	...	...	...	...	...	—	—	—	—	—	Burkina Faso
110	—	100.0	...	...	...	500	8	62	16	42	—	—	Burundi
													Cameroon
2,637	98,220	24.4	57,558	20.6[2]	79.4[2]	6,786	12	586	467	1,856	23,564	99,700	Canada
...	...	...	...	...	...	...	...	—	—	—	—	—	Cape Verde
...	...	...	...	...	...	...	...	—	—	—	—	—	Cayman Islands
...	...	...	...	...	...	...	...	—	—	—	—	—	Central African Republic
												—	Chad
118	1,020	46.7	903	97.4	2.6	257	29	9	39	147	1,540	...	Chile
1,000	13,750	15.2	14,047	...	...	22,000	22	982	786	2,200	7,600	...	China
...	...	...	...	...	...	...	...	—	—	—	—	—	Christmas Island
114	4,140	19.8	4,928	4.8	95.2	2,028	16	126	88	227	4,935	...	Cocos (Keeling) Islands
													Colombia
73	34[8]	51.3	2	...	...	710	14	49	4	21	25	...	Comoros
—	—	38.9	—	—	—	...	...	—	—	—	—	—	Congo
100	—	58.8	—	—	—	120	26	4.7	5	16	176	...	Cook Islands
									13	60			Costa Rica
													Côte d'Ivoire
...	22	91.1	23	...	...	...	...	—	54	160	—	—	Cuba
—	—	62.1	—	...	...	...	...	—	4	17	—	—	Cyprus
14	870	32.4	11,632	...	...	19	19	1	126	455	2,948	9,016	Czechoslovakia
120	2,390	25.6	1,475	...	...	541	15	35	52	177	688	1,005	Denmark
...	...	...	...	...	...	...	...	—	—	—	—	—	Djibouti
...	...	25.4	...	...	...	...	...	—	11	47	—	—	Dominica
113	80	22.7	55	—	100.0[4]	1,350	12	113	33	123	104	...	Dominican Republic
332	6,920	13.6	4,343	37.1	62.9	4,644	15	311	164	489	2,158	...	Ecuador
		92.0				...	...	—	5	17	1,767	...	Egypt
											—	—	El Salvador

Energy (continued)

country	installed capacity, 1987 ('000 kW)	production capacity ('000,000 kW-hr)	production amount ('000,000 kW-hr)	fossil fuel (%)	hydro-power (%)	nuclear fuel (%)	exports ('000,000 kW-hr)	imports ('000,000 kW-hr)	consumption amount, 1987 ('000,000 kW-hr)	per capita, 1987 (kW-hr)	residential, 1986 (%)	non-residential, 1986 (%)	coal reserves, latest ('000,000 metric tons)	coal production, 1987 ('000 metric tons)	coal consumption, 1987 ('000 metric tons)
Equatorial Guinea	5	44	17	88.2	11.8	—	—	—	17	41	...	...	11	—	—
Ethiopia	363	3,180	810	19.8	80.2	—	—	—	810	18	...	...	...	—	—
Faeroe Islands	68	596	180	72.2	27.8	—	—	—	180	3,830	...	...	...	—	—
Falkland Islands	1	9	3	100.0	—	—	—	—	3	1,000	...	...	...	...	...
Fiji	200	1,752	430	18.6	81.4	—	—	—	430	601	26.4	73.6	...	...	16
Finland	11,661	102,150	53,464	37.5	25.8	36.7	507	6,104	59,061	11,961	18.6[2]	81.3[2]	...	—	5,239
France	97,600[12]	854,976[12]	356,200[12]	10.4[12]	19.1[12]	70.5[12]	38,400[12]	8,700[12]	326,500[12]	5,870[12]	30.3[7]	69.7[7]	381	19,077[12]	31,747[12]
French Guiana	89	780	249	100.0	—	—	—	—	249	2,862	...	58.7[2,13]	...	...	...
French Polynesia	79	692	225	84.4	15.6	—	—	—	225	1,316	...	...	...	...	...
Gabon	200	1,752	876	22.9	77.1	—	—	—	876	827	57.7	42.3	...	...	...
Gambia, The	11	96	44	100.0	—	—	—	—	44	56	...	...	...	...	...
Gaza Strip	...	...	...	...	...	...	...	...	...	...	...	...	...	...	...
Germany, East	23,525	206,079	114,180	88.7	1.5	9.8	3,664	7,451	117,967	7,089	31.7[11]	68.3[11]	23,000	302,976	310,390
Germany, West	84,110	736,804	415,812	63.7	4.6	31.7	18,370	22,177	419,619	6,900	26.3[7]	73.7[7]	65,120	191,232	195,759
Ghana	1,185	10,381	4,758	1.7	98.3	—	281	—	4,477	327	...	...	—	—	3
Gibraltar	21	184	70	100.0	—	—	—	—	70	2,333	...	...	...	...	...
Greece	10,198	89,334	30,087	90.8	9.2	—	362	977	30,702	3,072	30.6[7]	69.4[7]	3,300	44,612	44,425
Greenland	88	771	188	100.0	—	—	—	—	188	3,418	34.1	65.9	...	...	...
Grenada	8	70	25	100.0	—	—	—	—	25	250	46.8[4]	53.2[4]	...	...	...
Guadeloupe	103	902	462	100.0	—	—	—	—	462	1,367	...	32.9[13]	...	...	...
Guam	302	2,646	1,000	100.0	—	—	—	—	1,000	8,475	36.9[7]	63.1[7]	...	...	...
Guatemala	785	6,877	1,770	61.6	38.4	—	—	—	1,770	210	27.0[2]	73.0[2]	...	...	...
Guernsey	...	...	...	...	...	...	...	...	...	...	...	...	...	...	...
Guinea	176	1,542	500	66.6	33.4	—	—	—	500	78	...	...	...	...	...
Guinea-Bissau	7	61	14	100.0	—	—	—	—	14	15	...	...	...	...	...
Guyana	168	1,472	385	98.7	1.3	—	—	—	385	389	32.5[14]	67.5[14]	13[1]	...	...
Haiti	146	1,279	450	28.9	71.1	—	—	—	450	65	...	...	21[1]	...	...
Honduras	285	2,497	1,085	18.9	81.1	—	2	160	1,243	266	52.7	47.3	...	—	8,010
Hong Kong	6,614	57,939	23,753	100.0	—	—	1,362	—	22,391	3,988	66.2	33.8	4,920	22,844	25,515
Hungary	6,629	58,070	29,749	62.5	0.6	36.9	1,997	12,610	40,362	3,805	30.7[3]	69.3[3]	1,740	1,730	2,914
Iceland	951	8,331	4,210	0.1	94.0	5.9[5]	—	—	4,210	16,976	20.9[2]	79.1[2]	...	—	60
India	58,433	511,873	217,500	70.9	26.6	2.5	30	16	217,486	271	40.9	59.1	23,232[1]	185,355	183,301
Indonesia	10,430	91,367	34,810	78.5	20.9	0.6[5]	—	—	34,810	202	59.1	40.9	193	1,240	1,440
Iran	13,404	117,419	37,910	83.1	16.9	—	—	—	37,910	739	21.1[11]	78.9[11]	...	...	...
Iraq	3,700	32,412	22,860	97.3	2.7	—	—	—	22,860	1,340	...	...	...	...	...
Ireland	3,880	33,989	12,636	91.2	8.8	—	—	—	12,636	3,493	41.4[7]	58.6[7]	15	45	3,253
Isle of Man	...	...	188[4]	100.0	—	—	—	—	172	2,530[3]	48.1[7]	51.9[7]	...	...	...
Israel	4,137	36,240	17,491	100.0	—	—	359	—	17,132	3,918	66.6	33.4	39	—	3,397
Italy	56,403[15]	494,090[15]	198,292[15]	78.5[15]	19.9[15]	0.9[15]	1,672[15]	24,818[15]	221,438[15]	3,867[15]	25.0[7]	75.0[7]	...	1,656[15]	22,916[15]
Jamaica	740	6,482	2,385	94.8	5.2	—	—	—	2,385	990	23.6	76.4	...	...	...
Japan	176,419	1,545,430	698,970	60.6	12.0	27.2	—	—	698,970	5,733	20.8[2]	79.2[2]	1,120	13,049	102,512
Jersey	...	...	337[4]	...	...	...	...	...	368	4,720	...	...	...	...	...
Jordan	983	8,611	3,486	99.5	0.5	—	364	—	3,122	823	71.3	28.7	...	...	...
Kampuchea (Cambodia)	35	307	70	57.1	42.9	—	—	—	70	9	...	...	...	...	...
Kenya	575	5,037	2,629	13.7	72.7	13.6[5]	—	176	2,805	127	40.0	60.0	...	—	91
Kiribati	2	18	7	100.0	—	—	—	—	7	104	...	...	...	...	...
Korea, North	8,900	77,964	50,200	42.0	58.0	—	—	—	50,200	2,347	...	...	600	52,000	54,450
Korea, South	20,982	183,802	80,250	44.4	6.7	48.9	—	—	80,250	1,905	31.5	68.5	132	24,274	41,911
Kuwait	6,060	53,086	18,400	100.0	—	—	—	—	18,400	9,887	93.5	6.5	...	...	...
Laos	225	1,971	1,100	4.5	95.5	—	755	20	365	97	...	...	...	...	...
Lebanon	819	7,174	4,600	86.7	13.3	—	—	40	4,640	1,679	...	...	—	10	10
Lesotho	10	10	10	10	10	10	10	10	10	10	10	10	10	10	10
Liberia	325	2,847	825	61.3	38.7	—	—	—	825	355	...	...	...	—	2
Libya	2,000	17,520	14,260	100.0	—	—	—	—	14,260	3,492	...	...	...	—	16
Liechtenstein	16	16	16	16	16	16	16	16	16	16	16	16	16	16	16
Luxembourg	1,238	10,845	573	82.5	17.5	—	440	4,003	4,136	11,239	15.3[7]	84.7[7]	...	—	198
Macau	159	1,393	616	100.0	—	—	—	40	656	1,540	75.0[4]	25.0[4]	...	—	8
Madagascar	102	894	504	46.4	53.6	—	—	—	504	46	...	...	1,075[1]	—	26
Malawi	185	1,621	578	2.4	97.6	—	1	—	577	76	55.1	44.9	12	—	...
Malaysia	4,490	39,332	17,387	71.8	28.2	—	23	—	17,364	1,072	56.4	43.6	7	—	475
Maldives	4	35	13	100.0	—	—	—	—	13	66	50.9[3]	49.1[3]	...	...	...
Mali	87	762	204	20.6	79.4	—	—	—	204	24	...	...	...	—	182
Malta	252	2,208	944	100.0	—	—	—	—	944	2,728	25.1[11]	74.9[11]	...	...	...
Martinique	65	569	276	100.0	—	—	—	—	276	836	...	40.9[13]	...	...	6
Mauritania	114	999	120	79.2	20.8	—	—	—	120	64	...	...	...	...	30
Mauritius	279	2,444	488	71.3	28.7	—	—	—	488	458	...	...	...	...	...
Mayotte	6	53	10	100.0	—	—	—	—	8	105	...	...	...	...	...
Mexico	26,788	234,663	104,791	78.3	17.6	4.1[5]	2,042	117	102,866	1,239	17.4[11]	82.6[11]	2,110	11,137	10,528
Monaco	12	12	12	12	12	12	12	12	12	12	12	12	12	12	12
Mongolia	877	7,683	3,153	100.0	—	—	—	70	3,223	1,589	29.8[3]	70.2[3]	24,000[1]	7,765	7,224
Montserrat	4	35	13	100.0	—	—	—	—	13	1,000	38.6[4]	61.4[4]	...	...	...
Morocco	2,236	19,587	7,120	91.3	8.7	—	...	...	7,120	305	68.4	31.6	45	760	1,570
Mozambique	1,803	15,794	500	88.0	12.0	—	—	330	830	57	...	...	240	43	63
Myanmar (Burma)	1,001	8,769	2,279	50.8	49.2	—	—	—	2,279	58	...	59.1[2,13]	2	81	121
Nauru	10	88	29	100.0	—	—	—	—	29	3,222	...	...	...	...	...
Nepal	203	1,778	538	4.8	95.2	—	21	32	549	31	53.4	46.6	497	—	85
Netherlands, The	17,386	152,301	68,411	94.8	—	5.2	21	3,644	72,034	4,935	25.0[4]	75.0[4]	...	—	11,455
Netherlands Antilles	200	1,752	625	100.0	—	—	—	—	625	3,374	...	...	...	...	...
New Caledonia	391	3,425	1,004	74.4	25.6	—	—	—	1,004	6,314	...	...	2	—	155
New Zealand	7,434	65,122	27,030	23.0	72.9	4.1[5]	—	—	27,030	8,183	37.5[4]	62.5[4]	243	2,260	1,960
Nicaragua	395	3,460	1,063	46.6	25.2	28.2[5]	10	200	1,253	358	69.8	30.2	5[1]	65	65
Niger	63	552	157	100.0	—	—	—	135	292	45	61.5	38.5	169	145	100
Nigeria	4,040	35,390	9,905	77.7	22.3	—	100	—	9,805	96	80.6	19.4	...	—	...
Niue	1	9	3	100.0	—	—	—	—	3	750	...	...	...	...	...
Norfolk Island	...	...	6	100.0	...	...	...	...	...	...	...	...	...	...	...

natural gas — published proved reserves, 1989 ('000,000,000 cu m)	production — natural gas, 1988 ('000,000 cu m)	production — manufactured gas, 1987 (% of total gas consumption)	consumption — amount, 1987 ('000,000 cu m)	consumption — residential, 1986 (%)	consumption — non-residential, 1986 (%)	crude petroleum reserves, 1989 — published proved ('000,000 barrels)	years to exhaust proved reserves	production, 1988 ('000,000 barrels)	consumption, 1987 ('000,000 barrels)	refining capacity, 1989 ('000 barrels per day)	pipelines (latest)[a] — length (km)	pipelines — traffic ('000,000 metric ton-km)	country
...	...	115.9	...	...	...	...	...	—	...	—	—	—	Equatorial Guinea
...	—		—	...	...	...	...	—	6	18	—	—	Ethiopia
...	...		...	...	...	...	...	—	—	—	—	—	Faeroe Islands
...	—	100.0[8]	—	—	—	...	...	—	—	—	—	—	Falkland Islands
...	...	...	...	...	...	...	...	—	—	—	—	—	Fiji
30	—	28.8	1,573	0.6[7]	99.4[7]	...	...	—	78	241	—	—	Finland
	3,170	22.3[12]	28,026[12]	32.4[7]	67.6[7]	206	8	25	478[12]	1,876	7,546	25,859	France
...	—	...	...	...	...	...	...	—	—	—	—	—	French Guiana
...	...	...	...	...	...	...	...	—	—	—	—	—	French Polynesia
16	100	3.3	172	23.2	76.8	930	15	64	8	24	284	...	Gabon
...	...	...	...	...	...	...	...	—	—	—	—	—	Gambia, The
...	...	...	...	...	...	...	...	—	—	—	—	—	Gaza Strip
175	12,000	38.9	8,165	...	...	4.4	22	0.2	154	470	1,801	4,300	Germany, East
188	16,670	22.1	63,015	36.6[7]	63.4[7]	408	15	28	490	1,518	5,789	8,676	Germany, West
—		79.8				1	10	0.1[8]	7	27	3	...	Ghana
...	...	...	...	...	...	...	...	—	—	—	—	—	Gibraltar
6	120	97.1	133	...	...	20	3	8	110	385	573	...	Greece
...	...	...	...	...	...	...	...	—	—	—	—	—	Greenland
...	...	...	...	...	...	...	...	—	—	—	—	—	Grenada
...	...	...	...	...	...	...	...	—	—	—	—	—	Guadeloupe
...	—	100.0[8]	...	...	...	...	...	—	...	...	...	...	Guam
...	...	10.1	...	...	...	81	58	1.4	4	16	275	...	Guatemala
24	...	...	...	...	...	...	...	—	—	—	—	—	Guernsey
...	...	...	...	...	...	...	...	—	—	—	—	—	Guinea
...	...	...	...	...	...	...	...	—	—	—	—	—	Guinea-Bissau
...						...	...	—	...	—	—	—	Guyana
—	—	28.5	—	—	—	...	...	—	2	14	—	—	Haiti
		58.6				...	...	—			—	—	Honduras
...	...					...	...	—					Hong Kong
112	6,300	10.8	10,969	14.0[7]	86.0[7]	280	20	14	61	220	1,804	2,819	Hungary
—	—					...	...	—	...	...	—	—	Iceland
1,050	8,660	27.8	6,241	51.1	48.9	4,464	19	231	348	1,051	5,200	...	India
2,464	38,020	16.1	6,493	—	100.0	8,250	20	415	233	714	2,961	...	Indonesia
14,200	20,000	7.6	15,807	—	100.0[4]	63,000	78	806	213	530	9,800	...	Iran
2,690	5,730	34.3	999	...	...	100,000	102	978	125	319	5,075	...	Iraq
49	2,020	2.9	1,574	13.9[7]	86.1[7]	...	...	—	11	56	—	—	Ireland
...	...	...	...			...	...	—	...	...	—	—	Isle of Man
1	40	100.3	41	—	100.0	1.6	16	0.1	52	180	998	...	Israel
290	16,630	17.7[15]	36,302[15]	45.6[7]	54.4[7]	739	22	34	518[15]	2,450	3,851	11,315	Italy
—	—	48.5	—	...	...	...	...	—	7	34	10	—	Jamaica
38	2,100	45.7	41,865	61.3[14]	38.7[14]	55	12	4.5	1,147	4,363	406	...	Japan
...	...	...	...			...	...	—	—	—	—	—	Jersey
28	—	89.2	—	...	...	...	...	0.2	18	100	209	—	Jordan
...	...	104.0	...	—	...	...	...	—	—	—	—	—	Kampuchea (Cambodia)
—	...	...	—			...	...	—	15	90	483	—	Kenya
...	...	...	...			...	...	—	...	...	...	—	Kiribati
...	...	28.7	2,256	...	...	...	...	—	21	42	37	—	Korea, North
		39.1	7,871	23.1	76.9			—	211	880	294	...	Korea, South
1,378	6,490					91,920	200	458	216	817	917	—	Kuwait
...	...	...	...			...	...	—			136	—	Laos
—	—	21.1	...	...	...	...	...	—	9	37	72	...	Lebanon
...	...					...	...	—	10		—	—	Lesotho
—		50.5[8]				...	...	—		15	—	—	Liberia
722	5,500	16.9	3,564[16]			22,380	66	340	56	329	4,826	...	Libya
—		16				...	...	—			—	—	Liechtenstein
—	—	50.6	409	48.0[7]	52.0[7]	...	...	—	9	—	48	—	Luxembourg
2	—	100.0[8]	...	...	...	...	...	—	2	16	—	—	Macau
—	—	100.0[8]	—	—	—	...	...	—	—	—	—	—	Madagascar
—	...					...	...	—			—	—	Malawi
1,472	16,450	12.5	4,479	13.2	86.8	3,379	17	197	53	209	1,307	...	Malaysia
...	...	...	...			...	...	—	—	—	—	—	Maldives
...	...	...	...			...	...	—	—	—	—	—	Mali
—	—	214.1	...	...	...	...	...	—	3	13	—	—	Malta
						...	...	—	7		—	—	Martinique
						...	...	—			—	—	Mauritania
...	...	...	...			...	...	—	—	—	—	—	Mauritius
...	...	...	...			...	...	—	—	—	—	—	Mayotte
2,078	26,140	24.6[12]	22,895	3.9[11]	96.1[11]	54,110	59	922	452[12]	1,354	12,726	—	Mexico
...	...	...	...			...	...	—	12	—	—	—	Monaco
...	...	...	...			...	...	—	—	—	—	—	Mongolia
...	...	...	...		64.6[2,13]	...	...	—	...	...	—	—	Montserrat
3	60	40.4	86	—	100.0	2.6	26	0.1	34	155	362	—	Morocco
65	—	—				...	...	—			289	...	Mozambique
267	1,040	0.4	1,136	—	100.0[4]	195	39	5	7	26	1,343	...	Myanmar (Burma)
...	...	...	...			...	...	—	—	—	—	—	Nauru
...	...	...	...			...	...	—	—	—	—	—	Nepal
1,730	68,000	14.7	49,438	46.8[4]	53.4[4]	170	5	31	351	1,381	1,383	4,287	Netherlands, The
—	—	75.0	—	...	...	...	...	—	71	320	—	—	Netherlands Antilles
...	...	...	...			...	...	—			—	—	New Caledonia
145	4,570	1.7	3,254	4.8[4]	95.2[4]	158	16	10	24	88	310	...	New Zealand
—	—	93.6	—	—	—	...	...	—	4	15	56	—	Nicaragua
...	...	...	...			...	...	—			—	—	Niger
2,476	3,800	1.7	3,700	—	100.0	16,000	32	496	50	415	5,042	...	Nigeria
...	...	...	...			...	...	—	—	—	—	—	Niue
...	...	...	...			...	...	—	—	—	—	—	Norfolk Island

Energy (continued)

country	installed capacity, 1987 ('000 kW)	production, 1987 capacity ('000,000 kW-hr)	production, 1987 amount ('000,000 kW-hr)	power source, 1987 fossil fuel (%)	power source, 1987 hydro-power (%)	power source, 1987 nuclear fuel (%)	trade, 1987 exports ('000,000 kW-hr)	trade, 1987 imports ('000,000 kW-hr)	consumption amount, 1987 ('000,000 kW-hr)	consumption per capita, 1987 (kW-hr)	consumption residential, 1986 (%)	consumption non-residential, 1986 (%)	coal reserves, latest ('000,000 metric tons)	coal production, 1987 ('000 metric tons)	coal consumption, 1987 ('000 metric tons)
Norway	25,646	224,659	103,810	0.5	99.5	—	3,311	2,932	103,431	24,756	27.0[2]	73.0[2]	30	399	870
Oman	1,200	10,512	3,793	100.0	—	—	—	—	3,793	2,841	...	...	...	...	...
Pacific Is., Trust Territory of the	57	499	169	82.2	17.8	—	...	...	169	1,037	...	...	...	...	...
Marshall Islands	...														
Micronesia, Fed. States of	...														
Northern Mariana Islands															
Palau	...	...	...				...	...							
Pakistan	6,653	58,280	33,475	52.9	45.6	1.5	—	—	33,475	301	67.6	32.4	102	2,419	3,218
Panama	898	7,866	2,902	30.0	70.0	—	—	—	2,902	1,276	26.8[11]	73.2[11]	...	—	5
Papua New Guinea	469	4,108	1,797	75.6	24.4	—	—	—	1,797	485	21.4	78.6	...	—	1
Paraguay	3,350	29,346	2,825	0.2	99.8	—	—	10	2,835	722	...	...	...	—	—
Peru	3,675	32,193	14,195	22.2	77.8	—	—	—	14,195	685	38.8	61.2	28[1]	150	140
Philippines	6,375	55,845	23,852	59.1	21.9	19.0[5]	—	—	23,852	411	66.0	34.0	82	1,171	2,094
Pitcairn Island															
Poland	30,110	263,764	145,832	97.2	2.8	—	8,703	10,422	147,551	3,909	33.5[3]	66.5[3]	47,080	266,205	236,652
Portugal	6,851	60,015	20,101	54.5	45.5	—	675	3,700	23,126	2,261	36.4[2]	63.6[2]	52	254	2,759
Puerto Rico	4,200	36,792	13,757	98.1	1.9	—	—	—	13,757	3,870	31.0[11]	69.0[11]	...	—	200
Qatar	1,005	8,804	4,420	100.0	—	—	—	—	4,420	13,517	83.1	16.9	...	...	...
Réunion	151	1,323	682	22.3	77.7	—	—	—	682	1,205	...	...	...	...	...
Romania	20,200	176,952	73,090	82.8	17.2	—	—	3,100	76,190	3,322	23.6[3]	76.4[3]	3,970[1]	47,300	52,600
Rwanda	60	526	174	2.3	97.7	—	3	8	179	27	...	...	...	...	...
St. Helena and Ascension	2	18	2	100.0	—	—	—	—	2	286	...	...	...	...	...
St. Kitts and Nevis	15	131	36	100.0	—	—	—	—	36	735	...	...	...	...	...
St. Lucia	20	175	74	100.0	—	—	—	—	74	561	26.6[3]	73.4[3]	...	...	...
St. Pierre and Miquelon	24	210	38	100.0	—	—	—	—	38	5,429	...	...	...	...	...
St. Vincent and the Grenadines	10	88	31	38.7	61.3	—	—	—	31	290	45.3[4]	54.7[4]	...	...	...
San Marino	15	15	15	15	15	15	15	15	15	15	...	...	...	15	15
São Tomé and Principe	6	53	15	46.7	53.3	—	—	—	15	144	...	...	...	...	...
Saudi Arabia	14,970	131,137	37,100	100.0	—	—	—	—	37,100	2,953	67.1	32.9	...	...	...
Senegal	207	1,813	752	100.0	—	—	—	—	752	111	...	...	...	...	...
Seychelles	19	166	67	100.0	—	—	—	—	67	985	...	...	...	...	...
Sierra Leone	110	964	196	100.0	—	—	—	—	196	51	...	...	...	...	...
Singapore	3,371	29,530	11,814	100.0	—	—	—	—	11,814	4,514	49.6	50.4	...	—	1
Solomon Islands	13	114	30	100.0	—	—	—	—	30	102	77.6	22.4	...	...	...
Somalia	60	526	255	100.0	—	—	—	—	255	37	...	...	...	...	...
South Africa	24,732[10]	216,652[10]	122,465[10]	96.2[10]	0.6[10]	3.2[10]	300[10]	—	122,165[10]	3,196[10]	...	...	64,380	177,282[10]	134,532[10]
Bophuthatswana	...														
Ciskei	...														
Transkei	...														
Venda	...														
South West Africa/Namibia	[10]	[10]	[10]	[10]	[10]	[10]	[10]	[10]	[10]	[10]	...	...	...	[10]	[10]
Spain	36,044	315,745	133,168	48.0	21.0	31.0	4,704	3,171	131,635	3,383	16.7[2]	83.2[2]	883	34,953	45,452
Sri Lanka	1,071	9,382	2,707	19.6	80.4	—	—	—	2,707	163	58.5	41.5	...	—	—
Sudan, The	450	3,942	1,055	51.1	48.9	—	—	—	1,055	46	...	...	...	—	—
Suriname	415	3,635	1,330	29.7	70.3	—	—	—	1,330	3,437	...	...	...	—	1
Swaziland	[10]	[10]	[10]	[10]	[10]	[10]	[10]	[10]	[10]	[10]	18.7[14]	81.3[14]	1,000	[10]	[10]
Sweden	33,455	293,066	146,625	4.6	49.3	46.1	6,185	2,169	142,609	17,079	26.4[2]	73.6[2]	1	25	4,168
Switzerland	15,250[16]	133,590[16]	56,976[16]	1.7[16]	60.2[16]	38.1[16]	20,314[16]	10,859[16]	47,521[16]	7,275[16]	26.6[7]	73.4[7]	...	—	521[16]
Syria	2,918	25,562	7,161	79.1	20.9	—	130	...	7,031	626	21.2[7]	78.8[7]	...	—	—
Taiwan	17,721	155,236	70,701	40.6	10.9	48.5	—	—	59,175	3,008	26.3	73.7	174	1,499	...
Tanzania	439	3,846	874	30.2	69.8	—	—	—	874	36	...	...	200	3	3
Thailand	7,801	68,337	29,992	86.4	13.6	—	18	416	30,390	570	54.0	46.0	879	6,901	7,099
Togo	34	298	40	90.0	10.0	—	—	238	278	88	...	...	...	...	...
Tokelau	...														
Tonga	6	53	16	100.0	—	—	—	—	16	139	...	...	...	...	...
Trinidad and Tobago	985	8,629	3,315	100.0	—	—	—	—	3,315	2,708	39.9	60.1	...	—	—
Tunisia	1,414	12,387	4,549	97.5	2.5	—	3	—	4,546	596	44.2	55.8	—	—	16
Turkey	12,493	109,439	44,353	57.9	42.0	0.1[5]	—	572	44,925	856	14.2[11]	85.8[11]	5,350	46,988	48,504
Turks and Caicos Islands	8	70	9	100.0	—	—	—	—	9	1,000	43.1	56.9	...	...	...
Tuvalu	...														
Uganda	163	1,428	655	1.7	98.3	—	107	—	548	33	...	...	...	...	...
U.S.S.R.	332,266	2,910,650	1,664,924	75.6	13.2	11.2	35,000	300	1,630,224	5,792	21.6[3]	78.4[3]	269,760	712,299	694,897
United Arab Emirates	4,420	38,719	13,100	100.0	—	—	—	—	13,100	9,003	...	...	...	...	...
United Kingdom	64,772	567,403	300,247	80.3	1.3	18.4	37	11,672	311,882	5,477	35.4[7]	64.6[7]	5,070	104,435	117,187
United States	743,377	6,511,983	2,685,627	73.0	9.5	17.0	4,995	46,826	2,727,458	11,204	34.9[7]	65.1[7]	290,840	831,754	751,840
Uruguay	1,449	12,693	4,526	7.0	93.0	—	6	—	4,520	1,478	61.4	38.6	...	...	...
Vanuatu	11	96	26	100.0	—	—	—	—	26	171	...	...	...	...	...
Venezuela	17,092	149,726	54,704	55.9	44.1	—	—	—	54,704	2,994	49.4	50.6	372	62	112
Vietnam	1,260	11,038	5,300	62.3	37.7	—	—	—	5,300	84	36.4[3]	63.6[3]	150	5,600	5,100
Virgin Islands (U.S.)	316	2,768	963	100.0	—	—	—	—	963	8,835	40.2[4]	59.8[4]	...	...	...
Wallis and Futuna	...														
West Bank															
Western Sahara	56	491	81	100.0	—	—	—	—	81	491	...	...	...	...	...
Western Samoa	17	149	46	60.9	39.1	—	—	—	46	275	...	...	...	...	...
Yemen (Aden)	160	1,402	465	100.0	—	—	—	—	465	205	...	...	...	...	...
Yemen (Şan'ā')	490	4,292	718	100.0	—	—	—	—	718	98	...	...	1[1]	—	—
Yugoslavia	16,150	141,474	80,792	57.7	32.5	5.6	2,208	2,583	81,167	3,465	26.1[2]	73.9[2]	18,230	71,133	75,080
Zaire	2,541	22,259	5,295	2.6	97.4	—	110	3	5,188	159	...	89.1[2],[13]	600	95	136
Zambia	2,436	21,339	8,479	0.4	99.6	—	1,500	20	6,999	925	33.0	67.0	72	463	458
Zimbabwe	1,539	13,482	7,645	67.4	32.6	—	—	1,350	8,995	1,017	44.0	56.0	734	4,843	4,818

natural gas — published proved reserves, 1989 ('000,000,000 cu m)	production — natural gas, 1988 ('000,000 cu m)	production — manufactured gas, 1987 (% of total gas consumption)	consumption — amount, 1987 ('000,000 cu m)	consumption — residential, 1986 (%)	consumption — non-residential, 1986 (%)	crude petroleum reserves, 1989 — published proved ('000,000 barrels)	reserves, 1989 — years to exhaust proved reserves	production, 1988 ('000,000 barrels)	consumption, 1987 ('000,000 barrels)	refining capacity, 1989 ('000 barrels per day)	pipelines (latest)[a] — length (km)	pipelines (latest)[a] — traffic ('000,000 metric ton-km)	country
2,298	29,830	48.0	1,561	...	...	11,039	28	390	66	239	53	4,511	Norway
283	2,450	76.0	2,178	...	...	4,142	19	218	15	77	1,300	...	Oman
...	...	...	...	...	...	...	...	—	—	—	—	—	Pacific Is., Trust Territory of the Marshall Islands
...	...	...	...	...	...	...	...	—	—	—	—	—	Micronesia, Fed. States of
...	...	...	...	...	...	...	...	—	...	—	—	—	Northern Mariana Islands / Palau
651	12,590	1.3	10,128	36.4	63.6	158	9	17	42	131	1,135	...	Pakistan
—	—	44.5	—	—	—	...	...	—	10	100	130	—	Panama
128		100.0[8]	—	—	—	200	...	—	—	—	—	—	Papua New Guinea
—	—	10.7	...	...	...	...	...	—	2	8	—	—	Paraguay
340	1,250	24.0	734	59.6	40.4	457	9	52	64	172	800	—	Peru
18	—	77.1	—	—	—	16	5	3.4	69	254	357	...	Philippines
													Pitcairn Island
158	5,700	33.7	13,035	...		12	10	1.2	104	385	2,346	16,996	Poland
—		57.5	...	...	...	...	...	—	58	313	69	—	Portugal
—		74.1	...	...	...	...	...	—	35	123			Puerto Rico
4,621	6,470	15.9	4,725	—	100.0	3,150	25	127	11	62	235		Qatar
—			...	...	...	...	...	—	...	—			Réunion
162	33,000	7.9	40,953	...		1,231	18	68	192	617	4,229	4,481	Romania
57	—		1					—	—	—	—	—	Rwanda
...	...	...	...	...	...	...	...	—	—	—	—	—	St. Helena and Ascension
...	...	...	...	...	...	...	...	—	—	—	—	—	St. Kitts and Nevis
...	...	...	...	...	...	...	...	—	—	—	...	...	St. Lucia
...	...	...	...	...	...	...	...	—	—	—	...	...	St. Pierre and Miquelon
...	...		...	...		...		—		—	—	—	St. Vincent and the Grenadines
...	...	15	15	...		...		—	15	—	—	—	San Marino
—			—			...		—		—	—	—	São Tomé and Príncipe
5,020	29,100	45.3	23,239	9.8	90.2	169,970	99	1,719	445	1,375	6,550	—	Saudi Arabia
—		10.5						—	4	30	—	...	Senegal
...	...	...	...	...		...		—		—	—	—	Seychelles
—			—			...		—	2	10	—	—	Sierra Leone
—		134.7	—	—	—	...		—	254	852	—	—	Singapore
6			...			...		—		—	—	—	Solomon Islands
—			...			...		—	2	10	15	—	Somalia
50	—	100.0[10]	—	...		115[6]	...	—	117[10]	434	2,679	...	South Africa
—			...			...		—	—	—	...	...	Bophuthatswana
—			...			...		—	—	—	...	...	Ciskei
—			...			...		—	—	—	...	...	Transkei
—			...			...		—	—	—	...	...	Venda
57		10						—	10	—	—	...	South West Africa/Namibia
23	920	55.2	3,025	—	—	44	4	11	337	1,285	2,059	3,165	Spain
—		96.4	—	—	—	...		—	13	50	62	...	Sri Lanka
85	—	50.1	...			300		—	7	21	815	...	Sudan, The
...			...			29	32	0.9	1	—	—	...	Suriname
...		10	...			...		—		—	—	—	Swaziland
—		50.7	283			...		—	118	427	—	—	Sweden
—		17.8[16]	1,659[16]	38.3[7]	61.7[7]	...		—	28[16]	132	314	1,161	Switzerland
113	720	34.2	190	...		1,730	17	100	84	244	1,819	...	Syria
24	680	...	...			8	9	0.9		570	615	...	Taiwan
118	—	100.0	...			...		—	4	14	982	...	Tanzania
212	5,460	12.5	4,391	—	100.0	231	17	14	64	191	67	...	Thailand
—			...			...		—	—	—	—	—	Togo
...			...			...		—	—	—	—	—	Tokelau
...			...			...		—	—	—	—	—	Tonga
470	4,360	4.7	4,066	—	100.0	528	10	54	36	300	1,051	...	Trinidad and Tobago
88	350	5.8	649	6.0	94.0	1,790	47	38	12	34	883	...	Tunisia
33	100	72.2	284	...		381	21	18	166	725	5,797	31,936	Turkey
...			...			...		—	—	—	—	—	Turks and Caicos Islands
...			...			...		—	—	—	—	—	Tuvalu
...			...			...		...			...	...	Uganda
42,500	770,000	9.5	650,686	...		58,500	13	4,554	3,692	12,300	81,500	1,312,500	U.S.S.R.
5,664	18,640	20.5	13,529	...		56,230	98	573	54	180	830	...	United Arab Emirates
590	45,750	13.7	65,233	52.7[7]	47.3[7]	5,175	6	867	502	1,803	3,926	10,561	United Kingdom
5,150	472,490	19.7	498,847	33.4[11]	66.6[11]	26,500	9	2,981	4,680	15,419	275,800	827,541	United States
—	—	91.8	—			...		...	9	33	—	—	Uruguay
...			...			...		—	—	—	—	—	Vanuatu
3,000	19,680	14.0	20,460	7.4	92.6	58,084	96	605	299	1,201	6,850	—	Venezuela
—	—	100.0	...			...		—	—	—	150	...	Vietnam
...			...			...		...	71	545	...		Virgin Islands (U.S.)
...			...			...		—	...	—	—	—	Wallis and Futuna
...			...			...		—	—	—	—	—	West Bank
...			...			...		—	—	—	—	—	Western Sahara
...			—			...		—	...	—	32	...	Western Samoa
142	—	100.0[8]	—			1,000	17	58	25	162			Yemen (Aden)
156			...			548	119	4.6	3	10	424	—	Yemen (Şanʿāʾ)
90	3,020	24.3	5,739	...		211	8	27	107	609	1,523	2,504	Yugoslavia
1	—	100.0	—			96	9	11	2	17	390	...	Zaire
...		100.0	—			...		...	4	21	1,724	...	Zambia
...	—	93.5	—			...		...			8		Zimbabwe

[1]Estimated reserves in place. [2]1981. [3]1985. [4]1984. [5]Geothermally generated electricity. [6]1987. [7]1983. [8]1986. [9]Belgium includes Luxembourg. [10]South Africa includes Botswana, Lesotho, South West Africa/Namibia, and Swaziland. [11]1982. [12]France includes Monaco. [13]Transportation and industry only; excludes agricultural, commercial, and public service sectors. [14]1980. [15]Italy includes San Marino. [16]Switzerland includes Liechtenstein.

Transportation

This table presents data on the transportation infrastructure of the various countries and dependencies of the world and on their commercial passenger and cargo traffic. Most states have roads and airports, with services corresponding to the prevailing level of economic development. A number of states, however, lack railroads or inland waterways, because of either geographic constraints or lack of development capital and technical expertise. Pipelines, one of the oldest means of bulk transport if aqueducts are considered, are today among the most narrowly developed transportation modes worldwide for shipment of bulk materials. Because the principal contemporary application of pipeline technology is to facilitate the shipment of hydrocarbon liquids and gases, coverage of pipelines will be found in the "Energy" table. It is, however, also true that pipelines now find increasing application for slurries of coal or other raw materials.

While the United Nations' *Statistical Yearbook* and *Monthly Bulletin of Statistics* provide much data on infrastructure and traffic and have established basic definitions and classifications for transportation statistics, the number of countries covered is limited. Several commercial publications maintain substantial data bases and publishing programs for their particular areas of interest: Highway and vehicle statistics are provided by the International Road Federation's annual *Road and Motor Vehicle Statistics* and *World Road Statistics;* the International Union of Railways' *International Railway Statistics* and Jane's *World Railways* provide similar data

for railways; Lloyd's *Register of Shipping Statistical Tables* summarizes the world's merchant marine; the *Official Airline Guide,* the International Civil Aviation Organization's *Digest of Statistics: Commercial Air Carriers,* and the International Air Transport Association's *World Air Transport Statistics* have also been used to supplement and update data collected by the UN. Because several of these agencies are commercially or insurance-oriented, their data tend to be more complete, accurate, and timely than those of intergovernmental organizations, which depend on periodic responses to questionnaires or publication of results in official sources. All of these international sources have been extensively supplemented by national statistical sources to provide additional data. Such diversity of sources, however, imposes limitations on the comparability of the statistics from country to country because the basis and completeness of data collection and the frequency and timeliness of analysis and publication may vary greatly. Data shown in italic are from 1984 or earlier.

The categories adopted in the table also have special problems of comparability. Total road length is subject to wide international variation of interpretation, as "roads" can mean anything from mere tracks to highly developed highways. Each country also has individual classifications that differ according to climate, availability of road-building materials, traffic patterns, administrative responsibility, and so on. "Paved roads," by contrast, is a much more tightly definable category, but the proportion of paved to total roads may be distorted by the less comparable total road

Transportation

country	roads and motor vehicles (latest)								railroads (latest)						
	roads			motor vehicles			cargo		track length		traffic				
	length		paved (per-cent)	auto-mobiles	trucks and buses	persons per vehicle	short ton-mi ('000,-000)	metric ton-km ('000,-000)	mi	km	passengers		cargo		
	mi	km									passen-ger-mi ('000,000)	passen-ger-km ('000,000)	short ton-mi ('000,000)	metric ton-km ('000,000)	
Afghanistan	13,670	22,000	...	*31,000*	*31,700*	220	*1,993*	*2,910*	6	10	...	...	430.9	629.1	
Albania	10,377	16,700	40	*3,500*	*11,200*	146	...	...	316	509	411.1	661.6	...	...	
Algeria	50,734	81,648	59	712,700	471,500	18	*2,148*	*3,136*	2,337[2]	3,761[2]	1,225	1,972	2,012	2,937	
American Samoa	217	350	43	4,119	276	8.3	...	...	—	—	—	—	—	—	
Andorra	*137*	*220*	55	25,000	6,250	1.5	...	...	—	—	—	—	—	—	
Angola	45,877	73,830	51	56,625	50,000	82	...	...	1,739[2]	2,798[2]	203	326	1,178	1,720	
Anguilla	68	109	63	973	239	5.4	...	...	—	—	—	—	—	—	
Antigua and Barbuda	724	1,161	33	11,188	3,321	5.6	...	...	21,233[2]	34,172[2]	7,740	12,456	6,000	8,760	
Argentina	131,338	211,369	27	3,898,000	1,434,700	5.8	...	...	—	—	—	—	—	—	
Aruba	236	380	100	23,568	537	2.5	...	...	—	—	—	—	—	—	
Australia	500,016	804,700	50	8,770,899	1,231,359	1.6	*32,964*	*48,127*	24,084[2,9]	38,760[2,9]	1,359	2,187	33,120	48,357	
Austria	66,799	107,503	100	2,684,780	221,139	2.6	*5,949*	*8,685*	4,125	6,638	4,575	7,363	7,537	11,004	
Bahamas, The	2,548	4,100	40	88,000	5,600	2.4	...	...	—	—	—	—	—	—	
Bahrain	182	293	...	81,872	25,475	4.1	...	...	—	—	—	—	—	—	
Bangladesh	63,730	102,564	10	41,894	25,202	1,569	...	...	1,785[2]	2,872[2]	3,825	6,155	351	512	
Barbados	1,020	1,642	79	34,740	7,332	6.0	...	...	—	—	—	—	—	—	
Belgium	79,622	128,139	96	3,497,818	312,510	2.6	*13,099*	*19,124*	2,248[2]	3,618[2]	3,959	6,372	5,269	7,692	
Belize	1,865	3,001	13	*3,707*	*1,855*	29	...	...	—	—	—	—	—	—	
Benin	4,626	7,445	11	2,740	567	1,191	...	...	360	580	85.5	137.6	121.1	176.8	
Bermuda	150	240	100	17,852	2,768	2.8	...	...	—	—	—	—	—	—	
Bhutan	1,412	2,273	76	1,587	916	524	*1,133*	*1,654*	2,264[2]	3,643[2]	313	504	345	503	
Bolivia	25,468	40,987	4	78,160	142,976	31	...	...	442	712	...	...	0.9	1.3	
Botswana	7,154	11,514	14	16,426	24,786	27	...	...	18,503[2]	29,777[2]	10,167	16,362	68,401	99,863	
Brazil	881,349	1,418,396	9	10,516,000	1,067,000	12	*158,085*	*230,800*	...	...	...	...	...	...	
British Virgin Islands	70	113	62	—— 4,706 ——		2.6	...	...	—	—	—	—	—	—	
Brunei	1,156	1,860	50	84,527	11,051	2.4	...	...	12[16]	19[16]	...	...	...	...	
Bulgaria	23,555	37,908	91	1,138,433	588,600	5.2	*5,175*	*7,556*	2,672	4,300	5,018	8,075	12,220	17,842	
Burkina Faso	6,979	11,231	12	*21,182*	*5,729*	272	...	...	342	550	422	680	322	470	
Burundi	3,666	5,900	7	9,892	8,685	269	...	...	—	—	—	—	—	—	
Cameroon	32,444	52,214	6	86,800	32,700	87	*175*	*255*	729[2]	1,173[2]	268	432	518	756	
Canada	174,140	280,251	57	11,118,071	3,095,243	1.8	*29,033*	*42,388*	74,600	120,000	1,193	1,920	174,264	255,264	
Cape Verde	1,398	2,250	29	*3,000*	*1,343*	70	...	...	—	—	—	—	—	—	
Cayman Islands	110	177	68	9,055	1,856	2.3	...	...	—	—	—	—	—	—	
Central African Republic	12,600	20,278	2	1,035	20,000	125	*2.8*	*4.1*	—	—	—	—	—	—	
Chad	24,855	40,000	1	2,741	4,000	744	...	...	—	—	—	—	—	—	
Chile	49,227	79,223	13	660,000	278,000	13	*179,524*	*262,100*	5,037[2]	8,107[2]	729	1,174	1,097	1,601	
China	610,336	982,243	83	1,114,622	2,812,068	270	...	...	40,364	64,960	203,000	326,000	676,400	987,600	
Christmas Island	20	32	...	759	383	2.9	...	...	15	24	...	...	...	...	
Cocos (Keeling) Islands	15	24	...	...	...	...	*6,745*	*9,848*	2,011[2]	3,236[2]	92	148	318	464	
Colombia	66,001	106,218	10	840,776	391,433	24	...	...	—	—	—	—	—	—	
Comoros	466	750	53	*3,600*	*2,000*	68	...	...	—	—	—	—	—	—	
Congo	6,835	11,000	5	*30,500*	*78,600*	15	*46*	*67*	498	802	283	456	367	536	
Cook Islands	174	280	...	689	728	12	...	...	—	—	—	—	—	—	
Costa Rica	21,970	35,357	15	134,954	89,641	13	...	...	435[2]	700[2]	56	90	102.7	150.0	
Côte d'Ivoire	34,175	55,000	9	*182,956*	*52,491*	41	...	...	341	549	533[19]	858[19]	363[19]	530[19]	
Cuba	21,100	34,000	30	200,100	164,500	27	*1,208*	*1,763*	3,140	5,053	1,629	2,622	1,674	2,445	
Cyprus	5,708	9,186	...	142,569	56,500	3.6	...	...	—	—	—	—	—	—	
Czechoslovakia	45,733	73,601	100	2,694,994	425,174	5.0	*8,584*	*12,533*	8,141	13,102	12,445	20,029	46,563	67,985	
Denmark	43,614	70,190	100	1,587,419	287,532	2.7	*6,884*	*10,050*	1,539	2,476	2,974	4,787	1,151	1,680	
Djibouti	1,799	2,895	7	12,049	951	33	...	...	66	106	...	...	90.1	131.6	
Dominica	489	787	60	2,713	1,250	21	...	...	—	—	—	—	—	—	
Dominican Republic	7,084	11,400	49	99,952	59,892	40	...	...	88	142	13	20.9	3.8	5.6	
Ecuador	22,486	36,187	16	256,812	36,691	33	...	...	600[2]	965[2]	...	...	...	...	
Egypt	20,034[22]	32,241[22]	52[22]	783,306	371,699	42	*16,500*	*24,090*	3,327	5,355	17,616	28,350	2,005	2,927	
El Salvador	7,558	12,164	14	138,276	23,381	31	...	...	374[2]	602[2]	3.1	5.0	16.7	24.4	

statistics. Automobile and truck and bus fleet statistics, which are usually based upon registration, are relatively accurate, though some countries round off figures, and unregistered vehicles may cause substantial undercount. There is also inconsistent classification of vehicle types; in some countries a vehicle may serve variously as an automobile, a truck, or a bus, or even as all three on certain occasions. Relatively few countries collect and maintain commercial road traffic statistics.

Data on national railway systems are generally given for railway track length rather than the length of routes, which may be multitracked. Siding tracks usually are not included, but some countries fail to distinguish them. The United States data include only class 1 railways, which account for about 94 percent of total track length. Passenger traffic is usually calculated from tickets sold to fare-paying passengers. Such statistics are subject to distortion if there are large numbers of nonpaying passengers, such as military personnel, or if season tickets are sold and not all the allowed journeys are utilized. Railway cargo traffic is calculated by weight hauled multiplied by the length of the journey. Changes in freight load during the journey should be accounted for but sometimes are not, leading to discrepancies.

Merchant fleet and tonnage statistics collected by Lloyd's registry service for vessels over 100 gross tons are quite accurate. Cargo statistics, however, reflect the port and customs requirements of each country and the reporting rules of each country's merchant marine authority (although these, increasingly, reflect the recommendations of the International Maritime Organization); often, however, they are only estimates based on customs declarations and the count of vessels entered and cleared. Even when these elements are reported consistently, further uncertainties may be introduced because of ballast, bunkers, ships' stores, or transshipped goods included in the data.

Airport data are based on scheduled flights reported in the commercial *Official Airline Guide* and are both reliable and current. The comparability of civil air traffic statistics suffers from differing characteristics of the air transportation systems of different countries; data for an entire country may be two to three years behind those for a single airport.

Outside of Europe, where standardization of data on inland waterways is necessitated by the volume of international traffic, comparability of national data declines markedly. Calculations as to both the length of a country's waterway system (or route length of river, lake, and coastal traffic) and the makeup of its stock of commercially significant vessels (those for which data will be collected) are largely determined by the nature and use of the country's hydrographic net—its seasonality, relief profile, depth, access to potential markets—and inevitably differ widely from country to country. Data for coastal or island states may refer to scheduled coastwise or interisland traffic.

merchant marine				air								canals and inland waterways (latest)				country
fleet, 1988 (vessels over 100 gross tons)	total dead-weight tonnage, 1988 ('000)	international cargo (latest)		airports with sched-uled flights, 1989	traffic (latest)							length		cargo		
		loaded metric tons ('000)	off-loaded metric tons ('000)		passengers		cargo					mi	km	short ton-mi ('000,000)	metric ton-km ('000,000)	
					passenger-mi ('000,000)	passenger-km ('000,000)		short ton-mi ('000,000)	metric ton-km ('000,000)							
20	79.9	1,077	626	2	108.5[1]	174.7[1]		5.5[1]	8.1[1]			750	1,200	...	...	Afghanistan
148	1,052.6	50,543	15,450	1	...	...		...	...			27	43	...	...	Albania
2	4	195	574	24	1,397[3]	2,248[3]		7.3[3]	10.6[3]			...	...	...	...	Algeria
—	—	—	—	3	...	...		...	...			...	...	...	...	American Samoa
—	—	—	—	—	—	—		—	—			—	—	—	—	Andorra
110	121.9	10,140	980	18	606[5]	975[5]		23.2[5]	33.9[5]			805	1,295	...	...	Angola
12	5.4	...	18	1	...	...		...	...			...	...	...	...	Anguilla
190	555.1	16	347	2	...	...		...	...			...	...	...	...	Antigua and Barbuda
451	2,834.0	22,320	9,144	66	4,837[6]	7,785[6]		127[6]	186[6]			6,800	11,000	19,326	28,215	Argentina
927[7]	8	...	...	1	...	...		...	...			...	...	...	...	Aruba
709	3,648.9	264,096	29,208	441	16,285	26,208		2,640	3,855			5,200	8,368	...	...	Australia
32	350.6	1,846	5,418	6	1,022	1,644		16	23.4			277	446	1,090	1,591	Austria
572	15,020.8	9,325	8,710	21	135[10]	218[10]		0.1	0.2			...	...	...	...	Bahamas, The
89	67.9	12,258	3,261	1	814[11]	1,418[11]		24.7[11]	36[11]			...	...	...	...	Bahrain
289	611.9	1,132	7,393	7	1,235	1,987		50.9	74.3			5,000	8,046	...	...	Bangladesh
38	8.8	211	460	1	93[12]	149[12]		0.8[13]	1.1[13]			...	...	...	...	Barbados
344	3,401.0	45,485	82,407	4	3,714	5,977		368	538			1,269	2,043	3,468	5,063	Belgium
3	0.8	136	144	8	...	...		...	...			513	825	...	...	Belize
13	4.8	173	1,095	1	129.6[14]	208.6[14]		24.1[14]	35.2[14]			...	...	...	...	Benin
116	6,874.2	112	462	1	...	...		...	...			...	...	...	...	Bermuda
1	15.8	—	—	1	2.7	4.4		...	...			—	—	—	—	Bhutan
—	—	...	...	19	628	1,011		16.2	23.7			6,214	10,000	90	132	Bolivia
—	—	...	...	8	14[15]	22[15]		0.1[15]	0.1[15]			...	...	...	...	Botswana
719	10,103.8	169,392	58,080	110	15,176	24,423		840	1,226			31,069	50,000	60,960	89,000	Brazil
29	6.8	2	52	3	...	...		...	...			...	...	...	...	British Virgin Islands
34	345.0	18,627	672	1	207	333		4.1	6			130	209	...	...	Brunei
201	1,984.3	3,930	25,377	13	2,223	3,578		28.6	41.7			292	470	40,167	58,643	Bulgaria
—	—	...	...	3	132.8	213.7		24.7	36.1			...	...	...	...	Burkina Faso
1	0.4	39	182	2	...	...		...	...			...	...	...	...	Burundi
46	71.8	1,056	2,520	10	360	580		76	111			1,299	2,090	...	...	Cameroon
1,225	3,379.4	158,938	68,106	61	32,709	52,641		838.6	1,224			1,860	3,000	...	...	Canada
35	25.9	108	286	8	16.1	26.0		1.6	2.3			...	...	...	...	Cape Verde
235	664.3	677	671	3	...	...		...	...			...	...	...	...	Cayman Islands
—	—	...	...	1	132.8[17]	213.7[17]		24.7[17]	36.1[17]			500	800	...	...	Central African Republic
—	—	...	...	1	132.8	213.7		24.7	36.1			1,240	2,000	...	...	Chad
287	912.7	15,144	5,952	18	1,516	2,440		318.4	464.8			450	725	5,629	8,218	Chile
1,841	19,359.7	69,564	71,136	80	13,300	21,400		507	740			68,244	109,829	181,937	292,800	China
—	—	1,202	44	1	...	...		...	...			...	...	...	...	Christmas Island
—	—	...	...	1	...	...		...	...			...	...	...	...	Cocos (Keeling) Islands
97	584.6	16,416	6,036	69	2,490	4,008		98.9	144.4			8,900	14,300	1,921	2,804	Colombia
4	1.5	10	95	3	...	...		...	...			...	...	...	...	Comoros
21	10.8	8,369	660	6	132.8	213.7		24.7	36.1			696	1,120	...	...	Congo
2	—	10	28	6	...	...		...	...			...	...	...	...	Cook Islands
25	14.0	1,500	1,653	8	489[18]	787[18]		22.7[18]	33.2[18]			454	730	...	...	Costa Rica
56	149.3	4,658	4,874	15	198.9[17]	320.1[17]		35.8[17]	52.2[17]			609	980	...	...	Côte d'Ivoire
412	1,218.8	2,820	2,148	12	1,696	2,729		26.8	39.2			149	240	...	...	Cuba
1,352	32,810.6	2,040	3,960	1	1,337	2,151		155	226			...	...	...	...	Cyprus
18	231.7	...	...	14	1,518	2,443		43.1	63			295	475	3,471	5,067	Czechoslovakia
944	6,332.9[20]	13,476	30,504	12	2,210[21]	3,556[21]		88.5[21]	129.2[21]			259	417	1,438	2,100	Denmark
7	2.7	155	466	3	...	...		...	...			...	...	...	...	Djibouti
6	4.2	33	51	2	...	...		...	...			...	...	...	...	Dominica
36	78.1	2,234	3,844	5	128.1	206.1		2.1	3			...	...	...	...	Dominican Republic
154	609.0	13,543	2,458	16	555	893		29.2	42.6			932	1,500	...	...	Ecuador
431	1,821.3	12,792	27,852	10	3,423	5,508		83.5	121.9			2,175	3,500	1,716	2,505	Egypt
14	3.3	288	1,920	1	521[23]	838[23]		4.4[23]	6.5[23]			...	...	...	...	El Salvador

Transportation (continued)

country	roads length mi	km	paved (per-cent)	auto-mobiles	trucks and buses	persons per vehicle	cargo short ton-mi ('000,000)	metric ton-km ('000,000)	track length mi	km	passengers passenger-mi ('000,000)	passenger-km ('000,000)	cargo short ton-mi ('000,000)	metric ton-km ('000,000)
Equatorial Guinea	1,691	2,721	12	4,000	3,000	40	...	...	—	—	—	—	—	—
Ethiopia	24,225	38,987	45	41,000	19,000	769	...	...	485[24]	781[24]	217	350	86	125
Faeroe Islands	269	433	...	14,179	3,462	2.6	...	...	—	—	—	—	—	—
Falkland Islands	317	510	6	1,000	500	1.3	...	...	—	—	—	—	—	—
Fiji	2,996	4,821	13	34,380	24,318	12	...	...	660[16]	1,062[16]	...	...	...	...
Finland	47,453	76,369	54	1,795,908	238,258	2.4	15,000	21,900	5,553	8,936	1,989	3,201	5,354	7,816
France	500,165	804,940	92	21,970,000	3,982,000	2.1	81,508	119,000	21,528[2]	34,647[2]	39,302	63,250	35,814	52,287
French Guiana	691	1,112	65	27,010	1,120	3.2	...	...	—	—	—	—	—	—
French Polynesia	492	792	33	— 54,979 —		3.3	...	...	416	670	12	19	71	103
Gabon	4,682	7,535	8	16,093	10,503	43	...	...	—	—	—	—	—	—
Gambia, The	1,484	2,388	21	5,200	720	129	...	...	—	—	—	—	—	—
Gaza Strip			...	16,666	3,911	26	...	...	—	—	—	—	—	—
Germany, East	75,940	122,214	...	3,600,450	434,864	4.1	5,448	7,954	8,704	14,008	14,020	22,563	40,288	58,823
Germany, West	305,242	491,240	99	27,908,200	1,375,500	2.1	97,604	142,500	41,965	67,536	27,470	44,208	41,039	59,916
Ghana	17,600	28,300	20	52,864	23,375	163	...	...	592[2]	953[2]	241.9	389.3	86.0	125.5
Gibraltar	31	50	100	15,576	1,320	1.8	...	...	—	—	—	—	—	—
Greece	64,191	103,306	83	1,526,863	717,448	4.5	...	...	1,540[2]	2,479[2]	1,204	1,938	410	599
Greenland	50	80	...	2,009	1,591	15	...	...	—	—	—	—	—	—
Grenada	621	1,000	66	4,784	981	16	...	...	—	—	—	—	—	—
Guadeloupe	1,314	2,115	80	95,962	28,134	2.7	...	...	—	—	—	—	—	—
Guam	419	674	100	55,147	16,828	1.7			—	—	—	—	—	—
Guatemala	10,700	17,300	17	188,100	58,500	31			561[2]	903[2]	...	...	...	...
Guernsey			...	9,948	9,992	284			—	—	—	—	—	—
Guinea	17,600	28,400	4	3,000	2,000	175			584[2]	940[2]	...	...	...	...
Guinea-Bissau	3,143	5,058	8						—	—	—	—	—	—
Guyana	5,524	8,890	9	25,541	7,648	24			65	109	...	...	...	...
Haiti	2,299	3,700	17	34,669	11,658	113			—	—	—	—	—	—
Honduras	11,152	17,947	12	77,556	17,078	45			624[2]	1,004[2]	...	...	49	72
Hong Kong	891	1,434	100	182,621	118,405	19			21	34	1,469	2,364		
Hungary	18,455	29,701	99	1,789,600	218,744	5.3	4,721	6,892	8,171	13,150	7,153	11,512	14,423	21,057
Iceland	7,067	11,373	15	120,456	13,102	1.8	318	464	—	—	—	—	—	—
India	1,101,000	1,772,000	47	1,895,000	1,214,000	258	55,500	81,000	38,407[2]	61,810[2]	161,186	259,404	151,342	220,956
Indonesia	136,572	219,791	39	1,191,231	1,284,278	70	17,000	25,000	4,090	6,583	4,556	7,332	995	1,452
Iran	86,599	139,368	48	2,246,143	434,944	17	46,750	68,250	2,837[2]	4,567[2]	1,570	2,526	2,645	3,861
Iraq	20,653	33,238	72	491,800	246,700	21	...	...	1,516[2]	2,439[2]	624	1,005	886	1,294
Ireland	57,354	92,303	94	711,087	106,285	4.3	...	...	1,835	2,953	746.9	1,202	385.7	563.1
Isle of Man	357	574	58	31,594	3,574	1.8	...	...	37[2]	59[2]	...	...	...	...
Israel	7,968	12,823	100	696,712	140,352	5.3	...	...	328[2]	528[2]	107.7	173.4	673.7	983.6
Italy	187,223	301,307	100	22,342,000	1,918,800	2.4	103,185	150,648	12,156	19,563	25,721	41,395	12,621	18,427
Jamaica	7,680	12,360	39	52,886	23,032	31	...	...	183	294	41.8	67.4	116.8	170.5
Japan	682,800	1,098,900	65	28,653,692	19,091,587	2.6	148,026	216,115	16,016	25,776	211,972	341,136	13,907	20,304
Jersey			...	58,424	6,814	1.2	...	...	—	—	—	—	—	—
Jordan	3,495	5,625	73	158,892	73,469	12	19,133	27,934	409[2]	658[2]	3.7	6.0	864	1,262
Kampuchea (Cambodia)	8,296	13,351	20	700	1,800	2,600	...	...	380	612	34	54	6.8	10
Kenya	33,700	54,200	12	133,335	110,806	89	134	196	1,649[2]	2,654[2]	422.5	680.0	1,252	1,828
Kiribati	398	640	5	307	130	147	...	...	—	—	—	—	—	—
Korea, North	13,670	22,000	2				...	...	5,280	8,500	...	...	...	...
Korea, South	33,982	54,689	57	844,350	746,906	26	5,737	8,376	3,939	6,340	15,197	24,457	8,946	13,061
Kuwait	2,405	3,871	100	424,554	115,361	3.6	...	...	—	—	—	—	—	—
Laos	8,067	12,983	31	15,800	3,000	200	...	...	—	—	—	—	—	—
Lebanon	4,579	7,370	85	473,372	49,560	5.0	...	...	138	222	5.3	8.6	29	42
Lesotho	2,640	4,250	12	5,129	11,962	82	...	...	1	2	...	...	...	...
Liberia	5,011	8,064	9	12,747	8,288	100	...	...	304[2]	490[2]	...	...	1,746[15]	2,549[15]
Libya	11,992	19,300	56	428,000	216,000	5.9	...	...	—	—	—	—	—	—
Liechtenstein	201	323	...	15,889	1,801	1.6	...	...	12	19	...	...	...	...
Luxembourg	3,160	5,085	99	177,011	16,776	1.9	164	239	169[2]	272[2]	172	276	436	636
Macau	56	90	100	20,391	4,099	18	...	...	—	—	—	—	—	—
Madagascar	11,560	18,610	30	21,860	14,542	283	...	...	549[2]	883[2]	127	205	138	201
Malawi	7,590	12,215	21	15,339	15,755	246	—	—	515[2]	829[2]	64.0	102.9	67.4	98.5
Malaysia	24,276	39,069	80	1,504,208	338,980	9.0	...	...	1,381	2,222	947[35]	1,524[35]	912[35]	1,332[35]
Maldives	...	...	...	401	234	308	...	...	—	—	—	—	—	—
Mali	11,185	18,000	8	29,436	7,556	207	...	...	401	646	480.1	772.8	213.3	429.3
Malta	860	1,385	93	86,298	18,546	3.3	...	...	—	—	—	—	—	—
Martinique	1,185	1,907	85	135,269	7,328	2.3	...	...	429[2]	690[2]	4.4	7.0	4,207	6,142
Mauritania	5,064	8,150	17	15,017	2,188	96	...	...	—	—	—	—	—	—
Mauritius	1,108	1,783	92	24,365	6,178	34	...	...	—	—	—	—	—	—
Mayotte	143	230	49	— 1,528 —		40	...	...	—	—	—	—	—	—
Mexico	145,222	233,712	45	5,176,714	2,282,431	10	...	...	16,254[2]	26,158[2]	4,082	6,569	28,011	40,895
Monaco	30	48	100	15,709	3,260	1.5	...	...	1	2	...	...	...	...
Mongolia	30,600	49,200	2	...	...	...	1,438	2,099	1,128	1,815	303	487	4,233	6,180
Montserrat	180	290	73	1,217	215	8.3	...	...	—	—	—	—	—	—
Morocco	36,767	59,171	47	554,059	255,149	29	830	1,212	1,176[2]	1,893[2]	1,286	2,069	3,236	4,725
Mozambique	16,215	26,095	20	99,400	24,700	100	...	...	2,182	3,512	65.0	104.6	170.5	248.9
Myanmar (Burma)	14,416	23,200	17	43,300	44,700	386	...	...	1,949[2]	3,137[2]	2,707	4,356	378	552
Nauru	17	27	78	— 1,788 —		4.0	...	...	2	4	—	—	—	—
Nepal	3,918	6,306	44	14,201	9,988	574	984	1,437	33[2]	53[2]	...	...	...	...
Netherlands, The	71,714	115,413	87	5,118,000	477,000	2.6	13,853	20,225	1,745	2,809	5,838	9,396	2,055	3,000
Netherlands Antilles	510	820	...	54,140	10,174	2.9	...	...	—	—	—	—	—	—
New Caledonia	4,037	6,497	18	42,000	2,500	3.3	...	...	—	—	—	—	—	—
New Zealand	57,868	93,130	55	1,393,326	305,208	2.0	...	...	2,692	4,332	285	458	2,168	3,165
Nicaragua	9,319	14,997	10	46,184	30,535	44	...	...	214	344	15.8	25.5	47	68
Niger	24,836	39,970	8	8,981	22,727	222	...	...	—	—	—	—	—	—
Nigeria	77,000	124,000	48	262,550	90,731	241	...	...	2,178	3,505	1,689	2,718	566.7	827.4
Niue	142	229	54	261	73	9.7	...	...	—	—	—	—	—	—
Norfolk Island	50	80	75	1,802	90	1.1	...	...	—	—	—	—	—	—

merchant marine				air					canals and inland waterways (latest)				country
fleet, 1988 (vessels over 100 gross tons)	total dead-weight tonnage, 1988 ('000)	international cargo (latest)		airports with sched-uled flights, 1989	traffic (latest)				length		cargo		
		loaded metric tons ('000)	off-loaded metric tons ('000)		passengers		cargo		mi	km	short ton-mi ('000,000)	metric ton-km ('000,000)	
					passenger-mi ('000,000)	passenger-km ('000,000)	short ton-mi ('000,000)	metric ton-km ('000,000)					
2	6.7	144	51	2	4	7	0.7	1.0	...	...	...	...	Equatorial Guinea
26	94.1	711	1,955	37	346.9	558.3	71.1	103.8	...	...	...	...	Ethiopia
214	20	201	444	1	...	...	...	...	...	...	...	...	Faeroe Islands
5	4.1	4	6	1	...	...	...	...	...	...	...	...	Falkland Islands
57	36.8	480	576	18	336	540	13.1	19.1	126	203	...	...	Fiji
259	810.9	23,352	31,872	21	2,470	4,034	73.9	107.9	4,148	6,675	2,877	4,200	Finland
811	6,854.1[25]	57,120	171,960	69	24,857[26]	40,004[26]	2,514[26]	3,670[26]	9,278	14,932	4,110	6,000	France
7	27	27	249	7	...	...	...	...	286	460	...	...	French Guiana
37	27	12	523	31	...	...	...	...	...	...	...	...	French Polynesia
27	29.3	5,868	968	23	259.5	417.6	18.6	27.2	994	1,600	...	...	Gabon
7	5.1	78	167	1	...	...	...	...	250	400	...	...	Gambia, The
—	—	...	...	—	...	...	...	...	...	...	...	...	Gaza Strip
369	1,800.3	11,982	13,141	4	1,768	2,846	54	78.8	1,441	2,319	1,669	2,437	Germany, East
1,233	4,994.5	44,016	94,164	27	21,132	34,008	2,478	3,617	3,245	5,222	32,877	48,000	Germany, West
136	122.5	1,036	2,496	4	168.4	271.0	23.1	33.7	803	1,293	...	...	Ghana
107	5,795.8	5	405	1	...	...	...	...	...	...	...	...	Gibraltar
1,874	39,718.6	24,252	30,696	29	4,437	7,140	78.1	114.1	50	80	585	854	Greece
82	20	291	280	19	163	26.3	0.23	0.34	...	...	...	...	Greenland
2	0.5	27	52	2	...	...	...	...	...	...	...	...	Grenada
11	27	396	1,224	7	...	...	...	...	...	...	...	...	Guadeloupe
5	4	239	793	1	...	...	...	...	...	...	...	...	Guam
5	6.5	1,381	2,307	3	102.3	164.7	7.8	11.4	162	260	...	...	Guatemala
—	—	...	...	1	...	...	...	...	...	...	...	...	Guernsey
19	2.9	10,106	489	2	17.9	28.8	1.7	2.5	805	1,295	...	...	Guinea
17	2.8	33	129	1	6	9	0.7	1.0	...	...	...	...	Guinea-Bissau
75	13.3	1,548	636	18	104	168	12	18	3,700	6,000	...	...	Guyana
2	0.2	169	680	2	...	...	...	...	60	100	...	...	Haiti
587	873.0	1,392	1,138	9	242.6[28]	390.5[28]	9.8[28]	14.3[28]	289	465	...	...	Honduras
394	12,352.1	27,720[29]	53,376[29]	1	...	...	...	...	...	...	...	...	Hong Kong
15	108.0	...	...	4	835	1,344	8.0	11.6	1,008	1,622	1,112	1,623	Hungary
396	148.3	932	1,643	31	1,462	2,353	19.2	28.1	...	...	58	84	Iceland
797	9,922.8	24,668	39,490	95	11,080	17,832	459.2	670.4	10,054	16,180	...	...	India
1,736	2,956.6	147,552	40,596	134	6,905	11,112	230.8	337.0	13,409	21,579	17,000	25,000	Indonesia
375	7,939.3	78,667	12,205	13	3,363	5,412	469.8	685.9	562	904	...	...	Iran
135	1,675.9	97,830	8,638	3	746	1,200	36	52	631	1,015	...	...	Iraq
169	172.8	5,373	13,316	6	1,700	2,736	57.6	84.1	...	...	...	...	Ireland
—	—	6	203	1	...	...	...	...	...	...	...	...	Isle of Man
66	655.7	7,740	11,700	5	4,526[30]	7,284[30]	443.9[30]	648.1[30]	...	...	...	...	Israel
1,583	11,867.3	36,864	208,836	36	9,715[31]	15,636[31]	715.6[31]	1,045[31]	994	1,600	138	201	Italy
12	21.3	5,485	3,672	6	1,202	1,935	15.5	22.6	...	...	...	...	Jamaica
9,804	48,413.6	80,724	666,864	65	52,024	83,724	2,865	4,182	1,100	1,770	135,587	197,953	Japan
—	—	...	...	1	...	...	...	...	...	...	...	...	Jersey
4	47.7	11,268	8,748	3	2,440	3,927	138.0	201.5	...	...	19,202	28,035	Jordan
3	3.8	10	100	1	...	...	...	...	2,300	3,700	...	...	Kampuchea (Cambodia)
28	4.8	1,878	4,437	16	468.5[32]	754.0[32]	68.4[32]	99.9[32]	...	...	...	...	Kenya
7	2.8	10	25	17	6.2	10.0	0.03	0.04	3	5	...	...	Kiribati
77	581.7	609	4,640	3	...	...	...	...	1,400	2,253	...	...	Korea, North
1,930	11,524.1	54,300	144,192	6	9,007	14,496	1,133	1,654	1,000	1,609	9,249	13,503	Korea, South
206	1,011.0	43,973	7,253	1	2,094	3,370	231.7	338.2	...	...	...	...	Kuwait
—	—	—	—	7	6	9	0.7	1.0	2,850	4,587	...	...	Laos
201	634.5	143	2,311	1	399.0	642.2	12.4	18.2	...	...	...	...	Lebanon
—	—	...	...	14	6.8	11.0	0.9	1.3	—	—	—	—	Lesotho
1,507	93,987.1	14,640	1,729	1	11	17	0.07	0.10	—	—	—	—	Liberia
107	1,463.2	47,172	6,975	11	900[33]	1,447[33]	2.4[33]	3.5[33]	—	—	—	—	Libya
—	—	—	—	—	—	—	—	—	...	...	...	...	Liechtenstein
1	2.5	—	—	1	57	92	606.9	886.1	23	37	208	304	Luxembourg
6	34	313	502	—	—	—	—	—	...	...	...	...	Macau
77	117.2	468	1,596	51	262.6	422.6	26.0	38.0	...	...	...	...	Madagascar
1	0.3	...	...	4	53.0	86.9	6.6	9.7	891	1,434	6.7	9.8	Malawi
499	2,265.8	15,876[36]	24,468[36]	38	5,339	8,592	264.3	385.9	4,534	7,296	...	...	Malaysia
41	165.4	20	70	2	...	...	...	...	...	...	...	...	Maldives
—	—	...	...	2	68	110	0.4	0.6	1,128	1,815	18	27	Mali
356	4,518.5	192	1,668	1	395	636	3.6	5.2	...	...	...	...	Malta
6	27	338	1,014	1	...	...	...	...	...	...	...	...	Martinique
112	19.6	9,956	486	9	147.6	237.6	26.3	38.5	...	...	...	...	Mauritania
33	223.4	876	1,236	2	732.8	1,179	97.0	141.6	...	...	...	...	Mauritius
—	—	...	...	1	...	...	...	...	...	...	...	...	Mayotte
659	1,985.3	89,580	11,244	78	16,353[37]	26,317[37]	114[37]	166[37]	1,800	2,900	...	...	Mexico
—	—	—	—	1	...	...	...	...	...	...	...	...	Monaco
—	—	—	—	1	229	368	5.5	8.1	247	397	2.9	4.3	Mongolia
1	1.0	34	1	1	...	...	...	...	...	...	...	...	Montserrat
335	593.0	19,632	14,460	15	1,378	2,218	34.9	50.9	...	...	2,622	3,828	Morocco
106	27.8	2,110	2,427	2	242.1	389.6	30.8	44.9	2,330	3,750	...	...	Mozambique
120	412.5	1,124	475	21	142	229	16	23	7,954	12,800	...	...	Myanmar (Burma)
6	83.8	1,483	59	1	148[38]	238[38]	1.1[38]	1.6[38]	...	...	...	...	Nauru
—	—	—	—	5	209[33]	336[33]	4.0[33]	5.9[33]	...	...	...	...	Nepal
1,173	4,698.5[39]	82,716	249,576	4	13,687	22,027	1,186	1,731	3,939	6,340	22,455	32,784	Netherlands, The
7	7	12,032	11,529	5	234[40]	377[40]	1.2[40]	1.8[40]	...	...	...	...	Netherlands Antilles
11	27	1,335	813	9	53[41]	112[41]	0.3	0.5	...	...	...	...	New Caledonia
131	378.1	9,619	7,405	36	6,666	10,728	229.3	334.8	1,000	1,609	1,503	2,195	New Zealand
23	18.2	333	1,453	1	...	...	...	...	1,379	2,220	...	...	Nicaragua
—	—	...	...	1	147.6	237.6	26.3	38.5	186	300	...	...	Niger
220	851.9	62,830	11,490	14	1,014	1,632	25.5	37.2	5,328	8,575	...	...	Nigeria
—	—	—	—	1	...	...	...	...	...	...	...	...	Niue
—	—	—	—	1	...	...	...	...	...	...	...	...	Norfolk Island

Transportation (continued)

country	roads length (mi)	roads length (km)	roads paved (per-cent)	motor vehicles automobiles	motor vehicles trucks and buses	persons per vehicle	road cargo short ton-mi ('000,000)	road cargo metric ton-km ('000,000)	track length (mi)	track length (km)	passenger-mi ('000,000)	passenger-km ('000,000)	rail cargo short ton-mi ('000,000)	rail cargo metric ton-km ('000,000)
Norway	53,938	86,805	68	1,623,137	280,070	2.2	4,842	7,069	2,622[2]	4,219[2]	1,359	2,187	1,933	2,822
Oman	12,893	20,749	20	120,367	106,097	5.9	...	...	—	—	—	—	—	—
Pacific Is., Trust Terr. of the														
Marshall Islands	...	...	...	...	...	...	...	...	—	—	—	—	—	—
Micronesia, Fed. States of	140	226	17	...	...	...	...	...	—	—	—	—	—	—
Northern Mariana Islands	186	300	18	...	...	...	...	...	—	—	—	—	—	—
Palau	16	26	...	1,687		7.2	...	...	—	—	—	—	—	—
Pakistan	68,430	110,128	52	540,835	158,895	159	...	...	7,842	12,620	11,000	17,000	5,300	7,800
Panama	6,039	9,719	33	134,339	46,545	12	...	...	149[2]	240[2]	...	...	...	...
Papua New Guinea	12,263	19,736	6	18,748	30,497	69	...	...	—	—	—	—	—	—
Paraguay	9,186	14,783	13	84,986	41,986	26	...	...	274[2]	441[2]	14	22	24	34
Peru	43,460	69,942	11	377,424	233,389	34	...	...	2,144[2]	3,451[2]	321.2	517.0	697.5	1,018
Philippines	98,058	157,810	14	773,242	110,192	63	...	...	658[2]	1,059[2]	142	228	41	60
Pitcairn Island	4	6	—	1		59	...	...	—	—	—	—	—	—
Poland	211,384	340,191	63	4,231,700	953,668	7.2	25,468	37,183	16,551	26,637	30,003	48,285	83,139	121,381
Portugal	32,282	51,953	86	2,571,457	189,822	3.7	4,950	7,220	2,241[2]	3,607[2]	3,670	5,907	1,106	1,615
Puerto Rico	5,810	9,351	87	1,297,098	257,554	2.1	...	...	—	—	—	—	—	—
Qatar	671	1,080	...	131,044	3,710	2.8	...	...	—	—	—	—	—	—
Réunion	1,684	2,710	81	138,081	45,017	2.1	...	...	384[2]	614[2]	...	...	...	...
Romania	45,235	72,799	64	250,000	130,000	58	4,080	5,957	7,006	11,275	20,820	33,506	53,476	78,074
Rwanda	7,500	12,070	7	7,109	10,026	381	140	200	—	—	—	—	—	—
St. Helena and Ascension	118	190	89	953	391	5.4	...	...	—	—	—	—	—	—
St. Kitts and Nevis	190	305	41	3,540	690	11	...	...	—	—	—	—	—	—
St. Lucia	464	747	79	7,049	2,084	22	...	...	—	—	—	—	—	—
St. Pierre and Miquelon	75	120	50	1,920	774	2.3	...	...	—	—	—	—	—	—
St. Vincent and the Grenadines	463	745	58	4,946	2,407	15	...	...	—	—	—	—	—	—
San Marino	147	237	...	18,304	1,851	1.1	...	...	—	—	—	—	—	—
São Tomé and Príncipe	199	320	66	1,774	265	41	...	...	—	—	—	—	—	—
Saudi Arabia	57,664	92,802	36	2,245,042	2,023,365	2.9	...	...	544[2]	875[2]	57.4	92.3	322.0	470.1
Senegal	9,315	15,000	30	76,142	37,105	58	375	547	562[2]	905[2]	18.9	30.5	316	462
Seychelles	164	264	61	3,531	1,277	14	...	...	—	—	—	—	—	—
Sierra Leone	5,200	8,370	17	23,500	6,763	121	36	53	52	84	...	...	...	...
Singapore	1,669	2,686	96	251,414	117,401	7.2	...	...	16	26	...	...	...	...
Solomon Islands	1,300	2,100	8	1,350	1,708	92	...	...	—	—	—	—	—	—
Somalia	10,697	17,215	15	17,754	9,533	234	...	...	—	—	—	—	—	—
South Africa	113,691	182,968	29	3,107,031	1,217,214	6.7	...	...	14,669[2]	23,607[2]	9,442	15,196	62,803	91,691
Bophuthatswana	3,900	6,300	13	...	...	...	...	...	165	265	...	...	...	...
Ciskei	1,867	3,004	15	...	...	...	...	...	60	96	...	...	...	...
Transkei	5,468	8,800	...	...	...	...	...	...	174	280	...	...	...	...
Venda	762	1,226	4.1	...	...	...	...	...	8	13	...	...	...	...
South West Africa/Namibia	34,230	55,088	9	103,715		11	...	...	1,481	2,383	...	...	3,356	4,900
Spain	197,609	318,022	56	10,318,526	1,864,475	3.2	81,434	118,891	7,898[2]	12,710[2]	9,768	15,720	8,030	11,724
Sri Lanka	12,858	20,693	41	147,837	243,913	42	...	...	1,208	1,944	1,286	2,069	156	228
Sudan, The	4,100	6,599	59	99,400	17,211	203	...	...	2,974[2]	4,786[2]	714	1,149	1,096	1,600
Suriname	5,541	8,917	26	35,052	14,600	8.1	...	...	320	515	...	...	73	107
Swaziland	1,773	2,853	18	20,883	7,271	24	15,487	22,611	320	515	...	...	12,444	18,168
Sweden	80,897	130,191	70	3,366,570	259,576	2.3	4,552	6,646	7,279	11,715	3,706	5,964	5,137	7,500
Switzerland	44,128	71,018	96	2,732,720	228,757	2.2	1,075	1,570	3,117	5,016	6,744	10,853	970	1,416
Syria	18,770	30,208	94	112,595	127,420	46	7,251	10,586	1,275	2,052	559	900	1,560	2,278
Taiwan	12,393	19,945	85	1,579,121	524,144	9.4	...	...	2,983	4,800	5,116	8,233	...	...
Tanzania	51,023	82,114	4	49,000	33,000	266	...	...	1,616	2,600	2,125	3,420	857	1,248
Thailand	52,670	84,764	40	572,107	898,310	36	...	...	2,321[2]	3,735[2]	5,954	9,583	1,874	2,736
Togo	4,689	7,547	22	47,083	22,230	50	...	...	250	403	65	105	11	16
Tokelau	...	...	...	...	...	...	...	...	—	—	—	—	—	—
Tonga	269	433	65	1,561	3,397	19	...	...	—	—	—	—	—	—
Trinidad and Tobago	4,909	7,900	46	241,595	82,361	3.6	...	...	—	—	—	—	—	—
Tunisia	17,008	27,371	57	281,201	193,963	16	658	960	1,314[2]	2,115[2]	630	1,014	1,477	2,156
Turkey	198,300	319,133	19	1,193,121	559,220	30	40,296	58,831	5,076[2]	8,169[2]	3,833	6,168	4,973	7,260
Turks and Caicos Islands	75	121	20	2,331		6	...	...	—	—	—	—	—	—
Tuvalu	5	8	...	...	...	...	...	...	—	—	—	—	—	—
Uganda	17,605	28,332	22	32,155	5,646	400	...	...	799[2]	1,286[2]	...	...	...	...
U.S.S.R.	603,500	971,200	74	11,737,100	9,613,600	13	97,000	141,000	90,809	146,144	250,000	402,300	2,619,500	3,824,700
United Arab Emirates	2,709	4,360	61	61,146	16,618	18	...	...	—	—	—	—	—	—
United Kingdom	218,906	352,295	100	17,421,000	2,437,000	2.9	71,303	104,100	23,900[53]	38,464[53]	19,983[53]	32,160[53]	9,912[53]	14,472[53]
United States	3,879,538	6,243,340	88	139,041,000	41,948,000	1.3	698,642	1,020,000	184,235	296,497	12,000	19,200	976,000	1,424,900
Uruguay	32,311	52,000	23	190,000	100,000	10	500	730	1,859[2]	2,991[2]	87.4	140.6	145	212
Vanuatu	660	1,062	24	3,087	2,500	8.4	...	...	—	—	—	—	—	—
Venezuela	62,492	100,571	33	2,300,000	1,248,000	5.0	...	...	273[2]	439[2]	13.8	22.2	12.2	17.8
Vietnam	53,250	85,700	11	...	...	...	1,168	1,705	2,000	3,218	3,016	4,854	686	1,001
Virgin Islands (U.S.)	660	1,062	100	52,922		2.0	...	...	—	—	—	—	—	—
Wallis and Futuna	75	120	13	...	...	...	...	...	—	—	—	—	—	—
West Bank	...	...	...	36,290	13,173	17	...	...	—	—	—	—	—	—
Western Sahara	3,790	6,100	22	6,284	424	20	...	...	—	—	—	—	—	—
Western Samoa	1,296	2,085	19	1,757	2,593	37	...	...	—	—	—	—	—	—
Yemen (Aden)	6,793	10,932	18	25,600	29,200	40	...	...	—	—	—	—	—	—
Yemen (Ṣan'ā')	23,168	37,285	6	125,464	183,582	27	...	...	—	—	—	—	—	—
Yugoslavia	75,029	120,747	59	3,023,693	290,466	7.1	15,302	22,340	5,760	9,270	7,172	11,542	17,406	25,413
Zaire	91,031	146,500	2	24,523	60,528	349	...	...	3,623	5,252	205[57]	330[57]	1,223[57]	1,785[57]
Zambia	23,214	37,359	19	105,783	94,780	30	...	...	1,340	2,157	347	558	1,072	1,565
Zimbabwe	48,421	77,927	17	253,470	28,839	29	...	...	2,109[2]	3,394[2]	...	...	7,698	11,239

[1] Bakhtar Afghan Airlines only. [2] Route length. [3] Air Algérie international flights only. [4] United States data include American Samoa, Guam, Trust Territory of the Pacific Islands, Puerto Rico, and the U.S. Virgin Islands. [5] TAAG airline only. [6] Aerolineas Argentinas only. [7] Includes Netherlands Antilles. [8] Included with The Netherlands. [9] Government railways only. [10] Bahamasair only. [11] Apportionment of ¼ of international flights of Gulf Air (jointly run by Bahrain, Oman, Qatar, and United Arab Emirates) only. [12] Caribbean Airways only. [13] Caribbean Air Cargo only. [14] Cotonou airport traffic only. [15] Air Botswana only. [16] For industrial purposes only. [17] Air Afrique only. [18] Lasca only. [19] Traffic between Ouagadougou, Burkina Faso, and Abidjan, Côte d'Ivoire. [20] Includes Faeroe Islands and Greenland. [21] Apportionment of 2⁄7 of SAS operations only. [22] National roads only. [23] TACA airline only. [24] Includes 100 km of the Chemin de Fer Djibouti-Ethiopien (CDE) in Djibouti. [25] Includes French overseas territories. [26] Air France, UTA, and Air Inter only. [27] Included with France. [28] TAN and SAHSA airlines only. [29] Includes transshipments.

merchant marine: fleet, 1988 (vessels over 100 gross tons)	merchant marine: total deadweight tonnage, 1988 ('000)	international cargo (latest): loaded metric tons ('000)	international cargo (latest): off-loaded metric tons ('000)	air: airports with scheduled flights, 1989	traffic passengers: passenger-mi ('000,000)	traffic passengers: passenger-km ('000,000)	traffic cargo: short ton-mi ('000,000)	traffic cargo: metric ton-km ('000,000)	canals length: mi	canals length: km	canals cargo: short ton-mi ('000,000)	canals cargo: metric ton-km ('000,000)	country
2,078	15,235.1	57,408	20,544	49	5,485[21]	8,828[21]	622.4[21]	908.6[21]	980	1,577	8,378	12,232	Norway
32	16.4	22,143	4,028	6	814[11]	1,418[11]	24.7[11]	36.0[11]	...	...	...	...	Oman
24	[4]												Pacific Is., Trust Terr. of the
		26	117	2									Marshall Islands
				4									Micronesia, Fed. States of
				3									Northern Mariana Islands
		2	56	1									Palau
73	526.2	4,308	17,604	32	4,789	7,707	246.7	360.2					Pakistan
5,022	71,476.0	1,120	2,023	6	313.9	505.2	6.3	9.3	497	800	...	...	Panama
82	46.3	2,052	1,749	177	306	492	6.6	9.7	6,798	10,940	...	...	Papua New Guinea
39	44.3	...	...	1	542.3	872.7	4.2	6.2	1,900	3,100	...	...	Paraguay
621	896.9	7,766	4,919	24	1,581	2,544	210.1	306.8	5,300	8,600	...	...	Peru
1,483	15,485.1	12,984	24,696	18	5,377[42]	8,653[42]	187.7[42]	274.1[42]	2,000	3,219	...	...	Philippines
—													Pitcairn Island
714	4,666.8	32,040	18,180	12	2,075	3,340	13.4	19.5	2,479	3,989	1,040	1,519	Poland
300	1,581.6[34]	6,168	18,561	20	3,094[43]	4,980[43]	93.2[43]	136.0[43]	510	820	...	...	Portugal
28	[4]	[4]	[4]	8									Puerto Rico
65	463.4	13,527	2,127	1	814[11]	1,418[11]	24.7[11]	36.0[11]					Qatar
6	[27]	325	1,466	1									Réunion
462	5,356.5	11,863	31,055	15	2,394	3,852	43.2	63.0	1,071	1,724	1,819	2,656	Romania
2	2.8	1	32	2									Rwanda
1	0.6	33	37	1									St. Helena and Ascension
7	2.1	195	281	2									St. Kitts and Nevis
8	[27]	20	56	1									St. Lucia
													St. Pierre and Miquelon
237	1,420.1	86	211	4									St. Vincent and the Grenadines
—													San Marino
3	1.2	11	19	1	3.8	6.1	0.07	0.10	—	—	—	—	São Tomé and Príncipe
320	3,802.5	163,766	37,521	23	9,280	14,935	335.5	489.9					Saudi Arabia
155	37.6	2,327	2,733	10	129.6[33]	208.6[33]	24.1[33]	35.2[33]	603	970	...	...	Senegal
6	2.5	6	215	6									Seychelles
40	8.7	1,216	607	1	68.3[44]	109.9[44]	1.4[44]	2.0[44]	500	800	447	652	Sierra Leone
715	11,793.5	57,792	84,168	1	15,502	24,948	889.5	1,299					Singapore
36	6.8	40	141	17	7[45]	11[45]	0.02[45]	0.04[45]					Solomon Islands
26	15.9	233	1,006	14	181.4	291.9	2.7	3.9					Somalia
241	522.7	75,756	10,440	39	5,674[46]	9,132[46]	281.9[46]	411.5[46]					South Africa
—	—	—	—	1	—								Bophuthatswana
—	—	—	—	1									Ciskei
—		—		1	...	...	...	...					Transkei
—	—	—	—										Venda
—		483	260	7									South West Africa/Namibia
2,343	7,263.2	41,280	105,624	30	13,802	22,212	431.5	630	649	1,045	21,836[47]	31,880[47]	Spain
111	557.6	3,324	5,400	1	1,511	2,431	193.8	282.9	267	430	...	...	Sri Lanka
25	127.7	663	2,286	10	292.5[48]	470.7[48]	6.4[48]	9.3[48]	3,300	5,310	...	...	Sudan, The
23	13.7	1,828	1,681	5	248.9[49]	400.0[49]	33.9[49]	49.5[49]	746	1,200	...	...	Suriname
—		—	—	1	14	22	1.5	2.2					Swaziland
633	1,926.6	44,592	55,176	43	3,549[50]	5,712[50]	120.9[50]	176.5[50]	1,275	2,052	6,200	9,000	Sweden
25	434.0	...	...	5	8,901	14,325	557.1	813.4	40	65	108	158	Switzerland
59	97.4	8,832	6,528	5	526.8	847.8	61.5	89.8	418	672	...	...	Syria
617	6,810.6	18,086	83,014	9	10,942	17,609	2,205	3,219					Taiwan
39	33.6	635	2,602	19	155	249	1,709	2,495					Tanzania
258	776.7	19,008[51]	24,444[51]	23	8,359	13,452	358.6	523.5	2,300	3,701	...	...	Thailand
12	74.7	195	1,254	1	132.8	213.7	24.7	36.1	30	50	...	...	Togo
—													Tokelau
16	18.0	12	55	6	3.4	5.5	0.01	0.02					Tonga
51	13.7	8,327	4,267	2	1,339[52]	2,155[52]	8.6[52]	12.6[52]					Trinidad and Tobago
72	447.4	6,108	10,020	6	1,475	2,375	14.8	21.5					Tunisia
872	5,441.3	84,324	61,776	14	1,627	2,618	31.1	45.5	750	1,200	*35*	*51*	Turkey
14	5.5	164	156	5									Turks and Caicos Islands
2	0.5	...	...	1									Tuvalu
3	8.6	...	...	4	59.7	96.1	16.0	23.4					Uganda
6,741	29,199.3	164,670	84,830	52	132,458	213,171	1,865	2,723	76,118	122,500	179,113	261,500	U.S.S.R.
241	1,311.9	57,865	7,097	5	1,882[11]	3,029[11]	65.9[11]	96.2[11]					United Arab Emirates
2,142	11,113.5	129,096	159,744	47	36,783	59,196	1,417	2,068	1,424	2,291	35,206	51,400	United Kingdom
6,380	29,920.4[4]	361,152[54]	461,364[54]	834	390,934	629,148	11,066	16,156	25,482	41,009	432,884	632,000	United States
87	282.2	596[55]	1,518[55]	7	241.9	389.3	25.3	37.0	1,000	1,600	...	...	Uruguay
127	1,429.7	59	61	27									Vanuatu
286	1,428.6	72,267	14,902	29	2,200	3,540	77.5	113.2	4,400	7,100	...	...	Venezuela
164	501.5	304	1,359	3	6,454	10,387	4.1	6.0	11,000	17,702	...	...	Vietnam
3	[4]	105.5	648.3	6									Virgin Islands (U.S.)
7	[27]	—	—	2									Wallis and Futuna
—	—												West Bank
		42	15	1									Western Sahara
6	34.8	43	87	3									Western Samoa
22	12.4	1,299	4,659	9	*62*	*100*	*1.2*	*1.7*					Yemen (Aden)
11	408.5	237	2,426	5	363.2[56]	584.5[56]	41.3[56]	60.3[56]					Yemen (San'ā')
499	5,487.7	8,472	25,524	17	5,511	8,869	95.1	138.9	1,616	2,600	3,116	4,550	Yugoslavia
30	75.9	2,057	779	22	237.5[58]	382[58]	8.3[58]	12.2[58]	9,300	15,000	*678*	*990*	Zaire
—	—	—	—	9	378.4	609.0	17.6	25.7	1,398	2,250	...	...	Zambia
		—	—	8	403	648	6.3	9.1					Zimbabwe

[30]El Al only. [31]Alitalia only. [32]Kenya Airways only. [33]International traffic only. [34]Included with Portugal. [35]Peninsular Malaysia and Singapore. [36]Peninsular Malaysia only. [37]Aeronaves de Mexico and Mexicana only. [38]Air Nauru only. [39]Includes Netherlands Antilles and Aruba. [40]Antillean Airlines only. [41]Air Caledonie only. [42]PAL only. [43]TAP only. [44]Sierra Leone Airlines international traffic only. [45]Solair only. [46]SAA only. [47]Coastal shipping only. [48]Sudan Airways only. [49]Suriname Airways only. [50]Apportionment of 3/7 of SAS operations only. [51]Port of Bangkok only. [52]BWIA international traffic only. [53]British Railways only; excludes Northern Ireland. [54]Includes Puerto Rico. [55]Port of Montevideo only. [56]Yemen Airways only. [57]Zaire National Railways only. [58]Air Zaire only.

Communications

Virtually all the states of the world have a variety of communications services available to their citizens: newspapers (although only daily papers are included in this table), radio broadcast systems, and telephone, post office, and telegraph facilities; most also have television and telex. The focus of this table, therefore, is on the relative density and distribution of communications services. Unfortunately, the availability of information about the infrastructure and traffic volume of these national systems often runs behind the capabilities of the systems themselves. Certain countries publish no information about themselves; others publish data analyzed according to a variety of fiscal, calendar, religious, or other years; still others, while they possess such data almost simultaneously with the end of the business year, may not see them published except in company reports of limited distribution. Even when they are published in national statistical summaries, it may be only after a delay of up to several years.

The data also differ in their completeness and reliability. Data for some kinds of communications apparatus and traffic are relatively easy to collect; telephones, for example, even mobile, must be installed, and service recorded so that it may be charged. But in most countries radios may be purchased by anyone and turned on whenever desired; car radios are seldom enumerated or licensed separately. As a result, data on distribution and use of radio and television apparatus may be collected in a variety

of ways—on the basis of numbers of subscribers, licenses issued, periodic sample surveys, census or housing surveys, or private consumer surveys.

The United Nations Educational, Scientific and Cultural Organization (Unesco) publishes in its *Statistical Yearbook* extensive data on newspapers, radio, and television that have been collected from standardized questionnaires. The quality and recency of its data, however, depend on the completion and timely return of each questionnaire by national authorities, and response rates depend on a variety of factors. In general, however, response rates for inquiries by international organizations in communications are better than in other fields because these organizations and the responsible authorities in each country must conduct day-to-day business and, hence, have a better ongoing relationship.

Newspaper statistics are especially difficult to collect and compare. Newspapers continually are founded, cease publication, merge, or change frequency of publication. Data on circulation, sales, and readership are often incomplete, slow to be aggregated at the national level, or regarded as proprietary for either private or governmental publications. In some countries circulation data are virtually nonexistent. In others no daily newspaper exists.

The commercially published annual *World Radio TV Handbook* (A. G. Sennitt, editor) is a valuable source of information on broadcast media

Communications

country	daily newspapers (latest) number	daily newspapers (latest) total circulation ('000)	daily newspapers (latest) circulation per 1,000 population	radio, 1988 transmitters (latest)	radio, 1988 receivers (all types) ('000)	radio, 1988 persons per receiver	television, 1988 transmitters (latest)	television, 1988 receivers (all types) ('000)	television, 1988 persons per receiver	telephones, 1987 receivers ('000)	telephones, 1987 persons per receiver	traffic ('000 calls) local	traffic ('000 calls) long-distance	traffic ('000 calls) international
Afghanistan	14	151	10	5	150[1]	93[1]	1	20[2]	709[2]	31[3]	443[3]	—————110[4]—————		18[4]
Albania	2	135	48	32	500[2]	6.2[2]	216	246	13	4.8[7]	580[7]	—————14,986—————		
Algeria	6	1,082	47	55	5,436[2]	4.2[2]	44	1,550[2]	15[2]	889	26	—1,692,830[8]——		1,148,700[8]
American Samoa	2	8	235	1	17	2.1	3	8.0	4.5	7.3[1]	5.0[1]	...	...	798[1]
Andorra	—	—	—	9	8.0[1]	5.8[1]	54	4.0[1]	12[1]	21[3]	1.9[3]	...	...	...
Angola	4	112	14	73	435	22	3	41	228	77	122	66,140[11]	260[11]	320[11]
Anguilla	—	...	...	4	2.5	2.8	—	...	...	1.4[1]	4.8[1]	————1,211[1]————		58[1]
Antigua and Barbuda	1	6	66	5[13]	23	3.4	2	27	2.9	11[3]	7.2[3]	36,400[3, 8]	3,600[3, 8]	3,223[6, 14]
Argentina	227	...	...	175	21,582	1.5	183	7,165	4.5	3,655	8.7	33,509,639[8]	21,743[19]	6,110
Aruba	2	9	131	8	40	1.6	1	19	3.3	23	2.7	————73,397[14]————		5,858[14]
Australia	61	4,740	308	335	7,169	2.3	400	6,000	2.8	8,727[6]	1.8[6]	7,796,866	1,405,781	56,570
Austria	33	...	...	604	4,699	1.6	951	2,688	2.8	3,979	1.9	———27,840,391[14]———		366,827[14]
Bahamas, The	3	28	118	6	124	2.0	1	54	4.6	119	2.0	929,270	2,840	3,915
Bahrain	5	21	50	5	248	1.7	2	186	2.3	122	3.4	————244,407[8]————		40,565[14]
Bangladesh	59	848	8	25	4,449	24	11	426	244	164[1]	627[1]	————347,600[22]————		84[14, 22]
Barbados	2	39	154	4	223	1.1	1	66	3.9	94	2.7	————483,000[10]————		2,052
Belgium	39	1,930	195	41	4,521[2]	2.2[2]	32	3,050[2]	3.2[2]	4,719	2.1	2,458,000[8]	2,778,000[8]	121,609
Belize	—	—	—	11	95	1.9	2	12	15	9.7[6]	17[6]	...	7,103[6, 14]	844[6, 14]
Benin	1	12	3	7	327	14	1	16	272	16	277	55,206	...	1,959[14]
Bermuda	1	18	310	6	100[1]	0.6[1]	2	67	0.9	84	0.7	...	...	3,784
Bhutan	—	—	—	1	22	64	...	0.2[10]	6,180[10]	1.9[6]	684[6]	481,700	44,509[1, 14]	3,795[1, 14]
Bolivia	13	311	50	191	3,939	1.8	42	447	16	323	21	77,580[1, 8]	1,031[1, 14]	8,908[14]
Botswana	1	30	22	11	149	8.1	...	...	...	40	29	34,400,000[8]	1,800,000	16,000
Brazil	279	8,528	62	1,729	58,867	2.5	137	36,000	4.0	13,162	11	————4,000[3, 8]————		2,150[6, 14]
British Virgin Islands	—	—	—	1	7.0	1.7	1	2.7	4.4	3.7[6]	3.2[6]	...	...	...
Brunei	—	—	—	8	78[1]	3.0[1]	2	50[1]	4.7[1]	40	6.1	...	22,720[8, 11]	9,306[14]
Bulgaria	17	2,834	316	39	1,983[2]	4.5[2]	266	2,073[2]	5.3[2]	1,876[1]	4.8[1]	25,800[10]	60010]	6,130[10]
Burkina Faso	2	7	0.8	9	311[1]	26[1]	2	42	205	171	482[1]	————16,132[3, 8]————		1,675[14]
Burundi	1	20	4	13	230[1]	21[1]	1	4.5	1,180	7.9[1]	622[1]	1,205[10]	533[10]	635[1, 14]
Cameroon	1	66	6	25	1,007	11	32	5.0	2,216	62	179	...	...	22,905[6, 14]
Canada	110	5,700	225	1,607	22,578	1.1	2,002	15,709	1.7	20,126	1.3	36,510,528	2,117,842	37,406
Cape Verde	—	—	—	5	50[1]	6.8[1]	—	5.0[2]	70[2]	4.4[6]	76[6]	————126[3]————		377[3]
Cayman Islands	2	14	624	4	20[1]	1.1[1]	1	1.2[1]	19[1]	25	1.0	————16,353[3, 8]————		4,412[6, 14]
Central African Republic	1	0.2	0.1	4	125[1]	22[1]	1	1.4[10]	1,817[10]	11	247	6,142	20	2
Chad	1	2	0.3	7	1,268	4.3	...	...	...	4.7[1]	1,114[1]	4,379[1, 14]	109[1, 14]	269[1, 14]
Chile	33	1,145	91	302	4,219	3.0	131	2,330	5.5	815	16	1,435,482	557,076	22,154[14]
China	222	...	...	571	121,212	8.9	c. 5,400	126,000	8.6	8,057	134	————903,200[1]————		17,660[1]
Christmas Island	—	—	—	1	2.5[6]	0.9[6]	1	...	...	0.18[10]	3.1[10]	...	...	...
Cocos (Keeling) Islands	—	—	—	1	0.2	3.5	...	...	...	0.50[10]	12	8,952,600[8]	1,554,521[14]	46,003[14]
Colombia	30	1,862	61	439	7,980[1]	3.5[1]	49	5,500	5.6	2,438	12	————940[5]————		145
Comoros	—	—	—	4	100[2]	4.2[2]	1	5.8	375	19	111	11,261	4,570	490
Congo	3	24	11	10	229	9.4	...	...	...	3.1	5.5	...	36[1]	584[14]
Cook Islands	1	2	105	5	5.0	3.6	12	470	6.1	409	6.9	787,652[1, 14]	445,062[1, 14]	20,199[14]
Costa Rica	6	308	110	80	253	11	11	625	19	88[4]	97[4]	...	...	...
Côte d'Ivoire	2	130	12	25	1,478	7.9	...	...	...	...	...	————150,200————		1,625
Cuba	17	1,290	126	160	3,435	3.0	78	2,069	5.0	564	18	————903,379[8]————		7,817
Cyprus	10	86	157	6	198	3.7	29	165	4.4	272	2.6	6,272,000	461,000	8,500
Czechoslovakia	30	4,372	280	126	4,258	3.7	81	4,387	3.6	3,838	4.1	2,629,000	1,713,000	76,000
Denmark	48	1,881	366	48	2,118	2.4	34	1,932	2.7	4,434	1.2	————22,498[2]————		3,023[14]
Djibouti	—	—	—	2	30[2]	16[2]	1	14	35	8.7	55	...	...	...
Dominica	—	—	—	4	35	2.4	...	...	...	6.9[6]	12[6]	————6,000[3, 8]————		779[6, 14]
Dominican Republic	8	294	44	126	1,141	6.0	19	556	12	311	22	...	16,541	4,832
Ecuador	7	538	57	370	2,987	3.4	27	600[2]	17[2]	355	28	...	...	2,066
Egypt	17	...	...	154	13,669[2]	3.6[2]	74	3,860[2]	13[2]	1,455	34	1,300,000	70,000	6,300
El Salvador	5	253	52	79	1,937	2.6	5	425	12	136	36	394,560[8]	263,040[8]	24,117[14]
Equatorial Guinea	2	1	3	5	97	3.5	1	2.5	134	1.4[7]	209[7]	382,604[8]	4,741	3,081[14]
Ethiopia	3	47	1	8	2,000[1]	22[1]	18	70	679	181	2.6[1]	...	...	447
Faeroe Islands	—	—	—	4	18	2.6	23	10	4.7	0.58	3.4	————47————		596[14]
Falkland Islands	—	—	—	2	11[1]	1.9[1]	1	...	...	60	12	————176,190[8]————		4,750[14]
Fiji	2	53	74	14	431	1.7	...	...	...					

and has complete and timely coverage. It depends on data received from broadcasters, but because some do not respond, local correspondents and monitors are used in many countries, and some unconfirmed or unofficial data are included as estimates. Data on transmitters may be complicated by new or changing technology in areas like the use of low-powered relays (secondary, or repeater installations) for local rebroadcast or use of satellite relays.

The statistics on telephones, telegraph, and telex are derived mainly from the UN-affiliated International Telecommunication Union's (ITU's) *Yearbook of Common Carrier Telecommunication Statistics* with additional data from American Telephone and Telegraph's *The World's Telephones* and from a variety of national and regional intergovernmental sources. A number of countries report incomplete telephone data: the national total may exclude figures for some telephone companies, or some portion of the national territory; some countries supply statistics only on telephone exchange lines; some island states report only radio telephones. A number of countries omit data on public coin-box telephones; their statistics, thus, reflect an undercount. The traffic data for telephone calls may represent any one of three quantities: "pulses," a measure of mechanical activity rather than an enumeration of actual conversations; minutes of connect time; or "calls," the practical equivalent of a conversation between in-

dividuals. Depending on a country's metering system, multiple counting of a single call may occur. Telegraph traffic is reported predominantly as "messages," or sometimes in words; telex traffic is usually reported in minutes of connect time, but, depending on the national metering system, it may also be given as "pulses," or minutes.

Post office statistics are compiled mainly from the Universal Postal Union's annual summary *Statistique des services postaux*. Postal services, unlike the other media discussed above, tend most often to be operated by a single national service, to cover a country completely, and to record traffic data according to broadly similar schemes (although the details of *classes* of mail handled may differ). Some countries do not enumerate domestic traffic or may record only international traffic requiring handling charges.

Unesco surveys, the diverse industry sources cited above, and scores of national statistical sources have also been used in the compilation of this table because no single source is complete.
... Not available.
—None, nil, or not applicable.

post offices, 1987			telegraph, 1987			telex, 1987				country
number	persons per office	pieces of mail handled ('000)	total traffic ('000)	national traffic ('000)	international outgoing traffic ('000)	subscriber lines	traffic ('000 minutes)			
							total	national	international outgoing	
3495[5]	36,400[5]	11,218[5]	183[4]	95[4]	88[4]	125[6]	...	...	169[6]	Afghanistan
613	5,029	13,763	3,748	...	...	...	...	...	...	Albania
2,472	9,830	366,312	2,502[9]	2,328[9]	174[9]	8,244	31,658[1]	26,141	8,415[1]	Algeria
...	...	...	14[1]	—	14[1]	80[1]	101[1]	...	...	American Samoa
...	...	3,483[10]	...	...	...	...	...	...	...	Andorra
133	64,700	9,460	198[11]	154[11]	44[11]	1,000	5,218	925	4,293	Angola
22	320	435	0.9[10]	0.004[10]	33[6,9]	36[1]	...	...	101[1,12]	Anguilla
15[5]	5,330[5]	2,262[15,16,17,18]	...	...	315[6,9]	108[6]	...	...	189[6]	Antigua and Barbuda
5,776	5,450	677,978[1]	12,587	12,379	208	12,169	...	230,940[8]	9,272	Argentina
20	20	20	6.4	4.0	2.4	203	231	16	215	Aruba
4,537[1]	3,450[1]	3,396,433[1]	1,986	1,678	308	45,025[1]	55,897[12]	40,805[12]	15,092[12]	Australia
2,650[6,21]	2,850[6,21]	2,915,155[6]	1,388	1,179	209	25,954	113,344[6]	76,321[6]	34,726	Austria
127	1,650	52,397	25[1]	12[1]	13[1]	555	817	62	755	Bahamas, The
10	35,100	42,600	114	17	97	1,870	8,643	2,054	6,589	Bahrain
7,735	13,600	298,733	3,998[22]	3,470[22]	528[22]	1,090[6]	...	90[12,22]	2,437[6]	Bangladesh
16	15,900	16,971	...	...	22	341	762	15	747	Barbados
1,840	5,360	3,110,984	748	553	195	27,620	134,030	61,348	72,682	Belgium
112[1]	1,520[1]	3,096[1]	20[10]	10[10]	270[6,9]	976	...	...	138[6]	Belize
180	20,700	5,127	...	53[6]	...	284[1]	14,294[1,8]	76[6]	330[1]	Benin
15[5]	3,330[5]	...	...	...	572[6,9]	530[6]	...	...	1,616[6]	Bermuda
81[5]	16,700[5]	...	...	...	...	...	...	...	...	Bhutan
458[5]	11,600[5]	54,609[5]	197[1]	173[1]	24[1]	1,170[1]	2,743[1]	1,496[1]	1,248[1]	Bolivia
72	16,700	57,000	...	...	292[1,9]	651[1]	2,672[1]	1,159[1]	1,513[1]	Botswana
12,347	11,400	3,177,365[23]	27,715[1]	27,624[1]	91[1]	93,300	500,000	480,000	20,000	Brazil
9[1]	1,220[1]	96[6,24]	...	...	144[6,9]	58[3]	...	...	77[6]	British Virgin Islands
13	17,400	10,637	23	1.5	22	496	...	...	743	Brunei
2,857[5]	3,100[5]	...	7,593[10]	7,393[10]	199[10]	6,030[10]	30,733[10]	27,463[10]	3,270[10]	Bulgaria
76	105,000	22,891[1]	...	...	30	336	...	...	711	Burkina Faso
24	208,000	1,955[15,18]	5.1[1]	1.6[1]	3.5[1]	191[1]	...	...	293[1]	Burundi
261[6]	33,800[6]	...	917[3]	889[3]	28[3]	1,940	...	...	3,002[6]	Cameroon
14,554	1,780	7,716,501[23]	...	...	445[25]	43,900	...	...	13,234	Canada
592[1]	5,730[21]	2,345	52[3]	41[3]	11[3]	806	170[3]	0.6[3]	210[6]	Cape Verde
16	1,500	3,725	...	...	396[6,9]	246[1]	...	...	463[6]	Cayman Islands
76	34,900	...	73[1]	48[1]	25[1]	154[1]	...	...	380[1]	Central African Republic
35	148,000	1,771	750[1,9]	71[1,9]	679[1,9]	110[1]	292[1]	11[1]	282[1]	Chad
1,074	10,500	174,810[23]	2,338	2,278	60	7,923	27,988	22,456	5,532	Chile
50,934	21,100	5,478,932[16,18,23]	203,021[1]	197,498[1]	5,523[1]	6,919	...	...	12,884	China
2[10]	1,600[10]	...	...	...	...	...	...	...	...	Christmas Island
4[10]	150[10]	...	...	...	...	...	...	...	...	Cocos (Keeling) Islands
1,644	16,900	194,848	18,047	17,984	63	6,570	30,427	24,836	5,591	Colombia
9[5]	38,900[5]	...	...	175	...	61[6]	...	...	83[6]	Comoros
133[6]	14,400[6]	19,770[6]	215	196	19	498	...	...	685	Congo
12[1]	1,460[1]	1,815[1]	36[3]	26[3]	120[9]	72	...	117	57[12]	Cook Islands
329	8,560	29,039[6]	273[6]	228[6]	45[6]	1,639	2,553[1]	583[1]	1,960	Costa Rica
1,141	8,760	114,154[15,16,18]	581[4]	508[4]	73[4]	1,821[6]	...	...	3,304[6]	Côte d'Ivoire
885	11,600	6,925	...	17,171	6,573[9]	4,840	35,710	33,891	1,819	Cuba
748	910	39,802[15,16]	132	91	41	3,752	6,790	2,424	4,366	Cyprus
6,635	2,350	82,765[24]	9,189	8,926	263	11,395	...	70,100[8]	6,850	Czechoslovakia
1,282	4,000	1,728,470	137	64	73	13,042	70,013	24,679	45,334	Denmark
5[10]	60,000[10]	1,623[10]	19[1]	0.2[1]	16	201	560[1]	24[1]	455	Djibouti
63[10]	1,270[10]	2,051[10]	...	...	244[6,9]	49[6]	...	...	82[6]	Dominica
201	32,400	4,609	...	...	...	...	...	...	...	Dominican Republic
476	20,800	26,369	...	...	38	3,152	6,771	3,311	3,460	Ecuador
8,884	5,660	414,023	10,587[1]	9,880[1]	707[1]	6,446	17,985[1]	8,300[1]	9,700	Egypt
378	14,600	20,483	2,090	2,077	13	906	5,796	4,906	890	El Salvador
20	15,600	276[26]	...	...	...	...	...	...	...	Equatorial Guinea
908	50,800	33,957	332	308	14	794	2,004	824	1,180	Ethiopia
...	...	...	28[1]	—	28[1]	200[1]	...	...	...	Faeroe Islands
...	...	...	...	...	0.9	25	58	0.6	58	Falkland Islands
235	3,040	24,865[16]	134	126	8	680	1,904	921	983	Fiji

Communications (continued)

country	daily newspapers (latest)			radio, 1988			television, 1988			telephones, 1987		traffic ('000 calls)		
	number	total circulation ('000)	circulation per 1,000 population	transmitters (latest)	receivers (all types) ('000)	persons per receiver	transmitters (latest)	receivers (all types) ('000)	persons per receiver	receivers ('000)	persons per receiver	local	long-distance	international
Finland	68	2,719	551	115	4,922	1.0	214	1,851	2.7	3,028[6]	1.6[6]	2,771,000	456,000	23,200
France	95	11,369	205	840	49,009	1.1	10,670	21,968	2.5	37,120	1.5	—95,099,270[8]—		146,542[8]
French Guiana	2	17	191	15	441	1.91	14	6.5	14	28	3.2	—63,031[8]—		3,854[14]
French Polynesia	3	23	126	14	90	2.1	15	27[2]	6.9[2]	44	4.4	13,560[8,10]	34,800[8,10]	288,000[8,10]
Gabon	2	33	35	34	103	12	8	37	33	14[10]	81[10]			
Gambia, The	1	2	3	7	134	6.1	...	...	...	3.6[1]	216[1]	3,600[1]	600[1]	400[1]
Gaza Strip					...	...								
Germany, East	39	9,070	545	130	6,758	2.5	576	6,199	2.7	3,875	4.3	1,390,100	815,796	14,441
Germany, West	356	25,255	413	446[28]	26,341	2.3	5,718	23,011	2.7	40,288	1.5	18,764,430	11,046,661	514,931
Ghana	4	460	33	17	2,920	4.7	6	175[2]	77[2]	75	181	201[19]	319[19]	111[19]
Gibraltar	1	3	103	2	10	3.0	4	7.0	4.3	13	2.3			1,388
Greece	142	...	...	67	4,085[2]	2.4[2]	372	1,755[2]	5.7[2]	4,126	2.4	5,904,757	675,118	31,243
Greenland	—	—	—	38	15	3.6	7	12	4.6	12[3]	4.4[3]			
Grenada	—	—	—	1	45	2.4	1	...	...	6.6	16	—148[10]—		1,124[6,14]
Guadeloupe	1	51	150	20	100[2]	3.4[2]	21	150	2.3	100	3.4	—421,748[8]—		
Guam	1	18	149	5	105	1.2	2	83	1.5	37	3.5	...	...	...
Guatemala	9	...	...	104	407	21	24	475	18	128[6]	63[6]	8,583[6]	12,468[6]	2,301[6]
Guernsey	1	16	277	1	...	...	1	50	131	55	1.1	—51,014—		473
Guinea	—	—	—	9	200[1]	31[1]	...	...	...	16[11]	310[11]	...	96[10,14]	986[10,14]
Guinea-Bissau	1	6	7	2	31	30	...	...	...	3.0[1]	297[1]			
Guyana	1	58	77	13	308	2.5	3	40	19	30	25	—88,458[6,8]—		311
Haiti	6	22	4	35	132	41	4	25	218	82[1]	65[1]	41,137	1,293	1,960
Honduras	7	218	47	209	1,847	2.6	39	140	34	56	84	270,900[14]	196,000[14]	16,300[14]
Hong Kong	68	3,189	602	24	2,750	2.1	52	1,357[2]	4.1[2]	2,662	2.1	—4,100,000[6]—		253,156[14]
Hungary	29	2,570	242	51	6,093	1.7	109	4,215	2.5	1,609	6.6	1,378,655[8]	1,828,609[8]	914,221[8]
Iceland	6	127	516	34	153	1.6	130	76	3.3	125[10]	1.9[10]			2,123
India	1,802	12,896	26	191	53,937	15	174	13,200	62	4,420	180	16,484,000[8]	229,300	2,410
Indonesia	97	3,049	18	745	21,785	8.0	207	7,112	24	890	193	—7,266,568[8]—		6,841
Iran	17	...	...	349	11,093	4.7	585	2,250	23	2,079	24	11,340,148[1]	276,970[1]	5,716[1]
Iraq	6	328	21	46	3,222[2]	5.3[2]	35	972[2]	18[2]	937	18	—5,339,151[8]—		13,329[6,14]
Ireland	7	709	200	26	2,113	1.7	77	937	3.8	942[6]	3.8[6]	—2,286,467[1,8]—		46,394[14,29]
Isle of Man	—	—	—	1	22[11]	3.0[11]	...	22[10]	3.0[10]	...	...			
Israel	25	1,148	263	63	2,055	2.2	56	655	6.9	2,065	2.2	2,250,000[8]	3,490,000[8]	73,575[14]
Italy	99	...	...	2,179	14,817	3.9	2,711	14,605	3.9	28,052	2.0	13,449,900	6,213,291	164,316
Jamaica	2	90	38	20	907	2.6	8	387	6.1	161	15	...	14,459	5,682
Japan	124	70,669	578	1,134	96,703	1.3	13,119	30,250	4.1	66,636[6]	1.8[6]	54,800,000	21,100,000	413,000[14]
Jersey	1	24	300	1	...	...	1	...	...	80	1.0	57,553	9,115	977
Jordan	5	185	65	17	1,100	2.7	46	250	12	212	14	—136,479[14]—		24,557[14]
Kampuchea (Cambodia)	...	280	13	6	753	10	2	49	141	7.3[11]	790[11]			
Kenya	5	...	...	33	1,815	12	4	192	118	316	70	8,360[19]	13,492[19]	11,977[14,19]
Kiribati	—	—	—	2	10	6.8	...	11[7]	5.5[7]	1.4	48	67[14]	34[14]	103[14]
Korea, North	16	...	...	32	3,697	5.8	11	215	99	10[10]	2,000[10]			
Korea, South	26	11,000	265	214	41,959	1.0	144	8,643[2]	4.9[2]	10,732	3.9	47,571,823[8]	1,906,976	22,983
Kuwait	7	418	223	14	1,100	1.8	10	800	2.4	330	5.8	...	...	11,295
Laos	3	13	4	18	367[2]	10[2]	2	32[2]	118[2]	8.1[6]	450[6]	3,879[6]	2[6]	23[6]
Lebanon	39	573	212	22	2,198	1.3	18	838	3.4	150	18	...	...	...
Lesotho	3	44	28	3	462	36[2]	3	1.5[2]	1,085[2]	146	117[6]	1,100[8]		336
Liberia	7	...	...	14[30]	566	4.4	5	43[1]	55[1]	28	86	...	...	14,689[14]
Libya	1	40	10	30	1,007	3.9	13	295	13	500	7.8	9,386	4,536	8,559[14]
Liechtenstein	2	15	546	...	9.4[2]	2.9[2]	...	8.9[2]	3.1[2]	41	0.7			
Luxembourg	6	130	365	7	229[1]	1.6[2]	3	92[2]	4.0[2]	157[1]	2.3[1]	—174,026—		101,193[14]
Macau	14	242	568	5	150	3.0	4	80	5.6	69	6.3	—162,171—		8,930
Madagascar	5	116	11	29	2,108	5.3	41	100	112	46	239	23,540[1]	4,890[1]	378
Malawi	2	32	5	16	1,907	4.3	...	...	...	47	172			2,348[14]
Malaysia	42	...	...	83	7,091	2.4	65	1,465	11	1,501	11	—8,490,642[1,8]—		6,871
Maldives	2	...	...	2	22	9.2	1	4.6	44	2.5[6]	75[6]	3,600[6]	68[6,14]	260[6,14]
Mali	1	40	5	8	300[1]	25[1]	1	0.9	8,642	9.5[3]	760[3]	...	907	977
Malta	4	81	235	3	107	3.2	1	132	2.6	164	2.1	—119,834—		1,925
Martinique	1	30	90	46	55[1]	6.0[1]	10	45	7.5	107	3.1	—349,187[8]—		
Mauritania	1	...	...	4	233	8.1	1	1.1	1,722	4.8[10]	350[10]	7,712[8,10]	85[10,14]	310[10,14]
Mauritius	8	90	86	5	200[1]	5.2[1]	4	128	8.2	67[31]	15[31]	—79,855[31]—		4,973[14,31]
Mayotte	1	...	...	1	30[1]	2.3[1]	...	...	...					
Mexico	392	11,256	142	887	16,311	5.1	430	9,500	8.7	8,237	10	2,978,969	724,668	30,348
Monaco	2	11	408	9	10.6	2.6	5	18	1.6	376	0.86	—14,402[8]—		144,769[8]
Mongolia	2	179	90	22	212[2]	9.4[2]	20	111[2]	18[2]	491	38[1]			
Montserrat	—	—	—	5[32]	4.5	2.9	1	1.3	10	3.5[6]	3.4[6]	—4,674[6,8]—		688[6,14]
Morocco	11	305	13	34	4,395	5.4	77	1,206[2]	19[2]	343	69	—1,048,306[8]—		501
Mozambique	2	81	6	40	479	31	1	35	425	63	235	—89,000[8]—		2,680[14]
Myanmar (Burma)	6	533	14	6	3,174	13	2	68	592	62	624			72[10]
Nauru	—	—	—	1	4.0	2.0	...	...	...	1.6[1]	5.1[1]	—1,800[1]—		300[1]
Nepal	59	...	...	4	2,012[1]	8.5[1]	7	27	667	26	686	—4,479[14]—		1,583[14]
Netherlands, The	43	4,579	315	50	12,146[2]	1.2[2]	29	4,703[2]	3.2[2]	9,410	1.6	3,401,000	2,830,000	160,000
Netherlands Antilles	5	66	375	18[33]	150	1.2	3	32	5.7	101	1.8	116,677[8]	5,716[14]	16,514[14]
New Caledonia	2	24	158	25	90	1.7	35	36[2]	4.3[2]	32[10]	4.6[10]	—31,512[8]—		3,703[14]
New Zealand	32	1,055	324	102	3,053[2]	1.1[2]	740	978[2]	3.5[2]	2,403	1.4	...	197,852	15,608
Nicaragua	4	219	62	44	883	4.1	7	210	17	50[3]	64[3]	—272,503[3,8]—		5,069[3,14]
Niger	1	5	0.7	17	357	19	12	25	277	12[6]	563[6]	—597,740[6]—		2,231[6,14]
Nigeria	26	...	...	77	9,558	12	61	5,600	20	265[1]	397[1]	86,947[6,8]	1,140[6,19]	25,257[6,14]
Niue	—	—	—	1	1.0	3.0	—	0.69	3.5					11
Norfolk Island	—	—	—	2	0.9	2.2	1	0.43	4.7[3]	1.0[2]	2.0[1]	402[1,14]		23[1,14]
Norway	84	2,268	540	855	3,285	1.3	1,486	1,466	2.9	2,579[3]	1.6[3]	—7,691,764[8]—		228,660[14]
Oman	3	30	24	14	888	1.6	34	1,000	1.4	8.0	17	—374,133[8]—		4,258
Pacific Is., Trust Terr. of the														
Marshall Islands	—	—	—	2	...	...	...	...	...	...	...			...
Micronesia, Fed. States of	—	—	—	4	17	5.8	3	1.13	90	...	...			...
Northern Mariana Islands	—	—	—	3	10.5	2.0	1	4.1	5.1	4.9	4.4	...	147	344
Palau	—	—	—	1	9.0	1.6	1	1.6	8.8	1.1	13			
Pakistan	125	1,321	12	51	9,775	11	19	1,509	73	679	159	—3,480,391[8]—		3,145
Panama	9	197	89	85	900[1]	2.5[1]	14	476	4.9	240	9.6	788,969	134,372	4,212
Papua New Guinea	1	28	8	54	230	15	10	230[6]	14[6]	72	48	93,458	55,083	3,554

post offices, 1987 number	persons per office	pieces of mail handled ('000)	telegraph, 1987 total traffic ('000)	national traffic ('000)	international outgoing traffic ('000)	telex, 1987 subscriber lines	traffic ('000 minutes) total	national	international outgoing	country
3,632[10]	1,340[10]	1,098,005[10]	577	520	57	7,800	22,413	8,346	14,067	Finland
17,089[27]	3,230[27]	17,635,400[27]	11,708	10,376	1,332	143,916	572,023	427,171	144,852	France
...	...	...	19[1]	16[1]	3[1]	308	734	619	115	French Guiana
92	1,840	14,569	48	41	7	317	811	53	758	French Polynesia
...	...	13,435[5]	272[10]	146[10]	126[10]	801[6]	2,721[10]	876[10]	2,286[6]	Gabon
...	...	...	10.7[1]	1.7[1]	9.0[1]	120[1]	151[1]	1[1]	150[1]	Gambia, The
										Gaza Strip
11,976	1,390	1,490,399	13,936	11,198	2,738	17,020	...	...	9,857	Germany, East
17,748	3,440	14,848,904	5,298	3,832	1,496	165,246	528,145	350,595	177,550	Germany, West
1,004	12,200	121,810	...	17	1,232[9]	477	1,321	121	1,200	Ghana
4	7,430	6,271	10.4[6]	4.5[6]	5.9[6]	188[6]	436[6]	8[6]	428[6]	Gibraltar
1,226[21]	8,140[21]	432,684	2,849	2,642	207	23,605	56,701	33,946	22,755	Greece
51[5]	2,160[5]	...				53[6]			117[6]	Greenland
44[5]	7,500[5]	...		0.2[7]	29[6]		1,182	1,004	178	Grenada
			40	38	2	785				Guadeloupe
540	14,100	47,092	...	...	2,907[6,9]	1,182[6]	...	...	...	Guam
18	3,110	12,931[23]	1.2	0.7	0.5	327	...	...	597[6,12]	Guatemala
75	78,300	14,897	50[10]	21[10]	29[10]	195[10]	...	...	415[10]	Guernsey
...	...	...								Guinea
										Guinea-Bissau
131[1]	6,490[1]	32,272[1]	...	...	1,391	142[1]	365[1,12]	52[1,12]	313[1,12]	Guyana
132[5]	33,100[5]	1,046,472[17]				827	4,818	3,659	1,159	Haiti
508[5]	7,260[5]	60,689[5]	1,265	15	1,250	29,700	83,239	38,577	44,662	Honduras
147	38,500	682,228	798	7	791	11,960	...	78,195[8]	9,674	Hong Kong
3,220	3,290	1,711,406	12,780	12,358	422					Hungary
139[21]	1,790	61,461	599	587	12	576	1,821	296	1,525	Iceland
143,987	5,490	12,673,108	62,131	60,861	1,270	34,044	...	358,349[8]	25,169	India
19,722	8,650	463,090	11,147	11,090	57	13,453	...	780,382[8]	11,180	Indonesia
3,815[6]	12,400[6]	256,751[6,15,16,18]	5,768[1]	5,701[1]	671	5,497	3,014[12]	861[12]	6,496	Iran
288[10]	49,000[10]	193,996[10]	...	844[10]	426[6]	2,187[6]	7,668[6]	1,652[6]	6,016[6]	Iraq
2,118	1,670	482,153[16,17]	152[1]	82	30[1]	6,637	31,695	19,439	12,256	Ireland
37	1,750	24,049								Isle of Man
1,496	2,950	423,900	528[1]	380[1]	148[1]	6,425	24,749	18,500	6,249	Israel
14,461	3,970	6,086,263	24,336	23,239	1,097	74,406	334,407	215,298	119,109	Italy
788[6]	2,780[6]		273[3]	195[3]	78[3]	506[6]	...	...	1,007[6]	Jamaica
23,778	5,140	19,368,082	41,510	41,040	470	42,000	165,822[11]	111,103[11]	39,069	Japan
24	3,360	44,692	...	...	...	531	...	...	1,525[3]	Jersey
792	3,660	104,228	...	...	3,790[9]	2,592	...	...	3,563	Jordan
...	...									Kampuchea (Cambodia)
853	29,900	210,639[1]	1,368[1]	1,410	156[1]	2,531	4,619	1,326	3,293	Kenya
5[5]	10,800[5]	...	855[9]	808[9]	47[9]	32	107[3]	57[3]	106	Kiribati
3,095[21]	13,600[21]	1,572,733[23]	12,084	11,979	105	10,304	9,692[12]	2,660[12]	7,032[12]	Korea, North
55	30,900	108,543[15,16,18]	471	121	350	3,192	9,898	3,691	6,207	Korea, South
105	37,100	12,781	5,066[6,9]	4,894[6,9]	172[6,9]	376	...	...	47[6]	Kuwait
										Laos
...	...	...	84	48	36					Lebanon
137	10,900	26,039	563	73	49[3]	219[3]	287[3]	142[10]	166[10]	Lesotho
45	33,800	15,843[15,16,18]	...	...	...	49				Liberia
317	10,900	71,672[15,16,24]	70	35	35	2,600	...	...	2,893	Libya
12	2,310	16,134[23]	...	...	...					Liechtenstein
106	3,480	167,453	37	14	23	2,731	12,079	1,973	10,106	Luxembourg
15	28,800	7,533	27	0.5	26	645	422[12]	49[12]	373[12]	Macau
8,910	1,230	49,355	183[1]	172[1]	11[1]	387[1]	988[1]	127[1]	861[1]	Madagascar
263[6]	23,800[6]	113,975[6]	182	146	36	592	...	...	665	Malawi
5,733	2,880	788,465	962	818	144	11,228	...	...	6,119	Malaysia
28	6,480	1,759	...	...	5.6[6]	150[6]			256[6]	Maldives
122[1]	66,300[1]	8,578[1]								Mali
165[5]	22,500[5]	37,366[5]	45[6]	22[6]	20[1]	928[1]	2,692[1]	342[1]	2,350[1]	Malta
44[5]	7,270[5]	...	98[1]	93[1]	5[1]	641	948	807	141	Martinique
...	...	3,035[5]	42[10]	28[10]	14[10]	231[6]	...	3,560[8,10]	192[6]	Mauritania
112	9,440	31,939	...	...	36	702	2,377	414	1,963	Mauritius
...	...	...	0.026[1]	0.022[1]	0.004[1]	45	...	...	...	Mayotte
7,075[1]	10,950[1]	742,093[15,16]	25,142	24,902	240	24,526	77,858	64,102	13,756	Mexico
...	...	...	12[6]	7[6]	5[6]	672[6]	...	...	2,338[6]	Monaco
382[5]	3,900[5]	...								Mongolia
11[6]	1,090[6]	394[6]	...	2.8[3]	...	33[6]	...	...	31[6]	Montserrat
1,160	19,600	180,566[16]	987	875	112	7,112	5,648[12]	3,509[12]	2,139[12]	Morocco
322	45,800	26,441	170[22]	117[22]	19	783	...	1,500[8]	1,900	Mozambique
1,114	33,700	67,040[15,16,18]	1,028[10]	997[10]	31[10]	130[1]	...	...	472[1]	Myanmar (Burma)
1[6]	7,000[6]	168[6]			22[1]	17[1]	54[1]	0.3[1]	54[1]	Nauru
...	...	...	1,203	1,134	69	405	...	...	809	Nepal
2,624	5,610	5,694,900	708	423	285	38,600	...	375,705[6,8]	82,600	Netherlands, The
14[6,20]	19,500[6,20]	14,045[6,20]	...	...	978[10,20]	635[1]	...	...	1,307[1]	Netherlands Antilles
262	670	19,012	34[1]	9[1]	25[1]	229	6,682[8]	262[8]	6,420[8]	New Caledonia
1,242[1]	2,550[1]	838,656[1,15]	569	314	255	5,320	16,689	9,482	7,207	New Zealand
...	...	...	770[3]	755[3]	15[3]	391[11]	1,572[3]	425[3]	1,147[3]	Nicaragua
283	25,300	6,763	621[6]	598[6]	23[6]	297[6]	...	...	529[6]	Niger
3,583	28,200	1,123,891	484[6]	431[6]	53[6]	4,848[6]	...	11,502[6,8]	3,661[6]	Nigeria
...	...	...	9[6]	...	...	24[1]	...	...	...	Niue
1[1]	2,000[1]	919[1]	0.7[1]	—	0.7[1]	24[1]	2[1]	—	2[1]	Norfolk Island
2,723	1,540	1,803,593	245	156	89	10,731	36,836	18,392	18,444	Norway
70	21,400	35,813[24]	178[1]	11[1]	3,933[9]	1,459	3,334	1,317	2,017	Oman
...	...	...	...	...	...	...	...	...	...	Pacific Is., Trust Terr. of the Marshall Islands
...	...	...	...	...	...	...	...	...	...	Micronesia, Fed. States of
...	...	...	...	...	...	...	...	...	...	Northern Mariana Islands Palau
12,336	7,960	678,499[23]	3,521	3,240	281	7,180	...	87[12]	9,138	Pakistan
268	7,460	24,585	503	479	24	1,843	4,043	885	2,158	Panama
114	34,200	40,202[1]	41	25	16	1,360	3,072	1,746	1,326	Papua New Guinea

Communications (continued)

country	daily newspapers (latest) number	total circulation ('000)	circulation per 1,000 population	radio, 1988 transmitters (latest)	receivers (all types) ('000)	persons per receiver	television, 1988 transmitters (latest)	receivers (all types) ('000)	persons per receiver	telephones, 1987 receivers ('000)	persons per receiver	traffic ('000 calls) local	long-distance	international
Paraguay	4	123	32	48	753	5.4	5	350	12	100	40	352,360[8]		1,477
Peru	66	…	…	413	4,374	4.9	138	1,600[2]	13[2]	805	26	2,399,679[1,14]	215,238[1,14]	25,699[1,14]
Philippines	25	2,379	44	295	3,953	15	67	6,700	8.8	820[6]	67[6]	17,463[3]		7,804
Pitcairn Island	—	—	—	—	—	—	—	—	—	0.016	3.6	…	…	0.5
Poland	45	7,250	192	107	10,845	3.5	230	9,868	3.8	4,618	8.2	…	1,386,106	5,638
Portugal	30	…	…	92	2,173[2]	4.7[2]	23	1,618[2]	6.4[2]	2,072	5.0	8,068,762[8]		
Puerto Rico	5	599	183	68	2,000	1.7	19	830	4.0	907	3.6	1,882,523	162,810	4,022
Qatar	5	52	147	11	160	2.5	9	160	2.5	121	3.3	370,350		27,000[14]
Réunion	3	55	99	15	150	3.8	32	90	6.4	133	4.3	379,820[8]		…
Romania	36	3,109	137	91	3,150[2]	7.3[2]	344	3,801[2]	6.0[2]	1,963[6]	11[6]	…	…	…
Rwanda	1	…	…	8[32]	412	16	—	—	—	10	652	8,129[1,8]	487[1,14]	983[14]
St. Helena and Ascension	—	—	—	2	3.0	2.5	—	—	—	1.06	7.06	…	…	1,065[6,14]
St. Kitts and Nevis	—	—	—	1	23	1.9	1	7.0	6.2	3.86	126	…	…	353[6]
St. Lucia	—	—	—	3	99	1.5	…	5.0[1]	28[1]	14[1]	10[1]	13,073[3,8]		
St. Pierre and Miquelon	—	—	—	5	3.0	2.0	8	2.0	3.1	4.1	1.5	16,483[8]		
St. Vincent and the Grenadines	—	—	—	2	58	2.0	1	10	11	8.5[6]	13[6]	5,500[3,8]		1,169[6,14]
San Marino	—	—	—	1	13	1.8	…	6[1]	3.7[1]	14	1.6	6,910		3,604
São Tomé and Príncipe	—	—	—	5	30	3.9	…	…	…	2.6	44	2,710	71	34
Saudi Arabia	11	587	47	58	3,997	3.3	120	3,750	3.5	1,513	8.5	2,825,563[8]	287,158	57,589
Senegal	1	31	5	19	824	8.7	3	234	31	34[6]	192[6]	…	…	11,461[14]
Seychelles	2	7	104	1	27	2.4	7	5.5	12	13	5.0	18,125[8]		900[14]
Sierra Leone	1	10	3	4	936	4.1	2	34	114	15[1]	253[1]	…	…	1,025[14]
Singapore	7	701	268	21	746	3.5	8	538	4.9	1,164	2.3	3,420,000	30,800	30,797
Solomon Islands	—	—	…	5	65	4.6	…	…	…	5.5	54	7,308	522	126
Somalia	1	…	…	4	362	20	1	…	…	6.06	9716	…	…	…
South Africa	21	1,162	41	301	10,000[34]	3.6[34]	465	2,629[34]	14[34]	4,236	7.0	…	64,536	17,862
Bophuthatswana	—	—	—	16	[34]	[34]	9	[34]	[34]	32	59	…	126,211[8]	…
Ciskei	—	—	—	2	[34]	[34]	…	[34]	[34]	20	41	4,344[7,8]	1,281[7]	…
Transkei	—	—	—	14	[34]	[34]	6	6.0	619	…	…	…	…	…
Venda	—	—	—	6	[34]	[34]	…	[34]	[34]	…	…	…	…	…
South West Africa/Namibia	3	21	18	c. 40	220[2]	5.8[2]	13	25[1]	48[1]	66	18	…	22,555[14]	35,502[8]
Spain	106	2,970	76	264	11,820	3.4	1,027	14,871	2.6	15,477	2.5	13,445,364	3,311,651	117,299
Sri Lanka	15	850	53	59	2,721	6.1	12	500	33	133	124	660,000[6]		6,395[14]
Sudan, The	6	105	5	6	5,737	4.6	20	1,166	23	76	338	66,693	641	363
Suriname	2	…	…	14	248	1.7	6	40	11	39	11	133,419[8]		3,777[14]
Swaziland	2	16	24	8	115	6.3	11	13	58	21	34	60,274[14]	9,081[14]	1,146[1,14]
Sweden	186	4,902	586	355	7,272[2]	1.2[2]	845	3,292[2]	2.5[2]	7,410[3]	1.1[3]	27,276,300[8]		8,578,000[8]
Switzerland	102	3,229	491	196	2,554	2.6	1,077	2,316	2.9	9,283	0.7	1,515,650	1,364,803	920,430[14]
Syria	9	201	19	29	2,000[1]	5.3[1]	40	400[1]	27[1]	653	17	690,000	87,000[14]	15,800[14]
Taiwan	31	3,500	179	61	13,594	1.5	38	6,085[2]	3.2[2]	6,549	3.0	35,857,980	9,139	34,446
Tanzania	3	101	5	15	2,000	12	2	10	2,300	123	186	5,400[19]	4,400[19]	507
Thailand	31	…	…	207	9,567	5.7	48	4,819[1]	11[1]	1,000[1]	53[1]	1,626,789[8]	89,362	8,065
Togo	2	…	…	6	693	5.0	4	23	152	13[1]	263[1]	4,572[7,8]	437[14]	5,199[14]
Tokelau	—	—	—	…	…	…	…	…	…	0.003[7]	525[7]	…	…	…
Tonga	—	—	—	2	80	1.2	…	…	…	4.0[3]	243	1,566[3]	603	716[3]
Trinidad and Tobago	4	166	136	5	401	3.1	5	345	3.6	200	6.2	165,864	355,514	16,946
Tunisia	6	230	33	12	1,694	4.7	20	500[2]	15[2]	312	25	742,592[8]		545,049[8]
Turkey	338	4,188	81	55	7,093	7.8	325	8,075	6.8	4,827	11	12,664,509[8]		93,942[14]
Turks and Caicos Islands	—	—	—	2	4.0	2.0	…	…	…	1.66	5.26	4,564[6,8]		587[6,14]
Tuvalu	—	—	—	1	4.0	2.2	…	…	…	0.16	54	481[13]		17[13]
Uganda	2	49	3	8	345	46	9	90	178	59	266	78,034		274
U.S.S.R.	727	96,414	345	…	187,846	1.5	2,882	90,000	3.2	41,800	6.7	…	1,454,400[7]	4,965
United Arab Emirates	12	291	174	15[35]	378	4.7	15[35]	150	12	404	4.3	…	472,287[14]	135,435[14]
United Kingdom	107	25,159	443	705	57,456[2]	1.0[2]	1,643	18,953[2]	3.0[2]	29,518[3]	1.9[3]	20,448,200	5,830,800	302,800
United States	1,646	64,986	266	11,561	515,496	0.5	6,837	195,795	1.3	181,091[3]	1.3[3]	379,884,264	53,215,072	561,998
Uruguay	21	…	…	115	1,780	1.7	33	500	6.0	437	6.8	465,592	65,443	5,376
Vanuatu	—	—	—	5	20	7.5	…	…	…	7	21	12,000		200
Venezuela	61	2,739	163	221	8,026	2.3	63	2,760[2]	6.6[2]	1,677	11	9,659,732[14]	1,311,815[14]	73,132[14]
Vietnam	4	2,250	38	38	6,600[2]	10[2]	20	2,200[1]	30[1]	115[1]	537[1]	7,528[11]		1,239[1,14]
Virgin Islands (U.S.)	2	19	181	8	90	1.2	2	32	3.4	55	1.9	168,149[14]	8,216[14]	894[14]
Wallis and Futuna	—	—	—	1	…	…	2	…	…	0.34	45	16	1	27
West Bank	—	—	—	—	…	…	…	…	…	1.07	143[7]	…	…	…
Western Sahara	—	—	—	…	…	…	…	5.0[6]	32[6]	6.3[6]	25[6]	…	78[7]	208[7]
Western Samoa	—	—	—	8	72	2.3	5	47[2]	49[2]	16[3]	131[3]	40[7]	18[7]	71[7]
Yemen (Aden)	2	26	11	7	171	14	…	…	…	63[3]	104[3]	…	…	2,514
Yemen (Ṣanʿāʾ)	2	…	…	5	150	57	17	150[2]	57[2]	6,937	3.4	2,884	63,136	2,403
Yugoslavia	28	2,586	110	919	4,772[2]	4.9[2]	1,061	4,089[2]	5.7[2]	396[6]	791[6]	788[6]	1,020[6]	3,685[6]
Zaire	4	45	2	13	3,349	9.7	18	16	2,035	81	95	259[14]	2,517[14]	6,893[14]
Zambia	2	105	15	31	1,000[1]	7.0[1]	9	200	39	278	32	277,772[8]	481,916[8]	403,907[8]
Zimbabwe	3	191	23	73	421	23	14	137	71					

[1]1986. [2]1987. [3]1984. [4]1980. [5]1978. [6]1985. [7]1982. [8]Number of pulses ('000). [9]Number of words ('000). [10]1983. [11]1981. [12]Number of calls ('000). [13]Excludes transmitters of the BBC, "Deutsche Welle," and Voice of America. [14]Number of minutes ('000). [15]Excludes postcards. [16]Excludes small packets. [17]1977. [18]Excludes printed matter. [19]Operator-controlled calls only. [20]Netherlands Antilles includes Aruba. [21]Permanent post offices only. [22]1979. [23]Domestic and foreign sent only. [24]Foreign received and foreign sent only. [25]Excludes traffic to the U.S.

post offices, 1987			telegraph, 1987			telex, 1987				country
number	persons per office	pieces of mail handled ('000)	total traffic ('000)	national traffic ('000)	inter-national outgoing traffic ('000)	sub-scriber lines	traffic ('000 minutes) total	national	international outgoing	
383	10,200	6,424	333	264	69	988	1,161[1]	2,158[8]	1,346	Paraguay
2,633[1]	7,680[1]	53,307[1]	12,822[1]	12,779[1]	41	4,170[1]	28,512[1]	22,330[1]	6,182[1]	Peru
2,100	27,100	845,690[16,18]	13,457[3]	13,243[3]	214[3]	8,792[6]	11,782[3]	3,463[3]	7,435[6]	Philippines
1	60	...	...	...	...	...	...	...	...	Pitcairn Island
8,342	4,530	1,719,123	16,693	15,967	726	31,920	...	...	9,427	Poland
8,117	1,270	561,342	997	926	71	24,339	84,806	60,887	23,919	Portugal
124[5]	24,700[5]	...	...	...	...	...	...	...	...	Puerto Rico
25	10,000	31,970[24]	107	8	99	1,033	2,658	910	1,748	Qatar
50[5]	10,340[5]	...	28	24	4	664	1,543	1,277	266	Réunion
5,046[5]	4,430[5]	795,199[17]	5,393[22]	5,150[22]	243[22]	6,750[11]	...	...	3,683[11]	Romania
27	239,000	16,489	17	15	2	100	625[11]	522[11]	255	Rwanda
10	600	100	4.6[6]	...	4.6[6]	116	...	...	416	St. Helena and Ascension
9[5]	5,000[5]	6,381[5]	...	10[6]	172[6,9]	59[6]	...	...	118[6]	St. Kitts and Nevis
54	1,850	3,804	19[11]	—	285[6,9]	166[1]	...	...	233[6]	St. Lucia
...	...	1,714[16,17]	0.9	0.8	0.1	47	86	58	28	St. Pierre and Miquelon
51	2,530	...	...	...	208[6,9]	93[6]	...	...	127[6]	St. Vincent and the Grenadines
10	2,350	...	6.2	5.0	1.2	105	135	10	125	San Marino
11	10,900	222	2.9	0.4	2.5	39	86	0.6	85	São Tomé and Príncipe
443	15,800	477,066	1,466	859	607	14,962	12,637[12]	6,818[12]	5,819[12]	Saudi Arabia
136[21]	49,700[21]	44,391[10]	413	287	126	1,094	...	...	2,311	Senegal
98[1,21]	38,500[1,21]	29,986	...	...	6.7	188	389	104	285	Seychelles
133	19,800	378,488[1]	...	204	13	310	584	44	540	Sierra Leone
113	2,610	1,894	256	9.5	246	17,949	61,969	31,835	30,134	Singapore
...	...	...	10.1	7.6	2.5	119	264[6]	15[6]	226	Solomon Islands
...	...	...	...	...	...	...	...	...	...	Somalia
2,227[5,34]	13,500[5,34]	1,678,751[5,34]	8,007	7,748	259	33,537	...	254,233[8]	13,999	South Africa
34	34	34	34	34	34	...	...	...	...	Bophuthatswana
34[3,34]	34	34	34	34	34	...	...	...	...	Ciskei
34	34	34	34	34	34	...	...	...	...	Transkei
34	34	34	34	34	34	...	...	...	...	Venda
81[5]	12,914[5]	...								South West Africa/Namibia
12,985	2,960	4,434,262	5,590	5,321	269	41,956	119,755	71,057	48,698	Spain
3,789	4,320	574,612	...	1,870[7]	146[1]	1,439	1,826[3,12]	252[3,12]	5,005	Sri Lanka
782	30,900	32,632[16]	...	...	...	775[7]	...	...	1,379[7]	Sudan, The
...	...	...	62[3]	6[3]	56[6]	345	1,361[1]	84	1,209[1]	Suriname
69	9,800	10,295	35	33	2.2	353	776	274	502	Swaziland
4,877	1,730	3,541,873[26]	218	104	114	19,660	44,097	15,627	28,470	Sweden
3,774	1,750	4,579,510	1,637[1]	1,018[1]	619[1]	40,129[1]	159,146[1]	85,320[1]	73,826[1]	Switzerland
570	19,200	23,208	224	155	69	2,402	...	...	1,819	Syria
12,553[1]	1,540[1]	1,446,694[1]	885	799	86	...	...	...	...	Taiwan
795	30,200	172,439	1,222	1,200	22	1,327	6,800	3,100	3,700	Tanzania
3,996	13,500	451,000	7,967	7,878	89	6,164	12,657	4,842	7,815	Thailand
389[1]	8,100[1]	...	84	45	39	487	933	284	649	Togo
...	...	...	...	...	...	...	...	...	...	Tokelau
...	...	...	153[3]	82[3]	71[3]	80[6]	...	...	89[6]	Tonga
230	5,290	16,723[23]	...	217[7]	...	267[10]	...	...	1,053[10]	Trinidad and Tobago
593[1]	12,000[1]	179,726[1]	451	373	78	2,898	7,431	2,757	4,674	Tunisia
38,445[21]	1,370[21]	1,226,816	6,662	6,570	92	20,491	...	158,498[8]	20,715	Turkey
7	1,360	371[15,16]	...	0.1[6]	40[6,9]	70[6]	...	...	90[6]	Turks and Caicos Islands
8	1,030	115[24]	74[9]	24[9]	50[9]	5	...	...	30	Tuvalu
361	36,000	13,592	...	44	212[9]	880	262[10,12]	114[10,12]	122[12]	Uganda
98,445	2,890	61,788,000[23]	541,012[7]	540,110[7]	902[7]	1,704[6]	...	...	9,581[3]	U.S.S.R.
155	10,500	235,464	439	64	375	6,262	17,815	8,032	9,782	United Arab Emirates
21,071	2,680	14,068,100	2,836[10]	886[10]	836[1]	111,505[1]	218,746[10,12]	110,296[10,12]	345,095[1]	United Kingdom
40,030	5,660	153,360,253[23]	19,314	17,066	2,248	78,421	...	...	156,463	United States
1,277[5]	2,320[5]	35,356[17]	1,164	1,120	44	1,881	2,822	150	2,672	Uruguay
6[10]	20,800[10]	3,000[10]	...	...	3.5	98[1]	264[1]	23[1]	240[1]	Vanuatu
662	27,600	66,725[16]	3,244[6]	2,928[6]	316[6]	18,327	208,546	199,433	9,112	Venezuela
...	...	...	...	51[1]	275[1]	...	...	10[11,12]	788[1]	Vietnam
5[5]	23,200[5]	...	...	...	...	22	...	...	194	Virgin Islands (U.S.)
2	6,800	282	5.4	0.3	5.1	4	...	...	20	Wallis and Futuna
...	...	...	...	...	...	...	...	...	...	West Bank
47[6]	3,330[6]	2,087[6,15,24]	...	...	...	...	...	...	...	Western Sahara
120	19,500	3,106	...	177	...	...	...	...	...	Western Samoa
						100[6]	371[7]	47	433[6]	Yemen (Aden)
143	64,900	17,081	...	...	50	1,009	576	120	456	Yemen (Şan'ā')
3,892[1]	6,000[1]	1,232,839[1]	12,388[1]	11,504[1]	884[1]	12,999[1]	...	298,733[1,8]	17,344[1]	Yugoslavia
365	95,900	25,505	53[6]	43[6]	10[6]	1,697[6]	2,068[6]	66[6]	2,002[6]	Zaire
422[1]	15,200[1]	28,160[1]	19,999[1]	18,882[9]	1,109[9]	1,708	5,036	3,510	1,526	Zambia
311	24,300	192,728	542	514	28	2,480	6,901	5,052	1,849	Zimbabwe

[26]Domestic only. [27]Includes overseas departments. [28]Excludes foreign armed services network transmitters. [29]Excludes traffic to the U.K. [30]Excludes Voice of America transmitters. [31]Excludes Rodriguez. [32]Excludes transmitters of "Deutsche Welle." [33]Excludes transmitters of Transworld Radio and "Radio Nederland." [34]South Africa includes Bophuthatswana, Ciskei, Transkei, and Venda. [35]Abu Dhabi only.

Trade: external

The following table presents comparative data on the international, or foreign, trade of the countries of the world. The table analyzes data for both imports and exports in two ways: (1) into several major commodity groups defined in accordance with the United Nations system called the Standard International Trade Classification (SITC) and (2) by direction of trade for each country with major world trading blocs and partners. These commodity groupings are defined by the SITC code numbers beneath the column headings. The single-digit numbers represent broad SITC categories (in the SITC, called "sections"); the double-digit numbers represent subcategories ("divisions") of the single-digit categories (27 is a subcategory of 2), the three-digit is a subcategory ("group") of the double-digit (667 is a subcategory of 66). Where a plus or minus sign is used before one of these SITC numbers, the SITC category or subcategory is being added to or subtracted from the aggregate implied by the total of the preceding sections. The SITC commodity aggregations used here are listed in the table at the end of this headnote. The full SITC commodity breakdown—some 3,118 basic headings—is presented in the 1986 United Nations publication *Standard International Trade Classification, Revision 3* (though many countries still report according to revision 2).

The SITC was developed by the United Nations through its Statistical Commission as an outgrowth of the need for a standard system of aggregating commodities of external trade to provide international comparability of foreign trade statistics. All member nations of the United Nations are urged to use the SITC system as far as possible in reporting their external trade statistics. The United Nations Statistical Commission has defined external merchandise trade as "all goods whose movement into or out of the customs area of a country compiling the statistics adds to or subtracts from the material resources of the country." Goods passing through a country for transport only are excluded, but goods entering for reexport, or deposited (as in a bonded warehouse, or free trade area) for reimport, are included. Statistics in this table refer only to goods and exclude purely financial transactions that are covered in the "Finance" and "National product and accounts" tables.

For purposes of comparability of data, total value of imports and exports is given in this table in U.S. dollars; conversions from other currencies are determined according to International Monetary Fund (IMF) average rates for the year for which data are supplied. The commodity categories are given in terms of percentages of the total value of the country's import or export trade (with the exclusions noted above). Value is based on transaction value: for imports, the value at which the goods were

Trade: external

country	year	imports total value U.S.$ (000,000)	food and agricultural raw materials (0+1+2−27−28+4)	mineral ores and concentrates (27+28+667)	fuels and other energy (3)	manufactured goods total[a] (5+6−667+7+8+9)	of which chemicals and related products (5)	of which machinery and transport equipment (7)	of which other[a] (6−667+8+9)	from EEC[b]	from United States	from U.S.S.R. and Eastern Europe[c]	from Japan	from all other[d]
Afghanistan	1987[1]	1,025.6	16.4[2]	0.5[2]	18.0[2]	65.1[2]	4.5[2]	24.8[2]	35.8[2]	7.1	0.8	39.3	12.7	40.1
										28.0	4.3	42.4	0.1	25.2
Albania	1983[3]	274.3	...	...	33.3[2]	...	16.6[2]	22.2[2]	23.4	60.3	7.0	3.7	3.9	25.0
Algeria	1987	7,028.7	31.0	1.0	2.3	65.7	13.7	28.6	23.4	0.1[7]	77.6[7]	—[7]	9.7[7]	12.7[7]
American Samoa	1985[4]	296.2	53.7	0.1[5]	16.4	29.9[6]	0.9	7.5	21.5[6]	84.9	2.8	0.2	6.3	5.9
Andorra	1987	700.4	—28.3[5]—		3.7	68.0[6]	7.3	19.9	40.8[8]					
Angola	1981	1,678.4	31.7	0.2	0.8	67.3	12.1	20.9	34.3	56.8	9.8	5.2	4.5	23.7
Anguilla	1987	10.3	...	...										
Antigua and Barbuda	1984	131.9	24.6	...	25.0	50.4	6.4	21.8	22.2	10.6	37.8	—	—	51.6
Argentina	1987	5,817.8	8.8	3.5	11.5	76.2	20.0	37.8	18.4	31.8	16.4	2.7	7.6	41.5
Aruba	1986	191.9	32.9	0.1	3.0	64.0	9.2	14.6	40.2	25.4	37.4	0.1	3.3	33.8
Australia	1987	26,914.5	7.8	1.0	4.9	86.3	9.9	40.2	36.2	23.4	21.1	0.3	19.3	36.0
Austria	1987	32,674.2	9.6	1.6	7.2	81.6	10.3	34.7	36.5	68.0	3.5	6.8	4.4	17.4
Bahamas, The	1986	3,288.9	6.4	0.1	73.7	19.8	4.0	6.1	9.7	15.2	25.3	0.1	0.9	58.5
Bahrain	1987	2,713.6	10.1	0.3	53.4	36.2	5.6	13.5	17.0	24.3[3]	8.3[3]	...	4.8[3]	62.6[3]
Bangladesh	1987	2,572.7	33.2	1.0	13.8	52.0	8.3	17.2	26.5	13.1	9.1	2.8	12.0	63.0
Barbados	1986	593.2	17.6	0.5	10.2	71.6	8.7	35.9	27.0	20.6	40.0	0.1	5.6	33.7
Belgium[8]	1988	92,104.4	13.8	9.5	7.2	69.5	11.5	23.7	34.3	73.1	4.3	2.0	2.4	23.7
Belize	1986	122.0	27.4	0.1	13.9	58.6	8.4	18.0	32.2	16.4	57.4	0.1	2.4	23.7
Benin	1982	475.5	25.4	0.4	4.7	69.4	5.3	22.2	41.9	60.5	5.1	2.3	5.5	26.7
Bermuda	1985	402.5	20.5	0.1	14.3	65.1	9.2	19.9	36.0	16.5	60.1	0.2	3.4	19.8
Bhutan	1983	39.0[9]	14.5	0.3	21.4	63.9	3.4	29.7	30.8	12.0	0.3		4.6	83.1[10]
Bolivia	1985	693.0	19.5[12]	0.3[12]	0.5[12]	79.7[12]	12.7[12]	41.0[12]	26.0[12]	17.4	20.3	...	9.6	52.8
Botswana	1984	706.8	20.8	1.9	10.3	67.1	6.8	29.2	31.0		1.9	...	0.3	97.8[13]
Brazil	1987	16,578.6	10.4	2.9	32.5	54.2	15.6	26.0	12.5	21.9	20.7	2.8	5.7	49.0
British Virgin Islands	1982	58.5	28.2	0.4	10.6	60.8	4.3	33.0	23.6	7.8	42.9	—	0.1	49.2
Brunei	1985	610.5	20.8	0.9	1.8	76.5	7.2	34.1	35.2	17.6	15.7	—	19.9	46.8
Bulgaria	1987	16,210.9	8.6	—40.5[16]—		50.9[17]	5.8	39.7	5.4[17]	9.8	0.7	77.0	1.0	11.5
Burkina Faso	1985	325.5	—39.8[5]—		12.8	47.3[6]	10.1	19.6	17.6[6]	37.9	15.0	0.5	2.9	43.7
Burundi	1987	211.5	9.9	1.6	9.7	78.9	11.1	31.1	36.7	51.7	1.6	1.2	8.1	37.5
Cameroon	1987	1,749.0	15.0	2.1	1.4	81.5	14.8	35.8	30.9	64.7	3.5	1.4	8.2	22.2
Canada	1987	87,577.9	7.9	2.0	4.9	85.3	6.1	54.7	24.4	11.6	68.1	0.3	6.5	13.5
Cape Verde	1984		—36.1[5]—		12.7	51.2[6]	6.3	20.4	24.5[6]	70.1	2.1	3.3	1.7	22.8
Cayman Islands	1987	195.1	—22.1[5]—		9.4	68.5[6]	5.9	29.4	33.2[6]	8.9	74.0		4.3	12.9
Central African Republic	1984	87.4	—29.1[5]—		22.0	48.9[6]	6.0	30.4	12.6[6]	59.3	4.6	...	5.3	30.8
Chad	1984	181.4	15.9[21]	0.6[21]	14.2[21]	69.3[21]	16.4[21]	28.8[21]	24.1[21]	39.3[3]	11.2[3]	...	0.1[3]	49.4[3]
Chile	1986	2,964.0	8.4	1.3	14.9	75.4	16.4	35.7	23.3	22.7	21.6	0.3	10.0	45.3
China	1988	55,250.7	15.8	1.0[5]	1.4	81.8[6]	16.5	30.2	35.1[6]	14.7	12.0	7.0	20.0	46.2
Christmas Island	...	...	...	...	...	...	...	...	...	...	...	...	...	...
Cocos (Keeling) Islands	...	...	...	...	...	...	...	...	...	...	...	...	...	...
Colombia	1986	3,852.1	12.7	1.1	4.0	82.2	22.0	36.7	23.5	23.2	36.1	1.6	9.1	30.1
Comoros	1985	36.7	—47.1[5,22]—		13.1[22]	39.8[6,22]	3.5[22]	17.6[22]	18.8[6,22]	53.2[3]	3.4[3]	—	0.8[3]	42.6[3]
Congo	1985	580.2	19.5	0.5	3.1	76.8	8.4	35.4	33.0	72.1	6.6	1.1	3.4	16.7
Cook Islands	1987	33.7	—29.3[5]—		11.4	59.3[6]	7.0	18.3	34.0[6]	7.2[24]	4.2[24]	—24	10.4[24]	78.1[24]
Costa Rica	1984	1,086.2	11.4	0.7	15.3	72.5	22.9	20.3	29.3	14.0	36.2	0.3	7.5	41.9
Côte d'Ivoire	1985	1,733.8	18.2	0.7	22.0	59.1	12.8	22.2	24.0	54.1	6.9	1.1	5.0	33.0
Cuba	1986	9,172.9	14.0	0.3[5]	33.5	52.2[6]	5.7	30.8	15.7	6.2	—	82.4	3.5	7.8
Cyprus	1987	1,479.9	15.2	0.7	12.3	71.8	9.6	24.5	37.7	56.9	4.5	5.9	10.2	22.4
Czechoslovakia	1987	23,290.1	10.2	3.2	27.9	58.7	6.7	35.7	16.3	10.6	0.2	74.2	0.4	14.6
Denmark	1987	25,348.2	16.0	0.5	7.9	75.5	10.9	29.9	34.7	51.9	5.1	2.5	4.4	36.1
Djibouti	1985	200.7	43.9	0.9	9.8	45.4	5.8	19.9	19.8	52.2[24]	1.8[24]	—24	7.6[24]	38.4[24]
Dominica	1987	66.4	28.3	0.2	6.6	64.9	13.8	18.6	32.5	24.1	20.4	0.1	...	55.4
Dominican Republic	1985	1,247.9	13.7	0.3	35.2	50.7	11.7	23.2	15.9	10.3	34.7	—	6.3	48.6
Ecuador	1984	1,715.7	15.4	0.8	1.6	82.2	21.0	35.3	26.0	18.5	30.8	1.1	14.1	35.5
Egypt	1987	16,225.8	32.7	0.8	2.8	63.8	12.1	28.5	23.1	41.2	13.7	9.5	6.4	29.2
El Salvador	1984	1,314.0	14.5	0.4	37.8	47.3	16.9	10.5	19.8	7.6	23.9	0.2	3.1	65.1
Equatorial Guinea	1984	25.0	—28.6[5]—		20.1	51.3[6]	4.3	25.4	21.6[6]	73.8[3]	0.7[3]	—3	0.8[3]	24.7[3]
Ethiopia	1985	988.6	32.8	0.3	14.8	52.2	7.4	28.7	16.1	35.6	16.1	20.0	6.0	22.3
Faeroe Islands	1987	513.3	11.6	0.5	6.3	81.6	3.6	50.9	27.1	49.1	1.5	0.8	3.9	44.7
Falkland Islands	1986	13.9	...	...		...			...	100.0	—		—	—
Fiji	1986	436.0	18.0	0.3	16.6	65.1	8.4	23.5	33.2	11.5	4.8	0.2	14.4	69.1

purchased by the importer plus the cost of transportation and insurance to the frontier of the importing country (c.i.f. [cost, insurance, and freight] valuation); for exports, the value at which the goods were sold by the exporter, including the cost of transportation and insurance to bring the goods onto the transporting vehicle at the frontier of the exporting country (f.o.b. [free on board] valuation).

The largest part of the information presented here comes from the United Nations' *Commodity Trade Statistics* (including microfiche format) and *International Trade Statistics Yearbook*. These publications, however, cannot always provide the most recent data for all countries listed in this table and must be supplemented by national and regional sources.
a. Also includes any unallocated commodities.
b. EEC of 12 countries (Belgium, Denmark, France, West Germany, Greece, Ireland, Italy, Luxembourg, The Netherlands, Portugal, Spain, and the United Kingdom).
c. Includes Albania, Bulgaria, Czechoslovakia, East Germany, Hungary, Poland, and Romania.
d. May include value of trade shown as not available (...) in any of the four preceding columns.
... Not available.

— None, less than 0.05%, or not applicable.
Detail may not add to 100.0 or indicated subtotals because of rounding.

SITC category codes:

0	food and live animals.
1	beverages and tobacco.
2	crude materials, inedible, except fuels.
27	crude fertilizers and crude minerals (excluding coal, petroleum, and precious stones).
28	metalliferous ores and metal scrap.
3	mineral fuels, lubricants, and related materials (including coal, petroleum, natural gas, and electric current).
4	animal and vegetable oils, fats, and waxes.
5	chemicals and related products not elsewhere specified.
6	manufactured goods classified chiefly by material.
667	pearls, precious and semiprecious stones, unworked or worked.
7	machinery and transport equipment.
8	miscellaneous manufactured articles.
9	commodities and transactions not classified elsewhere.

exports total value U.S.$ (000,000)	food and agricultural raw materials (0+1+2 −27 −28 +4)	mineral ores and concentrates (27+28 +667)	fuels and other energy (3)	manufactured goods total [a] (5+6 −667 +7+8 +9)	of which chemicals and related products (5)	of which machinery and transport equipment (7)	of which other [a] (6 −667 +8+9)	to EEC [b]	to United States	to U.S.S.R. and Eastern Europe [c]	to Japan	to all other [d]	country
511.9	44.4[2]	—[2]	39.3[2]	16.3[2]	1.7[2]	—[2]	14.6[2]	10.1	0.8	73.3	0.2	15.7	Afghanistan
252.4	...	26.2[2]	40.3[2]	...	...	...	...	22.9	1.5	43.6	4.8	27.2	Albania
8,185.9	0.4	0.4	97.5	1.7	0.8	0.3	0.7	71.0	19.2	0.6	1.5	7.7	Algeria
200.6	100.0	—	—	—	—	—	—		98.2	—	1.5	0.3	American Samoa
24.6	29.6[5]		—	70.4[6]	7.2	10.9	52.4[6]	99.9	—	—	—	0.1	Andorra
1,874.5	5.4	12.1	82.1	0.4	—	—	0.4	26.6	37.2	2.0	1.3	32.9	Angola
1.4	...							...	...	...	...	...	Anguilla
17.6	6.2	—	11.5	82.3	7.5	30.1	44.7	3.4	17.9	—	—	78.7	Antigua and Barbuda
6,360.2	64.6	0.4	1.5	33.5	6.4	6.4	20.7	28.2	14.6	13.0	3.5	40.6	Argentina
23.7	44.0	1.0	0.1	54.9	6.0	10.3	38.6	3.3	3.8	—	0.2	92.8	Aruba
26,486.1	37.3	13.3	19.1	30.3	2.0	7.2	21.1	15.1	9.4	2.7	24.0	48.8	Australia
27,171.0	7.9	0.9	1.8	89.4	9.0	33.4	47.0	63.4	3.6	9.0	1.2	22.9	Austria
2,701.6	1.3	0.4	87.5	10.7	9.9	0.5	0.4	1.8	88.8	—	2.0	7.5	Bahamas, The
2,384.3	0.3	0.2	85.3	14.2	2.2	0.5	11.5	5.9[3]	2.7[3]	...	11.7[3]	79.6[3]	Bahrain
1,194.5	25.2	—	1.3	73.6	0.3	1.4	71.9	24.1	31.9	4.8	5.5	33.6	Bangladesh
277.4	15.6	0.4	16.2	67.8	5.4	47.7	14.7	13.7	44.8	1.4	1.2	39.0	Barbados
91,957.4	11.4	7.6	3.5	77.5	14.1	25.7	37.8	74.2	5.0	1.2	1.2	18.4	Belgium[8]
92.6	69.7	—	2.9	27.4	0.9	3.6	23.0	28.4	56.5	1.0	0.1	14.1	Belize
42.6	48.4	—	3.9	47.7	0.4	3.7	43.5	32.9	—	—	6.9	60.2	Benin
23.1	1.8	—	—	98.2	57.1	1.2	39.9	34.2	22.8	—	—	43.0	Bermuda
13.9[9]	32.1	—	—	67.9	16.5	—	51.4	0.4	—	—	0.2	99.4[11]	Bhutan
672.5	4.9	17.9	55.7	21.5	—	—	21.5	20.9	14.1	2.8	0.4	61.7	Bolivia
673.9	10.2	80.2	—	9.5	0.5	2.3	6.7	...	8.2	...	0.1	91.8[14]	Botswana
26,225.0	39.5[15]	7.5[15]	6.3[15]	46.7[15]	6.6[15]	15.2[15]	24.9[15]	26.9[15]	27.2[15]	4.0[15]	5.5[15]	36.4[15]	Brazil
1.2	78.1	2.7	1.5	17.7	0.1	10.2	7.4	4.6	57.4	—	—	38.0	British Virgin Islands
2,972.0	0.2	—	98.5	1.3	0.1	0.8	0.4	0.1	7.3	—	61.2	31.4	Brunei
15,905.1	16.2	7.1[16]		76.7[17]	4.9	60.6	11.2[17]	4.9	0.1	79.9	0.2	14.9	Bulgaria
69.4	72.7[5]		—	27.3[6]	0.3	2.4	24.5[6]	41.6	0.1	—	2.0	56.3	Burkina Faso
84.3	82.8	—	—	17.2	—	—	17.2	61.9[18]	5.2[18]	—[18]	1.5[18]	31.5[18]	Burundi
829.4	55.6	0.2	17.5	26.7	2.4	9.9	14.4	68.3	7.2	1.6	1.2	21.7	Cameroon
94,402.4	20.1	4.5	10.0	65.3	5.0	38.1	22.3	7.4	75.5	0.8	5.4	10.9	Canada
49.7	4.5	0.5	86.1	8.9	—	7.3	1.6	2.5	—	—	—	97.5[19]	Cape Verde
2.2	2.1[20]	2.2[20]	—[20]	95.8[20]	94.1[20]	0.5[20]	1.2[20]	—[20]	100.0[20]	—[20]	—[20]	—[20]	Cayman Islands
84.7	62.5[5]		—	36.7[6]	0.7	—	36.7[6]	77.2	0.9	...	0.1	21.8	Central African Republic
131.3	83.1[21]	0.8[21]	7.9[21]	8.2[21]	0.5[21]	—	5.4[21]	64.4[3]	0.1[3]	...	4.3[3]	31.3[3]	Chad
4,165.5	37.7	20.5	0.1	41.7	2.5	1.6	37.7	34.7	20.0	1.0	10.2	34.0	Chile
47,540.3	20.1	1.9[5]	8.4	69.6[6]	6.1	5.8	57.7[6]	9.9	7.1	6.5	16.7	59.8	China
...	...	...	...	...	...	...	...	...	...	...	...	...	Christmas Island
...	...	...	...	...	...	...	...	...	...	...	...	...	Cocos (Keeling) Islands
5,107.9	71.1	0.8	13.0	15.0	2.7	1.2	11.1	39.7	30.0	3.5	4.9	22.0	Colombia
15.7	64.5[23]	—[23]	—[23]	35.5[23]	18.1[23]	—[23]	17.4[23]	53.6[3]	39.7[3]	...	...	6.6[3]	Comoros
1,087.2	3.1	1.1	93.3	2.5	—	0.2	2.3	34.5	60.0	0.2	...	5.2	Congo
7.1	24.3	—	—	75.7	0.1	4.4	71.2	1.8	0.1	—	9.5	88.5	Cook Islands
951.3	74.0	—	1.9	24.1	6.3	3.1	14.6	25.6	37.6	3.3	0.5	32.9	Costa Rica
2,670.0	79.8	0.1	9.7	10.3	2.5	1.8	6.1	57.5	12.6	5.8	1.1	22.9	Côte d'Ivoire
6,297.6	86.2	6.3[5]	5.0	2.5[6]	0.4	0.7	1.4[6]	4.6	—	86.8	2.1	6.5	Cuba
619.9	33.2	2.0	5.2	59.6	4.7	9.8	45.2	41.0	1.8	5.0	0.5	51.6	Cyprus
23,012.5	5.3	0.3	3.6	90.9	6.4	55.2	29.3	9.7	0.4	73.7	0.3	15.9	Czechoslovakia
24,708.3	34.9	0.6	3.0	61.5	9.1	24.2	28.1	46.8	7.0	1.4	3.7	41.1	Denmark
14.0	6.1[25]	—[25]		93.9[25]	0.1[25]	—	1.4[25]	42.1[20]	5.9[20]	0.1[20]	—[20]	52.0[20]	Djibouti
48.0	72.9	—	—	27.1	18.2	0.1	8.9	67.7	2.8	—	—	29.4	Dominica
738.5	75.7[24]	0.3[24]	—[24]	24.1[24]	4.0[24]	4.5[24]	15.6[24]	13.4	77.1	3.0	2.4	4.2	Dominican Republic
2,582.5	29.6	—	69.6	0.8	0.3	—	0.5	3.5	64.1	0.7	0.7	31.0	Ecuador
4,351.5	21.8	0.2	35.7	42.3	2.1	0.1	40.1	37.9	7.7	22.0	2.2	30.3	Egypt
615.0	70.4	0.3	2.7	26.7	6.0	1.6	19.1	24.4	34.9	2.5	5.4	32.8	El Salvador
23.5	76.5[5]		0.2	23.3[6]	0.1	0.5	22.7[6]	83.8[3]	2.3[3]	—[3]	1.1[3]	12.8[3]	Equatorial Guinea
337.5	88.9	0.2	9.8	1.1	0.6	—	0.5	48.9	10.5	8.7	10.3	21.7	Ethiopia
344.7	80.0	—	—	20.0	—	19.9	0.1	76.7	10.2	0.6	2.0	10.5	Faeroe Islands
17.9[26]	100.0	—	—	—	—	—	—	100.0	—	—	—	—	Falkland Islands
276.0	59.3	0.1	15.1	25.5	0.8	3.1	21.6	35.5	4.7	—	1.7	58.1	Fiji

Trade: external (continued)

country	year	imports total value U.S.$ (000,000)	food and agricultural raw materials (0+1+2−27−28+4)	mineral ores and concentrates (27+28+667)	fuels and other energy (3)	manufactured goods total[a] (5+6−667+7+8+9)	of which chemicals and related products (5)	of which machinery and transport equipment (7)	of which other[a] (6−667+8+9)	from European Economic Community (EEC)[b]	from United States	from U.S.S.R. and Eastern Europe[c]	from Japan	from all other[d]
Finland	1988	21,093.2	8.7	3.1	9.6	78.6	10.8	39.2	28.6	43.5	6.4	14.6	7.4	28.2
France[27]	1987	157,914.1	14.2	1.3	10.8	73.7	10.7	31.6	31.4	61.1	7.2	2.8	3.8	25.2
French Guiana	1987	394.4	22.4	0.1	10.1	67.4	5.9	31.9	29.6	74.9	4.3	0.4	3.2	17.3
French Polynesia	1983	538.3	21.4	0.3	11.9	66.3	5.3	30.1	30.9	57.9	15.8	0.1	4.3	21.9
Gabon	1983	685.6	18.5	1.0	1.8	78.8	7.5	38.5	32.7	74.6	11.0	0.4	7.4	6.6
Gambia, The	1987[28]	113.6	—34.8[5]—		7.1	58.1[6]	7.0	21.1	29.9[6]	55.6[3]	7.1[3]	3.3[3]	4.9[3]	29.0[3] 100.0[30]
Gaza Strip	1987	412.1	...	...	...	48.9	9.1	34.1	5.7	13.2[32]	0.3[32]	64.8[32]	0.8[32]	20.8[32]
Germany, East	1987	28,786.1	—51.1—							51.7	6.6	3.6	6.5	31.6
Germany, West[33]	1988	250,533.6	15.2	2.3	8.5	74.9	9.7	29.2	36.1	48.1	9.1	1.2	4.3	37.3
Ghana	1983	542.3	17.0	0.1	10.1	72.7	10.3	32.5	30.0					
Gibraltar	1988	257.9	—24.4[5]—		20.7	54.9[6]	4.3	21.4	29.2[6]	73.4[34]	5.4[34]	...[34]	10.4[34]	10.8[34]
Greece	1987	12,930.3	23.0	1.3	13.8	61.9	11.0	24.5	26.4	61.0	2.8	5.2	4.2	26.8
Greenland	1987	507.1	21.7	0.4	3.7	74.2	3.9	32.7	37.6	78.4	3.7	0.2	4.4	13.2
Grenada	1986	83.5	—35.5[2,5]—		13.3[2]	51.2[2,6]	10.0[2]	14.8[2]	26.4[2,6]	24.2	25.6	—	7.1	43.1
Guadeloupe	1987	1,040.2	24.2	0.2	4.7	70.9	9.2	29.6	32.0	80.1	3.3	0.4	2.7	13.6
Guam	1983	610.7	16.9	0.1	46.9	36.2	2.3	19.1	14.8		23.4		19.9	56.6
Guatemala	1984	1,472.2	8.9	0.2	33.0	57.8	21.7	15.2	20.9	12.0	28.8	0.4	4.6	54.2
Guernsey[36]	...	...	...	...	...	...	...	...	...	...	...	...	...	...
Guinea	1980	204.4	—10.0[5]—		30.3	59.7[6]	3.0	39.8	16.9[6]	71.0[3]	10.2[3]	5.8[3]	1.7[3]	11.3[3]
Guinea-Bissau	1984	38.7	20.1[23]	2.2[23]	6.2[23]	71.5[23]	5.6[23]	36.4[23]	29.5[23]	51.9	8.8	15.2	0.2	23.8
Guyana	1983	246.1	5.6	0.5	43.2	50.7	9.4	23.2	18.1	20.1	21.6	0.7	1.6	56.0
Haiti	1987[4]	406.9	—32.3[5]—		11.7	56.0[6]	10.3	18.3	27.4[6]	16.8[3]	45.6	0.3[3]	6.9	30.4[3]
Honduras	1985	873.7	9.7	0.3	25.9	64.2	17.6	21.4	25.2	12.9	32.9	0.3	5.9	48.0
Hong Kong	1988	63,937.3	11.0	3.0	1.9	84.1	8.9	28.8	46.4	10.4	8.5	0.4	18.8	61.9
Hungary	1987	9,855.6	12.2	1.6[5]		69.2[6]	15.0	30.7	23.4[6]	24.6	2.5	47.4	1.5	23.9
Iceland	1987	1,581.5	10.1	2.0	7.4	80.5	7.1	38.3	35.0	52.1	7.1	5.8	8.2	26.8
India	1987[1]	15,717.0	10.7	11.9	15.1	62.4	13.1	31.2	18.1	32.6	9.4	7.1	12.9	38.0
Indonesia	1988	13,248.5	13.0	2.5	7.2	77.2	19.2	38.5	19.6	18.9	13.1	0.8	25.6	41.6
Iran	1985	11,635.0	—20.9[5]—		2.1	77.1[6]	12.8	37.6	26.7[6]	38.5[3]	0.7[3]	7.2[3]	12.9[3]	40.8[3]
Iraq	1986	10,190.0	17.6[37]	0.2[37]	0.3[37]	81.9[37]	7.5[37]	39.8[37]	34.6[37]	31.4[37]	5.7[37]	3.4[37]	20.4[37]	39.1[37]
Ireland	1988	15,568.0	14.0	0.9	5.6	79.5	12.3	34.4	32.9	66.2	15.9	1.1	4.9	12.0
Isle of Man[36]	...	...	...	...	...	...	...	...	...	...	...	...	...	...
Israel	1988	12,870.0[38]	11.0	21.7	7.3	60.0	9.1	27.3	23.6	52.0	16.6	0.5	3.7	27.3
Italy[39]	1987	125,075.8	20.2	2.0	13.7	64.2	10.9	27.2	26.1	56.5	5.3	4.1	2.1	31.9
Jamaica	1988	1,434.6	20.9	0.1	13.6	65.3	11.4	21.3	32.7	15.3	48.1	0.8	3.5	32.3
Japan	1987	146,048.0	25.8	6.3	27.1	40.8	7.8	11.4	21.6	11.9	21.7	1.6	—	64.7
Jersey	1980	537.1	23.9	0.4	9.3	66.5	6.5	24.8	35.2	...	...	...	...	100.0[40]
Jordan	1987	2,705.2	21.1	1.3	17.2	60.5	10.0	20.5	30.0	31.4	10.2	5.3	6.1	47.1
Kampuchea (Cambodia)	...	...	...	...	...	...	...	...	...	...	...	...	...	...
Kenya	1987	1,739.3	9.5	0.5	20.1	70.0	17.8	34.3	17.8	43.5	7.1	0.5	10.9	38.1
Kiribati	1987	17.6	38.1	0.1	10.6	51.1	5.0	20.8	25.4		4.3	—	11.9	82.2
										8.3[3]	—[3]	56.0[3]	9.8[3]	25.9[3]
Korea, North	1987	2,500.0[3]	...	...	...	...	...	...	...	11.2	21.4	—	33.3	34.1
Korea, South	1987	41,017.2	14.5	4.3	14.7	66.5	11.2	34.4	20.9	31.3	12.3	1.0	23.6	31.8
Kuwait	1986	5,691.2	18.6	0.6	0.5	80.3	6.0	38.9	35.5	3.1[3]	—[3]	...	7.0[3]	89.8[3]
Laos	1986	205.0	32.1[43]	0.2[43]	11.2[43]	56.4[43]	6.1[43]	25.7[43]	24.7[43]					
Lebanon	1987	1,929.7[3]	—17.3[5,24]—		3.6[24]	79.1[6,24]	7.8[24]	29.3[24]	42.0[6,24]	40.6[3]	5.5[3]	...	3.1[3]	50.9[3]
Lesotho	1981	504.9	25.1	0.8[5]	9.6	64.5	6.4	17.0	41.1	1.5	0.2	...	...	98.2[44]
Liberia	1984	363.2	25.5	0.9	19.8	53.9	6.7	26.8	20.5	40.0	22.3	1.1	8.1	28.5
Libya	1982	7,175.5	17.1	0.4	1.4	81.1	3.9	36.8	40.4	63.5	4.2	5.4	5.1	21.9
Liechtenstein	1986	265.4	5.1	0.3[5]	0.4	94.3[6]	4.9	32.1	57.3[6]	...	...	...	...	...
Luxembourg	1986	4,020.2	13.2	3.4	10.1	73.3	14.2	24.5	34.6	91.4	2.2		0.6	5.7
Macau	1988	1,291.5	15.5	1.1	4.2	79.2	5.1	13.1	61.1	6.8	4.5	0.6	10.5	77.6
Madagascar	1986	373.6	17.0	0.4	23.1	59.5	11.7	28.8	19.0	48.6	10.7	10.3	6.5	23.8
Malawi	1984	270.1	—10.8[5]—		16.5	72.7[6]	22.0	23.3	27.3[6]	23.8	4.2	—	8.2	63.9
Malaysia	1988	16,576.5	12.3	2.1	5.3	80.3	11.2	44.6	24.4	13.4	17.7	0.5	23.4	45.1
Maldives	1985	52.7	37.4	1.8	15.5	45.4	7.3	17.5	20.6	10.4[3]	—[3]	—[3]	25.4[3]	64.1[3]
Mali	1982	401.8	21.3	0.7	27.5	50.4	9.2	18.4	22.8	43.8	2.4	0.9	1.3	51.6
Malta	1987	1,116.5	15.0	0.7	6.5	77.8	8.0	33.2	36.5	67.7	10.9	3.9	2.0	15.4
Martinique	1987	1,120.1	21.8	0.2	8.2	69.9	8.7	31.1	30.1	83.6	2.2	0.2	2.5	11.5
Mauritania	1984	246.0	30.3[23]	4.5[16,23]	14.0[23]	51.2[17,23]	4.3[23]	27.0[23]	19.9[23]	70.0[3]	8.6[3]	...	1.5[3]	19.9[3]
Mauritius	1987	1,012.8	15.7	1.5	7.5	75.3	6.4	22.1	46.8	64.0	1.7	...	9.8	24.4
Mayotte	1985	21.8	—34.0—		11.9	54.2	10.0	18.4	25.7	...	...	...	...	100.0[45]
Mexico	1985	16,151.8	16.6	2.6	4.4	76.5	13.9	43.5	19.2	11.8	69.6	0.3	5.2	13.1
Monaco[27]	...	...	...	...	...	...	...	...	...	...	...		96.7	3.3
Mongolia	1986	1,732.0[3]	9.7	—28.3[16]—		62.0[17]	6.8	36.1	19.1[17]	...	...	...	...	...
Montserrat	1987	25.2	27.9	0.1	8.3	63.6	6.2	28.0	29.4	19.6[47]	38.5[47]	—[47]	4.7[47]	37.1[47]
Morocco	1987	4,228.7	20.4	6.2	17.5	55.8	10.6	23.5	21.8	52.6	9.1	5.1	1.2	32.0
Mozambique	1984	487.2	—25.0[5]—		18.7	56.4[6]	4.6	17.3	34.4[6]	32.1	5.8	25.7	3.2	33.2
Myanmar (Burma)	1987[1]	552.3	—17.9—			82.1		49.9	...	23.1[3]	1.3[3]	11.7[3]	28.8[3]	35.2[3]
Nauru	1986[48]	10.7	—35.8[5]—		2.1	62.1	2.7	8.6	50.8[6]	...	...	...	...	...
Nepal	1985[28]	442.1	16.2	0.6	11.6	71.6	13.4	19.6	38.6	7.0	1.3	0.7	11.8	79.2
Netherlands, The	1988	99,801.7	18.2	1.8	9.4	70.6	10.5	29.0	31.1	63.7	7.5	2.1	3.2	23.6
Netherlands Antilles	1987[49]	1,501.8	7.6	0.1	69.9	22.4	3.1	8.1	11.2	48.0[24]	10.2[24]	0.1[24]	5.6[24]	36.1[24]
New Caledonia	1985	342.3	22.1	0.3[5]	25.1	52.5[6]	5.5	24.4	22.6[6]	23.1	16.1	0.3	18.8	41.8
New Zealand	1987	7,255.1	8.1	2.4	6.7	82.8	12.4	39.8	30.5	16.3	16.2	21.3	2.9	43.2
Nicaragua	1984	825.9	14.1	0.2	17.7	68.0	20.7	27.8	19.5	48.0	3.7	0.4	2.5	45.4
Niger	1981	509.7	24.8	1.9	14.8	58.4	6.9	25.7	25.8	56.4	8.3	5.0	9.0	21.3
Nigeria	1987	3,918.7	12.8	2.7	0.4	84.1	16.9	38.2	29.0	—	0.1	—	13.3	86.6
Niue	1985	1.9	40.5	0.1	19.9	39.5	3.7	19.6	16.2	...	...	...	...	100.0[50]
Norfolk Island	1987[28]	17.4	19.5	0.2	6.1	74.3	5.5	14.5	54.2	46.2	6.6	2.3	4.6	40.3
Norway	1988	23,186.6	8.6	4.6	3.6	83.2	8.2	39.6	35.4	31.6	8.8	0.1	16.8	42.6
Oman	1988	2,200.4	20.4	0.6	1.5	77.4	6.1	33.4	37.9	—[52]	34.7[52]	—[52]	25.2[52]	40.1[52]
Pacific Is., Trust Territory of the	1978[28]	38.9	—46.2[5]—		12.9	40.9[6]	4.8	12.5	23.5[6]		31.6	—	14.5	53.9
Marshall Islands	1983	17.5	—36.2[2,5]—		18.2[2]	45.5[2,6]	3.4[2]	9.7[2]	32.4[2,6]	...	...	...	...	...
Micronesia, Fed. States of	1986	40.4	—49.7[5]—		...	50.3[6]	6.2	12.6	31.5[6]	...	...	...	...	...

exports

total value U.S.$ (000,000)	food and agricultural raw materials (0+1+2-27-28+4)	mineral ores and concentrates (27+28+667)	fuels and other energy (3)	manufactured goods total[a] (5+6-667+7+8+9)	of which chemicals and related products (5)	of which machinery and transport equipment (7)	of which other[a] (6-667+8+9)	to European Economic Community (EEC)[b]	to United States	to U.S.S.R. and Eastern Europe[c]	to Japan	to all other[d]	country
21,720.8	13.9	0.4	1.7	84.0	5.7	27.4	50.9	44.2	5.8	16.4	1.8	31.8	Finland
143,401.5	18.3	0.9	2.3	78.5	14.3	35.4	28.8	60.4	7.3	2.2	1.5	28.6	France[27]
53.8	77.0	0.1	0.1	22.9	0.9	5.6	16.3	40.9	21.9	—	10.7	26.4	French Guiana
41.2	14.4	15.2	—	70.4	2.4	17.2	50.7	70.4	12.6	—	4.9	12.1	French Polynesia
1,475.4	7.5	7.0	79.5	6.0	1.2	0.6	4.1	54.6	25.6	1.8	0.3	17.6	Gabon
29.0	86.1[29]	—[29]	—[29]	13.9[29]	...	...	13.9[29]	36.6[3]	0.3[3]	...[3]	9.9[3]	53.3[3]	Gambia, The
157.1	...	...	...	...	...	...	...	...	...	...	...	100.0[31]	Gaza Strip
29,870.4		—23.5—		76.5	12.5	48.0	16.0	...[32]	...[32]	...[32]	...[32]	...[32]	Germany, East
323,333.5	6.2	0.8	1.2	91.8	13.6	48.1	30.1	54.3	8.0	3.5	2.3	31.9	Germany, West[33]
462.8	52.9	1.8	16.5	28.8	—	—	28.8	32.7	6.7	9.7	7.4	43.4	Ghana
82.1		—8.2[5]—	51.5	40.3[6]	2.8	18.1	19.4[6]	22.2	...	...	...	77.8[35]	Gibraltar
6,489.5	33.1	3.4	6.7	56.8	3.1	2.7	51.0	67.3	6.8	4.3	0.9	20.6	Greece
346.2	83.5	12.1	0.8	3.6	—	3.3	0.3	94.6	—	—	—	5.4	Greenland
28.7	84.5[2,29]	—[2,29]	—[2,29]	15.5[2,29]	—[2,29]	—[2,29]	15.5[2,29]	61.0	3.7	—	—	35.3	Grenada
91.7	78.2	0.3	0.2	21.3	3.0	9.8	8.5	68.7	0.4	—	—	30.9	Guadeloupe
39.2	23.5	2.7	3.5	70.3	5.6	11.5	53.2	...	24.9	...	4.8	70.4	Guam
1,094.6	73.9	0.2	2.4	23.5	9.8	1.1	12.6	15.0	38.3	0.1	4.5	42.1	Guatemala
466.7	3.0	96.8	...	0.2	—	—	0.2	45.4[3]	23.5[3]	21.4[3]	—[3]	9.6[3]	Guernsey[36]
18.9	87.1[23]	0.3[23]	—[23]	12.6[23]	0.3[23]	—[23]	12.3[23]	64.4	—	—	—	35.6	Guinea
													Guinea-Bissau
188.7	52.9	36.4	0.2	10.5	2.7	3.4	4.4	37.1	17.3	4.0	8.0	33.6	Guyana
210.6	37.1[12]	—[12]	—[12]	62.9[12]	3.2[12]	—[12]	59.7[12]	37.9[3]	52.7	0.1[3]	0.5	8.8[3]	Haiti
699.4	90.8	4.5	0.9	3.9	1.1	0.1	2.7	26.6	48.9	3.9	6.7	13.9	Honduras
63,175.4	6.3	1.6	0.4	91.6	5.8	26.9	58.9	15.9	24.8	0.3	5.9	53.2	Hong Kong
9,571.3	21.8	0.9[5]	4.2	73.1[6]	11.6	33.9	27.6[6]	20.0	3.0	50.1	0.7	26.2	Hungary
1,375.1	80.0	0.9	—	19.1	—	1.5	17.5	57.3	18.3	4.7	7.8	11.9	Iceland
9,738.7	27.9	21.8	3.4	47.0	3.9	6.7	36.4	22.0	18.7	18.6	10.7	30.0	India
19,218.5	23.9	3.5	40.2	32.4	1.8	0.7	29.9	11.2	16.0	0.6	41.7	30.5	Indonesia
13,328.0	...	...	98.0	...	...	...	2.0	35.5[3]	5.2[3]	5.2[3]	17.2[3]	36.9[3]	Iran
16,575.7	0.4	—	99.6[3]	—	—	—	—	37.4[3]	5.7[3]	0.2[3]	11.7[3]	45.0[3]	Iraq
18,738.4	27.6	2.3	0.5	69.5	12.8	31.2	25.5	74.2	7.7	0.5	1.9	15.7	Ireland
...	...	...	...	...	...	...	...	...	...	...	...	...	Isle of Man[36]
9,605.6	11.6	30.6	0.6	57.3	14.0	25.4	17.8	33.2	30.7	0.3	6.7	29.1	Israel
116,602.1	7.7	0.4	2.4	89.5	7.5	34.8	47.1	56.1	9.6	3.1	1.6	29.6	Italy[39]
833.5	25.5	50.3	2.3	22.0	2.5	2.4	17.1	30.2	36.5	3.9	1.0	28.3	Jamaica
229,054.5	1.3	0.2	0.4	98.2	5.0	70.6	22.6	16.6	36.8	1.4	—	45.2	Japan
209.2	27.6	4.3[41]	—	68.0	1.2	31.1	35.7	...	...	...	...	100.0[42]	Jersey
927.6	13.2	28.8	0.2	57.8	22.4	13.5	21.9	8.3	1.9	5.5	2.7	81.7	Jordan
...	...	...	...	...	...	...	...	...	...	...	...	...	Kampuchea (Cambodia)
960.1	70.1	2.5	13.1	14.4	4.1	2.5	7.8	42.4	5.4	0.9	0.9	50.4	Kenya
2.0	71.5	1.5	—	27.0	—	—	27.0	38.2	11.6	—	1.8	48.4	Kiribati
1,600.0[3]	...	...	...	...	...	...	...	7.0[3]	—[3]	48.4[3]	13.9[3]	30.6[3]	Korea, North
47,206.6	5.3	0.3	1.6	92.8	2.8	35.8	54.2	14.0	38.9	—	17.8	29.3	Korea, South
9,052.0	1.3	0.2	84.4	14.1	2.1	6.6	5.4	26.6[3]	3.6[3]	0.2[3]	13.8[3]	55.7[3]	Kuwait
58.0	84.0[43]	11.9[43]	—[43]	4.1[43]	—[43]	—[43]	4.1[43]	1.7[3]	0.5[3]	...	2.3[3]	95.5[3]	Laos
600.6[3]		—14.4[5,24]—	—[24]	85.6[6,24]	1.1[24]	18.2[24]	66.2[6,24]	15.2[3]	5.2[3]	...	0.3[3]	79.3[3]	Lebanon
49.6	28.8	42.6	0.1	28.5	0.9	3.3	24.3	10.3	0.1	...	...	89.6	Lesotho
449.1	34.1	64.8	—	1.1	0.1	0.3	0.8	70.5	20.2	1.9	1.3	6.1	Liberia
13,953.7	—	—	99.9	0.1	...	...	...	65.5[3]	3.5[3]	2.3[3]	0.3[3]	28.5[3]	Libya
688.8	0.3	0.15	0.2	99.5[6]	5.7	46.5	47.3[6]	40.1	...	...	...	59.9	Liechtenstein
3,720.5	6.7	1.1	0.2	92.0	18.2	13.2	60.6	79.3	5.2	...	0.1	15.4	Luxembourg
1,494.1	1.6	—	—	98.3	0.9	2.7	94.7	35.6	34.1	0.4	3.5	26.3	Macau
316.6	84.6	5.7	2.2	7.5	1.3	1.9	4.4	58.2	14.8	3.6	10.9	12.4	Madagascar
311.8		—95.1[5]—	4.9	[6]	0.5	1.7	2.7[6]	57.2	8.6	—	3.0	31.2	Malawi
21,129.4	37.3	1.0	15.9	45.8	2.2	28.3	15.3	14.4	17.4	0.9	17.0	50.4	Malaysia
23.0	67.4	0.1	—	32.5	—	—	32.5	3.4	24.3	—	10.1	62.2	Maldives
233.5	97.2	...	...	2.8	—	—	2.7	29.4	—	—	1.6	69.0	Mali
603.1	5.7	1.0	2.2	91.1	1.8	30.1	59.2	67.8	7.7	3.6	0.2	20.7	Malta
193.5	69.1	0.3	14.5	16.1	3.4	3.9	8.8	70.3	0.3	—	—	29.4	Martinique
297.3	50.2	49.1	—	0.7	—	—	0.7	64.7[3]	0.3[3]	...	12.5[3]	22.5[3]	Mauritania
934.5		—40.9—	—	59.1	0.6	0.6	57.9	79.3	14.6	0.3	0.1	5.7	Mauritius
0.6	24.6	—	—	75.4	41.5	...	33.9	...	...	...	...	100.0[46]	Mayotte
24,364.5	8.9	2.1	60.1	28.9	3.1	15.9	9.9	16.6	65.1	0.2	7.1	11.0	Mexico
...	...	...	...	...	...	...	...	...	...	94.2	...	...	Monaco[27]
675.0[3]	40.5		—40.1[16]—	15.4[17]	...	—	15.4[17]	...	...	94.2	...	5.8	Mongolia
2.9[15]	5.8[15]	—[15]	0.3[15]	93.9[15]	0.2[15]	20.5[15]	73.2[15]	...	55.6[15,29]	...	...	44.4[15,29]	Montserrat
2,806.9	30.6	16.2	2.7	50.4	20.7	1.8	27.9	61.3	1.6	5.0	4.3	27.8	Morocco
86.4	79.3	1.4[5]	6.3	13.0[6]	—	—	13.0[6]	26.9	14.6	15.4	11.9	31.2	Mozambique
352.7	69.9	6.2	...	23.9	...	...	...	5.9[3]	2.2[3]	5.5[3]	6.1[3]	80.3[3]	Myanmar (Burma)
54.8	—	100.0	...	...	...	...	...	...	...	...	...	...	Nauru
128.5	40.7	0.2	—	59.1	3.5	—	55.6	15.2	21.7	4.2	0.5	58.4	Nepal
103,559.1	25.2	1.5	8.6	64.7	16.7	22.0	26.1	70.6	3.9	1.2	0.8	23.6	Netherlands, The
1,307.6	0.7	0.5	95.2	3.6	1.4	0.9	1.3	7.1	23.6	—	4.1	65.4	Netherlands Antilles
277.2	1.1[29]	82.8[29]	—[29]	16.1[29]	—[29]	—[29]	16.1[29]	47.1[24]	6.9[24]	—[24]	23.7[24]	22.3[24]	New Caledonia
6,963.6	71.0	0.5	0.9	27.6	4.7	4.2	18.7	22.5	15.4	1.9	16.6	43.6	New Zealand
386.7	91.7	—	—	8.3	4.6	—	3.7	36.2	12.6	3.0	24.7	23.4	Nicaragua
454.8	17.1	79.7	0.9	2.3	—	0.5	1.8	46.6	—	—	17.7	35.7	Niger
7,383.4	3.7	—	95.4	0.9	0.2	—	0.7	41.4	47.0	—	0.1	11.5	Nigeria
0.1	61.9	—	—	38.1	—	—	38.1	—	1.3	—	—	98.7	Niue
1.9	38.7	—	—	61.3	0.3	15.2	45.8	—	—	—	—	100.0[51]	Norfolk Island
22,503.0	11.2	1.5	36.5	50.7	8.2	15.0	27.5	65.2	6.1	1.3	1.9	25.5	Norway
2,992.0	3.0	0.1	86.6	10.3	0.2	6.0	4.1	10.4[3]	3.0[3]	—[3]	51.3[3]	35.4[3]	Oman
19.3		—96.5[6]—	—	3.5[6]	—	—	3.5[6]	...	...	...	...	...	Pacific Is., Trust Territory of the Marshall Islands
3.1	99.1	—	—	0.9	—	—	0.9	...	79.4	—	—	20.6	
...	...	...	...	...	...	...	...	...	...	...	...	...	Micronesia, Fed. States of

Trade: external (continued)

country	year	imports total value U.S.$ (000,000)	Standard International Trade Classification (SITC) categories (percent)							direction of trade (percent)				
			food and agricultural raw materials (0 + 1 + 2 − 27 − 28 + 4)	mineral ores and concentrates (27 + 28 + 667)	fuels and other energy (3)	manufactured goods total[a] (5 + 6 − 667 + 7 + 8 + 9)	of which chemicals and related products (5)	of which machinery and transport equipment (7)	of which other[a] (6 − 667 + 8 + 9)	from European Economic Community (EEC)[b]	from United States	from U.S.S.R. and Eastern Europe[c]	from Japan	from all other[d]
Northern Mariana Islands	1985	45.3	60.1	—[5]	13.6	26.3[6]	3.3	12.0	11.0	—	61.9	—	23.5	14.6
Palau	1984	25.1[53]	28.9	0.1[5]	0.9[53]	70.0[6]	4.0	24.5	41.5[6]	—	41.8	—	38.2	20.0
Pakistan	1987	5,829.5	18.4	2.3	17.7	61.6	17.2	28.5	15.9	25.8	9.4	2.1	15.9	46.8
Panama	1985	1,383.3	12.5	0.2	21.2	66.1	12.3	23.5	30.3	8.3	31.7	0.2	8.9	50.9
Papua New Guinea	1985	1,006.0	19.5	0.4[5]	17.6	62.6[6]	7.5	30.0	25.1[6]	5.4[3]	9.9	—[3]	17.4	67.2[3]
Paraguay	1986	578.1	10.0	0.6	21.4	67.9	8.7	32.6	26.6	18.0	13.6	0.1	6.0	62.4
Peru	1986	2,391.2	25.6	0.9	2.9	70.6	20.8	30.9	19.0	21.9	27.4	0.8	9.0	40.9
Philippines	1987	7,187.6	12.0	1.4	18.2	68.4	14.0	16.6	37.8	11.6	22.1	0.7	16.6	49.0
Pitcairn Island	...	...	...	...	...	...	...	...	...	...	...	...	...	...
Poland	1987	10,843.7	16.1	3.6	17.3	63.0	11.4	32.2	19.4	22.7	1.3	40.8	1.1	34.2
Portugal	1987	13,441.2	18.2	1.0	11.6	69.1	10.6	33.4	25.1	63.4	4.9	0.8	4.0	27.0
Puerto Rico	1986[28]	10,098.9	20.0	0.9	14.9	64.2	14.3	22.0	27.8	6.3	60.6	0.1	8.9	24.1
Qatar	1987	1,134.0	20.4	1.9	0.8	76.9	6.3	40.4	30.2	39.3	11.9	0.4	16.3	32.1
Réunion	1987	1,464.6	22.2	0.2	4.5	73.0	9.3	30.3	33.4	80.2	0.3	—	2.6	16.8
Romania	1985	11,266.9	10.6	—56.1[16]—		33.3[17]	6.8	22.2	4.3[17]	10.2	3.1	43.1	1.1	42.6
Rwanda	1985	295.7	24.1	1.4	15.2	59.3	6.2	21.6	31.6	39.4	6.6	0.6	9.4	44.1
St. Helena and Ascension	1984	4.3	39.0	—	11.7	49.2	6.8	15.7	26.7	57.0			0.2	42.8
St. Kitts and Nevis	1983	51.9	25.1	0.1	10.0	64.8	8.5	19.2	37.1	20.7	40.5	—	3.4	35.4
St. Lucia	1986	154.8	25.7	0.2	7.7	66.5	12.2	19.8	34.5	24.4	34.1	0.2	6.9	34.4
St. Pierre and Miquelon	1984	43.9	19.4	0.1	29.9	50.6	4.3	27.4	18.8	46.1	0.3	—		53.5
St. Vincent and the Grenadines	1986	87.3	27.1	0.2[5]	6.6	66.0[6]	13.3	18.1	34.6[6]	25.6	34.1	0.3	4.1	36.0
San Marino[39]	...	...	...	...	...	...	...	...	...	...	...	...	...	...
São Tomé and Principe	1984	11.0	46.5[52]	3.0[16, 52]	1.9[52]	45.7[17, 52]	10.1[52]	12.8[52]	22.8[17, 52]	69.3[3]	—[3]	5.0[3]	3.3[3]	22.4[3]
Saudi Arabia	1985	23,622.4	15.6	0.4	0.5	83.5	6.5	35.8	41.3	35.2	17.0	0.6	19.0	28.2
Senegal	1984	1,009.7	29.6	—	28.0	42.4	8.4	16.8	17.3	44.1	5.1	0.7	1.7	48.5
Seychelles	1986	105.6	20.8	0.1	17.0	62.2	5.7	27.5	28.9	47.6	2.3	1.8	6.3	41.9
Sierra Leone	1986	276.5	—32.9[5]—		11.1	55.9[6]	8.8	27.1	20.1	45.6	9.9	1.2	6.4	36.8
Singapore	1988	43,861.8	10.2	0.6	14.1	75.1	6.6	43.4	25.2	12.0	15.6	0.6	21.9	49.9
Solomon Islands	1987	80.8	19.1	0.3	14.7	66.0	6.7	29.1	30.2	6.6	2.9	—	19.1	71.4
Somalia	1981	512.9	26.6	—	2.3	71.1	2.0	50.0	19.1	66.0	4.3	0.1	1.8	27.8
South Africa[54]	1985	10,311.4	8.5	2.2	0.6[55]	88.7[56]	12.2	39.5	37.0[56]	42.4	14.0	0.1	10.0	33.4
Bophuthatswana[54]	...	...	...	...	...	...	...	...	...	...	...	...	...	...
Ciskei[54]	...	...	...	...	...	...	...	...	...	...	...	...	...	...
Transkei[54]	...	...	...	...	...	...	...	...	...	...	...	...	...	...
Venda[54]	...	...	...	...	...	...	...	...	...	...	...	...	...	...
South West Africa/Namibia[54]	...	...	...	...	...	...	...	...	...	...	...	...	...	...
Spain	1986	637.7												
	1988	60,556.5	15.5	3.0	11.4	70.2	10.1	39.1	20.9	56.8	8.9	2.6	5.1	26.6
Sri Lanka	1986	1,831.6	19.4	2.0	12.6	66.1	11.1	22.7	32.3	15.2	7.3	1.4	17.1	59.0
Sudan, The	1985	909.1	18.2	0.1	37.8	43.9	10.0	17.9	16.0	38.3[24]	9.1[24]	1.5[24]	3.2[24]	47.9[24]
Suriname	1987	294.3	13.2	6.8[5]	23.2	56.8[6]	15.2	20.8	20.8[6]	27.2	31.2	0.1	1.3	40.2
Swaziland	1987[1]	359.6	12.2	0.6	15.4	71.9	6.5	15.4	50.0	4.9	0.8	—	1.3	93.0[58]
Sweden	1988	45,642.9	9.2	1.9	6.8	82.0	10.0	39.6	32.4	56.0	7.5	3.7	6.4	26.4
Switzerland	1988	56,385.2	9.1	5.2	3.7	82.0	11.6	32.3	38.1	71.3	5.5	1.2	5.0	17.0
Syria	1987	4,260.2	17.5	0.9	19.8	61.7	12.5	25.1	24.1	35.3	5.3	17.0	3.0	39.4
Taiwan	1988	49,726.1	12.4	2.4	7.9	77.2	12.7	32.9	31.6	12.4	26.2	0.5	29.8	31.1
Tanzania	1984	781.7	12.3	1.7[5]	20.1	65.9[6]	13.1	32.2	20.7[6]	44.6	3.9	1.1	9.8	40.6
Thailand	1987	12,972.3	10.4	3.9	13.4	72.3	14.4	32.1	25.9	15.6	12.5	1.8	26.0	44.1
Togo	1984	271.2	—30.0—		11.4	58.6	10.8	20.0	27.9	63.3	4.3	0.7	5.3	26.5
Tokelau	1982	0.6	55.7	—	33.4	11.1	5.7	1.1	4.3	—	—	—	—	100.0[59]
Tonga	1986	40.0	31.6	0.7	12.3	55.4	8.7	15.3	31.4	4.0	3.8	—	11.4	80.7
Trinidad and Tobago	1988	1,127.0	20.8	2.9	11.9	64.4	12.0	25.1	27.2	19.8	38.0	0.6	5.2	36.5
Tunisia	1987	3,023.4	16.7	5.4	10.8	67.0	11.2	22.0	33.9	67.8	6.0	4.2	0.9	21.1
Turkey	1987	14,162.6	11.2	3.1	22.4	63.3	15.2	28.6	19.5	40.0	9.7	5.5	6.1	38.7
Turks and Caicos Islands	1988[1]	33.2	—24.8[5]—		8.8	66.5[6]	...	...	...	6.5	74.7[12]	...	5.9	25.3[12]
Tuvalu	1985	2.9	32.5	0.1	12.5	55.0	5.0	20.3	29.6	6.5	0.4	—	5.9	87.2
Uganda	1986	344.1[3]	8.7[22]	0.7[22]	29.6[22]	61.0[22]	11.1[22]	26.8[22]	23.0[22]	37.6[3]	1.3[3]	...	5.0[3]	56.1[3]
U.S.S.R.	1987	97,185.3	—18.6[5]—		2.7	78.8[6]	7.9	41.4	29.5[6]	11.4	1.5	56.5	2.7	27.9
United Arab Emirates	1984	7,062.1	16.1	1.2	7.7	74.9	5.6	32.1	37.2	34.9	12.0	0.7	17.8	34.5
United Kingdom[36]	1988	189,563.9	14.0	3.5	4.8	77.8	8.8	37.6	31.4	52.4	10.1	1.5	6.1	29.8
United States[61]	1988	441,282.4	7.8	2.0	9.3	80.8	4.4	44.7	31.7	19.3	—	0.5	20.4	59.9
Uruguay	1987	1,141.9	12.7	1.0	15.7	70.6	20.9	30.9	18.8	21.0	8.0	1.0	3.2	66.8
Vanuatu	1984	66.3	26.6	0.2	10.3	62.9	7.0	23.1	32.8	13.5	1.3	—	12.8	72.4
Venezuela	1987	8,711.2	—17.9[5]—		1.8	80.3[6]	17.9	44.7	17.6[6]	27.3	43.9	0.6	6.1	22.2
Vietnam	1987	3,096.0[3]	...	...	...	...	...	...	...	2.8[3]	0.8[3]	79.3[3]	6.4[3]	10.6[3]
Virgin Islands (U.S.)	1986	2,652.7	...	...	66.2	...	...	...	...	...	54.5	...	...	...
Wallis and Futuna	1984	8.1	—34.9[5]—		11.8	53.2[6]	—	17.5	35.7[6]	...	...	...	...	100.0[63]
West Bank	1987	639.1	...	...	...	...	...	...	...	...	...	...	...	...
Western Sahara	...	...	...	...	...	...	...	...	...	...	...	...	...	...
Western Samoa	1983	52.6	24.3	0.3	17.5	57.9	7.4	22.9	27.6	5.5	11.0	—	11.4	72.2
Yemen (Aden)	1986	483.2	—38.6[5]—		15.3	46.2[6]	6.2	20.5	19.5[6]	22.9[3]	3.3[3]	22.2[3]	3.1[3]	48.5[3]
Yemen (San'ā')	1987	1,027.3	36.0	0.3[5]	2.4	61.2[6]	7.9	18.9	34.3	49.2	9.3	1.1	10.3	30.1
Yugoslavia	1988	13,153.8	13.3	3.8	18.1	64.8	17.4	27.5	19.8	38.5	5.5	27.2	1.3	27.4
Zaire	1984	794.2	22.4[65]	1.2[65]	7.6[65]	68.8[65]	10.3[65]	31.7[65]	26.9[65]	50.6	9.0	1.3	2.7	36.5
Zambia	1984	740.8	6.9	0.6	29.7	62.7	13.6	28.7	20.4	24.5	6.4	0.3	3.3	65.4
Zimbabwe	1987	1,208.9	6.2	2.8	13.8	77.2	17.8	36.4	23.1	35.4	10.4	1.9	4.4	47.9

[1]Year ending March.　[2]1982.　[3]Estimated based on trading partners' information.　[4]Year ending September 30.　[5]Excluding precious stones, etc. (667).　[6]Including precious stones, etc. (667).　[7]Excluding fish imported for canneries.　[8]Figures for Belgium–Luxembourg Economic Union (Luxembourg is also shown separately).　[9]1987–88: imports $110.3, exports $60.8.　[10]Includes 82.1% from India.　[11]Includes 97.5% to India.　[12]1984.　[13]Includes 78.1% from rest of Customs Union of Southern Africa.　[14]Includes 71.9% to Switzerland.　[15]1985.　[16]Including metals.　[17]Excluding metals.　[18]1986.　[19]Includes 94.7% for ships' bunkers and stores.　[20]1981.　[21]1975.　[22]1976.　[23]1980.　[24]1983.　[25]1979.　[26]Excluding fish caught under license; for 1988 this totaled $234 million, with estimated direction as follows: EEC 36.7% United States 0.0%, U.S.S.R. and Eastern Europe 17.6%, Japan 26.2%, other 19.5%.　[27]Figures for France include Monaco.　[28]Year ending June 30.　[29]Domestic exports only.　[30]Includes 92.3% from Israel.　[31]Includes 91.2% to Israel.　[32]Import figures refer to total trade turnover (figures are not available separately for imports and for exports).　[33]Excluding trade with East Germany (1.5% of total imports and 1.3% of total exports).　[34]Excluding petroleum products.　[35]Includes 51.5% for ships' bunkers.　[36]Figures for United Kingdom include Guernsey, Isle of Man, and Jersey (the latter is also shown separately).　[37]Commercial imports only (excluding oil companies' imports).　[38]Excluding imported military goods of $2,160.5 million.

exports total value U.S.$ (000,000)	SITC: food and agricultural raw materials (0+1+2−27−28+4)	SITC: mineral ores and concentrates (27+28+667)	SITC: fuels and other energy (3)	manufactured goods total (5+6−667+7+8+9)	of which chemicals and related products (5)	of which machinery and transport equipment (7)	of which other (6−667+8+9)	to EEC	to United States	to U.S.S.R. and Eastern Europe	to Japan	to all other	country
12.3	—	—	—	100.0	—	—	100.0	—	100.0	—	—	—	Northern Mariana Islands
0.5	69.1	—	—	30.9	—	—	30.9	—	8.0	—	58.8	33.2	Palau
4,105.1	26.9	0.4	0.7	72.0	0.3	0.3	71.4	31.3	11.1	4.3	11.6	41.7	Pakistan
301.2	78.2	1.1	7.2	13.5	3.3	0.1	10.1	16.1	64.1	0.2	0.1	19.5	Panama
917.3	45.6[29]	34.5[5,29]	—[29]	19.9[6,29]	—[29]	—[29]	19.9[6,29]	41.4[3]	4.0	0.6[3]	22.1	31.9[3]	Papua New Guinea
232.5	90.9	—	—	9.1	3.3	—	5.7	20.5	4.0	—	0.8	74.7	Paraguay
2,530.6	20.3[12]	19.2[12]	25.8[12]	34.7[12]	1.3[12]	1.4[12]	31.9[12]	24.6	29.8	5.0	10.5	30.1	Peru
5,720.2	28.3	4.1	1.7	65.9	4.3	10.5	51.1	18.9	36.1	0.5	17.2	27.4	Philippines
...	...	...	...	...	...	...	...	...	...	...	...	...	Pitcairn Island
12,204.8	14.0	2.7	11.3	72.0	7.2	33.6	31.3	25.8	2.6	35.0	0.6	36.0	Poland
9,167.0	16.6	1.3	1.9	80.2	5.4	16.4	58.3	71.2	6.5	1.0	0.7	20.7	Portugal
11,571.4	16.7	1.5	3.2	78.6	34.7	22.1	21.8	3.5	87.3	—	0.3	8.8	Puerto Rico
1,984.6	—[20]	—[20]	93.9[20]	6.1[20]	3.9[20]	—[20]	2.2[20]	11.9[3]	0.2[3]	—[3]	38.5[3]	49.4[3]	Qatar
148.3	88.8	0.1	0.2	10.9	2.9	4.6	3.3	89.3	0.2	—	2.7	7.8	Réunion
12,167.3	12.6	28.3[16]		59.0[17]	10.7	29.9	18.4[17]	24.1	5.8	36.1	0.6	33.5	Romania
131.0	90.9	7.5	—	1.6	—	—	1.6	91.6	2.8	—	0.2	5.4	Rwanda
0.04	100.0	—	—	—	—	—	—	...	...	...	...	...	St. Helena and Ascension
18.4	67.9	—	—	32.1	0.4	10.1	21.6	19.6	51.7	...	...	28.5	St. Kitts and Nevis
82.9	75.6	—	0.1	24.4	0.3	4.7	19.3	69.2	12.1	—	0.3	18.7	St. Lucia
7.8	99.9	—	—	0.1	—	—	0.1	7.7	74.3	—	—	18.0	St. Pierre and Miquelon
63.8	85.9	—[5]	—	14.1[6]	1.0	3.8	9.3[6]	31.2	9.4	—	—	59.4	St. Vincent and the Grenadines
12.2	99.8[52]	—[52]	—[52]	0.2[52]	...	—[52]	0.1[52]	56.6[3]	—[3]	34.7[3]	—[3]	8.7[3]	San Marino[39]
...	...	...	...	...	...	...	...	...	...	...	...	...	São Tomé and Príncipe
27,487.1	0.5	0.1	94.4	5.0	2.8	1.4	0.8	22.3[3]	6.7[3]	1.7[3]	34.1[3]	35.2[3]	Saudi Arabia
534.4	63.3		18.5	18.2	9.0	2.6	6.7	48.0	0.2	—	1.6	50.2	Senegal
18.4	14.1	0.2	71.9	13.9	0.4	7.5	6.0	8.6	4.3	0.1	1.2	85.8	Seychelles
275.0	33.1[24]	62.0[24]	3.9[24]	1.1[24]	0.1[24]	—[24]	1.0[24]	91.0[24]	2.4[24]	—[24]	—[24]	6.6[24]	Sierra Leone
39,304.9	10.5	0.7	12.8	76.0	6.6	48.0	21.4	13.0	23.8	0.6	8.6	53.9	Singapore
64.0	94.0	—	—	6.0	—	—	6.0	22.2	5.3	—	35.6	36.9	Solomon Islands
152.0	99.4	—	0.2	0.4	—	0.1	0.2	6.2	—	—	—	93.7	Somalia
16,419.4	8.6	11.5	8.9	71.1[57]	2.8	2.5	65.8[57]	21.4	8.4	0.1	7.8	62.4	South Africa[54]
...	...	...	...	...	...	...	...	...	...	...	...	...	Bophuthatswana[54]
...	...	...	...	...	...	...	...	...	...	...	...	...	Ciskei[54]
...	...	...	...	...	...	...	...	...	...	...	...	...	Transkei[54]
...	...	...	...	...	...	...	...	...	...	...	...	...	Venda[54]
878.4	9.7	82.6	...	7.7	...	...	7.7	...	...	...	...	...	South West Africa/Namibia[54]
40,466.6	20.0	1.2	4.7	74.1	8.8	33.5	31.8	65.6	7.9	1.3	1.2	24.1	Spain
1,194.2	48.5	6.8	6.9	37.8	0.9	3.3	33.6	23.4	26.1	2.9	5.5	42.0	Sri Lanka
240.5	93.0	0.4	—	6.6	0.1	4.6	2.0	25.2[24]	2.0[24]	7.7[24]	5.4[24]	59.7[24]	Sudan, The
306.0	32.0	65.5[5]	0.3	2.3[6]	0.1	0.5	1.8[6]	31.4	20.1	—	13.0	35.5	Suriname
286.2	67.2	0.1	6.3	26.4	0.2	0.5	25.7	...	...	...	...	...	Swaziland
49,742.4	9.7	1.5	2.2	86.6	7.2	42.8	36.6	52.3	9.9	2.1	1.8	34.0	Sweden
50,733.9	3.7	4.9	0.1	91.3	21.6	32.4	37.3	56.0	8.5	3.3	4.3	27.8	Switzerland
2,476.8	12.8	4.1	51.8	31.3	10.7	0.5	20.1	47.4	0.6	36.2	0.1	15.7	Syria
60,451.8	6.5	0.2	0.6	92.7	3.5	35.2	54.0	14.6	38.6	0.1	14.5	32.3	Taiwan
376.7	77.5	3.4[5]	4.4	14.8	1.1	0.6	13.2[6]	50.0	2.7	1.3	5.4	40.6	Tanzania
11,659.2	45.2	4.6	0.7	49.5	1.7	11.9	35.9	22.2	18.6	0.5	14.9	43.8	Thailand
191.3	41.0	49.0	1.4	8.6	0.5	2.3	5.8	62.5	0.8	10.6	0.7	25.4	Togo
0.1	100.0	—	—	—	—	—	—	...	...	...	...	...	Tokelau
6.4	77.8	—	—	22.2	0.2	3.6	18.4	2.1	16.5	...	0.2	81.2	Tonga
1,412.0	6.0	0.6	60.5	33.0	20.9	1.3	10.8	8.7	57.3	0.1	0.5	33.3	Trinidad and Tobago
2,152.4	13.5	2.4	23.6	60.4	18.1	5.8	36.5	78.1	1.8	3.2	0.1	16.8	Tunisia
10,189.7	27.6	2.7	2.3	67.4	6.6	10.7	50.1	47.8	7.0	3.1	1.5	40.6	Turkey
4.1	99.5	—	—	0.5	—	—	0.5	—[12]	100.0[12]	—[12]	—[12]	—	Turks and Caicos Islands
0.1	100.0	—	—	—	—	—	—	—	—	—	—	100.0[60]	Tuvalu
429.7[3]	96.6[22]	0.2[22]	0.8[22]	2.4[22]	—[22]	—[22]	2.4[22]	56.3[3]	29.5[3]	...	3.9[3]	10.3[3]	Uganda
109,026.9	6.7	2.3[5]	46.4	44.5[6]	3.0	15.5	26.0[6]	14.4	0.4	50.4	1.4	33.3	U.S.S.R.
13,869.2	1.7	0.2	87.5	10.6	0.5	3.4	6.7	15.2[3]	6.3[3]	—[3]	38.2[3]	40.3[3]	United Arab Emirates
145,141.8	8.3	3.6	7.1	81.0	13.9	39.1	27.9	50.2	12.9	1.5	2.1	33.2	United Kingdom[36]
320,465.4	16.5	2.2	2.6	78.7	9.9	44.5	24.3	23.3	—	1.1	11.7	63.9	United States[61]
1,191.1	44.1	0.3	0.2	55.5	7.8	3.0	44.6	28.1	14.9	5.8	1.5	49.8	Uruguay
43.9	99.5[29]	—[29]	—[29]	0.5[29]	—[29]	—[29]	0.5[29]	52.0	—	—	9.1	38.9	Vanuatu
8,402.0	0.7[24]	1.2[24]	94.4[24]	3.8[24]	0.4[24]	0.2[24]	3.1[24]	21.4[24]	32.6[24]	—[24]	2.8[24]	43.1[24]	Venezuela
978.0[3]	...	...	...	...	...	...	...	3.8[3]	—[3]	58.8[3]	13.5[3]	23.9[3]	Vietnam
2,119.0	...	...	92.6	...	...	...	...	...	96.8	...	...	...	Virgin Islands (U.S.)
0.02	100.0	—	—	—	—	—	—	—	—	—	—	100.0[62]	Wallis and Futuna
228.2	...	...	...	...	...	...	...	...	...	...	...	100.0[64]	West Bank
...	...	...	...	...	...	...	...	...	...	...	...	...	Western Sahara
18.6	90.6			9.4	—	5.8	3.6	11.6	31.7	—	3.6	53.1	Western Samoa
290.1	...	...	95.9[12]	...				6.2[3]	0.1[3]	2.4[3]	10.3[3]	81.0[3]	Yemen (Aden)
47.5	46.3	—	35.7	18.1	...	...	...	21.0[3]	6.8[3]	—	3.5[3]	68.6[3]	Yemen (Şan'ā')
12,597.2	12.9	1.1	1.8	84.2	9.2	30.7	44.3	36.7	5.8	33.6	0.7	23.4	Yugoslavia
1,003.4	13.0[24]	70.8[24]	11.1[24]	5.0[24]	...	...	...	55.8[3]	29.3[3]	—[3]	4.7[3]	10.2[3]	Zaire
659.8	2.7[5]		1.8	95.5[6]	—	0.2	95.4[6]	32.2	9.6	0.7	23.5	34.0	Zambia
1,427.7	40.5	23.7	0.3	35.5	1.1	1.2	33.2	40.4	6.8	3.2	5.0	44.5	Zimbabwe

[39] Figures for Italy include San Marino. [40] Includes 84.9% from United Kingdom. [41] Including coins. [42] Includes 67.3% to United Kingdom. [43] 1974. [44] Includes 97.1% from rest of Customs Union of Southern Africa. [45] Includes 56.1% from France. [46] Includes 70.2% to France. [47] 1984. [48] Based on trade with Australia and New Zealand only. [49] Curaçao and Bonaire only. [50] Includes 54.8% from Australia. [51] Includes 58.0% to Australia. [52] 1977. [53] Excluding bulk imports of fuels. [54] Figures for South Africa refer to Customs Union of Southern Africa (includes South Africa, Botswana, Lesotho, and Swaziland, also shown separately; also South West Africa/Namibia, Bophuthatswana, Ciskei, Transkei, and Venda). [55] Excluding crude oil. [56] Including crude oil (included in "special transactions" accounting in total for 17.7%). [57] Including gold (included in "special transactions" accounting in total for 51.2%). [58] Includes 90.1% from rest of Customs Union of Southern Africa. [59] All from South Pacific countries. [60] All to the South Pacific region. [61] Figures for United States include American Samoa, Guam, Puerto Rico, and Virgin Islands (U.S.), also shown separately. [62] All to Northern Mariana Islands. [63] Includes 90.9% from Israel. [64] Includes 70.3% to Israel, 29.1% to Jordan. [65] 1978.

Trade: domestic

The following table presents data relating to domestic wholesale and retail trade for the countries of the world. The section on wholesale trade is based for the most part on establishments engaged primarily in selling goods to retailers and distributors for resale or to purchasers who buy for business and farm uses. The retail trade section is based on businesses engaged in selling merchandise for personal or household consumption; restaurants are, when possible, included, hotels excluded.

The data presented here are based on information received from a variety of direct country and international sources. The direct country sources include such items as correspondence, statistical abstracts, annual reports, and censuses of business and trade. Among the more useful international sources are the various compilations of the United Nations dealing with domestic trade and Euromonitor's *Retail Trade International* (2 vols.).

Since there is no single published source or common international methodology for the compilation of data on wholesale and retail trade, nor a single current year on which, by common agreement, the various national reports would be based, allowance must be made for variations in the meaning and recency of the information provided for any single country and for its comparability internationally. Variations occur in part because of the ways in which countries define wholesale and retail trade; the conventional capitalist, or free-enterprise, distinctions between wholesale and retail activity (of a single enterprise or an entire national trade sector) may not exist in the business practice of some countries, and data may overlap in their final reports. Variations also exist in the kind and level of detail reported. For example, countries may design surveys differently according to the size (number of employees, sales, surface area) of establishments surveyed, their profitability, or other less direct criteria, such as ownership or location. The depth of analysis to which the data are subjected may also vary. The structure of a national trade sector is also affected by the degree of government involvement, which may range from total control of wholesale distribution in some socialist countries, to partial involvement in some strategic sectors, or to relative noninvolvement in fully private trade sectors of capitalist countries. In some smaller countries data may refer to a single trading enterprise.

At the table's extreme left, preceding the year to which the trade data refer, the combined value of the country's wholesale and retail trade as a percentage of gross domestic product or net material product is given. Unless otherwise noted, GDP data include restaurants and exclude hotels.

Both the wholesale and retail sections of the table provide similar detail: establishments or outlets, employees, sales, and derived values for relationships among these measures; the retail section provides an additional breakdown of sales by an end-use classification of retail sales outlets.

Although all sales figures are given in U.S. dollars, the comparability of these dollar figures may differ considerably; for instance, the purchasing power of various national currencies in domestic transactions may bear only a distant relationship to the exchange rate of the same currency in international transactions. The price of goods may also vary, depending on the degree to which they are subject to direct subsidies and artificial cost controls such as tax, investment, or free-trade preferences by a central government seeking to influence social or economic conditions.

Trade: domestic

country	domestic trade as percentage of GDP, 1986	year	wholesale trade — establishments[a]	employees[b]	sales[c] $'000,000	employees per establishment	sales per establishment $'000	retail trade — outlets[a]	employees[b]	sales[c] $'000,000
Afghanistan	10.2[1,2,3]	1981–82	...	[4]	...	...	...	11,140[6]	126,100[4]	...
Albania	9.5[5]	1987	...	[4]	...	...	...	3,600[7]	36,200[4]	1,260
Algeria	15.7	1971	...	[4]	...	...	...	404	65,917[4,8]	12,607[9]
American Samoa	...	1986	40	77[10]	...	...	...	592	499[10]	...
Andorra	25.2[11]	1972	...					...	2,264	...
Angola	10.1[2,3]	1973	[4]	[4]	...	[4]	...	29,138[4]	...	...
Anguilla	34.1[2]	1984	[4]	[4]	...	...	...	92[4]	403[4]	...
Antigua and Barbuda	20.8[2]	1980	25	350	...	14.0	...	199	1,000	23[9]
Argentina	14.5	1974	45,700	275,000[12]	10,922[13]	6.0[12]	...	445,798[14]	930,000[12,14]	15,540[9]
Aruba	...	1983	...	[4]	...	...	...	...	3,192[4,15]	16
Australia	17.3[2]	1988	39,319[17]	361,000[12,17]	84,798[15]	9.2[12,17]	2,157[15]	110,500[10]	737,378[10,12]	73,626
Austria	15.7[2]	1985	13,019	150,800[12]	38,400	11.6[12]	2,950	36,039	223,500[12]	14,870
Bahamas, The[19]	26.2[2]	1980	23	1,066	143	46.3	6.235	132	4,059	257[11]
Bahrain	14.8[18]	1983	[4]	[4]	...	[4]	...	255[4]	12,551[4]	1,601
Bangladesh	8.5[2]	1985	...	[4]	...	...	...	...	3,610,000[4]	4,800
Barbados	26.9[2]	1986	...	[4]	...	...	...	1,911[20]	25,300[4]	264[9]
Belgium	18.2[2]	1984	60,589	160,600	65,110	2.6	1,075	135,534	193,500	20,957
Belize	15.2[2]	1983	...	[4]	...	...	...	...	4,558[4]	23
Benin	19.2[2]	1979	...	...	...	...	...	170[7]	1,910[7,12]	150[9]
Bermuda	32.8[20]	1985	60[20]	820	...	...	...	310[7,21]	4,342[14]	116[14,18]
Bhutan	10.8[2]	1982	...	[4]	...	...	...	...	9,000[4,12]	...
Bolivia	20.4	1983	...	[4]	...	...	...	1,660	128,800[4,11]	1,818
Botswana	16.7	1983–84	205	3,500	494[9]	...	...	...	10,700	165[9]
Brazil	13.8[2]	1984	45,969[10]	370,000[10]	91,331[10]	8.0[10]	1,987[10]	1,030,000	3,450,000	40,090
British Virgin Islands	26.7[2,5]	1982	...	...	...	...	...	...	366	5[21]
Brunei	11.5	1986	[4]	[4]	...	[4]	...	833[4,25]	4,261[4,25]	...
Bulgaria	4.6[1,2]	1987	...	7,700[3]	...	...	...	41,339[14]	79,820[14]	34,700[19]
Burkina Faso	10.0[2,3]	1975	...	[4]	...	...	...	...	19,354[4,12]	445
Burundi	7.9[2]	1981	...	...	...	...	...	1,312[7]	1	753[9]
Cameroon	14.7[2,18]	1980	...	...	...	...	...	...	13,776[7,12]	...
Canada	11.7	1985	...	[4]	139,110[18]	...	...	...	2,082,000[4,26]	103,410
Cape Verde	...	1980	...	[4]	...	...	...	...	3,851[4]	...
Cayman Islands	17.0[15]	1979	...	[4]	...	...	...	...	1,518[4]	...
Central African Republic	21.3[2]	1978[2]	4	[4]	[4]	...	[4]	102[4,7]	26,659[4,12,27]	252[4,7]
Chad	26.6[3]	1983	...	[4]	[4]	...	...	...	1,661[4,7,28]	497[4]
Chile	18.3[2,10]	1983	561[7]	15,300[7]	2,312[7]	27.2[7]	4,121[7]	1,125[7,14]	21,700[7,14]	1,403[7,14]
China	9.8[2]	1987	67,000	1,089,000[12]	...	16.2[12]	...	8,814,000[14]	20,125,000[12,14]	156,363[14]
Christmas Island	...	1981	—	[4]	...	—	...	5	65[4]	...
Cocos (Keeling) Islands	...	1981	...	[4]	...	...	...	1	13[4]	...
Colombia	13.6[2]	1985	...	...	...	...	...	1,110[30]	49,000[30]	1,690[30]
Comoros	25.0[2]	1980	...	[4]	...	...	...	...	1,873[4,7]	...
Congo	16.3[2]	1980	...	...	...	...	...	109[4]	369[4]	31[4]
Cook Islands	24.0[3,5]	1982[31]	4	[4]	[4]	...	[4]	9,713	26,486	475[9]
Costa Rica	16.8	1975	332[32]	4,073[32]	35[32]	12.3[32]	104[32]	2,023[7]	16,720[7]	1,548[4,9]
Côte d'Ivoire	18.2[2,10]	1981	...	...	...	[4]	...	...	...	...
Cuba	30.9[1]	1987	...	14,440	...	...	...	56,916[3]	230,000[3,12]	11,831
Cyprus	18.2[2]	1986	1,559[18]	12,400	225	5.3[18]	720[18]	8,474[18]	20,100[12,14]	268[14]
Czechoslovakia	16.2[1,2]	1987	63,110[3]	251,000[3]	40,083[3]	4.0[3]	635[3]	62,901	257,691	57,240
Denmark	13.0[2]	1984	13,946	126,174	36,865	9.0	2,643	32,534	150,082	16,042
Djibouti	15.6[2,18]	1985	28	371[11]	...	...	...	431	1,877[11]	...
Dominica	13.5[2]	1983	...	[4]	...	...	...	...	1,597[4,21]	4
Dominican Republic	15.5	1983	670	...	3,136	...	4,681	11,220[11]	...	1,259[11]
Ecuador	17.6	1983	402	15,900	1,396	39.6	3,473	501	17,400	1,068
Egypt	13.2[2,33]	1983–84	2,552	45,500[12]	4,492	18.0[12]	1,760	2,545[18]	55,800[12,18]	3,252[18]
El Salvador	28.5[2]	1983	396	6,400	1,038	16.2	2,621	1,416	10,700	485

The data on distribution of retail sales by kind of consumer goods may have their origin in several different types of data or analysis: One country may aggregate sales data by kind of establishment only (this may be perfectly satisfactory in a country of small, independent outlets); another may aggregate data directly by kind of goods (most easily done in a country with well-developed statistical, tax-reporting, and commercial systems). Other countries may find it impolitic to publish data that reflect the poverty of their distribution network or their supply of consumer goods and may aggregate or publish data for only a few sectors: food or nonfood goods, for example. For countries with only a few trading enterprises in a particular sector, detail must often be withheld to preserve the confidentiality of individual businesses.

The notes that follow further define the various headings.

a. The number of establishments or outlets refers to economic units that operate at a single physical location in one principal kind of activity, whether singly owned or part of a multiunit firm. Such units are not necessarily identical with a company or enterprise.

b. Number of employees refers to full-time and part-time paid workers, including salaried managers and officers; it usually excludes owner-operators, partners, vendors, and unpaid relatives.

c. Total sales (also called turnover) includes the value of merchandise sold for cash or credit; amounts received from customers for layaway purchases; receipts from rental or leasing of vehicles, equipment, tools, instruments, etc.; receipts for delivery, installation, maintenance, repair, alteration, storage, and other services.

d. Outlets engaged primarily in the sale of food and nonalcoholic beverages, such as grocery stores, meat and fish markets, and bakeries.

e. Outlets engaged primarily in the sale of clothing and shoes; also includes outlets that sell accessory items, such as millinery, furs, and leather goods.

f. Outlets engaged primarily in the sale of home furnishings, including furniture, draperies, floor coverings, household appliances, and home entertainment equipment.

g. Outlets that primarily serve food and drink, including restaurants, lunchrooms, cafeterias, social caterers, refreshment places, contract feeders, ice cream parlors, and bars and taverns.

h. Outlets engaged primarily in the sale of pharmaceuticals, cosmetics, and perfumes.

i. Outlets engaged primarily in the sale of building materials, hardware, garden supplies, paint, electrical supplies, and farm equipment.

j. Outlets engaged primarily in the sale of motor vehicles, motorcycles, bicycles, and tires, batteries, and other automotive supplies and parts; includes service stations.

k. Outlets engaged in the sale of multiple lines of merchandise, such as department stores, variety stores, and rural general stores.

l. Miscellaneous specialized outlets such as those engaged primarily in the sale of liquors, sporting goods, books, jewelry, photographic and optical goods, gifts, flowers, tobacco products, home fuels, and newspapers.

retail trade (continued)

food[d]	clothing, shoes[e]	home furnishings[f]	eating, drinking[g]	drugs, pharmaceuticals[h]	building materials[i]	automobile parts[j]	general merchandise[k]	other[l]	employees per outlet	sales per outlet $'000	population per outlet	country
61.9	...	...	...	—38.1—	...	...	...	...	...	...	...	Afghanistan
...	...	...	...	...	...	...	...	...	...	113[6]	277[6]	Albania
...	...	...	...	...	...	...	...	...	5.0[7]	...	5,146[7]	Algeria
...	...	...	...	...	...	...	...	...	3.8	...	90	American Samoa
...	...	...	...	...	...	...	...	...	...	...	39	Andorra
...	...	...	...	...	...	...	...	...	4.3[4]	...	73[4]	Angola
...	...	...	...	...	...	...	...	...	5.0	100	...	Anguilla
...	...	...	...	...	...	...	...	...	2.1[12, 14]	...	378	Antigua and Barbuda
...	...	...	...	...	...	...	...	...	...	...	58[14]	Argentina
...	...	...	...	...	...	...	...	...	...	...	...	Aruba
36.1	9.8	3.2	17.2[2]	3.6	5.8	...	12.4	11.9	6.7[10, 12]	398[10]	1,321[10]	Australia
30.0[18]	14.5[18]	10.3[18]	...	4.8[18]	...	13.7[18]	10.1[18]	16.6[18]	6.2[12]	413	210	Austria
24.4[11]	7.7[11]	7.1[11]	—	3.7[11]	8.4[11]	30.1[11]	7.6[11]	11.0[11]	30.8	1,881	1,026	Bahamas, The[19]
...	...	...	...	...	...	...	...	...	49.2[4]	...	1,507[4]	Bahrain
...	...	...	...	...	...	...	...	...	...	...	...	Bangladesh
35.1	...	...	...	—64.9—	...	...	...	...	...	...	130[20]	Barbados
...	...	...	...	...	...	...	...	...	1.4	155	73	Belgium
...	...	...	...	...	...	...	...	...	...	...	...	Belize
...	...	...	...	...	...	...	...	...	11.3[7, 12]	...	19,871[7]	Benin
...	...	...	...	...	...	...	...	...	11.0[9, 14]	...	1787[7, 21]	Bermuda
...	...	...	...	...	...	...	...	...	...	...	...	Bhutan
...	...	...	...	...	...	...	...	...	...	...	...	Bolivia
15.0[22]	7.2	13.0[23]	...	4.7	[23]	27.3[24]	19.3	13.5	6.4	99.4	3221[8]	Botswana
...	...	...	...	...	...	...	...	...	3.4	39	129	Brazil
...	...	...	...	...	...	...	...	...	...	...	...	British Virgin Islands
50.9	10.9	3.4	...	5.9	...	...	0.2	28.7	5.1[4, 25]	...	2794[4, 25]	Brunei
...	...	...	...	...	...	...	...	...	1.9[14]	839[14]	217[14]	Bulgaria
...	...	...	...	...	...	...	...	...	...	...	...	Burkina Faso
...	...	...	...	...	...	...	...	...	...	...	...	Burundi
...	...	...	...	...	...	...	...	...	10.5[7, 12]	...	6,481[7]	Cameroon
22.8	5.1	2.3	8.3	3.8	0.8	29.8	12.8	14.3	...	...	...	Canada
...	...	...	...	...	...	...	...	...	...	...	...	Cape Verde
...	...	...	...	...	...	...	...	...	...	...	...	Cayman Islands
...	...	...	...	...	...	...	...	...	...	2,471[4, 7]	21,774[4, 7]	Central African Republic
...	...	...	...	...	...	...	...	...	...	...	...	Chad
28.3[11]	29	5.0[11]	1.6[11]	5.4[11]	4.7[11]	18.0[11]	17.1[11, 29]	19.9[11]	19.3[7, 14]	1,247[7, 14]	10,210[7, 14]	Chile
54.0	17.2	—28.8—							2.3[12, 14]	18[14]	120[14]	China
...	...	...	...	...	...	...	...	...	...	...	662	Christmas Island
...	...	...	...	...	...	...	...	...	...	...	569	Cocos (Keeling) Islands
...	...	...	...	...	...	...	...	...	44.1[30]	1,522[30]	...	Colombia
...	...	...	...	...	...	...	...	...	...	...	...	Comoros
...	...	...	...	...	...	...	...	...	...	...	...	Congo
37.7	13.5	6.9	...	8.2	7.0	15.1	5.9	5.7	3.4[4]	284[4]	84[4]	Cook Islands
...	...	...	...	...	...	...	...	...	2.7	59	202	Costa Rica
...	...	...	...	...	...	...	...	...	8.3[7]	...	4,257[7]	Côte d'Ivoire
37.0	...	...	28.8	3.4	...	2.8	...	28.0	4.0[3, 12]	184[3]	177[3]	Cuba
21.9[3, 32]	17.7[3]	8.6[3]	...	3.2[3]	9.0[3]	29.7[3]	...	9.9[3]	1.0[18]	124[18]	77[18]	Cyprus
46.9	14.7	12.0	...	3.7	2.2	7.9	...	12.6	4.1	910	248	Czechoslovakia
41.2[26]	5.1[26]	11.4[26]	9.6[26]	2.7[26]	...	19.1[26]	1.6[26]	9.3[26]	4.6	493	157	Denmark
...	...	...	...	...	...	...	...	...	...	...	998	Djibouti
...	...	...	...	...	...	...	...	...	...	...	...	Dominica
24.2[10]	29.1[10]	8.1[10]	3.0[10]	4.8[10]	4.0[10]	17.8[10]	3.4[10]	5.6[10]	...	112[11]	519[11]	Dominican Republic
...	...	...	...	...	...	...	...	...	34.7	2,131	79	Ecuador
11.9[8, 34]	7.6[8, 34]	16.2[8, 34]	...	7.9[8, 34]	6.3[8, 34]	12.4[8, 34]	28.2[8, 34]	9.5[8, 34]	21.9[12]	1,278	17,756	Egypt
...	...	...	...	...	...	...	...	...	7.6	342	3,336	El Salvador

Trade: domestic (continued)

country	domestic trade as percentage of GDP, 1986	year	wholesale trade					retail trade		
			establishments[a]	employees[b]	sales[c] $'000,000	employees per establishment	sales per establishment $'000	outlets[a]	employees[b]	sales[c] $'000,000
Equatorial Guinea	5.0[2]	...	...	...	...	8.5	...	7,416	17,100	201
Ethiopia	9.6[2]	1973[7,35]	375	3,200	...	19	241	430	1,484[2,4,10]	38
Faeroe Islands	15.4[33]	1987	78	[4]	...	...	...	21	...	...
Falkland Islands	...	1976	2	...	...	...	...	...	...	...
Fiji	15.2[2]	1983	138[7]	2,000[7]	248[7]	14.5[7]	1,797[7]	578[7]	6,000[7]	351[7]
Finland	10.2[2]	1987	10,001[18]	82,719[18]	26,223[18]	8.3[18]	2,622[18]	36,600[26]	147,697[26]	29,760
France	12.3	1988	176,271	1,066,566[33]	238,044[26]	6.4[33]	1,481[26]	559,808	1,230,399[33]	151,522[26]
French Guiana	12.3[20]	1988	139	[4]	...	...	...	588	2,737[4,26]	...
French Polynesia	14.0[18]	1986	[4]	[4]	...	...	...	947[4]	5,038[4]	...
Gabon	13.4	1982	...	...	...	...	...	...	12,683[4,12,21]	...
Gambia, The	28.6[2]	1983	...	[4]	...	...	...	...	3,732[4]	...
Gaza Strip	...	1986	...	[4]	...	...	...	...	13,400[4]	...
Germany, East	9.0[1,2]	1987	...	...	...	...	...	102,900[9]	882,800	66,252
Germany, West	8.6	1986	41,909	990,800[12]	365,236	23.6[12]	8,715	168,230	2,099,600[12]	222,333
Ghana	22.8[2]	1977[7]	460	1,100	115	2.4	250	2,182	5,700	237
Gibraltar	...	1986	...	601	...	...	...	...	1,857	...
Greece	11.7[2,3]	1984	23,218	73,812	...	3.2	...	184,892	301,318	12,263[5]
Greenland	8.0[20]	1988	...	[4]	149	[4]	...	...	2,214[4,33]	173
Grenada	19.9[2]	1983	...	[4]	[4]	...	...	7,408[4]	2,813[4,21]	6[4]
Guadeloupe	18.3[2,10]	1988	[4]	[4]	...	...	...	802	9,561[4,26]	212[9]
Guam	51.5[11]	1982	89	981	165	11.0	1,853	802	5,400	413
Guatemala	24.9	1985	...	[4]	...	...	...	88,200[11]	178,741[4]	712[9]
Guernsey	...	1986	...	[4]	...	...	...	...	4,413[4]	...
Guinea	21.5[3]	1979	...	[4]	...	...	...	...	12,808[4,37]	...
Guinea-Bissau	...	1979	[4]	[4]	...	...	...	685[4,8]	5,085[4]	44[4,28]
Guyana	6.9[2]	1980	...	[4]	...	...	...	147[7]	14,690[4]	93[9]
Haiti	17.7	1983	...	[4]	...	...	...	653[7,27]	303,353[4]	174
Honduras	12.0[2]	1984	...	[4]	...	...	...	...	107,292[4]	401[9]
Hong Kong	20.6[2]	1987	14,843	67,055	10,712	4.5	722	58,406	347,095	16,549[38]
Hungary	13.0[1,2]	1988	206[11]	122,600[11]	13,121[21]	595[11]	...	55,045[39]	259,900[39]	11,992[39]
Iceland	9.1[2]	1986	1,509[9,40]	5,132[21]	598[9,40]	...	396[40]	1,868[40]	9,056[40,41]	967[40]
India	10.9[2]	1980	[4]	[4]	[4]	[4]	[4]	3,132,000[4,14]	3,615,000[4,14]	108,300[9]
Indonesia	16.7[2]	1980	[4]	[4]	[4]	...	...	54,632[4]	85,400[4]	3,451[4]
Iran	19.9[2,3]	1972–73	18,210	31,688	2,429	1.7	133	218,132	80,055	27,814[9]
Iraq	11.0[2,3]	1975–76	1,532[25]	2,700[25]	...	1.8[25]	...	77,766[25]	106,800[25]	11,378[9]
Ireland	12.2[2,3]	1984	3,073[8]	40,584[8]	4,593[8]	13.2[8]	1,495[8]	32,332[8]	79,870[8]	5,110
Isle of Man	12.0[10]	1981	...	775	...	...	...	...	3,146	...
Israel	13.0[2]	1983	3,836[8]	44,700[26]	...	8.7[8]	...	43,112	91,200[26]	10,578
Italy	19.2[2]	1983	...	[4]	...	...	...	1,033,725	1,369,200[4]	122,978
Jamaica	23.6[2]	1979	...	[3]	...	...	...	10,150[10]	125,100[3,27]	1,457[9]
Japan	13.2[2]	1988	436,502	4,331,601[12]	2,221,892[3]	9.9[12]	5,379[3]	1,619,599[14]	6,850,478[12,14]	889,253[12,14]
Jersey	...	1986	...	855	...	...	...	...	7,046	...
Jordan	15.1	1977	78[7]	1,075[7]	...	13.8[7]	...	189[7]	2,436[7]	2,210[9]
Kampuchea (Cambodia)	...	...	...	...	...	...	...	...	...	...
Kenya	10.9[2]	1985	2,018	27,481	[4]	13.6	...	4,969	34,628	638[2,4]
Kiribati	12.3	1987	...	[4]	...	...	...	30	1,127[3,4]	[4]
Korea, North	...	...	...	...	...	...	...	749,538	1,467,286	20,889
Korea, South	13.1[2]	1982	45,568	112,400	9,693	2.5	213	14,600	59,527[12]	6,622
Kuwait	8.6[2]	1985	3,087	26,122[12]	3,915	8.5[12]	1,268	...	...	...
Laos	12.1[18]	...	...	...	...	...	...	...	...	...
Lebanon	28.0[18]	1986	...	[4]	...	...	...	...	114,706[4]	1,662[9]
Lesotho	14.3[2]	...	...	...	...	...	...	...	46,850[4]	...
Liberia	5.5[2]	1984	...	[4]	...	...	...	26,825	44,605[12]	9,205[9]
Libya	7.4[2,18]	1973	1,126	4,148[12]	...	3.7[12]	...	228	740	...
Liechtenstein	...	1975	67	216	...	3.2	...	...	...	...
Luxembourg	16.0[2,3]	1986	1,538	7,830[11]	3,152	6.8[11]	2,051	3,750	12,867[11]	2,311
Macau	...	1981	...	482[12]	...	...	...	...	13,652[12]	...
Madagascar	29.0[2,3]	1976	1,104	...	...	...	...	1,570	...	696[21]
Malawi	13.0	1984	439	23,000	522	52	1,189	500	8,600	127
Malaysia	11.6	1980	19,663	116,200	15,461	5.9	786	95,993	73,000	6,099
Maldives	14.8[2]	1977	...	[4]	...	...	...	...	1,341[4,12]	...
Mali	15.6[3]	1979	...	[4]	...	...	...	...	5,200[4]	...
Malta	13.2[2]	1983	3	[4]	...	1.0	...	47	11,936[4,26]	2.3
Martinique	17.4[2,11]	1983	...	[4]	...	...	333	59	3,518[4,21]	234
Mauritania	12.8[2,18]	1971[7]	23	100	102	4.3	4,445	...	700	103
Mauritius	11.7[2]	1986	[4]	[4]	...	[4]	...	207[2,4,7]	10,107[2,4,7]	164[2,4,7]
Mayotte	...	1983	[4]	[4]	[4]	...	[4]	41[4]	597[3,4]	27[4]
Mexico	23.8	1975	11,652	130,939[12]	6,739	11.2[12]	578	463,612	987,089[12]	17,062[9]
Monaco	...	...	...	...	...	...	...	4,828	21,100	1,088
Mongolia	31.6[1,3]	1983[4,43]	...	...	...	...	...	...	...	...
Montserrat	18.0[2]	1980	...	...	...	...	...	160	200	11[21]
Morocco	13.4[2,3]	1972	...	...	...	...	...	4,000[7]	20,000[7]	4,727[9]
Mozambique	...	1980	...	[4]	...	...	...	...	63,058[4]	2,116
Myanmar (Burma)	22.7[2]	1983	...	...	...	...	...	...	...	...
Nauru	...	...	...	...	...	...	...	...	...	...
Nepal	4.2[2]	1983	...	[4]	...	...	...	85,955	119,000[4,12,21]	736
Netherlands, The	13.1[2]	1986	38,309	255,300[9]	110,204	...	2,877	...	336,000[9]	35,409
Netherlands Antilles	18.3[3]	1986	...	[4]	...	...	...	...	16,390[4]	149[9,16]
New Caledonia	24.7[18]	1981	...	[4]	...	...	...	324	4,524[4]	...
New Zealand	17.7[2]	1984	8,263[44]	76,664[44]	16,295[44]	9.3[44]	1,972[44]	29,961[14,44]	116,301[14,44]	11,263
Nicaragua	23.9	1987	...	[4]	...	...	...	20,610[11]	94,600[4]	356[9]
Niger	13.5[2,18]	...	...	...	...	...	...	...	...	...
Nigeria	19.7[2,3]	1983[7]	154	16,000	2,220	104	14,415	421	20,000	2,202
Niue	...	1982	[4]	[4]	...	...	...	22[4]	82[4]	...
Norfolk Island	...	1986	...	[4]	...	...	...	...	275[4]	...

retail trade (continued)

percent breakdown of sales

food[d]	clothing, shoes[e]	home furnishings[f]	eating, drinking[g]	drugs, pharmaceuticals[h]	building materials[i]	automobile parts[j]	general merchandise[k]	other[l]	employees per outlet	sales per outlet $'000	population per outlet	country
...	...	...	...	...	...	...	...	...	2.3	27	...	Equatorial Guinea
...	...	...	...	...	...	...	...	...	...	89	109	Ethiopia
...	...	...	...	...	...	...	...	...	...	...	95	Faeroe Islands
...	...	...	...	...	...	...	...	...	...	...	...	Falkland Islands
27.8[28]	10.4[28]	1.7[28]	...	1.0[28]	2.6[28]	17.1[28]	22.7[28]	16.7[28]	10.4[7]	607[7]	1,163[7]	Fiji
23.8	5.7	1.8	...	2.3	8.2	26.0	20.3	11.9	4.0[26]	613[26]	134[26]	Finland
54.6[26]	10.2[26]	6.9[26]	7.9[26]	4.0[26]	3.6[26,36]	4.6[26]	...	8.2[26]	2.2[33]	270[26]	98[33]	France
...	...	...	...	...	...	...	...	...	...	...	156	French Guiana
50.5	9.6	...	...	...	33.8	6.1	...	...	...	...	...	French Polynesia
...	...	...	...	...	...	...	...	...	5.3[4]	...	188[4]	Gabon
...	...	...	...	...	...	...	...	...	...	...	...	Gambia, The
49.4	15.8	5.8	—	5.7	6.8	...	...	16.5	8.7[9,12]	380[9]	162[9]	Gaza Strip
29.2	10.5	13.1	—	6.8	...	15.8	16.5	8.1	12.5[12]	1,322	363	Germany, East
...	...	...	...	...	...	...	...	...	2.6	108	4,738	Germany, West
...	...	...	...	...	...	...	...	...	...	...	...	Ghana
60.0[5]	18.1[5]	9.5[5]	...	...	...	...	...	12.4[5]	1.6	...	54	Gibraltar
...	...	...	...	...	...	...	...	...	...	...	...	Greece
...	...	...	...	...	...	...	...	...	...	...	...	Greenland
...	...	...	...	...	...	...	...	...	...	...	...	Grenada
...	...	...	...	...	...	...	...	...	...	...	...	Guadeloupe
16.3	4.3	3.1	9.2	0.6	4.2	32.6	7.4	22.3	6.7	515	138	Guam
...	...	...	...	...	...	...	...	...	...	...	83[11]	Guatemala
...	...	...	...	...	...	...	...	...	...	...	...	Guernsey
...	...	...	...	...	...	...	...	...	...	...	...	Guinea
...	...	...	...	...	...	...	...	...	0.8[4,8]	...	1,080[4,8]	Guinea-Bissau
9.7	18.9	13.8	4.5	2.8	17.7	18.6	...	14.0	...	743	5,884	Guyana
...	...	...	...	...	...	...	...	...	...	...	7,034[7,27]	Haiti
23.7[18]	8.8[18]	...	...	...	...	...	5.0[18]	62.5[18]	...	...	...	Honduras
29.8	6.1	12.3	10.2	2.4	7.6	7.8	10.2	13.6	5.9	289	96	Hong Kong
...	...	...	...	...	...	...	...	...	4.7[39]	218[39]	192[39]	Hungary
24.6[9]	8.8[9]	10.1[9]	—	5.6[9]	—	—	31.1[9]	19.8[9]	4.8[40,41]	518[40]	130[40]	Iceland
...	...	...	...	...	...	...	...	...	1.2[4,14]	...	219[4,14]	India
...	...	...	...	...	...	...	...	...	1.6[4]	63[4]	2,681[4]	Indonesia
...	...	...	...	...	...	...	...	...	0.4	...	141	Iran
...	...	...	...	...	...	...	...	...	1.4[25]	...	148[25]	Iraq
40.0	12.4	...	15.8	3.4	...	6.0	6.0	16.4	2.5[8]	129[8]	99[8]	Ireland
22.0	7.0	11.0	...	...	...	10.0	6.0	44.0	2.1	...	...	Isle of Man
50.8	15.1	...	...	3.4	...	...	...	30.7	...	245	95	Israel
...	...	...	...	...	...	...	...	...	...	119	55	Italy
...	...	...	...	...	...	...	...	...	...	...	214[10]	Jamaica
27.8	9.7	5.0	—	...	...	10.3	14.6	32.6	4.2[12,14]	549[12,14]	7.8[14]	Japan
...	...	...	...	...	...	...	...	...	...	...	...	Jersey
...	...	...	...	...	...	...	...	...	12.9[7]	...	792[7]	Jordan
...	...	...	...	...	...	...	...	...	...	...	...	Kampuchea (Cambodia)
...	...	...	...	...	...	...	...	...	7.0	128[2,4]	4,092	Kenya
...	...	...	...	...	...	...	...	...	...	127	2,226	Kiribati
29.4[20,22]	13.1[20]	8.9[20]	18.9[20]	5.0[20]	2.4[20]	5.4[20]	1.2[20]	15.6[20]	...	...	...	Korea, North
11.0	13.7	14.4	...	2.2	6.7	27.4	11.1	13.5	2.0	28	53	Korea, South
...	...	...	...	...	...	...	...	...	4.1	454	117	Kuwait
...	...	...	...	...	...	...	...	...	...	...	...	Laos
...	...	...	...	...	...	...	...	...	...	...	...	Lebanon
...	...	...	...	...	...	...	...	...	...	...	...	Lesotho
...	...	...	...	...	...	...	...	...	...	...	...	Liberia
...	...	...	...	...	...	...	...	...	1.7[12]	...	84	Libya
...	...	...	...	...	...	...	...	...	3.2	...	105	Liechtenstein
30.5[22]	12.1	10.4	...	3.6	...	35.7	...	7.7	3.3[11]	616	98	Luxembourg
...	...	...	...	...	...	...	...	...	...	...	4,977	Macau
...	...	...	...	...	...	...	...	...	17.2	254	14,196	Madagascar
32.9[42]	7.3[42]	10.8[42]	...	2.5[42]	1.1[42]	33.3[24,42]	4.4[42]	7.7[42]	...	...	...	Malawi
...	...	...	...	...	...	...	...	...	0.8	64	143	Malaysia
...	...	...	...	...	...	...	...	...	...	...	...	Maldives
...	...	...	...	...	...	...	...	...	...	...	...	Mali
...	...	...	...	...	...	...	...	...	...	578[7]	83,378[7]	Malta
...	...	...	...	...	...	...	...	...	...	...	...	Martinique
...	...	...	...	...	...	...	...	...	11.9	1,742	20,300	Mauritania
...	...	...	...	...	...	...	...	...	48.8[2,4,7]	792[2,4,7]	4,976[2,4,7]	Mauritius
...	...	...	...	...	...	...	...	...	...	652[3]	1,477[3]	Mayotte
17.8	7.3	5.8	...	2.8	7.3	24.5	16.6	17.9	2.1[12]	41	138	Mexico
...	...	...	...	...	...	...	...	...	...	...	...	Monaco
...	...	...	...	...	...	...	...	...	4.3	225	372	Mongolia
...	...	...	...	...	...	...	...	...	1.2	c. 70	73	Montserrat
...	...	...	...	...	...	...	...	...	5.0[7]	...	c. 4,000[7]	Morocco
...	...	...	...	...	...	...	...	...	...	...	...	Mozambique
...	...	...	...	...	...	...	...	...	...	...	...	Myanmar (Burma)
...	...	...	...	...	...	...	...	...	...	...	...	Nauru
43.9	11.9	15.3	...	1.8	...	5.0	...	22.1	3.7	412	170	Nepal
...	...	...	...	...	...	...	...	...	...	...	...	Netherlands, The
...	...	...	...	...	...	...	...	...	...	...	143[11]	Netherlands Antilles
...	...	...	...	...	...	...	...	...	...	...	439	New Caledonia
17.9	4.7	7.1	4.0[45]	2.3	1.6	41.4	5.4	15.7[46]	3.9[14,44]	346[14,44]	106[14,44]	New Zealand
...	...	...	...	...	...	...	...	...	...	...	143[11]	Nicaragua
...	...	...	...	...	...	...	...	...	...	...	...	Niger
...	...	...	...	...	...	...	...	...	47.5	5,230	226,615	Nigeria
...	...	...	...	...	...	...	...	...	3.7[4]	...	144[4]	Niue
...	...	...	...	...	...	...	...	...	...	...	...	Norfolk Island

Trade: domestic

country	domestic trade as percentage of GDP, 1986	year	wholesale trade establishments[a]	employees[b]	sales[c] $'000,000	employees per establishment	sales per establishment $'000	retail trade outlets[a]	employees[b]	sales[c] $'000,000
Norway	12.1[2]	1987	15,722	111,022[41]	48,042	7.1[41]	3,056	38,556	135,263[41]	26,292
Oman	13.7[2]	1986		[4]				4,731[2,4,5]	123,000[4]	2,449[9]
Pacific Is., Trust Terr. of the										
Marshall Islands		1980		148[12]					395[2,12]	
Micronesia, Fed. States of	29.6[9]	1980		348[12]					489[2,12]	
Northern Mariana Islands		1982	11	364	29	33	2,595	258	1,490	57
Palau		1983		114[12]					226[2,12]	
Pakistan	14.8[2]	1983						276,701[27]	501,773[12,27]	12,848
Panama	13.7[2]	1982[47]	560	13,115	1,491	23.4	2,662	7,561	15,765[7]	1,334
Papua New Guinea	7.9[9]	1985		[10]					91,900[8,12]	1,186
Paraguay	26.7[2]	1983						103,010	72,200	2,015
Peru	18.4[2,3]	1973	4,210	34,100	2,163	8.1	514	279,968	241,872	4,836
Philippines	19.2[2]	1981	20,642	122,717	4,538	5.9	220			
Pitcairn Island		1982	—	—	—	—	—	1		
Poland	16.0[1,2]	1985		119,600[41]	33,482			256,869	606,700[41]	31,009
Portugal	20.4	1983[7]	4,522	135,400[12]	9,260	29.9[12]	2,048	4,889	74,400[12]	3,057
Puerto Rico	14.8[3]	1985	2,327	18,000	7,365	7.7	3,165	35,918	127,000	7,206
Qatar	6.3[2]	1983	268					2,848		1,943
Réunion	15.6[9]	1988	[4]	[4]				6,409[4]	21,562[4]	
Romania	6.3[1,9]	1985						82,707	457,800	16,164
Rwanda	13.8[2]	1978							8,014[2,4]	
St. Helena and Ascension		1976		[4]					954[12]	
St. Kitts and Nevis	18.9[2]	1984		[4]					940[4]	
St. Lucia	22.1[2]	1980		[4]					4,770[2,4,12]	
St. Pierre and Miquelon		1982		[4]					279[2,4,12]	
St. Vincent	10.9[2]		102[26]	[4]				867[26]	1,704[4]	
San Marino		1988		[4]					1,994[4]	
São Tomé and Príncipe	9.8[18]	1981		[4]				80,266	174,187[12]	36,574[9]
Saudi Arabia	8.4[2,33]	1981	4,460	31,481[12]		7.1[12]		510[8]	24,789[4]	664[9]
Senegal	37.4[2]	1982		[4]						
Seychelles	24.8[2]	1985	[4]	[4]		[4]		131[4]	1,298[4]	
Sierra Leone	12.8[2,3]	1983–84							7,211[4,37]	177[9]
Singapore	17.1[2]	1983	20,103	98,900	30,772	4.9	1,531	16,029[14]	42,800	4,741
Solomon Islands	7.7[14,15]	1986		[4]					3,300[4]	
Somalia	5.6[3]									
South Africa	13.2[2,49]	1988			37,451			58,100[9,49]	373,200[9,49]	22,197
Bophuthatswana	[49]	1979[4]						1,248	4,195	110
Ciskei	[49]	1979[4]						682	1,632	36
Transkei	[49]	1977[4]							5,580[12]	
Venda	[49]	1978[4]						485		
South West Africa/Namibia	11.2	1977	222	5,035	377	22.7	1,698	1,284	7,569	254
Spain	20.5[2,3]	1984	40,000[20]					710,865[20]	1,400,000[20]	54,777
Sri Lanka	19.0[2]	1983[7]	190	15,000		78.9		1,348	44,300	1,116[4,18]
Sudan, The	23.4[3]	1981								3,278
Suriname	15.5[2]	1984		[4]					12,840[4]	189[9]
Swaziland	10.4[2]	1984	67	1,000		14.9		656	3,700	23[26]
Sweden	11.4[2]	1986	31,960[18]	167,800[18]	37,518[18]	5.2[18]	1,174[18]	70,431	220,035	35,540
Switzerland	17.4[3]	1985	15,019	143,470		9.6		53,465	259,674	23,620[18]
Syria	20.0[2]	1983	2,827[27]					75,865[27]	110,000[12,27]	5,696
Taiwan	13.7[2]	1987	55,654[9]	169,100	7,572[3]	2.9[9]	101[9]	355,760[9]	181,200	14,291[3]
Tanzania	12.2[2,3]	1983						1,620[7]	16,524[7]	945
Thailand	22.6[2]	1980[7,52]	5,647	187,737	21,693	33.2	3,842	11,280	113,408	3,945
Togo	22.0[9]	1980						181[7]	1,815[7]	112
Tokelau		1984						3	821	
Tonga	14.8[2,9]	1976		14[12]					654[12]	
Trinidad and Tobago	14.3[2,3]	1977	124	6,786	509	54.7	4,102	370	15,986	812[9]
Tunisia	19.4[2]	1984		[3]				23,027	153,860[3,4]	2,814
Turkey	17.1[2]	1984	12,623	53,500	7,311	4.2	579		100,400	8,585
Turks and Caicos Islands		1983		[4]					288[2,4]	
Tuvalu	34.0[20]	1979		[4]					113[4,12]	
Uganda	5.2[11]	1977	226	4,100		18.1		251	3,200	5,285[21]
U.S.S.R.	17.3[1,2]	1985		2,371,000	259,220			1,041,400	7,660,000	421,460
United Arab Emirates	11.3[2]	1983	[4]			[4]		13,906[2,4,8]	121,278[4,8]	5,093[9]
United Kingdom	12.2[2]	1988	108,392[18,54]	877,000[9,54]	212,577[18,54]	8.4[9,54]	1,961[18,54]	343,387	2,334,000	204,400[14,54]
United States	17.3[2]	1987	415,829[11]	4,984,880[11]	1,997,895[11]	12.0[11]	4,805[11]	1,503,593	17,779,942	1,493,309
Uruguay	10.4[2]	1984						256	1,439[12]	5,397[14]
Vanuatu		1983[55]	18	187[12]		10.4[12]			161,596	13,366[9]
Venezuela	18.4[2]	1979							447,000[4,26]	7,485[8]
Vietnam	11.7[1,9]	1979	2,400[56]	[4]				1,191[56]	6,980	489
Virgin Islands (U.S.)		1982	104	1,363	197	13.1	1,196			
Wallis and Futuna		1983		[4]					123[4,12]	
West Bank		1986		[4]					23,000[4]	
Western Sahara				[4]						
Western Samoa	18.4[2]	1981		[4]					1,821[2,4]	
Yemen (Aden)	12.3[9]	1986		[4]					47,373[4]	
Yemen (Şan'ā')	13.1[2]	1986		[4]					201,606[4]	2,195[9]
Yugoslavia	11.1[2]	1986	9,146	54,818	6,332	6.0	692	92,200[38]	219,775	54,065[38]
Zaire	18.6[18]	1981						3,036[7]	33,398[7]	3,300[9]
Zambia	10.7[2]	1974	494[7]	15,500[7]	977[7]	31.4[7]	1,978[7]	1,636[7]	13,700[7]	768[9]
Zimbabwe	11.3[2]	1985		[4]					78,800[4]	693

[1]Percent of net material product. [2]Includes hotels. [3]1985. [4]Retail trade data include wholesale trade. [5]1978. [6]Excludes retail trade network of the agricultural cooperatives. [7]Data refer to larger establishments only. [8]1977. [9]1983. [10]1980. [11]1982. [12]All persons engaged including proprietors. [13]1973. [14]Excludes restaurants (eating and drinking establishments). [15]1972. [16]Netherlands Antilles includes Aruba. [17]1981–82. [18]1984. [19]Data refer to New Providence Island only. [20]1979. [21]1981. [22]Includes alcohol and tobacco. [23]Home furnishings includes building materials. [24]Includes all fuels. [25]Privately owned establishments only. [26]1986. [27]1975. [28]1976. [29]General merchandise includes clothing, shoes. [30]For 12 major cities only. [31]Rarotonga only. [32]Wholesalers selling directly to the public only. [33]1987. [34]Selected outlets in urban areas only. [35]Excludes Addis Ababa and Asmera. [36]Motorcycles, bicycles, motor fuel, lubricants, and tires only.

retail trade (continued)

percent breakdown of sales

food[d]	clothing, shoes[e]	home furnishings[f]	eating, drinking[g]	drugs, pharma-ceuticals[h]	building materials[i]	automobile parts[j]	general merchandise[k]	other[l]	employees per outlet	sales per outlet $'000	population per outlet	country
31.2[22]	9.7	12.2	...	...	...	31.9	5.2	9.8	3.5[41]	682	109	Norway
...	...	...	...	...	...	...	...	...	...	...	188[2,4,5]	Oman
...	...	...	...	...	...	...	...	...	...	...	...	Pacific Is., Trust Terr. of the Marshall Islands
...	...	...	...	...	...	...	...	...	...	...	...	Micronesia, Fed. States of
25.1	1.4	1.0	10.4	...	6.2	20.5	6.6	28.8	5.8	220	71	Northern Mariana Islands
64.0	12.0	4.0	...	...	...	...	...	20.0	1.8[12,27]	...	273[27]	Palau
33.5[48]	10.9[48]	9.5[48]	...	...	...	...	...	46.1[48]	13.9[7]	176	270	Pakistan
...	...	...	7.1[2]	...	...	26.0	...	66.9	...	...	...	Panama
...	...	...	...	...	...	...	...	...	...	...	...	Papua New Guinea
...	...	...	...	...	...	...	...	...	0.7	20	145	Paraguay
25.4[22]	12.3	6.7	...	...	11.3	29.5[24]	...	14.8	0.9	17	177	Peru
...	...	...	...	...	...	...	...	...	...	...	...	Philippines
...	...	...	...	...	...	...	...	...	...	...	54	Pitcairn Island
31.1[39]	9.9[39]	11.1[39]	...	2.0[39]	4.9[39]	6.7[39]	...	34.3[39]	2.4[41]	121	144	Poland
21.5[5]	14.1[5]	11.2[5]	...	3.3[5]	5.6[5]	35.2[5]	—38.5—		15.3[12]	625	2,047	Portugal
30.5[11]	9.9[11]	4.5[11]	7.5[11]	4.3[11]	5.9[11]	23.2[11]	8.9[11]	5.3[11]	3.5	201	91	Puerto Rico
...	...	...	...	...	...	...	...	...	...	682	99	Qatar
...	...	...	...	...	...	...	...	...	3.4[4]	...	90[4]	Réunion
30.0	10.0	5.9	25.0	1.6	0.8	...	...	26.7	5.5	195	275	Romania
...	...	...	...	...	...	...	...	...	...	...	...	Rwanda
...	...	...	...	...	...	...	...	...	...	...	...	St. Helena and Ascension
...	...	...	...	...	...	...	...	...	...	...	...	St. Kitts and Nevis
...	...	...	...	...	...	...	...	...	...	...	...	St. Lucia
...	...	...	...	...	...	...	...	...	...	...	...	St. Pierre and Miquelon
...	...	...	...	...	...	...	...	...	...	...	...	St. Vincent
...	...	...	...	...	...	...	...	...	...	...	26[26]	San Marino
...	...	...	...	...	...	...	...	...	...	...	...	São Tomé and Príncipe
...	...	...	...	...	...	...	...	...	2.2[12]	...	120	Saudi Arabia
...	...	...	...	...	...	...	...	...	11.0[7]	...	11,839[7]	Senegal
...	...	...	...	...	...	...	...	...	9.9[4]	...	498[4]	Seychelles
...	...	...	...	...	...	...	...	...	...	...	...	Sierra Leone
1.2	4.3	10.2	10.5	0.7	0.3	22.1	—50.7—		2.7[14]	296[14]	156[14]	Singapore
...	...	...	...	...	...	...	...	...	...	...	...	Solomon Islands
...	...	...	...	...	...	...	...	...	...	...	...	Somalia
43.6	16.0	9.8	3.8	4.0	...	...	14.7	8.1	6.4[9,49]	383[9,49]	c. 540[9,49]	South Africa
...	...	...	...	...	...	...	...	...	3.4	88	1,041	Bophuthatswana
...	...	...	...	...	...	...	...	...	2.4	53	972	Ciskei
...	...	...	...	...	...	...	...	...	...	...	...	Transkei
...	...	...	...	...	...	...	...	...	...	...	621	Venda
31.4	11.9	5.3	...	2.8	1.7	...	41.9	5.0	5.9	198	713	South West Africa/Namibia
39.2	10.5	16.7	...	...	...	4.2[50]	...	29.4	2.0[20]	119[20]	52[20]	Spain
...	...	...	...	...	...	...	...	...	32.9	...	11,436	Sri Lanka
...	...	...	...	...	...	...	...	...	...	...	...	Sudan, The
...	...	...	...	...	...	...	...	...	...	...	...	Suriname
52.5[26]	25.1[26]	22.4[26]	...	...	...	...	...	...	5.6	...	969	Swaziland
30.7[9]	8.0[9]	8.6[9]	9	2.3[9]	2.3[9]	21.2[9]	10.5[9]	16.3[9]	3.1	505	119	Sweden
46.4[18]	13.5[18]	...	4.0[18]	...	...	...	...	36.1[18]	4.9	...	122	Switzerland
16.0	2.5	...	...	3.5	12.3	39.5[51]	3.5	22.7	1.4[12,27]	...	97[27]	Syria
21.5[21]	3.2[21]	8.8[21]	...	4.1[21]	3.1[21]	8.7[21,24]	3.1[21]	47.5[21]	0.3[9]	33[9]	52[9]	Taiwan
2.6	2.7	10.8	...	1.3	10.8	57.8	5.5	8.5	10.0[7]	...	12,600[7]	Tanzania
...	...	...	...	...	...	...	...	...	10.1	350	4,163	Thailand
...	...	...	...	...	...	...	...	...	10.0[7]	...	15,600[7]	Togo
...	...	...	...	...	...	...	...	...	...	...	533	Tokelau
...	...	...	...	...	...	...	...	...	...	...	...	Tonga
18.6	...	8.5	2.7	...	10.7	28.2	15.3	15.9	43.2	1,467	2,798	Trinidad and Tobago
...	...	...	...	...	...	...	...	...	...	...	...	Tunisia
24.8	12.3	15.4	...	3.7	8.8	11.2[53]	0.6	23.2[24]	4.4	373	2,130	Turkey
...	...	...	...	...	...	...	...	...	...	...	...	Turks and Caicos Islands
...	...	...	...	...	...	...	...	...	...	...	...	Tuvalu
42.6	23.9	7.4	8.7	1.2	1.1	5.6	...	9.5	12.7	...	47,200	Uganda
...	...	...	...	...	...	...	...	...	7.4	405	267	U.S.S.R.
35.8	10.4	18.2[23]	...	1.8[24]	...	...	17.9	15.9	...	...	49[2,4,8]	United Arab Emirates
20.2	5.2	5.0	10.0	3.6	5.5	29.1	21.1	9.3	6.8[12,14,54]	400[14,26,54]	165[14,26,54]	United Kingdom
...	...	...	...	...	...	...	...	...	11.8	912	162	United States
...	...	...	...	...	...	...	...	...	...	...	...	Uruguay
50.2	10.1	7.6	...	...	...	5.0	...	27.1	5.6[12]	...	484	Vanuatu
...	...	...	...	...	...	...	...	...	...	...	...	Venezuela
26.5	7.1	3.7	8.6	2.2	3.8	13.1	4.6	30.4	25.0[56]	...	26,300[56]	Vietnam
...	...	...	...	...	...	...	...	...	5.9	411	97	Virgin Islands (U.S.)
...	...	...	...	...	...	...	...	...	...	...	...	Wallis and Futuna
...	...	...	...	...	...	...	...	...	...	...	...	West Bank
...	...	...	...	...	...	...	...	...	...	...	...	Western Sahara
...	...	...	...	...	...	...	...	...	...	...	...	Western Samoa
...	...	...	...	...	...	...	...	...	...	...	...	Yemen (Aden)
35.1	16.1	...	...	...	5.8	...	...	43.1	5.3	407	557	Yemen (Şan'ā')
...	...	...	...	...	...	...	...	...	11.0[7]	...	9,676[7]	Yugoslavia
...	...	...	...	...	...	...	...	...	8.4[7]	359[7]	2,873[7]	Zaire
...	...	...	...	...	...	...	...	...	...	...	...	Zimbabwe

[37]Includes wage earners in finance and insurance.   [38]1988.   [39]Socialist sector only.   [40]Excludes fuels, automobiles, alcohol and tobacco, and building materials.   [41]Full-time equivalents.   [42]Peninsular Malaysia only.   [43]State- and cooperative-owned establishments including public catering.   [44]1982–83.   [45]Excludes bars.   [46]Includes bars and hotels.   [47]Excludes Colón Free Trade Zone.   [48]1971.   [49]South Africa includes Bophuthatswana, Ciskei, Transkei, and Venda.   [50]Motor vehicles only.   [51]Includes machinery, transport equipment, and petroleum products.   [52]Excludes combined wholesale/retail outlets.   [53]Excludes all fuels.   [54]Excludes motor vehicles.   [55]Urban establishments only.   [56]State sector only.

Finance

This table presents major statistical aggregates comprising national financial structure or constituting a basis for certain international financial comparisons. It includes such data as international reserves, money supply, central banking activity and discount rates, commercial (or "deposit money") banking activity, and external indebtedness of the central government. The country models are broadly similar and permit comparison of internal structure and external position at a high level of generalization.

One of the principal financial criteria of the relative economic position of a country is the size of its international reserves. International reserves as represented in this table comprise the sum of a country's (1) reserve position in the International Monetary Fund (IMF), a quota subscribed in the country's own currency, constituting a level up to which transactions may be effected within the IMF system, (2) holdings of foreign exchange, (3) holdings of gold, and (4) holdings of Special Drawing Rights (SDRs; an unconditional credit allocation, within a quota system set by the IMF, of currency needed by a country to maintain stability of foreign exchange transactions or markets). At appropriate accounting intervals these four elements are valued in a single unit of account (the SDR) and summed. The portion of this reserve total comprised by foreign exchange is very significant as an indication of the country's international liquidity (ability to pay its debts immediately in hard, or convertible, currencies). The ratio of external debt to total reserves, however, is less susceptible of interpretation in isolation: a low ratio, for example, may characterize the situation of a country with little need to borrow or of one with substantial debt but also the means to repay it. Much higher ratios, on the other hand, may be manageable, despite small reserves, if a country's export earnings are also high.

The section on money supply for the country, both as a total and as a per capita amount, refers to one particular measure of money in circulation: M1, the sum of money in private sector demand deposit accounts and outside banks in circulation; it is distinguished from a broader measure of supply, M2, which is roughly M1 plus "quasi-money" (the time, savings, and foreign-currency deposits of residents).

The section of the table outlining banking activity and the principal monetary aggregates encompasses both central bank authorities and commercial (deposit) banks. For both, the principal component aggregates are grouped under assets and liabilities. For certain countries, the four principal aggregates under assets and liabilities do not comprise the entire total, and the percentages shown, therefore, may add to less than 100% (occasionally more, when the net of other liabilities [capital, reserves, undistributed profits, checks, and other transit items] is negative, reducing the total against which these percentages are calculated). The items excluded by the choice of categories are the least significant worldwide but may be important locally; they include such items as quasi-money, money seasonally adjusted, unused bank overdrafts, and so on. In the case of the central bank authority, data are also provided for the central bank discount rate, generally the controlling interest rate for banking and commercial activity in the country.

The largest share of assets in the case of both central and commercial banks is usually either claims on government and government agencies

Finance

country	international reserves, 1989[a]: total ('000,000 SDRs)	% foreign exchange	ratio of external debt to total reserves, 1987[b]	money supply, 1988[b]: stock ('000,000 national currency)	M1 per capita	central bank authority, 1988[b] assets (%): claims on government	claims on private sector	claims on banks	claims on foreign assets	liabilities (%): reserve money	government deposits	foreign liabilities	capital accounts	central bank discount rate, 1989[a]
Afghanistan	231	79.2	4.5[1]	131.4[2]	9,170[2]	83.9[2,3]	0.3[2]	1.3[2]	14.5[2]	70.5[2]	8.3[2]	4.5[2]	7.6[2]	...
Albania	...	...	...	223.869[2]	9,530[2]	81.2	0.1	13.2	5.6	89.7	0.1	0.2	—	...
Algeria	952	78.5	10.0	...	...	...	...	...	...	...	...	...	...	...
American Samoa	...	...	...	...	...	...	...	...	...	...	...	...	...	...
Andorra	...	...	...	...	...	...	...	...	...	...	...	...	...	...
Angola	...	...	...	...	...	...	...	...	...	...	...	...	...	...
Anguilla		...	...	0.128	1,640	34.9	—	—	65.1	104.5	—	—	—	7.0[7]
Antigua and Barbuda	21[6]	100.0[6]	4.6[1,5]	12.580[2]	400[2]	31.2[8]	—	35.2[8]	33.6[8]	39.2[8]	0.3[8]	21.6[8]	8.9[8]	61.2[9,10]
Argentina	2,652[6]	94.2[6]	25.9	0.181	2,900	—	—	—	100.0	77.0	9.5	—	11.5	9.5
Aruba	70	100.0												15.9
Australia	10,104	92.4	...	36.161	2,210	21.4	—	—	78.6	70.1	—	—	33.0	5.0
Austria	6,911	82.8	...	232.2	30,600	3.0	—	32.9	64.1	71.8	0.1	—	27.9	9.0
Bahamas, The	142	94.4	1.1	0.292	1,180	19.5	—	8.7	71.7	70.0	1.7	—	30.2	9.5[11]
Bahrain	903	94.6	0.81	0.239	560		—		100.0	24.2	49.2	5.1	5.3	10.8
Bangladesh	673	94.7	10.5	49.996[9]	480[9]	13.4[3]	—	40.8	45.8	61.9	1.2	40.2		
Barbados	87	97.7	3.4	0.524	2,060	25.2	6.7	0.9	67.2	75.2	20.8	20.8	7.9	8.0
Belgium	8,908	79.7	3.1	1,151.1	117,000	19.5	—	—	80.5	88.2	—	—	—	9.3
Belize	48	95.8	3.1	0.082	450	24.5	—	—	75.5	49.8	—	12.2	—	10.0
Benin	4	25.0	218.3	72.0	15,900	20.7	—	77.7	1.6	34.5	5.4	54.9	—	8.5
Bermuda		...	...	0.317[2]	230[2]	...	...	...	...	...	...	...	...	11.0[6,13]
Bhutan	116	73.3	32.4	0.661	90	66.3	—	16.1	17.6	13.7	77.5	25.9	—	6.5
Bolivia	2,026	98.2	0.3	0.407	330	—	—	—	100.0	9.1	53.7	—	19.0	443.5
Botswana	4,381[6]	98.4[6]	14.3	106.1[5]	770[5]	32.3[3,5]	17.3[5]	4.3[5]	46.1[5]	14.1[5]	23.7[5]	67.1[5]	—	5.9[2,10]
Brazil		...	...	0.026[2,14]	2,100[2,14]	...	...	...	...	...	...	...	...	...
British Virgin Islands	...	...	...	...	...	...	...	...	...	...	...	...	...	...
Brunei		...	...	1.092[9]	4,700[9]	...	...	...	...	...	...	...	...	...
Bulgaria	224	94.2	2.5	101.1	11,700	14.5	—	3.7	81.8	79.7	3.6	14.6	—	8.5
Burkina Faso	86	88.4	11.8	19.970	3,830	54.2[3]	0.7	9.4	35.7	39.5	11.2	16.8	19.8	7.0
Burundi	112	99.1	42.7	389.1	34,300	23.7	—	66.4	9.9	38.7	27.4	29.5	—	9.5
Cameroon		...	...			26.3	—	—	73.7	96.1	—	—	—	12.3
Canada	12,561	84.2	...	90.8	3,480	...	...	...	...	...	...	...	...	...
Cape Verde		...	...	0.045	1,790	...	...	...	...	...	...	...	...	...
Cayman Islands		...	...	51.8	18,600	34.9	—	13.8	51.4	61.6	8.7	23.3	—	9.5
Central African Republic	93	92.5	5.3	64.6	11,800	17.2	—	51.2	31.6	75.3	8.4	9.0	—	9.5
Chad	49	89.8	5.1	...	...	...	...	...	...	...	...	...	...	...
Chile	2,659	98.0	6.0	116.2[8]	9,670[8]	14.6[8]	11.0[8]	48.1[8]	26.3[8]	5.8[8]	1.8[8]	35.3[8]	11.3[8]	26.1[6,10]
China	12,554	90.7	1.4	548.8	500	12.7	7.2	74.0	6.1	87.6	6.0	0.8	5.8	...
Christmas Island	...	...	...	...	...	...	...	...	...	...	...	...	...	...
Cocos (Keeling) Islands	...	...	...	...	...	...	...	...	...	...	...	...	...	...
Colombia	2,360	93.9	4.4	1,282.0	41,500	24.7	3.1	15.4	56.8	47.4	18.0	9.1	10.4	30.0
Comoros	14[9]	100.0[9]	6.1	8.879	20,200	18.4	—	—	81.6	62.8	18.6	3.8	20.5	8.5[6]
Congo	2	50.0	864.4	95.0	41,600	55.9	—	41.5	2.6	53.8	3.8	37.1	—	9.5
Cook Islands	...	...	...	...	...	...	...	...	...	...	...	...	...	...
Costa Rica	571	99.8	7.4	65.267	22,500	42.6[3]	—	17.2	40.2	29.9	7.0	128.9	4.5	31.5
Côte d'Ivoire	7	71.4	744.5	578.0	48,600	35.3	—	64.3	0.4	45.0	0.2	51.8	—	8.5
Cuba	...	...	...	...	...	...	...	...	...	...	...	...	...	...
Cyprus	751	95.7	1.6	0.359	640	24.1	—	12.1	63.8	85.0	3.5	1.6	—	6.0
Czechoslovakia		...	...	235.4[2]	45,900[2]	6.4	23.0	1.2	69.3	27.8	42.4	1.5	—	7.0
Denmark	6,154	92.5	...	26.310	53,600	—	—	19.6	80.4	69.8	27.2	—	6.5	...
Djibouti		...	2.4	...	...	...	...	...	...	...	...	...	...	6.5[7]
Dominica	10[6]	100.0[6]	14.5[1,5]	0.061	770	52.5	—	—	47.5	68.9	—	30.1	—	...
Dominican Republic	99	100.0	16.1	2.609[2]	380[2]	33.4[3]	—	27.1	39.5	97.6	—	241.8	-13.9	...
Ecuador	317	95.0	17.6	396.5	38,300	61.5[3]	2.3	14.3	21.9	24.3	16.7	148.9	2.0	14.0
Egypt	1,156	91.3	23.0	20.579	400	80.3[3]	—	11.0	8.6	62.2	4.1	28.7	—	...
El Salvador	153	88.9	7.6	3.425	680	41.0[3]	0.1	39.3	19.5	47.2	17.5	28.6	8.2	...

or foreign assets and holdings, though some of the latter, such as the large outstanding loans to socialist and less developed countries, have become the chief liabilities. The chief liability of a central bank is usually reserve money (the currency and notes issued by the bank). When government deposits represent a substantial share, budgetary surpluses have usually been deposited by the central government. Large foreign liabilities imply extensive foreign investment. Among the deposit money banks, loans to the private sector normally represent the largest share of assets; occasionally, a trade- or banking-oriented country such as Belgium or Hong Kong will show major foreign assets. The chief liabilities of these banks will usually be savings deposits. If the country commands a high degree of confidence internationally, foreign liabilities may comprise a substantial share of liabilities.

Because the majority of the world's countries are in the less developed bloc, and because their principal financial concern is external debt and its service, data are given for outstanding external public and publicly guaranteed long-term debt rather than for total public debt, which is the major concern in the developed countries. For comparability, the data are given in U.S. dollars. The volume of debt by itself does not create external payment problems. If the country's external debt service (interest payments plus principal repayment) needs can be met by a strong, dependable export market, by export of services, or, occasionally, by direct remittances from abroad (by residents working abroad and sending wages home in foreign currencies, for example), no debt problem need exist. Countries whose debt service ratio (total debt service as a percent of

exports of goods and services) is relatively high, however, must often base their external borrowing policy on maintenance of domestic conditions of strict efficiency and, sometimes, austerity. The failure to adhere to such policies may lead to eventual crises of financial liquidity, deflation, and slower growth.

Ideally, the data presented here should be obtained by utilizing a single international methodology to provide a universally comparable set of international statistics. No international agency, however, can collect such data for all countries because of differences, both overall and in detail, in national definitions of financial aggregates, in accounting methodology, and in the completeness with which it is possible to survey a country's financial activity. The greater part of the data presented in the table comes from the IMF's *International Financial Statistics* and the World Bank's *World Debt Tables*. These sources are supplemented by other recent data from national, regional, or other international sources. In a few cases the desired data are negligible or unavailable, as noted.

Detailed percentages may not add to 100.0 because of rounding, statistical discrepancy, or nonaccounting of negligible quantities.
—None, less than half the last significant figure, or not applicable.
... Not available.
a. Latest month.
b. Year-end.

deposit money banks, 1988[b]										external public debt outstanding (long-term, disbursed only), 1987[b]							country
assets (%)				liabilities						total ('000,000 U.S.$)	creditors (%)		debt service				
loans to govern-ment	loans to private sector	re-serves	foreign assets	deposits ('000,000,000 national currency)	composition (%)						offi-cial	private	total ('000,000 U.S.$)	repayment (%)		debt service ratio (%)	
					demand depos.	savings depos.	govt. depos.	foreign liabilities						princi-pal	inter-est		
2.6[2,3]	46.0[2]	21.2[2]	30.2[2]	26.771[2]	21.1[2]	45.7[2,4]	0.3[2]	5.2[2]		1,482[1]	...	...	49[1]	18.4[1]	81.6[1]	9.6[1]	Afghanistan
9.8[2]	87.0[2]	2.6[2]	0.6[2]	207.541[2]	50.0[2]	16.4[2]	5.0[2]	19.8[2]		19,240	17.0	83.0	4,920	72.0	28.0	46.0	Albania
...	...	...	...	...	...	...	...	...		...	...	...	...	...	...	...	Algeria
...	...	...	...	...	...	...	...	...		...	...	...	...	...	...	...	American Samoa
																	Andorra
...	...	...	...	...	...	...	...	...		1,283[1]	...	...	259[1]	72.2[1]	27.8[1]	13.2[1,5]	Angola
14.1[3]	61.1	9.7	15.1	0.678	11.3	55.4	—	21.8		76[1,5]	...	...	6[1,5]	...	...	...	Anguilla
24.3[2]	63.7[2]	5.6[2]	6.4[2]	76.658[2]	4.3[2]	46.8[2,4]	8.5[2]	38.9[2]		47,451	15.0	85.0	3,894	13.0	87.0	4.7[1,5]	Antigua and Barbuda
1.9	59.2	11.9	27.1	0.722	18.9	44.4	0.3	29.9		...	...	...	...	...	...	45.3	Argentina
																	Aruba
14.6[3]	77.4	4.3	3.8	196.344	12.2	57.5	0.2	8.1		...	...	...	...	...	...	...	Australia
33.9[3]	38.4	1.8	25.9	2,652.9	5.0	43.0	2.2	28.1		...	...	...	...	...	...	...	Austria
20.8[3]	88.0	7.4	−16.1	0.983	21.7	69.8[4]	1.9	...		174.7	18.5	81.5	49.7	72.6	27.4	2.7[9]	Bahamas, The
7.6	32.5	3.2	56.6	1.511	10.2	50.9	22.1	10.6		958[1]	...	...	147[1]	51.7[1]	48.3[1]	6.3[1]	Bahrain
31.7[3,9]	56.0[9]	6.8[9]	5.5[9]	152.340[9]	20.3[9]	54.3[9]	3.5[9]	2.4[9]		8,851	97.5	2.5	323	59.1	40.9	16.5	Bangladesh
23.9	58.5	8.5	9.1	1.650	20.0	61.9	5.1	13.1		501	47.3	52.7	71	54.3	45.7	7.4[9]	Barbados
23.6[3]	18.3	0.2	57.9	9,681.3	7.7	16.2[4]	...	71.9		...	...	...	...	...	...	...	Belgium
16.5[3]	68.5	10.2	4.8	0.289	14.8	58.9	10.9	7.3		113.0	88.8	11.2	11.1	64.0	36.0	7.3	Belize
10.0	84.4	1.2	4.4	125.7	33.6	20.6	17.7	16.2		929	57.5	42.5	34	55.9	44.1	15.9	Benin
...	...	...	...	7.024[2]	...	...	...	...		316[1]	...	...	66[1]	59.1[1]	40.9[1]	95.8[1,5]	Bermuda
...	78.7	16.6	4.7	1.128[2]	...	...	...	...		40.7	100.0	—	0.5	—	100.0	...	Bhutan
—	45.8	42.0	8.8	2.079	6.5	49.1[4]	—	5.7		4,599	76.4	23.6	137	54.4	45.6	22.1	Bolivia
3.5[3]	41.4[2]	14.4[2]	3.8[2]	0.747	41.6	45.5	—	6.2		514.4	91.5	8.5	69.6	54.2	45.8	3.7	Botswana
40.3[2,3]	...	...	...	6,693.6[2]	10.9[2]	12.8[2]	1.4[2]	14.1[2]		91,653	27.5	72.5	7,656	38.4	61.6	26.7	Brazil
—	38.1[2]	1.0[2]	60.9[2]	0.229[2]	8.0[2]	49.8[2]	—	37.6[2]		91.5	...	...	0[1,5]	...	...	...	British Virgin Islands
—17.9[9]—		0.7[9]	...	3.433[9]	—82.5[9]—			...		27[1]	...	...	5[1]	20.0[1]	80.0[1]	...	Brunei
...	...	...	...	...	...	...	...	...		6,100[15]	...	...	...	...	...	...	Bulgaria
4.2	64.3	25.8	5.7	164.2	28.8	29.1	35.3	8.4		794	95.2	4.8	31	54.8	45.2	8.8[9]	Burkina Faso
39.2[3]	54.4	2.0	4.5	17.871	46.1	17.9	2.6	6.7		718	97.2	2.8	42	64.3	35.7	38.5	Burundi
6.9	81.4	2.3	9.4	1,257.2	17.7	24.5	20.5	7.8		2,785	80.0	20.0	336	60.4	39.6	15.8	Cameroon
6.8[3]	76.5	1.9	14.8	356.5	20.3	49.5[4]	0.5	21.5		...	...	...	...	...	...	...	Canada
...	...	...	...	...	...	...	...	...		120.6	97.6	2.4	6.9	50.7	49.3	...	Cape Verde
...	...	...	...	202.663	...	...	...	...		145[1,5]	...	...	39[1,5]	...	...	...	Cayman Islands
0.7	87.2	0.8	11.2	35.2	30.8	23.2	7.8	7.7		520	95.0	5.0	22	59.1	40.9	12.0	Central African Republic
1.1	86.0	7.3	5.6	84.9	26.5	5.1	13.0	4.7		296.6	84.2	15.8	6.5	50.8	49.2	3.8	Chad
9.7[8]	81.6[8]	2.6[8]	6.0[8]	1,331.0[8]	3.9[8]	29.1[8]	7.0[8]	64.2[8]		15,536	25.5	74.5	1,367	13.6	86.4	21.1	Chile
—	81.4[2]	15.2[2]	3.4[2]	1,139.6[2]	23.4[2]	29.3[2]	...	3.3[2]		23,659	40.3	59.7	2,842	62.4	37.6	7.1	China
...	...	...	...	...	...	...	...	...		...	...	...	...	...	...	...	Christmas Island
3.9	67.9	21.8	6.5	2,622.7	27.6	31.2[4]	—	15.1		13,828	59.8	40.2	2,372	53.3	46.7	30.7	Colombia
2.6	65.3	16.5	16.0	10.488	36.7	34.1	0.8	18.3		187.7	99.9	0.1	1.2	25.0	75.0	4.1	Comoros
17.4	75.2	1.2	6.2	233.3	17.9	18.3	19.5	9.3		3,679	43.4	56.6	195	76.9	23.1	18.6	Congo
...	...	...	...	...	...	...	...	...		21.5	...	...	0[1,5]	...	...	...	Cook Islands
8.8[3]	46.0	40.0	5.2	131.222	30.6	64.2[4]	1.2	3.1		3,629	55.1	44.9	182	33.5	66.5	12.1	Costa Rica
7.8	84.3	4.5	3.4	1,374.3	20.3	26.6	8.3	15.7		8,450	56.0	44.0	710	40.6	59.4	19.6	Côte d'Ivoire
...	...	...	...	...	...	...	...	...		8,369[1]	...	...	462[1]	51.7[1]	48.3[1]	5.5[1,5]	Cuba
12.0	62.8	17.6	7.6	1.856	10.8	58.4	1.9	18.0		1,419	66.3	33.7	260	63.8	36.2	13.4	Cyprus
...	...	...	...	...	...	...	...	...		5,900[15]	...	...	...	...	...	...	Czechoslovakia
6.3[2]	63.7[2]	0.8[2]	29.2[2]	574.1[2]	38.5[2]	31.8[2]	—	27.7[2]		...	...	...	...	...	...	...	Denmark
0.8[3]	50.0	1.3	47.9	73.020	23.8	34.6	2.0	22.0		152.4	97.9	2.1	12.5	72.8	27.2	...	Djibouti
5.4[3]	45.7	10.4	38.5	0.281	13.6	52.8	—	15.8		48[1,5]	...	...	1[1,5]	...	...	4.1[1,5]	Dominica
17.7[2,3]	66.0[2]	14.1[2]	2.1[2]	5.678[2]	22.3[2]	40.3[2]	8.5[2]	1.6[2]		2,938	72.2	27.8	162	42.0	58.0	16.3[9]	Dominican Republic
—	76.1	19.0	5.0	549.6	42.3	32.4	—	...		9,026	35.0	65.0	494	45.1	54.9	20.7	Ecuador
30.3[3]	28.1	16.4	25.2	67.410	12.3	50.4[4]	2.1	12.6		34,515	82.3	17.7	1,495	52.1	47.9	12.7	Egypt
5.3	71.8	18.7	4.3	8.448	22.8	61.6[4]	...	1.7		1,597	94.9	5.1	180	58.9	41.1	19.4	El Salvador

Finance (continued)

country	international reserves, 1989[a] total ('000,000 SDRs)	% foreign exchange	ratio of external debt to total reserves, 1987[b]	money supply, 1988[b] stock ('000,000,000 national currency)	M1 per capita	assets (%) claims on government	claims on private sector	claims on banks	claims on foreign assets	liabilities (%) reserve money	government deposits	foreign liabilities	capital accounts	central bank discount rate, 1989[a]
Equatorial Guinea	4	100.0	306.8	5.9	17,400	55.2	—	30.4	14.4	37.7	16.9	71.3	—	9.5
Ethiopia	53	84.9	15.7	3.722	80	55.9	—	40.1	4.0	69.2	8.7	4.3	7.1	3.0
Faeroe Islands	...	...	...	...	...	...	...	...	...	...	...	...	...	...
Falkland Islands	...	...	...	0.280	380	0.5[3]	—	—	99.5	60.8	12.0	—	23.2	8.0
Fiji	140	82.9	2.5	...	...	...	...	...	...	...	...	...	...	7.5
Finland	5,068	92.2	...	35.921	7,250	2.1	10.4	24.1	63.4	63.4	3.8	0.5	12.6	7.5
France	22,755	78.4	...	1,366.0	24,400	7.1	—	41.6	51.3	52.3	—	1.0	—	9.5
French Guiana	...	...	...	2.977	32,100	...	...	...	...	...	...	...	...	...
French Polynesia	...	...	...	41.203	217,000	...	...	...	...	...	...	...	...	9.5
Gabon	46	89.1	125.7	146.3	119,000	59.1	—	21.4	19.5	49.1	12.1	48.7	—	16.0
Gambia, The	24	100.0	3.9	0.214	260	22.4[3]	—	24.4	53.1	44.1	53.8	137.2	16.1	16.0
Gaza Strip	...	...	...	...	...	...	...	...	...	...	...	...	...	...
Germany, East	...	...	...	408.3	6,680	8.6	—	51.2	40.2	78.2	1.2	9.4	—	5.0
Germany, West	47,533	85.1	...	122.0	8,760	65.9[3]	—	2.5	31.5	42.1	5.8	91.2	—	26.0
Ghana	145	93.8	10.6	...	...	...	...	...	...	...	...	...	...	...
Gibraltar	...	...	...	1,000.0[2]	100,000[2]	55.2[2]	0.3[2]	16.5[2]	28.0[2]	80.5[2]	3.3[2]	—	—	19.0
Greece	2,212	90.6	6.1	...	...	...	...	...	...	...	...	...	...	...
Greenland	...	...	...	0.083	780	43.8	—	—	56.2	92.0	—	3.8	—	6.5[7]
Grenada	13[6]	100.0[6]	2.9	5.304	15,600	...	...	...	...	...	...	...	...	...
Guadeloupe	...	...	...	...	...	...	...	...	...	...	...	...	...	...
Guam	...	...	...	...	...	...	...	...	...	...	...	...	...	...
Guatemala	257	90.3	7.5	2.019	230	74.4[3]	—	8.5	17.1	90.9	35.1	44.0	6.2	13.0
Guernsey	...	...	...	...	...	...	...	...	...	...	...	...	...	...
Guinea	...	...	...	22.5[9]	3,660[9]	...	...	...	...	...	...	...	...	...
Guinea-Bissau	...	...	...	...	...	...	...	...	...	...	...	...	...	...
Guyana	3[6]	100.0[6]	102.7	2.095	2,780	99.9	—	—	0.1	27.8	—	53.0	12.2	14.0[6]
Haiti	13	92.3	36.5	2.098[2]	390[2]	83.5[2,3]	9.3[2]	2.2[2]	5.0[2]	64.7[2]	12.5[2]	33.6[2]	6.3[2]	24.0
Honduras	25	96.0	25.2	1.244	250	55.1[3]	—	38.2	6.6	29.3	22.7	50.8	16.3	...
Hong Kong	...	...	...	88.834	15,500	...	...	...	...	...	...	...	...	10.5
Hungary	1,318	95.8	6.8	308.8	29,200	43.4[3]	—	43.0	13.7	26.5	2.8	70.7	1.7	38.0
Iceland	283	97.9	...	44.231	176,000	53.1	1.5	1.1	44.4	50.6	14.1	6.1	7.0	10.0
India	3,677	73.2	5.4	576.2	710	79.2	—	11.4	9.4	73.1	0.2	5.1	7.0	11.1[11]
Indonesia	3,861	95.3	7.2	14,392.0	82,100	11.3[3]	5.1	53.9	29.7	21.2	26.4	13.2	9.2	...
Iran	...	...	...	3,922.0[16]	89,400[16]	85.0[3,16]	—	2.1[16]	12.8[16]	68.2[16]	17.9[16]	1.6[16]	3.9[16]	...
Iraq	...	...	...	...	...	...	...	...	...	...	...	...	...	...
Ireland	3,178	91.2	...	2.826	800	13.3	—	—	86.7	57.2	23.8	—	23.2	10.0
Isle of Man	...	...	...	...	...	...	...	...	...	...	...	...	...	27.8[6]
Israel	4,276	99.2	3.0	3.725	820	46.8	—	18.2	34.9	71.2	23.8	0.3	—	13.5
Italy	34,175	87.9	...	368,261.0[2]	6,416,000[2]	63.8[2]	—	0.9[2]	35.4[2]	70.0[2]	—	—	—	21.0
Jamaica	117	100.0	20.1	3.445	1,440	75.5	—	3.9	20.7	96.3	95.1	211.8	7.8	3.3
Japan	69,122	92.3	...	111,844.0	910,000	34.1	—	32.8	33.1	110.9	14.1	—	—	...
Jersey	...	...	...	...	...	...	...	...	...	...	...	...	...	6.2[6]
Jordan	237	88.6	7.4	1.668	390	65.5	—	—	34.5	95.3	—	—	—	...
Kampuchea (Cambodia)	...	...	...	...	...	...	...	...	...	...	...	...	...	16.0
Kenya	237	92.4	17.3	19.160	820	73.1	—	—	26.9	59.8	—	41.3	5.1	...
Kiribati	...	...	...	...	...	...	...	...	...	...	...	...	...	...
Korea, North	...	...	...	...	...	...	...	...	...	...	...	...	...	8.0
Korea, South	13,247	99.1	6.8	12,152.0	288,000	12.0[3]	—	57.5	30.5	35.1	20.8	0.1	—	6.0
Kuwait	1,860	80.2	0.1[1]	0.958	480	—	—	—	100.0	77.1	158.6	—	49.7	...
Laos	...	...	...	...	...	...	...	...	...	...	...	...	...	21.8[2]
Lebanon	1,183	70.8	0.3	30.326[9]	11,100[9]	25.7[2]	0.2[2]	0.3[2]	73.8[2]	12.4[2]	20.8[2]	—	—	16.5
Lesotho	41	95.1	3.5	0.220	130	45.0	—	—	55.0	92.7	-8.6	1.9	10.7	5.1[10]
Liberia	1	100.0	2,258.8	0.189	80	98.9[3]	0.2	0.8	0.1	33.8	2.6	47.2	-1.5	5.0[2]
Libya	3,472	82.7	0.1[1]	3.012	750	32.3	1.8	—	65.9	98.8	39.2	—	—	...
Liechtenstein	...	...	...	...	...	...	...	...	...	...	...	...	...	5.0[10]
Luxembourg	...	...	...	54.5[2]	146,000[2]	...	...	...	...	...	...	...	...	...
Macau	...	...	...	5.712[2]	13,200[2]	...	...	...	...	...	...	...	...	11.5
Madagascar	176	100.0	16.8	455.0	41,100	78.4[3]	—	0.6	20.9	14.6	36.8	145.1	0.6	11.0
Malawi	75	96.0	22.0	0.436	50	57.5[3]	—	—	42.5	56.9	19.2	37.4	—	4.1[6]
Malaysia	5,071	92.6	2.5	18.730	1,090	10.6	—	—	89.4	58.0	5.4	—	—	7.0[11]
Maldives	21	100.0	7.3	0.230	1,120	49.5	—	0.1	50.4	82.2	23.2	1.9	4.5	8.5
Mali	39	74.4	108.5	114.0	14,500	68.6	—	23.1	8.3	65.8	—	18.5	—	5.5
Malta	967	90.2	0.1	0.361	1,040	—	—	—	100.0	80.5	8.8	—	—	...
Martinique	...	...	...	4.991	14,800	...	...	...	...	...	...	...	...	...
Mauritania	34[6]	94.1[6]	25.8	20.858	10,900	30.5	—	40.4	29.2	49.1	1.1	86.3	23.1	6.5[6]
Mauritius	357	98.3	1.6	3.704	3,500	15.8	—	1.6	82.6	45.2	7.6	19.0	4.4	10.0
Mayotte	...	...	...	0.346	4,520	...	...	...	...	...	...	...	...	...
Mexico	3,985	88.4	6.6	20,744.0	249,000	68.3	—	2.0	29.7	40.6	—	21.5	—	51.8[11]
Monaco	...	...	...	...	...	...	...	...	...	...	...	...	...	...
Mongolia	...	...	...	...	...	...	...	...	...	...	...	...	...	...
Montserrat	...	...	...	...	...	...	...	...	...	...	...	...	...	8.5[6]
Morocco	292	91.4	41.5	62.032	2,560	41.6	19.8	24.7	13.9	78.5	1.4	25.1	—	...
Mozambique	128	93.0	107.2	16.337[9]	420[9]	-26.5[9]	—	124.7[9]	1.8[9]	69.5[9]	—	5.3[9]	—	1.5[2,10]
Myanmar (Burma)	...	...	...	...	...	...	...	...	...	...	...	...	...	...
Nauru	...	...	...	...	...	...	...	...	...	...	...	...	...	...
Nepal	188	93.6	4.9	9.801	540	58.1	1.7	6.2	33.9	42.4	18.4	8.5	18.2	11.0
Netherlands, The	14,164	81.7	...	111.3	7,530	6.3	—	8.8	84.9	54.9	4.3	—	9.5	6.0
Netherlands Antilles	201	90.5	4.2[1]	0.665	3,640	19.6	—	—	80.4	77.9	7.1	—	—	6.0
New Caledonia	...	...	...	40.877	261,000	...	...	...	...	...	...	...	...	...
New Zealand	2,091	98.7	...	6.667[2]	1,990[2]	34.8	0.5	0.3	64.4	20.1	50.4	12.2	—	14.6
Nicaragua	...	...	...	10.937[16]	3,520[16]	74.3[16]	—	17.9[16]	7.8[16]	34.9[16]	-0.9[16]	84.5[16]	1.3[16]	...
Niger	149	93.3	5.0	73.2[2]	10,300[2]	27.3	—	21.3	51.4	58.1	15.4	22.4	—	8.5
Nigeria	823	97.0	21.4	21.446	190	81.7	4.0	4.6	9.7	41.4	18.7	0.1	4.3	15.0[2]
Niue	...	...	...	...	...	...	...	...	...	...	...	...	...	...
Norfolk Island	...	...	...	...	...	...	...	...	...	...	...	...	...	...

deposit money banks, 1988[b] — assets (%) and liabilities · **external public debt outstanding (long-term, disbursed only), 1987[b]**

loans to government	loans to private sector	reserves	foreign assets	deposits ('000,000,000 national currency)	demand depos.	savings depos.	govt. depos.	foreign liabilities	total ('000,000 U.S.$)	official	private	debt service total ('000,000 U.S.$)	principal	interest	debt service ratio (%)	country
5.2	69.9	12.7	12.1	10.3	31.0	.5.4	6.8	—	174.9	95.0	5.0	9.1	65.9	34.1	23.0	Equatorial Guinea
57.8[3]	11.6	27.1	3.6	4.164	42.2	37.7	3.6	3.1	2,434	83.3	16.7	180	72.2	27.8	28.4	Ethiopia
...	...	...	...	...	...	...	...	...								Faeroe Islands
...	...	...	...	...	...	...	...	...	0[1,5]			0[1,5]				Falkland Islands
20.5[3]	54.8	17.5	7.2	0.751	28.2	60.4	3.5	6.2	334.2	83.8	16.2	62.3	58.5	41.5	12.1	Fiji
0.7[2]	74.0[2]	5.1[2]	20.2[2]	367.057[2]	6.3[2]	45.0[2]	3.2[2]	35.4[2]								Finland
4.7[9]	60.0[9]	1.4[9]	34.0[9]	3,997.0[9]	18.2[9]	27.6[9]	—	32.2[9]								France
...	...	...	...	...	...	...	...	...	18[1,5]	...	...	1[1,5]	...	...	1.7[1,5]	French Guiana
...	...	...	...	...	...	...	...	...	365[1]	...	...	6[1]	—	100.0[1]	7.3[1]	French Polynesia
27.0	68.5	1.2	3.3	372.5	25.4	27.4	11.6	9.8	1,605	39.8	60.2	71	18.6	81.4	5.1	Gabon
35.3[3]	51.0	6.3	7.5	0.409	23.9	44.2	—	2.1	272.9	93.9	6.1	14.8	67.1	32.9	12.9	Gambia, The
...	...	...	...	...	...	...	...	...								Gaza Strip
18.9[3]	63.6	3.1	14.3	2,858.1	9.3	30.6	7.3	8.2	20,400[15]	...	...	...	...	...	...	Germany, East
16.0[3]	43.8	31.6	8.6	75.3	43.0	43.8	4.0	17.3	2,207	87.7	12.3	173	67.6	32.4	19.2	Germany, West
— 17.4[9] —			0.9[9]	...	0.401[9]	— 79.0[9] —			80[1]	...	...	17[1]	64.7[1]	35.3[1]	...	Ghana
33.7[2]	38.7[2]	22.3[2]	5.3[2]	4,425.7[2]	5.4[2]	71.1[2]	...	23.8[2]	17,437	27.6	72.4	3,435	66.8	33.2	29.9	Gibraltar
...	...	...	...	...	...	...	...	...								Greece
13.6[3]	59.0	11.4	16.0	0.360	13.4	60.9	—	11.5	66.8	96.0	4.0	5.5	67.3	32.7	6.6[9]	Greenland
...	...	...	...	...	...	...	...	...	57[1]	...	...	0[1]	...	...	...	Grenada
...	...	...	...	...	...	...	...	...								Guadeloupe
1.5	72.8	24.5	1.1	4.272	21.4	69.7	—	3.5	2,345	69.3	30.7	292	50.3	49.7	24.9	Guam
...	...	...	...	...	...	...	...	...								Guatemala
...	...	...	...	...	...	...	...	...	1,616	93.9	6.1	111	68.5	31.5	...	Guernsey
...	...	...	...	...	...	...	...	...	390.7	79.0	21.0	8.8	53.4	46.6	37.1	Guinea
																Guinea-Bissau
22.6[3]	27.6	46.9	2.9	5.744	17.9	57.7	—	2.5	874	77.5	22.5	25	36.0	64.0	9.4[5]	Guyana
0.9[2]	50.4[2]	42.5[2]	6.2[2]	1.900[2]	34.7[2]	62.3[2]	—	0.4[2]	673	89.9	10.1	22	60.9	39.1	5.1	Haiti
21.7	71.7	6.0	0.6	3.251	19.0	48.4[4]	—	2.8	2,681	81.3	18.7	229	62.3	37.7	23.0	Honduras
...	...	...	81.5	3,286.4	...	...	...	81.8	4,710[1]	10.9	89.1	1,157[1]	63.1[1]	36.9[1]	4.6[1]	Hong Kong
44.9[3]	36.2	14.5	4.4	873.9	16.0	34.5[4]	—	11.0	15,931	...	...	3,228	65.0	35.0	26.7	Hungary
3.6	83.4	9.6	3.4	133.613	31.1	32.2	—	26.1								Iceland
22.1	63.4	14.6	—	1,367.5	15.9	71.2	—		37,325	82.4	17.6	3,296	62.2	37.8	16.9	India
12.3[3]	65.1	8.6	14.0	59,887.0	13.4	46.0[4]	3.7	1.9	41,284	60.4	39.6	5,434	57.0	43.0	27.9	Indonesia
19.3[8]	44.6[8]	33.6[8]	2.5[8]	6,117.8[8]	37.5[8]	48.8[8]	—	1.0[8]	1,397[1]	...	...	953[1]	88.6[1]	11.4[1]	6.2[1,5]	Iran
...	...	...	...	...	...	...	...	...	9,645[1]	...	...	2,445[1]	79.0[1]	21.0[1]	13.2[1,5]	Iraq
16.6	62.5	4.8	16.1	12.880	10.3	48.6	0.8	25.5	...	...	...	...	...	...	...	Ireland
...	...	...	...	...	...	...	...	...								Isle of Man
37.1	40.8	11.5	10.5	109.119	1.9	40.1	5.1	15.7	17,767	72.9	27.1	2,451	44.0	56.0	17.8	Israel
21.6[2]	54.2[2]	13.8[2]	10.3[2]	691,494.0[2]	43.8[2]	32.6[2]	—	15.0[2]								Italy
14.9[3]	50.6	25.5	9.0	6.025	35.8	108.1	4.3	14.1	3,511	83.6	16.4	437	48.3	51.7	25.8	Jamaica
11.1[3]	76.2	1.4	11.3	564,949.0	14.2	52.7	—	17.2	...	...	...	...	...	...	...	Japan
...	...	...	...	...	...	...	...	...								Jersey
12.8	55.8	9.5	21.9	2.618	13.5	55.7	4.2	21.1	3,518	67.6	32.4	518	64.6	35.4	16.1	Jordan
...	...	...	...	...	...	...	...	...	564[1]	...	...	9[1]	0.0[1]	100.0[1]	45.8[1,5]	Kampuchea (Cambodia)
20.2[3]	70.1	7.8	2.0	43.824	26.4	54.1[4]	4.8	3.6	4,482	82.6	17.4	502	58.0	42.0	28.8	Kenya
...	...	...	...	...	...	...	...	...	10[1,5]	...	...	0[1,5]	...	...	3.1[1,5]	Kiribati
...	...	...	...	...	...	...	...	...	610[1]							Korea, North
6.4	74.8	11.5	7.3	79,809.0	8.9	46.1[4]	5.4	7.8	24,541	47.5	52.5	12,299	85.0	15.0	21.9	Korea, South
—	70.4	0.5	29.1	8.497	7.2	48.3	1.1	12.1	511[1]	...	...	932[1]	96.9[1]	3.1[1]	9.9[1]	Kuwait
...	...	...	...	...	...	...	...	...	736	99.5	0.5	13	84.6	15.4	...	Laos
9.0[9]	30.7[9]	2.3[9]	57.9[9]	413.4[9]	3.8[9]	71.0[4,9]	0.2[9]	15.7[9]	236.2	92.5	7.5	29.8	55.7	44.3	...	Lebanon
26.1[3]	24.8	32.4	16.7	0.586	30.4	46.1	2.9	5.6	237.0	93.0	7.0	14.6	64.4	35.6	4.4	Lesotho
23.0[3]	25.9	43.2	7.9	0.292	31.7	22.7	6.9	12.0	1,152	82.9	17.1	11	45.5	54.5	2.5	Liberia
—	70.9	25.8	3.3	3.280	60.4	34.1	4.2	4.7	445[1]	...	...	249[1]	96.8[1]	3.2[1]	5.9[1,5]	Libya
...	...	...	...	...	...	...	...	...								Liechtenstein
—	2.5	—	97.5	8,925.3	1.4	5.8	—	85.9	...	...	...	...	...	...	...	Luxembourg
— 31.6[2] —			64.2[2]	33.421[2]	16.3[2]	25.9[2]	—	44.9[2]	128[1]	...	...	12[1]	41.7[1]	58.3[1]	1.3[1,5]	Macau
2.1	74.9	9.5	13.4	700.0	40.5	11.1	8.9	5.0	3,113	91.2	8.8	147	43.5	56.5	35.5	Madagascar
17.1[3]	38.4	42.2	2.2	0.685	33.7	54.9	—	6.6	1,155	95.8	4.2	71	63.4	36.6	23.3	Malawi
13.0	74.7	3.2	9.1	80.059	12.0	51.7	9.4	6.4	19,065	23.9	76.1	2,974	59.1	40.9	14.3	Malaysia
20.5[3]	38.8	30.1	10.6	0.451	14.5	42.5	0.6	26.6	61.8	87.1	12.9	6.4	75.0	25.0	14.4[9]	Maldives
3.7	66.9	21.5	7.9	114.3	42.8	22.8	14.8	23.1	1,847	96.7	3.3	32	59.4	40.6	9.9	Mali
12.0	53.0	17.6	17.4	0.588	6.1	75.5	—	11.5	112.3	100.0	—	12.9	82.9	17.1	1.0	Malta
...	...	...	...	...	...	...	...	...	30[1]	...	...	0[1]	...	...	...	Martinique
0.7	86.0	3.0	10.3	23.957	33.7	16.6	1.1	27.7	1,868	93.2	6.8	86	67.4	32.6	18.2	Mauritania
30.9	53.6	8.2	7.4	16.687	10.1	80.2	—	0.7	545	83.5	16.5	75	60.0	40.0	6.2	Mauritius
...	...	...	...	...	...	...	...	...								Mayotte
38.9[3]	45.9	8.9	6.2	95,385.0	7.5	22.0[4]	0.2	20.1	82,771	19.3	80.7	8,972	36.2	63.8	30.1	Mexico
...	...	...	...	...	...	...	...	...								Monaco
...	...	...	...	...	...	...	...	...	6,500[1]	...	...	140[1]	—	100.0[1]	...	Mongolia
...	...	...	...	...	...	...	...	...	4.1[1,5]	...	...	0[1,5]	...	...	5.9[1,5]	Montserrat
38.6[5]	52.7[5]	1.6[5]	7.1[5]	43.934[5]	54.4[5]	37.8[5]	—	1.1[5]	18,468	73.4	26.6	1,270	51.4	48.6	23.4	Morocco
93.1[3,9]	5.7[9]	1.2[9]	—	52.909[9]	2.1[9]	14.1[4,9]	9.1[9]	14.5[9]	1,610[1]	...	...	141[1]	68.1[1]	31.9[1]	81.0[1,5]	Mozambique
...	...	...	...	...	...	...	...	...	4,257	91.5	8.5	182	62.3	37.7	59.3	Myanmar (Burma)
...	...	...	...	...	...	...	...	...	27[1,5]	...	...	14[1,5]	...	...	...	Nauru
31.1[3]	48.3	7.4	13.2	18.469	13.9	72.5	—	4.0	902	96.1	3.9	34	58.8	41.2	9.7	Nepal
17.0[3]	50.3	0.3	32.4	743.2	10.2	34.6[4]	—	29.6								Netherlands, The
0.3[3]	47.0	9.8	43.0	2.393	13.9	42.0[4]	0.5	40.1	1,012[1]	...	...	167[1]	65.9[1]	34.1[1]	12.8[1]	Netherlands Antilles
19.8[2]	73.4[2]	1.3[2]	5.6[2]	24.963[2]	22.4[2]	57.9[2]	—	6.2[2]	359[1]	...	...	10[1]	10.0[1]	90.0[1]	4.1[1]	New Caledonia
...	...	...	...	...	...	...	...	...								New Zealand
—	84.4[16]	13.8[16]	1.8[16]	20.709[16]	26.2[16]	20.5[4,16]	21.6[16]	6.5[16]	6,150	78.3	21.7	34	64.7	35.3	10.9[9]	Nicaragua
13.5[2]	64.2[2]	20.2[2]	2.1[2]	144.2[2]	24.9[2]	28.6[2]	13.9[2]	26.6[2]	1,259	81.7	18.3	107	43.9	56.1	33.5	Niger
22.7	57.3	6.3	13.7	37.102	26.6	45.7	6.0	0.9	25,707	45.2	54.8	779	30.7	69.3	10.0	Nigeria
...	...	...	...	...	...	...	...	...								Niue
...	...	...	...	...	...	...	...	...								Norfolk Island

Finance (continued)

country	international reserves, 1989[a] — total ('000,000 SDRs)	% foreign exchange	ratio of external debt to total reserves, 1987[b]	money supply, 1988[b] — stock ('000,000,000 national currency)	M1 per capita	central bank authority, 1988[b] — assets (%) claims on government	claims on private sector	claims on banks	claims on foreign assets	liabilities (%) reserve money	government deposits	foreign liabilities	capital accounts	central bank discount rate, 1989[a]
Norway	10,486	92.2	...	187.1	44,500	10.0	—	42.3	47.7	17.7	63.5	—	—	10.0
Oman	766	93.7	1.7	0.315	230	18.0	—	—	82.0	35.7	18.3	0.2	21.3	7.7[10]
Pacific Is., Trust Terr. of the	...	...	...	...	...	...								
Marshall Islands	...	...	...	...	...	...								
Micronesia, Fed. States of	...	...	...	...	...	...								
Northern Mariana Islands	...	...	...	...	...	...								
Palau														10.0
Pakistan	497	83.1	22.0	189.834	1,720	59.3	—	26.5	14.2	69.8	10.4	10.4	—	10.0
Panama	52	100.0	47.7	0.410[5]	190[5]	74.6[3]	20.5	—	4.9	9.9	35.2	45.8	8.5	8.8
Papua New Guinea	322	96.3	3.3	0.322	90	21.3	—	—	78.7	28.2	34.3	1.1	34.6	
Paraguay	301	78.7	4.4	328.488	80,900	38.4[3]	0.8	23.8	37.0	91.7	12.5	2.2	10.5	
Peru	566	88.7	18.6	42.713[9]	2,090[9]	35.7[3,9]	—	25.5[9]	38.7[9]	72.2[9]	12.3[9]	21.1[9]	11.5[9]	9.0
Philippines	419	69.9	20.2	59.7	1,010	37.8[3]	—	21.5	40.7	62.6	52.6	34.2	—	
Pitcairn Island														
Poland	1,547	98.9	23.4	5,748	152,000	18.3	—	64.7	17.0	76.3	15.6	3.4	1.0	6.0[6]
Portugal	5,615	88.7	3.5	1,783.1	172,000	41.6[3]	—	1.0	57.4	35.7	5.5	0.1	18.3	14.5
Puerto Rico	...	...	...	4.778[2]	11,700[2]	—	—	0.2[2]	99.8[2]	70.3[2]	12.8[2]	—	4.0[2]	7.0[6,10]
Qatar	400[6]	80.0[6]	0.3[1]	7.382	12,800									
Réunion	590[9]	80.7[9]	7.4[9]	179.7[9]	7,860[9]	—	42.1[9]	55.9[9]	2.1[9]	28.2[9]	28.7[9]	2.9[9]	—	
Rwanda	60	76.7	3.3	18.332	2,650	32.8	1.0	19.3	46.9	55.9	12.0	9.6	—	9.0
St. Helena and Ascension	...	...	...	...	...									
St. Kitts and Nevis	8[6]	100.0[6]	...	...	...									7.0[7]
St. Lucia	24[6]	100.0[6]	2.6[1,5]	0.141	960	27.5	—	—	72.5	99.2	—	—	—	
St. Pierre and Miquelon	...	...	...	0.189	30,400									
St. Vincent and the Grenadines	16[6]	100.0[6]	1.8	0.063	550	16.7	—	—	83.3	98.2	—	—	—	6.5[7]
San Marino	...	...	...	...	...									
São Tomé and Príncipe	...	...	...	105.7	7,930	—	—	—	100.0[2]	18.3[2]	30.3[2]	—	—	
Saudi Arabia	14,723	59.9	0.2[1]	214.9	29,900	46.7	—	52.5	0.9	35.6	2.7	56.7	—	8.5
Senegal	10	80.0	270.3	...	...									
Seychelles	6	100.0	5.9	0.188	2,800	73.6	—	8.4	17.9	52.7	35.6	—	5.5	6.0
Sierra Leone	2	100.0	90.4	4.630	1,180	89.5[9]	—	—	10.5[9]	63.8[9]	0.6[9]	398.2[9]	—	16.0
Singapore	14,394	98.9	0.2	11.958	4,490	—	—	—	100.0	26.8	23.1	—	—	5.2[11]
Solomon Islands	27	96.3	2.3	0.049	160	12.8	—	11.1	76.1	29.6	30.1	5.4	39.0	11.0[7]
Somalia	10	90.0	268.8	45.436	7,070	73.4[3]	—	13.5	13.0	58.9	16.5	165.1	11.1	45.0
South Africa	648	78.7	...	39.934	1,070	10.2	—	20.3	69.5	117.0	65.2	31.1	...	17.0
Bophuthatswana	...	...	...	...	...									
Ciskei	...	...	...	...	...									
Transkei	...	...	...	...	...									
Venda	...	...	...	...	...									
South West Africa/Namibia	...	...	...	...	...									13.8
Spain	32,472	94.1	...	10,573.0	271,000	36.4	—	11.0	52.6	98.7	2.8	—	5.6	10.0
Sri Lanka	116	98.3	14.6	32.155	1,920	74.8	—	7.4	17.8	55.0	9.1	2.0	31.1	
Sudan, The	34	100.0	694.0	11.218	420	96.8	—	2.5	0.7	79.8	—	95.8	1.8	
Suriname	11	81.8	2.5[1]	1.562[2]	3,720[2]	96.7[2]	—	—	3.3[2]	86.0[2]	0.8[2]	—	3.0[2]	
Swaziland	114	99.1	2.1	0.143	190	1.1	—	0.2	98.7	47.3	26.2	4.0	7.5	12.0
Sweden	7,483	90.8	...	115.4[2]	13,700[2]	57.3	—	10.4	32.3	49.8	—	—	—	9.5
Switzerland	19,442	84.7	...	86.4	13,000	7.2	—	6.1	86.7	67.4	5.0	—	—	5.5
Syria	186[2]	84.4[2]	13.8	67.821[2]	6,080[2]	93.7[2,3]	—	1.1[2]	5.2[2]	77.2[2]	10.0[2]	16.0[2]	0.2[2]	5.0[2]
Taiwan	58,103	...	—[1]	1,950.5	98,000	0.2	—	0.4	99.4	36.9	9.5	—	—	4.5
Tanzania	36	100.0	130.3	64.126	2,740	39.3	—	49.7	11.0	40.9	—	97.2	—	12.5[6]
Thailand	6,260	97.7	3.4	148.5	2,700	15.8	—	24.3	59.9	44.8	5.0	5.6	46.2	8.0
Togo	169	100.0	2.9	64.4	18,100	36.4	—	3.3	60.3	73.8	1.1	22.9	—	8.5
Tokelau	...	...	...	...	...									
Tonga	...	...	...	...	...									
Trinidad and Tobago	117	86.3	8.6	2.187[2]	1,760[2]	47.7[2]	—	—	52.3[2]	52.3[2]	14.9[2]	—	38.0[2]	7.5[6]
Tunisia	646	97.8	11.6	2.494	310	3.6	—	40.3	56.1	63.1	8.8	18.5	4.2	9.2[2]
Turkey	2,298	92.8	17.1	11,211.0	204,000	59.6[3]	—	5.7	34.7	23.7	0.9	69.7	1.1	54.0
Turks and Caicos Islands	...	...	...	...	...									
Tuvalu	...	...	...	...	...									
Uganda	4	100.0	20.7	6.062[9]	400[9]	92.1[3,9]	—		7.9[9]	91.0[9]	47.3[9]	69.3[9]	—	45.0
U.S.S.R.	...	...	...	...	...	0.2	—	5.9	94.0	59.5	24.6	—	14.4	
United Arab Emirates	3,427	92.8	0.3[1]	10.753	5,970	−14.8	—	—	114.8	60.0	—	42.0	—	13.9[11]
United Kingdom	30,445	90.6	...	105.1	1,840	33.5	—	—	66.5	347.3	28.2	0.6	—	7.0
United States	49,870	53.0	...	804.3	3,250									76.0[10]
Uruguay	488	76.8	4.6	135.2[2]	45,500[2]	49.0	4.2	13.1	33.7	14.9	47.1	52.3	—	7.0[11]
Vanuatu	27	92.6	0.4	3.395	22,400	—	—	0.1	99.9	31.6	51.3	0.6	14.6	37.0
Venezuela	2,917	83.9	3.9	166.076	8,740	9.7	—	15.3	75.0	53.6	8.8	—	54.4	
Vietnam	...	...	...	...	...									
Virgin Islands (U.S.)	...	...	...	...	...									
Wallis and Futuna	...	...	...	0.764	50,400									
West Bank	...	...	...	...	...									
Western Sahara	...	...	...	...	...									
Western Samoa	39	97.4	1.9	0.030	190	−16.5	—	6.8	109.8	53.0	22.9	10.5	—	12.0[10]
Yemen (Aden)	45	80.0	16.8	0.472	200	96.0	—	—	4.0	94.5	—	1.8	—	9.5[10]
Yemen (Ṣan'ā')	155	89.0	4.0	27.342	3,130	93.6[3]	—	—	6.4	75.7	9.9	1.3	0.5	
Yugoslavia	1,716	96.1	18.3	24,069.0	1,018,000	2.4	4.1	30.5	62.9	188.9	3.1	84.9	—	372.0
Zaire	115	87.0	35.7	210.673	6,390	85.9[3]	0.8	0.9	12.5	32.6	1.7	61.1	−51.2	26.0[2]
Zambia	100[6]	100.0[6]	39.9	5.246	660	83.4	0.5	—	16.1	44.8	0.1	169.0	—	15.0
Zimbabwe	172	91.3	10.9	1.603	180	45.2[3]	—	—	54.8	89.1	—	20.5	—	9.0

deposit money banks, 1988[b]									external public debt outstanding (long-term, disbursed only), 1987[b]							country
assets (%)				liabilities					total ('000,000 U.S.$)	creditors (%)		debt service				
loans to government	loans to private sector	reserves	foreign assets	deposits ('000,000,000 national currency)	composition (%)					official	private	total ('000,000 U.S.$)	repayment (%)		debt service ratio (%)	
					demand depos.	savings depos.	govt. depos.	foreign liabilities					principal	interest		
10.8[3]	81.4	0.5	7.4	561.9	26.0	29.9[4]	0.9	22.0	...	...	...	...	...	...	...	Norway
2.9	66.7	6.1	24.4	1.147	12.1	57.4	7.4	10.5	2,474	16.0	84.0	612	71.2	28.8	11.2[9]	Oman
...	...	...	...	...	...	...	...	...	43[1]	...	...	17[1]	82.4[1]	17.6[1]	...	Pacific Is., Trust Terr. of the
...	...	...	...	...	...	...	...	...	...	...	...	...	...	...	...	Marshall Islands
...	...	...	...	...	...	...	...	...	...	...	...	...	...	...	...	Micronesia, Fed. States of
...	...	...	...	...	...	...	...	...	...	...	...	...	...	...	...	Northern Mariana Islands
...	...	...	...	...	...	...	...	...	...	...	...	...	...	...	...	Palau
25.5[3]	61.3	8.0	5.2	296.167	32.6	30.2	0.3	12.6	13,150	95.0	5.0	1,173	67.5	32.5	17.5	Pakistan
1.4[5]	9.0[5]	—	89.6[5]	25.184[5]	1.4[5]	5.5[5]	...	88.9[5]	3,722	39.1	60.9	383	41.3	58.7	6.5	Panama
19.2	76.5	2.1	2.2	1.108	18.1	58.7	1.7	8.2	1,471	55.7	44.3	176	56.3	43.7	13.0	Papua New Guinea
—	55.1	40.3	4.6	509.916	32.3	39.7	—	1.6	2,218	60.9	39.1	223	57.4	42.7	21.3	Paraguay
1.0[9]	50.1[9]	44.3[9]	4.6[9]	49.383[9]	32.0[9]	43.9[4,9]	—	3.2[9]	12,485	51.3	48.7	448	56.0	44.0	12.5	Peru
19.5	48.4	9.8	22.3	265.6	7.1	69.2	4.5	26.1	22,321	46.8	53.2	2,142	36.3	63.7	22.7	Philippines
...	...	...	...	...	...	...	...	...	...	...	...	...	...	...	...	Pitcairn Island
34.4	51.3	9.9	4.4	32,229.0	10.0	19.7	0.2	51.8	35,569	64.4	35.6	1,922	50.1	49.9	14.3	Poland
30.6[3]	38.7	21.0	9.8	6,409.1	19.7	70.4	4.0	4.6	14,922	18.6	81.4	4,832	75.4	24.6	30.1	Portugal
—	47.8[2]	2.5[2]	49.7[2]	20.848[17] 18.289[2]	19.3[2]	48.5[2]	1.8[2]	14.6[2]	216[1]	...	...	59[1]	62.7[1]	37.3[1]	3.0[1]	Puerto Rico
...	...	...	...	...	...	...	...	...	...	...	...	...	...	...	...	Qatar
30.4[9]	66.1[9]	1.1[9]	2.5[9]	670.2[9]	6.5[9]	25.0[9]	—	14.2[9]	601[1]	...	...	0[1]	...	...	...	Réunion
...	...	...	...	...	...	...	...	...	5,425	60.0	40.0	1,631	69.2	30.8	12.1[9]	Romania
28.5[3]	58.4	3.5	9.6	27.923	29.5	44.7	9.4	3.5	544.4	97.9	2.1	19.9	65.8	34.2	11.3	Rwanda
...	...	...	...	...	...	...	...	...	...	...	...	...	...	...	...	St. Helena and Ascension
6.4[3]	62.0	9.5	22.0	0.648	13.1	67.8	...	8.0	121[1,5]	...	...	0[1,5]	...	...	1.1[1,5]	St. Kitts and Nevis
...	...	...	...	...	...	...	...	...	341[1,5]	...	...	11[1,5]	...	...	1.0[1,5]	St. Lucia
...	...	...	...	...	...	...	...	...	...	...	...	...	...	...	...	St. Pierre and Miquelon
17.9[3]	44.7	11.5	26.0	0.357	10.5	67.8	—	11.0	36.0	99.2	0.8	2.9	55.2	44.8	3.1[9]	St. Vincent and the Grenadines
...	...	...	...	...	...	...	...	...	...	...	...	...	...	...	...	San Marino
—	36.0	5.5	58.6	196.0	29.3	43.1[4]	0.4	14.7	83.9	99.3	0.7	3.8	55.4	44.6	41.2	São Tomé and Príncipe
...	...	...	...	...	...	...	...	...	3,687[1]	...	...	1,232[1]	92.1[1]	7.9[1]	5.3[1]	Saudi Arabia
5.0	83.6	7.9	3.5	500.2	23.4	23.9	7.6	13.7	3.068	91.6	8.4	274	58.8	41.2	21.2	Senegal
70.9	15.4	6.0	7.7	0.631	14.5	55.7	9.5	6.2	84.2	84.9	15.1	10.1	70.3	29.7	6.9[9]	Seychelles
22.9[3]	23.7	43.6	9.8	4.538	51.4	27.3	—	0.9	513	83.0	17.0	5	80.0	20.0	9.7[9]	Sierra Leone
6.5	48.7	3.5	41.3	83.705	7.1	36.0	4.3	40.4	2,543	12.3	87.7	503	61.0	39.0	1.4	Singapore
26.7	59.0	10.1	4.3	0.121	23.9	66.0	3.4	2.1	85.0	79.5	20.5	8.1	74.1	25.9	2.6[5]	Solomon Islands
-10.7[3]	65.3	11.9	33.6	45.413	50.3	30.9	—	—	2,288	92.7	7.3	9	55.6	44.4	8.3	Somalia
7.5	87.1	3.4	2.0	88.057	37.9	45.3	...	5.6	...	...	...	...	...	...	...	South Africa
...	...	...	...	...	...	...	...	...	...	...	...	...	...	...	...	Bophuthatswana
...	...	...	...	...	...	...	...	...	...	...	...	...	...	...	...	Ciskei
...	...	...	...	...	...	...	...	...	...	...	...	...	...	...	...	Transkei
...	...	...	...	...	...	...	...	...	...	...	...	...	...	...	...	Venda
0.2[8]	50.5[8]	23.0[8]	—	0.810[8]	—64.7[8]—		24.6[8]	0.4[8]	...	...	...	...	...	...	...	South West Africa/Namibia
23.0[3]	59.2	11.7	6.2	45,224.0	15.3	37.8	4.0	9.3	...	...	...	...	...	...	...	Spain
23.5[3]	56.9	8.0	11.6	84.965	15.9	44.1	5.9	10.7	4,109	82.5	17.5	339	64.6	35.4	16.1	Sri Lanka
0.6	45.0	32.0	22.5	10.024	47.3	27.5	10.8	6.1	7,876	78.7	21.3	48	62.5	37.5	6.8	Sudan, The
5.9	42.6	50.6	0.8	2.168	52.6	34.9	0.4	5.1	45[1]	...	...	11[1]	54.5[1]	45.5[1]	3.7[1]	Suriname
2.0	46.3	24.6	27.2	0.564	19.6	56.6	2.7	6.9	272.7	96.5	3.5	30.8	60.7	39.3	6.1	Swaziland
13.0[2]	72.9[2]	1.9[2]	12.1[2]	803.2	7.7[2]	51.8[2]	—	26.7[2]	...	...	...	...	...	...	...	Sweden
1.9	64.9	1.4	31.8	665.7	6.6	38.4	—	23.2	...	...	...	...	...	...	...	Switzerland
44.9[2,3]	14.9[2]	38.7[2]	1.6[2]	60.265[2]	38.9[2]	19.1[2]	6.5[2]	8.5[2]	3,648	80.9	19.1	365	69.3	30.7	14.9	Syria
8.1[3]	62.1	25.9	4.0	4,809.4	33.9	47.9	5.3	7.5	2,940[1]	...	...	1,957[1]	85.6[1]	14.4[1]	3.7[1]	Taiwan
84.0[3]	8.5	5.2	2.4	94.862	34.7	24.9	1.3	84.3	4,068	89.4	10.6	83	55.4	44.6	18.5	Tanzania
13.1[3]	79.8	3.0	4.1	1,063.5	4.5	75.9	2.7	5.6	14,023	61.5	38.5	1,947	56.6	43.4	13.6	Thailand
0.6	52.8	33.8	12.8	185.6	21.7	43.1	20.7	14.4	1,042	92.1	7.9	63	55.6	44.4	13.9	Togo
...	...	...	...	...	...	...	...	...	24[1,5]	...	...	...	...	...	...	Tokelau
...	...	...	...	...	...	...	...	...	...	...	...	11[1,5]	...	...	7.0[1,5]	Tonga
14.8[2,3]	72.4[2]	9.5[2]	3.3[2]	8.471[2]	16.0[2]	74.6[2]	1.7[2]	3.9[2]	1,635	23.5	76.5	384	68.5	31.5	17.8[9]	Trinidad and Tobago
11.8	80.3	1.6	6.4	5.539	28.8	35.9	4.3	9.4	6,189	71.4	28.6	913	64.7	35.3	24.1	Tunisia
26.8[3]	45.5	14.5	13.3	44,766.0	16.5	32.4	17.3	25.4	30,490	59.6	40.4	4,576	59.9	40.1	27.8	Turkey
...	...	...	...	...	...	...	...	...	32[1,5]	...	...	0[1,5]	...	...	...	Turks and Caicos Islands
...	...	...	...	...	...	...	...	...	...	...	...	...	...	...	...	Tuvalu
2.0	65.8	16.7	15.4	16.504	96.6	19.6	2.9	6.4	1,116	94.8	5.2	70	65.7	34.3	18.9	Uganda
...	...	...	...	...	...	...	...	...	41,200[15]	...	...	...	...	...	...	U.S.S.R.
6.8[3]	38.0	6.2	48.9	116.313	6.2	40.8	5.4	19.4	1,463[1]	...	...	468[1]	76.7[1]	23.3[1]	4.5[1,5]	United Arab Emirates
1.3[3]	38.9	0.5	59.3	816.2	11.1	19.7[4]	—	62.7	...	...	...	...	...	...	...	United Kingdom
9.0[3]	82.5	2.8	5.7	4,331.9	13.4	50.1	1.0	6.8	...	...	...	...	...	...	...	United States
13.1[3,9]	47.3[9]	18.0[9]	21.5[9]	760.2[9]	5.4[9]	46.8[4,9]	2.2[9]	27.5[9]	3,048	21.3	78.7	404	33.2	66.8	24.4	Uruguay
2.9[3]	21.9	1.8	73.4	19.904	12.3	60.1[4]	1.6	20.4	14.6	89.0	11.0	1.4	64.3	35.7	1.3[9]	Vanuatu
3.5[3]	79.4	12.0	5.1	337.230	37.6	56.3[4]	5.9	3.4	25,245	4.5	95.5	2,869	42.1	57.9	22.4	Venezuela
...	...	...	...	...	...	...	...	...	9,574[1]	...	...	353[1]	15.3[1]	84.7[1]	...	Vietnam
...	...	...	...	...	...	...	...	...	...	...	...	...	...	...	...	Virgin Islands (U.S.)
...	...	...	...	...	...	...	...	...	3[1,5]	...	...	0[1,5]	...	...	...	Wallis and Futuna
...	...	...	...	...	...	...	...	...	...	...	...	...	...	...	...	West Bank
...	...	...	...	...	...	...	...	...	...	...	...	...	...	...	...	Western Sahara
11.4[3]	42.8	33.3	12.4	0.093	20.9	60.8	5.0	2.0	71.8	96.8	3.2	4.5	71.1	28.9	6.6	Western Samoa
5.8[3]	3.7	82.5	8.0	0.440	35.5	42.2	13.4	8.8	1,669	100.0	—	71	78.9	21.1	14.5	Yemen (Aden)
3.2[3]	28.3	61.9	6.6	16.801	28.1	49.9	1.3	11.7	2,155	96.4	3.6	145	69.0	31.0	12.9	Yemen (Şan'ā')
—	53.9	39.2	6.9	157,959.0	11.4	47.5[4]	2.9	36.3	14,446	47.4	52.6	2,118	47.0	53.0	13.3	Yugoslavia
3.7[2]	33.4[2]	39.0[2]	24.0[2]	83.079[2]	37.3[2]	8.2[2,4]	1.6[2]	7.6[2]	7,334	88.0	12.0	247	51.4	48.6	12.8	Zaire
23.4	37.0	27.3	12.2	11.637	29.9	41.9	3.3	4.3	4,354	86.0	14.0	129	56.6	43.4	13.5	Zambia
37.7[3]	49.8	11.0	1.5	3.749	29.3	49.6	3.2	3.2	2,044	58.5	41.5	383	71.5	28.5	23.2	Zimbabwe

[1]Includes long-term private debt not guaranteed by the government.   [2]1987.   [3]Includes claims on nonfinancial government (public) enterprises and/or local governments.   [4]Includes foreign currency deposits.   [5]1985.   [6]1988.   [7]Treasury bill rate.   [8]1984.   [9]1986.   [10]Short-term deposit rate.   [11]Money market rate.   [12]Notes and coins only.   [13]Long-term deposit rate.   [14]Cash and demand deposits at local banks only.   [15]Gross hard currency debt to the West.   [16]1983.   [17]June 30.

Housing and construction

The present table summarizes data about the housing stock and the construction industries of the countries of the world. The principal focus is on the elements that are most comparable internationally: the age of the housing (by decade, so far as possible), the legal tenure of the householder, construction of exterior walls, principal physical amenities, sanitary arrangements, and the amount of space both absolutely (total area of the average dwelling in square metres [1 square metre equals 1.20 square yards, or 10.76 square feet]) and relatively (persons per room). The data on construction characterize the industry in terms of: (1) the portion of national gross domestic product (GDP) represented by each country's construction industry, (2) the number of new dwelling units constructed annually, their area, and the rate (in years) required to replace the total national stock of dwellings shown on the extreme left of the table, and (3), for nonresidential construction, the number of buildings or portions of buildings built for nonresidential purposes and their area in square metres.

Because housing patterns differ greatly from country to country, the portion of each country's housing stock for which data are compared

was defined as specifically as possible. In general, the numbers refer to permanent, private dwelling units that are usually occupied year-round, whether or not actually occupied on the date of the housing census or survey. That definition implies the exclusion of certain housing that is often part of national housing censuses: vacation homes, second homes occupied less than half the year, collective or communal dwellings, and so on. The housing unit to which the data on tenure refer may be either the individual dwelling or the household, according to the reporting practice of the country concerned.

The data are collected mostly from national housing censuses and surveys. The majority of countries combine the housing census with the population census at five- to ten-year intervals. Some countries, however, can conduct a meaningful housing census only in the capital city or in the few largest cities; others may be able to collect and process data for only a few of the most important housing characteristics even when national coverage is complete. These choices may be dictated by the lack of funding to collect data for the entire country or by the perception, particularly in a tropical, rural country where adequate dwellings can be

Housing and construction

country	housing stock								tenure[c] (percent)			construction of exterior walls (percent)			
	year	dwelling units[a]	median age[b] (years)	decade built (percent)					owned	rented	collective, vacant, other	traditional materials	sawn/ framed wood	masonry or cement	other
				1939 or earlier	1940–49	1950–59	1960–69	1970 or later							
Afghanistan	1979	3,940,000[1]	...	...	...	...	...	...	55.2	23.5	21.3	...	...	...	...
Albania	1979	463,333	...	...	...	...	...	...	63.0	24.6	12.4	...	...	...	...
Algeria	1985	3,013,271	...	...	...	...	23.7	...	71.2	25.1	3.7	4.1	56.3	34.9	4.7
American Samoa	1980	4,688	13.4	4.2	4.8	7.7	38.4	44.9	...	...	...	...	...	...	...
Andorra	...	...	...	...	...	...	...	...	...	...	...	...	...	...	...
Angola	...	...	...	...	...	...	...	...	...	...	...	—	8.1	91.2	0.7
Anguilla	1984	1,840	...	...	...	...	...	...	55.9	40.4	3.7	...	...	...	...
Antigua and Barbuda	1970	15,405[9]	11.1	13.8	9.7	31.4	46.1	—	67.7	14.8	17.5	6.1	6.7	84.2	3.0
Argentina	1980	7,103,853	21.6	9.1	14.9	17.3	22.0	36.7	49.0	51.0	—	...	9.4	87.7	2.9
Aruba	1981	14,929	29.0	28.2	— 34.2 —		14.9	22.7	...	...	...	...	...	...	...
Australia	1981	5,285,571[10]	26.1	— 37.9 —		10.4	18.6	33.1	61.6	22.6	15.8	...	...	...	...
Austria	1981	3,150,600[10]	63.6	— 35.7[14,15] —		— 34.0[15,16] —		30.3[15]	47.7	36.2	16.1	...	...	...	...
Bahamas, The	1980	54,308	30.7	— 54.7 —			25.6	19.7	51.4	37.4	11.2	4.0[17]	32.3	54.7	9.0
Bahrain	1981	52,810	15.2	41.2	17.1	14.5	— 27.2 —		49.6	30.0	20.4	2.1[12]	—	95.1[12]	2.8[12]
Bangladesh	1981	14,790,000	...	...	...	...	...	...	89.7	5.0	5.3	20.0	11.6	5.0	63.4
Barbados	1980	67,138	18.9	— 51.3 —			20.6	28.1	70.2	21.5	8.3	0.1	68.9[18]	26.3	4.7
Belgium	1981	3,997,100[13]	35.2	48.4[19]	— 17.2[20] —		14.2	16.0	59.2	38.1	2.7	...	...	...	...
Belize	1980	27,298	...	— 24.6 —			30.0	41.0	56.1	27.2	16.7	7.5	73.4	14.0	5.1
Benin	1979	612,041	...	...	...	...	...	...	...	...	...	...	...	...	...
Bermuda	1980	20,350	31.2	— 67.9 —			16.6	15.5	39.4	53.7	6.9	—	1.7[15]	95.1	3.2
Bhutan	...	...	...	...	...	...	...	...	...	...	...	...	...	...	...
Bolivia	1976	1,040,704	...	...	...	...	47.4	...	69.3	15.1	15.6	...	...	...	...
Botswana	1981	170,262	...	...	...	...	...	...	59.9	17.1	23.0	65.5	—	28.0	6.5
Brazil	1986	31,100,180	...	...	...	...	...	...	64.1	21.6	14.3	...	...	...	...
British Virgin Islands	1980	3,287	21.6	— 39.8 —		— 31.2 —		29.0	47.4	43.0	9.6	—	21.6	68.0	10.4
Brunei	1981	28,676	...	...	...	...	...	...	83.8	11.8	4.4	0.2	54.8	36.5	8.5
Bulgaria	1975	3,214,500[10]	17.9	47.0	— 34.9 —		11.1	7.0	77.3	22.7	—	...	...	...	...
Burkina Faso	...	...	...	...	...	...	...	...	...	...	...	...	...	...	...
Burundi	1979[28]	938,000	...	...	...	...	...	...	98.7	1.1	0.2	...	...	...	...
Cameroon	1976	1,390,896	...	...	...	...	...	...	83.4	11.2	5.4	75.5	13.9	9.5	1.1
Canada	1981	9,057,533[10]	14.6	— 41.2 —		13.8	17.9	27.1	62.1	37.9	—	57.7	—	36.5	5.8
Cape Verde	1980	59,919	...	...	...	...	17.3[29]	14.1[30]	...	15.4	...	1.0	24.0	74.0	1.0
Cayman Islands	1979	4,426	...	— 52.0 —			...	48.0	67.8	32.2	—	82.2	7.1	2.5	8.2
Central African Republic	1975	405,399	...	...	...	...	...	...	...	...	...	...	...	...	...
Chad	...	...	...	...	...	...	...	...	...	...	...	...	...	...	...
Chile	1982	2,510,275	20.4	— 46.2 —			21.1	32.7	63.1	18.7	18.2	13.0	44.4	41.6	1.0
China	1986	249,270,175	...	...	...	...	...	...	18.5[2,6]	81.5[2,6]	...	...	...	...	...
Christmas Island	1984	1,231	14.0[7]	— 32.2 —			27.2[7]	40.6[7]	—	86.4[31]	13.6[31]	—	1.7[31]	74.7[31]	23.6[31]
Cocos (Keeling) Islands	1981	150	...	...	...	...	33.3	...	— 80.7 —		19.3	—	6.0	52.0	42.0
Colombia	1985	5,266,581	20.6[33]	46.7[33]	7.9[33]	26.2[33]	19.2[33]	—	67.6	23.6	8.8	16.7	7.0	75.6	0.7
Comoros	1980	81,791	...	— 5.3 —		7.7	21.3	63.7	87.4	3.1	9.5	73.5	1.8	16.9	7.8
Congo	1984	363,140	...	...	...	...	...	...	61.0	34.6	4.4	15.0	20.0	52.8	12.2
Cook Islands	1986	3,315[5]	14.0[31]	5.9[31]	5.7[31]	16.8[31]	48.6[31]	23.0[31]	85.3[11]	9.4[11]	5.3[11]	...	...	...	...
Costa Rica	1984	500,788	...	...	...	...	36.4[33]	...	65.8	20.7	13.5	1.1	60.1	35.6	3.2
Côte d'Ivoire	1985	1,146,370[35]	...	...	...	...	...	...	...	...	...	1.4	37.1	61.5	—
Cuba	1981	2,363,364	24.6	15.0[36]	8.2[37]	21.3[38]	21.6	25.6	...	...	...	11.9	—	87.6	0.5
Cyprus	1982	194,300[10]	22.8	— 39.9 —			15.4	44.7	60.0	16.5	23.5	...	2.9	93.8	3.3
Czechoslovakia	1980	5,747,000[10]	36.7	— 40.0[19] —		15.1[20]	20.3	24.6	44.7	41.7	13.6	...	...	...	...
Denmark	1988	2,306,836	36.3	39.3	6.4	10.2	16.9	27.2	55.4	43.5	1.1	...	73.0[39]	22.5	4.5
Djibouti	1982	25,000	27.6	...	...	...	...	...	...	...	...	...	...	...	...
Dominica	1981	17,307	...	— 58.4[21] —		16.9[21]	21.1[21]	3.6[21]	64.7[21]	26.6[21]	8.7[21]	0.2[21]	88.8[21]	10.2[21]	0.8[21]
Dominican Republic	1981	1,114,833[9]	...	— 12.4 —			— 87.6 —		72.0	17.0	11.0	31.8[21]	46.2[21]	15.3[21]	6.7[21]
Ecuador	1982	1,576,441	...	...	...	...	...	...	66.7	22.9	10.4	46.9	9.3	41.4	2.4
Egypt	1986	9,732,728	...	17.2[2]	— 19.9[2] —		— 62.9[2] —		64.0	27.2	8.8	...	...	...	...
El Salvador	1971	680,456	...	...	...	...	...	...	56.7[34]	22.3[34]	21.0[34]	37.9	9.6	46.9	5.6
Equatorial Guinea	...	...	...	...	...	...	...	...	...	...	...	...	...	...	...
Ethiopia	1984	9,300,000	...	...	...	...	...	...	84.5	9.9	5.6	—	43.9	53.5	2.6
Faeroe Islands	1977	11,172	32.5	33.7	— 26.4 —		21.8	15.0	38.9	16.6	44.5	—	86.4	10.9	2.7
Falkland Islands	1980	589	...	...	...	...	...	...	74.4	14.6	11.0	9.0	26.4	29.8	34.8
Fiji	1986	124,098	...	...	...	...	...	...	...	...	...	...	...	...	...
Finland	1985	1,887,710	17.0	19.1	5.8	13.7	18.1	43.3	69.0	26.0	5.0	14.0[43]	81.8[43]	— 4.2[43] —	
France	1982	19,590,400	31.0[34]	— 71.9[34] —			12.7[34]	15.4[34]	50.7	41.0	8.3	...	...	...	...
French Guiana	1982	21,063	...	...	...	...	23.2[21]	...	34.5	54.0	11.5	29.4[45]	— 70.6 —		
French Polynesia	1983	...	13.6	— 5.0 —		9.0	30.0	56.0	...	...	...	38.0	— 62.0 —		
Gabon	1967[47]	15,886	...	...	...	...	...	...	— 87.0 —		13.0	...	...	...	...

built by hand, that no urgent housing problem exists. These choices may be complex, however, as planners are always aware that much housing is physically inadequate to protect dwellers from the elements, is disadvantageously placed in relation to tainted or disease-infested water supply or to the outfall of unprocessed sewage, or is built of materials (mud, skins, thatch, etc.) that may harbour pests or disease. In the developed countries, median age and the distribution of physical amenities provide strong indicators of the quality and availability of housing.

The data for the construction industry refer to the most recent year in which a broad range of countries could be surveyed.

The broadest indication of total activity in a national construction industry is its contribution to the national gross domestic product, since that figure, in addition to construction of buildings, also includes civil-engineering projects, such as dams, roads and other transportation infrastructure, recreational facilities, irrigation and land reclamation works, and the like. The scope of the data relating to construction of buildings may be limited in several respects. It may be confined to activity capable of being surveyed in the modern or urban sectors only, may be limited to

private new construction only or to government and government-financed activity only, or may refer to construction mortgaged or financed through certain organizations only. Depending on national data-collection systems, it usually excludes remodeling of old premises but may include extensions or enlargements of existing buildings. The data for new construction are usually of two principal types of data: authorized new construction or certification after construction that newly built structures meet building and fire codes and the like. Data for construction completed are naturally more meaningful but are not available for every country, necessitating the substitution of authorized construction data, which are usually available only for areas regulated by certain types of governmental authorities.

a. Data refer to permanent, private dwelling units that are usually occupied year-round, whether or not occupied on the census date.

b. Data are estimates unless specifically provided by a country source.

c. Data may be either for dwellings or for households, depending on country reporting practice.

d. Data may be either for construction completed or for construction authorized, depending on country reporting practice.

physical amenities (percent)			sewage disposal (percent)			space[b]				construction industry (1986)						country
piped water	electricity	inside toilet or WC	closed public sewer or septic tank	open public sewer	other	average area (sq m)	rooms per dwelling unit	persons per room	percent of GDP	new residential[d]			new nonresidential[d]		
										total no. of dwellings	floor area ('000 sq m)	years to replace nat'l stock	number of units	floor area ('000 sq m)	
25.3[2]	66.5[2]	5.5[2]	5.5	77.9	16.6	...	5.5	2.1	4.0[3]	...	...	...	...	...	Afghanistan
45.8[5]	73.3	...	51.0	22.8	26.2	...	...	...	6.4[3, 4]	15,049	...	30.8	...	...	Albania
77.4	96.2	...	83.5		16.5	...	2.8	2.5	17.2	...	...	...	...	...	Algeria
—	—	—	—		—	...	3.0	2.3	...	218	...	21.5	...	...	American Samoa
									13.4[6]	...	91[7]		14[7]	47.5[7]	Andorra
36.9	64.1	30.1[8]	55.7	—44.3—		...	4.8	0.8	4.2	...	585[7]	...	210[7]	164.5[7]	Angola
85.4			17.0	—83.0—		...	3.1	...	...	...	...	...	...	...	Anguilla
72.9	86.8	95.1	77.1	—22.9—		...	3.9	1.3	9.4	764	...	20.2	...	...	Antigua and Barbuda
98.7	98.7	89.2	...			...	4.3	1.1	3.3	...	...	...	...	...	Argentina
56.8									5.7	266		56.1	127		Aruba
97.1[11]	98.4[12]	92.2	99.0	—1.0—		...	5.1	0.6	6.9	119,770	21,360[13]	44.1	23,340[13]	8,123[13]	Australia
95.0		85.5	94.3		5.7	76.5	4.3[10]	0.6[10]	6.6	38,838	3,790	81.1	500[13]	100[13]	Austria
63.9	77.9		63.2	2.2	34.6	...	4.0	1.2	3.1	1,612	3,790	33.7	72	...	Bahamas, The
97.5	98.2	...	44.7		55.3	...	3.0[12]	2.3[12]	7.5	1,919	...	27.5	1,444	...	Bahrain
56.8			1.3	—98.7—		...	2.0	2.9	5.7	...	...	...	...	...	Bangladesh
82.4	83.0	43.6	95.8	0.7	3.5	...	4.2	0.8	4.9	1,960	...	34.3	...	...	Barbados
95.3	100.0	79.0	62.5[21]	—37.5[21]—		82.1	5.5[13]	0.4[13]	5.1	29,565	18,430[22]	136.1	7,284	25,376[22]	Belgium
60.1	59.4	19.7	21.1	—78.9—		...	2.5[23]	1.9[23]	5.4	102[24]		24	...	...	Belize
...	...	...	...			...	...	...	4.7[13]	...	...	...	...	...	Benin
97.4		96.7	96.7	—3.3—		...	3.2	0.7	4.9[25]	486	...	41.9	...	...	Bermuda
37.9	33.0		12.5	—87.5—		...	...	...	8.7	...	...	...	1[1]	...	Bhutan
56.1	5.4	25.4	8.6	20.4	71.0	...	...	...	5.0	...	...	...	...	...	Bolivia
70.8	83.2		55.9	—44.1—		...	5.1[7]	0.9[7]	2.9	...	81.9[13]	...	472[13]	97.6[13]	Botswana
62.3	90.2	65.1	65.1	25.3	9.6	...	3.9	1.1	5.9	115,914[24]		24	5,017[13]	3,771[13]	Brazil
									10.1[25]	95[26]		34.6	...	...	British Virgin Islands
90.3	64.2	94.2	57.4	—42.6—		...	4.2	1.6	4.0	...	...	...	5[27]	...	Brunei
74.6	99.8	33.2	33.2	—67.8—		...	2.5[10]	1.1[10]	9.5	...	5,174[13]	...	...	...	Bulgaria
...	...	...	...			...	...	...	1.4[27]	...	...	...	...	...	Burkina Faso
11.0	0.6	...	1.6	—98.4—		...	...	...	5.3	...	...	...	...	...	Burundi
22.0	5.9	2.2	2.2	70.4	27.6	...	4.1	1.2	6.0[27]	...	230[1]	...	53[1]	51.1[1]	Cameroon
99.5	100.0	98.9	98.9	—1.1—		...	5.7	0.5	7.0	184,605	...	49.1	14,846[13]	...	Canada
7.1	13.7	14.8	—3.4—		96.6	...	1.8	2.8	20.3[31]	...	31[6]	...	3[6]	...	Cape Verde
99.0	96.0	83.7	57.0	—43.0—		...	4.0	1.1	9.6	236[26]		18.8[26]	...	0.5[6]	Cayman Islands
...	...	...	...			...	1.1[32]	3.4[32]	2.5[13]	...	7[27]	...	16[27]	...	Central African Republic
...	...	...	...			...	...	...	1.7[13]	...	...	...	...	...	Chad
81.4	84.7		63.2	36.4	0.4	...	3.6	1.3	5.5	52,082	2,897	48.2	...	1,144	Chile
89.4[2, 6]		25.2[2, 6]	47.0[2, 6]	—53.0[2, 6]—		37.0[6]	2.26	1.8[6]	6.3[3]	...	95,651[13]	...	...	75,761[13]	China
100.0	100.0	100.0	100.0			...	5.7	1.0	...	...	...	...	...	...	Christmas Island
35.6	100.0	100.0	100.0	—		...	6.1	0.6	...	...	...	...	...	...	Cocos (Keeling) Islands
70.5	78.5	77.9	69.6	—30.4—		...	3.3	1.6	3.7	...	7,404[13]	...	1,442[13]	1,224[13]	Colombia
12.9	5.7		2.1	—97.9—		33.7	2.5	2.1	11.5[6]	...	...	...	...	...	Comoros
30.5	8.8	16.6	—86.2[2]—		13.8[2]	...	3.7[2]	1.7[2]	6.1	...	...	...	...	...	Congo
70.8	86.4	77.9	36.7[11]	—63.3[11]—		...	4.5	1.2	4.5[34]	...	...	...	24[13]	...	Cook Islands
86.9	97.3	...	66.5	—33.5—		...	4.0	1.4	4.6	...	760[13]	...	2,868[13]	178[13]	Costa Rica
23.0	39.6	23.9	—68.5—		31.5	...	...	...	2.2[27]	...	...	...	...	...	Côte d'Ivoire
74.1	82.9	45.2	60.9	9.0	30.1	...	4.1	1.0	8.7[3]	70,914	...	33.3	469[13]	1,803[13]	Cuba
100.0	98.1	74.5	95.6	—4.4—		...	4.6	0.8	10.1	7,034	979	...	1,103[13]	411[13]	Cyprus
91.6	100.0	70.8	91.2	—8.8—		68.0	3.5	0.9	10.7[3]	112,420[13]	8,100[13]	51.1[13]	...	...	Czechoslovakia
100.0	100.0	99.2	98.6[31]	—1.4[31]—		98.0	4.7	0.5	5.6	28,489	3,218	74.4	15,309[13]	5,748	Denmark
45.0	58.0	82.0	26.0	23.0	51.0	...	1.9	6.9	7.5[10]	91[24]	20.7	...	46[13]	21.7[13]	Djibouti
91.1[1]	...	12.3[1]	12.3[1]	—87.7[1]—		...	2.8[1]	1.7[1]	7.4	...	...	...	...	...	Dominica
49.3	36.7[21]	14.1	52.1[21]	22.6[21]	25.3[21]	...	2.8[21]	1.5[21]	6.9	...	467	...	819	422	Dominican Republic
51.8	47.3	32.7	34.9	13.3	51.8	...	2.8	1.8	4.6	...	3,825[13]	...	596[13]	412.7[13]	Ecuador
73.1	87.0	...	...			...	3.3	1.5	4.8	166,577[6]	...	58.4[6]	...	...	Egypt
48.0[40]	34.1	6.3[12]	20.0[40]	—80.0[40]—		...	1.5[34]	3.3[34]	3.1	...	341[13]	...	8[13]	0.7[13]	El Salvador
...	...	...	...			...	...	...	9.1	...	...	...	...	...	Equatorial Guinea
...	...	...	...			...	...	2.7[41]	4.0	...	157.7[13]	...	92[1]	46.9[1]	Ethiopia
99.7	99.5	95.0	89.7	8.1	2.2	...	5.5	1.1	10.2[8]	292	...	38.3	...	...	Faeroe Islands
98.8		98.8	98.0[42]	—2.0[42]—		...	7.4[42]	0.4[42]	...	...	...	...	...	...	Falkland Islands
73.7	48.5	56.0	35.4[5]	—64.6[5]—		...	3.3	1.8	5.3	...	67	...	106	45	Fiji
93.9	95.9[43]	91.1	95.9	—4.1—		73.9	3.6	0.7	6.6	41,910	3,367	45.0	32,886[13]	28,265[13, 22]	Finland
99.2	98.8[44]	85.0	73.8[35]	—26.2[35]—		77.0[34]	3.8[27]	0.6[27]	5.3	236,600	...	82.8	...	31,956	France
67.7	80.4	59.1	34.3	—65.7—		...	2.8	1.3	8.2[40]	880	...	23.9	...	28.5[13]	French Guiana
86.0	76.0	76.0	2.0	67.0	31.0	...	3.4	1.7[5]	11.5	...	98[46]	...	214[13]	46	French Polynesia
	50.5	...	...			...	3.0	1.3	9.0	...	216.1[35]	...	75[35]	119.4[35]	Gabon

Housing and construction (continued)

country	year	dwelling units[a]	median age[b] (years)	1939 or earlier	1940–49	1950–59	1960–69	1970 or later	owned	rented	collective, vacant, other	traditional materials	sawn/framed wood	masonry or cement	other
					decade built (percent)					tenure[c] (percent)			construction of exterior walls (percent)		
Gambia, The	1983	202,199	...	...	...	...	...	...	63.9	21.9	14.2	82.9	—	12.9	4.2
Gaza Strip	1985	66,819[48]	...						89.1[49]	7.6[49]	3.3[49]	...	...	...	...
Germany, East	1981	6,910,700[10]	...	—62.4—		6.1	10.1	21.4	36.3	63.7	—[35]	...	...	...	...
Germany, West	1987	25,492,554	...	30.6[50]	15.2[51]	23.6[52]	19.8[53]	10.8[54]	39.0	60.3	0.7	...	...	...	...
Ghana	1984	1,216,677	...						47.7[35]	25.3[35]	27.0[35]	...	...	...	...
Gibraltar	1986	7,846	...	...	...	...	...	...	5.9	94.1	—	...	...	...	...
Greece	1981	3,999,332	29.2	—30.2[19]—		27.4[20]	20.7	21.5	73.1[8]	26.9[8]	—	...	...	...	...
Greenland	1985	16,096	10.8[11]	—11.9[11]—		18.8[11]	46.5[11]	22.8[11]	39.3	—60.7—		...	...	...	...
Grenada	1970	19,642	18.3	—48.0—		29.0	22.2	0.8	76.5	14.0	9.5	0.4	80.8	17.8	1.0
Guadeloupe	1982	85,629	...					8.1[8]	64.3	29.9	5.8	29.5[45]		—70.5—	
Guam	1980	28,091	...					44.6	40.8	47.6	11.6[42]	...	...	...	...
Guatemala	1981	1,259,598	12.5	—62.0—			10.0	28.0	64.7	11.3	24.0	55.6	21.1	19.3	4.0
Guernsey	1986	18,632	...	...	...	...	...	...	69.1	30.9	...	...	...	...	...
Guinea	1983	674,152	...	...	...	...	...	...	...	...	...	...	...	...	...
Guinea-Bissau	1979	123,936	...	...	...	...	...	...	...	...	...	95.7	0.1	2.3	1.9
Guyana	1980	149,734	...	—43.5—			19.4	37.1	56.1	27.1	16.8		74.8	17.1	8.1
Haiti	1982	1,130,795	...					24.1	82.9[11]	4.8[11]	12.3[11]	...	...	...	...
Honduras	1988	809,263	...	—43.1[8]—			37.9[8]		71.8[8]	16.5[8]	12.7[8]	61.0[8]	26.4[8]	11.7[8]	0.9[8]
Hong Kong	1986	1,205,900	...	...	...	...	13.6[31]	38.3[31]	35.1	58.1	6.8	...	...	...	...
Hungary	1984	3,890,600[10]	36.2	—40.6[19]—		12.8[38]	16.9	29.7	75.1	24.7	0.2	30.8	14.3	54.8	0.1
Iceland	1984	82,200[10]	25.6	18.5	—27.5—		—54.1—		70.3[23]	—29.7[23]—		...	...	71.9[23]	...
India	1981	142,954,921	...	...	...	...	...	...	84.6[12]	15.4[12]		...	...	...	...
Indonesia	1980	30,263,273	...	...	...	...	...	...	87.0[12]	5.0[12]	8.0[12]	...	...	...	...
Iran	1986	8,112,650	...	—82.5[11]—				17.5[11]	77.0	12.2	9.8	...	...	...	...
Iraq	1956	741,000	...	...	...	...	...	...	83.0	12.8	4.2	...	...	...	...
Ireland	1981	985,300[13]	47.2	44.6	—16.4—		12.8	26.2	67.9	20.9	11.2	...	...	...	...
Isle of Man	1981	27,042	...	—9.5[55]—		—90.5[56]—			62.5	36.5	1.0	...	...	...	...
Israel	1983	1,104,270	...	...	...	...	...	...	72.9	24.6	2.5	...	...	...	...
Italy	1981	17,542,000	19.4	—30.8[19]—		19.7[20]	27.5[57]	22.0	58.9	35.5	5.6	...	...	...	...
Jamaica	1982	517,297	...	—33.6—			26.8	39.6	46.7	29.5	23.8	7.1	28.4	54.4	10.1
Japan	1983	34,704,500	13.0	—13.5—		9.7	24.0	52.1	62.4	37.3	0.3	—	77.4	21.5	1.1
Jersey	1986[58]	29,201	...						49.9	48.0	2.1	...	...	...	...
Jordan	1979	378,815[60]	...						62.6	30.8	6.6	...	...	...	...
Kampuchea (Cambodia)															
Kenya	1979	2,956,369	...												
Kiribati	1978	10,093[13,58]	...	...	...	...	...	...	68.2	17.9	13.9	64.4	—35.6—		
Korea, North															
Korea, South	1985	6,104,210	19.0[7]	—26.1[7]—		15.8[7]	18.2[7]	39.9[7]	83.8	12.8	3.4	11.8[7]	38.8[7]	49.2[7]	0.2[7]
Kuwait	1985	228,781	14.5[7]	—12.2[7]—			38.8[7]	34.5[7]	38.2	53.6	8.2	46.5[43]	—	36.5[43]	17.0[43]
Laos															
Lebanon	1970	483,908[9]	...	—30.1[62]—		40.2[63]	29.4		...	...	...	...	...	...	...
Lesotho	1986[58]	330,035	...						...	...	...	...	...	...	...
Liberia	1974[47]	263.333	...						...	...	...	...	...	...	...
Libya	1984	569,679	...	...	...	...	...	...	62.5[33]	28.0[33]	9.5[33]	...	...	...	...
Liechtenstein	1980	8,421	29.4	—27.1[62]—		15.0[63]	27.1	30.8	53.6	41.7	4.7	...	...	...	...
Luxembourg	1981	128,281[58]	...	—62.1[55]—		11.8[64]	7.8	18.3	59.2	—40.8—		...	...	...	...
Macau	1981	45,158	...						71.8[21]	28.2[21]	—	—	0.5[21]	99.3[21]	0.2[21]
Madagascar	1975	1,671,473	...												
Malawi	1977	1,834,118	...						39.6	—60.4—		...	...	...	...
Malaysia	1980	2,332,563	...						64.0	23.0	13.0	...	...	...	...
Maldives	1985	29,818	...												
Mali	1976[58]	1,253,802	...												
Malta	1985	101,509	...	—81.8[66]—			18.2[67]	—	53.9	43.0	3.1	93.0[48]		92.9[48]	0.21[48]
Martinique	1982	85,265	...						64.1	31.3	7.3	20.4[45]		—79.6—	
Mauritania	1977	246,462	...												
Mauritius	1983[68]	158,215	...	—19.7—			24.3[69]	56.0[70]	73.2	12.5	14.3		4.2	66.8	28.9
Mayotte	1985	13,142	...						88.1[34]	6.2[34]	5.7[34]	67.7	—16.7—		15.6
Mexico	1980	12,216,462	...	—51.4—			15.4	33.2	66.8	—33.2—		28.2	9.6	56.2	6.0
Monaco	1975	12,625	28.5	—51.4—		22.7	—25.8—		...	...	...	...	...	...	...
Mongolia	1969	242,000	...						100.0	—	—	...	...	...	...
Montserrat	1980	3,706	...	—47.4—			24.5	28.1	69.2	21.9	8.8	—	60.9	39.0	0.1
Morocco	1982[58]	3,419,282	...						40.8[2]	43.7[2]	15.5[2]	24.5	—73.5—		1.8
Mozambique	1980	2,712,439	...									86.5	2.3	8.3	2.9
Myanmar (Burma)	1983	6,750,884	...									83.5	14.8	—	1.7
Nauru	1977	508[71]	...	—88.6[71]—				11.4[71]	11.0[41]	80.6[41]	8.4[41]	...	...	...	...
Nepal	1961[24]	37,122	...						75.3	10.7	14.0	...	...	...	...
Netherlands, The	1985	5,588,600[4]	20.0[5]	7.1	8.8[72]	15.4[73]	19.8	38.4	43.2	56.8		...	...	...	...
Netherlands Antilles	1981	41,101	21.0	22.4	—27.4—		19.7	30.3	45.3	54.7		—	21.6	75.7	2.7
New Caledonia	1983	35,107	15.8	—9.8—		11.2	32.1	46.9	53.0	31.1	15.9	6.3	21.0	58.1	14.6
New Zealand	1986	1,167,826	...	—64.6[31]—			19.2[31]	16.2[37]	74.1	23.1	2.8	...	...	...	...
Nicaragua	1971	330,422	...						64.4	20.3	15.3	30.8	45.6	21.8	1.8
Niger	1960	611,070[58]	...						66.5			...	...	...	...
Nigeria	1961[47]	92,900	...						8.0	80.9	11.1	...	...	...	...
Niue	1986	549	...						75.2	7.5	17.3	...	...	...	...
Norfolk Island	1986	787	14.8[31]	—32.8[31]—			32.5[31]	34.7[31]	55.0	34.1	10.9	—	46.4	3.8	49.8
Norway	1980	1,720,000[10]	25.3	35.1	6.9	16.8	18.7	22.5	66.6	23.5	9.9	...	...	...	...
Oman	1982	2,469	...	...	...	...	...	...	...	...	...	...	...	...	...
Pacific Is., Trust Terr. of the															
Marshall Islands	1980	4,163	...	3.4	3.1	13.3	24.7	55.5	60.0	33.0	7.0	10.7	63.5	15.9	9.9
Micronesia, Fed. States of	1980	11,562	...	1.7	2.1	5.2	21.3	69.7	51.8	39.2	9.0	6.0	41.8	14.6	37.6
Northern Mariana Islands	1980	3,373	...	0.8	3.7	8.4	29.4	57.7	53.6	36.1	10.3	0.0	6.1	33.4	60.5
Palau	1980	2,265	...	2.5	3.1	8.6	29.8	56.0	78.0	12.1	9.9	0.7	23.1	16.7	59.5
Pakistan	1980	12,587,648	17.2[74]	...	17.1[62,74]	36.7[74,75]	24.9[74,76]	21.3[74,77]	78.4[74]	7.7[74]	13.9[74]	49.2[74]	2.4[74]	41.4[74]	7.1[74]
Panama	1980	364,726	18.0	—47.4—		12.8	18.1	21.7	70.1	21.1	8.8	37.1	—	52.2	10.7
Papua New Guinea	1980	556,519[58]	...						40.0[35]	—60.0[35]—		...	...	...	...

physical amenities (percent)			sewage disposal (percent)			space[b]			percent of GDP	construction industry (1986) new residential[d]			new nonresidential[d]		country
piped water	electricity	inside toilet or WC	closed public sewer or septic tank	open public sewer	other	average area (sq m)	rooms per dwelling unit	persons per room		total no. of dwellings	floor area ('000 sq m)	years to replace nat'l stock	number of units	floor area ('000 sq m)	
21.9	...	...	...	...	...	...	2.0	2.0	3.3	...	...	...	14[35]	...	Gambia, The
97.2	93.5	97.3	...	...	...	...	2.6	2.4	22.2	1,404	203	...	...	41.3	Gaza Strip
98.2	100.0	60.1	90.8	—9.2—	...	63.0	2.8[10]	0.9[10]	7.2	215,690	7,202	32.0	...	...	Germany, East
100.0	99.7[42]	98.3	97.1[7]	—2.97—		85.6	4.4	0.5	5.2	251,940	24,284	101.2	41,860	23,483	Germany, West
34.0[40]	...	...	...	...	...	...	...	...	2.4	...	...	...	...	...	Ghana
96.7[31]	100.0[31]	98.8[31]	100.0[31]	—		...	3.2[31]	1.2[31]	6.4	...	...	...	...	...	Gibraltar
81.3[12]	89.0[12]	93.0[12]	...	...	...	138.4[10]	3.3[10]	0.9[12]	...	109,643	39,724	36.5	11,471[13]	12,887[13,22]	Greece
62.7[11]	84.2[11]	39.1[11]	39.1[11]	—60.9[11]—		...	2.8	1.2	27.4[40]	753	41.5[13]	21.4	...	12.3[13]	Greenland
86.5	...	23.0	23.0	—77.0—		...	2.9	1.6	9.0	...	...	23.7	...	...	Grenada
69.4	77.2	55.4	24.6	—75.4—		...	3.5	1.1	4.47	3,620	...	...	...	166	Guadeloupe
99.5	...	96.5	97.5	—2.5—		...	4.7	0.7	7.96	292	...	64.9	297	...	Guam
52.0	37.0	14.3	20.1	3.4	76.5	...	2.4	2.2	1.7	...	269[13]	...	...	144.0[13]	Guatemala
96.5[11]	...	88.8[11]	49.3[11]	—50.7[11]—		...	5.5[11]	0.5	...	...	...	...	...	...	Guernsey
...	...	...	...	...	...	...	...	...	6.4[13]	...	...	...	...	...	Guinea
3.7	3.9	25.6	25.8	—74.2—		...	1.4	4.5	3.1[13]	...	...	...	...	...	Guinea-Bissau
38.1	69.0	29.0	10.4	—89.6—		...	2.9	1.8	7.0	...	...	...	56[7]	...	Guyana
12.0[40]	1.1[12]	...	2.0[40]	—98.0[40]—		...	2.2[12]	2.1[12]	6.0	...	...	...	...	...	Haiti
55.0[40]	25.0[8]	13.0[8]	14.4[8]	—85.6[8]—		...	2.4[8]	2.3[8]	4.6	1,442[24]	214	[24]	148	98	Honduras
85.7[31]	...	69.2[33]	65.4[33]	—34.6[33]—		53.2[12]	3.1[33]	2.8[33]	4.5	67,925	1,178	20.6	269	1,352	Hong Kong
81.2	98.8	65.9	79.5	—20.5—		65.0	3.6[10]	0.8[10]	10.3	69,428	...	56.0	3,433[13]	21,886[13,20]	Hungary
99.1[23]	94.6[23]	93.6[23]	86.5[23]	—13.5[23]—		...	4.8[23]	0.9[23]	6.4	...	...	756.0[13,22]	...	926.5[13,22,27]	Iceland
67.0[33]	53.5[2,33]	20.0[33]	...	...	...	...	2.0[12]	2.6[12]	5.4	...	...	...	13,908[13,27]	...	India
11.0	14.2	26.6	22.8[12]	—77.2[12]—		59.0	3.3	1.7[12]	5.4	...	...	...	...	...	Indonesia
46.8[11]	83.1	26.7[11]	...	...	...	60.0[11]	2.7[11]	2.0[11]	7.3[13]	124,891[13]	18,608[13]	65.0[13]	5,235[13]	1,466[13]	Iran
20.8	17.1	...	...	...	...	...	2.4	...	7.5[13]	...	8,330[13]	...	11,799[13]	1,960[13]	Iraq
94.8	94.7[12]	93.0	72.3[12]	—27.7[12]—		...	3.7	1.0[13]	6.4[27]	23,948	...	41.1	...	840	Ireland
...	...	96.8	...	...	...	...	3.0	0.4	9.8	64	...	157.7	...	...	Isle of Man
96.5[12]	96.5[12]	98.8	99.0[8]	—1.0[8]—		...	3.0	1.2	3.8	21,000	2,770	52.6	...	1,130	Israel
98.7	99.0[12]	94.0	95.7[12]	—4.3[12]—		85.3	4.0[13]	0.8	5.6	132,844	12,009	131.4	28,542	86,880[22]	Italy
76.9	48.6	35.2	...	...	...	...	2.4[21]	4.3	7.7	2,180	...	237.3	...	...	Jamaica
94.0	...	58.2	61.2	—38.8—		85.9	4.7	0.7	6.7	1,364,609	111,004	25.4	...	96,678	Japan
94.0[59]	...	93.0[31]	96.0[59]	...	...	...	5.5	0.5	...	307	...	95.1	...	...	Jersey
77.2	77.3	55.4[41]	15.7	—84.3—		...	...	...	7.0	6,292	1,709	60.2	820	557	Jordan
...	...	...	...	...	...	...	...	...	5.3[61]	...	...	...	...	...	Kampuchea (Cambodia)
...	...	...	...	...	...	...	...	...	5.2	...	154	...	85	184	Kenya
21.3	23.7	15.5	...	...	...	...	...	...	5.1	...	...	...	...	...	Kiribati
34.0	49.9[21]	33.1	...	...	...	73.0	3.5	1.8	7.8	288,000	22,518	34.2	36,801	21,024	Korea, North
53.9[7]	99.5[7]	...	35.9[7]	—64.1[7]—		...	4.0[7]	1.8[7]	3.1	9,735[26]	1,755	23.5[26]	550	1,224	Korea, South
...	...	...	...	...	...	...	...	...	5.1[27]	...	...	...	...	...	Kuwait
...	...	...	...	...	...	...	...	...	...	...	...	...	...	...	Laos
...	93.4	82.9	...	...	...	...	...	...	5.3[27]	...	...	...	...	...	Lebanon
...	...	...	...	...	...	...	...	...	8.9	...	...	...	52	...	Lesotho
70.1[33]	72.1[33]	40.6[33]	40.6[33]	—59.4[33]—		...	2.3[58]	1.7	2.8	...	...	...	...	...	Liberia
96.5	96.6	86.7	90.2	—9.8—		102.0	3.3[33]	1.8[33]	10.9[27]	...	...	...	...	...	Libya
...	...	...	...	...	...		3.0	1.4	...	...	197[22]	...	...	283[22]	Liechtenstein
99.4[21]	...	97.2	93.0[21]	—7.0[21]—		86.4[21]	5.4	0.5	5.8	1,417	995	90.5	45	458	Luxembourg
95.7	99.3	68.9	...	...	...	...	3.2[27]	2.5[27]	...	4,331	294	10.4	35	375	Macau
...	...	...	...	...	...	...	...	...	4.5[1]	...	19.7	...	38	5.7	Madagascar
12.4	15.7[48]	33.0[48]	33.0[48]	—67.0[48]—		...	2.1	1.7	4.1	102[24]	...	[24]	77[13]	...	Malawi
65.0	64.4	...	56.4	4.4	39.2	...	2.3[21,65]	2.6[21,65]	4.3	...	2,670	...	...	293	Malaysia
...	9.8[5]	...	2.5[5]	—97.5[5]—		...	2.3[5]	2.7[5]	8.1	...	...	...	...	...	Maldives
...	...	...	...	...	...	...	...	...	4.9[27]	...	...	...	...	...	Mali
98.0	98.0	98.8	98.0	15.4[48]	6.1[48]	...	3.2[48]	1.3[48]	3.6[6]	2,132[43]	...	47.6[43]	2,319	...	Malta
55.4	70.5	41.8	41.8	—58.2—		...	3.4	1.1	7.9[27]	1,278	...	66.7	...	56.2[13]	Martinique
...	...	...	...	...	...	...	...	...	...	...	...	...	...	...	Mauritania
79.7	92.6	51.1	51.1	—48.9—		...	5.4	...	5.6	...	414	...	490	159	Mauritius
27.4[34]	...	4.4	54.7[34]	—45.3[34]—		...	4.1	2.5	...	616	...	21.3	...	...	Mayotte
66.2	74.6	45.0	49.2	—50.8—		...	2.3	2.5	4.8	...	...	...	61,386[13,31]	...	Mexico
100.0	100.0	98.4	98.4	—1.6—		...	2.8	0.4	...	...	...	...	...	...	Monaco
0.3	47.5	...	...	...	...	...	...	...	5.1[6]	...	379[13]	...	...	113.3[7,13]	Mongolia
78.6	72.1	49.3	49.3	30.4	20.4	...	3.5	0.9	7.1	50[26]	...	74.1[26]	...	...	Montserrat
30.5	37.2	50.2	...	...	...	...	2.7	2.2	5.5	51,911	2,156[13]	65.9	1,014[13]	457[13]	Morocco
12.7	4.2	...	...	...	...	...	...	...	11.0	—145[35]—		51.7[35]	20[35]	25.0[35]	Mozambique
...	...	...	...	...	...	...	3.6[41]	1.6[41]	1.6	...	...	...	1,483	...	Myanmar (Burma)
...	49.2	...	...	...	...	...	...	...	...	...	...	...	...	...	Nauru
47.7	30.2	6.1	...	...	...	...	3.7	2.0	6.3	...	...	...	...	...	Nepal
100.0	94.8[2,12]	100.0	89.8[2,12]	—10.2[2,12]—		...	4.1	0.7	5.4	103,330	...	53.1	15,091[13]	49,968[13,22]	Netherlands, The
79.6	96.9	79.6	...	...	...	...	4.2	1.0	9.0[7]	415	...	99.0	483	...	Netherlands Antilles
85.1	79.0[25]	68.3	69.2	—30.8—		...	3.3	1.3	4.6[1]	...	46	...	1[13,27]	...	New Caledonia
92.7[12]	...	97.1[12]	...	...	...	...	5.6	0.5	5.7	23,035	2,848	50.7	8,398	3,228	New Zealand
27.9	40.9	19.3	19.2	—80.8—		...	2.2	2.1	3.5	...	43	...	28[13,27]	19.6[13,27]	Nicaragua
...	...	...	...	...	...	...	...	...	2.1	...	...	...	...	...	Niger
...	81.3	7.0	...	...	...	...	1.4	3.0	5.1[13]	...	...	...	1,592[7,13]	...	Nigeria
93.0	98.0	44.0	14.1	—85.9—		...	4.0[31]	1.2[31]	...	6[13]	...	...	...	...	Niue
8.0	98.3	...	94.2	—	5.8	...	6.2	2.5	...	...	...	...	...	...	Norfolk Island
97.5[21]	...	86.8	86.8	—13.2—		83.5	5.1[10]	0.5[10]	5.9	25,784	4,756	67.0	4,954[13]	3,322	Norway
...	...	...	...	...	...	...	...	...	10.8	1,043	...	...	266	...	Oman
															Pacific Is., Trust Terr. of the
46.3	48.9	...	28.6	—71.4—		...	...	...	...	...	...	...	...	...	Marshall Islands
40.0	28.3	...	8.0	—92.0—		...	...	...	...	...	...	...	...	...	Micronesia, Fed. States of
92.5	94.1	...	54.8	—45.2—		...	...	...	...	...	...	...	...	...	Northern Mariana Islands
70.8	75.7	...	19.6	—80.4—		...	...	...	...	...	...	...	...	...	Palau
20.3[74]	30.6[74]	25.1[74]	43.9	—56.1—		...	1.9[74]	3.3[74]	6.6	...	34[13]	...	90[13]	142.5[13]	Pakistan
80.7	65.7	74.3	...	...	...	...	2.6	1.8	5.0	...	...	...	...	...	Panama
50.0	56.0	40.0	...	...	...	...	...	...	4.3[1]	587	...	...	...	...	Papua New Guinea

Housing and construction (continued)

country	year	dwelling units[a]	median age[b] (years)	1939 or earlier	1940–49	1950–59	1960–69	1970 or later	owned	rented	collective, vacant, other	traditional materials	sawn/ framed wood	masonry or cement	other
					decade built (percent)					tenure[c] (percent)			construction of exterior walls (percent)		
Paraguay	1982	580,810[9]	21.1		56.0		17.0	27.0	80.4	10.5	9.1	21.5	29.7	47.6	1.2
Peru	1981	3,257,100	...		30.9		69.1		68.5	14.8	14.8	47.4	7.0	33.1	12.5
Philippines	1980	8,607,187	...	...	...	...	21.5[21]	...	80.2	12.4	7.4	36.3	33.6	23.8	6.3
Pitcairn Island	1986	15	...	46.7	20.0	13.3	—	20.0	100.0	—	—		100.0		
Poland	1978	11,205,000[4]	...	42.1[14]		38.8[16]		19.1					14.1	85.9	
Portugal	1981	3,235,630	33.7		53.3		17.5	29.2	56.7	38.8	4.6	—	0.7	61.0	38.3
Puerto Rico	1980	969,611	15.8	5.7	6.5	15.0	31.6	41.2	65.7	23.8	10.5	—	19.7	77.4	2.9
Qatar	...	...	...	...	...	...	...	...	...	...	...	...	...	...	...
Réunion	1982	141,123	...	...	...	...	21.2[8]	...	54.6	34.5	10.9	...	...	...	...
Romania	1966	5,380,299	...												
Rwanda	1979	1,055,950	...	...	...	...	...	...	74.7	19.5	5.8				
St. Helena and Ascension	1987	1,429	23.4[11]	...	...	...	...	...	54.7	31.4	13.9		76.2[18]	20.8	3.0
St. Kitts and Nevis	1980	11,615	24.2		63.5		17.9	14.7	64.7	26.0	9.3	0.1	83.6[18]	12.4	3.9
St. Lucia	1980	26,919	...		36.8		21.5	41.7	77.3	17.8	4.9				
St. Pierre and Miquelon	1982	1,760	11.3		69.0		13.8	17.2							
St. Vincent and the Grenadines	1970	16,940	...	—		...	...	...	74.7	16.5	7.9	8.9	64.1	26.1	0.8
San Marino	1979	7,000	...	...	...	...	...	...	73.5	21.9	4.6	...	...	...	...
São Tomé and Príncipe	1981	25,197[78]	...	...	...	...	...	...				...	...	...	...
Saudi Arabia	...	...	...	...	...	...	...	...	84.6		15.4				
Senegal	1955[47,79]	13,000	...	...	...	...	...	...	46.6	53.4		4.1	57.2	38.7	—
Seychelles	1977	12,315	...	...	...	...	...	...							
Sierra Leone	...	...	...		63.2		36.8		55.0	39.6	5.4	4.7		95.3	
Singapore	1980	513,224	...						27.4[11]	43.0[11]	29.6[11]				
Solomon Islands	1979[47]	3,423	...												
Somalia	...	...	...												
South Africa	1970	1,354,520	18.6	24.6	16.0	24.2	35.2	—							
Bophuthatswana	...	...	...	...	...	...	...	...							
Ciskei	...	...	...	...	...	...	...	...							
Transkei	...	...	...	...	...	...	...	...							
Venda	...	...	...	...	...	...	...	...							
South West Africa/Namibia	...	...	...												
Spain	1984	15,332,900	39.4[7,43]	39.2[7,43]	23.4[7,43]		18.5[7,43]	18.9[7,43]	57.2[43]	24.4[43]	18.3[43]				
Sri Lanka	1981	2,811,406	...	...	...	...	11.1[12]	...	69.4	10.1	20.5	76.5	4.4	16.7	2.4
Sudan, The	1966[2]	253,060	...		52.4		47.6		59.2	28.3	12.6	38.9[80]		61.1[80]	
Suriname	1980	77,658	...									65.9		34.1	
Swaziland	1986	122,369	...	25.9	10.4	15.2	23.1	25.4	38.9[7]	56.0[7]	5.1[7]	98.7[7]			
Sweden	1985	3,863,439	24.0		58.1		22.6	19.3	29.9	67.1	3.0	...	...	...	...
Switzerland	1980	2,969,000[10]	...	...	...	...	8.7[21]	...	81.6[21]	15.5[21]	2.8[21]	...	...	...	...
Syria	1987	1,836,195	...	13.8[19]		14.0[20]	42.4[81]	29.8[82]	79.1	11.8	9.1	...	...	...	...
Taiwan	1980	3,171,876[9]	15.3						75.4	19.4	5.2	83.0	—	16.3	0.7
Tanzania	1978	3,554,793	...		17.0		83.0		83.4	9.1	7.5	15.1	70.0	6.3	8.6
Thailand	1980	8,414,648	...	22.0[21]		25.0[21]	53.0[21]	—							
Togo	1958–60[2]	22,274	...	...	...	...	...	...	97.7[42]	2.3[42]	—	49.6	28.2	12.3	9.9
Tokelau	1982	284	...	...	...	...	...	...	85.1	2.5	12.4	35.1	45.4	15.3	4.2
Tonga	1976	15,091[10,58]	22.5	52.7	6.7[83]		20.3[84]	20.3[85]	64.6	34.0	1.4	3.3	32.6	53.8	10.3[18]
Trinidad and Tobago	1980	231,436	...		56.3		14.5	29.2	78.9	12.6	8.5				
Tunisia	1984	1,313,200	...	...	...	...	...	...	76.2[86]	22.0	1.8	0.7[58]		99.3[58]	
Turkey	1986	10,855,495	...		45.1		15.5	39.4	68.6	22.8	8.6	—	36.8	59.9	3.3
Turks and Caicos Islands	1980	1,644	20.0	...	...	...	...	...	81.6	12.1	6.6	64.9	4.2	31.0	—
Tuvalu	1979	1,079	...	...	...	...	...	...							
Uganda	...	...	...	...	...	...	...	...	42.1	57.9	...				
U.S.S.R.	1984	79,285,700[58]	...						36.2	45.2	18.6	2.9	7.3	87.3	2.5
United Arab Emirates	1980	153,009	15.0	—	0.8	1.3	11.4	86.5	51.1	40.3	8.6	...	...	...	...
United Kingdom	1981[87]	22,611,700[10]	32.6	54.0		13.0	16.6	16.4	63.5	32.3	4.2	...	...	...	...
United States	1985	99,888,000[10]	25.0	24.0	8.9	14.0	16.6	36.5				...	...	...	...
Uruguay	1985	852,400	...	...	...	...	...	...	59.0[86]	23.9	17.1	61.4	7.7	13.6	17.2
Vanuatu	1979	22,513	...	...	...	...	...	...	40.9[47]	25.7[47]	33.4[47]	11.8	2.1	78.9	7.2
Venezuela	1981	2,708,674	...	...	...	...	...	...	75.1	17.8	7.1	...	...	...	...
Vietnam	1979	9,977,316	...	...	...	...	...	...	34.6	52.2	13.2	...	...	...	...
Virgin Islands (U.S.)	1980	32,650	14.7	6.5	3.5	8.9	42.7	38.4							
Wallis and Futuna	1983	1,389	14.4	8.0		11.0	24.0	57.0	94.4[11]	0.6[11]	5.0[11]	67.0	31.0		2.0
West Bank	1985	119,165[48]	...	...	...	...	...	...	86.2[49]	11.5[49]	2.3[49]	...	...	...	...
Western Sahara	1982	19,559	...	...	...	...	...	...	32.2[44]	62.3[44]	5.5[44]	...	...	...	...
Western Samoa	1981	33,402	...	...	...	...	...	...	80.1	2.0	17.9	62.3	24.4	8.6	4.7
Yemen (Aden)	1973	74,261[43]	...												
Yemen (Şan'ā')	1975	863,109	...	...	...	...	...	...	85.3	7.0	7.7			82.6	17.4
Yugoslavia	1981	6,786,700[13]	...	31.1		12.7	26.8	29.4	67.1	25.0	7.9	...	...	...	...
Zaire	1967[47]	168,000	...	...	...	...	...	...	47.4	38.3	14.3	...	...	...	...
Zambia	1980	1,128,300	...	...	...	...	...	...	78.8[89]	21.1[89]		55.9[91]		44.1[91]	
Zimbabwe	1969	925,581	...						65.1[90]	32.6[90]	2.3[90]				

[1]1983. [2]Urban areas only. [3]Percent of net material product. [4]1987. [5]1977. [6]1982. [7]1980. [8]1974. [9]Occupied dwellings only; may include seasonal and temporary housing. [10]1986. [11]1976. [12]1971. [13]1985. [14]1944 and earlier. [15]In 1988. [16]1945–70. [17]Stucco. [18]Includes wood and brick, and wood and concrete. [19]1945 and earlier. [20]1946–60. [21]1970. [22]Volume in cubic metres. [23]1960. [24]National coverage substantially incomplete; no meaningful replacement rate could be calculated. [25]1983–85 average. [26]Average annual gain in housing stock during intercensal interval preceding last census. [27]1984. [28]Data refer to rugos, which usually contain two or three dwellings each. [29]1970–75. [30]1976–80. [31]1981. [32]1959–60; data refer to households and are based on a demographic survey of the African population excluding Bangui town, East Dubangi, and the nomad population. [33]1973. [34]1978. [35]1975. [36]1933 and earlier. [37]1934–45. [38]1946–59. [39]Includes corrugated steel. [40]1979. [41]1961. [42]1972. [43]Data refer to buildings, not dwellings. [44]1968. [45]Traditional houses (usually constructed of fragile tropical materials and lacking modern

physical amenities (percent)			sewage disposal (percent)			space[b]			construction industry (1986)	new residential[d]			new nonresidential[d]		
piped water	electricity	inside toilet or WC	closed public sewer or septic tank	open public sewer	other	average area (sq m)	rooms per dwelling unit	persons per room	percent of GDP	total no. of dwellings	floor area ('000 sq m)	years to replace nat'l stock	number of units	floor area ('000 sq m)	country
...	...	26.4					2.2[42]	2.4[42]	6.0	2,254[4,24]	...	24	2,715[4]	365[4]	Paraguay
73.4	89.5	78.0	58.1	—41.9—		42.4	2.6	2.0	4.6	...	952	...			Peru
41.4	46.0	35.0	44.1	—55.9—			2.4[42]	2.3[42]	3.6		2,124[13]		2,807[13]	2,170[13]	Philippines
100.0	100.0	—	—	—100.0—		100.0	5.0	0.4							Pitcairn Island
69.7	96.2	41.4	67.0	—33.0—		53.9	4.0[10]	0.9[10]	12.9[3]				62,041[13]		Poland
73.4	77.6	67.7	75.5	—24.5—			5.0[27]	0.8	5.6	37,274	2,750	86.8	6,238	1,649	Portugal
95.2	97.4	89.7	89.6	—10.4—			4.8	0.8	1.7		1,798		900[13]	41.0[13]	Puerto Rico
									6.9	1,184			258		Qatar
70.6	81.6	50.7	52.4	—47.6—			3.6	1.2	4.7[7]	5,216					Réunion
	48.6		12.2	—87.8—			2.6	1.4	7.6	105,610[13]	8,591[13]	50.9[13]			Romania
91.9	78.6	73.6					2.2	1.7	6.0				63[27]		Rwanda
96.6	58.3	33.5	31.8[21]	—68.2[21]—			3.0	1.3	9.8	171[26]		68.0[26]			St. Helena and Ascension
79.5	36.1[21]		11.0[21]	—89.0[21]—			3.2	1.6	7.5	471[43]	18	57.2[43]			St. Kitts and Nevis
99.7	99.8	99.2	97.6	—2.4—			4.6	0.7		54		32.6	121	10.3	St. Lucia
															St. Pierre and Miquelon
95.0[1]			22.0[1]	—78.0[1]—			2.8	1.8	10.6		307				St. Vincent and the Grenadines
99.8	100.0	98.3	98.3	—1.7—			4.5	0.8		171		46.4	82		San Marino
									3.3[1]						São Tomé and Príncipe
									12.3						Saudi Arabia
87.7	95.9						2.3	1.5	6.5	873[24]	235	24	39	38	Senegal
77.5	46.8	33.1	33.1	—66.9—			3.6	1.4	5.8	4,802[5,46]			46		Seychelles
									2.6[1]						Sierra Leone
90.6[21]	98.3	63.6[21]	63.6[21]	—36.4[21]—			1.8[21]	2.5[21]	8.2	43,692	9,222[13]	11.7	992[13]	2,790	Singapore
92.7[11]	79.6[11]	89.2	89.2[11]	—10.8[11]—		10.8[11]	2.3[11]	2.0[11]							Solomon Islands
									3.2[13]						Somalia
							3.4		3.1	33,284	4,905	40.7		2,581	South Africa
															Bophuthatswana
															Ciskei
															Transkei
															Venda
90.5[7,43]	94.7[7,43]		87.9[7,43]	—12.1[7,43]—			4.4[19]		2.2						South West Africa/Namibia
18.2	14.9	4.7	4.7	—95.3—		18.6[21]	2.5	2.1	6.8	193,410		79.4			Spain
63.9	26.4	70.2	2.6	—97.4—			2.2	2.5	7.8	59,637		47.2			Sri Lanka
62.9	82.0	40.4	19.6[80]	—80.4[80]—			2.1	1.9	4.4						Sudan, The
									6.2		355[13,22]		161[13]		Suriname
33.4[11]	11.6	21.4							3.5				28[27]		Swaziland
100.0	96.2[7]	98.0	96.3[7]	—3.7[7]—			3.2	0.7	6.7	28,791		134.2			Sweden
100.0		93.3	92.2	—	7.8	86.0	3.8[10]	0.6[10]	7.6[13]	42,570		69.8	8,109	3,818[13,27]	Switzerland
40.2[1]	41.7[1]		36.0[1]	—64.0[1]—		93.0	3.0	2.0	7.0	55,568	7,573	33.0			Syria
79.4	99.7	94.2	69.3			85.9	3.7	1.5	4.1		25,959			692	Taiwan
37.2	6.3						2.5	1.9	1.9						Tanzania
17.3	43.0	40.9	40.9[11]	9.8[11]	49.3[11]		1.9[11]	1.9	5.1		5,812			4,356	Thailand
4.1	10.3		—	—100.0—			1.8	3.4	2.9[1]						Togo
2.3[42]	60.9	2.3[42]													Tokelau
61.3	20.9	42.3	11.2	—88.8—					3.9[1]						Tonga
64.3	83.3	41.1	41.0	—59.0—			3.3	1.4	9.0	2,046[24]	344	24	69	39	Trinidad and Tobago
26.4	63.4	43.3	51.8	—41.2—			1.9	2.4	5.7						Tunisia
68.0	56.8[35]	70.6	42.0	52.0	6.0		2.4[13]	2.2[21]	4.1	168,597	17,963	64.4	3,933	4,335	Turkey
19.9	47.6		70.5	—29.5—			3.5	1.1	8.5	56		19.3	25		Turks and Caicos Islands
65.4	7.4	37.3							13.0[40]						Tuvalu
90.8[2]	100.0[2]	88.7[2]	88.7[2]	—11.3[2]—					0.3[6]				65[42]	26.8[42]	Uganda
30.9[44]	24.2[44]	84.5					2.8	1.8	12.0	2,100,000	119,800	37.8			U.S.S.R.
		99.0					3.8	0.6	10.8				133[13,27]		United Arab Emirates
98.5	96.9	98.2	99.2	—0.8—		147.1	5.2	0.5	6.1	208,095		106.2			United Kingdom
									4.7		214,900			140,100	United States
88.9	84.7	73.3	...	92.0			3.4	1.7	1.7		160[13]		105[13]	21.4[13]	Uruguay
13.7	11.7	19.1							2.0[6]		5.7			15.3	Vanuatu
85.3	88.6	84.4	71.3	—28.7—			3.9[12]	1.5[12]	3.5	91,666	4,904	29.5	678	1,067	Venezuela
									3.0[1,3]				53[27]	59.3[27]	Vietnam
96.3	98.1	86.0	93.6	—6.4—			4.2	0.8					262[13,40]		Virgin Islands (U.S.)
23.0		9.0	24.0	—	7.6		1.8[11]	4.0[11]		39[13]		35.6[13]			Wallis and Futuna
75.2	91.2	90.1						2.7	14.1	5,229	660	22.8			West Bank
78.5	95.3						4.5	1.2						161.4	Western Sahara
80.7	37.7	71.0	16.6	—83.4—			3.9[11,79]	1.5[11,79]	1.9	132[13]			118[13]		Western Samoa
							2.0	3.0	10.2[1]						Yemen (Aden)
5.7	4.6						2.0	2.8	4.2						Yemen (Şan'ā')
67.8	95.7	53.3				60.7	2.6[13]	1.3[13]	6.9	129,996	13,845	52.2	17,800	4,554	Yugoslavia
									5.1[27]				73[13]	39[13]	Zaire
12.4[89]	27.5[23]	15.1[89]			82.3[89]		1.9[89]	2.6[89]	2.5						Zambia
	9.3[91]						2.8	1.9							Zimbabwe

conveniences). [46]Residential includes nonresidential. [47]Capital city only. [48]1967. [49]Excludes refugee camps. [50]1948 or earlier. [51]1949–57. [52]1958–68. [53]1969–78. [54]1979 or later. [55]1947 and earlier. [56]1948–83. [57]1961–71. [58]Data refer to households. [59]Minimum. [60]Includes nonconventional housing units. [61]1966. [62]1946 and earlier. [63]1947–60. [64]1948–60. [65]Peninsular Malaysia only. [66]1957 and earlier. [67]1958–67. [68]Excluding Rodrigues and lesser outlying islands. [69]1960–68. [70]1969–83. [71]Dwellings of indigenous population. [72]1931–44. [73]1945–59. [74]Excludes Islāmābad, North-West Frontier, and Federally Administered Tribal Areas. [75]1947–65. [76]1966–75. [77]1976–80. [78]De jure population. [79]European-style dwellings only. [80]1964. [81]1961–75. [82]1976 and later. [83]1939–56. [84]1956–66. [85]1966–70. [86]Includes squatters. [87]Data exclude Northern Ireland. [88]Preliminary. [89]1969. [90]Dwellings occupied by Europeans, Coloured, and Asians only. [91]Dwellings occupied by Africans only.

Household budgets and consumption

This table provides international data on household income, on the consumption expenditure of households for goods and services, and on the principal object of such expenditure (in most countries), food consumption (by kind). For purposes of this compilation, income comprises pretax monetary payments and payment in kind. The first part of the table provides data on distribution of income by households and by sources of income; the second part analyzes the largest portion of income use—consumption expenditure. Such expenditure is defined as the purchase of goods and services to satisfy current wants and needs. This definition excludes income expended on taxes, debts, savings and investments, and insurance policies. The third and last part of the table focuses on food, which usually, and often by a wide margin, represents the largest share of consumer spending worldwide. The data provided include daily available calories per capita and consumption of major food groups.

For both sources of income and consumption expenditure, the primary basis of analysis for most countries is the household, an economic unit that can be as small as a single person or as large as an extended family. For some of the countries that do not compile information by household, the table provides data on personal income and personal expenditure, i.e., the income and expenditure of all the individuals constituting a society's households. When no expenditure data at all is available, the table reports the weights of each major class of goods and services comprising a given country's consumer (or retail) price index (CPI). The weighting of the components of the CPI usually reflects household spending patterns within the country, its principal urban or rural areas, though sometimes only in the country's capital city or major cities.

The data on distribution of income show, collectively for an entire country, the proportion of total income earned by households comprising the lowest quintile and highest decile (poorest 20% and wealthiest 10%) within the country. These figures show the degree to which either group represents a disproportionate share of poverty or wealth.

The data on sources of income illuminate patterns of economic structure in the gaining of an income. They indicate, for example, that in poor, agrarian countries income often derives largely from self-employment (usually farming) or that in industrial countries, with well-developed systems of salaried employment and social welfare, income derives mainly from wages and salaries and secondarily from transfer payments (see headnote a). Because household sizes and numbers of income earners vary so greatly internationally, and because the frequency and methodology of household and CPI surveys do not permit single-year comparisons for more than a few countries at once, no summary of total household income or expenditure was possible. Instead, U.S. dollar figures are supplied for per capita private final consumption expenditure (for a single, recent year) that are more comparable internationally and refer to the same date. The figures on distribution of consumption expenditure by end use reveal patterns of personal and family use of disposable income and indicate, inter alia, that in developing countries food may absorb 50% or more of disposable income, while in the larger household budgets of the developed countries, by contrast, food purchases may account for only 20–30% of spending. In either type of country, the cost of transportation often rivals that of housing, once the more basic need. Each category of expenditure betrays similar complexities of local habit, necessity, and aspiration.

The reader should exercise caution when using these data to make intercountry comparisons. Most of the information comes from single-country surveys, which often differ markedly in their coverage of economically or demographically stratified groups, in sample design, or in the methods

Household budgets and consumption

country	income (latest) percent received by — lowest 20% of households	highest 10% of households	by source (percent) wages, salaries	self-employment	transfer payments[a]	other[b]	consumption expenditure per capita private final, U.S.$ 1987	food[c]	housing[d]	clothing[e]	health care	energy, water	education
Afghanistan	...	...	20.7	28.0	8.2	43.1	100[1]	33.9	3.0	...	1.1	0.7	...
Albania	...	...	...	...	...	...	1,500	55.7	11.7	9.2	3.1	...	[2]
Algeria	...	...	...	...	...	...		44.3	23.4[3]	5.8	...	...	...
American Samoa	...	...	...	...	...	...		...	...	...	...	...	...
Andorra	...												
Angola	...	...	...	...	...	...	560	...	...	...	...	...	...
Anguilla	...	...					1,460	...	...	...	...	...	...
Antigua and Barbuda							2,170[4]	42.9	23.3	7.5	...	5.5	...
Argentina	4.4	35.2	...	...	...	...	1,410[5]	46.3	7.2	10.9	4.5	4.1	[2]
Aruba	...						6	24.5	18.4	8.4	2.9	...	[2]
Australia	4.7	28.4	60.3	7.4	25.7	6.6	7,330	20.8	21.9	6.2	6.4	2.4	[2]
Austria	4.0	28.7	56.0	19.4	24.6	—	8,670	17.1	13.1	10.4	4.6	5.4	0.2
Bahamas, The	3.6	32.1	...	...	...	...	4,250[4]	17.1	15.1	5.1	4.1	...	[2]
Bahrain							4,150[4]	32.4	21.2	5.9	2.3	2.2	2.3
Bangladesh	6.6	29.5	26.1	50.8	0.5	22.6	150[4]	63.3	8.8	5.9	1.1	8.4	1.2
Barbados	6.8						3,760	45.2	13.1	5.1	...	6.2	...
Belgium	7.9[7]	21.5[7]	51.9	10.4	20.7	17.0	7,230[4]	23.5	16.7	8.4	...	6.3	...
Belize	...	...	84.1	——15.9——			790[4]	51.5[8]	2.3	11.1	3.4	6.0	1.5
Benin	8.0	39.0					390	72.3	...	21.2	...	3.7	...
Bermuda	7.2	24.7	72.2	6.7	2.4	18.7	12,690[9]	17.3	20.8	5.3	4.1	4.0	2.8
Bhutan	4.0	...	...	...	...	...	640[4]	41.7	12.6	9.8	4.6	0.7	1.2
Bolivia	...	...	...	...	...	...	850	40.1[8]	13.6[11]	10.8	1.3	[11]	...
Botswana	4.3[7,10]	42.0[7,10]	70.6	16.6	12.8	—	330[4]	49.0[8,12]	8.6[12]	6.4[12]	5.3[12]	11.7[12]	2.2[12]
Brazil	2.3	48.3	...	...	...	...	2,880[4]	34.1	21.0	8.2	3.1	4.5	3.2
British Virgin Islands	...							45.1	5.0[11]	6.1	...	[11]	[2]
Brunei	9.7	22.5	54.3	11.1	18.3	16.3	1,610	43.5	7.4	9.8	2.1	[11]	3.4
Bulgaria	...	...	...	...	...	...	210	38.7[13]	5.1[13]	4.4[13]	5.2[13]	13.7[13]	[2]
Burkina Faso	...						260	59.6[13]	4.4[13]	11.1[13]	...	5.8[13]	...
Burundi	...						1,050	33.6[13]	14.6[13]	16.3[13]	5.0[13]	...	...
Cameroon	...							...	...	...	...	...	...
Canada	6.0	30.1	64.2	8.2	15.1	12.5	9,360	15.6	23.1[3]	6.3	3.8	[3]	2.9
Cape Verde	...						530	63.4[13]	...	9.2[13]	...	...	...
Cayman Islands	...						410	70.5[13]	0.6[13]	9.5[13]	1.0[13]	6.5[13]	...
Central African Republic	...						220	45.3[13]	...	3.5[13]	11.9[13]	5.8[13]	...
Chad	8.0	30.0						...	...	...	...	...	...
Chile	4.4	34.8	40.8	...	8.1	51.2	840	41.9	13.3	7.6	...	...	[2]
China	8.5[15]	37.7[15,16]	81.2[17]	...	15.2[17]	3.6[17]	140	55.2[15]	14.5[15]	8.6[15]	...	4.8[15]	[2]
Christmas Island	...							...	...	...	...	...	...
Cocos (Keeling) Islands	...						760[4]	38.4	20.0	9.2	3.8	4.6	2.9
Colombia	4.0	43.5	49.3	36.6	6.2	7.9	340	56.0	...	10.0	5.0	14.4	...
Comoros	...	...	25.6	64.5	8.7	1.2	790	51.6[8,13]	...	8.2[13]	2.6[13]	5.4[13]	...
Congo	7.0	43.5						58.4	3.1	12.4	...	...	...
Cook Islands	...						1,030	40.8[13,18]	12.3[13,18]	10.0[13,18]	—	6.6[13,18]	[2]
Costa Rica	3.9[17]	39.8[17]	44.9	49.9	——5.2——		980	48.0[13]	7.8[13]	10.1[13]	0.7[13]	8.5[13]	...
Côte d'Ivoire	2.4	43.7						...	...	...	...	...	...
Cuba	...		57.3	...	...	42.7	1,440	25.6	...	...	...	2.4	...
Cyprus	7.9[17]	...					2,650[4]	30.5	6.2	9.5	3.1	2.7	1.2
Czechoslovakia	10.0[19]	21.8[19]	62.8	—	20.1	17.1	4,680	26.4	...	8.5	...	...	1.5
Denmark	3.8	25.2	65.5	8.8	12.4	13.3	10,680	16.6	24.9	6.0	1.9	6.2	...
Djibouti	...		51.6	36.0	10.5	1.9	930	50.3	6.4	1.7	2.4	13.1	...
Dominica	...						730[20]	43.1	16.1[3]	6.5	...	5.4	...
Dominican Republic	4.5[7]	41.7[7]	41.7	31.8	1.5	25.0	620[4]	51.7[8]	23.9	6.0	...	...	...
Ecuador	2.9	51.5	23.2	71.7	0.5	4.6	760	33.4	11.6[11]	10.2	4.5	[11]	...
Egypt	5.8	33.2					600	49.7[17]	8.8[17]	14.2[17]	1.8[17]	3.6[17]	2.1[17]
El Salvador	5.5[7]	29.5[7]					760	42.7	6.0	9.8	4.1	2.1	1.2

employed for collection, classification, and tabulation of data. Further, the reference period of the data varies greatly; while a significant portion of the data is from 1979 or later, information for some countries dates from the early and mid-1970s. This older information is typeset in italic. Finally, intercountry comparisons of annual personal consumption expenditure may be misleading because of the distortions of price and purchasing power present when converting a national currency unit into U.S. dollars.

The table's food consumption data include total daily available calories per capita (food supply), which amounts to domestic production and imports minus exports, animal feed, and nonfood uses, and a percentage breakdown of the major food groups that make up food supply.

The data for daily available calories per capita provide a measure of the nutritional adequacy of each nation's food supply. The following list, based on estimates from the United Nations Food and Agriculture Organization (FAO), indicates the regional variation in recommended daily minimum nutritional requirements, which are defined by factors such as climatic ambience and average body weight: Africa (2,320 calories), Centrally Planned Asia (2,300 calories), Far East (2,240 calories), Latin America (2,360 calories), Near East (2,440 calories).

The breakdown of diet by food groups describes the character of a nation's food supply. A typical breakdown for a low-income country might show a diet with heavy intake of vegetable foods, such as cereals, potatoes, or cassava. In the high-income countries, a relatively larger portion of total calories derives from animal products (meat, eggs, and milk). The reader should note, however, that these data refer to total national *supply* and do not reflect the dietary differences that often exist between socioeconomic groups within a single country.

In compiling this table, Britannica editors rely on both numerous national reports and principal secondary sources such as the International Bank for Reconstruction and Development's *World Development Report* (annual), the International Labour Organisation's *Household Income and Expenditure Statistics 1968–1976* and *Statistical Sources and Methods, vol. 1 Consumer Price Indices* (2nd ed.); the UN's *Yearbook of National Accounts Statistics* (annual) and *National Accounts Statistics: Compendium of Income Distribution Statistics;* and the FAO's *Food Balance Sheets 1979–81* and *1984–86*.

The following terms further define the column headings:
a. Includes pensions, family allowances, unemployment payments, remittances from abroad, and social security and related benefits.
b. Includes interest and dividends, rents and royalties, and all other income not reported under the three preceding categories.
c. Includes alcoholic and nonalcoholic beverages and meals away from home when identifiable. Excludes tobacco except as noted.
d. Rent, maintenance of dwellings, and taxes only; excludes energy and water (heat, light, power, and water) and household durables (furniture, appliances, utensils, and household operations), shown separately.
e. Includes footwear.
f. Furniture, appliances, and utensils; usually includes expenditure on household operation.
g. Includes expenditure on cultural activities other than education.
h. May include data not shown separately in preceding categories, including meals away from home (see note c).
i. Represents pure fats and oils only.
j. Consists mainly of peas, beans, and lentils; spices; stimulants; sugars and honey; and nuts and oilseeds.

transportation, communications	household durable goods[f]	recreation[g]	personal effects, other[h]	food consumption									country
				daily available calories per capita	percent of total calories derived from								
					cereals	potatoes, cassava	meat, poultry	fish	eggs, milk	fruits, vegetables	fats, oils[i]	other[j]	
...	...	...	61.3	*1,896*	*81.5*	*1.4*	*3.3*	*—*	*3.6*	*2.4*	*3.1*	*4.7*	Afghanistan
6.7	6.4	3.4[2]	3.8	*2,657*	*66.4*	*2.6*	*5.2*	*0.1*	*6.2*	*4.7*	*6.4*	*8.4*	Albania
14.9	3		11.6	*2,688*	*57.1*	*2.1*	*2.2*	*0.3*	*7.5*	*4.2*	*13.5*	*13.1*	Algeria
...	...	...	...	...	...	...	...	...	...	...	...	...	American Samoa
													Andorra
...	...	...	...	*2,141*	*35.3*	*33.8*	*3.2*	*0.9*	*1.9*	*4.2*	*7.2*	*13.5*	Angola
10.0	...	...	10.8	...	...	...	...	...	...	...	...	...	Anguilla
8.7	5.2	6.4[2]	6.7	*2,089*	*35.3*	*0.4*	*9.6*	*2.4*	*11.7*	*7.2*	*12.8*	*20.7*	Antigua and Barbuda
17.4	9.1	5.0[2]	14.3	3,191	30.9	2.7	20.7	0.3	8.6	4.3	11.9	19.5	Argentina
6	6	6	6	6	6	6	6	6	6	6	6	6	Aruba
13.4	6.7	3.9[2]	18.3	3,326	23.3	2.7	18.0	0.8	11.7	4.8	15.1	23.5	Australia
16.3	6.8	5.6	20.5	3,416	20.0	3.3	14.5	0.5	11.2	5.7	22.7	22.1	Austria
15.9	5.2	6.3[2]	31.2	2,609	24.5	2.2	19.2	0.8	7.1	8.4	10.3	27.5	Bahamas, The
8.5	9.8	6.4	9.0	...	...	...	...	...	...	...	...	...	Bahrain
0.9	...	...	10.4	*1,922*	*83.9*	*0.9*	*0.7*	*0.8*	*1.4*	*1.3*	*5.1*	*6.0*	Bangladesh
4.6	9.6	...	16.2	3,181	30.1	2.4	15.1	2.1	7.1	2.6	12.8	27.9	Barbados
12.8	9.3	9.8	13.2	3,850	19.4	5.0	19.4	0.7	8.9	4.8	23.4	18.6	Belgium
6.5	10.1	2.2	5.4	2,585	34.9	0.7	9.2	0.6	9.3	7.2	10.5	27.5	Belize
...	...	...	...	*2,181*	*32.4*	*20.9*	*2.7*	*0.6*	*1.0*	*3.2*	*11.5*	*27.7*	Benin
10.6	11.9	5.4	17.8	*2,545*	*26.7*	*1.4*	*20.2*	*2.4*	*10.8*	*8.1*	*11.4*	*19.1*	Bermuda
...	0.7	...	2.1	*2,028*	*85.2*	*2.4*	*0.4*	*0.1*	*0.6*	*1.4*	*5.3*	*4.6*	Bhutan
12.6	8.9	3.1	4.8	*2,128*	*46.2*	*9.4*	*8.7*	*0.1*	*2.8*	*6.2*	*7.1*	*19.5*	Bolivia
10.5	13.7	...	10.0	*2,230*	*60.9*	*0.3*	*4.8*	*0.3*	*7.4*	*1.4*	*5.1*	*19.9*	Botswana
6.3[12]	...	2.1[12]	8.4[12]	*2,644*	*39.4*	*7.0*	*5.7*	*0.4*	*6.1*	*4.9*	*10.5*	*26.1*	Brazil
2.3	13.1	1.6	8.9	...	...	...	...	...	...	...	...	...	British Virgin Islands
17.2	8.3	8.9[2]	9.4	2,850	45.7	1.3	10.3	1.6	6.9	4.3	7.2	22.7	Brunei
6.8	4.3	7.4	15.3	3,634	40.6	1.6	9.6	0.5	8.9	5.3	14.7	18.9	Bulgaria
18.6[13]	3.0[13]	2.3[2, 13]	9.0[13]	*2,049*	*68.0*	*0.6*	*2.3*	*0.1*	*2.0*	*1.0*	*4.6*	*21.3*	Burkina Faso
...	6.0[13]	...	13.1[13, 14]	*2,270*	*26.5*	*8.2*	*1.0*	*0.3*	*0.9*	*7.9*	*1.5*	*53.8*	Burundi
10.5[13]	...	5.1[13]	14.9[13]	*2,040*	*35.5*	*7.2*	*3.4*	*0.6*	*0.8*	*9.7*	*10.2*	*32.7*	Cameroon
15.9	8.8	7.6	16.0	3,425	20.2	3.2	16.7	1.0	10.0	5.7	18.9	24.3	Canada
...	...	...	20.7[13]	*2,729*	*53.4*	*1.6*	*1.9*	*1.7*	*2.5*	*2.7*	*12.8*	*23.4*	Cape Verde
4.1[13]	0.8[13]	1.3[13]	5.7[13]	*1,940*	*18.7*	*33.3*	*7.0*	*0.5*	*0.4*	*5.6*	*7.1*	*27.4*	Cayman Islands
...	...	...	33.5[13]	*1,762*	*57.2*	*11.2*	*3.2*	*1.6*	*2.6*	*2.9*	*3.3*	*18.0*	Central African Republic
11.8	7.8	8.2[2]	9.4	2,573	49.2	4.0	6.8	0.8	6.2	4.5	8.7	19.9	Chad
...	...	5.1[2, 15]	11.8[15]	2,628	71.3	0.9	6.5	0.4	1.1	2.3	4.6	12.9	Chile
...	...	...	...	...	...	...	...	...	...	...	...	...	China
6.8	7.5	3.8	6.4	2,550	33.1	8.6	7.0	0.2	5.8	8.6	9.1	27.5	Christmas Island
													Cocos (Keeling) Islands
6.6	...	3.0	5.0	*2,110*	*42.5*	*26.0*	*2.0*	*1.2*	*1.4*	*6.5*	*4.8*	*15.7*	Colombia
...	6.9[13]	...	25.3[13]	*2,599*	*19.5*	*37.9*	*2.4*	*3.3*	*1.1*	*7.6*	*13.0*	*15.4*	Comoros
5.7	9.6	...	10.8	...	...	...	...	...	...	...	...	...	Congo
6.5[13, 18]	8.2[13, 18]	9.2[2, 13, 18]	6.4[13, 18]	*2,781*	*37.3*	*0.8*	*5.9*	*0.2*	*8.5*	*6.2*	*11.5*	*29.4*	Cook Islands
12.2[13]	3.4[13]	0.6[13]	8.7[13]	2,550	40.3	8.5	2.9	1.0	1.8	7.9	9.1	28.6	Costa Rica
5.7	...	...	66.3	3,107	36.5	3.2	7.4	1.2	8.4	3.9	8.9	30.5	Côte d'Ivoire
15.1	11.1	5.9	14.7	3,054	40.0	2.5	*13.7*	0.4	7.9	7.0	*10.1*	18.4	Cuba
...	5.0	...	60.1	3,473	30.2	4.2	*13.7*	0.4	9.8	4.0	17.0	20.7	Cyprus
17.1	7.0	8.1	10.7	3,512	20.4	3.8	22.2	1.3	9.5	4.0	17.3	21.4	Czechoslovakia
...	1.5	...	24.6	...	...	...	...	...	...	...	...	...	Denmark
													Djibouti
...	3	...	34.3	2,649	28.8	0.8	7.8	1.0	5.9	9.6	6.6	39.6	Dominica
...	...	...	18.4	2,464	32.3	1.7	4.9	0.4	6.3	14.7	4.9	26.8	Dominican Republic
11.5	5.8	...	23.0	*2,058*	*34.1*	*4.9*	*5.8*	*1.9*	*7.9*	*9.7*	*12.6*	*23.1*	Ecuador
5.2[17]	3.6[17]	1.3[17]	9.7[17]	3,313	61.5	1.4	2.7	0.3	2.2	5.7	13.0	13.2	Egypt
11.2	13.2	3.4	6.3	*2,048*	*56.9*	*0.9*	*2.4*	*0.2*	*5.3*	*4.7*	*8.4*	*21.3*	El Salvador

Household budgets and consumption   (continued)

country	income (latest)		by source (percent)				consumption expenditure	by kind or end use (percent of household or personal budget; latest)					
	percent received by						per capita private final, U.S.$ 1987						
	lowest 20% of households	highest 10% of households	wages, salaries	self-employment	transfer payments[a]	other[b]		food[c]	housing[d]	clothing[e]	health care	energy, water	education
Equatorial Guinea	...	...	0.6[15]	87.8[15]	—[15]	11.6[15]	130	66.7[15]	0.5[15]	6.8[15]	3.1[15]	15.9[15]	2.5[15]
Ethiopia	...	...	...	...	...	...	100	43.8	8.5	8.0	...	18.9	...
Faeroe Islands	...	...	...	...	...	...	...	46.0[13]	10.0[13]	13.0[13]	...	5.0[13]	...
Falkland Islands	...	...	81.5	9.1	—	9.4	1,050	33.9	18.6	6.3	...	4.9	...
Fiji	3.7	37.8	...	...	...	...	...	...	...	...	...	...	...
Finland	3.6	26.8	68.1	15.0	14.4	2.5	9,850	20.0	15.0	5.2	2.6	3.3	[2]
France	5.5	26.4	50.4	15.0	28.9	5.8	9,630	19.6	18.2[11]	6.3	13.9	4.1	0.4
French Guiana	...	...	74.6	...	25.4		4,660[1]	50.0	7.3	8.4	2.2	4.1	...
French Polynesia	...	...	48.0	40.9	9.4	1.6	2,230	36.5	5.9	9.0	1.0	8.6	[2]
Gabon	3.3	54.4	...	...	...	...	520	54.7[8,13,21]	13.0[13,21]	17.5[13,21]	1.9[13,21]	...	...
Gambia, The	...	...	...	...	...	...	720[5]	...	...	...	...	...	...
Gaza Strip	...	...	...	...	...	...	4,800	58.0[22]	5.1[22]	17.5[22]	...	...	5.4[22]
Germany, East	12.2[7,23]	17.5[7,23]	68.3	...	31.7	...	...	42.9[8]	3.3	14.6	...	2.1	4.3
Germany, West	6.0	24.0	60.3	[24]	23.5	16.2[24]	10,130	24.1	19.0	8.8	2.9	6.9	[2]
Ghana	...	...	41.6[25]	47.1[25]	—	11.3[25]	390	57.4	11.5[11]	14.3	1.3	[11]	[2]
Gibraltar	...	...	...	...	...	...	...	39.1	12.6	11.0	...	...	...
Greece	...	...	43.0	[24]	17.5	39.5[24]	2,650[4]	37.4	8.6	8.5	3.0	3.2	0.6
Greenland	...	...	...	...	...	...	940[4]	32.4	7.7	10.0	0.3	5.4	[2]
Grenada	...	...	76.8		23.2		3,450[9]	59.0	6.5	8.0	...	6.0	[11]
Guadeloupe	...	...	...	...	...	...	...	29.8	8.2	26.3[3,11]	4.6	[11]	...
Guam	...	...	...	...	...	...	...	24.1	28.6	10.6	4.8	...	0.3
Guatemala	5.3	42.1	76.8	...	...	23.2	710	64.4	16.0[11]	3.1	0.6	[11]	...
Guernsey	...	...	...	...	...	...	260	23.7	12.2	7.5	...	8.2	...
Guinea	...	...	...	...	...	...	210	61.5	7.3[11]	7.9	11.1	[11]	...
Guinea-Bissau	...	...	...	...	...	...	...	...	...	...	...	...	...
Guyana	...	...	73.0	...	6.3	20.7	140	42.5[8]	21.4	8.6	...	5.2	[2]
Haiti	...	...	...	...	...	...	400[4]	77.9	8.3	3.2	...	[11]	[2]
Honduras	3.2	50.6	52.7	...	1.7	45.6	680	44.4	22.3[11]	9.1	6.9	[11]	1.2
Hong Kong	4.3[19]	37.3[19]	65.9	34.1			5,080	18.3	15.6[11]	20.0	6.2	[11]	...
Hungary	6.9[7]	20.5[7]	...	...	...	...	1,400	31.4	8.7	10.5	...	4.7	...
Iceland	4.0	27.6	80.0		20.0		13,920	22.6	12.3	7.6	2.3	3.4	[2]
India	5.0	34.9	42.2	39.7	...	18.1	200[4]	54.8	2.7	10.1	1.9	4.6	2.6
Indonesia	6.6	34.0	42.1	41.5	2.5	13.9	250	61.2[8]	17.4[11]	4.9	...	[11]	...
Iran	3.8	41.7	40.8	28.2	3.7	27.3	2,070[4]	43.3[8]	22.8[11]	9.6	4.3	4.0	...
Iraq	2.1	...	...	...	...	...	1,050[26]	53.2[8]	20.6[3]	10.0	1.7	4.0	...
Ireland	4.6	26.5	59.8	12.7	20.3	7.2	2,180	37.1	5.9	7.4	...	5.7	[2]
Isle of Man	6.4	26.6	64.1	6.6	16.9	12.4	...	31.0	7.9	7.0	...	11.0	...
Israel	8.4	23.2	90.8	0.8	8.4		5,000	27.4[8]	18.0	8.0	...	3.3	[2]
Italy	6.2	28.1	49.5	19.9	20.6	10.0	6,550[4]	25.5	13.7	8.4	2.0	5.1	0.2
Jamaica	2.2	...	60.7	14.3	15.2	9.8	680[4]	35.1	6.7	3.4	2.3	5.5	...
Japan	9.1[19]	22.7[19]	57.5	12.3	19.0	11.1	11,290	26.8	4.7	7.1	2.5	6.3	3.9
Jersey	...	...	...	...	...	...	...	28.3	14.9	8.3	...	6.5	...
Jordan	...	...	...	...	...	...	1,530	37.5	6.3[11]	5.5	4.0	[11]	3.3
Kampuchea (Cambodia)	...	...	22.4	...	...	77.6	330	46.5	10.0	7.7	2.2	2.6	1.0
Kenya	2.6	45.8	...	...	...	...	...	50.0	1.0	7.5	...	3.6	...
Kiribati	...	...	69.7	21.4	6.0	2.9	370[27]	46.5[28]	0.6[28]	29.9[28]	...	3.3[28]	...
Korea, North	...	...	...	...	...	...	...	34.8	4.3	7.8	7.5	6.2	[2]
Korea, South	8.0[17,29]	24.5[17,29]	50.7	38.2	11.1		1,520	27.5[8]	26.1[11]	8.3	0.5	[11]	[2]
Kuwait	...	...	53.8	20.8	25.4		5,350	...	...	...	...	...	...
Laos	...	...	...	...	...	...	...	...	...	...	...	...	...
Lebanon	5.0	45.0	27.9	...	3.0	69.1	705[20]	42.8[13]	16.8[13]	8.6[13]	7.2[13]	4.5[13]	3.9[13]
Lesotho	...	...	42.0	51.6	6.4		760	34.0[17]	9.7[17]	19.3[17]	1.8[17]	4.8[17]	4.1[17]
Liberia	5.3	...	...	...	...	...	350	34.4[13]	14.9[13]	13.8[13]	...	5.0[13]	...
Libya	10.1	...	...	...	...	...	3,749	37.2	32.2[11]	6.9	3.3	[11]	[2]
Liechtenstein	...	...	92.9[30]	7.1[30]	...	...	...	21.3[8]	18.0	6.6	7.7	4.4	[2]
Luxembourg	...	...	88.6	9.1	2.3	—	7,980[4]	16.6	12.6	6.7	6.9	7.4	[2]
Macau	...	...	...	...	...	...	...	44.2[8]	22.8	7.3	...	4.8	...
Madagascar	5.2	...	58.8[13,31]	14.1[13,31]	...	27.1[13,31]	300	60.4	...	8.6	...	9.1	...
Malawi	10.4	40.1	83.3	6.0	—	11.7	160	39.3[8,32]	13.3[32]	10.7[32]	...	...	[2]
Malaysia	3.5	39.8	...	...	...	...	910	41.1[8]	18.2[11]	4.7	1.3	[11]	[2]
Maldives	...	...	...	...	...	...	260[4]	...	...	...	...	...	...
Mali	...	...	...	...	...	...	320	31.5	5.0[33]	8.5	3.5	2.3[33]	[2]
Malta	...	...	49.9	17.4	14.2	18.5	3,590	34.8	5.3	10.2	16.1	1.9	...
Martinique	...	...	74.2	...	...	25.8	4,770[9]	61.0[13]	24.0[13]	5.2[13]	...	...	...
Mauritania	...	...	...	...	...	...	510	...	...	...	...	...	...
Mauritius	4.0	46.7	52.3	32.3	6.0	9.4	1,320	50.4[8]	4.0	10.5	3.0	6.4	2.9
Mayotte	...	...	...	...	...	...	...	...	79.5	...	...	...	...
Mexico	2.9	40.6	52.4	23.6	5.6	18.4	1,100[4]	35.8[8]	8.2[11]	10.3	5.0	[11]	[2]
Monaco	...	...	...	...	...	...	...	...	...	...	...	...	...
Mongolia	...	...	...	...	...	...	...	...	...	...	...	...	...
Montserrat	...	...	...	...	...	...	3,200[4]	54.1[8]	0.7	17.9	...	1.8	...
Morocco	4.0	...	...	...	...	...	840	54.0	7.0	8.5	...	3.0	...
Mozambique	...	...	...	...	...	...	210	...	...	...	...	...	...
Myanmar (Burma)	8.0	...	...	...	...	...	180[4]	49.1[13]	10.4[13]	15.3[13]	2.4[13]	4.0[13]	5.9[13]
Nauru	...	...	...	...	...	...	...	...	...	...	...	...	...
Nepal	3.1	50.7	39.2[13]	60.8[13]			120	57.4[13]	11.4[1,13]	10.5[13]	4.2[13]	[11]	[2]
Netherlands, The	8.3	21.5	40.0	20.8	24.7	14.5	8,850	18.7	18.5[11]	7.5	12.6	[11]	[2]
Netherlands Antilles	...	...	...	...	...	...	3,520[6,27]	24.4[8,34]	18.8[34]	8.7[34]	2.2[34]	—	[2]
New Caledonia	...	...	63.1	23.9	13.0	...	3,660[20]	34.8	15.7	6.4	...	2.7	...
New Zealand	5.1[19]	28.7[19]	68.1	9.1	12.7	10.1	4,950[4]	17.4	22.4	5.9	1.8	2.7	0.6
Nicaragua	3.1[15]	...	...	...	...	...	1,070	68.4[8,13]	12.2[3,11,13]	11.6[13]	...	[11]	...
Niger	...	...	...	...	...	...	290	50.5	19.1[13]	7.3	...	...	...
Nigeria	...	...	36.2	49.4	4.3	10.1	810	53.0[8]	...	6.0	...	11.4	...
Niue	...	...	...	...	...	...	...	43.0	5.0	5.0	...	...	...
Norfolk Island	...	...	...	...	...	...	...	...	...	...	...	...	...

transportation, communications	household durable goods[f]	recreation[g]	personal effects, other[h]	daily available calories per capita	cereals	potatoes, cassava	meat, poultry	fish	eggs, milk	fruits, vegetables	fats, oils[i]	other[i]	country
0.7[15]	2.1[15]	0.1[15]	1.6[15]	1,793	68.8	3.9	4.2	—	2.9	0.8	2.2	17.2	Equatorial Guinea
...	6.6	...	14.2	3,135	29.3	5.5	15.8	3.9	7.0	3.3	18.0	17.2	Ethiopia
...	5.0[13]	...	21.0[13]	...	...	...	...	...	...	...	...	...	Faeroe Islands
11.3	7.6	...	17.4	2,901	38.8	7.3	4.5	2.5	3.0	1.8	8.9	33.2	Falkland Islands
													Fiji
17.4	6.8	8.8[2]	20.9	3,080	23.1	6.1	16.1	2.5	15.2	3.8	14.6	18.8	Finland
13.8	8.3	6.0	13.5	3,273	23.1	4.3	14.0	1.1	12.9	5.3	18.1	21.2	France
7.5	6.7	4.9	8.9	2,748	35.3	2.8	16.4	2.6	7.0	5.5	7.6	22.8	French Guiana
13.1	9.2	8.6[2]	8.1	2,896	35.8	3.5	10.4	2.2	5.0	3.6	16.4	23.2	French Polynesia
6.3[13,21]	...	...	6.6[13,21]	2,428	24.2	24.3	6.2	1.9	2.8	13.8	8.3	18.5	Gabon
...	...	...	14.0[22]	2,367	60.8	1.2	2.7	1.5	2.1	0.6	11.3	19.9	Gambia, The
...	...	...	...	2,596	50.4	1.6	4.2	0.2	4.9	9.0	13.8	15.9	Gaza Strip
1.4	4.1	...	27.3	3,800	25.1	7.1	14.6	0.9	9.2	4.2	18.3	20.6	Germany, East
15.8	8.7	9.9[2]	3.9	3,475	21.2	4.1	15.4	0.6	10.5	5.9	19.3	23.1	Germany, West
3.3	3.8	3.9[2]	4.5	1,733	27.8	27.0	2.3	2.3	0.4	8.3	8.5	23.4	Ghana
13.3	10.0	...	14.0	...	...	...	...	...	...	...	...	...	Gibraltar
14.9	7.7	3.8	12.3	3,686	30.5	3.4	12.7	0.9	10.3	8.9	17.1	16.2	Greece
8.1	13.3	8.4[2]	14.4	...	...	...	...	...	...	...	...	...	Greenland
4.0	6.5	...	10.0	2,409	32.7	0.6	6.9	1.1	10.2	7.9	7.7	32.8	Grenada
13.3	3	5.2	12.6	2,674	34.6	1.5	11.3	3.4	9.0	7.6	10.4	22.3	Guadeloupe
18.0	...	5.1	8.8	...	...	...	...	...	...	...	...	...	Guam
7.0	5.0	0.9	2.7	2,297	58.0	0.6	2.2	0.1	4.6	3.7	7.0	24.0	Guatemala
15.7	8.3	...	24.6	...	...	...	...	...	...	...	...	...	Guernsey
5.1	2.9	4.1	0.1	1,782	41.2	12.5	1.8	0.7	1.2	15.9	12.8	13.9	Guinea
...	...	...	...	2,326	57.7	8.2	3.9	0.3	2.3	5.4	12.6	9.6	Guinea-Bissau
4.8	2.9	6.4[2]	8.2	2,456	56.0	0.0	3.7	2.9	3.7	2.9	5.6	25.2	Guyana
...	4.0	...	6.6	1,902	39.5	3.4	3.1	0.4	1.5	10.1	5.7	36.4	Haiti
3.0	8.3	2.4[2]	3.5	2,078	55.6	0.4	3.3	0.1	5.8	7.9	8.2	18.8	Honduras
8.1	12.6	8.3	9.7	2,779	36.3	0.6	20.2	3.4	4.3	4.7	14.4	16.1	Hong Kong
10.3	8.0	8.0	10.3	3,540	30.2	2.6	13.7	0.3	8.2	4.3	19.1	21.7	Hungary
19.8	7.4	11.3	13.3	3,146	18.4	3.6	15.6	6.3	18.7	2.9	11.8	22.6	Iceland
11.8	4.2	1.1	6.2	2,204	64.2	1.6	0.3	0.3	4.4	3.3	7.2	18.8	India
...	2.9	...	13.6	2,513	66.4	6.5	1.0	1.1	0.5	2.3	6.7	15.6	Indonesia
6.0	6.3	1.0[2]	6.7	2,986	64.1	1.2	3.8	—	2.8	4.7	8.4	15.0	Iran
...	3	1.7	8.8	2,155	60.6	0.5	3.9	0.2	3.6	6.3	5.9	19.0	Iraq
12.1	6.6	9.7[2]	15.5	3,689	24.0	6.6	17.3	1.3	10.6	3.5	15.2	21.7	Ireland
14.9	5.7	...	22.5	...	...	...	...	...	...	...	...	...	Isle of Man
4.0	6.4	...	32.9	3,037	33.2	2.1	8.2	0.8	10.5	8.3	17.9	19.1	Israel
15.7	7.5	6.0[2]	16.1	3,494	32.3	2.0	11.1	0.9	10.4	6.9	19.3	17.2	Italy
13.2	5.4	2.2	26.0	2,581	36.4	0.9	5.5	0.4	5.4	8.2	13.0	30.3	Jamaica
9.0	4.1	9.0	26.6	2,858	42.1	1.8	7.0	6.2	5.8	4.4	12.2	20.5	Japan
13.9	7.1	...	21.0	...	...	...	...	...	...	...	...	...	Jersey
5.8	4.7	3.0	29.9	2,107	61.8	1.6	3.7	0.3	5.2	2.9	9.1	15.4	Jordan
...	...	...	15.0	1,925	80.5	1.1	3.7	1.2	0.4	3.6	1.9	7.6	Kampuchea (Cambodia)
8.4	9.4	3.1	9.1	2,140	60.3	5.0	2.8	0.4	3.7	2.7	5.1	20.0	Kenya
8.0	2.9	...	27.0	2,936	25.1	0.0	2.3	5.9	0.8	5.4	10.2	50.2	Kiribati
...	3.8[28]	...	15.9	3,199	68.4	4.0	2.9	3.4	0.9	4.1	2.5	13.9	Korea, North
6.6	5.3	10.7[2]	27.5	2,876	62.3	0.5	4.8	3.0	1.7	6.1	6.4	15.1	Korea, South
12.7	11.3	3.9[2]	9.7	3,076	38.0	1.2	11.1	0.4	10.1	7.5	12.7	18.9	Kuwait
...	...	...	...	1,929	83.4	1.4	5.5	0.6	1.3	2.5	1.1	4.2	Laos
5.4[13]	2.6[13]	1.9[13]	6.3[13]	2,495	52.7	2.0	3.6	0.2	3.9	6.0	8.0	23.6	Lebanon
9.5[17]	6.9[17]	3.1[17]	6.8[17]	2,296	74.4	0.0	3.8	0.3	2.5	1.7	3.2	14.2	Lesotho
...	6.1[13]	...	25.8[13]	2,358	46.8	18.8	2.4	1.2	0.9	5.1	15.5	9.3	Liberia
9.4	4.6	8.5[2]	2.5	3,611	42.1	1.4	7.7	0.1	6.8	7.8	18.2	15.9	Libya
13.3	5.8	16.3[2]	6.6	...	...	...	...	...	...	...	...	...	Liechtenstein
16.8	9.3	3.6[2]	20.1	3,950	19.4	5.0	19.4	0.7	8.9	4.8	23.4	18.6	Luxembourg
4.9	2.9	...	13.1	2,205	40.2	0.6	17.9	2.1	5.2	4.8	11.8	17.6	Macau
...	2.4	...	19.5	2,413	59.6	16.0	6.3	0.4	0.5	4.1	2.6	10.5	Madagascar
17.6[32]	9.6[32]	...	9.5[32]	2,372	67.8	4.3	1.6	0.7	0.7	4.2	2.8	17.9	Malawi
16.6	5.9	6.7[2]	5.5	2,723	47.3	2.6	6.2	3.0	5.2	3.9	13.7	18.2	Malaysia
...	...	...	...	1,765	42.5	6.4	0.8	12.4	—	6.3	7.7	23.9	Maldives
15.2	8.7	6.1[2]	21.3	2,021	78.5	1.3	3.9	0.7	2.2	0.9	3.7	8.9	Mali
9.7	8.1	...	13.9	2,878	32.3	1.3	12.2	1.0	11.5	5.8	15.4	20.6	Malta
...	...	...	9.8[13]	2,780	33.7	1.1	10.3	2.9	5.5	7.6	7.1	31.9	Martinique
...	...	...	...	2,283	48.5	0.1	4.4	8.2	16.3	2.2	7.0	13.4	Mauritania
10.0	6.4	—	6.4	2,736	52.3	1.3	2.4	1.1	6.3	1.2	11.3	24.1	Mauritius
...	...	...	20.5	...	...	...	...	...	...	...	...	...	Mayotte
12.4	12.0	4.9[2]	11.5	3,148	48.7	0.6	8.5	0.6	5.9	3.5	10.5	21.8	Mexico
...	...	...	...	...	...	...	...	...	...	...	...	...	Monaco
...	...	...	...	2,830	56.6	2.7	21.9	0.1	3.3	0.6	5.8	9.1	Mongolia
...	10.2	...	15.3	...	...	...	...	...	...	...	...	...	Montserrat
6.9	3.6	...	17.0	2,864	65.6	1.1	2.5	0.6	2.0	2.9	9.6	15.8	Morocco
...	...	...	...	1,607	34.1	42.0	1.8	0.5	1.0	2.0	10.9	7.8	Mozambique
3.8[13]	0.5[13]	1.1[13]	7.5[13]	2,592	77.1	0.5	2.0	1.7	1.1	2.5	6.7	8.3	Myanmar (Burma)
...	...	...	...	...	...	...	...	...	...	...	...	...	Nauru
2.1[13]	—	7.9[2,13]	6.5[13]	2,050	81.5	1.6	1.5	0.0	4.2	0.9	4.3	6.0	Nepal
11.5	7.9	9.6	13.7	3,258	19.7	4.7	11.9	0.8	13.0	5.2	23.3	21.4	Netherlands, The
19.4[34]	10.0[34]	5.9[3,34]	10.6[34]	2,922[6]	29.2[6]	2.1[6]	16.5[6]	1.4[6]	11.4[6]	7.0[6]	13.2[6]	19.2[6]	Netherlands Antilles
9.7	18.5	6.3[2]	8.6	2,984	35.8	2.2	10.2	1.9	7.5	4.3	12.4	25.8	New Caledonia
17.6	11.6	5.2	14.8	3,405	22.0	2.7	16.8	1.6	14.4	5.4	15.5	21.6	New Zealand
...	3	...	7.8[13]	2,446	40.5	1.2	6.1	0.4	7.7	5.1	9.7	29.3	Nicaragua
...	3	...	23.1	2,349	69.4	3.4	3.6	0.1	2.6	1.7	4.4	14.9	Niger
4.7	3.8	...	21.1	2,115	40.9	12.0	1.7	0.5	0.8	3.7	10.9	29.5	Nigeria
17.5	13.0	...	16.5	...	...	...	...	...	...	...	...	...	Niue
...	...	...	...	...	...	...	...	...	...	...	...	...	Norfolk Island

Household budgets and consumption   (continued)

country	income (latest)						consumption expenditure						
	percent received by		by source (percent)				per capita private final, U.S.$ 1987	by kind or end use (percent of household or personal budget; latest)					
	lowest 20% of households	highest 10% of households	wages, salaries	self-employment	transfer payments[a]	other[b]		food[c]	housing[d]	clothing[e]	health care	energy, water	education
Norway	4.0	25.4	62.0	17.7	20.3	—	10,450	23.4	11.1	7.6	4.2	6.8	0.4
Oman	...	...	...	...	...	...	2,910[4]	...	...	...	...	...	...
Pacific Is., Trust Territory of the													
Marshall Islands	...	...	...	...	...	...	...	57.7	15.6[3,11]	12.0	...	11	...
Micronesia, Federated States of	...	...	...	...	...	...	...	73.5					
Northern Mariana Islands	...	...	...	...	...	...	...	36.9	7.4	...	3.1	6.3	3.7
Palau	...	...	...	...	...	...	...	...	...	...	...	5.6	2
Pakistan	8.0	...	28.9	49.1	1.6	20.4	250[4]	48.6[8]	11.2	7.5	...	5.6	2
Panama	2.0	44.2	85.3	...	9.2	5.5	1,340	47.3	12.7[11]	4.8	4.9	11	2
Papua New Guinea	...	...	72.7	2.5	...	24.8	470[4]	40.9	12.5[3]	6.2	...	4.9	...
Paraguay	...	...	37.5	...	2.5	60.0	870	48.7	16.4	9.7	3.4	—	1.5
Peru	5.9[17]	28.4[17]	...	...	...	...	900[4]	55.4	10.4[11]	7.5	4.6	11	2
Philippines	5.2	37.0	—95.7—		...	4.3	440	54.0	...	6.5	...	4.7	...
Pitcairn Island	...	...	...	...	...	...	...						
Poland	10.1[18]	20.6[18]	74.3	...	11.0	14.7	930	43.5	13.3	13.8	3.0	2.6	...
Portugal	5.2	33.4	42.4	[24]	21.8	35.8[24]	1,570[4]	34.8	3.2	11.2	4.3	2.7	0.8
Puerto Rico	3.2	34.7	56.0	6.4	28.0	9.6	5,100[4]	26.9	15.9[11]	8.4	6.0	11	2.2
Qatar	...	...	...	...	...	...	4,110[4]	39.1	10.7	4.4	0.2	0.8	1.6
Réunion	3.1[19]	51.4[19]	66.4	17.1	12.4	3.8	3,700[9]	22.4	10.6	7.9	2.3	2.2	2
Romania	...	...	62.6	—37.4—			1,340	62.7[35]	—	13.8[35]	0.7[35]	9.2[35]	2
Rwanda	...	...	16.5	71.0	9.5	3.0	240	77.9[8]	1.0	1.0	8.2	...	...
St. Helena and Ascension	...	...	...	...	...	...	1,050[20]	55.6[8]	7.6	7.5	...	6.6	...
St. Kitts and Nevis	...	...	...	...	...	...	740[20]	46.8	.13.5	6.5	2.3	4.5	2
St. Lucia	...	...	...	...	...	...	...						
St. Pierre and Miquelon	...	...	...	...	...	...	...						
St. Vincent and the Grenadines	...	...	...	...	...	...	700[4]	62.6[8]	6.3	7.7	...	6.2	...
San Marino	...	...	...	...	...	...	...	30.4[8]	9.7[11]	8.8	5.1	11	2
São Tomé and Príncipe	...	...	...	...	...	...	370						
Saudi Arabia	...	...	...	...	...	...	2,730[4]	52.2[17,36]	17.2[17,36]	6.6[17,36]	2.1[17,36]	1.8[17,36]	1.1[17,36]
Senegal	5.5	45.4	51.6	—48.4—			570	56.0[13]	8.7[13]	11.9[13]	...	5.8[13]	...
Seychelles	4.1	35.6	77.2	3.8	3.2	15.8	1,410	53.9	13.6	4.2	0.4	9.1	...
Sierra Leone	5.6	37.8	27.9	61.6	...	10.5	310	54.8[8]	13.2[11]	6.4	1.6	11	2
Singapore	6.5	34.4	75.4	18.7	2.0	3.9	3,600	23.0	10.3	8.7	3.7	11	2
Solomon Islands	...	...	74.1	—25.9—			550[1]	51.0	12.5[3,11]	4.9	...	11	...
Somalia	...	...	...	...	...	...	310	62.3[8,13]	15.3[13]	5.6[13]	...	4.3[13]	...
South Africa	1.9	39.4	78.6	[24]	6.0	15.4[24]	970[4,37]	33.8	12.4[11]	7.7	4.2	11	—
Bophuthatswana	...	...	...	...	...	...	...	38.6[8]	10.8	12.2	2.8	...	1.8
Ciskei	...	...	...	...	...	...	...						
Transkei	3.4	43.8	...	...	...	...	...	51.2	4.3	11.2	0.5	4.5	1.9
Venda	...	...	56.2	4.8	32.9	6.1							
South West Africa/Namibia	...	...	72.8	...	3.3	23.9	37						
Spain	6.9[7]	24.5[7]	52.3	28.6	16.8	2.3	3,760[4]	27.6[8]	15.2[11]	7.2	3.7	11	2
Sri Lanka	5.9	35.2	54.0	[24]	11.6	34.4[24]	310[4]	49.7	2.8	7.1	1.6	3.1	1.2
Sudan, The	4.0	34.6	35.8	53.0	...	11.2	290	61.3	9.8	5.7	5.3	4.4	0.8
Suriname	9.3	...	74.6	...	3.2	22.2	1,070	39.9[13]	4.4[13]	11.0[13]	3.6[13]	6.9[13]	2.6[13]
Swaziland	2.8	54.5	...	...	...	...	1,138	39.3[8,38]	...	10.0[38]	8.0[38]	6.5[38]	...
Sweden	5.1	22.9	60.7	11.2	22.0	6.1	9,970	24.0[8]	25.8[11]	7.7	1.6	11	2
Switzerland	6.0[39]	27.0[39]	64.0	[24]	14.7	21.3[24]	15,250	21.3[8]	18.0	6.6	7.7	4.4	2
Syria	6.0	...	...	...	...	...	2,110	48.8[8]	17.7	9.1	...	4.6	2
Taiwan	8.4	22.8	59.4	22.6	6.1	11.9	1,590[4]	36.5[8]	23.0[11]	6.0	5.4	11	2
Tanzania	5.8	35.6	33.8	59.8	...	6.4	340	53.8[8]	8.6	10.8	4.5	6.6	0.8
Thailand	5.1	42.8	36.7	29.7	6.0	27.6	510[4]	37.4	23.1[11]	6.4	...	11	2
Togo	8.0	30.5	...	...	...	...	280	60.9	9.9[11]	7.7	1.6	11	0.6
Tokelau	...	...	...	...	...	...	860[20]	49.3	10.5	5.6	0.3	2.7	...
Tonga	...	...	...	...	...	...	...						
Trinidad and Tobago	2.6	33.6	...	...	...	...	2,160[4]	27.7	22.7	15.5	2.2	1.1	1.5
Tunisia	4.1	37.6	...	...	...	...	1,254	39.0	10.7	6.0	3.0	5.1	1.8
Turkey	3.5[7]	41.5[7]	38.9[17]	46.8[17]	9.4[17]	4.9[17]	780[4]	41.2[17]	25.2[17]	14.8[17]	3.3[17]	...	...
Turks and Caicos Islands	...	...	...	...	...	...	...						
Tuvalu	...	...	17.9	76.1	...	6.0	...	45.5	11.5[3]	7.5	...	...	...
Uganda	6.2	...	88.3[13,40]	1.8[13,40]	—9.9[13,40]—		240	58.0[13,36]	...	14.0[13,36]	...	6.0[13,36]	...
U.S.S.R.	...	...	79.1	3.3	9.3	8.3	2,640	40.6	3.2[41]	20.8	41	0.3[41]	41
United Arab Emirates	...	...	...	...	...	...	5,000[4]						
United Kingdom	5.8	24.8	64.3	7.7	17.3	10.7	6,010[4]	24.2	16.8	7.5	...	5.9	...
United States	4.2	28.2	59.5	8.2	14.5	17.8	12,230	17.5	15.5	7.4	13.4	4.2	7.5
Uruguay	6.0[7,17]	29.3[7,17]	53.5	20.8	—30.1—		1,920	39.9	17.6[11]	7.0	9.3	11	1.3
Vanuatu	...	...	59.0	33.7	...	7.3	...	45.8	10.2[3]	14.1	...	...	...
Venezuela	3.0	35.7	...	...	...	...	1,760	51.8	8.5[11]	4.7	4.9	11	2
Vietnam	...	...	65.7	2.6	13.0	12.7	...	25.3[42]	24.9[42]	5.4[42]	...	6.5[42]	...
Virgin Islands (U.S.)	...	...	...	...	...	...	...	48.2	...	6.8	...	...	...
Wallis and Futuna	...	...	...	...	...	...	...						
West Bank	...	...	...	...	...	...	1,080[20]						
Western Sahara	...	...	...	...	...	...	...						
Western Samoa	...	...	49.4	22.8	...	27.8	590[20]	58.8	5.1[3]	4.2	...	5.0	...
Yemen (Aden)	...	...	...	...	...	...	430[4]						
Yemen (San'ā')	...	...	12.2	74.1	13.4	0.3	560[4]	65.0[8]	6.1	5.8	4.0	7.2	0.9
Yugoslavia	7.2	24.7	56.9	...	18.9	24.2	500	38.3	8.5[11]	10.2	3.4	11	2
Zaire	...	...	...	...	...	...	350	61.7	11.5[11]	9.7	2.6	11	2
Zambia	3.4	46.4	79.9	17.8	1.3	1.0	430	37.7[8]	11.0	8.3	1.0	—	2.1
Zimbabwe	3.0	55.5	...	...	...	...	380	33.4[8]	6.3	18.8	1.8	7.6	3.7

1 1982. 2 Recreation includes education. 3 Housing includes household durable goods. 4 1986. 5 1983. 6 Netherlands Antilles includes Aruba. 7 Based on post-tax income. 8 Includes tobacco. 9 1985. 10 Rural wage earners only. 11 Housing includes energy and water. 12 Middle-income families in São Paulo. 13 Capital city only. 14 Includes wage taxes. 15 Rural only. 16 Highest 20%. 17 Urban areas only. 18 Low- and middle-income families only. 19 Based on post-tax per capita income. 20 1984. 21 Wage earners only. 22 Low-income population in Banjul and Kombo St. Mary only. 23 Excludes property income and pensions. 24 Other includes self-employment. 25 Urban areas of eastern region only. 26 1981. 27 1980. 28 Workers and clerical workers only.

transportation, communications	household durable goods[f]	recreation[g]	personal effects, other[h]	daily available calories per capita	cereals	potatoes, cassava	meat, poultry	fish	eggs, milk	fruits, vegetables	fats, oils[i]	other[i]	country
17.8	7.9	7.8	13.0	3,215	24.4	4.6	11.3	3.1	14.9	4.5	18.5	18.7	Norway
...	...	...	...	...	...	...	...	...	...	...	...	...	Oman
...	[3]	...	14.7										Pacific Is., Trust Territory of the Marshall Islands
...	...	...	26.5										Micronesia, Federated States of
18.2	7.5	4.0	12.9										Northern Mariana Islands
													Palau
4.5	2.0	2.8[2]	17.8	2,245	60.1	0.4	2.2	0.2	5.5	2.7	13.6	15.3	Pakistan
6.8	8.5	5.8[2]	9.2	2,439	39.9	1.8	9.0	0.4	5.6	4.5	12.8	25.9	Panama
13.0	[3]	...	22.5	2,269	15.4	34.5	6.3	1.9	0.6	23.7	4.4	13.2	Papua New Guinea
4.5	6.2	2.3	7.3	2,843	32.2	14.0	13.4	0.1	4.1	8.6	7.0	20.7	Paraguay
8.6	4.6	6.9[2]	2.0	2,192	46.7	7.5	4.8	1.5	4.6	4.7	7.2	23.1	Peru
3.1	13.9	...	16.8	2,354	62.2	3.0	5.0	3.2	1.4	6.5	4.2	14.6	Philippines
													Pitcairn Island
5.5	...	9.7	8.6	3,298	34.7	6.0	9.6	1.3	12.3	3.5	14.6	18.1	Poland
14.6	10.0	3.9	14.5	3,134	39.7	5.5	10.7	2.4	5.1	4.9	14.4	17.4	Portugal
16.8	6.3	4.3	13.2										Puerto Rico
3.7	24.4	——15.1——											Qatar
23.6	9.9	10.1[2]	11.0	3,011	46.3	1.1	10.2	1.5	4.8	3.5	12.3	20.4	Réunion
3.7[35]	4.7[35]	3.0[2,35]	2.2[35]	3,358	43.2	3.9	8.8	0.7	9.1	6.5	12.0	15.9	Romania
				1,880	12.9	13.2	1.4	—	1.8	13.3	2.0	55.3	Rwanda
0.8	0.7	...	10.4										St. Helena and Ascension
4.3	9.4	...	9.0	2,349	26.3	1.0	11.0	2.0	11.2	2.9	10.2	35.3	St. Kitts and Nevis
6.3	5.8	3.2[2]	8.3	2,499	26.9	1.1	13.3	1.5	7.0	12.3	9.7	28.3	St. Lucia
													St. Pierre and Miquelon
3.7	6.6	...	6.9	2,776	38.0	1.8	7.7	0.6	3.6	3.7	9.0	35.6	St. Vincent and the Grenadines
14.5	7.5	8.1[2]	15.9										San Marino
4.5[17,36]	5.9[17,36]	...	8.6[17,36]	2,385	36.4	3.9	1.6	2.8	1.0	3.7	18.2	33.1	São Tomé and Príncipe
				3,031	41.9	0.5	8.8	0.5	8.7	10.5	13.5	15.7	Saudi Arabia
5.4[13]	1.7[13]	...	10.5[13]	2,336	68.9	0.4	3.0	1.3	2.5	1.2	11.8	11.0	Senegal
6.4	6.6	1.4	4.4										Seychelles
15.0	4.7	3.2[2]	1.1	1,868	56.3	4.8	1.2	1.8	0.5	3.9	18.1	13.4	Sierra Leone
12.2	9.3	13.7[2]	19.1	2,854	36.0	1.9	16.9	2.5	6.1	6.9	5.2	24.5	Singapore
6.6	[3]	...	25.0	2,163	23.0	0.5	3.7	5.5	0.8	3.1	8.0	55.6	Solomon Islands
			12.1[13]	2,088	44.2	0.9	11.7	0.5	16.0	2.4	12.1	12.3	Somalia
17.5	9.7	5.7	9.0	2,941	53.0	1.5	8.1	0.6	4.7	2.4	8.3	21.4	South Africa
													Bophuthatswana
8.5	7.7	1.2	16.3										Ciskei
				2,450									Transkei
5.4	11.9	0.9	8.2										Venda
				2,183	47.7	14.2	13.8	—	4.8	1.8	10.0	7.7	South West Africa/Namibia
13.7	6.9	6.7	19.0	3,365	25.1	5.8	15.2	1.5	9.8	7.0	17.2	18.4	Spain
16.4	4.7	3.6	9.8	2,436	58.3	3.2	0.3	1.4	2.2	4.2	5.2	25.1	Sri Lanka
2.4	4.7	0.3	5.3	2,077	46.0	0.9	7.3	0.1	13.2	3.5	11.0	17.9	Sudan, The
9.5[13]	12.3[13]	5.8[13]	4.0[13]	2,713	52.6	1.7	6.1	1.8	4.8	2.7	8.2	22.1	Suriname
15.3[38]	9.0[38]	9.9	11.9[38]	2,550	51.9	0.5	6.6	—	4.0	2.9	7.6	26.6	Swaziland
16.4	6.6	9.9[2]	8.4	3,048	22.3	4.3	10.4	2.1	16.2	4.4	19.1	21.2	Sweden
13.3	5.8	16.3[2]	6.6	3,431	19.6	2.6	19.0	0.6	13.7	6.5	17.1	21.0	Switzerland
3.8	5.1	3.1[2]	7.8	3,259	46.6	1.6	3.8	0.1	6.3	8.3	12.9	20.5	Syria
8.5	4.4	10.1[2]	5.6	2,749									Taiwan
6.4	6.3	1.6	0.6	2,214	46.2	18.4	2.4	1.0	2.1	8.2	5.0	16.7	Tanzania
10.7	...	4.3[2]	18.1	2,329	63.4	2.0	4.0	1.5	1.4	6.3	2.6	19.0	Thailand
8.2	3.9	0.4	6.8	2,224	45.7	16.8	2.4	1.0	0.6	1.5	6.8	25.4	Togo
													Tokelau
5.8	10.6	0.5	14.7	2,942	15.5	—	10.4	1.4	1.1	4.2	6.1	61.3	Tonga
13.2	8.8	1.4	5.9	3,058	34.3	1.8	7.1	1.0	9.7	4.4	13.8	28.0	Trinidad and Tobago
9.0	11.2	7.1	7.1	2,941	57.5	1.3	3.0	0.7	4.2	5.8	13.1	14.4	Tunisia
5.5[17]	...	6.1[17]	3.9[17]	3,148	52.7	3.5	2.9	0.5	3.7	9.1	13.0	14.6	Turkey
													Turks and Caicos Islands
10.5	[3]	...	25.0										Tuvalu
10.0[13,36]	...	...	12.0[13,36]	2,225	22.0	23.4	2.6	1.2	1.9	13.1	1.3	34.5	Uganda
[41]	11.6	8.6	14.9	3,394	37.2	5.8	9.9	2.0	8.6	3.8	12.7	19.9	U.S.S.R.
				3,714	34.4	0.6	7.4	2.7	7.4	12.2	14.2	21.1	United Arab Emirates
14.3	7.8	...	22.9	3,218	19.9	5.9	15.4	0.8	11.6	4.2	19.1	23.0	United Kingdom
12.4	7.9	7.4	6.8	3,642	18.8	2.7	18.5	0.8	11.3	5.2	17.4	25.4	United States
10.4	6.3	3.1	5.1	2,676	33.0	2.6	19.3	0.3	11.5	3.9	10.5	18.9	Uruguay
9.8	[3]	...	20.1	2,344	26.3	0.1	13.6	2.6	2.4	3.5	8.2	43.5	Vanuatu
10.8	6.3	6.8[2]	6.2	2,532	37.9	1.7	9.1	1.1	9.1	6.1	11.9	23.1	Venezuela
				2,135	72.9	8.6	4.8	2.2	0.1	2.6	2.0	6.8	Vietnam
11.7[42]	4.3[42]	...	21.9[42]										Virgin Islands (U.S.)
			45.0										Wallis and Futuna
				2,905	44.4	1.9	6.1	0.1	6.2	11.0	12.5	17.8	West Bank
9.0	[3]	...	17.9	2,463	18.9	0.4	11.5	4.0	1.0	13.1	7.8	43.3	Western Sahara
				2,275	63.4	0.7	3.1	2.4	5.7	4.0	6.7	14.0	Western Samoa
													Yemen (Aden)
3.2	7.8	—	—	2,331	63.5	2.4	4.4	0.3	4.4	3.6	6.7	14.8	Yemen (San'ã')
11.8	8.2	4.0[2]	15.6	3,542	46.0	2.7	7.8	0.3	8.2	3.7	15.6	15.8	Yugoslavia
5.9	4.8	3.8[2]	...	2,160	16.2	54.0	2.1	0.6	0.2	7.4	7.2	12.4	Zaire
4.3	—	—	35.6	2,125	71.6	4.3	2.6	1.0	1.5	1.6	4.5	12.9	Zambia
4.0	14.8	0.6	9.0	2,120	62.9	1.5	2.4	0.2	1.7	1.2	8.7	21.4	Zimbabwe

[29]Excludes single-person households and self-employed. [30]Earned income only. [31]Malagasy households only. [32]Balantyre and Lilongwe only. [33]Housing includes water. [34]Curaçao and Bonaire only. [35]Rural cooperatives only. [36]Middle-income population only. [37]South Africa includes South West Africa/Namibia. [38]Middle- to high-income families only. [39]Excludes transfers and property income. [40]Unskilled African workers only. [41]Mostly paid by state subsidies. [42]St. Thomas only.

Health services

The provision of health services in most countries is both a principal determinant of the quality of life and a large and growing sector of the national economy. This table summarizes the basic indicators of: health manpower; hospitals, by kind and utilization; mortality rates that are most indicative of general health services; external controls on health (adequacy of food supply and availability of safe drinking water); and sources and amounts of expenditure on health care. Each datum refers more or less directly to the availability or use of a particular health service in a country, and, while each may be an accurate measure at a national level, each may also conceal considerable differences in availability of the particular service to different segments of a population or regions of a country. In the United States, for example, the availability of physicians ranges from about one per 800 persons in the least well-served states to one per 300 in the best-served, with a rate of one per 175 in the national capital. Such disparities are even more pronounced in most other countries, unless the government has made some special effort to achieve a more even distribution of manpower and facilities. In addition, even when trained manpower exists and facilities have been created, the country may lose health professionals via the "brain drain" to foreign countries; or low levels of financial support at the national level may leave facilities underserved; or lack of good transportation may prevent those most in need from reaching a clinic or hospital that could help them.

Definitions and limits of data have been made as specific as possible in the compilation of this table. For example, despite wide variation worldwide in the nature of the qualifying or certifying process that permits an individual to represent himself as a physician, organizations such as the World Health Organization (WHO) try to institute international standards for training and qualification. International statistics presented here for "physicians" refer to persons qualified according to WHO standards and exclude traditional health practitioners, whatever the local custom with regard to the designation "doctor." Statistics for health manpower in this table uniformly include all those actually working in the health service field, whether in the actual provision of services or in teaching, administration, research, or other tasks. One group of practitioners for whom this type of guideline works less well is that of midwives, whose training and qualifications vary enormously from country to country but who must be included, as they represent, after nurses, perhaps the largest and most important category of health auxiliary worldwide. The statistics here refer to those midwives working in some kind of institutional setting (a hospital, clinic, community health-care centre, or the like) and exclude rural noninstitutional midwives and traditional birth attendants.

Hospitals also differ considerably worldwide in terms of staffing and services. In this tabulation, the term hospital refers generally to a permanent facility offering inpatient services and/or nursing care and staffed by at least one physician. Establishments offering only outpatient or custodial care are excluded. These statistics are broken down into data for general hospitals (those providing care in more than one specialty), specialized facilities (with care in only one specialty), local medical centres, and rural health-care centres; the last two generally refer to institutions that provide a more limited range of medical or nursing care, often less than full-time. Hospital data are further analyzed into three categories of administrative

Health services

country	health personnel							hospitals		kinds (%)				ownership (%)			hospital beds per 10,000 pop.
	year	physicians	dentists	nurses	pharmacists	midwives	population per physician	year	number	general	specialized	medical centres	rural	government	private non-profit	private for profit	
Afghanistan	1987	2,957	329	2,135	206[1]	529[1]	4,797	1982	68	66.2	16.2	—	17.6	86.8	13.2	—	5
Albania	1987	6,308	1,033	6,801[5]	772	9,936	489	1987	872	—18.1—		—81.9—		100.0	—	—	55
Algeria	1987	17,760	5,648	24,700[9]	1,752	3,800[9]	1,302	1984	447	—44.3—		55.7	—	85.3[10]	4.4[10]	10.3[10]	27[11]
American Samoa	1984	25	4	18[13]	1[6]	13	1,398	1986	1	100.0	—	—	—	100.0	—	—	37
Andorra	1984	53	...	...	2	...	784	1984	1	100.0	—	—	—	100.0	—	—	31
Angola	1986	655	...	9,528	...	1,237	13,489	1986	24	...	...	...	...	...	...	...	15
Anguilla	1987	4	1	19[3]	1[16]	11[16]	1,683	1987	1	—	—	—	100.0	100.0	—	—	36
Antigua and Barbuda	1987	48	7	207	27[18]	160[5]	1,606	1986	2	50.0	50.0	—	—	100.0	—	—	51
Argentina	1984	81,260	6,620	14,150	681	...	370	1980	3,189	84.2	15.8	—	—	41.9	3.6	54.5	54
Aruba	1988	64	16	287	9	3	949	1988	2	50.0	—	50.0	—	100.0	—	—	55
Australia	1986	36,610	5,721[1]	139,434[13]	9,800[20]	...[13]	438	1987	1,053[19]	...	...	...	...	68.4[19]—31.6[19]—			54
Austria	1988	20,502	3,069	28,480	1,919	806	370	1988	340	37.9	62.1	—	—	...	...	...	109
Bahamas, The	1986	296	31[3]	952[9]	37[22]	120[22]	799	1985	5	60.0	20.0	20.0	—	60.0	—40.0—		43
Bahrain	1985	518	19	1,148[13]	68[1]	13	771	1986	12	42.7	58.3	—	—	75.0	16.7	8.3	34
Bangladesh	1987	16,929	447[18]	7,000	...	5,837	6,219	1987	875	68.9[18]	5.11[18]	23.11[18]	2.9[18]	69.5	—30.5—		3
Barbados	1984	213	25	760	...	436	1,183	1982	11	27.3	18.2	—	54.5	81.8	—	18.2	84[3]
Belgium	1986	29,776	5,760	91,263[1]	10,792	4,920[1]	331	1982	531	53.3	46.7	—	—	36.3	—63.7—		92[18]
Belize	1987	85	12	230	7	175	2,061	1987	12[10]	58.3[10]	25.0[10]	—	16.7[10]	100.0[10]	—	—	33
Benin	1983	238	13[22]	1,317	55[22]	323	16,025	1980	131	4.6	9.9	80.9	4.6	87.8	12.2	—	13[1]
Bermuda	1987	77	20	561	31	...	751	1987	2	50.0	50.0	—	—	...	...	...	69
Bhutan	1986	134	...	252	63	171	9,791	1986	28								7
Bolivia	1984	4,032	319	1,066	1,902[28]	...	1,551	1983	400[29]	18.0[29]	5.5[29]	42.5[29]	34.0[29]	...	...	...	18
Botswana	1986	156	14	1,530	10[22]	714[22]	7,218	1984	22	—63.6—		36.4	—	72.7	—27.3—		23
Brazil	1985	198,329	56,015[22]	306,411[22]	5,129[22]	2,526[22]	684	1986	23,314[1]	22.6[1]	13.31	—64.1[1]—		64.0[1]	—36.0[1]—		36
British Virgin Islands	1987	11	2	81	2[17]	1[17]	1,109	1987	1	100.0	—	—	—	100.0	—	—	41
Brunei	1986	171	28	779	8	185	1,323	1986	8	87.5	—	—	12.5	87.5	12.5	—	39
Bulgaria	1987	27,107	5,921	60,102	4,147	7,642	331	1987	244	77.5	22.5	—	—	...	...	...	95
Burkina Faso	1988	280	17	1,993	104	292	29,914	1988	66	3.0	—	83.4	13.6	100.0	—	—	7[3]
Burundi	1985[31]	178	9	559	9	36[3]	26,494	1985[23]	220	—13.6—		86.4—		...	...	...	12
Cameroon	1986	833	17[1]	3,216[1]	96[1]	399[1]	12,540	1988	629	—27.0—		—73.0—		72.3	—27.7—		27[3]
Canada	1985	51,966	13,027	250,458	18,813	...	491	1978	1,226	65.8	26.9	7.3	—	93.4	—	6.6	75[22]
Cape Verde	1984	60	3[22]	186	7[22]	10	5,440	1980	21	9.5	4.8	61.9	23.8	100.0	—	—	21
Cayman Islands	1988	35	9	120	8	15	711	1988	2	100.0	—	—	—	100.0	—	—	29
Central African Republic	1988	164	6[3]	710[3]	25	171	16,788	1988	133	—21.1—		—78.9—		79.7	—20.3—		17
Chad	1980	94	4[17, 31]	933[17, 31]	9[17, 31]	96[17, 31]	47,640	1978	4	100.0	—	—	—	—	—	100.0	8
Chile	1986	12,334	1,774[31]	26,389[31]	2023[1]	2,021[31]	983	1986	219	51.4[1]	19.0[1]	—	29.6[1]	82.2	—17.8—		27
China	1987	1,482,000[33]	...	718,000	33,800[9]	76,000[9]	724[33]	1987	60,429	14.7[9]	5.6[9]	—	79.5[9]	100.0[9]	—	—	25
Christmas Island	1986	2	1	5[20]	1	...	1,013	1986	1	100.0	—	—	—	100.0	—	—	197
Cocos (Keeling) Islands	1987	1	—	4	—	...	672	1987	2	50.0	—	50.0	—	100.0	—	—	74
Colombia	1984	23,250	10,080	44,520	...	...	1,229	1983	946	—79.6—		—20.4—		82.1[22]	17.9[22]	—	17
Comoros	1984	31	4	168[13]	3	13	12,237	1980	17	17.7	—	23.5	58.8	100.0	—	—	23[1]
Congo	1988	500	2[17]	2,500[1]	28[17]	246[1]	4,334	1978	473	0.6	0.2	97.3	1.9	94.9	5.1	—	17[35]
Cook Islands	1986	15	8[1, 31]	57[13]	2[20, 31]	13	1,146	1981	8	12.5	—	—	87.5	100.0	—	—	87
Costa Rica	1984	2,539	790	1,300	702	...	1,011	1980	39	48.7	28.2	—23.1—		92.3	—	7.7	27[18]
Côte d'Ivoire	1982	502	36[17]	3,052[17]	76[17]	615[17]	17,847	1978	61[16]	13.1[16]	3.3[16]	—	83.6[16]	98.4	—1.6—		9[35]
Cuba	1987	28,060	5,923	53,595	650[18]	...	369	1986	261	28.0	—47.1—		24.9	...	...	...	57[11]
Cyprus	1987[36]	1,195	330[18]	2,211[13, 18]	93[18]	13	570	1986[36]	124[1]	3.2[1]	—89.5[1]—		7.3[1]	12.1[1]	0.8[1]	87.1[1]	63
Czechoslovakia	1988	48,711	8,285	146,952[11]	7,375[11]	6,792[1]	312	1987	383	60.1	39.9	—	—	100.0	—	—	101
Denmark	1987	13,144	4,795	31,757	1,476	915[9]	390	1987	127[1]	87.4[1]	12.6[1]	—	—	91.3[1]	8.7[1]	—	63[11]
Djibouti	1987	89	8	359[3]	13	175[3]	5,427	1987[29]	18	—16.7—		22.2	61.1	100.0	...	...	25
Dominica	1987	25	3	202	5[18]	47[17]	3,248	1983	48	2.1	2.1	91.6	4.2	100.0	—	—	40[18]
Dominican Republic	1985	3,056	199	4,287	129	...	2,100	1985	101	—45.5—		—54.5—		...	...	...	10
Ecuador	1984	11,033	4,292	14,794	505[10]	...	826	1984	337	16.6	7.1	49.6	26.7	53.7[10]	1.9[10]	44.4[10]	17
Egypt	1984	73,300	8,218[1]	34,371[20]	12,458[9]	9,004[1, 31]	616	1982	1,521	32.3	13.2	15.9	38.6	83.1	3.8	13.1	20[18]
El Salvador	1984	1,664	599	5,038	597	...	2,872	1979	82	15.8	17.1	15.9	51.2	69.5	1.2	29.3	9[9]

classification: public, private nonprofit, and private for profit. Statistics on number of beds refer to beds that are maintained and staffed on a full-time basis for a succession of inpatients to whom care is provided.

Data on hospital utilization refer to institutions defined as above. Admission and discharge, the two principal points at which statistics are normally collected, are the basis for the data on the amount and distribution of care by kind of facility. The data on numbers of patients exclude babies born during a maternal confinement but include persons who die before being discharged. The bed-occupancy and average length-of-stay statistics depend on the concept of a "patient-day," which is the annual total of daily censuses of inpatients. The bed-occupancy rate is the ratio of total patient-days to potential days based on the number of beds; the average length-of-stay rate is the ratio of total patient-days to total admissions. Bed-occupancy rates may exceed 100% because stays of partial days are counted as full days.

Two measures that give health planners and policy makers an excellent indication of the level of ordinary health care are those for mortality of children under age five and for maternal mortality. The former is the probability of a newborn infant dying before age five. The latter refers to deaths attributable to delivery or complications of pregnancy, childbirth, the puerperium (the period immediately following birth), or abortion.

Levels of nutrition and access to safe drinking water are two of the most basic limitations imposed by the physical environment in which health-care activities take place. The nutritional data are based on recommendations of the United Nations' Food and Agriculture Organization for the necessary daily intake (in calories) for a moderately active person of

average size in a climate of a particular kind (fewer calories are needed in a hot climate) to remain in average good health. Excess intake in the many developed countries ranges to more than 40% above the minimum required to maintain health (the excess usually being construed to diminish, rather than raise, health). The range of deficiency is less dramatic numerically but far more critical to the countries in which deficiencies are chronic, because the deficiencies lead to overall poor health (raising health service needs and costs), to decreased productivity in nearly every area of national economic life, and to the loss of social and economic potential through early mortality. By "safe" water is meant only water that has no substantial quantities of chemical or biological pollutants, i.e., quantities sufficient to cause "immediate" health problems.

Two principal kinds of public health-care finance data are given: health insurance and central government expenditure. The data on insurance refer to public programs only and identify the mandated basis or extent of responsibility for costs or funding required under the relevant law of the principal participants (individuals, employers, and government). Data on public health-care expenditure refer to a consolidated statement of expenditure, budgetary and otherwise, by all elements of the central government but exclude expenditure by other levels (state, city, etc.). In a number of countries significant government expenditures for health-care services are made at these other levels, amounting to 2, 10, and sometimes 20 times the level of central government expenditure. These expenditures may include costs for national health insurance, family-planning programs, and workmen's compensation. Expenditures at the national level for social security are excluded.

admissions or discharges					bed occu-pancy rate (%)	aver-age length of stay (days)	mortality		popu-lation with access to safe water (latest) (%)	food supply (% of FAO require-ment) 1984–86	financing of public health care, latest year					country
	by kinds of hospital (%)						under age 5 per 1,000 live newborn 1985–90	maternal mortality per 100,000 live births 1980–84			health-care insurance			public health expendi-tures (% of natl. budget)	public health expendi-tures per capita (U.S.$)	
rate per 10,000 pop.	general	special-ized	medical centres	rural							indiv. (% of earn-ings)	em-ployer (% of payroll)	govt. (% of covered earnings)			
76[2]	52.8[2]	46.7[2]	—	0.5[2]	58.0[2]	8[2]	318	640.0	21	91[3]	—	—	—	—	2.10[4]	Afghanistan
	...	...	...	...			48		92	121[6]	—	8.0[7]	8	...	32.10[4]	Albania
568[3]	...	...	...	...	64.1[10, 12]	10[10, 12]	105	129.0	85	112	4.5[7]	5.5[7]	...	...	58.30[4]	Algeria
1,253	100.0	—	—	—	40.0	4.3	30[14]	...	...	...	...	...	...	17.6	237.10	American Samoa
...	...	...	...	...	...	...	17[14]		100	...	...	...	...	...	...	Andorra
260	—	—	—	...	44.5[15]	16[15]	232	...	33	84[3]	...	...	...	...	10.90[4]	Angola
1,097[1]	—	—	—	100.0[1]	52.3[17]	6[17]	27[14]	...	...	...	...	...	...	8.3	88.00	Anguilla
63[19]	...	...	...	...	49.9[19]	7[19]	27[14]	...	100	86	3.0[7]	5.0[7]	—	13.1	66.60[4]	Antigua and Barbuda
...	...	...	...	...	...	...	38	69.0	57	136	3.0	4.5	—	1.9	10.30	Argentina
...	...	...	...	...	...	...	27[14]	...	...	...	...	...	...	...	...	Aruba
2,196[11]	...	...	...	...	83.2[11]	15[11]	10	8.9	99	125	21	—	8	9.5	316.20	Australia
979[23]	77.0	—23.0—		...	...	...	12	10.9	100	142	3.2[21]	3.2[21]	...	12.5	772.60	Austria
1,104[1]	74.0[1]	26.0[1]	—	—	72.6[19]	9[19]	27[14]	19.3[3]	100	112	1.7[7, 24]	7.3[7, 25]	—	13.4	274.40	Bahamas, The
853	...	...	...	...	...	...	32	...	100	...	—	—	—	7.7	205.70	Bahrain
	...	...	...	...			188	600.0	40	83	...	...	...	5.0	0.90	Bangladesh
842	93.9	4.6	—	1.5	89.8[23]	34[23]	14	22.3	99	131	1.0	1.0	—	11.3	183.70	Barbados
1,552	91.0	9.0	—	—	85.3	19	12	7.5	94	146	1.8	3.8	...	1.7	78.10	Belgium
...	...	...	...	...	...	...	...	34.0	64	114	3.0[7]	4.1[7]	8	9.0	30.80	Belize
1,330	93.2	6.8	—	—	81.8	9.8[19]	184	1,680.0	20	95	—	0.2[26]	—	5.6	2.20[4]	Benin
	...	...	...	...			11[14]	...	...	105	...	...	...	15.1	686.80[4]	Bermuda
4,149[27]	...	...	...	...	...	...	196	...	8	90[22]	...	...	...	5.6	2.90	Bhutan
	...	...	...	...			171	480.0	37	89	2.0	8.0	—	1.5	5.20	Bolivia
691[22]	89.1[22]	6.7[22]	4.2[22]		90.0[19]	10[19]	92	300.0	53	96	—	—	—	5.9	25.60	Botswana
868[22]	100.0[22]	—	—	—	75.0[22]	8[22]	86	154.0	71	111	21	21	21	6.4	26.80	Brazil
	...	...	...	...			29	...	90	...	...	...	...	10.3	198.70	British Virgin Islands
1,069[1]	98.5[1]	—	—	1.5[1]	38.0[1]	4[1]	...	...	90	127	...	...	...	3.4	186.80	Brunei
2,118[1]	...	...	...	...	84.4[1]	16[1]	19	20.1	96	145	—	30.0[7]	8	...	159.90[4]	Bulgaria
665[5, 12]	...	...	...	...	63.7[5, 12]	12[5, 12]	235	1,500.0	30	86	—	11.5[30]	—	5.8	2.10	Burkina Faso
109	...	...	...	...	...	...	191	...	24	97	...	...	...	...	1.60[4]	Burundi
	...	...	...	...			153	141.0	32	80	—	7.0[30]	—	3.5	9.90	Cameroon
1,677	93.9	6.0	0.1	—	75.7[1]	13[1]	9	4.8	97	129	21	21	21	6.3	211.70	Canada
279[32]	...	...	...	...	71.7[32]	11[32]	86	107.3[22]	50	116	8.0	15.0	...	...	...	Cape Verde
1,271	100.0	—	—	—	58.7	5	27[14]	...	99	...	...	...	...	12.3	428.70	Cayman Islands
326[3]	43.9[10]	1.0[10]	37.9[10]	17.2[10]	41.9[3]	7[3]	223	600.0	16	86	—	12.0[26, 30]	—	5.1	3.30	Central African Republic
...	...	...	...	...	...	...	223	...	30	63[3]	—	6.0[30]	—	3.8	0.60	Chad
1,039[1]	84.9[22]	9.3[22]	—	5.8[22]	75.2[9]	8[9]	24	53.5	84	105	6.0	—	—	6.0	24.40	Chile
182[9]	...	...	...	...	82.7[9]	16[9]	44	44.0	50	111	—	34	—	...	4.20[4]	China
923	...	...	...	...	...	...	10[14]	...	100	...	...	...	...	...	...	Christmas Island
744	76.0	—	24.0	—	4.9	2	10[14]	...	100	...	...	...	...	...	...	Cocos (Keeling) Islands
385[1]	88.9[17]	11.1[17]	—	—	59.3[1]	6[1]	68	126.0	92	110	2.3	4.7	—	4.5	9.10	Colombia
510[17]	63.7[17]	—	—	36.3[17]	67.9[17]	11[17]	127	...	...	90	...	...	...	7.3	12.10	Comoros
	...	...	...	...			115	...	25	117	—	0.2	—	...	17.30[4]	Congo
1,352	70.7	—	—	29.3	43.6[19]	9[19]	30[14]	...	92	...	...	...	...	...	...	Cook Islands
1,192	77.8	16.7	—5.5—		75.7	8	22	27.4	84	124	5.5	9.3	1.3	19.3	82.80	Costa Rica
171[16]	...	...	...	...	...	...	148	...	66	110	—	5.5[30]	—	4.0	8.40	Côte d'Ivoire
1,619	32.3	—64.2—		3.5	74.4[1]	11[1]	18	51.6	82	135	—	10.0	8	...	62.70[4]	Cuba
759	94.3	1.5	—	4.2	77.7[19]	7[19]	16	...	100	140[3]	6.0[7, 36]	6.0[7, 36]	8.36	6.7[36]	131.20[36]	Cyprus
1,801	95.6	4.4	—	—	80.1	16	16	10.2	100	141	—	20.0[7]	8	...	278.20[4]	Czechoslovakia
2,050	97.9[18]	2.1[18]	—	—	81.1	9	9	5.6	100	131	—	—	8	1.3	59.40	Denmark
...	...	...	...	...	...	...	188[14]	...	45	...	...	...	...	5.8	19.50	Djibouti
729	...	...	...	...	...	...	33[14]	57.5	77	109	3.0[7]	5.0[7]	—	8.8	22.70	Dominica
437	...	...	...	...	55.4	5	82	56.0	62	109	2.5[7]	7.0[7]	2.5[7]	9.0	8.90	Dominican Republic
471	—85.0[10, 37]—		15.0[10]	37	60.4	8	87	162.0	59	90	5.0[7]	1.0	—	7.3	18.80	Ecuador
...	...	...	...	...	...	...	124	80.0	90	132	1.0	4.0	—	2.5	13.00	Egypt
378[19]	...	...	...	...	77.1[19]	7[19]	84	72.5	55	94[3]	2.5	6.3	...	7.4	8.60	El Salvador

Health services (continued)

country	health personnel							hospitals		kinds (%)				ownership (%)			hospital beds per 10,000 pop.
	year	physicians	dentists	nurses	pharmacists	midwives	population per physician	year	number	general	specialized	medical centres	rural	government	private non-profit	private for profit	
Equatorial Guinea	1985	5	—	248[16]	...	2[16]	61,000	1982	65[5]	...	...	—	...	...	...	...	112
Ethiopia	1986–87	1,241	16[22]	12,016[13]	282	13	36,660	1986–87	86	32.6[22]	18.6[22]	—	48.8[22]	88.4[22]	9.3[22]	2.3[22]	3
Faeroe Islands	1987	82	39	236	8[18]	20	569	1987	3	33.3	—	—	66.7	100.0	—	—	79
Falkland Islands	1987	4	1	12	—	5	500	1987	1	100.0	—	—	—	100.0	—	—	145
Fiji	1987	271	48	1,543	44[22]	...	2,649	1984	27	11.1	33.3	—	55.6	92.6	7.4	—	24[11]
Finland	1987	10,889	4,093	47,067[13]	7,060[18]	13	453	1985	367	79.8	20.2	—	—	94.9	—5.1—		123[18]
France	1986	138,825	34,946	294,260	45,521	9,725	399	1986	3,730	—90.9—		—	9.1	28.4	—71.6—		130
French Guiana	1987	237	51	499	33	29	374	1986	6	16.7[1]	—	66.7[1]	16.7[1]	33.3[3]	—66.7[3]—		97
French Polynesia	1985	214	51[1]	394[13]	241	13	815	1981	34	8.8	5.9	52.9	32.4	94.1	—	5.9	55[6]
Gabon	1983	328	205	823[5]	285	99[38]	3,390	1985	105	—26.7—		—73.3—		100.0	—	—	45
Gambia, The	1981	60	6[17]	179[17]	2[17]	90[17]	10,900	1978	16	18.8	12.5	...	68.7	87.5	12.5	...	12[20]
Gaza Strip								1986	7	...	...	...	...	85.7	14.3	...	17
Germany, East	1988	40,516	12,527	116,600[9]	4,049	...	411	1987	541	...	...	...	...	85.2	—14.8—		101
Germany, West	1987	165,015	38,055	315,090	33,025	5,518	370	1987	3,071	44.7[22]	55.3[22]	—	—	35.4	34.0	30.6	110
Ghana	1984	1,900	95[20]	17,758[20]	611[20]	6,728[20]	6,640	1979	329	2.7	4.9	54.7	37.7	78.4	13.1	8.5	18[20]
Gibraltar	1988	28	2	297	3	8	1,067	1986[23]	2	50.0	50.0	—	—	100.0	—	—	64
Greece	1985	29,103	8,737	22,550	...	1,907	341	1985	552	50.0	50.0	—	—	23.0	—77.0—		53[18]
Greenland	1987	65	29	534	...	13	833	1987	16	6.3	—	—	93.7	100.0	—	—	102
Grenada	1987	42	7	315	1[17]	107[17]	2,462	1982	39	7.7	7.7	69.2	15.4	100.0	—	—	35[11]
Guadeloupe	1986	491	114	1,169	153	95	682	1986	29[9]	60.0[17]	30.0[17]	—	10.0[17]	37.9[9]	—62.1[9]—		101
Guam	1986	147	23[1]	594[13]	30[1]	13	823	1982	4	25.0	25.0	50.0	—	50.0	—50.0—		21[10]
Guatemala	1984	3,544	810	9,093	411	...	2,256	1985	159[40]	38.4[40]	25.8[40]	32.7[40]	3.1[40]	76.7[40]	—	23.3[40]	12
Guernsey	1982	53	21	592	15	31	1,094	1982	5	20.0	80.0	—	—	100.0	—	—	91
Guinea	1988	635	22	243	261	343	10,300	1988	38	—100.0—		...	...	100.0	—	—	6
Guinea-Bissau	1985	122	2[22]	674	3[22]	111	7,164	1981	17	11.8	—	...	88.2	100.0	—	—	19[6]
Guyana	1987	142	19	887[3]	21[3]	546[10]	5,307	1979	55	20.0	12.7	27.3	40.0	87.3	3.6	9.1	49[9]
Haiti	1985	803	92	657	6[10,31]	100[10]	6,539	1981	72	—77.8—		—	22.2	61.1	—38.9—		9[9]
Honduras	1987	2,087	446	972	729	...	2,100	1987	46	59.1[1]	11.4[1]	—	29.5[1]	45.7	—54.3—		12
Hong Kong	1987[41]	5,484	1,240	17,215	623	981	1,024	1982	71	43.7	15.5	39.4	1.4	50.7	26.8	22.5	44[11]
Hungary	1988	31,516	4,543	44,524	4,569	2,709	336	1988	...	...	...	...	...	...	...	...	99
Iceland	1986	632	197[9]	2,868[9,13]	178[9]	13	385	1986	46[22]	54.3[22]	41.4[22]	4.3[22]	—	71.6	—28.4—		116
India	1985[41]	297,200	9,598[3]	165,000	155,621[20]	168,493[33]	2,522	1981	25,452	26.7	0.3	65.8	7.2	30.2[17]	23.0[17]	46.8[17]	8[18]
Indonesia	1986	20,768	2,304[1]	122,945[1,13]	3,587[1]	13	8,010	1986	1,408	14.7[17]	8.3[17]	39.4[17]	37.6[17]	66.4	13.9	19.7	7
Iran	1987	16,918	2,488	43,291	2,650[6]	2,202[6]	2,992	1982	581	71.1	15.5	9.8	3.6	95.7	—	4.3	16
Iraq	1984	4,428	984	6,082[1]	952	2,267[1]	3,324	1982	230[9]	48.3	33.8	2.1	15.8				18[9]
Ireland	1984	5,180	1,131	25,261	2,068[20]	13	681	1986	181	65.7	34.3	—	—	69.1	—30.9—		82
Isle of Man	1988	86	19[1,31]	750[1,31]	30[1]	61[1,31]	745	1986	3	33.3	33.3	—	33.3	100.0	—	—	109[20]
Israel	1983	11,895	2,900	14,785	2,540	12,110	345	1986	150	29.3	70.7	—	—	30.0	30.0	40.0	63
Italy	1986	245,116	3,697	186,335[13]	43,500[22]	13	234	1985	1,798	73.5	26.5	—	—	63.2	—36.8—		82
Jamaica	1987[31]	330	55	2,505	76	470	7,186	1987	36	83.3	16.7	—	—	80.6	—19.4—		25
Japan	1986	191,346	66,797	621,451	135,990	24,056	635	1986	9,699	88.8	11.2	—	—	15.3	—84.7—		125
Jersey	1987	86	41[1]	646[1]	22[1]	27[20]	941	1987	6	16.7	83.3	—	—	100.0	—	—	93
Jordan	1986	3,114	623[3]	2,596[3,13]	800[3]	13	881	1986	41[3]	80.0[3]	20.0[3]	—	—	39.0[3]	—61.0[3]—		19
Kampuchea (Cambodia)	1984	200	...	...	130	...	36,000	1984	146	84.9	15.1	—	—	...	...	...	23
Kenya	1985	2,842	384	20,625	231	...	7,122	1985	512	—47.5—		—52.5—		...	...	...	15
Kiribati	1986	16	1[9]	125[9,13]	3[9]	13	4,094	1982	34	2.9	—	97.1	—	100.0	—	—	43[18]
Korea, North	1987	57,800	...	...	...	...	370	1982	7,924	19.3	12.4	—68.3—		...	...	...	130
Korea, South	1987	34,185	6,761	69,829	32,855	6,513[18]	1,216	1987	1,032	—49.4—		50.6		...	...	...	21
Kuwait	1987	2,799	329	8,802	843	82	669	1986	24	...	...	...	...	66.7	—33.3—		29[23]
Laos	1985	558	15[45]	6,753[13]	16[45]	13	6,495	1985	38[16]	...	...	...	...	...	...	...	27
Lebanon	1986	3,509	730[10]	3,681[10]	1,002[10]	614[10]	771	1982	130[40]	...	...	...	...	...	...	...	38
Lesotho	1982	114	6	452	7	...	12,265	1985	136	—14.7—		—85.3—		40.9[5]	59.1[5]		16
Liberia	1985	89	5	908	4[22]	443	24,600	1981	85[22]	...	...	...	...	60.0[22]	—40.0[22]—		15
Libya	1983	5,019	400	5,924[13]	618	13	694	1982	64	68.8	31.2	—	—	100.0	—	—	48
Liechtenstein	1987	29	10	...	2	...	950	1985	1	...	...	...	...	...	...	...	37
Luxembourg	1987	666	175	1,469[20]	274	112	557	1987	32	56.3	43.7	—	—	40.0	—60.0—		126
Macau	1987	518	105[20]	989[13]	5[20]	13	831	1987	10	—100.0—		—	—	100.0	—	—	29
Madagascar	1982	1,233	94[20]	3,813	87[20]	1,323	7,451	1978	749	0.8	1.1	75.7	22.4	100.0	—	—	23[1]
Malawi	1984	262	12[6]	1,286[13]	12[6]	13	27,094	1986	371	12.9	0.8	—86.3—		67.7	—32.3—		17
Malaysia	1986	5,394	1,050[3]	29,358[6]	815[3]	14,525[6]	2,986	1981[46]	163	20.2	50.4	—	29.4	39.9	—	60.1	20
Maldives	1985	23	...	74	13	141	7,957	1985	4	100.0	—	—	—	100.0	—	—	7
Mali	1983	349	15	2,058	58	305	20,474	1983	162	0.5[5]	81.3[5]	—	18.2[5]	100.0	—	—	6
Malta	1982	413	57	2,962	369	225	799	1983	7	28.6	71.4	—	—	100.0	—	—	101
Martinique	1986	519	110	1,121	160	134	641	1986	17	17.6[10]	11.9[10]	17.6[10]	52.9[10]	76.5	—23.5—		93
Mauritania	1984	170	8	582	16	129	9,547	1984	13	8.3[5]	—	—	91.7[5]	100.0	—	—	8
Mauritius	1987	801	120	2,258[13,31]	100[18]	13	1,298	1986	19	36.8	21.1	31.6	10.5	89.5	—10.5—		28[23]
Mayotte	1980	9	1	51	1	2	5,567	1985	2	100.0	—	—	—	100.0	—	—	17
Mexico	1984	66,373[1]	3,207	36,443	112[28]	634[28]	1,102[1]	1974	1,575	47.3	10.6	26.2	15.9	...	...	...	9[3]
Monaco	1986	53	32[1]	208[1]	56[1]	6[1]	538	1982	1	100.0	—	—	—	100.0	—	—	152[16]
Mongolia	1987[31]	5,000	200	7,932[6]	400	963[20]	403	1981	1,659	2.1	5.4	71.9	20.6	100.0	—	—	114[11]
Montserrat	1987	7	1	71	4[3]	32[17]	1,700	1986	1	100.0	—	—	—	100.0	—	—	58
Morocco	1987	4,908	467	22,207	1,351	79	4,725	1987[29]	180	50.0	—	50.0	—	100.0	—	—	11
Mozambique	1986	279	96[22,31]	2,694	8[22,31]	971	50,817	1986	250	4.0	0.8	84.4	10.8	100.0	—	—	11
Myanmar (Burma)	1986	10,031	410[1]	6,978[1,28]	80[1,28]	15,543[1]	3,797	1986	614[15]	49.7[15]	2.4[15]	—	47.9[15]	100.0[15]	—	—	7
Nauru	1980	11	2[38]	61[13,38]	1[38]	13	700	1980	2[38]	100.0[38]	—	—	—	50.0[38]	50.0[38]		250
Nepal	1987	863[33]	...	742[18]	427[18]	1,845	20,356[33]	1987	91	88.2[22]	11.8[22]	—	—	82.4[22]	17.6[22]		2
Netherlands, The	1988	37,144	7,585	34,500[13]	2,103	1,046	396	1987	308	64.3	35.7	—	—	...	...	...	64
Netherlands Antilles	1985	184	35	...	21	12	950	1985	11	—100.0—		—	—	...	...	...	85
New Caledonia	1987	253	33[9]	283[20]	42[9]	27[9]	608	1981	38	10.5	7.9	39.5	42.1	92.1	—	7.9	83[6]
New Zealand	1987	6,390	1,238	42,661[13]	3,403	13	522	1987	344	...	...	...	...	49.7	—50.3—		90
Nicaragua	1984	2,172	222	5,649	...	...	1,456	1985	52	55.1	8.2	36.7	...	46.2[45]	—	53.8[45]	16
Niger	1985	160	10[17]	1,080[17]	12[17]	192	38,534	1978	212	1.9	0.5	94.8	2.8	97.2	2.8	—	6[10]
Nigeria	1985	14,757	899	57,108	3,567	47,052	6,900	1985	11,588	6.6	0.5	—92.9—		100.0	—	—	9
Niue	1986[31]	3	3	27	...	7	858	1986	1	100.0	—	—	—	100.0	—	—	97
Norfolk Island	1987[31]	2	1	8[20]	19	1[20]	1,002	1987	1	100.0	—	—	—	100.0	—	—	110

admissions or discharges — rate per 10,000 pop.	general	specialized	medical centres	rural	bed occupancy rate (%)	average length of stay (days)	under age 5 per 1,000 live newborn 1985–90	maternal mortality per 100,000 live births 1980–84	population with access to safe water (latest) (%)	food supply (% of FAO requirement) 1984–86	indiv. (% of earnings)	employer (% of payroll)	govt. (% of covered earnings)	public health expenditures (% of natl. budget)	public health expenditures per capita (U.S.$)	country
...	...	...	...	...	...	...	214	...	...	...	...	...	...	...	...	Equatorial Guinea
1,812[18]	76.6[18]	—	—	24.3[18]	67.0	11[18]	252	...	15	72[3]	—	—	...	3.6	1.00	Ethiopia
1,790[20]	100.0[20]	—	—	—	41.7[20]	8[20]	10[14]	...	...	...	—	—	...	13.1	1,112.70[4]	Faeroe Islands
997[20]	59.4[20]	10.2[20]	—	30.4[20]	77.1[20]	8[20]	...	...	...	...	...	...	...	...	...	Falkland Islands
...	...	...	...	...	...	...	31	41.9[19]	83	127	—	—	—	9.1	42.10	Fiji
2,139	58.9[22]	40.8[22]	—0.3[22]—		84.6	18	7	3.1	100	114	1.0	1.4	8	10.5	462.90	Finland
2,252	...	...	...	...	79.4	17	10	14.3	100	130	5.5	8.0	...	20.8	882.60	France
2,060[29]	82.2[1,29]	—	—	17.8[1,29]	63.4[29]	9[29]	...	...	...	121	...	...	...	...	...	French Guiana
1,472	70.9	...	3.2	25.9	51.7	8	30[14]	...	50	127	...	...	...	...	...	French Polynesia
258[20]	...	...	...	...	23.6[20]	13[20]	169	124.0	50	104[3]	...	4.0	...	...	55.50[4]	Gabon
437[19]	...	...	...	...	...	...	281	...	45	99	...	...	...	8.0	8.20	Gambia, The
1,312	...	...	...	...	68.4	3	100[14]	...	...	...	...	...	...	...	...	Gaza Strip
1,383[6]	42.8[4]	57.2[4]	—	—	74.0[6]	21[6]	12	15.6	100	145	10.0[7]	12.5[7,39]	8	...	228.30[4]	Germany, East
1,871[3]	80.5[6]	19.5[6]	—	—	84.8[3]	18[3]	11	16.3	100	130	3.5[24]	3.5[24]	...	18.4	579.10	Germany, West
...	...	...	...	...	...	...	145	1,074.0	49	75	5.0[7]	11.5[7]	...	8.3	4.20	Ghana
1,597	...	...	...	...	55.4	8	17[14]	...	...	...	...	...	...	10.4	308.50	Gibraltar
1,190	67.3	32.7	...	...	69.3	12	16	13.1	95	148	3.7	3.7	...	10.5	160.80	Greece
2,525[9]	23.1[9]	—	—	76.9[9]	59.9	10[9]	...	...	...	100	...	...	...	...	...	Greenland
749[12]	...	...	...	...	...	...	33[14]	...	85	100	4.0[7]	4.0[7]	...	15.6	21.90	Grenada
2,420[3]	58.1[9,23]	41.9[9,23]	—	...	87.1[3]	15[3]	17	106.4[17]	...	110	...	...	...	...	...	Guadeloupe
738[10]	97.6[10]	2.4[10]	—	—	78.8[10]	8[10]	...	...	100	...	...	...	...	12.9	177.70	Guam
284	...	...	...	...	57.7	9	99	92.0	51	105	2.0	4.0	...	7.6	8.90	Guatemala
977	89.0	11.0	...	...	83.9	28	11	...	...	...	...	...	...	...	...	Guernsey
...	...	...	...	...	...	...	249	...	20	77	—	3.2	...	...	3.10[4]	Guinea
326	59.8	—	—	40.2	57.5	11	223	400.0	31	84[3]	...	...	...	5.4	4.50	Guinea-Bissau
123	...	...	...	...	...	...	37	104.0	76	108	4.9[7]	7.4[7]	—	5.7	28.00	Guyana
429[22]	75.6[22]	16.7[22]	—	7.7[22]	70.2[22]	8[22]	170	156.0	33	84	2.0[24]	4.0[25]	1.2	...	3.60[4]	Haiti
1,494	93.6	3.2	3.2	—	82.4	8	106	82.0	69	92	2.5	5.0	2.5	8.0	10.90	Honduras
2,264	...	...	...	...	77.1	12	10	6.0	100	121	—	34	—	9.7	117.30[4]	Hong Kong
...	...	...	...	...	...	...	19	19.2	99	135	3.0[24]	24.0	8	3.6	51.40	Hungary
2,087[9]	84.0[22]	14.2[22]	1.8[22]	—	101.0[9]	19[1]	7	0.0	100	118	2.0	—	8	22.8	764.30	Iceland
66[17,19]	...	...	...	...	55.1[17,19]	9[17,19]	148	500.0	54	100	2.2	4.4	25.0	1.9	1.00	India
...	...	...	...	...	...	...	117	800.0	33	116	2.0	5.0	—	1.5	1.40	Indonesia
592	65.5	26.4	7.0	1.1	60.3	6	155	...	71	130[3]	7.0[7]	20.0[7]	3.0[7]	6.0	54.10	Iran
...	...	...	...	...	...	...	94	...	80	121[3]	5.0[7]	12.0[7,42]	—	4.6	58.20	Iraq
1,754	82.1	17.9	—	—	...	7[43]	11	7.2	97	147	1.0	1.0	8	13.0	481.10	Ireland
1,274[20]	83.9[20]	7.0[20]	—	9.1[20]	81.2[20]	25[20]	10[14]	...	...	...	...	...	...	26.0	522.00	Isle of Man
1,688	96.0	4.0	—	—	88.5	13	16	3.1	98	118	0.8	5.7	—	3.2	165.70	Israel
1,660	91.1	8.9	—	—	69.1	12	12	11.3	99	139	1.2	11.9[24]	...	9.6	651.30	Italy
627	83.0	17.0	—	—	77.0	7	23	102.0	96	115	2.5[7]	2.5[7]	...	7.8	44.40	Jamaica
643[1]	97.9[1]	2.1[1]	—	—	83.3[1]	56[1]	8	17.8	98	122	4.3	4.3	16.4	...	623.10[4]	Japan
1,821	81.3	18.7	—	—	86.8[6]	24[6]	10[14]	...	...	...	...	...	...	18.4	660.30	Jersey
1,061	93.6[1]	6.4[1]	—	—	61.8	4	57	...	93	120[3]	—	—	...	4.2	30.00	Jordan
...	...	...	...	...	...	...	192	...	3	95[3]	...	...	...	...	...	Kampuchea (Cambodia)
...	...	...	...	...	...	...	113	168.0	27	93	...	...	...	6.6	5.40	Kenya
633	47.6	—	52.4	—	58.0	15	36[14]	...	44	129	—	...	—	15.5	32.10	Kiribati
...	...	...	...	...	...	...	31	41.0	100	137	...	...	...	...	12.30[4]	Korea, North
2779[9,44]	97.8[9,44]	2.2[9,44]	—	...	68.1	...	31	12.1[9]	83	122	1.5[24]	1.5[24]	...	2.3	14.20	Korea, South
1,041[23]	...	...	...	...	71.7[1]	8[1]	23	11.3	100	127	...	...	...	7.6	385.30	Kuwait
96[16]	...	...	...	...	19.7[16]	7[16]	160	...	21	100[3]	—	—	—	...	...	Laos
...	...	...	...	...	...	...	49	...	92	121[3]	1.5	5.5	...	...	28.00[4]	Lebanon
410[5]	20.8[5]	0.4[5]	6.2[5]	72.6[5]	79.6[5,19]	10[5,19]	135	...	36	101	...	...	...	6.9	5.30	Lesotho
...	...	...	...	...	...	...	206	...	37	102	...	...	...	7.1	8.00	Liberia
719	...	...	...	...	52.7	13	118	80.0	90	153	1.0	1.4	1.6	...	165.60[4]	Libya
...	...	...	...	...	...	...	10[14]	...	...	...	...	...	...	...	...	Liechtenstein
1,941	94.4	5.6	—	—	80.2	19	10	0.0	100	146	4.1	4.1	...	2.3	98.80	Luxembourg
445	...	...	...	...	45.6	11	31[14]	...	...	96	...	...	...	...	...	Macau
699[19]	...	...	...	...	57.9[19]	2[19]	90	...	20	106	—	8.3[30]	...	4.2	1.90	Madagascar
420[6]	...	...	...	...	53.0[6]	8[6]	263	250.0	65	102	—	—	...	7.1	3.70	Malawi
635[23]	...	...	...	...	...	...	35	59.0	71	122	—	—	8	4.4	29.90	Malaysia
291	100.0	—	—	...	57.5[47]	5[47]	...	...	17	92[3]	...	...	...	3.6	9.40	Maldives
1,785	54.9[5]	37.5[5]	—	7.6[5]	58.8[5]	7[5]	291	...	16	86	—	2.0	...	1.7	0.80	Mali
1,569[1]	...	...	...	...	83.7[1]	19[1]	13	17.9	100	116	8.3[7]	8.3[7]	8.3[7]	9.4	134.40	Malta
1,732	69.0[10]	6.0[10]	11.3[10]	13.7[10]	70.9	14	19	...	...	115	...	...	...	...	...	Martinique
115[5]	...	...	...	...	97.8[5]	5[5]	214	...	37	99	...	2.0	...	2.8	4.50	Mauritania
1,139[9,23]	...	...	...	...	84.5[22,23]	8[22,23]	28	52.0	99	123	—	—	—	8.0	36.10	Mauritius
778	100.0	—	...	...	74.8	6	...	...	...	...	...	...	...	...	...	Mayotte
...	...	...	...	...	...	...	68	92.0	74	135	2.3	5.6	...	1.1	6.20	Mexico
2,630	100.0	—	...	...	77.6	14	10[14]	...	100	116	...	...	...	...	...	Monaco
2,508	25.9	33.0	1.1	40.0	89.1	14	58	140.0	100	116	...	...	...	...	11.30[4]	Mongolia
718[20]	100.0[20]	—	—	...	30.7[20]	5[20]	27[14]	...	100	...	...	...	...	...	...	Montserrat
210	92.4[48]	—	7.6[48]	—	54.5	10	118	327.0	57	118	0.2	0.4	—	2.9	6.30	Morocco
92[19,22]	...	...	...	...	70.2[19,22]	9[19,22]	241	300.0	9	69	...	...	...	6.6	3.20	Mozambique
289[15]	75.7[15]	10.1[15]	—	14.2[15]	78.1[15]	9[15]	85	135.0	21	120	1.0	2.0	1.0	7.7	2.20	Myanmar (Burma)
2,660[38]	100.0[38]	—	—	—	...	...	36[14]	...	...	...	...	—	8	14.2	178.50	Nauru
46[19,22]	...	...	...	...	61.5[19,22]	7[19,22]	196	850.0	16	93	—	—	—	5.0	1.30	Nepal
1,066	97.7	2.3	...	...	80.0	18	9	7.4	100	121	5.9	14.1	...	11.0	925.70	Netherlands, The
...	...	...	...	...	...	...	27[14]	...	...	121	...	...	...	5.4	84.60	Netherlands Antilles
1,468	77.9	3.0	3.2	15.9	57.6	16	39[14]	...	...	131	...	...	...	...	...	New Caledonia
1,344[23]	...	...	...	...	77.7[23]	15[23]	12	11.8	100	129	—	—	8	12.4	600.90	New Zealand
634	—91.7—		8.3	...	...	...	93	65.0	56	108[3]	4.0	11.0	0.5	14.6	33.10	Nicaragua
83[19]	...	...	...	...	62.0[19]	9[19]	228	420.0	36	100	—	11.0[26,30]	—	4.1	3.40	Niger
...	...	...	...	...	...	...	173	1,500.0	36	90	6.0[7]	6.0[7]	—	0.8	0.50	Nigeria
1,674[9]	100.0[9]	—	—	—	56.7[22]	14[22]	...	...	100	...	...	...	...	9.6	136.10	Niue
...	...	...	...	...	37.7[9]	9[9]	10[14]	...	...	...	...	...	...	7.5	123.30	Norfolk Island

Health services (continued)

country	year	physicians	dentists	nurses	pharmacists	midwives	population per physician	year	number	general (%)	specialized (%)	medical centres (%)	rural (%)	government (%)	private non-profit (%)	private for profit (%)	hospital beds per 10,000 pop.
Norway	1985	10,110	4,397	44,353[13]	3,041[6]	[13]	411	1987	1,206	6.1	93.9	—	—	100.0	...	...	158
Oman	1987	1,243	83	3,497	227	33[6]	1,071	1987	174	—28.7—		—71.3—		100.0	...	...	30
Pacific Is., Trust Terr. of the																	
Marshall Islands	1985	17	2	51	...	...	2,111	1985	2	100.0	—	—	—	100.0	...	...	15
Micronesia, Fed. States of	1985	36	13	257	7	...	2,542	1985	4	100.0	—	—	—	100.0	...	...	36
Northern Mariana Islands	1986	23	4	103	2	2	898	1988	1	100.0	—	—	—	100.0	...	...	34
Palau	1986[31]	10	3	82	1	...	1,397	1986	1	100.0	—	—	—	100.0	...	...	49
Pakistan	1987	51,020	2,050	16,722	2,785[18]	10,650	2,086	1987	895[1,12]	62.3[1]	6.1[1]	—	31.6[1]	82.2[1]	1.1[1]	16.7[1]	6
Panama	1987	2,722	514	2,456	157[17]	13	836	1986	58	...	...	...	...	85.7[4,8]	—14.3[4,8]—		34[11]
Papua New Guinea	1987	283	16[22]	3,941[3,13]	9[22]	13	11,904	1980	390	5.1	—	53.6	41.2	46.2	53.8	—	45[3]
Paraguay	1984	2,453	195	3,584	860[10]	783[10]	1,458	1985	143[16]	63.6[16]	4.9[16]	—	31.5[16]	91.6[16]	8.4[16]	—	9
Peru	1987	20,198	4,826	15,464	4,995	3,468	1,026	1986	1,341	—26.3—		—73.7—		34.4	—65.6—		16
Philippines	1982	46,579	1,090[20,31]	9,644[20,31]	539[20,31]	9,470[20,31]	1,090	1985	1,814	...	...	...	...	...	...	...	16
Pitcairn Island	1985	...	...	1[31]	...	...	...		...	...	...	...	...	...	...	...	53
Poland	1988	77,496	17,679	183,919	16,004	21,614	487	1987	714	61.1	38.9	—	—	...	...	...	48
Portugal	1988	26,381	1,073	29,525[9]	5,525	824[9]	388	1987	595	24.7	13.8	61.5	—	85.5	—14.5—		48
Puerto Rico	1984	7,560	741[22]	14,392[22]	1,436[22]	199[22]	433	1980	111	72.1	27.9	—	—	48.6	19.8	31.5	38[3]
Qatar	1986	543	66	1,672	135[31]	70[20,31]	696	1985	3	33.0	67.0	—	—	100.0	—	—	29[18]
Réunion	1988	959	244	1,942[18]	184	102[18]	599	1984	21	36.4[5]	18.1[5]	—	45.5[5]	74.2[4,8]	—25.8[4,8]—		68[11]
Romania	1987[31]	41,059	7,212	81,031[1]	6,517	12,248[1]	559	1987	437[20]	56.8[20]	32.5[20]	—	10.8[20]	...	...	...	93
Rwanda	1985[31]	178	9	559	9	616[20]	21,943	1985[23]	220	—13.6—		—86.4—		100.0	...	...	9
St. Helena and Ascension	1986	3	1	53	...	...	2,367	1986	8	12.5	12.5	75.0	—	100.0	...	...	76
St. Kitts and Nevis	1987	22	5	231	7[9]	123[22]	1,974	1987	4	...	...	...	...	...	...	...	56
St. Lucia	1987	54	5	303	13[3]	...	2,636	1986	5	20.0	20.0	—	60.0	...	...	...	36
St. Pierre and Miquelon	1986	13	3	205	...	15	473	1986	1	100.0	—	—	—	100.0	...	...	163
St. Vincent	1987	39	2	218	15[3]	...	2,874	1987	9	11.1	22.2	11.1	55.6	88.9	—11.1—		31
San Marino	1987	60	...	...	...	...	375	1987	...	...	...	...	...	...	...	...	66
São Tomé and Príncipe	1985	53	—	344[6]	1[6]	10[6]	2,035	1978	16	12.5	—	87.5	—	...	...	...	78
Saudi Arabia	1986	12,707	1,084	24,955	479	...	950	1986	181	...	...	...	...	77.9	—22.1—		23
Senegal	1984	432	69	839[31]	110	501[31]	14,808	1984	87	18.4	29.9	51.7	—	100.0	—	—	10[1]
Seychelles	1987	37[4,9]	8[9]	275	3[9]	131[10]	1,794[4,9]	1987	6[9]	16.7[9]	16.7[9]	66.7[9]	—	100.0	—	—	56
Sierra Leone	1984	262	18	1,318[13]	14	13	13,737	1984	109	5.5	5.5	54.1	34.9	89.9	—10.1—		13
Singapore	1987	2,941	653	9,129	487	650[9]	888	1987	21	...	...	...	...	42.9	—57.1—		37
Solomon Islands	1986	38	15[9]	487	...	556	7,402	1986	8	100.0	—	—	—	75.0	25.0	—	53
Somalia	1986	450	2	1,834	180	...	13,315	1985	...	...	...	...	...	...	...	...	9
South Africa	1986[41]	22,525	3,704	88,795	7,557	...	1,510	1980	595	...	...	...	...	40.7	—59.3—		41
Bophuthatswana	1987	106	...	2,672	...	...	18,300	1987	163	—6.7—		—93.3—		...	...	...	33
Ciskei	1986[31]	283	7	3,855	10	54	3,080	1986	97	5.2	1.0	92.8	1.0	99.0	1.0	—	41
Transkei	1985	240	...	4,112[17]	...	...	14,200	1987	31	...	...	...	...	...	...	...	21
Venda	1985	25	...	839	...	...	18,400	1985	54	5.5	1.9	—92.6—		...	...	...	34
South West Africa/Namibia	1988	281	41	3,390	70	...	4,450	1988	61	...	...	...	...	...	...	...	60
Spain	1987	135,406	7,304	142,960	32,307	5,763	287	1984	935	46.1	53.9	—	—	41.3	16.6	42.1	47
Sri Lanka	1986[31]	2,222	301[9]	8,019	441[1]	3,255[9]	7,253	1982	493	5.9	31.4	20.7	42.0	100.0	—	—	28[18]
Sudan, The	1981[31]	2,169	334	13,693	58	376	9,369	1981	160	21.9	5.6	—	72.5	...	...	...	9
Suriname	1985	219	22[3]	1,400[3]	13[17]	88[17]	1,798	1980	17	29.4	17.6	47.1	5.9	58.8	29.4	11.8	50[9]
Swaziland	1984	80	13	377[6]	4[6]	731[17]	7,971	1984	23	30.4	8.7	—60.9—		56.5	—43.5—		25
Sweden	1986	23,154	9,000	64,437[9]	4,475[11]	4,321	362	1986	1,000[6]	10.3[6]	89.7[6]	—	—	...	...	...	72
Switzerland	1986	10,602	3,110	40,000[10]	...	1,650[10]	620	1983	372	52.7	47.3	—	—	...	...	...	102
Syria	1987	8,146	2,456	9,786	2,960	3,049	1,347	1987	206	79.6	20.4	—	—	22.8	—77.2—		11
Taiwan	1987	19,396	4,150	30,174	9,259	2,380	1,010	1987	1,086	6.3	5.5	88.2	—	...	...	...	44
Tanzania	1984	1,065	18[17]	8,291[1]	25[5]	2,887[1]	19,775	1982	3,032	4.9	—	87.2	7.9	...	...	...	11[3]
Thailand	1986	9,464	1,395	29,860	3,356	6,373	5,564	1986	944	89.8	10.2	—	—	74.4	—25.6—		16
Togo	1985	230	5[3]	1,116	50	712[3]	12,992	1979	65	10.8	4.6	61.5	23.1	96.9	3.1	—	13[1]
Tokelau	1987[31]	3	1	...	...	...	567	1987	3	—	—	—	100.0	100.0	—	—	212
Tonga	1987	47	11	216	2	27	2,020	1982	9	44.4	—	55.6	—	100.0	—	—	32[11]
Trinidad and Tobago	1985	1,103	129	3,344[13]	496	13	1,071	1985	31	8.0[10]	16.0[10]	40.0[10]	36.0[10]	60.0[10]	—	40.0[10]	35
Tunisia	1987	3,474	550[18]	9,778	1,264	...	2,198	1987	148	—16.9—		—83.1—		100.0	—	—	21
Turkey	1987	38,829	8,589	34,855	13,668	21,982	1,361	1987	756	77.8	9.7	—12.6—		84.7	—15.3—		27
Turks and Caicos Islands	1987[31]	5	1[3]	36[13]	...	13	2,063	1987	5	20.0	—	—	80.0	100.0	—	—	36
Tuvalu	1986[31]	3	2[9]	26[13]	1[9]	13	2,798	1985	8	11.1	—	—	88.9	100.0	—	—	...
Uganda	1984	700	17[20]	6,778[13,20]	27[20]	13	20,300	1985	485	15.5	1.2	83.3	—	84.5	15.5	—	15[6]
U.S.S.R.	1988	1,232,600[4,9]	...	2,880,000[1,13]	91,000[9]	13	232[4,9]	1988	23,700	...	...	...	...	100.0	—	—	131
United Arab Emirates	1985	2,361	242	6,090	190	...	659	1985	20[6]	50.0[20]	27.3[20]	4.5[20]	18.2[20]	95.5[20]	4.5[20]	—	37
United Kingdom	1981	92,172	17,472	182,897	17,589	...	611	1986	2,501[20]	...	...	...	...	100.0	—	—	72
United States	1987	594,000	158,000	1,593,000	156,960[9]	2,700[18]	413	1986	6,841	84.9	15.1	—	—	32.3	51.4	16.3	53
Uruguay	1986	6,529	2,799	3,000[3]	560	282	397	1986	48[21]	—29.2—		—	70.8	100.0	—	—	30
Vanuatu	1986	27	21	303[13]	31	13	5,191	1980	21	14.3	—	52.4	33.3	47.6	52.4	—	35[6]
Venezuela	1987	28,400	961	54,500	4,063[10]	...	643	1987	541	...	...	...	...	42.5	—57.5—		26
Vietnam	1988	20,100[4,9]	...	83,401[18]	12,100[11]	18,047[18]	3,140[4,9]	1984	10,768	14.6	6.5	78.9	—	100.0	—	—	34[3,5]
Virgin Islands (U.S.)	1985	167	...	241[28]	...	...	622	1985	...	...	...	...	...	...	...	...	49
Wallis and Futuna	1981[27]	4	1	27	1	5	2,800	1982	3	33.3	—	—	66.7	100.0	—	—	77
West Bank	...	...	...	...	2[1]	...	13,000	1986	17	...	...	...	...	52.9	—47.1—		16
Western Sahara[50]	...	...	...	...	...	...	...	1982[29]	2	50.0	—	50.0	—	100.0	—	—	9
Western Samoa	1987	44	7[20]	344[20]	4[20]	42[20,31]	3,665	1984	30	3.3	—	—	96.7	100.0	—	—	42[11]
Yemen (Aden)	1986	652	18[20]	1,733[3]	29[20]	261[3]	3,416	1986	54	12.2[22]	16.4[22]	34.7[22]	36.7[22]	98.0[22]	2.0[22]	—	20
Yemen (San'ā')	1986	1,234	52	2,965[13]	107	13	6,637	1984	34	63.3[1]	3.3[1]	—	33.3[1]	86.7[1]	13.3[1]	—	7[18]
Yugoslavia	1986	32,691	9,574	82,617	6,146	8,636	712	1985	425[22]	32.5[22]	30.3[22]	37.2[22]	—	40.9[10]	44.6[10]	14.5[10]	61
Zaire	1982	2,000	58[10]	14,661[10]	414[10]	3,043[10]	14,092	1982	942[10]	37.3[10]	38.9[10]	23.8[10]	—	80.9	19.1	—	26
Zambia	1984	798	42	5,167	44	1,392	8,076	1987	965	8.2	0.3	19.0	72.5	72.5	—27.5—		32[3]
Zimbabwe	1986	1,257	124	12,391	313	2,320	6,687	1984	1,202	3.7	1.3	—95.0—		72.5	—27.5—		23

[1]1982. [2]Excludes four specialized hospitals. [3]1984. [4]May include expenditures at the intermediate and local levels of government and/or the costs of additional services such as national health insurance and family-planning programs. [5]1977. [6]1983. [7]Includes funds for old-age retirement, incapacitating disability, work injury, and life insurance. [8]Government provides remainder of the cost of benefits. [9]1985. [10]1979. [11]1987. [12]Excludes medical centres. [13]Nurses includes midwives. [14]Regional average. [15]Excludes specialized hospitals and medical centres. [16]1975. [17]1978. [18]1986. [19]General hospitals only. [20]1981. [21]Amounts vary internally. [22]1980. [23]Government hospitals only. [24]Minimum on a graduated scale. [25]Maximum on a graduated scale. [26]Employed women only. [27]Includes outpatients. [28]1974. [29]Public sector only. [30]Includes family allowances. [31]Government-employed health personnel only. [32]1972. [33]Includes physicians

admissions or discharges					mortality				population with access to safe water (latest) (%)	food supply (% of FAO requirement) 1984–86	financing of public health care, latest year					country
rate per 10,000 pop.	by kinds of hospital (%)				bed occupancy rate (%)	average length of stay (days)	under age 5 per 1,000 live newborn 1985–90	maternal mortality per 100,000 live births 1980–84			health-care insurance			public health expenditures (% of natl. budget)	public health expenditures per capita (U.S.$)	
	general	specialized	medical centres	rural							indiv. (% of earnings)	employer (% of payroll)	govt. (% of covered earnings)			
1,637	86.7	13.3	—	...	85.6	9[19]	9	3.9	99	120	4.47	16.87	4.97	10.5	542.00	Norway
1,248[19]	...	...	...	...	83.0[19]	5[19]	157	...	53	...	...	...	...	4.8	123.40	Oman
																Pacific Is., Trust Terr. of the
...	...	...	...	...			36[14]							26.1	120.20	Marshall Islands
2,171	100.0	...	...	...			36[14]								100.00	Micronesia, Fed. States of
1,550	100.0	—	—	—	54.7	4	36[14]								511.60	Northern Mariana Islands
1,233	...						36[14]								229.00	Palau
							165	600.0	44	97	—	7.0	—	0.9	0.60	Pakistan
692	...	...	...	...	64.5[6]	7[6]	33	66.0	62	106	1.0	8.0	0.8[7]	15.5	115.60	Panama
253[19]	...	...	...	...			84	1,000.0	16	82[3]				9.7	23.70	Papua New Guinea
							61	469.0	25	123	9.57	16.57	1.57	3.1	3.50	Paraguay
416[1]	...	...	...	...	88.2[1]	14[1]	122	314.0	52	93	2.5	5.0	—	6.2	12.90	Peru
							72	80.0	52	104	1.3	1.3	[8]	4.2	4.00	Philippines
											—	33.0[7]	[8]	15.4	303.00	Pitcairn Island
1,262	...	...	...	...	90.6	14	19	14.2	67	126				12.2	92.40	Poland
910	—93.5—		6.5	—	65.1	12	20	18.7	92	128	8.07	21.07	...	8.1	71.10	Portugal
1,227	95.0	5.0	—	—	64.8	8	17	10.4								Puerto Rico
1,328[20]	54.3[20]	45.7[20]	—	—			38		95					0.8	70.00	Qatar
836[5,19]	...	...			82.0[5,19]	12[5,19]	14			133						Réunion
...	...	...					28	152.0	77	127		7.0[24]	[8]	0.8	5.00	Romania
85[44]	...	...	...	...	42.8[44]	7[44]	205	210.0	60	80	—	—	—	4.5	1.50	Rwanda
1,028[19,22]					58.9[19,22]	10[19,22]	27[14]	90.9[20]	75	97				11.3	70.60	St. Helena and Ascension
916							33[14]		70	103	5.07	5.07	—			St. Kitts and Nevis
							11[14]									St. Lucia
																St. Pierre and Miquelon
629[18,19]					64.5[18,19]	7[18,19]	33[14]		75	115	—	—	—	12.8	46.00	St. Vincent
1,435[22]					69.5	11[22]	17[14]			100						San Marino
1,733	76.1	—	23.9		68.7	12	178[14]		52	100						São Tomé and Príncipe
757[23]							98		93	125					257.30[4]	Saudi Arabia
378[5,17]	34.2[5]	—	54.8[5]	11.0[5]	75.1[5,17]	9.6[5,17]	222	530.0	43	103	3.0[25]	3.0[25]	—	4.0	4.20	Senegal
1,507[19]					65.0[19]	6[19]	188[14]		82	100	5.07	10.07	—	13.1	43.40	Seychelles
13[19,22]					77.1[19,22]	18[19,22]	291	450.0	24	81	—	—	—	7.5	3.70	Sierra Leone
1,200			—		73.0[20]	10[20]	11	9.6	100	124	—	—	[8]	4.1	82.40	Singapore
							39[14]		27	95	—	—		6.2	13.60	Solomon Islands
							252	1,100.0	33	90				3.2	2.20	Somalia
							96			120	—	—	[8]	9.4	69.40	South Africa
488					79.0	16	103[14]							5.4	26.00	Bophuthatswana
							103[14]									Ciskei
1,130					102.4	11	103[14]									Transkei
							103[14]									Venda
914[20]	91.7[20]	8.3[20]	—	—	73.0[20]	15	176			83[3]						South West Africa/Namibia
1,623	39.9	15.0	0.8	44.3	88.3	6	11	10.0	95	137	4.87	25.87	...	12.7	185.10	Spain
81[19]							43	90.0	37	110	—	—	[8]	5.8	7.50	Sri Lanka
820	83.6	2.4	8.0	6.0	41.6	15	175		40	88	—	—	—	1.3	0.80	Sudan, The
							37	75.0	89	120			...	3.7	47.60	Suriname
506							173		38	110	—	—	—	7.5	17.50	Swaziland
1,848					76.6	11	7	4.3	100	113	—	9.5	...	1.2	82.20	Sweden
1,278	85.9	14.1			80.8	24	8	6.7	99	128	—	—	—	13.1	384.70	Switzerland
456					55.7	5	63	280.0	71	131			—	1.4	12.40	Syria
											1.47	5.67	3.27	1.4	7.80	Taiwan
706	66.5	—	13.1	20.4			174	370.0	52	95	5.07	5.07	—	5.7	3.50	Tanzania
							49	270.0	70	105				6.1	10.10	Thailand
965[1]	—	—	—	100.0[1]	12.0[1]	11[1]	152	84.0	34	97	—	2.0[26]	—	3.8	4.60	Togo
									100							Tokelau
718	97.6	—	2.4	—	56.8	10	30[14]		75	129				3.9	70.30	Tonga
980[10,15]					88.6[10,15]	5[10,15]	23	56.3	98	126	2.87	5.67	[8]	5.9	113.90	Trinidad and Tobago
652[3]					65.5[3]	8[3]	99		89	123	5.0	15.0	—	6.5	29.20	Tunisia
540	78.3[20]	19.1[20]	—	2.6[20]	44.1[20]	9[20]	92	207.0	67	125	5.0	6.0	—	2.4	6.70	Turkey
							27[14]							9.1	137.00	Turks and Caicos Islands
1,368	40.9			59.1	51.5[19]	12.2[19]	36[14]							3.1	34.30	Tuvalu
							169	300.0	16	95	—	—	—	2.4	0.50	Uganda
							27		100	133		4.4[24]			269.20[4]	U.S.S.R.
1,032[1]	78.4[20]	15.4[20]	0.8[20]	5.4[20]	69.6[1]	7[1]	38		93	154				6.2	185.00	United Arab Emirates
1,401	80.6	15					11	7.0	100	128	9.0	11.45	...	13.1	501.20	United Kingdom
1,458	96.9[3]	3.1[3]	—	—	68.4	7	12	8.3	100	138	1.3	1.3	...	12.2	525.60	United States
442					70.8	18	30	44.8	83	100	3.0	4.0	...	4.8	23.70	Uruguay
912	40.5	...	14.0	45.5	33.6	8	39[14]		55	103			1.57	12.4	34.50	Vanuatu
1,587	12.4	8.1	56.6	22.9	80.7	7	43		83	103	2.0	4.25[24]	1.5[24]	10.0	73.30	Venezuela
							91	110	41	104[3]						Vietnam
							27[14]							15.7	349.70	Virgin Islands (U.S.)
1,100	76.0	—	—	24.0	49.4	13	30[14]									Wallis and Futuna
901					73.9	5	100[14]									West Bank
226	98.2	...	1.8		36.9	5	105[14]									Western Sahara[50]
823	62.0	—	—	38.0	25.4	7	30[14]		95	108	—	—	—	9.3	18.50	Western Samoa
277[3]							196	100.0	46	97					8.10[4]	Yemen (Aden)
95	89.0	0.4	—	10.6	73.4	18	196		31	94				3.6	6.30	Yemen (Ṣanʿāʾ)
1,273	52.1[51]	23.5[51]	24.4[51]		85.7	15	28	21.0	68	139	8.7				156.70[4]	Yugoslavia
474[10,19]					71.6[10,19]	12[10,19]	161	800.0	18	97	—			3.2	2.10	Zaire
1,249	—75.7—		—24.3—		68.5	7	127	109.0	48	92	5.0[25]	5.0[24]	—	4.7	4.80	Zambia
867	35.4	24.8	—39.8—		69.7	7	113	145.0	52	89				6.1	13.50	Zimbabwe

practicing dentistry and 279,000 doctors of traditional Chinese medicine. [34]Employer provides entire cost. [35]1988. [36]Republic of Cyprus only. [37]General hospitals includes specialized and rural hospitals. [38]1971. [39]Excludes hazardous occupations such as mining. [40]1973. [41]Registered personnel: all may not be present and working in the country. [42]Excludes oil field operations. [43]Excludes mental hospitals. [44]General and specialized hospitals only. [45]1976. [46]Peninsular Malaysia only. [47]Central Hospital only. [48]Based on bed ownership. [49]Includes dentists. [50]Settlements of Smara, Boujdour, and El Aaiún only. [51]Based on patient-days.

Social protection

This table summarizes three principal areas of social protective activity for the countries of the world: social security, crime and law enforcement, and military affairs. Because the administrative structure, financing, manning, and scope of programmed tasks in these fields vary so greatly from country to country, no well-accepted body of statistical comparisons exists in international convention to permit evaluation of all three of these subjects against each other, either from the perspective of a single country, or internationally. The data provided within any single subject area do, however, represent the most consistent approach to problems of international comparison found in the published literature for that field.

The provision of social security programs to answer specific social needs, for example, is summarized simply in terms of the existence or nonexistence of a specific benefit program because of the great complexity of national programs in terms of eligibility, coverage, term, age limits, financing, payments, and so on. Activities connected with a particular type of benefit often take place at more than one governmental level or through more than one agency at the same level. The data shown here are summarized from the U.S. Social Security Administration's *Social Security Programs Throughout the World* (biennial). A bullet symbol (●) indicates that a country has at least one program within the defined

area; in some cases it may have several. A blank space indicates that no program existed providing the benefit shown; ellipses [...] indicate that no information was available as to whether a program existed.

Data given for social security expenditure as a percentage of total central governmental expenditure are taken from the International Monetary Fund's *Government Finance Statistics Yearbook,* which provides the most comparable analytical series on the consolidated accounts of central governments, governmentally administered social security funds, and independent national agencies, all usually separate accounting entities, through which these services may be provided in a given country.

Data on the finances of social security programs are taken in large part from the International Labour Office's *The Cost of Social Security* (triennial), supplemented by national data sources.

Figures for criminal offenses known to police, usually excluding civil offenses and minor traffic violations, are taken in part from Interpol's *International Crime Statistics* (biennial) and a variety of national sources. Statistics are based on the number of offenses, not the number of offenders; attempted offenses are counted as the offense that was attempted. A person identified as having committed multiple offenses is counted only under the most serious offense. Murder refers to all acts involving

Social protection

country	social security						finances										
	programs available, 1987					expenditures, 1986 (% of total central govt.)	year	receipts					expenditures			
	old-age invalidity, death	sickness and maternity[a]	work injury	unemployment	family allowances			total ('000,000 natl. cur.)	insured persons (%)	employers (%)	government (%)	other (%)	total ('000,000 natl. cur.)	benefits (%)	administration (%)	other (%)
Afghanistan	●	●	●			...	...	...	...	...	...	...	1,171.0	...	...	...
Albania	●	●	●		●	...	1987	...	...	...	...	...	20,468.0	93.3	5.8	0.9
Algeria	●	●	●		●	...	1986	22,075.0	...	...	...	...	0.6	100.0	—	...
American Samoa	...	...	...	...	...	...	1980	2.3	29.3	40.9	...	29.7	...	...	...	...
Andorra	...	...	...	...	...	...		...	...	...	...	...	...	...	...	...
Angola	...	...	...	...	...	...		...	...	...	...	...	0.1	...	...	...
Anguilla						...	1986	...	...	...	...	...	4.2	66.1	33.9	—
Antigua and Barbuda	●	●	●		●	...	1983	13.0	29.2	48.7	—	22.1	58.9	78.9	3.4	17.7
Argentina	●	●	●	●	●	31.0	1983	60.5	29.5	23.2	30.8	16.5	37.1			
Aruba						6	1987	33.6								
Australia	●	●		●	●	25.4	1982–83	25,638.4	13.5	13.3	69.3	3.9	23,084.9	95.6	4.0	0.4
Austria	●	●	●	●	●	45.7[7]	1983	303,603.0	28.6	46.5	21.5	3.4	295,799	95.2	2.5	2.3
Bahamas, The	●	●	●			9.3	1983	48.5	23.2	38.0	5.1	33.7	19.9	77.0	21.8	1.2
Bahrain	●		●			2.2[7]	1983	47.1	24.9	49.9	—	25.2	9.3	61.5	16.5	22.0
Bangladesh	...	●	●			9.8[7,8]	1983	29.0	19.4	43.4	4.3	32.9	13.0	94.9	5.1	—
Barbados	●	●	●			18.8	1983	135.5	35.0	36.2	3.3	25.5	78.3	92.7	4.6	2.7
Belgium	●	●	●	●	●	39.5[8]	1983	1,180,799.7	19.6	38.1	38.0	4.4	1,172,396.4	94.6	4.3	1.2
Belize	●	●	●			5.5	1983	11.5	7.3	77.3	3.0	12.3	5.7	89.1	10.7	0.2
Benin	●	●	●		●	8.7[7,10]	1983	7,001.7	21.3	78.6	—	0.1	6,200.2	95.0	5.0	...
Bermuda	...					...		...	...	...	...	...	...	...	...	...
Bhutan						...	1984						7.7			
Bolivia	●	●	●		●	4.9[2]	1983	41,325.3	25.5	34.8	24.2	15.5	31,679.2	84.8	14.6	0.7
Botswana						3.3[7]	1986	—					30.1[7]			
Brazil	●	●	●		●	20.7[8]	1983	6,823,360.0	15.2	74.7	8.0	2.2	6,753,246.0	93.0	6.9	0.1
British Virgin Islands	...					...	1982	...	...	...	...	...	0.2	...	...	...
Brunei	●		●		●	...	1984						39.5			
Bulgaria	●	●	●		●	...	1983	2,953.7	...	...	...	...	2,953.7	100.0	...	...
Burkina Faso	●	●	●		●	8.2[7,8]	1983	9,322.8	23.4	74.1	0.1	2.4	5,891.2	67.3	27.2	5.5
Burundi	●		●		●	0.7[11]	1983	890.0	32.1	41.0	11.2	15.7	502.5	77.9	18.4	3.7
Cameroon	●		●		●	4.5	1983	42,817.0	11.1	69.0	—	19.9	16,536.0	91.2	—	8.8
Canada	●	●	●	●	●	28.7	1983	65,451.7	11.3	15.3	63.7	9.7	60,701.0	96.5	2.6	0.9
Cape Verde	●	●	●		●	...		...	...	...	...	...	...	...	...	...
Cayman Islands						2.3[7]	1987									
Central African Republic	●		●		●	6.2[2,7]	1983	2,283.5	9.9	88.7	—	1.4	1,922.0	55.8	35.9	8.3
Chad	●		●		●	1.9[13]	1983	230.9	13.8	84.8	—	1.4	203.5	23.1	75.3	1.6
Chile	●	●	●	●	●	36.4	1983	262,412.6	30.8	2.1	48.5	18.6	224,473.7	90.3	8.2	1.5
China	●	●	●			...		...	...	...	...	...	...	...	...	...
Christmas Island						...		...	...	...	...	...	...	...	...	...
Cocos (Keeling) Islands	●	●	●		●	...	1985	0.2	...	...	...	...	0.2	...	...	...
Colombia	●	●	●			19.6[2]	1983	78,006.0	22.9	49.3	10.8	17.0	67,996.0	88.3	11.6	0.1
Comoros	...				●	...	1983	40.7	100.0	—	—	—	54.3	17.4	62.3	20.3
Congo	●	●	●		●	0.4[17]	1983	15,272.8	12.1	80.2	—	7.7	7,256.7	66.6	21.3	12.1
Cook Islands	●					19.2	1983	11,702.1	28.4	47.0	18.5	6.1	7,780.5	88.8	5.1	6.1
Costa Rica	●	●	●		●	3.6[2]	1983	29,125.0	61.9	17.7	—	20.4	16,337.7	78.4	9.1	12.5
Côte d'Ivoire	●		●		●		1983	1,491.5	—	44.3	55.7	—	1,491.5	96.6	—	3.4
Cuba	●	●	●			...	1983	95.0	28.6	42.4	20.4	8.6	56.6	98.1	1.7	0.2
Cyprus[18]	●	●	●	●		19.1	1983	105,190.0	—	3.7	94.6	1.7	105,190.0	99.7	0.3	—
Czechoslovakia	●	●			●	33.3[8]	1983	149,307.6	3.3	8.1	85.9	2.7	143,850.2	97.1	2.9	—
Denmark	●	●	●	●	●	8.3[10]	1979	1,352.2	...	...	...	...	1,115.7	...	...	...
Djibouti						...		...	...	...	...	...	...	...	...	...
Dominica	●	●	●			1.4[10]	1980	7.1	27.4	45.6	—	27.0	2.0	56.7	43.3	—
Dominican Republic	●	●	●			7.0[8]	1980	136.8	...	...	43.6	4.4	123,852	87.2	8.0	4.8
Ecuador	●	●	●			0.9[7,8]	1983	30,616.0	28.9	39.9	0.8	30.4	23,344.0	64.6	22.5	12.9
Egypt	●	●	●	●		10.9	1987	2,257.0	39.0	60.9	—	—	1,904.0	...	...	...
El Salvador	●	●	●			2.8	1983	288.7	27.9	35.9	12.2	24.2	178.0	86.3	13.7	—
Equatorial Guinea	...				●	...	1983	43.0	4.7	95.3	—	—	20.0	30.0	70.0	—
Ethiopia	●					4.4[12]	1983	126.5	31.6	65.3	—	3.1	106.3	98.1	1.9	—
Faeroe Islands	●	●		●	●	...		...	...	...	...	...	...	...	...	...
Falkland Islands	●					...		...	...	...	...	...	...	...	...	...
Fiji	●		●			4.0	1983	92.7	26.5	26.8	9.1	37.6	33.1	74.3	4.6	21.1

the voluntary taking of life, including infanticide, but excluding abortion, or involuntary acts such as those normally classified as manslaughter. Assault includes "serious," or aggravated assault—that involving injury, endangering life, or perpetrated with the use of a dangerous instrument. Burglary involves theft from the premises of another; although Interpol statistics are reported as "breaking and entering," national data may not always distinguish cases of forcible entry. Automobile theft excludes brief use of a car without the owner's permission, "joyriding," and implies intent to deprive the owner of the vehicle permanently. Criminal offense data for certain countries refer to cases disposed of in court, rather than to complaints. Police manpower figures refer, for the most part, to full-time, paid professional staff, excluding clerical support and volunteer staff. Personnel in military service who perform police functions are presumed to be employed in their principal activity, military service.

The figures for military manpower refer to full-time, active-duty military service and exclude reserve, militia, paramilitary, and similar organizations. Because of the difficulties attached to the analysis of data on military manpower and budgets (including problems such as data withheld on national security grounds, or the publication of budgetary data specifically intended to hide actual expenditure, or the complexity of long-term

financing of purchases of military matériel [how much was actually spent as opposed to what was committed, offset by nonmilitary transfers, etc.]), extensive use is made of the principal international analytical tools: publications such as those of the International Institute for Strategic Studies (*The Military Balance* and *Strategic Survey*) and the U.S. Arms Control and Disarmament Agency (*World Military Expenditures and Arms Transfers*), both annuals.

The data on military expenditures are from the sources identified above, as well as from the IMF's *Government Finance Statistical Yearbook* and country statistical publications.
a. Sickness and maternity refers to cash benefits for sickness and maternity. Countries must provide both benefits to be included. In many countries medical care and hospital coverage are also provided for sickness and maternity.
b. A police officer is a full-time, paid professional, performing domestic security functions. Data include administrative staff but exclude clerical employees, volunteers, and members of paramilitary groups.
c. Includes all active-duty personnel, regular and conscript, performing national security functions. Excludes reserves, paramilitary forces, border patrols, and gendarmeries.

crime and law enforcement (latest)					population per police officer[b]	military protection								country
offenses reported to the police per 100,000 population						manpower, 1988[c]		expenditure, 1987				arms trade, 1987 ('000,000 U.S.$)		
total	personal		property			total ('000)	per 1,000 population	total '000,000	per capita[e]	% of central government expenditure	% of GDP or GNP	imports	exports	
	murder	assault	burglary	automobile theft										
...	...	...	...	...	540[1]	55.0	3.8	287[2]	21[2]	64.4[2]	7.7[2]	1,300	0	Afghanistan
...	...	...	...	...	550	42.0	13.3	151	49	11.1	5.1	0	0	Albania
1,768	...	123	...	...	840	139.0	5.8	1,930	82	8.3	3.0	700	0	Algeria
6,393	5.5	1,266	623	33.1	460	—	[3]	...	...	...	...	...	...	American Samoa
3,009	...	...	...	...	220	—	—	...	...	...	...	...	...	Andorra
294	7.4	...	...	0.1	14[4]	100.0	10.7	690[5]	99[5]	25.0[5]	8.7[5]	1,600	0	Angola
2,102	...	...	...	...	100	—	[3]	—	—	—	—	...	...	Anguilla
2,718	...	...	...	...	120	0.7[5]	8.9[5]	...	...	...	...	...	...	Antigua and Barbuda
181	0.2	0.6	—	17.6	1,270	95.0	3.0	1,100	35	12.0	1.4	30	20	Argentina
3,659	34.6	342.4	...	...	...	—	[3]	...	...	...	...	...	...	Aruba
7,264	4.2	81.3	1,787.3	838.8	450	70.5	4.3	4,986	310	9.2	2.5	625	30	Australia
5,279	2.4	1.4	767.7	15.0	470	54.7	7.2	1,447	191	3.1	1.2	10	10	Austria
6,437	29.0	66.0	2,571.4	...	150	0.6	2.4	9[2]	40[2]	2.5[2]	0.5[2]	...	...	Bahamas, The
2,335	1.4	464.3	63.5	...	180	2.9	6.8	160	346	13.9	4.1	280	0	Bahrain
53	2.1	...	...	...	2,560	101.5	0.9	321	3	26.4	1.8	10	0	Bangladesh
3,230	4.0	85.0	183.8	6.7	280	...	...	8[9]	32[9]	1.8[9]	0.6[9]	20	0	Barbados
2,572	3.1	89.4	554.9	169.6	640	88.3	9.0	4,163	422	5.6	3.0	140	20	Belgium
1,869	...	573.8	420.2	...	290	0.7	3.9	4[2]	25[2]	4.0[2]	2.0[2]	...	...	Belize
1,234	...	...	...	...	3,250	4.4	1.0	34[9]	8[9]	15.5[9]	2.1[9]	0	0	Benin
7,413	10.8	154.6	2,092.3	...	370	—	[3]	—	—	—	—	...	...	Bermuda
...	...	...	...	...	...	4.0[8]	3.1[8]	...	...	...	...	...	...	Bhutan
...	...	...	...	...	...	27.6	3.9	127	20	16.6	3.0	0	0	Bolivia
3,567	10.3	401.1	442.8	...	750	3.3	2.7	24	21	3.8	2.2	0	0	Botswana
116	...	...	...	...	...	319.2	2.2	2,200	15	6.2	0.8	100	600	Brazil
1,865	...	...	...	...	190	—	[3]	—	—	—	—	...	...	British Virgin Islands
...	...	...	...	...	100	4.0	16.0	305[2]	1,398[2]	24.5[2]	8.1[2]	...	...	Brunei
...	...	...	...	...	...	157.8	17.6	6,656	743	22.9	10.3	600	480	Bulgaria
41	0.2	4.1	—	—	...	8.7	1.0	51	6	17.6[2]	3.1	0	0	Burkina Faso
108	4.9	18.2	...	...	...	7.2	1.4	37	7	12.7	3.1	20	0	Burundi
...	...	...	...	...	1,170	11.6	1.0	246	24	8.4	1.9	5	0	Cameroon
11,169	5.7	124.0	1,426.8	334.4	8,640	84.6	3.3	8,835	342	9.4	2.2	150	120	Canada
13,340	20	375.0	2,140.0	...	110	1.2	3.3	12[12]	471[12]	13.5[12]	11.8[12]	5	0	Cape Verde
...	...	...	...	...	110	—	[3]	...	...	...	...	...	...	Cayman Islands
...	...	...	...	...	2,740[1]	6.5	2.3	11[5]	55	10.8[5]	2.0[5]	0	0	Central African Republic
...	...	...	...	...	990	17.0	3.2	34	7	40.1	3.5	100	0	Chad
1,485	6.0	129.6	...	5.7	470	101.0	7.9	683	55	12.7	4.0	30	170	Chile
52	1.1	1.7	...	...	1,360[14]	3,200.0	2.9	20,660	19	20.4	4.4	380	1,000	China
790[15]	...	...	...	...	190	—	[3]	—	—	—	—	...	...	Christmas Island
...	...	...	...	...	...	—	[3]	—	—	—	—	...	...	Cocos (Keeling) Islands
622	...	...	...	...	420	86.3	2.8	371	12	7.4	1.1	10	0	Colombia
...	...	...	...	...	960	—	[16]	...	...	...	...	...	...	Comoros
17	0.8	0.5	...	...	870	8.8	3.9	105	51	12.5	4.6	5	0	Congo
...	...	...	...	...	...	—	[3]	—	—	—	—	...	...	Cook Islands
870	5.3	12.0	...	...	480	9.5	3.6	26	9	...	0.6	0	0	Costa Rica
286	2.1	50.4	21.9	4.8	4,640	7.1	0.6	178	17	4.4[2]	1.9	0	0	Côte d'Ivoire
...	...	...	...	...	650	180.5	17.3	1,600[8]	154[8]	...	5.4[8]	1,800	0	Cuba
698	2.6	13.3	213.2	...	180	13.0	18.1	35	51	2.9	0.9	260	0	Cyprus[18]
...	...	...	...	...	640	197.0	12.6	10,320	662	21.8	6.8	900	975	Czechoslovakia
10,058	5.8	130.9	2,475.9	647.8	600	29.3	5.7	2,141	418	5.5	2.2	100	10	Denmark
...	...	...	...	...	...	4.2	8.7	27[2]	67[2]	22.4[2]	8.1[2]	...	...	Djibouti
22,432	9.3	47.0	1,025.0	11.0	300	...	...	...	...	...	...	...	...	Dominica
3,843	9.2	61.3	220.8	34.8	580	20.8	3.0	64	9	10.9	1.4	5	0	Dominican Republic
333	5.1	4.0	...	4.3	260	40.0	3.9	250	25	15.3	2.6	70	0	Ecuador
2,378	...	...	...	...	580	445.0	8.9	6,527	126	22.3	9.2	1,500	70	Egypt
...	...	...	...	...	1,000	55.0	10.8	178	34	30.3	3.9	50	0	El Salvador
...	...	...	...	...	190	1.4	4.2	2[19]	9[19]	21.0[19]	...	0	0	Equatorial Guinea
119	7.4	25.2	1.7	...	1,100	315.8	6.7	442	9	24.0	8.5	1,000	0	Ethiopia
...	...	...	...	...	...	—	[3]	...	...	...	...	...	...	Faeroe Islands
...	...	...	...	—	330	—	[3]	—	—	—	—	...	...	Falkland Islands
1,962	2.0	263.4	418.7	...	440	3.5	4.7	14[9]	20[9]	4.1[9]	1.2[9]	0	0	Fiji

Social protection (continued)

country	social security					expenditures, 1986 (% of total central govt.)	finances									
	programs available, 1987						year	receipts					expenditures			
	old-age invalidity, death	sickness and maternity[a]	work injury	unemployment	family allowances			total ('000,000 natl. cur.)	insured persons (%)	employers (%)	government (%)	other (%)	total ('000,000 natl. cur.)	benefits (%)	administration (%)	other (%)
Finland	●	●	●	●	●	35.07	1983	61,869.5	7.1	39.6	46.5	6.8	56,564.8	96.0	4.0	—
France	●	●	●	●	●	8.78	1983	1,246,605.6	20.5	48.0	24.2	7.3	1,216,861.4	90.4	4.0	5.6
French Guiana	●	...	●	...	●	...	...	...					...	...	...	...
French Polynesia	●	...	●	...	●	...	...	...					...	...	...	...
Gabon	●	...	●		●	...	1983	39,632.0	16.0	65.1	12.8	6.1	33,350.0	81.0	12.1	6.9
Gambia, The	●		●			3.520	1982	—	...				5.6	...	...	...
Gaza Strip	...	...	...	...	...	—										
Germany, East	●	●	●	●	●	...	1983	30,829.5	23.1	29.5	47.3	0.1	30,829.5	99.7	0.3	—
Germany, West	●	●	●	●	●	50.22,7	1983	408,738.0	35.5	33.9	27.2	3.4	409,569.0	96.6	2.6	0.8
Ghana	●		●			4.8	1987	...					...	...	...	...
Gibraltar	●	●	●	●	●	...										
Greece	●	●	●	●	●	28.812	1983	572,741.0	28.2	41.9	23.0	6.9	542,909.0	93.4	6.0	0.6
Greenland	●	●	●		●	...										
Grenada	●	●				5.07,11	1983	8.6	20.2	64.7	5.5	9.6	5.2	82.8	3.8	13.4
Guadeloupe	●		●		●	...		...					...	...	...	...
Guam	●		●			...										
Guatemala	●	●	●			2.610	1983	124.2	29.5	51.0	3.6	15.9	90.2	88.7	11.3	—
Guernsey	●	●		●	●	...		...					...	...	...	...
Guinea	●	●	●		●	...	1983	166.3	78.7	21.3	—	—	44.7	74.6	25.4	...
Guinea-Bissau	●		●			3.6	1983	28.2	25.5	44.1	—	30.4	47.8	3.4	19.3	77.3
Guyana	●	●	●			3.75	1983	136.3	22.7	28.0	1.0	48.3	26.6	71.9	26.2	1.9
Haiti	●	●	●			5.12	1977	60.5	—26.6—		69.9	3.5	52.4	92.7	7.3	—
Honduras	●	●	●			4.510	1983	77.5	25.6	47.2	7.1	20.1	54.8	81.5	17.9	0.6
Hong Kong	●			●			1985	...					895.6	...	...	...
Hungary	●	●	●		●	21.8	1983	138,375.0	14.9	47.1	38.0	—	138,375.0	99.5	0.5	—
Iceland	●	●	●	●	21	14.08	1985	1,475.0	—	56.7	43.3	—	4,173.7	...	...	...
India	●	●	●			—	1983	46,228.3	14.1	67.0	2.1	16.8	24,262.5	97.4	1.9	0.7
Indonesia	●		●			—	1983	56.3	16.5	48.4	—	35.1	15.9	29.8	64.0	6.2
Iran	●	●	●		●	14.2	1983	301,532.0	17.4	49.8	25.9	6.9	107,519.0	93.3	6.7	—
Iraq	●	●	●			...	1977	107.8	9.9	55.6	21.9	12.6	71.0	94.0	2.4	3.6
Ireland	●	●	●	●	●	13.9	1983	3,384.4	13.1	24.6	60.6	1.7	3,426.0	94.6	4.9	0.5
Isle of Man	●	●	●	●	●	17.2	1985	...					14.4	...	...	...
Israel	●	●	●	●	●	15.9	1983	100,258.8	18.9	37.5	34.1	9.5	91,205.3	86.6	8.9	4.5
Italy	●	●	●	●	●	27.5	1983	143,008.0	15.3	48.0	33.8	2.9	139,511.0	93.0	3.6	3.4
Jamaica	●	●	●			3.211	1983	191.7	18.6	22.3	31.9	27.3	96.8	87.1	12.8	0.1
Japan	●	●	●	●	●	...	1983	40,946,872.0	26.2	28.7	29.0	16.0	32,661,494.0	90.1	1.8	8.1
Jersey	●	●	●	...	●	9.8	1984	31.3	—58.9—		30.3	10.8	...	...	...	...
Jordan	●		●			6.8	1983	30.3	30.7	59.0	—	10.3	3.4	74.6	24.5	0.9
Kampuchea (Cambodia)	...	...	●		●	...										
Kenya	●		●			0.2	1983	600.4	25.3	25.3	—	49.4	55.5	72.8	27.2	—
Kiribati	●		●			...		...					...	...	...	...
Korea, North	...	...	...	...	...	...		...					...	...	...	...
Korea, South	●		●			7.0	1988	926,000.0	31.6	68.4	—	—	1,344,000.0	...	...	...
Kuwait	●		●	●		7.2	1983	213.0	9.0	17.7	39.9	33.4	92.8	95.1	4.6	0.3
Laos	...	...	●		...	...		...					...	...	...	...
Lebanon	●	●	●		●	...		...					...	...	...	...
Lesotho	●		●			1.08	1985	—					2.7	...	...	...
Liberia	●	●	●			0.7	1983	2.9	—	69.0	13.8	17.2	2.6	54.4	45.6	—
Libya	●	●	●			...	1977	192.9	9.1	28.7	58.7	3.5	128.2	96.2	3.2	0.5
Liechtenstein	●		●	●	●	...		...					...	...	...	...
Luxembourg	●	●	●	●	●	49.28	1983	51,234.3	24.3	32.0	25.8	17.9	48,230.8	85.5	2.4	12.1
Macau	●					...	1981	...					...	...	...	...
Madagascar	●		●		●	10.324	1983	9,536.1	5.3	69.6	—	25.1	6,609.0	100.0	—	—
Malawi	●		●			0.7	1986	...					5.4	...	...	...
Malaysia	●		●			2.612	1983	4,376.6	24.3	45.4	0.6	29.7	3,138.4	96.3	3.6	0.1
Maldives	...	...	...	...	...	1.38	1985	—					2.4	...	...	...
Mali	●	●	●		●	6.17,8	1983	5,781.6	10.8	59.5	1.5	28.2	5,628.9	50.9	27.3	21.8
Malta	●	●	●	●	●	39.4	1983	70.1	27.6	33.2	39.2	—	67.2	99.1	0.9	—
Martinique	●		●	...	●	...		...					...	...	...	...
Mauritania	●		●		●	3.710	1983	1,210.3	9.2	56.9	29.7	4.2	1,076.3	87.8	6.0	6.2
Mauritius	●		●		●	16.27	1983	454.4	10.1	20.2	54.3	15.4	262.1	95.4	4.5	0.1
Mayotte	●		●		●	...		...					...	...	...	...
Mexico	●	●	●			8.2	1983	526,385.0	21.7	57.5	8.1	12.7	471,840.0	66.6	17.1	16.3
Monaco	●	●	●	●	●	...		...					...	...	...	...
Mongolia	●				●	...		...					...	...	...	...
Montserrat	●	...	...	...	...	...										
Morocco	●	●	●		●	6.07	1983	1,451.6	8.4	78.4	—	13.2	818.1	93.3	6.7	...
Mozambique	●		●			...	1983	154.0	99.8	—	—	0.2	83.0	21.4	37.0	41.6
Myanmar (Burma)	●	●	●			0.38	1983	37.1	19.9	59.8	17.8	2.4	25.5	70.2	18.5	11.4
Nauru	●		●			...		...					...	...	...	...
Nepal	●		●			0.78	1985	—					59.3	...	...	...
Netherlands, The	●	●	●	●	●	34.3	1983	146,960.0	38.0	30.5	17.6	13.9	126,547.0	92.2	3.3	4.5
Netherlands Antilles	●	●	●	...	●	16.46	19877	130.0	98.5	—	—	1.5	126.0	...	...	...
New Caledonia	●		●		●	...		...					...	...	...	...
New Zealand	●	●	●	●	●	28.3	1983	5,822.1	2.2	4.4	91.6	1.8	5,711.2	98.1	1.8	0.1
Nicaragua	●	●	●			3.319	1983	832.9	20.4	53.5	10.4	15.7	427.5	65.5	28.5	6.0
Niger	●		●		●	1.77,19	1983	6,116.3	8.4	80.6	—	11.0	4,619.9	38.3	18.2	43.5
Nigeria	●		●			2.527	1983	78.4	28.2	20.1	—	51.7	11.3	45.6	54.4	...
Niue	...	...			...	...										
Norfolk Island	●				●	...										
Norway	●	●	●	●	●	35.17,8	1983	91,154.6	20.9	32.1	45.1	1.9	87,863.0	97.6	2.4	—
Oman	●					—	1987	...					...	...	...	...
Pacific Is., Trust Territory of the Marshall Islands	●	...	...	...	...	...		...					...	...	...	...
Micronesia, Fed. States of	...	...	...	...	...	...		...					...	...	...	...

crime and law enforcement (latest)					population per police officer[b]	military protection								country
offenses reported to the police per 100,000 population						manpower, 1988[c]		expenditure, 1987				arms trade, 1987 ('000,000 U.S.$)		
total	personal		property			total ('000)	per 1,000 population	total '000,000	per capita[e]	% of central government expenditure	% of GDP or GNP	imports	exports	
	murder	assault	burglary	automobile theft										
7,324	1.1	36.9	902.9	199.7	640	35.2	7.1	1,324[9]	269[9]	5.1[9]	1.7[9]	40	0	Finland
5,956	4.1	66.1	741.4	472.2	630	456.9	8.2	34,830	626	9.0	4.0	220	2,600	France
...	...	...	...	...	...	—	[3]	—	—	—	—	...	...	French Guiana
170	1.3	7.6	36.3	7.7										French Polynesia
					1,290	3.0	2.5	165[9]	141[9]	7.6[9]	4.8[9]	0	0	Gabon
...					3,310	0.6	0.7	2[12]	3[12]	3.6[12]	1.3[12]	0	0	Gambia, The
4,355	...	...	...	...										Gaza Strip
666						172.0	10.4	14,440	870	12.7	7.3	220	210	Germany, East
7,154	4.5	105.0	1,910.9	115.1		488.7	8.0	34,130	560	10.0	3.0	420	1,800	Germany, West
...	...	...	...	...	620	10.6	0.8	45	3	6.2	0.9	10	0	Ghana
8,140	...	...	...	...	170	—	[3]	—	—	—	—	...	...	Gibraltar
2,953	1.5	53.8	151.8	...	380	214.0	21.3	2,902	291	12.0	6.2	150	40	Greece
12,460	...	...	...	...	340	—	[3]	—	—	—	—	...	...	Greenland
6,248	10.9	928.1	525.4	...	230	—	—	—	—	—	—	...	...	Grenada
...	...	...	...	...	...	—	[3]	—	—	—	—	...	...	Guadeloupe
3,454														Guam
...	...	...	...	...	670	42.0	4.8	104	12	13.1	1.5	5	0	Guatemala
...	...	...	...	...	...	—	[3]	—	—	—	—	...	...	Guernsey
...	...	...	...	...	1,140	9.9	1.5	60[2]	10[2]	...	3.2[2]	50	0	Guinea
...	...	...	...	...	...	9.2	9.9	4	4	4.1	3.2	40	0	Guinea-Bissau
1,980	15.6	28.1	434.7	...	190	5.5	7.3	34[8]	43[8]	5.9[5]	8.9[8]	0	0	Guyana
701					400	7.6	1.4	40	6	9.6	1.8	0	0	Haiti
	9.4	7.7		3.3	1,040	18.7	3.9	133	28	13.3	3.7	60	60	Honduras
1,474	1.3	141.3	216.0	7.6	220	—	[3]	—	—	—	—	...	...	Hong Kong
1,719	4.2	58.1	250.7	47.8	710	99.0	9.4	4,525	427	12.0	5.2	360	220	Hungary
1,550	0.9	64.3	704.8	112.8	940	—	—	—	—	—	—	0	0	Iceland
179	3.4	...	16.4	...	820	1,362.0	1.7	9,632	12	16.9	3.9	3,200	5	India
142	1.0	7.1	28.7	4.0	1,340	284.0	1.6	1,367	8	8.7	2.1	250	0	Indonesia
...	...	...	...	...		604.5	11.8	21,120[8]	499[8]	34.1[8]	7.9[8]	1,500	0	Iran
518	12.9	216.4	40.8	1.42	140	1,000.0	60.1	16,710[8]	1,098[8]	50.8[20]	30.7	5,600	5	Iraq
2,448	0.6	3.3	856.8	33.6	310	13.2	3.7	447	126	3.0	1.9	5	0	Ireland
...	...	...	...	...		—	[3]	—	—	—	—	...	...	Isle of Man
5,247	4.6	21.7	1,081.7	...	210	141.0	31.3	5,536	1,311	24.7	16.6	1,600	360	Israel
2,452	4.3	28.1		292.6	680	386.0	6.7	18,350	320	4.6	2.5	170	210	Italy
1,980	18.0	29.2	358.3	14.9	430	2.5	1.0	26	10	1.8[8]	1.1	5	0	Jamaica
1,409	1.4	17.4	243.9	28.4	480	245.0	2.0	24,320	199	6.5	1.0	725	80	Japan
...	...	...	...	...		—	[3]	—	—	—	—	...	...	Jersey
700	2.3	18.1	49.4	14.7	630	85.3	28.8	646	235	22.0	13.9	320	0	Jordan
...	...	...	...	...	1,980	60.0	7.62	68[22]	18[22]	...	11.0[22]	350	0	Kampuchea (Cambodia)
448	5.4	20.7	60.0	14.5	1,500	23.0	1.0	182	8	8.0	2.4	10	0	Kenya
2,472					330									Kiribati
...	...	...	...	...	460	842.0	38.4	5,800	270	...	22.4	420	410	Korea, North
1,989	1.4	60.3	62.0	...	420	629.0	14.8	5,626	133	25.5	4.8	550	30	Korea, South
667	5.3	21.8	57.0	11.1	80	20.3	5.3	1,330	714	13.7	5.2	150	0	Kuwait
...	...	...	...	...	280	55.5	14.4	55[8]	15[8]	21.3[2]	10.5[2]	110	0	Laos
366	13.2	14.1	65.7	67.3	530	—	—	429[5]	135[5]	20.0[5]	8.2[5]	5	0	Lebanon
1,896	51.1	204.3	201.3	...	1,130	—	—	11	7	9.4	2.3	0	0	Lesotho
...	...	...	...	...	1,570	5.8	2.4	40	17	14.2	3.8	10	0	Liberia
852	1.3	3.6	...	...		71.5	16.6	3,063	799	40.0[2]	11.1	625	30	Libya
...	...	...	...	...	660	—	[23]	—	—	—	—	...	...	Liechtenstein
4,463	7.0	66.3	695	95.8	730	0.8	2.2	73	200	2.2[8]	0.8	10	0	Luxembourg
823	...	...	...	...		—	[3]	—	—	—	—	...	...	Macau
...	...	...	...	...	2,900	21.0	1.9	44	4	8.0[8]	2.4	30	0	Madagascar
971	3.1	129.3	22.0	0.3	1,670	5.3	0.6	18	3	5.1	1.4	0	0	Malawi
606	...	...	...	...	760	113.0	6.7	937	58	9.7	3.2	60	0	Malaysia
3,747	2.2	3.9	...	...	35,710	—	—	...	...	...	...	...	...	Maldives
33	—	1.1	3.9	—	160	7.3	0.9	47	6	7.9[5]	2.5	40	0	Mali
1,861	3.3	4.9	7.9	204.2	230	1.2	3.5	26	70	3.7	1.5	0	0	Malta
...	...	...	...	...		—	[3]	—	—	—	—	...	...	Martinique
...	...	...	...	...	710	11.0	5.8	37	20	25.0[8]	4.2	0	0	Mauritania
2,544	2.6	14.7	66.5	...	240	—	—	3	3	0.8	0.2	0	0	Mauritius
...	...	...	...	...		—	[3]	—	—	—	—	...	...	Mayotte
110	7.4	3.5	...	...		138.0	1.7	726	9	2.3	0.5	240	0	Mexico
3,180	...	57.6	618.7	100.7		—	—	...	...	...	...	...	...	Monaco
...	...	...	...	...	120	24.5	12.0					0	0	Mongolia
5,626[15]	...	...	...	...	110	—	[3]	—	—	—	—	...	...	Montserrat
769	1.5	170.5	...	...	840	203.5	8.6	1,114	46	15.0[8]	7.1	130	0	Morocco
...	...	...	...	...		36.7	2.5	103	7	34.6	8.4	120	0	Mozambique
404	5.0	39.7	...	—	650	186.0	4.7	281	7	...	3.0	10	0	Myanmar (Burma)
...	...	...	...	...	110	—	—	...	...	...	...	...	...	Nauru
11	1.7	0.4	0.6	...	1,000	35.0	1.9	33	2	5.0	1.2	0	0	Nepal
7,444	1.2	117.9	2,776.0	164.4	510	106.1	7.2	6,543	447	5.5	3.1	550	180	Netherlands, The
4,684[25]	...	...	...	...	330	—	[3]	—	—	—	—	...	...	Netherlands Antilles
...	...	...	...	...		—	[3]	—	—	—	—	...	...	New Caledonia
13,247	4.1	136.9	2,477.6	1,026.4	630	12.8	3.8	755	228	5.0	2.2	30	0	New Zealand
...	...	...	...	...	90[4]	77.0	21.3	5,225	1,597[8]	26.2	17.2	500	0	Nicaragua
32	0.2	2.5	1.0	0.1	2,350[26]	3.3	0.5	178	3[8]	5.7[8]	0.7[8]	10	10	Niger
312	...	...	...	...	1,140	94.5	0.8	180	2	2.7	0.8	60	0	Nigeria
...	...	...	...	...	270	—	[3]	—	—	—	—	...	...	Niue
...	...	...	...	...	750	—	[3]	—	—	—	—	...	...	Norfolk Island
3,950	0.9	27.4	116.7	499.3	660	35.8	8.5	2,775	664	7.4	3.4	200	5	Norway
162	...	...	...	...	430	25.5	18.6	1,516	1,235	43.4	23.3	30	0	Oman
2,273	...	...	...	...	400	—	[28]	—	—	—	—	...	...	Pacific Is., Trust Territory of the
						—	[28]	—	—	—	—	...	...	Marshall Islands
...	...	...	...	...										Micronesia, Fed. States of

Social protection (continued)

Programs available, 1987 columns: old-age invalidity, death / sickness and maternity[a] / work injury / unemployment / family allowances. Finances columns under receipts and expenditures are '000,000 natl. cur. with percentage breakdowns.

country	old-age invalidity, death	sickness and maternity[a]	work injury	unemployment	family allowances	expenditures, 1986 (% of total central govt.)	year	receipts total	insured persons (%)	employers (%)	government (%)	other (%)	expenditures total	benefits (%)	administration (%)	other (%)
Northern Mariana Islands	•	...	...	...	...	...	...	...	...	...	...	...	...	...	...	...
Palau	•	...	...	...	...	0.2	1983	2,587.2	...	62.8	33.1	4.1	2,249.7	97.8	1.7	0.5
Pakistan	•	•	•	...	...	9.9	1983	455.8	27.3	43.3	3.2	26.2	339.9	86.0	7.8	6.2
Panama	•	•	•	...	...	0.1	1983	45.0	40.5	32.1	8.0	19.4	9.4	82.3	9.7	8.0
Papua New Guinea	•	...	...	...	...											
Paraguay	•	•	•	...	...	29.4	1986	30,021.0					24,280.0			
Peru	•	•	•	...	...	0.2[5]	1983	567.3	—88.4—		—	11.6	605.2	88.5	11.5	—
Philippines	•	•	•	...	...	1.0	1983	6,762.8	26.0	36.1	—	37.9	2,850.3	83.6	14.0	2.4
Pitcairn Island	...	...	...	...	•	...										
Poland	•	•	•	•	•	...	1980	325,454.0	2.1	52.2	44.2	1.5	304,600.0	98.8	0.5	0.7
Portugal	•	•	•	•	•	24.3[5,7]	1983	228,867.6	27.9	61.6	10.1	0.4	231,782.7	94.7	5.3	—
Puerto Rico	•	•	•	•	...		1980	...	...	...	...	...	1,041.3	100.0	—	—
Qatar	...	...	...	...	...	...										
Réunion	•	•	•	...	•	...										
Romania	•	•	•	...	•	21.8[8]	1983	72,064.9	—	54.0	46.0	...	63,927.5	100.0	—	—
Rwanda	•	...	•	...	•	2.9[7,20]	1977	1,440.5	26.9	44.8	—	28.3	384.9	58.3	41.7	...
St. Helena and Ascension	•	...	...	...	•								3.0			
St. Kitts and Nevis	•	•	•	...	...	9.0[7,8]	1985	11.1	...	...	...	...	3.0	...	...	...
St. Lucia	•	•	•	...	...	...	1983	6.9	43.5	43.5	...	13.0	2.2	45.5	54.5	—
St. Pierre and Miquelon	...	...	...	...	...	...										
St. Vincent and the Grenadines	•	•	•	...	•	2.1[7]	1987	—	...	...	...	...	—	...	...	...
San Marino	•	•	•	•	•	...	1983	51,673.0	12.0	48.7	36.1	3.2	46,179.0	95.7	3.7	0.6
São Tomé and Príncipe	•	•	•	...	•	...	1983	82.9	40.0	59.7	—	0.3	19.7	100.0	—	—
Saudi Arabia	•	...	•	...	...	2.6[2,7]	1983	7,914.0	—	93.2	—	6.8	6,085.0	79.0	19.4	1.6
Senegal	•	•	•	...	•	5.3[11]	1983	69.1	30.1	60.2	—	9.7	42.7	69.6	4.9	25.5
Seychelles	•	...	•	...	...	1.7[2]	1983	10.5	—26.7—		73.3	—	10.0	100.0	...	...
Sierra Leone	•	...	•	...	...	1.5	1977	...	...	...	...	...	...	...	...	...
Singapore	•	...	•	...	...	0.9[7]	1983	4,935.1	38.7	42.7	0.1	18.6	2,226.3	59.7	0.9	39.4
Solomon Islands	•	...	•	...	...	1.7[7,27]	1983	7.5	30.3	45.5	—	24.2	1.5	78.2	21.8	—
Somalia	•	...	•	...	...		1978	—	...	...	...	...	...	...	...	...
South Africa	•	•	•	•	•	...	1985	387.0	—	100.0	—	—	...	...	...	...
Bophuthatswana	...	...	...	...	...	...	1984	...	...	...	...	...	...	...	...	...
Ciskei	...	...	...	...	...	...							21.9	...	...	...
Transkei	...	...	...	...	...	...										
Venda	...	...	...	...	...	...										
South West Africa/Namibia	•	...	•	...	•											
Spain	•	•	•	•	•	38.3[10]	1983	4,021,128.7	16.1	59.1	22.9	2.0	4,044,425.8	96.0	2.6	1.4
Sri Lanka	•	•	•	...	...	9.2[6]	1983	4,800.0	19.1	20.4	37.8	22.7	2,695.3	97.9	1.8	0.3
Sudan, The	•	...	•	...	...	2.2[20]	1983	33.2	16.8	37.4	—	45.8	7.5	35.8	64.2	—
Suriname	•	...	...	...	...	6.0	1983	125.8	35.8	26.5	36.6	1.1	106.3	98.1	1.9	—
Swaziland	•	...	•	...	...		1983	11.1	29.5	40.8	—	29.7	4.6	52.6	24.6	22.8
Sweden	•	•	•	•	•	41.5	1983	252,244.1	1.0	43.8	46.0	9.2	234,574.4	97.8	2.2	—
Switzerland	•	•	•	•	•	49.9[2]	1983	33,854.7	41.4	25.8	23.9	8.9	29,831.6	93.3	2.9	3.8
Syria	•	...	•	...	...	4.1	1986	—	...	...	...	...	1,538.0	...	...	...
Taiwan	•	•	•	...	...	18.2[2,7]										
Tanzania	•	•	•	...	...	0.5[8]	1983	394.7	32.2	32.2	—	35.6	201.3	32.1	22.2	45.7
Thailand	•	•	•	...	...	3.2	1983	1,832.5	—	93.1	0.7	6.2	1,609.4	99.2	0.8	—
Togo	•	•	•	...	•	6.5	1983	7,167.0	9.7	73.5	—	16.8	3,315.0	69.7	26.3	4.0
Tokelau	...	...	...	...	...	...										
Tonga	...	...	...	...	...	...										
Trinidad and Tobago	•	•	•	...	•	5.3[12]	1983	680.5	12.6	27.3	47.1	13.0	456.9	91.3	8.7	—
Tunisia	•	•	•	...	•	6.2[2]	1984	214.7	41.9	41.3	...	...	206.8	90.0[11]	6.1[11]	3.9[11]
Turkey	•	•	•	•	...	0.4	1983	556,419.0	32.1	41.6	7.6	18.7	432,858.0	96.1	3.4	0.5
Turks and Caicos Islands	...	...	...	...	...	...							0.1	67.6	32.4	—
Tuvalu	...	...	...	...	...	...	1981	...	...	...	...	...	...	...	...	...
Uganda	•	...	•	...	...	2.1	1983	171.0	24.3	24.3	—	51.4	56.2	5.7	94.3	—
U.S.S.R.	•	•	•	...	•		1983	75,789.0	—	—	97.2	2.8	75,789.0	100.0	—	—
United Arab Emirates	...	...	...	...	...	3.8[2,7]	1981	...	...	...	...	...	...	...	...	...
United Kingdom	•	•	•	•	•	29.8[7]	1983	58,456.0	17.9	23.9	55.6	2.6	56,523.0	95.3	2.9	1.8
United States	•	•	•	•	...	23.2	1983	517,050.0	22.5	34.1	34.7	8.7	454,283.0	95.3	3.1	1.6
Uruguay	•	•	•	•	•	45.0	1983	23,129.0	24.7	24.6	47.9	2.8	20,424.0	92.5	5.5	2.0
Vanuatu	...	...	...	...	...	0.9	1986	—	...	...	...	...	36.9	...	...	...
Venezuela	•	•	•	...	•	6.9	1983	5,109.0	—67.9—		13.7	18.4	4,449.0	82.4	17.6	...
Vietnam	•	•	•	...	...	...										
Virgin Islands (U.S.)	•	...	...	...	...	...										
Wallis and Futuna	...	...	...	...	...	...										
West Bank	...	...	...	...	...	...										
Western Sahara	...	...	...	...	...	...							—	...	...	...
Western Samoa	•	...	•	...	...	...	1984	—	...	...	...	...	—	...	...	...
Yemen (Aden)	...	...	...	...	...	—	1987	—	...	...	...	...	—	...	...	...
Yemen (Şan'ā')	...	...	...	...	...											
Yugoslavia	•	•	•	•	•	9.0	1983	488,529.9	63.2	23.2	6.9	6.7	486,099.8	86.8	2.8	10.4
Zaire	•	•	•	...	•	—	1983	145.9	...	...	...	...	104.6	...	...	...
Zambia	•	...	•	...	...	1.3[8]	1983	94.3	38.5	28.5	—	33.0	44.0	70.3	29.7	—
Zimbabwe	•	...	•	...	...	2.9	1983	167.0	25.9	7.6	64.2	2.3	112.2	93.7	6.2	0.1

Column groups: **crime and law enforcement (latest)** — offenses reported to the police per 100,000 population (total; personal: murder, assault; property: burglary, automobile theft). **population per police officer[b]**. **military protection** — manpower, 1988[c] (total '000, per 1,000 population); expenditure, 1987 (total '000,000, per capita[e], % of central government expenditure, % of GDP or GNP); arms trade, 1987 ('000,000 U.S.$) (imports, exports).

total	murder	assault	burglary	automobile theft	population per police officer[b]	manpower total ('000)	manpower per 1,000 pop.	expenditure total '000,000	per capita[e]	% of central govt. exp.	% of GDP or GNP	imports	exports	country
...	...	...	323	...	...	—	[3]	—	—	—	—	...	...	Northern Mariana Islands
221	5.6	0.1	9.1	4.1	720	...	...	...	...	...	...	...	...	Palau
711	4.7	2.6	...	92.8	180	480.6	4.4	2,226	21	25.4	6.5	150	5	Pakistan
700	8.5	37.3	107.7	9.1	720	7.3	3.1	105	46	3.7[8]	2.0	5	0	Panama
...	...	...	...	...	...	3.2	0.9	399	12[9]	4.1	1.5	0	0	Papua New Guinea
244	1.2	10.5	130.6	8.0	310	16.0	4.0	47	11	11.2	1.0	0	0	Paraguay
309	38.7	46.4	...	...	730	118.0	5.6	2,198	106	24.8	4.9	430	0	Peru
...	...	...	...	...	1,160	147.5	2.5	458	7	7.8	1.3	40	0	Philippines
...	...	...	...	...	...	—	[3]	—	...	...	...	...	...	Pitcairn Island
1,292	...	...	...	...	370	406.0	10.7	17,950	476	31.7	6.9	725	800	Poland
757	450	9.6	29.2	52.5	660	73.9	7.1	1,131	110	9.7	3.2	20	50	Portugal
5,484	...	...	...	...	380	...	[3]	...	...	...	...	...	...	Puerto Rico
1,434	2.4	3.9	1.5	30.3	220	7.0	16.7	608[19]	2,638[19]	20.1	9.3	80	0	Qatar
...	...	...	...	...	...	—	[3]	...	...	...	...	...	...	Réunion
...	...	...	...	...	...	179.5	7.8	7,609	332	14.1	5.2	110	190	Romania
359	9.7	137.8	1.4	0.2	4,650	5.2	0.8	42	6	12.0	2.0	0	0	Rwanda
...	...	...	...	5,150	170	—	[3]	—	...	...	...	...	...	St. Helena and Ascension
4,289	10.7	575.7	778.6	...	300	—	—	...	...	...	...	...	...	St. Kitts and Nevis
...	...	...	...	...	430	—	...	...	...	...	...	...	...	St. Lucia
...	...	...	...	...	...	—	[3]	...	...	...	...	...	...	St. Pierre and Miquelon
...	...	...	...	...	250	—	—	...	...	...	...	...	...	St. Vincent and the Grenadines
...	...	...	...	...	400	—	—	...	...	...	...	...	...	San Marino
204	1.0	0.2	...	11.6	280	...	...	1[19]	7[19]	2.5[19]	1.6[19]	5	5	São Tomé and Príncipe
264	1.2	27.7	14.8	0.6	730	72.3	5.6	10,490	710	30.0	12.8	3,800	20	Saudi Arabia
...	...	...	...	...	...	9.7[29]	1.4[29]	97	14	6.7	2.2	5	5	Senegal
5,735	6.0	729.3	718.8	...	120	1.3	19.4	8[2]	124[2]	7.4[2]	5.6[2]	...	...	Seychelles
...	...	...	...	...	600	3.1	0.8	5[9]	1[9]	5.0[8]	0.5[9]	0	0	Sierra Leone
1,552	2.6	4.4	116.0	19.4	230	55.5	21.0	1,008[9]	389[9]	15.1[9]	5.5[9]	180	10	Singapore
144	1.5	8.0	31.2	...	620	—	—	...	...	...	...	...	...	Solomon Islands
...	...	...	...	...	540	65.0	10.3	43[9]	6[9]	30.0[9]	3.2[9]	20	20	Somalia
...	...	...	...	...	870	103.5	2.8	3,400	99	14.7	4.4	0	0	South Africa
...	...	...	...	...	...	...	...	...	...	...	...	...	...	Bophuthatswana
...	...	...	...	...	...	...	...	...	...	...	...	...	...	Ciskei
...	...	...	...	...	...	...	...	...	...	...	...	...	...	Transkei
...	...	...	...	...	...	...	...	...	...	...	...	...	...	Venda
3,347	2.3	26.8	1,220.1	349.6	580	—	[3]	...	...	...	...	...	...	South West Africa/Namibia
66.5	...	...	...	...	860	309.5	7.9	6,906	177	6.8	2.4	875	100	Spain
649	5.0	35.2	107.7	6.9	740	22.0	1.3	204	12	9.4	3.1	40	40	Sri Lanka
...	...	...	...	...	...	57.7	2.2	231	10	12.9[8]	2.7	50	0	Sudan, The
...	...	...	...	...	...	3.0	7.1	30[9]	74[9]	4.9[9]	2.6[9]	5	0	Suriname
...	...	...	...	...	610	—	...	8[2]	11	5.1	1.3	0	0	Swaziland
13,069	6.4	24.8	1,820.3	661.3	330	67.0	8.0	4,434	529	6.7	2.9	60	160	Sweden
5,093	2.1	50.0	1,031.3	1,626.4[30]	640	3.5	0.5	3,726	567	10.8	2.1	850	180	Switzerland
52	2.1	0.1	19.7	3.4	1,970	404.0	35.6	3,364	302	32.0	11.9	1,900	0	Syria
481	...	...	...	...	720	405.5	20.4	4,701	238	41.5	4.6	600	0	Taiwan
79	8.8	...	16.8	0.7	1,330	40.1	1.7	85[8]	4[8]	14.0[8]	3.3[8]	110	0	Tanzania
314	12.4	18.5	9.5	2.4	530	256.0	4.8	1,657	31	18.3	3.7	350	0	Thailand
11	...	...	...	...	1,970	5.9	1.7	40	12	13.3	3.3	0	0	Togo
...	...	...	...	...	210	—	[3]	—	...	...	...	...	...	Tokelau
1,278	...	...	...	...	330	—	[31]	—	...	...	...	...	...	Tonga
4,187	8.1	28.0	714.0	...	280	2.8	2.2	204[2]	175[2]	6.0[2]	2.7[2]	0	0	Trinidad and Tobago
1,240	2.1	134.0	143.6	11.1	340	38.0	4.8	289	38	9.0	3.1	50	0	Tunisia
179	1.4	16.3	...	6.6	1,570	635.3	11.7	2,890	55	19.4	4.4	925	10	Turkey
5,066	...	317.6	2,177.7	...	130	—	[3]	—	—	...	...	...	...	Turks and Caicos Islands
...	...	...	...	...	290	—	—	—	...	...	...	...	...	Tuvalu
...	...	...	...	...	1,090	35.0	2.2	51[8]	3[8]	15.6	1.4	40	0	Uganda
1,377	2.7	11.3	...	...	1,050[32]	5,096.0	17.8	303,000	1,067	45.9	12.3	625	21,200	U.S.S.R.
...	...	...	...	...	140	43.0	24.2	1,580[9]	944[9]	36.9[9]	7.4[9]	260	0	United Arab Emirates
7,603	1.6	244.7	1,875.8	823.4	420	316.7	5.6	31,580	556	12.5	4.7	380	2,100	United Kingdom
5,480	8.6	346.1	1,344.6	507.8	345	2,163.2	8.8	296,200	1,215	28.0	6.5	625	12,600	United States
...	...	...	...	...	170	24.4	8.2	165[9]	55[9]	10.1[9]	2.5[9]	0	0	Uruguay
...	...	...	...	...	450	—	—	—	...	...	...	...	...	Vanuatu
988	8.4	134.9	...	125.3	320	69.0	3.7	1,379	75	10.7	3.6	90	0	Venezuela
...	...	...	...	...	...	1,252.0	19.6	2,400[9]	39[9]	40.7[9]	19.4[9]	1,900	5	Vietnam
3,798	...	...	...	...	240	—	[3]	...	...	...	...	...	...	Virgin Islands (U.S.)
2,226	...	...	...	...	...	—	—	—	—	—	—	...	...	Wallis and Futuna
...	...	...	...	...	...	—	[3]	—	...	...	...	...	...	West Bank
...	...	...	...	...	...	—	[3]	—	...	...	...	...	...	Western Sahara
...	...	...	...	...	...	—	[31]	—	...	...	...	...	...	Western Samoa
...	...	...	...	...	1,440	27.5	11.7	196[9]	88[9]	21.0[5]	22.0	300	0	Yemen (Aden)
1,135	5.4	35.5	...	...	500	36.6	4.3	324	50	21.5	7.2	390	0	Yemen (Şan'ā')
...	...	...	...	...	140	188.0	8.0	1,317	56	27.1	2.2	210	160	Yugoslavia
...	...	...	...	...	910	51.0	1.6	155[9]	5[9]	18.2[9]	3.0[9]	5	0	Zaire
2,088	8.3	17.5	406.8	18.6	540	16.2	2.2	167[2]	26[2]	20.9[2]	6.6[2]	0	0	Zambia
3,715	12.1	169.1	353.2	30.4	750	47.0	5.3	283	30	11.6	5.0	80	0	Zimbabwe

[1] Rural areas only. [2] 1984. [3] Political dependency; defense is the responsibility of the administering country. [4] Includes civilian militia. [5] 1983. [6] Netherlands Antilles includes Aruba. [7] Includes welfare. [8] 1985. [9] 1986. [10] 1979. [11] 1977. [12] 1981. [13] 1976. [14] Local officers only. [15] Offenses disposed of in court. [16] Military defense is the responsibility of France. [17] 1971. [18] Republic of Cyprus only. [19] 1980. [20] 1982. [21] Coverage is through tax system. [22] 1975. [23] Military defense is the responsibility of Switzerland. [24] 1974. [25] Curaçao only. [26] Includes paramilitary forces. [27] 1978. [28] Military defense is the responsibility of the United States. [29] Includes The Gambia. [30] Includes bicycles and motorcycles. [31] Military defense is the responsibility of New Zealand. [32] MVD (internal security) only.

Education

This table presents international data on education analyzed to provide maximum comparability among the different educational systems in use among the nations of the world. The principal data are, naturally, numbers of schools, teachers, and students, arranged by four principal levels of education—the first, or primary; general second level (secondary); vocational second level; and third level (higher). Whenever possible, data referring to preprimary education programs have been excluded from this compilation. The ratio of students to teachers is calculated for each level. These data are supplemented at each level by a figure for enrollment ratio, an indicator of each country's achieved capability to educate the total number of children potentially educable in the age group usually represented by that level. At the first and second levels this is given as a net enrollment ratio and at the third level as a gross enrollment ratio. Two additional comparative measures are given at the third level: students per 100,000 population and proportion (percent) of adults age 25 and over who have achieved some level of higher or postsecondary education. Data in this last group are confined as far as possible to those who have completed their educations and are no longer in school. No enrollment ratio is provided for vocational training at the second level because of the great variation worldwide in the academic level at which vocational training takes place, in the need of countries to encourage or direct students into vocational programs (to support national development), and, most particularly, in the age range of students who normally constitute a national vocational system (some will be as young as 14, having just completed a primary cycle; others will be much older).

At each level of education, differences in national statistical practice, in national educational structure, public-private institutional mix, training and deployment of teachers, and timing of cycles of enrollment or completion of particular grades or standards all contribute to the problems of comparability among national educational systems.

Reporting the number of schools in a country is not simply a matter of counting permanent red-brick buildings with classrooms in them. Often the resources of a less developed country are such that temporary or outdoor facilities are all that can be afforded, while in a developed but sparsely settled country students might have to travel 80 km (50 mi) a day to find a classroom with 20 students of the same age, leading to the institution of measures such as traveling teachers, radio or televisual instruction at home under the supervision of parents, or similar systems. According to UNESCO definitions, therefore, a "school" is defined only as "a body of students . . . organized to receive instruction."

Such difficulties also limit the comparability of statistics on numbers of teachers, with the further complications that many at any level must work part-time, or that the institutions in which they work may perform a mixture of functions that do not break down into the tidy categories required by a table of this sort. In certain countries teacher training is confined to higher education, in others as a vocational form of secondary training, and so on. For purposes of this table, teacher training at the secondary level has been treated as vocational education. At the higher level, teacher training is classified as one more specialization in higher education itself.

Education

country	year	first level (primary)					general second level (secondary)					vocational second level[a]	
		schools	teachers[c]	students[d]	student/teacher ratio	net enroll-ment ratio	schools	teachers[c]	students[d]	student/teacher ratio	net enroll-ment ratio	schools	teachers[c]
Afghanistan	1989	553	16,756	586,014	35.0	15[1]	819	5,715	271,000	47.4	...	33	556
Albania	1987	1,668	27,297	543,000	19.9	...	446	8,442	124,000	14.7	...	406	6,640
Algeria	1988	11,843	139,875	3,801,651	27.2	88[2]	2,479	110,738	2,082,646	18.8	45[1]	71[3]	2,528[4]
American Samoa	1989	122[5]	454[1]	10,209[5]	17.0[1]	...	7	203[1]	3,097	16.5[1]	...	1	4[6]
Andorra	1987	13	214[2]	5,344	24.8[2]	...	10	53[2]	2,253	20.5[2]	...	5	37[2]
Angola	1984	6,308[9]	32,004[9]	870,410	...	66[3]	...	3,870[3]	151,759	...	...	...	410[3]
Anguilla	1986	6	66	1,483	22.5	...	1	39	634	16.3	...	...	...
Antigua and Barbuda	1988	43	446	9,097	20.4	...	15	319	4,413	13.8	...	2[4]	56[4]
Argentina	1986	20,865	238,818	4,778,264	20.0	96[11]	1,987[7,12]	95,869[12]	761,601[12]	7.9[12]	42[11]	3,117[7,12]	142,342[12]
Aruba	1988	30	323	6,303	19.5	...	10	166	2,976	17.9	...	15	225
Australia	1987	8,442[13]	108,253	1,687,390	15.6	97[2]	1,637	123,489	1,295,337	10.5	87[2]	234[2]	52,587[2]
Austria	1988	3,394	28,652	350,907	12.2	86[7]	2,048	57,233	462,975	8.1	68[14]	1,392[4]	22,662[4]
Bahamas, The	1987	183	1,677	36,003	21.5	...	39	1,285	23,280	18.1	...	9	707
Bahrain	1988	131	3,673	60,519	16.5	94[2]	35	1,563	33,148	21.2	67[2]	157[2]	8,952
Bangladesh	1987	43,992	188,369	11,263,000	59.8	53	8,983	100,865	2,962,000	29.4	17[1]		
Barbados	1985	130	1,464	30,792	21.0	99[3]	36	1,449	28,815	19.9	89[7]	3	154
Belgium	1987	4,294	45,261[7]	727,647	...	95[2]	2,227[1]	56,719[9]	441,879	...	87[2]	209[9]	6,864[9]
Belize	1988	226	1,578	39,779	25.2	...	24[4]	297	7,326	24.7	...	5[4,16]	...
Benin	1985	2,715	13,452	444,163	33.1	51	133[3]	2,409[7]	112,267[7]	46.6[7]	13[2]	30[3]	609[9]
Bermuda	1988	18	252	5,334	21.2	...	18[17]	293[17]	3,949[17]	13.5[17]	...	18	18
Bhutan	1987	148	1,398	36,628	28.3	8[19]	30	640	15,299	23.9	...	8	18
Bolivia	1987	9,758	51,376	888,182	17.3	79[2]	724	8,258	211,519	25.6	26[2]	47	1,805
Botswana	1986	537	7,324	235,941	32.2	89	73	1,619	35,966	22.2	24	22	317
Brazil	1988	201,541	1,055,170[4]	26,821,134	24.9[4]	82[1]	10,244	206,111[2]	3,339,090	14.6[2]	15[1]	—	—
British Virgin Islands	1988	27	108[8]	1,921[8]	17.8[8]	...	3	84	1,113	13.3	...	8	414[16]
Brunei	1986	146	2,225	36,983	16.6	...	29	1,636	18,714	11.4	...	8	414[16]
Bulgaria	1988	2,935	62,054	1,091,089	17.0	97[7]	554	9,837	164,157	16.7	78[7]	537	19,035
Burkina Faso	1986	1,758	6,091	351,807	57.8	27[1]	107	1,519	48,875	32.2	41	18	421
Burundi	1986	1,171	7,256	452,424	62.3	42	62	857	16,789	19.6	3	47	1,051
Cameroon	1987	5,920	35,431	1,723,024	48.6	75[19]	388	9,289	288,515	31.1	15[6]	220	4,449
Canada	1988	15,512[21]	273,190[21]	4,959,000[21]	18.1[21]	97[2]	[21]	[21]	[21]	[21]	92[2]	...	...
Cape Verde	1987	347	1,464	49,703	34.0	88[2]	16	321	10,304	32.1	9[2]	3	53
Cayman Islands	1989	16	303[21]	2,150	14.6[21]	...	6	[21]	2,262	[21]	...	1	10
Central African Republic	1985	986	4,502	294,312	65.4	51[2]	41	914	45,166	49.4	...	4	127
Chad	1988	1.231	4,494	288,479	64.2	25[22]	...	590[14]	43,053	...	...	...	...
Chile	1988	8,767	62,746[3]	2,004,710[1]	...	92[7]	1,694	...	601,760	...	46[9]	1,262	...
China	1987	984,181	6,085,000	146,437,000	24.1	95[2]	92,857	2,870,000	49,481,000	17.2	...	12,294	395,000
Christmas Island	1989	1[21]	15	202	13.5	...	[21]	7	51	7.3	...	—	—
Cocos (Keeling) Islands	1986	2	8	105	13.1	...	1	5	30	6.0	...	23	23
Colombia	1987	36,109	130,375	3,903,019	29.9	73[2]	5,884[23]	95,077[23]	1,973,025[23]	20.8[23]	...	4[24]	41[4]
Comoros	1986	257	1,901	66,084	34.8	59	32[24]	432[24]	20,541	31.3[24]	...	4[24]	41[4]
Congo	1985	1,522	7,612	458,338	60.2	...	247	5,188	199,073	38.4	...	19	1,073
Cook Islands	1986	30	165	3,183	19.3	...	8	146	2,156	14.8	...	...	...
Costa Rica	1988	3,207	11,113	409,621	36.9	88[2]	169	6,052	116,488	19.2	36[2]	76	2,260
Côte d'Ivoire	1984	5,976	28,561	1,179,456	41.3	...	218[6]	4,569[4]	245,043	...	...	38[6]	1,947[24]
Cuba	1988	9,617	59,819	936,914	15.7	95[2]	1,321	65,796	775,345	11.8	69[2]	791	35,912
Cyprus[25]	1988	379	2,562	56,530	22.1	88[2]	95	2,886	38,785	13.4	80[2]	10	444
Czechoslovakia	1987	6,274	97,385	2,088,750	21.4	...	343	9,723	134,103	13.8	...	561	17,044
Denmark	1988	2,523	34,744[2]	380,049	11.6[2]	...	3,218	38,821[2]	319,034	8.7[2]	83[1]	340	23
Djibouti	1987	59	559	27,136	48.5	...	21[23]	302[23]	8,003[23]	26.5[23]	...	23	23
Dominica	1988	66	646	16,105	24.9	...	9	171	3,264	19.1	...	...	27[2]
Dominican Republic	1987	6,299[2]	31,275	1,296,366	41.5	79	...	9,963	426,962	42.9	...	...	...
Ecuador	1987	16,146	59,820	1,871,287	31.3	87[19]	2,027[23]	49,749[23]	744,373[23]	15.0[23]	28[11]	519[9]	48,605[9]
Egypt	1986	13,223	194,929	6,002,850	30.8	...	20,106	128,616	2,704,371	21.0	...	179[9]	667[9]
El Salvador	1985	2,883	24,295	1,049,100[2]	38.7	62[7]	285	3,880	90,900[2]	23.3	14[7]	23	23

The number of students may conceal great variation in what each country defines as a particular educational "level." Many countries do, indeed, have a primary system comprised of grades 1 through 6 (or 1 through 8) that passes students on to some kind of postprimary education. But the age of intake, the ability of parents to send their children or to permit them to finish that level, or the need to withdraw the children seasonally for agricultural work all make even a simple enrollment figure difficult to assess in isolation. All of these difficulties are compounded when a country has instruction in more than one language, or when its educational establishment is so small that higher, sometimes even secondary, education cannot take place within the country. Enrollment figures in this table may, therefore, include students enrolled outside the country.

Student-teacher ratio, however, usually provides a good measure of the ratio of trained educators to the enrolled educable. In general, at each level of education both students and teachers have been counted on the basis of full-time enrollment or employment, or full-time equivalent when country statistics permit. At the primary and secondary levels, net enrollment ratio is the ratio of the number of children within the usual age group for a particular level who are actually enrolled to the total number of children in that age group ($\times$ 100). This ratio is usually less than (occasionally, equal to) 100 and is the most accurate measure of the completeness of enrollment at that particular level. It is not always, however, the best indication of utilization of teaching staff and facilities. Utilization, provided here for higher education only, is best seen in a gross enrollment ratio, which compares total enrollment (of all ages) to the population within the normal age limits for that level. For a country with substantial adult literacy or general educational programs, the difference may be striking: typically, for a less developed country with a good net enrollment ratio of 90 to 95, the gross enrollment ratio may be 20, 25, even 30% higher, indicating the heavy use made by the country of facilities and teachers at that level.

Literacy data provided here have been compiled as far as possible from data for the population age 15 and over for the best comparability internationally. Standards as to what constitutes literacy may also differ markedly; sometimes completion of a certain number of years of school is taken to constitute literacy; elsewhere it may mean only the ability to read or write at a minimal level testable by a census taker; in other countries studies have been undertaken to distinguish among degrees of functional literacy.

Finally, the data provided for public expenditure on education are complete in that they include all levels of public expenditure (national, state, local) but are incomplete for certain countries in that they do not include data for private expenditure; in some countries this fraction of the educational establishment may be of significant size. Occasionally data for external aid to education may be included in addition to domestic expenditure.

a. Usually includes teacher training at the second level.
b. Latest.
c. Full-time.
d. Full-time; may include students registered in foreign schools.

| students[d] | student/ teacher ratio | third level (higher) | | | | | | percent of population age 25 and over with post-secondary education[b] | literacy[b] | | | | public expenditure on education (percent of GNP)[b] | country |
		institutions	teachers[c]	students[d]	student/ teacher ratio	gross enroll-ment ratio	students per 100,000 popula-tion[b]		over age	total (%)	male (%)	female (%)		
8,537	15.4	5	198	1,419	7.5	1.4[2]	129	3.0	15	23.7	38.9	7.8	1.8	Afghanistan
82,000	12.3	8	1,625	19,000	11.7	7.2[2]	719	...	15	100.0	...	...	...	Albania
98,000[4]	38.8[4]	15[3]	17,581	160,195	12.3	7.4[2]	690	0.3	15	44.7	57.3	31.7	6.1	Algeria
157	11.2[6]	2	48[7]	909[8]	35.7[7]	...	...	12.6	15	95.9	95.6	96.3	8.2	American Samoa
1,248	18.7[2]	...	...	...	...	...	...	...	15	100.0	...	...	...	Andorra
7,147	...	1[9]	316[9]	4,493	...	0.6	53	...	15	28.0	36.2	19.3	5.2	Angola
...	...	...	...	...	...	...	...	6.8[10]	15	94.7	94.6	94.8	...	Anguilla
631[4]	11.3[4]	—	...	...	...	...	...	...	15	90.0	...	...	2.7	Antigua and Barbuda
1,167,969[12]	8.2[12]	1,251[7]	69,985	902,882	12.9	38.7	2,911	6.1	15	94.9	95.5	94.4	1.8	Argentina
2,807	12.5	1	20	180	9.0	...	...	...	15	95.0	...	...	...	Aruba
886,679	16.3[2]	95	26,385	393,734	14.9	28.9[2]	2,453	21.5	15	99.5	...	...	5.6	Australia
364,264[4]	16.1[4]	18	10,517	183,795	17.5	27.9[2]	2,398	3.3	15	100.0	100.0	100.0	6.0	Austria
...	...	1	127	4,932	38.8	...	...	...	15	89.0	...	...	5.1	Bahamas, The
7,478	10.6	4	539	5,529	10.3	10.1[1]	967	3.8	15	75.1	82.0	63.5	5.0	Bahrain
277,000	30.9	854	22,309	709,055	31.8	4.9[2]	445	1.3	15	33.1	43.3	22.2	2.1	Bangladesh
3,592	23.3	1	108	1,617	15.0	19.4[7]	2,065	3.3	15	98.0[15]	98.3[15]	97.7[15]	6.1	Barbados
371,112	...	17[1]	5,349	103,505	19.4	31.9[2]	2,546	...	...	100.0	...	...	5.5	Belgium
834[4,16]	...	16	...	...[16]	...	...	...	2.3	15	93.0	...	...	...	Belize
6,784[7]	...	1[9]	803[9]	6,818[9]	8.5[9]	2.1[9]	179	0.3	15	27.9	39.8	16.6	5.1	Benin
18	...	1[18]	68[2,18]	561[18]	...	...	...	7.4	15	96.9	96.7	97.0	3.2	Bermuda
18	18	2	145[18]	604[18]	4.2[18]	0.2[7]	17	...	15	18.0	31.0	9.0	...	Bhutan
15,947	8.8	10	3,555	97,153	27.3	19.0[1]	1,648	5.0	15	65.8	65.9	65.8	0.5	Bolivia
3,217	10.1	1	249	1,700	6.8	2.0	175	0.5	15	70.8	72.6	69.5	6.0	Botswana
...	...	855[2]	122,486[2]	1,418,196[2]	11.6[2]	11.3[9]	1,140	5.0	15	79.3	80.4	78.3	3.3	Brazil
—	—	—	—	—	—	—	—	8.5	15	98.3	98.1	98.5	4.7	British Virgin Islands
1,688	4.1	1[20]	33[20]	176[20]	5.3[20]	...	...	9.4	15	80.3	86.5	72.8	2.0	Brunei
238,633	12.5	30	15,941	116,407	7.3	20.3[2]	1,381	5.2	15	95.5	...	...	7.1	Bulgaria
4,808	11.4	1	325	3,869	11.9	0.7[7]	57	...	15	13.2	20.7	6.1	2.5	Burkina Faso
13,280	12.6	8	468	2,783	5.9	0.7[1]	59	...	10	33.8	42.8	25.7	2.7	Burundi
93,857	21.1	5	975	19,586	20.1	2.2[7]	185	0.3	15	55.2	70.2	41.0	2.6	Cameroon
...	...	266	59,300	795,730	13.4	54.6[2]	4,853	37.4	14	95.6	95.6	95.7	7.4	Canada
211	4.0	...	...	—	—	—	—	...	15	49.3	55.3	43.4	2.8	Cape Verde
85	8.5	1	9	156	17.3	...	...	2.9	15	97.5	97.5	97.6	...	Cayman Islands
2,233	17.6	...	105[7]	2,133[7]	20.3[7]	1.2	103	...	15	40.0	53.0	29.0	2.8	Central African Republic
2,559	...	1	141	1,643	11.6	0.4	34	...	15	17.8	35.6	0.5	1.9	Chad
133,941	...	201	15,131[7]	233,148	...	15.9[1]	1,640	7.2	15	94.3	...	...	4.5	Chile
4,550,000	11.5	1,063	385,000	1,959,000	5.1	1.7[2]	184	1.0	15	72.6	83.5	61.2	2.7	China
9	9.0	—	—	—	—	—	—	...	15	80.0	...	...	...	Christmas Island
23	23	...	...	...	...	...	...	...	...	...	...	...	...	Cocos (Keeling) Islands
...	...	235	47,990	457,680	9.5	13.1[2]	1,423	3.3	18	69.1	...	...	2.9	Colombia
334[4]	14.6[4]	—	—	—	—	...	...	...	15	46.3	54.2	39.0	5.2	Comoros
5,477	22.2	1	...	9,385	...	6.9[3]	572	...	15	62.9	71.4	55.4	4.9	Congo
...	...	...	41[6]	360[6]	8.8[6]	...	...	2.1	15	91.8	92.1	91.4	...	Cook Islands
26,576	11.8	8[2]	5,211[12]	50,033[2]	9.6[2]	23.8[2]	2,498	5.8	15	92.6	92.6	92.6	5.2	Costa Rica
21,758	...	1[6]	1,204[3]	19,660	...	2.5	208	...	15	57.3	...	...	6.7	Côte d'Ivoire
367,792	10.2	35	22,492	262,225	11.7	22.5[2]	2,526	5.9	15	96.0	...	...	6.3	Cuba
3,406	7.7	19	359	4,247	11.8	7.0[2]	621	...	15	94.5	...	...	3.7	Cyprus[25]
257,968	15.1	36	19,459	169,011	8.7	15.7[2]	1,088	6.0	15	100.0	100.0	100.0	5.2	Czechoslovakia
181,682	...	96	...	109,504	...	29.3[1]	2,271	...	15	100.0	100.0	100.0	7.7	Denmark
23	23	—	—	161[7]	...	...	...	...	14	11.9	...	...	3.9	Djibouti
259[2]	9.6[2]	2	...	...	...	...	...	1.7	15	94.9	...	...	...	Dominica
24,758	...	...	6,539[2]	123,748[2]	18.9[2]	19.3[1]	1,982	1.9	15	77.3	77.7	76.8	1.6	Dominican Republic
23	23	21	12,647	261,913	20.7	33.1[7]	3,078	7.6	15	69.1	86.8	56.9	3.4	Ecuador
951,986	...	12	33,200[9]	659,945	...	21.2[1]	1,918	3.4	15	44.9	57.6	31.8	5.5	Egypt
9,505	...	34	4,789[2]	74,024[2]	15.5[2]	14.1[2]	1,292	...	15	69.0	73.2	65.3	2.5	El Salvador

Education (continued)

country	year	first level (primary)					general second level (secondary)					vocational second level[a]	
		schools	teachers[c]	students[d]	student/ teacher ratio	net enroll-ment ratio	schools	teachers[c]	students[d]	student/ teacher ratio	net enroll-ment ratio	schools	teachers[c]
Equatorial Guinea	1981	511	647	40,110	62.0	...	14[23]	288[23]	3,013[23]	10.5[23]	...	[23]	[23]
Ethiopia	1986	7,900	50,922	2,448,778	48.1	...	1,209	15,218	655,517	43.1	...	...	390[1]
Faeroe Islands	1988	67[21]	592[21]	5,536	14.4[21]	...	[21]	[21]	2,995	[21]	...	9	...
Falkland Islands	1988	8[4]	21	245	11.7	...	1	12	130	10.8	...	—	—
Fiji	1987	672[2]	4,436	136,567	30.8	100[1]	140[2]	2,646	43,942	16.6	...	44[2]	246
Finland	1986	4,233	25,140	380,509	15.1	...	1,093	22,360	300,748	13.4	...	574[4, 16]	22,869[4, 16]
France	1986	67,504	331,040	6,944,849	21.0	100	11,589[23]	373,605[23]	5,584,233[23]	14.9[23]	86[2]	[23]	177[1]
French Guiana	1983	51	409	9,780	23.9	...	11[1]	470[1]	6,468[2]	...	...	17	362[1]
French Polynesia	1989	270	1,337[1]	43,300	20.5[1]	...	24	804[1]	18,610[23]	16.9[1]	...	29	720
Gabon	1985	940	3,837	178,811	46.6	...	51	1,894	25,815	13.6	...	...	...
Gambia, The	1985	189	2,640	66,257	25.1	68	8	235	4,348	18.5	17	16	502
Gaza Strip	1987	305[21]	4,087[21]	107,809	40.8[21]	...	[21]	[21]	58,993	[21]	...	[21]	[21]
Germany, East	1988	5,683	57,158	945,720	16.5	...	5,727	105,346	1,061,015	10.1	...	4,678	53,792
Germany, West	1987	24,282	302,097	4,221,948	14.0	81[1]	5,312	188,541	2,670,458	14.2	70[1]	7,568	89,829
Ghana	1986	9,180	67,261	1,567,778	23.3	...	5,702	44,578	768,347	17.2	...	137	2,887
Gibraltar	1989	14	92	2,937	31.9	...	2	124	1,694	13.7	...	1	29
Greece	1986	8,657	37,994	887,735	23.4	92[7]	2,654	41,782	704,119	16.8	79[7]	480	8,138
Greenland	1989	90[21]	1,110[21]	7,435	8.1[21]	...	[21]	[21]	1,508	[21]	...	8[4]	110[4]
Grenada	1988	58	761	19,963	26.2	...	18	297	6,437	21.7	...	49	[23]
Guadeloupe	1988	333[5]	1,927[2]	39,991	22.2[2]	...	50	3,015[7, 23]	34,360	...	...	...	...
Guam	1987	31	822	14,471	17.6	...	24	944	15,281	16.2	...	3	117
Guatemala	1987	8,481	31,441	1,097,851	34.9	62[9]	...	16,333[23]	241,053[23]	14.8[23]	14[3]	1	[23]
Guernsey[27]	1989	25	248	4,423	17.8	...	9	297	3,535	11.9	...	31	58
Guinea	1987	2,204	7,493	270,140	36.0	22[2]	225	3,577	76,493	21.4	7[1]	4	758
Guinea-Bissau	1985	668	3,153	81,444	25.8	53[7]	12	650	11,710	18.0	3[9]	...	107
Guyana	1987	425	3,948	112,501	28.5	90[24]	92	2,700	73,418	27.2	...	7	...
Haiti	1986	3,734	23,200	872,500	37.6	44[7]	376	6,978	139,422	20.0	...	36	...
Honduras	1987	7,054	21,476	840,057	39.1	87[7]	438	7,618	142,679	18.7	20[7]	...	...
Hong Kong	1987	714	19,368	531,993	27.5	95[7]	397	18,323	434,145	23.7	64[7]	27	1,174
Hungary	1989	3,526	90,620	1,242,700	13.7	96[2]	186	8,368	127,679	15.3	68[2]	758	22,467
Iceland	1987	187	2,600[9]	25,108	9.6[9]	...	122	...	20,664	...	...	43	...
India	1986	528,079	...	86,465,189	...	...	195,388	...	43,230,690	...	...	5,494[16]	...
Indonesia	1988[28]	144,561	1,107,100	26,649,890	24.1	98[2]	26,367	583,527	8,793,056	15.1	37[2]	3,460	95,777
Iran	1987	53,342	219,330	6,788,323	31.0	96[2]	11,803	125,589[11, 19]	2,046,800	...	...	1,045	[11, 19]
Iraq	1989	7,930	122,089	3,012,028	24.7	87[2]	2,387	42,829	981,409	22.9	43[2]	258	9,323
Ireland	1987	3,450	21,611	576,197	26.7	89[3]	596	14,546	257,959	17.7	79[3]	260	6,572
Isle of Man	1987	33	240[9]	5,063	...	...	7	276[9]	5,107	...	...	1	32[11]
Israel	1988	2,004	45,351	761,385	16.8	92[9]	609	26,378	236,358	9.0	...	378	...
Italy	1988	26,643	215,039	3,370,709	15.7	97[7]	10,032	127,274	2,618,679	20.6	70[7]	7,702	125,054
Jamaica	1987[8]	787	9,419	332,636	35.3	94[9]	131	7,447	226,288	30.4	57[6]	10	501
Japan	1988	24,901	445,000	9,872,000	22.2	100[2]	16,778	569,000	11,430,000	21.0	96[2]	1	...
Jersey	1986	30	294	5,717[30]	19.1	...	10	378	4,482[30]	12.4	...	52[4]	1,152[4]
Jordan	1988	1,884[5]	19,133[5]	605,777[5]	31.7[5]	88[9]	1,681	21,729	357,475	16.5	71[3]	13	278
Kampuchea (Cambodia)	1984	3,629[3]	45,000[4]	1,900,000[4]	42.2[4]	...	207	4,494	145,730	32.4	...	44	1,743
Kenya	1987	13,392	142,807	4,843,432	33.9	86[6]	2,417	22,296	458,712	20.6	11[11]	6	52
Kiribati	1988	112	458	13,868	30.3	...	8	140	2,437	17.4	...	...	...
Korea, North	1982	4,700[22]	...	2,500,000	...	...	600[4, 23]	100,000[23]	2,500,000[23]	25.0[23]	...	[23]	[23]
Korea, South	1988	6,531	130,142	4,771,722	36.7	92[4]	3,454	120,834	4,055,089	33.6	76[3]	688	32,016
Kuwait	1988	295	10,125	181,844	18.0	80[2]	431	19,996	255,566	12.8	74[3]	117[2]	2,326
Laos	1985	7,470	18,070	584,000	27.4	...	563	5,815	91,356	15.7	...	...	586
Lebanon	1985	1,116	31	329,340	...	...	1,405[3]	53,450[3, 31]	230,934	...	...	181[3]	3,506
Lesotho	1987	1,174	5,880	331,858	56.4	72[7]	164	1,891	41,138	21.8	13[7]	10	183
Liberia	1980	1,232	9,099	208,045[1]	...	...	419	1,129	52,514[1]	...	...	6	63
Libya	1983	2,744	42,202	741,502	17.6	...	1,555	25,044	301,415	12.0	...	195	3,883
Liechtenstein	1989	14[30]	102	1,807	17.7	...	9[30]	107	1,686	15.8	...	1	74[32]
Luxembourg	1987	...	1,745[2]	24,381	14.0[2]	83[9]	...	3,482[9, 32, 33]	7,772	...	65[1]	2[34]	26[34]
Macau	1987	74	1,118	31,914	28.5	...	30	851	14,913	17.5	...	126	1,302
Madagascar	1984	13,973	42,462	1,625,216	38.3	46[1]	104[35]	10,383	288,543	27.8	...	12	234
Malawi	1988	2,660	16,885	1,066,642	63.1	...	79	1,258	26,396	21.0	...	54	1,969
Malaysia	1987	6,691	102,356	2,274,452	22.2	...	1,165	60,390	1,302,048	21.6	...	...	...
Maldives	1986	243	1,138	41,812	36.7	...	9	291	3,581	12.3	...	10	52
Mali	1983	1,558	10,912	348,373	31.9	15[7]	20	3,870	64,148	16.6	...	11	890
Malta	1988	125	1,603	36,564	22.8	87[2]	42	1,762	22,341	12.7	70[2]	26	690
Martinique	1987	218	2,024[7]	33,492	19.3[7]	...	...	2,745[23]	45,247[23]	16.5[23]	...	...	[23]
Mauritania	1986	878	2,629[7]	140,871	45.4[7]	30[7]	44	1,013[7]	34,674	27.6[7]	...	6	372[7]
Mauritius	1987	277	6,504	144,130	22.2	91[2]	127	3,683	71,059	19.3	34[11]	77	693
Mayotte	1987	28	366	15,632	42.7	...	2[23]	65[23]	1,392[23]	21.4[23]	...	[23]	[23]
Mexico	1988	80,518	455,693	14,875,000	32.6	97[2]	16,999	224,732[2]	4,401,000	...	46[2]	5,811[2]	139,391[2]
Monaco	1987	6	...	4,484[21]	...	...	3	[21]	...	...	...	...	...
Mongolia	1988	[31]	[31]	[31]	[31]	95[2]	712[31]	18,400[31]	443,000[31]	24.1[31]	84[19]	28	1,300
Montserrat	1988	14	67	1,403	20.9	...	1	71	984	13.9	...	1[4]	12[4]
Morocco	1988	3,752	80,833[8]	2,182,348	26.0[8]	63[2]	1,241	63,478[8]	1,348,670	20.2[8]	24[1]	696[37]	5,705[37]
Mozambique	1987	3,927[38]	20,884[38]	1,286,961[38]	61.6[38]	48[2]	198	3,163	103,322	32.7	4[24]	30	852
Myanmar (Burma)	1988	31,499	188,417	5,369,641	28.5	65[14]	2,429	61,556	1,591,927	25.9	16[14]	146	1,536
Nauru	1989	3	61	1,367	22.4	...	2	34	629	18.5	...	1	3
Nepal	1987	12,186	53,405	1,857,658	34.8	56[7]	5,140	21,785	540,049	24.8	18[7]	52	117[2]
Netherlands, The	1988	9,502	102,388[2]	1,536,000	15.3[2]	87[7]	1,338	53,361[2]	747,000	15.1[2]	85[1]	1,693	55,931[2]
Netherlands Antilles	1986	91	1,145	24,600	21.5	...	22	630	8,600	13.7	...	3	50
New Caledonia	1987	276	1,564	32,205	20.6	...	47	1,179	13,540	11.5	...	28	200
New Zealand	1987	2,575	19,113	432,972	22.7	100[2]	396	13,490	232,307	17.2	83[1]	28	3,130[2]
Nicaragua	1988	4,624[5]	24,127[5]	678,937[5]	28.1[5]	75[2]	328[23]	7,167[23]	172,108[23]	24.0[23]	20[7]	[23]	[23]
Niger	1986	1,976	7,690	293,512	38.2	27[1]	64[24]	1,963[1]	51,448[1]	26.2[1]	4[6]	8[6]	120[6]
Nigeria	1985	35,181	359,701[7]	13,612,765	35.4[9]	...	5,826	82,749[7]	3,169,624[7]	38.3[7]	...	479	15,738[7]
Niue	1987	8	31	392	12.6	...	1	21	310	14.8	...	—	—
Norfolk Island	1989	2	9	239	26.6	...	1	10	87	8.7	...	—	—

students[d]	student/teacher ratio	third level (higher) institutions	teachers[c]	students[d]	student/teacher ratio	gross enrollment ratio	students per 100,000 population[b]	percent of population age 25 and over with post-secondary education[b]	literacy over age	total (%)	male (%)	female (%)	public expenditure on education (percent of GNP)[b]	country
[23]	[23]	—	—	—	—	3.8	324	...	...	31.5	46.0	17.0	...	Equatorial Guinea
4,969[1]	12.7[1]	11[7]	1,314[1]	18,436	...	0.7[1]	63	...	...	3.7	...	...	3.9	Ethiopia
1,387	...	1	...	94	...	...	...	...	15	99.0	...	...	...	Faeroe Islands
—	—	—				...	...	...	15	99.5	...	...	...	Falkland Islands
2,723	11.1	5[9]	320[2]	2,211[2]	6.9[2]	3.2[2]	314	4.5	15	85.5	90.2	80.9	6.7	Fiji
113,117[4]	10.8[4,16]	16		133,933[4]	16	34.5	2,733	13.8	15	100.0	100.0	100.0	5.9	Finland
[23]	[23]	1,094[24]	46,648[1]	1,163,903[1]	25.0[1]	30.2	2,358		15	98.8	98.9	98.7	6.1	France
2,623	...							6.4	16	82.0	82.5	81.3	19.2	French Guiana
[23]	9.5[1]	1		180[7]					15	95.0	94.9	95.0	9.7	French Polynesia
13,529	18.8	1[7]	616[7]	3,228[7]	5.2[7]	4.3[2]	349		15	77.0			4.5	Gabon
10,102	20.1	9	177	1,489	8.4	—		0.2	15	24.9	35.6	15.1	4.3	Gambia, The
831	21	1[9]	303	2,387[9]				9.5[26]						Gaza Strip
364,370	6.8	53[4]	30,500[4]	437,919		31.1[2]	2,608	17.3	15	100.0	100.0	100.0	5.3	Germany, East
2,600,822	30.0	110	336,996	1,366,057	4.0	29.8[1]	2,546	4.3	15	100.0	100.0	100.0	4.6	Germany, West
40,485	14.0	9	1,316	10,225	7.8	1.5[1]	125	0.4	15	53.2	64.1	42.8	2.6	Ghana
352[2]	14.1[2]	—		—	—				15	99.0	99.0	99.0	6.0	Gibraltar
109,415	13.4	89	11,878	181,901	15.3	23.5[7]	1,709	7.6	14	93.8	97.3	90.6	2.6	Greece
650[4]	5.9[4]	2[4]	35[4]	200[4]	5.7[4]				15	100.0	100.0	100.0		Greenland
		2	195	850	4.4			1.5	15	85.0			5.6	Grenada
17,757	...	2		5,835				5.2	15	90.1	89.7	90.5	15.0	Guadeloupe
2,410	20.6	1	206	2,208	10.7			34.4	15	96.4	96.4	96.5	8.5	Guam
[23]	[23]	1[20]	3,007[20]	50,000[20]	16.6[20]	8.6[2]	779	1.2	15	55.0	62.6	47.1	1.8	Guatemala
84	1.4	—							15	100.0	100.0	100.0		Guernsey[27]
4,929	6.5	23	946	7,470	7.9	1.3[2]	109		15	28.3	39.7	17.2	3.3	Guinea
1,027	9.6	...							15	31.4	46.2	17.3	3.3	Guinea-Bissau
...		2		1,023		2.1[1]	244	1.8	15	95.9	97.0	94.8	10.1	Guyana
14,437	...	16	818[1]	6,288[1]	6.7[1]	1.1[7]	101	0.7	15	41.5	44.0	39.2	1.2	Haiti
95,956		7[1]	2,692[1]	34,478[1]	14.0[1]	9.5[1]	838	3.3	15	59.5	60.7	58.4	5.0	Honduras
21,593	18.4	11	3,530	34,434	9.8	12.8[7]	1,410	7.1	15	88.1	94.7	80.9	2.8	Hong Kong
398,488	17.7	58	16,242	103,041	6.3	15.4[2]	923	7.0	15	98.9	99.2	98.6	5.7	Hungary
7,491	...	4	280[9]	4,744	17.1[9]	22.1[1]	2,040	3.7	15	99.0			4.0	Iceland
3,196,963[16]		16		[16]		8.9[9]	776	2.5	15	40.8	54.8	25.7	3.6	India
1,447,278	15.1	792	115,359	1,179,489	10.2	6.5[7]	600	0.8	15	74.1	83.0	65.4	2.0	Indonesia
252,620		116	14,341	167,971	11.7	5.1[2]	478		15	61.8	71.0	52.1	3.8	Iran
153,647	16.5	25[4]	8,327[4]	142,496[4]	17.1[4]	10.0[9]	856		15	45.9	65.9	26.0	3.8	Iraq
85,814	13.1	51	4,396	56,579	12.9	21.6[7]	1,888	7.9	15	100.0	100.0	100.0	6.7	Ireland
383	...													Isle of Man
105,324		7[20]	8,112[2]	98,821[29]		33.3[2]	2,746	23.1	15	91.8	95.0	88.7	10.2	Israel
2,719,334	21.7	47[4]	51,264[4]	1,004,509[4]	19.6[4]	24.7[2]	1,989	4.1	15	97.0	97.9	96.3	4.0	Italy
8,778	17.5	17		17,791		4.2[2]	508	2.0	14	88.6	88.2	89.1	5.8	Jamaica
		1,123	142,000	2,496,000	17.6	28.8[2]	1,987	14.3	15	100.0	100.0	100.0	5.1	Japan
283[4]	...												4.1	Jersey
50,138[4]	43.5[4]	3	1,430	36,149	25.3	37.4[9]	1,992	0.8	15	79.4	81.7	73.9	7.1	Jordan
7,334	26.4	2		586[9]					15	48.0				Kampuchea (Cambodia)
23,496	13.6	4[20]		9,888[20]		1.3[1]	106		15	59.2	69.6	49.2	6.7	Kenya
568	10.9					—			15	90.0			8.7	Kiribati
[23]	[23]	245[4]	9,244	200,000	21.6	—			15	90.0			3.6	Korea, North
857,624	26.8	442	35,753	1,340,381	37.5	33.9[4]	3,606	8.9	15	92.7	97.5	87.9	4.5	Korea, South
11,388	19.4	1	863	15,751	18.2	15.5[1]	1,307	10.1	15	75.1	78.7	69.6	4.2	Kuwait
19,358	8.3	6	452[9]	2,399		1.5	131		15	83.9	92.0	75.8	1.0	Laos
37,036	10.6	18[3]	7,460	70,510	9.4	27.4[7]	2,634	3.1	15	77.0	85.7	68.9		Lebanon
2,567	14.0	1	132	1,081	8.2	1.8[7]	158	0.1	15	73.6	62.4	84.5	3.5	Lesotho
2,322	36.9	3	190	3,955[1]		2.5[19]	203	1.5	15	22.4	27.4	18.4	5.7	Liberia
50,363	12.9	8[3]	1,340[6]	25,700[3]		10.6[1]	832	1.0	10	74.4	85.0	62.0	7.5	Libya
147	...	—	—	—	—			5.4	15	100.0	100.0	100.0		Liechtenstein
15,217			33	795		2.9[7]	232		15	100.0	100.0	100.0	5.2	Luxembourg
61[34]	2.3[34]	5	70	6,891	98.4	—		1.4	10	61.3	76.4	46.2		Macau
11,041	8.5	3	1,059	37,746	35.6	4.6[1]	383		15	67.5	73.7	61.6	3.5	Madagascar
3,634	15.5	4	306	2,330	7.6	0.7[2]	59	0.2	15	41.2			3.3	Malawi
23,145	11.8	42[2]	10,347[2]	109,545[2]	10.6[2]	6.0[1]	599		15	72.6	82.2	63.2	7.8	Malaysia
462	8.9							0.4	15	81.1	80.2	82.0	0.6	Maldives
12,612	14.2	7	499	5,792	11.6	1.0[2]	81	0.2	15	10.1	18.6	1.8	2.8	Mali
6,465	9.4	1	147	1,147	9.8	4.8[2]	377	2.4	15	96.0	96.2	95.9	3.3	Malta
[23]	[23]	17	407	1,220[7]	30.5[7]				15	92.5	91.8	93.2	13.5	Martinique
4,336	9.6[7]	7[7]	25[24]	4,434		0.4	248		15	28.0	38.0	17.0	7.9	Mauritania
444[7]	...	2[7]	184[3]	344		1.0[2]	119	3.6	15[36]	81.8[36]	89.0[36]	74.8[36]	3.4	Mauritius
[23]	[23]								15	31.8				Mayotte
2,088,292[2]	15.0[2]	1,347[2]	98,061[2]	1,072,764[2]	13.7[2]	15.7[2]	1,508	5.3	15	90.3	92.3	88.3	2.1	Mexico
1,218[3]								6.8						Monaco
22,200	17.1	8	1,500	22,600	15.1	21.7[2]	1,991		15	89.5	93.4	85.5	7.0	Mongolia
72[4]	6.0[4]	...						5.8					3.5	Montserrat
70,075[37]	12.3[37]	29	6,320	189,422	30.0	8.8[1]	820		15	70.7	82.4	58.7	7.9	Morocco
9,066	10.6	3	354	1,862	5.3	0.1[1]	10		15	16.6	20.0	13.3	1.2	Mozambique
17,000	11.1	35	7,191	255,866	35.6	5.1[24]	489	0.2	15	78.5	85.8	71.6	1.6	Myanmar (Burma)
30	10.0	1[39]		c. 200[39]					15	99.0				Nauru
648[2]	5.5[2]	116[2]	4,165[2]	67,555[2]	16.2	4.6[7]	397	6.8	15	20.7	31.9	9.2	3.0	Nepal
594,000	11.4[2]	453[2]	30,952[2]	307,537[2]	9.9[2]	32.0[1]	2,792	7.2	15	100.0	100.0	100.0	6.9	Netherlands, The
650	13.0	2	80	700	8.8			6.4	15	95.0			10.1	Netherlands Antilles
5,887	29.4	6	40	853	21.3				14	89.4	90.1	88.7	13.4	New Caledonia
130,483[40]	42.1[2]	7[20]	2,775[20]	37,074[20]	13.4[20]	33.0[20]	3,066	30.6	15	100.0	100.0	100.0	5.3	New Zealand
[23]	[23]	13	1,484	25,478	17.2	8.7[2]	791		15	74.0			6.6	Nicaragua
2,208[1]	19.6[6]	3[30]	310[30,41]	4,101[30,41]	13.2[30,41]	0.6[7]	48		15	9.8	14.0	5.8	3.1	Niger
336,868	24.9[7]	80[7]	10,038	126,285	12.6	2.9[2]	239		15	42.4	53.8	31.5	1.8	Nigeria
—	—	—	—	—	—	—		1.9	15	99.8	99.7	99.9		Niue
—	—	—	—	—	—				15	100.0	100.0	100.0		Norfolk Island

886 Britannica World Data

Education (continued)

country	year	first level (primary)					general second level (secondary)					vocational second level[a]	
		schools	teachers[c]	students[d]	student/teacher ratio	net enrollment ratio	schools	teachers[c]	students[d]	student/teacher ratio	net enrollment ratio	schools	teachers[c]
Norway	1987	3,500	33,005	593,767	18.0	97[1]	940[23]	18,135[23]	206,086[23]	11.4[23]	87[1]	[23]	[23]
Oman	1988	367	8,080	212,328	26.3	80[2]	311	4,332	56,394	13.0	14[24]	23	702
Pacific Is., Trust Territory of the													
Marshall Islands	1986	89	507[21]	9,906	22.9[21]	...	7	[21]	1,727	[21]	...	...	...
Micronesia, Fed. States of	1984	151	1,051	23,345	22.2	...	14	314	4,159	13.2	...	...	...
Northern Mariana Islands	1989	18	240	4,882	20.3	...	9[23]	163[23]	2,075[23]	12.7[23]	...	23	23
Palau	1987	26	289[21]	2,784	13.1[21]	...	6	[21]	1,009	[21]	...	1[7]	36[7]
Pakistan	1988	84,307	194,200	7,687,000	39.6	...	11,361	147,300	2,809,000	19.1	...	299	4,502
Panama	1987	2,617	13,698	346,137	25.3	89[2]	341	10,068	189,771	18.8	48[2]	50	624
Papua New Guinea	1986	2,461	12,318	374,950	30.4	...	122	2,025	49,974	24.7	...	112	745
Paraguay	1988	4,318	24,729	627,190	25.4	85[2]	780[23]	9,444[23]	164,086[23]	17.4[23]	25[2]	23	23
Peru	1987	23,486	119,750	3,763,730	31.4	97[1]	4,189	76,373	1,732,466	22.7	...	1,071	7,995
Philippines	1987	33,607	292,602	9,204,168	31.5	95[2]	5,388[1]	101,082	3,420,921	33.8	52[2]	18	18
Pitcairn Island	1988	1[21]	1[21]	10	12.0[21]	...	[21]	[21]	2	[21]	...	—	—
Poland	1989	17,264	263,026	5,087,005	19.3	99[1]	903	21,912	393,532	18.0	73[1]	6,224	73,071
Portugal	1987	12,692	75,456	1,234,293	16.4	97[9]	1,509[2]	53,881[2]	647,391[2]	12.0	38[7]	345[7]	2,971[7]
Puerto Rico	1986	1,542	18,359	427,582	23.3	...	395	13,612	334,661	24.6	...	52	...
Qatar	1987	122	3,141	42,502	14.0	100[2]	69	2,801	22,518	8.0	55[2]	3	113
Réunion	1987	351	3,917	73,526	18.8	...		3,263	57,699	17.7	...		719
Romania	1988	13,895	141,609	3,027,196	21.4	...	981	43,805	1,228,490	28.0	...	764	12,419
Rwanda	1986	1,612	16,003	904,378	56.5	64[2]	...	1,479[23]	8,577	...	2[2]	...	23
St. Helena and Ascension	1987	8	36	675	18.8	...	4	38	455	12.0	...	1	13
St. Kitts and Nevis	1988	27[8]	263[8]	6,457[8]	24.6[8]	...	6	273	4,115	15.1	...	1[4]	18[4]
St. Lucia	1988	81	1,060	32,809	31.0	...	12	351	6,284	17.9	...	4[4]	...
St. Pierre and Miquelon	1986	5	37	556	15.0	...	3[19]	55	548	10.0	...	2[19]	16
St. Vincent and the Grenadines	1988	61	1,261	24,541	19.5	...	21	371	6,447	17.4	...	...	...
San Marino	1987	13	171	1,363	8.0	...	5	179	1,222	6.8	...	...	...
São Tomé and Príncipe	1985	63	517	19,086	36.9	...	11	300	6,186	20.6	...	2	35
Saudi Arabia	1988	7,682	88,314	1,484,663	16.8	56[2]	3,031	43,358	620,238	14.3	31[2]	32	3,295
Senegal	1986	2,171	11,513	583,507	41.2	44[1]	162	2,346[7]	113,653	...	...	5	...
Seychelles	1988	25[4]	702	14,522	20.7	...	4[2]	162	2,643	16.3	...	1[2]	147
Sierra Leone	1985	1,219	10,451	350,160	33.5	...	171	3,829	81,879	21.4	...	12	406
Singapore	1988	288	10,795	278,348	25.8	100[7]	157	8,967	200,185	22.3	58[19]	17	1,565
Solomon Islands	1987	462	2,124	42,374	20.0	...	20	300	5,604	18.7	...	2[7]	63[7]
Somalia	1985	1,121	14,521	274,610	18.9	14	80	2,522	65,186	25.8	4	23	725
South Africa	1988	19,310[4,21]	286,228[21]	7,163,987[21]	25.0[21]	...	[21]	[21]	[21]	[21]	...	132[1]	19,219
Bophuthatswana	1986	1,293	10,153[8]	498,585	35.1[8]	...	1,282[8]	16,178[8]	553,848[8]	34.2[8]	...	8[8]	261[8,34]
Ciskei	1987	545	4,369	200,752	45.9	...	158	1,809	59,414	32.8	...	1	20
Transkei	1987	1,387	12,617	778,825	61.7	...	1,854	10,245	217,842	21.3	...	16[29]	349[29]
Venda	1986	400	4,039	139,822	34.6	...	155	2,081	51,078	24.5	...	1	42
South West Africa/Namibia	1986	1,074[21]	11,121[21]	273,500	31.5[21]	...	[21]	[21]	76,580[21]	[21]	...	5	81
Spain	1987	23,105[9]	220,980	5,575,519	25.2	98[1]	2,632	74,918	1,278,206	17.1	75[3]	2,184	50,933
Sri Lanka	1986	9,325	146,356	2,304,499	15.7	100	5,629[9]	113,148[9]	2,930,070[9]	25.9[9]	...	28	1,101[1]
Sudan, The	1985	6,707	47,750	1,653,491	34.6	...	2,167	17,591	490,583	27.9	...	98	1,513[7]
Suriname	1985	...	2,809	71,454	25.4	98[7]	63	1,047	18,612	17.8	...	64	1,283
Swaziland	1987	477	4,462	147,743	33.1	86	113	1,760	32,942	18.7	34	7	181
Sweden	1988	4,674	99,030	928,009	9.4	96[24]	484	29,080	285,116	9.8	81[24]	...	...
Switzerland	1988	...	...	375,300	...	...	...	...	362,900	...	...	...	...
Syria	1987	9,315	85,583	2,158,594	25.2	100[2]	1,922	52,074	855,453	16.4	53[2]	143	7,245
Taiwan	1988	2,447	75,826	2,392,750	31.6	...	838	61,034	1,254,460	20.6	...	208	17,259
Tanzania	1986	10,147	93,000	3,160,000	34.0	52[2]	193[1]	4,329[1]	83,098[1]	19.2[1]	...	41	1,277
Thailand	1986	32,683	356,844	7,160,494	20.1	...	1,437[6]	107,493	1,829,559	17.0	...	1,528[6]	17,893[7]
Togo	1987	2,345	10,209	474,998	46.5	73[2]	248[3]	3,985[7]	88,327	...	...	18	198
Tokelau	1983	3[6]	39	482	15.8	...	3[6]	6[6]	806	13.3[6]	...	...	12[6]
Tonga	1985	112	744	17,019	22.9	...	50[7]	770	14,644	19.0	...	12[7]	70
Trinidad and Tobago	1989	469	7,686	182,764	23.8	90[1]	89[4]	4,878	91,808	18.8	50[1]	10	...
Tunisia	1989	3,676	43,921	1,326,150	30.2	96[2]	485	23,300	447,795	19.2	32[7]	...	229[34]
Turkey	1987	49,714	216,859	6,703,528	30.9	85[2]	5,734[2]	100,431	2,412,347	24.0	35[2]	2,075[2]	46,368
Turks and Caicos Islands	1988	14[44]	80[44]	1,484[44]	18.6[44]	...	4[44]	69[44]	810[44]	11.7[44]	...	—	—
Tuvalu	1984	11	61	1,349	22.1	100[3]	1	15[9]	243	16.7[9]	...	8[9]	16[9]
Uganda	1984	6,420	58,377	1,908,564	32.7	40[3]	297	5,603	114,828	20.5	...	118	1,039
U.S.S.R.	1988	67,100	2,807,000[21]	37,900,000	15.2[21]	...	63,200	[21]	4,700,000	[21]	...	4,508	251,800
United Arab Emirates	1987	354[21]	6,793	165,463	24.4	88[2]	27	4,464	67,621	15.1	...	9[2]	372
United Kingdom	1987	24,609	208,700	4,550,300	21.8	97[1]	5,091	253,800	3,902,400	15.4	81[1]	729[45]	93,000[1,45]
United States	1988	101,050[21]	1,517,000	31,704,000	20.9	97[2]	[21]	1,075,000[23]	13,734,000[23]	12.8[23]	90[2]	23	23
Uruguay	1987	2,382	16,568	354,177	21.4	92[2]	276	12,244	175,710	14.4	55[7]	94	...
Vanuatu	1986	265	1,036	23,856	23.0	...	21[12]	133[12]	2,904[12]	21.8[12]	...	12	12
Venezuela	1987	19,868[2]	112,157	2,880,333	25.7	86[1]	2,277[2,23]	61,671[23]	1,058,058[23]	17.2[23]	38[1]	23	23
Vietnam	1987	13,731[21]	426,000[21]	12,483,000[21]	29.3[21]	86[1]	[21]	[21]	[21]	[21]	...	292	11,300
Virgin Islands (U.S.)	1987[46]	41	781[47]	14,723	...	...	10	506[47]	10,903	...	...	3[2]	27[2]
Wallis and Futuna	1983	13[48]	134[3]	3,962	...	...	...	...	150[3,42]	...	...	...	...
West Bank	1987[49]	1,142[21]	8,972[21]	181,804	31.7[21]	...	[21]	[21]	102,659	[21]	...	21	21
Western Sahara	1985	24	428	13,943	32.6	...	7	237	4,560	19.2	...	...	...
Western Samoa	1983	164	1,502[50]	31,447[50]	20.9	...	38[7]	520	20,404	39.2	...	4	69
Yemen (Aden)	1984	924	11,281	294,028	26.1	...	51	1,493	29,205	19.6	...	29	453
Yemen (Şan'ā')	1986	5,814	16,115	907,480	56.3	22[11]	942	5,988	122,022	20.4	3[11]	73	736
Yugoslavia	1987	12,069	139,167	2,833,231	20.4	78[1]	1,248	63,711	901,351	14.1	76[6]	...	...
Zaire	1986	10,065[7]	112,077[7]	4,993,523	44.6	75[9]	3,972[7]	49,459[7]	3,198,051	...	49[7]	205[51]	...
Zambia	1986	3,164	29,841	1,365,926	45.8	87[7]	276	5,627	150,298	26.8	...	28	1,055
Zimbabwe	1988	4,471	57,566	2,220,967	38.6	100[2]	1,484	23,899	653,353	27.3	...	21	1,224

[1]1985. [2]1986. [3]1982. [4]1987. [5]Includes preschool. [6]1980. [7]1984. [8]Public schools only. [9]1983. [10]Age 30 and over. [11]1975. [12]General second level includes teacher training at the second level. [13]Includes special education. [14]1977. [15]National literacy standard based solely on school attendance. [16]Vocational second level includes third level. [17]Includes four special schools for primary and secondary students. [18]Third level includes vocational second level. [19]1979. [20]Universities only. [21]First level includes second level. [22]1976. [23]General second level includes vocational second level. [24]1981. [25]Republic of Cyprus only. [26]Includes East Jerusalem. [27]Excludes Sark. [28]Schools under the Department of Education and Culture only. [29]Includes postsecondary teacher training. [30]1988. [31]General second level includes first level. [32]Includes part-time teachers. [33]General second level includes vocational second level and third level.

students[d]	student/teacher ratio	third level (higher) institutions	teachers[c]	students[d]	student/teacher ratio	gross enrollment ratio	students per 100,000 population[b]	percent of population age 25 and over with post-secondary education[b]	literacy[b] over age	total (%)	male (%)	female (%)	public expenditure on education (percent of GNP)[b]	country
23	23	227	7,002	103,111	14.7	27.9[1]	2,124	11.9	15	100.0	100.0	100.0	6.9	Norway
5,922	8.4	1	203	1,138	5.6	2.1[2]	168		6	38.0	55.0	20.0	4.3	Oman
														Pacific Is., Trust Territory of the
...	...	...	...	...	...	...	...	7.8	25	86.3	89.1	83.2	...	Marshall Islands
...	...	...	...	920	...	...	...	8.0	15	76.7	67.0	87.2	...	Micronesia, Fed. States of
23	23	1	102	1,097	10.8	...	...	21.9	15	96.3	96.9	95.6	...	Northern Mariana Islands
382[7]	10.6[7]	...	...	...	...	...	...	16.8	25	92.7	94.4	91.0	...	Palau
63,000	14.0	705	39,233	567,805	14.5	5.1[2]	487	1.9	15	25.6	36.0	15.2	2.1	Pakistan
9,853	15.8	8	3,317	55,633	16.8	28.2[2]	2,787	8.3	15	88.2	89.0	87.7	5.0	Panama
10,078	13.5	2	400	3,029	7.6	2.0	178		15	42.3	52.4	31.3	4.7	Papua New Guinea
23	23	2	2,694[1]	28,737	10.8[1]	9.7[7]	929	2.0	15	85.7	88.7	82.9	1.5	Paraguay
206,137	25.8	46	23,480	409,654	17.4	24.6[2]	2,339	10.1	15	87.0	93.5	79.9	2.9	Peru
18	18	1,178[1,18]	33,935[1,18]	1,127,968[1,18]	33.2[1,18]	38.0[1]	3,621	15.2	15	88.7	89.9	87.5	1.7	Philippines
									15	100.0	100.0	100.0	...	Pitcairn Island
1,357,579	18.6	92	59,142	272,531	4.6	16.9[2]	1,205	5.7	15	99.2	...	...	3.8	Poland
27,946[7]	9.4[7]	221	10,179	109,190	10.7	12.6[7]	1,112	1.6	15	84.0	88.8	79.7	4.4	Portugal
149,191	...	45	9,045	156,818	17.3	48.1[24]	4,100	18.4	15	89.1	89.7	88.5	8.2	Puerto Rico
856	7.6	1	452	4,931	10.9	18.9[2]	1,619		15	74.7	76.8	72.5	5.6	Qatar
11,903	16.6	...	...	4,135	...	...	...		15	78.6	76.5	80.5	15.1	Réunion
278,003	22.4	44	12,036	157,041	13.0	11.2[1]	694	4.6	15	95.8	...	...	2.1	Romania
12,295	...	3[1]	331[1]	1,987[1]	6.0[1]	0.4[1]	33	0.3	15	49.4	62.2	37.2	3.3	Rwanda
43	3.3	...	...	...	...	...	...		12	96.9	96.4	97.5	...	St. Helena and Ascension
166[4]	9.2[4]	1[4,8]	9[4,8]	55[4,8]	6.1[4,8]	...	...	2.1	15	90.0	...	...	6.6	St. Kitts and Nevis
817[4]	...	1[4]	16[4]	123[4]	7.7[4]	...	...	1.3	15	90.0	...	...	7.6	St. Lucia
252	15.8	—	—	—	—	—	—	7.5	15	99.5	99.5	99.5	...	St. Pierre and Miquelon
744[42]	—	...	...	332[42]	...	...	...	1.4	15	85.0	...	...	5.0	St. Vincent and the Grenadines
370	10.6	...	...	700[9,42]	...	...	...		15	98.0	98.2	97.7	...	San Marino
...	...	...	...	...	...	...	...		15	54.2	70.2	39.1	6.4	São Tomé and Príncipe
31,354	9.5	78	9,950	114,516	11.5	13.4[2]	1,097	0.3	12	57.2	69.7	35.1	10.6	Saudi Arabia
3,515	...	7	497[7]	13,450	...	2.4[1]	209		15	22.5	31.0	14.2	4.7	Senegal
1,405	9.6	...	...	...	...	...	...	2.6	15	57.3	54.9	59.6	9.0	Seychelles
4,774	11.8	2	296	2,445	8.3	0.6[6]	55		15	23.6	31.2	16.5	3.8	Sierra Leone
26,911	17.2	6	4,018	46,904	11.7	11.8[9]	1,406	3.4	15	82.9	91.6	74.0	4.3	Singapore
1,142[7]	18.1[7]	—	—	—	—	—	—	1.6	15	54.1	62.4	44.9	5.2	Solomon Islands
10,203	14.1	1	262[24]	3,405	...	3.9[2]	330		10	54.8	60.9	47.9	1.4	Somalia
170,656	8.9	84[1]	28,478	267,608	9.4	...	...	3.7	15	79.3	80.6	78.0	3.8	South Africa
4,939[8]	13.0[8,34]	1	187	3,282	17.6	...	...		15	75.0	...	...		Bophuthatswana
174	8.7	3[43]	97[43]	1,677[43]	17.3[43]	...	...		15	72.0	...	...		Ciskei
6,363[29]	18.2[29]	1	...	4,350	...	...	...		...	...	...	...		Transkei
422	10.0	5	119[7]	5,135	24.0[7]	...	...		...	...	...	...		Venda
1,200	14.8	3	137	537	3.9	...	...		15	72.5	74.2	70.8	1.9	South West Africa/Namibia
751,995	14.8	33[1]	34,378[2]	826,306	...	31.8[2]	2,627	7.1	15	92.8	95.9	89.9	3.2	Spain
21,771	18.9[1]	8[20]	2,549	59,377	23.3	3.9[2]	364	1.1	15	86.1	90.8	81.2	3.5	Sri Lanka
30,973	...	16	1,464[9]	35,648	...	2.0	173		15	21.6	36.5	6.5	4.8	Sudan, The
15,996	12.5	...	373	2,914	7.8	7.7[2]	890		15	79.2	83.8	74.8	10.4	Suriname
1,280	7.1	1	178	1,270	7.1	3.9[2]	328		15	67.0	69.0	65.0	5.8	Swaziland
...	...	...	25,400	336,995	13.3	36.8[2]	2,635	15.4	15	100.0	100.0	100.0	7.6	Sweden
240,600	...	...	...	121,700	...	22.6[2]	1,789		15	100.0	100.0	100.0	4.8	Switzerland
56,664	7.8	4[20]	...	138,743[20]	...	17.4[1]	1,665	1.3	15	61.1	76.5	45.5	6.6	Syria
445,747	25.8	107	22,924	464,664	20.3	...	2,225		15	91.2	96.0	86.0	3.6	Taiwan
13,956	10.9	2	877[1]	3,342	...	0.3[2]	26		15	85.0	...	...	4.3	Tanzania
390,640[7]	21.8[7]	62[6]	30,905[1]	1,026,952[1]	33.2[1]	19.6[1]	1,998	2.9	15	88.8	93.2	84.5	3.9	Thailand
5,050	25.5	1	308	4,500	14.6	1.8[7]	156	1.3	15	39.1	51.7	27.5	5.2	Togo
197[6]	16.4[6]	—	—	32[42]	—	—	—		15	99.8	99.8	99.8	...	Tokelau
591	8.4	1[3]	...	705	...	...	...		15	92.8	92.9	92.8	4.4	Tonga
7,103	...	1[20]	241[20]	2,488[20]	10.3[20]	4.2[1]	464	2.9	15	95.1	96.7	93.6	5.9	Trinidad and Tobago
4,183	18.3	...	3,901	54,466	14.0	5.5[2]	564	2.8	15	48.2	60.4	35.7	5.9	Tunisia
676,136	14.6	310[2]	24,382	505,091	20.7	10.2[2]	1,003	3.6	15	65.6	81.3	49.8	2.1	Turkey
—	—	—	—	—	—	—	—	7.7	15	86.7	85.0	88.0	...	Turks and Caicos Islands
354[9]	22.1[9]								15	95.5	95.5	95.5	...	Tuvalu
23,335	22.5	14	934	8,216	8.8	0.8[1]	65	0.1	15	57.3	69.7	45.3	2.7	Uganda
2,911,000	11.6	898	370,000	2,675,000	7.2	21.6[2]	1,814	11.5	15	99.0	...	...	7.0	U.S.S.R.
2,614	7.0	...	449[1]	7,640	14.1[1]	8.4[1]	603	6.0	15	73.0	74.5	68.4	2.3	United Arab Emirates
529,791[45]	...	46[20]	31,432[20]	360,809[20]	11.5[20]	22.4[1]	1,806		15	100.0	100.0	100.0	5.2	United Kingdom
23	23	3,406	722,000	7,117,000	9.9	59.3[2]	5,167	32.2	15	95.5	95.7	95.3	7.5	United States
52,766	...	1	5,490	61,367	11.2	41.6[2]	3,357	6.3	15	95.0	94.5	95.4	3.1	Uruguay
12	12								15	52.9	57.3	47.8	...	Vanuatu
23	23	82[2]	32,404	441,734	13.6	26.4[1]	2,559	7.0	15	89.6	91.4	87.8	6.8	Venezuela
156,000	13.8	96	19,200	127,000	6.6	2.2[6]	212		15	94.0	...	...	3.0	Vietnam
775[2]	28.7[2]	1	97	757	8.3	...	...	17.6	15	90.0	...	...	7.4	Virgin Islands (U.S.)
—	—	—	—	—	—	—	...	1.0[10]	20	48.9	51.4	46.6	...	Wallis and Futuna
								8.1	...	...	...	...	...	West Bank
1,225	21	4[9]	483[19]	7,066[9]	...	—	...		15	...	...	...	...	Western Sahara
651	9.4	6	37	562	15.2	...	...	2.2	15	97.8	97.8	97.9	5.9	Western Samoa
5,602	12.4	1	486[9]	6,256[2]	...	2.3[24]	177		15	38.9	66.6	10.9	7.4	Yemen (Aden)
12,507	17.0	1	245	9,024	36.8	1.2[6]	76		15	18.9	38.5	3.1	5.6	Yemen (Şan'ā')
...	...	91	25,673	346,587	13.5	19.2[2]	1,509	6.8	15	89.6	95.5	83.9	3.8	Yugoslavia
319,805	...	36	3,072	37,706	12.3	1.6[1]	137		15	61.2	78.6	44.7	3.4	Zaire
9,687	9.2	2	575	3,831	6.7	1.5[2]	128	0.4	15	68.6	79.3	58.3	5.4	Zambia
40,854	33.4	1	561	7,699	13.7	3.9[2]	330	0.6	15	76.0	81.5	66.8	7.9	Zimbabwe

[34]Teacher training only. [35]1972. [36]Island of Mauritius only. [37]Vocational only. [38]Includes Portuguese language initiation classes. [39]University of the South Pacific extension centre. [40]Includes part-time students. [41]Université de Niamey and École Nationale d'Administration du Niger only. [42]Students registered abroad. [43]Excludes the University of Fort Hare. [44]Government schools only. [45]Third level vocational and teacher training. [46]Excludes 19 combined primary-secondary schools. [47]Public-school teachers only. [48]Includes intermediate education (ages 12–14). [49]Excludes East Jerusalem. [50]Includes some secondary teachers. [51]1978.

Cultural institutions

This table supplies worldwide statistics for the principal and most comparable elements of cultural activity: publishing, libraries, cinema, performing arts, museums, and nature preservation. For the most part, the data that can be compiled and compared are those measures produced as a result of governmental activity or expenditure, such as copyright and deposit, public funding, taxation, and land-use policy.

International comparisons of such data, however, should be approached with caution. In older, more prosperous nations, where the physical necessities of life are in secure supply, more money is available for cultural activities—and, indeed, for collecting data on them—than in less developed countries. Yet a developing country with an embryonic statistical system may have a flourishing cultural life that includes theatrical performance, live music, or the practice of arts no longer central to the Western experience, such as oral storytelling, ceremonial dance, traditional community ritual, or puppetry. Such activities may be more fully integrated into the life of the people than the more measurable cultural pursuits of a developed society.

The statistics actually reported may include books published (copyrighted), cultural facilities, library holdings, seating capacities of theatres and cinemas, attendance (tickets sold), and so on. Even when these figures are recalculated on a per capita basis, apparent differences among countries may be more a function of each country's statistical reporting system than of differences in the cultural habits and preferences of the people.

Furthermore, some kinds of data cannot be given meaningfully. For example, available data on government expenditures for cultural activi-

ties represent a wide variety of government policies. Some governments provide no support for cultural activities at any level; others subsidize or support them directly. Some offer tax incentives; others employ artists as teachers, performers, scholars, or archivists. Most national data on manpower engaged in cultural activities are collected on the basis of the individual's main source of income, without regard for his or her aspirations or avocations, part-time paid or unpaid activities, or other less convenient measures. A substantial part of the data presented were obtained from periodic surveys by Unesco, and they refer to a wide range of years. Throughout the table, data given in roman type are from 1985 or later; those in italic are from before 1985.

Figures for book production generally include all works published in separate bindings except advertising works, timetables, telephone directories, price lists, catalogs of businesses or exhibitions, musical scores, maps, atlases, and the like. The figures include government publications, school texts, theses, offprints, series works, and illustrated works, even those consisting principally of illustrations. Figures refer to works actually published during the year of survey, usually by a registered publisher, and deposited for copyright. A book is defined as a work of 49 or more pages, a pamphlet as a work of from 5 to 48 pages. A work published simultaneously in more than one country is counted as having been published in each. Data for newspapers are given in the "Communications" table beginning on page 834.

Data on libraries are for public libraries and exclude other types of collections, such as national (except when it is the sole *public* library), school

Cultural institutions

country	book publishing								public libraries			
	number of titles				number of copies ('000)				number	volumes ('000)	registered borrowers ('000)	loans per 1,000 population
	books		periodicals	pamphlets	books		periodicals	pamphlets				
	total	of which school textbooks			total	of which school textbooks						
Afghanistan	415[3]	108[3]	51	...	5,981[3]	...	1,094	...	55	350	11	...
Albania	1,091	564	8	52	7,972	3,377	2,894	380	45	3,723	...	...
Algeria	551	39	27	167	1,300[5]	1,194	476	...	35	165	...	...
American Samoa	98[3]	24[3]	16	1[3]	333.8	...	8	1[3]	1	251	...	5,400
Andorra	...	...	15	...	...	...	15	...	1	26	...	631
Angola	14	...	...	12	116	...	81	191	2	41	...	...
Anguilla	...	...	...	...	...	...	...	...	1	...	...	...
Antigua and Barbuda	...	...	...	10	13,526[10]	1,289[10]	...	10	1,528	9,532	4,201	360
Argentina	4,818[10]	...	...	...	...	...	...	...	12	12	12	12
Aruba	12	...	...	12	...	...	...	...				
Australia	1,954	165	3,534	649	...	...	...	...	350	24,500	...	...
Austria	9,786	210	2,364	907	...	...	...	...	2,081	7,442	802	1,800
Bahamas, The	...	...	...	...	...	...	...	...	37	60	...	...
Bahrain	46	46	...	...	858	858	237	49	13	205	327	722
Bangladesh	1,022	...	171	...	...	...	737	...	69	500	...	...
Barbados	18	...	120	69	...	...	...	...	1[14]	173	64	2,212
Belgium	8,327[10]	...	11,256	10	...	...	...	...	705	16,612	1,731	4,300
Belize	—	—	...	12[5]	—	...	...	156[5]	1	100	...	...
Benin	13	...	...	—	18	...	...	...	1	32	...	...
Bermuda	...	...	...	...	...	...	...	...	1	149	3	...
Bhutan	...	...	...	...	...	...	...	...	99[18]	125	1,120	37
Bolivia	274	4[3]	106	27	...	...	153	33	1	108	30	190
Botswana	70[3]	...	20	27[3]	35	...	979,842	114,289	4,175	11,517	10,694	58
Brazil	15,845	...	3,782	5,339	178,813	...	23	...	3	35	10	2,939
British Virgin Islands	20	...	20	—	3	...	...	...				
Brunei	15	4	19	—	38	240	128	—	1	97	6	230
Bulgaria	3,756	966	1,758	797	50,181	10,768	10,211	7,460	5,502	56,500	2,155	5,045
Burkina Faso	4	...	...	...	9	...	...	...				
Burundi	54	9	...	17	274	229	...	174	2	34	...	...
Cameroon	22[3]	7[3]	41	...	94[3]	7[3]	...	...	5	6	...	...
Canada	8,600	...	1,382	429	...	...	59,071	...	760	53,673	...	6,347
Cape Verde	10	...	4	—	13	...	...	...	—	—	...	—
Cayman Islands	5	...	—	...	...	...	...	...	1	6	2	2,300
Central African Republic	...	...	...	...	...	...	...	...	1	4	0.3	...
Chad	...	...	4	...	...	...	...	...				
Chile	1,162	101	118	337	15,118	1,500	909	4,770	179	783	18	367
China	52,000[10]	6,159[10]	3,100	10	5,280,000[10]	2,488,460[10]	2,380,000	10	2,406	261,000	117,000	154
Christmas Island	...	...	...	...	...	...	...	...	1	13	3	8,000
Cocos (Keeling) Islands	...	...	...	...	...	...	...	...	1	...	...	...
Colombia	6,500	2,570	1,034	8,541	48,005	25,750	...	70,749	974	2,381	...	...
Comoros	...	...	...	...	...	...	...	...	2	8	...	...
Congo	9	...	...	118	285	...	...	1,471	1	11	14	22
Cook Islands	...	...	3	...	...	...	4	...	1	15	3	1,100
Costa Rica	801	825	274	6	641	...	163	...	18	707	...	...
Côte d'Ivoire	46	11	12	...	3,766	3,517	325	...	1	25	2	3
Cuba	1,848	972	47	326	41,511	23,282	2,279	2,979	327	4,800	554	1,290
Cyprus	82[30]	71[30]	35	110[30]	603[30]	597[30]	93	7[30]	130[18]	180	...	230
Czechoslovakia	8,745	2,470[31]	1,050	1,275	76,621	19,986[31]	22,480	14,485	9,247	57,891	2,949	6,300
Denmark	7,493	907[32]	3,493	3,636	...	...	1	...	250	35,079	...	16,500
Djibouti	...	...	2	...	...	...	...	...	2	16	...	64
Dominica	...	...	...	...	...	...	...	...	2	15	4	660
Dominican Republic	1,504	...	...	715	3,017	...	...	1,320	15	9	533	120
Ecuador	...	...	284	...	...	...	...	...	97	324	...	...
Egypt	1,192	286	216	85	57,716	45,332	2,188	2,404	223	1,329	6	10
El Salvador	37[3]	6[3]	...	8	170	...	66	...	113	111	...	...

and university, private, professional, business, or government libraries, even though these may play a significant role locally or nationally. Public libraries were thought to provide the most representative set of figures. Data for "volumes" may reflect either actual holdings or an estimate based on length of occupied shelving.

Statistics on commercial cinema attendance may originate from a variety of screening facilities, including fixed, mobile, or drive-in facilities. Seating capacity is given for fixed facilities only. The data on long (or feature) films may refer to prints with a length of from 1,000 to 3,000 metres, depending on the reporting practices of the individual country. However, there is some consensus among reporting countries on a standard length (for classification purposes) of 2,000 metres.

In the performing arts, many countries (if they report such data at all) include not only the familiar Western performance modes—music, theatre, opera, musical theatre, dance—but also other types of live performance, such as traditional, ceremonial, seasonal, festival, or holiday observances and such entertainments as circuses and puppet and shadow theatre. Data on number of performances and attendance refer to both amateur and professional performances unless footnoted. Statistics on the number of theatres refer to theatre buildings and open-air theatres intended mainly for theatrical and other dramatic performances. Premises only occasionally or partly used for performances of this type, such as cultural centres, cultural houses, youth centres, sports establishments, concert halls, cinemas, university and school premises, open-air grounds, antique theatres, historic buildings, and ancient sites, are excluded.

Museum data are derived in large part from surveys by Unesco and the International Council of Museums (ICOM). The number of museums and museum attendance refer to public and private institutions whose exhibits and collections are devoted primarily to art, archaeology and history, natural history and natural science and technology, or ethnology and anthropology; they may be specialized (single theme), regional, or general. National parks and nature reserves, zoos, aquariums, and botanical gardens have not been counted with museums since they are included in the nature conservation section of the table.

Data on nature preservation facilities generally refer to those operated by the national conservation authority (though in some countries, particularly those with federal systems, authority may be lodged with other governmental levels). The data on number of facilities cover all types of facilities operated by the relevant authority, including national parks and monuments, scientific reserves, game reserves, protected landscapes, resource and anthropological reserves, and multiple-use management areas. Data on surface extent usually include only those facilities with an area of more than 10 sq km (4 sq mi).

The data on national parks and nature reserves are derived from information compiled by the International Union for Conservation of Nature and Natural Resources (IUCN) and from Britannica's holdings of published and unpublished national data. The data on zoos, aquariums, and botanical gardens are mainly from the International Species Inventory System (zoos and aquariums) and the International Association of Botanical Gardens.

cinema					performing arts				museums				nature preservation			country
annual attendance (all cinemas)		fixed cinemas		number of long films produced	number of facilities	number of performances	annual attendance		number	annual attendance		national parks and nature reserves		zoos, botanical gardens, etc. (number[2])	
number ('000,-000)	per 1,000 population	number	seating capacity ('000)				number ('000)	per 1,000 population		number ('000)	per 1,000 population	number	square metres per capita[1]		
4.9	300	34	19	3	...	...	...	...	7	7	0.5	6	120	1	Afghanistan
	1,300	103[4]	28[4]	14	13	25,280	8,654	2,884	2,034			6	110	1	Albania
20.5[6]	900[6]	216	110	2	6	786	389		117	385[7]	177	5	100	4	Algeria
0.1	3,200	6	6	...	...	...			1	52	1,700	1	4,300	...	American Samoa
0.2	6,900	5	2	...	—	14[9]	6[9]	190[9]	2	9	300	—	—	...	Andorra
3.5	380	42	32	1	3	48	41	5	13	185	21	5	1,800	1	Angola
...	...	...	...	...	...	...	...	...	3	...	...	...	...	...	Anguilla
		1										1	250	1	Antigua and Barbuda
49.9[4,6]	1,700[4,6]	919[4]	622[4]	15	399	330[9]	4,136[9]	160[9]	318	5,215[11]	200[11]	29	850	16	Argentina
...	...	...	...	...	...	...	...	12	...	...	...	—	—	12	Aruba
35.5	2,216	703	333	28	90	1,419[9]			16	5,279[13]	360[13]	580	22,500	41	Australia
11.5	1,500	444	103	18	36	6,014[9]	6,854[9]	905[9]	209	6,852	906	27	390	2	Austria
1.0	2,400	13	6	...	...	...			7	30	77	4	5,300	1	Bahamas, The
		313		...	...	...			2	30	77	...	...	1	Bahrain
		681	363	75	...	...			38			3	3	1	Bangladesh
1.2	5,200	6	5	...	5	1118[15]	12[15]	47[15]	1	30	120	1	10	...	Barbados
20.5[6]	2,100[6]	472	...	14	30	6,000[9]	1,430[9]	145[9]	132[16]	3,454[16]	350[16]	4	12	12	Belgium
1.3[6]	320[6]	74		...	...	...			1	1	6	2	320	16	Belize
0.2	2,700	4	2	...	3	63[15]	15[15]	280[15]	5	8[17]	217	2	2,100	3	Benin
									14	...	...	10	5	1	Bermuda
31.1[6]	5,700[6]	12	5						1	16	13	11	6,700	...	Bhutan
0.1[4]	200[4]	209	160	2	13	500[9]	123[9]	22[9]	28	52	59	12	7,300	4	Bolivia
99.1	730	1[4]	0.8[4]	...	...	29			2	52	59	8	107,000	...	Botswana
35.3[19]	3,300	1,403	708	73	302	22,599	7,043	52	895	20,082	148	50	880	31	Brazil
		1	0.4	...	...	3	4	330	1	1	85	7	800	1	British Virgin Islands
2.6	13,000	7	6	...	—	78	9	41	3	112	510	...	...	1	Brunei
85.1	9,500	3,305	702	35	66	18,302[9]	5,912[9]	660[9]	210	15,426	1,700	10	95	5	Bulgaria
4.0	600	12	14	...	...	...			1	...	...	6	1,000	...	Burkina Faso
0.1	24	7	3	...	13	79[15]	77[15]	19[15]	2[20]	620	120	7	210	...	Burundi
...	...	66	40	2	...	44[21]	39[21]	5[21]	12	4,641	560	15	2,300	2	Cameroon
79.7	3,200	788	568	32	476	30,720[9,22]	9,468[9,22]	374[9,22]	661	16,165[23]	640[23]	78	9,000	117	Canada
					...	...			...	...	...	...	...	...	Cape Verde
0.2[6]	11,700[6]	4	1	...	...	...			...	...	...	...	...	...	Cayman Islands
25.2	6,000	...	...	...	4	120[24]	7[24]	1[24]	7	...	...	4	15,000	8	Central African Republic
		13	12	...					5	3[25]	0.6[25]	1	230	...	Chad
12.6[6]	1,000[6]	177	107	2	20	2,513[9]	872[9]	72[9]	69			64	10,500	10	Chile
18,250	18,100	143,650[26]	...	140	1,756	743,891[9]	723,222[9]	690[9]	900			62	22	47	China
		2										1	7,000		Christmas Island
												1			Cocos (Keeling) Islands
56.1[6]	2,000[6]	586	277	9	14	159[9]	90[9]	3[9]	73	1,442[27]	57[27]	30	1,400	...	Colombia
...	...	...	...	1	1	74			5	57[28]	29[28]	10	7,800	1	Comoros
									1	6	320	1	7,800	...	Congo
0.2[6]	100[6]	104		2	9	347[9]	50[9]	24[9]	16	473[29]	200[29]	21	1,700	1	Cook Islands
7.0	900	72	42	2	...	...			1	...	...	10	1,800	2	Costa Rica
															Côte d'Ivoire
76.5	7,600	510	276	17	42	51,638	25,600	2,559	241	8,159	816	4	24	7	Cuba
		...	...	2	12	793	206	330	26	95	150	—	—	1	Cyprus
73.8[6]	4,730[6]	2,785	810	55	82	21,939[9]	8,665[9]	545[9]	263	21,606	1,390	28	750	42	Czechoslovakia
11.0	2,200	397	67	11	89[33]	10,139[9,33]	2,455[9,33]	478[9,33]	278	7,538	1,470	23	250	5	Denmark
0.6	5,200	4	6	...	...	...			...	...	...	—	—	...	Djibouti
7.0[4,6]	1,500[4,6]	3			2	41	74	14	6	...	...	1	810	1	Dominica
		834	46[4]									5	350	1	Dominican Republic
31.9	700	330		52	75	148			23	...	...	12	3,000	1	Ecuador
15.9[6]	3,700[6]	185	164		30	1,941	364	9	34	2,076	46	1	4	12	Egypt
		79	52.1	...	30	620	341	65	20	1,333	290	—	—	1	El Salvador

Cultural institutions (continued)

country	number of titles: books — total	of which school textbooks	periodicals	pamphlets	number of copies ('000): books — total	of which school textbooks	periodicals	pamphlets	public libraries: number	volumes ('000)	registered borrowers ('000)	loans per 1,000 population
Equatorial Guinea	...	...	...	...	...	...	...	...	3[18]	12	...	...
Ethiopia	100	60	3	127	270	180	2	381	3	80	...	...
Faeroe Islands	113	9	3	...	11	1	...	...	15	151	7	3,210
Falkland Islands	...	...	3	...	...	...	2	...	...	...	...	...
Fiji	10[3]	6[3]	13	3	20[3]	12[3]	...	6	9	91	33	520
Finland	8,694	528	4,275	1,886	...	...	195,381	...	461	30,330	2,084	16,290
France	30,424	4,573	22,443	11,741	365	69	6	1	1,426	64,379	6,094	1,957
French Guiana	1[3]	—	7	—	2[3]	—	25	10	1	19	0.7	210
French Polynesia	56	8	17	16	92	40	...	...	1	17	1	220
Gabon	...	...	...	...	...	...	...	...	—	—	...	...
Gambia, The	65[3]	30[3]	3	7	40[3]	...	...	5	1	89	2	29
Gaza Strip	...	...	...	...	...	...	...	...	...	...	...	...
Germany, East	5,636	181	542	850	110,296	19,711	21,520	32,760	6,912	46,631	3,964	5,470
Germany, West	63,679	3,419	6,197	12,821	...	...	275,494	...	13,945[18]	75,660	6,174	3,195
Ghana	338	27	74	12	163	...	254	91	9	1,119	55	54
Gibraltar	...	...	15	...	...	...	4	...	1	20	6	1,541
Greece	4,651[10]	114	821	10	...	...	80,400	...	498[18]	...	...	...
Greenland	...	...	...	8[3]	...	...	...	9[3]	73[35]	345[35]	0.7	5,040[35]
Grenada	2[3]	...	45	...	2[3]	...	142	...	1	28	...	...
Guadeloupe	...	...	...	...	...	...	...	...	1	90	15	410
Guam	12[3]	...	28	...	2[3]	...	...	...	8	188	17	...
Guatemala	312	...	...	181	...	...	...	...	1	27	...	...
Guernsey	...	...	1	...	...	...	...	...	1	12	...	...
Guinea	...	...	...	...	...	...	...	...	—	...	...	...
Guinea-Bissau	...	...	...	...	...	...	...	...	...	...	...	...
Guyana	16	1[3]	65	39	...	...	53	...	1	10	...	...
Haiti	...	...	...	...	...	...	...	...	1	12	...	...
Honduras	...	...	...	...	...	...	...	...	1	20	...	5
Hong Kong	3,642	538	495	2,039	27,483	7,771	...	16,829	48	2,277	1,601	1,900
Hungary	7,562	1,343	1,721	1,549	99,300	27,600	17,294	13,700	9,049[39]	51,808[39]	2,207[39]	4,525[39]
Iceland	1,180	23	...	...	...	...	...	...	234	1,637	...	8,000
India	11,529	608	19,937	1,014	...	...	50,094	...	17,024[18]	...	...	...
Indonesia	2,105	153	1,767	385	...	...	...	...	275	468	2,768	...
Iran	5,568	...	180	...	...	...	...	...	492	3,250	8,179	77
Iraq	82	...	...	...	452	...	...	...	15	240	17	...
Ireland	628	13	252	2,051	...	...	2,958	...	31	8,221	651	4,254
Isle of Man	...	...	...	...	...	...	...	10	...	...	...	...
Israel	4,161	1,189	890	243	8,872[10]	5,263[10]	...	...	983[40]	12,603	1,063	4,776
Italy	24,262	1,265	8,943	1,576	132,766	45,964	3,836	7,835	8,686	24,058	3,553	...
Jamaica	23[3]	3[3]	...	48	...	...	...	380	14	1,170	656	980
Japan	44,686	3,798	2,503	—	710,815	218,190	36,293	—	1,028	103,968	10,367	1,579
Jersey	...	...	41	...	...	...	211	...	65	70	1	6
Jordan	...	...	3	...	...	...	...	...	...	...	...	...
Kampuchea (Cambodia)	...	...	...	...	...	...	...	...	2	511	98	34
Kenya	238[3]	30[3]	...	...	331[3]	60[3]	...	...	1	40	...	...
Kiribati	...	...	...	...	...	...	...	...	...	...	...	...
Korea, North	...	...	...	...	...	...	...	9,151	159	3,255	13,565	200
Korea, South	33,743	3,396	870	2,094	114,971	50,293	...	...	25	738	585	50
Kuwait	222	...	50	28	6,083	...	982	24	...	...	...	...
Laos	...	...	...	...	...	...	...	...	...	...	...	...
Lebanon	...	...	2	...	...	...	10	...	6	94	...	...
Lesotho	...	...	...	...	...	...	...	...	1	...	3	14
Liberia	...	...	...	10	...	...	...	10	3	78	...	...
Libya	48[10]	...	...	...	2,405[10]	...	...	...	5	100	...	...
Liechtenstein	...	...	...	...	...	...	...	...	1	...	11	1,276
Luxembourg	339	6	337	126	...	...	...	...	4	250	120	...
Macau	...	...	...	...	...	...	...	158	56	76	69	2
Madagascar	321	44	...	79	335	100	166	1,605	2	28	6	51
Malawi	134	38	43	59	1,500	1,160	1,689	4,377	20	2,785	811	329
Malaysia	1,984	658	1,631	1,413	7,830	4,985	6	—	1	8	...	...
Maldives	3[3]	...	22	...	—	—	...	92[5]	46	552	...	...
Mali	160	...	264	160[5]	...	...	...	...	2	204	46	1,200
Malta	252	6	8	94	103[3]	...	17	33	1	120	...	...
Martinique	3[3]	...	...	18	...	...	...	...	1	26	...	...
Mauritania	21	21	...	20	...	...	...	...	...	...	...	...
Mauritius	110	23	...	47	88	34	...	50	4	210	...	...
Mayotte	...	...	...	...	...	...	...	...	...	...	...	...
Mexico	4,897	...	232	...	792[10]	...	792	10	557	3,720	8,492	174
Monaco	105[10]	...	105	10	6,923[10]	...	7,200	10	1	150	...	...
Mongolia	889[10]	...	38	10	...	...	...	...	404	9,600	...	...
Montserrat	...	...	63	...	...	...	145	...	1	...	...	...
Morocco	...	...	...	...	...	...	...	...	8	448	...	...
Mozambique	29	19	...	37	3,130	3,085	823	360	2	105	...	...
Myanmar (Burma)	673	...	26	—	...	...	...	...	6	154	...	...
Nauru	...	...	...	...	...	...	...	...	...	...	...	...
Nepal	43	—	94	—	70	—	...	—	400[18]	...	...	...
Netherlands, The	13,368[10]	2,385	...	10	...	...	...	...	471	42,919	4,177	12,029
Netherlands Antilles	28[12]	...	...	24[12]	...	...	...	...	7[12]	100[12]	10[12]	990[12]
New Caledonia	8[3]	...	15	7	7[3]	...	27	1	1	60	...	...
New Zealand	1,601	14	5,788	1,851	...	...	...	...	185	6,062	2,666	8,000
Nicaragua	26	...	...	...	146	...	...	...	41	...	...	...
Niger	...	4	...	...	8	8	...	0.1	18	481	206	2
Nigeria	1,415	453	...	798	...	...	...	...	1	6	1	3.359
Niue	...	...	...	...	...	...	3	1	1	5	0.2	6,000
Norfolk Island	—	—	2	1	—	—	...	...	...	...	...	...

cinema — annual attendance (all cinemas): number ('000,000)	per 1,000 population	fixed cinemas: number	seating capacity ('000)	number of long films produced	performing arts: number of facilities	number of performances	annual attendance: number ('000)	per 1,000 population	museums: number	annual attendance: number ('000)	per 1,000 population	nature preservation — national parks and nature reserves: number	square metres per capita[1]	zoos, botanical gardens, etc. (number[2])	country
0.5	1,600	10	4	...	...	219[9]	16[9]	47[9]	1	...	...	...	...	...	Equatorial Guinea
...	1,000	46	38	...	3	705	808	17	1[7]	67	0.17	10	700	3	Ethiopia
18.9[19]	10,500	5	1	...	...	...	...	...	3	11	238	...	...	...	Faeroe Islands
0.3	500	2	0.5	...	...	...	...	...	1	...	...	...	...	...	Falkland Islands
...	...	50	40	...	3	255	57	90	1	40	58	2	76	1	Fiji
6.3[6]	1,280[6]	344	72	13	48	11,100[9]	2,495[9]	506[9]	180	3,653	741	33	1,600	53	Finland
163.4	2,950	7,195	1,231	151	...	20,394[9,34]	6,042[9,34]	110[9,34]	1,434[20]	13,237[7]	239[7]	26	270	79	France
0.1[6]	600[6]	3	1	...	2	33[9]	14[9]	99[9]	1	12	190	—	...	...	French Guiana
1.1	2,100	18	7	...	...	...	...	...	3	...	...	2	220	...	French Polynesia
...	...	...	...	...	...	...	...	...	1	...	...	5	14,000	...	Gabon
...	...	...	...	...	...	...	...	...	...	...	...	1	32	...	Gambia, The
...	...	...	...	...	...	...	...	...	...	...	...	...	...	...	Gaza Strip
70.8	4,260	2,163	346	16	200	84,693[9]	29,155[9]	582[9]	714	34,322	2,070	13	12	119	Germany, East
105.2	1,720	3,262	643	69	280	61,316[9]	29,494[9]	483[9]	1,763	62,432	1,022	45	87	126	Germany, West
3.9[6]	340[6]	7	9	1	8	3,672	653	61	4	69	6	8	920	3	Ghana
0.2	5,900	4	2	...	3	39	15	450	1	17	590	...	...	...	Gibraltar
57.4	5,900	...	...	33	88	8,500[9]	2,000[9]	200[9]	83	3,541	354	14	63	3	Greece
...	...	...	...	...	...	...	...	...	11	...	...	2	36	...	Greenland
1.2	12,500	6	4	...	1	4[15]	10[15]	104[15]	1	8	86	1	140	2	Grenada
0.8	2,650	...	...	...	...	92	44	130	5	31[25]	95[25]	1	680	...	Guadeloupe
...	...	...	...	...	1	...	...	...	4	...	...	1	510	...	Guam
7.9[6]	1,000[6]	115	72	3	1	206[37]	50[37]	7[37]	18	58[38]	7[38]	2	75	14	Guatemala
...	...	...	...	...	...	...	...	...	9	...	...	...	...	1	Guernsey
2.6[6]	400[6]	29	61.2	...	...	...	...	...	5	21	4	1	24	1	Guinea
...	...	...	...	...	17	181	167	191	...	...	...	...	...	...	Guinea-Bissau
13.3[6]	14,700[6]	50	40	4	3	...	...	...	2	97[25]	130[25]	1	120	2	Guyana
2.1[6]	400[6]	28	14	...	...	...	...	...	4	73[17]	16[17]	2	10	...	Haiti
58.0	10,700	90	103	105	8	556[9]	297[9]	60[9]	3	22	7	4	970	3	Honduras
51.0	4,800	2,943	462	35	41	12,105[9]	5,545[9]	523[9]	5	565	130	...	...	3	Hong Kong
...	...	...	...	...	...	...	...	...	734	18,335	1,730	36	500	14	Hungary
1.3[6]	9,000[6]	20[4]	5[4]	1	5	765	162	667	59	232	954	21	32,000	2	Iceland
4,920.0	6,500	12,696	6,030	912	...	...	...	...	422	...	...	239	140	42	India
144.9[6]	1,000[6]	1,833[4]	959[4]	63	22	20,695	2,084	12	100	7,171	45	140	830	10	Indonesia
78	1,000	253[4]	144[4]	192	19	849[9]	...	...	44	...	...	24	680	3	Iran
...	...	84	65	1	132	609	204[9]	16[9]	13	63	4	...	...	1	Iraq
11.6	3,200	125	53	2	14	10,260[9]	...	...	49	...	...	3	57	5	Ireland
...	...	...	...	...	...	...	...	...	4	...	...	...	...	2	Isle of Man
24.2	6,600	214	152	19	5	275[9]	...	...	83	8,085	1,900	5	79	13	Israel
124.8	2,170	4,431	...	73	261	95,522[9]	24,470[9]	426[9]	1,122	23,469	409	34	91	57	Italy
...	...	...	...	...	16	868[15]	1,143[15]	540[15]	5	44[17]	22[17]	2[41]	2	5	Jamaica
143.9	1,170	2,053[4]	...	286	543	39,768[9]	...	...	676	109,167	910	50	180	97	Japan
...	...	...	...	...	...	...	...	...	5	...	...	...	...	1	Jersey
15.0	4,900	41	20	31	5	64	180	84	16	147[42]	58[42]	2	130	2	Jordan
9.2	600	40	20	...	...	...	...	...	2	...	...	1	15	...	Kampuchea (Cambodia)
...	...	...	...	...	...	...	...	...	6	531	27	28	1,500	5	Kenya
...	...	...	...	...	4	23[15]	...	...	...	...	...	2	870	2	Kiribati
187	9,200	1,178	653	37	—	...	...	...	17	...	...	...	...	...	Korea, North
48.1[6]	1,200[6]	482	...	81	16	3,449	402	10	146	665[43]	16[43]	14	120	4	Korea, South
0.9	500	14	15	...	5	...	95	66	3	326	174	...	...	1	Kuwait
...	...	...	...	...	...	...	...	...	...	...	...	...	...	...	Laos
...	...	...	...	...	...	...	...	...	7	...	...	...	...	1	Lebanon
1.5	800	13	9	...	...	...	...	...	1	...	...	1	45	...	Lesotho
10.2	3,500	49	22	2	14	439	160	51	7	...	...	1	590	1	Liberia
...	...	...	...	...	...	...	...	...	26	50	16	2	340	2	Libya
...	...	...	...	...	...	...	...	...	2	41	1,500	6	410	...	Liechtenstein
1.1	3,000	...	...	...	3	375[9]	258[9]	696[9]	14	225	630	4	3,100	...	Luxembourg
3.0	9,300	8	9	...	4	84	...	...	1	18	55	...	...	...	Macau
...	...	...	...	...	...	140[15]	60[15]	7[15]	47	217[17]	27[17]	14	670	3	Madagascar
1.5	300	4	2	...	2	...	...	...	2	80	12	9	1,500	11	Malawi
19.0	1,120	118	...	8	10	1,303	312	25	27	...	...	34	1,000	10	Malaysia
...	...	7	3	...	11	...	...	...	1	3	17	...	...	...	Maldives
0.9	2,570	18	13	1	...	...	...	...	20	603	1,770	6	1,100	1	Mali
1.1	3,450	...	...	...	...	...	...	...	5	...	...	2	1.1	1	Malta
...	...	19	8	...	...	136	36	38	...	...	...	1	2,100	...	Martinique
...	...	...	...	...	...	...	...	...	...	...	...	2	9,000	...	Mauritania
10.0	9,500	44	40	...	6	136	36	38	3	237	236	3	39	1	Mauritius
...	...	...	...	...	2	...	...	...	...	...	...	...	...	...	Mayotte
212.5	2,730	1,775	...	83	11	17,069[44]	6,549[44]	97[44]	87	12,388	160	29	120	11	Mexico
0.1	3,800	3	1	...	3	31	13	500	2	154	6,200	...	...	2	Monaco
17.7	9,400	59	...	6	21	...	3,600	1,700	4	7,400	4,400	4	24,000	...	Mongolia
...	...	1	...	...	1	16	4	360	1	2	170	2	17	1	Montserrat
39.0[6]	1,900[6]	267	162	12	...	...	...	...	11	1,580	74	6	1,300	5	Morocco
9.6[6]	700[6]	70	27	...	...	...	...	...	12	...	...	6	1,300	4	Mozambique
...	...	175[4]	136[4]	28	...	...	...	...	...	...	...	5	87	2	Myanmar (Burma)
...	...	...	...	...	...	...	...	...	...	...	...	...	...	...	Nauru
15.5	1,050	451	108.5	1	16	65	...	5	9	...	...	10	590	1	Nepal
...	...	...	...	12	451	36,125	8,600	590	538	15,879	1,096	47	100	36	Netherlands, The
0.3	2,000	8	2	...	3	61	22	147	1	20	147	3	625	2[12]	Netherlands Antilles
...	...	...	...	...	...	...	...	...	...	...	...	7	3,300	1	New Caledonia
...	...	172	103	9	...	2,287[9]	515[9]	120[9]	110	...	...	147	8,300	15	New Zealand
5.2	1,800	127	74	1	1	...	...	...	9	...	...	2	53	1	Nicaragua
8.6	100	240	...	20	23	...	...	...	17	600[7]	110[7]	3	590	...	Niger
...	...	...	...	...	...	...	...	...	18	...	...	3	90	8	Nigeria
...	...	...	...	...	...	...	...	...	...	...	...	...	...	...	Niue
10[19]	5,000	1	0.1	...	1	7	2	1,000	1	20	10,000	1	...	1	Norfolk Island

Cultural institutions (continued)

country	book publishing — number of titles: books total	books of which school textbooks	periodicals	pamphlets	number of copies ('000): books total	books of which school textbooks	periodicals	pamphlets	public libraries: number	volumes ('000)	registered borrowers ('000)	loans per 1,000 population
Norway	2,769	...	4,010	515	...	...	...	...	1,374	17,585	1,218	4,250
Oman	...	...	14	...	...	...	...	...	1	20	...	...
Pacific Is., Trust Terr. of the	93[3]	26	...	40[3]	47	11	...	80	5[18]	16	...	...
Marshall Islands	...	...	...	...	...	...	...	...	...	...	...	...
Micronesia, Fed. States of	...	...	...	...	...	...	...	...	...	...	...	...
Northern Mariana Islands	...	...	...	...	...	...	...	...	...	...	...	...
Palau	...	...	...	...	...	...	1,404	...	98	1,340	...	6
Pakistan	1,600	...	1,623	...	38[3]	...	...	5[3]	18	26	...	29
Panama	114	93	...	57	...	...	...	...	24	186	...	...
Papua New Guinea	...	...	72	...	...	...	...	...	15	45	...	...
Paraguay	...	...	...	...	...	...	...	...	...	...	...	...
Peru	560	59	507	75	...	...	...	...	557	1,950	...	123
Philippines	726	120	...	78	14,516[5]	14,464	...	202[5]	507[18]	...	194	...
Pitcairn Island	...	...	...	...	...	...	...	...	...	...	...	...
Poland	8,399	367	3,031	2,017	212,507	44,075	43,546	55,104	10,129	128,946	7,795	4,148
Portugal	9,052	970[32]	1,148	1,730	33,505	8,587[32]	...	2,804	178	7,546	...	513
Puerto Rico	...	...	...	...	...	...	...	...	121[40]	715	...	...
Qatar	316	219	8	21	2,100	1,533	191	105	7	273	10	53
Réunion	41	13	53	32	...	...	110	10	3	315	...	...
Romania	5,276[10]	...	435	10	64,335[10]	...	226,452	10	7,181	69,559	5,094	2,474
Rwanda	61	28	8	43	737	727	2	3	5	...	...	...
St. Helena and Ascension	...	2	...	...	...	...	...	2[3]	2	8	1	...
St. Kitts and Nevis	2[3]	—	...	3[3]	...	...	...	...	1	...	...	...
St. Lucia	44	25	...	19	89	84	7	18	3	15	...	...
St. Pierre and Miquelon	...	...	...	...	...	...	...	...	...	...	...	...
St. Vincent	...	...	...	...	...	...	...	...	1	...	...	...
San Marino	14	...	14	1	...	...	...	...	1	...	...	...
São Tomé and Príncipe	207	—	58	11	...	...	...	...	28	36	...	...
Saudi Arabia	42[3,10]	8[3,10]	29	10	169[3,10]	70[3,10]	...	10	1	7	...	...
Senegal	...	...	...	...	...	...	...	...	...	...	...	1,672
Seychelles	2[3]	...	2	31[3]	...	...	2	...	1	35	...	...
Sierra Leone	16	16	...	44[3]	93	43	...	12[3]	11	392	...	...
Singapore	1,524[49]	389[49]	1,786	403[49]	8,947[49]	4,081	4	2,179[49]	1	2,322	834	2,747
Solomon Islands	...	...	2	...	...	...	...	...	8	22	5	...
Somalia	...	...	...	...	...	...	...	...	...	...	...	...
South Africa	...	...	...	...	...	...	...	...	85	7,857	...	...
Bophuthatswana	...	...	...	...	...	...	...	...	...	...	...	...
Ciskei	...	...	...	...	...	...	...	...	...	...	...	...
Transkei	...	...	...	...	...	...	...	...	1	10	3	11
Venda	...	...	...	...	...	...	...	...	18	...	...	...
South West Africa/Namibia	...	...	3	...	...	...	...	...	8	157	...	170
Spain	31,694	2,889	6,711	6,711	199,760	34,522	48,936	48,937	1,677	11,730	1,308	...
Sri Lanka	957	93	454	1,411	8,853	6,832	42,511	4,750	650	...	197	...
Sudan, The	...	138[52]	25	...	...	12,905[52]	195	—	7	36	...	...
Suriname	...	...	22	...	...	...	44	...	2	268	54	2,100
Swaziland	...	...	1	...	...	...	2,600	...	1	51	...	...
Sweden	11,655[10]	260	43	10	...	...	5,680	...	383	45,713	...	8,940
Switzerland	11,626[10]	259[32]	1,533	10	...	...	31,773	...	79[53]	24,000[53]	...	1,400
Syria	57	...	48	—	...	...	454	—	14	365	618	563
Taiwan	12,046	...	3,418	...	...	...	...	...	198	1,084	...	...
Tanzania	166	12[3]	69	197	...	...	646	...	18[18]	428	11	9
Thailand	7,620	440	1,189	108	...	...	...	...	375	1,599	31	...
Togo	...	...	...	...	...	...	...	...	1	8	...	...
Tokelau	...	...	...	...	...	...	...	...	1	0.2	...	...
Tonga	33	5	...	287	0.4	0.1	...	...	...	...	...	...
Trinidad and Tobago	101	7	...	85	...	...	...	...	3	246	73	345
Tunisia	336	38	230	204	...	6,000	...	...	280	1,315	65	174
Turkey	6,382	192	2,856	654	...	...	...	...	726	6,878	486	40
Turks and Caicos Islands	...	...	...	...	...	...	...	...	1	26	3	1,641
Tuvalu	...	...	...	...	...	...	...	...	...	...	...	...
Uganda	...	...	...	...	...	...	...	...	1	73	157	31
U.S.S.R.	55,565	2,096[32]	5,295	28,411	1,530,337	296,000[32]	3,885,000	620,397	134,080	2,162,991	146,000	16,000
United Arab Emirates	41	41	8	—	2,215	2,215	25	16	7	15	...	...
United Kingdom	62,063	1,429	6,408	3,964	...	...	...	...	167	131,338	...	11,300
United States	47,489[57]	979	3,731	...	...	...	...	...	9,094	509,250	...	4,300
Uruguay	625	44	351	316	...	...	...	...	72	166	...	...
Vanuatu	...	...	...	...	...	...	...	...	1	12	0.7	...
Venezuela	3,596	...	160	604	1,194	...	4,649	...	195	2,031	66	669
Vietnam	2,100[10]	300[10]	173	10	52,000[10]	10	323	10	571	22,400	...	...
Virgin Islands (U.S)	...	...	...	...	...	...	...	...	1	90	10	707
Wallis and Futuna	...	...	...	...	...	...	...	...	...	...	...	...
West Bank	...	...	...	...	...	...	...	...	...	...	...	...
Western Sahara	...	...	...	...	...	...	...	...	...	...	...	...
Western Samoa	79	...	...	156	39	...	...	43	1	61	...	...
Yemen (Aden)	...	...	...	...	...	...	...	...	2	40	...	...
Yemen (Şan'ā')	...	...	40	...	...	...	...	...	...	...	...	...
Yugoslavia	9,000	1,489	1,659	1,734	45,397	20,221	4,127	7,886	2,012	28,060	...	1,600
Zaire	194[3]	53	106	37	...	...	225	...	11	177	9	1
Zambia	454	215[3]	...	—	235[60]	...	...	—	11	240	18	28
Zimbabwe	185	119	...	168	2,017	...	...	134	6	523	18	74

[1]Calculations based on statutory areas, whether of land or water. [2]Excludes zoological and aquatic collections in museums. [3]First editions only. [4]16-millimetre data not available. [5]School textbooks, university theses, and government publications only. [6]Excludes drive-ins, mobile units, or both. [7]National museums only. [8]Excludes school textbooks and children's books. [9]Professional only. [10]Books include pamphlets. [11]214 reporting. [12]Netherlands Antilles includes Aruba. [13]14 reporting. [14]The public library also serves as the national library. [15]Amateur only. [16]Ministry of Flemish Culture museums only. [17]3 reporting. [18]Library service points. [19]Attendance in '000's. [20]National and public museums only. [21]Drama, ballet, and dance only. [22]Drama, opera, ballet, and dance only. [23]644 reporting. [24]Amateur ballet, dance, and drama only. [25]1 reporting. [26]Film projection units. [27]57 reporting. [28]4 reporting. [29]11 reporting. [30]Excludes some Turkish publications. [31]Includes university theses. [32]Includes school pamphlets. [33]Royal theatre and regional theatres only. [34]Drama and opera only. [35]Includes national library and school

cinema					performing arts				museums			nature preservation			country
annual attendance (all cinemas) number ('000,000)	annual attendance per 1,000 population	fixed cinemas number	fixed cinemas seating capacity ('000)	number of long films produced	number of facilities	number of performances	annual attendance number ('000)	annual attendance per 1,000 population	number	annual attendance number ('000)	annual attendance per 1,000 population	national parks and nature reserves number	square metres per capita[1]	zoos, botanical gardens, etc. (number[2])	
11.1[6]	3,000[6]	449	121	7	13	4,877[9]	1,131[9]	270[9]	434	5,661	1,350	55	2,900	7	Norway
0.9	1,100	24	—	...	...	35[45]	5[45]	5[45]	1	...	...	1	190	...	Oman
...	...	52	...	...	...	...	...	...	5	...	...	1	93	...	Pacific Is., Trust Terr. of the
...	...	...	...	...	...	...	...	...	...	...	...	...	...	...	Marshall Islands
...	...	...	...	...	...	...	...	...	...	...	...	—	...	...	Micronesia, Fed. States of
...	...	...	...	...	...	...	...	...	...	...	...	2	370	...	Northern Mariana Islands
...	...	...	...	...	...	...	...	...	...	...	...	—	...	...	Palau
182.0	2,200	650[4]	455	67	11	18	169[9]	2[9]	10	2,052	21	52	650	6	Pakistan
7.1	4,800	...	...	...	1	55	...	...	10	...	...	6	3,000	2	Panama
...	...	...	...	...	7	122	265	91	2	100	32	2	9	3	Papua New Guinea
33.0	1,900	425	...	1	28	134[21]	185[21]	9[21]	18	201	10	9	3,300	1	Paraguay
...	...	...	...	...	6[52]	...	...	...	12	...	...	11	1,200	2	Peru
...	...	...	...	152	...	121[46]	29[46]	0.6[46]	61	...	...	26	72	5	Philippines
...	...	...	...	...	...	...	...	...	...	...	...	...	...	...	Pitcairn Island
95.3	2,500	1,728	459	40	152	113,511[9]	32,137[9]	850[9]	545	23,022	610	15	30	26	Poland
18.4	1,800	373[4]	179[4]	5	37	3,209[9]	594[9]	58[9]	228	5,675	556	12[47]	380[47]	10	Portugal
0.2	580	165	...	...	8	...	12[48]	...	24	...	...	2	1	8	Puerto Rico
...	...	4	3.8	1	...	...	1[48]	5[48]	1	60	300	1	...	1	Qatar
...	...	...	...	...	...	654	122	220	2	79	150	...	...	...	Réunion
208	9,082	5,454	257	29	150	47,714[9]	18,552[9]	809[9]	436	17,891	780	9	43	9	Romania
0.5	100	34	9.3	1	9	31[15]	58[15]	12[15]	4	...	...	2	430	...	Rwanda
53.0[19]	8,800	2	1	...	...	1[15]	1[15]	170[15]	1	...	...	...	...	1	St. Helena and Ascension
...	...	3	...	...	1	6[15]	...	...	...	...	...	...	...	...	St. Kitts and Nevis
...	...	8	...	...	...	...	...	...	1	7	58	1	120	...	St. Lucia
...	...	...	...	...	...	...	...	...	1	4	640	...	...	...	St. Pierre and Miquelon
0.1	4,500	7	3	...	1	26[9]	10[9]	460[9]	8	647	29,000	...	...	1	St. Vincent
...	...	2	...	...	...	...	...	...	...	...	...	...	...	...	San Marino
...	...	...	...	...	94	141[15]	18[15]	2[15]	1	40	4	1	400	2	São Tomé and Príncipe
3.6[6]	700[6]	60[4]	...	...	105	122[9]	52[9]	9[9]	4	55	10	9	3,300	4	Saudi Arabia
...	...	...	...	...	...	...	...	...	...	...	...	...	...	...	Senegal
...	...	...	...	...	2	6[15]	3[15]	40[15]	1	8	130	3	3,400	...	Seychelles
27.4	10,800	51	58	25	3	552	645	270	19	178[25]	55[25]	1	250	1	Sierra Leone
0.1[6]	300[6]	2	1	...	—	3	1	5	3	940	390	1	10	2	Singapore
...	...	...	...	...	...	...	...	...	1	29	150	1	46	...	Solomon Islands
...	...	...	...	...	...	...	...	...	1	...	...	1	570	...	Somalia
31.2	1,200	260	...	12	51	3,597[50]	1,348[50]	54[50]	22[51]	2,477[51]	96[51]	136	2,000	35	South Africa
...	...	...	...	...	...	...	...	...	...	...	...	2	380	...	Bophuthatswana
...	...	...	...	...	...	...	...	...	...	...	...	8	360	...	Ciskei
...	...	...	...	...	...	...	...	...	1	...	...	2	22	...	Transkei
...	...	...	...	...	...	...	...	...	1	...	...	1	75	...	Venda
...	...	...	...	...	...	...	...	...	9	...	...	9	60,000	1	South West Africa/Namibia
85.7[6]	2,210[6]	2,234	...	62	301	18,862	6,702	180	554	11,697	320	56	440	22	Spain
36.5	2,300	318	201	18	22	1,002[15]	600[15]	41[15]	9	466	34	37	400	4	Sri Lanka
13.0	600	56	97	2	...	333	134	340	7	221	10	3	810	2	Sudan, The
...	...	...	...	...	7	...	...	...	3	...	...	9	15,000	1	Suriname
...	...	4	...	...	...	...	...	...	1	...	...	4	610	...	Swaziland
17.5	2,080	1,112	232	27	27	11,460	2,301	274	199	16,557	1,971	67	1,800	18	Sweden
19.0	2,300	428	122	44	67	12,617	1,747[9]	270[9]	419	7,607	1,164	19	190	32	Switzerland
11.6	1,060	85	48	1	9	281	61	6	21	514	47	...	...	...	Syria
128.0	6,500	602	516	235	...	...	...	...	10	...	...	28	84	3	Taiwan
4.0	200	34	15	...	5	21	15	1	6	119[54]	7[54]	15	4,900	...	Tanzania
...	...	577[4]	400[4]	134	...	...	...	...	64	...	...	45	530	51	Thailand
...	...	...	...	...	...	...	...	...	1	48	21	7	1,600	...	Togo
0.1	1,000	3	2	—	...	...	...	...	...	...	...	...	...	...	Tokelau
...	...	...	...	...	...	...	...	...	...	...	...	5	320	...	Tonga
...	...	72	57	...	...	49[15]	...	...	1	8	7	8	140	1	Trinidad and Tobago
4.4	700	79	38	...	22	781	164	26	35	367[55]	52[55]	3	46	1	Tunisia
40.2	800	675	402	162	31	3,816[9,56]	1,218[9,56]	249[9,56]	133	6,637	129	15	58	7	Turkey
...	...	3	1	...	...	3	0.6	100	...	...	...	...	...	...	Turks and Caicos Islands
...	...	...	...	...	...	...	...	...	...	...	...	...	...	...	Tuvalu
2.3[6]	200[6]	174[4]	104[4]	...	...	...	...	...	16	...	...	18	900	2	Uganda
3,775.0	13,300	143,433	25,975	323	658[9]	282,100[9]	122,800[9]	429[9]	2,121	199,300	690	163	660	144	U.S.S.R.
7.1	10,300	74	29	...	18	37[37]	...	...	2	...	...	...	...	2	United Arab Emirates
62.0	1,100	1,327	505	39	404	...	40,242[9,22]	720[9,22]	1,768	52,000	920	57	270	155	United Kingdom
1,053.1	4,500	16,032	5,611	396	...	21,596	40,200	170	4,440	329,083	1,500	354	1,327	532	United States
6.2	2,100	120	80	1	25	3,097	...	...	19	17[58]	6[58]	6	100	4	Uruguay
0.1	1,000	3	1	...	...	...	...	...	...	...	...	...	...	...	Vanuatu
12.6[6]	680[6]	392	169	12	39	4,445	6,189	338	134	...	...	34	4,000	79	Venezuela
375.0	6,300	430	178	35	81	...	57,400[9]	1,000[9]	9	1,918[59]	375[59]	12	27	2	Vietnam
...	...	...	...	...	...	...	...	...	5	811	7,700	2	660	3	Virgin Islands (U.S.)
...	...	...	...	...	...	...	...	...	...	...	...	4	...	...	Wallis and Futuna
...	...	...	...	...	...	...	...	...	...	...	...	...	...	...	West Bank
0.5	3,200	6	6	...	...	9	2	11	...	...	...	...	...	...	Western Sahara
3.9[6]	2,000[6]	24	24	...	...	...	...	...	...	...	...	1	180	1	Western Samoa
...	...	...	...	...	...	...	...	...	5	...	...	...	...	...	Yemen (Aden)
14.5[6]	2,500[6]	35	28	...	...	...	...	...	...	...	...	...	...	...	Yemen (Ṣan'ā)
70.8	3,000	1,254	429	30	123	19,496[9]	5,610[9]	240[9]	379	10,649	497	20	140	19	Yugoslavia
...	...	...	...	...	4	98	22	18	4	...	...	9	2,700	4	Zaire
1.6	300	12	4	...	...	...	...	...	6	175	26	19	10,000	19	Zambia
2.5	600	32	...	...	...	...	...	...	9	162[61]	20[61]	17	3,400	4	Zimbabwe

libraries. [36]13,400,000 square metres per capita; a single national park comprises about one-third of the area of Greenland. [37]Drama only. [38]12 reporting. [39]Public educational libraries include service points and trade union libraries. [40]Includes 9 mobile libraries. [41]Marine parks only. [42]10 reporting. [43]58 reporting. [44]Excludes amateur opera and musical comedy. [45]Drama and folk dance only. [46]Metropolitan Manila only. [47]Excludes the Azores and Madeira. [48]Folk dance only. [49]Excludes government publications. [50]Performances of state-subsidized regional performing arts councils only. [51]Museums designated "declared cultural institutions" only. [52]Includes children's books. [53]Public libraries with 50,000 or more volumes only. [54]5 reporting. [55]32 reporting. [56]State theatres only. [57]Excludes government publications, books sold only by subscription, dissertations, and pamphlets. [58]2 reporting. [59]8 reporting. [60]School textbooks and government publications only. [61]6 reporting.

BIBLIOGRAPHY AND SOURCES

The following list indicates the principal sources used in the compilation of *Britannica World Data*. It is by no means a complete list, either for international or for national sources, but is indicative only of the range of materials to which reference has been made in preparing this compilation. For example, in addition to the kinds of works cited below, reference has also been made to the constitutions of each country, to the publications of its central or commercial banks, to unpublished information received in correspondence from the countries, and to other more specialized sources.

International Statistical Sources

Africana Publishing Co. *Africa Contemporary Record* (Colin Legum, ed. [annual]).

Angus & Robertson Publishers. *Pacific Islands Year Book* (irreg.).

Asian Development Bank. *Key Indicators of Developing Member Countries of ADB* (annual, with supplements).

Billboard Ltd. *World Radio TV Handbook* (annual).

Caribbean Development Bank. *Annual Report.*

Council for Mutual Economic Assistance (Comecon). *Statistichesky Yezhegodnik Stran-Chlenov Soveta Economicheskoy Vzaimopomoshchi* (Statistical Yearbook of the Council for Mutual Economic Assistance).

Eastern Caribbean Central Bank. *Report and Statement of Accounts* (annual).

Europa Publications Ltd. *Africa South of the Sahara* (annual); *The Europa Year Book* (2 vol.); *The Far East and Australasia* (annual); *The Middle East and North Africa* (annual); *South America, Central America, and the Caribbean* (annual); *Western Europe* (annual).

Food and Agriculture Organization. *Food Balance Sheets* (irreg.); *Production Yearbook; Trade Yearbook; World Census of Agriculture* (decennial); *Yearbook of Fishery Statistics; Yearbook of Forest Products.*

Her Majesty's Stationery Office. *The Commonwealth Yearbook.*

Holmes & Meier Publishers. *Latin America and Caribbean Contemporary Record* (Abraham F. Lowenthal, ed. [annual]); *Middle East Contemporary Survey* (Itamar Rabinovich and Haim Shaked, eds. [annual]).

Instituts d'Émission d'Outre-Mer et des Départements d'Outre-Mer (France). *Rapports d'Activité* (annual); *Bulletin trimestriel* (quarterly).

Inter-American Development Bank. *Economic and Social Progress in Latin America* (annual).

Inter-Parliamentary Union. *World Directory of Parliaments* (annual).

International Air Transport Association. *World Air Transport Statistics* (annual).

International Bank for Reconstruction and Development/The World Bank. *World Bank Atlas* (annual); *World Debt Tables* (annual); *World Development Report* (annual); *World Tables* (irreg.).

International Civil Aviation Organization. *Civil Aviation Statistics of the World* (annual); *Digest of Statistics.*

International Institute for Strategic Studies. *The Military Balance* (annual).

International Labour Organisation. *Year Book of Labour Statistics; The Cost of Social Security: Basic Tables* (triennial).

International Monetary Fund. *Annual Report on Exchange Arrangements and Exchange Restrictions; Government Finance Statistics Yearbook; International Financial Statistics* (monthly, with supplements and yearbook).

International Road Federation. *World Road Statistics* (annual).

Jane's Publishing Co., Ltd. *Jane's World Railways* (annual).

Lloyd's Register of Shipping. *Lloyd's Register of Shipping: Statistical Tables* (annual).

Longman Group U.K. Ltd. *Keesing's Record of World Events* (monthly).

Macmillan Press Ltd. *The Statesman's Year-Book.*

Middle East Economic Digest Ltd. *Africa Economic Digest* (semimonthly); *Middle East Economic Digest* (semimonthly).

Mining Journal. *Mining Annual Review.*

Nordic Council. *Yearbook of Nordic Statistics.*

Official Airline Guides, Inc. *Official Airline Guide* (monthly).

Organization of Eastern Caribbean States. *Annual Digest of Statistics.*

Organization for Economic Cooperation and Development. *Economic Surveys* (annual); *Financing and External Debt of Developing Countries* (annual); *National Accounts of Developing Countries* (irreg.).

Oxford University Press. *World Christian Encyclopedia* (David B. Barrett, ed. [1982]).

PennWell Publishing Co. *International Petroleum Encyclopedia* (annual).

René Moreux et Cie. *Marchés tropicaux & Méditerranéens* (semimonthly).

South Pacific Commission. *Key Economic Indicators* (occasional); *South Pacific Economies: Statistical Summary* (biennial).

United Nations (UN). *Compendium of Human Settlements Statistics* (irreg.); *Construction Statistics Yearbook; Demographic Yearbook; International Trade Statistics Yearbook; Energy Statistics Yearbook; Industrial Statistics Yearbook* (2 vol.); *Monthly Bulletin of Statistics; Population Studies* (irreg.); *National Accounts Statistics* (3 vol.; annual); *Population and Vital Statistics Report* (quarterly); *Statistical Yearbook; Supplement to the Statistical Yearbook and the Monthly Bulletin of Statistics* (irreg.); *World Population Prospects 19*** (biennial).

UN: Conference on Trade and Development. *Handbook of International Trade and Development Statistics* (annual); *The Least Developed Countries* (annual).

UN: Economic Commission for Africa. *African Socio-Economic Indicators* (annual); *African Statistical Yearbook; Demographic and Related Socio-Economic Data Sheets for ECA Member States* (1986); *Survey of Economic and Social Conditions in Africa* (irreg.).

UN: Economic Commission for Europe. *Annual Bulletin of Housing and Building Statistics for Europe; Annual Bulletin of Transport Statistics for Europe.*

UN: Economic Commission for Latin America. *Economic Survey of Latin America* (2 vol.; annual); *Statistical Yearbook for Latin America.*

UN: Economic and Social Commission for Asia and the Pacific. *Foreign Trade Statistics of Asia and the Pacific* (annual); *Statistical Indicators for Asia and the Pacific* (quarterly); *Statistical Yearbook for Asia and the Pacific.*

UN: Economic and Social Commission for Western Asia. *Demographic and Related Socio-Economic Data Sheets* (irreg.); *Population Bulletin* (irreg.); *The Population Situation in the ECWA Region* (irreg.); *Statistical Abstract of the Region of the Economic and Social Commission for Western Asia* (annual).

UN: Educational, Scientific, and Cultural Organization. *Statistical Yearbook.*

United States: Central Intelligence Agency, *The World Factbook* (annual); Dept. of Commerce, *Foreign Economic Trends* (irreg.), *Overseas Business Reports* (annual), *World Population* (annual); Dept. of Energy, *International Energy Annual;* Dept. of Health and Human Services, *Social Security Programs Throughout the World* (biennial); Dept. of Interior, *Minerals Year-book* (3 vol.); Dept. of State, *Background Notes* (irreg.).

Vatican (Central Statistics Office of the Church). *Statistical Yearbook of the Church.*

West India Committee and FT International. *The Caribbean Handbook* (annual).

World Health Organization. *World Health Statistics Annual.*

World Tourism Organization. *World Tourism Statistics* (annual).

National Statistical Sources

Afghanistan. *First Seven-Year Economic and Social Development Plan, 1355–1361* (March 1976–March 1983); *Preliminary Results of the First Afghan Population Census, 1979; Review of the General Socio-economic Situation in the Democratic Republic of Afghanistan During 1358* (21 March 1979–20 March 1980).

Albania. *Report on the Directives of the 9th Congress of the Party for the 8th Five-Year Plan (1986–1990) of the Development of the Economy and Culture of the People's Socialist Republic of Albania; Portrait of Albania* (1982); *Vjetari statistikori R.P.S. të Shqipërisë* (Statistical Yearbook of the People's Socialist Republic of Albania [annual]); *40 années d'Albanie socialiste* (1984).

Algeria. *Annuaire statistique; Recensement général de la population et de l'habitat, 1987.*

American Samoa. *American Samoa Statistical Digest* (annual); *Population of American Samoa* (ESCAP; Country Monograph Series No. 7.1 [1979]); *1980 Census of Population and Housing* (U.S.).

Andorra. *Recull Estadístic* (1985).

Angola. *Informação Estatística* (annual); *Recenseamento Geral da População, 1960; Situação Econômica e Financeira de Angola* (annual).

Anguilla. *Abstract of Statistics, 1960–1982; Anguilla Census of Population 1984.*

Antigua. *Statistical Yearbook.*

Argentina. *Anuario estadístico de la República Argentina; Boletín estadístico trimestral* (quarterly); *Censo nacional de población y vivienda, 1980; Encuesta permanente de hogares* (irreg.).

Aruba. *Monthly Statistical Report: International Tourism to Aruba; Statistical Yearbook.*

Australia. *Census of Manufacturing Establishments: Summary of Operations by Industry Subdivision, Australia* (annual); *Monthly Summary of Statistics, Australia; National Income and Expenditure* (annual); *Foreign Trade Australia: Comparative and Summary Tables* (annual); *Social Indicators* (irreg.); *Year Book Australia; 1986 Census of Population and Housing.*

Austria. *Österreichisches Jahrbuch* (annual); *Sozialstatistische Daten 1986; Statistisches Handbuch* (annual); *Volkszählung, 1981.*

Bahamas, The. *Quarterly Statistical Summary; Statistical Abstract* (annual); *Vital Statistics Report* (annual); *1980 Census of Population and Housing.*

Bahrain. *Statistical Abstract* (annual); *1981 Census of Bahrain.*

Bangladesh. *Bangladesh Population Census, 1981; Population of Bangladesh* (ESCAP; Country Monograph Series No. 8 [1981]); *Statistical Yearbook of Bangladesh.*

Barbados. *Barbados Economic Report* (annual); *Monthly Digest of Statistics; Report on the Census of Production, 1981.*

Belgium. *Annuaire statistique de la Belgique; Recensement de la population et des logements au 1er mars 1981.*

Belize. *Abstract of Statistics* (annual); *Belize Economic Survey* (annual); *Labour Force Survey* (1983–84); *1980–81 Population Census of the Commonwealth Caribbean, Belize.*

Benin. *Annuaire statistique; Recensement des Entreprises 1980* (2 parts); *Recensement général de la population et de l'habitation* (1979).

Bermuda. *Bermuda Digest of Statistics* (annual); *Report of the Population Census, 1980; Report of the Manpower Survey* (annual).

894

Bhutan. *Development in a Himalayan Kingdom* (A World Bank Country Study [1983]); *Statistical Yearbook of Bhutan* (annual).

Bolivia. *Censo Nacional de población y vivienda de 1976; Compendio Estadistico* (annual); *Estadísticas Económicas* (annual); *Resumen estadístico* (annual).

Botswana. *National Development Plan 1985–91; 1981 Population and Housing Census; Statistical Abstract* (annual).

Brazil. *Anuário Econômico-Fiscal; Anuário Estatístico do Brasil; Foreign Trade of Brazil* (annual); *IX Recenseamento Geral do Brasil, 1980.*

British Virgin Islands. *Census of the British Virgin Islands, 12th May 1980* (*Provisional*); *Statistical Abstract* (irreg.).

Brunei. *Brunei Statistical Yearbook; Report on the Census of Population, 1981.*

Bulgaria. *Prebroyavane—1975; resultati, perspektivi* (Census of Population—1975: Results, Perspectives); *Statisticheskii godishnik* (Statistical Yearbook).

Burkina Faso. *Annuaire Statistique; Recensement général de la population du 10 au 20 decembre 1985; Statistiques Sociales* (annual).

Burundi. *Annuaire statistique; Recensement général de la population, 16–30 août 1979.*

Cameroon. *Note annuelle de statistique; Recensement général de la population et de l'habitat d'avril 1976; Tableaux économiques du Cameroun* (1983).

Canada. *Canada Year Book* (irreg.); *Census of Agriculture, 1981; National Income and Expenditure Accounts* (quarterly); *Census Canada 1986: Population.*

Cape Verde. *Boletím Trimestral Estatística* (quarterly); *1.º Recenseamento Geral da População e Habitação—1980.*

Cayman Islands. *Cayman Islands Population Census 1979; Statistical Abstract of the Cayman Islands* (annual).

Central African Republic. *Annuaire statistique; Recensement général de la population de décembre 1975.*

Chad. *Annuaire statistique.*

Chile. *Chile XV censo nacional de población y de vivienda, 21 de abril 1982; Compendio estadístico* (annual); *Cuentas nacionales de Chile, 1960–1980; Plan nacional indicativo de desarrollo* (quinquennial).

China, People's Republic of. *Almanac of China's Economy* (irreg.); *China: A Statistics Survey in 19*** (annual); *People's Republic of China Year-Book; Major Figures by 10 Percent Sampling on the 1982 Census of the People's Republic of China; Statistical Yearbook of China; Yearbook of the Encyclopedia of China.*

Christmas Island. *Annual Report; Census of Population and Housing, 30 June 1981.*

Cocos (Keeling) Islands. *Annual Report; Census of Population and Housing, 30 June 1981.*

Colombia. *Colombia estadística* (annual); *XV Censo nacional de población y IV de vivienda* (1985).

Comoros. *Plan interimaire de développement économique et sociale (1983–1986); Recensement général de la population et de l'habitat 15 septembre 1980.*

Congo, People's Republic of the. *Annuaire statistique; Recensement général de la population de 1974.*

Cook Islands. *Cook Islands Census of Population and Dwellings, 1986; Cook Islands Quarterly Statistical Bulletin.*

Costa Rica. *Anuario estadístico; Censos Nacionales de 1973; Plan Nacional de Desarrollo, 1986–90* (2 vol.).

Côte d'Ivoire. *Annuaire statistique; La Côte d'Ivoire en chiffres* (irreg.); *L'Économie Ivoirienne* (irreg.); *Enquête permanente aupres des menages: resultats provisoires 1985.*

Cuba. *Anuario estadístico; Censo de población y viviendas, 1981; Compendio estadístico de Cuba* (annual); *Cuba Quarterly Economic Report.*

Cyprus. *Census of Industrial Production* (annual); *Economic Report* (annual); *Statistical Abstract* (annual).

Czechoslovakia. *Statistická ročenka Československé Socialistické Republiky* (Statistical Yearbook of the Czechoslovak Socialist Republic); *Sčítání lidu, domů a bytů 1980* (Census of Population and Housing).

Denmark. *Folke- og boligtaellingen, 1981* (Population and Housing Census); *Statistisk årbog* (Statistical Yearbook).

Djibouti. *Annuaire statistique de Djibouti.*

Dominica. *Statistical Digest.*

Dominican Republic. *República Dominicana en cifras* (annual); *VI Censo nacional de población y vivienda, 1981.*

Ecuador. *Encuesta anual de manufactura y minería; Serie estadística* (quinquennial); *IV Censo de población: III de vivienda resultados anticipados por muestreo* (1982).

Egypt. *Population, Housing, and Establishment Census, 1986; Statistical Yearbook.*

El Salvador. *Anuario estadístico; Censos económicos, 1979* (*Manufactura diversa; Agroindustrias; Comercio y servicios; Electricidad, construcción, transporte comercial*); *El Salvador en cifras* (annual).

Equatorial Guinea. *Censos Nacionales, I de Población y I de Vivienda—4 al 17 de Julio de 1983.*

Ethiopia. *Ethiopia 1984 Population and Housing Census; Ethiopia Statistical Abstract* (annual).

Faeroe Islands. *Árbog for Faerøerne* (Yearbook for the Faeroe Islands).

Fiji. *Annual Employment Survey; Census of Industries* (annual); *Current Economic Statistics* (quarterly); *1986 Census of the Population.*

Finland. *Annual Statistics of Agriculture; Economic Survey* (annual); *1985 Population and Housing Census; Statistical Yearbook of Finland.*

France. *Annuaire statistique de la France; Données sociales* (triennial); *Recensement général de la population de 1982; Métropole; Tableaux de l'Economie Française* (annual).

French Guiana. *Annuaire statistique de la Guyane; Recensement général de la population dans les Départements d'outre-mer en 9 mars 1982, Guyane; Tableaux economiques regionaux: Guyane* (annual).

French Polynesia. *Bilan statistique de l'année; Résultats du recensement de la population de la Polynésie Française, 15 Octobre 1983; Tableaux de l'economie polynesienne* (irreg.); *Te avei'a: Bulletin d'information statistique* (quarterly).

Gabon. *Situation économique, financière et sociale de la République Gabonaise* (annual).

Gambia, The. *The Gambia since Independence: 1965–1980, 15 years of Nationhood.*

Gaza Strip. *Judaea, Samaria, and Gaza Area Statistics Quarterly; Palestinian Statistical Abstract* (annual).

Germany, East. *Statistisches Jahrbuch der Deutschen Demokratischen Republik; Volks-, Berufs-, Wohnraum-, und Gebäude zahlung 1981.*

Germany, West. *Statistisches Jahrbuch für die Bundesrepublik Deutschland; Volkszählung vom 27 Mai 1970* (Census of Population).

Ghana. *Economic Survey* (annual); *Ghana: An Official Handbook* (1977); *Industrial Statistics* (annual); *Population Census of Ghana, 1984.*

Gibraltar. *Abstract of Statistics* (annual); *Census of Gibraltar, 1981.*

Greece. *Recensement des industries manufacturières: Artisanat, du commerce et autres services* (1978); *Recensement de la population et des habitations, 1981; Statistical Yearbook of Greece.*

Greenland. *Grønland* (annual); *Grønlands befolkning* (Greenland Population [annual]).

Grenada. *Abstract of Statistics* (annual).

Guadeloupe. *Annuaire statistique de la Guadeloupe; Recensement général de la population dans les Departements d'Outre-mer en 9 mars 1982, Guadeloupe; Tableaux economiques regionaux: Guadeloupe* (annual).

Guam. *Guam Annual Economic Review; 1980 Census of Population and Housing.*

Guatemala. *Anuario estadístico; Censos nacionales, 1981: IX de población—IV de habitación.*

Guernsey. *Guernsey Census 1986; Statistical Digest* (annual).

Guinea, Republic of. *Situation Économique et Conjoncturelle au 31 decembre 1985 et éléments sur la mise en oeuvre de la réform économique au cours du première trimestre 1986.*

Guinea-Bissau. *Boletim Trimestral de Estatística; Recenseamento Geral da População e da Habitação, 16 de Abril de 1979.*

Guyana. *Annual Statistical Abstract.*

Haiti. *Bulletin trimestriel de statistique; Haiti: A Country Profile* (1981); *Résultats préliminaires du recensement général (Septembre 1982).*

Honduras. *Anuario estadístico; Censo nacional de Población, 1974; Honduras en cifras* (annual); *Plan nacional de desarrollo, 1987–90.*

Hong Kong. *Annual Digest of Statistics; Hong Kong* (annual); *Hong Kong 1986 By-Census; Hong Kong in Figures* (annual); *Hong Kong Social and Economic Trends* (irreg.).

Hungary. *Statisztikai évkönyv* (Statistical Yearbook); *1980, Évi népszámlálás* (Census of Population).

Iceland. *Hagtidhindi* (monthly); *Tölfraedihandbók* (Statistical Abstract of Iceland [irreg.]); *Verslunarskýrslur* (External Trade [annual]).

India. *Census of India, 1981; Economic Survey* (annual); *India: A Reference Annual; Statistical Abstract* (annual).

Indonesia. *Indonesia: An Official Handbook* (1989); *Sensus penduduk Indonesia, 1980* (Census of Population); *Statistical Yearbook of Indonesia.*

Iran. *General Census of Population and Housing, November 1976; A Statistical Reflection of the Islamic Republic of Iran* (annual); *Statistical Yearbook of the Islamic Republic of Iran.*

Iraq. *Iraq: A Country Study* (1979); *Statistical Abstract* (annual).

Ireland. *Census of Population of Ireland, 1986; National Income and Expenditure* (annual); *Statistical Abstract* (annual).

Isle of Man. *Isle of Man 1981 Census Report; Isle of Man Digest of Economic and Social Statistics* (annual).

Israel. *1983 Census of Population and Housing; Statistical Abstract* (annual).

Italy. *Annuario di statistica agraria: Annuario di statistiche demografiche; Annuario di statistiche industriali; Annuario statistico dell'istruzione; Annuario statistico Italiano; Statistiche forestale* (annual); *Statistiche sociali* (1981); *12 Censimento general della popolazione, 1981.*

Jamaica. *Economic and Social Survey* (annual); *Statistical Abstract* (annual); *Statistical Yearbook of Jamaica.*

Japan. *Establishment Census of Japan, 1981; Japan Statistical Yearbook; Statistical Indicators on Social Life* (annual); *1985 Population Census of Japan.*

Jersey. *Report of the Census for 1986; Statistical Digest* (annual).

Jordan. *Census 1979; Family Expenditure Survey* (1980); *National Accounts* (irreg.); *Statistical Yearbook.*

Kenya. *Economic Survey* (annual); *Kenya Statistical Digest* (quarterly); *Statistical Abstract* (annual).

Kiribati. *Annual Abstract of Statistics; National Development Plan, 1979–1982; Report on the 1985 Census of Population.*

Korea, North. *North Korea: A Country Study* (1981).

Korea, South. *Korea Statistical Yearbook; Social Indicators in Korea* (irreg.); *The 5th Five-Year Economic and Development Plan, 1982–1986; 1980 Population and Housing Census.*

Kuwait. *Annual Statistical Abstract; Economic Report* (annual); *General Census of Population and Housing and Buildings 1985.*

Lesotho. *Annual Statistical Bulletin; 1976 Population Census Report.*

Liberia. *Economic Survey* (annual); *1974 Census of Population and Housing.*

Libya. *The Five-Year Development Plan 1981–85; Libya Population Census, 1973; Statistical Abstract for Libya* (annual).

Liechtenstein. *Statistisches Jahrbuch; Volkszählung, 2 Dezember 1980* (Census of Population).

Luxembourg. *Annuaire statistique; Bulletin du STATEC* (monthly); *Recensement général de la population du 31 mars 1981.*

Macau. *Anuário Estatístico; Inquerito Industrial* (annual); *XII Recenseamento Geral da População, 1981.*

Madagascar. *Recensement général de la population et des habitats, 1975; Situation économique* (annual).

Malawi. *Malawi Population and Housing Census, 1987; Malawi Statistical Yearbook; Malawi Yearbook.*

Malaysia. *Fifth Malaysia Plan, 1986–1990; Malaysia Official Year Book; Malaysian Annual Statistical Bulletin; 1980 Population and Housing Census.*

Maldives. *National Development Plan 1985–1987* (2 vols.); *Population and Housing Census, 1985; Statistical Year Book of Maldives.*

Mali. *Annuaire statistique du Mali; Recensement de la population, 1–16 décembre 1976.*

Malta. *Annual Abstract of Statistics; Census of Industrial Production Report for 19*** (annual); *Malta Year Book* (annual).

Martinique. *Annuaire statistique de la Martinique; Bulletin de statistique* (quarterly); *Recensement de la population dans les départements d'outre-mer, 9 mars 1982—Martinique; Tableaux economiques regionaux: Martinique* (annual).

Mauritania. *Annuaire Statistique.*

Mauritius. *Bi-annual Digest of Statistics; 1983 Housing and Population Census of Mauritius.*

Mayotte. *Recensement général de la population, 1978.*

Mexico. *Anuario estadístico; X Censo general de población y vivienda, 1980; La Economia Mexi-*

cana en Cifras (1986); *Informe de Gobierno: Estadístico* (annual).

Mongolia. *National Economy of the MPR, 1921–86* (1986; quinquennial?).

Montserrat. *Caribbean Population Census, May 12, 1980; Statistical Digest* (annual).

Morocco. *Annuaire statistique du Maroc; Economic and Social Development Report, 1981; Recensement général de la population et de l'habitat de 1982.*

Mozambique. *Informação Estatística* (annual); *1º Recenseamento Geral da População, 1980.*

Myanmar (Burma). *Report to the Pyithu Hluttaw on the Financial, Social, and Economic Conditions for 19*** (annual); *1983 Population Census.*

Nepal. *Census of Manufacturing Establishments of Nepal, 1981–82; Economic Survey* (annual); *Population Monograph of Nepal* (1987); *The Sixth Plan (1980–85); Statistical Pocket Book* (irreg.); *Statistical Yearbook of Nepal.*

Netherlands, The. *Statistical Yearbook of the Netherlands; 14e Algemene volkstelling, 28 februari 1971* (14th General Population Census).

Netherlands Antilles. *Tweede Algemene Volks- en Woningtelling Nederlandse Antillen: toestand per 1 Februari 1981; Statistical Yearbook of the Netherlands Antilles.*

New Caledonia. *Annuaire statistique; Enquête socio-économique, 1980–1981; Resultats du Recensement de la population, 15 Avril 1983; Tableaux de l'economie Caledonienne* (annual).

New Zealand. *1986 New Zealand Census of Population and Dwellings; New Zealand Official Yearbook.*

Nicaragua. *Anuario estadístico de Nicaragua; Nicaragua: A Country Study* (1982); *Plan Económico, 1987* (irreg.).

Niger. *Annuaire statistique; Les comptes de la nation: années 1978–1979–1980* (1984); *Données de base* (1979).

Nigeria. *Annual Abstract of Statistics; Fourth National Development Plan* (1981); *Nigeria: A Country Study* (1981).

Niue. *Abstract of Statistics* (annual); *Census of Population and Housing, 1976; Niue National Development Plan, 1980–1985.*

Norfolk Island. *Annual Report; Census of Population and Housing, 30 June 1986.*

Norway. *Folke- og boligtelling 1980* (Population and Housing Census); *Industristatistikk* (annual); *Statistisk årbok* (Statistical Yearbook).

Oman. *Statistical Year Book; The Second Five-Year Plan of Development, 1981–1985.*

Pacific Islands, Trust Territory of the. *Report of the Trusteeship Council to the Security Council on the Trust Territory of the Pacific Islands* (annual); *Report to the United Nations* (annual).

Pakistan. *Economic Survey* (annual); *Pakistan Statistical Yearbook; Population Census of Pakistan, 1981; Some Socio-Economic Trends* (annual); *10 Years of Pakistan in Statistics, 1972–1982* (1983).

Panama. *Indicadores económicos y sociales* (annual); *Octavo censo de población: Cuarto censo de vivienda, 11 de mayo de 1980; Panama en cifras* (annual); *Situacion económica: Cuentas nacionales* (annual); *Situacion económica: Industria* (annual).

Papua New Guinea. *Abstract of Statistics* (quarterly); *National Accounts Statistics—Statistical Bulletin* (quarterly); *Population of Papua New Guinea (ESCAP;* Country Monograph Series No. 7.2 [1982]); *Social Indicators of Papua New Guinea, 1980–85; Summary of Statistics* (annual); *1980 National Population Census.*

Paraguay. *Anuario estadístico del Paraguay; Censo nacional de población y viviendo, 1982.*

Peru. *Censos nacionales; VIII de población: III de vivienda, 12 de julio de 1981; Compendio estadístico* (annual); *Informe estadístico* (annual).

Philippines. *Philippine Statistical Yearbook; Philippine Yearbook; 1980 Census of Population.*

Poland. *Narodowy spis powszechny z dnia 7 XII 1978 r.* (Census of Population); *Rocznik statystyczny* (Statistical Yearbook).

Portugal. *Anuário Estatístico; Estatísticas Agricolas* (annual); *Estatísticas do Comercio Externo* (annual); *Estatísticas Demograficas* (annual); *Estatísticas Industriais* (2 vol.; annual); *Estatísticas Monetarias e Financeiras* (annual); *Recenseamento Agricola, 1979; XII Recenseamento Geral da População: II Recenseamento Geral da Habitação, 1981.*

Puerto Rico. *Anuario estadístico; Estadisticas socioeconomicas* (annual); *Informe económico al gobernador* (Economic Report to the Governor [annual]); *1980 Census of Population* (U.S.).

Qatar. *Annual Statistical Abstract; Economic Survey of Qatar* (annual); *Qatar Year Book.*

Réunion. *l'Economie de la Réunion* (annual); *Faits et chiffres réunionnaise* (1985); *Panorama de l'Économie de la Réunion* (annual); *Recensement général de la population en 1974: Départements d'outre-mer—Réunion.*

Romania. *Anuarul statistic al Republicii Socialiste România; Recensământul populaţiei şi al locuinţelor, din 5 ianuarie 1977; Romania Yearbook.*

Rwanda. *Bulletin de Statistique: Supplement Annuel; IIIème Plan de Developpement Economique, Social et Culturel 1982–86.*

St. Kitts and Nevis. *Annual Digest of Statistics; St. Christopher and Nevis: Economic Report* (World Bank Country Study) (1985).

St. Lucia. *Annual Statistical Digest.*

St. Pierre and Miquelon. *Résultats du recensement de la population dans les départements d'outre-mer, 9 mars 1982.*

St. Vincent and the Grenadines. *Digest of Statistics* (annual).

San Marino. *Annuario statistico, 1981–84* (4 vol.?; irreg.); *3 Censimento generale dell agricoltura* (1977); *5 Censimento generale della popolazione* (1979).

Saudi Arabia. *The Statistical Indicator* (annual); *Statistical Summary* (Saudi Arabian Monetary Agency [annual]); Statistical Year Book.

Senegal. *Le Sénégal en chiffres* (irreg.); *Situation économique du Senegal* (annual).

Seychelles. *National Development Plan, 1985–89; Statistical Abstract* (annual); *1977 Census Report.*

Sierra Leone. *Sierra Leone: 12 Years of Economic Achievement and Political Consolidation under the APC and Dr. Siaka Stevens, 1968–80.*

Singapore. *Census of Population, 1980; Economic and Social Statistics, 1960–1982; Report on the Census of Industrial Production* (annual); *Singapore Yearbook; Yearbook of Statistics Singapore.*

Solomon Islands. *Solomon Islands 1986 Population Census; Statistical Yearbook.*

Somalia. *Statistical Abstract* (annual).

South Africa. *Population Census 1985; South Africa: Official Yearbook of the Republic of South Africa; South African Statistics* (biennial).

South West Africa/Namibia. *Budget 19**–19*** (annual); *Statistical/Economic Review* (annual).

Spain. *Anuario estadístico; Censo de población de 1981.*

Sri Lanka. *Census of Population and Housing, 1981; Report on the Survey on Manufacturing Industries, 1979; Sri Lanka Year Book; Statistical Pocketbook of the Democratic Socialist Republic of Sri Lanka* (annual).

Sudan, The. *Third Population Census, 1983.*

Suriname. *Statistisch Jaarboek van Suriname.*

Swaziland. *Annual Statistical Bulletin; Report on the 1976 Swaziland Population Census.*

Sweden. *Folk- och bostadsräkningen, 1980* (Population and Housing Census); *Statistisk årsbok för Sverige* (Statistical Abstract of Sweden [annual]).

Switzerland. *Recensement fédéral de la population, 1980; Statistisches Jahrbuch* (Statistical Yearbook).

Syria. *Census of Agriculture, 1981; General Census of Housing and Inhabitants, 1981; Statistical Abstract* (annual).

Taiwan. *Industry of Free China* (monthly); *Social Indicators of the Republic of China* (annual); *Statistical Abstract* (annual); *Statistical Yearbook of the Republic of China; Taiwan Statistical Data Book* (annual); *Yearbook of Labor Statistics; 1980 Census of Population and Housing.*

Tanzania. *Tanzania Statistical Abstract* (irreg.); *1978 Population Census.*

Thailand. *Report of the Survey of Business Trade and Services* (biennial); *Foreign Trade Statistics* (monthly); *Report of the Industrial Survey, Whole Kingdom* (biennial); *Report of the Labor Force Survey: Whole Kingdom* (quarterly); *Statistical Handbook of Thailand* (annual); *Statistical Yearbook; 1980 Population and Housing Census.*

Togo. *Annuaire statistique; Plan de développement économique & social, 1981–1985; Recensement général de la population, 1970.*

Tokelau. *Census of Population, 1981; Report of the Administrator of Tokelau for the Year Ended: 31 March 19*** (annual).

Tonga. *Population Census, 1986; Statistical Abstract* (irreg.).

Trinidad and Tobago. *Population Census, 1980; Annual Statistical Digest.*

Tunisia. *Annuaire statistique de la Tunisie; Recensement général de la population et des logements, 30 mars 1984.*

Turkey. *Diş Ticaret İstatistikleri* (Annual Foreign Trade Statistics); *Genel Sanayi ve İşyerleri Sayımı* (Census of Industry and Business Establishments [1980]); *Genel Nüfus Sayımı, 12. 10. 1985* (Census of Population); *Genel Tarım Sayımı, 1980* (Census of Agriculture); *İnşaat İstatistikleni* (Construction Statistics [annual]); *Türkiye İstatistik Yilliği* (Statistical Yearbook of Turkey).

Turks and Caicos Is. *Statistical Yearbook of the Turks and Caicos Islands.*

Tuvalu. *Abstract of Statistics* (irreg.); *Census of the Population, 1979.*

Union of Soviet Socialist Republics. *Narodnoye Khozyaystvo SSSR* (National Economy of the USSR [annual]); *Promyshlennost SSSR* (Industry USSR [irreg.]); *Trud v SSSR* (Labour in the USSR [irreg.]).

United Arab Emirates. *Statistical Yearbook* (Abu Dhabi) (annual).

United Kingdom. *Annual Abstract of Statistics; Britain: An Official Handbook* (annual); *National Income and Expenditure* (annual); *Census 1981; Report on the Census of Production: Summary Tables* (annual).

United States. *Agricultural Statistics* (annual); *Annual Energy Review; Current Population Reports* (Series P-20, P-23, P-25, P-26, P-27, P-28, P-60); *Digest of Education Statistics* (annual); *Minerals Yearbook* (3 vol.; annual); *National Transportation Statistics* (annual); *Statistical Abstract* (annual); *U.S. Exports: SIC-Based Products* (annual); *U.S. Imports: SIC-Based Products* (annual); *Vital and Health Statistics* (series 1–20); *1987 Census of Construction Industries; 1987 Census of Manufacturing; 1987 Census of Retail Trade; 1987 Census of Wholesale Trade; 1987 Census of Agriculture; 1980 Census of Population and Housing.*

Uruguay. *Anuario Estadístico; Censo General: VI de población: IV de viviendas, Octubre 1985. Encuesta Nacional de Hogares* (annual).

Vanuatu. *Recensement de la population, 1979; Vanuatu Statistical Yearbook.*

Venezuela. *Anuario estadístico; Encuesta de hogares por muestreo* (annual); *Encuesta industrial* (annual); *IX Censo general de población y vivienda, 20 de octubre 1981.*

Virgin Islands of the United States. *Annual Report; Economic Review, 1986; 1980 Census of Population* (U.S.).

Wallis and Futuna. *Résultats du Recensement de la Population, 15 Février 1983.*

West Bank. *Judaea, Samaria, and Gaza Area Statistics Quarterly; Palestinian Statistical Abstract* (annual).

Western Sahara. *Recensement General de la Population et de l'Habitat* (1982 [Morocco]).

Western Samoa. *Annual Statistical Abstract; Census of Population and Housing, 1976.*

Yemen, People's Democratic Republic of. *The Yemens: Country Studies* (1986).

Yemen Arab Republic. *The Housing and Population Census, February 1975; Statistical Year Book.*

Yugoslavia. *Popis stanovištva i stanova od 31. marta 1981* (Census of Population and Housing as of March 31, 1981); *Statistički godišnjak Jugoslavije* (Statistical Yearbook of Yugoslavia).

Zaire. *Annuaire statistique;* Conjoncture Economique (annual); *Recensement Scientifique de la Population du 1er juillet 1984.*

Zambia. *Country Profile: Zambia 1985; Monthly Digest of Statistics; Third National Development Plan, 1979–83; 1980 Census of Population and Housing.*

Zimbabwe. *1982 Population Census: Main Demographic Features of the Population of Zimbabwe; Statistical Year-book.*

Index

This index covers both *Britannica Book of the Year* (cumulative for ten years) and *Britannica World Data.*

Entries in dark type are titles of articles in the *Book of the Year;* **an accompanying year in dark type gives the year the reference appears, and the accompanying page number** in light type shows where the article appears. For example, "Archaeology **90**:143; **89**:125; **88**:125; **87**:141; **86**:164; **85**:165; **84**:176; **83**:177; **82**:183; **81**:183" indicates that the article "Archaeology" appeared every year from 1981 through 1990. Other references that appear with a page number but without a year refer to references from the current yearbook.

Indented entries in light type that follow dark type article titles refer by page number to other places in the text where the subject of the article is discussed. Light type entries that are not indented refer by page number to subjects that are not themselves article titles. Names of people covered in biographies and obituaries are followed by the abbreviation "(biog.)" or "(obit.)" with the year in dark type and a page number in light type, *e.g.,* Ailey, Alvin (obit.) **90**:103; or Reagan, Ronald Wilson (biog.) **89**:82; **88**:80; **87**:93; **86**:108; **85**:110; **84**:95; **83**:89; **82**:90; **81**:88. In cases where a person has both a biography and an obituary, the words appear as subentries under the main entry and are alphabetized accordingly, *e.g.,*:

Berlin, Irving
biography **89**:66
obituary **90**:105

References to illustrations are by page number and are preceded by the abbreviation *il.*

The index uses word-by-word alphabetization (treating a word as one or more characters separated by a space from the next word). Names beginning with "Mc" and "Mac" are alphabetized as "Mac"; "St." is treated as "Saint."

E

H

J

U

U.A.E.: *see* United Arab Emirates
UAL Corp. (Am. co.)
  stock exchanges 190
UAW (Am. org.): *see* United Automobile
  Workers
UBP: *see* United Bermuda Party
UCR (pol. party, Arg.): *see* Unión Cívica
  Radical
UDF (pol. party, Fr.): *see* Union pour la
  Démocratic Françoise
UDP: *see* United Democratic Party
Ueberroth, Peter V. (biog.) **85**:115
UEFA Cup
  association football 338
Uemura, Naomi (obit.) **85**:147
Uganda **90**:418; **89**:402; **88**:401; **87**:440;
  86:474; **85**:478; **84**:678; **83**:678;
  82:680; **81**:676
  see also WORLD DATA
UGT (Sp. labour union): *see* Unión Gen-
  eral de Trabajadores
Uhlenbeck, George Eugene (obit.) **89**:111
Uhlman, Fred (obit.) **86**:146
Ullmann, Liv Johanne (biog.) **86**:116
ultraviolet radiation, *or* UV
  Antarctica 538
Ulusu, Bulent (biog.) **81**:95
UMA (pol. org., Af.): *see* Arab Maghreb
  Union
Umberto II (obit.) **84**:133
UMW (Am. org.): *see* United Mine
  Workers
UN: *see* United Nations
UNDP (pol. party, Ant.): *see* United Na-
  tional Democratic Party
unemployment
  developing countries 193
  economic affairs 177
  social security 317
UNEP: *see* United Nations Environment
  Program
Unesco: *see* United Nations Educational,
  Scientific and Cultural Organization
UNICEF: *see* United Nations Children's
  Fund
Union Carbide Corp. (Am. co.)
  Bhopal settlement 216
  India 449
Unión Cívica Radical, *or* UCR (pol. party,
  Arg.)
  Argentina 509
Unión General de Trabajadores, *or* UGT
  (Sp. labour union)
  Spain 477
Union Maghreb Arabe (pol. org., Af.): *see*
  Arab Maghreb Union
Union of Soviet Socialist Republics
  90:492; **89**:474; **88**:473; **87**:517;
  86:547; **85**:552; **84**:679; **83**:679;
  82:681; **81**:677
  agriculture
    fisheries 137
    food processing 141
  Antarctic research 538
  arts
    dance 166
    exhibitions 150
    motion pictures 284
    theatre 386
  business and industry
    aerospace 228
    automobiles 229
    chemicals 233
    cotton 243
    strikes 249
    wine production 231
  crime and law enforcement 161
  economic affairs 187
  education 201
  energy 203, 239
  environment 211
  international affairs 392
    Afghanistan 447
    African affairs 400
      Egypt 426
      Ethiopia 405
    China 441
    Eastern European affairs 484
      Czechoslovakia 487
      Hungary 489
    Finland 464
    Iran 428
    Japan 443
    Mongolia 445
    Southeast Asian affairs 452
      Vietnam 460
    Syria 436
    United Nations 394
    United States 500
    Western European affairs 461
      West Germany 469
  life expectancy statistics 24
  migration 299
  military affairs 271, 273
  newspaper publishing 300
  photo essay 12
  prisons and penology 164
  railroad disasters 171, *il.*

religion 306
  Churches of Christ 310
  Islam 316
  Lutheran Communion 311
  Orthodox Church 313
  Seventh-day Adventist Church 312
space exploration 320
special report **88**:474
sports and games
  aerial sports 322
  boxing 333
  chess 334
  field hockey 337
  gymnastics 344
  ice hockey 348
  swimming 355
  volleyball 360
  weight lifting 360
  wrestling 360
television and radio 380
  see also WORLD DATA
Union pour la Démocratic Françoise, *or*
  UDP (pol. party, Fr.)
  France 465
Uniroyal Goodrich (Am. co.)
  rubber 241
UNITA: *see* National Union for the Total
  Independence of Angola
Unitarian Churches, *or* Unitarian Universalist Churches, *or* Universalist
  Churches 312
Unitarian Universalist Association,
  or UUA
  Unitarian Churches 312
United Airlines (Am. co.)
  air travel 228
United Arab Emirates, *or* U.A.E. **90**:437;
  89:420; **88**:420; **87**:462; **86**:492;
  85:497; **84**:683; **83**:684; **82**:685; **81**:681
  see also WORLD DATA
United Automobile Workers, *or* UAW
  (Am. org.)
  Nissan bid *il.* 248
United Bermuda Party, *or* UBP (pol.
  party, Ber.)
  dependent states 534
United Church of Canada 312
United Church of Christ 310, 313
United Democratic Party, *or* UDP
  Belize 511
United Kingdom **90**:480; **89**:464; **88**:464;
  87:509; **86**:537; **85**:542; **84**:684;
  83:684; **82**:685; **81**:682
  arts
    architecture 146
    dance 166
    exhibitions 149
    literature 260
    motion pictures 283
    museums 286
    theatre 384
  business and industry
    automobiles 228
    building and construction 232
    electrical 233
    gemstones 235
    insurance 236
    labour 248
    publishing 301, 302
    shipbuilding 242
    spirits 231
    television 380
  economic affairs 180
  education 199, 201
  energy 202, 239
  engineering projects
    bridges 204
    channel tunnel 208
    roads 208
  environment 210
  food safety (special report) 140
    consumer affairs 159
  immigration 299
  international affairs
    Argentina 507, 509
    Commonwealth of Nations 395
    dependent states 534
    international law 251
    Ireland 472
    Nigeria 412
    Oman 433
    Pakistan 451
    United Arab Emirates 437
    United Nations 394
    U.S.S.R. 495
    West Germany 468
    Western European affairs 460
    Zimbabwe 421
  law 250
  mental health 224
  military affairs 276
  prisons and penology 163
  race relations 304
  religion 312
  social security 317
  special report **81**:686
  sports and games
    aerial sports 322
    association football 338
    cricket 335
    field hockey 337
    golf 343
    ice hockey 349
    rugby 339
  stock exchanges 195
  terrorism 161
  see also WORLD DATA
United Mine Workers, *or* UMW (Am.
  org.)
  labour-management relations 248

United National Democratic Party, *or*
  UNDP (pol. party, Ant.)
  Antigua and Barbuda 508
United Nations **90**:393; **89**:376; **88**:376;
  87:415; **86**:447; **85**:448; **84**:688;
  83:688; **82**:690; **81**:688
  Afghanistan 447
  Canada 16
  environmental issues 209
  Namibia 535
  "Operation Lifeline Sudan" *il.* 417
  San Marino 477
  Somalia 414
  South Africa 416
  special report **85**:450
United Nations Children Fund, *or*
  UNICEF
  health care 21
United Nations Educational, Scientific and
  Cultural Organization, *or* Unesco
  special report **85**:450
United Nations Environment Program, *or*
  UNEP
  decisions 209
  greenhouse effect 211
United Nations Human Rights Commis-
  sion
  Romania 491
United Nations Peacekeeping Forces
  (biog.) **89**:85
United Nations Population Fund
  demography 297
United States **90**:499; **89**:482; **88**:481;
  87:526; **86**:557; **85**:561; **84**:691;
  83:691; **82**:694; **81**:690
  agriculture 129
    fisheries 137
    food processing 138
    food safety (special report) 140
  archaeology 144
  arts
    architecture 146
    dance 164
    exhibitions 149
    jazz 290
    literature 261
    motion pictures 282
    museums 286
    photography 293
    theatre 386
  business and industry 226
    advertising 227
    aerospace 227
    automobiles 229
    beer 231
    building and construction 232
    ceramics 232
    chemicals 233
    computers 246
    electrical 233
    furniture 234
    furs 234
    glass 236
    insurance 236
    iron and steel 237
    labour 248
    lumber exports 245
    microelectronics 238
    nuclear power 239
    paints and varnishes 240
    photography 293
    publishing 301, 303
    rubber 241
    telecommunications 242
    television and radio 379
    tourism 245
  coins and paper money 292
  consumer affairs 159
  crime and law enforcement 160
    prisons and penology 163
  Earth science
    geophysics 174
    hydrology 174
    meteorology 175
  economic affairs 178
  education 198
  energy 202
  engineering projects
    bridges 205
    roads 207
    tunnels 208
  environment 209, 211
    Antarctica 537
    Arctic regions 538
  freight and pipelines 390
  health and disease 220
    mental health 223
  international affairs
    Afghanistan 447
    Bahamas 510
    Bangladesh 447
    Bolivia 511
    Canada 13, 498
    China 441
    Colombia 514
    Cuba 516
    dependent states 535
    Egypt 426
    El Salvador 518
    France 466
    Gambia 406
    Honduras 520
    international law 251
    Israel 430
    Japan 443
    Jordan 431
    Kampuchea 455
    Korea 444
    Lebanon 432
    Liberia 409

Libya 432
Mexico 521
Middle East and North Africa 421
Nicaragua 522
Pakistan 450
Panama 522, *il.* 53
Philippines 457
Saudi Arabia 434
Singapore 458
Southeast Asian affairs 452
Syria 436
United Kingdom 482
United Nations 393
U.S.S.R. 495
Vietnam 459
West Germany 468
Western European affairs 462
libraries 253
military affairs 271, 272
mining 280
population
  demography 297
  immigration 299
  life expectancy 24
  race relations 305
religion 307
  Islam 316
  Lutheran Communion 311
  Orthodox Church 314
social security 318
space exploration 319
special reports **89**:144, 483; **85**:563;
  84:327, 698; **83**:698; **82**:287; **81**:697
sports and games
  aerial sports 321
  automobile racing 323
  baseball 325
  basketball 328
  bowling 331
  chess 334
  contract bridge 335
  cycling 336
  field hockey 337
  football
    college 340
    professional 341
  golf 342
  horse racing 344
  ice hockey 347
  polo 351
  rowing 351
  sailing 352
  swimming 355
  tennis 357
  track and field 357
    marathon and cross country 360
  volleyball 360
  wrestling 360
stamps 292
stock exchanges 191
zoology 253
  see also WORLD DATA
United States Commerce Committee
  television and radio 379
United States Air Force
  military affairs 273
United States Army
  military affairs 273
United States Census Bureau
  demography 297
United States Department of Energy
  nuclear industry 239
United States Institute of Mental Health
  mental health 224
United States Marine Corps
  military affairs 273
United States Navy
  military affairs 273
United States Supreme Court
  court decisions 249
United States v. Monsanto (law case)
  court decisions 250
United States v. Sokolow (law case)
  court decisions 250
Universalist Churches: *see* Unitarian
  Churches
University Boat Race (U.K.)
  rowing 352
University Hospital (hospital, Lund,
  Swed.)
  breast cancer study 222
University Hospital (hospital, Uppsala,
  Swed.)
  breast cancer study 222
UNO (pol. org., Nic.): *see* National Oppo-
  sition Union
Uno, Sosuke
  Japan 442, *il.* 180
Unser, Al, Jr. 323
UP (pol. org., Colom.): *see* Patriotic Union
Upper Argen (viaduct, W.Ger.)
  construction problems 204
Upper Volta: *see* Burkina Faso
Upshaw, Gene (biog.) **88**:84
"UpTime: The Disk Monthly" (mag.)
  introduction 302
uranium-lead dating
  geochronology 173
Uranus
  special report **87**:152
urban habitat
  bird adaptation 255
urban mass transit 391
Urbanek, Karel
  Czechoslovakia 487
Urey, Harold Clayton (obit.) **82**:124
Urrutia Lleo, Manuel (obit.) **82**:125
Uruguay **90**:526; **89**:510; **88**:509; **87**:556;
  86:587; **85**:588; **84**:719; **83**:719;
  82:719; **81**:718